1 MONTH OF
FREE
READING

at

www.ForgottenBooks.com

By purchasing this book you are eligible for one month membership to ForgottenBooks.com, giving you unlimited access to our entire collection of over 1,000,000 titles via our web site and mobile apps.

To claim your free month visit:

www.forgottenbooks.com/free848426

ISBN 978-0-484-31496-1
PIBN 10848426

THE GOSPEL MESSENGER.

"Set for the Defense of the Gospel."

Vol. 30, Old Series.   Mt. Morris, Ill., and Huntingdon, Pa., Jan. 5, 1892.   No. 1.

The Gospel Messenger.

H. B. BRUMBAUGH, Editor,

And Business Manager of the Eastern House, Box 50,
Huntingdon, Pa.

Table of Contents.

BRO. W. J. SWIGART, on his return from the New Enterprise, Pa., church, informed us that, though the meetings held were interesting, the attendance was somewhat affected by the very general prevalence of sickness, the *Grippe* having taken hold of quite a large number of the citizens.

THE NEW YEAR.

EVERYTHING that belongs to this life grows old and passes away, and because we cannot retain the old, we always greet the new with pleasure and gladness. Indeed, it is a very pleasant thought that, since we cannot hold the old, we can accept the new. We are interested in time, no matter how fleeting it be, and we always have more reference to that which we expect, than we do to that which we have used, and did we ever stop to think that we receive it all as a matter of faith?

As we pen these thoughts, we are yet in the old year, but we already are living in the new. While the few short days that still remain are being used in preparation for the new year, the old year is practically gone. Yes, we are glad that the new follows the old, so it always has been and always will be, and the most encouraging thought of all is, the new may be better than the old.

Since the light of sin has nipped the freshness and vigor of our world and lives, things have grown old. They fade as a leaf, and, as the flower, they pass away, but for six thousand years our good Father has been replacing the old with a new that is better.

The clouds of night have been hanging over this world of ours, but the break of day is streaking the eastern shore and soon it will be day,—a new day upon which the sun of peace and life will no more set.

Though this may not be the first day of the year 1892, yet it will come, and happy, yea, thrice happy will be those who can greet it with songs of gladness and words of praise. May the days and years that may come to each of us, between this and then, be days of preparation and peace, so that, when the Master comes, we may be found ready.

BIBLE TERM.

THERE is a considerable inquiry on the part of the ministers and Bible workers, as to the courses that will be pursued at our "Bible Terms." Some of the schools have already given a partial program of the course, and as ours at Huntingdon does not open until the first of February, we will now give an idea of what we expect to do. Our object is to pursue a course that will give the greatest possible amount of Biblical instruction in the short time that will be given to the work. Parts of it must necessarily be methods rather than matter, and yet it is surprising to know how much real solid and practical information can be given and received in the time allotted.

Among the important things for Bible teachers to learn is, to properly and intelligently *read* the Scriptures. Much of the Bible-reading done fails to be instructive to the hearers, because of the manner in which the reading is done. The same may be said of hymn-reading. A little instruction and practice in this direction will add greatly to the efficiency of those who are the church workers.

Another very important help is the study of Bible History. This knowledge not only helps to confirm our faith in the truthfulness and power of the Bible, but greatly aids in the interpretation of Bible truths. To study the lives and the customs of the people who lived at the times when the Bible narratives, as given, transpired, and as understood when they were written, gives us a key to their interpretations that cannot be had in any other way. These are facts that must be apparent to every careful Bible student.

Again, much depends on the manner in which the Bible is studied, whether it be in catches, dips, by piecemeal or consecutively. Of all the books in the world, there are none so miserably read as the Bible. This may seem to be putting the matter a little strong, but is it not a truth? We feel that we ought not to read the Bible, just as if the mere reading would answer the purpose,—no matter whether we open on the sixth chapter of Matthew or the third chapter of John, or in Revelations or Genesis,—no matter where, only so we read the Bible. What knowledge would we get of any other book or history, if we would read them in this way? Very little indeed, and yet much of the Bible-reading is done in this way.

That our readers, and especially those who are interested in Bible study, may have an idea of what is done at these "Bible Terms," we give the following outline of the work or course that will be pursued:

1. BIBLE HISTORY.—This embraces a knowledge of the Bible Lands, their location, their people, customs, languages and usages as they were in the times when the different narratives were acted out and written.

2. OLD AND NEW TESTAMENT EXEGESIS, or the consecutive and critical study of the Books of the Old and New Testament.

3. THE LIFE OF CHRIST, as given in the four Gospels, and the light thrown upon it by history, etc.

4. THE PROPAGATION OF THE GOSPEL, or Christianity, as set forth in the Acts and the epistolary writings.

5. EVIDENCES OF CHRISTIANITY, as shown outside of the Bible, in favor of the truthfulness of the doctrines taught.

6. HOMILETICS, or some instructions on the preparation and delivery of sermons.

7. ELOCUTION, or Scripture and hymn-reading. These are all important studies to those who are now, or may expect to, engage in Bible work, and are intended for the help of ministers, Bible-teachers, Sunday-school workers and all who are interested in Bible study.

The Term opens at Huntingdon Feb. 1, and will continue for four weeks.

From this work none of the schools expect any pay. The teaching is done *free*. A charge of $3.00 per week is made to cover the cost of board, room, etc. This includes good board, pleasant, steam-heated rooms and good beds.

The "Term" was originated to accommodate such ministers, and others, interested in Bible study, as cannot take the regular "school course," and is held in the winter season, because it is thought to be the most suitable time for our people to attend.

From present indications, the coming "Term" will be largely attended, as a number have already expressed their intention of being present. All are invited,—ministers, teachers, Bible students, old and young, brethren and sisters. Come and spend a few weeks in the best of all works,— the study of the best of all books. As soon as you determine on coming, let us know, that we may make the necessary preparations, as we wish to make your stay with us both profitable and pleasant. Address, H. B. Brumbaugh, Huntingdon, Pa.

THE GOSPEL MESSENGER.

"Set for the Defense of the Gospel."

Vol. 30, Old Series.   Mt. Morris, Ill., and Huntingdon, Pa., Jan. 5, 1892.   No. 1.

The Gospel Messenger.

H. B. BRUMBAUGH, Editor,

And Business Manager of the Eastern House, Box 50,
Huntingdon, Pa.

Table of Contents.

BRO. W. J. SWIGART, on his return from the New Enterprise, Pa., church, informed us that, though the meetings held were interesting, the attendance was somewhat affected by the very general prevalence of sickness, the *Grippe* having taken hold of quite a large number of the citizens.

THE NEW YEAR.

EVERYTHING that belongs to this life grows old and passes away, and because we cannot retain the old, we always greet the new with pleasure and gladness. Indeed, it is a very pleasant thought that, since we cannot hold the old, we can accept the new. We are interested in time, no matter how fleeting it be, and we always have more reference to that which we expect, than we do to that which we have used, and did we ever stop to think that we receive it all as a matter of faith?

As we pen these thoughts, we are yet in the old year, but we already are living in the new. While the few short days that still remain are being used in preparation for the new year, the old year is practically gone. Yes, we are glad that the new follows the old, so it always has been and always will be, and the most encouraging thought of all is, the new may be better than the old.

Since the blight of sin has nipped the freshness and vigor of our world and lives, things have grown old. They fade as a leaf, and as the flower, they pass away, but for six thousand years our good Father has been replacing the old with a new that is better.

The clouds of night have been hanging over this world of ours, but the break of day is streaking the eastern shore and soon it will be day,—a new day upon which the sun of peace and life will no more set.

Though this may not be the first day of the year 1892, yet it will come, and happy, yea, thrice happy will be those who can greet it with songs of gladness and words of praise. May the days and years that may come to each of us, between this and then, be days of preparation and peace, so that, when the Master comes, we may be found ready.

BIBLE TERM.

THERE is a considerable inquiry on the part of the ministers and Bible workers, as to the courses that will be pursued at our "Bible Terms." Some of the schools have already given a partial program of the course, and as ours at Huntingdon does not open until the first of February, we will now give an idea of what we expect to do. Our object is to pursue a course that will give the greatest possible amount of Biblical instruction in the short time that will be given to the work. Parts of it must necessarily be methods rather than matter, and yet it is surprising to know how much real solid and practical information can be given and received in the time allotted.

Among the important things for Bible teachers to learn is, to properly and intelligently *read* the Scriptures. Much of the Bible-reading done fails to be instructive to the hearers, because of the manner in which the reading is done. The same may be said of hymn-reading. A little instruction and practice in this direction will add greatly to the efficiency of those who are the church workers.

Another very important help is the study of Bible History. This knowledge not only helps to confirm our faith in the truthfulness and power of the Bible, but greatly aids in the interpretation of Bible truths. To study the lives and the customs of the people who lived at the times when the Bible narratives, as given, transpired, and as understood when they were written, gives us a key to their interpretations that cannot be had in any other way. These are facts that must be apparent to every careful Bible student.

Again, much depends on the manner in which the Bible is studied, whether it be in catches, dips, by piecemeal or consecutively. Of all the methods in the world, there are none so miserably read as the Bible. This may seem to be putting the matter a little strong, but is it not applying the same to any other book or history, if we would read them in this way? Very little indeed, and yet much of the Bible-reading is done in this way.

That our readers, and especially those who are interested in Bible study, may have an idea of what is done at these "Bible Terms," we give the following outline of the work or course that will be pursued:

1. BIBLE HISTORY.—This embraces a knowledge of the Bible Lands, their location, their people, customs, languages and usages as they were acted out and written.

2. OLD AND NEW TESTAMENT EXEGESIS, or the consecutive and critical study of the Books of the Old and New Testament.

3. THE LIFE OF CHRIST, as given in the four Gospels, and the light thrown upon it by history, etc.

4. THE PROPAGATION OF THE GOSPEL, or Christianity, as set forth in the Acts and the epistolary writings.

5. EVIDENCES OF CHRISTIANITY, as shown outside of the Bible, in favor of the truthfulness of the doctrines taught.

6. HOMILETICS, or some instructions on the preparation and delivery of sermons.

7. ELOCUTION, or Scripture and hymn-reading. These are all important studies to those who are now, or may expect to, engage in Bible work, and are intended for the help of ministers, Bible-teachers, Sunday-school workers and all who are interested in Bible study.

The Term opens at Huntingdon Feb. 1, and will continue for four weeks.

From this work none of the schools expect any pay. The teaching is done *free*. A charge of $3.00 per week is made to cover the cost of board, room, etc. This includes good board, pleasant, steam-heated rooms and good beds.

The "Term" was originated to accommodate such ministers, and others, interested in Bible study, as cannot take the regular "school course," and is held in the winter season, because it is thought to be the most suitable time for our people to attend.

From present indications, the coming "Term" will be largely attended, as a number have already expressed their intention of being present. All are invited,—ministers, teachers, Bible students, old and young, brethren and sisters. Come and spend a few weeks in the best of all works,—the study of the best of all books. As soon as you determine on coming, let us know, that we may make the necessary preparations, as we wish to make your stay with us both profitable and pleasant. Address, H. B. Brumbaugh, Huntingdon, Pa.

of Christ, and calls all Christians, dogs (*Cowan*). Yet it claims to teach all the principles "that the soul of man desires," both for time and eternity.

One of the arguments used, to sustain the time-honored lodge, is, that Solomon is its founder, and built the first temple. Granting · that he was, though for this there is no evidence, we fail to see the benefit he derived from it, for, after the building of the temple, he fell into the vanities of sinful pleasures from which the "beauties of the secret order" did not redeem him.

Another claim is that Christ himself was a member of the lodge. Now, if he was, he could only have taken the "Entered Apprentice" degree, for he says, "In secret have I said nothing," and in all the degrees, except the first, each member is required to be active.

Again he says, "Swear not at all," but in taking each degree, the candidate is required to forswear himself by the taking of blood-curdling oaths, which increase in horribleness as they advance in degrees.

Now the *religion* of Jesus Christ is entirely a different thing. It is to be told, not in darkness, but in the light. It is to be published, not in secret chambers, but upon the housetops. It is to be told not to a select few, but to the world.

The doors to Christ's kingdom are not chained with iron-clad oaths, but stand wide open. The invitation is not alone to the wealthy, but "whosoever will let him come and take of the water of life freely."

Sin every-where is closely followed by secrecy, for men do not want their vices published to the world. The saloon-keeper screens his door, the gambler his window, and the lodge men take an upper room, and bolt the door. Great men are admitted,—men at the head of governments, men, high in profession,—the LL. D., the M. D., the Rev. D. D., as well as the drunkard, the infidel, the skeptic and the pagan. All are on one common level,—"yoked together." There they revel at the dead hour of night, perpetuating some heathen myth, brought up from the dark ages, shrouded in mystery. Man,—the noblest work of God's creation,—is playing the murderer in darkness. Secrecy and sin, born together; they are stalking up and down, as roaring lions. Through the world they are going together, and together they must perish.

Feed the one and the other will fatten; slay the one and the other will die.

Columbus, Ohio.

TEMPERANCE ARITHMETIC.

COMPILED BY JOHN KNISLEY.

1. There are 115,000 saloons in the United States, and 64,000 public schools. How many more saloons than schools? If I am correctly informed, there are 51,000 more saloons than schools.

2. The people of the United States pay $80,-000,000 yearly for the support of the public schools, and $1,485,000,000 for the support of the saloons, or $1,405,000,000 more than the schools.

3. The value of the food products of our country, for a single year, is about $600,000,000. The cost of alcoholic drinks is about $1,485,000,000. How much more does the liquor cost than the food and clothing? I answer, $885,000,000.

4. The 3,000 saloons of San Francisco take in daily an average of $10 each. That is $30,000 daily.

5. There are about 600,000 drunkards in the United States. How many cities of 40,000 inhabitants each would these drunkards make?

6. In the City of Oakland, the Athens of California, there are 200 saloons. If every saloonist

sells 40 drams a day, how many drams are drank daily? *Answer.*—About 8,000.

7. If a family spends 15 cents a day for beer, how much is expended in four weeks and how many loaves of bread, at 10 cents a loaf, could be bought for the same money?

8. A smoker spends 29 cents a day for cigars; will you calculate how many dollars he will spend in one-half year, and how many pairs of shoes, at $2.00 per pair, he could purchase with this wasted money?

Dear brethren and sisters, let us warn all those who have become habituated to the liquor habit, and also those who use tobacco so greatly. No one should indulge in either of these unbecoming habits. It does not only destroy souls, but it brings many to an untimely grave. O, how many die from the effect of the use of strong drink! O, that all would abstain from such injurious habits, and spend the money, thus saved, for the upbuilding of the church of God!

The apostle Paul, in 1 Cor. 3: 16, 17, says, "Know ye not that ye are the temple of God, and that the Spirit of God dwelleth in you? If any man defile the temple of God, him shall God destroy, for the temple of God is holy, which temple ye are." No wonder that the Savior said, "Watch and pray," Matt. 26: 41. He well knew that there are many things whereby we can become defiled, and, not knowing what moment we will be called away, we should watch and pray continually, to keep our garments white. Let us all daily renew our baptismal covenants. Mine I made fifty-five years ago, and I hope, by a faithful life, to meet all the dear members in that heavenly home where we will part no more.

"It is the hope, the blessed hope,
The hope that Christ has given,—
The hope, when days and years are past,
We all shall meet in heaven."

Teegarden, Ind.

HE SAW ANGELS.

BY LIZZIE HILARY.

I have often heard young members,—when giving the reason for growing cold and indifferent toward the church,—say that they did not receive the encouragement from the older members that they should have had. I fear this may be the case in many instances, and the older ones should be more guarded about the young. We, too often, forget that we were once young. I well remember that, when I united with the church, another young sister and I were the only young members of that congregation, but we never felt lonely, because the older ones paid great attention to us, and kept us encouraged to go on in the good work.

Oh, how I did love to get in company with some of our good old sisters who now rest beneath the sod! Never shall I forget the good counsel they gave me, and I thank God to-night that I have never felt like going back, but want to press on, though there may be trials and difficulties for us to encounter. If we are faithful, the crown is over there!

Dear young pilgrims, let me, as one that loves you, encourage you to be faithful! Try always to let your light shine! Do not be ashamed of what you profess, for the world will soon see that you are ashamed of your religion. Never be afraid to defend the cause of Christ. Though you may be young in years, yet you can speak a word for Jesus.

Permit me to relate a circumstance which took place but a short time ago, here in the West. Five young members, — three sisters and two brethren,—went to a feast, about thirty or forty miles distant. On their way home one of the sisters lost her shawl and they went back to find it,

and night overtook them before they were near their journey's end. If I mistake not, just before dark they stopped to feed their team, and fell in to a conversation with the man of the house, and I am glad to say, their conversation was on religion. The man asked them if they belonged to some church. Of course he noticed by their appearance, that they were not trying to follow the fashions of this world.

These members were all young in years, and the young brother that did the talking was only fifteen years of age, and was not yet in the church quite a year. After they had discussed the doctrine of the Brethren church pretty well, the man said to them, "Well, if you are Christians, come in and let us have worship before you go."

It was then nearly dark, and they had twelve miles yet to go. How many would have excused themselves and went on, but these did not do so. They went in, as the man had requested, and, after the sisters had put their neat caps on, and were ready for worship, the man gave them the Bible. One of the young sisters read a chapter, and the young brother then made some remarks on it, after which he led in prayer.

When they arose, the man asked them if they had ever seen angels. They said, "No." "Well," said he, "I have." Do you not think their light shone brightly to that man?

May God help us all to let our light shine before the world, is my prayer!

MINISTERIAL MEETING OF NORTH-EASTERN OHIO.

BY T. C. WEAND.

This meeting was held Nov. 24, 1891, in the Wooster church, Wayne County, Ohio. The exceedingly stormy weather kept many from attending, yet the interest was good. Many instructive and inspiring thoughts were given for the strength of the soul by our dear brethren, who did not stop for the unpleasant weather. The greater the sacrifice, the greater the blessing, seemed to be verified in this meeting.

The meeting was organized by electing brethren Noah Longenecker and Jno. Kahler, Moderators; T. C. Wieand and J. J. Hoover, Clerks. The following are some of the thoughts expressed:

1. *True Revivals.*—These depend on the principles of the Gospel. The minister should be equipped, "rooted and grounded in the truth," present the Truth, teach the people, awaken them to a sense of their condition and duty to God. He should feel like Paul: "Woe be unto me if I preach not the Gospel."

2. *Church Government.* — "Tell it unto the church," of Matt. 18, was referred to, showing the judicial and executive power of the church. Most troubles in church government arise from not having been properly "taught" or not having been "transformed by the renewing of the mind."

3. *The Minister's Inner Life.*—The minister should have pure motives. "Out of the abundance of the heart the mouth speaketh." He should guard his thoughts; "as he thinketh so is he." Thoughts form character, and character "will out."

4. *Pastoral Visits.*—Pastoral visits should be made according to advice by the General Brotherhood, to reach the isolated and poor, and show some regard for their children.

5. *Preparation of Sermons.*—A minister who does not keep to his subject, does not preach a sermon, but only makes a speech. Paul, in 2 Tim. 3: 16, gives an outline for a series of sermons. The minister needs inspiration, prayer, study of meaning and connection of words. He should "study to show himself approved unto

of Christ, and calls all Christians, dogs (*Cowan*). Yet it claims to teach all the principles "that the soul of man desires," both for time and eternity.

One of the arguments used, to sustain the time-honored lodge, is, that Solomon is its founder, and built the first temple. Granting that he was, though for this there is no evidence, we fail to see the benefit he derived from it, for, after the building of the temple, he fell into the vanities of sinful pleasures from which the "beauties of the secret order" did not redeem him.

Another claim is that Christ himself was a member of the lodge. Now, if he was, he could only have taken the "Entered Apprentice" degree, for he says, "In secret have I said nothing," and in all the degrees, except the first, each member is required to be active.

Again he says, "Swear not at all," but in taking each degree, the candidate is required to forswear himself by the taking of blood-curdling oaths, which increase in horribleness as they advance in degrees.

Now the *religion* of Jesus Christ is entirely a different thing. It is to be told, not in darkness, but in the light. It is to be published, not in secret chambers, but upon the housetops. It is to be told not to a select few, but to the world.

The doors to Christ's kingdom are not chained with iron-clad oaths, but stand wide open. The invitation is not alone to the wealthy, but "whosoever will let him come and take of the water of life freely."

Sin every-where is secretly followed by secrecy, for men do not want their vices published to the world. The saloon-keeper screens his door, the gambler his window, and the lodge men take an upper room, and bolt the door. Great men are admitted,—men at the head of governments, men, high in the profession,—the LL. D., the M. D., the Rev'. D. D., as well as the drunkard, the infidel, the skeptic and the pagan. All are on one common level,—"yoked together." There they revel at the dead hour of night, perpetuating some heathen myth, brought up from the dark ages, shrouded in mystery. Man,—the noblest work of God's creation,—is playing the murderer in darkness. Secrecy and sin, born together; they are stalking up and down, as roaring lions. Through the world they are going together, and together they must perish.

Feed the one and the other will fatten; slay the one and the other will die.

Columbus, Ohio.

TEMPERANCE ARITHMETIC.

COMPILED BY JOHN KNISLEY.

1. THERE are 115,000 saloons in the United States, and 64,000 public schools. How many more saloons than schools? If I am correctly informed, there are 51,000 more saloons than schools.

2. The people of the United States pay $80,-000,000 yearly for the support of the public schools, and $1,485,000,000 for the support of the saloons, or $1,405,000,000 more than the schools.

3. The value of the food products of our country, for a single year, is about $600,000,000. The cost of alcoholic drinks is about $1,485,000,000. How much more does the liquor cost than the food and clothing? I answer, $885,000,000.

4. The 3,000 saloons of San Francisco take in daily an average of $10 each. That is $30,000 daily.

5. There are about 600,000 drunkards in the United States. How many cities of 40,000 inhabitants each would these drunkards make?

6. In the City of Oakland, the Athens of California, there are 200 saloons. If every saloonist sells 40 drams a day, how many drams are drunk daily? Answer.—About 8,000.

7. If a family spends 15 cents a day for beer, how much is expended in four weeks and how many loaves of bread, at 10 cents a loaf, could be bought for the same money?

8. A smoker spends 20 cents a day for cigars; will you calculate how many dollars he will spend in one-half year, and how many pairs of shoes, at $2.00 per pair, he could purchase with this wasted money?

Dear brethren and sisters, let us warn all those who have become habituated to the liquor habit, and also those who use tobacco so greatly. No one should indulge in either of these unbecoming habits. It does not only destroy souls, but it brings many to an untimely grave. O, how many die from the effect of the use of strong drink!- O, that all would abstain from such injurious habits, and spend the money, thus saved, for the upbuilding of the church of God!

The apostle Paul, in 1 Cor. 3: 16, 17, says, "Know ye not that ye are the temple of God, and that the Spirit of God dwelleth in you? If any man defile the temple of God, him shall God destroy, for the temple of God is holy, which temple ye are." No wonder that the Savior said, "Watch and pray," Matt. 26: 41. He well knew that there are many things whereby we can become defiled, and, not knowing what moment we will be called away, we should watch and pray continually, to keep our garments white. Let us all daily renew our baptismal covenants. Mine I made fifty-five years ago, and I hope, by a faithful life, to meet all the dear members in that heavenly home where we will part no more.

"It is the hope, the blessed hope,
The hope that Christ has given,—
The hope, when days and years are past,
We all shall meet in heaven."

Teegarden, Ind.

HE SAW ANGELS.

BY LIZZIE HILARY.

I HAVE often heard young members,—when giving the reason for growing cold and indifferent toward the church,—say that they did not receive the encouragement from the older members that they should have had. I fear this may be the case in many instances, and the older ones should be more guarded about the young. We, too often, forget that we were once young. I well remember that, when I united with the church, another young sister and I were the only young members of that congregation, but we never felt lonely, because the older ones paid great attention to us, and kept us encouraged to go on in the good work.

Oh, how I did love to get in company with some of our good old sisters who now rest beneath the sod! Never shall I forget the good counsel they gave me, and I thank God to-night that I have never felt like going back, but want to press on, though there may be trials and difficulties for us to encounter. If we are faithful, the crown is over there!

Dear young pilgrims, let me, as one that loves you, encourage you to be faithful! Try always to let your light shine! Do not be ashamed of what you profess, for the world will soon see that you are ashamed of your religion. Never be afraid to defend the cause of Christ. Though you may be young in years, yet you can speak a word for Jesus.

Permit me to relate a circumstance which took place but a short time ago, here in the West. Five young members, — three sisters and two brethren,—went to a feast, about thirty or forty miles distant. On their way home one of the sisters lost her shawl and they went back to find it,

and night overtook them before they were near their journey's end. If I mistake not, just before dark they stopped to feed their team, and fell in-to a conversation with the man of the house, and I am glad to say, their conversation was on religion. The man asked them if they belonged to some church. Of course he noticed by their appearance, that they were not trying to follow the fashions of the world.

These members were all young in years, and the young brother that did the talking was only fifteen years of age, and was not yet in the church quite a year. After they had discussed the doctrine of the Brethren church pretty well, the man said to them, "Well, if you are Christians, come in and let us have worship before you go."

It was then nearly dark, and they had twelve miles yet to go. How many would have excused themselves and went on, but these did not do so. They went in, as the man had requested, and, after the sisters had put their neat caps on, and were ready for worship, the man gave them the Bible. One of the young sisters read a chapter, and the young brother then made some remarks on it, after which he led in prayer.

When they arose, the man asked them if they had ever seen angels. They said, "No." "Well," said he, "I have." Do you not think their light shone brightly to that man?

May God help us all to let our light shine before the world, is my prayer!

MINISTERIAL MEETING OF NORTH-EASTERN OHIO.

BY T. C. WIEAND.

THIS meeting was held Nov. 24, 1891, in the Wooster church, Wayne County, Ohio. The exceedingly stormy weather kept many from attending, yet the interest was good. Many instructive and inspiring thoughts were given for the strength of the soul by our dear brethren, who did not stop for the unpleasant weather. The greater the sacrifice, the greater the blessing, seemed to be verified in this meeting.

The meeting was organized by electing brethren Noah Longenecker and Jno. Kahler, Moderators; T. C. Wieand and J. J. Hoover, Clerks. The following are some of the thoughts expressed:

1. *True Revivals.*—These depend on the principles of the Gospel. The minister should be equipped, "rooted and grounded in the truth," present the Truth, teach the people, awaken them to a sense of their condition and duty to God. He should feel like Paul: "Woe be unto me if I preach not the Gospel."

2. *Church Government.* — "Tell it unto the church," of Matt. 18, was referred to, showing the judicial and executive power of the church. Most trouble in church government arise from not having been properly "taught" or not having been "transformed by the renewing of the mind."

3. *The Minister's Inner Life.*—The minister should have pure motives. "Out of the abundance of the heart the mouth speaketh." He should guard his thoughts; "as he thinketh so is he." Thoughts form character, and character "will out."

4. *Pastoral Visits.*—Pastoral visits should be made according to advice by the General Brotherhood, to reach the isolated and poor, and show some regard for their children.

5. *Preparation of Sermons.*—A minister who does not keep to his subject, does not preach a sermon, but only makes a speech. Paul, in 2 Tim. 3: 16, gives an outline for a series of sermons. The minister needs inspiration, prayer, study of meaning and connection of words. He should "study to show himself approved unto

lent suggestions were offered, as to the most feasible and effective methods for overcoming the difficulties, for removing the hindrances and supplying the deficiencies, etc.

MINISTERS AND THEIR DUTIES.

This topic brought out lines of thought that cannot fail to encourage and help the ministers who were present.

1. It was thought good for all ministers to read and study carefully the instructions given in the Bible by an old, experienced preacher to younger preachers, as found in the letters of Paul to Timothy and Titus, and take them as a rule of action as much as possible. Such points as the following were brought out:

1. The minister should study to show himself approved unto God.

2. To be a workman that need not be ashamed. On this line it becomes necessary for ministers to avoid doing some things that are sometimes done by ministers, and to learn to do some other things in a little different way.

3. He should also study to rightly divide the Word of Truth. Upon this line it is good to follow the Lord's plan of dividing it.

1. It consists of the Old and the New Testaments, and may properly be so classed. Another part of it is history, giving an account of the creation, the ark, the flood, the call of Abraham, the sojourn in Egypt, the rise and fall of individuals and nations, the birth, life and resurrection of Christ, etc. Another part of it is law; a third, prophecy; a fourth part, poetry. It may further be divided by applying that part which is for the regulation of the members of the church where it belongs, and that which is intended to awaken the sinner and bring him to Christ, etc., also to where it belongs.

2. A minister should flee youthful lusts, and follow righteousness, faith, charity and peace. He must not strive, but be gentle unto all men, be apt to teach, patient. In all things he should show himself a pattern of good works, uncorruptness, gravity, sincerity, using sound speech that cannot be condemned, etc., and, so far as possible, he should free himself from the entanglement of this life, that he may please him who has chosen him to be a soldier.

The Sunday-school and its relations to the church was ably discussed; also the relation of the ministers to the Sunday-school and prayer-meeting received a due share of attention. The meeting adjourned on the evening of Dec. 17 with the feeling on the part of all, so far as known to the writer, that it was good to be there.

McPherson, Kans.

SOME OF THE EVILS OF SCOWLING.

BY JONATHAN HAHN.

I WANT to say to those in the habit of scolding the children or any one else, that scolding carries away your religious influence. It makes you seem harsh. It spoils your face. Please take an old brother's advice and quit scowling. Before you know it your face will resemble a small railroad map. There is a grand trunk line from your cowlick to the bridge of your nose, intersected by parallel lines, running east and west, with curves arching your eyebrows: and, oh, how much older you look for it!

Scowling steals upon us unawares. We frown when the light is too strong and when it is too weak. We tie our brows into a knot when we are thinking, and knit them even more tightly when we cannot think.

There is no denying, there are plenty of things to scowl about. The baby in the cradle frowns when something fails to suit. The little one who likes sugar on his bread and butter tells his trouble in the same way when you leave the sugar off. "Cross," we say about the children, and "worried to death," about the grown folks, and as for ourselves,—we can't help it. But we must. Its reflex influence makes others unhappy; for face answereth to face in life as well as in water. It belies our religion. We should possess our souls in such peace that it will reflect itself in placid countenance. If our foreheads be rigid with wrinkles before forty, what will they be at seventy?

There is one consoling thought about these marks of time and trouble,—the death angel almost always erases them. Even the extremely aged in death often wear a smooth and peaceful brow, which leaves our memories of them calm and tranquil. But, my dear brethren and sisters, our business is with life. Scowling is a kind of silent scolding. It shows that our souls need sweetening. For pity's sake let us take a sad-iron or a glad-iron or the Lord's smoothing tools, and straighten those creases out of our faces, before they become indelibly engraven upon our visage! Love thinketh no evil and never scolds, but always admonishes with a pleasant and cheerful face!

Van Wert, Ohio.

CALL FOR A PREACHER.

IN his remarks on an appeal by Bro. E. B. Hoff, of Waterloo, in the MESSENGER of Nov. 30, our editor says that many of the ministering brethren have not means to locate among the isolated members. If some good brother, who is firm in the faith, would come among us, we would be glad to help him get a comfortable living for his family, and I think it is so in other places where a few of our brethren are located. We are not wealthy, for it is now as in olden times,—the common people hear the Word of God gladly, but, though our means would seem small to many of our eastern brethren, our hearts are large.

Those who live in large congregations, cannot realize what temptations we, who live isolated, have to endure. Many of us are young in years and Christian experience and have been brought up in a different faith. Often our Brethren's wives and families can preach as loud in a community as the husband and father can in the congregation. Do not be afraid, dear brethren, to come out to the fertile prairies of Northern and Western Iowa, for the same Father will care for you here, as among your kinsfolk and friends.

M. WOODARD.

Farnhamville, Calhoun Co., Iowa.

REMARKS.

We trust that some faithful minister will respond to this practical call, for a church that is willing to help hold up a minister's hands certainly deserves a faithful shepherd, and there are no people in the Union who appreciate sound, earnest preaching like these isolated members. By offering to help a minister, they make it possible for a minister of limited means to not only procure a living for his family, but also to make himself useful to the cause.

More than likely we have a hundred ministers, in limited circumstances, who might be induced to locate with isolated congregations, if the necessary financial help could be offered them. Furthermore, there is nothing wrong about aiding a minister in locating at a point where he can make himself useful in feeding the flock of God. Some of the most faithful elders we have in the Brotherhood have been thus aided, and the cause prospered in their hands. We have now in mind several able ministers who were aided by the churches needing help in the ministry, and the aid thus given, proved a blessing to the church, as well as the ministers.

We also trust that ministers who respond to calls of this kind, will do so in all good faith, realizing that these isolated members need good, spiritual food and the very best of care, hence the importance of being well rooted and grounded in the faith, and in full sympathy with the church and her doctrine. J. H. M.

CHOICE SELECTIONS.

"To overcome adverse influences, is no unimportant part of life's conflict."

* * *

"It would be a different world to-day, if all who claim to be 'the salt of the earth' were as eager to repress injustice in its smaller and meaner forms, as to make money or influential friends."

* * *

"GOOD impulses may be the very voice of God, stirring whatever is noble and generous within us. Nor are they accidental; loving and brave emotions belong to warm and courageous hearts. They come of themselves, like song birds, but they come surely where sunshine and still grove invite them,—not into clamor and foul air."

* * *

"It is the duty of every man, to whom a special vocation presents itself, to set opposite each other two considerations. 'Dare I undertake this task?' —is a solemn question, but so is this: 'Dare I let this task go past me? Am I prepared for the responsibility of allowing it to drift into weaker hands?' These are days when the church of Christ is calling for the help of every one capable of aiding her, and we ought to hear it said more often, that one is afraid not to teach in Sunday-school, and another dares not refuse a proffered district, and a third fears to leave charitable tasks undone. To him that knoweth to do good, and doeth it not, to him it is sin; and we hear too much about the terrible responsibility of working for God, but too little about the still graver responsibility of refusing to work for him when called."

The Gospel Messenger

Is the recognized organ of the German Baptist or Brethren's church, and advocates the form of doctrine taught in the New Testament and pleads for a return to apostolic and primitive Christianity.

It recognizes the New Testament as the only infallible rule of faith and practice, and maintains that Faith toward God, Repentance from dead works, Regeneration of the heart and mind, baptism by Trine Immersion for remission of sins unto the reception of the Holy Ghost by the laying on of hands, are the means of adoption into the household of God,—the church militant.

It also maintains that Feet-washing, as taught in John 13, both by example and command of Jesus, should be observed in the church.

That the Lord's Supper, instituted by Christ and as universally observed by the apostles and the early Christians, is a full meal, and, in connection with the Communion, should be taken in the evening or after the close of the day.

That the Salutation of the Holy Kiss, or Kiss of Charity, is binding upon the followers of Christ.

That War and Retaliation are contrary to the spirit and self-denying principles of the religion of Jesus Christ.

That the principle of Plain Dressing and of Non-conformity to the world, as taught in the New Testament, should be observed by the followers of Christ.

That the Scriptural duty of Anointing the Sick with Oil, in the Name of the Lord, James 5:14, is binding upon all Christians.

It also advocates the church's duty to support Missionary and Tract Work, thus giving to the Lord for the spread of the Gospel and for the conversion of sinners.

In short, it is a vindicator of all that Christ and the apostles have enjoined upon us, and aims, amid the conflicting theories and discords of modern Christendom, to point out ground that all must concede to be infallibly safe.

☞ The above principles of our Fraternity are set forth on our "Brethren's Envelopes." Use them! Price, 15 cents per package; 40 cents per hundred.

lent suggestions were offered, as to the most feasible and effective methods for overcoming the difficulties, for removing the hindrances and supplying the deficiencies, etc.

MINISTERS AND THEIR DUTIES.

This topic brought out lines of thought that cannot fail to encourage and help the ministers who were present.

1. It was thought good for all ministers to read and study carefully the instructions given in the Bible by an old, experienced preacher to younger preachers, as found in the letters of Paul to Timothy and Titus, and take them as a rule of action as much as possible. Such points as the following were brought out:

i. The minister should study to show himself approved unto God.

2. To be a workman that need not be ashamed. On this line it becomes necessary for ministers to avoid doing some things that are sometimes done by ministers, and to learn to do some other things in a little different way.

3, He should also study to rightly divide the Word of Truth. Upon this line it is good to follow the Lord's plan of dividing it.

1. It consists of the Old and the New Testaments, and may properly be so classed. Another part of it is history, giving an account of the creation, the ark, the flood, the call of Abraham, the sojourn in Egypt, the rise and fall of individuals and nations, the birth, life and resurrection of Christ, etc. Another part of it is law; a third, prophecy; a fourth part, poetry. It may further be divided by applying that part which is for the regulation of the members of the church where it belongs, and that which is intended to awaken the sinner and bring him to Christ, etc., also to where it belongs.

2. A minister should flee youthful lusts, and follow righteousness, faith, charity and peace. He must not strive, but be gentle unto all men, be apt to teach, patient. In all things he should show himself a pattern of good works, uncorruptness, gravity, sincerity, using sound speech that cannot be condemned, etc., and, so far as possible, he should free himself from the entanglement of this life, that he may please him who has chosen him to be a soldier.

The Sunday-school and its relations to the church was ably discussed; also the relation of the ministers to the Sunday-school and prayer-meeting received a due share of attention. The meeting adjourned on the evening of Dec. 17 with the feeling on the part of all, so far as known to the writer, that it was good to be there.

McPherson, Kans.

SOME OF THE EVILS OF SCOWLING.

BY JONATHAN HAUN.

I WANT to say to those in the habit of scolding the children or any one else, that scolding carries away your religious influence. It makes you seem harsh. It spoils your face. Please take an old brother's advice and quit scowling. Before you know it your face will resemble a small railroad map. There is a grand trunk line from your cowlick to the bridge of your nose, intersected by parallel lines, running east and west, with curves arching your eyebrows: and, oh, how much older you look for it!

Scowling steals upon us unawares. We frown when the light is too strong and when it is too weak. We tie our brows into a knot when we are thinking, and knit them even more tightly when we cannot think.

There is no denying, there are plenty of things to scowl about. The baby in the cradle frowns when something fails to suit. The little one who likes sugar on his bread and butter tells his trouble in the same way when you leave the sugar off. "Cross," we say about the children, and as for ourselves,—we can't help it. But we must. Its reflex influence makes others unhappy; for face answereth to face in life as well as in water. It belies our religion. We should possess our souls in such peace that it will reflect itself in placid countenance. If our foreheads be rigid with wrinkles before forty, what will they be at seventy?

There is one consoling thought about these marks of time and trouble,—the death angel almost always erases them. Even the extremely aged in death often wear a smooth and peaceful brow, which leaves our memories of them calm and tranquil. But, my dear brethren and sisters, our business is with life. Scowling is a kind of silent scolding. It shows that our souls need sweetening. For pity's sake let us take a sad-iron or a glad-iron or the Lord's smoothing tools, and straighten those creases out of our faces, before they become indelibly engraven upon our visage! Love thinketh no evil and never scolds, but always admonishes with a pleasant and cheerful face!

Van Wert, Ohio.

CALL FOR A PREACHER.

IN his remarks on an appeal by Bro. E. B. Hoff, of Waterloo, in the MESSENGER of Nov. 30, our editor says that many of the ministering brethren have not means to locate among the isolated members. If some good brother, who is firm in the faith, would come among us, we would be glad to help him get a comfortable living for his family, and I think it is so in other places where a few of our brethren are located. We are not wealthy, for it is now as in olden times,—the common people hear the Word of God gladly, but, though our means would seem small to many of our eastern brethren, our hearts are large.

Those who live in large congregations, cannot realize what temptations we, who live isolated, have to endure. Many of us are young in years and Christian experience and have been brought up in a different faith. Often our Brethren's wives and families can preach as loud in a community as the husband and father can in the congregation. Do not be afraid, dear brethren, to come out to the fertile prairies of Northern and Western Iowa, for the same Father will care for you here, as among your kinsfolk and friends.

M. WOODARD.

Farnhamville, Calhoun Co., Iowa.

REMARKS.

We trust that some faithful minister will respond to this practical call, for a church that is willing to help hold up a minister's hands certainly deserves a faithful shepherd, and there are no people in the Union who appreciate sound, earnest preaching like these isolated members. By offering to help a minister, they make it possible for a minister of limited means to not only procure a living for his family, but also to make himself useful to the cause.

More than likely we have a hundred ministers, in limited circumstances, who might be induced to locate with isolated congregations, if the necessary financial help could be offered them. Furthermore, there is nothing wrong about aiding a minister in locating at a point where he can make himself useful in feeding the flock of God. Some of the most faithful elders we have in the Brotherhood have been thus aided, and the cause prospered in their hands. We have now in mind several able ministers who were aided by the churches needing help in the ministry, and the aid thus given, proved a blessing to the church, as well as the ministers.

We also trust that ministers who respond to calls of this kind, will do so in all good faith, realizing that these isolated members need good, spiritual food and the very best of care, hence the importance of being well rooted and grounded in the faith, and in full sympathy with the church and her doctrine.
J. H. M.

CHOICE SELECTIONS.

"To overcome adverse influences, is no unimportant part of life's conflict."

⁎ ⁎ ⁎

"It would be a different world to-day, if all who claim to be 'the salt of the earth' were as eager to repress injustice in its smaller and meaner forms, as to make money or influential friends."

⁎ ⁎ ⁎

"Good impulses may be the very voice of God, stirring whatever is noble and generous within us. Nor are they accidental; loving and brave emotions belong to warm and courageous hearts. They come of themselves, like song birds, but they come surely where sunshine and still grove invite them,—not into clamor and foul air."

⁎ ⁎ ⁎

"It is the duty of every man, to whom a special vocation presents itself, to set opposite each other two considerations. 'Dare I undertake this task?' —is a solemn question, but so is this: 'Dare I let this task go past me? Am I prepared for the responsibility of allowing it to drift into weaker hands?' These are days when the church of Christ is calling for the help of every one capable of aiding her, and we ought to hear it said more often, that one is afraid not to teach in Sunday-school, and another dares not refuse a proffered district, and a third fears to leave charitable tasks undone. To him that knoweth to do good, and doeth it not, to him it is sin; and we hear too much about the terrible responsibility of working for God, but too little about the still graver responsibility of refusing to work for him when called."

The Gospel Messenger

Is the recognized organ of the German Baptist or Brethren's church, and advocates the form of doctrine taught in the New Testament and pleads for a return to apostolic and primitive Christianity.

It recognizes the New Testament as the only infallible rule of faith and practice, and maintains that Faith toward God, Repentance from dead works, Regeneration of the heart and mind, baptism by Trine Immersion for remission of sins unto the reception of the Holy Ghost by the laying on of hands, are the means of adoption into the household of God,—the church militant.

It also maintains that Feet-washing, as taught in John 13, both by example and command of Jesus, should be observed in the church.

That the Lord's Supper, instituted by Christ and as universally observed by the apostles and the early Christians, is a full meal, and, in connection with the Communion, should be taken in the evening or after the close of the day.

That the Salutation of the Holy Kiss, or Kiss of Charity, is binding upon the followers of Christ.

That War and Retaliation are contrary to the spirit and self-denying principles of the religion of Jesus Christ.

That the principle of Plain Dressing and of Non-conformity to the world, as taught in the New Testament, should be observed by the followers of Christ.

That the Scriptural duty of Anointing the Sick with Oil, in the Name of the Lord, James 5: 14, is binding upon all Christians.

It also advocates the church's duty to support Missionary and Tract Work, thus giving to the Lord for the spread of the Gospel and for the conversion of sinners.

In short, it is a vindicator of all that Christ and the apostles have enjoined upon us, and aims, amid the conflicting theories and discords of modern Christendom, to point out ground that all must concede to be infallibly safe.

☞ The above principles of our Fraternity are set forth on our "Brethren's Envelopes." Use them! Price, 15 cents per package; 40 cents per hundred.

SHOULD A BROTHER BE EXCUSED FROM THE MINISTRY UPON HIS OWN REQUEST?

Whenever it is proven beyond the possibility of a doubt that the church made a mistake in calling a brother to the ministry, the known fact that such mistake was made would already annul such action. But where shall we go for such positive proof? There is none in reach. Therefore, when a brother is called by the church as a minister, there is none able to say, knowingly, that God did not co-operate in the church's action. If, then, the church would reverse its own action, without such proof, the last action would be guess work and if the first action was not a mistake, the last would be. Therefore, in consideration of such circumstances,

IS IT RIGHT FOR A BROTHER TO ASK THE CHURCH TO RELIEVE HIM,

and at the same time say that he is not fit for the place and that, if the church does not relieve him, he will not serve any way?

It is not right because he is not obedient to the church, which is violating one of the conditions by which he was admitted into the church, i. e., he is not willing to hear the church. He is really setting up his own, private judgment against the judgment of the church without any authority to do so, in a matter in which the church acted with all the authority that there is.

Again, it is not right because it is a violation of Matt. 7: 12, "All things whatsoever ye would that men should do to you, do ye even so to them." He would not be willing to allow any other brother such liberty on any other matter as he is using in this. For example: Suppose there is a difference between him and his brother of $100 which they cannot settle, after which the church makes a decision that his brother rightfully owes him the $100 and that he shall pay him that amount,—if that brother should refuse to pay him, he would immediately complain against him to the church, for not hearing the church; yet, indeed, such a case would be of minor importance, when compared with the refusal to try to fulfill his office, which was imposed upon him by also a majority of the same church.

Therefore, we would advise, as a safe course, do what you can, no matter how little that may appear to you or to others, Jesus Christ will crown you.

Hagerstown, Ind.

DENMARK FROM 1840 TO 1890.

BY G. HOPE.

IN 1840 the country was settled mainly in small villages; now nearly all have built where their main body of land lies. Then the houses were mainly built of lumber, filled out in the open spaces with clay. Now the fine, pressed bricks take the place of the latter and the straw roof passes away for tile, slate and shingles.

Then the country was full of swamps where peat was dug and watery holes left,—now these swamps are transformed into regularly irrigated, fruitful meadows. The barren waste land is transformed into farm land, or planted to pine or other forest trees. Even the quicksand hills, on the shores of the North Sea, are transformed into promising pineries, and the farmers, even in North Jutland, surround their houses with beautiful groves and orchards, where before was a treeless plain, as far as the eye could see the landscape. Even the battle with the North Sea is carried on with success, to stop its continual washing and undermining the land, and transforming it into ocean bottom and flying quicksand hills. Stone barriers of an expensive nature are built in the sea to keep off the destroying current, and a peculiar grass is planted every year, to stop the ever-drifting quicksand from moving in over the fruitful land.

In 1840 there were in the little kingdom 1,296,000 inhabitants. In 1890 they had increased 889,000, not counting the emigration, which has been considerable.

The capital, Copenhagen, with its suburbs, had, in 1840, 125,368 inhabitants; in 1890 it had 375,251; that is in fifty years it increased threefold.

Aarhus has grown from 7,073 to 33,308, Odense from 9,198 to 30,277. The increase has not only been in the great centers, but Herning, in North Jut-land, which in 1840 had but twenty-one inhabitants, all surrounded by unfruitful waste land, has now 3,343 inhabitants and is surrounded by farm lands and great forests and so all along the railroad the stations are centers for promising and thrifty villages.

The cities have, in those fifty years, had a growth from 262,000 to 633,000 inhabitants or 400,000 more than formerly. The farm population has grown with an addition of 500,000; or three persons for every two persons in 1840,—an increase in the population of 20,000 yearly, not counting emigration.

Denmark contains 693 square miles and had, in 1801, 1,348 persons on a square mile; in 1890 it supported 3,153 to the square mile. The Danish mile is four times as large as an English mile.

The last ten years have been very depressing for the farmer. Prices are continually going down; there are difficulties to get hired help; on account of emigration, and the change from grain raising to dairy and fattening cattle and hogs; but the Danish farmer knows how to economize, if need compel. He employs married hands in the place of unmarried, that seek foreign countries.

The farmer gets about ten cents per pound of pork sold to packing companies. Beef sells for about 15 cents per pound; fatted calves, 15 cents per pound; sheep, 14 cents per pound; salted pork, 14 cents per pound; fresh pork, 12 to 14 cents per pound; geese, 15 cents per pound; ducks, 54 cents a piece; chickens, 25 cents a piece; eggs, 35 cents for 20; butter, 40 to 50 cents per pound; rye bread, unbolted, 18 cents for 8 pounds; potatoes, 75 cents per bushel.

Copenhagen is now the only fortified place in Denmark. The fortifications are a network of strong, modern forts. A deep ditch and a high, earthen wall surround the whole city, in half a circle, from ocean to ocean, situated several miles outside of the city limits, and built by the Government contrary to law and against the will of the majority of the people. The harbor is enlarged to about double its size, and will now have a free trade department for all nations. The new harbor also presents strong fortifications on the seaside. The entrance affords only a small opening for vessels to pass through, and is guarded by strong forts and formidable cannons. For several miles out at sea there is but one channel to enter into the harbor, or approach the city, and on that very point there is now building a strong fort, constructed by sinking large blocks of cement until this foundation rises above the surface of the water. By this fortification any vessel will have to pass so closely that you can reach it with a long pole.

Thus little Denmark works on, and perhaps this sketch will be of some interest to our friends who keep on asking for letters, wondering why I do not write for the paper. I have had no time, before to-day, which I dedicate to you.

MISSION WORK

For my part is now closed in Sweden and Copenhagen. All that remains is to bid them good-bye, there and in Malmo. I start for America, if the Lord will, in January, '92. Since our dear brother, D. L. Miller, and wife, left, I have held fifty-one meetings in Sweden and ten in Copenhagen, and have not had proper rest or regular living, since I left home, July 25, 1891.

In Sweden the work seems going forward. There are several requests made for baptism at several places, as soon as some hindrances and obstacles are removed. At several places our Baptist friends are earnestly counting the cost, and investigating their standing. One Baptist church in South Sweden has changed entirely to our practice in every point except baptism. We (Bro. Olsson and I), spent a night with them, in talking and exchanging of ideas. We told them what we knew of trine immersion and our own life, which was listened to with interest, without a single objection. It was indeed one of the most loving receptions I ever had. May God bless them to go on in the good work.

Many express uncertainty in their standing and admit that we do as the Bible reads. Hence the preachers' alarm and hostility to us, and especially to me, whom they hate as the first cause of the planting of the church there, and of the trouble they now have on hand. In Malmo and Linhamn some disowned members said they would return again, and they showed us much kindness.

In Copenhagen four or five have returned to the fold and promise to work for peace. More would like to come, but could not yet get down low enough to make needed confession of their faults, though the church gladly did her part, and on a few points retraced her steps to the line of the Brotherhood, where they, not knowing better, had gone a little too far.

Copenhagen, like all large cities, is a hard place, but the church there has now, in Bro. Hanson, a quiet, loving, patient brother, whom, all the members admit, is a good, consistent man, and if they all will work with him, and with one another, and not against each other, better days may dawn for that place yet. On the whole I can but recommend the work and the cause to our Brotherhood for earnest prayer and good care, as well as needed assistance for the future.

The new tract, by Bro. D. L. Miller, is doing good work and is liked by all. The Danish Brethren long to have it printed, which, so far, has not been done, as they have not heard from the Tract Committee. The churches have fond hopes that Bro. D. L. Miller will return, if he can not go on to Palestine, which, we hope, he may still do for the good of all.

I stop here a few days, doing business to have the Danish meeting-house transferred to the General Brotherhood. From here I go North to Eld. Eskildsen, and will work in his district till about New Year. I do not consider it prudent to stay longer, as the churches will then have got needed assistance, some comfort, and able to go on without me. I would like to visit a few places east, along the B. & O. R. R., and see some of those of like precious faith, and be home in time for spring work, if the Lord will.

Returning home I have promised to stop at Bro. Isaac Culp's, Grater's Ford, Pa., in order to see those who so tenderly nursed my dear companion in her sickness, when we started to Denmark the first time. Letters may reach me there from the middle to the latter part of January.

This may be my last letter for this year. Thanks to any and all for their prayers, their letters, and their kindness to me and family. May God bless you with a New Year of grace, peace, joy and mercy, and with fervent love to each other, and, above all, with thankful hearts to God, our Heavenly Father, CHRISTIAN HOPE.

Aalborg, Nov. 23, 1891.

SHOULD A BROTHER BE EXCUSED FROM THE MINISTRY UPON HIS OWN REQUEST?

Whenever it is proven beyond the possibility of a doubt that the church made a mistake in calling a brother to the ministry, the known fact that such mistake was made would already annul such action. But where shall we go for such positive proof? There is none in reach. Therefore, when a brother is called by the church as a minister, there is none able to say, knowingly, that God did not co-operate in the church's action. If, then, the church would reverse its own action, without such proof, the last action would be guess work and if the first action was not a mistake, the last would be. Therefore, in consideration of such circumstances,

IS IT RIGHT FOR A BROTHER TO ASK THE CHURCH TO RELIEVE HIM,

and at the same time say that he is not fit for the place and that, if the church does not relieve him, he will not serve any way?

It is not right because he is not obedient to the church, which is violating one of the conditions by which he was admitted into the church, i. e., he is not willing to hear the church. He is really setting up his own, private judgment against the judgment of the church without any authority to do so, in a matter in which the church acted with all the authority that there is.

Again, it is not right because it is a violation of Matt. 7: 12, "All things whatsoever ye would that men should do to you, do ye even so to them." He would not be willing to allow any other brother such liberty on any other matter as he is using in this. For example: Suppose there is a difference between him and his brother of $100 which they cannot settle, after which the church makes a decision that his brother rightfully owes him the $100 and that he shall pay him that amount,—if that brother should refuse to pay him, he would immediately complain against him to the church, for not hearing the church; yet, indeed, such a case would be of minor importance, when compared with the refusal to try to fulfill his office, which was imposed upon him by also a majority of the same church.

Therefore, we would advise, as a safe course, do what you can, no matter how little that may appear to you or to others, Jesus Christ will crown you.

Hagerstown, Ind.

DENMARK FROM 1840 TO 1890.

BY C. HOPE.

In 1840 the country was settled mainly in small villages; now nearly all have built where their main body of land lies. Then the houses were mainly built of lumber, filled out in the open spaces with clay. Now the fine, pressed bricks take the place of the latter and the straw roof passes away for tile, slate and shingles.

Then the country was full of swamps where peat was dug and watery holes left,—now those swamps are transformed into regularly irrigated, fruitful meadows. The barren waste land is transformed into farm land, or planted to pine or other forest trees. Even the quicksand hills, on the shores of the North Sea, are transformed into promising pineries, and the farmers, even in North Jutland, surround their houses with beautiful groves and orchards, where before was a treeless plain, as far as the eye could see the landscape. Even the battle with the North Sea is carried on with success, to stop its continual washing and undermining the land, and transforming it into ocean bottom and flying quicksand hills. Stone barriers of an expensive nature are built in the sea to keep off the destroying current, and a peculiar grass is planted every year, to stop the ever-drifting quicksand from moving in over the fruitful land.

In 1840 there were in the little kingdom 1,296,000 inhabitants. In 1890 they had increased 889,000, not counting the emigration, which has been considerable.

The capital, Copenhagen, with its suburbs, had, in 1840, 125,268 inhabitants; in 1890 it had 375,251; that is in fifty years it increased threefold.

Aarhus has grown from 7,078 to 33,308, Odense from 9,198 to 30,277. The increase has not only been in the great centers, but Herning, in North Jut-land, which in 1840 had but twenty-one inhabitants, all surrounded by unfruitful waste land, has now 3,343 inhabitants and is surrounded by farm lands and great forests and so all along the railroad the stations are centers for promising and thrifty villages.

The cities have, in those fifty years, had a growth from 263,000 to 633,000 inhabitants or 400,000 more than formerly. The farm population has grown with an addition of 500,000; or three persons for every two persons in 1840,—an increase in the population of 20,000 yearly, not counting emigration.

Denmark contains 693 square miles and had, in 1801, 1,348 persons on a square mile; in 1890 it supported 3,153 to the square mile. The Danish mile is four times as large as an English mile.

The last ten years have been very depressing for the farmer. Prices are continually going down; there are difficulties to get hired help, on account of emigration, and the change from grain raising to dairy and fattening cattle and hogs; but the Danish farmer knows how to economize, if need compel. He employs married hands in the place of unmarried, that seek foreign countries.

The farmer gets about ten cents per pound of pork sold to packing companies. Beef sells for 15 cents per pound; fatted calves, 15 cents per pound; sheep, 14 cents per pound; salted pork, 14 cents per pound; fresh pork, 12 to 14 cents per pound; geese, 15 cents per pound; ducks, 54 cents a piece; chickens, 25 cents a piece; eggs, 35 cents for 20; butter, 40 to 50 cents per pound; rye bread, unbolted, 18 cents for 8 pounds; potatoes, 75 cents per bushel.

Copenhagen is now the only fortified place in Denmark. The fortifications are a network of strong, modern forts. A deep ditch and a high, earthen wall surround the whole city, in half a circle, from ocean to ocean, situated several miles outside of the city limits, and built by the Government contrary to law and against the will of the majority of the people. The harbor is enlarged to about double its size, and will now have a free trade department for all nations. The new harbor also presents strong fortifications on the seaside. The entrance affords only a small opening for vessels to pass through, and is guarded by strong forts and formidable cannons. For several miles out at sea there is but one channel to enter into the harbor, or approach the city, and on that very point there is now building a strong fort, constructed by sinking large blocks of cement until this foundation rises above the surface of the water. By this fortification any vessel will have to pass so closely that you can reach it with a long pole.

Thus little Denmark works on, and perhaps this sketch will be of some interest to our friends who keep on asking for letters, wondering why I do not write for the paper. I have had no time, before to-day, which I dedicate to you.

MISSION WORK

For my part is now closed in Sweden and Copenhagen. All that remains is to bid them good-bye, there and in Malmo. I start for America, if the Lord will, in January, '92. Since our dear brother, D. L. Miller, and wife, left, I have held fifty-one meetings in Sweden and ten in Copenhagen, and have not had proper rest or regular living, since I left home, July 25, 1891.

In Sweden the work seems going forward. There are several requests made for baptism at several places, as soon as some hindrances and obstacles are removed. At several places our Baptist friends are earnestly counting the cost, and investigating their standing. One Baptist church in South Sweden has changed entirely to our practice in every point except baptism. We (Bro. Olsson and I), spent a night with them, in talking and exchanging of ideas. We told them what we knew of trine immersion and our own life, which was listened to with interest, without a single objection. It was indeed one of the most loving receptions I ever had. May God bless them to go on in the good work.

Many express uncertainty in their standing and admit that we do as the Bible reads. Hence the preachers' alarm and hostility to us, and especially to me, whom they hate as the first cause of the planting of the church there, and of the trouble they now have on hand. In Malmo and Linhamn some disowned members said they would return again, and they showed us much kindness.

In Copenhagen four or five have returned to the fold and promise to work for peace. More would like to come, but could not yet get down low enough to make needed confession of their faults, though the church gladly did her part, and on a few points retraced her steps to the line of the Brotherhood, where they, not knowing better, had gone a little too far.

Copenhagen, like all large cities, is a hard place, but the church there has now, in Bro. Hanson, a quiet, loving, patient brother, whom, all the members admit, is a good, consistent man, and if they all will work with him, and with one another, and not against each other, better days may dawn for that place yet. On the whole I can but recommend the work and the cause to our Brotherhood for earnest prayer and good care, as well as needed assistance for the future.

The new tract, by Bro. D. L. Miller, is doing good work and is liked by all. The Swedish Brethren long to have it printed, which, so far, has not been done, as they have not heard from the Tract Committee. The churches have food hopes that Bro. D. L. Miller will return, if he can not go on to Palestine, which, we hope, he may still do for the good of all.

I stop here a few days, doing business to have the Danish meeting-houses transferred to the General Brotherhood. From here I go North to Eld. Eskildsen, and will work in his district till about New Year. I do not consider it prudent to stay longer, as the churches will then have got needed assistance, some comfort, and able to go on without me. I would like to visit a few places east, along the B. & O. R. R., and see some of those of like precious faith, and be home in time for spring work, if the Lord will.

Returning home I have promised to stop at Bro. Isaac Culp's, Grater's Ford, Pa., in order to see those who so tenderly nursed my dear companion in her sickness, when we started to Denmark the first time. Letters may reach me there from the middle to the later part of January.

This may be my last letter for this year. Thanks to any and all for their prayers, their letters, and their kindness to me and family. May God bless you with a New Year of grace, peace, joy and mercy, and with fervent love to each other, and, above all, with thankful hearts to God, our Heavenly Father, CHRISTIAN HOPE.

Aalborg, Nov. 22, 1891.

THE *Christian Leader* says the best way to reform a bad boy is to begin with his grandmother. There is much truth in this, and it will be well for all of those who have the good of the race at heart to give it due consideration. This nation is in need of good mothers. The mothers of our land are now moulding the future condition of generations to come. Mothers are also moulding the church for the future. The fathers are helping, but the greater influence is on the side of the mothers. Like mothers, like church, may prove as true as ," Like priest, like people."

IT is strange how thoughtless intelligent men may become, respecting their own personal interest. It is said that Geo. W. Allen, better known as the " Land Bill " Allen, spent $60,000 in an attempt to secure one hundred and sixty acres of land for each early settler in Ohio, and at the age of eighty-three was driven to the poor-house, having been so intent on providing for others that he neglected to make any provisions for himself. The minister of the Gospel is exposed to the same danger, for in his zeal to save others he may so neglect his own personal piety as to make shipwreck of his own faith and thereby be a cast-away.

A WRITER truthfully remarks that a large per cent of the converts at protracted meetings are children, and there are not so many men and women of mature years as was the case a generation ago. The facts as stated cannot be denied, but there must be some reason for it worthy of consideration. Sunday-schools have been the means of leading many children to embrace religion even without protracted meetings, and prepared others for the influence of sensational preaching, of which we have an unusual amount of late years. In fact, most of the preaching done at protracted meetings is of the sensational character, and of course reaches the young more than those of mature years. We need more solid, doctrinal preaching, in order to reach men and women of thought, and it is really astonishing how little sound doctrinal preaching is heard in these days, especially in fashionable churches. We have no reason for discouraging the ingathering of the young, wishing to encourage it as much as possible, but we certainly ought not to neglect those of mature years. Then, while we are gathering the young into the flock, special efforts should be made to properly care for them. This, we fear, is being greatly neglected in some localities. The subject deserves our prayerful consideration.

THE ANCIENT LANDMARKS.

WITH this issue we enter upon the work of another year. The past is forever gone, and it is wholly to the future that we must now look for all of our opportunities. As a church we have a grand work before us, and should enter upon it with a deep sense of our responsibilities.

Our field is greatly enlarging and the work is becoming more diversified as well as more perplexing. This is an age requiring skill in the handling of the Word as well as great faithfulness, for it is also an age of much religious deception. Hence we think it wise to pause and consider the ancient landmarks set by our fathers. Prov. 22: 28. A well-maintained landmark insures peace and justice respecting boundary lines. All civilized nations have their lands carefully marked, in order that the owners of the soil may know their limits, and for this purpose the ancient, or original, lines and corners should be duly respected.

There are also spiritual landmarks that deserve our most serious consideration, and unless we keep them fresh in our minds, all traces of them may eventually be lost. A very important line at this time is the one existing between the church and the world, the line that marks the separation between the kingdom of this world and the kingdom of Christ. It was here that our fathers set certain ancient marks that are likely to be removed unless great care is taken to preserve them. These ancient landmarks were not the inventions of our fathers, but were found by them in the Scriptures. When they inaugurated their reformatory movement in Germany, they set up these landmarks for the guidance of their own as well as for future generations, and all the churches in America that have duly respected them have certainly made their work a success. It is indeed encouraging to go into a large congregation where the landmarks, set by our fathers, have been well preserved. It enables both the church and the world to see where one kingdom begins and the other ends. But it is certainly lamentable to see whole congregations entirely ignoring these landmarks, so much so, that no one can tell the church from the world. If our intention is to be just like the world, what is the use of having any marks at all! Our fathers searched the Scriptures for the old, apostolic landmarks, and, after finding them, set them up in their faith and practice, and then transmitted them to us, and we may now, appropriately as well as earnestly, exhort our Brethren not to remove the ancient landmarks which were set by our fathers.

Among the marks set up by them we may name honesty, purity, truthfulness, prayerfulness, plainness, meekness, brotherly love, non-resistance, abstaining from politics, places of amusement and many other things of the same character. Non-conformity to the world in dress and customs was a conspicuous mark with them and served a very important part in their reformatory movement. But we are sorry to say that this mark is becoming obliterated in some parts of our beloved Zion. With our fathers the family altar was the cornerstone of every home, and no one thought of serving God without daily offering his gift thereon.

Our fathers restored the ancient form of Christian baptism, as well as the proper observances of feet-washing, the Lord's Supper and the Communion. They also brought to light the salutation of the holy kiss, and other duties, which a semi-worldly Christianity had permitted to pass entirely out of use. In this manner they set up the ancient landmarks that had been neglected for centuries.

In earnest support of these old landmarks the MESSENGER enters upon the work of another year, trusting that in our efforts we may have the aid as well as the prayers and sympathies of the entire Brotherhood. Attempts are being made to remove many of these landmarks and it becomes us as a people to see that they are fully respected on every hand. Popular Christianity has removed so many of the landmarks set by the apostles that it is now extremely difficult to locate the boundary lines. Our people certainly do not desire to follow the popular course in this respect, but, on the other hand, these ancient boundary lines must be distinctly pointed out and maintained in every department of our church work, and the Lord being our helper we hope to do something in this direction the present year, hence crave an interest in the prayers and sympathies of all those who want to see the apostolic order of things prevail.

J. H. M.

[Copyrighted.]

EDITORIAL WANDERINGS IN THE OLD WORLD.

BY D. L. MILLER.

Number Fourteen.

IN our last letter we gave some illustrations, taken from the ancient records of Nineveh, showing a wonderful agreement with the Bible. Indeed the similarity in the records is remarkable, and so strongly do they verify the Bible and corroborate its statements, that no one who is at all acquainted with the facts, in the case, will, for a moment, doubt the truth of the Book. Some there are, who will refuse to investigate, and continue to doubt, but the fair-minded man will examine to see whether these things are true. Those who refuse to do this, show a hardness of heart and a deep-seated prejudice against the truth that always comes to those who turn away from its influence.

As an illustration of how some men investigate, and then criticise the Bible, the following incident is given. A few days ago we met a party who had been to Egypt and Palestine, and, being deeply interested in those countries, we conversed with one of them who seemed to be a leader. We found that they had made a flying trip through Europe, gone to Egypt and the Holy Land, and had taken less than two months for the entire tour. They had gone to Jaffa, rode over to Jerusalem, and then to, the Valley of the Jordan, spent one night there, and then back to Jerusalem and to Jaffa, where they took a steamer for Europe. They had spent four days in riding across the country in one of the most interesting lands in the world. As a result, they had but a very limited and superficial knowledge of the places they visited. We should have thought nothing more of the talk, had it not been that we afterwards overheard the leader telling some one else of their trip to the Holy Land, and criticising the Bible. During the talk the question was asked, "Did you see Jacob's well?" "Oh yes," was the reply; "we had a place pointed out as the well of Jacob, but there is nothing authentic about it." Now the fact is, the man had not been within nearly 100 miles of Shechem and Jacob's well, and we concluded that he had a very confused idea of what he did see, or else he willfully misrepresented the facts, to sneer as he did at the Bible. This man will return to America and say that he has visited Palestine, and that the Bible is not true, and those who hear him will credit his statements. The fact is, there is no place in the world better authenticated than is Jacob's well. We have direct historical testimony, covering a period of over fifteen hundred years, as to its location, and it agrees so exactly with the account of it in the Gospel, that there cannot be the slightest doubt as to the place, and this fact is recognized by all travelers and scholars, but our modern investigator, after spending four days in searching the country, declares that it is not authentic. Could self-assurance and misrepresentation be carried farther than this?

Our readers will pardon this digression, but it illustrates so clearly the disposition found in a class of unbelievers, to shut their eyes to the truth, that we give it as it occurred.

We now return to the records, and give one that throws an important side-light upon a statement made in the Bible. After recording the invasion of Judea, by the king of Assyria, he is dis-

sermon on the subject "How to Read and Study God's Word," which was very instructive to all, especially to young ministers. He closed his sermon by calling the attention of the members to the duty they owe to their ministers. This we feel, was very appropriate on the present occasion. Nov. 29 our meetings closed and Bro. Deeter went to other fields.   J. A. Weaver.

A Word to the Solicitors of the Old Folks' Home, Mexico, Ind.

We trust you are all interested in the welfare of the Home, and that you will take pains to collect our interest promptly, for which favor we will be grateful. All solicitors who have not received blank receipts, will please address us at once, as we want the solicitors to give a receipt to every one that pays.

We do not want our solicitors to slight any who are well-wishers of the Home, even if they have not given notes. Take as many new notes as you can; we would like to increase our Endowment.

Try to collect your money by the first of the year, and send the same to Bro. Levi Miller, Treasurer of the Home and he will receipt promptly.   F. Fisher.

From the Blue Creek Church, Ohio.

Nov. 8 I attended the dedicatory services of the new house, built by the Blue Creek church, Ohio. The rainy morning hindered many from coming, but quite a large congregation gathered, and manifested much interest in the services. At this meeting I had the pleasure of meeting Eld. Geo. Worst, of Ashland County, Ohio, and Eld. S. Neher, of Wells County, Ind. The latter has the care of the Blue Creek church. I also met Bro. Beigle, of the Pleasant Dale church, Ind. The members at Blue Creek have built a very good house and deserve much credit for the great effort and sacrifice necessary to obtain the house. Their Communion was Nov. 10, and was an excellent meeting. I remained with those members for ten days. Much of the time it rained; so that the meeting could not be as well attended as would have been the case with more favorable weather and roads. Bro. Stump, of the Palestine church, Ohio, came Nov. 10, and remained till the close of the meeting, and assisted in the preaching.

This church is located on the eastern boundary of the Middle District of Indiana and has passed through some severe trials. There are several points that I visited on the eastern boundary of this State District. They are isolated from the main body of the church, and, as they are newly-organized churches, they need encouragement. Cannot some of our faithful elders and ministers of Indiana pay them a visit this winter? I will name a few of those churches: Bear Creek, Blue Creek, Pleasant Dale. In all these churches you will find a hearty welcome and a large field for preaching the Gospel to an interested people. We left for our home Nov. 17, in order to reach the Ministerial Meeting Nov. 20, at Pittsburgh, Ohio. It was a glorious meeting.   Silas Gilbert.
Lightsville, Ohio.

On the Way.

On Sunday evening, Nov. 29, I commenced a series of meetings at the Forest Grove church, in the Rock Run District, Elkhart Co., Ind. In this section of country there are only a few members living, but there are plenty of Omish, Mennonites and Lutherans.

Our meetings lasted two weeks, with a growing interest. I never held a meeting where all denominations attended so regularly. Three-made

---

the good confession and were baptized. There were four other applicants for baptism, but some of them were sick with La Grippe and preferred waiting until they got better. Many more expressed themselves willing to go with us, but were waiting for the consent of their companions.

This place has been somewhat neglected, by too many disappointments, etc. I do not know of any other way to break down a meeting faster than to disappoint congregations, and permit a little rain to keep the preacher at home. Promptness, on the part of the minister, will make others prompt.   J. H. Miller.
Goshen, Ind., Nov. 13.

From Boon River Church, Iowa.

It has been a long time since our elder, Wm. Ikenberry, has been with us, so that we appreciated his presence all the more during his late visit to us. We felt greatly built up by his preaching. Bro. Harvey Eikenberry was also with us, and preached one week, beginning Nov. 14. At the close of his meeting, Bro. Harvey was met by Bro. O. J. Beaver, from Chickasaw, Iowa. These two brethren went from here to Lyons County, Iowa, to hold some meetings. On their return home, Bro. Beaver stopped off with us, and preached a few soul-cheering sermons. These two brethren are young in the ministry, but full of zeal and energy for the good cause. Nov. 14 the members of the Boon River church met in council. The meeting passed off very pleasantly. Among the business before the meeting was a desire to learn, whether we could build a meeting-house. We decided in favor of building. We are now organized, and feel that we have much need of a church-house. Bro. George Aschenbrenner and Elias Long were chosen as solicitors for the church work.   Daniel Aschenbrenner.
Stilson, Iowa, Dec. 13.

Wayside Notes.

In my last report I was with the Brethren in the Stony Creek church. We had a very pleasant meeting. The inclement weather militated somewhat against our meeting. We closed on the evening of Dec. 7. Two were baptized, and one reclaimed. From this place, on the morning of Dec. 8, in company with Bro. Dan Smeltzer, and wife, I went to the Arcadia church, to attend the Brethren's Ministerial Meeting of the Southern District of Indiana. It was the first meeting of the kind, ever held in the District, and very well attended. Everything passed off pleasantly. We had a three days' session, and I heard several express themselves as being well pleased, and that these were the most profitable three days they had ever spent. I hope these meetings may grow in favor, and bring about more of a union among us. The meetings closed in the afternoon of the 10th, at 2 P. M. I remained until Dec. 12. Bro. R. R. Goshorn preached on the evening of the 10th, on the "Design of Baptism," which was delivered in a very logical way. There were two baptized.

On the 12th inst., I came to the Middle Fork church, Clinton Co., where I am trying to hold up the banner of King Immanuel. May the labors of God's servants be blessed!

Last evening, after the close of the services, a report of a revolver was heard, and the groans of a young man soon told the sad tale that some one was shot. On examination it was found that a young man was shot in the face. How seriously he was hurt we are not able to say, as he was taken away by his friends. The father of the son that did the shooting is opposed to Sunday-schools, and denounces them in a most radical manner. I am of the opinion that a boy, brought

---

up in the Sunday-school, will not carry such weapons.

We were forcibly impressed with the Scripture, found in the book of Job: "When the sons of God came to present themselves before the Lord and Satan came also among them." So, while the servants of the Lord are at work, the adversary is lurking around as a roaring lion, seeking whom he may devour. May we buckle on the armor of our warfare, and fight more valiantly the battle of the Lord. Brethren, train up your child in the way he should go, and we have the assurance that "he will not depart from it." Our children should go to church and Sunday-school, learn to reverence and respect the people of God, and to read God's Word. This is the way they should go, and we, as their parents, are to lead them into that way. May the Lord help us to do our duty towards our children and our God!
     Geo. L. Studebaker.
Shideler, Ind., Dec. 14.

From Cartersville, Va.

Our series of meetings, conducted by Bro. Bowser, closed last night. On account of the illness of mother and myself, we could not attend. He expects to leave here Dec. 17, if nothing prevents. We are, indeed, very sorry to give him up, for he gave good satisfaction here in every respect, and awakened a great interest. The prospects seem brighter than ever for the cause to prosper. I believe the Lord sent him among us.

I trust the good Lord will send some one to us while the fire is kindled, that the flame may not die out.

There are only a few of us in number, and we cannot work by ourselves. The Brethren have kindly sent me a lot of the missionary number of the Gospel Messenger, which I expect to distribute, trusting that some good may be done through them. Pray for us, and if any one can send us a shepherd, we will be made quite happy.
     Florida E. Etter.
Dec. 13.

From Holyoke, Colorado.

We are somewhat isolated here, in the Far West, and your weekly visit to us is looked for anxiously, as it is full of good news from far distant States, telling of the good meetings the dear brethren are having, and what good things the Lord is doing for them. Our Communion meeting was held Nov. 14 and 15. The attendance was small, as the weather was somewhat stormy. There were only seven,—three brethren and four sisters,—around the table of the Lord, but we had a soul-refreshing little meeting. Our dear young brother, A. C. Snowberger, officiated at our meeting and many were the words of comfort and encouragement he gave us. How sorry we feel that he cannot be with us oftener, but his field of labor now is in Southern Colorado, as he has moved to the San Luis Valley, near Monte Vista. Our elder, John S. Snowberger, is called away quite often, to help in other parts of this great West, to preach to the scattered sheep. I do not think there is an elder, west of the Missouri River, that has made more of a sacrifice for the cause or that has worked as hard and exposed himself so much in all kinds of weather.   D. A. Fickel.

From Covina, Cal.

The writer of this has now spent several days in the land of sunshine and oranges. But these are not all the good things to be found here. There are plenty of lemons, too, so that if you wish to enjoy a glass of lemonade and do not get it, you can blame yourself for it. Well, this is not

sermon on the subject "How to Read and Study God's Word," which was very instructive to all, especially to young ministers. He closed his sermon by calling the attention of the members to the duty they owe to their ministers. This we feel, was very appropriate on the present occasion. Nov. 29 our meetings closed and Bro. Deeter went to other fields.　　　　　J. A. Weaver.

A Word to the Solicitors of the Old Folks' Home, Mexico, Ind.

We trust you are all interested in the welfare of the Home, and that you will take pains to collect our interest promptly, for which favor we will be grateful. All solicitors who have not received blank receipts, will please address us at once, as we want the solicitors to give a receipt to every one that pays.

We do not want our solicitors to slight any who are well-wishers of the Home, even if they have not given notes. Take as many new notes as you can; we would like to increase our Endowment.

Try to collect your money by the first of the year, and send the same to Bro. Levi Miller, Treasurer of the Home and he will receipt promptly.　　　　　F. Fisher.

From the Blue Creek Church, Ohio.

Nov. 8 I attended the dedicatory services of the new house, built by the Blue Creek church, Ohio. The rainy morning hindered many from coming, but quite a large congregation gathered, and manifested much interest in the services. At this meeting I had the pleasure of meeting Eld. Geo. Worst, of Ashland County, Ohio, and Eld. S. Noher, of Wells County, Ind. The latter has the care of the Blue Creek church. I also met Bro. Beigle, of the Pleasant Dale church, Ind. The members at Blue Creek have built a very good house and deserve much credit for the great effort and sacrifice necessary to obtain the house. Their Communion was Nov. 10, and was an excellent meeting. I remained with those members for ten days. Much of the time it rained; so that the meeting could not be as well attended as would have been the case with more favorable weather and roads. Bro. Stump, of the Palestine church, Ohio, came Nov. 10, and remained till the close of the meeting, and assisted in the preaching.

This church is located on the eastern boundary of the Middle District of Indiana and has passed through some severe trials. There are several points that I visited on the eastern boundary of this State District. They are isolated from the main body of the church, and, as they are newly-organized churches, they need encouragement. Cannot some of our faithful elders and ministers of Indiana pay them a visit this winter? I will name a few of those churches: Bear Creek, Blue Creek, Pleasant Dale. In all these churches you will find a hearty welcome and a large field for preaching the Gospel to an interested people. We left for our home Nov. 17, in order to reach the Ministerial Meeting Nov. 20, at Pittsburgh, Ohio. It was a glorious meeting.　　Silas Gilbert.

Lightsville, Ohio.

On the Way.

On Sunday evening, Nov. 29, I commenced a series of meetings at the Forest Grove church, in the Rock Run District, Elkhart Co., Ind. In this section of country there are only a few members living, but there are plenty of Omish, Mennonites and Lutherans.

Our meetings lasted two weeks, with a growing interest. I never held a meeting where all denominations attended so regularly. Three made the good confession and were baptized. There were four other applicants for baptism, but some of them were sick with *La Grippe* and preferred waiting until they got better. Many more expressed themselves willing to go with us, but were waiting for the consent of their companions.

This place has been somewhat neglected, by too many disappointments, etc. I do not know of any other way to break down a meeting faster than to disappoint congregations, and permit a little rain to keep the preacher at home. Promptness, on the part of the minister, will make others prompt.　　　　　J. H. Miller.

Goshen, Ind., Nov. 13.

From Boon River Church, Iowa.

It has been a long time since our elder, Wm. Ikenberry, has been with us, so that we appreciated his presence all the more during his late visit to us. We felt greatly built up by his preaching. Bro. Harvey Eikenberry was also with us, and preached one week, beginning Nov. 14. At the close of his meeting, Bro. Harvey was met by Bro. O. J. Beaver, from Chickasaw, Iowa. These two brethren went from here to Lyons County, Iowa, to hold some meetings. On their return home, Bro. Beaver stopped off with us, and preached a few soul-cheering sermons. These two brethren are young in the ministry, but full of zeal and energy for the good cause. Nov. 14 the members of the Boon River church met in council. The meeting passed off very pleasantly. Among the business before the meeting was a desire to learn, whether we could build a meeting-house. We decided in favor of building. We are now organized, and feel that we have much need of a church-house. Bro. George Aschenbrenner and Elias Long were chosen as solicitors for the church work.　　Daniel Aschenbrenner.

Shison, Iowa, Dec. 13.

Wayside Notes.

In my last report I was with the Brethren in the Stony Creek church. We had a very pleasant meeting. The inclement weather militated somewhat against our meeting. We closed on the evening of Dec. 7. Two were baptized, and one reclaimed. From this place, on the morning of Dec. 8, in company with Bro. Dan Smeltzer, and wife, I went to the Arcadis church, to attend the Brethren's Ministerial Meeting of the Southern District of Indiana. It was the first meeting of the kind, ever held in the District, and very well attended. Everything passed off pleasantly. We had a three days' session, and I heard several express themselves as being well pleased, and that these were the most profitable three days they had ever spent. I hope these meetings may grow in favor, and bring about more of a union among us. The meetings closed in the afternoon of the 10th, at 2 P. M. I remained until Dec. 12. Bro. R. R. Goshorn preached on the evening of the 10th, on the "Design of Baptism," which was delivered in a very logical way. There were two baptized.

On the 12th inst., I came to the Middle Fork church, Clinton Co., where I am trying to hold up the banner of King Immanuel. May the labors of God's servants be blessed!

Last evening, after the close of the services, a report of a revolver was heard, and the groans of a young man soon told the sad tale that some one was shot. On examination it was found that a young man was shot in the face. How seriously he was hurt we are not able to say, as he was taken away by his friends. The father of the son that did the shooting is opposed to Sunday-schools, and denounces them in a most radical manner. I am of the opinion that a boy, brought up in the Sunday-school, will not carry such weapons.

We were forcibly impressed with the Scripture, found in the book of Job: "When the sons of God came to present themselves before the Lord and Satan came also among them." So, while the servants of the Lord are at work, the adversary is lurking around as a roaring lion, seeking whom he may devour. May we buckle on the armor of our warfare, and fight more valiantly the battle of the Lord. Brethren, train up your child in the way he should go, and we have the assurance that "he will not depart from it." Our children should go to church and Sunday-school, learn to reverence and respect the people of God, and to read God's Word. This is the way they should go, and we, as their parents, are to lead them into that way. May the Lord help us to do our duty towards our children and our God!

　　　　　Geo. L. Studebaker.
Shideler, Ind., Dec. 14.

From Cartersville, Va.

Our series of meetings, conducted by Bro. Bowser, closed last night. On account of the illness of mother and myself, we could not attend. He expects to leave here Dec. 17, if nothing prevents. We are, indeed, very sorry to give him up, for he gave good satisfaction here in every respect, and awakened a great interest. The prospects seem brighter than ever for the cause to prosper. I believe the Lord sent him among us.

I trust the good Lord will send some one to us while the fire is kindled, that the flame may not while the above expires.

There are only a few of us in number, and we cannot work by ourselves. The Brethren have kindly sent me a lot of the missionary number of the Gospel Messenger, which I expect to distribute, trusting that some good may be done through them. Pray for us, and if any one can send us a shepherd, we will be made quite happy.

　　　　　Florida E. Etter.
Dec. 13.

From Holyoke, Colorado.

We are somewhat isolated here, in the Far West, and your weekly visit to us is looked for anxiously, as it is full of good news from far distant States, telling of the good meetings the dear brethren are having, and what good things the Lord is doing for them. Our Communion meeting was held Nov. 14 and 15. The attendance was small, as the weather was somewhat stormy. There were only seven,—three brethren and four sisters,—around the table of the Lord, but we had a soul-refreshing little meeting. Our dear young brother, A. C. Snowberger, officiated at our meeting and many were the words of comfort and encouragement he gave us. How sorry we feel that he cannot be with us oftener, but his field of labor now is in Southern Colorado, as he has moved to the San Luis Valley, near Monte Vista. Our elder, John S. Snowberger, is called away quite often, to help in other parts of this great West, to preach to the scattered sheep. I do not think there is an elder, west of the Missouri River, that has made more of a sacrifice for the cause or that has worked as hard and exposed himself so much in all kinds of weather.　　D. A. Fiorel.

From Covina, Cal.

The writer of this has now spent several days in the land of sunshine and oranges. But these are not all the good things to be found here. There are plenty of lemons, too, so that if you wish to enjoy a glass of lemonade and do not get it, you can blame yourself for it. Well, this is not

Campbell, Mich.—The District Meeting, of the State District of Michigan, will be held with the brethren and sisters of the Black River church, Van Buren Co., Mich., on Saturday, Feb. 20, 1892, at 10 A. M. sharp. Those coming from the north and east will come to Grand Rapids, and from there take the Chicago and West Michigan R. R. to Bangor, where they will be met the day before meeting. A full delegation is desired.—*E. M. Smith, Clerk, Dec. 2.*

North Beatrice, Nebr.—On the evening of Nov. 30, Bro. J. E. Young, of Beatrice, came to us and began a series of meetings, preaching each evening and also each Sunday, closing on the evening of Dec. 20. Bro. Young labored zealously and faithfully. As a result one young man came out on the Lord's side. Bro. Young has promised to hold another series of meetings in the near future. The North Beatrice church is very much in need of ministerial aid.—*J. E. Bryant, Dec. 23.*

Brainerd, Kans.—We are few in number, but are still striving, by the grace of God, to work for the Master. When Bro. Studebaker came down to Butler County to fill his appointments, we felt sad that his health is so bad that he could not preach for us. This was a disappointment to all. We trust his health will improve sufficiently, so that he can fill his next appointment. Bro. Chas. M. Yearout was with us recently and preached eleven sermons for us.—*Laura Thomas, Dec. 22.*

Canton, Ohio.—I am on my way from the Mahoning church, near the town of Columbiana, Ohio, where I have just closed a pleasant series of meetings with six accessions and one applicant. I expect to commence meetings this evening at the Eden church-house, in the Tuscarawas congregation, six miles from Canton. The GOSPEL MESSENGER, with its encouraging words and glad news from the churches, is very helpful to us. May God continue to bless it in saying souls!—*I. D. Parker, Dec. 21.*

Beaver Creek, Md.—Dec. 15 we closed our series of meetings, held in the Long Meadow meeting-house. Our elder, D. F. Stouffer, commenced the meetings Nov. 28. He preached several sermons and was then called to other fields of labor. Bro. Wilbur Stover, of Edgemont, Md., continued the meetings in a very creditable manner, and as an immediate result ten dear souls were received into church-fellowship. The members were strengthened, and impressions made on many which, we hope, will induce them to make the good choice.—*John Rowland.*

Bremen, Ind.—Bro. Daniel Snell, of Sidney, Ind., came to the Yellow River church, Ind. Nov. 28, and commenced a series of meetings, which he continued until Dec. 16, preaching in all twenty-nine very interesting and impressive sermons. Bro. Snell faithfully discharged his duty in holding forth the Word of Life in its purity. We also feel confident that there were lasting impressions made on the minds of the people. As an immediate result of the meetings, one dear young brother was added to our number by baptism.—*Belle Hoffhein.*

Fredonia, Kans.—The Fredonia Brethren's Sunday-school and church was closed Nov. 29, on account of the scarlet fever, raging in town and vicinity. The disease was spreading rapidly when the Board of Health closed all schools, Sunday-schools, churches, and all gatherings for worship or amusement. We were made to rejoice on Dec. 16, when one precious soul made her wants known and was baptized, we trust, to walk in newness of life. May the Lord help us all to walk in that straight and narrow path that leads to life eternal. *Ida Thompson, Dec. 17.*

Purchase Line, Pa.—Dec. 12 the members of the Manor congregation, Pa., met in the Crooked Creek meeting-house in church council. One sister was received by letter. As there was but little business before the meeting, most of the time was occupied by the members in friendly talks on things of church interest. After this we agreed to take up a subscription to help some of the poor, and, as a result, $4.95 was raised for the Home Mission; $6 for the Rockton poor fund; $6.15 for the poor in Denmark, and $145 for the General Mission Work.—*Lizzie Fyock, Cor. Sec.*

Dayton, Ohio.—Bro. J. Bennett Trout, of New Carlisle, Ohio, began a series of meetings in the Bear Creek church, Montgomery Co., Ohio, Dec. 5, continuing until Dec. 16. He preached, in all, eighteen sermons. Owing to an attack of La Grippe, he had to close the meetings sooner than was anticipated, for which we all felt sorry. Bro. Trout is not afraid to preach the Whole Truth, and did so in such a way that both saint and sinner were edified and set to thinking. While there were no immediate accessions, yet there were good impressions made. We hope he will soon be able to resume his work.—*Josiah Eby.*

New Hope Church, Kans.—We are still trying to press forward and labor for the upbuilding of Christ's kingdom here on earth. Bro. Henry Shideler came to us Dec. 5, and preached two very acceptable sermons. Dec. 6 Bro. J. H. Neher came and preached two sermons which were very edifying. He was working in behalf of the Old Folks' Home. Dec. 8 Bro. Samuel Edgecomb came and labored until Sunday evening, Dec. 20. Bro. Edgecomb did us much good while with us, in telling the members of the duties, devolving upon them, as well as presenting to the sinner the way of life. Although there were no additions to the church, yet we feel that some are considering the matter of salvation.—*A. B. Lichtenwalter.*

Veganville, Pa.—We have just closed a series of meetings at the Blue Ball meeting-house in the Conestoga church, Lancaster Co., Pa. This was the third series of meetings for this fall. Dec. 5 brethren John and Samuel Utz, of Union Bridge and New Market, Md., came to us and jointly labored one week, when Bro. John left for Lexington, in the West Conestoga congregation. Bro. Samuel remained until Dec. 19. These brethren labored very earnestly and acceptably, and while there were no additions, yet we have reason to believe that some seed has fallen upon good ground, and in God's own time, it may spring up and bring forth fruit. The church has been encouraged and inspired with new zeal, to labor more earnestly in the cause of Christ. May the Lord reward them for their labors!—*I. W. Taylor, Dec. 21.*

Friedens, Pa.—Bro. Geo. S. Rairigh, of Johnstown, Pa., commenced a series of meetings in the Sipesville church (Quemahoning congregation), Somerset Co., Pa., on Thursday evening, Dec. 10, and continued until Sunday evening, Dec. 20, preaching in all, thirteen sermons. Though there were none added to the church, we felt that the spirit of the Lord was present. May our light burn brighter in the days to come, and may we show greater activity in our spiritual life! Bro. Rairigh is a faithful and earnest worker, and our prayer is that the Lord may grant him health and strength, so that he may yet do much good service for the Master. Bro. Rairigh also preached the funeral sermon (assisted by Bro. R. Hull) for sister Maggie Maust, at the above-named church, on Saturday, Dec. 12. She passed into rest at the early age of twenty-two years, but death had no terrors for her.—*J. D. Baer, Dec. 21, 1891.*

Manor Church, Md.—On the evening of Dec. 5, according to appointment, Bro. Silas Hoover, of Somerset County, Pa., came to us and began a series of meetings. The meetings at first were small, but the roads being nice and the weather fine, caused people to turn out. Then followed good preaching, which caused saint and sinner to awaken to a full sense of the duty they owe to God. The interest grew as the meetings continued. Brethren and sisters were made stronger in the Lord. Seventeen dear souls were made to feel the "love of God" in their day of grace, and joined in with God's children to walk in newness of life. Many more are counting the cost. The meetings closed Dec. 16. May many more such good meetings be enjoyed throughout the Brotherhood!—*Samuel H. Neikirk.*

Burr Oak, Kans.—The quarterly council in the Burr Oak church was held Nov. 28. All the business was transacted in love and union. Our elder, John Hollinger, and also Eld. C. S. Holsinger were with us. The church is in love and union. Eld. C. S. Holsinger commenced a series of meetings on the evening of Nov. 28. He preached at the church for two weeks, and then moved the meetings eight miles north-east to a school-house. Good interest and good order were manifested during our meetings. Bro. Holsinger preached twenty-three discourses in all. He gave us rich food for the soul. At the close of our meetings three precious souls were received by baptism. May they be bright and shining lights in this world! It would be well if our brother could be kept at work in the western field; he could do much good. May the Lord ever go with him, on his journey from place to place!—*Emma Hackenberry.*

Rome, Ohio.—Thanksgiving services were held in the Oak Grove church at 10:30 in the forenoon. We had short, but very interesting, addresses by all the ministers present. In the evening Bro. Weidman conducted Thanksgiving services in the Pleasant Grove church. At the close of these meetings contributions were received for the General Mission Work. Our series of meetings began at the Pleasant Grove church, Dec. 5. Bro. J. M. Mohler, of Pennsylvania, is with us, to present the *Gospel plan of salvation* to all who will come to hear him. If the Lord wills, we expect to continue our meetings at this point a week or ten days. Then we will commence meetings at the Oak Grove church, and continue as long as Bro. Mohler can remain with us. We ask an interest in the prayers of the faithful, for the success of these meetings. Our invitation is Rev. 22: 17. Bro. Dickey is with the Brethren in the Logan church at this writing.—*M. A. Dickey, Aleada, Ohio, Dec. 7.*

Mitchell, Kans.—There is great rejoicing in the Kansas Centre church, Kansas. Dec. 10 Bro. Isaac H. Crist and wife, of Gardner, Kansas, came among us and preached at a school-house, three miles north-east of Mitchell, wielding the Sword of the Spirit skillfully. He preached in all fourteen sermons, and as a result six were received by baptism, and one was reclaimed. One young man said, when his wife made application, that, in being baptized, she would risk her life, as it was dangerous to baptize in the winter time. But two days afterwards, like Saul of Tarsus, he was stricken down and wanted to be received into fellowship the next day. He is now rejoicing in hope of eternal life. The interest of the meeting increased from the beginning to the close. The doctrine of the Brethren church was ably defended and the church builds up. We hope all will be inspired with greater diligence to serve the Master and at last receive the crown.—*Isaac S. Brubaker, Dec. 21.*

Campbell, Mich.—The District Meeting, of the State District of Michigan, will be held with the brethren and sisters of the Black River church, Van Buren Co., Mich., on Saturday, Feb. 20, 1892, at 10 A. M. sharp. Those coming from the north and east will come to Grand Rapids, and from there take the Chicago and West Michigan R. R. to Bangor, where they will be met the day before meeting. A full delegation is desired.—S. M. Smith, Clerk, Dec. 2.

North Beatrice, Nebr.—On the evening of Nov. 30, Bro. J. E. Young, of Beatrice, came to us and began a series of meetings, preaching each evening and also each Sunday, closing on the evening of Dec. 20. Bro. Young labored zealously and faithfully. As a result one young man came out on the Lord's side. Bro. Young has promised to hold another series of meetings in the near future. The North Beatrice church is very much in need of ministerial aid.—J. E. Bryant, Dec. 28.

Brainerd, Kans.—We are few in number, but are still striving, by the grace of God, to work for the Master. When Bro. Studebaker came down to Butler County to fill his appointments, we felt sad that his health is so bad that he could not preach for us. This was a disappointment to all. We trust his health will improve sufficiently, so that he can fill his next appointment. Bro. Chas. M. Yearout was with us recently and preached eleven sermons for us.—Laura Thomas, Dec. 22.

Canton, Ohio.—I am on my way from the Mahoning church, near the town of Columbiana, Ohio, where I have just closed a pleasant series of meetings with six accessions and one applicant. I expect to commence meetings this evening at the Eden church-house, six miles from Canton. The GOSPEL MESSENGER, with its encouraging words and glad news from the churches, is very helpful to us. May God continue to bless us in saying souls!—I. D. Parker, Dec. 21.

Beaver Creek, Md.—Dec. 15 we closed our series of meetings, held in the Long Meadow meeting-house. Our elder, D. F. Stouffer, commenced the meetings Nov. 28. He preached several sermons and was then called to other fields of labor. Bro. Wilbur Stover, of Edgemont, Md, continued the meetings in a very creditable manner, and as an immediate result ten dear souls were received into church-fellowship. The members were strengthened, and impressions made on many which, we hope, will induce them to make the good choice.—John Rowland.

Bremen, Ind.—Bro. Daniel Snell, of Sidney, Ind., came to the Yellow River church, Ind., Nov. 28, and commenced a series of meetings, which he continued until Dec. 16, preaching in all twenty-nine very interesting and impressive sermons. Bro. Snell faithfully discharged his duty in holding forth the Word of Life in its purity. We also feel confident that there were lasting impressions made on the minds of the people. As an immediate result of the meetings, one dear young brother was added to our number by baptism.—Belle Hoffhein.

Fredonia, Kans.—The Fredonia Brethren's Sunday-school and church was closed Nov. 29, on account of the scarlet fever, raging in town and vicinity. The disease was spreading rapidly when the Board of Health closed all schools, Sunday-schools, churches, and all gatherings for worship or amusement. We were made to rejoice on Dec. 16, when one precious soul made her wants known, and was baptized, we trust, to walk in newness of life. May the Lord help us all to walk in that straight and narrow path that leads to life eternal. Ida Thompson, Dec. 17.

Purchase Line, Pa.—Dec. 12 the members of the Manor congregation, Pa., met in the Crooked Creek meeting-house in church council. One sister was received by letter. As there was but little business before the meeting, most of the time was occupied by the members in friendly talks on things of church interest. After this we agreed to take up a subscription to help some of the poor, and, as a result, $4.95 was raised for the Home Mission; $6 for the Rockton poor fund; $6.15 for the poor in Denmark, and $145 for the General Mission Work.—Lizzie Fyock, Cor. Sec.

Dayton, Ohio.—Bro. J. Bennett Trout, of New Carlisle, Ohio, began a series of meetings in the Bear Creek church, Montgomery Co., Ohio, Dec. 5, continuing until Dec. 16. He preached, in all, eighteen sermons. Owing to an attack of La Grippe, he had to close the meetings sooner than was anticipated, for which we all felt sorry. Bro. Trout is not afraid to preach the Whole Truth, and did so in such a way that both saint and sinner were edified and set to thinking. While there were no immediate accessions, yet there were good impressions made. We hope he will soon be able to resume his work.—Josiah Eby.

New Hope Church, Kans.—We are still trying to press forward and labor for the upbuilding of Christ's kingdom here on earth. Bro. Henry Shideler came to us Dec. 5, and preached two very acceptable sermons. Dec. 6 Bro. J. H. Neher came and preached two sermons which were very edifying. He was working in behalf of the Old Folks' Home. Dec. 8 Bro. Samuel Edgecomb came and labored until Sunday evening, Dec. 20. Bro. Edgecomb did us much good while with us, in telling the members of the duties, devolving upon them, as well as presenting to the sinner the way of life. Although there were no additions to the church, yet we feel that some are considering the matter of salvation.—A. B Lichtenwaller.

Voganville, Pa.—We have just closed a series of meetings at the Blue Ball meeting-house in the Conestoga church, Lancaster Co., Pa. This was the third series of meetings for this fall. Dec. 5 brethren John and Samuel Utz, of Union Bridge and New Market, Md., came to us and jointly labored one week, when Bro. John left for Lexington, in the West Conestoga congregation. Bro. Samuel remained until Dec. 19. These brethren labored very earnestly and acceptably, and while there were no additions, yet we have reason to believe that some seed has fallen upon good ground, and in God's own time, it may spring up and bring forth fruit. The brethren has been encouraged and inspired with new zeal, to labor more earnestly in the cause of Christ. May the Lord reward them for their labors!—I. W. Taylor, Dec. 21.

Friedens, Pa.—Bro. Geo. S. Rairigh, of Johnstown, Pa., commenced a series of meetings in the Sipesville church (Quemahoning congregation), Somerset Co., Pa., on Thursday evening, Dec. 10, and continued until Sunday evening, Dec. 20, preaching in all, thirteen sermons. Though there were none added to the church, we felt that the spirit of the Lord was present. May our light burn brighter in the days to come, and may we show greater activity in our spiritual life! Bro. Rairigh is a faithful and earnest worker, and our prayer is that the Lord may grant him health and strength, so that he may yet do much good service for the Master. Bro. Rairigh also preached the funeral sermon (assisted by Bro. R. Hull) for sister Maggie Maust, at the above-named church, on Saturday, Dec. 12. She passed into rest at the early age of twenty-two years, but death had no terrors for her.—J. D. Baer, Dec. 21, 1891.

Manor Church, Md.—On the evening of Dec. 5, according to appointment, Bro. Silas Hoover, of Somerset County, Pa., came to us and began a series of meetings. The meetings at first were small, but the roads being nice and the weather fine, caused people to turn out. Then followed good preaching, which caused saint and sinner to awaken to a full sense of the duty they owe to God. The interest grew as the meetings continued. Brethren and sisters were made stronger in the Lord. Seventeen dear souls were made to feel the "love of God" in their day of grace, and joined in with God's children to walk in newness of life. Many more are counting the cost. The meetings closed Dec. 16. May many more such good meetings be enjoyed throughout the Brotherhood!—Samuel H. Neikirk.

Burr Oak, Kans.—The quarterly council in the Burr Oak church was held Nov. 28. All the business was transacted in love and union. Our elder, John Hollinger, and also Eld. C. S. Holsinger were with us. The church is in love and union. Eld. C. S. Holsinger commenced a series of meetings on the evening of Nov. 28. He preached at the church for two weeks, and then moved the meetings eight miles north-east to a school-house. Good interest and good order were manifested during our meetings. Bro. Holsinger preached twenty-three discourses in all. He gave us rich food for the soul. At the close of our meetings three precious souls were received by baptism. May they be bright and shining lights in this world! It would be well if our brother could be kept at work in the western field; he could do much good. May the Lord ever go with him, on his journey from place to place!—Emma Hackenberry.

Rome, Ohio.—Thanksgiving services were held in the Oak Grove church at 10: 30 in the forenoon. We had short, but very interesting, addresses by all the ministers present. In the evening Bro. Weidman conducted Thanksgiving services in the Pleasant Grove church. At the close of these meetings contributions were received for the General Mission Work. Our series of meetings began at the Pleasant Grove church, Dec. 5. Bro. J. M. Mohler, of Pennsylvania, is with us, to present the Gospel plan of salvation to all who will come to hear him. If the Lord wills, we expect to continue our meetings at this point a week or ten days. Then we will commence meetings at the Oak Grove church, and continue as long as Bro. Mohler can remain with us. We ask an interest in the prayers of the faithful, for the success of these meetings. Our invitation is Rev. 22: 17. Bro. Dickey is with the Brethren in the Logan church at this writing.—M. A. Dickey, Alvada, Ohio, Dec. 7.

Mitchell, Kans.—There is great rejoicing in the Kansas Centre church, Kansas. Dec. 10 Bro. Isaac H. Crist and wife, of Gardner, Kansas, came among us and preached at a school-house, three miles north-east of Mitchell, wielding the Sword of the Spirit skillfully. He preached in all fourteen sermons, and as a result six were received by baptism, and one was reclaimed. One young man said, when his wife made application, that, in being baptized, she would risk her life, as it was dangerous to baptize in the winter time. But two days afterwards, like Saul of Tarsus, he was stricken down and wanted to be received into fellowship the next day. He is now rejoicing in hope of eternal life. The interest of the meeting increased from the beginning to the close. The doctrine of the Brethren church was ably defended and the church built up. We hope all will be inspired with greater diligence to serve the Master and at last receive the crown.—Isaac S. Brubaker, Dec. 21.

PIPER.—In the Hopewell church, Pa., Nov. 28, 1891, Sist. Laura Piper, wife of friend Samuel Pipes, aged 35 years, 5 months and 11 days.

Deceased left home a few weeks prior to her death for the benefit of her health. She still continued to grow worse until the time above stated, when she breathed her last, far from home. Her body was brought back and buried in the home graveyard. Funeral services conducted by Rev. Schyler, of the Presbyterian church.

LEONARD.—At the same place, Dec. 3, 1891, Wm. Leonard, son of John and Margaret Leonard, aged about 22 years.

Deceased leaves a father, mother, four brothers and three sisters to mourn their loss. Though he made no profession, he has one sister who is the wife of a minister in the Brethren church.

CORNELIUS.—At the same place, Dec. 1, 1891, Martin Cornelius, aged about 60 years. The subject of this notice had taken too much morphine, and never wakened. He died about eighteen hours after taking the poison.   DANIEL RITCHEY.

JULIUS.—In the Kaskaskia church, Fayette Co., Ill., Nov. 21, 1891, of typhus malaria fever, Bro. James Julius, aged 44 years, 7 months and 15 days.

Bro. Julius was born in Virginia. With his parents he moved to Indiana in early life and later on to Illinois. He united with the Brethren in 1886 and was a zealous brother and kind neighbor. He leaves a wife and three children to mourn their loss. Services by the writer from 2 Cor. 5: 1.
GRANVILLE NEVINGER.

SIMPKINS.—At the same place, Nov. 28, 1891, sister Elvira Simpkins, aged 81 years and 1 month.

Sister Simpkins passed about seventy years of her life in Ohio, where she raised a family. The last ten years she spent at the kind home of her son,—Bro. James Simpkins, who, with his excellent wife, rendered the old sister's last days very pleasant. Services by the writer from Rev. 14: 13.
GRANVILLE NEVINGER.

McCLERGE.—In the Lancaster congregation, Ind., Bro. John McClerge, aged 69 years, 8 months and 7 days.

On the morning of Dec. 5 he came very unexpectedly to his death. He went into a pen where there was a vicious hog, which attacked him and caused his death in less than five minutes. A battery was severed which caused stoppage of the heart. He was a faithful brother. A large concourse of people was in attendance at the funeral services, which were conducted by the writer from these words, " There is but a step between me and death."   DORSEY HODGDEN.

BOWERS.—At Martinsburg, Blair Co., Pa., Nov. 27, 1891, Mrs. Nancy Bowers, wife of John Bowers, deceased, aged 71 years, 6 months and 5 days.

Deceased retired in her usual health. By 4 o'clock in the morning she was paralyzed, not being able to utter one word. She lived but four days in this condition. She was a faithful member of the River Brethren church for about fifty-two years. She leaves seven children, four sons and three daughters. One daughter preceded her in death.
MRS. J. KLEPSER.

TABER.—In the Black River church, Mich., Dec. 8, 1891, sister Isabel Taber, aged 56 years, 8 months and 23 days.

Her maiden-name was Porter. In 1856 she was married to David Taber. She was a widow thirty years. Funeral services by Bro. Thurston Miller. Text, 2 Cor. 5: 1.
A. B. WALLICK.

VOWELS.—In the Dry Creek church, Iowa, Nov. 30, 1891, of diphtheria, Harley, son of Joseph and sister Flora Vowels, aged 3 years, 2 months and 24 days.

Death, in a few short days, called for another victim. Dora, 2, Tommy S. passed away, after suffering from the same terrible disease. Thus two precious jewels were, in so short a time, taken from the family circle. While

the heart-stricken parents feel almost overcome with grief, they have the blessed assurance that their dear children now dwell with the angels of light. O, how sweet it shall be to meet these dear ones around God's throne above, when this short life is over!
ANNA F. BOSSERMAN.

EBIE.—In the Spring River church, Jasper Co., Mo., Sept. 1, 1891, Bro. John H. Ebie, aged 48 years, 5 months and 11 days.

Bro. John came to this place from Stark County, Ohio, in November, 1889, and remained here until the time of his death. He was a sufferer for many years with Brights' disease. He was anointed with oil in the name of the Lord several months before his death. He served in the office of deacon a number of years. He leaves a sorrowing wife and six children, to mourn the loss of one that was near and dear to them, but we hope that their loss is his gain. His funeral was largely attended and the services conducted by Eld. George Barnhart from the words, "What is man?"   CHRISTIAN HOLDEMAN.

EBERSOLE.—In the Yellow Creek church, Pa., Aug. 3, 1891, Mary Esther, daughter of Bro. Gideon and sister Susan Ebersole, aged 1 year, 2 months and 15 days.

Funeral services conducted by Bro. P. S. Myers and others.   BARBARA HOLSINGER.

BROADWATER.—In the Root River congregation, Minn., Dec. 9, 1891, Amanda A. Broadwater, aged 44 years, 9 months and 26 days.

Deceased leaves a kind husband, two daughters, one son and many other relatives to mourn her departure. This Visitation of God's providence has cast a gloom over our pathway, but may the grief-stricken family look to the One who doeth all things well. Funeral services by Bro. John W. Sadler from 1 Thess. 4: 14, to a large and sympathizing congregation.   ELLA M, ORR.

CRAFT.—In Johnson County, Nebr., Catharine (Hardrock) Craft.

Deceased was born March 22, 1836, in Germany. When three years of age she came with her parents to Washington County, Md., where she grew to womanhood. From there she came to Shelby County, Ohio, but having very poor health, she came west to Illinois. In 1878 she, with her family, moved to Johnson County, Nebr., where she spent the remaining days of her life. For about forty years she has been a faithful follower of Christ, having become a member of the German Baptist church in her youth. In 1862 she was united in marriage to Jacob Craft, and three children were given them.
A. BERKEYBILE.

BLOUGH.—In Quemahoning Township, Somerset Co., Pa., Dec. 11, 1891, of dropsy of the heart, Katie May, little daughter of friend Samuel and Sarah Blough, aged 4 years, 5 months and 16 days.

Funeral services were held at the Blough Mennonite church by Samuel Gindlesperger and Simon Lehman from Job 14: 1, 2.
ABNER BOMGARDNER.

WINELAND.—In the Solomon's Creek District, at Milford Junction, Ind., Oct. 31, 1891, Bro. Jacob Wineland, aged 64 years, 3 months and 26 days.

Deceased was born in Knox County, Ohio, and was a consistent member. His conversation was generally concerning the Bible and the great beyond.

Several years ago he quit using tobacco and donated the tobacco money to the missionary cause. Funeral services by Davis Younce, of Syracuse, assisted by Daniel Wysong, of Nappanee.   L. A. NEFF.

ARNOLD.—In the Iowa River church, Marshall Co., Iowa, Dec. 6, 1891, of cancer, Elizabeth Arnold, aged 52 years, 10 months and 8 days.

Funeral services by Bro. John Calkins, assisted by Bro. Frank Wheeler. Bro. William has lost an affectionate wife, the children a devoted mother and the church a loving sister. She bore her affliction with Christian patience. If we all prove faithful, we shall meet her again.   ELLEN M, NICHOLSON.

PIPER.—In the Hopewell church, Pa., Nov. 28, 1891, Mrs. Laura Piper, wife of friend Samuel Piper, aged 35 years, 5 months and 11 days.

Deceased left home a few weeks prior to her death for the benefit of her health. She still continued to grow worse until the time above stated, when she breathed her last, far from home. Her body was brought back and buried in the home graveyard. Funeral services conducted by Rev. Schyler, of the Presbyterian church.

LEONARD.—At the same place, Dec. 2, 1891, Wm. Leonard, son of John and Margaret Leonard, aged about 22 years.

Deceased leaves a father, mother, four brothers and three sisters to mourn their loss. Though he made no profession, he has one sister who is the wife of a minister in the Brethren church.

CORNELIUS.—At the same place, Dec. 1, 1891, Martin Cornelius, aged about 60 years.

The subject of this notice had taken too much morphine, and never wakened. He died about eighteen hours after taking the poison.   DANIEL RITCHEY.

JULIUS.—In the Kaskaskia church, Fayette Co., Ill., Nov. 21, 1891, of typhus malaria fever, Bro. James Julius, aged 44 years, 7 months and 15 days.

Bro. Julius was born in Virginia. With his parents he moved to Indiana in early life and later on to Illinois. He united with the Brethren in 1886 and was a zealous brother and kind neighbor. He leaves a wife and three children to mourn their loss. Services by the writer from 2 Cor. 5: 1.
                        GRANVILLE NEVINGER.

SIMPKINS.—At the same place, Nov. 28, 1891, sister Elvira Simpkins, aged 81 years, and 1 month.

Sister Simpkins passed about seventy years of her life in Ohio, where she raised a family. The last ten years she spent at the kind home of her son,—Bro. James Simpkins, who, with his excellent wife, rendered the old sister's last days very pleasant. Services by the writer from Rev. 14: 13.
                        GRANVILLE NEVINGER.

McCLERGE.—In the Lancaster congregation, Ind., Geo. John McClerge, aged 69 years, 8 months and 7 days.

On the morning of Dec. 5 he came very near death to his death. He went into a room where there was a vicious dog, which attacked him and caused his death in less than five minutes. An artery was severed which caused stoppage of the heart. He was a faithful brother. A large concourse of people was in attendance at the funeral services, which were conducted by the writer from these words, "There is but a step between me and death."   DORSEY HODGDEN.

BOWERS.—At Martinsburg, Blair Co., Pa., Nov. 27, 1891, Mrs. Nancy Bowers, wife of John Bowers, deceased, aged 71 years, 6 months and 5 days.

Deceased retired in her usual health. By 4 o'clock in the morning she was paralyzed, not being able to utter one word. She lived four days in this condition. She was a faithful member of the River Brethren church for about fifty-two years. She leaves seven children, four sons and three daughters. One daughter preceded her in death.
                        MRS. J. KLEPSER.

TABER.—In the Black River church, Mich., Dec. 8, 1891, sister Isabel Taber, aged 56 years, 8 months and 23 days.

Her maiden-name was Porter. In 1856 she was married to David Taber. She was a widow thirty years. Funeral services by Bro. Thurston Miller. Text, 2 Cor. 5: 1.
                        A. B. WALLICK.

VOWELS.—In the Dry Creek church, Iowa, Nov. 30, 1891, of diphtheria, Harley, son of Joseph and sister Flora Vowels, aged 3 years, 2 months and 24 days.

Death, in a few short days, called for another victim. Dec. 2, Tommy S. passed away, after suffering from the same terrible disease. Thus two precious jewels were, in so short a time, taken from the family circle. White

the heart-stricken parents feel almost overcome with grief, they have the blessed assurance that their dear children now dwell with the angels of light. O, how sweet it shall be to meet these dear ones around God's throne above, when this short life is over!
                        ANNA F. BOSSERMAN.

EBIE.—In the Spring River church, Jasper Co., Mo., Sept. 1, 1891, Bro. John H. Ebie, aged 48 years, 5 months and 11 days.

Bro. John came to this place from Stark County, Ohio, in November, 1887, and remained here until the time of his death. He was a sufferer for many years with Brights' disease. He was anointed with oil in the name of the Lord several months before his death. He served in the office of deacon a number of years. He leaves a sorrowing wife and six children, to mourn the loss of one that was near and dear to them, but we hope that their loss is his gain. His funeral was largely attended and the services conducted by Eld. George Barnhart from the words, "What is man?" CHRISTIAN HOLDERMAN.

EBERSOLE.—In the Yellow Creek church, Pa., Aug. 3, 1891, Mary Esther, daughter of Bro. Gideon and sister Susan Ebersole, aged 1 year, 9 months and 15 days.

Funeral services conducted by Bro. P. S. Myers and others.   BARBARA HOLSINGER.

BROADWATER.—In the Root River congregation, Minn., Dec. 9, 1891, Amanda A. Broadwater, aged 44 years, 9 months and 26 days.

Deceased leaves a kind husband, two daughters, one son and many other relatives to mourn her departure. This visitation of God's providence has cast a gloom over our pathway, but may the grief-stricken family look to the One who doeth all things well, Funeral services by Bro. John W. Sadler from 1 Thess. 4: 14, to a large and sympathizing congregation.   ELLA M. ORR.

CRAFT.—In Johnson County, Nebr., Catharine (Hasdnock) Craft.

Deceased was born March 22, 1836, in Germany. When three years of age she came with her parents to Washington County, Md., where she grew to womanhood. From there she came to Shelby County, Ohio, but having very poor health, she came west to Illinois. In 1878 she, with her family, moved to Johnson County, Nebr., where she spent the remaining days of her life. For about forty years she has been a faithful follower of Christ, having become a member of the German Baptist church in her youth. In 1861 she was united in marriage to Jacob Craft, and three children were given them.
                        A. BERKEYBILE.

BLOUGH.—In Quemahoning Township, Somerset Co., Pa., Dec. 11, 1891, of dropsy of the heart, Katie May, little daughter of friend Samuel and Sarah Blough, aged 4 years, 5 months and 16 days.

Funeral services were held at the Blough Mennonite church by Samuel Gindlesperger and Simon Lehman from Job 14: 1, 2.
                        ABNER BOMGARDNER.

WINELAND.— In the Solomon's Creek District, at Milford Junction, Ind., Oct. 31, 1891, Bro. Samuel Wineland, aged 64 years, 3 months and 26 days.

Deceased was born in Knox County, Ind., and was a consistent member. This conversation was generally concerning the Bible and the great beyond.

Several years ago he united using tobacco and donated the tobacco money to the missionary cause. Funeral services by Davis Younce, of Syracuse, assisted by Daniel Wysong, of Nappanee.   L. A. NEFF.

ARNOLD.—In the Iowa River church, Marshall Co., Iowa, Dec. 6, 1891, of cancer, Elizabeth Arnold, aged 72 years, 10 months and 8 days.

Funeral services by Bro. John Cakerion, assisted by Bro. Frank Wheeler. Bro. William has lost an affectionate wife, the children a devoted mother and the church a loving elder. She bore her affliction with Christian patience. If we all prove faithful, we shall meet her again. ELLEN M. NICHOLSON.

THE GOSPEL MESSENGER.

"Set for the Defense of the Gospel."

Vol. 30, Old Series.　　　　Mt. Morris, Ill., and Huntingdon, Pa., Jan. 12, 1892.　　　　No. 2.

The Gospel Messenger.

H. B. BRUMBAUGH, Editor,
And Business Manager of the Eastern House, Box 50.
Huntingdon, Pa.

Table of Contents.

WE had a very pleasant call from Bro. Isaac Frantz, of Ohio, who stopped over on his return from the eastern churches, where he had been canvassing in the interest of the Tract Work. We were glad to learn that he was fairly successful, and, and had he not been unexpectedly called home, he would have given the "Endowment Fund" quite a lift. Bro. Frantz has been giving much of his time and talent to this work and the ministry, and it should be fully appreciated by the church, as he seems to have a peculiar fitness for work of this kind.

WE are informed that the Ministerial Meeting, held at Waynesborough, Pa., was largely attended and of unusual interest. It was our intention to be present, but, through a mistake of dates, got ready to go a week after the time. For this we were sorry, as we would have much enjoyed meeting with the ministering brethren of the southern part of our District. These meetings are becoming quite general among us, and, we hope, will prove a power for good to our ministers and also to the churches. We are glad to believe that there is a very general awakening, as to the work of the ministry.

PROGRAM OF BIBLE TERM

To be held at Huntingdon, Pa., commencing Feb. 1 and continue four weeks. That those who are interested in this work may have an idea of what will be done during the Bible Term, we give the following program:

1. Bible History, as found in the Pentateuch, or the historical books of the Bible, including Sacred Geography and Biblical Antiquities.

2. The Propagation of Christianity, as given in the Acts and the Epistolary Writings, including the Geography and the Journeys of Paul.

3. Biblical Hermeneutics, or the Rules for Biblical Interpretations. Teacher, H. B. Brumbaugh.

(1) *Exegetical Study.*—1 Timothy.

(2) *Homiletics.*—Bible Authority for Preaching; Purpose of Preaching; Matter for Preaching; Methods of Preaching; Selection of Texts and Subjects; Preparation and Delivery of Sermons; The Preacher's Motive for Preaching; The Aid of the Holy Spirit in Preaching; Practice and Exercise in the Treatment of Texts and Subjects.

(3) *Elocution.*— General Expression; Voice; Natural and Speaking; Clear and Correct Thinking the Basis of Clear and Correct Expressing; Bible and Hymn Reading; Hints on Common Class-room and Pulpit Faults, etc. Teacher, W. J. Swigart.

(1) Life of Christ studied Chronologically; The Years of Preparation and the First and Second Years of his Ministry.

(2) Exegetical Study of one of the Gospels with the attending Geography and Biblical Antiquities.

(3) Sunday-school work, such as the occasion may demand. Teacher, J. B. Brumbaugh.

In addition to the above work there will be excellent opportunities afforded for instruction in sacred music, voice culture, etc.

During the Term sermons and lectures will be given on the doctrines of the Bible, as believed and accepted by the church. We hope to have with us brethren who have given the work special preparation and will be able to profitably entertain and instruct all who may come, old and young, ministers, officials, and lay members. All are invited.

ANNUAL MEETING OF 1892.

BY GALEN B. BOYER.

As is already generally known, our next Annual Meeting, the Lord willing, will be held at Cedar Rapids, Iowa, the place selected by the Middle District of that State. The brethren, composing the Committee of Arrangements, are earnest and conscientious workers, and are doing all in their power to make the Meeting of 1892 in every way a success. The Committee and its organization stands as follows: Eld. John Zuck, Clarence, Chairman; Eld. J. S. Snyder, Brooklyn, Secretary; Bro. G. W. Hopwood, Deep River, Treasurer. Upon my arrival in the City, Dec. 28, 1891, I was met and warmly welcomed by Bro. Tisdale, who resides in the City, the Commissioner of Arrangements, Mr. John S. Ely, President of the Commercial Association, and Mr. Brewer, a representative of the *Cedar Rapids Republican*, one of the daily papers of the City. That the Meeting is located at this point is due to the untiring efforts of Bro. Tisdale, and the liberal offer made by the Commercial Association. This Association consists of business men of the City, to further its interests, and, from what I could learn, they are doing good work in that direction.

The day was busily, though pleasantly, spent in viewing the proposed grounds for the Meeting, and the City and its principal industries. During the afternoon Mr. Ely kindly accompanied us and used every means to make the visit entertaining and pleasant. Among the special favors received from him, was a ride over the new Electric Railway between Cedar Rapids and Marion, six miles distant. This was the first day the cars were running regularly, and the trip was a most enjoyable one.

CEDAR RAPIDS,

A city, having a population between twenty and twenty-five thousand, and covering an area of about fourteen square miles, is situated near the centre of the State, on the Cedar River, a stream famous in the State for its clear water and picturesque and shady banks. From a standpoint of population, Cedar Rapids ranks seventh in the State, but it ranks among the first in enterprise and advantages. The streets, a number of which are paved with cedar and brick, fringed with shade trees and bordered with sodded lawns, clean and orderly. Many of the business blocks are built of cream-colored brick or red superior stone, while the residences are brick or frame buildings, constructed in good modern taste. Besides the industries, common to all cities and especially active in this place, here are the headquarters of the Burlington, Cedar Rapids and Northern Railroad. Here is also situated one of the largest packing houses and the largest oatmeal mill in the United States, and three wide-awake educational institutions in addition to the well-managed public schools.

The City has a morning and an evening paper, daily, except Sunday, and a number of weekly and monthly newspapers. The water-works have a pumping capacity of 6,000,000 gallons every twenty-four hours and supply the City with good water from three Artesian wells of from 1,440 to 2,225 feet deep.

The City is lighted by electricity and gas, and all the principal portions are connected by the latest improved electric street railway. Including the line, recently built to Marion, about fifteen miles are now in operation. The cars move along rapidly each way every fifteen minutes, making it possible to reach any part of the City in a short time.

RAILROADS.

According to Russell's Railway Guide for Iowa, Cedar Rapids has "more passenger trains entering and leaving during twenty-four hours than any other city in Iowa." The Burlington, Cedar Rapids and Northern, Chicago and North-western, Chicago, Milwaukee and St. Paul, and Illinois Central Railroads all pass through the City, giving it through trains to Chicago, Springfield, Ill., St. Louis, Kansas City, Omaha and Sioux City. These points are all about equally distant (nearly 200 miles) from Cedar Rapids, and the trains are run so that a passenger may leave in

(*Concluded on page 31.*) .

THE GOSPEL MESSENGER.

"Set for the Defense of the Gospel."

Vol. 30, Old Series. Mt. Morris, Ill., and Huntingdon, Pa., Jan. 12, 1892. No. 2.

The Gospel Messenger.

H. B. BRUMBAUGH, Editor,

And Business Manager of the Eastern House, Box 50,
Huntingdon, Pa.

Table of Contents.

WE had a very pleasant call from Bro. Isaac Frantz, of Ohio, who stopped over on his return from the eastern churches, where he had been canvassing in the interest's of the Tract Work. We were glad to learn that he was fairly successful, and, had he not been unexpectedly called home, he would have given the "Endowment Fund" quite a lift. Bro. Frantz has been giving much of his time and talent to this work and the ministry, and it should be fully appreciated by the church, as he seems to have a peculiar fitness for work of this kind.

WE are informed that the Ministerial Meeting, held at Waynesborough, Pa., was largely attended and of unusual interest. It was our intention to be present, but, through a mistake of dates, got ready to go a week after the time. For this we were sorry, as we would have much enjoyed meeting with the ministering brethren of the southern part of our District. These meetings are becoming quite general among us, and, we hope, will prove a power for good to our ministers and also to the churches. We are glad to believe that there is a very general awakening, as to the work of the ministry.

PROGRAM OF BIBLE TERM.

To be held at Huntingdon, Pa., commencing Feb. 1 and continue four weeks. That those who are interested in this work may have an idea of what will be done during the Bible Term, we give the following program:

1. Bible History, as found in the Pentateuch; or the historical books of the Bible, including Sacred Geography and Biblical Antiquities.

2. The Propagation of Christianity, as given in the Acts and the Epistolary Writings, including the Geography and the Journeys of Paul.

3. Biblical Hermeneutics, or the Rules for Biblical Interpretations. Teacher, H. B. Brumbaugh.

(1) *Exegetical Study.*—1 Timothy.

(2) *Homiletics.*—Bible Authority for Preaching; Purpose of Preaching; Matter for Preaching; Methods of Preaching; Selection of Texts and Subjects; Preparation and Delivery of Sermons; The Preacher's Motive for Preaching; The Aid of the Holy Spirit in Preaching; Practice and Exercise in the Treatment of Texts and Subjects.

(3) *Elocution.*— General Expression; Voice; Natural and Speaking; Clear and Correct Thinking the Basis of Clear and Correct Expressing; Bible and Hymn Reading; Hints on Common Class-room and Pulpit Faults, etc. Teacher, W. J. Swigart.

(1) Life of Christ studied Chronologically; The Years of Preparation and the First and Second Years of his Ministry.

(2) Exegetical Study of one of the Gospels with the attending Geography and Biblical Antiquities.

(3) Sunday-school work, such as the occasion may demand. Teacher, J. B. Brumbaugh.

In addition to the above work there will be excellent opportunities afforded for instruction in sacred music, voice culture, etc.

During the Term sermons and lectures will be given on the doctrines of the Bible, as believed and accepted by the church. We hope to have with us brethren who have given the work special preparation and will be able to profitably entertain and instruct all who may come, old and young, ministers, officials, and lay members. All are invited.

ANNUAL MEETING OF 1892.

BY GALEN B. ROYER.

As is already generally known, our next Annual Meeting, the Lord willing, will be held at Cedar Rapids, Iowa, the place selected by the Middle District of that State. The brethren, composing the Committee of Arrangements, are earnest and conscientious workers, and are doing all in their power to make the Meeting of 1892 in every way a success. The Committee and its organization stands as follows: Eld. John Zuck, Clarence, Clearman; Eld. J. S. Snyder, Brooklyn, Secretary; Bro. G. W. Hopwood, Deep River, Treasurer.

Upon my arrival in the City, Dec. 28, 1891, I was met and warmly welcomed by Bro. Tisdale, who resides in the City, the Committee of Arrangements, Mr. John S. Ely, President of the Commercial Association, and Mr. Brewer, a representative of the *Cedar Rapids Republican*, one of the daily papers of the City. That the Meeting is located at this point is due to the untiring efforts of Bro. Tisdale, and the liberal offer made by the Commercial Association. This Association consists of business men of the City, to further its interests, and, from what I could learn, they are doing good work in that direction.

The day was busily, though pleasantly, spent in viewing the proposed grounds for the Meeting, and the City and its principal industries. During the afternoon Mr. Ely kindly accompanied us and used every means to make the visit entertaining and pleasant. Among the special favors received from him, was a ride over the new Electric Railway between Cedar Rapids and Marion, six miles distant. This was the first day the cars were running regularly, and the trip was a most enjoyable one.

CEDAR RAPIDS,

A city, having a population between twenty and twenty-five thousand, and covering an area of about fourteen square miles, is situated near the centre of the State, on the Cedar River, a stream famous in the State for its clear water and picturesque and shady banks. From a standpoint of population, Cedar Rapids ranks seventh in the State, but it ranks among the first in enterprise and advantages. The streets, a number of which are paved with cedar and brick, fringed with shade trees and bordered with sodded lawns between the drive-way and the sidewalk, are kept clean and orderly. Many of the business blocks are built of cream-colored brick or red superior stone, while the residences are brick or frame buildings, constructed in good modern taste. Besides the industries, common to all cities and especially active in this place, here are the headquarters of the Burlington, Cedar Rapids and Northern Railroad. Here is also situated one of the largest packing houses and the largest oatmeal mill in the United States, and three wide-awake educational institutions in addition to the well-managed public schools.

The City has a morning and an evening paper, daily, except Sunday, and a number of weekly and monthly newspapers. The water-works have a pumping capacity of 6,000,000 gallons every twenty-four hours and supply the City with good water from three Artesian wells of from 1,440 to 2,225 feet deep.

The City is lighted by electricity and gas, and all the principal portions are connected by the latest improved electric street railway. Including this line, reconstructed by Marion, about fifteen miles are now in operation. The cars move along rapidly each way every fifteen minutes, making it possible to reach any part of the City in a short time.

RAILROADS.

According to Russell's Railway Guide for Iowa, Cedar Rapids has "more passenger trains entering and leaving during twenty-four hours than any other city in Iowa." The Burlington, Cedar Rapids and Northern, Chicago and North-western, Chicago, Milwaukee and St. Paul, and Illinois Central Railroads all pass through the City, giving it through trains to Chicago, Springfield, Ill., St. Louis, Kansas City, Omaha and Sioux City. These points are all about equally distant (nearly 200 miles) from Cedar Rapids, and the trains are run so that a passenger may leave in

(*Concluded on page 21.*).

good place for you to meet the Master when he appears.

Now, my friends, I do not know when Christ is coming. If Jesus Christ were to come while I am living, I would like him to find me right at my desk, hard at work. If I were on the farm, I would like him to find me at my post, doing my duty. Were I in school, I would like the Master to find me hard at work on my studies. Were I in any kind of honorable business, I would like him to find me engaged right in that kind of business; because, whatever we do, we ought to be willing that the Lord should find us in that business.

Brethren, do not get the idea that, when the Lord comes, you must quit your business, in order to get ready to meet him. We want to get ready to meet the Lord *right now*, and then, when he does come, we will be ready for him, whether we be at home or abroad. If we are from home, it will be just as well for us as though we were at home. The wife wants to be ready to meet her Master when her husband is absent, as well as when he is at home. The students here at school want to be as much prepared to meet Jesus in this building, as they would be were they at home under their parents' roof.

In Isa. 65: 20-22 we have this language: "There shall be no more thence an infant of days, nor an old man that hath not filled his days: for the child shall die a hundred years' old; but the sinner being a hundred years old shall be accursed. And they shall build houses, and inhabit them; and they shall plant vineyards, and eat the fruit of them. They shall not build, and another inhabit; they shall not plant, and another eat: for as the days of a tree are the days of my people, and mine elect shall long enjoy the work of their hands." Now in those 1,000 years this world will move right on. The earth will be inhabited during that period, and the people will support themselves. They must have houses in which to live. They shall plant vineyards and build houses, and shall live in them. They shall plant vineyards and enjoy the fruit thereof, and thus reap the reward of their own toil. During that Millennium period there is going to be a great change in this world, but not to the degree that some people are looking for. People must have something to eat; somebody must raise it. There must be clothes to wear, and somebody must make them; houses to live in, and somebody to build them. The people will go up to Jerusalem once a year to worship God. There must be ways of traveling. There will be thousands of ocean vessels, and people will travel during that period more than they do now. We will need all those vessels upon the ocean. We will need our telegraphic lines and our mail facilities. We will need our schools; we will need much during that period. I don't think it will be a period of idleness; it will be a busy period. True, it will be a period of rest, but a rest from sin. It will be a rest from everything that is disagreeable, but I want to tell you that it is going to be an active period, and one in which there is going to be some great development.

I am under the impression that our modern inventions and discoveries are only preparing us for that period. During that 1,000 years the child shall die a hundred years old. If a child die at one hundred years, how old will a man and woman be? And if they do not die under a hundred years of age, it will not be long until there will be a mighty population upon the globe. There will be people all over these valleys and these hills and mountain sides, and on all the islands. It will be a grand period,—a period when our land must be made to produce more. It will be a period when more people will live up.

on the globe than have ever been here before. The saints who are living when Christ comes, will be changed and have their place with the resurrected saints. But there will be others in the flesh to make up this great population.

It will not be a sinful period, for Satan will be under control, and many changes are going to take place. I want to mention some of them. All the saloons and distilleries will be done away with. There will be no liquor manufacturing during that period. There will be no saloons here to influence men and women to drink. During that Millennium period Madame Fashion will be destroyed. She will not be able to reign from Paris as she now does.

Have you ever stopped to think how much money would be saved, were it not for all the foolish fashions of the world? I have figured a little on it, and I think it would save the United States six hundred million dollars a year. That is a sum that would go far towards helping people to live. The United States is using six hundred million dollars worth of tobacco every year. Now that evil will be wiped out, and that amount will be saved. Besides that, we have the enormous expense of keeping a standing army, and keeping up the police force of our country,—two hundred million dollars per year,—which would thus be saved in the United States. That is nothing in comparison to the great sums that will be saved in Europe. And then consider the poor and the insane which we now care for; two hundred million dollars more will be saved in the United States. Look at the gambling dens, the horse-races, and the hundreds of other evils that I cannot now mention, that will be done away with in that period. I have the total amount on my paper, that will be saved during the Millennium in one year,—about three billion dollars. Carry these estimates to the rest of the world, and you will observe that we will save money enough to keep another world like this.

During that period the globe shall produce as it never produced before. The people also will have better laws and know better how to live. It will be a matter of absolute joy and happiness to live here during that period. There will be no strife between labor and capital, because Christ, who will administer the government, will give such laws as will make a proper harmony between labor and capital, between brain and brawn, between the ruler and his subject, between the teacher and his pupil. It will be a government of uniform principle throughout, when people can enjoy all the happiness there is to be enjoyed. Oh, my friends, I long for that period to come; I would like to live in it.

But I want to allude to another line of thought. During that period, like David, we will study the stars which God has made, and if men now, in the short period of only fifty years, can make such discoveries as some of them are making, what may men not do who live five hundred years? Edison is not yet forty years old, but has revolutionized the world in a short time; what may a man not do who lives two or three hundred years, with a brilliant and cultivated mind? Men shall then study science under the influence of what is right and just.

I want to say to you, students, do not stop studying because you think Jesus Christ will come. Keep right on in your studies, because another field will open up to you beyond that period. But you, who have not yet named the name of Christ, you who have not yet given your heart to Jesus, turn away from your sins and give your heart to him, for the time is coming when Christ will come to take vengeance upon them that know not God, and obey not the Gospel of our Lord and Savior Jesus Christ. We will want

to enjoy that period; so get ready for it now. We want to get ready to meet our Master in the shop, in the kitchen, in the parlor, on the street, or any place else. If any of my hearers are engaged in a business they do not care for the Lord to find them in, get out of it at once, and do something that is honorable. So let us all prepare to meet our Lord!

PEN PICTURES.

BY J. S. FLORY.

[This article was unintentionally overlooked. It should have appeared in November last.—ED.]

GENIUS, with the pen of imagery, dipped in the coloring of passing events, might give us an interesting landscape scene with heavenly rays of shimmering light, taking for the foundation the following outlines of sketch work. The canvas, the earth's surface, from where Atlantic's foaming waves beat upon the eastern shore, to where the great Pacific's waters lave the western confines of the American continent. Time, Oct. 17, 1891.*

The sun is hiding behind the Alleghany Mountains. The full moon begins to shine with its wanton lustre, ten thousand of the professed followers of the Meek and Lowly Redeemer have already, or are contemplating a close scrutiny of self in the exercise of self-examination. It is six o'clock. Old veterans of the cross arise from supper, lay aside their upper garments, and wash one another's feet. Why not, when there comes that heaven-horn echo: "If I, then, your Lord and Master, have washed your feet, ye also *ought* to wash one another's feet, for I have given you an *example* that ye *should* do as I have done to you."

The work, thus commenced, goes on. Congregation after congregation catches up, as it were, the Master's words, and, following up the shadows of the retreating sun, the work goes on. An hour later the same blessed work is going on out in the "Western Country." And still it goes on,—farther and farther. The six o'clock shadows move westward another hour later, and where the shadows of the great Rocky Mountains are cast over the valley of the St. Vrain, the faithful from over the State of Colorado are walking in "heavenly places," there in the old stone sanctuary. Beyond the mountains the shadows fly; another hour has gone and there in the land of flowers and almost eternal spring, where the roar of the ocean's waves can be almost heard, the children of a King are washing one another's feet.

We go back to commence another sketch line, the supper is being eaten, the mind is contemplating in sweet joy the final fulfillment of this,—*the Lord's Supper;* then the solemn and soul-reviving Communion of the body and blood of our Savior takes place. As in the first line of sketch work, we continue those lines in unbroken modulations, until hours after they reach the Pacific slope. While just commencing here, those in the Far East are going to their homes, and long before the exercises are through, those where the work first commenced, are sleeping the sleep of the obedient, and perchance dreaming of the blessed land "over there."

The outlines are thus drawn, a glance at the canvas, that takes in the whole, portrays a grand picture of obedience and love for the Truth. Six hours of universal union work in one evening, ten thousand voices sending up praises to God over the length and breadth of our Land,—ten thousand of the church of the Living God joining in

*Taking the notices in the GOSPEL MESSENGER of the feasts to be held Oct. 17, and numbers of others, not so given, we think it is safe to say there were from forty to fifty feasts held that evening, at which probably ten thousand members took part. The difference in time would extend the time, from the first to the close of the last, about six hours.

is one of the many things she has borrowed from paganism.

We read in this chapter, "They that dwell upon the earth shall rejoice over them and make merry, and shall send gifts one to another, because these two prophets tormented them that dwelt on the earth." The Papal adherents will be so delighted that these faithful witnesses are at length silenced, that they will give the most extravagant expression to their joy. And we find, by referring to history, that at the close of this council, which had pronounced the death of the witnesses, the warmest congratulations, accompanied by the most costly presents, were sent to the Pope by the princes of Europe, especially from the king of Portugal. In return the Pope conferred on the king half the Eastern world. The most splendid fetes and the most luxurious dinners were given, toasts were drunk, eloquent speeches were made, and the subject of joy, says the historian, was the total reduction of the heretics, and healing of the French schism. Dean Waddington, writing of this time, says: "At this moment the pillars of the Papal strength seemed visible and palpable, and Rome surveyed them with exaltation from golden palaces."

REMARKS ON JAMES 5: 14.

BY NOAH LONGANECKER.

BEFORE reading this article, the reader is requested to re-read the "New Testament Greek," number eleven, by James M. Neff, on page 611, of No. 39, last volume. With the exception of his "opinion" attached to the close of said article, it will bear re-printing and careful study. Because of said article we consider said number worth its weight in gold. We shall consider the subject from another stand-point

We understand "elders," as used in James 5: 14, as "a term of rank or office." When Christ established his church, "he ordained twelve, that they should be with him, and that he might send them forth to preach, and to have power to· heal sickness." Mark 3: 14, 15. When he sent them forth, "he sent them forth by two and two." Mark 6: 7. He commanded them to "heal the sick." Matt. 10: 8.

We are informed that after they were ordained apostles and were sent forth by two and two, "they went out and preached that men should repent. And they cast out many devils, and anointed with oil many that were sick, and healed them." Mark 6: 12, 13.

The healing of the sick was associated with the anointing of oil. Summary: Christ organized his church by ordaining twelve. He sent them out by two and two. They were to preach the Gospel and heal the sick. They preached the Gospel and anointed with oil the sick and healed them.

Again; when local churches were established in the time of the apostles, "they ordained them elders in every church." Acts 14: 23. Here we have the practice of the apostles. "They ordained them elders in every church." Not an elder, but elders. Hence they could go forth on their mission "by two and two," as Christ gave them example. Churches were anciently established in cities. Paul, in writing to Titus, says, "for this cause left I thee in Crete, that thou shouldest set in order the things that are wanting, and ordain elders in every city, as I had appointed thee." Thus we see that the teaching of the apostles agreed with their practice; and their teaching and practice agreed with the example of Christ, if not also his command. There were then, in the apostolical churches, elders, officially, in every church.

Now, referring to James 5: 14, we read, "Is any sick among you? let him call for the elders of the church; and let them pray over him, anointing him with oil in the name of the Lord," etc. "In the name of the Lord," signifies, "according to his direction or authority." The apostles, according to the command of Christ, anointed the sick with oil and healed them. James, in writing "to the twelve tribes which are scattered abroad," enjoins the anointing of the sick by the elders of the church, with oil, in the name of the Lord. Annual Council has always decided that the elders referred to in James 5: 14, are the "ordained elders." Of course, in more modern councils the opinion was added that "if ordained elders can not be had, those less in office will do." This opinion is founded on 1 Tim. 5: 1, 2, where Paul writes about the more aged brethren and sisters, and calls them elder brethren and elder women; therefore, if the ordained elders cannot be had, those elder brethren and elder women will do. In 1 Tim. 5: 1, and 1 Pet. 5: 5, we have the terms "elder," one singular and the other plural in form, but we cannot substitute "elders" for "elder," unless we change the sense. It will not do to say that because Paul writes about elder men and elder women, therefore, Peter, in 1 Pet. 5: 1, exhorts elder men and elder women. Such an opinion would exclude the greater part of the ministers from assisting in the anointing; for they are not of the "elder" by way of age, nor of the "elders" by way of ordination. But the article by Bro. Neff, to our mind, settles this part of the question, and therefore we forbear to continue this train of thought.

ANNUAL MEETING OF 1892.

(Continued from first page.)

the evening and the next morning be in one of the cities named, or vice versa. Thus it will be seen there is easy access from any direction. The reputation for a good service on the part of these roads, is so well known as to need no further comment. It is hoped that the Western Passenger Association will grant the usual rate, one fare for the round trip, and as soon as the rate is settled, it will be announced through the GOSPEL MESSENGER.

The depots of these four roads are so near to each other that they form practically a union depot in the centre of the City. Near these will be erected a suitable building for a General Information Bureau where the Lodging Committee will be located, and information concerning trains, the places of lodging, the Meeting, the City, etc., may be had during either night or day. This certainly will be a great convenience to all.

THE GROUNDS

Where the Meeting is to be held, are about one mile from the depots, and may be reached either by the Electric Railway, which has a double track from the depots to within one block of the Grounds, or by ample sidewalks, leading to the Grounds. The street cars will carry passengers from the Meeting to any part of the City for five cents per person, including baggage. The Grounds are large enough for the Meeting, sufficiently rolling to give a fair waterfall, in case of rain, and the larger part is covered with a grove which will afford agreeable shade in case of warm weather.

When it comes to the buildings and conveniences for the Meeting, the Commercial Association have certainly made a very liberal offer to help carry the burden of expense. In fact, they carry nearly all of it. While the contract is carefully itemized in every particular, the force of it is this: "Tell us what you want to hold your Meeting, and we will put it there for your free use, on the conditions that when your Meeting is over, all we put there comes back to us again." All they ask is that the Committee will appoint some one to superintend the arrangement of the Grounds and the building, and they will furnish all material and do the work. In accordance with this the Committee have ordered

A TABERNACLE

To be erected, 120 feet square, and closed at the one end where the Moderator will stand. It is to seat 5,000 people. A platform, sixteen by eighty feet across the closed end, will be made for the use of the Standing Committee and about one hundred old brethren that usually cannot get close enough in front to hear. The part set aside for the delegates, shall be made· comfortable, and in fact the whole building will be built with the express purpose of comfort during the long sessions. The Tabernacle, as well as all the other buildings, will have a water-tight roof.

STANDING COMMITTEE ROOM AND OTHER BUILDINGS.

There is now on the Grounds a building suitable for the Standing Committee room. Here the Committee is to meet and have board and furnished FREE. The Dining Hall is to have a seating capacity of 1,000, and provided with a kitchen containing suitable arrangements. Adjoining it will be a lunch stand, 16x140 feet. In addition to these there will be suitable buildings for baggage room, ticket-office, post-office, GOSPEL MESSENGER office, Tract office and such others as may be needed. Artesian water will be piped to any point the Committee may direct, and the Grounds and buildings will be lighted by electricity. All other things needed, such as convenient hitching-grounds, police force, etc., will be supplied.

LODGING.

The Grounds are within the city limits and in the best residont part of the City. The citizens will open their houses to our people, and do all they can to make the brethren comfortable while there. The rooms will be assigned near the Grounds first, and as the demand requires, move farther back until all are accommodated. With the excellent street car system, it will make little difference whether one is near or far from the Meeting.

In conclusion, after looking carefully over the plans of the Committee, as far as they are matured, and hearing them explained in the detail, in reading what the Commercial Association proposes to do, and the natural advantages the town offers for holding such a meeting, I feel assured that, if the Lord permits us to gather together there, to do business in his house, we shall find the accommodations agreeable and everything done to make the Meeting a pleasant and successful one. To that end I pray our Father's blessing.

The Gospel Messenger

Is the recognized organ of the German Baptist or Brethren's church, and advocates the form of doctrine taught in the New Testament and pleads for a return to apostolic and primitive Christianity.

It recognizes the New Testament as the only infallible rule of faith and practice, and maintains that Faith toward God, Repentance from dead works, Regeneration of the heart and mind, baptism by Trine Immersion for remission of sins unto the reception of the Holy Ghost by the laying on of hands, are the means of adoption into the household of God,—the church militant.

It also maintains that Feet-washing, as taught in John 13, both by example and command of Jesus, should be observed in the church.

That the Lord's Supper, instituted by Christ and as universally observed by the apostles and the early Christians, is a full meal, and, in connection with the Communion, should be taken in the evening or about the close of the day.

That the Salutation of the Holy Kiss, or Kiss of Charity, is binding upon the followers of Christ.

That War and Retaliation are contrary to the spirit and self-denying principles of the religion of Jesus Christ.

That the principle of Plain Dressing and of Non-conformity to the world, as taught in the New Testament, should be observed by the followers of Christ.

That the Scriptural duty of Anointing the Sick with Oil, in the Name of the Lord, James 5: 14, is binding upon all Christians.

It also advocates the church's duty to support Missionary and Tract Work, thus giving to the Lord for the spread of the Gospel and for the conversion of sinners.

In short, it is a vindicator of all that Christ and the apostles have enjoined upon us, and aims, amid the conflicting theories and discords of modern Christendom, to point out ground that all must concede to be infallibly safe.

☞ The above principles of our Fraternity are set forth on our "Brethren's Envelopes." Use them! Price, 15 cents per package; 50 cents per hundred.

is one of the many things she has borrowed from paganism.

We read in this chapter, "They that dwell upon the earth shall rejoice over them and make merry, and shall send gifts one to another, because these two prophets tormented them that dwelt on the earth." The Papal adherents will be so delighted that these faithful witnesses are at length silenced, that they will give the most extravagant expression to their joy. And we find, by referring to history, that at the close of this council, which had pronounced the death of the witnesses, the warmest congratulations, accompanied by the most costly presents, were sent to the Pope by the princes of Europe, especially from the king of Portugal. In return the Pope conferred on the king half the Eastern world. The most splendid fetes and the most luxurious dinners were given, toasts were drunk, eloquent speeches were made, and the subject of joy, says the historian, was the total reduction of the heretics, and healing of the French schism. Dean Waddington, writing of this time, says: "At this moment the pillars of the Papal strength seemed visible and palpable, and Rome surveyed them with exaltation from golden palaces."

REMARKS ON JAMES 5: 14.

BY NOAH LONGANECKER.

BEFORE reading this article, the reader is requested to re-read the "New Testament Greek," number eleven, by James M. Neff, on page 611, of No. 39, last volume. With the exception of his "opinion" attached to the close of said article, it will bear re-printing and careful study. Because of said article we consider said number worth its weight in gold. We shall consider the subject from another stand-point

We understand "elders," as used in James 5: 14, as "a term of rank or office." When Christ established his church, "he ordained twelve, that they should be with him, and that he might send them forth to preach, and to have power to heal sickness." Mark 3: 14, 15. When he sent them forth, "he sent them forth by two and two." Mark 6: 7. He commanded them to "heal the sick." Matt. 10: 8.

We are informed that after they were ordained apostles and were sent forth by two and two, "they went out and preached that men should repent. And they cast out many devils, and anointed with oil many that were sick, and healed them." Mark 6: 12, 13.

The healing of the sick was associated with the anointing of oil. Summary: Christ organized his church by ordaining twelve. He sent them out by two and two. They were to preach the Gospel and heal the sick. They preached the Gospel and anointed with oil the sick and healed them.

Again; when local churches were established in the time of the apostles, "they ordained them elders in every church." Acts 14: 23. Here we have the practice of the apostles. "They ordained them elders in every church." Not an *elder*, but *elders*. Hence they could go forth on their mission "by two and two," as Christ gave them example. Churches were anciently established in cities. Paul, in writing to Titus, says, "for this cause left I thee in Crete, that thou shouldest set in order the things that are wanting, and ordain elders in every city, as I had appointed thee." Thus we see that the *teaching* of the apostles agreed with their *practice;* and their *teaching* and *practice* agreed with the *example* of Christ, if not also his command. There were then, in the apostolical churches, elders, officially, in every church.

Now, referring to James 5: 14, we read, "Is any sick among you? let him call for the elders of the church; and let them pray over him, anointing him with oil in the name of the Lord," etc. "In the name of the Lord," signifies, "according to his direction or authority." The apostles, according to the command of Christ, anointed the sick with oil and healed them. James, in writing "to the twelve tribes which are scattered abroad," enjoins the anointing of the sick by the elders of the church, with oil, in the name of the Lord. Annual Council has always decided that the elders referred to in James 5: 14, are the "*ordained elders*." Of course, in more modern councils the opinion was added that "if ordained elders can not be had, those less in office will do." This opinion is founded on 1 Tim. 5: 1, 2, where Paul writes about the more aged brethren and sisters, and calls them elder brethren and elder women; therefore, if the ordained elders cannot be had, those elder brethren and elder women will do. In 1 Tim. 5: 1, and 1 Pet. 5: 5, we have the terms "elder," one singular and the other plural in form, but we cannot substitute "elders" for "elder," unless we change the sense. It will not do to say that because Paul writes about elder men and elder women, therefore, Peter, in 1 Pet. 5: 1, exhorts elder men and elder women. Such an opinion would exclude the greater part of the ministers from assisting in the anointing; for they are not of the "elder" by way of age, nor of the "elders" by way of ordination. But the article by Bro. Neff, to our mind, settles this part of the question, and therefore we forbear to continue this train of thought.

ANNUAL MEETING OF 1892.

(Continued from first page.)

the evening and the next morning be in one of the cities named, or *vice versa*. Thus it will be seen there is easy access from any direction. The reputation for a good service on the part of these roads, is so well known as to need no further comment. It is hoped that the Western Passenger Association will grant the usual rate, one fare for the round trip, and as soon as the rate is settled, it will be announced through the GOSPEL MESSENGER.

The depots of these four roads are so near to each other that they form practically a union depot in the centre of the City. Near them will be erected a suitable building for a General Information Bureau where the Lodging Committee will be located, and information concerning trains, the places of lodging, the Meeting, the City, etc., may be had during either night or day. This certainly will be a great convenience to all.

THE GROUNDS

Where the Meeting is to be held, are about one mile from the depots, and may be reached either by the Electric Railway, which has a double track from the depots to within one block of the Grounds, or by ample sidewalks, leading to the Grounds. The street cars will carry passengers from the Meeting to *any part* of the City for five cents per person, including baggage. The street cars are large enough for the Meeting, sufficiently rolling to give a fair waterfall, in case of rain, and the larger part is covered with a grove which will afford agreeable shade in case of warm weather.

When it comes to the buildings and conveniences for the Meeting, the Commercial Association have certainly made a very liberal offer to help carry the burden of expense. In fact, they carry nearly all of it. While the contract is carefully itemized in every particular, the force of it is this: "Tell us what you want to hold your Meeting, and we will put it there for your *free use*, on the conditions that when your Meeting is over, all we put there comes back to us again." All they

ask is that the Committee will appoint some one to superintend the arrangement of the Grounds and the building, and they will furnish all material and do the work. In accordance with this the Committee have ordered

A TABERNACLE

To be erected, 120 feet square, and closed at the one end where the Moderator will stand. It is to seat 5,000 people. A platform, sixteen by eighty feet across the closed end, will be made for the use of the Standing Committee and about one hundred old brethren that usually cannot get close enough in front to hear. The part set aside for the delegates, shall be made comfortable, and in fact the whole building will be built with the express purpose of comfort during the long sessions. The Tabernacle, as well as all the other buildings, will have a water-tight roof.

STANDING COMMITTEE ROOM AND OTHER BUILDINGS.

There is now on the Grounds a building suitable for the Standing Committee room. Here the Committee is to meet and have good beds furnished FREE. The Dining Hall is to have a seating capacity of 1,000, and provided with a kitchen containing suitable arrangements. Adjoining it will be a lunch stand, 16x140 feet. In addition to these there will be suitable buildings for baggage room, ticket-office, post-office, GOSPEL MESSENGER office, Tract office and such others as may be needed. Artesian water will be piped to any point the Committee may direct, and the Grounds and buildings will be lighted by electricity. All other things needed, such as convenient hitching-grounds, police force, etc., will be supplied.

LODGING.

The Grounds are within the city limits and in the best resident part of the City. The citizens will open their houses to our people, and do all they can to make the brethren comfortable while there. The rooms will be assigned near the Grounds first, and as the demand requires, move farther back until all are accommodated. With the excellent street car system, it will make little difference whether one is near or far from the Meeting.

In conclusion, after looking carefully over the plans of the Committee, as far as they are matured, and hearing them explained in the detail, in reading what the Commercial Association proposes to do, and the natural advantages the town offers for holding such a meeting, I feel assured that, if the Lord permits us to gather together there, to do business in his house, we shall find the accommodations agreeable and everything done to make the Meeting a pleasant and successful one. To that end I pray our Father's blessing.

The Gospel Messenger

Is the recognized organ of the German Baptist or Brethren's church, and advocates the form of doctrine taught in the New Testament and pleads for a return to apostolic and primitive Christianity.

It recognizes the New Testament as the only infallible rule of faith and practice, and maintains that Faith toward God, Repentance from dead works, Regeneration of the heart and mind, baptism by Trine immersion for remission of sins unto the reception of the Holy Ghost by the laying on of hands, are the means of adoption into the household of God,—the church militant.

It also maintains that Feet-washing, as taught in John 13, both by example and command of Jesus, should be observed in the church.

That the Lord's Supper, instituted by Christ and as universally observed by the apostles and the early Christians, is a full meal, and, in connection with the Communion, should be taken in the evening or after the close of the day.

That the Salutation of the Holy Kiss, or Kiss of Charity, is binding upon the followers of Christ.

That War and Retaliation are contrary to the spirit and self-denying principles of the religion of Jesus Christ.

That the principles of Plain Dressing and of Non-conformity to the world, as taught in the New Testament, should be observed by the followers of Christ.

That the Scriptural duty of Anointing the Sick with Oil, in the Name of the Lord, James 5: 14, is binding upon all Christians.

It also advocates the church's duty to support Missionary and Tract Work, thus giving to the Lord for the spread of the Gospel and for the conversion of sinners.

In short, it is a vindicator of all that Christ and the apostles have enjoined upon us, and aims, amid the conflicting theories and discords of modern Christendom, to point out ground that all must concede to be infallibly safe.

☞ The above principles of our Fraternity are set forth on our "Brethren's Envelopes." Use them! Price, 15 cents per package; 40 cents per hundred.

of the Southern District of Illinois, at the Cerro Gordo church, Dec. 16 and 17, 1891:

1. After the devotional exercises, Bro. Geo. W. Cripe stated the object of the meeting.

2. On motion Bro. Dan. Vaniman was chosen temporary chairman.

3. The following rules were adopted to govern the meeting:

(a) The organization shall consist of Moderator, Clerk and Treasurer, who shall be elected by a majority ballot of the ministers present, belonging to the Southern District of Illinois, and shall hold their offices for one year, or until their successors shall be appointed.

(b) The Moderator shall keep order, decide who is entitled to the floor, require each speaker to confine his remarks to the subject before the meeting; decide when the speakers' time expires, and when the discussion on any subject shall close.

(c) The Moderator, with the assistance of the elders present, shall designate who shall fill the places of those brethren whose names appear on the programme but are not present.

(d) It shall be the duty of the Clerk to take notes of the proceedings of the meeting, and make true entries, in a journal provided for the purpose, of all the business transacted by the meeting. He shall read all papers which shall be ordered to be read, have the custody of all papers belonging to the meeting, and perform such other duties as usually belong to such offices.

(e) It shall be the duty of the Treasurer to take charge of the funds belonging to the assembly, and pay out only when ordered to do so by the meeting. He shall render an account of all funds received and expended, as often as requested to do so by the meeting.

(f) No one shall speak without first addressing the Moderator and being recognized by him.

(g) No one shall be entitled to more than two speeches on the same subject (without the consent of the meeting), the first limited to fifteen minutes, and the second to five minutes.

(h) Any one using personalities in his speech, shall be called to order by the Moderator.

(i) All the members present (whether belonging to the Southern District of Illinois or not), are permitted to take part in the speaking.

4. ORGANIZATION. The meeting was organized by electing D. B. Gibson, Moderator; Chas. Gibson, Clerk; John S. Kuns, Treasurer.

5. CARRYING OUT THE PROGRAMME.

(a) "The Church, its Mission and Relation to its Ministers." Discussed by David Troxel and T. B. Lyon; followed by Michael Flory, A. J. Bowers, Daniel Vaniman, G. W. Cripe and Thomas Keiser.

(b) "What will Make our Churches Prosper?" Discussed by T. D. Lyon and A. J. Bowers, followed by Bro. Frederick, of Indiana; G. W. Cripe, A. J. Nickey, Daniel Vaniman, D. B. Studebaker and Thomas Keiser.

(c) "The Minister and his Duties." Discussed by G. W. Cripe and D. B. Gibson; followed by brethren Frederick, Vaniman, Nickey, Troxel and Bowers.

(d) "Missionary Work and How to Make it more Effective." Discussed by G. W. Cripe and Menno Stouffer; followed by J. H. Brubaker, David Troxel and Daniel Vaniman.

(e) "The Relation of Ministers to the Sunday-school and Prayer-meeting." Discussed by Michael Flory and J. H. Brubaker, followed by A. J. Bowers and D. B. Studebaker.

(f) "The Sunday-school and its Relation to the Church." Discussed by D. B. Gibson and A. J. Nickey; followed by Michael Flory.

6. On motion the officers of the meeting were authorized to appoint a committee to prepare a

---

programme for the next Ministerial Meeting; also a committee to select a time and place for next meeting.

7. Committee on Programme, Geo. W. Cripe, D. B. Gibson and William Landis. Committee on time and place, Geo. W. Cripe, D. B. Gibson and William Landis.

8. A collection was held to meet the expenses of the meeting, amounting to $7.32.

9. On motion the Clerk was instructed to purchase a journal and such other stationery as he may need, and the Treasurer is instructed to pay the bill.

10. The Treasurer is instructed to pay the Clerk of the Committee on Programme for this meeting when he shall receive the order, signed by the Clerk of this meeting.

11. The Committee on Programme for next meeting extend an invitation to the members of Southern Illinois, to send questions they desire to have on the programme to G. W. Cripe, Cerro Gordo, Ill. They also request the churches, desiring the next Ministerial Meeting, to send in their calls to G. W. Cripe, foreman of Committee.

12. Calls for next Ministerial Meeting were made by the Hudson church and by the Cerro Gordo church.

13. Resolved that this assembly tender the Cerro Gordo church a vote of thanks for the kindness, generosity and hospitality given us during this meeting.

14. On motion it was decided to send a copy of the Minutes to the MESSENGER Office for publication.

15. The Minutes of the Meeting were read and approved.

Girard, Ill.

ON THE WAY.

BY J. H. MILLER.

I AM now at Plevna, Howard Co., Ind., in the Greentown church, holding a series of meetings. This congregation is in Southern Indiana, and has four ministers, with a medium-sized church of members. Bro. Aaron Moss, from the Howard church, was at their last council. I formed an agreeable acquaintance with him and the ministers of the Greentown church.

I am much worried over a constant pressure of business. In a late article in the MESSENGER I presented the idea that an elder made a very poor evangelist, and vice versa, and I have of late made a special failure of both. I am trying to take care of four churches, and let myself be used as an evangelist. I see that my work does not give the best result in that way. While in the field's work, I frequently receive letters, calling me home to attend to some church work, thus often causing me to spoil a good series of meetings, when souls are nearing the kingdom. How often have members come to me and said, "Bro. Miller, you have just worked up an interest, and now you are leaving us just when we think of doing something."

My heart, not long since, was moved, who two sisters came to me with tears in their eyes, and lamented this sad state of affairs. I have given the subject much thought, and I feel, more than ever, that every congregation should have her own elder. Then let those ministers who can, and are willing, go out as missionaries and evangelists.

I have asked counsel of some of the dear brethren whether I should give up my evangelistic work, or the charge of so many churches. One or the other I must do. The answer of nearly all, so far, has been, "Let some one else take charge of those churches, while you prepare yourself more fully for evangelistic work."

I do wonder what the editors of our church paper have to say on this subject. A word of counsel to a "pilgrim soldier" would be like a brace in a building. Moses, in fighting the battles of the Lord, had to have some one to stay his hands. Ex. 17: 9–12.

Dec. 23.

REMARKS.

We have long been of the opinion that elders should be ordained in every church, so as to avoid the necessity of one elder being burdened with the care of many churches. In case a congregation does not have suitable material of which to make an elder, it should be placed in charge of an elder who will give special attention to preparing material for that purpose. This may be done by proper teaching on this line of work. It is to be feared that we do not give special attention to the way of instructing our members in regard to the qualifications and duties of church officers. More attention given to this line of work might bring forward more men, qualified to lead the flock of God.

Men who are qualified to do evangelistic work by all means ought to do the "work of an evangelist," and spend their time working up the cause at isolated points. He who does this aright will have no time to look after other congregations. Furthermore, it is very unwise for a man to undertake more than he can do well. It is far better to work in more laborers, and so to divide up the burdens as well as the honors. J. H. M.

WHAT DO THESE THINGS SUGGEST?

BY B. E. KESLER.

RECENTLY I took it upon myself to compare the MESSENGER in price and in reading matter with other church papers. The results showed that the MESSENGER is not only more entirely devoted to religious matter, but is lower in price, everything considered.

While, after all, a paper is what its publishers make it, I know that it is a great help to them always to have on hand neat, well-written articles and notes from correspondents, to help in making the paper interesting to its readers. Then, again, a paper cannot be published without proper support and encouragement, and no church can prosper as well without us with a paper.

What, then, do these facts suggest? They tell us that every member who can, should take the paper, and that those who can write should employ their talent in that direction. Let all, now and then, drop the editors a word of approval. It encourages us in any undertaking to know that our efforts and our labors are appreciated. With what eagerness we put forth increased effort when we know we have the sympathy of our fellow-men!

Again, when any business, pertaining to the Lord's work, is to be done, how slow we are to take hold, and how sparingly we now, when we have taken hold! We see this when calls are made for contributions for the poor, for church expenses, or for helping to build up churches. We don't act that way when a business, pertaining to our own work is at stake. Supposing Bro. A. or Bro. B. wants a good horse, a fine house, a hundred acres of land, or anything else for his own convenience, what do you think he would say, were you to tell him the Lord needed means for any of the above-named purposes? "I'm too poor." Well, how long do you think he would do without that horse, or that house, or that land, or any other convenience? You don't know? Well, what do these things suggest? They tell us that every one should give as the Lord has prospered him.

Furthermore, suppose a church has a large ter-

WORK.

OAKER.

ntion of the members
Illinois to the fact that
l soon be placed in the
tion. Let all consider
er. The object of the
h,
of Illinois has a large
get the best results we
o draw. By having a
interest only, we will
at will last as long as
fund of this kind, if
ted to do an immense

o thus helping to move
There are members
old, and have considera-
, and before they pass
pportunity to bequeath,
alth to the work of the
having a lot or part in
t of us cannot do much,
nat we can. We, in no
and our work will fol-
passed away. No mat-
fifty, one hundred dol-
still will be doing work
sandor.
lled to the necessity of
se duty will be to can-
which they live, and for-
ass of the solicitors to the
Missionary Committee.
x 224, Virden, Ill.,
l 10 of Minutes of 1801.
of churches have this at-
ticable.

ORDER OF COMMITTEE.

AL MEETING.

GIBSON.

acord of the proceedings
og, held by the ministers

---

of the Southern District of Illinois, at the Cerro
Gordo church, Dec. 16 and 17, 1891:

1. After the devotional exercises, Bro. Geo. W.
Cripe stated the object of the meeting.

2. On motion Bro. Dan. Vaniman was chosen
temporary chairman.

3. The following rules were adopted to govern
the meeting:

(a) The organization shall consist of Moderator, Clerk and Treasurer, who shall be elected by
a majority ballot of the ministers present, belonging to the Southern District of Illinois, and shall
hold their offices for one year, or until their successors shall be appointed.

(b) The Moderator shall keep order, decide
who is entitled to the floor, require each speaker
to confine his remarks to the subject before the
meeting, decide when the speakers' time expires,
and when the discussion on any subject shall
close.

(c) The Moderator, with the assistance of the
elders present, shall designate who shall fill the
places of those brethren whose names appear on
the programme but are not present.

(d) It shall be the duty of the Clerk to take
notes of the proceedings of the meeting, and make
true entries, in a journal provided for the purpose, of all the business transacted by the meeting.
He shall read all papers which shall be ordered to be read, have the custody of all papers
belonging to the meeting, and perform such other
duties as usually belong to such offices.

(e) It shall be the duty of the Treasurer to take
charge of the funds belonging to the assembly,
and pay out only when ordered to do so by the
meeting. He shall render an account of all funds
received and expended, as often as requested to
do so by the meeting.

(f) No one shall speak without first addressing
the Moderator and being recognized by him.

(g) No one shall be entitled to more than two
speeches on the same subject (without the consent of the meeting), the first limited to fifteen
minutes, and the second to five minutes.

(h) Any one using personalities in his speech,
shall be called to order by the Moderator.

(i) All the members present (whether belonging to the Southern District of Illinois or not),
are permitted to take part in the speaking.

4. ORGANIZATION. The meeting was organized
by electing D. B. Gibson, Moderator; Chas. Gibson, Clerk; John S. Kuns, Treasurer.

5. CARRYING OUT THE PROGRAMME.

(a) "The Church, its Mission and Relation to
its Ministers." Discussed by David Troxel and
T. B. Lyon; followed by Michael Flory, A. J.
Bowers, Daniel Vaniman, G. W. Cripe and Thomas Keiser.

(b) "What will Make our Churches Prosper?"
Discussed by T. D. Lyon and A. J. Bowers, followed by Bro. Frederick, of Indiana; G. W.
Cripe, A. J. Nickey, Daniel Vaniman, D. B. Studebaker and Thomas Keiser.

(c) "The Minister and his Duties." Discussed
by G. W. Cripe and D. B. Gibson; followed by
brethren Frederick, Vaniman, Nickey, Troxel
and Bowers.

(d) "Missionary Work and How to Make it
more Effective." Discussed by G. W. Cripe and
Menno Stouffer; followed by J. H. Brubaker, David Troxel and Daniel Vaniman.

(e) "The Relation of Ministers to the Sunday-
school and Prayer-meeting." Discussed by Michael Flory and J. H. Brubaker, followed by A.
J. Bowers and D. B. Studebaker.

(f) "The Sunday-school and its Relation to the
Church." Discussed by D. B. Gibson and A. J.
Nickey; followed by Michael Flory.

6. On motion the officers of the meeting were
authorized to appoint a committee to prepare a

---

programme for the next Ministerial Meeting; also a committee to select a time and place for next
meeting.

7. Committee on Programme, Geo. W. Cripe,
D. B. Gibson and William Landis. Committee
on time and place, Geo. W. Cripe, D. B. Gibson
and William Landis.

8. A collection was held to meet the expenses
of the meeting, amounting to $7.32.

9. On motion the Clerk was instructed to purchase a journal and such other stationery as he
may need, and the Treasurer is instructed to pay
the bill.

10. The Treasurer is instructed to pay the
Clerk of the Committee on Programme for this
meeting when he shall receive the order, signed
by the Clerk of this meeting.

11. The Committee on Programme for next
meeting extend an invitation to the members of
Southern Illinois, to send questions they desire to
have on the programme to G. W. Cripe, Cerro
Gordo, Ill. They also request the churches, desiring the next Ministerial Meeting, to send in
their calls to G. W. Cripe, foreman of Committee.

12. Calls for next Ministerial Meeting were
made by the Hudson church and by the Cerro
Gordo church.

13. Resolved that this assembly tender the Cerro Gordo church a vote of thanks for the kindness, generosity and hospitality given us during
this meeting.

14. On motion it was decided to send a copy of
the Minutes to the MESSENGER Office for publication.

15. The Minutes of the Meeting were read and
approved.

Girard, Ill.

ON THE WAY.

BY J. H. MILLER.

I AM now at Plevna, Howard Co., Ind., in the
Greentown church, holding a series of meetings.
This congregation is in Southern Indiana, and
has four ministers, with a medium-sized church
of members. Bro. Aaron Moss, from the Howard
church, was at their last council. I formed an
agreeable acquaintance with him and the ministers of the Greentown church.

I am much worried over a constant pressure of
business. In a late article in the MESSENGER I
presented the idea that an elder made a very poor
evangelist, and vice versa, and I have of late
made a special failure of both. I am trying to
take care of four churches, and let myself be
used as an evangelist. I see that my work does
not give the best result in that way. While in
the field at work, I frequently receive letters, calling me home to attend to some church work, thus
often causing me to spoil a good series of meetings, when souls are nearing the kingdom. How
often have members come to me and said, "Bro.
Miller, you have just worked up an interest, and
now you are leaving us just when we think of doing something."

My heart, not long since, was moved, while
two sisters came to me with tears in their eyes,
and lamented this sad state of affairs. I have
given the subject much thought, and I feel, more
than ever, that every congregation should have
her own elder. Then let those ministers who can,
and are willing, go out as missionaries and evangelists.

I have asked counsel of some of the dear brethren whether I should give up my evangelistic
work, or the charge of so many churches. One
or the other I must do. The answer of nearly all,
so far, has been, "Let some one else take charge
of those churches, while you prepare yourself
more fully for evangelistic work."

I do wonder what the editors of our chuuh paper have to say on this subject. A word of counsel to a "pilgrim soldier" would be like a brace
in a building. Moses, in fighting the battles of
the Lord, had to have some one to stay his hands.
Ex. 17: 9–12.

Dec. 23.

REMARKS.

We have long been of the opinion that elders
should be ordained in every church, so as to avoid
the necessity of one elder being burdened with
the care of many churches. In case a congregation does not have suitable material of which to
make an elder, it should be placed in charge of an
elder who will give special attention to preparing material for that purpose. This may be done
by proper teaching on this line of work. It is to
be feared that we do not give special attention to
the way of instructing our members in regard to
the qualifications and duties of church officers.
More attention given to this line of work might
bring forward more men, qualified to lead the flock
of God.

Men who are qualified to do evangelistic work
by all means ought to do the "work of an evangelist," and spend their time working up the
cause at isolated points. He who does this
aright will have no time to look after other congregations. Furthermore, it is very unwise for a
man to undertake more than he can do well. It is
far better to work in more laborers, so as to divide
up the burdens as well as the honors. J. H. M.

WHAT DO THESE THINGS SUGGEST?

BY B. E. KESLER.

RECENTLY I took it upon myself to compare the
MESSENGER in price and in reading matter with
other church papers. The results showed that
the MESSENGER is not only more entirely devoted
to religious matter, but is lower in price, everything considered.

While, after all, a paper is what its publishers
make it, I know that it is a great help to them always to have on hand neat, well-written articles
and notes from correspondents, to help in making
the paper interesting to its readers. Then, again,
a paper cannot be published without proper support and encouragement, and no church can prosper as well without us WITH a paper.

What, then, do these facts suggest? They tell
us that every member who can, should take the
paper, and that those who can write should employ their talent in that direction. Let all, now
and then, drop the editors a word of approval.
It encourages us in any undertaking to know that
our efforts and our labors are appreciated. With
what eagerness we put forth increased effort when
we know we have the sympathy of our fellow-men!

Again, when any business, pertaining to the
Lord's work, is to be done, how slow we are to take
hold, and how sparingly we sow, when we have tak-
en hold! We see this when calls are made for
contributions for the poor, for church expenses, or
for helping to build up churches. We don't act
that way when a business, pertaining to our own
work is at stake. Supposing Bro. A. or Bro. B.
wants a good horse, a fine house, a hundred acres
of land, or anything else for his own convenience,
what do you think he would say, were you to tell
him the Lord needed means for any of the above-
named purposes? "I'm too poor." Well, how
long do you think he would do without that horse,
or that house, or that land, or any other convenience? You don't know? Well, what do these
things suggest? They tell us that every one
should give as the Lord has prospered him.

Furthermore, suppose a church has a large ter-

---

capital of France, last November, that we should meet with the Committee in January and again enjoy the blessing of our own home.

Had our plans been carried out, we should, at this time, be wandering in the land of the Pharaohs or crossing the desert on our pilgrimage to Jerusalem. As it is, we are at home, and oh, what a meaning the word has to the weary travelers! How little we know of the future and what it is to bring to us! How we plan and arrange and then the paths we have marked out are never pressed by our feet.

But we are fully persuaded that the Lord rules in human affairs. Long ago we committed our going and coming to him and we submit without a murmur to what might have the appearance of a great disappointment. We can only know now that for some cause our trip to the East had to be abandoned and deferred. Why a combination of circumstances occurred to bring about this result, we cannot now know, and here we rest the case, knowing that all things work together for good to them that love the Lord.

To our readers we give the following explanation of the causes which led us to defer, for the present, our trip to the East. Soon after reaching London we received notice that the cholera was raging in the East, and that it had broken out in Damascus. Later came the information that all the ports in Syria including the Palestine seaports were quarantined, and that the various steamer lines on the Mediterranean had stopped running to Syria and Palestine. Here was an obstacle in the way which we could not overcome. We, however, concluded to wait, hoping for a favorable issue. We went to Paris, and while there met the general manager of the continental and eastern lines of travel. He was very kind to us and gave us much valuable information. Just before we left Paris he said to us, "I shall advise you not to attempt to visit Palestine this winter. The cholera is there now; it may abate later in the season, but you are entirely unused to the climate, the seeds of the disease will be there, and if you come in contact with the disease you will fall a victim to it." This advice we decided to follow.

We then thought of spending the winter in Europe, and had some hopes of returning to Denmark and Sweden, to labor in the mission there, but owing to the failure of wife's health, and after advising with those competent to give advice in the case, we concluded that it would be best for us to return to our home. In coming to this conclusion, we sought the guidance of the Divine Hand, and as the way was closed to us in Asia, and open for us to America, we took the open way, as it appeared to us, at the time, by the Lord's direction.

We spoke of the disappointment. At first we felt it keenly. We had spent a good deal of time and money in preparing for the trip. Over one hundred volumes of the best works on Egypt and Palestine had been purchased, and many of them carefully read and studied. We had left our home at a great sacrifice to both of us, and much greater to wife than we realized at the time. We had braved the dangers of an ocean voyage, had purchased tickets for at least a part of the eastern trip, and after all the way was closed. To give up a work upon which the heart is set; is not always easy to do. But we had placed it all in the hands of the Lord, and are glad to say that we have not a single regret, personal to ourselves. While we felt the disappointment, it has never caused us a moment's worry.

But there is to us a matter of regret in the thought that others may be disappointed. Some, we know, were quite anxious to have the series of letters from the East, and some may have subscribed for the MESSENGER to secure them. There will, no doubt, be some disappointment felt by these, and, on their account, we are sorry and wish we might have been enabled to go on with our journey, but we trust that they will bear with the slight loss. They are not alone in this. Counting the cost of the trip to Europe, and return, and the tickets for the eastern trip, still unused, a good portion of the entire expense of the trip to the East had been met, and the meeting of the expense has been a matter entirely personal to ourselves We only refer to this to show our readers that we have tried to do our part.

As to what is to come, we have notes from which, if the Lord will, a number of letters will be written, covering the ground of our wanderings in the Old World. Some letters will also be given, outside of our line of travel. These letters will run through a portion of the current volume of the MESSENGER. We believe they will be interesting and instructive. If, however, when the letters close, any who were induced to subscribe for the paper on account of the promised letters, feel dissatisfied, they will notify us, and the money for the unexpired part of their subscription will be refunded. We believe but few will make this demand when all the circumstances are taken into consideration, but we feel that it is but just and right that this offer be made.

Our trip to the East and the Lands of the Bible is simply deferred for the present. If the Lord so wills it, and the way opens, we still have the desire to go on with the work. If not, we express the hope that, what has already been accomplished in that direction, may be an inspiration to others to take up the work. It rests to-day, so far as we are concerned, where it has rested these many years, in the hands of the Lord, and there we leave it, knowing right well that he will direct it all for our good.

Our home-coming was pleasant to us. We sailed from Bremerhaven Dec. 15, in company with Bro. Hope and Prof. Cravens. After a rough winter voyage we landed in New York Dec. 24, and reached home Jan. 2, just six months, less two days, from the time we started on our wanderings, and now we are at home. Another journey ended! When we met those we loved at the depot, and received their warm greeting and hearty welcome home, we were so glad and happy, and then we thought of the end of another journey, of another home-coming, of another welcome and greeting. If the greeting of loved ones brings joy to our hearts here, "oh, what will it be over there!" To the weary traveler and the tired wanderer, home is doubly dear. So to those who are but pilgrims here, who seek a better country, the desire to go home becomes stronger as they plod on their weary way, and when the summons comes, how glad they are to go! How joyfully they cross over the river, and how they can sing as they go home:

> "Friends fondly cherished, have passed on before;
> Waiting, they watch me approaching the shore;
> Singing to cheer me through death's chilling gloom;
> Joyfully, joyfully haste to thy home.
> Sounds of sweet melody fall on my ear;
> Harps of the blessed, your voices I hear!
> Rings with the harmony heaven's high dome—
> Joyfully, joyfully haste to thy home."

May the Lord help us all to be ready, so that, when the summons comes to go home, we may joyfully and gladly go!   D. L. M.

[Copyrighted.]

EDITORIAL WANDERINGS IN THE OLD WORLD.

BY D. L. MILLER.

Number Fifteen.

London.—St. Paul's Cathedral.—Westminster Abbey.

THREE weeks in London enabled us to see something of the great city outside of the various collections of antiquities in which we were so much interested and of which we have written at considerable length. Among other places we visited and spent some time in St. Paul's Cathedral and Westminster Abbey; both of these churches are of great historical interest and well worth a visit. We also spent considerable time in the London Tower, a fortress, a prison, and a palace, in which have been enacted scenes of such horrible cruelty that it would seem that the very stones would have cried out against the inhumanity of some of the kings and queens of England. From the Tower we went to Windsor Castle, the favorite residence of Queen Victoria, who has been on the throne fifty-four years.

As a rule, we do not care to spend much time in writing descriptions of palaces, picture galleries, and fine buildings. We are much more interested in the study of the home life of the common people. The former have been the subject of newspaper and magazine articles by the thousand. Over and over again the towns and cities have been described, but very little has been written as to how the masses of the people live. Of course, our stay in England was much too short to give attention to the customs of the people, and we shall not attempt to write upon them. But there are a number of places in great centers of population, like London and Paris, around which cluster so many important historical events that we think well to give our readers a brief sketch of them, and we devote this letter to London and a few of its most important places of interest.

ST. PAUL'S CATHEDRAL

is London's most important building. Standing, as it does, in the very heart of the great metropolis, it has been, not unaptly, called the capitol of the city. The site upon which the present building stands was occupied by a church, built by the early Christians during the Roman period, which was destroyed by the Saxon Pagans and rebuilt by king Ethelbert A. D. 610. This was burned down in 961 and restored within a year. Again the edifice suffered from fire, and it was not until 1675 that the present building was begun and carried to completion in 1710, at a cost of nearly four million dollars. It is built in the form of a cross and is 500 feet long; the arms of the cross, or transepts are 250 feet in length and 118 feet in width. The dome is 112 feet in diameter and 225 feet high inside. The area is about 8,500 square yards.

Some idea of the vast extent of the building may be formed by the following comparison. The school buildings at Mt. Morris, three in number, could be placed in one end of the cathedral and would take up less than one-third of its length, in the other end the Huntingdon school buildings could be placed and there would be a distance of 200 feet between them and Mt. Morris. McPherson College would find ample room in one arm and Lordsburg in the other, and Bridgewater could be easily accommodated in the center under the vast dome. After these were all thus placed

capital of France, last November, that we should meet with the Committee in January and again enjoy the blessing of our own home.

Had our plans been carried out, we should, at this time, be wandering in the land of the Pharaohs or crossing the desert on our pilgrimage to Jerusalem. As it is, we are at home, and oh, what a meaning the word has to the weary travelers! How little we know of the future and what it is to bring to us! How we plan and arrange and then the paths we have marked out are never pressed by our feet.

But we are fully persuaded that the Lord rules in human affairs. Long ago we committed our going and coming to him and we submit without a murmur to what might have the appearance of a great disappointment. We can only know now that for some cause our trip to the East had to be abandoned and deferred. Why a combination of circumstances occurred to bring about this result, we cannot now know, and here we rest the case, knowing that all things work together for good to them that love the Lord.

To our readers we give the following explanation of the causes which led us to defer, for the present, our trip to the East. Soon after reaching London we received notice that the cholera was raging in the East, and that it had broken out in Damascus. Later came the information that all the ports in Syria including the Palestine seaports were quarantined, and that the various steamer lines on the Mediterranean had stopped running to Syria and Palestine. Here was an obstacle in the way which we could not overcome. We, however, concluded to wait, hoping for a favorable issue. We went to Paris, and while there met the general manager of the continental and eastern lines of travel. He was very kind to us and gave us much valuable information. Just before we left Paris he said to us, "I shall advise you not to attempt to visit Palestine this winter. The cholera is there now; it may abate later in the season, but you are entirely unused to the climate, the seeds of the disease will be there, and if you come in contact with the disease you will fall a victim to it." This advice we decided to follow.

We then thought of spending the winter in Europe, and had some hopes of returning to Denmark and Sweden, to labor in the mission there, but owing to the failure of wife's health, and after advising with those competent to give advice in the case, we concluded that it would be best for us to return to our home. In coming to this conclusion, we sought the guidance of the Divine Hand, and as the way was closed to us in Asia, and open for us to America, we took the open way, as it appeared to us, at the time, by the Lord's direction.

We spoke of the disappointment. At first we felt it keenly. We had spent a good deal of time and money in preparing for the trip. Over one hundred volumes of the best works on Egypt and Palestine had been purchased, and many of them carefully read and studied. We had left our home at a great sacrifice to both of us, and much greater to wife than we realized at the time. We had braved the dangers of an ocean voyage, had purchased tickets for at least a part of the eastern trip, and after all the way was closed. To give up a work upon which the heart is set; is not always easy to do. But we had placed it all in the hands of the Lord, and are glad to say that we have not a single regret, personal to ourselves. While we felt the disappointment, it has never caused us a moment's worry.

But there is to us a matter of regret in the thought that others may be disappointed. Some, we know, were quite anxious to have the series of letters from the East, and some may have subscribed for the MESSENGER to secure them. There will, no doubt, be some disappointment felt by these, and, on their account, we are sorry and wish we might have been enabled to go on with our journey, but we trust that they will bear with the slight loss. They are not alone in this. Counting the cost of the trip to Europe, and return, and the tickets for the eastern trip, still unused, a good portion of the entire expense of the trip to the East had been met, and the meeting of the expense has been a matter entirely personal to ourselves. We only refer to this to show our readers that we have tried to do our part.

As to what is to come, we have notes from which, if the Lord will, a number of letters will be written, covering the ground of our wanderings in the Old World. Some letters will also be given, outside of our line of travel. These letters will run through a portion of the current volume of the MESSENGER. We believe they will be interesting and instructive. If, however, when the letters close, any who were induced to subscribe for the paper on account of the promised letters, feel dissatisfied, they will notify us, and the money for the unexpired part of their subscription will be refunded. We believe but few will make this demand when all the circumstances are taken into consideration, but we feel that it is but just and right that this offer be made.

Our trip to the East and the Lands of the Bible is simply deferred for the present. If the Lord so will it, and the way opens, we still have the desire to go on with the work. If not, we express the hope that, what has already been accomplished in that direction, may be an inspiration to others to take up the work. It rests to-day, so far as we are concerned, where it has rested these many years, in the hands of the Lord, and there we leave it, knowing right well that he will direct it all for our good.

Our home-coming was pleasant to us. We sailed from Bremerhaven Dec. 15, in company with Bro. Hope and Prof. Cravens. After a rough winter voyage we landed in New York Dec. 24, and reached home Jan. 2, just six months, less two days, from the time we started on our wanderings, and now we are at home. Another journey ended! When we met those we loved at the depot, and received their warm greeting and hearty welcome home, we were so glad and happy, and then we thought of the end of another journey, of another home-coming, of another welcome and greeting. If the greeting of loved ones brings joy to our hearts here, "oh, what will it be over there!" To the weary traveler and the tired wanderer, home is doubly dear. So to those who are but pilgrims here, who seek a better country, the desire to go home becomes stronger as they plod on their weary way, and when the summons comes, how glad they are to go! How joyfully they cross over the river, and how they can sing as they go home:

> "Friends fondly cherished, have passed on before;
> Waiting, they watch me approaching the shore;
> Singing to cheer me through death's chilling gloom;
> Joyfully, joyfully haste to thy home.
> Sounds of sweet melody fall on my ear;
> Harps of the blessed, your voices I hear!
> Rings with the harmony heaven's high dome—
> Joyfully, joyfully haste to thy home."

May the Lord help us all to be ready, so that when the summons comes to go home, we may joyfully and gladly go!   D. L. M.

EDITORIAL WANDERINGS IN THE OLD WORLD.

BY D. L. MILLER.

Number Fifteen.

London.—St. Paul's Cathedral.—Westminster Abbey.

THREE weeks in London enabled us to see something of the great city outside of the various collections of antiquities in which we were so much interested and of which we have written at considerable length. Among other places we visited and spent some time in St. Paul's Cathedral and Westminster Abbey; both of these churches are of great historical interest and well worth a visit. We also spent considerable time in the London Tower, a fortress, a prison, and a palace, in which have been enacted scenes of such horrible cruelty that it would seem that the very stones would have cried out against the inhumanity of some of the kings and queens of England. From the Tower we went to Windsor Castle, the favorite residence of Queen Victoria, who has been on the throne fifty-four years.

As a rule, we do not care to spend much time in writing descriptions of palaces, picture galleries, and fine buildings. We are much more interested in the study of the home life of the common people. The former have been the subject of newspaper and magazine articles by the thousand. Over and over again the towns and cities have been described, but very little has been written as to how the masses of the people live. Of course, our stay in England was much too short to give attention to the customs of the people, and we shall not attempt to write upon them. But there are a number of places in great centers of population, like London and Paris, around which cluster so many important historical events that we think well to give our readers a brief sketch of them, and we devote this letter to London and a few of its most important places of interest.

ST. PAUL'S CATHEDRAL

is London's most important building. Standing, as it does, in the very heart of the great metropolis, it has been, not unaptly, called the capitol of the city. The site upon which the present building stands was occupied by a church, built by the early Christians during the Roman period, which was destroyed by the Saxon Pagans and rebuilt by king Ethelbert A. D. 610. This was burned down in 961 and restored within a year. Again the edifice suffered from fire, and it was not until 1675 that the present building was begun and carried to completion in 1710, at a cost of nearly four million dollars. It is built in the form of a cross and is 500 feet long; the arms of the cross, or transepts are 250 feet in length and 118 feet in width. The dome is 112 feet in diameter and 225 feet high inside. The area is about 8,500 square yards.

Some idea of the vast extent of the building may be formed by the following comparison. The school buildings at Mt. Morris, three in number, could be placed in one end of the cathedral and would take up less than one-third of its length, in the other end the Huntingdon school buildings could be placed and there would be a distance of 200 feet between them and Mt. Morris. McPherson College would find ample room in one arm and Lordsburg in the other, and Bridgewater could be easily accommodated in the center under the vast dome. After these were all thus placed

and I shall long remember their kindness to me, a stranger among them. This church is under the eldership of Bro. J. H. Caylor, assisted in the ministry by brethren Smeltzer and Bercham.

I write this for the benefit of any brethren or sisters, that may be living or stopping for a while in or about Indianapolis. They can have the privilege of church fellowship and service by taking the Lake Erie & Western R. R., twenty-two miles north-east to Noblesville, where you will be cared for by first notifying Bro. J. H. Caylor, Noblesville, Ind.　　　JOHN BENNETT.

Elbinsville, Pa., Dec. 17.

From Ogden Centre, Lenawee Co., Mich.

WE are few in number, but are still striving, by the grace of God, to work for the Master. We held a series of meetings at Ogden Centre, in the Advent church. Eld. Perry McKimmy did the preaching. He preached the Word in its purity and with power. Three precious souls were made willing to forsake sin and join in with the children of God, to help spread the glad tidings of the Gospel. Others were near the kingdom, and we hope that the good seed sown may be as bread cast upon the waters. On account of not having a house of our own, we discontinued our meetings after the first week. The doctrines of the Gospel becoming too strong for our Advent elder, he said that we could have the house next evening only on condition that the brother would preach from the subject which he would give. The proposition was accepted. At the close of the meeting the subject that he gave was on the change of the Sabbath. This the brother explained satisfactorily to a well-filled house, but not so satisfactorily to our Advent elder. The questions asked were all promptly answered.　　　J. N. McKIMMY.

Call for a Minister.

THE little band of members at this place is isolated, and would like very much if some brother, who is able to defend the cause, as taught by the Brethren, would locate among us. We are few in number, and in limited circumstances, but are willing to assist as far as able. Our church is known as the Sampson Hill church. For further particulars address the writer.

HENRY TRANTER.

Shoals, Martin Co., Ind.

REMARKS.

Here is another opportunity for a minister of limited means to make himself useful. This practical way of calling for ministerial aid, we trust, will result in great good, both spiritually and temporally.

A Trip to South Dakota.

I BOARDED the 2 A. M. train at New Hampton, Iowa, for Kimball, S. D., where I was met at 6 P. M., by Bro. Peterson, of the Bijou Hills church. The next morning I started with Bro. Peterson in a lumber wagon for Bijou Hills,—a distance of twenty-five miles, nearly South-west from Kimball. I reached Bro. W. G. Cook's about one o'clock P. M., where we were kindly received by Bro. and sister Cook. After a little rest we started with Bro. Cook and family for the place of meeting, where we found the dear brethren and sisters assembled to celebrate the suffering and death of our blessed Lord. It was a feast to all present. The meetings were continued until the inclemency of the weather forbade further work.

There are about forty members in this church, and a more active, zealous and devoted member ship is seldom seen. Bro. W. G. Cook has the

oversight of the little flock and is aided in the ministry by brethren John McLean and W. E. Root,—both worthy brethren, young in the ministry, but bidding fair to become efficient workmen in the house of the Lord. These two brethren were forwarded to the second degree of the ministry, while I was there, and one deacon was elected. The church is in a good working condition.

The brethren here are laboring under many disadvantages. They had short crops and a long way to market. Failures in crops have kept them down financially, but the last year's bountiful harvest has helped them considerably. One of the greatest difficulties, with which they have to contend, is the lack of a suitable place wherein to hold meetings. Their school-houses are too small, and having no meeting-house, they rent a Grand Army Hall for summer use. Being poorly constructed, it cannot be kept comfortable in cold weather, and even this Hall can only be rented for a month at a time, and the result is they are obliged to discontinue their regular meetings during the winter.　　　M. H. FOWLER.

Fredericksburg, Iowa.

From Cartersville, Va.

BRO. BOWSER and family left us last Thursday, which makes us feel quite sad, as we thought that this was the place for him, but we give all things over into the hands of him who doeth all things well. A good work can be done here. Who will respond? There is plenty of work here for two ministers. I read in the GOSPEL MESSENGER some time ago a sketch, written by Bro. F. M. Bowers, of New Stark, Ohio, and others, wishing to locate in South-eastern Virginia. We would be glad to have them among us. We have a church-house, but very few members. Bro. Mallory wrote to him as soon as he read the article, and yesterday received the letter again from the Dead Letter Office. I take this method of letting him know our need, and trust that he will respond to the call.　　　FLORIDA J. E. ETTER.

Dec. 19.

From Cherry Grove, Ill.

BRO. Samuel Lehman, from Lee County, Ill., has been holding meetings with us during the past week. The meetings closed last night with good and growing interest. Sinners have been warned of the great danger, and old soldiers of the cross have been made to feel that it is good to wait on the Lord. The church has been much revived and we believe God's name has been glorified. We hope our brother will come again and help to cheer us on our earthly pilgrimage. Messages from the East and West this morning tell us of much sickness and many deaths among the young and the old. The question comes forcibly to our mind, "Are we God's children and are we living for heaven and happiness?"

JAS. H. LARKINS.

Dec. 21.

From Wichita, Kans.

WE came here last spring to take charge of the church, and are now trying to hold regular meetings in the city. We meet with much that is in the way. We have no meeting-house in the city, but are trying to raise funds to build or buy one. Most of the members here are in limited circumstances. Then, too, some in the church are not favorable to having meetings or Sunday-school in the city.

Bro. Eby was with us a short time ago in council. He was called here to assist in forwarding brethren A. L. Snowberger and Charles Delp to the second degree of the ministry. All passed off

satisfactorily. Bro. Eby preached two forcible discourses in the city, on Christian work, that were calculated to stir up drones, unless, indeed, they were too far gone to be moved by human instrumentality.

We have rented, for the present, the Congregational church on Fifteenth Street, where we hold Sunday-school and meetings. Brethren, passing through here, will be kindly taken care of if they will stop over.　　　WILLIAM JOHNSON.

From the Mission Field in Idaho and Washington.

OUR Communion meeting at Moscow, Oct. 24, was one of unusual interest. We also had a good meeting on Thanksgiving Day. We cannot report as many additions as we would like, still, additions are not always a proof of success. To maintain order, peace, love and fellowship is most essential to prosperity. When such is the case, additions will be the natural outgrowth.

We have now been at Moscow one year, and have learned something of the magnitude of mission work in this broad field, which is becoming larger all the time. Calls come from all directions, where there are one or more members at a place. They say, "Come; we have not heard a brother preach for years. We want our children that we have not had time to visit since. The field is large, and the workers are few. I would rejoice if our Mission Board could send two good missionaries to this field. One is needed in the north; one in the south. Men are needed, sound in faith, sound in principle, able and willing to maintain the principles of our great Brotherhood. We want men for new fields that are sociable to all classes,—men that hold forth the Truth with boldness; men who know no surrender and are not easily discouraged. New fields require time and patience, and men who will settle down to the work and stay until the work is permanently established. We like visitors, but their stay is too short to accomplish much.　　　SIDNEY HODGDEN.

Moscow, Idaho, Dec. 22.

Notes of Travel.

WIFE and I left home Dec. 1, *en route* for the Salt River Valley, Arizona, of which we had heard much, concerning its mild climate, fruit productions, etc. In company with about twenty of our friends and acquaintances we left Kansas City over the M. K. & T. R. R., and arrived at Fort Worth, Tex., on the evening of the 2nd. Here we had some time to wait, which we spent in looking about the City. Among the many things of interest I will only mention one, the Natatorium, supplied with water by an artesian well, 1,400 feet deep, sending forth a stream about six inches in diameter. Here one can take any kind of bath he may wish. Proceeding to El Paso, where we again have some time for sightseeing, we cross the Rio Grande River into the old town of Paso del Norte, Mex. Here we inspect the old Catholic church, erected about 300 years ago, and are now living in a good state of preservation. Here is to be seen the embalmed body of the priest, who met a violent death a great many years ago. Blood on his temple and face can be plainly seen.

Leaving El Paso, we are again carried over the desert. Along the way we see some giant cactus, fifteen feet high, with large arms extending laterally. This, in addition to smaller kinds of cactus and sage brush, is about all one sees until we reach the Valley, which is a veritable garden of verdure, wherever it is brought under cultivation,

and I shall long remember their kindness to me, a stranger among them. This church is under the eldership of Bro. J. H. Caylor, assisted in the ministry by brethren Smeltzer and Bercham.

I write this for the benefit of any brethren or sisters, that may be living or stopping for a while in or about Indianapolis. They can have the privilege of church fellowship and service by taking the Lake Erie & Western R. R., twenty-two miles north-east to Noblesville, where you will be cared for by first notifying Bro. J. H. Caylor, Noblesville, Ind.   JOHN BENNETT.

Elbinsville, Pa., Dec. 17.

From Ogden Centre, Lenawee Co., Mich.

WE are few in number, but are still striving, by the grace of God, to work for the Master. We held a series of meetings at Ogden Centre, in the Advent church. Eld. Perry McKimmy did the preaching. He preached the Word in its purity and with power. Three precious souls were made willing to forsake sin and join in with the children of God, to help spread the glad tidings of the Gospel. Others were near the kingdom, and we hope that the good seed sown may be as bread cast upon the waters. On account of not having a house of our own, we discontinued our meetings after the first week. The doctrines of the Gospel becoming too strong for our Advent elder, he said that we could have the house next evening only on condition that the brother would preach from the subject which he would give. The proposition was accepted. At the close of the meeting the subject that he gave was on the change of the Sabbath. This the brother explained satisfactorily to a well-filled house, but not so satisfactorily to our Advent elder. The questions asked were all promptly answered.   J. N. McKIMMY.

Call for a Minister.

THE little band of members at this place is isolated, and would like very much if some brother, who is able to defend the cause, as taught by the Brethren, would locate among us. We are few in number, and in limited circumstances, but are willing to assist as far as able. Our church is known as the Sampson Hill church. For further particulars address the writer.   HENRY TRANTER.

Shoals, Martin Co., Ind.

REMARKS.

Here is another opportunity for a minister of limited means to make himself useful. This practical way of calling for ministerial aid, we trust, will result in great good, both spiritually and temporally.

A Trip to South Dakota.

I BOARDED the 2 A. M. train at New Hampton, Iowa, for Kimball, S. D., where I was met at 5 P. M., by Bro. Peterson, of the Bijou Hills church. The next morning I started with Bro. Peterson in a lumber wagon for Bijou Hills,—a distance of twenty-five miles, nearly South-west from Kimball. I reached Bro. W. G. Cook's about one o'clock P. M., where we were kindly received by Bro. and sister Cook. After a little rest we started with Bro. Cook and family for the place of meeting, where we found the dear brethren and sisters assembled to celebrate the sufferings and death of our blessed Lord. It was a feast to all present. The meetings were continued until the inclemency of the weather forbade further work.

There are about forty members in this church, and a more active, zealous and devoted membership is seldom seen. Bro. W. G. Cook has the oversight of the little flock and is aided in the ministry by brethren John McLean and W. E. Root,—both worthy brethren, young in the ministry, but bidding fair to become efficient workmen in the house of the Lord. These two brethren were forwarded to the second degree of the ministry, while I was there, and one deacon was elected. The church is in a good working condition.

The brethren here are laboring under many disadvantages. They had short crops and a long way to market. Failures in crops have kept them down financially, but the last year's bountiful harvest has helped them considerably. One of the greatest difficulties, with which they have to contend, is the lack of a suitable place wherein to hold meetings. Their school-houses are too small, and having no meeting-house, they rent a Grand Army Hall for summer use. Being poorly constructed, it cannot be kept comfortable in cold weather, and even this Hall can only be rented for a month at a time, and the result is they are obliged to discontinue their regular meetings during the winter.   M. H. FOWLER.

Fredericksburg, Iowa.

From Cartersville, Va.

BRO. BOWSER and family left us last Thursday, which makes us feel quite sad, as we thought that this was the place for him, but we give all things over into the hands of him who doeth all things well. A good work can be done here. Who will respond? There is plenty of work here for two ministers. I read in the GOSPEL MESSENGER some time ago a sketch, written by Bro. F. M. Bowers, of New Stark, Ohio, and others, wishing to locate in South-eastern Virginia. We would be glad to have them among us. We have a church-house, but very few members. Bro. Mallory wrote to him as soon as he read the article, and yesterday received the letter again from the Dead Letter Office. I take this method of letting him know our need, and trust that he will respond to the call.   FLORIDA J. E. ETTER.

Dec. 19.

From Cherry Grove, Ill.

BRO. Samuel Lehman, from Lee County, Ill., has been holding meetings with us during the past week. The meetings closed last night with good and growing interest. Sinners have been warned of the great danger, and old soldiers of the cross have been made to feel that it is good to wait on the Lord. The church has been much revived and we believe God's name has been glorified. We hope our brother will come again and help to cheer us on our earthly pilgrimage. Messages from the East and West this morning tell us of much sickness and many deaths among the young and the old. The question comes forcibly to our mind, "Are we God's children and are we living for heaven and happiness?"   JAS. H. LARKINS.

Dec. 21.

From Wichita, Kans.

WE came here last spring to take charge of the church, and are now trying to hold regular meetings in the city. We meet with much that is in the way. We have no meeting-house in the city, but are trying to raise funds to build or buy one. Most of the members here are in limited circumstances. Then, too, some in the church are not favorable to having meetings or Sunday-school in the city.

Bro. Eby was with us a short time ago in council. He was called here to assist in forwarding brethren A. L. Snowberger and Charles Delp to the second degree of the ministry. All passed off satisfactorily. Bro. Eby preached two forcible discourses in the city, on Christian work, that were calculated to stir up drones, unless, indeed, they were too far gone to be moved by human instrumentality.

We have rented, for the present, the Congregational church on Fifteenth Street, where we hold Sunday-school and meetings. Brethren, passing through here, will be kindly taken care of if they will stop over.   WILLIAM JOHNSON.

From the Mission Field in Idaho and Washington.

OUR Communion meeting at Moscow, Oct. 24, was one of unusual interest. We also had a good meeting on Thanksgiving Day. We cannot report as many additions as we would like, still, additions are not always a proof of success. To maintain order, peace, love and fellowship is most essential to prosperity. When such is the case, additions will be the natural outgrowth.

We have now been at Moscow one year, and have learned something of the magnitude of mission work in this broad field, which is becoming larger all the time. Calls come from all directions, where there are one or more members at a place. They say, "Come; we have not heard a brother preach for years. We want our children to hear the Gospel in its purity."

There are points of interest we visited last May that we have not had time to visit since. The field is large, and the workers are few. I would rejoice if our Mission Board could send two good missionaries to this field. One is needed in the north; one in the south. Men are needed, sound in faith, sound in principle, able and willing to maintain the principles of our great Brotherhood. We want men for new fields that are sociable to all classes,—men that hold forth the Truth with boldness; men who know no surrender and are not easily discouraged. New fields require time and patience, and men who will settle down to the work and stay until the work is permanently established. We like visitors, but their stay is too short to accomplish much.   SIDNEY HODGDEN.

Moscow, Idaho, Dec. 22.

Notes of Travel.

WIFE and I left home Dec. 1, *en route* for the Salt River Valley, Arizona, of which we had heard much, concerning its mild climate, fruit productions, etc. In company with about twenty of our friends and acquaintances we left Kansas City over the M. K. & T. R. R., on the evening of the 2nd. Here we had some time to wait, which we spent in looking about the City. Among the many things of interest I will only mention one, the Natatorium, supplied with water by an artesian well, 1,400 feet deep, sending forth a stream about six inches in diameter. Here one can take any kind of bath he may wish. Proceeding to El Paso, where we again have some time for sight-seeing, we cross the Rio Grande River into the old town of Paso del Norte, Mex. Here we inspect the old Catholic church, erected about 300 years ago, and which is in a good state of preservation. Here is to be seen the embalmed body of the priest, who met a violent death a great many years ago. Blood on his temple and face can be plainly seen.

Leaving El Paso, we are again carried over the desert. Along the way we see some giant cactus, fifteen feet high, with large arms extending later, ally. This, in addition to smaller kinds of cactus and sage brush, is about all one sees until we reach the Valley, which is a veritable garden of verdure, wherever it is brought under cultivation,

Upon his return he and his mother started for Chamberlain, but sister Cook could only remain until Sunday afternoon, when she had to return home because they left the two little boys sick. Bro. Cook reports that he cannot be moved for a week or more.

There was one death from *La Grippe* in our vicinity. At this writing my folks are some better, and I am able to sit up and make this report, though I am very nervous. Dear saints, remember us and also Bro. Cook's family in your prayers!   B. F. MILLER.

Dec. 30.

Lower Stillwater Notes.

LAST night closed a very interesting series of meetings with us. Dec. 12 Bro. L. W. Teeter, of Hagerstown, Ind., came to us and began meetings, which continued each night until Dec. 28. Some day meetings were also held.

The inquiring mind wonders why the day meetings are not better attended during such a series. The minister leaves his home affairs for weeks at a time, and comes into a community because of his general interest in the welfare of the church and the salvation of souls. Why, then, can we not have special interest in our own children, neighbors and friends, and unite in the special effort with our presence and prayers?

As an immediate result one young sister chose the good part with the people of God. Others are near,—so near that it takes all their power to keep them out.

We do not feel to measure the success of the meeting by the number of accessions alone. The members have been much built up and established.

We are keeping up an evergreen Sunday-school this winter. Instead of closing in the fall, as usual, we re-organized, choosing as Superintendent, Bro. W. W. Barnhart, who, since our last report, has been called to the ministry.

Our force has also been increased by Bro. Wm. Bowser, who has been laboring in Eastern Virginia the past year. Jan. 30 we intend to commence a series of meetings in our Upper house. Bro. Dan. P. Shively, of Peru, Ind., will be with us.   L. A. BOOKWALTER.

Trotwood, Ohio, Dec. 29.

From Ladoga, Ind.

WITHIN the last year there have been forty-six additions to the church at this place. Twenty-one were baptized as a result of the efforts of our home ministers, and nineteen during our protracted meetings. Two were reclaimed and four were received by letter. This shows the result of a more systematic work on the part of our ministers than they had been doing heretofore. There has also been one death in the church, and two members have withdrawn. Our home ministers will begin a series of meetings at the Bethel church-house, Jan. 30.

Bro. Charlie Campbell came to us Dec. 12, and began a series of meetings at Mt. Pleasant. He preached earnestly until Dec. 22, when he was called home to preach a funeral. Next day he returned and continued meetings until Dec. 25, when the meetings closed with one addition by baptism.   CHARITY HIMES.

Death of Eld. William McWhorter.

THE subject of this notice lived in the Four Mile congregation, and died of pneumonia, aged fifty-four years, two months and six days.

Deceased was born in Franklin County, Ind., Oct. 17, 1837. He was a remarkably devout child, and in his youth united with the church. He was called to the ministry Sept. 16, 1876, and to the eldership June 20, 1891. He was loved and respected by all who knew him. Nov. 1, 1866, he was married to Martha M. Stephens. To this union were born three children, one son and two daughters.

He was married a second time Nov. 2, 1876, to Catherine Speer. The son having gone to rest four years ago, Bro. William now leaves a wife, two daughters and a great number of friends who mourn their loss, which, we trust, is his eternal gain. During his four days of illness, he called for the elders of the church, and was anointed with oil in the name of the Lord.

The funeral services were conducted at his residence by Eld. Jacob life from 1 Thess. 4: 13, 14, to a large concourse of people.   EDWARD M. COBB.

Bath, Ind.

From the Spring Creek Church, Ind.

BRO. GORMAN HEETER, of North Manchester, Ind., came to us, to fill a few appointments at Sidney, in the absence of our home ministers. Seeing that there was a good interest, the brethren thought it advisable to continue the meetings a few evenings. Thus we continued for two weeks, closing on Christmas evening with the very best of interest. Good attention was paid to the brother's remarks during the entire meeting. This was Bro. Heeter's first effort to hold a series of meetings alone, but after hearing him, we can truly say that he is "a workman that needeth not to be ashamed." We had no accessions to the church, but we hope that many good impressions were made.   E. MILLER.

To Texas and Return.

NOV. 10th wife and I started for Texas. At Kansas City we met Bro. A. M. Dickey, of Melbourne, Iowa. How thankful we felt that we, as Brethren, may know each other!

South of Kansas City I opened my satchel and took out a roll of tracts and MESSENGERS, which I distributed in several cars. They raised quite an excitement and got us into quite a discussion with a Campbellite and an elderly lady of the Advent faith, but we felt that the doctrine of the Brethren could be readily maintained. We arrived at Miami, Texas, Dec. 13 at 11 P. M. Our five weeks' stay in Texas was in the Counties of Gray, Donley, Wheeler and Lipscomb. We preached but once, and then the congregation was small, on account of rough winds or "Northerners" as the people call them.

The best way to preach in this part of Texas in the winter is according to Matt. 10: 12, 13; Luke 10: 5, 6, 7. The people seem to take much interest in the preaching of the true Gospel.

In Gray County Bro. John Stump's home is located. He is a minister in the second degree, with about eight members in that neighborhood. We found them strong in the faith and in good hopes of getting an organization soon.

I had a desire to visit the Lipscomb church (it being the nearest point where there are Brethren), so Bro. Stump and I started for that point, taking with us the needed provisions, etc. After traveling about seventy miles, we found a brother and sister by the name of N. A. Gray, near Hickings, Texas. I need not tell you of the joy that our visit brought to them, as they had not seen any Brethren for nearly three years. They are the only members that are left in that part of the country. They live about twenty-five miles from Lipscomb, where the Brethren have a good church-house, which, however, is not in use now. Gray County is now the place where the Brethren are locating, and, I think, with a good effort on their part, and some help from the Mission Board,

in the way of a missionary, to work up an organization, much good could be accomplished. Here is a grand place for a young minister, who is able and willing to live a pioneer life. There is no other minister of the Brethren closer than 130 miles of Bro. John Stump. The people are very kind and generous. Write to Bro. John Stump, Miami, Texas, and he will gladly answer all inquiries.

We left Miami, Texas, Dec. 10, and upon our arrival home, Dec. 23, found our family well.
     JOSEPH WEAVER.

Ligonier, Ind.

Notes from Our Correspondents.

"As cold water to a thirsty soul, so is good news from a far country."

Mahoning Church.—Bro. I. D. Parker began a series of meetings at the Zion Hill church, Dec. 6, and continued till Dec. 21. During that time we held our quarterly council, at which five were received into the church by baptism. One was reclaimed and there is one applicant for baptism. A letter of membership was granted to a sister, and the members greatly strengthened. The weather and roads were all that could be expected for this time of the year, which made it very pleasant for those who wished to attend church. Bro. Parker is an able expounder of God's Word.
—*Anna Nettrour, Leetonia, Ohio.*

Greene, Iowa.—A series of meetings at this place closed Dec. 13, after two weeks' duration. Bro. Jacob Delp, of Yellow Creek, Ill., and Bro. Frank Myers, of Mt. Carroll, Ill., came to us Nov. 28, and preached in all twenty-seven sermons. Although some seemed to be counting the cost, yet none came out on the Lord's side. We believe there were some good impressions made. The Brethren also gave the members some good admonitions, reminding all of their duty toward God and man, and we think that the church in general feels built up, ready to go forward with more zeal in the Master's work than ever before.—*J. L. Shook, Dec. 14.*

Mount Storm, W. Va.—The Brethren of the Alleghany church commenced a series of meetings Dec. 10, lasting about one week. Through the efficient ministerial labors of our brethren Tobias and Aaron Fike, of Eglon, W. Va., the members were much edified, and two more were added to the army of the Lord, and others made to fear and tremble. After this the above-named brethren commenced preaching for us at the Striped school-house with increased interest, but after a few days' meetings we had to close on account of the sudden illness of our ministering brethren, one of whom, at this writing, is unable to go home. May the Lord bless them for their labor of love!—*Raphael Baker, Dec. 23.*

Roann, Ind.—On Saturday, Dec. 12, Bro. Jacob S. Snell, of Collamer, Ind., came to us to conduct a series of meetings. He continued preaching until Dec. 5, and preached in all sixteen sermons. The attention was commendable, and the congregations were large until interfered with by the inclemency of the weather, dark nights and bad roads. Deep impressions were made on the minds of many. One dear soul came out on the Lord's side and was baptized according to the commission given by Christ. We feel sure that others are counting the cost, and we hope they will, before it is eternally too late, get the consent of their minds and join in with the people of God. Our dear brother labored earnestly and ably for us, pointing out to us all the duties we owe to God. The church feels much strengthened and built up. May God bless our dear brother in other fields of labor!—*Joseph John, Dec. 25.*

Upon his return he and his mother started for Chamberlain, but sister Cook could only remain until Sunday afternoon, when she had to return home because they left the two little boys sick. Bro. Cook reports that he cannot be moved for a week or more.

There was one death from 'La Grippe in our vicinity. At this writing my folks are some better, and I am able to sit up and make this report, though I am very nervous. Dear saints, remember us and also Bro. Cook's family in your prayers!　　　B. F. MILLER.

Dec. 30.

Lower Stillwater Notes.

LAST night closed a very interesting series of meetings with us. Dec. 12 Bro. L. W. Teeter, of Hagerstown, Ind., came to us and began meetings, which continued each night until Dec. 28, Some day meetings were also held.

The inquiring mind wonders why the day meetings are not better attended during such a series. The minister leaves his home affairs for weeks at a time, and comes into a community because of his general interest in the welfare of the church and the salvation of souls. Why, then, can we not have special interest in our own children, neighbors and friends, and unite in the special effort with our presence and prayers?

As an immediate result one young sister chose the good part with the people of God. Others are near,—so near that it takes all their power to keep them out.

We do not feel to measure the success of the meeting by the number of accessions alone. The members have been much built up and established.

We are keeping up an evergreen Sunday-school this winter. Instead of closing in the fall, as usual, we re-organized, choosing as Superintendent, Bro. W. W. Barnhart, who, since our last report, has been called to the ministry.

Our force has also been increased by Bro. Wm. Bowser, who has been laboring in Eastern Virginia the past year. Jan. 30 we intend to commence a series of meetings in our Upper house. Bro. Dan. P. Shively, of Peru, Ind., will be with us.　　　I. A. BOOKWALTER.

Trotwood, Ohio, Dec. 29.

From Ladoga, Ind.

WITHIN the last year there have been forty-six additions to the church at this place. Twenty-one were baptized as a result of the efforts of our home ministers, and nineteen during our protracted meetings. Two were reclaimed and four were received by letter. This shows the result of a more systematic work on the part of our ministers than they had been doing heretofore. These has also been one death in the church, and two members have withdrawn. Our home ministers will begin a series of meetings at the Bethel church-house, Jan. 30.

Bro. Charlie Campbell came to us Dec. 12, and began a series of meetings at Mt. Pleasant. He preached earnestly until Dec. 22, when he was called home to preach a funeral. Next day he returned and continued meetings until Dec. 25, when the meetings closed with one addition by baptism.　　　CHARITY HIMES.

Death of Eld. William McWhorter.

THE subject of this notice lived in the Four Mile congregation, and died of pneumonia, aged fifty-four years, two months and six days.

Deceased was born in Franklin County, Ind., Oct. 17, 1837. He was a remarkably devout child, and in his youth united with the church. He was called to the ministry Sept. 16, 1876, and to the eldership June 20, 1891. He was loved and respected by all who knew him. Nov. 1, 1868, he was married to Martha M. Stephens. To this union were born three children, one son and two daughters.

He was married a second time Nov. 2, 1876, to Catherine Speer. The son having gone to rest four years ago, Bro. William now leaves a wife, two daughters and a great number of friends who mourn their loss, which, we trust, is his eternal gain. During his four days of illness, he called for the elders of the church, and was anointed with oil in the name of the Lord.

The funeral services were conducted at his residence by Eld. Jacob life from 1 Thess. 4: 13, 14, to a large concourse of people.

EDWARD M. COBB.

Bath, Ind.

From the Spring Creek Church, Ind.

BRO. GORMAN HEETER, of North Manchester, Ind., came to us, to fill a few appointments at Sidney, in the absence of our home ministers. Seeing that there was a good interest, the brethren thought it advisable to continue the meetings a few evenings. Thus we continued for two weeks, closing on Christmas evening with the very best of interest. Good attention was paid to the brother's remarks during the entire meeting. This was Bro. Heeter's first effort to hold a series of meetings alone, but after hearing him, we can truly say that he is "a workman that needeth not to be ashamed." We had no accessions to the church, but we hope that many good impressions were made.　　　E. MILLER.

To Texas and Return.

Nov. 10th wife and I started for Texas. At Kansas City we met Bro. A. M. Dickey, of Melbourne, Iowa. How thankful we felt that we, as Brethren, may know each other!

South of Kansas City I opened my satchel and took out a roll of tracts and MESSENGERS, which I distributed in several cars. They raised quite an excitement and got us into quite a discussion with a Campbellite and an elderly lady of the Advent faith, but we felt that the doctrine of the Brethren could be readily maintained. We arrived at Miami, Texas, Dec. 13 at 11 P. M. Our five weeks' stay in Texas was in the Counties of Gray, Donley, Wheeler and Lipscomb. We preached but once, and then the congregation was small, on account of rough winds or "Northerners" as the people call them.

The best way to preach in this part of Texas in the winter is according to Matt. 10: 12, 13; Luke 10: 5, 6, 7. The people seem to take much interest in the preaching of the true Gospel.

In Gray County Bro. John Stump's home is located. He is a minister in the second degree, with about eight members in that neighborhood. We found them strong in the faith and in good hopes of getting an organization soon.

I had a desire to visit the Lipscomb church (it being the nearest point where there are Brethren), so Bro. Stump and I started for that point, taking with us the needed provisions, etc. After traveling about seventy miles, we found a brother and sister by the name of N. A. Gray, near Hickings, Texas. I need not tell you of the joy that our visit brought to them, as they had not seen any Brethren for nearly three years. They are the only members that are left in that part of the country. They live about twenty-five miles from Lipscomb, where the Brethren have a good church-house, which, however, is not in use now. Gray County is now the place where the Brethren are locating, and I think, with a good effort on their part, and some help from the Mission Board,

in the way of a missionary, to work up an organization, much good could be accomplished. Here is a grand place for a young minister,—who is able and willing to live a pioneer life. There is no other minister of the Brethren closer than 130 miles of Bro. John Stump. The people are very kind and generous. Write to Bro. John Stump, Miami, Texas, and he will gladly answer all inquiries.

We left Miami, Texas, Dec. 10, and upon our arrival home, Dec. 23, found our family well.

JOSEPH WEAVER.

Ligonier, Ind.

Notes from Our Correspondents.

"As cold water to a thirsty soul, so is good news from a far country."

Mahoning Church.—Bro. I. D. Parker began a series of meetings at the Zion Hill church, Dec. 6, and continued till Dec. 21. During that time we held our quarterly council, at which five were received into the church by baptism. One was reclaimed and there is one applicant for baptism. A letter of membership was granted to a sister, and the members greatly strengthened. The weather and roads were all that could be expected for this time of the year, which made it very pleasant for those who wished to attend church. Bro. Parker is an able expounder of God's Word.—Anna Nettrour, Leetonia, Ohio.

Greene, Iowa.—A series of meetings at this place closed Dec. 13, after two weeks' duration. Bro. Jacob Delp, of Yellow Creek, Ill., and Bro. Frank Myers, of Mt. Carroll, Ill., came to us Nov. 28, and preached in all twenty-seven sermons. Although some seemed to be counting the cost, yet none came out on the Lord's side. We believe there were some good impressions made. The Brethren also gave the members some good admonitions, reminding all of their duty toward God and man, and we think that the church in general feels built up, ready to go forward with more zeal in the Master's work than ever before.—J. L. Shook, Dec. 14.

Mount Storm, W. Va.—The Brethren of the Alleghany church commenced a series of meetings Dec. 10, lasting about one week. Through the efficient ministerial labors of our brethren Tobias and Aaron Fike, of Eglon, W. Va., the members were much edified, and two more were added to the army of the Lord, and others made to fear and tremble. After this the above-named brethren commenced preaching for us at the Striped school-house with increased interest, but after a few days' meetings we had to close on account of the sudden illness of our ministering brethren, one of whom, at this writing, is unable to go home. May the Lord bless them for their labor of love!—Raphael Baker, Dec. 23.

Reann, Ind.—On Saturday, Dec. 12, Bro. Jacob S. Snell, of Collamer, Ind., came to us to conduct a series of meetings. He continued preaching until Dec. 5, and preached in all sixteen sermons. The attention was commendable, and the congregations were large until interfered with by the inclemency of the weather, dark nights and bad roads. Deep impressions were made on the minds of many. One dear soul came out on the Lord's side and was baptized according to the commission given by Christ. We feel sure that others are counting the cost, and we hope they will, before it is eternally too late, get the consent of their minds and join in with the people of God. Our dear brother labored earnestly and ably for us, pointing out to us all the duties we owe to God. The church feels much strengthened and built up. May God bless our dear brother in other fields of labor!—Joseph John, Dec. 25.

THOMAS.—In the Quemahoning congregation, Pa., Sept. 24, 1891, of diphtheria, Clarence Cloyd Thomas, son of friend Silas and sister Lovina Thomas, aged 1 year, 5 months and 5 days.

Funeral services by Samuel Gindiesparer (Mennonite), and the undersigned.
    S. P. ZIMMERMAN.

ZOOK.—In the Slate Creek church, Sumner Co., Kans., Nov. 14, 1891, of typhoid feVer, Bro. John Zook, aged 58 years, 9 months and 4 days.

Deceased was married to Miss Sarah Teeter Dec. 21, 1855, at the age of tWenty-two years. Nine children were born to them, seven of whom surViVe their father. He united with the church at the age of thirty-one years. Since that time he has been a faithful, deVoted member. Funeral sermon by the undersigned from 1 Tim. 4:7, 8.
    JOHN WISE.

MINICK.—In the Kansas Center church, Kans., Oct. 30, 1891, of typhoid feVer, sister Lydia Minick, aged 43 years, 3 months and 3 days.

· She, with her husband, joined the Brethren church about four years ago. Funeral discourse by Eld. Jonathan Brubaker.
    ISAAC S. BRUBAKER.

LONG.—In the bounds of the Wichita church, Sedgwick Co., Kans., Nov. 9, 1891, Aletha, wife of Bro. Peter Long (formerly of Washington County, Md.), aged 62 years, 9 months and 22 days.

She was a member of the EVangelical Lutheran church. For about eight weeks preVious to her death she was confined to her bed. She suffered intensely at times but bore her affliction with Christian fortitude, and longed for the end to come. She leaVes a husband, three children, two step-children, and a large circle of friends to mourn their loss. Funeral discourse by Eld. John Wise, of Conway Springs, from Num. 23: 10.
    J. WISE.

NEHER.—In Conway Springs, Kans., Dec. 12, 1891, sister Sarah, wife of Bro. John Neher, formerly of Macoupin County, Ill., aged 66 years, 9 months and 18 days.

Deceased leaVes a husband, five children and a large number of friends to mourn their loss. Funeral serVices by brethren John Wise and Jacob Troxel from 1 Thess. 4: 12–18.
    JOHN WISE.

FIKE.—At Eglon, W. Va., Dec. 16, 1891, Florence Ethel Fike, aged 9 months and 7 days.

Deceased was the only child and daughter of Bro. Noah and sister Maggie Fike. The funeral serVices were conducted by Bro. Isaac W. Abernathy from Job 14: 1, 2.
    RACHEL WEIMER.

BRUBAKER.—In the Washington Creek church, Douglas Co., Kans., Dec. 16, 1891, Eld. Peter Brubaker, aged 81 years, 7 months and 21 days.

Deceased was born in Franklin County, Pa., April 25, 1810. He united with the Brethren June 5, 1859, and was elected to the office of deacon in the fall of the same year. He was called to the ministry in 1860 and serVed in that office till 1874, when he was ordained to the eldership. In that office he serVed faithfully until death. He was loVed and respected by all who knew him, as was manifested by the large attendance at his funeral. Elders James Hilkey and Samuel Harshman deliVered the funeral discourse from the latter part of Ps. 7.
    S. M. MILLER.

OVERHOLSER.—At Locke, Elkhart Co., Ind., Sept. 26, 1891, of paralysis, sister Dorotha OVerholser, wife of Daniel OVerholser, deceased, aged 74 years and 9 months.

Sister OVerholser, whose maiden name was Sala, was a natiVe of PennsylVania but partially reared in Montgomery County, Ohio, Where she united in marriage with Daniel OVerholser. They were blessed With eight children, seVen of whom are yet liVing. FiVe of them are members of the body of Christ. Our sister, With her companion, serVed in the deacon's office many years. She made choice of her text and seVeral hymns, to be used at her funeral, which was improVed by Bro. Lemuel Hillery and others,·from 2 Cor. 5: 1–4 inclusiVe.
    J. R. MILLER.

FRIEND—In the Canton church, Stark Co., Ohio, Sept. 25, 1891, sister Mary E. Friend, aged 32 years.

Sister Friend passed away after fiVe days of suffering. She was a faithful member of the German Baptist church for six years and leaVes a husband and two children to mourn their loss. Of the twin girls born, one has been taken and the other left.

Funeral services conducted by the undersigned from 1 Thess. 4: 14–18.
    WM. H. QUINN.

HASELET.—In the 'Mt. Etna church, six miles west of Cumberland, Cass Co., Iowa, Nov. 30, 1891, Margaret Ann Haselet, wife of Bro. Joe Haselet, aged 52 years, 2 months and 20 days.

The deceased was a member of the Brethren church since 1886 and liVed a Very consistent life. She leaVes a husband, a large family of children, friends and neighbors to mourn their loss. The writer was called to anoint her Nov. 5, and her improVement in health led us to hope for a speedy recoVery, but Nov. 28, she suddenly grew worse and ended her useful life on the day aboVe giVen. Funeral serVices by the writer.
    ISAAC BARTO.

HESTER.—In the Blue Ridge church, Piatt Co., Ill., Dec. 17, 1891, of consumption, Bro. Andrew J. Hester, aged 22 years and 3 days.

Deceased united with the German Baptist Brethren church when about sixteen years of age. Though called away in early life, he seemed to be fully resigned to the will of God and requested us all to meet him in that better land. A short while before he died he called for the elders of the church and was anointed according to James 5: 14, after which he expressed a willingness to go and be at rest. In his sickness he bore his afflictions with patience and Christian fortitude until the death angel came in the early morn and said, "It is enough; come up higher!" Death renders the home lonely, but we trust that the bereft mother, brother and sister, will be consoled with the hope that he whom they loVed is now at rest. Funeral serVices by the writer.
    C. BARNHART.

BOSTON—In the bounds of the Turkey Creek church, Benton Co., Mo., Dec. 5, 1891, L. W. Boston, aged 42 years, 6 months and 20 days.

By request the funeral was preached by Bro. Charles Masters to a large congregation of sympathizing friends. Deceased leaVes a widow and eight children to mourn the loss of a kind father and husband.
    ISAAC GADBERRY.

MILLER—In the Canton church, Stark Co., Ohio, Nov. 29, 1891, sister Mary Ellen Miller, aged 18 years, 2 months and 5 days.

Ella was a deVoted and faithful sister, haVing entered the church in her tender years. Shortly before her departure she was, by her request, anointed with oil in the name of the Lord, after which she was resigned to the will of the LoVing Master. We feel assured that the change is indeed a happy one. Funeral serVices improVed by J. F. and Eld C. Kahler.
    JOHN T. KAHLER.

HAINES.—In the Pleasant Valley church, Elkhart Co., Ind., Nov. 18, 1891, Franklin Orlando Haines, son of brother and sister A. Haines, aged 15 years, 9 month and 1 day.

Deceased was much respected by all who knew him. He was only sick a few days before he closed his eyes in death. He told his brother, sisters and cousins to prepare to meet him in heaVen. FiVe weeks preVious to his death one of his sisters was buried, aged 9 years and 1 day, leaVing father and mother, one son and two daughters to mourn their loss. Funeral services Nov. 22 by J. L. Berkey at the Forest GroVe church from Matt. 18: 3.
    LEVI E. WEAVER.

THOMAS.—In the Quemahoning congregation, Pa., Sept. 24, 1891, of diphtheria, Clarence Cloyd Thomas, son of friend Silas and sister Lovina Thomas, aged 1 year, 5 months and 5 days.

Funeral services by Samuel Gindlesparger (Mennonite), and the undersigned.
S. P. ZIMMERMAN.

ZOOK.—In the Slate Creek church, Sumner Co., Kans., Nov. 14, 1891, of typhoid fever, Bro. John Zook, aged 58 years, 9 months and 4 days.

Deceased was married to Miss Sarah Teeter Dec. 21, 1855, at the age of twenty-two years. Nine children were born to them, seven of whom survive their father. He united with the church at the age of thirty-one years. Since that time he has been a faithful, devoted member. Funeral sermon by the undersigned from 1 Tim. 4: 7, 8.
JOHN WISE.

MINICK.—In the Kansas Center church, Kans., Oct. 30, 1891, of typhoid fever, sister Lydia Minick, aged 43 years. 3 months and 3 days.

She, with her husband, joined the Brethren church about four years ago. Funeral discourse by Eld. Jonathan Brubaker.
ISAAC S. BRUBAKER.

LONG.—In the bounds of the Wichita church, Sedgwick Co., Kans., Nov. 9, 1891, Aleatha, wife of Bro. Peter Long (formerly of Washington County, Md.), aged 62 years, 9 months and 22 days.

She was a member of the Evangelical Lutheran church. For about eight weeks previous to her death she was confined to her bed. She suffered intensely at times but bore her affliction with Christian fortitude, and longed for the end to come. She leaves a husband, three children, two step-children, and a large circle of friends to mourn their loss. Funeral discourse by Eld. John Wise, of Conway Springs, from Num. 23: 10.
J. WISE.

NEHER.—In Conway Springs, Kans., Dec. 12, 1891, sister Sarah, wife of Bro. John Neher, formerly of Macoupin County, Ill., aged 66 years, 9 months and 18 days.

Deceased leaves a husband, five children and a large number of friends to mourn their loss. Funeral services by brethren John Wise and Jacob Troxel from 1 Thess. 4: 12–18.
JOHN WISE.

FIKE.—At Eglon, W. Va., Dec. 16, 1891, Florence Ethel Fike, aged 9 months and 2 days.

Deceased was the only child and daughter of Bro. Noah and sister Maggie Fike. The funeral services were conducted by Bro. Isaac W. Abernathy from Job 14: 1, 2.
RACHEL WEIMER.

BRUBAKER.—In the Washington Creek church, Douglas Co., Kans., Dec. 16, 1891, Eld. Peter. Brubaker, aged 81 years, 7 months and 21 days.

Deceased was born in Franklin County, Pa., April 25, 1810. He united with the Brethren June 5, 1859, and was elected to the office of deacon in the fall of the same year. He was called to the ministry in 1860 and served in that office till 1874, when he was ordained to the eldership. In that office he served faithfully until death. He was loved and respected by all who knew him, as was manifested by the large attendance at his funeral. Elders James Hilkey and Samson Harshman delivered the funeral discourse from the latter part of Ps. 7.
S. M. MILLER.

OVERHOLSER.—At Locke, Elkhart Co., Ind., Sept. 26, 1891, of paralysis, sister Dorotha Overholser, wife of Daniel Overholser, deceased, aged 74 years and 9 months.

Sister Overholser, whose maiden name was Sala, was a native of Pennsylvania but partially reared in Montgomery County, Ohio, where she united in marriage with Daniel Overholser. They were blessed with eight children, seven of whom are yet living. Five of them are members of the body of Christ. Our sister, with her companion, served in the

deacon's office many years. She made choice of her text and several hymns, to be used at her funeral, which was improved by Bro. Lemuel Hillery and others, from 2 Cor. 5: 1–4 inclusive.
J. R. MILLER.

FRIEND.—In the Canton church, Stark Co., Ohio, Sept. 15, 1891, sister Mary E. Friend, aged 32 years.

Sister Friend passed away after five days of suffering. She was a faithful member of the German Baptist church for six years and leaves a husband and two children to mourn their loss. Of the twin girls born, one has been taken and the other left.

Funeral services conducted by the undersigned from 1 Thess. 4: 14–18.
WM. H. QUINN.

HASELET.—In the Mt. Etna church, six miles west of Cumberland, Cass Co., Iowa, Nov. 30, 1891, Margaret Ann Haselet, wife of Bro. Joe Haselet, aged 52 years, 2 months and 20 days.

The deceased was a member of the Brethren church since 1886 and lived a very consistent life. She leaves a husband, a large family of children, friends and neighbors to mourn their loss. The writer was called to anoint her Nov. 5, and her improvement in health led us to hope for a speedy recovery, but Nov. 28, she suddenly grew worse and ended her useful life our the day above given. Funeral services by the writer.
ISAAC BARTO.

HESTER.—In the Blue Ridge church, Platt Co., Ill., Dec. 17, 1891, of consumption, Bro. Andrew J. Hester, aged 22 years and 3 days.

Deceased united with the German Baptist Brethren church when about sixteen years of age. Though called away in early life, he seemed to be fully resigned to the will of God and requested us all to meet him in that better land. A short while before he died he called for the elders of the church and was anointed according to james 5: 14, after which he expressed a willingness to go and be at rest. In his sickness he bore his afflictions with patience and Christian fortitude until the death angel came in the early morn and said, "It is enough; come up higher!" Death renders the home lonely, but we trust that the bereft mother, brother and sister, will be consoled with the hope that he whom they loved is now at rest. Funeral services by the writer.
C. BARNHART.

BOSTON.—In the bounds of the Turkey Creek church, Benton· Co., Mo., Dec. 5, 1891, L. W. Boston, aged 42 years, 6 months and 20 days.

By request the funeral was preached by Bro. Charles Masters to a large congregation of sympathizing friends. Deceased leaves a widow and eight children to mourn the loss of a kind father and husband.
ISAAC GADBERRY.

MILLER.—In the Canton church, Stark Co., Ohio, Nov. 29, 1891, sister Mary Ellen Miller, aged 18 years, 2 months and 5 days.

Ella was a devoted and faithful sister, having entered the church in her tender years. Shortly before her departure she was, by her request. anointed with oil in the name of the Lord, after which she was resigned to the will of the Loving Master. We feel assured that the change is indeed a happy one. Funeral services improved by J. F. and Eld. C. Kahler.
JOHN T. KAHLER.

MAINES.—In the Pleasant Valley church, Elkhart Co., Ind., Nov. 18, 1891, Franklin Orlando Haines, son of brother and sister A. Haines, aged 15 years, 7 month and 1 day.

Deceased was much respected by all who knew him. He was only sick a few days before he closed his eyes in death. He told his brother, sisters and cousins to prepare to meet him in heaven. Five weeks previous to his death one of his sisters was buried, aged 9 years and 1 day, leaving father and mother, one son and two daughters to mourn their loss. Funeral services Nov. 22 by J. L. Berkey at the Forest Grove church from Matt. 18: 3.
LEVI E. WEAVER.

THE GOSPEL MESSENGER.

"Set for the Defense of the Gospel."

Vol. 30, Old Series.   Mt. Morris, Ill., and Huntingdon, Pa., Jan. 19, 1892.   No. 3.

The Gospel Messenger.

H. B. Brumbaugh, Editor,

And Business Manager of the Eastern House, Box 50.
Huntingdon, Pa.

Table of Contents.

You have only one life of probation to live, and the magnitude of its value no mortal can compute. If you are wise, you will redeem the time with every possible effort.

Bro. J. B. Brumbaugh is now with the Brethren of the Green Tree church, holding a series of meetings. This is an evergreen church in growth and we hope that the ingathering may always continue.

At last the long-wished-for snow has come and on our streets is heard the merry jingling of the sleigh bells. Well, nature wants her rest and we are glad that our Good Father so kindly lays over her the mantle of white that she may take her sleep, protected from the snapping and biting frosts that claim their rights during the wintry months. All is well that the Father doeth.

Every one is peculiarly blest. It would be a difficult matter for any one to look around him and not see others in more trying circumstances than he. If he has had losses, he can find those who have suffered greater losses; if he has had bodily afflictions, he can find those who have been more sorely afflicted. In one way or another he has escaped that to which his neighbor has fallen victim, the mere thought of which makes him shudder. There never is a time in any life when thanksgiving cannot appropriately be the chief portion of prayer.

Bro. Michael Claar gave us a short call last week on his way to Lewistown, Pa., where he is now holding a series of meetings. May abundant success attend his efforts!

Sister Grow, of Sharpsburg, Md., is a visitor in the Normal. Her whole family, two daughters and one son, are attending our school and sister Grow is here to see as to their welfare. Bro. Hess, of Chambersburg, Pa., also brought his two daughters and made a short stay. We are always pleased to have parents, who have children with us, come and see our school and work.

THOUGHT FLASHES.

Reader, did any one ever ask you what you were good for? The question is often put to the children and from them we sometimes have very pretty and thoughtful answers. But we, as children of a larger growth, don't exercise such familiarities, and did we do so, what would our answers be?

As the old year went out and the new one came in, this thought came to us seriously, perhaps, for the first time, and we were puzzled as we were never before. The thought came to us: Supposing some one were to ask us this question, what answer could we give? Children answer, "To love mama or papa, or to help them, or to do good." But these answers will not do for us,—the last one should, but we are not at all sure that it would suit our case. In taking our retrospect we, seemingly, see nothing. My, O, my! what a worthless creature! Building on the good foundation and yet good for nothing! Can it be?

Reader, apply this question to yourself once and see how well you can dispose of it. Perhaps you can dispose of it more readily. Some can do it better than others. We all may be good for something, and ought to be, and it will be well for us to try and determine just what that thing is, and then do it.

For years we have been trying to learn to think a great deal, and to wait a long time before we speak or write, when the blood is warm and the passions are moving. Sometimes, we think we are good for this kind of work, but then even this may be overdone, and things may spoil for want of speaking.

Again; we sometimes think that we are good for emergencies. When others weaken and are ready to give up we get stronger, and in this way become useful and helpful. But then this may be accounted for, outside of our personality, in two ways. First, it is natural to strengthen as others weaken. Emergencies develop latent energies and make persons strong who, at other times, seem weak. Again, occasions show us the magnitude of the strength needed, and the little we have, of ourselves, to use, and are thus caused to go to the Source from which all strength comes, so that we are made strong, not so much in utilizing the strength we have as the using of the strength that is given us. There, now, we have "given ourselves away," and yet have not told you clearly what we are good for,—neither did we intend to do so; we only gave these few suggestions, thinking that they may be helpful in solving an answer to the question as it may come to you.

At our late time of public prayer a request came to us from a devoted daughter that earnest, fervent prayer should be made for her mother whose husband had been suddenly stricken down by death. The writer, as well as many others, having been personally acquainted with the wife and husband, our sympathies were deeply moved towards the stricken sister. But the thought came to us, what does this mean? What does it mean? you may ask. Yes, that was the question as it came to us, and the thought is a very serious one, too. Of course the request would be granted, because, to offer a prayer is such an easy thing to do. If no one would ask of us harder things than this, we would clap our hands and be glad.

But the thought came to us, Why will we do this? If we can have no higher motive in the doing than to accord to the asking, our wording would be as empty before God as the sounds of an instrument, touched by unsanctified hands. A prayer to God, either for ourselves or others, means more than the uttering of words. It must be the intelligent desire of the heart, actuated by love and an unflinching faith in God and his willingness to give. The manner of our prayer has much to do with the answering of it. It is a wonderful thought that, for our sake, God will do, or not do, and yet it is a truth. Lot would not have been saved from the burning of Sodom for his own sake. It was the appeal of faithful Abraham that saved Lot and his daughters. The prayer of the righteous availeth much, and God does hear the prayers of the good in behalf of others. This we ought to believe and feel to be successful petitions to our Heavenly Father.

One of our wise men once said: "It is a good thing to make a beginning. It is a better thing to go on, and best of all, to continue to the end." This is a thought flash for us all just now, as we have entered the threshold of the New Year. Many beginnings for the better have been made. This is right, but unless these beginnings are continued, where will the good be? A lost good is worse to us than no good at all, as has been fully illustrated in the cases of those who had been rich and through loss or profligacy lost all. Their knowledge of the good they once enjoyed forever unfitted them for any enjoyment in their less fortunate condition. Our *better* and *best* must come from an increase of the good, or the beginning, and all good, if properly husbanded, will increase until the fullness of all good culminates in perpetual enjoyment. Nothing is good but that which tends towards our lasting and eternal good. To this one thing all other things must be subordinated if we will enjoy God and heaven forever.

THE GOSPEL MESSENGER.

"Set for the Defense of the Gospel."

Vol. 30, Old Series.　　Mt. Morris, Ill., and Huntingdon, Pa., Jan. 19, 1892.　　No. 3.

The Gospel Messenger.

H. B. BRUMBAUGH, Editor,

And Business Manager of the Eastern House, Box 50,
Huntingdon, Pa.

Table of Contents.

You have only one life of probation to live, and the magnitude of its value no mortal can compute. If you are wise, you will redeem the time with every possible effort.

BRO. J. B. BRUMBAUGH is now with the Brethren of the Green Tree church, holding a series of meetings. This is an evergreen church in growth and we hope that the ingathering may always continue.

AT last the long-wished-for snow has come and on our streets is heard the merry jingling of the sleigh bells. Well, nature wants her rest and we are glad that our Good Father so kindly lays over her the mantle of white that she may take her sleep, protected from the snapping and biting frosts that claim their rights during the wintry months. All is well that the Father doeth.

EVERY one is peculiarly blest. It would be a difficult matter for any one to look around him and not see others in more trying circumstances than he. If he has had losses, he can find those who have suffered greater losses; if he has had bodily afflictions, he can find those who have been more sorely afflicted. In one way or another he has escaped that to which his neighbor has fallen victim, the mere thought of which makes him shudder. There never is a time in any life when thanksgiving cannot appropriately be the chief portion of prayer.

BRO. MICHAEL CLAAR gave us a short call last week on his way to Lewistown, Pa., where he is now holding a series of meetings. May abundant success attend his efforts!

SISTER GROW, of Sharpsburg, Md., is a visitor in the Normal. Her whole family, two daughters and one son, are attending our school and sister GROW is here to see as to their welfare. Bro. Hass, of Chambersburg, Pa., also brought his two daughters and made a short stay. We are always pleased to have parents, who have children with us, come and see our school and work.

THOUGHT FLASHES.

READER, did any one ever ask you what you were good for? The question is often put to the children and from them we sometimes have very pretty and thoughtful answers. But we, as children of a larger growth, don't exercise such familiarities, and did we do so, what would our answers be?

As the old year went out and the new one came in, this thought came to us seriously, perhaps, for the first time, and we were puzzled as we were never before. The thought came to us: Supposing some one were to ask us this question, what answer could we give? Children answer, "To love mama or papa, or to help them, or to do good." But these answers will not do for us,—the last one should, but we are not at all sure that it would suit our case. In taking our retrospect we, seemingly, see nothing. My, O, my! what a worthless creature! Building on the good 'foundation and yet good for nothing! Can it be?

Reader, apply this question to yourself once and see how well you can dispose of it. Perhaps you can dispose of it more readily. Some can do it better than others. We all may be good for something, and ought to be, and it will be well for us to try and determine just what that thing is, and then do it.

For years we have been trying to learn to *think* a great deal, and to wait a long time before we speak or write, when the blood is warm and the passions are moving. Sometimes, we think we are good for this kind of work, but then even this may be overdone, and things may spoil for want of speaking.

Again; we sometimes think that we are good for emergencies. When others weaken and are ready to give up we get stronger, and in this way become useful and helpful. But then this may be accounted for, outside of our personality, in two ways. First, it is natural to strengthen as others weaken. Emergencies develop latent energies and make persons strong who, at other times, seem weak. Again, occasions show us the magnitude of the strength needed, and the little we have, of ourselves, to use, and are thus caused to go to the Source from which all strength comes, so that we are made strong, not so much in utilizing the strength we have as the using of the strength that is given us. There, now, we have "given ourselves away," and yet have not told you clearly what we are good for,—neither did we intend to do so; we only gave these few suggestions, thinking that they may be helpful in solving an answer to the question as it may come to you.

At our late time of public prayer a request came to us from a devoted daughter that earnest, fervent prayer should be made for her mother whose husband had been suddenly stricken down by death. The writer, as well as many others, having been personally acquainted with the wife and husband, our sympathies were deeply moved towards the stricken sister. But the thought came to us, what does this mean? What does it mean? you may ask. Yes, that was the question as it came to us, and the thought is a very serious one, too. Of course the request would be granted, because, to offer a prayer is such an easy thing to do. If no one would ask of us harder things than this, we would clap our hands and be glad.

But the thought came to us, Why will we do this? If we can have no higher motive in the doing than to accord to the asking, our wording would be as empty before God as the sounds of an instrument, touched by unsanctified hands. A prayer to God, either for ourselves or others, means more than the uttering of words. It must be the intelligent desire of the heart, actuated by love and an unflinching faith in God and his willingness to give. The manner of our prayer has much to do with the answering of it. It is a wonderful thought that, for our sake, God will do, or not do, and yet it is a truth. Lot would not have been saved from the burning of Sodom for his own sake. It was the appeal of faithful Abraham that saved Lot and his daughters. The prayer of the righteous availeth much, and God does hear the prayers of the good in behalf of others. This we ought to believe and feel to be successful petitions to our Heavenly Father.

One of our wise men once said: "It is a good thing to make a beginning. It is a better thing to go on, and best of all, to continue to the end." This is a thought flash for us all just now, as we have entered the threshold of the New Year. Many beginnings for the better have been made. This is right, but unless these beginnings are continued, where will the good be? A lost good is worse to us than no good at all, as has been fully illustrated in the cases of those who had been rich and through loss or profligacy lost all. Their knowledge of the good they once enjoyed forever unfitted them for any enjoyment in their less fortunate condition. Our *better* and *best* must come from an increase of the good, or the beginning, and all good, if properly husbanded, will increase until the fullness of all good culminates in perpetual enjoyment. Nothing is good but that which tends towards our lasting and eternal good. To this one thing all other things must be subordinated if we will enjoy God and heaven forever.

his priests on the other, not to hear either one to the hurt of the other. For this he lost his life.

At this time Rome, the fourth kingdom of Daniel's prophecy, comes upon the scene, and steps between these parties. In reality it takes control of Palestine, while Antipater, mentioned in a previous lesson, became really governor, subservient to Rome. Antipater had four sons, Phasael, Herod, Joseph, Pheroras, and a daughter named Salome. Herod became king B. C. 37, and reigned until the time of Christ. He is called "Herod the Great." His object was to set up an independent monarchy, connected with Judaism. Thus arose a party, called Herodians. Herod was a Jew by profession, although an Idumean by birth. In the year 31 B. C., there was a destructive earthquake in Judea, in which between 10,000 and 20,000 persons lost their lives. In the year 25 B. C., there was a very severe famine in Palestine. Herod made great sacrifices to purchase provisions for the people.

The greatest event of Herod's life, from a Jewish stand-point, was his rebuilding of the temple. He announced his intention to the Jews at the passover, about 19 B. C., but they were afraid he would pull down the old one, and not be able to rebuild it. So he agreed that he would prepare everything for the new one before he would pull down the old one. This required about two years, so that about the year 16 B. C., he began to build the new temple. He was about eight or nine years in completing his work, although repairs and additions were continually made, so that the Jews told Christ that the temple had then been forty-six years in building, and, it is said not ·to have been completely finished until about five years before it was destroyed in the general destruction of Jerusalem, wherein Christ's prophecy was fulfilled,—"Not one stone shall be left upon another." This was in 70 A. D., about forty years after the death of Christ.

Herod, being a Jew by profession, did many things to retain the ·favor of the Jews, while at the same time, he leaned toward the idolatrous worship of Rome. He built a great city on the coast of the Mediterranean Sea, and called it Cæsarea, in honor of Cæsar. He also set up some images in accordance with Roman worship. His intention, probably, was to make it his capital sometime. It became a noted place later on. It was here that Paul was kept bound two years, and appeared before Agrippa and Festus.

Herod was a very cruel man, and his domestic life is one of tragedy. His first wife was named Doris, by whom he had one son named Antipater. He divorced her and married a woman named Mariamne, by whom he had two sons. Through groundless jealousy he had Mariamne put to death, and later had her two sons put to death. His eldest son, Antipater, conspired against Herod's life, and he had him executed just five days before his own death. At one time Augustus Cæsar remarked, "It is better to be Herod's hog than his son." Some time before his death, Herod was attacked with a very painful and loathsome disease in the form of ulcerations on his body, which were not benefited by baths which he took in a famous spring at Athens called Callirhoe. He gave orders that representatives of the chief families of Judea be shut up in prison at Jericho and put to death as soon as he died, so that his funeral would not want mourners. Just about this time came the wise men from the east, seeking for "the King of the Jews." This enraged and troubled Herod. We all know the circumstances, as recorded by Matthew. Herod died shortly after, aged· seventy years, having reigned thirty-seven years. He died a miserable, conscience-stricken man, after having attempted suicide.

THE GREAT QUESTION.

BY J. F. BRITTON.

" The great day of his wrath is come; and who shall be able to stand?"—Rev. 6: 17.

There are periods when God speaks after the the manner of men, embracing thousands of years that we might call days. God's days are not like our days, for a thousand years in his sight are but as yesterday, when it is passed, and as a watch in the night. There was the day of creation. I do not know how long God was making this world, or any other world, nor does it make any difference. It is enough for me to know that he made it. He said, "Let there be light, and there was light," and the grass grew, and the flowers bloomed, and the birds sang, and the earth brought forth her fruits, and the clouds sent down their refreshing showers. God did it all, and he looked upon the work of his hands, and said that it was good.

There was another period that we might call the day of gloom, when man broke God's law and fell from his high estate. The clouds gathered over the heads of the unhappy pair, as they walked out of the Garden of Eden,—transgressors,—with the way of the transgressor before them. The inhabitants of the world increased, and, as they multiplied in numbers, they grew worse in wickedness, and darker was the day. Prophets came and declared the will of the Lord, and angels from heaven appeared on the scene and warned men, but they continued in their sins, and the day grew still darker and darker, until it merged into a moonless and starless night, for the tempest of sin, like a great pall, had covered the earth. However, there was one star,—the star of Bethlehem, the morning-star,—that foretold the coming of another day. It was the day of mercy. When the angels came with their shout of joy, they said, "Glory to God in the highest; on earth peace and good will to men." When Jesus Christ entered the world, he declared the day of God's mercy. We live in the noontide of that day.

The heralds of the cross are penetrating to every country and every clime, and the blessed news of salvation is being told by many of the Lord's messengers. They proclaim the day of mercy, and yet there are people all through the country, who set at naught God's mercy. One of the most painful verses in the Bible, to my mind, is this: "He came to his own, and his own received him not." We read about the crucifixion and our minds dwell with horror upon the scene. As the meek and lowly Jesus, bending under the burden of his cross, is made to climb the Hill of Calvary, we feel like putting our hands to our ears, as we hear them taunting him: "If thou be the Son of God, come down from the cross!" See them wag their heads! As he bleeds and dies upon the cross, we turn away heartsick, and say, "Men must have been turned into beasts, and reason must have forsaken her throne, when Jesus died on the cross by wicked hands." We dwell upon the horrible scene and express ourselves as though we would not have done the same thing, and yet there are scores of men and women, who, up to this very day, have turned away from Jesus,—have closed the door of mercy in their own faces, and despised the love that would woo and win them to the heart of him who died that they might live.

Thank God, the day of mercy has not ended yet. The Sun of Righteousness shines with· unclouded splendor in our sky to-day, and the Word speaks of mercy to one and to all, "Whosoever will, let him take the water of life freely." But this day of mercy will close after a while, and what will the next day be? What ought it to be? If there had been a starving family in your neighborhood, and you had sent your son with bread, meat and clothing, and the perishing ones had seized him, beaten, bruised and slain him, what would you have felt like doing? What should the next day be? The text tells us. The great day of his wrath is come, and who shall be able to stand? There is a day of mercy, and we live in it. There is also a day of wrath, and we are approaching it. It will be a great day,—the day for which all other days were made,—the day when every one of us must give an account of himself to God, and must stand or fall according to that account. This day is great in its circumstances,—great in its events,—great in its consequences! It will be a·day too,—not night. Some may wish that it could be night, so that they might crouch in some corner of the great temple of justice, and cry for rocks and mountains to fall on them, but no, it will be broad day.

John saw it so clearly,—his vision is so unclouded that he speaks of it as already come: "The great day of his wrath is come." He looks upon it as at hand,—as if, in his ears, at that very moment, the trump of the archangel were ringing out the blast, declaring that time shall be no more, and he asks the question of all questions, "Who shall stand?" Will the man who has looked in the face of nature and given her the lie,—the man who has trampled the Word of God under foot, and stifled his own conscience, and ruined his own soul,—will he be able to stand? What about the man who is going through life, defiling the very air around him with his hideous oaths, violating that name that is above every name, giving emphasis to his language by coupling with it such oaths as shock the stoutest nerve,—will the blasphemer be able to stand? Will the drunkard be able to stand? He cannot stand here; much less there. He reels and staggers along the·road of life, how shall he stand in that great day? The man that has lived a moral life, and feels that he is better than other people, and is trusting in his morality, instead of the blood of Jesus Christ, which is the only true hope of heaven.—will the moralist be able to stand? Those who have tasted the Bread of Life, and have gone off now to live upon the husks of sin,— will the backslider be able to stand? If the righteous shall scarcely be saved, how shall the indolent, indifferent and ungodly church members be able to stand?

The great day of his wrath is come, and who will be able to stand? Ah, this is the great question of that great day, Who will be able to stand? The answer is plain. We are looking at this question in the light of God's own Word, and he tells that those who accept Jesus Christ as their Savior, and with all their heart, mind and strength, endeavor to adorn their lives with all the requisitions of the Gospel, ever looking unto him as their all, and in all, shall stand in that great day, and not only stand, but shall ·stand at the right hand of God forever.

Dalinsville, Va.

"Friendship tests character. Friendship is a standard by which one's truest self is tested. In order to be a real friend, one must put himself out of sight; for unselfishness is the very soul of friendship. In any planning or doing for a friend, the question for every one of us must be, not "What would I like?" nor "What would be for my interest?" but "What would my friend prefer?" and "What would be for the interest of my friend?" Unless we give our friend the first place in our thinking and wishing and doing for that friend, we cannot fairly claim to be swayed in our course by friendship.

his priests on the other, not to hear either one to the hurt of the other. For this he lost his life.

At this time Rome, the fourth kingdom of Daniel's prophecy, comes upon the scene, and steps between these parties. In reality it takes control of Palestine, while Antipater, mentioned in a previous lesson, became really governor, subservient to Rome. Antipater had four sons, Phasael, Herod, Joseph, Pheroras, and a daughter named Salome. Herod became king B. C. 37, and reigned until the time of Christ. He is called "Herod the Great." His object was to set up an independent monarchy, connected with Judaism. Thus arose a party, called Herodians. Herod was a Jew by profession, although an Idumean by birth. In the year 31 B. C., there was a destructive earthquake in Judea, in which between 10,000 and 20,000 persons lost their lives. In the year 25 B. C., there was a very severe famine in Palestine. Herod made great sacrifices to purchase provisions for the people.

The greatest event of Herod's life, from a Jewish stand-point, was his rebuilding of the temple. He announced his intention to the Jews at the passover, about 19 B. C., but they were afraid he would pull down the old one, and not be able to rebuild it. So he agreed that he would prepare everything for the new one before he would pull down the old one. This required about two years, so that about the year 16 B. C., he began to build the new temple. He was about eight or nine years in completing his work, although repairs and additions were continually made, so that the Jews told Christ that the temple had then been forty-six years in building, and, it is said not to have been completely finished until about five years before it was embraced in the general destruction of Jerusalem, wherein Christ's prophecy was fulfilled,—"Not one stone shall be left upon another." This was in 70 A. D., about forty years after the death of Christ.

Herod, being a Jew by profession, did many things to retain the favor of the Jews, while at the same time, he leaned toward the idolatrous worship of Rome. He built a great city on the coast of the Mediterranean Sea, and called it Cæsarea, in honor of Cæsar. He also set up some images in accordance with Roman worship. His intention, probably, was to make it his capital sometime. It became a noted place later on. It was here that Paul was kept bound two years, and appeared before Agrippa and Festus.

Herod was a very cruel man, and his domestic life is one of tragedy. His first wife was named Doris, by whom he had one son named Antipater. He divorced her and married a woman named Mariamne, by whom he had two sons. Through groundless jealousy he had Mariamne put to death, and later had her two sons put to death. His eldest son, Antipater, conspired against Herod's life, and he had him executed just five days before his own death. At one time Augustus Cæsar remarked, "It is better to be Herod's hog than his son." Some time before his death, Herod was attacked with a very painful and loathsome disease in the form of ulcerations on his body, which were not benefited by baths which he took in a famous spring at Athens called Callirhoe. He gave orders that representatives of the chief families of Judea be shut up in prison at Jericho and put to death as soon as he died, so that his funeral would not want mourners. Just about this time came the wise men from the east, seeking for "the King of the Jews." This enraged and troubled Herod. We all know the circumstances, as recorded by Matthew. Herod died shortly after, aged seventy years, having reigned thirty-seven years. He died a miserable, conscience-stricken man, after having attempted suicide.

THE GREAT QUESTION.

BY J. F. BRITTON.

"The great day of his wrath is come; and who shall be able to stand?"—Rev. 6: 17.

THERE are periods when God speaks after the the manner of men, embracing thousands of years that we might call days. God's days are not like our days, for a thousand years in his sight are but as yesterday, when it is passed, and as a watch in the night. There was the day of creation. I do not know how long God was making this world, or any other world, nor does it make any difference. It is enough for me to know that he made it. He said, "Let there be light, and there was light," and the grass grew, and the flowers bloomed, and the birds sang, and the earth brought forth her fruits, and the clouds sent down their refreshing showers. God did it all, and he looked upon the work of his hands, and said that it was good.

There was another period that we might call the day of gloom, when man broke God's law and fell from his high estate. The clouds gathered over the heads of the unhappy pair, as they walked out of the Garden of Eden,—transgressors,—with the way of the transgressor before them. The inhabitants of the world increased, and, as they multiplied in numbers, they grew worse in wickedness, and darker was the day. Prophets came and declared the will of the Lord, and angels from heaven appeared on the scene and warned men, but they continued in their sins, and the day grew still darker and darker, until it merged into a moonless and starless night, for the tempest of sin, like a great pall, had covered the earth. However, there was one star,—the star of Bethlehem, the morning-star,—that foretold the coming of another day. It was the day of mercy. When the angels came with their shout of joy, they said, "Glory to God in the highest; on earth peace and good will to men." When Jesus Christ entered the world, he declared the day of God's mercy. We live in the noontide of that day.

The heralds of the cross are penetrating to every country and every clime, and the blessed news of salvation is being told by many of the Lord's messengers. They proclaim the day of mercy, and yet there are people all through the country, who set at naught God's mercy. One of the most painful verses in the Bible, to my mind, is this: "He came to his own, and his own received him not." We read about the crucifixion and our minds dwell with horror upon the scene. As the meek and lowly Jesus, bending under the burden of his cross, is made to climb the Hill of Calvary, we feel like putting our hands to our ears, as we hear them taunting him: "If thou be the Son of God, come down from the cross!" See them wag their heads! As he bleeds and dies upon the cross, we turn away heartsick, and say, "Men must have been turned into beasts, and reason must have forsaken her throne, when Jesus died on the cross by wicked hands." We dwell upon the horrible scene and express ourselves as though we would not have done the same thing, and yet there are scores of men and women, who, up to this very day, have turned away from Jesus,—have closed the door of mercy in their own faces, and despised the love that would woo and win them to the heart of him who died that they might live.

Thank God, the day of mercy has not ended yet. The Sun of Righteousness shines with unclouded splendor in our sky to-day, and the Word goes forth to one and to all, "Whosoever will, let him take the water of life freely." But this day of mercy will close after a while, and what will the next day be? What ought it to be? If there

had been a starving family in your neighborhood, and you had sent your son with bread, meat and clothing, and the perishing ones had seized him, beaten, bruised and slain him, what would you have felt like doing? What should the next day be? The text tells us. The great day of his wrath is come, and who shall be able to stand? There is a day of wrath, and we are approaching it. It will be a great day,—the day for which all other days were made,—the day when every one of us must give an account of himself to God, and must stand or fall according to that account. This day is great in its circumstances,—great in its events,—great in its consequences! It will be a day too,—not night. Some may wish that it could be night, so that they might crouch in some corner of the great temple of justice, and cry for rocks and mountains to fall on them, but no, it will be broad day.

John saw it so clearly,—his vision is so unclouded that he speaks of it as already come: "The great day of his wrath is come." He looks upon it as at hand,—as if, in his ears, at that very moment, the trump of the archangel were ringing out the blast, declaring that time shall be no more, and he asks the question of all questions, "Who shall stand?" Will the man who has looked in the face of nature and given her the lie,—the man who has trampled the Word of God under foot, and stifled his own conscience, and ruined his own soul,—will he be able to stand? What about the man who is going through life, defiling the very air around him with his hideous oaths, violating that name that is above every name, giving emphasis to his language by coupling with it such oaths as shock the stoutest nerve,—will the blasphemer be able to stand? He cannot stand here; much less there. He reels and staggers along the road of life, how shall he stand in that great day? The man that has lived a moral life, and feels that he is better than other people, and is trusting in his morality, instead of the blood of Jesus Christ, which is the only true hope of heaven,—will the moralist be able to stand? Those who have tasted the Bread of Life, and have gone off now to live upon the husks of sin,—will the backslider be able to stand? If the righteous shall scarcely be saved, how shall the indolent, indifferent and ungodly church members be able to stand?

The great day of his wrath is come, and who will be able to stand? Ah, this is the great question of that great day, Who will be able to stand? The answer is plain. We are looking at this question in the light of God's own Word, and he tells that those who accept Jesus Christ as their Savior, and with all their heart, mind and strength, endeavor to adorn their lives with all the requisitions of the Gospel, ever looking unto him as their all, and in all, shall stand in that great day, and not only stand, but shall stand at the right hand of God forever.

Dalinsville, Va.

"FRIENDSHIP tests character. Friendship is a standard by which one's truest self is tested. In order to be a real friend, one must put himself out of sight; for unselfishness is the very soul of friendship. In any planning or doing for a friend, the question for every one of us must be, not "What would I like?" nor "What would be for my interest?" but "What would my friend prefer?" and "What would be for the interest of my friend?" Unless we give our friend the first place in our thinking and wishing and doing for that friend, we cannot fairly claim to be swayed in our course by friendship.

about and tell the first brother I meet what I have seen. Do I do right? No. I don't love that brother as I should, or I would not talk about him, to the still further injury of his character.

In all cases of individual and public grievances, we should, in trying to correct the wrongs in others, be clothed with the gentle and loving spirit of the Master, and thus being clothed, I will proceed in a matter like case 1, by going to my brother or sister with the object of gaining them, for I see they are going astray. I will talk to them kindly, and admonish them as to their wrongs, and in all probability, I can get them to see their error, and get them to promise to be more careful.

Of course, if good admonitions are not heeded, and the party will persist in their wrong course, it will be the duty of the church to send them a visit and then it becomes public.

In case 2 it is my duty when a brother becomes sober, to tell him what I have seen, and with the loving spirit of Christ, try to get him to see the sin committed, and in all probability he will say he did wrong and confess it to me, but that will not be sufficient, because it was a trespass against the body. Then I would advise him to come before the church at the first opportunity, state his own case and ask the church to forgive him, but if he will not do this, then the church will be under obligation to send brethren to visit him, try to get him to see the wrong, and ask him to appear before the church for a hearing.

In the supposed cases, above alluded to, we have first an individual, and secondly a public trespass, and neither case should be allowed to be brought into open council before the party, first aggrieved, had done his duty.

The above was suggested by the thought that it is to be greatly feared, that many of us, professing to be children of God, do not exercise sufficient love for the erring ones who have gone astray. See Matt. 18: 12.

> "Speak gently to the erring ones;
> Ye know not all the power,
> With which the dark temptation came,
> In some unguarded hour.

> "Speak gently to the erring ones;
> O do not thou forget,
> However darkly stained by sin,
> He is thy brother yet."

Mt. Carroll, Ill.

RESURRECTION.

BY NOAH LONGANECKER.

By resurrection here we mean "the rising again from the dead; the resumption of life." There are three kinds of life mentioned in the Bible,—natural, spiritual and eternal. Natural life consists in the union of the soul and body. Spiritual life consists in the union of the soul and God. Eternal life consists in the communion of the body and soul with God in the realms of glory.

Corresponding to these three kinds of life, there are three kinds of death,—natural, spiritual and eternal. Natural death is the separation of soul and body. Spiritual death is the separation of the soul and God. Eternal death is the separation of body and soul from God in the world to come.

We have said that natural death is the separation of soul and body. Permit a few passages as proof-texts. "As her soul was in departing, (for she died)." Gen. 35: 18. "O Lord, my God, I pray thee, let this child's soul come into him again. And the soul of the child came into him again, and he revived." 1 Kings 17: 21, 22. The soul of the child had departed from the body, which was death. It came into him again, which

was life. Stephen prayed, "Lord Jesus, receive my spirit."

Paul taught the same doctrine: "We are confident, I say, and willing rather to be absent from the body, and to be present with the Lord." Since resurrection is the rising again from the dead, and the resumption of life, the reader will at once see the force of the remarks above. Whether our works are good or wicked, they are done while our souls are in the body, and, therefore, soul and body must again be united when we receive our reward, whether good or bad.

A certain writer presents this truth as follows: "The divine laws are the rule of duty to the entire man, and not to the soul only; and they are obeyed or violated by the soul and body in conjunction; the soul designs, the body executes. Carnal affections deprave the soul, corrupt the mind and mislead it. The heart is the fountain of profaneness, and the tongue expresses it. Thus the members are instruments of iniquity, and the body is obedient to the holy soul in doing and suffering for God, and denies its sensual appetites and satisfactions in compliance with reason and grace; the members are instruments of righteousness. Hence it follows that there will be a universal resurrection, that the rewarding goodness of God may appear in making the bodies of his servants gloriously happy with their souls, and their souls completely happy in union with their bodies, to which they have a natural inclination, and his revenging justice may be manifest in punishing the bodies of the wicked with eternal torments, answerable to their guilt." (Craden's Complete Concordance, page 487.)

If death is a separation, then resumption of life is a bringing together again. This fact is proven in 1 Kings 17: 21, 22, where Elijah resurrected the child. Hence, in the resurrection of the dead, their bodies and souls must again be united. "For I know that my Redeemer liveth, and that he shall stand at the latter day upon the earth: and though after my skin worms destroy this body, yet in my flesh shall I see God." Job 19: 25, 26. "Many of them that sleep in the dust of the earth shall awake." Dan. 12: 2.

We have shown that at death the soul leaves the body and is not buried with it in the dust. Christ's body that was buried in the grave, came forth again. As the first-fruit is, so will the general harvest be. Permit an illustration: "And the graves were opened; and many bodies of the saints which slept arose, and came out of the graves after his resurrection." Matt. 27: 52, 53.

It is generally believed that these saints were resurrected to die no more. They, no doubt, were translated to heaven. "Marvel not at this: for the hour is coming, in the which all that are in the graves shall hear his voice, and shall come forth; they that have done good, unto the resurrection of life; and they that have done evil, unto the resurrection of damnation." John 5: 28, 29.

"If the Spirit of him that raised up Jesus from the dead dwell in you, he that raised up Christ from the dead shall also quicken your mortal bodies by his Spirit that dwelleth in you." Rom. 8: 11. The *mortal bodies* of the saints shall be quickened, and the resurrection of Christ shall be the pattern after which they shall be raised. Of course Christ's body saw no corruption, because he had no sin, but still it had to go wherever our bodies were, in order to redeem them from the grave.

"But," says some one, "Christ's body was changed, at his ascension, to a spiritual body." Some Bible students fail to make the proper distinction between a *spiritual body* and a *spirit*, and, hence, destroy the doctrine of future recognition. They do not understand the "*transfigura-*

tion" lesson fully. "We ourselves groan within ourselves, waiting for the adoption, to wit, the redemption of our body." Rom. 8: 23. Paul said that they had the first-fruits of the Spirit, but were anxiously waiting for the redemption of the body. I have been aware for years, that there are those who do not believe that our human bodies will ever be resurrected from the grave; but of late I learned that some of the ministers of our church entertain the same view. They believe that the Lord will bring new, spiritual bodies from heaven. We believe in a *complete* Redeemer,—a Redeemer of body and soul. "O grave, where is thy victory?" It will be swallowed up by the resurrection of the body. Yea, we will say, *is swallowed* up, for the "*first-fruits*" have already appeared by the resurrection of Christ's body.

Do you doubt the general harvest? Then look at the resurrection of the many bodies of the saints. Resurrection is more than the coming forth of the body from the grave. It is also the bringing together of body and soul, which is the resumption of life. In 1 Cor. 15: 35, we have the following question: "How are the dead raised up, and with what body do they come?" Paul answers the question by a similitude: "Thou fool, that which thou sowest is not quickened, except it die, and that which thou sowest, thou sowest not that body that shall be, but bare grain; it may chance of wheat, or of some other grain." The expression, "Thou sowest not that body that shall be," is one of the passages that lead many to believe that the human body will not be resurrected. True, the grain that is sown decomposes, yet it *produces* and nourishes root, stalk, leaves and full corn in the ear.

Let us notice Paul's explication of the similitude; "It is sown in corruption; it is raised in incorruption; it is sown in dishonor; it is raised in glory: it is sown in weakness; it is raised in power; it is sown a natural body; it is raised a spiritual body." In this explication Paul declares four times that the *body that is sown is raised.* Who dare deny? Some one may say, the contrast between the body that is sown and the one that is raised is so great that it cannot be the same. On the same ground we might say that the soul that is regenerated, created anew, or redeemed from sin, is not the same as when it was dead in trespasses and sins. The beautiful butterfly is from the caterpillar. This beautiful white paper is from refuse or filthy rags. But much greater will be the contrast between man, as he appears by nature, and as he will appear when both body and soul are redeemed from sin and death. But how about the wicked? True, their bodies will come forth, too, to be united with their souls, but neither being redeemed from sin, before the judgment, they must go to be judged according to the deeds done in the body. If they were "dogs, and sorcerers, and whoremongers, and murderers, and idolaters, and liars, and extortioners, and drunkards," etc., in this world, and were not regenerated, as such they will go before the judgment. What a contrast, then, between the righteous and wicked! Then "he that is unjust, let him be unjust still: and he which is filthy, let him be filthy still: and he that is righteous, let him be righteous still: and he that is holy, let him be holy still."

Here we let the curtain drop. Let us all meditate seriously.

"A DROP of ink is a very small thing, yet dropped into a tumbler of clear water it blackens the whole; and so the first oath, the first lie, the first glass, may seem very trivial, but they leave a dark stain upon one's character. Look out for the first stain."

about and tell the first brother I meet what I have seen. Do I do right? No. I don't love that brother as I should, or I would not talk about him, to the still further injury of his character.

In all cases of individual and public grievances, we should, in trying to correct the wrongs in others, be clothed with the gentle and loving spirit of the Master, and thus being clothed, I will proceed in a matter like case 1, by going to my brother or sister with the object of gaining them, for I see they are going astray. I will talk to them kindly, and admonish them as to their wrongs, and in all probability, I can get them to see their error, and get them to promise to be more careful. . . .

Of course, if good admonitions are not heeded, and the party will persist in their wrong course, it will be the duty of the church to send them a visit and then it becomes public.

In case 2 it is my duty when a brother becomes sober, to tell him what I have seen, and with the loving spirit of Christ, try to get him to see the sin committed, and in all probability he will say he did wrong and confess it to me, but that will not be sufficient, because it was a trespass against the body. Then I would advise him to come before the church at the first opportunity, state his own case and ask the church to forgive him, but if he will not do this, then the church will be under obligation to send brethren to visit him, try to get him to see the wrong, and ask him to appear before the church for a hearing.

In the supposed cases, above alluded to, we have first an individual, and secondly a public trespass, and neither case should be allowed to be brought into open council before the party, first aggrieved, had done his duty.

The above was suggested by the thought that it is to be greatly feared, that many of us, professing to be children of God, do not exercise sufficient love for the erring ones who have gone astray. See Matt. 18: 12.

"Speak gently to the erring ones;
  Ye know not all the power,
With which the dark temptation came,
  In some unguarded hour.

"Speak gently to the erring ones;
  O do not thou forget,
However darkly stained by sin,
  He is thy brother yet."

Mt. Carroll, Ill.

RESURRECTION.

BY NOAH LONGANECKER.

By resurrection here we mean "the rising again from the dead; the resumption of life." There are three kinds of life mentioned in the Bible,—natural, spiritual and eternal. Natural life consists in the union of the soul and body. Spiritual life consists in the union of the soul and God. Eternal life consists in the communion of the body and soul with God in the realms of glory.

Corresponding, to these three kinds of life, there are three kinds of death,—natural, spiritual and eternal. Natural death is the separation of soul and body. Spiritual death is the separation of the soul and God. Eternal death is the separation of body and soul from God in the world to come.

We have said that natural death is the separation of soul and body. Permit a few passages as proof-texts. "As her soul was in departing, (for she died)." Gen. 35: 18. "O Lord, my God, I pray thee, let this child's soul come into him again. And the soul of the child came into him again, and he revived." 1 Kings 17: 21, 22. The soul of the child had departed from the body, which was death. It came into him again, which

was life. Stephen prayed, "Lord Jesus, receive my spirit."

Paul taught the same doctrine: "We are confident, I say, and willing rather to be absent from the body, and to be present with the Lord." Since resurrection is the rising again from the dead, and the resumption of life, the reader will at once see the force of the remarks above. Whether our works are good or wicked, they are done while our souls are in the body, and, therefore, soul and body must again be united when we receive our reward, whether good or bad.

A certain writer presents this truth as follows: "The divine laws are the rule of duty to the entire man, and not to the soul only; and they are obeyed or violated by the soul and body in conjunction; the soul designs, the body executes. The senses are the open ports to admit temptations. Carnal affections deprave the soul, corrupt the mind and mislead it. The heart is the fountain of profaneness, and the tongue expresses it. Thus the members are instruments of iniquity, and the body is obedient to the holy soul in doing and suffering for God, and denies its sensual appetites and satisfactions in compliance with reason and grace; the members are instruments of righteousness. Hence it follows that there will be a universal resurrection, that the rewarding goodness of God may appear in making the bodies of his servants gloriously happy with their souls, and their souls completely happy in union with their bodies, to which they have a natural inclination, and his revenging justice may be manifest in punishing the bodies of the wicked with eternal torments, answerable to their guilt." (Cruden's Complete Concordance, page 487.)

If death is a separation, then resumption of life is a bringing together again. This fact is proven in 1 Kings 17: 21, 22, where Elijah resurrected the child. Hence, in the resurrection of the dead, their bodies and souls must again be united. "For I know that my Redeemer liveth, and that he shall stand at the latter day upon the earth: and though after my skin worms destroy this body, yet in my flesh shall I see God." Job 19: 25, 26. "Many of them that sleep in the dust of the earth shall awake." Dan. 12: 2.

We have shown that at death the soul leaves the body and is not buried with it in the dust. Christ's body that was buried in the grave, came forth again. As the first-fruit is, so will the general harvest be. Permit an illustration: "And the graves were opened; and many bodies of the saints which slept arose, and came out of the graves after his resurrection." Matt. 27: 52, 53.

It is generally believed that these saints were resurrected to die no more. They, no doubt, were translated to heaven. "Marvel not at this: for the hour is coming, in the which all that are in the graves shall hear his voice, and shall come forth; they that have done good, unto the resurrection of life; and they that have done evil, unto the resurrection of damnation." John 5: 28, 29.

"If the Spirit of him that raised up Jesus from the dead dwell in you, he that raised up Christ from the dead shall also quicken your mortal bodies by his Spirit that dwelleth in you." Rom. 8: 11. The *mortal bodies* of the saints shall be quickened, and the resurrection of Christ shall be the pattern after which they shall be raised. Of course Christ's body saw no corruption, because he had no sin, but still it had to go wherever our bodies were, in order to redeem them from the grave.

"But," says some one, "Christ's body was changed, at his ascension, to a spiritual body." Some Bible students fail to make the proper distinction between a *spiritual body* and a *spirit*, and, hence, destroy the doctrine of future recognition. They do not understand the "*transfigura-*

tion" lesson fully. "We ourselves groan within ourselves, waiting for the adoption, to wit, the redemption of our body." Rom. 8: 23. Paul said that they had the first-fruits of the Spirit, but were anxiously waiting for the redemption of the body. I have been aware for years, that there are those who do not believe that our human bodies will ever be resurrected from the grave; but of late I learned that some of the ministers of our church entertain the same view. They believe that the Lord will bring new, spiritual bodies from heaven. We believe in a *complete* Redeemer,—a Redeemer of body and soul. "O grave, where is thy victory?" It will be swallowed up by the resurrection of the body. Yes, we will say, is *swallowed up*, for the "*first-fruits*" have already appeared by the resurrection of Christ's body.

Do you doubt the general harvest? Then look at the resurrection of the many bodies of the saints. Resurrection is more than the coming forth of the body from the grave. It is also the bringing together of body and soul, which is the resumption of life. In 1 Cor. 15: 35, we have the following question: "How are the dead raised up, and with what body do they come?" Paul answers the question by a similitude: "Thou fool, that which thou sowest is not quickened, except it die, and that which thou sowest, thou sowest not that body that shall be, but bare grain; it may chance of wheat, or of some other grain." The expression, "Thou sowest not that body that shall be," is one of the passages that lead many to believe that the human body will not be resurrected. True, the grain that is sown decomposes, yet it produces and nourishes root, stalk, leaves and full corn in the ear.

Let us notice Paul's explication of the similitude; "It is sown in corruption; it is raised in incorruption; it is sown in dishonour; it is raised in glory: it is sown in weakness; it is raised in power; it is sown a natural body; it is raised a spiritual body." In this explication Paul declares four times that the *body* that is *sown* is *raised.* Who dare deny? Some one may say, the contrast between the body that is sown and the one that is raised is so great that it cannot be the same. On the same ground we might say that the soul that is regenerated, created anew, or redeemed from sin, is not the same as when it was dead in trespasses and sins. The beautiful butterfly is from the caterpillar. This beautiful white paper is from refuse or filthy rags. But much greater will be the contrast between man, as he appears by nature, and as he will appear when both body and soul are redeemed from sin and death. But how about the wicked? True, their bodies will come forth, too, to be united with their souls, but neither being redeemed from sin, before the judgment, they must go to be judged according to the deeds done in the body. If they were "dogs, and sorcerers, and whoremongers, and murderers, and idolators, and liars, and extortioners, and drunkards," etc., in this world, and were not regenerated, as such they will go before the judgment. What a contrast, then, between the righteous and wicked! Then "he that is unjust, let him be unjust still: and he which is filthy, let him be filthy still: and he that is righteous, let him be righteous still: and he that is holy, let him be holy still."

Here we let the curtain drop. Let us all meditate seriously.

"A drop of ink is a very small thing, yet dropped into a tumbler of clear water it blackens the whole; and so the first oath, the first lie, the first glass, may seem very trivial, but they leave a dark stain upon one's character. Look out for the first stain."

Lewistown church, Pennsylvania,.......	6 25
Missionary Meeting of North-eastern Ohio, ...	11 74
Maple Grove church, Ohio,............	39 05
Sandy church, Ohio,....................	5 00
Mahoning church, Ohio,...............	6 00
Fanny Hoover, Cambridge City, Ind.,...	5 00
Sally Clapper, Mooreland, Ind.,.........	1 00
Mrs. S. J. Morgan, Centerville, Ia.,.....	1 00
Mr. and Mrs. S. C. Kindy, Elkhart, Ind.,	10 00
Middle District of Indiana,.............	42 00
Bethel church Sunday-school, Nebr.,.....	5 35
Effie Rothrock (deceased,),...............	29
District of California,..................	5 50
Sisters of West Dayton church, Ohio,...	5 35
U. T. Farhey, Waterbury, Nebr........	5 00
St. Joseph Sunday-school, Ind.,.........	5 75
Salem church, Ohio,....................	25 05
Sallie M. Pretzman, Springfield, Ohio,..	2 00
Back Creek church, Pennsylvania,......	5 00
Daniel Barrick, Byron, Ill,...........	2 00
Jas. Keffer, New Virginia, Iowa,.......	1 25
Mary R. Mohler, Clyde, Kansas,.......	1 00
Hopewell church, Pennsylvania,........	1 00
Emmanuel Henry and wife, Garden Grove, Iowa,.......................	1 00
Lewis M. Kob and wife, Garden Grove, Iowa, ...	
A sister,..............................	2 00
A. J. Kreps, McVeytown, Pa.,.........	5 00
Albright congregation of Clover Creek church, Pa.,......................	3 00
Joseph F. Emmert, Waynesborough, Pa,.	11 12
Mrs. Amanda Harris, Mount Morris, Ill,	3 00
J. A. Murray, Winfield, Kans,.........	25
Pyrmont church, Indiana,...............	4 50
Esterly church, Louisiana,..............	8 70
Mingo church, Pennsylvania,...........	12 50
Covington church, Ohio,................	20 33
Leah T. Miller,.......................	1 00
Nettle Creek church, Indiana,..........	2 00
David Kilhefner and wife, Ephratah, Pa.,	1 00
Kate Buttesbaugh, McPherson, Kans.,..	3 00
A brother, Overbrook, Kans.,...........	10 00
A brother and sister, Hagerstown, Ind.,	5 00
A brother, Pottstown, Pa.,.............	10 00
Mariet Reed, Easton, W. Va.,..........	5 00
M. W. Reed, Easton, W. Va.,..........	10 00
O. W. Reed, Easton, W. Va.,..........	2 50
Clara Reed, Easton, W. Va.,..........	2 50
Grandma and her grandson,.............	1 00
A sister, Cameron, Mo.,................	5 00
Smithfork Sunday-school, Clinton County, Missouri,......................	3 00
Anna Wright, Kiowa, Kans,............	2 00
J. E. Gnagey, Accident, Md.,..........	10 00
Sarah Muse, Vinton, Va,..............	1 50
Daniel Fiant and family, Connersville, Ind.,.............................	5 00
Tropico church, California,.............	10 60
Johnstown church, Pennsylvania,.......	34 00
Baugo church, Indiana,................	2 80
W. H. Hall, Nocona, Texas,............	5 20
Samuel Oblinger, Waterville, Minn.,....	1 50
Two sisters, Salem, Oregon,...........	2 00
C. C. Stemen and family, Lacona, Ia.,..	1 69
Brother and sister, in Jennings, La.,....	5 00
S. H. Moyer, Philadelphia, Pa.,........	1 00
Mrs. Jincy Harshbarger, Garland, Ohio,	15
Mary G. Reiff, Roseville, Ind.,.........	1 25
Rome church, Ohio,....................	18 00
A brother, Rockton, Pa.,..............	1 00
South Bend church, Indiana,...........	28 50
Wolf Creek church, Ohio,..............	17 57
A sister, Orimora Station, Pa.,.........	1 50
Levi and Florence Ulrich, River, Ind.,..	2 00
English River church, Iowa,............	13 19
S. W. Bail, South Strabane, Pa.,.......	50
Pleasant Hill church, Iowa,............	2 10
Mound church, Missouri,..............	2 20

Yellow River church, Indiana,..........	20 25
Lizzie Barndollar, Everett, Pa ,....:....	5 00
J. S. Hershberger, Everett, Pa.,........	5 00
Logan church, Ohio,..................	29 50
Botetourt church, Virginia,............	18 00
P. A. and Clarinda Moore, Roanoke, Ill.,	2 50
John Gable and wife, New Sharon, Iowa,	5 00
Southern District of Illinois,...........	27 20
Okaw church, Illinois,.................	13 50
Arnold's Grove church, Illinois	11 25
Two-thirds proceeds of last Annual Meeting, at Hagerstown, Md............	2,000 00
Burr Oak church, Kansas,..........?...	1 50
Mary M. Mullendore, Claggett's, Md.,...	2 00
Margaret Calhoun, Everett, Pa.,........	10 00
Greene church, Iowa,..................	6 20
Monitor church, Kansas,...............	4 05
Minnie and Ella Sanger, Gatewood, W. Va.,................................	2 00
Elizabeth Johnson, Old Frame, Pa.,.....	2 15
Moses Walker, Boone, Ia.,.............	5 00
Michael Weckert, Salmon, Oregon,.....	1 00
Ezra Flora (deceased), Divernon, Ill.,...	100 00
A sister, Missouri,....................	1 00
Loramie's church, Ohio,...............	2 00
A brother and sister, Liberty, Ohio, ...	5 00
D., Winona, Minnesota, ...	10 00
Tropico church, California,............	4 30
Soalger Creek church, Kansas,.........	5 00
Sugar Creek church, Ohio,............	63 90
N. E. O., Chippewa church,...........	16 61
Keuka church, Florida,................	3 12
E. A. Staard, Indiana,.................	25
Isaac Grady, Indiana,.................	50
D. Rothenberger, Indiana,.............	25
John Shrock, Indiana,.................	1 00
A. Miller, Mexico, Ind.,..............	7 50
A reader of GOSPEL MESSENGER, Michigan, ...	1 00
Garrison church, Iowa,................	8 00
Green Spring church, Ohio,............	5 40
Lick Creek church, Ohio,..............	13 00
Sisters of West Dayton church, Ohio,...	5 16
South Waterloo church, Iowa,..........	45 00
Big Creek church, Illinois,.............	2 10
A brother, Chicago, Ill,...............	2 00
K. Leonard, Aurelia, Ia.,..............	1 00
James Mowery, Arcadia, Nebr.,.........	80
May Wilson, Belle Plaine, Ia.,.........	5 00
Levi Simmons, Carrollton, Ohio,......	1 00
A. J. Strickler, Brazil, Ia.,............	50
Elizabeth Hiner, Doe Hill, Va,.......	2 00
O. H. Elliott, Gambier, Ohio,.........	1 50
Christian Wirt, Lewistown, Minn.,.....	1 00
Walnut church, Indiana,..............	2 00
Mrs. Sarah M. Hornish, Jewel, Ohio,....	5 00
James Hossack, Leask Dale, Ont,......	5 00
George Hossack, Leask Dale, Ont·......	5 00
Jenny Hossack, Leask Dale, Ont,.......	5 00
A brother and sister, Enterprise, Kans.,.	3 00
Brother and sister Phineas L. Fike, Dobbin, Ia.,..........................	1 00
Falling Spring church, Pennsylvania....	20 00
Susan Clapper, Carey, Ohio,...........	10 00
Michael G. Domer, Baltic, Ohio,.......	1 00
Malinda A. Keller, Dallas Centre, Ia.,...	50
J. F. Ross, Simpson, W. Va.,...........	1 00
Catherine Boge, Lookout, Iowa,........	2 15
F. C. Cunningham, Ottawa, Kans,......	3 00
D. B. Heiny and wife, McCool Junction, Nebr.,..............................	1 04
Lexington church, ...	1 25
Quemahoning church, Pennsylvania,....	10 00
Susan Rothrock, Carlisle, Nebr.,........	2 50
Brethren's Sunday-school of Woodbury, Md...............................	4 90
A. Z. Gates, Beattie, Kans,............	1 08
Coquille Valley church, Oregon,........	17 10
Caroline Smith, Grelton, Ohio,........	2 00
A brother and sister, Saline City, Ind,,,,	5 00

G. W. Kephart, Altoona, Pa,..........	2 50
Abram Hack, Mowerville, Pa.,........	1 40
E. B., Nocona, Texas,.................	5 00
Geo. S. Rowland, Mountville, Pa.,......	5 00
Dorrance church, Kansas,.............	3 25
Levi Summer, Campbellsville, Ky.,.....	10 00
Catherine Biggs, Clearmount, Mo,.....	75
Susan Owen, River, Ind.,..............	50
A sister of Upper Cumberland church, Pennsylvania,......................	5 00
M. K. G., Pennsylvania,..............	2 00
John Leedy, Andrews, Ind.,...........	2 00
Levi Burch, Byron, Ill,...............	50
Jacob's Creek church, Pennsylvania,...	4 00
M. Snyder, Conrad Grove, Ia.,.......	5 00
George J. Klein, Conrad Grove, Ia.,....	10 00
Eliza Quagy, Grantsville, Md.,........	3 40
Levi and Sarah Stoner, Avion, Ohio,....	2 50
Northern District of Illinois,..........	111 16
Sale of Miller and Sommer Debate Book,	1 50
Interest on Loans from Endowment Fund,..........................	60 50
Interest on Loans from Mission Fund,...	30 00
Interest on Endowment Notes,........	690 46

GALEN B. ROYER, Sec.

MINISTERIAL MEETINGS.

BY J. S. MOHLER.

THE following is the program for the Ministerial Meeting to be held in the Olathe church, Kans., Tuesday, preceding the second Wednesday of April, 1892:

1. "Christian Perfection, from a Bible Standpoint."

2. "What are the Leading Points, Essential to Successful Church Government?"

3. "The General Deportment of Ministers when out, as well as in the Pulpit."

4. "The Selecting of Subjects for Preaching by which the Congregation may be most Edified. Is this a Point that should be Studied?"

5. "Advantages Gained by Frequent Exchanges of Visits by the Ministry."

6. "The Right Relation of Each Member to the Body,—the Church,—and how to Maintain that Relation."

7. "How Shall we best Care for the Young Members of the Church, so as to Nourish them in Divine Life?"

8. "Would not the Bible alone be a More Efficient Help in the Sunday-school than the Quarterlies?"

By order of Committee on Program.

Morrill, Kans.

WHO WILL RESPOND?

DURING these long winter evenings, I do wish that some of the MESSENGER contributors would write for our valuable paper, carefully-prepared articles on some of these subjects:

"How may we Obtain a Baptism of the Holy Ghost?"

"How may we make our Prayers of More Effect?"

"How may we Best Grow Spiritually?"

"What are our 'Tests of Membership?'"

"How can a Layman Best Aid the Great Cause of Missions?"　　　A MARYLAND BROTHER.

"WHOEVER would be Christ-like should be willing to wear Christ's crown; and the crown in which he was revealed to us was not silver nor gold, studded with gems. The crown which Christ wore was worthy of him. He came by suffering to redeem this world from suffering. Shall the servant be greater than the Master? Shall Christ suffer and you not?"

Lewistown church, Pennsylvania	6 25
Missionary Meeting of North-eastern Ohio,	11 74
Maple Grove church, Ohio,	39 05
Sandy church, Ohio,	5 00
Mahoning church, Ohio,	6 00
Fanny Hoover, Cambridge City, Ind.,	5 00
Sally Clapper, Mooreland, Ind.,	1 00
Mrs. S. J. Morgan, Centerville, Is.,	1 00
Mr. and Mrs. S. C. Kindy, Elkhart, Ind.,	10 00
Middle District of Indiana,	42 00
Bethel church Sunday-school, Nebr.,	5 85
Effie Rothrock (deceased,)	29
District of California,	5 50
Sisters of West Dayton church, Ohio,	5 35
U. T. Farhey, Waterbury, Nebr.,	5 00
St. Joseph Sunday-school, Ind.,	5 75
Salem church, Ohio,	25 05
Sallie M. Pretzman, Springfield, Ohio,	2 00
Back Creek church, Pennsylvania,	5 00
Daniel Barrick, Byron, Ill	2 00
Jas. Keffer, New Virginia, Iowa,	1 25
Mary R. Mobler, Clyde, Kansas,	1 00
Hopewell church, Pennsylvania,	1 00
Emmanuel Henry and wife, Garden Grove, Iowa,	1 00
Lewis M. Kob and wife, Garden Grove, Iowa,	2 00
A sister,	5 00
A. J. Kreps, McVeytown, Pa.,	3 00
Albright congregation of Clover Creek church, Pa.,	11 12
Joseph F. Emmert, Waynesborough, Pa.,	3 00
Mrs. Amanda Harris, Mount Morris, Ill,	25
J. A. Murray, Winfield, Kans.,	25
Pyrmont church, Indiana,	4 50
Esterly church, Louisiana,	8 70
Mingo church, Pennsylvania,	12 50
Covington church, Ohio,	20 33
Leah T. Miller,	1 00
Nettle Creek church, Indiana,	2 00
David Kilhefner and wife, Ephratah, Pa.,	1 00
Kate Buttosbaugh, McPherson, Kans.,	3 00
A brother, Overbrook, Kans.,	10 00
A brother and sister, Hagerstown, Ind.,	10 00
A brother, Pottstown, Pa.,	10 00
Mariet Reed, Easton, W. Va.,	5 00
M. W. Reed, Easton, W. Va.,	10 00
O. W. Reed, Easton, W. Va.,	2 50
Clara Reed, Easton, W. Va.,	2 50
Grandma and her grandson,	1 00
A sister, Cameron, Mo.,	5 00
Smithfork Sunday-school, Clinton County, Missouri,	3 00
Anna Wright, Kiowa, Kans.,	2 00
J. E. Gnagey, Accident, Md.,	10 00
Sarah Muse, Vinton, Iowa,	1 50
Daniel Fiant and family, Connersville, Ind.,	5 00
Tropico church, California,	10 60
Johnstown church, Pennsylvania,	34 00
Baugo church, Indiana,	2 80
W. H. Hall, Nocona, Texas,	5 20
Samuel Oblinger, Waterville, Minn.,	1 50
Two sisters, Salem, Oregon,	2 00
C. C. Stemen and family, Lacona, Is.,	1 69
Brother and sister, in Jennings, La.,	5 00
S. H. Moyer, Philadelphia, Pa.,	1 00
Mrs. Jinoy Harshbarger, Garland, Ohio,	1 25
Mary G. Reiff, Rossville, Ind.,	1 25
Rome church, Ohio,	18 00
A brother, Rockton, Pa.,	1 00
South Bend church, Indiana,	28 50
Wolf Creek church, Ohio,	17 57
A sister, Crimora Station, Va.,	1 50
Levi and Florence Ulrich, River, Ind.,	2 00
English church church, Iowa,	13 19
S. W. Bail, South Strabane, Pa.,	50
Pleasant Hill church, Iowa,	2 10
Mound church, Missouri,	2 20

Yellow River church, Indiana,	20 25
Lizzie Barndollar, Everett, Pa.,	5 00
J. S. Hershberger, Everett, Pa.,	5 00
Logan church, Ohio,	20 50
Botetourt church, Virginia,	18 00
P. A. and Clarinda Moore, Roanoke, Ill.	2 50
John Gable and wife, New Sharon, Iowa,	5 00
Southern District of Illinois,	27 26
Okaw church, Illinois,	13 50
Arnold's Grove church, Illinois	11 25
Two-thirds proceeds of last Annual Meeting, at Hagerstown, Md.,	2,000 00
Burr Oak church, Kansas,	1 50
Mary M. Mullendore, Claggett's, Md.,	2 00
Margaret Calhoun, Everett, Pa.,	10 00
Greene church, Iowa,	6 20
Monitor church, Kansas,	4 05
Minnie and Ella Sanger, Gatewood, W. Va.,	2 00
Elizabeth Johnson, Old Frame, Pa.,	2 15
Moses Walker, Boone, W. Va.,	5 00
Michael Weekert, Salmon, Oregon,	1 00
Ezra Flora (deceased,) Divernon, Ill.,	100 00
A sister, Missouri,	1 00
Loranie's church, Ohio,	2 00
A brother and sister, Liberty, Ohio,	5 00
D., Winona, Minnesota,	10 00
Tropico church, California,	4 30
Soaiger Creek church, Kansas,	5 00
Sugar Creek church, Ohio,	63 90
N. E. O., Chippewa church,	16 61
Keuka church, Florida,	3 12
E. A. Steard, Indiana,	25
Isaac Grady, Indiana,	50
D. Rothenberger, Indiana,	25
John Shrock, Indiana,	1 00
A. Miller, Mexico, Ind.,	7 50
A reader of GOSPEL MESSENGER, Michigan,	1 00
Garrison church, Iowa,	8 00
Green Spring church, Ohio,	5 40
Lick Creek church, Ohio,	13 00
Sisters of West Dayton church, Ohio,	5 16
South Waterloo church, Iowa,	45 00
Big Creek church, Illinois,	2 10
A brother, Chicago, Ill.,	2 00
K. Leonard, Aurelia, Ia.,	1 00
James Mowery, Arcadia, Nebr.,	80
May Wilson, Belle Plaine, Is.,	5 00
Levi Simmons, Carrollton, Ohio,	1 00
A. J. Strickler, Brazil, Ia.,	50
Elizabeth Hiuer, Doe Hill, Va.,	2 00
O. H. Elliott, Gambier, Ohio,	1 50
Christian Wirt, Lewistown, Minn.,	1 00
Walnut church, Indiana,	2 00
Mrs. Sarah M. Hornish, Jewel, Ohio,	5 00
James Hossack, Leask Dale, Ont.,	5 00
George Hossack, Leask Dale, Ont.	5 00
Jenny Hossack, Leask Dale, Ont.,	5 00
A brother and sister, Enterprise, Kans.,	3 00
Brother and sister Phineas L. Fike, Dobbin, Ia.,	1 00
Falling Spring church, Pennsylvania,	20 00
Susan Clapper, Carey, Ohio,	10 00
Michael G. Domer, Baltic, Ohio,	1 00
Malinda A. Keller, Dallas Centre, Ia.,	50
J. F. Ross, Simpson, W. Va.,	1 00
Catherine Boge, Lookout, Iowa,	2 15
F. C. Cunningham, Ottawa, Kans.,	3 00
D. B. Heiny and wife, McCool Junction, Nebr.,	1 04
Lexington church,	1 25
Quemahoning church, Pennsylvania,	10 00
Susan Rothrock, Carlisle, Nebr.,	2 50
Brethren's Sunday-school of Woodbury, Md.,	4 90
A. Z. Gates, Beattie, Kans,	1 08
Coquille Valley church, Oregon,	17 10
Caroline Smith, Grelton, Ohio,	2 00
A brother and sister, Saline City, Ind.,	5 00

G. W. Kephart, Altoona, Pa.,	2 50
Abram Hack, Mowersville, Pa.,	1 40
E. R., Nocona, Texas,	5 00
Geo. S. Rowland, Mountville, Pa.,	5 00
Dorrance church, Kansas,	3 25
Levi Summer, Campbellsville, Ky.,	10 00
Catherine Biggs, Clearmount, Mo	75
Susan Owen, River, Ind.,	50
A sister of Upper Cumberland church, Pennsylvania,	5 00
M. K. G., Pennsylvania,	2 00
John Leedy, Andrews, Ind.,	2 00
Levi Burch, Byron, Ill,	50
Jacob's Creek church, Pennsylvania,	4 00
M. Snyder, Conrad Grove, Is.,	5 00
George J. Klein, Conrad Grove, Is.,	10 00
Eliza Quagy, Grantsville, Md.,	3 40
Levi and Sarah Stoner, Avlon, Ohio,	2 50
Northern District of Illinois,	111 16
Sale of Miller and Sommer Debate Book,	1 50
Interest on Loans from Endowment Fund,	60 50
Interest on Loans from Mision Fund,	20 00
Interest on Endowment Notes,	690 46

GALEN B. ROYER, Sec.

MINISTERIAL MEETINGS.

BY J. S. MOHLER.

THE following is the program for the Ministerial Meeting to be held in the Olathe church, Kans., Tuesday, preceding the second Wednesday of April, 1892:

1. "Christian Perfection, from a Bible Standpoint."

2. "What are the Leading Points, Essential to Successful Church Government?"

3. "The General Deportment of Ministers when out, as well as in the Pulpit."

4. "The Selecting of Subjects for Preaching by which the Congregation may be most Edified. Is this a Point that should be Studied?"

5. "Advantages Gained by Frequent Exchanges of Visits by the Ministry."

6. "The Right Relation of Each Member to the Body,—the Church,—and how to Maintain that Relation."

7. "How Shall we best Care for the Young Members of the Church, so as to Nourish them in Divine Life?"

8. "Would not the Bible alone be a More Efficient Help in the Sunday-school than the Quarterlies?"

By order of Committee on Program.

Morrill, Kans.

WHO WILL RESPOND?

DURING these long winter evenings, I do wish that some of the MESSENGER contributors would write, for our valuable paper, carefully-prepared articles on some of these subjects:

"How may we Obtain a Baptism of the Holy Ghost?"

"How may we make our Prayers of More Effect?"

"How may we Best Grow Spiritually?"

"What are our 'Tests of Membership?'"

"How can a Layman Best Aid the Great Cause of Missions?"   A MARYLAND BROTHER.

"WHOEVER would be Christ-like should be willing to wear Christ's crown; and the crown in which he was revealed to us was not silver nor gold, studded with gems. The crown which Christ wore was worthy of him. He came by suffering to redeem this world from suffering. Shall the servant be greater than the Master? Shall Christ suffer and you not?"

BRO. WILBUR B. STOVER, of Edgemont, Md., has decided to go to Germantown, Pa.; and labor for the interest of the little church at that place. He feels that he is entering upon an important work, and it is to be hoped that he may not only keep alive the fire that has long been burning on the sacred altar at that place, but that he may, in a measure, be the means of greatly reviving the work of Zion, so as to restore this congregation to something like its former greatness and usefulness in the Brotherhood.

NEAR the center of Africa is Lake Victoria Nyanza, a body of water nearly 600 miles in circumference, and very deep. To this point the missionaries have penetrated and seem to be doing a very successful work. A steel steamer has just been completed in England for use on this lake. It will likely be transported over land, about 800 miles, and is to be employed in the interest of missionaries and commerce. A few years ago this part of the Dark Continent was peopled by savages, but in a short time this lake will be covered with steamers and civilization will take the sway.

BRETHREN R. H. Miller and I. D. Parker are with us at this time, doing some excellent preaching. If health permits, they may deliver about twenty discourses on doctrine and church government. We hope to be able to publish some of these sermons in the MESSENGER. The discourses are all prepared especially for these meetings and are, listened to with profound interest by hundreds who seem to greatly appreciate the efforts which our preachers are making. It is indeed a rich feast for those who are seeking further information concerning the great truths of the Bible.

A SISTER hands us this beautiful extract, the prayer of a devout wife for her husband. Would it not be wise for husbands, as well as wives, to often pray such prayers? "Lord, bless and preserve that dear person whom thou hast chosen to be my husband. Let his life be long and blessed, comfortable and holy, and let me also become a great blessing and comfort unto him—a sharer in all his sorrows, a meet helper in all his accidents and changes in the world. Make me amiable forever in his eyes and forever dear to him. Unite his heart to me in the dearest love and holiness, and mine to him in all sweetness, clarity and compliance. Keep me from all ungentleness and discontentedness and unreasonableness, and make me humble and obedient, useful and observant, that we may delight in each other according to thy Blessed Word and both of us may rejoice in thee, having our portion in the love and service of God forever. Amen."

WE have just printed the Minutes of the District Meeting of Tennessee, North Carolina and Florida. From it we glean a few items that may be of general interest. This District is composed of thirty congregations and nine of these are in North Carolina, one in Florida and the remaining twenty in Tennessee. Bro. G. C. Bowman represents the District on the next Standing Committee. Looking over the missionary reports we notice that during the past year Bro. F. W. Dove traveled 8,700 miles, held nearly seventy meetings, received by baptism thirty-six and reclaimed seven. Bro. A. J. Vines assisted him in part of the work. Bro. G. C. Bowman reported nearly 5,000 miles traveled, organized one church, attended 173 meetings and received twenty-three into the church, making a total of sixty six received into the church by baptism and restoration. Twenty-one of these united with the church in Missouri. The report shows that our Southern brethren are by no means idle, and that there is a grand opening for our people in the South.

I wish you would make an editorial concerning the use of some phrases. I have been recently in sections where outsiders make much sport of our ministers for the use of threadbare terms like these: "I wish liberty," "Brethren, be free," "The poet says," "I want to make a few remarks" and "I will now give it over to the Brethren." In themselves these phrases are full of meaning, but by excessive use they become almost by-words for some. This is a cause for offense or sport that might be avoided. It pains me at times when I see such causes for sport

The above comes from a brother who is deeply concerned for the church. We think the mere publishing of his request will be a sufficient suggestion to those who have never given these phrases the thought that our brother has. A hint to the wise is generally sufficient.

A BROTHER wishes to know whether sisters may, with propriety, speak in prayer-meetings and teach in Sunday-schools? Certainly they may. We have sisters that superintend Sunday-schools, hundreds teach in Sunday-schools, and all of them may, with perfect propriety, speak in prayer-meeting, or even lead, if called on to do so. They are also permitted to speak in our regular council-meetings. Years ago we had a sister in Ohio, sister Sarah Major, who often preached in a most acceptable manner. So far as Sunday-school work and prayer-meetings are concerned, we have always encouraged our sisters to use freely the privileges granted them to speak, teach or lead. This is in perfect harmony with the faith and practice of the Brethren church so far as we know.

MEETING OF THE GENERAL MISSION BOARD.

WE did not have space in last issue to say much concerning the work of the General Mission Board which met here the first week in January. The more we see of the doings of this Board, the more do we become convinced that it has an important undertaking before it, and is doing its utmost to carry forward the work which the General Brotherhood has placed in its hands. The Board is composed of men of sound judgment, who are extremely cautious regarding every department of their work. We only wish our people knew of the care and prudence the Board is exercising in all of its undertakings.

We wish to impress upon the minds of our members the fact that the more aggressive the District Mission Boards are in States where missionary work is needed, the more our General Board can accomplish, for much of their work must be done through these District Boards. Not so much work is being accomplished as we would like to see, but under the circumstances we could hardly expect more. As our ministers become better skilled in this line of work, and more of them can be induced to enter the field fully equipped for the duties and privations of the mission field, we may look for greater results. And yet we must say that the outlook is real encouraging.

The work in Denmark received a good deal of attention at this meeting, and we feel confident that our brethren across the waters are doing a noble work. Steps will be taken to build another meeting-house at the place mentioned by Bro. Hope several weeks ago. Some have already sent in donations to aid in the construction of this house, and others who feel to help in the work can send their contributions to Bro. Galen B. Royer. The Brethren in Denmark are not only having a hard struggle, but they are working earnestly, and it is no more than right that we encourage them in their difficult labors. They labor under difficulties unknown in this country, and our Mission Board is acting wisely in giving them the needed and substantial encouragement.　　— J. H. M.

THE FOUNDATION.

CHRIST is the real foundation of the Christian church. Paul says, "Other foundation can no man lay than that is laid, which is Jesus Christ." 1 Cor. 3: 11. Paul also refers to Christ when, in the preceding verse, he says, "I have laid the foundation and another buildeth thereon." From this Scripture we learn that the foundation may be laid by man. Preaching Christ is the laying of the foundation in the hearts of the people. The minister who proclaims the death, burial, resurrection and ascension of Christ, and demonstrates to the people that Jesus was crucified, buried and arose from the dead on the third day, and then ascended to the Father, lays the foundation of Christianity in the hearts of the people, and thus prepares them to receive his teachings. That is the way Paul laid the foundation of Christianity at Corinth. He was a "wise master builder" and knew how to lay a foundation. Wherever the apostles traveled they proclaimed the resurrection of Christ. Peter, on Pentecost, as well as Paul at Athens, proclaimed boldly the resurrection of Jesus, maintaining that God had raised him from the dead.

The whole question hinged on that one point, viz., the resurrection of Christ from the dead. If God raised him from the dead he must be a true prophet, for God would not raise a false prophet from the tomb. If he be a true prophet then he must be the Son of God, and therefore all he said and commanded must be true and should be obeyed. The man who believes in his heart that God raised Christ from the dead must, of necessity, believe that he is divine. Therefore it was all-important for the apostles to make it clear to the minds of the people that Christ really did arise from the dead. Well may Paul have said, "If Christ be not risen, then is our preaching vain, and your faith is vain also." 1 Cor. 15: 14. Thus it was that the foundation was laid in the hearts of the people by demonstration to them that Jesus really did arise from the dead, and was therefore the Son of God, authorized to make known the law of heaven to the children of men.

It is upon Christ that the church is founded. Without Christ there could be no Christian church, for he is both the head and foundation of it as well as the chief corner-stone thereof. And it is upon this foundation that the whole Christian church must rest. As previously quoted, Paul could lay the foundation, but others built thereon. In Ephesians it is declared that the saints "are built upon the foundation of the apostles and prophets, Jesus Christ himself being the chief corner stone." Eph. 2: 20. Christ is the foundation of both the apostles and prophets. The latter preach Christ in prophecy while the former preached him in fact. The prophets, in olden times, laid the foundation of Christ in prophecy by proclaiming his coming, and all those who believed their teachings had the foundation laid in their hearts. "Believest thou the prophets?" was the keen question that Paul put to King Agrippa. To believe the prophets was to believe that Christ arose from the dead, for they prophesied concerning his resurrection. But after he arose, then the apostles and others went every-where, proclaiming in fact what the prophets had proclaimed in prophecy. Christ is, therefore, the foundation of both the apostles and prophets. It is upon Christ that they rest, for upon him their faith is founded. They are no foundation

BRO. WILBUR B. STOVER, of Edgemont, Md., has decided to go to Germantown, Pa., and labor for the interest of the little church at that place. He feels that he is entering upon an important work, and it is to be hoped that he may not only keep alive the fire that has long been burning on the sacred altar at that place, but that he may, in a measure, be the means of greatly reviving the work of Zion, so as to restore this congregation to something like its former greatness and usefulness in the Brotherhood.

NEAR the center of Africa is Lake Victoria Nyanza, a body of water nearly 600 miles in circumference, and very deep. To this point- the missionaries have penetrated and seem to be doing a very successful work. A steel steamer has just been completed in England for use on this lake. It will likely be transported over land, about 600 miles, and is to be employed in the interest of missionaries and commerce. A few years ago this part of the Dark Continent was peopled by savages, but in a short time this lake will be covered with steamers and civilization will take the away.

BRETHREN R. H. Miller and I. D. Parker are with us at this time, doing some excellent preaching. If health permits, they may deliver about twenty discourses on doctrine and church government. We hope to be able to publish some of these sermons in the MESSENGER. The discourses are all prepared especially for these meetings and are listened to with profound interest by hundreds who seem to greatly appreciate the efforts which our preachers are making. It is indeed a rich feast for those who are seeking further information concerning the great truths of the Bible.

A SISTER hands us this beautiful extract, the prayer of a devout wife for her husband. Would it not be wise for husbands, as well as wives, to often pray such prayers? "Lord, bless and preserve that dear person whom thou hast chosen to be my husband. Let his life be long and blessed, comfortable and holy, and let me also become a great blessing and comfort unto him—a sharer in all his sorrows, a meet helper in all his accidents and changes in the world. Make me amiable forever in his eyes and forever dear to him. Unite his heart to me in the dearest love and fondness, and mine to him in all sweetness, charity and compliance. Keep me from all ungentleness and discontentedness and unreasonableness, and make me humble and obedient, useful and observant, that we may delight in each other according to thy Blessed Word and both of us may rejoice in thee, having our portion in the love and service of God forever. Amen."

WE have just printed the Minutes of the District Meeting of Tennessee, North Carolina and Florida. From it we glean a few items that may be of general interest. This District is composed of thirty congregations and nine of these are in North Carolina, one in Florida and the remaining twenty in Tennessee. Bro. G. C. Bowman represents the District on the next Standing Committee. Looking over the missionary reports we notice that during the past year Bro. F. W. Dove traveled 3,700 miles, held nearly seventy meetings, received by baptism thirty-six and reclaimed seven. Bro. A. J. Vines assisted him in part of the work. Bro. G. C. Bowman reported nearly 5,000 miles traveled, organized one church, attended 173 meetings and received twenty-three into the church, making a total of sixty six received into the church by baptism and restoration. Twenty-one of these united with the church in Missouri. The report shows that our Southern brethren are by no means idle, and that there is a grand opening for our people in the South.

I wish you would make an editorial concerning the use of some phrases. I have been recently in sections where outside remarks make much sport of our ministers for the use of threadbare terms like these: "I wish liberty," "Brethren, be free," "The poet says," "I want to make a few remarks" and "I will now give it over to the Brethren." In themselves these phrases are full of meaning, but by excessive use they become almost by-words for some. This is a cause for offense or sport that might be avoided. It pains me at times when I see such causes for sport.

The above comes from a brother who is deeply concerned for the church. We think the mere publishing of his request will be a sufficient suggestion to those who have never given these phrases the thought that our brother has. A hint to the wise is generally sufficient.

A BROTHER wishes to know whether sisters may, with propriety, speak in prayer-meetings and teach in Sunday-schools? Certainly they may. We have sisters that superintend Sunday-schools, hundreds teach in Sunday-schools, and all of them may, with perfect propriety, speak in prayer-meeting, or even lead, if called on to do so. They are also permitted to speak in our regular council-meetings. Years ago we had a sister in Ohio, sister Serah Major, who often preached in a most acceptable manner. So far as Sunday-school work and prayer-meetings are concerned, we have always encouraged our sisters to use freely the privilege granted them to speak, teach or lead. This is in perfect harmony with the faith and practice of the Brethren church so far as we know.

MEETING OF THE GENERAL MISSION BOARD.

WE did not have space in last issue to say much concerning the work of the General Mission Board which met here the first week in January. The more we see of the doings of this Board, the more do we become convinced that it has an important undertaking before it, and is doing its utmost to carry forward the work which the General Brotherhood has placed in its hands. The Board is composed of men of sound judgment, who are extremely cautious regarding every department of their work. We only wish our people knew of the care and prudence the Board is exercising in all of its undertakings.

We wish to impress upon the minds of our members the fact that the more aggressive the District Mission Boards are in States where missionary work is needed, the more our General Board can accomplish, for much of their work must be done through these District Boards. Not so much work is being accomplished as we would like to see, but under the circumstances we could hardly expect more. As our ministers become better skilled in this line of work, and more of them can be induced to enter the field fully equipped for the duties and privations of the mission fields, we may look for greater results. And yet we must say that the outlook is real encouraging.

The work in Denmark received a good deal of attention at this meeting, and we feel confident that our brethren across the waters are doing a noble work. Steps will be taken to build another meeting-house at the place mentioned by Bro. Hope several weeks ago. Some have already sent in donations to aid in the construction of this house, and others who feel to help in the work can send their contributions to Bro. Galen B. Royer. The Brethren in Denmark are not only having a hard struggle, but they are working earnestly, and it is no more than right that we encourage them in their difficult labors. They labor under difficulties unknown in this country, and our Mission Board is acting wisely in giving them the needed and substantial encouragement.   J. H. M.

THE FOUNDATION.

CHRIST is the real foundation of the Christian church. Paul says, "Other foundation can no man lay than that is laid, which is Jesus Christ." 1 Cor. 3: 11. Paul also refers to Christ when, in the preceding verse, he says, "I have laid the foundation and another buildeth thereon." From this Scripture we learn that the foundation may be laid by man. Preaching Christ is the laying of the foundation in the hearts of the people. The minister who proclaims the death, burial, resurrection and ascension of Christ, and demonstrates to the people that Jesus was crucified, buried and arose from the dead on the third day, and then ascended to the Father, lays the foundation of Christianity in the hearts of the people, and thus prepares them to receive his teachings. That is the way Paul laid the foundation of Christianity at Corinth. He was a "wise master-builder" and knew how to lay a foundation. Wherever the apostles traveled they proclaimed the resurrection of Christ. Peter, on Pentecost, as well as Paul at Athens, proclaimed boldly the resurrection of Jesus, maintaining that God had raised him from the dead.

The whole question hinged on that one point, viz., the resurrection of Christ from the dead. If God raised him from the dead he must be a true prophet, for God would not raise a false prophet from the tomb. If he be a true prophet then he must be the Son of God, and therefore all he said and commanded must be true and should be obeyed. The man who believes in his heart that God raised Christ from the dead must, of necessity, believe that he is divine. Therefore it was all-important for the apostles to make it clear to the minds of the people that Christ really did arise from the dead. Well may Paul have said, "If Christ be not risen, then is our preaching vain, and your faith is vain also." 1 Cor. 15: 14. Thus it was that the foundation was laid in the hearts of the people by demonstration to them that Jesus really did arise from the dead, and was therefore the Son of God, authorized to make known the law of heaven to the children of men.

It is upon Christ that the church is founded. Without Christ there could be no Christian church, for he is both the head and foundation of it as well as the chief corner-stone thereof. And it is upon this foundation that the whole Christian church must rest. As previously quoted, Paul could lay the foundation, but others build thereon. In Ephesians it is declared that the saints "are built upon the foundation of the apostles and prophets, Jesus Christ himself being the chief corner stone." Eph. 2: 20. Christ is the foundation of both the apostles and prophets. The latter preach Christ in prophecy while the former preached him in fact. The prophets, in olden times, laid the foundation of Christ in prophecy by proclaiming his coming, and all those who believed their teachings had the foundation laid in their hearts. "Believest thou the prophets?" was the keen question that Paul put to King Agrippa. To believe the prophets was to believe that Christ arose from the dead, for they prophesied concerning his resurrection. But after he arose, then the apostles and others went every-where, proclaiming in fact what the prophets had proclaimed in prophecy. Christ is, therefore, the foundation of both the apostles and prophets. It is upon Christ that they rest, for upon him their faith is founded. They are no foundation

CORRESPONDENCE.

"Write what thou seest, and send it unto the churches."

☞Church News solicited for this Department. If you have had a good meeting, send a report of it, so that others may rejoice with you. In writing give name of church, County and State. Be brief. Notes of Travel should be as short as possible. Land Advertisements are not solicited for this Department. We have an advertising page, and, if necessary, will issue supplements.

From Darkesville, W. Va.

BRO. ABRAHAM ROWLAND, of Hagerstown, Md., came to this place Dec. 21, and preached that evening, and also the following evening. We contemplate holding a series of meetings in the near future. Our Methodist friends asked us to have meetings, and they also gave us the use of their church. Some of them expressed themselves as not satisfied with their present church relations, and say that we do as we are taught in the Scriptures. There seems to be quite a stir among the people in this part of the country.

J. O. BUTTERBAUGH.

Dec. 24.

From the Macoupin Creek Church, Montgomery County, Ill.

THE members of this church met Dec. 18 to do some work in the house of the Lord. The business that came before the meeting was transacted very pleasantly. After the general church business was over, the ordination of Bro. Michael Flory to the eldership took place. Our elder, M. J. McClure, being absent on account of sickness in his family, sent Eld. David Frantz of Cerro Gordo to us, who took charge of the ordination. May God be with the brother now forwarded, that he may be a shining example to the flock wherever he may chance to be called, is our prayer.

To-day, Dec. 27, we had the opportunity of listening to a very practical sermon, preached at Pleasant Hill by Eld. Daniel Vaniman.

S. W. STUTZMAN.

Dec. 27.

From Moscow, Idaho.

BRO. DANIEL COSNER, wife, and family of ten children, came from Virginia eight years ago and settled fifty miles north of Spokane. Having recently moved to the City of Spokane, the children said, "Mother, let us try to get a minister of the Brethren to come and give us some meetings on Christmas Day. We would rather spend Christmas in that way than in the way it is generally spent."

Sister Cosner wrote, and the writer consented to go. How the family did rejoice to see us! We had five very happy and, we trust, profitable meetings with the family and others that met with us. Think of it, you that have the privilege of meeting once a week and oftener! Three of the children manifested a desire to unite with the church. Bro. Cosner and wife gave me their letters of recommendation, which state that he is a minister in the second degree. They expressed a desire to move where there is an organized church, and we hope they will do so. The work moves slowly in this country, but our labor is not in vain. God will give the increase!

SIDNEY HODGDEN.

Dec. 31.

A Happy New Year to You All.

I MEAN to all the friends and readers of the MESSENGER. This New Year's morning finds the writer in Glendora, Cal., and in as good health as he has enjoyed for many years. The winter, thus far, has been rather different from what is the rule here,—so say the people who have been living here a number of years. The heavy wind of Dec. 10, was very much out of the normal condi-

tion of things in this country. Frost has been seen here several mornings and ice was to be seen at different times. To-day (New Year's Day) the weather is beautiful. The sun shines with all its beauty,—for we had a heavy rain only two days ago, and that seems to add new beauty to all nature around. I am doing as well as I could expect; the mildness of the climate is greatly in my favor. We are having meetings regularly ever since I arrived. The attendance is not very large, but very regular. The people are generally good listeners, but not all full believers. I have hopes that I will be able to get through the winter in such condition as to be able to continue the good work when I get home.

A. HUTCHISON.

On the Way.

I CLOSED a two weeks' series of meetings, held in the Greentown District, Howard Co., Ind. During the last week of our meeting, the roads were almost impassable. One sister was baptized. She came, notwithstanding much opposition, but her bravery carried her through. The Brethren in the Greentown church are weak in the ministry, and need help. Will Southern Indiana come and help them? I was called to see an old lady (Patsy Sayers), whose children tell me, she is 110 years old. She does not look so old, and some of the neighbors are doubtful of her being of the age she claims. Many years ago the records of the whole family were burned up. None of them can read or write. This aged lady can hear well, and can thread a needle without glasses. She was born near Culpeper, Stafford Co., Va. Her mother lived to attain the age of 108 years. For twenty years she desired to join the church, but felt herself too feeble to attend to this noble work, being old and childish. We think the Brethren should have urged her to her duty.

On the way home I stopped off at North Manchester and found Bro. S. Bowman in bed, sick. He is old and feeble, and may be near his journey's end. I called on Bro. R. H. Miller and family. They, with others I called upon, were happy and cheerful. Some of the ministers in the North Manchester District were making arrangements to go to Mount Morris, to attend the "Bible Term." Some of the brethren were getting money ready, that those brethren might defray their expenses. That is the right way to make useful and active ministers. Often young ministers are called to the ministry with but limited education, no books, and no Bible knowledge. Often they are in limited circumstances and have to work hard to keep their families from getting into want. Perhaps they have a burden upon them which makes a minister's road hard to travel. By giving our young ministers a chance to more fully prepare themselves for the work, and occasionally helping them along, the church will have better talent for the work,—sermons can be delivered to edify all present, and a general growing interest is easily manifested. We should grow in grace and in the knowledge of the Truth, and also bear one another's burdens, and so fulfill the law of Christ.

J. H. MILLER.

Goshen, Ind.

Chips From The Work-House.

OLD PEOPLE.

WHILE holding some meetings in Marion and Dickinson Counties, Kansas, Dec. 13, Eld. Jacob Shirk and the writer drove out into the country, about five miles, to visit Samuel Zarms, who was born in Norfolk, Eng., Aug. 15, 1785, and is therefore one hundred six years old. He clearly remembers some things that occurred over one hundred years ago. He says that he has not been in

bed one week in all his life, on account of sickness. When asked whether he could see to read, he said, "Yes, but I cannot read." He remembers that when a little boy, he would run away from school; and hence he never learned to read. When he was five years old he was sent to help to drive a flock of turkeys. When returning, he met two girls who told him that his father was dead. This he would not admit as true until he reached home and could no longer deny it. He never wore glasses, and thinks he sees as clearly as in his youth.

Dec. 28, while travelling through the State of Illinois, I visited brother and sister Reed, who have, for many years, lived in Lincoln, Illinois. Bro. John is in his ninety-sixth year, and the old sister, his second wife, is in her eighty-fourth year. His oldest son, seventy-three years of age (living in Kossuth County, Iowa), with his wife; also the youngest son, sixty-three years of age (of Marshalltown, Iowa), were visiting their aged parents. The aged couple are rather feeble, but are still leaning upon the great and precious promises of the Gospel, looking forward to the time of meeting Abraham, Isaac and Jacob, the prophets and apostles, the many faithful and loved ones, who have gone before, and above all Jesus, the Author and Finisher of their faith. All of them they soon expect to join beyond the river, in the sweet by and by.

DANIEL VANIMAN.

McPherson, Kans.

Death of Jacob J. Blickenstaff and Wife.

IN the Salem church, Marion County, Ill., Dec. 1, 1891, Bro. Jacob J. Blickenstaff, aged 43 years, 9 months and 8 days.

His wife, Sister Anna, took sick two weeks after his death, and died Dec. 23, 1891, aged 43 years and 15 days.

Death always brings sorrow to those who are left behind, but when we see a loving father and mother both taken so near the same time, our grief becomes greatly intensified. They leave four children to mourn their loss, three of whom are small. The oldest, a daughter, is a member of the church. May God, in his infinite mercy, care for the children, and give them homes where they may have the good influence they lost in their parents.

The relatives have taken the children away, and nothing now remains of what, a short time ago, was a happy and well-organized family.

Bro. Jacob was a minister in the second degree. He and sister Anna were both zealous workers in the cause of Christ, earnestly contending for the faith once delivered to the saints.

They were known only to be loved, both in the church and out of it. The church has sustained a loss from which it does not seem possible to recover, but we trust in him who doeth all things well, believing that our departed brother and sister left an influence which shall be as bread cast on the waters, to be gathered many days hence. The funeral services on both occasions were conducted by Eld. John Hershberger.

S. S. FOUTS.

Salem, Ill.

Our Ministerial Meeting.

THE following is the programme of the Brethren's Ministerial Meeting for the Northern District of Iowa, Minnesota and South Dakota, to be held in the Greene church, Iowa, Thursday, Feb. 18 and 19, 1892, commencing at 9 A. M.:

1, Sermon on church organization by J. A. Murray and Wm. Ikenberry, to be preached on the evening of Feb. 17.

2. Opening on Thursday morning by the ministers of the Greene church.

3. "Object of Ministerial Meetings."—W. G. Cook and O. J. Beaver,

CORRESPONDENCE.

"Write what thou seest, and send it unto the churches."

☞"Church News solicited for this Department. If you have had a good meeting, send a report of it, so that others may rejoice with you. In writing give name of church, County and State. Be brief. Notes of Travel should be as short as possible. Land Advertisements are not solicited for this Department. We have an advertising page, and, if necessary, will issue supplements.

From Darkesville, W. Va.

BRO. ABRAHAM ROWLAND, of Hagerstown, Md., came to this place Dec. 21, and preached that evening, and also the following evening. We contemplate holding a series of meetings in the near future. Our Methodist friends asked us to have meetings, and they also gave us the use of their church. Some of them expressed themselves as not satisfied with their present church relations, and say that we do as we are taught in the Scriptures. There seems to be quite a stir among the people in this part of the country.

J. O. BUTERBAUGH.

Dec. 24.

From the Macoupin Creek Church, Montgomery County, Ill.

THE members of this church met Dec. 18 to do some work in the house of the Lord. The business that came before the meeting was transacted very pleasantly. After the general church business was over, the ordination of Bro. Michael Flory to the eldership took place. Our elder, M. J. McClure, being absent on account of sickness in his family, sent Eld. David Frantz of Cerro Gordo to us, who took charge of the ordination. May God be with the brother now forwarded, that he may be a shining example to the flock wherever he may chance to be called, is our prayer.

To-day, Dec. 27, we had the opportunity of listening to a very practical sermon, preached at Pleasant Hill by Eld. Daniel Vaniman.

S. W. STUTZMAN.

Dec. 27.

From Moscow, Idaho.

BRO. DANIEL COSNER, wife, and family of ten children, came from Virginia eight years ago and settled fifty miles north of Spokane. Having recently moved to the City of Spokane, the children said, "Mother, let us try to get a minister of the Brethren to come and give us some meetings on Christmas Day. We would rather spend Christmas in that way than in the way it is generally spent."

Sister Cosner wrote, and the writer consented to go. How the family did rejoice to see us! We had five very happy and, we trust, profitable meetings with the family and others that met with us. Think of it, you that have the privilege of meeting once a week and oftener! Three of the children manifested a desire to unite with the church. Bro. Cosner and wife gave me their letters of recommendation, which state that he is a minister in the second degree. They expressed a desire to move where there is an organized church, and we hope they will do so. The work moves slowly in this country, but our labor is not in vain. God will give the increase! SIDNEY HODGDEN.

Dec. 31.

A Happy New Year to You All.

I MEAN to all the friends and readers of the MESSENGER. This New Year's morning finds the writer in Glendora, Cal., and in as good health as he has enjoyed for many years. The winter, thus far, has been rather different from what is the rule here,—so say the people who have been living here a number of years. The heavy wind of Dec. 10, was very much out of the normal condi-

tion of things in this country. Frost has been seen here several mornings and ice was to be seen at different times. To-day (New Year's Day) the weather is beautiful. The sun shines with all its beauty,—for we had a heavy rain only two days ago, and that seems to add new beauty to all nature around. I am doing as well as I could expect; the mildness of the climate is greatly in my favor. We are having meetings regularly ever since I arrived. The attendance is not very large, but very regular. The people are generally good listeners, but not all full believers. I have hopes that I will be able to get through the winter in such condition as to be able to continue the good work when I get home. A. HUTCHISON.

On the Way.

I CLOSED a two weeks' series of meetings, held in the Greentown District, Howard Co., Ind. During the last week of our meeting, the roads were almost impassable. One sister was baptized. She came, notwithstanding much opposition, but her bravery carried her through. The Brethren in the Greentown church are weak in the ministry, and need help. Will Southern Indiana come and help them? I was called to see an old lady (Patsy Sayers), whose children tell me, she is 110 years old. She does not look so old, and some of the neighbors are doubtful of her being of the age she claims. Many years ago the records of the whole family were burned up. None of them can read or write. This aged lady can hear well, and can thread a needle without glasses. She was born near Culpeper, Stafford Co., Va. Her mother lived to attain the age of 108 years. For twenty years she desired to join the church, but felt herself too feeble to attend to this noble work, being old and childish. We think the Brethren should have urged her to her duty.

On the way home I stopped off at North Manchester and found Bro. S. Bowman in bed, sick. He is old and feeble, and may be near his journey's end. I called on Bro. R. H. Miller and family. They, with others I called upon, were happy and cheerful. Some of the ministers in the North Manchester District were making arrangements to go to Mount Morris, to attend the "Bible Term." Some of the brethren were getting money ready, that those brethren might defray their expenses. That is the right way to make useful and active ministers. Often young ministers are called to the ministry with but limited education, no books, and no Bible knowledge. Often they are in limited circumstances and have to work hard to keep their families from getting into want. Perhaps they have a burden upon them which makes a minister's road hard to travel. By giving our young ministers a chance to more fully prepare themselves for the work, and occasionally helping them along, the church will have better talent for the work,—sermons can be delivered to edify all present, and a general growing interest is easily manifested. We should grow in grace and in the knowledge of the Truth, and also bear one another's burdens, and so fulfill the law of Christ.

J. H. MILLER.

Goshen, Ind.

Chips From The Work-House.

OLD PEOPLE.

WHILE holding some meetings in Marion and Dickinson Counties, Kansas, Dec. 13, Eld. Jacob Shirk and the writer drove out into the country, about five miles, to visit Samuel Zarms, who was born in Norfolk, Eng., Aug. 15, 1785, and is therefore one hundred six years old. He clearly remembers some things that occurred over one hundred years ago. He says that he has not been in

bed one week in all his life, on account of sickness. When asked whether he could see to read, he said, "Yes, but I cannot read." He remembers that, when a little boy, he would run away from school; and hence he never learned to read. When he was five years old he was sent to help to drive a flock of turkeys. When returning, he met two girls who told him that his father was dead. This he would not admit as true until he reached home and could no longer deny it. He never wore glasses, and thinks he sees as clearly as in his youth.

Dec. 28, while travelling through the State of Illinois, I visited brother and sister Reed, who have, for many years, lived in Lincoln, Illinois. Bro. John is in his ninety-sixth year, and the old sister, his second wife, is in her eighty-fourth year. His oldest son, seventy-three years of age (living in Kossuth County, Iowa), with his wife; also the youngest son, sixty-three years of age (of Marshalltown, Iowa), were visiting their aged parents. The aged couple are rather feeble, but are still leaning upon the great and precious promises of the Gospel, looking forward to the time of meeting Abraham, Isaac and Jacob, the prophets and apostles, the many faithful and loved ones, who have gone before, and above all Jesus, the Author and Finisher of their faith. All of them they soon expect to join beyond the river, in the sweet by and by. DANIEL VANIMAN.

McPherson, Kans.

Death of Jacob J. Blickenstaff and Wife.

IN the Salem church, Marion County, Ill., Dec. 1, 1891, Bro. Jacob J. Blickenstaff, aged 43 years, 9 months and 8 days.

His wife, Sister Anna, took sick two weeks after his death, and died Dec. 28, 1891, aged 43 years and 15 days.

Death always brings sorrow to those who are left behind, but when we see a loving father and mother both taken so near the same time, our grief becomes greatly intensified. They leave four children to mourn their loss, three of whom are small. The oldest, a daughter, is a member of the church. May God, in his infinite mercy, care for the children, and give them homes where they may have the good influence they lost in their parents.

The relatives have taken the children away, and nothing now remains of what, a short time ago, was a happy and well-organized family.

Bro. Jacob was a minister in the second degree. He and sister Anna were both zealous workers in the cause of Christ, earnestly contending for the faith once delivered to the saints.

They were known only to be loved, both in the church and out of it. The church has sustained a loss from which it does not seem possible to recover, but we trust in him who doeth all things well, believing that our departed brother and sister left an influence which shall be as bread cast on the waters, to be gathered many days hence. The funeral services on both occasions were conducted by Eld. John Hershberger.

S. S. FOOTE.

Salem, Ill.

Our Ministerial Meeting.

THE following is the programme of the Brethren's Ministerial Meeting for the Northern District of Iowa, Minnesota and South Dakota, to be held in the Greene church, Iowa, Thursday, Feb. 18 and 19, 1892, commencing at 9 A. M.:

1. Sermon on church organization by J. A. Murray and Wm. Ikenberry, to be preached on the evening of Feb. 17.

2. Opening on Thursday morning by the ministers of the Greene church.

3. "Object of Ministerial Meetings."—W. G. Cook and O. J. Beaver;

Frederick, Md.—Bro. Henry C. Early, from Virginia, held a series of meetings for us Nov. 1, which was kept up for ten days with the best of interest. One came out on the Lord's side, and was received by baptism. We still hope that the good seed sown may bring forth much fruit!—*P. D. Fahrney.*

Marsh Creek, Pa.—Bro. H. C. Early, of Meyerheoffer's Store, Va., arrived here on the evening of Jan. 2, too late for the appointment of the evening. His introductory sermon was delivered yesterday to an appreciative audience. The meetings will possibly be continued until the last of next week. From here he goes to his native State, to spend sometime at Bridgewater College, for which he feels much interest.—*B. F. Kittinger.*

Farmington, Ill.—Since my last report three have been added to the fold by baptism. Others are not far from the kingdom. Sept. 26, 1891, our dear sister, Catherine Eshelman, who was truly a light to the world, crossed over the silent river. She was in her seventy-eighth year, and an exemplary sister. A short time before her death I had a conversation with her, at which time she expressed herself as fully depending on the will of the Lord.—*Solomon Bucklew.*

Bethlehem, Va.—We commenced a series of meetings Dec. 23, which we continued until Dec. 31. Bro. George Barnhart, of Missouri, did the preaching. He preached, in all, at this place, fourteen sermons, add as a result of his labors eight dear souls were made willing to be baptised. They were all quite young, save one who was in his seventy-eighth year. Many good impressions were made that, we hope, will not soon be forgotten, while saints were encouraged and made to rejoice.—*Nancy M. Bowman.*

Lewistown, Pa.—Through the efforts of brother and sister Shellenberger, who reside in Bonnerville, within the bounds of the Lewistown congregation, the brethren have built a meeting-house in that village. On Sunday, Jan. 3, the house was dedicated to the Lord. Bro. Andrew Bashor preached the dedicatory sermon, assisted by Abram Myers and our home ministers. In the evening we held a love-feast which was something new in that community. The house was full, the best of order prevailed, and all seemed anxious to see the solemn ordinances performed. We hope that some good impressions have been made on the people, and that there may be an ingathering of precious souls at that place, and that those of us that were permitted to enjoy another Communion, have been benefitted, and resolved to live a life more devoted to our Blessed Savior.—*Sarah Spangle, Jan. 7.*

Lima, Ohio.—Dec. 12 Bro. Jesse Stutsman came to the Sugar Creek church, Allen Co., Ohio, and began a series of meetings. He remained with us until Dec. 26, preaching in all twenty-two soul-stirring sermons. Bro. Stutsman had intended to stay with us over the following Sunday, but was called home on account of sickness in his family. A few days later we received the welcome news, that his wife was rapidly improving. Bro. Jesse earnestly contends for the faith once delivered to the saints. One precious soul came out on the Lord's side and many others, we believe, could say with one of old, "Almost thou persuadest me to be a Christian." We believe the good seed sown will yet produce a bountiful harvest in the near future. Bro. J. M. Mohler is to hold a series of meetings for us in the Pleasant View church, in a few weeks, where Bro. Stutsman held forth the Word of Life last winter. May the Lord abundantly bless and reward all who are thus engaged in their labor of love in the upbuilding of Zion!—*David Byerly, Jan. 4.*

Middle Creek, Iowa.—Brother and Sister Hipes came to us on a mission of love, Dec. 4, at which time Bro. Hipes commenced a series of meetings which he continued till the 10th, with good interest. Bro. Hipes has been laboring in the good cause since last June. Our best wishes go with them to other fields of labor.—*Elizabeth Gable.*

Pleasant View, Kans.—Bro. Lugenbeel, of Hubbell, Nebr., was called to hold a series of meetings for us Dec. 12. He preached in all eleven sermons. Bro. Lugenbeel is an able expounder of the Gospel, as believed and practiced by the Brethren. He gave us many good admonitions. There was one applicant for baptism at the close of the meeting. The ordinance was administered the following Sunday.—*Sylvester Workman.*

Centropolis, Kans.—On Monday, Dec. 28, 1891, Bro. George Wise came to the Appanoose church, Kans., to work in the interest of the Old Folks' Home (located near Booth, Reno Co., Kans). Bro. Wise labored faithfully, with encouraging results. He and Bro. Moses Brubaker remained with us until Jan. 4, 1892, preaching each evening until Sunday. One young sister was buried in the liquid stream, to walk in newness of life.—*James T. Kinzie, Jan. 5.*

Hartford City, Ind.—The members of this church have again passed through a season of rejoicing. Bro. M. L. Hahn, of Ohio, came to us Dec. 12, and conducted a series of meetings. He preached with much power. As an immediate result, four precious souls were received by baptism, and one reclaimed. Though the weather was very inclement, our meetings were well attended, and the interest was great. May the Good Lord bless our dear brother in his labors, and keep us all very humble, prayerful and faithful!—*L. Winklebleck.*

Accident, Md.—Bro Jonas Fike, of West Virginia, conducted a very interesting series of meetings in the Bear Creek congregation, commencing Dec 24, and continuing until Jan. 3. During the meetings four precious souls,—a father, mother and two young brethren united with the church. May they become useful in the service of Christ! Our dear brother held forth the Word of Life with zeal and energy. May the Lord ever bless his labors, and may he be instrumental in bringing many into the fold of Christ!—*Mary M. Bidinger, Jan. 4.*

Mount Ida, Kans.—Bro. A. I. Heestand, of Galesburg, Kans., came to the Cedar Creek church, Kans, and commenced a series of meetings. He held forth the Word of God in its purity. Good order prevailed throughout the meetings. The weather was all that could be wished for, and we had good roads, hence the meetings were well attended. As an immediate result two were buried with Christ in baptism, to walk in newness of life. The meetings closed on the evening of Dec. 26, and were said to be the best meetings this church has held for a number of year.—*Lafayette Watkins.*

Ottobine, Va.—Our series of meetings, at Franklin, in the Beaver Creek congregation, Va., came to a sudden halt. Not a minister was present at the last meeting on account of *La Grippe* having prostrated the entire ministerial force,—five in all. Another meeting that was to commence tonight at Dry River, has been recalled for the same reason. Your correspondent has been disabled with *La Grippe* for three weeks. There are but few families that are exempt from it, and a number of deaths have occurred. There were four burials to-day, not far from here. At our last council the writer was appointed correspondent for the MESSENGER from this arm of the church.—*G. W. Wine, Jan. 3.*

Bristolville, Ohio.—Eld. W. Murray, of Ashland, Ohio, came to us Dec. 5, and held a short series of meetings, closing with a Communion. Bro. Murray preached with more than his usual zeal and earnestness, and these meetings will long be remembered as among the best and most solemn we have ever had the privilege to enjoy. May we remember the kind words of encouragement and admonition, and live more faithful, more consecrated, and more Christ-like, and finally meet in the "many mansions."—*M. Strom.*

Dalton, Ohio.—On the evening of Dec. 12, Bro. Noah Longanecker came to the West Nimishillen church, Ohio, and began meetings at our Sippo Valley meeting-house. He continued the meetings until Dec. 20, preaching in all twelve sermons. We had good attendance, and great interest was manifested. The brethren and sisters were greatly built up in the most holy faith, and many lasting impressions were made. We had no successions, but feel that the Spirit has pleaded with many to turn to Christ.—*Abraham Horst.*

Alvada, Ohio.—Bro. J. M. Mohler, of Lewistown, Pa., came to the Oak Grove church, Hancock Co., Ohio, and held a series of meetings, commencing Dec. 14, and closing Dec. 27. He preached, in all, twenty-four sermons. Bro. L. H. Dickey, of Alvada, Ohio, delivered one sermon the evening before Bro. Mohler came to our assistance. Bro. Mohler preached the Word very plainly. He also contributed greatly to the interest of the Sunday-school. There were no additions, but we pray that the labors of our dear brother will not be in vain. Bro. Mohler has now gone to Green Spring church, Seneca Co., Ohio, to hold a series of meetings.—*Solomon Schubert.*

Clay Hill, Pa.—I was called to York, Pa., on business, and while there I was permitted to be with our dear brethren over Sunday and attended the preaching service on Sunday morning. It was well attended, and all seemed interested in the preaching. Bro. A. Meyers preached in the German language. This was quite a treat to me, as I love to hear a sermon in the German language sometimes; it seems homelike. The Sabbath-school, at 2: 30 P. M., I also attended. It was a pleasure to me to see the interest manifested by the old brethren and sisters in the training of their dear little ones. Here I saw the kind of a Bible class that should be in every well-organized Sunday-school,—the silver-haired fathers and mothers setting a good example and using their influence in the right direction. It is a power for good, the influence of which we can only know in eternity. I certainly enjoyed my visit.—*Jacob Kurtz, Dec. 27.*

Lordsburg, Cal.—In this sunny clime we enjoyed a Christmas Day close to the Savior's bleeding side. We celebrated the day here, in Lordsburg College, in a love-feast service. We are informed it was the largest feast held in California. About 150 communed. Many were from different parts of the Union. The evening services were held in the dining hall, a very large, spacious room. It was a beautiful sight. Many young members communed. Our dear brother, A Hutchison, officiated. Here, on this shore, as in all places, so far away from home, we are glad to see old friends. It seemed like meeting one of our own family to meet him, as we lived side by side for a number of years in Missouri. He and my husband worked harmoniously together in church work. Now he is here and husband, at present, is in Ohio, both working in the field. The school work is going on. There are prospects for a number of new students the next term.—*Amanda Wilmore, Dec. 26.*

Frederick, Md.—Bro. Henry C. Early, from Virginia, held a series of meetings for us Nov. 1, which was kept up for ten days with the best of interest. One came out on the Lord's side, and was received by baptism. We still hope that the good seed sown may bring forth much fruit!—*P. D. Fahrney.*

Marsh Creek, Pa.—Bro. H. C. Early, of Meyerheoffer's Store, Va., arrived here on the evening of Jan. 2, too late for the appointment of the evening. His introductory sermon was delivered yesterday to an appreciative audience. The meetings will possibly be continued until the last of next week. From here he goes to his native State, to spend sometime at Bridgewater College, for which he feels much interest.—*B. F. Kittinger.*

Farmington, Ill.—Since my last report three have been added to the fold by baptism. Others are not far from the kingdom. Sept 26, 1891, our dear sister, Catherine Eshelman, who was truly a light to the world, crossed over the silent river. She was in her seventy-eighth year, and an exemplary sister. A short time before her death I had a conversation with her, at which time she expressed herself as fully depending on the will of the Lord.—*Solomon Bucklew.*

Bethlehem, Va.—We commenced a series of meetings Dec. 23, which we continued until Dec. 31. Bro. George Barnhart, of Missouri, did the preaching. He preached, in all, at this place, fourteen sermons, and as a result of his labors eight dear souls were made willing to be baptized. They were all quite young, save one who was in his seventy-eighth year. Many good impressions were made that, we hope, will not soon be forgotten, while saints were encouraged and made to rejoice.—*Nancy M. Bowman.*

Lewistown, Pa.—Through the efforts of brother and sister Shellenberger, who reside in Bonnerville, within the bounds of the Lewistown congregation, the brethren have built a meeting-house in that village. On Sunday, Jan. 3, the house was dedicated to the Lord. Bro. Andrew Bashor preached the dedicatory sermon, assisted by Abram Myers and our home ministers. In the evening we held a love-feast which was something new in that community. The house was full, the feast of order prevailed, and all seemed anxious to see the solemn ordinances performed. We hope that some good impressions have been made on the people, and that there may be an ingathering of precious souls at that place, and that those of us that were permitted to enjoy another Communion, have been benefitted, and resolved to live a life more devoted to our Blessed Savior.—*Sarah Spanogle, Jan. 7.*

Lima, Ohio.—Dec. 12 Bro. Jesse Stuteman came to the Sugar Creek church, Allen Co., Ohio, and began a series of meetings. He remained with us until Dec. 26, preaching in all twenty-two soul-stirring sermons. Bro. Stuteman had intended to stay with us, over the following Sunday, but was called home on account of sickness in his family. A few days later we received the welcome news, that his wife was rapidly improving. Bro. Jesse earnestly contends for the faith once delivered to the saints. One precious soul came out on the Lord's side and many others, we believe, could say with one of old, " Almost thou persuadest me to be a Christian.". We believe the good seed sown will yet produce a bountiful harvest in the near future. Bro. J. M. Mohler is to hold a series of meetings for us in the Pleasant View church, in a few weeks, where Bro. Stutzman held forth the Word of Life last winter. May the Lord abundantly bless and reward all who are thus engaged in their labor of love in the upbuilding of Zion!—*David Byerly, Jan. 4.*

Middle Creek, Iowa.—Brother and Sister Hipes came to us on a mission of love, Dec. 4, at which time Bro. Hipes commenced a series of meetings which he continued till the 16th, with good interest. Bro. Hipes has been laboring in the good cause since last June. Our best wishes go with them to other fields of labor.—*Elizabeth Gable.*

Pleasant View, Kans.—Bro. Lugenbeel, of Hubbell, Nebr., was called to hold a series of meetings for us Dec. 12. He preached in all eleven sermons. Bro. Lugenbeel is an able expounder of the Gospel, as believed and practiced by the Brethren. He gave us many good admonitions. There was one applicant for baptism at the close of the meeting. The ordinance was administered the following Sunday.—*Sylvester Workman.*

Centropolis, Kans.—On Monday, Dec. 28, 1891, Bro. George Wise came to the Appanoose church, Kans., to work in the interest of the Old Folks' Home (located near Booth, Reno Co., Kans). Bro. Wise labored faithfully, with encouraging results. He and Bro. Moses Brubaker remained with us until Jan. 4, 1892, preaching each evening until Sunday. One young sister was buried in the liquid stream, to walk in newness of life.—*James T. Kinzie, Jan. 5.*

Hartford City, Ind.—The members of this church have again passed through a season of rejoicing. Bro. M. L. Hahn, of Ohio, came to us Dec. 12, and conducted a series of meetings. He preached with much power. As an immediate result, four precious souls were received by baptism, and one reclaimed. Though the weather was very inclement, our meetings were well attended, and the interest was great. May the Good Lord bless our dear brother in his labors, and keep us all very humble, prayerful and faithful!—*L. Winklebleck.*

Accident, Md.—Bro. Jonas Fike, of West Virginia, conducted a very interesting series of meetings in the Bear Creek congregation, commencing Dec 24, and continuing until Jan. 3. During the meetings four precious souls,—a father, mother and two young brethren united with the church. May they become useful in the service of Christ! Our dear brother held forth the Word of Life with zeal and energy. May the Lord ever bless his labors, and may he be instrumental in bringing many into the fold of Christ!—*Mary M. Biddinger, Jan. 4.*

Mount Ida, Kans.—Bro. A. I. Heestand, of Galesburg, Kans., came to the Cedar Creek church, Kans., and commenced a series of meetings. He held forth the Word of God in its purity. Good order prevailed throughout the meetings. The weather was all that could be wished for, and we had good roads, hence the meetings were well attended. As an immediate result two were buried with Christ in baptism, to walk in newness of life. The meetings closed on the evening of Dec. 26, and were said to be the best meetings this church has held for a number of year.—*Lafayette Watkins.*

Ottobine, Va.—Our series of meetings, at Franklin, in the Beaver Creek congregation, Va., came to a sudden halt. Not a minister was present at the last meeting on account of La Grippe having prostrated the entire ministerial force,—five in all. Another meeting that was to commence to-night at Dry River, has been recalled for the same reason. Your correspondent has been disabled with La G,rippe for three weeks. There are but few families that are exempt from it, and a number of deaths have occurred. There were four burials to-day, not far from here. At our last council the writer was appointed correspondent for the MESSENGER from this arm of the church.—*G. W. Wine, Jan. 3.*

Bristolville, Ohio.—Eld. W. Murray, of Ashland, Ohio, came to us Dec. 5, and held a short series of meetings, closing with a Communion. Bro. Murray preached with more than his usual zeal and earnestness, and these meetings will long be remembered as among the best and most solemn we have ever had the privilege to enjoy. May we remember the kind words of encouragement and admonition, and live more faithful, more consecrated, and more Christ-like, and finally meet in the " many mansions."—*M. Strom.*

Dalton, Ohio.—On the evening of Dec. 12, Bro. Noah Longanecker came to the West Nimishillen church, Ohio, and began meetings at our Sippo Valley meeting-house. He continued the meetings until Dec. 20, preaching in all twelve sermons. We had good attendance, and great interest was manifested. The brethren and sisters were greatly built up in the most holy faith, and many lasting impressions were made. We had no accessions, but feel that the Spirit has pleaded with many to turn to Christ.—*Abraham Horst.*

Alvada, Ohio.—Bro. J. M. Mohler, of Lewistown, Pa., came to the Oak Grove church, Hancock Co., Ohio, and held a series of meetings, commencing Dec. 14, and closing Dec. 27. He preached, in all, twenty-four sermons. Bro. L. H. Dickey, of Alvada, Ohio, delivered one sermon the evening before Bro. Mohler came to our assistance. Bro. Mohler preached the Word very plainly. He also contributed greatly to the interest of the Sunday-school. There were no additions, but we pray that the labors of our dear brother will not be in vain. Bro. Mohler has now gone to Green Springs church, Seneca Co., Ohio, to hold a series of meetings.—*Solomon Schubert.*

Clay Hill, Pa.—I was called to York, Pa., on business, and while there I was permitted to be with our dear brethren over Sunday and attended the preaching service on Sunday morning. It was well attended, and all seemed interested in the preaching. Bro. A. Meyers preached in the German language. This was quite a treat to me, as I love to hear a sermon in the German language sometimes; it seems homelike. The Sabbath school, at 2:30 P. M., I also attended. It was a pleasure to me to see the interest manifested by the old brethren and sisters in the training of their dear little ones. Here I saw the kind of a Bible class that should be in every well-organized Sunday-school, — the silver-haired fathers and mothers setting a good example and using their influence in the right direction. It is a power for good, the influence of which we can only know in eternity. I certainly enjoyed my visit.—*Jacob Kurtz, Dec. 27.*

Lordsburg, Cal.—In this sunny clime we enjoyed a Christmas Day close to the Savior's bleeding side. We celebrated the day here, in Lordsburg College, in a love-feast service. We are informed it was the largest feast held in California. About 160 communed. Many were from different parts of the Union. The evening services were held in the dining hall, a very large, spacious room. It was a beautiful sight. Many young members communed. Our dear brother, A. Hutchison, officiated. Here, on this shore, as in all places, so far away from home, we are glad to see old friends. It seemed like meeting one of our own family to meet him, as we lived side by side for a number of years in Missouri. He and my husband worked harmoniously together in church work. Now he is here and husband, at present, is in Ohio, both working in the field. The school work is going on. There are prospects for a number of new students the next term.—*Amanda Witmore, Dec. 26.*

BROWN.—At her home in Franklin Grove, Ill., Dec. 20, 1891, Mrs. Nancy E. Brown, aged 64 years, 10 months and 6 days.

Mrs. Nancy E. (Brace) Brown was born in Erie County, Pa., Feb. 14, 1827. She came west in 1848, first to Kane County, Illinois, and was married to J. G. Brown, April 6, 1851, after which they returned east again. After several years' residence there, she again came west with her husband, and settled on the farm north of this village in 1855. They left the farm last spring and came to the village, hoping to spend their declining years in ease and quiet. Mrs. Brown was the mother of two daughters, sister Alithetta Ostrander and Mrs. Addie V. Keith.

KEITH.—At her home, two miles north-east of Franklin Grove, Ill., Mrs. Addie V. (Brown) Keith, aged 36 years, 6 months and 13 days.

Deceased came west with her parents the same year she was born. She was married to Roscoe Keith in February, 1874. Six children were born to them, four of whom preceded her. Mother and daughter died on the same day, several hours apart, of pneumonia. Both of the corpses were taken to the Brethren's church. Funeral sermon from the woods, "What is your life?" by brethren L. Trostle and J. C. Murray, Dec. 23, 1891. Both were interred in one lot, but in separate graves.   C. H. HAWBECKER.

RYCHEN.—At her daughter's, Mrs. Rose Nicholson, in the Pine Creek church, Ind., Dec. 23, 1891, Mrs. Mary A. Rychen, aged 60 years and 2 months.

Deceased was born in Switzerland, Oct. 23, 1831, and emigrated to America with her parents in 1832. She settled at Bleecker, Fulton Co., New York, where she spent her childhood days.

In 1848 she married John B. Hanan, of the same place. To them four children were born,—one son and three daughters. In 1861 they settled in Indiana. She was a kind, affectionate wife, a loving mother, and a devoted Christian.

CRIPE.—In the Rock Run church, Goshen, Ind., Dec. 28, 1891, of diphtheria, Esther Adeline, beloved daughter of Bro. Allen and sister Emma Cripe, aged 7 years, 7 months and 10 days.   SARAH CRIPE.

MOHLER.—At her home, near Shendun, Va., Dec. 1, 1891, sister Elisabeth, wife of Abram Mohler, aged 80 years, 2 months , and 11 days.

Deceased leaves a husband, three sons and one daughter to mourn her departure. In her death the husband loses a devoted wife, the children a loving mother and the church a consistent and faithful member. Interment at Mt. Horeb church (Presbyterian), and funeral at Mill Creek from Ps. 119: 75.   H. C. EARLY.

REITZ.—In the Brothers' Valley congregation, Somerset Co., Pa., Dec. 26, 1891, Bro. Christian Reitz, aged 50 years, 10 months and 28 days.

Bro. Reitz was a dutiful deacon for a number of years. A wife and seven children survive him. Funeral services by Bro. D. H. Walker and Eld. Michael Weyand.

SIVITS.—In the same congregation, Dec. 27, 1891, Willie Sivits, son of John and Ida Sivits, aged 6 months. Funeral discourse by the writer.   D. H. WALKER.

MUSSER.—Also in the same congregation, Dec. 30, Bro. Christian Musser, aged 67 years, 1 month and 22 days. Funeral discourse by the undersigned.
    D. H. WALKER.

LEAMAN.—In the Maple Grove church, Ashland Co., Ohio, Ira J. Leaman, aged 8 years, 7 months and 6 days.

Ira was a very promising boy, the son of Bro. Samuel Leaman. Death robbed him of a mother's care at the age of 4 months and other hands kindly cared for him until he was re-united with his mother on the evergreen shore. Bro. David Umbaugh's family, who had so tenderly administered to all his wants, miss him as one of their own. He took sick at school on Wednesday, and died on Mon-

day. He is supposed to have died of scarlet fever. Funeral services from Ps. 23: 3, 4 by D. N. Workman.   D. N. W.

BECHTEL.—In the Chippewa congregation, Wayne Co., Ohio, Nov. 14, 1891, sister Lizzie M. Bechtel, aged 22 years, 8 months and 29 days.

Deceased was the daughter of Eld. Fred. erick Wenner. She was born at Dawson Station, Fayette Co., Pa., Feb. 15, 1869, and was married to W. K. Bechtel June 14, 1891. She died very suddenly. She was found very sick at her home, by her husband, on return, ing from his school on Friday evening, and she died on the evening of the next day. The cause of her death was poison, taken by her own hands. She stated to her husband as her last words on earth, " I did not do it purposely; I made a mistake. I think too much of you and my friends to do such a thing purposely."

Her friends accepted her dying statement and all feel to be thankful that she was allowed to utter those dying words. She lived twenty-four hours longer, but unconscious and unable to speak.

Sister Lizzie was always a very social and lively girl, which disposition she manifested on the day that she took the fatal dose, while being visited by her sister, who left her in good spirits not over a half hour before being found by her husband.

A very large congregation of sympathetic and loving friends and neighbors gathered at the Beech Grove meeting-house to pay a last tribute of respect to one whom they loved. Funeral services from John 11: 14, by Eld. D. N. Workman, assisted by Eld. I. D. Park, er.   D. N. WORKMAN.

BECKNER.—In the Dry Creek church, Linn Co., Iowa, Bro. John Beckner, aged nearly 88 years.

Deceased was born in Franklin County, Pa., Jan. 15, 1804. He was married, in 1826, to Miss Elizabeth Mentzer, and in 1845 they moved to Marion, Iowa, where he died. He leaves a wife, seven daughters and two sons to mourn the loss of a kind husband and father. Sixty-five years he and sister Beckner traveled life's journey together. Funeral services were held in the Disciple church in Marion, Iowa, by the Brethren, assisted by Rev. A. S. Marshall, and attended by a large circle of friends and old settlers. Text, Rev. 21: 4.   THOS. G. SNYDER.

CROUSE.—At the home of his parents, near Mayview, Jewell Co., Kans., Dec. 4, 1891, John Clinton, son of Henry and Christina Crouse, aged 31 years, 6 months and 15 days.

Deceased leaves a wife, one child, father, mother, three brothers, four sisters and many relatives and friends to mourn his departure. Funeral conducted by Rev. H. G. Breed, of the M. E. church, from Luke 12: 55, 56, and part of verse 37, to a large and sympathizing audience.   H. C.

NAILL.—In the bounds of the Middletown Valley congregation, Md., Dec. 23, 1891, Samuel C. Naill, aged 71 years, 3 months and 13 days. Funeral services conducted by John M. Bussard and Geo. S. Harp.
    MARTIN GROSNICKLE.

REIFF.—In the South Beatrice church, Gage Co., Nebr., of inflammation of the bowels, Raleigh Melvin, son of Bro. John and sister Susan Reiff, aged 4 years, 4 months and 16 days. Funeral discourse by Eld. Owen Peters from James 4: 14.
    M. L. SPIRE.

KEEVER.—In the Monticello church, White Co., Ind., sister Lucy Keever, wife of Thomas Keever, aged about 55 years.

Deceased leaves a husband and one daughter to mourn their loss. Funeral discourse by A. B. Bridge and the writer.
    A. S. CULP.

SHATTO.—In the Harrington congregation, Kans., Dec. 22, 1891, of La Grippe and pneumonia, Caroline Shatto, aged 64 years, 3 months and 12 days.

Funeral services conducted from Rev. 14: 13, by Bro. Geo. Wine and the writer.
    J. E. KELLER.

Jan. 19, 1892. THE GOSPEL MESSENGER. 47

BROWN.—At her home in Franklin Grove, Ill., Dec. 20, 1891, Mrs. Nancy E. Brown, aged 64 years, 10 months and 6 days.

Mrs. Nancy E. (Brace) Brown was born in Erie County, Pa., Feb. 14, 1827. She came west in 1848, first to Kane County, Illinois, and was married to J. Q. Brown, April 6, 1851, after which they returned east again. After several years' residence there, she again came west with her husband, and settled on the farm north of this village in 1855. They left the farm last spring and came to the village, hoping to spend their declining years in ease and quiet. Mrs. Brown was the mother of two daughters, sister Althetta Ostrander and Mrs. Addie V. Keith.

KEITH.—At her home, two miles north-east of Franklin Grove, Ill., Mrs. Addie V. (Brown) Keith, aged 36 years, 6 months and 13 days.

Deceased came west with her parents the same year she was born. She was married to Roscoe Keith in February, 1874. Six children were born to them, four of whom preceded her. Mother and daughter died on the same day, several hours apart, of pneumonia. Both of the corpses were taken to the Brethren's church. Funeral sermon from the words, "What is your life?" by brethren L. Trostle and J. C. Murray, Dec. 23, 1891. Both were interred in one lot, but in separate graves. C. H. HAWBECKER.

RYCHEN.—At her daughter's, Mrs. Ross Nicholson, in the Pine Creek church, Ind., Dec. 23, 1891, Mrs. Mary A. Rychen, aged 60 years and 2 months.

Deceased was born in Switzerland, Oct. 23, 1831, and emigrated to America with her parents in 1832. She settled at Bleecker, Fulton Co., New York, where she spent her childhood days.

In 1848 she married John B. Hanan, of the same place. To them four children were born,—one son and three daughters. In 1861 they settled in Indiana. She was a kind, affectionate wife, a loving mother, and a devoted Christian.

CRIPE.—In the Rock Run church, Goshen, Ind., Dec. 28, 1891, of diphtheria, Esther Adeline, beloved daughter of Bro. Allen and sister Emma Cripe, aged 9 years, 7 months and 10 days. SARAH CRIPE.

MOHLER.—At her home, near Shendun, Va., Dec. 1, 1891, sister Elizabeth, wife of Abram Mohler, aged 80 years, 2 months and 11 days.

Deceased leaves a husband, three sons and one daughter to mourn her departure. In her death the husband loses a devoted wife, the children a loving mother and the church a consistent and faithful member. Interment at Mt. Horeb church (Presbyterian), and funeral at Mill Creek from Ps. 119: 75.

H. C. EARLY.

REITZ.—In the Brothers' Valley congregation, Somerset Co., Pa., Dec. 26, 1891, Bro. Christian Reitz, aged 50 years, 10 months and 28 days.

Bro. Reitz was a dutiful deacon for a number of years. A wife and seven children survive him. Funeral services by Bro. D. H. Walker and Eld. Michael Weyand.

SIVITS.—In the same congregation, Dec. 27, 1891, Willie Sivits, son of John and Ida Sivits, aged 6 months. Funeral discourse by the writer. D. H. WALKER.

MUSSER.—Also in the same congregation, Dec. 30, Bro. Christian Musser, aged 67 years, 1 month and 22 days. Funeral discourse by the undersigned.

D. H. WALKER.

LEAMAN.—In the Maple Grove church, Ashland Co., Ohio, Ira J. Leaman, aged 8 years, 7 months and 6 days.

Ira was a very promising boy, the son of Bro. Samuel Leaman. Death robbed him of a mother's care at the age of 4 months and other hands kindly cared for him until he was re-united with his mother on the evergreen shore. Bro. David Umbaugh's family, who had so tenderly administered to all his wants, miss him as one of their own. He took sick at school on Wednesday, and died on Monday. He is supposed to have died of scarlet fever. Funeral services from Ps. 23: 3, 4 by D. N. Workman. D. N. W.

BECHTEL.—In the Chippewa congregation, Wayne Co., Ohio, Nov. 14, 1891, sister Lizzie M. Bechtel, aged 22 years, 8 months and 29 days.

Deceased was the daughter of Eld. Frederick Wenner. She was born at Dawson Station, Fayette Co., Pa., Feb. 15, 1869, and was married to W. K. Bechtel June 14, 1891. She died very suddenly. She was found very sick at her home, by her husband, on returning from his school on Friday evening, and she died on the evening of the next day. The cause of her death was poison, taken by her own hands. She stated to her husband as her last words on earth, "I did not do it purposely; I made a mistake. I think too much of you and my friends to do such a thing purposely."

Her friends accepted her dying statement and all feel to be thankful that she was allowed to utter those dying words. She lived twenty-four hours longer, but unconscious and unable to speak.

Sister Lizzie was always a very social and lively girl, which disposition she manifested on the day that she took the fatal dose, while being visited by her sister, who left her in good spirits not over a half hour before being found by her husband.

A very large congregation of sympathetic and loving friends and neighbors gathered at the Beech Grove meeting-house to pay a last tribute of respect to one whom they loved. Funeral services from John 11: 14, by Eld. D. N. Workman, assisted by Eld. I. D. Parker. D. N. WORKMAN.

BECKNER.—In the Dry Creek church, Linn Co., Iowa, Bro. John Beckner, aged nearly 88 years.

Deceased was born in Franklin County, Pa., Jan. 15, 1804. He was married, in 1826, to Miss Elizabeth Mentzer, and in 1845 they moved to Marion, Iowa, where he died. He leaves a wife, seven daughters and two sons to mourn the loss of a kind husband and father. Sixty-five years he and sister Beckner traveled life's journey together. Funeral services were held in the Disciple church in Marion, Iowa, by the Brethren, assisted by Rev. A. S. Marshall, and attended by a large circle of friends and old settlers. Text, Rev. 21: 4. THOS. G. SNYDER.

CROUSE.—At the home of his parents, near Mayview, Jewell Co., Kans., Dec. 4, 1891, John Clinton, son of Henry and Christina Crouse, aged 31 years, 6 months and 15 days.

Deceased leaves a wife, one child, father, mother, three brothers, four sisters and many relatives and friends to mourn his departure. Funeral conducted by Rev. H. G. Breed, of the M. E. church, from Luke 12: 55, 36, and part of verse 37, to a large and sympathizing audience. H. C.

NAILL.—In the bounds of the Middletown Valley congregation, Md., Dec. 23, 1891, Samuel C. Naill, aged 71 years, 2 months and 12 days. Funeral services conducted by John M. Bussard and Geo. S. Harp.

MARTIN GROSSNICKLE.

REIFF.—In the South Beatrice church, Gage Co., Nebr., of inflammation of the bowels, Raleigh Melvin, son of Bro. John and sister Susan Reiff, aged 4 years, 4 months and 16 days. Funeral discourse by Eld. Owen Peters from James 4: 14.

M. L. SPIRE.

KEEVER.—In the Monticello church, White Co., Ind., sister Lucy Keever, wife of Thomas Keever, aged about 55 years.

Deceased leaves a husband and one daughter to mourn their loss. Funeral discourse by A. B. Bridge and the writer.

A. S. CULP.

SHATTO.—In the Herrington congregation, Kans., Dec. 22, 1891, of *La Grippe* and pneumonia, Caroline Shatto, aged 64 years, 2 months and 12 days.

Funeral services conducted from Rev. 14: 13, by Bro. Geo. Wine and the writer.

J. E. KELLER.

PUBLICATIONS

The following books, Sunday-school supplies, etc., are for sale by the BRETHREN'S PUBLISHING CO., Mt. Morris, Ill., or Huntingdon, Pa., to whom all orders should be addressed.

The Brethren's Quarterly.

For Sunday-school teachers and scholars this publication is of the greatest benefit. Look at our prices.

Single subscription, one year,	35 cents.
Single subscription, per quarter,	10 cents.
Three copies, per quarter,	25 cents.
Eight copies, per quarter,	40 cents.
Twenty copies and over,	4 cents each.

Hymn Books.

New Tune and Hymn Books.

Half leather, per copy, post-paid,	$ 75
Morocco, per copy, post-paid,	1 00
Morocco, gilt edge, per copy, post-paid,	1 25

Hymn Books.

Morocco, per copy, post-paid,	$ 75
Morocco, gilt edge, per copy, post-paid,	85
Arabesque, per copy, post-paid,	40
Fine Limp, per copy, post-paid,	75
Fine Limp, gilt edge, per copy, post-paid,	85
German and English, per copy, post-paid,	75

Sunday-School Requisites.

The following list of things is needed in all Sunday-schools:

Testaments, Flexible, red edge, per dozen,	$1 00
Minute Books, each,	40
Class Books, per dozen,	75
S. S. Primers, with fine engravings, per dozen,	70

New and Beautiful Sunday-School Cards.

"The Gem," 50 picture cards, each with Bible text, verse of hymn,	35
250 Reward Tickets—verse of Scripture—red or blue,	20

The Young Disciple.

THE YOUNG DISCIPLE is a neatly printed weekly, published especially for the moral benefit and religious instruction of our young folks.

Single copy, one year,	$ 50
Six copies (the sixth to the agent),	2 50
Ten copies,	4 00

For Three Months or Thirteen Weeks.

20 copies to one address,	$1 70
30 " " " "	2 50
40 " " " "	3 35
50 " " " "	3 80
75 " " " "	5 20
100 " " " "	7 00

For Six Months or Twenty-Six Weeks.

20 copies to one address,	$ 3 35
30 " " " "	5 00
40 " " " "	6 60
50 " " " "	7 50
75 " " " "	10 20
100 " " " "	13 75

Our paper is designed for the Sunday-school and the home circle. We desire the name of every Sunday-school Superintendent in the Brotherhood, and want an agent in every church. Send for sample copies.

Certificates of Membership

WE have just printed a new edition of these very convenient certificates. Several improvements over the old style are noticeable, such as perforated stubs, firm, yet smooth, paper, etc. Price only 50 cents per book. Every congregation should have one. Address this office.

The Monon Route.

This road is running a fine line of Pullman Buffet Sleepers between Chicago and Indianapolis, Cincinnati and Louisville, in connection with the fast Florida express trains.

For full information, address, E. O. McCORMICK, General Passenger Agent, Adams Express Building, Chicago. (City Ticket Office, 73 Clark St.)

Send for our new Bible Catalogue. Prices to suit the times. We have a large variety and the most durable as well as ornamental binding.

GOOD BOOKS FOR ALL.

ANY book in the market furnished at publishers' lowest retail price by the Brethren's Publishing Company, Mt. Morris, Ill. *Special prices* given when books are purchased in quantities. When ordering books, not on our list, if possible give title, name of author, and address of publishers.

Family Bible, with Notes and Instructions.—Contains the harmony of the Gospels, Chronology, Maps, Tables of Weights and Measures, Family Record, eight elegant illustrations, etc. Price, substantially bound, $4.50.

German and English Testaments.—American Bible Society Edition. Price, 90 cents.

Homiletics and Pastoral Theology.—By W. G. T. Shedd. Cloth, $2.50.

Lectures on Preaching.—By Rev. Phillips Brooks. Cloth, 16mo, $1.50.

New Testament and Psalms with Notes.—Invaluable for Bible students, Sunday-school teachers, etc. Price, cloth, $2.00; without Psalms, $1.00.

Quinter and McConnell Debate.—A debate on Trine Immersion, the Lord's Supper, and Feet-washing, between Eld. James Quinter (German Baptist) and Eld. N. A. McConnell (Christian) held at Dry Creek, Iowa, 1867. Price, $1.50.

Popular Commentary on the New Testament.—Edited by Philip Schaff. Four volumes, 8vo. Matthew, Mark and Luke: $6.00. John and the Acts: $6.00. Romans to Philemon: $5.00. Hebrews to Revelation: $5.00.

Sabbatism.—By M. M. Eshelman. Treats the Sabbath question, showing that the first day of the week is the day for assembling in worship. Price 10 cents; 15 copies, $1.00.

Bunyan's Pilgrim's Progress.—An excellent edition of this good work, printed on good paper, finely illustrated with forty engravings, at the low price of $1.00 per copy.

Close Communion.—By Landon West. Treats this important subject in a simple though conclusive manner. Price, 50 cents.

In the Volume of the Book.—By Geo. F. Pentecost. Cloth, 60 cents.

Key to the Knowledge and Use of the Holy Bible.—By J. H. Blunt. Cloth, 16 mo, 75 cents.

Lange's Commentary.—Edited by Philip Schaff. Twenty-five vols. 8vo. Per vol., $3.00.

New and Complete Bible Commentary.—By Jamieson, Fausset and Brown. It is far in advance of other works. It is critical, practical, and explanatory. It is compendious and comprehensive in its character. It has a critical introduction to each Book of Scripture, and is by far the most practical, suggestive, scientific, and popular work of the kind in the English language. In four large 12mo volumes of about 1,000 pages each. In extra fine English cloth, sprinkled edges, the full set, $8.00; half Morocco, the full set, $10.00.

Sacred Geography and Antiquities.—A practical, helpful work for Bible students, ministers and Sunday-school teachers. Price, $2.25.

The Origin and Growth of Religion.—Hibbert Lectures. By T. W. R. Davids. Cloth, 8vo, $2.50.

Our Library on Christian Evidences.—This collection of works embraces the best books to be had on that subject: "Paley's Evidences of Christianity," New Edition, $1.50; "Nelson on Infidelity," 75 cents; "Manual of Christian Evidences," 75 cents; "Many Infallible Proofs," $1.25; "The Divine Demonstration," $1.50; "The Bible in the Nineteenth Century," 40 cents; "Grounds of Theistic and Christian Belief," $2.50. Price of the entire set, if ordered at one time, $8.00; special terms to ministers furnished upon application.

Bible Work, or Bible Reader's Commentary on the New Testament.—By J. G. Butler. Two. vols. 8vo, $10.00.

Biblical Antiquities.—By John Nevin. Gives a concise account of Bible times and customs; invaluable to all students of Bible subjects. Price, $1.50.

Biblical Theology of the Old Testament.—By R. F. Weidner. Cloth, $1.25.

Campbell and Owen Debate.—Contains a complete investigation of the evidences of Christianity. Price, $1.50.

Classified Minutes of Annual Meeting.—A work of rare interest for all who desire to be well informed in the church work, from the early days of our Brethren until the present. Price, cloth, $1.50; leather, $2.00.

Companion to the Bible.—This valuable work is so full of instruction that it can not fail to be of great benefit to every Christian. Price, $1.75.

Hours with the Bible.—By Cunningham Geikie. Old Testament Series—six volumes. Per volume, 90 cents.

Europe and Bible Lands.—By D. L. Miller. A book for the people,—more comprehensive and thorough than many higher-priced works. Price, cloth, $1.50; leather, $2.00.

Ecclesiastical History.—By Eusebius. Bohn Library. Cloth, $2.00.

Ecclesiastical History.—By Mosheim. 2 vols. 8vo., $4.00.

Early Days of Christianity.—By F. W. Farrar. Author's edition, cloth, 12mo, $1.25.

THE GOSPEL MESSENGER.

"Set for the Defense of the Gospel."

Vol. 30, Old Series.　　　Mt. Morris, Ill., and Huntingdon, Pa., Jan. 26, 1892.　　　No. 4.

The Gospel Messenger.

H. B. Brumbaugh, Editor,

And Business Manager of the Eastern House, Box 50.
Huntingdon, Pa.

Table of Contents.

Our friends can much oblige us by sending us good copies of the following numbers of the Gospel Messenger: Nos. 17, 22, 23 and 35. Address, Brethren's Publishing Company, Huntingdon, Pa.

THE GOOD FOUNDATION.

The subject for our first prayer-meeting of the year was, "The Importance of having a Good Foundation on which to Build our Spiritual House."

The first thoughts presented were as to the necessity of this foundation, as we are all builders.

The second, what is really meant by the foundation and a discrimination between the building and that upon which it is built. The foundation here is the rock on which the whole building, wall and all, is founded.

The third thought called attention to the time of establishing this foundation and the disappointments that follow if this work is not attended to early in life.

The fourth called special attention to the manner of reading the text (Luke 6: 46-48), and called attention to the fact that both men were builders and may have built the same kind of houses, yet the one was a foolish man and the other was called wise. The difference may not have been in the building, but in the forethought,

exercised in the starting,—the one on the rock, the other on the sand.

The last thought presented was, the advantages of building on the sure foundation, Christ Jesus, referring to 1 Cor. 3: 11-15. Those who build on this foundation,—works represented by silver, gold and precious stones,—shall receive a reward. Those who are so unfortunate as to build thereon hay, stubble, etc., will have their work consumed and they shall suffer loss,— that is, all they have done will be burned, but they, themselves, shall be saved. They still have the foundation upon which to stand,—they are still saved, though as by fire. This, though not the most desirable situation, is greatly to be desired rather than being eternally lost. These meetings, if rightly conducted, can be made great helps in keeping alive a proper interest in the church and her work.

BIBLICAL INTERPRETATIONS.

We have been asked to give the design or object of Biblical interpretations or hermeneutics. Perhaps the shortest way to do this will be to define the terms.

It is taken for granted that words, as used, convey ideas, and while the ideas themselves may be of a general character, the words to convey them may be subject to local interpretations. One man may use a certain word to convey an idea, while another man may use the same word to convey a different idea. Then, again, two men may use different words to convey the same idea. As an illustration, take the word *bottle*, as used in Luke 5: 37.

In order to get the true idea and meaning in this case, an interpretation is needed, and the manner by which the interpretation is made, is called hermeneutics.

If all men, in all time, had used exactly the same words to convey the same ideas, hermeneutics, as a system, would not be needed, as in that case there could be no misunderstanding as to facts described, or ideas conveyed. But this not being the case, interpretations are necessary. If a man who used the English language two hundred years, were to arise from the dead and get hold of some of our works on the arts and sciences, he would not be able to understand them, from the fact that the inventions alone, made within the last century have introduced into our language over one thousand new words, while some of the words, then used, have become obsolete and others used in their place. Even to-day, though we are an English-speaking people, in our own country different customs, circumstances and developments have made, to some extent, a sectional people, differing in our mode of thought, and, as a result, there is a difference in expression and feeling. To enable us to fully understand each other, we bring into use a system of hermeneutics, —in other words, we acquaint ourselves with each other's circumstances, mode of life, feelings and

forms of expression. Having learned these, we are enabled to understand each other, or interpret each other's language and feelings.

This can be done after this manner when both parties live in the same time and can get together, but hermeneutics are more especially applied to the writings of those who have written in past ages or different countries. If we wish to fully understand the writings of other countries, we must either go there and become familiar with their manner of living and mode of thought, or we must study or learn it through those who have been there. By so doing we may be able to interpret their writings. If the writings are those of past ages we must not only go to the place where the writings were made, but we must go back to the time, and become acquainted with the customs and mode of life of the people as they then lived. These are the laws of interpretation, as applied to writings of a general character, and precisely the same laws must be applied to the writings of the Bible. The Bible is a collection of books in human speech, and must be interpreted the same as other books, made in human language. The secret of interpreting any book is to understand fully what the author says. To interpret the Bible, we must understand the language of those who wrote it, and to do this we must go back to the time and place of the writing and become fully acquainted with the respective writers, the object of the writings and the circumstances by which the writer was surrounded.

Again, we refer to the circumstance, as recorded in Luke 5: 37. Accept the rendering as we have it in our common version with our present use of language, and we have nonsense, but go back to the days of the writer and we have an important truth, beautifully illustrated.

Not long since we received a letter from a lady of intelligence, stating that she had always been in love with the church of the Brethren and her doctrines, until a year ago. She then attended a series of meetings, held by one of our Brethren, who, among other subjects, preached on the "covering," and took the position that in no case could the hair form a covering, such as Paul names in Corinthians. His argument was that the hair could not be a covering, "for how could a woman take her hair off and put it on again? Any simpleton ought to know better than that." She became so disgusted with such reasoning and the man who did it, that she refused to go to hear him any further.

That the hair was used as a covering and can still be so used on the part of women is not denied by us as a church. But what we have been teaching is that the particular covering, here referred to by Paul, was a special covering then in common use by the Jewish Christians and here recommended by Paul to be used by all Christian women in times of religious services. And had this brother, if correctly reported, been governed by the

(Continued on page 53.)

THE GOSPEL MESSENGER.

"Set for the Defense of the Gospel."

Vol. 30, Old Series. Mt. Morris, Ill., and Huntingdon, Pa., Jan. 26, 1892. No. 4.

The Gospel Messenger.

H. B. Brumbaugh, Editor,
And Business Manager of the Eastern House, Box 50.
Huntingdon, Pa.

Table of Contents.

Our friends can much oblige us by sending us good copies of the following numbers of the Gospel Messenger: Nos. 17, 22, 32 and 35. Address, Brethren's Publishing Company, Huntingdon, Pa.

THE GOOD FOUNDATION.

The subject for our first prayer-meeting of the year was, "The Importance of having a Good Foundation on which to Build our Spiritual House."

The first thoughts presented were as to the necessity of this foundation, as we are all builders.

The second, what is really meant by the foundation and a discrimination between the building and that upon which it is built. The foundation here is the rock on which the whole building, wall and all, is founded.

The third thought called attention to the time of establishing this foundation and the disappointments that follow if this work is not attended to early in life.

The fourth called special attention to the manner of reading the text (Luke 6: 46-48), and called attention to the fact that both men were builders and may have built the same kind of houses, yet the one was a foolish man and the other was called wise. The difference may not have been in the building, but in the forethought,

exercised in the starting,—the one on the rock, the other on the sand.

The last thought presented was, the advantages of building on the sure foundation, Christ Jesus, referring to 1 Cor. 3: 11-15. Those who build on this foundation,—works represented by silver, gold and precious stones,—shall receive a reward. Those who are so unfortunate as to build thereon hay, stubble, etc., will have their work consumed and they shall suffer loss,—that is, all they have done will be burned, but they, themselves, shall be saved. They still have the foundation upon which to stand,—they are still saved, though as by fire. This, though not the most desirable situation, is greatly to be desired rather than being eternally lost. These meetings, if rightly conducted, can be made great helps in keeping alive a proper interest in the church and her work.

BIBLICAL INTERPRETATIONS.

We have been asked to give the design or object of Biblical interpretations or hermeneutics. Perhaps the shortest way to do this will be to define the terms.

It is taken for granted that words, as used, convey ideas, and while the ideas themselves may be of a general character, the words to convey them may be subject to local interpretations. One man may use a certain word to convey an idea, while another man may use the same word to convey a different idea. Then, again, two men may use different words to convey the same idea. As an illustration, take the word *bottle*, as used in Luke 5: 37.

In order to get the true idea and meaning in this case, an interpretation is needed, and the manner by which the interpretation is made, is called hermeneutics.

If all men, in all time, had used exactly the same words to convey the same ideas, hermeneutics, as a system, would not be needed, as in that case there could be no misunderstanding as to facts described, or ideas conveyed. But this not being the case, interpretations are necessary. If a man who used the English language two hundred years ago, were to arise from the dead and get hold of some of our works on the arts and sciences, he would not be able to understand them, from the fact that the inventions alone, made within the last century have introduced into our language over one thousand new words, while some of the words, then used, have become obsolete and others used in their place. Even to-day, though we are an English-speaking people, in our own country different customs, circumstances and developments have made, to some extent, a sectional people, differing in our mode of thought, and, as a result, there is a difference in expression and feeling. To enable us to fully understand each other, we bring into use a system of hermeneutics, —in other words, we acquaint ourselves with each other's circumstances, mode of life, feelings and

forms of expression. Having learned these, we are enabled to understand each other, or interpret each other's language and feelings.

This can be done after this manner when both parties live in the same time and can get together, but hermeneutics are more especially applied to the writings of those who have written in past ages or different countries. If we wish to fully understand the writings of other countries, we must either go there and become familiar with their manner of living and mode of thought, or we must study or learn it through those who have been there. By so doing we may be able to interpret their writings. If the writings are those of past ages we must not only go to the place where the writings were made, but we must go back to the time, and become acquainted with the customs and mode of life of the people as they then lived. These are the laws of interpretation, as applied to writings of a general character, and precisely the same laws must be applied to the writings of the Bible. The Bible is a collection of books in human speech, and must be interpreted the same as other books, made in human language. The secret of interpreting any book is to understand fully what the author says. To interpret the Bible, we must understand the language of those who wrote it, and to do this we must go back to the time and place of the writing and become fully acquainted with the respective writers, the object of the writings and the circumstances by which the writer was surrounded.

Again, we refer to the circumstance, as recorded in Luke 5: 37. Accept the rendering as we have it in our common version with our present use of language, and we have nonsense, but go back to the days of the writer and we have an important truth, beautifully illustrated.

Not long since we received a letter from a lady of intelligence, stating that she had always been in love with the church of the Brethren and her doctrines, until a year ago. She then attended a series of meetings, held by one of our Brethren, who, among other subjects, preached on the "covering," and took the position that in no case could the hair form a covering, such as Paul names in Corinthians. His argument was that the hair could not be a covering, "for how could a woman take her hair off and put it on again? Any simpleton ought to know better than that." She became so disgusted with such reasoning and the man who did it, that she refused to go to hear him any further.

That the hair was used as a covering and can still be so used on the part of women is not denied by us as a church. But what we have been teaching is that the particular covering, here referred to by Paul, was a special covering then in common use by the Jewish Christians and here recommended by Paul to be used by all Christian women in times of religious services. And had this brother, if correctly reported, been governed by the

(Continued on page 58.)

tained, we are referred to the fact that the apostles, in their epistles to the churches, say nothing about feet-washing.

Sure enough, when we consult the two, written by Peter, we find not a word on that subject. Then we turn to John, and read carefully the three epistles written by him, and we still find nothing. Next we take up the epistle general of James, and the desired information is not yet found. Lastly, we go to Jude, and with all our care in reading and our ardent desire to find the much-coveted proof, it still is wanting.

Now, what is to be done? We are at the end of the list, for these four are the only ones among the twelve apostles, that wrote to the churches. Shall we take it for granted, because there is nothing in those epistles, that, therefore, there was nothing said by them on that subject? Before we form our final conclusion, on this feature of the case, let us examine the same epistles, to find out if they taught anything on the subject of the Communion of the body and blood of the Lord?

We are surprised to find nothing. Now what think ye? We were ready to conclude, since none of them said anything about feet-washing in their epistles to the churches, that they did not teach feet-washing at all, and if their silence on that subject is to be regarded as proof that they did not teach it, the same would hold good on the Communion too. But we all seem to think those faithful ambassadors for Christ would not have neglected to teach such an important part, as the observance of the holy Communion, for Jesus says, "Except ye eat the flesh of the Son of Man, and drink his blood, ye have no life in you." John 6: 53.

Let us notice, in this connection, what he said to Peter about feet-washing: "If I wash thee not, thou hast no part with me." John 13: 8. Now where is the difference? We plainly read, "Except ye eat of the flesh and drink of the blood of Jesus, ye have no life in you." He made the penalty just as hard on Peter, when he refused to have his feet washed. Since the apostles said nothing in their epistles to the churches, on either of these,—the above-named points,—upon what mode of reasoning shall we rest our plea, if we say that they taught the Communion, and did not teach feet-washing? And where have we a promise, if we do not obey the all things, as given by the Head of the church?

But if silence is to be promoted to the position of an argument, would we not have a good deal of argument in favor of their having taught feet-washing?—for we are bound to admit that Jesus taught them to wash one another's feet. See John 13: 14, 15. We are also bound to admit that Jesus commanded them to teach the nations just what he had taught them. For he says, "Teaching them to observe all things, whatsoever I have commanded you." Matt. 28: 20. Here is where the promise came to the apostles, just as they were faithful to the all things, and we, their successors, claim the promise, but wish to leave the apostles to perform their duty. It is unreasonable, to say the least of it. We must fail in line with the duties, and then we have some showing for our claim to the promises.

But, after all, we are told that, in reference to the bread and cup of Communion, Jesus said, "This do in remembrance of me," making it binding upon us, as his followers, while in feet-washing he only says, "Ye ought" to do that. It is claimed that ought is not imperative, but leaves the matter at the option of the individual, to do or not to do, as he may feel. This, however, makes the feelings of the individual to be the authority for the action, and leaves Christ's authority out of the question.

Let us look at that a little. There was a certain man who had received one talent, and because he looked upon his master as being an austere man, because he gathered where he had not sown, etc., he allowed his feelings to control his actions, and hid his talent. He was informed later that he ought to have put it where it would have been yielding an income, and because he did not do what he ought to have done, he was bound and cast into outer darkness. Ought seems to be binding.

It is claimed however, that Paul comes to our relief, on the question of the Communion,—if the other apostles do say nothing about it, in their epistles to the churches. That is true. In 1 Cor. 10: 16, Paul speaks of the bread and cup of Communion. And in 1 Cor. 11: 23-26, he speaks of both the Supper and Communion, and tells plainly from whence his authority came, etc.

In 1 Tim. 5: 10, he also mentions feet-washing, and in Philpp. 4: 9, he says, "Those things, which ye have both learned, and received, and heard, and seen in me, do: and the God of peace shall be with you." If you do what Paul taught, the God of peace shall be with you, and that is just what Jesus said should follow, if they teach the all things. So Paul must have taught the all things, etc. See 2 Cor. 2: 9, also, 1 Tim. 6: 3. Here he brings in the words of Jesus Christ, and surely feet-washing belongs to the words of Jesus. To offset the "hot-country" theory, as taught in John 13: 18, here it positively says it was cold on the very night that Jesus washed the disciples' feet.

"ESAU."

BY E. N. GOSHORN.

WHILE studying the many characters which are prominent in the history of the world in general, we are astonished at the faithfulness, fidelity, and untiring zeal of the few, and the deception, sickleness, and comparative indifference of the many. In no history of any nation is that unselfishness exhibited in the biography of its great men, so in the Bible. There we find the evil deeds of individuals represented in detail; as well as the good. There we find not only David's righteousness, but also his great sins set forth with greater accuracy than human agency alone is able to accomplish. A man will scarcely speak evil of his fellows unless he hate them, and if so, he enlarges until more than truth is told.

Among the many characters, represented in the history of the Bible, we come to one whose life is not so prominently set forth as others, but who, nevertheless, possessed many interesting qualities. This is Esau. And since his acts are of little consequence in the history of God's people, we know very little about him except as a result of the conflicts of his life with the life of Jacob, his younger brother.

Besides other interesting incidents, connected with the birth of these two, we have this prophecy spoken of them, "The elder shall serve the younger." And as time passed, the affection of Rebekah, their mother, was bestowed upon Jacob, who was thus more attached to his home than Esau, who was comparatively shunned by his mother. Jacob's work, therefore, was more domestic, while Esau came to be of a roving character. "Esau was a cunning hunter,—a man of the field: and Jacob was a plain man, dwelling in tents. And Isaac loved Esau because he ate of his venison: but Rebekah loved Jacob." Gen. 25: 27, 28. As a result, we find both of them striving for supremacy.

According to the customs of God's people at that age, there were certain privileges conferred upon the oldest son,—such as lordship, the right to receive the blessing, and bestow it again, the right of inheritance, and the right to act as priest. These were called the birthright. This caused the conflicts between Esau and Jacob. The latter used every opportunity to wrest this from Esau. As Esau returns from the field, comparatively exhausted from severe exercise and hunger, we find him imploring Jacob for a morsel to eat. Jacob, taking advantage of the depressed condition of his brother, refused him food, except for his birthright. Esau feeling as if his life was near its close, accepts the fatal offer. This is the beginning of the failures and disasters of Esau. He becomes a gross sensualist, "a profane person," Heb. 12: 16, grieving his parents by associating with the daughters of the Canaanites. Finally he is denied the blessing, bestowed by the father upon the older son.

Why was he thus? In the first place he was not loved by his mother. If there is any one thing that stands decidedly above others in the formation of the character of an individual, it is a mother's love. There is no love so constant and unfailing as that of a mother. Without it, I dare say, very few ever attain to any excellency of character. To it we have attributed the success of the ablest men the world has ever produced.

Then, why should we wonder at the recklessness with which Esau plunged into a dissolute life, or should we not rather regard it as a natural consequence of the conduct of his parents? Again, can we censure him for selling his birthright? A man who is almost starving for food and who, if not supplied, will die, cares little for aught save that which will preserve life at the present; for how can he need anything, if not supplied with that?

This was the condition under which Esau was placed. Starving for sustenance, he was forced to part with all he had,—his birthright,—to obtain it. He reasoned thus: "Behold, I am at the point of death, and what profit shall this birthright do to me." Gen. 25: 32. We can only think that, though Esau acted foolishly, he did what any other man, not assisted by Divine Power, would have done. Nor was it because he esteemed his birthright lightly, for he afterwards repented bitterly when he was deprived of the blessing. These misfortunes were enough to drive almost any man to desperation. Is it any wonder his brother had to flee to escape his wrath, after having so shamefully deceived both him and his father? And even now I can scarcely help admiring his self-will, when in great distress because of the failure to receive the blessing, and when, in the height of anger, he delayed his evil intentions. Men now may do well to follow Esau's example in this respect. His intention was to kill his brother, but having curbed his desire for a more favorable opportunity, his wrath subsided, and when the opportunity presented itself, the desire was gone. Ever afterwards he was a friend to him whom he had sought to kill.

We have now given a short sketch of the life of Esau, as far as his immediate life is of interest to us, but in the prophecy to which we have alluded, there was the promise of two separate nations to arise from the two sons. This also was spoken concerning Esau. "And by thy sword thou shalt live." Gen. 37: 40. Thus we find that Esau was to become a great and warlike nation, "and his name is Edom." Gen. 37: 1. The Edomites did become a great nation, maintaining their nationality by the sword. We find them spoken of frequently in the Bible, and as we have to-day nations which trace their origin to Jacob, so we have a nation, supposed to have descended from Esau. Compare the Arabs with the Edomites, and we find traces of similarity.

tained, we are referred to the fact that the apostles, in their epistles to the churches, say nothing about feet-washing.

Sure enough, when we consult the two, written by Peter, we find not a word on that subject. Then we turn to John, and read carefully the three epistles written by him, and we still find nothing. Next we take up the epistle general of James, and the desired information is not yet found. Lastly, we go to Jude, and with all our care in reading and our ardent desire to find the much-coveted proof, it still is wanting.

Now, what is to be done? We are at the end of the list, for these four are the only ones among the twelve apostles, that wrote to the churches. Shall we take it for granted, because there is nothing in those epistles, that, therefore, there was nothing said by them on that subject? Before we form our final conclusion, on this feature of the case, let us examine the same epistles, to find out if they taught anything on the subject of the Communion of the body and blood of the Lord?

We are surprised to find nothing. Now what think ye? We were ready to conclude, since none of them said anything about feet-washing in their epistles to the churches, that they did not teach feet-washing at all, and if their silence on that subject is to be regarded as proof that they did not teach it, the same would hold good on the Communion too. But we all seem to think those faithful ambassadors for Christ would not have neglected to teach such an important part, as the observance of the holy Communion, for Jesus says, "Except ye eat the flesh of the Son of Man, and drink his blood, ye have no life in you." John 6: 53.

Let us notice, in this connection, what he said to Peter about feet-washing: "If I wash thee not, thou hast no part with me." John 13: 8. Now where is the difference? We plainly read, "Except ye eat of the flesh and drink of the blood of Jesus, ye have no life in you." He made the penalty just as hard on Peter, when he refused to have his feet washed. Since the apostles said nothing in their epistles to the churches, on either of these,—the above-named points,—upon what mode of reasoning shall we rest our plea, if we say that they taught the Communion, and did not teach feet-washing? And where have we a promise, if we do not obey the all things, as given by the Head of the church?

But if silence is to be promoted to the position of an argument, would we not have a good deal of argument in favor of their having taught feet-washing?—for we are bound to admit that Jesus taught them to wash one another's feet. See John 13: 14, 15. We are also bound to admit that Jesus commanded them to teach the nations just what he had taught them. For he says, "Teaching them to observe all things, whatsoever I have commanded you." Matt. 28: 20. Here is where the promise came to the apostles, just as they were faithful to the all things, and we, their successors, claim the promise, but wish to leave the apostles to perform their duty. It is unreasonable, to say the least of it. We must fall in line with the duties, and then we have some showing for our claim to the promises.

But, after all, we are told that, in reference to the bread and cup of Communion, Jesus said, "This do in remembrance of me," making it binding upon us, as his followers, while in feet-washing he only says, "Ye *ought*" to do that. It is claimed that ought is not imperative, but leaves the matter at the option of the individual, to do or not to do, as he may feel. This, however, makes the feelings of the individual to be the authority for the action, and leaves Christs's authority out of the question.

Let us look at that a little. There was a certain man who had received one talent, and because he looked upon his master as being an austere man, because he gathered where he had not sown, etc., he allowed his feelings to control his actions, and hid his talent. He was informed later that he *ought* to have put it where it would have been yielding an income, and because he did not do what he *ought* to have done, he was bound and cast into outer darkness. *Ought* seems to be binding.

It is claimed however, that Paul comes to our relief, on the question of the Communion,—if the other apostles do say nothing about it, in their epistles to the churches. That is true. In 1 Cor. 10: 16, Paul speaks of the bread and cup of Communion. And in 1 Cor. 11: 23-26, he speaks of both the Supper and Communion, and tells plainly from whence his authority came, etc.

In 1 Tim. 5: 10, he also mentions feet-washing, and in Philpp. 4: 9, he says, "Those things, which ye have both learned, and received, and heard, and seen in me, do: and the God of peace shall be with you." If you do what Paul taught, the God of peace shall be with you, and that is just what Jesus said should follow, if they teach the all things. So Paul must have taught the all things, etc. See 2 Cor. 2: 9, also, 1 Tim. 6: 3. Here he brings in the words of Jesus Christ, and surely feet-washing belongs to the words of Jesus. To offset the " hot-country " theory, as taught in John 13: 18, here it positively says it was *cold* on the very night that Jesus washed the disciples' feet.

"ESAU."

BY E. N. GOSHORN.

WHILE studying the many characters which are prominent in the history of the world in general, we are astonished at the faithfulness, fidelity, and untiring zeal of the few, and the deception, fickleness, and comparative indifference of the many. In no history of any nation is that unselfishness exhibited in the biography of its great men, as in the Bible. There we find the evil deeds of individuals represented in detail; as well as the good. There we find not only David's righteousness, but also his great sins set forth with greater accuracy than human agency alone is able to accomplish. A man will scarcely speak evil of his fellows unless he hate them, and if so, he enlarges until more than truth is told.

Among the many characters, represented in the history of the Bible, we come to one whose life is not so prominently set forth as others, but who, nevertheless, possessed many interesting qualities. This is Esau. And since his acts are of little consequence in the history of God's people, we know very little about him except as a result of the conflicts of his life with the life of Jacob, his younger brother.

Besides other interesting incidents, connected with the birth of these two, we have the prophecy spoken of them, "The elder shall serve the younger." And as time passed, the affection of Rebekah, their mother, was bestowed upon Jacob, who was thus more attached to his home than Esau, who was comparatively shunned by his mother. Jacob's work, therefore, was more domestic, while Esau came to be of a roving character. "Esau was a cunning hunter,—a man of the field; and Jacob was a plain man, dwelling in tents. And Isaac loved Esau because he ate of his venison: but Rebekah loved Jacob." Gen. 25: 27, 28. As a result, we find both of them striving for supremacy.

According to the customs of God's people at that age, there were certain privileges conferred

upon the oldest son,—such as lordship, the right to receive the blessing, and bestow it again, the right of inheritance, and the right to act as priest. These were called the birthright. This caused the conflicts between Esau and Jacob. The latter used every opportunity to wrest this from Esau. As Esau returns from the field, comparatively exhausted from severe exercise and hunger, we find him imploring Jacob for a morsel to eat. Jacob, taking advantage of the depressed condition of his brother, refused him food, except for his birthright. Esau feeling as if his life was near its close, accepts the fatal offer. This is the beginning of the failures and disasters of Esau. He becomes a gross sensualist, "a profane person," Heb. 12: 16, grieving his parents by associating with the daughters of the Canaanites. Finally he is denied the blessing, bestowed by the father upon the older son.

Why was he thus? In the first place he was not loved by his mother. If there is any one thing that stands decidedly above others in the formation of the character of an individual, it is a mother's love. There is no love so constant and unfailing as that of a mother. Without it, I dare say, very few ever attain to any excellency of character. To it we have attributed the success of the ablest men the world has ever produced.

Then, why should we wonder at the recklessness with which Esau plunged into a dissolute life, or should we not rather regard it as a natural consequence of the conduct of his parents? Again, can we censure him for selling his birthright? A man who is almost starving for food and who, if not supplied, will die, cares little for aught save that which will preserve life at the present; for how can he need anything, if not supplied with that?

This was the condition under which Esau was placed. Starving for sustenance, he was forced to part with all he had,—his birthright,—to obtain it. He reasoned thus: "Behold, I am at the point of death, and what profit shall this birthright do to me." Gen. 25: 32. We can only think that, though Esau acted foolishly, he did what any other man, not assisted by Divine Power, would have done. Nor was it because he esteemed his birthright lightly, for he afterwards repented bitterly when he was deprived of the blessing. These misfortunes were enough to drive almost any man to desperation. Is it any wonder his brother had to flee to escape his wrath, after having so shamefully deceived both him and his father? And even now I can scarcely help admiring his self-will, when in great distress because of the failure to receive the blessing, and when, in the height of anger, he delayed his evil intentions. Men now may do well to follow Esau's example in this respect. His intention was to kill his brother, but having curbed his desire for a more favorable opportunity, his wrath subsided, and when the opportunity presented itself, the desire was gone. Ever afterwards he was a friend to him whom he had sought to kill.

We have now given a short sketch of the life of Esau, so far as his immediate life is of interest to us, but in the prophecy to which we have alluded, there was the promise of two separate nations to arise from the two sons. This also was spoken concerning Esau. " And by thy sword thou shalt live." Gen. 37: 40. Thus we find that Esau was to become a great and warlike nation, "and his name is Edom." Gen. 37: 1. The Edomites did become a great nation, maintaining their nationality by the sword. We find them spoken of frequently in the Bible, and as we have to-day nations which trace their origin to Jacob, so we have a nation, supposed to have descended from Esau. Compare the Arabs with the Edomites, and we find traces of similarity.

But Satan is a deceiver, and he who wears his clothes will be deceived. There is One whose eyes can and will see all the holes and spots that are about the garments. you receive of this old man. Paul tells us, " Be not deceived; God is not mocked." Gal. 6: 7.

This old man is not particular about us putting on the whole garment he offers us. If he can only get us to wear one piece of the garment he offers us, he is satisfied; for he knows, then, that he has his work accomplished. He knows that he who seeth all things, hath said, " Whosoever shall keep the whole law, and yet offend in one point, he is guilty of all." James 2: 10.

And now, dear reader, let us examine ourselves, and see if we have about us even one piece of the garment, offered by this king. If so, then we are subjects of his kingdom, and cannot be subjects of the other kingdom. Paul tells us there is no concord between the two. 2 Cor. 6: 15. Now, as there is no concord between the two kings or their subjects, let us hasten to examine and see which is the best kingdom, and having found it, let us abide therein.

The subjects belonging to the kingdom of the old man are provided with garments or clothes that are the reverse of those that belong to the kingdom of the new man.

One of the garments offered by this old man is an attachment for the unbridling of the tongue. Dear reader, have we made use of this attachment for the unbridling of the tongue? If so, we are then in the kingdom of this old man. James, in his third chapter, speaks much about this, and shows us what great harm comes by the unbridling of the tongue. When speaking ill of our neighbor, or members, have we used this attachment so as to tell the untruth, that things may appear different? Remember, that God hath said that no liar can enter heaven, but "shall have their part in the lake which burneth with fire and brimstone." " Rev. 21: 8.

Seeing, then, the final end of those that wear garments offered by this old man; it is high time that we examine ourselves, to see if we are wearing any of the garments which this old man is insisting on us receiving, and if we find we are in possession of clothes from his manufactory, let us hasten to cast them far from us, and take the advice that James gives us: "Resist the devil and he will flee from you." James 4: 7.

Covina, Cal.

REFORM IN DRESS.

BY S. Z. SHARP.

REFORMATIONS mature slowly and come at long intervals. The great religious reformation, of the sixteenth century, had its origin several centuries before its consummation.

The anti-slavery movement had a small beginning among obscure persons. Its opponents embraced the forces of wealth, politics, and religion. The wealthy regarded this peculiar institution as necessary to their happiness. Aristocracy demanded it to maintain its appearance in public. This brought it into politics, and even religion was invoked in its defense, and the Bible was freely quoted to prove that it had the sanction of heaven. Denominations were divided, but all the efforts of the combined forces of earth and Satan could not resist the enlightened public sentiment, the spirit of the Gospel and the power of an unseen Hand, which crushed it forever.

Now we are in the midst of the temperance reform. The same forces of wealth, power and even religion, are marshalled against it. The Bible is freely quoted by the rum power, in its defense, but the same Power that annihilated slavery, can also overthrow the rum power.

While this last conflict is going on we see another reform advancing in a quiet way. Some of the same old enemies, — wealth and aristocracy,—are its opponents. We refer to the reform in dress.

All know that there is such a reform begun who are familiar with the best current literature and some of our most able lecturers, educators, and pulpit orators. Like all other great reforms, it may have a weak and obscure beginning, but the Judge of all the earth who doeth right, will be its defender.

The public mind is being enlightened on this subject. Educators are elevating, in many places, the youthful mind to a nobler sphere and a better practice. Ministers cry out against the sin and tyranny of fashion. Public lecturers denounce it. One of America's great educators and lecturers lately stated the following: " No true artist would choose to paint a noble character, in the garb of modern fashion. Artists, like poets, are guided by a kind of inspiration and express on canvas what their souls have received from a higher power." ,

An examination of the works of the greatest masters that ever lived, will show that the above statement is correct. The word and the spirit of God never contradict each other. The former says in regard to adorning the body, " Let it not be that outward adorning of plaiting the hair and of wearing of gold or of putting on of apparel." The latter only expresses in visible forms on canvas what the former teaches by precept. Many of our readers have seen the representation of Christ and his apostles at the last supper, and have noticed the propriety of each garment. The transfiguration, by Raphael, Christ before Pilate, by Michael Munkacsy, or any painting of a great master, no matter in what age it was produced, invariably presents its characters clothed in simple garments. This is the strongest proof that in every age the most enlightened taste was in favor of simplicity of dress.

An effort to bring about a reform in dress is going on. The progress may be slow, like that of the anti-slavery movement, but ti has God on its side. In the anti slavery and temperance movements the Brethren were pioneers. In the cause of simplicity of dress, the Brethren have ever been its strong defenders. They have a mission to fill in battling against the sin and tyranny of fashion.

OUR LIFE.

TALK of life as we may, trample upon it, despise it, reject it, still it is wonderful. There is something about it that bears the impress of greatness. There is something about the reality of the soul, more awe-inspiring than all the gorgeous splendors of the skies. There is a grandeur in its very repose that bespeaks its kinship with the Infinite and the Eternal. God made it, and looked upon it with a smile, and dignified it with his own glorious likeness. We cannot trifle with life without incurring guilt and the deepest shame. It is God's rarest and most wonderful gift. If we throw it away, all the universe will spurn us, and eternity itself cannot exhaust our suffering.—*Sel.*

" WE live in the midst of blessings, till we are utterly insensible of their greatness and of the source from whence they flow. We speak of our civilization, our arts, our freedom, our laws, and forget how large a share of all is due to Christianity. Blot Christianity out of the page of man's history, and what would our laws have been— what his civilization? Christianity is mixed up with our very being, and our daily life. There is not a familiar object around us, which has not been benefited by the light of Christian hope."

BIBLICAL INTERPRETATIONS.

(*Concluded from first page.*)

laws of hermeneutics he would have known that Paul knew what he was talking about, and that according to the customs of the times it would have been a very easy matter to use their hair for a covering. The meaning of the word, as then used, conveys the same truth as given by Paul. *Kalupto*, to cover, hide, conceal; *Kata*, downward. Put the two together, we have *Kata Kalupto*, to cover or veil by putting the hair down and forward. In this way the ladies of that time used their hair for a covering as Paul says, and in addition to this covering he here recommends and urges the veil, or artificial covering, to be used by all Christian women during times of prayer and religious worship.

There is much in Paul's writings that cannot be interpreted by present customs and usages. In these interpretations we must be governed by precisely the same laws as we would in interpreting any other book. We must get with the writer at the time he wrote and become familiar with all the surrounding and attending circumstances.

Some of you may think it strange that we thus write, and that a study of this kind is a new thing among us. But it is not. There is not a minister among us, of any note, who has not, to some extent, made use of the science of hermeneutics in his Biblical interpretations. He has either himself made it a study or unconsciously gotten it from his general reading and intercourse with others.

We sometimes foolishly deny certain things, because we fail to interpret our own language and the words we use. A good old brother once stated before a congregation that he never studied theology an hour during all his life. Of course he did not tell the truth, as he was a fair Scripturian and had studied theology during all his ministry. The trouble with him was, he had attached to the word a wrong meaning. And right here, in this case, we have a beautiful illustration of the use of hermeneutics as a help to a proper interpretation. He was a man who used certain words to convey his ideas to other persons. To him, and perhaps a few of his hearers, they meant one thing, while to others they meant quite a different thing. To those who understood the word in its true meaning, his declaration was unintelligible, and they could not understand his meaning unless they would first learn to know the man and his use of language. Just so it is in all cases of interpretation. To understand and be understood means to know each other, manner of life, modes of thought and use of language. If we wish to interpret Isaiah's writings, we must get back to his time, learn the modes of thought and manner of expression, with all the attending circumstances. In other words, we must place ourselves by his side and among the people to whom he spake. The same is true of the writings of the apostles and Paul. A good rule for all people and especially ministers of the Gospel, is, never to condemn a thing until we first know exactly what it is. Don't get frightened at such words as theology, homiletics, hermeneutics, etc., until you first consult a good dictionary and learn their exact meaning. By so doing you will be enabled to avoid repeating the blunders made by others who lacked that wisdom that should be possessed by those who claim to be teachers for God.

But Satan is a deceiver, and he who wears his clothes will be deceived. There is One whose eyes can and will see all the holes and spots that are about the garments. you receive of this old man. Paul tells us, "Be not deceived; God is not mocked." Gal. 6: 7.

This old man is not particular about us putting on the whole garment he offers us. If he can only get us to wear one piece of the garment he offers us, he is satisfied; for he knows, then, that he has his work accomplished. He knows that he who seeth all things, hath said, "Whosoever shall keep the whole law, and yet offend in one point, he is guilty of all." James 2: 10.

And now, dear reader, let us examine ourselves, and see if we have about us even one piece of the garment, offered by this king. If so, then we are subjects of his kingdom, and cannot be subjects of the other kingdom. Paul tells us there is no concord between the two. 2 Cor. 6: 15. Now, as there is no concord between the two kings or their subjects, let us hasten to examine and see which is the best kingdom, and having found it, let us abide therein.

The subjects belonging to the kingdom of the old man are provided with garments or clothes that are the reverse of those that belong to the kingdom of the new man.

One of the garments offered by this old man is an attachment for the unbridling of the tongue. Dear reader, have we made use of this attachment for the unbridling of the tongue? If so, we are then in the kingdom of this old man. James, in his third chapter, speaks much about this, and shows us what great harm comes by the unbridling of the tongue. When speaking ill of our neighbor, or members, have we used this attachment so as to tell the untruth, that things may appear different? Remember, that God hath said that no liar can enter heaven, but "shall have their part in the lake which burneth with fire and brimstone." Rev. 21: 8.

Seeing, then, the final end of those that wear garments offered by this old man; it is high time that we examine ourselves, to see if we are wearing any of the garments which this old man is insisting on us receiving, and if we find we are in possession of clothes from his manufactory, let us hasten to cast them far from us, and take the advice that James gives us: "Resist the devil and he will flee from you." James 4: 7.

Covina, Cal.

REFORM IN DRESS.

BY S. Z. SHARP.

Reformations mature slowly and come at long intervals. The great religious reformation, of the sixteenth century, had its origin several centuries before its consummation.

The anti-slavery movement had a small beginning among obscure persons. Its opponents embraced the forces of wealth, politics, and religion. The wealthy regarded this peculiar institution as necessary to their happiness. Aristocracy demanded it to maintain its appearance in public. This brought it into politics, and even religion was invoked in its defense, and the Bible was freely quoted to prove that it had the sanction of heaven. Denominations were divided, but all the efforts of the combined forces of earth and Satan could not resist the enlightened public sentiment, the spirit of the Gospel and the power of an unseen Hand, which crushed it forever.

Now we are in the midst of the temperance reform. The same forces of wealth, power and even religion, are marshalled against it. The Bible is freely quoted by the rum power, in its defense, but the same Power that annihilated slavery, can also overthrow the rum power.

While this last conflict is going on we see another reform advancing in a quiet way. Some of the same old enemies, — wealth and aristocracy,—are its opponents. We refer to the reform in dress.

All know that there is such a reform begun who are familiar with the best current literature and some of our most able lecturers, educators, and pulpit orators. Like all other great reforms, it may have a weak and obscure beginning, but the Judge of all the earth who doeth right, will be its defender.

The public mind is being enlightened on this subject. Educators are elevating, in many places, the youthful mind to a nobler sphere and a better practice. Ministers cry out against the sin and tyranny of fashion. Public lecturers denounce it. One of America's great educators and lecturers lately stated the following: "No true artist would choose to paint a noble character, in the garb of modern fashion. Artists, like poets, are guided by a kind of inspiration and express on canvas what their souls have received from a higher power."

An examination of the works of the greatest masters that ever lived, will show that the above statement is correct. The word and the spirit of God never contradict each other. The former says in regard to adorning the body, "Let it not be that outward adorning of plaiting the hair and of wearing of gold or of putting on of apparel." The latter only expresses in visible forms on canvas what the former teaches by precept. Many of our readers have seen the representation of Christ and his apostles at the last supper, and have noticed the propriety of each garment. The transfiguration, by Raphael, Christ before Pilate, by Michael Munkacsy, or any painting of a great master, no matter in what age it was produced, invariably presents its characters clothed in simple garments. This is the strongest proof that in every age the most enlightened taste was in favor of simplicity of dress.

An effort to bring about a reform in dress is going on. The progress may be slow, like that of the anti-slavery reform, but it has God on its side. In the anti slavery and temperance movements the Brethren were pioneers. In the cause of simplicity of dress, the Brethren have ever been its strong defenders. They have a mission to fill in battling against the sin and tyranny of fashion.

OUR LIFE.

Talk of life as we may, trample upon it, despise it, reject it, still it is wonderful. There is something about it that bears the impress of greatness. There is something about the reality of the soul, more awe-inspiring than all the gorgeous splendors of the skies. There is a grandeur in its very repose that bespeaks its kinship with the Infinite and the Eternal. God made it, and looked upon it with a smile, and dignified it with his own glorious likeness. We cannot trifle with life without incurring guilt and the deepest shame. It is God's rarest and most wonderful gift. If we throw it away, all the universe will spurn us, and eternity itself cannot exhaust our suffering.—*Sel.*

"We live in the midst of blessings, till we are utterly insensible of their greatness and of the source from whence they flow. We speak of our civilization, our arts, our freedom, our laws, and forget how large a share of all is due to Christianity. Blot Christianity out of the page of man's history, and what would our laws have been— what his civilization? Christianity is mixed up with our very being, and our daily life. There is not a familiar object around us, which has not been benefited by the light of Christian hope."

BIBLICAL INTERPRETATIONS.

(Concluded from first page.)

laws of hermeneutics he would have known that Paul knew what he was talking about, and that according to the customs of the times it would have been a very easy matter to use their hair for a covering. The meaning of the word, as then used, also conveys the same truth as given by Paul. *Kalupto*, to cover, hide, conceal; *Kata*, downward. Put the two together, we have *Kata Kalupto*, to cover or veil by putting the hair down and forward. In this way the ladies of that time used their hair for a covering as Paul says, and in addition to this covering he here recommends and urges the veil, or artificial covering, to be used by all Christian women during times of prayer and religious worship.

There is much in Paul's writings that cannot be interpreted by present customs and usages. In these interpretations we must be governed by precisely the same laws as we would in interpreting any other book. We must get with the writer at the time he wrote and become familiar with all the surrounding and attending circumstances.

Some of you may think it strange that we thus write, and that a study of this kind is a new thing among us. But it is not. There is not a minister among us, of any note, who has not, to some extent, made use of the science of hermeneutics in his Biblical interpretations. He has either himself made it a study or unconsciously gotten it from his general reading and intercourse with others.

We sometimes foolishly deny certain things, because we fail to interpret our own language and the words we use. A good old brother once stated he did not tell the truth, as he was a fair Scripturian and had studied theology during all his ministry. The trouble with him was, he had attached to the word a wrong meaning. And right here, in this case, we have a beautiful illustration of the use of hermeneutics as a help to a proper interpretation. He was a man who used certain words to convey his ideas to other persons. To him, and perhaps a few of his hearers, they meant one thing, while to others they meant quite a different thing. To those who understood the word in its true meaning, his declaration was unintelligible, and they could not understand his meaning unless they would first learn to know the man and his use of language. Just so it is in all cases of interpretation. To understand and be understood means to know each other, manner of life, modes of thought and use of language. If we wish to interpret Isaiah's writings, we must get back to his time, learn the modes of thought and manner of expression, with all the attending circumstances. In other words, we must place ourselves by his side and among the people to whom he spake. The same is true of the writings of the apostles and Paul. A good rule for all people and especially ministers of the Gospel, is, never to condemn a thing until we first know exactly what it is. Don't get frightened at such words as theology, homiletics, hermeneutics, etc., until you first consult a good dictionary and learn their exact meaning. By so doing you will be enabled to avoid repeating the blunders made by others who lacked that wisdom that should be possessed by those who claim to be teachers for God.

Lesson X.

With many, an erroneous idea prevails, concerning the number of children slain by Herod at Bethlehem, supposing there were likely hundreds of them; but a calculation, concerning the place and surroundings, would bring one to the conclusion that there could not have been many. Some writers say not more than ten or twelve. We do not know how many, but I have no doubt that the number was much smaller than is generally supposed.

Herod died in the year B. C. 4, although he died after the birth of Christ. This brings out the fact that, by some means, there was an error made in computing time from the birth of Christ. He was really born four years earlier than what is generally considered the commencement of the Christian era; so, in reality, we should now be in the year 1896 instead of 1892.

In studying the New Testament, it is very beneficial for us to have a proper understanding of the house of Herod, as several are mentioned. Herod had ten wives, but as it is sons, whose history we are following, we will not name the wives.

SONS OF HEROD.

1. Antipater, who was slain five days before his father's death.

2. Aristobulus.

3. Alexander.

These two were executed by Herod while he was alive.

4. Herod Philip I., who married Herodias, his niece, the daughter of Aristobulus. This Herodias is the one who caused the death of John the Baptist.

5. Herod Antipas, who, while having a living wife, married Herodias, the. wife of his brother Philip while her husband still lived. John reproved Herod Antipas for his unlawful marriage. The history of the transaction is found in Matt. 16 and Mark 6. This is the Herod who was at Jerusalem at the time of Christ's death, and as he was ruler over Galilee, Pilate sent Jesus to him.

6. Archelaus. This is the one that was ruler in Judea when Joseph and Mary, with Jesus, returned from Egypt. They turned aside into Galilee which was ruled over by Herod Antipas, who, Joseph thought, was not of so cruel a disposition as Archelaus.

7. Herod Philip II., who was tetrarch of the northern part of the country, east of the Jordan. He built Cæsarea Philippi at the upper waters of the Jordan. This is the northern limit of Christ's journeys. It was near here that the transfiguration took place. Herod Philip II married Salome, the daughter of Herodias and Herod Philip I. She is the one who danced before Herod Antipas and asked for the head of John.

The above are the seven sons of Herod. Aristobulus, the second one mentioned, had a son named Herod Agrippa. This is the Herod we read of in Acts 12: 1, who killed James and imprisoned Peter. He is also the person mentioned in Acts 12: 20, who was eaten by worms.

Herod Agrippa I. had a son who was called Herod Agrippa II. This is the Agrippa before whom Paul appeared and caused him to say, "Almost thou persuadest me to be a Christian." Agrippa had two sisters, Drusilla, the wife of Felix, named in Acts 24: 24, and Bernice, mentioned in Acts 25: 23.

McPherson, Kans.

"THE greatest loss of time is delay and expectation which depends upon the future. We let go the present which we have in our power, and look forward to that which depends upon chance, and so relinquish a certainty for an uncertainty."

DID JUDAS COMMUNE?

BY S. S. GARMAN.

I WISH to offer a few remarks in connection with Bro. Andrew Hutchison's article as to Jesus communing with Judas Iscariot.

If Jesus communed with Judas, the traitor, after instituting the Communion, he must have gone to the supper again, in order to give the sop to Judas after he had dipped it. It is not very reasonable to me that he did so.

Another point Bro Hutchison made was, why say, "Drink ye all of it, if one had gone out." That makes no difference. If all but six had gone out, Jesus could still have said, "Drink ye all of it," meaning all that were there. Judas was never called a disciple after Jesus gave him the sop.

Another point. Jesus says, "But I say unto you, I will not drink henceforth of this fruit of the vine, until that day when I drink is new with you in my Father's kingdom." Matt. 26: 29. It is not reasonable to me that Jesus should promise *Judas* to drink with him in his Father's kingdom.

CLOSE TO THE WORK.

BY JNO. CALVIN BRIGHT.

IN looking over the past year, I remember one circumstance, perhaps, more distinctly than any other. Anyhow, the impression made occurs quite frequently to my mind, and it has been the source of much profitable meditation.

It occurred at the last feast held in our beautiful valley. We had been fed on spiritual manna by those who are "eloquent in the Scriptures." After the services we had baptism in the stream close by the sanctuary. The congregation wended its way thither. In company with a dear brother, we arrived a little late The introductory exercises were held on the opposite side of the stream. I remarked, "We can stay on this side and have a good view of the ceremony." "No," said he, gently and firmly, "We want to go right over to where the services are held, as long as there is room." I always like to get as CLOSE TO THE WORK as possible." We went.

Multum in parvo. i. e, much in few words, thought I. And how appropriate to any occasion or any church work! No one ever succeeds in any calling if afraid of his work. The successful workers are closely united to their profession. I thought:

1. When baptism is performed, let all who can find room, join the baptismal party, and join in the singing, and bow and pray with them. After the ceremony is over, receive the baptized with the hand of fellowship and kiss of love. Wait until the meeting is dismissed, and do not hurry off without ceremony.

2 When services are held by the church, whether the regular meetings or the Communion service, or the meetings for council, let every member be *close to the work* and give what assistance he can. In all of our meetings let the members be united closely together, as well as close to the work, and their souls will be blessed as well as their labors. And when means are needed to assist the poor or meet the expenses of the church in its missionary and other departments, let all be so closely allied to the work that they will freely give to the Lord as he has prospered them.

We need not look very far until we see that, when our spiritual life was at its lowest ebb, we were too distant from the work. The enemy of

souls will overcome all stragglers. But when we dwell under his throne, and are led by his Spirit, one shall chase a hundred, and ten shall put a thousand to flight.

If the elder "rules well" and fulfills the outline as drawn by the inspired penman, he will be a close worker. If the deacon would purchase the degree of boldness and usefulness, delineated in God's Word, he is likewise diligent in his calling. And as they are ensamples to the flock, it follows that they are workers together with God.

God has given "every man his work." He has given him his field, and then he has given every one the talents necessary to be a successful worker in his vineyard. He rewards with "a hundredfold in this life, and in the world to come everlasting life." He invites "whosoever will." He says, "My yoke is easy and my burden is light," and he declares, "My reward is sure." Who would not give him a diligent service?

New Lebanon, Ohio.

"Not man's thoughts about God, but God's thoughts about man, are the charm and the comfort of all true religion. Man cannot by searching find out God, but God can without searching find out man and reveal himself to him. All of man's thoughts about God, in all the ages, amount to nothing in comparison with a single sentence of revelation, such as 'Herein is love, not that we loved God, but that he loved us, and sent his Son to be the propitiation for our sins.' Maurice calls attention to the fact that the brightest and busiest thinkers on earth without a revelation make no progress in religious knowledge or attainment. He says: 'The Hindoo, in action the idlest, is in imagining, dreaming, combining, the most busy of all human creatures.' But the Hindoo's thinking brings only added evidence of the restless longing of the soul for religious knowledge, and of the hopelessness of the soul's unaided search for religious knowledge. 'I ask nothing more,' adds Maurice, 'than the Hindoo system and the Hindoo life as evidence that there is that in man which demands a revelation—that there is not that in him which makes the revelation.' Nor is the Hindoo thinker a better illustration than the English and American thinker of this same great truth.'

The Gospel Messenger

Is the recognized organ of the German Baptist or Brethren's church, and advocates the form of doctrine taught in the New Testament and pleads for a return to apostolic and primitive Christianity.

It recognizes the New Testament as the only infallible rule of faith and practice, and maintains that Faith toward God, Repentance from dead works, Regeneration of the heart and mind, baptism by Trine Immersion for remission of sins unto the reception of the Holy Ghost by the laying on of hands, are the means of adoption into the household of God,—the church militant.

It also maintains that Feet-washing, as taught in John 13, both by example and command of Jesus, should be observed in the church.

That the Lord's Supper, instituted by Christ and as universally observed by the apostles and the early Christians, is a full meal, and, in connection with the Communion, should be taken in the evening or after the close of the day.

That the Salutation of the Holy Kiss, or Kiss of Charity, is binding upon the followers of Christ.

That War and Retaliation are contrary to the spirit and self-denying principles of the religion of Jesus Christ.

That the principle of Plain Dressing and of Non-conformity to the world, as taught in the New Testament, should be observed by the followers of Christ.

That the Scriptural duty of Anointing the Sick with Oil, in the Name of the Lord, James 5: 14, is binding upon all Christians.

It also advocates the church's duty to support Missionary and Tract Work, thus giving to the Lord for the spread of the Gospel and for the conversion of sinners.

In short, it is a vindicator of all that Christ and the apostles have enjoined upon us, and aims, amid the conflicting theories and discords of modern Christendom, to point out ground that all must concede to be infallibly safe.

☞ The above principles of our Fraternity are set forth on our "Brethren's Envelopes." Use them! Price, 15 cents per package; 40 cents per hundred.

Lesson X.

With many, an erroneous idea prevails, concerning the number of children slain by Herod at Bethlehem, supposing there were likely hundreds of them; but a calculation, concerning the place and surroundings, would bring one to the conclusion that there could not have been many. Some writers say not more than ten or twelve. We do not know how many, but I have no doubt that the number was much smaller than is generally supposed.

Herod died in the year B. C. 4, although he died after the birth of Christ. This brings out the fact that, by some means, there was an error made in computing time from the birth of Christ. He was really born four years earlier than what is generally considered the commencement of the Christian era; so, in reality, we should now be in the year 1896 instead of 1892.

In studying the New Testament, it is very beneficial for us to have a proper understanding of the house of Herod, as several are mentioned. Herod had ten wives, but as it is sons, whose history we are following, we will not name the wives.

SONS OF HEROD.

1. Antipater, who was slain five days before his father's death.
2. Aristobulus.
3. Alexander.

These two, were executed by Herod while he was alive.

4. Herod Philip I., who married Herodias, his niece, the daughter of Aristobulus. This Herodias is the one who caused the death of John the Baptist.

5. Herod Antipas, who, while having a living wife, married Herodias, the wife of his brother Philip while her husband still lived. John reproved Herod Antipas for his unlawful marriage. The history of the transaction is found in Matt. 16 and Mark 6. This is the Herod who was at Jerusalem at the time of Christ's death, and as he was ruler over Galilee, Pilate sent Jesus to him.

6. Archelaus. This is the one that was ruler in Judea when Joseph and Mary, with Jesus, returned from Egypt. They turned aside into Galilee which was ruled over by Herod Antipas, who, Joseph thought, was not of so cruel a disposition as Archelaus.

7. Herod Philip II., who was tetrarch of the northern part of the country, east of the Jordan. He built Cæsarea Philippi at the upper waters of the Jordan. This is the northern limit of Christ's journeys. It was near here that the transfiguration took place. Herod Philip II married Salome, the daughter of Herodias and Herod Philip I. She is the one who danced before Herod Antipas and asked for the head of John.

The above are the seven sons of Herod. Aristobulus, the second one mentioned, had a son named Herod Agrippa. This is the Herod we read of in Acts 12: 1, who killed James and imprisoned Peter. He is also the person mentioned in Acts 12: 20, who was eaten by worms.

Herod Agrippa I. had a son who was called Herod Agrippa II. This is the Agrippa before whom Paul appeared and caused him to say, "Almost thou persuadest me to be a Christian." Agrippa had two sisters, Drusilla, the wife of Felix, named in Acts 24: 24, and Bernice, mentioned in Acts 25: 23.

McPherson, Kans.

"THE greatest loss of time is delay and expectation which depends upon the future. We let go the present which we have in our power, and look forward to that which depends upon chance, and so relinquish a certainty for an uncertainty."

DID JUDAS COMMUNE?

BY S. S. GARMAN.

I WISH to offer a few remarks in connection with Bro. Andrew Hutchison's article as to Jesus communing with Judas Iscariot.

If Jesus communed with Judas, the traitor, after instituting the Communion, he must have gone back to the supper again, in order to give the sop to Judas after he had dipped it. It is not very reasonable to me that he did so.

Another point Bro Hutchison made was, why say, "Drink ye all of it, if one had gone out." That makes no difference. If all but six had gone out, Jesus could still have said, "Drink ye all of it," meaning all that were there. Judas was never called a disciple after Jesus gave him the sop.

Another point. Jesus says, "But I say unto you, I will not drink henceforth of this fruit of the vine, until that day when I drink it new with you in my Father's kingdom." Matt. 26: 29. It is not reasonable to me that Jesus should promise *Judas* to drink with him in his Father's kingdom.

CLOSE TO THE WORK.

BY JNO. CALVIN BRIGHT.

IN looking over the past year, I remember one circumstance, perhaps, more distinctly than any other. Anyhow, the impression made occurs quite frequently to my mind, and it has been the source of much profitable meditation.

It occurred in our beautiful valley. We had been fed on spiritual manna by those who are "eloquent in the Scriptures." After the services we had baptism in the stream close by the sanctuary. The congregation wended its way thither. In company with a dear brother, we arrived a little late. The introductory exercises were held on the opposite side of the stream. I remarked, "We can stay on this side and have a good view of the ceremony." "No," said he, gently and firmly, "We want to go right over to where the services are held, as long as there is room. I always like to get as CLOSE TO THE WORK as possible." We went.

Multum in parvo, i. e., much in few words, thought I. And how appropriate to any occasion or any church work! No one ever succeeds in any calling if afraid of his work. The successful workers are closely united to their profession. I thought:

1. When baptism is performed, let all who can find room, join the baptismal party, and join in the singing, and bow and pray with them. After the ceremony is over, receive the baptized with the hand of fellowship and kiss of love. Wait until the meeting is dismissed, and do not hurry off without ceremony.

2 When services are held by the church, whether the regular meetings or the Communion service, or the meetings for council, let every member be *close to the work* and give what assistance he can. In all of our meetings let the members be united closely together, as well as close to the work, and their souls will be blessed as well as their labors. And when means are needed to assist the poor or meet the expenses of the church in its missionary and other departments, let all be so closely allied to the work that they will freely give to the Lord as he has prospered them.

We need not look very far until we see that, when our spiritual life was at its lowest ebb, we were too distant from the work. The enemy of

---

souls will overcome all stragglers. But when we dwell under his throne, and are led by his Spirit, one shall chase a hundred, and ten shall put a thousand to flight.

If the elder "rules well" and fulfills the outline as drawn by the inspired penman, he will be a close worker. If the deacon would purchase the degree of boldness and usefulness, delineated in God's Word, he is likewise diligent in his calling. And as they are ensamples to the flock, it follows that they are workers together with God.

God has given "every man his work." He has given him his field, and then he has given every one the talents necessary to be a successful worker in his vineyard. He rewards with "a hundredfold in this life, and in the world to come everlasting life." He invites "whosoever will." He says, "My yoke is easy and my burden is light," and he declares, "My reward is sure." Who would not give him a diligent service?

New Lebanon, Ohio.

"Not man's thoughts about God, but God's thoughts about man, are the charm and the comfort of all true religion. Man cannot by searching find out God, but God can without searching find out man and reveal himself to him. All of man's thoughts about God, in all the ages, amount to nothing in comparison with a single sentence of revelation, such as 'Herein is love, not that we loved God, but that he loved us, and sent his Son to be the propitiation for our sins.' Maurice calls attention to the fact that the brightest and busiest thinkers on earth without a revelation make no progress in religious knowledge or attainment. He says: 'The Hindoo, in action the idlest, is in imagining, dreaming, combining, the most busy of all human creatures.' But the Hindoo's thinking brings only added evidence of the restless longing of the soul for religious knowledge, and of the hopelessness of the soul's unaided search for religious knowledge. 'I ask nothing more,' adds Maurice, 'than the Hindoo system and the Hindoo life as evidence that there is that in man which demands a revelation—that there is *not* that in him which makes the revelation.' Nor is the Hindoo thinker a better illustration than the English and American thinker of this same great truth.'

The Gospel Messenger

Is the recognized organ of the German Baptist or Brethren's church. and advocates the form of doctrine taught in the New Testament and pleads for a return to apostolic and primitive Christianity.

It recognizes the New Testament as the only infallible rule of faith and practice, and maintains that Faith toward God, Repentance from dead works, Regeneration of the heart and mind, baptism by Trine Immersion for remission of sins unto the reception of the Holy Ghost by the laying on of hands, are the means of adoption into the household of God,—the church militant.

It also maintains that Feet-washing, as taught in John 13, both by example and command of Jesus, should be observed in the church.

That the Lord's Supper, instituted by Christ and as universally observed by the apostles and the early Christians, is a full meal, and, in connection with the Communion, should be taken in the evening or after the close of the day.

That the Salutation of the Holy Kiss, or Kiss of Charity, is binding upon the followers of Christ.

That War and Retaliation are contrary to the spirit and self-denying principles of the religion of Jesus Christ.

That the principle of Plain Dressing and of Non-conformity to the world, as taught in the New Testament, should be observed by the followers of Christ.

That the Scriptural duty of Anointing the Sick with Oil, in the Name of the Lord, James 5: 14, is binding upon all Christians.

It also advocates the church's duty to support Missionary and Tract Work, thus giving to the Lord for the spread of the Gospel and for the conversion of sinners.

In short, it is a vindicator of all that Christ and the apostles have ordained upon us, and aims, amid the conflicting theories and discords of modern Christendom, to point out ground that all must concede to be infallibly safe.

☞ The above principles of our Fraternity are set forth on our "Brethren's Envelopes." Use them! Price, 15 cents per package: 40 cents per hundred.

Bro. C. S. Holsinger, who has been with us about two weeks, returned to his home at Pigeon Creek, Illinois, last week. He is now preparing to move to Kansas and make that State his field of labor for the future. While we greatly regret to lose him, for he is certainly needed in the field here, we are nevertheless glad that he is settling at a place where his services will be in demand.

QUERISTS' DEPARTMENT.

What is the proper way to fast, one or two meals a day, or for twenty-four hours? Please tell us something about it through the Messenger. Geo. Renner.

It would seem that the Savior instituted no particular fast, but left it optional with each individual, saying, "Can the children of the bride-chamber mourn, as long as the bridegroom is with them? but the days will come when the bride-groom shall be taken from them, and then shall they fast." Matt. 9: 15. To the disciples those days finally came, and "as they ministered to the Lord and fasted, the Holy Ghost said, Separate me Barnabas and Saul for the work whereunto I have called them. And when they had fasted and prayed, and laid their hands on them, they sent them away." Acts 13: 2, 3. We find them fasting on another occasion. "And when they had ordained them elders in every church, and had prayed with fasting, they commended them to the Lord, on whom they believed." Acts 14: 23.

Fasting is "to abstain from food; to omit to take nourishment in whole or in part; to go hungry."—Webster. As a religious exercise, or duty, it means to abstain from food voluntarily on account of some great sorrow or affliction, and may serve to subdue the will, or carnal passions, and prepare the mind for important religious or mental duties. Properly observed, it tends to subdue, in the mind and body, that which is liable to lead astray, and lead us near to God. What meals to omit in fasting should probably be left to the discretion of the individual. Whatever tends to subdue the will, and prepares us for a closer walk with God will meet the design of fasting. Some abstain from food an entire day, others one or two meals,—some even longer. Others deny themselves the use of certain articles of diet for a time. Either method is fasting, and, if done with the right motive, may result in good.

An occasional fast among our American people would be good for health, to say nothing of religion. As a people, we certainly do eat too much.

Who invented the mourner's bench? When and where was it invented? Geo. Renner.

Some years ago we saw an account of its invention, but the date of its origin was so recent that we did not think it worth remembering. It has not been in use, probably, over sixty years. You may rest assured that it is not apostolic. In that age the people were pointed to Christ, in whom they were taught to believe, and then repent of their sins and be baptized in the name of the Lord Jesus for the remission of their sins. That kind of preaching requires no mourner's bench.

Was Eve the only one who sinned, or did Adam sin too? God commanded the man only not to eat, but they both did eat. Phebe Smith.

Adam being the head of the family, it was sufficient for the purpose that the command be given to him. He certainly told Eve what the Lord commanded, for she told Satan, "But of the fruit of the tree which is in the midst of the garden, God hath said, Ye shall not eat of it, neither shall ye touch it, lest ye die." Gen. 3: 3. From this we may safely infer that she knew as much about the command as Adam. She was, therefore, without excuse. Hence both of them sinned knowingly.

Will you please explain Matt. 23: 15, which reads: "Woe unto you, scribes and Pharisees, hypocrites! for ye compass sea and land to make one proselyte; and when he is made, ye make him twofold more the child of hell than yourselves." How could they make him twofold more the child of hell than themselves? Meda Caskey.

A proselyte is a gentile convert, converted from heathenism to the Jewish religion. The reason for being twofold more the child of hell than the scribes and Pharisees is this,—the Pharisees were not only hypocrites, but they held, practiced and taught that which was wrong. The heathen proselyte not only accepted these errors but brought with him into his new relation additional errors, and in this manner he was just that much worse off than the Pharisees—hence twofold worse. Coming from one wrong system with his errors, and uniting with another, having other errors, gave him double the amount. He would have been just as well off, so far as the future is concerned, if he had remained in heathen idolatry.

This is a strong point in favor of ministers being sound in the Gospel faith, and preaching only that which is in keeping with the Gospel. If they hold to errors, and these errors are accepted by their converts, who come into the church with additional errors of their own, the last stage of the convert is not only worse than the first, but he proves a positive injury to the church in particular, as well as the cause of religion in general, while the church, in turn, can be of no real benefit to him.

Where is the Garden of Eden on earth? Did any person ever live there since Adam and Eve were driven out? A. Nelson Graybill.

The location of the Garden of Eden is absolutely unknown, and yet there is scarcely any end to the numerous conjectures concerning it. One author even claims that the home of our first parents was at the North Pole. A majority of those who have made the subject a study seem to agree on the southern part of Armenia as being the probable location of Eden, in a land where the River Euphrates takes its rise. At some suitable place in Eden the garden was located, probably not a very large one, but it was well watered and must have been in a genial clime. A few writers hold that the garden is now covered by the Mount of Olives on the east of Jerusalem, and when the mountain shall cleave, part passing towards the East and the other to the West, the garden will be exposed to view in the valley thus formed. Zach. 14: 4. But this is mere conjecture. After our first parents were driven from the garden, it was closed, and probably was never afterwards entered by a human being. This was 1,500 years before the flood. So long a period of neglect would likely obliterate all traces of the garden. Then came the flood, and possibly some geological changes, sufficient to alter the face of that part of the country enough so as to render it impossible to determine the location of Eden in any manner. So, after all, we do not know where it is, nor does its location out any figure respecting our welfare, spiritually or temporally. If it could be found, the world would make an idol of it, and spend more money visiting the place than is used for spreading the Gospel. It is well that we are pointed to the paradise above, where all the faithful may enter to enjoy the tree of life forever.
J. H. M.

EDITORIAL WANDERINGS IN THE OLD WORLD.

BY D.-L. MILLER.

Number Sixteen.—The London Tower.

Our last letter was mainly devoted to a brief description of two of the most noted churches, in many respects, to be found in Europe. Our purpose was to include in that letter, a description of the historic Tower of London, but we found so much to say about St. Paul's and Westminster Abbey, that our space was fully occupied, and the former place was crowded out. This letter will be devoted to a description of the Tower, and to some reflections suggested by the associations connected with the place. We do not propose to enter into a detailed description of the place. Several letters might be written without exhausting the subject.

Leaving St. Paul and Westminster Abbey,—both of these churches dedicated to the worship of God, and both transformed into great temples of fame and galleries of sculpture, ill befitting the sacred object for which they were constructed,—we wander through the busy streets of the great, bustling City, and finally reach the Tower, which is, historically, one of the most interesting spots in England. We had read so often of it, and our sympathies had so many times been drawn out toward those who had suffered and died within its dark walls, that at last, when we entered its portal, it was hard to realize that we were really in the old prison Tower of London. It seemed more like a dream than a reality, but the real soon asserted itself. The deep moat, the dark, heavy walls, the great tower, with walls fifteen feet thick, the dark, gloomy prison cells were all there; and we were made conscious of the fact that we were standing in the place where so many terrible incidents occurred, which darken the pages of English history, and give us an insight into the cruel spirit of the age which has passed away,—may we not fondly hope?—never more to return.

Perhaps no place in Europe, certainly none in England, has witnessed so many sad scenes, and been marked with so many evidences of "man's inhumanity to man," and woman's, too, for that matter, than this same old moated Tower, whose grim and gloomy walls overhang the River Thames in the City of London. Could these stones, upon which we tread as we enter the Tower, speak, what a history of human sorrow and cruelty they could reveal, but they are as silent as are the victims who suffered here in the years that have gone by. Silent and gloomy the old Tower keeps its story, and he that would learn must read the history of the past.

And what a history that is! It is not, however, within the scope or purpose of these "Wanderings" to enter into historical details to any but a very limited extent, and we shall not attempt it in this instance, for the history of the Tower of London is the history of England for many centuries. In turn it has served as a palace for the sovereigns of England, a strong fortress for the City of London, and a dark and gloomy prison over the doors of which, at one time, might well have been written, "He who enters here leaves all hope behind." Kings and queens, bishops and noblemen, warriors and statesmen, women and children, court favorites for a brief season, have passed through the Tower gate as State prisoners, and died within its dark walls without

Bro. C. S. Holsinger, who has been with us about two weeks, returned to his home at Pigeon Creek, Illinois, last week. He is now preparing to move to Kansas and make that State his field of labor for the future. While we greatly regret to lose him, for he is certainly needed in the field here, we are nevertheless glad that he is settling at a place where his services will be in demand.

QUERISTS' DEPARTMENT.

What is the proper way to fast, one or two meals a day, or for twenty-four hours? Please tell us something about it through the MESSENGER. GEO. RENNER.

It would seem that the Savior instituted no particular fast, but left it optional with each individual, saying, "Can the children of the bride-chamber mourn, as long as the bridegroom is with them? but the days will come when the bride-groom shall be taken from them, and then shall they fast." Matt. 9: 15. To the disciples those days finally came, and "as they ministered to the Lord and fasted, the Holy Ghost said, Separate me Barnabas and Saul for the work whereunto I have called them. And when they had fasted and prayed, and laid their hands on them, they sent them away." Acts 13: 2, 3. We find them fasting on another occasion. "And when they had ordained them elders in every church; and had prayed with fasting, they commended them to the Lord, on whom they believed." Acts 14: 23.

Fasting is "to abstain from food; to omit to take nourishment, in whole or in part; to go hungry."—Webster. As a religious exercise, or duty, it means to abstain from food voluntarily on account of some great sorrow or affliction, and may serve to subdue the will, or carnal passions, and prepare the mind for important religious or mental duties. Properly observed, it tends to subdue, in the mind and body, that which is liable to lead astray, and lead us near to God. What meals to omit in fasting should probably be left to the discretion of the individual. Whatever tends to subdue the will, and prepares us for a closer walk with God will meet the design of fasting. Some abstain from food an entire day, others one or two meals,—some even longer. Others deny themselves the use of certain articles of diet for a time. Either method is fasting, and, if done with the right motive, may result in good.

An occasional fast among our American people would be good for health, to say nothing of religion. As a people, we certainly do eat too much.

Who invented the mourner's bench? When and where was it invented? GEO. RENNER.

Some years ago we saw an account of its invention, but the date of its origin was so recent that we did not think it worth remembering. It has not been in use, probably, over sixty years. You may rest assured that it is not apostolic. In that age the people were pointed to Christ, in whom they were taught to believe, and then repent of their sins and be baptized in the name of the Lord Jesus for the remission of their sins. That kind of preaching requires no mourner's bench.

Was Eve the only one who sinned, or did Adam sin too? God commanded the man only not to eat, but they both did eat. PHEBE SMITH.

Adam being the head of the family, it was sufficient for the purpose that the command be given to him. He certainly told Eve what the Lord commanded, for she told Satan, "But of the fruit of the tree which is in the midst of the garden, God hath said, Ye shall not eat of it, neither shall ye touch it, lest ye die." Gen. 3: 3. From this we may safely infer that she knew as much about the command as Adam. She was, therefore, without excuse. Hence both of them sinned knowingly.

Will you please explain Matt. 23: 15, which reads: "Woe unto you, scribes and Pharisees, hypocrites! for ye compass sea and land to make one proselyte; and where he is made, ye make him twofold more the child of hell than yourselves." How could they make him twofold more the child of hell than themselves? MEDA CASKEY.

A proselyte is a gentile convert, converted from heathenism to the Jewish religion. The reason for being twofold more the child of hell than the scribes and Pharisees is this,—the Pharisees were not only hypocrites, but they held, practiced and taught that which was wrong. The heathen proselyte not only accepted these errors but brought with him into his new relation additional errors, and in this manner he was just that much worse off than the Pharisees—hence twofold worse. Coming from one wrong system with his errors, and uniting with another, having other errors, gave him double the amount. He would have been just as well off, so far as the future is concerned, if he had remained in heathen idolatry.

This is a strong point in favor of ministers being sound in the Gospel faith, and preaching only that which is in keeping with the Gospel. If they hold to errors, and these errors are accepted by their converts, who come into the church with additional errors of their own, the last stage of the convert is not only worse than the first, but he proves a positive injury to the church in particular, as well as the cause of religion in general, while the church, in turn, can be of no real benefit to him.

Where is the Garden of Eden on earth? Did any person ever live there since Adam and Eve were driven out? A. NELSON GRAYBILL.

The location of the Garden of Eden is absolutely unknown, and yet there is scarcely any end to the numerous conjectures concerning it. One author even claims that the home of our first parents was at the North Pole. A majority of those who have made the subject a study seem to agree on the southern part of Armenia as being the probable location of Eden, in a land where the River Euphrates takes its rise. At some suitable place in Eden the garden was located, probably not a very large one, but it was well watered and must have been in a genial clime. A few writers hold that the garden is now covered by the Mount of Olives on the east of Jerusalem, and when the mountain shall cleave, part passing towards the East and the other to the West, the garden will be exposed to view in the valley thus formed. Zech. 14: 4. But this is mere conjecture. After our first parents were driven from the garden, it was closed, and probably was never afterwards entered by a human being. This was 1,500 years before the flood. So long a period of neglect would likely obliterate all traces of the garden. Then came the flood, and possibly some geological changes, sufficient to alter the face of that part of the country enough so as to render it impossible to determine the location of Eden in any manner. So, after all, we do not know where it is, nor does its location cut any figure respecting our welfare, spiritually or temporally. If it could be found, the world would make an idol of it, and spend more money visiting the place than is used for spreading the Gospel. It is well that we are pointed to the paradise above, where all the faithful may enter to enjoy the tree of life forever.

J. H. M.

EDITORIAL WANDERINGS IN THE OLD WORLD.

BY D. L. MILLER.

Number Sixteen.—The London Tower.

Our last letter was mainly devoted to a brief description of two of the most noted churches, in many respects, to be found in Europe. Our purpose was to include in that letter, a description of the historic Tower of London, but we found so much to say about St. Paul's and Westminster Abbey, that our space was fully occupied, and the former place was crowded out. This letter will be devoted to a description of the Tower, and to some reflections suggested by the associations connected with the place. We do not propose to enter into a detailed description of the place. Several letters might be written without exhausting the subject.

Leaving St. Paul and Westminster Abbey,—both of these churches dedicated to the worship of God, and both transformed into great temples of fame and galleries of sculpture, ill befitting the sacred object for which they were constructed,—we wander through the busy streets of the great, bustling City, and finally reach the Tower, which is, historically, one of the most interesting spots in England. We had read so often of it, and our sympathies had so many times been drawn out toward those who had suffered and died within its dark walls, that, at last, when we entered its portal, it was hard to realize that we were really in the old prison Tower of London. It seemed more like a dream than a reality, but the real soon asserted itself. The deep moat, the dark, heavy walls, the great tower, with walls fifteen feet thick, the dark, gloomy prison cells were all there; and we were made conscious of the fact that we were standing in the place where so many terrible incidents occurred, which darken the pages of English history, and give us an insight into the cruel spirit of the age which has passed away,—may we not fondly hope?—never more to return.

Perhaps no place in Europe, certainly none in England, has witnessed so many sad scenes, and been marked with so many evidences of "man's inhumanity to man," and woman's, too, for that matter, than this same old moated Tower, whose grim and gloomy walls overhang the River Thames in the City of London. Could these stones, upon which we tread as we enter the Tower, speak, what a history of human sorrow and cruelty they could reveal, but they are as silent as are the victims who suffered here in the years that have gone by. Silent and gloomy the old Tower keeps its story, and he that would learn must read the history of the past.

And what a history that is! It is not, however, within the scope or purpose of these "Wanderings" to enter into historical details to any but a very limited extent, and we shall not attempt it in this instance, for the history of the Tower of London is the history of England for many centuries. In turn it has served as a palace for the sovereigns of England, a strong fortress for the City of London, and a dark and gloomy prison over the doors of which, at one time, might well have been written, "He who enters here leaves all hope behind." Kings and queens, bishops and noblemen, warriors and statesmen, women and children, court favorites for a brief season, have passed through the Tower gate as State prisoners, and died within its dark walls without

ance, and all present seemed to be much interested in the meeting. We had three sessions, the last one closing after nine o'clock P. M.

SUBJECTS DISCUSSED.

"The Ministry Fifty Years Ago and Now." First speaker was John Metzger.

"Orthodox Loyalty" was assigned to P. S. Myers, but he being unable to attend, A. Hutchison led off on this subject.

"Practice What You Preach." Discussion on this was opened by D. A. Norcross.

"The Preacher in the Pulpit." J. S. Flory.

"Systematic Preaching." B. F. Masterson.

"Ministerial Qualifications." S. G. Lehmer.

"Sunday-schools, Social Meetings and the Ministry: Their Relation to Each Other." J. F. Neher.

Several volunteer questions were introduced. All the ministers present, as well as other members, took active part in the discussions. The impression seemed to be that the meeting was one out of which much good will result. Sunday following, at 10 P. M., 'Bro. Hutchison preached in the chapel. Saturday, Jan. 2, we attended the quarterly council at Covina. A number of letters were read, several queries discussed and sent to District Meeting. Brethren Peter Overholser and D. A. Norcross were elected delegates to District Meeting.

At a called council of the Lordsburg church, held a few days prior to Christmas, something like a score of members were received by letter, Eld. Isaac Gibble, of Illinois, being one of the number.

The regular quarterly council convened at Lordsburg, Jan. 4. Several more members were received by letter. Brethren Dr. Garst and Peter Hartman were chosen as delegates to District Meeting.

The school is starting out in the second session with quite a number of new students. The long looked-for rains have come at last and everybody seems to be in a mood for rejoicing.

J. S. FLORY.

McPherson Notes.

ON January 2 we had our quarterly council. The attendance was large and all the business was disposed of in a short time, in love and harmony. It was then decided to hold an election for a minister on the following Saturday, when elders and ministers from other congregations should be present to attend the Bible course. To-day the election was held and the result was that two young brethren received nearly the entire vote of the church and nearly the same number of votes. The church decided to call them both to the ministry. The lot fell on Francis Vaniman, son of Eld. Daniel Vaniman, and James Gilbert. Bro. Gilbert finished several courses of study at Mt. Morris and now continues his studies with us. Brother Moses Zigler, who is also attending school from the Chapman congregation, was elected by the congregation in his absence and a unanimous request sent to this congregation, to install him here, which was also done. All are worthy young brethren and may do noble service for the Lord. At the same time this church advanced Bro. Edward Frantz to the second degree in the ministry.

We feel that not only this congregation, but others have been strengthened by this action. The ministerial force here in the West is entirely too small, and a heavy draft is made upon the McPherson church to minister to other congregations and to care for five mission stations.

Elder John Forney delivered the charge to the ministers installed, and Eld. Charles Yearout to the church. We are specially impressed with the propriety of charging the church to perform her duty when she lays unsolicited burdens upon some of her members.

The special Bible class was organized this week with a much larger attendance over t' e beginning last year. The study of the Bible is delightful and the time allotted is much too short for the recitation. One hopeful feature of the class is the interest manifested by the students, not only by the members, but also by those who are not.

The new year has brought in many new students, and the attendance at the college is quite large. We greatly need more means to finish the main building. We think there are many members who have plenty of means, if they knew the self-sacrifice of the members here and the work that is being done, they would be willing and anxious to help the work along.

Last Sunday another precious soul was received into the church by baptism.	S. Z. SHARP.

Baltimore Bible School.

THE following is the report of the Girls and Boys' Bible School, Baltimore, Md., for the fourth quarter, ending Dec. 31, 1891:

RECEIPTS.

Jacob Priser, Silver Lake, Ind.,	$ 50
Little folks, Eel River Sunday-school, Ind.,	2 27
South Waterloo Sunday-school, per Anna Miller,	6 00
A sister, Crimora, Va.,	1 00
A sister, Funkstown, Md.,	2 00
Lick Creek, Sunday-school, per C. L. Newcomer,	1 67
J. S. Harshbarger, Grantsville, Md.,	1 00
Enoch H. Eby, Summerville, Kans.,	1 00
Bene Rober, Waynesborough, Pa.,	1 00
Two sisters, Pasadena, Cal.,	15 00
Nappanee, Ind., Sunday-school, per J. C. Millinger,	3 91
Canton church, Ohio, Thanksgiving offering, per Henry Royer,	5 43
A sister, Gapland, Md.,	1 00
Mary Kuns, McPherson, Kans.,	1 42
Ministerial Meeting, Middle District, Pa., through W. J. Swigart,	12 15
Sisters' Mission, Huntingdon, Pa., through Lizzie B. Howe,	5 00
Abraham Steele, Pa.,	1 32
Miss Nan Smith, Pa.,	1 00
Brethren's Sunday-school, Melrose Centre, Iowa, per Hannah Schwark,	16 00
Midland church, Va., through Abraham Conner,	4 00
A sister, Manassas, Va.,	1 00
A brother and family and friends,	2 00
Total receipts,	$85 67

EXPENDITURES.

Balance from last report,	$11 62
Rent, October, November and December,	21 00
Christmas presents,	7 75
Clothing,	7 50
Fuel and light,	5 18
Helping a brother,	6 00
Medicine,	1 80
Total expenditures,	$60 75
Balance in bank,	$24 92

JAMES T. QUINLAN, Supt.

1315 Light St.

Impressions by the Way.

BY request of the Executive Committee of the Book and Tract Work I visited some of the churches in Eastern Pennsylvania, starting on my trip Nov. 20.

It is true, we are known by the company we keep, and by the study of our associations we learn many useful lessons. If we study with true and honest hearts, we may see what is objectionable and commendable in our comrades and may improve by adopting their good traits, and rejecting that which is objectionable. Be it remembered that a prejudiced mind is not teachable, for unless we bring our likes and dislikes into judgment, we may reject our highest interest.

As we speed on our way, almost at lightning speed during the night, many of the passengers are careless, indifferent and sleeping, even though the next moment may be their last. It presents a sad picture of the human family! How many are rushing on through life, spiritually careless and asleep, not heeding the truth that at any moment God may call them hence! If we, as a church, were to know that ahead there are inevitable causes of death and suffering, how earnest, active, and willing would we be to make almost any sacrifice, to give the warning voice and save the perishing? But what are we doing? What sacrifices are we making to save the poor, perishing sinner? Father, increase our zeal!

Our first work was in the Chiques church, which has a' membership of over 500 members. Here the true merits of Tract Work, as adopted by the church, were not so well known, but, I am thankful to say, due respect was paid to my weak efforts and here, as in my entire trip, when the merits of the Work were known, encouragement and financial aid were given, and I am convinced that the same will be the result all over the Brotherhood, if we all do our duty. One of the salutary influences here is the fact that the elders are loyal to the church and said, "Our heart is in the work." This is as it should be for the lambs will be strong according as they are fed by the shepherds.

I was also impressed by their comfortable, neat and clean houses of worship. As a people, we take great pains to have our meeting-houses attractive, neat and comfortable, which is a Christian duty, for by so doing we create a desire in the hearts of those in whom we are interested, to long for a home with the people of God. In like manner will church-going become desirable, in proportion to the interest manifested by the church, and the more home-like, the greater the attraction, for what is more repulsive than a neglected, poorly-lighted house, with a few cold-hearted people! It is not the mansion that makes home, but the united interest of the inmates. Therefore it is not the rich churches that may be thus blessed, but even our isolated poor may have their wants met, for we are all one family.

While in the depot in Philadelphia, waiting for the train, we noticed the provisions made for reading matter on the Prohibition question, and as I thought on the effect this may have on the rum question, I felt to thank God for the provision the church has made to counteract the effects of sin by its publications. With the provisions made to furnish reading matter to the inmates of hospitals, the depositing of well-chosen tracts in those places may tell in eternity.

The scope of our responsibility was impressed on my mind while in the mint. Here an automatic balance will condemn a coin, if it is found the 1,300dredth part of a grain too light. This weight is so small that it can scarcely be seen by the naked eye, unless on a white ground. When we are placed in the balance of equity, will we be found wanting?—is an individual question to answer.

Our next visit, at the home of our aged and afflicted Eld. Kulp, presented a lesson of blessings, secured only by faith and confidence in Christ. Though sorely afflicted for some time, he is cheerful and patient, trusting in his Father's love. May he, as all other afflicted ones, be remembered in our prayers!

At the Green Tree and Coventry churches our mind was much impressed with the words, "The memory of the just is blest," by the repeated ref-

ance, and all present seemed to be much interested in the meeting. We had three sessions, the last one closing after nine o'clock P. M.

SUBJECTS DISCUSSED.

"The Ministry Fifty Years Ago and Now." First speaker was John Metzgar.

"Orthodox Loyalty" was assigned to P. S. Myers, but he being unable to attend, A. Hutchison led off on this subject.

"Practice What You Preach." Discussion on this was opened by D. A. Norcross.

"The Preacher in the Pulpit." J. S. Flory.

"Systematic Preaching." B. F. Masterson.

"Ministerial Qualifications." S. G. Lehmer.

"Sunday-schools, Social Meetings and the Ministry: Their Relation to Each Other." J. F. Neher.

Several volunteer questions were introduced. All the ministers present, as well as other members, took active part in the discussions. The impression seemed to be that the meeting was one out of which much good will result. Sunday following, at 10 P. M., Bro. Hutchison preached in the chapel. Saturday, Jan. 2, we attended the quarterly council at Covina. A number of letters were read, several queries discussed and sent to District Meeting. Brethren Peter Overholser and D. A. Norcross were elected delegates to District Meeting.

At a called council of the Lordsburg church, held a few days prior to Christmas, something like a score of members were received by letter, Eld. Isaac Gibble, of Illinois, being one of the number.

The regular quarterly council convened at Lordsburg, Jan. 4. Several more members were received by letter. Brethren Dr. Garst and Peter Hartman were chosen as delegates to District Meeting.

The school is starting out in the second session with quite a number of new students. The long looked-for rains have come at last and everybody seems to be in a mood for rejoicing.

J. S. FLORY.

McPherson Notes.

ON January 2 we had our quarterly council. The attendance was large and all the business was disposed of in a short time, in love and harmony. It was then decided to hold an election for a minister on the following Saturday, when elders and ministers from other congregations should be present to attend the Bible course. To-day the election was held and the result was that two young brethren received nearly the entire vote of the church and nearly the same number of votes. The church decided to call them both to the ministry. The lot fell on Francis Vaniman, son of Eld. Daniel Vaniman, and James Gilbert. Bro. Gilbert finished several courses of study at Mt. Morris and now continues his studies with us. Brother Moses Zigler, who is also attending school from the Chapman congregation, was elected by the congregation in his absence and a unanimous request sent to this congregation, to install him here, which was also done. All are worthy young brethren and may do noble service for the Lord. At the same time this church advanced Bro. Edward Frantz to the second degree in the ministry.

We feel that not only this congregation, but others have been strengthened by this action. The ministerial force here in the West is entirely too small, and a heavy draft is made upon the McPherson church to minister to other congregations and to care for five mission stations.

Elder John Forney delivered the charge to the ministers installed, and Eld. Charles Yourout to the church. We are specially impressed with the propriety of charging the church to perform her duty when she lays unsolicited burdens upon some of her members.

The special Bible class was organized this week with a much larger attendance over the beginning last year. The study of the Bible is delightful and the time allotted is much too short for the recitation. One hopeful feature of the class is the interest manifested by the students, not only by the members, but also by those who are not.

The new year has brought in many new students, and the attendance at the college is quite large. We greatly need more means to finish the main building. We think there are many members who have plenty of means, if they knew the self-sacrifice of the members here and the work that is being done, they would be willing and anxious to help the work along.

Last Sunday another precious soul was received into the church by baptism.   S. Z. SHARP.

Baltimore Bible School.

THE following is the report of the Girls' and Boys' Bible School, Baltimore, Md., for the fourth quarter, ending Dec. 31, 1891:

RECEIPTS.

Jacob Priser, Silver Lake, Ind.,........$	50
Little folks, Eel River Sunday-school, Ind.,	2 27
South Waterloo Sunday-school, per Anna Miller, ...	6 00
A sister, Orimora, Va., ...	1 00
A sister, Funkstown, Md., ...	2 00
Lick Creek, Sunday-school, per C. L. Newcomer, ...	1 67
J. S. Harshbarger, Grantsville, Md., ...	1 00
Enoch H. Eby, Summerville, Kans., ...	1 00
Bene Roher, Waynesborough, Pa., ...	1 00
Two sisters, Pasadena, Cal., ...	15 00
Nappanee, Ind., Sunday-school, per J. C. Millinger, ...	3 91
Canton church, Ohio, Thanksgiving offering, per Henry Royer, ...	5 43
A sister, Gapland, Md., ...	1 00
Mary Kuns, McPherson, Kans., ...	1 42
Ministerial Meeting, Middle District, Pa., through W. J. Swigart, ...	12 15
Sisters' Mission, Huntingdon, Pa., through Lizzie B. Howe, ...	5 00
Abraham Steele, Pa., ...	1 32
Miss Nan Smith, Pa., ...	1 00
Brethren's Sunday-school, Melrose Centre, Iowa, per Hannah Schwark, ...	16 00
Midland church, Va., through Abraham Conner, ...	4 00
A sister, Manassas, Va., ...	1 00
A brother and family and friends, ...	2 00
Total receipts, ...$85 67	

EXPENDITURES.

Balance from last report, ...$11 52	
Rent, October, November and December,..	21 00
Christmas presents, ...	7 75
Clothing, ...	7 50
Fuel and light, ...	5 18
Helping a brother, ...	6 00
Medicine, ...	1 80
Total expenditures, ...$60 75	
Balance in bank, ...$24 92	

JAMES T. QUINLAN, Supt.

1315 Light St.

Impressions by the Way.

BY request of the Executive Committee of the Book and Tract Work I visited some of the churches in Eastern Pennsylvania, starting on my trip Nov. 20.

It is true, we are known by the company we keep, and by the study of our associations we learn many useful lessons. If we study with true and honest hearts, we may see what is objection-

able and commendable in our comrades and may improve by adopting their good traits, and rejecting that which is objectionable. Be it remembered that a prejudiced mind is not teachable, for unless we bring our likes and dislikes into judgment, we may reject our highest interest.

As we speed on our way, almost at lightning speed during the night, many of the passengers are careless, indifferent and sleeping, even though the next moment may be their last. It presents a sad picture of the human family! How many are rushing on through life, spiritually careless and asleep, not heeding the truth that at any moment God may call them hence! If we, as a church, were to know that ahead there are inevitable causes of death and suffering, how earnest, active, and willing would we be to make almost any sacrifice, to give the warning voice and save the perishing! But what are we doing? What sacrifices are we making to save the poor, perishing sinner? Father, increase our zeal!

Our first work was in the Chiques church, which has a membership of over 500 members. Here the true merits of Tract Work, as adopted by the church, were not so well known, but, I am thankful to say, due respect was paid to my weak efforts and here, as in my entire trip, when the merits of the Work were known, encouragement and financial aid were given, and I am convinced that the same will be the result all over the Brotherhood, if we all do our duty. One of the salutary influences here is the fact that the elders are loyal to the church and said, "Our heart is in the work." This is as it should be for the lambs will be strong according as they are fed by the shepherds.

I was also impressed by their comfortable, neat and clean houses of worship. As a people, we take great pains to have our meeting-houses attractive, neat and comfortable, which is a Christian duty, for by so doing we create a desire in the hearts of those in whom we are interested, to long for a home with the people of God. In like manner will church-going become desirable, in proportion to the interest manifested by the church, and the more home-like, the greater the attraction, for what is more repulsive than a neglected, poorly-lighted house, with a few cold-hearted people! It is not the mansion that makes home, but the united interest of the inmates. Therefore it is not the rich churches that may be thus blessed, but even our isolated poor may have their wants met, for we are all one family.

While in the depot in Philadelphia, waiting for the train, we noticed the provisions made for reading matter on the Prohibition question, and as I thought on the effect this may have on the rum question, I felt to thank God for the provision the church has made to counteract the effects of its publications. With the provisions made to furnish reading matter to the inmates of hospitals, the depositing of well-chosen tracts in those places may tell in eternity.

The scope of our responsibility was impressed on my mind while in the mint. Here an automatic balance will condemn a coin, if it is found the 1,300dredth part of a grain too light. This weight is so small that it can scarcely be seen by the naked eye, unless on a white ground. When we are placed in the balance of equity, will we be found wanting?—is an individual question to answer.

Our next visit, at the home of our aged and afflicted Eld. Kulp, presented a lesson of resignation, secured only by faith and confidence in Christ. Though sorely afflicted for some time, he is cheerful and patient, trusting in his Father's love. May he, as all other afflicted ones, be remembered in our prayers!

At the Green Tree and Coventry churches our mind was much impressed with the words, "The memory of the just is blest," by the repeated ref-

could soon be a large congregation built up. Any one wishing to learn more about the locality, will please address Bro. Isaac Brown, Ollie, Keokuk Co., Iowa. There is certainly a very kindhearted congregation of dear brethren and sisters there; also a community of warm friends to the Brethren.

At present I am at a point fifteen miles north of the City of Des Moines, where I commenced meetings last night. The weather is cold and stormy, but we hope for the best.

WM. C. HIPES.

Jan. 8.

From River, Ind.

ON the morning of Jan. 12 wife and I were called to Bro. Levi Hoover's, to see their sick son, twenty-three years of age, who has been under medical treatment for about ten months, for consumption. He is very much reduced, and not improving at all. We had visited him several times before, and conversed with him, in regard to his future state. He could not fully decide what to do till yesterday. After asking and answering some important questions, he firmly decided to be baptized.

Arrangements were made to take him to a creek near by, on, what we call, a "mud boat." On this the applicant was taken to the creek. After baptism he was taken back to the house again, where already some preparations had been made for a Communion in the evening.

Examination services commenced a little before 6 o'clock. Nine brethren and nine sisters communed. It was, indeed, a feast to the soul to the dear young brother, as well as the rest of us. After the feast, the young brother was anointed with oil in the name of the Lord. This was one of the most solemn occasions of the many that I have witnessed. Soon after this, nearly all present went to their homes, no doubt with much solemnity in their hearts, and praising God for what they had seen and felt. Wife and I remained till morning, when we left for our home. At that time the young brother was feeling quite comfortable, for which we praise the Lord.

We are having solid winter weather at present. Several times the thermometer has fallen below zero.

My health is not good at this time, but I thank the Lord that it is as well with me as it is.

SAMUEL MURRAY.

Notes from Our Correspondents.

"As cold water to a thirsty soul, so is good news from a far country."

Wyman, Ark.—The death messenger visited our house last night again, and took from us wife's dear mother (Ann M. Cosner), widow of Eld. Martin Cosner). Truly a Christian mother has gone home. She was in every respect a noble Christian. The cause of her death was pneumonia, from which she suffered only one week. Let us all prepare to meet the saints!—*Samuel Weimer, Jan. 14.*

Brownsville, Md.—We contemplate holding a series of meetings at the Brownsville meeting-house, beginning Feb. 6. Bro. Silas Hoover is expected to do the preaching, and if the weather is favorable, we anticipate a good meeting. We trust that the brethren and sisters will make the matter a subject of fervent prayer, that the weak may be strengthened and that some of the wandering sheep may be gathered into the fold. Some of us have dear ones away from Christ, for whom we feel a deep concern, and if we work in the Lord's way, their conversion will be accomplished.—*G. W. Kaetzel.*

Eagle's Mills, Md.—Bro. Jonas Fike, of Eglon, W. Va., commenced a series of meetings in the Bear Creek congregation, Garrett Co., Md., on the evening before Christmas. He preached each evening, and also on Christmas and New Year's Day at 10:30 A. M., until Jan. 3. Four united with the church, and were baptized during the meetings. The extent of the good, accomplished at the meetings, will only be known in the great beyond.—*S. A. Miller.*

Jones Mills, Pa.—We are in the midst of a glorious series of meetings. Bro. D. H. Walker, of Lull, Somerset Co., Pa., came to us on the evening of Jan. 2, and preached thirteen sermons. As an immediate result twelve dear souls were added to the church by baptism and one was reclaimed. There are three more applicants for baptism at this writing, and the meetings are still going on. As Bro. Walker had to go home, Bro. Robert Hull, of Bakersville, came to assist us in the good work.—*D. D. Horner, Jan. 12.*

Salem, Ohio.—We commenced a series of meetings on the evening of Jan. 7. Bro. Henry Frantz was to do the preaching for us, but was taken sick with *La Grippe,* and, therefore, not able to come, so the home ministers conducted the meeting until last evening, when Bro. Daniel Snell, of Indiana, came to us. He intends preaching for us until Sunday evening. We hope by that time Bro. Frantz will be well enough to labor for us. We are having good meetings. May the Lord bless our efforts!—*Jesse K. Brumbaugh, Jan. 13.*

Grater's Ford, Pa.—We have just closed a series of very interesting meetings in our chapel. Bro. Hope stopped with us on his return from Denmark. He came to us *filled* with the spirit, and dealt out to us the Bread of Life in such measure as to greatly build up and strengthen the saints: While there were no additions to the church, still we feel his visit to us has been of benefit. Bro. Hope is an able man, and can "give a reason for the hope there is in him." May God greatly bless his labors for the Lord's cause!—*Emma Kulp, Jan. 12.*

Aurelia, Iowa.—The Maple Valley church, Iowa, has been much strengthened and built up through the preaching of Bro. Reeves, from Spencer, and Bro. Albright, from Grundy Center. These brethren came to us Dec. 24, and conducted meetings both day and evening for one week. They are both young in years, but, by their earnestness and zeal for the Master's cause, they showed us an example which we may safely follow. Although there were no additions to the church, we think there were good impressions made, and we feel that these meetings did us much good, by way of binding us closer into the bonds of Christian fellowship and love. Dear brethren, let us press on in God's service, for we surely will be doubly rewarded in the end!—*Norman S. Eby.*

Reann, Ind.—Bro. Aaron Moss, from Ridgeway, Howard Co., Ind., came to us and began a series of meetings at the Enterprise meeting-house, Jan. 2, and continued until the evening of the 12th. He delivered, in all, twelve discourses, to fair congregations, considering the rough roads and the inclement weather. Many are confined to their rooms, on account of bad colds and *La Grippe,* and are thus deprived of enjoying the meetings. Bro. Moss is a fearless expounder of the Gospel. He gave us much spiritual food, and impressed upon us the great duty we owe to God. As a result of these meetings a middle-aged father was baptized, and others are near the kingdom. The Lord be praised for all the good!—*Joseph John, Jan. 13.*

Belleville, Pa.—The brethren of the Kishacoquillas Valley held a very interesting series of meetings in Gibboney's school-house, near Belleville, commencing Jan. 2, and closing Jan 10. The meetings were conducted by Bro. Brice Sell, of Newry, Blair Co., Pa. On Sunday, Jan. 10, Bro. Sell preached in the Belleville Methodist church to a large and appreciative audience.—*E. B. Grassmyer.*

To the Churches of Middle Indiana.—By order of District Meeting, the churches were to raise two hundred dollars for building a church-house at Kewana, and as I was placed on the building committee, and made treasurer of the same, I would be glad to have all the funds for building forwarded as soon as possible, as we desire to order material. I hope that all will respond soon.—*S. M. Aukerman, Somerset, Ind.*

Fergy, Ohio.—I have had a severe attack of *La Grippe* recently, which confined me to the house for nearly three weeks. This caused me to miss all of the series of meetings at Donald's Creek, with the exception of four meetings. Our meetings will close by to-morrow evening. Wife and daughter, who were also afflicted with *La Grippe,* are somewhat better. I hope that I may soon be able to fill the calls for meetings, for which I had made previous arrangements. — *Henry Frantz, Jan. 9.*

Somerset, Ind.—Bro. D. P. Shively, of Peru, Ind., began a series of meetings Dec. 26, and continued until Jan. 9. During this time we had some very unfavorable weather and bad roads, as well as some sickness in the neighborhood, but, with all these disadvantages, we had a glorious season of worship. We had good attendance, the best of order and a good interest. All seemed to awaken to a sense of their duty. As an immediate result four were baptized and others seemed to be seriously impressed. We have reasons to believe that much good will result from these meetings.—*S. M. Aukerman.*

Lower Miami, Ohio.—We have just closed a very interesting series of meetings. Bro. Daniel Bock, of Ridgeway, Ind., came to us on Christmas eve, and continued meetings until Jan. 1, when he was assisted by Bro. Joseph Holder, of Deweyville, Ohio. These dear brethren did not shun to declare the whole counsel of God, and while none were added to the church, yet we think many good impressions were made. On account of sickness in the neighborhood, these meetings were not as well attended as they otherwise would have been. At the close of the meetings, Jan. 10, a young brother, who has been very sick, requested to be anointed, which was attended to by the Brethren. We hope the Lord may spare his life. May he ever bless and prosper these brethren for their labors of love while among us!—*Lizzie Van-scoyk.*

Rossville, Ind.—Eld. D. S. Caylor, of Wabash County, Ind., came to the North Fork church, Carroll Co., Ind., Dec. 17, and commenced preaching the same evening in the upper meeting-house, near Owasco. Here he continued the meetings each evening until the 27th. Bro. Caylor, though not well part of the time, preached the Word with power. Though there were no immediate accessions, we feel that good and lasting impressions were made. The meetings at this place closed with an increased interest. On the evening of Dec. 28, Bro. Caylor commenced meetings in the Ockley school-house. If sinners will not be saved, we feel that our brethren have done their duty. There were no accessions at this place, but there is a time to sow and a time to reap. The meetings here closed Dec. 31.—*D. A. Hufford, Jan. 15.*

could soon be a large congregation built up. Any one wishing to learn more about the locality, will please address Bro. Isaac Brown, Ollie, Keokuk Co., Iowa. There is certainly a very kind-hearted congregation of dear brethren and sisters there; also a community of warm friends to the Brethren.

At present I am at a point fifteen miles north of the City of Des Moines, where I commenced meetings last night. The weather is cold and stormy, but we hope for the best.

Jan. 8.   WM. C. HIPES.

From River, Ind.

ON the morning of Jan. 12 wife and I were called to Bro. Levi Hoover's, to see their sick son, twenty-three years of age, who has been under medical treatment for about ten months, for consumption. He is very much reduced, and not improving at all. We had visited him several times before, and conversed with him, in regard to his future state. He could not fully decide what to do till yesterday. After asking and answering some important questions, he firmly decided to be baptized.

Arrangements were made to take him to a creek near by on, what we call, a "mud boat." On this the applicant was taken to the creek. After baptism he was taken back to the house again, where already some preparations had been made for a Communion in the evening.

Examination services commenced a little before 6 o'clock. Nine brethren and nine sisters communed. It was, indeed, a feast to the soul to the dear young brother, as well as the rest of us. After the feast, the young brother was anointed with oil in the name of the Lord. This was one of the most solemn occasions of the many that I have witnessed. Soon after this, nearly all present went to their homes, no doubt with much solemnity in their hearts, and praising God for what they had seen and felt. Wife and I remained till morning, when we left for our home. At that time the young brother was feeling quite comfortable, for which we praise the Lord.

We are having solid winter weather at present. Several times the thermometer has fallen below zero.

My health is not good at this time, but I thank the Lord that it is as well with me as it is.

SAMUEL MURRAY.

Notes from Our Correspondents.

"A cold water to a thirsty soul, so is good news from a far country."

Wyman, Ark.—The death messenger visited our house last night again, and took from us wife's dear mother (Ann M. Cosner, widow of Eld. Martin Cosner). Truly a Christian mother has gone home. She was in every respect a noble Christian. The cause of her death was pneumonia, from which she suffered only one week. Let us all prepare to meet the saints!—Samuel Weimer, Jan. 14.

Brownsville, Md.—We contemplate holding a series of meetings at the Brownsville meeting-house, beginning Feb. 6. Bro. Silas Hoover is expected to do the preaching, and if the weather is favorable, we anticipate a good meeting. We trust that the brethren and sisters will make the matter a subject of fervent prayer, that the weak may be strengthened and that some of the wandering sheep may be gathered into the fold. Some of us have dear ones away from Christ, for whom we feel a deep concern, and if we work in the Lord's way, their conversion will be accomplished.—G. W. Kaetzel.

Eagle's Mills, Md.—Bro. Jonas Fike, of Eglon, W. Va., commenced a series of meetings in the Bear Creek congregation, Garrett Co., Md., on the evening before Christmas. He preached each evening, and also on Christmas and New Year's Day at 10:30 A. M., until Jan. 3. Four united with the church, and were baptized during the meetings. The extent of the good, accomplished at the meetings, will only be known in the great beyond.—S. A. Miller.

Jones Mills, Pa.—We are in the midst of a glorious series of meetings. Bro. D. H. Walker, of Lull, Somerset Co., Pa., came to us on the evening of Jan. 2, and preached thirteen sermons. As an immediate result twelve dear souls were added to the church by baptism and one was reclaimed. There are three more applicants for baptism at this writing, and the meetings are still going on. As Bro. Walker had to go home, Bro. Robert Hull, of Bakersville, came to assist us in the good work.—D. D. Horner, Jan. 12.

Salem, Ohio.—We commenced a series of meetings on the evening of Jan. 7. Bro. Henry Frantz was to do the preaching for us, but was taken sick with La Grippe, and, therefore, not able to come, so the home ministers conducted the meeting until last evening, when Bro. Daniel Snell, of Indiana, came to us. He intends preaching for us until Sunday evening. We hope by that time Bro. Frantz will be well enough to labor for us. We are having good meetings. May the Lord bless our efforts!—Jesse K. Brumbaugh, Jan. 13.

Grater's Ford, Pa.—We have just closed a series of very interesting meetings in our chapel. Bro. Hope stopped with us on his return from Denmark. He came to us filled with the spirit, and dealt out to us the Bread of Life in such measure as to greatly build up and strengthen the saints. While there were no additions to the church, still we feel his visit to us has been of benefit. Bro. Hope is an able man, and can "give a reason for the hope there is in him." May God greatly bless his labors for the Lord's cause!—Emma Kulp, Jan. 12.

Aurelia, Iowa.—The Maple Valley church, Iowa, has been much strengthened and built up through the preaching of Bro. Reeves, from Spencer, and Bro. Albright, from Grundy Center. These brethren came to us Dec. 24, and conducted meetings both day and evening for one week. They are both young in years, but, by their earnestness and zeal for the Master's cause, they showed us an example which we may safely follow. Although there were no additions to the church, we think there were good impressions made, and we feel that these meetings did us much good, by way of binding us closer into the bonds of Christian fellowship and love. Dear brethren, let us press on in God's service, for we surely will be doubly rewarded in the end!—Norman S. Eby.

Reams, Ind.—Bro. Aaron Moss, from Ridgeway, Howard Co., Ind., came to us and began a series of meetings at the Enterprise meeting-house, Jan. 2, and continued until the evening of the 19th. He delivered, in all, twelve discourses, to fair congregations, considering the rough roads and the inclement weather. Many are confined to their rooms, on account of bad colds and La Grippe, and are thus deprived of enjoying the meetings. Bro. Moss is a fearless expounder of the Gospel. He gave us much spiritual food, and impressed upon us the great duty we owe to God. As a result of those meetings a middle-aged father was baptized, and others are near the kingdom. The Lord be praised for all the good!—Joseph John, Jan. 13.

Belleville, Pa.—The brethren of the Kishacoquillas Valley held a very interesting series of meetings in Gibboney's school-house, near Belleville, commencing Jan. 2, and closing Jan. 10. The meetings were conducted by Bro. Brice Sell, of Newry, Blair Co., Pa. On Sunday, Jan. 10, Bro. Sell preached in the Belleville Methodist church to a large and appreciative audience.—E. B. Grassmyer.

To the Churches of Middle Indiana.—By order of District Meeting, the churches were to raise two hundred dollars for building a church-house at Kewana, and as I was placed on the building committee, and made treasurer of the same, I would be glad to have all the funds for building forwarded as soon as possible, as we desire to order material. I hope that all will respond soon.—S. M. Aukerman, Somerset, Ind.

Fergy, Ohio.—I have had a severe attack of La Grippe recently, which confined me to the house for nearly three weeks. This caused me to miss all of the series of meetings at Donald's Creek, with the exception of four meetings. Our meetings will close by to-morrow evening. Wife and daughter, who were also afflicted with La Grippe, are somewhat better. I hope that I may soon be able to fill the calls for meetings, for which I had made previous arrangements.—Henry Frantz, Jan. 9.

Somerset, Ind.—Bro. D. P. Shively, of Peru, Ind., began a series of meetings Dec. 26, and continued until Jan. 9. During this time we had some very unfavorable weather and bad roads, as well as some sickness in the neighborhood, but, with all these disadvantages, we had a glorious season of worship. We had good attendance, the best of order and a good interest. All seemed to awaken to a sense of their duty. As an immediate result four were baptized and others seemed to be seriously impressed. We have reasons to believe that much good will result from these meetings.—S. M. Aukerman.

Lower Miami, Ohio.—We have just closed a very interesting series of meetings. Bro. Daniel Bock, of Ridgeway, Ind., came to us on Christmas eve, and continued meetings until Jan. 1, when he was assisted by Bro. Joseph Holder, of Deweyville, Ohio. These dear brethren did not shun to declare the whole counsel of God, and while none were added to the church, yet we think many good impressions were made. On account of sickness in the neighborhood, these meetings were not as well attended as they otherwise would have been. At the close of the meetings, Jan. 10, a young brother, who has been very sick, requested to be anointed, which was attended to by the Brethren. We hope the Lord may spare his life. May he ever bless and prosper those brethren for their labors of love while among us!—Lizzie Van scoyk.

Rossville, Ind.—Eld. D. S. Caylor, of Wabash County, Ind., came to the North Fork church, Carroll Co., Ind., Dec. 17, and commenced preaching the same evening in the upper meeting-house, near Owasco. Here he continued the meetings each evening until the 27th. Bro. Caylor, though not well part of the time, preached the Word with power. Though there were no immediate accessions, we feel that good and lasting impressions were made. The meetings at this place closed with an increased interest. On the evening of Dec. 28, Bro. Caylor commenced meetings in the Ockley school-house. If sinners will not be saved, we feel that our brethren have done their duty. There were no accessions at this place, but there is a time to sow and a time to reap. The meetings here closed Dec. 31.—D. A. Hufford, Jan. 15.

the age of twenty-one years he was married to Mary Ann Keltner, after which time they moved to Elkhart County, Ind., in the year 1855. They reared a family of eight children,—four sons and four daughters, all of whom were present to witness the departure of the aged father. The mother and wife preceded him to the tomb about three years. Twenty-three grandchildren and one great-grandchild are still living. Funeral services by D. Shively. J. H. MILLER.

KREIDER.—In the bounds of the Lower Cumberland church, near Hagerstown, Pa., Dec. 26, 1891, Mary Edna Kreider, infant daughter of Emmanuel and Lizzie Kreider, aged 5 months and 4 days.

; Services by the writer, from Matt. 19: 14. Interment at Miller's church near Sterrett's Gap. HENRY BEELMAN.

MILLER.—In the Valley church, Augusta Co., Va., Dec. 23, 1891, sister Fannie Miller, wife of Eld' John Miller, deceased, aged 71 years, 1 month and 29 days.

Deceased leaves seven children and many relatives and friends to mourn their loss, which, we believe, was her eternal gain. Sister Miller was a great' sufferer from rheumatism and dropsy for some years and unable to walk for nearly two years, but she was never heard to murmur, and bore her afflictions with Christian fortitude.

She was a devoted Christian mother, her life being an exemplary one, and will long be remembered by those to whom she was near and dear.

Deceased was a sister of elders Jacob Brower, of South English, Iowa, and John Brower, of Derrance, Kans.

Eld. John preceded her to the spirit world a little over four years. May the children prepare themselves to be again re-united in the kingdom of heaven! The funeral services were conducted by brethren A. D. Garber and Daniel Miller from 1 Pet. 2: 7.

DANIEL MILLER.

ARNOLD.—At Marcus, Iowa, Nov. 15, '1891' of consumption, Bro. Franklin D. Arnold, aged 54 years, 6 months and 1 day.

Deceased leaves a mother, wife and nine children, one brother, three sisters and a large circle of friends to mourn their loss. Truly, a righteous man has fallen asleep. He was unit d in marriage to Miss Mary Lehman Nov. 1, 1860, both of Defiance, Ohio. He was baptized into Christ in 1861 and lived a devoted Christian life. As in business, so in spiritual matters, he set his house in order, and testified to all that enquired into his welfare that all was well. He was fully resigned to the Lord's will.

Funeral services conducted by Rev. T. E. Carter, of the M. E. church, from Rev. 14: 13. H. B. LEHMAN.

HILE.—In the Lower Cumberland church, Pa., Dec. 29, 1891, Mary Hile, wife of John Hile, aged about 33 years.

Deceased, with her husband, came to our place March 26, both claiming to be members of the church. DAVID NIESLY.

MILLER.—In the Indian Creek congrega- tion, Fayette Co., Pa., Dec. 24, 1891, Free- man Miller, aged 17 years, 5 months and 11 days.

The subject of the above notice was a son of Bro. Amos M. and' sister Mary Miller. He, with an older brother, went out to cut down timber for a new barn. In felling the first tree, a limb broke and flew back, killing him instantly. Funeral services conducted by the writer, assisted by the home pastor, to a very large audience. D. D. HORNER.

HORN.—In the bounds of the Libertyville church, Van Buren Co., Iowa, Samuel Glenn, son of friend Frank and Nora Horn, aged 1 month and 18 days.

Funeral services conducted by the writer to a large and sympathizing congregation.

ABRAHAM WOLF.

HARSHBERGER.—In the Middle District, Miami Co., Ohio, Dec. 18, 1891, Elizabeth Ann' Harshberger, last daughter and child of Bro. Henry and sister Sarah Harshberg- er, aged 57 years, 7 months and 16 days.

Deceased fell victim to that much-dread- ed disease, consumption, from witch she suf- fered for several years. However slowly, yet surely it did Its work. Owing to the afflic- tion of the surviving parent, the funeral serv- ice took place at the home, by the under- signed, from 2 ings 20: 1. D. S. FILBRUN.

HARSHBERGER.—In the same congrega- tion and family, Dec. 24, 1891, Bro. Henry Harshberger, aged 81 years, 10 months and 12 days.

The subject of this notice is the one above alluded to. Bro. Harshberger was born in Rockingham County, Va., Feb. 12, 1810. He was one of the pioneers of Miami County, Ohio, having settled within its then wild bor- ders about the year 1830. Many, and some- times severe, were his trials, anxieties and dis- appointments in life, and many times, since the death of his companion, which occurred about five years ago, and the affliction of his daughter, did he express himself as wishing to remain in this world only so long as his daughter was permitted to remain. He said, "When Lizzie is gone I have nothing more for which to live here." When I bade him farewell on Sunday morning, after the funer- al service of his daughter, he said, " Bro. Dav- id, I am so lonely, but it won't be long and I am ready."

Bro. Harshberger was a kind father and husband, a devoted and consistent member for many years. Funeral occasion improved by the undersigned from 2 Tim. 4: 6, 7, 8.

D. S. FILBRUN.

DILLER.—In Churchtown, Pa., Dec. 30, 1891, Mrs. Solomon Diller, aged 82 years.

DAVID NIESLY.

WILLIAMS.—In Everett, Pa., Dec. 18, 1891, of La Grippe, J. B. Williams, aged about 60 years.

He leaves a wife and seven children to mourn their loss. He was the leading mer- chant of Everett. His remains were interred in the Everett cemetery.

CARRIE RITCHEY.

NEGLY—At Farmington, Ill., Nov. 13, 1891, Bro. David L. Negley, aged 20 years, 7 months and 28 days.

Deceased was a son of Bro. J. A. and sis- ter Sarah Negley, and was an exemplary young man, liked by all who knew him. Knowing that, owing to sickness, he must soon cross the river of death, he became deep- ly concerned about his soul's salvation and requested to be baptized. Bro. on Oct. 20, 1891, we complied with his request and he arose, rejoicing in the hope of eternal life and expressed himself, at different times, as being satisfied and ready to go.' Funeral services by the writer to a large audience.

He leaves a sorrowing father and mother, three brothers and two sisters.

SOLOMON BUCKLEW.

CUSHWA.—In the Hickory Grove church, Miami Co., Ohio; Dec. 4, 1881, Corn Ann Cushwa, daughter of friend James Cushwa, aged 24 years, 1 month and 7 days.

The deceased, while away from home, took ill and died of hemorrhage. Funeral services conducted by the writer from Rom. 8: 1. D. S. FILBRUN.

SEIGHMAN.—In the same church, Dec. 9, 1891, Bro. Jacob Seighman, aged 80 years, 10 months and 21 days.

Deceased was born in Lancaster County, Pa., Jan. 18, 1809, and was married to Catha- rine Bashor, of McAllisterville, Juniata Co., Pa., about fifty-nine years ago. He emigrat- ed to this State, to the place near where his death occurred, fifty-three years ago. His wife, two children, eleven grandchildren and nine great-grandchildren survive him. Bro. Seighman was a consistent member of the Brethren church Funeral occasion improved by the writer, assisted by Bro. Henry Gump, from 1 Thess. 4: 14. D. S. FILBRUN.

CHARLES.—In the bounds of the Rockton church, Pa., Jan. 1, 1892, Mrs. Samantha Charles, wife of Rodney Charles, aged 41 years, 7 months and 19 days. Funeral serv- ices conducted by the writer from 1 Cor. 15: 19-22. J. H. BEER.

→PUBLICATIONS←

☞The following books, Sunday-school supplies, etc., are for sale by the BRETH- REN'S PUBLISHING CO., Mt. Morris, Ill., or Huntingdon, Pa., to whom all orders should be addressed.

The Brethren's Quarterly.

For Sunday-school teachers and scholars this publi- cation is of the greatest benefit. Look at our prices:
Single subscription, one year, ... 35 cents.
Single subscription, per quarter, ... 10 cents.
Three copies, per quarter, ... 25 cents.
Eight copies, per quarter, ... 20 cents
Twenty copies and over, ... 2 cents each.

Hymn Books.

New Tune and Hymn Books.

Half leather, per copy, post-paid, ... $ 75
Morocco, per copy, post-paid, ... 1 00
Morocco, gilt edge, per copy, post-paid, ... 1 25

Hymn Books.

Morocco, per copy, post-paid, ... $ 75
Morocco, gilt edge, per copy, post-paid, ... 85
Arabesque, per copy, post-paid, ... 40
Morocco, per copy, post-paid, ... 75
Fine Limp, gilt edge, per copy, post-paid, ... 85
Fine Limp, gilt edge, per copy, post-paid, ... 75
German and English, per copy, post-paid, ... 75

Sunday-School Requisites.

The following list of things is needed in all Sunday- schools:
Testaments, Flexible, red edge, per dozen, ... $1 00
Minute Books, each, ... 40
Class Books, per dozen, ... 75
S. S. Primers, with fine engravings, per dozen, .. 20

New and Beautiful Sunday-School Cards.

" The Gem," in picture cards, each with Bible text, verse of hymn, ... 35
250 Reward Tickets—verse of Scripture—red or blue, ... 15

The Young Disciple.

The YOUNG DISCIPLE is a neatly printed weekly, published especially for the moral benefit and reli- gious instruction of our young folks.
Single copy, one year, ... 50
Six copies (the sixth to the agent), ... 2 50
Ten copies, ... 4 00

For Three Months or Thirteen Weeks.

10 copies to one address, ... $1 20
20 " " " 2 25
30 " " " 3 35
40 " " " 3 50
50 " " " 5 00
100 " " " 7 00

For Six Months or Twenty-Six Weeks.

20 copies to one address, ... $ 3 35
30 " " " 5 00
50 " " " 6 50
75 " " " 7 50
100 " " " 13 75

Our paper is designed for the Sunday-school and the home circle. We desire the name of every Sunday- school Superintendent in the Brotherhood, and want an agent in every church. Send for sample copies.

Certificates of Membership

We have just printed a new edition of these very convenient certificates. Several improvements over the old style are notice- able, such as perforated stubs, firm, yet smooth, paper, etc. Price only 50 cents per book. Every congregation should have one. Address this office.

The Monon Route.

This road is running a fine line of Pullman Buffet Sleepers between Chicago and Indian- apolis, Cincinnati and Louisville, in connec- tion with the fast Florida express trains.

For full information, address, E. O. Mc- CORMICK, General Passenger Agent, Adams Express Building, Chicago. (City Ticket Of fice, 75 Clark St.)

Send for our new Bible Catalogue. Prices to suit the times. We have a large variety and the most durable as well as ornamental binding.

the age of twenty-one years he was married to Mary Ann Keltner, after which time they moved to Elkhart County, Ind., in the year 1855. They reared a family of eight children,—four sons and four daughters, all of whom were present to witness the departure of the aged father. The mother and wife preceded him to the tomb about three years. Twenty-three grandchildren and one great-grandchild are still living. Funeral services by D. Shively.　　　　J. H. MILLER.

KREIDER.—In the bounds of the Lower Cumberland church, near Hagerstown, Pa., Dec. 26, 1891, Mary Edna Kreider, infant daughter of Emmanuel and Lizzie Kreider, aged 5 months and 4 days.

Services by the writer from Matt. 19: 14. Interment at Miller's church near Sterrett's Gap.　　　　HENRY BEELMAN.

MILLER.—In the Valley church, Augusta Co., Va., Dec. 22, 1891, sister Fannie Miller, wife of Eld' John Miller, deceased, aged 71 years, 1 month and 29 days.

Deceased leaves seven children and many relatives and friends to mourn their loss, which, we believe, was her eternal gain. Sister Miller was a great sufferer from rheumatism and dropsy for some years and unable to walk for nearly two years, but she was never heard to murmur, and bore her afflictions with Christian fortitude.

She was a devoted Christian mother, her life being an exemplary one, and will long be remembered by those to whom she was near and dear.

Deceased was a sister of elders Jacob Brower, of South English, Iowa, and John Brower, of Dorrance, Kans.

Eld. John preceded her to the spirit world a little over four years. May the children prepare themselves to be again re-united in the kingdom of heaven! The funeral services were conducted by brethren A. D. Garber and Daniel Miller from 1 Pet. 2: 7.
　　　　　　DANIEL MILLER.

ARNOLD.—At Marcus, Iowa, Nov. 15, 1891, of consumption, Bro. Franklin D. Arnold, aged 34 years, 6 months and 1 day.

Deceased leaves a mother, wife and nine children, one brother, three sisters and a large circle of friends to mourn their loss. Truly, a right-eous man has fallen asleep. He was unit'd in marriage to Miss Mary Lehman Nov. 1, 1860, both of Defiance, Ohio. He was baptised into Christ in 1861 and lived a devoted Christian life. As in business, so in spiritual matters, he set his house in order, and testified to all that enquired into his welfare that'all was well. He was fully resigned to the Lord's will.

Funeral services conducted by Rev. T. E. Carter, of the M. E. church, from Rev. 14: 13.　　　　H. B. LEHMAN.

HILE.—In the Lower Cumberland church, Pa., Dec. 29, 1891, Mary Hile, wife of John Hile, aged about 33 years.

Deceased, with her husband, came to our church March 26, both claiming to be members of that church.　　　　DAVID NIESLY.

MILLER.—In the Indian Creek congregation, Fayette Co., Pa., Dec. 24, 1891, Freeman Miller, aged 17 years, 5 months and 15 days

The subject of the above notice was a son of-Bro. Amos M. and sister Mary Miller. He, with an older brother, went out to cut down timber for a new barn. In felling the first tree, a limb broke and flew back, killing him instantly. Funeral services conducted by the writer, assisted by the home pastor, to a very large audience.　　　　D. D. HORNER.

HORN.—In the bounds of the Libertyville chuch, Van Buren Co., Iowa, Samuel Glenn, son of friend Frank and Nora Horn, aged 5 months and 18 days.

Funeral services conducted by the writer to a large and sympathizing congregation.
　　　　　　ABRAHAM WOLF.

HARSHBERGER.—In the Middle District, Miami Co., Ohio, Dec. 18, 1891, Elizabeth Ann Harshberger, last daughter and child of Bro. Henry and sister Sarah Harshberger, aged 57 years, 7 months and 16 days.

Deceased fell victim to that much-dreaded disease, consumption, from which she suffered for several years. However slowly, yet surely it did its work. Owing to the affliction of the surviving parent, the funeral services took place at the home, by the undersigned, from 2 ings 20: 1.
　　　　　　D. S. FILBRUN.

HARSHBERGER.—In the same congregation and family, Dec. 24, 1891, Bro. Henry Harshberger, aged 81 years, 10 months and 12 days.

The subject of this notice is the one above alluded to. Bro. Harshberger was born in Rockingham County, Va., Feb. 12, 1810. He was one of the pioneers of Miami County, Ohio, having settled within its them wild borders about the year 1830. Many, and sometimes severe, were his trials, anxieties and disappointments in life, and many times, since the death of his companion, which occurred about five years ago, and the affliction of his daughter, did he express himself as wishing to remain in this world only so long as his daughter was permitted to remain. He said, "When Lizzie is gone I have nothing more for which to live here." When I bade him farewell on Sunday morning, after the funeral service of his daughter, he said, " Bro. David, I am so lonely, but it won't be long and I am ready."

Bro. Harshberger was a kind father and husband, a devoted and consistent member for many years. Funeral occasion improved by the undersigned from 2 Tim. 4: 6, 7, 8.
　　　　　　D. S. FILBRUN.

DILLER.—In Churchtown, Pa., Dec. 30, 1891, Mrs. Solomon Diller, aged 82 years.
　　　　　　DAVID NIESLY.

WILLIAMS.—In Everett, Pa., Dec. 28, 1891, of La Grippe, J. B. Williams, aged about 60 years.

He leaves a wife and seven children to mourn his loss. He was the leading merchant of Everett. His remains were interred in the Everett cemetery.
　　　　　　CARRIE RITCHEY.

NEGLY.—At Farmington, Ill., Nov. 13, 1891, Bro. David L. Negley, aged 30 years, 7 months and 28 days.

Deceased was a son of Bro. J. A. and sister Sarah Negley, and was an exemplary young man, liked by all who knew him. Knowing that, owing to sickness, he must soon cross the river of death, he became deeply concerned about his soul's salvation and requested to be baptized. So, on Oct. 20, 1891, we complied with his request and he arose, rejoicing in the hope of eternal life and expressed himself, at different times, as being satisfied and ready to go. Funeral services by the writer to a large audience.

He leaves a sorrowing father and mother, three brothers and two sisters.
　　　　　　SOLOMON BUCKLEW.

CUSHWA.—In the Hickory Grove church, Miami Co., Ohio, Dec. 4, 1891, Cora Ann Cushwa, daughter of friend James Cushwa, aged 24 years, 1 month and 7 days.

The deceased, while away from home, took ill and died of hemorrhage. Funeral services conducted by the writer from Rom. 8: 1.　　　　D. S. FILBRUN.

SEIGHMAN.—In the same church, Dec. 9, 1891, Bro. Jacob Seighman, aged 82 years, 10 months and 21 days.

Deceased was born in Lancaster County, Pa., Jan. 18, 1809, and was married to Catharine Basher, of McAllisterville, Juniata Co., Pa., about fifty-nine years ago. He emigrated to this State to the place near where his death occurred, fifty-three years ago. His wife, two children, eleven grandchildren and nine great-grandchildren survive him. Bro. Seighman was a consistent member of the Brethren church Funeral occasion improved by the writer, assisted by Eld. Henry Gump, from 1 Thess. 4: 14.　　　D. S. FILBRUN.

CHARLES.—In the bounds of the Rockton church, Pa., Jan. 1, 1892, Mrs. Samantha Charles, wife of Rodney Charles, aged 41 years, 7 months and 19 days. Funeral services conducted by the writer from 1 Cor. 15: 19-22.　　　　J. H. BEER.

THE GOSPEL MESSENGER.

"Set for the Defense of the Gospel."

Vol. 30, Old Series.   Mt. Morris, Ill., and Huntingdon, Pa., Feb. 2, 1892.   No. 5.

The Gospel Messenger.

H. B. BRUMBAUGH, Editor,

And Business Manager of the Eastern House, Box 50,
Huntingdon, Pa.

Table of Contents.

THOUGHT FLASHES.

IT has been truly said: "An honest man is a sample of God's best work." The word honest needs an enlarged definition and means much more than we are in the habit of giving it. It is a grand thing to be honest with our fellow-man and ourselves, but it is still a greater thing to be honest before God. We are so fettered by customs, traditions and creeds that there are but few, indeed, who are honest to their convictions of right.

There are times when we feel like trying to do as did Samson, when bound with cords,—shaking ourselves until the shackles would break and fall at our feet. Why not?

* * *

"Observer" says: "I noticed an article on page 7, No. 1, and it brought this thought to me: 'Can a church disown a minister without a just cause when he wishes to remain in the church?'" We suppose there is no church that would wish to do such a thing. But likely the query hinges on "a just cause," and the only way to decide the question is to determine who shall decide the justness of the cause. Shall it be the man who is to be disowned, or the church that is to do the disowning? If the former is to be the judge, there will be no disowning done, because we, of ourselves, seldom give a just cause for church discipline. We are always right and the church wrong. Such a course would be fatal to church government and, as a result, every one would take his own way and there could be no church. The church, as a body, must be allowed the right of acting out its own

convictions and making its own decisions, and our only recourse, when we feel that we have been wronged, is patience, reason, and appeal. It is possible for a church to make mistakes in the decisions she makes but a true, humble, Christian spirit on the part of the one wronged, seldom fails to bring the desired reconciliation. We admire the man who is true to his convictions of right, but there are times when we all must submit our judgments. This we can afford to do if done through the proper spirit.

* * *

A brother who had been with us during a former Bible Term writes us:

I would like so much to be with you during your coming Bible Term, but don't think I can. I had to spend so much time during the summer in church work that I am financially sinking and must now try and take care of the little I have, or after awhile I may grow in want. I spent about three months of my time last year in preaching, for which I received no compensation. I not only lost this time but had to pay out money, in addition, for traveling expenses.
I would gladly come and spend a month with you if I could see how to make my ends meet. The term I spent with you did me much good and was a great help to me in my ministry, etc.

We give this extract to show what sacrifices our ministers make and, seemingly, how little their efforts are appreciated by those for whom they are made. This is not an isolated case.—They can be counted by the score. We now think of a large number of ministers, who greatly desire to attend these Bible Terms that they may the better prepare themselves for the work the church has placed upon them, but they are not able to do so. Their living, for themselves and families, depends on the labor of their own hands, and, therefore, they must remain at home, or their families will suffer. The thought comes to us most forcibly, "Is this right?" The churches want good preaching and complain of some of their home ministers because they do not preach better sermons. Some are willing to raise funds and send away for a good preacher to come and preach for them. Why not spend this money on your home preachers? Encourage them to make some preparation and they may do better work for you than those you send away for. We have some splendid talent in our ministry and all that is needed in many of the cases is encouragement, possibilities and development.

Let us look again at the one from whose letter we quoted. He is a man of very moderate means, has been called by the church to preach, but not equipped. He is full of zeal and desires to become an efficient worker for the church and the Master. To assist him in this he spends a month, at his own expense, at the Bible Term. This is a month not only of loss, but of cost. While thus studying to make himself approved of God and man, his soul becomes more fully imbued with the importance of the work and the responsibilities weighing upon him, and he goes home and during the year gives three months in active service, financially, time lost in addition to other expenses.

Brethren, what do you think of such men? We hear you say, "They are good and faithful brethren." Others say, "They will get their reward in heaven." If they do, don't you think they will get a tremendously large one, or that yours will

be tremendously small? Would it not be better for you to divide up a little now, so that in the day of accounts the Lord can divide a little with you?

Don't be mistaken. As sure as there is a God, a heaven, and a promised reward, there will be an evening up some time. If you do not see that it is done in this life, the Lord will see that it is done in the life to come.

There is nothing that our ministry needs to-day, more than encouragement to efficiency in their work. This lack is causing hundreds to lag by the way and only fill the place when they must. The pressure for good preaching in the church, and out of it, is so great, that those who do not have some opportunities for preparation are growing discouraged,—and who is to blame? We need, hesitatingly say, "The church." Our ministers, on the whole, old and young, are the best class of men in the world. They are devoted, self-sacrificing and zealous beyond—appreciation. Pardon the word, but it is the only one we can think of that expresses the thought.

Now, brethren, a little bit of praise and we close our thoughts for this time. We are glad to believe that many of you are looking at this matter in a better light. You are becoming more practical in your Christian work and in some cases the evening-up system is being practiced. Some of our needy ministers are being remembered in the work and we shall not be at all surprised, if several of such are sent to the Bible Term and others encouraged in other ways. This is right. God bless you still more.

Just now we open a letter from a good old elder and he says: "Prepare for six or eight from our church." Best of all, he will be one of the number. Yes, indeed, will we prepare and he shall have one of the Normal's spare rooms. We are glad to have the fathers with us. The presence of such will gladden the hearts of many, and then they will be a safeguard thrown around the work that is always needful.

Of course, there are those among us who shake their heads at these things because they are different from the ways in which they went. Yes, this may be very true, as we can truly attest in our own starting out, but we do not despise a good thing because it was not to be had when we were young. In farming and all the different occupations in life there have been many improvements in means to ends, but the ends to be accomplished are not changed. The wheat, the corn, and all other products are the same under modern culture as they were under the ways of the past. The difference is, the times require a greater product at a less outlay of labor and time. So it is in church work. The times require more skilled labor and a greater preparation. The products will be the same in quality but ought to be more in quantity.

We must adapt our ways and means to the wants of the times if we will be successful in the ends to be reached. These are facts so patent to every candid and thinking mind that no arguments are necessary to establish them, and if we wish to perpetuate the church and save sinners, we must accept the facts as we meet them. God's ways are in harmony with human reason and all we have to do to meet the emergencies that are forced upon us is to be reasonable. That our preparation must correspond with the character of the work to be done is both rational and reasonable.

THE GOSPEL MESSENGER.

"Set for the Defense of the Gospel."

Vol. 30, Old Series.   Mt. Morris, Ill., and Huntingdon, Pa., Feb. 2, 1892.   No. 5.

The Gospel Messenger.

H. B. BRUMBAUGH, Editor,

And Business Manager of the Eastern House, Box 50. Huntingdon, Pa.

Table of Contents.

THOUGHT FLASHES.

It has been truly said: "An honest man is a sample of God's best work." The word honest needs an enlarged definition and means much more than we are in the habit of giving it. It is a grand thing to be honest with our fellow-man and ourselves, but it is still a greater thing to be honest before God. We are so fettered by customs, traditions and creeds that there are but few, indeed, who are honest to their convictions of right.

There are times when we feel like trying to do as did Samson, when bound with cords,—shaking ourselves until the shackles would break and fall at our feet. Why not?

"Observer" says: "I noticed an article on page 7, No. 1, and it brought this thought to me: "Can a church disown a minister without a just cause when he wishes to remain in the church?" We suppose there is no church that would wish to do such a thing. But likely the query hinges on "a just cause," and the only way to decide the question is to determine who shall decide the justness of the cause. Shall it be the man who is to be disowned, or the church that is to do the disowning? If the former is to be the judge, there will be no disowning done, because we, of ourselves, seldom give a just cause for church discipline. We are always right and the church wrong. Such a course would be fatal to church government and, as a result, every one would take his own way and there could be no church. The church, as a body, must be allowed the right of acting out its own convictions and making its own decisions, and our only recourse, when we feel that we have been wronged, is patience, reason, and appeal. It is possible for a church to make mistakes in the decisions she makes but a true, humble, Christian spirit on the part of the one wronged, seldom fails to bring the desired reconciliation. We admire the man who is true to his convictions of right, but there are times when we all must submit our judgments. This we can afford to do if done through the proper spirit.

* * *

A brother who had been with us during a former Bible Term writes us:

I would like so much to be with you during your coming Bible Term, but don't think I can. I had to spend so much time during the summer in church work that I am financially sinking and must now try and take care of the little I have, or after awhile I may grow in want. I spent about three months of my time last year in preaching, for which I received no compensation. I not only lost this time but had to pay out money, in addition, for traveling expenses.

I would gladly come and spend a month with you if I could see how to make my ends meet. The term I spent with you did me much good and was a great help to me in my ministry, etc.

We give this extract to show what sacrifices our ministers make and, seemingly, how little their efforts are appreciated by those for whom they are made. This is not an isolated case. They can be counted by the score. We now think of a large number of ministers, who greatly desire to attend these Bible Terms that they may the better prepare themselves for the work the church has placed upon them, but they are not able to do so. Their living, for themselves and families, depends on the labor of their own hands, and, therefore, they must remain at home, or their families will suffer. The thought comes to us most forcibly, "Is this right?" The churches want good preaching and complain of some of their home ministers because they do not preach better sermons. Some are willing to raise funds and send away for a good preacher to come and preach for them. Why not spend this money on your home preachers? Encourage them to make some preparation and they may do better work for you than those you send away for. We have some splendid talent in our ministry and all that is needed in many of the cases is encouragement, possibilities and development.

Let us look again at the one from whose letter we quoted. He is a man of very moderate means, has been called by the church to preach, but not equipped. He is full of zeal and desires to become an efficient worker for the church and the Master. To assist him in this he spends a month, at his own expense, at the Bible Term. This is a month not only of loss, but of cost. While thus studying to make himself approved of God and man, his soul becomes more fully imbued with the importance of the work and the responsibilities weighing upon him, and he goes home and during the year gives three months more in active service, financially, time lost in addition to other expenses.

Brethren, what do you think of such men? We hear you say, "They are good and faithful brethren." Others say, "They will get their reward in heaven." If they do, don't you think they will get a tremendously large one, or that yours will be tremendously small? Would it not be better for you to divide up a little now, so that in the day of accounts the Lord can divide a little with you?

Don't be mistaken. As sure as there is a God, a heaven, and a promised reward, there will be an evening up some time. If you do not see that it is done in this life, the Lord will see that it is done in the life to come.

There is nothing that our ministry needs to-day, more than encouragement to efficiency in their work. This lack is causing hundreds to lag by the way and only fill the place when they meet. The pressure for good preaching in the church, and out of it, is so great, that those who do not have some opportunities for preparation are growing discouraged,—and who is to blame? We unhesitatingly say, "The church." Our ministers, on the whole, old and young, are the best class of men in the world. They are devoted, self-sacrificing and zealous beyond—appreciation. Pardon the word, but it is the only one we can think of that expresses the thought.

Now, brethren, a little bit of praise and we close our thoughts for this time. We are glad to believe that many of you are looking at this matter in a better light. You are becoming more practical in your Christian work and in some cases the evening-up system is being practiced. Some of our needy ministers are being remembered in the work and we shall not be at all surprised, if several of such are sent to the Bible Term and others encouraged in other ways. This is right. God bless you still more.

Just now we open a letter from a good old elder and he says: "Prepare for six or eight from our church." Best of all, he will be one of the number. Yes, indeed, will we prepare and he shall have one of the Normal's spare rooms. We are glad to have the fathers with us. The presence of such will gladden the hearts of many, and then they will be a safeguard thrown around the work that is always needful.

Of course, there are those among us who shake their heads at these things because they are different from the ways in which they went. Yes, this may be very true, as we can truly attest in our own starting out, but we do not despise a good thing because it was not to be had when we were young. In farming and all the different occupations in life there have been many improvements in means to ends, but the ends to be accomplished are not changed. The wheat, the corn, and all other products are the same under modern culture as they were under the ways of the past. The difference is, the times require a greater product at a less outlay of labor and time. So it is in church work. The times require more skilled labor and a greater preparation. The products will be the same in quality but ought to be more in quantity.

We must adapt our ways and means to the wants of the times if we will be successful in the ends to be reached. These are facts so patent to every candid and thinking mind that no arguments are necessary to establish them, and if we wish to perpetuate the church and save sinners, we must accept the facts as we meet them. God's ways are in harmony with human reason and all we have to do to meet the emergencies that are forced upon us is to be reasonable. That our preparation must correspond with the character of the work to be done is both rational and reasonable.

But who shall separate the Christian from the love of Christ? Shall tribulations, or distress, or persecution? Nay, in all these things we are more than conquerors through him that loved us. Rom. 8: 37. If sorrow comes, and we are bowed down in grief, what can lift the weight from the soul quicker than to bow ourselves at the feet of Jesus, and ask him in prayer to help us in our time of trouble! My unconverted readers, who are out in the cold world, are there no shadows out there; is your pathway not clouded? O pause, think, and ask yourselves the question: "Whom am I serving?"

Let me advise you to serve Satan no longer, for he promises what he never gives,—lasting pleasure, and gives what he never promised,—everlasting pain.

If our Father permits a trial to come, it is because that is needful and best for our spiritual development, and we must accept it as from his hand.

The trial itself may be severe, and we may not like nor enjoy the suffering of it; but we can and must love the will of God in these trials, for his will is always best, whether in joy or sorrow. Job said, "Shall we receive good at the hand of God, and shall we not receive evil?" Shall this life be one perpetual day without a cloud? Ah, no! it is reserved for heaven to be the land of day without night; of light without darkness. Our meetness for heaven is finished in this vale of tears; our growth and development is to be consummated in the eternal city of which "The Lamb is the light thereof."

Disease may darken the vision of mortal sight, close the lips, still the pulse, and lay low these clay houses, but can go no further. Death was conquered in the tomb, and out of death's darkness we shall awake with spiritual vision unclouded forever.

Central City, Iowa.

THE MILLENNIUM.

BY JAS. Y. HECKLER.

Part One.

FROM time to time I read articles in the MESSENGER under the above heading, generally varying some in their line of thought and argument, but they generally come to the same, or nearly the same conclusion by quoting some dark passages of Scripture, which generally are not well understood, but are used to prop up their theory which has been derived from some other person, and by the time the article is finished, they have God a respecter of persons, and Christ at the head of the Jewish Kingdom.

Now, if you will patiently hear me, I will show you that this is an old theory and an improbable one. The apostles and early Christians had no idea that it would be a thousand or two thousand years until Christ would come again, and we do not know but what it may be a thousand or two thousand years more until he does come. We positively know less about the future than they did, and but very little about the past. Our knowledge is very limited, indeed, very limited. The apostles and disciples of Christ thought he would restore the kingdom to Israel, (Luke 24: 21) in the similitude of David's kingdom, not so much in his righteousness as in his power, while he was with them, and after his resurrection from the dead, they asked him, "Lord, wilt thou at this time restore the kingdom to Israel?" Acts 1: 6.

You will see it was still the Jewish Kingdom. After his ascension into heaven, they had all things common, and were waiting for the second coming of Christ, and trying to convert as many people as they could, and the converts believed that Christ would soon come to "restore the kingdom to Israel," and sold their property, and brought the money to the apostles, because they expected that Christ would come, and undoubtedly they thought they would have no further need of the money.

Now this was just an example of what we hear of occurring every few years at some place, where some party of Adventists, believing that Christ will come at some specified time, give their money away. All this is only a repetition of what has often occurred before. The apostles and early Christians lived in Jerusalem for thirty or more years yet, after the ascension of Christ, but after the first fruits had been gathered into the church at that place, the money did not flow into the treasury so freely any more, and they became quite poor. After the terrible desolation of Jerusalem, by the Roman army, when the apostles were out in other parts of the world, they recollected that the Savior had told them that their city would be trodden down by the Gentiles until the times of the Gentiles should be fulfilled, and Luke inserted this declaration into his Gospel. The apostle Paul to the Romans (11: 25) refers to the same thing, but, it appears, he still has the Jewish Kingdom in view.

After Jerusalem was in desolation, a heap of ruins, the early Christians believed that Christ would come to reign a thousand years in Jerusalem, that the City would be rebuilt with beautiful architecture, and that Christ would reign as their immortal King in the New Jerusalem. The Jews had a tradition among themselves that the Messiah would come in the sixth chiliad, and they did not look for him to come as the lowly Nazarene.

Now, according to the chronology of the Septuagint, Josephus, and other writers on chronology, Christ did come in the sixth chiliad, and we are now already in the eighth chiliad, notwithstanding our present chronology.

In the year A. D. 127, the Emperor Adrian, to please the Jews, gave orders to rebuild Jerusalem. No sooner was this order granted than the Jews collected there in great numbers, and the City was rebuilt with great expedition. At that time they accepted a false Messiah whose name was Coziba, but who changed his name to Barochebas and titled himself "King of the Jews." No sooner had he done this than the Jews under their false Christ fell upon the Christians and other inhabitants of the cities and towns, and butchered them unmercifully. When the Emperor Adrian, away over at Rome, got to hear of those things, he sent a large body of men against them, and, after a bloody conflict, which continued about two years, in which over one hundred of their best towns were destroyed, with the loss of nearly six hundred thousand men in battle, the Jewish insurrection was quelled. Then all those Jews who yet remained, were, by a public decree, banished from the country and forbidden ever to return. In A. D. 326, the Empress Helena, the aged mother of Constantine, visited Jerusalem and ordered churches and memorials to be built to those sacred places, for there were many nominal Christians residing there.

Again, about the year A. D. 362, the Emperor Julian, the apostate, wishing to please the Jews, gave orders that the temple in Jerusalem should be rebuilt. Extravagant preparations were made by the Jews who flocked together there for that purpose, and spades and pickaxes of silver were provided for the occasion. But an insulted Providence did not suffer the work to proceed, for the workmen were scorched by the flames that issued out of the earth, and drove them from their unwise design. Jerusalem belonged to the Romans until the Roman Empire went to pieces, when it was conquered by the Persians under Cosroes II., A. D. 614. But, after a struggle of fourteen years, it was again taken by a nominal Christian General, whose name was Heraclius. But it was again surrendered by the Patriarch Saphronius to Caliph Omar, the Saracen General, under the banner of Mahomet, A. D. 637, and the Mosque of Omar was built in the reign of Caliph Abd-el-Melek, between the years 688 and 693. By this time Popery had been established and the Christian religion had lost its vitality. The Dark Ages had commenced. Notwithstanding the darkness of the times, the nominal Christians still believed that Christ would come to establish his kingdom in Jerusalem, and it became not only a custom, but a duty for Christians to make pilgrimages to the Holy Land, to visit the sacred places there.

As Christ had not come to establish his kingdom in Jerusalem, as it was believed he would by the early Christians, and as time passed on, there gradually arose an almost universal impression in the church, that in just one thousand years after the first advent of Christ, the world would come to an end. A certain historian says, "As the year 999 drew near its end, men almost held their breath to watch the result. For a whole generation, all the pulpits in Christendom had been ringing with the text, Rev. 20: 1, 2, 3, notwithstanding the emphatic declaration of Jesus, that not even the angels in heaven know the period of his second coming. Through all the ages of the church individuals have been appearing who have fixed upon a particular year when Christ was to come in clouds of glory. The year of our Lord 999 was one of very solemn import. There was a deep-seated impression throughout all Christendom that it was to be the last year of time, and, indeed, all the signs in the heavens above and on the earth beneath indicated that event. There was almost universal anarchy,—no law, no government, no safety, anywhere. There were wars and rumors of wars. Sin abounded. There were awful famines, followed by the fearful train of pestilence and death. The land was left untilled. There was no motive to plant when the harvest could not be gathered.

It will thus be seen how people can be in error and still be sincere in their belief, even in matters of religion. They thought the end of time and the universal conflagration were at hand, but they were mistaken. Nearly a hundred years later, when another generation was living, Peter, the Hermit, arose and went around, preaching and prophesying that Christ would soon come to establish his kingdom in Jerusalem; and, because that city was then in the hands of the infidels, as they called the Mohammedans, he preached up a Crusade, or Holy War, against the infidels, to subdue them and to take the Holy City out of their hands. I suppose you have often read about the Crusades, and the great gatherings that were held with popes, prelates, cardinals and great men at the head of them, to inaugurate them, and therefore I will merely say that, after a fierce conflict, the Crusaders took possession of Jerusalem in the year 1099, because they believed that Christ would soon come. They held the City eighty-eight years, but in 1187 it was again taken under the banner of Mahomet, by Saladin, the Sultan of Egypt. Since then the City and country have changed owners several times, but always under the Koran; excepting that the City was taken by Napoleon Bonaparte in 1799, but was not held long by him.

"AN hour's industry will do more to produce cheerfulness, suppress vile humors, and relieve your affairs, than a month's moaning."

But who shall separate the Christian from the love of Christ? Shall tribulations, or distress, or persecution? Nay, in all these things we are more than conquerors through him that loved us. Rom. 8: 37. If sorrow comes, and we are bowed down in grief, what can lift the weight from the soul quicker than to bow ourselves at the feet of Jesus, and ask him in prayer to help us in our time of trouble! My unconverted readers, who are out in the cold world, are there no shadows out there; is your pathway not clouded? O pause, think, and ask yourselves the question: "Whom am I serving?"

Let me advise you to serve Satan no longer, for he promises what he never gives,—lasting pleasure, and gives what he never promised,—everlasting pain.

If our Father permits a trial to come, it is because that is needful and best for our spiritual development, and we must accept it as from his hand.

The trial itself may be severe, and we may not like nor enjoy the suffering of it; but we can and must love the will of God in these trials, for his will is always best, whether in joy or sorrow. Job said, "Shall we receive good at the hand of God, and shall we not receive evil?" Shall this life be one perpetual day without a cloud? Ah, no! it is reserved for heaven to be the land of day without night; of light without darkness. Our meetness for heaven is finished in this vale of tears; our growth and development is to be consummated in the eternal city of which "The Lamb is the light thereof."

Disease may darken the vision of mortal sight, close the lips, still the pulse, and lay low these clay houses, but can go, no further. Death was conquered in the tomb, and out of death's darkness we shall awake with spiritual vision unclouded forever.

Central City, Iowa.

THE MILLENNIUM.

BY JAS. Y. HECKLER.

Part One.

FROM time to time I read articles in the MESSENGER under the above heading, generally varying some in their line of thought and argument, but they generally come to the same, or nearly the same conclusion by quoting some dark passages of Scripture, which generally are not well understood, but are used to prop up their theory which has been derived from some other person, and by the time the article is finished, they have God a respecter of persons, and Christ at the head of the Jewish Kingdom.

Now, if you will patiently hear me, I will show you that this is an old theory and an improbable one. The apostles and early Christians had no idea that it would be a thousand or two thousand years until Christ would come again, and we do not know but what it may be a thousand or two thousand years more until he does come. We positively know less about the future than they did, and but very little about the past. Our knowledge is very limited, indeed, very limited. The apostles and disciples of Christ thought he would restore the kingdom to Israel, (Luke 24: 21) in the similitude of David's kingdom, not so much in his righteousness as in his power, while he was with them, and after his resurrection from the dead, they asked him, "Lord, wilt thou at this time restore the kingdom to Israel?" Acts 1: 6.

You will see it was still the Jewish Kingdom. After his ascension into heaven, they had all things common, and were waiting for the second coming of Christ, and trying to convert as many people to him as they could, and the converts believed that Christ would soon come to "restore the kingdom to Israel," and sold their property, and brought the money to the apostles, because they expected that Christ would come, and undoubtedly they thought they would have no further need of the money.

Now this was just an example of what we hear of occurring every few years at some place, where some party of Adventists, believing that Christ will come at some specified time, give their money away. All this is only a repetition of what has often occurred before. The apostles and early Christians lived in Jerusalem for thirty or more years yet, after the ascension of Christ, but after the first fruits had been gathered into the church at that place, the 'money did not flow into the treasury so freely any more, and they became quite poor. After the terrible desolation of Jerusalem, by the Roman army, when the apostles were out in other parts of the world, they recollected that the Savior had told them that their city would be trodden down by the Gentiles until the times of the Gentiles should be fulfilled, and Luke inserted this declaration into his Gospel. The apostle Paul to the Romans (11: 25) refers to the same thing, but, it appears, he still has the Jewish Kingdom in view.

After Jerusalem was in desolation, a heap of ruins, the early Christians believed that Christ would come to reign a thousand years in Jerusalem, that the City would be rebuilt with beautiful architecture, and that Christ would reign as their immortal King in the New Jerusalem. The Jews had a tradition among themselves that the Messiah would come in the sixth chiliad, and they were looking for him when he did come, but they did not look for him to come as the lowly Nazarene.

Now, according to the chronology of the Septuagint, Josephus, and other writers on chronology, Christ did come in the sixth chiliad, and we are now already in the eighth chiliad, notwithstanding our present chronology.

In the year A. D. 127, the Emperor Adrian, to please the Jews, gave orders to rebuild Jerusalem. No sooner was this order granted than the Jews collected there in great numbers, and the City was rebuilt with great expedition. At that time they accepted a false Messiah whose name was Coziba, but who changed his name to Barochebas and titled himself "King of the Jews." No sooner had he done this than the Jews under their false Christ fell upon the Christians and other inhabitants of the cities and towns, and butchered them unmercifully. When the Emperor Adrian, away over at Rome, got to hear of those things, he sent a large body of men against them, and, after a bloody conflict, which continued about two years, in which over one hundred of their best towns were destroyed, with the loss of nearly six hundred thousand men in battle, the Jewish insurrection was quelled. Then all those Jews who yet remained, were, by a public decree, banished from the country and forbidden ever to return. In A. D. 326, the Empress Helena, the aged mother of Constantine, visited Jerusalem and ordered churches and memorials to be built to those sacred places, for there were many nominal Christians residing there.

Again, about the year A. D. 362, the Emperor Julian, the apostate, wishing to please the Jews, gave orders that the temple in Jerusalem should be rebuilt. Extravagant preparations were made by the Jews who flocked together there for that purpose, and spades and pickaxes of silver were provided for the occasion. But an insulted Providence did not suffer the work to proceed, for the workmen were scorched by the flames that issued out of the earth, and drove them from their unwise design. Jerusalem belonged to the Romans until the Roman Empire went to pieces, when it was conquered by the Persians under Cosroes II., A. D. 614. But, after a struggle of fourteen years, it was again taken by a nominal Christian General, whose name was Heraclius. But it was again surrendered by the Patriarch Sophronius to Caliph Omar, the Saracen General, under the banner of Mahomet, A. D. 637, and the Mosque of Omar was built in the reign of Caliph Abd-el-Melek, between the years 688 and 693. By this time Popery had been established and the Christian religion had lost its vitality. The Dark Ages had commenced. Notwithstanding the darkness of the times, the nominal Christians still believed that Christ would come to establish his kingdom in Jerusalem, and it became not only a custom, but a duty for Christians to make pilgrimages to the Holy Land, to visit the sacred places there.

As Christ had not come to establish his kingdom in Jerusalem, as it was believed he would by the early Christians, and as time passed on, there gradually arose an almost universal impression in the church, that in just one thousand years after the first advent of Christ, the world would come to an end. A certain historian says, "As the year 999 drew near its end, men almost held their breath to watch the result. For a whole generation, all the pulpits in Christendom had been ringing with the text, Rev. 20: 1, 2, 3, notwithstanding the emphatic declaration of Jesus, that not even the angels in heaven know the period of his second coming. Through all the ages of the church individuals have been appearing who have fixed upon a particular year when Christ was to come in clouds of glory. The year of our Lord 999 was one of very solemn import. There was a deep-seated impression throughout all Christendom that it was to be the last year of time, and, indeed, all the signs in the heavens above and on the earth beneath indicated that event. There was almost universal anarchy,—no law, no government, no safety, anywhere. There were wars and rumors of wars. Sin abounded. There were awful famines, followed by the fearful train of pestilence and death. The land was left untilled. There was no motive to plant when the harvest could not be gathered.

It will thus be seen how people can be in error and still be sincere in their belief, even in matters of religion. They thought the end of time and the universal conflagration were at hand, but they were mistaken. Nearly a hundred years later, when another generation was living, Peter, the Hermit, arose and went around, preaching and prophesying that Christ would soon come to establish his kingdom in Jerusalem; and, because that city was then in the hands of the infidels, as they called the Mohammedans, he preached up a Crusade, or Holy War, against the infidels, to subdue them and to take the Holy City out of their hands. I suppose you have often read about the Crusades, and the great gatherings that were held with popes, prelates, cardinals and great men at the head of them, to inaugurate them, and therefore I will merely say that, after a fierce conflict, the Crusaders took possession of Jerusalem in the year 1099, because they believed that Christ would soon come. They held the City eighty-eight years, but in 1187 it was again taken under the banner of Mahomet, by Saladin, the Sultan of Egypt. Since then the City and country have changed owners several times, but always under the Koran; excepting that the City was taken by Napoleon Bonaparte in 1799, but was not held long by him.

"AN hour's industry will do more to produce cheerfulness, suppress vile humors, and relieve your affairs, than a month's moaning."

power was a prominent feature of the Holy Spirit's presence in the apostolic church, it was not more prominent or more valued than the ordinary offices of the divine Paraclete, available to the church and to believers in all ages. We have more to do with these ordinary offices, as the extraordinary have been discontinued since Divine Revelation has been completed and established. There is danger that even the ordinary offices of the Holy Spirit may be, in a measure, discontinued through the very general indifference and unbelief which prevails on the subject, not to mention the open denial of one or two of the most prominent and most precious, which is now and then proclaimed by the adherents of a certain school of so-called religious teaching.

That the Holy Spirit was the animating agency of ancient prophecy, we have already seen, but that it was always to be peculiar to the prophets alone, is not true. Some of them possessed a larger measure of it than others, for this is one of the prominent facts in connection with this subject, that varying degrees of the Spirit were conferred upon different men, some having more or less than others. Among the prophets, Moses, Elijah, and Isaiah had a larger measure than any of the others, but it was simply a measure which even these received. To One only was the Holy Spirit given "without measure" and that was He who received its dove-like symbol on his sacred head. He alone possessed all its boundless resources of wisdom, knowledge, power, and love. But out of the interesting history of the Spirit's operation, in the ages preceding the Gospel, shines a radiant promise that this divine gift, so exclusively bestowed here and there, should, in the last days, be poured out upon "all flesh."

It was to be one of the peculiar, distinguishing, and glorious features of the new dispensation, making it infinitely better than the first, by a wide diffusion of those gifts and blessings which, in the first, were confined to only a few. The beginning of this fulfillment was the astounding miracle of the Pentecost, when not simply one of the most prominent, or most favored, but every one, from the least to the greatest, who sat within that celebrated hall, wherein the primitive church was gathered, were filled, overwhelmed, and transformed by the invisible Power, and from whence they went out to transform the world.

In his promise of this outpouring, our Savior mentioned several of its most important offices, as a "Comforter," a Guide "into all truth." He would bring to their remembrance all things which he, their Master, had said unto them. There were other important offices and gifts which the Spirit would bestow, such as a gift of tongues, and the gift of miracles, but our Savior did not particularly specify them. He only mentioned those offices which were adapted to meet a universal necessity, and would, therefore, remain with the church throughout all time.

As long as humanity, as long as the church militant remains in this world of darkness and trouble, there will be urgent, imminent, pathetic need of an ever-present Divine Comforter and Infallible Guide. Not that the Word is an insufficient guide, but the Spirit is necessary to "bring it to remembrance,"—to make timely and effective application of it to our minds and hearts, and continually help our weak understanding.

The evangelistic and apostolic writings abound with positive teaching of the personal indwelling of the Holy Spirit in the hearts of all true believers. It is only necessary to cite a few pertinent quotations. It is the definite purpose of God to give his Holy Spirit to all his believing children: "If ye then, being evil, know how to give good gifts unto your children; how much more shall your Heavenly Father give the Holy Spirit to them that ask him?" Luke 11: 13. He even claims the body for his habitation: "What! know ye not that your body is the temple of the Holy Ghost, which ye have of God?" 1 Cor. 6: 19.

Dwelling in us the Holy Ghost is our guide in the sense of helping our understanding of the Word, revealing truth to the mind, applying it to the heart, and disposing the will to submission and obedience. John 14: 26; 16: 13; 1 John 2: 27. He is the Comforter, making us sensible of reconciliation and peace with God, through faith in the Lord Jesus Christ, and supporting us under manifold trials and afflictions, with abundant and seasonable inward consolations. John 14: 16, 26; 15: 26; 16: 7; Acts 9: 31; Rom. 14: 17. He is the sanctifier, removing the dross of sin, and inspiring all holy desires and affections, continually lifting up the heart to seek after God. 1 Thess. 2: 13; 1 Peter 1: 2. How could he guide, or comfort, or sanctify any one unless he dwelt in them as a personal presence and power?

The universal need of guidance, instruction, consolation and sanctification, and our total inability to satisfy these needs, is proof, if proof were needed, of the universal application to the church of all these precious Scriptures. They are the priceless heritage of the saints until the end of time. No argument is needed by those who have tested the true Christian experience. The "joy of the Holy Ghost" is sufficiently convincing to all those who have realized it. Nothing could be more fatal to the spiritual life than that perversion of truth which is laid at the door of Campbellism, namely, that the Holy Spirit does not dwell in us in the sense of a guide, comforter, or sanctifier. Our object is to warn the earnest disciples of Jesus against this dangerous error, and to awaken a livelier interest in our inheritance, through Christ, of the blessed Holy Spirit. Let us pray that, as individual Christians, and as churches, we may receive a more abundant measure of this great gift, yes, that we may be "filled with the Holy Ghost!"

THE JUDGMENT.

BY A. HUTCHISON.

" He that judgeth me is the Lord."—1 Cor. 4: 4.

Do we realize how much there is in that short sentence? It has been said that, if the Lord is to judge us, it will go well with us, for they tell us that he is so full of mercy that he will not condemn us. But while it is all very true that the Lord is full of mercy and tender compassion, yet we must remember again that he has said, "I judge no man. But the word that I have spoken, the same shall judge him in the last day."

Now it seems necessary that we get this matter clearly before our minds. Jesus is represented to us in the Scriptures as being the judge of quick and dead, and it is doubtless true that he is. Notwithstanding who says, "I judge no man." He judges, not of himself, but by the words which he had previously spoken, and which, by the guidance of the Holy Ghost, were written in a book. Then, when the time for judgment shall have come, the books shall be opened, and what is found written in the book which we call the New Testament, will then be brought out, and will serve as so many witnesses. For Jesus has said, and it is recorded in that book, that "this Gospel of the kingdom shall be preached in all the world for a witness unto all nations; and then shall the end come." Matt. 24: 14.

The order of things, then, seems to be something like the following: Christ will be seated upon the throne of his judgment, and before him the nations will be assembled. Being thus in readiness, the next thing in order will be to open the books. The books being opened, each individual will next be summoned, each person in turn,— for when we look into our book, we find that it reads thus: "For we must all appear before the judgment seat of Christ, that every one may receive the things done in his body, according to that he hath done, whether it be good or bad." 2 Cor. 5: 10. Now we notice that each one is to receive the fruit, just after the kind of seed which that one has sown. Will there not be a good deal of anxiety just then about the kind of seed which we have sown? And O, what a joyful time that will be, when we shall hear the Judge say, "You are free,—the witnesses set you free." We are again reminded that the Record says, "If the Son therefore shall make you free, ye shall be free indeed." John 8: 36. O glorious thought, O happy hour! Shall it, can it ever be mine to enjoy? If Jesus says so, it can. And I know he will say it, if I have obeyed his Word. Christ has said, "Ye are my friends, if ye do whatsoever I command you." John 15: 14. Again we read that he will say, "Friend, go up higher." Then the whole case will depend upon the life that we live while here. For we read again, that "there is no work, nor device, nor knowledge, nor wisdom, in the grave whither thou goest." Eccl. 9: 10.

But another question arises here in the minds of some. What shall become of the millions who have all mouldered back to dust? We will call the revelator to the stand, and he will answer the question. He says, "And I saw the dead, small and great, stand before God; and the books were opened, etc." Not only the dead who were buried in the earth are included in this, for he further says, "And the sea gave up the dead which were in it; and death and hell delivered up the dead which were in them, and they were judged every man according to their works." Rev. 20: 12, 13. Now we have the testimony abundant that all must come to judgment, and that each one must be judged according to his or her own life and character. Then each of us can readily adopt the language of Paul, as given at the head of this article, and say, "He that judgeth me is the Lord." If we shall hear him say, "Depart from me, ye workers of iniquity, we will then realize what Watts meant in the following lines:

" O wretched state of deep despair,
To see my God remove,
And fix my doleful station, where
I must not taste his love."

Why will not all obey the Lord, and be saved now?

McPherson, Kans.

(To be Continued.)

TRUE PITY.

We overheard some persons speaking of a poor woman who had recently lost her husband, and one of them, after drawing a picture of the sad lot of the woman who was left with several small children, said: "I pity her from the bottom of my heart." We wonder if such pity as that ever did any good. That is not the right place for pity to come from. Pity that comes from the bottom of the heart is not as good as pity that comes from the bottom of the pocket-book. True pity helps. We do not deny that pity is a beautiful word on human lips, or a beautiful feeling in the human heart, but the sentiment for the unfortunate poor that takes the shape of a dollar is truer than that which takes the form of a tear. How are we to know that people have pity? By their words or their deeds? Pity that ends in charity, in assistance, that finds the way to the pocket, is real, genuine, true. No one doubts that. But pity that comes only from the bottom of the heart does not come from the right place.

power was a prominent feature of the Holy Spirit's presence in the apostolic church, it was not more prominent or more valued than the ordinary offices of the divine Paraclete, available to the church and to believers in all ages. We have more to do with these ordinary offices, as the extraordinary have been discontinued since Divine Revelation has been completed and established. There is danger that even the ordinary offices of the Holy Spirit may be, in a measure, discontinued through the very general indifference and unbelief which prevails on the subject, not to mention the open denial of one or two of the most prominent and most precious, which is now and then proclaimed by the adherents of a certain school of so-called religious teaching.

That the Holy Spirit was the animating agency of ancient prophecy, we have already seen, but that it was always to be peculiar to the prophets alone, is not true. Some of them possessed a larger measure of it than others, for this is one of the prominent facts in connection with this subject, that varying degrees of the Spirit were conferred upon different men, some having more or less than others. Among the prophets, Moses, Elijah, and Isaiah had a larger measure than any of the others, but it was simply a measure which even these received. To One only was the Holy Spirit given "without measure" and that was He who received its dove-like symbol on his sacred head. He alone possessed all its boundless resources of wisdom, knowledge, power, and love. But out of the interesting history of the Spirit's operation, in the ages preceding the Gospel, shines a radiant promise that this divine gift, so exclusively bestowed here and there, should, in the last days, be poured out upon "all flesh."

It was to be one of the peculiar, distinguishing, and glorious features of the new dispensation, making it infinitely better than the first, by a wide diffusion of those gifts and blessings which, in the first, were confined to only a few. The beginning of this fulfillment was the astounding miracle of the Pentecost, when not simply one of the most prominent, or most favored, but every one, from the least to the greatest, who sat within that celebrated hall, wherein the primitive church was gathered, were filled, overwhelmed, and transformed by the invisible Power, and from whence they went out to transform the world.

In his promise of this outpouring, our Savior mentioned several of its most important offices, as a "Comforter," a Guide "into all truth." He would bring to their remembrance all things which he, their Master, had said unto them. There were other important offices and gifts which the Spirit would bestow, such as a gift of tongues, and the gift of miracles, but our Savior did not particularly specify them. He only mentioned those offices which were adapted to meet a universal necessity, and would, therefore, remain with the church throughout all time.

As long as humanity, as long as the church militant remains in this world of darkness and trouble, there will be urgent, imminent, pathetic need of an ever-present Divine Comforter and Infallible Guide. Not that the Word is an insufficient guide, but the Spirit is necessary to "bring it to remembrance,"—to make timely and effective application of it to our minds and hearts, and continually help our weak understanding.

The evangelistic and apostolic writings abound with positive teaching of the personal indwelling of the Holy Spirit in the hearts of all true believers. It is only necessary to cite a few pertinent quotations. It is the definite purpose of God to give his Holy Spirit to all his believing children: "If ye then, being evil, know how to give good gifts unto your children; how much more shall your Heavenly Father give the Holy Spirit to them that ask him?" Luke 11: 13. He even claims the body for his habitation: "What! know ye not that your body is the temple of the Holy Ghost, which ye have of God?" 1 Cor. 6: 19.

Dwelling in us the Holy Ghost is our guide in the sense of helping our understanding of the Word, revealing truth to the mind, applying it to the heart, and disposing the will to submission and obedience. John 14: 26; 16: 13; 1 John 2: 27. He is the Comforter, making us sensible of reconciliation and peace with God, through faith in the Lord Jesus Christ, and supporting us under manifold trials and afflictions, with abundant and seasonable inward consolations. John 14: 16, 26; 15: 26; 16: 7; Acts 9: 31; Rom. 14: 17. He is the sanctifier, removing the dross of sin, and inspiring all holy desires and affections, continually lifting up the heart to seek after God. 1 Thess. 2: 13; 1 Peter 1: 2. How could he guide, or comfort, or sanctify any one unless he dwelt in them as a personal presence and power?

The universal need of guidance, instruction, consolation and sanctification, and our total inability to satisfy those needs, is proof, if proof were needed, of the universal application to the church of all these precious Scriptures. They are the priceless heritage of the saints until the end of time. No argument is needed by those who have tested the true Christian experience. The "joy of the Holy Ghost" is sufficiently convincing to all those who have realized it. Nothing could be more fatal to the spiritual life than that perversion of truth which is laid at the door of Campbellism, namely, that the Holy Spirit does not dwell in us in the sense of a guide, comforter, or sanctifier. Our object is to warn the earnest disciples of Jesus against this dangerous error, and to awaken a livelier interest in our inheritance, through Christ, of the blessed Holy Spirit. Let us pray that, as individual Christians, and as churches, we may receive a more abundant measure of this great gift, yea, that we may be "filled with the Holy Ghost!"

THE JUDGMENT.

BY A. HUTCHISON.

"He that judgeth me is the Lord."—1 Cor. 4: 4.

Do we realize how much there is in that short sentence? It has been said that, if the Lord is to judge us, it will go well with us, for they tell us that he is so full of mercy that he will not condemn us. But while it is all very true that the Lord is full of mercy and tender compassion, yet we must remember again that he has said, "I judge no man. But the word that I have spoken, the same shall judge him in the last day."

Now it seems necessary that we get this matter clearly before our minds. Jesus is represented to us in the Scriptures as being the judge of quick and dead, and it is doubtless true that he is. Notwithstanding he says, "I judge no man." He judges, not of himself, but by the words waich he had previously spoken, and which, by the guidance of the Holy Ghost, were written in a book. Then, when the time for judgment shall have come, the books shall be opened, and what is found written in the book which we call the New Testament, will then be brought out, and will serve as so many witnesses. For Jesus has said, and it is recorded in that book, that "this Gospel of the kingdom shall be preached in all the world for a witness unto all nations; and then shall the end come." Matt. 24: 14.

The order of things, then, seems to be something like the following: Christ will be seated upon the throne of his judgment, and before him the nations will be assembled. Being thus in readiness, the next thing in order will be to open the books. The books being opened, each individual will next be summoned,—yes, we must all come,—for when we look into our book, we find that it reads thus: "For we must all appear before the judgment seat of Christ, that every one may receive the things done in his body, according to that he hath done, whether it be good or bad." 2 Cor. 5: 10. Now we notice that each one is to receive the fruit, just after the kind of seed which that one has sown. Will there not be a good deal of anxiety just then about the kind of seed which we have sown? And O, what a joyful time that will be, when we shall hear the Judge say, "You are free,—the witnesses set you free." We are again reminded that the Record says, "If the Son therefore shall make you free, ye shall be free indeed." John 8: 36. O glorious thought, O happy hour! Shall it, can it ever be mine to enjoy? If Jesus says so, it can. And I know he will say it, if I have obeyed his Word. Christ has said, "Ye are my friends, if ye do whatsoever I command you." John 15: 14. Again we read that he will say, "Friend, go up higher." Then the whole case will depend upon the life that we live while here. For we read again, that "there is no work, nor device, nor knowledge, nor wisdom, in the grave whither thou goest." Eccl. 9: 10.

But another question arises here in the minds of some. What shall become of the millions who have all mouldered back to dust? We will call the revelator to the stand, and he will answer the question. He says, "And I saw the dead, small and great, stand before God; and the books were opened, etc." Not only the dead who were buried in the earth are included in this, for he further says, "And the sea gave up the dead which were in it; and death and hell delivered up the dead which were in them, and they were judged every man according to their works." Rev. 20: 12, 13. Now we have the testimony abundant that all must come to judgment, and that each one must be judged according to his or her own life and character. Then each of us can readily adopt the language of Paul, as given at the head of this article, and say, "He that judgeth me is the Lord." If we shall hear him say, "Depart from me, all ye workers of iniquity, we will then realize what Watts meant in the following lines:

"O wretched state of deep despair,
To see my God remove,
And fix my doleful station, where
I must not taste his love."

Why will not all obey the Lord, and be saved now?

McPherson, Kans.

(To be Continued.)

TRUE PITY.

We overheard some persons speaking of a poor woman who had recently lost her husband, and one of them, after drawing a picture of the sad lot of the woman who was left with several small children, said: "I pity her from the bottom of my heart." We wonder if such pity as that ever did any good. That is not the right place for pity to come from. Pity that comes from the bottom of the heart is not as good as pity that comes from the bottom of the pocket-book. True pity helps. We do not deny that pity is a beautiful word on human lips, or a beautiful feeling in the human heart, but the sentiment for the unfortunate poor that takes the shape of a dollar is truer than that which takes the form of a tear. How are we to know that people have pity? By their words or their deeds? Pity that ends in charity, in assistance, that finds the way to the pocket, is real, genuine, true. No one doubts that. But pity that comes only from the bottom of the heart does not come from the right place.

us, the rising generation, with examples of men from the creation of the world to the present time, who, having found the purpose for which they were created, made it their life-work to attain to that end, glorifying God in their lives, for every thought and deed was given in earnest, and the purpose being a noble one, the results must be equally ennobling.

To be thoroughly in earnest, we must first fully comprehend the responsibility and importance of the work we are to engage in. Abel was in earnest when he offered to God the gift, so acceptable, yet the offering of it and its acceptance, cost him his life. Noah realized the responsibility of his work, and breathed forth the earnestness of his soul in those last antediluvian days.

Though Moses trembled at first at the magnitude of the work, to which God called him, yet, never doubting God's power to strengthen him, he became interested and earnest, and was enabled to lead the Children of Israel out of the land of Egypt, against all opposing elements. Lot was in earnest, when he went about the wicked city, warning the inmates of impending danger, and though his work was ineffectual, he had done his part, and will receive his reward.

John the Baptist was in earnest in fulfilling his mission of preparing the way for the Light of the World.

Paul, that zealous apostle, was the very embodiment of earnestness and devotion, from his conversion to his death.

O, the depth of meaning in the monuments which these noble men have left behind them for the benefit of the world! All had great trials to contend with; Abel, the bitterness of a jealous brother; Noah, the scorn and derision of an unbelieving world; Moses, all the opposition which King Pharaoh and his army could invent; Lot, the wickedness and hard-heartedness of his own family; John, the darkness and ignorance of the time; and Paul, all manner of afflictions, and even martyrdom at last; yet all felt that God was their All in all, and soul, mind, and strength, went to fulfill the mission he had given them to do.

Dear young fellow-soldiers, how are we profiting by these bright examples? Do we ponder daily upon the great purpose of life, the opportunities to be improved, the great responsibility of our own missions, and the influence we are wielding upon those around us, or did we accept Christianity under a sudden impulse, and have we ever since been trying to live a Christian life simply because our associates are in the church? Have we been acting from motive rather than principle?

Are we often carried away, by the frivolities of our youthful natures, or are we so thoroughly in earnest, intent on being a true, model Christian, at all times, that we can be happy only when thinking on those things, mentioned in Philpp. 4: 8?

In the work in which we are engaged temporally, we often ask ourselves these questions solemnly at night: How many wrong or false impressions have my looks, thoughts, words, or actions, made this day upon the tender minds, and confiding hearts in our care? Then we almost tremble at the thought of answering some day for all the wrong impressions made, and for duty undone; but then this thought invariably comes to us:

"'Tis working with our heart and soul,
That makes our duty pleasure."

We feel that so long as we are truly in earnest, we cannot fail to do what God requires of us, and the rest he will take care of.

If earnestness is so important in temporal things, it is vastly more important in spiritual things. Let us then, who have put our hands to the Gospel plow, not turn back. "Though the plowshare cut through the flowers of life to its fountains, though it pass o'er the graves of the dead, and the hearts of the living, it is the will of the Lord, and his mercy endureth forever."

THE VALUE OF CEREMONIES.

BY JOHN E. MOHLER.

THE popular religious belief of to-day, re-acting from the grave danger of substituting the form for the spirit, has encountered what is, perhaps, no less a danger, namely, forgetting that all spirit must have form. That many evils are likely to result from this inclination, is apparent to some of the world's deepest religious thinkers.

Before discarding an established usage it is wise to consider, as far as possible, the advantages in the line of its purpose; especially so when the practice is of divine authority. God recognizes the great importance of demonstration in the work of evangelizing the world, and, therefore, has appointed special ways by which our spiritual relations to each other and to him should be manifested. Not only has he designated the manner by which these relations are to be made known, but this manner is their natural mode of expression. By natural mode of expression, I mean that method to which all humanity would most likely attach, instinctively, the same meaning. All the ceremonies, enjoined upon us, in the New Testament Scriptures, are of this nature. Being of this character, do they not demand our favor?

It is strange that those forms, which illustrate spiritual relations the most clearly, should be severely ridiculed by popular so called Christianity. Among these forms are,

(1) Feet-washing.—a practice most suggestive of humility or servitude. *How many blessings follow humility?*

(2) The salutation of the holy kiss,—the most natural token of love, which is greater than either faith or hope. 1 Cor. 13: 13.

(3) Non-conformity to the world,—suggesting a mind not of the world. Other examples might be given, but these will suffice.

The value of the Gospel ordinances, in the enlarging of our Christian influence, may be clearly seen. Not only do we thus show by our works that we have "the faith once delivered to the saints," but we are indeed made "epistles, known and read of all men."

We cannot rightly discard usage, which, in addition to enhancing our own spiritual growth, is a means of adding strength to missionary work, neither let us confine to privacy from the world that which may do good in public. Our nature, as shown by these God appointed means, reveals to the world the nature of the kingdom of God. Thereby every child of God is made an "ambassador for Christ," and he can easily preach the *Good News,*—nay, he cannot help it.

HOW MISSIONARIES ARE MADE.

DR. CYRUS HAMLIN has told in a five-minute speech how he came to be a missionary. He said: "In the vast majority of cases missionaries are made by the influence of the family. My widowed mother made me a missionary. She had me read every Sunday out of the *Panoplist,* and then later out of the *Missionary Herald.* We had, in those days, in our town a missionary contribution box, a cent box, and we were encouraged to earn some special cents for that box. I remember well one occasion which was, I think, a turning-point in my experience.

When the fall muster came, every boy had a pocketful of cents to spend. My mother gave me seven cents, saying, as she gave them, 'Perhaps you will put a cent or two in the contribution box in Mrs. Farrar's porch on the common.' So I began to think as I went along, Shall I put in one or shall it be two? Then I thought two cents was pretty small, and I came up to three,—three cents for the heathen and four cents for gingerbread; but that did not sound right, did not satisfy me, so I turned it the other way, and said four cents shall go for the heathen. Then, I thought, the boys will ask me how much I have to spend, and three cents is rather too small a sum to talk about. 'Hang it all,' I said, 'I'll put the whole in.' So in it all went. When I told my mother some years after that I was going to be a missionary, she broke down and said, 'I have always expected it.'"—*Missionary Review.*

FISHING.

A MINISTER, very fond of fishing, when away on his vacation, often tried to persuade his wife to join him in a day's sport, but without success. She could see no pleasure in it. At last, one day, to please him, she went. He prepared for her a rod and line, and a carefully-baited hook. She had not held the rod long before it began to shake and bend, and, after great excitement she landed a pickerel weighing five and three-quarters pounds. The minister says that since that time it has been a difficult task for him to go fishing often enough to satisfy his wife. Many Christians have little zeal in trying to win others to follow Christ, but if, in a single case, they could taste the joy of success, they would be enthusiastic winners of souls. It is sometimes a greater service to help a brother into successful work for others than even to save a soul from death.

"How prone we are to think that we belong where we want to be, instead of thinking that we ought to want to be where we belong? If our inclinations and supposed interests point in one direction, it is quite likely to seem to us that this is the direction of our duty. But if our duty seems to point in an opposite direction from our desires and our immediate gain, we are hardly ready to admit that the best place in the world for us is the place that we shrink from. We wish that our duty could lie in the direction of our wishes, instead of wishing that our wishes could go out in the direction of our duty.

The Gospel Messenger

In the recognized organ of the German Baptist or Brethren's church, and advocates the form of doctrine taught in the New Testament and pleads for a return to apostolic and primitive Christianity.

It recognizes the New Testament as the only infallible rule of faith and practice, and maintains that Faith toward God, Repentance from dead works, Regeneration of the heart and mind, baptism by Trine Immersion for remission of sins unto the reception of the Holy Ghost by the laying on of hands, are the means of adoption into the household of God,—the church militant.

It also maintains that Feet-washing, as taught in John 13, both by example and command of Jesus, should be observed in the church.

That the Lord's Supper, instituted by Christ and as universally observed by the apostles and the early Christians, is a full meal, and, in connection with the Communion, should be taken in the evening or after the close of the day.

That the Salutation of the Holy Kiss, or Kiss of Charity, is binding upon the followers of Christ.

That War and Retaliation are contrary to the spirit and self-denying principles of the religion of Jesus Christ.

That the principle of Plain Dressing and of Non-conformity to the world, as taught in the New Testament, should be observed by the followers of Christ.

That the Scriptural duty of Anointing the Sick with Oil, in the Name of the Lord, James 5: 14, is binding upon all Christians.

It also advocates the church's duty to support Missionary and Tract Work, thus giving to the Lord for the spread of the Gospel and for the conversion of sinners.

In short, it is a vindicator of all that Christ and the apostles have enjoined upon us, and alone, amid the conflicting theories and discords of modern Christendom, to point out ground that all must concede to be infallibly safe.

☞ The above principles of our Fraternity are set forth on our "Brethren's Envelopes." Use them! Price, 15 cents per package; 40 cents per hundred.

us, the rising generation, with examples of men from the creation of the world to the present time, who, having found the purpose for which they were created, made it their life-work to attain to that end, glorifying God in their lives, for every thought and deed was given in earnest, and the purpose being a noble one, the results must be equally ennobling.

To be thoroughly in earnest, we must first fully comprehend the responsibility and importance of the work we are to engage in. Abel was in earnest when he offered to God the gift, so acceptable, yet the offering of it and its acceptance, cost him his life. Noah realized the responsibility of his work, and breathed forth the earnestness of his soul in those last antediluvian days.

Though Moses trembled at first at the magnitude of the work, to which God called him, yet, never doubting God's power to strengthen him, he became interested and earnest, and was enabled to lead the Children of Isreal out of the land of Egypt, against all opposing elements. Lot was in earnest, when he went about the wicked city, warning the inmates of impending danger, and though his work was ineffectual, he had done his part, and will receive his reward.

John the Baptist was in earnest in fulfilling his mission of preparing the way for the Light of the World.

Paul, that zealous apostle, was the very embodiment of earnestness and devotion, from his conversion to his death.

O, the depth of meaning in the monuments which these noble men have left behind them for the benefit of the world! All had great trials to contend with; Abel, the bitterness of a jealous brother; Noah, the scorn and derision of an unbelieving world; Moses, all the opposition which King Pharaoh and his army could invent; Lot, the wickedness and hard-heartedness of his own family; John, the darkness and ignorance of the time; and Paul, all manner of afflictions, and even martyrdom at last; yet all felt that God was their All in all, and soul, mind, and strength, went to fulfill the mission he had given them to do.

Dear young fellow-soldiers, how are we profiting by these bright examples? Do we ponder daily upon the great purpose of life, the opportunities to be improved, the great responsibility of our own missions, and the influence we are wielding upon those around us, or did we accept Christianity under a sudden impulse, and have we ever since been trying to live a Christian life simply because our associates are in the church? Have we been acting from motive rather than principle?

Are we often carried away, by the frivolities of our youthful natures, or are we so thoroughly in earnest, intent on being a true, model Christian, at all times, that we can be happy only when thinking on those things, mentioned in Philpp. 4: 8?

In the work in which we are engaged temporally, we often ask ourselves these questions solemnly at night: How many wrong or false impressions have my looks, thoughts, words, or actions, made this day upon the tender minds, and confiding hearts in our care? Then we almost tremble at the thought of answering some day for all the wrong impressions made, and for duty undone; but then this thought invariably comes to us:

"'Tis working with our heart and soul,
That makes our duty pleasure."

We feel that so long as we are truly in earnest, we cannot fail to do what God requires of us, and the rest he will take care of.

If earnestness is so important in temporal things, it is vastly more important in spiritual things. Let us then, who have put our hands to the Gospel plow, not turn back. "Though the plowshare cut through the flowers of life to its fountains, though it pass o'er the graves of the dead, and the hearts of the living, it is the will of the Lord, and his mercy endureth forever."

THE VALUE OF CEREMONIES.

BY JOHN E. MOHLER.

THE popular religious belief of to-day, re-acting from the grave danger of substituting the form for the spirit, has encountered what is, perhaps, no less a danger, namely, forgetting that all spirit must have form. That many evils are likely to result from this inclination, is apparent to some of the world's deepest religious thinkers.

Before discarding an established usage it is wise to consider, as far as possible, the advantages in the line of its purpose; especially so when the practice is of divine authority. God recognizes the great importance of demonstration in the work of evangelizing the world, and, therefore, has appointed special ways by which our spiritual relations to each other and to him should be manifested. Not only has he designated the manner by which these relations are to be made known, but this manner is their natural mode of expression. By natural mode of expression, I mean that method to which all humanity would most likely attach, instinctively, the same meaning. All the ceremonies, enjoined upon us, in the New Testament Scriptures, are of this nature. Being of this character, should their careful observance not demand our favor?

It is strange that these forms, which illustrate spiritual relations the most clearly, should be severely ridiculed by popular so called Christianity. Among these forms are,

(1) Feet-washing.—a practice most suggestive of humility or servitude. *How many blessings follow humility?*

(2) The salutation of the holy kiss,—the most natural token of love, which is greater than either faith or hope. 1 Cor. 13: 13.

(3) Non-conformity to the world,—suggesting a mind not of the world. Other examples might be given, but these will suffice.

The value of the Gospel ordinances, in the enlarging of our Christian influence, may be clearly seen. Not only do we thus show by our works that we have "the faith once delivered to the saints," but we are indeed made "epistles, known and read of all men."

We cannot rightly discard usage, which, in addition to enhancing our own spiritual growth, is a means of adding strength to missionary work, neither let us confine to privacy from the world that which may do good in public. Our nature, as shown by those God-appointed means, reveals to the world the nature of the kingdom of God. Thereby every child of God is made an "ambassador for Christ," and he can easily preach the *Good News*,—nay, he cannot help it.

HOW MISSIONARIES ARE MADE.

DR. CYRUS HAMLIN has told in a five-minute speech how he came to be a missionary. He said: "In the vast majority of cases missionaries are made by the influence of the family. My widowed mother made me a missionary. She had me read every Sunday out of the *Panoplist*, and then later out of the *Missionary Herald*. We had, in those days, in our town a missionary contribution box, a cent box, and we were encouraged to earn some special cents for that box. I remember well one occasion which was, I think, a turning-point in my experience.

When the fall muster came, every boy had a pocketful of cents to spend. My mother gave me seven cents, saying, as she gave them, 'Perhaps you will put a cent or two in the contribution box in Mrs. Farrar's porch on the common.' So I began to think as I went along, Shall I put in one or shall it be two? Then I thought two cents was pretty small, and I came up to three,—three cents for the heathen and four cents for gingerbread; but that did not sound right, did not satisfy me, so I turned it the other way, and said four cents shall go for the heathen. Then, I thought, the boys will ask me how much I have to spend, and three cents is rather too small a sum to talk about. 'Hang it all,' I said, 'I'll put the whole in.' So in it all went. When I told my mother some years after that I was going to be a missionary, she broke down and said, 'I have always expected it.'"—*Missionary Review.*

FISHING.

A MINISTER, very fond of fishing, when away on his vacation, often tried to persuade his wife to join him in a day's sport, but without success. She could see no pleasure in it. At last, one day, to please him, she went. He prepared for her a rod and line, and a carefully-baited hook. She had not held the rod long before it began to shake and bend, and, after great excitement she landed a pickerel weighing five and three-quarters pounds.

The minister says that since that time it has been a difficult task for him to go fishing often enough to satisfy his wife. Many Christians have little zeal in trying to win others to follow Christ, but if, in a single case, they could taste the joy of success, they would be enthusiastic winners of souls. It is sometimes a greater service to help a brother into successful work for others than even to save a soul from death.

"How prone we are to think that we belong where we want to be, instead of thinking that we ought to want to be where we belong? If our inclinations and supposed interests point in one direction, it is quite likely to seem to us that this is the direction of our duty. But if our duty seems to point in an opposite direction from our desires and our immediate gain, we are hardly ready to admit that the best place in the world for us is the place that we shrink from. We wish that our duty could lie in the direction of our wishes, instead of wishing that our wishes could go out in the direction of our duty.

The Gospel Messenger

Is the recognized organ of the German Baptist or Brethren's church, and advocates the form of doctrine taught in the New Testament and pleads for a return to apostolic and primitive Christianity.

It recognizes the New Testament as the only infallible rule of faith and practice, and maintains that Faith toward God, Repentance from dead works, Regeneration of the heart and mind, baptism by Trine Immersion for remission of sins unto the reception of the Holy Ghost by the laying on of hands, are the means of adoption into the household of God,—the church militant.

It also maintains that Feet-washing, as taught in John 13, both by example and command of Jesus, should be observed in the church.

That the Lord's Supper, instituted by Christ and as universally observed by the apostles and the early Christians, is a full meal, and, in connection with the Communion, should be taken in the evening or after the close of the day.

That the Salutation of the Holy Kiss, or Kiss of Charity, is binding upon the followers of Christ.

That War and Retaliation are contrary to the spirit and self-denying principles of the religion of Jesus Christ.

That the principle of Plain Dressing and of Non-conformity to the world, as taught in the New Testament, should be observed by the followers of Christ.

That the Scriptural duty of Anointing the Sick with Oil, in the Name of the Lord, James 5: 14, is binding upon all Christians

It also advocates the church's duty to support Missionary and Tract Work, thus giving to the Lord for the spread of the Gospel and for the conversion of sinners.

In short, it is a vindicator of all that Christ and the apostles have enjoined upon us, and aims, amid the conflicting theories and discords of modern Christendom, to point out ground that all must concede to be infallibly safe.

☞ The above principles of our Fraternity are set forth on our "Brethren's Envelopes." Use them! Price, 15 cents per package; 40 cents per hundred.

[Copyrighted.]

EDITORIAL WANDERINGS IN THE OLD WORLD.

BY D. L. MILLER.

Number Seventeen.—An Important Question.

In No. 12 of this series of letters, published in the MESSENGER Dec. 8, 1891, reference was made to the tombs of Rachel, Jacob's best-loved wife, and her illustrious son who, in everything but in name, ruled for some years in the land of Egypt. We give below an extract from the letter in question:

I close this letter with a digression, suggested by the last paragraph. Jacob was buried in the tomb of his fathers, Abraham and Isaac. Gen. 50: 13. There also Sarah, Rebekah and Leah were buried. Gen. 49: 31. Why was it that Rachel, Jacob's best beloved wife, was buried over by the way as you go to Bethlehem, not more than twelve miles from the family tomb at Hebron, while Joseph, his best beloved and most illustrious son, is entombed within a mile of Jacob's well, near Shechem? We visited these places when in Palestine, and the question naturally suggests itself, Why were these two excluded from the family burying-ground? This question has suggested itself to others, and the following answer has been given:

May this not be a silent, though strong, protest against polygamy which was practiced at that time? Notice that Sarah was Abraham's first and only legal wife. She sleeps her last sleep with the father of the faithful. Isaac and his one legal wife rest in the same tomb. Jacob and his first wife, Leah, not the one he loved best, however, lay side by side in the same family burial-place, while Rachel and her great son were laid by the Wayside. It seems to us that this is a striking protest against a plurality of wives, as only the first wife was legally bound to her husband by the law of God. She only could receive admission to the tomb of her husband. The Bible does not teach polygamy; it simply records the fact that it was practiced and allowed because of the hardness of the hearts of the Israelites. The Master fully explains the original marriage law in the following words: " Have ye not read, that he which made them at the beginning, made them male and female, and said, " For this cause shall a man leave father and mother, and shall cleave to his wife: and they twain shall be one flesh? Wherefore they are no more twain but one flesh. What therefore God hath joined together, let not man put asunder." Matt. 19: 4-6.

Several of our readers have written us in regard to the suggestions contained in the foregoing extract. Naturally, a number of queries are suggested which show a marked sympathy for Rachel, the wife whom Jacob loved best, and of repugnance at the duplicity of Laban who deceived the young lover and gave him Leah instead of Rachel. Hence the question arises as to whether Leah really was Jacob's legal wife, as well as the other query as to why God permitted the practice of polygamy among the patriarchs. Instead of giving our readers a further account of our wanderings in this letter, we will turn it to a brief consideration of these and other questions involved.

All Bible readers are acquainted with the fact that the practice of polygamy was quite common among the people in Old Testament times, and to some it seems strange that even a record of this evil should be given in the Bible. Some one asks, Why is it that the Bible gives such a full record of the polygamous practices of the patriarchs and the kings of Israel? The answer to this question is not hard to find. The Bible, written by inspiration, is the Book of Truth. It gives not only the bright side of human nature but the dark side as well. It sets down the sins and weaknesses of such men as Aaron, Moses, Eli, David, Solomon and Peter. It is a truthful record and gives the facts. It was not written as men write books. Had it been the work of human agency, many of the dark sins committed by men who were counted among God's servants, would have been omitted. The deception practiced by Jacob and Laban, the weakness of Moses and Eli, the sins of David and Solomon, the betrayal of Christ by Peter, and even the dispute between Paul and Barnabas which became so serious that they separated, are given in all of their details, and these are only evidences of the truth of the Book.

In looking at these facts we must not fall into the too common error that because we have a detailed record of the evil in the lives of the Bible characters that, therefore, God looked with allowance upon such things, that, because some of the men of the Bible did these things, therefore there cannot be so much evil in them. No one, who is acquainted with the Bible and is searching for the truth, will make such a claim. The Mormons, to give some excuse to their practice, assert this claim, but they might as well cite the slaying of the Egyptian by Moses, as an excuse for murder.

In all ages of the world men have violated God's laws just as they are violating them to-day. The first great law of marriage was violated in the olden time just as it is being violated to-day. Polygamy is practiced to-day under the cover of the divorce laws of our States, which are a disgrace to civilization, just as it was practiced in violation of God's law ever since sin came into the world. The same is true of murder; ever since Cain slew his brother, men have killed each other. But because of this can we say that God permits these things? His law stands against all evil, and he will most surely judge and punish all these sins.

Take the Law of God as to marriage, set forth in the words of our Master: " Have ye not read, that he which made them at the beginning made them male and female, and said, For this cause shall a man leave his father and mother, and shall cleave to his wife: and they twain shall be one flesh? Wherefore they are no more twain, but one flesh. What therefore God hath joined together, let not man put asunder." This is God's law in regard to marriage. It was promulgated in the Garden of Eden, for in the very act of creating man and woman, the one for the other, the Creator established the great law of monogamy, as against polygamy. Men may reason on this subject and may, as did the Jews, secure, because of the hardness of their hearts, "a writing of divorcement," but the eternal law of God stands against them, for " from the beginning it was not so." Shall we say because men to-day, as did the Jews, violate God's law that he permits these things? Surely such a claim would be unjust and unreasonable.

In looking at this, as well as at all other great moral questions, we must not lose sight of the age and of the moral standards which prevailed at that time among the people. Ignorance, when it is unavoidable, may be offered as a partial excuse for violated law. In God's dealing with men there has been a gradual development from the lower to a higher standard of morality and of spiritual life. Our first parents occupied a very high plane. They were very close to God spiritually, so close that they walked and talked with him. Then came the fall and with it all of its terrible consequences. Sin and degradation, with the loss of spiritual life resulted. But the work of redemption and restoration began. The call of Abraham, from an idolatrous nation followed, and the great plan of salvation, which was to include the nation in Jesus Christ and the cross was inaugurated. Then came the law of Moses, which was far in advance of the morals of the age in which it was given. Its tendency was to bring men and women to a higher plane of morality and spirituality, and thus bring them nearer to God. But it was not perfect. It served its purpose in preparing the way for Christ. In this sense it was what Paul called it a school-master to bring us to Christ. Then came the higher and the perfect law of the Gospel, which, if obeyed, brings to the human race all that was lost in Adam.

It was the condition of the human race before the advent of Christ to which Paul refers in Acts 17: 30, "And the times of this ignorance God winked at, but now commandeth all men everywhere to repent." And again at Lystra, when the people, in their ignorance, would have done sacrifice to Paul and Barnabas, the apostle, in his efforts to restrain them, pointed them to the God of heaven " who, in times past, suffered all nations to walk in their own ways."

In looking at this subject we should not forget that God looked upon the sins of the world with long-suffering and forbearance; not that he condoned evil, or that he permitted sin in the sense that he could look upon it with any degree of allowance. He saw the depths into which the race had fallen and had compassion upon them because of their ignorance and helplessness. It was because of this, coupled with the hardness of heart, the result of ignorance, that Moses gave the writing of divorcement, and in this light we must view the polygamy of the patriarchs.

But through all their polygamy they seem to have kept inviolate the sacred right of the first wife and to have retained the idea of God's first great law of marriage. There seems to have been a silent recognition of this great law, giving the first wife precedence over the others. This was made apparent not only in the right accorded her of a last resting place in the sepulcher of the fathers, which was most highly prized, but also in the line of hereditary succession. Abraham had a number of wives but the line goes down through Isaac, the son of Sarah, his first wife, and this follows in like manner to Jacob, the son of Rebekah, Isaac's legal wife, and again the same honor falls upon Judah, the son of Leah, Jacob's first wife. Thus the right of Leah is established to the title of wifehood under God's first law, for in the line of direct descent we have the house of David, and then, in the fullness of time, Jesus, the son of Mary. And the words of prophecy are thus fulfilled: " The sceptre shall not depart from Judah nor a lawgiver from between his feet, until Shiloh come; and unto him shall the gathering of the people be." Gen. 49: 10.

There are other phases of this question that press for consideration, but space forbids more at this time. As much as our sympathy goes out to the lonely grave by the highway, as you come to Bethlehem, intensified as it is by the sad words of the old patriarch, as he leaned on his staff, ready to be gathered to the tomb of his father, when his heart went back to the first love of his young manhood and he said with so much tender pathos: " And as for me, when I came from Padan, Rachel died by me in the land of Canaan in the way, when yet there was but a little way to come to Ephrath: and I buried her there in the way of Ephrath: the same is Bethlehem," yet we must accord to Leah the honor of wifehood according to God's law of marriage and of being remotely the mother of the line of royalty, of which, in due time, Christ was born.

We learn through Bro. G. W. Fesler this week that a church has been organized eight miles east of Fort Collins, Colo.

EDITORIAL WANDERINGS IN THE OLD WORLD.

BY D. L. MILLER.

Number Seventeen.—An Important Question.

IN No. 12 of this series of letters, published in the MESSENGER Dec. 8, 1891, reference was made to the tombs of Rachel, Jacob's best-loved wife, and her illustrious son who, in everything but in name, ruled for some years in the land of Egypt. We give below an extract from the letter in question:

I close this letter with a digression, suggested by the last paragraph. Jacob was buried in the tomb of his fathers, Abraham and Isaac. Gen. 50:13. There also Sarah, Rebekah and Leah were buried. Gen. 49:31. Why was it that Rachel, Jacob's best beloved wife, was buried over the way as you go to Bethlehem, not more than twelve miles from the family tomb at Hebron, while Joseph, his best beloved and most illustrious son, is entombed within a mile of Jacob's Well, near Shechem? We visited these places when in Palestine, and the question naturally suggests itself, Why were these two excluded from the family burying-ground? This question has suggested itself to others, and the following answer has been given:

May this not be a silent, though strong, protest against polygamy which was practiced at that time? Notice that Sarah was Abraham's first and only legal wife. She sleeps her last sleep with the father of the faithful. Isaac and his one legal wife rest in the same tomb. Jacob and his first wife, Leah, not the one he loved best, however, lay side by side in the same family burial-place, while Rachel and her great son were laid by the wayside. It seems to us that this is a striking protest against a plurality of wives, as only the first wife was legally bound to her husband by the law of God. She only could receive admission to the tomb of her husband. The Bible does not teach polygamy; it simply records the fact that it was practiced and allowed because of the hardness of the hearts of the Israelites. The Master fully explains the original marriage law in the following words: " Have ye not read, that he which made them at the beginning, made them male and female, and said, " For this cause shall a man leave father and mother, and shall cleave to his wife: and they twain shall be one flesh? Wherefore they are no more twain but one flesh. What therefore God hath joined together, let not man put asunder." Matt. 19:4-6.

Several of our readers have written us in regard to the suggestions contained in the foregoing extract. Naturally, a number of queries are suggested which show a marked sympathy for Rachel, the wife whom Jacob loved best, and of repugnance at the duplicity of Laban who deceived the young lover and gave him Leah instead of Rachel. Hence the question arises as to whether Leah really was Jacob's legal wife, as well as the other query as to why God permitted the practice of polygamy among the patriarchs. Instead of giving our readers a further account of our wanderings in this letter, we will turn it to a brief consideration of these and other questions involved.

All Bible readers are acquainted with the fact that the practice of polygamy was quite common among the people in Old Testament times, and to some it seems strange that even a record of this evil should be given in the Bible. Some one asks, Why is it that the Bible gives such a full record of the polygamous practices of the patriarchs and the kings of Israel? The answer to this question is not hard to find. The Bible, written by inspiration, is the Book of Truth. It gives not only the bright side of human nature but the dark side as well. It sets down the sins and weaknesses of such men as Aaron, Moses, Eli, David, Solomon and Peter. It is a truthful record and gives the facts. It was not written as men write books. Had it been the work of human agency, many of the dark sins committed by men who were counted among God's servants, would have been omitted. The deception practiced by Jacob and Laban, the weakness of Moses and Eli, the sins of David and Solomon, the betrayal of Christ by Peter, and even the dispute between Paul and Barnabas which became so serious that they separated, are given in all of their details, and these are only evidences of the truth of the Book.

In looking at these facts we must not fall into the too common error that because we have a detailed record of the evil in the lives of the Bible characters that, therefore, God looked with allowance upon such things, that, because some of the men of the Bible did these things, therefore there cannot be so much evil in them. No one, who is acquainted with the Bible and is searching for the truth, will make such a claim. The Mormons, to give some excuse to their practice, assert this claim, but they might as well cite the slaying of the Egyptian by Moses, as an excuse for murder. In all ages of the world men have violated God's laws just as they are violating them to-day. The first great law of marriage was violated in the olden time just as it is being violated to-day. Polygamy is practiced to-day under the cover of the divorce laws of our States, which are a disgrace to civilization, just as it was practiced in violation of God's law ever since sin came into the world. The same is true of murder; ever since Cain slew his brother, men have killed each other. But because of this can we say that God permits these things? His law stands against all evil, and he will most surely judge and punish all these sins.

Take the Law of God as to marriage, set forth in the words of our Master: "Have ye not read, that he which made them at the beginning made them male and female, and said, For this cause shall a man leave his father and mother, and shall cleave to his wife: and they twain shall be one flesh? Wherefore they are no more twain, but one flesh. What therefore God hath joined together, let not man put asunder." This is God's law in regard to marriage. It was promulgated in the Garden of Eden, for in the very act of creating man and woman, the one for the other, the Creator established the great law of monogamy, as against polygamy. Men may reason on this subject and may, as did the Jews, secure, because of the hardness of their hearts, "a writing of divorcement," but the eternal law of God stands against them, for " from the beginning it was not so." Shall we say because men to-day, as did the Jews, violate God's law that he permits these things? Surely such a claim would be unjust and unreasonable.

In looking at this, as well as at all other great moral questions, we must not lose sight of the age and of the moral standards which prevailed at that time among the people. Ignorance, when it is unavoidable, may be offered as a partial excuse for violated law. In God's dealing with men there has been a gradual development from the lower to a higher standard of morality and of spiritual life. Our first parents occupied a very high plane. They were very close to God spiritually, so close that they walked and talked with him. Then came the fall and with it all of its terrible consequences. Sin and degradation, with the loss of spiritual life resulted. But the work of redemption and restoration began. The call of Abraham, from an idolatrous nation followed, and the great plan of salvation, which was to find its culmination in Jesus Christ and the cross was inaugurated. Then came the law of Moses, which was far in advance of the morals of the age in which it was given. Its tendency was to bring men and women to a higher plane of morality and spirituality, and thus bring them nearer to God. But it was not perfect. It served its purpose in preparing the way for Christ. In this sense it was what Paul called it a school-master to bring us to Christ. Then came the higher and the perfect law of the Gospel, which, if obeyed, brings to the human race all that was lost in Adam.

It was the condition of the human race before the advent of Christ to which Paul refers in Acts 17: 50, "And the times of this ignorance God winked at, but now commandeth all men everywhere to repent." And again at Lystra, when the people, in their ignorance, would have done sacrifice to Paul and Barnabas, the apostle, in his efforts to restrain them, pointed them to the God of heaven " who, in times past, suffered all nations to walk in their own ways."

In looking at this subject we should not forget that God looked upon the sins of the world with long-suffering and forbearance; not that he condoned evil, or that he permitted sin in the sense that he could look upon it with any degree of allowance. He saw the depths into which the race had fallen and had compassion upon them because of their ignorance and helplessness. It was because of this, coupled with the hardness of heart, the result of ignorance, that Moses gave the writing of divorcement, and in this light we must view the polygamy of the patriarchs.

But through all their polygamy they seem to have kept inviolate the sacred right of the first wife and to have retained the idea of God's first great law of marriage. There seems to have been a silent recognition of this great law, giving the first wife precedence over the others. This was made apparent not only in the right accorded her of a last resting place in the sepulcher of the fathers, which was most highly prized, but also in the line of hereditary succession. Abraham had a number of wives but the line goes down through Isaac, the son of Sarah, his first wife, and this follows in like manner to Jacob, the son of Rebekah, Isaac's legal wife, and again the same honor falls upon Judah, the son of Leah, Jacob's first wife. Thus the right of Leah is established to the title of wifehood under God's first law, for in the line of direct descent we have the house of David, and then, in the fullness of time, Jesus, the son of Mary. And the words of prophecy are thus fulfilled: "The sceptre shall not depart from Judah nor a lawgiver from between his feet, until Shiloh come; and unto him shall the gathering of the people be." Gen. 49: 10.

There are other phases of this question that press for consideration, but space forbids more at this time. As much as our sympathy goes out to the lonely grave by the highway, as you come to Bethlehem, intensified as it is by the sad words of the old patriarch, as he leaned on his staff, ready to be gathered to the tomb of his father, when his heart went back to the first love of his young manhood and he said with so much tender pathos: " And as for me, when I came from Padan, Rachel died by me in the land of Canaan in the way, when yet there was but a little way to come to Ephrath: and I buried her there in the way of Ephrath: the same is Bethlehem," yet we must accord to Leah the honor of wifehood according to God's law of marriage and of being remotely the mother of the line of royalty, of which, in due time, Christ was born.

WE learn through Bro. G. W. Fesler this week that a church has been organized eight miles east of Fort Collins, Colo.

Rebecca Linginfelter, Canton, Ill.,......	1 50
Mrs. H. A. Stahl, Gebhart's, Pa.,........	1 00
Nancy Martin, Mercersburg, Pa,........	5 00
South Keokuk church, Iowa,...........	7 25
Grundy County church, Iowa,...........	22 28
David Bidinger, Accident, Md,...........	5 00
Two sisters, Accident, Md.,..............	7 00
Susan Rowland, Dallas Centre, Iowa,....	1 00
Reuben Zug, Schaefferstown, Pa,........	1 00
Green Tree church, Pennsylvania, ...	15 00
Mary E. Leedy, Larwill, Ind	1 00
M. C. Caigane, Auburn, West Virginia,..	3 50
George Quickel, Mulberry, Pa,..........	8 50
Katie Replogle, Farragut, Iowa,.........	40
Emma E. Kindig, Ocarga, Ill.,..........	50
John Rudy, Liscomb, Iowa,.............	5 55
Mary Croft, Bradford, Ohio,...........	50
A brother, Colorado,....................	5 00
G. T., and Kate E. Leatherman, Burling-	
ton, West Virginia,..................	5 00
English River church, Iowa,............	1 50
Nannie Smouse, Pennsylvania..........	1 00
Jos. B. Replogle, Pennsylvania,........	90
Sister B. S. Kindig, Benson, Ill.,.......	5 00
Levi Stump and wife, Ligonier, Ind.,.....	14 00

Impressions by the Way.

(Continued.)

Our short stay at Ephratah was made pleasant and profitable by the zeal of the members in the meeting then in progress. Here we were impressed by the convenient preparations for baptizing. Often has my heart been pained and the good cause hindered by the want of a proper place to administer the sacred rite. 1 Cor. 14: 40. Here they have a place walled in and steps leading down to the running water. This is much more inviting than the mud and inconvenience we often encounter. It is not only in this, but in many things that the good work may be hindered by us not studying to show ourselves approved workmen.

The preparation of the tables at the time of our love-feasts is often too carelessly done. Unsightly dishes, that would be rejected at our own homes, provoke levity and criticism by the world. Our children hear it, and obstacles are thus placed in their way of accepting Christ, by our own want of care.

I suggest to all the practice of some of our churches, that a white cloth be spread over the prepared tables until after feet-washing. This cloth can then be removed until after the eating of the Supper. Covering the table again after Supper, will put it in an inviting condition for the Communion. In this way the clearing of the tables, which always destroys the solemnity of the meeting, is rendered unnecessary until after the services. To study what may be done in honor to God and for the promotion of his cause, is not only a duty but is productive of much good.

The Sunday-school at Ephratah, started by the efforts of a young sister, shows what may be done by individual efforts. Over one hundred are now in attendance and when we saw the aged veterans, as Eld. Samuel Harley, and others, encouraging the work by their aid and presence, we knew the reason why they are so successful.

As a matter for improvement I suggest and hope that our Sunday-schools will adopt and use our own literature exclusively. Some outside help that is used is not only deficient in teaching the Truth, but deceptive in its teaching. If we lack anything to meet our wants in the line of helps, let us provide the same.

The reading matter of our Sunday-schools and families will influence for good or evil. I am associated with many families in my work, and the importance and usefulness of the Gospel Messen-

ger is made very apparent to me. It is not only a medium of instruction, but a creating power, in citing an interest in the hearts and minds of our children for the church. It is a matter that should be second to none in the minds of professed Christians. Our children are the twigs that soon shall be the trees, and as they are cultivated, the fruit will be. Eph. 4: 1.

　　　　　　　　　　　　　ISAAC FRANTZ.
Pleasant Hill, Ohio.

From Sheridan, Mo.

I HAVE been preaching here in the Honey Creek church, in North-western Missouri, for the past ten days. Owing to unpleasant weather and bad roads, the congregations were not large, but the interest seems good. Some are counting the cost and are now almost persuaded, and are very near the kingdom. The Brethren are much revived, but express a regret that they have not the necessary ministerial force to ably maintain the cause, and gather wandering sheep into the fold.

I go this evening about six miles west, to the outskirts of the congregation, to labor for a while, where we will hold our meetings in a school-house among the Brethren that could not attend, owing to bad roads and unpleasant weather.

The weather here has been cold, and the mercury has been as low as 26 degrees below zero. I expect to work a while for the Whitesville church, Andrew Co., Mo., before I return home.

Bro. Wm. Clark, who was so suddenly taken ill with *La Grippe* early in December, is slowly improving, but not yet able to get out of the house. This leaves me enjoying the best of health, for which I am thankful.

May God's blessings attend you all! It is while on these trips that we learn to appreciate the value of our paper.　　　　　H. W. STRICKLER.

From Lordsburg, Cal.

THIS being my fifty-sixth "birthday," I thought I would use the columns of the MESSENGER as a medium through which to address its readers. I have just been reading Bro. D. L. Miller's explanation, as to their trip in the East, etc. I felt both glad and disappointed,—glad because they were at their own home (for few persons know more of what that word *home* means than our dear brother and sister Miller).

Then, again, I felt disappointed, to think that they were not permitted to carry into effect their desire and purpose, which prompted them to make the effort. The information which the Brotherhood would have obtained through that medium, would have been of inestimable value, but I feel like fully submitting to the directing hand of a kind Providence. I realize that we can much better afford to forego the pleasure of that knowledge, than to give up our brother and sister to the ravages of cholera.

So I say "Amen" to what seems to have been the guiding of the hand of our Father in heaven. May we all ever yield to the movement of that hand, to lead in all things!

I will next give some of my thoughts and experiences since I am in California. First I will say that the sins and temptations to which people are exposed here, do not differ very materially from those of other places. Their name is legion, however, and the persons who steer clear of all, or any of them, have great reason to be happy. A great many people come from the East to this country,—each one prompted by some inducement which has been held out to him or her. Some seem to be fully satisfied with their findings here, while others find little or nothing suited to their ideas of things. Not a few come with the

desire to find a place where they can enjoy better health, etc. Some of that class are well satisfied, and others are sadly disappointed. Some were prompted to come, because they understood there were no wind-storms here, but Dec. 10, 1891, took all of that idea out of them,—when they saw houses by the scores demolished, trees uprooted, and things turned up generally.

When viewing the situation, after the storm was over, and seeing houses of various kinds which had been blown down, the thought occurred that the gale of the wind must have been much stronger than I had realized at the time. (You know we don't take much note of wind in Kansas.) But when I came to examine the character of the buildings, I found them to have been built in a very temporary manner at first. They had built these houses a good deal like some people build their spiritual houses,—the outside looked fairly well, but inside they lacked the necessary braces, and so, when the storm came, destruction came upon them.

But after all, I thought again, what good would the braces and inside supports do in a storm, if the outside were not solid? The final conclusion was, that we need a good inside, and have that well protected by a genuine outer finish, before we will be able to stand in the storm at the last day. The solid interior must be put up first, and then the outer,—either will be of little value without the other.

If those who want it all outside, and such as seem to see nothing but the inside, could only meet on half-way ground, and get both, the outer and the inner all right, the world would be greatly benefited by the result. Well, I suppose that is enough of that, for the present.

Many very dear ones wish to know how the writer is getting along here on the Pacific Slope. I answer, that I am doing as well as I could reasonably expect. There seems to be a call for the plain, simple truths of the Bible to be taught in this country, as well as in the East. There is a vacuum in the needs of the human soul which cannot be fully satisfied with anything short of the unadulterated Word of. God. Hence the various organizations of a moral character, which, while they are good so far as they go, yet cannot fully meet the demands of the soul. I am as well as I have been for many years. The mildness of this climate suits me well; I am preaching daily. Address me at Lordsburg, Cal., in care of Dr. S. S. Garst.　　　　　　　　　A. HUTCHISON.

Death of Eld. Jacob Beughly.

JAN. 11 we were called to the Marklesburg congregation, to pay the last tribute of respect to another aged and much esteemed veteran of the cross.

Bro. Jacob Beughly, of Marklesburg, Fayette Co., Pa., was born July 18, 1808. At the age of twenty-two, Bro. Beughly was married to Justina Horner. Soon after this union they, by mutual consent, united with the church in holy baptism. There were born unto them seven children,—one son, and six daughters. The son, Jeremiah Beughly, is an elder in the church, and has charge of two congregations,—"Bear Creek" and "Maple Grove,"—in Garrett County, Md. Four daughters are still living.

Bro. Beughly was elected to the ministry about fifty years ago. I well remember of hearing my grandfather (Eld. Jacob M. Thomas, deceased) speak of him and Bro. Beughly traveling on horseback over several counties in West Virginia, Maryland and Pennsylvania, preaching to isolated members, and establishing churches.

Jan. 27, 1857, Justina, wife of Bro. Beughly, departed this life, in a full hope of a blest immor-

Rebecca Linginfelter, Canton, Ill.,	1 50
Mrs. H. A. Stahl, Gebhart's, Pa.,	1 00
Nancy Martin, Mercersburg, Pa.,	5 00
South Keokuk church, Iowa,	7 25
Grundy County church, Iowa,	22 23
David Bidinger, Accident, Md.,	5 00
Two sisters, Accident, Md.,	7 00
Susan Rowland, Dallas Centre, Iowa,	1 00
Reuben Zug, Schaefferstown, Pa.,	1 00
Green Tree church, Pennsylvania,	15 00
Mary E. Leedy, Larwill, Ind.,	1 00
M. C. Czigans, Auburn, West Virginia,	3 50
George Quickel, Mulberry, Pa.,	3 50
Katie Replogle, Farragut, Iowa,	40
Emma E. Kindig, Ocarga, Ill.,	50
John Rudy, Liscomb, Iowa,	5 55
Mary Croft, Bradford, Ohio,	50
A brother, Colorado,	5 00
G. T., and Kate E. Leatherman, Burlington, West Virginia,	5 00
English River church, Iowa,	1 50
Nannie Smouse, Pennsylvania,	1 00
Jos. B. Replogle, Pennsylvania,	90
Sister B. S. Kindig, Benson, Ill.,	5 00
Levi Stump and wife, Ligonier, Ind.,	14 00

Impressions by the Way.

(Continued.)

OUR short stay at Ephratah was made pleasant and profitable by the zeal of the members in the meeting then in progress. Here we were impressed by the convenient preparations for baptizing. Often has my heart been pained and the good cause hindered by the want of a proper place to administer the sacred rite. 1 Cor. 14: 40. Here they have a place walled in and steps leading down to the running water. This is much more inviting than the mud and inconvenience we often encounter. It is not only in this, but in many things that the good work may be hindered by us not studying to show ourselves approved workmen.

The preparation of the tables at the time of our love-feasts is often too carelessly done. Unsightly dishes, that would be rejected at our own homes, provoke levity and criticism by the world. Our children hear it, and obstacles are thus placed in their way of accepting Christ, by our own want of care.

I suggest to all the practice of some of our churches, that a white cloth be spread over the prepared tables until after feet-washing. This cloth can then be removed until after the eating of the Supper. Covering the table again after Supper, will put it in an inviting condition for the Communion. In this way the clearing of the tables, which always destroys the solemnity of the meeting, is rendered unnecessary until after the services. To study what may be done in honor to God and for the promotion of his cause, is not only a duty but is productive of much good.

The Sunday-school at Ephratah, started by the efforts of a young sister, shows what may be done by individual efforts. Over one hundred are now in attendance and when we saw the aged veterans, as Eld. Samuel Harley, and others, encouraging the work by their aid and presence, we knew the reason why they are so successful.

As a matter for improvement I suggest and hope that our Sunday-schools will adopt and use our own literature exclusively. Some outside help that is used is not only deficient in teaching the Truth, but deceptive in its teaching. If we lack anything to meet our wants in the line of helps, let us provide the same.

The reading matter of our Sunday-schools and families will influence for good or evil. I am associated with many families in my work, and the importance and usefulness of the GOSPEL MESSEN-

GER is made very apparent to me. It is not only a medium of instruction, but a creating power, inciting an interest in the hearts and minds of our children for the church. It is a matter that should be second to none in the minds of professed Christians. Our children are the twigs that soon shall be the trees, and as they are cultivated, the fruit will be. Eph. 4: 1.

ISAAC FRANTZ.

Pleasant Hill, Ohio.

From Sheridan, Mo.

I HAVE been preaching, here in the Honey Creek church, in North-western Missouri, for the past ten days. Owing to unpleasant weather and bad roads, the congregations were not large, but the interest seems good. Some are counting the cost and are now almost persuaded, and are very near the kingdom. The Brethren are much revived, but express a regret that they have not the necessary ministerial force to ably maintain the cause, and gather wandering sheep into the fold.

I go this evening about six miles west, to the outskirts of the congregation, to labor for a while, where we will hold our meetings in a school-house among the Brethren that could not attend, owing to bad roads and unpleasant weather.

The weather here has been cold, and the mercury has been as low as 28 degrees below zero. I expect to work a while for the Whitesville church, Andrew Co., Mo., before I return home.

Bro. Wm. Clark, who was so suddenly taken ill with *La Grippe* early in December, is slowly improving, but not yet able to get out of the house. This leaves me enjoying the best of health, for which I am thankful.

May God's blessings attend you all! It is while on these trips that we learn to appreciate the value of our paper.   H. W. STRICKLER.

From Lordsburg, Cal.

THIS being my fifty-sixth " birthday," I thought I would use the columns of the MESSENGER as a medium through which to address its readers. I have just been reading Bro. D. L. Miller's explanation, as to his trip in the East, etc. I felt both glad and disappointed,—glad because they were at their own home (for few persons know more of what that word *home* means than our dear brother and sister Miller).

Then, again, I felt disappointed, to think that they were not permitted to carry into effect their desire and purpose, which prompted them to make the effort. The information which the Brotherhood would have obtained through that medium, would have been of inestimable value, but I feel like fully submitting to the directing hand of a kind Providence. I realize that we can much better afford to forego the pleasure of that knowledge, than to give up our brother and sister to the ravages of cholera.

So I say " Amen " to what seems to have been the guiding of the hand of our Father in heaven. May we all ever yield to the movement of that hand, to lead in all things!

I will next give some of my thoughts and experiences since I am in California. First I will say that the aims and temptations to which people are exposed here, do not differ very materially from those of other places. Their name is legion, however, and the persons who steer clear of all, or any of them, have great reason to be happy. A great many people come from the East to this country,—each one prompted by some inducement which has been held out to him or her. Some seem to be fully satisfied with their findings here, while others find little or nothing suited to their ideas of things. Not a few come with the

desire to find a place where they can enjoy better health, etc. Some of that class are well satisfied, and others are sadly disappointed. Some were prompted to come, because they understood there were no wind-storms here, but Dec. 10, 1891, took all of that idea out of them,—when they saw houses by the scores demolished, trees uprooted, and things turned up generally.

When viewing the situation, after the storm was over, and seeing houses of various kinds which had been blown down, the thought occurred that the gale of the wind must have been much stronger than I had realized at the time. (You know we don't take much note of wind in Kansas.) But when I came to examine the character of the buildings, I found them to have been built in a very temporary manner at first. They had built these houses a good deal like some people build their spiritual houses,—the outside looked fairly well, but inside they lacked the necessary braces, and so, when the storm came, destruction came upon them.

But after all, I thought again, what good would the braces and inside supports do in a storm, if the outside were not solid? The final conclusion was, that we need a good inside, and have that well protected by a genuine outer finish, before we will be able to stand in the storm at the last day. The solid interior must be put up first, and then the outer,—either will be of little value without the other.

If those who want it all outside, and such as want to see nothing but the inside, could only meet on half-way ground, and get both, the outer and the inner all right, the world would be greatly benefited by the result. Well, I suppose that is enough of that, for the present.

Many very dear ones wish to know how the writer is getting along here on the Pacific Slope. I answer, that I am doing as well as I could reasonably expect. There seems to be a call for the plain, simple truths of the Bible to be taught in this country, as well as in the East. There is a vacuum in the needs of the human soul which cannot be fully satisfied with anything short of the unadulterated Word of God. Hence the various organizations of a moral character, which, while they are good so far as they go, yet cannot fully meet the demands of the soul. I am as well as I have been for many years. The mildness of this climate suits me well; I am preaching daily. Address me at Lordsburg, Cal., in care of Dr. S. S. Garst.   A. HUTCHISON.

Death of Eld. Jacob Beeghly.

JAN. 11 we were called to the Marklesburg congregation, to pay the last tribute of respect to another aged and much esteemed veteran of the cross.

Bro. Jacob Beeghly, of Marklesyburg, Fayette Co., Pa., was born July 18, 1808. At the age of twenty-two, Bro. Beeghly was married to Justina Horner. Soon after this union they, by mutual consent, united with the church in holy baptism. There were born unto them seven children,—one son, and six daughters. The son, Jeremiah Beeghly, is an elder in the church, and has charge of two congregations,—" Bear Creek " and " Maple Grove,"—in Garrett County, Md. Four daughters are still living.

Bro. Beeghly was elected to the ministry about fifty years ago. I well remember of hearing my grandfather (Eld. Jacob M. Thomas, deceased) speak of him and Bro. Beeghly traveling on horseback over several Counties in West Virginia, Maryland and Pennsylvania, preaching to isolated members, and establishing churches.

Jan. 27, 1857, Justina, wife of Bro. Beeghly, departed this life, in a full hope of a blest immor-

Notes from Our Correspondents.

"As cold water to a thirsty soul, so is good news from a far country."

Lakeside, Ind.—The Winnimac church, Ind., is enjoying an interesting series of meetings, conducted by Bro. L. M. Hahn. Thus far the meetings have resulted in one addition by baptism.—*Oliver Capron.*

Saline Valley, Kans.—We commenced meetings at the Freedom school-house, Lincoln Co., Kans., on the outskirts of the Saline Valley church, on the evening of Dec. 22. Bro. Wm. Himes, of the Dorrance church, preached the first three evenings, and then went home, the congregations being rather small on account of not being properly announced. I then continued the meetings each evening until Jan. 3, with crowded houses, good interest, and the best of order. Part of the time they could not all get into the house. Some were much interested, but it seemed they could not get the full consent of their minds. Somebody will be responsible in the day of judgment.—*L. W. Fitzwater, Jan. 14.*

Rockton, Iowa.—The Iowa River church met in quarterly council Jan. 10. All business that came before the church was transacted in a kind and brotherly way. We are trying to work for the good of souls, and ask the prayers of God's faithful ones, that we may do more work in God's service. Our church decided to hold a series of meetings, to be conducted by our home ministers. The meetings commenced on the evening of the tenth, and continued till the evening of the seventeenth. Although we had no accessions, we do believe that all who came went away with something to think upon. Our church decided to hold services every Sunday evening, alternately, at the stone church, and a school-house, about three and one-half miles north-west of the church.—*Ellen Nicholson, Jan. 19.*

York, Pa.—The members of this place have just enjoyed an interesting series of meetings. Eld. D. F. Stouffer, of Benevola, Washington County, Md., came to us Jan. 5 and remained until the 13th. During that time he preached nine sermons with more than his usual zeal and earnestness, and these meetings will long be remembered as among the best and most solemn we have ever had the privilege of enjoying. May we remember the kind words of encouragement and admonition, and live more faithful, more consecrated, and more Christ-like, and finally meet in the many mansions. Although there were no accessions, we trust that many good and lasting impressions were made, and that the good seed which was sown may bring forth good fruit in the future!—*A. M. Brodbeck.*

Nocona, Texas.—The Nocona church, Texas, met in quarterly council Jan. 2, at the house of Eld. Abe Molsbee. All the business before the meeting was considered and disposed of apparently with the best of feelings. Wm. H. Hall and wife, having recently moved among us from Erath County, were received as members of this charge, though not by letter, as there was no organized body to give one. Sister Mary Hall was appointed solicitor for District Mission Funds. It was decided that we continue the Sunday-school at the house of Eld. Abe Molsbee, for the next three months on Sunday afternoon. It has been held in Eld. H. Brubaker's house since it was too cold to hold it in the arbor. Sister Molsbee has been confined in bed with "*La Grippe,*" also one of her daughters. Bro. Joe Brubaker has been sick for some time. The weather for this climate has been the coldest we have experienced since in Texas.—*A. J. Wine, Jan. 15.*

Elmwood, Nebr.—The home ministers commenced a series of meetings Jan. 3 at the Fair View school-house. Bro. Jacob Ryan, after preaching four sermons, took sick. Bro. Jesse Y. Heckler then preached four more sermons, but had to close on account of other appointments. The best of order prevailed all through the meeting. The interest and attendance were good.—*J. J. Miller.*

Pleasant Grove, Kans.—Dec. 7 we commenced a series of meetings, and continued them until the evening of Dec. 21. They were conducted by Bro. T. G. Winey, one of our home ministers. Two, as an immediate result, were persuaded to forsake the ranks of sin, and to join the army of the Lord. The one is an aged brother, the other a young sister. She was baptized on her sixteenth birthday. Others were almost persuaded, but decided to defer for the present.—*J. W. Baker, Jan. 12.*

McComb, Ohio.—Eld. Ed. Loomis commenced a series of meetings in the Sugar Ridge church, Hancock Co., Ohio, Dec. 13, and closed on the night of Dec. 27. During the twenty-six discourses that he delivered, marked attention was paid to the Word preached. We had no accessions to the church, but we hope that many good impressions were made. At this writing we have pleasant winter weather with some snow. Health is not so good here. *La Grippe* is prevailing in this vicinity and city.—*D. W. C. Rau.*

McPherson, Kans.—The Monitor church met in quarterly council Dec. 31. All the business was transacted harmoniously, and the time passed pleasantly. We much regretted that Bro. J. D. Trostle, our elder, could not be with us because of his afflictions, as we have learned to enjoy his loving admonitions and councils. May God be with him in his trials! The two applicants previously reported, and one new applicant have been received by baptism since my last report. May they be faithful workers for the Master!—*S. E. Lantz, Jan. 18.*

Linganore, Md.—On the evening of Jan. 2, Bro. Henry Light, of Lancaster, Pa., commenced a series of meetings in the Locust Grove church, and continued until the 14th. The attendance was good, considering the inclement weather and *La Grippe.* Bro. Light is a very pleasant, interesting and instructive speaker, and does not shun to declare the whole Truth. Many deep and lasting impressions were made on both saint and sinner. As an immediate result of his labors, one dear young lamb was made willing to follow Christ, and others were "almost persuaded." May the Lord strengthen and encourage him, and bless his labors for good!—*Maggie E. Ecker.*

Longmont, Colo.—According to previous arrangements the Brethren, now composing the Powder Valley church, eight miles east of Ft. Collins, Colo., met at the Cascos school-house Jan. 16, and effected an organization. All the members were present but three, but all expressed themselves as being willing to labor for the upbuilding of the cause of Christ, and in harmony with the General Brotherhood. May the prayers of God's children go up in their behalf that they may grow in grace as well as in numbers. Feeling the need of official help, they elected Bro. D. M. Glick to the ministry, and brethren Samuel Pye and Samuel Glick to the office of deacon. All felt the great responsibility that is being placed upon them, and an unusual solemnity prevailed. May they all be instruments in the hands of God for good! May good, faithful minister, wishing to enjoy the pure air of Colorado, might find it to his advantage to correspond with the above brethren at Ft. Collins, Colo.—*G. W. Feeler.*

Wallace, Nebr.—In Messenger No. 50, of last volume, Bro. Cornelius Kessler speaks of the great value of the "Biographical Sketches" by Bro. B. F. Moomaw. Permit me to suggest that these "Sketches" be published in pamphlet form, so that they may be preserved for future generations.—*J. K. Shively.*

Whitfield, Ohio.—Bro. D. Bock, of Ridgeway, Mont. gomery Co., Ohio, Dec. 26, and began a series of meetings, which he continued until Jan. 1, when he was assisted by Bro. Holder, of Deweyville, Ohio. These brethren labored together until Dec. 4, when Bro. Bock left for home. Bro. Holder continued the meetings until Jan. 10, and then closed, having delivered twenty-one sermons. The Brethren labored earnestly, and although there were no accessions, we believe there were many good impressions made, and the church was much encouraged in the good cause. May the blessings of God rest upon our dear brethren who labored so zealously for us!—*E. Hyer, Jan. 18.*

Salem, Ohio.—Our meeting closed night before last. It was a very interesting one, and good attention was paid to the Word preached. Our large house was entirely filled the last night of our meeting. Many were sorry that the meetings closed so soon. The home ministers conducted the meetings until the 12th, after which Bro. Daniel Snell, of Indiana, preached for us. As yet we have had no accessions to the church since our meetings. Our brother left for home yesterday. May the Lord go with him! Our missionary solicitors, Bro. S. B. Christian and sister Christian, are making their semi-annual solicitation for the missionary cause. May the brethren and sisters contribute liberally to the good cause! Our tract solicitors, Bro. and sister John Rinehart have been soliciting for the Tract Work. Brethren and sisters, let us all be up to our duty, as we all have a work to do. Then, if we are faithful, we will receive a crown at the end of our race.—*Jesse K. Brumbaugh, Jan. 19.*

Pioneer, Ohio.—On Saturday evening, Dec. 21, the members of the Silver Creek church, Williams Co., Ohio, commenced a series of meetings in the Hickory Grove church, conducted by Bro. W. L. Desenberg. He preached at this place twenty-four sermons, we believe to the edification of all present. The weather was very inclement at the beginning of the meeting. On this account the attendance was not as large as it otherwise would have been. As the meeting progressed, and the weather became more favorable, the meetings grew in interest and number until we had good congregations. During these meetings one dear soul said he was tired of sin and desired to cast his lot with the people of God. He was baptized according to the instructions given by our Savior. Although young in years we hope he may hold out faithful to the end. From here we went to the west end of our District, and commenced meetings in the house owned by the Christian Union Society. As there are but few members living here, the doctrine, as understood and practiced by the Brethren, is somewhat new. Here our brother preached twenty-four sermons. We never saw a more attentive people than we met at this place. Although the roads were very bad, the house was filled with people, eager to hear the Word preached in its purity. At this place there was one added to the church, an old brother, past his three score and ten years. Others were almost persuaded, and with tears flowing down their cheeks, they said we should come again and, like the Bereans, they are searching the Scriptures to see whether these things are so. Thus we see the old and young starting together for the land of pure delight.—*J. W. Keiser.*

Notes from Our Correspondents.

"As cold water to a thirsty soul, so is good news from a far country."

Lakeside, Ind.—The Winnimac church, Ind., is enjoying an interesting series of meetings, conducted by Bro. L. M. Hahn. Thus far the meetings have resulted in one addition by baptism.—*Oliver Capron.*

Saline Valley, Kans.—We commenced meetings at the Freedom school-house, Lincoln Co., Kans., on the outskirts of the Saline Valley church, on the evening of Dec. 22. Bro. Wm. Himes, of the Dorrance church, preached the first three evenings, and then went home, the congregations being rather small on account of not being properly announced. I then continued the meetings each evening until Jan. 3, with crowded houses, good interest, and the best of order. Part of the time they could not all get into the house. Some were much interested, but it seemed they could not get the full consent of their minds. Somebody will be responsible in the day of judgment.—*L. W. Fitzwater, Jan. 14.*

Beckton, Iowa.—The Iowa River church met in quarterly council Jan. 10. All business that came before the church was transacted in a kind and brotherly way. We are trying to work for the good of souls, and ask the prayers of God's faithful ones, that we may do more work in God's service. Our church decided to hold a series of meetings, to be conducted by our home ministers. The meetings commenced on the evening of the tenth, and continued till the evening of the seventeenth. Although we had no accessions, we do believe that all who came went away with something to think upon. Our church decided to hold services every Sunday evening, alternately, at the stone church, and a school-house, about three and one-half miles north-west of the church.—*Ellen Nicholson, Jan. 19.*

York, Pa.—The members of this place have just enjoyed an interesting series of meetings. Eld. D. F. Stouffer, of Benevola, Washington County, Md., came to us Jan. 5 and remained until the 13th. During that time he preached nine sermons with more than his usual zeal and earnestness, and these meetings will long be remembered as among the best and most solemn we have ever had the privilege of enjoying. May we remember the kind words of encouragement and admonition, and live more faithful, more consecrated, and more Christ-like, and finally meet in the many mansions. Although there were no accessions, we trust that many good and lasting impressions were made, and that the good seed which was sown may bring forth good fruit in the future!—*A. M. Brodbeck.*

Nocona, Texas.—The Nocona church, Texas, met in quarterly council Jan. 2, at the house of Eld. Abe Molsbee. All the business before the meeting was considered and disposed of apparently with the best of feelings. Wm. H. Hall and wife, having recently moved among us from Erath County, were received as members of this church, though not by letter, as there was no organized body to give one. Sister Mary Hall was appointed solicitor for District Mission Funds. It was decided that we continue the Sunday-school at the house of Eld. Abe Molsbee, for the next three months on Sunday afternoon. It has been held in Eld. H. Brubaker's house since it was too cold to hold it in the arbor. Sister Molsbee has been confined in bed with "*La Grippe*;" also one of her daughters. Bro. Joe Brubaker has been sick for some time. The weather for this climate has been the coldest we have experienced since in Texas.—*A. J. Wine, Jan. 15.*

Elmwood, Nebr.—The home ministers commenced a series of meetings Jan. 3 at the Fair View school-house. Bro. Jacob Ryan, after preaching four sermons, took sick. Bro. Jesse Y. Heckler then preached four more sermons, but had to close on account of other appointments. The best of order prevailed all through the meetings. The interest and attendance were good.—*J. J. Miller.*

Pleasant Grove, Kans.—Dec. 7 we commenced a series of meetings, and continued them until the evening of Dec. 21. They were conducted by Bro. T. G. Winey, one of our home ministers. Two, as an immediate result, were persuaded to forsake the ranks of sin, and to join the army of the Lord. The one is an aged brother, the other a young sister. She was baptized on her sixteenth birthday. Others were almost persuaded, but decided to defer for the present.—*J. W. Baker, Jan. 12.*

McComb, Ohio.—Eld. Ed. Loomis commenced a series of meetings in the Sugar Ridge church, Hancock Co., Ohio, Dec. 13, and closed on the night of Dec. 27. During the twenty-six discourses that he delivered, marked attention was paid to the Word preached. We had no accessions to the church, but we hope that many good impressions were made. At this writing we have pleasant winter weather with some snow. Health is not so good here. *La Grippe* is prevailing in this vicinity and city.—*D. W. C. Rau.*

McPherson, Kans.—The Monitor church met in quarterly council Dec. 31. All the business was transacted harmoniously, and the time passed pleasantly. We much regretted that Bro. J. D. Trostle, our elder, could not be with us because of his afflictions, as we have learned to enjoy his loving admonitions and councils. May God be with him in his trials! The two applicants previously reported, and one new applicant have been received by baptism since my last report. May they be faithful workers for the Master!—*S. E. Lantz, Jan. 18.*

Linganore, Md.—On the evening of Jan. 2, Bro. Henry Light, of Lancaster, Pa., commenced a series of meetings in the Locust Grove church, and continued until the 14th. The attendance was good, considering the inclement weather and *La Grippe*. Bro. Light is a very pleasant, interesting and instructive speaker, and does not shun to declare the whole Truth. Many deep and lasting impressions were made on both saint and sinner. As an immediate result of his labors, one dear young lamb was made willing to follow Christ, and others were "almost persuaded." May the Lord strengthen and encourage him, and bless his labors for good!—*Maggie E. Ecker.*

Longmont, Colo.—According to previous arrangements the Brethren, now composing the Powder Valley church, eight miles east of Ft. Collins, Colo., met at the Caccus school-house Jan. 16, and effected an organization. All the members were present but three, but all expressed themselves as being willing to labor for the upbuilding of the cause of Christ, and in harmony with the General Brotherhood. May the prayers of God's children go up in their behalf that they may grow in grace as well as in numbers. Feeling the need of official help, they elected Bro. D. M. Glick to the ministry, and brethren Samuel Pye and Samuel Glick to the office of deacon. All felt the great responsibility that is being placed upon them, and an unusual solemnity prevailed. May they all be instruments in the hands of God for good! Any good, faithful minister, wishing to enjoy the pure air of Colorado, might find it to his advantage to correspond with the above brethren at Ft. Collins, Colo.—*G. W. Fesler.*

Wallace, Nebr.—In MESSENGER No. 50, of last volume, Bro. Cornelius Kessler speaks of the great value of the "Biographical Sketches" by Bro. B. F. Moomaw. Permit me to suggest that these "Sketches" be published in pamphlet form, so that they may be preserved for future generations.—*J. K. Shively.*

Whitfield, Ohio.—Bro. D. Bock, of Ridgeway, Ind., came to the Lower Miami church, Montgomery Co., Ohio, Dec. 25, and began a series of meetings, which he continued until Jan. 1, when he was assisted by Bro. Holder, of Deweyville, Ohio. These brethren labored together until Dec. 4, when Bro. Bock left for home. Bro. Holder continued the meetings until Jan. 10, and then closed, having delivered twenty-one sermons. The Brethren labored earnestly, and although there were no accessions, we believe there were many good impressions made, and the church was much encouraged in the good cause. May the blessings of God rest upon our dear brethren who labored so zealously for us!—*E. Hyer, Jan. 18.*

Salem, Ohio.—Our meeting closed night before last. It was a very interesting one, and good attention was paid to the Word preached. Our large house was entirely filled the last night of our meeting. Many were sorry that the meetings closed so soon. The home ministers conducted the meetings until the 12th, after which Bro. Daniel Snell, of Indiana, preached for us. As yet we have had no accessions to the church since our meetings. Our brother left for home yesterday. May the Lord go with him! Our missionary solicitors, Bro. S. B. Christian and sister Christian, are making their semi-annual solicitation for the missionary cause. May the brethren and sisters contribute liberally to the good cause! Our tract solicitors, Bro. and sister John Rinehart have been soliciting for the Tract Work. Brethren and sisters, let us all be up to our duty, as we all have a work to do. Then, if we are faithful, we will receive a crown at the end of our race.—*Jesse K. Brumbaugh, Jan. 19.*

Pioneer, Ohio.—On Saturday evening, Dec. 21, the members of the Silver Creek church, Williams Co., Ohio, commenced a series of meetings in the Hickory Grove church, conducted by Bro. W. L. Desenberg. He preached at this place twenty-four sermons, we believe to the edification of all present. The weather was very inclement at the beginning of the meeting. On this account the attendance was not as large as it otherwise would have been. As the meeting progressed, and the weather became more favorable, the meetings grew in interest and number until we had good congregations. During these meetings one dear soul said he was tired of sin and desired to cast his lot with the people of God. He was baptized according to the instructions given by our Savior. Although young in years we hope he may hold out faithful to the end. From here we went to the west end of our District, and commenced meetings in the house owned by the Christian Union Society. As there are but few members living here, the doctrine, as understood and practiced by the Brethren, is somewhat new. Here our brother preached twenty-four sermons. We never saw a more attentive people than we met at this place. Although the roads were very bad, the house was filled with people, eager to hear the Word preached in its purity. At this place there was one added to the church, an old brother, past his three score and ten years. Others were almost persuaded, and with tears flowing down their cheeks, they said we should come again and, like the Bereans, they are searching the Scriptures to see whether these things are so. Thus we see the old and young starting together for the land of pure delight.—*J. W. Keiser.*

BOURRIS.—In the same congregation, Dec. 30, 1891, of lung feVer, sister Elizabeth Bourris, aged 52 years, 1 month and 1 day.

Deceased leaVes a husband and fiVe daughters to mourn their loss. Sister Bourris liVed a consistent Christian life. Funeral serVices by the Brethren.

　　　　　　DAVID H. NICCUM.

MYER.—In the same congregation, Jan. 16, 1892, Bro. Isaac Myer, aged 46 years, 10 months and 14 days.

Deceased leaVes a wife and six children to mourn their loss.

Bro. Myer serVed in the office of deacon for about seVen years and was always at his post. His loss will be greatly felt by the church. Funeral serVices by the Brethren.

　　　　　　DAVID H. NICCUM.

FETTERS.—In the Tippecanoe church, Kosciusko Co., Ind., Nov. 20, 1891, sister Sarah Fetters, aged 73 years, 10 months and 20 days.

She was born in Tuscarawas County, Ohio. A few months before her death she united with the church and died in the triumphs of a liVing faith. Funeral serVices from Num. 23: 10.

　　　　　　DANIEL ROTHENBERGER.

SHOCK.—At the same place, Jan. 6, 1892, after six days of suffering from heart disease and lung feVer, sister Sarah (Harnish) Shock, aged 70 years, 7 months and 5 days.

Deceased was born in Montgomery County, Ohio. She was married to John Shock, with whom she enjoyed a happy life of many years. Besides her husband and three children (all members of the church), she leaVes many other relatiVes. She was truly a mother in Israel.

Funeral serVices from Isaiah 57: 1, 2, to a large and sympathizing congregation.

　　　　　　DANIEL ROTHENBERGER.

ELLABARGER.—In the bounds of the Nettle Creek church, near Hagerstown, Ind., Dec. 2, 1891, Henry Ellabarger, aged 89 years, 9 months and 19 days.

Deceased was born in Lancaster County, Pa., Feb. 13, 1802. In the spring of 1833 he left the place of his birth and came to Wayne County, Ind. He was married to Magdalena Breneman, Sept. 22, 1825. To them were born three children,—two sons and one daughter. The wife and daughter preceded him to the spirit land, leaving two sons to mourn their loss. Deceased had, in the latter end of his life, at least, not identified himself with any church, but held to the faith and teachings of the old Mennonites. The close of this long career was that of a life well spent. Shortly before his death he expressed his wish that the Lord would receiVe his soul. Few of us who yet remain can expect to attain to the ripe old age of this father, but may we be encouraged to liVe better and nobler liVes by his example and precept.

Funeral serVices at the Locust Grove church. Dec. 4, by brethren Abram Bowman and J. HooVer from the text, "Therefore, be ye also ready, for in such an hour as ye think not the Son of man cometh."

　　　　　　CYNTHIA ELLABARGER.

BARRICK.—In the, bounds of the Pipe Creek church, Carroll Co., Md., sister Rhoda Barrick, aged about 26 years.

On New Year's Day her remains were laid away in the graVe. Her funeral was largely attended and the occasion improVed by the writer and Eld. David Stoner, from Philipp. 1: 21.　　E. W. STONER.

CATNER.—In the Indian Creek congregation, Westmoreland Co., Pa., Jan. 8, 1892, Mary Catner, aged 73 years, 6 months and 29 days.

Funeral serVices by the writer from Isa. 38: 1, to a large audience. D. D. HORNER.

TURNEY.—In the Rockton church, Pa., Jan. 8, 1892, sister Elizabeth Turney, aged about 70 years.

Deceased has been a sufferer for seVeral years, haVing had three strokes of paralysis. ServVices by the Writer from Heb. 9: 27, 28.

　　　　　　. J. H. BEER.

BOVEY.—In Chicago, Ill., Jan. 9 1891, sister Mary (Funk) Bovey, aged 70 years, 4 months and 1 day.

Her remains were brought to Mt Morris; thence to Pine Creek church,—her former home. She was born near Hagerstown, Md., and moved to Illinois in 1841. She became a member of the Brethren church fifty years ago, being the first person baptized in said church. She liVed a consistent life. She desired to be anointed with oil according to James 5, which being attended to, she expressed herself as being ready to depart. Funeral sermon by the writer, assisted by Edmund Forney, from Rom. 8: 1, 2.

　　　　　　J. C. LAHMAN.

HELSINGER.—In Woodland Township, Carroll Co., Ill., Jan. 2, 1892, of pneumonia, Elizabeth Helsinger, wife of Joseph Helsinger, aged 48 years, 11 months and 3 days. Funeral serVices conducted by the writer in the U. B. church from Acts 20: 24.

　　　　　　FRANKLIN MYERS.

SEARS.—At their home, near Leon, Decatur Co., Iowa, Jan. 15, 1892, sister Ellen Sears (maiden name, Gittinger), aged 32 years, 5 months and 4 days.

The death of our sister was a very sad occurrence indeed, as she leaVes a tender babe, only three weeks old. The husband also is sorely afflicted, haVing sustained seVere injuries from the kick of a horse, some time ago. She died in the triumphs of a liVing faith, exhorting and admonishing all her friends to meet her "oVer there." Funeral serVices at the church, Jan. 17, by the writer. Text, Matt. 24: 44; I Thess. 4: 14.　L. M. KOB.

PUTERBAUGH.—In the bounds of the Ozawkie congregation, Kans., Jan. 12, 1892, Viola, daughter of Bro. Aaron and Mary Puterbaugh, aged 15 years, 8 months and, 26 days. Funeral serVices by the Brethren from James 4: 14, to a large circle of relatiVes and friends.　　C. C. ROOT.

GRAYBILL.—In the Ten Mile church, Washington Co., Pa., Jan. 6, 1892, Bro. Joseph G. Graybill, aged 77 years, 4 months and 29 days.

Deceased was a sufferer for many years with Bright's disease. He leaVes a sorrowing wife and seVen children,—three sons and four daughters,—to mourn the loss of one who was near and dear to them, but we hope that their loss is his eternal gain. The church here has lost a Very faithful and consistent member, the neighborhood a quiet and peaceable citizen. He was a member of this church for about forty-five years, and served the church in the office of deacon a number of years. Funeral serVices were held at his house by the writer, assisted by ReV. Himes of the M. E. church, from 1 Thess. 4: 13, 14, to a full house of sorrowing friends and others.

　　　　　　N. B. CHRISTNER.

HILL.—Near Brallsville, Washington Co., Pa., Dec. 2, 1891, of pneumonia, OliVer S., son of Thomas T. and Elizabeth Hill, aged 23 years.

Funeral serVices held at the house of his parents by Rev. Hunter, of the M. E. church, assisted by Rev. Smith, of the M. E. church, Hillsborough, Pa.　- N. B. CHRISTNER.

DULANEY.—In Floyd County, Va, Dec. 30, 1891, Charlie Quinter Dulaney, son of Bro. Wm. B. and sister Mary Dulaney, aged 3 years, 7 months and seVeral days.

The sufferings of the little one were great, but he has gone where he will suffer no more, but will dwell in that eternal bliss, where loVe and peace shall reign forever!

BURNETT.—In the same neighborhood, Jan. 1, 1892, Benjamin Early Burnett, son of Bro. Josiah and sister Elizabeth Burnett, aged 2 years, 10 months and 6 days.

Thus one by one we see passing away and the thought comes to us, "Are we prepared to meet our Creator in peace?" May the blessings of God comfort the grief-stricken parents, that they may not weep as those that haVe no hope, but that they may remember that they now haVe a bright angel in heaven. Funeral serVices by the Brethren.

　　　　　　CEPHAS D. REED.

GOOD BOOKS FOR ALL.

ANY book in the market furnished at publishers' lowest retail price by the Brethren's Publishing Company, Mt. Morris, Ill, *Special prices* given when books are purchased in quantities. When ordering books, not on our list, if possible giVe title, name of author, and address of publishers.

Family Bible, with Notes and Instructions.—Contains the harmony of the Gospels, Chronology, Maps, Tables of Weights and Measures, Family Record, eight elegant illustrations, etc. Price, substantially bound, $4.50.

German and English Testaments.—American Bible Society Edition. Price, 60 cents.

Homiletics and Pastoral Theology.—By W. G. T. Shedd. Cloth, $2.50.

Lectures on Preaching.—By Rev. Phillips Brooks. Cloth, 12mo. $1.50.

New Testament and Psalms with Notes.—Invaluable for Bible students. Sunday-school teachers, etc. Price, cloth, $1.00; without limbers, $1.00.

Quinter and McConnell Debate.—A debate on Trine Immersion, the Lord's Supper, and Feet-washing, between Eld. James Quinter (German Baptist) and Eld. N. A. McConnell (Christian) held at Dry Creek, Iowa, 1867. Price, $1.50.

Popular Commentary on the New Testament.—Edited by Philip Schaff. Four volumes, 8vo. Matthew, Mark and Luke, $6.00. John and the Acts, $6.00. Romans to Philemon, $6.00. Hebrews to Revelation, $5.00.

Sabbatism.—By M. M. Eshelman. Treats the Sabbath question, showing that the first day of the week is the day for assembling in worship. Price, in cents; 15 copies, $1.00.

Bunyan's Pilgrim's Progress.—An excellent edition of this good work, printed on good paper, finely illustrated with forty engravings, at the low price of $1.00 per copy.

Close Communion.—By Landon West. Treats this important subject in a simple though conclusive manner. Price, 50 cents.

In the Volume of the Book.—By Geo. F. Pentecost. Cloth, 60 cents.

Key to the Knowledge and Use of the Holy Bible.—By J. H. Brett. Cloth, 16 mo, 75 cents.

Lange's Commentary.—Edited by Philip Schaff. Twenty-five vols. Per vol., $3.00.

New and Complete Bible Commentary.—By Jamieson, Fausset and Brown. It is far in advance of other works. It is critical, practical, and explanatory. It is compendious and comprehensive in its character. It has a critical introduction to each Book of Scripture, and is by far the most practical, suggestive, scientific, and popular work of the kind in the English language. In four large 12mo volumes of about 1,000 pages each. In extra fine English cloth, sprinkled edges, the full set, $8.00; half Morocco, the full set, $12.00.

Sacred Geography and Antiquities.—A practical, helpful work for Bible students, ministers and Sunday-school teachers. Price, $2.25.

The Origin and Destiny of Religion.—Hibbert Lectures. By T. W. M. Davids. Cloth, 8vo, $2.50.

Our Library on Christian Evidences.—This collection of works embraces the best books to be had on that subject: "Paley's Evidences of Christianity," New Edition, $1.50; "Nelson on Infidelity," 75 cents; "Manual of Christian Evidences," 75 cents; "Many Infallible Proofs," $1.25; "The Divine Demonstration," $1.50; "The Bible in the Nineteenth Century," 20 cents; "Grounds of Theistic and Christian Belief," $2.50. Price of the entire set, if ordered at one time, $8.00; special terms to ministers furnished upon application. -

Bible Work, or Bible Reader's Commentary on the New Testament.—By J. G. Butler. Two, vols. 8vo, $10.00.

Biblical Antiquities.—By John Nevin. GiVes a concise account of Bible times and customs; invaluable to all students of Bible subjects. Price, $1.50.

Biblical Theology of the Old-Testament.—By R. F. Weidner. Cloth, $2.25.

Campbell and Owen Debate.— Contains a complete investigation of the evidences of Christianity. Price, $1.50.

Classified Minutes of Annual Meeting.—A work of rare interest for all who desire to be well informed in the church work from the early days of our Brethren until the present. Price, cloth, $1.50; leather, $2.00.

Companion to the Bible.—This valuable work is so full of instruction that it can not fail to be of great benefit to every Christian. Price, $1.15.

Hours with the Bible.—By Cunningham Geikie. Old Testament Series—six volumes. Per volume, 90 cents.

Europe and Bible Lands.—By D. L. Miller. A book for the people,—more comprehensive and thorough than many higher-priced works. Price, cloth, $1.50; leather, $2.00.

Ecclesiastical History.—By Eusebius. Bohn Library. Cloth, $2.00.

Ecclesiastical History.—By Mosheim. 2 vols. 8vo, $4.00.

Early Days of Christianity.—By F. W. Farrar. Author's edition, cloth, 12mo, $1.25.

→PUBLICATIONS←

☞ The following books, Sunday-school supplies, etc., are for sale by the BRETHREN'S PUBLISHING CO., Mt. Morris, Ill., or Huntingdon, Pa., to whom all orders should be addressed.

The Brethren's Quarterly.

For Sunday-school teachers and scholars this publication is of the greatest benefit. Look at our prices:
Single subscription, one year.............................25 cents.
Single subscription, per quarter,.....................10 cents.
Three copies, per quarter......................................25 cents.
Eight copies, per quarter.....................................60 cents.
Twenty copies and over,................................4 cents each.

Hymn Books.

New Tune and Hymn Books.

Half leather, per copy, post-paid,.......................$ 75
Morocco, per copy, post-paid,............................1 00
Morocco, gilt edge, per copy, post-paid,...........1 25

Hymn Books.

Morocco, per copy, post-paid,.............................$ 75
Morocco, gilt edge, per copy, post-paid,...........75
Arabesque, per copy, post-paid,.........................50
Fine Limp, per copy, post-paid,..........................75
Fine Limp, gilt edge, per copy, post-paid,........85
German and English, per copy, post-paid,........75

Sunday-School Requisites.

The following list of things is needed in all Sunday-school:
Testaments, Flexible, red edge, per dozen,.......$1 00
Minute-Books, each, ...10
Class Books, per dozen,...40
S. S. Primers, with fine engravings, per dozen,...70

New and Beautiful Sunday-School Cards.

"The Gem," 50 picture cards, each with Bible text, verse of hymn,..35
250 Reward Tickets—verse of Scripture—red or blue,..20

The Young Disciple.

The YOUNG DISCIPLE is a neatly printed weekly, published especially for the moral benefit and religious instruction of our young folks.
Single copy, one year,...$ 50
Six copies (the sixth to the agent),.....................2 50
Ten copies,..4 00

For Three Months or Thirteen Weeks.

20 copies to one address,.....................................$0 70
30 " " " " 2 50
40 " " " " 3 60
75 " " " " 5 00
100 " " " " 6 00

For Six Months or Twenty-Six Weeks.

20 copies to one address,.....................................$ 3 75
30 " " " " 5 00
40 " " " " 6 50
50 " " " " 7 50
75 " " " " 10 00
100 " " " " 13 75

Our paper is designed for the Sunday-school and the home circle. We desire the same of every Sunday school Superintendent in the Brotherhood, and want an agent in every church. Send for sample copies.

Certificates of Membership

We haVe just printed a new edition of these Very conVenient certificates. SeVeral improVements oVer the old style are noticeable, such as perforated stubs, firm, yet smooth, paper, etc. Price only 50 cents per book. EVery congregation should haVe one. Address this office.

The Monon Route.

This road is running a fine line of Pullman Buffet Sleepers between Chicago and Indianapolis, Cincinnati and LouisVille, in connection with the fast Florida express trains.

For full information, address, E. O. McCORMICK, General Passenger Agent, Adams Express Building, Chicago. (City Ticket Office, 7 S. Clark St.)

BOURRIS.—In the same congregation, Dec. 30, 1891, of lung fever, sister Elizabeth Bourris, aged 52 years, 3 month, and 1 day.

Deceased leaves a husband and five daughters to mourn their loss. Sister Bourris lived a consistent Christian life. Funeral services by the Brethren.

DAVID H. NICCUM.

MYER.—In the same congregation, Jan. 16, 1892, Bro. Isaac Myer, aged 46 years, 10 months and 14 days.

Deceased leaves a wife and six children to mourn their loss.

Bro. Myer served in the office of deacon for about seven years and was always at his post. His loss will be greatly felt by the church. Funeral services by the Brethren.

DAVID H. NICCUM.

FETTERS.—In the Tippecanoe church, Kosciusko Co., Ind., Nov. 20, 1891, sister Sarah Fetters, aged 73 years, 10 months and 20 days.

She was born in Tuscarawas County, Ohio. A few months before her death she united with the church and died in the triumphs of a living faith. Funeral services from Num. 23: 10.

DANIEL ROTHENBERGER.

SHOCK.—At the same place, Jan. 6, 1892, after six days of suffering from heart disease and lung fever, sister Sarah (Harnish) Shock, aged 70 years, 7 months and 5 days.

Deceased was born in Montgomery County, Ohio. She was married to John Shock, with whom she enjoyed a happy life of many years. Besides her husband and three children (all members of the church), she leaves many other relatives. She was truly a mother in Israel.

Funeral services from Isaiah 57: 1, 2, to a large and sympathizing congregation.

DANIEL ROTHENBERGER.

ELLABARGER.—In the bounds of the Nettle Creek church, near Hagerstown, Ind., Dec. 2, 1891, Henry Ellabarger, aged 89 years, 9 months and 19 days.

Deceased was born in Lancaster County, Pa., Feb. 13, 1802. In the spring of 1833 he left the place of his birth and came to Wayne County, Ind. He was married to Magdalena Breneman, Sept. 22, 1825. To them were born three children,—two sons and one daughter. The wife and daughter preceded him to the spirit land, leaving two sons to mourn their loss. Deceased had, in the latter end of his life, at least, not identified himself with any church, but held to the faith and teachings of the old Mennonites. The close of this long career was that of a life well spent. Shortly before his death he expressed his wish that the Lord would receive his soul. Few of us who yet remain can expect to attain to the ripe old age of this father, but may we be encouraged to live better and nobler lives by his example and precept.

Funeral services at the Locust Grove church Dec. 4, by brethren Abram Bowman and J. Hoover from the text, "Therefore, be ye also ready, for in such an hour as ye think not the Son of man cometh."

CYNTHIA ELLABARGER.

BARRICK.—In the bounds of the Pipe Creek church, Carroll Co., Md., sister Rhoda Barrick, aged about 26 years.

On New Year's Day her remains were laid away in the grave. Her funeral was largely attended and the occasion improved by the writer and Eld. David Stoner, from Philipp. 1: 21.

E. W. STONER.

CATNER.—In the Indian Creek congregation, Westmoreland Co., Pa., Jan. 8, 1892, Mary Catner, aged 73 years, 6 months and 29 days.

Funeral services by the writer from Isa. 38: 1, to a large audience. D. D. HORNER.

TURNEY.—In the Rockton church, Pa., Jan. 8, 1892, sister Elizabeth Turney, aged about 70 years.

Deceased has been a sufferer for several years, having had three strokes of paralysis. Services by the writer from Heb. 9: 27, 28.

J. H. BUBB.

BOVEY.—In Chicago, Ill., Jan. 9, 1892, sister Mary (Funk) Bovey, aged 79 years, 4 months and 1 day.

Her remains were brought to Mt. Morris; thence to Pine Creek church,—her former home. She was born near Hagerstown, Md., and moved to Illinois in 1841. She became a member of the Brethren church fifty years ago, being the first person baptized in said church. She lived a consistent life. She desired to be anointed with oil according to James 5, which being attended to, she expressed herself as being ready to depart. Funeral sermon by the writer, assisted by Edmund Forney, from Rom. 8: 1, 2.

J. C. LAHMAN.

HELSINGER.—In Woodland Township, Carroll Co., Ill., Jan. 2, 1892, of pneumonia, Elizabeth Helsinger, wife of Joseph Helsinger, aged 48 years, 11 months and 3 days.

Funeral services conducted by the writer in the U. B. church from Acts 20: 24.

FRANKLIN MYERS.

SEARS.—At their home, near Leon, Decatur Co., Iowa, Jan. 15, 1892, sister Ellen Sears (maiden name, Gittinger), aged 32 years, 5 months and 4 days.

The death of our sister was a very sad occurrence indeed, as she leaves a tender babe, only three weeks old. The husband also is sorely afflicted, having sustained severe injuries from the kick of a horse, some time ago. She died in the triumphs of a living faith, exhorting and admonishing all her friends to meet her "over there." Funeral services at the church, Jan. 17, by the writer. Text, Matt. 24: 44; 1 Thess. 4: 14. L. M. Kob.

PUTERBAUGH.—In the bounds of the Ozawkie congregation, Kans., Jan. 12, 1892, Viola, daughter of Bro. Aaron and Mary Puterbaugh, aged 15 years, 8 months and 26 days. Funeral services by the Brethren from James 4: 14, to a large circle of relatives and friends. C. C. ROOT.

GRAYBILL.—In the Ten Mile church, Washington Co., Pa., Jan. 6, 1892, Bro. Joseph G. Graybill, aged 77 years, 4 months and 27 days.

Deceased was a sufferer for many years with Bright's disease. He leaves a sorrowing wife and seven children,—three sons and four daughters,—to mourn the loss of one who was near and dear to them, but we hope that their loss is his eternal gain. The church here has lost a very faithful and consistent member, the neighborhood a quiet and peaceable citizen. He was a member of this church for about forty-five years, and served the church in the office of deacon a number of years. Funeral services were held at his house by the writer, assisted by Rev. Humes of the M. E. church, from 1 Thess. 4: 13, 14, to a full house of sorrowing friends and others.

N. B. CHRISTNER.

HILL.—Near Beallsville, Washington Co., Pa., Dec. 2, 1891, of pneumonia, Oliver S., son of Thomas T. and Elizabeth Hill, aged 23 years.

Funeral services held at the house of his parents by Rev. Humes, of the M. E. church, assisted by Rev. Smith, of the M. E. church, Hillsborough, Pa. - N. B. CHRISTNER.

DULANEY.—In Floyd County, Va., Dec. 20, 1891, Charlie Quinter Dulaney, son of Bro. Wm. B. and sister Mary Dulaney, aged 3 years, 7 months and several days.

The sufferings of the little one were great, but he has gone where he will suffer no more, but will dwell in that eternal bliss, where love and peace shall reign forever!

BURNETT.—In the same neighborhood, Jan. 1, 1892, Benjamin Early Burnett, son of Bro. Josiah and sister Elizabeth Burnett, aged 2 years, 10 months and 6 days.

Thus one by one we see passing away and the thought comes to us, "Are we prepared to meet our Creator in peace?" May the blessings of God comfort the grief-stricken parents, that they may not weep as those that have no hope, but that they may remember that they now have a bright angel in heaven. Funeral services by the Brethren.

CEPHAS D. REED.

GOOD BOOKS FOR ALL.

Any book in the market furnished at publishers' lowest retail price by the Brethren's Publishing Company, Mt. Morris, Ill., *Special prices* given when books are purchased in quantities. When ordering books, not on our list, if possible give title, name of author, and address of publishers.

Family Bible, with Notes and Instructions.—Contains the harmony of the Gospels, Chronology, Maps, Tables of Weights and Measures, Family Record, eight elegant illustrations, etc. Price, substantially bound, $4.50.

German and English Testaments.—American Bible Society Edition. Price, 60 cents.

Homiletics and Pastoral Theology.—By W. G. T. Shedd, 12mo, $2.50.

Lectures on Preaching.—By Rev. Phillips Brooks. Cloth, 12mo, $1.50.

New Testament and Psalms with Notes.—Invaluable for Bible students, Sunday-school teachers, etc. Price, cloth, $1.00; without flexible, $1.00.

Quinter and McConnell Debate.—A debate on Trine Immersion, the Lord's Supper, and Feet-washing, between Eld. James Quinter (German Baptist) and Eld. N. A. McConnell (Christian) held at Dry Creek, Iowa, 1867. Price, $1.50.

Popular Commentary on the New Testament.—Edited by Philip Schaff. Four volumes, 8vo. Matthew, Mark and Luke: $6.00. John and the Acts: $6.00. Romans to Philemon: $6.00. Hebrews to Revelation: $6.00.

Sabbatism.—By M. M. Eshelman. Treats the Sabbath question, showing that the first day of the week is the day for assembling to worship. Price, in cloth, 25 cents. $1.00.

Bunyan's Pilgrim's Progress.—An excellent edition of this good work, printed on good paper, finely illustrated with forty engravings, at the low price of $1.00 per copy.

Close Communion.—By Landon West. Treats this important subject in a simple though conclusive manner. Price, 50 cents.

In the Volume of the Book.—By Geo. F. Pentecost. Cloth. 60 cents.

Key to the Knowledge and Use of the Holy Bible.—By J. H. Blunt. Cloth, 16mo, 75 cents.

Lange's Commentary.—Edited by Philip Schaff. Twenty-five vols. 8vo. Per vol., $5.00.

New and Complete Bible Commentary.—By Jamieson, Faussett and Brown. It is far in advance of otherworks. It is critical, practical, and explanatory. It is comprehensive and comprehensive in its character. It has a critical Introduction to each Book of Scripture, and fit by far the most practical, suggestive, scientific, and popular work of the kind in the English language. In four large 12mo volumes of about 1,000 pages each. In extra fine English cloth, sprinkled edges, the full set, $8.00; half Morocco, the full set, $12.00.

Sacred Geography and Antiquities.—A practical, helpful work for Bible students, ministers and Sunday-school teachers. Price, $2.25.

The Origin and Growth of Religion.—By T. W. H. Davids. Cloth, 8vo, $2.50.

Our Library on Christian Evidences.—This collection of works embraces the best books to be had on that subject: "Paley's Evidences of Christianity," New Edition, $1.50; "Nelson on Infidelity," 75 cents; "Manual of Christian Evidences," 75 cents; "Many Infallible Proofs," $1.25; "The Divine Demonstration," $1.50; "The Bible in the Nineteenth Century," 20 cents; "Grounds of Theistic and Christian Belief," $2.50. Price of the whole library at one time, $8.00; special terms to ministers furnished upon application.

Bible Work, or Bible Reader's Commentary on the New Testament.—By J. G. Butler. Two volumes, 8vo, $6.00.

Biblical Antiquities.—By John Nevin. Gives a complete account of Bible times and customs, invaluable to all students of Bible subjects. Price, $1.50.

Biblical Theology of the Old Testament.—By R. F. Weidner. Cloth, $2.50.

Campbell and Owen Debate.—Contains a complete investigation of the evidences of Christianity. Price, $1.50.

Classified Minutes of Annual Meeting.—A work of rare interest for all who desire to be well informed in the church work, from the early days of our Brethren until the present. Price, cloth, $1.50; leather, $2.00.

Companion to the Bible.—This valuable work is so full of instruction that it can not fail to be of great benefit to every Christian. Price, $1.75.

Hours with the Bible.—By Cunningham Geikie. Old Testament Series—six volumes. Per volume, 90 cents.

Europe and Bible Lands.—By D. L. Miller. A book for the people,—more comprehensive and thorough than many higher-priced works. Price, cloth, $1.50; leather, $2.00.

Ecclesiastical History.—By Eusebius. John Library. Cloth, $2.00.

Ecclesiastical History.—By Mosheim. 2 vols. 8vo, $4.00.

Early Days of Christianity.—By F. W. Farrar. Author's edition, cloth, 12mo, $1.25.

THE GOSPEL MESSENGER.

"Set for the Defense of the Gospel."

Vol. 30, Old Series.   Mt. Morris, Ill., and Huntingdon, Pa., Feb. 9, 1892.   No. 6.

The Gospel Messenger.

H. B. BRUMBAUGH, Editor,

And Business Manager of the Eastern House, Box 50,
Huntingdon, Pa.

Table of Contents.

THE Huntingdon Bible Term opens on Monday, Feb. 1. At present writing the prospects are good for a large attendance, if the prevailing sickness does not change present purposes.

A VERY enjoyable members' meeting was held in the Normal parlor last week. An occasional meeting of this kind greatly aids in developing the social feeling that should exist between members of the same family.

J. B. BRUMBAUGH has returned from a three weeks' course of labor among the Eastern churches. We are glad to learn that Germantown, the mother church of this country, has now a minister who is laboring to build up again that which, through neglect and other causes, was almost dead. Our prayer is that Bro. Stover may be abundantly blessed and that the old Germantown church may have a most glorious revival.

SOME of our contributors seem to be careless about signing their names to their writings. In a number of cases we are able to determine the writer by being familiar with the handwriting, etc., but others go into the waste-basket or wait for developments, and in some cases they come in with a vengeance. Of course, we are blamed for the trouble that grows out of such neglect and it is a real satisfaction to see how such persons mellow down when they are informed that they neglected to give their name and address in their former letter. In writing for the press, on business or for anything else, be sure to close with your name and address.

WE have on hand a number of queries that we would gladly attend to had we the time. We hope to be able to consider some of them in the near future.

Those who wish a copy of the "Brethren's Church Manual,"—and it is an excellent thing for every member to have,—should order now. In it will be found the very things that you ought to know as to the faith, practice and government of the church. It is a convenient pocket companion and an ever-ready book for reference. Nicely bound in cloth, only 30 cents post-paid.

A BROTHER suggests that a fund should be provided for the benefit of the widows of poor ministers. Yes, we think so too. But would it not be well to do a little more for them before they become widows? The poor minister would enjoy a little appreciation before he passes over, and perhaps it would soften his dying pillow if he could feel that he as well as his were not forgotten.

THE MINISTERIAL RELATION.

"Feed my sheep."—John 21: 16.

THE relation of the minister to his people, or the flock over which he is placed by the church, is not only an important one, but is also a very peculiar one. This relation is frequently illustrated by the shepherd and the sheep, and to understand it, we must first understand the relation of the shepherd to the sheep of his flock or fold. Of course, the interpretation must not be made too literal and needs some modification. Christ says to Peter, "Feed my sheep." As this relation had been taught to the disciples previous to this time, Peter had no trouble in interpreting the language used and therefore was in no danger of making an over-literal application.

While in some ways the similarity is very striking, in other ways it is not, but there could be no choice of subjects made in which the similarity would reach so far and at the same time so fully exemplify the truth which he wished to teach. The relation existing between the shepherd and the sheep must essentially be different from the relation between the minister and his people. In the first place we have the rational and his relative duty to the animal. In the second, we have the rational as related to the rational. Hence, our relation to the human being must essentially be different from that to the animal, and to make the application too literal would frustrate the whole code of Christ's teaching.

But while there may be some danger of pushing the literal application too far, is not the greater danger in not going far enough? The danger, on our part, seems to be in the direction of getting too far away from the shepherd idea and because of this unburden ourselves of many of the duties that belong to the relation.

"Feed my sheep," —while we may over-literalize it, needs a larger definition, as "feeding" expresses only a part of the duties that belong to the relation. There must be a fold and the green pastures. There must be watching also, and the caring for the sheep. These are duties belonging to the relations that are more important than the simple feeding, and are among the striking similarities between the shepherd and the minister. It is a good thing to prepare and give food to the sheep, but if they are left unprotected from the dangers of the prowling wolves, what good will the feeding do? Life means more than food and raiment,—so with the child placed under the shepherd's care.

We received a letter the other day from a brother who asks how the lambs of the flock should be nourished and he continues by saying that in their church some young sisters, ranging in age from fifteen to seventeen, who violated some of the rules of the church, were, much against their wishes, cut off or expelled. He now wants to know if this is the proper way to nourish and feed the lambs.

These are cases that frequently come before the shepherds of the church for a passage and often it becomes a serious question for decision between church rules and the duties that grow out of the ministerial relation. The duty of the shepherd is dual in its character. First, obedience to the wishes of those by whom they are called or employed. Second, their duty towards those for whom employed. This is true, as well, of the shepherd of souls.

Much depends on understanding fully what is the relation of the minister to his people. In this case the shepherd is called by God, through the church, and if the church that calls is in full sympathy with the one who calls, there will be no restrictions placed on the shepherd that will militate against the great object which God has in view,—the salvation of souls. And therefore the legitimate relations between pastor and people will not be restricted.

Supposing this to be the condition of all ministers, we are now prepared to look at the relation that is or should be between the minister and the people placed under his charge. "Feed my sheep, feed my lambs," and "care for the flock," covers the whole ground growing out of the relation. Can we determine the relation by understanding the duties which the position imposes? We think so. And further, we learn it better than we can in any other way. "Am I my brother's keeper?" The duties that grew out of the position of the two brothers had taught Cain the relation between them and that he was his brother's keeper. But because he hated him, he despised the duties and therefore slew him. The relation is more readily seen than our disposition to fill or accept the duties that grow out of it.

The first thought, in this connection, is: The shepherd is greater than the sheep, and in saying this, we give "greater" its enlarged definition,—greater in strength, in wisdom, in experience and

(Concluded on page 85.)

THE GOSPEL MESSENGER.

"Set for the Defense of the Gospel."

Vol. 30, Old Series.   Mt. Morris, Ill., and Huntingdon, Pa., Feb. 9, 1892.   No. 6.

The Gospel Messenger.

H. B. BRUMBAUGH, Editor,

And Business Manager of the Eastern House, Box 50,
Huntingdon, Pa.

Table of Contents.

THE Huntingdon Bible Term opens on Monday, Feb. 1. At present writing the prospects are good for a large attendance, if the prevailing sickness does not change present purposes.

A VERY enjoyable members' meeting was held in the Normal parlor last week. An occasional meeting of this kind greatly aids in developing the social feeling that should exist between members of the same family.

J. B. BRUMBAUGH has returned from a three weeks' course of labor among the Eastern churches. We are glad to learn that Germantown, the mother church of this country, has now a minister who is laboring to build up again that which, through neglect and other causes, was almost dead. Our prayer is that Bro. Stover may be abundantly blessed and that the old Germantown church may have a most glorious revival.

SOME of our contributors seem to be careless about signing their names to their writings. In a number of cases we are able to determine the writer by being familiar with the handwriting, etc., but others go into the waste-basket, or wait for developments, and in some cases they come in with a vengeance. Of course, we are blamed for the trouble that grows out of such neglect and it is a real satisfaction to see how such persons mellow down when they are informed that they neglected to give their name and address in their former letter. In writing for the press, on business or for anything else, be sure to close with your name and address.

WE have on hand a number of queries that we would gladly attend to had we the time. We hope to be able to consider some of them in the near future.

Those who wish a copy of the "Brethren's Church Manual,"—and it is an excellent thing for every member to have,—should order now. In it will be found the very things that you ought to know as to the faith, practice and government of the church. It is a convenient pocket companion and an ever-ready book for reference. Nicely bound in cloth, only 30 cents post-paid.

A BROTHER suggests that a fund should be provided for the benefit of the widows of poor ministers. Yes, we think so too. But would it not be well to do a little more for them before they become widows? The poor minister would enjoy a little appreciation before he passes over, and perhaps it would soften his dying pillow if he could feel that *he* as well as *his* were not forgotten.

THE MINISTERIAL RELATION.

" Feed my sheep."—John 21: 16.

THE relation of the minister to his people, or the flock over which he is placed by the church, is not only an important one, but is also a very peculiar one. This relation is frequently illustrated by the shepherd and the sheep, and to understand it, we must first understand the relation of the shepherd to the sheep of his flock or fold. Of course, the interpretation must not be made too literal and needs some modification. Christ says to Peter, "Feed my sheep." As this relation had been taught to the disciples previous to this time, Peter had no trouble in interpreting the language used and therefore was in no danger of making an over-literal application.

While in some ways the similarity is very striking, in other ways it is not, but there could be no choice of subjects made in which the similarity would reach so far and at the same time so fully exemplify the truth which he wished to teach. The relation existing between the shepherd and the sheep must essentially be different from the relation between the minister and his people. In the first place we have the rational and his relative duty to the animal. In the second, we have the rational as related to the rational. Hence, our relation to the human being must essentially be different from that to the animal; and to make the application too literal would frustrate the whole code of Christ's teaching.

But while there may be some danger of pushing the literal application too far, is not the greater danger in not going far enough? The danger, on our part, seems to be in the direction of getting too far away from the shepherd idea and because of this unburden ourselves of many of the duties that belong to the relation.

"Feed my sheep,"—while we may over-literalize it, needs a larger definition, as "feeding" expresses only a part of the duties that belong to the relation. There must be a fold and the green pastures. There must be watching also, and the caring for the sheep. These are duties belonging to the relations that are more important than the simple feeding, and are among the striking similarities between the shepherd and the minister. It is a good thing to prepare and give food to the sheep, but if they are left unprotected from the dangers of the prowling wolves, what good will the feeding do? Life means more than food and raiment,—so with the child placed under the shepherd's care.

We received a letter the other day from a brother who asks how the lambs of the flock should be nourished and he continues by saying that in their church some young sisters, ranging in age from fifteen to seventeen, who violated some of the rules of the church, were, much against their wishes, cut off or expelled. He now wants to know if this is the proper way to nourish and feed the lambs.

These are cases that frequently come before the shepherds of the church and often it becomes a serious question for decision between church rules and the duties that grow out of the ministerial relation. The duty of the shepherd is dual in its character. *First*, obedience to the wishes of those by whom they are called or employed. *Second*, their duty towards those for whom employed. This is true, as well, of the shepherd of souls.

Much depends on understanding fully what is the relation of the minister to his people. In this case the shepherd is called by God, through the church, and if the church that calls is in full sympathy with the one who calls, there will be no restrictions placed on the shepherd that will militate against the great object which God has in view,—the salvation of souls. And therefore the legitimate relations between pastor and people will not be restricted.

Supposing this to be the condition of all ministers, we are now prepared to look at the relation that is or should be between the minister and the people placed under his charge. "Feed my sheep, feed my lambs," and "care for the flock," covers the whole ground growing out of the relation. Can we determine the relation by understanding the duties which the position imposes? We think so. And further, we learn it better than we can in any other way. "Am I my brother's keeper?" The duties that grew out of the position of the two brothers had taught Cain the relation between them and that he was his brother's keeper. But because he hated him, he despised the duties and therefore slew him. The relation is more readily seen than our disposition to fill or accept the duties that grow out of it.

The first thought, in this connection, is: The shepherd is greater than the sheep, and in saying this, we give "greater" its enlarged definition,—greater in strength, in wisdom, in experience and

(*Concluded on page 85.*)

plaining my sudden change of mind, which was brought about in the following manner:

Not long since, in conversation with some brethren upon religious topics, these questions were asked:

1. "In case of separation for the cause of fornication, could the offending companion repent, and turning again to the path of virtue, be forgiven by God?"

Answer.—"Yes; for all sins may be forgiven, except the blaspheming of the Holy Ghost."

2. Well, then, if this penitent should seek a reconciliation with the one from whom he, or she, had separated, bringing fruits of genuine repentance, ask to be forgiven, and again restored to former marriage relations, would the innocent party be bound to forgive, and restore? *Answer.* —"Yes," again.

Now if this last answer be correct, imagine the dilemma in which the latter is placed, should he or she have married another. No wonder the disciples said, "If the case of the man be so with his wife, it is not good to marry."

So now, after looking at it from this standpoint, whatever meaning may seem to be conveyed in the language referred to, I do not believe it was intended to teach that a second companion may be taken while the other lives, and surely this is a reasonable conclusion, for if God can forgive, and receive the truly penitent, what is man that he should refuse?

Gross sin was the cause of separation, and while that cause existed, the separation was justifiable,—I am not ready to say obligatory,—but now, through repentance, pardon is obtained, and pardon implies absolution, and as absolution means freedom, the cause of separation no longer exists; hence all the obligations and conditions, that formerly existed, and constituted them "one flesh," are now revived and restored in fact, whether the parties ever live together again or not.

Therefore the "wife is bound to her husband" and may not marry another, "so long as he liveth," and *vice versa*, no difference what the cause of separation may be.

The Scripture cited above is the only passage in the New Testament that can, by any fair interpretation, be construed into a grant that a second companion may be taken while the former is living. Mark, in recording the same identical circumstance, omits the exception, which, I think harmonizes better with the laws of repentance and pardon than does Matthew (see Mark 10: 11, 12), except that Matthew's record be construed to mean simply, that there is but one justifiable cause for putting away a wife (or a husband), and that cause is fornication, and that, in any case, the taking another amounts to adultery.

La Porte, Ind.

REMARKS.—While we deem it proper to give space for the above explanation, we, however, do not wish to open our columns to a discussion of this perplexing question. It is likely to long remain an unsettled question among our people.—ED.

THE SOUL, OR "INNER MAN."

BY DANIEL HAYS.

THE highest authorities say that the "soul is *the thinking, spiritual, and immortal* BEING in *man.*" This has been and still is the accepted meaning of the word. The term, when traced etymologically to its source, comes from a root which means *to think,* and is applied to that part of man's nature which enables him to think and reason.

THE OUTER MAN.—Man's physical body is the "outer man." This was made first in the order of man's creation, according to the law, "first the natural, afterward the spiritual." 1 Cor. 15: 46. The "outer man" was formed "of the dust of the ground," as the tenement, or house for the higher, spiritual BEING to live in. "And the Lord God formed man of the dust of the ground, and breathed into his nostrils the breath of life; and man became a living soul." Man formed of the dust *was* man,—the "outer man." But by the in-breathing of Divinity man became something more; he *became,*—"passed from one state to another,"—from the natural to the spiritual. He was a spiritual, immortal being within the natural,—a "living soul."

We must not confound the word "soul" with the word "mind" or "spirit." The soul is a real being. The mind is a power, or faculty of the soul,—the power by which we perceive, think, or reason. Secondarily the mind has faculties,—perception, memory, recollection, imagination, understanding, and reason. The word spirit has a wide range of meaning. If by it we mean the renewed nature of man, we should say so. If by it we mean the immortal part of man we should say so. Or if by it we mean the prevailing disposition of man, good or evil, we should say so.

Then the word "soul" may include the entire man; and, in some rare instances, it may seemingly apply to the outward, visible man. In 1 Thess. 5: 23 we have the threefold nature of man clearly stated: "I pray God your whole spirit, and soul, and body, be preserved blameless unto the coming of our Lord Jesus Christ."

Man's physical body contains the organs of physical life, not of spiritual life. All the organs of the body have a distinct function, each subordinated to the organs of mind,—the brain. But the brain is not the mind. The power behind the brain is infinitely greater than the brain. The brain is simply the instrument of the mind. It is by the brain, through the senses, that the mind holds communication with the physical world. If the brain be impaired, weakened, or diseased, the mind is not injured. Communication is interrupted,—we cannot work well with an imperfect instrument. The brain does not see, nor feel, nor think, neither does the heart love. The seat of the affections is in the mind.

THE INNER MAN.—Man's spiritual nature is the "inner man." It is the power that thinks all we think, that knows all we know, and yet, of its nature and organization, we know but little, simply because the mind in our present state is directly related through the senses to the world of matter. In our contracted views we erroneously attribute volition to the brain, and emotion to the heart, instead of tracing them to their higher source in the mind, and the "heart of hearts."

If the intellect be a faculty of the mind which receives and comprehends ideas, collected through the senses, and these ideas, thus received, be held by the memory, reproduced at will, and, under color of the imagination, held up before the understanding, and, under the power of reason, sifted, classified and compared, till all the facts are clearly seen, and higher fields of truth open to the mind in the realms of faith:—if all this and much more be carried on in the mind, we know that there is an organization beyond the brain, higher than this natural life. That organization is the soul of man. It is in the soul that the heart, the seat of the affections of Scripture, is placed. Love is a power of the soul, as the intellect is a faculty of the mind.

PAUL'S ARGUMENT.—In 1 Cor. 13 Paul brings in an argument that forever settles the question as to the nature and destiny of man. In the mind of the inspired writer, charity is an imperishable quality of all the Christian graces,—a thing of

life, without which a man is an empty shadow,—but with which a man is enabled to reach the highest aims of Christian character and holiness. Charity is not an emotion of our sensual nature,—not a passion which some mistake for love. It is the highest and purest form of friendship, a union of minds based upon mutual esteem and priceless worth, that moves the hand to works of mercy and acts of kindness, and enlists the soul in a life of obedience to God.

The heart may cease to beat, the brain may lie a shapeless mass within its casket, but "*charity never faileth.*" Love is stronger than death. Love survives the tomb. Then the soul, the source and centre of this vital energy, continues ever. It is not the charity outside of us that Paul speaks of, but the charity within us. It is individual, personal, real. The time will come when prophecies shall cease, and knowledge shall vanish away, because our knowledge and preaching are imperfect and temporary: "For we know in part, and we prophesy in part." But a glorious trinity remains, — three eternal principles: Faith, hope, charity. Since, then, these principles abide, it follows, as an unavoidable conclusion, that the soul being a unit in essence and organization, and inseparably related to each of these undying principles, must and shall abide forever.

The problem of man's redemption would have been a matter of easy solution if death ends all. Let a pestilence sweep man from the face of the earth, and the question is solved. But the redemption of man was the one great problem of the universe, one which the angels desired to look into, and one which the mind of God alone could solve. This stands as an unanswerable argument for the soul's immortality. The spark of divinity in man, the being created in the image of God, was the object of such concern, such mercy, and such love as to cause the Eternal Father to send his only Son into the world to die that man might be redeemed.

Now measure the value of the human soul. Will you estimate it in the scope of its powers, in its capacity for improvement, in the endless nature of its existence, or in all three?

Moore's Store, Va.

LOVE TESTED.

BY S. N. M'CANN.

"If a man love me, he will keep my words."—John 14: 23.

GOD'S love to the sinner is unquestionably great, long-suffering, and strongly manifested. It flowed out from the great heart of God to you, sinner, before the world began in a bright and precious promise, even the promise of eternal life. Titus 1: 2. Jesus Christ, the Son of God, received the promise, and began to suffer before the world was that you might be delivered from this present evil world, according to the will of God. Gal. 1: 4. "O, Father, glorify thou me with thine own self, with the glory which I had with thee before the world was." John 17: 5.

Think of it! Christ suffering for over four thousand years for you, sinner, he had purchased your redemption, for "as in Adam all die, even so in Christ shall all be made alive." 1 Cor. 15: 22. Christ suffered the penalty, obtained universal redemption and, as a consequence, universal quickening or universal resurrection, for "all that are in the graves shall hear his voice, and shall come forth; they that have done good unto the resurrection of life; and they that have done evil to the resurrection of damnation." John 5: 28.

God's love still abounds. Though redemption was brought nigh, he knew our frame; he knew

plaining my sudden change of mind, which was brought about in the following manner:

Not long since, in conversation with some brethren upon religious topics, these questions were asked:

1. "In case of separation for the cause of fornication, could the offending companion repent, and turning again to the path of virtue, be forgiven by God?"

Answer.—"Yes; for all sins may be forgiven, except the blaspheming of the Holy Ghost."

2. Well, then, if this penitent should seek a reconciliation with the one from whom he, or she, had separated, bringing fruits of genuine repentance, ask to be forgiven, and again restored to former marriage relations, would the innocent party be bound to forgive, and restore? *Answer.*—"Yes," again.

Now if this last answer be correct, imagine the dilemma in which the latter is placed, should he or she have married another. No wonder the disciples said, "If the case of the man be so with his wife, it is not good to marry."

So now, after looking at it from this standpoint, whatever meaning may seem to be conveyed in the language referred to, I do not believe it was intended to teach that a second companion may be taken while the other lives, and surely this is a reasonable conclusion, for if God can forgive, and receive the truly penitent, what is man that he should refuse?

Gross sin was the cause of separation, and while that cause existed, the separation was justifiable;—I am not ready to say obligatory,—but now, through repentance, pardon is obtained, and pardon implies absolution, and as absolution means freedom, the cause of separation no longer exists; hence all the obligations and conditions, that formerly existed, and constituted them "one flesh," are now revived and restored in fact, whether the parties ever live together again or not.

Therefore the "wife is bound to her husband" and may not marry another, "so long as he liveth," and *vice versa*, no difference what the cause of separation may be.

The Scripture cited above is the only passage in the New Testament that can, by any fair interpretation, be construed into a grant that a second companion may be taken while the former is living. Mark, in recording the same identical circumstance, omits the exception, which, I think harmonizes better with the laws of repentance and pardon than does Matthew (see Mark 10: 11, 12), except that Matthew's record be construed to mean simply, that there is but one justifiable cause for putting away a wife (or a husband), and that cause is fornication, and that, in any case, the taking another amounts to adultery.

La Porte, Ind.

REMARKS.—While we deem it proper to give space for the above explanation, we, however, do not wish to open our columns to a discussion of this perplexing question. It is likely to long remain an unsettled question among our people.—ED.

THE SOUL, OR "INNER MAN."

BY DANIEL HAYS.

THE highest authorities say that the "soul is *the thinking, spiritual, and immortal* BEING *in man.*" This has been and still is the accepted meaning of the word. The term, when traced etymologically to its source, comes from a root which means *to think,* and is applied to that part of man's nature which enables him to think and reason.

THE OUTER MAN.—Man's physical body is the "outer man." This was made first in the order of man's creation, according to the law, "first the natural, afterward the spiritual." 1 Cor. 15: 46. The "outer man" was formed "of the dust of the ground," as the tenement, or house for the higher, spiritual BEING to live in. "And the Lord God formed man of the dust of the ground, and breathed into his nostrils the breath of life; and man became a living soul." Man formed of the dust *was* man,—the "outer man." But by the in-breathing of Divinity man became something more; he *became,*—passed from one state to another,"—from the natural to the spiritual. He was a spiritual, immortal being within the natural,—a "living soul."

We must not confound the word "soul" with the word "mind" or "spirit." The soul is a real being. The mind is a power, or faculty of the soul,—the power by which we perceive, think, or reason. Secondarily the mind has faculties,—perception, memory, recollection, imagination, understanding, and reason. The word spirit has a wide range of meaning. If by it we mean the renewed nature of man, we should say so. If by it we mean the immortal part of man we should say so. Or if by it we mean the prevailing disposition of man, good or evil, we should say so. Then the word "soul" may include the entire man; and, in some rare instances, it may seemingly apply to the outward, visible man. In 1 Thess. 5: 23 we have the threefold nature of man clearly stated: "I pray God your whole spirit, and soul, and body, be preserved blameless unto the coming of our Lord Jesus Christ."

Man's physical body contains the organs of physical life, not of spiritual life. All the organs of the body have a distinct function, each subordinate to the organ of mind,—the brain. But the brain is not the mind. The power behind the brain is infinitely greater than the brain. The brain is simply the instrument of the mind. It is by the brain, through the senses, that the mind holds communication with the physical world. If the brain be impaired, weakened, or diseased, the mind is not injured. Communication is interrupted,—we cannot work well with an imperfect instrument. The brain does not see, nor feel, nor think, neither does the heart love. The seat of the affections is in the mind.

THE INNER MAN.—Man's spiritual nature is the "inner man." It is the power that thinks all we think, that knows all we know, and yet, of its nature and organization, we know but little, simply because the mind in our present state is directly related through the senses to the world of matter. In our contracted views we erroneously attribute volition to the brain, and emotion to the heart, instead of tracing them to their higher source in the mind, and the "heart of hearts."

If the intellect be a faculty of the mind which receives and comprehends ideas, collected through the senses, and these ideas, thus received, be held by the memory, reproduced at will, and, under color of the imagination, held up before the understanding, and, under the power of reason, sifted, classified and compared, till all the facts are clearly seen, and higher fields of truth open to the mind in the realms of faith:—if all this and much more be carried on in the mind, we know that there is an organization beyond the brain, higher than this natural life. That organization is the soul of man. It is in the soul that the heart, the seat of the affections of Scripture, is placed. Love is a power of the soul, as the intellect is a faculty of the mind.

PAUL'S ARGUMENT.—In 1 Cor. 13 Paul brings in an argument that forever settles the question as to the nature and destiny of man. In the mind of the inspired writer, charity is an impersonation of all the Christian graces,—a thing of life, without which a man is an empty shadow,—but with which a man is enabled to reach the highest aims of Christian character and holiness. Charity is not an emotion of our sensual nature,—not a passion which some mistake for love. It is the highest and purest form of friendship, a union of minds based upon mutual esteem and priceless worth, that moves the hand to works of mercy and acts of kindness, and enlists the soul in a life of obedience to God.

The heart may cease to beat, the brain may lie a shapeless mass within its casket, but "*charity never faileth.*" Love is stronger than death. Love survives the tomb. Then the soul, the source and centre of this vital energy, continues ever. It is not the charity outside of us that Paul speaks of, but the charity within us. It is individual, personal, real. The time will come when prophecies shall cease, and knowledge shall vanish away, because our knowledge and preaching are imperfect and temporary: "For we know in part, and we prophesy in part." But a glorious trinity remains,—three eternal principles: Faith, hope, charity. Since, then, these principles abide, it follows, as an unavoidable conclusion, that the soul being a unit in essence and organization, and inseparably related to each of these undying principles, must and shall abide forever.

The problem of man's redemption would have been a matter of easy solution if death ends all. Let a pestilence sweep man from the face of the earth, and the question is solved. But the redemption of man was the one great problem of the universe, one which the angels desired to look into, and one which the mind of God alone could solve. This stands as an unanswerable argument for the soul's immortality. The spark of divinity in man, the being created in the image of God, was the object of such concern, such mercy, and such love as to cause the Eternal Father to send his only Son into the world to die that man might be redeemed.

Now measure the value of the human soul. Will you estimate it in the scope of its powers, in its capacity for improvement, in the endless nature of its existence, or in all three?

Moore's Store, Va.

LOVE TESTED.

BY S. N. M'CANN.

" If a man love me, he will keep my WORDS."—John 14: 23.

GOD'S love to the sinner is unquestionably great, long-suffering, and strongly manifested. It flowed out from the great heart of God to you, sinner, before the world began in a bright and precious promise, even the promise of eternal life. Titus 1: 2. Jesus Christ, the Son of God, received the promise, and began to suffer before the world was that you might be delivered from this present evil world, according to the will of God. Gal. 1: 4. "O, Father, glorify thou me with thine own self, with the glory which I had with thee before the world was." John 17: 5.

Think of it! Christ suffering for over four thousand years for you, sinner! He has purchased your redemption, for "as in Adam all die, even so in Christ shall all be made alive." 1 Cor. 15: 22. Christ suffered the penalty, obtained universal redemption and, as a consequence, universal quickening or universal resurrection, for "all that are in the graves shall hear his voice, and shall come forth; they that have done good unto the resurrection of life; and they that have done evil to the resurrection of damnation." John 5: 28.

God's love still abounds. Though redemption was brought nigh, he knew our frame; he knew

dress, but peculiar in a good many ways. I imagined, the other evening, at the love-feast, that the outsiders thought, "What a peculiar people." I saw some of them laugh when the brethren saluted each other with the kiss of charity. They thought we were peculiar when we washed one another's feet. We might call your attention to a number of things in which we are peculiar, and I am glad it is so. Would you not like to belong to the family of Christ?—For a moment, just think of it! What a family! What a large family! Another thought. The family of Christ is a loving family. The very first of the foundation of the family of Christ was from God. "For God so loved the world, that he gave his only begotten Son, that whosoever believeth in him should not perish, but have everlasting life." Again, "By this shall all men know that ye are my disciples, if ye have love one for another." Thank God! O ask the mother why she kisses that babe, and she will say, "Because I love it." Christ gave his life that we could live, and should live in the family of Christ. Why did he give his life? What for? Why, for genuine love.

We should love God above all others. I often think, brethren and sisters, that I don't love God as I should. Young brethren and sisters, love him above all things in this world!

Then, again, the family of Christ is a family of peace. They cannot go to war; they cannot fight. No, the family of Christ cannot do this. You remember that terrible war we passed through. Some of the children of Christ were arrested, and led out on the battle field. They could march them around, and make them carry the gun and the sword, but they could not make them fight.

That dear old brother, John Cline, who used to live in those days, was a child of Christ. He proved to be a true Christian, and after all was over, after he went back to Virginia, they took his life. He was a true Christian. It is evident that the family of Christ cannot fight, for it is a family of peace.

I want to call your attention to something that should not be, but I sometimes fear it is the case. It is this: "The children of Christ should not quarrel." That outsider back there says, "They cannot quarrel when they are a family of peace." No, it should not be. I again call your attention to the children of Christ being a rich family. David says, "The earth is the Lord's, and the fullness thereof; the world; and they that dwell therein." If we have a brother here from the country that is a farmer, I would say that you are only a renter; it is the Lord's land that you are cultivating.

The family of Christ is a scattered family. It is scattered all over the United States, and that is not all. You go over the briny deep, and you find a part of this family, and that is not all. You find a part of this family in the upper world, and we are looking up there and trusting that finally that will be our home. Yes, Christ is there; and the holy angels, and we are glad to know, or feel quite sure, there are a great many loved ones over there in the other world. Some have mothers and fathers over there, and some of us have children over there. But I thank God that the time is coming when this family will be reunited. If I were as young as some of you, I would almost wish I could live till Jesus comes. He will come down to this lower world and gather us home. Then we, which are alive, shall be caught up together with them in the cloud, to meet the Lord in the air, and so shall we ever be with the Lord."

When Christ comes with an innumerable band of angels, we will be judged in a moment of time, in the twinkling of an eye. Just think of it! I sometimes think the time is not far distant when the Lord will come, and they that are sleeping in

Jesus, shall come forth and shall be changed. "For this corruptible must put on incorruption, and this mortal must put on immortality."

Now, dear brethren and sisters, I must close. I hope and pray that, when it goes well with you, you will think of the old brethren and sisters.

Mt. Morris, Ill.

THE JUDGMENT.

BY A. HUTCHISON.

Number Two.

THE question is asked in Holy Writ, "For the great day of his wrath is come; and who shall be able to stand?" David would answer, "He that hath clean hands, and a pure heart." Psa. 24: 4. This seems to be a direct answer, and the only way in which we can have clean hands or a pure heart, is by having them washed in the blood of the Lamb. This can only be done by obedience to the truth. Jesus said to his disciples, "Now ye are clean through the word which I have spoken unto you." John 15: 3. We certainly cannot expect to be made clean by or through his Word, unless we make an application of it, as directed by the Word itself.

This we have clearly indicated by the following language: "Seeing ye have purified your souls in obeying the Truth through the Spirit," etc. 1 Pet. 1: 22. This purifying must be done while we are here in this life, for there is a time coming when we cannot make the necessary preparation, but can only say in the language as given by the prophet Jeremiah: "The harvest is past, the summer is ended, and we are not saved." Jer. 8: 20.

Dear reader, did you ever think, that it is possible that you might be one of the number, included in that little pronoun we? It will be applied to every one who has not obeyed the Truth from the heart. Head or shell work *alone*, will not do, when the great day of his wrath is come. A heart filled with the love of God, is all that will pass the solemn test. Let us not be misied as to what the love of God is. Suppose we let an apostle define it for us, and then we will take no risk upon ourselves. He says, "This is the love of God, that we keep his commandments." 1 John 5: 3. Now we have it in a very short and comprehensive manner. There is nothing, in any sense, dark or mysterious about it, since the case is so clearly laid out before us, if we do not accept of it. We may, then, expect that the language of Isaiah will be true in our case: "And they shall go into the holes of the rocks, and into the caves of the earth, for fear of the Lord, and for the glory of his majesty, when he ariseth to shake terribly the earth." Isa. 2: 19.

When men allow themselves to give this question anything like a serious thought, they are wont to put it off, and look upon it as being a long way off, but if we are not on the look-out for it, we will find that it is like giving our obligation for the payment of a debt at a certain time. Notwithstanding we know the time, and the amount, yet it comes upon us before we are ready, and when this is the case, we are in distress; still we may make some shift, by which the case may be prolonged for a time. But in this other case, we know not the day nor the hour, for this is kept from us, therefore we ought always to be ready, and he to whom we are indebted does not require of us anything that we need to put off, not even for a day. Then he would have us act now, and carry no risk. But in view of all this, if we refuse, and procrastinate the time of our accepting Christ, and entering into his service, we then may expect to find the language, which we now quote, to be fearfully true, in our case. Listen to them: "And they shall say to the mountains, Cover us;

and to the hills, Fall on us." Hos. 10: 8. Again, in the language of him who had such a vivid picture before him of what was to come hereafter, we have the following, "And in those days shall men seek death, and shall not find it; and shall desire to die, and death shall flee from them." Rev. 9: 6. This is a gloomy picture, but it is precisely what Jesus said would be, when he was speaking of the things which should take place in the time that was coming. Here are his words: "Then shall they begin to say to the mountains, Fall on us; and to the hills, Cover us." Luke 23: 30. O how much each one, who is found in that condition, will feel like applying to himself the language of the following:

> "Jesus! I throw my arms around,
> And hang upon thy breast;
> Without a gracious smile from thee,
> My spirit cannot rest.

> "O tell me that my worthless name
> Is graven on thy hands,
> Show me some promise in thy book,
> Where my salvation stands."

Let us all say, like David of old: "And now, Lord, what wait I for? My hope is in thee." Psa. 39: 7.

McPherson, Kans.

(*To be Continued.*)

THE MINISTERIAL RELATION.

(*Continued from first page.*)

responsibilities. Do we, as ministers, feel that we really are this? If we cannot so feel ourselves, how can others feel it? And if others cannot feel it, why a shepherd? Why try to fill a position for which we have no fitness? And how can we care for and feed those who can care for and feed themselves better or even as well as we ourselves? There can be no possible advantage of sheep having a shepherd, no stronger, no greater than themselves. They would be at the mercy of the wolf and in danger of starvation, just the same as if they had no shepherd. So with the church. If the minister is in no way better or greater than his people,—spiritually we mean,—then there is no need of such minister, as he could not give what the people need. In caring for, directing and feeding the flock spiritually, the relation of the minister to the people is the same as that of the shepherd to the sheep, or as the parent to the child. Perhaps the latter brings the relation more clearly to us because we are more familiar with it. The fraternal relation is a very close and sacred one, and it will be well for us, as ministers, to study it well and then determine how well we are performing our duties in filling the relation that we sustain to our people. Do we labor as assiduously and conscientiously for the good of those who place themselves under our care, religiously, as we do for our children? Do we exercise towards them the same degree of patience, forbearance and charity as a religious father does towards his children? If not, are we performing the duties fully, that the relation demands?

To be a shepherd of souls is a grave and responsible charge and it behooves us, not only to understand the duties that the relation imposes, but to faithfully carry them out.

While we have presented these thoughts as to the relation of the minister to his people, we have also been impressed with the importance of the church learning more fully the relation that should be felt between herself and the minister. Of this relation we may speak at some future time.

dress, but peculiar in a good many ways. I imagined, the other evening, at the love-feast, that the outsiders thought, "What a peculiar people." I saw some of them laugh when the brethren saluted each other with the kiss of charity. They thought we were peculiar when we washed one another's feet. We might call your attention to a number of things in which we are peculiar, and I am glad it is so. Would you not like to belong to the family of Christ? For a moment, just think of it! What a family! What a large family!

Another thought. The family of Christ is a loving family. The very first of the foundation of the family of Christ was from God. "For God so loved the world, that he gave his only begotten Son, that whosoever believeth in him should not perish, but have everlasting life." Again, "By this shall all men know that ye are my disciples, if ye have love one for another." Thank God! O ask the mother why she kisses that babe, and she will say, "Because I love it." Christ gave his life that we could live, and should live in the family of Christ. Why did he give his life? What for? Why, for genuine love.

We should love God above all others. I often think, brethren and sisters, that I don't love God as I should. Young brethren and sisters, love him above all things in this world!

Then, again, the family of Christ is a family of peace. They cannot go to war; they cannot fight. No, the family of Christ cannot do this. You remember that terrible war we passed through. Some of the children of Christ were arrested, and led out on the battle field. They could march them around, and make them carry the gun and the sword, but they could not make them fight.

That dear old brother, John Cline, who used to live in those days, was a child of Christ. He proved to be a true Christian; and after all was over, after he went back to Virginia, they took his life. He was a true Christian. It is evident that the family of Christ cannot fight, for it is a family of peace.

I want to call your attention to something that should not be, but I sometimes fear it is the case. It is this: "The children of Christ should not quarrel." That outsider back there says, "They cannot quarrel when they are a family of peace." No, it should not be. I again call your attention to the children of Christ being a rich family. David says, "The earth is the Lord's, and the fullness thereof; the world, and they that dwell therein." If we have a brother here from the country that is a farmer, I would say that you are only a renter; it is the Lord's land that you are cultivating.

The family of Christ is a scattered family. It is scattered all over the United States, and that is not all. You go over the briny deep, and you find a part of this family, and that is not all. You find a part of this family in the upper world, and we are looking up there and trusting that finally that will be our home. Yes, Christ is there; and the holy angels, and we are glad to know, or feel quite sure, there are a great many loved ones over there in the other world. Some have mothers and fathers over there, and some of us have children over there. But I thank God that the time is coming when this family will be reunited. If I were as young as some of you, I would almost wish I could live till Jesus comes. He will come down to this lower world and gather us home. Then we, which are alive, shall be caught up together with them in the cloud, to meet the Lord in the air, and so shall we ever be with the Lord.

When Christ comes with an innumerable band of angels, we will be judged in a moment of time, in the twinkling of an eye. Just think of it! I sometimes think the time is not far distant when the Lord will come, and they that are sleeping in Jesus, shall come forth and shall be changed. "For this corruptible must put on incorruption, and this mortal must put on immortality."

Now, dear brethren and sisters, I must close. I hope and pray that, when it goes well with you, you will think of the old brethren and sisters.

Mt. Morris, Ill.

THE JUDGMENT.

BY A. HUTCHISON.

Number Two.

THE question is asked in Holy Writ, "For the great day of his wrath is come; and who shall be able to stand?" David would answer, "He that hath clean hands, and a pure heart." Psa. 24: 4. This seems to be a direct answer, and the only way in which we can have clean hands or a pure heart, is by having them washed in the blood of the Lamb. This can only be done by obedience to the truth. Jesus said to his disciples, "Now ye are clean through the word which I have spoken unto you." John 15: 3. We certainly cannot expect to be made clean by or through his Word, unless we make an application of it, as directed by the Word itself.

This we have clearly indicated by the following language: "Seeing ye have purified your souls in obeying the Truth through the Spirit," etc. 1 Pet. 1: 22. This purifying must be done while we are here in this life, for there is a time coming when we cannot make the necessary preparation, but can only say in the language as given by the prophet Jeremiah: "The harvest is past, the summer is ended, and we are not saved." Jer. 8: 20.

Dear reader, did you ever think, that it is possible that you might be one of the number, included in that little pronoun we? It will be applied to every one who has not obeyed the Truth from the heart. Head or shell work *alone*, will not do, when the great day of his wrath is come. A heart filled with the love of God, is all that will pass the solemn test. Let us not be misled as to what the love of God is. Suppose we let an apostle define it for us, and then we will take no risk upon ourselves. He says, "This is the love of God, that we keep his commandments." 1 John 5: 3. Now we have it in a very short and comprehensive manner. There is nothing, in any sense, dark or mysterious about it, since the case is no clearly laid out before us, if we do not accept of it. We may, then, expect that the language of Isaiah will be true in our case: "And they shall go into the holes of the rocks, and into the caves of the earth, for fear of the Lord, and for the glory of his majesty, when he ariseth to shake terribly the earth." Isa. 2: 19.

When men allow themselves to give this question anything like a serious thought, they are wont to put it off, and look upon it as being a long way off, but if we are not on the look-out for it, we will find that it is like giving our obligation for the payment of a debt at a certain time. Notwithstanding we know the time, and the amount, yet it comes upon us before we are ready, and when this is the case, we are in distress; still we may make some shift, by which the case may be prolonged for a time. But in this other case, we know not the day nor the hour, for this is kept from us, therefore we ought always to be ready, and he to whom we are indebted does not require of us anything that we need to put off, not even for a day. Then he would have us act now, and carry no risk. But in view of all this, if we refuse, and procrastinate the time of our accepting Christ and entering into his service, we then may expect to find the language, which we now quote, to be fearfully true, in our case. Listen to them: "And they shall say to the mountains, Cover us; and to the hills, Fall on us." Hos. 10: 8. Again, in the language of him who had such a vivid picture before him of what was to come hereafter, we have the following, "And in those days shall men seek death, and shall not find it; and shall desire to die, and death shall flee from them." Rev. 9: 6. This is a gloomy picture, but it is precisely what Jesus said would be, when he was speaking of the things which should take place in the time that was coming. Here are his words: "Then shall they begin to say to the mountains, Fall on us; and to the hills, Cover us." Luke 23: 30. O how much each one, who is found in that condition, will feel like applying to himself the language of the following:

"Jesus! I throw my arms around,
    And hang upon thy breast;
Without a gracious smile from thee,
    My spirit cannot rest.

"O tell me that my worthless name
    Is graven on thy hands,
Show me some promise in thy book,
    Where my salvation stands."

Let us all say, like David of old: "And now, Lord, what wait I for? My hope is in thee." Psa. 39: 7.

McPherson, Kans.

(*To be Continued.*)

THE MINISTERIAL RELATION.

(*Continued from first page.*)

responsibilities. Do we, as ministers, feel that we really are this? If we cannot so feel ourselves, how can others feel it? And if others cannot feel it, why a shepherd? Why try to fill a position for which we have no fitness? And how can we care for and feed those who can care for and feed themselves better or even as well as we ourselves? There can be no possible advantage of sheep having a shepherd, no stronger, no greater than themselves. They would be at the mercy of the wolf and in danger of starvation, just the same as if they had no shepherd. So with the church. If the minister is in no way better or greater than his people,—spiritually we mean,—then there is no need of such minister, as he could not give those who place themselves under our care, religiously, as we do for our children? Do we exercise towards them the same degree of patience, forbearance and charity as a religious father does towards his children? If not, are we performing the duties fully, that the relation demands?

To be a shepherd of souls is a grave and responsible charge and it behooves us, not only to understand the duties that the relation imposes, but to faithfully carry them out.

While we have presented these thoughts as to the relation of the minister to his people, we have also been impressed with the importance of the church learning more fully the relation that should be felt between herself and the minister. Of this relation we may speak at some future time.

Missionary and Tract Work Department.

"Upon the first day of the week, let every one of you lay by him in store as God hath prospered him, that there be no gatherings when I come."—1 Cor. 16: 2.

"Every man as he purposeth in his heart, so let him give. Not grudgingly or of necessity, for the Lord loveth a cheerful giver."—9 Cor. 9: 7.

HOW MUCH SHALL WE GIVE?

"Every man *according to his ability*." "Every one *as God hath prospered him*." "Every man, *according as he purposeth in his heart*, so let him give." "For if there be first a willing mind, it is accepted *according to that a man hath*, and not according to that he hath not."—2 Cor. 8: 12.

Organization of Missionary Committee.

DANIEL VANIMAN, Foreman, · · ·   McPherson, Kans
D. L. MILLER, Treasurer, · · ·   Mt. Morris, Ill.
GALEN B. ROYER, Secretary, · · ·   Mt. Morris, Ill.

Organization of Book and Tract Work.

S. W. HOOVER, Foreman, · · ·   Dayton, Ohio.
S. BOCK, Secretary and Treasurer, · · ·   Dayton, Ohio.

☞All donations intended for Missionary Work should be sent to GALEN B. ROYER, Mt. Morris, Ill.

☞All money for Tract Work should be sent to S. BOCK, Dayton, Ohio.

☞Money may be sent by Money Order, Registered Letter, or Drafts on New York or Chicago. Do not send personal checks, or drafts on interior towns, as it costs 25 cents to collect them.

☞Solicitors are requested to faithfully carry out the plan of Annual Meeting, that all our members be solicited to contribute at least twice a year for the Mission and Tract Work of the Church.

☞Notes for the Endowment Fund can be had by writing to the Secretary of either Work.

TAKE all your legal wants and wishes to God in prayer. "Ask," says the Savior, "and it shall be given you; seek, and ye shall find; knock, and it shall be opened unto you." There is great efficacy in prayer. The Christian can not live long acceptably without prayer, nor can he succeed in his religious work. A straight line is the shortest distance between two points; so is prayer the shortest distance to God. Every member should associate deep, earnest prayer with all his undertakings and efforts, in every branch and line of Christian work, to which the Holy Spirit has called him. Prayer, accompanied with faith in God and one's work, becomes a mighty, living, active power for success.—R.

ENCOURAGING.

THE Tract Work is steadily moving forward in the cause. Many new points of interest of a practical and encouraging character are constantly opening up in this work. The excellent spirit of many workers is, in one way or another, almost daily becoming more manifest, seeking expression in loving words and deeds. Many more brethren and sisters, both old and young, are coming forward and taking hold.

We work as we learn. Indeed the true spirit of our being, as well as character,—virtuous, benevolent, energetic or otherwise,—cannot long remain in obscurity. Our deeds become manifest. Precisely the same thing is true of the church and its membership, respecting her spirit and energies, but in a more extended sense. *Her works* are manifest. If not wholly so to us, they are to God. This makes the matter weighty and doubly important to all.

This excellent spirit, we believe, is prompting many additional workers to come forward and take a liberal interest in the work, taking hold with their energies, their hands, and their prayers, and by giving of their means. This is as it should be. May God be praised for it and all his works more and more! But this is not written in praise merely for what we have already done, but very much more to encourage us all to do still more. This we easily can and ought to do, "if there first be a willing mind." But there is just where the trouble is. Ordinarily, when once the *mind be-*comes *willing*, but few obstacles will ever be found in the way of true benevolence and progress; mountains will become as mere mole hills, and excuses vanish as the morning dew. True Christian benevolence is more generally measured by the spirit we possess, and in which we give and in which we work, than by either our wealth or our strength. Let your offering be ever so small, if it be given with a willing spirit, it will be most thankfully received into the Lord's treasury to carry on his work. If but a "widow's mite," it is much better than nothing at all, and far more precious in the sight of the Lord.

It is astonishing what united efforts, spirit and enterprise will accomplish in the cause. I append a few points and figures from a late report of the "American Tract Society," showing the immense amount of work they are doing in this line. "Its publications have reached the number of 444,201,-394, of which 30,431,191, were volumes, the rest being tracts, leaflets, cards, etc., and in 150 languages and dialects. These were carried directly to the homes of the people, for the most part destitute of moral and religious reading, by the house to house visits of its missionaries at various localities throughout the country. One hundred and sixty-five men were thus employed during the last year. These took the Gospel unto 118,697 homes, held 6,413 public meetings, distributed among them 103,913 volumes of saving-truth, and organized a large number of Sabbath and Bible schools for both adults and children. This entire work has been accomplished through voluntary contributions and about one thousand dollars a week were used in the gratuitous distribution of its literature among the needy."

May the Lord strengthen his Zion and bless both our hearts and our hands to do his will in all things!   S. W. H.

TRACTS—THEIR MISSION.

BY N. D. UNDERHILL.

TRACTS are, in some respects, like angels. Little white-winged messengers, bearing words of truth and loving counsel, they flit about here and there, going where the servant of God sends them, always on a mission of love, always telling the earnest truth, always pointing out the way to heaven.

Tracts are meek, gentle, harmless messengers, never disturbing any one's peace, never betraying any one's faults, but silently appealing to the eye, the mind, the heart of the soul to whom Christ would speak. They are like letters from Heaven, bearing words of grace and life to all who will receive and heed them, but are easily torn, burned or trodden under foot by the heedless, heartless soul who loves not God, and hates to be encumbered by his messages, his earnest, loving appeals, his sad but firm condemnations. They should be like snow-flakes, pure, white, clean (and as we believe they are), flying swiftly through the air in great showers; by the thousands and by the millions, clothing the earth with beauty, refreshing the tender plants (young converts) and thirsty streams (of good thoughts), cleansing the impure and soiled buildings (souls who, by contact with thoughts or actions), penetrating every crack and crevice (entering into every little opening), melting and sinking deep in the earth (people's hearts) to moisten, soften, cleanse and cause seeds to sprout (words to take root), plants to grow (actions to improve) and trees to bear fruit (Christians to do good deeds). Rising again in other forms, mist and vapor (sympathy and love) to form other clouds (of thought) and descend upon other plants, and into other hearts, it keeps on working, doing, moving, going, melting, chang-ing, multiplying and saving souls, who, without guides, would be lost and without refreshment, and thus perish.

There are many ways to use tracts. One way is to stand on the street corner and offer one to every person who passes. Another is to enclose a suitable tract in every letter we write. Another is, to stand at the door of a church or school-house and give one to every person who comes out.

There are many ways of distributing tracts, which are probably better than any of the above, but no one should confine his good deeds to a particular method or form. It is better to use all means possible, every way conceivable to plant good seeds in the hearts of human souls. We know of two sisters who, living on a public road, often keep travelers over night. When the travelers depart, they frequently find a tract or two in their overcoat pockets, which they are sure to examine, wondering meanwhile whence they came, what they are, etc. Persons who keep hotels, or those who sell, repair, make or clean clothing, have this opportunity of sowing seeds of Truth, while the receivers are much more likely to read and meditate upon them, than if they were handed to them in public, like a worthless and despised circular or advertisement. However, we do not wish to depreciate even the indiscriminate and public ways of giving, for the sower must scatter his seeds broad-cast, if he would reap a rich harvest.

When the two sisters, above mentioned, are visited by tramps, they think of the Savior who tramped here on earth so long ago and of His words, "Give to him that asketh thee, "I was a hungered and ye fed me," etc. So they prepare a good lunch, consisting of bread, butter, meat, cake, boiled eggs and so on, and with a large cup of good coffee, or rich sweet milk, they give it to the poor traveler, trying always to speak some kind words at the same time. When these tramps open their lunch they find good food for both body and soul, for their lunches are wrapped in a good religious paper, within a suitable tract is inclosed a little salt or sugar.

We know such people are not always ignorant or heartless, and we have seen them reading the papers within others, who ate their lunch at the house, afterward carefully folded the papers and tracts and put them in their pockets. We always fold small parcels in tracts and larger ones in good religious papers, knowing how curious-people are and how carefully they examine nearly every bit of paper that comes in their way, though many of them would scorn to be seen reading a tract, if boldly asked to do so.

We expect this year to send some tracts through the mails, accompanied by Christmas cards. We have known a poor person to receive replies (from distant strangers) to public appeals, in the form of a bundle of tracts, in which was inclosed a small donation of cash.

Tracts ought to be kept in all reading rooms. It is well for teachers, school-mates and others to obtain tracts, printed in the form of little books, in poems, on beautiful, tinted paper, and in many other attractive forms, to give away as presents on the last day of school and at other times. Such gifts will usually be kept as beautiful souvenirs, read, reread, and remembered. Their influence often extends throughout life and eternity. We know by experience that this is true.

Another good way is to have some tracts printed on letter paper in script, in exact imitation of a friendly letter, inclosed in envelopes and sent to the address of persons for whom they are suitable. They are sure to be read. It is well, as far as possible, to use judgment or discretion even in giving tracts. If your neighbor is a Pedobaptist, do not pounce upon him the first thing with a

Missionary and Tract Work Department.

HOW MUCH SHALL WE GIVE?

"Every man *according to his ability.*" "Every one *as God hath prospered him.*" "Every man, *according as he purposeth in his heart,* so let him give." "For if there be first a willing mind, it is accepted according *to that a man hath,* and not according to that he hath not."—2 Cor. 8:12.

Organization of Missionary Committee.

DANIEL VANIMAN, Foreman,				McPherson, Kans.
D. L. MILLER, Treasurer,				Mt. Morris, Ill.
GALEN B. ROYER, Secretary.				Mt. Morris, Ill.

Organization of Book and Tract Work.

S. W. HOOVER, Foreman,				Dayton, Ohio.
S. BOCK, Secretary and Treasurer,			Dayton, Ohio.

☞All donations intended for Missionary Work should be sent to GALEN B. ROYER, Mt. Morris, Ill.

☞All money for Tract Work should be sent to S. BOCK, Dayton, Ohio.

☞Money may be sent by Money Order, Registered Letter, or Drafts on New York or Chicago. Do not send personal checks, or drafts on interior towns, as it costs 25 cents to collect them.

☞Solicitors are requested to faithfully carry out the plan of Annual Meeting, that all our members be solicited to contribute at least twice a year for the Mission and Tract Work of the Church.

☞Notes for the Endowment Fund can be had by writing to the Secretary of either Work.

TAKE all your legal wants and wishes to God in prayer. "Ask," says the Savior, "and it shall be given you; seek, and ye shall find; knock, and it shall be opened unto you." There is great efficacy in prayer. The Christian can not live long acceptably without prayer, nor can he succeed in his religious work. A straight line is the shortest distance between two points; so is prayer the shortest distance to God. Every member should associate deep, earnest prayer with all his undertakings and efforts, in every branch and line of Christian work, to which the Holy Spirit has called him. Prayer, accompanied with faith in God and one's work, becomes a mighty, living, active power for success.—H.

ENCOURAGING.

THE Tract Work is steadily moving forward in the cause. Many new points of interest of a practical and encouraging character are constantly opening up in this work. The excellent spirit of many workers is, in one way or another, almost daily becoming more manifest, seeking expression in loving words and deeds. Many more brethren and sisters, both old and young, are coming forward and taking hold.

We work as we learn. Indeed the true spirit of our being, as well as character,—virtuous, benevolent, energetic or otherwise,— cannot long remain in obscurity. Our deeds become manifest. Precisely the same thing is true of the church and its membership, respecting her spirit and energies, but in a more extended sense. *Her works* are manifest. If not wholly so to us, they are to God. This makes the matter weighty and doubly important to all.

This excellent spirit, we believe, is prompting many additional workers to come forward and take a liberal interest in the work, taking hold with their energies, their hands, and their prayers, and by giving of their means. This is as it should be. May God be praised for it and all his works more and more! But this is not written in ease merely, for what we have already done, but very much more to encourage us all to do still more. This we easily can and ought to do, "if there first be a willing mind." But there is just where the trouble is. Ordinarily, when once the *mind be-*

comes willing, but few obstacles will ever be found in the way of true benevolence and progress; mountains will become as mere mole hills, and excuses vanish as the morning dew. True Christian benevolence is more generally measured by the spirit we possess, and in which we give and in which we work, than by either our wealth or our strength. Let your offering be ever so small, if it be given with a willing spirit, it will be most thankfully received into the Lord's treasury to carry on his work. If but a "widow's mite," it is much better than nothing at all, and far more precious in the sight of the Lord.

It is astonishing what united efforts, spirit and enterprise will accomplish in the cause. I append a few points and figures from a late report of the "American Tract Society," showing the immense amount of work they are doing in this line. "Its publications have reached the number of 444,201,- 394, of which 30,481,191, were volumes, the rest being tracts, leaflets, cards, etc., and in 150 languages and dialects. These were carried directly to the homes of the people, for the most part destitute of moral and religious reading, by the house to house visits of its missionaries at various localities throughout the country. One hundred and sixty-five men were thus employed during the last year. These took the Gospel into 118,697 homes, held 4,418 public meetings, distributed among them 108,913 volumes of saving truth, and organized a large number of Sabbath and Bible schools for both adults and children. This entire work has been accomplished through voluntary contributions and about one thousand dollars a week were used in the gratuitous distribution of its literature among the needy."

May the Lord strengthen his Zion and bless both our hearts and our hands to do his will in all things!					S. W. H.

TRACTS—THEIR MISSION.

BY N. D. UNDERHILL.

TRACTS are, in some respects, like angels. Little white-winged messengers, bearing words of truth and loving counsel, they flit about here and there, going where the servant of God sends them, always on a mission of love, always telling the earnest truth, always pointing out the way to heaven.

Tracts are meek, gentle, harmless messengers, never disturbing any one's peace, never betraying any one's faults, but silently appealing to the eye, the mind, the heart of the soul to whom Christ would speak. They are like letters from Heaven, bearing words of grace and life to all who will receive and heed them, but are easily torn, burned or trodden under foot by the heedless, heartless soul who loves not God, and hates to be instructed by his messages, his earnest, loving appeals, his sad but firm condemnations. They should be like snow-flakes, pure, white, clean (and as we believe they are), flying swiftly through the air in great showers, by the thousands and by the millions, clothing the earth with beauty, refreshing the tender plants (young converts) and thirsty streams (of good thoughts), cleansing the impure and soiled buildings (souls who, by contact with the world have become addicted to evil speech, thoughts or actions), penetrating every crack and crevice (entering into every little opening), melting and sinking deep in the earth (people's hearts) to moisten, soften, cleanse and cause seeds to sprout (words to take root), plants to grow (actions to improve) and trees to bear fruit (Christians to do good deeds). Raising again in other forms, mist and vapor (sympathy and love) to form other clouds (of thought) and descend upon other plants, and into other hearts, it keeps on working, doing, moving, going, melting, chang-

ing, multiplying and saving souls, who, without guides, would be lost and without refreshment, and thus perish.

There are many ways to use tracts. One way is to stand on the street corner and offer one to every person who passes. Another is to enclose a suitable tract in every letter we write. Another is, to stand at the door of a church or school-house and give one to every person who comes out.

There are many ways of distributing tracts, which are probably better than any of the above, but no one should confine his good deeds to a particular method or form. It is better to use all means possible, every way conceivable to plant good seeds in the hearts of human souls. We know of two sisters who, living on a public road, often keep travelers over night. When the travelers depart, they frequently find a tract or two in their overcoat pockets, which they are sure to examine, wondering meanwhile whence they came, what they are, etc. Persons who keep hotels, or those who sell, repair, make or clean clothing, have this opportunity of sowing seeds of Truth, while the receivers are much more likely to read and meditate upon them, than if they were handed to them in public, like a worthless and despised circular or advertisement. However, we do not wish to depreciate even the indiscriminate and public ways of giving, for the sower must scatter his seeds broad-cast, if he would reap a rich harvest.

When the two sisters, above mentioned, are visited by tramps, they think of the Savior who tramped here on earth so long ago and of His words, "Give to him that asketh thee, "I was a hungered and ye fed me," etc. So they prepare a good lunch, consisting of bread, butter, meat, cake, boiled eggs and so on, and with a large cup of good coffee, or rich sweet milk, they give it to the poor traveler, trying always to speak some kind words at the same time. When those tramps open their lunch they find good food for both body and soul, for their lunches are wrapped in a good religious paper, while within a suitable tract is inclosed a little salt or sugar.

We know such people are not always ignorant or heartless, and we have seen them reading the papers, while others, who ate their lunch at the house, afterward carefully folded the papers and tracts and put them in their pockets. We always fold small parcels in tracts and larger ones in good religious papers, knowing how curious people are and how carefully they examine nearly every bit of paper that comes in their way, though many of them would scorn to be seen reading a tract, if boldly asked to do so.

We expect this year to send some tracts through the mails, accompanied by Christmas cards. We have known a poor person to receive replies (from distant strangers) to public appeals, in the form of a bundle of tracts, in which was inclosed a small donation of cash.

Tracts ought to be kept in all reading rooms. It is well for teachers, school-mates and others to obtain tracts, printed in the form of little books, in poems, on beautiful, tinted paper, and in many other attractive forms, to give away as presents on the last day of school and at other times. Such gifts will usually be kept as beautiful souvenirs, read, reread, and remembered. Their influence often extends throughout life and eternity. We know by experience that this is true.

Another good way is to have some tracts printed on letter paper in script, in exact imitation of a friendly letter, inclosed in envelopes and sent to the address of persons for whom they are suitable. They are sure to be read. It is well, as far as possible, to use judgment or discretion even in giving tracts. If your neighbor is a Pedobaptist, do not pounce upon him the first thing with a

We are in receipt of a card from Bro. J. C. Lahman, stating that he and his wife reached Hawthorn, Fla., Jan. 29, requiring a run of just forty-eight hours from Mt. Morris. They found the weather warm and pleasant. Until further notice his address will be Hawthorn, Fla.

Bro. S. W. Hoover, of the Book and Tract Work, Dayton, Ohio, dropped in on us very unexpectedly last week. He also preached one very interesting sermon in the Chapel. We were glad to have Bro. Hoover call on us; it gave us an opportunity to remind him that our readers would appreciate an occasional article from him. He promises to write more for the Messenger. He also reports the Tract Work in an encouraging condition, stating that they are doing about twice the amount of work this year as compared with former years. We are glad to learn that they are not only doing a good work but have some very important improvements in contemplation.

They that measure themselves by themselves, and compare themselves among themselves are not wise, says Paul, and yet there are those who grade themselves in that manner. What they see other professing Christians do, they think they can do also. They reason, "If it is no harm for others to do so, I can too." Usually they compare themselves with those who are more or less defective, and in this way lower their own condition. We should look to a higher standard with a view of becoming better. If we must compare ourselves with others, select those of the better class and imitate only the better qualities found in them. Paul recognized this principle when he exhorted the brethren "to be followers of him even as he was of the Lord Jesus. In order to keep up the standard of Christianity, we must look higher than our ordinary associates. We should look to Jesus and the apostles and labor to imitate the good qualities so clearly set forth in them and thus be the means of elevating not only ourselves but others also.

THE KISS OF CHARITY AND FEET-WASHING.

Some time before his death we received from Eld. Jesse Crosswhite a communication, stating that in the early part of their movement some of the Disciple churches practiced feet-washing. We have heard similar reports from other sources, and now find it confirmed in a late number of the *Christian Standard*. J. S. Lamar is writing the "Life of Isaac Errett," the founder and former editor of the *Standard*. Speaking of the period in which Isaac Errett's father (Henry) figured, he says:

"It was but natural that these churches, thus going their way towards the light, should sometimes blunder; that in many cases they should attach undue importance to the circumstantial and transitory; and, especially that prevailing errors and abuses should drive them into opposite extremes. We are not surprised, therefore, to find that in a few of these churches such things as the kiss of charity and feet-washing were regarded as ecclesiastical obligations and binding upon the church as a church. It is interesting to note the shrewdness and, as I must think, the latent humor of Henry Errett in dealing with such things. He states the position of the New York church as follows: 'The kiss of charity, the washing of feet, and the entertainment of disciples, being things the performance of which arise from special occasions exemplified in the New Testament—we deem of importance to be attended to on such occasions. * * * As the salutation of the kiss is of no value

unless it be truly and evidently the fruit of love, flowing freely from the heart, they (the New York church) conceive that the brethren *should be at liberty* to manifest this mark of affection towards each other *whenever they feel disposed to do so.*'"

Thus it is seen how these early Disciple churches were induced to depart from two of the most clearly-stated commandments in the New Testament. The method adopted is what Mr. Lamar would call "shrewdness" and "humor," a very successful method indeed by which to lead away from the light those not thoroughly rooted and grounded in the Truth as it is recorded in the sacred writings. The quotation does, however, confirm what many of our aged brethren have repeatedly said in regard to feet-washing having been practiced by some of the early Disciple churches, a fact that we do not remember to have seen in print before this time. As they, and others, were induced to turn from the light, they, of course, dropped these institutions out of their minds, and finally out of their practice. Left to the Gospel alone, many religious bodies might have retained more of the primitive order in their practice, but "shrewdness" and "humor" have always played havoc with Christian simplicity, especially among those who are not fully established in the Gospel order. Our aim is not to offer many comments concerning the facts referred to, but to simply place the facts on record for the benefit of our readers.　　　J. H. M.

QUERISTS' DEPARTMENT.

Is it right, according to the Gospel, and the principles held by the Brethren, for a brother to belong to the Grand Army of the Republic, or any other similar institution? If not right, what should be done in such a case? It is claimed that there is no secrecy connected with such institutions.

HENRY M. SHERKY.

Our Brethren have always held that members should not become identified with organizations of this class. The Grand Army of the Republic is a military institution, based solely upon military operations in the past, such as our members could not take part in and retain their fellowship in the church. It is also, in character, a purely worldly institution, and sustains no relation whatever to that Christianity which discourages war and preaches the Gospel of peace. The simple fact that it is not a secret institution does not remove the objectionable character. There is no necessity, whatever, for our members to unite with any of these worldly institutions. They should rather give their time, influence and means to the furtherance of the principles which we, as a church, hold; principles which we know to be clearly set forth in the Gospel. Members, who have identified themselves with these worldly organizations, should be carefully, prayerfully and patiently admonished to withdraw from them. This should be done in a fatherly manner so as to save them if possible. If such kind treatment proves of no avail, then it would be proper to deal with them according to 2 Thess. 3: 6, which says, "Now we command you brethren, in the name of our Lord Jesus Christ, that ye withdraw yourselves from every brother that walketh disorderly." Walking with a worldly organization, contrary to the wishes of the Brethren, is certainly walking disorderly.

That the salutation, or holy kiss, is a divine injunction is a fact undeniable. Therefore, why do not the Brethren observe it at public gatherings, such as sales, educational meetings, etc., as well as on meeting days? Surely, if we breathe in the full sense of Matt. 5: 16 it will prompt us to act at all times alike.

PERRY B. FITZWATER.

Matt. 5: 16 is referred to. It reads as follows: "Let your light so shine before men, that they may see your good works and glorify your Father which is in heaven." There are several ways of saluting those we meet, such as the shake of the hand, the use of the kiss, or merely speaking, all of which may be used by the Christian, but the one specially recommended in the Gospel is the holy kiss, or kiss of charity. There are times and occasions when it seems in good keeping with the spirit of the Scriptures for Christian neighbors to salute each other by merely speaking, saying "Good morning," or something of the kind. Not only so, but we all do this way, from one end of the land to the other, without thinking it in the least unbecoming even the most devout. We thus meet and salute each other on the street, at places of business, etc. In these business and everyday relations we often shake hands, and sometimes salute with the kiss, governed largely by the feelings and circumstances. We need not be so formal in saluting those we meet so often in our everyday life. Besides, we should avoid using the kiss in a manner that will tend to destroy its sacred meaning, or lower it to a commonplace affair. If at a sale, or any other place of business, we should meet those with whom we are quite familiar in every-day life, we see no more use in insisting on the holy kiss then, than we would in ordinary neighborly greetings, and yet if two, who had not met for a time, should feel to embrace each other as Christian brethren, that, too, would seem quite appropriate. Certainly we should let our light shine, but not in such a way as to cause our good to be evil spoken of. At sales, or any other place of the kind, let brethren approach each other with a becoming degree of confidence, and not stand off and shake hands as though they were afraid to get near each other. At all of our religious and social gatherings we admire a free use of the salutation of the holy kiss, but at other places and under other circumstances let it be used becomingly. Let everything be done decently and in order.

Please tell us why it is that among the Brethren one leads in a prayer and another closes with the Lord's prayer? Give us Scripture for the practice. I do not like to practice what I may not understand.　　　E. F. BURROW.

We can give no special Scriptural reason for the practice, but the habit, if not abused, is at least in harmony with the spirit of the Scriptures throughout. The practice was adopted very early in the history of our people, and there is probably no reason for discontinuing it. Some have suggested that the Lord's prayer might be used only at the close of public meetings and omitted in the opening exercises. This, it would seem, has been left to the discretion of the church, Christ only saying to his disciples, "When ye pray, say, Our Father," etc. The church having adopted the practice of using this model prayer at the close of all public prayers, we feel like insisting upon the practice being continued in good faith. While there may be no Scripture directly demanding the use of it at the close of all others, there is certainly none discouraging its use, and there is probably no good reason for any one to decline following our long-established practice in this respect. It is, however, very important that we have our minds in proper condition to use the prayer when occasion demands it. He who understands the meaning of the Lord's prayer, and is in the proper frame of mind to use it, need not fear to repeat it at any time that the general usages of the Brotherhood call for it,　　　J. H. M.

WE are in receipt of a card from Bro. J. C. Lahman, stating that he and his wife reached Hawthorn, Fla., Jan. 29, requiring a run of just forty-eight hours from Mt. Morris. They found the weather warm and pleasant. Until further notice his address will be Hawthorn, Fla.

BRO. S. W. HOOVER, of the Book and Tract Work, Dayton, Ohio, dropped in on us very unexpectedly last week. He also preached one very interesting sermon in the Chapel. We were glad to have Bro. Hoover call on us; it gave us an opportunity to remind him that our readers would appreciate an occasional article from him. He promises to write more for the MESSENGER. He also reports the Tract Work in an encouraging condition, stating that they are doing about twice the amount of work this year as compared with former years. We are glad to learn that they are not only doing a good work but have some very important improvements in contemplation.

THEY that measure themselves by themselves, and compare themselves among themselves are not wise, says Paul, and yet there are those who grade themselves in that manner. What they see other professing Christians do, they think they can do also. They reason, "If it is no harm for others to do so, I can too." Usually they compare themselves with those who are more or less defective, and in this way lower their own condition. We should look to a higher standard with a view of becoming better. If we must compare ourselves with others, select those of the better class and imitate only the better qualities found in them. Paul recognized this principle when he exhorted the brethren "to be followers of him even as he was of the Lord Jesus. In order to keep up the standard of Christianity, we must look higher than our ordinary associates. We should look to Jesus and the apostles and labor to imitate the good qualities so clearly set forth in them and thus be the means of elevating not only ourselves but others also.

THE KISS OF CHARITY AND FEET-WASHING.

SOME time before his death we received from Eld. Jesse Crosswhite a communication, stating that in the early part of their movement some of the Disciple churches practiced feet-washing. We have heard similar reports from other sources, and now find it confirmed in a late number of the Christian Standard. J. S. Lamar is writing the "Life of Isaac Errett," the founder and former editor of the Standard. Speaking of the period in which Isaac Errett's father (Henry) figured, he says:

"It was but natural that these churches, thus going their way towards the light, should sometimes blunder; that in many cases they should attach undue importance to the circumstantial and transitory; and especially that prevailing errors and abuses should drive them into opposite extremes. We are not surprised, therefore, to find that in a few of these churches such things as the kiss of charity and feet-washing were regarded as ecclesiastical obligations and binding upon the church as a church. It is interesting to note the shrewdness and, as I must think, the latent humor of Henry Errett in dealing with such things. He states the position of the New York church as follows: 'The kiss of charity, the washing of feet, and the entertainment of disciples, being things the performance of which arise from special occasions exemplified in the New Testament—we deem of importance to be attended to on such occasions. * * * As the salutation of the kiss is of no value

unless it be truly and evidently the fruit of love, flowing freely from the heart, they (the New York church) conceive that the brethren should be at liberty to manifest this mark of affection towards each other whenever they feel disposed to do so.'

Thus it is seen how these early Disciple churches were induced to depart from two of the most clearly-stated commandments in the New Testament. The method adopted is what Mr. Lamar would call "shrewdness" and "humor," a very successful method indeed by which to lead away from the light those not thoroughly rooted and grounded in the Truth as it is recorded in the sacred writings. The quotation does, however, confirm what many of our aged brethren have repeatedly said in regard to feet-washing having been practiced by some of the early Disciple churches, a fact that we do not remember to have seen in print before this time. As they, and others, were induced to turn from the light, they, of course, dropped these institutions out of their minds, and finally out of their practice. Left to the Gospel alone, many religious bodies might have retained more of the primitive order in their practice, but "shrewdness" and "humor" have always played havoc with Christian simplicity, especially among those who are not fully established in the Gospel order. Our aim is not to offer many comments concerning the facts referred to, but to simply place the facts on record for the benefit of our readers.

J. H. M.

QUERISTS' DEPARTMENT.

Is it right according to the Gospel, and the principles held by the Brethren, for a brother to belong to the Grand Army of the Republic, or any other similar institution? If not right, what should be done in such a case? It is claimed that there is no secrecy connected with such institutions.

HENRY M. SHERRY.

OUR Brethren have always held that members should not become identified with organizations of this class. The Grand Army of the Republic is a military institution, based solely upon military operations in the past, such as our members could not take part in and retain their fellowship in the church. It is also, in character, a purely worldly institution, and maintains no relation whatever to that Christianity which discourages war and preaches the Gospel of peace. The simple fact that it is not a secret institution does not remove the objectionable character. There is no necessity, whatever, for our members to unite with any of these worldly institutions. They should rather give their time, influence and means to the furtherance of the principles which we, as a church, hold; principles which we know to be clearly set forth in the Gospel. Members, who have identified themselves with these worldly organizations, should be carefully, prayerfully and patiently admonished to withdraw from them. This should be done in a fatherly manner so as to save them if possible. If such kind treatment proves of no avail, then it would be proper to deal with them according to 2 Thess. 3: 6, which says, "Now we command you brethren, in the name of our Lord Jesus Christ, that ye withdraw yourselves from every brother that walketh disorderly." Walking with a worldly organization, contrary to the wishes of the Brethren, is certainly walking disorderly.

That the salutation, or holy kiss, is a divine injunction is a fact undeniable. Therefore, why do not the Brethren observe it at public gatherings, such as sales, educational meetings, etc., as well as on meeting days? Surely, if we breathe in the full sense of Matt. 5: 16 it will prompt us to act at all times alike.

PERRY B. FITZWATER.

Matt. 5: 16 is referred to. It reads as follows: "Let your light so shine before men, that they may see your good works and glorify your Father which is in heaven." There are several ways of saluting those we meet, such as the shake of the hand, the use of the kiss, or merely speaking, all of which may be used by the Christian, but the one specially recommended in the Gospel is the holy kiss, or kiss of charity. There are times and occasions when it seems in good keeping with the spirit of the Scriptures for Christian neighbors to salute each other by merely speaking, saying "Good morning," or something of the kind. Not only so, but we all do this way, from one end of the land to the other, without thinking it in the least unbecoming even the most devout. We thus meet and salute each other on the street, at places of business, etc. In these business and everyday relations we often shake hands, and sometimes salute with the kiss, governed largely by the feelings and circumstances. We need not be so formal in saluting those we meet so often in our everyday life. Besides, we should avoid using the kiss in a manner that will tend to destroy its sacred meaning, or lower it to a commonplace affair. If at a sale, or any other place of business, we should meet those with whom we are quite familiar in every-day life, we see no more use in insisting on the holy kiss then, than we would in ordinary neighborly greetings, and yet if two, who had not met for a time, should feel to embrace each other as Christian brethren, that, too, would seem quite appropriate. Certainly we should let our light shine, but not in such a way as to cause our good to be evil spoken of. At sales, or any other place of the kind, let brethren approach each other with a becoming degree of confidence, and not stand off and shake hands as though they were afraid to get near each other. At all of our religious and social gatherings we admire a free use of the salutation of the holy kiss, but at other places and under other circumstances let it be used prudently. Let everything be done decently and in order.

Please tell us why it is that among the Brethren one leads in a prayer and another closes with the Lord's prayer? Give us Scripture for the practice. I do not like to practice what I may not understand.

E. F. BURROW.

We can give no special Scriptural reason for the practice, but the habit, if not abused, is at least in harmony with the spirit of the Scriptures throughout. The practice was adopted very early in the history of our people, and there is probably no reason for discontinuing it. Some have suggested that the Lord's prayer might be used only at the close of public meetings and omitted in the opening exercises. This, it would seem, has been left to the discretion of the church, Christ only saying to his disciples, "When ye pray, say, Our Father," etc. The church having adopted the practice of using this model prayer at the close of all public prayers, we feel like insisting upon the practice being continued in good faith. While there may be no Scripture directly demanding the use of it at the close of all others, there is certainly none discouraging its use, and there is probably no good reason for any one to decline following our long-established practice in this respect. It is, however, very important that we have our minds in proper condition to use the prayer when occasion demands it. He who understands the meaning of the Lord's prayer, and is in the proper frame of mind to use it, need not fear to repeat it at any time that the general usages of the Brotherhood call for it.

J. H. M.

wife's illness and death, he was not permitted to be with us so very often, and the result was that we were, at times, left alone. The meeting closed Jan. 17. Notwithstanding a great deal of sickness in the community and some inclement weather, and, at times, bad roads, the attendance kept up fairly well. The interest was very good and the meetings closed with nearly a full house. As a result of the meetings, we had five additions, four of whom are to be baptized in the near future. One was restored to the fold. The brethren and sisters expressed themselves as having been much revived and strengthened. We, in company with the brethren, did considerable visiting, and certainly enjoyed it much. They were all very kind to us. We entertain the fond hope that, if we may never meet again on earth, we may meet in heaven.

The Brethren of the Back Creek congregation, adjoining the one in which the foregoing meeting was held, desire that we help them in a series of meetings in the Upton church Jan. 24, which we have agreed to do. T. F. IMLER.

Jan. 21.

From the Spring Creek Church, Ind.

BRO. WM. H. DEETER, of Milford, Ind., is now conducting a series of meetings at our Center house, near Dodgertown. The meeting has been running one week, with large congregations and the very best of attention. We hope to be able to send you a favorable report when the meetings close. We hope that many may "be added unto the church, both men and women."

There is a good deal of sickness here just now. Bro. Lewis Workman has been confined to his house for five weeks, and part of the time to his bed. I am happy to say that he is now much better.

LATER.—We had two applicants for baptism, and others said that they would soon come. May God help them to come! E. MILLER.

Sidney, Ind.

Notes by the Way.

I AM glad to say that I have about recovered from *La Grippe* and that I hope to be able, by next week, to resume my ministerial labors again. I have several series of meetings to hold yet this winter, if health permits.

Just one month has elapsed since I came home sick, but I was able to talk some last Sunday and to preach a funeral on Monday. Bro. Daniel Snell's meetings closed at the Bachelor's Creek church on the evening of Jan. 10 with good interest. The attendance at this series of meetings was not as large as usual on account of so much La Grippe. Two precious souls were baptized. May God help them to be shining lights! I feel sure the meeting was a good one. Though I could not attend but a few meetings, yet, from the reports I had each day, I am sure the Gospel was preached in its primitive purity. Bro. Snell is not afraid nor ashamed to hew to the line and to the plummet. The church received much good counsel that we can all profit by, if we are willing to apply it to ourselves and not give it all away.

I feel that we need a stirring up in the church as well as outside. If the church is cold and cannot get warm, it will be hard to make much impression on the unconverted. At least that has been my experience.

We expect Bro. G. L. Studebaker, of Indiana, to commence a series of meetings in New Carlisle, Feb. 14. I hope I may be permitted to attend that series of meetings, and enjoy the blessings of home with him, while he is with us. I expect to hold some meetings at two isolated points in our own district the latter part of March and April, as

the outskirts must be looked after as well as the main body of the church. The poor are too often neglected. HENRY FRANTZ.

Forgy, Ohio, Jan. 20.

From Sweden and Denmark.

I AM always glad to hear through the MESSENGER from the various churches in America. It gladdens us all to see that so many are coming to the church and our prayer is, that they all may be faithful to the end.

Now as the year has closed, we praise the Lord for all his goodness bestowed upon us during the past year, and especially in sending our dear brother and sister Miller to us. Their intention was to go to Palestine, but the Lord would have them to come here and no farther, for this time. His ways are wonderful, but he would teach us to take it all with patience. In the end he will show us that all is for our good.

Oct. 1 to Nov. 15 Bro. Hope and I held many good meetings at several places. All our members, the new as well as the old, were glad to hear him preach. By his labors they were much strengthened in their faith, and comforted in their trials. Bro. Hope has a special gift in that respect. When he left us, he went to Denmark to hold meetings. He left Tindal Dec. 9. I met him in Copenhagen and together we went to Bremen, to say farewell to brother and sister Miller who had asked me to come down, so we could speak together about the mission work before they left Europe.

Before Bro. Hope left Tindal, three were baptized there, and the last evening we were together with the members in Copenhagen, a sister was baptized at that place. All the members met in Bro. Hansen's home to say farewell to our dear brother before he left them, and they all promised to be faithful to the end, and to work together according to our beloved church order. Dec. 13 we reached Bremen at 12 o'clock in the night. We had a very rough voyage on the sea and were a day late.

If I may tell you my opinion about the MESSENGER, then I will say, that it is the best and cheapest paper I have ever seen. Containing as it does, sound doctrine, well edited, and filled with good news from all parts of our beloved Brotherhood, it is, therefore, well worth $1.50. It is wonderful that it has not yet found its way to all our Brethren's homes who are able to read English.

Right here I will say that we are very glad to see in its pages that our dear brethren are giving so freely to the poor brethren here in Scandinavia. I will hereby say to all the noble givers that the Lord will give you manifold again, and you may rest assured that the means will be properly used, because the brethren on the committee are good, responsible, and well-to-do. May God bless all the cheerful givers!

After I had said farewell to our dear brother and sister Miller and Bro. Hope on board the large and comfortable ship, "Havel," I left Bremen, Hamburg, Lübeck and Rostock for Copenhagen, which place I reached at 7 o'clock P. M., Dec. 17. I then went directly to Bro. O. L. Johansen's home, where I found the members assembled in a prayer-meeting. Many warm prayers were sent up in behalf of our dear brethren and our sister who were then on the great ocean. The next day we had a good meeting with the members in Malmo and Limhamn, and from there I went to Kjeflinge and Hör, at which places I had some very good meetings. At all places the travelers on the sea were remembered, and we asked the good Lord to deliver them from every danger.

I reached my dear home in safety the day before Christmas, glad to see that the Lord had protect-

ed my family and all the members from all danger and evil. On Christmas Day we had a good love-feast in my home, two applicants from Hör were baptized, and also a sister from Wanneberga. The Lord has richly blessed the church at this place during this year. At the feast we had last Christmas, there were only six members, now we number twenty-six. Twenty members have been baptized this year in and around Wanneberga. The Lord be praised.

Dec. 28, I went to Hör again and held two good meetings. As a result a sister was baptized there yesterday. In Hör we now have seven members. That place is twenty miles west from my home and is within the bounds of my district. The members belong to the church here in Wanneberga.

Beloved brethren and sisters in America, do not forget the young members in Sweden in your prayers, that they all may prove faithful to the end. Our desire is, that we may all live more for His glory this coming year then ever before. God grant that this may be the case!

We all send much love to you, and are very thankful for all you are doing for us. God bless you all! JOHN OLSSON.

From the Middle Creek Congregation, Pa.

BRO. RAIRIGH, of Cambria County, Pa., came to us Jan. 2 and commenced a series of meetings at the Pleasant Hill church, which were continued till Jan. 17. Bro. Rairigh's sermons were all interesting to both saint and sinner. He presented the Word of the Lord very forcibly. Three persons were buried with Christ in baptism, and arose from the watery grave to walk in newness of life. Others seemed to be almost persuaded to become Christians. Many lasting impressions were made during that series of meetings. All felt that it was time profitably spent. Bro. Rairigh has made many warm friends outside of the Brotherhood. All seemed delighted with the unbroken chain by which he had his sermons connected, and were pleased to see how nicely the Holy Scriptures harmonize when properly illustrated. J. W. WEGLEY.

Somerset, Pa.

From Bridgewater, Va.

OUR Bible session is moving along with good interest. We have four regular classes, besides the work done by Bro. Hayes on Saturday and Sunday.

Our Bible Term will close Jan. 29 and 30, with four questions for discussion. Each one of the questions is assigned to ministers for discussion. The questions are, "How Can we Obtain the best Results in Home Missions?" "How Can we Best Overcome the Dangerous Influence of Church Festivals, Lawn Parties, etc.?" "How Shall we Win our Children to the Church?" "How Shall We Best Impress Individual Responsibility on the Members of the Church?"

It will be a blessing to our church, if our Bible sessions do no more than inspire our ministers to a more devoted study of the Word, and the wants of the church.

May God bless them to that end! S. N. McCANN.

Jan. 22.

From Hagerstown, Md.

OUR series of meetings, which were conducted by Bro. Geo. S. Arnold, of Arlington, W. Va., have closed. These meetings commenced Jan. 10. Bro. Arnold preached, in all, eighteen very impressive sermons, and although the weather was very inclement, the attendance was fairly good. The weather always affects a congregation in the

wife's illness and death, he was not permitted to be with us so very often, and the result was that we were, at times, left alone. The meeting closed Jan. 17. Notwithstanding a great deal of sickness in the community and some inclement weather, and, at times, bad roads, the attendance kept up fairly well. The interest was very good and the meetings closed with nearly a full house. As a result of the meetings, we had five additions, four of whom are to be baptized in the near future. One was restored to the fold. The brethren and sisters expressed themselves as having been much revived and strengthened. We, in company with the brethren, did considerable visiting, and certainly enjoyed it much. They were all very kind to us. We entertain the fond hope that, if we may never meet again on earth, we may meet in heaven.

The Brethren of the Back Creek congregation, adjoining the one in which the foregoing meeting was held, desire that we hold in a series of meetings in the Upton church Jan. 24, which we have agreed to do.   T. F. IMLER.

Jan. 21.

From the Spring Creek Church, Ind.

BRO. WM. H. DEETER, of Milford, Ind., is now conducting a series of meetings at our Center house, near Dodgetown. The meeting has been running one week, with large congregations and the very best of attention. We hope to be able to send you a favorable report when the meetings close. We hope that many may "be added unto the church, both men and women."

There is a good deal of sickness here just now. Bro. Lewis Workman has been confined to his house for five weeks, and part of the time to his bed. I am happy to say that he is now much better.

LATER.—We had two applicants for baptism, and others said that they would soon come. May God help them to come!   E. MILLER.

Sidney, Ind.

Notes by the Way.

I AM glad to say that I have about recovered from La Grippe, and that I hope to be able, by next week, to resume my ministerial labors again. I have several series of meetings to hold yet this winter, if health permits.

Just one month has elapsed since I came home sick, but I was able to talk some last Sunday and to preach a funeral on Monday. Bro. Daniel Snell's meetings closed at the Donald's Creek church on the evening of Jan. 10 with good interest. The attendance at this series of meetings was not as large as usual on account of so much La Grippe. Two precious souls were baptized. May God help them to be shining lights! I feel sure the meeting was a good one. Though I could not attend but a few meetings, yet, from the reports I had each day, I am sure the Gospel was preached in its primitive purity. Bro. Snell is not afraid nor ashamed to hew to the line and to the plummet. The church received much good counsel that we can all profit by, if we are willing to apply it to ourselves and not give it all away.

I feel that we need a stirring up in the church as well as outside. If the church is cold and cannot get warm, it will be hard to make much impression on the unconverted. At least that has been my experience.

We expect Bro. G. L. Studebaker, of Indiana, to commence a series of meetings in New Carlisle, Feb. 14. I hope I may be permitted to attend that series of meetings, and enjoy the blessings of home with him, while he is with us. I expect to hold some meetings at two isolated points in our own district the latter part of March and April, as

the outskirts must be looked after as well as the main body of the church. The poor are too often neglected.   HENRY FRANTZ.

Forgy, Ohio, Jan. 30.

From Sweden and Denmark.

I AM always glad to hear through the MESSENGER from the various churches in America. It gladdens us all to see that so many are coming to the church and our prayer is, that they all may be faithful to the end.

Now as the year has closed, we praise the Lord for all his goodness bestowed upon us during the past year, and especially in sending our dear brother and sister Miller to us. Their intention was to go to Palestine, but the Lord would have them to come here and no farther, for this time. His ways are wonderful, but he would teach us to take it all with patience. In the end he will show us that all is for our good.

Oct. 1 to Nov. 15 Bro. Hope and I held many good meetings at several places. All our members, the new as well as the old, were glad to hear him preach. By his labors they were much strengthened in their faith, and comforted in their trials. Bro. Hope has a special gift in that respect. When he left us, he went to Denmark to hold meetings. He left Tindal Dec. 9. I met him in Copenhagen and together we went to Bremen, to say farewell to brother and sister Miller who had asked me to come down, so we could speak together about the mission work before they left Europe.

Before Bro. Hope left Tindal, three were baptized there, and the last evening we were together with the members in Copenhagen, a sister was baptized at that place. All the members met in Bro. Hansen's home to say farewell to our dear brother before he left them, and they all promised to be faithful to the end, and to work together according to our beloved church order. Dec. 18 we reached Bremen at 12 o'clock in the night. We had a very rough voyage on the sea and were a day late.

If I may tell you my opinion about the MESSENGER, then I will say, that it is the best and cheapest paper I have ever seen. Containing as it does, sound, doctrine, well edited, and filled with good news from all parts of our beloved Brotherhood, it is, therefore, well worth $1.50. It is wonderful that it has not found its way to all our Brethren's homes who are able to read English.

Right here I will say that we are very glad to see in its pages that our dear brethren are giving so freely to the poor brethren here in Scandinavia. I will hereby say to all the noble givers that the Lord will give you manifold again, and you may rest assured that the means will be properly used, because the brethren on the committee are good, responsible, and well-to-do. May God bless all the cheerful givers!

After I had said farewell to our dear brother and sister Miller and Bro. Hope on board the large and comfortable ship, "Havel," I left Bremen, Hamburg, Lubeck and Rostock for Copenhagen, which place I reached at 7 o'clock P. M., Dec. 17. I then went directly to Bro. O. L. Johansen's home, where I found the members assembled in a prayer-meeting. Many warm prayers were sent up in behalf of our dear brethren and our sister who were then on the great ocean. The next day we had a good meeting with the members in Malmo and Limhamn, and from there I went to Kjeflinge and Hör, at which places I had some very good meetings. At all places the travelers on the sea were remembered, and we asked the good Lord to deliver them from every danger.

I reached my dear home in safety the day before Christmas, glad to see that the Lord had protect-

ed my family and all the members from all danger and evil. On Christmas Day we had a good love, feast in my home, two applicants from Hör were baptized, and also a sister from Wanneberga. The Lord has richly blessed the church at this place during this year. At the feast we had last Christmas, there were only six members, now we number twenty-six. Twenty members have been baptized this year in and around Wanneberga. The Lord be praised.

Dec. 28, I went to Hör again and held two good meetings. As a result a sister was baptized there yesterday. In Hör we now have seven members. That place is twenty miles west from my home and is within the bounds of my district. The members belong to the church here in Wanneberga.

Beloved brethren and sisters in America, do not forget the young members in Sweden in your prayers; that they all may prove faithful to the end. Our desire is, that we may all live more for His glory this coming year than ever before. God grant that this may be the case!

We all send much love to you, and are very thankful for all you are doing for us. God bless you all!   JOHN OLSSON.

From the Middle Creek Congregation, Pa.

BRO. RAIRIGH, of Cambria County, Pa., came to us Jan. 2 and commenced a series of meetings at the Pleasant Hill church, which were continued till Jan. 17. Bro. Rairigh's sermons were all interesting to both saint and sinner. He presented the Word of the Lord very forcibly. Three persons were buried with Christ in baptism, and arose from the watery grave to walk in newness of life. Others seemed to be almost persuaded to become Christians. Many lasting impressions were made during that series of meetings. All felt that it was time profitably spent. Bro. Rairigh has made many warm friends outside of the Brotherhood. All seemed delighted with the unbroken chain by which he had his sermons connected, and were pleased to see how nicely the Holy Scriptures harmonize when properly illustrated.   J. W. WEGLEY.

Somerset, Pa.

From Bridgewater, Va.

OUR Bible session is moving along with good interest. We have four regular classes, besides the work done by Bro. Hayes on Saturday and Sunday.

Our Bible Term will close Jan. 29 and 30, with four questions for discussion. Each one of the questions is assigned to ministers for discussion. The questions are, "How Can we Obtain the best Results in Home Missions?" "How Can we Best Overcome the Dangerous Influence of Church Festivals, Lawn Parties, etc.?" "How Shall we Win our Children to the Church?" "How Shall We Best Impress Individual Responsibility on the Members of the Church?"

It will be a blessing to our church, if our Bible sessions do no more than inspire our ministers to a more devoted study of the Word, and the wants of the church.

May God bless them to that end!   S. N. McCANN.

Jan. 22.

From Hagerstown, Md.

OUR series of meetings, which were conducted by Bro. Geo. S. Arnold, of Arlington, W. Va., have closed. These meetings commenced Jan. 10. Bro. Arnold preached, in all, eighteen very impressive sermons, and although the weather was very inclement, the attendance was fairly good. The weather always affects a congregation in the

evening of Jan. 24; delivering, in all, fourteen sermons. He gave us many good instructions, and, though there were no immediate accessions, yet, we feel that many good impressions were made and the church much encouraged. We hope the Lord may ever bless those brethren for their labors of love while among us.

Jan. 26.　　　　　　　　MICHAEL KELLER.

"Messenger" Poor Fund.

Henry Willand, Ohio,...............	$2 15
Rachel Broadwater, Maryland,........	50
A. B. Smith, Pennsylvania,..........	50
Black River church, Ohio,...........	4 00
D. P. Keefer, Oregon,...,..........	40
Ross Workman, Minnesota,..:.......	25
C. Snyder, Ohio,...,..............	1.00
J. W. Wine, Virginia,..............	3 00
George Renner, Washington,.........	2 40
E. E. Riddlesberger,...............	1 00
Elijah Horner, Ohio,...............	6 25
Byron Pennell and wife, Michigan,...	1 00
Z. Arnold, Illinois,...............	2 15
Harrison Copp, Virginia,...........	2 00
J. B. Clapper, Ohio,...............	1 50
John H. Stifler, Pennsylvania,......	75
Eliza A. Seabrook, Iowa,...........	1 50
James' Glotfelty, Iowa,............	2 00
George Hossack, Ontario,..........	1 00
Noah Smith, Ohio,................	75
Rachel Fox, Pennsylvania,..........	40
Daniel Mohler, Illinois,...........	50
J. B. Clapper, Ohio,..............	2 35
James Kurtz, Pennsylvania,.........	50
Philip Phillips, Indiana,..........	25
Levi Summer, Kentucky,............	6 50
Samuel Rairigh, Pennsylvania,......	50
Henry Bollinger, Pennsylvania,.....	75
J. R. Royer, Pennsylvania,.........	40
J. W. Bowman, Pennsylvania,.......	40
James McBride, Illinois,...........	40
W. H. Gift, Illinois,.............	90
Mrs. J. D. Myers, Indiana,.........	50
Joseph Reiff, Indiana,............	40
A sister, California,..............	1 00
N. H. Wallace, Iowa,.............	1 00
Mary Croft, Ohio,...............	1 00
Rock River church, Illinois,.......	36 25
Rachel Tombaugh, Pennsylvania,....	40
Lewis E. Smith, Ohio,............	40
A. N. Huffman, Washington,.......	40
E. Miller, Indiana,..............	1 00
Lizzie High, Pennsylvania,.........	40
D. G. Hendricks, Pennsylvania,.....	2 00
Hannah H. Bean, Pennsylvania,.....	50
Covington church, Ohio,...........	5 55

Funds for Western Sufferers.

A brother, Ottobine, Virginia,.....	$1 75
Unknown,......................	2 50
Mary Carl, Bourbon, Ind.,.........	50
Eliza A. Baxter, Bourbon, Ind.,....	50
Infant class and teachers of Keuka Sunday-school, Fla.,................	50

Missionary Report.

THE following is a report of the Home Mission of the Middle District of Pennsylvania, from Oct. 13, 1891 to Jan. 22, 1892:

Lost Creek,...................	$8 00
Lewistown,....................	6 87
Falling Spring,................	13 00
New Enterprise,................	9 26
Antietam,.....................	17 00

Total,..............	$53 63

ANDREW BASHORE, Treas.
Oakland Mills, Pa., Jan. 25.

Notes from Our Correspondents.

"As cold water to a thirsty soul, so is good news from a far country."

Leysburg, Pa. — Bro. Zimmerman, of Somerset County, came to the Koontz church on Friday evening, Jan. 8, and continued his meetings until the 17th. Our brother's preaching made good impressions among the people of this place. There were no additions, but we think many are counting the cost.—*Minnie Guyer, Jan. 20.*

Dublin, Ind. — We have just closed a series of meetings at the Locust Grove church, Nettle Creek congregation. Bro. Isaac Frantz came to us on the evening of Jan. 9, and preached, in all, twenty-seven sermons to large congregations of eager listeners. He held forth the Gospel in its primitive purity. Though there were no immediate accessions, we feel that good and lasting impressions were made.—*Charles W. Miller, Jan. 25.*

Fredonia, Kans. — The Fredonia Brethren Sunday-school and church were re-opened Jan. 3. Five weeks ago we had to close on account of the scarlet fever. There are still some few cases of it in the country, while in the towns it has been checked. A goodly number of the brethren and sisters met at the river to-day, Jan. 26, to see one precious soul received by baptism. May the Lord help him to hold out faithful, is my prayer!—*Ida Thompson, Jan. 26.*

Big Rapids, Mich. — I write while waiting here for a train home. When I last wrote I was holding meetings in Mecosta County, in the Chippewa Creek church. Since we left home, Jan. 2, we have held thirty meetings, baptized two, and reclaimed one. Oh, that there were more workers to send into the vineyard, as the harvest is truly ripe! We see the need of earnest workers who are willing to go out into the by-ways and seek after the lost.—*G. E. Stone, Jan. 25.*

East Nimishillen, Ohio. — Dec. 17 Bro. J. A. Sell, of Pennsylvania, came to us and held a series of meetings for us in the Lake meeting-house, giving us fifteen very interesting sermons. Jan. 11 Stephen Yoder, of Nebraska, came to us and held a series of meetings in the Brick meeting-house, continuing until Jan. 22, and giving us twenty instructive sermons. Two were added by baptism during his meetings. Jan. 23 Bro. Yoder went to the West Nimishillen church, where he expects to preach the Word for a week or more.—*A. Brumbaugh, Jan. 25.*

Keuka, Fla. — We are still staying at Keuka, Fla., and find it a very pleasant place to live. The church facilities are good. We have had some cold weather and the leaves are nipped on some of the young orange trees, but the wood is not injured. Part of the last year's crop of oranges is on the trees yet, awaiting a better market. Wife has had an attack of La Grippe in a mild form, but is better at this time. I think she has been benefited by coming to this mild climate to spend the winter. The health is good in and around town.—*W. H. H. Sawyer, Jan. 19.*

Chicago, Ill. — The Brethren of the Chicago church held their Communion Jan. 14. Bro. J. C. Murray, of Indiana, officiated, assisted by Bro. D. L. Miller, of Mt. Morris. I must say it was as impressive a feast as I ever attended. The attendance was not so large, owing to the prevalence of La Grippe. About thirty-four members communed. The best attention prevailed throughout the congregation. The Brethren appreciate the presence of the adjoining members, and invite any who can, to be with them often and encourage them.—*S. B. Kuhn, Naperville, Ill.*

Bethlehem, Va. — At our council-meeting, Jan. 23, one young sister was received by baptism. Two of our number had to be disowned. Let us, as brethren and sisters, try to let our light so shine before them, that they may soon see the error of their way and return to the fold.—*Isaac Bowman.*

Lewistown, Pa. — Jan. 3 Bro. M. Claar commenced a series of meetings in the Dry Valley church, in the Lewistown congregation, and continued the meetings until the evening of Jan. 14. The attendance and the interest were good, and we hope there were some good impressions made.—*Sarah Spanogle, Jan. 23.*

Wade's Branch, Kans. — Bro. I. H. Crist came to us on the evening of Jan. 9, to dedicate our new meeting-house. The dedication services occurred Jan. 10, after which he held forth the Word of Truth with power for one week following. Sinners were made to tremble, and one made the good confession.—*P. M. Lawver, Jan. 25.*

Shannon, Ill. — Jan. 9 Bro. S. E. Yundt, of Mt. Morris, began a series of meetings in the Shannon church. In all he preached fifteen sermons, giving a warning voice to sinners, and urging them to repent. He admonished the members to faithfulness and zeal in the Master's cause. While there were no immediate accessions, some were seriously impressed, but delayed until some other time. We feel assured that the good impressions made will not be soon forgotten.—*D. Rowland.*

District Meeting. — The District Meeting of Nebraska for 1892 will be held in the Juniata congregation on Friday, April 8, commencing at 9 A. M. A missionary meeting will be held the day before, to commence at 10 A. M. All near the B. M. R. R. will come to Juniata the day before, where they will be met by the brethren and taken to the place of meeting. Trains from the East arrive at 4:37 P. M., and from the West at 9:30 A. M. Those living near the K. C. & O. R. R. will be met at Roseland the day before the meeting.—*Eld. David Bechtelheimer.*

Nappanee, Ind. — The Union Center church met in council Dec. 12. All business passed off pleasantly. We thank God for the spirit manifested by the members. Since our last quarterly council we received fifteen members by baptism, but have had no series of meetings up to this time. Four of these came when Bro. I. J. Rosenberger preached at Nappanee; two when he preached at Yellow Creek, and the rest at our regular meetings. We think honor is due our Sunday-school for part of the work. We have great reason to rejoice that the good spirit is still at work. My prayer is that they may all be faithful and become workers in the church.—*Alex. Miller.*

Farmersville, Ohio. — According to previous arrangements, I boarded the train at Farmersville, Ohio, on the morning of Jan. 8, en route to the Pleasant Valley church, Darke Co., Ohio. At Rossville I was met by our esteemed brother, Silas Gilbert, and conveyed to the Jordan house in the evening, where we found an attentive congregation. Our meetings continued each evening with a number of day meetings, and with an increasing interest until the close, which was on the evening of Jan. 24, having, in all, twenty-seven meetings. The immediate visible results of the meeting were seven accessions to the church by baptism. This church is a newly-organized one, and is presided over by Eld. Wm. Simmons, of the Union City church. The ministers are Silas Gilbert, Abraham Young and Benjamin Sharp, assisted by an earnest corps of deacons and a wide-awake laity. May the Lord abundantly bless and keep them all in the way of truth!—*Daniel M. Garver, Jan. 25.*

evening of Jan. 24, delivering, in all, fourteen sermons. He gave us many good instructions, and, though there were no immediate accessions, yet we feel that many good impressions were made and the church much encouraged. We hope the Lord may ever bless those brethren for their labors of love while among us.

Jan. 26.   MICHAEL KELLER.

"Messenger" Poor Fund:

Henry Willand, Ohio,.....	$ 2 15
Rachel Broadwater, Maryland,..........	50
A. B. Smith, Pennsylvania,...........	50
Black River church, Ohio,.........	4 00
D. P. Keefer, Oregon,.............	40
Ross Workman, Minnesota,..........	25
C. Snyder, Ohio,..............	1 00
J. W. Wine, Virginia,.............	3 00
George Benner, Washington,........	2 40
E. B. Riddlesberger,.............	1 00
Elijah Horner, Ohio,.............	6 25
Byron Pennell and wife, Michigan,.....	1 00
Z. Arnold, Illinois,..............	2 15
Harrison Copp, Virginia,..........	2 00
J. B. Clapper, Ohio,.............	1 50
John H. Stifler, Pennsylvania,........	75
Eliza A. Seabrook, Iowa,..........	1 50
James Glotfelty, Iowa,............	2 00
George Hossack, Ontario,..........	1 00
Noah Smith, Ohio,..............	75
Rachel Fox, Pennsylvania,.........	40
Daniel Mohler, Illinois,...........	50
J. B. Clapper, Ohio,.............	2 35
James Kurtz, Pennsylvania,........	50
Philip Phillips, Indiana,..........	25
Levi Summer, Kentucky,...........	6 50
Samuel Rairigh, Pennsylvania,.......	50
Henry Bollinger, Pennsylvania,......	75
J. R. Royer, Pennsylvania,.........	40
J. W. Bowman, Pennsylvania,.......	40
James McBride, Illinois,...........	40
W. H. Gift, Illinois,.............	80
Mrs. J. D. Myers, Indiana,.........	50
Joseph Reiff, Indiana,............	40
A sister, California,.............	1 00
N. H. Wallace, Iowa,.............	1 00
Mary Croft, Ohio,..............	1 00
Rock River church, Illinois,.........	36 25
Rachel Tombaugh, Pennsylvania,.....	40
Lewis E. Smith, Ohio,............	40
A. N. Huffman, Washington,........	4 00
E. Miller, Indiana,.............	1 00
Lizzie High, Pennsylvania,.........	2 00
D. G. Hendricks, Pennsylvania,......	2 00
Hannah H. Bean, Pennsylvania,......	50
Covington church, Ohio,...........	5 55

Funds for Western Sufferers.

A brother, Ottobine, Virginia,......	$1 75
Unknown,.................	2 50
Mary Carl, Bourbon, Ind.,..........	50
Eliza A. Baxter, Bourbon, Ind.,......	50
Infant class and teachers of Keuka Sunday-school, Fla.,...............	50

Missionary Report.

The following is a report of the Home Mission of the Middle District of Pennsylvania, from Oct. 13, 1891 to Jan. 22, 1892:

Lost Creek,...............	$ 8 00
Lewistown,...............	6 37
Falling Spring,..............	13 00
New Enterprise,.............	9 26
Antietam,................	17 00
Total,...............	$53 63

ANDREW BASHORE, Treas.
Oakland Mills, Pa., Jan. 25.

Notes from Our Correspondents.

" As cold water to a thirsty soul, so is good news from a far country."

Loysburg, Pa.—Bro. Zimmerman, of Somerset County, came to the Koontz church on Friday evening, Jan. 8, and continued his meetings until the 17th. Our brother's preaching made good impressions among the people of this place. There were no additions, but we think many are counting the cost.—*Minnie Guyer, Jan. 20.*

Dublin, Ind.—We have just closed a series of meetings at the Locust Grove church, Nettie Creek congregation. Bro. Isaac Frantz came to us on the evening of Jan. 9, and preached, in all, twenty-seven sermons to large congregations of eager listeners. He held forth the Gospel in its primitive purity. Though there were no immediate accessions, we feel that good and lasting impressions were made.—*Charles W. Miller, Jan. 25.*

Fredonia, Kans.—The Fredonia Brethren Sunday-school and church were re-opened. Jan. 3. Five weeks ago we had to close on account of the scarlet fever. There are still some few cases of it in the country, while in the towns it has been checked. A goodly number of the brethren and sisters met at the river to-day, Jan. 26, to see one precious soul received by baptism. May the Lord help him to hold out faithful, is my prayer! —*Ida Thompson, Jan. 26.*

Big Rapids, Mich.—I write while waiting here for a train home. When I last wrote I was holding meetings in Mecosta County, in the Chippewa Creek church. Since we left home, Jan. 2, we have held thirty meetings, baptized two, and reclaimed one. Oh, that there were more workers to send into the vineyard, as the harvest is truly ripe! . We see the need of earnest workers who are willing to go out into the by-ways and seek after the lost.—*G. E. Stone, Jan. 25.*

East Nimishillen, Ohio.—Dec. 17 Bro. J. A. Sell, of Pennsylvania, came to us and held a series of meetings for us in the Lake meeting-house, giving us fifteen very interesting sermons. Jan. 11 Stephen Yoder, of Nebraska, came to us and held a series of meetings in the Brick meeting-house, continuing until Jan. 22, and giving us twenty instructive sermons. Two were added by baptism during his meetings. Jan. 23 Bro. Yoder went to the West Nimishillen church, where he expects to preach the Word for a week or more.—*A. Brumbaugh, Jan. 25.*

Keuka, Fla.—We are still staying at Keuka, Fla, and find it a very pleasant place to live. The church facilities are good. We have had some cold weather and the leaves are nipped on some of the young orange trees, but the wood is not injured. Part of the last year's crop of oranges is on the trees yet, awaiting a better market. Wife has had an attack of *La Grippe* in a mild form, but is better at this time. I think she has been benefited by coming to this mild climate to spend the winter. The health is good in and around town.—*W. H. H. Sawyer, Jan. 19.*

Chicago, Ill.—The Brethren of the Chicago church held their Communion Jan. 14. Bro. J. C. Murray, of Indiana, officiated, assisted by Bro. D. L. Miller, of Mt. Morris. I must say it was as impressive a feast as I ever attended. The attendance was not so large, owing to the prevalence of *La Grippe*. About thirty-four members communed. The best attention prevailed throughout the congregation. The Brethren appreciate the presence of the adjoining members, and invite any who can, to be with them often and encourage them.—*S. B. Kuhn, Naperville, Ill.*

Bethlehem, Va.—At our council-meeting, Jan. 23, one young sister was received by baptism. Two of our number had to be disowned. Let us, as brethren and sisters, try to let our light so shine before them, that they may soon see the error of their way and return to the fold.—*Isaac Bowman.*

Lewistown, Pa.—Jan. 3 Bro. M. Claar commenced a series of meetings in the Dry Valley church, in the Lewistown congregation, and continued the meetings until the evening of Jan. 14. The attendance and the interest were good, and we hope there were some good impressions made.—*Sarah Spanogle, Jan. 23.*

Wade's Branch, Kans.—Bro. I. H. Crist came to us on the evening of Jan. 9, to dedicate our new meeting-house. The dedication services occurred Jan. 10, after which he held forth the Word of Truth with power for one week following. Sinners were made to tremble, and one made the good confession.—*G. M. Lawver, Jan. 25.*

Shannon, Ill.—Jan. 9 Bro. S. E. Yundt, of Mt. Morris, began a series of meetings in the Shannon church. In all he preached fifteen sermons, giving a warning voice to sinners, and urging them to repent. He admonished the members to faithfulness and zeal in the Master's cause. While there were no immediate accessions, some were seriously impressed, but delayed until some other time. We feel assured that the good impressions made will not be soon forgotten.—*D. Rowland.*

District Meeting.—The District Meeting of Nebraska for 1892 will be held in the Juniata congregation on Friday, April 8, commencing at 9 A. M. A missionary meeting will be held the day before, to commence at 10 A. M. All hope the B. M. R. R. will come to Juniata the day before, where they will be met by the brethren and taken to the place of meeting. Trains from the East arrive at 4:37 P. M., and from the West at 9:30 A. M. Those living near the K. C. & O. R. R. will be met at Roseland the day before the meeting.—*Eld. David Bechtelheimer.*

Nappanee, Ind.—The Union Center church met in council Dec. 12. All business passed off pleasantly. We thank God for the spirit manifested by the members. Since our last quarterly council we received fifteen members by baptism, but have had no series of meetings up to this time. Four of these came when Bro. I. J. Rosenberger preached at Nappanee; two when he preached at Yellow Creek, and the rest at our regular meetings. We think honor is due our Sunday-school for part of the work. We have great reason to rejoice that the good spirit is still at work. My prayer is that they may all be faithful and become workers in the church.—*Alex. Miller.*

Farmersville, Ohio.—According to previous arrangements, I boarded the train at Farmersville, Ohio, on the morning of Jan. 8, en route to the Pleasant Valley church, Darke Co., Ohio. At Rossville I was met by our esteemed brother, Silas Gilbert, and conveyed to the Jordan house in the evening, where we found an attentive congregation. Our meetings continued each evening with a number of day meetings, and with an increasing interest until the close, which was on the evening of Jan. 24, having, in all, twenty-seven meetings. The immediate visible results of the meeting were seven accessions to the church by baptism. This church is a newly-organized one, and is presided over by Eld. Wm. Simmons, of the Union City church. The ministers are Silas Gilbert, Abraham Young and Benjamin Sharp, assisted by an earnest corps of deacons and a wide-awake laity. May the Lord abundantly bless and keep them all in the way of truth!—*Daniel M. Garver, Jan. 25.*

WRIGHTSMAN.—In Anderson County, Kans., Jan. 17, 1892, Bro. Samuel Wrightsman, aged 74 years, 1 month and 2 days.

Bro. Wrightsman took La Grippe about ten days before he died, which, settling on his lungs, was the cause of his death. He called for the elders of the church a short time before his death and was anointed according to the instruction of the apostle. Bro. Wrightsman moved from Virginia to Macoupin County, Ill., where he lived a number of years. In March of 1891 he moved to Anderson County, Kansas, with his two sons. His funeral services were preached in the Bethel meeting-house at this place from Matt. 24: 44, after which his body was conveyed to Cerro Gordo, Ill., where it was buried by the side of his companion, who preceded him to the spirit world several years ago. He left five sons and many other relatives to mourn their loss, but we believe that their loss is his eternal gain.　　　PETER HACK.

WERTZ.—In Bryan, Williams Co., Ohio, Jan. 8, 1892, Bro. John P. Wertz, only son of Henry and Julia Wertz, aged 69 years, 1 month and 17 days.

Deceased was born in Hesse, Germany, Nov. 22, 1822. He emigrated to America in 1840, married Margaret G. Grindle in October, 1849, who died Jan. 6, 1892. There were born to this union eight children,—seven sons and one daughter, all of whom are yet living, together with seventy grandchildren. Bro. Wertz was a faithful member of the Brethren church for upwards of forty years, and for many years served as deacon.

Funeral services conducted by Bro. J. V. Felthouse, of Indiana, assisted by the writer.
G. W. SELLERS.

DAUGHERTY.—In the Dry Fork church, Jasper Co., Mo., Jan. 5, 1892, Mary E. Daugherty, daughter of Bro. Abraham Replogle, aged 21 years, 6 months and 26 days. Funeral services improved by the undersigned, assisted by Bro. Wm. Brydt.
W. M. HARVEY.

MILLER.—In Jewell City, Jewell Co., Kans., Aug. 15, 1891, Mary Miller, wife of John L. Miller, aged about 50 years.

Deceased was a member of the Brethren church, and was faithful until death.
K. G.

GOODYEAR.—In the Falling Spring congregation, Franklin Co., Pa., Jan. 13, 1892, sister Catharine Goodyear, aged 60 years, 1 month and 3 days.

The subject of the above notice entered the service of her Master in her early years, and devoted her life to the cause she so much loved. We believe she has left an influence which shall be as bread cast upon the waters, to be gathered many days hence. Previous to her departure she contributed a fair share of her earthly possessions to the work of the church. May others learn to do likewise! Funeral services by the writer, assisted by the Brethren.　　　WM. C. KOONTZ.

KENDIG.—Near Benson, Ill., Jan. 21, 1892, John M., son of Bro. J. J. and sister Phebe Kendig, aged 34 years and 9 months.

He was married to sister Ella Lantz, Nov. 21, 1889. He leaves, besides a wife and four small children, an aged father and mother, two brothers and one sister to mourn his departure. Friend John had made no preparation for the high calling, but may it be a warning to those who have not made their peace with God.

Funeral services were conducted by Bro. P. A. Moore at the Brethren's church, two miles east of Roanoke, from Mark 13: 37.
I. N. GISH.

HERTZLER.—In the Olathe church, Kans., Jan. 11, 1892, sister Sallie, wife of Bro. E. R. Hertzler, aged about 36 years.

Deceased joined the Brethren church Feb. 9, 1888. A few days before her death she requested to be anointed and expressed herself as ready to go. Eld. Geo. Myers preached the funeral sermon to a large congregation from Philipp. 1: 21. Bro. Hertzler buried his first wife Jan. 22, 1890. Both died of the same disease, La Grippe.
ALBERT SHARP.

TEETER.—In the Yellow Creek church, Pa., Dec. 17, 1891, sister Susan Teeter, aged 45 years, 1 month and 2 days.

About four years ago the subject of this notice followed her husband to the city of the dead, and was left to care for seven children. Now they are left to mourn the loss of an affectionate father and mother. Funeral services by Bro. J. L. Holsinger and the writer from Heb. 11: 10.　　　L. F. HOLSINGER.

MILLER.—At Davenport, Nebr., Ralph L. Miller, son of Bro. H. M. and sister Clara Miller, aged 5 months and 7 days.

Funeral occasion improved by the Brethren at the Christian church-house in Davenport.　　　D. H. FORNEY.

SAILOR.—In the Price's Creek church, Preble Co., Ohio, Dec. 20, 1891, Harley, son of Bro. Norman and sister Kate Sailor, aged 10 years, 6 months and 6 days.

On the morning of Dec. 19, he went with his mother and sister to town. As he was walking along on the sidewalk, he dropped down, and did not know anything after that, and the next day was brought home a corpse. Funeral services by Bro. Joseph Longanecker to a large and sympathizing congregation.
MALINDA LONGANECKER.

BASHOR.—In the bounds of the South Beatrice church, Nebr., Jan. 19, 1892, sister Mary Bashor, aged 73 years, 11 months and 23 days.

Mother Bashor, as she was usually called, was a consistent member of the White Horn church, Hawkins Co., Tenn., for nearly thirty years. She moved to this congregation with her family about two years ago. She was afflicted for a long time with paralysis but was patient in her affliction. A good deal of the time she was entirely helpless and had to be carried in the arms of her children, who did all in their power to make her last days happy and cheerful. She often called on the brethren and sisters to sing and pray with her, and in such exercises she received much spiritual strength. She leaves five children, three sons and two daughters, all members of the church here. Funeral services from Prov. 31: 27 by Eld. Owen Peters, assisted by brethren T. W. Graham and Isaac Dell.
M. L. SPIRE.

JEHNZEN.—In the Chippewa Creek church, Mecosta Co., Mich., Jan. 8, 1892, sister Augusta Jehnsen, wife of Bro John Jehnsen.

Sister Jehnsen was sick about eight hours. She leaves six little children, to be cared for by the grief-stricken husband. We have the assurance that the meeting on the other shore will be one of joy and happiness. Funeral services by the writer, Jan. 10, at the home of the deceased. GEO. E. STOUT.

PRICE.—In the Monticello church, White Co., Ind., Jan. 19, 1892, Asenath Price, aged 89 years, 2 months and 4 days.

Deceased was a faithful and consistent member of the church for many years. Funeral services conducted by the writer and the Methodist minister.　　　A. S. CULP.

BRIGE.—In the Rockton church, Clearfield Co., Pa., Jan. 12, 1892, sister Amanda Brige, aged nearly 69 years.

John Brige, her husband, died a little over one year ago. She said she would soon follow her husband. Funeral discourse from James 4: 14, middle clause, by Warren Charles and the writer.　　　PETER BEER.

McCLURG.—In the Lancaster church, Huntingdon Co., Ind., Jan. 16, 1892, Elnora McClurg, wife of John McClurg, deceased, aged 62 years, 6 months and 7 days.

Deceased was a sufferer for about eight years. Funeral services by the writer.
DORSEY HODGDEN.

FIKE.—Near Burns' Corner, in the Maple Grove church, Ashland Co., Ohio, Jan. 12, 1892, Anna Fike, aged 62 years, 1 month and 12 days.

Her death was caused by La Grippe. Funeral services by the undersigned.
WM. A. MURRAY.

GOOD BOOKS FOR ALL.

WRIGHTSMAN.—In Anderson County, Kans., Jan. 17, 1892, Bro. Samuel Wrightsman, aged 74 years, 1 month and 2 days.

Bro. Wrightsman took *La Grippe* about ten days before he died, which, settling on his lungs, was the cause of his death. He called for the elders of the church a short time before his death and was anointed according to the instruction of the apostle. Bro. Wrightsman moved from Virginia to Macoupin County, Ill., where he lived a number of years. In March of 1891 he moved to Anderson County, Kansas, with his two sons. His funeral services were preached in the Bethel meeting-house at this place from Matt. 24: 44, after which his body was conveyed to Cerro Gordo, Ill., where it was buried by the side of his companion, who preceded him to the spirit world several years ago. He left five sons and many other relatives to mourn their loss, but we believe that their loss is his eternal gain.   PETER HECK.

WERTZ.—In Bryan, Williams Co., Ohio, Jan. 6, 1892, Bro. John P. Werts, only son of Henry and Julia Werts, aged 69 years, 1 month and 17 days.

Deceased was born in Hesse, Germany, Nov. 22, 1822. He emigrated to America in 1840, married Margaret G. Grindle in October, 1849, who died Jan. 7, 1872. There were born to this union eight children,—seven sons and one daughter, all of whom are yet living, together with seventy grandchildren. Bro. Wertz was a faithful member of the Brethren church for upwards of forty years, and for many years served as deacon.

Funeral services conducted by Bro. J. v. Felthouse, of Indiana, assisted by the writer.   G. W. SELLERS.

DAUGHERTY.—In the Dry Fork church, Jasper Co., Mo., Jan. 5, 1892, Mary E. Daugherty, daughter of Bro. Abraham Replogle, aged 21 years, 6 months and 26 days. Funeral services improved by the undersigned, assisted by Bro. Wm. Bradt.   W. M. HARVEY.

MILLER.—In Jewell City, Jewell Co., Kans., Aug. 15, 1891, Mary Miller, wife of John L. Miller, aged about 59 years.

Deceased was a member of the Brethren church, and was faithful until death.   K. G.

GOODYEAR.—In the Falling Spring congregation, Franklin Co., Pa., Jan. 13, 1892, sister Catharine Goodyear, aged 60 years, 1 month and 3 days.

The subject of the above notice entered the service of her Master in her early years, and devoted her life to the cause she so much loved. We believe she has left an influence which shall be as bread cast upon the waters, to be gathered many days hence. Previous to her departure she contributed a fair share of her earthly possessions to the work of the church. May others learn to do likewise! Funeral services by the writer, assisted by the Brethren.   WM. C. KOONTZ.

KENDIG.—Near Benson, Ill., Jan. 21, 1892, John M., son of Bro. J. J. and sister Phebe Kendig, aged 34 years and 2 months.

He was married to sister Ella Lantz, Nov. 21, 1880. He leaves, besides a wife and four small children, an aged father and mother, two brothers and one sister to mourn his departure. Friend John had made no preparation for the high calling, but may it be a warning to those who have not made their peace with God.

Funeral services were conducted by Bro. P. A. Moore at the Brethren's church, two miles east of Roanoke, from Mark 13: 37.   I. N. GISH.

HERTZLER.—In the Olathe church, Kans., Jan. 11, 1892, sister Sallie, wife of Bro. E. R. Hertzler, aged about 36 years.

Deceased joined the Brethren church Feb. 9, 1888. A few days before her death she requested to be anointed and expressed herself as ready to go. Eld. Geo. Myers preached the funeral sermon to a large congregation from Philpp. 1: 21. Bro. Hertzler buried his first wife Jan. 22, 1890. Both died of the same disease, *La Grippe*.   ALBERT SHARP.

TEETER.—In the Yellow Creek church, Pa., Dec. 17, 1891, sister Susan Teeter, aged 45 years, 1 month and 2 days.

About four years ago the subject of this notice followed her husband to the city of the dead, and was left to care for seven children. Now they are left to mourn the loss of an affectionate father and mother. Funeral services by Bro. J. L. Holsinger and the writer from Heb. 11: 10.   L. F. HOLSINGER.

MILLER.—At Davenport, Nebr., Ralph L. Miller, son of Bro. H. M. and sister Clara Miller, aged 5 months and 7 days.

Funeral occasion improved by the Brethren at the Christian church-house in Davenport.   D. H. FORNEY.

SAILOR.—In the Price's Creek church, Preble Co., Ohio, Dec. 20, 1891, Harley, son of Bro. Norman and sister Kate Sailor, aged 10 years, 6 months and 6 days.

On the morning of Dec. 19, he went with his mother and sister to town. As he was walking along on the sidewalk, he dropped down, and did not know anything after that, and the next day was brought home a corpse. Funeral services by Bro. Joseph Longanecker to a large and sympathizing congregation.   MALINDA LONGANECKER.

BASHOR.—In the bounds of the South Beatrice church, Nebr., Jan. 19, 1892, sister Mary Bashor, aged 73 years, 11 months and 23 days.

Mother Bashor, as she was usually called, was a consistent member of the White Horn church, Hawkins Co., Tenn., for nearly thirty years. She moved to this congregation with her family about two years ago. She was afflicted for a long time with paralysis but was patient in her affliction. A good deal of the time she was entirely helpless and had to be carried in the arms of her children, who did all in their power to make her last days happy and cheerful. She often called on the brethren and sisters to sing and pray with her, and in such exercises she received much spiritual strength. She leaves five children, three sons and two daughters, all members of the church here. Funeral services from Prov. 31: 27 by Eld. Owen Peters, assisted by brethren T. W. Graham and Isaac Dell.   M. L. SPIRE.

JEHNZEN.—In the Chippewa Creek church, Mecosta Co., Mich., Jan. 8, 1892, sister Augusta Jehnzen, wife of Bro John Jehnzen.

Sister Jehnzen was sick only about eight hours. She leaves six little children, to be cared for by the grief-stricken husband. We have the assurance that the meeting on the other shore will be one of joy and happiness. Funeral services by the writer, Jan. 10, at the home of the deceased.   GEO. E. STOUT.

PRICE.—In the Monticello church, White Co., Ind., Jan. 19, 1892, Asenath Price, aged 89 years, 2 months and 4 days.

Deceased was a faithful and consistent member of the church for many years. Funeral services conducted by the writer and the Methodist minister.   A. S. CULP.

BRIGE.—In the Rockton church, Clearfield Co., Pa., Jan. 12, 1892, sister Amanda Brige, aged nearly 69 years

John Brige, her husband, died a little over one year ago. She said she would soon follow her husband. Funeral discourse from James 4: 14, middle clause, by Warren Charles and the writer.   PETER BEER.

McCLURG.—In the Lancaster church, Huntingdon Co., Ind., Jan. 16, 1892, Elnora McClurg, wife of John McClurg, deceased, aged 62 years, 6 months and 7 days.

Deceased was a sufferer for about eight years. Funeral services by the writer.   DORSEY HODGDEN.

FIKE.—Near Burns' Corner, in the Maple Grove church, Ashland Co., Ohio, Jan. 12, 1892, Anna Fike, aged 69 years, 1 month . and 12 days.

Her death was caused by *La Grippe*. Funeral services by the undersigned.   WM. A. MURRAY.

THE GOSPEL MESSENGER.

"Set for the Defense of the Gospel."

Vol. 30, Old Series.   Mt. Morris, Ill., and Huntingdon, Pa., Feb. 16, 1892.   No. 7.

The Gospel Messenger.

H. B. BRUMBAUGH, Editor,

And Business Manager of the Eastern House, Box 50,
Huntingdon, Pa.

Table of Contents.

REASONS WHY THE BRETHREN DO NOT JOIN SECRET, OATH-BOUND SOCIETIES.

Preached in the McPherson, Kans., College Chapel,
by Daniel Vaniman.

1. BECAUSE it is not necessary. The law of the Lord being perfect, the testimony of the Lord sure, and the statutes of the Lord right, Ps. 19, they contain every obligation required; therefore, whatever other obligation the secret order enjoins upon the Christian is necessarily human, schismatical, and dangerous, for we may neither add to nor diminish from the Bible.

2. Because we have already pledged our fidelity to Christ's law, which embraces the whole duty of man. It is therefore impossible for us to pledge our fidelity to another institution, differing from the church of Christ, and enjoining duties not found in the Bible, and maintain our fidelity to both. Wherein the secret order requires more than the Bible, it requires too much, where less, not enough. Wherein it differs from the Bible, it is not right. If just like the Bible, then it is unnecessary, because the Bible is enough.

3. The Brethren do not join secret societies, because they are wrong, which is proven:

(a) By the fact that they contradict the teachings of Christ in requiring an oath of admission, while Christ forbids his disciples to take oaths. The plain language of the Master on this point is, "I say unto you, Swear not at all; neither by heaven; for it is God's throne: nor by the earth;

for it is his footstool: neither by Jerusalem; for it is the city of the great King. Neither shalt thou swear by thy head, because thou canst not make one hair white or black. But let your communication be, Yea, yea; Nay, nay: for whatsoever is more than these cometh of evil." Matt. 5: 34-37. James 5: 12 reads, "Above all things, my brethren, swear not, neither by heaven, neither by the earth, neither by any other oath: but let your yea be yea; and your nay, nay; lest ye fall into condemnation."

(b) It is further proven that they are wrong by the fact that their secrecy is contrary both to the teaching and example of Christ. Christ taught: "What I tell you in darkness, that speak ye in light: and what ye hear in the ear, that preach ye from the housetops." Matt. 10: 27. When brought before Caiaphas, the high-priest, he said, "I spake openly to the world; I ever taught in the synagogue, and in the temple, whither the Jews always resort; and in secret have I said nothing." John 18: 20. His plan was to work openly, in the city and in the country, in the temple and in the synagogue, in the homes of the poor, as well as of the rich; in the desert and by the seaside,—every-where open to the inspection of all did he teach and work for the good of all. Secret organizations plan and work in secret, behind barred and guarded doors, where their members are bound by unscriptural oaths not to reveal outside, the secrets and plans by which only the few who belong to the lodge, and have money enough to keep their dues paid up, are benefited, leaving the millions of moneyless poor outside, to be cared for by the broader charity of Christ through his church, which can be entered without oath or initiation fees. Christ taught both by precept and example that his blessings are for the poor as well as the rich. "As we have therefore opportunity, let us do good unto all men," is the broad principle of Christianity. "Do good to my brother only" is the narrow principle of the lodge. Christ taught his disciples, "The poor ye have with you always," and that he would reward them for doing good to the needy ones, even as if done to himself, and if neglected he would regard it the same as if he himself were hungry, destitute, sick, or in prison, and would be neglected by them.

(c) It is still further proven that they are wrong by the fact that they take away the Christian's time and money which belong to the Lord and which, the Lord requires, should be used for the general good, thus using their means to build up the interests of a few, a ring, a lodge, a monopoly, sometimes composed largely of Jews, Mohammedans, pagans and infidels. When the Christian joins these he violates 2 Cor. 6: 14, by becoming unequally yoked together with unbelievers, where he is required to pay (1) his initiation fee; (2) degree fees; (3) weekly or monthly dues, which must be promptly kept up, or he loses his standing in the lodge and with it all that he has before paid in. After this money is paid to the lodge, it is beyond his control and is appropriated as this worldly institution sees fit, often to build costly lodges and to decorate them, not for the general good, but for the benefit of the few who

meet there. From these meetings even the wife and children, who helped to earn the money, are excluded.

Another part of the money is spent for regalia, badges, emblems, etc., which, in some cases, are decorated with gold, silver, and other costly decorations. All this is worn for outward adornment and worldly display, which misses the revealed will of the Lord nearly as far as did the appropriation of gold for Aaron's calf.

(d) It is still further proven that they are wrong from the fact that they take a man away from his wife and children to a place where he cannot take them with him because the order forbids it. The Word of God requires the Christian to bring up his children in the nurture and admonition of the Lord. God has ordained the church as the place where the Christian can take his wife and children that they may be brought under the hallowed influence of the house of the Lord and be edified and encouraged in the good things of the Lord. How very different is all this from the lodge, where the husband of the wife and father of the children alone can go, leaving the wife to take care of the family and still worse in many cases,—he pays out the money the wife has helped to earn, against her wish, all of which has a tendency to lessen the endearments of home, and leads, in many cases, to estrangement and serious consequences,—just the opposite of the true teaching of the Gospel.

An old negro preacher about hit it when, on being asked by the editor of the *Thomasville Times* how his church was getting along, he answered: "Mighty poor, mighty poor. De societies are drawing all the fatness out of the body. There is the Lyceum Society, with sister Jones and Bro. Brown to run it. Sister Williams must march in front of the Daughters of Rebecca. Then there are the Dorcases, the Marthas, the Daughters of Ham, the Liberian Ladies, the Masons, the Odd Fellows, the Sons of Ham, the Oklahoma Land-promised Pilgrims, etc. Why, Brudder, by the time the brudders and sisters pay all the dues, and tends all these meetings, there is nothing left for Mt. Pisgah church but just the cob. The corn has been all shelled off and throwed to these speckled chickens."

(e) The Brethren do not join secret societies, because they contain the old and dangerous error of substituting something more or something less for what the Lord commanded. This old error of doing something more or something less than God commanded, began in Eden's Garden. It brought Adam and Eve into trouble. It brought Moses and Saul, and all who ever tried it into trouble, and will just as certainly bring all who will, in the future, try it, into trouble, for God himself has declared the penalty for adding to, or diminishing from, his Word. Setting aside the commandments of God and doing something more or something less than is commanded in the Gospel, is the besetting sin of our race. It is the great sin of Papalism and every other ism of our day. It has led the children of God away from the simplicity of the Gospel and into the commandments of men. The Brethren, therefore, do well by rejecting every form and ceremony and service that is not commanded in the Gospel, and holding above all else, the law of the Lord, which is in their hearts the ruling power, to the exclusion of all the human devices, services and ceremonies of the lodge.

THE GOSPEL MESSENGER.

"Set for the Defense of the Gospel."

Vol. 30, Old Series.   Mt. Morris, Ill., and Huntingdon, Pa., Feb. 16, 1892.   No. 7.

The Gospel Messenger.

H. B. Brumbaugh, Editor,

And Business Manager of the Eastern House, Box 50,
Huntingdon, Pa.

Table of Contents.

REASONS WHY THE BRETHREN DO NOT JOIN SECRET, OATH-BOUND SOCIETIES.

Preached in the McPherson, Kans., College Chapel, by Daniel Vaniman.

1. BECAUSE it is not necessary. The law of the Lord being perfect, the testimony of the Lord sure, and the statutes of the Lord right, Ps. 19, they contain every obligation required; therefore, whatever other obligation the secret order enjoins upon the Christian is necessarily human, schismatical, and dangerous, for we may neither add to nor diminish from the Bible.

2. Because we have already pledged our fidelity to Christ's law, which embraces the whole duty of man. It is therefore impossible for us to pledge our fidelity to another institution, differing from the church of Christ, and enjoining duties not found in the Bible, and maintain our fidelity to both. Wherein the secret order requires more than the Bible, it requires too much, where less, not enough. Wherein it differs from the Bible, it is not right. If just like the Bible, then it is unnecessary, because the Bible is enough.

3. The Brethren do not join secret societies, because they are wrong, which is proven:

(a) By the fact that they contradict the teachings of Christ in requiring an oath of admission, while Christ forbids his disciples to take oaths. The plain language of the Master on this point is, "I say unto you, Swear not at all; neither by heaven; for it is God's throne; nor by the earth; for it is his footstool: neither by Jerusalem; for it is the city of the great King. Neither shalt thou swear by thy head, because thou canst not make one hair white or black. But let your communication be, Yea, yea; Nay, nay: for whatsoever is more than these cometh of evil." Matt. 5: 34-37. James 5: 12 reads, "Above all things, my brethren, swear not, neither by heaven, neither by the earth, neither by any other oath: but let your yea be yea; and your nay, nay; lest ye fall into condemnation."

(b) It is further proven that they are wrong by the fact that their secrecy is contrary both to the teaching and example of Christ. Christ taught: "What I tell you in darkness, that speak ye in light: and what ye hear in the ear, that preach ye from the housetops." Matt. 10: 27. When brought before Caiaphas, the high-priest, he said, "I spake openly to the world; I ever taught in the synagogue, and in the temple, whither the Jews always resort; and in secret have I said nothing." John 18: 20. His plan was to work openly, in the city and in the country, in the temple and in the synagogue, in the homes of the poor, as well as of the rich, in the desert and by the seaside,—every-where open to the inspection of all did he teach and work for the good of all. Secret organizations plan and work in secret, behind barred and guarded doors, where their members are bound by unscriptural oaths not to reveal outside, the secrets and plans by which only the few who belong to the lodge, and have money enough to keep their dues paid up, are benefited, leaving the millions of moneyless poor outside, to be cared for by the broader charity of Christ through his church, which can be entered without oath or initiation fees. Christ taught both by precept and example that his blessings are for the poor as well as the rich. "As we have therefore opportunity, let us do good unto all men," is the broad principle of Christianity. "Do good to my brother only" is the narrow principle of the lodge. Christ taught his disciples, "The poor ye have with you always," and that he would reward them for doing good to the needy ones, even as if done to himself, and if neglected he would regard it the same as if he himself were hungry, destitute, sick, or in prison, and would be neglected by them.

(c) It is still further proven that they are wrong by the fact that they take away the Christian's time and money which belong to the Lord and which, the Lord requires, should be used for the general good, thus using their means to build up the interests of a few, a ring, a lodge, a monopoly, sometimes composed largely of Jews, Mohammedans, pagans and infidels. When the Christian joins these he violates 2 Cor. 6: 14, by becoming unequally yoked together with unbelievers, where he is required to pay (1) his initiation fee; (2) degree fees; (3) weekly or monthly dues, which must be promptly kept up, or he loses his standing in the lodge and with it all that he has before paid in. After this money is paid to the lodge, it is beyond his control and is appropriated as this worldly institution sees fit, often to build costly lodges and to decorate them, not for the general good, but for the benefit of the few who meet there. From these meetings even the wife and children, who helped to earn the money, are excluded.

Another part of the money is spent for regalia, badges, emblems, etc., which, in some cases, are decorated with gold, silver, and other costly decorations. All this is worn for outward adornment and worldly display, which misses the revealed will of the Lord nearly as far as did the appropriation of gold for Aaron's calf.

(d) It is still farther proven that they are wrong from the fact that they take a man away from his wife and children to a place where he cannot take them with him because the order forbids it. The Word of God requires the Christian to bring up his children in the nurture and admonition of the Lord. God has ordained the church as the place where the Christian can take his wife and children that they may be brought under the hallowed influence of the house of the Lord and be edified and encouraged in the good things of the Lord. How very different is all this from the lodge, where the husband of the wife and father of the children alone can go, leaving the wife to take care of the family and still worse in many cases,—he pays out the money the wife has helped to earn, against her wish, all of which has a tendency to lessen the endearments of home, and leads, in many cases, to estrangement and serious consequences,—just the opposite of the true teaching of the Gospel.

An old negro preacher about hit it when, on being asked by the editor of the *Thomasville Times* how his church was getting along, he answered: "Mighty poor, mighty poor. De societies are drawing all the fatness out of the body. There is the Lyceum Society, with sister Jones and Bro. Brown to run it. Sister Williams must march in front of the Daughters of Rebecca. Then there are the Dorcases, the Marthas, the Daughters of Ham, the Liberian Ladies, the Masons, the Odd Fellows, the Sons of Ham, the Oklahoma Land-promised Pilgrims, etc. Why, Brudder, by the time the brudders and sisters pay all the dues, and tends all these meetings, there is nothing left for Mt. Pisgah church but just the cob. The corn has been all shelled off and throwed to these speckled chickens."

(e) The Brethren do not join secret societies, because they contain the old and dangerous error of substituting something more or something less for what the Lord commanded. This old error of doing something more or something less than God commanded, began in Eden's Garden. It brought Adam and Eve into trouble. It brought Moses and Saul, and all who ever tried it into trouble, and will just as certainly bring all who will, in the future, try it, into trouble, for God himself has declared the penalty for adding to, or diminishing from, his Word. Setting aside the commandments of God and doing something more or something less than is commanded in the Gospel, is the besetting sin of our race. It is the great sin of Papalism and every other ism of our day. It has led the children of God away from the simplicity of the Gospel and into the commandments of men. The Brethren, therefore, do well by rejecting every form and ceremony and service that is not commanded in the Gospel, and holding, above all else, the law of the Lord, which is in their hearts the ruling power, to the exclusion of all the human devices, services and ceremonies of the lodge.

circumstance. Had we more energy and more faith, and, above all, "LOVE FOR THE SPIRIT," to do his will, as had Philip, what a mighty work we might do for Christ,—not over in Europe or some heathen land, but right here in our own City, community and homes!

Again, the salvation of souls and the serving of our Heavenly Father are matters of the highest importance to us all. We cannot pass them by indifferently, because each individual is included and has a soul to be saved or lost. The time is short and passing by swiftly. The greatest possible activity is required, of course, consistent with the principles of the Gospel, to make good our profession, and prove successful in our ·life-work, in the Master's service, both as doers of the Word, as well as instructors and examples to others.

We all exert more or less influence over others. This truth many of us are slow to comprehend, and frequently still slower to put into practice,—much slower I feel than we ought to be. Let none fear they will do too much or do it too quickly. Promptness shows a ready and willing mind. May we all, therefore, take to us a lesson of profit from the exceeding promptness and activity of the apostle, and his love for the Spirit.

When told what to do, he ran. You ask, "Why all this haste?" I answer, "Because a soul was hanging in the balance." The same thing is true of us and of those around us. How many more inquiring and wandering souls, still unpardoned, might, by our exertions, be brought into the church and saved, had we more of this living, active spirit and faith!

I next wish to call your attention to the necessity, of having a thorough knowledge of the Scriptures, that we may know what and how to do, and, doing it, we may please God, receive the Spirit, and have a hope of heaven. We have the answer in 1 Pet. 3: 15. But this is not all. Turn to 1 John 4: 1, where he says, "Believe not every spirit, but try the spirits (prove them) whether they are of God: because many false prophets are gone out·into the world."

The apostle may here refer more directly to teachers, but all true teachers must surely be under the power and influence of the Holy Spirit, which, dwelling in them, will direct them aright and to the purpose, that no one may be led into error, but that all be led into the Truth. The Holy Spirit does not mislead anybody.

But how are we to know the Spirit of God? We cannot know without proving. This can only be done by the WORD of TRUTH. It cannot be done in any other way. If you are in harmony with this Word, you will have the Witness,—this personal Instructor and Guide. If you have an important matter, on which you want light, pray God to give it by his Spirit, that you may go aright, for without this Spirit, no great work can be done. But not only have many false prophets gone out into the world, but there are also many false doctrines taught, whereby many are deceived. Thus is seen· the necessity of a correct understanding of the Scriptures, that we may be qualified to judge between the genuine and the spurious.

First in this catalogue of false spirits is that of the devil,—that old serpent. He was a deceiver from the beginning. As such he intrudes himself into your presence, and, if not upon your guard, will enter your minds and corrupt your hearts. Thousands of men and women, on every side, and all over the world,'are constantly falling victims to his hypocrisy and lies. He is ever on the alert, seeking whom he may overcome. Be earnest, considerate and zealous. Watch unto prayer! Satan spoke to·Adam and Eve, perverting the Truth. God had told Adam that if he should eat of a certain forbidden tree he should surely die, but Satan said, "Thou shalt not surely die." They ate and fell under condemnation. Let us not be mistaken, my friends, as to the purposes and powers of this evil spirit, and of the many other evil spirits that have gone out to deceive the people, for God will bring every evil work into judgment.

I bring before you another circumstance, which is a sad one indeed,—that of Ananias and Sapphira, whom Satan tempted to deceive the apostles, relative to the sale and disposition of the proceeds of a certain possession of theirs. He was asked, "Ananias, why hath Satan filled thine heart to lie to the Holy Ghost?" Acts 5: 3. Death was the immediate result.

The enormity of this sin, you will observe, consisted in its being committed AGAINST THE HOLY GHOST. In this is seen the "sin against the Holy Ghost,—hypocrisy and willful lying. Truthfulness, therefore, is all-important. ?No liar shall inherit the kingdom of heaven." Persons who are untruthful and wicked, it is clear, are deceived, and, therefore, under the power of an evil spirit. On the other hand, the GOOD are possessed and kept by the Spirit of God, who wills and acts to please him. You will please furthermore note that I have not, relative to this circumstance, been talking about an influence or a power, but of the Spirit himself. It was not directly to such, as you will observe, that Ananias and Sapphira lied, but it was to the Holy Spirit. In consequence of this, they immediately fell victims to death. In like manner may we, if we become indifferent and unwatchful in regard to the TRUTH, die the spiritual death. 'If you all want to live happy in the world to come, you must ever be truthful in word and faithful in life.

It is said·that a dying young man made the following request: "Gather up my influence and bury it with me." At this late hour, alas, this man realized that he had been following an evil spirit. Doubtless he had lived wickedly, and now seeing what was before him, he did not want his influence to lead others in the same evil course. No good man would make a request like that. Good men and good women want good acts to remain and live as examples to others. Christ did not take his disciples with him when he went away, but left them here, and sent them the Spirit to direct their walk and their work in building up the kingdom.

We should all love the Holy Spirit. He is not only the personal Comforter and Companion of all of our Heavenly Father's spiritual children, but he also beareth them witness that such are his, and if children, then heirs; heirs of God and joint heirs with Christ. Rom. 8.

In conclusion, the "FRUIT OF THE SPIRIT is love, joy, peace, longsuffering, gentleness, goodness, faith, meekness, temperance: against such there is no law. If we live in the Spirit, let us also walk in the Spirit." Gal. 5: 22, 23, 25.

Let us all pray that we may· have this Spirit, and thank our Heavenly Father for all his goodness and love!

CHRISTIAN UNITY.

BY G. W. LOWRY.

"That they may be one as we are."—John 17: 11.

As·unit means one, unity means oneness; hence unity is the opposite of division. Paul, in writing to Romans, (15: 5), says, "Now the God of patience and consolation grant you to be likeminded one toward another according to Christ Jesus." The reason assigned is (verse 6), "that ye may, with one mind and one mouth, glorify God even the Father of our Lord Jesus Christ."

If unity to the extent of one mind and one mouth was essential to glorifying God then, is it now changed to suit existing circumstances?

Paul, in writing to the Philippians, (2: 1, 2) says, "If there be therefore any consolation in Christ, if any comfort of love, if any fellowship of the spirit . . . . fulfill ye my joy."

Dear reader, there is consolation in Christ, there is comfort in love, there is fellowship of the spirit In all these things our joy may be full. Paul says: "Be ye like-minded, having the same love, being of one accord, of one mind." Here Christian unity is plainly set forth to the church at Philippi.

Paul, in his admonition to Euodias and Syntiche (Philipp. 4: 2), tells them to be of the same mind in the Lord. As to the world, it did not matter,—one might have been a seamstress, and the other something else, but in the Lord there must be unity of mind,—sameness.

Peter, in his first epistle (3: 8) says: "Finally be ye all of one mind, having compassion one for another; love as brethren, be pitiful, be courteous." Here Christian unity is certainly set forth as a characteristic of the church, established by Jesus Christ.

Paul, in writing to the Corinthians, beseeches them (see 1 Cor. 1: 10) that, through the name of the Lord Jesus Christ (very high authority indeed), they should all speak the same thing, and that·there be no divisions among you (them), but that they be perfected together in the same mind, and in the same judgment. In 1 Cor. 11: 18, Paul speaks of divisions, and in verse 19 says, "There must also be heresies among you." Now, heresies are natural consequences of division, and in Romans 16: 17 Paul beseeches the brethren to mark them that cause division and avoid them. In verse 18 he tells why. "For they serve not the Lord Jesus Christ, but their own belly; and by .good words and fair speeches deceive the hearts of the simple. In speaking of the simple, Paul does not mean the idiot, but such as cannot read or do not read the Word, hence not able to judge for themselves.

· Paul, in writing to the Ephesians (4: 3-6) says: "There is·one body (church; see Eph. 1: 22, 23; Col. 1: 18) and one spirit even as ye were called in one hope of your calling. One Lord, one faith, one baptism." Hence

All have unity of headship,—one Lord.

Unity of belief,—one faith.

Unity of sacrament,—one baptism (not one immersion).

Unity of hope,—one hope of calling.

Unity of love,—unity of the Spirit in the bonds of peace.

Unity of organization,—one body or church, composed of many congregations.

The ties of Christian unity are so strong that everything gives way before it. (See Gal. 3: 28.) There is neither Jew nor Greek; there is neither bond nor free; there is neither male nor female, for ye are all one in Christ Jesus. Verse 27 tells us how: "For as many of you as have been baptized into Christ, have put on Christ." Where, dear reader, is there a passage which sanctions division?

Solomon, in Prov. 6, says: "These six things doth the Lord hate; yea, seven are an abomination unto him." The seventh is he that soweth. discord among brethren. Sowing discord destroys Christian unity, and that is abominable to God. Paul tells us to mark those that cause division, and to avoid them, and this is in harmony with the above, and according to John 2 we are not to receive them into our house, nor bid them God-speed, lest we partake of their evil doings.

The spirit manifests itself in union with Christ, and certainly not in disunion with one another,

circumstance. Had we more energy and more faith, and, above all, "LOVE FOR THE SPIRIT," to do his will, as had Philip, what a mighty work we might do for Christ,—not over in Europe or some heathen land, but right here in our own City, community and homes!

Again, the salvation of souls and the serving of our Heavenly Father are matters of the highest importance to us all. We cannot pass them by indifferently, because each individual is included and has a soul to be saved or lost. The time is short and passing by swiftly. The greatest possible activity is required, of course, consistent with the principles of the Gospel, to make good our profession, and prove successful in our life-work, in the Master's service, both as doers of the Word, as well as instructors and examples to others.

We all exert more or less influence over others. This truth many of us are slow to comprehend, and frequently still slower to put into practice,— much slower I feel than we ought to be. Let none fear they will do too much or do it too quickly. Promptness shows a ready and willing mind. May we all, therefore, take to us a lesson of profit from the exceeding promptness and activity of the apostle, and his love for the Spirit.

When told what to do, he ran. You ask, "Why all this haste?" I answer, "Because a soul was hanging in the balance." The same thing is true of us and of those around us. How many more inquiring and wandering souls, still unpardoned, might, by our exertions, be brought into the church and saved, had we more of this living, active spirit and faith!

I next wish to call your attention to the necessity of having a thorough knowledge of the Scriptures, that we may know what and how to do, and, doing it, we may please God, receive the Spirit, and have a hope of heaven. We have the answer in 1 Pet. 3: 15. But this is not all. Turn to 1 John 4: 1, where he says, "Believe not every spirit, but try the spirits (prove them) whether they are of God: because many false prophets are gone out into the world."

The apostle may here refer more directly to teachers, but all true teachers must surely be under the power and influence of the Holy Spirit, which, dwelling in them, will direct them aright and to the purpose, that no one may be led into error, but that all be led into the Truth. The Holy Spirit does not mislead anybody.

But how are we to know the Spirit of God? We cannot know without proving. This can only be done by the WORD of TRUTH. It cannot be done in any other way. If you are in harmony with this Word, you will have the Witness,—this personal Instructor and Guide. If you have an important matter, on which you want light, pray God to give it by his Spirit, that you may go aright, for without this Spirit, no great work can be done. But not only have many false prophets gone out into the world, but there are also many false doctrines taught, whereby many are deceived. Thus is seen the necessity of a correct understanding of the Scriptures, that we may be qualified to judge between the genuine and the spurious.

First in this catalogue of false spirits is that of the devil,—that old serpent. He was a deceiver from the beginning. As such he intrudes himself into your presence, and, if not upon your guard, will enter your minds and corrupt your hearts. Thousands of men and women, on every side, and all over the world, are constantly falling victims to his hypocrisy and lies. He is ever on the alert, seeking whom he may overcome. Be earnest, considerate and zealous. Watch unto prayer! Satan spoke to Adam and Eve, perverting the Truth. God had told Adam that if he

should eat of a certain forbidden tree he should surely die, but Satan said, "Thou shalt not surely die." They ate and fell under condemnation. Let us not be mistaken, my friends, as to the purposes and powers of this evil spirit, and of the many other evil spirits that have gone out to deceive the people, for God will bring every evil work into judgment.

I bring before you another circumstance, which is a sad one indeed,—that of Ananias and Sapphira, whom Satan tempted to deceive the apostles, relative to the sale and disposition of the proceeds of a certain possession of theirs. He was asked, "Ananias, why hath Satan filled thine heart to lie to the Holy Ghost?" Acts 5: 3. Death was the immediate result.

The enormity of this sin, you will observe, consisted in its being committed AGAINST THE HOLY GHOST. In this is seen the "sin against the Holy Ghost,—hypocrisy and willful lying. Truthfulness, therefore, is all-important. ?No liar shall inherit the kingdom of heaven." Persons who are untruthful and wicked, it is clear, are deceived, and, therefore, under the power of an evil spirit. On the other hand, the GOOD are possessed and kept by the Spirit of God, who wills and acts to please him. You will please furthermore note that I have not, relative to this circumstance, been talking about an influence or a power, but of the Spirit himself. It was not directly to such, as you will observe, that Ananias and Sapphira lied, but it was to the Holy Spirit. In consequence of this, they immediately fell victims to death. In like manner may we, if we become indifferent and unwatchful in regard to the Truth, die the spiritual death. If you all want to live happy in the world to come, you must ever be truthful in word and faithful in life.

It is said that a dying young man made the following request: "Gather up my influence and bury it with me." At this late hour, alas, this man realized that he had been following an evil spirit. Doubtless he had lived wickedly, and now seeing what was before him, he did not want his influence to lead others in the same evil course. No good man would make a request like this! Good men and good women want good acts to remain and live as examples to others. Christ did not take his disciples with him when he went away, but left them here, and sent them the Spirit to direct their walk and their work in building up the kingdom.

We should all love the Holy Spirit. He is not only the personal Comforter and Companion of all of our Heavenly Father's spiritual children, but he also beareth them witness that such are his, and if children, then heirs; heirs of God and joint heirs with Christ. Rom. 8.

In conclusion, the "FRUIT OF THE SPIRIT is love, joy, peace, longsuffering, gentleness, goodness, faith, meekness, temperance: against such there is no law. If we live in the Spirit, let us also walk in the Spirit." Gal. 5: 22, 23, 25.

Let us all pray that we may have this Spirit, and thank our Heavenly Father for all his goodness and love!

CHRISTIAN UNITY.

BY G. W. LOWRY.

"That they may be one as we are."—John 17: 11.

As unit means one, unity means oneness; hence unity is the opposite of division. Paul, in writing to Romans, (15: 5), says, "Now the God of patience and consolation grant you to be like-minded one toward another according to Christ Jesus." The reason assigned is (verse 6), "that ye may, with one mind and one mouth, glorify God even the Father of our Lord Jesus Christ."

If unity to the extent of one mind and one mouth was essential to glorifying God then, is it now changed to suit existing circumstances? Paul, in writing to the Philippians, (2: 1, 2) says, "If there be therefore any consolation in Christ, if any comfort of love, if any fellowship of the spirit . . . . fulfill ye my joy."

Dear reader, there is consolation in Christ, there is comfort in love, there is fellowship of the spirit. In all these things our joy may be full. Paul says: "Be ye like-minded, having the same love, being of one accord, of one mind." Here Christian unity is plainly set forth to the church at Philippi.

Paul, in his admonition to Euodias and Syntiche (Philipp. 4: 2), tells them to be of the same mind in the Lord. As to the world, it did not matter,—one might have been a seamstress, and the other something else, but in the Lord there must be unity of mind,—sameness.

Peter, in his first epistle (3: 8) says: "Finally be ye all of one mind, having compassion one for another; love as brethren, be pitiful, be courteous." Here Christian unity is certainly set forth as a characteristic of the church, established by Jesus Christ.

Paul, in writing to the Corinthians, beseeches them (see 1 Cor. 1: 10) that, through the name of the Lord Jesus Christ (very high authority indeed), they should all speak the same thing, and that there be no divisions among you (them), but that they be perfected together in the same mind, and in the same judgment. In 1 Cor. 11: 18, Paul speaks of divisions, and in verse 19 says, "There must also be heresies among you." Now, heresies are natural consequences of division, and in Romans 16: 17 Paul beseeches the brethren to mark them that cause division and avoid them. In verse 18 he tells why. "For they serve not the Lord Jesus Christ, but their own belly; and by good words and fair speeches deceive the hearts of the simple. In speaking of the simple, Paul does not mean the idiot, but such as cannot read or do not read the Word, hence are left to judge for themselves.

Paul, in writing to the Ephesians (4: 3-6) says: "There is one body (church; see Eph. 1: 22, 23; Col. 1: 18) and one spirit even as ye were called in one hope of your calling. One Lord, one faith, one baptism." Hence

All have unity of headship,—one Lord.

Unity of belief,—one faith.

Unity of sacrament,—one baptism (not one immersion).

Unity of hope,—one hope of calling.

Unity of love,—unity of the Spirit in the bonds of peace.

Unity of organization,—one body or church, composed of many congregations.

The ties of Christian unity are so strong that everything gives way before it. (See Gal. 3: 28.) There is neither Jew nor Greek; there is neither bond nor free; there is neither male nor female, for ye are all one in Christ Jesus. Verse 27 tells us how: "For as many of you as have been baptized into Christ, have put on Christ." Where, dear reader, is there a passage which sanctions division?

Solomon, in Prov. 6, says: "These six things doth the Lord hate; yea, seven are an abomination unto him." The seventh is he that soweth discord among brethren. Sowing discord destroys Christian unity, and that is abominable to God. Paul tells us to mark those that cause division, and to avoid them, and this is in harmony with the above, and according to John 2 we are not to receive them into our house, nor bid them God-speed, lest we partake of their evil doings.

The spirit manifests itself in union with Christ, and certainly not in disunion with one another.

to God from the bottom of their hearts, "God be merciful to me, a sinner."

If you can live without earnest prayer to God for mercy, habitually neglecting it, you give a full proof that you are alienated from the life of God through the ignorance that is in you, as if you were living in the grossest immoralities.

But when it pleases God to fasten conviction on the heart of a man, and to awaken his conscience, then his mind is stirred up as one out of a natural sleep. He sees a light he never saw before. He realizes that it is an evil and bitter thing to sin against God and his Holy Law. He reads in the Word of Truth, "that the wicked shall be turned into hell, and all the nations that forget God." Ps. 9: 17. He acknowledges, "I have forgotten God and sinned against him," and being convinced that the wages of sin is death, he asks very earnestly, "How shall I escape the damnations of hell?" Such a man is in deep earnestness when he makes the inquiry, "What must I do to be saved?" He feels that his all for eternity is at stake. The world, with all its pleasures and honors, becomes tasteless and insipid. It cannot give ease to his aching heart nor heal his wounded conscience. He now begins to pray. His prayer is the real language of his heart,—not the formal, unmeaning service it was before. A sense of his danger drives him to the throne of grace.

The Word of God he now reads as the decision of Eternal Truth; and he reads it as having an interest in every line. Dear sinner, has this inquiry ever been yours: "What must I do to be saved?" If not, yours is a very pitiable state. In youth is the time you should make the inquiry,—not wait until old age, for then you may never come and make the inquiry as the jailer did, and when the inquiry was made, Paul, as it were in a flash of lightning, told him what he ought to do to be saved.

Gebhart's, Pa.

THE VALUE OF CEREMONIES TO THE CHRISTIAN.

BY JOHN B. MOHLER.

THE zealous, careful, trusting, conscientious Christian does not question the duty of perfect obedience to the Word of God in all things. Not so every professor. Proof, aside from the divine blessing, of good resulting from the literal observance of the Lord's commandments may be of service to them, as well as to the unconverted. This proof must be drawn from the law that, "as all spirit has a form of expression peculiar to each of its states, so the repetition of each of these representative forms of expression, suggests, and tends to quicken, its respective spiritual source."

The observance of the Gospel ordinances is, therefore, in effect, *first*, suggestive, constituting perpetual object lessons, which serve to remind us of our spiritual growth; *second*, stimulating spiritual growth. The intelligent, sincere observance, literally, of every New Testament ordinance has these two distinct effects upon the disciple engaging therein. *Is not this true?* "Ah," says one, "I can obey the ordinances spiritually, and receive as much benefit as to obey them also literally." Can you? Remember he who made the heart said, "The heart is deceitful above all things." It is true, some persons seem able to maintain a tolerably healthy, spiritual growth *mentally*, while others would perceptibly fall under the same practice. But, rest assured that none of us are created so perfect, spiritually, that faithful obedience to God, in all his provisions, will not increase our strength and influence.

May God help us to use all the means he has appointed for our spiritual growth!

Warrensburgh, Mo.

TEACH THE CHILDREN.

BY GERTRUDE A. FLORY.

Number One.

THIS is a subject that lies very close to my heart. Upon the proper training and teaching of our children depends the future prosperity of the church. Besides that, I love the children. In all this world, there is nothing so pure, so sweet, so lovely and lovable, as a little child, and it is sad to see one growing up under a bad system of training, and sadder still, to see, in mature years, the effects of unrestrained evil in the spring-time of life. Parents too often forget that the seed sown in childhood will bear fruit in manhood or womanhood. If Gospel seed is sown in young and fertile minds, the mature life will produce the Gospel fruit, provided the seed has received the care it needed till it was able to bear fruit. It must not be planted, and allowed to germinate, among weeds which will choke it to death. The weeds must be rooted out, and the good seed properly watered, nourished and cultivated in clean soil, and the fruit will follow as a natural result.

Observation teaches that there is a great lack of religious teaching among our children. Not long since a brother and sister's daughter, aged thirteen years, told me that she knew nothing about anointing the sick with oil,—had never even heard of it. Another daughter, aged eleven years, had never been to a Communion meeting, nor did she know anything of the services of those meetings. One still older than either of these, had never seen our people baptize. Here were children that should have been lambs of the fold, but who, for the want of teaching, were ignorant of the requirements of the Gospel, yet they lived in an organized church, where meetings were held almost every Sunday throughout the year.

Once a five-year-old boy asked me, what a picture meant that hangs in a conspicuous place in our living room, because I love it best of all paintings. I told him, "It is a picture of Jesus blessing little children." "Who is Jesus?"—he then inquired, "Have you never heard," I asked, "how Jesus blessed the little children?" and he answered, "No." Deeply pained that a child should have lived five years in a Christian family, and then not be familiar with the name of Jesus, and that sweetest of all Bible stories, I related to him how Jesus, the Son of God, came to seek the sinning, and how he loved and blessed little children while he was on earth, and how he still loves them because "of such is the kingdom of heaven."

While I talked, he gazed intently at the painting, his face aglow with the light of interest. Then, turning to me his delighted, smiling face, he said: "That is what you sing about." "Yes," I replied, He had frequently heard me sing that beautiful song—that all mothers ought to sing to their little ones, "Little Ones Like Me," and he readily saw the connection between the song and the picture.

Such intelligence as this child manifested could readily grasp a great deal of Bible knowledge, if it were made simple enough for the child mind to understand.

Are there not hundreds of instances like those just mentioned? And is it not lamentable that such golden opportunities go unimproved? My dear fathers and mothers, you who neglect the early religious teaching of your children, God has given into your keeping, are missing pleasures and privileges, yea, *duties* that shall be as a poi-

soned arrow in your remembrance in later years. "Bring up your children in the nurture and admonition of the Lord" was not said for naught. It is a divine command, and they who do not feed their children on the bread of the living Gospel, will not be found guiltless before God. The only way to keep the dear children from drifting away from us, is to get them to love Jesus so much that they will not want the pleasures the world affords. This can only be done by a Gospel "nurture and admonition" begun in infancy, and continued through life, for where the parents' control ceases, the church's should begin.

It is a mistaken idea that man's *real* state of purity and religious advancement, can not equal the ideal. Man's grandest, loftiest ideal cannot excel the Bible standard of holiness. "Be ye therefore perfect, even as your Father which is in heaven is perfect." Matt. 5: 48. If we, as Christian parents, would make that divine stature our aim, and teach our children to aim also, to reach that high standing, there would be less mourning for wayward children than there is now. We fail oftentimes, simply because we *expect* to fail in what we undertake. But parents who undertake the sacred task of training immortal souls for glory, should never think of failure. Faith never fails nor falters. She is founded upon the Rock,—Jesus Christ,—in whom is strength for every emergency. Here the true parent rests the hope of the children's Christian attainments, and labors, both in teaching and example, that their lives shall be an honor to God and his holy cause.

"And these words I command thee this day, shall be in thine heart: and thou shalt teach them diligently unto thy children, and thou shalt talk of them when thou sittest in thine house, and when thou walkest by the way, and when thou liest down, and when thou risest up." Deut. 6: 6, 7. "That the generation to come might know them, even the children which should be born: who should arise and declare them to their children: that they might set their hope in God, and not forget the works of God, but keep his commandments." Psa. 78: 6, 7. This was a divine command to our fathers, to teach their children the statutes of Israel, that they might not forget the good way set before the fathers, and it is no less a command to-day. "Bring up your children in the nurture and admonition of the Lord," Eph. 6: 4, means nothing less than: "Teach them what Jesus taught you and, admonish them as he has admonished you," to "cleave to that which was good," and "abstain from all appearance of evil," "perfecting holiness in the fear of God," that ye may stand perfect and complete in all the will of God." Rom. 12: 9; 1 Thess. 5: 22; 2 Cor. 7: 1; Col. 4: 12.

La Porte, Ind., Box 515.

(To be Continued.)

SOMEBODY asks, "Do not those who strive to get what they call their own rights, generally, by their conduct, prevent Christ from getting his?" Christ's first right is to be the center from which those who are his shall act and think. That is the very meaning of the kingdom of Christ. When that ideal is in any measure realized, "our own rights" begin to seem a very small matter. At best we think of them as things we hold in trust for others, and for society at large.—*Sel.*

"THE fountain of content must spring up in the mind, and he who has so little knowledge of human nature as to seek happiness by changing anything but his own disposition, will waste his life in fruitless efforts and multiply the griefs that he proposes to remove."

to God from the bottom of their hearts, "God be merciful to me, a sinner."

If you can live without earnest prayer to God for mercy, habitually neglecting it, you give ample proof that you are alienated from the life of God through the ignorance that is in you, as if you were living in the grossest immoralities.

But when it pleases God to fasten conviction on the heart of a man, and to awaken his conscience, then his mind is stirred up as one out of a natural sleep. He sees a light he never saw before. He realizes that it is an evil and bitter thing to sin against God and his Holy Law. He reads in the Word of Truth, "that the wicked shall be turned into hell, and all the nations that forget God." Ps. 9: 17. He acknowledges, "I have forgotten God and sinned against him," and being convinced that the wages of sin is death, he asks very earnestly, "How shall I escape the damnations of hell?" Such a man is in deep earnestness when he makes the inquiry, "What must I do to be saved?" He feels that his all for eternity is at stake. The world, with all its pleasures and honors, becomes tasteless and insipid. It cannot give ease to his aching heart nor heal his wounded conscience. He now begins to pray. His prayer is the real language of his heart,—not the formal, unmeaning service it was before. A sense of his danger drives him to the throne of grace.

The Word of God he now reads as the decision of Eternal Truth; and he reads it as having an interest in every line. Dear sinner, has this inquiry ever been yours: "What must I do to be saved?" If not, yours is a very pitiable state. In youth is the time you should make the inquiry,—not wait until old age, for then you may never come and make the inquiry as the jailer did, and when the inquiry was made, Paul, as it were in a flash of lightning, told him what he ought to do to be saved.

Gebhart's, Pa.

THE VALUE OF CEREMONIES TO THE CHRISTIAN.

BY JOHN E. MOHLER.

THE zealous, careful, trusting, conscientious Christian does not question the duty of perfect obedience to the Word of God in all things. Not so every professor. Proof, aside from the divine blessing, of good resulting from the literal observance of the Lord's commandments may be of service to them, as well as to the unconverted. This proof must be drawn from the law that "as all spirit has a form of expression peculiar to each of its states, so the repetition of each of these representative forms of expression suggests, and tends to quicken, its respective spiritual source."

The observance of the Gospel ordinances is, therefore, in effect, *first*, suggestive, constituting perpetual object lessons, which serve to remind us of our spiritual duties; *second*, quickening, in stimulating spiritual growth. The intelligent, sincere observance, literally, of every New Testament ordinance has these two distinct effects upon the disciple engaging therein. *Is not this true?* "Ah," says one, "I can obey the ordinances spiritually, and receive all much benefit as to obey them also literally." Can you? Remember he who made the heart said, "The heart is deceitful above all things." It is true, some persons seem able to maintain a tolerably healthy, spiritual growth *mentally*, while others would perceptibly fall under the same practice. Yet, rest assured that none of us are created so perfect, spiritually, that faithful obedience to God, in all his provisions, will not increase our strength and influence.

May God help us to use all the means he has appointed for our spiritual growth!

Warrensburgh, Mo.

TEACH THE CHILDREN.

BY GERTRUDE A. FLORY.

Number One.

THIS is a subject that lies very close to my heart. Upon the proper training and teaching of our children depends the future prosperity of the church. Besides that, I love the children. In all this world, there is nothing so pure, so sweet, so lovely and lovable, as a little child, and it is sad to see one growing up under a bad system of training, and sadder still, to see, in mature years, the effects of unrestrained evil in the spring-time of life. Parents too often forget that the seed sown in childhood will bear fruit in manhood or womanhood. If Gospel seed is sown in young and fertile minds, the mature life will produce the Gospel fruit, provided the seed has received the care it needed till it was able to bear fruit. It must not be planted, and allowed to germinate, among weeds which will choke it to death. The weeds must be rooted out, and the good seed properly watered, nourished and cultivated in clean soil, and the fruit will follow as a natural result.

Observation teaches that there is a great lack of religious teaching among our children. Not long since a brother and sister's daughter, aged thirteen years, told me that she knew nothing about anointing the sick with oil,—had never even heard of it. Another daughter, aged eleven years, had never been to a Communion meeting, nor did she know anything of the services of those meetings. One still older than either of these, had never seen our people baptize. Here were children that should have been lambs of the fold, but who, for the want of teaching, were ignorant of the requirements of the Gospel, yet they lived in an organized church, where meetings were held almost every Sunday throughout the year.

Once a five-year-old boy asked me, what a picture meant that hangs in a conspicuous place in our living room, because I love it best of all paintings. I told him, "It is a picture of Jesus blessing little children." "Who is Jesus?"—he then inquired, "Have you never heard," I asked, "how Jesus blessed the little children?" and he answered, "No." Deeply pained that a child should have lived five years in a Christian family, and then not be familiar with the name of Jesus and that sweetest of all Bible stories, I related to him how Jesus, the Son of God, came to seek the sinning, and how he loved and blessed little children while he was on earth, and how he still loves them because "of such is the kingdom of heaven."

While I talked, he gazed intently at the painting, his face aglow with the light of interest. Then, turning to me his delighted, smiling face, he said: "That is what you sing about." "Yes," I replied. He had frequently heard me sing that beautiful song—that all mothers ought to sing to their little ones, "Little Ones Like Me," and he readily saw the connection between the song and the picture.

Such intelligence as this child manifested could readily grasp a great deal of Bible knowledge, if it were made simple enough for the child mind to understand.

Are there not hundreds of instances like those just mentioned? And is it not lamentable that such golden opportunities go unimproved? My dear fathers and mothers, you who neglect the early religious teaching of your children, God has given into your keeping, are missing pleasures and privileges, yes, *duties* that shall be as a poi-

soned arrow in your remembrance in later years.

"Bring up your children in the nurture and admonition of the Lord" was not said for naught. It is a divine command, and they who do not feed their children on the bread of the living Gospel, will not be found guiltless before God. The only way to keep the dear children from drifting away from us, is to get them to love Jesus so much that they will not want the pleasures the world affords. This can only be done by a Gospel "nurture and admonition" begun in infancy, and continued through life, for where the parents' control ceases, the church's should begin.

It is a mistaken idea that man's *real* state of purity and religious advancement, can not equal the ideal. Man's grandest, loftiest ideal cannot excel the Bible standard of holiness. "Be ye therefore perfect, even as your Father which is in heaven is perfect." Matt. 5: 48. If we, as Christian parents, would make that divine stature our aim, and teach our children to aim also, to reach that high standing, there would be less mourning for wayward children than there is now. We fail oftentimes, simply because we *expect* to fail in what we undertake. But parents who undertake the sacred task of training immortal souls for glory, should never think of failure. Faith never fails nor falters. She is founded upon the Rock,—Jesus Christ,—in whom is strength for every emergency. Here the true parent rests the hope of the children's Christian attainments, and labors, both in teaching and example, that their lives shall be an honor to God and his holy cause.

"And these words I command thee this day, shall be in thine heart: and thou shalt teach them diligently unto thy children, and thou shalt talk of them when thou sittest in thine house, and when thou walkest by the way, and when thou liest down, and when thou risest up." Deut. 6: 6, 7. "That the generation to come might know them, even the children which should be born: who should arise and declare them to their children: that they might set their hope in God, and not forget the works of God, but keep his commandments." Psa. 78: 6, 7. This was a divine command to our fathers, to teach their children the statutes of Israel, that they might not forget the good way set before the fathers, and it is it no less a command to-day. "Bring up your children in the nurture and admonition of the Lord," Eph. 6: 4, means nothing less than: "Teach them what Jesus taught you and, admonish them as he has admonished you," to "cleave to that which was good," and "abstain from all appearance of evil," "perfecting holiness in the fear of God," that ye may stand perfect and complete in all the will of God." Rom. 12: 9; 1 Thess. 5: 22; 2 Cor. 7: 1; Col. 4: 12.

La Porte, Ind., Box 515.

(*To be Continued.*)

SOMEBODY asks, "Do not those who strive to get what they call their own rights, generally, by their conduct prevent Christ from getting his?" Christ's first right is to be the center from which those who are his shall act and think. That is the very meaning of the kingdom of Christ. When that ideal is in any measure realized, "our own rights" begin to seem a very small matter. At best we think of them as things we hold in trust for others, and for society at large.—*Sel.*

"THE fountain of content must spring up in the mind, and he who has so little knowledge of human nature as to seek happiness by changing anything but his own disposition, will waste his life in fruitless efforts and multiply the griefs that he proposes to remove."

came from the lips of a Christian professor. I now ask the question: Can I have an anti-missionary spirit, and exhibit the Christ-life at the same time?" To have an anti-missionary spirit is not to walk as Jesus walked, not follow him, neither in example nor command. It is to deny the power of God,—it is to say, "Divinity dwells not in me." I tell you, my brethren, when we possess divinity, divinity possesses us,—divinity moves us,—divinity controls us,—we are not our own. Then all of our actions and movements and forms are in unison with the Christ-life; we are "living epistles" of Christianity, "living stones" in God's spiritual house. 1 Pet. 2: 5.

It is universally conceded that the great end of the Incarnation was to *reveal God*, so the chief end and object of the Christian is to reveal the Christ.

If our lives fail to reflect and reveal the Christ-life, it is because he does not abide in us. *Christ cannot be hid.* Mark 7: 24. These are not mere assertions, but they are statements, predicated upon the Word of God.

From these facts, then, we deduce the following rule: Professed Christians who do not exhibit Christ deny the power of God. Substantially this would place a person in a worse condition than an infidel. 1 Tim. 5: 8. To deny God's power is not less criminal than to deny the faith.

How very careful, then, should we be to have "Christ in us, the hope of glory." Col. 1: 27. Permit me here to say that if we take care of Christ, he will take care of the "form of godliness," and he will take care of his church, too. But let us be careful that we do not spend our time in cleaning "the outside of the cups and platters (Luke 11: 39), to the *exclusion* of the cleansing of the interior department. The devil always admires a "*big profession*," if it lacks its spiritual counterpart. Nothing pleases him more than to see an uncleansed soul washing cups and platters, or tithing "mint and rue, and all manner of herbs," and passing over "judgment and the love of God." Luke 11: 42. Let each now ask the question, "*Is it I?*"

Union Bridge, Md.

SUCH AS I HAVE.

BY LEAH REPLOGLE.

"SILVER and gold have I none," was the language of Peter to the beggar, and it is the heart's language of many a saint to-day.

"Silver and gold have I none," sighs many a willing heart, as it approaches the Beautiful Gate, the entrance to the "Royal Path of Life," that leads to the memorial temple, where the good deeds of the merciful are recorded. Many willing hearts are waiting with hands extended to distribute the silver and gold that never comes within their reach.

The royal commandment, "Give to him that asketh of thee," Matt. 5: 42, is heard by many a loyal subject, and echoed back in the language of Peter: "Silver and gold have I none," but Peter did not sigh for the silver and gold that he did not have; he gave such as he had,—a gift worth more than all the silver and gold in the world. His hands and his purse were empty, but his heart was full of compassion, and he was full of the Spirit and power of God. Freely he had received these heavenly treasures, and freely did he give.

Silver and gold are good, and ought to be given freely by those who have them. They who are rich in silver and gold, can, in deed and in truth, visit the widows and fatherless in their affliction, and turn their sorrow into joy. They can turn the darkness of the poor man's home into light

by their lamp of benevolence. No wonder, then, that we still hear the sad refrain, "Silver and gold have I none."

But those who have not silver and gold, need not withhold such as they have. "Such as I have, give I thee," let this be our motto. Let us drop our gifts into the great stream of benevolence. They may reach cultivated soil and bring forth fruit.

"Such as I have." What have I? Let each one take an inventory of the good things in his possession. Let us search the heavenly storehouse. "Let there be search made in the King's treasure-house." Let us see what we will have to give in this new year. We will find much besides silver and gold, with which to replenish our contribution box. Perhaps the reason our vessels of charity get empty, is, because we do not trade with the treasures they contain. Some of us have our treasuries filled with evil things, unkind words and evil deeds, and oh, how ready we are to distribute these! Let us covet earnestly the best gifts! Let us always be ready to give the fruits of the Spirit! Let us give kindness to the erring, comfort to the sorrowing, and sympathy to the suffering! A tear of sympathy is more precious in the sight of God than a diamond set in gold. May the Dear Lord enrich us with temporal and spiritual blessings to give to those who need them, and then, like Peter, let us give such as we have!

WAYS OF WORKING.

BY JOHN H. BOSSERMAN.

1. WE believe that the desire to give for the spreading of the Gospel of Jesus Christ exists in the heart of every true child of God.

2. We believe that giving is a creature of education.

3. We believe that the proper time to instill this grand principle is in youth.

4. We believe there are many who desire to share the blessings that attend the cheerful giver.

5. We believe the time is here when all who do not know how to give, should learn.

Let us begin with the children, and do not let so many of us think we are too large to be children. Some think they can see no way to work, and that as they are not ministers, there is no work for them. Another will say, "I am not even an official. Certainly, no work lies in my path. I am willing to work if I just knew the way." The old saying, "Where there is a will, there is a way," comes to us. We now proceed to offer

OUR WAY.

After trying to teach the beauties of giving in a Sunday-school lesson last year, we made the following proposition: To any and all who will accept the terms, we will give five cents, to be invested in any way they might see proper,—they to farm, harvest and market whatever raised and the proceeds to go to the Mission Board of the District in which we reside. Soon a band of twenty had enlisted and were at work for the Master. When the day came to report their investments and success, quite a variety of ways of working were developed. Some invested in eggs and raised chickens; others planted onion sets, some planted turnips, while others raised seeds,—corn, peas and pop-corn, receiving their share of patronage. The result was that quite a handsome sum was turned over to the Mission Fund. "Ah, but," some one will say, "Where is the nickel to come from?" We answer, Let some one who knows he has not been giving the Lord the tenth, or, perhaps, even the hundredth, raise the nickels for the children, or if all have given the tenth to the Lord, let it come out of the church treasury.

Now say what you please of the way, that is human,—but don't condemn the object, that is divine. Parents, let us teach our children by precept and example the beautiful lessons of giving for the Lord's cause, and, while looking for a better way, let us encourage the children to go to work, and inside of a year we will have three evangelists continually employed in each District in the Brotherhood. Let us consider this matter at our next quarterly councils, and get the way of working on foot.

McPherson, Kans., Jan. 20.

LOST AND SAVED.

MEN are lost. Only truth can save them. Those who continue ignorant, continue unsaved; but those who reject truth are doubly lost. "This is the condemnation, that light is come into the world, and men loved darkness rather than light."

Men are lost. Only love can save them; for the central truth which brings salvation, and in obeying which the soul is purified, is the message of Divine love. "We have known and believed the love that God hath to us." "He that loveth not, knoweth not God; for God is love."

Men are lost. Only Christ can save them; for it is in him that the truth and the love of God are manifested. "No man hath seen God at any time; the only-begotten Son, who is in the bosom of the Father, he hath declared him." "Hereby perceive we the love of God" (St. John simply says "the love,"—as though there were no love but this) "because he laid down his life for us." —*Sel.*

LOOK on the bright side. It is the right side. The times may be hard, but it will make them no easier to wear a gloomy and sad countenance. It is the sunshine and not the cloud that makes the flower. The sky is blue, ten times where it is black once. You have troubles; so have others. None are free from them. Trouble gives sinew and tone to life—fortitude and courage to man. That would be a dull sea, and the sailors would never get skill, where there was nothing to disturb the surface of the ocean. What though things look a little dark? The lane will turn, and night will end in a broad day. There is more virtue in a sunbeam than in a whole hemisphere of cloud and gloom.—*Sel.*

The Gospel Messenger

Is the recognized organ of the German Baptist or Brethren's church, and advocates the form of doctrine taught in the New Testament and pleads for a return to apostolic and primitive Christianity.

It recognizes the New Testament as the only infallible rule of faith and practice, and maintains that Faith toward God, Repentance from dead works, Regeneration of the heart and mind, baptism by Trine Immersion for remission of sins unto the reception of the Holy Ghost by the laying on of hands, are the means of adoption into the household of God,—the church militant.

It also maintains that Feet-washing, as taught in John 13, both by example and command of Jesus, should be observed in the church.

That the Lord's Supper, instituted by Christ and as universally observed by the apostles and the early Christians, is a full meal, and, in connection with the Communion, should be taken in the evening or after the close of the day.

That the Salutation of the Holy Kiss, or Kiss of Charity, is binding upon the followers of Christ.

That War and Retaliation are contrary to the spirit and self-denying principles of the religion of Jesus Christ.

That the principle of Plain Dressing and of Non-conformity to the world, as taught in the New Testament, should be observed by the followers of Christ.

That the Scriptural duty of Anointing the Sick with Oil, in the Name of the Lord, James 5: 14, is binding upon all Christians.

It also advocates the church's duty to support Missionary and Tract Work, thus giving to the Lord for the spread of the Gospel and for the conversion of sinners.

In short, it is a vindication of all that Christ and the apostles have enjoined upon us, and aims, amid the conflicting theories and discords of modern Christendom, to point out ground that all must concede to be infallibly safe.

The above principles of our Fraternity are set forth on our "Brethren's Envelopes." Use them! Price, 15 cents per package; 40 cents per hundred.

came from the lips of a Christian professor. I now ask the question: Can I have an anti-missionary spirit, and exhibit the Christ-life at the same time?" To have an anti-missionary spirit is not to walk as Jesus walked, not follow him, neither in example nor command. It is to deny the power of God,—it is to say, "Divinity dwells not in me." I tell you, my brethren, when we possess divinity, divinity possesses us,—divinity moves us,—divinity controls us,—we are not our own. Then all of our actions and movements and forms are in unison with the Christ-life; we are "living epistles" of Christianity, "living stones" in God's spiritual house. 1 Pet. 2: 5.

It is universally conceded that the great end of the Incarnation was to *reveal God, so* the chief end and object of the Christian is to reveal the Christ.

If our lives fail to reflect and reveal the Christ-life, it is because he does not abide in us. *Christ cannot be hid.* Mark 7: 24. These are not mere assertions, but they are statements, predicated upon the Word of God.

From these facts, then, we deduce the following rule: Professed Christians who do not exhibit Christ deny the power of God. Substantially this would place a person in a worse condition than an infidel. 1 Tim. 5: 8. To deny God's power is not less criminal than to deny the faith.

How very careful, then, should we be to have "Christ in us, the hope of glory." Col. 1: 27. Permit me here to say that if we take care of Christ, he will take care of the "form of godliness," and he will take care of his church, too. But let us be careful that we do not spend our time in cleaning "the outside of the cups and platters (Luke 11: 39), to the *exclusion* of the cleansing of the interior department. The devil always admires a "*big profession,*" if it lacks its spiritual counterpart. Nothing pleases him more than to see an uncleansed soul washing cups and platters; or tithing "mint and rue, and all manner of herbs," and passing over "judgment and the love of God." Luke 11: 42 Let each now ask the question, "*Is it I?*"

Union Bridge, Md.

SUCH AS I HAVE.

BY LEAH REPLOGLE.

"SILVER and gold have I none," was the language of Peter to the beggar, and it is the heart's language of many a saint to-day.

"Silver and gold have I none," sighs many a willing heart, as it approaches the Beautiful Gate, the entrance to the "Royal Path of Life," that leads to the memorial temple, where the good deeds of the merciful are recorded. Many willing hearts are waiting with hands extended to distribute the silver and gold that never comes within their reach.

The royal commandment, "Give to him that asketh of thee," Matt. 5: 42, is heard by many a loyal subject, and echoed back in the language of Peter: "Silver and gold have I none,"- but Peter did not sigh for the silver and gold that he did not have; he gave such as he had,—a gift worth more than all the silver and gold in the world. His hands and his purse were empty, but his heart was full of compassion, and he was full of the Spirit and power of God. Freely he had received these heavenly treasures, and freely did he give.

Silver and gold are good, and ought to be given freely by those who have them. They who are rich in silver and gold, can, in deed and in truth, visit the widows and fatherless in their affliction, and turn their sorrow into joy. They can turn the darkness of the poor man's home into light

by their lamp of benevolence. No wonder, then, that we still hear the sad refrain, "Silver and gold have I none."

But those who have not silver and gold, need not withhold such as they have. "Such as I have, give I thee," let this be our motto. Let us drop our gifts into the great stream of benevolence. They may reach cultivated soil and bring forth fruit.

"Such as I have." What have I? Let each one take an inventory of the good things in his possession. Let us search the heavenly store-house. "Let there be search made in the King's treasure-house." Let us see what we will have to give in this new year. We will find much besides silver and gold, with which to replenish our contribution box. Perhaps the reason our vessels of charity get empty, is, because we do not trade with the treasures they contain. Some of us have our treasures filled with evil things, unkind words and evil deeds, and oh, how ready we are to distribute these! Let us covet earnestly the best gifts! Let us always be ready to give the fruits of the Spirit! Let us give kindness. to the erring, comfort to the sorrowing, and sympathy to the suffering! A tear of sympathy is more precious in the sight of God than a diamond set in gold. May the Dear Lord enrich us with temporal and spiritual blessings to give to those who need them, and then, like Peter, let us give such as we have!

WAYS OF WORKING.

BY JOHN H. BOSSERMAN.

1. WE believe that the desire to give for the spreading of the Gospel of Jesus Christ exists in the heart of every true child of God.

2. We believe that giving is a creature of education.

3. We believe that the proper time to instill this grand principle is in youth.

4. We believe there are many who desire to share the blessings that attend the cheerful giver.

5. We believe the time is here when all who do not know how to give, should learn.

Let us begin with the children, and do not let so many of us think we are too large to be children. Some think they can see no way to work, and that as they are not ministers, there is no work for them. Another will say, "I am not even an official. Certainly, no work lies in my path. I am willing to work if I just knew the way." The old saying, "Where there is a will, there is a way," comes to us. We now proceed to offer

OUR WAY.

After trying to teach the beauties of giving in a Sunday-school lesson last year, we made the following proposition: To any and all who will accept the terms, we will give five cents, to be invested in any way they might see proper,—they to farm, harvest and market whatever raised and the proceeds to go to the Mission Board of the District in which we reside. Soon a band of twenty had enlisted and were at work for the Master. When the day came to report their investments and success, quite a variety of ways of working were developed. Some invested in eggs and raised chickens; others planted onion sets, some planted turnips, while others raised seeds,—corn, peas and pop-corn, receiving their share of patronage. The result was that quite a handsome sum was turned over to the Mission Fund. "Ah, but," some one will say, "Where is the nickel to come from?" We answer, Let some one who knows he has not been giving the Lord the tenth, or, perhaps, even the hundredth, raise the nickels for the children, or if all have given the tenth to the Lord, let it come out of the church treasury.

Now say what you please of the *way*, that is human,—but don't condemn the object, that is divine. Parents, let us teach our children by precept and example the beautiful lessons of *giving* for the Lord's cause, and, while looking for a better way, let us encourage the children to go to work, and inside of a year we will have three evangelists continually employed in each District in the Brotherhood. Let us consider this matter at our next quarterly councils, and get the way of working on foot.

McPherson, Kans., Jan. 20.

LOST AND SAVED.

MEN are lost. Only truth, can save them. Those who continue ignorant, continue unsaved; but those who reject truth are doubly lost. "This is the condemnation, that light is come into the world, and men loved darkness rather than light."

Men are lost. Only love can save them; for the central truth which brings salvation, and in obeying which the soul is purified, is the message of Divine love. "We have known and believed the love that God hath to us." "He that loveth not, knoweth not God; for God is love."

Men are lost. Only Christ can save them; for it is in him that the truth and the love of God are manifested. "No man hath seen God at any time: the only-begotten Son, who is in the bosom of the Father, he hath declared him." "Hereby perceive we the love of God" (St. John simply says "the love,"—as though there were no love but this) "because he laid down his life for us." —*Sel.*

LOOK on the bright side. It is the right side. The times may be hard, but it will make them no easier to wear a gloomy and sad countenance. It is the sunshine and not the cloud that makes the flower. The sky is blue, ten times where it is black one. You have troubles; so have others. None are free from them. Trouble gives sinew and tone to life — fortitude and courage to man. That would be a dull sea, and the sailors would never get skill, where there was nothing to disturb the surface of the ocean. What though things look a little dark? The lane will turn, and night will end in a broad day. There is more virtue in a sunbeam than in a whole hemisphere of cloud and gloom.—*Sel.*

The Gospel Messenger

Is the recognized organ of the German Baptist or Brethren's church, and advocates the form of doctrine taught in the New Testament and pleads for a return to apostolic and primitive Christianity.

It recognizes the New Testament as the only infallible rule of faith and practice, and maintains that Faith toward God, Repentance from dead works, Regeneration of the heart and mind, baptism by Trine Immersion for remission of sins unto the reception of the Holy Ghost by the laying on of hands, are the means of adoption into the household of God,—the church militant.

It also maintains that Feet-washing, as taught in John 13, both by example and command of Jesus, should be observed in the church.

That the Lord's Supper, instituted by Christ and as universally observed by the apostles and the early Christians, is a full meal, and, in connection with the Communion, should be taken in the evening or after the close of the day.

That the Salutation of the Holy Kiss, or Kiss of Charity, is binding upon the followers of Christ.

That War and Retaliation are contrary to the spirit and self-denying principles of the religion of Jesus Christ.

That the principle of Plain Dressing and of Non-conformity to the world, as taught in the New Testament, should be observed by the followers of Christ.

That the Scriptural duty of Anointing the Sick with Oil, in the Name of the Lord, James 5: 14, is binding upon all Christians.

It also advocates the church's duty to support Missionary and Tract Work, thus giving to the Lord for the spread of the Gospel and for the conversion of sinners.

In short, it is a vindicator of all that Christ and the apostles have enjoined upon us, and aims, amid the conflicting theories and discords of modern Christendom, to point out ground that all must concede to be infallibly safe.

☞ The above principles of our Fraternity are set forth on our "Brethren's Envelopes." Use them! Price, 15 cents per package; 40 cents per hundred.

THE WORD AND SPIRIT.

Do the Scriptures teach that in conversion the Holy Spirit comes into immediate contact with the sinner's heart?

C. W. DAVIS.

WE do not understand that the Spirit comes into immediate contact with the sinner's heart independent of the Word of Truth, or the Gospel. The Word and Spirit are united in their work. We cannot conceive of a case of conversion in the absence of either the Word or the Spirit. In Eph. 6: IT Paul tells us that the Word is the Sword of the Spirit; that is, the instrument the Spirit uses to accomplish its work. In Rom. 1: 16 this Word, or Gospel, is said to be "the power of God unto salvation to every one that believeth." It is the means God has used, through the Spirit, to bring about the conversion of sinners. The Word of God, or the Gospel, is the seed. See the parable of the sower in Matt. 13. Some of the seed fell by the wayside, some on stony ground, etc., and some on good ground. The latter grew and produced fruit. By the term "good ground" is meant honest hearts (Luke 8: 15). The seed sown in this parable is the Word of God (Luke 8: 11), which entered the hearts of the people, and where the hearts were honest, or in proper condition to receive it, the seed grew and produced fruit. The Word of God, or the Gospel, may be denominated as the seed of the kingdom of heaven, it being the means that is to be employed to regenerate or convert the people. In James 1: 18 we have this language: "Of his own will begat he us with the Word of Truth." Paul asserts the same doctrine when he says: "In Christ Jesus I have begotten you through the Gospel." 1 Cor. 4: 15. The "Gospel" and "Word of Truth" refer to the same thing. By this Word the people were begotten, or made believers.

And we may add that there is no other way of making believers. The Spirit helps, but does not do all the work. It enters the heart, but does not go alone. It comes in contact with the heart through the instrumentality of the Word, using the Word as the means by which to convert the sinner. In this way the Word becomes the Sword or instrument of the Spirit. This doctrine which teaches that the Spirit, independent of the Word, enters the sinner's heart and converts him, is false, unreasonable and unscriptural.

On the day of Pentecost, Peter and the other apostles preached the Word to the people with such power that it took a firm hold on them, and led to their conversion. In the case of the eunuch, Philip preached unto him Jesus, and this led him to the confession, saying, "I believe that Jesus Christ is the Son of God." This resulted in his being baptized and going on his way rejoicing. When Saul fell to the earth on his way to Damascus, he said, "Lord, what wilt thou have me to do?" The Lord told him to "Arise, and go into the city, and it shall be told thee what thou must do." In the City, Ananias came to him and told him what to do. One more case in this line will suffice. Cornelius was a devout man in his way, but not in a saved state. An angel appeared unto him and said, "Send men to Joppa, and call for Simon, whose surname is Peter; who will tell thee words, whereby thou and all thy house shall be saved." Acts 12: 13, 14.

In all these cases the Word was used as the instrument by which the conversions were accomplished, and without the Word not one of the persons referred to was brought into the kingdom. In the language of James, as quoted above, they were begotten with the Word of Truth. This Word of Truth, by preaching, was deposited in their hearts; they receiving it in good and honest hearts. After that Word was received into their hearts, then we understand that the Spirit nourished it, perhaps brooded over it as it did over the waters in the creation (see Gen. 1: 2 where brooding is the original meaning). In the Word is life, but this Word needs the care of the Spirit to cause it to take hold and grow. The growing of the Word produces faith, then repentance, and then brings about the new birth, which results in a new creature in Christ Jesus. Thus the sinner has been regenerated,—made over. A new man is made of him in the likeness of Jesus. The entire work started from the seed, the Word of Truth, which was received into a good and honest heart. From the time this seed enters the heart, we conceive that the Spirit influences it until the conversion is completed, and then the same Spirit becomes a personal comforter and guide to help the new-born Christian live a life of faithfulness until death. Thus it is seen that both the Word and Spirit enter the heart and work together in producing or bringing about genuine, Gospel conversion.

In the spiritual kingdom, the same as in the kingdom of nature, like begets like. The nature of the plant depends upon the seed from which it originates. By planting corn we produce corn. The same truth is known concerning wheat, oats or other grains. The Mormon doctrine, or seed—for every doctrine is a seed—planted in the heart where it is sincerely received, will produce a Mormon. The Mormon doctrine is the instrument used to make Mormons, and without this doctrine, people, holding that faith, could not be had. The same rule holds good concerning Mohammedanism. By this doctrine Mohammedans are produced. The work starts from the planting of these doctrines in the hearts of the people. Since like begets like, it is made clear that Mohammedans cannot be made by preaching Mormonism, and vice versa.

This principle, which we find underlying nature, applies with force to the Word of Truth, or the Gospel. It being the Word of God, begets its kind when received into good and honest hearts. One who is begotten by this Word—or made a believer—is born of God, because the seed is from God, and has in it a living principle, capable of development, until the believer becomes a man of full stature in Christ Jesus. Any one who will pause to study the principles, underlying the question, cannot help comprehending the reasonableness of the facts stated above, as well as their exact harmony with all that we can gather from the Scriptures concerning the process of conversion. The work is begun and consummated by the Word and Spirit working together. They are, however, distinct characters, yet in conversion do not work independent of each other.

There is nothing in this subject which space will not permit us to give at this time, but we think enough has been given to answer the question at the head of the article.

J. H. M.

IN this issue is a report from the Ludlow church, Darke Co., Ohio, by C. E. Culp, that is interesting because it is for the entire year. These yearly reports, well prepared and condensed, would prove profitable reading. We commend the plan. The church at Ludlow has by no means been idle,

EDITORIAL WANDERINGS IN THE OLD WORLD.

BY D. L. MILLER.

Number Eighteen.—The Crown Jewels.

IN our last letter we gave a brief description of the London Tower, one of the most interesting places, from a historical stand-point, in the City of London. Volumes might be written, descriptive of the place, for it enters largely into the history of the rulers of England. We have space in these wanderings for a description of only one more of its many interesting features, and then we shall invite our readers to go with us on a visit to Windsor Palace, the favorite residence of England's popular Queen.

After entering the narrow doorway with its massive masonry, which gives one an idea of the great strength of the Tower, we were shown into a strongly-built, vaulted chamber, situated in the center of one of the inner towers. In order to reach this strong and well-guarded chamber, we passed into entrances that looked like mere narrow openings cut into the heavy masonry, and then, after treading our way along a dark, narrow passage, arched over with heavy cut stone, we were admitted into the inner chamber, known as the Jewel room. In a double inner cage, made very strong, standing in the center of the room, are to be seen the crown jewels and regalia of the sovereigns of England. They are in charge of an officer, appointed by the sovereign, and can only be removed, when they are required to be worn on State occasions, by the keeper of crown jewels. Two trusty Britons constantly keep watch over the kingly treasures in the jewel room, for they are valued at millions of dollars. There is more money shut up in that small, vaulted chamber, in diamonds and pearls set in solid gold, than all the churches in America and England raise annually for foreign mission work,—more money spent to adorn the body of an earthly queen, than to save and adorn the souls of the millions who are dying without a knowledge of the Gospel of Christ.

The coronation crown of Queen Victoria occupies the center, and the highest place in the case. It was used for her coronation when she ascended to the throne in 1838. It is considered as being the most gorgeous and tasteful crown in Europe. It weighs three pounds and a quarter, and is adorned with no less than two thousand seven hundred and eighty-three diamonds. A brief description will no doubt be interesting.

The band or circlet which forms the base of the crown, and which fits the head of the Queen, is of pure gold, studded with many brilliant diamonds. It is apparently about an inch and a half wide, and inside of it is fitted a crimson velvet cap, bordered with royal ermine. Rising from the band, and supported by it, are four golden branches which meet together and form two arches, thus making the upper part of the crown. From the center of the arches rises an orb, or globe, of about two inches in diameter, made of diamonds of the first water. From the center of the globe rises a cross, also composed of diamonds with a magnificent sapphire in the center. On the band, or circlet, at the points from which the arches rise, are four Maltese crosses. The first is on the front of the crown, and contains seventy-five brilliants, surrounding the ancient, famous ruby which was given to the "Black Prince" in 1366 by the King of Castile. The other crosses

THE WORD AND SPIRIT.

Do the Scriptures teach that in conversion the Holy Spirit comes into immediate contact with the sinner's heart?

C. W. DAVIS.

WE do not understand that the Spirit comes into immediate contact with the sinner's heart independent of the Word of Truth, or the Gospel. The Word and Spirit are united in their work. We cannot conceive of a case of conversion in the absence of either the Word or the Spirit. In Eph. 6: 17 Paul tells us that the Word is the Sword of the Spirit; that is, the instrument the Spirit uses to accomplish its work. In Rom. 1: 16 this Word, or Gospel, is said to be "the power of God unto salvation to every one that believeth." It is the means God has used, through the Spirit, to bring about the conversion of sinners. The Word of God, or the Gospel, is the seed. See the parable of the sower in Matt. 13. Some of the seed fell by the wayside, some on stony ground, etc., and some on good ground. The latter grew and produced fruit. By the term "good ground" is meant honest hearts (Luke 8: 15). The seed sown, in this parable is the Word of God (Luke 8: 11), which entered the hearts of the people, and where the hearts were honest, or in proper condition to receive it, the seed grew and produced fruit. The Word of God, or the Gospel, may be denominated as the seed of the kingdom of heaven, it being the means that is to be employed to regenerate or convert the people. In James 1: 18 we have this language: "Of his own will begat he us with the Word of Truth." Paul asserts the same doctrine when he says: "In Christ Jesus I have begotten you through the Gospel." 1 Cor. 4: 15. The "Gospel" and "Word of Truth" refer to the same thing. By this Word the people were begotten, or made believers.

And we may add that there is no other way of making believers. The Spirit helps, but does not do all the work. It enters the heart, but does not go alone. It comes in contact with the heart through the instrumentality of the Word, using the Word as the means by which to convert the sinner. In this way the Word becomes the Sword or instrument of the Spirit. This doctrine which teaches that the Spirit, independent of the Word, enters the sinner's heart and converts him, is false, unreasonable and unscriptural.

On the day of Pentecost, Peter and the other apostles preached the Word to the people with such power that it took a firm hold on them, and led to their conversion. In the case of the eunuch, Philip preached unto him Jesus, and this led him to the confession, saying, "I believe that Jesus Christ is the Son of God." This resulted in his being baptized and going on his way rejoicing. When Saul fell to the earth on his way to Damascus, he said, "Lord, what wilt thou have me to do?" The Lord told him to "Arise, and go into the city, and it shall be told thee what thou must do." In the City, Ananias came to him and told him what to do. One more case in this line will suffice. Cornelius was a devout man in his way, but not in a saved state. An angel appeared unto him and said, "Send men to Joppa, and call for Simon, whose surname is Peter; who will tell thee words, whereby thou and all thy house shall be saved." Acts 12: 13, 14.

In all these cases the Word was used as the instrument by which the conversions were accomplished, and without the Word not one of the persons referred to was brought into the kingdom. In the language of James, as quoted above, they were begotten with the Word of Truth. This Word of Truth, by preaching, was deposited in their hearts; they receiving it in good and honest hearts. After that Word was received into their hearts, then we understand that the Spirit nourished it, perhaps brooded over it as it did over the waters in the creation (see Gen. 1: 2 where brooding is the original meaning). In the Word is life, but this Word needs the care of the Spirit to cause it to take hold and grow. The growing of the Word produces faith, then repentance, and then brings about the new birth, which results in a new creature in Christ Jesus. Thus the sinner has been regenerated,—made over. A new man is made of him in the likeness of Jesus. The entire work started from the seed, the Word of Truth, which was received into a good and honest heart. From the time this seed enters the heart, we conceive that the Spirit influences it until the conversion is completed, and then the same Spirit becomes a personal comforter and guide to help the now-born Christian live a life of faithfulness until death. Thus it is seen that both the Word and Spirit enter the heart and work together in producing or bringing about genuine, Gospel conversion.

In the spiritual kingdom, the same as in the kingdom of nature, like begets like. The nature of the plant depends upon the seed from which it originates. By planting corn we produce corn. The same truth is known concerning wheat, oats or other grains. The Mormon doctrine, or seed for every doctrine is a seed—planted in the heart where it is sincerely received, will produce a Mormon. The Mormon doctrine is the instrument used to make Mormons, and without this doctrine, people, holding that faith, could not be had. The same rule holds good concerning Mohammedanism. By this doctrine Mohammedans are produced. The work starts from the planting of these doctrines in the hearts of the people. Since like begets like, it is made clear that Mohammedans cannot be made by preaching Mormonism, and vice versa.

This principle, which we find underlying nature, applies with force to the Word of Truth, or the Gospel. It being the Word of God, begets its like when received into good and honest hearts. One who is begotten by this Word—or made a believer—is born of God, because the seed is from God, and has in it a living principle, capable of development, until the believer becomes a man of full stature in Christ Jesus. Any one who will pause to study the principles, underlying the question, cannot help comprehending the reasonableness of the facts stated above, as well as their act harmony with all that we can gather from the Scriptures concerning the process of conversion. The work is begun and consummated by the Word and Spirit working together. They are, however, distinct characters, yet in conversion do not work independent of each other.

There is much more in this subject which space will not permit us to give at this time, but we think enough has been given to answer the question at the head of the article.　　J. H. M.

IN this issue is a report from the Ludlow church, Darke Co., Ohio, by C. E. Culp, that is interesting because it is for the entire year. These yearly reports, well prepared and condensed, would prove profitable reading. We commend the plan. The church at Ludlow has by no means been idle.

EDITORIAL WANDERINGS IN THE OLD WORLD.

BY D. L. MILLER.

Number Eighteen.—The Crown Jewels.

IN our last letter we gave a brief description of the London Tower, one of the most interesting places, from a historical stand-point, in the City of London. Volumes might be written, descriptive of the place, for it enters largely into the history of the rulers of England. We have space in these wanderings for a description of only one more of its many interesting features, and then we shall invite our readers to go with us on a visit to Windsor Palace, the favorite residence of England's popular Queen.

After entering the narrow doorway with its massive masonry, which gives one an idea of the great strength of the Tower, we were shown into a strongly-built, vaulted chamber, situated in the center of one of the inner towers. In order to reach this strong and well-guarded chamber, we passed into entrances that looked like mere narrow openings cut into the heavy masonry, and then, after treading our way along a dark, narrow passage, arched over with heavy cut stone, we were admitted into the inner chamber, known as the Jewel room. In a double inner cage, made very strong, standing in the center of the room, are to be seen the crown jewels and regalia of the sovereigns of England. They are in charge of an officer, appointed by the sovereign, and can only be removed, when they are required to be worn on State occasions, by the keeper of crown jewels. Two trusty Britons constantly keep watch over the kingly treasures in the jewel room, for they are valued at millions of dollars. There is more money shut up in that small, vaulted chamber, in diamonds and pearls set in solid gold, than all the churches in America and England raise annually for foreign mission work,—more money spent to adorn the body of an earthly queen, than to save and adorn the souls of the millions who are dying without a knowledge of the Gospel of Christ.

The coronation crown of Queen Victoria occupies the center, and the highest place in the case. It was used for her coronation when she ascended to the throne in 1838. It is considered as being the most gorgeous and tasteful crown in Europe. It weighs three pounds and a quarter, and is adorned with no less than two thousand seven hundred and eighty-three diamonds. A brief description will no doubt be interesting.

The band or circlet which forms the base of the crown, and which fits the head of the Queen, is of pure gold, studded with many brilliant diamonds. It is apparently about an inch and a half wide, and inside of it is fitted a crimson velvet cap, bordered with royal ermine. Rising from the band, and supported by it, are four golden branches which meet together and form two arches, thus making the upper part of the crown. From the center of the arches rises an orb, or globe, of about two inches in diameter, made of diamonds of the first water. From the center of the globe rises a cross, also composed of diamonds with a magnificent sapphire in the center. On the band, or circlet, at the points from which the arches rise, are four Maltese crosses. The first is on the front of the crown, and contains seventy-five brilliants, surrounding the ancient, famous ruby which was given to the "Black Prince" in 1366 by the King of Castile. The other crosses

house, and the weather so pleasant as to admit of the outside door being open.

Since Nov. 10 we spent but little time at home. We have been soliciting for our Kansas Home, and holding an occasional short series of meetings. In the mean time I attended the special District Meeting of Middle Iowa by request.

The Home for the poor saints in Kansas is progressing very slowly,—just in proportion to the forthcoming means will we add. We will not run in advance of the means, and those must come from the members in Kansas, and not from the trustees, though I think that they will give as liberally as any others, to say nothing of their time spent, etc., gratuitously.

Some of the members seem to be impressed with the idea that we, who are living near the home, should do so much more than those more remote. I fail to see the reason for such a conclusion, but rather the reverse. I could assign good reasons for this. This I found, as usual,—some gave beyond their ability, and others much less than the Scripture requires, but as every one is accountable to God for his giving, and not to the trustees, we will say no more, only that the next meeting of the trustees will be, the Lord willing, the first Monday in March, 1892, at the Pleasant View church, Reno Co., Kans., at which time and place we hope all the solicitors, and all others, who feel in sympathy with our work, will be able to report favorably, so that the work can go forward. The Scriptures teach, that as we have opportunity we should do good unto all men, especially to the household of faith. We offer a rare opportunity for an exceeding great reward. Who will accept it?   ENOCH EBY.

Booth, Kans.

From California.

THERE are about one hundred members in the Lordsburg church, including four elders, four ministers and five deacons. They hold two meetings every Sunday in the chapel, morning and evening. Their Sunday-school convenes at eleven, and their prayer-meeting is held each Tuesday evening. All those services are well attended.

Jan. 10 Bro. A. Hutchison commenced a series of meetings and at this writing is still preaching to a very attentive audience. His preaching is full of Gospel truths. Such sermons will reach the hearts, as is made manifest already by two coming out on the side of the Lord. We truly hope that others will follow their example!

The weather, at present, is fine. Farmers are still busy plowing and seeding. Some of the wheat and barley fields look green. The oranges are now getting ripe. Hundreds of boxes were blown off by the storm, Dec. 19.

The MESSENGER is read by many in California and many hearts are made glad, in reading about the many coming out on the side of the Lord, all over the Brotherhood. We are saving the MESSENGERS and distributing them to such as do not subscribe for it.   J. W. METZGER.

Lordsburg, Cal.

From the Ludlow Church, Darke Co., Ohio.

WITHIN the year, beginning with January, 1891, and ending with January, 1892, four series of meetings were held at as many points in this church district. One was conducted by Bro. Bennet Trout, at Painter Creek, and one at Arcanum, by Bro. I. J. Rosenberger. Another has just been closed by Bro. Bennet Trout, at Pittsburgh. Bro. Henry Frantz also held a meeting for the Brethren in their joint house in George-town. The immediate fruits of these meetings resulted in greatly encouraging and strengthening the brethren and sisters in their Christian work,

and second, in the conversion of about sixty souls. What the future results may be, it is now impossible to say.

This church also enjoys the advantages of three Sunday-schools. These schools are conducted throughout the more favorable season of the year, and enjoy an average attendance of over one hundred pupils each. The Bible is made the text-book. Teacher's meetings are held once each week during the school sessions. At the close of the schools, these meetings are continued in the capacity of a Bible class.

While some have been added to the church, some have also been taken away. Some have removed to other parts, a few have proved unfaithful, and perhaps as many as ten have gone to eternity.   C. E. CULP.

Arcanum, Ohio, Jan. 30.

From Lordsburg, Cal.

BRO. Andrew Hutchison has been laboring with us for some time, and the results consequent upon his good work for the Master are becoming manifest. Four young men and two young women decided that they would come out on the Lord's side and were immersed in the large fountain, in front of the College, and coming "straightway up out of the water," imitated the example of Jesus in Jordan, nearly nineteen centuries ago.

May the good work, so prosperously begun, move on till it eventuates in the conversion and salvation of all our dear young people!

Bro. Hutchison wields the Sword of the Spirit with great skill. His logical deductions, from the premises, are beyond refutation.

May the Lord bless our efforts at this place in behalf of those who need salvation!

S. S. GARST.

From Union City Church, Ind.

WE just closed another very interesting series of meetings at our large meeting-house, conducted by Bro. I. J. Rosenberger. La Grippe was prevailing throughout our country at the time and scarcely a family escaped an attack. This materially interfered with the attendance. During the meetings the members were faithfully exhorted to their duty. The inconsistencies of the wayward, worldly and carnally-minded professor were held forth in the light of revelation, and the downward course of the sinner was pointed out. Eight dear souls were received by baptism as a partial result of the meeting. All of them are young persons. We feel they were kept near the church by the pious lives of parents and Sunday-school influences. May they be kept from evil!

We felt that the meetings should have continued a few days longer, as there were others apparently near the kingdom, but other engagements took Bro. Rosenberger away.   W. K. SIMMONS.

From the Mt. Hope Church, Oaklahoma Ter.

THIS church, I think, is in a condition at present, to do much good with the proper effort. We are centrally located, in a country where we can get food and raiment, and are all in union. Bro. Geo. Landis is our minister in the second degree. He is a good and valiant soldier of the cross. He is not only willing but able to preach the Gospel of the kingdom, though very poor in this world's goods. He ought to have some assistance to enable him to do more and better work.

Bro. Appleman, of the Paradise Prairie church, will be our future elder. We expect to begin a series of meetings the fifth Sunday in January. Bro. Appleman is expected to come to our assistance on Thursday following, and to bring some good helpers with him. If we can get into the proper spirit, the good Lord will surely meet with

us, and the Mt. Hope church will receive a blessing.

We are greatly in need of ministerial help here. Bro. Landis has three different appointments, two at home, and others seven miles distant. He has filled every appointment in 1891, excepting one. He has preached twice each Sunday besides officiating at funerals, and other meetings. There are good homes that may be had here, with timber, water and good land, for from five to eight hundred dollars, close to the organization. I hope the good Lord will put it in the heart of some good minister to locate among us. I have never lived in a place where the demand for preaching was so great. It will not be long, if the Lord gives us good crops, until we can offer special inducements to ministers to settle among us.

The Brethren's Mission and Tract Work was kind enough to send me one hundred of the missionary number of the MESSENGER. Nearly every number has been distributed to the unconverted, and I think they are doing much good. I have distributed since I am here over 400 Brethren's tracts. "The House we Live in" never fails to stir up the people. I would like to be kept supplied with good tracts, treating on the peculiar features of our people.   A. J. FEEBLER.

Crescent, I. T., Jan. 20.

From the Spring Creek Church, Kosciusko Co., Ind.

OUR series of meetings in this church, closed last evening. Bro. Wm. B. Deeter, of Milford, Ind., came to our place Jan. 11 and commenced meetings the same evening at our Center house, where he preached every night, and also held some day meetings to large and attentive congregations. He preached, in all, twenty-four discourses and as an immediate result, eight precious souls came out on the Lord's side and put on the Lord Jesus in the holy ordinance of Christian baptism. May God help them to adorn their holy profession! From here Bro. Deeter goes to the Mexico church, Miami Co., Ind., after a few days' rest. Bro. Deeter handles his subjects in an able manner. The members were much encouraged to go on in the service of their Master, and others are almost persuaded to join in with the people of God.

There is much sickness here at present. La Grippe is the common complaint. Our dear brother, Lewis Workman, had been down with La Grippe for six weeks, but is now able to be out again.   E. MILLER.

Jan. 28.

From Dayton, Ohio.

THE new year has brought with it much energy and zeal in the hearts of all people, we trust, who are trying to work out their soul's salvation, as was manifested in our little meeting last Sunday. Owing to a change we are deprived of the use of our church-house in East Dayton at the present time. Being urged by friends who attended our meetings to continue the work, we have procured a hall on Fifth Street, in which to hold meetings occasionally.

At the discontinuation of our Sunday-school, there was left a small surplus of means. Some of the little girls were asked if they would like to make a quilt or something for the Old Folks' Home. They readily assented to this plan, and an effort will now be made to contribute to the comfort of the aged ones in far-off Kansas.

The way at times would seem rather dark to the weary pilgrims, traveling to the better land, if it were not for the consolation of the Blessed Word. The primitive Christians had troubles and trials on the way, and the poet tells us that our troubles and trials here, will only make us richer in the great beyond.   MARY B. STITELY.

Jan. 18.

house, and the weather so pleasant as to admit of the outside door being open.

Since Nov. 10 we spent but little time at home. We have been soliciting for our Kansas Home, and holding an occasional short series of meetings. In the mean time I attended the special District Meeting of Middle Iowa by request.

The Home for the poor saints in Kansas is progressing very slowly,—just in proportion to the forthcoming means will we add. We will not run in advance of the means, and those must come from the members in Kansas, and *not* from the trustees, though I think that they will give as liberally as any others, to say nothing of their time spent, etc., gratuitously.

Some of the members seem to be impressed with the idea that we, who are living near the home, should do so much more than those more remote. I fail to see the reason for such a conclusion, but rather the reverse. I could assign good reasons for this. This I found, as usual,—some gave beyond their ability, and others much less than the Scripture requires, but as every one is accountable to God for his giving, and not to the trustees, we will say no more, only that the next meeting of the trustees will be, the Lord willing, the first Monday in March, 1892, at the Pleasant View church, Reno Co., Kans., at which time and place we hope all the solicitors, and all others, who feel in sympathy with our work, will be able to report favorably, so that the work can go forward. The Scriptures teach, that as we have opportunity we should do good unto all men, especially to the household of faith. We offer a rare opportunity for an exceeding great reward. Who will accept it?   ENOCH EBY.

Booth, Kans.

From California.

THERE are about one hundred members in the Lordsburg church, including four elders, four ministers and five deacons. They hold two meetings every Sunday in the chapel, morning and evening. Their Sunday-school convenes at eleven, and their prayer-meeting is held each Tuesday evening. All those services are well attended.

Jan. 10 Bro. A. Hutchison commenced a series of meetings and at this writing is still preaching to a very attentive audience. His preaching is full of Gospel truths. Such sermons will reach the hearts, as is made manifest already by two coming out on the side of the Lord. We truly hope that others will follow their example!

The weather, at present, is fine. Farmers are still busy plowing and seeding. Some of the wheat and barley fields look green. The oranges are now getting ripe. Hundreds of boxes were blown off by the storm, Dec. 19.

The MESSENGER is read by many in California and many hearts are made glad, in reading about the many coming out on the side of the Lord, all over the Brotherhood. We are saving the MESSENGERS and distributing them to such as do not subscribe for it.   J. W. METZGER.

Lordsburg, Cal.

From the Ludlow Church, Darke Co., Ohio.

WITHIN the year, beginning with January, 1891, and ending with January, 1892, four series of meetings were held at as many points in this church district. One was conducted by Bro. Bennet Trout, at Painter Creek, and one at Arcanum, by Bro. I. J. Rosenberger. Another has just been closed by Bro. Bennet Trout, at Pittsburgh. Bro. Henry Frantz also held a meeting for the Brethren in their joint house in Georgetown. The immediate fruits of these meetings resulted in greatly encouraging and strengthening the brethren and sisters in their Christian work,

and second, in the conversion of about sixty souls. What the future results may be, it is now impossible to say.

This church also enjoys the advantages of three Sunday-schools. These schools are conducted throughout the more favorable season of the year, and enjoy an average attendance of over one hundred pupils each. The Bible is made the text-book. Teacher's meetings are held once each week during the school sessions. At the close of the schools, these meetings are continued in the capacity of a Bible class.

While some have been added to the church, some have also been taken away. Some have removed to other parts, a few have proved unfaithful, and perhaps as many as ten have gone to eternity.   C. E. CULP.

Arcanum, Ohio, Jan. 30.

From Lordsburg, Cal.

BRO. Andrew Hutchison has been laboring with us for some time, and the results consequent upon his good work for the Master are becoming manifest. Four young men and two young women decided that they would come out on the Lord's side and were immersed in the large fountain, in front of the College, and coming "straightway up out of the water," imitated the example of Jesus in Jordan, nearly nineteen centuries ago.

May the good work, so prosperously begun, move on till it eventuates in the conversion and salvation of all our dear young people!

Bro. Hutchison wields the Sword of the Spirit with great skill. His logical deductions, from the premises, are beyond refutation.

May the Lord bless our efforts at this place in behalf of those who need salvation!   S. S. GARST.

From Union City Church, Ind.

WE just closed another very interesting series of meetings at our large meeting-house, conducted by Bro. I. J. Rosenberger. *La Grippe* was prevailing throughout our country at the time and virtually a family escaped an attack. This materially interfered with the attendance. During the meetings the members were faithfully exhorted to their duty. The inconsistencies of the wayward, worldly and carnally-minded professor were held forth in the light of revelation, and the downward course of the sinner was pointed out. Eight dear souls were received by baptism as a partial result of the meeting. All of them are young persons. We feel they were kept near the church by the pious lives of parents and Sunday-school influences. May they be kept from evil!

We felt that the meetings should have continued a few days longer, as there were others apparently near the kingdom, but other engagements took Bro. Rosenberger away.   W. K. SIMMONS.

From the Mt. Hope Church, Oaklahoma Ter.

THIS church, I think, is in a condition at present, to do much good with the proper effort. We are centrally located, in a country where we can get food and raiment, and are all in union. Bro. Geo. Landis is our minister in the second degree. He is a good and valiant soldier of the cross. He is not only willing but able to preach the Gospel of the kingdom, though very poor in this world's goods. He ought to have some assistance to enable him to do more and better work.

Bro. Appleman, of the Paradise Prairie church, will be our future elder. We expect to begin a series of meetings the fifth Sunday in January. Bro. Appleman is expected to come to our assistance on Thursday following, and to bring some good helpers with him. If we can get into the proper spirit, the good Lord will surely meet with

us, and the Mt. Hope church will receive a blessing.

We are greatly in need of ministerial help here. Bro. Landis has three different appointments, two at home, and others seven miles distant. He has filled every appointment in 1891, excepting one. He has preached twice each Sunday besides officiating at funerals, and other meetings. There are good homes that may be had here, with timber, water and good land, for from five to eight hundred dollars, close to the organization. I hope the good Lord will put it in the heart of some good minister to locate among us. I have never lived in a place where the demand for preaching was so great. It will not be long, if the Lord gives us good crops, until we can offer special inducements to ministers to settle among us.

The Brethren's Mission and Tract Work was kind enough to send me one hundred of the missionary number of the MESSENGER. Nearly every number has been distributed to the unconverted, and I think they are doing much good. I have distributed since I am here over 400 Brethren's tracts. "The House we Live in" never fails to stir up the people. I would like to be kept supplied with good tracts, treating on the peculiar features of our people.   A. J. PEEBLER.

Crescent, I. T., Jan. 30.

From the Spring Creek Church, Kosciusko Co., Ind.

OUR series of meetings in this church, closed last evening. Bro. Wm. R. Deeter, of Milford, Ind., came to our place Jan. 11 and commenced meetings the same evening at our Center house, where he preached every night, and also held some day meetings to large and attentive congregations. He preached, in all, twenty-four discourses and as an immediate result, eight precious souls came out on the Lord's side and put on the Lord Jesus in the holy ordinance of Christian baptism. May God help them to adorn their holy profession! From here Bro. Deeter goes to the Mexico church, Miami Co., Ind., after a few days' rest. Bro. Deeter handles his subjects in an able manner. The members were much encouraged to go on in the service of their Master, and others are almost persuaded to join in with the people of God.

There is much sickness here at present. *La Grippe* is the common complaint. Our dear brother, Lewis Workman, had been down with *La Grippe* for six weeks, but is now able to be out again.   E. MILLER.

Jan. 28.

From Dayton, Ohio.

THE new year has brought with it much energy and zeal in the hearts of all people, we trust, who are trying to work out their soul's salvation, as was manifested in our little meeting last Sunday. Owing to a change we are deprived of the use of our church-house in East Dayton at the present time. Being urged by friends who attended our meetings to continue the work, we have procured a hall on Fifth Street, in which to hold meetings occasionally.

At the discontinuation of our Sunday-school, there was left a small surplus of means. Some of the little girls were asked if they would like to make a quilt or something for the Old Folks' Home. They readily assented to this plan, and an effort will now be made to contribute to the comfort of the aged ones in far-off Kansas.

The way at times would seem rather dark to the weary pilgrims, traveling to the better land, if it were not for the consolation of the Blessed Word. The primitive Christians had troubles and trials on the way, and the poet tells us that our troubles and trials here, will only make us richer in the great beyond.   MARY B. STITELY.

Jan. 15.

From Hiawatha, Nebr.

ELD. Owen Peters, of Holmesville, Gage County Nebr., came to us on Jan. 2, to hold a series of meetings, commencing the same evening, and continuing for eight days. He preached nine sermons. Our congregations were not as large as at other times, yet we had good order and the best of attention. Bro. Peters is an able speaker and, I think, did much good while here. He closed the meetings sooner than anticipated, on account of cold, stormy weather. If we could have had a few more meetings, there would have been some accessions to the church.

Bro. J. S. Snowberger stopped with us Jan. 23rd and preached three sermons. He was on his way home from Kansas. Brethren, think of us here, in our isolated condition, without any minister! Do not let the good seed that has been sown, perish for the want of proper attention. We are in hopes that Bro. Peters will be with us again in the near future, and hope that the Lord may spare his life. May he ever bless and prosper those brethren for their labors of love while among us!

R. C. SHORT.

Feb. 1.

Ministerial Meeting.

THE following, is the program for Ministerial Meeting of North-Western Kansas, and Northern Colorado, to be held April 28, 1892, in the Burr Oak church, Jewell Co., Kans, to commence at ten A. M., the day before the District Meeting:

1. Devotional Exercises.

2. Object of the meeting, John Hollinger.

3. Organization and adoption of rules to govern the same.

4. " The Church, its Mission and what Methods of Work are best Adapted to Enable her to Fulfill the Same."—C. S. Hillery, Isaac Lerew.

5. " Preparations of Sermons."—G. W. Fessler, A. C. Daggett.

6. " Missionary Work and how to Make it more Effective."—B. B. Whitmer, L. W. Fitzwater.

7. " Pastoral Visits and how to Conduct them." —Eli Renner, John R. Garber.

8. " How may Bible Class, Social and Prayer-meetings be made a Greater Power for good in the Church?"—J. W. Jarboe, Wm. Lugenbeel.

9. Sermons on Church Government.— C. S. Holsinger, J. Ikenberry.

> JOHN HOLLINGER,　}
> P. B. PORTER,　　} Committee.
> S. L. MYERS,　　}

JOHN HOLSINGER, Secretary.

Notes from Our Correspondents.

"As cold water to a thirsty soul, so is good news from a far country."

Pleasant Valley, Ind.—Bro. Alexander Miller, of Nappanee, Ind., came to us and began a series of meetings on the evening of Jan. 9, and continued until Jan. 25, preaching, in all, twenty-four sermons. Bro. Miller held forth the Word of God in its primitive purity. We had good interest and great interest was manifested. The brethren and sisters were greatly built up in the most holy faith and many lasting impressions were made. During the meetings five precious souls, a husband and wife, and three young sisters, from twelve to fourteen years of age, were buried with Christ in baptism. Others were made to feel the need of a Savior. Our aged elder, Bro. Hoover, and Bro. C. Shrock were not permitted to be at all the meetings on account of feebleness. Bro. Miller's health was not the best during the meetings. He returned home to rest up, and then go into other fields.—*Levi E. Weaver.*

Derry, Pa.—The Lord is working wonderfully among us: Jan. 2 the Brethren commenced a series of meetings, and brethren Amos Hottenstein and John Whitmer came to us Jan. 4, at the Spring Creek meeting-house and preached for us nearly two weeks. Ten young souls came out on the Lord's side. The brethren preached the Word with power.—*Cyrus Westhenffer, Jan 26*

Dawson, Ohio.—The members of the Loramie church held a short series of meetings of ten sermons, including one children's meeting, which was enjoyed, we think, by all. The preaching was done by Bro. Isaiah Rairigh, of Michigan. We think much good seed was sown which, we hope, will bring much fruit to the honor and glory of God. Much to our regret our elder could not be with us all the time, on account of sickness in his family. May God's blessings go with our brother and sister for their labors of love!—*Jonathan Hoover, Feb. 2.*

Derby, Iowa.—Bro. M. Myers, from Creston, Iowa, came to us Jan. 14, and commenced a series of meetings the same evening at the Park school-house. After a few meetings at Derby, the meetings were moved back again to the Park-school-house, five miles south-east of Derby, where Bro. Myers preached thirteen sermons. The attendance was small on account of La Grippe, but all were very attentive to the Word preached. Bro Myers preached the Word with power. He impressed upon us the great duty we owe to God.—*Martin Heisel, Jan. 28.*

Wakarusa, Ind.—We have just closed a very interesting series of meetings. Bro. George W. Cripe, of Illinois, came to us Jan. 16, and continued until Jan. 31. Bro. Cripe did not shun to declare the whole counsel of God, and while none were added to the church, yet, we think, many good impressions were made. On account of sickness in the neighborhood, these meetings were not as well attended as they otherwise would have been, but still the attendance was fair. Bro. Cripe delivered, in all, nineteen discourses. It is to be regretted that he did not continue longer, for the interest was excellent. Deep impressions were made on the minds of many.—*David M. Wise, Feb. 2.*

Ollie, Iowa.—Dec. 19 Bro. and Sister Hipes, of Greene, Iowa, came to the South Keokuk church, Iowa, and commenced a series of meetings. They remained with us until Jan. 2, preaching, in all, eighteen sermons. Bro. Hipes preached the Word very plainly. The attendance was good and as a result two young sisters were added to the church by baptism. One who had wandered away from the fold was reclaimed. As we only have meeting here once a month, the preaching was much appreciated. May the Lord grant that the good seed which was sown may bring forth good fruit in the future. May the Lord continue to bless brother and sister Hipes in their labors.—*Mollie Heilman.*

Spring Run, Pa.—On the evening of Jan. 16 Bro. Michael Claar, of Claysburgh, Pa., commenced a series of meetings in the Spring Run church, and continued until Jan. 29, preaching every evening and some during the day,—in all, twenty sermons. Bro. Claar sets forth the Truth in a plain, clear way, and as a result, nineteen precious souls came out on the Lord's side. May the Good Lord guide and keep them in the narrow way, that leads to joys on high. May God bless our dear brother, and may he have many stars added to his crown of glory! He was called home on account of sickness in his family. May the Lord restore the afflicted one to health again!—*R. T. Myers, Feb. 3.*

Query and Answer.—Some time since, the query was asked, "Why does a writer or speaker use the plural *we* when he only refers to himself?". The editor answered it as far as editors are concerned. The reason given by grammarians and lexicographers, is the following: "We is often used in place of I, when the speaker or writer wishes to avoid the appearance of egotism."—*Noah Longanecker.*

East Nimishillen, Ohio.—Bro. Stephen Yoder, from Nebraska, has been holding meetings with us, commencing Jan. 9 and closing on the 23nd, delivering twenty-two sermons in all. Our meetings were largely attended, with growing interest, and resulted in two additions. The church has been much revived and we believe God's name has been glorified. We hope, Bro. Yoder will long be spared to work for the Lord.—*Samuel Markley.*

Randall, Kans.—I left home Jan. 28 for Burr Oak, Kans., to assist in holding a council and to make arrangements for a ministerial meeting, District Meeting and love-feast. The council occurred on Saturday, Jan. 30. There was a good attendance and considerable business was done. We gave four church letters and received three. I saw never at a council where there was more love and union manifested than in the Burr Oak church on said day. I am now, Feb. 3, at Bro. Zebts's, and will commence a series of meetings to-night at the Fair Play school-house, Jewell Co., Kans. I do not know how long the meetings will be kept up. Yesterday we visited Bro. John and sister Elliott, near Randall. Their eighteen-year-old son is very sick.—*John Hollinger.*

Hampton, Pa.—Bro. Albert Hollinger, of Huntsdale, Cumberland Co., Pa., commenced a series of meetings at the Brick church, Hampton, Adams Co., Pa., on Thursday evening, Jan. 14. He labored earnestly, preaching the Word with power, during the evenings, and spending the day in visiting. Our meetings increased in interest and many precious souls gave evidence of their deep conviction. Two precious souls were led into the stream by Bro. Hollinger, and were buried with Christ in baptism. We accompanied our brother on Sunday, Jan. 24, to Granite Hill, where, after services, we gave him the parting hand. We are continuing these meetings, and have also enlisted the sympathy of the Marsh Creek Brethren in our behalf. We are looking forward to the return of Bro. Hollinger to labor in our field a little while longer. Truly, we have a season of refreshing from the presence of the Lord. Good is being accomplished in the name of the Master!—*Samuel B. Miller, Jan. 25.*

New Stark, Ohio.—Bro. J. M. Mohler, of Lewistown, Pa., came to the Eagle Creek church, Ohio, Jan. 11, and remained with us until Jan. 25, preaching, in all, twenty-three sermons. We had good roads and fair congregations throughout our meetings. Quite a number could not attend on account of La Grippe. Bro. Mohler is a faithful expounder of the Word, and it does not pay any one long to learn that he does not preach to gain the esteem of men, but to honor God. While with us he held three children's meetings, prior to the evening services. We were much impressed with the importance of teaching the Gospel to our children while young, and we could easily see what could be accomplished in this direction, by parents, if the proper effort were made in time,—while they are, say from four to twelve years of age. There was one precious soul added to the church and the church otherwise built up and forcibly impressed with the importance of living up more faithfully to our principles of non-conformity to the world.—*J. R. Spacht, Feb. 1.*

From Hiawatha, Nebr.

ELD. Owen Peters, of Holmesville, Gage County Nebr., came to us on Jan. 2, to hold a series of meetings, commencing the same evening, and continuing for eight days. He preached nine sermons. Our congregations were not as large as at other times, yet we had good order and the best of attention. Bro. Peters is an able speaker and, I think, did much good while here. He closed the meetings sooner than anticipated, on account of cold, stormy weather. If we could have had a few more meetings, there would have been some accessions to the church.

Bro. J. S. Snowberger stopped with us Jan. 23rd and preached three sermons. He was on his way home from Kansas. Brethren, think of us here, in our isolated condition, without any minister! Do not let the good seed that has been sown, perish for the want of proper attention. We are in hopes that Bro. Peters will be with us again in the near future, and hope that the Lord may spare his life. May he ever bless and prosper those brethren for their labors of love while among us!

R. C. SHORT.

Feb. 1.

Ministerial Meeting.

THE following is the program for Ministerial Meeting of North-Western Kansas, and Northern Colorado, to be held April 28, 1892, in the Burr Oak church, Jewell Co., Kans., to commence at ten A. M., the day before the District Meeting:

1. Devotional Exercises.
2. Object of the meeting, John Hollinger.
3. Organization and adoption of rules to govern the same.
4. "The Church, its Mission and what Methods of Work are best Adapted to Enable her to Fulfill the Same."—C. S. Hillery, Isaac Lerew.
5. "Preparations of Sermons."—G. W. Fessler, A. C. Daggett.
6. "Missionary Work and how to Make it more Effective."—B. B. Whitmer, L. W. Fitzwater.
7. "Pastoral Visits and how to Conduct them." —Eli Renner, John R. Garber.
8. "How may Bible Class, Social and Prayer-meetings be made a Greater Power for good in the Church?"—J. W. Jarboe, Wm. Lugenbeel.
9. Sermons on Church Government.— C. S. Holsinger, J. Ikenberry.

JOHN HOLLINGER,
P. B. PORTER, } Committee.
S. L. MYERS,

JOHN HOLSINGER, Secretary.

Notes from Our Correspondents.

"As cold water to a thirsty soul, so is good news from a far country."

Pleasant Valley, Ind.—Bro. Alexander Miller, of Nappanee, Ind., came to us and began a series of meetings on the evening of Jan. 9 and continued until Jan. 26, preaching, in all, twenty-four sermons. Bro. Miller held forth the Word of God in its primitive purity. We had good attendance, and great interest was manifested. The brethren and sisters were greatly built up in the most holy faith and many lasting impressions were made. During the meetings five precious souls, a husband and wife, and three young sisters, from twelve to fourteen years of age, were buried with Christ in baptism. Others were made to feel the need of a Savior. Our aged elder, Bro. Hoover, and Bro. C. Shrock were not permitted to be at all the meetings on account of feebleness. Bro. Miller's health was not the best during the meetings. He returned home to rest up, and then go into other fields.—Levi E. Weaver.

Berry, Pa.—The Lord is working wonderfully among us. Jan. 2 the Brethren commenced a series of meetings, and brethren Amos Hottenstein and John Whitmer came to us Jan. 4, at the Spring Creek meeting-house and preached for us nearly two weeks. Ten young souls came out on the Lord's side. The brethren preached the Word with power.—Cyrus Westhenffer, Jan 26.

Dawson, Ohio.—The members of the Loramie church held a short series of meetings of ten sermons, including one children's meeting, which was enjoyed, we think, by all. The preaching was done by Bro. Isaiah Rairigh, of Michigan. We think much good seed was sown which, we hope, will bring much fruit to the honor and glory of God. Much to our regret our elder could not be with us all the time, on account of sickness in his family. May God's blessings go with our brother and sister for their labors of love!—Jonathan Hoover, Feb. 2.

Derby, Iowa. — Bro. M. Myers, from Creston, Iowa, came to us Jan. 14, and commenced a series of meetings the same evening at the Park school-house. After a few meetings at Derby, the meetings were moved back again to the Park school-house, five miles south-east of Derby, where Bro. Myers preached thirteen sermons. The attendance was small on account of La Grippe, but all were very attentive to the Word preached. Bro. Myers preached the Word with power. He impressed upon us the great duty we owe to God.—Martin Helsel, Jan. 28.

Wakarusa, Ind.—We have just closed a very interesting series of meetings. Bro. George W. Cripe, of Illinois, came to us Jan. 16, and continued until Jan. 31. Bro. Cripe did not shun to declare the whole counsel of God, and while none were added to the church, yet, we think, many good impressions were made. On account of sickness in the neighborhood, these meetings were not as well attended as they otherwise would have been, but still the attendance was fair. Bro. Cripe delivered, in all, nineteen discourses. It is to be regretted that he did not continue longer, for the interest was excellent. Deep impressions were made on the minds of many.—David M. Wise, Feb. 2.

Ollie, Iowa.—Dec. 19 Bro. and Sister Hipes, of Greene, Iowa, came to the South Keokuk church, Iowa, and commenced a series of meetings. They remained with us until Jan. 2, preaching, in all, eighteen sermons. Bro. Hipes preached the Word very plainly. The attendance was good and as a result two young sisters were added to the church by baptism. One who had wandered away from the fold was reclaimed. As we only have meeting here once a month, the preaching was much appreciated. May the good seed which was sown may bring forth good fruit in the future. May the Lord continue to bless brother and sister Hipes in their labors.—Mollie Heilman.

Spring Run, Pa.—On the evening of Jan. 16 Bro. Michael Claar, of Claysburgh, Pa., commenced a series of meetings in the Spring Run church, and continued until Jan. 29, preaching every evening and some during the day,—in all, twenty sermons. Bro. Claar sets forth the Truth in a plain, clear way, and as a result, nineteen precious souls came out on the Lord's side. May the Good Lead guide and keep them in the narrow way, that leads to joys on high. May God bless our dear brother, and may he have many stars added to his crown of glory! He was called home on account of sickness in his family. May the Lord restore the afflicted one to health again!—R. T. Myers, Feb. 3.

Query and Answer.—Some time since, the query was asked, "Why does a writer or speaker use the plural we when he only refers to himself?" The editor answered it as far as editors are concerned. The reason given by grammarians and lexicographers, is the following: "We is often used in place of I, when the speaker or writer wishes to avoid the appearance of egotism."—Noah Longaneeker.

East Nimishillen, Ohio.—Bro. Stephen Yoder, from Nebraska, has been holding meetings with us, commencing Jan. 9 and closing on the 22nd, delivering twenty-two sermons in all. Our meetings were largely attended, with growing interest, and resulted in two additions. The church has been much revived and we believe God's name has been glorified. We hope. Bro. Yoder will long be spared to work for the Lord.—Samuel Markley.

Randall, Kans.—I left home Jan. 28 for Burr Oak, Kans., to assist in holding a council and to make arrangements for a ministerial meeting, District Meeting and love-feast. The council occurred on Saturday, Jan. 30. There was a good attendance and considerable business was done. We gave four church letters and received three. I was never at a council where there was more love and union manifested than in the Burr Oak church on said day. I am now, Feb. 3, at Bro. Zebra's, and will commence a series of meetings to-night at the Fair Play school-house, Jewell Co., Kans. I do not know how long the meetings will be kept up. Yesterday we visited Bro. John and sister Elliott, near Randall. Their eighteen-year-old son is very sick.—John Hollinger.

Hampton, Pa.—Bro. Albert Hollinger, of Huntsdale, Cumberland Co., Pa., commenced a series of meetings at the Brick church, Hampton, Adams Co., Pa, on Thursday evening, Jan. 14. He labored earnestly, preaching the Word with power, during the evenings, and spending the day in visiting. Our meetings increased in interest and many precious souls gave evidence of their deep conviction. Two precious souls were led into the stream by Bro. Hollinger, and were buried with Christ in baptism. We accomplished our brother on Sunday, Jan. 24, to Granite Hill, where, after services, we gave him the parting hand. We are continuing these meetings, and have also enlisted the sympathy of the Marsh Creek Brethren in our behalf. We are looking forward to the return of Bro. Hollinger to labor in our field a little while longer. Truly, we have a season of refreshing from the presence of the Lord. Good is being accomplished in the name of the Master!—Samuel B. Miller, Jan. 25.

New Stark, Ohio.—Bro. J. M. Mohler, of Lewistown, Pa., came to the Eagle Creek church, Ohio, Jan. 11, and remained with us until Jan. 25, preaching, in all, twenty-three sermons. We had good roads and fair congregations throughout our meetings. Quite a number could not attend on account of La Grippe. Bro. Mohler is a faithful expounder of the Word, and it does not take any one long to learn that he does not people to gain the esteem of men, but to honor God. While with us he held three children's meetings, prior to the evening services. We were much impressed with the importance of teaching the Gospel to our children while young, and we could easily see what could be accomplished in this direction, by parents, if the proper effort were made in time,—while they are, say from four to twelve years of age. There was one precious soul added to the church, and the church otherwise built up and forcibly impressed with the importance of living up more faithfully to our principles of nonconformity to the world.—J. R. Spacht, Feb. 1.

of the daughters are members. God help the other children to fully prepare to meet their God. The cause of his death was paralysis. Funeral services from 2 Tim. 1: 12 by L. M. Kob.

SWISSHELM.—In the May Hill church, Adams Co, Ohio, Jan. 23, 1892, Lizzie Swisshelm, daughter of Joseph and Mary Ellenberger, aged 22 years, 2 months and 28 days.

Deceased united with the German Baptist Brethren church at the age of sixteen years, and was a bold and an earnest advocate of the faith she professed till death came. Her disease was lung trouble, and though she seemed to suffer much, yet she bore it patiently. She leaves a sorrow-stricken husband, who is yet out of the church, a darling little boy, a kind father and mother, four sisters, one brother and many friends to mourn their loss. Funeral services conducted by Bro. Allen Ockerman, from these words: "But some are fallen asleep." W. Q. CALVERT.

REAM.—In the bounds of the Pleasant View church, Phillips Co., Kans, Oct. 12, 1891, Irvin Ream, infant son of Bro. Daniel and Martha Ream, aged 5 days.
MARTHA WORKMAN.

SHOCK.—In the Clear Creek congregation, Huntingdon Co., Ind., Jan. 24, of paralysis, Adam Shock, aged 84 years, 7 months and 18 days.

Deceased was born in Huntingdon County, Pa., June 6, 1807, and came to Montgomery County, Ohio, with his parents when six years old. In August, 1864, he removed to Huntington County, Ind., where he remained until his death. He served the church as a deacon and was always found at his post of duty. Funeral services by the writer to a large concourse of friends and neighbors from the words, "What is your life?"
DORSEY HODGDEN.

SAYLER.—In the Middle Fork church, Clinton Co., Ind., Jan. 25, 1892, Bro. Sanford H. Sayler, aged 67 years, 3 months and 12 days.

Deceased was born in Ripley County, Ind., Oct. 13, 1824. The funeral services were conducted in the Pleasant View church, Oct. 27, by elders Isaac Cripe and Solomon Blickenstaff from 2 Tim. 4: 7, 8, to a large congregation. Our brother leaves a wife and six children.

Bro. Sayler was baptized in 1874, elected to the ministry in 1879 and ordained elder in 1889. He served the church faithfully until God called him home. This church feels her loss keenly, but realizes that God doeth all things well. JOHN E. METZGER.

FISHER.—In the Moggadee congregation, Franklin Co., Va., Jan. 17, 1892, Peter Fisher, aged 78 years and 6 months.

Deceased was baptized about five days before his death. After living nearly fourscore years outside of the church, he did not feel willing to die outside of the church. Funeral services by the Brethren from John 14: 1, 2. ISAAC BOWMAN.

HOFF.—In the bounds of the Pipe Creek church, Carroll Co., Md., Jan. 21, sister Elizabeth Hoff, aged about 88 years.

Interment in the cemetery adjoining the Beaver Dam church. Services by the Brethren. E. W. STONER.

COOLEY.—In Adeline, Ill., Jan. 21, 1892, John B. Cooley, aged 76 years, 11 months and 22 days.

Deceased was born in Down County, Ireland, Jan. 29, 1815. He was of a family of three children, one daughter and two sons. Alexander Cooley, the younger brother, still survives, and still lives in Ireland.

J. B. Cooley left Ireland, May 10, 1837, and reached America in the following month. He became well known in and around Mt. Morris. He hauled a large part of the stone in the first seminary building at that place and also aided in the erection of said building. He was married to Maria Brown Jan. 30, 1845. This union was blessed with four children,—three sons and one daughter, all of whom survive. The mother died Aug. 10, 1887. He joined the U. B. church in January, 1846, and remained a consistent member of that church until his death. L. H. COOLEY.

WYLAND.—In the Yellow Creek church, Elkhart Co, Ind, Jan. 2, 1892, infant child of friend Absalom Wyland, aged 3 months and 15 days. Services by the writer from 2 Kings 4: 26. JOHN METZLER.

CRULL.—In the Baugo church, Ind, Jan. 14, 1892, sister Elizabeth (Goodlander) Crull, aged 86 years, 3 months and 16 days.

Deceased was born at Brownsville, Pa, in 1805. In 1814 she moved, with her parents, to Dayton, Ohio, and in 1822 to Fayette County, Ind. In 1827 she was married to Daniel Crull and in 1834 they moved to St. Joseph County, Ind. Her husband died thirty-six years ago. She united with the church in 1857. Services by the writer from Num. 23: 10. JOHN METZLER.

SLUSHER.—In Falcon, Floyd Co, Va., Dec. 4, 1891, of *La Grippe*, sister Sarah Jane Slusher, aged 36 years, 10 months and 13 days.

Deceased was the wife of M. F. Slusher, son of the writer. She united with the Brethren church about sixteen years ago and lived a consistent Christian life until her death. She leaves four children and a broken-hearted husband to mourn their loss. Funeral services from Rev. 14: 13 by C. D. and J. Hylton and others. J. H. SLUSHER.

SNIDER.—In Garrison, Iowa, Jan. 21, 1892, of *La Grippe*, Bro. D. W. Snider, aged 64 years, 11 months and 22 days.

The funeral services were held Jan. 23 to a full house and conducted by the undersigned from 1 Cor. 15: 22

Deceased was born in the State of Ohio. When one year old he moved with his parents Bedford County, Pa. In 1851 he married Deborah Garretson. To them were born three children, one son and two daughters. One daughter preceded him to the spirit world. In October, 1864, they moved to Iowa. In 1866 he joined the Brethren church of which he was a consistent member till the last.

His wife, sister Snider, and both of the children were sorely afflicted with the same disease. This occurred in the bounds of the Garrison church. PETER FORNEY.

EMMERT.—In Hagerstown, Md., Jan. 19, 1892, of cancer of the breast, sister Sarah Emmert, aged 66 years, 4 months and 25 days.

Deceased was the wife of Bro. Leonard Emmert, deceased, a minister of the Beaver Creek congregation. She leaves two daughters and one son,—Bro David Emmert, Superintendent of the Orphans' Home of our city. Her life was exemplary,—a bright and shining light for those left behind. To know her was to love her. Her afflictions were often so severe that she longed to be gone, but her earnest prayer was that she might patiently await the summons of the Lord. Services by Bro. D. F. Stouffer and others from Job 14: 14. The church has lost a sincere sister, the family a loving and devoted mother. May our loss be her great gain!
W. S. REICHARD.

Seven Great Monarchies.—By George Rawlinson. In three volumes, cloth. Per volume, $1.00.

Mental Science and Methods of Mental Culture.—By Edward Brooks. Cloth, $1.75.

Manual of Jewish History and Literature.—By D. Cassel. Cloth, 75 cents.

Every Day Christian Life.—By F. W. Farrar. Cloth, 12mo, $1.25.

Every Day Religion.—By James Freeman Clarke. Cloth, 12mo, $1.50.

Faiths of the World.—A concise history of the great religious systems of the world. Cloth, 8vo, $2.00.

A Manual of Bible History.—By Wm. G. Blaikie. Cloth, $1.50.

Reason and Revelation.—By. R. Milligan. Should be in the hands of every Bible student. Price, $2.00.

The House We Live In.—By Daniel Vaniman. It gives a concise account of the faith and practice of the Brethren. Price, 100 copies, 60 cents.

The People's Bible.—By Joseph Parker. An excellent work. In twenty-four volumes, 8vo, cloth. Per volume, $1.50.

GOOD BOOKS FOR ALL.

ANY book in the market furnished at publishers' lowest retail price by the Brethren's Publishing Company, Mt. Morris, Ill, *Special prices* given when books are purchased in quantities. When ordering books, not on our list, if possible give title, name of author, and address of publishers.

Family Bible, with Notes and Instructions.—Contains the harmony of the Gospels, Chronology, Maps, Tables of Weights and Measures, Family Record, eight elegant illustrations, etc. Price, substantially bound, $4.50.

German and English Testaments.—American Bible Society Edition. Price, 60 cents.

Homiletics and Pastoral Theology.—By W. G. T. Shedd. Cloth, $2.50

Lectures on Preaching.—By Rev. Phillips Brooks. Cloth, 16mo, $1.50.

New Testament and Psalms with Notes.—Invaluable for Bible students, Sunday-school teachers, etc. Price, cloth, $2.00; without Psalms, $1.00.

Quinter and McConnell Debate.—A debate on Trine Immersion, the Lord's Supper, and Feet-washing, between Eld. James Quinter (German Baptist) and Eld. N. A. McConnell (Christian) held at Dry Creek, Iowa, 1867. Price, $1.50.

Popular Commentary on the New Testament.—Edited by Philip Schaff. Four volumes, 8vo. Matthew, Mark and Luke: $6.00. John and the Acts: $6.00. Romans to Philemon: $5.00. Hebrews to Revelation: $5.00.

Sabbatism.—By M. M. Eshelman. Treats the Sabbath question, showing that the first day of the week is the day for assembling in worship. Price, 10 cents; 15 copies, $1.00.

Bunyan's Pilgrim's Progress.—An excellent edition of this good work, printed on good paper, finely illustrated with forty engravings, at the low price of $1.00 per copy.

Close Communion.—By Landon West. Treats this important subject in a simple though conclusive manner. Price, 50 cents.

In the Volume of the Book.—By Geo. F. Pentecost. Cloth, 60 cents.

Key to the Knowledge and Use of the Holy Bible.—By J. H. Blunt. Cloth, 16 mo, 75 cents.

Lange's Commentary.—Edited by Philip Schaff. Twenty-five vols. 8vo. Per vol., $3.00

New and Complete Bible Commentary.—By Jamieson, Fausset and Brown. It is far in advance of other works. It is critical, practical, and explanatory. It is compendious and comprehensive in its character. It has a critical introduction to each Book of Scripture, and is by far the most practical, suggestive, scientific, and popular work of the kind in the English language. In four large 12mo volumes of about 1,000 pages each. In extra fine English cloth, sprinkled edges, the full set, $8.00; half Morocco, the full set, $10.00.

Sacred Geography and Antiquities.—A practical, helpful work for Bible students, ministers and Sunday-school teachers. Price, $2.25.

The Origin and Growth of Religion.—Hibbert Lectures. By T. W. R. Davids. Cloth, 8vo, $2.50.

Our Library on Christian Evidences.—This collection of works embraces the best books to be had on that subject: "Paley's Evidences of Christianity," New Edition, $1.50; "Nelson on Infidelity," 75 cents; "Manual of Christian Evidences," 75 cents; "Many Infallible Proofs," $1.25; "The Divine Demonstration," $1.50; "The Bible in the Nineteenth Century," 40 cents; "Grounds of Theistic and Christian Belief," $2.50. Price of the entire set, if ordered at one time, $8.00; special terms to ministers furnished upon application

Bible Work, or Bible Reader's Commentary on the New Testament.—By J. G. Butler. Two. vols. 8vo, $10.00.

Biblical Antiquities.—By John Nevin. Gives a concise account of Bible times and customs; invaluable to all students of Bible subjects. Price, $1.50.

Biblical Theology of the Old Testament.—By R. F. Weidner. Cloth, $1.25.

Campbell and Owen Debate.—Contains a complete investigation of the evidences of Christianity. Price, $1.50.

Classified Minutes of Annual Meeting.—A work of rare interest for all who desire to be well informed in the church work, from the early days of our Brethren until the present. Price, cloth, $1.50; leather, $2.00.

Companion to the Bible.—This valuable work is so full of instruction that it can not fail to be of great benefit to every Christian. Price, $1 15.

Hours with the Bible.—By Cunningham Geikie. Old Testament Series—six volumes. Per volume, 90 cents.

Europe and Bible Lands.—By D. L. Miller. A book for the people,—more comprehensive and thorough than many higher-priced works. Price, cloth, $1.50; leather, $2.00.

Ecclesiastical History.—By Eusebius. Bohn Library. Cloth, $2.00.

Ecclesiastical History.—By Mosheim. 2 vols. 8vo., $4.00.

Early Days of Christianity.—By F. W. Farrar. Author's edition, cloth, 12mo, $1.25.

→PUBLICATIONS←

☞ The following books, Sunday-school supplies, etc., are for sale by the BRETHREN'S PUBLISHING CO., Mt. Morris, Ill., or Huntingdon, Pa., to whom all orders should be addressed.

The Brethren's Quarterly.

For Sunday-school teachers and scholars this publication is of the greatest benefit. Look at our prices:

Single subscription, one year,	35 cents.
Single subscription, per quarter,	10 cents.
Three copies, per quarter,	25 cents.
Eight copies, per quarter,	40 cents.
Twenty copies and over,	4 cents each.

Hymn Books.

New Tune and Hymn Books.

Half leather, per copy, post-paid,	$ 75
Morocco, per copy, post-paid,	1 00
Morocco, gilt edge, per copy, post-paid,	1 25

Hymn Books.

Morocco, per copy, post-paid,	$ 75
Morocco, gilt edge, per copy, post-paid,	85
Arabesque, per copy, post-paid,	40
Fine Limp, per copy, post-paid,	75
Fine Limp, gilt edge, per copy, post-paid,	85
German and English, per copy, post-paid,	75

Sunday-School Requisites,

The following list of things is needed in all Sunday-schools:

Testaments, Flexible, red edge, per dozen,	$1 00
Minute Books, each,	40
Class Books, per dozen,	75
S. S. Primers, with fine engravings, per dozen,	70

New and Beautiful Sunday-School Cards.

"The Gem," 50 picture cards, each with Bible text, verse of hymn,	35
250 Reward Tickets—verse of Scripture—red or blue,	20

The Young Disciple.

The YOUNG DISCIPLE is a neatly printed weekly, published especially for the moral benefit and religious instruction of our young folks.

Single copy, one year,	$ 50
Six copies (the sixth to the agent),	2 50
Ten copies,	4 00

For Three Months or Thirteen Weeks.

20 copies to one address,	$1 70
30 " " " "	2 50
40 " " " "	3 35
50 " " " "	3 80
75 " " " "	5 20
100 " " " "	7 00

For Six Months or Twenty-Six Weeks.

20 copies to one address,	$ 3 35
30 " " " "	5 00
40 " " " "	6 60
50 " " " "	7 50
75 " " " "	10 20
100 " " " "	13 75

Our paper is designed for the Sunday-school and the home circle. We desire the name of every Sunday-school Superintendent in the Brotherhood, and want an agent in every church. Send for sample copies.

Certificates of Membership

WE have just printed a new edition of these very convenient certificates. Several improvements over the old style are noticeable, such as perforated stubs, firm, yet smooth, paper, etc. Price only 50 cents per book. Every congregation should have one. Address this office.

Send for our new Bible Catalogue. Prices to suit the times. We have a large variety and the most durable as well as ornamental binding.

of the daughters are members. God help the other children to fully prepare to meet their God. The cause of his death was paralysis. Funeral services from 2 Tim. 1 : 12 by L. M. Kob.

SWISSHELM.—In the May Hill church, Adams Co., Ohio, Jan. 23, 1892, Lizzie Swisshelm, daughter of Joseph and Mary Ellenberger, aged 22 years, 2 months and 28 days.

Deceased united with the German Baptist Brethren church at the age of sixteen years, and was a bold and an earnest advocate of the faith she professed till death came. Her disease was lung trouble, and though she seemed to suffer much, yet she bore it patiently. She leaves a sorrow-stricken husband, who is yet out of the church, a darling little boy, a kind father and mother, four sisters, one brother and many friends to mourn their loss. Funeral services conducted by Bro. Allen Ockerman, from these words: "But some are fallen asleep."   W. Q. CALVERT.

REAM.—In the bounds of the Pleasant View church, Phillips Co., Kans., Oct. 12, 1891, Irvin Ream, infant son of Bro. Daniel and Martha Ream, aged 5 days.

                    MARTHA WORKMAN.

SHOCK.—In the Clear Creek congregation, Huntingdon Co. Ind., Jan. 24, of paralysis, Adam Shock, aged 84 years, 7 months and 18 days.

Deceased was born in Huntingdon County, Pa., June 6, 1807, and came to Montgomery County, Ohio, with his parents when six years old. In August, 1864, he removed to Huntington County, Ind., where he remained until his death. He served the church as a deacon and was always found at his post of duty. Funeral services by the writer to a large concourse of friends and neighbors from the words, "What is your life?"

                    DORSEY HODGDEN.

SAYLER.—In the Middle Fork church, Clinton Co., Ind., Jan. 25, 1892, Bro. Sanford H. Sayler, aged 67 years, 3 months and 12 days.

Deceased was born in Ripley County, Ind., Oct. 13, 1824. The funeral services were conducted in the Pleasant View church, Oct. 27, by elders Isaac Cripe and Solomon Blickenstaff from 2 Tim. 4 : 7, 8, to a large congregation. Our brother leaves a wife and six children.

Bro. Sayler was baptized in 1874, elected to the ministry in 1879 and ordained elder in 1889. He served the church faithfully until God called him home. This church feels her loss keenly, but realizes that God doeth all things well.   JOHN E. METZGER.

FISHER.—In the Moggsdee congregation, Franklin Co., Va., Jan. 17, 1892, Peter Fisher, aged 78 years and 6 months.

Deceased was baptized about five days before his death. After living nearly fourscore years outside of the church, he did not feel willing to die outside of the church. Funeral services by the Brethren from John 14 : 1, 2.   ISAAC BOWMAN.

HOFF.—In the bounds of the Pipe Creek church, Carroll Co., Md., Jan. 21, sister Elizabeth Hoff, aged about 88 years.

Interment in the cemetery adjoining the Beaver Dam church. Services by the Brethren.   E. W. STONER.

COOLEY.—In Adeline, Ill., Jan. 21, 1892, John B. Cooley, aged 76 years, 11 months and 22 days.

Deceased was born in Down County, Ireland, Jan. 29, 1815. He was of a family of three children, one daughter and two sons. Alexander Cooley, the younger brother, still survives, and still lives in Ireland.

J. B. Cooley left Ireland, May 10, 1837, and reached America in the following month. He became well known in and around Mt. Morris. He hauled a large part of the stone in the first seminary building at that place and also aided in the erection of said building. He was married to Maria Brown Jan. 30, 1845. This union was blessed with four children,—three sons and one daughter, all of whom survive. The mother died Aug. 10, 1887. He

joined the U. B. church in January, 1846, and remained a consistent member of that church until his death.   L. H. COOLEY.

WYLAND.—In the Yellow Creek church, Elkhart Co., Ind., Jan. 2, 1892, infant child of friend Absalom Wyland, aged 3 months and 15 days. Services by the writer from 2 Kings 4 : 26.   JOHN METZLER.

CRULL.—In the Baugo church, Ind., Jan. 14, 1892, sister Elizabeth (Goodlander) Crull, aged 86 years, 3 months and 16 days.

Deceased was born at Brownsville, Pa., in 1805. In 1814 she moved, with her parents, to Dayton, Ohio, and in 1812 to Fayette County, Ind. In 1827 she was married to Daniel Crull and in 1834 they moved to St. Joseph County, Ind. Her husband died thirty-six years ago. She united with the church in 1857. Services by the writer from Num. 23 : 10.   JOHN METZLER.

SLUSHER.—In Falcon, Floyd Co., Va., Dec. 4, 1891, of La Grippe, sister Sarah Jane Slusher, aged 36 years, 10 months and 13 days.

Deceased was the wife of M. F. Slusher, son of the writer. She united with the Brethren church about sixteen years ago and lived a consistent Christian life until her death. She leaves four children and a broken-hearted husband to mourn their loss. Funeral services from Rev. 14 : 13 by C. D. and J. Hylton and others.   J. H. SLUSHER.

SNIDER.—In Garrison, Iowa, Jan. 21, 1892, of La Grippe, Bro. D. W. Snider, aged 64 years, 11 months and 12 days.

The funeral services were held Jan. 23 to a full house and conducted by the undersigned from 1 Cor. 15 : 22.

Deceased was born in the State of Ohio. When one year old he moved with his parents to Bedford County, Pa. In 1857 he married Deborah Garretson. To them were born three children, one son and two daughters. One daughter preceded him to the spirit world. In October, 1864, they moved to Iowa. In 1866 he joined the Brethren church of which he was a consistent member till the last.

His wife, sister Snider, and both of the children were sorely afflicted with the same diseases. This occurred in the bounds of the Garrison church.   PETER FORNEY.

EMMERT.—In Hagerstown, Md., Jan. 19, 1892, of cancer of the breast, sister Sarah Emmert, aged 66 years, 4 months and 25 days.

Deceased was the wife of Bro. Leonard Emmert, deceased, a minister of the Beaver Creek congregation. She leaves two daughters and one son,—Bro. David Emmert, Superintendent of the Orphans' Home of our city. Her life was exemplary,—a bright and shining light for those left behind. To know her was to love her. Her afflictions were often so severe, that she longed to be gone, but her earnest prayer was that she might patiently await the summons of the Lord. Services by Bro. D. F. Stouffer and others from Job 14 : 14. The church has lost a sincere sister, the family a loving and devoted mother. May our loss be her great gain!   W. S. REICHARD.

Seven Great Monarchies.—By George Rawlinson. In three volumes, cloth. Per volume, $1.00.

Mental Science and Methods of Mental Culture.—By Edward Brooks. Cloth, $1.75.

Manual of Jewish History and Literature.—By D. Cassel. Cloth, 75 cents.

Every Day Christian Life.—By F. W. Farrar. Cloth, izmo, $1.25.

Every Day Religion.—By James Freeman Clarke. Cloth, izmo, $1.50.

Paths of the World.—A concise history of the great religious systems of the world. Cloth, 8vo, $2.00.

A Manual of Bible History.—By Wm. G. Blaikie. Cloth, $1.50.

Reason and Revelation.—By R. Milligan. Should be in the hands of every Bible student. Price, $2.00.

The House We Live In.—By Daniel Vanizase. It gives a concise account of the faith and practice of the Brethren. Price, 100 copies, 60 cents.

The People's Bible.—By Joseph Parker. An excellent work. In twenty-four volumes, 8vo, cloth. Per volume, $1.50.

THE GOSPEL MESSENGER.

"Set for the Defense of the Gospel."

Vol. 30, Old Series.　　Mt. Morris, Ill., and Huntingdon, Pa., Feb. 23, 1892.　　No. 8.

The Gospel Messenger.

H. B. BRUMBAUGH, Editor,

And Business Manager of the Eastern House, Box 50,
Huntingdon, Pa.

Table of Contents.

"The gardener knows that where he puts the knife there will follow fruit. And blessed are they whom the Heavenly Husbandman prunes; if, when he cuts, there is a bud behind the knife."

WE would be pleased to give the names of all who were present with us during the Bible Term, but fearing that it might not be of general interest, we forbear, but assure those not named that their presence was none the less appreciated.

"That which you would wish you had said to a friend if you heard that the friend was dead, is the very thing for you to say to that friend to-day; for the friend who is alive to-day may be dead to-morrow. To-day is the only accepted time for any duty that must be done at some time."

"It is, of course, always better to be one's self, than to try to be some one else. One's personality is, in a peculiar sense, the special gift of God. It is that which secures to one the possibility of being and of doing. In it lies all his possibility of being what no one else can be, of doing what no one else can do. Our personality, as such, is therefore the last thing that we ought to be willing to surrender. And yet, one's very best personality may be exhibited in his power to lose himself in the personality of another; and, in many a case, he is most truly himself who most truly forgets himself—in his loving service of another's self."

ELD. J. W. BRUMBAUGH, of Clover Creek, Pa., has been a Normal guest during the Bible Term, and evidently is enjoying the work, as he has been taking in all the sessions. We are glad to note that he is improving in health and has been doing some ministerial labor. His presence among us is being enjoyed by all.

"IT is a blessed thought that nothing done for Christ is lost. No act of any child of his is too small for his notice. The kind word, the generous appreciation of another's effort, the trifling act of self-denial, even though unheeded by any other, is always dear and precious to our Lord, and as truly acceptable to him as the costly box of ointment, broken at his feet in love."

WE have been having a course of doctrinal sermons, preached by Eld. Jas. A. Sell. Up to this writing the order is as follows: Two sermons on Church Government, one on Repentance, Baptism, Trine Immersion, Feet-washing, the Lord's Supper, and Non-conformity. His discourses are received with marked attention and, we hope, will be productive of much good. These sermons are given in the evening, in connection with our Bible work.

DURING the former part of our Bible Term we had the pleasure of hearing a number of interesting sermons from our Ohio brethren, Isaac Frantz, I. J. Rosenberger, D. M. Irvin and J. F. Kahler. We were glad to have these brethren among us and hope that their visits may be repeated. They all attended the Bible Term except Bro. Rosenberger, who stopped off only a few days on his way east, where he was going to conduct a series of meetings.

ELD. J. F. OLLER, of Waynesborough, Pa., came to us with a delegation of about fourteen, including a part of his own family. If many of our churches would turn out in this way, it would make us feel around for more room,—and we would do it with pleasure, as these are the kind of delegations we most heartily welcome. As far as possible, we are trying to make it home-like for those who come to us, and if they enjoy their being with us as much as we enjoy having them here, we are sure that our joy is mutual.

"IF a professed disciple would not have his secular business become as a millstone about his neck, to drown him in perdition, he must be a man of prayer; he must daily secure spiritual communion with God. If he suffers his business to consume his time and spirits, so as to deprive him of opportunities for prayer, reading the Bible, and real communion with God, he must decay in piety, and his service of mammon eat up his service of God. No one who believes that God answers prayer, will think of omitting either secret or family devotion for want of time, even when business is unusually urgent. Which is worth most to you or your family, an additional period of your unblessed labors, or the blessing of God on your efforts, won by spending that time in pleading with Him in prayer? The plea of want of time is essentially atheistical; none should urge it but those

who regard prayer as an empty mockery, that never receive an answer from the Lord. Let the day begin with communion with God, let the disciple pass the whole day in the spirit of prayer, and all its duties will become spiritual duties, and all its scenes be inscribed with 'Holiness to the Lord.'"

AN EXPLANATION.

H. B. BRUMBAUGH,

Dear Brother:—

I would be pleased to have something more definite with respect to what you have said on the covering question in No. 4, of 1892, in which you state:

"In this way the ladies of that time used their hair for a covering as Paul says, *i. e.*, by putting the hair down and forward,—*v. c.*, down over their faces."

Do you mean to say those were Christian women, and that the hair was the only covering worn by them in public worship?

You also say, "That the hair was used as a covering and can still be used on the part of women, is not denied by us as a church."

Of course, we understand you to have reference to sisters in the church and not to unconverted women. I ask for information, as I want an accurate idea of your production.

J. M. MOHLER,

Lewistown, Pa.

IF we can add anything to more fully explain what we said about the covering, we will gladly do so. That it may be seen exactly what we did say, we repeat it again:

That the hair was used as a covering and can still be so used on the part of women is not denied by us as a church. But what we have been teaching is that the particular covering, here referred to by Paul, was a special covering then, in common use by the Jewish Christians and here recommended by Paul to be used by all Christian women in times of religious services. And had this brother, if correctly reported, been governed by the laws of hermeneutics he would have known that Paul knew what he was talking about, and that, according to the customs of the times, it would have been a very easy matter to use their hair for a covering. The meaning of the word, as then used, also conveys the same truth as given by Paul. *Kalupto*, to cover, hide, conceal; *Kata*, down-ward. Put the two together, we have *Kata Kalupto*, to cover or veil by putting the hair down and forward. In this way the ladies of that time used their hair for a covering as Paul says, and in addition to this covering he here recommends and urges the veil, or artificial covering, to be used by all Christian women during times of prayer and religious worship.

We really do not see how we can make the matter plainer than we have it, as we say exactly what Paul says: "But if a woman have long hair, it is a glory to her; for her hair is given her for a covering—a veil." If the Lord gave woman long hair for a covering we do not see why Christian women, as well as others, cannot wear their hair for a covering. It will be noticed that Paul speaks of two coverings or veilings. The one is her hair and it is an honor for her to wear it, because Paul says it is her glory. The other is the covering, or veil, which is to be used as a veil during praying or prophesying.

We don't see how there can be any misunderstanding about this. Our interpretation is almost exactly the same as was given by Bro. Yearout at the McPherson Bible Term. (See editorial on page 88, GOSPEL MESSENGER No. 6.) The covering subject is very simple and plain, if we don't add confusion to it by wrong interpretations.

THE GOSPEL MESSENGER.

"Set for the Defense of the Gospel."

Vol. 30, Old Series.   Mt. Morris, Ill., and Huntingdon, Pa., Feb. 23, 1892.   No. 8.

The Gospel Messenger.

H. B. Brumbaugh, Editor,

And Business Manager of the Eastern House, Box 50,
Huntingdon, Pa.

Table of Contents.

"The gardener knows that where he puts the knife there will follow fruit. And blessed are they whom the Heavenly Husbandman prunes; if, when he cuts, there is a bud behind the knife."

We would be pleased to give the names of all who were present with us during the Bible Term, but fearing that it might not be of general interest, we forbear, but assure those not named that their presence was none the less appreciated.

"That which you would wish you had said to a friend if you heard that the friend was dead, is the very thing for you to say to that friend to-day: for the friend who is alive to-day may be dead to-morrow. To-day is the only accepted time for any duty that must be done at some time."

"It is, of course, always better to be one's self, than to try to be some one else. One's personality is, in a peculiar sense, the special gift of God. It is that which secures to one the possibility of being and of doing. In it lies all his possibility of being what no one else can be, of doing what no one else can do. Our personality, as such, is therefore the last thing that we ought to be willing to surrender. And yet, one's very best personality may be exhibited in his power to lose himself in the personality of another; and, in many a case, he is most truly himself who most truly forgets himself—in his loving service of another's self."

Eld. J. W. Brumbaugh, of Clover Creek, Pa., has been a Normal guest during the Bible Term, and evidently is enjoying the work, as he has been taking in all the sessions. We are glad to note that he is improving in health and has been doing some ministerial labor. His presence among us is being enjoyed by all.

"It is a blessed thought that nothing done for Christ is lost. No act of any child of his is too small for his notice. The kind word, the generous appreciation of another's effort, the trifling act of self-denial, even though unheeded by any other, is always dear and precious to our Lord, and as truly acceptable to him as the costly box of ointment, broken at his feet in love."

We have been having a course of doctrinal sermons, preached by Eld. Jas. A. Sell. Up to this writing the order is as follows: Two sermons on Church Government, one on Repentance, Baptism, Trine Immersion, Feet-washing, the Lord's Supper, and Non-conformity. His discourses are received with marked attention and, we hope, will be productive of much good. These sermons are given in the evening, in connection with our Bible work.

During the former part of our Bible Term we had the pleasure of hearing a number of interesting sermons from our Ohio brethren, Isaac Frantz, I. J. Rosenberger, D. M. Irvin and J. F. Kahler. We were glad to have these brethren among us and hope that their visits may be repeated. They all attended the Bible Term except Bro. Rosenberger, who stopped off only a few days on his way east, where he was going to conduct a series of meetings.

Eld. J. F. Oller, of Waynesborough, Pa., came to us with a delegation of about fourteen, including a part of his own family. If many of our churches would turn out in this way, it would make us feel around for more room,—and we would do it with pleasure, as these are the kind of delegations we most heartily welcome. As far as possible, we are trying to make it home-like for those who come to us, and if they enjoy their being with us as much as we enjoy having them here, we are sure that our joy is mutual.

"If a professed disciple would not have his secular business become as a millstone about his neck, to drown him in perdition, he must be a man of prayer; he must daily secure spiritual communion with God. If he suffers his business to consume his time and spirits, so as to deprive him of opportunities for prayer, reading the Bible, and real communion with God, he must decay in piety, and his service of mammon eat up his service of God. No one who believes that God answers prayer, will think of omitting either secret or family devotion for want of time, even when business is unusually urgent. Which is worth most to you or your family, an additional period of your unblessed labor, or the blessing of God on your efforts, won by spending that time in pleading with Him in prayer? The plea of want of time is essentially atheistical; none should urge it but those

who regard prayer as an empty mockery, that never receives an answer from the Lord. Let the day begin with communion with God, let the disciple pass the whole day in the spirit of prayer, and all its duties will become spiritual duties, and all its scenes be inscribed with 'Holiness to the Lord.'"

AN EXPLANATION.

H. B. Brumbaugh,

Dear Brother:—

—I would be pleased to have something more definite with respect to what you have said on the covering question in No. 4, of 1892, in which you state:

"In this way the ladies of that time used their hair for a covering as Paul says, *i. e.,* by putting the hair down and forward,—*i. e.,* down over their faces."

Do you mean to say those were Christian women, and that the hair was the only covering worn by them in public worship?

You also say, "That the hair was used as a covering and can still be to used on the part of women, is not denied by us as a church."

Of course, we understand you to have reference to sisters in the church and not to unconverted women. I ask for information, as I want an accurate idea of your production.

J. M. Mohler,

Lewistown, Pa.

If we can add anything to more fully explain what we said about the covering, we will gladly do so. That it may be seen exactly what we did say, we repeat it again:

That the hair was used as a covering and can still be so used on the part of women is not denied by us as a church. But what we have been teaching is that the particular covering, here referred to by Paul, was a special covering then, in common use by the Jewish Christians and here recommended by Paul to be used by all Christian women in times of religious services. And had this before it, if correctly reported, been governed by the laws of hermeneutics he would have known that Paul knew what he was talking about, and that, according to the customs of the times, it would have been a very easy matter to use their hair for a covering. The meaning of the word, as then used, also conveys the same truth as given by Paul. *Kalupto,* to cover, hide, conceal; *Kata,* down-ward. Put the two together, we have *Kata Kalupto,* to cover or veil by putting the hair down and forward. In this way the ladies of that time used their hair for a covering as Paul says, and in addition to this covering he here recommends and urges the veil, or artificial covering, to be used by all Christian women during times of prayer and religious worship.

We really do not see how we can make the matter plainer than we have it, as we say exactly what Paul says: "But if a woman have long hair, it is a glory to her; for her hair is given her for a covering—a veil." If the Lord gave woman long hair for a covering we do not see why Christian women, as well as others, cannot wear their hair for a covering. It will be noticed that Paul speaks of two coverings or veilings. The one is her hair and it is an honor for her to wear it, because Paul says it is her glory. The other is the covering, or veil, which is to be used as a veil during praying or prophesying.

We don't see how there can be any misunderstanding about this. Our interpretation is almost exactly the same as was given by Bro. Yearout at the McPherson Bible Term. (See editorial on page 88, Gospel Messenger No. 6.) This covering subject is very simple and plain, if we don't add confusion to it by wrong interpretations.

power and influence again. The French convention repealed its atheistic laws, and acknowledged Christianity as the religion of the State. The resurrected witnesses were in sackcloth no more. The age of religious toleration had come, and there is no Catholic country now that prohibits the reading of the Bible, and the preaching of the Gospel. The Bible is now translated into every written tongue of earth. The sackcloth is laid aside, and the witnesses are taken up to heaven. This signifies not their removal, but exaltation to a power and glory unknown for 1,260 years.

In the preparation of this article we are indebted to the following authors: Johnson's "Lectures on the Apocalypse," D'Aubigne's "Reformation," and Gibbon's "Rome."

Dego, Ind.

DID JUDAS PARTAKE OF THE BREAD AND WINE?

BY LANDON WEST.

IN GOSPEL MESSENGER No. 48, I see an essay by our brother, A. Hutchison, headed: "Did Judas Go Out While they were Eating the Supper?" If I get the thought of Bro. Hutchison correctly, he takes the position that Judas did not go out, until after the passing of the bread and wine. His position is based upon what Luke says in 22: 15, 20, and because verse 21 says: "Behold the hand of him that betrayeth me, is with me on the table," our brother takes the position that Judas was at the table at Communion. He, in order to satisfy those who criticise the Brethren, would have all of us correct our little mistake, and not say any more that Judas went out while they were eating the Supper.

To satisfy critics is not so easily done, when they are found on two sides of the question, and I think the Truth should have the preference, and then let critics take their chances for satisfaction. Let the facts show.

That Judas came in and sat down at the table is certain. That he was still there at feet-washing, and while the Supper was being eaten, is also certain, but that he was yet there at the passing of the bread and the cup, is not certain, for we hear nothing of his presence there after the sop, for John says: "He then having received the sop, went immediately out and it was night." John 13: 30. But we have some other statements, to condemn the idea that he was present when the emblems of Communion were passed.

At feet-washing Jesus said that Judas was not clean, "for he knew who should betray him, therefore said he, Ye are not all clean." John 13: 11. John the Baptist said of Jesus "that he will thoroughly purge his floor." Matt. 3: 12.

Now, I say that Jesus will give the Communion to none, known and pointed out as unclean, and unfit for that service, is to say that our Master would not thoroughly cleanse his table, let alone his floor. It is to say that Jesus was not so particular as to the purity of his people and service as the Spirit would have Paul to be at Corinth, and the saints now to be in all parts of the world. I feel confident, that there is not a church of the Brethren in Europe or America that would knowingly allow a member to come to her Communion tables who had betrayed and sold another to his enemies, as did Judas. The Spirit forbids eating or keeping company with one who is called a brother, who is "covetous or an idolater," which would have excluded Judas at Corinth, and why not at Jerusalem from whence the Law of Righteousness was to go to all the world?

How can we reconcile the Master's words in Matt. 7: 6 with his practice, if we say Judas was allowed to commune with the Lord himself? Jesus says: "Give not that which is holy unto the dogs." And where is there a stronger case of holy things being given to a dog, and that, too, by our Savior's own hand, than here, if we allow Judas a place and part in the Lord's Communion? Why need any of us advocate close Communion, if we allow Judas all of it, he could ask for?

Paul tells of the fearful consequences of unworthily partaking of the Lord's body and blood, and says that those who do so, crucify him afresh. Our Savior said nothing as to fitness for it, more than to state, as to who was clean, and who was not, and to get the unclean one out of the room. So the Supper went on, and with it came the bread and the wine. We must not hold that all the events, given by Luke or the others, occurred in the order of time in which they are named, for Luke says that the query as to who should betray him, was passed after the Communion, 22: 23, while both Matthew and John give it at the Supper and, of course, before the Communion. Matt. 26: 21, 25; John 13: 21, 27. Mark also says it was before the taking of the bread and wine. Mark 14: 18, 21.

From what John says, it appears that Judas went out soon after the eating of the Supper began,—and the time taken by him to show his plan to the priests, and also the further delay in collecting and sending their forces with lanterns, torches and weapons,—was employed by Jesus in going on with the Supper, in giving the bread and wine to the disciples then with him. After his farewell sermon, as given in John 14, 15 and 16, his prayer of John 17, they sang a hymn and went out. The events are given most orderly and concisely by John and Matthew, who were both eye-witnesses of what they tell, while Mark and Luke give theirs from hearsay. To show that Luke did not give the events he names, in their order of time, as they occurred, I cite all of our readers to what he says of the baptism of Jesus, and the imprisonment of John the Baptist. (See Luke 3: 19–20.) There, in three verses, he shows his irregularity in naming events as plainly as can be seen. He says that Herod, because he was reproved by John the Baptist, put John in prison; and in the next verse he says Jesus came to him and was baptized. This statement cannot be correct as to order of time, for the other evangelists say, and we must all know, that the baptism occurred before John was cast into prison, for it is plain, that Jesus was not baptized in a prison, but in Jordan.

Lanier, Ohio.

THE ANTI-CHRISTIAN DOCTRINES OF CERTAIN FORMS OF ADVENTISM.

BY HENRY BIBLER.

THIS seems to be a serious charge to bring against a large body of professing Christians. Let us see if it is true, or false.

I except, of course, those who do not hold the views given below, or similar ones. I speak of the system, as we have it, spreading itself around us here. The second coming of Christ is a precious doctrine of the Word. Much of modern Adventism is the result of Satan's efforts to bring into disrepute the Truth, the progress of which he cannot withstand.

1. It denies the Gospel. They teach that no one can get eternal life until the resurrection. This is the fruit of materialism, which confounds eternal life with existence. Eternal Life, in Scripture, is, to know the only true God, and Jesus Christ, whom he has sent. All else is death, not only in the future, but now. Christ says, in John 5: 24, "Verily, verily, I say unto you, He

that heareth my word, and believeth on him that sent me, hath everlasting life, and shall not come into condemnation, but is passed from death unto life." "He that hath the Son hath life, and he that hath not the Son of God hath not life." Therefore, in John 5, there is resurrection to life as well as the judgment, as also in Rev. 20; and this is the constant teaching of the New Testament.

2. Adventists teach also, that believers are under the law. Scripture teaches that "as many as are of the works of the law are under the curse." Gal. 3: 10. We are told that the believer is dead to the law, that he might live to God, and that sin shall not have dominion over him, because he is not under the law, but under grace. Everywhere law and grace are contrasted, as opposite ways, in which God has dealt with man. Law is the testing of the creature under responsibility, and therefore the ministration of death and condemnation. Grace is the revelation of God in Christ, meeting the need of his fallen creatures with the work of redemption,—the grace that brings salvation, teaching him to deny ungodliness and worldly lusts, etc. Titus 2: 11, 12. To refer to all the proofs of this, would be to quote much of the New Testament. One part of them has returned openly to the Sabbath; but do they keep it, as required in the Levitical law? From their stand-point, however, it is consistent. They should remember that to gather sticks upon the Sabbath, or to light a fire in their habitations, is to have broken it and to have earned a curse. To be quite consistent, however, they should remain to circumcision, and then they would indeed be debtors to the whole law. Gal. 5: 1-4.

3. Another feature of the system is, the denial of the heavenly calling and hope of the church. For them John 17 can have no meaning, unless the glory that Christ had with the Father before the world was, in earthly glory, for, having returned to it as man, he shares it with his beloved and red-emed people. The truth in Ephesians and Colossians, etc., can have no place in their system. Indeed, the whole of the New Testament is full of the development of the heavenly things, consequent on the rejection of Christ by the heirs of the earthly inheritance, and the coming of the Holy Ghost, whilst it also fully recognizes the giving to the earthly people Israel, in grace, the inheritance promised ("for the gifts and calling of God are without repentance").

4. They also deny the Restoration of Israel, foretold in all the Prophets, and in the New Testament also; because they (the Adventists) have taken their place, and adopted, in part, the hopes of the nation, saying, as we are warned in Rev. 3, would be done by the opposers of the revival of the power of truth in the last days, "that they are Jews, and are not, but do lie."

5. They deny the immortality of the soul, and the consequent endurance of punishment by the finally impenitent. They oppose the teaching of Scripture as to this with the childish question, "Where is hell?"—thinking to puzzle their listeners with a talk about Hades and Sheol, which for them is the grave, and nothing more. Man is for them nothing but matter which breathes, but soul and spirit distinct from the body they will not allow. "Absent from the body; . . . present with the Lord." "At home in the body, absent from the Lord," has no real significance for them. The rich man in hell (Hades), lifting up his eyes in torment, is only a parable to teach something very undefinable about Jews and Gentiles; and the lake of fire, the second death, is extinction of existence. And yet, strangely enough, the Old Testament judgments, which are not the lake of fire, afford their main texts to prove annihilation. "Let us eat and drink and be merry, for to-mor-

power and influence again. The French convention repealed its atheistic laws, and acknowledged Christianity as the religion of the State. The resurrected witnesses were in sackcloth no more. The age of religious toleration had come, and there is no Catholic country now that prohibits the reading of the Bible, and the preaching of the Gospel. The Bible is now translated into every written tongue of earth. The sackcloth is laid aside, and the witnesses are taken up to heaven. This signifies not their removal, but exaltation to a power and glory unknown for 1,260 years.

In the preparation of this article we are indebted to the following authors: Johnson's "Lectures on the Apocalypse," D'Aubigne's "Reformation," and Gibbon's "Rome."

Dego, Ind.

DID JUDAS PARTAKE OF THE BREAD AND WINE?

BY LANDON WEST.

In Gospel Messenger No. 48, I see an essay by our brother, A. Hutchison, headed: "Did Judas Go Out While they were Eating the Supper?" If I get the thought of Bro. Hutchison correctly, he takes the position that Judas did not go out, until after the passing of the bread and wine. His position is based upon what Luke says in 22: 15, 20, and because verse 21 says: "Behold the hand of him that betrayeth me, is with me on the table," our brother takes the position that Judas was at the table at Communion. He, in order to satisfy those who criticise the Brethren, would have all of us correct our little mistake, and not say any more that Judas went out while they were eating the Supper.

To satisfy critics is not so easily done, when they are found on two sides of the question, and I think the Truth should have the preference, and then let critics take their chances for satisfaction. Let the facts show.

That Judas came in and sat down at the table is certain. That he was still there at feet-washing, and while the Supper was being eaten, is also certain, but that he was yet there at the passing of the bread and the cup, is not certain, for we hear nothing of his presence there after the sop, for John says: "He then having received the sop, went immediately out and it was night." John 13: 30. But we have some other statements, to condemn the idea that he was present when the emblems of Communion were passed.

At feet-washing Jesus said that Judas was not clean, "for he knew who should betray him, therefore said he, Ye are not all clean." John 13: 11. John the Baptist said of Jesus "that he will thoroughly purge his floor." Matt. 3: 12.

Now, I say that Jesus will give the Communion to one, known and pointed out as unclean, and unfit for that service, is to say that our Master would not thoroughly cleanse his table, let alone his floor. It is to say that Jesus was not so particular as to the purity of his people and service as the Spirit would have Paul to be at Corinth, and the saints now to be in all parts of the world. I feel confident, that there is not a church of the Brethren in Europe or America that would knowingly allow a member to come to her Communion tables who had betrayed and sold another to his enemies, as did Judas. The Spirit forbids eating or keeping company with one who is called a brother, who is "covetous or an idolater," which would have excluded Judas at Corinth, and why not at Jerusalem from whence the Law of Righteousness was to go to all the world?

How can we reconcile the Master's words in Matt. 7: 6 with his practice, if we say Judas was allowed to commune with the Lord himself? Jesus says: "Give not that which is holy unto the dogs." And where is there a stronger case of hc- ly things being given to a dog, and that, too, by our Savior's own hand, than here, if we allow Judas a place and part in the Lord's Communion? Why need any of us advocate close Communion, if we allow Judas all of it, he could ask for?

Paul tells of the fearful consequences of unworthily partaking of the Lord's body and blood, and says that those who do so, crucify him afresh. Our Savior said nothing as to fitness for it, more than to state, as to who was clean, and who was not, and to get the unclean one out of the room. So the Supper went on, and with it came the bread and the wine. We must not hold that all the events, given by Luke or the others, occurred in the order of time in which they are named, for Luke says that the query as to who should betray him, was passed after the Communion, 22: 23, while both Matthew and John give it at the Supper and, of course, before the Communion. Matt. 26: 21, 25; John 13: 21, 27. Mark also says it was before the taking of the bread and wine. Mark 14: 18, 21.

From what John says, it appears that Judas went out soon after the eating of the Supper began,—and the time taken by him to show his plan to the priests, and also the further delay in collecting and sending their forces with lanterns, torches and weapons,—was employed by Jesus in going on with the Supper, in giving the bread and wine to the disciples then with him. After his farewell sermon, as given in John 14, 15 and 16, his prayer of John 17, they sang a hymn and went out. The events are given most orderly and concisely by John and Matthew, who were both eye-witnesses of what they tell, while Mark and Luke give theirs from hearsay. To show that Luke did not give the events he names, in their order of time, as they occurred, I cite all of our readers to what he says of the baptism of Jesus, and the imprisonment of John the Baptist. (See Luke 3: 19-20.) There, in three verses, he shows his irregularity in naming events as plainly as can be seen. He says that Herod, because he was reproved by John, the Baptist, put John in prison; and in the next verse he says Jesus came to him and was baptized. This statement cannot be correct as to order of time, for the other evangelists say, and we must all know, that the baptism occurred before John was cast into prison, for it is plain, that Jesus was not baptized in a prison, but in Jordan.

Lanier, Ohio.

THE ANTI-CHRISTIAN DOCTRINES OF CERTAIN FORMS OF ADVENTISM.

BY HENRY BIBLER.

This seems to be a serious charge to bring against a large body of professing Christians. Let us see if it is true, or false.

I except, of course, those who do not hold the views given below, or similar ones. I speak of the system, as we have it, spreading itself around us here. The second coming of Christ is a precious doctrine of the Word. Much of modern Adventism is the result of Satan's efforts to bring into disrepute the Truth, the progress of which he cannot withstand.

1. It denies the Gospel. They teach that no one can get eternal life until the resurrection. This is the fruit of materialism, which confounds eternal life with existence. Eternal Life, in Scripture, is, to know the only true God, and Jesus Christ, whom he has sent. All else is death, not only in the future, but now. Christ says, in John 5: 24, "Verily, verily, I say unto you, He

that heareth my word, and believeth on him that sent me, hath everlasting life, and shall not come into condemnation, but is passed from death unto life." "He that hath the Son hath life, and he that hath not the Son of God hath not life." Therefore, in John 5, there is resurrection to life as well as the judgment, as also in Rev. 20; and this is the constant teaching of the New Testament.

2. Adventists teach also, that believers are under the law. Scripture teaches that "as many as are of the works of the law are under the curse." Gal. 3: 10. We are told that the believer is dead to the law, that he might live to God, and that sin shall not have dominion over him, because he *is not under the law,* but under grace. Everywhere law and grace are contrasted, as opposite ways, in which God has dealt with man. Law is the testing of the creature under responsibility, and therefore the ministration of death and condemnation. Grace is the revelation of God in Christ, meeting the need of his fallen creatures with the work of redemption,—the grace that brings salvation, teaching him to deny ungodliness and worldly lusts, etc. Titus 2: 11, 12. To refer to all the proofs of this, would be to quote much of the New Testament. One part of them has returned openly to the Sabbath; but do they keep it, as required in the Levitical law? From their stand-point, however, it is consistent. They should remember that to gather sticks upon the Sabbath, or to light a fire in their habitations, is to have broken it and to have earned a curse. To be quite consistent, however, they should return to circumcision, and then they would indeed be debtors to the whole law. Gal. 5: 1-4.

3. Another feature of the system is, the denial of the heavenly calling and hope of the church. For them John 17 can have no meaning, unless the glory that Christ had with the Father before the world was, in earthly glory, for, having returned to it as man, he shares it with his beloved and redeemed people. The truth in Ephesians and Colossians, etc., can have no place in their system. Indeed, the whole of the New Testament is full of the development of the heavenly things, consequent on the rejection of Christ by the heirs of the earthly inheritance, and the coming of the Holy Ghost, whilst it also fully recognizes the giving to the earthly people Israel, in grace, the inheritance promised ("for the gifts and calling of God are without repentance").

4. They also deny the Restoration of Israel, foretold in all the Prophets, and in the New Testament also; because they (the Adventists) have taken their place, and adopted, in part, the hopes of the nation, saying, as we are warned in Rev. 3, would be done by the opposers of the revival of the power of truth in the last days, "that they are Jews, and are not, but do lie."

5. They deny the immortality of the soul, and the consequent endurance of punishment by the finally impenitent. They oppose the teaching of Scripture as to this with the childish question, "Where is hell?"—thinking to puzzle their listeners with a talk about Hades and Sheol, which for them is the grave, and nothing more. Man is for them nothing but matter which breathes, but soul and spirit distinct from the body they will not allow. "Absent from the body; . . . present with the Lord." "At home in the body, absent from the Lord," has no real significance for them. The rich man in hell (Hades), lifting up his eyes in torment, is only a parable to teach something very undefinable about Jews and Gentiles; and the lake of fire, the second death, is extinction of existence. And yet, strangely enough, the Old Testament judgments, which are not the lake of fire, afford their main texts to prove annihilation. "Let us eat and drink and be merry, for to-mor-

and,—but the world's roll of great soldiers, authors, musicians, painters, poets, philosophers and financiers contains more Hebrew names than I could recite in many hours.

Are you looking for an aristocracy of wealth? The combined financial power of the Jews in Europe can prevent the floating of almost any national loan which may be put upon the markets of the world!

It is a spurious, false Christianity that hates Jews. The mystery of the Incarnation found expression in the flesh and blood of a Jew, and therefore, in a sense, we worship a Jew. We get our Ten Commandments—through the Jews. We sing Jewish psalms, are uplifted by the passion and poetry of Jewish prophets, and rely on Jewish biographies for the only history we have of Christ. We get our Pauline theology from a Jew, and we catch our clearest glimpse of the next world through the sublime apocalyptic vision of a Jew. Then, forsooth, we Christians turn about and sneer at Jews!

I have conversed with teachers of philosophy who spoke slightingly of the Jews, and yet were teaching with enthusiasm ideas which they have absorbed from Maimonides and Spinoza, the two greatest philosophers, omitting Kant, since Plato's day—both of them Jews.

I have heard musicians denounce Jews, and then spend days and nights trying to interpret the beauties of Rossini, Meyerbeer, and Mendelssohn,—all Jews.

I talked the other day with a gifted actress, and heard both her and her husband sweepingly condemn, confidentially, of course, the whole race of Jews, and yet that woman would give half her remaining life if she could reach the heights which the great queen of tragedy, Rachel, trod with such majesty and power — and Rachel was a Jewess.

Here in Washington I have heard aspiring politicians, when beyond the reach of the reporter's pencil, sneer at the Jews, and yet it was a Jew who made England's Queen Empress of India, and it was a Jew who was for years the adroit and sagacious chairman of the National Committee of one of our great political parties. The brainiest man in the Southern Confederacy was Judah P. Benjamin, a Jew, and Chase, when managing our national finances in a perilous time, owed much of his success to the constant advice of a New York Jew.

That you never see a Jew tramp or a Jew drunkard is a proverb, that you never meet a Jew beggar is a commonplace, and it is a statistical fact that there are relatively fewer inmates of our hospitals, jails, and work-houses furnished by the Jews than any other race contributes.

Convert the Jews! Let us first convert our modern Christians to genuine Christianity. Suppress the Jews! A score of Russian czars cannot do it. Every people on earth has tried it and failed. They have outlived the Tudors and the Plantagenets, the Romanoffs, the tyranny of Spain, the dynasties of France, Charlemagne, Constantine, the Cæsars, the Babylonian kings and the Egyptian Pharaohs. It was God's own race for 4,000 years, and the awful persecution it has survived for 2,000 more, stamps it as a race still bearing some mysterious relation to the plans of the Eternal. The beauty and fidelity of Jewish women command my homage, and among wealthy and educated Jews the exquisite refinement of Jewesses, their culture and high breeding, blended with a sort of Oriental grace and dignity, put them among the most charming women in the world.

But the Jew is tricky! Is he? Were you never taken in by a Methodist class leader on a real estate trade? Did you ever get into close quarters with a Presbyterian speculator? Did you ever buy mining stock on the representations of an Episcopalian broker? Did you ever take a man's word any quicker because he was a Baptist or a Roman Catholic? Did you ever see a stone weighing twenty pounds concealed in a bale of cotton grown by a Southerner? Did you never find lard in the butter sold by a New England Puritan?

The belief that the Jew is more dishonest than the Gentile is one half nonsense and the other half prejudice and falsehood. The anti-Jewish feeling which now seems to be rising again is unchristian, inhuman, and unamerican. No man can share it who believes in the universal fatherhood of God and the universal brotherhood of man.—*Geo. R. Wendling.*

FAITHFUL MINISTERS.

BY J. H. MILLER.

THE Bible sets forth the idea of God's Word being committed into the hands of faithful men. Paul while in bonds, Eph. 6: 20, made known his affairs to his Ephesian brethren by a faithful servant, namely, Tychicus, a beloved brother and faithful minister in the Lord.

In all ages of the world, the church prospered when carefully presided over by those who were called "faithful men." "The Lord is faithful, who will establish you and keep you from evil." 2 Thess. 3: 3 The church at Colossia had faithful brethren. Col. 1: 2. Paul had need of their faith and prayed for them.

If it took faithful men in the early Christian church, to prosper the Lord's work, why is it not just as necessary now? Paul speaks of Abraham, saying, "In thee shall all nations be blessed." So then they which be of faith are blessed with faithful Abraham. Gal. 3: 8, 9. We now refer to the old Israelitish church. Whenever the leaders, or men, proved unfaithful, the church lost her power. See 1 Sam. 15; Josh. 7. The church should have faithful men to carry on the Lord's work. Ministers who are not faithful to the trust, will not do good service for the Lord. The Master gave us ministers as well as apostles. He also commanded us to "go into all the world and preach the Gospel." This work should be placed in the hands of "none but faithful men."

Ministers, evangelists and missionaries should be faithful workers; if not, the work will be crippled and they will sustain loss. Ministers who do evangelistic work should dismiss, as much as possible, the cares of this life. I am made to feel happy that our Annual Meeting has guarded the evangelistic and missionary work so well. In 1877 a query came before that body, saying: "Will District Meeting petition Annual Conference to suggest to all the churches the necessity of restraining Brethren from traveling among the churches, when said evangelists will not, both by precept and example, faithfully maintain and urge the adoption of the recognized order of the General Brotherhood in the matter of dress, including also fully the doctrine of non-conformity to the world, as held by our faithful brethren, and thus have each branch of the church watchful in guarding against sowing the seeds of discord among Brethren? And we do petition that the Annual Meeting grant the foregoing petition to the District Meeting." (Classified Minutes, page 133.)

Our State District Mission Boards should be very careful whom they select and send out into new fields of labor. If a minister is sent out who is out of order, and will not hold up the established order of the church, his converts will pattern after him, for indeed he cannot stamp the plain Gospel order upon the hearts of any of his converts, if he is out of order himself.

Should some brother enforce discipline upon that church, the response would be, "We were converted by brother A. He dressed after the fashion of the world, and neither will we promise to change."

Such came under my notice some years ago. A minister, who did not have the appearance of a brother, was called into a congregation to hold a series of meetings. Several were added to the church. Soon after that, the annual visit was paid. Several deacons came to the house of those new converts to visit them. They refused, saying, "No one can visit us but that preacher who converted and baptized us." The preacher's appearance not indicating faithfulness, and he having tolerated things that the church could not endorse, caused all this trouble.

Although twenty years have elapsed, the church has not recovered from that shock. That unfaithful minister, who, perhaps, was born of the flesh, found his way back into the world again. The churches should be careful whom they call as evangelists to do their preaching. The Home Mission Board should look well to this one particular. I presume the General Mission Board keeps an open eye in that direction. The Annual Meeting of 1890 accepted the request and plan for securing suitable brethren on missionary work. I feel as though it should be published in the GOSPEL MESSENGER for the benefit of all concerned. It reads as follows:

"Let churches, having brethren possessing the necessary qualifications, from time to time hold elections to increase our ministry, with a view of meeting the growing demand for preaching the Gospel, both at home and in all the various localities of the missionary field of the world. And let all ministers, when elected, be advised and urged to hold themselves in readiness as much as possible, to be used by the church wherever they may be needed."

If such lessons as we get from the Bible and the General Brotherhood, would be more closely observed, our local churches would be in better working order. A steady, healthy growth is commendable. By getting the right men in the right place, the church will prosper and God's name glorified.

Goshen, Ind.

"IF your cup seems too bitter, if your burden seems too heavy, be sure that it is the wounded hand that is holding the cup, and that it is he who carried the cross that is carrying the burden."

The Gospel Messenger

Is the recognized organ of the German Baptist or Brethren's church, and advocating the form of doctrine taught in the New Testament and pleads for a return to apostolic and primitive Christianity.

It recognizes the New Testament as the only infallible rule of faith and practice, and maintains that Faith toward God, Repentance from dead works, Regeneration of the heart and mind, baptism by Trine immersion for remission of sins unto the reception of the Holy Ghost by the laying on of hands, are the means of adoption into the household of God,—the church militant.

It also maintains that Feet-washing, as taught in John 13, both by example and command of Jesus, should be observed in the church.

That the Lord's Supper, instituted by Christ and as universally observed by the apostles and the early Christians, is a full meal, and, in connection with the Communion, should be taken in the evening or after the close of the day.

That the Salutation of the Holy Kiss, or Kiss of Charity, is binding upon the followers of Christ.

That War and Retaliation are contrary to the spirit and self-denying principles of the religion of Jesus Christ.

That the principle of Plain Dressing and of Non-conformity to the world, as taught in the New Testament, should be observed by the followers of Christ.

That the Scriptural duty of Anointing the Sick with Oil, in the Name of the Lord, James 5: 14, is binding upon all Christians.

It also advocates the church's duty to support Missionary and Tract Work, thus giving to the Lord for the spread of the Gospel and for the conversion of sinners.

In short, it is a vindicator of all that Christ and the apostles have enjoined upon us, and aims, amid the conflicting theories and discords of modern Christendom, to point out ground that all must concede to be infallibly safe.

☞ The above principles of our Fraternity are set forth on our "Brethren's Envelopes." Use them! Price, 15 cents per package; 40 cents per hundred.

and,—but the world's roll of great soldiers, authors, musicians, painters, poets, philosophers and financiers contains more Hebrew names than I could recite in many hours.

Are you looking for an aristocracy of wealth? The combined financial power of the Jews in Europe can prevent the floating of almost any national loan which may be put upon the markets of the world!

It is a spurious, false Christianity that hates Jews. The mystery of the Incarnation found expression in the flesh and blood of a Jew, and therefore, in a sense, we worship a Jew. We get our Ten Commandments—the very foundation of our civilization—through the Jews. We sing Jewish psalms, are uplifted by the passion and poetry of Jewish prophets, and rely on Jewish biographies for the only history we have of Christ. We get our Pauline theology from a Jew, and we catch our clearest glimpse of the next world through the sublime apocalyptic vision of a Jew. Then, forsooth, we Christians turn about and sneer at Jews!

I have conversed with teachers of philosophy who spoke slightingly of the Jews, and yet were teaching with enthusiasm ideas which they have absorbed from Miamonides and Spinoza, the two greatest philosophers, omitting Kant, since Plato's day—both of them Jews.

I have heard musicians denounce Jews, and then spend days and nights trying to interpret the beauties of Rossini, Meyerbeer, and Mendelssohn,—all Jews.

I talked the other day with a gifted actress, and heard both her and her husband sweepingly condemn, confidentially, of course, the whole race of Jews, and yet that woman would give half her remaining life if she could reach the heights which the great queen of tragedy, Rachel, trod with such majesty and power — and Rachel was a Jewess.

Here in Washington I have heard aspiring politicians, when beyond the reach of the reporter's pencil, sneer at the Jews, and yet it was a Jew who made England's Queen Empress of India, and it was a Jew who was for years the adroit and sagacious chairman of the National Committee of one of our great political parties. The brainiest man in the Southern Confederacy was Judah P. Benjamin, a Jew, and Chase, when managing our national finances in a perilous time, owed much of his success to the constant advice of a New York Jew.

That you never see a Jew tramp or a Jew drunkard is a proverb, that you never meet a Jew beggar is a commonplace, and it is a statistical fact that there are relatively fewer inmates of our hospitals, jails, and poor-houses furnished by the Jews than any other race contributes.

Convert the Jews! Let us first convert our modern Christians to genuine Christianity. Suppress the Jews! A score of Russian czars cannot do it. Every people on earth has tried it and failed. They have outlived the Tudors and the Plantagenets, the Romanoffs, the tyranny of Spain, the dynasties of France, Charlemagne, Constantine, the Cæsars, the Babylonian kings and the Egyptian Pharaohs. It was God's own race for 4,000 years, and the awful persecution it has survived for 2,000 more, stamps it as a race still bearing some mysterious relation to the plans of the Eternal. The beauty and fidelity of Jewish women command my homage, and among wealthy and educated Jews the exquisite refinement of Jewesses, their culture and high breeding, blended with a sort of Oriental grace and dignity, put them among the most charming women in the world.

But the Jew is tricky! Is he? Were you never taken in by a Methodist class leader on a real estate trade? Did you ever get into close quar-

ters with a Presbyterian speculator? Did you ever buy mining stock on the representations of an Episcopalian broker? Did you ever take a man's word any quicker because he was a Baptist or a Roman Catholic? Did you ever see a stone weighing twenty pounds concealed in a bale of cotton grown by a Southerner? Did you never find lard in the butter sold by a New England Puritan?

The belief that the Jew is more dishonest than the Gentile is one half nonsense and the other half prejudice and falsehood. The anti-Jewish feeling which now seems to be rising again is unchristian, inhuman, and unamerican. No man can share it who believes in the universal fatherhood of God and the universal brotherhood of man.—*Geo. R. Wendling.*

FAITHFUL MINISTERS.

BY J. H. MILLER.

THE Bible sets forth the idea of God's Word being committed into the hands of faithful men. Paul while in bonds, Eph. 6: 20, made known his affairs to his Ephesian brethren by a faithful servant, namely, Tychicus, a beloved brother and faithful minister in the Lord.

In all ages of the world, the church prospered when carefully presided over by those who were called "faithful men." "The Lord is faithful, who will establish you and keep you from evil." 2 Thess. 3: 3. The church at Colossia had faithful brethren. Col. 1: 2. Paul had need of their faith and prayed for them.

If it took faithful men in the early Christian church, to prosper the Lord's work, why is it not just as necessary now? Paul speaks of Abraham, saying, "In thee shall all nations be blessed." So then they which be of faith are blessed with faithful Abraham. Gal. 3: 8, 9. We now refer to the old Israelitish church. Whenever the leaders, or men, proved unfaithful, the church lost her power. See 1 Sam. 15; Josh. 7. The church should have faithful men to carry on the Lord's work. Ministers who are not faithful to the trust, will not do good service for the Lord. The Master gave us ministers as well as apostles. He also commanded us to "go into all the world and preach the Gospel." This work should be placed in the hands of "none but faithful men."

Ministers, evangelists and missionaries should be faithful workers; if not, the work will be crippled and they will sustain loss. Ministers who do evangelistic work should dismiss, as much as possible, the cares of this life. I am made to feel happy that our Annual Meeting has guarded the evangelistic and missionary work so well. In 1877 a query came before that body, saying: "Will District Meeting petition Annual Conference to suggest to all the churches the necessity of restraining Brethren from traveling among the churches, when said evangelists will not, both by precept and example, faithfully maintain and urge the adoption of the recognized order of the General Brotherhood in the matter of dress, including also fully the doctrine of non-conformity to the world, as held by our faithful brethren, and thus have each branch of the church watchful in guarding against sowing the seeds of discord among Brethren? And we do petition that the Annual Meeting grant the foregoing petition to the District Meeting." (Classified Minutes, page 183.)

Our State District Mission Boards should be very careful whom they select and send out into new fields of labor. If a minister is sent out who is out of order, and will not hold up the established order of the church, his converts will pattern after him, for indeed he cannot stamp the plain Gospel order upon the hearts of any of his converts, if he is out of order himself.

Should some brother enforce discipline upon that church, the response would be, "We were converted by brother A. He dressed after the fashion of the world, and neither will we promise to change."

Such came under my notice some years ago. A minister, who did not have the appearance of a brother, was called into a congregation to hold a series of meetings. Several were added to the church. So far that, the annual visit was paid. Several deacons came to the house of those new converts to visit them. They refused, saying, "No one can visit us but that preacher who converted and baptized us." The preacher's appearance not indicating faithfulness, and he having tolerated things that the church could not endorse, caused all this trouble.

Although twenty years have elapsed, the church has not recovered from that shock. That unfaithful minister, who, perhaps, was born of the flesh, found his way back into the world again. The churches should be careful whom they call as evangelists to do their preaching. The Home Mission Board should look well to this one particular. I presume the General Mission Board keeps an open eye to that direction. The Annual Meeting of 1890 accepted the request and plan for securing suitable brethren on missionary work. I feel as though it should be published in the GOSPEL MESSENGER for the benefit of all concerned. It reads as follows:

"Let churches, having brethren possessing the necessary qualifications, from time to time hold elections to increase our ministry, with a view of meeting the growing demand for preaching the Gospel, both at home and in all the various localities of the missionary field of the world. And let all ministers, when elected, be advised and urged to hold themselves in readiness as much as possible, to be used by the church wherever they may be needed."

If such lessons as we get from the Bible and the General Brotherhood, would be more closely observed, our local churches would be in better working order. A steady, healthy growth is commendable. By getting the right men in the right place, the church will prosper and God's name glorified.

Goshen, Ind.

"IF your cup seems too bitter, if your burden seems too heavy, be sure that it is the wounded hand that is holding the cup, and that it is he who carried the cross that is carrying the burden."

The Gospel Messenger

Is the recognized organ of the German Baptist or Brethren's church, and advocates the form of doctrine taught in the New Testament and pleads for a return to apostolic and primitive Christianity.

It recognizes the New Testament as the only infallible rule of faith and practice, and maintains that Faith toward God, Repentance from dead works, Regeneration of the heart and mind, baptism by Trine immersion for remission of sins unto the reception of the Holy Ghost by the laying on of hands, are the means of adoption into the household of God,—the church militant.

It also maintains that Feet-washing, as taught in John 13, both by example and command of Jesus, should be observed in the church.

That the Lord's Supper, instituted by Christ and as universally observed by the apostles and the early Christians, is a full meal, and, in connection with the Communion, should be taken in the evening or after the close of the day.

That the Salutation of the Holy Kiss, or Kiss of Charity, is binding upon the followers of Christ.

That War and Retaliation are contrary to the spirit and self-denying principles of the religion of Jesus Christ.

That the principle of Plain Dressing and of Non-conformity to the world, as taught in the New Testament, should be observed by the followers of Christ.

That the Scriptural duty of Anointing the Sick with Oil, in the Name of the Lord, James 5: 14, is binding upon all Christians.

It also advocates the church's duty to support Missionary and Tract Work, thus giving to the Lord for the spread of the Gospel and for the conversion of sinners.

In short, it is a vindicator of all that Christ and the apostles have enjoined upon us, and aims, amid the conflicting theories and discords of modern Christendom, to point out ground that all must concede to be scripturally safe.

☞ The above principles of our Fraternity are set forth on our "Brethren's Envelopes." Use them! Price, 15 cents per package; 40 cents per hundred.

to their little ones, and it is always like a blow from an angry hand to me. I look up and see Jesus, around him myriads of children, clinging to his knees, his arms, his neck, his lips, and then back to these, repulsed by those who should love them best of any on earth, and I wonder if that blessed child-lover's words, "Suffer little children to come unto me, and forbid them not, for of such is the kingdom of heaven," have lost their hallowing influence over parents' hearts! The only difference between those who bask in the light of his glorious smiles and these that we call ours, is: Those have passed beyond the reach of sin, while these may have sin's fiery way to pass. O, then, let them have a blessed staff of love to lean upon while passing through!

(To be Continued.)

La Porte, Ind.

NON-CONFORMITY.

BY DAVID E. CRIPE.

JESUS says, "That which is highly esteemed among men is abomination in the sight of God." Nothing is more highly esteemed among the high, the proud, the unregenerated men of the world, than fine and fashionable attire. Unless there is some very strong reason why we should follow the fashions of the world, it is well to stop and ask if this is not one of those things which is an abomination in the sight of God.

If we would be followers of the meek and lowly Lamb of God, we cannot follow the world, "For the friendship of the world is enmity with God. Whosoever therefore will be a friend of the world is the enemy of God." James 4: 4. There is no half-way ground. We cannot serve two masters; we cannot be the friend of both God and the world. "Choose you this day whom you will serve."

God has always warned his people against idolatry, and fearfully punished them for worshiping idols. Loving fashion and following her dictates is as much idolatry as the worship of Baal ever was. The child of God should have nothing to do with it. Paul commands us to "present our bodies a living sacrifice, holy, acceptable unto God." To do this our bodies must be made pure, presented unto God on the altar of his service, and if he accepts them, they are his forever. We can never get them back again, while we serve him. "Ye are not your own, but are bought with a price."

If, then, our bodies belong to God, we have no right whatever to lend them to fashion, in order that she might make a display upon them of her gaudy array. If they are his, they must be clothed for him in humility.

Again Paul says, "Be not conformed to this world: but be ye transformed by the renewing of your minds." The mind must be renewed, the affections must be changed. The things we once loved we now dislike; the things we once hated we now love. This change of mind will bring about this transformation. Transform is the changing of the form, as transfigure is the changing of the form or figure. The two terms are almost the same. The transfiguration of Christ upon the mount is a beautiful figure of the transformation every one must undergo when he becomes a child of God, and receives the comforting of heavenly messengers. His face lost all stain of earth, all traces of pain, of care and sorrow, and became "bright as the sun," while he communed with Moses and Elias. His raiment became "white and glistening," "white as the light." All the material parts of his raiment which partook of the impurities of earth, were removed, else it could not have been white as the light.

So, too, should we put away from our garments everything that bears the stain of impure desires of the lust of the eye and the pride of life. Our garment should be as pure and free from all taint of worldliness, as that was which was white as the light. After the Savior's comforters left him, his face and raiment resumed their natural appearance. But, as we are promised that the Comforter shall never forsake us, we should continually be transformed both in face and attire.

"Ye are a chosen generation, a royal priesthood, a holy nation, a peculiar people; that ye should shew forth the praises of him who hath called you out of darkness into his marvellous light." 1 Pet. 2: 9. The priests under the Mosaic Law were required to wear a certain, prescribed garment, so every one could recognize them as priests. The garment was unlike that worn by the common people, but that of itself was not sufficient. It was not enough that it should be just a little different from the fashionable dress of the day, but it must be made after a certain pattern. The-priests of the same rank must all be dressed alike. Peter says if we follow Christ, we are priests, and priests of the highest lineage,—"royal priests." Then we, too, should wear a priestly garment, entirely different from the world, so that all can recognize us by sight as a "peculiar people." In this way can we show to the world more readily than any other, that we have heeded the call, "Come ye out from among them, and be ye a separate people," and that we are not ashamed to have every one know that we profess to follow Christ, even down into the valley of humiliation.

Akron, Ind.

A POWERLESS RELIGION.—2 Tim. 3: 5.

BY W. M. LYON.

Number Two.

SINCE our last letter I trust we have compared closely and critically our "form of godliness" with the actual expressions of our lives. If so, what has been the result? Does my *life* express more for Christ than it does for the world?

The church is a great orchard and the world's estimate of its value is based on the quality and quantity of its fruit. The question is not, "How many leaves are on that tree," or "What is the shape of its leaves," but "How much and what *kind of fruit* does it bear?"

"Herein is my Father glorified that ye bear much fruit; so shall ye be my disciples." John 15: 8. In John 15: 5 he refers to both quantity and quality. "ABIDE IN ME." Abiding in Christ is for the branch to draw sap from the true vine. That means a prolific bearer of Christian fruit. A large, leafy tree, with no fruit, is the professor of godliness, but not the possessor. The sign hangs out conspicuously, but the luscious counterpart is lacking. It is deceptive, misleading.

A large pile of leaves and no fruit makes a very soft bed for infidels to lie down on. Analyze the leafy, fruitless professor and the product is: A POWERLESS RELIGION,—a "form of godliness," but no power.

Now let us take another step. Did anybody ever see or hear of a person going to an orchard for a load of fruit, and through mistake, gather a load of leaves? Religiously, we find many such,—people who lug along a great load of leaves and think it fruit, or at least, actions would so speak for them. They cry, Pharisaically, "Fruit, fruit," while the world passes along and says, "Leaves! Leaves! Nothing but leaves! You make a splendid shade; we can *rest* under it, but we can't *live* on shade."

I have said that many mistake leaves for fruit. Can this be possible? Yes. Please turn to Matt.

7. Verses 16 and 20 demand fruit. Verse 15 tells of leaves and no fruit. Verses 21 and 22 show these great leafy professors making their final claim. Now turn to Matt. 25: 34-40 and mark the contrast. Here we have *fruit*.

But let us now make a closer and more critical application of our subject.

1. *As a collective body.*

2. *As individuals.*

First, notice the collective body as engaged on love-feast occasions. How very significant is each part of these solemn services! Look at those who stoop to wash each other's feet. Here we have the rich and the poor, the great and the small, the high and the low, all declaring themselves to be "one in Christ Jesus." Distinction here is said to be a stranger. The world looks on with admiration and respect. They say, "Surely a tree with such beautiful foliage should produce the most delightful fruit in abundance." The scene now changes and the bystanders now behold this same body emphasizing their former declarations by eating together. And again, as though to place still greater emphasis on this same central truth, they bind themselves together with the Christian salutation, and then partake of the sacred symbols of the broken body and shed blood of him who has promised to be their life and salvation. The solemn drama now ended and the world now starts out to search for the fruit that should be expected on the branches of this promising tree. We now reach the second division: *As individuals.*

I here venture the assertion that, if, upon investigation, the fruit be found to correspond with the foliage, we would not have much trouble to win souls to Christ. But what may we expect, when, upon investigation, it is found otherwise?

Suppose the world follow up brother A. and look for fruit. He is a wealthy brother. At love-feast, in stooping to wash the feet of Bro. B., who is a very poor brother, he said, "I hereby manifest a disposition to place myself on an equality with my poor brother, and, if necessary, to stoop down and lift him up." A few days after, when Bro. A., in company with others, meets Bro. B. on the street, somehow he does not recognize him.

A little later Bro. B. unfortunately becomes a subject for charity, but when the subscription is passed around, the action of the pencil on the paper tells a different tale from that of Bro. A. as he sat at the love-feast table with Bro. B., neither did it correspond with that act of Christian salutation which, being interpreted, means: "I solemnly pledge myself to be your helper in time of need and love you even as Christ has loved me." Here, then, we have drawn another picture of a powerless religion, a "form of godliness," but denying the power,—leaves, but no fruit. The world says, "Show me your fruit and then I'll cease talking about your leaves." Christ makes the same demand. Let us not be deceived. How much of Gal. 5: 22, 23 do we bear?

Union Bridge, Md.

»GOD having in this world placed us in a sea, and troubled the sea with a continual storm, hath appointed the church for a ship, and religion to be the stern, but there is no .port but death. Death is that harbor whither God hath designed every one, that he 'may find rest from the trouble of his soul."

»THERE is as much difference between the sufferings of the saints and those of the ungodly, as there is between the cords with which an executioner pinions a condemned malefactor and the bandages wherewith a tender surgeon binds his patient.

to their little ones, and it is always like a blow from an angry hand to me. I look up and see Jesus, around him myriads of children, clinging to his knees, his arms, his neck, his lips, and then back to these, repulsed by those who should love them best of any on earth, and I wonder if that blessed child-lover's words, "Suffer little children to come unto me, and forbid them not, for of such is the kingdom of heaven," have lost their hallowing influence over parents' hearts! The only difference between those who bask in the light of his glorious smiles and those that we call ours, is: Those have passed beyond the reach of sin, while these may have sin's fiery way to pass. O, then, let them have a blessed staff of love to lean upon while passing through!

(To be Continued.)

La Porte, Ind.

NON-CONFORMITY.

BY DAVID B. CRIPE.

JESUS says, "That which is highly esteemed among men is abomination in the sight of God." Nothing is more highly esteemed among the high, the proud, the unregenerated men of the world, than fine and fashionable attire. Unless there is some very strong reason why we should follow the fashions of the world, it is well to stop and ask if this is not one of those things which is an abomination in the sight of God.

If we would be followers of the meek and lowly Lamb of God, we cannot follow the world. "For the friendship of the world is enmity with God. Whosoever therefore will be a friend of the world is the enemy of God." James 4: 4. There is no half-way ground. We cannot serve two masters; we cannot be the friend of both God and the world. "Choose you this day whom you will serve."

God has always warned his people against idolatry, and fearfully punished them for worshiping idols. Loving fashion and following her dictates is as much idolatry as the worship of Baal ever was. The child of God should have nothing to do with it. Paul commands us to "present our bodies a living sacrifice, holy, acceptable unto God." To do this our bodies must be made pure, presented unto God on the altar of his service, and if he accepts them, they are his forever. We can never get them back again, while we serve him. "Ye are not your own, but are bought with a price."

If, then, our bodies belong to God, we have no right whatever to lend them to fashion, in order that she might make a display upon them of her gaudy array. If they are his, they must be clothed for him in humility.

Again Paul says, "Be not conformed to this world: but be ye transformed by the renewing of your minds." The mind must be renewed, the affections must be changed. The things we once loved we now dislike; the things we once hated we now love. This change of mind will bring about this transformation. Transform is the changing of the form, as transfigure is the changing of the form or figure. The two terms are almost the same. The transfiguration of Christ upon the mount is a beautiful figure of the transformation every one must undergo when he becomes a child of God, and receives the comforting of heavenly messengers. His face lost all stain of earth, all traces of pain, of care and sorrow, and became "bright as the sun," while he communed with Moses and Elias. His raiment became "white and glistening," "white as the light." All the material parts of his raiment which partook of the impurities of earth, were removed, else it could not have been white as the light.

So, too, should we put away from our garments everything that bears the stain of impure desires of the lust of the eye and the pride of life. Our garment should be as pure and free from all taint of worldliness, as that which was white as the light. After the Savior's comforters left him, his face and raiment resumed their natural appearance. But, as we are promised that the Comforter shall never forsake us, we should continually be transformed both in face and attire.

"Ye are a chosen generation, a royal priesthood, a holy nation, a peculiar people; that ye should shew forth the praises of him who hath called you out of darkness into his marvellous light." 1 Pet. 2: 9. The priests under the Mosaic Law were required to wear a certain, prescribed garment, so every one could recognize them as priests. The garment was unlike that worn by the common people, but that of itself was not sufficient. It was not enough that it should be just a little different from the fashionable dress of the day, but it must be made after a certain pattern. The priests of the same rank must all be dressed alike. Peter says if we follow Christ, we are priests, and priests of the highest lineage,—"royal priests." Then we, too, should wear a priestly garment, entirely different from the world, so that all can recognize us by sight as a "peculiar people." In this way can we show to the world more readily than any other, that we have heeded the call, "Come ye out from among them, and be ye a separate people," and that we are not ashamed to have every one know that we profess to follow Christ, even down into the valley of humiliation.

Akron, Ind.

A POWERLESS RELIGION.—2 Tim. 3: 5.

BY W. M. LYON.

Number Two.

SINCE our last letter I trust we have compared closely and critically our "form of godliness" with the actual expressions of our lives. If so, what has been the result? Does my life express more for Christ than it does for the world?

The church is a great orchard and the world's estimate of its value is based on the quality and quantity of its fruit. The question is not, "How many leaves are on that tree," or "What is the shape of its leaves," but "How much and what kind of fruit does it bear?"

"Herein is my Father glorified that ye bear much fruit; so shall ye be my disciples." John 15: 8. In John 15: 5 he refers to both quantity and quality. "ABIDE IN ME." Abiding in Christ is for the branch to draw sap from the true vine. That means a prolific bearer of Christian fruit. A large, leafy tree, with no fruit, is the professor of godliness, but not the possessor. The sign hangs out conspicuously, but the luscious counterpart is lacking. It is deceptive, misleading.

A large pile of leaves and no fruit makes a very soft bed for infidels to lie down on. Analyze the leafy, fruitless professor and the product is: A POWERLESS RELIGION,—a "form of godliness," but no power.

Now let us take another step. Did anybody ever see or hear of a person going to an orchard for a load of fruit, and through mistake, gather a load of leaves? Religiously, we find many such,—people who lug along a great load of leaves and think it fruit, or at least, actions would so speak for them. They cry, Pharisaically, "Fruit, fruit," while the world passes along and says, "Leaves! Leaves! Nothing but leaves! You make a splendid shade; we can rest under it, but we can't live on shade."

I have said that many mistake leaves for fruit. Can this be possible? Yes. Please turn to Matt.

7. Verses 16 and 20 demand fruit. Verse 15 tells of leaves and no fruit. Verses 21 and 22 show these great leafy professors making their final claim. Now turn to Matt. 25; 34-40 and mark the contrast. Here we have fruit.

But let us now make a closer and more critical application of our subject.

1. As a collective body.
2. As individuals.

First, notice the collective body as engaged on love-feast occasions. How very significant is each part of these solemn services! Look at those who stoop to wash each other's feet. Here we have the rich and the poor, the great and the small, the high and the low, all declaring themselves to be "one in Christ Jesus." Distinction here is said to be a stranger. The world looks on with admiration and respect. They say, "Surely a tree with such beautiful foliage should produce the most delightful fruit in abundance." The scene now changes and the bystanders now behold this same body emphasizing their former declarations by eating together. And again, as though to place still greater emphasis on this same central truth, they bind themselves together with the Christian salutation, and then partake of the sacred symbols of the broken body and shed blood of him who has promised to be their life and salvation. The solemn drama now ended and the world now starts out to search for the fruit that should be expected on the branches of this promising tree. We now reach the second division: As individuals.

I here venture the assertion that, if, upon investigation, the fruit be found to correspond with the foliage, we would not have much trouble to win souls to Christ. But what may we expect, when, upon investigation, it is found otherwise?

Suppose the world follow up brother A. and look for fruit. He is a wealthy brother. At love-feast, in stooping to wash the feet of Bro. B., who is a very poor brother, he said, "I hereby manifest a disposition to place myself on an equality with my poor brother, and, if necessary, to stoop down and lift him up." A few days after, when Bro. A., in company with others, meets Bro. B. on the street, somehow he does not recognize him.

A little later Bro. B. unfortunately becomes a subject for charity, but when the subscription is passed around, the action of the pencil on the paper tells a different tale from that of Bro. A. as he sat at the love-feast table with Bro. B., neither did it correspond with that act of Christian salutation which, being interpreted, means: "I solemnly pledge myself to be your helper in time of need and love you even as Christ has loved me." Here, then, we have drawn another picture of a powerless religion, a "form of godliness," but denying the power,—leaves, but no fruit. The world says, "Show me your fruit and then I'll cease talking about your leaves." Christ makes the same demand. Let us not be deceived. How much of Gal. 5: 22, 23 do we bear?

Union Bridge, Md.

"GOD having in this world placed us in a sea, and troubled the sea with a continual storm, hath appointed the church for a ship, and religion to be the stern, but there is no port but death. Death is that harbor whither God hath designed every one, that he may find rest from the trouble of his soul."

"THERE is as much difference between the sufferings of the saints and those of the ungodly, as there is between the cords with which an executioner pinions a condemned malefactor and the bandages wherewith a tender surgeon binds his patient.

A BROTHER and sister who live at an isolated point where they can enjoy preaching by the Brethren only a few times during the year, have sent $75.00 to Bro. Galen B. Royer, to be used for charitable purposes, part of it going to the sufferers in Russia. God will certainly bless these acts of charity.

QUERISTS' DEPARTMENT.

"What would be the duty of a deacon, in case there were applicants for baptism, and no ministering brother could be had in a reasonable time? Should we advise the applicants to wait, or would it be the duty of a deacon to baptize them?
    E. MILLER.

IN a regular way only elders, and ministers in the second degree, are authorized to administer the ordinance of baptism. In case of special necessity a minister in the first degree may also baptize, but it must be by the permission of one higher in office, or the advice of such members as it may be possible for him to consult. If the case is an urgent one, and the work must be attended to, and the members so advise, then it will be in harmony with our practice for one in the first degree to administer the sacred rite. Concerning a deacon baptizing, we have never known a case of that kind among our people. But if there are applicants for baptism, and it is deemed necessary that the work should be attended to at once, and no minister can be had within reasonable time, we would then advise that the members present be consulted, and if they decide that the rite may be administered by one of the deacons present, we should not think it improper for him to do so, being careful, however, to fully carry out the regulations of the general Brotherhood in regard to laying the order of the church before the applicants, and thus pursue the course usually followed by the Brethren. We can see nothing wrong about a course of this kind. It might not be out of place for the brethren, where the case referred to occurred, to seek the advice of the Annual Meeting on the question.

Will you please answer the following question: Where ought the wine for the Communion to be kept in time of the love-feast, on the table, or away from the Supper, in a basket, while the Supper is being eaten?   JOHN FRIEDLY.

This is one of the questions concerning which we have different usages among us. In this part of the Brotherhood it is our practice to place the Communion bread and wine on the table, and nestly cover them, before commencing feet-washing. After the close of the Supper, and during the reading of the chapter treating of the death and sufferings of Christ, the bread is uncovered and laid in order. The wine is not uncovered until the bread has been eaten. Then the wine is uncovered, two cups are filled and thanks returned. In some parts of the Brotherhood the bread and wine are not put on the table until after thanks have been returned for the Supper. A careful reading of that part of the Gospels, speaking of the instituting of the Lord's Supper, has always impressed us with the idea that both the bread and wine were on the table at the time the Savior partook of the Supper with his disciples. Since there is a slight difference of opinion on this question, it becomes us to exercise forbearance towards each other and live in peace. Whatever will bring about general peace in your congregation is the thing that we recommend. Peace and love in a congregation is a grand thing, and the church that abounds in this attainment will soon be blessed with sufficient wisdom to see alike on all similar questions of difference,

What is the usual order of conducting Sunday-schools among the Brethren? Some years ago we used the Brethren, we think with good success, but last year we used the Bible only, without any helps, but it seems to not have given the best of satisfaction. If we cannot do better I think we would better not open the school again next summer. Will you please give us some advice.   * * *

The brother, writing the above, requests us to withhold his name. This is something that we are not in the habit of doing, but will do so in this instance.

First of all we want to say, Do not think of abandoning your Sunday-school work. Make up your minds to open your school next summer, quarterlies or no quarterlies. Do not permit a difference of that kind to stop the school. We are decidedly in favor of quarterlies, and know that they are a great help, but if we lived in a neighborhood where they were not wanted, we would still enter the Sunday-school and work with earnestness. Paul says: "I am made all things to all men, that I might by all means save some." 1 Cor. 9: 22. This wisdom will come in good play here. Live in peace and keep the Sunday-school alive. It will want the quarterlies after awhile.

Concerning the order of the church in regard to the use of quarterlies,—that is left optional with the churches and Sunday-schools. Some use them and others do not. A very large majority of the schools, we think, use the quarterlies, and in the course of a few years we may expect all of our schools to use them. We have been engaged in Sunday-school work more or less for twenty-seven years, and our experience, as well as observation, teaches us that quarterlies are a great help indeed, where properly used. They are a great aid in helping the pupils to understand the lessons, to say nothing of the system they bring out in the line of study. These lesson helps, however, ought to be used in connection with the Bible and a good Bible map. In the use of helps much depends upon the teacher. The teacher who must look on the book for every question and also for each answer, is not likely to make the very best use of quarterlies, nor to teach his pupils the best method of studying the Bible.

Please explain John 5: 28, 29. What is in the grave—with the body until the resurrection that shall hear the Voice? Is the soul in the grave with the body until the resurrection? Many of us here would like to know.   D. B. HENRY.

The Scripture referred to reads as follows: "Marvel not at this: for the hour is coming, in the which all that are in the graves shall hear his voice, and shall come forth; they that have done good, unto the resurrection of life; and they that have done evil, unto the resurrection of damnation." John 5: 28, 29. We know that the soul does not go with the body to the grave, for Solomon says: "Then shall the dust return to the earth as it was, and the spirit shall return to God who gave it." Eccl. 12: 7. The term spirit here refers to the immortal part of man the same as the term soul does in the sense used by our querist. Under the altar John saw "the souls of them that were slain for the Word of God and for the testimony which they held." Rev. 6: 9. The first resurrection had not yet taken place when John saw these souls under the altar, hence the bodies still remained in the grave, while the souls were with God. In 1 Kings 17: 21, 22 we have a very clear statement concerning the soul leaving the body at death: "And he stretched himself upon the child three times, and cried unto the Lord, and said, O Lord my God, I pray thee, let this child's soul come into him again, And the Lord

heard the voice of Elijah; and the soul of the child came into him again, and he revived."

Concerning the death of Jesus Luke says: "And when Jesus had cried with a loud voice, he said, Father, into thy hands I commend my spirit: and having said thus, he gave up the ghost." Luke 23: 46. Here Jesus committed his spirit into the care of his Father, while his body went to the tomb. Stephen, being full of the Holy Ghost, held the same view concerning the spirit of man going to God at death, for when he was dying he said, "Lord Jesus, receive my spirit." Acts 7: 59. As additional evidence, to show that the soul and body are separated at death, we quote from the Revised Version, Acts 2: 27: "Because thou wilt not leave my soul in Hades, neither wilt thou permit thine holy one to see corruption." Hades means the abode of departed spirits. The language is quoted by Peter from Ps. 16: 8 and refers to the Savior, applying to his condition during death. His soul was not left in Hades with other spirits, but came forth and reunited with the body on the third day. From all these Scriptures we are led to infer that the soul, or spirit, does not go to the grave with the body, but is in the care of God while the body is resting in the grave.

The voice that calls the nations from the dead will be heard not only by the bodies that are in the graves, but also by the spirits that are in the care of God.

The following query and answer which we clip from the *Christian Standard*, will throw some light on a question that is occasionally sent us:

If Jesus was crucified on Friday, as has been commonly taught, how can the following statement be harmonized with the Friday idea? "To-day is the third day *since* these things were done" (Luke 24: 21). The above passage was spoken on Sunday following the crucifixion. If Sunday was the third day *since* the occurrence, would not Thursday be crucifixion day, Friday "the first day, Saturday the second and Sunday "the third day *since* these things were done"?
    CHAS. H. WARNER.

"The mere reading of Matt. 27: 62-64 will throw light on the way in which the people of the New Testament times spoke of the days since which certain things were done, which was to count the day on which an act was performed the first day, and the next day after, the second day. 'Now the next day, that followed the day of the preparation, the chief priests and Pharisees came together unto Pilate, saying, Sir, we remember that that deceiver said while he was yet alive, After three days I will rise again. Command therefore that the sepulcher be made sure until the third day, lest his disciples come by night and steal him away, and say unto the people, He is risen from the dead.' 'Until the third day' explains what they understood by 'after three days.' •

"Jesus said that he would 'be raised again the third day.' Matt. 16: 21. Mark makes him say that 'after three days' he would rise again. These seemingly differing expressions passed in those days as equivalents and would not be misunderstood by any. It is said, in Gen. 42: 17, that Joseph put his brethren into ward 'three days'; and in the next verse we learn that they were released 'on the third day.' To the people who asked Rehoboam to make their burdens lighter, he said, 'Depart ye for three days, then come again to me.' They went away, and it is said that they 'came again the third day as the king had appointed.' 2 Kings 12: 5, 12. In the light of the current use of the language referred to, there is no difficulty in harmonizing the different forms of expression."
    J. H. M.

A BROTHER and sister who live at an isolated point where they can enjoy preaching by the Brethren only a few times during the year, have sent $75.00 to Bro. Galen B. Boyer, to be used for charitable purposes, part of it going to the sufferers in Russia. God will certainly bless these acts of charity.

QUERISTS' DEPARTMENT.

"What would be the duty of a deacon, in case there were applicants for baptism, and no ministering brother could be had in a reasonable time? Should we advise the applicants to wait, or would it be the duty of a deacon to baptize them?
E. MILLER.

IN a regular way only elders, and ministers in the second degree, are authorized to administer the ordinance of baptism. In case of special necessity a minister in the first degree may also baptize, but it must be by the permission of one higher in office, or the advice of such members as it may be possible for him to consult. If the case is an urgent one, and the work must be attended to, and the members so advise, then it will be in harmony with our practice for one in the first degree to administer the sacred rite. Concerning a deacon baptizing, we have never known a case of that kind among our people. But if there are applicants for baptism, and it is deemed necessary that the work should be attended to at once, and no minister can be had within reasonable time, we would then advise that the members present be consulted, and if they decide that the rite may be administered by one of the deacons present, we should not think it improper for him to do so, being careful, however, to fully carry out the regulations of the general Brotherhood in regard to laying the order of the church before the applicants, and thus pursue the course usually followed by the Brethren. We can see nothing wrong about a course of this kind. It might not be out of place for the brethren, where the case referred to occurred, to seek the advice of the Annual Meeting on the question.

Will you please answer the following question: Where ought the wine for the Communion to be kept in time of the love-feast, on the table, or away from the Supper, in a basket, while the Supper is being eaten?. JOHN FRIEDLY.

This is one of the questions concerning which we have different usages among us. In this part of the Brotherhood it is our practice to place the Communion bread and wine on the table, and neatly cover them, before commencing feet-washing. After the close of the Supper, and during the reading of the chapter treating of the death and sufferings of Christ, the bread is uncovered and laid in order. The wine is not uncovered until the bread has been eaten. Then the wine is uncovered, two cups are filled and thanks returned. In some parts of the Brotherhood the bread and wine are not put on the table until after thanks have been returned for the Supper. A careful reading of that part of the Gospels, speaking of the instituting of the Lord's Supper, has always impressed us with the idea that both the bread and wine were on the table at the time the Savior partook of the Supper with his disciples. Since there is a slight difference of opinion on this subject, it becomes us to exercise forbearance towards each other and live in peace. Whatever will bring about general peace in your congregation is the thing that we recommend. Peace and love in a congregation is a grand thing, and the church that abounds in this attainment will soon be blessed with sufficient wisdom to see alike on all similar questions of difference.

What is the usual order of conducting Sunday-schools among the Brethren? Some years ago we used the quarterlies, we think with good success, but last year we used the Bible only, without any helps, but it seems to not have given the best of satisfaction. If we cannot do better I think we would better not open the school again next summer. Will you please give us some advice.
* * *

The brother, writing the above, requests us to withhold his name. This is something that we are not in the habit of doing, but will do so in this instance.

First of all we want to say, Do not think of abandoning your Sunday-school work. Make up your minds to open your school next summer, quarterlies or no quarterlies. Do not permit a difference of that kind to stop the school. We are decidedly in favor of quarterlies, and know that they are a great help, but if we lived in a neighborhood where they were not wanted, we would still enter the Sunday-school and work with earnestness. Paul says: "I am made all things to all men, that I might by all means save some." 1 Cor. 9: 24. This wisdom will come in good play here. Live in peace and keep the Sunday-school alive. It will want the quarterlies after awhile.

Concerning the order of the church in regard to the use of quarterlies,—that is left optional with the churches and Sunday-schools. Some use them and others do not. A very large majority of the schools, we think, use the quarterlies, and in the course of a few years we may expect all of our schools to use them. We have been engaged in Sunday-school work more or less for twenty-seven years, and our experience, as well as observation, teaches us that quarterlies are a great help indeed, where properly used. They are a great aid in helping the pupils to understand the lessons, to say nothing of the system they bring out in the line of study. These lesson helps, however, ought to be used in connection with the Bible and a good Bible map. In the use of helps much depends upon the teacher. The teacher who must look on the book for every question and also for each answer, is not likely to make the very best use of quarterlies, nor to teach his pupils the best method of studying the Bible.

Please explain John 5: 28, 29. What is in the grave—will the body until the resurrection that shall hear the Voice? Is the soul in the grave with the body until the resurrection? Many of us here would like to know. D. B. HENRY.

The Scripture referred to reads as follows: "Marvel not at this: for the hour is coming, in the which all that are in the graves shall hear his voice, and shall come forth; they that have done good, unto the resurrection of life; and they that have done evil, unto the resurrection of damnation." John 5: 28, 29. We know that the soul does not go with the body to the grave, for Solomon says: "Then shall the dust return to the earth as it was, and the spirit shall return to God who gave it." Eccl. 12: 7. The term spirit here refers to the immortal part of man the same as the term soul does in the sense used by our querist. Under the altar John saw "the souls of them that were slain for the Word of God and for the testimony which they held." Rev. 6: 9. The first resurrection had not yet taken place when John saw these souls under the altar, hence the bodies still remained in the grave, while the souls were with God. In 1 Kings 17: 21, 22 we have a very clear statement concerning the soul leaving the body at death: "And he stretched himself upon the child three times, and cried unto the Lord, and said, O Lord my God, I pray thee, let this child's soul come into him again, And the Lord

heard the voice of Elijah; and the soul of the child came into him again, and he revived."

Concerning the death of Jesus Luke says: "And when Jesus had cried with a loud voice, he said, Father, into thy hands I commend my spirit: and having said thus, he gave up the ghost." Luke 23: 46. Here Jesus committed his spirit into the care of his Father, while his body went to the tomb. Stephen, being full of the Holy Ghost, held the same view concerning the spirit of man going to God at death, for when he was dying he said, "Lord Jesus, receive my spirit." Acts 7: 59. As additional evidence, to show that the soul and body are separated at death, we quote from the Revised Version, Acts 2: 27: "Because thou wilt not leave my soul in Hades, neither wilt thou permit thine holy one to see corruption." Hades means the abode of departed spirits. The language is quoted by Peter from Ps. 16: 8 and refers to the Savior, applying to his condition during death. His soul was not left in Hades with other spirits, but came forth and reunited with the body on the third day. From all these Scriptures we are led to infer that the soul, or spirit, does not go to the grave with the body, but is in the care of God while the body is resting in the grave.

The voice that calls the nations from the dead will be heard not only by the bodies that are in the graves, but also by the spirits that are in the care of God.

The following query and answer which we clip from the Christian Standard, will throw some light on a question that is occasionally sent us:

If Jesus was crucified on Friday, as has been commonly taught, how can the following statement be harmonized with the Friday idea? "To-day is the third day since these things were done" (Luke 24: 21). The above passage was spoken on Sunday following the crucifixion. If Sunday was the third day since the occurrence, would not Thursday be crucifixion day, Friday the first day, Saturday the second and Sunday "the third day since these things were done"?
CHAS. H. WARNER.

"The mere reading of Matt. 27: 62-64 will throw light on the way in which the people of the New Testament times spoke of the days since which certain things were done, which was to count the day on which an act was performed the first day, and the next day after, the second day. 'Now the next day, that followed the day of the preparation, the chief priests and Pharisees came together unto Pilate, saying, Sir, we remember that that deceiver said while he was yet alive, After three days I will rise again. Command therefore that the sepulcher be made sure until the third day, lest his disciples come by night and steal him away, and say unto the people, He is risen from the dead.' 'Until the third day' explains what they understood by 'after three days.' Jesus said that he would 'be raised again the third day.' Matt. 16: 21. Mark makes him say that 'after three days' he would rise again. These seemingly differing expressions passed in those days as equivalents and would not be misunderstood by any. It is said, in Gen. 42: 17, that Joseph put his brethren into ward 'three days'; and in the next verse we learn that they were released 'on the third day.' To the people who asked Rehoboam to make their burdens lighter, he said, 'Depart ye for three days, then come again to me.' They went away, and it is said that they 'came again the third day as the king had appointed.' 2 Kings 12: 5, 12. In the light of the current use of the language referred to, there is no difficulty in harmonizing the different forms of expression."
J. H. M.

CORRESPONDENCE.

" Write what thou seest, and send it unto the churches." '

☞Church News solicited for this Department. If you have had a good meeting, send a report of it, so that others may rejoice with you. In writing give name of church, County and State. Be brief. Notes of Travel should be as short as possible. Land Advertisements are not solicited for this Department. We have an advertising page, and, if necessary, will issue supplements.

Wayside Notes.

I HAVE just returned from my labors in the Cherry Grove church, North-western Missouri. I commenced preaching at that point to a small congregation in the Brethren's meeting-house, but owing to rough roads, and cold and stormy weather, the congregations were not large at any time. The interest was good with those who attended. I preached thirteen sermons here. Then the brethren moved the meetings seven miles west to a school-house, where I preached nine times to interested hearers.

While I was at that place, the weather, after being quite cold, suddenly turned warm and made muddy roads. There was much sickness and some deaths in the neighborhood. Our meetings were interfered with by literary societies which held claims upon the use of the school-house; then singing-schools and dances in the neighborhood also engaged the attention of the young people. These and other causes militated against the success of our meetings, yet we felt that the Lord had not forsaken us altogether, for we had very good attention to the Word preached. As is too often the case, however, these meetings were closed just when the prospects were brightening. We were sorry that Bro. W. H. Clark, the local minister, was unable to attend any of the meetings owing to a severe attack of La Grippe. Sister McLoughlin was also in a very critical condition, and could not attend the meetings.

Our sympathies were also aroused in behalf of sister Hunt, whose health has been impaired by affliction, to such an extent that she is only able to go about the house by being supported. The brethren thought best to hold a meeting at her house, which proved to be of much interest to those present. Though no immediate result seemed to follow, by way of ingathering, yet I felt that my work is not wholly lost, but that seed has been sown that will yet bring forth a rich harvest.

I had intended to go to the Whitesville church, Mo., but owing to sickness and other causes, I turned my face homeward where I found the loved ones in the enjoyment of good health, for which I thank God and take courage.

The Lord willing, I shall start in a few days to fill a call for a series of meetings in the Hadley Creek church, Pike Co., Ill.

The church here is in love and union and enjoying the benefit of an evergreen Sunday-school.

H. W. STRICKLER.

Loraine, Ill.

From Moscow, Idaho.

THE meetings at the Moscow church closed last night. We had meetings every night for two weeks. Three other denominations had meetings at the same time. Quite a number of the members were sick, and could not attend, still we had a fair congregation during the meetings, with good interest. The brethren preached the Word in its purity and simplicity, and there are some that are near the kingdom.

Our meetings were very profitable to all of us that had the privilege of attending them. We, as members of the church, often need revivals in our own hearts, that we may go on with renewed energy in the service of God. Why is it that so few, in looking for a new location, look for a place where they can be of service to God? Stop and

think, dear Brethren, what Christ has done for us! He did not seek for the place where he could live at ease, but he sought to do his Father's will. Let us be like him, and try to lead others to a higher and holier life. In so doing we will earn for ourselves everlasting life.

Our meetings were conducted by Eld. Sidney Hodgden and Bro. Jacob Gwin. These brethren are earnest workers in the Lord's vineyard.

J. U. G. STIVERSON.

Feb. 1.

Lexington Church Items.

A protracted meeting held with us by Bro. D. D. Wine, of Covington, Ohio, commenced on the evening of Jan. 9, 1892, and closed on Monday evening, Feb. 1. The meeting throughout was of great interest, and we had good sleighing about all the time. La Grippe kept some away, but, had the meeting been earlier, this would have been much worse. Two other protracted meetings were in progress at the same time, close by, and it was thought that we had more than our share of people. The interest manifested was splendid and the order good. Eight were baptized,—all young folks, and there are three applicants. One was also added by letter.

Bro. Wine did us good service. He labored in such a way that none could be offended.

At this place the District Meeting of South-eastern Ohio will be held. Notwithstanding we are few in number and isolated, yet we expect to do the best we can to accommodate all who may attend the meetings. Brethren, do not neglect the isolated churches, on the home mission work.

ALLEN OCKERMAN.

From the Grundy County Church, Iowa.

ON Monday, Jan. 11, Bro. M. Dierdorff, of Yale, Iowa, came to us to conduct a series of meetings. He continued preaching until Jan. 25, and preached, in all, fifteen sermons. The congregations were large, considering the inclemency of the weather, and the bad roads. We trust deep impressions were made on the minds of many. One dear soul was willing to come out on the Lord's side. We are sorry that our brother's stay with us was limited, for we feel sure that others are counting the cost. May they, before it is eternally too late, get the consent of their minds and join in with the people of God! Bro. Dierdorff labored earnestly and ably for us, and shunned not to declare the whole counsel of God. May God bless our brother in other fields of labor!

ALDA E. ALBRIGHT.

Steamboat Rock, Iowa.

From Hawthorn, Fla.

TO-DAY I attended preaching at 10:30 A. M., at the Orange Lane. Meeting with the dear Brethren in this part of God's moral vineyard, as we had been accustomed to do in time past, was indeed pleasant. Here I formed the acquaintance of Bro. Sawyer and wife, who had come up from Keuka. We shall have preaching this evening at Orange Creek, and we hope to have the privilege of hearing Bro. Sawyer talk to us. We have been requested to make regular appointments at the latter place, which we probably will. The meetings here were discontinued after Bro. Moore went away. Bro. Neher had more points to fill than his time would allow. Bro. Sawyer informs us that since he and others came to Florida for the winter, services have been held each Lord's Day in the church at Keuka, and at other points. One young brother was received by baptism two weeks ago and others are making inquiry.

One of the difficulties in the way here are the

secret organizations, of which almost all male adults are members. This is a barrier to our receiving them into our church. When shall men learn that the church of Christ is superior to all human institutions, and that it fills the wants of all other forms of associations? In fact, Christianity is the only hope for the future life, and fits men for all the responsible duties of the present. It will induce us to make more sacrifices for every human being, without respect of person, than any other organization. The worldly organizations minister to those that have earned what they get, but the salvation of God is a free gift. Christ gave his life for us all, and can we not fully trust him for all needed blessings here and hereafter? Let us lean upon his Word and walk in the light as he is in the light, and have fellowship one with the other. Then, and only then, can his blood cleanse us from all sin,—in the land of Florida as well as elsewhere.

We think of the many isolated places as we sit and pen these thoughts, while alone this beautiful, summer-like afternoon, where all nature seems to smile and betoken the goodness of God.

J. C. LAHMAN.

Feb. 7.

From the Mission Board of the South-eastern District of Kansas.

QUITE a number of calls for preaching have been made from the different isolated places. The Board has responded to some of them. There has been one church organized, and two other points have been visited by the District evangelist, who reports good interest and splendid openings for the Brethren. There are other calls, but we have not sufficient funds in the treasury to respond to those demands. The work has been greatly hindered on this account.

Now, brethren and sisters, would it not be well for the different churches of the District to respond to these calls by giving a small donation? We ask that each church solicitor endeavor to raise as much as possible and forward it to the Treasurer, Bro. Samuel Cornelius, Parsons, Kans. If any one knows of any money belonging to our District for mission purposes, he will please forward it to the Treasurer. The work is in the hands of the church; the Board is controlled by the amount of funds received. M. O. HODGDEN.

Galesburg, Kans., Feb. 3.

Contributors to Poor Fund.

S. L. Shaver, Troutville, Va.,	$ 50
Jacob D. Rosenberger,	1 75
Aaron Teeter, New Enterprise, Pa.,	25
Jno. H. Hoofstittier, Millersville, Pa.,	40
Mrs. J. F. Baily, Dillsburg, Pa.,	50
J. W. Wakeman,	1 00
David Keim, St. Peter's, Pa.,	50
Mrs, Lydia Hogentogler,	2 50
Henry Thompson, Kearney, Md.,	50
David Foltz, Rushville, Ohio,	40
Geo. W. Petre, Hagerstown, Md.,	4 90
Jno. W. Cook, Baltimore, Md.,	50
J. E. Reed, Pittsburg, Pa.,	1 25

An Experiment.

LAST spring, when we re-organized our Sunday-school, we re-adopted the penny collection for each Sunday as heretofore.

At that time I suggested, which was agreed to, that we have a penny collection each Sunday also for the missionary work of the Southern District of Indiana. As the church holds two Communion meetings each year, and as in this (the Mississinewa church) they are almost invariably held on Friday, continuing the preaching over Sunday, I

CORRESPONDENCE.

"Write what thou seest, and send it unto the churches."

☞ Church News solicited for this Department. If you have had a good meeting, send a report of it, so that others may rejoice with you. In writing give name of church, County and State. Be brief. Notes of Travel should be as short as possible. Land Advertisements are not solicited for this Department. We have an advertising page, and, if necessary, will issue supplements.

Wayside Notes.

I HAVE just returned from my labors in the Cherry Grove church, North-western Missouri. I commenced preaching at that point to a small congregation in the Brethren's meeting-house, but owing to rough roads, and cold and stormy weather, the congregations were not large at any time. The interest was good with those who attended. I preached thirteen sermons here. Then the brethren moved the meetings seven miles west to a school-house, where I preached nine times to interested hearers.

While I was at that place, the weather, after being quite cold, suddenly turned warm and made muddy roads. There was much sickness and some deaths in the neighborhood. Our meetings were interfered with by literary societies which held claims upon the use of the school-house; then singing-schools and dances in the neighborhood also engaged the attention of the young people. These and other causes militated against the success of our meetings, yet we felt that the Lord had not forsaken us altogether, for we had very good attention to the Word preached. As is too often the case, however, these meetings were closed just when the prospects were brightening.

We were sorry that Bro. W. H. Clark, the local minister, was unable to attend any of the meetings owing to a severe attack of *La Grippe.* Sister McLoughlin was also in a very critical condition, and could not attend the meetings.

Our sympathies were also aroused in behalf of sister Hunt, whose health has been impaired by affliction, to such an extent that she is only able to go about the house by being supported. The brethren thought best to hold a meeting at her house, which proved to be of much interest to those present. Though no immediate result seemed to follow, by way of ingathering, yet I felt that my work is not wholly lost, but that seed has been sown that will yet bring forth a rich harvest.

I had intended to go to the Whitesville church, Mo., but owing to sickness and other causes, I turned my face homeward where I found the loved ones in the enjoyment of good health, for which I thank God and take courage.

The Lord willing. I shall start in a few days to fill a call for a series of meetings in the Hadley Creek church, Pike Co., Ill.

The church here is in town and union and enjoying the benefit of an evergreen Sunday-school.

H. W. STRICKLER.

Loraine, Ill.

From Moscow, Idaho.

THE meetings at the Moscow church closed last night. We had meetings every night for two weeks. Three other denominations had meetings at the same time. Quite a number of the members were sick, and could not attend, still we had a fair congregation during the meetings, with good interest. The brethren preached the Word in its purity and simplicity, and there are some that are near the kingdom.

Our meetings were very profitable to all of us that had the privilege of attending them. We, as members of the church, often need revivals in our own hearts, that we may go on with renewed energy in the service of God. Why is it that so few, in looking for a new location, look for a place where they can be of service to God? Stop and

think, dear Brethren, what Christ has done for us! He did not seek for the place where he could live at ease, but he sought to do his Father's will. Let us be like him, and try to lead others to a higher and holier life. In so doing we will earn for ourselves everlasting life.

Our meetings were conducted by Eld. Sidney Hodgden and Bro. Jacob Gwin. These brethren are earnest workers in the Lord's vineyard.

J. U. G. STIVERSON.

Feb. 1.

Lexington Church Items.

A protracted meeting held with us by Bro. D. D. Wine, of Covington, Ohio, commenced on the evening of Jan. 9, 1892, and closed on Monday evening, Feb. 1 The meeting throughout was of great interest, and we had good sleighing about all the time. *La Grippe* kept some away, but had the meeting been earlier, this would have been much worse. Two other protracted meetings were in progress at the same time, close by, and it was thought that we had more than our share of people. The interest manifested was splendid and the order good. Eight were baptized,—all young folks, and there are three applicants. One was also added by letter.

Bro. Wine did us good service. He labored in such a way that none could be offended.

At this place the District Meeting of South-eastern Ohio will be held. Notwithstanding we are few in number and isolated, yet we expect to do the best we can to accommodate all who may attend the meetings. Brethren, do not neglect the isolated churches, on the home mission work.

ALLEN OCKERMAN.

From the Grundy County Church, Iowa.

On Monday, Jan. 11, Bro. M. Dierdorff, of Yale, Iowa, came to us to conduct a series of meetings. He continued preaching until Jan. 25, and preached, in all, fifteen sermons. The congregations were large, considering the inclemency of the weather, and the bad roads. We trust deep impressions were made on the minds of many. One dear soul was willing to come out on the Lord's side. We are sorry that our brother's stay with us was limited, for we feel sure that others are counting the cost. May they, before it is eternally too-late, get the consent of their minds and join in with the people of God! Bro. Dierdorff labored earnestly and ably for us, and shunned not to declare the whole counsel of God. May God bless our brother in other fields of labor!

ALDA E. ALBRIGHT.

Steamboat Rock, Iowa.

From Hawthorn, Fla.

TO-DAY I attended preaching at 10:30 A. M., at the Orange Lane. Meeting with the dear Brethren in this part of God's moral vineyard, as we had been accustomed to do in time past, was indeed pleasant. Here I formed the acquaintance of Bro. Sawyer and wife, who had come up from Keuka. We shall have preaching this evening at Orange Creek, and we hope to have the privilege of hearing Bro. Sawyer talk to us. We have been requested to make regular appointments at the latter place, which we probably will. The meetings here were discontinued after Bro. Moore went away. Bro. Neher had more points to fill than his time would allow. Bro. Sawyer informs us that since he and others came to Florida for the winter, services have been held each Lord's Day in the church at Keuka, and at other points. One young brother was received by baptism two weeks ago and others are making inquiry.

One of the difficulties in the way here are the

secret organizations, of which almost all male adults are members. This is a barrier to our receiving them into our church. When shall men learn that the church of Christ is superior to all human institutions, and that it fills the wants of all other forms of associations? In fact, Christianity is the only hope for the future life, and fits men for all the responsible duties of the present. It will induce us to make more sacrifices for every human being, without respect of person, than any other organization. The worldly organizations minister to those that have earned what they get, but the salvation of God is a free gift. Christ gave his life for us all, and can we not fully trust him for all needed blessings here and hereafter? Let us lean upon his Word and walk in the light as he is in the light, and have fellowship one with the other. Then, and only then, can his blood cleanse us from all sin,—in the land of Florida as well as elsewhere.

We think of the many isolated places as we sit and pen these thoughts, while alone this beautiful, summer-like afternoon, where all nature seems to smile and betoken the goodness of God.

J. C. LAHMAN.

Feb. 7.

From the Mission Board of the South-eastern District of Kansas.

QUITE a number of calls for preaching have been made from the different isolated places. The Board has responded to some of them. There has been one church organized, and two other points have been visited by the District evangelist, who reports good interest and splendid openings for the Brethren. There are other calls, but we have not sufficient funds in the treasury to respond to those demands. The work has been greatly hindered on this account.

Now, brethren and sisters, would it not be well for the different churches of the District to respond to these calls by giving a small donation? We ask that each church solicitor endeavor to raise as much as possible and forward it to the Treasurer, Bro. Samuel Cornelius, Parsons, Kans. If any one knows of any money belonging to our District for mission purposes, he will please forward it to the Treasurer. The work is in the hands of the church; the Board is controlled by the amount of funds received. M. O. HODGDEN.

Galesburg, Kans., Feb. 3.

Contributors to Poor Fund.

S. L. Shaver, Troutville, Va.,	$ 50
Jacob D. Rosenberger,	1 75
Aaron Teeter, New Enterprise, Pa.,	25
Jno. H. Hoofstittler, Millersville, Pa.,	40
Mrs. J. F. Baily, Dillsburg, Pa.,	50
J. W. Wakeman,	1 00
David Keim, St. Peter's, Pa.,	50
Mrs. Lydia Hogentogler,	2 50
Henry Thompson, Kearney, Md.,	50
David Fultz, Rushville, Ohio,	40
Geo. W. Petre, Hagerstown, Md.,	4 90
Jno. W. Cook, Baltimore, Md.,	50
J. E. Reed, Pittsburg, Pa.,	1 25

An Experiment.

LAST spring, when we re-organized our Sunday-school, we re-adopted the penny collection for each Sunday as heretofore.

At that time I suggested, which was agreed to, that we have a penny collection each Sunday also for the missionary work of the Southern District of Indiana. As the church holds two Communion meetings each year, and as in this (the Mississine-we church) they are almost invariably held on Friday, continuing the preaching over Sunday, I

Notes from Our Correspondents.

"As cold water to a thirsty soul, so is good news from a far country."

Washington, Kans.—Bro. A. C. Dagget, from Scandia, Republic Co., came here and staid one week. He is a faithful worker in the Lord and good impressions were made on many.—*I. R. Phillippi, Jan. 24.*

South Bend, Ind.—Bro. Hollinger, of Darke County, Ohio, commenced a series of meetings in the Portage church, Dec. 19, and closed on the night of the 27th. Our brother labored earnestly, and although there were no accessions, we believe there were some good impressions made. The church was much encouraged in the good cause. —*Noah Early.*

New Lebanon, Ohio.—The Wolf Creek church has, for the past ten days enjoyed some of the most soul-reviving meetings. We have had interesting truths of the Gospel were brought forth and explained. Oh, what unsearchable truths are contained in the Gospel of our Lord and Master! Some that have been for years looking into the fold, were led in the liquid stream and baptized, we hope to walk in newness of life.—*Wm. S. Gilbert.*

Alvid, Tex.—We are well and more than pleased with our new home. All of the Brethren here have bought land. People here seem very much pleased with the Brethren's doctrine. We have preaching every two weeks, and expect soon to organize our church. Bro. W. H. Leaman is our minister, and by the help of our Blessed Savior we hope to be able to build a comfortable meeting-house here in Alvin.—*J. J. Wassam, Feb. 5.*

Mercer, Ohio.—Bro. B. F. Honeyman, of Gettysburg, Ohio, came to us Jan. 23, and held a series of meetings. He closed Feb. 7, after preaching, in all, nineteen sermons. He preached with power and, demonstration of the Spirit, so that our little Mercer church got aroused from its lethargy and morbid condition. Six precious souls came out on the Lord's side, and a number were strongly impressed, but for some cause, did not enter the fold of Christ.—*John Shellaberger.*

Beaver Creek, Ind.—Bro. M. L. Hahn came to us Jan. 12. He was suffering from a severe cold, and therefore the home minister conducted the meeting that evening. He began holding meetings on the evening of Jan. 13. He held, altogether, eighteen meetings, one social meeting, one young people's meeting, and one children's meeting. His efforts resulted in four additions, all being young men. We felt that others were near the fold. May God bless them, that they may come to Christ ere it is too late.—*J. Hahn.*

Goshen, Ind.—Bro. L. Hillery came to us Jan. 27, and commenced preaching at the Goshen church, Elkhart Co., Ind. The meeting at first was not very well attended on account of so many being sick with *La Grippe;* but we had interested congregations. Bro. Hillery preached fourteen sermons, mostly to the members. We never had any plainer preaching; there was no uncertain sound about it. On Sunday, Feb. 7, he preached two sermons on the "Covering," removing all doubts as to the hair being the proper Scriptural covering, or that just anything would do. Bro. Hillery is a good expounder, and we hope that the Lord may lengthen his days, so that he can help to instruct others in those things that are wanting in so many churches. Two precious lambs were added to the church; one thirteen years old, whose mother came to me and wished to know if her daughter was not too young to come to the church. She is a bright child, and understood herself fully. I said, "No, let her come."—*J. H. Miller.*

Cartersville, Va.—We are now without a shepherd. I read a letter in the MESSENGER from Bro. Abraham Frantz, of West Virginia, wishing to locate in a milder climate and hope that he may respond to our call, if it is the Blessed Master's will. We feel quite at a loss since Bro. Bowser left us, but we are glad that we have a Good Shepherd that will never leave nor forsake us. Let us try to bear the cross, and live faithful, so as to gain an entrance into that everlasting city where we shall be happy forevermore!—*Florida E. Etter.*

Notice.—Bro. C. Hope, of Herrington, Kansas, offers for sale a farm, containing 120 acres, situated 80 rods from the R. R. station and school-house. About one-half of the land has been broken. Five acres are in orchard, and about forty of the apple trees are now bearing fruit. There are some peach trees. There is on the land a house 16 by 16, a story and a half high, with an addition 8 by 16; also a granary, corn-crib, sheds, pasture yards and corral. a good wind-mill, and a never-failing well. Bro. Hope is anxious to dispose of his property, so as to arrange to give more time to the mission work. Hence we give this notice a prominent place. Write him at once at Herrington, Kans.

Bremen, Ind.—Bro. Daniel Whitmer, of South Bend, came to us Jan. 30, and stayed till Feb. 8. He preached, in all, eleven soul-cheering sermons. On account of a revival being held by the United Brethren church, we had small congregations. Bad roads as well as some sickness in the neighborhood also interfered with the success of our meetings. With all these disadvantages we had a glorious season of worship. Three young sisters came out on the Lord's side. On Sunday, after preaching, a large crowd gathered at the River, where the applicants were baptized. Others, we think, are counting the cost, and we hope they will yet, as Mary of old, choose that good part which never can be taken away from them! —*Christiana Parker, Feb. 11.*

Alfont, Ind.—Our long-expected meetings commenced Jan. 9. Bro. Fadeley came to the Beech Grove church at that time and preached in all, ten sermons. He held forth the Word with power, so that both saint and sinner received warning and instruction. The brethren and sisters were much built up. As an immediate result, three dear ones made the confession, and were baptized. One was reclaimed and one united by letter since then. We were glad to have Bro. Fadely with us, but were sorry when he had to leave. He took sick first with *La Grippe* which terminated in typhoid fever. His condition had somewhat improved by Jan. 31. We expect to commence another series of meetings to-night. Bro. Isaac Branson of the Killbuck church, Delaware Co., Ind., will be with us.—*Luther Bedel, Feb. 8.*

Campbell, Mich.—The quarterly council of this church was held at the east house Jan 30, having been deferred one month, to give a better opportunity to transact business for our District Meeting. On account of sickness, there was not a full attendance. Considerable matter came up for consideration, which was harmoniously disposed of. Two queries go to District Meeting, in regard to our State mission work. The church decided to represent at District Meeting by two delegates. The time of holding our regular quarterly council was changed to the second Saturday of May, August, November and February. This church has not as yet held a series of meetings this winter. We were disappointed in getting outside help, and prevented by sickness of some of the home ministers and other members from having the desired meetings.—*Peter B. Messner, Feb. 9.*

Navarre, Kans.—Jan. 24, Bro. Hope came to the Abilene congregation and preached for us up to the evening of Feb. 1. Next day Bro. C. C. Root, of Ozawkie, Kans., arrived, and up to this time has preached nine sermons. Thus far nine dear souls have made the good profession, seven have been baptized, and the good work is still going on. Many others seem to be counting the cost, and the members are much awakened and encouraged. Since these meetings are going on, we meet from day to day, and from house to house, for Bible reading and prayer, and the Lord is greatly blessing us.—*Rebecca Gift, Feb. 11.*

Indian Creek Church, Iowa.—Bro. S. M. Goughen, our came among us Jan. 31, and remained until Feb. 4, preaching during that time six sermons. He failed not to declare the whole counsel of God. We wish he could have remained longer, but not feeling well he thought it best to close the meetings for the present. Though the roads were bad, yet the attendance was good. The Brethren never preached here before. It was something new to most of the people. While there were no additions, we hope the Word preached may be as bread cast upon the waters to be gathered many days hence.—*Henry Blue.*

Edna Mills, Ind.—The members of the Middle Fork church, Clinton Co., Ind., held their quarterly church meeting, Feb. 2. The business passed off pleasantly. We have repaired what was known as our Upper church, and to-day changed the name to "New Hope." There were two delegates elected to District Meeting and a committee of three brethren was appointed to make arrangements for a series of meetings in the future. Since my last report, Bro. David Neff, of Roann, Ind., held a series of meetings for us. Owing to sickness the attendance was small, but the preaching was good, and while there were no additions to the church, I believe some good was done.— *John E. Metzger, Feb. 8.*

Sidney, Ind.—I commenced meetings in the Union church, Marshall Co., Ind., on the evening of Jan. 21. I closed last night, Feb. 11, after preaching in all thirty-four sermons to attentive listeners. As an immediate result, two were reclaimed, four baptized, and there is one applicant for baptism. This makes seven precious souls, in all, that came out on the Lord's side during these meetings. Others, seemingly, were near the kingdom. The congregations were not very large at these meetings, owing to much sickness and some deaths. I had made arrangements to go from here to the Pine Creek church, Ind., but owing to much sickness they have withdrawn the meeting till some future time. This will allow me some rest, and the privilege of being with the family at home.—*Dan. Snell, Feb. 12.*

Girard, Ill.—To-day was the quarterly council in the Macoupin Creek church. Three were added by letter. Bro. Joseph Jones and family have moved here from Bond County, Ill. He is a minister in the second degree, and his labors are much needed with us. We hope our brother and family will enjoy their new relations. The quarterly contributions were made for the home treasury, and also the General Church, Southern Mission, and Book and Tract Work. Bro. Martin Brubaker was appointed as solicitor for endowments and bequests for the Mission Work of Southern Illinois. Our Communion meeting was appointed for Oct. 7. A committee was also chosen to engage a minister to hold a series of meetings about the time of the feast. Bro. A. D. Stutzman was elected Superintendent of our Sunday-school; Bro. John Leer, Assistant. We will conclude our organization on the third Sunday in March.—*Michael Flory, Feb. 6.*

Notes from Our Correspondents.

"As cold water to a thirsty soul, so is good news from a far country."

Washington, Kans.—Bro. A. C. Dagget, from Scandia, Republic Co., came here and staid one week. He is a faithful worker in the Lord and good impressions were made on many.—*I. R. Phillippi, Jan. 24.*

South Bend, Ind.—Bro. Hollinger, of Darke County, Ohio, commenced a series of meetings in the Portage church, Dec. 19, and closed on the night of the 27th. Our brother labored earnestly, and although there were no accessions, we believe there were some good impressions made. The church was much encouraged in the good cause.—*Noah Early.*

New Lebanon, Ohio.—The Wolf Creek church has, for the past ten days enjoyed some of the most soul-reviving meetings. The deeply-hidden truths of the Gospel were brought forth and explained. Oh, what unsearchable truths are contained in the Gospel of our Lord and Master! Some that have been for years looking into the fold, were led in the liquid stream and baptized, we hope to walk in newness of life.—*Wm. S. Gilbert.*

Alvid, Tex.—We are well and more than pleased with our new home. All of the Brethren here have bought land. People here seem very much pleased with the Brethren's doctrine. We have preaching every two weeks, and expect soon to organize our church. Bro. W. H. Leaman is our minister, and by the help of our Blessed Savior we hope to be able to build a comfortable meeting-house here in Alvin.—*J. J. Wassam, Feb. 5.*

Mercer, Ohio.—Bro. B. F. Honeyman, of Gettysburg, Ohio, came to us Jan. 29, and held a series of meetings. He closed Feb. 7, after preaching, in all, nineteen sermons. He preached with power and demonstration of the Spirit, so that our little Mercer church got aroused from its lethargy and morbid condition. Six precious souls came out on the Lord's side, and a number were strongly impressed, but for some cause, did not enter the fold of Christ.—*John Shellaberger.*

Beaver Creek, Ind.—Bro. M. L. Hahn came to us Jan. 12. He was suffering from a severe cold, and therefore the home minister conducted the meeting that evening. He began holding meetings on the evening of Jan. 13. He held, altogether, eighteen meetings, one social meeting, one young people's meeting, and one children's meeting. His efforts resulted in four additions, all being young men. We felt that others were near the fold. May God bless them, that they may come to Christ ere it is too late.—*J. Hahn.*

Goshen, Ind.—Bro. I. Hillery came to us Jan. 27, and commenced preaching at the Goshen church, Elkhart Co., Ind. The meeting at first was not very well attended on account of so many being sick with *La Grippe;* but we had interested congregations. Bro. Hillery preached fourteen sermons, mostly to the members. We never had any plainer preaching; there was no uncertain sound about it. On Sunday, Feb. 7, he preached two sermons on the "Covering," removing all doubts as to the hair being the proper Scriptural covering, or that just anything would do. Bro. Hillery is a good expounder, and we hope that the Lord may lengthen his days, so that he can help to instruct others in those things that are wanting in so many churches. Two precious lambs were added to the church; one thirteen years old, whose mother came to me and wished to know if her daughter was not too young to come to the church. She is a bright child, and understood herself fully. I said, "No, let her come."—*J. H. Miller.*

Cartersville, Va.—We are now without a shepherd. I read a letter in the MESSENGER from Bro. Abraham Frantz, of West Virginia, wishing to locate in a milder climate and hope that he may respond to our call, if it is the Blessed Master's will. We feel quite at a loss since Bro. Bowser left us, but we are glad that we have a Good Shepherd that will never leave nor forsake us. Let us try to bear the cross, and live faithful, so as to gain an entrance into that everlasting city where we shall be happy forevermore!—*Florida E. Eller.*

Notice.—Bro. C. Hope, of Herrington, Kansas, offers for sale a farm, containing 120 acres, situated 80 rods from the R. R. station and school-house. About one-half of the land has been broken. Five acres are in orchard, and about forty of the apple trees are now bearing fruit. There are some peach trees. There is on the land a house 16 by 16, a story and a half high, with an addition 8 by 16; also a granary, corn-crib, sheds, pasture yards and corral, a good wind-mill, and a never-failing well. Bro. Hope is anxious to dispose of his property, so as to arrange to give more time to the mission work. Hence we give this notice a prominent place. Write him at once at Herrington, Kans.

Bremen, Ind.—Bro. Daniel Whitmer, of South Bend, came to us Jan. 30, and stayed till Feb. 8. He preached, in all, eleven soul-cheering sermons. On account of a revival being held by the United Brethren church, we had small congregations. Bad roads as well as some sickness in the neighborhood also interfered with the success of our meetings. With all these disadvantages we had a glorious season of worship. Three young sisters came out on the Lord's side. On Sunday, after preaching, a large crowd gathered at the River, where the applicants were baptized. Others, we think, are counting the cost, and we hope they will yet, as Mary of old, choose that good part, which never can be taken away from them!—*Christiana Parker, Feb. 11.*

Allent, Ind.—Our long-expected meetings commenced Jan. 9. Bro. Fadeley came to the Beech Grove church at that time and preached in all, ten sermons. He held forth the Word with power, so that both saint and sinner received warning and instruction. The brethren and sisters were much built up. As an immediate result, three dear ones made the confession and were baptized. One was reclaimed and one united by letter since then. We were glad to have Bro. Fadely with us, but were sorry when he had to leave. He took sick first with *La Grippe* which terminated in typhoid fever. His condition had somewhat improved by Jan. 31. We expect to commence another series of meetings to-night. Bro. Isaac Branson of the Killbuck church, Delaware Co., Ind., will be with us.—*Luther Beidel, Feb. 8.*

Campbell, Mich.—The quarterly council of this church was held at the east house Jan 30, having been deferred one month, to give a better opportunity to transact business for our District Meeting. On account of sickness, there was not a full attendance. Considerable matter came up for consideration, which was harmoniously disposed of. Two queries go to District Meeting, in regard to our State mission work. The church decided to represent at District Meeting by two delegates. The time of holding our regular quarterly council was changed to the second Saturday of May, August, November and February. This church has not as yet held a series of meetings this winter. We were disappointed in getting outside help, and prevented by sickness of some of the home ministers and other members from having the desired meetings.—*Peter B. Messner, Feb. 9.*

Navarre, Kans.—Jan. 24, Bro. Hope came to the Abilene congregation and preached for us up to the evening of Feb. 1. Next day Bro. C. C. Root, of Ozawkie, Kans., arrived, and up to this time has preached nine sermons. Thus far nine dear souls have made the good profession, seven have been baptized, and the good work is still going on. Many others seem to be counting the cost, and the members are much awakened and encouraged. Since these meetings are going on, we meet from day to day, and from house to house, for Bible reading and prayer, and the Lord is greatly blessing us.—*Rebecca Gift, Feb. 11.*

Indian Creek Church, Iowa.—Bro. S. M. Goughenour came among us Jan. 31, and remained until Feb. 4, preaching during that time six sermons. He failed not to declare the whole counsel of God. We wish he could have remained longer, but not feeling well he thought it best to close the meetings for the present. Though the roads were bad, yet the attendance was good. The Brethren never preached here before. It was something new to most of the people. While there were no additions, we hope the Word preached may be as bread cast upon the waters to be gathered many days hence.—*Henry Blue.*

Edna Mills, Ind.—The members of the Middle Fork church, Clinton Co., Ind., held their quarterly church meeting, Feb. 2. The business passed off pleasantly. We have repaired what was known as our Upper church, and to-day changed the name to "New Hope." There were two delegates elected to District Meeting and a committee of three brethren was appointed to make arrangements for a series of meetings in the future. Since my last report, Bro. David Neff, of Roann, Ind., held a series of meetings for us. Owing to sickness the attendance was small, but the preaching was good, and while there were no additions to the church, I believe some good was done.—*John E. Metzger, Feb. 8.*

Sidney, Ind.—I commenced meetings in the Union church, Marshall Co., Ind., on the evening of Jan. 21. I closed last night, Feb. 11, after preaching in all thirty-four sermons to attentive listeners. As an immediate result, two were reclaimed, four baptized, and there is one applicant for baptism. This makes seven precious souls, in all, that came out on the Lord's side during these meetings. Others, seemingly, were near the kingdom. The congregations were not very large at these meetings, owing to much sickness and some deaths. I had made arrangements to go from here to the Pine Creek church, Ind., but owing to much sickness they have withdrawn the meeting till some future time. This will allow me some rest, and the privilege of being with the family at home.—*Dan. Snell, Fb. 12.*

Girard, Ill.—To-day was the quarterly council in the Macoupin Creek church. Three were added by letter. Bro. Joseph Jones and family have moved here from Bond County, Ill. He is a minister in the second degree, and his labors are much needed with us. We hope our brother and family will enjoy their new relations. The quarterly contributions were made for the home treasury, and also the General Church, Southern Mission, and Book and Tract Work. Bro. Martin Brubaker was appointed as solicitor for endowments and bequests for the Mission Work of Southern Illinois. Our Communion meeting was appointed for Oct. 7. A committee was also appointed to engage a minister to hold a series of meetings about the time of the feast. Bro. A. D. Stutzman was elected Superintendent of our Sunday-school; Bro. John Leer, Assistant. We will conclude our organization on the third Sunday in March.—*Michael Flory, Feb. 6.*

LAIRD.—In the Lanark church, Ill., Jan. 21, 1892, Bro. John Laird, aged 74 years, 7 months and 13 days.

Deceased spent his youth and early manhood in Ohio. He came to Carroll County, Ill., in 1840, and lived on a farm until seventeen years ago, when he moved to Lanark.

About three years ago he united with the Brethren church, and lived an humble Christian life. He was afflicted for about eight years, when an attack of *La Grippe* soon called him to his long home. Funeral services at the residence by the writer:
D. ROWLAND.

MILLER.—At her home in Jewell City, Kans., Aug. 14, 1892, of typhoid malaria, sister Mary, wife of John L. Miller, aged 58 years.

Deceased leaves a husband and three children to mourn their loss. She was an honorable sister for many years. With her family she came from Pennsylvania to Illinois a number of years ago and was a member of the Waddam's Grove church until some years ago, when they moved to Kansas. Her husband never was a member of the church; neither her two sons, but her daughter has been a sister for many years.
ALLEN BOYER.

GITTINGER.—At her parental home, five miles north-east of Leon, Iowa, Feb. 2, 1892, sister Agnes Gittinger, daughter of D. R. and S. E. Gittinger, aged 36 years, 7 months and 17 days.

Sister Agnes was a faithful, devoted and consistent member of the Brethren church here for about fourteen years. She was sick the greater part of the past year and confined to her bed seven months. Funeral services at the church from 2 Sam. 14: 14.
L. M. KOB.

WILLIAMS.—At Beechymire, Union Co., Ind., Jan. 29, 1892, Nora Mari Williams, daughter of John and Maria Hart, aged 31 years, 11 months and 15 days.

At the age of eighteen years she united with the German Baptist Brethren church, and has ever since, we believe, lived a devoted Christian life. Feb. 8, 1883, she became the wife of Howard B. Williams, to whom she has ever since been a loving, devoted companion. To them were born four sons, the oldest of whom preceded his mother to the land of rest about six years.

Three little, motherless boys, with the stricken husband, are mourning their irreparable loss.

Deceased suffered long, but not a murmur escaped her lips. Peacefully she passed away, strong in the faith and hope of a blessed life beyond. Funeral occasion improved by Eld. Wm. B. Self, assisted by the writer.
C. HARADER.

CASHMAN.—Near Baker's Summit, Bedford Co., Pa., Jan. 30, 1892, sister Annie Cashman, consort of Bro. John Cashman (deceased), aged 78 years, 10 months and 4 days.

Deceased leaves behind her two sons and one daughter to mourn the loss of a kind mother. May they prepare to meet her in a better world! Funeral services at her house, conducted by brethren S. L. Holsinger and J. D. Brumbaugh from 2 Tim. 4: 6, 7, " I have fought a good fight," etc., to a large and sympathizing congregation. She was buried beside her husband, in the old Bloomfield graveyard.
D. S. REPLOGLE.

FINK.—In the Baugo church, Elkhart Co., Ind., Feb. 2, 1892, Lydia Fink, aged 84 years, 5 months and 26 days.

Deceased was born in Lancaster County, Pa. In 1837, she, with her husband, Emmanuel Fink, moved to Stark County, Ohio. In 1842 they came to Elkhart County, Ind. She was a member of the German Lutheran church. Services by the writer from Amos 4: 12.
JOHN METZLER.

ASQUITH.—In the Cedar County church, Mo., Feb. 1, 1892, of pneumonia, sister Mary, wife of Bro. Charles Asquith, aged 70 years, 7 months and 14 days.

Sister Asquith was born in Bradford, Yorkshire, England, and emigrated to America in 1855. She has been a member of the church for twenty-four years. An only son was called here on account of his father's sickness, but instead of the father, the mother was called away, after being sick only one week. Her husband, a minister, has lost a kind wife, the son a loving mother and the church a faithful sister.

Funeral services in the Methodist church by brethren J. C. Mays and H. Tingley, from Rev. 14: 12, 13.
REBECCA MAYS.

JONES.—In McVeytown, in the Spring Run congregation, Mifflin Co., Pa., Jan. 28, 1892, sister Amanda J. Jones, aged 39 years, 6 months and 18 days.

She was the youngest daughter of Eld. Joseph R. and sister Mary Hanawalt, and the wife of Bro. Geo. W. Jones. She leaves a husband and five children. She was anointed, and sweetly fell asleep in Jesus. Funeral sermon by Eld. Abraham Myers from Philip. 1: 21.
EMMA BOLLINGER.

KACHEL.—In the Conestoga church, Lancaster Co., Pa., Jan. 30, 1892, sister Lizz Kachel, wife of Bro. John Kachel, aged 37 years, 3 months and 25 days.

Our sister was a member of the church for thirteen years and was zealous in the work. Her sickness was consumption from which she suffered for several years. She bore her affliction with Christian fortitude. Services by the Brethren from 2 Tim. 4: 6.
SALLIE PFOUTZ.

JOHN.—In the Salem church, Montgomery Co., Ohio, June 27, 1891, John John, aged 79 years, 1 month and 13 days.

Deceased was born near Canton, Stark Co., Ohio, May 14, 1812, and married Nancy Warner Feb. 14, 1833. He leaves ten children, thirty-three grandchildren and nine great-grandchildren. His companion and five children preceded him to the spirit world.
J. SOTSMAN.

KEESAMAN.—In the bounds of the Lower Cumberland church, Mechanicsburg, Pa., after a lingering illness of several months, friend John Keesaman, aged 74 years, 6 months and 13 days.

Interment at the Mohler meeting-house. Deceased leaves a wife (a sister) and two grandsons. Funeral services were held in the Presbyterian church in Mechanicsburg, by Bro. Levi S. Mohler and the writer, assisted by Rev. Foster, of the Presbyterian church, from Rev. 6: 17.
DANIEL LANDIS.

TAPPER.—In St. Joseph church, St. Joseph Co., Ind., at the home of Bro. Jacob Bowers, Jan. 31, 1892, Mary Tapper, mother of sister Bowers, aged 78 years, 7 months and 16 days.

Deceased was a kind, faithful and consistent member of the Mennonite church. Services by Noah Metzler and the writer from James 4: 14.
JOHN METZLER.

SPANOGLE.—At Phillips, Hamilton Co., Nebr., Jan. 14, 1892, of paralysis, Bro. A. J. Spanogle, aged 53 years, 8 months and 6 days.

Deceased was born in Huntingdon County, Pa., May 8, 1838. He united with the Brethren church in early life and lived a consistent life until his death. He was the oldest son of Eld. Jacob Spanogle, deceased, of Philadelphia. He leaves a wife and six children, an aged mother, three sisters and one brother.
EDNA S. HALDEMAN.

MYERS.—In the Clover Creek church, Pa., Jan. 15, 1892, sister Sarah Myers, aged 52 years, 3 months and 8 days.

Deceased was a member of the Brethren church for many years and tried to follow the Savior in his appointed way. She called for the elders and was anointed according to James 5: 14. In her sickness she bore her afflictions with patience and Christian fortitude until the death angel came in the age of life and said, " It is enough; come up higher." Death renders home lonely, but we trust that the bereft father and children will be consoled with the hope that she, whom they loved so well, is gone to rest. Funeral services were conducted by brethren A. B. Burger and F. B. Maddocks. J. B. BRUMBAUGH.

LAIRD.—In the Lanark church, Ill., Jan. 21, 1892, Bro. John Laird, aged 74 years, 7 months and 13 days.

Deceased spent his youth and early manhood in Ohio. He came to Carroll County, Ill., in 1840, and lived on a farm until seventeen years ago, when he moved to Lanark.

About three years ago he united with the Brethren church, and lived an humble Christian life. He was afflicted for about eight years, when an attack of La Grippe soon called him to his long home. Funeral services at the residence by the writer.

D. ROWLAND.

MILLER.—At her home in Jewell City, Kans., Aug. 14, 1892, of typhoid malaria, sister Mary, wife of John L. Miller, aged 58 years.

Deceased leaves a husband and three children to mourn their loss. She was an honorable sister for many years. With her family she came from Pennsylvania to Illinois a number of years ago and was a member of the Waddam's Grove church until some years ago, when they moved to Kansas. Her husband never was a member of the church, neither her two sons, but her daughters has been a sister for many years.

ALLEN BOYER.

GITTINGER.—At her parental home, five miles north-east of Leon, Iowa, Feb. 2, 1892, sister Agnes Gittinger, daughter of D. R. and S. E. Gittinger, aged 36 years, 7 months and 17 days.

Sister Agnes was a faithful, devoted and consistent member of the Brethren church here for about fourteen years. She was sick the greater part of the past year and confined to her bed seven months. Funeral services at the church from 2 Sam. 14: 14.

L. M. KOB.

WILLIAMS.—At Beechymire, Union Co., Ind., Jan. 29, 1892, Nora Hast Williams, daughter of John and Maria Hart, aged 31 years, 11 months and 15 days.

At the age of eighteen years she united with the German Baptist Brethren church, and has ever since, we believe, lived a devoted Christian life. Feb. 8, 1883, she became the wife of Howard B. Williams, to whom she has ever since been a loving, devoted companion. To them were born four sons, the eldest of whom preceded his mother to the land of rest about six years.

Three little, motherless boys, with the stricken husband, are mourning their irreparable loss.

Deceased suffered long, but not a murmur escaped her lips. Peacefully she passed away, strong in the faith and hope of a blessed life beyond. Funeral occasion improved by Eld. Wm. B. Self, assisted by the writer.

C. MARADER.

CASHMAN.—Near Baker's Summit, Bedford Co., Pa., Jan. 30, 1892, sister Annie Cashman, consort of Bro. John Cashman (deceased), aged 78 years, 10 months and 4 days.

Deceased leaves behind her two sons and one daughter to mourn the loss of a kind mother. May they prepare to meet her in a better world! Funeral services at her house, conducted by brethren J. L. Holsinger and J. D. Brumbaugh from 2 Tim. 4: 6, 7, "I have fought a good fight," etc., to a large and sympathizing congregation. She was buried beside her husband, in the old Bloomfield graveyard.

D. S. REPLOGLE.

FINK.—In the Baugo church, Elkhart Co., Ind., Feb. 2, 1892, Lydia Fink, aged 84 years, 5 months and 26 days.

Deceased was born in Lancaster County, Pa. In 1837, she, with her husband, Emmanuel Fink, moved to Stark County, Ohio. In 1843 they came to Elkhart County, Ind. She was a member of the German Lutheran church. Services by the writer from Amos 4: 12.

JOHN METZLER.

ASQUITH.—In the Cedar County church, Mo., Feb. 1, 1892, of pneumonia, sister Mary, wife of Bro. Charles Asquith, aged 70 years, 7 months and 14 days.

Sister Asquith was born in Bradford, Yorkshire, England, and emigrated to America in 1855. She has been a member of the church for twenty-four years. An only son was called here on account of his father's sickness, but instead of the father, the mother was called away, also being sick only one week. Her husband, a minister, has lost a kind wife, the son a loving mother and the church a faithful sister.

Funeral services in the Methodist church by brethren J. C. Maye and H. Tingley, from Rev. 14: 12, 13.

REBECCA MAYE.

JONES.—In McVeytown, in the Spring Run congregation, Mifflin Co., Pa., Jan. 28, 1892, sister Amanda J. Jones, aged 39 years, 6 months and 18 days.

She was the youngest daughter of Eld. Joseph R. and sister Mary Hanawalt, and the wife of Bro. Geo. W. Jones. She leaves a husband and five children. She was anointed, and sweetly fell asleep in Jesus. Funeral sermon by Eld. Abraham Myers from Philpp. 1: 21.

EMMA BOLLINGER.

KACHEL.—In the Conestoga church, Lancaster Co., Pa., Jan. 30, 1892, sister Liza Kachel, wife of Bro. John Kachel, aged 37 years, 5 months and 25 days.

Our sister was a member of the church for thirteen years and was zealous in the work. Her sickness was consumption from which she suffered for several years. She bore her affliction with Christian fortitude. Services by the Brethren from 2 Tim. 4: 6.

SALLIE PFOUTZ.

JOHN.—In the Salem church, Montgomery Co., Ohio, June 27, 1891, John John, aged 79 years, 1 month and 13 days.

Deceased leaves near Canton, Stark Co., Ohio, May 14, 1812, and married Nancy Warner Feb. 14, 1833. He leaves ten children, thirty-three grandchildren and nine great-grandchildren. His companion and five children preceded him to the spirit world.

J. STUTSMAN.

KEESAMAN.—In the bounds of the Lower Cumberland church, Mechanicsburg, Pa., after a lingering illness of several months, friend John Keesaman, aged 74 years, 6 months and 13 days.

Interment at the Mohler meeting-house. Deceased leaves a wife (a sister) and two grandsons. Funeral services were held in the Presbyterian church in Mechanicsburg, by Bro. Levi S. Mohler and the writer, assisted by Rev. Foster, of the Presbyterian church, from Rev. 6: 17.

DAMIEL LANDIS.

TAPPER.—In St. Joseph church, St. Joseph Co., Ind., at the home of Bro. Jacob Bowers, Jan. 31, 1892, Mary Tapper, mother of sister Bowers, aged 78 years, 7 months and 16 days.

Deceased was a kind, faithful and consistent member of the Mennonite church. Services by Noah Metzler and the writer from James 4: 14.

JOHN METZLER.

SPANOGLE.—At Phillips, Hamilton Co., Nebr., Jan. 14, 1892, of paralysis, Bro. A. J. Spanogle, aged 53 years, 8 months and 6 days.

Deceased was born in Huntington County, Pa., May 8, 1838. He united with the Brethren church in early life and lived a consistent life until his death. He was the oldest son of Eld. Jacob Spanogle, deceased, of Philadelphia. He leaves a wife and six children, an aged mother, three sisters and one brother.

EDNA S. HALDEMAN.

MYERS.—In the Clover Creek church, Pa., Jan. 15, 1892, sister Sarah Myers, aged 51 years, 3 months and 6 days.

Deceased was a member of the Brethren church for many years and tried to follow the Savior in his appointed way. She called for the elders and was anointed according to James 5: 14. In her sickness she bore her afflictions with patience and Christian fortitude until the death angel came in the name of life and said, " It is enough; come up higher." Death renders home lonely, but we trust that the bereft father and children will be consoled with the hope that she, whom they loved so well, is gone to rest. Funeral services were conducted by brethren A. B. Burger and F. B. Maddocks. J. B. BRUMBAUGH.

GOOD BOOKS FOR ALL.

THE GOSPEL MESSENGER.

"Set for the Defense of the Gospel."

Vol. 30, Old Series.   Mt. Morris, Ill., and Huntingdon, Pa., March 1, 1892.   No. 9.

The Gospel Messenger.

H. B. BRUMBAUGH, Editor,

And Business Manager of the Eastern House, Box 50.
Huntingdon, Pa.

Table of Contents.

THE church at Fort Scott, Kans., seems to be coming forward in work. We hope to see the Brethren succeed there as well as at other points. It is a place where we ought to have a good strong church.

REPORT OF COMMITTEE.

AT the Middle District Meeting of Pennsylvania, held at Hopewell, April 22, 1891, the following resolution was passed:

Resolved, That this Meeting appoint five brethren who shall carefully study the manner of conducting an "Old Folks' Home" and prepare a plan complete for its erection and maintenance, with constitution and by-laws, and that if be published before March 1, 1892, and that this report be examined, discussed, and acted upon by the next District Meeting, the churches instructing their delegates for or against the measure with suggestions for amendments, etc.

This resolution was accepted by the Meeting and the following committee appointed: J. F. Oller, Andrew Spanogle, M. R. Bashore, J. B. Fluke, and H. B. Brumbaugh.

In harmony with the above resolution, we, the Committee, make the following report:

Being interested in the work contemplated, and wishing to perform the duties entrusted to us, several meetings were called and at these meetings reports were made by the different members of such information as had been received person-

ally and by letter, from brethren connected with Homes of this kind, now in active operation. We had submitted to us their different plans, constitutions, by-laws, modes of running them and cost of maintaining the inmates, and we are glad to announce that all these reports are quite favorable, and that the friends of these institutions are greatly encouraged in their work.

From the information and encouragement thus received we have been doing all we could in pushing our work forward. We have prepared constitution and by-laws, are considering plans and looking up suitable locations and will be ready to report at the time named. There is nothing said in the resolution about location but it is inferred in the request for "plans complete for erection," as all plans depend somewhat on the location. The different locations, the amount, quality, price, water conveniences, railroad and church facilities should all be carefully noted and be presented to the coming District Meeting. This will be done by the Committee and can also be done by others interested in the work. That homes of this kind are needed, there can be no question, and we are glad to learn that, so far as they have been tried, they are proving to be a success, and therefore we hope that all of our churches will instruct their delegates in favor of a Home for the homeless.

CHURCH DIVISION.

Cause and Results.

IN looking over a late number of the Lancaster, Pa., *New Era*, we noticed a history given of the Mennonite church and, in connection with it, a brief history of our own church and her divisions. The sad part about this history is the large number of divisions for the small number of communicants, and the small shades of difference upon which the splits were made,—much less than we have given in the apostolic church, and yet they remained together as one body.

For the satisfaction of our readers we will give a synopsis of the history referred to.

The Mennonite Church.

The Mennonite church proper, was founded by Menno Simon, and that this country in 1683, thirty-six years before our own people came to America.

In the United States there are 41,541 members of the twelve Mennonite denominations, with church property valued at $643,800. Of this number 31,532 are in Pennsylvania, with $366,600 worth of church property. From this it will be seen that three-fourths of the members of the Mennonite family reside in Pennsylvania. There are more Mennonites in Lancaster County than any other County in the Union. The membership here is 7,382, with $149,800 church property.

This may be regarded as the parent body. It traces its origin back not only to Menno Simons, but through the Waldensians of the twelfth centu-

ry and through other churches holding the same faith to the earliest ages of the Christian era. It is the most numerous body of Mennonites in this country, having 246 organizations and 17,078 communicants. This body is represented in 17 States, but 10,077 of its communicants are to be found in the State of Pennsylvania, 5,365 in Lancaster County alone. Next to Pennsylvania, Ohio has the largest number, 1,736. Many of the organizations consist of very small companies, there being only 513 communicants in Kansas.

BRUEDERHOEF MENNONITES.

The next branch is known as the Bruederhoef Mennonite church. Jacob Huter, burned at the stake in 1536, at Innsbruck, in the Tyrol, was its founder. He instituted the Communistic idea. The followers first came to America in 1874, and settled in South Dakota, where they have 352 members.

THE AMISH MENNONITES.

The Amish go back in their history 200 years to their founder, Jacob Amen, who separated from the Mennonite church in consequence of differences concerning church discipline. The designation "Amish" came from his name. They have been noted for plainness and peculiarity of dress. The Amish constitute the second largest body of Mennonites, numbering 10,101 communicants. Of these, 2,305 are in Illinois, 2,234 in Pennsylvania, and 1,965 in Ohio. The rest are divided among eleven States. There are 1,326 members in Lancaster County.

What is known as the Old Amish branch is found in seven States, with 1,547 members—144 in Pennsylvania in Mifflin County. They are very strict in adherence to ancient forms and practices of their church.

The apostolic Mennonites are a branch of the Amish, came to this country fifty years ago, and number 209—all in Ohio.

THE REFORMED MENNONITES.

The Reformed Mennonites are the result of a movement begun in 1812 for the "restoration of purity in teaching and the maintenance of discipline." They regarded the Mennonite Church as "a corrupt and dead body." Rev. John Herr, of Lancaster County, was their leader. They are strict in their observances, severe in the use of the ban, and generally refuse to be present at religious services conducted by other denominations. They number 1,655 communicants, divided among nine States, 890 of them being found in Pennsylvania.

There are nine organizations of this branch in Lancaster County, with 600 members.

THE GENERAL CONFERENCE MENNONITES.

In 1848 a difficulty arose among the Mennonites in the eastern part of Pennsylvania in a matter of discipline. John Oberholtzer, a young minister, was charged by the older ministers with attempting to introduce new practices and a different teaching on some subjects. This led to the separation of Oberholtzer and a number of his followers from the church and to the organization of a

THE GOSPEL MESSENGER.

"Set for the Defense of the Gospel."

Vol. 30, Old Series.　　　Mt. Morris, Ill., and Huntingdon, Pa., March 1, 1892.　　　No. 9.

The Gospel Messenger.

H. B. BRUMBAUGH, Editor,
And Business Manager of the Eastern House, Box 50,
Huntingdon, Pa.

Table of Contents.

THE church at Fort Scott, Kans., seems to be coming forward in work. We hope to see the Brethren succeed there as well as at other points. It is a place where we ought to have a good strong church.

REPORT OF COMMITTEE.

AT the Middle District Meeting of Pennsylvania, held at Hopewell, April 22, 1891, the following resolution was passed:

Resolved, That this Meeting appoint five brethren who shall carefully study the manner of conducting an "Old Folks' Home" and prepare a plan complete for its erection and maintenance, with constitution and by-laws, and that it be published before March 1, 1892, and that this report be examined, discussed, and acted upon by the next District Meeting, the churches instructing their delegates for or against the measure with suggestions for amendments, etc.

This resolution was accepted by the Meeting and the following committee appointed: J. F. Oller, Andrew Spanogle, M. R. Bashore, J. B. Fluke, and H. B. Brumbaugh.

In harmony with the above resolution, we, the Committee, make the following report:

Being interested in the work contemplated, and wishing to perform the duties entrusted to us, several meetings were called and at these meetings reports were made by the different members of such information as had been received personally and by letter, from brethren connected with Homes of this kind, now in active operation. We had submitted to us their different plans, constitutions, by-laws, modes of running them and cost of maintaining the inmates, and we are glad to announce that all these reports are quite favorable, and that the friends of these institutions are greatly encouraged in their work.

From the information and encouragement thus received we have been doing all we could in pushing our work forward. We have prepared constitution and by-laws, are considering plans and looking up suitable locations and will be ready to report at the time named. There is nothing said in the resolution about location but it is inferred in the request for "plans complete for erection," as all plans depend somewhat on the location. The different locations, the amount, quality, price, water conveniences, railroad and church facilities should all be carefully noted and be presented to the coming District Meeting. This will be done by the Committee and can also be done by others interested in the work. That homes of this kind are needed, there can be no question, and we are glad to learn that, so far as they have been tried, they are proving to be a success, and therefore we hope that all of our churches will instruct their delegates in favor of a Home for the homeless.

CHURCH DIVISION.

Cause and Results.

IN looking over a late number of the Lancaster, Pa., *New Era,* we noticed a history given of the Mennonite church and, in connection with it, a brief history of our own church and her divisions. The sad part about this history is the large number of divisions for the small number of communicants, and the small shades of difference upon which the splits were made,—much less than we have given in the apostolic church, and yet they remained together as one body.

For the satisfaction of our readers we will give a synopsis of the history referred to.

The Mennonite Church.

The Mennonite church proper, was founded by Menno Simon, of Friesland, Holland, in the year 1536 and emigrated in part to this country in 1683, thirty-six years before our own people came to America.

In the United States there are 41,541 members of the twelve Mennonite denominations, with church property valued at $643,800. Of this number $1,532 are in Pennsylvania, with $366,600 worth of church property. From this it will be seen that three-fourths of the members of the Mennonite family reside in Pennsylvania. There are more Mennonites in Lancaster County than any other County in the Union. The membership here is 7,382, with $149,800 church property.

This may be regarded as the parent body. It traces its origin back not only to Menno Simons, but through the Waldensians of the twelfth century and through other churches holding the same faith to the earliest ages of the Christian era. It is the most numerous body of Mennonites in this country, having 246 organizations and 17,078 communicants. This body is represented in 17 States, but 10,077 of its communicants are to be found in the State of Pennsylvania, 5,365 in Lancaster County alone. Next to Pennsylvania, Ohio has the largest number, 1,736. Many of the organizations consist of very small companies, there being only 513 communicants in Kansas.

BRUEDERHOEF MENNONITES.

The next branch is known as the Bruederhoef Mennonite church. Jacob Huter, burned at the stake in 1536, at Innsbruck, in the Tyrol, was its founder. He instituted the Communistic idea. The followers first came to America in 1874, and settled in South Dakota, where they have 352 members.

THE AMISH MENNONITES.

The Amish go back in their history 200 years to their founder, Jacob Amen, who separated from the Mennonite church in consequence of differences concerning church discipline. The designation "Amish" came from his name. They have been noted for plainness and peculiarity of dress. The Amish constitute the second largest body of Mennonites, numbering 10,101 communicants. Of these, 2,305 are in Illinois, 2,234 in Pennsylvania, and 1,965 in Ohio. The rest are divided among eleven States. There are 1,326 members in Lancaster County.

What is known as the Old Amish branch is found in seven States, with 1,547 members—144 in Pennsylvania in Mifflin County. They are very strict in adherence to ancient forms and practices of their church.

The apostolic Mennonites are a branch of the Amish, came to this country fifty years ago, and number 209—all in Ohio.

THE REFORMED MENNONITES.

The Reformed Mennonites are the result of a movement begun in 1812 for the "restoration of purity in teaching and the maintenance of discipline." They regarded the Mennonite Church as "a corrupt and dead body." Rev. John Herr, of Lancaster County, was their leader. They are strict in their observances, severe in the use of the ban, and generally refuse to be present at religious services conducted by other denominations. They number 1,655 communicants, divided among seven States, 890 of them being found in Pennsylvania.

There are nine organizations of this branch in Lancaster County, with 600 members.

THE GENERAL CONFERENCE MENNONITES.

In 1848 a difficulty arose among the Mennonites in the eastern part of Pennsylvania in a matter of discipline. John Oberholtzer, a young minister, was charged by the older ministers with attempting to introduce new practices and a different teaching on some subjects. This led to the separation of Oberholtzer and a number of his followers from the church and to the organization of a

that no more than the twelve were present; but then none of the evangelists have said there were *not* more. Besides I think we can get an idea from the following Scripture, that others were present:" And as they sat and did eat, Jesus said, Verily I say unto you, One of you which eateth with me shall betray me. And they began to be sorrowful, and to say unto him one by one, Is it I? and another said, Is it I? And he answered and said unto them, It is one of the twelve, that dippeth with me in the dish." Mark 14: 18–20. Take notice that in the eighteenth verse Jesus says, "One of you which *eateth* with me shall betray me." Then, in the twentieth verse, in answer to their sorrowful inquiries, he says, "It is one of the *twelve*." If there had been no more than the twelve present, the answer in the twentieth verse would contain nothing more definite than his declaration in the eighteenth verse, and would appear more like mocking their sorrow, than an intelligent reply to their earnest question.

But when we assume that other disciples were present, we can see the propriety of the answer; that the culprit was one of the *twelve*, and that within that circle they must look for the betrayer.

Now, in concluding this little review of the question, I will state that certain professing Christians hold to the idea that the laity should not wash feet, but that the elders should not only wash each *other's* feet, but the feet of the laity also, claiming that none but the twelve apostles were present when feet-washing was instituted, that the bishops, or elders, stand related to the other members now, as did the apostles then; therefore, as the command to "wash one another's feet" was not given to any of the laity, that class should be excused from this service. And it is a fact that *none but the apostles* were present to receive the command and example from the Savior, their argument is not without some weight. But if it can be shown beyond a reasonable doubt that other disciples were present to receive the command, this one point at least is gained, that the laity have an equal privilege with the official body, in this special service.

Now to the MESSENGER readers in general, and to my dear Bro. Miller in particular, I will say: "Please do not regard this as an effort to introduce an unpleasant controversy upon an unimportant question. But if the change in my views, as indicated here, for which I have now given my reasons, has been from truth to error, please set me right again.

La Porte, Ind.

"OCCUPY TILL I COME."

BY ELIZABETH H. DELP.

GOD calls us to work for him. The day passes and the shadows of night gather, in which he will come, and we must be found ready and watching. Souls are perishing about us, and we must do what we can to bring them to Jesus, that they may also be ready.

Many efforts are being made for the furtherance of Christ's kingdom upon the earth; his servants are proclaiming his will "in all the world." Some are devoting their lives to this service. Perhaps the field of labor will be a foreign land, where, away from home and friends and all that makes life a pleasure in this world, the missionary toils, as a stranger on earth. He will not cease his labors, because, in the burning heat of persecution, or the barren soil of ignorance, there is little to encourage or reward him. Surely, in heaven our Lord will "make him ruler over ten cities."

"Be ye followers of me, even as I also am of Christ," said one of the apostles. They preached only Jesus Christ and him crucified. Nothing hindered them; evil reports, scourgings and imprisonment were all welcomed in the name of Jesus.

If we bear the cross, we need not suffer the death of a martyr. It may be our lot to occupy only a small place for him, but even then we must be faithful in "a little" till he come. We can strive to grow in his likeness, that, as he delayeth, he will find us with hearts looking anxiously unto him. And when his chastening hand is laid upon us, could we but then remember that the incrustation of evil and sinfulness in our nature, can only be removed by the furnace of affliction and suffering! Only Christ can help us then, and by these dark and bitter experiences, we shall be purified and the soft light of resignation will beam from our spirit, and the Lord will claim us in his day, as one of his jewels.

"Clouds and darkness round us press,
Would we have one sorrow less?
All the sharpness of the cross,
All that tells the world is loss,
Death, and darkness, and the tomb,
Pain us only 'Till he come!'"

INSTRUCTING APPLICANTS FOR BAPTISM.

AT the end of the first week of our late protracted meetings in the Chapel, there were fifteen young members to be baptized. At a called meeting on Saturday, a good audience assembled in the Chapel for the purpose of hearing the order laid before the fifteen applicants. We sometimes do this in public. The services were opened with prayer, after which, Bro. D. E. Price, our elder, addressed the applicants, substantially as follows:

The reason why the Brethren church deems it necessary to present, or to call the *especial* attention of applicants for baptism to those principles, is, because they are neglected and treated lightly, or indifferently, by the majority of professors of the Christian religion.

When persons present themselves to the church as subjects for baptism, we take it for granted that the internal work has been wrought; that they have thoroughly repented toward God for all of their former sins, and have experienced peace in believing on Jesus Christ as their Savior, or, according to Matt. 11: 28, have obtained *rest* by coming to him. Then, before they are initiated into the church by baptism, they agree to conform to the following Gospel principles:

1. *Non-swearing.*—For authority we give the teachings of Jesus. Matt. 5: 33–37. "Again, ye have heard that it hath been said by them of old time, Thou shalt not forswear thyself, but shalt perform unto the Lord thine oaths: but I say unto you, Swear not at all; neither by heaven; for it is God's throne: nor by the earth; for it is his footstool: neither by Jerusalem; for it is the city of the great King. Neither shalt thou swear by thy head, because thou canst not make one hair white or black. But let your communication be, Yea, yea; Nay, nay: for whatsoever is more than these cometh of evil." The apostle James testifies to the teaching of Jesus, and says, "But above all things, my brethren, swear not, neither by heaven, neither by the earth, neither by any other oath: but let your yea be yea; and your nay nay; lest ye fall into condemnation." James 5: 12. Some claim that this Scripture has reference to profane swearing; but they should remember that profane swearing was strictly prohibited under the former dispensation, while the legal oath was allowed; hence we must come to the conclusion that it refers to the oath administered by the officers of the civil law. But the civil authorities have made provision for us, so we need not violate the Holy Scriptures, but can simply *affirm* when we are called on by 'the higher powers, to bear testimony in any matter.

2. *Non-resistance.* — The Savior follows his teaching on prohibition of swearing, in the same connection, by the doctrine of *non-resistance.* Matt. 5: 38–45 says, "Ye have heard that it hath been said, An eye for an eye, and a tooth for a tooth: but I say unto you, That ye resist not evil: but whosoever shall smite thee on thy right cheek, turn to him the other also. And if any man will sue thee at the law, and take away thy coat, let him have thy cloak also. And whosoever shall compel thee to go a mile, go with him twain. Give to him that asketh thee, and from him that would borrow of thee turn not thou away. Ye have heard that it hath been said, Thou shalt love thy neighbour, and hate thine enemy. But I say unto you, Love your enemies, bless them that curse you, do good to them that hate you, and pray for them which despitefully use you, and persecute you; that ye may be the children of your Father which is in heaven: for he maketh his sun to rise on the evil and on the good, and sendeth rain on the just and on the unjust." We find the same doctrine taught in Rom. 12: 19, 20, 21, "Dearly beloved, avenge not yourselves, but rather give place unto wrath: for it is written, Vengeance is mine; I will repay, saith the Lord. Therefore if thine enemy hunger, feed him; if he thirst, give him drink: for in so doing thou shalt heap coals of fire on his head. Be not overcome of evil, but overcome evil with good."

From the above Scriptures, and many more that might be produced, you see clearly, that you cannot be allowed to return evil for evil, either in a personal or rational sense; hence you cannot take up carnal weapons against your fellow-men, under any circumstances. Under no circumstances will you be permitted to use the law against your brother, nor against those not members without first consulting the church. In all cases of doubtful propriety it will be found best not to move without the counsel of the church. Our Brethren have also advised against voting at political elections, it being understood however, that those who do vote, do so upon their own responsibility, but it is, and always has been, contrary to the rules of the church for any member to take an active part in political contests of any class.

3. *Secret Societies.*—You cannot unite with any of the *secret societies* of the world; it don't matter by what name they may be called; and if already belonging to any of them, you must abandon them before you can be received into church fellowship; because it is a violation of the Gospel of Christ. We will produce, from the many Scriptural testimonies, only one, 2 Cor. 6: 14–18, "Be ye not unequally yoked together with unbelievers: for what fellowship hath righteousness with unrighteousness? and what communion hath light with darkness? and what concord hath Christ with Belial? or what part hath he that believeth with an infidel? and what agreement hath the temple of God with idols? for ye are the temple of the living God; as God hath said, I will dwell in them, and walk in them; and I will be their God, and they shall be my people. Wherefore come out from among them, and be ye separate, saith the Lord, and touch not the unclean thing; and I will receive you, and will be a Father unto you, and ye shall be my sons and daughters, saith the Lord Almighty." Hence, to unite with any of said societies is being yoked with all classes of unbelievers, and, also, to join them you must, in violation of the Gospel, be sworn into their fellowship.

4. *Non-conformity.*—To introduce this important question, we refer you to Rom. 12: 1, 2. "I beseech you therefore, brethren, by the mercies

that no more than the twelve were present; but then none of the evangelists have said there were *not* more. Besides I think we can get an idea from the following Scripture, that others were present: "And as they sat and did eat, Jesus said, Verily I say unto you, One of you which eateth with me shall betray me. And they began to be sorrowful, and to say unto him one by one, Is it I? and another said, Is it I? And he answered and said unto them, It is one of the twelve, that dippeth with me in the dish." Mark 14: 18-20. Take notice that in the eighteenth verse Jesus says, "One of you which *eateth* with me shall betray me." Then, in the twentieth verse, in answer to their sorrowful inquiries, he says, "It is one of the *twelve*." If there had been no more than the twelve present, the answer in the twentieth verse would contain nothing more definite than his declaration in the eighteenth verse, and would appear more like mocking their sorrow, than an intelligent reply to their earnest question.

But when we assume that other disciples were present, we can see the propriety of the answer; that the culprit was one of the *twelve*, and that within that circle they must look for the betrayer.

Now, in concluding this little review of the question, I will state that certain professing Christians hold to the idea that the laity should not wash feet, but that the elders should not only wash each *other's* feet, but the feet of the laity also, claiming that none but the twelve apostles were present when feet-washing was instituted, that the bishops, or elders, stand related to the other members now, as did the apostles then; therefore, as the command to "wash one another's feet" was not given to any of the laity, that class should be excused from this service. And if it is a fact that *none but the apostles* were present to receive the command and example from the Savior, their argument is not without some weight. But if it can be shown beyond a reasonable doubt that other disciples were present to receive the command, this one point at least is gained, that the laity have an equal privilege with the official body, in this special service.

Now to the MESSENGER readers in general, and to my dear Bro. Miller in particular, I will say: "Please do not regard this as an effort to introduce an unpleasant controversy upon an unimportant question. But if the change in my views, as indicated here, for which I have now given my reasons, has been from truth to error, please set me right again.

La Porte, Ind.

"OCCUPY TILL I COME."

BY ELIZABETH H. DELP.

GOD calls us to work for him. The day passes and the shadows of night gather, in which he will come, and we must be found ready and watching. Souls are perishing about us, and we must do what we can to bring them to Jesus, that they may also be ready.

Many efforts are being made for the furtherance of Christ's kingdom upon the earth; his servants are proclaiming his will "in all the world." Some are devoting their lives to this service. Perhaps the field of labor will be a foreign land, where, away from home and friends and all that makes life a pleasure in this world, the missionary toils, as a stranger on earth. He will not cease his labors, because, in the burning heat of persecution, or the barren soil of ignorance, there is little to encourage or reward him. Surely, in heaven our Lord will "make him ruler over ten cities."

"Be ye followers of me, even as I also am of Christ," said one of the apostles. They preached only Jesus Christ and him crucified. Nothing hindered them; evil reports, scourgings and imprisonment were all welcomed in the name of Jesus.

If we bear the cross, we need not suffer the death of a martyr. It may be our lot to occupy only a small place for him, but even then we must be faithful in "a little" till he come. We can strive to grow in his likeness, that, as he delayeth, he will find us with hearts looking anxiously unto him. And when his chastening hand is laid upon us, could we but then remember that the incrustation of evil and sinfulness in our nature, can only be removed by the furnace of affliction and suffering! Only Christ can help us then, and by these dark and bitter experiences, we shall be purified and the soft light of resignation will beam from our spirit, and the Lord will claim us in his day, as one of his jewels.

"Clouds and darkness round us press,
Would we have one sorrow less?
All the sharpness of the cross,
All that tells the world is loss,
Death, and darkness, and the tomb,
Pain us only 'Till he come!'"

INSTRUCTING APPLICANTS FOR BAPTISM.

AT the end of the first week of our late protracted meetings in the Chapel, there were fifteen young members to be baptized. At a called meeting on Saturday, a good audience assembled in the Chapel for the purpose of hearing the order laid before the fifteen applicants. We sometimes do this in public. The services were opened with prayer, after which, Bro. D. E. Price, our elder, addressed the applicants, substantially as follows:

The reason why the Brethren church deems it necessary to present, or to call the *especial* attention of applicants for baptism to those principles, is, because they are neglected and treated lightly, or indifferently, by the majority of professors of the Christian religion.

When persons present themselves to the church as subjects for baptism, we take it for granted that the internal work has been wrought; that they have thoroughly repented toward God for all of their former sins, and have experienced peace in believing on Jesus Christ as their Savior, or, according to Matt. 11: 28, have obtained *rest* by coming to him. Then, before they are initiated into the church by baptism, they agree to conform to the following Gospel principles:

1. Non-swearing.—For authority we give the teachings of Jesus. Matt. 5: 33-37. "Again, ye have heard that it hath been said by them of old time, Thou shalt not forswear thyself, but shalt perform unto the Lord thine oaths: but I say unto you, Swear not at all; neither by heaven; for it is God's throne: nor by the earth; for it is his footstool: neither by Jerusalem; for it is the city of the great King. Neither shalt thou swear by thy head, because thou canst not make one hair white or black. But let your communication be, Yea, yea; Nay, nay: for whatsoever is more than these cometh of evil." The apostle James testifies to the teaching of Jesus, and says, "But above all things, my brethren, swear not, neither by heaven, neither by the earth, neither by any other oath: but let your yea be yea; and your nay nay; lest ye fall into condemnation." James 5: 12.

Some claim that this Scripture has reference to profane swearing; but they should remember that profane swearing was strictly prohibited under the former dispensation, while the legal oath was allowed; hence we must come to the conclusion that it refers to the oath administered by the officers of the civil law. But the civil authorities have made provision for us, so we need not violate the Holy Scriptures, but can simply *affirm* when we are called on by the higher powers, to bear testimony in any matter.

2. Non-resistance. — The Savior follows his teaching on prohibition of swearing, in the same connection, by the doctrine of *non-resistance.* Matt. 5: 38-45 says, "Ye have heard that it hath been said, An eye for an eye, and a tooth for a tooth: but I say unto you, That ye resist not evil: but whosoever shall smite thee on thy right cheek, turn to him the other also. And if any man will sue thee at the law, and take away thy coat, let him have thy cloak also. And whosoever shall compel thee to go a mile, go with him twain. Give to him that asketh thee, and from him that would borrow of thee turn not thou away. Ye have heard that it hath been said, Thou shalt love thy neighbour, and hate thine enemy. But I say unto you, Love your enemies, bless them that curse you, do good to them that hate you, and pray for them which despitefully use you, and persecute you; that ye may be the children of your Father which is in heaven: for he maketh his sun to rise on the evil and on the good, and sendeth rain on the just and on the unjust." We find the same doctrine taught in Rom. 12: 19, 20, 21, "Dearly beloved, avenge not yourselves, but rather give place unto wrath: for it is written, Vengeance is mine; I will repay, saith the Lord. Therefore if thine enemy hunger, feed him; if he thirst, give him drink: for in so doing thou shalt heap coals of fire on his head. Be not overcome of evil, but overcome evil with good."

From the above Scriptures, and many more that might be produced, you see clearly, that you cannot be allowed to return evil for evil, either in a personal or rational sense; hence you cannot take up carnal weapons against your fellow-men, under any circumstances. Under no circumstances will you be permitted to use the law against your brother, nor against those not members without first consulting the church. In all cases of doubtful propriety it will be found best not to move without the counsel of the church. Our Brethren have also advised against voting at political elections, it being understood however, that those who do vote, do so upon their own responsibility, but it is, and always has been, contrary to the rules of the church for any member to take an active part in political contests of any class.

3. Secret Societies.—You cannot unite with any of the *secret societies* of the world; it don't matter by what name they may be called; and if already belonging to any of them, you must abandon them before you can be received into church fellowship; because it is a violation of the Gospel of Christ. We will produce, from the many Scriptural testimonies, only one, 2 Cor. 6: 14-18, "Be ye not unequally yoked together with unbelievers: for what fellowship hath righteousness with unrighteousness? and what communion hath light with darkness? and what concord hath Christ with Belial? or what part hath he that believeth with an infidel? and what agreement hath the temple of God with idols? for ye are the temple of the living God; as God hath said, I will dwell in them, and walk in them; and I will be their God, and they shall be my people. Wherefore come out from among them, and be ye separate, saith the Lord, and touch not the unclean thing; and I will receive you, and will be a Father unto you, and ye shall be my sons and daughters, saith the Lord Almighty." Hence, to unite with any of said societies is being yoked with all classes of unbelievers, and, also, to join them you must, in violation of the Gospel, be sworn into their fellowship.

4. Non-conformity.—To introduce this important question, we refer you to Rom. 12: 1, 2. "I beseech you therefore, brethren, by the mercies

back to his embrace and to their allegiance to him. But in that bright abode, where everything is seen through a perfect medium, where there is no tempter to give us wrong impressions of things, and we are freed from all the frailties and imperfections that are incident to the flesh, we will have no need of the lessons taught by adversity. Then we will understand each other perfectly. No dark suspicions will cast their gloomy shadows athwart our minds. There will be perfect love, because of perfect confidence. Oh how the weary, foot-sore pilgrim longs for that blissful abode, where there will be entire freedom from all infirmities of the flesh! The most lofty imagination can draw but a faint picture of that place of which it is written, "Eye hath not seen, nor ear heard, neither have entered into the heart of man, the things which God hath prepared for them that love him." 1 Cor. 2: 9.

HOW THEY BAPTIZE IN GREECE.

BY E. J. BEEGHLY.

In looking over my scrap-book, I noticed the following, which I have taken out of the *Nemaha County Republican* about a year ago, which I think would be interesting to a great many who read it. The article in question is headed, "Presbyterian Dilemma."

"Dr. W. D. Powell writes from Greece to the Texas *Baptist Herald* that the Presbyterians in Greece practice immersion for baptism, it being impossible to persuade native Greeks that the word *baptizo* means anything but *immerse*. Greek is still a living language, spoken by the inhabitants of Greece, and they think they know what Greek words mean. In this country Presbyterians argue against immersion and pretend that *baptizo* has other meanings and that the right way to baptize is by sprinkling. Various ponderous volumes our Presbyterian brethren have published, to show that sprinkling is the proper act for baptism, and the arguments have not been without weight with those who were not acquainted with the Greek language.

"Presbyterian scholars, who are not polemical, frankly concede that *baptizo* does not mean sprinkling or pouring. American Presbyterians have planted three churches in Greece and have been compelled to practice immersion, because everybody there knows Greek and knows that *baptizo* does not mean sprinkling or pouring. Dr. Powell says: I found that all churches in Greece, Presbyterians included, are compelled to immerse candidates for baptism, for, as one of the professors remarked: 'The commonest day laborer understands nothing else for *baptizo* but immersion.' He also visited the great university at Athens, which has 3,000 students, and he says, 'I asked a professor what *baptizo* meant and he said, It has but one meaning, to submerge, — to immerse. Why do you ask?'

"We commend this to the *Christian Observer* of this City and to our Presbyterian brethren generally. How comes it that if *baptizo* means to sprinkle, the Greeks cannot be made to believe it? Can it be that the Greeks do not understand their own language?

"What would the *Observer* say if a Presbyterian church in Kentucky should adopt immersion? Are arguments which are valid in America, worthless in Greece? By all means let some champion of sprinkling be sent to Greece to explain to the Greeks the meaning of Greek words. If the Methodists can spare Dr. Ditzler, the Presbyterians might secure his services for this task. We wait to see what our genial neighbor will say."—*Western Recorder.*

Sabetha, Kans.

CHURCH DIVISIONS.

(*Concluded from first Page.*)

body called New Mennonites. They suffered some divisions among themselves, but after awhile they entered into a union with churches in Illinois and Iowa which had come from Germany, and the result was the formation of a general conference, wherefore the body is called General Conference Mennonites. These Mennonites are less strict in discipline than other branches and are endeavoring to provide themselves with an educated and a paid ministry.

The General Conference embraces 3 districts, the central, eastern and the western, and is represented in ten States, its chief strength being in Kansas and Pennsylvania.

This branch has 1,426 members in Pennsylvania, with $69,500 in church property. Bucks County has the largest number of members, 906. There are only 31 members in Lancaster County.

THE CHURCH OF GOD IN CHRIST.

John Holdeman is the founder of this branch, which began its existence in 1859. Holdeman believed he was called of God to the ministry by visions and dreams. He claims by the spirit of prophecy to "understand the foreknowledge of God, to know mysteries, to settle difficulties, to keep peace, and to interpret visions and dreams." His followers strive to keep as closely as possible to the teachings of Menno Simons, Dietrich Philip, and the martyrs of the Church in Europe. This branch has 471 communicants, some of whom, however, are in Pennsylvania. Dickinson County, Kansas, has one organization with 100 members.

The old Wisler Mennonites have maintained a distinct existence for 20 years. They separated from the main body of Mennonites because they are opposed to Sunday-schools and evening meetings, and other practices, which they regard as innovations. They are represented in three States, Ohio, Indiana and Michigan, with 610 members.

DIE BUNDES CONFERENCE DER MENNONITEN BRUEDER-GEMEINDE.

This body originated in Russia about 50 years ago and came to this country in 1873-'76. They differ from other Mennonites in being immersionists, lay particular stress on the evidences of conversion, and are active and zealous in the performance of their religious duties. They have twelve organizations, and 1,388 communicants. Five of their organizations are in Kansas.

Henry Egli was the founder of the Defenseless Mennonites, who are strictly a branch of the Amish. They emphasize the importance of conversion and regeneration, and claim to have separated from the Amish on this account. They are represented in five States, with 856 communicants.

THE MENNONITE BRETHREN IN CHRIST.

This is the newest branch of the Mennonites, having originated only ten or twelve years ago. It is Methodistic in its form of organization, in its usages, and in its discipline. They are open Communion Mennonites, and baptize in any form the applicant may prefer. There are two annual conferences of them in this country, and they also have churches in Canada. About one-half of them are in Pennsylvania.

The communicants number 1,113,—559 in Pennsylvania.

It no doubt would be interesting to have the supposed or given cause for all these divisions, and yet, from our own experience as a church, we can readily see how easy it is to divide and how hard it is to stop. A division, once commenced,

may go on to infinity; every succeeding one making the next one possible and more easy, because, as the divisions increase, the differences between them grow less.

A given or supposed cause for such divisions is not always the *real* cause. Indeed the cause generally comes from where we are the least willing to admit. In making practical the "Ultimate Rule of Right," it is said we must *bear and forbear*. This means much, and includes all the duties that we, as Christians, are to exercise towards ourselves and our fellows, and could we set these duties before us and practically carry them out, we are sure these divisions would be avoided. To say that these causes are always one-sided and that the dissenting part is wholly in the wrong, would only show our egotism, and that we have not yet learned to know human nature, much less the divine.

The same cause that divided the Mennonite church into twelve parts, may divide each of those parts into twelve more parts and so on, *ad infinitum*. The same may be said of our own divisions. Do we say too much if we would say that we have not a single church within our organization to-day that, under similar circumstances would not be susceptible to divisions? We think not. If there should be such churches then, are they better than the apostolical churches in the days of Peter and Paul? Do you ever read the Acts and the epistolary writings? If so, have you carefully studied the characteristics of the membership of those churches? Did they have any difficulties—any troubles, differences of opinion and disorders? Plenty of them. Paul and Barnabas had a regular quarrel and they separated. About circumcision the early ministers and people had a regular jangle and, to have a reconciliation, some were circumcised directly against the letter of the teachings of Christ.

There was cause for division there. Look at the character of the communicants which Jude names and calls them "spots" in their feasts. Why were they not expelled? Again; look at the report Paul gives of the Corinthian churches. Surely such a church ought to have been disfellowshipped. Knowing things, what did this man of God do? He directed that they should correct the very gross wrongs into which they had fallen, and the others he would set in order when he visited them.

What an easy thing it would have been to have had divisions,—final,—in the apostolical churches. But they did not,—and why not? It would be well for the churches of more modern times to study more carefully the apostolic form of church government. We would undoubtedly learn that in their exercising of the ultimate rule of right, there was much *bearing* and *forbearing* exercised and that the executive power was seldom resorted to, except for crimes of gross immorality and inexcusable sins. They patterned after the family government, which is God's own form and is intended to provide for and save the children. This is what the church is to do and there can be no better way. The cause, it seems to us, for these divisions is, that we too much determine to have *our* way, and the more we manifest this determination, the more the dissenting party will determine to have its way, and the more each party so determines, the farther they get apart, and a division is the result. In our next we may speak some of the results of these divisions.

back to his embrace and to their allegiance to him. But in that bright abode, where everything is seen through a perfect medium, where there is no tempter to give us wrong impressions of things, and we are freed from all the frailties and imperfections that are incident to the flesh, we will have no need of the lessons taught by adversity. Then we will understand each other perfectly. No dark suspicions will cast their gloomy shadows athwart our minds. There will be perfect love, because of perfect confidence. Oh how the weary, foot-sore pilgrim longs for that blissful abode, where there will be entire freedom from all infirmities of the flesh! The most lofty imagination can draw but a faint picture of that place of which it is written, "Eye hath not seen, nor ear heard, neither have entered into the heart of man, the things which God hath prepared for them that love him." 1 Cor. 2: 9.

HOW THEY BAPTIZE IN GREECE.

BY E. J. BEEGHLY.

In looking over my scrap-book, I noticed the following, which I have taken out of the *Nemaha County Republican* about a year ago, which I think would be interesting to a great many who read it. The article in question is headed, "Presbyterian Dilemma."

"Dr. W. D. Powell writes from Greece to the *Texas Baptist Herald* that the Presbyterians in Greece practice immersion for baptism, it being impossible to persuade native Greeks that the word *baptizo* means anything but *immerse*. Greek is still a living language, spoken by the inhabitants of Greece, and they think they know what Greek words mean. In this country Presbyterians argue against immersion and pretend that *baptizo* has other meanings and that the right way to baptize is by sprinkling. Various ponderous volumes our Presbyterian brethren have published, to show that sprinkling is the proper act for baptism, and the arguments have not been without weight with those who were not acquainted with the Greek language.

"Presbyterian scholars, who are not polemical, frankly concede that *baptizo* does not mean sprinkling or pouring. American Presbyterians have planted three churches in Greece and have been compelled to practice immersion, because everybody there knows Greek and knows that *baptizo* does not mean sprinkling or pouring. Dr. Powell says: I found that all churches in Greece, Presbyterians included, are compelled to immerse candidates for baptism, for, as one of the professors remarked: 'The commonest day laborer understands nothing else for *baptizo* but immersion.' He also visited the great university at Athens, which has 3,000 students, and he said, 'I asked a professor what *baptizo* meant and he said, it has but one meaning, to submerge, — to immerse. Why do you ask?'

"We commend this to the *Christian Observer* of this City and to ten of Presbyterian brethren generally. How comes it that if *baptizo* means to sprinkle, the Greeks cannot be made to believe it? Can it be that the Greeks do not understand their own language?

"What would the *Observer* say if a Presbyterian church in Kentucky should adopt immersion? Are arguments which are valid in America, worthless in Greece? By all means let some champion of sprinkling be sent to Greece to explain to the Greeks the meaning of Greek words. If the Methodists can spare Dr. Ditzler, the Presbyterians might secure his services for this task. We wait to see what our genial neighbor will say."—*Western Recorder*.

Sabetha, Kans.

CHURCH DIVISIONS.

(Concluded from first Page.)

body called New Mennonites. They suffered some divisions among themselves, but after awhile they entered into a union with churches in Illinois and Iowa which had come from Germany, and the result was the formation of a general conference, wherefore the body is called General Conference Mennonites. These Mennonites are less strict in discipline than other branches and are endeavoring to provide themselves with an educated and a paid ministry.

The General Conference embraces 3 districts, the central, eastern and the western, and is represented in ten States, its chief strength being in Kansas and Pennsylvania.

This branch has 1,426 members in Pennsylvania, with $69,500 in church property. Bucks County has the largest number of members, 906. There are only 31 members in Lancaster County.

THE CHURCH OF GOD IN CHRIST.

John Holdeman is the founder of this branch, which began its existence in 1859. Holdeman believed he was called of God to the ministry by visions and dreams. He claims by the spirit of prophecy to "understand the foreknowledge of God, to know mysteries, to settle difficulties, to keep peace, and to interpret visions and dreams." His followers strive to keep as closely as possible to the teachings of Menno Simons, Dietrich Philip, and the martyrs of the Church in Europe. This branch has 471 communicants, none of whom, however, are in Pennsylvania. Dickinson County, Kansas, has one organization with 100 members.

The old Wisler Mennonites have maintained a distinct existence for 20 years. They separated from the main body of Mennonites because they are opposed to Sunday-schools and evening meetings, and other practices, which they regard as innovations. They are represented in three States, Ohio, Indiana and Michigan, with 610 members.

DIE BUNDES CONFERENCE DER MENNONITEN BRUEDER-GEMEINDE.

This body originated in Russia about 50 years ago and came to this country in 1873-'76. They differ from other Mennonites in being immersionists, lay particular stress on the evidences of conversion, and are active and zealous in the performance of their religious duties. They have twelve organizations, and 1,388 communicants. Five of their organizations are in Kansas.

Henry Egli was the founder of the Defenceless Mennonites, who are strictly a branch of the Amish. They emphasize the importance of conversion and regeneration, and claim to have separated from the Amish on this account. They are represented in five States, with 856 communicants.

THE MENNONITE BRETHREN IN CHRIST.

This is the newest branch of the Mennonites, having originated only ten or twelve years ago. It is Methodistic in its form of organization, in its usages, and in its discipline. They are open Communion Mennonites, and baptize in any form the applicant may prefer. There are two annual conferences of them in this country, and they also have churches in Canada. About one-half of them are in Pennsylvania.

The communicants number 1,113,—559 in Pennsylvania.

It no doubt would be interesting to have the supposed or given cause for all these divisions, and yet, from our own experience, as a church, we can readily see how easy it is to divide and how hard it is to stop. A division, once commenced,

may go on to infinity; every succeeding one making the next one possible and more easy, because, as the divisions increase, the differences between them grow less.

A given or supposed cause for such divisions is not always the real cause. Indeed the cause generally comes from where we are the least willing to admit. In making practical the "Ultimate Rule of Right," it is said we must *bear and forbear*. This means much, and includes all the duties that we, as Christians, are to exercise towards ourselves and our fellows, and could we set these duties before us and practically carry them out, we are sure these divisions would be avoided. To say that these causes are always one-sided and that the dissenting part is wholly in the wrong, would only show our egotism, and that we have not yet learned to know human nature, much less the divine.

The same cause that divided the Mennonite church into twelve parts, may divide each of those parts into twelve more parts and so on, *ad infinitum*. The same may be said of our own divisions. Do we say too much if we would say that we have not a single church within our organization to-day that, under similar circumstances would not be susceptible to divisions? We think not. If there should be such churches then, are they better than the apostolical churches in the days of Peter and Paul? Do you ever read the Acts and the epistolary writings? If so, have you carefully studied the characteristics of the membership of those churches? Did they have any difficulties—any troubles, differences of opinion and disorders? Plenty of them. Paul and Barnabas had a regular quarrel and they separated. About circumcision the early ministers and people had a regular jangle and, to have a reconciliation, some were circumcised directly against the letter of the teachings of Christ.

There was cause for division there. Look at the character of the communicants which Jude names and calls them "spots" in their feasts. Why were they not expelled? Again; look at the report Paul gives of the Corinthian churches. Surely such a church ought to have been disfellowshipped. Knowing things, what did this man of God do? He directed that they should correct the very gross wrongs into which they had fallen, and the others he would set in order when he visited them.

What an easy thing it would have been to have had divisions,—final,—in the apostolical churches. But they did not,—and why not? It would be well for the churches of more modern times to study more carefully the apostolic form of church government. We would undoubtedly learn that in their exercising of the ultimate rule of right, there was much *bearing* and *forbearing* exercised and that the executive power was seldom resorted to, except for crimes of gross immorality and inexcusable sins. They patterned after the family government, which is God's own form and is intended to provide for and save the children. This is what the church is to do and there can be no better way. The cause, it seems to us, for these divisions is, that we too much determine to have *our* way, and the more we manifest this determination, the more the dissenting party will determine to have its way, and the more each party so manifests, the farther they get apart, and a division is the result. In our next we may speak some of the results of these divisions.

14: 7 tells us that we have the poor with us always, and "whensoever ye will ye may do them good." What a grand opportunity has at this time presented itself to us, here in the State of Kansas, to aid in erecting a permanent home for the poor! When we consider the grand and blessed promises, contained in the Bible, to those who remember the poor in this life, we should not hesitate to contribute liberally, and help on with the good work, for we are told that "Blessed is he that considereth the poor; the Lord will deliver him in time of trouble. The Lord preserves him and keeps him alive, and he shall be blessed upon the earth, and thou wilt not deliver him unto the will of his enemies. The Lord will strengthen him upon the bed of languishing. Thou 'wilt make his bed in time of sickness."

Let us remember that when we give to the poor, the Lord considers the act, and that he will pay us again according to his pleasure. "He that hath pity upon the poor, lendeth unto the Lord, and that which he hath given will he pay him again." Prov. 19: 7. Surely the Lord will bear in mind to repay those acts of kindness; he will not forget your work and labor of love, which "ye have showed toward his name in that ye have ministered to the saints, and do minister."

Upon the other hand, if we turn a deaf ear to the pressing cry of those in need, how will the Lord regard us? Will he hear us when we cry? Please read Prov. 21: 13, and you will find that whoso stoppeth his ears to the cry of the poor, he also shall cry himself, and shall not be heard.

There are some who are especially mentioned in the Bible as those who should be cared for and supported. Turn to Isa. 1: 17 and you will find that we should learn to do well, relieve the oppressed, judge the fatherless, and plead for the widows. How is this work designated in the New Testament? "Pure religion and undefiled before God and the Father is this, to visit the fatherless and widows in their affliction and keep himself unspotted from the world." James 1: 27.

There are those of us, dear brethren and sisters, who, while we have our tables spread in abundance with the rich productions of this earth, may be forgetful of the many poor, scattered over the land, who have scarcely anything to eat. Could we not save considerable each year if we would do with a little less on our tables? Might we not fast part of the time? I believe the Lord would be delighted with an act like this; for he says in Isa. 58: 6, 7, "Is not this the fast that I have chosen? . . . Is it not to deal thy bread to the hungry, and that thou bring the poor that are cast out to thy house? When thou seest the naked that thou cover him; and that thou hide not thyself from thine own flesh?"

Circumstances do not always permit us to bring the poor into our houses; then, why should we not use our means to help in securing a home for the worthy poor? There is a promise for those who do this work. "Then shalt thou call, and the Lord shall answer. Thou shalt cry and he shall say, Here am I."

If we do these things we shall not have darkness and discouragements in this life, for there shall be light in obscurity, and our darkness shall be as the noonday. Why should we not remember the poor, while the Lord has made such great Promises to those who care for the needy ones? Those promises we may be sure of, for the Lord shall guide us continually, and satisfy our soul in drouth. We shall be like a watered garden, and like a spring of water that faileth not.

When we give to the poor, we lend to the Lord, and in this way we lay up treasure in heaven. Let us remember what the Savior enjoined upon the rich young man, that he might have treasure in heaven. Jesus said unto him, "If thou wilt be

perfect, go and sell that thou hast, and give to the poor, and thou shalt have treasure in heaven, and come and follow me." Matt. 19: 21.

At that great day, when the Lord shall come again to gather his people to him, what will he say to those whom he calls to inherit the kingdom of glory? He will say, "I was an hungered and ye gave me meat; I was thirsty and ye gave me drink. I was a stranger and ye took me in; naked and ye clothed me," etc. Matt. 25: 35, 36. When the righteous shall ask, in surprise, regarding the time of those good deeds, the Savior will reply, "Verily, I say unto you, Inasmuch as ye have done it unto one of the least of these my brethren ye have done it unto me." Verse 40.

Let each one ask himself this question, "Is it true, then, that if we neglect a poor saint in any degree we thus neglect the Savior?" This is a positive fact, for to this class Christ will say, "Verily I say unto you, Inasmuch as ye did it not to one of the least of these ye did it not to me." Verse 45. Whoever turns his face away from the earnest appeals of the worthy poor, or even neglects, through lack of interest, to look up their case, reproaches and dishonors his God.

Booth, Kans.

OUR VISIT TO MOUNT MORRIS DURING THE BIBLE TERM OF 1892.

WE believe we do not exaggerate when we say it was truly a season of "refreshing from the presence of the Lord" to all in attendance, with, possibly, one exception, viz., that of Bro. R. H. Miller, whose condition we do not know at present writing. To him and family, as well as to others, it marks one of life's saddest disappointments, yet, surrounded by so many loving friends, and enjoying the "peace that passeth all understanding," he was contented and happy.

The Bible Term was a season of planting and watering, attended with much sacrifice, patient teaching, hard study and great responsibility that brings corresponding joys in the hope of a more glorious harvest. It was our pleasure to visit many of the happy homes of brethren whom we love more dearly, as we know them better.

The sacrifice and untiring efforts of the sisters and mothers in these homes, to make students and visitors welcome at the Mount, contributes in no small degree to the success of the good work at that place. One cannot fail to observe the same social, Christian spirit in calling upon students and Professors, either at their study or class-rooms. Students speak in terms of praise with reference to the instruction and management in every department, and it was very gratifying to see efficiency, order and push,—the three leading elements of success,—characterizing all their work; and above all else, that betokens future prosperity, and makes it a desirable home for all seeking a higher development of the moral and intellectual faculties, is the safe, healthful and inspiring religious spirit one constantly meets in being associated with the institution.

I note with much pleasure the rapidly-growing sentiment among us of educating under the auspices of the church, and more especially the interest that is being awakened in a thorough and systematic study of the Book of all books,—a work which now constitutes a prominent feature of all our schools. We cannot put too high an estimate on the value of this work, if properly managed, and I am very sure that few, if any of us, know the burden and sacrifice of a few brethren that this much-needed branch of education in our Brotherhood may be put on a safe footing.

We feel that this work at Mount Morris, under the care of brethren Price, Royer, Young, Miller, Moore, and others, is in safe and efficient hands,

and the churches can do a good work by sending students and money to push the work onward. Several churches assisted their needy ministers in getting the benefit of last term. Let me assure all such churches, that your help was appreciated, and that those you assisted made good use of time and opportunity afforded for advancement. If every local church could have a few weeks' drill in Normal Sunday-school Work and Music, each year, under such instructors as Bro. Young and sister Bixler, the preaching of the Word would be easier and more effectual.

May the Good Spirit stir us all up to a higher appreciation of the labors of others in our behalf, and a greater willingness to lend a helping hand to the noble work! Twenty thousand ($20,000) dollars is needed to build a ladies' dormitory, and repair the old College building, to meet the constantly increasing demand for room. While the students seem happy and contented with the new College building, and their present boarding quarters, yet their dormitories are by no means what the cause demands at the hands of those who have the means to furnish better.

I. D. PARKER.

Ashland, Ohio.

KINDNESS TO ANIMALS.

IN Proverbs 12: 10 the wise man says, "A righteous man regardeth the life of his beast." The following is a practical sermon from that text. Those acquainted with Southern life will appreciate it:

On the march from the Rapidan, in '64, an exemplary six-mule team in a long line of transportation got lodged in the mud, and delayed the whole line behind it. The wagonmaster came up to it with his accustomed oath and roar, and was swinging his murderous cowhide in the air, when the negro driver, with a fondness for his mules that he did not entertain for any human creatures, cried out, "Hole on dar, boss, don't whip dem mules."

He got down from his box, and, ostensibly examining the harness, patted the rump of each mule as he made the circuit of the team, saying to them, "Who curry dese mules down ebery morning? Who gib dem dere oats twice or day? Who takes 'em to der spring? What yer hitched to dis wagon for, anyhow? Jes you stop fooling, and take it out of dis mud good and quick." He mounted his box, drew his reins together, cracked his whip in the air, the mules tightened in their traces, gave a long and strong pull, and the team moved to its place in the line.

14: 7 tells us that we have the poor with us always, and "whensoever ye will ye may do them good." What a grand opportunity has at this time presented itself to us, here in the State of Kansas, to aid in erecting a permanent home for the poor! When we consider the grand and blessed promises, contained in the Bible, to those who remember the poor in this life, we should not hesitate to contribute liberally, and help on with the good work, for we are told that "Blessed is he that considereth the poor; the Lord will deliver him in time of trouble. The Lord preserves him and keeps him alive, and he shall be blessed upon the earth, and thou wilt not deliver him unto the will of his enemies. The Lord will strengthen him upon the bed of languishing. Thou wilt make his bed in time of sickness."

Let us remember that when we give to the poor, the Lord considers the act, and that he will pay "us again according to his pleasure. "He that hath pity upon the poor, lendeth unto the Lord, and that which he hath given will be pay him again." Prov. 19: 7. Surely the Lord will bear in mind to repay those acts of kindness; he will not forget your work and labor of love, which "ye have showed toward his name in that ye have ministered to the saints, and do minister."

Upon the other hand, if we turn a deaf ear to the pressing cry of those in need, how will the Lord regard us? Will he hear us when we cry? Please read Prov. 21: 13, and you will find that whoso stoppeth his ears to the cry of the poor, he also shall cry himself, and shall not be heard.

There are some who are especially mentioned in the Bible as those who should be cared for and supported. Turn to Isa. 1: 17 and you will find that we should learn to do well, relieve the oppressed, judge the fatherless, and plead for the widows. How is this work designated in the New Testament? "Pure religion and undefiled before God and the Father is this, to visit the fatherless and widows in their affliction and keep himself unspotted from the world." James 1: 27.

There are those of us, dear brethren and sisters, who, while we have our tables spread in abundance with the rich productions of this earth, may be forgetful of the many poor, scattered over the land, who have scarcely anything to eat. Could we not save considerable each year if we would do with a little less on our tables? Might we not fast part of the time? I believe the Lord would be delighted with an act like this; for he says in Isa. 58: 6, 7, "Is not this the fast that I have chosen? . . . Is it not to deal thy bread to the hungry, and that thou bring the poor that are cast out to thy house? When thou seest the naked that thou cover him; and that thou hide not thyself from thine own flesh?"

Circumstances do not always permit us to bring the poor into our houses; then, why should we not use our means to help in securing a home for the worthy poor? There is a promise for those who do this work. "Then shalt thou call, and the Lord shall answer. Thou shalt cry and he shall say, Here am I."

If we do these things we shall not have darkness and discouragements in this life, for there shall be light in obscurity, and our darkness shall be as the noonday. Why should we not remember the poor, while the Lord has made such great promises to those who care for the needy ones? Those promises we may be sure of, for the Lord shall guide us continually, and satisfy our soul in drouth. We shall be like a watered garden, and like a spring of water that faileth not.

When we give to the poor, we lend to the Lord, and in this way we lay up treasure in heaven. Let us remember what the Savior enjoined upon the rich young man, that he might have treasure in heaven. Jesus said unto him, "If thou wilt be

perfect, go and sell that thou hast, and give to the poor, and thou shalt have treasure in heaven, and come and follow me." Matt. 19: 21.

At that great day, when the Lord shall come again to gather his people to him, what will he say to those whom he calls to inherit the kingdom of glory? He will say, "I was an hungered and ye gave me meat; I was thirsty and ye gave me drink. I was a stranger and ye took me in; naked and ye clothed me." etc. Matt. 25: 35, 36. When the righteous shall ask, in surprise, regarding the time of those good deeds, the Savior will reply, "Verily, I say unto you, Inasmuch as ye have done it unto one of the least of these my brethren ye have done it unto me." Verse 40.

Let each one ask himself this question, "Is it true, then, that if we neglect a poor saint in any degree we thus neglect the Savior?" This is a positive fact, for to this class Christ will say, "Verily I say unto you, Inasmuch as ye did it not to one of the least of these ye did it not to me." Verse 45. Whoever turns his face away from the earnest appeals of the worthy poor, or even neglects, through lack of interest, to look up their case, reproaches and dishonors his God.

Booth, Kans.

OUR VISIT TO MOUNT MORRIS DURING THE BIBLE TERM OF 1892.

We believe we do not exaggerate when we say it was truly a season of "refreshing from the presence of the Lord" to all in attendance, with, possibly, one exception, viz., that of Bro. R. H. Miller, whose condition we do not know at present writing. To him and family, as well as to others, it marks one of life's saddest disappointments, yet, surrounded by so many loving friends, and enjoying the "peace that passeth all understanding," he was contented and happy.

The Bible Term was a season of planting and watering, attended with much sacrifice, patient teaching, hard study and great responsibility that brings corresponding joys in the hope of a more glorious harvest. It was our pleasure to visit many of the happy homes of brethren whom we love more dearly, as we know them better.

The sacrifice and untiring efforts of the sisters and mothers in these homes, to make students and visitors welcome at the Mount, contributes in no small degree to the success of the good work at that place. One cannot fail to observe the same social, Christian spirit in calling, upon students and Professors, either at their study or class-rooms. Students speak in terms of praise with reference to the instruction and management in every department, and it was very gratifying to see efficiency, order and push,—the three leading elements of success,—characterizing all their work; and above all else, that betokens future prosperity, and makes it a desirable home for all seeking a higher development of the moral and intellectual faculties, is the safe, healthful and inspiring religious spirit one constantly meets in being associated with the institution.

I note with much pleasure the rapidly-growing sentiment among us of educating under the auspices of the church, and more especially the interest that is being awakened in a thorough and systematic study of the Book of all books,—a work which now constitutes a prominent feature of all our schools. We cannot put too high an estimate on the value of this work, if properly managed, and I am very sure that few, if any of us, know the burden and sacrifice of a few brethren that this much-needed branch of education in our Brotherhood may be put on a safe footing.

We feel that this work at Mount Morris, under the care of brethren Price, Royer, Young, Miller, Moore, and others, is in safe and efficient hands,

and the churches can do a good work by sending students and money to push the work onward. Several churches assisted their needy ministers in getting the benefit of last term. Let me assure all such churches, that your help was appreciated, and that those you assisted made good use of time and opportunity afforded for advancement. If every local church could have a few weeks' drill in Normal Sunday-school Work and Music, each year, under such instructors as Bro. Young and sister Bixler, the preaching of the Word would be easier and more effectual.

May the Good Spirit stir us all up to a higher appreciation of the labors of others in our behalf, and a greater willingness to lend a helping hand to the noble work! Twenty thousand ($20,000) dollars is needed to build a ladies' dormitory, and repair the old College building, to meet the constantly increasing demand for room. While the students seem happy and contented with the new College building, and their present boarding quarters, yet their dormitories are by no means what the cause demands at the hands of those who have the means to furnish better.

I. D. Parker.

Ashland, Ohio.

KINDNESS TO ANIMALS.

In Proverbs 12: 10 the wise man says, "A righteous man regardeth the life of his beast." The following is a practical sermon from that text. Those acquainted with Southern life will appreciate it:

On the march from the Rapidan, in '64, an exemplary six-mule team in a long line of transportation got lodged in the mud, and delayed the whole line behind it. The wagonmaster came up to it with his accustomed oath and roar, and was swinging his murderous cowhide in the air, when the negro driver, with a fondness for his mules that he did not entertain for any human creature, cried out, "Hole on dar, boss, don't whip dem mules."

He got down from his box, and, ostensibly examining the harness, patted the rump of each mule as he made the circuit of the team, saying to them, "Who carry dese mules down ebery morning? Who gib dem dere oats twice er day? Who takes 'em to der spring? What yer hitched to dis wagon for, anyhow? Jes you stop fooling, and take it out of dis mud good and quick." He mounted his box, drew his reins together, cracked his whip in the air, the mules tightened in their traces, gave a long and strong pull, and the team moved to its place in the line.

would be no sense in Jesus asking the question he did. This conclusion is rather confirmed by the apostle John, who says: "There was a man sent from God whose name was John." 1: 6. Here we have a man sent from God, using a baptism that is from heaven. It requires only a little reasoning to conclude or infer that the formula used by John must have also been of divine appointment. Assuming that John, in his mission, was directed by God, and did just what he was appointed to do, there is no reason for any other inference. This would lead to the conclusion that all those whom John baptized received a baptism that was from heaven, and therefore valid. Jesus submitted to the same form, whatever that may have been.

Just before leaving the world to go to the Father, Jesus said to his disciples: "Go ye therefore, and teach all nations, baptizing them in the name of the Father, and of the Son, and of the Holy Ghost." Matt. 28: 19. This formula was intended for the followers of Christ in all ages, and of course it was from heaven. Not only so, but the form of baptism therein taught is likewise from heaven. This line of reasoning shows that the baptism taught by Jesus in the commission, as well as that practiced by John, was from heaven. They were both authorized by God. John commenced baptizing about four years before Jesus gave his great commission (Matt. 28: 19) to his disciples. Can any one conclude, with the least show of reason, that God would have sent one form of baptism for John to practice and another to Jesus to teach, only a few years apart?

Furthermore, Jesus must have received at the hands of John the same form of baptism that he afterwards taught and had his disciples to administer to others. Any other conclusion must appear unreasonable, to say the least of it. There are no reasons whatever for concluding that there was any difference in the form of immersion practiced by John, Jesus or any of his disciples. If we, in any way, can get a clear statement of the way one baptized, that settles the question concerning the mode used by all the rest. To find out what Jesus taught when he said: "Baptizing them in the name of the Father, and of the Son, and of the Holy Ghost," is to settle the whole question.

We have shown in former articles that this commission teaches trine immersion so clearly that the fact was never called into question until over 500 years after the ascension of Jesus. It has also been shown that single immersion originated about the year A. D. 360, having been introduced by a man named Eunomius. For the benefit of some who may not have read much concerning this fact, we give the following quotation from Sozomen, a church historian:

"Some say that Eunomius was the first who dared to bring forward the notion that divine baptism ought to be administered by a single immersion; and to corrupt the tradition which has been handed down from the apostles, and which is still observed by all."—*Chrystal's History of the Modes of Baptism*, p. 76.

The following from Theodoret, who wrote about the year 430, is a further confirmation of the fact stated:

"He (Eunomius) subverted the law of holy baptism, which had been handed down from the beginning from the Lord and from the apostles; and made a contrary law, asserting that it was not necessary to immerse the candidate for baptism thrice, nor to mention the name of the Trinity, but to immerse once only into the death of Christ."—*Ibid*, p. 78.

Not only was single immersion not introduced till past the middle of the fourth century, but it

was never used by any of the churches in Palestine till hundreds of years after the close of the apostolic age. These facts go to show that trine immersion is the only form of immersion reaching back to the times of Jesus and John the Baptist.

We have a little testimony bearing directly on the question, that we will make use of at this point. Dr. Wall, a noted writer, in his work on Infant Baptism, Vol. 1, page 578, has this language:

"In England there seems to have been some plea, as early as the year 816, that attempted to bring in the use of baptism by affusion in the public administration; for Spelman recites a canon of a council in that year, 'Let the priests know that when they administer holy baptism they must not pour the water on the head of the infant; but they must always be dipped in the fount, as the Son of God gave his own example to all believers, when he was thrice dipped in the waters of Jordan: so it is necessary by order to be kept and used."

This shows how this synod, in the year 816, considered Jesus was baptized, and it is of some value, especially so since there is nothing to the contrary in any history of note, so far as we know.

Judson, the noted Baptist missionary, in his work on Baptism has something to say on this line that is worth considering. We quote him at some length:

"Immersion, however, maintained its ground until the middle of the seventeenth century, when the Westminster Assembly of Divines voted, by a majority of one, that immersion and sprinkling were indifferent. Previous to that period, the Baptists had formed churches in different parts of the country; and having always seen infants, when baptized, taken in the hands of the administrator, and laid under the water, in the baptismal font, and not having much, if any, communication with the Baptists on the continent, they thought, of course, that a candidate for baptism, though a grown person, should be treated in the same manner and laid backward under the water. They were probably confirmed in this idea by the phrase, 'buried in baptism.' The consequence has been that all the Baptists in the world, who have sprung from the English Baptists, have practiced the backward posture. But from the beginning it was not so. In the apostolic times, the administrator placed his right hand on the head of the candidate, who then, under the pressure of the administrator's hand, bowed forward, aided by the genuflection which instinctively comes to one's aid, when attempting to bow in the practice, until his head was submerged, and rose by his own effort. This appears from the figures sculptured in bronze and mosaic work, on the walls of the ancient baptisteries of Italy and Constantinople. These figures represent John the Baptist leaning towards the river; his right hand on the head of the Savior, as if pressing him down into the water; while the Savior is about to bow down under the pressure of the hand of John.

"The same is evident from the practice of the Greeks, the Armenians, and all the Oriental churches, who have not, like the Christians, of countless once overspread with the Roman Catholic heresy, exchanged immersion for sprinkling. All these Oriental churches practice immersion to this day."—*Judson on Baptism*, pp. 112, 113.

All of these Greek, Armenian and Oriental churches, referred to by Mr. Judson, practice trine immersion and always have from the very earliest period of which we have any account of their manner of baptizing. There is much more evidence of a similar nature and import which we cannot give in a short newspaper article like this, but the above shows that there is no ground for even presuming that John practiced any other form of immersion than that taught by the Savior, and introduced into the eastern churches by the apostles and other preachers, who organized these congregations, and all the evidence in existence goes to show most conclusively that this form was *forward trine immersion*, that being the only form of baptism whose origin cannot be found this side of the apostolic age.

We have not space now to say more. In another issue we may have some additional remarks to offer concerning the baptismal formula used by John.
　　　　　　　　　　　　　　　　　　J. H. M.

EDITORIAL WANDERINGS IN THE OLD WORLD.

BY D. L. MILLER.

Number Nineteen.

The Royal Palace.—Windsor Castle.—A Magnificent Tomb.—Stables which Cost a Quarter of a Million.—Farewell to London.

TWENTY-ONE miles from the City of London, on the right bank of the river Thames is the ancient city of Windsor, dating back to the latter part of the tenth century. In the center of the city, upon an isolated hill stands Windsor Castle, the favorite home of Queen Victoria, and one of the largest and most magnificent royal residences in the world. It has been for centuries the chief residence of the sovereigns of England, and is rich in historical associations.

William the Conqueror erected a castle at Windsor during his reign in the eleventh century and thus made the place a residence for kings. Edward the Third, who was born here, conceived the idea of erecting a magnificent palace, and in the fourteenth century he had the old castle removed and replaced by a new one in harmony with his tastes. Succeeding monarchs, added to the buildings and beautified the grounds until the reign of George the Fourth, 1820. He began a series of extensive improvements and restorations which were finally carried to completion in the reign of the present sovereign, at a total cost of about five million dollars. This immense sum of money spent in improving the royal residence has made it a marvel of rich magnificence, and it is said no other palace in the world can compare with Windsor in splendor and magnificence.

We left London with its fog and smoke and its resistless, busy rush, glad to breathe the fresh, pure country air again, and spent a day at Windsor. The royal family was absent and the Palace was open to visitors, who had secured permission to visit the place from the Lord Chamberlain. We secured the necessary papers without difficulty and were admitted to the royal residence. We shall not attempt to describe the place, a volume would be necessary for that. We can only briefly allude to several of the most interesting places within the great palace walls.

In 1861 Prince Albert, husband of Queen Victoria, died, and since then she has lived in widowhood. For many years she secluded herself from society and mourned for her departed husband. In memory of him she has erected inside of the castle walls a memorial chapel, bearing her husband's name, and in which he sleeps his last sleep. The building is sixty-eight feet long, twenty-eight feet wide and sixty feet high, and is truly a royal and sumptuous memorial. The following description of the chapel will no doubt interest our readers.

"The interior, beautiful with colored marble, mosaics, sculpture, stained glass, precious stones and gilding in extraordinary profusion and richness, must certainly be numbered among the finest works of its kind in the world. The ceiling is fan-shaped and vaulted, and is composed of Venetian enamel mosaics, representing angels, bearing devices relating to the Prince, and with shields symbolical of the Passion. At the sides of the west entrance are two marble figures, representing the Angels of Life and Death. The walls are decorated with a series of pictures of Scriptural subjects, inlaid with colored marbles, in which twen-

would be no sense in Jesus asking the question he did. This conclusion is rather confirmed by the apostle John, who says: "There was a man sent from God whose name was John." 1: 6. Here we have a man sent from God, using a baptism that is from heaven. It requires only a little reasoning to conclude or infer that the formula used by John must have also been of divine appointment. Assuming that John, in his mission, was directed by God, and did just what he was appointed to do, there is no reason for any other inference. This would lead to the conclusion that all those whom John baptized received a baptism that was from heaven, and therefore valid. Jesus submitted to the same form, whatever that may have been.

Just before leaving the world to go to the Father, Jesus said to his disciples: " Go ye therefore, and teach all nations, baptizing them in the name of the Father, and of the Son, and of the Holy Ghost." Matt. 28: 19. This formula was intended for the followers of Christ in all ages, and of course it was from heaven. Not only so, but the form of baptism therein taught is likewise from heaven. This line of reasoning shows that the baptism taught by Jesus in the commission, as well as that practiced by John, was from heaven. They were both authorized by God. John commenced baptizing about four years before Jesus gave his great commission (Matt. 28: 19) to his disciples. Can any one conclude, with the least show of reason, that God would have sent one form of baptism to John to practice and another to Jesus to teach, only a few years apart?

Furthermore, Jesus must have received at the hands of John this same form of baptism that he afterwards taught and had his disciples to administer to others. Any other conclusion must appear unreasonable, to say the least of it. There are no reasons whatever for concluding that there was any difference in the form of immersion practiced by John, Jesus or any of his disciples. If we, in any way, can get a clear statement of the way one baptized, that settles the question concerning the mode used by all the rest. To find out what Jesus taught when he said: "Baptizing them in the name of the Father, and of the Son, and of the Holy Ghost," is to settle the whole question.

We have shown in former articles that this commission teaches trine immersion so clearly that the fact was never called into question until over 500 years after the ascension of Jesus. It has also been shown that single immersion originated about the year A. D. 360, having been introduced by a man named Eunomius. For the benefit of some who may not have read much concerning this fact, we give the following quotation from Sozomon, a church historian:

" Some say that this Eunomius was the first who dared to bring forward the notion that divine baptism ought to be administered by a single immersion; and to corrupt the tradition which has been handed down from the apostles, and which is still observed by all."—Chrystal's History of the Modes of Baptism, p. 76.

The following from Theodoret, who wrote about the year 430, is a further confirmation of the fact stated:

" He (Eunomius) subverted the law of holy baptism, which had been handed down from the beginning from the Lord and from the apostles; and made a contrary law, asserting that it was not necessary to immerse the candidate for baptism thrice, nor to mention the name of the Trinity, but to immerse once only into the death of Christ."—Ibid., p. 76.

Not only was single immersion not introduced till past the middle of the fourth century, but it

was never used by any of the churches in Palestine till hundreds of years after the close of the apostolic age. These facts go to show that trine immersion is the only form of immersion reaching back to the times of Jesus and John the Baptist.

We have a little testimony bearing directly on the question, that we will make use of at this point. Dr. Wall, a noted writer, in his work on Infant Baptism, Vol. 1, page 578, has this language:

" In England there seems to have been some priest, as early as the year 816, that attempted to bring in the use of baptism by affusion in the public administration; for Spelman recites a canon of a council in that year, ' Let the priests know that when they administer holy baptism they must not pour the water on the head of the infant; but they must always be dipped in the fount, as the Son of God gave his own example to all believers, when he was thrice dipped in the waters of Jordan; so it is necessary by order to be kept and used."

This shows how this synod, in the year 816, considered Jesus was baptized, and it is of some value, especially so since there is nothing to the contrary in any history of note, so far as we know.

Judson, the noted Baptist missionary, in his work on Baptism has something to say on this line that is worth considering. We quote him at some length:

" Immersion, however, maintained its ground until the middle of the seventeenth century, when the Westminster Assembly of Divines voted, by a majority of one, that immersion and sprinkling were indifferent. Previous to that period, the Baptists had formed churches in different parts of the country; and having always seen infants, when baptized, taken in the hands of the administrator, and laid under the water, in the baptismal font, and not having much, if any, communication with the Baptists on the continent, they thought, of course, that a candidate for baptism, though a grown person, should be treated in the same manner and laid backward under the water. They were probably confirmed in this idea by the phrase, ' buried in baptism.' The consequence has been that all the Baptists in the world, who have sprung from the English Baptists, have practiced the backward posture. But from the beginning it was not so. In the apostolic times, the administrator placed his right hand on the head of the candidate, who then, under the pressure of the administrator's hand, bowed forward, aided by the genuflection which instinctively comes to one's aid, when attempting to bow in the practice, until his head was submerged, and rose by his own effort. This appears from the figures sculptured in bronze and mosaic work, on the walls of the ancient baptisteries of Italy and Constantinople. These figures represent John the Baptist leaning towards the river; his right hand on the head of the Savior, as if pressing him down into the water; while the Savior is about to bow down under the pressure of the hand of John.

" The same is evident from the practice of the Greeks, the Armenians, and all the Oriental churches, who have not, like the Christians, of course once overspread with the Roman Catholic heresy, exchanged immersion for sprinkling. All these Oriental churches practice immersion to this day."—Judson on Baptism, pp. 112, 113.

All of these Greek, Armenian and Oriental churches, referred to by Mr. Judson, practice trine immersion and always have from the very earliest period of which we have any account of their manner of baptizing. There is much more evidence of a similar nature and import which we quote in a short newspaper article like this, but the above shows that there is no ground for even presuming that John practiced any other form of immersion than that taught by the Savior, and introduced into the eastern churches by the apostles and other preachers, who organized these congregations, and all the evidence in existence goes to show most conclusively that this form was forward trine immersion, that being the only form of baptism whose origin cannot be found this side of the apostolic age.

We have not space now to say more. In another issue we may have some additional remarks to offer concerning the baptismal formula used by John.

J. H. M.

EDITORIAL WANDERINGS IN THE OLD WORLD.

BY D. L. MILLER.

Number Nineteen.

The Royal Palace.—Windsor Castle.—A Magnificent Tomb.—Stables which Cost a Quarter of a Million. —Farewell to London.

TWENTY-ONE miles from the City of London, on the right bank of the river Thames is the ancient city of Windsor, dating back to the latter part of the tenth century. In the center of the city, upon an isolated hill stands Windsor Castle, the favorite home of Queen Victoria, and one of the largest and most magnificent royal residences in the world. It has been for centuries the chief residence of the sovereigns of England, and is rich in historical associations.

William the Conqueror erected a castle at Windsor during his reign in the eleventh century and thus made the place a residence for kings. Edward the Third, who was born here, conceived the idea of erecting a magnificent palace, and in the fourteenth century he had the old castle removed and replaced by a new one in harmony with his tastes. Succeeding monarchs added to the buildings and beautified the grounds until the reign of George the Fourth, 1820. He began a series of extensive improvements and restorations which were finally carried to completion in the reign of the present sovereign, at a total cost of about five million dollars. This immense sum of money spent in improving the royal residence has made it a marvel of rich magnificence, and it is said no other palace in the world can compare with Windsor in splendor and magnificence.

We left London with its fog and smoke and its restless, busy rush, glad to breathe the fresh, pure country air again, and spent a day at Windsor. The royal family was absent and the Palace was open to visitors, who had secured permission to visit the place from the Lord Chamberlain. We secured the necessary papers without difficulty, and were admitted to the royal residence. We shall not attempt to describe the place, a volume would be necessary for that. We can only briefly allude to several of the most interesting places within the great palace walls.

In 1861 Prince Albert, husband of Queen Victoria, died, and since then she has lived in widowhood. For many years she secluded herself from society and mourned for her departed husband. In memory of him she has erected inside of the castle walls a memorial chapel, bearing her husband's name, and in which he sleeps his last sleep. The building is sixty-eight feet long, twenty-eight feet wide and sixty feet high, and is truly a royal and sumptuous memorial. The following description of the chapel will no doubt interest our readers.

" The interior, beautiful with colored marble, mosaics, sculpture, stained glass, precious stones and gilding in extraordinary profusion and richness, must certainly be numbered among the finest works of its kind in the world. The ceiling is fan-shaped and vaulted, and is composed of Venetian enamel mosaics, representing angels, bearing devices relating to the Prince, and with shields symbolical of the Passion. At the sides of the west entrance are two marble figures, representing the Angels of Life and Death. The walls are decorated with a series of pictures of Scriptural subjects, inlaid with colored marbles, in which twen-

nothing to them. The thought makes me homesick, and lonely and sad. I believe my own dear father is living somewhere in this wide world and if he is, I mean to find him. You assist me if you will, but I can offer you no reward at present, only my gratitude and my blessing. If you are unable to give me any information regarding my father, please help me to publish and circulate this notice.

Sincerely yours,

RETA BAILEY.

San Bernardino, Cal.

~ (*Papers, please copy*).

To the Isolated Members and Churches of the North-Western District of Kansas and Colorado.

THIS will inform you that, on account of sore afflictions from *La Grippe* and other sources, I have been unable to fulfill my promises to be with you. At this writing I am no better, but I still hope to see most, if not all, the places under my care and charge, before spring, unless otherwise ordained. · · B. B. WHITMER.

From Chestnut Grove Church, W. Va.

WHEN the time appointed for our love-feast, Oct. 24, 1891, arrived, we were favored with the presence of brethren Jacob Thomas, George Hutchison, and A. M. Frantz. The attendance was large and attentive. The Brethren gave strong, Scriptural proof in support of our practice. We had, in all, twenty-one sermons, and, as an immediate result, six dear souls were buried with Christ by baptism. Four of that number were not more than twelve years old, one being the youngest son of the writer. Thus all of our children have chosen that good part excepting a little girl of seven. The Lord be praised!

Brethren, why can we not teach our children to love Jesus while young? The church called Bro. J. M. Crouse to the ministry and advanced two brethren to the second degree. A. B. DUNCAN.

Feb. 4.

From the English Prairie Church, Ind.

JAN. 19 Bro. J. C. Murray, of Nappanee, Ind., came to our place and conducted a series of meetings for us until Feb. 2, continuing for two weeks. He preached every night while with us, and part of the time in day-time. He had large congregations at times, but much sickness prevented many from attending the meetings. Nevertheless our brother did his work well, and as a result two souls came out on the Lord's side and were baptized,—one brother and one sister. The latter is young in years. May the good Lord have his guardian care over them! Bro. Murray is an able speaker, and well versed in the Bible. The members were very much built up in their Christian faith. May the Lord bless our dear brother for his faithful labor done for us, while he was with us, is our prayer! JOHN LONG.

Brighton, Ind., Feb. 3.

A Change in the Program.

How common it is to have the program of life changed! Perhaps there has not been a change of program so universally regretted all over the Brotherhood as that of Bro D. L. Miller and wife, when they had to defer their journey to the Holy Land. And while the change on my program, made this morning, about ten o'clock A. M., does not affect so large a number as Bro. Miller's, I have most keenly felt both the cause and effect.

While riding one horse to the stream, and allowing the other one to run loose, and enjoy herself in jumping and skipping over the lawn, having no apprehension of danger, the loose horse quietly passed along by the side of me, and with a steady aim, kicked me upon the ankle. Whether she did it with a malicious intent or for sport, I cannot exactly say; but the result is, I am now occupying the sofa, with an ankle joint twice as large as it ought to be, well saturated with ointment, by the hands of one of my ministering angels, who is gently saying, "Papa, this is another result of your carelessness"

Now a change in the program comes through earnest solicitations. I arranged a part of my program to conduct a series of meetings, beginning Feb. 7th, at a point along the outskirts of the Beaver Creek congregation, where a deep religious feeling is now agitating the minds of some. In view of this meeting, and the responsibilities falling upon those who would have charge of it, I spent many hours in deep meditation upon matter and thoughts best adapted to the wants of the people, anticipating a pleasant and profitable meeting, but the program is changed; and while it has caused a disappointment keenly felt by a number of others with myself, I humbly submit and bend and kiss the rod, dwelling upon the words of the Apostle which have carried solace into the hearts of thousands who have been afflicted and bereaved: "All things work together for good to them that love God."

I pause for a moment, and I relate to you the sad change of program, brought upon the family of Bro. Elhanan Engler, of New Windsor, Md. The curtain of deep gloom is hanging over the once unbroken family circle, as the lifeless form of a devoted husband and loving father is resting in the casket until the time appointed for the burial. He is one, with thousands of others, who fell victim to the destroying attacks of *La Grippe*. In the death of Bro. Engler, the church has lost a zealous worker, the community, a most excellent and worthy citizen, and the family, a loved one; but I say to the widowed sister, "Mary look up and trust all to God; throw yourself into the loving arms of him who hath proved himself as the widow's stay." To the dear children, who delighted in lavishing affections upon an earthly father, I would say, "Accept God as your father, the church as your mother, the Savior as your brother, and all will go well with you in this life, and in the world to come, you will have life everlasting." · D. F. STOUFFER.

Benevola, Md., Feb. 6, 1892.

From Weyer's Cave, Va.

WE had the privilege of attending the Bible Class at Bridgewater College, commencing Jan. 5, and continuing until Jan. 30. The classes were so arranged as to come the last two periods in the forenoon and the first two in the afternoon.

The "Evidences of Christianity" class was composed of seventeen and the "Bible Doctrine" of thirty-seven earnest workers. Geography and history were also very interesting. The only thing we could regret was that more of our brethren and friends could not be with us, to help in the grand and noble work. We feel the time could not have been spent more usefully or pleasantly: Many lessons were learned, never to be forgotten, and we were made to see beauties in the Scriptures that we had never seen before. All seemed to enjoy the work and we think all were impressed with the responsibility of knowing more of the Word of Truth. May the Lord bless the work done and help us to continue the study, and not weary in well doing.

The work closed with an able discussion of the following subjects: "How shall we best Overcome the Dangerous Influence of Church Festivals, Lawn Parties, etc?" "How can we Obtain the best Results in our Home Mission?" "How Shall we Win our Children to the Church?" "How shall we Best impress Individual Responsibility on the Members of the Church?" The chapel was crowded with eager listeners.

SARAH OLICK.

From Grundy Centre, Iowa.

BRO. MOSES DIERDORFF, of Yale, Guthrie Co., Iowa, came to us Jan. 9. Next day he preached for us in Grundy Centre and on Monday evening, Jan. 11, he commenced meetings at the Grundy County church, ten miles west of Grundy Centre, where he continued his labors until the evening of the 25th, closing the meetings with a deep interest and good attendance, notwithstanding the fact that other denominations were holding meetings in the same neighborhood. We had good attendance and the general feeling was that the meetings ought to continue longer. One came out on the Lord's side at these meetings.

On Tuesday evening Bro. Deardorff preached for us in Grundy Centre, and the same night, at 9·30, he boarded the train to return home.

Feb. 14. A. W. HAWBAKER.

Death of Eld. G. D. Reed.

ELD. G. D. Reed passed away in the Pleasant Valley church, Floyd County, Va., January 19, 1892, aged 44 years, 5 months and 15 days.

Bro. Reed joined the Brethren church, Sept. 25, 1874, was married Nov. 22, 1877, and elected to the deacon's office Nov. 17, 1879, elected to the ministry July 19, 1884, authorized to administer baptism Nov. 14, 1885, to celebrate the rites of matrimony, Jan. 15, 1887; ordained elder Oct. 13, 1887.

Death always brings sorrow to those who are left behind, but we should not grieve as those who have no hope. While we feel that we have sustained a great loss, and that we will miss our dear elder, we are made to rejoice, when we think of the example he has left behind, that our loss is his eternal gain. Deceased was known only to be loved, not only by the church, but by all who knew him.

We extend our heart-felt sympathy to the family, especially to the dear sister, who, it seemed, could not be comforted. He leaves a widow and four small children. May they, when they are older, follow the example of their father, and prepare to meet him in the beautiful beyond!

B. T. AKERS.

Alum Ridge, Va., Feb. 3, 1892.

From the Wood River Church, Nebr.

BRO. J. W. Jarboe, of Republican City, came to us Jan. 30, and began a series of meetings on Sunday, Jan. 31, and continued until Feb. 10. He preached, in all, twelve sermons. Owing to bad roads and stormy weather, the congregations were small, part of the time, but good attention was given to the Word preached. Bro. Jarboe did not shun to declare the whole Gospel, and pointed sinners to the Lamb of God that taketh away the sin of the world.

Saints were much encouraged and one dear soul came out on the Lord's side, and was buried with Christ in baptism, and arose, we hope, to walk in newness of life. Others, we believe, are seriously counting the cost. Our desire and prayer is that they will not put off their return to the Master until it is too late.

Our church is under the care of Eld. S. M. Forney, and as the field is too large for one minister to fill all the calls that are made for preaching, we would be glad to have some ministering brother, who is sound in the faith, to move among us and help to push forward the work of the Lord

Notes from Our Correspondents.

" As cold water to a thirsty soul, so is good news from a far country."

Sawyer, Kans.—We have a glorious meeting now in progress, and we feel that the Spirit of God is at work. We look for good results, of which we will inform you later.—*N. F. Brubaker, Feb. 16.*

Oak Level, Va.—I would like to correspond with some ministering brethren who would like to move to a southern home, where their services are needed, and where prospects are encouraging. —*B. E. Kessler, Feb. 16.*

Collins, Mo.—The Osceola congregation met in quarterly council Feb. 6. The business was attended to in harmony. The church sent Bro. A. Killingsworth as delegate to District Meeting. Four were received by letter.—*E. W. Tracey.*

Cartersville, Va.—Is there no minister that would like to come to a mild climate, where there is cheap land, and a large field for labor? We are isolated from the church, and have not heard any preaching since November. Only eleven members are residing at this place.—*Wm. Mallory, Feb. 12.*

Tuscarawas, Ohio.—We commenced a series of meetings in the Zion house on the evening of Jan. 9, and continued about two weeks. Bro. F. B. Weimer, of Sterling, Ohio, was called to do the preaching. He delivered twenty-one interesting sermons. Good impressions were made, and one soul was made willing to forsake sin.—*Reuben Shroyer, Pierce, Ohio.*

Bement, Ill.—We have a neat little chapel, here in Bement, and just enjoyed a two weeks' series of meetings, resulting in two being reclaimed. May the Good Lord continue to be with us! There were only four members here at the start, but now we number seven. Eld. D. B. Gibson is our pastor. The meetings were largely attended and good attention was given.—*E. M. Rittenhouse, Feb. 18.*

Adrian, Mo.—The Mound church met in quarterly council Feb. 11. The business was disposed of to the satisfaction of all present. The Lord willing we expect to hold a series of meetings, commencing Feb. 21. It was decided to have a lovefeast June 4. Ministering brethren on the way to Annual Meeting will please bear this in mind, and be with us at that time, if convenient.—*Hanna Blocher.*

Information Wanted.—Where is the Big Conawago church in Pennsylvania? Can any one give me the early history of its organization, and of the organization of the Amwell church, N. J.? You may wonder why this question. Anthony Dierdorff, Sr., with his three sons, came to America under Alex. Mack, A. D. 1729, and 1733 located in or near the Amwell church, N. J. Anthony's sons, Peter and John, assisted in organizing the Big Conawago church in 1741, and Peter preached there for fifty years, and with George Brown attended that church until death.—*D. M. Dierdorff, Waterloo, Iowa.*

Ida, Kans.—Dec. 12 I commenced meeting at the Pleasant View church, Phillips Co., Kans. The Brethren there are alive to the cause. There are about twenty members in that church. Bro. J. W. Jarboe is their minister. He is a faithful worker in God's cause. The Brethren are all very kind there. If any of our ministering brethren pass up the Republic River, on the B. & M. R. R. to Republic City, they should stop off and preach for them. You will be kindly cared for by all. I held a children's meeting while with them,—the first they ever saw. One came out on the Lord's side.—*Wm. Lugenbeel.*

Franklin Grove, Ill.—Feb. 6 Bro. D. L Miller came to the Franklin Grove church and delivered to us appreciative talks on "Bible Lands." May his talks do us all good, and confirm us the more that the Bible is God's own Book. He remained with us one week. Feb. 13 Bro. S. E Yundt came to us and preached one week. We appreciated being so kindly remembered by our Mt. Morris brethren.—*C. H Hawbecker.*

Roanoke, Va.—I have often heard of five or six preachers uniting to hold a revival, but never saw it succeed until the present. Meetings have been in progress for two weeks in Troutville Valley church. Eight ministers are doing the preaching, and, contrary to the usual results in such cases, thirteen dear souls have thus far confessed Christ. The meetings are still in progress, with prospects for many more.—*I. M. Gibson, Feb. 16.*

Elkhart, Iowa.—Bro. Hipes, of Greene, Iowa, commenced a series of meetings at the Nicodemus school-house, on Monday evening. Jan. 19, and closed on Thursday evening, Jan. 29 Bro. Hipes is an able and efficient expounder of God's Word. Although there were no immediate results, we have reason to believe that some were counting the cost. We were greatly built up and encouraged to press onward.—*Jefferson Mathis.*

Darksville, W. Va.—Bro. Jacob Bricker, of the Manor church, Md., came to the place of the undersigned Jan. 6, and preached until Sunday evening, Jan. 31, when the meetings closed with increasing interest. Though there were no additions to the church, we believe the seed sown will manifest itself in the near future. The Word was preached in such a way and manner that a waybuilding man could not err therein.—*J. O. Buterbaugh, Feb. 13.*

Spencer, Ohio.—After sending my last report to the MESSENGER, I learned that one brother made application for baptism at the close of our meetings in the Black River church, and was baptized the following Monday. We had gone when he decided to unite with the church, therefore did not report the good news. Brethren Loomis and Hoover held one week's meetings at Friendsville, Ohio, about seven miles from our church. We hope for good results in the future.—*Clara Woods.*

Dallas Center, Iowa.—Our church, here at Dallas Center, has again been revived by the earnest efforts of Bro. David Rowland, of Lanark, Ill. He came to us Jan. 30, and held two meetings at our church, east of Dallas Center, and on the evening of Jan. 31, began a series of meetings in the Presbyterian church in Dallas Center. We had, in all, fourteen very good and instructive sermons at this place. Although there were none added to the church, we hope to see, in the near future, some fruit from Bro. Rowland's labor, not only from those out of the church, but of us who claim to be church members, that we may be a better light to those on the broad road.—*Ella Royer, Feb 13.*

Iswell, Ohio.—Bro. Jacob Heistand, of Wetzel, Ohio, came to us Jan. 10 and remained until Jan. 22. He preached eleven sermons in all. Jan. 22 Bro. J. Holder, of Hagerstown, Ind., came to us and preached twelve sermons. We had good congregations and good order. Although there were no accessions to the church, we believe there was a great deal of good done, as the members seemed to be encouraged and very much built up. The ministers, as above stated, preached the Word with great power and reminded the members, as well as others, of their duty toward God, as taught by the Gospel. On the north side of this congregation, Bro. George W. Sellars, of Bryan, Ohio, also held several meetings.—*Della M. Long, Feb. 18.*

Kinsley, Kans.—We are now living at this place, and would like to know if there are any other members living in this County. If so, we would be very thankful for the information. We also wish to know the place of the nearest organized church, as we wish our membership to be as near this place as possible. We should like some minister to come and preach for us as often as convenient. Please notify us beforehand, that we may have the use of a house. By coming to Kinsley, they will be met by my father, Addison Fryfogle.—*Irilla Fryfogle, Feb. 13.*

Smithville, Ohio.—We are pleased to report an interesting series of meetings in this, the Chippewa congregation. Bro. Shroyer came to us on the evening of Jan. 22, and preached twenty-four interesting sermons for us. He labored earnestly and worked hard while with us, although he had some disadvantage to contend with, having suffered from an attack of sickness just before coming here. In the midst of the meetings, hearing of sickness in his home, also caused our brother much anxiety. As an immediate result of the meetings, four were received by confession and baptism. Others were almost persuaded, but are waiting for a more convenient season.—*M. C. Lichtenwalter, Feb. 12.*

Shideler, Ind.—Bro. Henry Frantz, of Ohio, began a series of meetings in the Mississinewa church, Jan. 30. We had the pleasure of attending these meetings until Feb. 13, when we had to say farewell once again to the dear ones at home and go to other fields of labor. Bro. Henry expected to remain over Sunday. There had been no additions yet, but we feel the church has been much encouraged and built up. Bro. Henry is an earnest worker, and his sermons are practical. May the Lord bless his endeavors wherever he goes! At present I am with the Brethren at New Carlisle, Ohio, in the bounds of the Donel's Creek church. Bro. Henry Frantz has charge of this church. He will be home to-day.—*Geo. L. Studebaker, Feb 15.*

Virden, Ill.—The Pleasant Hill church held her regular quarterly council Feb. 13, the associate elder presiding. Among the items of interest acted upon may be mentioned, the calling of our next Ministerial Meeting, the share of books and tracts for 1891 from the Tract Work, the adoption of unfermented wine for Communion purposes, the re-organization of the Sunday-school, the appointment of the solicitor of the District Missionary Endowment Fund, and the reception of three into membership, by letter. Great unanimity pervaded the council, and we feel that such efforts as these will be blessed to our mutual profit. In the evening Eld. M. J. McClure occupied the pulpit, and the sermon on "The Providence of God," as well as his sermon on Sunday, were highly appreciated.—*James Wirt, Feb. 13.*

Burlington, W. Va.—We commenced a series of meetings at the Welton school-house, Feb. 6, and closed Feb. 14. Bro. Jonas Fike, from Preston County, W. Va., did the preaching. He delivered, in all, nine sermons. Bro. Jonas is a zealous worker. He wielded the Sword of the Spirit with power. Saints were made to rejoice and sinners to tremble. Three were made willing to come out on the Lord's side, and we believe many good impressions were made. On account of sickness and bad weather, the attendance was not so large at the beginning, but gradually increased and at the close the house was filled to overflowing. We also had a very interesting children's meeting on Sunday morning. God bless Bro. Jonas! The above-named school-house is in the Beaver Run congregation, about ten miles west of the church.—*Peter Arnold.*

Notes from Our Correspondents.

" As cold water to a thirsty soul, so is good news from a far country."

Sawyer, Kans.—We have a glorious meeting now in progress, and we feel that the Spirit of God is at work. We look for good results, of which we will inform you later.—*N. F. Brubaker, Feb. 16.*

Oak Level, Va.—I would like to correspond with some ministering brethren who would like to move to a southern home, where their services are needed, and where prospects are encouraging.—*B. E. Kessler, Feb. 16.*

Collins, Mo.—The Osceola congregation met in quarterly council Feb. 6. The business was attended to in harmony. The church sent Bro. A. Killingsworth as delegate to District Meeting. Four were received by letter.—*E. W. Tracey.*

Cartersville, Va.—Is there no minister that would like to come to a mild climate, where there is cheap land, and a large field for labor? We are isolated from the church, and have not heard any preaching since November. Only eleven members are residing at this place.—*Wm. Mallory, Feb. 12.*

Tuscarawas, Ohio.—We commenced a series of meetings in the Zion house on the evening of Jan. 9, and continued about two weeks. Bro. F. B. Weimer, of Sterling, Ohio, was called to do the preaching. He delivered twenty-one interesting sermons. Good impressions were made, and one soul was made willing to forsake sin.—*Reuben Shroyer, Pierce, Ohio.*

Bement, Ill.—We have a neat little chapel, here in Bement, and just enjoyed a two weeks' series of meetings, resulting in two being reclaimed. May the Good Lord continue to be with us! There were only four members here at the start, but now we number seven. Eld. D. B. Gibson is our pastor. The meetings were largely attended and good attention was given.—*E. M. Rittenhouse, Feb. 18.*

Adrian, Mo.—The Mound church met in quarterly council Feb. 11. The business was disposed of to the satisfaction of all present. The Lord willing we expect to hold a series of meetings, commencing Feb. 21. It was decided to have a lovefeast June 4. Ministering brethren on the way to Annual Meeting will please bear this in mind, and be with us at that time, if convenient.—*Hanna Bloobor.*

Information Wanted.—Where is the Big Conawago church in Pennsylvania? Can any one give me the early history of its organization, and of the organization of the Amwell church, N. J.? You may wonder why this question. Anthony Dierdorff, Sr., with his three sons, came to America under Alex. Mack, A. D. 1729, and 1733 located in or near the Amwell church, N. J. Anthony's sons, Peter and John, assisted in organizing the Big Conawago church in 1741, and Peter preached there for fifty years, and with George Brown attended that church until death.—*D. M. Dierdorff, Waterloo, Iowa.*

Ida, Kans.—Dec. 12 I commenced meeting at the Pleasant View church, Phillips Co., Kans. The Brethren there are alive to the cause. There are about twenty members in that church. Bro. J. W. Jarboe is their minister. He is a faithful worker in God's cause. The Brethren are all very kind there. If any of our ministering brethren pass up the Republic River, on the B. & M. R. R. to Republic City, they should stop off and preach for them. You will be kindly cared for by all. I held a children's meeting while with them,—the first they ever saw. One came out on the Lord's side.—*Wm. Lugenbeel.*

Franklin Grove, Ill.—Feb. 6 Bro. D. L. Miller came to the Franklin Grove church and delivered to us appreciative talks on "Bible Lands." May his talks do us all good, and confirm us the more that the Bible is God's own Book. He remained with us one week. Feb. 13 Bro. S. E. Yundt came to us and preached one week. We appreciated being so kindly remembered by our Mt. Morris brethren.—*C. H Haubecker.*

Roanoke, Va.—I have often heard of five or six preachers uniting to hold a revival, but never saw it succeed until the present. Meetings have been in progress for two weeks in Troutville Valley church. Eight ministers are doing the preaching, and, contrary to the usual results in such cases, thirteen dear souls have thus far confessed Christ. The meetings are still in progress, with prospects for many more.—*I. M. Gibson, Feb. 16.*

Elkhart, Iowa.—Bro. Hipes, of Greene, Iowa, commenced a series of meetings at the Nicodemus school-house, on Monday evening, Jan. 19, and closed on Thursday evening, Jan. 29. Bro. Hipes is an able and efficient expounder of God's Word. Although there were no immediate results, we have reason to believe that some were counting the cost. We were greatly built up and encouraged to press onward.—*Jefferson Mathis.*

Barkesville, W. Va.—Bro. Jacob Bricker, of the Manor church, Md., came to the place of the undersigned Jan. 6, and preached until Sunday evening, Jan. 31, when the meetings closed with increasing interest. Though there were no additions to the church, we believe the seed sown will manifest itself in the near future. The Word was preached in such a way and manner that a' wayfaring man could not err therein.—*J. O. Buterbaugh, Feb. 13.*

Spencer, Ohio.—After sending my last report to the MESSENGER, I learned that one brother made application for baptism at the close of our meetings in the Black River church, and was baptized the following Monday. We had gone when he decided to unite with the church, therefore did not report the good news. Brethren Loomis and Hoover held one week's meetings at Friendsville, Ohio, about seven miles from our church. We hope for good results in the future.—*Clara Woods.*

Dallas Center, Iowa.—Our church, here at Dallas Center, has again been revived by the earnest efforts of Bro. David Rowland, of Lanark, Ill. He came to us Jan. 30, and held two meetings at our church, east of Dallas Center, and on the evening of Jan. 31, began a series of meetings in the Presbyterian church in Dallas Center. We had, in all, fourteen very good and instructive sermons at this place. Although there were none added to the church, we hope to see, in the near future, some fruit from Bro. Rowland's labor, not only from those out of the church, but of us who claim to be church members, that we may be a better light to those on the broad road.—*Ella Royer, Feb. 13.*

Jewell, Ohio.—Bro. Jacob Heistand, of Wetzel, Ohio, came to us Jan. 10 and remained until Jan. 22. He preached eleven sermons in all. Jan. 22 Bro. J. Holder, of Hagerstown, Ind., came to us and preached twelve sermons. We had good congregations and good order. Although there were no accessions to the church, we believe there was a great deal of good done, as the members seemed to be encouraged and very much built up. The ministers, as above stated, preached the Word with great power and reminded the members, as well as others, of their duty toward God, as taught by the Gospel. On the north side of this congregation, Bro. George W. Sellars, of Bryan, Ohio, also held several meetings.—*Della M. Long, Feb. 18.*

Kinsley, Kans.—We are now living at this place, and would like to know if there are any other members living in this County. If so, we would be very thankful for the information. We also wish to know the place of the nearest organized church, as we wish our membership to be as near this place as possible. We should like some minister to come and preach for us as often as convenient. Please notify us beforehand, that we may have the use of a house. By coming to Kinsley, they will be met by my father, Addison Fryfogle.—*Irilla Fryfogle, Feb. 13.*

Smithville, Ohio.—We are pleased to report an interesting series of meetings in this, the Chippewa congregation. Bro. Shroyer came to us on the evening of Jan. 23, and preached twenty-four interesting sermons for us. He labored earnestly and worked hard while with us, although he had some disadvantage to contend with, having suffered from an attack of sickness just before coming here. In the midst of the meetings, hearing of sickness in his home, also caused our brother much anxiety. As an immediate result of the meetings, four were received by confession and baptism. Others were almost persuaded, but are waiting for a more convenient season.—*M. C. Eichlenwalter, Feb. 12.*

Shideler, Ind.—Bro. Henry Frantz, of Ohio, began a series of meetings in the Mississinewa church, Jan. 30. We had the pleasure of attending these meetings until Feb. 13, when we had to say farewell once again to the dear ones at home and go to other fields of labor. Bro. Henry expected to remain over Sunday. There had been no additions yet, but we feel the church has been much encouraged and built up. Bro. Henry is an earnest worker, and his sermons are practical. May the Lord bless his endeavors wherever he goes! At present I am with the Brethren at New Carlisle, Ohio, in the bounds of the Donel's Creek church. Bro. Henry Frantz has charge of this church. He will be home to-day.—*Geo. L. Studebaker, Feb. 15.*

Virden, Ill.—The Pleasant Hill church held her regular quarterly council Feb. 13, the associate elder presiding. Among the items of interest acted upon may be mentioned, the calling of our next Ministerial Meeting, the share of books and tracts for 1891 from the Tract Work, the adoption of unfermented wine for Communion purposes, the re-organization of the Sunday-school, the appointment of the solicitor of the District Missionary Endowment Fund, and the reception of three into membership, by letter. Great unanimity pervaded the council, and we feel that such efforts as these will be blessed to our mutual profit. In the evening Eld. M. J. McClure occupied the pulpit, and the sermon on "The Providence of God," as well as his sermon on Sunday, were highly appreciated.—*James Wirt, Feb. 19.*

Burlington, W. Va.—We commenced a series of meetings at the Welton school-house, Feb. 6, and closed Feb. 14. Bro. Jonas Fike, from Preston County, W. Va., did the preaching. He delivered, in all, nine sermons. Bro. Jonas is a zealous worker. He wielded the Sword of the Spirit with power. Saints were made to rejoice and sinners to tremble. Three were made willing to come out on the Lord's side, and we believe many good impressions were made. On account of sickness and bad weather, the attendance was not so large at the beginning, but gradually increased and at the close the house was filled to overflowing. We also had a very interesting children's meeting on Sunday morning. God bless Bro. Jonas! The above-named school-house is in the Beaver Run congregation, about ten miles west of the church.—*Peter Arnold.*

Deceased was married to Elijah Meyer, April 18, 1847. Seven children were born to them, five of whom (all sons and heads of families) are yet living.

Sister Meyer was a member of the Brethren church for about forty years and was always considered a very exemplary member. Funeral services by Bro. Jacob Rife, in the Christian church at Cadis, from the latter part of I Thess. 4.　　D. F. HOOVER.

WELLS.—In the Waddam's Grove congregation, at Pleasant Hill, Stephenson Co., Ill., sister Ellen Wells, aged 48 years, 3 months and 27 days.

Sister Wells was sick but a short time and although naturally a rugged woman, she became the fatal victim of *La Grippe* and pneumonia. Beside a large number of relatives and friends she left a sorrowing husband and five children to mourn their loss. Funeral occasion improved by "L. H. Eby and the writer from Philpp. 1: 21, "For me to live is Christ and to die is gain."　　D. B. EBY.

MOFFET.—At his late residence, five miles south-west of Muncie, Delaware Co., Ind., Feb. 7, 1892, Lambert Moffett, aged 85 years, 1 month and 25 days.

Deceased was born in Granger County, Tenn., and came to Fayette County, Ind., in 1816. Five years later he was married to Maria McCray, near Connersville, where he remained until the fall of 1836, when he removed to his late residence, five miles southwest of Muncie, Delaware County.

Deceased was the father of eleven children, five sons and six daughters, the mother and two daughters having preceded him to the grave. These remain five sons and four daughters to mourn his departure. Funeral services were held at the house by the writer from John 11: 20.　.　D. F. HOOVER.

ESHELMAN.—In the Cole Creek congregation, Ill., Sept. 16, 1891, sister Catharine Eshelman, wife of Samuel Eshelman, aged 74 years.

Deceased was a devoted Christian and possessed a large amount of zeal for the Master's cause. She passed away in full assurance of faith and hope of eternal life. Funeral services by the writer to a large audience.
SOLOMON BUCKLEW.

LANDIS.—In the Conestoga church, Lancaster Co., Pa., Jan. 24, 1892, sister Lydia Landis, wife of Bro. Isaac Landis, aged 71 years.

Deceased leaves a husband and seven children,—four sons and three daughters. Sister Lydia was a member of the Brethren church for thirty years and she was always ready to give a helping hand in time of need. As such she will long be remembered by all. Services by the Brethren from Matt. 24: 44.
SALLIE PFOUTZ.

WESTERFIELD.—In the Cole Creek congregation, Ill., Feb. 5, 1892, sister Ida Westerfield, wife of Cary Westerfield, and daughter of Bro. Matthias Lingenfelter, aged 25 years, 1 month and 18 days.

Sister Ida gave her heart to God at the age of nineteen years, and lived a devoted life to God. She was a noble wife and a kind mother. She leaves four little children, a husband and many dear friends to mourn their loss. Her seat in the church was never vacant if it was possible for her to get there. Funeral services preached by the writer to a very attentive audience from Rev. 14: 13.
SOLOMON BUCKLEW.

SPICKLER.—At Lincoln, Ill., at the school for feeble-minded children, Jan. 10, 1892, Fannie Ellen Spickler, daughter of C. B. and Ellen Spickler, aged 14 years, 11 months and 3 days.

Deceased was brought to her home at Pine Creek, Ill., for interment where services were conducted by Eld. Edmund Forney.

In infancy Fannie was stricken with sickness from which she never recovered. Each year augmented her suffering. A promising bud, blighted on earth to bloom above!
D. L. F.

ADVERTISEMENTS.

Tract Work.

List of Publications for Sale,—Sent Postage Prepaid.

CLASS A.

No. 1. Golden Gleams or Family Chart, ...$ 85
No. 2. Diagram of Passover and Lord's Supper, per copy, ... 75

CLASS B.

Plain Family Bible, per copy, ...$4 70
Trine Immersion, Quinter, per copy, ... 1 25
Europe and Bible Lands, Miller, per copy, ... 1 50
Doctrine of the Brethren Defended, Miller, per copy, ... 1 50
Close Communion, West, per copy,............ 40
Missionary Hymn Book, per dozen, $1.00; per copy, 10

CLASS C.—(Tracts.)

No. 1. The Brethren or Dunkards, per 100, $1.50 per copy,............................... 02
No. 2. Path of Life, per 100; $4; per copy,.... 05
No. 3. How to Become a Child of God, per 100, $4; per copy,........................... 01
No. 4. Conversation, per 100, $2.50; per copy, .. 03
No. 5. Water Baptism, per 100, $2.50; per copy, 03
No. 6. Single Immersion, per 100, $1; per copy,. 02
No. 7. Sabbatism, per 100, $1.50; per copy, ... 02
No. 8. Trine Immersion Traced to the Apostles, per 100, $7; per copy,................... 03
No. 9. Sermon on Baptism, per 100, $2.50; per copy, 03
No.10. Glad Tidings of Salvation, per 100, $1.50; per copy,........................... 02
No.12. Life of Eld. S. S. Weir (Colored), per 100, $1.50; per copy,..................... 02
No.12. Ten Reasons for Trine Immersion, per 100, $1; per copy,................... 02
No.13. The Lord's Day and the Sabbath, per 100, $2.50; per copy,................. 03

CLASS D.

No. 1. The House We Live In, per 100, ...$ 45
No. 2. Plan of Salvation, per 100, ... 45
No. 3. Come Let Us Reason Together, per 100, . 45
No. 4. How Shall I know that my Sins are Pardoned? per 100, ... 45
No. 5. Intemperance, per 100, ... 45
No. 6. Plain Dressing, per 100, ... 45
No. 7. Which is the Right Church? per 100, ... 45
No. 8. The House We Live In (Swedish) per 100, 45
No. 9. The House We Live In (Danish), per 100, 45
No. 10. Paul Wetzel's Reasons (German), per 100, 45
No. 11. Sinner, Stop, per 100, ... 45
No. 12. Faith, per 100, ... 45
No. 13. The Light House, per 100, ... 45
No. 14. Close Communion, per 100, ... 45
No. 15. The Truth Shall Make You Free, per 100, 45
No. 16. Modern Skepticism, per 100, ... 45
No. 17. Infant Baptism Weighed, etc., per 100, . 45
No. 18. Repentance, per 100, ... 45
No. 19. Talk to N. R. Zinggowen, etc., per 100, 45
No. 20. Life and Death, per 100, ... 45
No. 21. The House We Live In (German), per 100, 45
No. 22. The Prayer Covering, per 100, ... 45
No. 23. The Lord's Supper, per 100, ... 45
No. 24. Shall I Swear or Affirm? per 100, ... 45
No. 25. Secret Societies, per 100, ... 45
No. 26. Church Entertainments, per 100, ... 45
No. 27. Conversion or the New Birth, per 100, . 45
No. 28. The Bible Service of Foot-washing, per 100, 45
No. 29. Scriptural Communion, per 100, ... 45

CLASS E.

No. 1. Pause and Think, per 100, ... 20
No. 2. What Do We Need? per 100, ... 20
No. 3. Right or Wrong Way, per 100, ... 20
No. 4. Why Am I Not a Christian? per 100, .. 20
No. 5. Saving Words, per 100, ... 20
No. 6. Christ and War, per 100, ... 20
No. 7. The Bond of Peace, per 100, ... 20
No. 8. The Kiss of Charity, per 100, ... 20
No. 9. The Evils of Intemperance, per 100, .. 20
No. 10. The Lost Opportunity, per 100, ... 20
No. 11. Are You a Christian? per 100, ... 20
No. 12. After, Get Thee Down, per 100, ... 20
No. 13. A Personal Appeal, per 100, ... 20
No. 14. Lying Among the Pots, per 100, ... 20
No. 15. Gold and Costly Array, per 100, ... 20
No. 16. The Brethren's Card, per 100, ... 20
No. 17. The Whole Gospel Must Be Obeyed, per 100, 20

Bibles, Testaments, Hymn Books of all styles, at publishers' lowest retail prices, which will be furnished on application. Address:
BRETHREN'S BOOK & TRACT WORK,
DAYTON, OHIO.

GOOD BOOKS FOR ALL.

ANY book in the market furnished at publishers' lowest retail price by the Brethren's Publishing Company, Mt. Morris, Ill, *Special prices* given when books are purchased in quantities. When ordering books, not on our list, if possible give title, name of author, and address of publishers.

Family Bible, with Notes and Instructions.—Contains the harmony of the Gospels, Chronology, Maps, Tables of Weights and Measures, Family Record, eight elegant illustrations, etc. Price, substantially bound, $4.50.

German and English Testaments.—American Bible Society Edition. Price, 60 cents.

Homiletics and Pastoral Theology.—By W. G. T. Shedd. Cloth, $2.50.

Lectures on Preaching.—By Rev. Phillips-Brooks. Cloth, $1.50.

New Testament and Psalms with Notes.—Invaluable for Bible students, Sunday-school teachers, etc. Price, cloth, $1.00; without Psalms, $1.00.

Quinter and McDonald Debate.—A debate on Trine Immersion, the Lord's Supper, and Feet-washing, between Eld. James Quinter (German Baptist) and Eld. N. A. McConnell (Christian) held at Dry Creek, Iowa, 1887. Price, $1.50.

Popular Commentary on the New Testament.—Edited by Philip Schaff. Four volumes, 8vo. Matthew, Mark and Luke: $6.00. John and the Acts: $6.00. Romans to Philemon: $5.00. Hebrews to Revelation $5.00.

Sabbatism.—By M. M. Eshelman. Treats the Sabbath question, showing that the first day of the week is the day for assembling in worship. Price to cents; 15 copies, $1.00.

Bunyan's Pilgrim's Progress.—An excellent edition of this good work, printed on good paper, finely illustrated with forty engravings, at the low price of $1.00 per copy.

Close Communion.—By Landon West. Treats this important subject in a simple though conclusive manner. Price, 50 cents.

In the Volume of the Book.—By Geo. F. d'Pontecost. Cloth, 60 cents.

Key to the Knowledge and Use of the Holy Bible.—By J. H. Blunt. Cloth, 16 mo, 75 cents.

Lange's Commentary.—Edited by Philip Schaff. Twenty-two vols 8vo. For full set, $100.00.

New and Complete Bible Commentary.—By Jamieson, Fausset and Brown. It is far in advance of other works. It is critical, practical, and explanatory. It is compendious and comprehensive in its character. It has a critical introduction to each Book of Scripture, and is by far the most practical, suggestive, scientific, and popular work of the kind in the English language. In four large volumes, of about 1000 pages each. Printed on fine English cloth, sprinkled edges, the full set, $8.00; half Morocco, the full set, $12.00.

Sacred Geography and Antiquities.—A practical, helpful work for Bible students, ministers and Sunday-school teachers. Price, $2.25.

The Origin and Growth of Religion.—Hibbert Lectures. By T. W. R. Davis. Cloth, 8vo, $2.50.

Our Library on Christian Evidences.—This collection of works embraces the best books to be had on that subject: "Paley's Evidences of Christianity," New Edition, $1.50; "Nelson on Infidelity," 75 cents; "Manual of Christian Evidences," 75 cents; "Many Infallible Proofs," $1.25; "The Divine Demonstration," $2.50; "The Bible in the Nineteenth Century," at cents; "Grounds of Theistic and Christian Belief," $2.50. Price of the entire set, if ordered at one time, $6.00 special terms to ministers furnished upon application.

Bible Work, or Bible Reader's Commentary on the New Testament.—By J. G. Butler. Two vols. 8vo. $10.00.

Biblical Antiquities.—By John Nevin. Gives a concise account of Bible lores and customs; invaluable to all students of Bible subjects. Price, $1.50.

Biblical Theology of the Old Testament.—By R. F. Weidner. Cloth. $1.25.

Campbell and Owen Debate.—Contains a complete investigation of the evidences of Christianity. Price, $1.50.

Classified Minutes of Annual Meeting.—A work of rare interest for all who desire to be well informed in the church work, from the early days of our Brethren until the present. Price, cloth, $1.50; leather/$2.00.

Companion to the Bible.—This valuable work is so full of instruction that it can not fail to be of great benefit to every Christian. Price, $1.75.

Hours with the Bible.—By Cunningham Geikie. Old Testament Series—six volumes. Per volume, 90 cents.

Europe and Bible Lands.—By D. L. Miller. A book for the people,—more comprehensive and thorough than many higher-priced works. Price, cloth, $1.50; leather, $2.00.

Ecclesiastical History.—By Eusebius. Bohn Library. Cloth, $1.50.

Ecclesiastical History.—By Mosheim. 2 vols. 8vo., $4.00.

Early Days of Christianity.—By F. W. Farrar. Author's edition, cloth, 12mo. $1.25.

PUBLICATIONS.

The Brethren's Quarterly.

For Sunday-school teachers and scholars this publication is of the greatest benefit. Look at our prices:

Single subscription, one year,..................	35 cents.
Single subscription, per quarter,...............	10 cents.
Three copies, per quarter,.....................	25 cents.
Six copies, per quarter,.......................	40 cents.
Twenty copies and over,.......................	4 cents each.

Hymn Books.

New Tune and Hymn Books.

Half leather, per copy, post-paid,.............	$ 75
Morocco, per copy, post-paid,................	1 00
Morocco, gilt edge, per copy, post-paid,......	1 25

Hymn Books.

Morocco, per copy, post-paid,................	$ 75
Morocco, gilt edge, per copy, post-paid,......	85
Arabesque, per copy, post-paid,..............	40
Fine Limp, per copy, post-paid,..............	75
Fine Limp, gilt edge, per copy, post-paid,....	90
German and English, per copy, post-paid, ...	75

Sunday-School Requisites.

The following list of things is needed in all Sunday-schools:

Testaments, Flexible, red edge, per dozen, ..	$1 00
Minute Books, each,..........................	40
Class Books, per dozen,.......................	75
S. S. Primers, with fine engravings, per dozen,..	70

New and Beautiful Sunday-School Cards.

"The Gem," 50 picture cards, each with Bible text, verse of hymn,..................... 35
150 Reward Tickets—verse of Scripture—red or blue,.. 20

The Young Disciple.

The YOUNG DISCIPLE is a neatly printed weekly, published especially for the moral benefit and religious instruction of our young folks.

Single copy, one year,........................	$ 50
Six copies (the sixth to the agent),...........	2 50
Ten copies,...................................	4 00

For Three Months or Thirteen Weeks.

20 copies to one address,.....................		$1 70
25 " " "		2 10
30 " " "		2 35
40 " " "		3 00
50 " " "		3 60
75 " " "		5 00
100 " " "		7 00

For Six Months or Twenty-Six Weeks.

20 copies to one address,.....................		$ 3 35
25 " " "		5 00
30 " " "		6 60
40 " " "		7 50
50 " " "		10 30
100 " " "		13 75

Our paper is designed for the Sunday-school and the home circle. We desire the name of every Sunday-school Superintendent in the Brotherhood, and want an agent in every church. Send for sample copies.

Certificates of Membership

WE have just printed a new edition of these very convenient certificates. Several improvements over the old style are noticeable, such as perforated stubs, firm, yet smooth, paper, etc. Price only 50 cents per book. Every congregation should have one. Address this office.

The Monon Route.

This road is running a fine line of Pullman Buffet Sleepers between Chicago and Indianapolis, Cincinnati and Louisville, in connection with the fast Florida express trains.

For full information, address, E. O. MCCORMICK, General Passenger Agent, Adams Express Building, Chicago. (City Ticket Office, 7 S. Clark St.)

Send for our fine Bible Catalogue. Prices to suit the times. We have a large variety and the most durable as well as ornamental binding.

Deceased was married to Elijah Meyer, April 18, 1847. Seven children were born to them, five of whom (all sons and heads of families) are yet living.

Sister Meyer was a member of the Brethren church for about forty years and was always considered a very exemplary member. Funeral services by Bro. Jacob Rhe, in the Christian church at Cadiz, from the latter part of 1 Thess. 4. D. F. HOOVER.

WELLS.—In the Waddam's Grove congregation, at Pleasant Hill, Stephenson Co., Ill., sister Ellen Wells, aged 48 years, 3 months and 27 days.

Sister Wells was sick but a short time and although naturally a rugged woman, she became the fatal victim of *La Grippe* and pneumonia. Beside a large number of relatives and friends she left a sorrowing husband and five children to mourn their loss. Funeral occasion improved by "L. H. Eby and the writer from Philipp. 1: 21, "For me to live is Christ and to die is gain." D. B. EBY.

MOFFET.—At his late residence, five miles south-west of Muncie, Delaware Co., Ind., Feb. 7, 1892, Lambert Maffett, aged 85 years, 1 month and 25 days.

Deceased was born in Granger County, Tenn, and came to Fayette County, Ind., in 1806. Five years later he was married to Maria McCray, near Connersville, where he remained until the fall of 1836, when he removed to his late residence, five miles southwest of Muncie, Delaware County.

Deceased was the father of eleven children, five sons and six daughters, the mother and two daughters having preceded him to the grave. There remain five sons and four daughters to mourn his departure. Funeral services were held at the house by the writer from John 11: 20. D. F. HOOVER.

ESHELMAN.—In the Cole Creek congregation, Ill., Sept. 26, 1891, sister Catharine Eshelman, wife of Samuel Eshelman, aged 74 years.

Deceased was a devoted Christian and possessed a large amount of zeal for the Master's cause. She passed away in full assurance of faith and hope of eternal life. Funeral services by the writer to a large audience. SOLOMON BUERLEW.

LANDIS.—In the Conestoga church, Lancaster Co., Pa., Jan. 24, 1892, sister Lydia Landis, wife of Bro. Isaac Landis, aged 71 years.

Deceased leaves a husband and seven children,—four sons and three daughters. Sister Lydia was a member of the Brethren church for thirty years and she was always ready to give a helping hand in time of need. As such she will long be remembered by all. Services by the Brethren from Matt. 24: 44. SALLIE POUTZ.

WESTERFIELD.—In the Cole Creek congregation, Ill., Feb. 5, 1892, sister Ida Westerfield, wife of Cary Westerfield, and daughter of Bro. Matthias Lingenfelter, aged 25 years, 1 month and 18 days.

Sister Ida gave her heart to God at the age of nineteen years, and lived a devoted life to God. She was a noble wife and a kind mother. She leaves four little children, a husband and many dear friends to mourn their loss. Near seat in the church was never vacant if it was possible for her to get there. Funeral services preached by the writer to a very attentive audience from Rev. 14: 13. SOLOMON BUCKLEW.

SPICKLER.—At Lincoln, Ill., at the school for feeble-minded children, Jan. 10, 1892, Fannie Ellen Spickler, daughter of C. B. and Ellen Spickler, aged 14 years, 11 months and 2 days.

Deceased was brought to her home at Pine Creek, Ill., for interment where services were conducted by Eld. Edmund Forney.

In infancy Fannie was stricken with sickness from which she never recovered. Each year augmented her suffering. A promising bud, blighted on earth to bloom above! D. L. F.

THE GOSPEL MESSENGER.

"Set for the Defense of the Gospel."

Vol. 30, Old Series. Mt. Morris, Ill., and Huntingdon, Pa., March 8, 1892 No. 10.

The Gospel Messenger.

H. B. BRUMBAUGH, Editor,

And Business Manager of the Eastern House, Box 50,
Huntingdon, Pa.

Table of Contents.

D. A. C.—The best work we have on organizing and conducting Sunday-schools, is the "Brethren's Manual," sent post-paid for thirty cents.

SPRING-TIME seems to be coming. Only yesterday we heard the notes of the blue bird, and though they were charming, we could not help feeling pity for the little songster, fearing that the time had not yet come for the chanting of spring-time songs.

AT this time, Feb. 25, our Bible Term is still in session, but will close to-morrow. There are some here who came in the beginning, and will remain to the close. Others have been coming and going, and, of course, did not realize the same benefits as those who attended during the full term. On the whole, it was the best attended and the most successful term yet held, and we have reason to believe that all who were with us, will go away feeling that their time was well spent. We have prayed and labored that such a feeling should go from us.

CHURCH DIVISIONS.

Number Two.—Their Results.

IF, in church divisions, the results stopped at the time when the troubles culminate in so sad an end, it would be a satisfaction to feel that all is now over and that the effects will forever cease. But is this so? Is it the end or is it only the be-

ginning? There is something in the contemplation of this subject that always gives us feelings of regret and disappointment, and because of this our voice has always been against any tendency in that direction. *Bear* and *forbear* is represented as the golden tie that binds the world together, and it is one of the attributes that is common to both state and church. But to divide in our church relations,—what does it mean? In our other associations a division may be made as a matter of convenience, or to enhance a common interest. It may look to an ultimate good. This, however, cannot be looked for in church divisions. It is a division of purposes, interests and ends, and the final result is an estrangement of feelings. This happens in families and communities, and a division of purposes naturally follows. A division of purpose means a division of possibilities and power, so that the opportunities for doing good are greatly lessened, thus defeating, in part, the great object for which we should live.

Again, divisions are the opening wedge for many other evils to follow, and they do follow.

First. It makes subsequent divisions not only possible but much more easily reached, as it decreases the distance to go, to accomplish the purpose.

When traveling, people go to the nearest station. If the road makes its stations ten miles apart, those living between will have to go to one or the other, but if intermediate stations are made, they will, as a matter of convenience, go to those that are the nearer, and the more of these intermediate stations are made, the greater will be the convenience and the more will the people be inclined to go to the intermediates.

You may ask, "What do you mean by this? We mean this: Take the Mennonite church as an illustration. At first there was but one church of this faith, and those who wished to accept its doctrines had but one place to go. If a little dissatisfaction, on the part of some of the members, would arise, there was but one choice, either to become reconciled to the condition of things, or go out without having a place to which they could go, where they could find a church home. This made division very difficult, as there was nothing that could give encouragement in that direction. After awhile a division was made, but the principles, in the main, were the same. This makes two stations on the same road. The one may be larger than the other and the inducements held out may be greater at the one than the other. But selfishness will discard this difference and take the more convenient. This applies to getting out, as well as to getting in. Now these two may represent the two extremes, and if we have the extremes, how easy it seems to be to get in between, or even beyond, either way.

So it was in this church until there are now twelve divisions,—mostly intermediates,—and do you not see how much nearer these stations must be to each other? or, in other words, how much

less the shades of difference between these divisions must necessarily be?

What is the result of these divisions? It is not only confounding to the earnest seekers but it makes church discipline almost an impossibility. The confounding is in the similarity,—in the *dis*-similarity, and the difficulty in the way of administering proper discipline is the matter of choice. This thought needs no elaboration. It is seen in practical operation most everywhere, and, unfortunately, we are having it to contend with in our own church. We are still inclined to feel that if we had exercised the two bears a little more, we might have avoided some of the sad results that are now entailed upon us. Had we not better done it?

Since then we have been compelled to exercise this spirit more than before, and with the increase of division will there be an increased necessity for the careful exercising of the spirit of Christian forbearance.

Peace gained by division cannot be permanent. At best it is only temporary, and like causes will continue to produce like effects.

After our own division, the Old Order Brethren boasted in the peace that they thus enjoyed, so did the Progressive Brethren, and did we not say the same thing? And was it not a truth? It was, in a sense. It could not be otherwise. But was it not a selfish peace, dearly bought? And where is the peace, thus gained, to-day?

The same cause that marred the peace of us all at that time, has since been at work, and to-day we have our dissimilarities, which, if forced to issues, would be sufficient cause for division, as before. If we are not mistaken, the Progressive Brethren have among them now, more internal discord than was ever experienced before the divisions took place, and the question might be, How many divisions would be necessary to produce a desirable harmony? We do not say this with a feeling of disrepect to the Progressive, as we all have more or less of the same troubles among us. But the question is, Where is the gain? Encourage the feeling of division, and what will be the result,—where the end?

Can we, by having the extremes, throw in enough intermediates to eliminate distance, or accommodate all, and then agree to own the line in common? This might be a possibility, could we limit the bounds. But as we cannot do this, the dangers are that the breathes will widen, and our only hope is in laboring for peace and union. This is the basis on which true Christianity is founded, and when we get away from this, we are treading on dangerous grounds. That we cannot all have our own way in matters of church government is very certain. There are times when we must submit our judgments and forego our preferences, and this we can and should do when we can do so without a violation of principle, and this, the church, on no occasion, should require of its membership.

THE GOSPEL MESSENGER.

"Set for the Defense of the Gospel."

Vol. 30, Old Series.　　　　　　Mt. Morris, Ill., and Huntingdon, Pa., March 8, 1892.　　　　　　No. 10.

The Gospel Messenger.

H. B. BRUMBAUGH, Editor,

And Business Manager of the Eastern House, Box 50.
Huntingdon, Pa.

Table of Contents.

D. A. C.—The best work we have on organising and conducting Sunday-schools, is the "Brethren's Manual," sent post-paid for thirty cents.

SPRING-TIME seems to be coming. Only yesterday we heard the notes of the blue bird, and though they were charming, we could not help feeling pity for the little songster, fearing that the time had not yet come for the chanting of spring-time songs.

AT this time, Feb. 25, our Bible Term is still in session, but will close to-morrow. There are some here who came in the beginning, and will remain to the close. Others have been coming and going, and, of course, did not realize the same benefits as those who attended during the full term. On the whole, it was the best attended and the most successful term yet held, and we have reason to believe that all who were with us, will go away feeling that their time was well spent. We have prayed and labored that such a feeling should go from us.

CHURCH DIVISIONS.

Number Two.—Their Results.

IF, in church divisions, the results stopped at the time when the troubles culminate in so sad an end, it would be a satisfaction to feel that all is now over and that the effects will forever cease. But is this so? Is it the end or is it only the be-

ginning? There is something in the contemplation of this subject that always gives us feelings of regret and disappointment, and because of this our voice has always been against any tendency in that direction. *Bear* and *forbear* is represented as the golden tie that binds the world together, and it is one of the attributes that is common to both state and church. But to divide in our church relations,—what does it mean? In our other associations a division may be made as a matter of convenience, or to enhance a common interest. It may look to an ultimate good. This, however, cannot be looked for in church divisions. It is a division of purposes, interests and ends, and the final result is an estrangement of feelings. This happens in families and communities, and a division of purposes naturally follows. A division of purpose means a division of possibilities and power, so that the opportunities for doing good are greatly lessened, thus defeating, in part, the great object for which we should live.

Again, divisions are the opening wedge for many other evils to follow, and they do follow.

First. It makes subsequent divisions not only possible but much more easily reached, as it decreases the distance to go, to accomplish the purpose.

When traveling, people go to the nearest station. If the road makes its stations ten miles apart, those living between will have to go to one or the other, but if intermediate stations are made, they will, as a matter of convenience, go to those that are the nearer, and the more of these intermediate stations are made, the greater will be the convenience and the more will the people be inclined to go to the intermediates.

You may ask, "What do you mean by this? We mean this: Take the Mennonite church as an illustration. At first there was but one church of this faith, and those who wished to accept its doctrines had but one place to go. If a little dissatisfaction, on the part of some of the members, would arise, there was but one choice, either to become reconciled to the condition of things, or go out without having a place to which they could go, where they could find a church home. This made division very difficult, as there was nothing that could give encouragement in that direction. After awhile a division was made, but the principles, in the main, were the same. This makes two stations on the same road. The one may be larger than the other and the inducements held out may be greater at the one than the other. But selfishness will discard this difference and take the more convenient. This applies to getting out, as well as to getting in. Now these two may represent the two extremes, and if we have the extremes, how easy it seems to be to get in between, or even beyond, either way.

So it was in this church until there are now twelve divisions,—mostly intermediates,—and do you not see how much nearer these stations must be to each other? or, in other words, how much

less the shades of difference between these divisions must necessarily be?

What is the result of these divisions? It is not only confounding to the earnest seekers but it makes church discipline almost an impossibility. The confounding is in the similarity,—in the *dissimilarity*, and the difficulty in the way of administering proper discipline is the matter of choice. This thought needs no elaboration. It is seen in practical operation most every-where, and, unfortunately, we are having it to contend with in our own church. We are still inclined to feel that if we had exercised the two *bears* a little more, we might have avoided some of the sad results that are now entailed upon us. Had we not better done it?

Since then we have been compelled to exercise this spirit more than before, and with the increase of division will there be an increased necessity for the careful exercising of the spirit of Christian forbearance.

Peace gained by division cannot be permanent. At best it is only temporary, and like causes will continue to produce like effects.

After our own division, the Old Order Brethren boasted in the peace that they thus enjoyed, so did the Progressive Brethren, and did we not say the same thing? And was it not a truth? It was, in a sense. It could not be otherwise. But was it not a selfish peace, dearly bought? And where is the peace, thus gained, to-day?

The same cause that marred the peace of us all at that time, has since been at work, and to-day we have our dissimilarities, which, if forced to issues, would be sufficient cause for division, as before. If we are not mistaken, the Progressive Brethren have among them now, more internal discord than was ever experienced before the divisions took place, and the question might be, How many divisions would be necessary to produce a desirable harmony? We do not say this with a feeling of disrespect to the organization, as we all have more or less of the same troubles among us. But the question is, Where is the gain? Encourage the feeling of division, and what will be the result,—where the end?

Can we, by having the extremes, throw in enough intermediate to eliminate distance, or accommodate all, and then agree to own the line in common? This might be a possibility, could we limit the bounds. But as we cannot do this, the dangers are that the breaches will widen, and our only hope is in laboring for peace and union. This is the basis on which true Christianity is founded, and when we get away from this, we are treading on dangerous grounds. That we cannot all have our own way in matters of church government is very certain. There are times when we must submit our judgments and forego our preferences, and this we can and should do when we can do so without a violation of principle, and this, the church, on no occasion, should require of its membership.

and have them put to death. Only a few hours previous to his conversion we find him "breathing out threatenings and slaughter against the disciples of the Lord." Did Paul have no harvest to reap? Yes, verily; he was no exception to the rule. Though his whole future life was consecrated to the cause which he had so bitterly opposed, the seeds of persecution had already taken root, and as years wore on, they yielded bountifully. In Paul's history we learn that he was persecuted in various ways,—stoned, imprisoned, beaten with many stripes, and finally delivered up to a martyr's death.

Examine the records of those wicked characters, Herod, Dives, Judas Iscariot, and all others, who sinned against God and their fellow-men, and you will learn that, at last, their iniquities blasted their own lives and cursed their souls. "Be not deceived; God is not mocked; for whatsoever a man soweth, that shall he also reap.

These are eternal words, and as true as God himself. We cannot evade the harvest of sins which we commit. It may be a long time coming,—it may take it years to ripen,—but it will come as surely as the seeds are sown. How often we are reminded of this truth! How many times the soul is overwhelmed and well-nigh crushed by a torrent of calamities and agonies,—the products of a, perhaps, long-accumulating harvest!

We need not refer to the pages of history for this. We can see it in the lives of men and women all around us. Indeed, we can see it in our lives.

The time will come when a voice shall cry from heaven to each of us: "Thrust in thy sickle and reap; for the time is come for thee to reap, for the harvest is ripe." If we have sown the seeds of truth and mercy and purity and love, the harvest shall be "a far more exceeding and eternal weight of glory." But if they have been seeds of deception and malice and envy and hatred and murder and licentiousness and strife, we must reap in anguish and everlasting shame and our harvest shall be "The damnation of hell"!

Kind reader, what are you sowing?

INSURANCE AND PROHIBITION.

BY MARY M. GIBSON.

This may seem a strange subject to write on, but nevertheless I feel that it is a timely one.

Most of us understand the meaning of insurance. When we insure we want to secure and save ourselves from the loss we may suffer by fire, flood or storm. Prohibition is to save and rescue the souls that are leading the downward road to ruin and degradation. Many of our brethren are insuring their property, or earthly possessions (and some, perhaps, insure their lives), that the loss may not be so great. Does this hinder from being made willing to trust wholly in God? Will it keep him from moulding us in humble submission to his will, as does the potter his clay? Can there be anything more sublime than to feel perfect safety in the hands of a just God? Will insurance prohibit the representation of the body of Christ, where there is more power than that of the legislature? My friends, there is no company so rich as that of perfect trust in the Trinity.

Here is one that will insure his or her property for one thousand dollars in some company but would emphatically say, "No, brother, you cannot secure or save that soul that is worth more than the world in that line. You are to give your time and strength and God-given powers to redeem him from his iniquity, elsewhere; you are not practicing as I think is best. You are drifting away from the body to which you belong. You are going out into the by-ways too much."

Yes, my dear Christian friends, are we not commanded to go out into the by-ways and hedges and bring them in? The more vile a soul is, the more need it has of a loving Savior. Souls by the thousands are starving because we are not going out into the by-ways enough. We might find sheaves there that are now decaying, that might bring a rich reward indeed.

People take us to be a Christian people, and they are expecting to see devoted love in showing forth our light, that some beams might shine brightly on them. Why, oh why, should we be selfish and hold back with pen, tongue and brain, when we know full well that God has given us talents for the bettering of humanity! We had better pause and think soberly, pray earnestly, and act wisely that we may be the means of saving a soul from being hurled into eternity, without sufficient support to resist the temptation that might be weighing them down to destruction.

We can give our help to the work of prohibition in many ways. This will only make us love the church and her doctrines all the better. It will help to make us stronger in the Lord and the power of his might. Can we not help bring about a state of safety by the aid we give, in even saying one word of encouragement! It might bring forth a bright star for our crown in the realms of eternal bliss.

The man that has to suffer the loss of a thousand dollars, feels his loss deeply, but, oh, compare that with the worth of the soul! The thousand dollars are only temporal while that of the soul is for eternity. God cannot afford to do without those precious souls, when he has placed sufficient means into some one's hands to redeem them from all the fiery darts of hell? God will hold us responsible at the day of judgment if we do not do all that is in our power to save the souls of fallen humanity. Shall we not press forward with might and main? Do we think he will possibly be pleased with us if we sit inactive when we know we can reach out and assist in one of the most sacred works of our land that has ever been on record? "In the last days," saith the Lord, "I shall pour out my spirit upon all flesh and your sons and your daughters shall prophesy." That time I think has come.

Christ's chosen ones are not of the letter but of the Spirit, and the Spirit giveth life. Yea, the sons and daughters and handmaids will all have a hand in the glorious work of saving souls from sin and debauchery. Many shall come forth that have been vile and full of sin, to whom those loving sons and daughters that have been made new creatures in Christ Jesus. Would to God that I might be the means of bringing at least one soul out of the darkness and sin of a drunkard's life into the marvelous light! God be praised, and hallowed be his name that one soul might meet me in eternity face to face with a hearty clasp of the hand, and say, "Of a truth you were the means of redeeming my soul from a drunkard's hell." I teach my children and my primary Sunday-school class that they might be the means of doing that very thing some time, and if they should, what a bright light that would be!

Dear co-workers, the leaven is at work and God is calling us to the front ranks on every hand. Are we not willing to go at his bidding? What a glorious kingdom we might have by getting every soul on fire with the love of God, that is now failing here and there by sin and its iniquity. My heart is made to feel the weight of perishing souls that are in want of some dear loving hand to guide them into the ways of all truth. They are keeping an eye upon the Christian. Are we now ready and willing to heed their cry?

My dear, loving friends, will we not say, "Amen" to those that can and will, and give them our aid and assistance by saying, "Push the work, as God in his goodness may direct." Think of the many little children to-night that are hungry, with tattered dress and bare feet, and no fire to warm them! Think of these children when they beg mother for a piece of bread, and hear her say with a heavy heart, a sad countenance and tear-stained cheeks, "Not a bit of bread, dear children!" Would they not eagerly grasp an ear of corn from our hands, an old dress and hard shoes, to satisfy their need? Think of some huddled up in an old goods box or out-house to sleep,—perhaps the sleep of death,—while their mother and father are lying in the ditch, worse than dead! I often think of the poor little barefoot orphan girl that had no home but lay at a rich man's door wrapped in a winding sheet of snow, begging for bread, but, before the morning dawned, her soul had fled to that home above where there is room and bread for the poor.

THE ULTIMATUM.

BY J. S. FLORY.

It seems, after all that has been said and published for the last eighteen hundred years on the subject of faith, that in the minds of many it is as much a vexed problem as ever, or, we might say, more so. The simple, child-like mind does not seem to worry over it so much as the would-be wise.

The reason why it is so may not be difficult of solution. Is it not a fact that the learned aim too high,—their ideal of theology partakes too much of vain philosophy? Those who pride themselves on worldly wisdom too often lack the essential element of humble simplicity. "Doctors of Divinity," and "Right Reverend Divines" of the present day, as of yore, like the pompous toad spoken of in the fable, become so completely filled with unreal matter as to finally explode. Many are giving up pet theories of the past and are looking about for a new theology.

As to faith the question is being asked, "How broad is it? Where, as a factor in religion, is its appropriate place?" Still further the querist wants to know if really anything else is needed, and goes so far as to say it is not a factor but the sum total of the Christian religion. The most remarkable thing of all is, that gaping crowds take it all in as true.

What an idea! Ignore the tree but glorify the fruit! Care not for the root but worship the branches!

Let us examine the subject from a Bible standpoint. There can be no such a thing as Christian faith unless it be based on God's Word. Faith, separated from the Gospel dies as surely as the vine severed from the ground. "Faith cometh by hearing, and hearing by the Word of God." Rom. 10: 17. Who dare say that the Word of God does not contain all the fundamental principles of salvation?

The Word of God is the will of God and in that will we have the union of the wisdom and power of God. The wisdom of God declares and decides what is to be; the power of God secures the performance. Faith is the medium through which Divine power comes to the believer. Faith takes up God's will, and appropriates it to the creature, and in this way he becomes a son of God.

As God "doeth according to his will," so the true believer doeth according to God's will,—"God in him to will and to do of his pleasure." By this law of appropriation, the believer is able to do "mighty works," because God's will, wisdom, and power are always so closely allied and back of

and have them put to death. Only a few hours previous to his conversion we find him "breathing out threatenings and slaughter against the disciples of the Lord." Did Paul have no harvest to reap? Yes, verily; he was no exception to the rule. Though his whole future life was consecrated to the cause which he had so bitterly opposed, the seeds of persecution had already taken root, and as years wore on, they yielded bountifully. In Paul's history we learn that he was persecuted in various ways,— stoned, imprisoned, beaten with many stripes, and finally delivered up to a martyr's death.

Examine the records of those wicked characters, Herod, Dives, Judas Iscariot, and all others, who sinned against God and their fellow-men, and you will learn that, at last, their iniquities blasted their own lives and cursed their souls. "Be not deceived; God is not mocked; for whatsoever a man soweth, that shall he also reap.

These are eternal words, and as true as God himself. We cannot evade the harvest of sins which we commit. It may be a long time coming,—it may take 16 years to ripen,—but it will come as surely as the seeds are sown. How often we are reminded of this truth! How many times the soul is overwhelmed and well-nigh crushed by a torrent of calamities and agonies,—the products of a, perhaps, long-accumulating harvest!

We need not refer to the pages of history for this. We can see it in the lives of men and women all around us. Indeed, we can see it in our lives.

The time will come when a voice shall cry from heaven to each of us: " Thrust in thy sickle and reap; for the time is come for thee to reap, for the harvest is ripe." If we have sown the seeds of truth and mercy and purity and love, the harvest shall be " a far more exceeding and eternal weight of glory." But if they have been seeds of deception and malice and envy and hatred and murder and licentiousness and strife, we must reap in anguish and everlasting shame and our harvest shall be " The damnation of hell " !

Kind reader, what are you sowing?

INSURANCE AND PROHIBITION.

BY MARY M. GIBSON.

This may seem a strange subject to write on, but nevertheless I feel that it is a timely one.

Most of us understand the meaning of insurance. When we insure we want to secure and save ourselves from the loss we may suffer by fire, flood or storm. Prohibition is to save and rescue the souls that are leading the downward road to ruin and degradation. Many of our brethren are insuring their property, or earthly possessions (and some, perhaps, insure their lives), that the loss may not be so great. Does this hinder from being made willing to trust wholly in God? Will it keep him from moulding us in humble submission to his will, as does the potter his clay? Can there be anything more sublime than to feel perfect safety in the hands of a just God? Will insurance prohibit the representation of the body of Christ, where there is more power than that of the legislature? My friends, there is no company so rich as that of perfect trust in the Trinity.

Here is one that will insure his or her property for one thousand dollars in some company but would emphatically say, "No, brother, you cannot secure or save that soul that is worth more than the world in that line. You are to give your time and strength and God-given powers to redeem him from his iniquity, elsewhere; you are not practicing as I think is best. You are drifting away from the body to which you belong. You are going out into the by-ways too much."

Yes, my dear Christian friends, are we not commanded to go out into the by-ways and hedges and bring them in? The more vile a soul is, the more need it has of a loving Savior. Souls by the thousands are starving because we are not going out into the by-ways enough. We might find sheaves there that are now decaying, that might bring a rich reward indeed.

People take us to be a Christian people, and they are expecting to see devoted love in showing forth our light, that some beams might shine brightly on them. Why, oh why, should we be selfish and hold back with pen, tongue and brain, when we know full well that God has given us talents for the bettering of humanity! We had better pause and think soberly, pray earnestly, and act wisely that we may be the means of saving a soul from being hurled into eternity, without sufficient support to resist the temptation that might be weighing them down to destruction.

We can give our help to the work of prohibition in many ways. This will only make us love the church and her doctrines all the better. It will help to make us stronger in the Lord and the power of his might. Can we not help bring about a state of safety by the aid we give, in even saying one word of encouragement! It might bring forth a bright star for our crown in the realms of eternal bliss.

The man that has to suffer the loss of a thousand dollars, feels his loss deeply, but, oh, compare that with the worth of the soul! The thousand dollars are only temporal while that of the soul is for eternity. God cannot afford to do without those precious souls, when he has placed sufficient means into some one's hands to redeem them from all the fiery darts of hell? God will hold us responsible at the day of judgment if we do not do all that is in our power to save the souls of fallen humanity. Shall we not press forward with might and main? Do we think he will possibly be pleased with us if we sit inactive when we know we can reach out and assist in one of the most sacred works of our land that has ever been on record? "In the last days," saith the Lord, "I shall pour out my spirit upon all flesh and your sons and your daughters shall prophesy." That time I think has come.

Christ's chosen ones are not of the letter but of the Spirit, and the Spirit giveth life. Yes, the sons and daughters and handmaids will all have a hand in the glorious work of saving souls from sin and debauchery. Many shall come forth that have been vile and full of sin, to bring forth good fruit to his name's honor and glory. They will be brought out from under the bondage by those loving sons and daughters that have been made new creatures in Christ Jesus. Would to God that I might be the means of bringing at least one soul out of the darkness and sin of a drunkard's life into the marvelous light! God be praised, and hallowed be his name that one soul might meet me in eternity face to face with a hearty clasp of the hand, and say, "Of a truth you were the means of redeeming my soul from a drunkard's hell." I teach my children and my primary Sunday-school class that they might be the means of doing that very thing some time, and if they should, what a bright light that would be!

Dear co-workers, the leaven is at work and God is calling us to the front ranks on every hand. Are we not willing to go at his bidding? What a glorious kingdom we might have by getting every soul on fire with the love of God, that is now falling here and there by sin and its iniquity. My heart is made to feel the weight of perishing souls that are in want of some dear loving hand to guide them into the ways of all truth. They are keeping an eye upon the Christian. Are we now ready and willing to heed their cry?

My dear, loving friends, will we not say, " Amen " to those that can and will, and give them our aid and assistance by saying, " Push the work, as God in his goodness may direct." Think of the many little children to-night that are hungry, with tattered dress and bare feet, and no fire to warm them! Think of these children when they beg mother for a piece of bread, and hear her say with a heavy heart, a sad countenance and tear-stained cheeks, "Not a bit of bread, dear children!" Would they not eagerly grasp an ear of corn from our hands, an old dress and hard shoes, to satisfy their need? Think of some huddled up in an old goods box or out-house to sleep,—perhaps the sleep of death,—while their mother and father are lying in the ditch, worse than dead! I often think of the poor little barefoot orphan girl that had no home but lay at a rich man's door wrapped in a winding sheet of snow, begging for bread, but, before the morning dawned, her soul had fled to that home above where there is room and bread for the poor.

THE ULTIMATUM.

BY J. S. FLORY.

It seems, after all that has been said and published for the last eighteen hundred years on the subject of faith, that in the minds of many it is as much a vexed problem as ever, or, we might say, more so. The simple, child-like mind does not seem to worry over it so much as the would-be. wise.

The reason why it is so may not be difficult of solution. Is it not a fact that the learned aim too high,—their ideal of theology partakes too much of vain philosophy? Those who pride themselves on worldly wisdom too often lack the essential element of humble simplicity. "Doctors of Divinity," and "Right Reverend Divines" of the present day, as of yore, like the pompous toad spoken of in the fable, become so completely filled with unreal matter as to finally explode. Many are giving up pet theories of the past and are looking about for a new theology.

As to faith the question is being asked, "How broad is it? Where, as a factor in religion, is its appropriate place?" Still further the querist wants to know if really anything else is needed, and goes so far as to say it is not a factor but the sum total of the Christian religion. The most remarkable thing of all is, that gaping crowds take it all in as true.

What an idea! Ignore the tree but glorify the fruit! Care not for the root but worship the branches!

Let us examine the subject from a Bible standpoint. There can be no such a thing as Christian faith unless it be based on God's Word. Faith, separated from the Gospel dies as surely as the vine severed from the ground. "Faith cometh by hearing, and hearing by the Word of God." Rom. 10: 17. Who dare say that the Word of God does not contain all the fundamental principles of salvation?

The Word of God is the will of God and in that will we have the union of the wisdom and power of God. The wisdom of God declares and decides what is to be; the power of God secures the performance. Faith is the medium through which Divine power comes to the believer. Faith takes up God's will, and appropriates it to the creature, and in this way he becomes a son of God.

As God "doeth according to his will," so the true believer doeth according to God's will,—"God in him to will and to do of his pleasure." By this law of appropriation, the believer is able to do "mighty works," because God's will, wisdom, and power are always so closely allied and back of

Peter and John went up together into the temple at the hour of prayer, being the ninth hour." Acts 3: 1. Again, "Peter went up upon the housetop to pray about the sixth hour." Acts 10: 9. This custom led Paul and Silas on the Sabbath Day "out of the city by a river-side where prayer was wont to be made." They followed this prayer service with a preaching service, with glorious results.

Conclusion.—This new Christian doctrine had the following gratifying results then, and it ought to be followed with the same results now:

(a) "They continued steadfastly in the apostles' doctrine;" "not carried about with every wind of doctrine." They were genuinely converted.

(b) They joined in fellowship, became members of the church, the body of Christ, according to 1 John 1: 7.

(c) They met together, not only in the temple, but socially from house to house, ate in common together, which is a clear mark of friendship and good will.

(d) Their lives were lives of prayer. They were "instant in prayer."

We entertain fears that, in general, those ancient fixed hours of prayer, so carefully observed by the early apostolic church, are too much neglected.   L. J. Rosenberger.

BROTHERLY KINDNESS.

BY JULIA A. ARNOLD.

Brotherly kindness is one of the eight Christian graces. The softening power of the Divine Spirit can create it between hearts that mutually hate. In 1 John 4: 21, we read "And this commandment have we from him, That he who loveth God love his brother also."

Let us love one another! This little sentence should be written on every heart, and stamped on every memory. It should be the golden rule practiced, not only in every household, but throughout the world. By possessing brotherly kindness we are keeping the command of God, and we are often led by this love to lend a helping hand to our brother, which not only removes thorns from the pathway, but makes us to feel a pleasure in our own hearts, knowing that we are doing our duty to a fellow-creature.

In Gal. 6: 10 we read, "As we have therefore opportunity, let us do good unto all men, especially unto them who are of the household of faith." If we do not love and do good to our brethren and sisters, we must be miserable; our pleasures must be few indeed, while, on the other hand, if we love one another, we will, as we should, show our love by lending a helping hand, or speaking an encouraging word, and feel it no loss to ourselves, yet a benefit to others.

Who has not felt the power of these two words, brotherly kindness? Who has not needed the love of a kind friend? How soothing, when perplexed with some task that is mysterious and burdensome, to feel a gentle hand on the shoulder, and hear a kind voice whispering, "Do not feel discouraged? I see your trouble. Let me help you." Have not all felt the need of such words? Let me ask what causes such words to fall from our lips? I believe every one would say that brotherly kindness is the foundation of such. If we have enemies, and those enemies persecute us, how very pleasant it is to possess brotherly kindness enough to go and speak in loving words to them and make them feel that we love them with a love recommended by our Heavenly Father! We believe such love would banish all envy as the sunshine dissolves the dew.

Then, dear brethren and sisters, let us love one another, and let us show our love by endeavoring to strengthen and to encourage one another,—and in many other ways which would be well in the sight of God. This will make our lives glide smoothly on, and the founts of bitterness will yield sweet waters, and he, whose willing hand is ever ready to aid us, will reward our humble endeavors, and every good deed will be as "bread cast upon the waters to return after many days."

Bridgewater, Va.

RECOGNITION.

BY LEAH REPLOGLE.

A good deal has been written on heavenly recognition and it is a pleasant subject to think about, but perhaps it would be more profitable for us to think a little more about earthly recognition. We love to sing "Shall we know each other there?" but "Shall we know each other here?" is a more practical question for us.

In our social intercourse with each other, as members of families, we seldom lose an opportunity to recognize each other. The family tie, the cord of love, that binds us together naturally produces the mutual desire for recognition. How is it in our spiritual relationship? Divine love is infinitely superior to human love, so the attachment between the members of the spiritual family ought to be stronger than that between the members of the human family. Love recognizes its object and where there is mutual love, there will be recognition. Sometimes we see so little recognition among our dear brethren and sisters, that we fear there is a lack of love.

Do we not sometimes manifest too much coldness toward each other in the public sanctuary? When we meet and part in a cold, formal way we miss a part of the design for which the meeting was intended. Our dear Lord commanded the assembling of ourselves together, not only that he might meet with us there but that we might be strengthened by our coming in contact with each other. He wants us to come together that we may receive spiritual magnetism from each other. A friendly greeting is always encouraging and helpful, while coldness is a hindrance.

I once happened (for a short time), to be in a city where there was a church of the Brethren. I attended their services twice, without receiving the slightest recognition, either as a member, or a stranger. The coldness so chilled me that it left an unfavorable impression on my mind for some time.

There is power in the Christian's greeting. I have seen whole congregations revived by the touch of a few warm-hearted Christians who shook hands with those around them, giving to each a few words of good cheer, of comfort, or encouragement. Yes, there is power in the grasp of the hand, there is power in a smile, a bow, even in a look of recognition. Our ministering brethren will never know how much good they do, or how much they might do through recognition.

This power of recognition reaches beyond the membership. It includes the stranger and the unconverted. Many a one has received his first impulse for holy living from the touch of a consecrated hand. May we be inspired with love for each other that will manifest itself in recognition.

"IN MY NAME."

BY JOHN E. MOHLER.

"And this is the confidence that we have in him, that if we ask anything according to his will, he heareth us."—1 John 5: 14.

This is the only condition upon which prayer is heard by God. "His will" means much and is encased in his Word, but is fully revealed only by the Holy Spirit. Rom. 8: 26, 27; 1 Cor. 2: 10-16.

In this article I shall consider what seems a violation of the plain will of God made, perhaps, thoughtlessly in many public prayers. "Hitherto have ye asked nothing in my name: ask, and ye shall receive, that your joy may be full." John 16: 24. This is the language of Christ. The Gospels are teeming with the expression "In his name" and the epistles are marked with the same idea. Yet fervent prayers are offered in which the name of the Redeemer is not so much as mentioned.

Some one may say, "But we always think of Christ as the Mediator between us and God in our petitions." Is it sufficient to *silently think* of the Son in the administration of baptism? Is this sufficient in prayer? Can we, in view of John 14: 13, 14, 15, 16 and 16: 23, 24, consider the Lord's Prayer, as recorded by Matthew and Luke, a perfect prayer for us, as it is often said to be, especially since the language referred to above was spoken *since* the Lord's Prayer was formulated? With due reverence for the custom, should our public prayers be closed with the Lord's Prayer *outside* of Christ's name? "Let him that is taught in the Word communicate unto him that" is untaught,—even me!

Warrensburgh, Mo.

[The latter part of the above contains a query for some one to answer.—Ed.]

HOLY LIVING.

A godly person through perseverance and industry had been able to build himself a house. But his chief boast was, that from his fireside he could see his father's house on a distant hill. "No matter the weather," said he, "whether winter or summer, spring or autumn—no matter the sky, whether cloudless or stormy—when I sit by my east window, father's roof and chimney-tops, the gleam of his lamp at night, are always visible to my sight."

His words contain the philosophy of life, and enclose, as in a nutshell, the principles of holy living. Enviable—yea, thrice enviable—is the man who can pierce the clouds of social darkness which surround our earthly homes and see his Father's house, with its many mansions, in the distant heaven. Let the winter wind sweep and the long rains pour, still from his mansion here the Christian, by faith, can see, through all the tempest and darkness, the light beaming from the mansions in heaven; and by-and-by, bidding farewell to the earthly, he shall take perpetual possession of his eternal home.—*Sel.*

"More hearts pine away in secret anguish for the want of kindness from those who should be their comforters, than from any other calamity in life. A word of kindness is a seed which springs up a flower. A kind word and a pleasant voice are gifts easy to give. Be liberal with them. They are worth more than money. If a word or two will render a man happy, said a Frenchman, he must be a wretch indeed who would not give it. Kindness is stored away in the heart like rose leaves in a drawer, to sweeten every object around them. Little drops of rain brighten the meadows, and little acts of kindness brighten the world. We can conceive of nothing more attractive than the heart, when filled with the spirit of kindness. Certainly nothing embellishes human nature as the practice of this virtue; a sentiment so genial and so excellent ought to be emblazoned upon every thought and act of our lives. The principle underlies the whole theory of Christianity, and in no other persons do we find it more happily exemplified than in the life of our Savior, who, while on earth, "went about doing good."

teacher we find him preparing his disciples to continue his important work, and sending them out to preach the Gospel to all nations.

We may feel assured that in his life and works his teachings were the most important and sacred lessons ever given to man. His recorded sayings do not cover much space, yet each word is a living seed, and vast libraries have been filled with lessons from them. More lives have been changed for good, more love created, more joy and peace assured by his teachings than by the works of any other. His wonderful Sermon on the Mount is enough to lift each soul to higher and nobler aspirations. These lessons, and the many others, compel us to believe that he is, the only perfect teacher.

One of Christ's first lessons was self-denial. By this we learn to renounce the world as master and use it as a servant. Like it was with Christ's cross, so ours may become a glory.

Some one has beautifully said, "Christ's cross is the sweetest burden I ever bore." It is such a burden as wings to a bird or sails to a ship. Christ being divine had the authority to teach things without proof. We must go to him for proof for all we would teach. In the depth of his simplicity consists the height of his eloquence. Nature itself is his book of illustration. He calls attention to the lilies clothing the fields with their beauty, the shepherd leading his flock, and the birds warbling their sweet songs in the tree-tops.

Such are the pictures which illuminate his speeches and make nature testify of God. He used the most common events and incidents to interpret his meaning. The house built upon the sand, the house-wife looking for the lost coin, the noble deed of the good Samaritan,—all these are made to reveal truths of infinite importance. They seem to be spoken without previous study, yet they are clothed in such picturesque beauty that they reach the inmost soul better than any man's rhetorical effort. Christ unfolded mysteries to those who sought to know them, and led his pupils from the known to the unknown.

Beginning with the Old Testament, he gave the facts concerning the New. Yet, with all his care even, many believed him not and he marveled at it. He does not wonder at other human actions, but he does marvel, on the one hand at faith, when it overcomes all obstacles, and, on the other hand, he wonders at unbelief when it can, in the face of divine manifestations, harden itself into a willful, persistent rejection of him. All unbelief of God's promises (forgetting his merciful gifts and all he has done to save) is unreasonable and ungrateful. It prevents God's best blessings from flowing through us to others, and thus leads the innocent, the weak, the trusting into sin. Though a great degree of patience was exercised in his teachings and many refused to obey him, yet he did not become discouraged, but ever kept on; for he knew his mission was divine.

Christ taught great lessons of divine love. His highest motive was no personal fondness but a sense of the infinite value of a soul. Greater love hath no man than he who laid down his life even for his enemies. This admirable characteristic appears on nearly every page of the Gospel. His teaching was a marked contrast to that of the Jewish teachers, who looked with contempt on the ignorant. His words glow with gentleness, and strangers wonder at their sweetness.

Christ treated all humanity with the deepest regard, and we clearly see the boundless grace of him who is willing to receive the youngest child as well as the oldest man. His power is divine and his hearers felt that his words were from God. He knew he was from God, therefore he taught with calmness and certainty, yet ever with the fer-

vor of one who was held by the greatness of the spiritual and eternal realities on which he looked.

Having received the "Holy Spirit without measure, Christ kindled enthusiasm in the hearts of his hearers. If he taught men to love one another, they knew he was love; if he spoke to them of God, they knew he was in the bosom of God the Father."

While the power of the Holy Spirit won the confidence of his disciples and his words had in them the grandeur of his character, yet he was more than what he taught. This power is beyond comprehension.

He saw the infinite value of each individual soul, and taught individuals with as much interest as multitudes.

He taught what most good men desire to know, the coming of the kingdom and its glorious future. He, then, is the perfect teacher and has no rival. No man ever spoke such words, exerted such influence, produced such results as he.

Girard, Ill.

WHAT AM I GOOD FOR?

BY LEAH REPLOGLE.

WHILE reading the editor's "Thought Flashes," in GOSPEL MESSENGER, No. 3, I stopped to ask myself the question, "What am I good for?" My first thought was, "Good for Nothing." I felt sad, and tried to think of something that I might be good for, and then consoled myself with the thought that I was good for some trifling services to the world, but this did not satisfy me. I still felt grieved, and wished I might be good for something better. I thought of the editor's remarks on the answer of a child to his question, "Good to love papa and mama," and instantly the thought flashed into my mind, "I am good to love my Heavenly Father; I am good to praise the Lord, and to glorify him." This thought brought peace to my mind, and I am satisfied that my lifework should be that of prayer and praise, and thanksgiving to the Lord.

I turned to the Psalms for expressions of praise, and almost instantly these lines began to flash into my mind:—

> I will praise thee, O Gracious Lord,
>   With all my heart, with all my soul,
> Let all my being, all my power,
>   Join thy great goodness to extol.
>
> I praise thee for thy marvelous works,
>   And for thy wonders in the sky,
> For all thy doings here on earth,
>   Praise be to thee, O thou most high.
>
> "O, Lord our Lord, in all the earth,
>   How excellent is thy great na me,"
> Above the Heavens, thy glory shines,
>   The moon and stars thy praise proclaims.
>
> "I will bless thee at all times, Lord,"
>   Thy praises shall my lips employ,
> My soul shall magnify thy name,
>   Thy great salvation be my joy.
>
> I praise thee for thy judgments, Lord,
>   For all things t ask thee o'er and o'er,
> I'll sing of all thy righteousness,
>   And yet will praise thee more and more.

Yes, dear brethren and sisters, we are all good to praise the Lord, if we make his praise the delight of our life. O, I am so glad that the Lord lets us praise him, and the most beautiful thought of all is, if we are good to praise the Lord now, we always will be. We will never wear out, we will never want for employment, and we will never lack opportunity for service. Yes, we are good to praise the Lord.

May the dear Lord bless our editor and give him many more "Thought Flashes" to send out through the MESSENGER, until all the readers become illuminated by the light of the Holy

Spirit and we will have one grand chorus of praise to the Lord.

THE GREAT PHYSICIAN.

BY WILL SHIVELY.

I AM at this writing administering to the wants of a sick wife, afflicted with a severe attack of *La Grippe*, accompanied by malaria. While administering to her wants, I am made to think of the "Great Physician," who, while on earth, prescribed different remedies to cure sin. Some of these remedies are very disagreeable to us, as they come in abrupt contact with our carnal nature, so much so that some people refuse to take them. In Matt. 5: 44, we are commanded to love our enemies, bless them that curse us, do good to them that hate us and pray for them that despitefully use us and persecute us.

God's remedies, if used as directed, will break down hatred in the heart of man. They will create an humble, contrite heart, something we all need.

In the Bible we have many incentives to a better life. We have many remedies prepared by God, that people are willing to accept; but it is not always the most pleasant remedy from which we derive the most benefit. All the dispensations of God's providence are medicine to our souls. That which rebels against human nature is just as essential as that which the popular world is willing to use take it *all* and be *sure* of a cure.

Chicago, Ill., Feb. 7.

"THE lines of suffering on almost every human countenance have been deepened, if not traced there, by unfaithfulness to conscience, by departures from duty. To do wrong is the surest way to bring suffering; no wrong deed ever failed to bring it. Those sins which are followed by no palpable pain are yet terribly avenged, even in this life. They abridge our capacity of happiness, impair our relish for innocent pleasure, and increase our sensibility to suffering. They spoil us of the armor of a pure conscience; and of trust in God, without which we are naked amid hosts of foes and are vulnerable by all the changes of life. Thus, to do wrong is to inflict the surest injury on our own peace. No enemy can do us equal harm with what we do ourselves whenever and however we violate any moral or religious obligation."

The Gospel Messenger

Is the recognized organ of the German Baptist or Brethren's church, and advocates the form of doctrine taught in the New Testament and pleads for a return to apostolic and primitive Christianity.

It recognizes the New Testament as the only infallible rule of faith and practice, and maintains that Faith toward God, Repentance from dead works, Regeneration of the heart and mind, baptism by Trine Immersion for remission of sins unto the reception of the Holy Ghost by the laying on of hands, are the means of adoption into the household of God,—the church militant.

It also maintains that Feet-washing, as taught in John 13, both by example and command of Jesus, should be observed in the church.

That the Lord's Supper, instituted by Christ and as universally observed by the apostles and the early Christians, is a full meal, and, in connection with the Communion, should be taken in the evening or after the close of the day.

That the Salutation of the Holy Kiss, or Kiss of Charity, is binding upon the followers of Christ.

That War and Retaliation are contrary to the spirit and self-denying principles of the religion of Jesus Christ.

That the principle of Plain Dressing and of Non-conformity to the world, as taught in the New Testament, should be observed by the followers of Christ.

That the Scriptural duty of Anointing the Sick with Oil, in the Name of the Lord, James 5: 14, is binding upon all Christians.

It also advocates the church's duty to support Missionally and Tract Work, thus giving to the Lord for the spread of the Gospel and for the conversion of sinners.

In short, it is a vindicator of all that Christ and the apostles have enjoined upon us, and alms, amid the conflicting theories and discords of modern Christendom, to point out ground that all must concede to be infallibly safe.

The above principles of our Fraternity are set forth on our "Brethren's Envelopes." Use them! Price, 15 cents per package; 40 cents per hundred.

teacher we find him preparing his disciples to continue his important work, and sending them out to preach the Gospel to all nations.

We may feel assured that in his life and works his teachings were the most important and sacred lessons ever given to man. His recorded sayings do not cover much space, yet each word is a living seed, and vast libraries have been filled with lessons from them. More lives have been changed for good, more love created, more joy and peace assured by his teachings than by the works of any other. His wonderful Sermon on the Mount is enough to lift each soul to higher and nobler aspirations. These lessons, and the many others, compel us to believe that he is, the only perfect teacher.

One of Christ's first lessons was self-denial. By this we learn to renounce the world as master and use it as a servant. Like it was with Christ's cross, so ours may become a glory.

Some one has beautifully said, "Christ's cross is the sweetest burden I ever bore." It is such a burden as wings to a bird or sails to a ship. Christ being divine had the authority to teach things without proof. We must go to him for proof for all we would teach. In the depth of his simplicity consists the height of his eloquence. Nature itself is his book of illustration. He calls attention to the lilies clothing the fields with their beauty, the shepherd leading his flock, and the birds warbling their sweet songs in the tree-tops.

Such are the pictures which illuminate his speeches and make nature testify of God. He used the most common events and incidents to interpret his meaning. The house built upon the sand, the house-wife looking for the lost coin, the noble deed of the good Samaritan,—all these are made to reveal truths of infinite importance. They seem to be spoken without previous study, yet they are clothed in such picturesque beauty that they reach the inmost soul better than any man's rhetorical effort. Christ unfolded mysteries to those who sought to know them, and led his pupils from the known to the unknown.

Beginning with the Old Testament, he gave the facts concerning the New. Yet, with all his care even, many believed him not and he marveled at it. He does not wonder at other human actions, but he does marvel, on the one hand at faith, when it overcomes all obstacles, and, on the other hand, he wonders at unbelief when it can, in the face of divine manifestations, harden itself into a willful, persistent rejection of him. All unbelief of God's promises (forgetting his merciful gifts and all he has done to save) is unreasonable and ungrateful. It prevents God's best blessings from flowing through us to others, and thus leads the innocent; the weak, the trusting into sin. Though a great degree of patience was exercised in his teachings and many refused to obey him, yet he did not become discouraged, but ever kept on; for he knew his mission was divine.

Christ taught great lessons of divine love. His highest motive was no personal fondness but a sense of the infinite value of a soul. Greater love hath no man than he who laid down his life even for his enemies. This admirable characteristic appears on nearly every page of the Gospel. His teaching was a marked contrast to that of the Jewish teachers, who looked with contempt on the ignorant. His words glow with gentleness, and strangers wonder at their sweetness.

Christ treated all humanity with the deepest regard, and we clearly see the boundless grace of him who is willing to receive the youngest child as well as the oldest man. His power is divine and his hearers felt that his words were from God. He knew he was from God, therefore he taught with calmness and certainty, yet ever with the fer-

vor of one who was held by the greatness of the spiritual and eternal realities on which he looked.

Having received the "Holy Spirit without measure, Christ kindled enthusiasm in the hearts of his hearers. If he taught men to love one another they knew he was love; if he spoke to them of God, they knew he was in the bosom of God the Father."

While the power of the Holy Spirit won the confidence of his disciples and his words had in them the grandeur of his character, yet he was more than what he taught. This power is beyond comprehension.

He saw the infinite value of each individual soul, and taught individuals with as much interest as multitudes.

He taught what most good men desire to know, the coming of the kingdom and its glorious future. He, then, is the perfect teacher and has no rival. No man ever spoke such words, exerted such influence, produced such results as he.

Girard, Ill.

WHAT AM I GOOD FOR?

BY LEAH REPLOGLE.

While reading the editor's "Thought Flashes," in Gospel Messenger, No. 8, I stopped to ask myself the question, "What am I good for?" My first thought was, "Good for Nothing." I felt sad, and tried to think of something that I might be good for, and then consoled myself with the thought that I was good for some trifling services to the world, but this did not satisfy me. I still felt grieved, and wished I might be good for something better. I thought of the editor's remarks on the answer of a child to his question, "Good to love papa and mamma," and instantly the thought flashed into my mind, "I am good to love my Heavenly Father; I am good to praise the Lord, and to glorify him." This thought brought peace to my mind, and I am satisfied that my life-work should be that of prayer and praise, and thanksgiving to the Lord.

I turned to the Psalms for expressions of praise, and almost instantly these lines began to flash into my mind:

I will praise thee, O Gracious Lord,
　With all my heart, with all my soul,
Let all my being, all my power,
　Join thy great goodness to extol.

I praise thee for thy marvelous works,
　And for thy wonders in the sky,
For all thy doings here on earth,
　Praise be to thee, O thou most high.

"O, Lord our Lord, in all the earth,
　How excellent is thy great na'ru,"
Above the Heavens, thy glory shines,
　The moon and stars thy praise proclaims.

"I will bless thee at all times, Lord,"
　Thy praises shall my lips employ,
My soul shall magnify thy name,
　Thy great salvation be my joy.

I praise thee for thy judgments, Lord,
　For all things thank thee o'er and o'er,
I'll sing of all thy righteousness,
　And yet will praise thee more and more.

Yes, dear brethren and sisters, we are all good to praise the Lord, if we make his praise the delight of our life. O, I am so glad that the Lord lets us praise him, and the most beautiful thought of all is, if we are good to praise the Lord now, we always will be. We will never wear out, we will never want for employment, and we will never lack opportunity for service. Yes, we are good to praise the Lord.

May the dear Lord bless our editor and give him many more "Thought Flashes" to send out through the Messenger, until all the readers become illuminated by the light of the Holy

Spirit, and we will have one grand chorus of praise to the Lord.

THE GREAT PHYSICIAN.

BY WILL SHIVELY.

I am at this writing administering to the wants of a sick wife, afflicted with a severe attack of *La Grippa*, accompanied by malaria. While administering to her wants, I am made to think of the "Great Physician," who, while on earth, prescribed different remedies to cure sin. Some of these remedies are very disagreeable to us, as they come in abrupt contact with our carnal nature, so much so that some people refuse to take them. In Matt. 5: 44, we are commanded to love our enemies, bless them that curse us, do good to them that hate us and pray for them that despitefully use us and persecute us.

God's remedies, if used as directed, will break down hatred in the heart of man. They will create an humble, contrite heart, something we all need.

In the Bible we have many incentives to a better life. We have many remedies prepared by God, that people are willing to accept; but it is not always the most pleasant remedy from which we derive the most benefit. All the dispensations of God's providence are medicine to our souls. That which rebels against human nature is just as essential as that which the popular world is willing to accept. Let us take it *all* and be *sure* of a cure.

Chicago, Ill., Feb. 7.

"The lines of suffering on almost every human countenance have been deepened, if not traced there, by unfaithfulness to conscience, by departures from duty. To do wrong is the surest way to bring suffering; no wrong deed ever failed to bring it. Those sins which are followed by no palpable pain are yet terribly avenged, even in this life. They abridge our capacity of happiness, impair our relish for innocent pleasure, and increase our sensibility to suffering. They spoil us of the armor of a pure conscience, and of trust in God, without which we are naked amid hosts of foes and are vulnerable by all the changes of life. Thus, to do wrong is to inflict the surest injury on our own peace. No enemy can do us equal harm with what we do ourselves whenever and however we violate any moral or religious obligation."

The Gospel Messenger

Is the recognized organ of the German Baptist or Brethren's church, and advocates the form of doctrine taught in the New Testament and pleads for a return to apostolic and primitive Christianity.

It recognizes the New Testament as the only infallible rule of faith and practice, and maintains that Faith toward God, Repentance from dead works, Regeneration of the heart and mind, baptism by Trine Immersion for remission of sins unto the reception of the Holy Ghost by the laying on of hands, are the means of adoption into the household of God,—the church militant.

It also maintains that Feet-washing, as taught in John 13, both by example and command of Jesus, should be observed in the church.

That the Lord's Supper, instituted by Christ and as universally observed by the apostles and the early Christians, is a full meal, and, in connection with the Communion, should be taken in the evening or after the close of the day.

That the Salutation of the Holy Kiss, or Kiss of Charity, is binding upon the followers of Christ.

That War and Retaliation are contrary to the spirit and self-denying principles of the religion of Jesus Christ.

That the principle of Plain Dressing and of Non-conformity to the world, as taught in the New Testament, should be observed by the followers of Christ.

That the Scriptural duty of Anointing the Sick with Oil, in the Name of the Lord, James 5: 14, is binding upon all Christians.

It also advocates the church's duty to support Missionary and Tract Work, thus giving to the Lord for the spread of the Gospel and for the conversion of sinners.

In short, it is a vindicator of all that Christ and the apostles have enjoined upon us, and aims amid the conflicting theories and discords of modern Christendom, to point out ground that all must concede to be infallibly safe.

☞ The above principles of our Fraternity are set forth on our "Brethren's Envelopes." Use if em! Price, 15 cents per package; 40 cents per hundred—

SISTER KATE JOHNSON, of Somerset, Pa , is the first one to report the number of additions as given in ·the MESSENGER during the year 1891. She gives the number 3,836. Of course, there were many not reported which, if included, would easily run the number to more than 4,000. While this is a good showing, being better than we had expected, still it is not what it ought to be. It is only·about two converts to each minister among us. But we feel that with proper efforts we may do still more in the future, and we trust that our ministers will consecrate themselves anew to the work, and labor most earnestly for the conversion of sinners. The harvest is great, the laborers are few and the soul is of great value.

JOHN'S BAPTISM.

(Continued)

RESUMING our remarks on John's baptism we wish to state that, in the primitive churches, there was no controversy concerning the mode or form of Christian baptism. In the language of Dr. Wall, "The way of true immersion, or plunging the head of the person three times into the water, was the general practice 'of all antiquity." *History of Infant Baptism, Vol. 1, p. 592.*

It was not till about the year A. D. 360 that single immersion was introduced. The controversy coňcerning the Trinity is what gave rise to it. It never made much headway until after the fourth Council of Toledo, in the year A. D. 630, at which time its validity was first admitted by the Roman Catholic church. The backward action, however, seems not to have been introduced until about A. D. 1592.

Sprinkling and pouring were introduced on account of sickness, being used where persons were thought to be too sick or delicate to stand immersion. They never came into much use until about the thirteenth century, and not into very general use until after the Reformation. These facts leave trine immersion as the only baptism that could have been used during the apostolic age, hence, as previously stated, it must have been the mode used by John and commanded by Jesus in his last commission to his disciples.

We now proceed to take a still more careful look at John's baptism as it was related to Christian baptism. Concerning Apollos it is said that he " taught diligently the things of the Lord, knowing only the baptism of John." Acts 18: 25. After this Aquila and Priscilla took him unto them, and expounded unto him the way of the Lord more perfectly (26). From this we must infer that there was something about John's baptism, not fully up to the standard of that taught later. This deficiency could not have been in regard to the mode, for Apollos was not re-baptized. He was, however, instructed in the way of the Lord more perfectly. This shows that the deficiency was in knowledge and not in practice. It is said *"knowing* only the baptism of John." That is as far as he knew. He knew what the mode was; he knew what the baptism was, but there was a still higher order of knowledge, connected with this "washing of regeneration," which he had not yet fully understood. It was in this line that Aquila and Priscilla taught him the way of the Lord more perfectly. It was not necessary to teach him more concerning the mode, for he was doubtless correct on that point. And the simple fact that he was not re-baptized shows that there was no difference between the form of the baptism taught by John and that taught by Jesus.

The difference was in the knowledge of that which was connected with baptism. John taught as far as he was authorized to teach, and this is as far as the knowledge of Apollos went. But Jesus went still further in his teaching, and his apostles, aided by the Holy Ghost, taught the people just as far as Jesus had advanced them. This is why Aquila and Priscilla knew the way of the Lord more perfectly than did Apollos.

Turning to Acts 19: 2-6 we have this account of Paul with certain disciples at Ephesus: "He said unto them, Have ye received the Holy Ghost since ye believed? And they said unto him, We have not so much as heard whether there be any Holy Ghost. And he said unto them, Unto what then were ye baptized? And they said, Unto John's baptism. Then said Paul, John verily baptized with the baptism of repentance, saying unto the people, that they should believe on him which should come after him, that is, on Christ Jesus. When they heard this, they were baptized in the name of the Lord Jesus. And when Paul had laid his hands upon them, the Holy Ghost came on them; and they spake with tongues and prophesied." These disciples confessed that they had never even heard whether there be any Holy Ghost. This at once led Paul to ask, "Unto what then were ye baptized?" This shows clearly that the apostles used the formula of baptism given by Jesus, "baptizing them in the name of the Father and of the Son, and of the Holy Ghost." And how they could be baptized in the name of the Holy Ghost and yet had not even heard whether there be any Holy Ghost, was something Paul could not understand. That is why he asked the question. They replied by saying, "We were baptized unto John's baptism." Paul then gave them to understand when John baptized persons with water, he taught them that they should believe on Christ who was to come. This shows clearly that these disciples had been deceived and baptized by some one who failed to teach John's baptism correctly. They were baptized, probably having faith in God only, but no faith in Jesus Christ or the Holy Ghost. Hence the baptism was illegal because it was not received in "the faith." Paul then baptized them in the name of the Lord Jesus,—that is, the way the Lord had directed in Matt. 28: 19, where the formula is given. Hands being laid on them, and they having received the Holy Ghost, the work was completed legally.

Apollos was probably baptized by John, who taught him to believe on both Christ and the Holy Spirit. Hence the baptism was legal, the faith, mode of baptism, and formula all being regular. The disciples at Ephesus did not have genuine faith, for they were not taught to believe in either Christ or the Holy Ghost and were likely baptized by some one who did not understand his business. Hence their baptism was illegal. The one doing the baptizing may have seen John baptize, so he knew just how it was done, but failed to get John's teachings on the subject. To retain the mode is the simple matter but much more difficult to have retained anything like a clear idea of the teaching. The mode of baptism was probably·correct but the faith was sadly deficient.

We come now to the baptismal formula used by John. We know what formula was used by the apostles, for Jesus told them to baptize "in the name of the Father, and of the Son, and of the Holy Ghost." Matt. 28: 19. We are of the impression that John used the same formula, and

will give our reason for so thinking. Turning to Matt. 3: 11 we have this language: "I indeed baptize you with water unto repentance: but he that cometh after me is mightier than I, whose shoes I am not worthy to bear: he shall baptize you with the Holy Ghost, and with fire."

Here we observe that John taught the people concerning both Christ and the Holy Ghost. They already knew of the Father. Not one of them was baptized without a knowledge of the three persons of the Trinity. Hence they believed in them, and when baptized they had genuine faith in the Father, Son and Holy Ghost. What would, therefore, be more natural and reasonable than for them to be baptized in the name of the three divine persons in whom they believed? What other formula could have so completely harmonized with their faith and the teachings of John the Baptist?

Be it remembered that John was "filled with the Holy Ghost even from his mother's womb," (Luke 1: 15) for the very purpose of guiding him aright in his teaching. His teaching concerning the Father, Son and Holy Ghost was in exact line with what Christ taught when he came. Hence all the disciples made by John had genuine faith, repentance and baptism, and were therefore ready to be numbered among the disciples of Christ without any additional preparations. All of them being baptized in the name of the Father, whom they had long known, and of Jesus Christ, who was soon to appear, and of the Holy Ghost, that they were soon to receive, not only fitted them to understand the clear manifestation of the three persons of the Trinity at the baptism of Jesus, but enabled them to accept Jesus as the Christ, the son of the true and living God. They could feel that they were baptized into the name of their leader, though they were baptized before they saw him.

Then, when Jesus told them to "Go and teach all nations, baptizing them in the name of the Father, and of the Son, and of the Holy Ghost,' they could feel that this formula, which they were to use among all nations, was the very one pronounced over them when they were baptized, thus giving them additional assurance that John was truly sent from God, that his baptism was from heaven, and his teachings were in line with the doctrine set forth by Jesus.

It is sometimes urged that Jesus would not have been baptized in his own name, and for that reason some hold that John did not use the baptismal formula given by Christ. There was nothing improper in Jesus being baptized in his own name, as we read in Heb. 6: 13: "For when God made promise to Abraham, because he could swear by no greater, he sware by himself." If God could swear by himself, certainly Jesus could have been baptized in his own name. At the time of his baptism he told John, "Thus it becometh us to fulfill all righteousness." That is, all right-doing or, as the Campbell, Macknight and Doddridge rendering has it, "Permit this at present; for thus ought we to ratify every institution." Christian baptism was an institution to be administered "in the name of the Father, and of the Son and of the Holy Ghost." Jesus ratified that institution by submitting to the entire process. Thus he passed through "the washing of regeneration," though he needed no regeneration. But the rite has been fully ratified by him, and therefore has behind it not only the command of Jesus but his example, as well as the sanction of heaven.　J. H. M.

SISTER KATE JOHNSON, of Somerset, Pa, is the first one to report the number of additions as given in the MESSENGER during the year 1891. She gives the number 3,636. Of course, there were many not reported which, if included, would easily run the number to more than 4,000. While this is a good showing, being better than we had expected, still it is not what it ought to be. It is only about two converts to each minister among us. But we feel that with proper efforts we may do still more in the future, and we trust that our ministers will consecrate themselves anew to the work, and labor most earnestly for the conversion of sinners. The harvest is great, the laborers are few and the soul is of great value.

JOHN'S BAPTISM.

(Continued.)

RESUMING our remarks on John's baptism we wish to state that, in the primitive churches, there was no controversy concerning the mode or form of Christian baptism. In the language of Dr. Wall, ".The way of true immersion, or plunging the head of the person three times into the water, was the general practice of all antiquity." *History of Infant Baptism, Vol. 1, p. 592.*

It was not till about the year A. D. 360 that single immersion was introduced. The controversy concerning the Trinity is what gave rise to it. It never made much headway until after the fourth Council of Toledo, in the year A. D. 630, at which time its validity was first admitted by the Roman Catholic church. The backward action, however, seems not to have been introduced until about A. D. 1592.

Sprinkling and pouring were introduced on account of sickness, being used where persons were thought to be too sick or delicate to stand immersion. They never came into much use until about the thirteenth century, and not into very general use until after the Reformation. These facts leave trine immersion as the only baptism that could have been used during the apostolic age, hence, as previously stated, it must have been the mode used by John and commanded by Jesus in his last commission to his disciples.

We now proceed to take a still more careful look at John's baptism as it was related to Christian baptism. Concerning Apollos it is said that he "taught diligently the things of the Lord, knowing only the baptism of John." Acts 18: 25. After this Aquila and Priscilla took him unto them, and expounded unto him the way of the Lord more perfectly (26). From this we must infer that there was something about John's baptism, not fully up to the standard of that taught later. This deficiency could not have been in regard to the mode, for Apollos was not re-baptized. He was, however, instructed in the way of the Lord more perfectly. This shows that the deficiency was in knowledge and not in practice. It is said "knowing only the baptism of John." That is as far as he knew. He knew what the mode was; he knew what the baptism was, but there was a still higher order of knowledge, connected with this "washing of regeneration," which he had not yet fully understood. It was in this line that Aquila and Priscilla taught him the way of the Lord more perfectly. It was not necessary to teach him more concerning the mode, for he was doubtless correct on that point. And the simple fact that he was not re-baptized shows that there was no difference between the form of the baptism taught by John and that taught by Jesus.

The difference was in the knowledge of that which was connected with baptism. John taught as far as he was authorized to teach, and this is as far as the knowledge of Apollos went. But Jesus went still further in his teaching, and his apostles, aided by the Holy Ghost, taught the people just as far as Jesus had advanced them. This is why Aquila and Priscilla knew the way of the Lord more perfectly than did Apollos.

Turning to Acts 19: 2-6 we have this account of Paul with certain disciples at Ephesus: "He said unto them, Have ye received the Holy Ghost since ye believed? And they said unto him, We have not so much as heard whether there be any Holy Ghost. And he said unto them, Unto what then were ye baptized? And they said, Unto John's baptism. Then said Paul, John verily baptized with the baptism of repentance, saying unto the people, that they should believe on him which should come after him, that is, on Christ Jesus. When they heard this, they were baptized in the name of the Lord Jesus. And when Paul had laid his hands upon them, the Holy Ghost came on them; and they spake with tongues and prophesied." These disciples confessed that they had never even heard whether there be any Holy Ghost. This at once led Paul to ask, "Unto what then were ye baptized?" This shows clearly that the apostles used the formula of baptism given by Jesus, "baptizing them in the name of the Father and of the Son, and of the Holy Ghost." And how they could be baptized in the name of the Holy Ghost and yet had not even heard whether there be any Holy Ghost, was something Paul could not understand. That is why he asked the question. They replied by saying, "We were baptized unto John's baptism." Paul then gave them to understand when John baptized persons with water, he taught them that they should believe on Christ who was to come. This shows clearly that these disciples had been deceived and baptized by some one who failed to teach John's baptism correctly. They were baptized, probably having faith in God only, but no faith in Jesus Christ or the Holy Ghost. Hence the baptism was illegal because it was not received in "the faith." Paul then baptized them in the name of the Lord Jesus,—that is, the way the Lord had directed in Matt. 28: 19, where the formula is given. Hands being laid on them, and they having received the Holy Ghost, the work was completed legally.

Apollos was probably taught by John, who taught him to believe on both Christ and the Holy Spirit. Hence the baptism was legal, the faith, mode of baptism, and formula all being regular. The disciples at Ephesus did not have genuine faith, for they were not taught to believe in either Christ or the Holy Ghost and were likely baptized by some one who did not understand his business. Hence their baptism was illegal. The one doing the baptizing may have seen John baptize, so he knew, just how it was done, but failed to get John's teachings on the subject. To retain the mode in the mind would have been an easy matter, but much more difficult to have retained anything like a clear idea of the teaching. The mode of baptism was probably correct but the faith was sadly deficient.

We come now to the baptismal formula used by John. We know what formula was used by the apostles, for Jesus told them to baptize "in the name of the Father, and of the Son, and of the Holy Ghost." Matt. 28: 19. We are of the impression that John used the same formula, and

will give our reason for so thinking. Turning to Matt. 3: 11 we have this language: "I indeed baptize you with water unto repentance: but he that cometh after me is mightier than I, whose shoes I am not worthy to bear: he shall baptize you with the Holy Ghost, and with fire."

Here we observe that John taught the people concerning both Christ and the Holy Ghost. They already knew of the Father. Not one of them was baptized without a knowledge of the three persons of the Trinity. Hence they believed in them, and when baptized they had genuine faith in the Father, Son and Holy Ghost. What would, therefore, be more natural and reasonable than for them to be baptized in the name of the three divine persons in whom they believed? What other formula could have so completely harmonized with their faith and the teachings of John the Baptist?

Be it remembered that John was "filled with the Holy Ghost even from his mother's womb," (Luke 1: 15) for the very purpose of guiding him aright in his teaching. His teaching concerning the Father, Son and Holy Ghost was in exact line with what Christ taught when he came. Hence all the disciples made by John had genuine faith, repentance and baptism, and were therefore ready to be numbered among the disciples of Christ without any additional preparations. All of them being baptized in the name of the Father, whom they had long known, and of Jesus Christ, who was soon to appear, and of the Holy Ghost, that they were soon to receive, not only fitted them to understand the clear manifestation of the three persons of the Trinity at the baptism of Jesus, but enabled them to accept Jesus as the Christ, the son of the true and living God. They could feel that they were baptized into the name of their leader, though they were baptized before they saw him.

Then, when Jesus told them to "Go and teach all nations, baptizing them in the name of the Father, and of the Son, and of the Holy Ghost,' they could feel that this formula, which they were to use among all nations, was the very one pronounced over them when they were baptized, thus giving them additional assurance that John was truly sent from God, that his baptism was from heaven, and his teachings were in line with the doctrine set forth by Jesus.

It is sometimes urged that Jesus would not have been baptized in his own name, and for that reason some hold that John did not use the baptismal formula given by Christ. There was nothing improper in Jesus being baptized in his own name, as we read in Heb. 6: 13: "For when God made promise to Abraham, because he could swear by no greater, he sware by himself." If God could swear by himself, certainly Jesus could have been baptized in his own name. At the time of his baptism he told John, "Thus it becometh us to fulfill all righteousness." That is, all right-doing or, as the Campbell, Macknight and Doddridge rendering has it, "Permit this at present; for thus ought we to ratify every institution." Christian baptism was an institution to be administered "in the name of the Father, and of the Son and of the Holy Ghost." Jesus ratified that institution by submitting to the entire process. Thus he passed through the "washing of regeneration," though he needed no regeneration. But the rite has been fully ratified by him, and therefore has behind it not only the command of Jesus but his example, as well as the sanction of heaven.   J. H. M.

From the Powder Valley Church, Colo.

As has been reported by our elder, G. W. Fesler, this church has been lately organized. We are aiming to build up the cause of our Master in this part of Colorado. Thinking it necessary to hold a special council, we met for that purpose last Saturday, Feb. 13. A good deal of business came up to be disposed of, all of which was done to the satisfaction of those present. The writer was chosen as correspondent to our church paper. We will gladly welcome into our midst any brethren or sisters who desire to walk according to the Gospel and general order of the Brethren.

We sometimes notice in our paper that ministers wish to locate where weak lungs might be favored. We know of no location better suited for weak lungs, than the pure, bracing air of Colorado. I can speak from experience, as I was affected in that way when I came here, but have not been troubled at all since I am living here.

Ministering brethren will be gladly welcomed in our part of the Brotherhood. "The harvest indeed is great, but the laborers are few."

D. M. CLICK.

Ft. Collins, Colo.

From the State Centre Church, Iowa.

On account of quite a number of the members of this church locating elsewhere this spring, we met in council Feb. 13. Bro. A. M. Dickey has been elder and minister here for a number of years, but he, with his family, will locate in Spencer, Clay Co. Bro. John Poff and family will go to Woodbury County; the writer and family to near Eagle Grove, Wright County, this State. This will take seven members from this church, and there will be but thirty-nine members left.

The business of the council was transacted pleasantly. Bro. Stephen Johnson was chosen as our elder, and Bro. George Thomas, of Ames, was chosen to fill the place of Bro. Dickey, as preacher, for the ensuing year. Brethren H. Wahl, J. Menser and Bro. Sanders, were chosen to fill the office of deacons. There was also money raised for the painting of our meeting-house. The church is now out of debt. On account of deaths and removals, our number has decreased during the last two years, but we believe there is a brighter future if all will work together.

T. H. PARKE.

McPherson Notes.

I HAVE been accused of neglecting these contributions to the MESSENGER. I confess the neglect and will try to be more prompt.

Our Bible Term during the month of January was one of unusual interest, though many could not attend for want of means, to pay hired help to care for the interests at home, and also to pay expenses in coming here. We are not wealthy here in Kansas, like the older churches farther east. Eight States are represented, and the influence going forth from this year's Bible course, will spread far and wide. The result of the work was very gratifying.

A. W. Vaniman, Charles Yearout, Daniel Vaniman, Enoch Eby, and John Forney all took their turn in giving able discourses on "Evidences of Christianity," and all the doctrines of the church, and on "Church Government." From the character of the speakers, the readers can judge that the discourses were able.

The Geography of the Bible, the authors of the four Gospels, and the people of Palestine were studied before the "Life of Christ," which was made one of the chief studies, as well as the "Life of the Apostles."

The principles of reading, as applied to the Bible and the hymn book, were carefully studied; also the best method of preparing one's self for the sermon and the sermon for the people.

Ten rules were laid down for this purpose, which every minister would do well to observe.

Many expressed themselves as being benefited far beyond anything they had anticipated, and one old brother who has made the Bible a special study for fifty years, remarked that if he had had such advantages when he was young, he could hardly tell how much he would have been profited, but even in his old age he would not take $25.00 for what he had learned in these few weeks.

The Spirit of God was at work while his Word was being studied, and four made the good confession and were baptized during the Bible Term, and one came since.

The attendance at school is larger than at any previous term.

S. Z. SHARP.

From Mexico, Ind.

I CLOSED a two weeks' series of meetings Feb. 17, in the Mexico church, Ind. During that time I preached twenty-three sermons, and made over thirty visits. As an immediate, visible result, two were baptized, and the members much encouraged. Sickness and bad roads were much against the success of the meetings. Many of the members were not able to attend. In this congregation is located "The Old Folks' Home and Orphanage" of Middle Indiana. It is located in the suburbs of the village of Mexico, and was built and presented by Bro. Levi Miller to the State District. Bro. Miller has the satisfaction of seeing his bequest do good while he lives. This certainly is better than to hoard up tens of thousands of dollars, and, after bequeathing the same to charitable purposes, to have the heirs endeavor to defeat the purpose of the testator. In such cases a large percentage of the donation has to be spent to establish the validity of the will, if it can be done at all.

Bro. Frank and sister Lillie Fisher preside over the Home as Superintendent and Matron, and one only needs to be around the Home a short time, to be made sensible of the fact that they are the right persons in the right place. I had my misgivings about an "Old Folks' Home," before I went there, caused by the fact that some old members, who were unable to provide for themselves, refused to go to a Home of that kind, but a two weeks' stay at this Home completely converted me on that point. This Home is a model for cleanliness and neatness, and the seventeen old people in the Home are cheerful and apparently happy. They are well fed, well clad, well housed and well bedded, besides they have their devotional services every morning, consisting of Scriptural reading, prayer, and an occasional song by one of the old brethren or sisters. It is to them a home indeed, and it would be a great blessing if we had more such Homes. We held one meeting in the Home for the benefit of these old members, as but few of them could attend the meeting at the church-house, and it made us happy to see how the dear brethren and sisters enjoyed it.

During the above meetings we held one Communion for the benefit of a sick sister, and anointed three sick sisters.

W. R. DEETER.

Milford, Ind.

From Navarre, Kans.

OUR church at Navarre, Dickinson Co., Kans., has just had a gracious refreshing. Bro. Hope came to us and began a good work. Then Bro. C. C. Root, according to previous appointment, commenced meetings Feb. 3 and continued with unabated zeal day and night. He preached every night, and held social meetings at private houses every afternoon, until the night of the 17th. Thirteen precious souls declared themselves for Christ and were baptized,—mostly from our Sunday-school,—ranging in age from seven to thirty-five years. Others are almost persuaded to accept the offers of salvation, for surely they are left without excuse.

Our dear brethren did the preaching faithfully. They preached Jesus and they who believed were baptized, and, we trust, have received the Holy Ghost. The Lord be praised for his saving Gospel!

P. R. WRIGHTSMAN.

Navarre, Kans., Feb. 19.

Notes from the Second District of West Virginia.

BRO. WM. T. SINES came to Thornton on the evening of Feb. 5, and next day Bro. Wm. R. Murphy came also. These brethren were called to come and preach a series of discourses for us. They preached for us, in all, fourteen sermons, and our brethren labored faithfully for the Master's cause. The interest was still growing until the close of the meeting. One was reclaimed and others said they were coming soon. May the Spirit of God overrule all, and may all bow to the sceptre of his Word!

We felt built up during our meetings, and our prayer to God is that we may never forget the lessons learned. May the blessings of God rest with our brethren, and may they have souls for their hire! Come again, brethren; we will welcome you. We ask an interest in the prayers of our Brotherhood, that we may carry the banner of the cross and earnestly contend for the faith once delivered to the saints. We have great opposition. The "all-right" doctrine is taught and believed by many,—i. e., "You are right, and so are we." The Gospel is the power of God unto salvation unto all that believe, and it is the only power. Rom. 1: 16; Heb. 5: 9. More anon.

Z. ANNON.

Thornton, W. Va., Feb. 19.

From Decatur, Burt Co., Nebr.

THE Golden Springs church held her council Feb. 4. There were present, our elder, G. W. Stambaugh and wife, of York County, and Bro. William Meck and wife, of Butler County. Although we had some unpleasant business before the council, everything was settled, we trust, satisfactorily to the church, and in the fear of the Lord.

On the evening of Feb. 6 we held a love-feast, at which there were twenty-three members present. It was the first feast for several of us, but it was an occasion long to be remembered.

We are located about twelve miles north of Tekamah, which is our nearest railroad station. Ministering brethren will please take notice of this, and if any one can stop and preach for us, at any time, we will be very thankful. If any one will address me at Decatur, Nebr., I will see that they get to and from the station.

JOHN BARE.

Feb. 9.

From Monmouth, Kans.

THE work of the Lord is still moving on in the Osage church. Five precious souls were added to our number by baptism recently, four from Pittsburgh and one from McCune, all of Crawford County. Brother and sister Hamer reside in Pittsburgh, a mining town, and by their distribution of tracts and the GOSPEL MESSENGER, and by their chaste conversation, they have persuaded four precious souls to walk with the people of God. Now, as valiant soldiers, they help to fight the battles of the Lord.

From the Powder Valley Church, Colo.

As has been reported by our elder, G. W. Fesler, this church has been lately organized. We are aiming to build up the cause of our Master in this part of Colorado. Thinking it necessary to hold a special council, we met for that purpose last Saturday, Feb. 13. A good deal of business came up to be disposed of, all of which was done to the satisfaction of those present. The writer was chosen as correspondent to our church paper.

We will gladly welcome into our midst any brethren or sisters who desire to walk according to the Gospel and general order of the Brethren.

We sometimes notice in our paper that ministers wish to locate where weak lungs might be favored. We know of no location better suited for weak lungs, than the pure, bracing air of Colorado. I can speak from experience, as I was affected in that way when I came here, but have not been troubled at all since I am living here.

Ministering brethren will be gladly welcomed in our part of the Brotherhood. "The harvest indeed is great, but the laborers are few."

D. M. CLICK.

Ft. Collins, Colo.

From the State Centre Church, Iowa.

On account of quite a number of the members of this church locating elsewhere this spring, we met in council Feb. 13. Bro. A. M. Dickey has been elder and minister here for a number of years, but he, with his family, will locate in Spencer, Clay. Co. Bro. John Foft and family will go to Woodbury County; the writer and family to near Eagle Grove, Wright County, this State. This will take seven members from this church, and there will be but thirty-nine members left.

The business of the council was transacted pleasantly. Bro. Stephen Johnson was chosen as our elder, and Bro. George Thomas, of Ames, was chosen to fill the place of Bro. Dickey, as preacher, for the ensuing year. Brethren H. Wahl, J. Menser and Bro. Sanders, were chosen to fill the office of deacons. There was also money raised for the painting of our meeting-house. The church is now out of debt. On account of deaths and removals, our number has decreased during the last two years, but we believe there is a brighter future if all will work together.

T. H. PARER.

McPherson Notes.

I HAVE been accused of neglecting these contributions to the MESSENGER. I confess the neglect and will try to be more prompt.

Our Bible Term during the month of January was one of unusual interest, though many could not attend for want of means, to pay hired help to care for the interests at home, and also to pay expenses in coming here. We are not wealthy here in Kansas, like the older churches farther east. Eight States were represented, and the influence going forth from this year's Bible course, will spread far and wide. The result of the work was very gratifying.

A. W. Vaniman, Charles Yearout, Daniel Vaniman, Enoch Eby, and John Forney all took their turn in giving able discourses on "Evidences of Christianity," and all the doctrines of the church, and on "Church Government." From the character of the speakers, the readers can judge that the discourses were able.

The Geography of the Bible, the authors of the four Gospels, and the people of Palestine were studied before the "Life of Christ," which was made one of the chief studies, as well as the "Life of the Apostles."

The principles of reading, as applied to the Bible and the hymn book, were carefully studied; also the best method of preparing one's self for the sermon and the sermon for the people.

Ten rules were laid down for this purpose, which every minister would do well to observe.

Many expressed themselves as being benefited far beyond anything they had anticipated, and one old brother who has made the Bible a special study for fifty years, remarked that if he had had such advantages when he was young, he could hardly tell how much he would have been profited, but even in his old age he would not take $25.00 for what he had learned in these few weeks.

The Spirit of God was at work while his Word was being studied, and four made the good confession and were baptized during the Bible Term, and one came since.

The attendance at school is larger than at any previous term. S. Z. SHARP.

From Mexico, Ind.

I CLOSED a two weeks' series of meetings Feb. 17, in the Mexico church, Ind. During that time I preached twenty-three sermons, and made over thirty visits. As an immediate, visible result, two were baptized, and the members much encouraged. Sickness and bad roads were much against the success of the meetings. Many of the members were not able to attend. In this congregation is located "The Old Folks' Home and Orphanage" of Middle Indiana. It is located in the suburbs of the village of Mexico, and was built and presented by Bro. Levi Miller to the State District. Bro. Miller has the satisfaction of seeing his bequest do good while he lives. This certainly is better than to hoard up tens of thousands of dollars, and, after bequeathing the same to charitable purposes, to have the heirs endeavor to defeat the purpose of the testator. In such cases a large percentage of the donation has to be spent to establish the validity of the will, if it can be done at all.

Bro. Frank and sister Lillie Fisher preside over the Home as Superintendent and Matron, and one only needs to be around the Home a short time, to be made sensible of the fact that they are the right persons in the right place. I had my misgivings about an "Old Folks' Home," before I went there, caused by the fact that some old members, who were unable to provide for themselves, refused to go to a Home of that kind, but a two-weeks' stay at this Home completely converted me on that point. This Home is a model for cleanliness and neatness, and the seventeen old people in the Home are cheerful and apparently happy. They are well fed, well clad, well housed and well bedded, besides they have their devotional services every morning, consisting of Scriptural reading, prayer, and an occasional song by one of the old brethren or sisters. It is to them a home indeed, and it would be a great blessing if we had more such Homes. We held one meeting in the Home for the benefit of these old members, as but few of them could attend the meeting at the church-house, and it made us happy to see how the dear brethren and sisters enjoyed it.

During the above meetings we held one Communion for the benefit of a sick sister, and anointed three sick sisters: W. R. DETER.

Milford, Ind.

From Navarre, Kans.

OUR church at Navarre, Dickinson Co., Kans., has just had a gracious refreshing. Bro. Hope came to us and began a good work. Then Bro. C. C. Root, according to previous appointment, commenced meetings Feb. 3 and continued with unabated zeal day and night. He preached every night, and held social meetings at private houses every afternoon, until the night of the 17th. Thirteen precious souls declared themselves for Christ and were baptized,—mostly from our Sunday-school,—ranging in age from seven to thirty-five years. Others are almost persuaded to accept the offers of salvation, for surely they are left without excuse.

Our dear brethren did the preaching faithfully. They preached Jesus and they who believed were baptized, and, we trust, have received the Holy Ghost. The Lord be praised for his saving Gospel! P. R. WRIGHTSMAN.

Navarre, Kans., Feb. 19.

Notes from the Second District of West Virginia.

BRO. WM. T. SINES came to Thornton on the evening of Feb. 5, and next day Bro. Wm. R. Murphy came also. These brethren were called to come and preach a series of discourses for us. They preached for us, in all, fourteen sermons, and our brethren labored faithfully for the Master's cause. The interest was still growing until the close of the meeting. One was reclaimed and others said they were coming soon. May the Spirit of God overrule all, and may all bow to the sceptre of his Word!

We felt built up during our meetings, and our prayer to God is that we may never forget the lessons learned. May the blessings of God rest with our brethren, and may they have souls for their hire! Come again, brethren; we will welcome you. We ask an interest in the prayers of our Brotherhood, that we may carry the banner of the cross and earnestly contend for the faith once delivered to the saints. We have great opposition. The "all-right" doctrine is taught and believed by many,—i. e., "You are right, and so are we." The Gospel is the power of God unto salvation unto all that believe, and it is the only power. Rom. 1: 16; Heb. 5: 9. More anon.

Z. ANNON.

Thornton, W. Va., Feb. 19.

From Decatur, Burt Co., Nebr.

THE Golden Springs church held her council Feb. 4. There were present, our elder, G. W. Stambaugh and wife, of York County, and Bro. William Meck and wife, of Butler County. Although we had some unpleasant business before the council, everything was settled, we trust, satisfactorily to the church, and in the fear of the Lord.

On the evening of Feb. 6 we held a love-feast, at which there were twenty-three members present. It was the first feast for several of us, but it was an occasion long to be remembered.

We are located about twelve miles north of Tekamah, which is our nearest railroad station. Ministering brethren will please take notice of this, and if any one can stop and preach for us, at any time, we will be very thankful. If any one will address me at Decatur, Nebr., I will see that they get to and from the station. JOHN BARE.

Feb. 9.

From Monmouth, Kans.

THE work of the Lord is still moving on in the Osage church. Five precious souls were added to our number by baptism recently, four from Pittsburgh and one from McCune, all of Crawford County. Brother and sister Hamer reside in Pittsburgh, a mining town, and by their distribution of tracts and the GOSPEL MESSENGER, and by their chaste conversation, they have persuaded four precious souls to walk with the people of God. Now, as valiant soldiers, they help to fight the battles of the Lord.

Webster, Ohio.—A man calling himself Samuel Quigler, and traveling throughout the Brotherhood, has been disfellowshiped by Oakland church, Feb. 17, 1892.—*C. Bigler.*

Lower Deer Creek, Ind.—We have just closed a series of meetings, conducted by Bro. D. C. Campbell. One precious soul was made willing to follow Jesus through the bath of regeneration. Bless the Lord for his abundant mercy!—*S. H. Bechtelheimer.*

Hope, Kans.—Eld. J. D. Trostle is now so impaired in health, that he is unable to do any preaching most of the time, but we are glad to say that his zeal and love for the cause of Christ and the prosperity of the Brotherhood is strong. Pray with us, that, if it is God's will, he may be restored to his usefulness in the church, and for the accomplishment of much good.—*J. E. Keller.*

Bethel, Mo.—Eld. Brown, of this place, began a series of meetings on the evening of Feb. 11, at the Fairview church-house, assisted by our other ministers. The meeting continued until Feb. 19, at which time it closed on account of the inclemency of the weather. There were good congregations and much interest. The members at that place were greatly strengthened. We regret that the meetings could not have been continued, as much good seed was being sown and the result the future alone can reveal.—*Jos. Amdes.*

Ridgely, Md.—In my report of the Clay Lick meeting, written from Upton, Pa, as published in GOSPEL MESSENGER No. 6, I made a mistake which I should like to have corrected, so as to read, that five were baptized, four more to be baptized in the near future, and one that had strayed away from the fold, to be, re-instated.—*T. F. Imler, Waynesborough, Pa., Feb. 14.*

Hatfield, Pa.—Bro. T. J. Rosenberger, of Covington, Ohio, came to the Hatfield church, Feb 3, He remained with us until Feb 16, and preached, in all, twenty-five sermons. Bro. Rosenberger is a faithful expounder of the Word. While with us he held two children's meetings before Sunday morning services, which the children all seemed to enjoy very much. An aged father was led into the stream by Bro. Rosenberger and buried with Christ in baptism. Others were made to defer until a more convenient season.—*Ella C. Souders.*

Bellefontaine, Ohio.—We the members of the Logan church, Logan Co., Ohio, commenced a protracted meeting (Bro. J. M. Mohler doing the preaching) on the evening of Feb. 8, continuing until the evening of Feb. 23, preaching, in all, twenty-seven soul-refreshing sermons. He also held two children's meetings. Saints were made to rejoice to think that we have our names written in the Lamb's Book of Life. As an immediate result, six dear souls were made willing to leave the ranks of Satan and join in with the people of God. All are young in years, the youngest eleven years of age.—*Sarah A. Miller.*

Valley Church, Tenn. — Our series of meetings, which were conducted by Bro. F. W. Dove, of Washington County, commenced Saturday evening. Feb. 6, and closed Feb. 14. Bro. Dove preached, in all, sixteen very impressive sermons. The attendance was very good, considering the inclemency of the weather. The church is much revived and encouraged, sinners have been faithfully warned and the way of righteousness has been set plainly before the people. Eight souls were made willing to take up the cross and follow our Blessed Master. Six were baptized and others were almost persuaded to unite with us. We still hope and pray that the good seed sown may bring forth fruit in the near future.—*M. M. Derrick, Feb. 19.*

Bill's Siding, Iowa.—Feb. 1 Bro. C. S. Holsinger, of Lacon, Ill., came to the Palestine school-house, Johnson County, Iowa, and commenced holding forth the Word with power. He continued until the evening of Feb. 13 with good interest. We feel that he did a good work, and we hope to reap from his sowing. May the Lord bless our brother in his labors!—*J. C. Seibert.*

Woodland, Mich.—At the request of my mother I will inform the many friends in Ohio, that father and mother arrived home in safety Feb. 8, and found all well. They had a very enjoyable visit with the members in all the various churches. All have our sincere thanks for their kindness to them. They were gone nearly nine weeks, and we were glad to see them return. Bro. John Smith and my father are at the Black River church, Mich., attending District Meeting.—*E. J. Rairigh, Feb. 21.*

Battle, Ohio.—Bro. Frederic B. Weimer came to the Sugar Creek church, Ohio, on the evening of Feb. 6, and commenced a series of meetings. He preached, in all, eighteen sermons, with increasing interest to the last. As an immediate result twenty souls were received into the church by baptism. Bro. Weimer left for home Feb. 18. Bro. Peter Long, from Lagrange County, Ind., is with us and will continue the meetings several days. We can truly say it was a refreshing season to the church and one long to be remembered by all. May we all prove valiant soldiers for Jesus, and at last receive a crown.—*Simon Hurshman, Feb. 18.*

Smithborough, Ill.—Our regular quarterly council in the Hurricane Creek church occurred to-day. The church came before the church and all passed off pleasantly. Eld. Henry Lilligh was present. Notwithstanding the gloomy weather and muddy roads, we had a fair attendance. One who had wandered away from the fold for a score of years was, by unanimous consent, restored. The church decided to have a Sunday-school through the spring and summer, to commence at the beginning of the second quarter, the writer to act as Superintendent. Since our last report we enjoyed a week's meetings, conducted by Bro. Michael Flory.—*Cornelius Kessler, Feb 20.*

Kearney, Nebr.—I have just returned from a meeting ten miles North-east of Miller, on the South Loup, where the Brethren have been holding some meetings under the direction of the Mission Board of Nebraska. We had, in all, about twenty meetings. Feb. 21 four were baptized, and we closed on Sunday night with three more applicants to be baptized at the next meeting in March. The interest in the Word preached is commendable, and the prospects for more to come soon, are good. We also had a good meeting of ten days' duration near Bro. U. Y. Snavely's, conducted by Bro. J. W. Jarboe, of Kansas. One dear soul was added to the church. May they all hold out faithful till death!—*S. U. Forney. Feb. 23.*

Waconda, Mo.—Our quarterly council was held Feb. 20. The attendance was good, considering the damp weather and almost impassable roads. Brotherly love prevailed, and matters were easily adjusted. It was decided to hold a love-feast May 11. Our business was mostly preparatory to District Meeting. Brethren S. B. Shirkey and G. W. Clemens were chosen delegates. Our church has been prospering ever since the Miller and Sommer debate, held here in 1889. The brethren and friends have been very anxious to have Bro. Miller come back and preach for us. We are sorry to learn that his health is much impaired this winter, but hope that he may yet regain his strength, and pay us a visit.—*J. H. Shirky.*

Wichita, Kans.—The Wichita church will, the Lord willing, hold a love-feast in the city on Saturday, May 14. We held our quarterly council Feb. 13. Everything was transacted in a quiet, business-like way, and to the general satisfaction of the church. Our meetings are well attended, but to make them a success here, a house of worship of our own is needed.—*Wm. Johnson, 1533 Orange St., Feb. 21.*

A Correction.—In my notes in GOSPEL MESSENGER, page 92, in second paragraph, I meant to say this, "The meetings were opend by Bro. George S. Arnold, and the writer spoke from these words, 'My house shall be called a house of prayer,' Matt. 21: 13, followed by Bro. D. B. Arnold, who made some very appropriate remarks." In the last paragraph read, "Two dollars and forty cents a *month*," instead of week, as I there gave it.—*Z. Annon.*

Batavia, Ill.—Bro. Wm. R. Miller, of Chicago, came to us on Saturday, Feb. 20, and gave us four meetings, one on Saturday evening and three upon the following Sunday. Although the gatherings were not large, as we have only a small flock at this place, still we enjoyed the meetings very much and were much benefited. It is both pleasant and profitable to meet and associate with those of like precious faith. Brethren, let us not be slack in supporting the hands of God's ministering servants! Let us do our part fully, and with willing hearts, and then, brethren, you, whom God has blessed with talent and ability, slack not your hands in going to the rescue of perishing souls. "They that be wise shall shine as the brightness of the firmament; and they that turn many to righteousness as the stars forever and ever."—*M. Connell, Feb. 23.*

Alexandria, Nebr.—We are living in a new place, where the Brethren never had meetings until last year. Bro. J. J. Hoover, during the summer, held a few meetings, and the people were well pleased with the way he preached the Gospel, and requested him to return. He commenced meetings again Dec. 18, preaching, in all, twenty-four sermons. Good impressions were made, though there were no additions to the church at the time. On the second Sunday in February Bro. Hoover came again, and preached two sermons. One dear soul came out on the Lord's side, and good impressions were left on others. Bro. Hoover is a good worker and should be kept in the field. May God bless his labors! This is my first effort. I am a young brother in Christ, only twelve years of age. If I see this in print I will write again.—*Richard V. Shook, Feb. 19.*

Lima, Ohio.—Bro J. M. Mohler, of Lewistown, Pa., came to the Sugar Creek congregation and began a series of meetings in the Pleasant View meeting-house. He preached, in all, twenty-three sermons while among us, including one funeral sermon at the Sugar Creek church. He also spent some time, on two different evenings, before the regular time for services, in talking to the children, and also gave us some good instructions in the way of teaching our children. He plainly showed us, that, as a rule, we, as parents, in the great struggle to educate and instruct our children in the affairs that pertain to this life, neglect to teach them "to seek first the kingdom of God." We should be as eager to instruct them in the way of truth and holiness, as we are in giving them a common-school education. What a power we could thus be for good! Although there were no immediate accessions during our meetings, yet we feel that the church was encouraged and many good impressions made on those who are still out of the fold. May the good seed sown yet produce a bountiful harvest!—*David Byerly, Feb. 14.*

Webster, Ohio.—A man calling himself Samuel Quigler, and traveling throughout the Brotherhood, has been disfellowshiped by Oakland church, Feb. 17, 1892.—*C. Bigler.*

Lower Deer Creek, Ind.—We have just closed a series of meetings, conducted by Bro. D. C. Campbell. One precious soul was made willing to follow Jesus through the bath of regeneration. Bless the Lord for his abundant mercy!—*S. H. Bechtelheimer.*

Hope, Kans.—Eld. J. D. Trostle is now so impaired in health, that he is unable to do any preaching most of the time, but we are glad to say that his zeal and love for the cause of Christ and the prosperity of the Brotherhood is strong. Pray with us, that, if it is God's will, he may be restored to his usefulness in the church, and for the accomplishment of much good.—*J. E. Keller.*

Bethel, Mo.—Eld. Brown, of this place, began a series of meetings on the evening of Feb. 11, at the Fairview church-house, assisted by our other ministers. The meeting continued until Feb. 19, at which time it closed on account of the inclemency of the weather. There were good congregations and much interest. The members at that place were greatly strengthened. We regret that the meetings could not have been continued, as much good seed was being sown and the result the future alone can reveal.—*Jos. Andes.*

Ridgely, Md.—In my report of the Clay Lick meeting, written from Upton, Pa., as published in GOSPEL MESSENGER No. 6, I made a mistake which I should like to have corrected, so as to read, that five were baptized, four more to be baptized in the near future, and one that had strayed away from the fold, to be re-instated.—*T. F. Imler, Waynesborough, Pa., Feb. 14.*

Hatfield, Pa.—Bro. I. J. Rosenberger, of Covington, Ohio, came to the Hatfield church, Feb 3. He remained with us until Feb 16, and preached, in all, twenty-two sermons. Bro. Rosenberger is a faithful expounder of the Word. While with us he held two children's meetings before Sunday morning services, which the children all seemed to enjoy very much. An aged father was led into the stream by Bro. Rosehberger and buried with Christ in baptism. Others were made to defer until a more convenient season.—*Ella C. Souders.*

Bellefontaine, Ohio.—We the members of the Logan church, Logan Co., Ohio, commenced a protracted meeting (Bro. J. M. Mohler doing the preaching) on the evening of Feb. 8, continuing until the evening of Feb. 23, preaching, in all, twenty-seven soul-refreshing sermons. He also held two children's meetings Saints were made to rejoice to think that we have our names written in the Lamb's Book of Life. As an immediate result, six dear souls were made willing to leave the ranks of Satan and join in with the people of God. All are young in years, the youngest eleven years of age.—*Sarah A. Miller.*

Valley Church, Tenn.—Our series of meetings, which were conducted by Bro. F. W. Dove, of Washington County, commenced Saturday evening, Feb. 6, and closed Feb. 14. Bro. Dove preached, in all, sixteen very impressive sermons. The attendance was very good, considering the inclemency of the weather. The church is much revived and encouraged, sinners have been faithfully warned and the way of righteousness has been set plainly before the people. Eight souls were made willing to take up the cross and follow our Blessed Master. Six were baptized and others were almost persuaded to unite with us. We still hope and pray that the good seed sown may bring forth fruit in the near future.—*M. M. Derrick, Feb. 19.*

Hill's Siding, Iowa.—Feb. 1 Bro. C. S. Holsinger, of Lacon, Ill., came to the Palestine school-house, Johnson County, Iowa, and commenced holding forth the Word with power. He continued until the evening of Feb. 13 with good interest. We feel that he did a good work, and we hope to reap from his sowing. May the Lord bless our brother in his labors!—*J. C. Seibert.*

Woodland, Mich.—At the request of my mother I will inform the many friends in Ohio, that father and mother arrived home in safety Feb. 3, and found all well. They had a very enjoyable visit with the members in all the various churches. All have our sincere thanks for their kindness to them. They were gone nearly nine weeks, and we were glad to see them return. Bro. John Smith and my father are at the Black River church, Mich., attending District Meeting.—*E. J. Rairigh, Feb. 21.*

Baltic, Ohio.—Bro. Frederic B. Weimer came to the Sugar Creek church, Ohio, on the evening of Feb. 6, and commenced a series of meetings. He preached, in all, eighteen sermons, with increasing interest to the last. As an immediate result twenty souls were received into the church by baptism. Bro. Weimer left for home Feb. 18. Bro. Peter Long, from Lagrange County, Ind., is with us and will continue the meetings several days. We can truly say it was a refreshing season to the church and one long to be remembered by all. May we all prove valiant soldiers for Jesus, and at last receive a crown.—*Simon Harshman, Fb. 18.*

Smithsborough, Ill.—Our regular quarterly council in the Hurricane Creek church occurred to-day. Not much business came before the church and all passed off pleasantly. Eld. Henry Lilligh was present. Notwithstanding the gloomy weather and muddy roads, we had a fair attendance. One who had wandered away from the fold for a score of years was, by unanimous consent, restored. The church decided to have a Sunday-school through the spring and summer, to commence at the beginning of the second quarter, the writer to act as Superintendent. Since our last report we enjoyed a week's meetings, conducted by Bro. Michael Flory.—*Cornelius Kessler, Feb 20.*

Kearney, Nebr.—I have just returned from a meeting ten miles North-east of Miller, on the South Loup, where the Brethren have been holding some meetings under the direction of the Mission Board of Nebraska. We had, in all, about twenty meetings. Feb. 21 four were baptized, and we closed on Sunday night with three more applicants to be baptized at the next meeting in March. The interest in the Word preached is commendable, and the prospects for more to come soon, are good. We also had a good meeting of ten days' duration near Bro. U. Y. Snavely's, conducted by Bro. J. W. Jarboe, of Kansas. One dear soul was added to the church. May they all hold out faithful till death!—*S. U. Forney. Feb 23.*

Waconda, Mo.—Our quarterly council was held Feb. 20. The attendance was good, considering the damp weather and almost impassable roads. Brotherly love prevailed, and matters were easily adjusted. It was decided to hold a love-feast May 11. Our business was mostly preparatory to District Meeting. Brethren S. B. Shirkey and G. W. Clemens were chosen delegates. Our church has been prospering ever since the Miller and Sommer debate, held here in 1889 The brethren and friends have been very anxious to have Bro. Miller come back and preach for us. We are sorry to learn that his health is much impaired this winter, but hope that he may yet regain his strength, and pay us a visit.—*J. H. Shirkey.*

Wichita, Kans.—The Wichita church will, the Lord willing, hold a love-feast in the city on Saturday, May 14. We held our quarterly council Feb. 13. Everything was transacted in a quiet, business-like way, and to the general satisfaction of the church. Our meetings are well attended, but to make them a success here, a house of worship of our own is needed.—*Wm. Johnson, 1533 Orange St., Feb. 21.*

A Correction.—In my notes in GOSPEL MESSENGER, page 92, in second paragraph, I meant to say this, "The meetings were opend by Bro. George S. Arnold, and the writer spoke from these words, 'My house shall be called a house of prayer,' Matt. 21: 13, followed by Bro. D. B. Arnold, who made some very appropriate remarks." In the last paragraph read, "Two dollars and forty cents a *month*," instead of week, as I there gave it.—*Z. Annon.*

Batavia, Ill.—Bro. Wm. R. Miller, of Chicago, came to us on Saturday, Feb. 20, and gave us four meetings, one on Saturday evening and three upon the following Sunday. Although the gatherings were not large, as we have only a small flock at this place, still we enjoyed the meetings very much and were much benefited. It is both pleasant and profitable to meet and associate with those of like precious faith. Brethren, let us not be slack in supporting the hands of God's ministering servants! Let us do our part fully, and with will. ing hearts, and then, brethren, you, whom God has blessed with talent and ability, slack not your hands in going to the rescue of perishing souls. "They that be wise shall shine as the brightness of the firmament; and they that turn many to righteousness as the stars forever and ever."—*M. Connell, Feb. 23.*

Alexandria, Nebr.—We are living in a new place, where the Brethren never had meetings until last year. Bro. J. J. Hoover, during the summer, held a few meetings, and the people were well pleased with the way he preached the Gospel, and requested him to return. He commenced meetings again Dec. 18, preaching, in all, twenty-four sermons. Good impressions were made, though there were no additions to the church at the time. On the second Sunday in February Bro. Hoover came again, and preached two sermons. One dear soul came out on the Lord's side, and good impressions were left on others. Bro. Hoover is a good worker and should be kept in the field. May God bless his labors! This is my first effort. I am a young brother in Christ, only twelve years of age. If I see this in print, I will write again.—*Richard V. Shook, Feb 19.*

Lima, Ohio.—Bro. J. M. Mohler, of Lewiston, Pa., came to the Sugar Creek congregation, and began a series of meetings in the Pleasant View meeting-house. He preached, in all, twenty-three sermons while among us, including one funeral sermon at the Sugar Creek church. He also spent some time, on two different evenings, before the regular time for services, in talking to the children, and also gave us some good instructions in the way of teaching our children. He plainly showed us, that, as a rule, we, as parents, in the great struggle to educate and instruct our children in the affairs that pertain to this life, neglect to teach them "to seek first the kingdom of God." We should be as eager to instruct them in the way of truth and holiness, as we are in giving them a common-school education. What a power we could thus be for good! Although there were no immediate accessions during our meetings, yet we feel that the church was encouraged and many good impressions made on those who are still out of the fold. May the good seed sown yet produce a bountiful harvest!—*David Byerly, Feb. 14.*

ed. She was the mother of eleven children. She was buried in the Brethren's burying-ground at Ashton, Ill., Jan. 18. Before she died she was anointed. Funeral services from Rev. 21: 5 by Eld. D. Dierdorff.

C. H. HAWBECKER.

HERSHBERGER.—In the Bunker Hill church, Ohio, Feb. 15, 1892, Ida Catharine Hershberger, aged 7 months and 22 days.

This little child was the daughter of Bro. Eli and sister Sarah Hershberger. Funeral by Bro. Josiah Hochstetler, assisted by Frederic Mast, of the Mennonite church, from Matt. 18.

SARAH MIDDAUGH.

MILLER.—In Purcell, Ind. Ter., Aug. 30, 1891, Bro. Jacob Miller, aged 65 years, 6 months and 22 days.

Deceased was born in Virginia and was married to Catharine Rife. To them were born six sons and four daughters. April 13, 1877, his wife died. Aug. 19, 1883, he was married to Martha Beaty. They had three children.

There being no minister of the Brethren near, short devotional exercises were held at the grave by a resident Presbyterian minister.

ISAAC H. MILLER.

HAINES.—In the Salem congregation, Reno Co., Kans., Sept. 28, 1891, sister Lucy Haines, aged about 67 years.

Deceased was born in Richland County, Ohio, in 1824. In 1841 she married Philip Haines, who died in 1877. To them were born eight children. She united with the Brethren about twenty years ago. She was anointed by Eld. E. Eby and the writer a short time before her death. Funeral services by the writer from Rev. 14: 13.

ISAAC H. MILLER.

HERRIMAN.—In the bounds of the Salem congregation, Reno Co., Kans., Nov. 3, 1891, Willie, son of Elias and sister Sarah R. Merriman, aged 6 years, 4 months and 23 days.

He was run over by some colts on Friday evening and died the next Tuesday. Funeral discourse by Bro. D. T. Dierdorff from James 4: 14

ISAAC H. MILLER.

BUTTERBAUGH.—In the Eel River congregation, Kosciusko Co., Ind., Jan. 28, 1892, Albert, son of Bro. Daniel and sister Barbara Butterbaugh, aged 9 years, 1 month and 5 days.

Deceased was the youngest of the family. Funeral services by Bro. Silas Gilbert and the writer.

SAMUEL LECKRONE.

HOOVER.—In the Salimony church, Huntington Co., Ind., Jan 27, 1892, of stomach and lung trouble, William Hoover, son of Bro. Levi and sister Lavina Hoover, aged 23 years and 29 days.

He leaves a father and mother, two brothers and two sisters. Funeral conducted by the Brethren.

SAMUEL MURRAY.

WELBORN.—In the Union church, Ind., Jan. 27, 1892, sister Margaret Olive Welborn, aged 34 years, 1 month and 8 days.

Deceased leaves a number of small children and a kind husband. She united with the church when young and lived faithful till death. Funeral services by Daniel Snell from Rev. 14: 13.

DANIEL SNELL.

HOFF.—Near Marion, Franklin Co., Pa., Feb. 8, 1892, Sarah Hoff, aged 87 years, 4 months and 21 days.

Deceased was a member of the church over sixty years. Funeral services by brethren Good and Benedict from 1 Cor. 15: 18.

EDWARD SHEFFER.

BEELMAN.—In the bounds of the Seneca church, Huron Co., Ohio, Feb. 18, 1892, Bro. George Beelman, aged 78 years, 7 months and 4 days.

Funeral occasion improved by the undersigned from Rev. 2: 10.

S. A. WALKER.

PAULUS.—Near Elkhart, Elkhart Co., Ind., Feb. 3, 1892, of *La Grippe*, George Riley Paulus, son of Bro. Henry and sister Susan Paulus, aged 25 years and 7 days.

Funeral services were held at the school-house near his home. Services were conducted by Bro. Joseph Culp, of the Elkhart Valley congregation.

PETER HUFFMAN.

ADVERTISEMENTS.

Rates per Inch each Insertion.

One time or more,	$1 50
One month (4 times),	1 30
Three months (12 times),	1 20
Six months (25 times),	1 00
One year (50 times),	70
No advertisement accepted for less than	1 00

Tract Work.

List of Publications for Sale,—Sent Postage Prepaid.

CLASS A.

No. 1.	Golden Gleams or Family Chart,	$ 85
No. 2.	Diagram of Passover and Lord's Supper, per copy,	75

CLASS B.

Plain Family Bible, per copy,	$2 70
Trine Immersion, Quinter, per copy,	1 25
Europe and Bible Lands, Miller, per copy,	1 50
Doctrine of the Brethren Defended, Miller, per copy,	1 50
Close Communion, West, per copy,	40
Missionary Hymn Book, per dozen, $1.00; per copy,	10

CLASS C.—(TRACTS.)

No. 1.	The Brethren or Dunkards, per 100, $1.50 per copy,	02
No. 2.	Path of Life, per 100, $4; per copy,	05
No. 3.	How to Become a Child of God, per 100, $4; per copy,	05
No. 4.	Conversion, per 100, $2.50; per copy,	03
No. 5.	Water Baptism, per 100, $1.50; per copy,	02
No. 6.	Single Immersion, per 100, $1; per copy,	01
No. 7.	Sabbatism, per 100, $1.50; per copy,	02
No. 8.	Trine Immersion Traced to the Apostles, per 100, $7; per copy,	08
No. 9.	Sermon on Baptism, per 100, $2; per copy,	03
No. 10.	Glad Tidings of Salvation, per 100, $1.50; per copy,	02
No. 11.	Life of Eld. S. Weir (Colored), per 100, $1.50; per copy,	02
No. 12.	Ten Reasons for Trine Immersion, per 100, $1; per copy,	01
No. 13.	The Lord's Day and the Sabbath, per 100, $2.50; per copy,	03

CLASS D.

No. 1.	The House We Live In, per 100,	$ 45
No. 2.	Plan of Salvation, per 100,	45
No. 3.	Come Let Us Reason Together, per 100,	45
No. 4.	How Shall I know that my Sins are Pardoned? per 100,	45
No. 5.	Intemperance, per 100,	45
No. 6.	Plain Dressing, per 100,	45
No. 7.	Which is the Right Church? per 100,	45
No. 8.	The House We Live In (Swedish), per 100,	45
No. 9.	The House We Live In (Danish), per 100,	45
No. 10.	Paul Wetzel's Reasons (German), per 100,	45
No. 11.	Sinner, Stop, per 100,	45
No. 12.	Faith, per 100,	45
No. 13.	The Light House, per 100,	45
No. 14.	Close Communion, per 100,	45
No. 15.	The Truth Shall Make You Free, per 100,	45
No. 16.	Modern Skepticism, per 100,	45
No. 17.	Infant Baptism Weighed, etc., per 100,	45
No. 18.	Repentance, per 100,	45
No. 19.	Talk to R. R. Employees, etc., per 100,	45
No. 20.	Life and Death, per 100,	45
No. 21.	The House We Live In (German), per 100,	45
No. 22.	The Prayer Covering, per 100,	45
No. 23.	The Lord's Supper, per 100,	45
No. 24.	Shall I Swear or Affirm? per 100,	45
No. 25.	Secret Societies, per 100,	45
No. 26.	Church Entertainments, per 100,	45
No. 27.	Conversion or the New Birth, per 100,	45
No. 28.	The Bible Service of Feet-washing, per 100,	45
No. 29.	Scriptural Communion, per 100,	45

CLASS E.

No. 1.	Pause and Think, per 100,	20
No. 2.	What Do We Need? per 100,	20
No. 3.	Right or Wrong Way, per 100,	20
No. 4.	Why Am I Not a Christian? per 100,	20
No. 5.	Saving Words, per 100,	20
No. 6.	Christ and War, per 100,	20
No. 7.	The Bond of Peace, per 100,	20
No. 8	The Kiss of Charity, per 100,	20
No. 9.	The Evils of Intemperance, per 100,	20
No. 10.	The Lost Opportunity, per 100,	20
No. 11.	Are You a Christian? per 100,	20
No. 12.	Arise, Get Thee Down, per 100,	20
No. 13.	A Personal Appeal, per 100,	20
No. 14.	Lying Among the Pots, per 100,	20
No. 15.	Gold and Costly Array, per 100,	20
No. 16.	The Brethren's Card, per 100,	20
No. 17.	The Whole Gospel Must Be Obeyed, per 100,	20

Bibles, Testaments, Hymn Books of all styles, at publishers' lowest retail prices, which will be furnished on application. Address:

BRETHREN'S BOOK & TRACT WORK,
DAYTON, OHIO.

HOT SHOT FIRED at Fashion's Follies and Society's Abominations. A book of over 560 octavo pages, full of bold and fearless hits at the Abominations of Modern Society. Price, in cloth, $2.50; in half Russia, $3.50. We offer liberal inducements to agents. Send 75 cents for outfit, and write for our terms. Address, JAS. M. NEFF, Covington, Ohio.

44t2

GOOD BOOKS FOR ALL.

ANY book in the market furnished at publishers' lowest retail price by the Brethren's Publishing Company, Mt. Morris, Ill. *Special prices* given when books are purchased in quantities. When ordering books, not on our list, if possible give title, name of author, and address of publishers.

Family Bible, with Notes and Instructions.—Contains the harmony of the Gospels, Chronology, Maps, Tables of Weights and Measures, Family Record, eight elegant illustrations, etc. Price, substantially bound, $4.50.

German and English Testaments.—American Bible Society Edition. Price, 60 cents.

Homiletics and Pastoral Theology.—By W. G. T. Shedd. Cloth, $2.50

Lectures on Preaching.—By Rev. Phillips Brooks. Cloth, 16mo, $1.50

New Testament and Psalms with Notes.—Invaluable for Bible students, Sunday-school teachers, etc. Price, cloth, $2.00; without Psalms, $1.00.

Quinter and McConnell Debate.—A debate on Trine Immersion, the Lord's Supper, and Feet-washing, between Eld. James Quinter (German Baptist) and Eld. N. A. McConnell (Christian) held at Dry Creek, Iowa, 1867. Price, $1.50.

Popular Commentary on the New Testament.—Edited by Philip Schaff. Four volumes, 8vo. Matthew, Mark and Luke: $6.00. John and the Acts: $6.00. Romans to Philemon: $5.00. Hebrews to Revelation: $5.00.

Sabbatism.—By M. M. Eshelman. Treats the Sabbath question, showing that the first day of the week is the day for assembling in worship. Price, 10 cents; 15 copies, $1.00.

Bunyan's Pilgrim's Progress.—An excellent edition of this good work, printed on good paper, finely illustrated with forty engravings, at the low price of $1.00 per copy.

Close Communion.—By Landon West. Treats this important subject in a simple though conclusive manner. Price, 50 cents.

In the Volume of the Book.—By Geo. F. Pentecost. Cloth, 60 cents.

Key to the Knowledge and Use of the Holy Bible.—By J. H. Blunt. Cloth, 16 mo, 75 cents.

Lange's Commentary.—Edited by Philip Schaff. Twenty-five vols. 4vo. Per vol., $3.00

New and Complete Bible Commentary.—By Jamieson, Fausset and Brown. It is far in advance of other works. It is critical, practical, and explanatory. It is compendious and comprehensive in its character. It has a critical introduction to each Book of Scripture, and is by far the most practical, suggestive, scientific, and popular work of the kind in the English language. In four large 12mo volumes of about 1,000 pages each. In extra fine English cloth, sprinkled edges, the full set, $8.00; half Morocco, the full set, $10.00.

Sacred Geography and Antiquities.—A practical, helpful work for Bible students, ministers and Sunday-school teachers. Price, $2.25.

The Origin and Growth of Religion.—Hibbert Lectures. By T. W. R. Davids. Cloth, 8vo, $2.50.

Our Library on Christian Evidences.—This collection of works embraces the best books to be had on that subject: "Paley's Evidences of Christianity," New Edition, $1.50; "Nelson on Infidelity," 75 cents; "Manual of Christian Evidences," 75 cents; "Many Infallible Proofs," $1.25; "The Divine Demonstration," $1.50; "The Bible in the Nineteenth Century," 40 cents; "Grounds of Theistic and Christian Belief," $2.50. Price of the entire set, if ordered at one time, $8.00; special terms to ministers furnished upon application.

Bible Work, or Bible Reader's Commentary on the New Testament.—By J. G. Butler. Two vols. 8vo, $10.00.

Biblical Antiquities.—By John Nevin. Gives a concise account of Bible times and customs; invaluable to all students of Bible subjects. Price, $1.50.

Biblical Theology of the Old Testament.—By R. F. Weidner. Cloth, $1.25.

Campbell and Owen Debate.—Contains a complete investigation of the evidences of Christianity. Price, $1.50.

Classified Minutes of Annual Meeting.—A work of rare interest for all who desire to be well informed in the church work, from the early days of our Brethren until the present. Price, cloth, $1.50; leather, $2.00.

Companion to the Bible.—This valuable work is so full of instruction that it can not fail to be of great benefit to every Christian. Price, $1.15.

Hours with the Bible.—By Cunningham Geikie. Old Testament Series—six volumes. Per volume, 90 cents.

Europe and Bible Lands.—By D. L. Miller. A book for the people,—more comprehensive and thorough than many higher-priced works. Price, cloth, $1.50; leather, $2.00.

Ecclesiastical History.—By Eusebius. Bohn Library. Cloth, $2.00.

Ecclesiastical History.—By Mosheim. 2 vols. 8vo., $4.00.

Early Days of Christianity.—By F. W. Farrar. Author's edition, cloth, 12mo, $1.25.

→PUBLICATIONS←

☞ The following books, Sunday-school supplies, etc., are for sale by the BRETHREN'S PUBLISHING CO., Mt. Morris, Ill., or Huntingdon, Pa., to whom all orders should be addressed.

The Brethren's Quarterly.

For Sunday-school teachers and scholars this publication is of the greatest benefit. Look at our prices:

Single subscription, one year,	35 cents.
Single subscription, per quarter,	10 cents.
Three copies, per quarter,	25 cents.
Eight copies, per quarter,	40 cents.
Twenty copies and over,	4 cents each.

Hymn Books.

New Tune and Hymn Books.

Half leather, per copy, post-paid,	$ 75
Morocco, per copy, post-paid,	1 00
Morocco, gilt edge, per copy, post-paid,	1 25

Hymn Books.

Morocco, per copy, post-paid,	$ 75
Morocco, gilt edge, per copy, post-paid,	85
Arabesque, per copy, post-paid,	40
Fine Limp, per copy, post-paid,	75
Fine Limp, gilt edge, per copy, post-paid,	85
German and English, per copy, post-paid,	75

Sunday-School Requisites.

The following list of things is needed in all Sunday-schools:

Testaments, Flexible, red edge, per dozen,	$1 00
Minute Books, each,	40
Class Books, per dozen,	75
S. S. Primers, with fine engravings, per dozen,	70

New and Beautiful Sunday-School Cards.

"The Gem," 50 picture cards, each with Bible text, verse of hymn,	35
250 Reward Tickets—verse of Scripture—red or blue,	20

The Young Disciple.

The YOUNG DISCIPLE is a neatly printed weekly, published especially for the moral benefit and religious instruction of our young folks.

Single copy, one year,	$ 50
Six copies (the sixth to the agent),	2 50
Ten copies,	4 00

For Three Months or Thirteen Weeks.

20 copies to one address,	$1 70
30 " " " "	2 50
40 " " " "	3 35
50 " " " "	3 80
75 " " " "	5 20
100 " " " "	7 00

For Six Months or Twenty-Six Weeks.

20 copies to one address,	$ 3 35
30 " " " "	5 00
40 " " " "	6 60
50 " " " "	7 50
75 " " " "	10 20
100 " " " "	13 75

Our paper is designed for the Sunday-school and the home circle. We desire the name of every Sunday-school Superintendent in the Brotherhood, and want an agent in every church. Send for sample copies.

Certificates of Membership

WE have just printed a new edition of these very convenient certificates. Several improvements over the old style are noticeable, such as perforated stubs, firm, yet smooth, paper, etc. Price only 50 cents per book. Every congregation should have one. Address this office.

The Monon Route.

This road is running a fine line of Pullman Buffet Sleepers between Chicago and Indianapolis, Cincinnati and Louisville, in connection with the fast Florida express trains.

For full information, address, E. O. McCORMICK, General Passenger Agent, Adams Express Building, Chicago. (City Ticket Office, 73 S. Clark St.)

Send for our new Bible Catalogue. Prices to suit the times. We have a large variety and the most durable as well as ornamental binding.

ed. She was the mother of eleven children. She was buried in the Brethren's burying-ground at Ashton, Ill., Jan. 18. Before she died she was anointed. Funeral services from Rev. 21:5 by Eld. D. Dierdorff.
C. H. HAWBECKER.

HERSHBERGER.—In the Bunker Hill church, Ohio, Feb. 15, 1892, Ida Catharine Hershberger, aged 7 months and 11 days.

This little child was the daughter of Bro. Eli and sister Sarah Hershberger. Funeral by Bro. Josiah Hochstetler, assisted by Frederic Mast, of the Mennonite church, from Matt. 18.
SARAH MIDDAUGH.

MILLER.—In Purcell, Ind. Ter., Aug. 30, 1891, Bro. Jacob Miller, aged 65 years, 6 months and 22 days.

Deceased was born in Virginia and was married to Catharine Rife. To them were born six sons and four daughters. April 13, 1877, his wife died. Aug. 19, 1883, he was married to Martha Beaty. They had three children.

There being no minister of the Brethren near, short devotional exercises were held at the grave by a resident Presbyterian minister.
ISAAC H. MILLER.

HAINES.—In the Salem congregation, Reno Co., Kans., Sept. 28, 1891, sister Lucy Haines, aged about 67 years.

Deceased was born in Richland County, Ohio, in 1824. In 1841 she married Philip Haines, who died in 1877. To them were born eight children. She united with the Brethren about twenty years ago. She was anointed by Eld. E. Eby and the writer a short time before her death. Funeral services by the writer from Rev. 14:13.
ISAAC H. MILLER.

HERRIMAN.—In the bounds of the Salem congregation, Reno Co., Kans., Nov. 3, 1891, Willie, son of Elias and sister Sarah R. Merriman, aged 6 years, 4 months and 23 days.

He was run over by some colts on Friday evening and died the next Tuesday. Funeral discourse by Bro. D. T. Dierdorff from James 4:14.
ISAAC H. MILLER.

BUTTERBAUGH.—In the Eel River congregation, Kosciusko Co., Ind., Jan. 28, 1892, Albert, son of Bro. Daniel and sister Barbara Butterbaugh, aged 9 years, 1 month and 5 days.

Deceased was the youngest of the family. Funeral services by Bro. Silas Gilbert and the writer.
SAMUEL LECKRONE.

HOOVER.—In the Sallmony church, Huntington Co., Ind., Jan. 27, 1892, of stomach and lung trouble, William Hoover, son of Bro. Levi and sister Lavina Hoover, aged 23 years and 29 days.

He leaves a father and mother, two brothers and two sisters. Funeral conducted by the Brethren.
SAMUEL MURRAY.

WELBORN.—In the Union church, Ind., Jan. 27, 1892, sister Margaret Olive Welborn, aged 34 years, 1 month and 8 days.

Deceased leaves a number of small children and a kind husband. She united with the church when young and lived faithful till death. Funeral services by Daniel Snell from Rev. 14:13.
DANIEL SNELL.

HOFF.—Near Marion, Franklin Co., Pa., Feb. 8, 1892, Sarah Hoff, aged 87 years, 4 months and 21 days.

Deceased was a member of the church over sixty years. Funeral services by brethren Good and Benedict from 1 Cor. 15:18.
EDWARD SHEFFER.

BEELMAN.—In the bounds of the Seneca church, Huron Co., Ohio, Feb. 18, 1892, Bro. George Beelman, aged 78 years, 7 months and 4 days.

Funeral occasion improved by the undersigned from Rev. 2:10.
S. A. WALKER.

PAULUS.—Near Elkhart, Elkhart Co., Ind., Feb. 3, 1892, of La Grippe, George Riley Paulus, son of Bro. Henry and sister Susan Paulus, aged 25 years and 7 days.

Funeral services were held at the schoolhouse near his home. Services conducted by Bro. Joseph Culp, of the Elkhart Valley congregation.
PETER HUFFMAN.

THE GOSPEL MESSENGER.

"Set for the Defense of the Gospel."

Vol. 30, Old Series.　　　　Mt. Morris, Ill., and Huntingdon, Pa., March 15, 1892.　　　　No. 11.

The Gospel Messenger.

H. B. BRUMBAUGH, Editor,

And Business Manager of the Eastern House, Box 50,
Huntingdon, Pa.

Table of Contents.

THE Bible Class of '92 have arranged to return again in '93; no providential interference. This is encouraging and we trust they may all be spared to carry out their expressed wishes.

ON last Sunday evening, after church, our strange ministering brethren and the students had quite an interesting parlor meeting, which, we were told, was impressive and profitable. One of the characteristics of true religion is sociality, and we are always glad to have it indicated in this way, as the results are always productive of good.

A FEW days ago spring-time seemed to be lingering around, ready to greet us with its warm sunshine and showers, but now we are visited by a two-foot snow, and winter has rallied in good earnest,—the weather prophets say, for three weeks. Of course, we don't have a deciding vote in the matter, and therefore, will continue on in the even tenor of our way.

THE *St. Louis Christian Advocate* says: "Paul recommended to Timothy that he use grape juice as a cure for his infirmities and for his stomach's sake." We are very much in favor of using the pure, unfermented grape juice in place of wine, but the reason for writing "grape juice" instead of "wine" is what we would like to have proof for. Not only so, but we would certainly prize some proof of that kind very highly.

UNSOLICITED SYMPATHY.

WE have occupied the editorial chair for twenty and two years, and during this time we have received considerable advice,—some wise and some otherwise, with lots of sympathy thrown in. Much of this was kindly appreciated. But some one,—we don't know who,—in a late number of the *Brethren's Evangelist*, suffering, we suppose, from an overload of kindly feelings towards us, proffers some words of advice and expressions of sympathy which we scarcely know how to take. The dose seems sugar-coated on one side and kind of brown-bitter on the other. However, we may be mistaken and therefore will look only at the sugar-coated side.

As to the advice given, don't fret about us. We have now all the positions we want, and are not aspiring after Annual Meeting positions, either to the right or left hand of the Moderator, or any other place. Those places are always well filled, but, should such a feeling arise in our breast, we don't feel that it would be a good thing to change our church relations to get the "oft-coveted gifts." There are too many over that way now for the supplicants before the throne. No, we are, as yet, satisfied to dwell among our own people.

As to pay for our ministry, we feel no special concern. The Lord has been very good. We do sometimes plead for our poor ones, but even they will be cared for without changing folds. Pardon our feeling to boast just a little. Look at our possibilities. Our missions only in their infancy, the General Mission, the Tract Work, with their endowments, our colleges at Huntingdon, Mt. Morris, McPherson, Bridgewater and Lordsburg, with their educational possibilities and their Bible work!

You say to our poor preachers, "Come over to us." What for? You say: "To get paid for preaching." No, not yet. This is not their greatest need. If it were, we would advise them to go to the wood-choppings or to the professions. They need more consecration of heart and devotement of mind, more preparation, more study. We are coming to all we need. Our brethren are opening their hands and our schools their doors.

It is true, our pasture has been a little short, but we have a good seed bed, and a little patience will bring a good crop. No, our poor ministers are *not* wrongshipped by remaining in a field that contains so much promise. Your sympathy is uncalled for. Take good care of what you have. Build up your down-trodden college,—endow it, and promise your preachers something better than "wages" and you will find quite enough to do. We say this in all kindness and sincerity of heart. We have been trying to study human nature for years and so far we have found it poor stuff,—very poor. And we very candidly confess that our investigation has somewhat liberalized our feelings towards our fellow-beings, and especially towards those who are so near to us in faith and

practice as those who have gone off from us and are now laboring in separate organizations. We entertain no bitter, no unkind feelings towards any who are zealous for the cause of the Master. Let us not foolishly turn our weapons of warfare towards each other. We have a common enemy, sin and the devil, who is a match for our united effort and demands all of our forces. The more we can unite in the struggle against sin and for the salvation of souls, the closer will our attachments for each other grow and the greater will be the good that we can accomplish. Factions in life and idleness are the hot-beds for dissensions and divisions. Out of the camp,—pull up the stakes and charge for the enemy and God will unite us in sacrifice and love, and the flags of victory will be unfurled over our heads.

NICODEMUS.

FROM sister Barbara Hanawalt, of Johnstown, we received the following, which we here insert by request:

I heard recently, in a sermon, an allusion to the circumstance of Nicodemus coming to Jesus by night," with the comment that he was like the Christians of to-day, who are ashamed or afraid to come out boldly with their views, etc. The intent of the speaker and the moral conclusion he wished to impress, were, of course, all right. But, as he was a man claiming considerable theological ability (not of our Fraternity), I was somewhat surprised at his ideas.

I have always been accustomed to think of Nicodemus as an exemplary, honest inquirer, who sought Jesus to satisfy the cravings of his conscience and questioned him in the spirit of pure, earnest inquiry, and that his "coming by night" is attributable to the fact that professional duties occupied his time during the day, and it might be that he was not safe in seeking the Lord by daylight, considering the enmity of the Jews and Pharisees to the followers of Jesus, "seeking to destroy them," or might he have chosen the long, still interval of night to discuss the weighty matters in greater privacy with the Lord?"

The other view of the case makes him out quite a different character. I am anxious to know the opinion of others about the matter.

Yes, a great many opinions have obtained in Christendom about this man Nicodemus, and many are the sermons that have been based on, "And he went to Jesus by night." Of course, the interpretations differ, but not a few coincide with the view named. And as there is no possible way of determining the exact character of Nicodemus, or what his motives were at that time, we will have to rest satisfied from the inferences that may be drawn from the narrative and the attending circumstances, and such as may be drawn from the history and the usages of the people at that time. There is one thing, however, that our Christianity demands in cases where there is no direct evidence, and that is, to give our decision on the side of charity. It is nowhere said that this man went to Jesus by night because he was ashamed to go by day, and those who so interpret it, may have made the decision as the result of their own experience. We often unwittingly do this, and our decisions thus made, indicate what we would do under similar circumstances, rather than what Nicodemus did do.

(Concluded on page 169.)

THE GOSPEL MESSENGER.

"Set for the Defense of the Gospel."

Vol. 30, Old Series.   Mt. Morris, Ill., and Huntingdon, Pa., March 15, 1892.   No. 11.

The Gospel Messenger.

H. B. BRUMBAUGH, Editor,

And Business Manager of the Eastern House, Box 50,
Huntingdon, Pa.

Table of Contents.

THE Bible Class of '92 have arranged to return again in '93, no providential interference. This is encouraging and we trust they may all be spared to carry out their expressed wishes.

ON last Sunday evening, after church, our strange ministering brethren and the students had quite an interesting parlor meeting, which, we were told, was impressive and profitable. One of the characteristics of true religion is sociality, and we are always glad to have it indicated in this way, as the results are always productive of good.

A FEW days ago spring-time seemed to be lingering around, ready to g,eet, us with its warm sunshine and showers, but now we are visited by a two-foot snow, and winter has rallied in good earnest,—the weather prophets say, for three weeks. Of course, we don't have a deciding vote in the matter, and therefore, will continue on in the even tenor of our way.

THE *St. Louis Christian Advocate* says: "Paul recommended to Timothy that he use grape juice as a cure for his infirmities and for his stomach's sake." We are very much in favor of using the pure, unfermented grape juice in place of wine, but the reason for writing "grape juice" instead of "wine" is what we would like to have proof for. Not only so, but we would certainly prize some proof of that kind very highly.

UNSOLICITED SYMPATHY.

WE have occupied the editorial chair for twenty and two years, and during this time we have received considerable advice,—some wise and some otherwise, with lots of sympathy thrown in. Much of this was kindly appreciated. But some one,—we don't know who,—in a late number of the *Brethren's Evangelist*, suffering, we suppose, from an overload of kindly feelings towards us, proffers some words of advice and expressions of sympathy which we scarcely know how to take. The dose seems sugar-coated on one side and kind of brown-bitter on the other. However, we may be mistaken and therefore will look only at the sugar-coated side.

As to the advice given, don't fret about us. We have now all the positions we want, and are not aspiring after Annual Meeting positions, either to the right or left hand of the Moderator, or any other place. Those places are always well filled, but, should such a feeling arise in our breast, we don't now feel that it would be a good thing to change our church relations to get the "oft-coveted gifts." There are too many over that way now for the suppliants before the throne. No, we are, as yet, satisfied to dwell among our own people.

As to pay for our ministry, we feel no special concern. The Lord has been very good. We do sometimes plead for our poor ones, but even they will be cared for without changing folds. Pardon our feeling to boast just a little. Look at our possibilities. Our missions only in their infancy, the General Mission, the Tract Work, with their endowments, our colleges at Huntingdon, Mt. Morris, McPherson, Bridgewater and Lordsburg, with their educational possibilities and their Bible work!

You say to our poor preachers, "Come over to us." What for? You say: "To get paid for preaching." No, not yet. This is not their greatest need. If it were, we would advise them to go to the wood-choppings or to the professions. They need more consecration of heart and decision of mind, more preparation, more study. We are coming to all we need. Our brethren are opening their hands and our schools their doors.

It is true, our pasture has been a little short, but we have a good seed bed, and a little patience will bring a good crop. No, our poor ministers are not wrongshipped by remaining in a field that contains so much promise. Your sympathy is uncalled for. Take good care of what you have. Build up your down-trodden college,—endow it, and promise your preachers something better than "wages" and you will find quite enough to do. We say this in all kindness and sincerity of heart. We have been trying to study human nature for years and so far we have found it poor stuff,—very poor. And we very candidly confess that our investigation has somewhat liberalized our feelings towards our fellow-beings, and especially towards those who are so near to us in faith and practice as those who have gone off from us and are now laboring in separate organizations. We entertain no bitter, no unkind feelings towards any who are zealous for the cause of the Master. Let us not foolishly turn our weapons of warfare towards each other. We have a common enemy, sin and the devil, who is a match for our united effort and demands all of our forces. The more we can unite in the struggle against sin and for the salvation of souls, the closer will our attachments for each other grow and the greater will be the good that we can accomplish. Factions in armies never take root in the heat of battle. Camp life and idleness are the hot-beds for dissensions and divisions. Out of the camp,—pull up the stakes and charge for the enemy and God will unite us in sacrifice and love, and the flags of victory will be unfurled over our heads.

NICODEMUS.

FROM sister Barbara Hanawalt, of Johnstown, we received the following, which we here insert by request:

I heard recently, in a sermon, an allusion to the circumstance of " Nicodemus coming to Jesus by night," with the comment that he was like the Christians of to-day, who are ashamed or afraid to come out boldly with their views, etc. The intent of the speaker and the moral conclusion he wished to impress, were, of course, all right. But, as he was a man claiming considerable theological ability (not of our Fraternity), I was somewhat surprised at his ideas.

I have always been accustomed to think of Nicodemus as an exemplary, honest inquirer, who sought Jesus to satisfy the cravings of his conscience and questioned him in the spirit of pure, earnest inquiry, and that his "coming by night" is attributable to the fact that professional duties occupied his time during the day, and it might be that he was not safe in seeking the Lord by daylight, considering the enmity of the Jews and Pharisees to the followers of Jesus, "seeking to destroy them," or might he have chosen the long, still interval of night to discuss the weighty matters in greater privacy with the Lord?"

The other view of the case makes him out quite a different character. I am anxious to know the opinion of others about the matter.

Yes, a great many opinions have obtained in Christendom about this man Nicodemus, and many are the sermons that have been based on, "And he went to Jesus by night." Of course, the interpretations differ, but not a few coincide with the view named. And as there is no possible way of determining the exact character of Nicodemus, or what his motives were at that time, we will have to rest satisfied from the inferences that may be drawn from the narrative and the attending circumstances, and such as may be drawn from the history and the usages of the people at that time. There is one thing, however, that our Christianity demands in cases where there is no direct evidence, and that is, to give our decision on the side of charity. It is nowhere said that this man went to Jesus by night because he was ashamed to go by day, and those who so interpret it, may have made the decision as the result of their own experience. We often unwittingly do this, and our decisions thus made, indicate what we would do under similar circumstances, rather than what Nicodemus did do.

(Concluded on page 165.)

enjoy to a greater degree civil and religious liberty.

The civil rulers of the nations wield an influence that would tell mightily in the upbuilding of Christian deportment and practical morality. May we not hope that the day is not far distant when a person need not expect a nomination for any important civil office, unless a good moral character, or even a devout and pious one may be sustained? An atheist or an infidel cannot hope to be a hero in any good work.

Perfection in our Christian work comes through heroic means. It is not taking things mildly as they come, but it is bending one's energies for the acquisition of future good. This the Gospel requires. A result obtained by these means,—self-denial and heroism, — is surely commendable. We are at present put on probation, so that we may be rightly disciplined, in order to develop Christian character. Without discipline we remain undeveloped babes in Christ. This is not the design. It is expected that we arrive at the full stature of men and women in Christ. Little tasks, well done, beget confidence and strengthen us for greater labors. If we have the mind of a hero, something will be done, and a commensurate reward will follow.

Inactivity ill becomes one who is being rescued from peril, and therefore Christians should be willing to save not only themselves, but also those around them.

True heroism will always find imitators. Urged onward by this cheering result, Christian activity invariably culminates in the accomplishment of heroic deeds, and the smiles of heaven will dwell upon the efforts thus consecrated. The command is to go forth conquering and to conquer, and as an inspiration we look at Christ, who set us the noblest example of heroism ever displayed. We do well to study his life, and learn to imitate him. By his heroism, life and immortality were brought to light through the Gospel. Now every member may become a hero by living faithful and doing those things that Christ commanded. "I can do all things through Christ which strengthens me," says Paul. Cannot we say so too?

THREE LINES OF SEVEN WONDERS.

BY I. J. ROSENBERGER.

Seven Wonders of the Old World.

1. *Nineveh* was fourteen miles long, eight miles wide, and forty-six miles around, with a wall one hundred feet high, and thick enough for three chariots abreast.

2. *Babylon* included a space of fifty square miles within its walls, which were seventy-five feet thick, and one hundred feet high, with one hundred brazen gates.

3. *The Temple of Diana at Ephesus* was four hundred and twenty feet to the support of the roof. It was one hundred years in building.

4. *The largest of the pyramids* was 481 feet high. The base covered eleven acres, and 350,000 men were employed in building it.

5. *The Labyrinth of Egypt* contained three hundred chambers and twelve halls.

6. *Thebes, in Egypt*, presents ruins twenty-seven miles in circumference; it contained 350,000 citizens and 400,000 slaves.

7. *The Temple of Delphos* was so rich in donations, that it was plundered of $50,000,000, and the Emperor Nero carried away from it two hundred statues.

Seven Wonders of the New World.

1. *The Falls of Niagara* are three-fourths of a mile in width. An immense column of water plunges over rocks to the depth of 170 feet.

2. *The Mammoth Cave* of Kentucky, in which you can travel a whole day, cross a subterranean river in a boat, and catch fish having no eyes.

3. *The Natural Bridge over Cedar Creek, Va.*, spans a chasm 80 feet in width and 250 feet in depth.

4. *Lake Superior, the largest body of fresh water on the globe.* Its length is 430 miles, and its depth is at least 1,000 feet.

5. *The Great Salt Lake of Utah.* Length, 110 miles; width, from 20 to 40 miles; contains 22 per cent salt.

6. *The Soda Lakes of Wyoming.* The two largest contain seventy-five acres each. By evaporation in hot summer, a crust is formed three or four feet thick, which is removed like so much ice, and loaded on cars. It is used for manufacturing glass and for domestic use. The value of this product is immense.

7. *Yellowstone Park,—the Wonder Land of America,*—contains 3,575 square miles. It is surrounded by snow-covered mountains, 1,200 feet high. Its canyons, geysers, beautiful lakes, rapid rivers, with their cascades and cataracts, are immense. The eruptions of the geysers are periodical, and ascend to the height of 150 feet.

Seven Wonders of the Religious World.

1. *It is a wonder that intelligence can doubt the existence of a great first cause, an Allwise Being, whom we call* GOD, when "the heavens declare the glory of God, and the firmament showeth his handywork."

2. *It is a wonder that men doubt the authenticity of the Bible,* when its height, its depth, its fitness, with its amazing simplicity, prove its authorship divine.

3. *It was a wonder that the then believing world rejected the person of Christ,* when he came, as to time, manner, and place, in the full sunlight of prophecy.

4. *It is a wonder that the doctrine of Christ was rejected,* when it was apparent that no man could do the miracles that Christ did, "except God be with him." The proofs of his divinity were many and infallible. Besides his life, his deeds were not done in a corner.

5. *It is a wonder that intelligent minds can, with seeming candor, in the face of the Scriptures, hold up and defend a divided Christianity,* when the facts are, that "Christ is not divided." "A house divided against itself cannot stand." "By one spirit we are all baptized into one body." We are to be "fitly framed together," "joined together," "knit together," etc. Christ's prayer for all his believers was, that "they might all be one as we are one." Will not this prayer be answered? Besides, division has not a single good fruit, "by their fruits ye shall know them."

6. *It is a wonder that intelligent minds can be led to believe that we can live Christians and stand acquitted, by obeying only a part of Christ's commandments.* The theory is, "*It is just as you believe.*" Let us test this theory. One omits water baptism. The next omits feet-washing. The next omits the supper. The next omits the Communion. May not the next omit prayer? It is apparent that this theory is a pure brand of modern skepticism.

7. *It is a wonder,—a marvel,—that brethren can be led to believe that plainness and the self-denying principles of humility, can be cultured and retained in the church, and extend to each member the liberty of setting his own limits as to his habits and apparel, and not have some fixed approximate bounds.* It is a fact without any exceptions that each organization that extended this liberty to her membership, has speedily gone to the ever-changing, wide world of fashion, while all the bodies, who retain their plainness, do so by

some fixed bounds. Besides, it is a painful truth, of which observation is clear proof, that with the loss of plainness and the self-denying principles of humility, goes well-nigh all government and general discipline of the church.

John Wesley and William Otterbein were founders of very humble, self-denying bodies. There was then power in their discipline. To-day every vestige of their former humility is gone,—vanished. With it has gone their power in church government. They are leaders to-day in the world, in her vanity, fashion and pleasure. Committees sent by Annual Meeting rarely control either churches or individuals who have gone with the world of fashion. With the growth of pride and fashion is sure to develop the stern spirit of insubordination and rebellion. It is simply raising the gates, by which the church becomes flooded with the world's looseness and corruption; but, of course, in a refined form. It was a noble act for Christ to break down the middle wall of partition between the Jews and Gentiles. The devil's mission to-day is to break down another wall,—the wall between the church and the world. His success is amazing, for while he is bombarding on the outside, he has a large army of prying people with their battering rams, helping him on the inside; hence the work of the humble people of God to-day is between fires. But thanks be to God, "We can do all things through Christ that doth strengthen us!"

Covington, Ohio.

THE CHIEF OF THE PUBLICANS.

BY ELIZABETH H. DELP.

THE office of the publican was scorned by the Jews. Loving their liberty and hating to pay the tax, it was natural that they should have the greatest contempt for the "chief of the publicans." The Pharisees, in their proud exclusiveness, gave vent to this scathing criticism of Christ, "He eateth with publicans."

Zaccheus, the chief of these despised people, had a desire to see Jesus. He had heard of the wonders and miracles that Christ had performed, and his curiosity was aroused. But it is one thing to know about Christ, his birth, his life and mission, and a very different thing to know him as your personal Savior. Zaccheus had an intellectual knowledge of Christ, which, if wrought upon by the Holy Ghost, would soon become a living reality.

It is a glorious thing to see the Lord! Simeon was ready to depart when he had seen Jesus; earth held nothing more for him; he was content. The great apostle of the Gentiles distinguished himself by this sign,—"Have I not seen Jesus Christ, our Lord?"

We must see him by the eye of faith. Our vision may be dimmed and obscured here, yet in heaven we shall know him, when we see the "King in his beauty." By keeping our gaze fixed steadily upon Jesus, we love him more, and we see less of the world. We grow to be more like him, our hope is brighter, our faith more serene, and we are happy in his service.

Even as the dying Israelite looked upon the serpent in the wilderness and was healed, so the soul that is perishing in sin, must look to Jesus for salvation. But how many poor souls walk securely, spurning Christ's proffered mercy! The day passes, and the shadows of the night of death gather, and they go forth into the great darkness alone.

The streets were thronged, and Zaccheus could not see the Lord, because of the multitude. But Jesus saw him on the sycamore tree and spoke to him. Zaccheus, with a glad heart, entertained his

enjoy to a greater degree civil and religious liberty.

The civil rulers of the nations wield an influence that would tell mightily in the upbuilding of Christian deportment and practical morality. May we not hope that the day is not far distant when a person need not expect a nomination for any important civil office, unless a good moral character, or even a devout and pious one may be sustained? An atheist or an infidel cannot hope to be a hero in any good work.

Perfection in our Christian work comes through heroic means. It is not taking things mildly as they come, but it is bending one's energies for the acquisition of future good. This the Gospel requires. A result obtained by these means,—self-denial and heroism, — is surely commendable. We are at present put on probation, so that we may be rightly disciplined, in order to develop Christian character. Without discipline we remain undeveloped babes in Christ. This is not the design. It is expected that we arrive at the full stature of men and women in Christ. Little tasks, well done, beget confidence and strengthen us for greater labors. If we have the mind of a hero, something will be done, and a commensurate reward will follow.

Inactivity ill becomes one who is being rescued from peril, and therefore Christians should be willing to save not only themselves, but also those around them.

True heroism will always find imitators. Urged onward by this cheering result, Christian activity invariably culminates in the accomplishment of heroic deeds, and the smiles of heaven will dwell upon the efforts thus consecrated. The command is to go forth conquering and to conquer, and as an inspiration we look at Christ, who set us the noblest example of heroism ever displayed. We do well to study his life, and learn to imitate him. By his heroism, life and immortality were brought to light through the Gospel. Now every member may become a hero by living faithful and doing those things that Christ commanded. "I can do all things through Christ which strengthens me," says Paul. Cannot we say so too?

THREE LINES OF SEVEN WONDERS.

BY I. J. ROSENBERGER.

Seven Wonders of the Old World.

1. *Nineveh* was fourteen miles long, eight miles wide, and forty-six miles around, with a wall one hundred feet high, and thick enough for three chariots abreast.

2. *Babylon* included a space of fifty square miles within its walls, which were seventy-five feet thick, and one hundred feet high, with one hundred brazen gates.

3. *The Temple of Diana at Ephesus* was four hundred and twenty feet to the support of the roof. It was one hundred years in building.

4. *The largest of the pyramids* was 481 feet high. The base covered eleven acres, and 350,000 men were employed in building it.

5. *The Labyrinth of Egypt* contained three hundred chambers and twelve halls.

6. *Thebes, in Egypt,* presents ruins twenty-seven miles in circumference; it contained 350,000 citizens and 400,000 slaves.

7. *The Temple of Delphos* was so rich in donations, that it was plundered of $50,000,000, and the Emperor Nero carried away from it two hundred statues.

Seven Wonders of the New World.

1. *The Falls of Niagara* are three-fourths of a mile in width. An immense column of water plunges over rocks to the depth of 170 feet.

2. *The Mammoth Cave* of Kentucky, in which you can travel a whole day, cross a subterranean river in a boat, and catch fish having no eyes.

3. *The Natural Bridge over Cedar Creek, Va.,* spans a chasm 80 feet in width and 250 feet in depth.

4. *Lake Superior, the largest body of fresh water on the globe.* Its length is 430 miles, and its depth is at least 1,000 feet.

5. *The Great Salt Lake of Utah.* Length, 110 miles; width, from 20 to 40 miles; contains 22 per cent salt.

6. *The Soda Lakes of Wyoming.* The two largest contain seventy-five acres each. By evaporation in hot summer, a crust is formed three or four feet thick, which is removed like so much ice, and loaded on cars. It is used for manufacturing glass and for domestic use. The value of this product is immense.

7. *Yellowstone Park,—the Wonder Land of America,*—contains 3,575 square miles. It is surrounded by snow-covered mountains, 1,200 feet high. Its canyons, geysers, beautiful lakes, rapid rivers, with their cascades and cataracts, are immense. The eruptions of the geysers are periodical, and ascend to the height of 150 feet.

Seven Wonders of the Religious World.

1. *It is a wonder that intelligence can doubt the existence of a great first cause, an Allwise Being, whom we call* GOD, when "the heavens declare the glory of God, and the firmament showeth his handywork."

2. *It is a wonder that men doubt the authenticity of the Bible,* when its height, its depth, its fitness, with its amazing simplicity, prove its authorship divine.

3. *It was a wonder that the then believing world rejected the person of Christ,* when he came, as to time, manner, and place, in the full sunlight of prophecy.

4. *It is a wonder that the doctrine of Christ was rejected,* when it was apparent that no man could do the miracles that Christ did, "except God be with him." The proofs of his divinity were many and infallible. Besides his life, his deeds were not done in a corner.

5. *It is a wonder that intelligent minds can, with seeming candor, in the face of the Scriptures, hold up and defend a divided Christianity,* when the facts are, that "Christ is not divided." "A house divided against itself cannot stand." "By one spirit we are all baptized into one body." We are to be "fitly framed together," "joined together," "knit together," etc. Christ's prayer for all his believers was, that "they might all be one as we are one." Will not this prayer be answered? Besides, division has not a single good fruit; "by their fruits ye shall know them."

6. *It is a wonder that intelligent minds can be led to believe that we can live Christians and stand acquitted, by obeying only a part of Christ's commandments.* "It is just as you believe." Let us test this theory. One omits water baptism. The next omits feet-washing. The next omits the supper. The next omits the Communion. May not the next omit prayer? It is apparent that this theory is a pure brand of modern skepticism.

7. *It is a wonder,—a marvel,—that brethren can be led to believe that plainness and the self-denying principles of humility, can be cultured and retained in the church, and extend to each member the liberty of setting his own limits as to his habits and apparel, and not have some fixed approximate bounds.* It is a fact without any exceptions that each organization that extended this liberty to her membership, has speedily gone to the ever-changing, wide world of fashion, while all the bodies, who retain their plainness, do so by

some fixed bounds. Besides, it is a painful truth, of which observation is clear proof, that with the loss of plainness and the self-denying principles of humility, goes well-nigh all government and general discipline of the church.

John Wesley and William Otterbein were founders of very humble, self-denying bodies. There was then power in their discipline. To-day every vestige of their former humility is gone,—vanished. With it has gone their power in church government. They are leaders to-day in the world, in her vanity, fashion and pleasure. Committees sent by Annual Meeting rarely control either churches or individuals who have gone with the world of fashion. With the growth of pride and fashion is sure to develop the stern spirit of insubordination and rebellion. It is simply raising the gates, by which the church becomes flooded with the world's looseness and corruption; but, of course, in a refined form. It was a noble act for Christ to break down the middle wall of partition between the Jews and Gentiles. The devil's mission to-day is to break down another wall,—the wall between the church and the world. His success is amazing, for while he is bombarding on the outside, he has a large army of prying people with their battering rams, helping him on the inside; hence the work of the humble people of God to-day is between fires. But thanks be to God, "We can do all things through Christ that doth strengthen us!"

Covington, Ohio.

THE CHIEF OF THE PUBLICANS.

BY ELIZABETH H. DELP.

THE office of the publican was scorned by the Jews. Loving their liberty and hating to pay the tax, it was natural that they should have the greatest contempt for the "chief of the publicans." The Pharisees, in their proud exclusiveness, gave vent to this scathing criticism of Christ, "He eateth with publicans."

Zaccheus, the chief of these despised people, had a desire to see Jesus. He had heard of the wonders and miracles that Christ had performed, and his curiosity was aroused. But it is one thing to know about Christ, his birth, his life and mission, and a very different thing to know him as your personal Savior. Zaccheus had an intellectual knowledge of Christ, which, if wrought upon by the Holy Ghost, would soon become a living reality.

It is a glorious thing to see the Lord! Simeon was ready to depart when he had seen Jesus; earth held nothing more for him; he was content. The great apostle of the Gentiles distinguished himself by this sign,—"Have I not seen Jesus Christ, our Lord?"

We must see him by the eye of faith. Our vision may be dimmed and obscured here, yet in heaven we shall know him, when we see the "King in his beauty." By keeping our gaze fixed steadily upon Jesus, we love him more, and we see less of the world. We grow to be more like him, our hope is brighter, our faith more serene, and we are happy in his service.

Even as the dying Israelite looked upon the serpent in the wilderness and was healed, so the soul that is perishing in sin, must look to Jesus alone for salvation. But how many poor souls walk securely, spurning Christ's proffered mercy! The day passes, and the shadows of the night of death gather, and they go forth into the great darkness alone.

The streets were thronged, and Zaccheus could not see the Lord, because of the multitude. But Jesus saw him on the sycamore tree and spoke to him. Zaccheus, with a glad heart, entertained his

lawful to offer their gifts in this way, or the Savior would not have recommended it.

Though we cannot purchase our way to heaven with our money, yet it is a means by which we may lay up TREASURES there. It is true the Gospel, in one sense, is offered without money and without price, but I am afraid this offer is made too general, and the Scripture, upon which it is based, is very often misquoted, and misapplied. I, for one, for many years thought it read just as it is usually quoted and applied. We find the quotation in Isaiah 55: 1, "Ho, every one that thirsteth, come ye to the waters, and he that hath no money; come ye, buy, and eat; yea, come buy wine and milk without money and without price." We see at once that the above Scripture only applies to those who have no money. To SUCH, and SUCH ONLY, is it offered without money and without price.

The question may then arise, since we need money to carry on and advance the work of God, By what principle shall we be governed in our giving to the Lord's cause? We answer, "As the Lord has prospered us.'" We find in the text, that many that were rich cast in much, but the poor widow cast in two mites, which make a farthing, which was a very small amount, compared with theirs: and yet Jesus said she cast in more than they all, for they still had *abundance* left, but she cast in all her living. To our *sorrow*, and their own *disadvantage*, we often see the rich cast into the offerings of the Lord, a very trifling amount, and then try to hide themselves behind the widow's mite.

Some years ago, when the first missionary Brethren were sent to Denmark, as the move originated in Northern Illinois, the greater part of the burden rested on them, and on the way to a special District Meeting, appointed before the departure of the Brethren, knowing that we would have to raise considerable means to defray expenses, that question was sprung on the way to said meeting. One brother said, "I suppose I *will have to give my mite.*" We replied, "You don't need to give that much; only give a half mite, and we will be fully satisfied."

I suppose all can easily see the point; he wanted to have the credit of giving as much as the widow did, irrespective of circumstances. If he had given in reality as much as she did, there would have been enough money for the occasion, without any further donation.

The apostle Paul gives us a beautiful rule for giving, which we would all do well to adopt. He says in 2 Cor. 8: 10, 11, 12, 13, 14, "And herein I give my advice: for this is expedient for you, who have begun before, not only to do, but also to be forward a year ago. Now therefore perform the doing of it; that as there was a readiness to will, so there may be a performance also out of that which ye have. For if there be first a willing mind, it is accepted according to that a man hath, and not according to that he hath not. For I mean not that other men be eased, and ye be burdened: But by an equality, that now at this time your abundance may be a supply for their want, that their abundance also may be a supply for your want; that there may be equality."

It would be well if the above advice were strictly adhered to in all of our church work. The greatest reason why it is not, comes from improper teaching. If ministers, and *even elders*, when the church decides to raise a certain amount to meet necessary expenses, say, "You don't need to give, if you don't want to," what may we expect? It requires very little indifference on the part of those in charge, to stop the flow of the LORD's MONEY into HIS TREASURY. Heretofore, and in many places yet, the burden of church expenses has been, and is yet, borne by few, while others give

comparatively nothing; and very often the ministry (who give their time and talent to the church, and often go at their own expense, even when invited), if there is a meeting-house to be built, or any other expense to be met, are expected to head the subscription with the largest amount, if at all able to do so. This, I think, is what Bro. Paul would call "some eased, and others burdened,"—anything else but equality.

The most equable plan adopted and recommended by Annual Meeting, is for every member to give in proportion to his financial wealth. In some places they are allowed to make their own assessment; in others the State taxes are made a basis by which to reach the desired result. Some, of course, are ready to object to this method of raising means, to replenish the Lord's treasury, claiming it is not a FREE-WILL OFFERING, and basing their argument, or authority, upon 2 Cor. 9: 5, 6, 7, which reads as follows, "Therefore I thought it necessary to exhort the brethren, that they would go before unto you, and make up beforehand your bounty, whereof ye had notice before, that the same might be ready, as a matter of bounty, and not as of covetousness. But this I say, He which soweth sparingly shall reap also sparingly; and he which soweth bountifully shall reap also bountifully. Every man according as he purposeth in his heart, so let him give; not grudgingly, or of necessity: for God loveth a cheerful giver."

According to the above reasoning, the blessing to the giver depends entirely on the manner in which it was given. If we give unwillingly or grudgingly, let it be much or little, what we give may answer the same purpose wherever applied, but the giver will lose the blessing. On the other hand, if we willingly consent for the church to make an equal distribution of our property for necessary church expenses, it undoubtedly is a free-will offering. And we further state, and base our assertion on the above text, that whoever refuses to make an equal distribution of his property towards necessary church expenses, gives evidence of a covetous disposition; and this is the ONLY MEANS by which we can make out a CASE of COVETOUSNESS.

Mt. Morris, Ill.

THE SHAMBERGER AND BOND DEBATE.

BY LEVI MOHLER.

THE debate was held in the Prairie View (Brethren) church, near St. Martin's, Morgan Co., Mo. It began at 10: 30 A. M., Monday, Feb. 22, and continued until Saturday evening, at four o'clock. Two sessions daily were held from 10 to 12 o'clock, and from 2 o'clock till 4. Four half hour speeches were made each session.

The weather had been unpleasant for several days. The rain, following a thaw, put the roads in the very worst condition. Nevertheless we had a good attendance, and a large section of the country was represented the first day. A very large attendance was present every day following, except Wednesday, when it rained hard all day, reducing the crowd about one-half. The weather, the remainder of the time, was very favorable. Bro. Enoch Eby, was Moderator for Bro. G. A. Shamberger, of Esterly, Ls., representing the Brethren. On account of other engagements, Bro. Eby left Friday morning, and was succeeded as Moderator by Bro. Jacob Witmore. Wm. Hughes served as Moderator for Rev. J. W. Bond, of Gleasted, Mo., representing the Methodist church.

The propositions discussed were published in GOSPEL MESSENGER for Feb. 2.

There was the deepest public interest in the debate, and the propositions involved. A number of denominations were well represented in the audience. The best of feeling prevailed, and the result of the work is most satisfactory to the Brethren.

The doctrine of the church, with its foundation on the Word of God, was set forth in the clearest light, and was sustained unshaken by convincing arguments, many of them new, and strong as the Truth from which they were drawn.

The Brethren feel thankful to the Lord for the demonstration of the truth of the doctrine of the church, and the good that will likely result therefrom.

They also feel thankful to Bro. Shamberger for his careful and efficient labors.

May the blessing of the Lord go with him to his distant home in the sunny south, and ever abide with him and his, as with all the faithful of the Lord.

Warrensburg, Mo.

MUSIC.

BY FANNY MORROW.

MUSIC is sometimes defined as the science of harmonious sounds, and ever since the morning stars sang together and the sons of God shouted for joy, at the dawn of creation, music is frequently mentioned as a prominent and peculiar factor in divine worship.

We read in the Old Testament of singing men and singing women by hundreds,—those who were skillful and those who were trained by singing masters. King David himself, styled the sweet singer of Israel, exhorts the people to "sing praise with understanding." Paul, filled with the Holy Spirit, declares, "I will sing with the spirit and I will sing with the understanding also."

Thus all who can avail themselves of opportunities for cultivation of vocal music, have Scriptural grounds for the same. Methinks earth never heard such music as greeted the ears of the shepherds on Bethlehem's plains, when the glory of the Lord shone around and a multitude of the heavenly host praised God. Never again will such be heard until the great voice of many people shall be heard in heaven, saying, "Alleluia, salvation, and glory, and honor, and power, unto the Lord our God." In perfect harmony their songs shall arise as the voice of a great multitude, and as the voice of many waters, and as the voice of many thunderings, saying, "Alleluia, for the Lord God Omnipotent reigneth."

Osborne, Kans.

NICODEMUS.

(Concluded from first page.)

We do not say that the narrative could not bear such an interpretation, but we do say that it will bear several more charitable ones, quite as well and, in our estimation, much better.

It is a common fault among ministers to wrest Scripture from its intended and more obvious meaning to that of something else, merely for the purpose of making it a suitable text on which to grind out our sermons. We are not at all sure that such a course is to be commended. If we wish to ventilate a subject for which we can find no suitable text, the better way is to stick to the subject and let the text alone. An irrelevant text can add no force to a subject, no matter how much we may wrest it or name it over.

Yes, sister Hanawalt, we are inclined to your views, and will continue to give Nicodemus credit for being an honest seeker after the Truth, until he is proven otherwise.

lawful to offer their gifts in this way, or the Savior would not have recommended it.

Though we cannot purchase our way to heaven with our money, yet it is a means by which we may lay up THREASURES there. It is true the Gospel, in one sense, is offered without money and without price, but I am afraid this offer is made too general, and the Scripture, upon which it is based, is very often misquoted, and misapplied. I, for one, for many years thought it read just as it is usually quoted and applied. We find the quotation in Isaiah 55: 1, "Ho, every one that thirsteth, come ye to the waters, and he that hath no money; come ye, buy, and eat; yea, come buy wine and milk without money and without price." We see at once that the above Scripture only applies to those who have no money. To SUCH, and SUCH ONLY, is it offered without money and without price.

The question may then arise, since we need money to carry on and advance the work of God, By what principle shall we be governed in our giving to the Lord's cause? We answer, "As 'the Lord has prospered us.'" We find in the text, that many that were rich cast in much, but the poor widow cast in two mites, which make a farthing, which was a very small amount, compared with theirs; and yet Jesus said she cast in more than they all, for they still had *abundance* left, but she cast in all her living. To our *sorrow*, and their own *disadvantage*, we often see the rich cast into the offerings of the Lord, a very trifling amount, and then try to hide themselves behind the widow's mite.

Some years ago, when the first missionary Brethren were sent to Denmark, as the move originated in Northern Illinois, the greater part of the burden rested on them, and on the way to a special District Meeting, appointed before the departure of the Brethren, knowing that we would have to raise considerable means to defray expenses, that question was sprung on the way to said meeting. One brother said, "I suppose I *will have to give my mite*." We replied, "You don't need to give that much; only give a half mite, and we will be fully satisfied."

I suppose all can easily see the point; he wanted to have the credit of giving as much as the widow did, irrespective of circumstances. If he had given in reality as much as she did, there would have been enough money for the occasion, without any further donation.

The apostle Paul gives us a beautiful rule for giving, which we would all do well to adopt. He says in 2 Cor. 8: 10, 11, 12, 13, 14, "And herein I give my advice: for this is expedient for you, who have begun before, not only to do, but also to be forward a year ago. Now therefore perform the doing of it; that as there was a readiness to will, so there may be a performance also out of that which ye have. For if there be first a willing mind, it is accepted according to that a man hath, and not according to that he hath not. For I mean not that other men be eased, and ye be burdened: But by an equality, that now at this time your abundance may be a supply for their want, that their abundance also may be a supply for your want; that there may be equality."

It would be well if the above advice were strictly adhered to in all of our church work. The greatest reason why it is not, comes from improper teaching. If ministers, and *even elders*, when the church decides to raise a certain amount to meet necessary expenses, say, "You don't need to give, if you don't want to," what may we expect? It requires very little indifference on the part of those in charge, to stop the flow of the LORD'S MONEY into HIS TREASURY. Heretofore, and in many places yet, the burden of church expenses has been, and is yet, borne by few, while others give

comparatively nothing; and very often the ministry (who give their time and talent to the church, and often go at their own expense, even when invited), if there is a meeting-house to be built, or any other expense to be met, are expected to head the subscription with the largest amount, if at all able to do so. This, I think, is what Bro. Paul would call "some eased, and others burdened,"—anything else but equality.

The most equable plan adopted and recommended by Annual Meeting, is for every member to give in proportion to his financial wealth. In some places they are allowed to make their own assessment; in others the State taxes are made a basis by which to reach the desired result. Some, of course, are ready to object to this method of raising means, to replenish the Lord's treasury, claiming it is not a FREE-WILL OFFERING, and basing their argument, or authority, upon 2 Cor. 9: 5, 6, 7, which reads as follows, "Therefore I thought it necessary to exhort the brethren, that they would go before unto you, and make up beforehand your bounty, whereof ye had notice before, that the same might be ready, as a matter of bounty, and not as of covetousness. But this I say, He which soweth sparingly shall reap also sparingly; and he which soweth bountifully shall reap also bountifully. Every man according as he purposeth in his heart, so let him give; not grudgingly, or of necessity: for God loveth a cheerful giver."

According to the above reasoning, the blessing to the giver depends entirely on the manner in which it was given. If we give unwillingly or grudgingly, let it be much or little, what we give may answer the same purpose wherever applied, but the giver will lose the blessing. On the other hand, if we willingly consent for the church to make an equal distribution of our *property* for necessary church expenses, it undoubtedly is a free-will offering. And we further state, and base our assertion on the above text, that whoever refuses to make an equal distribution of his properly towards necessary church expenses, gives evidence of a covetous disposition; and this is the ONLY MEANS by which we can make out a CASE of COVETOUSNESS.

Mt. Morris, Ill.

THE SHAMBERGER AND BOND DEBATE.

BY LEVI MOHLER.

THE debate was held in the Prairie View (Brethren) church, near St. Martin's, Morgan Co., Mo. It began at 10: 30 A. M., Monday, Feb. 22, and continued until Saturday evening, at four o'clock. Two sessions daily were held: from 10 to 12 o'clock, and from 2 o'clock till 4. Four half hour speeches were made each session.

The weather had been unpleasant for several days. The rain, following a thaw, put the roads in the very worst condition. Nevertheless we had a good attendance, and a large section of the country was represented the first day. A very large attendance was present every day following, except Wednesday, when it rained hard all day, reducing the crowd about one-half. The weather, the remainder of the time, was very favorable. Bro Enoch Eby, was Moderator for Bro. G. A. Shamberger, of Esterly, La., representing the Brethren. On account of other engagements, Bro. Eby left Friday morning, and was succeeded as Moderator by Bro. Jacob Witmore. Wm. Hughes served as Moderator for Rev. J. W. Bond, of Glensted, Mo., representing the Methodist church.

The propositions discussed were published in GOSPEL MESSENGER for Feb. 2.

There was the deepest public interest in the debate, and the propositions involved. A number of denominations were well represented in the audience. The best of feeling prevailed, and the result of the work is most satisfactory to the Brethren.

The doctrine of the church, with its foundation on the Word of God, was set forth in the clearest light, and was sustained unshaken by convincing arguments, many of them new, and strong as the Truth from which they were drawn.

The Brethren feel thankful to the Lord for the demonstration of the truth of the doctrine of the church, and the good that will likely result therefrom.

They also feel thankful to Bro. Shamberger for his careful and efficient labors.

May the blessing of the Lord go with him to his distant home in the sunny south, and ever abide with him and his, as with all the faithful of the Lord.

Warrensburg, Mo.

MUSIC.

BY FANNY MORROW.

MUSIC is sometimes defined as the science of harmonious sounds, and ever since the morning stars sang together and the sons of God shouted for joy, at the dawn of creation, music is frequently mentioned as a prominent and peculiar factor in divine worship.

We read in the Old Testament of singing men and singing women by hundreds,—those who were skillful and those who were trained by singing masters. King David himself, styled the sweet singer of Israel, exhorts the people to "sing praise with understanding." Paul, filled with the Holy Spirit, declares, "I will sing with the spirit and I will sing with the understanding also."

Thus all who can avail themselves of opportunities for cultivation of vocal music, have Scriptural grounds for the same. Methinks earth never heard such music as greeted the ears of the shepherds on Bethlehem's plains, when the glory of the Lord shone around and a multitude of the heavenly host praised God. Never again will such be heard until the great voice of many people shall be heard in heaven, saying, "Alleluia, salvation, and glory, and honor, and power, unto the Lord our God." In perfect harmony their songs shall arise as the voice of a great multitude, and as the voice of many waters, and as the voice of many thunderings, saying, "Alleluia, for the Lord God Omnipotent reigneth."

Osborne, Kans.

NICODEMUS.

(Concluded from first page.)

We do not say that the narrative could not bear such an interpretation, but we do say that it will bear several more charitable ones, quite as well and, in our estimation, much better.

It is a common fault among ministers to wrest Scripture from its intended and more obvious meaning to that of something else, merely for the purpose of making it a suitable text on which to grind out our sermons. We are not at all sure that such a course is to be commended. If we wish to ventilate a subject for which we can find no suitable text the better way is to stick to the subject and let the text alone. An irrelevant text can add no force to a subject, no matter how much we may wrest it or name it over.

Yes, sister Hanawalt, we are inclined to your views, and will continue to give Nicodemus credit for being an honest seeker after the Truth, until he is proven otherwise.

whether I have a worse set of members than my adjoining brother; and by the time the ground is talked over, I will see clearly where the fault lies; hence will know how to improve.

The apostle says, "For though you have ten thousand instructors in Christ, yet have ye not many fathers." 1 Cor. 4: 15. A brother, ordained to take charge of a church, assumes the position of a father; hence the qualification, "If he knows not how to rule his own house, how shall he take care of the church of God." A father's ability to rule can be measured by his children, to a great extent, and as many fathers cannot rule their own house, so there are many in the church who are not as successful as they would be, had they the advantage of such meetings as above alluded to, to get the experience and advice of others who are better gifted. I present this article to the Brotherhood for thought.

Booth, Kans.

MISSIONARY BREVITIES.

BY J. H. BOSSERMAN.

I SUPPOSE there are none but what have their temporal plans laid out for the year's operations. In all this, have you had an "eye single" to the observance of the command "Go ye"?

Have you set aside a portion of ground for your children to raise missionary funds that they may be thus nurtured in the admonition of the Lord?

Don't give the children a weedy patch in some shady out-of-the-way place, on which you could never raise anything yourself, but let it be in the middle of your best field, so that the Lord can have a fair chance to bless it and its surroundings.

In giving out the seeds to the children, don't throw in a handful or two and say, "There, that's a nickle's worth," but deal it out to them as you would measure is to any one else and see that they get "Gospel measure."

In our last year's missionary operations the smallest returns exceeded 300 per cent of gain on the investment, and some as much as 5,000 per cent of gain. How would it do to turn a large share of the farm to the missionary cause and farm it on the shares for the Lord? I believe it would pay, both temporally and spiritually, since it takes a pretty well-managed farm to return ten or twelve per cent. Who will try it?

Oh, brethren, you who are hoarding up your "filthy lucre" until your sons and daughters are ruined by it, and until you are compelled to apply to yourselves the lamentations of Jer. 3: 1-20, arouse from your manifest "ease in Zion," return a portion of that, wherewith God has blessed you, to having the Gospel preached to "every creature."

To pray "Thy kingdom come" and then not do what we can to bring it about, is practically "faith without works," or like saying, "Lord, Lord," but do not the things the Master says. When we do all we can to transform the kingdom of darkness into the kingdom of light, then and first we can we conscientiously say, "Thy kingdom come."

McPherson, Kans.

WHAT ARE THE DUTIES OF THE MINISTER AND THE CHURCH IN THEIR RELATION TO THE SABBATH-SCHOOL?

BY S. M. MILLER.

IN listening to the discussion upon the above topic at our Ministerial Meeting, held in the Sugar Creek church, Allen Co., Ohio, my mind was caused to search for a fundamental principle from which all duty must proceed or emanate. That fundamental principle I find to be individual responsibility. When God said to Adam, "In the day thou eatest thereof thou shalt surely die," he made him individually responsible, and from that responsibility proceeded the duty of obedience to the divine law. But Adam being disobedient, was compelled to pay the penalty of judgment annexed to his individual responsibility.

Under the law of Moses the penalty of judgment was annexed to individual responsibility. "Let us hear the conclusion of the whole matter; fear God and keep his commandments, for this is the whole duty of man" (not men or church, but individual MAN) "for God shall bring every work into judgment, with every secret thing, whether it be good, or whether it be evil." Eccl. 12: 13, 14. Every work and secret thing shall be judged. Then judgment must fall on the individual, for the part he has exerted in the work, given him to do. Since God will render to every man according to his works, Prov. 24: 12, this is, I think, conclusive evidence of our individual work.

Again, under the Gospel, we have this: "The Son of Man shall come in the glory of his Father with his angels; and then he shall reward every man according to his works." Matt. 16: 27. "And, behold, I come quickly; and my reward is with me, to give every man according as his works shall be." Rev. 22: 12. Hence, under the Gospel, also, individual responsibility is the source from which all duty must proceed.

Realizing this fact, the individual is prepared to receive the divine command "Go ye therefore and teach all nations," etc, not that every member of Christ's kingdom must be a preacher or missionary, and all go, and all preach, to all nations, but individually all the members can teach (1) by their godly life and the manifestation of the love of God shed abroad in their hearts. (2) by their assistance in sending preachers and missionaries into the world to preach the Gospel. "How shall they preach except they be sent?" Rom. 10: 15. (3) By their individual assistance and co-operation in the work of the Sunday-school, which is the only general and universal medium of teaching, available to the church, in which all can unite, participate and mingle their individual efforts in the work.

Then it is apparent that the duty of the church in her relation to the Sunday-school is simply the duty incumbent upon every individual member of the church by the great commission "Go ye therefore," which strikes every member just as forcibly as it did those disciples that received it directly from the Master's lips. Could every member realize this fact, and take upon himself the responsibility of the great work of teaching, as Christ placed it upon his disciples, the Sunday-school would be an ever-living and evergreen emblem of glory to the church, and Christ's words would be verified and exemplified in each of us: "As my father hath sent me, even so send I you." John 20: 21.

As Christ was sent to perform an individual work for the Father, even so are we sent to perform an individual work for Christ. "Now if any man have not the Spirit of Christ, he is none of his." Rom. 8: 9. Christ manifested no other spirit excepting to do the will of the Father. "Because I seek not mine own will, but the will of the Father which hath sent me." John 5: 30. "I do always those things that please him." John 8: 29.

Then, if we are Christ's, we MUST have the Spirit of Christ, and if we have the Spirit of Christ we WILL be found seeking his will, and doing the things that please him. There is no possibility of dodging the command, "Go ye, therefore;" no possibility of shirking responsibility by hiding behind the church or church officers. The all-penetrating eyes of God will as surely find us, as they did Adam when he tried to shirk responsibility by hiding among the trees.

It is sad, but true, that we are too often found hiding behind the church or church officers.

When there is duty to perform, the efforts of all the members are required. Especially does this apply to us in the Sunday-school work. We may be earnest advocates of the Sunday-school until a Sunday-school is organized with Bro. A. as Superintendent, and Bro. B, Secretary, etc., then, perhaps, by our actions we say to those officers, "Go ye, therefore." Because you have been elected, therefore go ye and do this work, while we recline in our easy chairs, entertaining company, or visiting neighbors.

Behold the contrast between what we are, and what Christ intended we should be when he said, "As my Father hath sent me, even so I send you!"

Right here I think we find the most important duty of the minister in his relation to the Sunday-school,—to keep the members alive and awakened, that we may be made to feel and realize the weight of responsibility that is resting upon us.

The spiritual slumbering and deadness in the church would not exist if we could all be sufficiently aroused and enlivened to heed Paul's admonition, "Awake thou that sleepest, and arise from the dead, and Christ shall give thee light." Eph. 5: 14.

Here we see the necessity of the minister using his utmost endeavors to awaken those that are spiritually asleep, to call to life those that are spiritually dead. When the individual becomes wrapped in spiritual slumber, or chilled in spiritual death, he cannot feel or realize his individual responsibility, and no amount of preaching to the church is likely to awaken or enliven him. But he must be preached to individually,—the responsibility incumbent upon him by the "Go ye, therefore" must be brought vividly to his understanding; then we may hope to see him discharge his individual duty. When each member is found discharging his duty, the church will be found discharging her whole duty, and the Sunday-school will be recognized only as a part of the church work, but also an important part of each individual's work. The "Go ye, therefore" will be the watch-word of every true Christian believer, prompting him to verify and exemplify, "As my Father hath sent me, even so send I you."

Waterloo, Iowa.

The Gospel Messenger

Is the recognized organ of the German Baptist or Brethren's church, and advocates the form of doctrine taught in the New Testament and pleads for a return to apostolic and primitive Christianity.

It recognizes the New Testament as the only infallible rule of faith and practice, and maintains that Faith toward God, Repentance from dead works, Regeneration of the heart and mind, baptism by Trine Immersion for remission of sins unto the reception of the Holy Ghost by the laying on of hands, are the means of adoption into the household of God,—the church militant.

It also maintains that Feet-washing, as taught in John 13, both by example and command of Jesus, should be observed in the church.

That the Lord's Supper, instituted by Christ and as universally observed by the apostles and the early Christians, is a full meal, and, in connection with the Communion, should be taken in the evening or after the close of the day.

That the Salutation of the Holy Kiss, or Kiss of Charity, is binding upon the followers of Christ.

That War and Retaliation are contrary to the spirit and self-denying principles of the religion of Jesus Christ.

That the principle of Plain Dressing and of Non-conformity to the world, as taught in the New Testament, should be observed by the followers of Christ.

That the Scriptural duty of Anointing the Sick with Oil, in the Name of the Lord, James 5: 14, is binding upon all Christians.

It also advocates the church's duty to support Missionary and Tract Work, thus giving to the Lord for the spread of the Gospel and for the conversion of sinners.

In short, it is a vindicator of all that Christ and the apostles have enjoined upon us, and aims, amid the conflicting theories and discords of modern Christendom, to point out ground that all must concede to be infallibly safe.

☞ The above principles of our Fraternity are set forth on our "Brethren's Envelopes." Use them! Price, 15 cents per package; 40 cents per hundred.

whether I have a worse set of members than my adjoining brother; and by the time the ground is talked over, I will see clearly where the fault lies; hence will know how to improve.

The apostle says, "For though you have ten thousand instructors in Christ, yet have ye not many fathers." 1 Cor. 4: 15. A brother, ordained to take charge of a church, assumes the position of a father; hence the qualification, "If he knows not how to rule his own house, how shall he take care of the church of God." A father's ability to rule can be measured by his children, to a great extent, and as many fathers cannot rule their own house, so there are many in the church who are not as successful as they would be, had they the advantage of such meetings as above alluded to, to get the experience and advice of others who are better gifted. I present this article to the Brotherhood for thought.

Booth, Kans.

MISSIONARY BREVITIES.

BY J. H. BOSSERMAN.

I SUPPOSE there are none but what have their temporal plans laid out for the year's operations. In all this, have you had an "eye single" to the observance of the command "Go ye"?

Have you set aside a portion of ground for your children to raise missionary funds that they may be thus nurtured in the admonition of the Lord?

Don't give the children a weedy patch in some shady out-of-the-way place, on which you could never raise anything yourself, but let it be in the middle of your best field, so that the Lord can have a fair chance to bless it and its surroundings.

In giving out the seeds to the children, don't throw in a handful or two and say, "There, that a nickle's worth," but deal it out to them as you would measure it to any one else and see that they get "Gospel measure."

In our last year's missionary operations the smallest returns exceeded 300 per cent of gain on the investment, and some as much as 5,000 per cent of gain. How would it do to turn a large share of the farm to the missionary cause and farm it on the shares for the Lord? I believe it would pay, both temporally and spiritually, since it takes a pretty well-managed farm to return ten or twelve per cent. Who will try it?

Oh, brethren, you who are hoarding up your "filthy lucre" until your sons and daughters are ruined by it, and until you are compelled to apply to yourselves the lamentations of Jer. 3: 1–20, arouse from your manifest "ease in Zion," return a portion of that, wherewith God has blessed you, to having the Gospel preached to "every creature."

To pray "Thy kingdom come" and then not do what we can to bring it about, is practically "faith without works," or like saying, "Lord, Lord," but do not the things the Master says. When we do all we can to transform the kingdom of darkness into the kingdom of light, then and fix... can we conscientiously say, "Thy kingdom ...

McPherson, Kans.

WHAT ARE THE DUTIES OF THE MINISTER AND THE CHURCH IN THEIR RELATION TO THE SABBATH-SCHOOL?

BY S. M. MILLER.

IN listening to the discussion upon the above topic at our Ministerial Meeting, held in the Sugar Creek church, Allen Co., Ohio, my mind was caused to search for a fundamental principle from which all duty must proceed or emanate. That fundamental principle I find to be individ-

ual responsibility. When God said to Adam, "In the day thou eatest thereof thou shalt surely die," he made him individually responsible, and from that responsibility proceeded the duty of obedience to the divine law. But Adam being disobedient, was compelled to pay the penalty of judgment annexed to his individual responsibility.

Under the law of Moses the penalty of judgment was annexed to individual responsibility. "Let us hear the conclusion of the whole matter: fear God and keep his commandments, for this is the whole duty of man" (not *men* or *church*, but individual MAN) "for God shall bring every work into judgment, with every secret thing, whether it be good, or whether it be evil." Eccl. 12: 13, 14. Every work and secret thing shall be judged. Then judgment must fall on the individual, for the part he has exerted in the work, given him to do. Since God will render to every man according to his works, Prov. 24: 12, this is, I think, conclusive evidence of our individual work.

Again, under the Gospel, we have this: "The Son of Man shall come in the glory of his Father with his angels; and then he shall reward every man according to his works." Matt. 16: 27. "And, behold, I come quickly; and my reward is with me, to give every man according as his works shall be." Rev. 22: 12. Hence, under the Gospel, also, individual responsibility is the source from which all duty must proceed.

Realizing that the individual is prepared to receive the divine command "Go ye therefore and teach all nations," etc, not that every member of Christ's kingdom must be a preacher or missionary, and all go, and all preach, to all nations, but individually all the members can teach (1) by their godly life and the manifestation of the love of God shed abroad in their hearts. (2) by their assistance in sending preachers and missionaries into the world to preach the Gospel. "How shall they preach except they be sent?" Rom. 10: 15. (3) By their individual assistance and co-operation in the work of the Sunday-school, which is the only general and universal medium of teaching, available to the church, in which all can unite, participate and mingle their individual efforts in the work.

Then it is apparent that the duty of the church in her relation to the Sunday-school is simply the duty incumbent upon every individual member of the church by the great commission "Go ye therefore," which strikes every member just as forcibly as it did those disciples that received it directly from the Master's lips. Could every member realize this fact, and take upon himself the responsibility of the great work of teaching, as Christ placed it upon his disciples, the Sunday-school would be an ever-living and evergreen emblem of glory to the church, and Christ's words would be verified and exemplified in each of us: "As my Father hath sent me, even so send I you." John 20: 21.

As Christ was sent to perform an individual work for the Father, even so are we sent to perform an individual work for Christ. "Now if any man have not the Spirit of Christ, he is none of his." Rom. 8: 9. Christ manifested no other spirit excepting to do the will of the Father. "Because I seek not mine own will, but the will of the Father which hath sent me." John 5: 30. "I do always those things that please him." John 8: 29.

Then, if we are Christ's, we MUST have the Spirit of Christ, and if we have the Spirit of Christ we WILL be found seeking his will, and doing the things that please him. There is no possibility of dodging the command, "Go ye, therefore;" no possibility of shirking responsibility by hiding behind the church or church officers. The all-penetrating eyes of God will as

surely find us, as they did Adam when he tried to shirk responsibility by hiding among the trees.

It is sad, but true, that we are too often found hiding behind the church or church officers.

When there is duty to perform, the efforts of all the members are required. Especially does this apply to us in the Sunday-school work. We may be earnest advocates of the Sunday-school until a Sunday-school is organized with Bro. A. as Superintendent, and Bro. B, Secretary, etc., then, perhaps, by our actions we say to those officers, "Go ye, therefore." Because you have been elected, therefore go ye and do this work, while we recline in our easy chairs, entertaining company, or visiting neighbors.

Behold the contrast between what we are, and what Christ intended we should be when he said, "As my Father hath sent me, even so I send you."

Right here I think we find the most important duty of the minister in his relation to the Sunday-school,—to keep the members alive and awakened, that we may be made to feel and realize the weight of responsibility that is resting upon us.

The spiritual slumbering and deadness in the church would not exist if we could all be sufficiently aroused and enlivened to heed Paul's admonition, "Awake thou that sleepest, and arise from the dead, and Christ shall give thee light." Eph. 5: 14.

Here we see the necessity of the minister using his utmost endeavors to awaken those that are spiritually asleep, to call to life those that are spiritually dead. When the individual becomes wrapped in spiritual slumber, or chilled in spiritual death, he cannot feel or realize his individual responsibility, and no amount of preaching to the church is likely to awaken or enliven him. But he must be preached to individually,—the responsibility incumbent upon him by the "Go ye, therefore" must be brought vividly to his understanding; then we may hope to see him discharge his individual duty. When each member is found discharging his duty, the church will be found discharging *her* whole duty, and the Sunday-school will be recognized only as a part of the church work, but also an important part of each individual's work. The "Go ye, therefore" will be the watch-word of every true Christian believer, prompting him to verify and exemplify, "As my Father hath sent me, even so send I you."

Waterloo, Iowa.

═══════════════════════════

The Gospel Messenger

Is the recognized organ of the German Baptist or Brethren's church, and advocates the faith of doctrine taught in the New Testament and pleads for a return to apostolic and primitive Christianity.

It recognizes the New Testament as the only infallible rule of faith and practice, and maintains that Faith toward God, Repentance from dead works, Regeneration of the heart and mind, baptism by Trine Immersion for remission of sins unto the reception of the Holy Ghost by the laying on of hands, are the means of adoption into the household of God,—the church militant.

It also maintains that Feet-washing, as taught in John 13, both by example and command of Jesus, should be observed in the church.

That the Lord's Supper, instituted by Christ and as universally observed by the apostles and the early Christians, is a full meal, and, in connection with the Communion, should be taken in the evening or after the close of the day.

That the Salutation of the Holy Kiss, or Kiss of Charity, is binding upon the followers of Christ.

That War and Retaliation are contrary to the spirit and self-denying principles of the religion of Jesus Christ.

That the principle of Plain Dressing and of Non-conformity to the world, as taught in the New Testament, should be observed by the followers of Christ.

That the Scriptural duty of Anointing the Sick with Oil, in the Name of the Lord, James 5: 14, is binding upon all Christians.

It also advocates the church's duty to support Missionary and Tract Work, thus giving to the Lord for the spread of the Gospel and for the conversion of sinners.

In short, it is a vindicator of all that Christ and the apostles have enjoined upon us, and shows, amid the conflicting theories and discords of modern Christendom, to point out ground that all must concede to be infallibly safe.

☞ The above principles of our Fraternity are set forth on our "Brethren's Envelopes." Use them! Price, 15 cents per package; 40 cents per hundred.

close of his life. About twelve years ago his wife died, leaving him with a family of children to care for. His family was very sickly and he met with reverses until he lost his farm. The loss of his wife, some of his children, and then his farm, was a sore trial for him, interfering much with his studies and work in the ministry. His wife died in March. In the fall of the same year he was elected President of the Ashland College (Ohio), to which place he removed his little family, and remained eighteen months.

September 15, 1881 he married sister Emma Norris, of Maryland, who has since been a faithful companion to him. In the Spring of 1882 he moved on a farm near North Manchester, Ind., where he labored very hard, both mentally and physically. It is said that he was as good a farmer as he was a preacher. He had the reputation of being one of the best farmers in that part of the country. During this time he was active and earnest in church work, did much able preaching, and held several public discussions requiring rare skill and learning.

Failing health, however, caused him to retire from the farm a few years ago. He lived a while in the City of North Manchester, and then located near the Brethren's large meeting-house, west of the city, where he had intended to make his home during the remainder of his earthly life.

Bro. Miller served a number of times on the Standing Committee, and very extensively on other committees. He was also Moderator of the Annual Meeting at Broadway, Va., in 1879. He was one of the ablest counselors in the church, and always stood firm for the principles of the church. We always knew just where to find him. There was no uncertain sound about anything he wrote or said. In the very beginning of his Christian career he unreservedly adopted the principles of the Brethren church, and unflinchingly maintained them until the close of his life. It seems that he never entertained any doubts concerning the church being founded upon the true principles of Christianity, as set forth by Christ and the apostles. When it came to defending the principles of the church be never knew what it was to flinch.

As a preacher he possessed rare gifts, and has for years been regarded as the ablest doctrinal preacher in the Brotherhood. He had not only a clear understanding of the Scriptures, but had the ability to make it clear to the minds of others. When preaching, he never lost sight of his subject. He never wandered. He always had clear, well-defined points before him, and bent all his energies to get them well fixed in the minds of his hearers. Few men put more work on their sermons than did Bro. Miller. He has been known to work for weeks on one discourse, with a view of not only getting the truths of the Scriptures well fixed in his memory, but to so arrange his subject that his hearers would be both edified and instructed.

He was exceedingly anxious about the discourse that he was to have delivered at Mt. Morris. He had put much work on it, and he remained well, no doubt would have given us a most interesting series of discourses. While on his death-bed, he expressed his great regrets that he was not permitted to finish his discourses. But we all feel that during his sickness here we have learned lessons in patience, godliness, piety and trust that will greatly aid us all through our Christian career.

It was, perhaps, as a debater that Bro. Miller showed his greatest ability. He probably held no less than twelve public discussions, some of them lasting as long as eight days. He held two discussions with Aaron Walker, a Disciple minister, thoroughly schooled in the art of debating. He also held a debate with a minister by the name of Jowell, another in Virginia, one in Southern Missouri, and one with Daniel Sommer, in Ray County, Missouri. This was his last discussion, and the only one that was fully reported and published. He also went to Southern Illinois to hold a discussion, but the other parties withdrew their man when they discovered Bro. Miller's ability. He held other discussions, of which we have no special information at this time. As a debater he was always cool and always ready. He was never known to become excited or to flinch. He always entered these discussions well prepared, made but few points and they were always his very best, and he defended them to the last. As a defender of the faith he was as bold as a lion, and yet as gentle as a lamb. He happily combined the rare elements of strength, firmness and goodness. As a debater, he probably never had an equal among us.

Bro. Miller was also a good writer, and has left behind him some productions that will always be highly prized by our people. His book, entitled "The Doctrine of the Brethren Defended," will always remain a standard work among us. As a defense of some of our doctrine, it is not excelled by any work written by any of our Brethren. He also occupied a position on the editorial staff of the *Brethren at Work*, and did much very able writing for that journal. At the time of his death he was on the Advisory Committee of the MESSENGER, where his name still remains. While Bro. Miller was a good writer, he was never in love with the pen. He rather dreaded to write, and that is probably why he has not written more for publication. His writings were always sought after, and he has been many times requested to write some books, containing his ripest thoughts, but somehow he never got at it. He preferred to talk rather than to write.

By his first wife Bro. Miller had eight children, the most of whom are dead. With sister Emma Miller he leaves four children, all bright boys, on whose shoulders, it is to be hoped, the mantle of the father may some day fall. Sister Miller, in her bereavement, has the prayers and sympathies of this entire community, and as this article is read, we feel that the united prayers of all our readers will go up in her behalf. It was a hard experience for her to leave three children at home in Indiana, to come here and see her husband die away from home. But she bore her affliction bravely, and we feel that God is sustaining her in these sore trials that have come to her home.

On Wednesday morning, at 8:30, memorial services were held over the remains in the College Chapel, conducted by brethren D. L. Miller and J. G. Royer. The services were very impressive, and left lasting impressions on the minds of the hundreds who filled the Chapel. At the close all were permitted to take a last look at all that was mortal of Bro. R. H. Miller. The remains were then sent to North Manchester, Ind., accompanied by sister Miller, brethren D. L. Miller and J. G. Royer and their wives. It was Bro. Miller's request that he might be buried in the Brethren's cemetery at North Manchester. Thus ended the days of a good and useful man, who will long be remembered as one of the ablest men with which our Brotherhood has ever been blessed.   J. H. M.

EDITORIAL WANDERINGS IN THE OLD WORLD.

BY D. L. MILLER.

Number Twenty.—Gleanings from Our Note-Book.

IN our wanderings from place to place, we jotted down each day, impressions made on the mind by passing events and occurrences, and this letter will be devoted to some of the entries found in our note-book.

A dear brother writing to us, after expressing, in kind words the interest taken in our wanderings, says, "I almost envy you the privileges you enjoy of seeing so much of the Old World." We thought of the words of our brother, and then we took a look at the other side, for journeying in a foreign land has two sides, as well as most all other things in this world, and we put it in this way: To leave a comfortable home, with a host of kind, loving friends, in whose society there is constant enjoyment; to leave church privileges, above all the blessed privilege of meeting in public worship with those of like precious faith; to brave the storms and dangers of a long ocean voyage; to endure the discomforts of hotel life; to meet no face with which you are familiar, or people who have a common interest with you; to sojourn with those who speak in an unknown tongue, to be, in the fullest sense of the term, strangers in a strange land; to feel the anxiety, when sickness comes, so far away from home, with no friend near to comfort and cheer the wanderers,—all these things are to be placed over against the sight-seeing, and we set it down, after having had considerable experience along this line, as our sober conclusion, that there is *no place like home.*

Our notes say that one of the saddest sights we saw in London, was a woman staggering along the streets in a state of intoxication. We saw women in other parts of Europe hitched with dogs to carts; we saw them dragging harrows across ploughed fields, but this did not touch our heart, as did the sight of the drunken woman of London. We have always given women a high place in the world, and have had a high appreciation of her worth and influence. After due reflection, at a time of life when mere sentiment enters not so largely into an estimate of the formative influences upon my own life, I set it down as my best judgment, that whatever good in the end may come of my having lived in this world, is largely due to the influence of two of the nearest and dearest friends I have ever known,—wife and mother. The one has long since gone to her rich reward, the other is still with me, my constant companion in all my wanderings, my ever-ready helper in time of need, in the fullest and truest sense of the word, my better half. How it saddens the heart to see a woman reeling from the dram shop! And why not? Does she not have the same right to drink, chew and smoke that her brother does? Abstractly the answer is yes, but we do thank God that a woman is so much purer, so much truer, and so much better in every way, that she stands immeasurably above man in these things. But when she does fall from her high place, what a fall there is!

At Paris we spent several days in the Louvre, examining the ancient relics brought from Egypt, Nineveh and Babylon. In many respects it is superior to the collection in the British Museum. In one department is a wall, built of glazed brick, taken from an old palace in Nineveh,

close of his life. About twelve years ago his wife died, leaving him with a family of children to care for. His family was very sickly and he met with reverses until he lost his farm. The loss of his wife, some of his children, and then his farm, was a sore trial for him, interfering much with his studies and work in the ministry. His wife died in March. In the fall of the same year he was elected President of the Ashland College (Ohio), to which place he removed his little family, and remained eighteen months.

September 15, 1881 he married sister Emma Norris, of Maryland, who has since been a faithful companion to him. In the Spring of 1882 he moved on a farm near North Manchester, Ind., where he labored very hard, both mentally and physically. It is said that he was as good a farmer as he was a preacher. He had the reputation of being one of the best farmers in that part of the country. During this time he was active and earnest in church work, did much able preaching, and held several public discussions requiring rare skill and learning.

Failing health, however, caused him to retire from the farm a few years ago. He lived a while in the City of North Manchester, and then located near the Brethren's large meeting-house, west of the city, where he had intended to make his home during the remainder of his earthly life.

Bro. Miller served a number of times on the Standing Committee, and very extensively on other committees. He was also Moderator of the Annual Meeting at Broadway, Va., in 1879. He was one of the ablest counselors in the church, and always stood firm for the principles of the church. We always knew just where to find him. There was no uncertain sound about anything he wrote or said. In the very beginning of his Christian career he unreservedly adopted the principles of the Brethren church, and unflinchingly maintained them until the close of his life. It seems that he never entertained any doubts concerning the church being founded upon the true principles of Christianity, as set forth by Christ and the apostles. When it came to defending the principles of the church he never knew what it was to flinch.

As a preacher he possessed rare gifts, and has for years been regarded as the ablest doctrinal preacher in the Brotherhood. He had not only a clear understanding of the Scriptures, but had the ability to make it clear to the minds of others. When preaching, he never lost sight of his subject. He never wandered. He always had clear, well-defined points before him, and bent all his energies to get them well fixed in the minds of his hearers. Few men put more work on their sermons than did Bro. Miller. He has been known to work for weeks on one discourse, with a view of not only getting the truths of the Scriptures well fixed in his memory, but to so arrange his subject that his hearers would be both edified and instructed.

He was exceedingly anxious about the discourse that he was to have delivered at Mt. Morris. He had put much work on them, and, had he remained well, no doubt would have given us a most interesting series of discourses. While on his death-bed, he expressed his great regrets that he was not permitted to finish his discourses. But we all feel that during his sickness here we have learned lessons in patience, godliness, piety and trust that will greatly aid us all through our Christian career.

It was, perhaps, as a debater that Bro. Miller showed his greatest ability. He probably held no less than twelve public discussions, some of them lasting as long as eight days. He held two discussions with Aaron Walker, a Disciple minister, thoroughly schooled in the art of debating. He also held a debate with a minister by the name of Jewell, another in Virginia, one in Southern Missouri, and one with Daniel Sommer, in Ray County, Missouri. This was his last discussion, and the only one that was fully reported and published. He also went to Southern Illinois to hold a discussion, but the other parties withdrew their man when they discovered Bro. Miller's ability. He held other discussions, of which we have no special information at this time. As a debater he was always cool and always ready. He was never known to become excited or to flinch. He always entered these discussions well prepared, made but few points and they were always his very best, and he defended them to the last. As a defender of the faith he was as bold as a lion, and yet as gentle as a lamb. He happily combined the rare elements of strength, firmness and goodness. As a debater, he probably never had an equal among us.

Bro. Miller was also a good writer, and has left behind him some productions that will always be highly prized by our people. His book, entitled "The Doctrine of the Brethren Defended," will always remain a standard work among us. As a defense of some of our doctrine, it is not excelled by any work written by any of our Brethren. He also occupied a position on the editorial staff of the *Brethren at Work*, and did much very able writing for that journal. At the time of his death he was a member of the Advisory Committee of the MESSENGER, where his name still remains. While Bro. Miller was a good writer, he was never in love with the pen. He rather dreaded to write, and that is probably why he has not written more for publication. His writings were always sought after, and he has been many times requested to write some books, containing his ripest thoughts, but somehow he never got at it. He preferred to talk rather than to write.

By his first wife Bro. Miller had eight children, the most of whom are dead. With sister Emma Miller he leaves four children, all bright boys, on whose shoulders, it is to be hoped, the mantle of the father may some day fall. Sister Miller, in her bereavement has the prayers and sympathies of this entire community, and as this article is read, we feel that the united prayers of all our readers will go up in her behalf. It was a hard experience for her to leave three children at home in Indiana, to come here and see her husband die away from home. But she bore her affliction bravely, and we feel that God is sustaining her in these sore trials that have come to her home.

On Wednesday morning, at 8:30, memorial services were held over the remains in the College Chapel, conducted by brethren D. L. Miller and J. G. Royer. The services were very impressive, and left lasting impressions on the minds of the hundreds who filled the Chapel. At the close all were permitted to take a last look at all that was mortal of Bro. R. H. Miller. The remains were then sent to North Manchester, Ind., accompanied by sister Miller, brethren D. L. Miller and J. G. Royer and their wives. It was Bro. Miller's request that he might be buried in the Brethren's cemetery at North Manchester. Thus ended the days of a good and useful man, who will long be remembered as one of the ablest men with which our Brotherhood has ever been blessed.   J. H. M.

EDITORIAL WANDERINGS IN THE OLD WORLD.

BY D. L. MILLER.

Number Twenty.—Gleanings from Our Note-Book.

In our wanderings from place to place, we jotted down each day, impressions made on the mind by passing events and occurrences, and this letter will be devoted to some of the entries found in our note-book.

A dear brother writing to us, after expressing in kind words the interest taken in our wanderings, says, "I almost envy you the privileges you enjoy of seeing so much of the Old World." We thought of the words of our brother, and then we took a look at the other side, for journeying in a foreign land has two sides, as well as most all other things in this world, and we put it in this way: To leave a comfortable home, with a host of kind, loving friends, in whose society there is constant enjoyment; to leave church privileges, above all the blessed privilege of meeting in public worship with those of like precious faith; to brave the storms and dangers of a long ocean voyage; to endure the discomforts of hotel life; to meet no face with which you are familiar, or people who have a common interest with you; to sojourn with those who speak in an unknown tongue, to be, in the fullest sense of the term, strangers in a strange land; to feel the anxiety, when sickness comes, so far away from home, with no friend near to comfort and cheer the wanderers,—all these things are to be placed over against the sight-seeing, and we set it down, after having had considerable experience along this line, as our sober conclusion, that there is *no place like home.*

Our notes say that one of the saddest sights we saw in London, was a woman staggering along the streets in a state of intoxication. We saw women in other parts of Europe hitched with dogs to carts; we saw them dragging harrows across ploughed fields, but this did not touch our heart, as did the sight of the drunken woman of London. We have always given women a high place in the world, and have had a high appreciation of her worth and influence. After due reflection, at a time of life when mere sentiment enters not so largely into an estimate of the formative influences upon my own life, I set it down as my best judgment, that whatever good in the end may come of my having lived in this world, is largely due to the influence of two of the nearest and dearest friends I have ever known,—wife and mother. The one has long since gone to her rich reward, the other is still with me, my constant companion in all my wanderings, my ever-ready helper in time of need, in the fullest and truest sense of the word, my better half. How it saddens the heart to see a woman reeling from the dram shop! And why not? Does she not have the same right to face, chew and smoke that her brother does? Abstractly the answer is yes, but we do thank God, that she is so much purer, so much truer, and so much better in every way, that she stands immeasurably above man in these things. But when she does fall from her high place, what a fall there is!

At Paris we spent several days in the Louvre, examining the ancient relics brought from Egypt, Nineveh and Babylon. In many respects it is superior to the collection in the British Museum. In one department is a wall, built of glazed brick, taken from an old palace in Nineveh,

to hear of the good work prospering. But if *all* God's dear people would only live holy lives, and take more interest in church work, how much more good might be done for our Heavenly Father's cause!

Bro. Joseph Long came to the Aughwick congregation in February, and preached for us eight sermons in all. As a result, members who attended, received a rich, spiritual feast and were built up and made stronger, and encouraged to work for the Master, while those who could, and did not attend, lost a golden opportunity to hear good preaching, and to obtain rich spiritual food. The attendance was not so good,—perhaps mainly on account of unfavorable weather and bad roads. Brethren, this ought not so to be. If a good brother leaves his home interests and his family, and comes many miles to labor for a church, and travels through mud, wet, and cold, to speak the Word of Truth, surely the membership ought to attend!

There were no additions at this time, but we think some were seriously considering the matter of turning from darkness to light. Our brother preached two strong sermons, on "Building of Character" and "The Reason we are Dunkards." We trust the good seed sown may yet bring forth much fruit to the honor and glory of God, and the salvation of souls, and that our brother may yet turn many to righteousness, to shine as the stars forever and ever in the saints' everlasting rest.   T. O. CLOYD.

Feb. 25.

From the Ridge Church, Highland County, Ohio.

A SERIES of meetings was begun at this place Jan. 30. It was carried on for one week by the home ministers. Bro. Geo. Wilkins, of Hollowtown, Ohio, then came and continued the meetings two weeks longer, closing Feb. 21.

The brethren and sisters all seemed to have the spirit of work, and the most of them took great interest in the meetings. Five dear souls were received by the holy ordinance of baptism, and eight, that had wandered away into the by-paths of sin, were brought back and welcomed into the fold. There are three applicants to be baptized in the near future. As a congregation we have many failures, and we fall far short of what we should be. But I pray the Lord that we may go forward and come nearer to the Great Exemplar. Our weekly prayer-meeting, which had been discontinued, has been re-established. May it continue and do much good!

Arrangements have been made to repair and improve our church-house, and in this work our Brethren show a commendable zeal.

                              ALBERT P. REED.
Feb. 23.

From the Libertyville Church, Jefferson County, Iowa.

ON Saturday, Feb. 20, we held our quarterly council at the Pleasant Hill church. We were glad to see so many of our members present. It shows that they have a zeal for the progress of the church. A considerable amount of business came before the meeting, which was disposed of seemingly to the satisfaction of all present. We have two church-houses, hence have quarterly meeting every six weeks. During the three years that I have lived here, and labored for the church, I have never heard an unkind word spoken in all of our deliberations.

At our last meeting Bro. James Glotfelty was elected as delegate to District Meeting. He will carry a request from this church to District Meeting. Though we have been laboring in love together as Brethren, yet ye cannot report as many accessions to the church as some of our sister churches. During the past year we have had

eight additions by confession and baptism. We have appointed May 27 for our Communion, commencing at 4 P. M., and to continue over Sunday. Brethren contemplating attending Annual Meeting, and passing over the Rock Island R. R., will please stop and preach for us. We will meet them at Libertyville if notified of their coming.

                              ABRAHAM WOLFE.
Feb. 22.

At Home Again.

HOME is a short word but carries with it a very extensive meaning. It has been my privilege to dwell in many pleasant homes during the last four months, spent in the service of my Master. It is useless to mention names, for they are many and I hope all feel that I did appreciate their kindness.

I arrived home Feb. 22, very much in need of rest, having spent the last two weeks with the Lancaster City congregation. I feel deeply interested in the little flock at that place, they having lately organized. This is much to their advantage. To build up a church in the City requires persistent work. The Lancaster City brethren and sisters seem to understand their situation, and realize the responsibility. By their united efforts and the proper encouragement from the adjoining churches, they certainly will succeed in building up a strong congregation. I hope the time is not far distant when the country churches will take a deep interest in the city mission work. The Lancaster City church is in need of a faithful minister. Eld. S. R. Zug, of Mastersonville, Pa., has charge of the church, and is much interested in the cause. He is anxious to have a ministering brother (sound in the faith) locate in the city. There is an opportunity to do a good work. The city is large, and a great field for the Master is white already to harvest. The brethren and sisters are plain and hospitable, and in full sympathy with the general Brotherhood. May God's choicest blessings ever attend the brethren and sisters of Lancaster City.

As stated, I arrived home Feb. 22 and found our brethren busy at work for the Master. Eld. S. R. Zug, of Mastersonville, Pa., was conducting a series of interesting meetings on the south side of Jacob Hollinger and Bro. Samuel M. Stouffer (our home brethren) were conducting a series of interesting meetings on the north side of our congregation, with five applicants for baptism at this date, and more expected.   ALBERT HOLLINGER.
Huntsdale, Pa.

From Tropico, Cal.

THE writer is still trying to tell the old story of salvation to every one who will accept of it upon the conditions of the Master. The people of this country seem to enjoy hearing of salvation by Christ, and also expect you to cite the hearer to the Bible. But, judging from indications, one would be inclined to the idea, that they would enjoy it fully as well, if the preacher would forbear itemizing too closely. The special duties, as required of man, when applied to the ordinances of the Lord's house, would better be left out, if you want all men to speak well of you.

We are very glad, however, to say that we find faithful representatives of the Gospel principles among the members in this valley (San Fernando). They have much to encounter in setting up the peculiarities of our people. This is, by no means, a proof that these principles are contrary to the Gospel. For Paul says, "The natural man receiveth not the things of the Spirit of God." 1 Cor. 2: 14. We need not be at any

loss to determine the case. Just let us inquire who it is that objects to the Gospel ordinances, and also to the rules and usages of the church, and we will always find it is the natural man that offers the objections. A little more conversion would be a good remedy in such cases. A little more crucifying of the world unto us, and of self unto the world, is needed all along the line. We ought all to examine our titles very carefully. A mistake in the matter of salvation is of too much importance for us to be indifferent about it. We must not entertain the idea, that, because we are in the church, therefore our passport to heaven is genuine.

On the night of Feb. 23 there was a very considerable earthquake shock felt here. Many people were very much alarmed over it, but when the great earthquake shall come, which will shake heaven also, then will be the time which will cause a mighty quaking among the children of men. "Blessed are they that do his commandments, that they may have right to the tree of life, and may enter in through the gates into the city." Rev. 22: 14. If we have a title of that kind, we are safe, in whatever country we may be; and if we have not, then again, it matters not in what country we may be found, we cannot enter the state of the saved. The great masses seem to be seeking earthly titles and crowns, such as earth can give.

It is my intention to try to be at home, any way, by April 10. Then I hope to be able to work some on Kansas soil. From several places there have been calls for preaching, — some in towns and some in the country. It is not likely that a series of meetings can be conducted at that time of the year, unless it might be in towns. I think of starting on my way toward the place of Annual Meeting, probably as soon as the early part of May, provided there are openings to work on the road, either the Union Pacific or Rock Island R. R. Should there be such places, please notify me at McPherson, Kans, sometime during the month of April. I do not want to be idle.

                              A. HUTCHISON.
Feb. 25.

From the Donald's Creek Church, Ohio.

BRO. G. L. STUDABAKER commenced a series of meetings in New Carlisle, Feb. 14. The meetings were interesting from the start. Owing to my absence from home, I was not able to attend the three first meetings. When I arrived I found the house well filled each evening with eager listeners. Thus the meetings continued for two weeks. Feb. 27 I had to leave for other fields. Up to that time three precious souls had already been baptized, to walk in newness of life. Another young lady made application to be baptized yesterday. I feel that our meetings were food to the soul. Our house was so crowded that the church concluded to build a new house, so that the people of New Carlisle could be accommodated. We hope by the time we hold another series of meetings, we will have a house large enough to seat all that may come. Should we not live to see it, may the Lord bless the work, to make more room, and encourage those that are willing to give of their means to the spreading of the Gospel, in building churches, and every other lawful way!

When I last communicated to your paper, I was laboring with the Brethren in the Mississinewa church, Ind. I closed my labors at said church on the evening of Feb. 14. While there were no immediate accessions to the church, the meeting will, I hope, be one that will result in much good.

Perhaps some are ready to ask, "Why did not Bro. Studabaker preach at home and Bro. Frantz likewise? Would that not have been just as

to hear of the good work prospering. But if *all* God's dear people would only live holy lives, and take more interest in church work, how much more good might be done for our Heavenly Father's cause!

Bro. Joseph Long came to the Aughwick congregation in February, and preached for us eight sermons in all. As a result, members who attended, received a rich, spiritual feast and were built up and made stronger, and encouraged to work for the Master, while those who could, and did not attend, lost a golden opportunity to hear good preaching, and to obtain rich spiritual food. The attendance was not so good,—perhaps mainly on account of unfavorable weather and bad roads. Brethren, this ought not so to be. If a good brother leaves his home interests and his family, and comes many miles to labor for a church, and travels through mud, wet, and cold, to speak the Word of Truth, surely the membership ought to attend!

There were no additions at this time, but we think some were seriously considering the matter of turning from darkness to light. Our brother preached two strong sermons, on "Building of Character" and "The Reason we are Dunkards." We trust the good seed sown may yet bring forth much fruit to the honor and glory of God, and the salvation of souls, and that our brother may yet turn many to righteousness, to shine as the stars forever and ever in the saints' everlasting rest.　　T. O. CLOYD.

Feb. 25.

From the Ridge Church, Highland County, Ohio.

A SERIES of meetings was begun at this place Jan. 30. It was carried on for one week by the home ministers. Bro. Geo. Wilkins, of Hollowtown, Ohio, then came and continued the meetings two weeks longer, closing Feb. 21.

The brethren and sisters all seemed to have the spirit of work, and the most of them took great interest in the meetings. Five dear souls were received by the holy ordinance of baptism, and eight, that had wandered away into the by-paths of sin, were brought back and welcomed into the fold. There are three applicants to be baptized in the near future. As a congregation we have many failures, and we fall far short of what we should be. But I pray the Lord that we may go forward and come nearer to the Great Exemplar. Our weekly prayer-meeting, which had been discontinued, has been re-established. May it continue and do much good!

Arrangements have been made to repair and improve our church-house, and in this work our Brethren show a commendable zeal.

ALBERT P. REED.

Feb. 23.

From the Libertyville Church, Jefferson County, Iowa.

ON Saturday, Feb. 20, we held our quarterly council at the Pleasant Hill church. We were glad to see so many of our members present. It shows that they have a zeal for the progress of the church. A considerable amount of business came before the meeting, which was disposed of seemingly to the satisfaction of all present. We have two church-houses, hence have quarterly meeting every six weeks. During the three years that I have lived here, and labored for the church, I have never heard an unkind word spoken in all of our deliberations.

At our last meeting Bro. James Glotfelty was elected as delegate to District Meeting. He will carry a request from this church to District Meeting. Though we have been laboring in love together as Brethren, yet we cannot report as many accessions to the church as some of our sister churches. During the past year we have had

eight additions by confession and baptism. We have appointed May 27 for our Communion, commencing at 4 P. M., and to continue over Sunday. Brethren contemplating attending Annual Meeting, and passing over the Rock Island R. R., will please stop and preach for us. We will meet them at Libertyville if notified of their coming.

ABRAHAM WOLFE.

Feb. 22.

At Home Again.

HOME is a short word but carries with it a very extensive meaning. It has been my privilege to dwell in many pleasant homes during the last four months, spent in the service of my Master. It is useless to mention names, for they are many and I hope all feel that I did appreciate their kindness.

I arrived home Feb. 22, very much in need of rest, having spent the last two weeks with the Lancaster City congregation. I feel deeply interested in the little flock at that place, they having lately organized. This is much to their advantage. To build up a church in the City requires persistent work. The Lancaster City brethren and sisters seem to understand their situation, and realize the responsibility. By their united efforts and the proper encouragement from the adjoining churches, they certainly will succeed in building up a strong congregation. I hope the time is not far distant when the country churches will take a deep interest in the city mission work. The Lancaster City church is in need of a faithful minister. Eld. S. R. Zug, of Mastersonville, Pa., has charge of the church, and is much interested in the cause. He is anxious to have a ministering brother (sound in the faith) locate in the city. There is an opportunity to do a good work. The city is large, and a great field for the Master is white already to harvest. The brethren and sisters are plain and hospitable, and in full sympathy with the general Brotherhood. May God's choicest blessings ever attend the brethren and sisters of Lancaster City.

As stated, I arrived home Feb. 22 and found our brethren busy at work for the Master. Eld. S. R. Zug, of Mastersonville, Pa., was conducting a series of interesting meetings on the south side of our congregation, and at the same time Eld. Jacob Hollinger and Bro. Samuel M. Stouffer (our home brethren) were conducting a series of interesting meetings on the north side of our congregation, with five applicants for baptism at this date, and more expected. ALBERT HOLLINGER.

Huntsdale, Pa.

From Tropico, Cal.

THE writer is still trying to tell the old story of salvation to every one who will accept of it upon the conditions of the Master. The people of this country seem to enjoy hearing of salvation by Christ, and also expect you to cite the hearer to the Bible. But, judging from indications, one would be inclined to the idea, that they would enjoy it fully as well, if the preacher would forbear itemizing too closely. The special duties, as required of man, when applied to the ordinances of the Lord's house, would better be left out, if you want all men to speak well of you.

We are very glad, however, to say that we find very faithful representatives of the Gospel principles among the members in this valley (San Fernando). They have much to encounter in setting up the peculiarities of our people. This is, by no means, a proof that these principles are contrary to the Gospel. For Paul says, "The natural man receiveth not the things of the Spirit of God." 1 Cor. 2: 14. We need not be at any

loss to determine the case. Just let us inquire who it is that objects to the Gospel ordinances, and also to the rules and usages of the church, and we will always find it is the natural man that offers the objections. A little more conversion would be a good remedy in such cases. A little more crucifying of the world unto us, and of self unto the world, is needed all along the line. We ought all to examine our titles very carefully. A mistake in the matter of salvation is of too much importance for us to be indifferent about it. We must not entertain the idea, that, because we are in the church, therefore our passport to heaven is genuine.

On the night of Feb. 23 there was a very considerable earthquake shock felt here. Many people were very much alarmed over it, but when the great earthquake shall come, which will shake heaven also, then will be the time which will cause a mighty quaking among the children of men. "Blessed are they that do his commandments, that they may have right to the tree of life, and may enter in through the gates into the city." Rev. 22: 14. If we have a title of that kind, we are safe, in whatever country we may be; and if we have not, then again, it matters not in what country we may be found, we cannot enter the state of the saved. The great masses seem to be seeking earthly titles and crowns, such as earth can give.

It is my intention to try to be at home, any way, by April 10. Then I hope to be able to work some on Kansas soil. From several places there have been calls for preaching,— some in towns and some in the country. It is not like-ly that a series of meetings can be conducted at that time of the year, unless it might be in towns. I think of starting on my way toward the place of Annual Meeting, probably as soon as the early part of May, provided there are openings to work on the road, either the Union Pacific or Rock Island R. R. Should there be such places, please notify me at McPherson, Kans., sometime during the month of April. I do not want to be idle.

A. HUTCHISON.

Feb. 25.

From the Donald's Creek Church, Ohio.

BRO. G. L. STUDABAKER commenced a series of meetings in New Carlisle, Feb. 14. The meetings were interesting from the start. Owing to my absence from home, I was not able to attend the three first meetings. When I arrived I found the house well filled each evening with eager listeners. Thus the meetings continued for two weeks. Feb. 27 I had to leave for other fields. Up to that time three precious souls had already been baptized, to walk in newness of life. Another young lady made application to be baptized yesterday. I feel that our meetings were food to the soul. Our house was so crowded that the church concluded to build a new house, so that the people of New Carlisle could be accommodated. We hope by the time we hold another series of meetings, we will have a house large enough to seat all that may come. Should we not live to see it, may the Lord bless the work, to make more room, and encourage those that are willing to give of their means to the spreading of the Gospel, in building churches, and every other lawful way!

When I last communicated to your paper, I was laboring with the Brethren in the Mississinewa church, Ind. I closed my labors at said church on the evening of Feb. 14. While there were no immediate accessions to the church, the meeting will, I hope, be one that will result in much good. Perhaps some are ready to ask, "Why did not Bro. Studabaker preach at home and Bro. Frantz likewise? Would that not have been just as

attention. We hope new tracts upon live topics will be presented and those, especially assigned by the committee, at Hagerstown, to certain writers. The time and place of committee meeting will be given later.

By order of Foreman,
I. D, PARKER, Sec.

From the Pine Creek Congregation, Ill.

FEB. 14 we commenced a series of meetings in Polo. Bro. Geo. Zollars preached nine sermons in all to very attentive congregations and we hope his labor may be the means of bringing some nearer to God, as well as strengthening those that have already made choice of the good part.

Bro. D. L. Miller came to us on the evening of Feb. 22, and, after preaching one sermon for us, commenced a series of Bible Talks,—five in all, which were not only interesting but very instructive, and, we believe, a means of reaching the minds of many that could not be reached in any other way. By these Talks many points of doubt were removed from the minds of the hearers. The house was filled to its fullest capacity, and the last evening some returned to their homes because they could not be accommodated with seats. Bro. Miller gives these Bible Talks free, so that no one need be deprived of hearing them, and the Lord will surely reward him for his labors. At the close of these Talks the opportunity was given to all to make a free-will offering for the Russian sufferers, and a liberal amount was raised for that purpose.　　·C· FARRNEY.

Notice to the Brethren of Kansas and Nebraska.

THE annual meeting of the Brethren's Mutual Aid and Insurance Association will be held in the Olathe church, Johnson Co., Kans., April 14, the day following District Meeting.

B. S. KATHERMAN, Sec.

Notes from Our Correspondents.

"As cold water to a thirsty soul, so is good news from a far country."

New Lebanon, Ohio.—One was restored to church fellowship in the Wolf Creek church Feb. 25, at a most harmonious council-meeting.—*Jno. Calvin Bright, March 3.*

Bremen, Ind.—March 5 we met in council at the Brick church. It passed off pleasantly. The congregation was small on account of a funeral in the District. Bro. J. Kauffman was selected as delegate for Annual Meeting.—*Simon P. Eversole.*

Long Meadow, Md.—Since my last report five more have united with the church, making, in all, seventeen, as the result of our series of meetings, previously reported. May the Lord help them to daily reflect the image of Christ, that they may be a light to the world!—*John Rowland, March 2.*

Wanted.—The address of Daniel Fouts. Any one who can give the desired information, will favor the church here and Bro. Fouts. The last heard of Bro. Fouts, he was at or near Fremont, Nebr., staying, I think, with his brothers, Solomon and Samuel. Address any information to J. R. Leatherman, Conway Springs, Kans.

La Place, Ill.—The members of the Okaw church held their quarterly meeting to-day. All business passed off pleasantly. Three letters of membership were given. One was received by letter. We decided to commence our Sunday-school in April. We appointed a Communion meeting for June 2, at 4 P. M. Bro. Eli Wolfe was appointed as solicitor for the District Endowment Fund.—*E. F. Wolfe, March 3.*

Peabody, Kans.—This church has just enjoyed a very pleasant council. Two 'came back to the church that had wandered away. May the good work go on! We also expect, the Lord willing, to hold a love-feast May 7, at 2 P. M.—*Katie Yost, March 3.*

Lacon, Ill.—By request I went to Johnson County, Iowa, March 1, and labored two weeks in the Palestine school-house. What the result of the meetings will be, the Lord only knows. This is a mission point in care of Bro. J. C. Seibert. We hope he may be able, by the help of the Lord, to build up a prosperous church at that place.—*C. S. Holsinger.*

South English, Iowa.—Our last quarterly council passed off Feb. 27, in the English River congregation, Keokuk Co., Iowa. Considerable business came before the church, but all was disposed of apparently harmoniously. The church made arrangements for some needed improvements on the old meeting-house in the near future. We hope it may be the means of furthering and enlarging God's kingdom. We are having very warm weather for this latitude at present. — *Peter Browar.*

Covington, Ohio.—A pleasant series of meetings was held in the Newton church at Pleasant Hill. Bro. I. D. Parker, of Ashland, Ohio, came to our assistance Feb. 6, and remained until the 23rd, when he had to leave us rather unexpectedly, to attend to some matter of importance at home. The meeting was interesting and largely attended throughout, and we were sorry to have it stop when it did. Bro. Parker did his part of the work well. Two were baptized and others, we think, are near the kingdom.—*D. D. Wine.*

Pleasant Valley, Va.—Bro. S. N. McCann began a series of meetings for us Feb. 3 and continued until Feb. 10, preaching, in all, nine sermons. The meetings were well attended, and the Word of God faithfully delivered. While there were no additions, some were made to see the error of their way, and on Sunday, Feb. 21, two precious young souls gave their hearts to Jesus, and were buried with him in baptism. May they ever prove bright and shining lights! Others are as one of old,—almost persuaded.—*Sarah Click, Weyer's Cave, Va.*

Pipe Creek Church, Ind.—We commenced a series of meetings on the evening of Jan. 12, and closed Jan. 24, with a good interest, Bro. Amsey Puterbaugh, of Oswego, Ind., did the preaching. He delivered seventeen sermons in all. There were no additions to the church, but, we think, much good was done to both members and outsiders. Quite a number of our members could not attend the meetings on account of La Grippe. Bro. Puterbaugh shunned not to declare all the counsel of God. He is an able expounder of the Gospel. May the Lord ever be with him!—*D. H. Long.*

Sawyer, Kans.—Bro. Brubaker commenced meetings at the Liberty school-house, five miles west of Sawyer, Jan. 26, and continued until the 31st, with good attendance and attention, but no accessions. Bro. Brubaker commenced another meeting, four and one-half miles north-west of Sawyer, Feb. 7, and continued until the 21st, with good interest. While there were no accessions, we hope that the good seed which may have its effect. May it be as bread cast upon the waters, to be gathered many days hence! Bro. Brubaker was assisted by Bro. Glick. Both are home ministers. I will further say that I have received a number of tracts and also a number of sample copies of the MESSENGER, for which I feel thankful. I distributed them to the best of my ability. I sent some to Massachusetts, where, I learn, the Brethren are not known.—*J. H. Miller.*

Avery, Mo.—The Spring Branch church met in council, Jan. 23, and held a choice for two ministers. The lot fell upon our dear young brethren, Barr E. Breshears and T. B. Ihrig. May the Lord give them grace that they may prove faithful to their high calling, and become workmen that need not be ashamed!—*R. S. Rust.*

Schuylkill, Pa.—Eld. H. A. Light came to us Feb. 8, and remained till Feb. 19, and preached fourteen sermons. The attendance was good. There were three additions by baptism. We have a substantial and convenient meeting-house and one preacher in the first degree. He is a good leader of the little flock, full of zeal and perseverance. Our two deacons assist in singing, exhorting and prayer, as liberty is given. Eld. J. Hartzler is our presiding elder.—*D. N. Yothers.*

Spring Run, Pa.—After the convalescence of the son of Eldr Michael Clear, Claysburgh, Blair Co., Pa., he returned to the Spring Run congregation, and preached thirteen sermons in the Pine Glen school-house; then came again to the Spring Run meeting-house and preached five sermons. Nineteen were baptized here, which have already been reported and there is one more applicant. The Dry Valley meetings, together with the ones here, make fifty-one sermons, with one week's intermission.—*Emma Bollinger, McVeytown, Pa.*

Lyons, Kans.—The Kansas Center church met in quarterly council Feb. 20. All business passed off pleasantly. Among the different items of business, delegates were chosen for District Meeting and a superintendent elected for our Sunday-school, which will open April 1. How enjoyable to the Christian to meet at God's house to do work for the Master, and how very necessary that we, as members, should all feel an interest in the work of the Lord's house, that we may keep our beloved Fraternity pure and prosperous! We appointed our love-feast for May 14 — *S. J. Dresher.*

Stanton Mills, Pa.—The Quemahoning congregation held three series of meetings during the present winter, at three different points. The first one was held at Sipesville by Bro. Geo. S. Rairigh; the second at Sugar Grove, by D. H. Walker; the third by Bro. Rairigh, at Pine Grove and Conemaugh. This made six weeks' solid service. At all of these meetings the attendance was good, excepting on a few, rainy nights. Marked attention was given to every branch of the service, and many excellent sermons were preached by both brethren. Often the audiences were deeply affected, and while a goodly number were almost persuaded, three openly declared themselves for Christ. The good seed sown, we hope, will yet produce fruit to the honor of God.—*E. J. Blough, Feb. 22.*

Progress, Colo.—We had no preaching by the Brethren at this place since last October, until Feb. 6, when Bro. J. Henricks, of Grant County, Kans., came and remained till the 22nd. He preached, in all, sixteen sermons. The interest and attendance during the meetings were very good, and we also had very favorable weather. While there were no additions, there seems to be quite an interest awakened. The success of a series of meetings does not always depend on additions. The members here are much encouraged. We are in need of a ministering brother to locate among us. We have thirteen members here. Bro. Henricks is our elder, and he lives about seventy-five miles away. There is a large field here, but the laborers are very few. We often think of our eastern churches, where, on each Sunday, there are as many as half a dozen ministers behind the table, when two or three could do the work.—*Mina Walker, Feb. 29.*

attention. We hope new tracts upon live topics will be presented and those, especially assigned by the committee, at Hagerstown, to certain writers. The time and place of committee meeting will be given later.

By order of Foreman,
I. D, PARKER, Sec.

From the Pine Creek Congregation, Ill.

FEB. 14 we commenced a series of meetings in Polo. Bro. Geo. Zollars preached nine sermons in all to very attentive congregations and we hope his labor may be the means of bringing some nearer to God, as well as strengthening those that have already made choice of the good part.

Bro. D. L. Miller came to us on the evening of Feb. 22, and, after preaching one sermon for us, commenced a series of Bible Talks,—five in all,—which were not only interesting but very instructive, and, we believe, a means of reaching the minds of many that could not be reached in any other way. By these Talks many points of doubt were removed from the minds of the hearers. The house was filled to its fullest capacity, and the last evening some returned to their homes because they could not be accommodated with seats. Bro. Miller gives these Bible Talks free, so that no one need be deprived of hearing them, and the Lord will surely reward him for his labors. At the close of these Talks the opportunity was given to all to make a free-will offering for the Russian sufferers, and a liberal amount was raised for that purpose.　　　C. FAHRNEY.

Notice to the Brethren of Kansas and Nebraska.

THE annual meeting of the Brethren's Mutual Aid and Insurance Association will be held in the Olathe church, Johnson Co., Kans, April 14, the day following District Meeting.

B. S. KATHERMAN, Sec.

Notes from Our Correspondents.

"As cold water to a thirsty soul, so is good news from a far country."

New Lebanon, Ohio.—Ono was restored to church fellowship in the Wolf Creek church Feb. 25, at a most harmonious council-meeting.—Jno. Calvin Bright, March 3.

Bremen, Ind.—March 5 we met in council at the Brick church. It passed off pleasantly. The congregation was small on account of a funeral in the District. Bro. J. Kauffman was selected as delegate for Annual Meeting.—Simon P. Eversole.

Long Meadow, Md.—Since my last report five more have united with the church, making, in all, seventeen, as the result of our series of meetings, previously reported. May the Lord help them to daily reflect the image of Christ, that they may be a light to the world!—John Rowland, March 2.

Wanted.—The address of Daniel Fouts. Any one who can give the desired information, will favor the church here and Bro. Fouts. The last heard of Bro. Fouts, he was at or near Fremont, Nebr., staying, I think, with his brothers, Solomon and Samuel. Address any information to J. R. Leatherman, Conway Springs, Kans.

La Place, Ill.—The members of the Okaw church held their quarterly meeting to-day. All business passed off pleasantly. Three letters of membership were given. One was received by letter. We decided to commence our Sunday-school in April. We appointed a Communion meeting for June 2, at 4 P. M. Bro. Eli Wolfe was appointed as solicitor for the District Endowment Fund.—E. F. Wolfe, March 3.

Peabody, Kans.—This church has just enjoyed a very pleasant council. Two came back to the church that had wandered away. May the good work go on! We also expect, the Lord willing, to hold a love-feast May 7, at 2 P. M.—Katie Yost, March 2.

Lacon, Ill.—By request I went to Johnson County, Iowa, March 1, and labored two weeks in the Palestine school-house. What the result of the meetings will be, the Lord only knows. This is a mission point in care of Bro. J. C. Seibert. We hope he may be able, by the help of the Lord, to build up a prosperous church at that place.—C. S. Holsinger.

South English, Iowa.—Our last quarterly council passed off Feb. 27, in the English River congregation, Keokuk Co., Iowa. Considerable business came before the church, but all was disposed of apparently harmoniously. The church made arrangements for some needed improvements at the old meeting-house in the near future. We hope it may be the means of furthering and enlarging God's kingdom. We are having very warm weather for this latitude at present. — Peter Brower.

Covington, Ohio.—A pleasant series of meetings was held in the Newton church at Pleasant Hill. Bro. I. D. Parker, of Ashland, Ohio, came to our assistance Feb. 6, and remained until the 23rd, when he had to leave us rather unexpectedly, to attend to some matter of importance at home. The meeting was interesting and largely attended throughout, and we were sorry to have it stop when it did. Bro. Parker did his part of the work well. Two were baptized and others, we think, are near the kingdom.—D. D. Wine.

Pleasant Valley, Va.—Bro. S. N. McCann began a series of meetings for us Feb. 3 and continued until Feb. 10, preaching, in all, nine sermons. The meetings were well attended, and the Word of God faithfully delivered. While there were no additions, some were made to see the error of their way, and on Sunday, Feb. 21, two precious young souls gave their hearts to Jesus, and were buried with him in baptism. May they ever prove bright and shining lights! Others are as one of old,—almost persuaded.—Sarah Click, Weyer's Cave, Va.

Pipe Creek Church, Ind.—We commenced a series of meetings on the evening of Jan. 12, and closed Jan. 24, with a good interest. Bro. Amsey Puterbaugh, of Oswego, Ind., did the preaching. He delivered seventeen sermons in all. There were no additions to the church, but, we think, much good was done to both members and outsiders. Quite a number of our members could not attend the meetings on account of La Grippe. Bro. Puterbaugh shunned not to declare all the counsel of God. He is an able expounder of the Gospel. May the Lord ever be with him!—D. H. Long.

Sawyer, Kans.—Bro. Brubaker commenced meetings at the Liberty school-house, five miles west of town Jan. 26, and continued until the 31st, with good attendance and attention, but no accessions. Bro. Brubaker commenced another meeting, four and one-half miles north-west of town Feb. 7, and continued until the 21st, with good interest. While there were no accessions, we hope that the good seed sown will have its effect. May it be as bread cast upon the waters, to be gathered many days hence! Bro. Brubaker was assisted by Bro. Glick. Both are home ministers. I will further say that I have received a number of tracts and also a number of sample copies of the MESSENGER, for which I feel thankful. I distributed them to the best of my ability. I sent some to Massachusetts, where, I learn, the Brethren are not known.—J. H. Miller.

Avery, Mo.—The Spring Branch church met in council, Jan. 23, and held a choice for two ministers. The lot fell upon our dear young brethren, Burr E. Brenhears and T. B. Ihrig. May the Lord give them grace that they may prove faithful to their high calling, and become workmen that need not be ashamed!—R. S. Rust.

Schuylkill, Pa.—Eld. H. A. Light came to us Feb. 8, and remained till Feb. 19, and preached four- teen sermons. The attendance was good. There were three additions by baptism. We have a substantial and convenient meeting-house and one preacher in the first degree. He is a good leader of the little flock, full of zeal and perseverance. Our two deacons assist in singing, exhorting and prayer, as liberty is given. Eld. J. Hartzler is our presiding older.—D. N. Yothers.

Spring Run, Pa.—After the convalescence of the son of Eld' Michael Claar, Claysburgh, Blair Co., Pa., he returned to the Spring Run congregation, and preached thirteen sermons in the Pine Glen school-house; then came again to the Spring Run meeting-house and preached five sermons. Nineteen were baptized here, which have already been reported and there is one more applicant The Dry Valley meetings, together with the ones here, make fifty-one sermons, with one week's intermission.—Emma Bollinger, McVeytown, Pa.

Lyons, Kans.—The Kansas Center church met in quarterly council Feb. 20. All business passed off pleasantly. Among the different items of business, delegates were chosen for District Meeting and a superintendent elected for our Sunday-school, which will open April 1. How enjoyable to the Christian to meet at God's house to do work for the Master, and how very necessary that we, as members, should all feel an interest in the work of the Lord's house, that we may keep our beloved Fraternity pure and prosperous! We appointed our love-feast for May 14. — S. J. Dresher.

Stanton Mills, Pa.—The Quemahoning congregation held three series of meetings during the present winter, at three different points. The first one was held at Sipesville by Bro. Geo. S. Rairigh; the second at Sugar Grove, by D. H. Walker; the third by Bro. Rairigh, at Pine Grove and Conemaugh. This made six weeks' solid service. At all of these meetings the attendance was good, excepting on a few rainy nights. Marked attention was given to every branch of the service, and many excellent sermons were preached by both brethren. Often the audiences were deeply affected, and while a goodly number were almost persuaded, three openly declared themselves for Christ. The good seed sown, we hope, will yet produce fruit to the honor of God.—E. J. Blough, Feb. 22.

Progress, Colo.—We had no preaching by the Brethren at this place since last October, until Feb. 6, when Bro. J. Henricks, of Grant County, Kans., came and remained till the 22nd. He preached, in all, sixteen sermons. The interest and attendance during the meetings were very good, and we also had very favorable weather. While there were no additions, there seems to be quite an interest awakened. The success of a series of meetings does not always depend on additions. The members here are much encouraged. We are in need of a ministering brother to locate among us. We have thirteen members here. Bro. Henricks is our elder, and he lives about seventy-five miles away. There is a large field here, but the laborers are very few. We often think of our eastern churches, where, on each Sunday, there are as many as half a dozen ministers behind the table, when two or three could do the work.—Mina Walker, Feb. 29.

DAUGHERTY.—Also, in the same congregation, Feb. 5, 1892, infant daughter of Mr. and Mrs. John and Zino Daugherty, aged 5 days. Funeral services by the writer.
A. A. WISE.

DAVENPORT.— Near Wakarusa, Elkhart Co., Ind., at the home of Martin Davenport, Feb. 20, 1892, sister Amanda Davenport, aged 20 years, 5 months and 2 days. Services by the writer, assisted by Bro. I. R. Miller from Num. 23: 10. JOHN METZLER.

GASKELL.—At his home near Fairmansville, Iowa, Feb. 23, 1892, Daniel Gaskell, aged 71 years, 10 months and 23 days. He was born in New Jersey and came to Calhoun County at an early day. Funeral services by D. G. Youker and R. P. Young from 1 Cor. 15: 55, 56. A. M. WHITE.

HOLLINGER.—At Clay Hill, Pa., Feb. 20, 1892, Emma A. Hollinger, aged 3 years, 6 months and 18 days. Funeral occasion improved from Matt. 18: 3 by the writer and Eld. Wm. C. Koontz. Interment at Brown's Mill. WM. A. ANTHONY.

BEAR.—In the bounds of the Lower Twin Creek church, Montgomery Co., Ohio, Feb. 10, 1892, David Bear, aged 75 years, 10 months and 4 days. Bro. Bear was born in Montgomery County, Ohio. April 16, 1816, and was united in marriage with Elizabeth Mullendore, Aug. 16, 1837. This union was blessed with thirteen children. Services by the Brethren from 1 Cor. 15: 35.
DANIEL M. GARVER.

SHOCK.—In the Tippecanoe church, Kosciusko Co., Ind., Feb. 17, 1892, Bro. Adam Shock, aged 69 years, 2 months and 6 days. He was born in Montgomery County, Ohio, and moved to Kosciusko County, Ind., forty years ago. He suffered with dropsy for sixteen months, but bore all with patience. Funeral services from Rev. 14: 12, 13.
DANIEL ROTHENBERGER.

HARMON.—In the Garrison church, Iowa, Feb. 20, 1892, of old age, sister Mary E. Harmon, aged 88 years, 21 months and 12 days. Sister Harmon (nee Festenbaur) was born in Baden, Germany, March 9, 1803. When about thirty-seven years old, she, with her first husband,——Trout, came to America. To them were born ten children. Her first husband died in Pennsylvania. She then married Henry Harmon. To them were born two children. About 1858 she was baptized by J. H. Fillmore, as the first fruits of the Brethren church in Benton County, Iowa. Funeral discourse from 1 Cor. 15: 21, 22, by the undersigned. PETER FORNEY.

HARVEY.—At Sodus, near Benton Harbor, Mich., Feb. 19, 1892, of old age, sister Lucena Harvey, aged 89 years, 2 months and 26 days. She was born Nov. 24, 1802, in Essex Co., New Hampshire, and was married to Oscar O. Harvey in the year 1838. In 1855 they moved to Gratiot County, Mich., and in 1860 settled on their farm at Sodus, Berrien County, Mich., where she died. Funeral sermon by the undersigned, assisted by Eld. Akin, of the Church of God, from 2 Tim. 4: 7, 8, and Ps. 17: 15.

PECK.—In McPherson, Kans., Feb. 13, 1892, Bro. Jacob Peck, aged 82 years, 3 months and 6 days. Bro. Peck was a faithful member of the Brethren church for more than fifty years and was ready to depart, having made due preparation, and was waiting the summons. Services conducted by Eld. Daniel Vaniman and the writer from Rev. 14: 14. S. Z. SHARP.

MARTIN.—At his father's residence, near Plymouth, Ind., Feb. 21, 1892, friend Lot Day Martin, eldest son of Daniel and Catharine Martin, aged 25 years, 4 months and 15 days. Funeral by J. H. Sellers.

ZIGLER.—At Timberville, Va., Bro. David Zigler, aged 71 years and 11 months. Deceased was never married. He was always in his place at church and came as near being at peace with all mankind as any one I ever knew. Services by D. Hays and the writer. S. H. MYERS.

DAUGHERTY.—Also, in the same congregation, Feb. 5, 1892, infant daughter of Mr. and Mrs. John and Zino Daugherty, aged 5 days. Funeral services by the writer.
A. A. WISE.

DAVENPORT.—Near Wakarusa, Elkhart Co., Ind., at the home of Martin Davenport, Feb. 20, 1892, sister Amanda Davenport, aged 20 years, 5 months and 2 days. Services by the writer, assisted by Bro. I. R. Miller from Num. 23: 10.
JOHN METZLER.

GASKELL.—At his home near Farnhamville, Iowa, Feb. 23, 1892, Daniel Gaskell, aged 71 years, 10 months and 23 days. He was born in New Jersey and came to Calhoun County at an early day. Funeral services by D. G. Yonker and R. P. Young from 1 Cor. 15: 55, 56.
A. M. WHITE.

HOLLINGER.—At Clay Hill, Pa., Feb. 20, 1892, Emma A. Hollinger, aged 3 years, 8 months and 18 days. Funeral occasion improved from Matt. 18: 3 by the writer and Eld. Wm. C. Koontz. Interment at Brown's Mill.
WM. A. ANTHONY.

BEAR.—In the bounds of the Lower Twin Creek church, Montgomery Co., Ohio, Feb. 20, 1892, David Bear, aged 75 years, 10 months and 4 days. Bro. Bear was born in Montgomery County, Ohio. April 16, 1816, and was united in marriage with Elizabeth Mullendore, Aug. 16, 1837. This union was blessed with thirteen children. Services by the Brethren from 1 Cor. 15: 35.
DANIEL M. GARVER.

SHOCK.—In the Tippecanoe church, Kosciusko Co., Ind., Feb. 17, 1892, Bro. Adam Shock, aged 69 years, 2 months and 6 days. He was born in Montgomery County, Ohio, and moved to Kosciusko County, Ind., forty years ago. He suffered with dropsy for sixteen months, but bore all with patience. Funeral services from Rev. 14: 12, 13.
DANIEL ROTHENBARGER.

HARMON.—In the Garrison church, Iowa, Feb. 20, 1892, of old age, sister Mary E. Harmon, aged 88 years, 11 months and 12 days. Sister Harmon (nee Festenbaur) was born in Baden, Germany, March 9, 1803. When about thirty-seven years old, she, with her first husband,—Trout, came to America. To them were born ten children. Her first husband died in Pennsylvania. She then married Henry Harmon. To them were born two children. About 1858 she was baptized by J. H. Fillmore, as the first fruits of the Brethren church in Benton County, Iowa. Funeral discourse from 1 Cor. 15: 21, 22, by the undersigned.
PETER FORNEY.

HARVEY.—At Sodus, near Benton Harbor, Mich., Feb. 19, 1891, of old age, sister Lucena Harvey, aged 89 years, 2 months and 26 days. She was born Nov. 24, 1802, in Essex Co., New Hampshire, and was married to Oscar O. Harvey in the year 1838. In 1855 they moved to Gratiot County, Mich., and in 1860 settled on their farm at Sodus, Berrien County, Mich., where she died. Funeral sermon by the undersigned, assisted by Eld. Akin, of the Church of God, from 2 Tim. 4: 7, 8, and Ps. 17: 15.

PECK.—In McPherson, Kans., Feb. 13, 1892, Bro. Jacob Peck, aged 82 years, 1 month and 6 days. Bro. Peck was a faithful member of the Brethren church for more than fifty years and was ready to depart, having made due preparation, and was waiting the summons. Services conducted by Eld. Daniel Vaniman and the Brethren from Rev. 14: 14.
S. Z. SHARP.

MARTIN.—At his father's residence, near Plymouth, Ind., Feb. 11, 1892, interred Lot Day Martin, oldest son of Daniel and Catharine Martin, aged 25 years, 4 months and 15 days. Funeral by J. H. Sellers.

ZIGLER.—At Timberville, Va., Bro. Daniel Zigler, aged 71 years and 11 months. Deceased was never married. He was always in his place at church and came as near being at peace with all mankind as any one I ever knew. Services by D. Hays and the writer.
S. H. MYERS.

THE GOSPEL MESSENGER.

"Set for the Defense of the Gospel."

Vol. 30, Old Series. Mt. Morris, Ill., and Huntingdon, Pa., March 22, 1892. No. 12.

The Gospel Messenger.

H. B. BRUMBAUGH, Editor,

And Business Manager of the Eastern House, Box 50,
Huntington, Pa.

Table of Contents.

AT this writing, March 11, our fields are still well covered with snow. We are anxiously awaiting the south wind and springtime's melting showers.

MARCH 24 will close an unusually full and successful Winter Term for the Normal College, with encouraging prospects for an overflowing Spring Term.

WE had the pleasure of meeting Eld. Wm. Howe the other day, on the train, on his way to the Snake Spring Valley church. He is called there to assist in adjusting some difficulties that have arisen among the membership. We hope that all will be satisfactorily settled.

A BROTHER writes us that he has ordered his paper stopped four times and yet it continues to come. This means that he has written us four postal cards, and every time he has neglected to give his post-office, and as the office from which he mails only *blots*, instead of stamping the name plainly, we are not able to get the office from the post-mark. Try it once more, and be sure to give your post-office, and your request will be promptly attended to.

THE James Creek brethren think that they have the most desirable location for the Old Folks' Home of any that can be offered in the Middle District of Pennsylvania. We went out to see it the other day, and after considering all the advantages, are inclined to believe that they are about right. The possibilities are there for making it a lovely place, and as the brethren, of late, have been purchasing the homes in that vicinity, we see no reason why their location should not receive a very favorable consideration.

MR. JAMES STRONG, of Philadelphia, has endowed a new professorship in the Pennsylvania College. The amount of the gift is $25,000, and the chair endowed is to be called "English Bible." We are glad to learn that other colleges, as well as ours own, are becoming awakened on the importance of more Bible work. Here is a grand opportunity for some of our brethren. Our Bible Department should have a good endowment, as we have hundreds of ministers and church workers who are anxious to take a course in Bible study, but are not able to do so. In making your bequests, don't forget this. To be sure that your wishes will be carried out, do it while you are yet living, and thus save it from shrewd lawyers and covetous relatives. It is time that we all learn that the Lord never intended to entrust his wealth into our hands, for us to lavish it on our children and relatives, often to their destruction. "Will a man rob God?" Yes, my brother, many of us are doing this very thing. How much of that which he is giving us, are we using for the promotion of his purposes? How much? Think it over, because an answer will be demanded in the judgment.

BE HONEST.

THE man who can truly say, "I would rather be right than be President," is a moral hero and the world should rise up and call him blessed. We sometimes say such things and try to make ourselves believe that we mean them. But on a closer examination we are made to doubt our own judgment and wonder if such a desire for the right is a possibility with us while still in the tenements of these fleshly houses.

There are times when we can all entertain such feelings as a wish, but how many of us can make them so-practical that others can believe that we are in earnest? The desire is a good thing, and we should labor to entertain it even if we should not be able to carry it out.

What made David a man after God's own heart? It was his honesty, and, by the way, this expression is, at times, much misinterpreted. It does not mean that David himself was in any way to be compared with the purity and goodness of God, but that David had a disposition which the Lord loved. Had we all this disposition, having, in addition to what David had, the guidance of the Holy Spirit, how good a people we would be! To be honest by ourselves and our God is a standard worthy of the best of us. It has been well said, "An honest man is God's nobleman." It is a word that is subject to a wonderful elaboration and we seldom look at it in its enlarged definition. It means more than giving full measure and weight, and paying what are termed our honest debts,—few do this much. True honesty goes back of all this. These things are only a few of the outcroppings. Honesty is an element of the soul and stands justified at the bar of reason. It is that which affirms to the ultimate good of our-

selves and our fellows, that beyond which there is no "if" or doubt.

What we need most in the world and in the church is more downright honesty,—that which is honest before an enlightened reason and before God. Before we can raise ourselves to this standard of morality and Christianity we must make an intelligent study of ourselves. We must learn to know ourselves. This is a great study, and as greatly neglected as it is great. We are inclined to study everything else. We want to know all about the heavens and the earth and all things contained therein, but how very indisposed we are to make ourselves the subject for investigation.

Let us make a start as close at home as we can well get,—in our home every-day life. Let us just now call into account the motives that have prompted us to plan and to do to-day,—in dealing with our children, our employees, our neighbors, and those with whom we are related in our life's work! Have the motives, away back of our actions, been honest before our own bar of reason, and before God? Now, think a moment and say yes or no. Be honest, right now, for once and speak it out! Make your own decision! It will do you good and give you impressions that will be helpful to you in all future life. Remember that honesty in our ordinary and every-day affairs is as important as in the more responsible relations. He that is honest in the little things, will also be honest in the greater things. It is not the thing or the things so much as the motive that is back of them.

We now go to prayer. Surely we will be honest when we come into the immediate presence of him who knows, whom we address and from whom we ask. Are we, or are our prayers mere forms? Our needs are many and we have become a praying people. We pray much and do little, and really expect less. We pray for the coming of the kingdom and are unwilling to be subject to its laws. We pray that the will of God may be done on earth, and our practices say it shall not be done.

We ask that our sins may be forgiven as we forgive others, and don't want it done in this way. We ask the Lord to lead us, and refuse to be led. We ask to be guided by the Holy Spirit and at the same time are determined to go our own way. Again, we ask for a decision. Are we honest? How is it? Say yes, if you can. If not, be honest and tell the truth,—say no.

Again, we come to the ministry. Certainly here we will find honesty. Well, so it should be, but before we decide it will be well to make a test. We will first look at the old way of preaching. Sunday morning has come and behind the table are seated three or four preachers without any arrangement as to who is to preach. The elder says, "Now, brethren, one of you be free and

(Concluded on page 181.)

THE GOSPEL MESSENGER.

"Set for the Defense of the Gospel."

Vol. 30, Old Series.　　　Mt. Morris, Ill., and Huntingdon, Pa., March 22, 1892.　　　No. 12.

The Gospel Messenger.

H. B. BRUMBAUGH, Editor,

And Business Manager of the Eastern House, Box 50,
Huntingdon, Pa.

Table of Contents.

At this writing, March 11, our fields are still well covered with snow. We are anxiously awaiting the south wind and springtime's melting showers.

MARCH 24 will close an unusually full and successful Winter Term for the Normal College, with encouraging prospects for an overflowing Spring Term.

WE had the pleasure of meeting Eld. Wm. Howe the other day, on the train, on his way to the Snake Spring Valley church. He is called there to assist in adjusting some difficulties that have arisen among the membership. We hope that all will be satisfactorily settled.

A BROTHER writes us that he has ordered his paper stopped four times and yet it continues to come. This means that he has written us four postal cards, and every time he has neglected to give his post-office, and as the office from which he mails only *blots*, instead of stamping the name plainly, we are not able to get the office from the post-mark. Try it once more, and be sure to give your post-office, and your request will be promptly attended to.

THE James Creek brethren think that they have the most desirable location for the Old Folks' Home of any that can be offered in the Middle District of Pennsylvania. We went out to see it the other day, and after considering all the advantages, are inclined to believe that they are about right. The possibilities are there for making it a lovely place, and as the brethren, of late, have been purchasing the homes in that vicinity, we see no reason why their location should not receive a very favorable consideration.

MR. JAMES STRONG, of Philadelphia, has endowed a new professorship in the Pennsylvania College. The amount of the gift is $25,000, and the chair endowed is to be called "English Bible." We are glad to learn that other colleges, as well as our own, are becoming awakened on the importance of more Bible work. Here is a grand opportunity for some of our brethren. Our Bible Department should have a good endowment, as we have hundreds of ministers and church workers who are anxious to take a course in Bible study, but are not able to do so. In making your bequests, don't forget this. To be sure that your wishes will be carried out, do it while you are yet living, and thus save it from shrewd lawyers and covetous relatives. It is time that we all learn that the Lord never intended to entrust his wealth into our hands, for us to lavish it on our children and relatives, often to their destruction. "Will a man rob God?" Yes, my brother, many of us are doing this very thing. How much of that which he is giving us, are we using for the promotion of his purposes? How much? Think it over, because an answer will be demanded in the judgment.

BE HONEST.

THE man who can truly say, "I would rather be right than be President," is a moral hero and the world should rise up and call him blessed. We sometimes say such things and try to make ourselves believe that we mean them. But on a closer examination we are made to doubt our own judgment and wonder if such a desire for the right is a possibility with us while still in the tenements of these fleshly houses.

There are times when we can all entertain such feelings as a wish, but how many of us can make them so-practical that others can believe that we are in earnest? The desire is a good thing, and we should labor to entertain it even if we should not be able to carry it out.

What made David a man after God's own heart? It was his honesty, and, by the way, this expression is, at times, much misinterpreted. It does not mean that David himself was in any way to be compared with the purity and goodness of God, but that David had a disposition which the Lord loved. Had we all this disposition, having, in addition to what David had, the guidance of the Holy Spirit, how good a people we would be! To be honest by ourselves and for God is a standard worthy of the best of us. It has been well said, "An honest man is God's nobleman." It is a word that is subject to a wonderful elaboration. We seldom look at it in its enlarged definition. It means more than giving full measure and weight, and paying what are termed our honest debts,—few do this much. True honesty goes back of all this. These things are only a few of the outcroppings. Honesty is an element of the soul and stands justified at the bar of reason. It is that which affirms to the ultimate good of our selves and our fellows, that beyond which there is no "if" or doubt.

What we need most in the world and in the church is more downright honesty,—that which is honest before an enlightened reason and before God. Before we can raise ourselves to this standard of morality and Christianity we must make an intelligent study of *ourselves*. We must learn to know ourselves. This is a great study, and as greatly neglected as it is great. We are inclined to study everything else. We want to know all about the heavens and the earth and all things contained therein, but how very indisposed we are to make ourselves the subject for investigation.

Let us make a start as close at home as we can well get,—in our home every-day life. Let us just now call into account the motives that have prompted us to plan and to do to-day,—in dealing with our children, our employees, our neighbors, and those with whom we are related in our life's work! Have the motives, away back of our actions, been honest before our own bar of reason, and before God? Now, think a moment and say *yes* or *no*. Be honest, right now, for *once* and speak it out! Make your own decision! It will do you good and give you impressions that will be helpful to you in all future life. Remember that honesty in our ordinary and every-day affairs is as important as in the more responsible relations. He that is honest in the little things, will also be honest in the greater things. It is not the thing or the things so much as the motive that is back of them.

We now go to prayer. Surely we will be honest when we come into the immediate presence of him who knows, whom we address and from whom we ask. Are we, or are our prayers mere forms? Our needs are many and we have become a praying people. We pray much and do little, and really expect less. We pray for the coming of the kingdom and are unwilling to be subject to its laws. We pray that the will of God may be done on earth, and our practices say it shall not be done.

We ask that our sins may be forgiven as we forgive others, and don't want it done in this way. We ask the Lord to lead us, and refuse to be led. We ask to be guided by the Holy Spirit and at the same time are determined to go our own way. We ask for a decision. Are we honest? How is it? Say yes, if you can. If not, be honest and tell the truth,—say no.

Again, we come to the ministry. Certainly here we will find honesty. Well, so it should be, but before we decide it will be well to make a test. Sunday morning has come and behind the table are seated three or four preachers without any arrangement as to who is to preach. The elder says, "Now, brethren, one of you be free and

(Concluded on page 161.)

this Scripture, gives license to the different denominations, and that it is the design of God, that there should be those different persuasions, so that all the people, with their different minds and consciences, might be accommodated with a home in the church. Of course this looks somewhat plausible, but yet it conflicts with the text, together with all the strong testimony in favor of the oneness of the church of Christ. Now, to harmonize this Scripture with the foregoing, we must look at it from a different stand-point. The Savior did not come to speak peace to a sinful world, while in their sins, but to testify to the world that the deeds thereof were evil, and to call sinners to repentance; hence he did not come to give peace or ease to the guilty consciences, "but rather divisions."

"How divisions?"—says one. Why, he came to separate a people from a sinful world, unto himself,—"a peculiar people, zealous of good works," etc., to draw a line of distinction between the church and the world, or between his kingdom and the kingdoms of this world; hence causing divisions in that sense. This is agreeable with the meaning of the text. More might be added, but let this suffice on that part of the subject.

3. "One Spirit," 1 Cor. 12: 13, signifies that all the children of God, in all nations, Jews or Gentiles, bond or free, by one Spirit were all baptized into one body. Again Paul, in Eph. 4: 3, writes to the children of God to endeavor to keep the unity of the Spirit in the bond of peace. If you read 1 Cor. 12: 4-11, you find that the different gifts given to the children of God, were all given by the same Spirit, which, we have reason to believe, was the Spirit of Christ, for the apostle says, in Rom. 8: 9, "Now if any man have not the Spirit of Christ, he is none of his," hence a perfect oneness, even in the Spirit, is to govern God's people.

4. "One Lord." Since there is but one kingdom of Christ recognized in the Gospel,—one "church of the living God, which is the pillar and ground of the truth," "one sheepfold," so that all the people that hear the voice of Jesus, and follow him, belong to the same flock, and must look to the same Good Shepherd, we see no need of more than one Lord to govern God's people. That Lord is Jesus Christ. In 1 Cor. 8: 6, Paul says, "Unto us there is but one Lord Jesus Christ, by whom are all things, and we by him." In John 13: 13, we have the Savior's own testimony, that he is Lord over God's heritage.

5. "One faith." Eph. 4: 13, 14 tells us to persevere "till we all come in the unity of faith," etc. Read both verses, which prove a unity of faith in the children of God. In John 17 Jesus prays in behalf of his disciples, that they might all be one, even as he and his Father are one. Of course he meant one in sentiment, one in judgment, one in faith, etc., or, as Paul declares, in 1 Cor. 1: 10, "Now I beseech you, brethren, by the name of our Lord Jesus Christ, that ye all speak the same thing, and that there be no divisions among you; but that ye be perfectly joined together in the same mind and in the same judgment." Hence it may be seen that there is a perfect unity of faith required of the followers of Christ.

6. "One baptism." This is used by some to prove single immersion, but when we examine it together with other Scriptures, we are led to the conclusion that it has no reference to the mode, but to the rite of baptism. The term "baptism" here does not specify any particular mode or manner of baptism, but simply alludes to the ordinance itself,—"one baptism," that is, one way to baptize. All believers were brought into the church the same way, as Paul intimates in 1 Cor. 12: 13, "For by one Spirit are we all baptized into one

body, whether we be Jews or Gentiles, whether we be bond or free; and have been all made to drink into one Spirit." The apostles baptized into the name of the Lord Jesus. That implies, "According to his directions," as shown in Matt. 28: 19, "Baptizing them in the name of the Father, and of the Son, and of the Holy Ghost."

The above formula indicates the number of actions in the ordinance. It is quite reasonable that one order in baptism is sufficient in the church of Christ, for there is but one church or body of Christ upon earth. One spirit suffices as its guide; one Lord governs it; one faith constitutes its aim; all believe alike and it would be utterly impossible to have more than one mode of baptism practiced among them.

I wish next to present another idea, in regard to some of the popular doctrines, as advocated in the world by some of the great preachers of to-day. They know as well as I do that the Gospel teaches there is but one true church upon earth and they will preach that doctrine to the people, yet they do not represent any particular church themselves, and will preach for any denomination, wherever they get the most for their labor. They will preach on the first principles of the Gospel, etc. They represent no particular church, so when they get people under conviction, they will advise them to make their own choice of a church, to go wherever they can feel at home. Now, after teaching the people that there is but one true church, and then advising them to join any church of their choice, they are bound to teach them something more to clear that up, which is this,— they teach them that all the prominent and faithful members of the different persuasions compose the church of Christ.

Now I want to show you that this popular theory does not comport with the teachings of the Scriptures. We all know that the different denominations have their public debates, and when they have their discussions they will select their ablest ministers and when they come together to discuss their differences, they will study and labor hard, almost night and day, to defeat their opponent and to build up their own theories.

I will now leave it to the judgment of my readers as to whether the above proceedings of the different churches will harmonize with the following Scripture, 1 Cor. 1: 10, "Now I beseech you, brethren, by the name of our Lord Jesus Christ, that ye all speak the same thing, and that there be no divisions among you; but that ye be perfectly joined together in the same mind and in the same judgment." I trust that the foregoing remarks are sufficient.

As I said in the onset, I hold that the Gospel teaches but one church of Christ. This I hope has been sufficiently proven in the foregoing testimony. The question might be asked, "If there is one church above all others, that God will accept as his, what church is it?" I will venture this answer, "It is the one that is the nearest right. God would certainly not reject the one that is the nearest right, to take some other that is farther away."

I will venture another question, "Who is the nearest right?" Answer, "It is the one that comes the nearest living up to the requirements of the Gospel." "Prove all things, hold fast to that which is good." 1 Thess. 5: 21.

THE *Raleigh Christian Advocate* says: "The woman who was up before a magistrate for getting drunk, very pertinently asked him why, if the law objected to people getting drunk, it issued licenses for the sale of liquor. Her question is yet unanswered."

THE DEBATE.

Affirmative Arguments and Thoughts by G. A. Shamberger, in the Shamberger–Bond Debate, held in the Prairie View Church, Morgan Co., Mo., with Notes by Levi Mohler, of Warrensburgh, Mo.

PROPOSITION.—WATER baptism is essential to the remission of the sins of the penitent believer.

NOTE.—"Penitent believer" has reference to one who is seeking membership in the body of Christ, not one who has it. We do not affirm that water baptism only is essential to remission of sins. There may be a number of things,—baptism is one of them.

STATEMENT 1.—The Scriptures teach that remission of sins is effected by a number of causes.
FIRST CAUSE.—2 Cor. 5: 17, 19; Eph. 2: 4, 5; Gracious cause.
SECOND CAUSE.—2 Cor. 5: 17-19; Heb. 6: 16-19; Meritorious cause.
THIRD CAUSE.—1 Tim. 6: 12; Heb. 6: 16, 19; Appropriating cause.
STATEMENT 2.—The Scriptures teach that sins are remitted when God is approached as follows:
1. By faith towards God. Heb. 11: 16.
2. By repentance towards God. Luke 24: 46, 47; Acts 17: 30.
3. By faith towards the Lord Jesus. John 4: 1; Acts 20: 20, 21.
4. By baptism as commanded by Jesus. Matt. 28: 19.

ARGUMENT 1.—The Scriptures teach that Christ is put on by baptism. Gal. 3: 27.
(1) We offer Christ as our righteousness. 2 Cor. 5: 21; Jer. 23: 6; 1 Cor. 1: 30.

NOTES.—Baptism is the appropriating act. By baptism we put on Christ. Clothing, when put on, is appropriated. We appropriate Christ, with his righteousness, when we put him on by baptism. We then appear before God, not in our own righteousness, which was as filthy rags, but in the righteousness of Christ, and are thereby well-pleasing in the sight of God.

THOUGHT 1.—Since we put on Christ in baptism, he is not put on before baptism.
THOUGHT 2.—Those that have put on Christ are freed from sin.
THOUGHT 3.—Baptism is the only way given under heaven or among men whereby we may put on Christ.

ARGUMENT 2.—The Scriptures teach that the body of Christ is cleansed by the washing of water by the Word. Eph. 5: 25-27; 1 Cor. 6: 11; body of Christ, 1 Cor. 12: 27, is the church.

NOTES.—When we have a penitent believer we are ready and God is ready to wash him and put him in the church. When we give him baptism, according to the Word, he is washed by the blood of Christ, whom he appropriates by baptism.

THOUGHT 1.—The church is not cleansed before it receives the washing of water.
THOUGHT 2.—When the church is washed it is cleansed.
THOUGHT 3.—Those who are cleansed have remission.

ARGUMENT 3.—The Scriptures teach that we are baptized into Christ. Gal. 3: 27; Rom. 6: 3; 1 John 5: 11, 12.

NOTES.—Our cleansing is by the blood of Christ in which we are washed when baptized into him. Our hope for acceptance with God is the righteousness of Christ, which we put on when we get into him.

Baptism itself does not remit sins but its God's appointed way into Christ,—to his blood. In that way it is essential to cleansing, being the means of access to the blood of Christ, by which we are cleansed.

Baptism is a literal rite of typical character, pointing and leading to spiritual blessings in Christ.

THOUGHT 1.—Since we are baptized into Christ we are not in him prior to baptism.

this Scripture gives license to the different denominations, and that it is the design of God, that there should be those different persuasions, so that all the people, with their different minds and consciences, might be accommodated with a home in the church. Of course this looks somewhat plausible, but yet it conflicts with the text, together with all the strong testimony in favor of the oneness of the church of Christ. Now, to harmonize this Scripture with the foregoing, we must look at it from a different stand-point. The Savior did not come to speak peace to a sinful world, while in their sins, but to testify to the world that the deeds thereof were evil, and to call sinners to repentance; hence he did not come to give peace or ease to the guilty consciences, "but rather divisions."

"How divisions?"—says one. Why, he came to separate a people from a sinful world, unto himself,— "a peculiar people, zealous of good works," etc., to draw a line of distinction between the church and the world, or between his kingdom and the kingdoms of this world, hence causing divisions in that sense. This is agreeable with the meaning of the text. More might be added, but let this suffice on that part of the subject.

3. "One Spirit," 1 Cor. 12: 13, signifies that all the children of God, in all nations, Jews or Gentiles, bond or free, by one Spirit were all baptized into one body. Again Paul, in Eph. 4: 3, writes to the children of God to endeavor to keep the unity of the Spirit in the bond of peace. If you read 1 Cor. 12: 4–11, you find that the different gifts given to the children of God, were all given by the same Spirit, which, we have reason to believe, was the Spirit of Christ, for the apostle says, in Rom. 8: 9, "Now if any man have not the Spirit of Christ, he is none of his," hence a perfect oneness, even in the Spirit, is to govern God's people.

4. "One Lord." Since there is but one kingdom of Christ recognized in the Gospel,—one "church of the living God, which is the pillar and ground of the truth," "one sheepfold," so that all the people that hear the voice of Jesus, and follow him, belong to the same flock, and must look to the same Good Shepherd, we see no need of more than one Lord to govern God's people. That Lord is Jesus Christ. In 1 Cor. 8: 6, Paul says, "Unto us there is but one Lord Jesus Christ, by whom are all things, and we by him." In John 13: 13, we have the Savior's own testimony, that he is Lord over God's heritage.

5. "One faith." Eph. 4: 13, 14 tells us to persevere "till we all come in the unity of faith," etc. Read both verses, which prove a unity of faith in the children of God. In John 17 Jesus prays in behalf of his disciples, that they might all be one, even as he and his Father are one. Of course he meant one in sentiment, one in judgment, one in faith, etc., or, as Paul declares, in 1 Cor. 1: 10, "Now I beseech you, brethren, by the name of our Lord Jesus Christ, that ye all speak the same thing, and that there be no divisions among you; but that ye be perfectly joined together in the same mind and in the same judgment." Hence it may be seen that there is a perfect unity of faith required of the followers of Christ.

6. "One baptism." This is used by some to prove single immersion, but when we examine it together with other Scriptures, we are led to the conclusion that it has no reference to the mode, but to the rite of baptism. The term "baptism" here does not specify any particular mode or manner of baptism, but simply alludes to the ordinance itself,— "one baptism," that is, one way to baptize. All believers were brought into the church the same way, as Paul intimates in 1 Cor. 12: 13, "For by one Spirit are we all baptized into one

body, whether we be Jews or Gentiles, whether we be bond or free; and have been all made to drink into one Spirit." The apostles baptized into the name of the Lord Jesus. That implies, "According to his directions," as shown in Matt. 28: 19, "Baptizing them in the name of the Father, and of the Son, and of the Holy Ghost."

The above formula indicates the number of actions in the ordinance. It is quite reasonable that one order in baptism is sufficient in the church of Christ, for there is but one church or body of Christ upon earth. One spirit suffices as its guide; one Lord governs it; one faith constitutes its aim; all believe alike and it would be utterly impossible to have more than one mode of baptism practiced among them.

I wish next to present another idea, in regard to some of the popular doctrines, as advocated in the world by some of the great preachers of to-day. They know as well as I do that the Gospel teaches there is but one true church upon earth and they will preach that doctrine to the people, yet they do not represent any particular church themselves, and will preach for any denomination, wherever they get the most for their labor. They will preach on the first principles of the Gospel, such as faith, repentance, conversion, new birth, etc. They represent no particular church, so when they get people under conviction, they will advise them to make their own choice of a church, to go wherever they can feel at home. Now, after teaching the people that there is but one true church, and then advising them to join any church of their choice, they are bound to teach them something more to clear that up, which is this,— they teach them that all the prominent and faithful members of the different persuasions compose the church of Christ.

Now I want to show you that this popular theory does not comport with the teachings of the Scriptures. We all know that the different denominations have their public debates, and when they have their discussions they will select their ablest ministers and when they come together to discuss their differences, they will study and labor hard, almost night and day, to defeat their opponent and to build up their own theories.

I will now leave it to the judgment of my readers as to whether the above proceedings of the different churches will harmonize with the following Scripture, 1 Cor. 1: 10, "Now I beseech you, brethren, by the name of our Lord Jesus Christ, that ye all speak the same thing, and that there be no divisions among you; but that ye be perfectly joined together in the same mind and in the same judgment." I trust that the foregoing remarks are sufficient.

As I said in the onset, I hold that the Gospel teaches but one church of Christ. This I hope has been sufficiently proven in the foregoing testimony. The question might be asked, "If there is one church above all others, that God will accept as his, what church is it?" I will venture this answer, "It is the one that is the nearest right. God would certainly not reject the one that is the nearest right, to take some other that is farther away."

I will venture another question, "Who is the nearest right?" Answer, "It is the one that comes the nearest living up to the requirements of the Gospel." "Prove all things, hold fast to that which is good." 1 Thess. 5: 21.

THE *Raleigh Christian Advocate* says: "The woman who was up before a magistrate for getting drunk, very pertinently asked him why, if the law objected to people getting drunk, it issued licenses for the sale of liquor. Her question is yet unanswered.

THE DEBATE.

Affirmative Arguments and Thoughts by G. A. Shamberger in the Shamberger-Bond Debate, held in the Prairie View Church, Morgan Co., Mo., with Notes by Levi Mohler, of Warrensburgh, Mo.

PROPOSITION.—Water baptism is essential to the remission of the sins of the penitent believer.

NOTE.—"Penitent believer" has reference to one who is seeking membership in the body of Christ, not one who has it. We do not affirm that water baptism only is essential to remission of sins. There may be a number of things,—baptism is one of them.

STATEMENT 1.—The Scriptures teach that remission of sins is effected by a number of causes.

FIRST CAUSE.—2 Cor. 5: 17, 19; Eph. 2: 4, 5; Gracious cause.

SECOND CAUSE.—2 Cor. 5: 17–19; Heb. 6: 16–19; Meritorious cause.

THIRD CAUSE.—1 Tim. 6: 12; Heb. 6: 16, 19; Appropriating cause.

STATEMENT 2.—The Scriptures teach that sins are remitted when God is approached as follows:
1. By faith towards God. Heb. 11: 16.
2. By repentance towards God. Luke 24: 46, 47; Acts 17: 30.
3. By faith towards the Lord Jesus. John 4: 1; Acts 20: 20, 21.
4. By baptism as commanded by Jesus. Matt. 28: 19.

ARGUMENT 1.—The Scriptures teach that Christ is put on by baptism. Gal. 3: 27.
(1) We offer Christ as our righteousness. 2 Cor. 5: 21; Jer. 23: 6; 1 Cor. 1: 30.

NOTES.—Baptism is the appropriating act. By baptism we put on Christ. Clothing, when put on, is appropriated. We appropriate Christ, with his righteousness, when we put him on by baptism. We then appear before God, not in our own righteousness, which is as filthy rags, but in the righteousness of Christ, and are thereby well-pleasing in the sight of God.

THOUGHT 1.—Since we put on Christ in baptism, he is not put on before baptism.

THOUGHT 2.—Those that have put on Christ are freed from sin.

THOUGHT 3.—Baptism is the only way given under heaven or among men whereby we may put on Christ.

ARGUMENT 2.—The Scriptures teach that the body of Christ is cleansed by the washing of water by the Word. Eph. 5: 25–27; 1 Cor. 6: 11; body of Christ, 1 Cor. 12: 27, is the church.

NOTES.—When we have a penitent believer we are ready and God is ready to wash him and put him in the church. When we give him baptism, according to the Word, he is washed by the blood of Christ, whom he appropriates by baptism.

THOUGHT 1.—The church is not cleansed before it receives the washing of water.

THOUGHT 2.—When the church is washed it is cleansed.

THOUGHT 3.—Those who are cleansed have remission.

ARGUMENT 3.—The Scriptures teach that we are baptized into Christ. Gal. 3: 27; Rom. 6: 3; 1 John 5: 11, 12.

NOTES.—Our cleansing is by the blood of Christ in which we are washed when baptized into him. Our hope for acceptance with God is the righteousness of Christ, which we put on when we get into him.

Baptism itself does not remit sins but it is God's appointed way into Christ,—to his blood. In that way it is essential to cleansing, being the means of access to the blood of Christ, by which we are cleansed.

Baptism is a literal rite of typical character, pointing and leading to spiritual blessings in Christ.

THOUGHT 1.—Since we are baptized into Christ, we are not in him prior to baptism.

3. 1 John 5: 1 in Revised Version reads: "Whosoever believeth that Jesus' is the Christ, is *begotten* of God." Old Version reads, "Is *born* of God." There is a great difference between begotten and born. Many are begotten children of God that are never born. Baptism pertains to birth,—faith, to begetting.

4. Christ could not be an example to us in baptism for the remission of sins, he being without sin. He is our Example so far as it was possible for him to be. He could not be our Example in ceasing from sin, or in repenting from it, for the same reason. We do not, therefore, conclude that we shall not cease from sin, or repent from sin because we have not Christ's example, neither do we conclude that we are not baptized for the remission of sins, because he was not.

PARENTS' MISTAKES.

BY J. E. BLOUGH.

It is not my intention, in this article, to enumerate or point out the mistakes of ungodly and wicked parents, but a few of those that are daily made by well-meaning Christian men and women.

It is no uncommon thing to hear parents relating, in the presence of children,—and often in a boastful manner,—the sports that they used to engage in when they were young. Some delight to tell how they fought at elections, how they drank in the harvest field, at barn-raisings, log-rollings, etc. Some even glory in relating the good times they had at parties and dances. These are things that ought to bring remorse to our conscience every time the memory recalls them, and the less our children know about them, the better for us, and certainly for them. If children know that their parents engaged in such wickedness, they will feel more at liberty to do the same, and parents will not have as much influence over them. Let us, then, be very careful in relating things of the past.

Another serious and often fatal mistake is made by storing in our cellars several barrels of cider for drinking purposes. Wherever this is done, the custom is to pass it round whenever a friend or neighbor calls. In this way it is sometimes offered to those not accustomed to it, and may create in them a desire for more or something stronger. This has been the beginning of many young men's ruin.

The best work against intemperance must be done in the home. Parents have it in their power to train their children to abhor that which is evil and cleave to that which is good, and they owe them this duty. They bring their children into existence. They hold them under their hand till the young life has taken a bias that will last through eternity. Usually the tiny, tilting craft has its prow turned toward heaven or hell before the parent's hand lets go the helm. This ought to startle careless people out of their indifference. It ought to drive them to lives of piety, for how can they teach that which they have not learned? How can they impart that which they do not possess?

Parents must teach by example. Precept has no authority, unless backed by example. For the sake of the children, liquors should be banished from the home. The story is most pitiful and quite too common to need repetition: "I learned to drink at my father's table. My mother's hand first passed me the cup that is working my damnation." One thing is certain,—if we really care much about abolishing this horrible traffic, we will see to it that our children have books and papers that will keep them in sympathy with the efforts made for its prohibition. How was it several years ago when the citizens of Pennsylvania had the privilege of voting for a Prohibitory Amendment to the Constitution? Many, professing Christianity, were violent in their language

against it. What can we expect of such parents' sons? By personal example, by look, by reading and by prayer, we may make an atmosphere that shall set and keep our households right on this great question. Only thus can we hope to save ourselves and those whom God has given to be with us, from the tide that sweeps to destruction so many of the noblest and best.

The same rule holds good in regard to tobacco. What reason is there in a parent, while using tobacco, to prohibit his sons from using it? Let the father first set a good example by quitting the filthy habit, then can he, with propriety, admonish his sons. What benefit is derived, anyway, from its use? I answer, "Not any, but a great deal of harm."

Parents also make a sad mistake when they dress their children in gay and fashionable clothing, either for the sake of admiration or of being in the latest fashion. Fond mothers often place things upon their innocent darlings that they would be ashamed to wear themselves. I hope, however, that in the majority of such cases it is done thoughtlessly. My advice to mothers would be not to put anything upon your children that you could not consistently wear yourself. In whatever way you may foster their pride, it will surely lead them to follow all the foolish fashions of the world. That will certainly be in their way of coming into the church. Mothers who dress their children fashionably and extravagantly, need not wonder why they do not join the church when they arrive at the proper age.

Many parents make mistakes in the government of their children. We must not watch them with a suspicious eye, frown at the merry outbursts of innocent hilarity or suppress their joyous laughter, or we will mould them into melancholy little models of octogenarian gravity. When they have been at fault, we must not simply punish them on account of the personal injury that we have chanced to suffer, in consequence of their fault, while disobedience, unattended by inconveniences to ourselves, passes without rebuke.

Wise government is not to overwhelm the little culprit with angry words, to stun him with a deafening noise, to call him by hard names, which do not express his misdeeds, to load him with epithets which would be extravagant if applied to a fault of tenfold enormity, or to declare, with passionate vehemence, that he is the worst child in the world and destined for the gallows. Thousands of children are daily treated in this way. Many a child's pride and ambition are hurt by being severely criticised or unjustly punished for crimes for which he is not responsible.

Reprove with calmness and composure, and not with angry irritation,—in a few words fitly chosen, not with a torrent of abuse. Punish as often as you threaten, and threaten only when you intend and can remember to perform. Say what you mean, and infallibly do as you say.

In our homes we must have industry and sympathy. In choosing amusements for the children, the latter element must be brought in. To fully understand the little ones, we must sympathize with them. When a child asks questions, do not meet it with, "Oh, don't bother me." A child is a living interrogation point. Every day it meets with new and strange objects. Tell it all it wants to know. The more inquisitive the child, the brighter are his prospects for the future. Never let your angry passions rise, no matter how much you may be tried. The child has a right to ask questions and to be fairly answered; not to be snubbed as if he were guilty of an impertinence, nor ignored as though his desire for information were of no consequence, nor misled, as if it did

not matter whether true or false impressions were made upon his mind.

Parents, make the home attractive, agreeable and cheerful! Supply the children with plenty of sound, chaste, entertaining literature! Sing, talk, read and pray with them and for them, and you can rest assured that the desire to leave the farm and country and go to the city will not enter their hearts. The country is flooded with cheap and trashy literature, which, if children are permitted to read, is certain to lead to vice and crime.

Last, but not least, if you want to educate your children, do not send them to colleges of other denominations, or to places where religious influences are wanting, but patronize one of our own schools, where they will be taught to respect the Bible and Christianity. Many a bright son and daughter has been lost to the church, because they were sent to some popular college where our doctrine is not treated with the proper degree of respect.

Scalp Level, Pa.

BE HONEST.

(Concluded from first page.)

preach to-day." The general response is: "I did not expect to preach to-day and am not at all prepared," and with one accord excuses are made. Nobody expected to preach,—nobody prepared. Is it true,—is it honest thus to speak? Perhaps every last one has a subject prepared and is elsmaching for a pressure sufficiently strong to make it proper (?) to get up. Finally, after it is found that no one has a subject and no one is prepared, one of the number takes the liberty,—gets up and tells the waiting people, "Brethren and sisters and friends, I did not expect to address you at this time and have made no preparation. I would much rather have kept my seat and heard Bro. B preach, who is much more able to talk to you than I am, but as it seems to be my duty, by the help of the Lord, I will do the best I can," etc. (Opens the Bible.) "I just happened to open at the fourth chapter of John, and, by the help of your prayers, I will use a short time and then give it over to my brethren," etc. Now, all this sounds very humble and dependent indeed,—but is it true, is it honest? Even under so unsystematized a form as this, is it possible that men who have been called to preach the Gospel, and on whose preaching and teaching the salvation of souls depends, could go up to the house of the Lord without any expectation or preparation? Do you not have a subject all "cut and dry" ready for use, if called upon? How is it, my brother? Was it only a chance that you opened on the fourth chapter of John? Was your dependence entirely on the Lord for the sermon you expected to preach, and did you really believe that the other brethren could do it *better* than yourself? If they had told you so, could you have gladly and honestly said Amen to it? In saying and doing such things, are you acting honestly before God and the people? And may not the same be said of the senseless and foolish excuses that are made and said by those who know that they are to preach? Again we ask, Is it honest? It is true, these things are largely form and habit, the outgrowth of a false show of humility, but are they justifiable?

These are things that it will be well for us to ponder carefully as the Scriptures call for men who have honest hearts, of honest report, and we are to walk and talk honestly before God and man.

3. 1 John 5: 1 in Revised Version reads: " Whosoever believeth that Jesus' is the Christ, is begotten of God." Old Version reads, " Is born of God." There is a great difference between begotten and born. Many are begotten children of God that are never born. Baptism pertains to birth,—faith, to begetting.

4. Christ could not be an example to us in baptism for the remission of sins, he being without sin. He is our Example so far as it was possible for him to be. He could not be our Example in ceasing from sin, or in repenting from it, for the same reason. We do not, therefore, conclude that we shall not cease from sin, or repent from sin because we have not Christ's example, neither do we conclude that we are not baptized for the remission of sins, because he was not.

PARENTS' MISTAKES.

BY J. R. BLOUGH.

IT is not my intention, in this article, to enumerate or point out the mistakes of ungodly and wicked parents, but a few of those that are daily made by well-meaning Christian men and women.

It is no uncommon thing to hear parents relating, in the presence of children,—and often in a boastful manner,—the sports that they used to engage in when they were young. Some delight to tell how they fought at elections, how they drank in the harvest field, at barn-raisings, log-rollings, etc. Some even glory in relating the good times they had at parties and dances. These are things that ought to bring remorse to our conscience every time the memory recalls them, and the less our children know about them, the better for us, and certainly for them. If children know that their parents engaged in such wickedness, they will feel more at liberty to do the same, and parents will not have as much influence over them. Let us, then, be very careful in relating things of the past.

Another serious and often fatal mistake is made by storing in our cellars several barrels of cider for drinking purposes. Wherever this is done, the custom is to pass it round whenever a friend or neighbor calls. In this way it is sometimes offered to those not accustomed to it, and may create in them a desire for more or something stronger. This has been the beginning of many young men's ruin.

The best work against intemperance must be done in the home. Parents have it in their power to train their children to abhor that which is evil and cleave to that which is good, and they owe them this duty. They bring their children into existence. They hold them under their hand till the young life has taken a bias that will last through eternity. Usually the tiny, tilting craft has its prow turned toward heaven or hell before the parent's hand lets go the helm. This ought to startle careless people out of their indifference. It ought to drive them to lives of piety, for how can they teach that which they have not learned? How can they impart that which they do not possess?

Parents must teach by example. Precept has no authority, unless backed by example. For the sake of the children, liquors should be banished from the home. The story is most pitiful and quite too common to need repetition: "I learned to drink at my father's table." My mother's hand first passed me the cup that is working my damnation." One thing is certain,—if we really care much about abolishing this horrible traffic, we will see to it that our children have books and papers that will keep them in sympathy with the efforts made for its prohibition. How was it several years ago when the citizens of Pennsylvania had the privilege of voting for a Prohibitory Amendment to the Constitution? Many, professing Christianity, were violent in their language

against it. What can we expect of such parents' sons? By personal example, by look, by reading and by prayer, we may make an atmosphere that shall set and keep our households right on this great question. Only thus can we hope to save ourselves and those whom God has given to be with us, from the tide that sweeps to destruction so many of the noblest and best.

The same rule holds good in regard to tobacco. What reason is there in a parent, while using tobacco, to prohibit his sons from using it? Let the father first set a good example by quitting the filthy habit, then can he, with propriety, admonish his sons. What benefit is derived, anyway, from its use? I answer, "Not any, but a great deal of harm."

Parents also make a sad mistake when they dress their children in gay and fashionable clothing, either for the sake of admiration or of being in the latest fashion. Fond mothers often place things upon their innocent darlings that they would be ashamed to wear themselves. I hope, however, that in the majority of such cases it is done thoughtlessly. My advice to mothers would be not to put anything upon your children that you could not consistently wear yourself. In whatever way you may foster their pride, it will surely lead them to follow all the foolish fashions of the world. That will certainly be in their way of coming into the church. Mothers who dress their children fashionably and extravagantly, need not wonder why they do not join the church when they arrive at the proper age.

Many parents make mistakes in the government of their children. We must not watch them with a suspicious eye, frown at the merry outbursts of innocent hilarity or suppress their joyous laughter, or we will mould them into melancholy little models of octogenarian gravity. When they have been at fault, we must not simply punish them on account of the personal injury that we have chanced to suffer, in consequence of their fault, while disobedience, unattended by inconveniences to ourselves, passes without rebuke.

Wise government is not to overwhelm the little culprit with angry words, to stun him with a deafening noise, to call him by hard names, which do not express his misdeeds, to load him with epithets which would be extravagant if applied to a fault of tenfold enormity, or to declare, with passionate vehemence, that he is the worst child in the world and destined for the gallows. Thousands of children are daily treated in this way. Many a child's pride and ambition are hurt by being severely criticised or unjustly punished for crimes for which he is not responsible.

Reprove with calmness and composure, and not with angry irritation,—in a few words fitly chosen, not with a torrent of abuse. Punish as often as you threaten, and threaten only when you intend and can remember to perform. Say what you mean, and infallibly do as you say.

In our homes we must have industry and sympathy. In choosing amusements for the children, the latter element must be brought in. To fully understand the little ones, we must sympathize with them. When a child asks questions, do not meet it with, "Oh, don't bother me." A child is a living interrogation point. Every day it meets with new and strange objects. Tell it all it wants to know. The more inquisitive the child, the brighter are his prospects for the future. Never let your angry passions rise, no matter how much you may be tried. The child has a right to ask questions and to be fairly answered; not to be snubbed as if he were guilty of an impertinence, nor ignored as though his desire for information were of no consequence, nor misled, as if it did

not matter whether true or false impressions were made upon his mind.

Parents, make the home attractive, agreeable and cheerful! Supply the children with plenty of sound, chaste, entertaining literature! Sing, talk, read and pray with them and for them, and you can rest assured that the desire to leave the farm and country and go to the city will not enter their hearts. The country is flooded with cheap and trashy literature, which, if children are permitted to read, is certain to lead to vice and crime.

Last, but not least, if you want to educate your children, do not send them to colleges of other denominations, or to places where religious influences are wanting, but patronize one of our schools, where they will be taught to respect the Bible and Christianity. Many a bright son and daughter has been lost to the church, because they were sent to some popular college where our doctrine is not treated with the proper degree of respect.

Scalp Level, Pa.

BE HONEST.

(Concluded from first page.)

preach to-day." The general response is: "I did not expect to preach to-day and am not at all prepared," and with one accord excuses are made. Nobody expected to preach,—nobody prepared. Is it true,—is it honest thus to speak? Perhaps every last one has a subject prepared and is almost aching for a pressure sufficiently strong to make it proper (?) to get up. Finally, after it is found that no one has a subject and no one is prepared, one of the number takes the liberty,—gets up and tells the waiting people, "Brethren and sisters and friends, I did not expect to address you at this time and have made no preparation. I would much rather have kept my seat and heard Bro. B preach, who is much more able to talk to you than I am, but as it seems to be my duty, by the help of the Lord, I will do the best I can," etc. (Opens the Bible.) "I just happened to open at the fourth chapter of John, and, by the help of your prayers, I will use a short time and then give it over to my brethren," etc. Now, all, this sounds very humble and dependent indeed,—but is it true, is it honest? Even under so unsystematized a form as this, is it possible that men who have been called to preach the Gospel, and on whose preaching and teaching the salvation of souls depends, could go up to the house of the Lord without any expectation or preparation? Do you not have a subject all "cut and dry" ready for use, if called upon? How is it, my brother? Was it only a chance that you opened on the fourth chapter of John? Was your dependence entirely on the Lord for the sermon you expected to preach, and did you really believe that the other brethren could do it better than yourself? If they had told you so, could you have gladly and honestly said Amen to it? In saying and doing such things, are you acting honestly before God and the people? And may not the same be said of the senseless and foolish excuses that are made and said by those who know that they are to preach? Again we ask, Is it honest? It is true, these things are largely form and habit, the outgrowth of a false show of humility, but are they justifiable?

These are things that it will be well for us to ponder carefully as the Scriptures call for men who have honest hearts, of honest report, and we are to walk and talk honestly before God and man.

take such injunctions of the spiritual law as the following: "Whether ye eat or drink, or whatsoever ye do, do all to the glory of God." 1 Cor. 10: 31. "Abstain from all appearance of evil." 1 Thess. 5: 22. "Have no fellowship with the unfruitful works of darkness." Eph. 5: 11.

Scores of other passages of like nature might be quoted, but why multiply words and arguments to prove what the universal conscience of enlightened mankind admits without question, that the Bible, as the Word of God, generally and specifically covers the whole ground of morals and religion, and that the very thought of human addendas and supplements is presumption. Let us all exalt and magnify that word, "not as the word of men, but as it is in truth, the Word of God." 1 Thess. 2: 18. The insufficiency is not in the Bible, but in us; but a diligent and prayerful study of its sacred pages will increasingly qualify us for more efficient service, in which, if we continue, we shall "both save ourselves and them that hear us."

Green Forest, Va.

THE SUNDAY-SCHOOL AND THE CHURCH.

BY S. Z. SHARP.

The Sunday-school should be a servant of the church, bringing souls to Christ by teaching them his Word, and strengthening them after they are in the fold. This requires qualified teachers and suitable means for instruction.

Teachers can impart only what they know and must themselves understand the Word of God before they can teach it to others. "First of all, the Sunday-school teacher should be a Christian," otherwise it will be "the blind leading the blind."

He must be a Christian in faith and experience, having his own lamp lighted at the altar of God, for how can he let his light shine before men when he is yet in darkness? 2 Peter 1: 21; Rom. 15: 24. He must be a Christian by example. 1 Tim. 6: 11.

He should be a church member and be loyal to the church, in its methods and doctrines, as well as in its work. 1 John 3: 14; Eph. 2: 10.

He must be an earnest Bible student. 2 Tim. 3: 16, 17.

He must be in sympathy with his work and his pupils. Phil. 1: 7; 1 Thess. 3: 12.

He must have wisdom as well as knowledge to do his work efficiently. James 1: 5; 1 Thess. 3: 7.

In many instances the influence of the Sunday-school teacher is greater than that of the preacher, since he comes more directly in contact with the minds which he instructs.

It is claimed that the Sunday-school work is more influential than the Missionary and Tract Work, the church paper, or the colleges. If these should be under the supervision of the General Conference, why should not the Sunday-school work be as well? What are we to think of a Sunday-school being taught, in part at least, by those not fully in sympathy with the church, either in doctrine or method, and we take no notice of the bad seed that is sown; then, when Sunday-school is over, public preaching begins by a minister who is placed under the strictest surveillance? Why are we so indifferent to the former and so careful with the latter?

Then look at the literature brought into our Sunday-schools and its erroneous teachings, imparted to our sons and daughters, and our Annual Meeting takes no notice of it.

Would it not be well for our Annual Conference to appoint a committee of five brethren who have long made Sunday-school work a study, whose duty it shall be to inquire into the needs of our Sunday-school work, and report to a subsequent Annual Meeting the wants of our Sunday-schools, and suggest a plan of putting them on a safe and efficient basis?

OUR BIBLE CLASS.

BY A. W. VANIMAN.

Practical Questions on Lesson XI.

Our previous lessons brought us to the time of Christ, from which point we will continue. The history of the New Covenant divides itself into two parts:

1. The revelation of the Gospel by Jesus Christ.

2. The propagation of the Gospel by his followers.

The first is contained in the four Gospels,—the latter in the Acts and Epistles.

In the latter part of the reign of *Herod the Great*, there lived in Judea an aged couple, named Zacharias and Elizabeth, but they were childless. Zacharias was a priest and, as we find, in 1 Chron. 24, the priests were divided into twenty-four courses. Each course took its turn, by going to Jerusalem, and officiating in their office for probably seven days. Then they returned to their homes to attend to other duties. While Zacharias was officiating at the altar one day, an angel stood by him, telling him that Elizabeth should bring forth a son whose name should be John. This child was to be a Nazarite from birth. When a person vowed the vow of a Nazarite, he was, during the continuance of the vow, not to drink any wine, or partake of the fruit of the vine in any form,—either to eat or drink. Furthermore, he was not to cut his hair. Num. 6: So we see that John never drank wine or cut his hair. We must not confound Nazarite with Nazarene. Christ was called a Nazarene, a resident of Nazareth, but this had no reference whatever, to being a Nazarite. It is very questionable whether the statement so often made, that wine was used at the Passover, is correct,—especially as a universal custom. In this event, one who had made the Nazarite vow could not partake.

Six months after the angel visited Zacharias, the same angel visited Mary, the cousin of Elizabeth, and informed her of the birth of the Savior. Mary then visited Elizabeth and remained with her three months. Mary was espoused to Joseph and he now finds, as he supposed, that Mary had proved untrue to him. The espousal was considered sacred, the same as the marriage vow, and infidelity during that period was considered the same as adultery, and, according to law, was punished with death. Joseph, being a kind-hearted man, concluded to put her away privily, but was hindered by what was told him in a dream.

In the birth of Jesus, as well as in many other things connected with Christ, we find such remarkable fulfillment of prophecy, that it would seem almost impossible for one to doubt, if he thoroughly study the matter. Joseph and Mary lived in Nazareth. The prophecy said Christ should be born in Bethlehem. This was accomplished by the Emperor of Rome issuing a decree that a census be taken of all the families in the Roman Empire.

A certain writer says: "He ordered all the citizens of Rome to register their estates according to their value in money, taking an oath in a form he prescribed, to deliver a faithful account, according to the best of their knowledge, specifying the names of their parents, their own age, the names of their wives and children, adding also what quarter of the city, or what town in the country they lived in. In this event the Jews would go to the proper places, so as to be enrolled in the tribe and family to which they belonged. It was not really necessary for Mary to go with Joseph away down to Bethlehem, and one would suppose she would have had good reason for remaining at home, but she went, and while there, the Savior of the world was born, in accordance with the prophecy, uttered over seven hundred years before. Jesus was born in a stable and laid in a manger. We need not, necessarily, conclude that his parents were too poor to secure a good place to stay, but the Bible tells us that it was because there was no room in the inn."

McPherson, Kans.

IMPORTANCE OF PRAYER.

Prayer is, in the plan of God, a vital force in the universe,—as truly a force in the moral world as electricity or gravitation is a force in the world of nature. It is, therefore, not enough to say that because our Father knoweth what things we have need of before we ask him, we shall gain nothing through an attempt to make known to him our needs and desires. God has chosen to condition certain gifts to us on our request for them, and, unless we pray accordingly, we have no right to expect to receive these gifts. The Son of God while he was Son of man realized the importance of prayer for himself and for his loved ones, and he enjoined on his disciples the duty and the privilege of prayer. If we would be blessed, we must pray for ourselves. If we would have others blessed, we must pray for them. It is often the case that we can do more for those whom we love by prayer in their behalf, than by any other mode of endeavor. And to know that those who love us are praying in our behalf, is something to be profoundly grateful for. God may honor the prayers for us of those whom we prize but lightly.—*Sel.*

The *Press* says that the introduction of a brass band of ten pieces at the evening services of the Eleventh street M. E. church, Philadelphia, was considered as a decided innovation, some of the congregation protesting, although it attracted hundreds to the church. But the minister, Garbutt Read, said from the pulpit that it was not sacrilegious, because the prodigal son had been welcomed by his brethren with a band of music. A man who can misrepresent Scripture in that style is not worthy to be called a *minister*, let alone a *reverend*. If this is not getting the world, with its sins, into the church then we do not understand the meaning of things.

The Gospel Messenger

Is the recognized organ of the German Baptist or Brethren's church, and advocates the form of doctrine taught in the New Testament and pleads for a return to apostolic and primitive Christianity.

It recognizes the New Testament as the only infallible rule of faith and practice, and maintains that Faith toward God, Repentance from dead works, Regeneration of the heart and mind, baptism by Trine Immersion for remission of sins unto the reception of the Holy Ghost by the laying on of hands, are the means of adoption into the household of God,—the church militant.

It also maintains that Feet-washing, as taught in John 13, both in precept and command of Jesus, should be observed in the church.

That the Lord's Supper, instituted by Christ and as universally observed by the apostles and the early Christians, is a full meal, and, in connection with the Communion, should be taken in the evening or after the close of the day.

That the Salutation of the Holy Kiss, or Kiss of Charity, is binding upon the followers of Christ.

That War and Retaliation are contrary to the spirit and self-denying principles of the religion of Jesus Christ.

That the principle of Plain Dressing and of Non-conformity to the world, as taught in the New Testament, should be observed by the followers of Christ.

That the Scriptural duty of Anointing the Sick with Oil, in the Name of the Lord, James 5: 14, is binding upon all Christians.

It also advocates the church's duty to support Missionary and Tract Work, thus giving to the Lord for the spread of the Gospel and for the conversion of sinners.

In short, it is a vindicator of all that Christ and the apostles have enjoined upon us, and aims, amid the conflicting theories and discords of modern Christendom, to point out ground that all must concede to be infallibly safe.

The above principles of our Fraternity are set forth on our "Brethren's Envelopes." Use them! Price, 15 cents per package; 40 cents per hundred.

take such injunctions of the spiritual law as the following: "Whether ye eat or drink, or whatsoever ye do, all to the glory of God." 1 Cor. 10: 31. "Abstain from all appearance of evil." 1 Thess. 5: 22. "Have no fellowship with the unfruitful works of darkness." Eph. 5: 11.

Scores of other passages of like nature might be quoted, but why multiply words and arguments to prove what the universal conscience of enlightened mankind admits without question, that the Bible, as the Word of God, generally and specifically covers the whole ground of morals and religion, and that the very thought of human addendas and supplements is presumption. Let us all exalt and magnify that word, "not as the word of men, but as it is in truth, the Word of God." 1 Thess. 2: 13. The insufficiency is not in the Bible, but in us; but a diligent and prayerful study of its sacred pages will increasingly qualify us for more efficient service, in which, if we continue, we shall "both save ourselves and them that hear us."

Green Forest, Va.

THE SUNDAY-SCHOOL AND THE CHURCH.

BY S. Z. SHARP.

The Sunday-school should be a servant of the church, bringing souls to Christ by teaching them his Word, and strengthening them after they are in the fold. This requires qualified teachers and suitable means for instruction.

Teachers can impart only what they know and must themselves understand the Word of God before they can teach it to others. "First of all, the Sunday-school teacher should be a Christian," otherwise it will be "the blind leading the blind."

He must be a Christian in faith and experience, having his own light at the altar of God, for how can he let his light shine before men when he is yet in darkness? 2 Peter 1: 21; Rom. 15: 24. He must be a Christian by example. 1 Tim. 6: 11.

He should be a church member and be loyal to the church, in its methods and doctrines, as well as in its work. 1 John 3: 14: Eph. 2: 10.

He must be an earnest Bible student. 2 Tim. 3: 16, 17.

He must be in sympathy with his work and his pupils. Phil. 1: 7; 1 Thess. 3: 12.

He must have wisdom as well as knowledge to do his work efficiently. James 1: 5; 1 Thess. 3: 7.

In many instances the influence of the Sunday-school teacher is greater than that of the preacher, since he comes more directly in contact with the minds which he instructs.

It is claimed that the Sunday-school work is more influential than the Missionary and Tract Work, the church paper, or the colleges. If these should be under the supervision of the General Conference, why should not the Sunday-school work be as well? What are we to think of a Sunday-school being taught, in part at least, by those not fully in sympathy with the church, either in doctrine or method, and we take no notice of the bad seed that is sown; then, when Sunday-school is over, public preaching begins by a minister who is placed under the strictest surveillance? Why are we so indifferent to the former and so careful with the latter?

Then look at the literature brought into our Sunday-schools and its erroneous teachings, imparted to our sons and daughters, and our Annual Meeting takes no notice of it.

Would it not be well for our Annual Conference to appoint a committee of five brethren who have long made Sunday-school work a study, whose duty it shall be to inquire into the needs of our Sunday-school work, and report to a subsequent Annual Meeting the wants of our Sunday-schools,

and suggest a plan of putting them on a safe and efficient basis?

OUR BIBLE CLASS.

BY A. W. VANIMAN.

Practical Questions on Lesson XI.

Our previous lessons brought us to the time of Christ, from which point we will continue. The history of the New Covenant divides itself into two parts:

1. The revelation of the Gospel by Jesus Christ.

2. The propagation of the Gospel by his followers.

The first is contained in the four Gospels,—the latter in the Acts and Epistles.

In the latter part of the reign of *Herod the Great,* there lived in Judea an aged couple, named Zacharias and Elizabeth, but they were childless. Zacharias was a priest and, as we find, in 1 Chron. 24, the priests were divided into twenty-four courses. Each course took its turn, by going to Jerusalem, and officiating in their office for probably seven days. Then they returned to their homes to attend to other duties. While Zacharias was officiating at the altar one day, an angel stood by him, telling him that Elizabeth should bring forth a son whose name should be John. This child was to be a Nazarite from birth. When a person vowed the vow of a Nazarite, he was, during the continuance of the vow, not to drink any wine, or partake of the fruit of the vine in any form,—either to eat or drink. Furthermore, he was not to cut his hair. Num. 6: So we see that John never drank wine or cut his hair. We must not confound Nazarite with Nazarene. Christ was called a Nazarene, a resident of Nazareth, but this had no reference whatever, to being a Nazarite. It is very questionable whether the statement so often made, that wine was used at the Passover, is correct,— especially as a universal custom. In this event, one who had made the Nazarite vow could not partake.

Six months after the angel visited Zacharias, the same angel visited Mary, the cousin of Elizabeth, and informed her of the birth of the Savior. Mary then visited Elizabeth and remained with her three months. Mary was espoused to Joseph and he now finds, as he supposed, that Mary had proved untrue to him. The espousal was considered sacred, the same as the marriage vow, and infidelity during that period was considered the same as adultery, and, according to law, was punished with death. Joseph, being a kind-hearted man, concluded to put her away privily, but was hindered by what was told him in a dream.

In the birth of Jesus, as well as in many other things connected with Christ, we find such remarkable fulfillment of prophecy, that it would seem almost impossible for one to doubt, if he thoroughly study the matter. Joseph and Mary lived in Nazareth. The prophecy said Christ should be born in Bethlehem. This was accomplished by the Emperor of Rome issuing a decree that a census be taken of all the families in the Roman Empire.

A certain writer says: "He ordered all the citizens of Rome to register their estates according to their value in money, taking an oath in a form he prescribed, to deliver a faithful account, according to the best of their knowledge, specifying the names of their parents, their own age, the names of their wives and children, adding also what quarter of the city, or what town in the country they lived in. In this event the Jews would go to the proper places, so as to be enrolled in the tribe and family to which they belonged. It was not really necessary for Mary to go with

Joseph away down to Bethlehem, and one would suppose she would have had good reason for remaining at home, but she went, and while there, the Savior of the world was born, in accordance with the prophecy, uttered over seven hundred years before. Jesus was born in a stable and laid in a manger. We need not, necessarily, conclude that his parents were too poor to secure a good place to stay, but the Bible tells us that it was because there was no room in the inn."

McPherson, Kans.

IMPORTANCE OF PRAYER.

Prayer is, in the plan of God, a vital force in the universe,—as truly a force in the moral world as electricity or gravitation is a force in the world of nature. It is, therefore, not enough to say that because our Father knoweth what things we have need of before we ask him, we shall gain nothing through an attempt to make known to him our needs and desires. God has chosen to condition certain gifts to us on our request for them, and, unless we pray accordingly, we have no right to expect to receive these gifts. The Son of God while he was Son of man realized the importance of prayer for himself and for his loved ones, and he enjoined on his disciples the duty and the privilege of prayer. If we would be blessed, we must pray for ourselves. If we would have others blessed, we must pray for them. It is often the case that we can do more for those whom we love by prayer in their behalf, than by any other mode of endeavor. And to know that those who love us are praying in our behalf, is something to be profoundly grateful for. God may honor the prayers for us of those whom we prize but lightly.—*Sel.*

The *Press* says that the introduction of a brass band of ten pieces at the evening services of the Eleventh street M. E. church, Philadelphia, was considered as a decided innovation, some of the congregation protesting, although it attracted hundreds to the church. But the minister, Garbutt Read, said from the pulpit that it was not sacrilegious, because the prodigal son had been welcomed by his brethren with a band of music. A man who can misrepresent Scripture in that style is not worthy to be called a *minister,* let alone a *reverend.* If this is not getting the world, into its sins, into the church then we do not understand the meaning of things.

The Gospel Messenger

Is the recognized organ of the German Baptist or Brethren's church, and advocates the faith of doctrine taught in the New Testament and pleads for a return to apostolic and primitive Christianity.

It recognizes the New Testament as the only infallible Rule of faith and practice, and maintains that Faith toward God, Repentance from dead works, Regeneration of the heart and mind, baptism by Trine Immersion for remission of sins unto the reception of the Holy Ghost by the laying on of hands, are the means of adoption into the household of God,—the church militant.

It also maintains that Feet-washing, as taught in John 13, both by example and command of Jesus, should be observed in the church.

That the Lord's Supper, instituted by Christ and as universally observed by the apostles and the early Christians, is a full meal, and, in connection with the Communion, should be taken in the evening or after the close of the day.

That the Salutation of the Holy Kiss, or Kiss of Charity, is binding upon the followers of Christ.

That War and Retaliation are contrary to the spirit and self-denying principles of the religion of Jesus Christ.

That the principle of Plain Dressing and of Non-conformity to the world, as taught in the New Testament, should be observed by the followers of Christ.

That the Scriptural duty of Anointing the Sick with Oil, in the Name of the Lord, James 5: 14, is binding upon all Christians.

It also advocates the church's duty to support Missionary and Tract Work, thus giving to the Lord for the spread of the Gospel and for the conversion of sinners.

In short, it is a vindicator of all that Christ and the apostles have enjoined upon us, and aims, amid the conflicting theories and discords of modern Christendom, to point out ground that all must concede to be infallibly safe.

The above principles of our Fraternity are set forth on our "Brethren's Envelopes." Use them! Price, 15 cents per package; 40 cents per hundred.

OUR quarterly church council, held in the Chapel, passed off very pleasantly a few days ago. An aged brother from the Old Order element was restored to fellowship. Bro. G. V. Goahorn was advanced to the second degree of the ministry. Much other work was done, all of which, we trust, will redound to the glory and honor of God.

CHRISTIANS who imagine that they cannot be of any value to the cause of Christ simply because they possess only ordinary talents, may receive encouragement from what Spurgeon one time said: "Simon Peter was worth ten Andrews, so far as we can gather from sacred history, and yet Andrew was instrumental in bringing him to Jesus. You may be deficient in talent, and yet be the means of drawing to Christ one who will become eminent in grace and service."

FANATICS, of whatever religion, seldom possess grace enough to keep them within reasonable bounds. They are always a dangerous element. Recently a mob, composed of fanatics, members of the Greek church at Athens, Greece, attacked, pillaged, and partly wrecked the Protestant church in that city. They also wrecked the parsonage, and everything belonging to the ministers residing in it, was destroyed. The chief minister is agent of the British and Foreign Bible Society, and intends to claim compensation for his losses from the government of Greece. Several members of the church, during the attack, fled to the British consulate, and were pursued to its very doors by the fanatics from whom they had escaped. Defeated in overtaking them, the mob demanded their surrender by the Consul, but, of course, in this they failed. They then waited at the Consulate to assault any who might leave it to return to their homes; but in this they were also foiled. The wrecked church was built with money subscribed by both Englishmen and Americans; and no reason can be assigned for its destruction except the virulence of sectarian prejudice.

A BROTHER sends us a copy of The Baptist Banner, published at Huntingdon, W. Va., Jan. 6, 1892, containing an article against trine immersion by Mr. Bibb, with a request that we reply to it. We think there is not much in the article to reply to. All the points in the article are derived, in a measure, from the "Quinter and McConnell Debate," and therefore contain nothing new unless it be the intimation that our people are few, and therefore our form of baptism has not numerical strength behind it. It may not be amiss to remind this Baptist writer, in the language of Hinton, one of the ablest Baptist historians in America that

"The practice of trine immersion prevailed, in the West as well as the East, till the fourth council of Toledo, which, acting under the advice of Gregory the Great, in order to settle some disputes which had arisen, decreed that henceforth only one immersion should be used in baptism; and from that time the practice of only one immersion gradually became general throughout the western or Latin Church."—Hinton's History of Baptism, p. 156.

We may further remind him that all the ancient Baptist churches, such as Waldenses, etc., practiced trine immersion. Our people still retain the same old practice. Furthermore, if there ever was any person baptized by backward single immersion before the year 1522, we would like some one to refer us to the book and page giving us an account of it. By the time the writer of the article referred to gets through replying to the quotation with which Baptist histories abound, he may, in the language of Robinson, the most noted Baptist historian of England, be ready to exclaim:

"It is not true that dipping was exchanged for sprinkling by choice before the Reformation (A. D. 1517), for, till after that period, the ordinary baptism was trine immersion."—Robinson's History of Baptism, p. 148.

SISTER ELIZABETH WITWER, of Chicago, Ill., is spending the winter with her son in Dallas, Texas. She seems well pleased with her visit. We make the following extract from the letter, as it contains a lesson that should not only be heeded by our members, but they should be urged to show more kindness towards the strangers who attend our meetings: "I think some of our members are too timid in not coming forward and getting acquainted with new members and strangers when they come among us. I have attended both Baptist and Methodist churches at Normal Park, Chicago. Their churches are very plain and they seem to notice strangers when they come in. After they are dismissed they come up and shake hands and introduce you to some others and invite you to come again, and it makes one feel more at home. I think this is the way we ought to do. It makes the strangers feel that we are interested in their welfare. Invite them to come again; find out where they live and call to see them if it is so you can. In this way we might often encourage each other."

GO AND SIN NO MORE.

WE clip the following from the Morning News, published at Lancaster, Pa:

"Rev. John Herr, a German Baptist Elder, who combines with his pastoral work the occupation of a farmer, awoke from his sleep to see two neighbors robbing his store-house where he kept his meat. One was found to be within, taking the plunder, while the other received it at the door. The man at the door soon left with his first load, but the preacher took his place quietly and simulated the departed thief's voice and manner. He received his own meat and carefully deposited it in the bag prepared by the marauders until all had been removed. At this point the second thief returned, and both were terror-stricken when they found themselves in the minister's presence.

He requested them to replace all the meat, then presented them with as much of it as they could carry, gave them his blessing and told them to "go and sin no more." They went with tears in their eyes and promised to do better.

BAPTIZED 3,000 IN ONE NIGHT.

ELD. J. B. BRINEY, a Disciple minister and writer of acknowledged ability, is writing the ablest series of articles for the Christian Evangelist on the forms of baptism that we have ever read. From article No. 22 we clip the following, which is worth preserving:

"On the 16th of April, A. D. 404, Chrysostom immersed three thousand people in Constantinople, dipping every person three times! Further, in his life of Chrysostom, as quoted by Dr. Christian, says: 'On Easter eve, April 16, the Church of Chrysostom and the friendly clergy met together, as was the custom, to spend the night in vigils and to greet the rays of the Easter morning. With them were assembled three thousand young Christians who were to receive baptism.' Chrysostom, as quoted by Dr. Christian, very plainly tells what he did in baptizing: 'For we sink our heads in the water as in some grave, the old man is buried and the whole man, having sunk entirely down, is concealed. Then we emerge him, the new man rises again. For as it is easy for us to be immersed and to emerge, so it is easy for God to bury the old man and bring to light the new.' This is done three times.' Of this transaction Dr. Christian well says: 'If Chrysostom could immerse three thousand converts in one night, when the soldiers threatened his life and drove him from his church, it would seem an easy thing for Peter to immerse a like number when he had

favor with all the people, as he did have on the day of Pentecost."

This John Chrysostom was for a number of years bishop of the church of Antioch, where the disciples were first called Christians. He was probably the finest Greek scholar of Christian antiquity. The above quotation shows the possibility of one man baptizing 3,000 persons in a short time, and also serves as additional proof in defense of trine immersion.

RAILROAD ARRANGEMENTS FOR OUR ANNUAL CONFERENCE TO BE HELD AT CEDAR RAPIDS, IOWA, BEGINNING JUNE 7, 1892.

THE Western and Central Passenger Associations have granted one fare for the round trip, as the following extracts from their circulars will show. The Western Association, under date of March 4, says:

Lines in this Association have agreed upon the following arrangement for the above-named Meeting, namely:

One fare for the round trip from all Association points to Cedar Rapids and return. Tickets to be sold May 30 to June 6, 1892, inclusive, good for return passage until and including June 30, 1892. Tickets to be good for going passage on date of sale only, and for continuous passage in each direction. Ordinary non-signature excursion tickets to be used, except that tickets used from terminals shall be of the ironclad signature form; such terminals to be understood to be Kansas City, Leavenworth, Atchison, St. Joseph, Omaha, Council Bluffs, Sioux City, St. Paul, Minneapolis, Milwaukee, Chicago, St. Louis and Peoria.

The above rates and arrangements are tendered for the use of connecting lines, and said connecting lines are notified that their tickets and orders which may reach these lines prior to May 29, 1892, or later than June 6, 1892, will not be accepted or exchanged; said connecting lines are further notified that in ticketing over these lines for this occasion, tickets or orders for same of the ironclad signature form must be used.

The Central Association, under date of March 9, says:

To ALL MEMBERS OF THE CENTRAL TRAFFIC ASSOCIATION.

Gentlemen:—
At the meeting of the Passenger Committee of this Association on the 2nd inst., it was

Resolved, That a rate of one lowest limited first-class fare for the round trip be authorized to the eastern termini of the Western Passenger Association, to be added to the rates the Western Passenger Association may establish; ticket conditions to conform to those adopted by that Association.

The Western Passenger Association have, in their Circular No. 34, dated March 4, 1892, authorized the following:

"One fare for the round trip from all Association Points to Cedar Rapids and return. Tickets to be sold May 30 to June 6, 1892, inclusive, good for return passage until and including June 30, 1892. Tickets to be good for going passage on date of sale only, and for continuous passage in each direction. Ordinary non-signature excursion tickets to be used, except that tickets used from terminals shall be of the ironclad signature form. Such terminals to be understood to be Kansas City, Leavenworth, Atchison, St. Joseph, Omaha, Council Bluffs, Sioux City, St. Paul, Minneapolis, Milwaukee, Chicago, St. Louis and Peoria.

The above rates and arrangements are tendered for the use of connecting lines, and said connecting lines are notified that their tickets and orders which may reach these lines prior to May 30, 1892, or later than June 6, 1892, will not be accepted or exchanged; said connecting lines are further notified that in ticketing over these lines for this occasion, tickets or orders for same of the ironclad signature form must be used."

The Trunk Line Association have promised to make a rate of one fare for the round trip. The Trans-Missouri and Southern Associations have not, as yet, been heard from, but it is hoped that they will respond favorably to the requests made. The Committee of Arrangements for our next Annual Meeting very kindly assisted us in making these arrangements and while we did not get all we hoped to obtain in the way of stop-over privileges, we have secured a low rate, as low as we ought to ask for. Our Brethren, and others interested, will please preserve this paper.

D. L. MILLER,
Chairman of Committee on Transportation.

OUR quarterly church council, held in the Chapel, passed off very pleasantly a few days ago. An aged brother from the Old Order element was restored to fellowship. ·Bro. G. V. Goshorn was advanced to· the second degree of the ministry. Much other work was done, all of which, we trust, will redound to the glory and honor of God.

CHRISTIANS who imagine that they cannot be of any value to the cause of Christ simply because they possess only ordinary talents, may receive encouragement from what Spurgeon one time said: "Simon Peter was worth ten Andrews, so far as we can gather from sacred history, and yet Andrew was instrumental in bringing him to Jesus. You may be deficient in talent, and yet be the means of drawing to Christ one who will become eminent in grace and service."

FANATICS, of whatever religion, seldom possess grace enough to keep them within reasonable bounds. They are always a dangerous element. Recently a mob, composed of fanatics, members of the Greek church at Athens, Greece, attacked, pillaged, and partly burned the Protestant church in that city. They also wrecked the parsonage, and everything belonging to the ministers residing in it, was destroyed. The chief minister is agent of the British and Foreign Bible Society, and intends to claim compensation for his losses from the government of Greece. Several members of the church, during the attack, fled to the British consulate, and were pursued to its very doors by the fanatics from whom they had escaped. Defeated in overtaking them, the mob demanded their surrender by the Consul, but, of course, in this they failed. They then waited at the Consulate to assault any who might leave it to return to their homes; but in this they were also foiled. The wrecked church was built with money subscribed by both Englishmen and Americans; and no reason can be assigned for its destruction except the virulence of sectarian prejudice.

A BROTHER sends us a copy of *The Baptist Banner*, published at Huntingdon, W. Va., Jan. 6, 1892, containing an article against trine immersion by Mr. Bibb, with a request that we reply to it. We think there is not much in the article to reply to. All the points in the article are derived, in a measure, from the "Quinter and McConnell Debate," and therefore contain nothing new unless it be the intimation that our people are few, and therefore our form of baptism has not numerical strength behind it. It may not be amiss to remind this Baptist writer, in the language of Hinton, one of the ablest Baptist historians in America that

"The practice of trine immersion prevailed, in the West as well as the East, till the fourth council of Toledo, which, acting under the advice of Gregory the Great, in order to settle some disputes which had arisen, decreed that henceforth only one immersion should be used in baptism; and from that time the practice of only one immersion gradually became general throughout the western or Latin Church."—*Hinton's History of Baptism*, p. 158.

We may further remind him that all the ancient Baptist churches, such as Waldenses, etc., practiced trine immersion. Our people still retain the same old practice. Furthermore, if there ever was any person baptized by backward single immersion before the year 1592, we would like some one to refer us to the book and page giving us an account of it. By the time the writer of the article referred to gets through replying to the quotation with which Baptist histories abound, he may, in the language of Robinson, the most noted Baptist historian of England, be ready to exclaim:

"It is not true that dipping was exchanged for sprinkling by choice before the Reformation (A. D. 1517), for, till after that period, the ordinary baptism was trine immersion."—*Robinson's History of Baptism*, p. 148.

SISTER ELIZABETH WITWER, of Chicago, Ill., is spending the winter with her son in Dallas, Texas. She seems well pleased with her visit. We make the following extract from the letter, as it contains a lesson that should not only be heeded by our members, but they should be urged to show more kindness towards the strangers who attend our meetings: "I think some of our members are too timid in not coming forward and getting acquainted with new members and strangers when they come among us. I have attended both Baptist and Methodist churches at Normal Park, Chicago. Their churches are very plain and they seem to notice strangers when they come in. After they are dismissed they come up and shake hands and introduce you to some others and invite you to come again, and it makes one feel more at home. I think this is the way we ought to do. It makes the strangers feel that we are interested in their welfare. Invite them to come again; find out where they live and call to see them if it is so you can. In this way we might often encourage each other."

GO AND SIN NO MORE.

WE clip the following from the *Morning News*, published at Lancaster, Pa :

"Rev. John Herr, a German Baptist Elder, who combines with his pastoral work the occupation of a farmer, awoke from his sleep to see two neighbors robbing his store-house where he kept his meat. One was found to be within, taking the plunder, while the other received it at the door.

The man at the door soon left with his first load, but the preacher took his place quietly and simulated the departed thief's voice and manner. He received his own meat and carefully deposited it in the bag prepared by the marauders until all had been removed. At this point the second thief returned, and both were terror-stricken when they found themselves in the minister's presence.

He requested them to replace all the meat, then presented them with as much of it as they could carry, gave them his blessing and told them to "go and sin no more." They went with tears in their eyes and promised to do better.

BAPTIZED 3,000 IN ONE NIGHT.

ELD. J. B. BRINEY, a Disciple minister and writer of acknowledged ability, is writing the ablest series of articles for the *Christian Evangelist* on the forms of baptism that we have ever read. From article No. 22 we clip the following, which is worth preserving:

"On the 16th of April, A. D. 404, Chrysostom immersed three thousand people in Constantinople, dipping every person *three times!* Perthes, in his life of Chrysostom, as quoted by Dr. Christian, says: 'On Easter ·eve, April 16, the Church of Chrysostom and the friendly clergy met together, as was the custom, to spend the night in vigils and to greet the rays of the Easter morning. With them were assembled three thousand young Christians who were to receive baptism.' Chrysostom, as quoted by Dr. Christian, very plainly tells what he did in baptizing: 'For we sink our heads in the water as in some grave, the old man is buried and the whole man, having sunk entirely down, is concealed. Then we emerge him, the new man rises again. For as it is easy for us to be immersed and to emerge, so it is easy for God to bury the old man and bring to light the new. This is done three times.' Of this transaction Dr. Christian well says: 'If Chrysostom could immerse three thousand converts in one night, when the soldiers threatened his life and drove him from his church, it would seem an easy thing for Peter to immerse a like number when' he had

---

favor with all the people, as he did have on the day of Pentecost."

This John Chrysostom was for a number of years bishop of the church of Antioch, where the disciples were first called Christians. He was probably the finest Greek scholar of Christian antiquity. The above quotation shows the possibility of one man baptizing 3,000 persons in a short time, and also serves as additional proof in defense of trine-immersion.

RAILROAD ARRANGEMENTS FOR OUR ANNUAL CONFERENCE TO BE HELD AT CEDAR RAPIDS, IOWA, BEGINNING JUNE 7, 1892.

THE Western and Central Passenger Associations have granted one fare for the round trip, as the following extracts from their circulars will show. The Western Association,· under date of March 4, says:

Lines in this Association have agreed upon the following arrangement for the above-named Meeting, namely:

One fare for the round trip from all Association points to Cedar Rapids and return. Tickets to be sold May 30 to June 6, 1892, inclusive, good for return passage until and including June 30, 1892. Tickets to be good for going passage on date of sale only, and for continuous passage in each direction. Ordinary non-signature excursion tickets to be used, except that tickets used from terminals shall be of the ironclad signature form; such terminals to be understood to be Kansas City, Leavenworth, Atchison, St. Joseph, Omaha, Council Bluffs, Sioux City, St. Paul, Minneapolis, Milwaukee, Chicago, St. Louis and Peoria.

The above rates and arrangements are tendered for the use of connecting lines, and said connecting lines are notified that their tickets and orders which may reach these lines prior to May 19, 1892, or later than June 6, 1892, will not be accepted or exchanged; said connecting lines are further notified that in ticketing over these lines for this occasion, tickets or orders for same of the ironclad signature form must be used.

The Central Association, under date of March 9, says:

TO ALL MEMBERS OF THE CENTRAL TRAFFIC ASSOCIATION.

Gentlemen:—

At the meeting of the Passenger Committee of this Association on the 2nd inst., it was

Resolved, That a rate of one lowest limited first-class fare for the round trip be authorized to the eastern terminal of the Western Passenger Association, to be added to the rates the Western Passenger Association may establish; ticket conditions to conform to those adopted by that Association.

The Western Passenger Association have, in their Circular No. 34, dated March 4, 1892, authorized the following:

"One fare for the round trip from all Association Points to Cedar Rapids and return. Tickets to be sold May 30 to June 6, 1892, inclusive, good for return passage until and including June 30, 1892. Tickets to be good for going passage on date of sale only, and for continuous passage in each direction. Ordinary non-signature excursion tickets to be used, except that tickets used from terminals shall be of the ironclad signature form. Such terminals to be understood to be Kansas City, Leavenworth, Atchison, St. Joseph, Omaha,· Council Bluffs, Sioux City, St. Paul, Minneapolis, Milwaukee, Chicago, St. Louis and Peoria.

The above rates and arrangements are tendered for the use of connecting lines, and said connecting lines are notified that their tickets and orders which may reach these lines prior to May 19, 1892, or later than June 6, 1892, will not be accepted or exchanged; said connecting lines are further notified that in ticketing over these lines for this occasion, tickets or orders for same of the ironclad signature form must be used."

The Trunk Line Association has promised to make a rate of one fare for the round trip. The Trans-Missouri and Southern Associations have not, as yet, been heard from, but it is hoped that they will respond favorably to the requests made. The Committee of Arrangements for our next Annual Meeting very kindly assisted us in making these arrangements and while we did not get all we hoped to obtain in the way of stop-over privileges, we have secured a low rate, as low as we ought to ask for. Our Brethren, and others interested, will please preserve this paper.

D. L. MILLER,

Chairman of Committee on Transportation.

CORRESPONDENCE.

"Write what thou seest, and send it unto the churches."

☞ Church News solicited for this Department. If you have had a good meeting, send a report of it, so that others may rejoice with you. In writing give name of church, County and State. Be brief. Notes of Travel should be as short as possible. Land Advertisements are not solicited for this Department. We have an advertising page, and, if necessary, will issue supplements.

From Lancaster, Pa.

SUNDAY evening, Feb. 21, we had the last of a series of meetings, commenced by the Brethren in the Lancaster church, Feb. 6, 1892. The meetings were conducted by Bro. Albert Hollinger, of Huntsdale, Cumberland Co., Pa. While with us, Bro. Hollinger labored earnestly, preaching, in all, nineteen sermons.

As an immediate result, the church was built up and the members strengthened. Two precious souls heeded the Savior's call and were baptized. Four others gave their consent to come in the near future, and one dear soul desires to be reclaimed.

We feel to thank God and take courage in regard to the work here. It is but a short time since we were organized into a separate church, and though few in number, our faith is strong in the Lord. We feel confident that the Lord is in the work and that we will be prospered, and be a power for good in the work of the Lord in this city. We have been organized to stay, but we are still needy and dependent, and desire the prayers of all who would have the cause of Christ prospered in our city. A. J. EVANS.

Feb. 23.

From the Franklin County Church, Iowa.

WE have just closed a short, yet very interesting and soul-cheering series of meetings. Feb. 20, Wm. Albright, of Grundy County, Iowa, commenced the work. Feb. 23 our elder, J. F. Eikenberry, of Greene, Iowa, came to his assistance. The meetings continued until Feb. 28. Bro. Albright did most of the preaching,—ten sermons in all. The congregations were fair, considering the dark and foggy nights and very muddy roads. As an immediate result nine precious young souls were buried with Christ in baptism. A number of others were deeply impressed. May they not put it off, but come to their Savior ere it is eternally too late!

Feb. 27 we met for a members' meeting. Here we received good admonitions and encouraging words from our dear elder. May we ever remember what we heard during these meetings, and may we live more faithful and consecrated lives, that we may be bright and shining lights to those who are yet on the broad road.

MARY C. ALLEN.

Hansell, Iowa.

From the Round Mountain Church, Ark.

AFTER the death of my mother-in-law which took place Jan. 14, caused by La Grippe and pneumonia, my whole family took the La Grippe. Some of the children soon got over it. The writer, however, took a relapse and was very sick. It was the severest attack of sickness I had for twenty-one years. At present writing I can walk out a little, but am not able to do anything yet. Wife was not so long getting over it. In the neighborhood so many had it that there were scarcely enough well persons to take care of the sick. Five adults died in this neighborhood from the effects of that dread disease. Three of them were members of the church. They will be much missed in church and Sunday-school. We have had no meetings for more than a month, but I hope that I will be able again, before long, to resume my labors in the

ministry, and that the work will move onward. It is through the mercies of God that we are spared; he saved us. Before I took sick, I was out in Madison County twice, about twenty-five miles distant, and preached several times for the people where Bro. Shower lives. There was quite an interest taken in the meetings. I had intended to hold a series of meetings there before this time, but was hindered through sickness. There are good prospects of several coming to the church there. It may build up a nucleus which may terminate in a church. I hope that I may yet be able, some time this spring, to give them a meeting, as I believe it will result in much good. The interest at our meetings and our social meetings has been very good. SAMUEL WEIMER.

Feb. 27.

From Warrensburgh, Mo.

THE Annual District Meeting of the Middle District of Missouri was held in the Warrensburgh church, Feb. 18 and 19, together with a Ministerial Meeting, March 17.

The Ministerial Meeting was well attended by the ministers of the District, as well as the members. There was the deepest interest taken in the proceedings by all present, making the Ministerial Meeting very pleasant and, undoubtedly, edifying and profitable.

The District Meeting occupied two days. Considerable time was taken up by missionary business, which is a growing work in this District. The regular quarterly council was held March 3. The business before the meeting and its disposal, indicated a healthful state of the membership. For this we are truly thankful, and pray the Lord that it may so continue.

Our Sunday-school for the summer was organized by electing Bro. John E. Mohler as Superintendent and Abram Weaver as Assistant. Our Sunday-school will commence the first Sunday in April. We also have preaching every Sunday through the summer. It is proposed to conduct the Sunday-school on the topic plan, using largely Bible characters for subjects. A teachers' meeting will be held every Sunday evening, preparatory to the next Sunday's work.

ALICE A. ROOP.

March 5.

A Sad Accident.

THE most shocking accident that ever happened in the bounds of the Price's Creek church, occurred Feb. 11, at 9 A. M. Mr. Jacob Kiesling, and his son William, and a hired hand, Mr. D. Shivadecker, were at work in a saw-mill. As William was turning the throttle, the boiler exploded, literally blowing things to atoms. William was killed instantly, but Mr. Shivadecker lived thirty minutes. Mr. Kiesling was thrown into the dust pit, consequently was not hurt much, excepting that his face and one arm were badly scalded. At this writing he is speedily recovering.

William Kiesling's age, at the time of his departure, was twenty-six years, two months and eight days. Mr. Shivadecker's age was twenty-nine years, two months and sixteen days. Both were unmarried. Mr. Shivadecker was a member of the Brethren church, but William Kiesling made no profession. JOS. LONGANECKER.

Manchester, Ohio.

From Lawrenceville, Va.

LAST Saturday, Feb. 27, we had a very enjoyable council-meeting. Bro. S. H. Myers, from Timberville, Va., was with us. On account of the inclemency of the weather not many members attended. One sister was received by letter. A considerable amount of business was transacted in

love and union. Among the business attended to was the establishing of a Sunday-school at the Valley Pike meeting-house the coming season. On motion Bro. John W. Leedy was appointed Superintendent. Eld. S. A. Shaver was elected on the Standing Committee, at the District Meeting, held at Elk Run, April 13 and 14. Brethren Joseph S. Gochenour and John Byman were our delegates. M. H. COPP.

From Gretna, Ohio.

WE have just passed through an interesting series of meetings. Bro. J. M. Mohler, of Lewistown, Pa., came to the Logan church Feb. 8, and and labored with us until the 23rd, preaching, in all, twenty-five sermons, and holding two children's meetings. Owing to inclement weather and bad roads, the congregations were not as large as we would like to have seen. Six came out and made the good confession, and set their faces Zionward. All were young people. Others were "almost persuaded." O may they not put off the one thing needful to their soul's salvation until it is too late, but say with the one of old, "'As for me and my house we will serve the Lord."

We held our regular quarterly council March 2. Bro. L. H. Dickey, of Alvada, Ohio, was with us. Everything passed off in peace and harmony. One query was sent to District Meeting. Eld. Abednego Miller was sent as delegate to Annual Meeting. We also elected our Sunday-school officers for the ensuing summer. Bro. L. E. Kauffman was chosen as Superintendent.

J. R. SNYDER.

A Favor Asked.

IF some brother or sister, in each congregation of our Brotherhood will be kind enough to write to me, answering the following questions, I shall consider it a great favor:

1. When was the last singing school held in your church, and by whom was it taught?

2. About how many members in your congregation can read the *character notes*, and how many the *round notes*?

3. What kind of books are used to sing from in your church services? What kind in the Sunday-school?

4. What can you say of the singing in your church?—is it good or poor?

My motive in making this request is to learn something of the status of the song worship in the Brotherhood. I am especially interested in this part of religious service, and have been, for a number of years, devoting my best energies to the improvement of the singing in the churches.

We, as a church, believe in congregational singing, and I believe that, upon the whole, we have better singing by the congregations than most other denominations, but there is much room for improvement. It is a sad fact that the teaching of the young folks to sing, and especially to sing church music, is greatly neglected. One great help in bringing children up in the nurture and admonition of the Lord is to teach them to sing, so that they can sing in the sanctuary and in the home. Many boys and girls, instead of spending the evenings at home, and attending church and Sunday-school services, go elsewhere, and often to questionable places, in search of enjoyment.

Brethren should see to it that they do not make home a prison house for their children, but a pleasant, enjoyable place; then the children will not care to seek pleasures away from home. Music, of the proper kind, is one of the best of home attractions. Especially ought children to be taught to sing and enjoy sacred music.

WM. BEERY.

Huntingdon, Pa.

CORRESPONDENCE.

"Write what thou seest, and send it unto the churches."

Church News solicited for this Department. If you have had a meeting, send a report of it, so that others may rejoice with you. ... give name of church, County and State. Be brief. Notes of ...should be as short as possible. Land Advertisements not for ... this Department. We have an advertising page, and, if neces. ... Issue supplements.

From Lancaster, Pa.

...NDAY evening, Feb. 21, we had the last of a ... of meetings, commenced by the Brethren in Lancaster church, Feb. 6, 1892. The meet-were conducted by Bro. Albert Hollinger, of ...adale, Cumberland Co., Pa. While with us, Hollinger labored earnestly, preaching, in ...ineteen sermons.

... an immediate result, the church was built ... the members strengthened. Two precious ... heeded the Savior's call and were baptized. ... others gave their consent to come in the future, and one dear soul desires to be re-...ed.

... feel to thank God and take courage in ...rd to the work here. It is but a short time ... we were organized into a separate church, though few in number, our faith is strong in Lord. We feel confident that the Lord is in ...work and that we will be prospered, and be a ...r for good in the work of the Lord in this ...

We have been organized to stay, but we are needy and dependent, and desire the prayers ... who would have the cause of Christ pros-...d in our city.　　A. J. EVANS.

...b. 23.

From the Franklin County Church, Iowa.

...E have just closed a short, yet very interesting ...soul-cheering series of meetings. Feb. 20, ... Albright, of Grundy County, Iowa, com-...ed the work. Feb. 23 our elder, J. F. Eiken-..y, of Greene, Iowa, came to his assistance. ... meetings continued until Feb. 28. Bro. Al-...it did most of the preaching,—ten sermons in ... The congregations were fair, considering the ... and foggy nights and very muddy roads. As ...mediate result nine precious young souls ... buried with Christ in baptism. A number ...hers were deeply impressed. May they not ... off, but come to their Savior ere it is eter-...too late!

...b. 27 we met for a members' meeting. Here ...ceived good admonitions and encouraging ... from our dear elder. May we ever remem-...hat we heard during these meetings, and ...e live more faithful and consecrated lives, ...e may be bright and shining lights to those ...re yet on the broad road.

...　　　MARY C. ALLEN.

...nsell, Iowa.

From the Round Mountain Church, Ark.

...EN the death of my mother-in-law which took ...Jan. 14, caused by La Grippe and pneumo-..y whole family took the La Grippe. Some ... children soon got over it. The writer, how-...ook a relapse and was very sick. It was the ...st attack of sickness I had for twenty-one ...

At present writing I can walk out a little, ... not able to do anything yet. Wife was not ... getting over it. In the neighborhood so ... had it that there were scarcely enough well ... to take care of the sick. Five adults died ... neighborhood from the effects of that dread ... Three of them were members of the ... They will be much missed in church and ...y-school. We have had no meetings for ...han a month, but I hope that I will be able ... before long, to resume my labors in the

---

ministry, and that the work will move onward. It is through the mercies of God that we are spared; he saved us. Before I took sick, I was out in Madison County twice, about twenty-five miles distant, and preached several times for the people where Bro. Shower lives. There was quite an in-terest taken in the meetings. I had intended to hold a series of meetings there before this time, but was hindered through sickness. There are good prospects of several coming to the church there. It may build up a nucleus which may ter-minate in a church. I hope that I may yet be able, some time this spring, to give them a meeting, as I believe it will result in much good. The interest at our meetings and our social meetings has been very good.　　　SAMUEL WEIMER.

Feb. 27.

From Warrensburgh, Mo.

THE Annual District Meeting of the Middle District of Missouri was held in the Warrens-burgh church, Feb. 18 and 19, together with a Ministerial Meeting, March 17.

The Ministerial Meeting was well attended by the ministers of the District, as well as the mem-bers. There was the deepest interest taken in the proceedings by all present, making the Minister-ial Meeting very pleasant, and, undoubtedly, edi-fying and profitable.

The District Meeting occupied two days. Con-siderable time was taken up by missionary business, which is a growing work in this District. The regular quarterly council was held March 3. The business before the meeting and its disposal, indi-cated a healthful state of the membership. For this we are truly thankful, and pray the Lord that it may so continue.

Our Sunday-school for the summer was organ-ized by electing Bro. John E. Mohler as Superin-tendent and Abram Weaver as Assistant. Our Sunday-school will commence the first Sunday in April. We also have preaching every Sunday through the summer. It is proposed to conduct the Sunday-school on the topic plan, using largely Bible characters for subjects. A teachers' meet-ing will be held every Sunday evening, prepara-tory to the next Sunday's work.

　　　ALICE A. ROOP.

March 5.

A Sad Accident.

THE most shocking accident that ever happened in the bounds of the Price's Creek church, oc-curred Feb. 11, at 9 A. M. Mr. Jacob Kissling, and his son William, and a hired hand, Mr. D. Shiv-adecker, were at work in a saw-mill. William was turning the throttle, the boiler exploded, lit-erally blowing things to atoms. William was killed instantly, but Mr. Shivadecker lived thirty minutes. Mr. Kissling was thrown into the dust pit, conse-quently was not hurt much, excepting that his face and one arm were badly scalded. At this writing he is speedily recovering.

William Kissling's age, at the time of his de-parture, was twenty-six years, two months and eight days. Mr. Shivadecker's age was twenty-nine years, two months and sixteen days. Both were unmarried. Mr. Shivadecker was a member of the Brethren church, but William Kissling made no profession.　　　JOS. LONGANECKER.

Manchester, Ohio.

From Lawrenceville, Va.

LAST Saturday, Feb. 27, we had a very enjoya-ble council-meeting. Bro. S. H. Myers, from Timberville, Va., was with us. On account of the inclemency of the weather not many members at-tended. One sister was received by letter. A considerable amount of business was transacted in

---

love and union. Among the business attended to was the establishing of a Sunday-school at the Valley Pike meeting-house the coming season. On motion Bro. John W. Leedy was appointed Superintendent. Eld. S. A. Shaver was elected on the Standing Committee, at the District Meet-ing, held at Elk Run, April 13 and 14. Brethren Joseph S. Gochenour and John Byman were our delegates.　　　M. H. COPP.

From Gretna, Ohio.

WE have just passed through an interesting se-ries of meetings. Bro. J. M. Mohler, of Lewis-town, Pa., came to the Logan church Feb. 8, and and labored with us until the 23rd, preaching, in all, twenty-five sermons, and holding two children's meetings. Owing to inclement weather and bad roads, the congregations were not as large as we would like to have seen. Six came out and made the good confession, and set their faces Zionward. All were young people. Others were "almost persuaded." O may they not put off the one thing needful to their soul's salvation until it is too late, but say with the one of old, "As for me and my house we will serve the Lord."

We held our regular quarterly council March 2. Bro. L. H. Dickey, of Alvada, Ohio, was with us. Everything passed off in peace and harmony. One query was sent to District Meeting. Eld. Abednego Miller was sent as delegate to Annual Meeting. We also elected our Sunday-school officers for the ensuing summer. Bro. L. E. Kauffman was chosen as Superintendent.

　　　J. R. SNYDER.

A Favor Asked.

IF some brother or sister, in each congregation of our Brotherhood will be kind enough to write to me, answering the following questions, I shall consider it a great favor:

1. When was the last singing school held in your church, and by whom was it taught?

2. About how many members in your congrega-tion can read the character notes, and how many the round notes?

3. What kind of books are used to sing from in your church services? What kind in the Sunday-school?

4. What can you say of the singing in your church?—is it good or poor?

My motive in making this request is to learn something of the status of the song worship in the Brotherhood. I am especially interested in this part of religious service, and have been, for a number of years, devoting my best energies to the improvement of the singing in the churches.

We, as a church, believe in congregational singing, and I believe that, upon the whole, we have better singing by the congregations than most other denominations, but there is much room for improvement. It is a sad fact that the teach-ing of the young folks to sing, and especially to sing church music, is greatly neglected. One great help in bringing children up in the nurture and admonition of the Lord is to teach them to sing, so that they can sing in the sanctuary and in the home. Many boys and girls, instead of spend-ing the evenings at home, and attending church and Sunday-school services, go elsewhere, and oft-en to questionable places, in search of enjoyment.

Brethren should see to it that they do not make home a prison house for their children, but a pleasant, enjoyable place; then the children will not care to seek pleasures away from home. Mu-sic, of the proper kind, is one of the best of home attractions. Especially ought children to be taught to sing and enjoy sacred music.

　　　WM. BERRY.

Huntingdon, Pa.

"The Life of Bro.
will bear re-reading
roug the Brethren.
service of love, is a
l food to the soul—

xeter church met in
avid Bechtelheimer
as settled, we hope,
brother will remain
us. May the Lord
—*Friedrich Wied.*

t met in quarterly
s great deal of busi-
all passed off pleas-
house of the Lord;
ns. Brethren John
elegates to District
as baptized on the
hel Weimer.

darch 5, in quarter-
business before the
ith a Christian-like
tey, and Eld. S. M.
ky Co., Ohio, were
arger will represent
District Meeting of
. *C. Rau, McComb.*

m of the Lafayette
menced a series of
, Mohler, of Lewis-
ings. He was with
thstanding the wet
ndance, to listen to
nd much good was
ord's side and others
ay the Lord's good

iller and Brubaker,
Feb. 13, and stayed
ave us sixteen inter-
e made to weep and
for his unspeakable
ult, three were bap-
the cost seriously.
to organize a Sun-
our house Wednes-

k and sisters of the
h quarterly council
b business came up
d off quietly. Bro.
delegate to Annual
alized our Sunday-
mmunion. May the
kers! To-day, Feb.
f the Yellow River
in public worship,
application for bap-
aries H. Sellers.

olderman came to us
ng at Liberty that
Sunday, and at the
ay night, with fair
y council was held
was commendable,
er we were having.
all the business was
anner. Eight mem-
nd two letters were
Harris and Leander
gates to the District
in the Shoal Creek
Matilda Holderread,

Garden Grove, Iowa.—I arrived safely home
March 5, and found all well. During my visit, in
the State of Indiana, from Oct. 22, 1891, to March
2, 1892 (with the exception of nine days in Ohio),
I had the pleasure of listening to fifty-six sermons. Thus I received much spiritual food,
which was highly appreciated by me.—*Jemima
Kob, March 9.*

Milmine, Ill.—We met in council March 10. As
the weather was very inclement, the attendance
was small. All business passed off very pleasantly. The writer was appointed correspondent for
this church. Elder D. B. Gibson was elected delegate to Annual Meeting. Bro. Philip Siders was
elected as trustee for our two meeting-houses, to
take the place of one removed. Our church has
suffered much through emigration in the last
few years, but our loss is the gain of other
churches.—*Mamie V. Gibson.*

Garrison, Iowa.—Bro. James L. Thomas, of Ames,
Iowa, came to us Feb. 27, and stayed till March 6.
He preached, in all, eleven sermons. He held
forth the Word with power, so that both saint
and sinner received warning and instruction.
Though we cannot report any added to the fold,
we believe there were some good impressions
made. Though the roads were almost impassable,
we never saw more interest manifested. We pray
that the good seed sown may be gathered ere
long.—*E. H. Stauffer, Feb. 7.*

Green Springs, Pa.—The members here were made
to rejoice, when, during a series of meetings, conducted by our home brethren, six precious souls
united with the church by baptism. May they be
bright, shining lights in the church! Another
young lady had made up her mind to go with us,
but was hindered by her mother. Notwithstanding the inclemency of the weather and the bad
roads, they had good meetings. May the good
work go on till many more give their hearts to
God!—*Leah T. Miller, Oakville, Pa.*

Chautauqua, Kans.—Bro. Caleb Fogle, of Independence, Kans, commenced a series of meetings
in our school-house Feb. 22, preaching, in all, ten
sermons. He closed March 1, with a growing interest. We had fair congregations, considering
the inclemency of the weather and sickness. As
an immediate result one came out on the Lord's
side, and was added to the church by baptism.
We think there were others near the kingdom.
May the Lord help us all to walk in that straight
and narrow path that leads to life eternal!—*Cathern Rogers, March 9.*

Pipe Creek, Ind.—The brethren and sisters of this
church assembled in council March 10. Everything passed off in peace and harmony. We appointed our love-feast for May 14, commencing at
10 A. M. Delegates were chosen for Annual and
District Meetings. Bro. Daniel Bowser was selected as delegate to Annual Meeting, and brethren Joseph Shepler and Daniel Long as delegates
to District Meeting. Bro. Daniel P. Nead was
re-elected Sunday-school Superintendent. Our
Sunday-school will commence in a few weeks.—
W. B. Dailey, Peru, Ind., March 12.

White Church, Ind.—Our quarterly council occurred March 2. A good deal of business came
before the meeting, but all went off very pleasantly. Bro. S. M. Dunbar was elected as delegate to
Annual Meeting, and Bro. Ira Fisher to the District Meeting. Bro. J. C. Murray commenced
meetings for us Feb. 15, and closed March 2. As
an immediate result of the meetings, seven were
baptized, three reclaimed, and the church much
built up. March 2 one was added to the church
by letter. This makes ten added to the fold since
our last report. The Lord be praised for all his
goodness!—*F. Johnson.*

Dayton, Ohio.—We are in the midst of a series of
meetings, with fair weather and good attendance
and attention. One has made the good choice
and was baptized to walk in newness of life.
Many more are counting the cost. Bro. Isaac
Frantz, of Pleasant Hill, Ohio, is doing the
preaching. Two applicants came forward this
evening.—*Elmer Wombold, March 7.*

Wolf Lake, Ind.—The Brethren of the Blue River
district, Whitley Co., Ind., met in quarterly
council March 5. Considerable business was before the meeting, but all was disposed of in a
Christian-like manner. We elected one delegate
to Annual Meeting, and also the needed officers
for our Sunday-school, which is to commence
soon. We agreed to hold our love-feast, the Lord
willing, June 18, to begin at 3 P. M.—*Levi Zumbrun, March 12.*

Bazleton, W. Va.—I left my home Feb. 28, and
went to Pine Grove, where I held a series of
meetings. I preached eight sermons and baptized four precious souls. Several more made the
good confession of faith, and will be baptized
in the near future. Others are counting the cost.
We had a very interesting meeting, and pray God
to still continue the good work, till all will return
to the Lord, and be saved on the easy terms of
the Gospel. Brethren, let us not forget to look to
the Father for help. Let us pray in behalf of the
poor soldiers who have enlisted in the service of
the Master!—*Joseph Guthrie.*

Navarre, Kans.—The Abilene church met in quarterly council March 3. Considerable business
came before the meeting, and was disposed of in a
Christian-like spirit. Bro. Daniel Vaniman was
with us and presided over the meeting, and also
preached a few evenings for us very acceptably.
We are glad to have the Brethren come and give
us such timely admonition. Bro. Geo. Manon
was elected delegate to District Meeting, and Bro.
Jacob Keller delegate to Annual Meeting, with
Eld. John Humbarger as alternate. The church
decided to hold a love-feast May 7, commencing
at 2 o'clock P. M.—*John J. Manon, Gypsum,
Kans.*

Williamsport, Ind.—Bro. Solomon Blickenstaff
visited us again Feb. 6, and remained until the
15th, preaching in all twelve sermons. There
was good attendance, and although there were no
more added to our small number, the meeting did
us all good. Quite a sad accident happened to
Bro. Jacob Frederick's oldest son. Two weeks
ago this Friday evening, as he was riding to town,
his pony became frightened at some obstruction
in the road, and threw him off, bruising him considerably about the head and face. He was unconscious for two or three days, and it was feared
something serious might result, but at last accounts he was better. Bro. Mohler paid us a
pleasant visit during our meetings.—*Geo. W. Mc-
Kinney.*

Huntington, Ind.—Eld. Joseph Spitzer commenced
a series of meetings in the Loon Creek house, of
the Salimony congregation, on the evening of
Feb. 22, and continued until the evening of March
4, when we closed on account of the inclement
weather and bad roads. Bro. Spitzer preached
the Word in unmistakable terms, and with a zeal
worthy of the cause, but the weather and roads
were so bad and the nights so dark that our congregations were small and irregular most of the
time. Two dear young sisters confessed Christ
and were buried with him in baptism, we trust to
walk in newness of life. Our quarterly council
was held March 5. A large amount of business
came before the meeting. We appointed our
love-feast for June 3, at 3 P. M.—*A. N. Snowberger, March 7.*

"The Life of Bro.
will bear re-reading
tong the Brethren.
service of love, is a
t food to the soul.—

lxeter church met in
avid Bechtelheimer
as settled, we hope,
brother will remain
us. May the Lord
!—*Friedrich Wied-*

t met in quarterly
a great deal of busi-
all passed off pleas-
house of the Lord.
ne. Brethren John
elegates to District
as baptized on 'the
hel *Weimer.*

March 5, in quarter-
business before the
ith a Christian-like
tey, and Eld. S. M.
ty Co., Ohio, were
rger will represent
District Meeting of
. *C. Rau, McComb,*

en of the Lafayette
imenced a series of
. Mohler, of Lewis-
ings. He was with
thstanding the wet
ndance, to listen to
nd much good was
.ord's side and others
ay the Lord's good

'ller and Brubaker,
Feb. 13, and stayed
ive us sixteen inter-
 made to weep and
for his unspeakable
ilt, three were bap-
the cost seriously,
to organize a Sun-
our house Wednes-

and sisters of the
 quarterly councoil
business came up
t off quietly. Bro.
lelegate to Annual
ized our Sunday-
munion. May the
ters! To-day, Feb.
t the Yellow River
in public worship,
pplication for bap-
ries *H. Sellers.*

lderman came to us
ig at Liberty that
Sunday, and at the
ay night, with fair
y council was held
was commendable,
er we were having.
all the business was
inner. Eight mem-
nd two letters were
arris and Leander
ates to the District
n the Shoal Creek
atilda *Holderread,*

Garden Grove, Iowa.—I arrived safely home March 5, and found all well. During my visit in the State of Indiana, from Oct. 22, 1891, to March 2, 1892 (with the exception of nine days in Ohio), I had the pleasure of listening to fifty-six sermons. Thus I received much spiritual food, which was highly appreciated by me.—*Jemima Kob, March 9*

Milmine, Ill.—We met in council March 10. As the weather was very inclement, the attendance was small. All business passed off very pleasantly. The writer was appointed correspondent for this church. Elder D. B. Gibson was elected delegate to Annual Meeting. Bro. Philip Siders was elected as trustee for our two meeting-houses, to take the place of one removed. Our church has suffered much through emigration in the last few years, but our loss is the gain of other churches.—*Mamie V. Gibson.*

Garrison, Iowa.—Bro. James L. Thomas, of Ames, Iowa, came to us Feb. 27, and stayed till March 6. He preached, in all, eleven sermons. He held forth the Word with power, so that both saint and sinner received warning and instruction. Though we cannot report any added to the fold, we believe there were some good impressions made. Though the roads were almost impassable, we never saw more interest manifested. We pray that the good seed sown may be gathered ere long.—*E. H. Stauffer, Feb. 7.*

Green Springs, Pa.—The members here were made to rejoice, when, during a series of meetings, conducted by our home brethren, six precious souls united with the church by baptism. May they be bright, shining lights in the church! Another young lady had made up her mind to go with us, but was hindered by her mother. Notwithstanding the inclemency of the weather and the bad roads, they had good meetings. May the good work go on till many more give their hearts to God!—*Leah T. Miller, Oakville, Pa.*

Chautauqua, Kans.—Bro. Caleb Fogle, of Independence, Kans., commenced a series of meetings in our school-house Feb. 22, preaching, in all, ten sermons. He closed March 1, with a growing interest. We had fair congregations, considering the inclemency of the weather and sickness. As an immediate result one came out on the Lord's side, and was added to the church by baptism. We think there were others near the kingdom. May the Lord help us all to walk in that straight and narrow path that leads to life eternal!—*Cathern Rogers, March 9.*

Pipe Creek, Ind.—The brethren and sisters of this church assembled in council March 10. Everything passed off in peace and harmony. We appointed our love-feast for May 14, commencing at 10 A. M. Delegates were chosen for Annual and District Meetings. Bro. Daniel Bowser was selected as delegate to Annual Meeting, and brethren Joseph Shepler and Daniel Long as delegates to District Meeting. Bro. Daniel P. Nead was re-elected Sunday-school Superintendent. Our Sunday-school will commence in a few weeks.—*W. B. Dailey, Peru, Ind., March 11.*

White Church, Ind.—Our quarterly council occurred March 2. A good deal of business came before the meeting, but all went off very pleasantly. Bro. S. M. Dunbar was elected as delegate to Annual Meeting, and Bro. Ira Fisher to the District Meeting. Bro. J. C. Murray commenced meetings for us Feb. 15, and closed March 2. As an immediate result of the meetings, seven were baptized, three reclaimed, and the church much built up. March 2 one was added to the church by letter. This makes ten added to the fold since our last report. The Lord be praised for all his goodness!—*F. Johnson.*

Dayton, Ohio.—We are in the midst of a series of meetings, with fair weather and good attendance and attention. One has made the good choice and was baptized to walk in newness of life. Many more are counting the cost. Bro. Isaac Frantz, of Pleasant Hill, Ohio, is doing the preaching. Two applicants came forward this evening.—*Elmer Wombold, March 7.*

Wolf Lake, Ind.—The Brethren of the Blue River district, Whitley Co., Ind., met in quarterly council March 5. Considerable business was before the meeting, but all was disposed of in a Christian-like manner. We elected one delegate to Annual Meeting, and also the needed officers for our Sunday-school, which is to commence soon. We agreed to hold our love-feast, the Lord willing, June 18, to begin at 3 P. M.—*Levi Zumbrun, March 12.*

Hazleton, W. Va.—I left my home Feb. 28 and went to Pine Grove, where I held a series of meetings. I preached eight sermons and baptized four precious souls. Several more made the good confession of faith, and will be baptized in the near future. Others are counting the cost. We had a very interesting meeting, and pray God to still continue the good work, till all will return to the Lord, and be saved on the easy terms of the Gospel. Brethren, let us not forget to look to the Father for help. Let us pray in behalf of the young soldiers who have enlisted in the service of the Master!—*Joseph Guthrie.*

Navarre, Kans.—The Abilene church met in quarterly council March 3. Considerable business came before the meeting, and was disposed of in a Christian-like spirit. Bro. Daniel Vaniman was with us and presided over the meeting, and also preached a few evenings for us very acceptably. We are glad to have the Brethren come and give us such timely admonition. Bro. Geo. Manon was elected delegate to District Meeting, and Bro. Jacob Keller delegate to Annual Meeting, with Eld. John Humbarger as alternate. The church decided to hold a love-feast May 7, commencing at 2 o'clock P. M.—*John J. Manon, Gypsum, Kans.*

Williamsport, Ind.—Bro. Solomon Blickenstaff visited us again Feb. 6, and remained until the 15th, preaching in all twelve sermons. There was good attendance, and although there were no more added to our small number, the meeting did us all good. Quite a sad accident happened to Bro. Jacob Frederick's oldest son. Two weeks ago this Friday evening, as he was riding to town, his pony became frightened at some obstruction in the road, and threw him off, bruising him considerably about the head and face. He was unconscious for two or three days, and it was feared something serious might result, but at last accounts he was better. Bro. Mohler paid us a pleasant visit during our meetings.—*Geo. W. McKinney.*

Huntington, Ind.—Eld. Joseph Spitzer commenced a series of meetings in the Loon Creek house, of the Salimony congregation, on the evening of Feb. 22, and continued until the evening of March 4, when we closed on account of the inclement weather and bad roads. Bro. Spitzer preached the Word in unmistakable terms, and with a zeal worthy of the cause, but the weather and roads were so bad and the nights so dark that our congregations were small and irregular most of the time. Two dear young sisters confessed Christ and were buried with him in baptism, we trust to walk in newness of life. Our quarterly council was held March 5. A large amount of business came before the meeting. We appointed our love-feast for June 2, at 3 P. M.—*A. N. Snowberger, March 7.*

Chatham, Ill.—The Sugar Creek congregation held her regular quarterly council, March 5, our elder, M. J. McClure, being present. All business passed off pleasantly, with one exception. Eld. M. J. McClure was elected as delegate to Annual Meeting. Our Communion meeting was appointed for S-pt 2 A committee was also chosen to secure a minister to hold a series of meetings about the time of the feast. Bro. Henry McKenzie was elected as Superintendent of our Sunday school. We will commence our Sunday-school the first Sunday in April.—*Martha R. Harnly, March 7.*

Middleton, Mich.—The members of the New Haven church met yesterday, March 5, in quarterly council. All business passed off pleasantly. A minister, his wife and daughter were received by letter. There were also three letters granted to members that are about moving to other parts of the Brotherhood. Thus we see we are shifting,—some coming and others going,—but our greatest concern should be that we may be properly prepared to pass over to that country from whence no traveler ever returns. At present peace and union prevail among us. May the Good Lord continue these blessings, not only on the New Haven church but upon the entire Brotherhood.—*Eleazar Bosserman, March 6.*

Literary Notes.

Ecclesiastical Amusements. By Rev. E. P. Marvin. Introduction by Drs. John Hall and Howard Crosby. Fiftieth thousand, revised and enlarged. 64 pp, 12mo, in handsome embossed card-board binding, 25 cts. Pamphlet edition, paper cover, 10 cts; 100 for $5.00, postpaid. Fifty thousand copies have been printed and sold in the last few months. Address A. W. Hall, Publisher, Syracuse, N. Y.

The Moral Crusader, William Lloyd Garrison. A Biographical Sketch. By Goldwin Smith, D. C. L. Cloth, 12mo, 200 pp., with portrait, $1.20. Funk & Wagnalls Company, New York and London.

We have here a terse biographical essay, in which Goldwin Smith has undertaken to reconcile character and conduct as presented in the life of the great Anti-Slavery Agitator, and with the exercise of keen analytical acumen he presents us with so shrewd an estimate of the man in all his strength and weakness, that his policy is rendered intelligible, when, without such side lights it appears inconsistent, if not inexplicable.

MATRIMONIAL.

"What therefore God hath joined together, let not man put asunder."

SWAB—BOWERS.—At the residence of Bro. John Eisenbise, Morrill, Kans., Feb. 25, 1892, by Eld. J. S. Mohler, Bro. Oliver A. Swab, of Lanark, Ill., and Miss Mary Bowers, of Morrill, Kans.   S. M. E.

MINNICH—BRUBAKER.—At the residence of the bride's parents, near Girard, Ill., Feb. 28, 1892, by G. W. Gibson, Bro. Jacob Minnich, of Eaton, Ind., and sister Lizzie Brubaker, of Girard, Ill. I. J. HARSHBARGER.

PIKE—SHROVE.—At the residence of the bride's parents, Denver, Colo., Feb. 28, 1892, by the undersigned, Mr. Charles Pike and sister Minnie Shrove, all of Denver, Colo.   D. H. WEAVER.

HENLY—MEADOR.—At the residence of the bride's parents, Dec. 24, 1891, by Rev. Paul Bradley, Mr. Hezekiah Henly, of Henrico County, and Miss Annie E. Meador, of Cumberland Co., Va.

DENLINGER—SMITH.—At the residence of the bride's parents, March 3, 1892, by Rev. Paul Bradley, Bro. Wilson C. Denlinger, of Ohio, and Miss Cora B. Smith, of Cumberland Co., Va.
                    FLORIDA J. E. ETTER.

SAPPELT—DANS.—At the residence of sister Shank, near Mechanicsburg, Cumberland Co., Pa., Feb. 23, 1892, by the undersigned, Mr. Maximilian Sappelt and sister Cora E. Dans.   DANIEL LANDIS.

GARVER—CLEAR.—At the residence of the undersigned, in Cherokee County, Iowa, March 6, 1892, Bro. J. J. Garver and sister Parmelia Clear.   JOHN EARLY.

FALLEN ASLEEP

"Blessed are the dead which die in the Lord."

JENNINGS.—In Middletown, Henry Co., Ind., Jan. 2, 1892, sister Eliza Jennings, aged about 58 years Sister Jennings was born in Hagerstown, Md. She was twice married. Her union with her first husband was blessed by eight children. In 1882 she was married to George L. Jennings. Funeral in the Brethren's church in Middletown by the writer, from 1 Cor. 15: 49. H. L. FADELY.

CULP.—At Sulphur Springs, Henry Co., Ind., Jan. 2, 1891, sister Culp, aged 79 years, 9 months and 26 days. Deceased was anointed about two weeks before she died. She leaves two sons and two daughters. Funeral by Bro. John McCarty, assisted by the writer.
                    HENRY L. FADELY.

SMITH.—In the bounds of the English church, Keokuk Co., Iowa, Feb. 18, 1892, friend Chri tian Smith, aged 79 years, 8 months and 8 days. Funeral by Rev. Samuel West in the Brethren church from Rom. 8: 17.   PETER BROWER.

LIGHTEL.—Within the limits of the Mt. Zion church, Tuscarawas Co., Ohio, Feb. 27, 1892, George Henry Lightel, aged 33 years, 1 month and 3 days. Deceased was a verification of his own text, "It is soon cut off." Ps. 90: 10.   EDWARD LOOMIS.

MILLS.—In the Licking Creek church, Ohio, Feb. 7, 1892, Bro. Benjamin Mills, aged 61 years, 9 months and 13 days. Bro. Mills has been ailing for a long time. He leaves before his death he was anointed. He leaves a wife and six children. Funeral by Bro. Jacob Weller, from 2 Cor. 5: 1, to a large congregation.   JACOB S. KELLER.

HULL.—In the same church, Feb. 14, 1892, sister Peggy Hull, aged 80 years, 5 months and 1 day. She leaves a husband and nine children. Funeral by Bro. Jacob Weller, from Isa. 38: 1.   JACOB S. KELLER.

BEARD.—In the Licking Creek congregation, Feb. 23, 1892, sister Nancy Beard, aged 81 years, 6 months and 16 days. She had been ailing for a long while. Funeral services will be in the near future.
                    JACOB S. KELLER.

WELLER.—Also in the same neighborhood, Feb. 24, 1892, Thomas P. Weller, aged 25 years. Funeral services conducted by Rev. Owens, from Ps. 96.
                    JACOB S. KELLER.

BRADT.—In the Dry Fork congregation, Jasper Co., Mo., Feb. 11, 1892, sister Ann Elizabeth Bradt, aged 47 years, 7 months and 6 days. She leaves a husband and eight children. Funeral by Bro. W. M. Harvey, assisted by the Brethren.
                    FRANCES HARVEY.

FOUST.—In the Jacob's Creek congregation, Westmoreland Co., Pa., Feb. 14, 1892, sister Fanny, wife of Bro. Amos C. Foust, aged 26 years and 4 days. She leaves a husband and two little children. Funeral discourse by Rev. DeVanie (as Bro. D. D. Horner was ill), from Philpp. 1: 21.
                    JEREMIAH FOUST.

SHIREMAN.—In the Eel River church, Kosciusko Co., Ind., Feb. 28, 1892, Esta E. Shireman, grandson of Bro. Abraham and Magdalena Montel, aged 9 years, 8 months and 7 days. Funeral by Bro. Samuel Leckrone and the writer.
                    EMMANUEL LECKRONE.

BRICKER.—In the Manor congregation, Md., Mary Naomi Irene, daughter of Bro. Jacob and sister Maggie Bricker, aged 11 months and 5 days. Funeral services by Eld. David Long, assisted by the brethren.
                    D. VICTOR LONG.

BOOP.—In the Buffalo church, Union Co., Pa., Feb. 22, 1892, sister Elizabeth Boop, relict of Conrad Boop, aged 85 years, 8 months and 18 days. She was a faithful member of the Brethren church for more than fifty years.   ADAM BEAVER.

CLEMMENS.—In the bounds of the Russell church, Russell Co., Kans., Jan. 23, 1892, Hattie A. Clemmens, aged 61 years, 8 months and 29 days. Deceased suffered much with heart disease, which ended her life. Funeral services by the writer from Heb. 9: 27.
                    JOHN HOLLINGER.

SAYLOR.—In the Middle Creek congregation, Somerset Co., Pa., Amanda Elizabeth Saylor, daughter of Bro. Wm. Saylor, aged 3 years, 9 months and 6 days. Funeral by the writer, assisted by Eld. Frederick Murray.   G. W. LOWRY.

ELLIOTT.—In the bounds of the Limestone church, Jewell Co., Kans., Feb. 4, 1892, Angie Elliott, son of Bro. John and sister Laura Elliott, aged 18 years, 10 months and 2 days. Funeral services Feb 6, by the writer from Job 14: 1, 2 and first part of fourteenth Verse.   JOHN HOLLINGER.

GARRETT.—In the Lower Cumberland church, Pa., Feb. 27, 1892, sister Sarah Garrett, aged 75 years and 3 months. Deceased was a consistent member of the church for over fifty years. Funeral services at her late home in Mechanicsburg by Bro. Daniel Landis and the writer from 1 Thess 4: 14.
                    HENRY BEELMAN.

HALTERMAN.—In the Lost River congregation, W. Va., Feb. 24, 1892, Bro. Silvanus Halterman, aged 24 years, 1 month and 2 days. Deceased, at the time of his death, was seventeen miles from home. While tending to his steam saw-mill, the belt flew off, and was wrapped in the fly-wheel. As he tried to throw it off, the fly-wheel, while it was running, struck him on the head and killed him instantly. Funeral services by Rev. L. D. Caldwell from 2 Tim. 4: 6-8.
                    J. F. CALDWELL.

GLASS.—In the Sandy church, Columbiana Co., Ohio, near North Georgetown, Feb. 28, 1892, sister Rebecca Glass, wife of Isaac L. Glass, aged 59 years, 8 months and 26 days. Funeral services were postponed on account of the illness of her companion, who was not able to attend services on the day of the funeral.   ELI STROUP.

BRITSCH.—In the Dry Fork church, Jasper Co., Mo., Dec 19. 1891, sister Susannah Britsch, wife of Wm. L. Britsch (*nee Horner*), aged 49 years, 7 months and 24 days. Deceased was born at Crawfordsville, Ind., in 1842. She was married Jan. 17, 1861, moved to Lamar, Mo., in 1883; was baptized Oct. 30, 1889, and was buried at White church, Montgomery Co., Ind. Funeral services by the writer.   D. C. CAMPBELL.

WINE.—In Moore's Store, Va., March 6, 1892, Ida Florence, infant daughter of Bro. D. P. Wine, aged 14 days. Brief services, reading the Scriptures, exhortation and prayer were held at the house of the bereaved family, sister Wine being ill. DANIEL HAYS.

SLIFER.—In the bounds of the Brownsville congregation, Md., at Broad Run, Frederick Co., March 8, 1892, Mary Ann Slifer, wife of the late Peter Slifer, aged 81 years. She was a faithful member of the Brethren church. Services by the writer and Bro. Eli Yourtee.   DAVID AUSHERMAN.

LAYMAN.—In the Upper Cumberland church, Pa., Dec. 4, 1891, Grandpa Layman, aged 73 years, 1 month and 8 days. Funeral services conducted by Eld. John F. Stany and Jacob Hollinger.   H. B. B.

MILLER.—Near Brownsville, Md., Jan. 9, 1892, Mary Ann Miller, wife of the late Peter Miller, of Washington County, Md., aged 69 years. Funeral services by the writer and C. D. Hylton.

GRIM.—In the Brownsville congregation, Md., Feb. 2, 1892, Abraham D. Grim, aged 59 years, 5 months and 7 days. He was a member of the Brethren's church for a number of years. Funeral services by David Ausherman.

JUDSON.—In the Monroe church, Monroe Co., Iowa, Jan. 26, 1892, sister Mercy Judson, aged 81 years, 3 months and 19 days She was born in Pennsylvania. She leaves four children. A short time before her death she was anointed. Funeral by the home ministers.   BARBARA A. MILLER.

MOUNTAN.—In the Montgomery church, Pa., Feb. 9, 1892, sister Rachel Mountan, wife of Bro. Sidney Mountan, aged 33 years, 7 months and 9 days. Services by the writer from Rev. 14: 13-15.

COENIHAN.—In the bounds of the Montgomery church, Pa., Feb. 17, 1892, Matthew Coenihan, aged 34 years, 9 months and 21 days. At the funeral Ps. 34 was read and prayer offered.   J.-H. BEER.

BRUNN.—In the bounds of the Irvin Creek church, Dunn Co., Wis., March 2, 1892, Nelly May Brunn, aged 18 years, 5 months and 1 day. Funeral services by the writer from 1 Pet. 1: 24, to a large congregation.   SAMUEL CRIST.

ERB.—In Mt. Carroll, Ill., Feb. 27, 1892, sister Erb, aged about 100 years. Services by the Brethren from Acts 20: 24.
                    FRANKLIN MYERS.

KNISLEY.—In Mechanicsburg, Cumberland Co., Pa., Feb. 14, 1892, Bro. David Knisley, aged 67 years, 2 months and 26 days. Bro. David called for the brethren a few days before his death and was anointed. His wife not being able to attend the services at the church on account of sickness, short services were held at the house before going to the union house in Mechanicsburg, where the funeral was preached. DANIEL LANDIS.

COOK.—In the Union church, Marshall Co., Ind., Feb. 23, 1892, sister J. C. Cook, aged 50 years, 11 months and 12 days. She leaves three children. Funeral by Daniel Snell from Num. 23: 10. DANIEL SNELL.

KAUFFMAN.—In the Quemahoning church, Somerset Co., Pa., Feb. 21, 1892, of hemorrhage of the brain, Kate Ann, daughter of friend John and sister Elizabeth Kauffman, aged 2 years, 9 months and 8 days. Services by the undersigned.
                    S. P. ZIMMERMAN.

WILKINSON.—In Owego, Ind., Feb. 5, 1892, Mrs. Elizabeth Wilkinson, aged 66 years, 9 months and 4 days. Services in Otwego by the writer, from Isa. 53: 11.

MOCK.—In the Tippecanoe church, Ind., Feb. 22, 1891, Bro. Geo. Mock, aged 72 years, 7 months and 9 days. Bro. George was a deacon. Services by the writer from John 16: 20, 22.

MOCK.—In the same church, Feb. 24, 1892, Jacob Mock, sr., aged 84 years, 3 months and 17 days. Services from Ps. 94: 22, by the writer.

DYE.—In the same church, Feb. 25, 1892, Nancy J. Dye, daughter of Jacob Mock, aged 56 years, 6 months and 28 days. Services by the writer. A. H. PUTTERBAUGH.

OVERLEESE.—In the South Beatrice church, Gage Co., Nebr., March 4, 1892, Martin A. Overleese, infant son of Bro. Perry, and sister Elizabeth Overleese, aged 2 months and 3 days.   MILLIE A. COHUN.

CRIPE.—In the Wallace congregation, Lincoln Co., Nebr., March 1, 1892, Pearly May Cripe, aged 4 months and 3 days. Funeral by the writer.
                    DAVID BECHTELHEIMER.

Chatham, Ill.—The Sugar Creek congregation held her regular quarterly council, March 5, our elder, M. J. McClure, being present. All business passed off pleasantly, with one exception. Eld. M. J. McClure was elected as delegate to Annual Meeting. Our Communion meeting was appointed for S-pt 2 A committee was also chosen to secure a minister to hold a series of meetings about the time of the feast. Bro. Henry McKenzie was elected as Superintendent of our Sunday-school. We will commence our Sunday-school the first Sunday in April.—*Martha R. Harnly, March 7.*

Middleton, Mich.—The members of the New Haven church met yesterday, March 6, in quarterly council. All business passed off pleasantly. A minister, his wife and daughter were received by letter. There were also three letters granted to members that are about moving to other parts of the Brotherhood. Thus we see we are shifting,—some coming and others going,—but our greatest concern should be that we may be properly prepared to pass' over to that country from whence no traveler ever returns. At present peace and union prevail among us. May the Good Lord continue these blessings, not only on the New Haven church but upon the entire Brotherhood.—*Eleasor Bossermon, March 6.*

Literary Notes.

Ecclesiastical Amusements. By Rev. E. P. Marvin. Introduction by Drs. John Hall and Howard Crosby. Fiftieth thousand, revised and enlarged. 64 pp.; 12mo, in handsome embossed card-board binding, 25 cts. Pamphlet edition, paper cover, 10 cts; 100 for $5.00, postpaid. Fifty thousand copies have been printed and sold in the last few months. Address A. W. Hall, Publisher, Syracuse, N. Y.

The Moral Crusader, William Lloyd Garrison. A Biographical Sketch. By Goldwin Smith, D. C. L. Cloth, 12mo, 200 pp., with portrait, $1.00. Funk & Wagnalls Company, New York and London.

We have here a terse biographical essay, in which Goldwin Smith has undertaken to reconcile character and conduct as presented in the life of the great Anti-Slavery Agitator, and with the exercise of keen analytical acumen he presents us with so shrewd an estimate of the man in all his strength and weakness, that his policy is rendered intelligible, when, without such side lights it appears inconsistent, if not inexplicable.

MATRIMONIAL.

" What therefore God hath joined together, let not man put asunder."

SWAB—BOWERS.—At the residence of Bro. John Eisenbise, Morrill, Kans., Feb. 25, 1892, by Eld. J. S. Mohler, Bro. Oliver A. Swab, of Lanark, Ill., and Miss Mary Bowers, of Morrill, Kans.
S. M. E.

MINNICH—BRUBAKER.—At the residence of the bride's parents, near Girard, Ill., Feb. 28, 1892, by G. W. Gibson, Bro. Jacob Minnich, of Easton, Ind , and sister Lizzie Brubaker, of Girard, Ill. I. J. HARSHBARGER.

PIKE—SHROVE.—At the residence of the bride's parents, Denver, Colo., Feb. 28, 1892, by the undersigned, Mr. Charles Pike and sister Minnie Shrove, all of Denver, Colo.
D. H. WEAVER.

HENLY—MEADOR.—At the residence of the bride's parents, Dec. 24, 1891, by Rev. Paul Bindley, Mr. Hezekiah Henly, of Henrico County, and Miss Annie E. Meador, of Cumberland Co , Va.

DENLINGER—SMITH.—At the residence of the bride's parent, March 3, 1892, by Rev. Paul Bindley, Bro. Wilson C. Denlinger, of Ohio, and Miss Cora B. Smith, of Cumberland Co , Va.
FLORIDA J. E. ETTER.

SAPPELT—DANS.—At the residence of sister Shank, near Mechanicsburg, Cumberland Co., Pa., Feb. 23, 1892, by the undersigned, Mr. Maximilian Sappelt and sister Cora E. Dans. DANIEL LANDIS.

GARVER—CLEAR.—At the residence of the undersigned, in Cherokee County, Iowa, March 6, 1892, Bro. J. J. Garver and sister Parmelia Clear. JOHN EARLY.

FALLEN ASLEEP

" Blessed are the dead which die in the Lord."

JENNINGS.—In Middletown, Henry Co., Ind., Jan. 2, 1892, sister Eliza Jennings, aged about 38 years Sister Jennings was both in Hagerstown, Md. She was twice married. Her union with her first husband was blessed by eight children. In 1882 she was married to George L. Jennings. Funeral in the Brethren's church in Middletown by the writer, from 1 Cor. 15: 49. H. L. FADELY.

CULP.—At Sulphur Springs, Henry Co., Ind , Jan. 2, 1892, sister Culp, aged 79 years, 9 months and 26 days. Deceased was anointed about two weeks before she died. She leaves two sons and two daughters. Funeral by Bro. John McCarty, assisted by the writer. HENRY L. FADELY.

SMITH.—In the bounds of the English River congregation, Keokuk Co., Iowa, Feb. 18, 1892, friend Chri tian Smith, aged 79 years, 8 months and 8 days. Funeral by Rev. Samuel West in the Brethren church from Rom. 8: 17. PETER BROWER.

LIGHTEL.—Within the limits of the Mt. Zion church, Tuscarawas Co., Ohio, Feb. 27, 1892, George Henry Lightel, aged 33 years, 1 month and 3 days. Deceased was a verification of his own text , " It is soon cut off." Ps. 90: 10. EDWARD LOOMIS

MILLS.—In the Licking Creek church, Feb. 7, 1892, Bro. Benjamin Mills, aged 61 years, 9 months and 13 days. Bro. Mills has been ailing for a long time. A few days before his death he was anointed. He leaves a wife and five children Funeral by Bro. Jacob Weller, from 2 Cor. 5: 1, to a large congregation. JACOB S. KELLER.

HULL.—In the same church, Feb. 14, 1892, sister Peggy Hull, aged 80 years, 5 months and 1 day. She leaves a husband and nine children. Funeral by Bro. Jacob Weller, from Isa. 38: 1. JACOB S. KELLER.

BEARD.—In the Licking Creek congregation, Feb. 23, 1892, sister Nancy Beard, aged 81 years, 6 months and 16 days. She had been ailing for a long while. Funeral services will be in the near future.
JACOB S. KELLER.

WELLER.—Also in the same neighborhood, Feb. 24, 1892, Thomas P. Weller, aged 25 years. Funeral services conducted by Rev. Cross, from Ps. 96. JACOB S. KELLER.

BRADT.—In the Dry Fork congregation, Jasper Co., Ind, Feb. 13, 1892, sister Ann Elizabeth Bradt, aged 47 years, 7 months and 6 days. She leaves a husband and eight children. Funeral by Bro. W. M. Harvey, assisted by the Brethren.
FRANCES HARVEY.

FOUST.—In the Jacob's Creek congregation, Westmoreland Co., Pa., Feb. 14, 1892, sister Fanny, wife of Bro. Amos C. Foust, aged 26 years and 4 days. She leaves a husband and two little children. Funeral discourse by Rev. Devanes (as Bro. D. D. Horner was ill), from Philipp. 1: 21.
JEREMIAH FOUST.

SHIREMAN.—In the Eel River church, Kosciusko Co., Ind., Feb. 28, 1892, Esta E. Shireman, grandson of Bro. Abraham and Magdalena Montel, aged 9 years, 8 months and 7 days. Funeral by Bro. Samuel Leckrone and the writer.
EMMANUEL LECKRONE.

BRICKER.—In the Manor congregation, Md , Mary Naomi Irene, daughter of Bro. Jacob and sister Maggie Bricker, aged 11 months and 5 days. Funeral services by Eld. David Long, assisted by the brethren.
D. VICTOR LONG.

BOOP.—In the Buffalo church, Union Co., Pa., Feb. 22, 1892, sister Elizabeth Boop, relict of Conrad Boop, aged 85 years, 8 months and 18 days. She was a faithful member of the Brethren church for more than fifty years. ADAM BEAVER.

CLEMMENS.—In the bounds of the Russell church, Russell Co., Kans , Jan. 23, 1892, Hattie A. Clemmens, aged 61 years, 8 months and 20 days. Deceased suffered much with heart disease, which ended her life. Funeral services by the writer from Heb. 9: 17.
JOHN HOLLINGER.

SAYLOR.—In the Middle Creek congregation, Somerset Co., Pa., Amanda Elizabeth Saylor, daughter of Bro. Wm. Saylor, aged 3 years, 9 months and 6 days. Funeral by the writer, assisted by Eld. Frederick Murray. G. W. LOWRY.

ELLIOTT.—In the bounds of the Limestone church, Jewell Co., Kans., Feb. 4, 1892, Angle Elliott, son of Bro. John and sister Laura Elliott, aged 18 years, 10 months and 2 days. Funeral services Feb 6, by the writer from Job 14: 1, 2 and first part of fourteenth verse. JOHN HOLLINGER.

GARRETT.—In the Lower Cumberland church, Pa., Feb. 27, 1892, sister Sarah Garrett, aged 75 years and 3 months. Deceased was a consistent member of the church for over fifty years. Funeral services at her late home in Mechanicsburg by Bro. Daniel Landis and the writer from 1 Thess 4: 14.
HENRY BERKMAN.

HALTERMAN.—In the Lost River congregation, W. Va., Feb. 24, 1892, Bro. Silvanus Halterman, aged 24 years, 1 month and 2 days. Deceased, at the time of his death, was seventeen miles from home. While tending to his steam saw-mill, the belt flew off, and was whipped in the fly-wheel. As he tried to throw it off, the fly-wheel, while it was running, struck him on the head and killed him instantly. Funeral services by Rev. L. D. Caldwell from 2 Tim. 4: 6-8.
J. F. CALDWELL.

GLASS.—In the Sandy church, Columbiana Co., Ohio, near North Georgetown, Feb. 28, 1892, sister Rebecca Glass, wife of Isaac L. Glass, aged 59 years, 8 months and 26 days. Funeral services were postponed on account of the illness of her companion, who was not able to attend services on the day of the funeral. ELI STROUP.

BRITSCH.—In the Dry Fork church, Jasper Co., Mo., Dec. 19, 1891, sister Susannah Britsch, wife of Wm. L. Britsch (nee Horner), aged 45 years, 7 months and 24 days. Deceased was born at Crawfordsville, Ind., in 1842. She was married Jan. 17, 1861, moved to Lamar, Mo., in 1883; was baptized Oct. 30, 1889, and was buried at White church, Montgomery Co., Ind. Funeral services by the writer. D. C. CAMPBELL.

WINE.—In Moore's Store, Va., March 6, 1892, Ida Florence, infant daughter of Bro. D. P. Wine, aged 24 days. Brief services, reading the Scriptures, exhortation and prayer were held at the house of the bereaved family, sister Wine being ill. DANIEL HAYS.

SLIFER.—In the bounds of the Brownsville congregation, Md., at Broad Run, Frederick Co., Md., March 6, 1892, Mary Ann Slifer, wife of the late Peter Slifer, aged 81 years. She was a faithful member of the Brethren church. Services by the writer and Eli Yourtee. DAVID AUSHERMAN.

LAYMAN.—In the Upper Cumberland church, Pa., Dec. 4, 1891, Grandpa Layman, aged 73 years, 1 month and 8 days. Funeral services conducted by Eld. John F. Stany and Jacob Hollinger. H. B. B.

MILLER.—Near Brownsville, Md., Jan. 9, 1892, Mary Ann Miller, wife of the late Peter Miller, of Washington County, Md., aged 69 years. Funeral services by the writer and C. D. Hylton.

GRIM.—In the Brownsville congregation, Md., Feb. 2, 1892, Abraham D. Grim, aged 59 years, 5 months and 7 days. He was a member of the Brethren's church for a number of years. Funeral services by David Ausherman.

JUDSON.—In the Monroe church, Monroe Co., Iowa, Jan. 26, 1892, sister Mercy Judson, aged 81 years, 3 months and 19 days She was born in Pennsylvania. She leaves four children. A short time before her death she was anointed. Funeral by the home ministers. BARBARA A. MILLER.

MOUNTAN.—In the Montgomery church, Pa., Feb. 9, 1892, sister Rachel Mountan, wife of Bro. Sidney Mountan, aged 33 years, 7 months and 9 days. Services by the writer from Rev. 14: 13-15.

COENIHAN. — In the bounds of · the Montgomery church, Pa., Feb. 17, 1892, Mathew Coenihan, aged 34 years, 9 months and 21 days. At the funeral Ps. 34 was read and prayer offered. J. H. BARR.

BRUNN.—In the bounds of the Irvin Creek church, Dunn Co., Wis., March 2, 1892, Nelly May Brunn, aged 18 years, 5 months and 1 day. Funeral services by the writer from 1 Pet. 1: 24, to a large congregation. SAMUEL CRIST.

· ERB.—In Mt. Carroll, Ill., Feb. 27, 1892, sister Erb, aged about 100 years. Services by the Brethren from Acts 20: 24.
FRANKLIN MYERS.

KNISLEY.—In Mechanicsburg, Cumberland Co., Pa., Feb. 14, 1892, Bro. David Knisley, aged 67 years, 2 months and 26 days. Bro. David called for the brethren a few days before his death and was anointed. His wife not being able to attend the services at the church on account of sickness, short services were held at the house before going to the union house in Mechanicsburg, where the funeral was preached. DANIEL LANDIS.

COOK.—In the Union church, Marshall Co., Ind., Feb. 23, 1892, sister J. C. Cook, aged 50 years, 11 months and 17 days. She leaves three children. Funeral by Daniel Snell from Num. 23: 10. DANIEL SNELL.

KAUFFMAN. — In the Quemahoning church, Somerset Co., Pa., Feb. 21, 1892, of hemorrhage of the brain, Katie Ann, daughter of friend John and sister Elizabeth Kauffman, aged 2 years, 9 months and 8 days. Services by the undersigned.
S. P. ZIMMERMAN.

WILKINSON.—At Oswego, Ind., Feb. 5, 1892, Mrs. Elizabeth Wilkinson, aged 66 years, 9 months and 4 days. Services in Oswego by the writer, from Isa. 53: 11.

MOCK.—In the Tippecanoe church, Ind., Feb. 22, 1891, Bro. Geo. Mock, aged 73 years, 7 months and 9 days. Bro. George was a deacon. Services by the writer from John 16: 20, 22.

MOCK.—In the same church, Feb. 24, 1892, Jacob Mock, sr., aged 84 years, 5 months and 17 days. Services from Ps. 94: 22, by the writer.

DYE.—In the same church, Feb. 27, 1892, Nancy J. Dye, daughter of Jacob Mock, aged 56 years, 6 months and 28 days. Services by the writer. A. H. PUTERBAUGH.

OVERLEESE.—In the South Beatrice church, Gage Co., Nebr., March 4, 1892, Martin A. Overleese, infant son of Bro. Perry, and sister Elizabeth Overleese, aged 2 months and 3 days. MILLIE A. COHUN.

CRIPE.—In the Wallace congregation, Lincoln Co., Nebr., March 1, 1892, Pearly May Cripe, aged 4 months and 3 days. Funeral by the writer.
DAVID BECHTELHEIMER.

Announcements.

DISTRICT MEETINGS.

March 22, 10.9 A. M., District Meeting of Southern Iowa, in the Middle Creek church, Mahaska Co., Iowa. Missionary meeting on the evening of the 29th. Those coming by railroad will come to Lacy day before and they will be met at 8:30 A. M., and 4:30 P. M., by notifying John Gable, New Sharon, Iowa.

April 2, Middle District of Indiana, in the Rossas church, Wabash Co., Ind. Delegates will please come prepared to pay their quota of expenses for the District, to defray the expenses of publishing District Meeting Minutes. They should also be ready to state how many copies of District Meeting Minutes will be needed to supply each family in their congregation with one copy.

April 8, 10.9 A. M., District of Nebraska, in the Junius congregation. Ministerial meeting the day before, at 10 A. M.

April 13, 10.9 A. M., District Meeting of Southern Indiana, in the Howard church, Howard Co., Ind., 12 miles west of Kokomo. Those coming by railroad will come to Kokomo the day before. Come on morning train. Arrangements will be made to convey all to place of Meeting.

April 13, 10.9 A. M., District Meeting for North-eastern Kansas in the Olathe church, 3 miles north-west of Gardner. Ministerial meeting April 12, 10.9 A M. Gardner is on the Southern Kansas Division of the A. T. & S. F. System, where all trains will be met on Monday, the 11th, but none later.

April 13, South-western District of Kansas, in the Salem church, Reno County, Kansas, 6×7×8 miles south of McPherIn.

April 14 and 15. North-western District of Ohio, in the Lafayette church, Allen Co., Ohio. Those coming on Thursday, April 14, to meet the Mission Board, and travelling by the Pittsburg and Ft. Wayne Road should stop off at Lafayette. The 4 traveling by the Chicago and Erie R. R., should get off at Harrod Station. There will be ample conveyance at either station by the brethren. All the brethren wishing conveyance either the Pittsburg & Ft. Wayne R. R., or the Chicago and Erie R. R., can get same by applying to A. N. Baker.

April 15 and 16, at 10 A. M., District Meeting of First District of Virginia, at Peter's Creek church.

April 19, at 9:30 A. M., Eastern District of Maryland, in the Middletown Valley church.

April 21, District Meeting of Western Maryland, at the Vanclevesville house, Berkeley Co., W. Va. Brethren coming on the B. & O. road will stop off at Vanclevesville Station.

April 29, at 10 A. M., District Meeting of North-eastern Kansas and North Colorado, in Burr Oak church, Burr Oak, Jewell Co., Kans. Every church is requested to be represented as far as possible, and we want every delegate to be prepared to meet expenses for the printing of the Minutes and expenses of delegate to Annual Meeting.

May 5, at 10 A. M., North District of Missouri, in the Bethel congregation, at the Squaw Creek meeting-house, Holt Co., Mo. Those coming by rail will be met at Mound City by addressing Jos. Andes at that place.

May 12, District Meeting of Southern Missouri and Arkansas, in the Shoal Creek church, Newton Co., Mo. Those coming by rail to Pierce City will be met on the morning of May 11, by notifying John Holder. read to Ergo. Those coming to Purdy will notify Leander Marsdef and will be met on the morning of May 11.

LOVE FEASTS.

April 30, 11.9 P. M., in the Burr Oak church, Jewell Co., Kans. Meetings to continue over Sunday. Any one coming by the Union Pacific R. R. from the West should come by way of Solomon City, then go to Delohl, and then there to Jamestown on the Missouri Pacific R. R. (Central Branch). Then go to Burr Oak on Burr Oak Branch. Those coming by the Rock Island R. R. should stop at Otego, where they will be met by addressing Eld. Eli Renner, Burr Oak.

Kans., or they can go to Mankato, Gore Clough cars to the Missouri Pacific on Burr Oak Branch; likewise to Burr Oak, where they will be met by addressing Lewis Huff, or Joel Kinzie, at Burr Oak, Kans.

May 7, at 9 A. M., in the Bethel congregation, at the Squaw Creek meeting-house, Holt Co., Mo.

May 7, at 9 P. M., Abilene, Kans.

May 9, at 5 P. M., Peabody church, Kans.

May 7 and 8, in the Vanity church, Jo..., at the residence of S. A. Butter. Place of meeting six miles west of Liberty.

May 17, at 10 A. M., Wolf Creek church, Montgomery Co., Ohio.

May 11, 11:1 P. M., in the Yellow Creek congregation, Bedford County, Pa.

May 13 and 14, 10 9 P. M., Silver Creek church, Ogle Co., Ill.

May 14, 10:1 P. M., in the Kansas Center church, 3 miles east of Lyons.

May 14, 10 A. M. Pine Creek congregation, Miami Co., Ind.

May 21, at 10 A. M., Mississinewa church, Delaware Co., Ind., 3 miles west of Shideler. Those coming by rail should come to Shideler and inquire for the brethren.

June 4, in the Yellow Creek church, Elkhart Co., Ind 3 miles south-west of Goshen.

June 3 and 5, at 5 P. M., Yellow Creek, Ill.

June 7, at 5 P. M., in the Okaw church, Piatt Co., Ill. Ministering brethren on their way to Annual Meeting will please stop with us.

June 17, 20, at 5 P. M., Yellow River congregation, Marshall Co., Ind.

June 18, Green Spring District, Seneca Co., Ohio.

To Close out

The few copies of the BRETHREN'S ALMANAC still on hand, we offer them at REDUCED PRICES. As long as the supply lasts, we will send them at the rate of five cents per copy post-paid, but to get them you should ORDER NOW.

Brethren's Quarterly.

Orders should be sent in at once for the Quarterly for the First Quarter of 1892. Price, three copies, 25 cents; eight copies, 40 cents; twenty copies and over, four cents each.

Juvenile Quarterly.

THIS is just the Quarterly for the little folks. Price; Three Copies, per Quarter, 20 Cents; 6 Copies, per Quarter, 25 Cents; 10 Copies and over, per Quarter, 3 Cents each.

The Hollinger Fence and Post.

Strong, Simple, Durable and Cheap! No More Cruelty to Stock!

Mother Morrison, Ind., Morrison 4, 1890. To Whom It May Concern:—This is to certify that we have examined the Hollinger wi e fence and are satisfied that it is an excellent fence, as it is superior to barbed wire, by which so many horses and cattle are cruelly injured. We are also pleased to recommend with the builder, Daniel Hollinger, and do not hesitate to recommend him as a self-dealing, honest man, believing he will faithfully carry out any promise he may make. D. N. Workman.

For full particulars call on or address as follows: Eld. Daniel Hollinger, Covington, Ohio; West of Ohio, D. Hollinger, Mt. Morris, Ill.

GOOD BOOKS FOR ALL.

Cruden's Concordance. — A very complete work. Price, cloth, $1.50; sheep, $3.00.

The Story of the Bible. — An excellent volume for old and young; will interest and instruct all those desiring a knowledge of the Scriptures. Price, $1.00.

Seven Great Monarchies. — By George Rawlinson. In three volumes, cloth. Per volume, $1.00.

Mental Science and Methods of Mental Culture. — By Edward Brooks. Cloth, $1.75.

Manual of Jewish History and Literature. — By D. Cassel. Cloth, 75 cents.

Every Day Christian Life. — By F. W. Farrar. Cloth, 12mo, $1.25.

Biblical Theology of the Old Testament. — By R. F. Weidner. Cloth, $2.25.

Campbell and Owen Debate. — Contains a complete investigation of the evidences of Christianity. Price, $1.50.

Classified Minutes of Annual Meeting. — A work of rare interest for all who desire to be well informed in the church work, from the early days of our Brethren until the present. Price, cloth, $1.50; leather, $2.00.

Europe and Bible Lands. — By D. L. Miller. A book for the people,—more comprehensive and thorough than many higher-priced works. Price, cloth, $1.50; leather, $2.00.

Ecclesiastical History. — By Eusebius. Bohn Library. Cloth, $2.00.

Ecclesiastical History. — By Mosheim. 2 vols. 8vo., $4.00.

Early Days of Christianity. — By F. W. Farrar. Author's edition, cloth, 12mo, $1.50.

New and Complete Bible Commentary. — By Jamieson, Fausset and Brown. It is far in advance of other works. It is critical, practical, and explanatory. It is compendious and comprehensive in its character. It has a critical introduction to each Book of Scripture, and is by far the most practical, suggestive, scientific, and popular work of the kind in the English language. In four large 12mo volumes of about 1,000 pages each. In extra fine English cloth, sprinkled edges, the full set, $8.00; half Morocco, the full set, $10.00.

Sacred Geography and Antiquities. — A practical, helpful work for Bible students, ministers and Sunday-school teachers. Price, $2.25.

The Origin and Growth of Religion. — Hibbert Lectures. By T. W. R. Davids. Cloth, 8vo, $2.50.

Our Library on Christian Evidences. — This collection of works embraces the best books to be had on that subject: "Paley's Evidences of Christianity," New Edition, $1.50; "Nelson on Infidelity," 75 cents; "Manual of Christian Evidences," 75 cents; "Many Infallible Proofs," $1.25; "The Divine Demonstration," $1.50; "The Bible in the Nineteenth Century," 20 cents; "Grounds of Theistic and Christian Belief," $2.50. Price of the entire set, if ordered at one time, $8.00; special terms to ministers furnished upon application.

Bible Work, or Bible Reader's Commentary on the New Testament. — By J. G. Butler. Two. volumes, 8vo, $10.00.

Biblical Antiquities. — By John Nevin. Gives a concise account of Bible times and customs; invaluable to all students of Bible subjects. Price, $1.50.

Quinter and McConnell Debate. — A debate on Trine Immersion, the Lord's Supper, and Feet-washing, between Eld. James Quinter (German Baptist) and Eld. N. A. McConnell (Christian) held at Dry Creek, Iowa, 1867. Price, $1.50.

Popular Commentary on the New Testament. — Edited by Philip Schaff. Four volumes, 8vo. Matthew, Mark and Luke; $6.00. John and the Acts, $6.00. Romans to Philemon; $6.00. Hebrews to Revelation; $6.00.

Sabbatism. — By M. M. Eshelman. Treats the Sabbath question, showing that the first day of the week is the day for assembling in worship. Price to cents; 15 copies, $1.00.

EGGS, EGGS FOR HATCHING

Send three stamps for mammoth Catalogue and Guide to Poultry Raisers. The finest book of the kind published. Containing valuable information for the poultry man and all who have poultry, either for pleasure or profit.
C. C. SHOEMAKER,
L. B. 1964. Freeport, Ill.

Windsor European Hotel

TRIBUNE BLOCK,

145 to 155 Dearborn St. S. Ganotorst, Prop.

Chicago, Ill.

This hotel is centrally located, and the most respectable House of its kind in the City. The Grand Depot is near us, one square to on station, 6:0 cars 5f rooms to $1.00 per day, per person. Thompson's Restaurant underneath. First-class Passenger Elevator.

Announcements.

DISTRICT MEETINGS.

March 26, at 9 A. M., District Meeting of Southern Iowa, in the Middle Creek church, Mahaska Co., Iowa. Missionary meeting on the evening of the 25th. Those coming by railroad will come to Lacy day before and they will be met at 8:00 A. M., and 4:30 P. M., by notifying John Gable, New Sharon, Iowa.

April 6, Middle District of Indiana, in the Rossm church, Wabash Co., Ind. Delegates will please come prepared to pay their quota of expenses for the District, to defray the expenses of publishing District Meeting Minutes. They should also be ready to state how many copies of District Meeting Minutes will be needed to supply each family in their congregations with one copy.

April 8, at 9 A. M., District of Nebraska, in the Juniata congregation. Ministerial meeting the day before, at 10 A. M.

April 12, at 9 A. M., District Meeting of Southern Indiana, in the Howard church, Howard Co., Ind., 21 miles west of Kokomo. Those coming by railroad will come to Kokomo the day before. Come on morning train. Arrangements will be made to convey all to place of Meeting.

April 13, at 9 A. M., District Meeting for North-eastern Kansas in the Ozake church, 8 miles north-west of Gardner. Ministerial meeting April 12, at 9 A. M. Gardner is on the Southern Kansas Division of the A. T. & S. R. System, where all trains will be met on Monday, the 11th, but none later.

April 13, South-western District of Kansas, in the Salem church, Reno County, 8 miles, several miles south of Nickerson.

April 14 and 15, North-western District of Ohio, in the Lafayette church, Allen Co., Ohio. Those coming on Thursday, April 14, to meet the Mission Board, and traveling by the Pittsburg and Ft. Wayne Road should stop off at Lafayette. Those traveling by the Chicago and Erie R. R., should get off at Harrod Station. There will be ample conveyance at either station by the brethren. All the brethren wishing trains taken off either the Pittsburg & Ft. Wayne R. R., or the Chicago and Erie R. R., can get same by applying to A. M. Baker.

April 15 and 16, at 10 A. M., District Meeting of First District of Virginia, at Peter's Creek church.

April 19, at 9:30 A. M., Eastern District of Maryland, in the Middletown Valley church.

April 21, District Meeting of Western Maryland, at the Vanclavesville house, Berkeley Co., W. Va. Brethren coming on the B. & O. road will stop off at Vanclavesville Station.

April 29, at 10 A. M., District Meeting of North-western Kansas and North Colorado, in Burr Oak church, Burr Oak, Jewell Co., Kans. Every church is requested to be represented as far as possible, and we want every delegate to be prepared to meet expenses for the printing of the Minutes and expenses of delegate to Annual Meeting.

May 5, at 10 A. M., North District of Missouri, in the Bethel congregation, at the Squaw Creek meeting-house, Holt Co., Mo. Those coming by rail will be met at Mound City by addressing John Miller at that place.

May 11, District Meeting of Southern Missouri and Arkansas, in the Shoal Creek church, Newton Co., Mo. Those coming by rail to Pierce City will be met on the morning of May 11, by notifying John Kreider, read at Ergo. Those coming to Purdy will notify Leander Harader and will be met on the morning of May 11.

LOVE FEASTS.

April 30, 11 P. M., in the Burr Oak church, Jewell Co., Kans. Meetings to continue over Sunday. Any one coming by the Union Pacific R. R. from the West should come by way of Solomon City, then go to Polate, and from there to Jamestown on the Missouri Pacific R. R. (Central Branch). Then go to Burr Oak on Burr Oak Branch. Those coming by the Rock Island R. R. should stop at Otago, when they will be met by addressing Eld. Eli Renner, Burr Oak.

Kans., or they can go to Mankato, there change cars to the Missouri Pacific on Burr Oak Branch; thence to Burr Oak, where they will be met by addressing Lewis Hoff, or Joel Kinzle, at Burr Oak, Kans.

May 7, 10 to A. M., in the Bethel congregation, at the Squaw Creek meeting-house, Holt Co., Mo.

May 7, at 3 P. M., Abilene, Kans.

May 7, at 2 P. M., Peabody church, Kans.

May 7 and 8, in the Esterly church, La., at the residence of S. A. Sutter. Place of meeting 1½ miles north-west of Esterly.

May 11, 10 A. M., Wolf Creek church, Montgomery Co., Ohio.

May 13, 1½4 P. M., in the Yellow Creek congregation, Bedford County, Pa.

May 13 and 14, at 4 P. M., Silver Creek church, Ogle Co., Ill.

May 14, at 2 P. M., in the Kansas Center church, 3 miles east of Lyons.

May 14, at 10 A. M., Mississinewa church, Delaware Co., Ind., 3 miles west of Shideler. Those coming by rail should come to Shideler and inquire for the brethren.

June 1, in the Yellow Creek church, Elkhart Co., Ind., 7 miles south-west of Goshen.

June 2 and 3, at 1 P. M., Yellow Creek, Ill.

June 2, at 4 P. M., in the Okaw church, Piatt Co., Ill. Ministering brethren on their way to Annual Meeting will please stop with us.

June 17, at 4 P. M., Yellow River congregation, Marshall Co., Ind.

June 18, Green Spring District, Seneca Co., Ohio.

To Close out

The few copies of the BRETHREN'S ALMANAC still on hand, we offer them at REDUCED PRICES. As long as the supply lasts, we will send them at the rate of five cents per copy post-paid, but to get them you should ORDER NOW.

Brethren's Quarterly.

Orders should be sent in at once for the Quarterly for the First Quarter of 1892. Price, three copies, 25 cents; eight copies, 40 cents; twenty copies and over, four cents each.

Juvenile Quarterly.

This is just the *Quarterly* for the little folks. Price, Three Copies, per Quarter, 20 Cents; 6 Copies, per Quarter, 25 Cents; 10 Copies and over, per Quarter, 3 Cents each.

The Hollinger Fence and Post.

Strong, Simple, Durable and Cheap! No More Cruelty to Stock!

MOUNT MORRIS, ILL., MARCH 4, 1892.

To Whom It May Concern:—This is to certify that we have examined the Hollinger wire fence and are satisfied that it is an excellent fence, in no wise superior to barbed wire, by which so many horses and cattle are cruelly injured. We are also personally acquainted with the builder, David Hollinger, and do not hesitate to recommend him as a fair-dealing, honest man, believing he will faithfully carry out any promise he may make.

D. L. MILLER,
D. N. WORKMAN.

For full particulars call on or address as follows: East of Ohio, I. K. Hollinger, Covington, Ohio; West of Ohio, D. Hollinger, Mt. Morris, Ill.

GOOD BOOKS FOR ALL.

Cruden's Concordance.—A very complete work. Price, cloth, $1.50; sheep, $3.00.

The Story of the Bible.—An excellent volume for old and young; will interest and instruct all those desiring a knowledge of the Scriptures. Price, $1.00.

Seven Great Monarchies.—By George Rawlinson. In three volumes, cloth. Per volume, $1.00.

Mental Science and Methods of Mental Culture.—By Edward Brooks. Cloth, $1.75.

Manual of Jewish History and Literature.—By D. Cassel. Cloth, 75 cents.

Every Day Christian Life. — By F. W. Farrar. Cloth, 12mo, $1.25.

Biblical Theology of the Old Testament.—By R. F. Weidom. Cloth, $1.25.

Campbell and Owen Debate. — Contains a complete investigation of the evidences of Christianity. Price, $1.50.

Classified Minutes of Annual Meeting.—A work of rare interest for all who desire to be well informed in the church work, from the early days of our Brethren until the present. Price, cloth, $1.50; leather, $2.00.

Europe and Bible Lands.—By D. L. Miller. A book for the people,—more comprehensive and thorough than many higher-priced works. Price, cloth, $1.50; leather, $2.00.

Ecclesiastical History.—By Eusebius. Bohn Library. Cloth, $2.00.

Ecclesiastical History.—By Mosheim. 2 vols. 8vo, $2.00.

Early Days of Christianity.—By F. W. Farrar. Author's edition, cloth. 12mo, $1.25.

New and Complete Bible Commentary.—By Jamieson, Fausset and Brown. It is far in advance of other works. It is critical, practical, and explanatory. It is compendious and comprehensive in its character. It has a critical Introduction to each Book of Scripture, and fix by far the most practical, suggestive, scientific, and popular work of the kind in the English language. In four large 12mo volumes of about 1,000 pages each. In extra fine English cloth, sprinkled edges, the full set, $8.00; half morocco, the full set, $12.00.

Sacred Geography and Antiquities.—A practical, helpful work for Bible students, ministers and Sunday-school teachers. Price, $2.25.

The Origin and Growth of Religion.—Hibbert Lectures. By T. W. R. Davids. Cloth, 8vo, $2.50.

Our Library on Christian Evidences.—This collection of works intended for the best books to be had on that subject: "Paley's Evidences of Christianity," New Edition, $1.50; "Nelson on Infidelity," 75 cents; "Manual of Christian Evidences," 75 cents; "Many Infallible Proofs," $1.25; "The Divine Demonstration," $1.50; "The Bible in the Nineteenth Century," 90 cents; "Grounds of Theistic and Christian Belief," $2.50. Price of the entire set, if ordered at one time, $8.00; special terms to ministers furnished upon application.

Bible Work, or Bible Reader's Commentary on the New Testament.—By J. G. Butler. Two. vols. 8vo, $10.00.

Biblical Antiquities.—By John Nevin. Gives a concise account of Bible times and customs; an invaluable to all students of Bible subjects. Price, $1.50.

Quinter and McConnell Debate.—A debate on Trine Immersion, the Lord's Supper, and Feet-washing, between Eld. James Quinter (German Baptist) and Eld. N. A. McConnell (Christian) held at Dry Creek, Iowa, 1867. Price, $1.50.

Popular Commentary on the New Testament.—Edited by Philip Schaff. Four volumes, 8vo. Matthew, Mark and Luke: $6.00. John and the Acts; $6.00. Romans to Philemon: $5.00. Hebrews to Revelation; $5.00.

Sabbatism.—By M. M. Eshelman. Treats the Sabbath question, showing that the first day of the week is the day for assembling in worship. Price, 10 cents; 15 copies, $1.00.

EGGS, EGGS FOR HATCHING

Send three stamps for mammoth Catalogue and Guide to Poultry Raisers. The finest book of the kind published. Containing valuable information for the poultry man and all who have poultry, either for pleasure or profit.

C. C. SHOEMAKER,
L. B. 1962. Freeport, Ill.

Windsor European Hotel

TRIBUNE BLOCK,

145 to 153 Dearborn St. S. Geauctras, Prop.

Chicago, Ill.

This hotel is centrally located, and the most respectable House of its class in the City. The charges are moderate, varying in price from 75 cents to $1.50 per day, per person. Thompson's Restaurant underneath. First-class Passenger Elevator.

✦ESSAYS✦

"Study to show thyself approved unto God; a workman that needeth not be ashamed, rightly dividing the Word of Truth."

THE LONELY GROVE.

[The following poem on the death of Eld. John Kline, was written and set to music by J. Senger many years ago. It has been sent to us for the MESSENGER.—ED.]

He once was young and bloomed in youth,
   As many in the present day;
Yet saw recorded in the Truth,
   That heav'n and earth must pass away.
He sought a place, a resting place,
   A place beyond this vale of tears,
Where he might see his Father's face—
   Where he might soothe his present fears.

He called aloud with tears of love,
   To know who'd join his company,
Which lasts through all eternity;
   Few here and there would join his band,
While passing through the wilderness:
   While Satan fought him hand to hand,
To drive him back in sad distress.

Though troubles here and trials there,
   Assailed him as they passed along:
Yet he would cry without despair,
   Oh, sinner, come and join our throng!
He often crossed the mountains high;
   And often journeyed prairies through,
To warn the flock of dangers nigh,
   And tell them what they ought to do.

He nobly fought to win the prize,
   That he might gain the mercy-seat;
But lo! he fell no more to rise,
   Or stand upon his mortal feet.
(While others died upon the bed,
   With sighing friends to weep around),
He in the distant grove lay dead,
   On naught but leaves and stones and ground.

A sudden blow took life and sense,
   While passing through that lonely grove,
Yet none could tell from whom nor whence,
   But He who lives in heav'n above.
My loss is great, I fell with pain,
   To know on earth we'll meet no more:
Yet hope my loss is his great gain,
   When he shall walk that happy shore.

MARRY ONLY IN THE LORD.

BY SAMUEL CHAMBERS.

I HAVE been waiting twenty-five years for some brother to write a good article, explaining what Paul meant where he said, "Be ye not unequally yoked together with unbelievers, for what fellowship hath righteousness with unrighteousness; and what communion hath light with darkness." They speak of it, as if it had reference only to secret societies. I think it means more than that. It also means marrying. This I will try to prove by Paul's own language. The Old Testament is a school-master to bring us to Christ. I will first refer you to Gen. 6: 2, "The sons of God saw the daughters of men that they were fair; and they took them wives of all which they chose,"—just as we do now. For this reason God sent the flood upon the earth. He wanted his sons and daughters to be separated from the world in marrying. The Jews were not allowed to marry other people, and we have the same God to deal with now.

Paul says, "Be ye not unequally yoked together." We understand him to mean marriage with unbelievers. Some one may ask: "What if a married woman should come to the church and her husband would not?" Paul answers that. "And the woman; which hath a husband that believeth not, and if he be pleased to dwell with her, let her not leave him." What liberty has she if her unbelieving husband dies? Paul says (verse 39), "The wife is bound by the law as long as her husband liveth; but if her husband be dead, she is at liberty to be married to whom she will; only in the Lord." That means in the church. Hear Peter, "Peace be with you all that are in Christ Jesus."

"Well," says one, "I have known some to marry those out of the church, and it was the means of bringing them into the church." Here let us remember that this never was God's way of bringing people into the church. Paul says, "For we dare not make ourselves of the number, or compare ourselves with some that commend themselves: but they, measuring themselves by themselves, and comparing themselves among themselves, are not wise." 2 Cor. 10: 12. "And we know that we are of God, and the whole world lieth in wickedness." 1 John 5: 19. James has something to say on that subject, too. "Know ye not that the friendship of this world is enmity with God? Whosoever, therefore, will be a friend of the world, is the enemy of God." Yet some will give away their strength as Samson did, and sometimes have no control of their children, and the church has but little control over them. So there is power lost to the church.

I see in the MESSENGER an item which says, "If you are in doubt about a thing being right or wrong, place yourself on the safe side of the doubt and watch developments." That is just what I am trying to have all do.

I once heard a dear old elder, in his preaching, say something in favor of what I am writing about. I asked some of the brethren after preaching, if they understood what he was alluding to. They said they did not. I told them that I understood the matter fully. I am no preacher, but I do think that brethren, when preaching, ought to explain so that others can understand them.

Many years ago, when I was seeking for the true church, I went to hear a Baptist. His text was, "If ye know these things, happy are ye if ye do them." I wondered what he would do with that! He did not touch the point. After meeting I went to him and asked why he did not explain what thing the Savior had reference to. He looked down, ran his fingers through his hair, and said, "I had no time to explain; I only spoke of things in general."

Let us hear Peter again, "Seeing ye have purified your souls in obeying the truth through the Spirit, unto unfeigned love of the brethren, see that ye love one another with a pure heart fervently." Brethren, don't you honestly think that our love for the members looks as though it were feigned when we go out of the church to get a companion for life?

I am nearly seventy-three years old. I spend my leisure time in reading and studying the Scriptures. I have looked over all my church papers to ascertain the number of marriages by members of the church. I find the record very discouraging. I find 216 where the parties were both members, and 232 where there was but one of them a member. Does that look as if we were trying to bring about what the Lord told his disciples to pray for, "Thy kingdom come; thy will be done on earth as it is done in heaven?"

Lima, Ohio.

DESULTORY REMARKS.

BY NOAH LONGANECKER.

No. 10 of GOSPEL MESSENGER comes brimful of good things. All true Israel cannot but be benefited by carefully reading "Immediate and Universal Knowledge of God." Then comes "Sowing and Reaping." Truly may sister Sadie say, "These are eternal words, and as true as God himself." I had once thought of taking up John E.

Mohler's suggestive "query." But again I thought, "Let some abler pen try it."

Multum-in parvo, much in little, may be said of the two selected articles on page 149. Thanks to the Editor for his remarks on "What Kind of a Mark Did the Lord Set on Cain?" Truly "there is a good moral in the lesson." "Anointing" contains things "new and old." The subject is an important one. It is a Gospel question, and is suitable for the GOSPEL MESSENGER. Such articles will certainly assist all inquiring minds. Said article suggested the following to my mind: (1) That the word "*ordained*," in Mark 3: 14, is used in the sense of "*appointed*." The Revised and American Versions both read "*appointed*." (2) That there is a wonderful similarity between the appointing of the "*twelve*" and of the "*seventy*." Read Matt. 9: 37, 38, and then Luke 10: 2, and you will find that Christ used the same language to both the twelve and the seventy.

What a wonderful similarity between their commissions! Read Matt. 10, Mark 3 and Luke 9, and then compare with Luke 10. Now read Luke 9: 1 and 10: 1, 19, and you will learn that Christ gave the seventy power and authority, as well as the twelve. Or, as Jamison, Fausset and Brown have it, "He both *qualified* and *authorized* them." What is the object of the "ordination of elders" as commanded in the Bible? Is it not that they might be both qualified and authorized to the work for which they were appointed?

That power and authority is still from the Lord, although he may use his servants as a means to it. As the Lord sent the twelve, so he sent the seventy forth, "two and two." Our translation of Luke 10: 1 is faulty. It reads, "After these things the Lord appointed other seventy also," as if he had appointed seventy before this time. The Revised Version reads, "Now after these things the Lord appointed seventy others." The American Version reads, "After these things the Lord appointed also seventy others." He had appointed the twelve before this time; now he also appointed seventy others.

Under the Jewish church there were twelve Patriarchs; one for each tribe. Under the Christian church there were twelve apostles,—one for each tribe. Paul was the apostle of the Gentiles, which were also to be gathered into the fold. Matthew filled the place of Judas. Read Acts 1: 26, 2: 14 and 1 Cor. 15: 5, 8. Under the Jewish church, Moses, — the lawgiver of the Jewish church,—appointed seventy elders, to assist him in the government of the Jewish church, so Christ, the Lawgiver of the Christian church, appointed seventy and sent them forth. Taking all things into consideration, is there not a remarkable similarity between Christ's appointing, qualifying and authorizing the twelve and seventy, and that of choosing and ordaining elders by the church? Verily there is. Of course, when Christ was here personally, he could do that without means, which he now does through means. But I am deviating from my subject.

The Huntingdon Editor makes some good hits on "Church Divisions." When asked for the causes of such divisions, the "Office Editor" truly gave the *one chief* cause. Here it is in capitals: "SELF-WILL AND A DISREGARD FOR THE WRITTEN WORD." "SELF-WILL is the one cause, which always leads to "a disregard for the Written Word." If any one doubts the statement, let him but carefully read sacred and profane history. The following editorial will bear reprinting:

"The best report we have heard from any congregation, is that given by Bro. Abraham Wolf, concerning the Libertyville church, Iowa. He says, during the three years he has lived there, he has not heard an unkind word in any of the deliber-

✦ESSAYS✦

"Study to show thyself approved unto God; a workman that needeth not to be ashamed, rightly dividing the Word of Truth."

THE LONELY GROVE.

[The following poem on the death of Eld. John Kline, was written and set to music by J. Senger many years ago. It has been sent to us for the MESSENGER.—EID.]

He once was young and bloomed in youth,
    As many in the present day;
Yet saw recorded in the Truth,
    That heav'n and earth must pass away.
He sought a place, a resting place,
    A place beyond this vale of tears,
Where he might see his Father's face—
    Where he might soothe his present fears.

He called aloud with teary of love,
    To know who'd join his company,
To seek a resting-place above,
    Which lasts through all eternity;
Few here and there would join his band,
    While passing through the wilderness:
While Satan fought him hand to hand,
    To drive him back in sad distress.

Though troubles here and trials there,
    Assailed him as they passed along;
Yet he would cry without despair,
    Oh, sinner, come and join our throng!
He often crossed the mountains high;
    And often journeyed prairies through,
To warn the flock of dangers nigh,
    And tell them what they ought to do.

He nobly fought to win the prize,
    That he might gain the mercy-seat;
But lo! he fell no more to rise,
    Or stand upon his mortal feet.
(While others died upon the bed,
    With sighing friends to weep around),
He in the distant grove lay dead,
    On naught but leaves and stones and ground.

A sudden blow took life and sense,
    While passing through that lonely grove,
Yet none could tell from whom nor whence,
    But He who lives in heav'n above.
My loss is great, I fell with pain,
    To know on earth we'll meet no more:
Yet hope my loss is his great gain,
    When he shall walk that happy shore.

MARRY ONLY IN THE LORD.

BY SAMUEL CHAMBERS.

I HAVE been waiting twenty-five years for some brother to write a good article, explaining what Paul meant where he said, "Be ye not unequally yoked together with unbelievers, for what fellowship hath righteousness with unrighteousness; and what communion hath light with darkness." They speak of it, as if it had reference only to secret societies. I think it means more than that. It also means marrying. This I will try to prove by Paul's own language. The Old Testament is a school-master to bring us to Christ. I will first refer you to Gen. 6: 2, "The sons of God saw the daughters of men that they were fair; and they took them wives of all which they chose,"—just as we do now. For this reason God sent the flood upon the earth. He wanted his sons and daughters to be separated from the world in marrying. The Jews were not allowed to marry other people, and we have the same God to deal with now.

Paul says, "Be ye not unequally yoked together." We understand him to mean marriage with unbelievers. Some one may ask: "What if a married woman should come to the church and her husband would not?" Paul answers that. "And the woman; which hath a husband that believeth not, and if he be pleased to dwell with her, let her not leave him." What liberty has she if her unbelieving husband dies? Paul says (verse 39), "The wife is bound by the law as long as her husband liveth; but if her husband be dead, she is at liberty to be married to whom she will; only in the Lord." That means in the church. Hear Peter, "Peace be with you all that are in Christ Jesus."

"Well," says one, "I have known some to marry those out of the church, and it was the means of bringing them into the church." Here let us remember that this never was God's way of bringing people into the church. Paul says, "For we dare not make ourselves of the number, or compare ourselves with some that commend themselves: but they, measuring themselves by themselves, and comparing themselves among themselves, are not wise."- 2 Cor. 10: 12. "And we know that we are of God, and the whole world lieth in wickedness." 1 John 5: 19. James has something to say on that subject, too. "Know ye not that the friendship of this world is enmity with God? Whosoever, therefore, will be a friend of the world, is the enemy of God." Yet some will give away their strength as Samson did, and sometimes have no control of their children, and the church has but little control over them. So there is power lost to the church.

I see in the MESSENGER an item which says, "If you are in doubt about a thing being right or wrong, place yourself on the safe side of the doubt and watch developments." That is just what I am trying to have all do.

I once heard a dear old elder, in his preaching, say something in favor of what I am writing about. I asked some of the brethren after preaching, if they understood what he was alluding to. They said they did not. I told them that I understood the matter fully. I am no preacher, but I do think that brethren, when preaching, ought to explain so that others can understand them.

Many years ago, when I was seeking for the true church, I went to hear a Baptist. His text was, "If ye know these things, happy are ye if ye do them." I wondered what he would do with that! He did not touch the point. After meeting I went to him and asked why he did not explain what things the Savior had reference to. He looked down, ran his fingers through his hair, and said, "I had no time to explain; I only spoke of things in general."

Let us hear Peter again, "Seeing ye have purified your souls in obeying the truth through the Spirit, unto unfeigned love of the brethren, see that ye love one another with a pure heart fervently." Brethren, don't you honestly think that our love for the members looks as though it were feigned when we go out of the church to get a companion for life?

I am nearly seventy-three years old. I spend my leisure time in reading and studying the Scriptures. I have looked over all my church papers to ascertain the number of marriages by members of the church. I find the record very discouraging. I find 216 where the parties were both members, and 232 where there was but one of them a member. Does that look as if we were trying to bring about what the Lord told his disciples to pray for, "Thy kingdom come; thy will be done on earth as it is done in heaven?"

Lima, Ohio.

DESULTORY REMARKS.

BY NOAH LONGANECKER.

No. 10 of GOSPEL MESSENGER comes brimful of good things. All true Israel cannot but be benefited by carefully reading "Immediate and Universal Knowledge of God." Then comes "Sowing and Reaping." Truly may sister Sadie say, "These are eternal words, and as true as God himself." I had once thought of taking up John E.

Mohler's suggestive "query." But again I thought, "Let some abler pen try it."

Multum-in parvo, much in little, may be said of the two selected articles on page 149. Thanks to the Editor for his remarks on "What Kind of a Mark Did the Lord Set on Cain?" Truly "there is a good moral in the lesson." "Anointing" contains things "new and old." The subject is an important one. It is a Gospel question, and is suitable for the GOSPEL MESSENGER. Such articles will certainly assist all inquiring minds. Said article suggested the following to my mind: (1) That the word "*ordained*," in Mark 3: 14, is used in the sense of "*appointed*." The Revised amd American Versions both read "*appointed*." (2) That there is a wonderful similarity between the appointing of the "*twelve*" and of the "*seventy*." Read Matt. 9: 37, 38, and then Luke 10: 2, and you will find that Christ used the same language to both the twelve and the seventy.

What a wonderful similarity between their commissions! Read Matt. 10, Mark 3 and Luke 9, and then compare with Luke 10. Now read Luke 9: 1 and 10: 1, 19, and you will learn that Christ gave the seventy power and authority, as well as the twelve. Or, as Jamison, Faussett and Brown have it, "He both *qualified* and *authorized* them." What is the object of the "ordination of elders" as commanded in the Bible? Is it not that they might be both qualified and authorized to the work for which they were appointed?

That power and authority is still from the Lord, although he may use his servants as a means to it. As the Lord sent the twelve, so he sent the seventy forth,. "two and two." Our translation of Luke 10: 1 is faulty. It reads, "After these things the Lord appointed other seventy also," as if he had appointed seventy before this time. The Revised Version reads, "Now after these things the Lord appointed seventy others." The American Version reads, "After these things the Lord appointed also seventy others." He had appointed the twelve before this time; now he also appointed seventy others.

Under the Jewish church there were twelve Patriarchs; one for each tribe. Under the Christian church there were twelve apostles,—one for each tribe. Paul was the apostle of the Gentiles, which were also to be gathered into the fold. Matthew filled the place of Judas. Read Acts 1: 26, 2: 14 and 1 Cor. 15: 5, 8. Under the Jewish church, Moses, — the lawgiver of the Jewish church,—appointed seventy elders, to assist him in the government of the Jewish church, so Christ, the Lawgiver of the Christian church, appointed seventy and sent them forth. Taking all things into consideration, is there not a remarkable similarity between Christ's appointing, qualifying and authorizing the twelve and seventy, and that of choosing and ordaining elders by the church? Verily there is. Of course, when Christ was here personally, he could do that without means, which he now does through means. But I am deviating from my subject.

The Huntingdon Editor makes some good hits on "Church Divisions." When asked for the causes of such divisions, the "Office Editor" truly gave the *one chief cause*. Here it is in capitals: "SELF-WILL AND A DISREGARD FOR THE WRITTEN WORD." "SELF-WILL is the *one* cause, which always leads to "a disregard for the Written Word." If any one doubts the statement, let him but carefully read sacred and profane history. The following editorial will bear reprinting:

"The best report we have heard from any congregation, is that given by Bro. Abraham Wolf, concerning the Libertyville church, Iowa. He says, during the three years he has lived there, he has not heard an unkind word in any of she deliber

clude that some other decree has gone forth,—something like this: "Go and tell twenty thousand readers now living, and preserve it that generations to come may know what great things I am doing for the Lord." The reports referred to are becoming a little monotonous. When we examine them and get the sum total of their contents we have about this and no more: "I left my home on a certain day. I went to the station. I boarded the train at a certain hour. I had a pleasant ride. I arrived at the destined point safely. I was met by Bro. so and so. I was taken to his hospitable home where I met his amiable wife, who did all she could to make me comfortable. After partaking of a bountiful repast, I was taken to the church where I had previously arranged to preach to the people. I met a good congregation, anxiously awaiting my arrival. I continued my meetings day and evening with increasing interest until a certain date, when I was compelled to close my meetings at this point, in order to meet my engagements, which I had made elsewhere. As an immediate result I baptized," etc. Possibly the Lord is not mentioned ones,—no room in the inn for him.

Some may think the above too strong, but we have a copy of the MESSENGER, with an article of about half a column, containing the personal pronoun seventeen times.

May we not kindly ask those who wish to report their work, to give us a little more of the Lord, and not quite so much of "I," and possibly the change will be hailed with joy by all, except, probably, a little family circle now and then. "Try the spirits whether they are of God." 1 John 4: 7. "If any man have not the spirit of Christ, he is none of his." Rom. 8: 9. "Whosoever shall exalt himself shall be abased." Matt. 23: 12.

THE SHAMBERGER-BOND DEBATE.

Negative Arguments of G. A. Shamberger, with Notes by Levi Mohler, Warrensburgh, Mc.

"PROPOSITION.—The penitent sinner is justified or pardoned by faith only."

NOTE. — "Pardoned" is understood in this proposition to qualify the meaning of "justified."

"ARGUMENT 1.—God justifies and pardons according to law. Rom. 3: 24, 27; Rom. 8: 1, 2; James 1: 22, 25."

NOTE.—This law is the law of the Spirit. Rom. 8: 2. The perfect law of liberty. James 1: 25. The law of faith. Rom. 3: 27.

The law, by which God justifies or pardons is given to us in the Gospel. He could not give a law, but what sacrifice was required to make it effective. The law was given through Christ. It was sealed and made powerful to save by his blood, which power the blood of beasts could not give.

This perfect law of liberty demands faith, repentance and baptism, in order to the remission of sins, and not faith only.

As far as a man follows that law of God, he is justified, and no farther. If from the heart he follows it in faith, he is justified, as far as the law provides that man is justified by simply believing.

If he continues through repentance to baptism, he is then justified to the extent that the law provides that he shall be, by faith, repentance and baptism,—which extent is to the pardon of sins and to acceptance as a child of God. He is then ready to go on to good works in a holy life, to grow in grace from a babe in Christ, to full stature in him, advancing in the divine life towards the perfection of God, for all of which the perfect law of liberty,—the Gospel,—provides, and towards which he advances, as he obeys that law.

In this view man is justified by faith and works prior to and after baptism, by believing and obeying the just law of God, revealed to him, but he is not therein justified in the sense of pardon from sin, but only in the sense of being made just or right, by obeying a just and righteous law.

His sins of the past, which render him a sinner before God, must be absolved by provisions outside of his own conduct or anything that he can do.

From his sins he can only be justified by the blood of Christ, when baptized into his death, where his blood flowed,—a fountain for cleansing from sin,—and by the righteousness of Christ, which he puts on when baptized into him. Continuing in Christ, his blood will ever avail and his righteousness may ever be worn for justification from sins that may be committed after baptism.

There is a difference in the grades of justification, as follows:

1. The justification that comes from obeying the laws of God, prior to and after baptism, which is secured by man through faith and works. Of this order was Abraham's justification and imputed righteousness.

2. Justification in the sense of pardon and of acceptance with God as a child of God.

This justification, man of himself cannot secure only so far as to believe and follow the law of God that leads to the blood of Christ, which alone washes away sin, and to the righteousness of Christ, in which alone he is made acceptable in the sight of God.

The law that leads man to the provisions made for pardon, in the blood and righteousness of Christ, is the law of baptism into Christ.

Abraham's justification was not of this kind, not to this degree. The law for justification from sin did not exist in the world in Abraham's time. The blood of Christ was not shed,—no other blood avails, or ever did avail for the pardon of sin. Abraham's sins were carried over until atonement should be made for sin. Then his sins had remission with the sins of all the faithful of God, who lived before Christ, Rom. 3: 25, by a law not revealed to us, of applying the atonement to those who lived before Christ.

But that they were not pardoned contrary to the law that requires "that the soul that sinneth shall die," is known by their sins being carried over to the atonement of Christ, in which is the only escape from the penalty of the law.

Abraham was justified in the sense of pardon, by the atonement according to law, the same as we.

"THOUGHT 1.—The law comes to us through a mediator."

"THOUGHT 2.—No law applies to a man who cannot obey it."

"ARGUMENT 2.—The Scriptures nowhere say we are pardoned or forgiven by *faith*."

"ARGUMENT 3.—The Scriptures nowhere say we are pardoned or justified by faith only."

NOTE.—Faith is something within one's self, and if man is pardoned by *faith only*, his hope for salvation is not in Christ or the Gospel, but in his faith.

Faith, then, has more merit and power than the blood of Christ and the Gospel.

Paul says, "The Gospel is the power of God unto salvation."

"ARGUMENT 4.—The Scriptures nowhere teach that penitent sinners are justified or pardoned by anything *only* done by them."

"ARGUMENT 5.—The Scriptures pointedly deny the faith-only doctrine. James 2: 24; Gal. 5: 6; Acts 5: 32."

"No righteousness takes away sin save Christ's. Rom. 3: 25."

"ARGUMENT 6. — The Scriptures teach that faith alone is dead. James 2: 17, 20."

"ARGUMENT 7.—The Scriptures teach that a man having faith alone is nothing. Sounding brass surely. 1 Cor. 13: 1; 1 John 2: 5 and 5: 3."

NOTE.—It is necessary to have love with faith. "This is the love of God that we keep his commandments." 1 John 5: 3.

"ARGUMENT 8. — The Scriptures teach that those who believe only, are not free. John 8: 30-32; Rom. 6: 17, 18, 22; John 12: 42, 43."

"ARGUMENT 9. — The Scriptures teach that faith is perfected by works. James 2: 21, 24; Gal. 5: 6, 7. James was not ignorant of the Scriptures in point."

NOTE.—An imperfect faith cannot be the basis of a perfect salvation or of pardon from sin.

Faith is capable of change, of advancement, of decline or of perversion to error. Works index the character of faith.

"ARGUMENT 10. — The Scriptures teach that penitent believers in Jesus are justified, but not wholly or fully. Rom. 5: 1; 4: 3-5; James 2: 23, 24."

NOTE.—The penitent believer is justified by his belief, as far as and like Abraham.

No faith of Abraham ever could of itself take away sin. Only the blood of Christ can do that. Man stops too soon when he says, "Faith only." We must have faith in its place, but it is not a sin-bearer or a washer-away of sins.

"ARGUMENT 11. — The Scriptures teach that justification is from sins that are past, and that it is perfected when Christ is put on. 1 Cor. 6: 11; Acts 13: 36. By him we are baptized into his name. Col. 2: 10, 12; Acts 10: 48,—through his name.

"On the divine side a number of means are used to justify. Is it strange? A number are on the human side. An imperfect faith is looking humanward, the basis of an imperfect justification. A perfect faith is the basis of a perfect justification. The same may be said of righteousness."

NOTE.—As to the justification which Christ gives when we put him on, it is perfect. There is no sin but what may be atoned for through the blood of Jesus. Washed in his blood, the soul is clean and white—justification is perfect.

"ARGUMENT 12.—The teachings of Christ were that the healing, cleansing power comes from him, though he says, 'Thy faith hath made thee whole.' Luke 8: 43, 48; Acts 3: 16 and 4: 10."

NOTE.—In Luke 8: 43, 48, we have a woman diseased, who hears of Jesus and believes, what she hears, as the sinner hears of the same physician. When she hears and believes, is she healed? No. She believes, goes to where Jesus is in the crowd. She tries to get to him, to touch him; yet she is not healed.

She touches him, and virtue went forth from him and it healed her, yet Jesus said, "Thy faith hath made thee whole." Her faith led her to act and appropriate the healing virtue in Christ. Faith acts in the same way to-day, and the healing virtue still comes from Jesus.

GENERAL NOTES.—We cannot find a case where the Spirit is the administrator of baptism. Water is the first element; the Spirit is the second. The Spirit is never the administrator.

Baptism, "into the name of Christ," "in him," "into his death," all mean the same thing. An infidel cannot be baptized into the name of Christ. You can perform the ceremony, but you cannot do it in the name of Christ. It takes faith and repentance, with baptism, for that.

clude that some other decree has gone forth,—something like this: "Go and tell twenty thousand readers now living, and preserve it that generations to come may know what great things I am doing for the Lord." The reports referred to are becoming a little monotonous. When we examine them and get the sum total of their contents we have about this and no more: "I left my home on a certain day. I went to the station. I boarded the train at a certain hour. I had a pleasant ride. I arrived at the destined point safely. I was met by Bro. so and so. I was taken to his hospitable home where I met his amiable wife, who did all she could to make me comfortable. After partaking of a bountiful repast, I was taken to the church where I had previously arranged to preach to the people. I met a good congregation, anxiously awaiting my arrival. I continued my meetings day and evening with increasing interest until a certain date, when I was compelled to close my meetings at this point, in order to meet my engagements, which I had made elsewhere. As an immediate result I baptized," etc. Possibly the Lord is not mentioned once,—no room in the inn for him.

Some may think the above too strong, but we have a copy of the MESSENGER, with an article of about half a column, containing the personal pronoun seventeen times.

May we not kindly ask those who wish to report their work, to give us a little more of the Lord, and not quite so much of "I," and possibly the change will be hailed with joy by all, except, probably, a little family circle now and then. "Try the spirits whether they are of God." 1 John 4: 7. "If any man have not the spirit of Christ, he is none of his." Rom. 8: 9. "Whosoever shall exalt himself shall be abased." Matt. 23: 12.

THE SHAMBERGER-BOND DEBATE.

Negative Arguments of G. A. Shamberger, with Notes by Levi Mohler, Warrensburgh, Mo.

"PROPOSITION.—The penitent sinner is justified or pardoned by faith only."

NOTE. — "Pardoned" is understood in this proposition to qualify the meaning of "justified."

"ARGUMENT 1.—God justifies and pardons according to law. Rom. 3: 24, 27; Rom. 8: 1, 2; James 1: 22, 25."

NOTE.—This law is called the law of the Spirit Rom. 8: 2. The perfect law of liberty. James 1: 25. The law of faith. Rom. 3: 27.

The law, by which God justifies or pardons is given to us in the Gospel. He could not give a law, but what sacrifice was required to make it effective. The law was given through Christ. It was sealed and made powerful to save by his blood, which power the blood of beasts could not give.

This perfect law of liberty demands faith, repentance and baptism, in order to the remission of sins, and not faith only.

As far as a man follows that law of God, he is justified, and no farther. If from the heart he follows it in faith, he is justified, as far as the law provides that man is justified by simply believing.

If he continues through repentance to baptism, he is then justified to the extent that the law provides that he shall be, by faith, repentance and baptism,—which extent is to the pardon of sins and to acceptance as a child of God. He is then ready to go on to good works in a holy life, to grow in grace from a babe in Christ, to full stature in him, advancing in the divine life towards the perfection of God, for all of which the perfect law of liberty,—the Gospel,—provides, and towards which he advances, as he obeys that law.

In this view man is justified by faith and works prior to and after baptism, by believing and obeying the just law of God, revealed to him, but he is not therein justified in the sense of pardon from sin, but only in the sense of being made just or right, by obeying a just and righteous law.

His sins of the past, which render him a sinner before God, must be absolved by provisions outside of his own conduct or anything that he can do.

From his sins he can only be justified by the blood of Christ, when baptized into his death, where his blood flowed,—a fountain for cleansing from sin,—and by the righteousness of Christ, which he puts on when baptized into him. Continuing in Christ, his blood will ever avail and his righteousness may ever be worn for justification from sins that may be committed after baptism.

There is a difference in the grades of justification, as follows:

1. The justification that comes from obeying the laws of God, prior to and after baptism, which is secured by man through faith and works. Of this order was Abraham's justification and imputed righteousness.

2. Justification in the sense of pardon and of acceptance with God as a child of God.

This justification, man of himself cannot secure only so far as to believe and follow the law of God that leads to the blood of Christ, which alone washes away sin, and to the righteousness of Christ, in which alone he is made acceptable in the sight of God.

The law that leads man to the provisions made for pardon, in the blood and righteousness of Christ, is the law of baptism into Christ.

Abraham's justification was not of this kind, not to this degree. The law for justification from sin did not exist in the world in Abraham's time. The blood of Christ was not shed,—no other blood avails, or ever did avail for the pardon of sin. Abraham's sins were carried over until atonement should be made for sin. Then his sins had remission with the sins of all the faithful of God, who lived before Christ, Rom. 3: 25, by a law not revealed to us, of applying the atonement to those who lived before Christ.

But that they were not pardoned contrary to the law that requires "that the soul that sinneth shall die," is known by their sins being carried over to the atonement of Christ, in which is the only escape from the penalty of the law.

Abraham was justified in the sense of pardon, by the atonement according to law, the same as we.

"THOUGHT 1.—The law comes to us through a mediator."

"THOUGHT 2.—No law applies to a man who cannot obey it."

"ARGUMENT 2.—The Scriptures nowhere say we are pardoned or forgiven by faith."

"ARGUMENT 3.—The Scriptures nowhere say we are pardoned or justified by faith only."

NOTE.—Faith is something within one's self, and if man is pardoned by faith only, his hope for salvation is not in Christ or the Gospel, but in his faith.

Faith, then, has more merit and power than the blood of Christ and the Gospel. Paul says, "The Gospel is the power of God unto salvation."

"ARGUMENT 4.—The Scriptures nowhere teach that penitent sinners are justified or pardoned by anything only done by them."

"ARGUMENT 5.—The Scriptures pointedly deny the faith-only doctrine. James 2: 24; Gal. 5: 6; Acts 5: 32."

"No righteousness takes away sin save Christ's. Rom. 3: 25."

"ARGUMENT 6. — The Scriptures teach that faith alone is dead. James 2: 17, 20."

"ARGUMENT 7.—The Scriptures teach that a man having faith alone is nothing. Sounding brass surely. 1 Cor. 13: 1; 1 John 2: 5 and 5: 3."

NOTE.—It is necessary to have love with faith. "This is the love of God that we keep his commandments." 1 John 5: 3.

"ARGUMENT 8. — The Scriptures teach that those who believe only, are not free. John 8: 30-32; Rom. 6: 17, 18, 22; John 12: 42, 43."

NOTE.—The Jews did believe on Jesus, John 8: 30, 32, and these believers are said not to be free from sin, but were found in sin. A person may believe and yet not be free. This disposes of the proposition, if true.

"ARGUMENT 9. — The Scriptures teach that faith is perfected by works. James 2: 21, 24; Gal. 5: 6, 7. James was not ignorant of the Scriptures in point."

NOTE.—An imperfect faith cannot be the basis of a perfect salvation or of pardon from sin.

Faith is capable of change, of advancement, of decline or of perversion to error. Works lude of the character of faith.

"ARGUMENT 10.—The Scriptures teach that penitent believers in Jesus are justified, but not wholly or fully. Rom. 5: 1; 4: 3-5; James 2: 22, 24."

NOTE.—The penitent believer is justified by his belief, as far as and like Abraham.

No faith of Abraham ever could of itself take away sin. Only the blood of Christ can do that. Man stops too soon when he says, "Faith only." We must have faith in its place, but it is not a sin-bearer or a washer-away of sins.

"ARGUMENT 11. — The Scriptures teach that justification is from sins that are past, and that it is perfected when Christ is put on. 1 Cor. 6: 11; Acts 13: 36. By him we are baptized into his name. Col. 2: 10, 12; Acts 10: 43,—through his name.

"On the divine side a number of means are said to justify. Is it strange? A number are on the human side. An imperfect faith is, looking humanward, the basis of an imperfect justification. A perfect faith is the basis of a perfect justification. The same may be said of righteousness."

NOTE.—As to the justification which Christ gives when we put him on, it is perfect. There is no sin but what may be atoned for through the blood of Jesus. Washed in his blood, the soul is clean and white—justification is perfect.

"ARGUMENT 12.—The teachings of Christ were that the healing, cleansing power comes from him, though he says, 'Thy faith hath made thee whole.' Luke 8: 43, 48; Acts 3: 16 and 4: 10."

NOTE.—In Luke 8: 43, 48, we have a woman diseased, who hears of Jesus and believes what she hears, as the sinner hears of the same physician. When she hears and believes, is she healed? No. She believes, goes to where Jesus is in the crowd. She tries to get to him, to touch him; yet she is not healed.

She touches him, and virtue went forth from him and it healed her, yet Jesus said, "Thy faith hath made thee whole." Her faith led her to act and appropriate the healing virtue in Christ. Faith acts in the same way to-day, and the healing virtue still comes from Jesus.

GENERAL NOTES.—We cannot find a case where the Spirit is the administrator of baptism. Water is the first element; the Spirit is the second. The Spirit is never the administrator.

Baptism, "into the name of Christ," "in him," "into his death," all mean the same thing. An infidel cannot be baptized into the name of Christ. You can perform the ceremony, but you cannot do it in the name of Christ. It takes faith and repentance, with baptism, for that.

Missionary and Tract Work Department.

"Upon the first day of the week, let every one of you lay by him in store as God hath prospered him, that there be no gatherings when I come."—1 Cor. 16: 2.

"Every man as he purposeth in his heart, so let him give. Not grudgingly or of necessity, for the Lord loveth a cheerful giver."—2 Cor. 9: 7.

HOW MUCH SHALL WE GIVE?

"Every man according to his ability." "Every one as God hath prospered him." "Every man, according as he purposeth in his heart, so let him give." "For if there be first a willing mind, it is accepted according to that a man hath, and not according to that he hath not."—2 Cor. 8: 12.

Organization of Missionary Committee.

DANIEL VANIMAN, Foreman, - - - McPherson, Kans.
D. L. MILLER, Treasurer, - - - - Mt. Morris, Ill.
GALEN B. ROYER, Secretary, - - - Mt. Morris, Ill.

Organization of Book and Tract Work.

S. W. HOOVER, Foreman, - - - - Dayton, Ohio.
S. BOCK, Secretary and Treasurer, - - Dayton, Ohio.

☞All donations intended for Missionary Work should be sent to GALEN B. ROYER, Mt. Morris, Ill.

☞All money for Tract Work should be sent to S. BOCK, Dayton, Ohio.

☞Money may be sent by Money Order, Registered Letter, or Drafts on New York or Chicago. Do not send personal checks, or drafts on interior towns, as it costs 25 cents to collect them.

☞Solicitors are requested to faithfully carry out the plan of Annual Meeting, that all our members be solicited to contribute at least twice a year for the Mission and Tract Work of the Church.

☞Notes for the Endowment Fund can be had by writing to the Secretary of either Work.

DID JUDAS, THE TRAITOR, PARTAKE OF THE COMMUNION?

BY CHAS. M. YEAROUT.

LET us examine, and harmonize the four Gospels upon the subject.

(a) As they were eating, Jesus said one of them (the apostles) should betray him. Matt. 26: 21; Mark 14: 18; Luke 22: 21; John 13: 21.

(b) The apostles enquired among themselves, and also asked Jesus who it was that should do this thing. Matt. 26: 22-25; Mark 14: 19; Luke 22: 23; John 13: 22-25.

(c) Jesus answers them: "He that dippeth with me in the dish, or he to whom I shall give a sop when I have dipped." Matt. 26: 23; Mark 14: 20; John 13: 26.

It is evident from the above that the traitor was made known while they were eating, or during the Supper. Matthew and Mark plainly teach that they were all dipping in a dish together. John says, that Jesus dipped a sop (a piece) and gave it to Judas Iscariot, by which he was made known as the traitor. Luke does not say anything about the dipping into the dish, or the sop, but says, "Behold the hand of him that betrayeth me is with me on the table." This agrees with the other evangelists, for how could he dip into a dish on the table without having his hands on the table?

The Communion was not instituted till after, or at the close of the Supper. Matt. 26: 26; Luke 22: 20; 1 Cor. 11: 24, 25. I offer as proof, that Jesus gave the sop to Judas during the time they were eating the Supper, John 21: 20. Here we learn that John "leaned on Jesus' breast at Supper."

I will now offer several reasons why Judas did not partake of the Communion.

(1) Because it is not reasonable that the Lord Jesus Christ, possessed of all knowledge and wisdom, would administer those sacred, life-giving emblems to a wicked person as Judas was. John 6: 70.

(2) Because Judas, after receiving the sop, went immediately out; and this sop was given during the Supper. John 13: 26-30; 21: 20. Hence Judas was not in the upper room when the Communion was instituted.

(3) Because he was not a fit subject to partake of the flesh and blood of the Son of God.

(4) Because he was a traitor, and had already sold the Lord for thirty pieces of silver. Matt. 26: 15, 16.

(5) Because ye cannot drink the cup of the Lord, and the cup of devils, 1 Cor. 10: 21, and had Jesus administered the Communion to Judas, he would have given a precedent for the admission of devils to the Lord's table.

(6) Because, in thus eating and drinking unworthily, he would have eaten and drank damnation to himself, 1 Cor. 11: 29, and the Lord would have knowingly administered his flesh and blood (which are designed for the support and growth of the spiritual life) to an unworthy person. John 6: 53, 54, 55, 56.

(7) Because Christ promised to again participate with those to whom he administered the Communion in the Father's kingdom. Matt. 26: 29.

(8) Because it is contrary to the teaching and tenor of the Gospel. We are not allowed to eat with the covetous, or idolaters, or drunkards, or extortioners. 1 Cor. 5: 11. We are to withdraw from those who walk disorderly, etc. 2 Thess. 3: 6. "For what fellowship hath righteousness with unrighteousness? and what communion hath light with darkness? And what concord hath Christ with Belial? or what part hath he that believeth with an infidel?" 2 Cor. 6: 14, 15.

Judas was covetous, worldly-minded, and treacherous, and in no sense worthy to partake of those sacred emblems.

Westphalia, Kans.

HOW MANY WERE PRESENT IN THAT UPPER ROOM?

BY J. H. MILLER.

IN GOSPEL MESSENGER No. 9, page 130, present volume, I notice that my position is called in question, in reference to an article I had written in Vol. 29, No. 48, page 762.

I never gave the subject any thought before as to how many of Christ's disciples were present in that upper room. Were there twelve beside the Savior, or more? The brother claimed for a long time that none but "the twelve" were present, but now is willing to change his mind. He refers to the following Scriptures: Acts 1: 21, 22, 23, 26, "Wherefore of these men, which have companied with us all the time that the Lord Jesus went in and out among us, beginning from the baptism of John, unto that same day that he was taken up from us, must one be ordained to be a witness with us of his resurrection. And they appointed two, Joseph called Barsabas, who was surnamed Justus, and Matthias. And they gave forth their lots; and the lot fell upon Matthias, and he was numbered with the eleven apostles."

The writer makes a strong point here, and claims because one was appointed, who had been with Christ and the apostles ALL the time, from the baptism of John, unto the same day that he was taken up, would include being in the "upper room," hence those two, in addition to the twelve must have been present.

He further claims that "even more than fourteen were present." "From the number of men which had companied with them all the time, two were appointed to be set before the Lord, that he might show which of the two he had chosen."

If these two were the only ones possessing the qualifications described by Peter, the church need not have appointed them. Peter could have informed the disciples that of "these two must one be ordained. True, the words used by Peter (these men) may not warrant the conclusion, that more than two are included, but the inference is strong that more are meant."

I am well pleased that our brother gets nothing stronger than inference. If these two were the only ones possessing the qualifications described by Peter, the church need not have appointed them. Peter could have informed the disciples that of "these two must one be ordained." I presume the church, in that early day, did as is done now,—let the church make the choice; Peter was a careful apostle, and would let the church do the work.

Peter, upon another occasion, well remembered where the power of God's Word lay, when he said to the lame man, "In the name of Jesus Christ, of Nazareth, rise up and walk." He might have said, "In my name do this," but he undoubtedly had read how Moses fell, when he took the glory of God unto himself, and did not sanctify the Lord before the people. Num. 20: 12. It is always safe to submit all weighty matters unto the Lord, and work through the church.

The apostle only wished to inform the members of the church to make choice of one who had a good knowledge of the work of Christ, and one who had companied with those holy men. It was not necessary that Matthias should be present upon all occasions. Even all the apostles did not see what Christ did upon the Mount of Transfiguration; none were present but Peter, James and John. Matt. 17: 1-13; Mark 9: 1-10.

None of the apostles were present at the raising of Jairus' daughter, but Peter, James and John. "And he suffered no man to follow him, save Peter, James and John. Mark 5: 37. Peter, James and John were called by the Savior to witness his suffering and prayer in the Garden of Gethsemane. He brought his disciples to the place "which was named Gethsemane: and he said to his disciples, Sit ye here, while I shall pray. And he taketh with him Peter, James and John, ... and went forward a little, and fell on the ground." Mark 14: 32-35.

Here we have found three places where even not all of the apostles were present. Then, why conclude, by inference, that more than the twelve were present at the Supper? "Now when the evening was come he sat down with the twelve." Matt. 26: 20. "And in the evening he cometh with the twelve." Mark 14: 17. "And when the hour was come, he sat down, and the twelve apostles with him." Luke 22: 14.

In searching the Scriptures, as referred to, I am unable to get any proof in favor of any being present excepting the twelve and Christ. It is a little strange that four men, at different periods of time, should write upon such an important subject, and agree so well upon all they have written, and then not mention, at even one time, that more were present besides the twelve.

Again, it seems strange to me, that the Savior would have other disciples present, and not invite them to the table, admitting this to be a fact, that a number of disciples were present, and none of them at the table but the twelve apostles. Many would now excuse themselves, claiming that the "Last Supper" only the twelve were invited to the table, and only the twelve took part in feet-washing, and if others could be excused so can we, etc., etc.

Goshen, Ind.

OUR BIBLE CLASS.

BY A. W. VANIMAN.

Practical Questions on Lesson XII.

1. INTO what two parts is the history of the New Covenant divided?

2. What was a Nazarite?

3. Where did prophecy say Christ would be born?

Missionary and Tract Work Department.

"Upon the first day of the week, let every one of you lay by him in store as God hath prospered him, that there be no gatherings when I come."—1 Cor. 16: 2.

"Every man as he purposeth in his heart, so let him give. Not grudgingly or of necessity, for the Lord loveth a cheerful giver."—2 Cor. 9: 7.

HOW MUCH SHALL WE GIVE?

"Every man *according to his ability*." "Every one *as God hath prospered him*." "Every man, *according as he purposeth in his heart*, so let him give." "For if there be first a willing mind, it is accepted *according to that a man hath*, and not according to that he hath not."—2 Cor. 8: 12.

Organization of Missionary Committee.

DANIEL VANIMAN, Foreman, - - - McPherson, Kans.
D. L. MILLER, Treasurer, - - - Mt. Morris, Ill.
GALEN B. ROYER, Secretary, - - - Mt. Morris, Ill.

Organization of Book and Tract Work.

S. W. HOOVER, Foreman, - - - Dayton, Ohio.
S. BOCK, Secretary and Treasurer, - - Dayton, Ohio.

☞ All donations intended for Missionary Work should be sent to GALEN B. ROYER, Mt. Morris, Ill.

☞ All money for Tract Work should be sent to S. BOCK, Dayton, Ohio.

☞ Money may be sent by Money Order, Registered Letter, or Drafts on New York or Chicago. Do not send personal checks, or drafts on interior towns, as it costs 25 cents to collect them.

☞ Solicitors are requested to faithfully carry out the plan of Annual Meeting, that all our members be solicited to contribute at least twice a year for the Mission and Tract Work of the Church.

☞ Notes for the Endowment Fund can be had by writing to the Secretary of either Work.

DID JUDAS, THE TRAITOR, PARTAKE OF THE COMMUNION?

BY CHAS. M. YEAROUT.

LET us examine, and harmonize the four Gospels upon the subject.

(a) As they were eating, Jesus said one of them (the apostles) should betray him. Matt. 26: 21; Mark 14: 18; Luke 22: 21; John 13: 21.

(b) The apostles enquired among themselves, and also asked Jesus who it was that should do this thing. Matt. 26: 22-25; Mark 14: 19; Luke 22: 23; John 13: 22-25.

(c) Jesus answers them: "He that dippeth with me in the dish, or he to whom I shall give a sop when I have dipped." Matt. 26: 23; Mark 14: 20; John 13: 26.

It is evident from the above that the traitor was made known while they were eating, or during the Supper. Matthew and Mark plainly teach that they were all dipping in a dish together. John says, that Jesus dipped a sop (a piece) and gave it to Judas Iscariot, by which he was made known as the traitor. Luke does not say anything about the dipping into the dish, or the sop, but says, "Behold the hand of him that betrayeth me is with me on the table." This agrees with the other evangelists, for how could he dip into a dish on the table without having his hands on the table?

The Communion was not instituted till after, or at the close of the Supper. Matt. 26: 26; Luke 22: 20; 1 Cor. 11: 24, 25. I offer as proof, that Jesus gave the sop to Judas during the time they were eating the Supper, John 21: 20. Here we learn that John "leaned on Jesus' breast at Supper."

I will now offer several reasons why Judas did not partake of the Communion.

(1) Because it is not reasonable that the Lord Jesus Christ, possessed of all knowledge and wisdom, would administer those sacred, life-giving emblems to a wicked person as Judas was. John 6: 70.

(2) Because Judas, after receiving the sop, went immediately out; and this sop was given during the Supper. John 13: 26-30; 21: 20. Hence Judas was not in the upper room when the Communion was instituted.

(3) Because he was not a fit subject to partake of the flesh and blood of the Son of God.

(4) Because he was a traitor, and had already sold the Lord for thirty pieces of silver. Matt. 26: 15, 16.

(5) Because ye cannot drink the cup of the Lord, and the cup of devils, 1 Cor. 10: 21, and had Jesus administered the Communion to Judas, he would have given a precedent for the admission of devils to the Lord's table.

(6) Because, in thus eating and drinking unworthily, he would have eaten and drank damnation to himself, 1 Cor. 11: 29, and the Lord would have knowingly administered his flesh and blood (which are designed for the support and growth of the spiritual life) to an unworthy person. John 6: 53, 54, 55, 56.

(7) Because Christ promised to again participate with those to whom he administered the Communion in the Father's kingdom. Matt. 26: 29.

(8) Because it is contrary to the teaching and tenor of the Gospel. We are not allowed to eat with the covetous, or idolaters, or drunkards, or extortioners. 1 Cor. 5: 11. We are to withdraw from those who walk disorderly, etc. 2 Thess 3: 6. "For what fellowship hath righteousness with unrighteousness? and what communion hath light with darkness? And what concord hath Christ with Belial? or what part hath he that believeth with an infidel?" 2 Cor. 6: 14, 15.

Judas was covetous, worldly-minded, and treacherous, and in no sense worthy to partake of those sacred emblems.

Westphalia, Kans.

HOW MANY WERE PRESENT IN THAT UPPER ROOM?

BY J. H. MILLER.

IN GOSPEL MESSENGER No. 9, page 130, present volume, I notice that my position is called in question, in reference to an article I had written in Vol. 29, No. 48, page 762.

I never gave the subject any thought before as to how many of Christ's disciples were present in that upper room. Were there twelve beside the Savior, or more? The brother claimed for a long time that none but "the twelve" were present, but now is willing to change his mind. He refers to the following Scriptures: Acts 1: 21, 22, 23, 26, "Wherefore of these men, which have companied with us all the time that the Lord Jesus went in and out among us, beginning from the baptism of John, unto that same day that he was taken up from us, must one be ordained to be a witness with us of his resurrection. And they appointed two, Joseph called Barsabas, who was surnamed Justus, and Matthias. And they gave forth their lots; and the lot fell upon Matthias, and he was numbered with the eleven apostles."

The writer makes a strong point here, and claims because one was appointed, who had been with Christ and the apostles ALL the time, from the baptism of John, unto the *same day* that he was taken up, would include being in the "upper room," hence those two, in addition to the twelve must have been present.

He further claims that "even more than fourteen were present." "From the number of men which had companied with them *all* the time, two were appointed to be set before the Lord, that he might show which of the two he had chosen."

If these two were the only ones possessing the qualifications described by Peter, the church need not have appointed them. Peter could have informed the disciples that of these *two* must one be ordained. True, the words used by Peter (these men) may not warrant the conclusion, that more than two are included, but the inference is strong that more are meant."

I am well pleased that our brother gets nothing stronger than *inference*. If these two were the only ones possessing the qualifications described by Peter, the church need not have appointed them. Peter could have informed the disciples that of "these two must one be ordained." I presume the church, in that early day, did as is done now,—let the church make the choice; Peter was a careful apostle, and would let the church do the work.

Peter, upon another occasion, well remembered where the power of God's Word lay, when he said to the lame man, "In the name of Jesus Christ, of Nazareth, rise up and walk." He might have said, "In my name do this," but he undoubtedly had read how Moses fell, when he took the glory of God unto himself, and did not sanctify the Lord before the people. Num. 20: 12. It is always safe to submit all weighty matters unto the Lord, and work through the church.

The apostle only wished to inform the members of the church to make choice of one who had a good knowledge of the work of Christ, and one who had companied with those holy men. It was not necessary that Matthias should be present upon all occasions. Even all the apostles did not see what Christ did upon the Mount of Transfiguration; none were present but Peter, James and John. Matt. 17: 1-13; Mark 9: 1-10.

None of the apostles were present at the raising of Jairus' daughter, but Peter, James and John. "And he suffered no man to follow him, save Peter, James and John. Mark 5: 37. Peter, James and John were called by the Savior to witness his suffering and prayer in the Garden of Gethsemane. He brought his disciples to the place "which was named Gethsemane: and he said to his disciples, Sit ye here, while I shall pray. And he taketh with him Peter, James and John, ... and went forward a little, and fell on the ground." Mark 14: 32-35.

Here we have found three places where even not all of the apostles were present. Then, why conclude, by inference, that more than the twelve were present at the Supper? "Now when the evening was come he sat down with the twelve." Matt. 26: 20. "And in the evening he cometh with the twelve." Mark 14: 17. "And when the hour was come, he sat down, and the twelve apostles with him." Luke 22: 14.

In searching the Scriptures, as referred to, I am unable to get any proof in favor of any being present excepting the twelve and Christ. It is a little strange that four men, at different periods of time, should write upon such an important subject, and agree so well upon all they have written, and then not mention, at even *one time*, that more were present besides the twelve.

Again, it seems strange to me, that the Savior would have other disciples present, and not invite them to the table, admitting this to be a *fact*, that a number of disciples were present, and none of them at the table but the twelve apostles. Many would now excuse themselves, claiming that at the "Last Supper" only the twelve were invited to the table, and only the twelve took part in feet-washing, and if others could be excused so can we, etc., etc.

Goshen, Ind.

OUR BIBLE CLASS.

BY A. W. VANIMAN.

Practical Questions on Lesson XII.

1. INTO what two parts is the history of the New Covenant divided?

2. What was a Nazarite?

3. Where did prophecy say Christ would be born?

The Gospel Messenger,

A Weekly at $1.50 Per Annum.

PUBLISHED BY

The Brethren's Publishing Co.

D. L. MILLER,	· · · · ·	Editor.
J. H. MOORE,	· · · · ·	Office Editor.
J. B. BRUMBAUGH,	} · · · ·	Associate Editors.
J. G. ROYER,	}	
JOSEPH AMICK,	· · · · ·	Business Manager.

ADVISORY COMMITTEE.
R. H. Miller, A. Hutchison, Daniel Hays.

☞Communications for publication should be legibly written with black ink on one side of the paper only. Do not attempt to interline, or to put on one page what ought to occupy two.

☞Anonymous communications will not be published.

☞Do not mix business with articles for publication. Keep your communications on separate sheets from all business.

☞Time is precious. We always have time to attend to business and to answer questions of importance, but please do not subject us to need less answering of letters.

☞The MESSENGER is mailed each week to all subscribers. If the address is correctly entered on our list, the paper must reach the person to whom it is addressed. If you do not get your paper, write us, giving particulars.

☞When changing your address, please give your former as well as your future address in full, so as to avoid delay and misunderstanding.

☞Always remit to the office from which you order your goods, no matter from where you receive them.

☞Do not send personal checks or drafts on interior banks, unless you send with them 25 cents each, to pay for collection.

☞Remittances should be made by Post-office Money Order, Drafts on New York, Philadelphia or Chicago, or Registered Letters, made payable and addressed to "Brethren's Publishing Co., Mount Morris, Ill.," or "Brethren's Publishing Co., Huntingdon, Pa."

☞Entered at the Post-office at Mount Morris, Ill., as second-class matter.

Mount Morris, Ill., · · · · March 29, 1892.

MUCH correspondence is crowded out this week. We will try and make room for all in next issue.

· BRO. DANIEL LANDIS, of Shiremanstown, Cumberland Co., Pa., has changed his address to Bowmansdale, same County and State.

BRO. LEONARD HYER, one of our ministers of Noble County, Indiana, called on us last week. We enjoyed his short call very much.

APRIL 13 and 14 is the time appointed for the District Meeting of the Second District of Virginia, to be held with the Brethren of the Elk Run church.

WRITING from Mexico, Ind., Bro. Frank Fisher says: "The Good Lord has truly blessed us at the Home. While we have had much sickness this winter, yet the Lord has brought us safely through all."

BRO. H. C. LONGANECKER, formerly of Yorkshire, Ohio, may now be addressed at North Star, same State. Aaron Moss has also changed his address from Ridgeway, Ind., to Landess, Grand Co., same State.

BRO. ENOCH EBY, of Booth, Kans., writes us that the contemplated "Old People's Home" at that place is to be commenced soon, as sufficient funds have been secured to justify the committee in proceeding with the buildings.

APRIL 15 and 16 is the time set for the District Meeting of the First District of West Virginia, to be held in the Sandy Creek church, Preston County. This ·notice ought to have appeared last week, but it reached us just after the paper was made up and sent to the press room.

AFTER an absence of over four months, preaching in Ohio and Indiana, Bro. J. M. Mohler has returned to his home at Lewistown, Pa. We trust that Bro. Mohler enjoyed his extended trip, and we feel confident that he has done much good by his plain, earnest manner of preaching.

To say you are as good as somebody else may be placing a very low estimate on yourself. That somebody may be the very person that you would not care for another to compare you with.

THE Brethren at Pittsburgh, Ohio, have decided to pull down their old meeting-house and erect a large one, the former having proved insufficient to accommodate the people who gather there to hear preaching.

THERE are sixteen members living in and near Denver, Colo., where there seems to be a good opening for some live minister. We trust our Brethren will look up these places where there are harvest fields ready for the laborers.

BRO. W. H. H. SAWYER and wife, who have been spending the winter at Keuka, Fla., expect to return to their home in Brown County, Kansas, this week. Bro. Sawyer reports the health of his wife greatly improved by their stay in the South.

BRO. JOHN ZUCK wishes us to announce that the Committee of Arrangements for Annual Meeting will meet at Cedar Rapids, Iowa, on Tuesday, April 5, at 9 A. M., and those having business with the Committee may be governed accordingly.

UNDER date of March 15 Bro. S. H. Myers, of Timberville, Va., says: "All the workers for the "Old Folks' Home" have but one opinion concerning it, and that is to make it a success. But it takes money. The snow here is eight inches deep."

WE learn that Bro. C. Delp, of Kansas, is preparing to locate at one of the mission points in Arkansas. We are glad to see our ministers pushing out into the frontier. About 500 might follow Bro. Delp's example to good advantage. We will have plenty of material left of which to make 500 more ministers if we need them. Just as fast as we find men suited to the work, we ought to encourage them to venture out into these new fields and battle for the Lord and his cause.

THE Christian people are truly the salt of the earth, and were it not for them the world would most assuredly retrograde far more rapidly than it now does. They are the great bulwarks of what is right. They are the great light-houses of the moral world and lead the masses to something higher than merely selfish considerations. By their influences they are saving the world from ruin. Whatever may be said of other forms of religion, and even morality, there is no ·saving power in the world like that of true Christianity. Drive Christianity from the face of the earth and our world will be ruined.

WE are asked to state how long a member, especially a minister, may hold his certificate of membership after locating in a new congregation. In our judgment he should hand it in the very first opportunity, and the longer he holds it after that first opportunity, the greater is the danger of him keeping it too long for the good of ·his reputation. If he is a minister, by all means should he hand in his letter at a very·early date, and if he does not within a reasonable time, the elder in charge should quietly inquire into the cause of the letter being withheld, and, if necessary, admonish him concerning his duty towards the church to which he has moved. While we can make all proper allowance for inexperienced private members, who may not know any better, we should require ministers to be very punctual in this respect, in order to set proper examples before others.

BRO. S. BOCK, of the Brethren's Tract Work, Dayton, Ohio, wishes us to state for them, that they are in receipt of a letter from Byron, Mich., on business, but the writer fails to give his name. If this meets his eye, he will please respond with his name.

BRO. I. J. ROSENBERGER'S very outspoken way of presenting the Gospel in the East, seems to have led him into a public discussion with an Adventist, by the name of Eld. Shrock, of Pennsylvania. Our correspondent gives us to understand that the truth lost nothing in Bro. Rosenberger's hands. The discussion, we presume, was on the Law and Sabbath question.

"HAPPINESS is inborn. It is not an outward trait. It· is generated in the soul. It is never bought or sold as an article of commerce. You may fill your house with all manner of beautiful and curious things, but you cannot lay in a stock of happiness in the same way. If you are happy, your happiness is that which you are able to make by the use of the mind itself. A fundamental condition of happiness in this world is activity, and that kind of activity which carries with it all the faculties."

ONE of our Methodist exchanges says:· ·
"The Baptist Church is very strong in the Southern States. In many communities it takes the lead. During the past twenty-five years it has made a wonderful advance in the education of its ministers and in other important particulars. We are not jealous of our 'submersionist' brethren, though we take exception to some of their exclusive ways. They preach a sound, honest Gospel, and go after the masses of the people. The only thing about which we are careful is, that they may not take our crown. Let the Methodists bestir themselves.'"

To this we may add that our Brethren will find a great field open for them, if they will only enter, and work with the earnestness that should characterize the advocates of primitive Christianity.

THE regular Bible Work at Mt. Morris closed last week. Its success has been far beyond expectation, and promises to be still greater next year. The attendance was good, and the interest taken in the different lines of Bible study very encouraging. A number of young members completed the work for the first year and will continue their studies at least another year. Among them were several young ministers who are preparing themselves for the work to which the church has called them. As these brethren enter upon their work in other fields, we hope to see them not only teach the grand truths learned from the Bible, but we pray that they may prove true to the church that has placed them in the ministry.

RAILROADS are penetrating the dark regions of Africa, and rum, too, is keeping pace with the rapid advance of art and civilization, but many missionaries are on hand to convert the heathens and counteract the influences of rum, while others are to follow. The early history of America is repeating itself in the Dark·Continent, and we may look for a long and even a shameful struggle in some particulars. If climatic obstacles do not prove too great, the country will open up quite rapidly and civilization will soon penetrate every portion of the great continent, capable of supporting human life. The struggle will, however, be between rum on the side of evil and Christianity on the side of right. Various religious bodies will push their missionaries into every nook and corner and thus the struggle will continue, with what result the Lord alone can see, but one thing is certain, here is a chance, as well as at other places, for the Christian soldier to demonstrate his patriotism for the cause of Christianity.

The Gospel Messenger,

A Weekly at $1.50 Per Annum.

PUBLISHED BY

The Brethren's Publishing Co.

D. L. MILLER,	Editor.
J. H. MOORE,	Office Editor.
J. B. BRUMBAUGH,	
J. G. ROYER,	Associate Editors.
JOSEPH AMICK,	Business Manager.

ADVISORY COMMITTEE.
R. H. Miller, A. Hutchison, Daniel Hays.

- ☞Communications for publication should be legibly written with black ink on one side of the paper only. Do not attempt to interline, or to put on one page what ought to occupy two.
- ☞Anonymous communications will not be published.
- ☞Do not mix business with articles for publication. Keep your communications on separate sheets from all business.
- ☞Time is precious. We always have time to attend to business and to answer questions of importance, but please do not subject us to need less answering of letters.
- ☞The MESSENGER is mailed each week to all subscribers. If the address is correctly entered on our list, the paper must reach the person to whom it is addressed. If you do not get your paper, write us, giving particulars.
- ☞When changing your address, please give your former as well as your future address in full, so as to avoid delay and misunderstanding.
- ☞Always remit to the office from which you order your goods, no matter from where you receive them.
- ☞Do not send personal checks or drafts on interior banks, unless you send with them 15 cents each, to pay for collection.
- ☞Remittances should be made by Post-office Money Order, Drafts on New York, Philadelphia or Chicago, or Registered Letters, made payable and addressed to "Brethren's Publishing Co., Mount Morris, Ill.," or "Brethren's Publishing Co., Huntingdon, Pa."
- ☞Entered at the Post-office at Mount Morris, Ill., as second-class matter.

Mount Morris, Ill., - - - - March 29, 1892.

MUCH correspondence is crowded out this week. We will try and make room for all in next issue.

BRO. DANIEL LANDIS, of Shiremanstown, Cumberland Co., Pa., has changed his address to Bowmansdale, same County and State.

BRO. LEONARD HYER, one of our ministers of Noble County, Indiana, called on us last week. We enjoyed his short call very much.

APRIL 13 and 14 is the time appointed for the District Meeting of the Second District of Virginia, to be held with the Brethren of the Elk Run church.

WRITING from Mexico, Ind., Bro. Frank Fisher says: "The Good Lord has truly blessed us at the Home. While we have had much sickness this winter, yet the Lord has brought us safely through all."

BRO. H. C. LONGANECKER, formerly of Yorkshire, Ohio, may now be addressed at North Star, same State. Aaron Moss has also changed his address from Ridgeway, Ind., to Landess, Grand Co., same State.

BRO. ENOCH EBY, of Booth, Kans., writes us that the contemplated "Old People's Home" at that place is to be commenced soon, as sufficient funds have been secured to justify the committee in proceeding with the buildings.

APRIL 15 and 16 is the time set for the District Meeting of the First District of West Virginia, to be held in the Sandy Creek church, Preston County. This notice ought to have appeared last week, but it reached us just after the paper was made up and sent to the press room.

AFTER an absence of over four months, preaching in Ohio and Indiana, Bro. J. M. Mohler has returned to his home at Lewistown, Pa. We trust that Bro. Mohler enjoyed his extended trip, and we feel confident that he has done much good by his plain, earnest manner of preaching.

To say you are as good as somebody else may be placing a very low estimate on yourself. That somebody may be the very person that you would not care for another to compare you with.

THE Brethren at Pittsburgh, Ohio, have decided to pull down their old meeting-house and erect a large one, the former having proved insufficient to accommodate the people who gather there to hear preaching.

THERE are sixteen members living in and near Denver, Colo., where there seems to be a good opening for some live minister. We trust our Brethren will look up these places where there are harvest fields ready for the laborers.

BRO. W. H. H. SAWYER and wife, who have been spending the winter at Keuka, Fla., expect to return to their home in Brown County, Kansas, this week. Bro. Sawyer reports the health of his wife greatly improved by their stay in the South.

BRO. JOHN ZUCK wishes us to announce that the Committee of Arrangements for Annual Meeting will meet at Cedar Rapids, Iowa, on Tuesday, April 5, at 9 A. M., and those having business with the Committee may be governed accordingly.

UNDER date of March 15 Bro. S. H. Myers, of Timberville, Va., says: "All the workers for the "Old Folks' Home" have but one opinion concerning it, and that is to make it a success. But it takes money. The snow here is eight inches deep."

WE learn that Bro. C. Delp, of Kansas, is preparing to locate at one of the mission points in Arkansas. We are glad to see our ministers pushing out into the frontier. About 500 might follow Bro. Delp's example to good advantage. We will have plenty of material left of which to make 500 more ministers if we need them. Just as fast as we find men suited to the work, we ought to encourage them to venture out into these new fields and battle for the Lord and his cause.

THE Christian people are truly the salt of the earth, and were it not for them the world would most assuredly retrograde far more rapidly than it now does. They are the great bulwarks of what is right. They are the great light-houses of the moral world and lead the masses to something higher than merely selfish considerations. By their influences they are saving the world from ruin. Whatever may be said of other forms of religion, and even morality, there is no saving power in the world like that of true Christianity. Drive Christianity from the face of the earth and our world will be ruined.

WE are asked to state how long a member, especially a minister, may hold his certificate of membership after locating in a new congregation. In our judgment he should hand it in the very first opportunity, and the longer he holds it after that first opportunity, the greater is the danger of him keeping it too long for the good of his reputation. If he is a minister, by all means should he hand in his letter at a very early date, and if he does not within a reasonable time, the elder in charge should quietly inquire into the cause of the letter being withheld, and, if necessary, admonish him concerning his duty towards the church to which he has moved. While we can make all proper allowance for inexperienced private members, who may not know any better, we should require ministers to be very punctual in this respect, in order to set proper examples before others.

BRO. S. BOCK, of the Brethren's Tract Work, Dayton, Ohio, wishes us to state for them, that they are in receipt of a letter from Byron, Mich., on business, but the writer fails to give his name. If this meets his eye, he will please respond with his name.

BRO. I. J. ROSENBERGER'S very outspoken way of presenting the Gospel in the East, seems to have led him into a public discussion with an Adventist, by the name of Eld. Shroek, of Pennsylvania. Our correspondent gives us to understand that the truth lost nothing in Bro. Rosenberger's hands. The discussion, we presume, was on the Law and Sabbath question.

"HAPPINESS is inborn. It is not an outward trait. It is generated in the soul. It is never bought or sold as an article of commerce. You may fill your house with all manner of beautiful and curious things, but you cannot lay in a stock of happiness in the same way. If you are happy, your happiness is that which you are able to make by the use of the mind itself. A fundamental condition of happiness in this world is activity, and that kind of activity which carries with it all the faculties."

ONE of our Methodist exchanges says:

"The Baptist Church is very strong in the Southern States. In many communities it takes the lead. During the past twenty-five years it has made a wonderful advance in the education of its ministers and in other important particulars. We are not jealous of our 'submersionist' brethren, though we take exception to some of their exclusive ways. They preach a sound, honest Gospel, and go after the masses of the people. The only thing about which we are careful is, that they may not take our crown. Let the Methodists bestir themselves.'"

To this we may add that our Brethren will find a great field open for them, if they will only enter, and work with the earnestness that should characterize the advocates of primitive Christianity.

THE regular Bible Work at Mt. Morris closed last week. Its success has been far beyond expectation, and promises to be still greater next year. The attendance was good, and the interest taken in the different lines of Bible study very encouraging. A number of young members completed the work for the first year and will continue their studies at least another year. Among them were several young ministers who are preparing themselves for the work to which the church has called them. As these brethren enter upon their work in other fields, we hope to see them not only teach the grand truths learned from the Bible, but we pray that they may prove true to the church that has placed them in the ministry.

RAILROADS are penetrating the dark regions of Africa, and rum, too, is keeping pace with the rapid advances of art and civilization, but many missionaries are on hand to convert the heathens and counteract the influences of rum, while others are to follow. The early history of America is repeating itself in the Dark Continent, and we may look for a long and even a shameful struggle in some particulars. If climatic obstacles do not prove too great, the country will open up quite rapidly and civilization will soon penetrate every portion of the great continent, capable of supporting human life. The struggle will, however, be between rum on the side of evil and Christianity on the side of right. Various religious bodies will push their missionaries into every nook and corner and thus the struggle will continue, with what result the Lord alone can see, but one thing is certain, here is a chance, as well as at other places, for the Christian soldier to demonstrate his patriotism for the cause of Christianity.

we saw the effects of the storm. The following is an extract from the *London Standard* of Oct. 15: "The effect of the storm at Dover has been very disastrous. The gale raged with the force of a hurricane throughout Tuesday night and until 9 or 10 o'clock yesterday morning, when it abated for a short time; but it blew from the south-southwest with great violence all yesterday. The worst part of the storm was early in the morning. The sea washed tons of boulders from the foreshore on to the Marine Promenades. But the wildest scene was at the Admiralty Pier, where the full force of the storm was felt. The sea broke over the pier, deluging the trains, and in two cases damage was done to the carriages. Damage to the extent of several thousand pounds (ten thousand dollars) has been done to the extension works. The whole of the extensive gauntree work has been swept away, although it had resisted all the severe gales of the last two or three years, and the huge piles are floating about the sea to the danger of navigation. Two of them were recovered on the shore at Dover yesterday afternoon; one had been snapped in two as though it were a match, and large iron shackles were twisted into curious shapes. An idea of the force of the sea, at the end of the pier, may be obtained from the fact that shots, weighing seventeen hundred pounds, which are used in the eighty-ton guns, and which are stacked on the pier, were shifted by the sea. The wind played curious antics with the movable things about the pier; several of the large wagon-barrows, used for carrying luggage to the boats, were smashed, and others were blown into the sea. All the Calais and Ostend mail packets made fearful passages in crossing the channel on Tuesday night and yesterday. The inward Ostend boat, due at 9 o'clock, did not arrive until an hour and twenty minutes later. Great anxiety was felt for the Ostend boat, Compte de Flanders, about which no tidings could be obtained until late in the afternoon. She left Dover on Tuesday night about 9 o'clock, being unable to reach the pier, and did not reach Ostend until noon yesterday, having experienced a terrible passage."

We referred, in a previous letter, to our landing at Dover on Tuesday night, Oct. 13, in the hurricane, and now, as we look over our notes, it all comes back again. It was a terrible night of storm and destruction and we shall never forget it. The English Channel is a treacherous body of water and many a good ship has been wrecked on its coasts. Only recently one of the large steamers, a companion of the *Aller* and *Havel*, was cast on the Aldergate ledge of rocks in the Channel and was wrecked. Fortunately the passengers and crew were all taken ashore and not a life was lost. Looking back to that night of storm, shipwreck and death, for on that night many a poor wanderer on the sea went down to a watery grave, we can only thank the dear, loving Father that he led us through it all in safety. We rejoice, too, to know that in the new heaven and new earth, the home of God's people, there shall be "no more sea."

To-day, as we cross the Channel, it is calm and smooth enough, and we land in France without even experiencing the choppy sea that is so common on the Channel and which often brings seasickness to old sailors.

What a change an hour's voyage makes in our surroundings! We are among a people, differing from the English in so many ways. A new language which, at first, seems a very Babel to us.

The few words of French, we had stored away for this occasion, don't seem to have a place among the strange sounds we hear. The question, "*Parles vous Francais?*" (Do you speak French?) does not sound, coming from a Frenchman's lips, anything like it is written. We listen and wait for a familiar sound, a word or phrase that we understand, and then give it up.

One phrase we had learned. Showing our ticket to a conductor we remarked, "*Defense fumare,*" and he at once took us to a compartment in one of the cars, set apart for those who do not smoke. On our railways at home cars are set apart for smokers. In Europe smoking is so general that compartments are provided for those who do not smoke, and a notice to the effect that smoking is forbidden is posted on the door. We learned, after enduring tobacco smoke for some time, to look for the compartment where smokers are not allowed to enter. So far as the phrases "No smoking" and "Smoking forbidden" are concerned, we became quite a linguist, and we give them in the different languages for the benefit of those who may have occasion to use them. Danish, *Ikke Rogere;* Swedish, *Rökning Forbjuden;* German, *Nicht Rauchen;* Holland, *Neit Roaken;* French, *Defense Fumare;* Italian, *Illa Fumaro.*

We pass over a greater part of our journey from Calais to Paris at night, reaching the capital of France in the darkness. We found some English friends who spoke French and who kindly assisted us, and we found a resting-place at a comfortable hotel, without difficulty. In our next we shall have something to say about Paris.

THE SENTENCE OF JESUS.

A CORRESPONDENT of *Notes and Queries* extracts from the *Zolnische Zeitung* what is called "A Correct Transcript of the Sentence of Death Pronounced Against Jesus Christ." The following is a copy of the most memorable judicial sentence which has ever been pronounced in the annals of the world:

"Sentence pronounced by Pontius Pilate, intendent of the province of lower Galilee, that Jesus of Nazareth shall suffer death by the cross. In the seventeenth year of the reign of the Emperor Tiberius and on the 25th of the month of March, in the most holy city of Jerusalem, during the pontificate of Annas and Caiaphas, Pontius Pilate, intendent of the province of lower Galilee, sitting in judgment in the presidency seat of the Prætors, sentences Jesus Christ of Nazareth to death on a cross between two robbers, as the numerous and notorious testimonials of the people prove:

"1. Jesus is a misleader.

"2. He has excited the people to sedition.

"3. He is an enemy of the law.

"4. He calls himself the son of God.

"5. He calls himself falsely the king of Israel.

"6. He went into the temple, followed by a multitude carrying palms in their hands. Orders: The first centurion, Quintus Cornelius, to bring him to the place of execution, forbids all persons, rich or poor, to prevent the execution of Jesus.

"The witnesses who have signed the execution against Jesus are: 1. Daniel Robani, Pharisee. 2. John Zorobabel. 3. Ralphael Robania. 4. Capet. Jesus to be taken out of Jerusalem through the gate of Tournea.

"The sentence is engraved on a plate of brass in the Hebrew language, and on its sides are the following words: "A similar plate has been sent to each tribe." It was discovered in the year 1280 in the city of Aquill [Aquilla (?)] in the King-

dom of Naples, by a search made for the discovery of Roman antiquities, and remained there until it was found by the commissaries of art in the French army of Italy. Up to the time of the campaign in Southern Italy it was preserved in the sacristy of the Carthusians, near Naples, where it was kept in a box of ebony. Since then the relic has been kept in the chapel of Caserta. The Carthusians obtained it by their petitions that the plate might be kept by them, which was an acknowledgment of the sacrifices they made for the French army. The French translation was made literally by members of the commission of arts. Dennon had a fac-simile of the plate engraved, which was bought by Lord Howard on the sale of his cabinet for 2,890 francs. There seems to be no historical doubt as to the authenticity of this. The reasons of the sentence correspond exactly with those of the Gospels."

The above "sentence," sent in by one of our contributors, is exceedingly interesting reading, but we cannot say that it is strictly authentic. The plate of brass, however, referred to, is still in existence, being preserved in one of the museums of the East.

SOLDIERS AT THE LOVE-FEAST.

BRO. P. R. Wrightsman, of Kansas, relates the following interesting incident:

"We well remember in times of the war in Tennessee when the old Limestone church had a love-feast appointed on Saturday, the day before a regiment of Confederate soldiers came and camped in our church-lot. On Saturday morning, when we convened for Divine services, to our astonishment and disgust, there were a thousand armed soldiers. In this event the church was in a dilemma, not knowing what to do for the best, whether to dismiss our meetings or go on, but finally the church in her wisdom concluded to go on with the meeting. The large house was packed to its utmost capacity and better order I never witnessed at a love-feast and we were led to believe that impressions were made then and there that have since ripened into Christianity. After the meeting was closed, many of the soldiers said to us, "When the war is over, come over into Georgia, Alabama and Carolina and preach for us. We never heard such preaching." We are happy to learn that, since then, our Brethren have established a number of churches far south of where they used to preach before the war. Yet those Southern requests have not near all been answered."

Doubtless there are other members who can recall interesting incidents of the kind that would prove profitable reading, if published. We are glad for Bro. Wrightsman's narrative, and we will thank him, or any one else, for accounts of similar incidents. Such experiences ought to be placed on record for the benefit of future generations.

THE ORDER AGAIN.

ON page 131 of the present volume we published our manner of laying the order before the applicants for baptism. One of our readers, in a letter, addressed to Bro. D. E. Price, says: "Why is it that, in telling them that going to fairs, picnics, etc., was conforming to the world, you missed the tobacco and picture-taking, which are also for the gratification of the flesh, and are considered to be in the same line by Annual Meeting as those mentioned? Just look at the enormous amount of money spent for these two items!"

In laying the order before the applicants, referred to, the tobacco clause was unintentionally

we saw the effects of the storm. The following is an extract from the *London Standard* of Oct. 15: "The effect of the storm at Dover has been very disastrous. The gale raged with the force of a hurricane throughout Tuesday night and until 9 or 10 o'clock yesterday morning, when it abated for a short time; but it blew from the south-southwest with great violence all yesterday. The worst part of the storm was early in the morning. The sea washed tons of boulders from the foreshore on to the Marine Promenades. But the wildest scene was at the Admiralty Pier, where the full force of the storm was felt. The sea broke over the pier, deluging the trains, and in two cases damage was done to the carriages. Damage to the extent of several thousand pounds (ten thousand dollars) has been done to the extension works. The whole of the extensive gauntree work has been swept away, although it had resisted all the severe gales of the last two or three years, and the huge piles are floating about the sea to the danger of navigation. Two of them were recovered on the shore at Dover yesterday afternoon; one had been snapped in two as though it were a match, and large iron shackles were twisted into curious shapes. An idea of the force of the sea, at the end of the pier, may be obtained from the fact that shots, weighing seventeen hundred pounds, which are used in the eighty-ton guns, and which are stacked on the pier, were shifted by the sea. The wind played curious antics with the movable things about the pier; several of the large wagon-barrows, used for carrying luggage to the boats, were smashed, and others were blown into the sea. All the Calais and Ostend mail packets made fearful passages in crossing the channel on Tuesday night and yesterday. The inward Ostend boat, due at 9 o'clock, did not arrive until an hour and twenty minutes later. Great anxiety was felt for the Ostend boat, Compte de Flandres, about which no tidings could be obtained until late in the afternoon. She left Dover on Tuesday night about 9 o'clock, being unable to reach the pier, and did not reach Ostend until noon yesterday, having experienced a terrible passage."

We referred, in a previous letter, to our landing at Dover on Tuesday night, Oct. 13, in the hurricane, and now, as we look over our notes, it all comes back again. It was a terrible night of storm and destruction and we shall never forget it. The English Channel is a treacherous body of water and many a good ship has been wrecked on its coasts. Only recently one of the large steamers, a companion of the Aller and Havel, was cast on the Aldergate ledge of rocks in the Channel and was wrecked. Fortunately the passengers and crew were all taken ashore and not a life was lost. Looking back to that night of storm, shipwreck and death, for on that night many a poor wanderer on the sea went down to a watery grave, we can only thank the dear, loving Father that he led us through it all in safety. We rejoice, too, to know that in the new heaven and new earth, the home of God's people, there shall be "no more sea."

To-day, as we cross the Channel, it is calm and smooth enough, and we land in France without even experiencing the choppy sea that is so common on the Channel and which often brings sea-sickness to old sailors.

What a change an hour's voyage makes in our surroundings! We are among a people, differing from the English in so many ways. A new language which, at first, seems a very Babel to us.

The few words of French, we had stored away for this occasion, don't seem to have a place among the strange sounds we hear. The question, "*Parles vous Francais?*" (Do you speak French?) does not sound, coming from a Frenchman's lips, anything like it is written. We listen and wait for a familiar sound, a word or phrase that we understand, and then give it up.

One phrase we had learned. Showing our ticket to a conductor we remarked, "*Defense fumare,*" and he at once took us to a compartment in one of the cars, set apart for those who do not smoke. On our railways at home cars are set apart for smokers. In Europe smoking is so general that compartments are provided for those who do not smoke, and a notice to the effect that smoking is forbidden is posted on the door. We learned, after enduring tobacco smoke for some time, to look for the compartment where smokers are not allowed to enter. So far as the phrases "No smoking" and "Smoking forbidden" are concerned, we became quite a linguist, and we give them in the different languages for the benefit of those who may have occasion to use them. Danish, *Ikke Rogere;* Swedish, *Rökning Forbjuden;* German, *Nicht Rauchen;* Holland, *Neil Roaken;* French, *Defense Fumare;* Italian, *Illa Fumaro.*

We pass over a greater part of our journey from Calais to Paris at night, reaching the capital of France in the darkness. We found some English friends who spoke French and who kindly assisted us, and we found a resting-place at a comfortable hotel, without difficulty. In our next we shall have something to say about Paris.

THE SENTENCE OF JESUS.

A CORRESPONDENT of *Notes and Queries* extracts from the Zolnische *Zeitung* what is called "A Correct Transcript of the Sentence of Death Pronounced Against Jesus Christ." The following is a copy of the most memorable judicial sentence which has ever been pronounced in the annals of the world:

"Sentence pronounced by Pontius Pilate, intendent of the province of lower Galilee, that Jesus of Nazareth shall suffer death by the cross. In the seventeenth year of the reign of the Emperor Tiberius and on the 25th of the month of March, in the most holy city of Jerusalem, during the pontificate of Annas and Caiaphas, Pontius Pilate, intendent of the province of lower Galilee, sitting in judgment in the presidential seat of the Prætors, sentence Jesus Christ of Nazareth to death on a cross between two robbers, as the numerous and notorious testimonials of the people prove:

"1. Jesus is a misleader.
"2. He has excited the people to sedition.
"3. He is an enemy of the law.
"4. He calls himself the son of God.
"5. He calls himself falsely the king of Israel.
"6. He went into the temple, followed by a multitude carrying palms in their hands. Orders: The first centurion, Quintus Cornelius, to bring him to the place of execution, forbid all persons, rich or poor, to prevent the execution of Jesus.

"The witnesses who have signed the execution against Jesus are: 1. Daniel Robani, Pharisee. 2. John Zorobabel. 3. Ralphael Robania. 4. Capel Jesus to be taken out of Jerusalem through the gate of Tournea.

"The sentence is engraved on a plate of brass in the Hebrew language, and on its sides are the following words: "A similar plate has been sent to each tribe." It was discovered in the year 1280 in the city of Aquill [Aquilla (?)] in the King-

dom of Naples, by a search made for the discovery of Roman antiquities, and remained there until it was found by the commissaries of art in the French army of Italy. Up to the time of the campaign in Southern Italy it was preserved in the sacristy of the Carthusians, near Naples, where it was kept in a box of ebony. Since then the relic has been kept in the chapel of Caserta. The Carthusians obtained it by their petitions that the plate might be kept by them, which was an acknowledgment of the sacrifices they made for the French army. The French translation was made literally by members of the commission of arts. Dennon had a fac-simile of the plate engraved, which was bought by Lord Howard on the sale of his cabinet for 2,890 francs. There seems to be no historical doubt as to the authenticity of this. The reasons of the sentence correspond exactly with those of the Gospels."

The above "sentence," sent in by one of our contributors, is exceedingly interesting reading, but we cannot say that it is strictly authentic. The plate of brass, however, referred to, is still in existence, being preserved in one of the museums of the East.

SOLDIERS AT THE LOVE-FEAST.

BRO. P. R. Wrightsman, of Kansas, relates the following interesting incident:

"We well remember in times of the war in Tennessee when the old Limestone church had a love-feast appointed on Saturday, that, the day before a regiment of Confederate soldiers came and camped in our church-lot. On Saturday morning, when we convened for Divine services, to our astonishment and disgust, there were a thousand armed soldiers. In this event the church was in a dilemma, not knowing what to do for the best, whether to dismiss our meetings or go on, but finally the church in her wisdom concluded. to go on with the meeting. The large house was packed to its utmost capacity and better order I never witnessed at a love-feast and we were led to believe that impressions were made then and there that have since ripened into Christianity. After the meeting was closed, many of the soldiers said to us, "When the war is over, come over into Georgia, Alabama and Carolina and preach for us. We never heard such preaching." We are happy to learn that, since then, our Brethren have established a number of churches far south of where they used to preach before the war. Yet those Southern requests have not near all been answered."

Doubtless there are other members who can recall interesting incidents of the kind that would prove profitable reading, if published. We are glad for Bro. Wrightsman's narrative, and we will thank him, or any one else, for accounts of similar incidents. Such experiences ought to be placed on record for the benefit of future generations.

THE ORDER AGAIN.

ON page 131 of the present volume we published our manner of laying the order before the applicants for baptism. One of our readers, in a letter, addressed to Bro. D. E. Price, says: "Why is it that, in telling them that going to fairs, picnics, etc., was conforming to the world, you missed the tobacco and picture-taking, which are also for the gratification of the flesh, and are considered to be in the same line by Annual Meeting as those mentioned? Just look at the enormous amount of money spent for these two items!"

In laying the order before the applicants, referred to, the tobacco clause was unintentionally

pressed themselves by saying, that surely all was in accordance with the Bible. The best of order prevailed throughout the entire services.

On Sunday, Bro. J. C. Lehman delivered a very able discourse to a large, attentive audience, on these words: "That Christ may dwell in your hearts by faith; that ye, being rooted and grounded in love, may be able to comprehend with all saints what is the breadth, and length, and depth, and height," etc. Eph. 3: 17, 18.

On Sunday night Bro. Sawyer again gave us a good talk on these words: "For God hath not given us the spirit of fear; but of power, and of love, and of a sound mind." 2 Tim. 1: 7.

J. I. MILLER.

March 14.

"Thrilling Incidents on Sea and Land."

SINCE the announcement of my new work, under the above title, was given in the MESSENGER, a great interest has been shown by many in its success. The response, to my request for advance subscribers, has exceeded my expectations, and encouraged me to go onward.

The success of canvassers for this work has been excellent, not only among members, but also among those not of our faith. One sister in Illinois took eleven orders for the book in less than an hour, and others are doing nearly as well. In localities where no agent has as yet been appointed, some one will please apply for the agency and give the work his earnest attention.

It is proposed, the Lord willing, to have the work ready for delivery by Aug. 1. Meanwhile let all make a strong effort to push the sale of the book, and report to me from time to time. Address all communications to me, as below.

GEORGE D. ZOLLERS.

Mount Carroll, Ill.

Jottings.

BRO. C. M. YEAROUT came to us from the McPherson Bible Normal, and preached for us two weeks to general satisfaction. We had excellent interest at our meetings, but out of fifteen or twenty lepers that should have cried, "Lord Jesus, have mercy on us," only two young sisters returned to give God the glory. Bro. Yearout did his duty, and none can say he did not give them fair warning.

Having a desire to visit our dear, afflicted brother, S. S. Mohler, and to attend the District Meeting of the Middle District of Missouri, near Warrensburgh, as well as the debate in Morgan County, as announced in GOSPEL MESSENGER, I accordingly left home Feb. 16, and arrived at Bro. Mohler's next day. After spending an hour or more, and enjoying some refreshments, I was taken to the Ministerial Meeting, which to me was very interesting, because of the interest manifested in the work of the ministry, and also to see so many active and zealous young ministers.

The next two days were spent in the work of the District. A more harmonious meeting would be hard to find. While all we saw and heard was commendable, we call special attention to two features, first, the large mission field, of which favorable reports were made by those in charge. Due attention was also given for the next year by giving every man his work, to occupy till the next meeting. The other feature to be admired was a strong effort to send nothing to the General Conference. The work having been finished in great peace and harmony, a letter of greeting, from Bro. S. S. Mohler was read, in behalf of its success. It was reciprocated, and also suggested that all present should unite in a season of prayer in his behalf, as well as to ask the blessing of God on the work of the meeting. This was done

with sighs, and groans, and tears, after which the meeting was dismissed. After an affectionate farewell, the members dispersed, feeling that it was good to be there. Returning to Bro. Mohler's, we spent another short season with him; then left to spend the night with Eld. D. M. Mohler, where we had the pleasure of a short visit with his father-in-law, John Hershy, who must soon go to his reward, according to the course of nature.

From here I went to the debate. Of this we might say a good deal, but to make a fair report, we might be censured with prejudice by some, and I am conscientious in making any other kind. I am very thankful, however, to say that the Truth lost nothing by the investigation. I learned more than ever that it is hard work to try to prop up a cause without it. I feel assured, that good seed has been sown by Bro. Shamberger's clear and logical style of argument,—seed that will, in the future, produce fruit to the honor of God, and his cause. I further remark, that the discussion was conducted in a Christian manner, with a friendly spirit.

On my return I intended to stop again with our dear brother, S. S. Mohler, but a failure in making connection frustrated my purposes. For this I felt sorry, for Bro. Mohler surely needs the sympathy of all his dear brethren and sisters, and the company of as many as can stop with him. I am glad I can say he is better than one year ago, and we entertain fond hopes that he will recover, and that the more rapidly as the weather becomes warmer. I also hope that he is daily realizing, more or less, the fact, that his brethren and sisters are praying for his restoration to health, and "will not God avenge his own elect which cry day and night unto him, though he bear long with them? He will avenge them speedily."

My next point was Springfield, Mo., where I visited two families of members, namely, brother and sister Rexroad, located at 976 Main St., formerly from Hutchinson, Kans., also Bro. Puterbaugh, formerly from Lanark, Ill. I do not remember his Street; I name these because they much desire to have some preaching by the Brethren. Here is a good mission point. I think there are more members in the City.

My next point was Navarre, Dickinson Co., Kans., whither I went to do some church work. Then I returned home to our quarterly council, where, among some very good things, we had, however, some evidence that Satan was not yet bound, as some understand it. If he is bound now, what would be the state of the world if he were loose?

March 7 and 8 the Trustees of our Kansas Home met and transacted the necessary business, for the further development of the Home. The amount of available means was ascertained, and a building committee appointed, with instructions to proceed at once, as fast as circumstances will permit. I would say to those who withheld their donations till they could see success, Send on; it is no longer doubtful. The house will be built, if the Lord permit. Send all donations to Bro. A. F. Miller, our treasurer, Booth, Reno Co., Kans. (See ministerial list in Brethren's Almanac.) I have received several letters recently, asking where to send funds; if you forget the name, send it to me, in the same letter you ask, and it will be all right. We live near by. Many members in Missouri gave us a strong evidence that they are in sympathy with our work. Some gave donations, others promised to do so in the near future. One dear young family, near Warrensburgh, has already made good their promise by sending $10. Though, as beginners, they have hard work to get a home, they also feel that they

should have a home in heaven. Some of the Elders said they would lay the matter before their churches at a suitable time, so as to give all an opportunity to do good. Some sisters spoke of donating bed-clothing, etc. The members in Missouri are looking around for an opportunity to work for the Lord, and surely this is a good one. A card yesterday, from Missouri, says, "I have donations; where shall I send them?" Who is next?

We have also been greatly encouraged by a brother and sister in Canada, who cheered us not by word alone, but by a $75 check. They did not say we should publish the name or amount. Any that should prefer, we will. We can not reciprocate, but the One to whom the donation is made, keeps the Book of Life, and will never forget to record the name, and pay back one hundred per cent, or more. Our object, in writing as we do, is, to encourage others to do good, and present an opportunity. Our work of soliciting in this State is done, but we lack means yet to finish and furnish the Home. We thought of other States who are more wealthy than Missouri, whose members might feel to lend something to the Lord. O how happy you can make us feel!

Just at this point the GOSPEL MESSENGER was handed to me, containing the article on the life and death of our much-lamented brother, R. H. Miller. Although we feel sure that our great loss is his gain, we could not restrain the unbidden tear when we remembered the very many days and nights we so pleasantly spent together in church work. While the church still needs his wise and safe counsels, on church government especially, the Holy Father saw different, and we humbly submit, with the resolution to improve life more to the service of God, so that we, too, may die the death of the righteous, and our last end be like theirs, is my prayer in Jesus' name! Amen.   ENOCH EBY.

Booth, Kans.

From Davenport, Nebr.

BRO. J. E. YOUNG, of Beatrice, Nebr., began a series of meetings at the Lichty school-house on the evening of Feb. 9, and continued until the 20th. This is a point in the Bethel congregation, where the Brethren have preaching every four weeks, and it was thought best to have a series of meetings. Bro. Young uses the Sword of the Spirit with power. He reproves sin sharply, and yet speaks in such a manner as to command the attention and respect of the people. This was our Savior's method of teaching, and this we must have to-day if we would win sinners to Christ.

At the close of these meetings Bro. Young was called home on account of sickness in his family. Considering the unpleasant weather and condition of the roads, and distance that some of our members live from the meetings, the attendance was good, and attention excellent. We can report no additions at this place. Before leaving for home, Bro. Young preached on Sunday evening at the Christian church-house in Davenport, to a large congregation.

After remaining at home one week, he returned to continue the meetings in Davenport, where he preached until March 8, delivering thirteen sermons, to good congregations. This is a point where a few members live, and our ministers have only occasionally given it a passing notice. Here, like in many towns, creeds and theories have taken the place of Gospel. During these meetings the people were introduced to some new lines of thought, and began to search whether these things were so, and although we can report no additions, as an immediate result, our doctrine has a stronger foot-hold in the hearts of the people than ever before, because they see that it more nearly approaches primitive Christianity. Surely "the harvest is great!"   D. H. FORNEY.

March 13.

pressed themselves by saying, that surely all was in accordance with the Bible. The best of order prevailed througout the entire services.

On Sunday, Bro. J. C. Lehman delivered a very able discourse to a large, attentive audience, on these words: "That Christ may dwell in your hearts by faith; that ye, being rooted and grounded in love, may be able to comprehend with all saints what is the breadth, and length, and depth, and height," etc. Eph. 3: 17, 18.

On Sunday night Bro. Sawyer again gave us a good talk on these words: "For God hath not given us the spirit of fear; but of power, and of love, and of a sound mind." 2 Tim. 1: 7.

J. L. MILLER.

March 14.

"Thrilling Incidents on Sea and Land."

SINCE the announcement of my new work, under the above title, was given in the MESSENGER, a great interest has been shown by many in its success. The response, to my request for advance subscribers, has exceeded my expectations, and encouraged me to go onward.

The success of canvassers for this work has been excellent, not only among members, but also among those not of our faith. One sister in Illinois took eleven orders for the book in less than an hour, and others are doing nearly as well. In localities where no agent has as yet been appointed, some one will please apply for the agency and give the work his earnest attention.

It is proposed, the Lord willing, to have the work ready for delivery by Aug. 1. Meanwhile let all make a strong effort to push the sale of the book, and report to me from time to time. Address all communications to me, as below.

GEORGE D. ZOLLERS.

Mount Carroll, Ill.

Jottings.

BRO. C. M. YEAROUT came to us from the McPherson Bible Normal, and preached for us two weeks to general satisfaction. We had excellent interest at our meetings, but out of fifteen or twenty lepers that should have cried, "Lord Jesus, have mercy on us," only two young sisters returned to give God the glory. Bro. Yearout did his duty, and none can say he did not give them fair warning.

Having a desire to visit our dear, afflicted brother, S. S. Mohler, and to attend the District Meeting of the Middle District of Missouri, near Warrensburgh, as well as the debate in Morgan County, as announced in GOSPEL MESSENGER, I accordingly left home Feb. 16, and arrived at Bro. Mohler's next day. After spending an hour or more, and enjoying some refreshments, I was taken to the Ministerial Meeting, which to me was very interesting, because of the interest manifested in the work of the ministry, and also to see so many active and zealous young ministers.

The next two days were spent in the work of the District. A more harmonious meeting would be hard to find. While all we saw and heard was commendable, we call special attention to two features, first, the large mission field, of which favorable reports were made by those in charge. Due attention was also given for the next year by giving every man his work, to occupy till the next meeting. The other feature to be admired was a strong effort to send nothing to the General Conference. The work having been finished in great peace and harmony, a letter of greeting, from Bro. S. S. Mohler was read, in behalf of its success. It was reciprocated, and also suggested that all present should unite in a season of prayer in his behalf, as well as to ask the blessing of God on the work of the meeting. This was done

with sighs, and groans, and tears, after which the meeting was dismissed. After an affectionate farewell, the members dispersed, feeling that it was good to be there. Returning to Bro. Mohler's, we spent another short season with him; then left to spend the night with Eld. D. M. Mohler, where we had the pleasure of a short visit with his father-in-law, John Hershy, who must soon go to his reward, according to the course of nature.

From here I went to the debate. Of this we might say a good deal, but to make a fair report, we might be censured with prejudice by some, and I am conscientious in making any other kind. I am very thankful, however, to say that the Truth lost nothing by the investigation. I learned more than ever that it is hard work to try to prop up a cause without it. I feel assured, that good seed has been sown by Bro. Shambarger's clear and logical style of argument,—seed that will, in the future, produce fruit to the honor of God, and his cause. I further remark, that the discussion was conducted in a Christian manner, with a friendly spirit.

On my return I intended to stop again with our dear brother, S. S. Mohler, but a failure in making connection frustrated my purposes. For this I felt sorry, for Bro. Mohler surely needs the sympathy of all his dear brethren and sisters, and the company of as many as can stop with him. I am glad I can say he is better than one year ago, and we entertain fond hopes that he will recover, and that the more rapidly as the weather becomes warmer. I also hope that he is daily realizing, more or less, the fact, that his brethren and sisters are praying for his restoration to health, and "will not God avenge his own elect which cry day and night unto him, though he bear long with them? He will avenge them speedily."

My next point was Springfield, Mo., where I visited two families of members, namely, brother and sister Rexroad, located at 976 Main St., formerly from Hutchinson, Kans., also Bro. Puterbaugh, formerly from Lanark, Ill. I do not remember his Street; I name these because they much desire to have some preaching by the Brethren. Here is a good mission point. I think there are more members in the City.

My next point was Navarre, Dickinson Co., Kans., whither I went to do some church work. Then I returned home to our quarterly council, where, among some very good things, we had, however, some evidence that Satan was not yet bound, as some understand it. If he is bound now, what would be the state of the world if he were loose?

March 7 and 8 the Trustees of our Kansas Home met and transacted the necessary business, for the further development of the Home. The amount of available means was ascertained, and a building committee appointed, with instructions to proceed at once, as fast as circumstances will permit. I would say to those who withheld their donations till they could see success, Send on; it is no longer doubtful. The house will be built if the Lord permit. Send all donations to Bro. A. F. Miller, our treasurer, Booth, Reno Co., Kans. (See ministerial list in Brethren's Almanac.) I have received several letters recently, asking where to send funds; if you forget the name, send it to me, in the same letter you ask, and it will be all right. We live near by. Many members in Missouri gave us a strong evidence that they are in sympathy with our work. Some gave donations, others promised to do so in the near future. One dear young family, near Warrensburgh, have already made good their promise by sending $10. Though, as beginners, they have hard work to get a home, they also feel that they

should have a home in heaven. Some of the Elders said they would lay the matter before their churches at a suitable time, so as to give all an opportunity to do good. Some sisters spoke of donating bed-clothing, etc. The members in Missouri are looking around for an opportunity to work for the Lord, and surely this is a good one. A card yesterday, from Missouri, says, "I have donations; where shall I send them?" Who is next?

We have also been greatly encouraged by a brother and sister in Canada, who cheered us not by word alone, but by a $75 check. They did not say we should publish the name or amount. Any that should prefer, we will. We can not reciprocate, but the One to whom the donation is made, keeps the Book of Life, and will never forget to record the name, and pay back one hundred per cent, or more. Our object, in writing as we do, is, to encourage others to do good, and present an opportunity. Our work of soliciting in this State is done, but we lack means yet to finish and furnish the Home. We thought of other States who are more wealthy than Missouri, whose members might feel to lend something to the Lord. O how happy you can make us feel!

Just at this point the GOSPEL MESSENGER was handed to me, containing the article on the life and death of our much-lamented brother, B. H. Miller. Although we feel sure that our great loss is his gain, we could not restrain the unbidden tear when we remembered the very many days and nights we so pleasantly spent together in church work. While the church still needs his wise and safe counsels, on church government especially, the Holy Father saw different, and we humbly submit, with the resolution to improve life more to the service of God, so that we, too, may die the death of the righteous, and our last end be like theirs, is my prayer in Jesus' name! Amen.

ENOCH EBY.

Booth, Kans.

From Davenport, Nebr.

BRO. J. E. YOUNG, of Beatrice, Nebr., began a series of meetings at the Lichty school-house on the evening of Feb. 9, and continued until the 20th. This is a point in the Bethel congregation, where the Brethren have preaching every four weeks, and it was thought best to have a series of meetings. Bro. Young uses the Sword of the Spirit with power. He reproves sin sharply, and yet speaks in such a manner as to command the attention and respect of the people. This was our Savior's method of teaching, and this we must have to-day if we would win sinners to Christ.

At the close of these meetings Bro. Young was called home on account of sickness in his family. Considering the unpleasant weather and condition of the roads, and distance that some of our members live from the meetings, the attendance was good, and attention excellent. We can report no additions at this place. Before leaving for home, Bro. Young preached on Sunday evening at the Christian church-house in Davenport, to a large congregation.

After remaining at home one week, he returned to continue the meetings in Davenport, where he preached until March 9, delivering thirteen sermons, to good congregations. This is a point where a few members live, and our ministers have only occasionally given it a passing notice. Here, like in many towns, creeds and theories have taken the place of Gospel. During these meetings the people were introduced to some new lines of thought, and began to search whether these things were so, and although we can report no additions, as an immediate result, our doctrine has a stronger foot-hold in the hearts of the people than ever before, because they see that it more nearly approaches primitive Christianity. Surely "the harvest is great!" D. H. FORNEY.

March 13.

Literary Notes.

The Treasury for Pastor and People for March is on our table. It contains many articles of sterling worth and of present as well as of permanent interest. To preachers, students and others this Magazine is invaluable. The portrait of Dr. H. M. Du Bose, of San Francisco, is given, with a view of the Methodist church in Los Angeles. His brief biographical sketch and sermon are worthy of careful reading. The three following articles are of inestimable value: One by Professor W. H. Green on The Anti-Biblical Phase of Higher Criticism; a sermon by Dr. Day on Preaching in Great Cities, and a paper by President Andrews on The Moral and Religious Value of Higher Education. Sermons in their Leading Thoughts are by Drs. Vandyke, Greer, Brown and Carson. Bishop Fox presents his View of The Attitude of the Church Toward Amusements. Dr. Barrow discourses on The Devil's Creed, and an article on One of the Apocalyptic Plagues, will be found exceedingly timely. Christian Training in Childhood, by Dr. Bradley; The Parsonage as an Aid to Christian Effort, by Rev. A. D. Adams, and The Devotional Side of the Pastor's Life—by Rev. G. B. Taylor, are each excellent; so also is God's Money and God's Work, by Dr. J. Corbett. A Day in Nazareth, by R. T. Cumming, is a bright, readable paper. Dr. Moment's light on the International Lessons is always bright. The editorials on The Cedar has Fallen, Be Sure of the Facts, "Hoist With Their Own Petard," and Manageable Groups are timely, suggestive and pointed. Yearly subscription, $4.50. Clergymen, $3.00. Single copies, 25 cents. E. B. Treat, Publisher, 5 Cooper Union, New York.

MATRIMONIAL.

" What therefore God hath joined together, let not man put asunder."

MOORE—GILLMORE.—At the residence of the bride's parents, near Blue Valley, York Co., Nebr., March 6, 1892, by Eld. G. W. Stambaugh, Mr. Perl Moore and Miss Stella Gillmore, all of York County, Nebr.

FRIEDRICH WIEDMAN.

HIATT—PRICHARD.—At the residence of the bride's parents, near Exeter, Nebr., Feb. 17, 1892, by Eld. G. W. Stambaugh, Mr. R. B. Hiatt and Miss Lizzie Prichard, all of York County, Nebr.

FRIEDRICH WIEDMAN.

SHEPLER—ROWLAND.—At the residence of the groom's parents, Feb. 21, 1892, by Bro. Geo. Strycher, Mr. Berlin Shepler and Miss Anna Rowland, both of Peabody, Marion Co., Kans. ESTHER SHEPLER.

COCHRAN—GODWIN.—At the home of the bride's parents, near Silver Lake, Kans., March 1, 1892, by Rev. E. B. Tucker, Bro. Harry V. Cochran, of Harvey County, Kans., and Miss Annie E. Godwin, of Shawnee County, Kans. SUSAN COCHRAN.

MISHLER—YODER.—At the residence of the bride's parents, in the bounds of the Monitor church, McPherson Co., Kans., Feb. 28, 1892, by Bro. Geo. E. Studebaker, Bro. Moses J. Mishler and sister Mary E. Yoder.

S. J. MILLER.

→ FALLEN ASLEEP ←

" Blessed are the dead which die in the Lord."

ENGLAR.—In the Sam's Creek congregation, Carroll Co., Md., March 1, 1892, Bro. Louis Englar, aged 43 years, 10 months and 23 days. He leaves a sorrowing widow, but no children. Funeral services by the writer.

WM. H. FRANKLIN.

MILLER.—At the home of his son-in-law, Mr. Fahrney, in Waynesborough, Pa., Feb. 29, 1892, of apoplexy, Bro. Jacob Miller, aged 80 years and 20 days. Deceased retired in usual health but next morning was found unconscious. He lived about one week more, but never spoke. He was a brother of Eld. Moses Miller and the last surviving one of a large family. He was married twice; leaves a widow, three sons and three daughters. His remains were brought to the Fogelsanger church and laid to rest by the side of his former wife. Services by Bro. J. F. Stamy, from Order) and Bro. S. M. Stouffer.

D. H. MILLER.

MOORE.—At Bufnsville, N. C., Feb. 20, 1892, Sarzeta Celesta Moore, aged 27 years, 10 months and 2 days. She was united in marriage with Wm. M. Moore, June 5, 1887. She was a woman of noble Christian qualities.

W. M. MOORE.

PENCE.—In the Exeter church, York Co., Nebr., Jan. 20, 1892, Elizabeth Pence, wife of Bro. Thomas Pence, aged 67 years, 8 months and 26 days. Funeral services at the home of the deceased by Eld. G. W. Stambaugh, D. B. Heiny and the writer, from Deut. 30: 19, 20.

SMITH.—Also in the same church, Feb. 18, 1892, sister Catharine Smith, aged about 14 years. Funeral services at the home of the deceased by Eld. G. W. Stambaugh, assisted by the writer, from 2 Tim. 4: 6, 7, 8.

FRIEDRICH WIEDMAN.

MILLER.—In the Monroe County church, Iowa, March 8, 1892, of croup, infant child of brother and sister Wesley Miller, aged about 3 years. Funeral services by the home ministers.

HIRAM BERKMAN.

OVERLISS.—In the South Beatrice congregation, Gage Co., Nebr., March 3, 1892, Marlin A., infant son of Bro. Petty and sister Bettie Overliss, aged 2 months and 3 days. Funeral discourse by Eld. Urias Shick, from 2 Cor. 5: 1.

M. L. SPIRE.

WARD.—In Philadelphia, Pa., Dec. 29, 1891, sister Mary Ward, aged 93 years. Funeral services by the writer from Heb. 10: 34.

HAUSE.—In Philadelphia, Pa., Feb. 19, 1892, Bro. John Hause, aged 83 years. Funeral services by the writer from 2 Cor. 5: 1. May they rest in peace. T. T. MYERS.

BRUMBAUGH.—Near New Baltimore, Ohio, Feb. 9, 1892, sister Catharine Brumbaugh, widow of Henry Brumbaugh, deceased, aged 79 years, 10 months and 14 days. She was as well as usual and able to be about her household duties, until the very instant of her death. She had just gone into another room, when she dropped over and died without a struggle, or saying a word. Deceased was born and raised in Blair County, Pa., came to Ohio, and settled in Portage County, in April, 1832, where she lived until her death. Funeral services by Bro. Noah Longanecker.

J. B. BLOUGH.

FELLER.—In the same vicinity, Feb. 15, 1892, Bro. Daniel Feller, aged 82 years, 1 month and 6 days. Bro. Feller came from Fayette County, Pa., in 1830. He married Esther Brumbaugh in 1834, who survives him. Funeral services by Bro. David Young.

A. BRUMBAUGH.

OAKS.—In the Shoal Creek church, near Grangeville, Newton Co., Mo., Jan. 3, 1892, of La Grippe and pneumonia fever, Daniel Oaks, aged 70 years, 8 months and 24 days. He was born in Montgomery County, Ohio, April 10, 1824, and married Lydia Kunz, Feb. 16, 1843. Twelve children were born to them. He leaves a sorrow-stricken wife, almost blind and helpless. He united with the Brethren church about forty years ago. His body was taken to Illinois and buried in the Moultry County graveyard, near Lovington. Funeral services at his house by J. T. Harris, from 2 Tim. 4: 6, 7, 8.

PERTHENIO EARLY.

WILLIAMS.—In the Monroe County church, Iowa, Jan. 7, 1892, Scott Williams, husband of sister Dora Williams, aged about 35 years. He was killed suddenly while helping to put a railroad engine back on the rails, that had been thrown from the track, owing to a broken rail. He leaves a wife and one child. Funeral by the home ministers.

HIRAM BERKMAN.

BEERY.—Within the bounds of the Rush Creek church, Hocking Co., Ohio, Jan. 30, 1892, sister Fannie Beery, aged 75 years, 1 month and 9 days. She was born Dec. 21, 1816. She was the mother of thirteen children. Her companion preceded her three months, lacking one day. Funeral services by the writer, assisted by Eld. Daniel Hendricks, of the P. B. church, from 2 Kings 20: 1.

J. C. BEERY.

SPICHER.—In the South Waterloo congregation, Black Hawk Co., Iowa, Feb. 23, 1892, Bro. William Spicher, aged 33 years, 11 months and 7 days. He leaves a sorrowing wife and two little girls. Services conducted by Eld. J. A. Murray and the writer from Ps. 103: 15 to a large congregation.

S. H. MILLER.

PRICE.—In the bounds of the Pleasant View church, Phillips Co., Kans., Feb. 6, 1892, Mrs. Martha Price, wife of friend Hansford Price. Funeral services conducted by the writer from Ps. 39: 4.

J. W. JARBOE.

KEISER.—In the Warrensburgh church, Johnson Co., Mo., March 5, of pneumonia, sister Mollie Keiser, aged about 36 years. The deceased leaves a sorrowing husband. Her body was taken to Woodford County, Ill., for interment. MARY MOWLER.

DEMOSS.—In the Monroe County church, Jan. —, 1892, of kidney trouble, Jackson Demoss, husband of sister ——Demoss, aged about 65 years. Funeral conducted by the home ministers. HIRAM BERKMAN.

WOODRUFF.—In the Monroe County church, March 8, 1892, Willis Woodruff, son of Thomas and sister Drusilla Woodruff, was killed in a coal bank Dec. 5, 1892, aged about 19 years. The day's work was done and all started home. For some reason little Willis went back. The shots had not all gone off but this he did not know and going too close to one, as it fired, some of the coal struck and killed him. Funeral by the home brethren to many weeping friends.

HIRAM BERKMAN.

HARSHBARGER.—In the White church, Ind., Jan. 8, 1892, Abraham Harshbarger, aged 47 years, 6 months and 5 days. He was married to Amanda Bowers, Aug. 20, 1860. To this union ten children were born. Funeral services by Bro. D. C. Campbell from 1 Cor. 15: 16. F. JOHNSON.

BERKLEY.—In the Quemahoning congregation, Somerset Co., Pa., Feb. 29, 1892, sister Cathrine Berkley, aged 65 years, 2 months and 4 days Disease, cancer and dropsy. During her illness she had a love-feast held in her room, and also was anointed. Funeral services by the undersigned and S. P. Zimmerman to a large audience.

E. J. BLOUGH.

HENSLEY.—In the Limestone church, Tenn., Feb. 11, 1891, Elizabeth Hensley, aged 86 years, 10 months and 13 days. In 1862 she united with the church of the Brethren.

J. B. PENCE.

MYERS.—In the Four Mile church, Fayette Co., Ind., Jan. 14, 1892, sister Sarah Myers, aged 86 years, 8 months and 14 days. Deceased was born in Botetourt County, Virginia, in 1809. She came to Union County, with her parents, in 1811. In 1829 she was married to Bro. Jacob Myers, who preceded her to the spirit land. She was a consistent member of the German Baptist church for fifty-eight years. Funeral occasion improved by the Brethren. JACOB MYERS.

HOUK.—In the bounds of the Lower Twin Creek congregation, Montgomery Co., Ohio, March 1, 1892, Susan Hazel Houk, aged 1 year, 1 months and 28 days. She was a daughter of friend George W. and Kate Houk, formerly of Madison County, Ind. Funeral by the writer from Psalms' 103: 15, 16. DANIEL M. GARVER.

KINSEY.—In the Lower Twin Creek church, Montgomery Co., Ohio, March 8, 1892, of paralysis, Bro. David Kinsey. Oct. 18, 1838, he was joined in marriage with Catharine Mullendore, and this union was blessed with eleven children. He was anointed two days previous to his departure. Funeral occasion improved from Ps. 17: 15, by the writer, assisted by elders Landon West and Jonas Horning. DANIEL M. GARVER.

BEEGHLEY.—In the Maple ——congregation, Cherokee Co., Iowa, Nov. 26, 1891, sister Sarah Beeghley, wife of Bro. Michael Beeghley, aged 58 years, 9 months and 10 days. Funeral services conducted by Eld. John Early from Rev. 14: 12.

ELIAS FORNEY.

NEUSBAUM.—In the New Haven church, Gratiot Co., Mich., Feb. 24, 1892, Bro. Abe Neusbaum, aged 51 years, 8 months and 3 days. He leaves a wife and five children. Funeral services by Bro. Geo. E. Stone.

JOHN STONE.

CRIPE.—At Los Angeles, Cal., Feb. 4, 1892, of consumption, sister Lizzie Cripe, wife of James Cripe, and daughter of John and Magdalena Franz, aged 25 years and 24 days. In poor health she came to California a few months before she died, thinking that the mild climate might benefit her. She leaves a husband and two children. She was married to James Cripe March 27, 1887. Funeral discourse by the writer from 2 Tim. 4: 7, 8.

JOHN METZGER.

ZUCK.—In the Cole Creek congregation, Fulton Co., Ill., Feb. 10, 1892, Mary Zuck, aged 86 years, 5 months and 13 days. She emigrated from Franklin County, Pa., in her early life. She was a member of the Brethren church for forty-five years. Funeral services by the writer from John 5: 24, 25.

SOLOMON BUCKLEW.

HUFFMAN.—In the Beaver Creek congregation, Va., Jan. 19, 1892, sister Elizabeth, wife of friend Marlin Huffman, aged 62 years, 9 months and 14 days. Funeral at Ottobine by Eld. J. Thomas.

FLEMMINGS.—In the same congregation, on Briery Branch, Feb. 25, 1892, of membraneous croup, Edgar L., son of friend William Flemmings, aged 4 years, 2 months and 7 days. Funeral at Ottobine by the writer from Matt. 18, first clause of verse 3.

RANDELL.—Near the same place, March 8, 1892, of catarrhal fever, Sarah M., daughter of Bro. Daniel Randell, aged 1 year, 8 months and 20 days. Funeral services at Beaver Creek by the writer from John 11, last clause of verse 28.

G. W. WINE.

VANCAMP.—In the Buckhannon congregation, Upshur Co., W. Va., January, 1892, Bro. Eliza Vancamp, aged about 72 years. Bro. Vancamp was a faithful Christian and a worthy deacon. He was never known to shun his duty. He possessed a sympathetic heart, and none were ever turned from his door. Whenever there was help needed, he was always first to respond. He leaves a wife and three daughters.

SHOCKEY.—In the same congregation, Feb. 10, 1892, Bro. Valentine Shockey, aged nearly 66 years. Bro. Shockey was born in Garrett County, Md., and was brought to Virginia by his parents at the age of eleven years. His mother was Christiana Markley, a daughter of Jacob Markley, of near Markleysburg, Pa. He leaves a wife and eight children.

VANCAMP.—In the same congregation, March 2, 1892, sister Mary Woodson, aged nearly 78 years. Sister Woodson was born and raised in Lynchburg, Va. Her maiden name was Golden. She was the mother of fourteen children.

PENCE.—Also, in the above congregation, Feb. 6, 1892, Harley Pence, the oldest son of Daniel and Mary Pence, aged 11 years.

DAVID J. MILLER.

SLIFER.—At Broad Run, Md., March 6, 1892, sister Mary Slifer, widow of Peter Slifer, aged about 82 years. Funeral services by Eld. D. Ausherman, assisted by Eld. Bill Yourtee.

LOIS.—In the Brownsville congregation, Pa., on the same day as above, sister Margaret Lois, widow of the late Joseph Lois, aged about 59 years. Funeral services were held in the Lutheran church in Sharpsburg, by Eld Yourtee. A. C. CASTLE.

Literary Notes.

The Treasury for Pastor and People for March is on our table. It contains many articles of sterling worth and of present as well as of permanent interest. To preachers, students and others this Magazine is invaluable. The portrait of Dr. H. M. Du Bose, of San Francisco, is given, with a view of the Methodist church in Los Angeles. His brief biographical sketch and sermon are worthy of careful reading. The three following articles are of incalculable value: One by Professor W. H. Green on The Anti-Biblical Phase of Higher Criticism; a sermon by Dr. Day on Preaching in Great Cities, and a paper by President Andrews on The Moral and Religious Value of Higher Education. Sermons in their Leading Thoughts are by Drs. Vandyke, Greer, Brown and Carson. Bishop Foss presents his view of The Attitude of the Church Toward Amusements. Dr. Barrow discourses on The Devil's Creed, and an article on One of the Apocalyptic Plagues, will be found exceedingly timely. Christian Training in Childhood, by Dr. Bradley; The Parsonage as an Aid to Christian Effort, by Rev. A. D. Adams, and The Devotional Side of the Pastor's Life, by Rev. G. B. Taylor, are each excellent; so also is God's Money and God's Work, by Dr. J. Corbett. A Day in Nazareth, by R. T. Cumming, is a bright, readable paper. Dr. Moment's light on the International Lessons is always bright. The editorials on The Cedar has Fallen, Be Sure of the Facts, "Hoist With Their Own Petard," and Manageable Groups are timely, suggestive and pointed. Yearly subscription, $1.50. Clergymen, $1.00. Single copies, 25 cents. E. B. TREAT, Publisher, 5 Cooper Union, New York.

MATRIMONIAL.

"What therefore God hath joined together, let not man put asunder."

MOORE—GILLMORE.—At the residence of the bride's parents, near Blue Valley, York Co., Nebr., March 6, 1892, by Eld. G. W. Stambaugh, Mr. Perl Moore and Miss Stella Gillmore, all of York County, Nebr.
FRIEDRICH WIEDMAN.

HIATT—PRICHARD.—At the residence of the bride's parents, near Exeter, Nebr., Feb. 17, 1892, by Eld. G. W. Stambaugh, Mr. R. B. Hiatt and Miss Lizzie Prichard, all of York County, Nebr.
FRIEDRICH WIEDMAN.

SHEPLER—ROWLAND.—At the residence of the groom's parents, Feb. 22, 1892, by Bro. Geo. Strycher, Mr. Bertin Shepler and Miss Anna Rowland, both of Peabody, Marion Co., Kans. ESTHER SHEPLER.

COCHRAN—GODWIN.—At the home of the bride's parents, near Silver Lake, Kans., March 1, 1892, by Rev. E. B. Tucker, Bro. Harry Y. Cochran, of Harvey County, Kans., and Miss Annie E. Godwin, of Shawnee County, Kans. SUSAN COCHRAN.

MISHLER—YODER.—At the residence of the bride's parents, in the bounds of the Monitor church, McPherson Co., Kans., Feb. 28, 1892, by Bro. Geo. E. Studebaker, Bro. Moses J. Mishler and sister Mary E. Yoder.
S. J. MILLER.

→ FALLEN ASLEEP ←

"Blessed are the dead which die in the Lord."

ENGLAR.—In the Sam's Creek congregation, Carroll Co., Md., March 1, 1892, Bro. Louis Englar, aged 43 years, 10 months and 23 days. He leaves a sorrowing widow, but no children. Funeral services by the writer.
WM. H. FRANKLIN.

MILLER.—At the home of his son-in-law, Mr. Fahrney, in Waynesborough, Pa., Feb. 29, 1892, of apoplexy, Bro. Jacob Miller, aged 60 years and 20 days. Deceased retired in usual health but next morning was found unconscious. He lived about one week more, but never spoke. He was a brother of Eld. Moses Miller and the last surviving one of a large family. He was married twice; leaves a widow, three sons and three daughters. His remains were brought to the Fogelsanger church and laid to rest by the side of his former wife. Services by Bro. J. F. Stamy, from Matt. 27: 44, followed by Mr. Mentzer (Old Order) and Bro. S. M. Stouffer.
D. H. MILLER.

MOORE.—At Burnsville, N. C., Feb. 20, 1892, Sarepta Celesta Moore, aged 27 years, 10 months and 2 days. She was united in marriage with Wm. M. Moore, June 5, 1887. She was a woman of noble Christian qualities. W. M. MOORE.

PENCE.—In the Exeter church, York Co., Nebr., Jan. 20, 1892, Elizabeth Pence, wife of Bro. Thomas Pence, aged 67 years, 8 months and 26 days. Funeral services at the home of the deceased by Eld. G. W. Stambaugh, D. B. Heiny and the writer, from Deut. 30: 19, 20. W. M. MOORE.

SMITH.—Also in the same church, Feb. 28, 1892, sister Catharine Smith, aged about 14 years. Funeral services at the home of the deceased by Eld. G. W. Stambaugh, assisted by the writer, from 2 Tim. 4: 6, 7, 8.
FRIEDRICH WIEDMAN.

MILLER.—In the Monroe County church, Iowa, March 3, 1892, of croup, infant child of brother and sister Warder Miller, aged about 3 years. Funeral services by the home ministers. HIRAM BERKMAN.

OVERLISS.—In the South Beatrice congregation, Gage Co., Nebr., March 3, 1892, Martin A., infant son of Bro. Perry and sister Bettie Overliss, aged 2 months and 3 days. Funeral discourse by Eld. Urias Shick, from 2 Cor. 5: 1. M. L. SPIRE.

WARD.—In Philadelphia, Pa., Dec. 29, 1891, sister Mary Ward, aged 29 years. Funeral services by the writer from Heb. 10: 34.

HAUSE.—In Philadelphia, Pa., Feb 19, 1892, Bro. John Hause, aged 23 years. Funeral services by the writer from 2 Cor. 5: 1. May they rest in peace. T. T. MYERS.

BRUMBAUGH.—Near New Baltimore, Ohio, Feb. 9, 1892, sister Catharine Brumbaugh, widow of Henry Brumbaugh, deceased, aged 79 years, 10 months and 14 days. She was as well as usual and able to be about her household duties, until the very instant of her death. She had just gone into another room, when she dropped over and died without a struggle, or saying a word. Deceased was born and raised in Blair County, Pa., came to Ohio, and settled in Portage County, in April, 1832, where she lived until her death. Funeral services by Bro. Noah Longanecker.
A. BRUMBAUGH.

FELLER.—In the same vicinity, Feb. 15, 1892, Bro. Daniel Feller, aged 81 years, 1 month and 6 days. Bro. Feller came from Fayette County, Pa., in 1830. He married Esther Brumbaugh in 1834, who survives him. Funeral services by Bro. David Young.
A. BRUMBAUGH.

OAKS.—In the Shoal Creek church, near Grangeville, Newton Co., Mo., Jan. 3, 1892, of La Grippe and pneumonia fever, Daniel Oaks, aged 70 years, 6 months and 24 days. He was born in Montgomery County, Ohio, April 10, 1824, and married Lydia Kuns, Feb. 16, 1843. Twelve children were born to them. He leaves a sorrow-stricken wife, almost blind and helpless. He united with the Brethren church about forty years ago. His body was taken to Lovington and buried in the Moultry County grave-yard, near Lovington, Ohio, March 1, 1892, Susan Hazel Houk, from 2 Tim. 4: 6, 7, 8.
PERTHENIO EARLY.

WILLIAMS.—In the Monroe County church, Iowa, Jan. 7, 1892, Scott Williams, husband of sister Dora Williams, aged about 35 years. He was killed suddenly while helping to put a railroad engine back on the rails, that had been thrown from the track, owing to a broken rail. He leaves a wife and one child. Funeral by the home ministers.
HIRAM BERKMAN.

BEERY.—Within the bounds of the Rush Creek church, Hocking Co., Ohio, Jan. 30, 1892, sister Fannie Beery, aged 75 years, 1 month and 9 days. She was born Dec. 21, 1816. She was the mother of thirteen children. Her companion preceded her three months, lacking one day. Funeral services by the writer, assisted by Eld. Daniel Hendricks, of the P. B. church, from 2 Kings 20: 1. J. C. BEERY.

SPICHER.—In the South Waterloo congregation, Black Hawk Co., Iowa, Feb. 23, 1892, Bro. William Spicher, aged 33 years, 11 months and 9 days. He leaves a sorrowing wife and two little girls. Services conducted by Eld. J. A. Murray and the writer from Ps. 103: 15 to a large congregation.
S. H. MILLER.

PRICE.—In the bounds of the Pleasant View church, Phillips Co., Kans., Feb. 6, 1892, Mrs. Martha Price, wife of friend Hansford Price. Funeral services conducted by the writer from Ps. 37: 4. J. W. JARBOE.

KEISER.—In the Warrensburgh church, Johnson Co., Mo., March 5, of pneumonia, sister Mollie Keiser, aged about 36 years. The deceased leaves a sorrowing husband. Her body was taken to Woodford County, Ill., for interment. MARY MOHLER.

DEMOSS.—In the Monroe County church, Jan. —, 1892, of kidney trouble, Jackson Demoss, husband of sister —Demoss, aged about 65 years Funeral conducted by the home ministers. HIRAM BERKMAN.

WOODRUFF.—In the Monroe County church, March 8, 1892, Willis Woodruff, son of Thomas and sister Drusilla Woodruff, was killed in a coal bank Dec. 5, 1890, aged about 19 years. The day's work was done and all started home. For some reason little Willis went back. The slate had not all gone off but this he did not know and going too close to one, as it fired, some of the coal struck and killed him. Funeral by the home brethren to many weeping friends.
HIRAM BERKMAN.

HARSHBARGER.—In the White church, Ind., Jan. 8, 1892, Abraham Harshbarger, aged 47 years, 6 months and 5 days. He was married to Amanda Bowers, Aug. 20, 1861. To this union ten children were born. Funeral services by Bro. D. C. Campbell from 1 Cor. 15: 16. F. JOHNSON.

BERKLEY.—In the Quemahoning congregation, Somerset Co., Pa., Feb. 29, 1892, sister Cathrine Berkley, aged 65 years, 7 months and 4 days Disease, cancer and dropsy. During her illness she had a loveliest faid in her room, and also was anointed. Funeral services by the undersigned and S. P. Zimmerman to a large audience.
E. J. BLOUGH.

HENSLEY.—In the Limestone church, Tenn., Feb. 11, 1891, Elizabeth Hensley, aged 66 years, 10 months and 13 days. In 1865 she united with the church of the Brethren.
J. B. PENCE.

MYERS.—In the Four Mile church, Fayette Co., Ind., Jan. 14, 1892, sister Sarah Myers, aged 86 years, 8 months and 14 days. Deceased was born in Botetourt County, Virginia, in 1805. She came to Union County, with her parents, in 1811. In 1829 she was married to Bro. Jacob Myers, who preceded her to the spirit land. She was a consistent member of the German Baptist church for fifty-eight years. Funeral occasion improved by the Brethren. JACOB RIFE.

HOUK.—In the bounds of the Lower Twin Creek congregation, Montgomery Co., Ohio, March 1, 1892, Susan Hazel Houk, aged 1 year, 1 months and 28 days. She was a daughter of friend George W. and Kate Houk, formerly of Madison County, Ind. Funeral by the writer from Psalms' 103: 15, 16. DANIEL M. GARVER.

KINSEY.—In the Lower Twin Creek church, Montgomery Co., Ohio, March 2, 1892, of paralysis, Bro. David Kinsey. Oct. 28, 1838, he was joined in marriage with Catharine Mullendore, and this union was blessed with eleven children. He was anointed two days previous to his departure. Funeral occasion improved from Ps. 17: 15, by the writer, assisted by elders Landon West and Jonas Horning. DANIEL M. GARVER.

BEEGHLEY.—In the Maple Valley congregation, Cherokee Co., Iowa, Nov. 16, 1891, sister Sarah Beeghley, wife of Bro. Michael Beeghley, aged 58 years, 9 months and 20 days. Funeral services conducted by Eld. John Early from Rev. 14: 12.
ELIAS FORNEY.

NEUSBAUM.—In the New Haven church, Gratiot Co., Mich., Feb. 24, 1892, Bro. Abe Neusbaum, aged 51 years, 8 months and 3 days. He leaves a wife and five children. Funeral services by Bro. Geo. E. Stone.
JOHN STORER.

CRIPE.—At Los Angeles, Cal., Feb. 4, 1892, of consumption, sister Lizzie Cripe, wife of James Cripe, and daughter of John and Magdalena Franz, aged 25 years and 24 days. In four health she came to California a few months before she died, thinking that the mild climate might benefit her. She leaves a husband and two children. She was married to James Cripe March 27, 1887. Funeral discourse by the writer from 2 Tim. 4: 7, 8.
JOHN METZGER.

ZUCK.—In the Cole Creek congregation, Fulton Co., Ill., Feb. 10, 1892, Mary Zuck, aged 86 years, 5 months and 13 days. She emigrated from Franklin County, Pa., in her early life. She was a member of the Brethren church for forty-five years. Funeral services by the writer from John 5: 24, 25.
SOLOMON BUCKLEW.

HUFFMAN.—In the Beaver Creek congregation, Va., Jan. 19, 1892, sister Elizabeth, wife of friend Martin Huffman, aged 62 years, 9 months and 14 days. Funeral at Ottobine by Eld. J. Thomas.

FLEMMINGS.—In the same congregation, on Briery Branch, Feb. 25, 1892, of membraneous croup, Edgar L., son of friend William Flemmings, aged 4 years, 2 months and 7 days. Funeral at Ottobine by the writer from Matt. 18, first clause of verse 3.

RANDELL.—Near the same place, March 8, 1892, of catarrhal fever, Sarah M., daughter of Bro. Daniel Randell, aged 1 year, 8 months and 20 days. Funeral services at Beaver Creek by the writer from John 11, last clause of verse 28. G. W. WINE.

VANCAMP.—In the Buckhannon congregation, Upshur Co., W. Va., January, 1892, Bro. Eliza Vancamp, aged 82 years. Bro. Vancamp was a faithful Christian and a worthy deacon. He was never known to shun his duty. He possessed a sympathetic heart, and none were ever turned from his door. Whenever there was help needed, he was always first to respond. He leaves a wife and three daughters.

SHOCKEY.—In the same congregation, Feb. 10, 1892, Bro. Valentine Shockey, aged nearly 66 years. Bro. Shockey was born in Garrett County, Md., and was brought to Virginia by his parents at the age of eleven years. His mother was Christiana Markley, a daughter of Jacob Markley, of near Markleysburg, Pa. He leaves a wife and eight children.

WOODSON.—In the same congregation, March 2, 1892, sister Mary Woodson, aged nearly 78 years. Sister Woodson was born and raised in Lynchburg, Va. Her maiden name was Golden. She was the mother of fourteen children.

PENCE.—Also, in the above congregation, Feb. 6, 1892, Harley Pence, the oldest son of Daniel and Mary Pence, aged 11 years.
DAVID J. MILLER.

SLIFER.—At Broad Run, Md., March 6, 1892, sister Mary Slifer, widow of Peter Slifer, aged about 81 years. Funeral services by Eld. D. Aushesman, assisted by Eld. Eli Yourtee.

LOIS.—In the Browneville congregation, Pa., on the-same day as above, sister Margaret Lois, widow of the late Joseph Lois, aged about 50 years. Funeral services were held in the Lutheran church in Sharpsburg, by Eli Yourtee. A. C. CASTLE.

Announcements.

DISTRICT MEETINGS.

April 6, Middle District of Indiana, in the Rossa church, Wabash Co., Ind. Delegates will please come prepared to pay their quota of expenses for the District, to defray the expenses of publishing District Meeting Minutes. They should also be ready to state how many copies of District Meeting Minute will be needed to supply each family in their congregation with one copy.

April 8, at 9 A. M., District of Nebraska, in the Juniata congregation. Ministerial meeting the day before, at 10 A. M.

April 13, at 9 A. M., District Meeting of Southern Indiana, in the Howard church, Howard Co., Ind., 11 miles west of Kokomo. Those coming by railroad will come to Kokomo the day before. Come on morning train. Arrangements will be made to convey all to place of Meeting.

April 13, District of Texas, Oklahoma, Indian Territory, and South-west Kansas, in the Salem congregation, two miles south and three miles west of Nickerson, Reno Co., Kans. Brethren are requested to come some time previous to District Meeting and hold a series or at least a few meetings for us. Whoever will favor us, will be met at Nickerson, by dropping a card to either F. Detter or F. Cross, Nickerson, Kans. Delegates to District Meeting will be met at Nickerson also.

April 15, at 9 A. M., District Meeting for North-eastern Kansas in the Olathe church, 3 miles north-west of Gardner. Ministerial meeting April 12, at 9 A. M. Gardner is on the Southern Kansas Division of the A. T. & S. F. System, where all trains will be met on Monday, the 11th, but none later.

April 15, South-western District of Kansas, in the Salem church, Reno County, Kansas, several miles south of Nickerson.

April 16 and 17, North-western District of Ohio, in the Lafayette church, Allen Co., Ohio. Those coming on Thursday, April 14, to meet the Mission Board, and conveying by the Pittsburg and Ft. Wayne Road should stop off at Lafayette. There traveling by the Chicago and Erie R. R., should get off at Harrod Station. There will be ample conveyance at either station by the brethren. All the brethren wishing time-tables of either the Pittsburg & Ft. Wayne R. R., or the Chicago and Erie R. R., can get same by applying to A. M. Baker.

April 15 and 16, First District of West Virginia, in Sandy Creek church, Preston Co., W. Va.

April 15 and 16, at 10 A. M., District Meeting of First District of Virginia, at Peter's Creek church.

April 20, at 9:30 A. M., Eastern District of Maryland, in the Middletown Valley church.

April 21, District Meeting of Western Maryland, at the Vanclevesville house, Berkeley Co., W. Va. Brethren coming on the B. & O. road will stop off at Vanclevesville Station.

April 29, at 10 A. M., District Meeting of North-western Kansas and North Colorado, in Burr Oak church, Burr Oak, Jewell Co., Kans. Every church is requested to be represented as far as possible, and we want every delegate to be prepared to meet expenses for the printing of the Minutes and payment of delegate to Annual Meeting.

May 5, at 10 A. M., North District of Missouri, in the Bethel congregation, at the Squaw Creek meeting-house, Holt Co., Mo. Those coming by rail will be met at Mound City by addressing Jos. Andes at that place.

May 10, at 8 A. M., District of Northern Illinois, in the Milledgeville church, Carroll Co., Ill.

May 21, District Meeting of Southern Missouri and Arkansas, in the Shoal Creek church, Newton Co., Mo. Those coming by rail to Pierce City will be met on the morning of May 11, by notifying John Holder, read at Ergo. Those coming to Purdy will notify Leander Harader and will be met on the morning of May 11.

LOVE FEASTS.

April 13 and 14, Second District of Virginia, at Elk Run church six en miles north of Staunton, Augusta Co., Va.

April 30, at 2 P. M., in the Oak church, Jewell Co., Kans. Meetings to continue over Sunday. Any one coming by the Union Pacific R. R from the West should come by way of Solomon City, then go to Jewell, and from there to Jamestown on the Missouri Pacific R. R. (Central Branch). Then go to Burr Oak, or Burr Oak Branch. Those coming by the Rock Island R. R. should stop at Otego, where they will be met by addressing the Elk Ranner, Burr Oak, Kans., or they can go to Mankato, three changes east, to the Missouri Pacific on Burr Oak Branch, thence to Burr Oak, where they will be met by addressing Lewis Hoff, or Joel Kinzie, at Burr Oak, Kans.

April 30, at 2 P. M., Walnut Valley church, Kansas, 7½ miles West and 2½ miles north of Great Bend, Kans.

May 7, at 10 A. M., in the Bethel congregation, at the Squaw Creek meeting-house, Holt Co., Mo.

May 7, 10, at 2 P. M., Abilene, Kans.

May 7, at 2 P. M., Peabody church, Kans.

May 7, at 10 A. M., Washington Creek church, Douglas Co., Kansas.

May 7 and 8, in the Flat Rock church, Va.

May 7 and 8, in the Knobly church, Va., at the residence of S. A. Sutter. Place of meeting 2½ miles south-west of Batavia.

May 13, 16, at 10 A. M., Wolf Creek Church, Montgomery Co., Ohio.

May 12, 13, at 2 P. M., in the Yellow Creek congregation, Bedford County, Pa.

May 13 and 14, at 2 P. M., Silver Creek church, Ogle Co., Ill.

May 14, 15, at 2 P. M., in the Kansas Center church, 5 miles east of Lyons.

May 14, at 2 P. M., Pleasant View church, Reno Co., Kans., 1¾ miles south-west of South.

May 14, 10 to A. M., Pipe Creek congregation, Miami Co., Ind.

May 20, at 10 A. M., Mexicotown church, Delaware Co., Ind., 4 miles west of Shideler. Those coming by rail should come to Shideler and inquire for the brethren.

May 21, at 3 P. M., in the Harlan congregation, four miles east of Harlan, Shelby Co., Iowa. Meetings to 3 continue over Sunday.

May 28, at 10 A. M., Hartford Church, Hartford City, Ind.

May 31 and June 1, Cherry Grove, Carroll Co., Ill.

June 1, in the Yellow Creek church, Elkhart Co., Ind., 7 miles south-west of Goshen.

June 1, at 2 P. M., 11 Pleis, Ind. Train that have from the south, at 10 A. M.

June 3, at 2 P. M., Walnut Level church, Wells Co., Ind.

June 9, at 2 P. M., in this Pleasant church, June Co., Ohio. Those coming from the East on their way to Annual Meeting will please take a note of this and stop off with us. Those coming on the Pennsylvania line will please stop off at Greenville and inform George Baker, Baker, Darke Co., Ohio. Those coming on the Big Four Line, will stop off at Savannah or Clark's Station and inform Moses Hollinger, New Madison, Darke Co., Ohio, or George Stamp, Baker, Darke Co., Ohio.

June 2, at 3 P. M., in the Shaw church, Platt Co., Ill. Ministering brethren on their way to Annual Meeting, will please stop with us.

June 2 and 3, at 2 P. M., Hickory Grove church, Carroll Co., Ind. Brethren going to Annual Meeting will please remember us.

June 3, at 3 P. M., Kingsley church, four miles south-east of Kingsley, Iowa.

June 17, at 2 P. M., Yellow River congregation, Marshall Co., Ind.

June 18, Green Spring District, Seneca Co., Ohio.

Announcements.

DISTRICT MEETINGS.

April 6. Middle District of Indiana, in the Rossen church, Wabash Co., Ind. Delegates will please come prepared to pay their quote of expenses for the District, to defray the expenses of publishing District Meeting Minutes. They should also be ready to state how many copies of District Meeting Minutes will be needed to supply each family in their congregation with one copy.

April 6, at 9 A. M., District of Nebraska, in the Juniata congregation. Ministerial meeting the day before, at 10 A. M.

April 12, at 9 A. M., District Meeting of Southern Indiana, in the Howard church, Howard Co., Ind., 11 miles west of Kokomo. Those coming by railroad will come to Kokomo the day before. Come on morning train. Arrangements will be made to convey all to place of Meeting.

April 13, District of Texas, Oklahoma, Indian Territory, and South-west Kansas, in the Salem congregation, two miles south and three miles east of Nickerson, Reno Co., Kans. Brethren are requested to come some time previous to District Meeting and hold a series or at least a few meetings for us. Whoever will favor us, will be met at Nickerson, by dropping a card to either F. Detter or F. Crow, Nickerson, Kans. Delegates to District Meeting will be met at Nickerson also.

April 13, at 9 A. M., District Meeting for North-eastern Kansas in the Olathe church, 1 mile north-west of Gardner. Ministerial meeting April 12, at 9 A. M. Gardner is on the Southern Kansas Division of the A. T. & S. F. System, where all trains will be met on Monday, the 11th, but none later.

April 13, South-western District of Kansas, in the Salem church, Reno County, Kansas, several miles north of Nickerson.

April 14 and 15. North-western District of Ohio, in the Lafayette church, Allen Co., Ohio. Those coming on Thursday, April 14, to meet the Mission Board, and traveling by the Pittsburg and Ft. Wayne Road should stop off at Lafayette. Those traveling by the Chicago and Erie R. R., should get off at Harrod Station. There will be ample conveyance at either station by the brethren. All the brethren wishing tune tables of either the Pittsburg & Ft. Wayne R. R., or the Chicago and Erie R. R., can get same by applying to A. M. Baker.

April 15 and 16, First District of West Virginia, in Sandy Creek church, Preston Co., W. Va.

April 19 and 16, at 10 A. M., District Meeting of First District of Virginia, in Peter's Creek church.

April 19, at 9:30 A. M., Eastern District of Maryland, in the Middletown Valley church.

April 21, District Meeting of Western Maryland, at the Vearintonsville house, Berkeley Co., W. Va. Brethren coming on the B. & B.O. road will stop off at Vearintonsville Station.

April 29, at 10 A. M., District Meeting of North-western Kansas and North Colorado, in Burr Oak church, Burr Oak, Jewell Co., Kans. Every church is requested to be represented so far as possible, and we want every delegate to be prepared to meet expenses for the printing of the Minutes and expenses of delegate to Annual Meeting.

May 5, at 10 A. M.. North District of Missouri, in the Bethel congregation, at the Squaw Creek meeting-house, Holt Co., Mo. Those coming by rail will be met at Mound City by addressing Jos. Amdon at that place.

May 10, 10 A. M., District of Northern Illinois, in the Milledgeville church, Carroll Co., Ill.

May 11, District Meeting of Southern Missouri and Arkansas, in the Shoal Creek church, Newton Co., Mo. Those coming by rail to Pierce City will be met on the morning of May 11, by notifying John Holderread at Kege. Those coming to Purdy will notify Leander Harader and will be met on the morning of May 11.

LOVE FEASTS.

April 23 and 24, Second District of Virginia, at Elk Run church six or eight miles north of Staunton, Augusta Co., Va.

April 30, at 2 P. M., in the Burr Oak church, Jewell Co., Kans. Meetings to continue over Sunday. Any one coming by the Union Pacific R. R. from the West should come by way of Salomon City, then go to Jewell, and from there to Jamestown on the Missouri Pacific R. R. (Central Branch). Those coming by the Burr Oak or Burr Oak Branch.—Those coming by the Rock Island R. R. should stop at Otega, where they will be met by addressing Eld. Eli Renner, Burr Oak, Kans., or they can go to Montclair, these change cars in the Missouri Pacific of Burr Oak Branch; thence to Burr Oak, where they will be met by addressing Lewis Hoff, or Joel Kimmle, at Burr Oak, Kans.

April 30, at 2 P. M., Walnut Valley church, Kansas, 3½ miles West and 2½ miles north of Great Bend, Kans.

May 7, at 10 A. M., in the Bethel congregation, at the Squaw Creek meeting-house, Holt Co., Mo.

May 7, at 2 P. M., Abilene, Kans.

May 7, at 2 P. M., Peabody church, Kans.

May 7, at 10 A. M., Washington Creek church, Douglas Co., Kansas.

May 12, Timberville, Va., in the Flat Rock church, Va.

May 7 and 8, in the Beaverly church, Ia., at the residence of S. A. Sanco. Place of meeting 2½ miles south-west of Beaverly.

May 10, 10 A. M., Wolf Creek church, Montgomery Co., Ohio.

May 13, at 4 P. M., in the Yellow Creek congregation, Bedford County, Pa.

May 13 and 14, at 2 P. M., Silver Creek church, Ogle Co., Ill.

May 14, at 9 P. M., in the Kansas Center church, 3 miles east of Kysner.

May 14, at 2 P. M., Pleasant View church, Reno Co., Kans., 1½ miles south-east of Booth.

May 14, at 10 A. M., Pipe Creek congregation, Miami Co., Ind.

May 20, at 10 A. M., Mineralsville church, Delaware Co., Ind., 3 miles west of Shideler. Those coming by rail should come to Shideler and inquire for the brethren.

May 21, at 2 P. M., in the Hatton congregation, four miles east of Hatton, Shelby Co., Iowa. Meetings to continue over Sunday.

May 28, at 10 A. M., Hartford Church, Hartford City, Ind.

May 31 and June 1, Cherry Grove, Carroll Co., Ill.

June 1, in the Yellow Creek church, Elkhart Co., Ind., 3 miles south-west of Goshen.

June 2, at 4 P. M., in Kum, Ind. Train line here from the south at 10 A. M.

June 3, at 2 P. M., in the Palestine church, Darke Co., Ohio. Those coming from the East on their way to Annual Meeting will please take a route of this and stop off with us. Those coming on the Pennsylvania line will please stop off at Greenville and inform George Biber, Baker, Darke Co., Ohio. Those coming on the Big Four Line, will stop off at Savannah or Clark's Station and inform Moses Hollinger, New Madison, Darke Co., Ohio, or George Stoup, Baker, Darke Co., Ohio.

June 9, at 4 P. M., in the Okaw church, Piatt Co., Ill. Ministering brethren on their way to Annual Meeting will please stop with us.

June 9 and 1, at 2 P. M., Hickory Grove church, Carroll Co., Ill. Brethren going to Annual Meeting will please remember us.

June 10, at 3 P. M., Kingsley church, four miles south-east of Kingsley, Iowa.

June 17, at 4 P. M., Silver River congregation, Marshall Co., Ind.

June 18, Green Spring District, Seneca Co., Ohio.

EGGS, EGGS FOR HATCHING

from three strains for mammoth Catalogue and Guide to Poultry Raisers. The finest book of the kind published. Containing valuable information for the poultry man and all who have poultry, either for pleasure or profit.

C. C. SHOEMAKER,
A. D. 1964. Freeport, Ill.

The Hollinger Fence and Post.

Strong, Simple, Durable and Cheap!
No More Cruelty to Stock!

MOUNT MORRIS, ILL., MARCH 3, 1892.

To Whom it May Concern:—This is to certify that we have examined the Hollinger wire fence and are satisfied that it is an excellent fence, much superior to barbed wire, by which so many horses and cattle are cruelly injured. We are also personally acquainted with the builder, David Hollinger, and do not hesitate to recommend him as a fair-dealing, honest man, believing he will faithfully carry out any promise he may make.

D. L. MILLER,
D. M WINGERT.

For full particulars call on or address as follows: East of Ohio, I. B. Hollinger, Covington, Ohio; West of Ohio, D. Hollinger, Mt. Morris, Ill.

To Close out

The few copies of the BRETHREN'S ALMANAC still on hand, we offer them at REDUCED PRICES. As long as the supply lasts, we will send them at the rate of five cents per copy post-paid, but to get them you should ORDER NOW.

The Pillar of Fire.—By J. H. Ingraham. Cloth. $1.50.

The Bible the Sunday-school Text-book.—By Alfred Holborn. Cloth. 75 cents.

Origin of Single Immersion.—By Eld. James Quinter. Price, 2 copies, 5 cents; 12 copies, 25 cents; 50 copies, $1.00.

Excursions to California.

Excursions in charge of M. M. Eshelman, Immigration Agent, will leave Chicago every day at 6:30 P. M. Tuesdays, and Kansas City Wednesdays, during the year 1892, on dates as follows:

Chicago, January 26, February 23, March 22, April 26, May 10, June 28, July 26, August 23, September 27, October 25, November 22, December 20.

Kansas City, January 27, February 24, March 23, April 27, May 20, June 29, July 27, August 24, September 28, October 26, November 23, December 21.

Parties wishing to avail themselves of the privileges of these excursions, should write M. M. Eshelman, North Fostoria, California, prior to the 25th of each month, and from the fifteenth to the end of the month, at 509 Union Avenue (opposite Union Depot), Kansas City, Mo., stating when and where they wish to join one of these excursions, and he will give them full information. And if desired will reserve berths in Tourist Sleeping Car for them. Do not fail to write him; he will do you good. The rate will be as low as the lowest made in the Pacific Coast.

GEORGE L. McDONAUGH,
TRAVELING AGENT.

Juvenile Quarterly.

THIS is just the *Quarterly* for the little folks. Price, Three Copies, 20 Cents; 6 Copies, per Quarter, 25 Cents; 10 Copies and over, per Quarter, 3 Cents each.

Brethren's Quarterly.

Orders should be sent in at once for the Quarterly for the First Quarter of 1892. Price, three copies, 25 cents; eight copies, 40 cents; twenty copies and over, four cents each.

For Sale!

GROCERY STORE & MEAT-MARKET

Being desirous of devoting most of my time to Church and Missionary Work, I offer for sale my entire stock and fixture of 519-521 West Van Buren Street, Chicago, Ill. About $1,000 capital will be required to purchase and conduct the business successfully. A good business chance for the right man. Address, W. R. Miller & Bro., 439-441 West Van Buren St., Chicago, Ill.

Windsor
European Hotel

TRIBUNE BLOCK.

145 to 155 Dearborn St. S. Gregory, Prop.

Chicago, Ill.

This hotel is centrally located, and the most respectable House of its class in the City. The charges are moderate, varying in price from 25 cents to $1.50 per day, per person. Thompson's Restaurant underneath. First-class Passenger Elevator.

ESSAYS

"Study to show thyself approved unto God; a workman that needeth not be ashamed, rightly dividing the Word of Truth."

"COME."

BY GERTRUDE A. FLORY.

" Is not this the Christ? "—John 4: 29.

How beautiful and fair!
In form and mien divine!
Like snow, his clustering hair,
His locks whitest and fine.

His eyes with crimson light
Like luminous fire glows;
His lips, like lilies white,
With righteousness o'erflows.

His voice is like the tones
Of flowing water's song;
His temples, palace thrones
Where virtue's beauties throng.

His wondrous face aflame,
Like vivid lightning gleams;
Around his stately frame
Celestial glory streams.

His feet are like fine brass
Burnished by furnace fire;
When sins beneath them pass
They burn with sacred ire.

In accents soft and mild,
To every soul oppressed,
He whispers: Weary child,
Come unto me and rest.

To fears, a holy calm
My spirit doth impart,
Comfort and fragrant balm
To every broken heart.

Come, in my rest is love;
And in my love is power;
For fledglings and the dove
I make a nestling bower.

Far greater is my care
For thee, O, faithless one!
Come, and my blessings share
Ere Time's swift sands are run.

To every sinning soul,
He comes with wooing voice
And pleads: Come, be made whole,
To-day, O, make thy choice!

I am the Way that leads
To life which shall not cease;
I am the Truth that feeds
Each seeking soul with peace.

I am a Living Fount
That quenches thirst and pain;
Up to its waters mount
And "never thirst again!"

Come, taste my grace sublime
And thou shalt hunger not;
I am a Fruitful Vine
Set in a goodly spot.

To thee, I bring employ
Of high and priceless worth;
Bliss, purity and joy,
Not found elsewhere on earth.

And through Time's changing scene,
By waters still and deep,
In pastures fresh and green,
I'll fold thee with my sheep.

Come, feed among the hills,
Where sin doth not alloy;
In valleys, cleft by rills
Of happiness and joy.

He speaks, and sweetest love
Beams in his tender eyes;
His deeds, rich blessings prove;
His life, a sacrifice.

La Porte, Ind., Oct. 19, 1891.

LOCAL OPTION.

BY WM. BIXLER.

APRIL 7 is the time set for giving the people of Springfield, Ohio, an opportunity to say whether they want saloons or not. I thought that, perhaps, a timely word, fitly spoken, might be the means of, at least, doing some good in removing the temptation from our boys and young men in our immediate vicinity. We need scarcely enumerate the evils caused, either directly or indirectly, by selling intoxicants over the bar. Our alms-houses, jails, and penitentiaries, are living witnesses of the heinous crimes resulting therefrom. Go to your County-seats and ask to be shown the records, and, to your surprise, you will find that by far the greater per cent of criminal cases, brought into your courts, originated in some saloon. Who pays the expenses of trying these cases? The tax-payer.

Are we responsible for these crimes and expenses? I say we are, as far as our power goes to prevent them. If, then, we are responsible, it should only be the work of a moment to decide what to do. If we could but fully realize what the consequences may be, of saying, "No, we want no saloon," and that by a silent, "Yes," we are helping establish the evil of all evils, in our midst,—an evil which has not one single thing in it, to recommend it to the public and especially to our children. It does not elevate the morals of a community, neither does it Christianize, but, all on the contrary, it degrades, unchristianizes, breaks up families, and last, but not least, it annually furnishes thousands of victims for a premature grave. It may even land their souls in the region of the damned. Is it not time that we look around us, meet the enemy, and strike the death blow when opportunity is afforded? If this does not find its way into the waste-basket, I hope the editor will kindly endorse what is set forth in this imperfect article.

North Springfield, Ohio.

REMARKS.

Bro. Bixler calls our attention to a very important question, one which we have given a good deal of thought, and have long since determined our course of action. We take no part in political elections. The Brethren have advised against it, and following this advice is not likely to lead any of us into trouble. But local option, where it is entirely free from politics, is another question, concerning which our people are left at liberty to exercise their judgment. At the Annual Meeting at Harrisonburgh, Va., in 1889, it was "*Resolved*, that this Annual Meeting recommend that all our brethren carefully maintain our position against the use, or toleration of intoxicants, whether to manufacture, to sell, or use as a beverage, and to the extent of our influence contribute our part to secure practical prohibition; but we advise against taking part in the public agitation of the subject. Acts 5."

This resolution places us absolutely on the side of prohibition, with instructions to use our influence to secure practical prohibition, but not 'to take part in the *public* agitation of the question. So far as we are concerned personally, we always vote in favor of prohibition whenever the question comes before the people separate and apart from politics. We regard liquor as the greatest curse on the face of the earth, and propose to use our own influence against it on every hand, so far as we can do so in harmony with Gospel principles. When it comes to local option, we never want to see any of our Brethren vote for license. If any of them are conscientiously opposed to voting we have nothing to say, but we hope no one, who calls himself a brother, would venture to endorse the liquor traffic by voting in favor of license. Some years ago the Northern District of Illinois decided that she could not permit any of her members to vote in favor of license. The decision was a good one, and, as far as we know, has been carried out.

This of course has reference mainly to local option, and places our Brethren on record on the right and safe side of that question. We hope never to see the time when our members will be permitted to cast their influence on the side of the gigantic evil that is leading so many of our young men to ruin. Whether our brethren should vote at the election, to which our brother calls attention, must be left optional with them. We are not acquainted with the circumstances and surroundings of that particular case, hence we can venture no advice, but we do say, that it is to the interest of every father and mother to see that they use their influence against saloons on every hand. When it comes to local option here at Mt. Morris, we are deeply concerned, especially on account of the many young people who attend school here. We are glad to say that this is a temperance town, and our Brethren are helping to make it so. They are all on the side of temperance, and though they take no part in the public agitation of the question, yet when it comes to voting on the question, those who wish to go quietly to the polls and cast their influence against saloons of every grade and order; and it so happens, fortunately, that all those connected with the MESSENGER office are among the number who cast their votes, as well as their influence, against the saloon curse.—EDS.

THE SHAMBERGER-BOND DEBATE.

Affirmative Arguments of G. A. Shamberger, with Notes by Levi Mohler, Warrensburgh, Mo.

NUMBER III.

" PROPOSITION.—The washing of the saints' feet is an ordinance of the church, and should be observed by all Christians."

NOTE.—The first case of feet-washing, is in Gen. 18: 4. The character of the Old Testament feet-washing is set forth in the following Scriptures: Gen. 19: 2; 24: 32; 43: 24; Judg. 19: 21; 1 Sam. 25: 41.

This is the ancient custom of feet-washing, and is of great antiquity.

"ARGUMENT 1.—The Scriptures teach that Christ washed the feet of his assembled disciples, and disciples only. John 3: 5. Notice the authority, John 3: 25; Matt. 10: 24, 27. The authority which Christ claimed, just before giving the great commission, he had when he gave the law of feet-washing.

"As early in his ministry as in John 3: 25, Christ said, 'The Father loveth the Son, and hath given all things into his hands.' This is sufficient to prove that Jesus had authority to deliver the Gospel, and establish its laws. They were not an ordinary company, who were with Christ on the night of feet-washing.

"Only twelve apostles were ordained to be with the Son of God during his ministry, to hear him, witness his life, and afterwards to preach him and his doctrine to all the world.

"It was this company whose feet Jesus washed, and to whom he gave the law to wash one another's feet."

"THOUGHT 1.—During three years' going in and out before his disciples, Christ had never before washed their feet."

"THOUGHT 2.—No church ordinance was instituted prior to this night."

✦ESSAYS✦

"Study to show thyself approved unto God; a workman that needeth not be ashamed, rightly dividing the Word of Truth."

"COME."

BY GERTRUDE A. FLORY.

"Is not this the Christ?"—John 4: 29.

How beautiful and fair!
  In form and mien divine!
Like snow, his clustering hair,
  His locks whitest and fine.

His eyes with crimson light
  Like luminous fire glows;
His lips, like lilies white,
  With righteousness o'er-flows.

His voice is like the tones
  Of flowing water's song;
His temples, palace thrones
  Where virtue's beauties throng.

His wondrous face aflame,
  Like vivid lightning gleams;
Around his stately frame
  Celestial glory streams.

His feet are like fine brass
  Burnished by furnace fire;
When sins beneath them pass
  They burn with sacred ire.

In accents soft and mild,
  To every soul oppressed,
He whispers: Weary child,
  Come unto me and rest.

To fears, a holy calm
  My spirit doth impart,
Comfort and fragrant balm
  To every broken heart.

Come, in my rest is love;
  And in my love is power;
For fledglings and the dove
  I make a nestling bower.

Far greater is my care
  For thee, O, faithless one!
Come, and my blessings share
  Ere Time's swift sands are run.

To every sinning soul,
  He comes with wooing voice
And pleads: Come, be made whole,
  To-day, O, make thy choice!

I am the Way that leads
  To life which shall not cease;
I am the Truth that feeds
  Each seeking soul with peace.

I am a Living Fount
  That quenches thirst and pain;
Up to its waters mount
  And "never thirst again!"

Come, taste my grace sublime
  And thou shalt hunger not;
I am a Fruitful Vine
  Set in a goodly spot.

To thee, I bring employ
  Of high and priceless worth;
Bliss, purity and joy,
  Not found elsewhere on earth.

And through Time's changing scene,
  By waters still and deep,
In pastures fresh and green,
  I'll fold thee with my sheep.

Come, feed among the hills,
  Where sin doth not alloy;
In valleys, cleft by rills
  Of happiness and joy.

He speaks, and sweetest love
  Beams in his tender eyes;
His deeds, rich blessings prove;
  His life, a sacrifice.

La Paris, Ind., Oct. 19, 1891.

LOCAL OPTION.

BY WM. BIXLER.

APRIL 7 is the time set for giving the people of Springfield, Ohio, an opportunity to say whether they want saloons or not. I thought that, perhaps, a timely word, fitly spoken, might be the means of, at least, doing some good in removing the temptation from our boys and young men in our immediate vicinity. We need scarcely enumerate the evils caused, either directly or indirectly, by selling intoxicants over the bar. Our alms-houses, jails, and penitentiaries, are living witnesses of the heinous crimes resulting therefrom. Go to your County-seats and ask to be shown the records, and, to your surprise, you will find that by far the greater per cent of criminal cases, brought into your courts, originated in some saloon. Who pays the expenses of trying these cases? The tax-payer.

Are we responsible for these crimes and expenses? I say we are, as far as our power goes to prevent them. If, then, we are responsible, it should only be the work of a moment to decide what to do. If we could but fully realize what the consequences may be, of saying, "No, we want no saloon," and that by a silent, "Yes," we are helping establish the evil of all evils, in our midst,—an evil which has not one single thing in it, to recommend it to the public and especially to our children. It does not elevate the morals of a community, neither does it Christianize, but, all on the contrary, it degrades, unchristianizes, breaks up families, and last, but not least, it annually furnishes thousands of victims for a premature grave. It may even land their souls in the region of the damned. Is it not time that we look around us, meet the enemy, and strike the death blow when opportunity is afforded? If this does not find its way into the waste-basket, I hope the editor will kindly endorse what is set forth in this imperfect article.

North Springfield, Ohio.

REMARKS.

BRO. Bixler calls our attention to a very important question, one which we have given a good deal of thought, and have long since determined our course of action. We take no part in political elections. The Brethren have advised against it, and following this advice is not likely to lead any of us into trouble. But local option, where it is entirely free from politics, is another question, concerning which our people are left at liberty to exercise their judgment. At the Annual Meeting at Harrisonburgh, Va., in 1889, it was "*Resolved,* that this Annual Meeting recommend that all our brethren carefully maintain our position against the use, or toleration of intoxicants, whether to manufacture, to sell, or use as a beverage, and to the extent of our influence contribute our part to secure practical prohibition; but we advise against taking part in the *public* agitation of the subject. Acts 5."

This resolution places us absolutely on the side of prohibition, with instruction to use our influence to secure practical prohibition, but not to take part in the *public* agitation of the question. So far as we are concerned personally, we always vote in favor of prohibition whenever the question comes before the people separate and apart from politics. We regard liquor as the greatest curse on the face of the earth, and propose to use our own influence against it on every hand, so far as we can do so in harmony with Gospel principles. When it comes to local option, we never want to see any of our Brethren vote for license. If any of them are conscientiously opposed to voting we have nothing to say, but we hope no one, who calls himself a brother, would venture to endorse the liquor traffic by voting in favor of license. Some years ago the Northern District of Illinois decided that she could not permit any of her members to vote in favor of license. The decision was a good one, and, as far as we know, has been carried out.

This of course has reference mainly to local option, and places our Brethren on record on the right and safe side of that question. We hope never to see the time when our members will be permitted to cast their influence on the side of the gigantic evil that is leading so many of our young men to ruin. Whether our brethren should vote at the election, to which our brother calls attention, must be left optional with them. We are not acquainted with the circumstances and surroundings of that particular case, hence we can venture no advice, but we do say, that it is to the interest of every father and mother to see that they use their influence against saloons on every hand. When it comes to local option here at Mt. Morris, we are deeply concerned, especially on account of the many young people who attend school here. We are glad to say that this is a temperance town, and our Brethren are helping to make it so. . They are all on the side of temperance, and though they take no part in the public agitation of the question, yet when it comes to voting on the question, those who wish to go quietly to the polls and cast their influence against saloons of every grade and order; and it so happens, fortunately, that all those connected with the MESSENGER office are among the number who cast their votes, as well as their influence, against the saloon curse.—EDS.

THE SHAMBERGER-BOND DEBATE.

Affirmative Arguments of G. A. Shamberger, with Notes by Levi Mohler, Warrensburgh, Mo.

NUMBER III.

"PROPOSITION.—The washing of the saints' feet is an ordinance of the church, and should be observed by all Christians."

NOTE.—The first case of feet-washing is in Gen. 18: 4. The character of the Old Testament feet-washing is set forth in the following Scriptures: Gen. 19: 2; 24: 32; 43: 24; Judg. 19: 21; 1 Sam. 25: 41.

This is the ancient custom of feet-washing, and is of great antiquity.

"ARGUMENT 1.—The Scriptures teach that Christ washed the feet of his assembled disciples, and disciples only. John 3: 5. Notice the authority, John 3: 25; Matt. 10: 24, 27. The authority which Christ claimed, just before giving the great commission, he had when he gave the law of feet-washing.

"As early in his ministry as in John 3: 25, Christ said, 'The Father loveth the Son, and hath given all things into his hands.' This is sufficient to prove that Jesus had authority to deliver the Gospel, and establish its laws. They were not an ordinary company, who were with Christ on the night of feet-washing.

"Only twelve apostles were ordained to be with the Son of God during his ministry, to hear him, witness his life, and afterwards to preach him and his doctrine to all the world.

"It was this company whose feet Jesus washed, and to whom he gave the law to wash one another's feet."

"THOUGHT 1.—During three years' going in and out before his disciples, Christ had never before washed their feet."

"THOUGHT 2.—No church ordinance was instituted prior to this night."

A FEW OF MY THOUGHTS.

BY A. HUTCHISON.

I HAVE just read Bro. Moore's account of the sickness and death of Bro. R. H. Miller, and to describe my thoughts and feelings while reading that article is beyond my power. One thought was, Who will take his place in the church and its work? I confess my inability to find the man, but the Lord's thoughts and ways are so far above, and beyond mine, that I try to be able to say, "The Lord's will be done." But when I look at the necessity for faithful men,—men of God, who are both able and willing to defend the principles of the Gospel, as understood by the church, I confess that I do not see my way to easily yield to what seems to be the inevitable. I can only pray for more faith and more grace. But the blessed thought comes to me that our brother was ready,—having fought a good fight, and thus finished his course, and then the *crown*. O for such a glorious death! May I be ready, too, when the time comes! May every brother and sister feel that the Lord is, by this dispensation, calling us to a greater responsibility, by permitting such faithful standard bearers to be taken from us.

I now introduce a different phase of the subject. While it was the privilege of brethren, sisters and friends to look upon the face of our dear brother, as he was wrestling with the disease, which was praying upon his vitals, and behold the waves rising higher and higher, which seemed to threaten the citadel, and again to recede; so that they could look upon the placid countenance of the man of God, telling them, "All is well,"—I was standing upon the beach, watching the waves of the great deep, as they rolled on toward the shore, until they would reach the beach, and be broken. Then they would recede, and, for a few moments, all would seem calm and serene. But soon another wave would come, even higher and more threatening than the other. This continued as long as we were looking,—causing the writer to form a new, and grand conception of what Isaiah meant when he said, "The wicked are like the troubled sea, when it cannot rest, whose waters cast up mire and dirt." Isa. 57: 20.

If the wicked are so continuously disturbed as the ocean is, it is no wonder that the prophet said, "There is no peace, saith my God, to the wicked." Isa. 57: 21.

And while there were a number of us looking at the same scenery, each one would seemingly have a view of something peculiar to him or herself. But each one could see the one Grand, Great, First Cause back of all that was visible to our natural vision. One only needs to look at the waters of the great deep a few moments, till he is impressed with the force of the expression, "The sea and the waves roaring." Luke 21: 25. It is a grand place to catch a new inspiration concerning the power and greatness of him who could say, "Peace, be still," and the great waves would obey.

As I stood upon the wharf, watching the massive waves roll on, and as I saw how they would lash the beach, and toss the skiffs up and down, and even cause the mighty steamer to sway to and fro, I could readily excuse Peter for his fears when he undertook to walk upon the water in a storm. Indeed I think the number who would do as well as he did, would be very small now. But the grand lesson to be learned is, to call upon Jesus for help in every time of need. He is ready to help.

I find that in every country, as far as I have been permitted to travel, there is every-where presented a medium through which to study the wisdom and power of the Author of our being.

In looking at the passenger steamer, as it approached the landing, the thought occurred, "How grand and beautiful,—how smoothly it glides along on the face of the placid waters! O how pleasant it must be to the inmates to thus approach the shore!" But as the wind seemed to rise higher and higher, it became a question among the spectators as to whether they would dare approach the wharf with the large steamer. Our anxieties were soon quelled when the captain, or mate, came up and signaled the people upon the wharf to stand back, "lest you be toppled over, if we strike the wharf with some force." But the skilled steersman at the helm seemed, to be master of the situation, and all came safely to land, to meet and greet their friends, who were in readiness to receive them and bid them welcome. So we feel that our dear elder, Bro. Miller, was aboard the vessel whose Captain, Steersman, and Mate all knew how to make a safe landing.

LYDIA'S CONVERSION.

BY J. S. FLORY.

THERE are some features in connection with the conversion of this woman of Thyatira, that stand out very prominently and are worthy of imitation. First we notice the two missionaries, Paul and Timotheus, going out to carry the Gospel into Macedonia. In the colony of Philippi they tarried, doubtless looking about for an opportunity to commence an aggressive work against the works of darkness.

On the Sabbath Day, hearing of a prayer-meeting, to be held in God's own ancient sanctuary, we imagine by the side of a beautiful stream, one, doubtless, said to the other, "Let us go out there." They knew a prayer-meeting was a good place to go to. I have no idea that Paul, for a moment, questioned the propriety of the meeting, because it was carried on by women; no, indeed, he always endorsed heartily the efforts of women engaged in the Master's work. He and his co-workers found opportunity to talk of the great salvation. It did not take Paul long to tell them of Christ and the way to get into him. Lydia, through the influence of the Spirit of God, that is always so closely allied to his Word, took heed to the glad tidings and was converted.

Now notice one feature as the outcome of her conversion. She had a heart, overflowing with true, genuine hospitality. Herself the guest of the Lord of lords and King of kings, how could she do otherwise than say to his servants, "Come and abide in my house?" Hers was none of that hollow hospitality that would say with the lips, "Come and see me," while at the threshold of the heart there lingered a hope that they would not. Nay, verily, but it was the very essence of true, genuine hospitality, that would *constrain* them to come, without, for a moment, considering whether everything at home was just in order to entertain them.

She knew and felt that the sweetness of the kindred ties of saintship would make her brothers or sisters welcome to what she had, and that they would enjoy her offerings, though they be but scanty. She felt that the same Blessed Spirit made them one in Christ, and heirs to what she had.

Sharing the one common salvation and the association of the one common brotherhood, why not have temporal things common, especially when engaged in religious work and religious associations? Oh for the day when God's people will show a more solid front of real, brotherly love *for* each other, by each other, and *among* each other! Our ancient sister Lydia's hospitality was not of that kind that seemed aglow with love in earnest entreaties to "Come and see me," "Now be sure and dine with us the first time you come our way," to prove, when the opportunity came, to be blind hospitality, passing by on the other side, cold as an iceberg. Her new-found love of that nature that would express with the lips her ardent devotion for the cause of Christ, while, at heart and in her actions, she would say, in reference to the ministers of God, "I admire your zeal and sacrifice. Go on and do the best you can, but as for me, I have just bought another farm, or built a new house, or bought a yoke of oxen. Then I have that bill to meet for the purpls that I bought last week; therefore I cannot do anything just now; but I shall pray for you."

Lydia's conversion was not of that kind. She had the kind that took Christ to abide in her heart; whether cold or hungry, naked or in prison; she was personally interested in him. She loved Christ, as he dwelt in others as well as in herself, and she would do to others as she would to herself. Therefore, having done it to the least of his disciples, she did it to him. How sad the thought that, in the day of final reckoning, many will be turned away because, in this life, they had opportunity to do good, neglected the opportunity, and did it not. Oh, the depth of meaning in the denunciation of the Divine Judge, "Depart from me; I never knew you!" While you so devotedly read your Bible and take it for granted that you *do* love your Blessed Master, be right sure you really do love his children also, as an evidence that you have passed from death to life.

THE COVERING.—1 Cor. 11: 16.

BY J. M. MOHLER.

THERE is not one command in the Gospel but what is more or less shrouded in mystery. "Love your enemies;" "Bless them that curse you;" "Do good to them that hate you;" "Pray for them that despitefully use you;" "Believe and be baptized;" "Ye must be born again;" eating the Lord's Supper; washing feet; Communion; abstaining from all appearance of evil; rendering evil to no man, and many other commands embody mysteries beyond the conception of the human or finite mind. As to the development of the soul, spiritually, by a literal obedience of the commands of Jesus, we know not, i. e., we cannot fully know how the soul is developed, *spiritually*, yet, in a measure, those commands are simple and plain, if, we do not add confusion by wrong interpretations.

What is true of one command is equally true of another. It is a very easy matter for one who is unprejudiced, or circumcised in heart and in ears, to know that the hair never was, neither can it be used for a covering on the part of Christian women in time of worship, so as to be approved and acceptable to God. Heathen ladies, in offering their sacrifices to Bacchus, who was the god of wine, and in general of earthly festivity, jollity and revelry, had their faces uncovered and their hair dishevelled, i. e., flowing around their faces, ears and heads, in disorder, loosely and in confusion. Corinth was celebrated for the great wealth of its temple of Venus, the goddess of love. Now those Corinthian or Christian women, in imitation of those heathen ladies, for the female sex is very fond and especially prone to follow the fashions, did cast off their coverings, or veils, and simply used their hair, in imitation of those heathen ladies. Thus they dishonored their own heads as well as their economical [domestic] head, or man. Hence the necessity of Paul correcting them, and teaching them that the religion of Jesus Christ was not built on manners, customs and fashions of heathens.- If the hair, as a covering for worship, would have been acceptable to God, there would have been no need of correction.

Is it possible that any person of intelligence can conceive that the hair can be worn as a covering acceptable to God in time of worship? Just

A FEW OF MY THOUGHTS.

BY A. HUTCHISON.

I HAVE just read Bro. Moore's account of the sickness and death of Bro. R. H. Miller, and to describe my thoughts and feelings while reading that article is beyond my power. One thought was, Who will take his place in the church and its work? I confess my inability to find the man, but the Lord's thoughts and ways are so far above, and beyond mine, that I try to be able to say, "The Lord's will be done." But when I look at the necessity for faithful men,—men of God, who are both able and willing to defend the principles of the Gospel, as understood by the church, I confess that I do not see my way to easily yield to what seems to be the inevitable. I can only pray for more faith and more grace. But the blessed thought comes to me that our brother was ready,—having fought a good fight, and thus finished his course, and then the crown. O for such a glorious death! May I be ready, too, when the time comes! May every brother and sister feel that the Lord is, by this dispensation, calling us to a greater responsibility, by permitting such faithful standard bearers to be taken from us.

I now introduce a different phase of the subject. While it was the privilege of brethren, sisters and friends to look upon the face of our dear brother, as he was wrestling with the disease, which was preying upon his vitals, and behold the waves rising higher and higher, which seemed to threaten the citadel, and again to recede, so that they could look upon the placid countenance of the man of God, telling them, "All is well,"—I was standing upon the beach, watching the waves of the great deep, as they rolled on toward the shore, until they would reach the beach, and be broken. Then they would recede, and, for a few moments, all would seem calm and serene. But soon another wave would come, even higher and more threatening than the other. This continued as long as we were looking,—causing the writer to have a new, and grand conception of what Isaiah meant when he said, "The wicked are like the troubled sea, when it cannot rest, whose waters cast up mire and dirt." Isa. 57: 20.

If the wicked are so continuously disturbed as the ocean is, it is no wonder that the prophet said, "There is no peace, saith my God, to the wicked." Isa. 57: 21.

And while there were a number of us looking at the same scenery, each one would seemingly have a view of something peculiar to him or herself. But each one could see the one Grand, Great, First Cause back of all that was visible to our natural vision. One only needs to look at the waters of the great deep a few moments, till he is impressed with the force of the expression, " The sea and the waves roaring." Luke 21: 25. It is a grand place to catch a new inspiration concerning the power and greatness of him who could say, " Peace, be still," and the great waves would obey.

As I stood upon the wharf, watching the massive waves roll on, and as I saw how they would lash the beach, and toss the skiffs up and down, and even cause the mighty steamer to sway to and fro, I could readily excuse Peter for his fears when he undertook to walk upon the water in a storm. Indeed I think the number who would do as well as he did, would be very small now. But the grand lesson to be learned is, to call upon Jesus for help in every time of need. He is ready to help.

I find that in every country, as far as I have been permitted to travel, there is every-where presented a medium through which to study the wisdom and power of the Author of our being.

In looking at the passenger steamer, as it approached the landing, the thought occurred, "How grand and beautiful,—how smoothly it glides along on the face of the placid waters! O how pleasant it must be to the inmates to thus approach the shore!" But as the wind seemed to rise higher and higher, it became a question among the spectators as to whether they would dare approach the wharf with the large steamer. Our anxieties were soon quelled when the captain, or mate, came up and signaled the people upon the wharf to stand back, "lest you be toppled over, if we strike the wharf with some force." But the skilled steersman at the helm seemed, to be master of the situation, and all came safely to land, to meet and greet their friends, who were in readiness to receive them and bid them welcome. So we feel that our dear elder, Bro. Miller, was aboard the vessel whose Captain, Steersman, and Mate all knew how to make a safe landing.

LYDIA'S CONVERSION.

BY J. S. FLORY.

THERE are some features in connection with the conversion of this woman of Thyatira, that stand out very prominently and are worthy of imitation. First we notice the two missionaries, Paul and Timotheus, going out to carry the Gospel into Macedonia. In the colony of Philippi they tarried, doubtless looking about for an opportunity to commence an aggressive work against the works of darkness.

On the Sabbath Day, hearing of a prayer-meeting, to be held in God's own ancient sanctuary, we imagine by the side of a beautiful stream, one, doubtless, said to the other, "Let us go out there." They knew a prayer-meeting was a good place to go to. I have no idea that Paul, for a moment, questioned the propriety of the meeting, because it was carried on by women; no, indeed, he always endorsed heartily the efforts of women engaged in the Master's work. He and his co-workers found opportunity to talk of the great salvation. It did not take Paul long to tell them of Christ and the way to get into him. Lydia, through the influence of the Spirit of God, that is always so closely allied to his Word, took heed to the glad tidings and was converted.

Now notice one feature as the outcome of her conversion. She had a heart, overflowing with true, genuine hospitality. Herself the guest of the Lord of lords and King of kings, how could she do otherwise than say to his servants, "Come and abide in my house?" Hers was none of that hollow hospitality that would say with the lips, "Come and see me," while at the threshold of the heart there lingered a hope that they would not. Nay, verily, but it was the very essence of true, genuine hospitality, that would constrain them to come, without, for a moment, considering whether everything at home was just in order to entertain them.

She knew and felt that the sweetness of the kindred ties of saintship would make her brothers or sisters welcome to what she had, and that they would enjoy her offerings, though they be but scanty. She felt that the same Blessed Spirit made them one in Christ, and heirs to what she had.

Sharing the one common salvation and the association of the one common brotherhood, why not have temporal things common, especially when engaged in religious work and religious associations? Oh for the day when God's people will show a more solid front of real, brotherly love for each other, by each other, and among each other! Our ancient sister Lydia's hospitality was not of that kind that seemed aglow with love in earnest entreaties to "Come and see me," "Now be sure and dine with us the first time you come our way," to prove, when the opportunity came, to be blind hospitality, passing by on the other side, cold as an iceberg. Her new-found love of that nature that would express with the lips her ardent devotion for the cause of Christ, while, at heart and in her actions, she would say, in reference to the ministers of God, "I admire your zeal and sacrifice. Go on and do the best you can, but as for me, I have just bought another farm, or built a new house, or bought a yoke of oxen. Then I have that bill to meet for the purple that I bought last week; therefore I cannot do anything just now; but I shall pray for you."

Lydia's conversion was not of that kind. She had the kind that took Christ to abide in her heart; whether cold or hungry, naked or in prison; she was personally interested in him. She loved Christ, as he dwelt in others as well as in herself, and she would do to others as she would to herself. Therefore, having done it to the least of his disciples, she did it to him. How sad the thought that, in the day of final reckoning, many will be turned away because, in this life, they had opportunity to do good, neglected the opportunity, and did it not. Oh, the depth of meaning in the denunciation of the Divine Judge, "Depart from me; I never knew you!" While you so devotedly read your Bible and take it for granted that you do love your Blessed Master, be right sure you really do love his children also, as an evidence that you have passed from death to life.

THE COVERING.—1 Cor. 11: 16.

BY J. M. MOHLER.

THERE is not one command in the Gospel but what is more or less shrouded in mystery. "Love your enemies;" "Bless them that curse you;" "Do good to them that hate you;" "Pray for them that despitefully use you;" "Believe and be baptized;" "Ye must be born again;" eating the Lord's Supper; washing feet; Communion; abstaining from all appearance of evil; rendering evil to no man, and many other commands embody mysteries beyond the conception of the human or finite mind. As to the development of the soul, spiritually, by a literal obedience of the commands of Jesus, we know not, i. e., we cannot fully know how the soul is developed, spiritually, yet, in a measure, those commands are simple and plain, if we do not add confusion by wrong interpretations.

What is true of one command is equally true of another. It is a very easy matter for one who is unprejudiced, or circumcised in heart and in ears, to know that the hair never was, neither can it be used for a covering on the part of Christian women in time of worship, so as to be approved and acceptable to God. Heathen ladies, in offering their sacrifices to Bacchus, who was the god of wine, and in general of earthly festivity, jollity and revelry, had their faces uncovered and their hair disheveled, i. e., flowing around their faces, ears and heads, in disorder, loosely and in confusion. Corinth was celebrated for the great wealth of its temple of Venus, the goddess of love. Now those Corinthian or Christian women, in imitation of those heathen ladies, for the female sex is very fond and exceedingly prone to follow the fashions, did cast off their coverings, or veils, and simply used their hair, in imitation of those heathen ladies. Thus they dishonored their own heads as well as their economical [domestic] head, or man. Hence the necessity of Paul correcting them, and teaching them that the religion of Jesus Christ was not built on manners, customs and fashions of heathens. If the hair, as a covering for worship, would have been acceptable to God, these would have been no need of correction.

Is it possible that any person of intelligence can conceive that the hair can be worn as a covering acceptable to God in time of worship? Just

Missionary and Tract Work Department.

"Upon the first day of the week, let every one of you lay by him in store as God hath prospered him, that there be no gatherings when I come."—1 Cor. 16: 2.

"Every man as he purposeth in his heart, so let him give. Not grudgingly or of necessity, for the Lord loveth a cheerful giver."—2 Cor. 9: 7.

HOW MUCH SHALL WE GIVE?

"Every man according to his ability." "Every one as God hath prospered him." "Every man, according as he purposeth in his heart, so let him give." "For if there be first a willing mind, it is accepted according to that a man hath, and not according to that he hath not."—2 Cor. 8: 12.

Organization of Missionary Committee.

DANIEL VANIMAN, Foreman, - - McPherson, Kans.
D. L. MILLER, Treasurer, - - - Mt. Morris, Ill.
GALEN B. ROYER, Secretary, - - - Mt. Morris, Ill.

Organization of Book and Tract Work.

S. W. HOOVER, Foreman, - - - Dayton, Ohio.
S. BOCK, Secretary and Treasurer, - - Dayton, Ohio.

☞All donations intended for Missionary Work should be sent to GALEN B. ROYER, Mt. Morris, Ill.

☞All money for Tract Work should be sent to S. BOCK, Dayton, Ohio.

☞Money may be sent by Money Order, Registered Letter, or Drafts on New York or Chicago. Do not send personal checks, or drafts on interior towns, as it costs 25 cents to collect them.

☞Solicitors are requested to faithfully carry out the plan of Annual Meeting, that all our members be solicited to contribute at least twice a year for the Mission and Tract Work of the Church.

☞Notes for the Endowment Fund can be had by writing to the Secretary of either Work.

BREAKING BREAD.

BY JOSEPH FAHNESTOCK.

IN GOSPEL MESSENGER No. 8, some reasons are given why the sisters should not be allowed to break the bread of Communion. It is claimed that the breaking of bread is an official work and that which is official is done or performed by an officer. Now, if breaking of bread is an official work, feet-washing is also. If they would be consistent, those who contend that it is an official work should also insist that the elders perform the work, just as Christ broke the bread to all the members and washed their feet.

It is claimed that all men are eligible to office and hence have a right to break bread. Paul (1 Tim. 3) shows us plainly that all men are not eligible, or suitable for office and can not be put into office. Paul tells us whose duty and privilege it is to break bread (1 Cor. 10: 16, 17). "The bread which we break; for we being many are one bread and one body." This includes the whole church, —male and female. The word we is not used here in the singular, as some writers use it, for themselves, but evidently means the whole church; therefore all have the right to break bread and engage in the other ordinances belonging to the church. The duty of the elders is to oversee things, that there be order and that all be done according to the Gospel, but nowhere does the Gospel show that there shall be any difference between the lay members, as regards the service, for they are all one in Christ, therefore the service must be the same for both. Another reason given for the present practice is, that man did not help to crucify Christ, but that man committed the crime. How can that best fit the man? Does sinning fit a person to serve the Lord? It is a strange idea to me.

Again it is argued that, inasmuch as the woman first sinned and handed life away, therefore the man must hand it back by the bread of Communion. This bread of the Communion is for another purpose. It is to represent Christ's broken body and to be taken in remembrance of him. Inasmuch as life was lost through the woman, God saw fit to send life back again through the woman. Through Mary a higher life was brought than that which was lost. How highly God honored her! But if she were here, would she be allowed to break bread? The decision of the church, as it now stands, would say, "No." Elizabeth, mother of John, would fare the same way. Let us look into the Old Dispensation and there see how God honored women by giving them prophetic gifts, that through them priest and king could hear from God. Miriam, Deborah and Hulda were prophets of God. Man is the head of the woman, but man has no right to take Scripture rights from her. Now, if Christ's death was not the same for the women as for the men, then there would be cause for difference, but I am satisfied that Christ died the same for the women as for the men, and as they are as near and dear to the Savior as the men, and as their hands are good enough to prepare the Communion bread, they ought all to share alike. True and genuine sisters are sisters to Christ, and to deny Christ's own sisters to break bread, I believe is wrong.

When Bro. Quinter honored me with a visit shortly before his death, he expressed himself as being strongly in favor of the sisters breaking bread, and said he did not feel like leaving the matter as it had been heretofore.

A HINT TO PREACHERS.

A STORY is told of a preacher who once went to a distinguished tragedian and asked of him why it was that actors, who recited fiction, could enchain the attention of an audience so much more closely than preachers, who spoke the truth. The well-known answer was: "It is because you speak truth as if it was fiction, while we actors speak fiction as if it was truth." We have often thought of this as we have listened to a minister in his public ministrations. Outside of the pulpit, in the social circle, we have found him simple, natural, and interesting, but as soon as he ascended the pulpit steps he would put off the man and put on the minister. Instead of his natural tones a clerical air and tone were assumed that were never witnessed outside of the pulpit. The reading was in an unnatural key, the prayer was spoken in tones that no mortal ever assumed when really engaged in earnest petition, and the discourse was delivered in a stilted, artificial style. The supposed holy tone and manner assumed showed that the preacher was acting. He was speaking truth as if it was fiction. On the other hand, the good actor conceals his acting and speaks fiction as though it was truth. It would be immeasurable gain if preachers would cease to advertise that they are actors. Let them be earnest, natural, themselves. It makes the irreligious think that religion may be a sham, to see that the preacher is shamming.—Christian Evangelist.

CORRESPONDENCE.

"Write what thou seest, and send it unto the churches."

☞Church News solicited for this Department. If you have had a good meeting, send a report of it, so that others may rejoice with you. In writing give name of church, County and State. Be brief. Notes of Travel should be as short as possible. Land Advertisements are not solicited for this Department. We have an advertising page, and, if necessary, will issue supplements.

Anointed with Oil in the Name of the Lord.

THIS was surely complied with in this case. Our elder, S. H. Bechtelheimer, of the Lower Deer Creek church, Middle Indiana, was taken down with lung fever, and being very sick, called for the elders, according to the directions of the apostle James. The elders called, were our aged brother, Hiel Hamilton, who is eighty-two years old, and our still older brother, John Shively, in his 87th year. Feb. 20 they were called, and at that time it rained all day. When we saw those two aged brethren come a distance of five miles through the rain, the thought suggested itself to us, if all of our brethren and sisters would discharge their duty as those old brethren did, the light would be so great that the world could not help but be constrained to glorify God. We realize that the prayers of faith have saved the sick, and that the Lord has raised him up. At this writing, March 14, our brother seems to be out of danger. The Lord be praised! ISAAC CRIPE.

Camden, Ind.

From Harleysville, Pa.

THE series of meetings, conducted by Bro. I. J. Rosenberger in Montgomery County, Pa., has now closed. His discourses were direct and tangible, and were freighted with Gospel commands and promises. Our brother wielded the Sword of the Spirit fearlessly, and the result was that saints rejoiced and resolved to press on toward the mark. Sinners pronounced their willingness to forsake sin and turn their feet toward the testimonies of the Lord. There was a general shaking of the dry bones.

An interesting feature of Bro. Rosenberger's work at this place was a discussion with Eld. Schrock, an Adventist Missionary, who is mystifying the minds of the people in our towns. Bro. Rosenberger made a clean sweep of all he undertook. He left not one stone unturned, thus proving that Christ is the end of the law and by it no flesh shall be justified. He proved that the keeping of Sabbaths, dreams, visions, etc., can never make the comers thereunto perfect, assuring us that we have come to Mt. Zion, the city of God, which speaketh better things. By the elder's display, we concluded he fully realized the critical position in which he was placed. He certainly was driven to the wall. May God bless our brother's labors and finally receive him into glory!

KATIE S. HARLEY.

March 16.

From the Cedar Lake Church, Ind.

MARCH 12 we held our quarterly council. The greater part of the business that came before the meeting was disposed of to the satisfaction of all. Our elder, James Barton, presided, assisted by Eld. Jacob Gump, of the Cedar Creek church. As is sometimes the case in church councils, we may not all see alike, but let us use charity towards others. Let us set our mark too low! What we, as a church, want, is more consecration. We want more vital piety, and we should have our hearts and lives dedicated to God. I firmly believe that the church is built on the Rock, Christ Jesus.

May God bless the MESSENGER! Eternity alone can tell the great amount of good that it is doing. We have appointed our love-feast for June 2.

J. H. ELSON.

Fairfield Center, Ind.

Ministerial Meeting.

THE following is the program of the Ministerial Meeting of Southern Ohio, to be held in the Lower Stillwater church (upper house) May 28, 1892, commencing at 9 o'clock A. M.:

1. "The Church and its Mission." — John Smith, J. C. Bright.

2. "Relations of the Ministry and Laity and their Relation to Each Other." — Bennett Trout, Jesse Kinsie.

3. "Sunday-school — How to Conduct — and its Relation to the Church." — D. D. Wine, E. B. Bagwell.

4. "What will Inspire our Churches with more Earnestness and Zeal?" — Tobias Kreider, Samuel Horning.

Missionary and Tract Work Department.

"Upon the first day of the week, let every one of you lay by him in store as God hath prospered him, that there be no gatherings when I come."—1 Cor. 16: 2.

"Every man as he purposeth in his heart, so let him give. Not grudgingly or of necessity, for the Lord loveth a cheerful giver."—2 Cor. 9: 7.

HOW MUCH SHALL WE GIVE?

"Every man *according to his ability.*" "Every one *as God hath prospered him.*" "Every man, *according as he purposeth in his heart*, so let him give." "For if there be first a willing mind, it is accepted *according to that a man hath*, and not according to that he hath not."—2 Cor. 8: 12.

Organization of Missionary Committee.

DANIEL VANIMAN, Foreman,	- - -	McPherson, Kans.
D. L. MILLER, Treasurer,	- - -	Mt. Morris, Ill.
GALEN B. ROYER, Secretary,	- - -	Mt. Morris, Ill.

Organization of Book and Tract Work.

S. W. HOOVER, Foreman,	- - -	Dayton, Ohio.
S. BOCK, Secretary and Treasurer,	- - -	Dayton, Ohio.

☞All donations intended for Missionary Work should be sent to GALEN B. ROYER, Mt. Morris, Ill.

☞All money for Tract Work should be sent to S. BOCK, Dayton, Ohio.

☞Money may be sent by Money Order, Registered Letter, or Drafts on New York or Chicago. Do not send personal checks, or drafts on interior towns, as it costs 25 cents to collect them.

☞Solicitors are requested to faithfully carry out the plan of Annual Meeting, that all our members be solicited to contribute at least twice a year for the Mission and Tract Work of the Church.

☞Notes for the Endowment Fund can be had by writing to the Secretary of either Work.

BREAKING BREAD.

BY JOSEPH FAHNESTOCK.

IN GOSPEL MESSENGER No. 8, some reasons are given why the sisters should not be allowed to break the bread of Communion. It is claimed that the breaking of bread is an official work and that which is official is done or performed by an officer. Now, if breaking of bread is an official work, feet-washing is also. If they would be consistent, those who contend that it is an official work should also insist that the elders perform the work, just as Christ broke the bread to *all* the members and washed their feet.

It is claimed that all men are eligible to office and hence have a right to break bread. Paul (1 Tim. 3) shows us plainly that all men are *not* eligible, or suitable for office and can not be put into office. Paul tells us whose duty and privilege it is to break bread (1 Cor. 10: 16, 17). "The bread which we break; for we being many are one bread and one body." This includes the whole church, —male and female. The word *we* is not used here in the singular, as some writers use it, for themselves, but evidently means the whole church; therefore all have the right to break bread and engage in the other ordinances belonging to the church. The duty of the elders is to oversee things, that there be order and that all be done according to the Gospel, but nowhere does the Gospel show that there shall be any difference between the lay members, as regards the service, for they are all one in Christ, therefore the service must be the same for both. Another reason given for the present practice is, that woman did not help to crucify Christ, but that man committed the crime. How can that best fit the men? Does sinning fit a person to serve the Lord? It is a strange idea to me.

Again it is argued that, inasmuch as the woman first sinned and handed life away, therefore the man must hand it back by the bread of Communion. This bread of the Communion is for another purpose. It is to represent Christ's broken body and to be taken in remembrance of him. Inasmuch as life was lost through the woman, God saw fit to send life back again through the woman. Through Mary a higher life was brought than that which was lost. How highly God honored

her! But if she were here, would she be allowed to break bread? The decision of the church, as it now stands, would say, "No." Elizabeth, mother of John, would fare the same way. Let us look into the Old Dispensation and there see how God honored women by giving them prophetic gifts, that through them priest and king could hear from God. Miriam, Deborah and Hulda were prophets of God. Man is the head of the woman, but man has no right to take Scripture rights from her. Now, if Christ's death was not the game for the women as for the men, then there would be cause for difference, but I am satisfied that Christ died the same for the women as for the men, and as they are as near and dear to the Savior as the men, and as their hands are good enough to prepare the Communion bread, they ought all to share alike. True and genuine sisters are sisters to Christ, and to deny Christ's own sisters to break bread, I believe is wrong.

When Bro. Quinter honored me with a visit shortly before his death, he expressed himself as being strongly in favor of the sisters breaking bread, and said he did not feel like leaving the matter as it had been heretofore.

A HINT TO PREACHERS.

A STORY is told of a preacher who once went to a distinguished tragedian and asked of him why it was that actors, who recited fiction, could enchain the attention of an audience so much more closely than preachers, who spoke the truth. The well-known answer was: "It is because you speak truth as if it was fiction, while we actors speak fiction as if it was truth." We have often thought of this as we have listened to a minister in his public ministrations. Outside of the pulpit, in the social circle, we have found him simple, natural, and interesting, but as soon as he ascended the pulpit steps he would put off the man and put on the minister. Instead of his natural tones a clerical air and tone were assumed that were never witnessed outside of the pulpit. The reading was in an unnatural key, the prayer was spoken in tones that no mortal ever assumed when really engaged in earnest petition, and the discourse was delivered in a stilted, artificial style. The supposed holy tone and manner assumed showed that the preacher was *acting.* He was speaking truth as if it was fiction. On the other hand, the good actor conceals his acting and speaks fiction as though it was truth. It would be immeasurable gain if preachers would cease to advertise that they are actors. Let them be earnest, natural, *themselves.* It makes the irreligious think that religion may be a sham, to see that the preacher is shamming.—*Christian Evangelist.*

CORRESPONDENCE.

"Write what thou seest, and send it unto the churches."

☞Church News solicited for this Department. If you have had a good meeting, send a report of it, so that others may rejoice with you. In writing give name of church, County and State. Be brief, Notes of Travel should be as short as possible. Land Advertisements are not solicited for this Department. We have an advertising page, and, if necessary, will issue supplements.

Anointed with Oil in the Name of the Lord.

THIS was surely complied with in this case. Our elder, S. H. Bechtelheimer, of the Lower Deer Creek church, Middle Indiana, was taken down with lung fever, and being very sick, called for the elders, according to the directions of the apostle James. The elders called, were our aged brother, Hiel Hamilton, who is eighty-two years old, and our still older brother, John Shively, in his 87th year. Feb. 29 they were called, and at that time it rained all day. When we saw those two aged brethren come a distance of five miles

through the rain, the thought suggested itself to us, if all of our brethren and sisters would discharge their duty as those old brethren did, the light would be so great that the world could not help but be constrained to glorify God. We realize that the prayers of faith have saved the sick, and that the Lord has raised him up. At this writing, March 14, our brother seems to be out of danger. The Lord be praised! ISAAC CRIPE.

Camden, Ind.

From Harleysville, Pa.

THE series of meetings, conducted by Bro. I. J. Rosenberger in Montgomery County, Pa., has now closed. His discourses were direct and tangible, and were freighted with Gospel commands and promises. Our brother wielded the Sword of the Spirit fearlessly, and the result was that saints rejoiced and resolved to press on toward the mark. Sinners pronounced their willingness to forsake sin and turn their feet toward the testimonies of the Lord. There was a general shaking of the dry bones.

An interesting feature of Bro. Rosenberger's work at this place was a discussion with Eld. Schrock, an Adventist Missionary, who is mystifying the minds of the people in our towns. Bro. Rosenberger made a clean sweep of all he undertook. He left not one stone unturned, thus proving that Christ is the end of the law and by it no flesh shall be justified. He proved that the keeping of Sabbaths, dreams, visions, etc., can never make the comers thereunto perfect, assuring us that we have come to Mt. Zion, the city of God, which speaketh better things. By the elder's display, we concluded he fully realized the critical position in which he was placed. He certainly was driven to the wall. May God bless our brother's labors and finally receive him into glory! KATIE S. HARLEY.

March 16.

From the Cedar Lake Church, Ind.

MARCH 12 we held our quarterly council. The greater part of the business that came before the meeting was disposed of to the satisfaction of all. Our elder, James Barton, presided, assisted by Eld. Jacob Gump, of the Cedar Creek church. As is sometimes the case in church councils, we may not all see alike, but let us use charity towards others. Let us not set our mark too low! What we, as a church, want, is more consecration. We want more vital piety, and we should have our hearts and lives dedicated to God. I firmly believe that the church is built on the Rock, Christ Jesus.

May God bless the MESSENGER! Eternity alone can tell the great amount of good that it is doing. We have appointed our love-feast for June 2.

J. H. ELSON.

Fairfield Center, Ind.

Ministerial Meeting.

THE following is the program of the Ministerial Meeting of Southern Ohio, to be held in the Lower Stillwater church (upper house) May 26, 1892, commencing at 8 o'clock A. M.:

1. "The Church and its Mission."—John Smith, J. C. Bright.

2. "Relations of the Ministry and Laity and their Relation to Each Other."—Bennett Trout, Jesse Kinzie.

3. "Sunday-school—How to Conduct—and its Relation to the Church."—D. D. Wine, E. B. Bagwell.

4. "What will Inspire our Churches with more Earnestness and Zeal?"—Tobias Kreider, Samuel Horning.

The Gospel Messenger,

A Weekly at $1.50 Per Annum.

PUBLISHED BY

The Brethren's Publishing Co.

D. L. MILLER,	. . . .	Editor.
J. H. MOORE,	. . . . .	Office Editor.
J. B. BRUMBAUGH, }	. . . . .	Associate Editors.
J. G. ROYER, }		
JOSEPH AMICK,	. . . .	Business Manager.

ADVISORY COMMITTEE.

R. H. Miller, A. Hutchison, Daniel Hays.

☞ Communications for publication should be legibly written with black ink on one side of the paper only. Do not attempt to interline, or to put on one page what ought to occupy two.

☞ Anonymous communications will not be published.

☞ Do not mix business with articles for publication. Keep your communications on separate sheets from all business.

☞ Time is precious. We always have time to attend to business and to answer questions of importance, but please do not subject us to need less answering of letters.

☞ The MESSENGER is mailed each week to all subscribers. If the address is correctly entered on our list, the paper must reach the person to whom it is addressed. If you do not get your paper, write us, giving particulars.

☞ When changing your address, please give your former as well as your future address in full, so as to avoid delay and misunderstanding.

☞ Always remit to the office from which you offer your goods, no matter from which you receive them.

☞ Do not send personal checks or drafts on interior banks, unless you send with them 25 cents each, to pay for collection.

☞ Remittances should be made by Post-office Money Order, Drafts on New York, Philadelphia or Chicago, or Registered Letters, made payable and addressed to " Brethren's Publishing Co., Mount Morris, Ill.," or " Brethren's Publishing Co., Huntingdon, Pa."

☞ Entered at the Post-office at Mount Morris, Ill., as second-class matter.

Mount Morris, Ill.,   · · · ·   April 5, 1892.

BRO. JACOB TOMBAUGH, of Gratiot County, Mich., has changed his post-office from New Haven Center to Middleton.

BRO. NOAH LONGANECKER may now be addressed at Hartville, Stark Co., Ohio, instead of North Industry, his former address.

WE feel to thank God that the most of our best preachers come from the humble walks of life. There is a chance for the poor to become useful.

BRO. B. F. MILLER, of Alpena, S. D., writes that Bro. J. W. Trostle, of Iowa, recently visited that place and preached two excellent sermons.

FROM the Southern Californian we learn, that Bro. John W. Metzger and wife, who have been spending the winter in California, will return to their home in Indiana, this week.

ELD. SAMUEL MURRAY, of River, Ind., we are informed, is quite sick, being affected with an abscess on the liver. When last heard from, he was suffering intensely. He desires the prayers of the members.

A CARD from Clayton, Ohio, informs us that Eld. John Sollenberger, of the Salem church, died on the morning of March 22. No particulars are given. We are promised a more extended notice of his death.

THE Boon River church, Iowa, is making arrangements to build a meeting-house the coming summer. The church is greatly in need of an English preacher. It is to be hoped that some one will locate there to help the good work along.

BRO. J. G. ROYER is spending a few weeks in the East. He will visit the places mentioned below as the dates are given: Loudenville, Ohio, April 2 to 5; New Berlin, Ohio, April 6 to 11; Rossville, Ohio, April 12 to 13; District Meeting of the First District of Virginia, April 15 and 18; District Meeting of Eastern Maryland, April 19.

"MANY lose the opportunity of saying a kind thing by waiting to weigh the matter too long."

THE church at Johnstown, Pa., seems to be moving along encouragingly. Eighteen have been received into the church there since the beginning of the present year.

A CARD from Bro. Landon West informs us that he is holding a series of meetings among the colored people at Washington C. H., Ohio, with considerable interest manifested. Two white men made the good confession and were baptized.

WE are in receipt of Minutes of the District Meeting of Middle Missouri. Considerable business was before the meeting. One query goes to the Annual Meeting. Bro. David Bowman will represent the District on the Standing Committee.

A VERY destructive cyclone passed through Cerro Gordo, Ill., the 27th of last month, doing considerable damage, but fortunately no lives were lost. Bro. Geo. W. Cripe will tell our readers about it next week. His communication reached us too late for this issue.

THE article in No. 11, page 167, credited to S. M. Miller, of Waterloo, Iowa, should have been West Cairo, Ohio. The article came to us without any post-office address attached, and thinking that it was from the Bro. S. M. Miller at Waterloo, we were led into the mistake which is hereby corrected.

WE are informed that the interesting story, going the rounds of the papers, about Bro. John Herr having caught two thieves in the act of stealing, etc., is unfounded. We are glad that the report is untrue, but the story was certainly an interesting one, and taught most excellent non-resistant Christian doctrine.

AN institution, known as the Woman's Mission Home, in Nashville, Tenn., has already rescued over two hundred and twenty-five young women from a life of infamy, and is now seeking to enlarge its capacity by erecting a building that is to cost $16,000. We feel like encouraging such enterprises, for they certainly prove a help to suffering humanity.

THE Ministerial Meeting for Southern Ohio has an excellent program for consideration. See notice in this issue. There will be but six subjects before the Meeting, and we hardly know which is the most important. We like the idea of having but few subjects, and then discuss them well. We hope other Districts will consider this suggestion.

WE are still receiving questions concerning John's baptism, all of which are clearly answered in the several articles we have written on that subject. We will be pleased to answer any new points, but do not care to repeat what we have already written. Some of the new questions we may answer when we can spare the space, but questions already answered we will not answer again.

THE committee appointed by the Annual Meeting Committee, to assist in the sale of the old meeting-house in East Dayton, Ohio, met March 21, and let the contract for a new brick house, 40 by 60 feet, to be heated by furnace. The building is to be of first-class material throughout, and when completed, will cost about $5,000. This cost includes the ground, which is said to be well located. This means a hew, and, we hope, prosperous era in the history of the East Dayton church.

ELD. DAVID BECHTELHEIMER, of Adams County, Nebr., after an absence of several months, traveling in Iowa, Illinois and Indiana, has returned to his home. He left home last November, and since then has done considerable preaching, and also visited the scenes of his early life. He found many changes had taken place since he was elected to the ministry forty-three years ago.

RECENTLY an entire edition of a paper in Arizona was thrown out of the mails under the Anti-lottery law; it had given an account of a piano raffle. What must be done with papers containing accounts of raffles at churches? It will be a sad comment on Christianity when the law of the land must take hold of churches and compel them to do what is right. Surely there is need of reformation in many of the churches.

SUNDAY is the Lord's Day, because he arose from the dead on that day. The day is therefore set apart in commemoration of his resurrection from the dead, and on that day we should not forsake the assembling of ourselves together, as the manner of some is. Under the Old Law the Sabbath, or Saturday, was the consecrated day, but a change of law, as well as a change in the priesthood, has brought into existence a new day, hence the Lord's Day, or the first day of the week, as it is sometimes called.

THERE are three baptisms distinctly taught in the New Testament. First, the baptism in water. This was first administered by John, but afterwards by the disciples of Christ, and is to be continued by the servants of Christ until the close of the present dispensation. It is the only baptism that man is authorized to administer. Second, the baptism in the Holy Ghost. This is done by Jesus and God alone, and is for the benefit of all the penitent ones who have been properly baptized in water. This baptism man cannot administer. It is reserved exclusively for divine hands. The third baptism is that of fire, intended for the wicked. The power to administer this is also entrusted exclusively to the power that is divine. Of these three baptisms, the one in water is the only one which man is authorized to administer, though he may pray for the performance of the second and warn the sinner of the danger of the third. He who properly receives and profits by the first and second, will escape the third, but he who ignores the first will be deprived of the second, and must then endure the horrors of the third.

"FIRST Principles and Perfection," by J. S. Lamar, is the title of an excellent, well-bound book of 288 pages, sent us by the Standard Publishing Co., Cincinnati, Ohio. The author discusses the first principles of the doctrine of Christ in a clear and forcible manner. Analytically it is the best treatise on that question that we have ever read, and as a general thing, is quite reliable, though somewhat conservative on a few points. The chapters on "Going on to Perfection" open up a line of thought new to most readers. We would urge a careful reading and study of this line of thought. Mr. Lamar simply opens up the subject, leaving a wide field for consideration, concerning which much more might be told. The author goes as far as his belief in the means of grace will permit. A more extended view of, "If ye know these things, happy are ye if ye do them," would enable one to greatly enlarge on what has been so well suggested. The book may be ordered from this office, and will prove a profitable work for any one who desires a better understanding of the First Principles of Christianity. Price, $1.50.

The Gospel Messenger,

A Weekly at $1.50 Per Annum.

PUBLISHED BY

The Brethren's Publishing Co.

D. L. MILLER, ... Editor.

J. H. MOORE, ... Office Editor.

J. B. BRUMBAUGH, }
J. G. ROYER,   } . . . . . Associate Editors.
JOSEPH AMICK, ... Business Manager.

ADVISORY COMMITTEE.

R. H. Miller, A. Hutchison, Daniel Hays.

☞ Communications for publication should be legibly written with black ink on one side of the paper only. Do not attempt to interline, or to put on one page what ought to occupy two.

☞ Anonymous communications will not be published.

☞ Do not mix business with articles for publication. Keep your communications on separate sheets from all business.

* ☞ Time is precious. We always have time to attend to business and to answer questions of importance, but please do not subject us to needless answering of letters.

☞ The MESSENGER is mailed each week to all subscribers. If the address is correctly entered on our list, the paper must reach the person to whom it is addressed. If you do not get your paper, write us, giving particulars.

☞ When changing your address, please give your former as well as your future address in full, so as to avoid delay and misunderstanding.

☞ Always remit to the office from which your ordered your goods, no matter from where you receive them.

☞ Do not send personal checks or drafts on interior banks, unless you send with them 15 cents each, to pay for collection.

☞ Remittances should be made by Post-office Money Order, Drafts on New York, Philadelphia or Chicago, or Registered Letter, made payable and addressed to "Brethren's Publishing Co., Mount Morris, Ill.," or "Brethren's Publishing Co., Huntingdon, Pa."

☞ Entered at the Post-office at Mount Morris, Ill., as second-class matter.

Mount Morris, Ill., ... April 5, 1892.

BRO. JACOB TOMBAUGH, of Gratiot County, Mich., has changed his post-office from New Haven Center to Middleton.

BRO. NOAH LONGANECKER may now be addressed at Hartville, Stark Co., Ohio, instead of North Industry, his former address.

WE feel to thank God that the most of our best preachers come from the humble walks of life. There is a chance for the poor to become useful.

BRO. B. F. MILLER, of Alpena, S. D., writes that Bro. J. W. Trostle, of Iowa, recently visited that place and preached two excellent sermons.

FROM the *Southern Californian* we learn, that Bro. John W. Metzger and wife, who have been spending the winter in California, will return to their home in Indiana, this week.

ELD. SAMUEL MURRAY, of River, Ind., we are informed, is quite sick, being affected with an abscess on the liver. When last heard from, he was suffering intensely. He desires the prayers of the members.

A CARD from Clayton, Ohio, informs us that Eld. John Sollenberger, of the Salem church, died on the morning of March 22. No particulars are given. We are promised a more extended notice of his death.

THE Boon River church, Iowa, is making arrangements to build a meeting-house the coming summer. The church is greatly in need of an English preacher. It is to be hoped that some one will locate there to help the good work along.

BRO. J. G. ROYER is spending a few weeks in the East. He will visit the places mentioned below, as the dates are given: Loudenville, Ohio, April 2 to 5; New Berlin, Ohio, April 6 to 11; Rossville, Ohio, April 12 to 13; District Meeting of the First District of Virginia, April 15 and 16; District Meeting of Eastern Maryland, April 19.

"MANY lose the opportunity of saying a kind thing by waiting to weigh the matter too long."

THE church at Johnstown, Pa., seems to be moving along encouragingly. Eighteen have been received into the church there since the beginning of the present year.

A CARD from Bro. Landon West informs us that he is holding a series of meetings among the colored people at Washington C. H., Ohio, with considerable interest manifested. Two white men made the good confession and were baptized.

WE are in receipt of Minutes of the District Meeting of Middle Missouri. Considerable business was before the meeting. One query goes to the Annual Meeting. Bro. David Bowman will represent the District on the Standing Committee.

A VERY destructive cyclone passed through Cerro Gordo, Ill., the 27th of last month, doing considerable damage, but fortunately no lives were lost. Bro. Geo. W. Cripe will tell our readers about it next week. His communication reached us too late for this issue.

THE article in No. 11, page 167, credited to S. M. Miller, of Waterloo, Iowa, should have been West Cairo, Ohio. The article came to us without any post-office address attached, and thinking that it was from the Bro. S. M. Miller at Waterloo, we were led into the mistake which is hereby corrected.

WE are informed that the interesting story, going the rounds of the papers, about Bro. John Herr having caught two thieves in the act of stealing, etc., is unfounded. We are glad that the report is untrue, but the story was certainly an interesting one, and taught most excellent nonresistant Christian doctrine.

AN institution, known as the Woman's Mission Home in Nashville, Tenn., has already rescued over two hundred and twenty-five young women from a life of infamy, and is now seeking to enlarge its capacity by erecting a building that is to cost $16,000. We feel like encouraging such enterprises, for they certainly prove a help to suffering humanity.

THE Ministerial Meeting for Southern Ohio has an excellent program for consideration. See notice in this issue. There will be but six subjects before the Meeting, and we hardly know which is the most important. We like the idea of having but few subjects, and then discuss them well. We hope other Districts will consider this suggestion.

WE are still receiving questions concerning John's baptism, all of which are clearly answered in the several articles we have written on that subject. We will be pleased to answer any new points, but do not care to repeat what we have already written. Some of the new questions we may answer when we can spare the space, but questions already answered we will not answer again.

THE committee appointed by the Annual Meeting Committee, to assist in the sale of the old meeting-house in East Dayton, Ohio, met March 21, and let the contract for a new brick house, 40 by 60 feet, to be heated by furnace. The building is to be of first-class material throughout, and when completed, will cost about $5,000. This cost includes the ground, which is to be well located. This means a new, and, we hope, prosperous era in the history of the East Dayton church.

ELD. DAVID BECHTELHEIMER, of Adams County, Nebr., after an absence of several months, traveling in Iowa, Illinois and Indiana, has returned to his home. He left home last November, and since then has done considerable preaching, and also visited the scenes of his early life. He found many changes had taken place since he was elected to the ministry forty-three years ago.

RECENTLY an entire edition of a paper in Arizona was thrown out of the mails under the Anti-lottery law; it had given an account of a piano raffle. What must be done with papers containing accounts of raffles at churches? It will be a sad comment on Christianity when the law of the land must take hold of churches and compel them to do what is right. Surely there is need of reformation in many of the churches.

SUNDAY is the Lord's Day, because he arose from the dead on that day. The day is therefore set apart in commemoration of his resurrection from the dead, and on that day we should not forsake the assembling of ourselves together, as the manner of some is. Under the Old Law the Sabbath, or Saturday, was the consecrated day, but a change of law, as well as a change in the priesthood, has brought into existence a new day, hence the Lord's Day, or the first day of the week, as it is sometimes called.

THERE are three baptisms distinctly taught in the New Testament. First, the baptism in water. This was first administered by John, but afterwards by the disciples of Christ, and is to be continued by the servants of Christ until the close of the present dispensation. It is the only baptism that man is authorized to administer. Second, the baptism in the Holy Ghost. This is done by Jesus and God alone, and is for the benefit of all penitent ones who have been properly baptized in water. This baptism man cannot administer. It is reserved exclusively for divine hands. The third baptism is that of fire, intended for the wicked. The power to administer this is, also, entrusted exclusively to the power that is divine. Of these three baptisms, the one in water is the only one which man is authorized to administer, though he may pray for the performance of the second and warn the sinner of the danger of the third. He who properly receives and profits by the first and second, will escape the third, but he who ignores the first will be deprived of the second, and must then endure the horrors of the third.

"FIRST Principles and Perfection," by J. S. Lamar, is the title of an excellent, well-bound book of 288 pages, sent us by the Standard Publishing Co., Cincinnati, Ohio. The author discusses the first principles of the doctrine of Christ in a clear and forcible manner. Analytically it is the best treatise on that question that we have ever read, and as a general thing, is quite reliable, though somewhat conservative on a few points. The chapters on "Going on to Perfection" open up a line of thought new to most readers. We would urge a careful reading and study of this line of thought. Mr. Lamar simply opens up the subject, leaving a wide field for consideration concerning which much more might be told. The author goes as far as his belief in the means of grace will permit. A more extended view of, "If ye know these things, happy are ye if ye do them," would enable one to greatly enlarge on what has been so well suggested. The book may be ordered from this office, and will prove a profitable work for any-one who desires a better understanding of the First Principles of Christianity. Price, $1.50.

QUERISTS' DEPARTMENT.

We, like most people, have our peculiar ways about some things, and one of them is this: Often, after a series of meetings, we publish concerning the minister, that "he failed not to declare the whole 'counsel of God'" Now I think it would require a long series of meetings to do that.

J. C. PACK.

THE phrase is often used rather loosely and is intended, perhaps, to mean less than what it really says. Certainly it would require a long while to declare the whole counsel of God, and yet, in a few discourses, a minister might tell enough to be the means of saving any one who will receive the Word in a good and honest heart. It is, however, better to say, of the minister and his work, that "he shunned not to declare the whole counsel of God." And it would perhaps be still more edifying to use expressions of the kind very sparingly, for they are used so frequently by our writers, when reporting series of meetings, that they cease to be impressive.

A minister was expelled from the church, and now wishes to be received back. Must he be received as a private member, or with his office?   J. B. S.

That depends upon the wishes of the church. The church can restore him to fellowship, either without or with his office, just as she judges proper. A majority of the church expelled him with his office, and a majority may also restore him with his office. If he is received back into the church without anything being said concerning his office, it would be understood that he is restored to his former place as a minister. If he was expelled for one of the gross crimes, mentioned in 1 Cor. 5: 11, he may be restored to membership by a majority of the members, but cannot be re-instated in his office excepting by the unanimous consent of the church. If the crime was an aggravating one, he cannot be restored to his office at all, though he may be received as a private member.

In GOSPEL MESSENGER, No. 8, current volume, page 11, center column, will find an anonymous query about using the quarterlies in the Sunday-school. In the answer given we find, near the center of the last paragraph, "that quarterlies are a great help indeed, where properly used." Please explain how they are used, when "properly used." J. W. VETTER.

Quarterlies should be used as helps in studying the lessons, but not as helps by which to recite. We have seen the teacher, with quarterly in hand, call off the questions, while the pupils would read the answers from the quarterlies. No one would ever think of teaching grammar or mathematics in that manner. By the aid of the quarterly the pupils ought to master their lessons sufficiently to answer most of the questions without looking on the book. The proper way is to first study the lesson directly from the Bible, looking up the references and connections with care. After that, study the comments, etc., found in the quarterlies and such other books as may prove helpful.

When, where, and by whom were Peter and the other apostles baptized?   A. N. GRAYBILL.

Peter was one of John's disciples, and was therefore baptized by him. See John 1: 35-42, where there are facts sufficient narrated to lead to this conclusion. All of the apostles were probably baptized in the early part of John's ministry, and therefore were numbered with his disciples, but afterwards followed Jesus as they were called. They were baptized in the River Jordan, where John administered the rite when he first commenced preaching and baptizing. Since John's baptism was from heaven, there could be no question about its legality. Then he who was good enough to immerse the Savior, was certainly qualified to baptize any one who accepted his teachings and brought forth fruit meet for repentance.

Please explain 2 Cor. 12: 7-9, which reads as follows: "And lest I should be exalted above measure through the abundance of the revelations, there was given to me a thorn in the flesh, the messenger of Satan to buffet me, lest I should be exalted above measure. For this thing I besought the Lord thrice, that it might depart from me. And he said unto me, My grace is sufficient for thee: for my strength is made perfect in weakness. Most gladly therefore will I rather glory in my infirmities, that the power of Christ may rest upon me." What is meant by thorn in the flesh?

D. CHAMBERS.

Commentators find this a perplexing question. Likely some local affliction in the flesh is referred to, which clung to the faithful apostle all of his life. The nature of the affliction cannot be determined. It may have been a defective eye, a crippled limb, or something of that character. It was an affliction that the Lord declined to remove, though asked to do so three times. He gave Paul to understand that the divine grace was sufficient to enable him to endure the affliction and make his work a success. Hundreds of good Christians to-day have their thorns in the flesh to endure. They should bear their afflictions patiently, knowing that Paul, the most favored of the apostles, had to also suffer.

Who was Melchisedec? My brother-in-law, who is not a member of the church, but who reads the MESSENGER, would like to read an article from you on the subject.

G. L. STUDEBAKER.

We cannot take space or time to write a long article just now. Let it suffice to say that Melchisedec is generally presumed to have been the king of the little town of Salem, which, in the time of Abraham, stood where Jerusalem is now located. He was also a true 'priest of the Most High God, and served as a type of Christ. We can do no more than refer to the seventh chapter of Hebrews and add, that being "without father, without mother, without descent, having neither beginning of days, nor end of life" does not refer to the facts of his history, but to the records of his genealogy. So far as the records were concerned, he was a priest of the Most High God without receiving his office from his ancestors before him. He was a priest by direct appointment of God. Paul's reference to Melchisedec was to show to the Jews that Jesus could also be our High Priest, after the order of Melchisedec, without belonging to the tribe of Levi. This is the real point that Paul had in view and it is well enough to keep it in mind when looking at the character of Melchisedec. But Christ is now our Melchisedec, and as Abraham rendered honor to the former, it becomes our duty to render all due honor to the latter.

We believe that Melchisedec was a real person, though in some manner he was specially favored by God, for he was authorized to receive a tenth of the spoils which Abraham had captured, and in turn blessed the great father of the Jewish race. Some suppose him to be Shem, who was still living at the time of the events referred to. Of course this is conjecture, and yet it would seem that if any one on earth was worthy to receive a tenth of the spoils, and in turn bless the father of the faithful, it would have been this grand old man, who lived long before the flood, and was therefore the most noted man then on the face of the globe. Paul says, "Now consider how great this man was, unto whom even the patriarch Abraham gave the tenth of his spoils." Heb. 7: 4.

It would be interesting, indeed, to read a carefully prepared history of such a remarkable personage, but the Bible, which is the Book of the ages, contains only a passing notice of the one who stood so high in the estimation of both God and man as to be called "King of Righteousness."

J. H. M.

CORRESPONDENCE.

"Write what thou seest, and send it unto the churches."

Church News solicited for this Department. If you have had a good meeting, send a report of it, so that others may rejoice with you. In writing give name of church, County and State. Be brief. Notes of Travel should be as short as possible. Land Advertisements are not solicited for this Department. We have an advertising page, and, if necessary, will issue supplements.

To the Members in Denmark and Sweden.

Dear Brethren and Sisters:—

I WILL now fulfill the promise I made you, before I left Europe, and write you through the MESSENGER:

Peace be multiplied! Nearly a year has passed since I left you, dear Brethren. I will never forget the blessed meetings which I had the happy privilege of enjoying with you, "especially in Wanneberga." I felt very happy during the time I was with you, to see that you were so happy in Jesus, and your gladness and willingness to follow his commandments. Your kind faces are ever before me, and I remember you with great pleasure. Although thousands of miles are between us, my thoughts often fly across the deep ocean to you. We are very far separated, and God knows, if we shall ever again meet here on earth, but O happy thought, we have a place where we can meet,—at the Throne of Grace. Let us often meet there!

Perhaps some of my travels will be of some interest to you. In Baltimore, Md., was my first stopping place in this country. This is a large city, with not far from 650,000 inhabitants. Here there are only a few members living, but in Woodberry,—about four miles from the city,—is a little church, with about forty members. During my stay in Baltimore, I went down to the wharf sometimes, and distributed a good many tracts among the sailors and emigrants, and had some pleasant conversation with them about Jesus' love to fallen humanity, and his willingness to save poor sinners.

Once, as I went out, I came to a little fort, where I found all kinds of people, from all parts of Europe, who had joined the forces of the U. S. A. There I met some Scandinavians, and had a good talk with them. I became especially acquainted with a Swedish soldier, and fell into an earnest conversation with him about the salvation of the soul. I told him to receive salvation before it would be too late. I left him much impressed.

Some time after, when I went down; I found him a believer. I told him about our faith and practice, that we should obey and follow what Jesus has commanded us to do, and that a Christian is not allowed to fight or go to war. He said "I wish to go out from it, but cannot under two years, unless I pay $120. Then I can go out whenever I please." Pray for him that he may soon obey the Lord in all things.

Last July I went farther west to a place, named McKeesport, Pa. There I found about four thousand Swedes. I saw many of my countrymen walking in sin, and I felt much compassion for them. I wished that I could do something for them in pointing them to Christ, who is willing to accept any one who will come. There are five Swedish churches, different denominations, at that place, I distributed some tracts, "The House

sion work? I like Bro. Gish's idea of calling for them. I believe they can do as much of it as the ministers, and we will say, as did Bro. Gish, that we have need of two good deacons. We have a small church and no deacons. Who will volunteer to come and help us with a little means and ambition? Anyone can get along and do well here.

If you have to sacrifice some things, for awhile at least, will not the Lord reward you? Will "I not open the windows of heaven, saith the Lord?"

We have had to leave our home here for nearly two years, on account of loss through a bank failure, but are glad to say that, by hard work, we are able to get back, and mean to work.

Oh, who will come and help us? Now is the time to work, while the whole field is open to us.
J. P. HARSHBARGER.

March 6.

From Sterling, Logan Co., Colo.

WE met with the people of this locality last Sunday for public worship, for the first time. A small congregation of eager listeners was in attendance. There are twelve of the Father's children here in this locality, which belongs to the Holyoke church, and is under the care of Bro. J. S. Snowberger, but isolated fifty miles from the main body.

Any of the ministering brethren from the West, going to Annual Meeting, are very cordially invited to stop with us, either going or coming, or both. We expect to have regular meetings in the future. We earnestly invite all members who wish to be governed by the teachings of the *Gospel*, and the *general* order of the Brotherhood, and who may be in need of a home, to locate with us. Nearly all of this large valley is under irrigation, and good locations can be bought for $12 to $18 per acre.
W. M. WISE.

From Covina, Cal.

WE are now permitted to look at Southern California, arrayed in her spring dress. So, when you consider all that enters into the make-up of this country, you will find reason to feel that it was a part of what was pronounced by its author as being "very good."

At present I feel that I shall have reason to bless the day when I visited this country. I speak in reference to my physical condition. I shall give particulars later, if I am allowed to realize what now seems to be in sight,—that is, to have my enfeebled circulation invigorated and equalized. Should such be my fortune, I shall never regret my visit to California. Many of the readers of the MESSENGER know how poor my circulation has been for years. The prospect is flattering, at present, for a change for the better, and to this end I crave the prayers of such as can pray in faith, believing that God is able and willing to bless, even to the warming of cold feet, as well as cold hearts. Cold feet are bad enough, but cold hearts are much worse. I have not been preaching every day for the past two weeks.
A. HUTCHISON.

March 18.

From the Lexington Church, Highland Co, Ohio.

THE Lexington church-house (the place of our District Meeting) is situated on a good pike, one mile south of Highland Station, place of stopping. This is on the B. & O. R. R., running from Cincinnati to Parkersburg. The best route from Dayton is through Washington C. H., to Musselman's station. There you strike our road from Springfield to Washington C. H. From there to Greenfield is our road. Our morning train is due at Highland Station at 8: 30. It leaves Musselman's after seven; Springfield at 8 A. M. Coming by way of Cincinnati, you get here at 9: 30 A. M. Unless special arrangements can be made with railroad companies you cannot get here in time for the meeting unless you come the day before. Trains arrive here from the East at half-past 4 o'clock P. M., and from the West at about 6 o'clock P. M. These trains will be met by the Brethren's conveyances as far as we are able. Hacks will be run at reasonable rates, also.

We are forty-five miles from Dayton, and those who wish to drive through, will have a good road all the way. Come by the way of Xenia, Lumberton, Wilmington, Antioch and Lexington. We would like to have preaching on Monday evening and Tuesday evening at three or four different points by the Brethren. Do not expect too much; as there are only eight or nine homes of the Brethren in reach of the church. If further information is desired, address me at Highland, Ohio. Let some of the Brethren confer with the railroad companies as to rates.
ALLEN OOKERMAN.

March 19.

From the Johnstown Congregation, Pa.

THE Johnstown church has had a season of refreshing from the presence of the Lord. Bro. George Rairigh, one of our home ministers, began a series of meetings in the Walnut Grove church, Feb. 26, and for more than three weeks expounded unto us the Truth. Sinners were made to tremble, and saints made strong in the doctrine of the Living God. As an immediate result of his efforts, thirteen precious souls knelt in the troubled waters, and arose to walk in the newness of life, the oldest a man whose hair is white with the frosts of many winters, and the youngest a sweet girl of ten. A dear sister who had wandered into "forbidden pastures," returned home amid great rejoicing. This makes eighteen souls that have been received into the Johnstown church this year. May God keep them faithful!

This church is in good working order. We have a large and interesting Sunday-school, which is kept active during the entire year. We have organized a Bible class under the name of "Walnut Grove Bible class," at which place we meet once a week in order to become better versed in the prophecies, and Bible history in general. Pray that we may accomplish much good in the name of Jesus!
SADIE BRALLIER NOFFSINGER.

From Maryland.

RECENTLY I attended a council in Talbot County, four miles south of Easton, in a small meeting-house. The business was all transacted in a Christian spirit, and when finished, a meal was furnished in the church free of charge to all present. I learned that the membership is growing considerably. Years ago, on such occasions, they could all get around an ordinary table, but this time the half could not get to the table. Members are moving in from Virginia and other places, and settling down in the vicinity of Cordova (the northern part of Talbot County). The membership is now larger there than around Easton. The result will be a new meeting-house in the near future at the former place.

While preaching the Gospel in Caroline County, Md., near Denton, for over ten days, I noticed that the Ridgely church is multiplying in membership quite fast. Some years ago we organized that church with twenty members. At present they number about seventy, and have since built two good meeting-houses, one near Denton, the other near Ridgely. Bro. King, their elder, is doing a good work there. Of late he got some new help, by election and immigration, L. Brumbaugh and L. Stucky, who will help to carry forward the work of Christ. The Conference of the Eastern District of Pennsylvania will be held in the Ridgely church on the Eastern shore of Maryland, May 11 and 14, 1892. Eld. King will give due notice before long.

I am glad that the Lord prospers his work in that section of the vineyard. We had good attendance while there. Apparently good seed was sown and under God's influence may produce a glorious harvest. We returned home March 21, and found all well, thank the Lord.
WM. HERTZLER.

The Fund for Russian Sufferers.

BELOW we give a report of the funds, received for the Russian Sufferers through the MESSENGER office, and also those received by the undersigned, up to March 29:

A brother and sister, Canada,	$25 00
Amanda R. Cassel, Pennsylvania,	2 00
B. C. Cripe, Goshen, Ind.,	2 00
S. M. Goughnour, Elkhart, Iowa,	1 00
M. E. Miller, Mt. Morris, Ill.,	1 00
J. A. & H. L. Weaver, Longmont, Colo.,	2 00
W. B. Youndt, University of Virginia,	5 00
Frances Arnold, Indiana,	1 50
Brethren and friends, Polo, Ill.,	25 00
A brother, Pleasant Hill, Pa.,	1 00
Mrs. A. C. Barr, Philadelphia, Pa.,	1 00
Monroe County church, Fredric, Iowa,	2 25
O. O. Button, Ramona, Kans.,	5 00
J. P. Strickler, Ramona, Kans.,	5 00
Noah Miller, North English, Iowa,	1 00
A sister, Long Meadow church, Md.,	25
T. B. Hersch, Jesup, Iowa,	2 00
J. M. Follis, Fredric Iowa,	45
Members at Mt. Morris, Silver Creek church, Ill.,	7 07
D. W. Badger, Panther, Iowa,	2 00
By the Wirt Brethren, Lewiston, Minn.,	3 00
F. W. Mower, Los Angeles, Cal.,	1 00
A sister, Cearfoss, Md.,	25
Yellow Creek, church, Ill.,	10 00
J. F. Emmert, Waynesborough, Pa.,	2 00
Cherry Grove church, Lanark, Ill.,	14 25
J. Johnson, Union Bridge, Md.,	1 00
S. F. Johnson, Union Bridge, Md.,	1 00
C. Johnson, Union Bridge, Md.,	1 00
Lanark church, Lanark, Ill.,	17 00
Hickory Grove church, Mt. Carroll, Ill.,	8 00
Walter S. Long, Shirleysburgh, Pa.,	1 00
Isaac Henricks, Virden, Ill.,	1 00
Arnold's Grove church, Ill.,	3 55

Of the above sum, $107.77 came in time, to be utilized in the purchase of flour, sent with the ship-load of provisions, of which previous mention was made. Messrs. McC. Reeve and W. C. Edgar, who were sent from this country, to personally supervise the distribution of the goods, have promised to write a communication for the MESSENGER concerning the actual condition of the suffering ones, as found on their arrival. This account will be accurate and reliable, and will also afford a means of knowing where the remainder of our funds may best be applied.

We here, again, mention the fact that ALL the work, connected with the shipping and distribution of the donations, was done *free of charge*, so that the entire amount contributed was applied to the purpose intended. Those who were kind enough to donate, will find their reward not only in the grateful hearts of those whom they befriended, but also in the promise of Him, who will reward every act of kindness, done in his name to the least of his children. L. A. PLATE.
Mt. Morris, Ill.

sion work? I like Bro. Gish's idea of calling for them. I believe they can do as much of it as the ministers, and we will say, as did Bro. Gish, that we have need of two good deacons. We have a small church and no deacons. Who will volunteer to come and help us with a little means and ambition? Anyone can get along and do well here.

If you have to sacrifice some things, for awhile at least, will not the Lord reward you? Will "I not open the windows of heaven, saith the Lord?"

We have had to leave our home here for nearly two years, on account of loss through a bank failure, but are glad to say that, by hard work, we are able to get back, and mean to work.

Oh, who will come and help us? Now is the time to work, while the whole field is open to us.

J. P. HARSHBARGER.

March 6.

From Sterling, Logan Co., Colo.

WE met with the people of this locality last Sunday for public worship, for the first time. A small congregation of eager listeners was in attendance. There are twelve of the Father's children here in this locality, which belongs to the Holyoke church, and is under the care of Bro. J. S. Snowberger, but isolated fifty miles from the main body.

Any of the ministering brethren from the West, going to Annual Meeting, are very cordially invited to stop with us, either going or coming, or both. We expect to have regular meetings in the future. We earnestly invite all members who wish to be governed by the teachings of the *Gospel*, and the *general* order of the Brotherhood, and who may be in need of a home, to locate with us. Nearly all of this large valley is under irrigation, and good locations can be bought for $12 to $18 per acre.

W. M. WISE.

From Covina, Cal.

WE are now permitted to look at Southern California, arrayed in her spring dress. So, when you consider all that enters into the make-up of this country, you will find reason to feel that it was a part of what was pronounced by its author as being "very good."

At present I feel that I shall have reason to bless the day when I visited this country. I speak in reference to my physical condition. I shall give particulars later, if I am allowed to realize what now seems to be in sight,—that is, to have my enfeebled circulation invigorated and equalized. Should such be my fortune, I shall never regret my visit to California. Many of the readers of the MESSENGER know how poor my circulation has been for years. The prospect is flattering, at present, for a change for the better, and to this end I crave the prayers of such as can pray in faith, believing that God is able and willing to bless, even to the warming of cold feet, as well as cold hearts. Cold feet are bad enough, but cold hearts are much worse. I have not been preaching every day for the past two weeks.

A. HUTCHISON.

March 18.

From the Lexington Church, Highland Co., Ohio.

THE Lexington church-house (the place of our District Meeting) is situated on a good pike, one mile south of Highland Station, place of stopping. This is on the B. & O. R. R., running from Cincinnati to Parkersburg. The best route from Dayton is through Washington C. H., to Musselman's station. There you strike our road from Springfield to Washington C. H. From there to Greenfield is our road. Our morning train is due at Highland Station at 8: 30. It leaves

Musselman's after seven; Springfield at 8 A. M. Coming by way of Cincinnati, you get here at 9: 30 A. M. Unless special arrangements can be made with railroad companies you cannot get here in time for the meeting unless you come the day before. Trains arrive here from the East at half-past 4 o'clock P. M., and from the West at about 6 o'clock P. M. These trains will be met by the Brethren's conveyances as far as we are able. Hacks will be run at reasonable rates, also.

We are forty-five miles from Dayton, and those who wish to drive through, will have a good road all the way. Come by the way of Xenia, Lumberton, Wilmington, Antioch and Lexington. We would like to have preaching on Monday evening and Tuesday evening at three or four different points by the Brethren. Do not expect too much; as there are only eight or nine homes of the Brethren in reach of the church. If further information is desired, address me at Highland, Ohio. Let some of the Brethren confer with the railroad companies as to rates.

ALLEN OCKERMAN.

March 19.

From the Johnstown Congregation, Pa.

THE Johnstown church has had a season of refreshing from the presence of the Lord. Bro. George Rairigh, one of our home ministers, began a series of meetings in the Walnut Grove church, Feb. 26, and for more than three weeks expounded unto us the Truth. Sinners were made to tremble, and saints made strong in the doctrine of the Living God. As an immediate result of his efforts, thirteen precious souls knelt in the troubled waters, and arose to walk in the newness of life, the oldest a man whose hair is white with the frosts of many winters, and the youngest a sweet girl of ten. A dear sister who had wandered into "forbidden pastures," returned home amid great rejoicing. This makes eighteen souls that have been received into the Johnstown church this year. May God keep them faithful!

This church is in good working order. We have a large and interesting Sunday-school, which is kept active during the entire year. We have organized a Bible class under the name of "Walnut Grove Bible class," at which place we meet once a week in order to become better versed in the prophecies, and Bible history in general. Pray that we may accomplish much good in the name of Jesus!

SADIE BRALLIER NOFFSINGER.

From Maryland.

RECENTLY I attended a council in Talbot County, four miles south of Easton, in a small meeting-house. The business was all transacted in a Christian spirit, and when finished, a meal was furnished in the church free of charge to all present. I learned that the membership is growing considerably. Years ago, on such occasions, they could all get around an ordinary table, but this time the half could not get to the table. Members are moving in from Virginia and other places, and settling down in the vicinity of Cordova (the northern part of Talbot County). The members at Ridgely are now larger there than around Easton. The result will be a new meeting-house in the near future at the former place.

While preaching the Gospel in Caroline County, Md., near Denton, for over ten days, I noticed the Ridgely church is multiplying in membership quite fast. Some years ago we organized that church with twenty members. At present they number about seventy, and have a nice built two good meeting-houses, one near Denton, the other near Ridgely. Bro. King, their elder, is doing a good work there. Of late he got some new help,

by election and immigration, L. Brumbaugh and L. Stucky, who will help to carry forward the work of Christ. The Conference of the Eastern District of Pennsylvania will be held in the Ridgely church on the Eastern shore of Maryland, May 11 and 14, 1892. Eld. King will give due notice before long.

I am glad that the Lord prospers his work in that section of the vineyard. We had good attendance while there. Apparently good seed was sown and under God's influence may produce a glorious harvest. We returned home March 21, and found all well, thank the Lord.

WM. HERTZLER.

The Fund for Russian Sufferers.

BELOW we give a report of the funds received for the Russian Sufferers through the MESSENGER office, and also those received by the undersigned, up to March 29:

A brother and sister, Canada,	$25 00
Amanda R. Cassel, Pennsylvania,	2 00
B. C. Cripe, Goshen, Ind.,	2 00
S. M. Goughnour, Elkhart, Iowa,	1 00
M. E. Miller, Mt. Morris, Ill.,	1 00
J. A. & H. L. Weaver, Longmont, Colo.,	2 00
W. B. Youndt, University of Virginia,	5 00
Frances Arnold, Indiana,	1 50
Brethren and friends, Polo, Ill.,	25 00
A brother, Pleasant Hill, Pa.,	1 00
Mrs. A. C. Barr, Philadelphia, Pa.,	1 00
Monroe County church, Fredric, Iowa,	3 25
O. O. Button, Ramona, Kans.,	5 00
J. P. Strickler, Ramona, Kans.,	5 00
Noah Miller, North English, Iowa,	1 00
A sister, Long Meadow church, Md.,	25
T. B. Hersch, Jesup, Iowa,	2 00
J. M. Follis, Fredric Iowa,	45
Members at Mt. Morris, Silver Creek church, Ill.,	7 07
D. W. Badger, Panther, Iowa,	2 00
By the Wirt Brethren, Lewiston, Minn.,	3 00
F. W. Mower, Los Angeles, Cal.,	1 00
A sister, Cearfoss, Md.,	25
Yellow Creek, church, Ill.,	10 00
J. F. Emmert, Waynesborough, Pa.,	2 00
Cherry Grove church, Lanark, Ill.,	14 25
J. Johnson, Union Bridge, Md.,	1 00
S. F. Johnson, Union Bridge, Md.,	1 00
C. Johnson, Union Bridge, Md.,	1 00
Lanark church, Lanark, Ill.,	17 00
Hickory Grove church, Mt. Carroll, Ill.,	8 00
Walter S. Long, Shirleysburgh, Pa.,	1 00
Isaac Henricks, Virden, Ill.,	1 00
Arnold's Grove church, Ill.,	3 65

Of the above sum, $107.77 came in time, to be utilized in the purchase of flour; sent with the ship-load of provisions, of which previous mention was made. Messrs. McC. Reeve and W. C. Edgar, who were sent from this country, to personally supervise the distribution of the goods, have promised to write a communication for the MESSENGER concerning the actual condition of the suffering ones, as found on their arrival. This account will be accurate and reliable, and will also afford a means of knowing where the remainder of our funds may be best applied.

We here, again, mention the fact that ALL the work, connected with the shipping and distribution of the donations, was done *free of charge*, so that the entire amount contributed was applied to the purpose intended. Those who were kind enough to donate, will find their reward not only in the grateful hearts of those whom they befriended, but also in the promise of Him, who will reward every act of kindness, done in his name to the least of his children. J. A. PLATE.

Mt. Morris, Ill.

Union City, Ind.—We held our quarterly council March 19. Quite a large amount of business was disposed of. The poor were remembered and the mission work encouraged in a substantial way. Delegates were elected to District and Annual Meetings, Sunday-school officers chosen, and two deacons elected and installed. —*W. K. Simmons.*

Notice.—The Missionary and District Meeting of Nebraska will be held in the town of Juniata. All that can come on the B. & M. R. R. should do so, as it will save twelve miles conveyance. Please bring ten cents from each member for the expenses of Delegates to Annual Meeting and for Minutes of Annual Meeting and also District Meeting.—*Eld. D. Bechtelheimer, Juniata, Nebr.*

Wichita, Kans.—Last night, March 14, we were called to Sedgwick, Kans., to anoint sister Stoner. We found her very low in body, but strong in faith, trusting in the Lord. The anointing was attended to in the fear of the Lord, Bro. C. Delp assisting. Bro. Delp is making arrangements to go with his family to one of the mission posts in Arkansas. We are sorry to have him leave us, as there is much work to do here for the Lord, but we pray the Lord to bless him in his new field. Bro. Sharp has promised to be at our feast, May 14. —*William Johnson, 1583 Orange St.*

Warrior's Mark, Pa.—The brethren and sisters of this congregation commenced a series of meetings, and after continuing over a week, Bro. Michael Claar, of Bedford Co., Pa., came to us and held forth the Word of Life. The meetings were very interesting, and five were added to the fold, and one was reclaimed. They are all young, and five of them are just starting out in life. Four of them are just beginning housekeeping, one is a young man, and the last is a little girl of eleven years,—a bright, tender lamb of the fold.—*S. S. Gray.*

Keuka, Fla.—We intend, the Lord willing, to start on our way north March 21. We intend to visit Sister Mary Wigfield at St. Augustine, and expect to reach our Kansas home about April 1. My wife has been greatly benefited in health by spending the winter in Florida. We have bought a home in Morrill, Kans., and will move there as soon as we can. We make this change to avail ourselves of the school and church privileges. We enjoyed a feast of love with the Keuka Brethren March 12 and 13. Bro. J. C. Lahman and wife, of Mt. Morris, were also present. —*W. H. H. Sawyer, March 18.*

French Broad, Tenn.—Brethren C. H. Diehl and P. D. Reed, of Washington Co., Tenn., came to us March 4, and held a series of meetings. Bro. Reed stayed until the 10th, and then returned home. Bro. Diehl remained until the 14th, and as a result nine

came out on the Lord's side and were baptized. Our Brethren labored faithfully for the Master's cause. The attendance was very good, notwithstanding the rainy weather at that time. We felt built up during our meetings, and our prayer to God is that we may never forget the many good lessons learned. May the blessings of God rest with our brethren, and may they have souls for their hire.—*Eva Bashor, March 21.*

Three Springs, Pa.—On the evening of Feb. 9 Bro. Joseph Snowberger of Williamsburgh, Pa., commenced a series of meetings at the Three Springs school-house and continued until Feb. 14. He preached in all eight sermons. On account of sickness, inclement weather and other meetings in the community the attendance was not as large as it otherwise would have been, but the attention was good. Bro. Snowberger preached the Word with spirit and with power, and we enjoyed the preaching very much, as we are somewhat isolated from the body of the church, and do not often have continued meetings. While there were no additions to the church, the members were highly admonished, and sinners were warned to flee the wrath to come.—*J. M. Mosemore.*

MATRIMONIAL.

" What therefore God hath joined together, let no man put asunder."

CROWL—GRIPE.—At the residence of the bride's parents, in the Upper Wood River church, Custer Co., Nebr., March 17, 1892, by the undersigned, John Crowl and sister Catharine Ora Gripe.   JOHN J. HOOVER.

MACEY—SHIRKY.—At the residence of the bride's parents, March 15, 1892, by Bro. S. B. Shirky, Bro. Louis Macey and sister Anna Shirky, all of the Wacanda congregation, Ray Co., Mo.   S. A. Rhoads.

SHOUP—BOYD.—At the residence of the bride's parents, Cherry Grove, Carroll Co., Ill., Jan. 26, 1892, Mr. Frank Shoup and Miss Ross Boyd.   HENRY M. MARTIN.

MAN—TARR.—At the home of the bride's parents, near Springdale, Leavenworth Co., Kans., March 16, 1892, by the undersigned, Franklin Man to Mary Tarr.   DAVID KIMMEL.

→FALLEN ASLEEP←

" Blessed are the dead which die in the Lord."

SMITH.—March 14, 1892, Luella Johnson, aged 18 years, 5 months and 8 days. She was married to John Smith, Jan. 3, 1891. In his case she leaves a two weeks' old infant. May God in his mercy spare his life to be one of usefulness. Funeral services conducted by Eld. Jacob Gripe from 1 Sam. 20: 3.

BERKEYBILE.—In the Shade Creek congregation, Somerset Co., Pa., Feb. 3, 1892, of old age, sister Christenia (Whetstone) Berkeybile, wife of Andrew Berkeybile (deceased), aged 87 years, 2 months and 11 days. Funeral services by Eld. Hiram Musselman. Sister Berkeybile was a faithful member of the Brethren church for many years. She was the mother of twelve children.
          FANNIE M. FAUST.

KEISER.—At Warrensburgh, Mo., March 5, 1892, of pneumonia, sister Mollie Keiser, wife of Bro. David A. Keiser, aged about 38 years. Deceased was born in Augusta County, Va. Funeral and burial at the Panther

Creek church, Ill. Funeral services by brethren Philip Moore and C. C. Brubaker.
          THOS. KEISER.

McKIMMY.—In the Swan Creek congregation, Ohio, March 17, 1892, of diphtheria, Sadie McKimmy, daughter of Bro. John and sister Ida McKimmy; aged 2 years, 6 months and 13 days.   JASPER McKIMMY.

HEAVNER.—In the bounds of the New Dale church, Hardy Co., W. Va., March 8, 1892, of consumption, Mrs. Elizabeth Heavner, aged 63 years, 2 months and 28 days. Funeral services by L. D. Caldwell in the New Dale church.

HALTERMAN.—In the Lost River congregation, Hardy Co., W. Va., March 10, 1892, Bro. Isanc Halterman, aged 40 years, 2 months and 6 days. He leaves a wife and four children. Funeral by brethren S. May and S. Mathias.

WHITMER.—In the bounds of the Linville Creek congregation, Rockingham Co., Va., March 14, 1892, Bro. Adam Whitmer, aged 47 years, 6 months and 4 days. He leaves a wife and six children. Funeral services by brethren J. P. Zigler, assisted by S. May.   L. D. CALDWELL.

BROWN.—Near Mulvane, Kans., Feb. 2, 1892, Gertrude Edith Ella Brown, aged 5 months and 23 days. This was one of the triplets born to Bro. Peter S. and sister —— Brown. Funeral services appropriate to the occasion.   WILLIAM JOHNSON.

SIMISON.—In the bounds of the Wichita church, Kans., Feb. 2, 1892, sister Barbara Simison, aged 91 years, 3 months and 26 days. The subject of this notice was born in Westmoreland County, Pa., and was married to Samuel Simison, April 5, 1817. Funeral services by the writer.   WM. JOHNSON.

BONEWITZ.—In the Coquille church, Coos Co., Ore., Urbin, infant son of Bro. John and sister Margaret Bonewitz, aged 4 months and 10 days. Funeral services by the Brethren.   THOMAS BARKLOW.

DAWSON.—Within the bounds of the Round Mountain church, Ark., Feb. 13, 1892, of La Grippe, Leonidas A. Dawson, aged 18 years, 4 months and 21 days. Services were held at his parents' house, after which he was buried in the grave-yard near the church.
          LINA DAWSON.

HARRIS.—In the Union City church, Ind., Jan. 8, 1892, of a paralytic stroke, sister Rebecca Harris, aged 87 years.

ARNOLD.—In the Union City church, Ind., Jan. 25, 1892, sister Mary Arnold, *nee* Pickett, *nee* Marquis, aged 67 years, 10 months and 26 days. Funeral discourse by Eld. J. Shatsman.

COOK.—In the same congregation, Feb. 3, 1892, of La Grippe, Bro. Amos Cook, aged 81 years, 3 months and 23 days. The day before his death he was anointed in the name of the Lord. He was a member of the church for forty-four years.

KUNKLE.—In the same congregation, March 16, 1892, sister Magdalena Kunkle, aged 77 years and 11 days. She was born in York County, Pa., came to Ohio in 1829, married Jacob P. Kunkle in 1838, and was a member of the church for 52 years.
          W. K. SIMMONS.

DECKER.—At Roseburg, Oregon, Feb. 29, 1892, of consumption, sister Rebecca Catharine Decker, wife of Bro. P. A. Decker, aged 54 years, 7 months and 4 days. She and her husband were the first two to unite with the Coquille church, in the fall of 1873. A year ago she and her husband went to California to relieve her lung trouble. Stopping awhile at that place, she came back to Roseburg, Oregon.   THOMAS BARKLOW.

BURGET.—At Louisville, Ohio, Feb. 23, 1892, Samuel Burget, aged 76 years and 11 months. He was born near Mapleton, Stark Co., Ohio, and married to Lydie Wass, June 15, 1845. To them were born six children. Funeral services by Rev. W. O. Baker.
          H. P. BRINKWORTH.

RIGGLE.—In the Elkhart church, near Goshen, Ind., March 17, 1891, sister Eve C. Riggle (wife of Eld. Daniel Riggle), aged 50 years, 11 months and 20 days. Her disease had the appearance of consumption and cancer in the stomach. She was the mother of ten children. She was anointed shortly before her death. Funeral services by the writer.   J. H. MILLER.

KNEE.—In the Mt. Etna congregation, Adams Co., Iowa, March 4, 1892, Frederic Knee, aged 83 years, 1 month and 15 days. Funeral discourse from Job 14: 10.   M. MYERS.

HOFF.—At her home in Dallas Center, Iowa, Feb. 12, 1892, after a long illness, sister Katie Hoff, born July 24, 1826. She was married three times. Her maiden name was Herring. Her first husband's name was Piper; second Swank and the third and last, Hoff.
          ELLA ROYER.

ENGLISH.—At his home in Miami Co., Ind., March 4, 1892, of La Grippe, Bro. Joseph Franklin English, aged 84 years, 3 months and 4 days. He was married to Edna Hopper, of Virginia, Jan. 10, 1833. To them were born eight children. Funeral services at the Court-er church, in the Mexico District, from Psa. 17: 15, by the writer.   FRANK FISHER.

CRANE.—At her home in Chicago, Ill., March 9, 1892, of La Grippe, Dolcines E. Crane, daughter of Joseph and Elizabeth Fisher, of Mexico, Ind., aged 40 years, 3 months and 10 days. She leaves two sons and an affectionate husband. A short time before she died she was sitting up in bed. She called her friends to her bedside, and bade them Good-bye.   FRANK FISHER.

GRANSTAFF.—In the Oak Hill church, Shenandoah Co., Va., Feb. 11, 1892, sister Mary E. Granstaff, aged 42 years, 4 months and 20 days. She was anointed with oil in the name of the Lord. She suffered intensely for about five months. Funeral services by the writer from James 4: 14.
          WILLIAM PETERS.

SMITH.—In the Oak Hill church, Shenandoah Co., Va., Feb. 18, 1892, sister Mary Smith, aged 81 years, 11 months and 3 days. She was sick but a short time. Funeral services by the writer from 2 Tim. 4: 6-8.
          WILLIAM PETERS.

GRIM.—At his home near Brownsville, Washington Co., Maryland, Feb. 3, 1892, after a brief attack of nervous trouble, Bro. A. D. Grim, aged 59 years, 5 months and 7 days. Funeral services by Bro. D. Ausherman. He leaves a pleasant family of sons and daughters, and a wife.   A. C. CASTLE.

HICKEY.—In the Whiteville congregation, Andrew Co., Mo., Feb. 27, 1892, of paralysis, sister Mary Hickey, wife of Bro. Levi M. Hickey, aged 60 years, 2 months and 1 day. Her maiden name was Barbour. She was born in Washington Co., Tenn., Dec. 26, 1831. Dec. 22, 1859, she was united in marriage with Levi M. Hickey. In 1865 they came to Missouri. In June, 1891, she had a stroke of paralysis, from which she never entirely recovered, and on Dec. 17, 1891, she had a second stroke. She leaves a kind husband and five children.   LINA HICKEY.

MILLER.—Near Greencastle, Pa., Feb. 15, 1892, Fannie M. Miller, only remaining daughter of Samuel G. and Sarah Miller, aged 18 years, 5 months and 12 days. Funeral services from 1 Cor. 15: 26, by J. D. Benedict and D. B. Mentzer.   J. K. MILLER.

RISLEY.—In the Salem congregation, Reno Co., Kans., March 3, 1892, sister Maggie Risley, aged about 45 years. Deceased leaves a husband and three children. Funeral services by Daniel T. Dierdorff.
          A. F. CROSS.

SHERRY.—In the Massissinewa church, Delaware Co., Ind., Feb. 27, 1892, sister Rachel Sherry, aged 84 years, 4 months and 16 days. Funeral services by elders J. U. Studebaker and Samuel Younce.

RARICK.—In the same church, Feb. 28, 1892, of scarlet fever, Raymond Arthur, son of Levi and Amanda Rarick, aged 4 years and 1 month.   JACOB W. RARICK.

Union City, Ind.—We held our quarterly council March 19. Quite a large amount of business was disposed of. The poor were remembered and the mission work encouraged in a substantial way. Delegates were elected to District and Annual Meetings, Sunday-school officers chosen, and two deacons elected and installed.—*W. K. Simmons.*

Notice.—The Missionary and District Meeting of Nebraska will be held in the town of Juniata. All that can come on the B. & M. R. R. should do so, as it will save twelve miles conveyance. Please bring ten cents from each member for the expenses of Delegates to Annual Meeting and for Minutes of Annual Meeting and also District Meeting.—*Eld. D. Bechtelheimer, Juniata, Nebr.*

Wichita, Kans.—Last night, March 14, we were called to Sedgwick, Kans., to anoint sister Stoner. We found her very low in body, but strong in faith, trusting in the Lord. The anointing was attended to in the fear of the Lord, Bro. C. Delp assisting. Bro. Delp is making arrangements to go with his family to one of the mission posts in Arkansas. We are sorry to have him leave us, as there is much work to do here for the Lord, but we pray the Lord to bless him in his new field. Bro. Sharp has promised to be at our feast, May 14.—*William Johnson, 1588 Orange St.*

Warrior's Mark, Pa.—The brethren and sisters of this congregation commenced a series of meetings, and after continuing over a week, Bro. Michael Claar, of Bedford Co., Pa., came to us and held forth the Word of Life. The meetings were very interesting, and five were added to the fold, and one was reclaimed. They are all young, and five of them are just starting out in life. Four of them are just beginning housekeeping, one is a young man, and the last is a little girl of eleven years,—a bright, tender lamb of the fold.—*S. S. Gray.*

Keuka, Fla.—We intend, the Lord willing, to start on our way north March 21. We intend to visit Sister Mary Wigfield at St. Augustine, and expect to reach our Kansas home about April 1. My wife has been greatly benefited in health by spending the winter in Florida. We have bought a home in Morrill, Kans., and will move there as soon as we can. We make this change to avail ourselves of the school and church privileges. We enjoyed a feast of love with the K-uka Brethren March 12 and 13. Bro. J. C. Lahman and wife, of Mt. Morris, were also present.—*W. H. H. Sawyer, March 18.*

French Broad, Tenn.—Brethren C. H. Diehl and P. D. Reed, of Washington Co., Tenn., came to us March 4, and held a series of meetings. Bro. Reed stayed until the 10th, and then returned home. Bro. Diehl remained until the 14th, and as a result nine came out on the Lord's side and were baptized. Our brethren labored faithfully for the Master's cause. The attendance was very good, notwithstanding the rainy weather at that time. We felt built up during our meetings, and our prayer to God is that we may never forget the many good lessons learned. May the blessings of God rest with our brethren, and may they have souls for their hire.—*Eva Bashor, March 21.*

Three Springs, Pa.—On the evening of Feb. 9 Bro. Joseph Snowberger of Williamsburgh, Pa., commenced a series of meetings at the Three Springs school-house and continued until Feb. 14. He preached in all eight sermons. On account of sickness, inclement weather and other meetings in the community the attendance was not so large as it otherwise would have been, but the attention was good. Bro. Snowberger preached the Word with spirit and with power, and we enjoyed the preaching very much, as we are somewhat isolated from the body of the church, and do not often have continued meetings. While there were no additions to the church, the members were highly admonished, and sinners were warned to flee the wrath to come.—*J. M. Masemore.*

MATRIMONIAL.

"What therefore God hath joined together, let not man put asunder."

CROWL–GRIPE.—At the residence of the bride's parents, in the Upper Wood River church, Custer Co., Nebr., March 17, 1892, by the undersigned, John Crowl and sister Catharine Ora Gripe. JOHN J. HOOVAR.

MACEY–SHIRKY.—At the residence of the bride's parents, March 15, 1892, by Bro. S. B. Shirky, Bro. Louis Macey and sister Anna Shirky, all of the Wacanda congregation, Ray Co., Mo. S. A. RHODES.

SHOUP–BOYD.—At the residence of the bride's parents, Cherry Grove, Carroll Co., Ill., Jan. 26, 1892, Mr. Frank Shoup and Miss Rose Boyd. HENRY M. MARTIN.

MAN–TARR.—At the home of the bride's parents, near Springdale, Leavenworth Co., Kans., March 16, 1892, by the undersigned, Franklin Man to Mary Tarr. DAVID KIMMEL.

✦ FALLEN ASLEEP ✦

"Blessed are the dead which die in the Lord."

SMITH.—March 14, 1892, Luella Johnson, aged 18 years, 5 months and 8 days. She was married to John Smith, Jan. 3, 1891. In his care she leaves a two weeks' old infant. May God in his mercy spare his life to be one of usefulness. Funeral services conducted by Eld. Jacob Cripe from 1 Sam. 20: 3. THOMAS BARKLOW.

BERKEYBILE.—In the Shade Creek congregation, Somerset Co., Pa., Feb. 3, 1892, of old age, sister Christenia (Whetstone) Berkeybile, wife of Andrew Berkeybile (deceased), aged 87 years, 2 months and 11 days. Funeral services by Eld. Hiram Musselman. Sister Berkeybile was a faithful member of the Brethren church for many years. She was the mother of twelve children.
FANNIE M. FAUST.

KEISER.—At Warrensburgh, Mo., March 5, 1892, of pneumonia, sister Mollie Keiser, wife of Bro. David A. Keiser, aged about 38 years. Deceased was born in Augusta County, Va. Funeral and burial at the Panther Creek church, Ill. Funeral services by brethren Philip Moore and C. C. Brubaker.
THOS. KEISER.

McKIMMY.—In the Swan Creek congregation, Ohio, March 17, 1892, of diphtheria, Sadie McKimmy, daughter of Bro. John and sister Ida McKimmy, aged 2 years, 6 months and 13 days. JASPER McKIMMY.

HEAVNER.—In the bounds of the New Dale church, Hardy Co., W. Va., March 8, 1892, of consumption, Mrs. Elizabeth Heavner, aged 63 years, 2 months and 28 days. Funeral services by L. D. Caldwell in the New Dale church.

HALTERMAN.—In the Lost River congregation, Hardy Co., W. Va., March 10, 1892, Bro. Isaac Halterman, aged 40 years, 2 months and 6 days. He leaves a wife and four children. Funeral by brethren S. May and S. Mathias.

WHITMER.—In the bounds of the Linville Creek congregation, Rockingham Co., Va., March 14, 1892, Bro. Adam Whitmer, aged 47 years, 6 months and 4 days. He leaves a wife and six children. Funeral services by brethren J. P. Zigler, assisted by S. May. L. D. CALDWELL.

BROWN.—Near Mulvane, Kans., Feb 2, 1892, Gertrude Edith Ella Brown, aged 5 months and 23 days. This was one of the triplets born to Bro. Peter S. and sister Brown. Funeral services appropriate to the occasion. WILLIAM JOHNSON.

SIMISON.—In the bounds of the Wichita church, Kans., Feb. 2, 1892, sister Barbara Simison, aged 91 years, 3 months and 26 days. The subject of this notice was born in Westmoreland County, Pa., and was married to Samuel Simison, April 5, 1827. Funeral services by the writer. WM. JOHNSON.

BONEWITZ.—In the Coquille church, Coos Co., Ore., Urbin, infant son of Bro. John and sister Margaret Bonewitz, aged 4 months and 10 days. Funeral services by the Brethren. THOMAS BARKLOW.

DAWSON.—Within the bounds of the Round Mountain church, Ark., Feb. 5, 1892, of La Grippe, Leonidas A. Dawson, aged 18 years, 4 months and 21 days. Services were held at his parents' house, after which he was buried in the grave-yard near the church. LENA DAWSON.

HARRIS.—In the Union City church, Ind., Jan. 8, 1892, of a paralytic stroke, sister Rebecca Harris, aged 87 years.

ARNOLD.—In the Union City church, Ind., Jan. 25, 1892, sister Mary Arnold, *nee* Pickett, *nee* Marquis, aged 67 years, 10 months and 26 days. Funeral discourse by Eld. J. Stuizman.

COOK.—In the same congregation, Feb. 3, 1892, of La Grippe, Bro. Amos Cook, aged 81 years, 3 months and 22 days. The day before his death he was anointed in the name of the Lord. He was a member of the church for forty-four years.

KUNKLE.—In the same congregation, March 16, 1892, sister Magdalena Kunkle, aged 77 years and 11 days. She was born in York County, Pa., came to Ohio in 1829, married Jacob P. Kunkle in 1838, and was a member of the church for 52 years. W. K. SIMMONS.

DECKER.—At Roseburg, Oregon, Feb. 29, 1892, of consumption, sister Catharine Decker, wife of Bro. P. A. Decker, aged 54 years, 7 months and 4 days. She and her husband were the first two to unite with the Coquille church, in the fall of 1873. A year ago she and her husband went to California to relieve her lung trouble. Stopping awhile at that place, she came back to Roseburg, Oregon. THOMAS BARKLOW.

BURGET.—At Louisville, Ohio, March 23, 1892, Samuel Burget, aged 76 years and 11 months. He was born near Mapleton, Starke Co., Ohio, and married to Lydia Wass, June 15, 1845. To them were born six children. Funeral services by Rev. W. O. Baker.
H. P. BRINKWORTH.

RIGGLE.—In the Elkhart church, near Goshen, Ind., March 17, 1892, sister Eve C. Riggle (wife of Eld. Daniel Riggle), aged 50 years, 11 months and 20 days. Her disease had the appearance of consumption and cancer in the stomach. She was the mother of ten children. She was anointed shortly before her death. Funeral services by the writer. J. H. MILLER.

KNEE.—In the Mt. Etna congregation, Adams Co., Iowa, March 4, 1892, Frederic Knee, aged 83 years, 1 month and 15 days. Funeral discourse from Job 14: 10. M. MYERS.

HOFF.—At her home in Dallas Center, Iowa, Feb. 12, 1892, after a long illness, sister Katie Hoff, born July 24, 1826. She was married three times. Her maiden name was Herring. Her first husband's name was piper; second Swank and the third and last, Hoff.
ELLA ROYER.

ENGLISH.—At his home in Miami Co., Ind., March 4, 1892, of La Grippe, Bro. Joseph Franklin English, aged 84 years, 3 months and 4 days. He was married to Edna Hopper, at Virginia, Jan. 10, 1833. To them were born eight children. Funeral services at the Court-er church, in the Mexico District, from Psa. 17: 15, by the writer. FRANK FISHER.

CRANE.—At her home in Chicago, Ill., March 9, 1892, of La Grippe, Dolcinea E. Crane, daughter of Joseph and Elizabeth Fisher, of Mexico, Ind., aged 40 years, 3 months and 10 days. She leaves two sons and an affectionate husband. A short time before she died she was sitting up in bed. She called her friends to her bedside, and bade them Goodbye. FRANK FISHER.

GRANSTAFF.—In the Oak Hill church, Shenandoah Co., Va., Feb. 11, 1892, sister Mary E. Granstaff, aged 42 years, 4 months and 20 days. She was anointed with oil in the name of the Lord. She suffered intensely for about five months. Funeral services by the writer from James 4: 14.
WILLIAM PETERS.

SMITH.—In the Oak Hill church, Shenandoah Co., Va., Feb. 28, 1892, sister Mary Smith, aged 81 years, 11 months and 3 days. She was sick but a short time. Funeral services by the writer from 2 Tim. 4: 6-8.
WILLIAM PETERS.

GRIM.—At his home near Brownsville, Washington Co., Maryland, Feb. 3, 1892, after a brief attack of nervous trouble, Bro. A. D. Grim, aged 59 years, 5 months and 7 days. Funeral services by Bro. D. Ausherman. He leaves a pleasant family of sons and daughters, and a wife. C. C. CASTLE.

HICKEY.—In the Whitesville congregation, Andrew Co., Mo., Feb. 27, 1892, of paralysis, sister Mary Hickey, wife of Bro. Levi M. Hickey, aged 60 years, 2 months and 1 day. Her maiden name was Bashor. She was born in Washington Co., Tenn., Dec. 26, 1831. Dec. 22, 1859, she was united in marriage with Levi M. Hickey. In 1865 they came to Missouri. In June, 1890, she had a stroke of paralysis, from which she never entirely recovered, and on Dec. 17, 1891, she had a second stroke. She leaves a kind husband and five children. LENA HICKEY.

MILLER.—Near Greencastle, Pa., Feb. 15, 1892, Fannie M. Miller, only remaining daughter of Samuel G. and Sarah Miller, aged 18 years, 5 months and 22 days. Funeral services from 1 Cor. 15: 26, by J. D. Brandiff and D. B. Mentzer. J. K. MILLER.

RISLEY.—In the Salem congregation, Reno Co., Kans., March 3, 1892, sister Mary Risley, aged about 45 years. Deceased leaves a husband and three children. Funeral services by Daniel T. Dierdorff.
A. F. CROSS.

SHERRY.—In the Massissinewa church, Delaware Co., Ind., Feb. 27, 1892, sister Rachel Sherry, aged 82 years, 4 months and 16 days. Funeral services by elders J. U. Studebaker and Samuel Younce.

RARICK.—Of scarlet fever, Raymond Arthur, son of Levi and Amanda Rarick, aged 4 years and 1 month. JACOB W. RARICK.

Announcements.

DISTRICT MEETINGS.

April 6, Middle District of Indiana, in the Rossa church, Wabash Co., Ind. Delegates will please come prepared to pay their quota of expenses for the District, to defray the expenses of publishing District Meeting Minutes. They should also be ready to state how many copies of District Meeting Minutes will be needed to supply each family in their congregation with one copy.

April 6, at 9 A. M., District of Nebraska, in the Juniata congregation. Ministerial meeting the day before, at 10 A. M.

April 13, at 9 A. M., District Meeting of Southern Indiana, in the Howard church, Howard Co., Ind., 11 miles west of Kokomo. Those coming by railroad will come to Kokomo the day before. Come on morning train. Arrangements will be made to convey all to place of Meeting.

April 13, District of Texas, Oklahoma, Indian Territory, and South-west Kansas, in the Salem congregation, nine miles south and three miles west of Nickerson, Reno Co., Kans. Brethren are requested to come some time previous to District Meeting and hold a series or at least a few meetings for us. Whoever will favor us, will be met at Nickerson, by dropping a card to either P. Deiter or F. Crosu, Nickerson, Kans. Delegates to District Meeting will be met at Nickerson also.

April 13, at 9 A. M., District Meeting for North-eastern Kansas in the Olathe church, 3 miles north-west of Gardner. Ministerial meeting April 12, at 9 A. M. Gardner is on the Southern Kansas Division of the A. T. & S. F. System, where all trains will be met on Monday, the 11th, but none later.

April 13, South-western District of Kansas, in the Salem church, Reno County, Kans., several miles south of Nickerson.

April 14 and 15, North-western District of Ohio, in the LaFayette church, Allen Co., Ohio. Those coming on Thursday, April 14, to meet the Miamis Board, and twelving by the Pittsburg and Ft. Wayne Road should stop off at Lafayette. The 1 traveling by the Chicago and Erie R. R., should get off at Harrod Station. There will be ample conveyance at either station by the Brethren. All the Brethren wishing to use tables of either the Pittsburg & Ft. Wayne R. R., or the Chicago and Erie R. R., can get same by applying to A. M. Baker.

April 15 and 16, First District of West Virginia, in Sandy Creek church, Preston Co., W. Va.

April 15 and 16, at 10 A. M., District Meeting of First District of Virginia, at Peter's Creek church.

April 19, at 9:30 A. M., Eastern District of Maryland, in the Middletown Valley church.

April 21, District Meeting of Western Maryland, at the Vanclevesville house, Berkeley Co., W. Va. Brethren coming on the B. & O. road will stop off at Vanclevesville Station.

April 29, at 10 A. M., District Meeting of North-western Kansas and North Colorado, in Burr Oak church, Jewell Co., Kans. Every church is requested to be represented as far as possible, and we want every delegate to be prepared to meet expenses for the printing of the Minutes and expenses of delegate to Annual Meeting.

May 5, at 10 A. M., North District of Missouri, in the Bethel congregation, at the Squaw Creek meeting-house, Holt Co., Mo. Those coming by rail will be met at Mound City by addressing Jos. Andes at that place.

May 10, at 8 A. M., District of Northern Illinois, in the Milledgeville church, Carroll Co., Ill.

May 11, District Meeting of Southern Missouri and Arkansas, in the Shoal Creek church, Newton Co., Mo. Those coming by rail to Pierce City will be met on the morning of May 11, by notifying John Holder, read at Ergo. Those coming to Purdy will notify I. N. H. under Haander and will be met on the morning of May 11.

LOVE-FEASTS.

April 23 and 24, Second District of Virginia, at Elk Run church, eleven miles north of Staunton, Augusta Co., Va.

April 30, at 2 P. M., in the Burr Oak church, Jewell Co., Kans. Meetings to continue over Sunday. Any one coming by the Union Pacific R. R. from the West should come by way of Solomon City, then go to Delia, and from there to Jamestown on the Missouri Pacific R. R. (Central Branch). Then go to Burr Oak on Burr Oak Branch. Those coming by the Rock Island R. R. should stop in Otego, where they will be met by addressing Eld. Ed. Brown, Burr Oak, Kans., or they can go to Mankato, there change cars to the Missouri Pacific on Burr Oak Branch; thence to Burr Oak, where they will be met by addressing Lewis Hall, or Jeef Kinzie, in Burr Oak, Kans.

April 30, at 2 P. M., Walnut Valley church, Kansas.

May 1 and 2, at 2 P. M., Chippewa church, Lancaster Co., Pa., at the Chippewa Hill meeting-house.

May 5, at 10 A. M., Wolf Creek church, Montgomery Co., Ohio.

May 14, at 4 P. M., in the Yellow Creek congregation, Bedford County, Pa.

May 13 and 14, at 2 P. M., River Creek church, Ogle Co., Ill.

May 14, at 2 P. M., in the Kansas Center church, 3 miles east of Lyons.

May 14, at 4 P. M., Pleasant View church, Reno Co., Kans., 2½ miles south-west of Buda.

May 14, at 10 A. M., Pipe Creek congregation, Miami Co., Ind.

May 14, at 4 P. M., in the Bear Creek church, Montgomery Co., Ohio.

May 20, at 10 A. M., Minstertown church, Delaware Co., Ind., 3 miles west of Shideler. Those coming by rail should come to Shideler and inquire for the brethren.

May 27, at 2 P. M., in the Harlan congregation, five miles east of Harlan, Shelby Co., Iowa. Meetings to continue over Sunday.

May 28, at 10 A. M., Hartford church, Hartford Co., Md.

May 31 and June 1, Cherry Grove, Carroll Co., Ill.

May 31, at 4 P. M., in the Belcher church, Elkhart Co., Ind., three miles north-west of Wakarusa, Ind.

May 28, at 2 P. M., Lordsonville, Grant Co., Ind.

June 1, at 4 P. M., Yellow Creek church, Elkhart Co., Ind.

June 2, in the Yellow Creek church, Elkhart Co., Ind., 3 miles south-west of Goshen.

June 2, at 4 P. M., South Beatrice church, Gage Co., Neb. Those coming via U. P. R. R., stop at Holmesville; the on the B. & M. R. R., should stop at Beatrice; via the Rock Island R. R., should stop at Rockford.

June 2, at 2 P. M., at Flora, Ind. Train due here from the south at 11 A. M.

June 3, at 10 P. M., Yellow Creek, Ill.

June 3, at 2 P. M., in the Palestine church, Darke Co., Ohio. Those coming from the East on their way to Annual Meeting will please take notice of this and stop off with us. Those coming on the Pennsylvania line will please stop off at Greenville and inform George Baker, Painter, Darke Co., Ohio. Those coming on the Big Four Line, will stop off at Savannah or Clark's Station and inform Moses Hollinger, New Madison, Darke Co., Ohio.

June 4, at 4 P. M., in the Okaw church, Piatt Co., Ill. Ministering brethren on their way to Annual Meeting will please stop with us.

June 4, at 10 A. M., Springfield congregation, Nevada, Ind.

June 4, at 4 P. M., Berkeley church, W. Va.

June 4 and 5, at 4 P. M., Hickory Grove church, Carroll Co., Ill. Brethren going to Annual Meeting will please remember us.

June 4 and 5, at 10 A. M., Lick Creek church, Williams Co., Ohio, 3 mile north-west of Bryan.

June 4, Palestine church, Ohio. Members will be met at New Madison and Clark's Station on the " Big Four R. R.," by notifying Moses Hollinger, New Madison, Ohio.

June 11, at 2 P. M., Cherub church, Ill., in the Stinking Branch of the Wabash R. R.

June 18, at 10 A. M., South Waterloo church, Waterloo, Iowa.

June 19, at 2 P. M., Ridgeley church, four miles north-east of Kingsley, Iowa.

June 19, at 4 P. M., Yellow River congregation, Marshall Co., Ind.

June 18, Green Spring District, Seneca Co., Ohio.

June 18 and 19, at 11 A. M., Middle Creek church, Mahaska Co., Iowa.

The Bible the Sunday-school Text-book.—By Allred Holsopple. Cloth, 75 cents.

Origin of Single Immersion.—By Eld. James Quinter. Price, 2 copies, 5 cents; 25 copies, 60 cents; 100 copies, $2.00.

To Close out

The few copies of the BRETHREN'S ALMANAC still on hand, we offer them at REDUCED PRICES. As long as the supply lasts, we will send them at the rate of five cents per copy post-paid, but to get them you should ORDER NOW.

CALIFORNIA.

CALIFORNIA is the most attractive and delightful section of the United States, if not of the world; and by many, beautiful resorts will be crowded with the best families of the East during the entire winter. It offers to the investor the best open opportunity for safe and large returns from its fruit lands. It offers the kindest climate in the world to the feeble and debilitated; and it is reached in the most comfortable manner over the Atchison, Topeka & Santa Fe Railroad. Pullman Vestibule Sleeping Cars leave Chicago by this line every day in the year and go, without change or transfer through to San Francisco, Los Angeles and San Diego. This is a feature not offered by any other line. Write to John J. Byrne, 601 Rialto Building, Chicago, Ill., if you desire any further information as to the country and the accommodations for reaching it.

EGGS, EGGS FOR HATCHING

Send three stamps for mammoth Catalogue and Guide to Poultry Raisers. This finest book of the kind published. Containing valuable information for the poultry man and all who have poultry, either for pleasure or profit.

C. C. SHOEMAKER,
L. B. 1064. Freeport, Ill.

Juvenile Quarterly.

This is just the *Quarterly* for the little folks. Price, Three Copies, per Quarter, 20 Cents; 6 Copies, per Quarter, 35 Cents; 10 Copies and over, per Quarter, 3 Cents each.

Brethren's Quarterly.

Orders should be sent in at once for the *Quarterly* for the First Quarter of 1892. Price, three copies, 25 cents; eight copies, 40 cents; twenty copies and over, four cents each.

The Hollinger Fence and Post.

Strong, Simple, Durable and Cheap!
No More Cruelty to Stock!

MOUNT MORRIS, ILL., March 4, 1892.

To William B. May, Concord.—This is to certify that we have examined the Hollinger wire fence and are satisfied that it is an excellent fence, much superior to barbed wire, for which so many horses and cattle are cruelly injured. We are also personally acquainted with the builder, Mr. Hollinger, and do not hesitate to recommend him as a fair-dealing, honest man, believing he will faithfully carry out any promise he may make.

D. L. MILLER,
D. N. WINGERT.

For full particulars call on or address the editor, East of Ohio, J. K. Hollinger, Covington, Ohio. West of Ohio, D. Hollinger, Mt. Morris, Ill.

Announcements.

DISTRICT MEETINGS.

April 6, Middle District of Indiana, in the Rossie church, Wabash Co., Ind. Delegates will please come prepared to pay their quota of expenses for the District, to defray the expenses of publishing District Meeting Minutes. They should also be ready to state how many copies of District Meeting Minutes will be needed to supply each family in their congregation with one copy.

April 6, at 9 A. M., District of Nebraska, in the Juniata congregation. Ministerial meeting the day before, at 10 A. M.

April 13, at 9 A. M., District Meeting of Southern Indiana, in the Howard church, Howard Co., Ind., 11 miles west of Kokomo. Those coming by railroad will come to Kokomo the day before. Come on morning train. Arrangements will be made to convey all to place of Meeting.

April 13, District of Texas, Oklahoma, Indian Territory, two miles south and three miles west of Nickerson, Reno Co., Kans. Brethren are requested to come some time previous to District Meeting and hold a series or at least a few meetings for us. Whoever will favor us, will be met at Nickerson, by dropping a card to either P. Detter or F. Crane, Nickerson, Kans. Delegates to District Meeting will be met at Nickerson also.

April 13, at 9 A. M., District Meeting for North-eastern Kansas in the Olathe church, 3 miles north-west of Gardner. Ministerial meeting April 12, at 9 A. M. Gardner is on the Southern Kansas Division of the A. T. & S. F. System, where all trains will be met on Monday, the 11th, for noon train.

April 13, South-western District of Kansas, in the Salem church, Reno County, Kansas, several miles south of Nickerson.

April 14 and 15, North-western District of Ohio, in the Lafayette church, Allen Co., Ohio. Those coming on Thursday, April 14, to meet the Mission Board, and traveling by the Pittsburg and Ft. Wayne Road should stop off at Lafayette. The 11 traveling by the Chicago and Erie R. R., should get off at Harrod Station. There will be ample conveyance at either station by the brethren. All the brethren wishing to take tithes of either the Pittsburg & Ft. Wayne R. R., or the Chicago and Erie R. R., can get same by applying to A. M. Baker.

April 19 and 16, First District of West Virginia, in Sandy Creek church, Preston Co., W. Va.

April 19 and 16, at 10 A. M., District Meeting of First District of Virginia, at Peter's Creek church.

April 19, at 9:30 A. M., Eastern District of Maryland, in the Middletown Valley church.

April 21, District Meeting of Western Maryland, at the Vanclevesville house, Berkeley Co., W. Va. Brethren coming on the B. & O. road will stop off at Vanclevesville Station.

April 29, at 10 A. M., District Meeting of North-western Kansas and North Colorado, in Burr Oak church, Burr Oak, Jewell Co., Kans. Every church is requested to be represented as far as possible, and we want every delegate to be prepared to meet expenses for the printing of the Minutes and expenses of delegates to Annual Meeting.

May 2, at 10 A. M., North District of Missouri, in the Bethel congregation, at the Squaw Creek meeting-house, Holt Co., Mo. Those coming by rail will be met at Mound City by addressing Jos. Andes at that place.

May 10, at 8 A. M., District of Northern District, in the Milfordville church, Carroll Co., Ill.

May 11, District Meeting of Southern Missouri and Arkansas, in the Shoal Creek church, Newton Co., Mo. Those coming by rail to Pierce City will be met on the morning of May 11, by notifying John Heidenreid at Ergo. Those coming to Purdy will notify Lander Harader and will be met on the morning of May 11.

LOVE-FEASTS.

April 13 and 14, Second District of Virginia, at Elk Run church, eleven miles north of Staunton, Augusta Co., Va.

April 30, at 2 P. M., in the Burr Oak church, Jewell Co., Kans. Meetings to continue over Sunday. Any one coming by the Union Pacific R. R. from the West should come by way of Solomon City, then go to Beloit, and from there to Jamestown on the Missouri Pacific R. R. (Central Branch). Then go to Burr Oak to Burr Oak church. Those coming by the Rock Island R. R. should stop at Osage, where they will be met by addressing Eld. Eli Renner, Burr Oak, Kans., or they can go to Mankato, there change cars to the Missouri Pacific, on Burr Oak Branch, thence to Burr Oak, where they will be met by addressing Lewis Heit, or Joel Kinzie, at Burr Oak, Kans.

April 30, at 5 P. M., Walnut Valley church, Kansas, 3½ miles West and 3½ miles north of Great Bend, Kans.

May 2 and 3, at 2 P. M., Chiques church, Lancaster Co., Pa., at the Chiques' Hill meeting-house.

May 7, at 10 A. M., in the Bethel congregation, at the Squaw Creek meeting-house, Holt Co., Mo.

May 7, at 2 P. M., Abilene, Kans.

May 7, at 2 P. M., Peabody church, Kans.

May 7, at 10 A. M., Walnut Creek church, Douglas Co., Kansas.

May 7, at Timberville, Va., in the Flat Rock church, Va.

May 7 and 8, in the Fatterly church, 3½ at the residence of S. A. Eaker. Place of meeting 2½ miles south-west of Fatterly.

May 10, at 10 A. M., Wolf Creek church, Montgomery Co., Ohio.

May 13, at 5 P. M., in the Yellow Creek congregation, Bedford County, Pa.

May 13 and 14, at 2 P. M., Silver Creek church, Ogle Co., Ill.

May 14, at 7 P. M., in the Kansas Center church, 3 miles east of Lyons.

May 14, at 2 P. M., Pleasant View church, Reno Co. Kans., 2½ miles south-east of Enoch.

May 14, at 10 A. M., Pipe Creek congregation, Miami Co., Ind.

May 14, at 4 P. M., in the Deer Creek church, Montgomery Co., Ohio.

May 20, at 10 A. M., Middletown church, Delaware Co., Ind., 4 miles west of Shidder. Those coming by rail should come to Shidder and inquire for the brethren.

May 21, at 3 P. M., in the Harlen congregation, four miles east of Harlen, Shelby Co., Iowa. Meetings to continue over Sunday.

May 28, at 10 A. M., Hartford church, Hartford City, Ind.

May 21 and June 1, Cherry Grove, Carroll Co., Ill.

May 31, 10 4 P. M., in the Rouge church, Elkhart Co., Ind., three miles north-west of Wakarusa, Ind.

June 1, at 2 P. M., Lecturesville, Grant Co., Ind.

June 1, at 4 P. M., Yellow Creek church, Elkhart Co., Ind.

June 1, in the Yellow Creek church, Elkhart Co., Ind., 3 miles south-west of Goshen.

June 3, at 4 P. M., South District church, Gage Co., Nebr. Those coming via U. P. R. R., stop at Holmesville; via the B. & M. R. R., should stop off at Beatrice; via the Rock Island R. R., should stop at Blakeford.

June 2, at 2 P. M., at Plum, Ind. Train 600 here from the north at 10 A. M.

June 4, at 2 P. M., Walnut Level church, Wells Co., Ind.

June 4 and 5, at 2 P. M., Yellow Creek, Ill.

June 7, at 2 P. M., in the Painviller church, Darke Co., Ohio. Those coming from the East on their way to Annual Meeting will please take a note of this and stop off with us. Those coming on the Pennsylvania line will please stop off at Greenville and return George Baker, Painville; Darke Co., Ohio. Those coming on the Big Four Line, will stop off at Bradford church, there is a station two miles above Holzinger, New Madison, Darke Co., Ohio, or George Stamp, Baker, Darke Co., Ohio.

June 8, at 2 P. M., in the Olive church, Platt Co., Ill. Ministerial brethren on their way to Annual Meeting will please stop with us.

June 4, at 10 A. M., Springfield congregation, Waveca, Ind.

June 4 and 5, at 2 P. M., Berkeley church, W. Va.

June 4 and 5, at 2 P. M., Hickory Grove church, Carroll Co., Ill. Brethren going to Annual Meeting will please remember us.

June 4, at 10 A. M., Lick Creek church, Williams Co., Ohio, 3 miles south-west of Bryan.

June 6, Painville church, Ohio. Members will be met at New Madison and Clark's Station on the "Big Four R. R." by notifying Moses Holzinger, New Madison, Ohio.

June 11, at 2 P. M., Carroll church, Ill. See the Sensler Branch of the Wabash R. R.

June 18, at 10 A. M., South Waterloo church, Waterloo, Iowa.

June 14, at 2 P. M., Kingsley church, four miles southwest of Kingsley, Iowa.

June 14, at 2 P. M., Yellow River congregation, Marshall Co., Ind.

June 18, Green Spring District, Seneca Co., Ohio.

June 18 and 19 at 2 P. M., Middle Creek church, Mercer, Junita Co., Iowa.

The Bible the Sunday-school Text-book.—By Alfred Hofborn. Cloth, 25 cents.

Origin of Single Immersion.—By Eld. James Quinter. Plain 3 copies, 5 cents; 20 copies, 25 cents; 50 copies, $1.00.

GENERAL NOTES.

Infant baptism binds religion on children, while they are yet unaccountable.

The ties that bind are, early training, parental influence and affection, association, the influence of friends, etc. All these are bonds of earth.

Take away the earthly ties, and how many would leave the Roman church who now remain firmly in it, bound by ties as strong as life, but earthly in character and origin!

Those whom Christ gives to God, are not born of corruptible, but of incorruptible seed. They are not bound to God and the church by earthly ties, but by heavenly,—by the Spirit of God, the Word of God, by an enlightened judgment, principle, love to God and to the church, bonds of heaven that shall never be broken.

There never was a church in the wilderness or before Christ in any special sense, in the form in which it now exists.

There were no terms of membership,—faith, repentance, or regeneration. Nothing is required but to be born or bought into the church,—a kind of politico-religious affair.

The two covenants. Read Gal. 4: 20-30. Abraham had two sons,—one of, the bond woman and one of the free. These are the two covenants. The covenant from Mt. Sinai gendereth to bondage.

The circumcision was its sign. This covenant was not developed beyond its sign till at Mt. Sinai, when it was developed into the law that governed Israel. The covenant of promise existed only as a promise, until it was developed by Christ in the Gospel. The covenant of circumcision, or the law, was in the same relation to the covenant of promise, as Ishmael to Isaac. Ishmael was cast out, as was the law when Christ came.

The Law of Moses has no more authority over the Gospel than had Ishmael over Isaac.

For its basis the Gospel is entirely independent of the law. The institutions of the law were cast out with it, and have now no authority whatever. They are gone forever. Ishmael never returned.

Not knowing what he said, Peter wanted Moses, Elias and Christ to dwell together. Luke 9: 30, 35. "Hear him." God says: "Make no tabernacles; for Moses and Elias,—the law and the prophets,—are gone."

THE COVERING.—1 Cor. 11: 16.

BY J. M. MOHLER.

Number Two.

It is a direct revelation from God, hence of divine authority, and not simply recommended by Paul. Matt. 7: 24. The importance of a divine command depends upon the Lord, and to disregard any known duty is virtually to reject divine authority. It is an established principle.

To demonstrate practically that the hair cannot be used acceptably to God, for the covering of the head in time of worship, I wish to illustrate by using an axiom. Two or more things which are equal to the same thing are equal to each other. If the covering, in verse 15, is the same as that alluded to in verses 4-6, then the word hair can be used in those verse, and make good sense. "Every man praying, etc., having his head covered, i. e., (having his hair on his head) dishonoreth his head. Every woman praying, etc., with her head uncovered, i. e., (with her hair off her head) dishonoreth her head,—for if the woman be not covered, i. e., (if she have no hair on her head) let her also be shorn or shaven. What unmeaning and senseless language!

Please allow me to illustrate. I say, this lamp is equal to that clock, and this table is equal to that clock. Here we have two things equal to

the same thing, which is the clock. If both the table and lamp are equal to the same thing, it is already proven that the lamp and table are equal to each other. This is called an axiom, which is a self-evident truth. Hence the word "hair," in verse 15, cannot be substituted for the words covered in verses 4 to 6, and make good sense. A fair degree of good common sense will teach us that the word hair in verse 15, and the word "covered" in verses 4 to 6, cannot be used interchangeably.

From the attention that was paid to this subject, it is evident that it must have occasioned considerable disturbance in the church of Corinth, and if it were possible for Paul to visit some of the churches of to-day, he would realize the painful necessity of correcting them, as he did the Corinthian church. God commanded the head to be covered,—not the face. We should cover the head and have the' face uncovered. To the best of my knowledge, in the Gospel is found the only divine authority for the covering and uncovering of the head in time of worship. Man had the prerogative to be immediately from God, but the woman was from the man. Man is the image and glory of God, i. e., the image, majesty, dominion and power shine forth most brightly in the man; therefore he ought to have his head uncovered.

"But," you ask, "is not the woman also created in the image of God?" We say, Yes. Considering the woman according to her specifical nature, as such, she was created after the image of God in righteousness and true holiness, as well as the man, but then, considering the woman according to her personal relation to the man, she is not the image of God, because dominion, which is the image of God, is man's privilege, and subjection the woman's duty.

Originally man was not made of the woman nor for the woman; hence, for those, and no doubt many other reasons, unknown to us, God has required the woman to cover her head in time of worship, that she may express her submission and subjection, according to the divine arrangement of God. Strictly speaking, it is not proper to name this covering a cap. Virtually it is more than a cap. It is a covering or a veiling of the head. All said,—pro and con,—the covering, as recognized by the General Brotherhood, is only a veiling of the head,—the most convenient way of covering the head in time of worship,—a covering specially worn as an honor to God, worn by a special people, on special occasions, and for a special purpose. It is an easy matter for us to know that God demands, on the part of the woman, an artificial covering in time of prayer, etc., and that the hair, in no case, will satisfy divine justice in time of worship. No process of reasoning or demonstration can make it plainer, therefore do not add confusion to it by using wrong interpretations.

Box 111, Lewistown, Pa.

SINGLE MODE.

BY C. D. HYLTON.

I am unable to see any good reason why the single mode of washing feet should not be the universal and only mode among us.

One of the characteristics of the Brethren is to follow God's Book where it leads, laying aside all creeds and traditions of men. Jesus says, "I have given you an example that ye should do as I have done to you." What was the example? He "began to wash the disciples' feet and to wipe them with the towel wherewith he was girded." I cannot follow my Lord's example unless I do like him. So, if I only wash, and let another brother wipe, as in the double mode, I cannot consistently say that I have done as Christ commanded me.

Christ did not wash the disciples' feet and tell one of them to follow with the towel. In the single mode every member can obey the command, while in the double mode many are deprived of the privilege.

We want harmony in practice but can never have it, excepting by the single mode. There is no danger in changes as long as we get nearer the Bible by them.

In some places the Brethren are censured for following two modes, and this should cause us to come closer to God's Word. If the Word make us free, we shall be free indeed. If God be for us, who can be against us?

THE NEGRO.

A residence of seven years in the South gave us a chance to learn more about the wants of the South than we can learn in a life-time from books and papers. There is a genius about the people of the South that cannot be expressed by either word or picture. One has to spend years in learning it, before he gets the correct idea. The future of the negro is one of the great questions of the South. It has long been an opinion that the power to improve his condition must come from his own ranks. This fact was clearly comprehended recently in a great Negro Convention, at Tuskegree, Ala. Among the resolutions passed were a number of special notes. The following, though not particularly religious, may prove interesting to our readers, and enable them to better understand the condition of the negro. This is the best thing we have yet seen, pertaining to the developing of this peculiar race of people.—ED.

In view of our general condition, we would suggest the following remedies: 1. That, as far as possible, we aim to raise at home our own meat and bread. 2. That, as fast as possible, we buy land, even though a very few acres at a time. 3. That a larger number of our young people be taught trades, and that they be urged to prepare themselves to enter as largely as possible all the various avocations of life. 4. That we especially try to broaden the field of labor for our women. 5. That we make every sacrifice, and practice every form of economy, that we may purchase land and free ourselves from our burdensome habit of living in debt. 6. That we urge our ministers and teachers to give more attention to the material condition and home life of the people. 7. We urge that our people do not depend entirely upon the State to provide school houses and lengthen the time of the schools, but that they take hold of the matter themselves, when the State leaves off, and by supplementing the public funds from their own pockets and by building school-houses, bring about the desired results. 8. We urge patrons to give earnest attention to the mental and moral fitness of those who teach their schools. 9. That we urge the doing away with all sectarian prejudice in the management of the schools.

As the judgment of this Conference, we would further declare: That we put on record our deep sense of gratitude to the good people of all sections for their assistance, and that we are glad to recognize a growing interest on the part of the best white people of the South in the education of the negro.

That we appreciate the spirit of friendliness and fairness shown us by the Southern white people in matters of business in all lines of material development.

We are esteemed quite as highly as we deserve even when we are misjudged unfavorably at some particular point. If we could have our own way about the estimate put upon us by others, we should have all our best qualities made prominent and all our worst qualities ignored. But that would not be a fair way of judging us, and we have no right to expect it. Yet how sure we are to wince under a sense of injustice when we happen to be thought ill of at a point where we are not quite as bad as we are supposed to be, and how little weight do we give to the fact that at many another point we are thought more highly of than we ought to be! Who of us can say that he would really be the gainer in the esteem of his best friend if he were seen just as he is, with all his defects standing out in their baldness? And if it be true that we are, on the whole, the gainers by the imperfect knowledge of us, possessed by those who love us best, why should we deem ourselves ill-treated when a single fault that is not ours is ascribed to us, while a dozen of our real faults are concealed from the knowledge of those whose good opinion we prize?—Sel.

GENERAL NOTES.

Infant baptism binds religion on children, while they are yet unaccountable.

The ties that bind are, early training, parental influence and affection, association, the influence of friends, etc. All these are bonds of earth.

Take away the earthly ties, and how many would leave the Roman church who now remain firmly in it, bound by ties as strong as life, but earthly in character and origin!

Those whom Christ gives to God, are not born of corruptible, but of incorruptible seed. They are not bound to God and the church by earthly ties, but by heavenly,—by the Spirit of God, the Word of God, by an enlightened judgment, principle, love to God and to the church, bonds of heaven that shall never be broken.

There never was a church in the wilderness or before Christ in any special sense, in the form in which it now exists.

There were no terms of membership,—faith, repentance, or regeneration. Nothing is required but to be born or bought into the church,—a kind of politico-religious affair.

The two covenants. Read Gal. 4: 20–30. Abraham had two sons,—one of, the bond woman and one of the free. These are the two covenants. The covenant from Mt. Sinai gendereth to bondage.

The circumcision was its sign. This covenant was not developed beyond its sign till at Mt. Sinai, when it was developed into the law that governed Israel. The covenant of promise existed only as a promise, until it was developed by Christ in the Gospel. The covenant of circumcision, or the law, was in the same relation to the covenant of promise, as Ishmael to Isaac. Ishmael was cast out, as was the law when Christ came.

The Law of Moses has no more authority over the Gospel than had Ishmael over Isaac.

For its basis the Gospel is entirely independent of the law. The institutions of the law were cast out with it, and have now no authority whatever. They are gone forever. Ishmael never returned.

Not knowing what he said, Peter wanted Moses, Elias and Christ to dwell together. Luke 9: 30, 36. "Hear him." God says: "Make no tabernacles; for Moses and Elias,—the law and the prophets,—are gone."

THE COVERING.—1 Cor. 11: 16.

BY J. M. MOHLER.

Number Two.

It is a direct revelation from God, hence of divine authority, and not simply recommended by Paul. Matt. 7: 24. The importance of a divine command depends upon the Lord, and to disregard any known duty is virtually to reject divine authority. It is an established principle.

To demonstrate practically that the hair cannot be used acceptably, to God, for the covering of the head in time of worship, I wish to illustrate by using an axiom. Two or more things which are equal to the same thing are equal to each other. If the covering, in verse 15, is the same as that alluded to in verses 4–6, then the word *hair* can be used in those verse, and make good sense. "Every man praying, etc., having his head covered, *i. e.*, (having his hair on his head) dishonoreth his head. Every woman praying, etc., with her head uncovered, *i. e.*, (with her hair off her head) dishonoreth her head,—for if the woman be not covered, *i. e.*, (if she have no hair on her head) let her also be shorn or shaven. What unmeaning and senseless language!

Please allow me to illustrate. I say, this lamp is equal to that clock, and this table is equal to that clock. Here we have two things equal to the same thing, which is the clock. If both the table and lamp are equal to the same thing, it is already proven that the lamp and table are equal to each other. This is called an axiom, which is a self-evident truth. Hence the word "hair," in verse 15, cannot be substituted for the words covered in verses 4 to 6, and make good sense. A fair degree of good common sense will teach us that the word hair in verse 15, and the word "covered" in verses 4 to 6, cannot be used interchangeably.

From the attention that was paid to this subject, it is evident that it must have occasioned considerable disturbance in the church of Corinth, and if it were possible for Paul to visit some of the churches of to-day, he would realize the painful necessity of correcting them, as he did the Corinthian church. God commanded the head to be covered,—not the face. We should cover the head and have the face uncovered. To the best of my knowledge, in the Gospel is found the only divine authority for the covering and uncovering of the head in time of worship. Man had the prerogative to be immediately from God, but the woman was from the man. Man is the image and glory of God, *i. e.*, the image, majesty, dominion and power shine forth most brightly in the man; therefore he ought to have his head uncovered.

"But," you ask, "is not the woman also created in the image of God?" We say, Yes. Considering the woman according to her specifical nature, as such, she was created after the image of God in righteousness and true holiness, as well as the man, but then, considering the woman according to her personal relation to the man, she is not the image of God, because dominion, which is the image of God, is man's privilege, and subjection the woman's duty.

Originally man was not made of the woman nor for the woman; hence, for those, and no doubt many other reasons, unknown to us, God has required the woman to cover her head in time of worship, that she may express her submission and subjection, according to the divine arrangement of God. Strictly speaking, it is not proper to use the covering a cap. Virtually it is more than a cap. It is a covering or a veiling of the head. All said,—*pro* and *con*,—the covering, as recognized by the General Brotherhood, is only a veiling of the head,—the most convenient way of covering the head in time of worship,—a covering specially worn as an honor to God, worn by a special people, on special occasions, and for a special purpose. It is an easy matter for us to know that God demands, on the part of the woman, an artificial covering in time of prayer, etc., and that the hair, in no case, will satisfy divine justice in time of worship. No process of reasoning or demonstration can make it plainer, therefore do not add confusion to it by using wrong interpretations.

Box 111, Lewistown, Pa.

SINGLE MODE.

BY O. D. HYLTON.

I AM unable to see any good reason why the single mode of washing feet should not be the universal and only mode among us.

One of the characteristics of the Brethren is to follow God's Book where it leads, laying aside all creeds and traditions of men. Jesus says, "I have given you an example that ye should do as I have done to you." What was the example? He "began to wash the disciples' feet and to wipe them with the towel wherewith he was girded." I cannot follow my Lord's example unless I do like him. So, if I only wash, and let another brother wipe, as in the double mode, I cannot consistently say that I have done as Christ commanded me.

Christ did not wash the disciples' feet and tell one of them to follow with the towel. In the single mode every member can obey the command, while in the double mode many are deprived of the privilege.

We want harmony in practice but can never have it, excepting by the single mode. There is no danger in changes as long as we get nearer the Bible by them.

In some places the Brethren are censured for following two modes, and this should cause us to come closer to God's Word. If the Word make us free, we shall be free indeed. If God be for us, who can be against us?

THE NEGRO.

A RESIDENCE of seven years in the South gave us a chance to learn more about the wants of the South than we can learn in a life-time from books and papers. There is a genius about the people of the South that cannot be expressed by either word or picture. One has to spend years in learning it, before he gets the correct idea. The future of the negro is one of the great questions of the South. It has long been an opinion that the power to improve his condition must come from his own ranks. This fact was clearly comprehended recently in a great Negro Convention, at Tuskegree, Ala. Among the resolutions passed were a number of special notes. The following, though not particularly religious, may prove interesting to our readers, and enable them to better understand the condition of the negro. This is the best thing we have yet seen, pertaining to the developing of this peculiar race of people.—ED.

In view of our general condition, we would suggest the following remedies: 1. That, as far as possible, we aim to raise at home our own meat and bread. 2. That, as fast as possible, we buy land, even though a very few acres at a time. 3. That a larger number of our young people be taught trades, and that they be urged to prepare themselves to enter as largely as possible all the various avocations of life. 4. That we especially try to broaden the field of labor for our women. 5. That we make every sacrifice, and practice every form of economy, that we may purchase land and free ourselves from our burdensome habit of living in debt. 6. That we urge our ministers and teachers to give more attention to the material condition and home life of the people. 7. We urge that our people do not depend entirely upon the State to provide school houses and lengthen the time of the schools, but that they take hold of the matter themselves, when the State leaves off, and by supplementing the public funds from their own pockets and no building school-houses, bring about the desired results. 8. We urge patrons to give earnest attention to the mental and moral fitness of those who teach their schools. 9. That we urge the doing away with all sectarian prejudice in the management of the schools.

As the judgment of this Conference, we would further declare: That we put on record our deep sense of gratitude to the good people of all sections for their assistance, and that we are glad to recognize a growing interest on the part of the best white people of the South in the education of the negro.

That we appreciate the spirit of friendliness and fairness shown us by the Southern white people in matters of business in all lines of material development.

WE are esteemed quite as highly as we deserve even when we are misjudged unfavorably at some, particular point. If we could have our own way about the estimate put upon us by others, we should have all our best qualities made prominent and all our worst qualities ignored. But that would not be a fair way of judging us, and we have no right to expect it. Yet how sure we are to wince under a sense of injustice when we happen to be thought ill of at a point where we are not quite as bad as we are supposed to be, and how little weight do we give to the fact that at many another point we are thought more highly of than we ought to be! Who of us can say that he would really be the gainer in the esteem of his best friend if he were seen just as he is, with all his defects standing out in their baldness? And if it be true that we are, on the whole, the gainers by the imperfect knowledge of us, possessed by those who love us best, why should we deem ourselves ill-treated when a single fault that is not ours is ascribed to us, while a dozen of our real faults are concealed from the knowledge of those whose good opinion we prize?—*Sel.*

nest where these young ones first formed the nucleus of a nation; how they had been directed by the "Pillar of Cloud" to the place where God desires them to prepare to meet his holy presence.

Moses has given God's message to the people who, with one voice, respond, "All that the Lord hath spoken we will do." When he has returned to the mountain with their speech, God tells him to "sanctify the people to-day and to-morrow, and let them wash their clothes, for the third day the Lord will come down in the sight of all the people upon Mt. Sinai."

Bounds were set unto the people around the mountain, lest they should touch it and die. The mandate was to be stoned or shot through, whether man or beast that should touch.

Moses had given them all the words of the Lord, and they had accepted the terms, had spent the two days in putting from them all that is unholy or unclean. They had washed themselves in the crystal fountain that God had brought from the rock to quench their burning thirst,—not their hands, or their feet only, but their whole bodies. The garments that were to last them from Egypt to Canaan might be soiled from their desert march; the same never-failing fountain was sufficient, and they were true to their covenant and cleansed their garments (for one's vestment is a kind of outer self), so that no sin may infest the assembly when they come before His Majesty.

All are cleansed, from the least unto the greatest; and they have forgotten their worldly hopes and ambitions in anticipation of seeing the holy presence of Him who had freed them from their misery and brought them through temptations, deprivations and suffering with the promise of full fruition in the land whither they are journeying. Have all these purified themselves from the sins committed by the way? They have answered God's purpose and we need not inquire further.

On the third day, clouds and smoke fill the holy place. The lightnings flash and thunders roll from Sinai's rugged heights and the people tremble and quake as they sit at the foot of the mountain and at the feet of God. Holy awe and reverence pervade this vast assembly, while God, the only one who ever spoke to so large an audience, speaks to the people concerning the laws that are to govern them through the generations to come. Thunders and lightnings are the introduction to this great sermon; the thunders, God's voice, the lightnings, the fire of his countenance, to awaken their attention, for the God of all the earth would speak to them.

While they were permitted thus to behold the manifestation of his presence, they dare not gaze upon him lest they die. How many of us are branded with that prying disposition that will not let us rest under the plain, simple truths of God! It was the sin of discontent in our first parents,— a desire for knowledge,—seeking more wisdom than God gave them, that caused their downfall, and has cursed so many fathers in Israel. Is it any wonder that God should take this precaution? The restraints and warnings of the divine law are all given for our good and to prevent the danger we might otherwise run into.

We constitute but a small part of God's creation; we have trials that are grievous to be borne; we fight some battles with this earth, and sometimes become thirsty and cry for water to cool our parched lips, but we want it sweetened; become hungry and cry for bread that will save our lives, and then want meat. We learn the sad fact that "nothing human is alien to us;" yet we are not willing to do as much as these benighted Hebrews.

It was at the mount that they decided to have Moses speak with God in their stead because they were unable to endure his presence. We do not

have Moses to be our intercessor, but we are happy in the contrast between God on Mt. Sinai, and his manifestations of Jesus the Christ. The blast of the trumpet does not now terrify, nor a mountain smoke with his presence and threaten death to those who touch, but we can come to the spiritual Mount Zion, where countless angels dwell; to the spirits of just men made perfect and to Jesus the Christ who is the Rock of our salvation. He is the messenger of the New Covenant and has told us what is necessary for us to do, if we would meet his approbation.

These washings and cleansings of the Old Testament are types of what we have revealed in the New. The washing at the mountain was to purify their outward beings, and the antitype is the washing we must undergo to become new creatures in Christ Jesus. As they purified their forms and garments, we must purify our hearts and lives.

If the English-speaking people are the Israel of to-day, what a time is coming when we must appear in the presence of our Creator! Then, if we have not bathed in some crystal stream, if we have not purified our vesture, we will not be ready when Gabriel shall sound the trumpet of the resurrection to meet our Father, and will cry for the rocks and hills to hide us from the presence of Him who sitteth upon the throne.

THE TONGUE.

BY ENOCH EBY.

"Even so the tongue is a little member, and boasteth great things. Behold, how great a matter a little fire kindleth!" James 3: 5.

The angel said unto John, "Eat the little book," Rev. 10: 9. A man does not live by "bread alone, but by every word that proceedeth out of the mouth of God."—Jesus. David says, "I keep thy word in my heart that I sin not." If we should keep the second chapter of James in our heart, it would be a great blessing to us, to the church and the neighborhood. About all the quarrels in families, neighborhoods, churches, and in the world, even wars, have their origin in the tongue. It is a world of iniquity. It is a fire. Set on the fire of hell, it setteth on fire the whole course of nature, but a fire will finally stop unless it gets fuel. Where there is no tale-bearer, the strife ceaseth. Prov. 26: 2. The fire would go out if there were no tale-bearer.

What is a tale-bearer? "One who impertinently communicates intelligence or anecdotes and makes mischief in society by his officiousness."— Webster. "A tale-bearer revealeth secrets." Prov. 11: 13. Whispering is a fruit of the tongue, and condemned by the apostle. 2 Cor. 12: 20. What kind of a character is that? A whisperer is a tattler;—one who tells secrets.—Webster. Backbiting is another evil fruit. What does it look like? In your absence, or better, behind your back, the backbiter will censure, slander, reproach, or speak evil of you.—Webster. 2 Cor. 12: 20, "Lord, who shall abide in thy tabernacle? He that backbiteth not with his tongue, nor doeth evil to his neighbor, nor taketh up a reproach against his neighbor." Ps. 15. Evil speaking is forbidden by the apostle; also foolish talking and jesting. The tongue is a very useful member, but it must be controlled, and governed like the ships, or the horse, as the Apostle James illustrates it. Some persons must have been double-tongued, or the Apostle would not have made it a qualification of a deacon. I suppose that means to tell the same thing two ways, or mixing truth and error like the serpent did (who has a forked tongue, a striking emblem of her work). It means speaking as a friend to your face, and as an enemy be-

hind your back, or it might be, as James says, "Therewith bless we God even the Father, and therewith curse we men, which are made after the similitude of God." That is done by thousands, but he shows that one fountain cannot bring forth two kinds of water.

Again, if any man among you seem to be religious, and bridleth not his tongue, but deceiveth his own heart, that man's religion is vain. James 1. His religion is useless,—worth nothing, hence the bridling of the tongue becomes to be a serious matter. If all the members of the body were kept in subjection, while the tongue is allowed to run like a vicious horse without a bridle, it will avail nothing in the judgment. No other member is so hard to control in a general way. No other member is so constantly employed.

It is considered a breach of good manners in society not to keep the tongue going. An assembly is called a Quaker meeting before silence reigns half as long as it did in heaven. If there is not enough intelligence or spirituality in the crowd to feed, or employ the tongue, it will run on gossip, and more rapidly, like a mill, when there is nothing in the hopper to grind.

There is another reason why the tongue should be bridled. No other member affects others so much in its work. When the unbridled horse, hitched to a buggy, runs away, not only the inmates are in danger, but many in the crowd. So with the tongue. It may, perchance, be at a quilting, log-rolling, sale, or raising, that it may be shown what a great little thing the tongue is.

"Death and life are in the power of the tongue: and they that love it shall eat the fruit thereof." Prov. 18: 21. When will that be? When the fruit is ripe, ready to harvest.

"When this feeble, falt'ring tongue
Lies silent in the grave."

In the judgment we will eat the fruit, either life or death, for the power of both is in the tongue. "Be not deceived, God is not mocked. Whatsoever a man soweth, that shall he reap." No member sows as much seed as the tongue; and he that soweth the wind shall reap the whirlwind. Hosea 8: 7. Whirlwinds are more destructive than winds. In the judgment the tongue will suffer. The rich man prayed for one drop of water to cool his tongue. I am impressed with the thought that he did the most wickedness with the tongue. The tongue is a good index to soul or body. The doctor says, "Let me see your tongue." The sick man does not complain of his tongue. The rich man did not call for water as a sick man does, because of thirst. It was the tongue, the tongue that is suffering. Remember it is set on fire in hell. He set it on fire in this life, while he was enjoying his good things, but he did not realize it. It was only a pleasant wind, but now he is reaping the whirlwind. "Behold, how great a matter a little fire kindleth."

O reader, pause for a moment! Will you feed the fire to reap such an end?

Again I refer to Rev. 16: 10 as an evidence that the tongue must suffer prominently. Whatever the judgment or plague was, matters not. They gnawed their tongues for pain, and in that pain the tongue still continued its work and blasphemed the God of heaven.

If all would bridle the tongue and control it as the Gospel demands, strife and uproars and commotions would cease in families, neighborhoods, churches and nations. May the Lord help his people to do so! Amen.

Booth, Kans.

"A HEART-MEMORY is better than a mere head-memory. It is better to carry away a little of the life of God in our souls than to be able to repeat every word of every sermon we have heard."

nest where these young ones first formed the nucleus of a nation; how they had been directed by the "Pillar of Cloud" to the place where God desires them to prepare to meet his holy presence.

Moses has given God's message to the people who, with one voice, respond, "All that the Lord hath spoken we will do." When he has returned to the mountain with their speech, God tells him to "sanctify the people to-day and to-morrow, and let them wash their clothes, for the third day the Lord will come down in the sight of all the people upon Mt. Sinai."

Bounds were set unto the people around the mountain, lest they should touch it and die. The mandate was to be stoned or shot through, whether man or beast that should touch.

Moses had given them all the words of the Lord; and they had accepted the terms, had spent the two days in putting from them all that is unholy or unclean. They had washed themselves in the crystal fountain that God had brought from the rock to quench their burning thirst,—not their hands, or their feet only, but their whole bodies. The garments that were to last them from Egypt to Canaan might be soiled from their desert march; the same never-failing fountain was sufficient, and they were true to their covenant and cleansed their garments (for one's vestment is a kind of outer self), so that no sin may infest the assembly when they come before His Majesty.

All are cleansed, from the least unto the greatest; and they have forgotten their worldly hopes and ambitions in anticipation of meeting the holy presence of Him who had freed them from their misery and brought them through temptations, deprivations and suffering with the promise of full fruition in the land whither they are journeying. Have all these purified themselves from the sins committed by the way? They have answered God's purpose and we need not inquire further.

On the third day, clouds and smoke fill the holy place. The lightnings flash and thunders roll from Sinai's rugged heights and the people tremble and quake as they sit at the foot of the mountain and at the feet of God. Holy awe and reverence pervade this vast assembly, while God, the only one who ever spoke to so large an audience, speaks to the people concerning the laws that are to govern them through the generations to come. Thunders and lightnings are the introduction to this great sermon; the thunders, God's voice; the lightnings, the fire of his countenance, to awaken their attention, for the God of all the earth would speak to them.

While they were permitted thus to behold the manifestation of his presence, they dare not gaze upon him lest they die. How many of us are branded with that prying disposition that will not let us rest under the plain, simple truths of God! It was the sin of discontent in our first parents,—a desire for knowledge,—seeking more wisdom than God gave them, that caused their downfall, and has cursed so many fathers in Israel. Is it any wonder that God should take this precaution? The restraints and warnings of the divine law are all given for our good and to prevent the danger we might otherwise run into.

We constitute but a small part of God's creation; we have trials that are grievous to be borne; we fight some battles with this earth, and sometimes become thirsty and cry for water to cool our parched lips, but we want it sweetened; become hungry and cry for bread that will save our lives, and then want meat. We learn the sad fact that "nothing human is alien to us;" yet we are not willing to do as much as these benighted Hebrews.

It was at the mount that they decided to have Moses speak with God in their stead because they were unable to endure his presence. We do not

have Moses to be our intercessor, but we are happy in the contrast between God on Mt. Sinai, and his manifestations of Jesus the Christ. The blast of the trumpet does not now terrify, nor a mountain smoke with his presence and threaten death to those who touch, but we can come to the spiritual Mount Zion, where countless angels dwell; to the spirits of just men made perfect and to Jesus the Christ who is the Rock of our salvation. He is the messenger of the New Covenant and has told us what is necessary for us to do, if we would meet his approbation.

These washings and cleansings of the Old Testament are types of what we have revealed in the New. The washing at the mountain was to purify their outward beings, and the antitype is the washing we must undergo to become new creatures in Christ Jesus. As they purified their forms and garments, we must purify our hearts and lives.

If the English-speaking people are the Israel of to-day, what a time is coming when we must appear in the presence of our Creator! Then, if we have not bathed in some crystal stream, if we have not purified our vesture, we will not be ready when Gabriel shall sound the trumpet of the resurrection to meet our Father, and will cry for the rocks and hills to hide us from the presence of Him who sitteth upon the throne.

THE TONGUE.

BY ENOCH EBY.

" Even so the tongue is a little member, and boasteth great things. Behold, how great a matter a little fire kindleth!" James 3 : 5.

THE angel said unto John, "Eat the little book," Rev. 10: 9. A man does not live by "bread alone, but by every word that proceedeth out of the mouth of God."—Jesus. David says, "I keep thy word in my heart that I sin not." If we should keep the second chapter of James in our heart, it would be a great blessing to us, to the church and the neighborhood. About all the quarrels in families, neighborhoods, churches, and in the world, even wars, have their origin in the tongue. It is a world of iniquity. It is a fire. Set on the fire of Hell, it setteth on fire the whole course of nature, but a fire will finally stop unless it gets fuel. Where there is no tale-bearer, the strife ceaseth. Prov. 26: 2. The fire would go out if there were no tale-bearer.

What is a tale-bearer? "One who impertinently communicates intelligence or anecdotes and makes mischief in society by his officiousness."—Webster. "A tale-bearer revealeth secrets." Prov. 11: 13. Whispering is a fruit of the tongue, and condemned by the apostle. 2 Cor. 12: 20. What kind of a character is that? A whisperer is a tattler,—one who tells secrets.—Webster.

Backbiting is another evil fruit. What does it look like? In your absence, or better, behind your back, the backbiter will censure, slander, reproach, or speak evil of you.—Webster. 2 Cor. 12: 20, "Lord, who shall abide in thy tabernacle? He that backbiteth not with his tongue, nor doeth evil to his neighbor, nor taketh up a reproach against his neighbor." Ps. 15. Evil speaking is forbidden by the apostle; also foolish talking and jesting. The tongue is a very useful member, but it must be controlled, and governed like the ships, or the horse, as the Apostle James illustrates it.

Some persons must have been double-tongued, or the Apostle would not have made it a qualification of a deacon. I suppose that means to tell the same thing two ways, or mixing truth and error like the serpent did (who has a forked tongue, a striking emblem of her work). It means speaking as a friend to your face, and as an enemy be-

hind your back, or it might be, as James says, "Therewith bless we God even the Father, and therewith curse we men, which are made after the similitude of God." That is done by thousands, but he shows that one fountain cannot bring forth two kinds of water.

Again, if any man among you seem to be religious, and bridleth not his tongue, but deceiveth his own heart, that man's religion is vain. James 1. His religion is useless,—worth nothing, hence the bridling of the tongue becomes to be a serious matter. If all the members of the body were kept in subjection, while the tongue is allowed to run like a vicious horse without a bridle, it will avail nothing in the judgment. No other member is so hard to control in a general way. No other member is so constantly employed.

It is considered a breach of good manners in society not to keep the tongue going. An assembly is called a Quaker meeting before silence reigns half as long as it did in heaven. If there is not enough intelligence or spirituality in the crowd to feed, or employ the tongue, it will run on gossip, and more rapidly, like a mill, when there is nothing in the hopper to grind.

There is another reason why the tongue should be bridled. No other member affects others so much in its work. When the unbridled horse, hitched to a buggy, runs away, not only the inmates are in danger, but many in the crowd. So with the tongue. It may, perchance, be at a quilting, log-rolling, sale, or raising, that it may be shown what a great little thing the tongue is.

"Death and life are in the power of the tongue; and they that love it shall eat the fruit thereof." Prov. 18: 21. When will that be? When the fruit is ripe, ready to harvest.

" When this feeble, falt'ring tongue
Lies silent in the grave."

In the judgment we will eat the fruit, either life or death, for the power of both is in the tongue. "Be not deceived, God is not mocked. Whatsoever a man soweth, that shall he reap." No member sows as much seed as the tongue; and he that soweth the wind shall reap the whirlwind. Hosea 8: 7. Whirlwinds are more destructive than winds. In the judgment the tongue will suffer. The rich man prayed for one drop of water to cool his tongue. I am impressed with the thought that he did the most wickedness with the tongue. The tongue is a good index to soul or body. The doctor says, "Let me see your tongue." The sick man does not complain of his tongue. The rich man did not call for water as a sick man does, because of thirst. It was the tongue, the tongue that is suffering. Remember it is set on fire in hell. He set it on fire in this life, while he was enjoying his good things, but he did not realize it. It was only a pleasant wind, but now he is reaping the whirlwind. "Behold, how great a matter a little fire kindleth." O reader, pause for a moment! Will you feed the fire to reap such an end?

Again I refer to Rev. 16: 10 as an evidence that the tongue must suffer prominently. Whatever the judgment or plague was, matters not. They gnawed their tongues for pain, and in that pain the tongue still continued its work and blasphemed the God of heaven.

If all would bridle the tongue and control it as the Gospel demands, strife and uproars and commotions would cease in families, neighborhoods, churches and nations. May the Lord help his people to do so! Amen.

Booth, Kans.

"A HEART-MEMORY is better than a mere head-memory. It is better to carry away a little of the life of God in our souls than to be able to repeat every word of every sermon we have heard."

is worthy of being a child of God, or perhaps is already one of the flock, we should put forth every effort to hold them sacred and dear, as Paul entreated his son Timothy. Yes, he wrote loving epistles and letters, and praised him for his good works. He told him that he had remembrance of him, "in his prayers night and day," greatly desiring to see him, "that he might be filled with joy." He was not afraid to tell him of his good qualities, and how he came to possess them.

Paul also told Timothy that "God had not given them the spirit of fear, but of power, and of love, and of a sound mind." Have we not Timothys to-day, that should be looked after with the same abounding love as they were looked after in Paul's day and time? We should certainly tell them, as he did, "to keep the good things, and be strong in the love and grace that is in Christ Jesus; yes, endure hardness as good soldiers of the cross."

Many Timothys are weak and faltering under the hard strokes of life's discipline, who would be able to bear up under much, if we had more Pauls among us, to help them rise above the strokes, by receiving loving epistles to guide them in the ways of truth and righteousness. They would soon begin to grow strong and crave more than milk. They would have a deeper insight, and would more readily comprehend the Blessed Word, and the Lord would give them understanding and wisdom in all things, for his sake.

There are mothers in Israel who have blessings to impart If no other way will answer, write it for the benefit of others, that a son Timothy or a daughter Phebe may receive it. Dear mother, you may be young in years, but it is the love and deep concern that you throw around your children, that makes you a mother in Israel. I commend you for your zeal. Press onward, wherever you see the need of your hallowed influence! Do not be afraid it will not have its proper effect.

It has been wisely said, "The only true wealth of parents is that of their children, because they are all they have that is for eternity." How important, then, that we raise our children in the nurture and admonition of the Lord, that there be no separation in time nor eternity!

This may not seem to be of interest to those to whom this article is addressed, but perhaps they are able to grasp more of it than we think. If we always address children as babes, they will not grasp anything deeper, but when we give them some of the deep things, they are ready to listen with eagerness, and often grasp the meaning.

In God's eyes some great things are small, and some things are very great. "A pure motive will multiply the value of a small deed many times, while a selfish motive will divide a great deed just as often." Could we but realize how large and bounteous the widow's mite appeared to be in the eyes of Jesus, and how small were the large gifts of the Pharisees, who gave for display! No matter how small a thing we do in his name, he takes particular notice of it. Do not be discouraged because your life and opportunities seem to be so meager. There are not enough people willing to serve in the low, humble places.

Do you want to make a worthy offering to God? Then give him yourself. Early piety will never hinder you in any line of work. Do you think God cares more for what you can do, or give, or say, than he does for you? Nay, verily. We should be so filled with the love of God in our hearts and minds that we could hardly wait to proclaim it to one another. Is not that the true idea? Christ is indeed willing to sanctify and receive the young child as well as the aged man. Often a little child has great power, in its innocence and humility. The influence of little children is often beyond our comprehension. In

them we can see great beauties that we cannot fathom. Their utter helplessness and dependency upon greater strength teaches the true Christian what he is desirous to know, for without God giving them aid sufficient, to live, move, and have their being, they could do nothing. Jesus taught his disciples a great lesson by taking up a little child, and placing it in their midst, with the words, "Except you become as this little child, you cannot enter the kingdom of heaven."

We wonder if they were not struck with amazement and wonder, why he should exalt such a little creature as that in their eyes. Are we ready ourselves, to believe this to be an excellent thing? It teaches us to love purity and truth, all of which is acceptable in the sight of God. What is to be the future history of our children? God can only tell. Should we not be wide-awake and much concerned about it? When they begin sowing their wild oats (as the saying is), they are traveling the downward road to ruin. We had better take them by the hand and gently lead them into the glories of Christ's kingdom. Yes, come, young man, young maiden and children. Jesus wants you; his labor is love, his voice is music, his service is sweet, his yoke is easy, and his burden is light. There is ample room for all. May God speed the day when we will know nothing but love, and Jesus Christ and him crucified!

Virden, Ill., Box 421.

CORRESPONDENCE.

"Write what thou seest, and send it unto the churches."

☞Church News solicited for this Department. If you have had a good meeting, send a report of it, so that others may rejoice with you. In writing give name of church, County and State. Be brief. Notes of Travel should be as short as possible. Land Advertisements are not solicited for this Department. We have an advertising page, and, if necessary, will issue supplements.

On the Way.

MARCH 19 I left home for a mission point about eighteen miles south-east of Goshen, Ind., called "Haw Patch." This is an isolated place. At one time, about twenty years ago, it was a good point for meetings. Bro. Jacob Berkey (deceased) built up a small church there, and equipped it with a corps of officers. By neglect and removal of some officers, the cause has gone down. One brother, who was elected to the ministry, soon left the district and about fifteen or eighteen members were left, with two deacons. Finally that body of members were attached to the Springfield district, but they were too far away, to receive proper attention Since then they have become discouraged, and requested that something should be done to keep their little flock together. They have been much neglected, and often some minister would send in an appointment, and fail to come. About eighteen years ago the Brethren built a house of worship in the little village of "Haw Patch," so that the minister who would come there to preach, would not need to be crowded into a school-house. By neglect the brethren became more discouraged, and finally made a request to be attached to the Shipshewana district, expecting, by so doing, to be better cared for. Much to their discouragement, however, there was no improvement. One brother (a deacon) told me he had about given up all hopes. The above-named districts had all they could do at home, and being some distance away, and some of its ministers in limited circumstances, has brought about some of this neglect. Last fall the school-house burned down, and having no place suitable for school-work, the trustees rented the church.

In the meantime the Mission Board, by the advice of some brethren, thought it advisable to assist those brethren some. Accordingly I was

sent there to hold meetings for them for nine days. At first our meetings were not largely attended, on account of muddy roads and dark nights, but towards the close we had good congregations. On account of school being held in the church, we could not hold any day services. Perhaps, by careful work, and being prompt in filling all appointments, the cause may be built up.

It is to be regretted that the cause was suffered to go down, as this place is one of the garden spots of Northern Indiana. "Haw Patch" is a beautiful plain of rich soil, six or seven miles square. For wheat growing there is nothing to excel it in the State. Most of this beautiful plain is owned by the Amish people. The large and substantial buildings, with well-fenced fields, show to the traveler the industry and careful work of its possessors. Before the land was brought under cultivation, a species of haw was found growing among the large forest timber, hence the name "Haw Patch."

The Free-will Baptists have built up a small congregation there. Lately they built a house of worship, and as they, with the Amish, have regular services in that country, and our people have been so much disappointed, they have taken away some members. The Savior tells us that if the shepherd leaves his flock, they will scatter. John 10: 12.

One difficulty that I see in some of our churches is, that there are not enough ministers to carry on the work. In some districts the ministers are old and worn out, and cannot preach any more. Why not call young men into the work? "But," says some good brother, "I see no timber suitable." Neither did David's brother or King Saul, see any man in all that large army of workers, able to meet the Philistine giant. The Lord had a youth who was able to meet all such opposition. "Old men for counsel and young men for war." Some church districts do not know how much talent they have, until put to trial. One good way to bring this matter to the proper test is, to have a a Bible class, a social meeting, or a good, lively Sunday-school. Then have all the members to engage in *active work.* It will not be long until you will see one or more go to the brook,—God's Word,—and select a few pebbles. Placing them in a sling (the power he receives from God), he will march on to victory. 　　J. H. MILLER.

Goshen, Ind.

The Gospel Messenger

Is the recognized organ of the German Baptist or Brethren's church, and advocates the form of doctrine taught in the New Testament and pleads for a return to apostolic and primitive Christianity.

It recognizes the New Testament as the only infallible rule of faith and practice, and maintains that Faith toward God, Repentance from dead works, Regeneration of the heart and mind, baptism by Trine Immersion for remission of sins unto the reception of the Holy Ghost by the laying on of hands, are the means of adoption into the household of God,—the church militant.

It also maintains that Feet-washing, as taught in John 13, both by example and command of Jesus, should be observed in the church.

That the Lord's Supper, instituted by Christ and as universally observed by the apostles and the early Christians, is a full meal, and, in connection with the Communion, should be taken in the evening or after the close of the day.

That the Salutation of the Holy Kiss, or Kiss of Charity, is binding upon the followers of Christ.

That War and Retaliation are contrary to the spirit and self-denying principles of the religion of Jesus Christ.

That the principle of Plain Dressing and of Non-conformity to the world, as taught in the New Testament, should be observed by the followers of Christ.

That the Scriptural duty of Anointing the Sick with Oil, in the Name of the Lord, James 5: 14, is binding upon all Christians.

It also advocates the church's duty to support Missionary and Tract Work, thus giving to the Lord for the spread of the Gospel and for the conversion of sinners.

In short, it is a vindicator of all that Christ and the apostles have enjoined upon us, and aims, amid the conflicting theories and discords of modern Christendom, to point out ground that all must concede to be infallibly safe.

☞The above principles of our Fraternity are set forth on our "Brethren's Envelopes." Use them! Price, 15 cents per package; 40 cents per hundred.

is worthy of being a child of God, or perhaps is already one of the flock, we should put forth every effort to hold them sacred and dear, as Paul entreated him to do. Yes, he wrote loving epistles and letters, and praised him for his good works. He told him that he had remembrance of him, "in his prayers night and day," greatly desiring to see him, "that he might be filled with joy." He was not afraid to tell him of his good qualities, and how he came to possess them.

Paul also told Timothy that "God had not given them the spirit of fear, but of power, and of love, and of a sound mind." Have we not Timothys to-day, that should be looked after with the same abounding love as they were looked after in Paul's day and time? We should certainly tell them, as he did, "to keep the good things, and be strong in the love and grace that is in Christ Jesus; yes, endure hardness as good soldiers of the cross."

Many Timothys are weak and faltering under the hard strokes of life's discipline, who would be able to bear up under much, if we had more Pauls among us, to help them rise above the strokes, by receiving loving epistles to guide them in the ways of truth and righteousness. They would soon begin to grow strong and crave more than milk. They would have a deeper insight, and would more readily comprehend the Blessed Word, and the Lord would give them understanding and wisdom in all things, for his sake.

There are mothers in Israel who have blessings to impart. If no other way will answer, write it for the benefit of others, that a son Timothy or a daughter Phebe may receive it. Dear mother, you may be young in years, but it is the love and deep concern that you throw around your children, that makes you a mother in Israel. I commend you for your zeal. Press onward, wherever you see the need of your hallowed influence! Do not be afraid it will not have its proper effect.

It has been wisely said, "The only true wealth of parents is that of their children, because they are all they have that is for eternity." How important, then, that we raise our children in the nurture and admonition of the Lord, that there be no separation in time nor eternity!

This may not seem to be of interest to those to whom this article is addressed, but perhaps they are able to grasp more of it than we think. If we always address children as babes, they will not grasp anything deeper, but when we give them some of the deep things, they are ready to listen with eagerness, and often grasp the meaning.

In God's eyes some great things are small, and some things are very great. "A pure motive will multiply the value of a small deed many times, while a selfish motive will divide a great deed just as often." Could we but realize how large and bounteous the widow's mite appeared to be in the eyes of Jesus, and how small were the large gifts of the Pharisees, who gave for display! No matter how small a thing we do in his name, he takes particular notice of it. Do not be discouraged because your life and opportunities seem to be so meager. There are not enough people willing to serve in the low, humble places.

Do you want to make a worthy offering to God? Then give him yourself. Early piety will never hinder you in any line of work. Do you think God care more for what you can do, or give, or say, than he does for you? Nay, verily. We should be so filled with the love of God in our hearts and minds that we could hardly wait to proclaim it to one another. Is not that the true idea? Christ is indeed willing to sanctify and receive the young child as well as the aged man. Often a little child has great power, in its innocence and humility. The influence of little children is often beyond our comprehension. In

them we can see great beauties that we cannot fathom. Their utter helplessness and dependency upon greater strength teaches the true Christian what he is desirous to know, for without God giving them aid sufficient, to live, move, and have their being, they could do nothing. Jesus taught his disciples a great lesson by taking up a little child, and placing it in their midst, with the words, "Except you become as this little child, you cannot enter the kingdom of heaven."

We wonder if they were not struck with amazement and wonder, why he should exalt such a little creature as that in their eyes. Are we ready ourselves, to believe this to be an excellent thing? It teaches us to love purity and truth, all of which is acceptable in the sight of God. What is to be the future history of our children? God can only tell. Should we not be wide-awake and much concerned about it? When they begin sowing their wild oats (as the saying is), they are traveling the downward road to ruin. We had better take them by the hand and gently lead them into the glories of Christ's kingdom. Yes, come, young man, young maiden and children. Jesus wants you; his labor is love, his voice is music, his service is sweet, his yoke is easy, and his burden is light. There is ample room for all. May God speed the day when we will know nothing but love, and Jesus Christ and him crucified!

Virden, Ill., Box 421.

CORRESPONDENCE.

"Write what thou seest, and send it unto the churches."

☞"Church News solicited for this Department. If you have had a good meeting, send a report of it, so that others may rejoice with you. In writing give name of church, County and State. Be brief. Notes of Travel should be as short as possible. Land Advertisements are not solicited for this Department. We have an advertising page, and, if necessary, will issue supplements.

On the Way.

MARCH 19 I left home for a mission point about eighteen miles south-east of Goshen, Ind., called "Haw Patch." This is an isolated place. At one time, about twenty years ago, it was a good point for meetings. Bro. Jacob Berkey (deceased) built up a small church there, and equipped it with a corps of officers. By neglect and removal of some officers, the cause has gone down. One brother, who was elected to the ministry, soon left the district and about fifteen or eighteen members were left, with two deacons. Finally that body of members were attached to the Springfield district, but they were too far away, to receive proper attention. Since then they have become discouraged, and requested that something should be done to keep their little flock together. They have been much neglected, and often some minister would send in an appointment, and fail to come. About eighteen years ago the Brethren built a house of worship in the little village of "Haw Patch," so that the minister who would come there to preach, would not need to be crowded into a school-house. By neglect the brethren became more discouraged, and finally made a request to be attached to the Shipshewana district, expecting, by so doing, to be better cared for. Much to their discouragement, however, there was no improvement. One brother (a deacon) told me he had about given up all hopes. The above-named districts had all they could do at home, and being some distance away, and some of its ministers in limited circumstances, has brought about some of this neglect. Last fall the school-house burned down, and having no place suitable for school-work, the trustees rented the church.

In the meantime the Mission Board, by the advice of some brethren, thought it advisable to assist those brethren some. Accordingly I was

sent there to hold meetings for them for nine days. At first our meetings were not largely attended, on account of muddy roads and dark nights, but towards the close we had good congregations. On account of school being held in the church, we could not hold any day services. Perhaps, by careful work, and being prompt in filling all appointments, the cause may be built up.

It is to be regretted that the cause was suffered to go down, as this place is one of the garden spots of Northern Indiana. "Haw Patch" is a beautiful plain of rich soil, six or seven miles square. For wheat growing there is nothing to excel it in the State. Most of this beautiful plain is owned by the Amish people. The large and substantial buildings, with well-fenced fields, show to the traveler the industry and careful work of its possessors. Before the land was brought under cultivation, a species of haw was found growing among the large forest timber, hence the name "Haw Patch."

The Free-will Baptists have built up a small congregation there. Lately they built a house of worship, and as they, with the Amish, have regular services in that country, and our people have been so much disappointed, they have taken away some members. The Savior tells us that if the shepherd leaves his flock, they will scatter. John 10: 12.

One difficulty that I see in some of our churches is, that there are not enough ministers to carry on the work. In some districts the ministers are old and worn out, and cannot preach any more. Why not call young men into the work? "But," says some good brother, "I see no timber suitable." Neither did David's brother or King Saul, see any man in all that large army of workers, able to meet the Philistine giant. The Lord had a youth who was able to meet all such opposition. "Old men for counsel and young men for war." Some church districts do not know how much talent they have, until put to trial. One good way to bring this matter to the proper test is, to have a Bible class, a social meeting, or a good, lively Sunday-school. Then have all the members to engage in active work. It will not be long until you will see one or more go to the brook,—God's Word,—and select a few pebbles. Placing them in a sling (the power he receives from God), he will march on to victory. J. H. MILLER.

Goshen, Ind.

The Gospel Messenger

Is the recognized organ of the German Baptist or Brethren's church, and advocates the form of doctrine taught in the New Testament and pleads for a return to apostolic and primitive Christianity.

It recognizes the New Testament as the only infallible rule of faith and practice, and maintains that Faith toward God. Repentance from dead works, Regeneration of the heart and mind, baptism by Trine Immersion for remission of sins unto the reception of the Holy Ghost by the laying on of hands, are the means of adoption into the household of God,—the church militant.

It also maintains that Feet-washing, as taught in John 13, both by example and command of Jesus, should be observed in the church.

That the Lord's Supper, instituted by Christ and as universally observed by the apostles and the early Christians, is a full meal, and, in connection with the Communion, should be taken in the evening or after the close of the day.

That the Salutation of the Holy Kiss, or Kiss of Charity, is binding upon the followers of Christ.

That War and Retaliation are contrary to the spirit and self-denying principles of the religion of Jesus Christ.

That the principle of Plain Dressing and of Non-conformity to the world, as taught in the New Testament, should be observed by the followers of Christ.

That the Scriptural duty of Anointing the Sick with Oil, in the Name of the Lord, James 5: 14, is binding upon all Christians.

It also advocates the church's duty to support Missionary and Tract Work, thus giving to the Lord for the spread of the Gospel and for the conversion of sinners.

In short, it is a vindicator of all that Christ and the apostles have enjoined upon us, and aims, amid the conflicting theories and discords of modern Christendom, to point out ground that all must concede to be infallibly safe.

☞ The above principles of our Fraternity are set forth on our "Brethren's EnVelopes." Use them! Price, 15 cents per package; 40 cents per hundred.

Bro. D. E. Brubaker went to Washburn, Woodford Co., last week, to assist in church work and hold some meetings. He reports the church in a peaceable and encouraging condition.

Bro. J. C. Lahman, who is spending the winter at Hawthorn, Fla., thinks of visiting some members in the southern part of the State before re. turning in May. There are a few members near Manatee, who have been there for nine years.

Some one writing us is puzzled concerning what the Scriptures declare in regard to John baptizing with water, but Jesus was to baptize with the Holy Ghost and fire. He thinks that with the death of John, water baptism ceased, and during the Christian Dispensation we have only the baptism of the Holy Ghost and fire. It re. quires only a limited knowledge of the Scriptures to prove that water baptism was still practiced during the time of the apostles. We read that Philip and the eunuch came to-s certain water, and that they both went down into the water, and Philip baptized the eunuch. It would not be possible to conceive of a case more clearly stated in support of water baptism than this. The Sa. maritans were baptized by Philip, some time be. fore they received the Holy Ghost, by the laying on of the hands of the apostles, showing that it was water baptism that they received at the hands of, Philip. We might refer to other circum. stances, but we will let this suffice. We, however, add that water baptism is to be performed by man, but Holy Ghost and fire baptism are to be administered by Jesus. So far as we know, Christ never baptized any one in water,—this he had done by the apostles,—but he did and will admin. ister the Holy Ghost and fire baptism, The Holy Ghost baptism is for those who become members of the kingdom of Christ, while fire baptism is for those who are members of Satan's kingdom.

On another page Bro. J. H. Miller suggests the right thing, when he advises that more young men be put to the ministry. It is true that some congregations do not know how much talent they have lying dormant. We know instances where congregations declined to call some of their tal. ented young brethren to the work, and, when these brethren located elsewhere, they were, elect. ed to the ministry, and to-day some of them are among the best workers we have in the church. By no means ought those in charge to permit the ministers to become aged and feeble without hav. ing younger ministers coming on to take their places. We have the material in abundance, and we ought to call it out. While we should be par. ticulas to commit the Word to none but faith. ful men, who will be able to teach others, we ought not to set our estimations so high as to overreach everything around us. In the early settlement of our country, school-teachers who could teach only reading, writing, spelling and a few other things, did a grand work for the future of the race, though we need far better teachers now. Just so in the Gospel work. We must take the best we can get until we can get better. Some very ordinary preachers will get credit in the coming kingdom for some good work done in this little world. If some of the early congrega. tions had looked for talented men to elect to the ministry, most of them would have still been waiting, But they put their men and two-talented men to work, giving them an opportunity to im. prove their talents, and that is why we now have some very trusty and skilled preachers. They were made of ordinary talent, but had a chance to commence young. So we repeat, Let us have more preachers! We need them. The field is large, and the harvest is ripe already.

TRUNK LINE RATES TO ANNUAL MEETING.

The following letter, written to Bro. E. W. Stoner, Union Bridge, Md., who has charge, by appointment of Annual Meeting, of the Trunk Line Association, by Mr. Bond, gives the action of the Lines east of the Ohio River:

I have much pleasure in advising you that the Trunk Line Association, at its meeting held in New York, March 16, acted upon your application, and authorized a rate of one lowest first class limited fare *per capita* for the round trip, on account of the next Annual Meeting, of the German Baptist Brethren, to be held at Cedar Rapids, Iowa, June 3 to 9, tick. ets to be of iron-clad signature form, and for continuous pas. sage in each direction, tickets to be sold only in the States of Pennsylvania (exclusive of the City of Philadelphia), Mary. land, Virginia and West Virginia, May 26 to June 4, good for going passage on date of sale only, and good returning any time until and including June 30.

We are receiving letters asking if stop-over privileges can be granted, and if the tickets can. not be placed on sale at an earlier date. We have used our endeavor, seconded by the Com. mittee of Arrangements and several General Pas. senger Agents, to get these favors, but up to this time have failed. If any other arrangements are effected, notice will be given. Bro. John Wise, of the Trans-Missouri, and Bro. Geo. Bowman, of the Southern Association, have not yet reported rates.

D. L. M.

VERY IMPORTANT.

We wish to call the attention of all State Dis. trict Clerks to the following, which passed the last Annual Meeting:

Will District Meeting of Middle Indiana, ask Annual Meeting to (rst) require the Clerks of the several State Dis. tricts to furnish the Writing Clerk of Annual Meeting a copy of the Minutes of District Meeting, with queries marked, in. tended for Annual Meeting? (2) Said District Meeting Min. utes shall be sent to Writing Clerk of Annual Meeting at least two weeks before Annual Meeting. (3) Requiring the Writ. ing Clerk of Annual Meeting to furnish a printed list of all the queries for the use of the delegates representing the sev. eral churches. *Ans.*—We do so require. Passed Annual Meeting.

It will thus be seen that it is the duty of all the District-Clerks to see that marked copies of these Minutes reach Bro. D. L. Miller at least two weeks before the Annual Meeting. Up to the present time Michigan, Northern Indiana and Southern Illinois are the only Districts that have sent in Minutes with queries marked for the An. nual Meeting. The clerks of all other Districts that have held their District Meetings, will send in theirs at once. It is not sufficient to send copies of your Minutes; they must be marked copies, so that no mistake will be made in select. ing that intended for the Annual Meeting. The Clerks of District Meetings, yet to be held, will not wait for their printed Minutes, but just as soon as the meetings are over, will please send to Bro. Miller copies of the queries intended for the Annual Meeting.

It is his duty to have all these queries printed on a sheet so they can be had by delegates and others at the Annual Meeting. This arrange. ment will enable all concerned to have a better understanding of the matters to be discussed in the open Conference. We trust that all the Dis. trict Clerks will attend to their part promptly, so there will be no delay or mistake about this mat. ter.

☞Clerks will not fail to send to us copies of their printed Minutes, to be kept on file in the of. fice, These, of course, need not be marked copies.

J. H. M.

EDITORIAL WANDERINGS IN THE OLD WORLD.

BY D. L. MILLER.

Number Twenty-Two.

The City of Paris, with a population of nearly two and a quarter million souls, may well be called the City of the Napoleons. Wandering through the streets of this modern city of splendor, one sees the impress of the Bonapartes on every hand, and you are again and again reminded of the first Consul and his ambitious nephew, Napoleon the Third. The fine streets and alleys, the grand boulevards and open squares, the beautiful gar. dens and magnificent palaces, and the splendid monuments and arches of triumph are what these rulers made them. Come what may to the City of Paris, short of destruction the name of Napoleon will live within her gates.

It was the ambition of Napoleon III. to make of Paris what Nebuchadnezzar succeeded in making of Babylon so many centuries ago,—the most beautiful and magnificent city in all the world. Such was his success, assisted by Hausman and other eminent engineers and artists, that the Cap. ital of France easily holds the palm and is. with. out rival either in the Old or New World.

Paris is, above all things, a city of pleasure and sin. Her ever-thronging and surging crowd of humanity is made up largely of pleasure-seekers. She sits as the mistress of fashion, and the man. dates of her man-milliner, Worth, are followed all over the civilized world with a zeal worthy of a better cause. Fashion rules and the people seem intent on having a good time. The streets, squares and public gardens are made to accommo. date the desire for pleasure. You may stand in one spot and count a hundred life-size marble figures adorning the palace of the Louvre. The garden of the Tuileries, in the heart of Paris, contains seventy-four acres. It is laid out in beau. tiful flower gardens. Its promenades, the finest in Europe, are lined with chestnut, linden and plane trees. It is adorned with numberless ba. sins, flowing fountains and statuary. Life-size, nude human figures, cut from pure white marble, abound on every hand. An eminent author says there is enough nude statuary exposed in Paris, to send, in a few years, "any city in Europe into the damnation of the foulest social hell." In Paris sin has no covering. It is open and brazen-front. ed. The very customs of society present it open. ly to the world. The drinking saloon has no screen before its door, or shades at its windows. Its doors are thrown wide open and much of the drinking is done at small tables under awnings on the side-walk. At some of the large drinking sa. loons you may often count more than a hundred men and women, seated promiscuously at these tables, drinking, laughing and having, as they call it, a good time. Men and women, who are outcasts from decent society at home, are here petted and flattered. The moral statistics show a state of affairs that "only suggest the enormity of the vice and shame covered by the show and splen. dor of this proud city of Napoleon that was."

The cause for all this social pollution is not hard to find. The teachings of Voltaire, Rousseau and other infidel writers had a wonderful influence on the minds of the French. The influence of Christianity was weakened, and Reason was en. throned as the god of Paris. One of the oldest and most noted churches in the city, Notre Dame, was converted into a "Temple of Reason" and within this temple of philosophy was raised aft.

BRO. D. E. BRUBAKER went to Washburn, Woodford Co., last week, to assist in church work and hold some meetings. He reports the church in a peaceable and encouraging condition.

BRO. J. C. LAHMAN, who is spending the winter at Hawthorn, Fla., thinks of visiting some members in the southern part of the State before returning in May. There are a few members near Manatee, who have been there for nine years.

SOME one writing us is puzzled concerning what the Scriptures declare in regard to John baptizing with water, but Jesus was to baptize with the Holy Ghost and fire. He thinks that with the death of John, water baptism ceased, and during the Christian Dispensation we have only the baptism of the Holy Ghost and fire. It requires only a limited knowledge of the Scriptures to prove that water baptism was still practiced during the time of the apostles. We read that Philip and the eunuch came to a certain water, and that they both went down into the water, and Philip baptized the eunuch. It would not be possible to conceive of a case more clearly stated in support of water baptism than this. The Samaritans were baptized by Philip, some time before they received the Holy Ghost, by the laying on of the hands of the apostles, showing that it was water baptism that they received at the hands of Philip. We might refer to other circumstances, but we will let this suffice. We, however, add that water baptism is to be performed by man, but Holy Ghost and fire baptism are to be administered by Jesus. So far as we know, Christ never baptized any one in water,—this he had done by the apostles,—but he did and will administer the Holy Ghost and fire baptism. The Holy Ghost baptism is for those who become members of the kingdom of Christ, while fire baptism is for those who are members of Satan's kingdom.

ON another page Bro. J. H. Miller suggests the right thing, when he advises that more young men be put to the ministry. It is true that some congregations do not know how much talent they have lying dormant. We know instances where congregations declined to call some of their talented young brethren to the work, and when these brethren located elsewhere, they were elected to the ministry, and to-day some of them are among the best workers we have in the church. By no means ought those in charge to permit the ministers to become aged and feeble without having younger ministers coming on to take their places. We have the material in abundance, and we ought to call it out. While we should be particular to commit the Word to none but faithful men, who will be able to teach others, we ought not to set our estimations so high as to overreach everything around us. In the early settlement of our country, school-teachers who could teach only reading, writing, spelling and a few other things, did a grand work for the future of the race, though we need far better teachers now. Just so in the Gospel work. We must take the best we can get until we can get better. Some very ordinary preachers will get credit in the coming kingdom for some good work done in this little world. If some of the early congregations had looked for talented men to elect to the ministry, most of them would have still been waiting. But they put their one and two-talented men to work, giving them an opportunity to improve their talents, and that is why we now have some very trusty and skilled preachers. They were made of ordinary talent, but had a chance to commence young. So we repeat, Let us have more preachers! We need them. The field is large, and the harvest is ripe already.

TRUNK LINE RATES TO ANNUAL MEETING.

THE following letter, written to Bro. E. W. Stoner, Union Bridge, Md., who has charge, by appointment of Annual Meeting, of the Trunk Line Association, by Mr. Bond, gives the action of the Lines east of the Ohio River:

I have much pleasure in advising you that the Trunk Line Association, at its meeting held in New York, March 16, acted upon your application, and authorized a rate of one lowest first class limited fare *per capita* for the round trip, on account of the next Annual Meeting of the German Baptist Brethren, to be held at Cedar Rapids, Iowa, June 310 9, tickets to be of iron-clad signature form, and for continuous passage in each direction, tickets to be sold only in the States of Pennsylvania (exclusive of the City of Philadelphia), Maryland, Virginia and West Virginia, May 28 to June 4, good for going passage on date of sale only, and good returning any time until and including June 30.

We are receiving letters asking if stop-over privileges can be granted, and if the tickets cannot be placed on sale at an earlier date. We have used our endeavor, seconded by the Committee of Arrangements and several General Passenger Agents, to get these favors, but up to this time have failed. If any other arrangements are effected, notice will be given. Bro. John Wise, of the Trans-Missouri, and Bro. Geo. Bowman, of the Southern Association, have not yet reported rates.

D. L. M.

VERY IMPORTANT.

WE wish to call the attention of all State District Clerks to the following, which passed the last Annual Meeting:

Will District Meeting of Middle Indiana ask Annual Meeting to (1st) require the Clerks of the several State Districts to furnish the Writing Clerk of Annual Meeting a copy of the Minutes of District Meeting, with queries marked, intended for Annual Meeting? (2) Said District Meeting Minutes shall be sent to Writing Clerk of Annual Meeting at least two weeks before Annual Meeting. (3) Requiring the Writing Clerk of Annual Meeting to furnish a printed list of all the queries for the use of the delegates representing the several churches. Ans.—We do so require. Passed District Meeting.

It will thus be seen that it is the duty of all the District-Clerks to see that *marked* copies of these Minutes reach Bro. D. L. Miller at least two weeks before the Annual Meeting. Up to the present time Michigan, Northern Indiana and Southern Illinois are the only Districts that have sent in Minutes with queries *marked* for the Annual Meeting. The clerks of all other Districts that have held their District Meetings, will send in theirs at once. It is not sufficient to send *copies* of your Minutes; they must be *marked* copies, so that no mistake will be made in selecting that intended for the Annual Meeting. The Clerks of District Meetings, yet to be held, will not wait for their printed Minutes, but just as soon as the meetings are over, will please send to Bro. Miller copies of the queries intended for the Annual Meeting.

It is his duty to have all these queries printed on a sheet so they can be had by delegates and others at the Annual Meeting. This arrangement will enable all concerned to have a better understanding of the matters to be discussed in the open Conference. We trust that all the District Clerks will attend to their part promptly, so there will be no delay or mistake about this matter.

Clerks will not fail to send to us copies of their printed Minutes, to be kept on file in this office. These, of course, need not be marked copies.

J. B. B.

EDITORIAL WANDERINGS IN THE OLD WORLD.

BY D. L. MILLER.

Number Twenty-Two.

THE City of Paris, with a population of nearly two and a quarter million souls, may well be called the City of the Napoleons. Wandering through the streets, of this modern city of splendor, one sees the impress of the Bonapartes on every hand, and you are again and again reminded of the first Consul and his ambitious nephew, Napoleon the Third. The fine streets and alleys, the grand boulevards and open squares, the beautiful gardens and magnificent palaces, and the splendid monuments and arches of triumph are what these rulers made them. Come what may to the City of Paris, short of destruction the name of Napoleon will live within her gates.

It was the ambition of Napoleon III. to make of Paris what Nebuchadnezzar succeeded in making of Babylon so many centuries ago,—the most beautiful and magnificent city in all the world. Such was his success, assisted by Hausman and other eminent engineers and artists, that the Capital of France easily holds the palm and is without rival either in the Old or New World.

Paris is, above all things, a city of pleasure and sin. Her ever-thronging and surging crowd of humanity is made up largely of pleasure-seekers. She sits as the mistress of fashion, and the mandates of her man-milliner, Worth, are followed all over the civilized world with a zeal worthy of a better cause. Fashion rules and the people seem intent on having a good time. The streets, squares and public gardens are made to accommodate the desire for pleasure. They are studded with costly monuments and statuary. You may count in one spot and count a hundred life-size marble figures adorning the palace of the Louvre. The garden of the Tuileries, in the heart of Paris, contains seventy-four acres. It is laid out in beautiful flower gardens. Its promenades, the finest in Europe, are lined with chestnut, linden and plane trees. It is adorned with numberless basins, flowing fountains and statuary. Life-size, nude human figures, cut from pure white marble, abound on every hand. An eminent author says there is enough nude statuary exposed in Paris, to send, in a few years, "any city in Europe into the damnation of the foulest social hell." In Paris sin has no covering. It is open and brazen-fronted. The very customs of society present it openly to the world. The drinking saloon has no screen before its door, or shades at its windows. Its doors are thrown wide open and much of the drinking is done at small tables under awnings on the side-walk. At some of the large drinking saloons you may often count more than a hundred men and women, seated promiscuously at these tables, drinking, laughing, and having, as they call it, a good time. Men and women, who are outcasts from decent society at home, are here petted and flattered. The moral statistics show a state of affairs that "only suggest the enormity of the vice and shame covered by the show and splendor of this proud city of Napoleon that was."

The cause for all this social pollution is not hard to find. The teachings of Voltaire, Rousseau and other infidel writers had a wonderful influence on the minds of the French. The influence of Christianity was weakened, and Reason was enthroned as the god of Paris. One of the oldest and most noted churches in the city, Notre Dame, was converted into a "Temple of Reason" and within this temple of philosophy was raised an al-

There are two organizations in Pittsylvania with two resident ministers, T. C. Wood and Daniel Duncan. In Henry County we have one organization of about thirty members with no minister, but two deacons. Bro. Henry Eikenberry has the oversight there this year. The Brethren are making arrangements to build a house this year, but will need help, which, we trust, they will get.

I am well pleased with Bro Eby's remarks on the duty of elders, on page 166, of No. 11. He has called our attention to the fact that there are elders in the Brotherhood who do not know what the established order of the Brotherhood is, in regard to the sisters' prayer-covering.

Did Paul authorize Timothy, or Titus, or any of their successors, to ordain men to office who were not sound in the faith, and who did not know how to administer the affairs of the church?

WM. ROBERSON.

A Sad Death.

BRO. WM. GOOCH, of this place, was shelling corn, when one of his fingers got caught in the sheller and was torn off at the first joint. The doctor happened to be in the house at the time, waiting on sister Gooch, and he attended to the case, and thought it would be all right. That evening Bro. Gooch did the milking, but the wound soon began to swell, and a large abscess formed on the top of his hand. When that broke, he began to go down very fast. The doctor pronounced it blood poisoning. His suffering was intense at times, but he bore it all with great patience. He died March 24, at the age of 61 years, 3 months and 21 days. He leaves a wife and three daughters to mourn their loss, which is his eternal gain. He was a member of the Brethren church six years, and it was seldom that his seat was vacant. His funeral was preached by Bro. J. S. Mohler to a large crowd of sympathizing friends.

LIZZIE HILARY.

Belleville, Kans.

From Oakland, Md.

FEB. 20, according to previous arrangement, I met in council with the Brethren of the Hopewell congregation, Pa., and preached three sermons at Beaver's Run to a large and attentive congregation. On Monday, Feb. 22, I returned to Hyndman, Pa. Here I met with Bro. Ed. Hostetler, who preached in the evening of the same day to the people at this place. On Tuesday, Feb. 23, the writer held a meeting. As an immediate result, three precious souls became willing to put on Christ in baptism.

Feb. 25 I returned home and on Sunday, Feb. 28, I went to visit a sick woman (my wife's sister), who has been very ill for quite a while. She requested baptism, and on Monday morning, Feb. 29, there being considerable snow, she was conveyed to the water's side in a sleigh, and from there carried into the water on a chair. Although it was necessary to remove some of the ice before baptism, I never baptized a more submissive applicant. Many of her friends claimed that it would result in her death, but to their surprise she grew better. Others claimed if this did not kill her, it would prove to their minds that baptism by immersion was the Lord's way, and they would follow her example.

March 19 we met in council. We decided to represent at District Meeting by letter. The Lord willing, we will have our love-feast June 18 and 19. In the evening of the day of the council our sick sister requested that we hold a Communion in her house. Her request was granted, and accordingly, at the time appointed, assisted by Bro. I. O. Thompson, we broke unto the little band of members present (eleven in number), the Bread of Life. Our sick sister seemed much encouraged, and we hope she may ever live faithful, and at last gain a home in heaven. On Sunday, March 20, Bro. Thompson preached for us from Rom. 1: 16. Pray for us, dear brethren, that we may ever prove faithful! WM. T. SINES.

From Appanoose, Kans.

WE are moving along quietly in this congregation, subject, however, to occasional disappointments on account of inclement weather. A special council was to be held Feb. 6, but as it rained all day, the council was held next day, after the regular services. Bro John A. Root, of Ozawkie, was with us and assisted in restoring a dear sister to full fellowship.

March 5 our quarterly council was to be held, but then it rained again all day, and the council was afterwards announced to be held to-day (March 26). This has, without doubt, been the most inclement day of the whole winter. After raining hard in the night, the weather turned somewhat colder, the wind blew a gale, and the snow flew thick. Then it changed to rain again, and all the streams are filled with water. The result is, another disappointment has occurred. If we can have all our disappointments in this life, we ought to bear them patiently and willingly. Like in all other places, La Grippe was prevalent here. Some members did not escape its attack, but none of them died; while a number of other citizens were taken away.

HIRAM S. GARST.

From the Lone Star State.

THE colony from Kansas, now located near Alvin, Tex., desiring to be organized, to more fully carry on the work, the Mission Board of Texas requested me to go there; hence, March 14, I boarded the train, in company with Bro. Philip Eby, for Alvin We arrived on the evening of the next day, and found, on arrival, that Bro. S. A. Honberger, of Esterly, La., had been preaching there for one week. On the evening of my arrival, the weather turned cold, so we could not have any more services until the evening of the 19th. There was no stove in the church they were using, hence they could not hold services. On the evening of the 19th we met at Bro. J. J. Wassam's house to organize. Seven members met, all with letters of membership and all desiring to be organized. They presented certificates of eight more members living about thirty miles north-west of them. These also wanted to unite with the new organization. One minister is the second degree and two deacons are among the number. All unanimously agreed to work in harmony with the Word of God and the counsel of the Brotherhood. They are taking hold of the work with a commendable zeal, and I ask the prayers of the church in their behalf.

There is a great work and field at that place with almost unlimited bounds. The prospect is so great between them and other organized churches that we did not limit the bounds. The work is truly hopeful, and the people seem to welcome our doctrine. They are mostly northern people, and they have a fruitful country and fertile soil. Best of all, I think the climate is healthful. Bro. Gish, of Fort Scott, Kans., arrived there March 21, with his family. He is a minister, and his wife and daughter are also members.

A commendable feature in their town, Alvin, is, that they have local option, and, consequently, a temperate town. I hope they will so continue. Tropical fruits, as far as has been tried, do exceedingly well. Blackberries and dewberries grow wild and are quite prolific. Strawberries, pears, plums, grapes and peaches also do finely. Corn and oats are said to do well. Vegetables of all kinds produce largely. On Monday, March 21, three other disciples and I went to Galveston for sight-seeing. The Gulf is indeed a grand sight for one who has never seen it. Oh the wonderful works of God! Vast sums of money are spent here on the jetties, to procure deep water. In the evening we returned to Alvin and stayed over night. March 23 I bade farewell to the faithful of Alvin, and started for home, where I arrived March 24 and found all well, excepting sister Molsbee, who was suffering severely from a second attack of La Grippe. May the Good Lord bless and restore her to health again!

HENRY BRUBAKER.

Nocona, Tex., March 25.

From Waterloo, Iowa.

ON March 11, I went to the Boon River church, Hancock Co., Iowa, and met with the church in council on Saturday, March 12. All business passed off pleasantly. The Boon River church is making arrangements to build a meeting-house this coming summer. This church has a membership of about twenty-five, in Hancock and Wright Counties, with good prospects for more moving in soon, and a very good interest among outsiders. They have only one minister,—Bro. George Aschenbrenner,—and two deacons. They have many calls for preaching. Bro. Aschenbrenner is a German, and there are calls enough for German preaching to keep him busy all of his time. Brethren, it is too bad that this German brother must preach in English, and let the German drop. Is there not a young. David somewhere in the Brotherhood who will volunteer to go and do the English preaching for the Boon River congregation? There would be plenty of work for two English ministers, but we will be glad to get only one. Who will come to our aid? Your help is needed.

Now, as there is occasionally a minister who is thinking of moving West, I would invite all such to take a look at Hancock County. They have good soil, their land is low in price, and convenient to the railroad. Take the Chicago, Milwaukee and St. Paul R. R., to Britt, then the Minneapolis & St. Louis to Stilson. Bro. Elias Long lives three miles South of Stilson. We do not only invite ministers but any of the Brethren and sisters who contemplate changing their location, to settle there and help to build up the cause of the Master. WM. IKENBERRY.

From Loraine, Ill.

THE little band of God's dear children at Loraine is still at work, and, seemingly, in good spirits. We have our regular preaching here every second and fourth Sundays in each month, at the hours of 11 A. M. and 7 P. M. Our Sunday-school meets every Sunday at 3 P. M.

We held our council on Saturday, March 12, and set the time for our spring Communion for Saturday, May 14. Bro. John Pool is expected with us at that time, and will probably be with us five or six days. Brethren and sisters, all who can, should come and make us a visit, especially is the young members' influence needed here. Ministers, come and feast with us! We would like one or two elders to assist us on Saturday at 2 P. M. H. W. STRICKLER.

Loraine, Ill.

From Lewiston, Minn.

WE are in usual health, both temporally and spiritually. We have been repairing our church house this winter, at an expense of about $200,

There are two organizations in Pittsylvania with two resident ministers, T. C. Wood and Daniel Duncan. In Henry County we have one organization of about thirty members with no minister, but two deacons. Bro. Henry Eikenberry has the oversight there this year. The Brethren are making arrangements to build a house this year, but will need help, which, we trust, they will get.

I am well pleased with Bro Eby's remarks on the duty of elders, on page 166, of No. 11. He has called our attention to the fact that there are elders in the Brotherhood who do not know what the established order of the Brotherhood is, in regard to the subject of prayer-covering.

Did Paul authorize Timothy, or Titus, or any of their successors, to ordain men to office who were not sound in the faith, and who did not know how to administer the affairs of the church?
WM. ROBERTSON.

A Sad Death.

BRO. WM. GOOCH, of this place, was shelling corn, when one of his fingers got caught in the sheller and was torn off at the first joint. The doctor happened to be in the house at the time, waiting on sister Gooch, and he attended to the case, and thought it would be all right. That evening Bro. Gooch did the milking, but the wound soon began to swell, and a large abscess formed on the top of his hand. When that broke, he began to go down very fast. The doctor pronounced it blood poisoning. His suffering was intense at times, but he bore it all with great patience. He died March 24, at the age of 61 years, 3 months and 21 days. He leaves a wife and three daughters to mourn their loss, which is his eternal gain. He was a member of the Brethren church six years, and it was seldom that his seat was vacant. His funeral was preached by Bro. J. S. Mohler to a large crowd of sympathizing friends.
LIZZIE HILARY.
Belleville, Kans.

From Oakland, Md.

FEB. 20, according to previous arrangement, I met in council with the Brethren of the Hopewell congregation, Pa., and preached three sermons at Beaver's Run to a large and attentive congregation. On Monday, Feb. 22, I returned to Hyndman, Pa. Here I met with Bro. Ed. Hostetler, who preached in the evening of the same day to the people at this place. On Tuesday, Feb. 23, the writer held a meeting. As an immediate result, three precious souls became willing to put on Christ in baptism.

Feb. 25 I returned home and on Sunday, Feb. 28, I went to visit a sick woman (my wife's sister), who has been very ill for quite a while. She requested baptism, and on Monday morning, Feb. 29, there being considerable snow, she was conveyed to the water's side in a chair, and from there carried into the water on a chair. Although it was necessary to remove some of the ice before baptism, I never baptized a more submissive applicant. Many of her friends claimed that it would result in her death, but to their surprise she grew better. Others claimed if this did not kill her, it would prove to their minds that baptism by immersion was the Lord's way, and they would follow her example.

March 19 we met in council. We decided to represent our District Meeting by letter. The Lord willing, we will have our love-feast June 18 and 19. In the evening of the day of the council our sick sister requested that we hold a Communion in her house. Her request was granted, and accordingly, at the time appointed, assisted by Bro. I. O. Thompson, we broke unto the little band of members present (eleven in number), the

Bread of Life. Our sick sister seemed much encouraged, and we hope she may ever live faithful, and at last gain a home in heaven. On Sunday, March 20, Bro. Thompson preached for us from Rom. 1: 16. Pray for us, dear brethren, that we may ever prove faithful! WM. T. SINES.

From Appanoose, Kans.

WE are moving along quietly in this congregation, subject, however, to occasional disappointments on account of inclement weather. A special council was to be held Feb. 6, but as it rained all day, the council was held next day, after the regular services. Bro John A. Root, of Ozawkie, was with us and assisted in restoring a dear sister to full fellowship.

March 5 our quarterly council was to be held, but then it rained again all day, and the council was afterwards announced to be held to-day (March 26). This has, without doubt, been the most inclement day of the whole winter. After raining hard in the night, the weather turned somewhat colder, the wind blew a gale, and the snow flew thick. Then it changed to rain again, and all the streams are filled with water. The result is, another disappointment has occurred. If we can have all our disappointments in this life, we ought to bear them patiently and willingly.

Like in all other places, *La Grippe* was prevalent here. Some members did not escape its attack, but none of them died; while a number of other citizens were taken away.
HIRAM S. GARST.

From the Lone Star State.

THE colony from Kansas, now located near Alvin, Tex., desiring to be organized, to more fully carry on the work, the Mission Board of Texas requested me to go there; hence, March 14, I boarded the train, in company with Bro. Philip Eby, for Alvin. We arrived on the evening of the next day; and found, on arrival, that Bro. S. A. Honberger, of Matterly, La., had been preaching there for one week. On the evening of my arrival, the weather turned cold, so we could not have any more services until the evening of the 19th. There was no stove in the church they were using, hence they could not hold services. On the evening of the 19th we met at Bro. J. J. Wassam's house to organize. Seven members met, all with letters of membership and all desiring to be organized. They presented certificates of eight more members living about thirty miles north-west of them. These also wanted to unite with the new organization. One minister in the second degree and two deacons are among the number. All unanimously agreed to work in harmony with the Word of God and the counsel of the Brotherhood. They are taking hold of the work with a commendable zeal, and I ask the prayers of the church in their behalf.

There is a great work and field at that place with almost unlimited bounds. The distance is so great between them and other organized churches that we did not limit the bounds. The work is truly hopeful, and the people seem to welcome our doctrine. They are mostly northern people, and they have a fruitful country and fertile soil. Best of all, I think the climate is healthful. Bro. Gish, of Fort Scott, Kans, arrived there March 21, with his family. He is a minister, and his wife and daughter are also members.

A commendable feature in their town, Alvin, is, that they have local option, and, consequently, a temperate town. I hope they will so continue. Tropical fruits, as far as has been tried, do exceedingly well. Blackberries and dewberries

grow wild and are quite prolific. Strawberries, pears, plums, grapes and peaches also do finely. Corn and oats are said to do well. Vegetables of all kinds produce largely. On Monday, March 21, three other disciples and I went to Galveston for sight-seeing. The Gulf is indeed a grand sight for one who has never seen it. Oh the wonderful works of God! Vast sums of money are spent here on the jetties, to procure deep water. In the evening we returned to Alvin and stayed over night. March 23 I bade farewell to the faithful of Alvin, and started for home, where I arrived March 24 and found all well, excepting sister Molsbee, who was suffering severely from a second attack of *La Gripps*. May the Good Lord bless and restore her to health again!
HENRY BRUBAKER.
Nocona, Tex., March 25.

From Waterloo, Iowa.

ON March 11, I went to the Boon River church, Hancock Co., Iowa, and met with the church in council on Saturday, March 12. All business passed off pleasantly. The Boon River church is making arrangements to build a meeting-house this coming summer. This church has a membership of about twenty-five, in Hancock and Wright Counties, with good prospects for more moving in soon, and a very good interest among outsiders. They have only one minister,—Bro. George Aschenbrenner,—and two deacons. They have many calls for preaching. Bro. Aschenbrenner is a German, and there are calls enough for German preaching to keep him busy all of his time. Brethren, it is too bad that this German brother must preach in English, and let the German drop. Is there not a young David somewhere in the Brotherhood who will volunteer to go and do the English preaching for the Boon River congregation? There would be plenty of work for two English ministers, but we will be glad to get only one. Who will come to our aid? Your help is needed.

Now, as there is occasionally a minister who is thinking of moving West, I would invite all such to take a look at Hancock County. They have good soil, their land is low in price, and convenient to the railroad. Take the Chicago, Milwaukee and St. Paul R. R., to Britt, then the Minneapolis & St. Louis to Stilson. Bro. Elias Long lives three miles South of Stilson. We do not only invite ministers but any of the Brethren and sisters who contemplate changing their location, to settle there and help to build up the cause of the Master. WM. IKENBERRY.

From Loraine, Ill.

THE little band of God's dear children at Loraine is still at work, and, seemingly, in good spirits. We have our regular preaching here every second and fourth Sundays in each month, at the hours of 11 A. M. and 7 P. M. Our Sunday-school meets every Sunday at 3 P. M.

We held our council on Saturday, March 19, and set the time for our spring Communion for Saturday, May 14. Bro. John Pool is expected with us at that time, and will probably be with us five or six days. Brethren and sisters, all who can, should come and make us a visit, especially is the young members' influence needed here. Ministers, come and feast with us! We would like one or two elders to assist us on Saturday at 2 P. M. H. W. STRICKLER.
Loraine, Ill.

From Lewiston, Minn.

WE are in usual health, both temporally and spiritually. We have been repairing our church house this winter, at an expense of about $200.

obtaining the desired information. Land ranges from $4 to $10 per acre, at each of these places, and they are within twelve to fourteen miles of each other, respectively.

We shall be glad to have you locate at either place. Come over into Macedonia and help us.

B. E. KESSLER.

Notes and Jottings.

OUR EASTERN VISIT.—NUMBER ONE.

I LEFT home Jan. 28, and arrived at Loudonville, Ohio, next day,. Here I remained apcd preached over the Lord's Day. I was sorry to find my mother-in-law, Workman, suffering seriously with brain trouble. It was in this church that I was called to the ministry, May, 1869. I was under the fostering ministerial care of father-in-law, Morgan Workman, for three years.

I arrived at Huntingdon, Pa., Feb. 1. This was my first visit to Huntingdon, and to me it was pleasant. They feel encouraged in their school work. Their government, as to morals and general religious instruction, seems to be all that could be asked for.

On the evening of Feb. 3, we met our appointment at the Hatfield church, Montgomery Co., Pa. The work here is in the care of brethren F. P. Cassel, assisted by Hillery Crouthamel and Wm. Frets. There seemed to be great harmony in their church work. Each morning sermon was followed with a social service, which seemed as manna to the hungry. Bro. Cassel has firmness and great kindness, combined with the requirements of 1 Tim. 3: 4, "having his children under subjection with all gravity," which gives him great power as an elder.

The children's meeting that preceded each Sunday morning service, seemed highly pleasing to both parents and children. The filled house at the close, on the evening of March 16, was evidence of the interest felt in the meeting. One was baptized,—David Rosenberger, a distant relative, with whom I had been corresponding on the subject of rebaptism. He has been a member of the River Brethren.

We next made Norristown a short visit The Brethren in this city have a commodious, substantial house of worship, but no resident minister. They are supplied by the adjoining ministers. About forty members reside in the city, but the greater portion hold their membership elsewhere. Unfortunately, some of the congregations east have no district lines. The place of membership is left to the taste or preference of the members. Think what the forty members could do for the good cause of the Master in Norristown, if they were united in the work at home, among their immediate neighbors.

I spent Sunday, Feb. 21, in Philadelphia. I attended Sunday-school and morning service in Germantown. I confess I felt a peculiar sensation, on entering the little, neat, old stone church, built by our pioneer Christian fathers a long time ago.

Here was once a flourishing church, organized Dec. 25, 1723. On that day four were baptized, and the first feast ever held in America, with Peter Becker as their elder. Bro. Stover, of Maryland, a young man of promise, has taken recent charge of the work at Germantown. My anxious prayer is that Bro. Stover may prove a Josiah in finding the book of the law, lost to so many souls.

At 3 P. M. I met with the brethren in a hall on Marshall Street. The Brethren held this as a mission point for some years. Of late it has been placed in the hands of Bro. Joel Reiner, as an organization. We followed their Sunday-school with a preaching service.

At 7 P. M. I met with the Brethren in their new house on the corner of Dauphin and Carlisle Streets. The attendance was encouraging. The condition and history of the church in Philadelphia is well known. I need not repeat it. In sympathy they seem to be approaching the General Brotherhood. Bro. T. T. Myers is yet in charge, and they seem to enjoy his labors. The church in this city was organized on Crown Street in 1815, with Bro. Peter Keiser as elder, who served in the ministry sixty years,—fifty years in the eldership. I. J. ROSENBERGER.

"RELIGION is the best armor a man can have, but the worst cloak."

Notes from Our Correspondents.

"As cold water to a thirsty soul, so is good news from a far country."

Summitville, Ind.—The members of the Oasis church held their quarterly council, March 10. Everything passed off in a loving spirit We like to go to the house of the Lord when all labor together as one. We agreed to hold our love-feast May 28, at 2 o'clock.—*Hulda Piow.*

Harlan, Iowa.—The members of this church assembled in council March 21. Everything passed off in peace and harmony. We appointed our love-feast for May 27, and will have meetings the entire week previous to the feast. We would be glad to have some of the brethren in the West, who are going to Annual Meeting, to stop with us at that time. We expect Bro. Dierdorff to be with us at our meetings.—*Nancy J. Miller.*

Mooreland, Ind.—The quarterly council of the Buck Creek church occurred March 26. Much business came before the council, but all was disposed of in a spirit of love. Our Sunday-school was organized on Sunday, following. Bro. Joseph Oxley was chosen as Superintendent, assisted by a full corps of officers. Our love-feast was appointed for May 27, beginning at 4 P. M. Eld. D. H. Replogle was elected delegate to District Meeting.—*Isaac Wike, March 26.*

Burr Oak, Ind.—We commenced a series of meetings in the Salem meeting-house, in the extreme South-west part of the Union church, Marshall Co., March 18, and continued until the 27th. Bro. Noah Fisher, of the Mexico church, did the preaching. As a result of the meetings two were baptized. Saints were encouraged and the church greatly revived. Could the meetings have been continued, many more would have joined in with the people of God.—*Joseph Burns, March 31.*

Barksville, W. Va.—We had our church council March 19. Considerable business came before the church, but as we believe it was all disposed of in a Christian-like manner. The church thought it necessary to elect a brother to the ministry, and one to the deacon's office. Bro. Joseph Utz was called to the ministry, and Bro. Daniel Sutton to the deacon's office. Bro. David Long presided over the meeting and installed the above brethren. Our love-feast will occur June 4, the Lord willing.—*J. O. Puterbaugh, March 25.*

Woodberry, Md.—Eld. E. W. Stoner, of Pipe Creek, Md., preached for us this morning, after which we retired to the water-side, and witnessed the baptism of one who came out on the Lord's side. May the grace of God ever guide our dear young brother in his Christian warfare. This is a good field for our ministering brethren. Do not fail to call and see us if you ever come to Baltimore. We are few in number, but will welcome you. Our Sunday-school is prospering, and we are also interested in missionary work. May the Lord help us to do more!—*John S. Geiser.*

A Correction.—In my "Notice to all Concerned," in GOSPEL MESSENGER No. 13, page 203, my language would seem to convey the idea that all of the work and results were due to myself. Please read, "During our efforts, etc.," as other Brethren did nobly in assisting in the work in Kansas City. Also, instead of 17,500 read 175,000 inhabitants.—*Isaac H. Crist, Gardner, Kans.*

Garrison, Iowa.—The brethren and sisters of the Garrison church met in quarterly council March 19, at which time one, who had strayed from the fold, was received back into fellowship. All other business before the meeting passed off quietly. The writer was chosen delegate to Annual Meeting. On Sunday, March 20, Eld. J. L. Snyder, of Brooklyn, preached for us in the forenoon and evening.—*E. H. Stouffer.*

Warsaw, Ind.—Our quarterly council convened on Saturday, Feb. 27, with a good attendance, considering the roads and weather. The business of the meeting passed off pleasantly, and a deep interest for the cause was manifested. The church concluded to elect the officers for the Sabbath-school for the ensuing year, beginning with the second quarter. Bro. John Johnson was elected Superintendent. We decided also to use the Brethren's literature. Great sorrow was caused among us by the death of our much-esteemed Bro. R. H. Miller, who had the care over us, and from whom the church had received much encouragement. Truly God's ways are not our ways.—*N. B. Heeter, March 22.*

Parahamville, Iowa.—The members of the Farnhamville church met in council March 19. Bro. M. H. Fowler, of Fredericksburgh, Iowa, presided. A great deal of business came before the church, which was adjusted in a good, brotherly spirit. We met the following Sunday morning to re-organize our Sunday-school, after which Bro. Fowler spoke on "Bible Truth" for about thirty minutes. Bro. Fowler continued with us until Thursday, March 24, during which time he preached six sermons, and two precious souls were resolved to walk in newness of life. May they ever prove faithful and gain the crown!—*A. M. White, March 27.*

Rock Creek, Colo.—Our quarterly council convened yesterday at the house of Bro. Henry Larioks. The members were all present but two who were detained at home on account of sickness. A considerable amount of business came before the meeting, but all was transacted in a spirit of love. A letter was read from our beloved brother, Eld. Enoch Eby. This did our hearts good. We love to get such letters from our dear brethren, for they establish our hearts and make us strong in the faith. The lumber is being put on the ground for our new church-house, and we look forward with eagerness to the time when we will be permitted to worship God in a house, dedicated to his service.—*A. C. Snowberger, March 27.*

Finley, Nebr.—In GOSPEL MESSENGER No. 10, page 152, I see an editorial item made as follows: "It has been discovered that there were, for the first time in nearly three hundred years, five Mondays in the month of February." By observation we find that the same day of the month falls on the same day of the week, every twenty-eight years; hence February had five Mondays in the years of 1808, 1836, 1864 and 1892.—*W. O. Beckner.* [Our item was made up from what was published in the Chicago *Evening Journal.* We are glad to be corrected whenever we make a mistake. Others have called our attention to the item, and we now stand corrected, without looking up the facts any further than what is contained in the letter, calling our attention to the mistake.—ED.]

obtaining the desired information. Land ranges from $4 to $10 per acre, at each of these places, and they are within twelve to fourteen miles of each other, respectively.

We shall be glad to have you locate at either place. Come over into Macedonia and help us.
B. E. KESSLER.

Notes and Jottings.

OUR EASTERN VISIT.—NUMBER ONE.

I LEFT home Jan. 28, and arrived at Loudonville, Ohio, next day,. Here, I remained and preached over the Lord's Day. I was sorry to find my mother-in-law, Workman, suffering seriously with brain trouble. It was in this church that I was called to the ministry, May, 1869. I was under the fostering ministerial care of father-in-law, Morgan Workman, for three years.

I arrived at Huntingdon, Pa., Feb. 1. This was my first visit to Huntingdon, and to me it was pleasant. They feel encouraged in their school work. Their government, as to morals and general religious instruction, seems to be all that could be asked for.

On the evening of Feb. 3, we met our appointment at the Hatfield church, Montgomery Co., Pa. The work here is in the care of brethren F. P. Cassel, assisted by Hillery Crouthamel and Wm. Fretz. There seemed to be great harmony in their church work. Each morning sermon was followed with a social service, which seemed as manna to the hungry: Bro. Cassel has firmness and great kindness, combined with the requirements of 1 Tim. 3: 4, "having his children under subjection with all gravity," which gives him great power as an elder.

The children's meeting that preceded each Sunday morning service, seemed highly pleasing to both parents and children. The filled house at the close, on the evening of March 16, was evidence of the interest felt in the meeting. One was baptized,—David Rosenberger, a distant relative, with whom I had been corresponding on the subject of rebaptism. He has been a member of the River Brethren.

We next made Norristown a short visit. The Brethren in this city have a commodious, substantial house of worship, but no resident minister. They are supplied by the adjoining ministers. About forty members reside in the city, but the greater portion hold their membership elsewhere. Unfortunately, some of the congregations east have no district lines. The place of membership is left to the taste or preference of the members. Think what the forty members could do for the good cause of the Master in Norristown, if they were united in the work at home, among their immediate neighbors.

I spent Sunday, Feb. 21, in Philadelphia. I attended Sunday-school and morning service in Germantown. I confess I felt a peculiar sensation, on entering the little, neat, old stone church, built by our pioneer Christian fathers a long time ago.

Here was once a flourishing church, organized Dec. 25, 1723. On that day four were baptized, and the first feast ever held in America, with Peter Becker as their elder. Bro. Stover, of Maryland, a young man of promise, has taken recent charge of the work at Germantown. My anxious prayer is that Bro. Stover may prove a Josiah in finding the book of the law, lost to so many souls.

At 3 P. M. I met with the brethren in a hall on Marshall Street. The Brethren held this as a mission point for some years. Of late it has been placed in the hands of Bro. Joel Reiner, as an organization. We followed their Sunday-school with a preaching service.

At 7 P. M. I met with the Brethren in their new house on the corner of Dauphin and Carlisle Streets. The attendance was encouraging. The condition and history of the church in Philadelphia is well known. I need not repeat it. In sympathy they seem to be approaching the General Brotherhood. Bro. T. T. Myers is yet in charge, and they seem to enjoy his labors. The church in this city was organized on Crown Street in 1815, with Bro. Peter Keiser as elder, who served in the ministry sixty years,—fifty years in the eldership.   I. J. ROSENBERGER.

" RELIGION is the best armor a man can have, but the worst cloak."

Notes from Our Correspondents.

"As cold water to a thirsty soul, so is good news from a far country."

Summitville, Ind.—The members of the Oasis church held their quarterly council, March 10. Everything passed off in a loving spirit. We like to go to the house of the Lord when all labor together as one. We agreed to hold our love-feast May 28, at 2 o'clock.—*Hulda Flora.*

Harlan, Iowa.—The members of this church assembled in council March 21. Everything passed off in peace and harmony. We appointed our love-feast for May 27, and will have meetings the entire week previous to the feast. We would be glad to have some of the brethren in the West, who are going to Annual Meeting, to stop with us at that time. We expect Bro. Dierdorff to be with us at our meetings.—*Nancy J. Miller.*

Mooreland, Ind.—The quarterly council of the Buck Creek church occurred March 26. Much business came before the council, but all was disposed of in a spirit of love. Our Sunday-school was organized on Sunday, following. Bro. Joseph Oxley was chosen as Superintendent, assisted by a full corps of officers. Our love-feast was appointed for May 27, beginning at 4 P. M. Eld. D. H. Replogle was elected delegate to District Meeting.—*Isaac Wike, March 26.*

Burr Oak, Ind.—We commenced a series of meetings in the Salem meeting-house, in the extreme South-west part of the Union church, Marshall Co., March 18, and continued until the 27th. Bro. Noah Fisher, of the Mexico church, did the preaching. As a result of the meetings two were baptized. Saints were encouraged and the church greatly revived. Could the meetings have been continued, many more would have joined in with the people of God.—*Joseph Burns, March 31.*

Darksville, W. Va.—We had our church council March 19. Considerable business came before the church, but we believe it was all disposed of in a Christian-like manner. The church thought it necessary to elect a brother to the ministry, and one to the deacon's office. Bro. Joseph Uts was called to the ministry, and Bro. Daniel Sutton to the deacon's office. Bro. David Long presided over the meeting and installed the above brethren. Our love-feast will occur June 4, the Lord willing.—*J. O. Puterbaugh, March 25.*

Woodberry, Md.—Eld. E. W. Stoner, of Pipe Creek, Md., preached for us this morning, after which we retired to the water-side, and witnessed the baptism of one who came out on the Lord's side. May the grace of God ever guide our dear young brother in his Christian warfare. This is a good field for our ministering brethren. Do not fail to call and see us if you ever come to Baltimore. We are few in number, but will welcome you. Our Sunday-school is prospering, and we are also interested in missionary work. May the Lord help us to do more!—*John S. Geiser.*

A Correction.—In my "Notice to all Concerned," in GOSPEL MESSENGER No. 13, page 203, my language would seem to convey the idea that all of the work and results were due to myself. Please read, "During our efforts, etc.," as other Brethren did nobly in assisting in the work in Kansas City. Also, instead of 17,500 read 175,000 inhabitants.—*Isaac H. Crist, Gardner, Kans.*

Garrison, Iowa.—The brethren and sisters of the Garrison church met in quarterly council March 19, at which time one, who had strayed from the fold, was received back into fellowship. All other business before the meeting passed off quietly. The writer was chosen delegate to Annual Meeting. On Sunday, March 20, Eld. J. L. Snyder, of Brooklyn, preached for us in the forenoon and evening.—*E. H. Stouffer.*

Warsaw, Ind.—Our quarterly council convened on Saturday, Feb. 27, with a good attendance, considering the roads and weather. The business of the meeting passed off pleasantly, and a deep interest for the cause was manifested. The church concluded to elect the officers for the Sabbath-school for the ensuing year, beginning with the second quarter. Bro. John Johnson was elected Superintendent. We decided also to use the Brethren's literature. Great sorrow was caused among us by the death of our much-esteemed Bro. R. H. Miller, who had the care over us, and from whom the church had received much encouragement. Truly God's ways are not our ways.—*N. B. Heeter, March 22.*

Farahamville, Iowa.—The members of the Farnhamville church met in council March 19. Bro. M. H. Fowler, of Fredericksburgh, Iowa, presided. A great deal of business came before the church, which was adjusted in a good, brotherly spirit. We met the following Sunday morning to re-organize our Sunday-school, after which Bro. Fowler spoke on "Bible Truth" for about thirty minutes. Bro. Fowler continued with us until Thursday, March 24, during which time he preached six sermons, and two precious souls were resolved to walk in newness of life. May they ever prove faithful and gain the crown!—*A. M. White, March 27.*

Rock Creek, Ohio.—Our quarterly council convened yesterday at the house of Bro. Henry Larioks. The members were all present but two who were detained at home on account of sickness. A considerable amount of business came before the meeting, but all was transacted in a spirit of love. A letter was read from our beloved brother, Eld. Enoch Eby. This did our hearts good. We love to get such letters from our dear brethren, for they establish our hearts and make us strong in the faith. The lumber is being put on the ground for our new church-house, and we look forward with eagerness to the time when we will be permitted to worship God in a house, dedicated to his service.—*A. C. Snowberger, March 27.*

Finley, Nebr.—In GOSPEL MESSENGER No. 10, page 152, I see an editorial item which reads as follows: "It has been discovered that there were, for the first time in nearly three hundred years, five Mondays in the month of February." By observation we find that the same day of the month falls on the same day of the week, every twenty-eight years; hence February had five Mondays in the years of 1808, 1836, 1864 and 1892—*W. O. Beckner.* [Our item was made up from what was published in the Chicago *Evening Journal.* We are glad to be corrected whenever we make a mistake. Others have called our attention to the item, and we now stand corrected, without looking up the facts any further than what is contained in the letter, calling our attention to the mistake.—ED.]

THE GOSPEL MESSENGER.

"Set for the Defense of the Gospel."

Vol. 30, Old Series.   Mt. Morris, Ill., and Huntingdon, Pa., April 19, 1892   No. 16.

The Gospel Messenger.

H. B. BRUMBAUGH, Editor,
And Business Manager of the Eastern House, Box 50,
Huntingdon, Pa.

RECENTLY a lady died in Virginia, at the age of ninety-nine years. Just a few days before her death, she applied for membership, but could be received only as an applicant. That was certainly a long time to put off calling on the name of the Lord.

FROM recent reports we learn that the Philadelphia church is in a prosperous condition and that frequent accessions are had by conversion and baptism. The Sunday-school is large and growing, so that more room will soon be needed. We are glad to note that success is attending the efforts of the members of this church and that Bro. Myers is giving excellent satisfaction.

A SISTER asks us if there is any virtue in *enforced* obedience. Yes, if we don't require it to be enforced too hard. This means to submit our wills against our inclinations, at the request or demand of others. To do this, is grace within itself and becomes, to us, a profitable discipline. The enforcement, here, we accept in its modified sense, and not resistance to compulsory and physical means.

THE Pennsylvania Railroads have favored all ministers residing along their line with half-fare rates by procuring the usual "Clerical Tickets." The privilege extends from Philadelphia in the East, to Chicago and St. Louis in the West. Of course, these half-fare tickets are not expected to be used for the transaction of business. Our brethren are expected to deal justly with railroads as well as with other people. Honesty makes no discriminations.

IS IT RIGHT?

A SISTER, who, for reasons known to herself, wishes to have her name withheld, asks: "Is it right for a lady who is a member of the church to marry a Catholic? He belongs to this church but is not a strong Catholic."

Whether this sister wants this advice for herself or for some one else, she does not say. But as the question is one of general importance, we shall give it a few thoughts. In advising people who are in love, we have learned a few things, and one of them is to first learn what kind of advice they wish, or rather, what they wish to do, and then tell them to go ahead and do it, because this is what is expected, and will render the better satisfaction for the time being.

Not long since we were asked if it would be wrong to marry a young man who drinks, part of the object being to reform him. Our advice was then, and still is, to reform him thoroughly first and do the marrying afterwards.

Our querist does not say it in so many words but we have the inference pretty strongly asserted in her saying that he is not a "strong Catholic," meaning, of course, that the possibilities for his conversion are rather encouraging. Now, if this is the thought or hope, to make it reasonably safe we advise, by all means, do the converting first, and do the marrying afterwards, as it is much easier to convert a drinker from the way of drunkenness than it is to convert a Catholic from his faith. At any rate, this is not the intention of the covenant of matrimony.

It is a noble work to convert people from bad to that which is better. But if it cannot be done without marrying, then we say, "Hands off." The commission is not, Go ye and marry people and then have them converted, but preach to them the Gospel. If the Gospel,—the Truth,—will not convert, we would not like to risk the marriage relation. There are thousands of ladies who have over-estimated their converting power through marriage, and were made to reap a bad harvest all through life.

The object of the marriage relation is too often lost sight of. Next to that of our religion it is the most sacred, and the nature of the union is such that to meet the true intention of it there must be a unity of feeling morally and spiritually, —especially the latter. As this cannot exist between a Protestant and a Catholic, there should be no intermarriage, no matter how strong may be the feelings of sexual love. There are many such marriages, but the ultimate of them all is either a conversion of one of the parties, connubial misery through life, or, divorce. And as Catholics are largely unyielding in their religion, the lady who marries one might as well decide to turn Catholic or lead a miserable life, for "how can two walk together unless they agree?" We would be pleased to elaborate this subject more fully, but have not the space and time now, be-cause there is another almost on the same line in an article that will appear next week.

AN OFF YEAR.

THIS seems, in some respects, to be a kind of off year in religious work, such at least appears to be the complaint among the churches in the country, and also in many of the towns and cities. For this there may be a cause, indeed, there must be a cause. But whether this cause is a justifiable one may be a question. There are circumstances that do interfere with holding religious meetings, over which we have no control, such as bad weather and sickness. All of these prevailed to some extent during the winter, and as a result, many of the meetings commenced were not continued as long as they would have been, had the circumstances been more favorable. And the fact that there has been less effort put forth by the church in having the Truth preached, may account for two things:

1. No conversions and additions to the church. Right here is a suggestive thought. Does the salvation of souls depend upon the personal efforts which we, as Christian workers and ministers, make? If so, is it not a wonderful thought, —that souls should be lost through our indifference and neglect? And yet, is it not true that the Lord has so ordained that through the foolishness of preaching the world shall be saved for Christ? It is surely a great thought, and as true as it is great. There is a wonderful responsibility lying somewhere and it will be well for us to try to determine where it is, as it is the will of God that all shall have, at least an opportunity, such as it is intended that we should have to be saved, and if his will is to be executed through us, we cannot be held guiltless unless we make the intended and necessary effort.

2. The lack of religious privileges has, or may have, a deadening effect upon our own religious feelings and lives, so we can readily see how this deadening comes about and grows. When we commence going back, all the attending circumstances combine to push in that direction.

But, then, it is encouraging to look on the other side and feel that when we start in the other direction, the combination works for the forward movement. It is still time for laboring and sowing and if there could now be a forward movement made, much might yet be done for a general advancement in the good cause. Some of our best meetings have been held in the springtime and early summer. Let our forces be organized and make a mighty effort to rescue the perishing before the time arrives when it will be said, "The harvest is past, and we are not saved."

If religiously, so far, we have had an "off year," there is no reason why it should so continue. The seeming causes having been removed, we should now make up for that which is lost by doubling our diligence and working with our might.

THE GOSPEL MESSENGER.

"Set for the Defense of the Gospel."

Vol. 30, Old Series.   Mt. Morris, Ill., and Huntingdon, Pa., April 19, 1892   No. 16.

The Gospel Messenger.

H. B. BRUMBAUGH, Editor,
And Business Manager of the Eastern House, Box 50,
Huntingdon, Pa.

Table of Contents.

RECENTLY a lady died in Virginia, at the age of ninety-nine years. Just a few days before her death she applied for membership, but could be received only as an applicant. That was certainly a long time to put off calling on the name of the Lord.

FROM recent reports we learn that the Philadelphia church is in a prosperous condition and that frequent accessions are had by conversion and baptism. The Sunday-school is large and growing, so that more room will soon be needed. We are glad to note that success is attending the efforts of the members of this church and that Bro. Myers is giving excellent satisfaction.

A SISTER asks us if there is any *virtue* in *enforced* obedience. Yes, if we don't require it to be enforced too hard. This means to submit our wills against our inclinations, at the request or demand of others. To do this, is a grace within itself and becomes, to us, a profitable discipline. The enforcement, here, we accept in its modified sense, and not resistance to compulsory and physical means.

THE Pennsylvania Railroads have favored all ministers residing along their line with half-fare rates by procuring the usual "Clerical Tickets." The privilege extends from Philadelphia in the East, to Chicago and St. Louis in the West. Of course, these half-fare tickets are not expected to be used for the transaction of business. Our brethren are expected to deal justly with railroads as well as with other people. Honesty makes no discriminations.

IS IT RIGHT?

A SISTER, who, for reasons known to herself, wishes to have her name withheld, asks: "Is it right for a lady who is a member of the church but is not a strong Catholic."

Whether this sister wants this advice for herself or for some one else, she does not say. But as the question is one of general importance, we shall give it a few thoughts. In advising people who are in love, we have learned a few things, and one of them is to first learn what kind of advice they wish, or rather, what they wish to do, and then tell them to go ahead and do it, because this is what is expected, and will render the better satisfaction for the time being.

Not long since we were asked if it would be wrong to marry a young man who drinks, part of the object being to reform him. Our advice was then, and still is, to reform him thoroughly first and do the marrying afterwards.

Our querist does not say it in so many words but we have the inference pretty strongly asserted in her saying that he is not a "strong Catholic," meaning, of course, that the possibilities for his conversion are rather encouraging. Now, if this is the thought or hope, to make it reasonably safe we advise, by all means, do the converting first, and do the marrying afterwards, as it is much easier to convert a drinker from the way of drunkenness than it is to convert a Catholic from his faith. At any rate, this is not the intention of the covenant of matrimony.

It is a noble work to convert people from bad to that which is better. But if it cannot be done without marrying, then we say, "Hands off." The commission is not, Go ye and marry people and then have them converted, but preach to them the Gospel. If the Gospel,—the Truth,—will not convert, we would not like to risk the marriage relation. There are thousands of ladies who have over-estimated their converting power through marriage, and were made to reap a bad harvest all through life.

The object of the marriage relation is too often lost sight of. Next to that of our religion it is the most sacred, and the nature of the union is such that to meet the true intention of it there must be a unity of feeling morally and spiritually, —especially the latter. As this cannot exist between a Protestant and a Catholic, there should be no intermarriage, no matter how strong may be the feelings of sexual love. There are many such marriages, but the ultimate of them all is either a conversion of one of the parties, connubial misery through life, or, divorce. And as Catholics are largely unyielding in their religion, the lady who marries one might as well decide to turn Catholic or lead a miserable life, for "how can two walk together unless they agree?" We would be pleased to elaborate this subject more fully, but have not the space and time now, because there is another almost on the same line in an article that will appear next week.

AN OFF YEAR.

THIS seems, in some respects, to be a kind of off year in religious work, such at least appears to be the complaint among the churches in the country, and also in many of the towns and cities. For this there may be a cause, indeed, there must be a cause. But whether this cause is a justifiable one may be a question. There are circumstances that do interfere with holding religious meetings, over which we have no control, such as bad weather and sickness. All of these prevailed to some extent during the winter, and as a result, many of the meetings commenced were not continued as long as they would have been, had the circumstances been more favorable. And the fact that there has been less effort put forth by the church in having the Truth preached, may account for two things:

1. No conversions and additions to the church. Right here is a suggestive thought. Does the salvation of souls depend upon the personal efforts which we, as Christian workers and ministers, make? If so, is it not a wonderful thought, —that souls should be lost through our indifference and neglect? And yet, is it not true that the Lord has so ordained that through the foolishness of preaching the world shall be saved for Christ? It is surely a great thought, and as true as it is great. There is a wonderful responsibility lying somewhere and it will be well for us to try to determine where it is, as it is the will of God that all shall have, at least an opportunity, such as it is intended that we should be to be saved, and if his will is to be executed through us, we cannot be held guiltless unless we make the intended and necessary effort.

2. The lack of religious privileges has, or may have, a deadening effect upon our own religious feelings and lives, so we can really see how this deadening comes about and grows. When we commence going back, all the attending circumstances combine to push in that direction.

But, then, it is encouraging to look on the other side and feel that when we start in the other direction, the combination works for the forward movement. It is still time for laboring and sowing and if there could now be a forward movement made, much might yet be done for a general advancement in the good cause. Some of our best meetings have been held in the springtime and early summer. Let our forces be organized and make a mighty effort to rescue the perishing before the time arrives when it will be said, "The harvest is past, and we are not saved."

If religiously, so far, we have had an "off year," there is no reason why it should so continue. The seeming causes having been removed, we should now make up for that which is lost by doubling our diligence and working with our might.

people *know* that I am rightly commissioned to be their leader and deliverer?" Signs enough being given him to convince the most skeptical, he throws aside his weakness, leans on the Invisible Arm and looks towards Egypt where this unswerving faith in the Invisible Jehovah is destined to nerve his arm for empire and make for him a name above every other name in Old Testament story,—a name we look up to and admire after the lapse of centuries,—a name second only to the Great Antitype that was heralded by angels and found by the Star of Bethlehem.

Whenever those moments of weakness overtake him in the future he falls back on the same arm and, in effect, says, "Lord, my steps falter, my arm fails, my feet grow weary; help thou me or I fail and fall."

My brother minister, did you ever feel this weakness, felt by Moses? Did you ever feel that your faltering tongue could not possibly deliver your Master's message,—that the people would require elegance of speech, subtle reasoning, philosophical research and logic beyond your power? Oh, yes, how often we have felt this, and we have hesitated, like Moses, when our tasks were much lighter than were his. When we could take the sure word of testimony in our hands that has been given us, as our message, we have felt in our weakness, often no doubt, that the people would require some sign, forgetting that we had the sign of the Sun of Righteousness,—of the Prophet Jonas. If we have been called to this holy office by the Invisible,—and our duty lies not here unless we have been,—we have the Invisible to support us.

My unconverted friend, have you ever had your moments of weakness? Are you not, in your present state, weak day by day? Ah, you know that you are. Conscience, that monitor of the soul, has told you to go into the Egyptian darkness of your heart and release your manhood and your immortal soul from the oppression of evil habit,—taking God's name in vain, tarrying at the wine cup, thinking evil thoughts, performing evil deeds. If you have tried to perform this without help, you have failed. You can only do it through the power of him who is invisible. Trust him, and he will give the desires of thine heart; trust him and he will bring it to pass; trust him and he will be a " lamp to thy feet and a light to thy pathway." Oh, that you could trust him now; cast yourself at his feet and be washed in a Savior's blood. Failing to do this you are lost.

3. Again, Moses trusted the Invisible in his seasons of disappointment. How disappointed he must have felt when the people rebelled against him in the wilderness,—when those, for whom he had labored so arduously, proved ungrateful. How disappointed he must have been when the people, whom God had promised to assist and guide, through him, to the earthly Canaan,—their future inheritance,—figuratively described as a land flowing with milk and honey, in contrast with the land of slavery they left behind,—how disappointed, I repeat, he must have been when they committed sin, thus increasing the difficulties of the journey and lengthening the road by devious wanderings, up and down the by-paths of the wilderness. Moses knew, had they deported themselves as reasonable and thankful people should have done, who were the recipients of the priceless boon of liberty and freedom,—that the journey would soon be over,—the earthly Canaan won and their organization, as an independent nation, consummated. How disappointed and grieved he must have been, then, at the folly and evil effects of their readiness to sin, and thus thwart their own happiness! May we not learn from this that sin causes us to wander in darkness,—

that it thwarts our happiness, lessens our joys and increases our sorrows? Then, why this persistent following in the paths of the destroyer? Why this rebellion against lawful authority and turning away from and refusing to obey the teachings of the Great Leader, typified by Moses, who is delivering us from the scourges of a harder task-master than Rameses, and offering us a more glorious inheritance than the great Prophet viewed from Pisgah's top?

Again, the disappointment of Moses must have been bitter when, on 'coming down from' the mount where he had received the stones inscribed with the Law, one clause of which read, "Thou shalt have no other gods before me," he found that, in his absence, the people had reverted to the worship of the false Gods of the Egyptians, taken their ornaments and made for themselves a golden calf. How his righteous soul must have been vexed as we see him almost in despair, breaking the tables of the Law he had just received. "Will these people never learn wisdom? Will they never be willing to lean on the Invisible, and trust in him?" As for himself, in this disappointment, he seeks the counsel of the Invisible, from whom the people had turned away. He can only "endure by still trusting him who had never left him nor forsaken him.

Let us take, as our motto, " *I will endure as seeing him who is invisible,*"—"Oh," you say, "it is so hard to get a living, abiding faith in the power of the Unseen,—in his interest in me." That is because we, like Thomas, want to see with our eyes and feel with our hands.

Why can we not repress and depress the things of earth, and exalt more those of heaven? We dwell too much upon the seen, too little upon the unseen. We walk too much by sight, too little by faith. We think too much of filling the storehouses upon our farms,—our earthly coffers,—too little about replenishing the more valuable storehouses of the spirit. We grasp too much after the things of time, forgetting the more momentous things of eternity,—are wedded too much to earth and not enough to heaven. Henceforth let it not be so!

Let us take warning from what has been revealed unto us of the deceitfulness of riches, the lust of the eye and the pride of life. Let us hear the voice ringing in our ears, " *This* night thy soul may be required of thee." If we must increase in goods, let it be those goods, the merchandise of which is better than the merchandise of silver and gold. Let us see God ever near us! Let us see ourselves acting as in the presence of the holy angels, and see with the eyes of faith which Moses exercised, the spiritual kingdom of which we may be a part, or to which we already belong. Then, from the mount of faith, as Moses from Pisgah, we can look across the swellings of Jordan and see our inheritance,—its streams more clear, its skies more fair, its mountains more beautiful, its Ruler more majestic than any inheritance this earth has ever afforded. There are no enemies upon the border land of that country, to destroy our cities or to make us afraid,—an inheritance wherein ignorance has fled, and knowledge is become perfect, where death enters not, but life evermore shall be ours! Is it not worth an effort to gain that home? Ah, yes, you feel that it is. You want that home, you expect it. It can be ours, the way is open, the home is waiting for us, and angels are ready to conduct us to it. Let us endure as seeing him who is invisible.

Roanoke, Va.

WHEN you hear people talk of the wickedness of mankind, partake not of their pleasure. When you hear people speak of the virtues of mankind, approve and rejoice therein.

THE SHAMBERGER-BOND DEBATE.

Affirmative Arguments and Thoughts of G. A. Shamberger, with Notes from Speeches by Levi Mohler, Warrensburgh, Mo.

NUMBER V.

" PROPOSITION.—The Scriptures teach that immersion is essential to Scripture baptism, and when there is no immersion, there is no Scripture baptism."

NOTE.—Received in its first definition immersion means to dip.—*Webster.* Baptism, from *baptein* means to dip in water. (Webster's first definition.)

" ARGUMENT 1.—God requires his command-ments to be kept as he gave them. Deut. 6; 24, 25; Heb. 2: 1, 3; 1 Sam. 15: 1, 3. The command to Saul is given in verses 7 to 9; what Saul did is stated in verses 10 and 11. God's judgment is given in verse 13. Saul's opinion is given in verses. 14 to 21. Saul seeks to justify himself in verses 22 and 23. General statement of the prophet.— "Intentions won't sanctify." Lev. 10: 1, 3."

NOTES.—It is most important to have impressed on the mind, a reverence for God's Word, as he delivered it to us, in its exact form of delivery. The public thought of to-day is: It don't make any difference how it is done, and, in many cases, whether it is done at all. In giving the law, Moses said: "As I command you." It makes a difference, is the idea.

In 1 Sam. 15 we have an explicit command of: God given to Saul, who obeys it nearly, so near, he thought he had obeyed it. For Saul's deviation from the commandment, he was denounced and rejected from being king.

"THOUGHT 1.—Israel's God is our God."

"THOUGHT 2.—He revealed to Israel his manner of treating his word."

"THOUGHT 3.—The things that happened to Israel are written for our learning."

"THOUGHT 4.—God speaks to us by his Son."

"THOUGHT 5.—The chances of escape are less to them who turn away from Christ than those who turned away from Moses."

" ARGUMENT 2.—No positive institution was ever given in the Law or Gospel, that can be kept, by a deviation from one form, unless allowance is made in the law of the institution. Ex. 12: 3, 10; Lev. 12: 5, 8 and 14: 1, 2; Num. 9: 6, 14; Ex. 12: 48, 49."

NOTES.—The Passover was a positive institution. Ex. 12: 3, 10. God gave a law for governing it. To keep it in deviation from one form, was not permitted, unless that deviation was provided for by the Lord.

A man, unclean from touching a dead body, enquired of Moses concerning his eating the Passover then at hand. Although Moses was the law-giver, he would not take it upon himself to say what should be done, but went to the Lord for directions. Lev. 9: 6, 11. He dared not, of himself, change the positive institution of God.

"THOUGHT 1.—Baptism is a positive institution."

" THOUGHT 2.—Since the law of baptism makes no allowance for choice of modes, it must always be administered in the same form."

"THOUGHT 3.—Any quarrel about inadaptability is with others and not with us."

" ARGUMENT 3.—All deviations in positive institutions, are expressed in different words. Lev. 12: 5, 8 and Lev. 14: 21, 22; Ex. 12: 5."

NOTE.—Whatever baptism may mean, it means one thing and only one. In giving positive institutions, God gave the deviations that could be made, and, unless plainly stated, no deviation was permitted.

For the Passover they could take a lamb of the sheep or goats, "or" give liberty of choice.

people *know* that I am rightly commissioned to be their leader and deliverer?" Signs enough being given him to convince the most skeptical, he throws aside his weakness, leans on the Invisible Arm and looks towards Egypt where this unswerving faith in the Invisible Jehovah is destined to nerve his arm for empire and make for him a name above every other name in Old Testament story,—a name we look up to and admire after the lapse of centuries,—a name second only to the Great Antitype that was heralded by angels and found by the Star of Bethlehem.

Whenever those moments of weakness overtake him in the future he falls back on the same arm and, in effect, says, "Lord, my steps falter, my and fails, my feet grow weary; help thou me or I fail and fall."

My brother minister, did you ever feel this weakness, felt by Moses? Did you ever feel that your faltering tongue could not possibly deliver your Master's message,—that the people would require elegance of speech, subtle reasoning, philosophical research and logic beyond your power? Oh, yes, how often we have felt this, and we have hesitated, like Moses, when our tasks were much lighter than were his. When we could take the sure word of testimony in our hands that has been given us, as our message, we have felt in our weakness, often no doubt, that the people would require some sign, forgetting that we had the sign of the Son of Righteousness,—of the Prophet Jonas. If we have been called to this holy office by the Invisible,—and our duty lies not here unless we have been,—we have the Invisible to support us.

My unconverted friend, have you ever had your moments of weakness? Are you, not, in your present state, weak day by day? Ah, you know, that you are. Conscience, that monitor of the soul, has told you to go into the Egyptian darkness of your heart and release your manhood and your immortal soul from the oppression of evil habit,—taking God's name in vain, tarrying at the wine cup, thinking evil thoughts, performing evil deeds. If you have tried to perform this without help, you have failed. You can only do it through the power of him who is invisible. Trust him, and he will give the desires of thine heart; trust him and he will bring it to pass; trust him and he will be a " lamp to thy feet and a light to thy pathway." Oh, that you could trust him now; cast yourself at his feet and be washed in a Savior's blood. Failing to do this you are lost.

3. Again, Moses trusted the Invisible in his seasons of disappointment. How disappointed he must have felt when the people rebelled against him in the wilderness,—when those, for whom he had labored so arduously, proved ungrateful. How disappointed he must have been when the people, whom God had promised to assist and guide, through him, to the earthly Canaan,—their future inheritance,—figuratively described as a land flowing with milk and honey, in contrast with the land of slavery they left behind,—how disappointed, I repeat, he must have been when they committed sin, thus increasing the difficulties of the journey and lengthening the road by devious wanderings, up and down the by-paths of the wilderness. Moses knew, had they deported themselves as reasonable and thankful people should have done, who were the recipients of the priceless boon of liberty and freedom,—that the journey would soon be over,—the earthly Canaan won and their organization, as an independent nation, consummated. How disappointed and grieved he must have been, then, at the folly and evil effects of their readiness to sin, and thus thwart their own happiness! May we not learn from this that sin causes us to wander in darkness,—

that it thwarts our happiness, lessens our joys and increases our sorrows? Then, why this persistent following in the paths of the destroyer? Why this rebellion against lawful authority and turning away from and refusing to obey the teachings of the Great Leader, typified by Moses, who is delivering us from the scourges of a harder task-master than Rameses, and offering us a more glorious inheritance than the great Prophet viewed from Pisgah's top?

Again, the disappointment of Moses must have been bitter when, on coming down from the mount where he had received the stones inscribed with the Law, one clause of which read, "Thou shalt have no other gods before me," he found that, in his absence, the people had reverted to the worship of the false Gods of the Egyptians, taken their ornaments and made for themselves a golden calf. How his righteous soul must have been vexed as we see him almost in despair, breaking the tables of the Law he had just received. "Will these people never learn wisdom? Will they never be willing to lean on the Invisible, and trust in him?" As for himself, in this disappointment, he seeks the counsel of the Invisible, from whom the people had turned away. He can only "endure by still trusting him who had never left him nor forsaken him.

Let us take as our motto, " *I will endure as seeing him who is invisible.*"—" Oh," you say, "it is so hard to get a living, abiding faith in the power of the Unseen,—in his interest in me." That is because we, like Thomas, want to see with our eyes and to feel with our hands.

Why can we not repress and depress the things of earth, and exalt more those of heaven? We dwell too much upon the seen, too little upon the unseen. We walk too much by sight, too little by faith. We think too much of filling the storehouses upon our farms,—our earthly coffers,—too little about replenishing the more valuable storehouses of the spirit. We grasp too much after the things of time, forgetting the more momentous things of eternity,—are wedded too much to earth and not enough to heaven. Henceforth let it not be so!

Let us take warning from what has been revealed unto us of the deceitfulness of riches, the lust of the eye and the pride of life." Let us hear the voice ringing in our ears, " *This* night thy soul may be required of thee." If we must increase in goods, let it be those goods, the merchandise of which is better than the merchandise of silver and gold. Let us see God ever near us! Let us see ourselves acting as in the presence of the holy angels, and see with the eyes of faith, which Moses exercised, the spiritual kingdom of which we may be a part, or to which we already belong. Then, from the mount of faith, as Moses from Pisgah, we can look across the swellings of Jordan and see our inheritance,—its streams more clear, its skies more fair, its mountains more beautiful, its Ruler more majestic than any inheritance this earth has ever afforded. There are no enemies upon the border land of that country, to destroy our cities or to make us afraid,—an inheritance wherein ignorance has part, and knowledge is become perfect, where death enters not, but life evermore shall be ours! Is it not worth an effort to gain that home? Ah, yes, you feel that it is. You want that home, you expect it. It can be ours, the way is open, the home is waiting for us, and angels are ready to conduct us to it. Let us endure as seeing him who is invisible.

Roanoke, Va.

When you hear people talk of the wickedness of mankind, partake not of their pleasure. When you hear people speak of the virtues of mankind, approve and rejoice therein.

THE SHAMBERGER-BOND DEBATE.

Affirmative Arguments and Thoughts of G. A. Shamberger, with Notes from Speeches by Levi Mohler, Warrensburgh, Mo.

NUMBER V.

" PROPOSITION.—The Scriptures teach that immersion is essential to Scripture baptism, and when there is no immersion, there is no Scripture baptism."

NOTE.—Received in its first definition immersion means to dip.—*Webster.* Baptism, from *baptein* means to dip in water. (Webster's first definition.)

" ARGUMENT 1.—God requires his command ments to be kept as he gave them. Deut. 6: 24, 25; Heb. 2: 1, 3; 1 Sam. 15: 1, 3. The command to Saul is given in verses 7 to 9; what Saul did is stated in verses 10 and 11. God's judgment is given in verse 13. Saul's opinion is given in verses 14 to 21. Saul seeks to justify himself in verses 22 and 23. General statement of the prophet.— "Intentions won't sanctify." Lev. 10: 1, 3."

NOTE.—It is most important to have impressed on the mind, a reverence for God's Word, as he. delivered it to us, in its exact form of delivery. The public thought of to-day is: It don't make any difference how it is done, and, in many cases, whether it is done at all. In giving the law, Moses said: " As I command you." It makes a difference, is the idea.

In 1 Sam. 15 we have an explicit command of God given to Saul, who obeys it nearly, so near, he thought he had obeyed it. For Saul's deviation from the commandment, he was denounced, and rejected from being king.

" THOUGHT 1.—Israel's God is our God."

" THOUGHT 2.—He revealed to Israel his manner of treating his word."

" THOUGHT 3.—The things that happened to Israel are written for our learning."

" THOUGHT 4.—God speaks to us by his Son."

" THOUGHT 5.—The chances of escape are less to them who turn away from Christ than those who turned away from Moses."

" ARGUMENT 2.—No positive institution was ever given in the Law or Gospel, that can be kept, by a deviation from one form, unless allowance is made in the law of the institution. Ex. 12: 3, 10; Lev. 12: 5, 8 and 14: 1, 2; Num. 9: 6, 14; Ex. 12: 48, 49."

NOTES.—The Passover was a positive institution. Ex. 12: 3, 10. God gave a law for governing it. To keep it in deviation from one form, was not permitted, unless that deviation was provided for by the Lord.

A man, unclean from touching, a dead body, enquired of Moses concerning his eating the Passover then at hand. Although Moses was the law-giver, he would not take it upon himself to say what should be done, but went to the Lord for directions. Lev. 9: 6, 11. He dared not, of himself, change the positive institution of God.

" THOUGHT 1.—Baptism is a positive institution."

" THOUGHT 2.—Since the law of baptism makes no allowance for choice of modes, it must always be administered in the same form."

" THOUGHT 3.—Any quarrel about inadaptability is with others and not with us."

" ARGUMENT 3.—All deviations in positive institutions, are expressed in different words. Lev. 12: 5, 8 and Lev. 14: 21, 22; Ex. 12: 5."

NOTE.—Whatever baptism may mean, it means one thing and only one. In giving positive institutions, God gave the deviations that could be made, and, unless plainly stated, no deviation was permitted.

For the Passover they could take a lamb of the sheep or goats, " or " give liberty of choice.

upon the inner chambers of our hearts, which necessity grows out of the very nature of things, our peculiar dispositions, our destiny and our duties and relations to one another and to our God. These considerations will receive further attention in the discussion of some of the subsequent points in this discourse.

2. Self-examination is necessary because it is so abundantly taught in the Word of God. The apostle's injunction to the church at Corinth by no means stands alone as Scriptural authority for the doctrine of self-examination.

Nor was the necessity of this spiritual introspection for the first time revealed to the writers of the New Testament, and by them made known to the world. Ever since God created and set a-beating the first human heart, there has existed the necessity of self-examination; and the duty is taught in the Old Testament as well as in the New.

Among the many wise things which the wise man so wisely said, is his exhortation of Prov. 4: 23: "Keep thy heart with all diligence; for out of it are the issues of life." This amounts to an exhortation to self-examination; for how can I keep my heart with all diligence without making it, its moral condition and peculiar tendencies the object of my diligent concern and watchfulness? And in view of the fact that out of it are the issues of my spiritual and eternal life, should I not pay the most diligent heed to the wise man's injunction? We dare not ignore it nor consider it lightly.

We also notice Psa. 119: 9, "Wherewithal shall a young man cleanse his way? By taking heed thereto according to thy word." Let the young man who has rushed wildly and thoughtlessly into sin, but who now grieves and sighs for a better life,—let him enter at once upon a course of diligent and rigid self-examination. Let him examine his ways,—what they have been and what they are; and if the examination be "according to thy word," the issue will be a glorious one, and all that he could desire. Woe to that man, be he young or old, rich or poor, high or low, who refuses to "take heed to his ways according to thy word!"

Without referring particularly to the many other Old Testament passages which bear more or less directly upon our subject, we now pass to a consideration of the New Testament teaching of self-examination.

The Master said in his Sermon on the Mount, "Judge not." That is, do not judge rashly and unjustly; especially do not judge or condemn others until you have first judged yourself. "And why beholdest thou the mote that is in thy brother's eye, but considerest not the beam that is in thine own eye?" Do not be examining your brother's heart to remove the comparatively small evils until you have examined your own heart, and at least removed the greater sins. "Thou hypocrite, first cast out the beam out of thine own eye; and then shalt thou see clearly to cast out the mote out of thy brother's eye." As the brethren at Corinth were more concerned about the power of Christ in Paul than in themselves, so a great many men to-day are apparently more concerned about the condition of the hearts of others than of their own; and as Paul warned his brethren to examine themselves instead of him, so now Christ would have us know that our first and essential chief duty is to examine our own hearts, get the beams out of our own eyes, by the grace of God endeavor to do more toward clearing ourselves of sin; and then will he accept us as servants fit for higher duties and more glorious work.

Covington, Ohio.

ACROSTIC.

Written on hearing of the Death of Bro. R. H. Miller.

This Weak and Imperfect Tribute, to the Memory of a Great and Good Man, is Affectionately Dedicated to Sister Emma Miller.

RINGING all sadly the funeral chime,
Of him who has gone to the heavenly clime.
BOUND for the mansions in glory above,
Entraptured by seraphs and heavenly love.
Ring sweetly the bells in heaven's high dome,
To welcome his soul to its beautiful home.
His battles are fought and victory won,
'Mid angels and saints he shall wear the bright crown.
In raptures so sweet his soul shall reign,
Listening to strains from the heavenly choir.
Look up, ye dear friends, your loved one has gone,
Earth's ties are now broken and you are alone.
Revere your blest Savior, you'll all meet at home.

McKee's Gap, Pa.   *Jno. A. Sell.*

COMMUNION.

BY H. C. EARLY.

In Two Chapters.—Number One.

THE Communion service, because of its sacred importance, John 6: 53, 54, should be engaged in understandingly and prayerfully. The time and manner of its institution by our Blessed Lord, the purpose attached to it, Luke 22: 19, the solemn language of Paul, 1 Cor. 11: 25–29, the warnings and barriers thrown around the Lord's table throughout the New Testament record,—all combine to show that it is a service requiring special condition of heart and life, and specific relation to Christ and his church. "For he that eateth and drinketh unworthily, eateth and drinketh damnation to himself, not discerning the Lord's body."

Some standard of fitness must be adopted and respected by the Lord's people. That all persons, irrespective of mental, moral and spiritual conditions, are entitled to the high and holy service of the Communion, none dare assert.

The *necessary qualifications* are embraced in the law of membership into the church and state of union, peace and love among her members. 1 Cor. 1: 10; Matt. 5: 23; 1 John 3: 14, 15, 16.

In the act of complying with the law of church membership the individual is admitted into the church,—the "one body by the one spirit," which implies, (1) unity of faith; (2) unity of doctrine; (3) unity of spirit, all of which go to make Communion possible. The Communion service is among the privileges of church life. It lies back of membership and is dependent upon it, and, therefore, any one, desiring the Communion, must expect to reach it in the *regular way.* Membership first; then the Communion.

The law of membership is a wall of protection to church privileges and fellowship. In this respect the church is like all other institutions. If we get the privileges and benefits of any institution, we first become identified with it. This is fundamental in all good government. To reverse this order would not only imperil government, but would, in fact, destroy the best government on earth. Why should not this be true in the church as well? The command to commune was given to Christians, — those who had secured membership in the church, not to those who had no membership,—as a commemorative service, not as a means of grace to sinners. Luke 22: 19, 20; 1 Cor. 11: 24, 25. After this manner the apostles labored. The Pentecostians were first taught, then baptized according to Christ's command, after which they engaged in the breaking of bread.

The law of church membership embraces teaching, faith, repentance, baptism, pardon of sin, and gift of the Holy Spirit. See Matt. 28: 19; Mark 16: 16; Luke 24: 47; Acts 2: 37, 38; 16: 30–33; 1 Cor. 12: 13; Heb. 11: 6. From these texts we deduce the following conclusions:

1. That teaching is necessary to faith.

---

2. That faith is necessary to repentance.
3. That repentance is necessary to baptism.
4. That baptism is necessary to pardon of sin.
5. That the pardon of sin is necessary to the gift of the Holy Spirit,—all of which are required by the law of church membership.

It is clear from the foregoing analysis that a person entitled to the privileges of the Communion, is one who has obtained membership in the church, having exercised true evangelical faith and repentance. He has been baptized by the "one baptism" into each name of the Holy Trinity (Matt. 28: 19); for the remission of sins (Acts 2: 38), and continues steadfast in the doctrine of the church and in peace with her members. Such individual membership makes the "one body" of the "one faith," "joined together in the same mind and in the same judgment," "speaking the same thing," having no divisions. 1 Cor. 1: 10.

Peace and love among the members, one with another, are absolutely essential in order to Communion. 1 Thess. 5: 13; Matt. 5: 24; 1 Cor. 5, 7, 8; 1 Pet. 1: 22; 1 John 4: 20. Brethren, united in faith and practice but not at peace and in love, one with another, dare not approach the Lord's table. Absence of peace and love makes absence of Communion. The highest service among men on earth requires the highest condition of heart. If peace and love be destroyed, reconciliation first, then the Communion,—union of service. Matt. 5: 24. If this be true of those of the same faith and practice, what may be said of those differing in faith and practice?

Now, for the sake of being better understood, we remark that the qualifications, preparatory to Communion are of two classes, individual and congregational. The individual is the act of the individual obtaining admission into the church through the law of church membership; and the congregational is the necessary state of love, peace and union throughout the membership of the church.

The sanctity of the Lord's table should be carefully guarded and preserved; for "we have an altar whereof they have no right to eat who serve the tabernacle." Heb. 13: 10. This throws positive restriction around the church altar or Lord's table. This closes the door against all who serve the flesh. God's ancient sanctuary and holy place were most rigidly guarded lest they be defiled; and if that which was but the shadow was so diligently kept from defilement, with what sacred care should we reverence and protect the church altar, consecrated by the blood of Jesus?

To show that this view of the teaching of the Scriptures is not only ours, we quote briefly from a view of the early Church Fathers and modern writers.

Justin Martyr, who wrote about fifty years after the death of St. John, says, "This food is called by us Eucharist, of which it is not lawful for any to partake but such as believe the things that are taught by us to be true, and have been baptized."

Jerome, who wrote about A. D. 400, says, "Catechumens cannot communicate at the Lord's table, being unbaptized." Austin, A. D. 500, Bede, A. D. 700, Theophylact, A. D. 1100, all say that no unbaptized person was admitted to the Communion.

Dr. Wall says, "Among all the absurdities that were ever held none ever maintained that any person should partake of the Communion before he was baptized." Dr. Adam Clarke says, "No person was permitted to come to the Eucharist till he had been baptized."

This was conceded and taught by both Baptists and Pedobaptists, at least until within the last century, and let it be borne in mind that a person not baptized, according to the Scriptures, is unbaptized.

Mayerhoeffer's Store, Va.

upon the inner chambers of our hearts, which necessity grows out of the very nature of things, our peculiar dispositions, our destiny and our duties and relations to one another and to our God. These considerations will receive further attention in the discussion of some of the subsequent points in this discourse.

2. Self-examination is necessary because it is so abundantly taught in the Word of God. The apostle's injunction to the church at Corinth by no means stands alone as Scriptural authority for the doctrine of self-examination.

Nor was the necessity of this spiritual intro-spection for the first time revealed to the writers of the New Testament, and by them made known to the world. Ever since God created and set a-beating the first human heart, there has existed the necessity of self-examination; and the duty is taught in the Old Testament as well as in the New.

Among the many wise things which the wise man so wisely said, is his exhortation of Prov. 4: 23: "Keep thy heart with all diligence; for out of it are the issues of life." This amounts to an exhortation to self-examination; for how can I keep my heart with all diligence without making it, its moral condition and peculiar tendencies the object of my diligent concern and watchfulness? And in view of the fact that out of it are the issues of my spiritual and eternal life, should I not pay the most diligent heed to the wise man's injunction? We dare not ignore it nor consider it lightly.

We also notice Psa. 119: 9, "Wherewithal shall a young man cleanse his way? By taking heed thereto according to thy word." Let the young man who has rushed wildly and thoughtlessly into sin, but who now grieves and sighs for a better life,—let him enter at once upon a course of diligent and rigid self-examination. Let him examine his ways,—what they have been and what they are; and if the examination be "according to thy word," the issue will be a glorious one, and all that he could desire. Woe to that man, be he young or old, rich or poor, high or low, who refuses to "take heed to his ways according to thy word!"

Without referring particularly to the many other Old Testament passages which bear more or less directly upon our subject, we now pass to a consideration of the New Testament teaching of self-examination.

The Master said in his Sermon on the Mount, "Judge not." That is, do not judge rashly and unjustly; especially do not judge or condemn others until you have first judged yourself. "And why beholdest thou the mote that is in thy brother's eye, but considerest not the beam that is in thine own eye?" Do not 'be examining your brother's heart to remove the comparatively small evils until you have examined your own heart, and at least removed the greater evils.

"Thou hypocrite, first cast out the beam out of thine own eye; and then shalt thou see clearly to cast out the mote out of thy brother's eye." As the brethren at Corinth were more concerned about the power of Christ in Paul than in themselves, so a great many men to-day are apparently more concerned about the condition of the hearts of others than of their own; and as Paul warned his brethren to examine themselves instead of him, so now Christ would have us know that our first and essential chief duty is to examine our own hearts, get the beams out of our own eyes, by the grace of God endeavor to do more toward clearing ourselves of sin; and then will he accept us as servants fit for higher duties and more glorious work.

Covington, Ohio.

COMMUNION.

BY H. C. EARLY.

In Two Chapters.—Number One.

THE Communion service, because of its sacred importance, John 6: 53, 54, should be engaged in understandingly and prayerfully. The time and manner of its institution by our Blessed Lord, the purpose attached to it, Luke 22: 19, the solemn language of Paul, 1 Cor. 11: 25–29, the warnings and barriers thrown around the Lord's table throughout the New Testament record,—all combine to show that it is a service requiring special condition of heart and life, and specific relation to Christ and his church. "For he that eateth and drinketh unworthily, eateth and drinketh damnation to himself, not discerning the Lord's body."

Some standard of fitness must be adopted and respected by the Lord's people. That all persons, irrespective of mental, moral and spiritual conditions, are entitled to the high and holy service of the Communion, none dare assert.

The *necessary qualifications* are embraced in the law of membership into the church and state of union, peace and love among her members. 1 Cor. 1: 10; Matt. 5: 23; 1 John 3: 14, 15, 16.

In the act of complying with the law of church membership the individual is admitted into the church,—the "one body by the one spirit," which implies, (1) unity of faith; (2) unity of doctrine; (3) unity of spirit, all of which go to make Communion possible. The Communion service is among the privileges of church life. It lies back of membership and is dependent upon it, and, therefore, any one, desiring the Communion, must expect to reach it in the *regular way*. Membership first; then the Communion.

The law of membership is a wall of protection to church privileges and fellowship. In this respect the church is like all other institutions. If we get the privilege and benefits of any institution, we first become identified with it. This is fundamental in all good government. To reverse this order would not only imperil government, but would, in fact, destroy the best government on earth. Why should not this be true in the church as well? The command to commune was given to Christians, — those who had secured membership in the church, not to those who had no membership,—as a commemorative service, not as a means of grace to sinners. Luke 22: 19, 20; 1 Cor. 11: 24, 25. After this manner the apostles labored. The Pentecostians were first taught, then baptized according to Christ's command, after which they engaged in the breaking of bread.

The law of church membership embraces teaching, faith, repentance, baptism, pardon of sin, and gift of the Holy Spirit. See Matt. 28: 19; Mark 16: 16; Luke 24: 47; Acts 2: 37, 38; 16: 30–33; 1 Cor. 12: 13; Heb. 11: 6. From these texts we deduce the following conclusions:

1. That teaching is necessary to faith.

2. That faith is necessary to repentance.

3. That repentance is necessary to baptism.

4. That baptism is necessary to pardon of sin.

5. That the pardon of sin is necessary to the gift of the Holy Spirit,—all of which are required by the law of church membership.

It is clear from the foregoing analysis that a person entitled to the privileges of the Communion, is one who has obtained membership in the church, having exercised true evangelical faith and repentance. He has been baptized by the "one baptism" into each name of the Holy Trinity (Matt. 28: 19); for the remission of sins (Acts 2: 38), and continues steadfast in the doctrine of the church and in peace with her members. Such individual membership makes the "one body" of the "one faith," "joined together in the same mind and in the same judgment," "speaking the same thing," having no divisions. 1 Cor. 1: 10.

Peace and love among the members, one with another, are absolutely essential in order to Communion. 1 Thess. 5: 13; Matt. 5: 24; 1 Cor. 5, 7, 8; 1 Pet. 1: 22; 1 John 4: 20. Brethren, united in faith and practice but not at peace and in love, one with another, dare not approach the Lord's table. Absence of peace and love makes absence of Communion. The highest service among men on earth requires the highest condition of heart. If peace and love be destroyed, reconciliation first, then the Communion, — union of service. Matt. 5: 24. If this be true of those of the same faith and practice, what may be said of those differing in faith and practice?

Now, for the sake of being better understood, we remark that the qualifications, preparatory to Communion are of two classes, individual and congregational. The individual is the act of the individual obtaining admission into the church through the law of church membership, and the congregational is the necessary state of love, peace and union throughout the membership of the church.

The sanctity of the Lord's table should be carefully guarded and preserved; for "we have an altar whereof they have no right to eat who serve the tabernacle." Heb. 13: 10. This throws positive restriction around the church altar or Lord's table. This closes the door against all who serve the flesh. God's ancient sanctuary and holy place were most rigidly guarded lest they be defiled; and if that which was but the shadow was so diligently kept from defilement, with what sacred care should we reverence and protect the church altar, consecrated by the blood of Jesus?

To show that this view of the teaching of the Scriptures is not only ours, we quote briefly from a view of the early Church Fathers and modern writers.

Justin Martyr, who wrote about fifty years after the death of St. John, says, "This food is called by us Eucharist, of which it is not lawful for any to partake but such as believe the things that are taught by us to be true, and have been baptized."

Jerome, who wrote about A. D. 400, says, "Catechumens cannot communicate at the Lord's table, being unbaptized." Austin, A. D. 500, Bede, A. D. 700, Theophylact, A. D. 1100, all say that no unbaptized person was admitted to the Communion.

Dr. Wall says, "Among all the absurdities that were ever held none ever maintained that any person should partake of the Communion before he was baptized." Dr. Adam Clarke says, "No person was permitted to come to the Eucharist till he had been baptized."

This was conceded and taught by both Baptists and Pedobaptists, at least until within the last century, and let it be borne in mind that a person not baptized, according to the Scriptures, is unbaptized.

Meyerhoeffer's Store, Va.

laid up in heaven, no sinner saved, upon E's plan, but hardness engendered, friends alienated, and the donor disgraced. Which will you imitate?

These Chips say, "Give by straight out endowment contract, and make sure work!" The following advantages are secured to the committee upon the endowment plan: (1) It is a permanent and regular income that can be depended upon; (2) it is easily collected; (3) it enables the committee to determine how much may be depended on from this source, and lay out work accordingly.

Not only should the Missionary and Book and Tract Work be largely endowed in this way, but also the Brethren's schools, the Old Folks and Orphans' Homes, as well as other institutions that are helping the Master's work forward.

McPherson, Kans.

IMPORTANT DISCOVERIES IN AFRICA.

THE Dark Continent is beginning to yield up its treasures and the remains of an unknown chapter in the world's history are coming to light. Mr. J. Theodore Bent, an English explorer, has recently returned from an expedition to Mashonaland or Makalangaland, a portion of Africa which fell to England in the partitioning out of the most promising portions of that continent among rival European powers, and he gives a most thrilling and interesting account of archaeological discoveries which he made in regions never before reached by Europeans. He found relics of a high civilization and some of the largest and most striking ruins in the world. A phallic temple at Zimbabwe consists of a large circular building on a gentle rise, with a net-work of inferior buildings, extending into the valley below, while on the summit of a hill, 400 feet above, is a labyrinthine fortress, consisting of a wall 16 feet thick and 30 feet in height, surmounted by monoliths, alternating with small, round towers. A second wall on the inside was separated from this by a narrow passage.

Mr. Brent found his principal treasures in a corner of the fortress, in what was evidently the temple of the stronghold, and which is now used by the petty chief on the hill as a cattle kraal. The temple was supported by an elaborate system of under-walls and was approached by a narrow passage and a stair-case of rare architecture. Its outer wall was decorated with birds, carved on the summits of soap-stone beams, five or six feet in height. Iron bells, of curious form, and which had evidently been used in religious worship, were found near the birds, while in the middle of the building stood an altar of small granite blocks, and near it were found quantities of soap-stone phalli.

There was found evidences of gold-smelting in that unwritten past and among those unknown people. A gold-smelting furnace, made of hard cement, was found underneath the temple, with crucibles of the same material and tools for crushing and burnishing. All gave evidence of the extent of the industry and of the gold craze of the past.

Many other interesting localities were visited and many long-hidden wonders of a strange and eventful past were brought to light. Some striking chapters of the world's history yet remain to be written. Who were the people who built these great monuments and temples?—*Christian Advocate.*

FOUR MILLION "CHRISTIAN" (?) MURDERERS.

THE Northern District of Illinois placed herself on the right and safe side of the record a few years ago when she decided that she would not permit any of her members to vote for license to sell intoxicants. If we vote for these licenses we certainly become a party to the awful crimes that are almost hourly committed in consequence of the sale and use of liquors. The following, which we clip from the *Voice*, tells a fearful story for our readers to consider.

"Times change, and we change with them. The pagans of old Rome used to pit man against man in the gladiatorial arena and bid them fight each other to the death, that the popular love for exciting sport might be gratified. For fifteen centuries Christians have been boasting that that sort of brutality was stopped by Christianity. It is about time that these boastings were laid on the table indefinitely.

"In the days of Luther a great revolt was instituted against the sale of indulgences, as carried on by Tetzel. For four centuries Protestants have been censuring the Roman Catholic Church for having sold indulgences to sin, for a price, and the Catholics have been protesting against the charges as false and unjust. It is about time that the dispute be laid on the table indefinitely.

"There never was, in the brutal, gladiatorial combats of Rome, anything to compare, in atrocity and cruelty, with the black record that lies to-day upon our four million 'Christian' voters of America; and the most sweeping charges brought against Tetzel and his times pale into insignificance beside the dark shame in which Catholics and Protestants are alike participating to-day. Where is the sense in Christians boasting about the cessation of the gladiatorial combats, when in their place we have 240,000 men commissioned to employ all the arts that money can command in pauperizing, crazing and poisoning their fellow men? Where is the sense in Protestants and Catholics disputing over the responsibility for a few indulgences six centuries ago when year after year they are jointly issuing for much smaller sums indulgences infinitely more villainous?

"When the gladiators fought, each man had something like an equal chance; to-day art is pitted against ignorance. Then it was sword against sword, trained skill against trained skill; now it is slow poison against unsuspecting and uninformed victims. Then it was a duel; now it is assassination. Then the public gazed upon slaves and barbarians fighting each other; to-day men are commissioned by Christian voters to weave nets about their own sons and daughters and drag them down to a living death. Then the responsibility rested upon an autocratic ruler and the pagan public merely cheered the contest; to-day people are, the rulers and four million church members are responsible for the infamy. Then the sport was continued to gratify the love for an exhibition of personal skill and courage; to-day our modern crime is perpetuated because 4,000,000 church members want a certain set of wily and scheming politicians to win. Then, at the most, a few hundreds perished in a year; now thousands perish every month. Then it was pagan darkness; now it is Christian enlightenment. Then the fatherhood of God and the brotherhood of man had not dawned upon the world; now the phrase is in nearly everybody's mouth.

"Four million 'Christian' murderers! Is the phrase the result of a heated imagination? Who, then, is responsible for these thousands that stagger into drunkards' graves each month? Are they responsible for their own deaths? In a measure, yes; but how many thousands of them went along the road to ruin, utterly ignorant of the physiological effects of liquor, believing to the last that beer is nourishing and whiskey is stimulating, and never knowing their danger until their system was diseased and minds enslaved past all hope? Who is responsible—the men who enticed them to drink and sold them the poison?" Those who helped him to the power have a fearful charge to answer for.

MISSIONARY WORK IN INDIA.

ONE of our exchanges says: "India is to-day the most hopeful mission field in the world, and is occupied by more missionary societies than any other section. Out of a total population of 288,159,672 the number of Christians is placed at 2,284,191. During the past decade, the rate of increase has been 22.6 per cent—more than double that of any other community. There are 37 organized missionary societies at work in India, with 1,727 missionaries and 2,961 native preachers. There are 1,605 churches, with 249,492 communicants; 294,167 pupils in the day-schools, and 124,608 in the Sabbath-schools. But these figures do not by any means include all the evangelistic agencies in the empire. The great British and Foreign Bible Society is at work in all parts of the country; a number of woman's boards are working independently; several independent missionary organizations are operating successfully, such as the Oxford Mission, conducted by the students of Oxford University, while evangelists like Dr. Pentecost are doing a great work among the Eurasians and other English-speaking people."

"MR. WILLIAM SAUSSER, a wealthy resident of Hannibal, Mo., who died recently, left his entire estate, valued at $150,000, to Westminster (Presbyterian) College at Fulton; except the homestead near Hannibal, and an annuity of $2,500 a year to his wife. This is a magnificent bequest and we congratulate our Presbyterian friends. It shows what others are doing for the cause of religion as they understand it."

"IT makes no kind of difference who said it, but some sensible man or woman wrote: 'Let us resolve first, to cultivate the grace of silence; second, to deem all fault-finding that does no good a sin, and to resolve, when we are ourselves happy, not to poison the atmosphere of our neighbors by calling upon them to remark every painful and disagreeable feature in their daily life; third, to practice the grace and virtue of praise.' Did we ever read anything more appropriate for these times."

The Gospel Messenger

In the recognized organ of the German Baptist or Brethren's church, and advocates the form of doctrine taught in the New Testament and pleads for a return to apostolic and primitive Christianity.

It recognizes the New Testament as the only infallible rule of faith and practice, and maintains that Faith toward God, Repentance from dead works, Regeneration of the heart and mind, baptism by Trine Immersion for remission of sins unto the reception of the Holy Ghost by the laying on of hands, are the means of adoption into the household of God,—the church militant.

It also maintains that Feet-washing, as taught in John 13, both by example and command of Jesus, should be observed in the church.

That the Lord's Supper, instituted by Christ and as universally observed by the apostles and the early Christians, is a full meal, and, in connection with the Communion, should be taken in the evening or after the close of the day.

That the Salutation of the Holy Kiss, or Kiss of Charity, is binding upon the followers of Christ.

That War and Retaliation are contrary to the spirit and self-denying principles of the religion of Jesus Christ.

That the principle of Plain Dressing and Non-conformity to the world, as taught in the New Testament, should be observed by the followers of Christ.

That the Scriptural duty of Anointing the Sick with Oil, in the Name of the Lord, James 5: 14, is binding upon all Christians.

It also advocates the church's duty to support Missionary and Tract Work, thus giving to the Lord for the spread of the Gospel and for the conversion of sinners.

In short, it is a vindicator of all that Christ and the apostles have enjoined upon us, and aims, amid the conflicting theories and discords of modern Christendom, to point out ground that all must concede to be infallibly safe.

☞ The above principles of our Fraternity are set forth on our "Brethren's Envelopes." Use them! Price, 15 cents per package; 40 cents per hundred.

laid up in heaven, no sinner saved, upon E's plan, but hardness engendered, friends alienated, and the donor disgraced. Which will you imitate?

These Chips say, "Give by straight out endowment contract, and make sure work!" The following advantages are secured to the committee upon the endowment plan: (1) It is a permanent and regular income that can be depended upon; (2) it is easily collected; (3) it enables the committee to determine how much may be depended on from this source, and lay out work accordingly.

Not only should the Missionary and Book and Tract Work be largely endowed in this way, but also the Brethren's schools, the Old Folks and Orphans' Homes, as well as other institutions that are helping the Master's work forward.

McPherson, Kans.

IMPORTANT DISCOVERIES IN AFRICA.

THE Dark Continent is beginning to yield up its treasures and the remains of an unknown chapter in the world's history are coming to light. Mr. J. Theodore Bent, an English explorer, has recently returned from an expedition to Mashonaland or Makalangaland, a portion of Africa which fell to England in the partitioning out of the most promising portions of that continent among rival European powers, and he gives a most thrilling and interesting account of archæological discoveries which he made in regions never before reached by Europeans. He found relics of a high civilization and some of the largest and most striking ruins in the world. A phallic temple at Zimbabwe consists of a large circular building on a gentle rise, with a net-work of inferior buildings, extending into the valley below, while on the summit of a hill, 400 feet above, is a labyrinthine fortress, consisting of a wall 16 feet thick and 30 feet in height, surmounted by monoliths, alternating with small, round towers. A second wall on the inside was separated from this by a narrow passage.

Mr. Brent found his principal treasures in a corner of the fortress, in what was evidently the temple of this stronghold, and which is now used by the petty chief on the hill as a cattle kraal. The temple was supported by an elaborate system of under-walls and was approached by a narrow passage and a stair-case of rare architecture. Its outer wall was decorated with birds, carved on the summits of soap-stone beams, five or six feet in height. Iron bells, of a curious form, and which had evidently been used in religious worship, were found near the birds, while in the middle of the building stood an altar of small granite blocks, and near it were found quantities of soap-stone phalli.

There were also found evidences of gold-smelting in that unwritten past and among those unknown people. A gold-smelting furnace, made of hard cement, was found underneath the temple, with crucibles of the same material and tools for crushing and burnishing. All gave evidence of the extent of the industry and of the gold craze of the past.

Many other interesting localities were visited and many long-hidden wonders of a strange and eventful past were brought to light. Some striking chapters of the world's history yet remain to be written. Who were the people who built these great monuments and temples?—*Christian Advocate.*

FOUR MILLION "CHRISTIAN" (?) MURDERERS.

THE Northern District of Illinois placed herself on the right and safe side of the record a few years ago when she decided that she would not permit any of her members to vote for license to sell intoxicants. If we vote for these licenses we certainly become a party to the awful crimes that are almost hourly committed in consequence of the sale and use of liquors. The following, which we clip from the *Voice*, tells a fearful story for our readers to consider.

"Times change, and we change with them. The pagans of old Rome used to pit man against man in the gladiatorial arena and bid them fight each other to the death, that the popular love for exciting sport might be gratified. For fifteen centuries Christians have been boasting that that sort of brutality was stopped by Christianity. It is about time that these boastings were laid on the table indefinitely.

"In the days of Luther a great revolt was instituted against the sale of indulgences, as carried on by Tetzel. For four centuries Protestants have been censuring the Roman Catholic Church for having sold indulgences to sin, for a price, and the Catholics have been protesting against the charges as false and unjust. It is about time that the dispute be laid on the table indefinitely.

"There never was, in the brutal, gladiatorial combats of Rome, anything to compare, in atrocity and cruelty, with the black record that lies to-day upon our four million 'Christian' voters of America; and the most sweeping charges brought against Tetzel and his times pale into insignificance beside the dark shame in which Catholics and Protestants are alike participating to-day. Where is the sense in Christians boasting about the cessation of the gladiatorial combats, when in their place we have 240,000 men commissioned to employ all the arts that money can command in pauperizing, crazing and poisoning their fellow men? Where is the sense in Protestants and Catholics disputing over the responsibility for a few indulgences six centuries ago when year after year they are jointly issuing for much smaller sums indulgences infinitely more villainous?

"When the gladiators fought, each man had something like an equal chance; to-day art is pitted against ignorance. Then it was sword against sword, trained skill against trained skill; now it is slow poison against unsuspecting and uninformed victims. Then it was a duel; now it is assassination. Then the public gazed upon slaves and barbarians fighting each other; to-day men are commissioned by Christian voters to weave nets about their own sons and daughters and drag them down to a living death. Then the responsibility rested upon an autocratic ruler and the pagan public merely cheered the contest; to-day people are the rulers and four million church members are responsible for the infamy. Then the sport was continued to gratify the love for an exhibition of personal skill and courage; to-day our modern crime is perpetuated because 4,000,000 church members want a certain set of wily-and scheming politicians to win. Then, at the most, a few hundreds perished in a year; now thousands perish every month. Then it was pagan darkness; now it is Christian enlightenment. Then the fatherhood of God and the brotherhood of man had not dawned upon the world; now the phrase is in nearly everybody's mouth.

"'Four million 'Christian' murderers! Is the phrase the result of a heated imagination? Who, then, is responsible for these thousands that stagger into drunkards' graves each month? Are they responsible for their own deaths? In a measure, yes; but how many thousands of them went along the road to ruin, utterly ignorant of the physiological effects of liquor, believing to the last that beer is nourishing and whiskey is stimulating, and never knowing their danger until their system was diseased and minds enslaved past all hope? Who is responsible—the men who enticed them to drink and sold them the poison?" Those who helped him to the power have a fearful charge to answer for.

MISSIONARY WORK IN INDIA.

ONE of our exchanges says: "India is to-day the most hopeful mission field in the world, and is occupied by more missionary societies than any other section. Out of a total population of 288,-159,672 the number of Christians is placed at 2,284,191. During the past decade, the rate of increase has been 22.6 per cent—more than double that of any other community. There are 37 organized missionary societies at work in India, with 1,227 missionaries and 2,961 native preachers. There are 1,605 churches, with 249,492 communicants; 294,167 pupils in the day-schools, and 124,603 in the Sabbath-schools. But these figures do not by any means include all the evangelistic agencies in the empire. The great British and Foreign Bible Society is at work in all parts of the country; a number of women's boards are working independently; several independent missionary organizations are operating successfully, such as the Oxford Mission, conducted by the students of Oxford University, while evangelists like Dr. Pentecost are doing a great work among the Eurasians and other English-speaking people."

"MR. WILLIAM SAUSSER, a wealthy resident of Hannibal, Mo., who died recently, left his entire estate, valued at $150,000, to Westminster (Presbyterian) College at Fulton; except the homestead near Hannibal, and an annuity of $2,500 a year to his wife. This is a magnificent bequest and we congratulate our Presbyterian friends. It shows what others are doing for the cause of religion as they understand it."

"IT makes no kind of difference who said it, but some sensible man or woman wrote: 'Let us resolve first, to cultivate the grace of silence; second, to deem, all fault-finding that does no good a sin, and to resolve, when we are ourselves happy, not to poison the atmosphere of our neighbors by calling upon them to remark every painful and disagreeable feature in their daily life; third, to practice the grace and virtue of praise.' Did we ever read anything more appropriate for these times."

The Gospel Messenger

In the recognized organ of the German Baptist or Brethren's church, and advocates the form of doctrine taught in the New Testament and pleads for a return to apostolic and primitive Christianity.

It recognizes the New Testament as the only infallible rule of faith and practice, and maintains that Faith toward God, Repentance from dead works, Regeneration of the heart and mind, baptism by Trine Immersion for remission of sins unto the reception of the Holy Ghost by the laying on of hands, are the means of adoption into the household of God,—the church militant.

It also maintains that Feet-washing, as taught in John 13, both by example and command of Jesus, should be observed in the church.

That the Lord's Supper, instituted by Christ and as universally observed by the apostles and the early Christians, is a full meal, and, in connection with the Communion, should be taken in the evening or after the close of the day.

That the Salutation of the Holy Kiss, or Kiss of Charity, is binding upon the followers of Christ.

That War and Retaliation are contrary to the spirit and self-denying principles of the religion of Jesus Christ.

That the principle of Plain Dressing and of Non-conformity to the world, as taught in the New Testament, should be observed by the followers of Christ.

That the Scriptural duty of Anointing the Sick with Oil, in the Name of the Lord, James 5: 14, is binding upon all Christians.

It also advocates the church's duty to support Missionary and Tract Work, thus giving to the Lord for the spread of the Gospel and for the conversion of sinners.

In short, it is a vindicator of all that Christ and the apostles have enjoined upon us, and aims, amid the conflicting theories and discords of modern Christendom, to point out ground that all must concede to be infallibly safe.

☞ The above principles of our Fraternity are set forth on our "Brethren's Envelopes." Use them! Price, 15 cents per package; 40 cents per hundred.

of his salvation. He fell with his armor on, battling for the cause he loved so well.

On the morning of his death, the sun rose bright and clear. The clouds, which had hung heavily overhead for several days, had disappeared, and it was a bright, beautiful morning. In the sick-chamber was our dear brother, the sands of his life almost run. His wan, sunken features told of the physical suffering he had endured. Around the bedside stood the sorrow-stricken wife and a number of brethren and sisters, who felt that a wise counselor, a father in Israel, a faithful servant of God, a loving brother was going away from them. A curtain at a window was drawn aside and the bright sunlight fell across his couch, but the light was too strong for his weakened eyes. The curtain was again replaced, and then the question was asked, "Is it not too dark?" and the sufferer said, "It is light enough for me." Yes. it was light enough for him, for in his soul was shining the light of the brightest hope that God gives his children in this world,— a light that gilds even the dark valley and shadow of death, and makes it but a pathway to glory. It was the hope of eternal life that cheered our brother, the hope of a mansion above, "A building of God, an house not made with hands, eternal in the heavens."

Soon after this he requested that we have a season of worship and devotion around his bedside. He indicated the position to be occupied by those present, and being asked if he had a Scripture reading to suggest, after a moment's thought he gave these words: "For we know that if our earthly house of this tabernacle were dissolved, we have a building of God, an house not made with hands, eternal in the heavens." After prayer, to which he most heartily responded, he left messages for absent loved ones, to his sons and daughter, and especially to his little boys who were so soon to be left fatherless. And then he composed himself and waited patiently for the end to come. He was ready and anxious to go home. As his feet were slipping over the brink, we heard the thrice-repeated prayer: "Oh that the Lord would come and take me," and with these words upon his lips, the last he was ever to utter in this world, the Lord took him home. "And he was not, for God took him." Such was the death of our beloved brother, R. H. Miller. A death like this must have inspired the prophet when he gave utterance to these words: "Let me die the death of the righteous, and let my last end be like his."

After the memorial services, which were held in the Chapel at this place, an account of which has already been given in the MESSENGER, we started on our sad journey to North Manchester, Ind., the earthly home of our departed brother, and where he requested that his body might be placed in the tomb. The journey was a sad one. Only a short time before, our brother had come to us, to labor in the ministry of the Word. Sickness had come to him, and then the devoted wife hastened to his bedside to care for him, and now we were going to his home with his lifeless body. While we were cheered by his glorious and triumphant death, yet we felt the personal loss which we all had sustained, and it was with sad hearts that we made the journey.

We reached North Manchester in the evening, in the midst of a heavy storm of wind and snow. A number of brethren and sisters were at the depot, and in every face was to be seen the evidence of the love all bore for Bro. Miller. Each one felt that in his death they had suffered a personal loss, and that his place would not be easily filled. Carriages were in waiting, and we were taken to the now desolate home of sister Miller, about two miles from North Manchester. The scene here was one to melt the hardest heart. The meeting between sister Miller and her now fatherless boys, we will not attempt to describe. It was a scene over which angels might well weep.

The next day at 11 A. M., the funeral was appointed, at the Brethren's new meeting-house, which had only recently been completed, and in the construction of which Bro. Miller had taken a great interest. The house is a very large one, yet, notwithstanding the fact that the roads were very bad, and that a heavy snow-storm prevailed the entire day, the large meeting-house was filled, thus showing that our brother had the respect of the community. Bro. J. G. Royer preached the funeral sermon. His text was taken from the chapter selected by our dear brother to be read the morning of his death, 2 Cor. 5: 10, "For we must all appear before the judgment seat of Christ; that every one may receive the things done in his body, according to that he hath done, whether it be good or bad." The sermon was a practical lesson to the living, and was made especially impressive on account of the occasion that called it forth. At the close the dying words of Bro. Miller to his children were repeated, and the scene was painfully impressive. A number of ministers were present from other congregations, and brethren William R. Deeter, Amasa Puterbaugh and the writer assisted Bro. Royer in the services.

We laid his body to rest in the silent grave, surrounded by a multitude of sorrowing friends, whose tears manifested the depth of their love and sorrow. Around that open grave the snow was eddying and drifting, driven by the fierce storm. As we stood there we thought of the quiet, peaceful rest our brother was then enjoying, in such strong contrast with the tempest that was raging all about us. Undisturbed by the driving storm he ceased his last sleep. The storms are past, the pains of death no more feared, life's labor and sorrow have ceased and the warfare is ended. His last battle has been fought. With his armor on, with his face to the foe, faithful unto death, he fell in the line of duty, and his soul has found rest and peace with God.

"Servant of God, well done!
Rest from thy lov'd employ;
The battle fought, the victory won,
Enter thy Master's joy."

Some one having been asked as to a monument to mark his last resting place, said, "Let me live in the hearts of my people. I ask for no other monument." We believe that our departed brother will live in the hearts of his people. The evidences, manifested at his funeral, were of such a character as to show that where he was best known, he was most loved. Strong men wept as they took a last look at his familiar face, and the members of the church at North Manchester and surrounding congregations showed that they felt they had lost a faithful shepherd and a kind, loving father.

But Bro. Miller's death is not simply a local loss. His influence and labor were not circumscribed by the lines of a local congregation, or by the bounds of a State District. His influence was felt over our entire Brotherhood, and his place in our Annual Conferences, as a wise counselor and a faithful adherent to the principles of the church, will not soon be filled. He was a man who had the courage of his convictions and manfully maintained them. He loved the church of his choice, and her principles were dear to his heart. He was a true champion and defender of the faith. He gave the best years of his life to her service, and died in the full vigor of ripening age. The last sermon he preached was marked by all the force and power which he knew so well how to use. He spoke over an hour and held the interest of his large audience to the very close. Some of us who had heard him often, felt that it was one of his best efforts. His life was a grand success, not as the world counts success, for he had but little of this world's goods, but in abundant and far-reaching labor for the church of God.

For some years we have been intimately associated with him in our work. As we came to know him well, our love for him, as a man and a brother, and our respect for his abilities and faithfulness to the church increased. He was a man you could depend upon, and you could always tell where to find him. The church was always first with him and to her interests he was true, first, last, and all the time. He was a warm-hearted friend, and to those who knew him well, there was a depth of love and earnestness, unknown to the casual observer. He had a kind heart, and to us he often spoke kindly of those who had gone away from the church, and no one regretted more than he, the causes which led to the final rupture. When it came he stood unflinchingly by the church, and defended her with all the rare ability with which God had endowed him. But he has gone. The church has lost one of her pillars, and those who know him best, a warm-hearted, loving brother and friend. May not his life of faithfulness be helpful to us? May it not prove an incentive to us all to be faithful unto death?

The story of his life of labor and love is written in the hearts of the people for whom he labored, but it should be written on paper and published for the encouragement of others, and we hope some one will undertake this labor of love. We give here, in closing, a few items of interest that came to us from Bro. William Harshbarger, of Ladoga, Ind.:

Bro. R. H. Miller was born in Kentucky, March 7, 1825, and reached the age of sixty-six years, nine months and one day. In 1867 he united with the church at Ladoga, Ind., and August 16, 1858, he was called to the ministry in the same church. The certificate of his election to the ministry shows that he received the entire vote of the church, thus evidencing that he had the confidence of his brethren and sisters. The certificate is signed by brethren Hiel Hamilton, Samuel Murray, Matthias Frantz, Daniel W. Himes and Wesley Burket. After a few years he was advanced to the eldership and had charge of the church at Ladoga until 1880, when he moved to Ashland, Ohio, where he spent two years, and then went to North Manchester, where he lived at the time of his death, and where his widow, with her four little fatherless boys, will continue to make her home. Brethren and sisters, let us not forget that humble home, where our dear sister Miller, bereft of the help and counsel of a beloved husband, is struggling alone to bring up her boys in the nurture and admonition of the Lord.

D. L. M.

of his salvation. He fell with his armor on, battling for the cause he loved so well.

On the morning of his death, the sun rose bright and clear. The clouds, which had hung heavily overhead for several days, had disappeared, and it was a bright, beautiful morning. In the sick-chamber lay our dear brother, the sands of his life almost run. His wan, sunken features told of the physical suffering he had endured. Around the bedside stood the sorrow-stricken wife and a number of brethren and sisters, who felt that a wise counselor, a father in Israel, a faithful servant of God, a loving brother was going away from them. A curtain at a window was drawn aside and the bright sunlight fell across his couch, but the light was too strong for his weakened eyes. The curtain was again replaced, and then the question was asked, "Is it not too dark?" and the sufferer said, "It is light enough for me." Yes, it was light enough for him, for in his soul was shining the light of the brightest hope that God gives his children in this world,—a light that gilds even the dark valley and shadow of death, and makes it but a pathway to glory. It was the hope of eternal life that cheered our brother, the hope of a mansion above, "A building of God, an house not made with hands, eternal in the heavens."

Soon after this he requested that we have a season of worship and devotion around his bedside. He indicated the position to be occupied by those present, and being asked if he had a Scripture reading to suggest, after a moment's thought he gave these words: "For we know that if our earthly house of this tabernacle were dissolved, we have a building of God, an house not made with hands, eternal in the heavens." After prayer, to which he most heartily responded, he left messages for absent loved ones, to his sons and daughter, and especially to his little boys who were so soon to be left fatherless. And then he composed himself and waited patiently for the end to come. He was ready and anxious to go home. As his feet were slipping over the brink, we heard the thrice-repeated prayer: "Oh that the Lord would come and take me," and with these words upon his lips, the last he was ever to utter in this world, the Lord took him home. "And he was not, for God took him." Such was the death of our beloved brother, R. H. Miller. A death like this must have inspired the prophet when he gave utterance to these words: "Let me die the death of the righteous, and let my last end be like his."

After the memorial services, which were held in the Chapel at this place, an account of which has already been given in the MESSENGER, we started on our sad journey to North Manchester, Ind., the earthly home of our departed brother, and where he requested that his body might be placed in the tomb. The journey was a sad one. Only a short time before, our brother had come to us, to labor in the ministry of the Word. Sickness had come to him, and then his devoted wife hastened to his bedside to care for him, and now we were going to his home with his lifeless body. While we were cheered by his glorious and triumphant death, yet we felt the personal loss which we all had sustained, and it was with sad hearts that we made the journey.

We reached North Manchester in the evening, in the midst of a heavy storm of wind and snow. A number of brethren and sisters were at the depot, and in every face was to be seen the evidence of the love all bore for Bro. Miller. Each one felt that in his death they had suffered a personal loss, and that his place would not be easily filled. Carriages were in waiting, and we were taken to the now desolate home of sister Miller, about two miles from North Manchester. The scene here was one to melt the hardest heart. The meeting between sister Miller and her now fatherless boys, we will not attempt to describe. It was a scene over which angels might well weep.

The next day at 11 A. M., the funeral was appointed, at the Brethren's new meeting-house, which had only recently been completed, and in the construction of which Bro. Miller had taken a great interest. The house is a very large one, yet, notwithstanding the fact that the roads were very bad, and that a heavy snow-storm prevailed the entire day, the large meeting-house was filled, thus showing that our brother had the respect of the community. Bro. J. G. Royer preached the funeral sermon. His text was taken from the chapter selected by our dear brother to be read the morning of his death, 2 Cor. 5: 10, "For we must all appear before the judgment seat of Christ; that every one may receive the things done in his body, according to that he hath done, whether it be good or bad." The sermon was a practical lesson to the living, and was made especially impressive on account of the occasion that called it forth. At the close the dying words of Bro. Miller to his children were repeated, and the scene was painfully impressive. A number of ministers were present from other congregations, and brethren William B. Deeter, Amasa Puterbaugh and the writer assisted Bro. Royer in the services.

We laid his body to rest in the silent grave, surrounded by a multitude of sorrowing friends, whose tears manifested the depth of their love and sorrow. Around that open grave the snow was eddying and drifting, driven by the fierce storm. As we stood there we thought of the quiet, peaceful rest our brother was then enjoying, in such strong contrast with the tempest that was raging all about us. Undisturbed by the driving storm he sleeps his last sleep. The storms are past, the pains of death no more feared, life's labor and sorrow have ceased and the warfare is ended. His last battle has been fought. With his armor on, with his face to the foe, faithful unto death, he fell in the line of duty, and his soul has found rest and peace with God.

"Servant of God, well done!
Rest from thy lov'd employ;
The battle fought, the victory won,
Enter thy Master's joy."

Some one having been asked as to a monument to mark his last resting place, said, "Let me live in the hearts of my people. I ask for no other monument." We believe that our departed brother will live in the hearts of his people. The evidences, manifested at his funeral, were of such a character as to show that where he was best known, he was most loved. Strong men wept as they took a last look at his familiar face, and the members of the church at North Manchester and surrounding congregations showed that they felt they had lost a faithful shepherd and a kind, loving father.

But Bro. Miller's death is not simply a local loss. His influence and labor were not circumscribed by the lines of a local congregation, or by the bounds of a State District. His influence was felt over our entire Brotherhood, and his place in our Annual Conferences, as a wise counselor and a faithful adherent to the principles of the church, will not soon be filled. He was a man who had the courage of his convictions and manfully maintained them. He loved the church of his choice, and her principles were dear to his heart. He was a true champion and defender of the faith. He gave the best years of his life to her service, and died in the full vigor of ripening age. The last sermon he preached was marked by all the force and power which he knew so well how to use. He spoke over an hour and held the interest of his large audience to the very close. Some of us who had heard him often, felt that it was one of his best efforts. His life was a grand success, not as the world counts success, for he had but little of this world's goods, but in abundant and far-reaching labor for the church of God.

For some years we have been intimately associated with him in our work. As we came to know him well, our love for him, as a man and a brother, and our respect for his abilities and faithfulness to the church increased. He was a man you could depend upon, and you could always tell where to find him. The church was always first with him and to her interests he was true, first, last, and all the time. He was a warm-hearted friend, and to those who knew him well, there was a depth of love and earnestness, unknown to the casual observer. He had a kind heart, and to ne he often spoke kindly of those who had gone away from the church, and no one regretted more than he, the causes which led to the final rupture. When it came he stood unflinchingly by the church, and defended her with all the rare ability with which God had endowed him. But he has gone. The church has lost one of her pillars, and those who know him best, a warm-hearted, loving brother and friend. May not his life of faithfulness be helpful to us? May it not prove an incentive to us all to be faithful unto death?

The story of his life of labor and love is written in the hearts of the people for whom he labored, but it should be written on paper and published for the encouragement of others, and we hope some one will undertake this labor of love. We give here, in closing, a few items of interest that came to us from Bro. William Harshbarger, of Ladoga, Ind.:

Bro. B. H. Miller was born in Kentucky, March 7, 1825, and reached the age of sixty-six years, nine months and one day. In 1857 he united with the church at Ladoga, Ind., and August 16, 1858, he was called to the ministry in the same church. The certificate of his election to the ministry shows that he received the entire vote of the church, thus evidencing that he had the confidence of his brethren and sisters. The certificate is signed by brethren Hiel Hamilton, Samuel Murray, Matthias Frantz, Daniel W. Himes and Wesley Burket. After a few years he was advanced to the eldership and had charge of the church at Ladoga until 1880, when he moved to Ashland, Ohio, where he spent two years, and then went to North Manchester, where he lived at the time of his death, and where his widow, with her four little fatherless boys, will continue to make her home. Brethren and sisters, let us not forget that humble home, where our dear sister Miller, bereft of the help and counsel of a beloved husband, is struggling alone to bring up her boys in the nurture and admonition of the Lord.

D. L. M.

very interesting to see and hear Bro. Abraham concerning his vast collection of books, ancient manuscripts and rare documents. There are two marvelous features we name: (1) How he could gather such a collection of literature with his disadvantages; (2) how he has acquired the ability to so readily communicate their vast information. I was sorry to find his sight and hearing seriously impaired.

Years ago the Brethren here and at Hatfield had Sunday-schools, but of late have none. A large majority are in favor of Sunday-schools and even attend elsewhere. I urged the necessity of a school in each church under the Brethren's care. Future engagements compelled me to close March 3 with encouraging prospects for additions.

March 4 my line of work took me to the church at Green Tree. Bro. Jacob Gotwalls has been in charge here for years, but at present the work largely falls on Bro. J. T. Meyers, whose labors seem to be appreciated. Bro. John Umstead was one of the early standard-bearers at this place, and the meek and humble principles of the Gospel flourished at his hand.

March 7 we returned to the Hatfield church. A meeting was arranged for in a large hall in Lonsdale, where Bro. Cassel lives. The Brethren have regular preaching in the town. We found a large and very interesting congregation. We regretted that our time was so short. In the congregation seemed to be many anxious seekers. For some weeks an Advent evangelist, Eld. J. S. Shrook, had been holding meetings at Lexington, near Lonsdale, in defense of their doctrine, especially on the Sabbath question. At length a package of our pamphlets, "Sabbath and Lord's Day," published by the Tract Work, was scattered in the neighborhood. To this pamphlet the elder replied one night, making some unwarranted assertions, and challenging the author of the pamphlet. The community was now in a good deal of confusion. The Brethren came to me and related the situation, inviting me to meet Eld. Shrock on the issue (the Sabbath). This I immediately consented to do, and met the elder on Thursday, March 10, at 3 P. M. To more fully accommodate us, they dismissed the school, as the hall we occupied was above the school-room. Eld. Shrock followed me with a reply. I took up the subject on the next evening, then told the congregation, after a brief outline, that we would leave the subject with them, as our engagements compelled us to leave. A number expressed themselves satisfied with our exposition of the subject.

On the evening of March 12 I met the congregation in Lancaster City. The church here is without a resident minister. Though they have had a house for twenty-eight years, they have a membership of only about fifty. Until recently they have had regular services only every six weeks. The cause can never prosper with such sparing efforts. They have recently gone into a separate organization. It is hoped that prosperity will dawn on the cause in Lancaster. They now have preaching every two weeks. We enjoyed our short visit with the dear members in Lancaster. Their future looked encouraging, and a number are near the kingdom.

My next stop was at Floria and Elizabethtown, in the limits of Bro. S. R. Zug's congregation. There seems to be much harmony here in church work. The congregations are large at this place. They have Sunday-school, but it is not so well supported as desirable. The necessity of a Sunday-school and children's meetings, as a means to mould the rising generation, is too apparent to meet with opposition. I reached home March 23 and found all well. Thank the Lord for his preserving care!

I. J. ROSENBERGER.

From Warrior's Mark, Pa.

THIS church has closed a very interesting and, we think, profitable series of meetings, which was begun Feb. 22, at which time Bro. Michael Claar was to be with us, but did not get here until March 8. As the brethren and sisters were not in favor of closing the meeting, when once started, on account of Bro. Claar not getting here, it was carried on by Bro. S. S. Gray, our home minister.

Upon the arrival of Bro. Claar, he preached every evening; also on Friday morning, March 11, when two came out and were buried by baptism, to walk in newness of life. On Friday evening another dear soul made application, and was received on Sunday. A sister who had gone out into the world was made willing to come back and was gladly received.

On Tuesday, March 15, two more were received by baptism, the one being but young in years,—not over eleven years of age. May they prove to be lights unto the church, and unto the world also. The meetings were continued until Sunday evening, when Bro. Claar preached his last sermon for the time being. Bro. Claar is an efficient laborer, and gave us some good instructions. Our meetings closed with five added to the church by baptism and one reclaimed.

B. F. NEARHOOF.

March 21.

From the Union Church, Marshall Co., Ind.

IT has been long since I last reported to the MESSENGER, and in the meantime we have experienced many sad changes. We also had great joy when six precious souls were born into the church of God during our meetings in January, conducted by Bro. Daniel Snell, of Sidney, Ind.

We had a very pleasant council-meeting March 12. The business passed off satisfactorily to all. Eld. Wm. G. Cook, of Bijou Hills, S. D., was with us. Bro. J. F. Appleman will represent our church at Annual Meeting. March 27, at 10: 30, we met to re-organize our Sunday-school, with Bro. Geo. Long as Superintendent, and a good corps of officers and teachers.

How blessed it would be, had we many more good Sunday-school workers in our Brotherhood. We feel that it is the strength of the church. Our social meetings on Sunday evenings are of great interest to young and old. We get many good thoughts from these meetings, and think that every church should have them. Bro. Jacob Fisher, of Mexico, Ind., has been holding some meetings in the south part of our District recently, resulting in two accessions to the church, and a general interest being aroused among the brethren and sisters. May God bless the good work every-where is our prayer! LAURA APPELMAN.

Plymouth, Ind., March 28.

From Shideler, Ind.

WE closed our meeting at Middletown, Ind., on the evening of March 27. The inclement weather militated somewhat against the success of the meetings. A very good interest was taken in the meetings, however, and we had good attendance and attention.

Two made the good confession and were baptized by Bro. D. F. Hoover. Others expressed themselves as being almost ready. We feel glad, however, that the door of the church is open, and that at any time, "whosoever *will* may come."

The quarterly church council took place while we were with the Brethren. Everything passed off pleasantly. This is as it should be. The council was presided over by Eld. D. F. Hoover, who has charge of the church. Eld. Abraham Bowman was also present.

The "Brethren's Home" is located in this church. Brother and sister McCarty preside over the "Home." They are certainly the right persons in the right place. We will be sorry to see them leave. GEO. L. STUDEBAKER.

To the Young Disciples in Mt. Morris College.

NUMBER ONE.

THE fact that Jesus "on the Sabbath day entered into the synagogue and taught" (Mark 1: 21), plainly shows that corruption in the church is not a sufficient reason for refusing to work in it. On the contrary, it is a very strong reason why we should show the kind of life and teaching that should prevail in the church, and put forth our best efforts to leaven it with the good old Gospel of Christ. Jesus used the best means at hand, even though they were sometimes misused by others. We should do likewise.

It is true he "taught as one that had authority," and not as an expounder of other men's opinions. His teaching carried with it the authority of the source of truth. He spoke with the authority of one who *knows*. He knew the way to heaven, for he had been there. He spoke, therefore, with the authority of conscious experience. It was this conscious experience, manifested in his conduct, his character, his holy life and his divine deeds, that gave him such great personal power in his teaching.

My beloved, you will speak "with authority," just in so far as the truth is *a part of your own being*. You make it a part of your being, not by merely reading the Word. There must be a spiritual assimilation of it. It is not the quantity of food eaten, but the part assimilated that builds up physically. The same is true spiritually. And it is this spiritual assimilation that makes available the personal power of the Holy Ghost,—a power more important to you, as disciples of Jesus, than all the book learning any college can afford.

Education, rightly applied, is a most desirable, because a very powerful agency in Christian work; but it can never answer as a substitute for the Holy Ghost. It is this power, more than any other one thing, that the church to-day needs. We need money, and men,—educated, trained men, to push forward the work of spreading the Gospel; but the greatest of all our needs,—a need of the laity, the preachers, and the elders, is the personal power of the Holy Spirit to discern the relative position of the world and the church. The world every-where makes demands of the church. She asks the church to conform to her aims, her precepts and her practices. She cries, "Compromise, *compromise!*" The Master, with outstretched arms, cries, "Separation, *separation!*"

The Lord help you, dear young brethren and sisters, to put yourselves into such an attitude as will insure you a double portion of his Spirit, is the prayer of your fellow-disciple.

I have enjoyed very pleasant visits with the Brethren of Ashland and Loudonville, Ohio. I have met a number of old students, and many friends of the school. Many are the prayers which ascend in your behalf from the altars of families represented in the school.

J. G. ROYER.

Loudonville, Ohio.

From Mansfield, Ill.

THE members of the Blue Ridge church held their quarterly council to-day, April 2. Considerable business came before the meeting and all was disposed of in a Christian-like spirit. Five members were received by letter. Eld. John Barnhart was elected to represent this church at An-

very interesting to see and hear Bro. Abraham concerning his vast collection of books, ancient manuscripts and rare documents. · There are two marvelous features we name: (1) How he could gather such a collection of literature with his disadvantages; (2) how he has acquired the ability to so readily communicate their vast information. I was sorry to find his sight and hearing seriously impaired.

Years ago the Brethren here and at Hatfield had Sunday-schools, but of late have none. A large majority are in favor of Sunday-schools and even attend elsewhere. I urged the necessity of a school in each church under the Brethren's care. Future engagements compelled me to close March 3 with encouraging prospects for additions.

March 4 my line of work took me to the church at Green Tree. Bro. Jacob Gotwalls has been in charge here for years, but at present the work largely falls on Bro. J. T. Meyers, whose labors seem to be appreciated. Bro. John Umstead was one of the early standard-bearers at this place, and the meek and humble principles of the Gospel flourished at his hand.

March 7 we returned to the Hatfield church. A meeting was arranged for in a large hall in Lonsdale, where Bro. Cassel lives. The Brethren have regular preaching in the town. We found a large and very interesting congregation. We regretted that our time was so short. In the congregation seemed to be many anxious seekers. For some weeks an Advent evangelist, Eld. J. S. Shrock, had been holding meetings at Lexington, near Lonsdale, in defense of their doctrine, especially on the Sabbath question. At length a package of our pamphlets, "Sabbath and Lord's Day," published by the Tract Work, was scattered in the neighborhood. To this pamphlet the elder replied one night, making some unwarranted assertions, and challenging the author of the pamphlet. The community was now in a good deal of confusion. The Brethren came to me and related the situation, inviting me to meet Eld. Shrock on the issue (the Sabbath). This I immediately consented to do, and met the elder on Thursday, March 10, at 3 P. M. To more fully accommodate us, they dismissed the school, as the hall we occupied was above the school-room. Eld. Shrock followed me with a reply. I took up the subject on the next evening, then told the congregation, after a brief outline, that we would leave the subject with them, as our engagements compelled us to leave. A number expressed themselves satisfied with our exposition of the subject.

On the evening of March 12 I met the congregation in Lancaster City. The church here is without a resident minister. Though they have had a house for twenty-eight years, they have a membership of only about fifty. Until recently they have had regular services only every six weeks. The cause can never prosper with such sparing efforts. They have recently gone into a separate organization. It is hoped that prosperity will dawn on the cause in Lancaster. They now have preaching every two weeks. We enjoyed our short visit with the dear members in Lancaster. Their future looked encouraging, and a number are near the kingdom.

My next stop was at Florin and Elizabethtown, in the limits of Bro. S. R. Zug's congregation. There seems to be much harmony here in church work. The congregations are large at this place. They have Sunday-school, but it is not so well supported as desirable. The necessity of a Sunday-school and children's meetings, as a means to mould the rising generation, is too apparent to meet with opposition. I reached home March 23 and found all well. Thank the Lord for his preserving care!　　　I. J. ROSENBERGER.

From Warrior's Mark, Pa.

THIS church has closed a very interesting and, we think, profitable series of meetings, which was begun Feb. 22, at which time Bro. Michael Claar was to be with us, but did not get here until March 8. As the brethren and sisters were not in favor of closing the meeting, when once started, on account of Bro. Claar not getting here, it was carried on by Bro. S. S. Gray, our home minister.

Upon the arrival of Bro. Claar, he preached every evening; also on Friday morning, March 11, when two came out and were buried by baptism, to walk in newness of life. On Friday evening another dear soul made application, and was received on Sunday. A sister who had gone out into the world was made willing to come back and was gladly received.

On Tuesday, March 15, two more were received by baptism, the one being but young in years,—not over eleven years of age. May they prove to be lights unto the church, and unto the world also. The meetings were continued until Sunday evening, when Bro. Claar preached his last sermon for the time being. Bro. Claar is an efficient laborer, and gave us some good instructions. Our meetings closed with five added to the church by baptism and one reclaimed.

　　　B. F. NEARHOOF.
March 21.

From the Union Church, Marshall Co., Ind.

IT has been long since I last reported to the MESSENGER, and in the meantime we have experienced many and changes. We also had great joy when six precious souls were born into the church of God during our meetings in January, conducted by Bro. Daniel Snell, of Sidney, Ind.

We had a very pleasant council-meeting March 12. The business passed off satisfactorily to all. Eld. Wm. G. Cook, of Bijou Hills, S. D., was with us. Bro. J. F. Appleman will represent our church at Annual Meeting. March 27, at 10: 30, we met to re-organize our Sunday-school, with Bro. Geo. Long as Superintendent, and a good corps of officers and teachers.

How blessed it would be, had we many more good Sunday-school workers in our Brotherhood. We feel that it is the strength of the church. Our social meetings on Sunday evenings are of great interest to young and old. We get many good thoughts from these meetings, and think that every church should have them. Bro. Jacob Fisher, of Mexico, Ind., has been holding some meetings in the south part of our District recently, resulting in two accessions to the church, and a general interest being aroused among the brethren and sisters. May God bless the good work every where is our prayer!　　　LAURA APPELMAN.
Plymouth, Ind., March 28.

From Shideler, Ind.

WE closed our meeting at Middletown, Ind., on the evening of March 27. The inclement weather militated somewhat against the success of the meetings. A very good interest was taken in the meetings, however, and we had good attendance and attention.

Two made the good confession and were baptized by Bro. D. F. Hoover. Others expressed themselves as being almost ready. We feel glad, however, that the door of the church is open, and that at any time, "whosoever *will* may come."

The quarterly church council took place while we were with the Brethren. Everything passed off pleasantly. This is as it should be. The council was presided over by Eld. D. F. Hoover, who has charge of the church. Eld. Abraham Bowman was also present.

The "Brethren's Home" is located in this church. Brother and sister McCarty preside over the "Home." They are certainly the right persons in the right place. We will be sorry to see them leave.　　　GEO. L. STUDEBAKER.

To the Young Disciples in Mt. Morris College.

NUMBER ONE.

THE fact that Jesus "on the Sabbath day entered into the synagogue and taught" (Mark 1: 21), plainly shows that corruption in the church is not a sufficient reason for refusing to work in it. On the contrary, it is a very strong reason why we should show the kind of life and teaching that should prevail in the church, and put forth our best efforts to leaven it with the good old Gospel of Christ. Jesus used the best means at hand, even though they were sometimes misused by others. We should do likewise.

It is true he "taught as one that had authority," and not as an expounder of other men's opinions. His teaching carried with it the authority of the source of truth. He spoke with the authority of one who *knows*. He knew the way to heaven, for he had been there. He spoke, therefore, with the authority of conscious experience. It was this conscious experience, manifested in his conduct, his character, his holy life and his divine deeds, that gave him such great personal power in his teaching.

My beloved, you will speak "with authority," just in so far as the truth is a *part of your own being*. You make it a part of your being, not by merely reading the Word. There must be a spiritual assimilation of it. It is not the quantity of food eaten, but the part assimilated that builds up physically. The same is true spiritually. And it is this spiritual assimilation that makes available the personal power of the Holy Ghost,—a power more important to you, as disciples of Jesus, than all the book learning any college can afford.

Education, rightly applied, is a most desirable, because a very powerful agency in Christian work; but it can never answer as a substitute for the Holy Ghost. It is this power, more than any other one thing, that the church to-day needs. We need money, and men,—educated, trained men, to push forward the work of spreading the Gospel; but the greatest of all our needs,—a need of the laity, the preachers, and the elders, is the personal power of the Holy Spirit to discern the relative position of the world and the church. The world every-where makes demands of the church. She asks the church to conform to her aims, her precepts and her practices. She cries, "Compromise, *compromise!*" The Master, with outstretched arms, cries, "Separation, *separation!*"

The Lord help you, dear young brethren and sisters, to put yourselves into such an attitude as will insure you a double portion of his Spirit, is the prayer of your fellow-disciple.

I have enjoyed very pleasant visits with the Brethren of Ashland and Loudonville, Ohio. I have met a number of old students, and many friends of the school. Many are the prayers which ascend in your behalf from the altars of families represented in the school.

　　　J. G. ROYER.
Loudonville, Ohio.

From Mansfield, Ill.

THE members of the Blue Ridge church held their quarterly council to-day, April 2. Considerable business came before the meeting and all was disposed of in a Christian-like spirit. Five members were received by letter. Eld. John Barnhart was elected to represent this church at An-

Mountain, lay the poor little boy, only five years and two days old when he left the school-house. The leaves under him were rotten and his clothes nearly so.

We had just begun meeting at the same school-house he had left nearly five months ago, when a man came to the window and said, he wanted to see Bro. Powell. Bro. Powell went out, and immediately came back, saying little Ottie was found dead out on the mountain. You may imagine the excitement was great. We at once dismissed the meeting. Quite a number went to the place. It was distant at least seven miles, over very rough rocky ridges. The remains were brought down to the school-house the same evening. On Monday morning they held an inquest and prepared to bury the remains on the place, at Bro. Powell's. Sister Powell being very poorly, not many were allowed to be in the house at once. As she desired that we have some exercises at the house, we invited the people to come in front of the house, where they stood very attentively, while we had a short service. The neighbors and friends, for ten miles had helped our dear brother search for his dear little one, but all in vain. Happy to say, the almost broken-hearted and sick mother seemed to be getting better from the time the news reached her that her child was found, though dead. A great load of suspense has been removed. We hope she may soon be well again.

J. M. OLINE.

Knightly, Va.

From Olpe, Kans.

THE Verdigris church met in quarterly council March 19. Considerable business came before the meeting and was disposed of in the spirit of the Gospel and, we hope, to the edifying of all. One thing was the missionary cause and the method of raising money to carry on the great work. We had, at one time, appointed solicitors and each member subscribed a certain amount per week, to be paid quarterly, but this did not prove satisfactory to some. One brother had adopted the plan of dropping pennies each week in a little box. Then, at some convenient time, he would turn the amount over to the solicitors according to Matt. 6: 3, "But when thou doest alms, let not thy left hand know what thy right hand doeth." Paul says, "Upon the first day of the week let every one of you lay by him in store, as God hath prospered him, that there be no gatherings when I come." 1 Cor. 16: 2.

After considering the above, we thought the plan of an individual or family contribution box a good one. Now, instead of two solicitors, we have a treasurer. Each member is expected to bring his contributions each quarter, in their box or purse, just as they have gathered it, and hand it in to the treasurer. He counts the money, reports the total, and forwards the amount to the Treasurer of the Mission Board.

Let us, dear brethren and sisters, not become weary in well-doing, but throw in our mite, be it much or little, and carry on this glorious work. Let us not wait till we get rich, so we will not miss it, for that is not acceptable with God. A sacrifice is wanted. Christ said that the poor widow cast in more than they all. Why? Because she made a sacrifice. I believe we should give until we have made a sacrifice,—let it be much or little. We have received one by baptism this winter, and a number by letter.

J. M. QUACKENBUSH.

March 13.

Annual Meeting Notice.

BRO. W. D. Tisdale, 535 East Avenue, Cedar Rapids, Iowa, has been appointed Corresponding Secretary of the Lodging Committee for our next Annual Meeting. Applications for lodging should be made to him. Make your applications early, stating for how many and for what time lodging is wanted. Information given on application. Preserve this notice.

By order of Committee of Arrangements.

JOHN ZUCK,
Foreman.

Notes from Our Correspondents.

"As cold water to a thirsty soul, so is good news from a far country."

Ourey, Ohio.—The members of the Pleasant Grove church met at their house of worship on their regular preaching day, and after listening to a very able sermon, delivered by Bro. Silas Weidman, followed by Bro. Samuel Thomas with some very good remarks, they proceeded to organize their Sunday-school, by electing Bro. Joseph S. Robison as Superintendent.—*Joseph S. Robison, April 4.*

Claysburg, Pa.—We, the members of the Claar congregation held our quarterly council April 2, 1892. A dark cloud has rested upon our church for some time, but now it is disappearing. The church is again in peace and love. All our business passed off in love and harmony. We decided to hold a love-feast, the Lord willing, May 7, at 4 P. M. It will be the first love-feast in our new meeting-house.—*C. F. Lingenfelter.*

Beech Grove, Ind.—The Beech Grove church met in council April 2, to do business in the house of the Lord. The deacons made the visit, but found all in peace and harmony. The church sends Eld. D. R. Richards to District Meeting. Bro. Richards is an able expounder of the Gospel. He has labored long and hard here, and now has a quiet little church of about seventy-five members, with a good corps of officers,—three deacons and one minister.—*Luther Bodel, April 2.*

Hawthorn, Fla.—Our love-feast at the above place will be held May 7, commencing at 3: 30 P. M., at the Methodist church, three miles north of Hawthorn, near Bro. John Teeter's on the Florida Central & Peninsular R. R. An invitation is given to all members, especially in Florida. Stop off at Hawthorn, on the Florida Southern or Florida Central & Peninsular R. R. Bro. Stover, Crumpacker and I live just one mile north of Hawthorn.—*J. C. Lahman, April 6.*

South Beatrice, Nebr.—Our quarterly council occurred March 19. Much business came before the church, but all went off pleasantly. The attendance was good. It seemed as if the members were glad to meet each other, there having been much bad weather for a number of Sundays, so that we could not get to meeting. Brethren Owen Peters and Thomas Graham were elected as delegates to Annual Meeting and brethren Stephen Yoder and James Gish to District Meeting. Bro. Thomas Graham was elected Sunday-school Superintendent. Our school will commence the second Sunday in April.—*Lydia Dell.*

Steamboat Rock, Iowa.—The members of the Grundy County church met in quarterly council April 2. Our elder, Stephen Johnson, of Garrison, was with us and conducted the meeting. Considerable business came before the meeting, but everything, we believe, was settled in harmony with the true Christian spirit of love and forbearance. Bro. A. W. Hawbaker was elected delegate to Annual Meeting. The church decided, the Lord willing, to begin a series of meetings May 15, and to end with a feast, June 2, beginning at four o'clock P. M. No providential hinderance, Bro. A. Hutchison, of McPherson, Kans, will conduct the meetings.—*Alda E. Albright, April 4.*

Beatrice, Nebr.—We have the promise of train service from Beatrice to Annual Meeting without a change of cars. There are three Traveling Agents living at Beatrice: Union Pacific, Rock Island and Chicago, Burlington & Quincy. They all make this promise and will give the best possible rates. All who contemplate going by the way of Beatrice, will please drop me a card, at least a week previous to the meeting, stating what day they would like to reach Cedar Rapids, Iowa.—*J. E Young, March 28.*

Alvada, Ohio.—The quarterly church council in the Rome church occurred March 12. The business before the meeting was very pleasantly disposed of. Among the work that was done, was the establishing of a church library. We elected Eld. L. H. Dickey delegate to Annual Meeting and brethren Silas Weidman and J. W. Chambers delegates to District Meeting of North-western Ohio. We send two queries to District Meeting. We also elected a Superintendent and Assistant for our Sunday-school this summer. We continued our Sunday-school during the winter, every alternate Sunday, when we had preaching, using the Testament.—*M. A. Dickey.*

Yale, Nebr.—Bro. John J. Hoover came to us March 19, and preached ten sermons. He is an able speaker and represented the Brethren's doctrine by precept and example. The attendance was not very large, the nights were dark and cold, but some were brought to a new light. Some said that they did not know there was such a denomination as the Brethren. Bro. John went west of Arcadia, close to Bro. J. B. Mowery's, and held about four meetings. We were sorry to have him leave us, for he could do a great work here. There is a good field here and if any of our brethren would like to come to this part of Nebraska, they should address the writer, or J. B. Mowery, of Arcadia, Nebr. We would gladly welcome them. We have a healthful climate here.—*D. M. Ross, April 2.*

Roaring Spring, Pa.—The brethren and sisters at Roaring Spring met in semi-annual council April 2. On account of the inclemency of the weather, the attendance was not so large. All business was transacted in a Christian-like manner. The church decided to hold a love-feast May 14, and also to have a series of meetings, to begin May 7. The meetings are to be conducted by Eld. G. W. Brumbaugh and A. B. Barket, two home ministers. The writer was advanced to the second degree of the ministry. We also elected two deacons, namely, Jor. P. Long and S. B. Albright, who were properly installed. Elders A. Sell and J. B. Replogle officiated. May the blessings of the Lord rest upon us so that we may prove to be faithful workers, is my prayer!—*J. R. Slayer, April 3.*

Homestead, Pa.—I have received and perused No. 13 of GOSPEL MESSENGER,—the first number that I have read this year, as I have been away from home since October last. My dear aunt (father's sister), Catharine Brumbaugh, of New Baltimore, Ohio, died recently, and her death notice appeared in the number referred to. Her death was a shock to me. I was then very low with *La Grippe*, erysipelas, etc. But the Lord was very gracious to me. I am able to go about again, but suffer much from my eyes and ears. I was feelingly affected when I read sister Vinie Mahorney's letter on page 203. She has been an invalid for four years, but is still so interested in the Lord's cause, and advocating the progress of the Sunday-school work. Yes, let us take her advice and establish Sunday-schools in every land. Dear sister, may God bless and comfort you in your afflictions!—*Emily R. Slifer, April 6.*

Mountain, lay the poor little boy, only five years and two days old when he left the school-house. The leaves under him were rotten and his clothes nearly so.

We had just begun meeting at the same school-house: he had left nearly five months ago, when a man came to the window and said, he wanted to see Bro. Powell. Bro. Powell went out, and immediately came back, saying little Ottie was found dead out on the mountain. You may imagine the excitement was great. We at once dismissed the meeting. Quite a number went to the place. It was distant at least seven miles, over very rough rocky ridges. The remains were brought down to the school-house the same evening. On Monday morning they held an inquest and prepared to bury the remains on the place, at Bro. Powell's. Sister Powell being very poorly, not many were allowed to be in the house at once. As she desired that we have some exercises at the house, we invited the people to come in front of the house, where they stood very attentively, while we had a short service. The neighbors and friends, for ten miles had helped our dear brother search for his dear little one, but all in vain. Happy to say, the almost broken-hearted and sick mother seemed to be getting better from the time the news reached her that her child was found, though dead. A great load of suspense has been removed. We hope she may soon be well again.

J. M. CLINE.

Knightly, Va.

From Olpe, Kans.

THE Verdigris church met in quarterly council March 19. Considerable business came before the meeting and was disposed of in the spirit of the Gospel and, we hope, to the edifying of all. One thing was the missionary cause and the method of raising money to carry on the great work. We had, at one time, appointed solicitors and each member subscribed a certain amount per week, to be paid quarterly, but this did not prove satisfactory to some. One brother had adopted the plan of dropping pennies each week in a little box. Then, at some convenient time, he would turn the amount over to the solicitors according to Matt. 6: 3, "But when thou doest alms, let not thy left hand know what thy right hand doeth." Paul says, "Upon the first day of the week let every one of you lay by him in store, as God hath prospered him, that there be no gatherings when I come." 1 Cor. 16: 2.

After considering the above, we thought the plan of an individual or family contribution box a good one. Now, instead of two solicitors, we have a treasurer. Each member is expected to bring his contributions each quarter, in their box or purse, just as they have gathered it, and hand it in to the treasurer. He counts the money, reports the total, and forwards the amount to the Treasurer of the Mission Board.

Let us, dear brethren and sisters, not become weary in well-doing, but throw in our mite, be it much or little, and carry on this glorious work. Let us not wait till we get rich, so we will not miss it, for that is not acceptable with God. A sacrifice is wanted. Christ said that the poor widow cast in more than they all. Why? Because she made a sacrifice. I believe we should give until we have made a sacrifice,—let it be much or little. We have received one by baptism this winter, and a number by letter.

J. M. QUACKENBUSH.

March 19.

Annual Meeting Notice.

BRO. W. D. Tisdale, 535 East Avenue, Cedar Rapids, Iowa, has been appointed Corresponding Secretary of the Lodging Committee for our next Annual Meeting. Applications for lodging should be made to him. Make your applications early, stating for how many and for what time lodging is wanted. Information given on application. Preserve this notice.

By order of Committee of Arrangements.

JOHN ZUCK,
Foreman.

Notes from Our Correspondents.

"As cold water to a thirsty soul, so is good news from a far country."

Carey, Ohio.—The members of the Pleasant Grove church met at their house of worship on their regular preaching day, and after listening to a very able sermon, delivered by Bro. Silas Weidman, followed by Bro. Samuel Thomas with some very good remarks, they proceeded to organize their Sunday-school, by electing Bro. Joseph S. Robison as Superintendent.—*Joseph S. Robison, April 4.*

Claysburg, Pa.—We, the members of the Claar congregation held our quarterly council April 2, 1892. A dark cloud has rested upon our church for some time, but now it is disappearing. The church is again in peace and love. All our business passed off in love and harmony. We decided to hold a love-feast, the Lord willing, May 7, at 4 P. M. It will be the first love-feast in our new meeting-house.—*C. F. Lingenfelter.*

Beech Grove, Ind.—The Beech Grove church met in council April 2, to do business in the house of the Lord. The deacons made the visit, but found all in peace and harmony. The church sends Eld. D. R. Richards to District Meeting. Bro. Richards is an able expounder of the Gospel. He has labored long and hard here, and now has a quiet little church of about seventy-five members, with a good corps of officers,—three deacons and one minister.—*Luther Bedel, April 3.*

Hawthorn, Fla.—Our love-feast at the above place will be held May 7, commencing at 3: 30 P. M., at the Methodist church, three miles north of Hawthorn, near Bro. John Teeter's on the Florida Central & Peninsular R. R. An invitation is given to all members, especially in Florida. Stop off at Hawthorn, on the Florida Southern or Florida Central & Peninsular R. R. Bro. Stover, Crumpacker and I live just one mile north of Hawthorn.—*J. C. Lahman, April 6.*

South Beatrice, Nebr.—Our quarterly council occurred March 19. Much business came before the church, but all went off pleasantly. The attendance was good. It seemed as if the members were glad to meet each other, there having been much bad weather for a number of Sundays, so that we could not get to meeting. Brethren Owen Peters and Thomas Graham were elected as delegates to Annual Meeting and brethren Stephen Yoder and James Gish to District Meeting. Bro. Thomas Graham was elected Sunday-school Superintendent. Our school will commence the second Sunday in April.—*Lydia Dell.*

Steamboat Rock, Iowa.—The members of the Grundy County church met in quarterly council April 2. Our elder, Stephen Johnson, of Garrison, was with us and conducted the meeting. Considerable business came before the meeting, but everything, we believe, was settled in harmony with the true Christian spirit of love and forbearance. Bro. A. W. Hawbaker was elected delegate to Annual Meeting. The church decided, the Lord willing, to begin a series of meetings May 15, and to end with a feast, June 2, beginning at four o'clock P. M. No providential hinderance, Bro. A. Hutchison, of McPherson, Kans, will conduct the meetings.—*Alda E. Albright, April 4.*

Beatrice, Nebr.—We have the promise of train service from Beatrice to Annual Meeting without a change of cars. There are three Traveling Agents living at Beatrice: Union Pacific, Rock Island and Chicago, Burlington & Quincy. They all make this promise and will give the best possible rates. All who contemplate going by the way of Beatrice, will please drop me a card, at least a week previous to the meeting, stating what day they would like to reach Cedar Rapids, Iowa.—*J. E. Young, March 28.*

Alvada, Ohio.—The quarterly church council in the Rome church occurred March 12. The business before the meeting was very pleasantly disposed of. Among the work that was done, was the establishing of a church library. We elected Eld. L. H. Dickey delegate to Annual Meeting and brethren Silas Weidman and J. W. Chambers delegates to District Meeting of North-western Ohio. We also elected a Superintendent and Assistant for our Sunday-school this summer. We continued our Sunday-school during the winter, every alternate Sunday, when we had preaching, using the Testament.—*M. A. Dickey.*

Yale, Nebr.—Bro. John J. Hoover came to us March 19, and preached ten sermons. He is an able speaker and represented the Brethren's doctrine by precept and example. The attendance was not very large; the nights were dark and cold, but some were brought to a new light. Some said that they did not know there was such a denomination as the Brethren. Bro. John went west of Arcadia, close to Bro. J. B. Mowery's, and held about four meetings. We were sorry to have him leave us, for he could do a great work here. There is a good field here and if any of our brethren would like to come to this part of Nebraska, they should address the writer, or J. B. Mowery, of Arcadia, Nebr. We would gladly welcome them. We have a healthful climate here.—*D. M. Ross, April 2.*

Roaring Spring, Pa.—The brethren and sisters at Roaring Spring met in semi-annual council April 2. On account of the inclemency of the weather, the attendance was not so large. All business was transacted in a Christian-like manner. The church decided to hold a love-feast May 14, and also to have a series of meetings, to begin May 7. The meetings are to be conducted by Eld. G. W. Brumbaugh and A. B. Burket, two home ministers. The writer was advanced to the second degree of the ministry. We also elected two deacons, namely, Jos. P. Long and S. E. Albright, who were properly installed. Elders A. Sell and J. B. Replogle officiated. May the blessings of the Lord rest upon us so that we may prove to be faithful workers, is my prayer!—*J. R. Stayer, April 3.*

Homestead, Pa.—I have received and perused No. 13 of GOSPEL MESSENGER,—the first number that I have read this year, as I have been away from home since October last. My dear aunt (father's sister), Catharine Brumbaugh, of New Baltimore, Ohio, died recently, and her death notice appeared in the number referred to. Her death was a shock to me. I was then very low with La Grippe, erysipelas, etc. But the Lord was very gracious to me. I am able to go about again, but suffer much from my eyes and ears. I was feelingly affected when I read sister Vinie Mahoney's letter on page 203. She has been an invalid for four years, but is still so interested in the Lord's cause, and advocating the progress of the Sunday-school work. Yes, let us take her advice and establish Sunday-schools in every land. Dear sister, may God bless and comfort you in your afflictions!—*Emily R. Slifer, April 6.*

THE GOSPEL MESSENGER.

"Set for the Defense of the Gospel."

Vol. 30, Old Series.   Mt. Morris, Ill., and Huntingdon, Pa., April 26, 1892.   No. 17.

The Gospel Messenger.

H. B. BRUMBAUGH, Editor,

And Business Manager of the Eastern House, Box 50,
Huntingdon, Pa.

Table of Contents.

No man will backslide as long as he keeps his face towards his Master. He may stumble, but he can get up and go straight ahead, and will reach his crown ultimately.

WE have passed through a cold snap of weather which would have done credit to the earlier winter months. Some fears are entertained about the earlier budding fruits, but we hope that there is no occasion for such fears.

· BRO. C. MYERS and family, of Warble, Pa., have moved to Huntingdon and made their home with us; also Bro. Levi Stoner and family, of Avlon, Ohio. They are both ministers who have come here to enjoy school and church privileges. We extend to them a hearty welcome.

BRO. LONG, a minister of the River Brethren church, from Center County, Pa., gave us a short call last week. He came to see about sending his daughter to our school. He says that she dresses plainly and he wishes to place her among plain people. We will be glad to have her come and hope that we can make her stay with us both pleasant and profitable.

WE were made sad in learning of the death of Bro. Evan Nearhoof, of the Warrior's Mark, Pa., church. He was one of their active deacons, and was also a good Sunday-school worker. He was a man of sterling integrity, and in his death the church and community have sustained quite a loss. His home was a Christian inn, where members always found a welcome. We extend to the family our sympathies.

WE had the pleasure of listening to a very interesting lecture, the other evening, by Dr. Green, President of Princeton College. His subject was "Biblical Criticism on the Authorship of the Pentateuch." He belongs to the conservative school of Bible Critics, and affirms strongly that Moses is the author. He produced some interesting thoughts, as held by the more liberal school, confining himself entirely to those who claim to be evangelical or orthodox Christians, naming those who claim that the Pentateuch is a compilation from four different manuscripts, or writings, whose authors are unknown, named respectively, G, E, P, D. These writings, it is claimed, were something like the four Gospels of the New Testament, and that the events of the four were harmonized so as to make but one continued narrative. This view he strongly antagonized, and gave some solid evidence in favor of the Mosaical authorship. It was quite a learned address and was very interesting to Bible students.

QUERISTS' DEPARTMENT.

THE RIGHT TO ORIGINATE.

An answer to the following question, through the GOSPEL MESSENGER, is earnestly desired: Has any local church, or the ministerial force, any right to originate a new question and present it to their members on the annual visit, requiring an answer, after the usual questions have been presented and answered, thereby causing trouble?   SAMUEL PRICE.

WE are not sure that we quite understand our querist. If he means a question of discipline, or order, we say no, as official members do not have the right to originate questions, apply them to the membership and exact promise, independent of the voice and wish of the church. All such requirements must first have the assent of the church before they can be made a rule of right, to be applied to others. Visiting officials, however, have a discretionary power that properly belongs to the office or position. This power, or authority, need not, necessarily, originate with them, but through their knowledge of the Truth, and the church's interpretation of this Truth. To get the end or object of the visit, they may ask questions to get the desired information and tender the necessary advice. Visiting brethren should not go beyond the scope of their office, neither is it in their province to administer discipline, but advice only. If this is not accepted, they should report to the church.

THE ETHIOPIAN.

Please give your idea of the following Scriptures: "Can the Ethiopian change his skin?" Jer. 13: 23. "I am black but comely." Cant. 1: 6. May we not infer from this language that the negro is a descendant of King Solomon?   W. H. RIDDLE.

No. These two Scriptures do not suggest national kinship. The first has reference to the Ethiopian as a race, the second refers to a white man, exposed to wind and sun, until his skin became dark or black through exposure. There are other instances in the Bible of this same kind that must be interpreted in the same way.

WOE OF THE PHARISEES.

Please explain through the MESSENGER Matt. 23: 13, 14, "But woe unto you scribes and Pharisees, hypocrites; for ye shut up the kingdom against men; for ye neither go in yourselves, neither suffer ye them that are entering to go in," etc.   M. E. MURPHY.

This should have a literal interpretation as to the people and the time. Christ had direct reference to the people that were before him and whom he was addressing. They were doing just what Christ charged them with. They would not themselves enter the kingdom of Christ, and because of their influence and professed wisdom, they hindered or stood in the way of those who had a desire to enter. In this way, they virtually shut up the kingdom against men. They have many descendants who are doing the same thing to-day. The things named in verse 14 are different results, growing out of the same spirit. And need we wonder that it is said of them, "Therefore ye shall receive the greater damnation?"

These were men that had large possibilities. To whom much is given, of him much will be required. Possibilities bring proportionate responsibilities, and we will be rewarded or punished according to this proportion. Let us be sure that we are not filling the places to-day that these men filled in the time of Christ. We are either helping to get people into the kingdom of Christ or we are keeping them out. Which?

A CHRISTIAN WITHOUT A CHURCH.

Dear Sir:—Here are some questions which I would like to have answered through your paper. I belong to no church but believe that the Brethren are right. Now I should like to be a Christian, but there is no church here. Do you think that a person could be a Christian and not belong to a church? And do you think that one could be a Christian and bring up a Christian family if one should marry a Catholic? He is a good moral fellow and not very strict, but still he holds to the Catholic church. I shall look anxiously for an answer.
A FRIEND.

We are sorry that you are living in this world of religious possibilities without being an active disciple of Jesus.

Again, we are glad that you have a love for the truth, and that you believe that the Brethren church hold and practice this truth, and that you would like to be a Christian and be a church member; yea, it should be a strong desire on your part to become a member of the body of Christ, and we hope that when your desire becomes sufficiently strong, the Lord will open a way for you. The Brethren have organized churches in your State and you should be willing to make some sacrifice to become an heir of salvation.

We do not see how any one can be a Christian in a saving sense, outside of the church. There is no such promise, and the soul is too precious to risk its salvation outside of the promise, "He that believeth and is baptized, shall be saved," etc.

As to your last question, you will find it partly answered under the head, "Is It Right?" We do not say that it would be impossible for a wom-

(Concluded on page 261.)

THE GOSPEL MESSENGER.

"Set for the Defense of the Gospel."

Vol. 30, Old Series.　　　Mt. Morris, Ill., and Huntingdon, Pa., April 26, 1892　　　No. 17.

The Gospel Messenger.

H. B. Brumbaugh, Editor,

And Business Manager of the Eastern House, Box 50,
Huntingdon, Pa.

Table of Contents.

No man will backslide as long as he keeps his face towards his Master. He may stumble, but he can get up and go straight ahead, and will reach his crown ultimately.

We have passed through a cold snap of weather which would have done credit to the earlier winter months. Some fears are entertained about the earlier budding fruits, but we hope that there is no occasion for such fears.

Bro. C. Myers and family, of Warble, Pa., have moved to Huntingdon and made their home with us; also Bro. Levi Stoner and family, of Avlon, Ohio. They are both ministers who have come here to enjoy school and church privileges. We extend to them a hearty welcome.

Bro. Long, a minister of the River Brethren church, from Center County, Pa., gave us a short call last week. He came to see about sending his daughter to our school. He says that she dresses plainly and he wishes to place her among plain people. We will be glad to have her come and hope that we can make her stay with us both pleasant and profitable.

We were made sad in learning of the death of Bro. Evan Nearhoof, of the Warrior's Mark, Pa., church. He was one of their active deacons, and was also a good Sunday-school worker. He was a man of sterling integrity, and in his death the church and community have sustained quite a loss. His home was a Christian inn, where members always found a welcome. We extend to the family our sympathies.

We had the pleasure of listening to a very interesting lecture, the other evening, by Dr. Green, President of Princeton College. His subject was "Biblical Criticism on the Authorship of the Pentateuch." He belongs to the conservative school of Bible Critics, and affirms strongly that Moses is the author. He produced some interesting thoughts, as held by the more liberal school, confining himself entirely to those who claim to be evangelical or orthodox Christians, naming those who claim that the Pentateuch is a compilation from four different manuscripts, or writings, whose authors are unknown, named respectively, G, E, P, D. These writings, it is claimed, were something like the four Gospels of the New Testament, and that the events of the four were harmonized so as to make but one continued narrative. This view he strongly antagonized, and gave some solid evidence in favor of the Mosaical authorship. It was quite a learned address and was very interesting to Bible students.

QUERISTS' DEPARTMENT.

THE RIGHT TO ORIGINATE.

An answer to the following question, through the Gospel Messenger, is earnestly desired: Has any local church, or the ministerial force, any right to originate a new question and present it to their members on the annual Visit, requiring an answer, after the usual questions have been presented and answered, thereby causing trouble?　　Samuel Price.

We are not sure that we quite understand our querist. If he means a question of discipline, or order, we say no, as official members do not have the right to originate questions, apply them to the membership and exact promises, independent of the voice and wish of the church. All such requirements must first have the assent of the church before they can be made a rule of right, to be applied to others. Visiting officials, however, have a discretionary power that properly belongs to the office or position. This power, or authority, need not, necessarily, originate with them, but through their knowledge of the Truth, and the church's interpretation of this Truth. To gain the end or object of the visit, they may ask questions to get the desired information and tender the necessary advice. Visiting brethren should not go beyond the scope of their office, neither is it in their province to administer discipline, but advice only. If this is not accepted, they should report to the church.

THE ETHIOPIAN.

Please give your idea of the following Scriptures: "Can the Ethiopian change his skin?" Jer. 13: 23. "I am black but comely." Cant. 1: 6. May we not infer from this language that the negro is a descendant of King Solomon?
W. H. Riddle.

No. These two Scriptures do not suggest national kinship. The first has reference to the Ethiopian as a race, the second refers to a white man, exposed to wind and sun, until his skin became dark or black through exposure. There are other instances in the Bible of this same kind that must be interpreted in the same way.

WOE OF THE PHARISEES.

Please explain through the Messenger Matt. 23: 13, 14. "But woe unto you scribes and Pharisees, hypocrites; for ye shut up the kingdom against men; for ye neither go in yourselves, neither suffer ye them that are entering to go in," etc.
M. E. Murphy.

This should have a literal interpretation as to the people and the time. Christ had direct reference to the people that were before him and whom he was addressing. They were doing just what Christ charged them with. They would not themselves enter the kingdom of Christ, and because of their influence and professed wisdom, they hindered or stood in the way of those who had a desire to enter. In this way, they virtually shut up the kingdom against men. They have many descendants who are doing the same thing to-day. The things named in verse 14 are different results, growing out of the same spirit. And need we wonder that it is said of them, "Therefore ye shall receive the greater damnation?"

These were men that had large possibilities. To whom much is given, of him much will be required. Possibilities bring proportionate responsibilities, and we will be rewarded or punished according to this proportion. Let us be sure that we are not filling the places to-day that these men filled in the time of Christ. We are either helping to get people into the kingdom of Christ or we are keeping them out. Which?

A CHRISTIAN WITHOUT A CHURCH.

Dear Sir:—Here are some questions which I would like to have answered through your paper. I belong to no church but believe that the Brethren are right. Now I should like to be a Christian, but there is no church here. Do you think that a person could be a Christian and not belong to a church? And do you think that one could be a Christian and bring up a Christian family if one should marry a Catholic? He is a good moral fellow and not very strict, but still he holds to the Catholic church. I shall look anxiously for an answer.
A Friend.

We are sorry that you are living in this world of religious possibilities without being an active disciple of Jesus.

Again, we are glad that you have a love for the truth, and that you believe that the Brethren church hold and practice this truth, and that you would like to be a Christian and be a church member; yes, it should be a strong desire on your part to become a member of the body of Christ, and we hope that when your desire becomes sufficiently strong, the Lord will open a way for you. The Brethren have organized churches in your State and you should be willing to make some sacrifice to become an heir of salvation.

We do not see how any one can be a Christian in a saving sense, outside of the church. There is no such promise, and the soul is too precious to risk its salvation outside of the promise, "He that believeth and is baptized, shall be saved," etc. As to your last question, you will find it partly answered under the head, "Is It Right?" We do not say that it would be impossible for a wom-

(Concluded on page 262.)

children? "Take heed, brethren," says the writer to the Hebrews (3: 12), "lest there be in any of you an evil heart of unbelief, in departing from the living God." By neglect of the duty of self-examination it is possible for us to wander even upon the verge of unbelief without knowing it. Will we not more carefully examine ourselves? "If we would judge ourselves (which we could not do without first examining ourselves) we should not be judged." 1 Cor. 11: 31.

II *When should we examine ourselves?*

1. There are special occasions, when our hearts should undergo especially prayerful examinations. Among the instructions and warnings which Paul gives with reference to the Lord's Supper is this: "Let a man examine himself." If there is ever a time in a Christian's life and experience when he should tremble with a feeling of his responsibility to God, it is when he comes to the Table of the Lord, and is about to engage in that service by which he declares his membership in the true kingdom of God, and professes to the world that he is in perfect and common union with all his fellow-members of Christ's body. And it is as a preparation for this solemn service that Paul would have our thoughts turned upon themselves, and would have us look within ourselves to see that no malice toward our brethren exists there, that our co _ union may be one in fact as well as in form. Thus only will God remove all impurities from our hearts, and enable us to be as "the pure in heart" who "shall see God," and in the emblems of which we are about to partake discern the Lord's body whose breaking the service commemorates. Thus only may we so far banish unhallowed thoughts as to properly reflect upon the goodness of God, and the greatness of the consequences of Christ's agony and death, as we should upon these occasions.

2. We should also examine ourselves daily. It is not sufficient that we only perform this duty just before engaging in a Communion service; nor is there any Scriptural authority to justify such a practice. On the other hand, it is implied in many of the passages of Scripture to which I have already referred, that it is a duty of a general character, obligatory alike at all times and upon all occasions. If it was a duty last week, it is just as much so this; if yesterday, none the less to-day. We have shown that self-examination is necessary to purity of heart, a confident faith in Jesus, and a constant nearness to him. And it need not be argued that these are as essential one day as another.

But if I enter into a thorough examination of my spiritual condition to-day and find myself right before God, may I not be assured that I shall remain so for many days? No; not so long as I remain a fallible creature. The Word of God answers, No. "The heart is deceitful above all things," says Jeremiah (17: 9). How often has man been denounced as "unstable," "double-minded," "driven by the wind and tossed!" How often has it been necessary to admonish and urge him to be "steadfast," "unmovable," and to "endure to the end!" Not only the Scriptures, but every sane man's consciousness and experience answers, "No; though I have found myself right to-day, within myself I have no assurance of being right to-morrow."

It is an experience that has been a thousand times repeated in the lives of Christian men and women, that the heart is one day filled to overflowing with the good things from above, and exalted with a consciousness of the presence of the Spirit of God; and perhaps the next day we are attacked by the Evil one, and, being thrown off our guard by the previous day's feeling of security, we yield to his seductions and are brought thereby to the lowest humiliation. My dear brother, it is well to set a guard to your heart to-day; but that is by no means sufficient for to-morrow. It is well for you to examine yourself to-day; but that can serve as no excuse for a neglect of the duty to-morrow.

Because of our ever-present proneness to sin; because of the untiring, unceasing efforts of Satan to lead us astray, self-examination becomes an every-day duty and necessity. May the sleep of no night overtake us until in mind we have re-traveled the past day's journey, inquired into the moral quality of our actions, and the motives that prompted them; and with thankfulness to God for the good we have been enabled to do, and a prayer for his pardon of the evil, and a humble resolve upon improvement in the future, may we fall asleep in peace!

Covington, Ohio.

THE UNWELCOME VISITOR.

SELECTED BY ALBERT MYERS.

Arad.—I see you are a stranger, and appear to be weary; come, rest yourself awhile in my humble home.

Stranger.—I accept your kind offer. You appear to have much comfort about your dwelling. Are you its only occupant?

A.—No; I have a wife and seven children,—two noble sons and five lovely daughters,—who are all absent; but I expect them to return very soon.

S.—I have a commission to summons one of the inhabitants of the town to great honor and dignity.

A.—O how happy I should be if your visit were directed to my humble abode!

S.—Would you, then, readily and willingly part with any one of your family for such a distinction?

A.—I should be very neglectful of their interest if I were to refuse.

S.—But what are their qualifications for court?

A.—My eldest son is bold, active, generous and sociable; the youngest is a scholar, and ambitious of distinction.

S.—What have you to say of your daughters?

A.—The eldest has prudence, judgment and sedateness; the second, a talent for literary pursuits; the third is benevolent and affectionate; the fourth, cheerful and gay; the youngest, serious and religious.

S.—But you have said nothing of your wife; do you not desire *her* advancement?

A.—She is aged and infirm, I could not spare her.

S.—There are no exemptions. My prince is absolute, and the individual whom I call must obey my summons. What are your powers to resist *Death?*

A.—Wretched man that I am! Instead of a friend, I behold the great destroyer of the human race before me!

S.—Which shall I take, the eldest boy or girl?

A.—O spare them! they are the props and stay of their parents. Their mother's feeble health, and my declining years require their active care.

S.—Your youngest son, can you not spare him?

A.—Pity a father's delight to see his opening qualities ripen into manhood; he is ambitious of eminence and renown.

S.—Can you give me, then, your youngest daughter?

A.—She is a blessing and an example to the family. Her devotional spirit shames our worldly feelings and pursuits.

S.—You are content, then, to resign your head?

A.—Rather the rest than her; by patience and gentleness she softened the ruggedness of my temper; and without her I should again become the rash and ill-natured being I was before I saw her.

S.—You are selfish in your excuses; what have you to urge against my taking *you?*

A.—I feel that I am not prepared. The thought of death recalls to remembrance the half-forgotten sins of early years; they crowd upon my memory, and fill my soul with anguish.

S.—Let them, then, recall thee to repentance; and, for thy present comfort, know that I am not sent to thee, nor to thy house at present. But be assured that I shall visit thee again. Be ready, therefore, against my return; set thy house in order, that, at my summons, both thou and thy family may be prepared to obey it.

Waddam's Grove, Ill.

A BEAUTIFUL DREAM.

BY D. E. BRUBAKER.

Not very long ago, as I was on my way to a meeting, I passed by the house of a blind, feeble, old brother. Just as I came opposite the little gate, in front of the humble little home, the thought came to me, "If you were old, and blind, and feeble, do you think you would like if your brethren would stop occasionally and give you a word of cheer and comfort?" I yielded at once to this impulse, and was soon in the little lonely room, and, oh, what exclamations of joy broke forth from the aged blind man! He stroked my hair, again and again, with his old, trembling hand, as he said, "O how glad I am; I cannot see you but I like to hear you talk." We had, as usual, a very pleasant visit.

I reminded the old brother that, if we proved faithful, bye and bye, in the glory world, we would receive better vision. This seemed to stir up many memories of the past, in the old man's life. He finally said, "O I must tell you about a beautiful dream I had, not long since, which has done me much good. I dreamed I was climbing a very high mountain, and when I had reached a very high point, the climbing was getting very steep. Finally I could get no farther. My little path seemed all closed up. My feet seemed to be on a rock, and for support I reached both of my hands above me to a small tree. I looked back, down into the dark valley below, and saw that I could not get back. I felt as if I certainly must fall. Just as I was about to give up, I looked and saw a beautiful white angel coming to me. He came right here, to my left side, and took hold of me. Another one came to my right side, and took hold, and still another one came up behind me, and they helped me, and kept me from falling. Just then I awoke, and O how much good that dream has done me."

I could not restrain the tears while this old pilgrim was relating this beautiful dream. For over eighty years he has been climbing the mountain of life. Thirty years ago, when I first knew him, he was a strong man, had good eyes, and climbing the rugged mountain was then comparatively easy. He is now poor in this world's goods; he is blind, his mind is feeble, and truly, he has made his way against much opposition to a high point in the mountain. I think he can almost get glimpses of the "Beulah Land" beyond.

The beautiful, white-robed angels of faith, hope and charity, stand by and support him, while the eternal rock, Christ Jesus, is beneath, and his old, feeble hands are firmly clasped to the Tree of Life. Who need fear to look down into the dark valley and shadow of death, with such mighty messengers of help, to keep us in the way? We may be kept from falling, though the climbing may be very difficult. Let us not forget, in our

he does not love Christ, yet it is clear that this good man, this honest man, this virtuous man, this much-respected man, makes Jesus a liar. How can you love Jesus and yet not believe him; love him and yet become angry, when you see the picture that you are constantly drawing of him? ' If a man love me he will keep my words."—*Je-sus.*

Interrogate the Greek church, the Roman Catholic church, or Protestantism, on this great question of love to God and his Son, Jesus Christ, and the answer is alike strong and emphatic, that they love Jesus.

Consult either of the multitudinous branches of Protestantism in regard to this vital question of love, and you get one and the same response from all. Each and every sect would consider any man unkind, to say the least, who would intimate such a thought as "coldness," "no love for Jesus," in regard to their doctrine.

All sects profess to love Jesus; all professors say that they love him, and, more, they all profess to know him, yet it is absolutely sure that they who keep not the commandments of Jesus are liars and the truth is not in them. 1 John 2: 4. It is true that Jesus had commands to be kept, else he could not have said, "If ye love me, keep my commandments." John 14: 15, 21. "He that hath my commandments, and keepeth them, he it is that loveth me," and "If ye keep my commandments ye shall abide in my love." John 15: 10.

Now, since Jesus has commands to be kept, and all that love him, all that abide in his love, keep them, how can we, who do not keep them, say the truth when we say we love them? Since all the sects of Protestantism, of Catholicism, and of the Greek church, say that they love Jesus, and even profess that they do love him, shall we believe each and every one of them, because of their sincerity and zeal thus manifested?

Shall we believe the evidence of one, and be so uncharitable and mean in the extreme as not to believe all? If we believe one, we are compelled to believe all. Even the moral man must be allowed his claim that he loves Jesus, and you cannot exclude the good, clever fellow, even though he is not so moral, when he says that he loves Jesus. You are selfish, you are self-righteous to exclude any man from the list who says he loves Jesus, when one that is not exclude every one that does not obey Jesus in all things. Shall we believe Jesus or shall we believe men? Shall we believe Jesus or shall we believe our feelings? Men say they love Jesus, when they do not keep his sayings. Good, moral men become insulted when told that they do not love Jesus, yet they do not keep his words. Good men, professors of religion, feel grieved and count you selfish to not give full credence to their claim of love. They do not keep the sayings of Jesus but they do claim to love him. I must either believe Jesus or disbelieve him,—there is no middle ground. If I give credence to the claim of one man that says he loves Jesus, and does not keep his "commands," his "words," his "sayings," I MUST, I am COMPELLED to give credence to every man who says so.

If I believe the claims of men, I do not believe Jesus. If I do not believe Jesus, I am condemned already, and it will not matter materially, what church I belong to, or whether I belong to any. The only true test of our love is our entire submission. Not my will but thine, is the constant prayer of the true child of God. "He that saith I know him, and keepeth not his commandments, is a liar, and the truth is not in him." 1 John 2: 4.

Bridgewater, Va.

"THEY never fall who die in a great cause."

BIBLE DANCING.

THE editor of *Zion's Watchman* has been asked to explain the "dance," mentioned in the two closing Psalms. Here is his answer:

"One of the striking things impressed upon our mind while in the Holy Land was, that its life and habits are to-day just what they were in the days of Abraham, of David, of Christ, and the Apostles. The fact is especially agreeable and helpful to the Bible student who seeks to find an agreement between the Book and the Land.

" We were invited to a wedding, while in Jerusalem, where the dancing was in progress during the eight days of the feast. But we found the men danced by themselves (in another part of the house), and the women by themselves. As a special favor, we asked to see the women dance, and they would not in our presence, being "shame-faced" (too modest to dance before men).

" David's dances are never in connection with women. The women that went out to meet Saul and David, returning from battle, sang and danced among themselves. (See 1 Samuel 18: 6–7.) Also remember, the faces of women are covered. Men never walk with women on the streets, or speak to them, or in any way recognize them. Not even husbands speak to their wives, should they meet them on the street.

"The social relations and freedom between the sexes among us are entirely unknown in the East. Yes, men dance, and women dance, but each sex dances by itself. Look at your Bible, and you will find our observation correct. If men and women dance because they find that men and women in the Bible danced, in all fairness, let them dance after the manner of Bible dancing. Let men hire a hall and dance till break of day, and let women dance in their rooms while men are "down town," and there will be no sin in it, but, on the contrary, a healthful exercise. But, never, never, take the Bible as authority for the modern dance, where men and women are locked in voluptuous embrace. Such obtrusive boldness and flaunting immodesty in public are entirely unknown to people in the East"

KEEP IN THE CURRENT.

THE negro preachers sometimes make good points. Here is one that is worth remembering:

"My bredren, God bless your souls, 'ligion is like the Alabama riber! In spring it comes fresh, an' bring all the ole logs, slabs, an' sticks dat hab been lyin' on de bank, an' carries dem down in de current. Bymeby de water go down—den de log cotch on dis island, deu slab get cotched on de sho', an' de sticks on de bushes—an' dare they lie, within' an dryin' till dare come 'noder fresh. Jus' so dare come 'rival of 'ligion—dis ole sinner brought in, dat ole blackslider brought back, an' all the folk seem comin, an' mighty good times. But breden, God bless your souls, bymeby 'rival gone—den dis ole sinner is stuck on his ole sin, den dat old blackslider is potched where he was afore, on jus' such a rook; den one after 'noder dat had got 'ligion lies all along de shore, an dare dey lie till 'noder 'rival. Belubed bredren, God bless your souls, keep in de current."

"THE true spirit of the Sabbath appointment is, not that we should condense the religion of the week into the Sabbath, but that we should carry from the Sabbath its hallowed impulses and feelings into the other days of the week, to elevate and sustain us amid its wearisome secularities and depressing cares. The Lord has given us the Sabbath, not to relieve us of our religion, but so to revive our religion on that day as to impel its healthy tide into the remotest nook and corner of every-day duty."

WELL SAID.

IT is said that the Bible has been upset twenty-seven times in the last five years, by those who do not receive it as a revelation from God. But the good Book is considerably like a cube of New England granite: when you upset it, you have only set it up; it is just as big one way as another, and just as big after it is tumbled down as it was before. Indeed "it stands four squares to every wind that blows."

OUR REWARD.

WHEN we have done that we came for, it is time for us to be gone. This earth is only made for action, not for fruition; the services of God's children should be ill rewarded if they must stay here always. Let no man think much that those are fetched away which are faithful to God; they should not change, if it were not to their preferment. It is our folly that we would have good men live forever, and account it a hard measure that they were. He that lends them to the world owes them a better turn than this earth can pay them. It were injurious to wish that goodness should hinder any man from glory. So is the death of God's saints precious, that is certain.

KIND WORDS.

A KIND word costs but little, but it may bless all day the one to whom it is spoken. Nay, have not kind words been spoken to you, which have lived in your heart through years, and borne fruit of joy and hope? Let us speak kindly to one another. We have burdens and worries, but let us not, therefore, rasp and irritate those near us, those we love, those whom Christ would have us to save. Speak kindly in the morning; it lightens the cares of the day, and makes the household and all its affairs move along smoothly. Speak kindly at night, for it may be before dawn some loved one may finish his or her space of life for this world, and it will be too late to ask forgiveness.

A CHRISTIAN WITHOUT A CHURCH.

(Concluded from first page.)

an to live with a Catholic husband and be a Christian, but while we say this, we feel that it would be wrong for you, or any one else, to marry a Catholic with this expectation.

As to bringing up a Christian family in such a relation, we do not see how it could be done. No, don't try it. See the Lord's Prayer and pray, "Lead us not into temptation." Dear friend, these are grave matters, and of yourself you cannot do it. They are too much for you. And you cannot ask the Lord's help when you knowingly go into forbidden paths. Marriage is intended for the highest good of the parties concerned. If you do not see this in it, hands off.

As to his being morally good and not very strict as to the Catholic faith, does not necessarily recommend him as a suitable man for a Christian woman to marry, unless you can feel that he is weakening in the Catholic faith and growing towards the Truth as you believe it. If this should be the case, then your better way will be to become a Christian yourself and then try to convert your friend to the truth before marrying him. Remember this *one* thing,—your influence over the man you love is as strong before marriage as it ever can be afterwards, and if you cannot have a reasonable assurance from him before marriage, don't run the risk, because a risk it will be,—one that you or no one else can afford to make. What-soever you do, do it to the honor and glory of God.

he does not love Christ, yet it is clear that this good man, this honest man, this virtuous man, this much-respected man, makes Jesus a liar. How can you love Jesus and yet not believe him; love him and yet become angry, when you see the picture that you are constantly drawing of him? ' If a man love me he will keep my words."—*Jesus.*

Interrogate the Greek church, the Roman Catholic church, or Protestantism, on this great question of love to God and his Son, Jesus Christ, and the answer is alike strong and emphatic, that they love Jesus.

Consult either of the multitudinous branches of Protestantism in regard to this vital question of love, and you get one and the same response from all. Each and every sect would consider any man unkind, to say the least, who would intimate such a thought as "coldness," "no love for Jesus," in regard to their doctrine.

All sects profess to love Jesus; all professors say that they love him, and, more, they all profess to know him, yet it is absolutely sure that they who keep not the commandments of Jesus are liars and the truth is not in them. 1 John 2: 4. It is true that Jesus had commands to be kept, else he could not have said, "If ye love me, keep my commandments." John 14: 15, 21. "He that hath my commandments, and keepeth them, he it is that loveth me," and "If ye keep my commandments ye shall abide in my love." John 15: 10.

Now, since Jesus has commands to be kept, and all that love him, all that abide in his love, keep them, how can we, who do not keep them, say the truth when we say we love them? Since all the sects of Protestantism, of Catholicism, and of the Greek church, say that they love Jesus, and even profess that they do love him, shall we believe each and every one of them, because of their sincerity and zeal thus manifested?

Shall we believe the evidence of one, and be so uncharitable and mean in the extreme as not to believe all? If we believe one, we are compelled to believe all. Even the moral man must be allowed his claim that he loves Jesus, and you cannot exclude the good, clever fellow, even though he is not so moral, when he says that he loves Jesus. You are selfish, you are self-righteous to exclude any man from the list who says he loves Jesus, when you do not exclude every one that does not obey Jesus in all things. Shall we believe Jesus or shall we believe men? Shall we believe Jesus or shall we believe our feelings? Men say they love Jesus, when they do not keep his sayings. Good, moral men become insulted when told that they do not love Jesus, yet they do not keep his words. Good men, professors of religion, feel grieved and count you selfish to not give full credence to their claim of love. They do not keep the sayings of Jesus but they do claim to love him. I must either believe Jesus or disbelieve him,—there is no middle ground. If I give credence to the claim of one man that says he loves Jesus, and does not keep his "commands," his "words," his "sayings," I MUST, I am COMPELLED to give credence to every man who says so.

If I believe the claims of men, I do not believe Jesus. If I do not believe Jesus, I am condemned already, and it will not matter materially, what church I belong to, or whether I belong to any. The only true test of our love is our entire submission. Not my will but thine, is the constant prayer of the true child of God. "He that saith I know him, and keepeth not his commandments, is a liar, and the truth is not in him." 1 John 2: 4.

Bridgewater, Va.

"THEY never fail who die in a great cause."

BIBLE DANCING.

THE editor of *Zion's Watchman* has been asked to explain the "dance," mentioned in the two closing Psalms. Here is his answer:

"One of the striking things impressed upon our mind while in the Holy Land was, that its life and habits are to-day just what they were in the days of Abraham, of David, of Christ, and the Apostles. The fact is especially agreeable and helpful to the Bible student who seeks to find an agreement between the Book and the Land.

"We were invited to a wedding, while in Jerusalem, where the dancing was in progress during the eight days of the feast. But we found the men danced by themselves (in another part of the house), and the women by themselves. As a special favor, we asked to see the women dance, and they would not in our presence, being "shame-faced" (too modest to dance before men).

"David's dances are never in connection with women. The women that went out to meet Saul and David, returning from battle, sang and danced among themselves. (See 1 Samuel 18: 6–7.) Also remember, the faces of women are covered. Men never walk with women on the streets, or speak to them, or in any way recognize them. Not even husbands speak to their wives, should they meet them on the street.

"The social relations and freedom between the sexes among us are entirely unknown in the East. Yes, men dance, and women dance, but each sex dances by itself. Look at your Bible, and you will find our observation correct. If men and women dance because they find that men and women in the Bible danced, in all fairness, let them dance after the manner of Bible dancing. Let men hire a hall and dance till break of day, and let women dance in their rooms while men are "down town," and there will be no sin in it, but, on the contrary, a healthful exercise. But, never, never, take the Bible as authority for the modern dance, where men and women are locked in voluptuous embrace. Such obtrusive boldness and flaunting immodesty in public are entirely unknown to people in the East."

KEEP IN THE CURRENT.

THE negro preachers sometimes make good points. Here is one that is worth remembering:

"My bredren, God bless your souls, 'ligion is like the Alabama riber! In spring it come fresh, an' bring all the ole logs, slabs, an' sticks dat hab been lyin' on dat bank, an' carries dem down in de current. Bymeby de water go down—den de log cotch on dis island, den slab get cotched on de sho', an' de sticks on de bushes—an' dare they lie, withrin' an dryin' till dare come 'noder fresh. Jus'- so dare come 'rival of 'ligion—dis ole sinner brought in, dat ole blackslider brought back, an' all the folk seem comin, an' mighty good times. But breden, God bless your souls, bymeby 'rival gone—den dis ole sinner is stuck on his ole sin, den dat old blackslider is potched where he was afore, on jus' such a rock; den one after 'noder dat had got 'ligion lies all along de shore, an dare dey lie till 'noder 'rival. Belubed bredren, God bless your souls, keep in de current."

"THE true spirit of the Sabbath appointment is, not that we should condense the religion of the week into the Sabbath, but that we should carry from the Sabbath its hallowed impulses and feelings into the other days of the week, to elevate and sustain us amid its wearisome secularities and depressing cares. The Lord has given us the Sabbath, not to relieve us of our religion, but so to revive our religion on that day as to impel its healthy tide into the remotest nook and corner of every-day duty."

WELL SAID.

IT is said that the Bible has been upset twenty-seven times in the last five years, by those who do not receive it as a revelation from God. But the good Book is considerably like a cube of New England granite: when you upset it, you have only set it up; it is just as big one way as another, and just as big after it is tumbled down as it was before. Indeed "it stands four squares to every wind that blows."

OUR REWARD.

WHEN we have done that we came for, it is time for us to be gone. This earth is only made for action, not for fruition; the services of God's children should be ill rewarded if they must stay here always. Let no man think much that those are fetched away which are faithful to God; they should not change, if it were not to their preferment. It is our folly that we would have good men live forever, and account it a hard measure that they were. He that lends them to the world owes them a better turn than this earth can pay them.! It were injurious to wish that goodness should hinder any man from glory. So is the death of God's saints precious, that is certain.

KIND WORDS.

A KIND word costs but little, but it may bless all day the one to whom it is spoken. Nay, have not kind words been spoken to you, which have lived in your heart through years, and borne fruit of joy and hope? Let us speak kindly to one another. We have burdens and worries, but let us not, therefore, rasp and irritate those near us, those we love, those whom Christ would have us to save. Speak kindly in the morning; it lightens the cares of the day, and makes the household and all its affairs move along smoothly. Speak kindly at night, for it may be before dawn some loved one may finish his or her space of life for this world, and it will be too late to ask forgiveness.

A CHRISTIAN WITHOUT A CHURCH.

(Concluded from first page.)

(Concluded from first page.)

an to live with a Catholic husband and be a Christian, but while we say this, we feel that it would be wrong for you, or any one else, to marry a Catholic with this expectation.

As to bringing up a Christian family in such a relation, we do not see how it could be done. No, don't try it. See the Lord's Prayer and pray, "Lead us not into temptation." Dear friend, these are grave matters, and of yourself you cannot do it. They are too much for you. And you cannot ask the Lord's help when you knowingly go into forbidden paths. Marriage is intended for the highest good of the parties concerned. If you do not see this in it, hands off.

As to his being morally good and not very strict as to the Catholic faith, does not necessarily recommend him as a suitable man for a Christian woman to marry, unless you can feel that he is weakening in the Catholic faith and growing towards the Truth as you believe it. If this should be the case, then your better way will be to become a Christian yourself and then try to convert your friend to the truth before marrying him. Remember this *one* thing,—your influence over the man you love is as strong before marriage as it ever can be afterwards, and if you cannot have a reasonable assurance from him before marriage, don't run the risk, because a risk it will be,—one that you or no one else can afford to make. Whatsoever you do, do it to the honor and glory of God.

Chiques church, Pa.,	20 50
A brother, Pottstown, Pa.,	18 00
Baby boy's orange tree, Florida,	2 20
J. E. Reed, Pittsburgh, Pa.,	1 00
Lower Miami church, Ohio,	12 00
A brother and sister, Sidney, Nebr.,	5 00
Estate of Martha A. Kreps, deceased, Pennsylvania,	15 00
Jas. H. Kirkham, Laconia, Ind.,	25
Woodland church, Mich.,	7 10
Isaac Rairigh, Campbell, Mich.,	1 00
Dry Valley church, Pa.,	3 10
G. E. Goughnour and wife, Maxwell, Iowa,	4 50
David Miller and family, Indiana,	2 52
Andrew Miller, Indiana,	10
Mary E. Weil, Indiana,	14
Hannah Souder, Indiana,	05
A sister, Philadelphia,	200 00
Sugar Creek church, Ohio,	5 00
Mary Rohrer, Canton, Ill.,	2 00
M. G. Hill, Hodgensville, Ky.,	2 50
Susan Hill, Hodgensville, Ky.,	2 50
Maggie Hill, Hodgensville, Ky.,	1 00
Martha E. Hill, Hodgensville, Ky.,	25
Addie Van Motts, Hodgensville, Ky.,	50
Bear Creek church, Ohio,	15 55
Our Quarterly Dues, Pennsylvania,	1 00
A sister, Missouri,	1 00
A brother, Astoria, Ill.,	2 00
Manor church, Pa.,	1 45
A sister, Martinsburgh, Pa.,	2 00
Anonymous, Clover Creek, Pa.,	1 40
Pleasant Dale church, Ind.,	5 00
Anna Wright, Kiowa, Kans.,	10 00
M. W. Light, Lightsty, Pa.,	2 00
Miller and Sommer Debate Book, J. L-K.,	1 50
A brother, Sebastapol, Ind.,	25
Two-thirds proceeds Annual Meeting at Hagerstown, Md.,	666 63
Duncan family, McMinnville, Tenn.,	35
J. M. Keeny, Fort Alleghany, Pa.,	1 55
The Lord's Tenth, Pennsylvania,	5 00
Howard church, Ind.,	8 40
Members in and around Stuttgart, Ark.,	3 25
Eliz. J. Bosserman, Dunkirk, Ohio,	2 00
A sister, Howard, Ind.,	1 00
Beaver Run church, W. Va.,	4 00
Almeeta Flory, Chili, Ind.,	1 00
M. E. Loudenslager, Defiance, Ohio,	1 50

MARCH.

Looney's Creek Sunday-school, W. Va.,	$2 85
J. C. Frang, West Virginia,	50
Chas. Hamstead, West Virginia,	75
Lower Stillwater church, Ohio,	15 73
Cherokee church, Kans.,	2 65
Abilene church, Kans.,	7 00
Sunday-school at Welty church, Md.,	10 00
"A sister," Wadsworth, Ohio,	5 00
Mrs. T. B. Hersh, Jesup, Iowa,	1 50
South-eastern District of Kansas,	8 75
Solomon's Creek church, Ind.,	6 71
Powell's Valley church, Oregon,	6 00
Unknown, Upper Strasburg, Pa.,	1 00
Members of East Dayton, Ohio,	2 00
Daniel Smith, Cuba, Kans.,	40
A friend, California,	20 00
Churches in Europe,	21 31
Tropico church, Cal.,	10 60
Big Swatara church, Pa.,	10 00
Spring Creek church, Pa.,	10 00
White Oak church, Pa.,	13 00
Tulpehocken church, Pa.,	15 04
A lover of the church, Roseville, Ohio,	1,000 00
S. A. Shaver, Maurertown, Va.,	40
A sister, Burkittville, Md	8 00
Box 36, Lima, Ohio,	10 00
Sisters of West Dayton church, Ohio,	4 00
J. Johnson, Union Bridge, Md.,	2 00

Wm. B. Wilson, Orbisonia, Pa.,	1 00
A few members near Harleysville, Pa.,	11 00
English River church, Iowa,	9 50
W. A. Manst, Lenora, Minn.,	10 00
Jesse Barrick, Byron, Ill.,	5 00
Knob Creek church, Tenn.,	3 00
Isolated sister of Missouri,	1 00
Walnut church, Ind.,	7 40
Stonelick church, Ohio,	3 00
E. N. and Rebecca Spillman, St. John, Kans.,	2 25
Miller and Sommer Debate Book, J. C. F.,	1 50
Middle Indiana,	42 00
Chapman Creek church, Kans.,	2 00
Bachelor Run church, Ind.,	10 65
John C. Richer, Peru, Ind.,	10 00
South Waterloo church, Iowa,	4 00
Esterly church, L-.,	45 00
A sister at Kirncofe, Va.,	1 00
Southern District of Illinois,	16 85
Salem church, Ohio,	19 17
Pleasant Grove church, Kans.,	2 40
Jesse E. Stremmel, Astoria, Ill.,	8 00
Juniata church, Nebr.,	1 00
Sunday-school at Hudson, Ill.,	3 40
Nocona church, Texas,	5 50
Northern District of Illinois,	129 07

Mt. Morris, Ill.

"LIGHT AND TRUTH."

BY S. W. HOOVER.

Number Three.

WE next come to Jesus, the Messiah of the world, to whom all power was given, both in heaven and upon earth. "In him was life; and the life was the light of men. That was the true Light, which lighteth every man that cometh into the world." John 1: 4; 9. On him, if one believes and repents, grace, pardon and peace will descend. Jesus was the "True Light," in comparison to all other teaching and teachers. He was the end of the law, and in him all righteousness was fulfilled. He was as much superior to Moses, as a lawgiver, as the Gospel is to the Law. The Law could only point the people to him "as the Lamb of God that taketh away the sin of the world." John 1: 29. He could point the world to the cross, and *himself as that Lamb,—*"sin's victim, sin's atonement, sin's sacrifice, sin's destruction, the abolisher of death, and the fountain of life." He was superior to John the Baptist and the prophets. These could only teach the way of eternal life, by pointing to him, but had no power to give it, whilst Jesus could both teach and bestow life. What a world of meaning there is contained in these words: "I am the way, the truth, and the life: no man cometh unto the Father, but by me." John 14: 6.

In order to heal the wounds which sin had made, and that we might have eternal life, Jesus opened up a new and living way, and to this end, presents the ultimatum of the new or spiritual birth, by the Word. By it we are born again, "not of corruptible seed, but of incorruptible, by the Word of God, which liveth and abideth forever." 1 Pet 1: 23. The Word of God is the life and seed of the new birth, the product a new creature or life in Christ. "Therefore if any man be in Christ, he is a new creature." 2 Cor. 5: 17. By the phrase "new creature," we understand, born into new or eternal life. Prophetically, Isaiah (9: 2) spoke of the coming of Jesus, "the Light of the world," thus, "The people that walked in darkness have seen a great light: they that dwell in the land of the shadow of death, upon them hath the light shined." The words do not refer to the person of Jesus as the light, although, as a man, he possessed all the elements and characteristics of purity and holiness, which he exhibited in word, actions and life, but to him, as the Messiah of the world, by whom salvation is come. "And this is the record, that God hath given to us eternal life, and this life is in his Son." 1 John 5: 11. And in the following verse, "He that hath the Son hath life; and he that hath not the Son of God hath not life."

After contemplating his personal work as the Messiah, Christ left the world and ascended to his Heavenly Father, but he left us his Word of Truth, which is still creating, his life as the light which is still shining, and sent believers the Holy Spirit to conduct the affairs of the kingdom, and lead his people in the way.

The characteristics of Jesus, manifested during his personal stay among the people, are now to be exhibited by his followers, who compose the militant church or body of Christ, and of whom he affirms, "Ye are the light of the world. A city that is set on a hill cannot be hid." Matt. 5: 14. For every one that doeth evil hateth the light, neither cometh to the light, lest his deeds should be reproved. But he that doeth truth cometh to the light, that his deeds may be made manifest, that they are wrought in God." John 3: 20, 21. Those who believe and have been brought into Christ, made heirs of an immortal inheritance and "walk in the light, as he is in the light," enjoy the greatest privileges, highest honors, and fullest promises, to which it is possible for a human soul to arrive, and the Divine Being confer, this side of eternity.

Slowly but surely, over land and sea, town and city, kingdom and nation, has the empire of light arisen, step by step, and borne onward, as upon angels' wings, the sweet and beautiful message of the Gospel of faith, and hope, and life. It is still moving onward. The Truth has lost none of its power, the light none of its glory, but, in its onward and upward movement, shineth more and more unto the perfect day.

Dayton, Ohio.

" THOSE who err in one direction always take care to let you know that they are quite free from error in the opposite direction. A boorish man thanks God very loudly that he is not insincere; nobody having ever thought of accusing him even of that small and wretched approach to politeness which is sometimes favored by insincerity."

The Gospel Messenger

Is the recognized organ of the German Baptist or Brethren's church, and advocates the form of doctrine taught in the New Testament and pleads for a return to apostolic and primitive Christianity.

It recognizes the New Testament as the only infallible rule of faith and practice, and maintains that Faith toward God, Repentance from dead works, Regeneration of the heart and mind, baptism by Trine Immersion for remission of sins unto the reception of the Holy Ghost by the laying on of hands, are the means of adoption into the household of God,—the church militant.

It also maintains that Feet-washing, as taught in John 13, both by example and command of Jesus, should be observed in the church.

That the Lord's Supper, instituted by Christ and as universally observed by the apostles and the early Christians, is a full meal, and, in connection with the Communion, should be taken in the evening or after the close of the day.

That the Salutation of the Holy Kiss, or Kiss of Charity, is binding upon the followers of Christ.

That War and Retaliation are contrary to the spirit and self-denying principles of the religion of Jesus Christ.

That the principle of Plain Dressing and of Non-conformity to the world, as taught in the New Testament, should be observed by the followers of Christ.

That the Scriptural duty of Anointing the Sick with Oil, in the Name of the Lord, James 5: 14, is binding upon all Christians.

It also advocates the church's duty to support Missionary and Tract Work, thus giving to the Lord for the spread of the Gospel and for the conversion of sinners.

In short, it is a vindicator of all that Christ and the apostles have enjoined upon us, and aims, amid the conflicting theories and discords of modern Christendom, to point out ground that all must concede to be infallibly safe.

The above principles of our Fraternity are set forth on our "Brethren's Envelopes." Use them! Price, 15 cents per package; 40 cents per hundred.

Ohiques church, Pa., 20 50
A brother, Pottstown, Pa., 18 00
Baby boy's orange tree, Florida, 2 20
J. E. Reed, Pittsburgh, Pa., 1 00
Lower Miami chnrch, Ohio, 12 00
A brother and sister, Sidney, Nebr., 5 00
Estate of Martha A. Kreps, deceased, Pennsylvania, 15 00
Jas. H. Kirkham, Laconia, Ind., 25
Woodland church, Mich, 7 10
Isaac Rairigh, Campbell, Mich, 1 00
Dry Valley church, Pa., 3 10
G. E. Goughnour and wife, Maxwell, Iowa, 4 50
David Miller and family, Indiana, 2 52
Andrew Miller, Indiana, 10
Mary E. Weil, Indiana, 14
Hannah Souder, Indiana, 05
A sister, Philadelphia, 200 00
Sugar Creek church, Ohio, 5 00
Mary Rohrer, Canton, Ill., 2 00
M. G. Hill, Hodgensville, Ky., 2 50
Susan Hill, Hodgensville, Ky., 2 50
Maggie Hill, Hodgensville, Ky., 1 00
Martha E. Hill, Hodgensville, Ky., 25
Addie Van Motts, Hodgensville, Ky., 50
Bear Creek church, Ohio, 15 55
Our Quarterly Dues, Pennsylvania, 1 00
A sister, Missouri, 1 00
A brother, Astoria, Ill., 2 00
Manor church, Pa., 1 45
A sister, Martinsburgh, Pa., 2 00
Anonymous, Clover Creek, Pa., 1 40
Pleasant Dale church, Ind., 5 00
Anna Wright, Kiowa, Kans., 10 00
M. W. Light, Lighety, Pa., 2 00
Miller and Sommer Debate Book, J. L K., 1 50
A brother, Sebastopol, Ind., 25
Two-thirds proceeds Annual Meeting at Hagerstown, Md., 666 63
Duncan family, McMinnville, Tenn., 35
J. M. Keeny, Port Alleghany, Pa., 1 55
The Lord's Tenth, Pennsylvania, 5 00
Howard church, Ind., 8 40
Members in and around Stuttgart, Ark., 3 25
Eliz. J. Bosserman, Dunkirk, Ohio, 2 00
A sister, Howard, Ind., 2 00
Beaver Run church, W. Va, 4 00
Almeeta Flory, Chili, Ind., 1 00
M. E. Loudenslager, Defiance, Ohio, 1 50

MARCH.

Looney's Creek Sunday-school, W. Va., 2 85
J. C. Frang, West Virginia, 50
Chas. Hamstead, West Virginia, 75
Lower Stillwater church, Ohio, 15 73
Cherokee church, Kans., 2 65
Abilene church, Kans., 7 00
Sunday-school at Welty church, Md., 10 00
"A sister," Wadsworth, Ohio, 5 00
Mrs. T. B. Hezah, Jesup, Iowa, 1 50
South-eastern District of Kansas, 8 75
Solomon's Creek church, Ind., 6 71
Powell's Valley church, Oregon, 5 00
Unknown, Upper Strasburg, Pa., 1 00
Members of East Dayton, Ohio, 2 00
Daniel Smith, Cuba, Kans., 40
A friend, California, 20 00
Churches in Europe, 21 31
Tropico church, Cal., 10 60
Big Swatara church, Pa., 10 00
Spring Creek church, Pa., 10 00
White Oak church, Pa., 13 00
Tulpehocken church, Pa., 16 04
A lover of the church, Roseville, Ohio, 1,000 00
S. A. Shaver, Maurertown, Va., 40
A sister, Burkittsville, Md, 8 00
Box 36, Lima, Ohio, 10 00
Sisters of West Dayton church, Ohio, 4 00
J. Johnson, Union Bridge, Md., 2 00

Wm. B. Wilson, Orbisonia, Pa., 1 00
A few members near Harleysville, Pa., 11 00
English River church, Iowa, 9 50
W. A. Manst, Lenora, Minn., 10 00
Jesse Barrick, Byron, Ill., 5 00
Knob Creek church, Tenn., 8 00
Isolated sister of Missouri, 1 00
Walnut church, Ind, 7 40
Stonelick church, Ohio, 3 00
E. N. and Rebecca Spillman, St. John, Kans., 2 25
Miller and Sommer Debate Book, J. C. F., 1 50
Middle Indiana, 42 00
Chapman Creek church, Kans., 2 00
Bachelor Run church, Ind., 10 65
John C. Richer, Peru, Ind., 10 00
South Waterloo church, Iowa, 40 00
Esterly church, L-, 4 50
A sister at Kiracofe, Va., 1 00
Southern District of Illinois, 16 85
Salem church, Ohio, 19 17
Pleasant Grove church, Kans, 2 40
Jesse E. Stremmel, Astoria, Ill., 3 00
Juniata church, Nebr., 1 00
Sunday-school at Hudson, Ill., 3 40
Nocona church, Texas, 5 50
Northern District of Illinois, 128 07

Mt. Morris, Ill.

"LIGHT AND TRUTH."

BY S. W. HOOVER.

Number Three.

We next come to Jesus, the Messiah of the world, to whom all power was given, both in heaven and upon earth. "In him was life; and the life was the light of men. That was the true Light, which lighteth every man that cometh into world." John 1: 4, 9. On him, if one believes and repents, grace, pardon and peace will descend. Jesus was the "True Light," in comparison to all other teaching and teachers. He was the end of the law, and in him all righteousness was fulfilled. He was as much superior to Moses, as a lawgiver, as the Gospel is to the Law. The Law could only point the people to him "as the Lamb of God that taketh away the sin of the world." John 1: 29. He could point the world to the cross, and himself as that Lamb,—' sin's victim, sin's atonement, sin's sacrifice, sin's destruction, the abolisher of death, and the fountain of life." He was superior to John the Baptist and the prophets. These could only teach the way of eternal life, by pointing to him, but had no power to give it, whilst Jesus could both teach and bestow life. What a world of meaning there is contained in these words: "I am the way, the truth, and the life: no man cometh unto the Father, but by me." John 14: 6.

In order to heal the wounds which sin had made, and that we might have eternal life, Jesus opened up a new and living way, and to this end, presents the ultimatum of the new or spiritual birth, by the Word. By it we are born again, "not of corruptible seed, but of incorruptible, by the Word of God, which liveth and abideth forever." 1 Pet 1: 23. The Word of God is the life and seed of the new birth, the product a new creature or life in Christ. "Therefore if any man be in Christ, he is a new creature." 2 Cor 5: 17. By the phrase "new creature," we understand, born into new or eternal life. Prophetically, Isaiah (9: 2) spoke of the coming of Jesus, "the Light of the world," thus, "The people that walked in darkness have seen a great light: they that dwell in the land of the shadow of death, upon them hath the light shined." The words do not refer to the person of Jesus as the light, although, as a man, he possessed all the elements and characteristics of purity and holiness, which he exhibited in word, actions and life, but to him, as the Messiah of the world, by whom salvation is come. "And this is the record, that God hath given to us eternal life, and this life is in his Son." 1 John 5: 11. And in the following verse, "He that hath the Son hath life; and he that hath not the Son of God hath not life."

After contemplating his personal work as the Messiah, Christ left the world and ascended to his Heavenly Father, but he left us his Word of Truth, which is still creating, his life as the light which is still shining, and sent believers the Holy Spirit to conduct the affairs of the kingdom, and lead his people in the way.

The characteristics of Jesus, manifested during his personal stay among the people, are now to be exhibited by his followers, who compose the militant church or body of Christ, and of whom he affirms, "Ye are the light of the world. A city that is set on a hill cannot be hid." Matt. 5: 14. For every one that doeth evil hateth the light, neither cometh to the light, lest his deeds should be reproved. But he that doeth truth cometh to the light, that his deeds may be made manifest, that they are wrought in God." John 3: 20, 21. Those who believe and have been brought unto Christ, made heirs of an immortal inheritance and "walk in the light, as he is in the light," enjoy the greatest privileges, highest honors, and fullest promises, to which it is possible for a human soul to arrive, and the Divine Being confer, this side of eternity.

Slowly but surely, over land and sea, town and city, kingdom and nation, has the empire of light arisen, step by step, and borne onward, as upon angels' wings, the sweet and beautiful message of the Gospel of faith, and hope, and life. It is still moving onward. The Truth has lost none of its power, the light none of its glory, but, in its onward and upward movement, shineth more and more unto the perfect day.

Dayton, Ohio.

"Those who err in one direction always take care to let you know that they are quite free from error in the opposite direction. A boorish man thanks God very loudly that he is not insincere; nobody having ever thought of accusing him even of that small and wretched approach to politeness which is sometimes favored by insincerity."

The Gospel Messenger

Is the recognized organ of the German Baptist or Brethren's church, and advocates the form of doctrine taught in the New Testament and pleads for a return to apostolic and primitive Christianity.

It recognizes the New Testament as the only infallible rule of faith and practice, and maintains that Faith toward God, Repentance from dead works, Regeneration of the heart and mind, baptism by Trine immersion for remission of sins unto the reception of the Holy Ghost by the laying on of hands, are the means of adoption into the household of God,—the church militant.

That the Lord's Supper, instituted by Christ and as universally observed by the apostles and the early Christians, is a full meal, and, in connection with the Communion, should be taken in the evening or after the close of the day.

That the Salutation of the Holy Kiss, or Kiss of Charity, is binding upon the followers of Christ.

That War and Retaliation are contrary to the spirit and self-denying principles of the religion of Jesus Christ.

That the principle of Plain Dressing and of Non-conformity to the world, as taught in the New Testament, should be observed by the followers of Christ.

That the Scriptural duty of Anointing the Sick with Oil, in the Name of the Lord, James 5: 14, is binding upon all Christians.

It also advocates the church's duty to support Missionary and Tract Work, thus giving to the Lord for the spread of the Gospel and for the conversion of sinners.

In short, it is a vindicator of all that Christ and the apostles have enjoined upon us, and aims, amid the conflicting theories and discords of modern Christendom, to point out ground that all must concede to be infallibly safe.

The above principles of our Fraternity are set forth on our "Brethren's Envelopes." Use them! Price, 15 cents per package; 40 cents per hundred.

WE are in receipt of the sad news, that Bro. John Lear, husband of sister Mattie A. Lear, of Urbana, Ill., died very suddenly a few weeks ago. In this bereavement sister Lear has the sympathies of our readers, as well as her many friends.

IT seems singular that the Mohammedans should undertake to convert the English people to their religion, but it is reported that they have raised a large sum of money for the purpose of supporting a Mohammedan Institution in Liverpool, with a view of planting and propagating their religion in England. To this may be added still another report on the same line, to the effect that an Arabic paper is to be started in New York, with an edition of 7,000 copies. There is also an Arabian colony in Chicago. By the way, Mohammedanism is the greatest foe Christianity has to fight. These Arabs are the descendants of Abraham through Ishmael. Through Isaac the Jews also sprang from Abraham, while the Christians are the children of Abraham by faith in Christ Jesus. Thus it may be seen that the descendants of that one man are a power in the world, second to none.

DRY figures are said to be usually void of interest, but it is surely interesting to study Bro. Royer's Quarterly Report in this issue. It shows the amount of money received by him for the General Mission Board, during the quarter past. While we may compute the amount in dollars and cents, we never can compute the power for good there may be in this money, nor can we understand the value of the prayers accompanying the donations. The first donation on the list is the Children's Mission. Well, we are glad to see the children lead off in so good a work. We trust these little ones will always be found in this line. We cannot stop to explain how the Board gets $215.00, as proceeds from a farm; but they own a farm, and the receipts obtained from it help preach the Gospel year after year. Running on down the long column we are led to wonder about that baby boy in Florida, who gave $2.20 from one orange tree. A sad story might be told of that little boy. Years ago his parents settled in the wilds of Florida, and though they can enjoy no preaching by the Brethren, they keep alive the religious interest in their souls. The little boy came to their home to cheer their hearts. They planted an orange tree in honor of the gift. The boy grew, and so did the tree. But the Lord took the little boy away, and the tree goes on bearing fruit, and the parents sell the fruit and send the money to the Mission Board. May that tree be the means of building up a church in that locality! As we pass on we find $200.00 from a sister who declines to give her name, and further on is another one, equally modest, who gives $1,000.00. Perhaps we would like to know the names of these two liberal saints. We need not concern ourselves about that, but we may and should admire their modesty and liberality, and those who are similarly blessed will do well to imitate them for the cause of Christ.

UNFERMENTED WINE.

Sometime ago you gave a receipt in the MESSENGER for making unfermented wine for Communion purposes. Some members are still opposed to the use of unfermented wine. Will you not give us Scriptural reasons for using the unfermented wine? Some say that the unfermented juice of the grape is not wine, and refer to where the Savior turned water into wine, and also to the case of Paul advising Timothy to use a little wine for the stomach's sake.
                        JOHN E. METZGER.

WINE may be either fermented or unfermented. The term wine may be applied to the fresh juice as it is pressed from the grapes. For proof of this we refer to Josephus, the great Jewish historian, who lived in the times of the apostles, and wrote his works while some of them were yet living, and therefore knew the current meaning of the word in question. In Book 2, Chapter 5, and Section 2, speaking of a dream that Joseph was called on to interpret, he says:

"He therefore said, That in his sleep he saw three clusters of grapes hanging upon three branches of a vine, large already and ripe for gathering, and that he squeezed them into a cup, which the king held in his hand; and when he had strained the wine, he gave it to the king to drink, and that he received it from him with a pleasant countenance. This, he said, was what he saw; and he desired Joseph, that if he had any portion of understanding in such matters, he would tell him what this vision foretold: who bid him be of good cheer, and expect to be loosed from his bonds in three days' time, because the king desired his service, and was about to restore him to it again; for he let him know that God bestows the fruit of the vine upon men for good; which wine is poured out to him, and is the pledge of fidelity and mutual confidence among men; and puts an end to their quarrels, takes away passion and grief out of the minds of them that use it, and makes them cheerful. Thou sayest that thou didst squeeze this wine from three clusters of grapes with thine hands, and that the king received it."

It will be noticed that in this quotation the fresh juice of the grape is repeatedly called wine. This ought to settle the right to call the unfermented juice wine. We will, however, further strengthen what Josephus says, by twenty-six proofs, which we find conveniently arranged in "The Old Faith Restated," pages 236, 237, where the definition of wine is given by a number of reliable authorities. We quote the following:

"1. Webster: 'Wine, the expressed juice of grapes.'

"2. Worcester: 'Must, the sweet or unfermented juice of the grape: new wine.'

"3. Liddell and Scott: 'Gleukos, sweet, new wine.'

"4. Groves: 'The fresh juice of the grape, must, new wine, and mead.'

"5. Parkhurst: 'Sweet wine, which distills of its own accord from the grapes.'

"6. Robinson: 'Must, grape juice unfermented.'

"7. Andrew: 'Mustum, new, or unfermented wine.'

"8. Leverett: 'Must, new wine.'

"9. Anthon: 'Young, new, fresh; must, new wine.'

"10. Dr. Ure: 'Juice newly expressed, and before it has begun to ferment is called must, and in common language, new wine.'

"11. Ainsworth: 'New wine, close shut up, and not allowed to work.'

"12. Littleton gives the same that Ainsworth does.

"13. Smith's Bible Dictionary, A. M. Ed.: 'It may be at once conceded that the Hebrew terms, translated wine, refer, occasionally, to an unfermented liquor.'

"14. Stuart: 'Facts show that the ancients not only preserved wine unfermented, but regarded it as of higher flavor and finer quality than fermented wine.'

"15. Barnes' Note on John 2: 10: 'That was the pure juice of the grape.'

"16. Kitto: 'Wine, asis, denotes the expressed juice of the grape, or other fruit.'

"17. Thayer: 'The numerous authorities already cited to show that unfermented grape juice is wine, also prove that unfermented wine existed.'

"18. Dr. E. Nott, late President of Union College: 'That unintoxicating wines existed from remote antiquity, and were held in high estimation by the wise and good, there can be no reasonable doubt. The evidence is unequivocal and plenary.'

"19. Roy. Dic. Lond.: 'Wine pressed from the grape but not fermented.'

"20. Dr. Hilbert: (Dic. Ger. Lond.): 'Wine pressed from the grape, but not fermented: new wine.'

"21. Littre: (Dic. de la language Francais): 'New wine not fermented.'

"22. Descherell: 'Wine which has just been made, and which has not yet fermented.'

"23. Scheller: (Lexicon 1832): 'Wine just pressed out and not strained.'

"24. Flugel: (Dic. Ger. and Eng.): 'Unfermonted wine.'

"25. Freund: (Leipsic 1878): "New or unfermented wine.'

"26. Dr. Adam Clark: (Com. vol. I., page 239, Lond. Ed., 1836, Note on Gen. 40: 11): 'From this we find that wine anciently was the mere expressed juice of the grape without fermentation.'"

After reading this array of testimony, it seems to us that no one has an excuse for saying that the unfermented juice of the grape may not very properly be called wine.

The wine made from water at the wedding in Cana of Galilee was most assuredly unfermented, for it was fresh, and had no time to ferment, any more than the juice just pressed from the grapes. It was made of water, and required the same power to make it that is required to make the juice found in the ripe grapes. Nature takes up water, and by means of the vine and fruit, transforms it into juice. The Savior did the same thing with the water at the wedding.

Furthermore, there is no reason for even presuming that the wine was intoxicating, for the Savior being a good man, would not have made the harmful drink when he could make the harmless just as easily. No good man, it would seem to us, would make an intoxicating drink when there was no occasion for it.

True, Paul did advise Timothy to take a little wine for his stomach's sake, and his oft infirmities. But this was medical advice and has nothing whatever to do with the question concerning the class of wine to be used on Communion occasions.

But, coming more directly to the question, there is not one word in the New Testament about using wine at the Communion table. The Savior calls it the "fruit of the vine," and the unfermented juice of the grape is certainly the fruit of the vine. The process of fermentation, which grape juice undergoes, frees it from the fruit element, and leaves remaining the alcoholic condition. If, therefore, the real fruit of the vine is desired, it must be had in the juice before fermentation takes place.

As we use unleavened bread to represent the broken body of Christ, consistency would teach us to also use unfermented wine to represent the shed blood.

Some of the wine purchased at drug-stores is said to be devoid of the fruit of the vine, as it is made of drugs, and certainly cannot fitly represent the shed blood of the Master. And since the unfermented wine is so easily made and kept, there is every reason for encouraging its use at all of our Communion services. In fact there is no reason whatever why it should not be used. We are glad to know that many congregations are adopting it.
                J. H. M.

WE are in receipt of the sad news, that Bro. John Lear, husband of sister Mattie A. Lear, of Urbana, Ill., died very suddenly a few weeks ago. In this bereavement sister Lear has the sympathies of our readers, as well as her many friends.

IT seems singular that the Mohammedans should undertake to convert the English people to their religion, but it is reported that they have raised a large sum of money for the purpose of supporting a Mohammedan Institution in Liverpool, with a view of planting and propagating their religion in England. To this may be added still another report on the same line, to the effect that an Arabic paper is to be started in New York, with an edition of 7,000 copies. There is also an Arabian colony in Chicago. By the way, Mohammedanism is the greatest foe Christianity has to fight. These Arabs are the descendants of Abraham through Ishmael. Through Isaac the Jews also sprang from Abraham, while the Christians are the children of Abraham by faith in Christ Jesus. Thus it may be seen that the descendants of that one man are a power in the world, second to none.

DRY figures are said to be usually void of interest, but it is surely interesting to study Bro. Royer's Quarterly Report in this issue. It shows the amount of money received by him for the General Mission Board, during the quarter past. While we may compute the amount in dollars and cents, we never can compute the power for good there may be in this money, nor can we understand the value of the prayers accompanying the donations. The first donation on the list is the Children's Mission. Well, we are glad to see the children lead off in so good a work. We trust these little ones will always be found in this line. We cannot stop to explain how the Board gets $215.00, as proceeds from a farm; but they own a farm, and the receipts obtained from it help preach the Gospel year after year. Running on down the long column we are led to wonder about that baby boy in Florida, who gave $2.20 from one orange tree. A sad story might be told of that little boy. Years ago his parents settled in the wilds of Florida, and though they can enjoy no preaching by the Brethren, they keep alive the religious interest in their souls. The little boy came to their home to cheer their hearts. They planted an orange tree in honor of the gift. The boy grew, and so did the tree. But the Lord took the little boy away, and the tree goes on bearing fruit, and the parents sell the fruit and send the money to the Mission Board. May that tree be the means of building up a church in that locality! As we pass on we find $200.00 from a sister who declines to give her name, and further on is another one, equally modest, who gives $1,000.00. Perhaps we would like to know the names of these two liberal saints. We need not concern ourselves about that, but we may and should admire their modesty and liberality, and those who are sufficiently blessed will do well to imitate them for the cause of Christ.

UNFERMENTED WINE.

Sometime ago you gave a receipt in the MESSENGER for making unfermented Wine for Communion purposes. Some members are still opposed to the use of unfermented wine. Will you not give us Scriptural reasons for using the unfermented Wine? Some say that the unfermented juice of the grape is not Wine, and refer to where the Savior turned water into wine, and also to the case of Paul advising Timothy to use a little wine for the stomach's sake.

JOHN E. METZGER.

WINE may be either fermented or unfermented. The term wine may be applied to the fresh juice as it is pressed from the grapes. For proof of this we refer to Josephus, the great Jewish historian, who lived in the times of the apostles, and wrote his works while some of them were yet living, and therefore knew the current meaning of the word in question. In Book 2, Chapter 5, and Section 2, speaking of a dream that Joseph was called on to interpret, he says:

"He therefore said, That in his sleep he saw three clusters of grapes hanging upon three branches of a vine, large already and ripe for gathering, and that he squeezed them into a cup, which the king held in his hand; and when he had strained the wine, he gave it to the king to drink, and that he received it from him with a pleasant countenance. This, he said, was what he saw; and he desired Joseph, that if he had any portion of understanding in such matters, he would tell him what this vision foretold: who bid him be of good cheer, and expect to be loosed from his bonds in three days' time, because the king desired his service, and was about to restore him to it again; for he let him know that God bestows the fruit of the vine upon men for good; which wine is poured out to him, and is the pledge of fidelity and mutual confidence among men; and puts an end to their quarrels, takes away passion and grief out of the minds of them that use it, and makes them cheerful. Thou sayest that thou didst squeeze this wine from three clusters of grapes with thine hands, and that the king received it."

It will be noticed that in this quotation the fresh juice of the grape is repeatedly called wine. This ought to settle the right to call the unfermented juice wine. We will, however, further strengthen what Josephus says, by twenty-six proofs, which we find conveniently arranged in "The Old Faith Restated," pages 236, 237, where the definition of wine is given by a number of reliable authorities. We quote the following:

"1. Webster: 'Wine, the expressed juice of grapes.'

"2. Worcester: 'Must, the sweet or unfermented juice of the grape: new wine.'

"3. Liddell and Scott: 'Gleukos, sweet, new wine.'

"4. Groves: 'The fresh juice of the grape, must, new wine, and mead.'

"5. Parkhurst: 'Sweet wine, which distills of its own accord from the grapes.'

"6. Robinson: 'Must, grape juice unfermented.'

"7. Andrew: 'Mustum, new, or unfermented wine.'

"8. Leverett: 'Must, new wine.'

"9. Anthon: 'Young, new, fresh; must, new wine.'

"10. Dr. Ure: 'Juice newly expressed, and before it has begun to ferment is called must, and in common language, new wine.'

"11. Ainsworth: 'New wine, close shut up, and not allowed to work.'

"12. Littleton gives the same that Ainsworth does.

"13. Smith's Bible Dictionary, A. M. Ed.: 'It may be at once conceded that the Hebrew terms, translated wine, refer, occasionally, to an unfermented liquor.'

"14. Stuart: 'Facts show that the ancients not only preserved wine unfermented, but regarded it as of higher flavor and finer quality than fermented wine.'

"15. Barnes' Note on John 2: 10: 'That was the pure juice of the grape.'

"16. Kitto: 'Wine, osis, denotes the expressed juice of the grape, or other fruit.'

"17. Thayer: 'The numerous authorities already cited to show that unfermented grape juice is wine, also prove that unfermented wine existed.'

"18. Dr. E. Nott, late President of Union College: 'That unintoxicating wines existed from remote antiquity, and were held in high estimation by the wise and good, there can be no reasonable doubt. The evidence is unequivocal and plenary.'

"19. Boy. Dic. Lond.: 'Wine pressed from the grape but not fermented.'

"20. Dr. Hilbert: (Dic. Ger. Lond.): 'Wine pressed from the grape, but not fermented: new wine.'

"21. Littre: (Dic. de la language Francais): 'New wine not fermented.'

"22. Descherell: 'Wine which has just been made, and which has not yet fermented.'

"23. Scheller: (Lexicon 1832): 'Wine just pressed out and not strained.'

"24. Flugel: (Dic. Ger. and Eng.): 'Unfermented wine.'

"25. Freund: (Leipsic 1878): "New or unfermented wine.'

"26. Dr. Adam Clark: (Com. vol. I., page 239, Lond. Ed., 1836, Note on Gen. 40: 11): 'From this we find that wine anciently was the mere expressed juice of the grape without fermentation.'"

After reading this array of testimony, it seems to us that no one has an excuse for saying that the unfermented juice of the grape may not very properly be called wine.

The wine made from water at the wedding in Cana of Galilee was most assuredly unfermented, for it was fresh, and had no time to ferment, any more than the juice just pressed from the grapes. It was made of water, and required the same power to make it that is required to make the juice found in the ripe grapes. Nature takes up water, and by means of the vine and fruit, transforms it into juice. The Savior did the same thing with the water at the wedding.

Furthermore, there is no reason for even presuming that the wine was intoxicating, for the Savior being a good man, would not have made the harmful drink when he could make the harmless just as easily. No good man, it would seem to us, would make an intoxicating drink when there was no occasion for it.

True, Paul did advise Timothy to take a little wine for his stomach's sake, and his oft infirmities. But this was medical advice and has nothing whatever to do with the question concerning the class of wine to be used on Communion occasions.

But, coming more directly to the question, there is not one word in the New Testament about using wine at the Communion table. The Savior calls it the "fruit of the vine," and the unfermented juice of the grape is certainly the fruit of the vine. The process of fermentation, which grape juice undergoes, frees it from the fruit element, and leaves remaining the alcoholic condition. If, therefore, the real fruit of the vine is desired, it must be had in the juice before fermentation takes place.

As we use unleavened bread to represent the broken body of Christ, consistency would teach us to also use unfermented wine to represent the shed blood.

Some of the wine purchased at drug-stores is said to be devoid of the fruit of the vine, as it is made of drugs, and certainly cannot fitly represent the shed blood of the Master. And since the unfermented wine is so easily made and kept, there is every reason for encouraging its use at all of our Communion services. In fact there is no reason whatever why it should not be used. We are glad to know that many congregations are adopting it.

J. H. M.

worldly kingdom with different ranks and official grades,—a kingdom with honors and upper seats. It was this that led them into that warm discussion about "who should be the greatest."

We do not think it strange that modern politicians should strive for positions, but to find those Galilean fishermen indulging in dreams of chief positions and first honors of the kingdom may be contrary to our expectations. And yet, why should not they aspire to "uppermost seats" as well as anybody else, since "to do the best we can in everything is our duty"? The mistake lay in their incorrect ideas of entering the kingdom, and their ignorance of the law leading to promotions. In Christ's kingdom it is not the *spirit of the law* that is to be followed, but the *spirit itself* as the law. The self-seeking spirit leads to promotions not in Christ's, but in Satan's kingdom. It is the spirit of hell, not of heaven. "To be first or nothing," leads downward, not upward. How different from the strong desire to improve, to attain to greater usefulness, to develop a greater degree of holiness and love. The self-seeking desire is entirely contrary to the spirit which is the law in Christ's kingdom, and hence "If any man desire to be first, the same shall be last of all." The law in the new kingdom is the spirit of love, of humility, of self-denial, of helpfulness to others, and all this for Jesus' sake, hence, the more one has of the desire to be first, the less he has of the law that leads to right-hand seats in the kingdom of heaven. The very desire to be first, therefore, necessarily makes him "last of all;" and he is the greatest who does the most for his fellow-men and claims the least for self. Nothing short of disinterested love can be truly great.

Allow me, my dear fellow-workers, to admonish you all to study to comprehend this law of the kingdom more fully. Your success in removing "the mote" at home that you may be qualified to "cast out the beam" away from home will be proportionate to your success in making this law of *disinterested* love the controlling spirit of your being, and will measure your power to "teach transgressors the way," and so "sinners be converted into the Lord."

My visit with the brethren at New Berlin, Ohio, (West Nimishillen church) has been an enjoyable one. This is the former home of two of our earnest workers in the college,—brethren E. S. and S. S. Young. Their parents are still living here and possess both the ability and will to make the wayfaring-one comfortable and happy.

J. G. BOYER.

April 11.

From Dodsonville, Jackson Co., Alabama.

WE are glad to announce the result of our series of meetings which closed March 26. Bro. J. G. Lewis, of Medina, Washington Co., Va., came to our place March 18, and commenced preaching on the 19th. He preached, in all, thirteen sermons. The result was four additions to the church by baptism. Bro. Lewis shunned not to declare the whole counsel of God.

March 26 a large crowd assembled to witness something never seen here, — tuine immersion. One man said he thought that was the right way to baptize. Others thought one action would do. There was little exception taken to Bro. Lewis' preaching. The preaching was done at three different points and calls were made for him to preach at three other places, but he could not fill the calls on account of his time being up. Who will be the next to come? If any of our ministers, passing on the Memphis & Charleston railroad, will send an appointment, we will meet them at Lime Rock eight miles north of where we live.

Lime Rock is ten or twelve miles west of Scottsborough, and about thirty miles east of Huntsville.   O. K. PARSONS.

Treasurer's Report.

REPORT of the Boys and Girls' Bible School, 1315 Light Street, Baltimore, Md., for the quarter ending March 31, 1892:

RECEIPTS.

Balance from last report,	$23 92
B. Beckone, Good's Mills, Va.,	2 00
Amy Hoffman, Mt. Zion, Va.,	1 00
A sister, Leipsic, Ohio,	1 25
J. F. Oller, Waynesborough, Pa.,	8 00
J. Y. Keeny, Elko, Md.,	1 00
Milledgeville, Sunday-school, Ill., per W. M. Fike,	10 67
Joseph Oller, Waynesborough, Pa.,	5 00
Lordsburg, Cal., Sunday-school, per Hettie A. Gibbol,	2 00
Balinda Riley, Tropico, Cal.,	3 00
A brother and sister, Canada,	15 00
A sister, New Paris, Pa.,	4 00
Effie Kuns,	25
Total receipts,	$77 09

EXPENSES.

Rent for quarter,	$21 00
Heating apparatus and pipe,	1 70
Doctor and medicine,	13 60
Shoes,	1 85
Stamps (for announcing our meetings),	1 25
Stationery, cards, etc., for children,	1 05
Clothes,	13 00
Helping a brother,	2 00
Car fare, taking scholars to meeting,	67
Oil,	25
Postage,	25
Stationery,	77
Charity,	2 00
Total expenses,	$58 89
Balance,	$18 20

CLAUDE SANSBURY, Treas.

Ministerial Meeting.

THE meeting was held at the Valley house of the Botetourt congregation, April 1 and 2. It was opened by singing hymn No. 273. Some appropriate remarks were offered by B. C. Moomaw, as to the object of the meeting and the need of divine aid in the work. He then called to prayer and invoked God for the aid of the Holy Spirit to direct us in our work of training.

The organization was then effected by the election of a Moderator and a Clerk.

Bro. C. E. Arnold, one of the professors of the Botetourt Normal, presided during the deliberations, we think to the satisfaction of all. A committee of five brethren was appointed to draft rules to govern the meeting. We used only a few, simple rules, to systematize the work and render fairness to all who chose to engage in the discussions.

At the request of the Moderator, Bro. B, F, Moomaw stated more fully the purpose of the program. (See GOSPEL MESSENGER No. 11, March 15, for a list of the subjects.)

"How shall we best Care for the Young Members of the Church," was dropped from the list, as none of the brethren assigned were present. The other seven subjects consumed the two days of four sessions, opening at 10 A. M. and closing at 4 P. M.

As the District Meeting is to be held in two weeks in an adjoining congregation, and some said they would not be able to attend both, the District was not so well represented.

This is the first experience of this kind of work for the church, and we hope to be able to make improvement in the future.

We are impressed with the importance of such ministerial training. Generals hold their councils of war to decide on the plan of attack and the part each one is expected to act. Teachers hold their institutes, attend their County and State Normals. Sunday-school teachers hold conventions and receive special instructions. Why should not ministers of the Gospel meet together to discuss the best means of saving souls, advancing the interests of the church of Christ and promoting the holy cause of God. Paul took Timothy and Titus, and kept them for a time under his own supervision. Afterwards he wrote some epistles for their special comfort. Methinks their greatest joy was to sit at the feet of the aged apostle to learn lessons suggested by his ripe age, mature judgment, and rich and varied experience. So should we gather all we can from the experience of our elder brethren in the ministry,—those whose care and burdens are telling on them and showing the frost of years.

By a pleasant interchanging of views with each other, the aged ones may partake of the warmth and buoyancy of the younger ministers, and thus bring about an equilibrium that may result in good to all. The attendance was large, though the weather was threatening.   T. C. DENTON.

From Belleville, Kansas.

THE church met in quarterly council Saturday April 9. Considerable business came before the meeting, but everything went off pleasantly. Bro. C. S. Holsinger, of Lacon, Ill., has moved among us, and the church here has chosen him as our elder, and we are all very much pleased with the thought of having him and his companion with us, to help us in the good cause. We have decided to hold our love-feast Saturday, June 11. We organised our Sunday-school by electing Daniel Holsinger, Superintendent. April 3, one dear young man was made willing to go down into the watery grave to rise and walk in newness of life. He is a very promising young brother, and we pray that his life may be the means of turning some one else from darkness to the marvelous light.

Last Sunday Bro. Wm. Lugenbeel, from Hubbel, Nebr., preached a very interesting discourse for us. At night Bro. Holsinger gave us a short discourse.

This church has had some discouragements for the past two years, but now we feel that the dark cloud is moving off, and we look forward to the dawning of a brighter day. May God help us all to be up and doing, while we have time to work, is my prayer.   LIZZIE HILARY

April 11.

Death of Eld. Hiram Peterson.

BRO. Hiram Peterson of the church at Brummett's Creek, Mitchell Co., N. C., passed away March 26, 1892. He lived to the age of eighty-one years, one month and eight days.

He was married in 1836 to Nancy Mashburn. His bereaved wife is still living. She belongs to the Brethren's church.

Bro. Hiram joined the church of the Brethren the same year in which he was married, and was always an orderly member, endeavoring to do exactly as the Bible taught him. He served as a deacon of the church for many years and always faithfully discharged his duty. Upon his election to the ministry, he studied the Bible carefully, to show himself a workman that needed not to be ashamed, and it was said by many that few had

worldly kingdom with different ranks and official grades,—a kingdom with honors and upper seats. It was this that led them into that warm discussion about "who should be the greatest."

We do not think it strange that modern politicians should strive for positions, but to find those Galilean fishermen indulging in dreams of chief positions and first honors of the kingdom may be contrary to our expectations. And yet, why should not they aspire to "uppermost seats" as well as anybody else, since "to do the best we can in everything is our duty"? The mistake lay in their incorrect ideas of entering the kingdom, and their ignorance of the law leading to promotions. In Christ's kingdom it is not the *spirit of the law* that is to be followed, but the *spirit itself* as the law. The self-seeking spirit leads to promotions not in Christ's, but in Satan's kingdom. It is the spirit of hell, not of heaven. "To be first or nothing," leads downward, not upward. How different from the strong desire to improve, to attain to greater usefulness, to develop a greater degree of holiness and love. The self-seeking desire is entirely contrary to the spirit which is the law in Christ's kingdom, and hence "If any man desire to be first, the same shall be last of all." The law in the new kingdom is the spirit of love, of humility, of self-denial, of helpfulness to others, and all this for Jesus' sake, hence, the more one has of the desire to be first, the less he has of the law that leads to right-hand seats in the kingdom of heaven. The very desire to be first, therefore, necessarily makes him "last of all;" and he is the greatest who does the most for his fellow-men and claims the least for self. Nothing short of disinterested love can be truly great.

Allow me, my dear fellow-workers, to admonish you all to study to comprehend this law of the kingdom more fully. Your success in removing "the mote" at home that you may be qualified to "cast out the beam" away from home will be proportionate to your success in making this law of *disinterested* love the controlling spirit of your being, and will measure your power to "teach transgressors the way," and so "sinners be converted into the Lord."

My visit with the brethren at New Berlin, Ohio, (West Nimishillen church) has been an enjoyable one. This is the former home of two of our earnest workers in the college,—brethren E. S. and S. S. Young. Their parents are still living here and possess both the ability and will to make the wayfaring one comfortable and happy.

J. G. ROYER.

April 11.

From Dodsonville, Jackson Co, Alabama.

WE are glad to announce the result of our series of meetings which closed March 26. Bro. J. G. Lewis, of Medina, Washington Co., Va., came to our place March 18, and commenced preaching on the 19th. He preached, in all, thirteen sermons. The result was four additions to the church by baptism. Bro. Lewis shunned not to declare the whole counsel of God.

March 26 a large crowd assembled to witness something never seen here, — taine immersion. One man said he thought that was the right way to baptize. Others thought one action would do. There was little exception taken to Bro. Lewis' preaching. The preaching was done at three different points and calls were made for him to preach at three other places, but he could not fill the calls on account of his time being up. Who will be the next to come? If any of our ministers, passing on the Memphis & Charleston railroad, will send an appointment, we will meet them at Lime Rock eight miles north of where we live.

Lime Rock is ten or twelve miles west of Scottsborough, and about thirty miles east of Huntsville.

O. K. PARSONS.

Treasurer's Report.

REPORT of the Boys' and Girls' Bible School, 1815 Light Street, Baltimore, Md., for the quarter ending March 31, 1892:

RECEIPTS.

Balance from last report,	$28 92
B. Beckons, Good's Mills, Va.,	2 00
Amy Hoffman, Mt. Zion, Va.,	1 00
A sister, Leipsic, Ohio,	1 25
J. F. Oller, Waynesborough, Pa.,	8 00
J. Y. Keeny, Elko, Md.,	1 00
Milledgeville, Sunday-school, Ill., per W. M. Fike,	10 67
Joseph Oller, Waynesborough, Pa.,	5 00
Lordsburg, Cal., Sunday-school, per Hettie A. Gibbel,	2 00
Belinda Riley, Tropico, Cal.,	3 00
A brother and sister, Canada,	15 00
A sister, New Paris, Pa.,	4 00
Effie Kuns,	25

Total receipts,	$77 09

EXPENSES.

Rent for quarter,	$21 00
Heating apparatus and pipe,	1 70
Doctor and medicine,	13 60
Shoes,	1 35
Stamps (for announcing our meetings),	1 25
Stationery, cards, etc, for children,	1 05
Clothes,	18 00
Helping a brother,	2 00
Car fare, taking scholars to meeting,	67
Oil,	25
Postage,	25
Stationery,	77
Charity,	2 00

Total expenses,	$58 89
Balance,	$18 20

CLAUDE SANSBURY, Treas.

Ministerial Meeting.

THE meeting was held at the Valley house of the Botetourt congregation, April 1 and 2. It was opened by singing hymn No. 273. Some appropriate remarks were offered by B. C. Moomaw, as to the object of the meeting and the need of divine aid in the work. He then called to prayer and invoked God for the aid of the Holy Spirit to direct us in our work of training.

The organization was then effected by the election of a Moderator and a Clerk.

Bro. C. E. Arnold, one of the professors of the Botetourt Normal, presided during the deliberations, we think to the satisfaction of all. A committee of five brethren was appointed to draft rules to govern the meeting. We need only a few, simple rules, to systematize the work and render fairness to all who chose to engage in the discussions.

At the request of the Moderator, Bro. B. F. Moomaw stated more fully the purpose of the program. (See GOSPEL MESSENGER No. 11, March 15, for a list of the subjects.)

"How shall we best Care for the Young Members of the Church," was dropped from the list, as none of the brethren assigned were present. The other seven subjects consumed the two days of four sessions, opening at 10 A. M. and closing at 4 P. M.

As the District Meeting is to be held in two weeks in an adjoining congregation, and some said they would not be able to attend both, the District was not so well represented.

This is the first experience of this kind of work for the church, and we hope to be able to make improvement in the future.

We are impressed with the importance of such ministerial training. Generals hold their councils of war to decide on the plan of attack and the part each one is expected to act. Teachers hold their institutes, attend their County and State Normals. Sunday-school teachers hold conventions and receive special instructions. Why should not ministers of the Gospel meet together to discuss the best means of saving souls, advancing the interests of the church of Christ and promoting the holy cause of God. Paul took Timothy and Titus, and kept them for a time under his own supervision. Afterwards he wrote some epistles for their special comfort. Methinks their greatest joy was to sit at the feet of the aged apostle to learn lessons suggested by his ripe age, mature judgment, and rich and varied experience.

So should we gather all we can from the experience of our elder brethren in the ministry,—those who are passing down the western slope of time, whose care and burdens are telling on them and showing the frost of years.

By a pleasant interchanging of views with each other, the aged ones may partake of the warmth and buoyancy of the younger ministers, and thus bring about an equilibrium that may result in good to all. The attendance was large, though the weather was threatening. T. C. DENTON.

From Belleville, Kansas.

THE church met in quarterly council Saturday April 9. Considerable business came before the meeting, but everything went off pleasantly. Bro. C. S. Holsinger, of Lacon, Ill., has moved among us, and the church here has chosen him as our elder, and we are all very much pleased with the thought of having him and his companion with us, to help us in the good cause. We have decided to hold our love-feast Saturday, June 11. We organized our Sunday-school by electing Daniel Holsinger, Superintendent. April 3, one dear young man was made willing to go down into the watery grave to rise and walk in newness of life. He is a very promising young brother, and we pray that his life may be the means of turning some one else from darkness to the marvelous light.

Last Sunday Bro. Wm. Lugenbeel, from Hubbel, Nebr., preached a very interesting discourse for us. At night Bro. Holsinger gave us a short discourse.

This church has had some discouragements for the past two years, but now we feel that the dark cloud is moving off, and we look forward to the dawning of a brighter day. May God help us all to be up and doing, while we have time to work, is my prayer. LIZZIE HILARY.

April 11.

Death of Eld. Hiram Peterson.

BRO. Hiram Peterson of the church at Brummett's Creek, Mitchell Co., N. C., passed away March 28, 1892. He lived to the age of eighty-one years, one month and eight days.

He was married in 1836 to Nancy Mashburn. His bereaved wife is still living. She belongs to the Brethren's church.

Bro. Hiram joined the church of the Brethren the same year in which he was married, and was always an orderly member, endeavoring to do exactly as the Bible taught him. He served as a deacon of the church for many years and always faithfully discharged his duty. Upon his election to the ministry, he studied the Bible carefully, to show himself a workman that needed not to be ashamed, and it was said by many that few had

in the school-houses. The dimensions of our church are 30 by 40 feet. It is a very plain building. We re-organized our Sunday-school March 27, the writer being elected as Superintendent. We have a very interesting school. The officers and teachers are trying to do their duty, and those that are not officers or teachers, manifest much interest. W. J. Long.

April 10.

From Sterling, Logan Co., Colo.

Our elder, Bro. John S. Snowberger, living near Holyoke, Phillips Co., Colo., came to us on Saturday, March 19, and held meetings on Sunday at 11 o'clock and also on Sunday night. On Monday the few members, living here in this part of the Good Hope church, assembled in council at the house of Bro. Joel H. Kinzie, and transacted some business pertaining to the welfare of the church, and the edification and spiritual growth of the members. We empowered Bro. Snowberger to represent us at District Meeting; also completed arrangements for two meetings a month near Sterling, one about five miles northeast of Sterling, the other six miles west, at Atwood, near where Bro. Hall lives. We were much encouraged by the good counsel our dear old brother gave us.

We cordially invite all loyal members of the church to come here and look at this country before locating elsewhere. We think we have good society, good schools, good land, good water, and a good country. Generally, water privileges for irrigating purposes, go with the land.

W. M. Wise.

April 13.

From Chicago, Ill.

The Chicago church met in quarterly council Monday, April 11. Nearly all the members, living in the city, were present, as well as some few from a distance. The meeting passed off pleasantly, under the supervision of Bro. W. R. Miller, the local minister.

A part of the business transacted was the election of delegates to District Meeting and the re-organization of the Sunday-school with Bro. J. J. Shively as Superintendent.

It was decided to represent the church at Annual Meeting by letter. Bro. Spare was chosen as delegate to District Meeting, with Bro. Andrew Emmert as alternate.

A report was read, showing a sum of $14.92 collected for the General Mission Fund. By this it may be seen that the little church planted here, in this great city, is bringing forth fruits to the honor and glory of God. O. F. Cripe.

Chicago, Ill., April 13.

Notes from Our Correspondents.

"As cold water to a thirsty soul, so is good news from a far country."

Jacob's Creek, Pa.—We held our semi-annual council March 26. Eld. A. Summy was elected delegate to District Meeting. We agreed to ask for some brother to locate with us to teach singing. Any one wishing further information will please write to W. H. Myers, Mt. Pleasant, Pa.—*J. K. Eicher.*

Gilman, Ind.—March 26 occurred our quarterly council in the Gilman church. Much business came before the meeting, but all was disposed of satisfactorily. Bro. I. E. Branson is delegate to District Meeting. Our Sunday-school was organized March 27 with the writer as Superintendent. —*H. E. Millepaugh.*

Medalo, Iowa.—The Soldier River church, Iowa, held its regular meetings April 9 and 10. Bro. Julius was here and preached two excellent sermons. There was not a very large audience present, but the Blessed Savior has said that where there are "two or three gathered together in my name, there will I be in the midst of them."—*Hester A. Stevens, April 12.*

Jonathan Creek, Ohio.—Our Sunday-school was organized by electing Bro. Q. Leckrone as Superintendent. After preaching services, one intelligent young brother came forward for baptism, which was performed the same day. We have regular preaching now. A flourishing Sunday-school is in progress, and there is a bright prospect for the future. We feel to thank God and take courage, to go on with more diligence.—*Benjamin Leckrone, April 10.*

Pipe Creek, Md.—Our spring council occurred April 15. Everything passed off pleasantly. The morning not being very pleasant, many of the members, living at a distance, were not present. A very good interest in the council was manifested. The work of building a new church house at Mechanicstown, Frederick Co., Md., is moving on. The foundation is about in readiness for the frame work. We also decided to hold our spring love-feast June 4 and 5, at 1: 30 P. M., at Rocky Ridge, Frederick Co., Md.—*Samuel Weybright.*

Gardner, Kan.—To-day at our regular meeting, one more was added to the Father's children at Ottawa, Kans., making five that have been baptized there since last July. There are good prospects for more in the near future. This is one of the many places where a live minister should be located. Any such, wanting to either engage in farming, or in business in the city, could do well. For further information write John Eshelman, Ottawa, Kans. There are twenty-three members in and near the city.—*I. H. Crist, April 3.*

Plymouth, Ohio.—The members of the Richland church met in council, Saturday, April 9. All the business brought up before the meeting passed off pleasantly. The visiting brethren found all in love and union. We decided to hold our love-feast June 11 and 12, the Lord willing, at Bro. John Kendall's, six miles north of Mansfield. Bro. Peter Heller is to represent our church at District Meeting. We expect to re-organize our Sunday-school April 24.—*Mary M. Helfer, April 11.*

Ireton, Iowa.—March 20, I went to Ireton, and held three meetings in the United Presbyterian church. There was a good attendance and a good interest, and many requests to come back again. I stopped at Sheldon, Iowa, from Saturday till Monday. Owing to rain and bad roads, we only held one meeting. Here, also, is a fine field. Our beloved elder, Tobias Myers, is working here, and I hope the good Lord will bless the work. May he send more laborers into that field, and may the Lord bless the labors of all his children!—*W. C. Hipes, Greene, Iowa, April 15.*

Lordsburg, Cal.—I expect soon to take my leave of this genial clime to greet the loved ones at home, at Centre View, Mo., where I can be addressed after April 15. I will make a few visits to different parts of California, and again to the grand ocean; then get ready for the journey. There are many beautiful things in California, and things not so beautiful. With the many beautiful and almost ever-blooming roses, there are also many thorns. So in our life there are many things to enjoy, and things we do not enjoy. It brings joy to the mind to think of meeting loved ones again. If it brings joy for friends to meet on earth, what must it be to meet above!—*Amanda Wilmore, April 8.*

Jeffersonville, Ill.—Our quarterly council, in the Martin's Creek church, was held March 26. We had a fair attendance of members, and the business passed off pleasantly, in love and good feeling. Our little band is still growing. Seven members have moved in since March 1. Bro. Nevinger, of Fayette County, was with us over the second Sunday in April, while Bro. J. Harshbarger filled Bro. Nevinger's appointments in Fayette.—*John Monck.*

Rocklon, Iowa.—The Iowa River church met in quarterly council April 9. Our elder, Stephen Johnson, of Garrison, was with us. He had not met with us for a long time, and I think his presence was appreciated by all. The business before the church was treated in a kind and brotherly way. Bro. A. W. Hausatus was elected delegate to our next Annual Meeting; Bro. Fetter Hall, alternate. Bro. Frank Wheeler was forwarded to the second degree of the ministry. We have preaching twice on Sunday; Sunday-school the year round, and prayer-meeting every Thursday evening. We are trying to work together for the good of souls, and we pray that God's smile may rest upon us.—*Ellen M. Nicholson, April 14.*

Roanoke, Va.—A series of meetings was conducted in the Roanoke congregation during the latter part of December and middle of January; at the Peter's Creek church first, and at the Back Creek church last. The attendance was fairly good, though the weather, in the main, during the time, was quite inclement. No additions are reported as yet from the first meeting, though we feel encouraged. At the last meeting there were fourteen baptized, including two shortly before the meeting. We find an increased and growing interest. Some have been found in attendance who have rarely attended our meetings. The preaching was done by the home brethren, and we felt that God blessed the efforts!—*F. S. Miller.*

Maxwell, Iowa.—The church met in council March 5. Eld. S. M. Goughnour presided over the meeting. There was considerable business before the meeting, but all was disposed of in a Christian spirit, and, so far as we know, all in love and union. The church desires to hold a love-feast June 25 and 26. We expect to commence a series of meetings in the town of Maxwell, June 11, to continue until June 24, to be conducted by Bro. A. Hutchison. We see many calls in the Gospel Messenger for ministerial help. This church here needs two good workers. The cause is suffering here for the want of ministerial help. Who will come and help? This church is located in the Middle District of Iowa. The Mission Board would like to locate some good workers in different places, and if poor, would help them.—*Thos. H. Higbe.*

Lanier, Ohio.—Since last October, ten have been baptized in Washington C. H., Ohio, and others are fully persuaded, but held back by various influences. A love-feast is now fixed for May 14, and the city authorities have donated the use of the city hall for Saturday and Sunday. The members at Frankfort and Circleville are looked for, and all our white brethren and sisters who love all the races, are invited to come and aid us in the work at this new point. Half-fare rates can be had from Dayton, Ohio, with low rates at a good hotel in Washington over Sunday. Those who wish to go on to District Meeting, can get half-fare rates for ten or more, and over the shortest route from Dayton. At Dayton, go to Third St. Depot, and take train on C. H. & D. R. R., for Washington C. H., at 8: 30 A. M. or 4: 15 P. M., and for District Meeting, leave Washington at 12: 05 P. M., and reach Highland after 4 P. M., via Greenfield Junction.—*Landon West, April 16.*

in the school-houses. The dimensions of our church are 30 by 40 feet. It is a very plain building. We re-organized our Sunday-school March 27, the writer being elected as Superintendent. We have a very interesting school. The officers and teachers are trying to do their duty, and those that are not officers or teachers, manifest much interest. W. J. LONG.

April 10.

From Sterling, Logan Co., Colo.

OUR elder, Bro. John S. Snowberger, living near Holyoke, Phillips Co., Colo., came to us on Saturday, March 19, and held meetings on Sunday at 11 o'clock and also on Sunday night. On Monday the few members, living here in this part of the Good Hope church, assembled in council at the house of Bro. Joel H. Kinzie, and transacted some business pertaining to the welfare of the church, and the edification and spiritual growth of the members. We empowered Bro. Snowberger to represent us at District Meeting; also completed arrangements for two meetings a month near Sterling, one about five miles northeast of Sterling, the other six miles west, at Atwood, near where Bro. Hall lives. We were much encouraged by the good counsel our dear old brother gave us.

We cordially invite all loyal members of the church to come here and look at this country before locating elsewhere. We think we have good society, good schools, good land, good water, and a good country. Generally, water privileges for irrigating purposes, go with the land.

W. M. WISE.

April 13.

From Chicago, Ill.

THE Chicago church met in quarterly council Monday, April 11. Nearly all the members, living in the city, were present, as well as some few from a distance. The meeting passed off pleasantly, under the supervision of Bro. W. R. Miller, the local minister.

A part of the business transacted was the election of delegates to District Meeting and the reorganization of the Sunday-school with Bro. J. J. Shively as Superintendent.

It was decided to represent the church at Annual Meeting by letter. Bro. Spare was chosen as delegate to District Meeting, with Bro. Andrew Emmert as alternate.

A report was read, showing a sum of $14.92 collected for the General Mission Fund. By this it may be seen that the little church planted here, in this great city, is bringing forth fruits to the honor and glory of God. O. F. CRIPE.

Chicago, Ill., April 13.

Notes from Our Correspondents.

" As cold water to a thirsty soul, so is good news from a far country."

Jacob's Creek, Pa.—We held our semi-annual council March 26. Eld. A. Summy was elected delegate to District Meeting. We agreed to ask for some brother to locate with us to teach singing. Any one wishing further information will please write to W. H. Myers, Mt. Pleasant, Pa.—*J. K. Eicher.*

Gilman, Ind.—March 26 occurred our quarterly council in the Gilman church. Much business came before the meeting, but all was disposed of satisfactorily. Bro. I. E. Branson is delegate to District Meeting. Our Sunday-school was organized March 27 with the writer as Superintendent. —*H. E. Millepaugh.*

Modale, Iowa.—The Soldier River church. Iowa, held its regular meetings April 9 and 10. Bro. Julius was here and preached two excellent sermons. There was not a very large audience present, but the Blessed Savior has said that where there are "two or three gathered together in my name, there will I be in the midst of them."—*Hester A. Stevens, April 12.*

Jonathan Creek, Ohio.—Our Sunday-school was organized by electing Bro. Q. Leckrone as Superintendent. After preaching services, one intelligent young brother came forward for baptism, which was performed the same day. We have regular preaching now. A flourishing Sunday-school is in progress, and there is a bright prospect for the future. We feel to thank God and take courage, to go on with more diligence.—*Benjamin Leckrone, April 10.*

Pipe Creek, Md.—Our spring council occurred April 15. Everything passed off pleasantly. The morning not being very pleasant, many of the members, living at a distance, were not present. A very good interest in the council was manifested. The work of building a new church house at Mechanicstown, Frederick Co., Md., is moving on. The foundation is about in readiness for the frame work. We also decided to hold our spring lovefeast June 4 and 5, at 1: 30 P. M., at Rocky Ridge, Frederick Co., Md.—*Samuel Weybright.*

Gardner, Kans.—To-day at our regular meeting, one more was added to the Father's children at Ottawa, Kans., making five that have been baptized there since last July. There are good prospects for more in the near future. This is one of the many places where a live minister should be located. Any such, wanting to either engage in farming, or in business in the city, could do well. For further information write John Eshelman, Ottawa, Kans. There are twenty-three members in and near the city.—*I. H. Crist, April 3.*

Plymouth, Ohio.—The members of the Richland church met in council, Saturday, April 9. All the business brought up before the meeting passed off pleasantly. The visiting brethren found all in love and union. We decided to hold our lovefeast June 11 and 12, the Lord willing, at Bro. John Kendall's, six miles north of Mansfield. Bro. Peter Helfer is to represent our church at District Meeting. We expect to re-organize our Sunday-school April 24.—*Mary M. Helfer, April 11.*

Ireton, Iowa.—March 20, I went to Ireton, and held three meetings in the United Presbyterian church. There was a good attendance and a good interest, and many requests to come back again. I stopped at Sheldon, Iowa, from Saturday till Monday. Owing to rain and bad roads, we only held one meeting. Here, also, is a fine field. Our beloved elder, Tobias Myers, is working here, and I hope the good Lord will bless the work. May he send more laborers into that field, and may the Lord bless the labors of all his children!—*W. C. Hipes, Greene, Iowa, April 15.*

Lordsburg, Cal.—I expect soon to take my leave of this genial clime to greet the loved ones at home, at Centre View, Mo., where I can be addressed after April 15. I will make a few visits to different parts of California, and again to the grand ocean; then get ready for the journey. There are many beautiful things in California, and things not so beautiful. With the many beautiful and almost ever-blooming roses, there are also many thorns. So in our life there are many things to enjoy, and things we do not enjoy. It brings joy to the mind to think of meeting loved ones again. If it brings joy for friends to meet on earth, what must it be to meet above!—*Amanda Wilmore, April 8.*

Jeffersonville, Ill.—Our quarterly council, in the Martin's Creek church, was held March 26. We had a fair attendance of members, and the business passed off pleasantly, in love and good feeling. Our little band is still growing. Seven members have moved in since March 1. Bro. Nevinger, of Fayette County, was with us over the second Sunday in April, while Bro. J. Harshbarger filled Bro. Nevinger's appointments in Fayette.—*John Monok.*

Bockton, Iowa.—The Iowa River church met in quarterly council April 9. Our elder, Stephen Johnson, of Garrison, was with us. He had not met with us for a long time, and I think his presence was appreciated by all. The business before the church was treated in a kind and brotherly way. Bro. A. W. Hausafus was elected delegate to our next Annual Meeting; Bro. Fetter, Hall, alternate. Bro. Frank Wheeler was forwarded to the second degree of the ministry. We have preaching twice on Sunday; Sunday-school the year round, and prayer-meeting every Thursday evening. We are trying to work together for the good of souls, and we pray that God's smile may rest upon us.—*Ellen M. Nicholson, April 14.*

Roanoke, Va.—A series of meetings was conducted in the Roanoke congregation during the latter part of December and middle of January; at the Peter's Creek church first, and at the Beck Creek church last. The attendance was fairly good, though the weather, in the main, during the time, was quite inclement. No additions are reported as yet from the first meeting, though we feel encouraged. At the last meeting there were fourteen baptized, including two shortly before the meeting. We find an increased and growing interest. Some have been found in attendance who have rarely attended our meetings. The preaching was done by the home brethren, and we felt that God blessed the efforts.—*P. S. Miller.*

Maxwell, Iowa.—The church met in council March 5. Eld. S. M. Goughnour presided over the meeting. There was considerable business before the meeting, but all was disposed of in a Christian spirit, and, so far as we know, all in love and union. The church desires to hold a love-feast June 25 and 26. We expect to commence a series of meetings in the town of Maxwell, June 11, to continue until June 24, to be conducted by Bro. A. Hutchison. We see many calls in the GOSPEL MESSENGER for ministerial help. The church here needs two good workers. The cause is suffering here for the want of ministerial help. Who will come and help? This church is located in the Middle District of Iowa. The Mission Board would like to locate some good workers in different places, and if poor, would help them.—*Thos. H. Higbs.*

Lanier, Ohio.—Since last October, ten have been baptized in Washington C. H., Ohio, and others are fully persuaded, but held back by various influences. A love-feast is now fixed for May 14, and the city authorities have donated the use of the city hall for Saturday and Sunday. The members at Frankfort and Circleville are looked for, and all our white brethren and sisters who love all the races, are invited to come and aid us in the work at this new point. Half-fare rates can be had from Dayton, Ohio, with low rates at a good hotel in Washington over Sunday. Those who wish to go on to District Meeting, can get halffare rates for ten or more, and over the shortest route from Dayton. At Dayton, go to Third St. Depot, and take train on C. H. & D. R. R., for Washington C. H., at 9: 30 A. M. or 4: 15 P. M., and for District Meeting, leave Washington at 12: 05 P. M., and reach Highland after 4 P. M., via Greenfield Junction.—*Landon West, April 16.*

THE GOSPEL MESSENGER.

"Set for the Defense of the Gospel."

| Vol. 30, Old Series. | Mt. Morris, Ill., and Huntingdon, Pa., May 3 1892 | No. 18. |

The Gospel Messenger.

H. B. BRUMBAUGH, Editor,

And Business Manager of the Eastern House, Box 50,
Huntingdon, Pa.

Table of Contents.

A COUNTRY WALK.

HAVING been requested to visit a sick lady down along the Juniata, several miles below town, we called upon Bro. C. Myers to go with us, and as he was not then engaged, he readily assented to walk with us. The morning was bright and pleasant, and add to this the things of interest by the way, we could not well help enjoying the occasion. Being confined closely to our desk, study and regular home duties, a walk of this kind, though only a short one, is always fraught with interest and pleasure.

While the study and the closet are welcome retreats for communing with the Father, yet where do we seem to get so doubly in relation to him as out in the open space, roofed by the blue sky, lighted by God's own lamp, and decorated by rivers, hills, mountains and forests. Then, to breathe in the pure morning air, as it comes fresh and sweet from the mountain heights beyond, is a treat, well worth appreciating.

When we reached the house, we found the lady quite ill, yet making preparations to go to Pittsburg for treatment on to-morrow morning. Her trouble is serious, and her father has formed the acquaintance of a physician who claimed powers for healing that are said to be almost miraculous.

The process of diagnosing cases, as described to us, is as follows: From the head of the patient must be clipped a lock of hair. This must not be touched by the hand, but cut off and left drop into a pure white paper. In this it is folded, and taken or sent to this physician, who, on examining it, makes his diagnosis of the disease and gives the treatment. From the sight and feel of the hair, he not only determines the character of the disease, but can also tell the age, sex, etc., of the patient. Is not this wonderful? It surely is wonderful, even bordering on the miraculous. The conclusion is thusly: A man who can know all this by simply seeing the hair of the person, does he not understand the nature of the disease? And if he fully—so fully, understands the disease, can he not cure it? This looks very reasonable, and why not believe?

Well, we hope it is all right, and that no disappointment may follow. Faith, in some cases, is better than medicine, and when this is so, we have no objections to offer.

We tried to introduce to the lady and family, the Great Physician who can heal both body and soul. The eighth chapter of Romans was read, followed with a season of prayer which seemed to be much appreciated by those present. Had we the time, these pastoral visits would be much enjoyed by us, as it affords us great pleasure to minister in holy things to those who are hungry and anxious to receive messages of truth and love from the Master. We have often been made to feel that we have too many business engagements to allow us to properly attend to the pastoral work that should be done. Others have expressed this same feeling, and though there are a number of ministers here, the work is not done as it should be. We are often impressed with this feeling, but just how to remedy the matter is not so plain, yet it should be done.

Our morning visit was a very pleasant one, and on our return we felt much refreshed for the work that we are now doing. As we thus come in contact with the home life of people, we are made conscious of the work that might be done for the Master and for souls, could we turn all of our energies in that direction. It brings the more forcibly to our mind the saying of the apostle Paul, "This one thing I do." After all, concentration to one purpose or thing is the great secret of success. We have a large number of men called to the ministry, but we have very few pastors. And yet, though we say this, we feel that our ministry is worthy of great praise, because hundreds of them do much more church work than the membership has a right to ask of them. It is a kind of gratuitous labor, thrown in by the laity, that the other part of the membership does not do.

THE WEEKLY PRAYER-MEETING.

THE Wednesday evening prayer-meeting is the middle of the week halting place to take in sup-

plies. And we are often made to feel that, without them, many of us would fall short before the Sabbath comes. Of course, we have our closets and family altars which, to the weary souls, are places and times of precious sweetness, but as a church, we need a place and time for general supplies where we can weigh and equalize each other's burdens, and thus make them easier and lighter for all. We have just returned from one of these meetings, and the peace of our own soul says that it was good to be there. The subject was, "Be careful for nothing," one of Paul's sweet admonitions, which, if taken from its legitimate relations would be meaningless; but when we consider that he was addressing Christian believers in the sense of children of the Heavenly Father, how sweet the admonition! The thought takes us back to the home-life when we were a part of the family, presided over and cared for by father and mother. We were careful or over anxious for nothing because all of our wants were supplied. It means children looking to, and trusting in, devoted parents. Though we had our duties and labors to perform, our minds wore not harassed with the cares and hardships of life as they are when we have no one to whom we can look when our heaviest needs press in upon us.

This is the thought that Paul wished to present to his Philippian brethren. He tells them that they are now the children of a Heavenly Father, and that all their wants will be supplied. That they should go forward, lovingly performing their duties, as they come to them, assured that the Lord will provide. It is simply a duplication of "Seek ye first the kingdom of God and all these things will be added." The meeting was a pleasant one and some seeds were dropped which, we hope, will grow and produce fruit.

After the close of the meeting, a young sister, who has been sick, called for the anointing, which was at once attended to, and the usual peace of mind followed. The anointing, as a means of grace and restoration, is a great privilege for the believing ones, and we are glad that many more, of late years, are desiring it, than formerly. This, we think, is because it is being more generally taught, by our ministers.

DISTRICT MEETING FOR MIDDLE PENNSYLVANIA.

As the notice of the District Meeting for Middle Pennsylvania, given by Bro. Neisley, does not seem to be fully understood, we add, that it will be held May 11, in the Lower Cumberland church, at the Mohler meeting-house. Delegates coming from Harrisburg, will take the Cumberland Valley R. R., to Mechanicsburgh. All delegates should come to Mechanicsburgh on Tuesday, May 10, where they will be met with conveyances. We are requested to state further, that a love-feast will be held at the Mohler meeting-house on Tuesday evening, May 10, to which the brethren and sisters are invited. The District Meeting will organize on Wednesday morning, May 11.

THE GOSPEL MESSENGER.

"Set for the Defense of the Gospel."

Vol. 30, Old Series.   Mt. Morris, Ill., and Huntingdon, Pa., May 8 1892   No. 18.

The Gospel Messenger.

H. B. BRUMBAUGH, Editor,

And Business Manager of the Eastern House, Box 50, Huntingdon, Pa.

Table of Contents.

A COUNTRY WALK.

HAVING been requested to visit a sick lady down along the Juniata, several miles below town, we called upon Bro. C. Myers to go with us, and as he was not then engaged, he readily assented to walk with us. The morning was bright and pleasant, and add to this the things of interest by the way, we could not well help enjoying the occasion. Being confined closely to our desk, study and regular home duties, a walk of this kind, though only a short one, is always fraught with interest and pleasure.

While the study and the closet are welcome retreats for communing with the Father, yet where do we seem to get so doubly in relation to him as out in the open space, roofed by the blue sky, lighted by God's own lamp, and decorated by rivers, hills, mountains and forests. Then, to breathe in the pure morning air, as it comes fresh and sweet from the mountain heights beyond, is a treat, well worth appreciating.

When we reached the house, we found the lady quite ill, yet making preparations to go to Pittsburg for treatment on to-morrow morning. Her trouble is serious, and her father has formed the acquaintance of a physician who claimed powers for healing that are said to be almost miraculous.

The process of diagnosing cases, as described to us, is as follows: From the head of the patient must be clipped a lock of hair. This must not be touched by the hand, but cut off and left drop into a pure white paper. In this it is folded, and taken or sent to this physician, who, on examining it, makes his diagnosis of the disease and gives the treatment. From the sight and feel of the hair, he not only determines the character of the disease, but can also tell the age, sex, etc., of the patient. Is not this wonderful? It surely is wonderful, even bordering on the miraculous. The conclusion is thusly: A man who can know all this by simply seeing the hair of the person, does he not understand the nature of the disease? And if he fully—so fully, understands the disease, can he not cure it? This looks very reasonable, and why not believe?

Well, we hope it is all right, and that no disappointment may follow. Faith, in some cases, is better than medicine, and when this is so, we have no objections to offer.

We tried to introduce to the lady and family, the Great Physician who can heal both body and soul. The eighth chapter of Romans was read, followed with a season of prayer which seemed to be much appreciated by those present. Had we the time, these pastoral visits would be much enjoyed by us, as it affords us great pleasure to minister in holy things to those who are hungry and anxious to receive messages of truth and love from the Master. We have often been made to feel that we have too many business engagements to allow us to properly attend to the pastoral work that should be done. Others have expressed this same feeling, and though there are a number of ministers here, the work is not done as it should be. We are often impressed with this feeling, but just how to remedy the matter is not so plain, yet it should be done.

Our morning visit was a very pleasant one, and on our return we felt much refreshed for the work that we are now doing. As we thus come in contact with the home life of people, we are made conscious of the work that might be done for the Master and for souls, could we turn all of our energies in that direction. It brings the more forcibly to our mind the saying of the apostle Paul, "This one thing I do." After all, concentration to one purpose or thing is the great secret of success. We have a large number of men called to the ministry, but we have very few pastors. And yet, though we say this, we feel that our ministry is worthy of great praise, because hundreds of them do much more church work than the membership has a right to ask of them. It is a kind of gratuitous labor, thrown in by them, that the other part of the membership does not do.

THE WEEKLY PRAYER-MEETING.

THE Wednesday evening prayer-meeting is the middle of the week halting place to take in supplies. And we are often made to feel that, without them, many of us would fall short before the Sabbath comes. Of course, we have our closets and family altars which, to the weary souls, are places and times of precious sweetness, but as a church we need a place and time for general supplies where we can weigh and equalize each other's burdens, and thus make them easier and lighter for all. We have just returned from one of these meetings, and the peace of our own soul says that it was good to be there. The subject was, "Be careful for nothing," one of Paul's sweet admonitions, which, if taken from its legitimate relations would be meaningless; but when we consider that he was addressing Christian believers in the sense of children of the Heavenly Father, how sweet the admonition! The thought takes us back to the home-life when we were a part of the family, presided over and cared for by father and mother. We were careful or over anxious for nothing because all of our wants were supplied. It means children looking to, and trusting in, devoted parents. Though we had our duties and labors to perform, our minds were not harassed with the cares and hardships of life as they are when we have no one to whom we can look when our heaviest needs press in upon us.

This is the thought that Paul wished to present to his Philippian brethren. He tells them that they are now the children of a Heavenly Father, and that all their wants will be supplied. That they should go forward, lovingly performing their duties as they come to them, assured that the Lord will provide. It is simply a duplication of "Seek ye *first* the kingdom of God and all these things will be added." The meeting was a pleasant one and some seeds were dropped which, we hope, will grow and produce fruit.

After the close of the meeting, a young sister, who has been sick, called for the anointing, which was at once attended to, and the usual peace of mind followed. The anointing, as a means of grace and restoration, is a great privilege for the believing ones, and we are glad that many more, of late years, are desiring it, than formerly. This, we think, is because it is being more generally taught, by our ministers.

DISTRICT MEETING FOR MIDDLE PENN-SYLVANIA.

As the notice of the District Meeting for Middle Pennsylvania, given by Bro. Neisley, does not seem to be fully understood, we add, that it will be held May 11, in the Lower Cumberland church, at the Mohler meeting-house. Delegates coming from Harrisburg, will take the Cumberland Valley R. R., to Mechanicsburgh. All delegates should come to Mechanicsburgh on Tuesday, May 10, where they will be met with conveyances. We are requested to state further, that a love-feast will be held at the Mohler meeting-house on Tuesday evening, May 10, to which the brethren and sisters are invited. The District Meeting will organize on Wednesday morning, May 11.

such, there will be no trouble about them coming to the order of the church, and observing all of Christ's commands. What a power for good is a church where the members are earnest and faithful in their profession! There are thousands of persons that are living in the vicinity of our churches, and yet are not acquainted with our church doctrine. Were they fully informed on this important subject, they would join in with us.

There are also many received into the church by baptism, who are not fully informed in regard to our church discipline. Afterwards they become dissatisfied, and are either disowned or leave the church, whereas, if they had been fully informed about "all things," they might prove faithful members. But the tendency with too many of our ministers is, to fall in with the ways of the ministers of the popular churches, that is, to preach such sermons as will draw persons to join our church, and taught in all the ordinances of the Lord's house.

Fort Scott, Kans.

BONNETS VERSUS HATS.

BY THURSTON MILLER.

In presenting this subject to the readers of the Gospel Messenger, the design is to instruct those who are yet unable to see the propriety of prohibiting sisters from wearing hats, and, instead, requiring the wearing of bonnets, and inasmuch as Gospel authority for such discriminations is frequently demanded, the writer feels justified in complying with requests to furnish an article in defense of the church's position on this question.

The Brotherhood and, no doubt, our editors, had confidently hoped that the time had passed when it was necessary to occupy space in the Messenger for such instructions, but recent information indicates that certain localities are sadly in need of just such teaching at the present time.

Therefore, in looking over the subject, with a view of omitting nothing that will be of value in helping all to a clear understanding of the reasons why the church has decided against the hat, and in favor of the bonnet for sisters, I find that, at a very early date in the history of God's people, it was designed that the sexes should be distinguished by their apparel; hence the following rule was given, by which they were to be governed in this matter: "The woman shall not wear that which pertaineth unto a man, neither shall a man put on a woman's garment: for all that do so are abomination unto the Lord thy God." Deut. 22: 5. The reader will not fail to notice the severe penalty indicated for those who should violate this rule. To become an abomination was equivalent to incurring the extreme hatred or detestation of God, which subjected the offender to extermination, or death. Hence the care necessary on the part of both male and female, in observing this rule.

Now it is clear that if the *hat* is a part of man's attire, it would be unlawful for a woman to adopt it as an ordinary covering for her head, as that would constitute her an abomination.

The same rule also applied to the man, should he adopt for himself the article ordinarily worn upon the woman's head. So then, if it can be shown that what was worn on the head distinguished sex in ancient times, the question is settled for Israel, at least.

By reading Isa. 3: 16 to close of chapter, you will find a long list of articles of female apparel, which comprised the whole of woman's attire, and as hats are not mentioned, but instead, *bonnets*

and *hoods*, these latter must have been a part of woman's apparel.

Now, by reading Dan. 3: 21, you will find that men wore *hats*, nor is it stated anywhere that men wore anything else at any time, as a protection for their heads, although it *is* found that, upon certain occasions, men wore *bonnets*, and this is sometimes urged as an offset, justifying hats for sisters.

But that this is no argument, will appear when it is remembered that this is a special command of God, to a special class, for a special service. See Ex. 28: 40; 29: 9; 39: 29; Lev. 8: 13; Ezek. 44: 18. These Scriptures prove (1) a special command to the priests, and *not* to the men in general; (2) that it was used by the priests, for a special service in the presence of God *alone*, and not to appear under any circumstances in this attire before the congregation.

Having now shown that, in the times of the prophets, the hat was an article of male attire, and that the *bonnet* and *hood* belonged to the woman, the reversing of which would subject the offenders to terrible penalties, the question may arise as to whether God is as exacting with the members of his church under the present dispensation, as he was with Israel, because this line of argument is rejected sometimes, the objectors claiming that we are governed *now* by the *New Testament*, and not by the Law of Moses. In answer to this, another question suggests itself, namely, "Does God tolerate, or approbate *now*, that which he condemned as abomination in the time of Moses?" It seems to me that every one who regards him as an unchangeable God, must answer, *No*.

But now, to show the relation between the Old and the New Testaments, the reader is referred to the Apostle Paul's declaration, "Wherefore the law was our schoolmaster to bring us unto Christ, that we might be justified by faith." Gal. 3: 24. The Apostle Peter understood this matter in that way when he exhorted wives to follow the example of the "holy women of old time, who trusted in God," referring them to Abraham's wife. 1 Pet. 3: 5, 6.

There is no doubt the church has decided this question more especially from the New Testament stand-point, which we will now examine. For a starting point in this line of argument, the reader is referred to our Savior's rebuke of the Pharisees, where he says, "Ye are they which justify yourselves before men; but God knoweth your hearts:" and then adds, "for that which is highly esteemed among men is abomination in the sight of God." Luke 16: 15. Now, with regard to woman's head-wear, is there anything that meets with more universal approbation, or is more highly esteemed among all classes than the *hat?* From her who begs rags from door to door, to the richest lady in the land, the *hat* is worn. From the most refined and virtuous woman of the *world* down to the *vilest* of her sex, regardless of what else may be afforded, the *hat* crowns the head, and from the baby girl of two or three years old, up through all ages, ranks and stations, the *hat*, in some form, is the head-wear. Hence, lest it should be regarded as an abomination in the sight of God, the hat is rejected by the church.

I am aware that some have held to the notion that the universal adoption of the hat by women should make it proper for our sisters to wear it also, or that custom should regulate such things. I know that sometimes, in the absence of written law, the civil courts will decide legal rights by custom, but God never intended that his church should be subject to any such regulations, as is plain from Paul's letter to the Romans, where he says, "I beseech you therefore, brethren, by the mercies of God, that ye present your bodies a liv-

ing sacrifice, holy, acceptable unto God, which is your reasonable service. And be not *conformed to this world:* but be ye transformed by the *renewing of* your mind, that ye may prove what is that good, and acceptable, and perfect will of God." Rom. 12: 1, 2.

For the reason just stated, the church decides it wrong for the members to either retain, or adopt the customs of the world in the matter of dress, and as the *hat* is, in the fullest sense, a worldly custom, it is rejected by her counsels. This decision is made very strong by the following inspired admonitions: "And be ye renewed in the spirit of your mind;" "and have no fellowship with the unfruitful works of darkness, but rather reprove them." Eph. 4: 23; 5: 11. "As obedient children, not fashioning yourselves according to the former lusts in your ignorance." 1 Pet. 1: 14. "Love not the world, neither the things that are in the world. If any man love the world, the love of the Father is not in him. For all that is in the world, the lust of the flesh, and the lust of the eyes, and the pride of life, is not of the Father, but is of the world." 1 John 2: 15, 16.

Paul, in writing to the Corinthians, reminds them of what the Lord has said, directly upon this subject, as follows: "Wherefore come out from among them, and be ye separate, saith the Lord, and touch not the unclean thing; and I will receive you, and will be a Father unto you, and ye shall be my sons and daughters, saith the Lord Almighty." 2 Cor. 6: 17, 18.

But enough has been quoted to show that we cannot, with Gospel consistency, retain or adopt any fashion or custom of the world; and now let us look at the subject from the stand-point of common sense, and compare the sisters' bonnet with the world's *hat.* Paul informs Timothy to instruct the women (sisters), to "adorn themselves in modest apparel, with shamefacedness and sobriety; not with braided hair, or gold, or pearls, or costly array; but (which becometh women professing godliness) with good works." 1 Tim. 2: 9, 10.

Please notice that shamefacedness and sobriety must characterize women *professing godliness*. Now, as shamefacedness means "bashfulness, or extreme modesty," cannot the most ordinary observer determine whether the sisters' bonnet or the world's *hat* is best suited to impart this appearance to the wearer?

You may test it in a hundred cases, and it will be on the side of the bonnet every time. The hat will, in every instance, favor the appearance of pride, boldness, or forwardness, as compared with the appearance produced by the bonnet, and you know it is said that "God resisteth the proud, but giveth grace unto the humble." James 4: 6.

It is also declared, "These six things doth the Lord hate; yea, seven are an abomination unto him: A proud look, a lying tongue, and hands that shed innocent blood, a heart that deviseth wicked imaginations, feet that be swift in running to mischief, a false witness that speaketh lies, and he that soweth discord among brethren." Prov. 6: 16, 17, 18, 19. The reader will notice that the *proud look* heads this list of seven things that are abomination unto the Lord, which includes liars, murderers, false witnesses, etc. This shows that it belongs to that class of offenses, if not the greatest. Then the proud look is to be avoided as an abomination, and who can possess the proud look, but those who *look* proud? Let common sense decide which that would be,—the face beneath the hat, or the one within the bonnet. Then, again, the sisters' bonnet is so becoming, because so completely harmonizing with her modest prayer-covering,—the cap.

such, there will be no trouble about them coming to the order of the church, and observing all of Christ's commands. What a power for good is a church where the members are earnest and faithful in their profession! There are thousands of persons that are living in the vicinity of our churches, and yet are not acquainted with our church doctrine. Were they fully informed on this important subject, they would join in with us.

There are also many received into the church by baptism, who are not fully informed in regard to our church discipline. Afterwards they become dissatisfied, and are either disowned or leave the church, whereas, if they had been fully informed about "all things," they might prove faithful members. But the tendency with too many of our ministers is, to fall in with the ways of the ministers of the popular churches, that is, to preach such sermons as will draw persons to join our church, before they are fully converted and taught in all the ordinances of the Lord's house.

Fort Scott, Kans.

BONNETS VERSUS HATS.

BY THURSTON MILLER.

In presenting this subject to the readers of the GOSPEL MESSENGER, the design is to instruct those who are yet unable to see the propriety of prohibiting sisters from wearing hats, and, instead, requiring the wearing of bonnets and, inasmuch as Gospel authority for such discriminations is frequently demanded, the writer feels justified in complying with requests to furnish an article in defense of the church's position on this question.

The Brotherhood and, no doubt, our editors, had confidently hoped that the time had passed when it was necessary to occupy space in the MESSENGER for such instructions, but recent sadly in need of just such teaching at the present time.

Therefore, in looking over the subject, with a view of omitting nothing that will be of value in helping all to a clear understanding of the reasons why the church has decided against the hat, and in favor of the bonnet for sisters, I find that, at a very early date in the history of God's people, it was necessary to see that the sexes should be distinguished by their apparel; hence the following rule was given, by which they were to be governed in this matter: "The woman shall not wear that which pertaineth unto a man, neither shall a man put on a woman's garment: for all that do so are abomination unto the Lord thy God." Deut. 22: 5. The reader will not fail to notice the severe penalty indicated for those who should violate this rule. To become an abomination is equivalent to incurring the extreme hatred or detestation of God, which subjected the offender to extermination, or death. Hence the care necessary on the part of both male and female, in observing this rule.

Now it is clear that if the *hat* is a part of man's attire, it would be unlawful for a woman to adopt it as an ordinary covering for her head, as that would constitute her an abomination.

The same rule also applied to the man, should he adopt for himself the article ordinarily worn upon the woman's head. So then, if it can be shown that what was worn on the head distinguished sex in ancient times, the question is settled for Israel, at least.

By reading Isa. 3: 16 to close of chapter, you will find a long list of articles of female apparel, which comprised the whole of woman's attire, and as hats are not mentioned, but, instead, *bonnets*

and *hoods*, these latter must have been a part of woman's apparel.

Now, by reading Dan. 3: 21, you will find that men wore *hats*, nor is it stated anywhere that men wore anything else at any time, as a protection for their heads, although it is found that, upon certain occasions, men wore *bonnets*, and this is sometimes urged as an offset, justifying hats for sisters.

But that this is no argument, will appear when it is remembered that this is a special command of God, to a special class, for a special service. See Ex. 28: 40; 29: 9; 39: 20; Lev. 8: 13; Ezek. 44: 18. These Scriptures prove (1) a special command to the priests, and *not* to the men in general; (2) that it was used by the priests, for a special service in the presence of God *alone*, and not to appear under any circumstances in this attire before the congregation.

Having now shown that, in the times of the prophets, the hat was an article of male attire, and that the *bonnet* and *hood* belonged to the woman, the reversing of which would subject the offenders to terrible penalties, the question may arise as to whether God is as exacting with the members of his church under the present dispensation, as he was with Israel, because this line of argument is rejected sometimes, the objectors claiming that we are governed *now* by the *New Testament*, and not *by* the Law of Moses. In answer to this, another question suggests itself, namely, "Does God tolerate, or approbate *now*, that which he condemned as abomination in the time of Moses?" It seems to me that every one who regards him as an unchangeable God, must answer, No.

But now, to show the relation between the Old and the New Testaments, the reader is referred to the Apostle Paul's declaration, "Wherefore the law was our schoolmaster to bring us unto Christ, that we might be justified by faith." Gal. 3: 24. The Apostle Peter understood this matter in that way when he exhorted wives to follow the example of the "holy women of old time, who trusted in God," referring them to Abraham's wife. 1 Pet. 3: 5, 6.

There is no doubt the church has decided this question more especially from the New Testament stand-point, which we will now examine. For a starting point in this line of argument, the reader is referred to our Savior's rebuke of the Pharisees, where he says, "Ye are they which justify yourselves before men; but God knoweth your hearts:" and then adds, "for that which is highly esteemed among men is abomination in the sight of God." Luke 16: 15. Now, with regard to woman's headwear, is there anything that meets with more universal approbation, or is more highly esteemed among all classes than the *hat*? From her who begs rags from door to door, to the richest lady in the land, the *hat* is worn. From the most refined and virtuous woman of the *world* down to the *vilest* of her sex, regardless of what else may be afforded, the *hat* crowns the head, and from the baby girl of two or three years old, up through all ages, ranks and stations, the *hat*, in some form, is the head-wear. Hence, lest it should be regarded as an abomination in the sight of God, the hat is rejected by the church.

I am aware that some have held to the notion that the universal adoption of the hat by women should make it proper for our sisters to wear it also, or that custom should regulate such things. I know that sometimes, in the absence of written law, the civil courts will decide legal rights by custom, but God never intended that his church should be subject to any such regulations, as is plain from Paul's letter to the Romans, where he says, "I beseech you therefore, brethren, by the mercies of God, that ye present your bodies a liv-

ing sacrifice, holy, acceptable unto God, which is your reasonable service. And be not *conformed to this world:* but be ye transformed by the *renewing of your mind,* that ye may prove what is that good, and acceptable, and perfect will of God." Rom. 12: 1, 2.

For the reason just stated, the church decides it wrong for the members to either retain, or adopt the customs of the world in the matter of dress, and as the *hat* is, in the fullest sense, a worldly custom, it is rejected by her counsels. This decision is made very strong by the following inspired admonitions: "And be ye renewed in the spirit of your mind;" "and have no fellowship with the unfruitful works of darkness, but rather reprove them." Eph. 4: 23; 5: 11. "As obedient children, not fashioning yourselves according to the former lusts in your ignorance," 1 Pet. 1: 14. "Love not the world, neither the things that are in the world. If any man love the world, the love of the Father is not in him. For all that is in the world, the lust of the flesh, and the lust of the eyes, and the pride of life, is not of the Father, but is of the world." 1 John 2: 15, 16.

Paul, in writing to the Corinthians, reminds them of what the Lord has said, directly upon this subject, as follows: "Wherefore come out from among them, and be ye separate, saith the Lord, and touch not the unclean thing; and I will receive you, and will be a Father unto you, and ye shall be my sons and daughters, saith the Lord Almighty." 2 Cor. 6: 17, 18.

But enough has been quoted to show that we cannot, with Gospel consistency, retain or adopt any fashion or custom of the world; and now let us look at the subject from the stand-point of common sense, and compare the sisters' bonnet with the world's *hat.* Paul informs Timothy to instruct the women (sisters), to "adorn themselves in modest apparel, with shamefacedness and sobriety; not with braided hair, or gold, or pearls, or costly array; but (which becometh women professing godliness) with good works." 1 Tim. 2: 9, 10.

Please notice that shamefacedness and sobriety must characterize women *professing godliness.* Now, as shamefacedness means "bashfulness, or extreme modesty," cannot the most ordinary observer determine whether the sisters' bonnet or the world's *hat* is best suited to impart this appearance to the wearer?

You may test it in a hundred cases, and it will be on the side of the bonnet every time. The hat will, in every instance, favor the appearance of pride, boldness, or forwardness, as compared with the appearance produced by the bonnet, and you know it is said that "God resisteth the proud, but giveth grace unto the humble." James 4: 6.

It is also declared, "These six things doth the Lord hate; yea, seven are an abomination unto him: A proud look, a lying tongue, and hands that shed innocent blood, a heart that deviseth wicked imaginations, feet that be swift in running to mischief, a false witness that speaketh lies, and he that soweth discord among brethren." Prov. 6: 16, 17, 18, 19. The reader will notice that the *proud look* heads this list of seven things that are abomination unto the Lord, which includes liars, murderers, false witnesses, etc. This shows that it belongs to that class of offenses, if not the greatest. Then the proud look is to be avoided as an abomination, and who can possess the proud look, but those who *look* proud? Let common sense decide which that would be,—the face beneath the hat, or the one within the bonnet. Then, again, the sisters' bonnet is so becoming, because so completely harmonizing with her modest prayer-covering,—the cap.

to a development, a growth. Every true Christian has been born again, old things have passed away, and he is a new creature in Christ, ready to combat sin, and act well his part in all the chances and changes of to-day.

"Jesus Christ, the same yesterday and to-day and forever." With a background of the most precious promises, this truth stands out in bold relief. There is rhythmic beauty in it, beyond that of rhyme or meter. From Matthew upto the Revelations we have a true record of his life, and we believe. To-day the soul of man is confronted by the same question, propounded when the Savior dwelt in the world, "What think ye of Christ?" He who died upon the cross as a ransom for the souls of men, he who cast out the evil spirits that were destroying those whom they inhabited,—the same Christ and the same power will save men to-day from their sins that would doom them to an eternity of woe.

The same Christ is walking with us to-day, as he journeyed with them to Emmaus, when as eventide they said, "Did not our hearts burn within us?" We can have the same blessed feeling of peace, and joy, and gladness, for Jesus will dwell in our hearts,—the same forever.

This is the ultimatum. Many souls have departed in ignorance and despair. They who walk with Jesus to-day, know that he will be the same forever. If we are but faithful to him who cannot change, we know that he has a mansion fitted up, a white robe, and a harp of gold, and, more blessed than all these,—we shall see him as he is!

Mainland, Pa.

THE SOUL.

BY CHAS. M. YEAROUT.

In Four Chapters.—Chapter One.

1. WHAT is the soul?

2. The soul can and does exist independent of the body after death.

3. "Dust thou art, and to dust thou shalt return," was never spoken of the soul.

4. The soul leaves the body at death.

5. Death means a separation.

6. The Scriptures do not teach that the souls of mankind go to the grave, neither do they teach they will come out of the grave.

7. The Word of God teaches the duality of man, or outward and inner man.

8. The children of God are now in possession of eternal life.

9. The intermediate state, or dwelling-place of the souls of men until the judgment.

10. Objections to the soul and its immortality examined and answered.

11. Evidence from other sources.

There are differences of opinion as to what the soul is. The materialist "teaches that life, soul, and spirit are nothing but a mode of molecular motion—a changing of position of the brain and nerve particles, and hence is insubstantial, having no entitative character or existence, separate from material organisms." Hence everything with them is material,—no eternal life abiding in them,—no immortality of the soul. All is subject to death and decay. The opposite extreme is spiritualism. Everything with them is spiritual,—many of them believing in the old pagan doctrine of the transmigration of the soul from one body to another. Neither of the above positions is sustained by the revealed will of God.

The soul is the exact counterpart of the physical body,—a substantial entity, an incorporeal organism, retaining its individuality after it leaves this earthly body, susceptible of enjoyment and happiness, or sorrow and suffering. These earthly bodies are the tabernacles or houses of the soul, as I shall prove by the Word of God farther on. "For what is a man profited, if he shall gain the whole world, and lose his own soul? or what shall a man give in exchange for his soul?" Matt. 16: 26. The Son of God realized the value and worth of the soul, and would have us understand, if we gain the whole world and lose our souls, we are poor, helpless and undone; for all the gold and silver and combined wealth of earth cannot purchase the salvation of one soul, or buy an entrance into heaven. When God formed man of the dust of the earth, he was a lifeless, inanimate lump of earth, until God breathed into his nostrils the breath of life, and man became a living soul. Gen. 2: 7.

When man dies, the body returns to the ground. "In the sweat of thy face shalt thou eat bread, till thou return unto the ground; for out of it wast thou taken: for dust thou art, and unto dust shalt thou return." Gen. 3: 19. God never said the soul should return to the ground, for it was not taken from the ground. God only said that should return to the ground which was taken out of it, and it is evident that nothing was taken out of the earth but a lifeless form. When the soul leaves the body, it is as Adam was, prior to God's breathing into his nostrils the breath of life,—dead, a lifeless, inanimate lump of flesh. Gen. 35: 18; 1 Kings 17: 20, 21, 22; Luke 12: 20. The Savior says, "Fear not them which kill the body, but are not able to kill the soul, but rather fear him which is able to destroy both soul and body in perpetual fire (Gehenna)."

If, as the materialist asserts, the body is the soul, why is it that killing the body does not affect the soul? This proves beyond doubt to those that believe Christ, that destroying the body does not destroy the soul. It is beyond the power of man to kill that immortal principle,—the soul,—because it is not subject to decay. That the soul can and does exist in a conscious state, independent of the body, is demonstrated by the appearance of Moses and Elias with Christ on the Mount of Transfiguration. "And, behold, there appeared unto them Moses and Elias, talking with him." Matt. 17: 3; Luke 9: 30, 31.

At the opening of the fifth seal, John saw under the altar "the souls of them that were slain by the word of God, and for the testimony which they held: and they (the souls) cried with a loud voice, saying, How long, O Lord, holy and true, dost thou not judge and avenge our blood on them that dwell on the earth? And white robes were given unto every one of them; and it was said unto them, that they should rest yet for a little season, until their fellow servants also and their brethren, that should be killed as they were, should be fulfilled." Rev. 6: 9, 10, 11; 3: 5.

How could these souls call on God, if they were unconscious? How could they wear white robes except they were organisms? How could they talk without tongues? How have desires, and express them without the senses?

The duality of man is recognized by the apostle Paul. In writing to the church at Corinth he says, "For we know that, if our earthly house of this tabernacle were dissolved, we have a building of God, a house not made with hands, eternal in the heavens. For in this we groan, earnestly desiring to be clothed upon with our house which is from heaven: therefore we are always confident, knowing that, whilst we are at home in the body, we are absent from the Lord: we are confident, I say, and willing rather to be absent from the body, and to be present with the Lord." 2 Cor. 5: 1, 2, 6, 8; Job 4: 19. "For I am in a strait betwixt two, having a desire to depart, and to be with Christ; which is far better: nevertheless to abide in the flesh is more needful for you." Philpp. 1; 23, 24. Peter speaks of putting off this tabernacle or house of flesh. 2 Pet. 1: 13, 14. "Though our outward man perish, yet the inner man is renewed day by day." 2 Cor. 4: 16; Eph. 3: 16. Though the outward man perish,—molder back to its mother earth,—the inner man, the soul, lives forever. For God is not the God of the dead, but of the living. "I am the God of Abraham, and the God of Isaac, and the God of Jacob," and he is not a God of the dead, but of the living, for all live unto him, or, as the Emphatic Diaglott has it, "To him all are alive." Matt. 22: 32; Luke 20: 37, 38. But are not Abraham, Isaac and Jacob dead? Why, then, are they represented as living? Death means a separation. God said to Adam, "Of every tree of the garden thou mayest freely eat: but of the tree of the knowledge of good and evil, thou shalt not eat of it: for in the day that thou eatest thereof thou shalt surely die." Gen. 2: 16, 17. Adam and Eve died the very day they partook of the forbidden tree, and not nine hundred years after. ward, as some, assert. They were driven out of the garden and separated from God. Gen. 3: 23, 24. The sinner is dead, Eph. 5: 14; separated from God and righteousness, having no hope or promise. Eph. 2: 12. The Christian is dead to sin, Rom. 6; 11; Col. 3: 3; separated from sin, having passed from death (*eis*) into life, John 5: 24; 1 John 3: 14. The wicked are finally separated from God, and cast into the lake of fire, which is represented as the second death or separation. They are punished with everlasting destruction from the presence of the Lord and the glory of his power. 1 Thess. 1: 8, 9; Rev. 20: 14, 15; Matt. 25: 46. The physical death is a separation of soul and body. When the soul leaves this body of clay, the body is dead. Gen. 35: 18; 1 Kings 17: 20, 21, 22; Matt 10: 28; Luke 12: 20; 16: 22, 23.

Westphalia, Kans.

"NOTHING is more unpleasing than to find that offense has been received when none was intended, and that pain has been given to those who were not guilty of any provocation. As the great end of society is mutual beneficence, a good man is always uneasy when he finds himself acting in opposition to the purposes of life; because, though his conscience may easily acquit him of *malice prepense*, of settled hatred, or contrivance of mischief, yet he seldom can be certain that he has not failed by negligence or indolence, that he has not been hindered from consulting the common interest by too much regard to his own ease, or too much indifference to the happiness of others."

"LIFE is eternal: by death and life Nature undergoes her annual revival; the trees burst into new life, the tender green shoots unfold; little wayside flowers struggle into existence; everywhere there are buds; all is brightness; the Spring permanently indicates that inherent power of yielding us the regular supply of healthy vigor and well-balanced strength in all departments of Nature; the young lambs, uncouth calves, yellow ducklings, etc., etc.,—briefly, the whole earth is full of young things; we see in Spring new life every.where, in all things, a countless creation of bright-eyed little things of every kind."

"To say that the same law runs through the kingdoms of nature and of grace, is simply to say that God is the law-giver for both those kingdoms. He who ordained, for the natural world, that whatsoever a man soweth that shall he also reap, ordained the same principle for the moral world. And thus it is that there is sure to be a correspondence between the disclosures of science and of revelation."

to a development, a growth. Every true Christian has been born again, old things have passed away, and he is a new creature in Christ, ready to combat sin, and act well his part in all the chances and changes of to-day.

"Jesus Christ, the same yesterday and to-day and forever." With a background of the most precious promises, this truth stands out in bold relief. There is rhythmic beauty in it, beyond that of rhyme or meter. From Matthew unto the Revelations we have a true record of his life, and we believe. To-day the soul of man is confronted by the same question, propounded when the Savior dwelt in the world, "What think ye of Christ?" He who died upon the cross as a ransom for the souls of men, he who cast out the evil spirits that were destroying those whom they inhabited,—the same Christ and the same power will save men to-day from their sins that would doom them to an eternity of woe.

The same Christ is walking with us to-day, as he journeyed with them to Emmaus, when at eventide they said, "Did not our hearts burn within us?" We can have the same blessed feeling of peace, and joy, and gladness, for Jesus will well in our hearts,—the same forever.

This is the ultimatum. Many souls have departed in ignorance and despair. They who walk with Jesus to-day, know that he will be the same forever. If we are but faithful to him who cannot change, we know that he has a mansion filled up, a white robe, and a harp of gold, and, more blessed than all these,—we shall see him as he is!

Mainland, Pa.

THE SOUL.

BY CHAS. M. YEAROUT.

In Four Chapters.—Chapter One.

1. WHAT is the soul?

2. The soul can and does exist independent of the body after death.

3. "Dust thou art, and to dust thou shalt return," was never spoken of the soul.

4. The soul leaves the body at death.

5. Death means a separation.

6. The Scriptures do not teach that the souls of mankind go to the grave, neither do they teach they will come out of the grave.

7. The Word of God teaches the duality of man, or outward and inner man.

8. The children of God are now in possession of eternal life.

9. The intermediate state, or dwelling-place of the souls of men until the judgment.

10. Objections to the soul and its immortality examined and answered.

11. Evidence from other sources.

There are differences of opinion as to what the soul is. The materialist "teaches that life, soul, and spirit are nothing but a mode of molecular motion—a changing of position of the brain and nerve particles, and hence is insubstantial, having no entitative character or existence, separate from material organisms." Hence everything with them is material,—no eternal life abiding in them,—no immortality of the soul. All is subject to death and decay. The opposite extreme is spiritualism. Everything with them is spiritual,—many of them believing in the old pagan doctrine of the transmigration of the soul from one body to another. Neither of the above positions is sustained by the revealed will of God.

The soul is the exact counterpart of the physical body,—a substantial entity, an incorporeal organism, retaining its individuality after it leaves this earthly body, susceptible of enjoyment and happiness, or sorrow and suffering. These earthly bodies are the tabernacles or houses of the soul, as I shall prove by the Word of God further on. "For what is a man profited, if he shall gain the whole world, and lose his own soul? or what shall a man give in exchange for his soul?" Matt. 16: 26. The Son of God realized the value and worth of the soul, and would have us understand, if we gain the whole world and lose our souls, we are poor, helpless and undone; for all the gold and silver and combined wealth of earth cannot purchase the salvation of one soul, or buy an entrance into heaven. When God formed man of the dust of the earth, he was a lifeless, inanimate lump of earth, until God breathed into his nostrils the breath of life, and man became a living soul. Gen. 2: 7.

When man dies, the body returns to the ground. "In the sweat of thy face shalt thou eat bread, till thou return unto the ground; for out of it wast thou taken: for dust thou art, and unto dust shalt thou return." Gen. 3: 19. God never said the soul should return to the ground, for it was not taken from the ground. God only said that should return to the ground which was taken out of it, and it is evident that nothing was taken out of the earth but a lifeless form. When the soul leaves the body, it is as Adam was, prior to God's breathing into his nostrils the breath of life,—dead, a lifeless, inanimate lump of flesh. Gen. 35: 18; 1 Kings 17: 20, 21, 22; Luke 12: 20. The Savior says, "Fear not them which kill the body, but are not able to kill the soul, but rather fear him which is able to destroy both soul and body in perpetual fire (Gehenna)."

If, as the materialist asserts, the body is the soul, why is it that killing the body does not affect the soul? This proves beyond doubt to those that believe Christ, that destroying the body does not destroy the soul. It is beyond the power of man to kill that immortal principle,—the soul,—because it is not subject to decay. That the soul can and does exist in a conscious state, independent of the body, is demonstrated by the appearance of Moses and Elias with Christ on the Mount of Transfiguration. "And, behold, there appeared unto them Moses and Elias, talking with him." Matt. 17: 3; Luke 9: 30, 31.

At the opening of the fifth seal, John saw under the altar "the souls of them that were slain by the word of God, and for the testimony which they held: and they (the souls) cried with a loud voice, saying, How long, O Lord, holy and true, dost thou not judge and avenge our blood on them that dwell on the earth? And white robes were given unto every one of them; and it was said unto them, that they should rest yet for a little season, until their fellow servants also and their brethren, that should be killed as they were, should be fulfilled." Rev. 6: 9, 10, 11; 3: 5.

How could those souls call on God, if they were unconscious? How could they wear white robes except they were organisms? How could they talk without tongues? How have desires, and express them without the senses?

The duality of man is recognized by the apostle Paul. In writing to the church at Corinth he says, "For we know that, if our earthly house of this tabernacle were dissolved, we have a building of God, a house not made with hands, eternal in the heavens. For in this we groan, earnestly desiring to be clothed upon with our house which is from heaven: therefore we are always confident, knowing that, whilst we are at home in the body, we are absent from the Lord: we are confident, I say, and willing rather to be absent from the body, and to be present with the Lord." 2 Cor. 5: 1, 2, 6, 8; Job 4: 19. "For I am in a strait betwixt two, having a desire to depart, and to be with Christ; which is far better: nevertheless to abide in the flesh is more needful for you." Philpp. 1; 23, 24. Peter speaks of putting off this tabernacle or house of flesh. 2 Pet. 1: 13, 14. "Though our outward man perish, yet the inner man is renewed day by day." 2 Cor. 4: 16; Eph. 3: 16. Though the outward man perish,—molder from its mother earth,—the inner man, the soul, lives forever. For God is not the God of the dead, but of the living. "I am the God of Abraham, and the God of Isaac, and the God of Jacob," and he is not a God of the dead, but of the living, for all live unto him, or, as the Emphatic Diaglott has it, "To him all are alive." Matt. 22: 32; Luke 20: 37, 38. But are not Abraham, Isaac and Jacob dead? Why, then, are they represented as living? Death means a separation. God said to Adam, "Of every tree of the garden thou mayest freely eat: but of the tree of the knowledge of good and evil, thou shalt not eat of it: for in the day that thou eatest thereof thou shalt surely die." Gen. 2: 16, 17. Adam and Eve died the very day they partook of the forbidden tree, and not nine hundred years afterward, as some assert. They were driven out of the garden and separated from God. Gen. 3: 23, 24. The sinner is dead, Eph. 5: 14; separated from God and righteousness, having no hope or promise. Eph. 2: 12. The Christian is dead to sin, Rom. 6: 11; Col. 3: 3; separated from sin, having passed from death (*sin*) into life, John 5: 24; 1 John 3: 14. The wicked are finally separated from God, and cast into the lake of fire, which is represented as the second death or separation. They are punished with everlasting destruction from the presence of the Lord and the glory of his power. 1 Thess. 1: 8, 9; Rev. 20: 14, 15; Matt. 25: 46. The physical death is a separation of soul and body. When the soul leaves this body of clay, the body is dead. Gen. 35: 18; 1 Kings 17: 20, 21, 22; Matt 10: 28; Luke 12: 20; 16: 22, 23.

Westphalia, Kans.

"NOTHING is more unpleasing than to find that offense has been received when none was intended, and that pain has been given to those who were not guilty of any provocation. As the great end of society is mutual beneficence, a good man is always uneasy when he finds himself acting in opposition to the purposes of life; because, though his conscience may easily acquit him of *malice prepense*, of settled hatred, or contrivances of mischief, yet he seldom can be certain that he has not failed by negligence or indolence, that he has not been hindered from consulting the common interest by too much regard to his own ease, or too much indifference to the happiness of others."

"LIFE is eternal: by death and life Nature undergoes her annual revival; the trees burst into new life, the tender green shoots unfold; little wayside flowers struggle into existence; everywhere there are buds; all is brightness; the Spring permanently indicates that inherent power of yielding us the regular supply of healthy vigor and well-balanced strength in all departments of Nature; the young lambs, uncouth calves, yellow ducklings, etc., etc.,—briefly, the whole earth is full of young things; we see in Spring new life every-where, in all things, a countless creation of bright-eyed little things of every kind."

"To say that the same law runs through the kingdoms of nature and of grace, is simply to say that God is the law-giver for both those kingdoms. He who ordained, for the natural world, that whatsoever a man soweth that shall he also reap, ordained the same principle for the moral world. And thus it is that there is sure to be a correspondence between the disclosures of science and of revelation."

Gospel is the written Word. The living Word interprets the written Word. Truth is the conformity of the object with the idea of the true. Jesus presents to the world the only consistent example of life and teaching. He not only taught the truth, but he also practiced it in his life. Again he affirms, "I am the life." He has given us a model life. Are we discouraged by bad example? There is ONE LIFE we can look up to with comfort, and take courage. There is power in the life of Christ. "For if when we were enemies, we were reconciled to God by the death of his Son; much more, being reconciled, *we shall be saved by his life*." Rom. 5: 10. Each one, as a branch, receives life from Christ the True Vine. There is a living connection between Christ and his Word; and there is a vital connection between the Holy Spirit and the Word. Those who are born of the Spirit are also born of the Word. 1 Pet. 1: 23; Jas. 1: 18. The Christian walks in the Truth. 3 John 4. The Truth is also in the Christian as a living reality. "Let the word of Christ DWELL in you richly in all wisdom." Col. 3: 16. The Holy Spirit is in the child of God. "But if the spirit of him that raised up Jesus from the dead dwell in you, he that raised up Jesus from the dead shall also quicken your mortal bodies by his spirit that dwelleth in you." Rom. 8: 11. The child of God is also in the Spirit. "If we live in the spirit, let us also walk in the spirit." Gal. 5: 25. In all this we have the threefold evidence of the unity of the Word and Spirit. Hence the Spirit guides into all truth by leading men and women into the observance of the Truth. The Holy Spirit will not only lead a man *to* the truth but onto of it into worldly organizations and the various worldly pleasures that gratify the carnal mind. We are to "try the spirits," and the only test is the standard of truth. The minister of the Gospel is not only to teach all nations, but he is also required to teach them *to observe all things*, for it is into *all truth* that the Holy Spirit is the guide.

Moore's Store, Va.

HOME MISSION WORK.

BY ARTEMAS SMITH.

I RECENTLY attended the District Meeting of the Southern District of Indiana and heard the discussion on the question of raising funds for missionary purposes and District expenses. It seems our brethren of Southern Indiana raise funds by a system of taxation, which it is not our purpose to discuss. We could not help, however, being impressed with the change that has come over the church of the Brethren in regard to the amount of money required to carry on the work of the church to-day or the church, as we remember it, thirty years ago. It would seem that the principal business of the meeting was to raise money.

We offer no comment or criticism, but our thoughts went back into the fifties, when our old pioneer brethren traveled through this country and established the nucleus of the churches of to-day. They did not get their way paid all the time. We do not plead for a return of those times. We think it right for the minister to have his way paid, but we are forced to wonder whether any of our ministers would make the sacrifices which our aged ministers made thirty years ago. They did not have the Home Mission Board to fall back upon, and yet, I think, there was more home mission preaching then than now, for the reason that the appointments were made in different portions of the country. The doctrine was preached in different localities, and, to some extent, a different audience each time, while to-day the Brethren preach at regular, stated intervals at the meeting-house. It is a rare occurrence that our Brethren preach in any of the numerous little villages, which have grown up in the country, and very many people know but little of the doctrine of the Brethren. Yet there is much more said about home mission work and the raising of funds than there was thirty years ago.

Now this state of affairs is not to be laid to the fault of the Mission Boards, by any means, but we suggest that the ministering brethren of each congregation thoroughly canvass their home territory, and preach at new points as often as convenient. We recommend this method in preference to a disposition shown by brethren, to await the call of the wealthy churches. We have an abiding faith in the doctrine of the Brethren preached to the outside world. A general effort in this direction, in addition to the work by the Mission Boards, would do much good. A practical living out the doctrine at home, by ministers and laity presenting a united front, is a power in our favor.

Dego, Ind.

WHY NOT WRITE IT "GRAPE JUICE?"

BY J. S. FLORY.

IN No. 11 of GOSPEL MESSENGER, current volume, our good brother wants a reason, with the proof, why the editor of the *St. Louis Christian Advocate*, in commenting on Paul's language to Timothy, uses the term "grape juice," instead of "wine." Our purpose in this article is to give a reason and back it up with a proof.

In taking the Hebrew, Greek, English, or any other language, that sets forth the true meaning of the Bible, it is evident to the mind of every unbiased searcher after the Truth, that there are two kinds of wine spoken of in the Bible, both the product of the vine. The idea held by some, that the juice of the vine is not wine until fermented, is preposterous, when looked at in the meaning of the Scriptures. In Matt. 9: 17 the phrase, "new wine into old bottles," cannot mean anything else but unfermented grape juice. Old skin bottles would hold new fermented wine just the same as old fermented wine without breaking, but not so with "new wine," unfermented juice of the grape, because those new bottles not being air-tight or free from leaven cells, as a result, fermentation would take place, the bottles being new would admit of expansion; not so with old bottles that had been expanded to their full tension. In Isa 16: 10 the juice of grapes, running from the press, is represented as wine. In Jer. 40, they gathered wine and summer fruits and oil.

In Jer. 48: 33 the idea is again presented that the grape juice, failing to come when they tread the grapes, it is the same meaning as to say the wine failed to come. Therefore the word wine being synonymous to saying grape juice, why not say grape juice, when, by so doing, the simple and true translation is given and cannot be misleading? Cider is cider, whether fermented or unfermented, so wine is wine, whether fermented or unfermented. One more verse, and we think it is settled forever, in the minds of our readers, that grape juice is wine long before it is fermented. Isa. 65: 8 says, "*New wine is found in the cluster*."

Such historians as Aristotle and Josephus, with many others, testify that the newly-pressed juice of grapes was called wine and did not intoxicate. It was a common beverage of the people, with their food, and for stomach ailments was recommended just as milk now is often prescribed. Under divine sanction this kind of wine was made and used, while nowhere between the lids of the Bible fermented wine (strong drink) was ever recommended by God, Christ, prophets, priests or apostles, but always condemned.

Where the word wine or new wine occurs and no other qualifying expression is used, how can we, with any show of propriety, put any construction other than that it means the pure, non-alcoholic juice of the grape. When it means fermented wine, there usually is a qualifying term that we may know what kind of wine is meant.

The Jews never use fermented wine in any of their religious services. Especially is this so when they keep the passover, because, say they, there must be no *leaven* of any kind in the house on such occasions. Would to God we could all see the inconsistency of using a *leavened* wine to represent the blood of our Blessed Master, who was without sin, while we contend for unleavened bread to represent his body. But we are rejoiced to see that light is springing up; we must learn to touch not the unclean thing, no matter under what form it comes.

In conclusion we say, Let us have a translation of the Scriptures on those mooted questions that is not misleading. It certainly is right to say Paul advised Timothy to use a little "grape juice" for his oft infirmities. The reason *why* we have shown.

THE HOLY BIBLE.

THE Bible should be to you not a book only, but a speaking trumpet, through which God speaks from afar to you, so that you may catch the very tones of his voice. You must read the Word of God to this end; for it is while reading, meditating and studying, and seeking to dip yourself into his spirit, that it seems suddenly to change from a written book into a talking book or phonograph. It whispers to you, or thunders at you as though God had hidden himself among the leaves and spoken to your condition,—as though Jesus, who feedeth among the lilies, has made the chapter to be lily beds, and had come to feed there. Ask Jesus to cause his Word to come fresh from his own mouth to your soul; and if it be so, and you thus live in daily communion with a personal Christ, you will make good speed in your pilgrim way to the eternal city.—*Sel.*

"BEAUTIFUL is the activity which works for good, and beautiful the stillness that waits for good; blessed the sacrifice of the one, and blessed the self-forgetfulness of the other."

The Gospel Messenger

Is the recognized organ of the German Baptist or Brethren's church, and advocates the form of doctrine taught in the New Testament and pleads for a return to apostolic and primitive Christianity.

It recognizes the New Testament as the only infallible Rule of faith and practice, and maintains that Faith toward God. Repentance from dead works, Regeneration of the heart and mind, baptism by Trine Immersion for remission of sins unto the reception of the Holy Ghost by the laying on of hands, are the means of adoption into the household of God,—the church militant.

It also maintains that Feet-washing, as taught in John 13, both by example and command of Jesus, should be observed in the church.

That the Lord's Supper, instituted by Christ and as universally observed by the apostles and the early Christians, is a full meal, and, in connection with the Communion, should be taken in the evening or after the close of the day.

That the Salutation of the Holy Kiss, or Kiss of Charity, is binding upon the followers of Christ.

That War and Retaliation are contrary to the spirit and self-denying principles of the religion of Jesus Christ.

That the principle of Plain Dressing and of Non-conformity to the world, as taught in the New Testament, should be observed by the followers of Christ.

That the Scriptural duty of Anointing the Sick with Oil, in the Name of the Lord. James 5: 14. is binding upon all Christians.

It also advocates the church's duty to support Missionary and Tract Work, thus giving to the Lord for the spread of the Gospel and for the conversion of sinners.

In short, it is a vindication of all that Christ and the apostles have enjoined upon us, and aims, amid the conflicting theories and discords of modern Christendom, to point out ground that all must concede to be infallibly safe.

☞ The above principles of our Fraternity are set forth on our "Brethren's Envelopes." Use them! Price, 15 cents per package; 40 cents per hundred.

Gospel is the written Word. The living Word interprets the written Word. Truth is the conformity of the object with the idea of the true. Jesus presents to the world the only consistent example of life and teaching. He not only taught the truth, but he also practiced it in his life. Again he affirms, "I am the life." He has given us a model life. Are we discouraged by bad example? There is ONE LIFE we can look up to with comfort, and take courage. There is power in the life of Christ. "For if when we were enemies, we were reconciled to God by the death of his Son; much more, being reconciled, *we shall be saved by his life.*" Rom. 5: 10. Each one, as a branch, receives life from Christ the True Vine. There is a living connection between Christ and his Word; and there is a vital connection between the Holy Spirit and the Word. Those who are born of the Spirit are also born of the Word. 1 Pet. 1: 23; Jas. 1: 18. The Christian walks in the Truth. 3 John 4. The Truth is also in the Christian as a living reality. "Let the word of Christ DWELL *in you* richly in all wisdom." Col. 3: 16. The Holy Spirit is *in* the child of God. "But if the spirit of him that raised up Jesus from the dead dwell in you, he that raised up Christ from the dead shall also quicken your mortal bodies by his spirit that dwelleth in you. Rom. 8: 11. The child of God is also in the Spirit. "If we live in the spirit, let us also walk in the spirit." Gal. 5: 25. In all this we have the threefold evidence of the unity of the Word and Spirit. Hence the Spirit guides into all truth by leading men and women into the observance of the Truth. The Holy Spirit will not only lead a man *to* the truth but *into* the truth, into *all* of it. It will not lead him out of it into worldly organizations and the various worldly pleasures that gratify the carnal mind. We are to "try the spirits;" and the only test is the standard of truth. The mission of the Gospel is not only to teach all nations, but he is also required to teach them *to observe all things*, for it is into *all truth* that the Holy Spirit is the guide.

Moore's Store, Va.

HOME MISSION WORK.

BY ARTEMAS SMITH.

I RECENTLY attended the District Meeting of the Southern District of Indiana and heard the discussion on the question of raising funds for missionary purposes and District expenses. It seems our brethren of Southern Indiana raise funds by a system of taxation, which it is not our purpose to discuss. We could not help, however, being impressed with the change that has come over the church of the Brethren in regard to the amount of money required to carry on the work of the church to-day or the church, as we remember it, thirty years ago. It would seem that the principal business of the meeting was to raise money.

We offer no comment or criticism, but our thoughts went back into the fifties, when our old pioneer brethren traveled through this country and established the nucleus of the churches of to-day. They did not get their way paid all the time. We do not plead for a return of those times. We think it right for the minister to have his way paid, but we are forced to wonder whether any of our ministers would make the sacrifices which our aged ministers made thirty years ago. They did not have the Home Mission Board to fall back upon, and yet, I think, there was more home mission preaching then than now, for the reason that the appointments were made in different portions of the country. The doctrine was preached in different localities, and, to some extent, a different audience each time, while to-day the Brethren preach at regular, stated intervals at the meeting-house. It is a rare occurrence that our Brethren preach in any of the numerous little villages, which have grown up in the country, and very many people know but little of the doctrine of the Brethren. Yet there is much more said about home mission work and the raising of funds than there was thirty years ago.

Now this state of affairs is not to be laid to the fault of the Mission Boards, by any means, but we suggest that the ministering brethren of each congregation thoroughly canvass their home territory, and preach at new points as often as convenient. We recommend this method in preference to a disposition shown by brethren, to await the call of the wealthy churches. We have an abiding faith in the doctrine of the Brethren preached to the outside world. A general effort in this direction, in addition to the work by the Mission Boards, would do much good. A practical living out the doctrine at home, by ministers and laity presenting a united front, is a power in our favor.

Dego, Ind.

WHY NOT WRITE IT "GRAPE JUICE!"

BY J. S. FLORY.

IN No. 11 of GOSPEL MESSENGER, current volume, our good brother wants a reason, with the proof, why the editor of the *St. Louis Christian Advocate*, in commenting on Paul's language to Timothy, uses the term "grape juice," instead of "wine." Our purpose in this article is to give a reason and back it up with a proof.

In taking the Hebrew, Greek, English, or any other language, that sets forth the true meaning of the Bible, it is evident to the mind of every unbiased searcher after the Truth, that there are two kinds of wine spoken of in the Bible, both the product of the vine. The idea held by some, that the juice of the vine is not wine until fermented, is preposterous, when looked at in the meaning of the Scriptures. In Matt. 9: 17 the phrase, "new wine into old bottles," cannot mean anything else but unfermented grape juice. Old skin bottles would hold new fermented wine just the same as old fermented wine without breaking, but not so with "new wine," unfermented juice of the grape, because those new bottles not being air-tight or free from leaven cells, as a result, fermentation would take place, the bottles being new would admit of expansion; not so with old bottles that had been expanded to their full tension. In Isa. 16: 10 the juice of grapes, running from the press, is represented as wine. In Jer. 40, they gathered wine and summer fruits and oil.

In Jer. 48: 33 the idea is again presented that the grape juice, failing to come when they tread the grapes, it is the same meaning as to say the wine failed to come. Therefore the word wine being synonymous to saying grape juice, why not say grape juice, when, by so doing, the simple and true translation is given and cannot be misleading? Cider is cider, whether fermented or unfermented, so wine is wine, whether fermented or unfermented. One more verse, and we think it is settled forever, in the minds of our readers, that grape juice is wine long before it is fermented. Isa. 65: 8 says, " *New wine is found in the cluster.*"

Such historians as Aristotle and Josephus, with many others, testify that the newly-pressed juice of grapes was called wine and did not intoxicate. It was a common beverage of the people, with their food, and for stomach ailments was recommended just as milk now is often prescribed. Under divine sanction this kind of wine was made and used, while nowhere between the lids of the Bible fermented wine (strong drink) was ever recommended by God, Christ, prophets, priests or apostles, but always condemned.

Where the word wine or new wine occurs and no other qualifying expression is used, how can we, with any show of propriety, put any construction other than that it means the pure, non-alcoholic juice of the grape. When it means fermented wine, there usually is a qualifying term that we may know what kind of wine is meant.

The Jews never use fermented wine in any of their religious services. Especially is this so when they keep the passover, because, say they, there must be no *leaven* of any kind in the house on such occasions. Would to God we could all see the inconsistency of using a *leavened* wine to represent the blood of our Blessed Master, who was without sin, while we contend for unleavened bread to represent his body. But we are rejoiced to see that light is springing up; we must learn to touch not the unclean thing, no matter under what form it comes.

In conclusion we say, Let us have a translation of the Scriptures on those mooted questions that is not misleading. It certainly is right to say Paul advised Timothy to use a little "grape juice" for his oft infirmities. The reason *why* we have showed.

THE HOLY BIBLE.

THE Bible should be to you not a book only, but a speaking trumpet, through which God speaks from afar to you, so that you may catch the very tones of his voice. You must read the Word of God to this end; for it is while reading, meditating and studying, and seeking to dip yourself into his spirit, that it seems suddenly to change from a written book into a talking book or phonograph. It whispers to you, or thunders at you as though God had hidden himself among its leaves and spoken to your condition,—as though Jesus, who feedeth among the lilies, has made the chapter to be lily beds, and had come to feed there. Ask Jesus to cause his Word to come fresh from his own mouth to your soul; and if it be so, and you thus live in daily communion with a personal Christ, you will make good speed in your pilgrim way to the eternal city.—*Sel.*

"BEAUTIFUL is the activity which works for good, and beautiful the stillness that waits for good; blessed the sacrifice of the one, and blessed the self-forgetfulness of the other."

The Gospel Messenger

Is the recognized organ of the German Baptist or Brethren's church, and advocates the form of doctrine taught in the New Testament and pleads for a return to apostolic and primitive Christianity.

It recognizes the New Testament as the only infallible rule of faith and practice, and maintains that Faith toward God, Repentance from dead works, Regeneration of the heart and mind, baptism by Trine Immersion for remission of sins unto the reception of the Holy Ghost by the laying on of hands, are the means of adoption into the household of God,—the church militant.

It also maintains that Feet-washing, as taught in John 13, both by example and command of Jesus, should be observed in the church.

That the Lord's Supper, instituted by Christ and as universally observed by the apostles and the early Christians, is a full meal, and, in connection with the Communion, should be taken in the evening or after the close of the day.

That the Salutation of the Holy Kiss, or Kiss of Charity, is binding upon the followers of Christ.

That War and Retaliation are contrary to the spirit and self-denying principles of the religion of Jesus Christ.

That the principle of Plain Dressing and of Non-conformity to the world, as taught in the New Testament, should be observed by the followers of Christ.

That the Scriptural duty of Anointing the Sick with Oil, in the Name of the Lord, James 5: 14, is binding upon all Christians.

It also advocates the church's duty to support Missionary and Tract Work, thus giving to the Lord for the spread of the Gospel and for the conversion of sinners.

In short, it is a vindicator of all that Christ and the apostles have enjoined upon us, and aims, amid the conflicting theories and discords of modern Christendom, to point out ground that all must concede to be infallibly safe.

☞ The above principles of our Fraternity are set forth on our "Brethren's Envelopes." Use them! Price, 15 cents per package; 40 cents per hundred.

PAUL was a teacher of good manners, as well as sound doctrine. In one of his letters he says, "Evil communications corrupt good manners." Many persons are careful to observe proper rules of politeness while in company, but act very rude in their own families. It seems to us that in our homes is the very place where the best of manners ought to be cultivated and sincerely practiced. People who learn to treat each other politely, learn to respect each other's feelings. They will also strive to respect the wishes and comforts of each other. A family that is careful to observe good manners at home, is almost certain to show proper training when in company. The example, however, should be set by those at the head of the family.

A BROTHER writes us that some of the poor churches in the West are not able to defray the expenses of delegates to their own District Meetings, and also to the Annual Meeting, and wishes to know of us which one should be preferred. Both meetings are important, and we would like to see all the churches represented at each and all of them, but by no means should the District Meetings be neglected. Religion and work, like charity, should commence at home. Our first duty is in our home congregations. Our next is the State District, and then the Annual Meeting. A live church at home will soon find its way to both of these meetings, hence we feel to encourage home zeal and punctuality.

THE center of population is rapidly moving west. It is now near Shelbyville, Ind., and in the course of a half century or less, may cross the Mississippi river. There will then be a power in the West, for a mighty population will wield a great influence over all this western country. We may now pause to ask, What will be the religion for this great population? If the right methods are employed, the power of our people will most assuredly be felt all over those great plains. Our work commenced in the East, and steadily we have been moving westward until now we have churches bordering on the Pacific. To widen out from all the points, where our scattering people have settled in the West, will unquestionably give us plenty of work to do. A great opening is before us, and it becomes us to make a good and wise use of all the opportunities and facilities at our command. We are also pushing southward where another mighty field is opening up, and calls loud for us to send workers to reap the harvest. Certainly our Brethren have no occasion for folding their arms in idleness.

THE following, clipped from one of our Methodist exchanges, shows how they sometimes handle important questions without gloves: "Something ought to be done to bring the Methodist people back to the habit of kneeling in prayer. A preacher tells us that he attended two revival services in city churches. In the Methodist revival the pastor stood and prayed, and the congregation sat. At the other meeting, not Methodist, the preacher and entire congregation knelt. That one church can keep its members in their Scriptural habit of worship is encouraging, as a proof of what can be done. Dr. Green used to tell how James Axley got a camp-meeting congregation to kneel. There were penitents, but no conversions, and spiritual matters were dragging, the straw was damp, and few would kneel square and go at it in earnest. Axley exhorted them till tired, and then said: ' We are going to pray; let every Christian pray, and every hypocrite squat.' There was no more squatting at that meeting. Our people do not even squat now. But we can remedy the evil. Let us do it."

ERROR may apologize, but truth should never. The men who comes before an audience with error may have reasons for offering apologies, but why should a minister, filled with the Holy Ghost, and having for his object the telling of nothing but heavenly truths, think of offering an apology? He can do his work with a clear conscience, and certainly he has no reason whatever for apologies of any kind. He should rather thank God that he is permitted to preach the truth.

THIS is most assuredly a missionary age. We have spoken of an attempt upon the part of the Mohammedans to establish their religion in England. We are now reminded that the Buddhist missionaries will attempt the conversion of Christians to their peculiar view of religion. In this age of religious liberty, men, of course, are left to worship as they think proper, at least in this and most of the European countries. A glance at what these religions have done ought to satisfy any one. The Mohammedan religion made Arabia what it is, hardly a safe place for a civilized white man to live, while Buddhism made China with all of its idolatry and miseries. The United States, the best nation on the globe, shows what Christianity may do where even only imperfectly taught and practiced. It might be suggested that none among us are so low in the scale of civilization as to be influenced by the religious systems prevalent in Arabia and China. Still there are a few that may be induced to accept most anything but the truth.

PARENTS should be exceedingly careful how they talk to their children. We mean the manner as well as the substance of the talk. You may think that because the children are yours, you have a right to speak to them as you please. This is a sad mistake. Every child in your family belongs to God, and it is only placed in your care for training, it being your duty to set before that child a proper example in conversation, as well as in other things. If your manner of talking is not that which becometh saints, you certainly ought to reform, not only for your good, but for the good of the children entrusted to your training and protection. No one has the right to spoil a child by training it to talk in an unbecoming manner. While children may learn to talk in a way that is not polite and respectable, be careful that they do not receive the example from you. There is a dignity and purity about careful conversation that parents should study and cultivate. All Christians should learn to use words that are fitly spoken.

THE following paragraph, concerning missionary work in the Disciple church, we clip from the *Christian Evangelist*. It contains a point or two that may be of some advantage to those among us who are greatly interested in the missionary movement: "This association was organized Oct. 24, 1849, and incorporated by the legislature of Ohio the year following. The first name, 'American Christian Missionary Society,' was changed to 'General Christian Missionary Convention' in 1869. It gave attention to both Home and Foreign Missions until 1875, when, on the organization of the Foreign Christian Missionary Society, it gave its attention exclusively to Home Missions. It does not, however, establish Missions in States where they have efficient State organizations. Its Missions will be found chiefly in the new States and Territories of the rapidly-growing West, and in the Atlantic and Gulf States. The Acting Board of Managers has charge of funds contributed for the support of pastors and evangelists, the distribution of tracts, and the support of superannuated and disabled ministers."

A PICTURE.

WE saw a young man starting out in life with a brave heart, full of hope for the future. He and his young wife had chosen the good part and united with the church. They were faithful Christians. They had but little money, but that gave them no great concern. They had good health, stout hearts and willing hands to labor. A farm was rented, and an indebtedness of one thousand dollars incurred to secure the necessary stock and implements to make farming a success. They commenced their farm life with promise of success, and they worked hard and saved at every point to pay off the debt.

The brother, by his exemplary and faithful life, won the confidence of all who knew him, both in and out of the church, and it was not long before a choice was held in his congregation for a minister and he was called by the church to labor in holy things. He was loath to accept the call, but it being urged upon him as duty and that he could not be faithful and refuse the call of the church, he accepted the important work. And now began a new life to him and his companion. God had blessed him with ability to preach the Word. He read and studied far into the night so that he might show himself approved unto God. The farm labor grew no less, and then came a loss of eight hundred dollars, and with several crop failures the debt increased, and the interest account grew heavier.

The brother was advanced to the second degree of the ministry, and then later to the eldership. He was called to do much work for the church. Sometimes his plow stood in the furrow while he was away preaching funerals, attending church work. He gave his time willingly and ungrudgingly, trusting that all would come right in the end. The years rolled on, church work increased, and the burden of debt in no way diminished, for there came the care of a large family, nine children having been given to the brother and sister. They were often oppressed and saddened with the outlook, but they labored on, hoping against hope, and struggling as best they could with the burden of debt resting upon them. Then there came the oversight of two churches, and the demands made upon the brother's time increased, and the debt also increased. It hung like a dark shadow over that home. Who can know the heart-aches and the hours of anxious, perplexing thought and care that came to that home, as the burden grew heavier and heavier, and at last the fact was pressed home to the minister and his faithful wife that they were unable to meet their obligations, and that insolvency was staring them in the face. They had now passed the meridian of life. They had worked hard together, lived scantily and saved wherever it was possible. They stood side by side, nobly struggling to avert the calamity they so much feared, but burdened as they were, it was a hopeless task. And at last the failure came. The only wonder is that it did not come sooner.

In the same congregation at least fifty brethren owned farms, prospered and grew wealthy. They gave their undivided time and attention to their work, and by looking after the one thing they succeeded and made money, while the minister with divided interest giving on occasion nearly half of his time to the church, failed to pay his debts. While others slept, he studied; while others

PAUL was a teacher of good manners, as well as sound doctrine. In one of his letters he says, "Evil communications corrupt good manners." Many persons are careful to observe proper rules of politeness while in company, but not very rude in their own families. It seems to us that in our homes is the very place where the best of manners ought to be cultivated and sincerely practiced. People who learn to treat each other politely, learn to respect each other's feelings. They will also strive to respect the wishes and comforts of each other. A family that is careful to observe good manners at home, is almost certain to show proper training when in company. The example, however, should be set by those at the head of the family.

A BROTHER writes us that some of the poor churches in the West are not able to defray the expenses of delegates to their own District Meetings, and also to the Annual Meeting, and wishes to know of us which one should be preferred. Both meetings are important, and we would like to see all the churches represented at each and all of them, but by no means should the District Meetings be neglected. Religion and work, like charity, should commence at home. Our first duty is in our home congregations. Our next is the State District, and then the Annual Meeting. A live church at home will soon find its way to both of these meetings, hence we feel to encourage home zeal and punctuality.

THE center of population is rapidly moving west. It is now near Shelbyville, Ind., and in the course of a half century or less, may cross the Mississippi river. There will then be a power in the West, for a mighty population will wield a great influence over all this western country. We may now pause to ask, What will be the religion for this great population? If the right methods are employed, the power of our people will most assuredly be felt all over those great plains. Our work commenced in the East, and steadily we have been moving westward until now we have churches bordering on the Pacific. To widen out from all the points, where our scattering people have settled in the West, will unquestionably give us plenty of work to do. A great opening is before us, and it becomes us to make a good and wise use of all the opportunities and facilities at our command. We are also pushing southward where another mighty field is opening up, and calls loud for us to send workers to reap the harvest. Certainly our Brethren have no occasion for folding their arms in idleness.

THE following, clipped from one of our Methodist exchanges, shows how they sometimes handle important questions without gloves: "Something ought to be done to bring the Methodist people back to the habit of kneeling in prayer. A preacher tells us that he attended two revival services in city churches. In the Methodist revival the pastor stood and prayed, and the congregation sat. At the other meeting, not Methodist, the preacher and entire congregation knelt. That one church can keep its members in their Scriptural habit of worship is encouraging, as a proof of what can be done. Dr. Green used to tell how James Axley got a camp-meeting congregation to kneel. There were penitents, but no conversions, and spiritual matters were dragging, the straw was damp, and few would kneel square and go at it in earnest. Axley exhorted them till tired, and then said: 'We are going to pray; let every Christian pray, and every hypocrite squat.' There was no more squatting at that meeting. Our people do not even squat now. But we can remedy the evil. Let us do it."

ERROR may apologize, but truth should never. The man who comes before an audience with error may have reasons for offering apologies, but why should a minister, filled with the Holy Ghost, and having for his object the telling of nothing but heavenly truths, think of offering an apology? He can do his work with a clear conscience, and certainly he has no reason whatever for apologies of any kind. He should rather thank God that he is permitted to preach the truth.

THIS is most assuredly a missionary age. We have spoken of an attempt upon the part of the Mohammedans to establish their religion in England. We are now reminded that the Buddhist missionaries will attempt the conversion of Christians to their peculiar view of religion. In this age of religious liberty, men, of course, are left to worship as they think proper, at least in this and most of the European countries. A glance at what these religions have done ought to satisfy any one. The Mohammedan religion made Arabia what it is, hardly a safe place for a civilized white man to live, while Buddhism made China with all of its idolatry and miseries. The United States, the best nation on the globe, shows what Christianity may do where even only imperfectly taught and practiced. It might be suggested that none among us are so low in the scale of civilization as to be influenced by the religious systems prevalent in Arabia and China. Still there are a few that may be induced to accept most anything but the truth.

PARENTS should be exceedingly careful how they talk to their children. We mean the manner as well as the substance of the talk. You may think that because the children are yours, you have a right to speak to them as you please. This is a sad mistake. Every child in your family belongs to God, and it is only placed in your care for training, it being your duty to set before that child a proper example in conversation, as well as in other things. If your manner of talking is not that which becometh saints, you certainly ought to reform, not only for your good, but for the good of the children entrusted to your training and protection. No one has the right to spoil a child by training it to talk in an unbecoming manner. While children may learn to talk in a way that is not polite and respectable, be careful that they do not receive the example from you. There is a dignity and purity about careful conversation that parents should study and cultivate. All Christians should learn to use words that are fitly spoken.

THE following paragraph, concerning missionary work in the Disciple church, we clip from the Christian Evangelist. It contains a point or two that may be of some advantage to those among us who are greatly interested in the missionary movement: "This association was organized Oct. 24, 1849, and incorporated by the legislature of Ohio the year following. The first name, 'American Christian Missionary Society,' was changed to 'General Christian Missionary Convention' in 1869. It gave attention to both Home and Foreign Missions until 1875, when, on the organization of the Foreign Christian Missionary Society, it gave its attention exclusively to Home Missions. It does not, however, establish Missions in States where they have efficient State organizations. Its Missions will be found chiefly in the new States and Territories of the rapidly-growing West and in the Atlantic and Gulf States. The Acting Board of Managers has charge of funds contributed for the support of pastors and evangelists, the distribution of tracts, and the support of superannuated and disabled ministers."

A PICTURE.

WE saw a young man starting out in life with a brave heart, full of hope for the future. He and his young wife had chosen the good part and united with the church. They were faithful Christians. They had but little money, but that gave them no great concern. They had good health, stout hearts and willing hands to labor. A farm was rented, and an indebtedness of one thousand dollars incurred to secure the necessary stock and implements to make farming a success. They commenced their farm life with promise of success, and they worked hard and saved at every point to pay off the debt.

The brother, by his exemplary and faithful life, won the confidence of all who knew him, both in and out of the church, and it was not long before a choice was held in his congregation for a minister and he was called by the church to labor in holy things. He was loath to accept the call, but it being urged upon him as duty and that he could not be faithful and refuse the call of the church, he accepted the important work. And now began a new life to him and his companion. God had blessed him with ability to preach the Word. He read and studied far into the night so that he might show himself approved unto God. The farm labor grew no less, and then came a loss of eight hundred dollars, and with several crop failures the debt increased, and the interest account grew heavier.

The brother was advanced to the second degree of the ministry, and then later to the eldership. He was called to do much work for the church. Sometimes his plow stood in the furrow while he was away preaching funerals, comforting the sorrowing, and attending to church work. He gave his time willingly and ungrudgingly, trusting that all would come right in the end. The years rolled on, church work increased, and the burden of debt in no way diminished, for there came the care of a large family, nine children having been given to the brother and sister. They were often oppressed and saddened with the outlook, but they labored on, hoping against hope, and struggling as best they could with the burden of debt resting upon them. Then there came the oversight of two churches, and the demands made upon the brother's time increased, and the debt also increased. It hung like a dark shadow over that home. Who can know the heart-aches and the hours of anxious, perplexing thought and care that came to that home, as the burden grew heavier and heavier, and at last the fact was pressed home to the minister and his faithful wife that they were unable to meet their obligations, and that insolvency was staring them in the face. They had now passed the meridian of life. They had worked hard together, lived scantily and saved wherever it was possible. They stood side by side, nobly struggling to avert the calamity they so much feared, but burdened as they were, it was a hopeless task. And at last the failure came. The only wonder is that it did not come sooner.

In the same congregation at least fifty brethren owned farms, prospered and grew wealthy. They gave their undivided time and attention to their work, and by looking after the one thing they succeeded and made money, while the minister with divided interest, giving on occasion nearly half of his time to the church, failed to pay his debts. While others slept, he studied; while others

Sterling is a pleasant and prosperous little city of several thousand inhabitants, situated on Rock River. On the opposite bank, and connected by a free bridge, is the City of Rock Falls. These cities have an excellent water power, and many large factories of different kinds are situated on either side, affording labor for many hundred hands. Sterling has a system of electric and gas lights, excellent water-works, free mail delivery, good railroad facilities, and an electric street railway under construction. It has also an excellent system of public schools, and there are many plain people, who are in sympathy with such a doctrine as the Bible teaches and the Brethren practice. We have a plain and comfortable meeting-house, lately built, and centrally located in the city. We have meetings regularly each Sunday, also Sunday-school and prayer-meeting.

We thought to lay these advantages before our brethren and sisters, and if there are such who are seeking a place to retire from active business life, or who would like to have the advantages of good schools to educate their children, or who desire to secure employment in a factory, and *especially* we call your attention to the opportunity of doing good and of building up the Lord's cause in this place. With such I will be glad to correspond. We are in need of a few faithful brethren and sisters, who are firmly established upon the doctrine of the Brethren, and are willing to spend and be spent for the cause of Christ,—brethren who are willing to let their light shine in the darkness, and especially in relation to the principles of our Fraternity, and, if need be, make some sacrifice for the cause of our Blessed Master. Who will respond?   P. R. KELTNER.

Sterling, Ill.

Caution.

PROBABLY a few words of advice to all of us who intend going to our Annual Meeting would not be out of place.

Brethren, and sisters, too, remember the time of our Annual Meeting is fast approaching and many of us will, no doubt, be thrown in large crowds, and crowded coaches. By-the-way, please remember,

1. Do not crowd to get on the cars. They will not leave until all are on.

2. Never occupy more space than necessary for your own comfort.

3. Do not turn a car seat, unless for three special friends.

4. Never place your boot nor shoe on the car seat; it is a bad habit.

5. Remember it is selfish to occupy a seat alone when others are standing.

6. Any filth you throw on the car floor is evidence of bad manners.

7. Please study the comforts of your fellow-passengers, and act accordingly; it will show refinement.

8. Show to all that this is not the first time you were away from home.

9. Do not change large money for strangers.

10. Do not assist strangers too readily.

11. Remember, if a stranger asks you to tell him the time of night, guess at it.

12. Never take a walk with strangers in some out-of-the-way place.

13. Above all, remember that as Christ has authority over all, and power to direct and govern all, they who put their trust in him will be forever safe. Ever remember that Christian brethren, and even pious, faithful ministers of the Gospel, may differ in judgment as to the best way of doing good, and while they exercise the right of private judgment, as to their own duty, they should cheerfully concede the same privilege to others,

The meeting and conference of Christians from different and distant places may be the means, not only of their own comfort, but of their increased usefulness to one another, and to their fellow-men generally, and in forming plans for future action we should ever remember our dependence on God. We should ever seek to understand his will and commit ourselves in well-doing to his merciful guidance and disposal. From all the occurrences of life we should endeavor to draw important instruction, and, as we have opportunity, we should communicate it for the benefit of others.

D. S. T. BUTTERBAUGH.

From Dubuque, Iowa.

IN reading the GOSPEL MESSENGER I noticed an article entitled, "City Preaching." We are members of the Dunkard church, and have been deprived of the privilege of attending our own church for a number of years. We feel an interest in getting a minister to come to this city to preach, and think a good work could be done here, and that we would have no trouble in getting a house in which to hold meetings.

Our brethren have been in the habit of coming as far as the outskirts of our city, but have not yet ventured into the city, where the work is so much needed. Send a minister here and we think there will be good results.

WILLIAM EMMERT.
LYDIA EMMERT.

April 18.

From Hawthorn, Fla.

BY a notice of the editor, the readers were informed of a contemplated trip by me to South Florida. I have just returned after having made a short visit to but two of the isolated members. On account of being unwell I did not see brother and sister Woodard, of Manatee. These members have lived for nine years in Florida, and in all that time have seen but two brethren. I much regretted not to be able to visit them.

My first stop was Tampa, second, Port Tampa, where I took a steam-boat to St. Petersburg, to visit sister William More and family. At that point I preached three times to small congregations, five miles out in the country.

Returning I took steamer to Manatee River to Braiden Town and stopped a few hours. Here I called on Bro. Neher, who has, with his son and daughter, been stopping at the above place during the winter for his health.

I might give the readers of the MESSENGER a more minute description of my observations of the people, customs and habits, and the prospects of building up churches in the South, but this part, I believe, can only be successfully done somewhat on the colonization plan. A number of families should locate, and then, if a minister can be found, suitable to the work, he should locate as shepherd of the flock to care for them, and to preach and establish our faith by living out our doctrine.

True, an evangelist may prepare the way by preaching and talking with the people, and distributing tracts, few ever having heard of our church, but it will require labor and time to introduce the self-denying doctrine of our Blessed Dord and Savior Jesus Christ. The habits of the native Floridian have been such as to render him largely indifferent to religious influence, and yet we do not find more, of what we might term, outright wickedness, if indeed as much, as in many places north.

We now desire to say something of the colored people. While the opportunities of education with them have been much improved, yet the possibilities of bringing them up to a standard of piety, measured by the Word of God, and the

doctrine taught by us, to my mind, are quite in the future. Their peculiar habits of mirthfulness are so prominent as to control the more reflective moments or thoughts, thus preventing steadfastness of purpose.

The race question is yet to be settled in the minds of many people of the South. There is yet a lingering sentiment or prejudice existing, and just how far this state of things is justifiable I am not prepared to say. The God that can control the destiny of men and nations, can bring even the colored man to a condition of fitness for his use in the future.   J. C. LAHMAN.

April 18.

Treasurer's Report.

THE following is the report of the Home Mission Fund of the District of Nebraska, from Oct. 1, 1891, to April 1, 1892:

RECEIPTS.

D. L. Miller,..........................	$350 00
South Beatrice church,.................	26 90
Sister Garman,.........................	25
Weeping Water church,..................	7 75
Bethel church,.........................	10 00
Perry Beckner,.........................	70
Pleasant Valley church,................	3 50
S. M. Forney and family,...............	8 00
South Beatrice church,.................	6 94
Blue River Valley church,..............	5 00

Total received from Oct. 1, 1891, to April 1, 1892,............................. $419 04

DISBURSEMENTS.

Owen Peters, mission work in Garfield County,..............................	$17 12
Owen Peters, mission work in Lincoln,..	3 50
B. F. Flory, mission work in Lincoln,...	3 50
J. J. Hoover, mission work at Minden,..	13 35
B. E. Whitmer, mission work in Lincoln,	8 75
M. L. Spire, expenses to meet mission board, ...	3 25
Isaac Dell, mission work in Lincoln,.....	3 55
Isaac Thomas, mission work in Otoe and Saline Counties,.....................	13 48
Jesse Y. Heckler, mission work in Lincoln and Dawson Counties, and one trip to City of Lincoln,..........	41 35
Urias Shick, mission work in Lincoln,....	5 00
Owen Peters, mission work in Dundy County, and one trip to City of Lincoln, ...	21 75
P. E. Whitmer, mission work in Nemaha County, ...	9 00
T. W. Graham, mission work in Lincoln,.	1 20
M. L. Spire, expenses to meet mission board, ...	4 47
Owen Peters, balance due expenses to Dundy County,.......................	5 61
Jesse Y. Heckler, mission work in Lincoln County,..........................	10 00
Isaac Dell, mission work in Lincoln,.....	4 80
T. W. Graham, mission work in Lincoln,.	3 00
Owen Peters, mission work in Lincoln,..	3 30
M. L. Spire, to meet mission board,.....	3 19
Perry Beckner, mission work at Elk Creek, ...	2 70
Isaac Thomas, mission work in Otoe and Saline Counties,.....................	13 36
S. M. Forney, mission work in Custer County, ...	26 00
To stamps and express orders,..........	60
Jesse Y. Heckler, mission work in Frontier County,............................	23 59
Urias Shick, mission work in Lincoln,....	2 50
J. J. Hoover, mission work in Custer County, ...	15 10
J. S. Ryan, mission work at Lincoln,.....	4 90
Perry Beckner, mission work at Elk Creek,	75

Total paid out from Oct. 1, 1891, to April 1, 1892,......................... $272 67

M. L. SPIRE, Treasurer.

Holmesville, Nebr., April 18, 1892.

Sterling is a pleasant and prosperous little city of several thousand inhabitants, situated on Rock River. On the opposite bank, and connected by a free bridge, is the City of Rock Falls. These cities have an excellent water power, and many large factories of different kinds are situated on either side, affording labor for many hundred hands. Sterling has a system of electric and gas lights, excellent water-works, free mail delivery, good railroad facilities, and an electric street railway under construction. It has also an excellent system of public schools, and there are many plain people, who are in sympathy with such a doctrine as the Bible teaches and the Brethren practice. We have a plain and comfortable meeting-house, lately built, and centrally located in the city. We have meetings regularly each Sunday, also Sunday-school and prayer-meeting.

We thought to lay these advantages before our brethren and sisters, and if there are such who are seeking a place to retire from active business life, or who would like to have the advantages of good schools to educate their children, or who desire to secure employment in a factory, and *especially* we call your attention to the opportunity of doing good and of building up the Lord's cause in this place. With such I will be glad to correspond. We are in need of a few faithful brethren and sisters, who are firmly established upon the doctrine of the Brethren, and are willing to spend and be spent for the cause of Christ,—brethren who are willing to let their light shine in the darkness, and especially in relation to the principles of our Fraternity, and, if need be, make some sacrifice for the cause of our Blessed Master. Who will respond? P. R. KELTNER.

Sterling, Ill.

Caution.

PROBABLY a few words of advice to all of us who intend going to our Annual Meeting would not be out of place.

Brethren, and sisters, too, remember the time of our Annual Meeting is fast approaching and many of us will, no doubt, be thrown in large crowds, and crowded coaches. By-the-way, please remember,

1. Do not crowd to get on the cars. They will not leave until all are on.

2. Never occupy more space than necessary for your own comfort.

3. Do not turn a car seat, unless for three special friends.

4. Never place your boot nor shoe on the car seat; it is a bad habit.

5. Remember it is selfish to occupy a seat alone when others are standing.

6. Any filth you throw on the car floor is evidence of bad manners.

7. Please study the comforts of your fellow-passengers, and act accordingly; it will show refinement.

8. Show to all that this is not the first time you were away from home.

9. Do not change large money for strangers.

10. Do not assist strangers too readily.

11. Remember, if a stranger asks you to tell him the time of night, guess at it.

12. Never take a walk with strangers in some out-of-the-way place.

13. Above all, remember that as Christ has authority over all, and power to direct and govern all, they who put their trust in him will be forever safe. Ever remember that Christian brethren, and even pious, faithful ministers of the Gospel, may differ in judgment as to the best way of doing good, and while they exercise the right of private judgment, as to their own duty, they should cheerfully concede the same privilege to others.

The meeting and conference of Christians from different and distant places may be the means, not only of their own comfort, but of their increased usefulness to one another, and to their fellow-men generally, and in forming plans for future action we should ever remember our dependence on God. We should ever seek to understand his will and commit ourselves in well-doing to his merciful guidance and disposal. From all the occurrences of life we should endeavor to draw important instruction, and, as we have opportunity, we should communicate it for the benefit of others.

D. S. T. BUTTERBAUGH.

From Dubuque, Iowa.

IN reading the GOSPEL MESSENGER I noticed an article entitled, "City Preaching." We are members of the Dunkard church, and have been deprived of the privilege of attending our own church for a number of years. We feel an interest in getting a minister to come to this city to preach, and think a good work could be done here, and that we would have no trouble in getting a house in which to hold meetings.

Our brethren have been in the habit of coming as far as the outskirts of our city, but have not yet ventured into the city, where the work is so much needed. Send a minister here and we think there will be good results.

WILLIAM EMMERT.
LYDIA EMMERT.

April 18.

From Hawthorn, Fla.

BY a notice of the editor, the readers were informed of a contemplated trip by me to South Florida. I have just returned after having made a short visit to but two of the isolated members. On account of being unwell I did not see brother and sister Woodard, of Manatee. These members have lived for nine years in Florida, and in all that time have seen but two brethren. I much regretted not to be able to visit them.

My first stop was Tampa, second, Port Tampa, where I took a steam-boat to St. Petersburg, to visit sister William More and family. At that point I preached three times to small congregations, five miles out in the country.

Returning I took steamer to Manatee River to Braiden Town and stopped a few hours. Here I called on Bro. Neher, who has, with his son and daughter, been stopping at the above place during the winter for his health.

I might give the readers of the MESSENGER a more minute description of my observations of the people, customs and habits, and the prospects of building up churches in the South, but this part, I believe, can only be successfully done somewhat on the colonization plan. A number of families should locate, and then, if a minister can be found, suitable to the work, he should locate as shepherd of the flock to care for them, and to preach and establish our faith by living out our doctrine.

True, an evangelist may prepare the way by preaching and talking with the people, and distributing tracts, few ever having heard of our church, but it will require labor and time to introduce the self-denying doctrine of our Blessed Lord and Savior Jesus Christ. The habits of the native Floridian have been such as to render him largely indifferent to religious influence, and yet we do not find more, of what we might term, outright wickedness, if indeed as much, as in many places north.

We now desire to say something of the colored people. While the opportunities of education with them have been much improved, yet the possibilities of bringing them up to a standard of piety, measured by the Word of God, and the doctrine taught by us, to my mind, are quite in the future. Their peculiar habits of mirthfulness are so prominent as to control the more reflective moments or thoughts, thus preventing steadfastness of purpose.

The race question is yet to be settled in the minds of many people of the South. There is yet a lingering sentiment or prejudice existing, and just how far this state of things is justifiable I am not prepared to say. The God that can control the destiny of men and nations, can bring even the colored man to a condition of fitness for his use in the future. J. C. LAHMAN.

April 18.

Treasurer's Report.

THE following is the report of the Home Mission Fund of the District of Nebraska, from Oct. 1, 1891, to April 1, 1892:

RECEIPTS.

D. L. Miller,	$350 00
South Beatrice church,	26 90
Sister Garman,	25
Weeping Water church,	7 75
Bethel church,	10 00
Perry Beckner,	70
Pleasant Valley church,	3 50
S. M. Forney and family,	8 00
South Beatrice church,	6 94
Blue River Valley church,	5 00

Total received from Oct 1, 1891, to April 1, 1892, $419 04

DISBURSEMENTS.

Owen Peters, mission work in Garfield County,	$ 17 12
Owen Peters, mission work in Lincoln,	2 50
B. F. Flory, mission work in Lincoln,	3 50
J. J. Hoover, mission work at Minden,	13 35
R. E. Whitmer, mission work in Lincoln,	8 75
M. L. Spire, expenses to meet mission board,	3 25
Isaac Dell, mission work in Lincoln,	3 55
Isaac Thomas, mission work in Otoe and Saline Counties,	13 48
Jesse Y. Heckler, mission work in Lincoln and Dawson Counties, and one trip to City of Lincoln,	41 35
Uriss Shick, mission work in Lincoln,	5 00
Owen Peters, mission work in Dundy County, and one trip to City of Lincoln,	21 75
P. E. Whitmer, mission work in Nemaha County,	9 00
T. W. Graham, mission work in Lincoln,	1 20
M. L. Spire, expenses to meet mission board,	4 47
Owen Peters, balance due expenses to Dundy County,	5 61
Jesse Y. Heckler, mission work in Lincoln County,	10 00
Isaac Dell, mission work in Lincoln,	4 80
T. W. Graham, mission work in Lincoln,	3 00
Owen Peters, mission work in Lincoln,	3 30
M. L. Spire, to meet mission board,	3 19
Perry Beckner, mission work at Elk Creek,	2 70
Isaac Thomas, mission work in Otoe and Saline Counties,	13 36
S. M. Forney, mission work in Custer County,	26 00
To stamps and express orders,	60
Jesse Y. Heckler, mission work in Frontier County,	23 59
Uriss Shick, mission work in Lincoln,	2 60
J. J. Hoover, mission work in Custer County,	15 10
J. S. Ryan, mission work at Lincoln,	4 90
Perry Beckner, mission work at Elk Creek,	75

Total paid out from Oct 1, 1891, to April 1, 1892, $272 67

M. L. SPIRE, Treasurer.

Holmesville, Nebr., April 18, 1892.

Notice Regarding Half-Fare Rates to District Meeting of Southern Ohio.

THIS meeting will be held at Highland, with the Lexington church, May 17. Arrangements have been made over the "Big Four," D. & M., O. & S., B. & O., by way of Springfield and Greenfield. Highland is twelve miles from Greenfield on the B. & O. Leaving Union City at 6: 35 A. M., you arrive at Highland at 3: 40 P. M. Leave Arcanum at 7: 20 A. M., by way of Troy; Dayton at 8: 53 A. M, by way of Springfield. Tickets will be on sale May 16, good to return May 18. Fare from Union City for the round trip, $3.60; Arcanum, $2.95; Pittsburgh, $2.95; New Carlisle, $2.25; Springfield, $1.85; Dayton, $2.20, by way of Springfield; $3.55, by way of Cincinnati. From Dayton we would advise all to go by way of Springfield, and save $1.35 in fare, as arrangements are completed. Change cars at Springfield and, perhaps, at Greenfield. The B. & O. people talk of taking us from Greenfield without change. If so, we would arrive at Highland at 1: 30, otherwise at 3: 40. Tickets at all stations on lines.

HENRY FRANTZ.

From Germantown, Pa.

I AM glad to say our work, here in the City, is progressing encouragingly. Four weeks ago closed a short series of meetings in the Philadelphia church. From then until the present time, ten have been added by baptism and others will be soon. During the same time two have been added by letter. The church has decided to be represented at both District and Annual Conference, and has chosen Bro. T. T. Myers as delegate. Plans are submitted for an addition to the present house of worship, and it is expected that structure will be completed during the summer. The progress and prospect of the work makes it very encouraging for any one in any way connected therewith.

Following the above mentioned revival we also had a short series of meetings in the Germantown church, Bro. Myers returning the favor for assistance given him. Three were baptized and others are manifestly near. The attendance and interest in the work are increasing gradually. Two weeks ago we began prayer-meeting. With earnest and careful work we have bright hopes for the future. Bro. Landon West hits the mark in his notes on city work. A little actual practice is sufficient to upset a good deal of theory.

WILBUR B. STOVER.

April 19, 1892.

From Ottawa, Kans.

THE labors of the District Meeting of Northeastern Kansas passed off very harmoniously. The attendance was good, considering the unpleasant weather. Bro. Wm. Davis, of Morrill, Brown Co., was chosen delegate to Annual Meeting. The work of the Mutual Aid Association, the constitution and by laws of the same were remodeled and improved. We closed our labors on Thursday evening.

I recently learned the whereabouts of my nephew, Wm. Pfouts, whose wife is a sister. They moved from North-western Nebraska to Neosho Co., Kans., two and one-half miles south of Carleton. I visited them, and they arranged for a meeting on Sunday night, in Carleton, where we had a large and attentive congregation. There we found other members, some of whom are aged, and, apparently, without a shepherd. Some of them had not been to a meeting of the Brethren for more than six years. We think they should be looked after and supplied with preaching

from the surrounding churches, and ministers traveling that way.

Let us pray more fervently that the Lord of the harvest may send more laborers. We are having considerable rain and wind this spring. The earth is being clothed with beauty.

J. D. TROSTLE.

Hope, Kans.

From the Slate Creek Church, Kansas.

MARCH 2 Bro. Charles M. Yearout, of Westphalia, Kans., began a series of meetings in the Slate Creek church, and continued until the evening of March 12, preaching in all thirteen sermons. During his stay with us thirteen precious souls started in the good work of serving their Lord and Master, several of which are very young. We hope and trust they may all be bright and shining lights in the church. Bro. Yearout does not shun to declare the Word in its primitive purity. His success in getting members into the church is not by telling exciting stories, but by preaching the Word in its purity, and so plain that children cannot help but understand it. May success follow him wherever he goes, is my prayer!　　　　J. B. THOMPSON.

Conway Springs, Kans.

From Naperville, Ill.

THE Brethren of the Naperville church met in council and spent about five hours in the interest of our church. Three members were received by letter, which gives joy to our little church. Considerable business was attended to, but we trust that all was transacted to the edifying of the church, and to the welfare of our souls.

As usual our semi-annual collection was taken for the Mission and Tract Work, which resulted in $9.75 for the Mission Work, and $3.65 for the Tract Work.

We hope to do better yet, as all were not present at the time of the collection.

Our love-feast will occur May 14, commencing at 2 P. M., and continuing over Sunday.

S. B. KUHN.

Notes from Our Correspondents.

"*As cold water to a thirsty soul, so is good news from a far country.*"

Blizzard, Tenn.—Bro. Dove and I went to Basemountain to do some church work. We held ten meetings. The Spirit of the Lord was with us and three were made willing to unite with the church, and one was restored to fellowship again. At the Pleasant Valley church, Washington County, we had twelve meetings. Eight dear souls were made willing to come to Christ. At South Watoga one young man, afflicted with consumption, made application and was visited and received as an applicant for baptism, but was too weak to be baptized. He died in a few weeks, "Be ye also ready, for in such an hour as ye think not the Son of man cometh."—*G. C. Bowman, April 21.*

Oshool, Mo.—The members of the Greenwood church are still laboring as best they can in the Master's service, and while great numbers are not being added to the church, we are nevertheless at work, and gaining some. During the winter two members were received into the church by baptism, and still others are interested. Our field of labor is widening. Calls are being made at new points that demand our attention. We find plenty to do, and if all our ministers were as active as they could be, much more might be done than there is. May God help us all to be more faithful to duty! Last Sunday, April 17, we re-organized our Sunday-school with a full corps of officers.—*J. J. Trozel, April 21.*

Clay County, Tex.—The Pleasant Valley church met in quarterly council April 11, and all business passed off very pleasantly. Our love-feast will be May 7. We have arranged for one week's series of meeting prior to the feast, commencing Saturday before the first Sunday in May.—*Mattie Bowman.*

Rockton, Pa.—We met in quarterly council April 9, to attend to the work necessary to keep God's house in order. Our moderator, Eld. Peter Beer, being present but not able to fill his office, he called on Bro. J. H. Beer to fill his place *pro tem.* Brethren Peter and J. H. Beer were selected to represent us at our next District Meeting. Bro. J. A. Brilhart was elected as trustee. We decided to hold our love-feast Sept. 2, at 4 P. M. A series of meetings was asked for and was unanimously granted, to commence the first Lord's Day in May.—*John A. Brilhart.*

Walton, Kans.—Bro. Hutchison, from McPherson, came to us last Saturday, and delivered four soul-stirring sermons in our school-house. He is an able expounder of the Gospel, and is sure to convince every honest heart of the truth as it is in Christ Jesus. The congregations were large and order good. I believe that all who heard him desired him to stay longer, but on account of busy times, chilly weather and his feeble health, he closed, promising us to come back some time in the future, and to give us a series of meetings, the Lord willing. We have an interesting Sunday-school at our school-house.—*Eliza G. Miller, April 19.*

Salem, Kans.—Our love-feast occurred April 11. The ministerial meeting was held next day and the District Meeting April 13. All these occasions were cheering to the soul. Bro. A. W. Vaniman remained with us a few days after the District Meeting and gave us five excellent sermons. We rejoice to know that as a result of the meetings two dear young souls came out on the Lord's side and were baptized, we hope, to walk in newness of life. One is a young lady in her teens, and a brother who is the head of a little family. May many more dear souls be brought to Christ before it is too late! Others are seriously count. ing the cost.—*Sadie Monts, April 18.*

North Manchester, Ind.—The members of the North Manchester church met at their new church-house west of town yesterday, and had a large and very interesting council. The report of the annual visit was made, and a considerable amount of business transacted very pleasantly, and with a good feeling by all. Our adjoining elders, David Neff, Samuel Leckrone, and Jacob Snell, were with us, and officiated in ordaining our worthy brother, Isaac Miller, to the full ministry. May God's good and unerring Spirit always accompany our dear brother, that he may ever prove faithful in his high calling! The brethren also appointed a Communion meeting for May 28 at 10 A. M.—*I. C. Cripe, April 22.*

Poudre Valley Church, Colo.—Our quarterly council occurred April 16. Eld. G. W. Fesler was present and presided over the meeting. Everything passed off satisfactorily. We were made to rejoice when a dear sister, who had strayed from the fold, returned and confessed her wrongs, and desired to walk with the people of God. May the Lord grant her grace to prove faithful! Our Sunday-school is progressing nicely, under the care of Bro. Samuel Fye. Should any ministering brethren pass through Ft. Collins, Colo., going to or from Annual Meeting, we would be pleased to have them stop and preach for us. They will be met by the writer, if notified a few days previous. Our church will be represented at District Meeting by letter.—*D. M. Click.*

Notice Regarding Half-Fare Rates to District Meeting of Southern Ohio.

THIS meeting will be held at Highland, with the Lexington church, May 17. Arrangements have been made over the "Big Four," D. & M., O. & S., B. & O., by way of Springfield and Greenfield. Highland is twelve miles from Greenfield on the B. & O. Leaving Union City at 6: 35 A. M., you arrive at Highland at 3: 40 P. M. Leave Arcanum at 7: 20 A. M., by way of Troy; Dayton at 8: 53 A. M, by way of Springfield. Tickets will be on sale May 16, good to return May 18. Fare from Union City for the round trip, $3.60; Arcanum, $2.95; Pittsburgh, $2.95; New Carlisle, $2.25; Springfield, $1.85; Dayton, $2.20, by way of Springfield; $3.55, by way of Cincinnati. From Dayton we would advise all to go by way of Springfield, and save $1.35 in fare, as arrangements are completed. Change cars at Springfield and, perhaps, at Greenfield. The B. & O. people talk of taking us from Greenfield without change. If so, we would arrive at Highland at 1: 30, otherwise at 3: 40. Tickets at all stations on lines.

HENRY FRANTZ.

From Germantown, Pa.

I AM glad to say our work, here in the City, is progressing encouragingly. Four weeks ago closed a short series of meetings in the Philadelphia church. From then until the present time, ten have been added by baptism and others will be soon. During the same time two have been added by letter. The church has decided to be represented at both District and Annual Conference, and has chosen Bro. T. T. Myers as delegate. Plans are submitted for an addition to the present house of worship, and it is expected that structure will be completed during the summer. The progress and prospect of the work makes it very encouraging for any one in any way connected therewith.

Following the above mentioned revival we also had a short series of meetings in the Germantown church, Bro. Myers returning the favor for assistance given him. Three were baptized and others are manifestly near. The attendance and interest in the work are increasing gradually. Two weeks ago we began prayer-meeting. With earnest and careful work we have bright hopes for the future. Bro. Landon West hits the mark in his notes on city work. A little actual practice is sufficient to upset a good deal of theory.

WILBUR B. STOVER.

April 19, 1892.

From Ottawa, Kans.

THE labors of the District Meeting of Northeastern Kansas passed off very harmoniously. The attendance was good, considering the unpleasant weather. Bro. Wm. Davis, of Morrill, Brown Co., was chosen delegate to Annual Meeting. The work of the Mutual Aid Association, the constitution and by laws of the same were remodeled and improved. We closed our labors on Thursday evening.

I recently learned the whereabouts of my nephew, Wm. Plouts, whose wife is a sister. They moved from North-western Nebraska to Neosho Co., Kans., two and one-half miles south of Carleton. I visited them, and they arranged for a meeting on Sunday night, in Carleton, where we had a large and attentive congregation. There we found other members, some of whom are aged, and, apparently, without a shepherd. Some of them had not been to a meeting of the Brethren for more than six years. We think they should be looked after and supplied with preaching from the surrounding churches, and ministers traveling that way.

Let us pray more fervently that the Lord of the harvest may send more laborers. We are having considerable rain and wind this spring. The earth is being clothed with beauty.

J. D. TROSTLE.

Hope, Kans.

From the Slate Creek Church, Kansas.

MARCH 2 Bro. Charles M. Yearout, of Westphalia, Kans., began a series of meetings in the Slate Creek church, and continued until the evening of March 12, preaching in all thirteen sermons. During his stay with us thirteen precious souls started in the good work of serving their Lord and Master, several of which are very young. We hope and trust they may all be bright and shining lights in the church. Bro. Yearout does not show to declare the Word in its primitive purity. His success in getting members into the church is not by telling exciting stories, but by preaching the Word in its purity, and so plain that children cannot help but understand it. May success follow him wherever he goes, is my prayer!

J. B. THOMPSON.

Conway Springs, Kans.

From Naperville, Ill.

THE Brethren of the Naperville church met in council and spent about five hours in the interest of our church. Three members were received by letter, which gives joy to our little church. Considerable business was attended to, but we trust that all was transacted to the edifying of the church, and to the welfare of our souls.

As usual our semi-annual collection was taken for the Mission and Tract Work, which resulted in $0.75 for the Mission Work, and $3.65 for the Tract Work.

We hope to do better yet, as all were not present at the time of the collection.

Our love-feast will occur May 14, commencing at 2 P. M., and continuing over Sunday.

S. B. KUHN.

Notes from Our Correspondents.

"An cold water to a thirsty soul, so is good news from a far country."

Blizzard, Tenn.—Bro. Dove and I went to Bearmountain to do some church work. We held ten meetings. The Spirit of the Lord was with us and three were made willing to unite with the church, and one was restored to fellowship again. At the Pleasant Valley church, Washington County, we had twelve meetings. Eight dear souls were made willing to come to Christ. At South Watoga one young man, afflicted with consumption, made application and was visited and received as an applicant for baptism, but was too weak to be baptized. He died in a few weeks. "Be ye also ready, for in such an hour as ye think not the Son of man cometh."—G. C. Bowman, April 21.

School, Mo.—The members of the Greenwood church are still laboring as best they can in the Master's service, and while great numbers are not being added to the church, we are nevertheless at work, and gaining some. During the winter two members were received into the church by baptism, and still others are interested. Our field of labor is widening. Calls are being made at new points that demand our attention. We find plenty to do, and if all our ministers were as active as they could be, much more might be done than there is. May God help us all to be more faithful to duty! Last Sunday, April 17, we re-organized our Sunday-school with a full corps of officers.—J. J. Trozel, April 21.

Clay County, Tex.—The Pleasant Valley church met in quarterly council April 11, and all business passed off very pleasantly. Our love-feast will be May 7. We have arranged for one week's series of meeting prior to the feast, commencing Saturday before the first Sunday in May.—Mattie Bowman.

Rockton, Pa.—We met in quarterly council April 9, to attend to the work necessary to keep God's house in order. Our moderator, Eld. Peter Beer, being present but not able to fill his office, he called on Bro. J. H. Beer to fill his place pro tem. Brethren Peter and J. H. Beer were selected to represent us at our next District Meeting. Bro. J. A. Brilhart was elected as trustee. We decided to hold our love-feast Sept. 3, at 4 P. M. A series of meetings was asked for and was unanimously granted, to commence the first Lord's Day in May.—John A. Brilhart.

Walton, Kans.—Bro. Hutchison, from McPherson, came to us last Saturday, and delivered four soul-stirring sermons in our school-house. He is an able expounder of the Gospel, and is sure to convince every honest heart of the truth as it is in Christ Jesus. The congregations were large and order good, I believe that all who heard him desired him to stay longer, but on account of busy times, chilly weather and his feeble health, he closed, promising us to come back some time in the future, and to give us a series of meetings, the Lord willing. We have an interesting Sunday-school at our school-house.—Eliza G. Miller, April 19.

Salem, Kans.—Our love-feast occurred April 11. The ministerial meeting was held next day and the District Meeting April 13. All these occasions were cheering to the soul. Bro. A. W. Vaniman remained with us a few days after the District Meeting and gave us five excellent sermons. We rejoice to know that as a result of the meetings two dear young souls came out on the Lord's side and were baptized, we hope, to walk in newness of life. One is a young lady in her teens, and a brother who is the head of a little family. May many more dear souls be brought to Christ before it is too late! Others are seriously counting the cost.—Sadie Monts, April 19.

North Manchester, Ind.—The members of the North Manchester church met at their new church-house west of town yesterday, and had a large and very interesting council. The report of the annual visit was made, and a considerable amount of business transacted very pleasantly, and with a good feeling by all. Our adjoining elders, David Neff, Samuel Leckrone, and Jacob Snell, were with us, and officiated in ordaining our worthy brother, Isaac Miller, to the full ministry. May God's good and unerring Spirit always accompany our dear brother, that he may ever prove faithful in his high calling! The brethren also appointed a Communion meeting for May 28 at 10 A. M.—I. C. Cripe, April 22.

Poudre Valley Church, Colo.—Our quarterly council occurred April 10. Eld. G. W. Fesler was present and presided over the meeting. Everything passed off satisfactorily. We were made to rejoice when a dear sister, who had strayed from the fold, returned and confessed her wrongs, and desired to walk with the people of God. May the Lord grant her grace to prove faithful! Our Sunday-school is progressing nicely, under the care of Bro. Samuel Pye. Should any ministering brethren pass through Ft. Collins, Colo., going to or from Annual Meeting, we would be pleased to have them stop and preach for us. They will be met by the writer, if notified a few days previous. Our church will be represented at District Meeting by letter.—D. M. Click.

Chicago & Iowa R. R.

If you desire to go anywhere and get there quickly and safely, take the Chicago & Iowa R. R.

The Short Line Between all Prominent Points

Through trains between
Chicago, St. Paul & Indianapolis,
Equipped with

Elegant Coaches, Dining and Sleeping Cars.

Everything provided to insure
COMFORT, SAFETY AND CONVENIENCE
For the traveling public.

Tickets on Sale to all Points in the United States, Canada or Mexico.

Baggage Checked Through, thus Saving Passengers the Annoyance of Rechecking.

For further information call on any agent, or address

H. D. JUDSON, Gen. Supt.,
Aurora, Ill.

CRUDEN'S
COMPLETE
CONCORDANCE

THIS excellent work, which we offer for sale to our readers, at the low price of $1.50 post-paid, is the only one of the kind that may be depended upon as being strictly reliable. Any verse in the Bible may be readily found by looking for any material word in the verse. Besides this there are given the significations of the principal words, by which their true, Scriptural meaning may be known. A full account of Jewish customs and ceremonies is given as well as a complete concordance of the proper names of the Bible and of the books called Apocrypha. Send all orders for the [illegible]

Brethren's Church Manual.

THIS is a small book, adapted to the wants of every member of the Church, and will be found especially useful to our ministers, deacons, Sunday-school officers and teachers and all who wish to be posted in the faith and practices of the church. Besides giving the faith, practices and duties of the church, it contains forms of Ordinations, Installings, Marriages, Burials, Prayers, etc. The work ends with a complete set of rules for conducting all kinds of public meetings, and is just the book every one interested in church work needs. Send for a copy. Only 30 cents for a copy, post-paid; per dozen, $3.00. Address Brethren's Publishing Co., Mt. Morris, Ill., or Huntingdon, Pa.

Excursions to California.

EXCURSIONS in charge of M. M. Eshelman, Immigration Agent, will leave Chicago over the "Santa Fe Route" Tuesdays, and Kansas City Wednesdays, during the year 1892, on dates as follows:

Chicago, January 26, February 23, March 22, April 26, May 24, June 28, July 26, August 23, September 27, October 25, November 22, December 27.

Kansas City, January 27, February 24, March 23, April 27, May 25, June 29, July 27, August 24, September 28, October 26, November 23, December 28.

Parties wishing to avail themselves of the privileges of these excursions, should write M. M. Eshelman, North Pomona, California, prior to the 15th of each month, and from the fifteenth to the end of the month, at 1050 Union Avenue (opposite Union Depot), Kansas City, Mo., stating when and where they wish to join one of these excursions, and he will give them full information, and if desired will reserve berths in Tourist Sleeping Car for them. Do not fail to write him; he will do you good. The rates will be as low as the lowest made to the Pacific Coast.

GEORGE L. MCDONAUGH,
TRAVELING AGENT.

ADVERTISEMENTS.

Rates per Inch each Insertion.

One time or more,	$1 50
One month (4 times),	1 30
Three months (12 times),	1 20
Six months (25 times),	1 00
One year (50 times),	70
No advertisement accepted for less than	1 00

Tract Work.

List of Publications for Sale,—Sent Postage Prepaid.

CLASS A.

No. 1. Golden Gleams or Family Chart,	$ 85
No. 2. Diagram of Passover and Lord's Supper, per copy,	75

CLASS B.

Plain Family Bible, per copy,	$2 70
Trine Immersion, Quinter, per copy,	1 25
Europe and Bible Lands, Miller, per copy,	1 50
Doctrine of the Brethren Defended, Miller, per copy,	1 50
Close Communion, West, per copy,	4
Missionary Hymn Book, per dozen, $1.00; per copy,	10

CLASS C.—(TRACTS.)

No. 1. The Brethren or Dunkards, per 100, $1.50 per copy,	02
No. 2. Path of Life, per 100, $4; per copy,	05
No. 3. How to Become a Child of God, per 100, $4; per copy,	05
No. 4. Conversion, per 100, $2.50; per copy,	03
No. 5. Water Baptism, per 100, $1.50; per copy,	02
No. 6. Single Immersion, per 100, $1; per copy,	01
No. 7. Sabbatism, per 100, $1.50; per copy,	02
No. 8. Trine Immersion Traced to the Apostles, per 100, $7; per copy,	08
No. 9. Sermon on Baptism, per 100, $2; per copy,	03
No. 10. Glad Tidings of Salvation, per 100, $1.50; per copy,	02
No. 11. Life of Eld. S. Weir (Colored), per 100, $1.50; per copy,	02
No. 12. Ten Reasons for Trine Immersion, per 100, $1; per copy,	01
No. 13. The Lord's Day and the Sabbath, per 100, $2.50; per copy,	03

CLASS D.

No. 1. The House We Live In, per 100,	$ 45
No. 2. Plan of Salvation, per 100,	45
No. 3. Come Let Us Reason Together, per 100,	45
No. 4. How Shall I know that my Sins are Pardoned? per 100,	45
No. 5. Intemperance, per 100,	45
No. 6. Plain Dressing, per 100,	45
No. 7. Which is the Right Church? per 100,	45
No. 8. The House We Live In (Swedish), per 100,	45
No. 9. The House We Live In (Danish), per 100,	45
No. 10. Paul Wetzel's Reasons (German), per 100,	45
No. 11. Sinner, Stop, per 100,	45
No. 12. Faith, per 100,	45
No. 13. The Light-House, per 100,	45
No. 14. Close Communion, per 100,	45
No. 15. The Truth Shall Make You Free, per 100,	45
No. 16. Modern Skepticism, per 100,	45
No. 17. Infant Baptism Weighed, etc., per 100,	45
No. 18. Repentance, per 100,	45
No. 19. Talk to R. R. Employees, etc., per 100,	45
No. 20. Life and Death, per 100,	45
No. 21. The House We Live In (German), per 100,	45
No. 22. The Prayer Covering, per 100,	45
No. 23. The Lord's Supper, per 100,	45
No. 24. Shall I Swear or Affirm? per 100,	45
No. 25. Secret Societies, per 100,	45
No. 26. Church Entertainments, per 100,	45
No. 27. Conversion or the New Birth, per 100,	45
No. 28. The Bible Service of Feet-washing, per 100,	45
No. 29. Scriptural Communion, per 100,	45

CLASS E.

No. 1. Pause and Think, per 100,	20
No. 2. What Do We Need? per 100,	20
No. 3. Right or Wrong Way, per 100,	20
No. 4. Why Am I Not a Christian? per 100,	20
No. 5. Saving Words, per 100,	20
No. 6. Christ and War, per 100,	20
No. 7. The Bond of Peace, per 100,	20
No. 8. The Kiss of Charity, per 100,	20
No. 9. The Evils of Intemperance, per 100,	20
No. 10. The Lost Opportunity, per 100,	20
No. 11. Are You a Christian? per 100,	20
No. 12. Arise, Get Thee Down, per 100,	20
No. 13. A Personal Appeal, per 100,	20
No. 14. Lying Among the Pots, per 100,	20
No. 15. Gold and Costly Array, per 100,	20
No. 16. The Brethren's Card, per 100,	20
No. 17. The Whole Gospel Must Be Obeyed, per 100,	20

Bibles, Testaments, Hymn Books of all styles, at publishers' lowest retail prices, which will be furnished on application. Address:

BRETHREN'S BOOK & TRACT WORK,
DAYTON, OHIO.

CATHOLICS The errors and dangers of their system, with a full account of their persecutions. A book of startling facts and forcible logic. Over 600 pages, illustrated. Cloth, $2.00; Leather, $2.50. "What to Read," our monthly magazine, one year free to every purchaser of a book. Liberal inducements to agents. Write for circulars and terms to Jas. M. Neff, Covington, Ohio.

PUBLICATIONS

☞ The following books, Sunday-school supplies, etc., are for sale by the BRETHREN'S PUBLISHING CO., Mt. Morris, Ill., or Huntingdon, Pa., to whom all orders should be addressed.

The Brethren's Quarterly.

For Sunday-school teachers and scholars this publication is of the greatest benefit. Look at our prices:

Single subscription, one year,	35 cents.
Single subscription, per quarter,	10 cents.
Three copies, per quarter,	25 cents.
Eight copies, per quarter,	40 cents.
Twenty copies and over,	4 cents each.

Hymn Books.

New Tune and Hymn Books.

Half leather, per copy, post-paid,	$ 75
Morocco, per copy, post-paid,	1 00
Morocco, gilt edge, per copy, post-paid,	1 25

Hymn Books.

Morocco, per copy, post-paid,	$ 75
Morocco, gilt edge, per copy, post-paid,	85
Arabesque, per copy, post-paid,	40
Fine Limp, per copy, post-paid,	75
Fine Limp, gilt edge, per copy, post-paid,	85
German and English, per copy, post-paid,	75

Sunday-School Requisites.

The following list of things is needed in all Sunday-schools:

Testaments, Flexible, red edge, per dozen,	$1 00
Minute Books, each,	40
Class Books, per dozen,	75
S. S. Primers, with fine engravings, per dozen,	70

New and Beautiful Sunday-School Cards.

"The Gem," 50 picture cards, each with Bible text, verse of hymn,	35
250 Reward Tickets—verse of Scripture—red or blue,	20

The Young Disciple.

The YOUNG DISCIPLE is a neatly printed weekly, published especially for the moral benefit and religious instruction of our young folks.

Single copy, one year,	$ 50
Six copies (the sixth to the agent),	2 50
Ten copies,	4 00

For Three Months or Thirteen Weeks.

20 copies to one address,	$1 70
30 " " " "	2 50
40 " " " "	3 35
50 " " " "	3 80
75 " " " "	5 20
100 " " " "	7 00

For Six Months or Twenty-Six Weeks.

20 copies to one address,	$ 3 35
30 " " " "	5 00
40 " " " "	6 60
50 " " " "	7 50
75 " " " "	10 20
100 " " " "	13 75

Our paper is designed for the Sunday-school and the home circle. We desire the name of every Sunday-school Superintendent in the Brotherhood, and want an agent in every church. Send for sample copies.

I INTEND Soon to issue a small monthly magazine to be published in the interests of all who buy books and read, at 50 cents per annum. But as a *special inducement* I will send it one year for 35 cents and give free a Handy and Reliable little Dictionary of 30,000 words and 320 pages, to all who send in their subscriptions at once. Address: Jas. M. Neff, Covington, Ohio.

JAMES T. QUINLAN,
SHIPPING & COMMISSION MERCHANT
Wool, Hay, Grain and Gen'l Produce,
305 South Charles St.,
BALTIMORE, - - MD.
8tf

Brethren's Quarterly.

Orders should be sent in at once for the **Quarterly** for the Second Quarter of 1892. Price, three copies, 25 cents; eight copies, 40 cents; twenty copies and over, four cents each.

LOOK AT THIS.

The Monon Route still reducing rates and offering better accommodations than ever before.

Commencing April 15, the fare from Chicago to Louisville, New Albany, Cincinnati, Hamilton, and Dayton will be $5.50; to Indianapolis $3.50. Round trip tickets good ten days at double the one way rate.

Parlor and Dining cars on day trains; Pullman Sleepers and Compartment Cars on night trains. A special Sleeper is run for Indianapolis business.

See that your tickets read via the MONON ROUTE.

JAMES BARKER, G. P. A.

The Conference at Cedar Rapids.

The Conference of German Baptist Brethren will be held at Cedar Rapids, Iowa, from June 3rd to 9th, and as the route used for the trip will prove an important factor in the general enjoyment of those who attend, the following facts in regard to the very favorable arrangements made by the Chicago & North-Western Ry. Co., will be of special interest.

Excursion tickets to Cedar Rapids and return will be sold from all stations on the North-Western Line, comprising over 8,000 miles of railway, at one-half regular rates (one fare for the round trip). Tickets will be sold at this rate from May 30th to June 6th, and will be good for return passage until and including June 30th.

The North-Western is the short line for delegates and visitors, destined to Cedar Rapids from either the East or West. Four through trains are run from Chicago and Omaha to Cedar Rapids, and among the advantages offered travelers are Solid, Vestibuled Trains of Palace Sleeping Cars, reclining chair cars (in which seats are free), modern day coaches, and superb dining cars.

Circulars giving detailed information will be mailed on application to W. A. Thrall, General Passenger and Ticket Agent, Chicago, or to any representative of the Company.

Church Entertainments: Twenty Objections.

By Rev. B. Carradine, D. D. 12mo, 100 pp. Paper cover, 30 cents. A strong book in defense of its position, written by a powerful pen, presenting the most candid and scriptural arraignment of unwarrantable methods for money-raising in the Church. The spirit of the book is highly devotional and cannot fail to inspire the reader with its seriousness.

Campbell and Owen Debate.—Contains a complete investigation of the evidences of Christianity. Price, $1.50.

THE NORTH WESTERN LINE
C. & N. W. R'Y.

With its thousands of miles of perfectly equipped road reaches the most important points in ILLINOIS, IOWA, WISCONSIN, NORTHERN MICHIGAN, MINNESOTA, NORTH and SOUTH DAKOTA, NEBRASKA and WYOMING.

SOLID VESTIBULED TRAINS

Between Chicago and St. Paul, Minneapolis, Council Bluffs, Omaha, Denver and Portland.

FREE RECLINING CHAIR CARS

Between Chicago, Council Bluffs, Omaha, Denver and Portland.

THROUGH SLEEPING CARS

Between Chicago and San Francisco without change.

SUPERB DINING CARS.

For Tickets, Time Tables and full information apply to Agents

CHICAGO & NORTH-WESTERN R'Y,
Or address the Gen'l Pass. and Ticket Ag't at Chicago.

W. H. NEWMAN, 3d Vice-Pres. J. M. WHITMAN, Gen'l Manager. W. A. THRALL, Gen'l Passenger and Ticket Agent.
N. A. No. 4-92.

THE GOSPEL MESSENGER.

"Set for the Defense of the Gospel."

Vol. 30, Old Series.   Mt. Morris, Ill., and Huntingdon, Pa., May 10, 1892.   No. 19

The Gospel Messenger.

H. B. Brumbaugh, Editor,

And Business Manager of the Eastern House, Box 50.
Huntingdon, Pa.

Table of Contents.

Since April 1 we have been well supplied in ministerial force. There are now seven of us, and with this number we ought to do considerable work, but whether it will be in proportion to the number, is yet to be seen. We are glad for the help, as we have a number of calls to fill which we could not do, had we not so much efficient help.

Some of our brethren don't seem to understand what loyalty to the church means. Those who are most loyal to the truth are the most loyal to the church. There is a sham loyalty that gives men a reputation at the expense of true Christian character. Men may err, but God cannot, therefore the truth must be respected though it may not always suit our wishes.

During this month the District Meetings of our State, Pennsylvania, will be held, and it is a matter of concern as to what the work of these meetings will be. If all of our District Meetings would do the work that it is their privilege to do, our Annual Meeting would be saved from a great deal of unnecessary care and labor. The "Old Folks' Home" will be before the Meeting of the Middle District, and we are informed that the Maryland Districts will have committees there to consider the propriety of uniting in this work and having but one Home for the three Districts.

Our last prayer-meeting, led by Bro. Reiff, was one of unusual interest. The subject was "Our Life," which opens a large field for thought and discussion.

Bro. Isaac Frantz, of Ohio, is with us. He was called on account of the illness of his daughter who is here attending school. At this time she is still seriously ill, but we hope that a change may be soon made for the better.

"An aged Christian who lately died, after a happy, well-spent life, said: "I was taught by my mother when a child to reckon each morning before I rose the blessings God had given me with which to begin the day. I was not merely to say:

> "When all thy mercies, O my God
> My rising soul surveys,
> Transported with the view I'm lost
> In wonder, love and praise."

But I was to count the mercies one by one, from the neat and serviceable shoes that covered my cold feet to the sunlight shining on the hill tops. My school friends, my play, my fun, mother's kiss, the baby sister in her cradle—all these I learned to consider separately, and of every one to say, 'He gave it to me.' This practice taught me the habit of thankfulness. It kept my heart near to him, kept it light and happy. These everyday blessings were not to be mere matters of course, but special loving touches from his paternal hand. No pain or sorrow could outwipe them."

CHURCH PRIVILEGES.

*Dear Brother:—*I am isolated from our own church and wish to know if it is wrong for me to attend the United Brethren church, which is quite near where I live. I enjoy attending their church service and Sunday-school. I also go to their prayer-meeting. Is it wrong for me to take part in such meetings? Please answer through the Messenger.

Charley Shock.

Junction, Ohio.

These are questions that come to us quite frequently and, we feel, require careful answering. We always feel to sympathize with our brethren and sisters who cannot enjoy church privileges of their choice. To be deprived of such privileges is a great loss, and the question is, What is the next best thing to do? To attend the services of other churches affords very important means of grace, provided the persons are well established in the faith,—so well that there can be no influence brought to bear upon them sufficiently strong to move them from the faith. The danger is in gradually falling in sympathy with that which is considered next best and becoming satisfied with it as the best.

No matter how much we may enjoy the good we may find in other churches, we should never allow ourselves to become satisfied with less than what we believe to be the whole truth.

We have had experiences of being away from our own services, and at such times we would attend the services of other churches, and did it to profit, without, in any way, affecting our faith or love for the church of our choice. We believe that others can do the same thing, if they are well grounded and established in the truth. In prayer-meeting we would take part if we felt like doing so. There is a vast difference in worshiping God in the spirit and worshiping him in a sectarian jacket. When we pray, we do not do it by rule or church form, but to God in the spirit and the truth. This can be done anywhere. In prayer we must be honest and ask God for just what we want and not for that which we believe it is wrong for us to ask him to do.

What is termed Christian courtesy often causes us to shape our prayers in a way to suit the circumstances, or please the people with whom we worship. There is no necessity for this, neither should we do so. There is a sense in which we are to pray for all men, and for the salvation of all we can pray anywhere.

We said that there is some danger in our affiliation in the services of other churches. But while this is so, is there not a greater danger in our remaining away from all religious services because we cannot attend those of our own? There are wrong tendencies on this side of the question as well. The danger is in our growing indifferent to religious services and in the train of this is an indifference to religion itself. The soul needs nourishment,—must be fed, and there must be a place to get this. For this we have churches and ministers,—so God ordained. And while we may get this nourishment in our homes and Bibles, it does not come in a way that makes it so readily received. The home means should never be neglected, no matter what our congregational privileges may be, but our nature seems to require more than this. "Feed my sheep," are the words of the Master, and if we are to be fed, there must be a feeder. If we should go to a feeder who does not give all good food, we ought to be able to take the good and reject the bad. If we are well grounded in the truth we can do this. It has been said of us, "Be ye not as horses and mules which have not understanding," and yet they pick the good hay from the briars and weeds. Can we not do it as well as horses and mules? We ought.

Again, by remaining away from religious services we set a bad influence in the community in which we live. Non-church going is not to be encouraged anywhere, and for us to be examples in this direction would not speak well for our religion.

Yes, go, but go in the fullness of Christ, bearing the truth and living the truth as you go, and when you go in this way you will not only gather strength for yourself but you will be able to give it to others. Let your light shine,—and doing this you will be safe anywhere. Of course, in thus going does not mean that you should unite with, or become a member of, that church. There can be no necessity for this, neither would it be right for us to do so. There can be no circumstances that will justify us in leaving the church of our choice.

THE GOSPEL MESSENGER.

"Set for the Defense of the Gospel."

Vol. 30, Old Series.　　　Mt. Morris, Ill., and Huntingdon, Pa., May 10, 1892.　　　No. 19

The Gospel Messenger.

H. B. BRUMBAUGH, Editor,

And Business Manager of the Eastern House, Box 50, Huntingdon, Pa.

Table of Contents.

SINCE April 1 we have been well supplied in ministerial force. There are now seven of us, and with this number we ought to do considerable work, but whether it will be in proportion to the number, is yet to be seen. We are glad for the help, as we have a number of calls to fill which we could not do, had we not so much efficient help.

SOME of our brethren don't seem to understand what loyalty to the church means. Those who are most loyal to the truth are the most loyal to the church. There is a sham loyalty that gives men a reputation at the expense of true Christian character. Men may err, but God cannot, therefore the truth must be respected though it may not always suit our wishes.

DURING this month the District Meetings of our State, Pennsylvania, will be held, and it is a matter of concern as to what the work of these meetings will be. If all of our District Meetings would do the work that it is their privilege to do, our Annual Meeting would be saved from a great deal of unnecessary care and labor. The "Old Folks' Home" will be before the Meeting of the Middle District, and we are informed that the Maryland Districts will have committees there to consider the propriety of uniting in this work and having but one Home for the three Districts.

OUR last prayer-meeting, led by Bro. Reiff, was one of unusual interest. The subject was "Our Life," which opens a large field for thought and discussion.

BRO. ISAAC FRANTZ, of Ohio, is with us. He was called on account of the illness of his daughter who is here attending school. At this time she is still seriously ill, but we hope that a change may be soon made for the better.

"AN aged Christian who lately died, after a happy, well-spent life, said: "I was taught by my mother when a child to reckon each morning before I rose the blessings God had given me with which to begin the day. I was not merely to say:

　"When all thy mercies, O my God
　　My rising soul surveys,
　Transported with the view I'm lost
　　In wonder, love and praise."

But I was to count the mercies one by one, from the neat and serviceable shoes that covered my cold feet to the sunlight shining on the hill tops. My school friends, my play, my fun, mother's kiss, the baby sister in her cradle—all these I learned to consider separately, and of every one to say, 'He gave it to me.' This practice taught me the habit of thankfulness. It kept my heart near to him, kept it light and happy. These everyday blessings were not to be mere matters of course, but special loving touches from his paternal hand. No pain or sorrow could outwipe them."

CHURCH PRIVILEGES.

*Dear Brother:—*I am isolated from our own church and wish to know if it is wrong for me to attend the United Brethren church, which is quite near where I live. I enjoy attending their church service and Sunday-school. I also go to their prayer-meeting. Is it wrong for me to take part in such meetings? Please answer through the MESSENGER.

CHARLEY SHOCK.

Junction, Ohio.

THESE are questions that come to us quite frequently and, we feel, require careful answering. We always feel to sympathize with our brethren and sisters who cannot enjoy church privileges of their choice. To be deprived of such privileges is a great loss, and the question is, What is the next best thing to do? To attend the services of other churches affords very important means of grace, provided the persons are well established in the faith,—so well that there can be no influence brought to bear upon them sufficiently strong to move them from the faith. The danger is in gradually falling in sympathy with that which is considered next best and becoming satisfied with it as the best.

No matter how much we may enjoy the good we may find in other churches, we should never allow ourselves to become satisfied with less than what we believe to be the whole truth.

We have had experiences of being away from our own services, and at such times we would attend the services of other churches, and did it to profit, without, in any way, affecting our faith or love for the church of our choice. We believe

that others can do the same thing, if they are well grounded and established in the truth. In prayer-meeting we would take part if we felt like doing so. There is a vast difference in worshiping God in the spirit and worshiping him in a sectarian jacket. When we pray, we do not do it by rule or church form, but to God in the spirit and the truth. This can be done anywhere. In prayer we must be honest and ask God for just what we want and not for that which we believe it is wrong for us to ask him to do.

What is termed Christian courtesy often causes us to shape our prayers in a way to suit the circumstances, or please the people with whom we worship. There is no necessity for this, neither should we do so. There is a sense in which we are to pray for all men, and for the salvation of all we can pray anywhere.

We said that there is some danger in our affiliation in the services of other churches. But while this is so, is there not a greater danger in our remaining away from all religious services because we cannot attend those of our own? There are wrong tendencies on this side of the question as well. The danger is in our growing indifferent to religious services and in the train of this is an indifference to religion itself. The soul needs nourishment,—must be fed, and there must be a place to get this. For this we have churches and ministers,—so God ordained. And while we may get this nourishment in our homes and Bibles, it does not come in a way that makes it so readily received. The home means should never be neglected, no matter what our congregational privileges may be, but our nature seems to require more than this. "Feed my sheep," are the words of the Master, and if we are to be fed, there must be a feeder. If we should go to a feeder who does not give all good food, we ought to be able to take the good and reject the bad. If we are well grounded in the truth we can do this. It has been said of us, "Be ye not as horses and mules which have not understanding," and yet they pick the good hay from the briars and weeds. Can we not do it as well as horses and mules? We ought.

Again, by remaining away from religious services we set a bad influence in the community in which we live. Non-church going is not to be encouraged anywhere, and for us to be examples in this direction would not speak well for our religion.

Yes, go, but go in the fullness of Christ, bearing the truth and living the truth as you go, and when you go in this way you will not only gather strength for yourself but you will be able to give it to others. Let your light shine,—and doing this you will be safe anywhere. Of course, in thus going does not mean that you should unite with, or become a member of, that church. There can be no necessity for this, neither would it be right for us to do so. There can be no circumstances that will justify us in leaving the church of our choice.

✦ESSAYS✦

'Study to show thyself approved unto God; a workman that needeth not be ashamed, rightly dividing the Word of Truth.'

CHRIST'S RESURRECTION.

BY J. S. MOHLER.

How sad was the night when the Savior lay dead,
Alone in death's chamber, a rock for his bed,
When Satan a season triumphantly reigned,
And Christ, by the powers of darkness was slain.

But hark! What is meant by this flashing of wings
Of angels from heaven? What tidings they bring
Of Jesus, who'd broken the bars of the grave
His captor led captive, the world might be saved.

The keepers affrighted, all fell to the ground
At the Voices of angels, while hovering around;
The rending of rocks, and the quaking of earth,
When Christ from the grave in great power came forth.

The keys of the grave, and of death he now holds,
Each house of the dead will forever unfold,
And death, and the grave, boast their vict'ry no more
When the grave, and the sea roll their millions to shore.

Then the saints of all ages in glory will reign,
Forever made free from all sorrow and pain,
With bodies like Christ's, in his glory arrayed,
Obtain their inheritance, never to fade.

By Christ to the fountains of waters be led,
With heavenly manna forever be fed.
With saints, and with angels, God's praises to sing
'Till the heavens with loud hallelujahs will ring.

Morrill, Kans.

THE THREE HEAVENS.

BY A. HUTCHISON.

IN 2 Cor. 12: 2 we read of the third heaven, and it is reasonable to suppose that if there is 'a third heaven, there must be a first and second. We find good reasons why such should be the case. In the Scriptures, God is represented to us as a triune God,—that is, three in one. These are named respectively, Father, Son and Holy Ghost. Now it is reasonable to suppose that where any one of these preside, that such a place might be called a heavenly place. Then, when we find a place for each of these to reign, then we will have found the three heavens. The first we will locate here, as being the church militant. Over this the Holy Spirit is to preside.

You will observe that when Christ had organized his church here, he left it, by giving the promise to the infant church, that the Comforter, which is the Holy Ghost, should come to it, and abide with the faithful disciples. Then, on the Day of Pentecost, he came as promised, and entered upon his work. This work is to continue until Christ shall come again. This is the preparatory period, getting the material ready for the Master's use when he comes. The Holy Spirit is superintending the work, and each one who will yield to the guidance of the Spirit will thus be made a partaker of the divine nature, and in this way be prepared for the great building, when Jesus comes. All who refuse to yield to the moulding and chiseling of the Holy Spirit, will be refused when the Master shall come. Jesus says, "Not every one that saith unto me, Lord, Lord, shall enter into the kingdom of heaven; but he that doeth the will of my Father which is in heaven." Matt. 7: 21.

You will notice that the work of the Spirit is, to lead into all truth. Then, since it is stated that God's Word is the truth, we may thereby know whether we are yielding to the operation of the Spirit or not. We are not to trust every spirit, for the apostle says, "Beloved, believe not every spirit, but try the spirits whether they are of God." 1 John 4: 1. It may require a good deal of hewing and dressing down, before we come to the Spirit's line and plummet, but to this we must come. For he is our Ruler, and to his teachings we must submit, or fail to reach the next heaven. Matt. 13: 47 says, "The kingdom of heaven is like unto a net, that was cast into the sea, and gathered of every kind," etc. This we apply to the church militant. Some get into the churches here, who do not submit themselves to the gentle wooing and guidance of the Holy Spirit, and therefore will be cast away, as stated in the next verse. Eph. 1: 3 says, "Blessed be the God and Father of our Lord Jesus Christ, who hath blessed us with all spiritual blessings in heavenly places in Christ." This we apply to the church here. All that is necessary, for us, to sit together in a heavenly place in Christ here, is for each one to rise up in rebellion against the evil one, and give ourselves fully up to the direction of the Holy Spirit. This will make a heavenly place, because, where the Holy Spirit (which came from heaven) rules, there must be a heavenly place. Again, Eph. 2: 6 says, "and has raised us up together, and made us sit together in heavenly places in Christ Jesus." Such I understand the first heaven to be, and here is where the third person in the Trinity reigns.

The second heaven I shall call the millennial reign. Over this Christ, the Son, presides. This shall begin when Christ shall come again. He will then enter upon his kingly ministry. For the time for his kingdom to come, and when he will reign as king, you will read 2 Tim. 4: 1, "I charge thee therefore before God, and the Lord Jesus Christ, who shall judge the quick and the dead at his appearing and his kingdom." Here you will notice that, when he appears, then his kingdom appears. Here is where we understand that he takes to himself the reigns of Government, calls to him those who have purified their robes under the influence of the Holy Spirit, in obeying the truth, and will these he reigns for one thousand years. The Holy Spirit having performed his part prior to this, he gives all over to Christ. We now have Christ to reign during this millennial period with his saints.

Now we will notice some of the things which shall take place when he comes. Luke 12: 37 says, "Blessed are those servants, whom the Lord, when he cometh, shall find watching: verily I say unto you, that he shall gird himself, and make them to sit down to meat, and will come forth and serve them." Then he says to the twelve apostles, "And I appoint unto you a kingdom, as my Father hath appointed unto me; that ye may eat and drink at my table in my kingdom, and sit on thrones judging the twelve tribes of Israel. Luke 22: 29, 30. Here he assigns to the twelve, their special work. To all other faithful ones he says, "To him that overcometh will I grant to sit with me in my throne, even as I also overcame, and am set down with my Father in his throne." Rev. 3: 21. This applies to every one, in every nation, who has yielded to the moulding influence of the Holy Spirit, during the probationary period. Rev. 7: 13, 14 says, "And one of the elders answered, saying unto me, What are these which are arrayed in white robes? and whence came they? And I said unto him, Sir, thou knowest. And he said unto me, These are they which came out of great tribulation, and have washed their robes, and made them white in the blood of the Lamb." This class has been made ready under the reign of the Holy Spirit, and they are now ready to go up higher,—even to the second heaven, there to serve as priests under Christ.

Now we pass to the third heaven. This is where God the Father reigns. Rev. 2: 7 says, "To him that overcometh will I give to eat of the tree of life, which is in the midst of the paradise of God." Again, Paul says, that he knew a man who was caught up into the third heaven. 2 Cor. 12: 2-4. Paul learned, what he knew of the Gospel, from Jesus Christ. Jesus had, prior to this, ascended to the right hand of the Father. He says, "But I certify you, brethren; that the Gospel which was preached of me is not after man, for I neither received it of man, neither was I taught it, but by the revelation of Jesus Christ. Gal. 1: 11, 12. Lastly, 1 Cor. 15: 28 says, "And when all things shall be subdued unto him, then shall the Son also be subject unto him that put all things under him, that God may be all in all." The Holy Spirit and Christ the Son both yield up all to God the Father, and then he will preside over all. This I understand to be the third heaven. If we ever attain to the third heaven, we must do so by taking our place in the lowest first, and then ascend the scale.

McPherson, Kans.

SELF-EXAMINATION.

BY JAS. M. NEFF.

In Four Chapters.—Chapter Four.

TEXT: Examine yourselves.—2 Cor. 13: 5.

WE have proposed two answers to the question, *How should we examine ourselves?* First, deliberately. Second, impartially. We here resume the discussion of the topic of impartial self-examination.

The only true standard of character is to be found in Jesus Christ, and the only infallible rule of conduct in the saving Gospel which he has left us. He who is satisfied to measure his character by anything below this divine standard, is satisfied with that which falls short of a strictly impartial self-examination.

The great question which ought to be of the profoundest concern to every human soul is not, Does my character compare favorably with that of my brother? nor, Is my life such as passes with my fellow-men as blameless? nor, Am I a Christian such as my father or brethren or elder would approve? but, How does my life compare with the standard left by Jesus Christ? Am I before God a man after his own heart?

And I would have us feel, brethren, that it is not sufficient that we search the Scriptures and acquaint ourselves with the rule of conduct, and the standard of character; but it is, perhaps, equally as essential that we search our own hearts, and ascertain how near we are living to the standard, how close we are walking to the rule.

"Remember that the time you have for self-examination is, after all, very short. Soon thou wilt know the great secret. I perhaps may not say words rough enough to rend off the mask which thou now hast upon thee, but there is one called Death who will stand no compliment. You may masquerade it out to-day in the dress of a saint, but death will soon strip you, and you must stand before the judgment-seat after death has discovered you in all your nakedness, be that naked innocence, or naked guilt. Remember, too, though you may deceive yourself, you will not deceive your God. You may have light weights, and the beam of the scale in which you weigh yourself may not be honest, and may not, therefore, tell the truth; but when God shall try you he will make no allowances; when the everlasting Jehovah grasps the balances of justice, and puts his law into one scale, ah, how wilt thou tremble when he shall put thee into the other; for unless Christ be thy Christ thou wilt be found light weight;—thou wilt be weighed in the balances and found wanting, and cast away forever."

God in his wisdom has seen fit to place us here in a world of sin,—in a world enshrouded in the

ESSAYS

CHRIST'S RESURRECTION.

BY J. S. MOHLER.

How sad was the night when the Savior lay dead,
Alone in death's chamber, a rock for his bed,
When Satan a season triumphantly reigned,
And Christ, by the powers of darkness was slain.

But hark! What is meant by this flashing of wings
Of angels from heaven? What tidings they bring
Of Jesus, who'd broken the bars of the grave
His captor led captive, the world might be saved.

The keepers affrighted, all fell to the ground
At the voices of angels, while hovering around;
The rending of rocks, and the quaking of earth,
When Christ from the grave in great power came forth.

The keys of the grave, and of death he now holds,
Each house of the dead will forever unfold,
And death, and the grave, boast their vict'ry no more
When the grave, and the sea roll their millions to shore.

Then the saints of all ages in glory will reign,
Forever made free from all sorrow and pain,
With bodies like Christ's, in his glory arrayed,
Obtain their inheritance, never to fade.

By Christ to the fountains of waters be led,
With heavenly manna forever be fed.
With saints, and with angels, God's praises to sing
'Till the heavens with loud hallelujahs will ring.

Morrill, Kans.

THE THREE HEAVENS.

BY A. HUTCHISON.

IN 2 Cor. 12: 2 we read of the third heaven, and it is reasonable to suppose that if there is a third heaven, there must be a first and second. We find good reasons why such should be the case. In the Scriptures, God is represented to us as a triune God,—that is, three in one. These are named respectively, Father, Son and Holy Ghost. Now it is reasonable to suppose that where any one of these presides, that such a place might be called a heavenly place. Then, when we find a place for each of these to reign, then we will have found the three heavens. The first we will locate here, as being the church militant. Over this the Holy Spirit is to preside.

You will observe that when Christ had organized his church here, he left it, by giving the promise to the infant church, that the Comforter, which is the Holy Ghost, should come to it, and abide with the faithful disciples. Then, on the Day of Pentecost, he came as promised, and entered upon his work. This work is to continue until Christ shall come again. This is the preparatory period, getting the material ready for the Master's use when he comes. The Holy Spirit is superintending the work, and each one who will yield to the guidance of the Spirit will thus be made a partaker of the divine nature, and in this way be prepared for the great building, when Jesus comes. All who refuse to yield to the moulding and chiseling of the Holy Spirit, will be refused when the Master shall come. Jesus says, "Not every one that saith unto me, Lord, Lord, shall enter into the kingdom of heaven; but he that doeth the will of my Father which is in heaven." Matt. 7: 21.

You will notice that the work of the Spirit is, to lead into all truth. Then, since it is stated that God's Word is the truth, we may thereby know whether we are yielding to the operation of the Spirit or not. We are not to trust every spirit, for the apostle says, "Beloved, believe not every spirit, but try the spirits whether they are of God." 1 John 4: 1. It may require a good deal of hewing and dressing down, before we come to the Spirit's line and plummet, but to this we must come. For he is our Ruler, and to his teachings we must submit, or fail to reach the next heaven. Matt. 13: 47 says, "The kingdom of heaven is like unto a net, that was cast into the sea, and gathered of every kind," etc. This we apply to the church militant. Some get into the churches here, who do not submit themselves to the gentle wooing and guidance of the Holy Spirit, and therefore will be cast away, as stated in the next verse. Eph. 1: 3 says, "Blessed be the God and Father of our Lord Jesus Christ, who hath blessed us with all spiritual blessings in heavenly places in Christ." This we apply to the church here. All that is necessary, for us, to sit together in a heavenly place in Christ here, is for each one to rise up in rebellion against the evil one, and give ourselves fully up to the direction of the Holy Spirit. This will make a heavenly place, because, where the Holy Spirit (which came from heaven) rules, there must be a heavenly place. Again, Eph. 2: 6 says, "and has raised us up together, and made us sit together in heavenly places in Christ Jesus." Such I understand the first heaven to be, and here is where the third person in the Trinity reigns.

The second heaven I shall call the millennial reign. Over this Christ, the Son, presides. This shall begin when Christ shall come again. He will then enter upon his kingly ministry. For the time for his kingdom to come, and when he will reign as king, you will read 2 Tim. 4: 1, "I charge thee therefore before God, and the Lord Jesus Christ, who shall judge the quick and the dead at his appearing and his kingdom." Here you will notice that, when he appears, then his kingdom appears. Here is where we understand that he takes to himself the reigns of Government, calls to him those who have purified their robes under the influence of the Holy Spirit, in obeying the truth, and with these he reigns for one thousand years. The Holy Spirit having performed his part prior to this, he gives all over to Christ. We now have Christ to reign during this millennial period with his saints.

Now we will notice some of the things which shall take place when he comes. Luke 12: 37 says, "Blessed are those servants, whom the Lord, when he cometh, shall find watching: verily I say unto you, that he shall gird himself, and make them to sit down to meat, and will come forth and serve them." Then he says to the twelve apostles, "And I appoint unto you a kingdom, as my Father hath appointed unto me; that ye may eat and drink at my table in my kingdom, and sit on thrones judging the twelve tribes of Israel. Luke 22: 29, 30. Here he assigns to the twelve, their special work. To all other faithful ones he says, "To him that overcometh will I grant to sit with me in my throne, even as I also overcame, and am set down with my Father in his throne." Rev. 3: 21. This applies to every one, in every nation, who has yielded to the moulding influence of the Holy Spirit, during the probationary period. Rev. 7: 13, 14 says, "And one of the elders answered, saying unto me, What are these which are arrayed in white robes? and whence came they? And I said unto him, Sir, thou knowest. And he said unto me, These are they which came out of great tribulation, and have washed their robes, and made them white in the blood of the Lamb." This class has been made ready under the reign of the Holy Spirit, and they are now ready to go up higher,—even to the second heaven, there to serve as priests under Christ.

Now we pass to the third heaven. This is where God the Father reigns. Rev. 2: 7 says, "To him that overcometh will I give to eat of the tree of life, which is in the midst of the paradise of God." Again, Paul says, that he knew a man who was caught up into the third heaven. 2 Cor. 12: 2-4. Paul learned, what he knew of the Gospel, from Jesus Christ. Jesus had, prior to this, ascended to the right hand of the Father. He says, "But I certify you, brethren, that the Gospel which was preached of me is not after man, for I neither received it of man, neither was I taught it, but by the revelation of Jesus Christ. Gal. 1: 11, 12. Lastly, 1 Cor. 15: 28 says, "And when all things shall be subdued unto him, then shall the Son also be subject unto him that put all things under him, that God may be all in all." The Holy Spirit and Christ the Son both yield up all to God the Father, and then he will preside over all. This I understand to be the third heaven. If we ever attain to the third heaven, we must do so by taking our place in the lowest first, and then ascend the scale.

McPherson, Kans.

SELF-EXAMINATION.

BY JAS. M. NEFF.

In Four Chapters.—Chapter Four.

TEXT: Examine yourselves.—2 Cor. 13: 5.

WE have proposed two answers to the question, *How should we examine ourselves?* First, deliberately. Second, impartially. We here resume the discussion of the topic of impartial self-examination.

The only true standard of character is to be found in Jesus Christ, and the only infallible rule of conduct in the saving Gospel which he has left us. He who is satisfied to measure his character by anything below this divine standard, is satisfied with that which falls short of a strictly impartial self-examination.

The great question which ought to be of the profoundest concern to every human soul is not, Does my character compare favorably with that of my brother? nor, Is my life such as passes with my fellow-men as blameless? nor, Am I a Christian such as my father or brethren or elder would approve? but, How does my life compare with the standard left by Jesus Christ? Am I before God a man after his own heart?

And I would have us feel, brethren, that it is not sufficient that we search the Scriptures and acquaint ourselves with the rule of conduct, and the standard of character; but it is, perhaps, equally as essential that we search our own hearts, and ascertain how near we are living to the standard, how close we are walking to the rule.

"Remember that the time you have for self-examination is, after all, very short. Soon thou wilt know the great secret. I perhaps may, not say words rough enough to rend off the mask which thou now hast upon thee, but there is one called Death who will stand no compliment. You may masquerade it out to-day in the dress of a saint, but death will soon strip you, and you must stand before the judgment-seat after death has discovered you in all your nakedness, he that naked innocence, or naked guilt. Remember, too, though you may deceive yourself, you will not deceive your God. You may have light weights, and the beam of the scale in which you weigh yourself may not be honest, and may not, therefore, tell the truth; but when God shall try you he will make no allowances; when the everlasting Jehovah grasps the balances of justice, and puts his law into one scale, ah, how wilt thou tremble when he shall put thee into the other; for unless Christ be thy Christ thou wilt be found light weight,—thou wilt be weighed in the balances and found wanting, and cast away forever."

God in his wisdom has seen fit to place us here in a world of sin,—in a world enshrouded in the

Gospel. Even so the Son of God stooped to our low condition. He hath been sent "to bind up the broken-hearted, to proclaim liberty to the captives, and the opening of the prison to them that are bound. Says the apostle to the Corinthians, "For ye know the grace of our Lord Jesus Christ, that though he was rich, yet for your sakes he became poor, that ye through his poverty might be rich,' and "forasmuch as the children are partakers of flesh and blood, he also himself, likewise, took part of the same; that through death he might destroy him that had the power of death, that is the devil.'

How he ennobled life and all its lawful labors! The first thirty years of his sojourn here were spent in a private station, and much of it was probably devoted to manual labor. But in this he glorified his Heavenly Father just as much as he did the last three years, when engaged in his public ministry. It is not the kind of work that is ennobling, but the manner in which it is done, hence the command, "Whatsoever thy hand findeth to do, do it with thy might," and the exhortation, "Let every man abide in the same calling wherein he was called."

Submission to the divine will is the highest and most perfect service that any being in any sphere can render to his Maker. If my lot in life is an humble one, my condition a painful one, my talents few, my sphere of action circumscribed, I need not complain. Right there I can best serve my Heavenly Father. That is the position I am best fitted to fill. The humblest laborer, if he does his work to the best of his ability, and conscientiously discharges his duties, with an entire submission to the divine will, is serving God just as much as the most talented divine in his calling. Among the vast hosts of heaven every will is in perfect accord with the divine will. There is not one discordant note. Christ came to re-establish such harmony on earth, and he taught us to pray, "Thy will be done on earth as in heaven." Man, in his natural state, is in a state of ceaseless rebellion against God, but when he is born from above, he learns submission to the behests of heaven. More and more this lesson is enforced, until the principle takes full possession of his heart.

What harmony there is in the service of Jehovah! The saints above and the saints on earth render to him the same acceptable homage. The former, in their glorified state, are standing before the throne, singing the song of Moses and the Lamb, offering, perhaps, a higher and more spiritual service, but not more real, or more pleasing to God. The service is the same in kind but not in degree. We are in the vestibule of the temple, while they have passed through the pearly gates. We see through a glass darkly, while they see face to face. We know in part, but they know as also they are known. But we are one family,—one in Christ. What distinguishing honor is ours as children of God! "Behold, what manner of love the Father hath bestowed upon us that we should be called the sons of God! But it doth not yet appear what we shall be; but we know that when he shall appear we shall be like him; for we shall see him as he is."

CHRYSOSTOM AND THE BREAKING OF BREAD.

BY DANIEL HAYS.

AFTER reading Bro. John Wise's article on "Breaking Bread of Communion," I present, by way of testimony, the following historical facts, as proof that the present practice of the church was the practice of the primitive fathers. Sozomon says, "Intinction, as the practice of steeping the body in the blood was called in the West, is thought by some to have been first adopted in consequence of a heretic at Constantinople, whom Chrysostom was communicating, having carried off the Eucharist which he had placed in her hand."

A writer in Christian Antiquities, Vol. 1, page 416, in commenting on the foregoing says, "The narrative in Sozomon of a transaction of Chrysostom's, describes a woman after receiving the bread into her hand, bowing her head as if to pray, and passing on the particle she had received to her maid-servant."

This occurred in the East, and in an age when the practice of the primitive Christians was scrupulously regarded. Chrysostom was one of the most profound Greek scholars, and stands out prominently as one of the great historical landmarks on the mode of Christian baptism. Neither does he stand alone as authority in the breaking of the bread of Communion by the elder, or officiating minister. There is abundant proof that the Eucharistic bread was, in ancient times, delivered into the hands of communicants. Basil says, "The presbyter delivers a portion of the Eucharist into the hand, and the communicant carries it to his mouth with his own hand."

In the primitive church it was regarded as the duty of the bishop, or elder, to break the bread of Communion. Ignatius, the martyr, says, "Apart from the bishop it is not lawful to baptize, or to celebrate an Agape."

The Savior anticipated the time when it would be made a question of preference. The question was raised among his disciples, "which of them should be accounted the greatest." Our Lord set the matter at rest for all time in the following words: "For whether is greater, he that sitteth at meat, or he that serveth? is not he that sitteth at meat? but I am among you as he that serveth." Luke 22: 27. Then the one that sits at meat and is served, has the place of honor. Then the minister that breaks the bread is the servant, and indeed this is the meaning of the word minister. As servant of all, Christ set the example at the first Communion. I will quote the language of Paul, for it is significant that he delivered the same practice to the Corinthians: "For I have received of the Lord that which also I delivered unto you, That the Lord Jesus, the same night in which he was betrayed, took bread: and when he had given thanks, he brake it, and said, Take, eat; this is my body, which is broken FOR you: this do in remembrance of me." 1 Cor. 11: 23, 24. In this we notice:

1. That Christ brake the bread for his disciples, and commanded them to eat it.

2. Paul received this practice from the Lord.

3. Paul delivered the same practice to the church at Corinth.

Moore's Store, Va.

THE LORD'S PRAYER.

BY B. E. KESLER.

IN No. 12, page 188, it is asked, "Why close our opening and closing prayer, at all our meetings with a repetition of the Lord's Prayer? Matt. 6: 7. A Gospel answer is wanted to this."

I answer: When it is shown that it is a *vain* repetition to use the Lord's Prayer as above, then we may well discontinue such usage, but as well may we say that the continuance of the Communion, feet-washing, the salutation, from time to time, is a vain repetition, or to say the use of the Lord's Prayer, as above, is a vain repetition. If are commands, and a repetition of either is not vain, if done in the proper spirit. But if a Gospel answer is wanted, we refer the brother to Luke 11: 2: "When ye pray, say, Our Father," etc. Now if we pray at the times alluded to in the query, the command, in Luke 11: 2, tells us what to say. If we do not pray at the times mentioned, then don't use the Lord's Prayer, of course. If we can be told how to obey the command without *doing* as commanded, let it be done, by all means.

Oak Level, Va.

NOT TIMOTHY.

"AND so ye have taken the teetotal pledge, have ye?" said an Irishman to his fellow-workman.

"Indade I have; and I'm not ashamed of it, either," was the reply of the bold teetotaler.

"But did not Paul tell Timothy to take a little wine for his stomach's sake?" queried the dram-drinker.

"So he did," rejoined the cold-water drinker; "but my name is not Timothy, and there is nothing the matter with my stomach."

"A LOVE of study or a love of knowledge is of advantage as a means to an end; but in itself it has no more value than a love of money-getting or a love of money. All gettings and all possessings have their true worth in the purpose of their applying, not in their mere achieving. That a man wants knowledge, and that he is willing to work for its obtaining, in order to its wise use for the good of others, is always to his credit. But the desire to study simply for the purpose of gaining knowledge, is only one phase of the spirit of curiosity; and the wish to have knowledge simply for the satisfaction of having it, is merely a form of mental miserliness. Much knowledge is worth no more than much flesh, unless its possessor makes it worth something by its using. It is better to have little flesh or little knowledge, while making it all effective for the advantage of others, than to be full-fleshed and learned without helping others through one's fullness."

"WE can have what we long for, if we long for the right thing. 'Blessed are they that hunger and thirst after righteousness: for they shall be filled.' There is nothing in the universe better than righteousness — right relations with God; and if this be our chief longing, we are sure of having what we long for."

The Gospel Messenger

Is the recognized organ of the German Baptist or Brethren's church, and advocates the form of doctrine taught in the New Testament and pleads for a return to apostolic and primitive Christianity.

It recognizes the New Testament as the only infallible rule of faith and practice, and maintains that Faith toward God, Repentance from dead works, Regeneration of the heart and mind, baptism by Trine Immersion for remission of sins unto the reception of the Holy Ghost by the laying on of hands, are the means of adoption into the household of God,—the church militant.

It also maintains that Feet-washing, as taught in John 13, both by example and command of Jesus, should be observed in the church.

That the Lord's Supper, instituted by Christ and as universally observed by the apostles and the early Christians, is a full meal, and, in connection with the Communion, should be taken in the evening or after the close of the day.

That the Salutation of the Holy Kiss, or Kiss of Charity, is binding upon the followers of Christ.

That War and Retaliation are contrary to the spirit and self-denying principles of the religion of Jesus Christ.

That the principle of Plain Dressing and of Non-conformity to the world, as taught in the New Testament, should be observed by the followers of Christ.

That the Scriptural duty of Anointing the Sick with Oil, in the Name of the Lord, James 5: 14, is binding upon all Christians.

It also advocates the church's duty to support Missionary and Tract Work, thus giving to the Lord for the spread of the Gospel and for the conversion of sinners.

In short, it is a Vindicator of all that Christ and the apostles have enjoined upon us, and aims amid the conflicting theories and discords of modern Christendom, to point out ground that all must concede to be infallibly safe.

☞ The above principles of our Fraternity are set forth on our "Brethren's Envelopes." Use them! Price, 15 cents per package; 40 cents per hundred.

Gospel. Even so the Son of God stooped to our low condition. He hath been sent "to bind up the broken-hearted, to proclaim liberty to the captives, and the opening of the prison to them that are bound. Says the apostle to the Corinthians, "For ye know the grace of our Lord Jesus Christ, that though he was rich, yet for your sakes he became poor, that ye through his poverty might be rich," and "forasmuch as the children are partakers of flesh and blood, he also himself, likewise, took part of the same; that through death he might destroy him that had the power of death, that is the devil."

How he ennobled life and all its lawful labor! The first thirty years of his sojourn here were spent in a private station, and much of it was probably devoted to manual labor. But in this he glorified his Heavenly Father just as much as he did the last three years, when engaged in his public ministry. It is not the kind of work that is ennobling, but the manner in which it is done, hence the command, "Whatsoever thy hand findeth to do, do it with thy might," and the exhortation, "Let every man abide in the same calling wherein he was called."

Submission to the divine will is the highest and most perfect service that any being in any sphere can render to his Maker. If my lot in life is an humble one, my condition a painful one, my talents few, my sphere of action circumscribed, I need not complain. Right there I can best serve my Heavenly Father. That is the position I am best fitted to fill. The humblest laborer, if he does his work to the best of his ability, and conscientiously discharges his duties, with an entire submission to the divine will, is serving God just as much as the most talented divine in his calling.

Among the vast hosts of heaven every will is in perfect accord with the divine will. There is not one discordant note. Christ came to re-establish such harmony on earth, and he taught us to pray, "Thy will be done on earth as in heaven." Man, in his natural state, is in a state of ceaseless rebellion against God, but when he is born from above, he learns submission to the behests of heaven. More and more this lesson is enforced, until the principle takes full possession of his heart.

What harmony there is in the service of Jehovah! The saints above and the saints on earth render to him the same acceptable homage. The former, in their glorified state, are standing before the throne, singing the songs of Moses and the Lamb, offering, perhaps, a higher and more spiritual service, but not more real, or more pleasing to God. The service is the same in kind but not in degree. We are in the vestibule of the temple, while they have passed through the pearly gates. We see through a glass darkly, while they see face to face. We know in part, but they know as also they are known. But we are one family,—one in Christ. What distinguishing honor is ours as children of God! "Behold, what manner of love the Father hath bestowed upon us that we should be called the sons of God! But it doth not yet appear what we shall be; but we know that when he shall appear we shall be like him; for we shall see him as he is."

CHRYSOSTOM AND THE BREAKING OF BREAD.

BY DANIEL HAYS.

AFTER reading Bro. John Wise's article on "Breaking Bread of Communion," I present, by way of testimony, the following historical facts, as proof that the present practice of the church was the practice of the primitive fathers. Sozomon says, "Intinction, as the practice of steeping the body in the blood was called in the West, is thought by some to have been first adopted in consequence of a heretic at Constantinople, whom Chrysostom was communicating, having carried off the Eucharist which he had placed in her hand."

A writer in Christian Antiquities, Vol. 1, page 416, in commenting on the foregoing says, "The narrative in Sozomon of a transaction of Chrysostom's, describes a woman after receiving the bread into her hand, bowing her head as if to pray, and passing on the particle she had received to her maid-servant."

This occurred in the East, and in an age when the practice of the primitive Christians was scrupulously regarded. Chrysostom was one of the most profound Greek scholars, and stands out prominently as one of the great historical landmarks on the mode of Christian baptism. Neither does he stand alone as authority in the breaking of the bread of Communion by the elder, or officiating minister. There is abundant proof that the Eucharistic bread was, in ancient times, delivered into the hands of communicants. Basil says, "The presbyter delivers a portion of the Eucharist into the hand, and the communicant carries it to his mouth with his own hand."

In the primitive church it was regarded as the duty of the bishop, or elder, to break the bread of Communion. Ignatius, the martyr, says, "Apart from the bishop it is not lawful to baptize, or to celebrate an Agape."

The Savior anticipated the time when it would be made a question of preference. The question was raised among his disciples, "which of them should be accounted the greatest." Our Lord set the matter at rest for all time in the following words: "For whether is greater, he that sitteth at meat, or he that serveth? is not he that sitteth at meat? but I am among you as he that serveth." Luke 22: 27. Then the one that sits at meat and is served, has the place of honor. Then the minister that breaks the bread is the servant, and indeed this is the meaning of the word minister. As servant of all, Christ set the example at the first Communion. I will quote the language of Paul, for it is significant that he delivered the same practice to the Corinthians: "For I have received of the Lord that which also I delivered unto you, That the Lord Jesus, the same night in which he was betrayed, took bread: and when he had given thanks, he brake it, and said, Take, eat; this is my body, which is broken for you: this do in remembrance of me." 1 Cor. 11: 23, 24. In this we notice:

1. That Christ brake the bread for his disciples, and commanded them to eat it.

2. Paul received this practice from the Lord.

3. Paul delivered the same practice to the church at Corinth.

Moore's Store, Va.

THE LORD'S PRAYER.

BY D. B. KESLER.

IN No. 12, page 188, it is asked, "Why close our opening and closing prayer, at all our meetings with a repetition of the Lord's Prayer? Matt. 6: 7. A Gospel answer is wanted to this."

I answer: When it is shown that it is a vain repetition to use the Lord's Prayer as above, then we may well discontinue such usage, but as well may we say that the continuance of the Communion, feet-washing, the salutation, from time to time, is a vain repetition, as to say the use of the Lord's Prayer, as above, is a vain repetition. All are commands, and a repetition of either is not vain, if done in the proper spirit. But if a Gospel answer is wanted, we refer the brother to Luke 11: 2: "When ye pray, say, Our Father," etc. Now if we pray at the times alluded to in the query, the command, in Luke 11: 2, tells us what to say. If we do not pray at the times mentioned, then don't use the Lord's Prayer, of course. If we can be told how to obey the command without doing as commanded, let it be done, by all means.

Oak Level, Va.

NOT TIMOTHY.

"AND so ye have taken the teetotal pledge, have ye?" said an Irishman to his fellow-workman.

"Indade I have; and I'm not ashamed of it, either," was the reply of the bold teetotaler.

"But did not Paul tell Timothy to take a little wine for his stomach's sake?" queried the dram-drinker.

"So he did," rejoined the cold-water drinker; "but my name is not Timothy, and there is nothing the matter with my stomach."

"A LOVE of study or a love of knowledge is of advantage as a means to an end; but in itself it has no more value than a love of money-getting or a love of money. All gettings and all possessings have their true worth in the purpose of their applying, not in their mere achieving. That a man wants knowledge, and that he is willing to work for its obtaining, in order to its wise use for the good of others, is always to his credit. But the desire to study simply for the purpose of gaining knowledge, is only one phase of the spirit of curiosity; and the wish to have knowledge simply for the satisfaction of having it, is merely a form of mental miserliness. Much knowledge is worth no more than much flesh, unless its possessor makes it worth something by its using. It is better to have little flesh or little knowledge, while making it all effective for the advantage of others, than to be full-fleshed and learned without helping others through one's fullness."

"WE can have what we long for, if we long for the right thing. 'Blessed are they that hunger and thirst after righteousness: for they shall be filled.' There is nothing in the universe better than righteousness—right relations with God; and if this be our chief longing, we are sure of having what we long for."

The Gospel Messenger

Is the recognized organ of the German Baptist or Brethren's church, and advocates the form of doctrines taught in the New Testament and pleads for a return to apostolic and primitive Christianity.

It recognizes the New Testament as the only infallible rule of faith and practice, and maintains that Faith toward God, Repentance from dead works, Regeneration of the heart and mind, baptism by Trine Immersion for remission of sins unto the reception of the Holy Ghost by the laying on of hands, are the means of adoption into the household of God,—the church militant.

It also maintains that Feet-washing, as taught in John 13, both by example and command of Jesus, should be observed in the church.

That the Lord's Supper, instituted by Christ and as universally observed by the apostles and the early Christians, is a full meal, and, in connection with the Communion, should be taken in the evening or after the close of the day.

That the Salutation of the Holy Kiss, or Kiss of Charity, is binding upon the followers of Christ.

That War and Retaliation are contrary to the spirit and self-denying principles of the religion of Jesus Christ.

That the principle of Plain Dressing and of Non-conformity to the world, as taught in the New Testament, should be observed by the followers of Christ.

That the Scriptural duty of Anointing the Sick with Oil, in the Name of the Lord, James 5: 14, is binding upon all Christians.

It also advocates the church's duty to support Missionary and Tract Work, thus giving to the Lord for the spread of the Gospel and for the conversion of sinners.

In short, it is a vindicator of all that Christ and the apostles have enjoined upon us, and aims, amid the conflicting theories and discords of modern Christendom, to point out ground that all must concede to be infallibly safe.

☞The above principles of our Fraternity are set forth on our "Brethren's Envelopes." Use them! Price, 15 cents per package; 40 cents per hundred.

Missionary and Tract Work Department.

"Upon the first day of the week, let every one of you lay by him in store as God hath prospered him, that there be no gatherings when I come."—1 Cor. 16: 2.

"Every man as he purposeth in his heart, so let him give. Not grudgingly or of necessity, for the Lord loveth a cheerful giver."—2 Cor. 9: 7.

HOW MUCH SHALL WE GIVE?

"Every man according to his ability." "Every one as God hath prospered him." "Every man, according as he purposeth in his heart, so let him give." "For if there be first a willing mind, it is accepted according to that a man hath, and not according to that he hath not."—2 Cor. 8: 12.

Organization of Missionary Committee.

DANIEL VANIMAN, Foreman,	McPherson, Kans.
D. L. MILLER, Treasurer,	Mt. Morris, Ill.
GALEN B. ROYER, Secretary,	Mt. Morris, Ill.

Organization of Book and Tract Work.

S. W. HOOVER, Foreman,	Dayton, Ohio.
S. BOCK, Secretary and Treasurer,	Dayton, Ohio.

☞All donations intended for Missionary Work should be sent to GALEN B. ROYER, Mt. Morris, Ill.

☞All money for Tract Work should be sent to S. BOCK, Dayton, Ohio.

☞Money may be sent by Money Order, Registered Letter, or Drafts on New York or Chicago. Do not send personal checks, or drafts on interior towns, as it costs 25 cents to collect them.

☞Solicitors are requested to faithfully carry out the plan of Annual Meeting, that all our members be solicited to contribute at least twice a year for the Mission and Tract Work of the Church.

☞Notes for the Endowment Fund can be had by writing to the Secretary of either Work.

PULPIT POWER, AND HOW OBTAINED.

Address delivered by B. C. Moomaw, at the Ministers' Meeting, in the Valley church, Botetourt Co., Va., April 1.

WHEN we consider the nature, magnitude, and difficulty of the work in which the preacher is engaged, we are ready to realize the necessity of employing all the helps which can in any way increase his efficiency, and enable him to achieve the very best results. No one is so perfect in any calling, who may not become more so by intelligent application and exercise; and if he has the elements of manhood in him, he will desire to make the most of his vocation. We see this honorable trait of human nature frequently illustrated in the various secular callings and professions, where all the resources and powers within human reach are bent to the one purpose of achieving the greatest possible success. How much more, then, should the preacher make the most of his vocation, since there is none other which can compare with it in importance and far-reaching results. It is necessary, therefore, in the first place, that we cultivate a high conception of the work to be done, and of the needful qualifications for that work. Something of the spirit of St. Paul should animate the preacher, when he said to the Romans, "I magnify mine office."

No preacher can succeed well, or wield any considerable power over the minds of men, who does not magnify his office. A low estimate of his calling will inevitably beget a fatal indolence and carelessness, detrimental alike in its effects upon the preacher and upon his hearers. Along with a high estimate of the ministerial calling should be found an equally high estimate of its essential qualifications. I think that just in this latter point can be located one of the most serious weaknesses of our ministerial system. We have too low an estimate of qualification, both as to its importance, and as to the elements which go to make it up. We have not studied carefully the lessons on this subject of history and experience. We do not sufficiently estimate those gifts and acquirements which are absolutely necessary to a high degree of efficiency in the ministry. It is true that the most important qualifications for the ministry are moral and spiritual, and it is for this reason that sometimes exceptionally good men in the pulpit wield a powerful influence, who only possess a moderate share of mental and educational qualifications; but this is no reason why the latter should be underestimated, or neglected. They are elements of pulpit power which may be compared to good mechanical implements. Take two farmers of equal ability. Give one of them the rude implements of a thousand years ago, and the other the wonderful machinery of the present day, and the latter will accomplish ten times as much as the former. This comparison will give us some idea of the advantages of a disciplined mind,—a mind trained to think connectedly, to reason logically, to classify and analyze correctly, and to express its views clearly and forcibly.

It is of the greatest importance that the preacher should have an abundant command of good language. Of what value to mankind would all the treasures of wisdom and knowledge be, locked behind lips which could not utter them? It takes the very highest cultivation and the severest training to enable one to speak or write with ease in plain, pure, simple English, but when the art is acquired, it is a mighty engine of power to its possessor. Those who have been so unfortunate as to acquire an ungrammatical habit, and have not been so fortunate as to receive the training of the schools, may correct their deficiencies to a large extent, and add materially to their fund of language and power of expression, by carefully studying the approved use, simple construction, and musical rhythm of standard English as it appears in our best authors, or as it appears in the St. James Bible, where it displays all its singular beauty and power.

Again, the preacher should have some idea of elocutionary and oratorical power. He should cultivate a strong, musical, well-modulated voice, an energetic but natural manner, good action, and appropriate gestures. A good sermon may be spoiled by a bad delivery, while an inferior sermon is improved by a good delivery. Nothing so weakens the effect of a discourse as a harsh voice, pitched on an unnatural key, or an affected manner, or indolent action, or awkward gestures. In all these things the preacher should study naturalness. As in painting the highest art is to reproduce, with perfect accuracy and faithfulness, the exact lineaments of nature as she appears in all the variety of hill and dale, light and shade, animate and inanimate, so in preaching, the highest art, so far as its elocutionary features are concerned, is to give perfectly natural, realistic, and sympathetic expression, in voice and manner, to every shade of thought and every variety of feeling.

It is true that the oratorical faculty is a natural gift, bestowed with great discrimination, and no amount of training will supply the total want of it; but different persons possess varying degrees of this faculty, some more, and some less, and in all there are defects which must be overcome by patient and intelligent training and cultivation. To overcome these defects will, in all cases, increase the attractiveness of a preacher, and this can be readily turn to account in the furtherance of his great object, namely, to gain a favorable hearing for the truth, and win men and women to a better life.

But while all these attainments and accomplishments are valuable helps to the preacher, which are not to be despised, or neglected, they are not the most important elements of pulpit power. These we have reserved for our last and most serious consideration. The first we will mention is

SIMPLICITY OF TREATMENT.

An ambiguous style, or one that is too much involved in philosophy, or mystery, or abstract speculation, or affected profundity, or one that in any direction goes beyond, or above, or beneath the comprehension of common men, is to be carefully avoided. The greatest thoughts can and should be clothed in the simplest manner. The preacher should study to clothe the greatest truths, and the profoundest theology in a garb which will at once introduce it to the plainest understanding. One of the most learned and eloquent preachers of this country said that the greatest compliment he ever received came from a pious, old negro woman, totally illiterate, who constantly attended upon his ministry. "De reason," she said, "why I likes to hear de doctor is kase I always kin make out what he is drivin at."

Some preachers put the Gospel hay so high in the rack that neither lambs nor sheep can reach it; but I have always observed that when you examine this high hay closely, you will find in it a great many dry sticks and stalks, totally drained of spiritual sap. The greatest preacher the world has seen since the days of Wesley and Whitefield, has just died in London. Since his death the civilized world has been meditating upon his unique character, and his wonderful power and success as a preacher. Almost the unanimous verdict of Christian scholarship the world over is, that one of the prime secrets of his pulpit power lay in his simplicity of doctrine and method of treatment. Hearing or reading Spurgeon's greatest sermons, a child might be attracted, instructed and edified. The most essential element of simplicity is

CLEARNESS.

The preacher should have a perfect understanding of what he intends to say. His subject, his ideas, his facts should be vividly alive in his own mind. They should take possession of it, and leap to the lips for utterance. Like David, let him "muse" over his message "until the fire burns." Burning thoughts will find burning words. Clear ideas will find clear language. Dim thoughts and dim methods of treatment will grope and stumble and stammer in obscure utterance, which confuses and confounds both speaker and hearer, and edifies nobody. By all means let the preacher get into his head a plain, straightforward comprehension of Gospel truth; let him have a plain, simple, natural way of presenting that truth; let him get a firm grip upon the special subject of each discourse; let the arrangement of parts be simple, and at the same time logical; let each thought stand in a clear sky, so that the light of heaven will shine through it, and illuminate it with a divine glory.

Do you want to study the most perfect illustrations of this kind of religious discourse? You will find them in the sermons of our Savior. From every stand-point of criticism they are the perfect models. Let your discourse be like his, and you will possess a truly marvelous and effective pulpit power. The

ABSENCE OF SELF-CONSCIOUSNESS

Is closely allied to simplicity and essential to pulpit power. Keep self out of sight in the pulpit! Do not be ambitious for fame! Avoid sky-scraping eloquence. Do not perorate. Do not send people away complimenting your grand sermon, but rather make them say, "Men and brethren, what shall we do?" Do not glorify yourself, your science, your learning, your eloquence, but glorify Christ, and in return he will glorify you by owning and blessing your ministry. Another element of simplicity is

CONCENTRATION,

The sermon should not be so crowded with diversified thought as to make no distinct impression of any. The central and most important

Missionary and Tract Work Department.

"Upon the first day of the week, let every one of you lay by him in store as God hath prospered him, that there be no gatherings when I come."—1 Cor. 16: 2.

"Every man as he purposeth in his heart, so let him give. Not grudgingly or of necessity, for the Lord loveth a cheerful giver."—2 Cor. 9: 7.

HOW MUCH SHALL WE GIVE?

"Every man *according to his ability.*" "Every one *as God hath prospered him.*" "Every man, *according as he purposeth in his heart,* so let him give." "For if there be first a willing mind, it is accepted *according to that a man hath,* and not according to *that he hath not.*"—2 Cor. 8: 12.

Organization of Missionary Committee.

DANIEL VANIMAN, Foreman,   · · ·   McPherson, Kans.
D. L. MILLER, Treasurer,   · · ·   Mt. Morris, Ill.
GALEN B. ROYER, Secretary,   · · ·   Mt. Morris, Ill.

Organization of Book and Tract Work.

S. W. HOOVER, Foreman,   · · ·   Dayton, Ohio.
S. BOCK, Secretary and Treasurer,   · · ·   Dayton, Ohio.

☞ All donations intended for Missionary Work should be sent to GALEN B. ROYER, Mt. Morris, Ill.

☞ All money for Tract Work should be sent to S. BOCK, Dayton, Ohio.

☞ Money may be sent by Money Order, Registered Letter, or Drafts on New York or Chicago. Do not send personal checks, or drafts on interior towns, as it costs 25 cents to collect them.

☞ Solicitors are requested to faithfully carry out the plan of Annual Meeting, that all our members be solicited to contribute at least twice a year for the Mission and Tract Work of the Church.

☞ Notes for the Endowment Fund can be had by writing to the Secretary of either Work.

PULPIT POWER, AND HOW OBTAINED.

Address delivered by B. C. Moomaw, at the Ministers' Meeting, in the Valley church, Botetourt Co., Va., April 1.

WHEN we consider the nature, magnitude, and difficulty of the work in which the preacher is engaged, we are ready to realize the necessity of employing all the helps which can in any way increase his efficiency, and enable him to achieve the very best results. No one is so perfect in any calling, who may not become more so by intelligent application and exercise; and if he has the elements of manhood in him, he will desire to make the most of his vocation. We see this honorable trait of human nature frequently illustrated in the various secular callings and professions, where all the resources and powers within human reach are bent to the one purpose of achieving the greatest possible success. How much more, then, should the preacher make the most of his vocation, since there is none other which can compare with it in importance and far-reaching results. It is necessary, therefore, in the first place, that we cultivate a high conception of the work to be done, and of the needful qualifications for that work. Something of the spirit of St. Paul should animate the preacher, when he said to the Romans, "I magnify mine office."

No preacher can succeed well, or wield any considerable power over the minds of men, who does not magnify his office. A low estimate of his calling will inevitably beget a fatal indolence and carelessness, detrimental alike in its effects upon the preacher and upon his hearers. Along with a high estimate of the ministerial calling should be found an equally high estimate of its essential qualifications. I think that just in this latter point can be located one of the most serious weaknesses of our ministerial system. We have too low an estimate of qualification, both as to its importance, and as to the elements which go to make it up. We have not studied carefully the lessons on this subject of history and experience. We do not sufficiently estimate those gifts and acquirements which are absolutely necessary to a high degree of efficiency in the ministry. It is true that the most important qualifications for the ministry are moral and spiritual, and it is for this reason that sometimes exceptionally good men in the pulpit wield a powerful influence, who only possess a moderate share of mental and educational qualifications; but this is no reason why the latter should be underestimated, or neglected. They are elements of pulpit power which may be compared to good mechanical implements. Take two farmers of equal ability. Give one of them the rude implements of a thousand years ago, and the other the wonderful machinery of the present day, and the latter will accomplish ten times as much as the former. This comparison will give us some idea of the advantages of a disciplined mind,—a mind trained to think connectedly, to reason logically, to classify and analyze correctly, and to express its views clearly and forcibly.

It is of the greatest importance that the preacher should have an abundant command of good language. Of what value to mankind would all the treasures of wisdom and knowledge be, locked behind lips which could not utter them? It takes the very highest cultivation and the severest training to enable one to speak or write with ease in plain, pure, simple English, but when the art is acquired, it is a mighty engine of power to its possessor. Those who have been so unfortunate as to acquire an ungrammatical habit, and have not been so fortunate as to receive the training of the schools, may correct their deficiencies to a large extent, and add materially to their fund of language and power of expression, by carefully studying the approved use, simple construction, and musical rhythm of standard English as it appears in our best authors, or as it appears in the St. James Bible, where it displays all its singular beauty and power.

Again, the preacher should have some idea of elocutionary and oratorical power. He should cultivate a strong, musical, well-modulated voice, an energetic but natural manner, good action, and appropriate gestures. A good sermon may be spoiled by a bad delivery, while an inferior sermon is improved by a good delivery. Nothing so weakens the effect of a discourse as a harsh voice, pitched on an unnatural key, or an affected manner, or indolent action, or awkward gestures. In all these things the preacher should study naturalness. As in painting the highest art is to reproduce, with perfect accuracy and faithfulness, the exact lineaments of nature as she appears in all the variety of hill and dale, light and shade, animate and inanimate, so in preaching, the highest art, so far as its elocutionary features are concerned, is to give perfectly natural, realistic, and sympathetic expression, in voice and manner, to every shade of thought and every variety of feeling.

It is true that the oratorical faculty is a natural gift, bestowed with great discrimination, and no amount of training will supply the total want of it; but different persons possess varying degrees of this faculty, some more, and some less, and in all there are defects which must be overcome by patient and intelligent training and cultivation. To overcome these defects will, in all cases, increase the attractiveness of a preacher, and this he can readily turn to account in the furtherance of his great object, namely, to gain a favorable hearing for the truth, and win men and women to a better life.

But while all these attainments and accomplishments are valuable helps to the preacher, which are not to be despised, or neglected, they are not the most important elements of pulpit power. These we have reserved for our last and most serious consideration. The first we will mention is SIMPLICITY OF TREATMENT.

An ambiguous style, or one that is too much involved in philosophy, or mystery, or abstract speculation, or affected profundity, or one that in any direction goes beyond, or above, or beneath the comprehension of common men, is to be carefully avoided. The greatest thoughts can and should be clothed in the simplest manner. The preacher should study to clothe the greatest truths, and the profoundest theology in a garb which will at once introduce it to the plainest understanding. One of the most learned and eloquent preachers of this country said that the greatest compliment he ever received came from a pious, old negro woman, totally illiterate, who constantly attended upon his ministry. "De reason," she said, "why I likes to hear de doctor is kase I always kin make out what he is drivin at."

Some preachers put the Gospel hay so high in the rack that neither lambs nor sheep can reach it; but I have always observed that when you examine this high hay closely, you will find in it a great many dry sticks and stalks, totally drained of spiritual sap. The greatest preacher the world has seen since the days of Wesley and Whitefield, has just died in London. Since his death the civilized world has been meditating upon his unique character, and his wonderful power and success as a preacher. Almost the unanimous verdict of Christian scholarship the world over is, that one of the prime secrets of his pulpit power lay in his simplicity of doctrine and method of treatment. Hearing or reading Spurgeon's greatest sermons, a child might be attracted, instructed and edified. The most essential element of simplicity is

CLEARNESS.

The preacher should have a perfect understanding of what he intends to say. His subject, his ideas, his facts should be vividly alive in his own mind. They should take possession of it, and leap to the lips for utterance. Like David, let him "muse" over his message "until the fire burns." Burning thoughts will find burning words. Clear ideas will find clear language. Dim thoughts and dim methods of treatment will grope and stumble and stammer in obscure utterance, which confuses and confounds both speaker and hearer, and edifies nobody. By all means let the preacher get into his head a plain, straightforward comprehension of Gospel truth; let him have a plain, simple, natural way of presenting that truth; let him get a firm grip upon the special subject of each discourse; let the arrangement of parts be simple, and at the same time logical; let each thought stand in a clear sky, so that the light of heaven will shine through it, and illuminate it with a divine glory.

Do you want to study the most perfect illustrations of this kind of religious discourse? You will find them in the sermons of our Savior. From every stand-point of criticism they are the perfect models. Let your discourse be like his, and you will possess a truly marvelous and effective pulpit power. The

ABSENCE OF SELF-CONSCIOUSNESS.

Is closely allied to simplicity and essential to pulpit power. Keep self out of sight in the pulpit! Do not be ambitious for fame! Avoid sky-scraping eloquence. Do not perorate. Do not send people away complimenting your grand sermon, but rather make them say, "Men and brethren, what shall we do?" Do not glorify yourself, your science, your learning, your eloquence, but glorify Christ, and in return he will glorify you by owning and blessing your ministry. Another element of simplicity is

CONCENTRATION,

The sermon should not be so crowded with diversified thought as to make no distinct impression of any. The central and most important

The Gospel Messenger,

A Weekly at $1.50 Per Annum.

PUBLISHED BY

The Brethren's Publishing Co.

D. L. MILLER,	· · · · · ·	Editor.
J. H. MOORE,	· · · · ·	Office Editor.
J. B. BRUMBAUGH,	}	ASSOCIATE EDITORS.
J. G. ROYER,		
JOSEPH AMICK,	· · · ·	Business Manager.

ADVISORY COMMITTEE.
R. H. Miller, A. Hutchison, Daniel Hays.

☞Communications for publication should be legibly written with black ink on one side of the paper only. Do not attempt to interline, or to put on one page what ought to occupy two.

☞Anonymous communications will not be published.

☞Do not mix business with articles for publication. Keep your communications on separate sheets from all business.

☞Time is precious. We always have time to attend to business and to answer questions of importance, but please do not subject us to need less answering of letters.

☞The MESSENGER is mailed each week to all subscribers. If the address is correctly entered on our list, the paper must reach the person to whom it is addressed. If you do not get your paper, write us, giving particulars.

☞When changing your address, please give your former as well as your future address in full, so as to avoid delay and misunderstanding.

☞Always remit to the office from which you order your goods, no matter from where you receive them.

☞Do not send personal checks or drafts on interior banks, unless you send with them 15 cents each, to pay for collection.

☞Remittances should be made by Post-office Money Order, Drafts on New York, Philadelphia or Chicago, or Registered Letters, made payable and addressed to "Brethren's Publishing Co., Mount Morris, Ill.," or "Brethren's Publishing Co., Huntingdon, Pa."

☞Entered at the Post-office at Mount Morris, Ill., as second-class matter.

Mount Morris, Ill.,   May 10, 1892.

$1.00 pays for the MESSENGER from now until Dec. 31, 1892. Subscribe now!

THE Second District of Virginia, will be represented on the Standing Committee this year by Daniel Hays.

IN this issue appears Bro. Hays' article entitled, "Chrysostom and the Breaking of Bread," which should have appeared in No. 16, but was unintentionally omitted.

BRO. JOHN J. HOOVER reports quite an awakening among the people at Crawford, Nebr. It is a mission point and six souls were gathered into the fold when last heard from.

THE Eastern District of Maryland sends several queries to the Annual Meeting. Bro. E. W. Stoner will represent the District on the Standing Committee.

BRO. JOSEPH HOLDER, of Hagerstown, Ind., may now be addressed at Anderson, Madison Co., same State. Those wishing his services for meetings, while on his way to and from the Annual Meeting, would better write him soon.

WE have just issued a new edition of the "Gospel Chimes," price 25 cents, or $2.50 per dozen. Our Sunday-school workers will find this excellent little song-book admirably adapted to their wants, and we hope to see them quite generally introduced.

ONE of our exchanges says: "This is to be a year full of political excitement, for it is the year of presidential election, and we hope our readers will not get so absorbed in politics as to backslide from God." By the way, there is not anything in the excitement of politics to keep any one from backsliding.

NEXT week, May 10, the members of Northern Illinois will meet with the Milledgeville church in District Conference. We hope to see a general attendance, as the meeting is an important one and ought to be largely attended by both the laity and the officials. We also learn that there is to be a love-feast the evening before.

QUERIES.

THE DISTRICT CLERKS, who have not yet sent in the queries from their respective Districts to the Annual Meeting, will please do so at once, so they can be printed according to the instructions of last Annual Meeting. The time is short and the work important. A number of Districts have not yet been heard from.

IN this issue is a real encouraging report in regard to church and Sunday-school work at Waynesborough, Pa. Those who have the oversight of congregations will do well to encourage such departments of religious exercises, as will prove edifying and instructive to both old and young. We hope to hear more concerning the good work of the Master at Waynesborough.

SPEAKING of the District Meeting at Roann, Ind., April 6, the North Manchest-r Journal says: "The financial report of the Old Folks' Home at Mexico was good. A sum total of $2,589.06 was received during the year and $1,538.77 expended, leaving balance on hand of $1,050 29. There are seventeen inmates, all old folks. S M. Aukerman, J. Snowberger, and W. S. Toney were re-elected on the home mission board and D. P. Shively as trustee of the Old Folks' Home. Jacob Snell was chosen on the Standing Committee at the Annual Meeting. The next Meeting will be held in the Monticello church, White County, on the first Wednesday in April, 1893."

A SHORT visit to Sterling last week, enabled us to enjoy some very pleasant meetings with the Brethren at that place. On Sunday morning, May 1, the house was well filled with a very intelligent and attentive audience. At the close of the services a sister was received by confession and baptism. A number of people assembled on the bank of the river, to witness the baptismal scene. Sterling is a city of probably ten thousand inhabitants, with a prosperous future before it. It is here that the Mission Board of Northern Illinois erected a substantial meeting-house in an excellent part of the city, at a time when only a few members lived there. For a time the preaching was done by adjoining ministers, but last July the Board placed the work in charge of Bro. P. B. Keltner, and arranged to sustain him while he would devote his entire time to the Sterling mission. In our judgment the Board did a very wise thing, and deserves credit for such an important undertaking. When Bro. Keltner commenced his work, there were one dozen members in the City. At the present time they number about twenty-three, showing a very healthy increase. Six of them were received by baptism, and the prospect of still more becoming quite encouraging. We are glad to see our brother and his wife so thoroughly interested in their work. They have not only accepted the work in good faith, but are falling into the right methods of doing city work, and find enough to occupy their entire time and attention. The members are also both hopeful, and in real earnest, and the indications are that a strong, orderly church is likely to be built up in Sterling. We were very much pleased with our trip, and greatly encouraged with the outlook. We wish to further say, that we are strongly impressed that the Mission Board is conducting the Sterling mission on the right plan, and ought to be encouraged in their efforts, and we will further add, with emphasis, that, in our opinion, this is the only successful method of building up new churches in cities, and the sooner we fall into it, the better it will be for the cause we are representing.

J. H. M.

BRO. I. D. PARKER requests us to say that all the members of the Examining Committee of the Tract Work are requested to meet at Mt. Morris, May 25, at 2 P. M. All those who have manuscript to come before the Committee will be governed accordingly.

NOW, brethren, since the Government has favored us with the new and enlarged postal cards, let us have short reports of church news from all the churches and plenty of them. Just a few lines from each church would make very interesting reading. Let every congregation send us some news every month, and oftener, if they have it.

ALL those who have friends in Denver, Colo., will please give attention to Bro. D. H. Weaver's letter impresses us we feel that he is going at the work in the right way. City work is so different from that usually performed in the rural districts that it requires some training for ministers to get into it just right. We hope our readers will assist in the Denver mission in the manner suggested.

"THE turning back of the fugitive Russian Jews from the German frontier, furnishes Europe with a pitiable spectacle. Even where ample security is offered by relief committees that the refugees will be supported and passed on, the authorities refuse and the poor creatures are mercilessly turned back. Still they come, for there is no way of notifying the swarming thousands of the prohibition to cross the German border. It is said that 400,000 Jews are now trying to fly from Russia, and Germany will need to police the whole frontier."

AFTER asking us to say to our readers, that in No. 17, p. 258, third column, third line from top, it should read forth-telling instead of "foretelling," Bro. Balabaugh adds: "I am glad you think the close of that article simple enough for simple people. My 'Biblical flights' are not very high, as I am not a bird of Pauline wing, and cannot yet mount above the dust and smoke and turmoil of this sin-smitten planet. My faith goes clean up to the Mercy-seat, but my understanding lags behind in many things. Faith is the telescope that sweeps the Empyrean of Grace. The child-heart knows what the philosophic mind cannot master. The child's feet stand on the philosopher's head."

RAILWAY ARRANGEMENTS.

The Trans-Missouri Passenger Association.

THE following letter from the above-named Association to Bro. John Wise will explain itself:

ELDER JOHN WISE,
      Box 157, Conway Springs, Kans.,

      DEAR SIR: In regard to your application for reduction of fares in favor of persons attending the Annual Meeting of German Baptist Brethren, to be held in Cedar Rapids, Ia., on June 3-9, I take pleasure in informing you that an open rate of one fare for the round trip has been agreed upon by the Railways designated in the following list.

This reduction will apply from all points in Kansas and Nebraska. Excursion tickets to be sold on June 1 to 3, inclusive, good to return until and including June 30, limited to continuous passage in each direction from date of sale or execution.   Yours truly,

       JAMES SMITH,
         Chairman.

Atchison, Topeka & Santa Fe Railroad,
    W. F. WHITE, P. T. M., Chicago, Ill.
    GEO. T. NICHOLSON, G. P. & T. A., Topeka, Kans.
Burlington & Missouri River Railroad in Nebraska,
    J. FRANCIS, G. P. & T. A., Omaha, Nebr.
Chicago, Rock Island & Pacific Railway,
    JOHN SEBASTIAN, G. T. & P. A., Chicago, Ill.
    T. J. ANDERSON, A. G. T. & P. A., Topeka, Kans.

The Gospel Messenger.

A Weekly at $1.50 Per Annum.

PUBLISHED BY

The Brethren's Publishing Co.

D. L. MILLER,	. . . . .	Editor.
J. H. MOORE,	. . . . .	Office Editor.
J. B. BRUMBAUGH,	. . . . .	Associate Editors.
J. G. ROYER,		
JOSEPH AMICK,	. . . . .	Business Manager.

ADVISORY COMMITTEE.

R. H. Miller, A. Hutchison, Daniel Hays.

Mount Morris, Ill., ... May 10, 1892.

$1.00 pays for the MESSENGER from now until Dec. 31, 1892. Subscribe now!

THE Second District of Virginia, will be represented on the Standing Committee this year by Daniel Hays.

IN this issue appears Bro. Hays' article entitled, "Chrysostom and the Breaking of Bread," which should have appeared in No. 16, but was unintentionally omitted.

BRO. JOHN J. HOOVER reports quite an awakening among the people at Crawford, Nebr. It is a mission point and six souls were gathered into the fold when last heard from.

THE Eastern District of Maryland sends several queries to the Annual Meeting. Bro. E. W. Stoner will represent the District on the Standing Committee.

BRO. JOSEPH HOLDER, of Hagerstown, Ind., may now be addressed at Anderson, Madison Co., same State. Those wishing his services for meetings, while on his way to and from the Annual Meeting, would better write him soon.

WE have just issued a new edition of the "Gospel Chimes," price 25 cents, or $2.50 per dozen. Our Sunday-school workers will find this excellent little song-book admirably adapted to their wants, and we hope to see them quite generally introduced.

ONE of our exchanges says: "This is to be a year full of political excitement, for it is the year of presidential election, and we hope our readers will not get so absorbed in politics as to backslide from God." By the way, there is not anything in the excitement of politics to keep any one from backsliding.

NEXT week, May 10, the members of Northern Illinois will meet with the Milledgeville church in District Conference. We hope to see a general attendance, as the meeting is an important one and ought to be largely attended by both the laity and the officials. We also learn that there is to be a love-feast the evening before.

QUERIES.

THE DISTRICT CLERKS, who have not yet sent in the queries from their respective Districts to the Annual Meeting, will please do so at once, so they can be printed according to the instructions of last Annual Meeting. The time is short and the work important. A number of Districts have not yet been heard from.

IN this issue is a real encouraging report in regard to church and Sunday-school work at Waynesborough, Pa. Those who have the oversight of congregations will do well to encourage such departments of religious exercises, as will prove edifying and instructive to both old and young. We hope to hear more concerning the good work of the Master at Waynesborough.

SPEAKING of the District Meeting at Roann, Ind., April 6, the North Manchester Journal says: "The financial report of the Old Folks' Home at Mexico was good. A sum total of $2,589.06 was received during the year and $1,538.77 expended, leaving balance on hand of $1,050 29. There are seventeen inmates, all old folks. S. M. Aukerman, J. Snowberger, and W. S. Toney were re-elected on the home mission board and D. P. Shively as trustee of the Old Folks' Home. Jacob Snell was chosen on the Standing Committee at the Annual Meeting. The next Meeting will be held in the Monticello church, White County, on the first Wednesday in April, 1893."

A SHORT visit to Sterling last week, enabled us to enjoy some very pleasant meetings with the Brethren at that place. On Sunday morning, May 1, the house was well filled with a very intelligent and attentive audience. At the close of the services a sister was received by confession and baptism. A number of people assembled on the bank of the river, to witness the baptismal scene. Sterling is a city of probably ten thousand inhabitants, with a prosperous future before it. It is here that the Mission Board of Northern Illinois erected a substantial meeting-house in an excellent part of the city, at a time when only a few members lived there. For a time the preaching was done by adjoining ministers, but last July the Board placed the work in charge of Bro. P. R. Keltner, and arranged to sustain him while he would devote his entire time to the Sterling mission. In our judgment the Board did a very wise thing, and deserves credit for such an important undertaking. When Bro. Keltner commenced his work, there were one dozen members in the City. At the present time they number about twenty-three, showing a very healthy increase. Six of them were received by baptism, and the prospect of still more seems quite encouraging. We are glad to see our brother and his wife so thoroughly interested in their work. They have not only accepted the work in good faith, but are falling into the right methods of doing city work, and find enough to occupy their entire time and attention. The members are also both hopeful, and in real earnest, and the indications are that a strong, orderly church is likely to be built up in Sterling. We were very much pleased with our trip, and greatly encouraged with the outlook. We wish to further say, that we are strongly impressed that the Mission Board is conducting the Sterling mission on the right plan, and ought to be encouraged in their efforts, and we will further add, with emphasis, that, in our opinion, this is the only successful method of building up new churches in cities, and the sooner we fall into it, the better it will be for the cause we are representing.

J. H. M.

BRO. I. D. PARKER requests us to say that all the members of the Examining Committee of the Tract Work are requested to meet at Mt. Morris, May 25, at 2 P. M. All those who have manuscript to come before the Committee will be governed accordingly.

Now, brethren, since the Government has favored us with the new and enlarged postal cards, let us have short reports of church news from all the churches and plenty of them. Just a few lines from each church would make very interesting reading. Let every congregation send us some news every month, and oftener, if they have it.

ALL those who have friends in Denver, Colo., will please give attention to Bro. D. H. Weaver's communication in this issue. We are glad the Brethren are making a special effort to establish a church in Denver, and the way Bro. Weaver's letter impresses us we feel that he is going at the work in the right way. City work is so different from that usually performed in the rural districts that it requires some training for ministers to get into it just right. We hope our readers will assist in the Denver mission in the manner suggested.

"THE turning back of the fugitive Russian Jews from the German frontier, furnishes Europe with a pitiable spectacle. Even where ample security is offered by relief committees that the refugees will be supported and passed on, the authorities refuse and the poor creatures are mercilessly turned back. Still they come, for there is no way of notifying the swarming thousands of the prohibition to cross the German border. It is said that 400,000 Jews are now trying to fly from Russia, and Germany will need to police the whole frontier."

AFTER asking us to say to our readers, that in No. 17, p. 258, third column, third line from top, it should read forth-telling instead of "foretelling," Bro. Balsbaugh adds: "I am glad you think the close of that article simple enough for simple people. My 'Biblical flights' are not very high, as I am not a bird of Pauline wing, and cannot yet mount above the dust and smoke and turmoil of this sin-smitten planet. My faith goes clean up to the Mercy-seat, but my understanding lags behind in many things. Faith is the telescope that sweeps the Empyrean of Grace. The child-heart knows what the philosophic mind cannot master. The child's feet stand on the philosopher's head."

RAILWAY ARRANGEMENTS.

The Trans-Missouri Passenger Association.

THE following letter from the above-named Association to Bro. John Wise will explain itself:

ELDER JOHN WISE,
Box 157, Conway Springs, Kans.,

DEAR SIR:

In regard to your application for reduction of fares in favor of persons attending the Annual Meeting of German Baptist Brethren, to be held in Cedar Rapids, Ia., on June 3-9, I take pleasure in informing you that an open rate of one fare for the round trip has been agreed upon by the Railways designated in the following list.

This reduction will apply from all points in Kansas and Nebraska. Excursion tickets to be sold on June 1 to 3, inclusive, good to return until and including June 30, limited to continuous passage in each direction from date of sale or execution.

Yours truly,
JAMES SMITH,
Chairman.

Atchison, Topeka & Santa Fe Railroad,
W. F. WHITE, P. T. M., Chicago, Ill.
GEO. T. NICHOLSON, G. P. & T. A., Topeka, Kans.
Burlington & Missouri River Railroad in Nebraska,
J. FRANCIS, G. P. & T. A., Omaha, Nebr.
Chicago, Rock Island & Pacific Railway,
JOHN SEBASTIAN, G. T. & P. A., Chicago, Ill.
T. J. ANDERSON, A. G. T. & P. A., Topeka, Kans.

Please explain Matt. 19: 10–12, "His disciples say unto him, If the case of the man be so with his wife, it is not good to marry. But he said unto them, All men cannot receive this saying, save they to whom it is given. For there are some eunuchs, which were so born from their mother's womb: and there are some eunuchs, which were made eunuchs of men: and there be eunuchs which have made themselves eunuchs for the kingdom of heaven's sake. He that is able to receive it, let him receive it." It says, "All men cannot receive this saying, save they to whom it is given." Who can receive it?
J. J. SHARP.

Those who can remain unmarried, and feel contented. There are those who cannot live contented and happy without a companion. Let such marry. There are others who could not, and would not enjoy marriage. They are the ones who can receive the doctrine of celibacy fully.

But there is another class who would enjoy the married life, but in order to become more useful in their calling, prefer to live in a state of celibacy. Paul and John the Baptist were of this number. The term *receive* does not refer to receiving the doctrine so much as the *capacity*, or *temperament*, to remain in the unmarried state. In ancient times some voluntarily entered upon a life of celibacy for the sake of greater usefulness, as it is well known that marriage is a hinderance to some lines of missionary work.

When, and on what grounds did the church set aside the rule of former years, which did not permit members to marry outsiders?   REBECCA WEAVER.

We are not aware that such a rule has been set aside, unless it be assumed that the New Testament teaches that members should not marry unbelievers. Our church does not forbid members marrying outsiders, but advises against it. And we feel that it would be well if the advice were more generally heeded. When two are agreed religiously, they can walk together in life more pleasantly.

Is it wrong for a minister to carry hymn books and Testaments to his place of preaching on Sunday and give them to his congregation and take money for them on Sunday, if the object is to advance the cause of Christ.
JASPER BARNTHOUSE.

If it is done with a view of making money, we consider it a wrong use of the Lord's day, but if it be solely for the good of the cause, we see no harm in it, and yet the more cautious we are about such things the better. We should not permit our good to be evil spoken of. Let us learn to do as little money business on Sunday as possible. In many places it is difficult to avoid transactions of this kind on Sunday, but we need not make a regular business of it.

Is it right or proper for the church, or any individual member, to report persons who make disturbance at a Communion or other meeting to the grand jury? J. H. FAHNESTOCK.

Brethren are generally advised not to use the law excepting in case of stern necessity. The law of the land protects us in our religious exercises, and any one who disturbs the services lays himself liable to the law. In case the disturbance should become so great as to interfere with the exercises, it would be well for the proper authorities to know it, and this can usually be done without going before the grand jury. We know of a case where bullets were fired into the meeting-house. The church appointed two of her deacons to consult with one of the County officers about it. The officer took the matter in hand, and that was the end of it. Some things are lawful, and yet not expedient. We must do our utmost to get along peaceably with all men, and if we are too greatly disturbed at our feasts, there are officers whose business it is to look after such cases if properly apprized of them. Our advice is that one of the

church officials consult with the proper officer privately.

How is it considered for brethren to go on the annual visit who do not conform to the order of the church; are members under obligations to accept such visits?   J. L. LESH.

All church officials are required to conform to the general order of the church, and they should be admonished to do so. This duty rests upon the visiting brethren as well as the other officials. But no one should refuse a visit just because the visiting official happens to be out of order in his general appearance. Receive the visit kindly, remembering that he is acting in his official and not in an individual capacity. By so doing strength and confidence may be gained sufficient to kindly admonish the official at the proper time. As long as a brother is an official it is our duty to respect him as such. If he is not doing right, it is the privilege of the church to handle him, but it is not the prerogative of any one member to interfere with or obstruct the work which the church requires him to do.

Can a brother serve as delegate to District or Annual Meeting and not conform to the order of the church in dress and abstaining from the use of tobacco?   J. L. LESH.

Many brethren who do not conform to the order are *permitted* to serve, but it is unfortunate that they cannot be induced to fall into the ways of the church more fully. Were the letter as well as the spirit of Annual Meeting decisions pressed, such delegates could likely be ruled out. We advise the sending of plainly-attired delegates when they can be had. This would be far better than making an effort to rule any one out. The more plainly-attired and well-informed delegates we can have at the Annual Meeting, the better it will be for the general good of the Brotherhood. The use of tobacco has not been made a test for delegates to District Meetings, but it has for the Annual Meeting. Delegates sent to Annual Meeting are usually rejected if they use tobacco.* The committee on credentials asks each delegate whether he uses tobacco.

TO THE YOUNG DISCIPLES IN MOUNT MORRIS COLLEGE.

NUMBER THREE.

To settle the dispute among the disciples as to "Who should be the greatest," the Savior gave them an object lesson. "He took a child and set him in the midst of them," and said, "Whosoever humbleth himself as this little child," not only "receiveth me," but "the same is the greatest in the kingdom of heaven." He was the greatest, not because of his sinlessness,—for if none but the sinless could enter the kingdom of heaven, that part which is on earth,—the church,—would be empty; but because of his possessing the qualities which are characteristic of childhood,—the qualities which make the ideal childhood. Humility, tender affection, perfect trust, unworldliness and a teachable spirit, are prominent among those qualities. It is these that make the life of the child a perfect life of faith.

Think of a little child! Unaided, what can it do? How absolutely dependent! It would be lost, if trusted alone. It would die for want, because it could not find the next meal. How is it, then, that childhood is the happy life it is? Simply because it is, as it were, instinctively a life of faith. It could not buy the next loaf, but it has a firm belief that "father" can. "So every disciple whose faith manifests itself by this child-like

spirit, says the Savior, "receiveth me," because he has taken into his heart the qualities of character which I love, and by which his life is so transformed that "all men know," that he is my disciple; and the act of receiving those qualities is the way by which such a disciple gives expression to his feelings of devotion to his Master. All who are in possession of this spirit are in the kingdom of heaven, and the more one has of it, the nearer he is to King Jesus, and the greater he is in the kingdom.

A willingness to be led by the world, and conform to its demands, dearly beloved, is an index both of the absence of this childhood faith, and of the transforming power by which your daily walk is adorned with heavenly radiance. May be, under whose shadow you sleep, before whom you eat your daily bread, and out of whose hand you draw your breath, enable you all to be "living epistles" which will speak "with authority" to the church of coming generations.

My visit to the Shenandoah and Roanoke Valleys, Va., afforded much which was highly interesting to me, and would have been equally interesting to you all, could you have been sharers with your brother.   J. G. ROYER.
Bridgewater, Va.

CORRESPONDENCE.

"Write what thou seest, and send it unto the churches."

☞ Church News solicited for this Department. If you have had a good meeting, send a report of it, so that others may rejoice with you. In writing give name of church, County and State. Be brief. Notes of Travel should be as short as possible. Land Advertisements are not solicited for this Department. We have an advertising page, and, if necessary, will issue supplements.

Antietam Sunday-Schools, Bible Class, Etc.

SOME time during the summer of 1872, Eld. Jacob F. Oller, of this congregation, then a minister in the second degree, organized the Waynesborough Sunday-school. Although the Brethren had a school as early as 1744 at Ephrata, Lancaster Co., Pa., this was the first school ever held in this part of the State.

The task was not an easy one. The then presiding elder, and some of the older members opposed it. It was feared the new innovation, as it was termed, would foster pride among the members and bring the church into disrepute. Had it not been for this, no objection would have been offered, by those opposing the school. They were zealous, laboring assiduously for the upbuilding of the church, but, to a certain degree, were not aggressive.

In 1857, fifteen years before the founding of our Waynesborough school, our General Conference granted Sunday-schools to be held wherever convenient, proving that this organization was no innovation and the good this and other schools in the Brotherhood have been doing, only proves the wisdom of Annual Conference in its decision.

Eld. Oller, for the sake of harmony, proceeded slowly at first, which, in time, proved the better way. He invited the old fathers and mothers with their children to attend and assist in the exercises. A majority complied, not one of whom, so far as we know, ever went away dissatisfied, for the order of the old brethren, the founders of our beloved Fraternity, was strictly observed. Instead of creating discord, as it was feared, there was love and union among old and young. Why was this? The answer, briefly told, is, plainness of dress was encouraged and only such lessons were taught that would agree with the Bible.

The government has never changed. Instead of the school being a barrier to the church it has fortified and strengthened it. Many young per-

Please explain Matt. 19: 10-12, "His disciples say unto him, If the case of the man be so with his wife, it is not good to marry. But he said unto them, All men cannot receive this saying, save they to whom it is given. For there are some eunuchs, which were so born from their mother's womb: and there are some eunuchs, which were made eunuchs of men: and there be eunuchs which have made themselves eunuchs for the kingdom of heaven's sake. He that is able to receive it, let him receive it." It says, "All men cannot receive this saying, save they to whom it is given." Who can receive it?
J. J. SHARP.

Those who can remain unmarried, and feel contented. There are those who cannot live contented and happy without a companion. Let such marry. There are others who could not, and would not enjoy marriage. They are the ones who can receive the doctrine of celibacy fully.

But there is another class who would enjoy the married life, but in order to become more useful in their calling, prefer to live in a state of celibacy. Paul and John the Baptist were of this number. The term *receive* does not refer to receiving the doctrine so much as the *capacity*, or *temperament*, to remain in the unmarried state. In ancient times some voluntarily entered upon a life of celibacy for the sake of greater usefulness, as it is well known that marriage is a hinderance to some lines of missionary work.

When, and on what grounds did the church set aside the rule of former years, which did not permit members to marry outsiders?
REBECCA WEAVER.

We are not aware that such a rule has been set aside, unless it be assumed that the New Testament teaches that members should not marry unbelievers. Our church does not forbid members marrying outsiders, but advises against it. And we feel that it would be well if the advice were more generally heeded. When two are agreed religiously, they can walk together in life more pleasantly.

Is it wrong for a minister to carry hymn books and Testaments to his place of preaching on Sunday and give them to his congregation and take money for them on Sunday, if the object is to advance the cause of Christ.
JASPER BARNTHOUSE.

It is done with a view of making money, we consider it a wrong use of the Lord's day, but if it be solely for the good of the cause, we see no harm in it, and yet the more cautious we are about such things the better. We should not permit our good to be evil spoken of. Let us learn to do as little money business on Sunday as possible. In many places it is difficult to avoid transactions of this kind on Sunday, but we need not make a regular business of it.

Is it right or proper for the church, or any individual member, to report persons who make disturbance at a Communion or other meeting to the grand jury?
J. H. FAHNESTOCK.

Brethren are generally advised not to use the law excepting in case of stern necessity. The law of the land protects us in our religious exercises, and any one who disturbs the services lays himself liable to the law. In case the disturbance should become so great as to interfere with the exercises, it would be well for the proper authorities to know it, and this can usually be done without going before the grand jury. We know of a case where bullets were fired into the meeting-house. The church appointed two of her deacons to consult with one of the County officers about it. The officer took the matter in hand, and that was the end of it. Some things are lawful, and yet not expedient. We must do our utmost to get along peaceably with all men, and if we are too greatly disturbed at our feasts, there are officers whose business it is to look after such cases if properly apprized of them. Our advice is that one of the

church officials consult with the proper officer privately.

How is it considered for brethren to go on the annual visit who do not conform to the order of the church; are members under obligations to accept such visits?
J. L. LUSH.

All church officials are required to conform to the general order of the church, and they should be admonished to do so. This duty rests upon the visiting brethren as well as the other officials. But no one should refuse a visit just because the visiting official happens to be out of order in his general appearance. Receive the visit kindly, remembering that he is acting in his official and not in an individual capacity. By so doing strength and confidence may be gained sufficient to kindly admonish the official at the proper time. As long as a brother is an official it is our duty to respect him as such. If he is not doing right, it is the privilege of the church to handle him, but it is not the prerogative of any one member to interfere with or obstruct the work which the church requires him to do.

Can a brother serve as delegate to District or Annual Meeting and not conform to the order of the church in dress and abstaining from the use of tobacco?
J. L. LUSH.

Many brethren who do not conform to the order are *permitted* to serve, but it is unfortunate that they cannot be induced to fall into the ways of the church more fully. Were the latter as well as the spirit of Annual Meeting decisions pressed, such delegates could likely be ruled out. We advise the sending of plainly-attired delegates when they can be had. This would be far better than making an effort to rule any one out. The more plainly-attired and well-informed delegates we can have at the Annual Meeting, the better it will be for the general good of the Brotherhood. The use of tobacco has not been made a test for delegates to District Meetings, but it has for delegates sent to the Annual Meeting. Delegates sent to Annual Meeting are usually rejected if they use tobacco. The committee on credentials asks each delegate whether he uses tobacco.
J. H. M.

TO THE YOUNG DISCIPLES IN MOUNT MORRIS COLLEGE.

NUMBER THREE.

To settle the dispute among the disciples as to "Who should be the greatest," the Savior gave them an object lesson. "He took a child and set him in the midst of them," and said, "Whosoever humbleth himself as this little child," not only "receiveth me," but "the same is the greatest in the kingdom of heaven." He was the greatest, not because of his sinlessness,—for if none but the sinless could enter the kingdom of heaven, that part which is on earth,—the church,—would be empty; but because of his possessing the qualities which are characteristic of childhood,—the qualities which make the ideal childhood. Humility, tender affection, perfect trust, unworldliness and a teachable spirit, are prominent among those qualities. It is these that make the life of the child a perfect life of faith.

Think of a little child! Unaided, what can it do? How absolutely dependent! It would be lost, if trusted alone. It would die for want, because it could not find the next meal. How is it, then, that childhood is the happy life it is? Simply because it is, as it were, instinctively a life of faith. It could not buy the next loaf, but it has a firm belief that "father" can. So every disciple whose faith manifests itself by this child-like

spirit, says the Savior, "receiveth me," because he has taken into his heart the qualities of character which I love, and by which his life is so transformed that "all men know," that he is my disciple; and the act of receiving those qualities is the way by which such a disciple gives expression to his feelings of devotion to his Master. All who are in possession of this spirit are in the kingdom of heaven, and the more one has of it, the nearer he is to King Jesus, and the greater he is in the kingdom.

A willingness to be led by the world, and conform to its demands, dearly beloved, is an index both of the absence of this childhood faith, and of the transforming power by which your daily walk is adorned with heavenly radiance. May be, under whose shadow you sleep, before whom you eat your daily bread, and out of whose hand you draw your breath, enable you all to be "living epistles" which will speak "with authority" to the church of coming generations.

My visit to the Shenandoah and Roanoke Valleys, Va., afforded much which was highly interesting to me, and would have been equally interesting to you all, could you have been sharers with your brother.
J. G. ROYER.
Bridgewater, Va.

CORRESPONDENCE.

"Write what thou seest, and send it unto the churches."

☞ Church News solicited for this Department. If you have had a good meeting, send a report of it, so that others may rejoice with you. In writing give name of church, County and State. Be brief. Notes of Travel should be as short as possible. Land Advertisements are not solicited for this Department. We have an advertising page, and, if necessary, will issue supplements.

Antietam Sunday-Schools, Bible Class, Etc.

Some time during the summer of 1872, Eld. Jacob F. Oller, of this congregation, then a minister in the second degree, organized the Waynesborough Sunday-school. Although the Brethren had a school as early as 1744 at Ephrata, Lancaster Co., Pa., this was the first school ever held in this part of the State.

The task was not an easy one. The then presiding elder, and some of the older members opposed it. It was feared the new innovation, as it was termed, would foster pride among the members and bring the church into disrepute. Had it not been for this, no objection would have been offered, by those opposing the school. They were zealous, laboring assiduously for the upbuilding of the church, but, to a certain degree, were not aggressive.

In 1857, fifteen years before the founding of our Waynesborough school, our General Conference granted Sunday-schools to be held wherever convenient, proving that this organization was no innovation and the good this and other schools is the Brotherhood have been doing, only proves the wisdom of Annual Conference in its decision.

Eld. Oller, for the sake of harmony, proceeded slowly at first, which, in time, proved the better way. He invited the old fathers and mothers with their children to attend and assist in the exercises. A majority complied, not one of whom, so far as we know, ever went away dissatisfied, for the order of the old brethren, the founders of our beloved Fraternity, was strictly observed. Instead of creating discord, as it was feared, there was love and union among old and young. Why was this? The answer, briefly told, is, plainness of dress was encouraged and only such lessons were taught that would agree with the Bible.

The government has never changed. Instead of the school being a barrier to the church it has fortified and strengthened it. Many young per-

April 21; we attended the District Meeting of Western Maryland which was organized by electing that old veteran of the .cross, Eld. David Long, Moderator; Bro. —— Beeghly, Reading Clerk, and Bro. D. F. Stouffer, Writing Clerk. It was a perfectly harmonious meeting, characterized by that love which thinketh no evil. The report of the Home Mission work was an attractive and prominent feature of the meeting. One hundred and twenty-one accessions were reported by baptism. This surely is a cause for rejoicing among the saints on earth, as it is among the angels in the heavenly mansions.

Bro. D. F. Stouffer was elected to Standing Committee. One query was sent to Annual Meeting as follows: "Inasmuch as the church has full control of the Missionary and Tract Societies, will not this District Meeting petition Annual Meeting to have the tract work done by specification and competitive bids, thinking in this manner to lessen cost very materially, and remove the general complaint against 'the price of our literature, provided that the bids for printing said literature be confined' to brethren who are engaged in the printing business." A similar query goes to Annual Meeting from Eastern Maryland.

There seems to be an idea among some (though it is *not* general as stated in the query) that our tracts cost too much money. This I believe to be a mistake. The .prices paid, especially after electrotyping, run very *low* for first-class work. The prices charged for printing circulars and ordinary advertising matter, for the most part printed upon cheap paper, and in numbers of 50,000 and 100,000 copies of a kind, must not be taken as a criterion for prices of first-class printing upon clean, strong paper, as that on which our tracts have been printed during the past year, and which certainly present a neat and tasty appearance. I don't think the Brethren in charge will object to giving the actual prices—they pay to the publishers for tracts, if such information is demanded at the proper time. Until these prices are given, they must be largely conjectured.

Another report made at this meeting had some commendable features; at least it showed that the brethren who directed the financial affairs of last Annual Meeting made a success of the work entrusted to them. They reported that the receipts of the Hagerstown meeting. were $4,810.00 above all expenses,—that two-thirds of this surplus had been sent to the "General Missionary Committee, and the .one-third to the "Book and Tract Work." We are glad those committees have the money thus entrusted to them, and hope that the application of it may be blessed by God to the conversion of many souls.   I. M. GIBSON.

Roanoke, Va.

From Denver, Colorado.

SINCE we have commenced meetings in Denver, we, have learned of parties living in the city who have once been members of our Fraternity, but have united with other denominations, because we had no church there. We have found several such, and believe that there may be many more. We appeal to the Brotherhood at large to assist us in the work of finding such parties. If any of our brethren or sisters have relatives or friends living in Denver, who, in former years, were friendly to the Brethren, or in the habit of attending the Brethren's meetings, they may help to build up the cause here and, perhaps, be instrumental in bringing some of their friends to Christ, by giving us their address (and number of street, if possible). This will enable us to find such persons and to visit them and, if possible, persuade them to attend our meetings and Sunday-school. You may also help the cause along by writing them encouraging letters, reminding them of the faith they once had in the church, and of the fact that there are brethren here, willing and anxious to help 'them to keep the faith once delivered to the saints.

Denver is a large city, and it is almost next to impossible to find persons here (unless they are permanently located and named in the directory) without knowing their street and number. Bro. Long and I rode perhaps ten miles in the city yesterday, to find three different parties, and succeeded in finding only one of the three.

It is our intention to visit all persons we can find .who have a friendly feeling towards our Fraternity, and, if possible, get them to'attend our meetings. Please address George Long, Villa Park, Colo., or the writer at Longmont. !After awhile I may ask you to help us another way.

D. H. WEAVER.

A Sad Accident.

ON the evening of April 8 Eld. John Stretch, in company with his son, Isaac, left Dowagiac, Mich., for his home, about three miles distant. They had gone but a short distance, when one of the single-trees became unfastened, which frightened the team.' The horses made a dash forward, leaving the wagon tongue drop to the ground, which soon ploughed its way into the earth, throwing brethren John S., and Isaac, about twelve or fifteen feet in the air. Bro. Isaac having hold of the lines, it seemed to help him. He escaped without being seriously hurt, but his father was seriously injured. Although no bones were broken, he fell on his chest with such force as to bruise his lungs very much. I was .called to his bed-side on Easter Sunday for the purpose of anointing him, which was attended to in the fear of the Lord. Last week he was a little better, but I received a letter from his son April 26, stating he is growing worse. Our prayer is that the good Lord will spare him, and raise him from his bed of affliction, but the Lord's will be done.

H. W. KRIEGHBAUM.

South Bend, Ind.

Annual Meeting Notes and Remarks.

The Committee of Arrangements met at Cedar Rapids, April 28, and transacted considerable business. Among the business transacted was the locating and staking out of the various buildings to be erected by the "Cedar Rapids Commercial Company," to locate water supplies, board pavements, street car platforms, etc.

Thus far everything is moving along· nicely. Work will soon commence on the buildings and be pushed to completion. We urge our brethren to send in their applications for lodging early. This is important. All is being done by the Committee and the Cedar Rapids people that can reasonably be expected of them, to insure the comfort of those who attend and to aid in making our coming Annual Meeting a pleasant one.

JOHN ZUCK.

Notes from Our Correspondents.

"As cold water to a thirsty soul, so is good news from a far country."

Salem, Ohio.—Our Sunday-school, under the care of brethren Andrew Gillman and G. W. Buntain, as Superintendents, is moving along pleasantly, and, we hope, profitably, as there are many children and also many 'brethren and sisters and friends attending it. Our church council, preparatory to District Meeting, will be held May 5. At our regular meeting last Sunday, we held a collection for the "Russian Sufferers," and $39.00 was donated by the members and friends.—*Jesse R. Brumbaugh, Union, Ohio, April 28.*

Bourbon, Ind.—After our meeting, April 24, one dear soul was baptized. In the afternoon we met again at 3 o'clock for children's meeting. We had a large attendance, with the best of order. After the meeting a collection for the Mission Board was taken to the amount of $7.56.—*Charlie H. Sellers.*

Weiser, Ark.—We, the brethren and sisters, met at Long Creek school-house in Poinsett County, Ark., and organized our Sunday-school for the summer with a full corps of officers. The writer was chosen Superintendent, and I ask all the brethren and sisters to remember me in their prayers that I may discharge the duties that are connected with the school.—*John Coyn.*

Montrose, Mo.—The members of the Deep Water church, Henry Co., Mo., held their quarterly council April 23. There was not much business, but all was disposed of, we believe, in a Christian spirit, and to the satisfaction of all present. We organized our Sunday-school by electing Bro. John Hougendougler, Superintendent, and also all other officers needed for our school. — *J. H. Falnestock, April 24.*

Information Wanted.—I would like to ask through the GOSPEL MESSENGER, if there are any brethren and sisters living near Medicine Lodge, or Kiowa, Kans. We live about fifteen miles south, and a few miles west of Medicine Lodge, and about a mile and a half from Mound Center school-house. I thought by sending this notice, some of the brethren might come to visit us and hold meetings in the district school-house. My husband is not a member of the Brethren church.— *Anna Wright.*

Johnstown, Pa.—As our District Meeting has not yet been announced, I will ask you to do so at once. The District Meeting for the Western District of Pennsylvania will be held May 11, in the Johnstown church, at Walnut Grove, two miles south of P. R. R., and B. & O. depots. 'Bus runs near to church.—*A. W. Myers, Box 161, April 2*. [We regret that this notice did not reach us one day sooner so it could have appeared in last issue, but the paper was on the press, and being printed, when the card, containing the announcement, came to hand.—ED]

Warsaw, Ind.—Our church prospects, are becoming more encouraging every day. The congregations at the various points are increasing and our Sunday-school, so far, is encouraging. We are glad to feel that the discord that has existed here, is fast dying away and that, in its stead, harmony and union prevail. If any of our brethren contemplate making a change in location, I should much desire a correspondence with them, as there are a number of farms'near our church for sa'e, on reasonable terms and convenient to good market.—*N. B. Heeter.*

Ottobine, Va.—After our annual visit in the Beaver Creek congregation we had our council April 8 and 9. The brethren's report showed the church to be in love and union, as much so, at least, as could be expected in so large a body of members. Quite an amount of business came before our District Meeting, which lasted two whole days. While there was considerable difference of sentiment on some points, nevertheless a spirit of Christian feeling and brotherly love characterized the whole meeting, which was pleasant indeed. Eld. Daniel Hays represents the Second District of Virginia at Annual Meeting. Elders I. Thomas and G. W. Wine are delegates from this church. We purpose, the Lord willing, to visit in the churches at Brooklyn and South English, Iowa, after the Annual Meeting. If those churches wish us to labor for them, we will be at their service.—*G. W. Wine, April 29.*

April 21, we attended the District Meeting of Western Maryland which was organized by electing that old veteran of the cross, Eld. David Long, Moderator; Bro. —— Beeghly, Reading Clerk, and Bro. D. F. Stouffer, Writing Clerk. It was a perfectly harmonious meeting, characterized by that love which thinketh no evil. The report of the Home Mission work was an attractive and prominent feature of the meeting. One hundred and twenty-one accessions were reported by baptism. This surely is a cause for rejoicing among the saints on earth, as it is among the angels in the heavenly mansions.

Bro. D. F. Stouffer was elected to Standing Committee. One query was sent to Annual Meeting as follows: "Inasmuch as the church has full control of the Missionary and Tract Societies, will not this District Meeting petition Annual Meeting to have the tract work done by specification and competitive bids, thinking in this manner to lessen cost very materially, and remove the general complaint against the price of our literature, provided that the bids for printing said literature be confined to brethren who are engaged in the printing business." A similar query goes to Annual Meeting from Eastern Maryland.

There seems to be an idea among some (though it is *not* general, as stated in the query) that our tracts cost too much money. This I believe to be a mistake. The prices paid, especially after electrotyping, run very low for first-class work. The prices charged for printing circulars and ordinary advertising matter, for the most part printed upon cheap paper, and in numbers of 50,000 and 100,000 copies of a kind, must not be taken as a criterion for prices of first-class printing upon clean, strong paper, as that on which our tracts have been printed during the past year, and which certainly present a neat and tasty appearance. I don't think the brethren in charge will object to giving the actual prices—*they* pay to the publishers for tracts, if such information is demanded at the proper time. Until these prices are given, they must be largely conjectured.

Another report made at this meeting had some commendable features; at least it showed that the brethren who directed the financial affairs of last Annual Meeting made a success of the work entrusted to them. They reported that the receipts of the Hagerstown meeting were $4,810.00 above all expenses,—that two-thirds of the surplus had been sent to the "General Missionary Committee, and the one-third to the "Book and Tract Work." We are glad these committees have the money thus entrusted to them, and hope that the application of it may be blessed by God to the conversion of many souls.   I. M. GIBSON.

Roanoke, Va.

From Denver, Colorado.

SINCE we have commenced meetings in Denver, we have learned of parties living in the city who have once been members of our Fraternity, but have united with other denominations, because we had no church there. We have found several such, and believe that there may be many more. We appeal to the Brotherhood at large to assist us in the work of finding such parties. If any of our brethren or sisters have relatives or friends living in Denver, who, in former years, were friendly to the Brethren, or in the habit of attending the Brethren's meetings, they may help to build up the cause here and, perhaps, be instrumental in bringing some of their friends to Christ, by giving us their address (and number of street if possible). This will enable us to find such persons and to visit them and, if possible, persuade them to attend our meetings and Sunday-school. You may also help the cause along

by writing them encouraging letters, reminding them of the faith they once had in the church, and of the fact that there are brethren here, willing and anxious to help them to keep the faith once delivered to the saints.

Denver is a large city, and it is almost next to impossible to find persons here (unless they are permanently located and named in the directory) without knowing their street and number. Bro. Long and I rode perhaps ten miles in the city yesterday, to find three different parties, and succeeded in finding only one of the three.

It is our intention to visit all persons we can find who have a friendly feeling towards our Fraternity, and, if possible, get them to attend our meetings. Please address George Long, Villa Park, Colo., or the writer at Longmont. After awhile I may ask you to help us another way.

D. H. WEAVER.

A Sad Accident.

ON the evening of April 8 Eld. John Stretch, in company with his son, Isaac, left Dowagiac, Mich., for his home, about three miles distant. They had gone but a short distance, when one of the single-trees became unfastened, which frightened the team. The horses made a dash forward, leaving the wagon tongue drop to the ground, which soon ploughed its way into the earth, throwing brethren John S., and Isaac, about twelve or fifteen feet in the air. Bro. Isaac having hold of the lines, it seemed to help him. He escaped without being seriously hurt, but his father was seriously injured. Although no bones were broken, he fell on his chest with such force as to bruise his lungs very much. I was called to his bed-side on Easter Sunday for the purpose of anointing him, which was attended to in the fear of the Lord. Last week he was a little better, but I received a letter from his son April 26, stating he is growing worse. Our prayer is that the good Lord will spare him, and raise him from his bed of affliction, but the Lord's will be done.

H. W. KRIEGHBAUM.

South Bend, Ind.

Annual Meeting Notes and Remarks.

The Committee of Arrangements met at Cedar Rapids, April 28, and transacted considerable business. Among the business transacted was the locating and staking out of the various buildings to be erected by the "Cedar Rapids Commercial Company," to locate water supplies, board pavements, street car platforms, etc.

Thus far everything is moving along nicely. Work will soon commence on the buildings and be pushed to completion. We urge our brethren to send in their applications for lodging early. This is important. All is being done by the Committee and the Cedar Rapids people that can reasonably be expected of them, to insure the comfort of those who attend and to aid in making our coming Annual Meeting a pleasant one.

JOHN ZUCK.

Notes from Our Correspondents.

"As cold water to a thirsty soul, so is good news from a far country."

Salem, Ohio.—Our Sunday-school, under the care of brethren Andrew Gillman and G. W. Bantain, as Superintendents, is moving along pleasantly, and, we hope, profitably, as there are many children and also many brethren and sisters and friends attending it. Our church council, preparatory to District Meeting, will be held May 5. At our regular meeting last Sunday, a collection for the "Russian Sufferers," and $39.00 was donated by the members and friends.—*Jesse R. Brumbaugh, Union, Ohio, April 28.*

Bourbon, Ind.—After our meeting, April 24, one dear soul was baptized. In the afternoon we met again at 3 o'clock for children's meeting. We had a large attendance, with the best of order. After the meeting a collection for the Mission Board was taken to the amount of $7.56.—*Charlie H. Sellers.*

Weiser, Ark.—We, the brethren and sisters, met at Long Creek school-house in Poinsett County, Ark., and organized our Sunday-school for the summer with a full corps of officers. The writer was chosen Superintendent, and I ask all the brethren and sisters to remember me in their prayers that I may discharge the duties that are connected with the school.—*John Coyn.*

Montrose, Mo.—The members of the Deep Water church, Henry Co., Mo., held their quarterly council April 23. There was not much business, but all was disposed of, we believe, in a Christian spirit, and to the satisfaction of all present. We organized our Sunday-school by electing Bro. John Hougendougler, Superintendent, and also all other officers needed for our school.—*J. H. Fahnestock, April 24.*

Information Wanted.—I would like to ask through the GOSPEL MESSENGER, if there are any brethren and sisters living near Medicine Lodge, or Kiowa, Kans. We live about fifteen miles south, and a few miles west of Medicine Lodge, and about a mile and a half from Mound Center school-house. I thought by sending this notice, some of the brethren might come to visit us and hold meetings in the district school-house. My husband is not a member of the Brethren church.—*Anna Wright.*

Johnstown, Pa.—As our District Meeting has not yet been announced, I will ask you to do so at once. The District Meeting for the Middle District of Pennsylvania will be held May 11, in the Johnstown church, at Walnut Grove, two miles south of P. R. R., and B. & O. depots. 'Bus runs near to church.—*A. W. Myers, Box 191, April 28.* [We regret that this notice did not reach us one day sooner so it could have appeared in last issue, but the paper was on the press, and being printed, when the card, containing the announcement, came to hand.—ED]

Warsaw, Ind.—Our church prospects are becoming more encouraging every day. The congregations at the various points are increasing and our Sunday-school, so far, is encouraging. We are glad to feel that the discord that has existed here, is fast dying away and that, in its stead, harmony and union prevail. If any of our brethren contemplate making a change in location, I should much desire a correspondence with them, as there are a number of farms near our church for sale, on reasonable terms and convenient to good market.—*N. B. Heeter.*

Ottobine, Va.—After our annual visit in the Beaver Creek congregation we had our council April 8 and 9. The brethren's report showed the church to be in love and union, as much so, at least, as could be expected in so large a body of members. Quite an amount of business came before our District Meeting, which lasted two whole days. While there was considerable difference of sentiment on some points, nevertheless a spirit of Christian feeling and brotherly love characterized the whole meeting, which was pleasant indeed. Eld. Daniel Hays represents the Second District of Virginia at Annual Meeting. Elders I. Thomas and G. W. Wine are delegates from this church. We purpose, the Lord willing, to visit in the churches at Brooklyn and South English, Iowa, after the Annual Meeting. If those churches wish us to labor for them, we will be at their service.—*G. W. Wine, April 29.*

Middle Creek, Pa.—We met in council, April 18. Rain and almost impassable roads prevented the attendance of some, yet there was a fair attendance. Elders Josiah Berkley and Valentine Blough are our delegates to Annual Meeting and J. C. Johnson and H. A. Stahl to District Meeting.—*Geo. W. Lowry.*

Jericho, Mo.—We met in quarterly council, April 23. Everything passed off in a loving spirit. We like to go to the house of the Lord when all labor together as one. The church sends two delegates to District Meeting,—brethren C. Haldeman and the writer. Bro. C. Haldeman is our delegate to Annual Meeting.—*Samuel Duncan, April 24.*

Lordsburg, Cal.—This will inform you that wife and I are still in our usual health. We think of starting for Cerro Gordo, Ill., the Lord willing, about May 2. How long we will stay there, time will tell. The weather is pleasant here. Strawberries are plenty. Prospects for fruit of all kind are good.—*John Metzger, April 21.*

Naperville, Ill.—In my last I omitted to mention the following: We send Bro. Jacob Sollenberger as delegate to Annual Meeting and Bro. H. M. Barkdoll to District Meeting. Any who may wish to be with us at our Communion will be met at the following stations: On the Northwestern R R., at Turner Junction; on the C. B. and Q. at Naperville or Aurora, by letting us know in time. Address me at Naperville. Remember our Communion May 14, at 2 P. M.—*S. B. Kuhn.*

Purchase Line, Pa.—The members of the Manor congregation met in council April 23, at the Purchase Line house. The day was pleasant and the attendance good. All the business was disposed of in a Christian spirit and brotherly love. We appointed our love-feast for June 9, commencing at 10 A. M. A series of meetings will be held at Purchase Line in October. Our Sunday-school will be re-organized May 1. Brethren Mark Minser and Joseph Holsopple are the delegates to District Meeting.—*Lizzie Fyock.*

McPherson, Kans. — The quarterly council of the Monitor church occurred April 8. Considerable business came before the council,—some of a painful nature, but we hope and trust that all was disposed of to the glory of God. Brethren Geo. E. Studebaker and J. W. Mishler were chosen delegates to District Meeting and Bro. S. J. Miller delegate to Annual Meeting. The time for our feast was set for June 11. The harvest, here in the West, being great and the laborers few, it was decided to hold an election on that date. We have an evergreen Sunday-school. The interest and attendance are encouraging. Eld. J. D. Trostle was with us and presided.—*S. E. Lantz, April 18.*

Monticello, Ind.—We held our quarterly church meeting on Saturday, April 23. The business all passed off pleasantly. We decided to hold our Communion meeting May 27.—*J. A. Weaver, April 25.*

Sheridan, Mo.—We, the members of the Honey Creek church, met in council, April 16, 1892, and had a very pleasant council. Two queries were sent to District Meeting. The church sends Bro. W. H. Clark to District Meeting. As we have had no regular preaching since Eld. W. B. Sell left us in March, 1891, we would like for some of the Brethren to stop off with us, either going to or from Annual Meeting, and give us some meetings. They will be met at the Sheridan Depot by notifying Bro. W. F. Dowis, or W. H. Clark. We live on the Diagonal road.—*E. Reddick, April 21.*

Crawford, Nebr.—I left home on the evening of April 19, having been sent to this place by the State Mission Board. It was raining when I left home, and on the way I found it had snowed. There is about one foot of snow on the ground, here at Crawford, and it has drifted so that I doubt whether the brethren will be able to come to town after me, as they live ten miles away. The country is quite rough in places, and the snow is drifted five or six feet deep in places. The snow is melting today and will settle a good deal. It has been hard on stock.—*John J. Hoover, April 21.*

Literary Notes.

"*Ethical Teachings in Old English Literature.*" By Theodore W. Hunt, Ph. D., Litt. D. Cloth, 12mo, 384 pp. $1.25. Funk & Wagnalls Company: New York, London, and Toronto.

In this discussion of Old English books and authors, Professor Hunt seeks to emphasize, in every legitimate way, that distinctively devout and Christian spirit which he has so clearly discerned in his study of these earlier eras. Special stress is also laid upon the fact that, in the teachings and influence of these older writers, those truths were established and diffused which went far to undermine the firmly-rooted principles of the Papacy, and to open the way, in part at least, for the great Elizabethan Reformation on behalf of English Protestantism.

"*The Hygienic Treatment of Consumption.*" In three parts. By M. L. Holbrook, M. D., Professor of Hygiene in the New York Medical College and Hospital for Women. A very great majority of all cases of consumption which have recovered have been cured by hygienic remedies and not by drug medication. In most cases the patients have applied these remedies themselves, often, perhaps, in a rude way; but even thus applied they have proved of the greatest advantage. Price by mail, $2.00. Dr. M. L. Holbrook, 46 East 21st St., New York, Publisher.

MATRIMONIAL.

"What therefore God hath joined together, let not man put asunder."

HARDMAN — WHITMER.— At Eld. Daniel Whitmer's residence, by the writer, Royal Hardman, of Washington, D. C., and sister Emma E. Whitmer, of St. Joseph County, Ind. — J. H. MILLER.

STRICKLER—BAGGERLY.— At the residence of D. A. Sevier, of Waverly, April 20, 1892, by the elder of the M. E. church South, Mr. Charles A. Strickler, of Loraine, Ill., and Miss Adda Baggerly, of Waverly, Ill. — H. W. STRICKLER.

RANDALL—SINCLAIR.—At the residence of the bride's parents, April 13, 1892, by the writer, Sanford H. Randall, of Crawford County, Kans., and Sarah J. Sinclair, of Cherokee County, Kans. — ANDREW NEHER.

→ FALLEN ASLEEP ←

"Blessed are the dead which die in the Lord."

BESTLE.—At Longmont, Colo., April 15, 1892, David Bestle, aged 71 years, 11 months and 10 days. Friend Bestle was born in Germany, and came to Colorado among the early settlers. Services by the writer to a large concourse of friends in the Brethren church.

LEEDY—Also at the same place, April 19, 1892, Robert Hugh Leedy, only son of Bro. Daniel Leedy, aged 13 years, 7 months and 21 days. — G. W. FESLER.

SLOSSIN.—In the bounds of the Greene church, Butler Co., Iowa at her residence, near Pearl Rock, Iowa, sister Lovina Slossin, aged about 67 years. Funeral services by the writer, assisted by Eld. J. F. Eikenberry. — WM. C. HIPES.

NICKEY.—In the Oakley church, Macon Co., Ill., April 20, 1892, Edith, infant daughter of Bro. A. J. Nickey. Services at the residence. — M. J. McCLURE.

ASHMAN.—At his residence, near Buswell, Garfield Co., Nebr., April 9, 1892, of pneumonia, Bro. J. B. Ashman. He was born in the City of New York, Sept. 9, 1831. From there he went to Roanoke, Woodford Co., Ill., where he was united in marriage to Miss Martha Rindig. To them were born eight children. He was a deacon in the church. Funeral services by Bro. Joseph Mast and Rev. Joseph Conner. — A. J. FREELAND.

WATKINS.—In the Rogan congregation, Wabash Co., Ind., Jan. 29, 1892, James Watkins, aged 45 years, 11 months and 25 days. He leaves a beloved companion (a sister), and five children. His body was consigned to the tomb in the Tombaugh cemetery. Funeral services by the Brethren from 2 Cor. 1:1, 9. — JOSEPH JOHN.

FANSLER.—At the residence of her son-in-law's, D. A. Vanscoy, near Keren's, W. Va., April 10, 1892, mother Elizabeth Fansler, aged 71 years, 6 months and 10 days. She was the wife of Peter Fansler, deceased, and the daughter of William and Teracy Workman. She was born in Allegheny County, Md., and moved to West Virginia with her parents in 1840. She was a member of the German Baptist church for forty years. She died very suddenly. She fell from the breakfast table. Her death was supposed to be heart disease. Burial services by Rev. J. P. Pigot, of the U. B. church. — D. A. VANSCOY.

MORTEN.—In the Shoal Creek church, Newton Co., Mo., April 1, 1892, Bro. John Morten, aged 76 years, 7 months and 21 days. Funeral services by Bro. L. B. Prickett, from Job 14: 14. — LEANDER HARADER.

BEANBLOSSOM.—In the Bethel church, Thayer Co., Nebr., April 20, 1892, after a long illness, sister Abbie V. Beanblossom, daughter of brother and sister William Beanblossom, aged 17 years, 3 months and 23 days. Funeral by the Brethren. — E. S. ROTHROCK.

THOMAS.—March 31, 1892, Elizabeth Thomas, aged 92 years, 6 months and 15 days. She was a faithful member of the Brethren church for forty-four years. Funeral services by the writer. — ELD. JOHN PROWANT.

VANPELT.—March 25, 1892, Delmer R. Vanpelt, aged 9 years, 6 months and 2 days.

VANPELT.—March 26, 1892, Mertie M. Vanpelt, aged 11 years, 2 months and 5 days. Funeral services held by the writer. — JOHN PROWANT.

BRALLIER.—In the Upper Deer Creek congregation, April 15, 1892, sister Sarah Elizabeth Brallier, aged 51 years, 3 months and 1 day. Funeral services by the writer, assisted by W. S. Toney from Rev. 14: 13. — JACOB CRIPE.

STONER.— In the Monticello church, White Co., Ind., April 16, 1892, sister Susan Stoner, aged 76 years, 5 months and 4 days. Funeral services by Bro. Jos. Amick, from Mt. Morris, Ill., assisted by the home ministers.

BIGLER.—In the Elkhart church, near Goshen, Ind., Jan. 18, 1892, Bro. Andrew Bigler, aged 75 years, 10 months and 25 days. Bro. Bigler was born in Washington County, Pa. He has been a minister for many years, and was an elder at the time of his death. — J. H. MILLER.

RHODES.— April 6, 1892, Mrs. Kate Rhodes, wife of Enos Rhodes (who preceded her to the grave seven years ago), aged 35 years, 9 months and 3 days. She was a consistent member of the Christian church. — S. J. REEDY.

KUSSMOUL.—Near Moats, Defiance Co., Ohio, Feb. 12, 1892, George E. Kussmoul, aged 22 years, 7 months and 23 days. The deceased had gone to convey saw logs to the farm of his brother, Jacob. The latter had been to a funeral, and on his return he saw the team standing in the woods. He went there and found George lying on his face,—dead,—and one log had soiled on him and the log chain was around his neck. How the chain got there, is not known. The deceased was the son of sister Susannah Kussmoul. He had made no profession. — FLORIDA ETTER.

DETRICK.—In the Marlow congregation, Chickasaw Nation, I. T., March 14, 1892, Georgie, son of Bro. Andrew and sister Emma Detrick, aged 9 years, 6 months and 13 days. Funeral services by Elihu Moore. — CORA MOORE.

WIDDERS.—In the Lower Cumberland congregation, Pa., March 18, 1892, Bro. Daniel Widders, aged 64 years, 1 month and 11 days. Bro. Daniel called for the elders and was anointed a short time before his death. He made choice of 2 Tim. 12: 2. Services by brethren Henry Beelman, L. S. Mohler and the writer. — DANIEL LANDIS.

ECHELBARGER.— In the Portage congregation, Wood Co., Ohio, April 21, 1892, Bro. John Echelbarger, aged 68 years, 3 months and 5 days. He was a deacon for a number of years. He leaved a wife and seven children. Funeral services from Rev. 14: 13 by Bro. J. C. Witmore. — J. W. BEEB.

BOYD.—April 19, 1892, Catharine Boyd, after an illness of six days with Bright's disease. She was a daughter of David Bueghly (deceased), and was born Jan. 26, 1833, in Somerset County, Pa. In 1853 she was married to Samuel Boyd. She became the mother of eleven children. In 1856 she united with the Brethren church and has ever since been consistent and steadfast in her belief. Funeral services were conducted by Rev. Hoskins, of the United Brethren from John 14: 13. — BELLE BOYD.

SHARES.—In the bounds of the Olathe church, Johnson Co., Kans., April 20, 1892, Chas. W. Shares, aged 55 years, 2 months and 26 days. Funeral by the Brethren in the Methodist church, in Edgerton. Text, 1 Sam. 20: 4. — ISAAC H. CRIST.

SMITH.—At his home, near Bissell, Pa., March 29, 1892, Israel Smith, aged 77 years, 9 months and 12 days. He was married to Hannah Grable March 27, 1839. He was blest with fifteen children. For fifty years he had been a faithful member of the Brethren or German Baptist church. Rev. P. M. Woods conducted the funeral services, assisted by Rev. Bovieh. — NETTIE MILLER.

Middle Creek, Pa.—We met in council, April 18. Rain and almost impassable roads prevented the attendance of some, yet there was a fair attendance. Elders Josiah Berkley and Valentine Blough are our delegates to Annual Meeting and J. C. Johnson and H. A. Stahl to District Meeting.—*Geo. W. Lowry.*

Jericho, Mo.—We met in quarterly council, April 23 Everything passed off in a loving spirit. We like to go to the house of the Lord when all labor together as one. The church sends two delegates to District Meeting,—brethren C. Haldeman and the writer. Bro. C. Haldeman is our delegate to Annual Meeting.—*Samuel Duncan, April 24.*

Lordsburg, Cal.—This will inform you that wife and I are still in our usual health. We think of starting for Cerro Gordo, Ill., the Lord willing, about May 2. How long we will stay there, time will tell. The weather is pleasant here. Strawberries are plenty. Prospects for fruit of all kind are good.—*John Metzger, April 21.*

Naperville, Ill.—In my last I omitted to mention the following: We send Bro. Jacob Sollenberger as delegate to Annual Meeting and Bro. H. M. Barkdoll to District Meeting. Any who may wish to be with us at our Communion will be met at the following stations: On the Northwestern R. E., at Turner Junction; on the C. B. and Q. at Naperville or Aurora, by letting us know in time. Address me at Naperville. Remember our Communion May 14, at 2 P. M.—*S. B. Kuhn.*

Purchase Line, Pa.—The members of the Manor congregation met in council April 23, at the Purchase Line house. The day was pleasant and the attendance good. All the business was disposed of in a Christian spirit and brotherly love. We appointed our love-feast for June 9, commencing at 10 A. M. A series of meetings will be held at Purchase Line in October. Our Sunday-school will be re-organized May 1. Brethren Mark Minser and Joseph Holsopple are the delegates to District Meeting.—*Lizzie Fyock.*

McPherson, Kans. — The quarterly council of the Monitor church occurred April 8. Considerable business came before the council,—some of a painful nature, but we hope and trust that all was disposed of to the glory of God. Brethren Geo. E. Studebaker and J. W. Mishler were chosen delegates to District Meeting and Bro. S. J. Miller delegate to Annual Meeting. The time for our feast was set for June 11. The harvest, here in the West, being great and the laborers few, it was decided to hold an election on that date. We have an evergreen Sunday-school. The interest and attendance are encouraging. Eld. J. D. Trostle was with us and presided.—*S. E. Lantz, April 18.*

Monticello, Ind.—We held our quarterly church meeting on Saturday, April 23. The business all passed off pleasantly. We decided to hold our Communion meeting May 27.—*J. A. Weaver, April 25.*

Sheridan, Mo.—We, the members of the Honey Creek church, met in council, April 16, 1892, and had a very pleasant council. Two queries were sent to District Meeting. The church sends Bro. W. H. Clark to District Meeting. As we have had no regular preaching since Eld. W. B. Sell left us in March, 1891, we would like for some of the Brethren to stop off with us, either going to or from Annual Meeting, and give us some meetings. They will be met at the Sheridan Depot by notifying Bro. W. F. Dowis, or W. H. Clark. We live on the Diagonal road.—*E. Reddick, April 21.*

Crawford, Nebr.—I left home on the evening of April 19, having been sent to this place by the State Mission Board. It was raining when I left home, and on the way I found it had snowed. There is about one foot of snow on the ground, here at Crawford, and it has drifted so that I doubt whether the brethren will be able to come to town after me, as they live ten miles away. The country is quite rough in places, and the snow is drifted five or six feet deep in places. The snow is melting today and will settle a good deal. It has been hard on stock.—*John J. Hoover, April 21.*

Literary Notes.

"*Ethical Teachings in Old English Literature.*" By Theodore W. Hunt, Ph. D., Litt. D. Cloth, 12mo, 384 pp. $1.25. Funk & Wagnalls Company: New York, London, and Toronto.

In this discussion of Old English books and authors, Professor Hunt seeks to emphasize, in every legitimate way, that distinctively devout and Christian spirit which he has so clearly discerned in his study of these earlier eras. Special stress is also laid upon the fact that, in the teachings and influence of these older writers, those truths were established and diffused which went far to undermine the firmly-rooted principles of the Papacy, and to open the way, in part at least, for the great Elizabethan Reformation on behalf of English Protestantism.

" *The Hygienic Treatment of Consumption.*" In three parts. By M. L. Holbrook, M. D., Professor of Hygiene in the New York Medical College and Hospital for Women. A very great majority of all cases of consumption which have recovered have been cured by hygienic remedies and not by drug medication. In most cases the patients have applied these remedies themselves, often, perhaps, in a rude way; but even thus applied they have proved of the greatest advantage. Price by mail, $2.00. Dr. M. L. Holbrook, 46 East 21st St., New York, Publisher.

STRICKLER—BAGGERLY. — At the residence of D. A. Sevier, of Waverly, April 20, 1892, by the elder of the M. E. church South, Mr. Charles A. Strickler, of Loraine, Ill., and Miss Adda Baggerly, of Waverly, Ill.
H. W. STRICKLER.

RANDALL—SINCLAIR.—At the residence of the bride's parents, April 13, 1892, by the writer, Sanford H. Randall, of Crawford County, Kans., and Sarah J. Sinclair, of Cherokee County, Kans.
ANDREW NEHER.

→ FALLEN ASLEEP ←

" Blessed are the dead which die in the Lord."

BESTLE.—At Longmont, Colo, April 15, 1892, David Bestle, aged 71 years, 11 months and 10 days. Friend Bestle was born in Germany, and came to Colorado among the early settlers. Services by the writer to a large concourse of friends in the Brethren church.

LEEDY.—Also at the same place, April 19, 1892, Robert Hugh Leedy, only son of Bro. Daniel Leedy, aged 13 years, 7 months and 21 days.
G. W. FESLER.

SLOSSIN.—In the bounds of the Greene church, Butler Co., Iowa at her residence, near Pearl Rock, Iowa, sister Lovina Slossin, aged about 67 years. Funeral services by the writer, assisted by Eld. J. F. Eikenberry.
WM. C. HIPES.

NICKEY.—In the Oakley church, Macon Co., Ill., April 22, 1892, Edith, infant daughter of Bro. A. J. Nickey. Services at the residence.
M. J. McCLURE.

ASHIMAN.—At his residence, near Burwell, Garfield Co., Nebr., April 9, 1892, of pneumonia, Bro. J. B. Ashiman. He was born in the City of New York, Sept. 9, 1831. From there he went to Roanoke, Woodford Co., Ill., where he was united in marriage to Miss Martha Rindig. To them were born eight children. He was a deacon in the church. Funeral services by Bro. Joseph Mast and Rev. Joseph Conner.
A. J. FREELAND.

WATKINS.—In the Rogue congregation, Wabash Co., Ind., Jan. 29, 1892, James Watkins, aged 45 years, 11 months and 14 days. He leaves a beloved companion (a sister), and five children. His body was consigned to the tomb in the Tombaugh cemetery. Funeral services by the Brethren from 2 Cor. 12:9.
JOSEPH DILL.

FANSLER.—At the residence of her son-in-law's, D. A. Vascoy, near Keres's, W. Va., April 10, 1892, mother Elizabeth Fansler, aged 71 years, 6 months and 10 days. She was the wife of Peter Fansler, deceased, and the daughter of William and Tracy Workman. She was born in Alleghany County, Md., and moved to West Virginia with her parents in 1840. She was a member of the German Baptist church for forty years. She died very suddenly. She fell from the breakfast table. Her death was supposed to be heart disease. Burial services by Rev. J. P. Piget, of the U. B. church.
D. A. VANSCOY.

MORTEN.—In the Shoal Creek church, Newton Co., Mo., April 1, 1892, Bro. John Morten, aged 60 years, 7 months and 11 days. Funeral services by Bro. L. E. Peickett, from Job 14: 14.
LEANDER HARADER.

BEANBLOSSOM.—In the Bethel church, Thayer Co., Nebr., April 10, 1892, after a long illness, sister Abbie V. Beanblossom, daughter of brother and sister William Beanblossom, aged 17 years, 5 months and 23 days. Funeral services by the Brethren.
E. S. ROTHROCK.

THOMAS.—March 31, 1892, Elizabeth Thomas, aged 67 years, 6 months and 15 days. She was a faithful member of the Brethren church for forty-four years. Funeral services by the writer. ELD. JOHN PROWANT.

VANPELT.—March 25, 1892, Delmer R. Vanpelt, aged 9 years, 6 months and 2 days.

VANPELT.—March 26, 1892, Mertie M. Vanpelt, aged 11 years, 2 months and 5 days. Funeral services held by the Writer.
JOHN PROWANT.

BRALLIER.—In the Upper Deer Creek congregation, April 15, 1892, sister Sarah Elizabeth Brallier, aged 51 years, 3 months and 1 day. Funeral services by the writer, assisted by W. S. Toney from Rev. 14: 13.
JACOB CRIPE.

STONER.—In the Monticello church, White Co., Ind., April 16, 1892, sister Susan Stoner, aged 76 years, 5 months and 2 days. Funeral services by Bro. Jos. Amick, from Mt. Morris, Ill., assisted by the home ministers.
J. H. MILLER.

BIGLER.—In the Elkhart church, near Goshen, Ind., Jan. 18, 1892, Bro. Andrew Bigler, aged 75 years, 10 months and 25 days. Bro. Bigler was born in Washington County, Pa. He has been a minister for many years, and was an elder at the time of his death.
RHODES.

RHODES.—April 6, 1892, Mrs. Kate Rhodes, wife of Elmos Rhodes (who preceded her to the grave seven years ago) aged 35 years, 9 months and 3 days. She was a consistent member of the Christian church.
S. J. REEDY.

KUSSMOUL.—Near Moats, Defiance Co., Ohio, Feb. 12, 1892, George E. Kussmoul, aged 22 years, 7 months and 23 days. The deceased had gone to convey saw logs to the farm of his brother, Jacob. The latter had been to a funeral, and on his return he saw the team standing in the woods. He went there and found George lying on his back, dead,—and one log had rolled on him and the log chain was around his neck. How the chain got there, is not known. The deceased was the son of sister Susannah Kussmoul. He had made no profession.
FLORIDA BYERS.

DETRICK.—In the Marlow congregation, Chickasaw Nation, I. T., March 14, 1892, Georgie, son of Bro. Andrew and sister Emma Detrick, aged 9 years, 6 months and 13 days. Funeral services by Elihu Moore.
CORA MOORE.

WIDDERS.—In the Lower Cumberland congregation, Pa., March 18, 1892, Bro. Daniel Widders, aged 64 years, 1 month and 11 days. Bro. Daniel called for the elders and was anointed a short time before his death. He made choice of 2 Tim. 12: 2. Services by brethren Henry Beelman, L. S. Mohler and the writer.
DANIEL LANDIS.

ECHELBARGER.—In the Portage congregation, Wood Co., Ohio, April 11, 1892, Bro. John Echelbarger, aged 68 years, 3 months and 3 days. He was a deacon for a number of years. He leaves a wife and seven children. Funeral services from Rev. 14: 13 by Bro. J. C. Witmore.
J. W. BEER.

BOYD.—April 19, 1892, Catharine Boyd, after an illness of six days with Bright's disease. She was a daughter of David Baughly (deceased), and was born Jan. 26, 1835, in Somerset County, Pa. In 1853 she was married to Samuel Boyd. She became the mother of eleven children. In 1856 she united with the Brethren church and has ever since been consistent and steadfast in her belief. Funeral services were conducted by Rev. Hoskins, of the United Brethren from John 14: 13.
BELLE BOYD.

SHARES.—In the bounds of the Olathe church, Johnson Co., Kans., April 20, 1892, Chas. W. Shares, aged 23 years, 2 months and 26 days. Funeral by the Brethren in the Methodist church, in Edgerton. Text, 1 Sam. 20: 4.
ISAAC H. CRIST.

SMITH.—At his home, near Blasell, Pa., March 29, 1892, Israel Smith, aged 77 years, 9 months and 12 days. He was married to Hannah Grable March 27, 1839. He was blest with fifteen children. For fifty years he had been a faithful member of the Brethren or German Baptist church. Rev. P. M. Woods conducted the funeral services, assisted by Rev. Bovier.
NETTIE MILLER.

Announcements.

DISTRICT MEETINGS.

May 10, District Meeting of Southern Missouri and Arkansas, in the Shoal Creek church. Newton Co., Mo. Those coming by rail to Pierce City will be met on the morning of May 11, by notifying John Halderman at Ergo. Those coming to Purdy will notify Leander Harader and will be met on the morning of May 11.

May 10, District Meeting for Eastern District of Pennsylvania and Eastern Shore of Maryland, in the Ridgely church, Caroline Co., Md. Delegates to be here by evening of May 11, and all elders the day before, as there will be an elders' meeting May 11, at 2 P. M. Excursion tickets can be had at all stations on the Pennsylvania R. R., east of the Susquehanna River, good from May 9 to 16, by presenting a card order, which can be obtained by addressing J. Y. King. Each elder will please order as many as needed in his church.

May 17, at 8 A. M., District of Southern Ohio, in the Lexington church, Highland Co., Ohio. Buy your ticket to Highland, Lexington Village, on the Cincinnati and Maritma Railway; go by way of Cincinnati.

May 21 and 23, South-western District of Kansas, to be held with the Brethren of Neosho County, near Galesburgh, on the M. K. & T. R. R., one mile north, and 1½ miles east of Galesburgh. Ministerial Meeting May 24.

LOVE-FEASTS.

May 10, at 10 A. M., Lower Cumberland Church, Cumberland Co., Pa., 3 miles east of Mechanicsburg. The following day the District Meeting will be held at the same place.

May 11, at the Rockingham meeting-house, Wiscondah congregation, Ray Co., Mo.

May 10, at 10 A. M., Wolf Creek church, Montgomery Co., Ohio.

May 13, at 4 P. M., in the Yellow Creek congregation, Bedford County, Pa.

May 13, at 3 P. M., Cedar Creek church, Anderson Co., Kans.

May 13 and 14, at 2 P. M., Silver Creek church, Ogle Co., Ill.

May 14, at 4 P. M., Middle Fork church, Clinton Co., Ind.

May 12 and 13, at 2 P. M., Welsh Run, Franklin Co., Pa.

May 12, at 5 P. M., Nettle Creek church, Hagerstown, Ind.

May 12, at 3 P. M., near Roaring Spring, in the Clear Creek congregation, Blair Co., Pa.

May 11, at 2 P. M., in the Kansas Center church, 3 miles east of Lyons.

May 12, at 10 A. M., Pipe Creek congregation, Miami Co., Ind.

May 14, Warrior's Mark, Pa.

May 14 and 15, at the Antietam meeting-house, Franklin Co., Pa. Stop off at Waynesborough.

May 14 and 15, in the Chapman Creek church, Dickinson Co., Kans., nine miles north and two miles east of Abilene.

May 11, at 4 P. M., in the Bear Creek church, Montgomery Co., Ohio.

May 10, at 5 P. M., Panther Creek church, Woodford Co., Ill. Meetings to continue over Sunday.

May 20, at 10 A. M., Mississinewa church, Delaware Co., Ind., 3 miles west of Shideler. Those coming by rail should count to Shideler and inquire for the brethren.

May 11, at 10 A. M., Bethel church, Nebr.

May 17, at 7 P. M., Pleasant View church, Reno Co., Kans., 2½ miles south-west of Booth.

May 21, at 3 P. M., McPherson, Kans.

May 11, Altoona church, Pa.

May 21 and 22, at 10 A. M., West Branch church, Ogle Co., Ill.

May 22, English Prairie church, Lagrange Co., Ind. A series of meetings will commence on Thursday previous to the Communion.

May 21, at 3 P. M., McPherson, Kans.

May 21, at 4 P. M., Turkey Creek congregation, at the Operation-house, Elkhart Co., Ind.

May 26 and 27, at 10 A. M., Pine Creek, Ogle Co., Ill.

May 21, 10 A. M., in the Kill-buck church, nine miles west of Muncie, Ind.

May 17, at 2 P. M., in the Harlem congregation, four miles east of Harlan, Shelby Co., Iowa. Meetings to continue over Sunday.

May 19, at 4 P. M., Rock Creek church, Ind.

May 16, at 2 A. M., Hartford church, Hartford Co., Ind.

May 26 and 28, at 2 P. M., Loss Creek congregation, Jennings Co., Pa., at Goshen.

May 17, at 2 P. M., Montiicello church, Ind.

May 18, at 2 P. M., Middle Creek congregation, Somerset Co., Pa.

May 26, in the North Manchester church, a mile west of the town of North Manchester, Ind.

May 28, at 2 P. M., Pleasant Valley church, Darke Co., Ohio. Meetings to continue over Sunday.

May 28, at 2 P. M., Lawrenceville, Grant Co., Ind.

May 26, at 10 A. M., Rome congregation, Oak Grove house, Hancock Co., Ohio.

May 28 and 29, at 2 P. M., Lanark church, Carroll Co., Ill.

May 28 and 29, at 10 A. M., in the Rock River congregation, Ill., at the Franklin Grove meeting-house.

May 19, at 4 P. M., Des Moines Valley church, Polk Co., Iowa. The 20 and 21 o'clock union will be met at Ankeny on the day of meeting.

May 20 and June 2, at 2 P. M., Cherry Grove, Carroll Co., Ill.

May 26, at 2 P. M., in the Sugar church, Elkhart Co., Ind., three miles north-west of Wakarusa, Ind.

May 31, at 2 P. M., Oakland church, Darke Co., Ohio.

May 30 and June 1, at 2 P. M., Buffalo Valley church, Union Co., Pa.

June 1, in the Yellow Creek church, Elkhart Co., Ind., 3 miles south-west of Goshen.

June 6, at 2 P. M., Yellow Creek church, Elkhart Co., Ind.

June 7, at 4 P. M., South Beatrice church, Gage Co., Nebr. Those coming via U. P. R. R., stop at Holmesville, via the B. & M. R. R.; should stop off at Beatrice via the Rock Island R. R.; should stop at Rockford.

June 1, at 2 P. M., at Pæa, Ind. Trains can come from the north-east 10 A. M.

June 2, at 4 P. M., White church, Montgomery Co., Ind., 2½ miles west of Coffee, Ind.

June 7, at 10 A. M., Rock Creek, Franklin Co., Pa., at the Shank meeting-house, 1½ miles south of Greencastle.

June 2 and 3, at 2 P. M., Yellow Creek, Ill.

June 2, at 4 P. M., in the Palmyra church, Darke Co., Ohio.

June 3, at 2 P. M., Upper Fall Creek church, 2 miles east of Middletown, Henry Co., Ind.

June 2, at 10 A. M., Ezel River church, Ind.

June 2, at 10 A. M., Cedar Lake congregation, near Corunna, DeKalb Co., Ind.

June 2 and 3, at 10 A. M., Arnott's church, Ill.

June 2, at 3 P. M., in the Salimony church, at Lancaster, 9 miles south of Huntington, Ind.

June 2, Palestine church, Darke. Members will be met at New Madison and Clark's Station on the "Big Four R. R." by notifying Moses Hollinger, New Madison, Ohio.

June 2, at 2 P. M., in the Chico church, Platt Co., Ill. Ministering brethren on their way to Annual Meeting will please stop with us.

June 3, at 2 P. M., Walnut Level church, Wells Co., Ind.

June 3, at 2 P. M., Blue Ridge church, Platt Co., Ill.

June 4, at 10 A. M., Springfield congregation, Wawaka, Ind.

June 2 and 3, at 2 P. M., Hickory Grove church, Carroll Co., Ill. Brethren going to Annual Meeting will please come over us.

June 2, at 2 P. M., Berkeley church, W. Va.

June 4, at 10 A. M., Lick Creek church, Williams Co., Ohio, 5 miles south-west of Bryan.

June 4, at 2 P. M., Brownsville, Md.

June 2, at 3 P. M., Maple Valley church, Iowa.

June 3, at 4 P. M., 3½ miles north-east of Summitville, Ind.

June 7, at 2 P. M., Carroll church, Ill., in the Sterling Branch of the Wabash R. R.

June 13 and 14, 10 A. M., Greene church, Greene, Iowa. There will be preaching on Friday evening previous.

June 12, at 2 P. M., Queenshoning church, Somerset Co., Pa.

June 14, at 3 P. M., Kingsley church, four miles southeast of Kingsley, Iowa.

June 15, at 2 P. M., in the Monitor church, 8 miles west and 4 miles south of McPherson, Kans.

June 15, at 4 to 6, 8 P. M., Hudson, Ill.

June 15, at 2 P. M., in the Bethel congregation, Reservoir Co., Ind., at the Pleasant View Chapel, three miles east of Milford.

June 15, at 10 A. M., in the west house, Indianapolis, Ind., via, Vale the D. L. & N. R. R., from Grand Rapids, Mich.; to Elkdale, where you will be met by notifying L. B. Fry, Eversole, Mich.

June 11, Pine Creek church, Pa. A series of meetings to begin the week previous. D. C. N. Bloyer is expected to be with us.

June 10, at 4 P. M., in the Shade Creek congregation, Somerset Co., Pa.

June 15 and 16, Pokin Center church, Iowa.

June 17, at 4 P. M., Yellow River congregation, Marshall Co., Ind.

June 16 and 17, Panther Creek, Dallas Co., Iowa.

June 16, at 10 A. M., South Waterloo church, Waterloo, Iowa.

June 16, Green Spring District, Seneca Co., Ohio.

June 12, at 2 P. M., Middle Creek church, Mahoning Co., Iowa.

June 22, at 10 A. M., the Van Wert church, seven miles north-east of Van Wert, Ohio. Those coming by rail will be met at Van Wert, day before the meeting by notifying Jacob Howland, or Joseph Longanecker, Wetzel, Ohio.

June 17 and 18, Indian Creek church, Polk Co., Iowa.

Annual Meeting Notice.

THE Illinois Central R. R. will have tickets on sale at Dixon, Polo, Forreston, Freeport, Lena, Waddam's Grove, Nora, and other points to Elloads, for the accommodation of our Brethren and friends who desire to attend our Annual Meeting at Cedar Rapids, Iowa, in June. The rate is one fare for the round trip. Fare from Polo and Forreston, $5.89.

Trains leave Polo 7:55 P. M., and 5:05 A. M., and arrive at Cedar Rapids at 11:05 P. M. and 12 A. M.

CANCERS, TUMORS, ETC.

Successfully treated by Dr. G. N. Boesler, of Waynesborough, Pa., where he has practiced for the last eleven years. Dr. Boesler is a graduate of the University of Maryland, at Baltimore City. References given and correspondence solicited. Address, Dr. G. W. Boesler, Waynesborough, Pa.

Announcements.

DISTRICT MEETINGS.

May 10, District Meeting of Southern Missouri and Arkansas, in the Shoal Creek church, Newton Co., Mo. Those coming by rail to Pierce City will be met on the morning of May 11, by notifying John Holderread at Ergo. Those coming to Purdy will notify Leander Hamilter and will be met on the morning of May 11.

May 11, District Meeting for Eastern District of Pennsylvania and Eastern Shore of Maryland, in the Ridgely church, Caroline Co., Md. Delegates to be here by evening of May 11, and all elders the day before, as there will be an elders' meeting May 11, at 2 P. M. Excursion tickets can be had at all stations on the Pennsylvania R. R., east of the Susquehanna River, good from May 9 to 16, by presenting a card order, which can be obtained by addressing J. Y. King. Each elder will please order as many as needed in his church.

May 17, 10 8 A. M., District of Southern Ohio, in the Lexington church, Highland Co., Ohio. Buy your ticket to Highland, Lexington Village, on the Cincinnati and Marietta Railway; go by way of Cincinnati.

May 24 and 25, South-eastern District of Kansas, to be held with the Brethren of Neosho County, near Galesburgh, on the M. K. & T. R. R., one mile north, and 1½ miles east of Galesburgh. Ministerial Meeting May 24.

LOVE-FEASTS.

May 10, at 10 A. M., Lower Cumberland Church, Cumberland Co., Pa., 3 miles east of Mechanicsburg. The following day the District Meeting will be held at the same place.

May 11, at the Rockingham meeting-house, Wacondah congregation, Ray Co., Mo.

May 11, at 10 A. M., Wolf Creek church, Montgomery Co., Ohio.

May 13, at 2 P. M., in the Yellow Creek congregation, Bedford County, Pa.

May 13 and 14, at 2 P. M., Cedar Creek church, Anderson Co., Kans.

May 13 and 14, at 2 P. M., Silver Creek church, Ogle Co., Ill.

May 14 and 15, at 2 P. M., Middle Fork church, Clinton Co., Ind.

May 14 and 16, at 2 P. M., Welsh Run, Franklin Co., Pa.

May 14, at 5 P. M., Mount Creek church, Hagerstown, Ind.

May 14, at 2 P. M., near Roaring Spring, in the Clar Creek congregation, Blair Co., Pa.

May 14, at 2 P. M., in the Kansas Center church, 3 miles east of Lyons.

May 14, at 10 A. M., Pipe Creek congregation, Miami Co., Ind.

May 14, Warrior's Mark, Pa.

May 14 and 15, at the Ashland meeting-house, Franklin Co., Pa. Stop off at Waynesborough.

May 14 and 15, in the Chapman Creek church, Dickinson Co., Kans., nine miles north and two miles east of Abilene.

May 14, at 4 P. M., in the Star Creek church, Montgomery Co., Ohio.

May 20, at 5 P. M., Panther Creek church, Woodford Co., Ill. Meetings to continue over Sunday.

May 20, at 10 A. M., Mississinewa church, Delaware Co., Ind., 3 miles west of Shideler. Those coming by rail should stop at Shideler and inquire for the brethren.

May 21, at 10 A. M., Bethel church, Nebr.

May 21, at 2 P. M., Pleasant View church, Reno Co., Kans., 1½ miles south-west of Booth.

May 21, at 3 P. M., McPherson, Kans.

May 21, Altoona church, Pa.

May 20 and 21, at 10 A. M., West Branch church, Ogle Co., Ill.

May 20, English Prairie church, Laġrange Co., Ind. A series of meetings will commence the Thursday previous to the Communion.

May 21, at 5 P. M., McPherson, Kans.

May 25, at 2 P. M., Turkey Creek congregation, at the Spring-dale house, Elkhart Co., Ind.

May 26 and 27, at 10 A. M., Pine Creek, Ogle Co., Ill.

May 27, at 10 A. M., in the Kishacoquillas church, nine miles west of Mattawana, Ind.

May 29, at 3 P. M., in the Mattaw congregation, four miles east of Mattaw, Shelby Co., Iowa. Meetings to continue over Sunday.

May 29, at 2 P. M., Back Creek church, Ind.

May 28, at 10 A. M., Hartford Church, Hartford City, Ind.

May 27 and 28, at 2 P. M., Lost Creek congregation, Juniata Co., Pa., at Goodwill.

May 27, at 2 P. M., Montecallo church, Ind.

May 28, at 2 P. M., Middle Creek congregation, Somerset Co., Pa.

May 28, in the North Manchester church, a mile east of the town of North Manchester, Ind.

May 28 and 29, at 2 P. M., Fairview Valley church, Darke Co., Ohio. Meetings to continue over Sunday.

May 28, at 2 P. M., Lewesville, Grant Co., Ind.

May 28, at 10 A. M., Rome congregation, Oak Grove house, Hancock Co., Ohio.

May 28 and 29, at 3 P. M., Libertb church, Carroll Co., Ill.

May 28 and 29, at 10 A. M., in the Rock River congregation, Ill., at the Franklin Grove meeting-house.

May 29, at 2 P. M., Des Moines Valley church, Polk Co., Iowa. The 30 and 31 o'clock train will be east of Ankeny on the day of meeting.

May 31 and June 2, at 2 P. M., Cherry Grove, Carroll Co., Ill.

May 31, at 2 P. M., in the Bango church, Elkhart Co., Ind., three miles south-west of Waterman, Ind.

May 31, at 2 P. M., Oakland church, Darke Co., Ohio.

May 31 and June 1, at 2 P. M., Buffalo Valley church, Union Co., Pa.

June 1, in the Yellow Creek church, Elkhart Co., Ind., 3 miles south-west of Goshen.

June 7, at 2 P. M., Yellow Creek church, Elkhart Co., Ind.

June 11, at 2 P. M., South Beatrice church, Gage Co., Nebr. Those coming via D. P. R. R., stop at Holmesville; via the B. & M. R. R., should stop off at Beatrice; via the Rock Island R. R., should stop at Rockford.

June 1, at 2 P. M., 400 Pleys, Ind. Train due here from the south at 10 A. M.

June 2, at 2 P. M., White church, Montgomery Co., Ind., 4½ miles west of Colfax, Ind.

June 2, 10 10 A. M., Buck Creek, Franklin Co., Pa., at the Black meeting-house, 1½ miles south of Greencastle.

June 2 and 3, at 2 P. M., Yellow Creek, Ill.

June 2, 10 2 P. M., in the Palestine church, Darke Co., Ohio.

June 2, 10 2 P. M., Upper Fall Creek church, 4 miles east of Middletown, Henry Co., Ind.

June 2, at 10 A. M., Red River church, Ind.

June 2, 10 10 A. M., Cedar Lake congregation, near Corunna, Dekalb Co., Ind.

June 2 and 3, 10 10 A. M., Astoria church, Ill.

June 3, 10 5 P. M., in the Salimony church, at Lancaster, 5 miles south of Huntington, Ind.

June 3, at 2 P. M., Palestine church, Ohio. Ministers will be met at New Madison and Clark's Station on the "Big Four R. R." by notifying Moses Holderz, New Madison, Ohio.

June 6, 10 4 P. M., in the Okaw church, Platt Co., Ill. Ministering brethren on their way to Annual Meeting will please stop with us.

June 3, at 5 P. M., Walnut Level church, Wells Co., Ind.

June 3, at 2 P. M., Blue Ridge church, Platt Co., Ill.

June 4, 10 10 A. M., Springfield congregation, Waukesha, Ind.

June 4 and 5, at 3 P. M., Hickory Grove church, Carroll Co., Ill. Brethren going to Annual Meeting will please remember us.

June 4, at 2 P. M., Berkeley church, W. Va.

June 4, at 2 P. M., Lick Creek church, Williams Co., Ohio, 7 miles south-east of Bryan.

June 4, 10 2 P. M., Brownsville, Md.

June 4, at 2 P. M., Maple Valley church, Iowa.

June 5, at 2 P. M., 5½ miles north-east of Summittville, Ind.

June 5 and 6, Bytheria, Pa.

June 11, at 2 P. M., Carroll church, Ill., on the Streator Branch of the Wabash R. R.

June 11 and 12, 10 10 A. M., Green church, Greene, Iowa. There will be preaching on Friday evening previous.

June 11, at 2 P. M., Quemahoning church, Somerset Co., Pa.

June 11, at 2 P. M., Kingsley church, four miles south-west of Kingsley, Iowa.

June 11, at 5 P. M., in the Morrison church, 8 miles west and 2 miles south of McPherson, Kans.

June 11, 10 10 A. M., Hudson, Ill.

June 11, 10 2 P. M., in the Bethel congregation, Kosciusko Co., Ind., in the Pleasant View Chapel, three miles east of Milford.

June 11, at 10 A. M., in the east house, Thornapple church, Mich. Take the U. D. & N. R. R. from Grand Rapids, Mich., to Kienzie, where you will be met by notifying L. D. Fry, Elmdale, Mich.

June 11, Pine Creek church, Ill. A series of meetings will begin one week previous. Eld. S. H. Myers is expected to be with us.

June 11, at 2 P. M., in the Shield Creek congregation, Scomerset Co., Pa.

June 15 and 16, Dallas Center church, Iowa.

June 17, at 2 P. M., Yellow River congregation, Marshall Co., Ind.

June 18 and 19, Panther Creek, Dallas Co., Iowa.

June 18, at 10 A. M., South Waterloo church, Waterloo, Iowa.

June 19, at 2 P. M., Green Spring District, Seneca Co., Ohio.

June 18 and 19, at 2 P. M., Middle Creek church, Mahoning Co., Iowa.

June 22, at 10 A. M., at Os Van Wert church, seven miles north-east of Van Wert, Ohio. Those coming by rail will be met at Van Wert; they notify the coming by notifying Jacob Holshend, or Joseph Longanecker, Wetzel, Ohio.

June 25 and 26, Twlan Creek church, Polk Co., Iowa.

Gospel Chimes.

BY WM. BEERY.

A new edition of this deservedly popular Sunday-school song-book has just been issued.

Bro. Beery has had a large experience in Sunday-school work, and the book which we offer to the Brethren, and the public in general, evinces the exercise of talent as well as good judgment. The religious purity of the hymns, contributed by sister Beery, adds much to the excellence of the book.

Price per single copy, 30 cts.; per dozen, by mail, $3.00; by express, $2.60. Lots of more than a dozen must be sent by express.

BRETHREN'S PUBLISHING CO.,
Or Huntingdon, Pa. — Mt. Morris, Ill.

Annual Meeting Notice.

THE Illinois Central R. R. will have tickets on sale at Dixon, Polo, Forreston, Freeport, Lena, Waddam's Grove, Nora, and other points in Illinois, for the accommodation of our Brethren and friends who desire to attend our Annual Meeting at Cedar Rapids, Iowa, in June. The rate is one fare for the round trip. Fare from Polo and Forreston, $3.80.

Trains leave Polo 2:33 P. M. and 3:22 A. M., and arrive at Cedar Rapids at 11:05 P. M. and 9:00 A. M.

CANCERS, TUMORS, ETC.

Successfully treated by Dr. G. N. Boxter, of Waynesborough, Pa., where he has practiced for the last sixteen years. Dr. Boxter is a graduate of the University of Maryland, at Baltimore City. References given and correspondence solicited. Address, DR. G. W. Boxter, Waynesborough, Pa.

CRUDEN'S COMPLETE CONCORDANCE

THIS excellent work, which we offer for sale to our readers, at the low price of $1.50, post-paid, is the only one of the kind that may be depended upon as being strictly reliable. Any one in the Bible may be readily found by looking for any material word in the verse. Besides this there are given the significations of the principal words, by which their true, Scriptural meaning may be known. A full account of Jewish customs and ceremonies is given as well as a complete concordance of the proper names of the Bible and of the books called Apocrypha. Send all orders for the above work to this office.

Our Library on Christian Evidences.—This collection of works constitutes the best books to be had on that subject: "Paley's Evidences of Christianity," New Edition, $1.50; "Notes on Infidelity," 75 cents; "Manual of Christian Evidences," 75 cents; "Many Infallible Proofs," $1.25; "The Divine Demonstration," $1.50; "The Bible in the Nineteenth Century," 25 cents; "Grounds of Theistic and Christian Belief," $2.50. Price of the entire set, if ordered at one time, $8.00; special terms to ministers furnished upon application.

"Study to show thyself approved unto God: a workman that needeth not be ashamed, rightly dividing the Word of Truth."

THE PRODIGAL.

BY M. M. SHERRICK.

"GIVE me my portion," cried a youth one day
    With glad hope in his eye, pride in his breast,
Tossing the curls his mother loved away,
    Back from the brow her lips so oft had pressed.

Down the long lane in uncurbed haste he strode
    Nor looked behind him where the rooftrees rise.
The orchard gained—then on the winding road
    He passed from sight of love and streaming eyes.

Out, out into the great world's mighty stream
    Where met the elements of all the raging years
And surge resistless as a midnight dream
    That breaks a heart or bathes a couch with tears.

Far, far he wandered from his father's lands.
    In vain he grasped for golden circlets bright
They changed to iron fetters for his hands—
    The daily chaplet was a scourge by night.

At last a meteor flash of inborn pride
    Shone bright above that hour, and to his eye
Revealed a thousand demons at his side,
    They meteor-like receded from the sky.

An angel form bent over him in love,
    With heaving breast and tear-dimmed, pitying eye.
Gave him the message from the court above
    And, blessing him, ascended to the sky.

"I will arise," he said, and with a bound
    He stood a man whose broken shackles lay.
The night-mare of his youth was gone, around
    Him fleeing shadows marked the coming day.

And with that day what splendor filled his soul!
    His life renewed—his former sins forgiven—
With joy entrancing, far beyond control
    He lost himself in that blest hope of heaven.

Once more he breathed the meadow-scented air
    That whispered in the trees about his home,
Once more the myriad ties of youth so fair
    Drew close around his heart and whispered "Come."

He goes. The yearnings of that wayward heart
    Cannot be stifled by the false alarms,
That make a slave, when once the fetters part.
    He goes, and finds his all in loving arms.

We all are prodigals and fondly chase,
    Our circling phantoms, in secluded rounds
Within the limits of terrestrial space—
    Time's middle-march between celestial bounds.

Why thus an exile from nativity—
    The soul's first boundless and eternal day?
Arise, for worlds untrodden wait for thee,
    Then loose thy bounds and, rising, lead the way,

Beyond the limits dimly seen in dreams
    To newer realms of thought and mines of truth
Untouched as yet,—where other sunlight beams
    Upon the circle of immortal youth

Behold what glowing splendors charm the eye—
    The glories of that home unlimited,
Where kings may live and, living, shall not die.
    Where Love beclouded mourns not for her dead.

Mt. Morris, Ill.

A GOOD SOLDIER.

BY J. F. BRITTON.

"Endure hardness, as a good soldier of Jesus Christ."—2 Tim. 2: 3.

THE phrase soldier implies warfare, and warfare implies stupendous labor, anxiety and hardships. There is a great difference between Christ's army, and the civil armies. The civil armies are made up of men between the ages of eighteen and forty-five. Christ's army is composed of men, women and children, old and young, but they are all volunteers. The Christian's cause is the highest and noblest that ever elicited the sympathies, or called forth the energies of the human heart. The Satanic powers have taken possession of our territory, and the heavenly mandate is, that we should go forth with all our heart, mind and strength to repossess it. Nothing stirs the blood in a man more than to have his home invaded. Not only our homes, but our hearts are invaded by the tyrant that takes away our happiness, injures our usefulness, and seeks to destroy us, both soul and body. Unlike other armies, our object is not to kill, but to make alive,—not to destroy men, but to save them.

Religion is a life-saving service. Along our shores are men, whose business it is to go out to a wrecked ship, and save the lives of those who are sinking beneath the waves. All around us in life's ocean souls are perishing beneath the waves of sin, and it is our imperative mission to go out after them, and try to save them. We are unlike other armies, in that our arms and equipments are not carnal. "For we fight not against flesh and blood, but against principalities, against powers, against the rulers of the darkness of this world, and against spiritual wickedness in high places. Therefore our weapons are the Sword of the Spirit, which is the Word of God."

When we look out upon the great battles of sin and righteousness, we behold wickedness arrayed against our holy religion. It is wonderful to see the soldiers of Satan, how active and dexterously they are at work, in the execution of their Master's cause! With these startling facts staring us in the face, should we not endure hardness, as good soldiers of Jesus Christ? The Christian's warfare is an endless battle, and if any man "thinketh he standeth, let him take heed lest he fall." When we think there is safety, there may come the vehement storms of misdemeanor and maltreatments, and unless we are skillful in the use of our sword, we will fall victims to the enemy. If they are defeated, they will change their tactics, and continue to seek after our degradation. They will propound to us all the fascinating allurements, which are congenial to our Adamstic natures, and it requires a great deal of endurance and energy to sustain us in the battles of self-denial, but if we are faithful and endure hardness, as good soldiers to the end, then a crown of unfading glory will be ours.

Our homes are another battle field. Temptations will come to us in form of a little private dance, or a harmless game of cards, or an innocent glass of wine and a pack of cigarettes. Take care, mother, they are trying to gain admission into your home. Meet them at the door, and resist them. The family altar is a strong defense against the enemy, all our Christian fathers and mothers should gather their families around the holy altar, at least once a day, and read a portion of Scripture, and then earnestly implore strength and guidance from the Holy Spirit, that they may withstand the battles of the day. Prayer is the Christian's greatest and strongest defense against the wiles of the enemy. The Christian's battle extends beyond heart and home,—out into the community. Each gambling den, liquor saloon and house of infamy is a strong fort of debauchery, and the divine edict is, that they should be demolished. Our Lord has said, "Go ye into all the world, and seek to liberate those who are in the Satanic bondage." The Christian soldier is never off duty, because the diabolical emissaries are ever on the alert to assault or decoy us, either in our places of business or out in society, hence it behooveth us to be watchful and assiduous in our antagonisms against the workers of atrocity.

Let all who may read these lines ask themselves the momentous and vital question, "What hardships am I enduring for Jesus?" Paul knew what hardness was. When they took up stones out of the street at Lystra, and pelted him till they thought he was dead; when the Jews laid many cruel stripes on him, and cast him in the inner prison, and made his feet fast in the stocks, —that was hardness. Ah, there are too many Christians nowadays, looking for flowery beds of ease. It seems to be quite easy for some to preach and write about going out into the highways and hedges, and tell the blessed story of Jesus and his love, but, ah, how few are willing to say, "Here am I, send me!" How few are willing to help in the sending! It looks as though some of our local churches are only battle tableaux, for there is no visible fight going on,—no enemy driven from the battle-field,—none, or very few, souls saved. It looks as though we were just *playing* soldiers, for there are but few or no sacrifices, no hardships, no long and weary marches, no death grapple, and no shout of victory.

If we are going to be Christ's soldiers, let us be *good* soldiers. The war may be long, the battle severe, but if we endure hardness, as good soldiers of Jesus Christ, victory will be ours at last. Then let us press on as the poet says,

"With shield and banner bright,
    We'll work for God, and battle for the right."

Let us ever trust in our Commander, Jesus Christ, the ever-conquering Immanuel. The keys of death and hell swing at his girdle, his garments are dyed in crimson, and his banner stained with blood. He is King of kings, and Lord of lords.

From victory unto victory,
    His army he shall lead,
Till every foe is vanquished
    And Christ is Lord indeed.

Dulinsville, Va.

CHRISTIAN SELF-DENIAL.

BY D. E. PRICE.

In Two Chapters.—Chapter One.

"And he said unto them all, If any man will come after me, let him deny himself, and take up his cross daily, and follow me."—Luke 9: 23; 14: 27; Matt. 10: 38; 16: 24; Mark 8: 34.

OUR Savior here only tells us to deny ourselves, but does not tell us what to deny ourselves of; and we would be left in doubt as to our practical observance of it, were there no other Scriptures that more fully define the subject. In Titus 2: 11-14, we have the following language: "For the grace of God that bringeth salvation hath appeared to all men, teaching us that denying ungodliness and worldly lusts, we should live soberly, righteously, and godly, in this present world; looking for that blessed hope, and glorious appearing of the great God, and our Savior Jesus Christ; who gave himself for us, that he might redeem us from all iniquity, and purify unto himself a peculiar people zealous of good works." In this quotation we are plainly told what to deny ourselves of,—*ungodliness* and *worldly lusts*, and then he tells us how to live: *Soberly, righteously* and *godly* in this present world.

The devil has always been an opposer of righteousness and true Christianity. He tried to destroy the Christian church in its infancy by fire and sword, and the most tortuous persecution his ingenuity could invent; but amidst all his opposition the church continued to prosper; and when he saw he was about to be defeated in his unhallowed purposes, he changed his tactics, and made it popular to profess Christianity, and became a professor, in part, himself, in order to deceive; and in this way he has succeeded wonderfully well, by uniting the *church* and the *world*, or by getting the world *into* the church. The *popular* church is making rapid strides towards being swallowed up by the world, and I fear the Breth-

red, at least to some extent, are following in the same channel. "Come out of her my people, and be not partakers of her sins, lest ye receive of her plagues."

Our Savior, whom we love to follow in the self-denying principles of the Gospel, says, John 15: 18, 19, "If the world hate you, ye know that it hated me before it hated you. If ye were of the world, the world would love its own, but because ye are not of the world, but I have chosen you out of the world, therefore the world hateth you." Hence, since the Christian is represented as not belonging to the world, it is inconsistent and unlawful for him to unite with the world in their unlawful pleasures. We read in 2 Cor. 11: 14, 15, "For Satan himself is transformed into an angel of light. Therefore it is no great thing if his ministers also be transformed as ministers of righteousness, whose end shall be according to their works." Therefore Satan, through his *ministers*, has introduced *ungodly games* of the world into the church, and invites the world to partake with them in their abominations. Jesus says, in Luke 16: 15, "That which is highly esteemed among men, is abomination in the sight of God." Again, in Eph. 5: 11, he says: "Have no fellowship with the unfruitful works of darkness, but rather reprove them." See 2 Cor. 6: 14-18.

Having the opportunity, a few years ago, to hear Henry Ward Beecher preach in his church at Brooklyn, N. Y., I heard him say, before he introduced his discourse, that "the Young Men's Christian Association, of Brooklyn, wanted to build a house. They wanted a good, substantial building, which they thought would cost about $250,000. One man had a standing bid of $60,000 for thirty days, providing the other $200,000 were raised in that time." He further stated, "They want a large audience room for religious worship, and some smaller rooms for games. We *want to take some of the devil's games and appropriate them to the Lord*." I am not sure that he used the word *some*, but I want to be on the safe side, hence give it in that way for fear of exaggeration.

The popular churches have run into such great extravagances in building their church-houses, and paying extortionate salaries to their ministers, that they are induced to resort to every possible method, whether *lawful* or *unlawful*, in order to get the world to unite with them in meeting their expenses. A certain writer says, "The church has become absolutely insane on the subject of entertaining men. Preachers are sought after who can amuse the people. Meetings of all kinds are devised to please and keep the congregation during the week, while the preacher, with anecdotes, sparkling wit and broad jest, must do the rest of the work on Sunday. Whatever happens, the people must be entertained, the idea being that, if not amused, they will all drift away and be lost. This whole idea of entertaining the people at God's house comes from Satan, and is one of the most subtile and dangerous of all his movements upon and against Christianity. He knows that if Christ is held before the people, and men look steadily at him, they will be saved. Hence, his idea is to divert the church from doing this wise, and heavenly, and powerful, and saving thing. He whispers that Christ alone is not enough to draw souls, that it takes Christ and jokes, Christ and lectures, Christ and entertainments. As he discovers his success in blinding the church, he becomes more aggressive, and whispers again that, if the naked cross be held up,—the simple, strict, holy life of Jesus be insisted on,—then all the young people will be driven away. He tells them that the young people are young people, and must be amused; and old people must be entertained, and entertain-

ment must be provided. So he tempts, and so he has succeeded in thousands of instances, in sidetracking the church. He has switched her off from one blessed, heavenly employment of crying, 'Behold the Lamb,' and she is now part lyceum, part theatre, and part kitchen. As you pass her doors to-day, you will hear the names of Socrates, Plato, Aristotle, Emerson, Tyndall, Darwin, and others, far more frequently than the name of Christ, while, instead of sobs and cries of 'What must I do to be saved?'—you will be greeted with clapping of hands, rattle of plates and bursts of uproarious applause. A sidetracked church! The church engaged in the noble, exalted, heavenly, spiritual and soul-saving employment of amusing the crowd!"

The same author, in another place says: "The church is called on to teach the men to deny the lust of the eye,—to crucify the flesh, mortify our members, subdue the appetites and every lust of the flesh. But, oh,—marvelous inconsistency! Here is the church, through its entertainments inviting men to gaze on the spectacular bordering on the theatrical, and, instead of subduing the appetites, to come up, and eat, and cram, and stuff, to the glory of God! And the more people stuff, the more money, of course, is made, and the better pleased is the church!"

Hear the same author in another place, "The church tells me I must not go to the theatre, and other places of worldly amusement, but the entertainment says, 'Come to me and I will give you very much the same, only under another er and softer name.' The church forbids my gambling, and warns me against the lottery; but the entertainment says in lieu of this, 'I will let you indulge in raffles, the grab bags, or the recent feature of voting,' which is only a milder form of a game of chance."

Who wonders that our children are found in places of worldly amusement, when we are all the time educating them in this direction, giving them, ourselves, a taste and relish for such things! Who wonders that, after we have blunted their spiritual sensibility, and familiarized their minds to such a life by contact with the more refined forms of worldliness outside of the church!

One more extract from the same author: "Now, if the church becomes assimilated to the world, is different, indeed, only by a few delicate shades of moral coloring, how will she be able to uplift her voice against the iniquity that is in the world? How can the pew and pulpit speak against the theatre, when we have things so much like it in our shows and festivals? How can the church denounce gambling and the lottery when she has grab bag and raffle and 'voting' within her sacred walls, and meeting with her smiling approval? The whole effect is to paralyze the tongue of preacher and layman in the presence of the great evils of the day."

Another writer says: "What if Moses had instituted a grand carnival or bazar to draw the surrounding heathen into his camp, and get means to build the tabernacle! How would it comport with the character of the early Christians, to read in one of Paul's epistles a suggestion that the saints at Corinth got up some amateur theatrical or Isthmian games to raise money for the poor saints at Jerusalem,—or an exhortation to Lydia to stir up the godly women of Philippi to get up a grand fair, festival, crazy tea, baby show, with fantastically-dressed Christian girls, and all our latest modern devices?

"Were the early meeting-houses bazars or restaurants? The Word of God and the ritual of our churches, teach that giving is an act of worship, as seen in Acts 10: 4, but these ecclesiastical vanity fairs are scenes of carnal revelry and ungodly mirth. Paul made tents, sold them in

legitimate trade, and gave the money to the Lord, but he did not beg the patronage of pagans for his cause, and then credit them with giving to the Lord. The early missionaries went forth, 'taking nothing of the gentiles.' Imagine Christ or Paul at a modern church fair, or strawberry festival! Men's methods may sometimes procure more money, but God's will procure the greatest blessing. No other way can be acceptable to him."

"O how unlike the complex works of man,
Heaven's simple, easy, unencumbered plan."

The ancient church had the Lord's Supper, as instituted by the Lord himself, but nearly all modern churches have laid it aside, and instead of those ancient and pious meetings, we see a class of social gatherings of quite a different character, such as picnics, church fairs, and all kinds of amusing entertainments, inaugurated and perpetuated for the special object of getting money and making fun. When interrogated on such proceedings as the above, the reply is: "Oh! it is for the benefit of the church!" Oh! where, or how, can we find any *denial of self* in such procedures as the above? Where is the cross that we are to bear daily, if we may unite with the world in all those worldly amusements? We are commanded to deny ourselves, and take up the cross daily. Self-denial and the cross both imply suffering. The Savior suffered on the Roman cross, and he bore it himself. Sometimes we hear it said we must bear the cross of Christ, which is a mistake. He commands us to bear our own.

Mt. Morris, Ill.

COVERED AND UNCOVERED IN PRAYER.

BY C. H. BALSBAUGH.

To a Sister in the West:—

I AM glad for your letter. Glad that you are interested in the principles that lie at the heart of phenomena and precepts and ordinances. Glad that you are eager to know the exact terms employed originally by the Holy Spirit, and the exact shade of meaning in each word. Glad for the stamps you inclosed, as I had used my last two-cent paster a few hours before your letter arrived. When I opened your letter and saw the fresh supply, my soul gratefully ejaculated, "The LORD is my Shepherd, I SHALL NOT WANT." Ps. 23: 1.

Our spiritual and material *needs* are *all* supplied ACCORDING TO HIS RICHES IN GLORY BY JESUS CHRIST." Eph. 3: 16. Philpp. 4: 19. Where there is any *real* need, and the supply is *sought in the* NAME OF JESUS, which means the consummation of His purpose in the incarnation and the cross, God has pledged His veracity to give it. To learn to pray in the name of Jesus is not only the fundamental condition, but the highest attainment of the Christian life.

We have not yet reached the bottom of the well of Truth and never will, for it has no bottom. Christ says, "*I am the Truth*," and Col. 2: 9, tells us how deep He is. We open new doors only to find a dozen, a score, a hundred other doors that want to be unlocked. Except we repent we perish. Luke 13: 3. "Without holiness no man shall see the Lord." Heb. 12: 14. Without love we are nothing. 1 Cor. 13: 1, 2, 3. Except we are born of God we cannot even see His kingdom. John 3: 3. Whose plummet is long enough to sound any of these mysteries? Who can tell how far the significance of baptism reaches? Who can give us the moral equivalents of the Eucharist? Who knows how large a sphere he enters, or how deeply he condemns himself, when he utters the first word in the Lord's Prayer. "OUR."

That means a love and sympathy, and patience and sacrifice, as high and deep, and wide and holy, as that displayed by Christ on the cross. Oh how many "lie to the Holy Ghost" in the very first word of their prayer! Even God's reason for a covering on the head of a female saint, has never been fully elucidated. But His *reasons* for His injunctions may exceed our comprehension. It is with His *authority* that we have directly to do. No matter whether we contend for cap or hair or veil or bonnet or hat, the mystery of the *why* remains the same. Two reasons are assigned in Scripture for the woman's covering in prayer: her constitutional relation to the man; and her higher relation to God and the angels. Her hair will not answer the purpose of either, but serve as a natural symbol of both.

The word "*also*," in 1 Cor. 11: 6, breaks the backbone of any argument that pleads for woman's long hair as the intended prayer-covering. I have seen not a few very fine logicians go to pieces by falling on that "stone of stumbling." The change of subject in verse 14, destroys the identity between the covering in verse 6, and that in verse 15. "Doth not even nature itself teach you," takes the apostle from the spiritual handling of his theme to its adumbration in the realm of matter. As a man is to keep his hair short, and a woman hers long, this is in the apostle's view, a confirmation of his argument in favor of a veil of special religious import.

The oriental veil, concerning which you make particular inquiry, was regarded indispensable among Eastern ladies. Even now, when a woman is caught with her veil removed, it is not uncommon to hear the exclamation "Oh, my misfortune!" They were worn of different sizes, and colors, and fabric. They were scooped over the head, or fastened to an extra head-piece, and sometimes reached nearly to the feet. Some wore them much shorter. The usual indoor veil was of thin muslin. They were also worn quite heavy, and not unfrequently jet black, and of fine, costly material. The modern cap is rather a light substitute, but may serve the original purpose well enough, provided God's two given reasons are the salient facts of the woman's life. Any covering that roots itself in the reasons assigned for it in the Sacred Record, is better than veil or cap worn simply as a traditional custom. Not a few who would think it sacrilege to kneel without a cap, do not think it a violation of divine order to rise from their devotional posture, and scold like furies if their wills are crossed. To pray unto God with uncovered head is pronounced a shame; "for that is even all one as if she were shaven," but to wear the symbol, and dishonor it by an unholy life, is a greater shame.

The covering for woman, and the not-covering for man, have the same obligations as to time and place and occasion. So far as the record goes, the woman's obligation is neither longer as to time, nor more imperative as to fact, than the man's. A woman's bare head, and a man's covered head, are equally dishonorable to God in that special posture or engagement, which is to express the elements and experience of the ordinary life. Reason can break in at many points with its clamorous why? why? but God knows, and *faith* says, Amen. The "*every*" of 1 Cor. 11: 4, 5, and the occasions specified, should set this hair—veil—cap—covering question forever at rest.

Had Paul made the slightest reference to custom as a reason for its observance, there might be a plea in this day for its being obsolete; but as it rests on principle inherent in the very constitution and relationship of human nature, we had better accept it, without quarreling about long or short, thin or heavy, black or white, coarse or fine. A just conception of 1 Cor. 11: 3, 11, 12, will

make us hot, only reverent toward God, but charitable towards each other. An old coffee-sack will answer if the relations to man and God and angel are adjusted and sustained by the Holy Spirit.

The Emphatic Diaglott does not differ from the best translations: "Her hair is given her *instead* of a covering." The word translated *instead* is a Greek term hard to catch and put in an English dress. It holds the sense, *indicative of, representative of*, so that our common version "*for* a covering," is as good as any, serving as a representative of something more spiritual, an added symbol of woman's relation to the race, and the sympathy and ministry of the higher world. So deep are the things of God, so vast, so intricate, so holy are our relations of life, and so wonderful and glorious and endless our destiny.

Union Deposit, Pa.

THE SOUL.

BY CHAS. M. YEAROUT.

In Four Chapters.—Chapter Three.

In *Truth Gleaner*, published at Waterloo, Iowa, issue of November, 1891, page 44, we have the following by the editor: "As a rule, the believers in the immortality of the soul are willing to stake their whole theory upon Gen. 2: 7, believing it says that God formed the body of the man of dust and put an immortal soul into that body . . . "And the Lord God breathed into his nostrils the breath of life; and man became a living soul."

Here is a clear statement of the facts, and all we have to do, is to accept each statement as the truth, the whole truth, and nothing but the truth. It says that the Lord God formed man of the dust of the ground; therefore that which was formed out of the dust of the ground was the man,—not a body into which a man was to be put. The statements, "The Lord God formed man of the dust of the ground," must, in and of itself, be true; and the next statement, following the conjunction "and" is the statement of another truth, namely, that God "breathed into his,— the man's—nostrils the breath of life; and this caused the man that had already been formed out of the dust of the ground, to become a living (not an immortal) soul. . . . It is clear that the soul came out of the earth."

It is plain that the editor does not believe in the doctrine taught by the apostles, of an outward and inner man. His materialistic vision cannot take in the beautiful, sublime teachings of the Savior. "Though a man may kill the body, he cannot kill the soul." Matt. 10: 28. I do not stake my belief in the immortality of the soul on Genesis, or any part of the Old Testament, although there is nothing in it that condemns the immortality of the soul.

The mechanic formed a steam engine of the iron of the earth, and it possessed all the parts of a complete engine,—steam-chests, pistons, pit-mans, cylinders, escapements, levers, etc., but it is of no earthly use to any one. What is wrong with it? It has the form of a perfect engine, but, behold, it is dead; as was the man. The parts are filled with steam, and we have a living engine. It wends its way through the country at almost lightning speed, pulling an enormous load. I say the mechanic formed the engine of the iron of the earth, therefore, that which was formed out of the earth was the engine, not a body into which the engine was to be put. The statement, "The mechanic formed the engine of the earth, must, in and of itself, be true; and the mechanic or engineer put steam into it,—the engine's chests,—and this caused the engine that had al-

ready been formed out of the iron of the ground to become a living engine. It is clear that the steam came not out of the earth.

The writer seems to put considerable stress on "become," "become,—to pass from one state to another; by assuming or receiving new properties or qualities, additional matter, or a new character."—*Webster.* Hence, when the lifeless man received the properties of soul and breath, he lived. It is clear, that the properties of soul, and breath did not come from the earth, but from God. Steam is the motive power that causes the engine to move (live). Take it away, and the engine stops,—is dead. The soul of man is the active, motive power that causes the man to act,—live. Take it away, and the man is dead.

"Many believers in the immortality of the soul contend that the soul was breathed into man when he received the breath of life."—*Ibid., Jan. 1892, page 55.* Do we have any account of man having a soul prior to God's breathing into his nostrils the breath of life? Is it anywhere stated that he was a dead soul, or soul at all, prior to this? What is the meaning of soul (*pseuche*)? Was it ever properly translated anything but life, the opposite of death? Then the materialist doctrine, "that life, soul, spirit, is nothing but a mode of molecular motion, having no entitative character or existence separate from organisms," is erroneous and anti-scriptural, and its consequent doctrine that the soul dies,—molders back to earth,—teaches that life is dead or extinct. Hence, if God desires creatures to worship and glorify his name, outside of the heavenly hosts, he will have to make a new creation, for all life is dead,—extinct, for there is no life in the grave.

"It is said that God breathed into the beasts the breath of life; therefore when the breath of life was breathed into man, he received an immortal soul, which the beasts did not receive. Now let us try the same syllogism in relation to the woman. . . . It is not said that God breathed into the woman the breath of life; therefore when the breath of life was breathed in to the man, he received an immortal soul, which the woman did not receive."—*Ibid, page 55.*

The above syllogism is weak in the extreme. Every one knows that the woman is above the brute creation; and is possessed of the nature and attributes of man, and was taken from man, hence is a part of man. Every one that is acquainted with Christ, and his precious teachings, knows that man is in possession of eternal life, and as soul means life, the soul is undying (John 5: 24; 3: 36; 6: 47–54; 10: 28; 1 John 5: 13.) Eternal is immortal, — without end,—and not subject to death. I am speaking of the children of God, for the sinner is now dead,—separated from God, and unless he repents and is converted to God, he will eventually forever be separated from God. "Whosoever liveth and believeth in Christ shall never die (never be separated from Christ), believest thou this?" John 11: 26; 6: 50. Does the Heavenly Master anywhere teach, that the beasts have everlasting life? Does he teach that they have passed from death unto life? Does the Bible anywhere teach, that the souls of the beasts will be saved? "We are not of them that draw back unto perdition; but of them that believe, to the saving of the soul." Heb. 10: 3. "And receive with meekness the engrafted word, which is able to save your souls," James 1: 21, was never spoken of beasts. Do the Scriptures teach that the souls of beasts shall "appear at the judgment seat of Christ, and not receive for that which they have done;" and "be rewarded according to their works?" If not, then why compare them with man, or the souls of men, the chief work of creation, created in the image and likeness of the eternal God, and possessed, in a certain degree,

That means a love and sympathy, and patience and sacrifice, as high and deep, and wide and holy, as that displayed by Christ on the cross. Oh how many "lie to the Holy Ghost" in the very first word of their prayer! Even God's reason for a covering on the head of a female saint, has never been fully elucidated. But His *reasons* for His injunctions may exceed our comprehension. It is with His *authority* that we have directly to do. No matter whether we contend for cap or hair or veil or bonnet or hat, the mystery of the *why* remains the same. Two reasons are assigned in Scripture for the woman's covering in prayer: her constitutional relation to the man; and her higher relation to God and the angels. Her hair will not answer the purpose of either, but serve as a natural symbol of both.

The word "*also*," in 1 Cor. 11: 6, breaks the backbone of any argument that pleads for woman's long hair as the intended prayer-covering. I have seen not a few very fine logicians go to pieces by falling on that "stone of stumbling." The change of subject in verse 14, destroys the identity between the covering in verse 6, and that in verse 15. "Doth not even nature itself 'teach you," takes the apostle from the spiritual handling of his theme to its adumbration in the realm of matter. As a man is to keep his hair short, and a woman hers long, this is in the apostle's view, a confirmation of his argument in favor of a veil of special religious import.

The oriental veil, concerning which you make particular inquiry, was regarded indispensable among Eastern ladies. Even now, when a woman is caught with her veil removed, it is not uncommon to hear the exclamation "Oh, my misfortune!" They were worn of different sizes, and colors, and fabric. They were scooped over the head, or fastened to an extra head-piece, and sometimes reached nearly to the feet. Some wore them much shorter. The usual indoor veil was of thin muslin. They were also worn quite heavy, and not unfrequently jet black, and of fine, costly material. The modern cap is rather a light substitute, but may serve the original purpose well enough, provided God's two given reasons are the salient facts of the woman's life. Any covering that roots itself in the reasons assigned for it in the Sacred Record, is better than veil or cap worn simply as a traditional custom. Not a few who would think it sacrilege to kneel without a cap, do not think it a violation of divine order to rise from their devotional posture, and scold like furies if their wills are crossed. To pray unto God with uncovered head is pronounced a shame; "for that is even all one as if she were shaven," but to wear the symbol, and dishonor it by an unholy life, is a greater shame.

The covering for woman, and the not-covering for man, have the same obligations as to time and place and occasion. So far as the record goes, the woman's obligation is neither longer as to time, nor more imperative as to fact, than the man's. A woman's bare head, and a man's covered head, are equally dishonorable to God in that special posture or engagement, which is to express the elements and experience of the ordinary life. Reason can break in at many points with its clamorous why? why? but GOD knows, and *faith* says, Amen. The "*every*" of 1 Cor. 11: 4, 5, and the occasions specified, should set this hair —veil—cap—covering question forever at rest.

Had Paul made the slightest reference to custom as a reason for its observance, there might be a plea in this day for its being obsolete; but as it rests on principles inherent in the very constitution and relationships of human nature, we had better accept it, without quarreling about long or short, thin or heavy, dark or white, coarse or fine. A just conception of 1 Cor. 11: 3, 11, 12, will

make us not only reverent toward God, but charitable towards each other. An old coffee-sack will answer if the relations to man and God and angel are adjusted and sustained by the Holy Spirit.

The Emphatic Diaglott does not differ from the best translations: "Her hair is given her *instead* of a covering." The word translated *instead* is a Greek term hard to catch and put in an English dress. It holds the sense, indicative of, representative of, so that our common version "*for* a covering," is as good as any, serving as a representative of something more spiritual, an added symbol of woman's relation to the race, and the sympathy and ministry of the higher world. So deep are the things of God, so vast, so intricate, so holy are our relations of life, and so wonderful and glorious and endless our destiny.

Union Deposit, Pa.

THE SOUL.

BY CHAS. M. YEAROUT.

In Four Chapters.—Chapter Three.

In *Truth Gleaner*, published at Waterloo, Iowa, issue of November, 1891, page 44, we have the following by the editor: "As a rule, the believers in the immortality of the soul are willing to stake their whole theory upon Gen. 2: 7, believing it says that God formed the body of the man of the dust of the ground, and put an immortal soul into that body . . . "And the Lord God formed man of the dust of the ground, and breathed into his nostrils the breath of life; and man became a living soul."

Here is a clear statement of the facts, and all we have to do, is to accept each statement as the truth, the whole truth, and nothing but the truth. It says that the Lord God formed man of the dust of the ground; therefore that which was formed out of the dust of the ground was the man,—not a body into which a man was to be put. The statement, "The Lord God formed man of the dust of the ground," must, in and of itself, be true; and the next statement, following the conjunction "and" is the statement of another truth, namely, that God "breathed into his,— the man's—nostrils the breath of life; and this caused the man that had already been formed out of the dust of the ground, to become a living (not an immortal) soul. . . . It is clear that the soul came out of the earth."

It is plain that the editor does not believe in the doctrine taught by the apostles, of an outward and inner man. His materialistic vision cannot take in the beautiful, sublime teachings of the Savior. "Though a man may kill the body, he cannot kill the soul." Matt. 10: 28. I do not stake my belief in the immortality of the soul on Genesis, or any part of the Old Testament, although there is nothing in it that condemns the immortality of the soul.

The mechanic formed a steam engine of the iron of the earth, and it possessed all the parts of a complete engine,—steam-chests, pistons, pit-mans, cylinders, escapements, levers, etc., but it is of no earthly use to any one. What is wrong with it? It has the form of a perfect engine, but, behold, it is dead; as was the man. The chests are filled with steam, and we have a living engine. It wends its way through the country at almost lightning speed, pulling an enormous load. I say the mechanic formed the engine of the iron of the earth, therefore, that which was formed out of the earth was the engine, not a body into which the engine was to be put. The statement, "The mechanic formed the engine of the earth, must, in and of itself, be true; and the mechanic or engineer put steam into it,—the engine's chests,—and this caused the engine that had al-

ready been formed out of the iron of the ground to become a living engine. It is clear that the steam came not out of the earth.

The writer seems to put considerable stress on "become," "become,—to pass from one state to another; by assuming or receiving new properties or qualities, additional matter, or a new character."—*Webster.* Hence, when the lifeless man received the properties of soul and breath, he lived. It is clear, that the properties of soul, and breath did not come from the earth, but from God. Steam is the motive power that causes the engine to move (live). Take it away, and the engine stops,—is dead. The soul of man is the active, motive power that causes the man to act,—live. Take it away, and the man is dead.

"Many believers in the immortality of the soul contend that the soul was breathed into man when he received the breath of life."—*Ibid., Jan. 1892, page 55.* Do we have any account of man having a soul prior to God's breathing into his nostrils the breath of life? Is it anywhere stated that he was a dead soul, or soul at all, prior to this? What is the meaning of soul (*pseuche*)? Was it ever properly translated anything but life, the opposite of death? Then the materialist doctrine, "that life, soul, spirit, is nothing but a mode of molecular motion, having no entitative character or existence separate from organisms," is erroneous and anti-scriptural, and its consequent doctrine that the soul dies,—molders back to earth,—teaches that life is dead or extinct. Hence, if God desires creatures to worship and glorify his name, outside of the heavenly hosts, he will have to make a new creation, for all life is dead,—extinct, for there is no life in the grave.

"It is said that God breathed into the beasts the breath of life; therefore when the breath of life was breathed into man, he received an immortal soul, which the beasts did not receive. Now let us try the same syllogism in relation to the woman. . . . It is not said that God breathed into the woman the breath of life; therefore when the breath of life was breathed into the man, he received an immortal soul, which the woman did not receive."—*Ibid, page 55.*

The above syllogism is weak in the extreme. Every one knows that the woman is above the brute creation; and is possessed of the nature and attributes of man, and was taken from man, hence is a part of man. Every one that is acquainted with Christ, and his precious teachings, knows that man is in possession of eternal life, and as soul means life, the soul is undying (John 5: 24; 3: 36; 6: 47-54; 10: 28; 1 John 5: 13.) Eternal is immortal,—without end,—and not subject to death. I am speaking of the children of God, for the sinner is now dead,—separated from God, and unless he repents and is converted to God, he will eventually forever be separated from God. "Whosoever liveth and believeth in Christ shall never die (never be separated from Christ), believest thou this?" John 11: 26; 6: 50. Does the Heavenly Master anywhere teach, that the beasts have everlasting life? Does he teach that they have passed from death unto life? Does the Bible anywhere teach, that the souls of the beasts will be saved? "We are not of them that draw back unto perdition; but of them that believe, to the saving of the soul." Heb. 10: 3. "And receive with meekness the engrafted word, which is able to save your souls," James 1: 21, was never spoken of beasts. Do the Scriptures teach that the souls of beasts shall "appear at the judgment seat of Christ, and not receive for that which they have done;" and "be rewarded according to their works?" If not, then why compare them with man, or the souls of men, the chief work of creation, created in the image and likeness of the eternal God, and possessed, in a certain degree,

Missionary and Tract Work Department.

"Upon the first day of the week, let every one of you lay by him in store as God hath prospered him, that there be no gatherings when I come."—1 Cor. 16: 2.

"Every man as he purposeth in his heart, so let him give. Not grudgingly or of necessity, for the Lord loveth a cheerful giver."—2 Cor. 9: 7.

HOW MUCH SHALL WE GIVE?

"Every man according to his ability." "Every one as God hath prospered him." "Every man, according as he purposeth in his heart, so let him give." "For if there be first a willing mind, it is accepted according to that a man hath, and not according to that he hath not."—2 Cor. 8: 12.

Organization of Missionary Committee.

DANIEL VANIMAN, Foreman, - - McPherson, Kans.
D. L. MILLER, Treasurer, - - Mt. Morris, Ill.
GALEN B. ROYER, Secretary, - - Mt. Morris, Ill.

Organization of Book and Tract Work.

S. W. HOOVER, Foreman, - - - Dayton, Ohio.
S. BOCK, Secretary and Treasurer, - Dayton, Ohio.

☞All donations intended for Missionary Work should be sent to GALEN B. ROYER, Mt. Morris, Ill.

☞All money for Tract Work should be sent to S. BOCK, Dayton, Ohio.

☞Money may be sent by Money Order, Registered Letter, or Drafts on New York or Chicago. Do not send personal checks, or drafts on interior towns, as it costs 15 cents to collect them.

☞Solicitors are requested to faithfully carry out the plan of Annual Meeting, that all our members be solicited to contribute at least twice a year for the Mission and Tract Work of the Church.

☞Notes for the Endowment Fund can be had by writing to the Secretary of either Work.

THE UNKIND WORDS.

CAN we not all peruse these truthful lines with profit:

If I had known in the morning,
How wearily all the day,
The word unkind
Would trouble my mind,
I said when you went away,
I had been more careful, darling,
Nor given you needless pain.
But we vex "our own,"
With look and tone,
We may never take back again.

For though in the quiet evening
You may give me the kiss of peace,
Yet, it might be,
That never for me
The pain of heart should cease.
How many go forth in the morning,
That never come home at night?
And hearts have broken
For harsh words spoken,
That sorrow can ne'er set right.

We have careful thoughts for the stranger,
And smiles for the sometime guest;
But oft for "our own"
The bitter tone, '
Though we love "our own" the best.
Ah! lips with the curve impatient!
Ah! brow with the look of scorn!
'Twere a cruel fate
Were the night too late
To undo the work of morn.

A FALLACY.

BY S. Z. SHARP.

WE have heard it advocated that no member of the church could be disfellowshipped, except for the crimes named in 1 Cor. 5: 11, which Scripture is as follows: "Now I have written unto you not to keep company, if any man that is called a brother be a fornicator, or covetous, or an idolater, or a railer, or a drunkard, or an extortioner; with such a one no not to eat."

The idea that we could not disown members except for the six crimes above named, being foreign to the general practice of our church, and I claim also opposed to the Gospel of Jesus Christ, the statement made a deep impression on my mind, for, if generally carried out, it would revolutionize our present church government. After careful study we are convinced that the above-named crimes do not include all for which members may be disowned. Our first proof is drawn from Matt. 18: 17: "If he neglect to hear the church, let him be unto thee as a heathen man and a publican."

This Scripture is certainly explicit enough to be obeyed. It is evident that a man cannot be a Christian and a heathen at the same time,—"to drink the cup of the Lord and the cup of devils." 1 Cor. 10: 21. In all our research we have found no testimony which does not decide in favor of excommunication in case Matt. 18: 15–17 is violated.

The true Christian church, ever since the beginning of the Christian era, has held the view that the above passage in Matthew taught excommunication and practiced accordingly, as we do now, and held the opposite view to be a fallacy.

Our second proof is drawn from 2 Thess. 3: 6, "Now we, command you, brethren, in the name of our Lord Jesus Christ, that ye withdraw yourselves from every brother that walketh disorderly, and not after the tradition which he received of us."

Here is a plain command to withdraw fellowship for disorderly conduct and no allusion is made to 1 Cor. 5: 11. Among the disorderly acts are named, "not working" and being "busybodies." The instruction is, "If any man obey not our word by this epistle, note that man, and have no company with him, that he may be ashamed."

Disorderly conduct would include lying. "For without are dogs, and sorcerers, and whoremongers, and murderers, and idolaters, and whosoever loveth and maketh a lie." Rev. 22: 15. "Also let none of you suffer as a thief." 1 Pet. 4: 15. Theft and robbery in the decalogue are classed with idolatry, lying, murder, adultery, and covetousness. Embezzlement is both a theft and a breach of trust, or an aggravated form of stealing.

From the above facts and Scripture proofs, it must be evident to any unbiased mind, that the church is authorized to disown members for other crimes than those named in 1 Cor. 5: 11, and failing to do so, she violates the plain command in 2 Thess. 3: 6.

McPherson, Kans.

THE CHILDREN'S MISSION.

BY MARY M. GIBSON.

Dear Children:

I SEAT myself this beautiful Wednesday morning to write you again. The sun is shining brightly, the little birds are pouring forth their lovely song, and all nature seems aglow with rapture. The earth is robed in its carpet of beautiful green, trees are putting forth their buds and blossoms and the wild flowers are springing forth from mother earth to gladden the heart of many a sweet child, that is roaming here and there over field and dale. While gathering some of them, we tread upon many that have not yet come forth. God has appointed a time for some much earlier than others. Thus we may have the full benefit of his wise provisions, to teach us of his goodness every day and hour we live.

I am made to wonder how many of us realize this fact, when we are out in the groves, fields, and meadows, searching for his blessed treasures! Can we make ourselves as bright and as beautiful as the pretty green plant and its lovely sweet flower? Yes, indeed we can, by the grace of God beaming forth in our very life. Yea, we have a much better chance than the little flower we tread upon, for God has given us wisdom and understanding and a whole life-time without intermission to make it so. May I ask you the question now: Are you doing this with all the power God has given you? Come, dear children, seek that you may excel in all the good things you possibly can. The apostle Paul tells us to do these things and why not you as well as grown people?

We learn many good lessons from you, when you thus direct yourself. Do you ever think of giving those lovely flowers you have plucked to another that they, too, might enjoy a portion of your pleasure? When you did so, have they not rendered unto you a pleasant "Thank you"? Just so, dear children, are you a tender plant for your Heavenly Father, and why should you not gladden him with your service by blooming forth into his glorious kingdom? Every soul that is made a new creature in Christ's kingdom, is a lovely blossom in his vineyard, and if not dwarfed, will bring forth good fruit to his name's honor and glory. Many of you say, "I am too small." Ah, the very hairs of our heads are all numbered. How small are they, compared to your soul, the very life you now live. Jesus is constantly watching you, in all you do or say, and do you know you often grieve him with your naughty words and actions? Ah, yes, dear children, we grieve him to do those things, and we should be very careful how or what we say and do in his sight, for he knows us every one, and is grieved because the offense we give him is as lasting as eternity, if we do not repent. If we do this, he is merciful and good to forgive. We should watch closely so as not to grieve Jesus, who has done more for us than we ever can do for him. No matter how much good, or how grievous anything may be, or how heavy a load to bear, or how burdensome to carry, he will be our constant helper, if we only ask and trust him. Remember he keeps sight of his hidden plants that have been stripped of their fragrant blossoms and green leaves, to seek shelter of mother earth, to prepare to come forth again by the aid of the warm rays of the sun, and the spring showers, after the autumn chills and wintery blasts have all disappeared, that they may gladden our hearts again and cheer us on our way Zionward. Is there not beauty for us in his hidden treasures? He sees and knows every one of us, and wants us to be his own dear children.

Every Sabbath we gather in the Lord's house, to learn of the precious truths contained in his Blessed Book. Sometimes our class is small; then again it is large, but we must try, by the help of God, just as hard to teach two or three, as thirty or forty. That is my experience. Some may say, "I cannot teach that many." Well, perhaps, you would be astonished to see the close attention given while reciting. It would do you good to hear the little three and four year old children, recite verses and answer questions. The warm weather and summer sunshine bring a larger number of attendants to the Lord's house that they may sit under the droppings of the sanctuary. Parents, come; we invite you to come and bring your children to the Sunday-school. They will learn that it is food for the soul, and the Bread of Life, to become children of his kingdom. It will help them to seek him early, to find him, and to remember their Creator in the days of their youth.

I love dearly to gather the children around me here on earth, and am made to wonder how it will be in eternity. Will they love to gather around me there, and twine their little arms about my neck? I never want to be any other way than to love the children. They are the greatest treasure of this world, and Jesus has said, "Theirs is the kingdom of heaven." Blessed be their names, and hallowed be their influence everywhere!

If the Lord will, I intend to go to our Annual Meeting this year. I want to go prepared to receive any donations that you may feel to give for

Missionary and Tract Work Department.

"Upon the first day of the week, let every one of you lay by him in store as God hath prospered him, that there be no gatherings when I come."—1 Cor. 16: 2.

"Every man as he purposeth in his heart, so let him give. Not grudgingly or of necessity, for the Lord loveth a cheerful giver."—2 Cor. 9: 7.

HOW MUCH SHALL WE GIVE?

"Every man according to his ability." "Every one as God hath prospered him." "Every man, according as he purposeth in his heart, so let him give." "For if there be first a willing mind, it is accepted according to that a man hath, and not according to that he hath not."—2 Cor. 8: 12.

Organization of Missionary Committee.

DANIEL VANIMAN, Foreman, - - McPherson, Kans.
D. L. MILLER, Treasurer, - - - Mt. Morris, Ill.
GALEN B. ROYER, Secretary, - - Mt. Morris, Ill.

Organization of Book and Tract Work.

S. W. HOOVER, Foreman, - - - Dayton, Ohio.
S. BOCK, Secretary and Treasurer, - Dayton, Ohio.

☞All donations intended for Missionary Work should be sent to GALEN B. ROYER, Mt. Morris, Ill.

☞All money for Tract Work should be sent to S. BOCK, Dayton, Ohio.

☞Money may be sent by Money Order, Registered Letter, or Drafts on New York or Chicago. Do not send personal checks, or drafts on interior towns, as it costs 25 cents to collect them.

☞Solicitors are requested to faithfully carry out the plan of Annual Meeting, that all our members be solicited to contribute at least twice a year for the Mission and Tract Work of the Church.

☞Notes for the Endowment Fund can be had by writing to the Secretary of either Work.

THE UNKIND WORDS.

CAN we not all peruse these truthful lines with profit:

If I had known in the morning,
How wearily all the day,
The word unkind
Would trouble my mind,
I said when you went away,
I had been more careful, darling,
Nor given you needless pain.
But we vex "our own,"
With look and tone,
We may never take back again.

For though in the quiet evening
You may give me the kiss of peace,
Yet, it might be,
That never for me
The path of heart should cease.
How many go forth in the morning,
That never come home at night?
And hearts have broken
For harsh words spoken,
That sorrow can ne'er set right.

We have careful thoughts for the stranger,
And smiles for the sometime guest;
But oft for "our own"
The bitter tone,'
Though we love "our own" the best.
Ah! lips with the curve impatient!
Ah! brow with the look of scorn!
'Twere a cruel fate
Were the night too late
To undo the work of morn.

A FALLACY.

BY S. Z. SHARP.

WE have heard it advocated that no member of the church could be disfellowshipped, except for the crimes named in 1 Cor. 5: 11, which Scripture is as follows: "Now I have written unto you not to keep company, if any man that is called a brother be a fornicator, or covetous, or an idolater, or a railer, or a drunkard, or an extortioner; with such a one no not to eat."

The idea that we could not disown members except for the six crimes above named, being foreign to the general practice of our church, and I claim also opposed to the Gospel of Jesus Christ, the statement made a deep impression on my mind, for, if generally carried out, it would revolutionize our present church government. After careful study we are convinced that the above-named crimes do not include all for which members may be disowned. Our first proof is drawn from Matt. 18: 17: "If he neglect to hear the church, let him be unto thee as a heathen man and a publican."

This Scripture is certainly explicit enough to be obeyed. It is evident that a man cannot be a Christian and a heathen at the same time,—"to drink the cup of the Lord and the cup of devils." 1 Cor. 10: 21. In all our research we have found no testimony which does not decide in favor of excommunication in case Matt. 18: 15–17 is violated.

The true Christian church, ever since the beginning of the Christian era, has held the view that the above passage in Matthew taught excommunication and practiced accordingly, as we do now, and held the opposite view to be a fallacy.

Our second proof is drawn from 2 Thess. 3: 6, "Now we, command you, brethren, in the name of our Lord Jesus Christ, that ye withdraw yourselves from every brother that walketh disorderly, and not after the tradition which he received of us."

Here is a plain command to withdraw fellowship for disorderly conduct and no allusion is made to 1 Cor. 5: 11. Among the disorderly acts are named, "not working" and being "busybodies." The instruction is, "If any man obey not our word by this epistle, note that man, and have no company with him, that he may be ashamed."

Disorderly conduct would include lying. "For without are dogs, and sorcerers, and whoremongers, and murderers, and idolaters, and whosoever loveth and maketh a lie." Rev. 22: 15. "Also let none of you suffer as a thief." 1 Pet. 4: 15. Theft and robbery in the decalogue are classed with idolatry, lying, murder, adultery, and covetousness. Embezzlement is both a theft and a breach of trust, or an aggravated form of stealing.

From the above facts and Scripture proofs, it must be evident to any unbiased mind, that the church is authorized to disown members for other crimes than those named in 1 Cor. 5: 11, and failing to do so, she violates the plain command in 2 Thess. 3: 6.

McPherson, Kans.

THE CHILDREN'S MISSION.

BY MARY M. GIBSON.

Dear Children:

I BEGIN myself this beautiful Wednesday morning to write you again. The sun is shining brightly, the little birds are pouring forth their lovely song, and all nature seems aglow with rapture. The earth is robed in its carpet of beautiful green, trees are putting forth their buds and blossoms and the wild flowers are springing forth from mother earth to gladden the heart of many a sweet child, that is roaming here and there over field and dale. While gathering some of them, we tread upon many that have not yet come forth. God has appointed a time for some much earlier than others. Thus we may have the full benefit of his wise provisions, to teach us of his goodness every day and hour we live.

I am made to wonder how many of us realize this fact, when we are out in the groves, fields, and meadows, searching for his blessed treasures! Can we make ourselves as bright and as beautiful as the pretty green plant and its lovely sweet flower? Yes, indeed we can, by the grace of God beaming forth in our very life. Yea, we have a much better chance than the little flower we tread upon, for God has given us wisdom and understanding and a whole life-time without intermission to make it so. May I ask you the question now: Are you doing this with all the power God has given you? Come, dear children, seek that you may excel in all the good things you possibly can. The apostle Paul tells us to do these things and why not you as well as grown people?

We learn many good lessons from you, when you thus direct yourself. Do you ever think of giving those lovely flowers you have plucked to another that they, too, might enjoy a portion of your pleasure? When you did so, have they not rendered unto you a pleasant "Thank you"? Just so, dear children, are you a tender plant for your Heavenly Father, and why should you not gladden him with your service by blooming forth into his glorious kingdom? Every soul that is made a new creature in Christ's kingdom, is a lovely blossom in his vineyard, and if not dwarfed, will bring forth good fruit to his name's honor and glory. Many of you say, "I am too small." Ah, the very hairs of our heads are all numbered. How small are they, compared to your soul, the very life you now live. Jesus is constantly watching you, in all you do or say, and do you know you often grieve him with your naughty words and actions? Ah, yes, dear children, we grieve him to do those things, and we should be very careful how or what we say and do in his sight, for he knows us every one, and is grieved because the offense we give him is as lasting as eternity, if we do not repent. If we do this, he is merciful and good to forgive. We should watch closely so as not to grieve Jesus, who has done more for us than we ever can do for him. No matter how much good, or how grievous anything may be, or how heavy a load to bear, or how burdensome to carry, he will be our constant helper, if we only ask and trust him. Remember he keeps sight of his hidden plants that have been stripped of their fragrant blossoms and green leaves, to seek shelter of mother earth, to prepare to come forth again by the aid of the warm rays of the sun, and the spring showers, after the autumn chills and wintery blasts have all disappeared, that they may gladden our hearts again and cheer us on our way Zionward. Is there not beauty for us in his hidden treasures? He sees and knows every one of us, and wants us to be his own dear children.

Every Sabbath we gather in the Lord's house, to learn of the precious truths contained in his Blessed Book. Sometimes our class is small; then again it is large, but we must try, by the help of God, just as hard to teach two or three, as thirty or forty. That is my experience. Some may say, "I cannot teach that many." Well, perhaps, you would be astonished to see the close attention given on while reciting. It would do you good to hear the little three and four year old children, recite verses and answer questions. The warm weather and summer sunshine bring a larger number of attendants to the Lord's house that they may sit under the droppings of the sanctuary. Parents, come; we invite you to come and bring your children to the Sunday-school. They will learn that it is food for the soul, and the Bread of Life, to become children of his kingdom. It will help them to seek him early, to find him, and to remember their Creator in the days of their youth.

I love dearly to gather the children around me here on earth, and am made to wonder how it will be in eternity. Will they love to cluster around me there, and twine their little arms about my neck? I never want to be any other way than to love the children. They are the greatest treasure of this world, and Jesus has said, "Theirs is the kingdom of heaven." Blessed be their names, and hallowed be their influence everywhere!

If the Lord will, I intend to go to our Annual Meeting this year. I want to go prepared to receive any donations that you may feel to give for

QUERIES.

THE DISTRICT CLERKS, who have not yet sent in the queries from their respective Districts to the Annual Meeting, will please do so at once, so they can be printed according to the instructions of last Annual Meeting. The time is short and the work important. A number of Districts have not yet been heard from.

IN this public manner we thank Bro. I. D. Parker for his early, well-prepared article concerning Bro. Geo. Irvin, trusting that in this way we may also impress others with the propriety of favoring our readers with similar notices, when elders and ministers of general usefulness pass away. Keep this suggestion in mind and at any time, when one of our public workers is called to the reward beyond, let us have a well-written sketch of his life and labors to encourage others who are engaged in the conflict with sin and Satan.

WE learn with pleasure that the West Dayton, Ohio, church is moving along encouragingly. On Saturday, April 30, they held their quarterly council, and all the business was pleasantly transacted. They decided to erect an addition to their church-house, for the accommodation of the Sunday-school children. They report an active force of officers and teachers, and that the number of regular attendants has increased considerably, the past four months. They also held an election for a minister. W. I. T. Hoover was chosen to fill this important position. S. W. Hoover will represent the church at Annual Meeting, and he and S. Book at District Meeting. They also decided to hold a love-feast in the near future.

SPECIAL RAILROAD ARRANGEMENTS.

THE BURLINGTON ROUTE has made special arrangements for the accommodation of our Brethren and friends who desire to visit in Northern Illinois on their way to the Conference at Cedar Rapids, Iowa. Half-fare permits for the round trip have been sent to all our ministers, enabling them to stop off when and where they wish. A great many have expressed a desire to visit Mt. Morris, and we shall be glad to have them with us. Come and you will be made welcome. The Burlington will place tickets on sale east of Chicago for the accommodation of those who want to come here and we trust a great many of our brethren and sisters will come this way. The Examining Committee of our Tract Work will meet here on the 25th inst., and we cordially invite others, who can do so, to come and see us.

A special train, composed of chair and day cars, will leave here on Saturday, June 4, and will be run according to the following time table:

Leave Forreston,	10:30 A. M.
" Maryland,	10:40 A. M.
" Mt. Morris,	11:00 A. M.
" Oregon,	11:10 A. M.
" Stratford,	11:25 A. M.
" Polo,	11:35 A. M.
" Hazelhurst,	11:45 A. M.
" Milledgeville,	11:53 A. M.
" Chadwick,	12:05 P. M.
" Daggetts,	12:15 P. M.
" Savanna,	12:30 P. M.
" Thomson,	1:10 P. M.
" Fulton,	1:25 P. M.
Arrive CEDAR RAPIDS,	5:00 P. M.

At the close of the Conference the special train will return to Mt. Morris, thus affording excellent opportunities to go to and return from Annual Meeting. As the Burlington has made this arrangement for the accommodation of our brethren and sisters, we trust it will be generally appreciated, and that all who can will take the special train. It will afford us a most pleasant way of going to and from Annual Meeting, and by taking this train, we will show the Burlington management that we fully appreciate its efforts in our behalf.

The fare for the round trip from all the stations named is $3.89 or a little over one cent a mile, a very low rate, indeed.

To reach Mt. Morris from Chicago, go to the Union Depot, Canal Street. Two trains leave daily for this place, at 8:50 A. M. and 6:10 P. M. The first runs through to Mt. Morris without change. On the latter passengers change at Oregon.   D. L. M.

OUR DISTRICT MEETING.

ON Monday, May 9th, a number of us left Mt. Morris en route for the District Meeting of Northern Illinois, held with the Brethren of the Milledgeville church. At Oregon our company was increased, but when we reached Polo our car was completely filled, so much so that some were obliged to stand. The day was a very disagreeable one, as it was raining most of the time and the roads were extremely muddy. We reached the Milledgeville church, which is two and one-half miles from the village of Milledgeville, at 4 P. M. A feast had been appointed for the evening, and the self-examination services had already commenced when we arrived. The feast was a very enjoyable one and was well attended from all parts of Northern Illinois, there being about twenty-five ministers present in addition to a number of other members. Bro. Daniel Dierdorff officiated.

The District Meeting opened the next morning at 8 A. M., with brethren Daniel Dierdorff, Moderator; D. L. Miller, Reading Clerk; Joseph Amick and Galen B. Royer, Writing Clerks. All the churches were represented by delegates with the exception of one in Wisconsin.

As is our custom, all the queries were then handed in and read, showing considerable business to come before the Meeting.

The missionary work and reports were first taken up. Bro. Levi Trostle reported that during the last year the District had raised for the General Missionary fund $985.15. Bro. C. P. Rowland's report showed that for home mission work he had collected $595.02; for the Chicago house, $405.25, and for the house at Sterling $278.30. This was followed by a report from Bro. D. R. Price who had received from the churches, for the care of the poor in the District, $1,148.40. The last report was made by Bro. Joseph Amick in behalf of the Old People's and Orphans' Home, showing that for the purpose of establishing the Home $5,963.65 had been collected. These reports were well arranged, clearly presented, and were exceedingly interesting and encouraging. They showed that during the last year Northern Illinois had raised for these various charitable and missionary purposes over $9,300.00, or, in round numbers, not far from $10,000 And from the general expression of the Meeting we would judge that not one, who helped to raise this amount, misses what he paid. We are glad to see our churches coming forward in this respect. The causes for which the money was raised are noble ones and we feel that God is blessing the churches in their liberal efforts.

Reports were made of the work at Chicago and Sterling, showing that considerable is being accomplished in these two cities, with encouraging prospects before them. Some reports were presented from other points, indicating the need of more missionary work, and the Meeting took steps to supply the calls in Wisconsin and other localities.

The Meeting now proceeded to consider the queries that came up from the churches. Four papers asked the Meeting to take the necessary steps to hold ministerial meetings in connection with the District Meetings. It was decided to hold our first ministerial meeting the day before the next District Meeting, and a committee of three brethren was appointed to prepare and publish the program.

A query concerning the Columbian Exposition was discussed, but failed to pass the Meeting. The Meeting then adjourned for dinner.

During the intermission the delegates retired and elected two members to serve on the Standing Committee. When the meeting resumed work at 1 P. M., the delegates reported elders Edmund Forney and D. B. Eby as the ones selected for that purpose. A number of other appointments were made, which we will not take space to give at this time.

A call was made for the Annual Meeting in 1893, or as soon thereafter as it can be granted.

Several other questions were before the Meeting, and discussed in the best of spirits. The Trustees of the Old Peoples' and Orphans' Home were authorized to push their enterprise, and the Meeting endorsed the plan of governing and operating the Home which the Trustees had drawn up and presented for consideration.

The Home Mission Board called for $800.00 to carry on their work during the next year. The amount was cheerfully appropriated.

It was also decided that the Chicago meeting-house, contemplated, should be deeded to the Trustees of the Chicago church, and the Sterling meeting-house be deeded to the Rock Creek congregation. The Mission Board was also instructed to incorporate under the laws of the State of Illinois, and thus better prepare themselves for holding church property.

The Meeting closed at 4:15, having been one of the very best District Meetings we ever witnessed. We never witnessed a better spirit in any Conference. We think that all the brethren went away greatly strengthened and encouraged, and fully resolved to enter upon the work of the coming year with renewed energy.

The Brethren of Milledgeville entertained us nobly, and provided for the wants of all who attended in a most satisfactory manner. The bad weather was against them, but it did not dampen their zeal.

Mr. A. H. Yancey, traveling agent of the Chicago, Burlington & Northern railroad also attended the meeting and did a favor that our people will not soon forget. He arranged for the 6 o'clock passenger train to stop opposite the meeting-house and let about one hundred of us get aboard without the inconvenience of going two and one-half miles to the station. Mr. Yancey has our thanks.

We reached home safely, feeling that the Lord was with us in our deliberations as well as our journey, and pray his blessings to rest upon the work that has been done.   J. H. M.

QUERIES.

THE DISTRICT CLERKS, who have not yet sent in the queries from their respective Districts to the Annual Meeting, will please do so at once, so they can be printed according to the instructions of last Annual Meeting. The time is short and the work important. A number of Districts have not yet been heard from.

In this public manner we thank Bro. I. D. Parker for his early, well-prepared article concerning Bro. Geo. Irvin, trusting that in this way we may also impress others with the propriety of favoring our readers with similar notices, when elders and ministers of general usefulness pass away. Keep this suggestion in mind and at any time, when one of our public workers is called to the reward beyond, let us have a well-written sketch of his life and labors to encourage others who are engaged in the conflict with sin and Satan.

We learn with pleasure that the West Dayton, Ohio, church is moving along encouragingly. On Saturday, April 30, they held their quarterly council, and all the business was pleasantly transacted. They decided to erect an addition to their church-house, for the accommodation of the Sunday-school children. They report an active force of officers and teachers, and that the number of regular attendants has increased considerably the past four months. They also held an election for a minister. W. I. T. Hoover was chosen to fill this important position. S. W. Hoover will represent the church at Annual Meeting, and he and S. Bock at District Meeting. They also decided to hold a love-feast in the near future.

SPECIAL RAILROAD ARRANGEMENTS.

THE BURLINGTON ROUTE has made special arrangements for the accommodation of our Brethren and friends who desire to visit in Northern Illinois on their way to the Conference at Cedar Rapids, Iowa. Half-fare permits for the round trip have been sent to all our ministers, enabling them to stop off when and where they wish. A great many have expressed a desire to visit Mt. Morris, and we shall be glad to have them with us. Come and you will be made welcome. The Burlington will place tickets on sale east of Chicago for the accommodation of those who want to come here and we trust a great many of our brethren and sisters will come this way. The Examining Committee of our Tract Work will meet here on the 25th inst., and we cordially invite others, who can do so, to come and see us.

A special train, composed of chair and day cars, will leave here on Saturday, June 4, and will be run according to the following time table:

Leave Forreston,	10:30 A. M.
"　Maryland,	10:40 A. M.
"　Mt. Morris,	11:00 A. M.
"　Oregon,	11:10 A. M.
"　Stratford,	11:25 A. M.
"　Polo,	11:35 A. M.
"　Hazelhurst,	11:45 A. M.
"　Milledgeville,	11:53 A. M.
"　Chadwick,	12:05 P. M.
"　Daggetts,	12:15 P. M.
"　Savanna,	12:30 P. M.
"　Thomson,	1:10 P. M.
"　Fulton,	1:25 P. M.
Arrive CEDAR RAPIDS,	5:00 P. M.

At the close of the Conference the special train will return to Mt. Morris, thus affording excellent opportunities to go to and return from Annual Meeting. As the Burlington has made this arrangement for the accommodation of our breth-

ren and sisters, we trust it will be generally appreciated, and that all who can will take the special train. It will afford us a most pleasant way of going to and from Annual Meeting, and by taking this train, we will show the Burlington management that we fully appreciate its efforts in our behalf.

The fare for the round trip from all the stations named is $3.89 or a little over one cent a mile, a very low rate, indeed.

To reach Mt. Morris from Chicago, go to the Union Depot, Canal Street. Two trains leave daily for this place, at 8:50 A. M. and 6:10 P. M. The first runs through to Mt. Morris without change. On the latter passengers change at Oregon.　　　　　　　　　　　　　　　D. L. M.

OUR DISTRICT MEETING.

ON Monday, May 9th, a number of us left Mt. Morris en route for the District Meeting of Northern Illinois, held with the Brethren of the Milledgeville church. At Oregon our company was increased, but when we reached Polo our car was completely filled, so much so that some were obliged to stand. The day was a very disagreeable one, as it was raining most of the time and the roads were extremely muddy. We reached the Milledgeville church, which is two and one-half miles from the village of Milledgeville, at 4 P. M. A feast had been appointed for the evening, and the self-examination services had already commenced when we arrived. The feast was a very enjoyable one and was well attended from all parts of Northern Illinois, there being about twenty-five ministers present in addition to a number of other members. Bro. Daniel Dierdorff officiated.

The District Meeting opened the next morning at 8 A. M., with brethren Daniel Dierdorff, Moderator; D. L. Miller, Reading Clerk; Joseph Amick and Galen B. Royer, Writing Clerks. All the churches were represented by delegates with the exception of one in Wisconsin.

As is our custom, all the queries were then handed in and read, showing considerable business to come before the Meeting.

The missionary work and reports were first taken up. Bro. Levi Trostle reported that during the last year the District had raised for the General Missionary fund $935.15. Bro. C. P. Rowland's report showed that for home mission work he had collected $596.02; for the Chicago house, $405.25, and for the house at Sterling $278.30. This was followed by a report from Bro. D. R. Price who had received from the churches, for the care of the poor in the District, $1,148.40. The last report was made by Bro. Joseph Amick in behalf of the Old People's and Orphans' Home, showing that for the purpose of establishing the Home $5,963.65 had been collected. These reports were well arranged, clearly presented, and were exceedingly interesting and encouraging. They showed that during the last year Northern Illinois had raised for these various charitable and missionary purposes over $9,300.00, or, in round numbers, not far from $10,000 And from the general expression of the Meeting we would judge that not one, who helped to raise this amount, misses what he paid. We are glad to see our churches coming forward in this respect. The causes for which the money was raised are noble ones and we feel that God is blessing the church so in their liberal efforts.

Reports were made of the work at Chicago and Sterling, showing that considerable is being accomplished in these two cities, with encouraging prospects before them. Some reports were presented from other points, indicating the need of more missionary work, and the Meeting took steps to supply the calls in Wisconsin and other localities.

The Meeting now proceeded to consider the queries that came up from the churches. Four papers asked the Meeting to take the necessary steps to hold ministerial meetings in connection with the District Meetings. It was decided to hold our first ministerial meeting the day before the next District Meeting, and a committee of three brethren was appointed to prepare and publish the program.

A query concerning the Columbian Exposition was discussed, but failed to pass the Meeting. The Meeting then adjourned for dinner.

During the intermission the delegates retired and elected two members to serve on the Standing Committee. When the meeting resumed work at 1 P. M., the delegates reported elders Edmund Forney and D. B. Eby as the ones selected for that purpose. A number of other appointments were made, which we will not take space to give at this time.

A call was made for the Annual Meeting in 1893, or as soon thereafter as it can be granted.

Several other questions were before the Meeting, and discussed in the best of spirits. The Trustees of the Old Peoples' and Orphans' Home were authorized to push their enterprise, and the Meeting endorsed the plan of governing and operating the Home which the Trustees had drawn up and presented for consideration.

The Home Mission Board called for $800.00 to carry on their work during the next year. The amount was cheerfully appropriated.

It was also decided that the Chicago meeting-house, contemplated, should be deeded to the Trustees of the Chicago church, and the Sterling meeting-house be deeded to the Rock Creek congregation. The Mission Board was also instructed to incorporate under the laws of the State of Illinois, and thus better prepare themselves for holding church property.

The Meeting closed at 4:15, having been one of the very best District Meetings we ever attended. We never witnessed a better spirit in any Conference. We think that all the brethren went away greatly strengthened and encouraged, and fully resolved to enter upon the work of the coming year with renewed energy.

The Brethren of Milledgeville entertained us nobly, and provided for the wants of all who attended in a most satisfactory manner. The bad weather was against them, but it did not dampen their zeal.

Mr. A. H. Yancey, traveling agent of the Chicago, Burlington & Northern railroad also attended the meeting and did a favor that our people will not soon forget. He arranged for the 6 o'clock passenger train to stop opposite the meeting-house and let about one hundred of us get aboard without the inconvenience of going two and one-half miles to the station. Mr. Yancey has our thanks.

We reached home safely, feeling that the Lord was with us in our deliberations as well as our journey, and pray his blessings to rest upon the work that has been done.　　　　　　　J. H. M.

WANTED—A MINISTER.

[Our people do not have to depend upon hired pastors, yet it may do some of them good to learn of the troubles other churches must sometimes endure, in order to obtain a very much needed shepherd.]

We have been without a pastor
Some eighteen months or more,
And though candidates are plenty—
We've had at least a score,
All of them "tip-top preachers,"
Or so their letters ran—
We are just as far as ever
From settling on the man.

The first who came among us
By no means was the worst,
But then we did not think of him
Because he was the first;
It being quite the custom
To sacrifice a few,
Before the church in earnest,
Determines what to do.

There was a smart young fellow
With serious, earnest way,
Who, but for one great blunder,
Had surely won the day;
Who left so good impression,
On Monday one or two
Went round among the people,
To see if he would do.

The pious, goodly portion,
Had not a fault to find;
His clear and searching preaching
They thought the very kind,
And all went smooth and pleasant,
Until they heard the views
Of some influential sinners
Who rent the highest pews.

On these, his pungent sealing
Made but a sorry hit;
The cost of Gospel teaching
Was quite too tight to fit.
Of course his fate was settled,
Attend, ye parsons all!
And preach to please the sinners,
If you would get a call.

Next came a spruce young dandy
Who wore his hair too long,
Another's coat was shabby,
And his voice not over strong;
And one New Haven student
Was worse than all those,
We couldn't hear the sermon
For thinking of his nose.

Then, wearying of candidates,
We looked the country through,
'Mid doctors and professors,
To find one that would do.
And after much discussion
On who should bear the ark,
With tolerable agreement,
We fixed on Dr. Park.

Here then we thought it settled,
But were amazed to find
Our flattering invitation,
Respectfully declined;
We turned to Dr. Hopkins
To help us in the lurch,
Who strangely thought that college
Had claims above "our church."

Next we dispatched committees,
By twos and threes, to urge
The labors for a Sabbath
Of the Rev. Shallow Splurge.
He came—a marked sensation,
So wonderful his style,
Followed the creaking of his boots
As he passed up the aisle.

His tones were so affecting,
His gesture so divine,
A lady fainted in the hymn,
Before the second line.
And on that day he gave us,
In accents clear and loud,
The greatest prayer ever addressed
To an enlightened crowd.

He preached a double sermon,
And gave us angel's food,
On such a lovely topic,
"The joys of solitude."

All full of sweet descriptions,
Of flowers and pearly streams,
Of warbling birds and moon-lit groves
And golden sunset beams;

Of faith and true repentance,
He nothing had to say,
He rounded all the corners,
And smoothed the rugged way;
Managed with great adroitness,
To entertain and please,
And leave the sinner's conscience
Completely at its ease.

Six hundred is the salary
We gave in former days,
We thought it very liberal,
And found it hard to raise;
But where we took the paper,
We had no need to urge,
To raise a cool two thousand
For the Rev. Shallow Splurge.

In vain were all our efforts,
We had no chance at all,
We found ten city churches
Had given him a call;
And he in prayerful waiting,
Was keeping all in tow,
But where they bid the highest,
'Twas whispered he would go.

And now, good Christian brothers,
We ask your earnest prayers
That God would send a shepherd,
To guide our church affairs:
With this clear understanding,
A man to meet our views
Must preach to-please the sinners,
And fill the vacant pews.

A RECOGNITION OF MERIT.

MR. W. S. REICHARD, Secretary of the Executive Committee of Arrangements for the Annual Conference of the Brethren, held at Hagerstown, Md., May 28 to June 4, 1891, has written upon authority of the Committee the following letter to Mr. E. F. Bond, Division Passenger Agent of the Baltimore and Ohio Railroad Company, who represented that Company in perfecting arrangements for the transportation of Brethren to the Conference. Mr. Reichard's letter is dated at Hagerstown, Md., April 26, last, and reads as follows:

"It is with extreme pleasure that in summing up and closing our business as the Executive Committee of Arrangements for the Annual Conference of the German Baptists, or Brethren, held at Hagerstown, Md., May 28 to June 4, 1891, I am authorized, as Secretary of that Committee, to notify the officials of the Baltimore and Ohio Railroad that a vote of thanks has been extended to them for the thoroughly efficient and masterly manner in which your Company handled the Brethren and their families attending the Conference from points both on and off its System, both going and returning, and take pride in recommending the Baltimore and Ohio System to the Brethren at large, believing that their elegantly equipped train service, the courteous treatment of their gentlemanly officials and their prompt and rapid transit will give them comfort and satisfaction.   Respectfully yours,
W. S. REICHARD,
Secretary.

Mr. Bond has acknowledged receipt of the letter with a kind and courteous note.

THE GRAVE OF THE INFIDEL COUNTESS.

WE have before us a photograph, just received from abroad, of a section of a grave-yard in Hanover. It is a winter scene apparently; the great trees are leafless, the sky dull and leaden, and an appreciable gloom has settled down over this "city of the dead." Directly in the foreground is a somewhat pretentious monument, composed of a huge block of granite, resting upon a square base of the same material, to which it is secured by heavy iron clamps, the whole thing built evidently with an idea of great permanency. Upon one of the sides is this most singular inscription, "This burial place, purchased to all eternity, must never be opened." But Nature has defied art, and wrenched the great blocks of stone asunder, and the monument that was to endure to eternity is at present an unsightly ruin.

What is the history of this remarkable grave, with its strange inscription? Many years ago, there died in the City of Hanover a young Countess, of pronounced infidel proclivities. She denied the doctrine of the resurrection in toto, and perhaps in a vain effort to defy any supernatural power that she thought might have a possible existence, she ordered that her body should be laid beneath the solid, and, in her judgment, impregnable structure our picture represents. Her wishes were strictly carried out, and there seemed a reasonable expectation that the pile would remain intact for many generations at least, and the bones of the skeptical countess rest in the oblivion she desired. But it was strangely ordered otherwise. A tiny seed shared this woman's resting place, and in its resurrection might had burst its shell, sent its small roots into the ground, and slowly gathering strength and proportions with the years, had wrenched open its prison doors, severed in twain the massive granite slabs, and having reached the light had spread itself heavenward, until it has become a great tree. The people of Hanover regard it with almost a superstitious awe, and tell with bated breath the tale of the wicked Countess and her futile efforts to defeat God's laws.

CORRESPONDENCE.

"Write what thou seest, and send it unto the churches."

Church News solicited for this Department. If you have had a good meeting, send a report of it, so that others may rejoice with you. In writing give name of church, County and State. Be brief. Notes of Travel should be as short as possible. Land Advertisements are not solicited for this Department. We have an advertising page, and, if necessary, will issue supplements.

A Report.

FOR the satisfaction of those who may be curious to know something about the nature of the answers that have been sent in response to my "Favor Asked," and for the purpose of showing, approximately, the condition of, and the interest taken in the singing in the congregations of our church, I make this report. This includes all the answers received to date, and it is not likely that any more will be sent in now.

Some of the letters received answered all the questions asked and others answered only some of them. The following are the churches heard from:

Rock River church, Franklin Grove, Ill.; Girard, Ill.; Ephrata, Pa.; Lititz, Pa.; Scalp Level, Pa.; Rockton, Pa.; Duncanaville, Pa.; Walnut Grove church, Johnstown, Pa.; Pioneer, Ohio; Covington, Ohio; Mahoning church, Columbiana, Ohio; New Philadelphia, Ohio; Lexington church, Samantha, Ohio; Ridgeway, Ind.; Pyrmont, Ind.; Dego, Ind.; Montgomery church, Hilledale, Ind.; New Haven church; Sebiton, Mich.; Monad church, Adrian, Mo.; Warrensburgh, Mo.; Ergo, Mo.; Cherokee church, Monmouth, Kans.; Pleasant View church, Booth, Kans.; Ozawkie, Kans.; Scott Valley church, Westphalia, Kans.; Conway Springs church, Kans.; South English, Iowa; Garden Grove, Iowa; Maxwell, Iowa; Greene, Iowa; Panora, Iowa; Lewistown, Minn.; Falls City, Nebr.; Rushville, Nebr.; Lado, Va.; Pipe Creek church, Linwood, Md.; Grater's Ford, Pa.; Penn Run, Pa.

To the question as to when the last singing-school was taught in the respective congregations, these are the answers: "We never had a singing school in our church," seven; "Twenty years ago," one; "Eighteen years ago," one; "Twelve years ago," one; "Eight years ago," two; "Six years

WANTED—A MINISTER.

[OUR people do not have to depend upon hired pastors, yet it may do some of them good to learn of the troubles other churches must sometimes endure, in order to obtain a very much needed shepherd.]

We have been without a pastor
Some eighteen months or more,
And though candidates are plenty—
We've had at least a score,
All of them "tip-top preachers,"
Or so their letters ran—
We are just as far as ever
From settling on the man.

The first who came among us
By no means was the worst,
But then we did not think of him
Because he was the first;
It being quite the custom
To sacrifice a few,
Before the church in earnest,
Determines what to do.

There was a smart young fellow
With serious, earnest way,
Who, but for one great blunder,
Had surely won the day;
Who left so good impression,
On Monday one or two
Went round among the people,
To see if he would do.

The pious, goodly portion,
Had not a fault to find;
His clear and searching preaching
They thought the very kind,
And all went smooth and pleasant,
Until they heard the views
Of some influential sinners
Who rent the highest pews.

On these, his pungent sealing
Made but a sorry lift;
The cost of Gospel teaching
Was quite too tight to fit
Of course his fate was settled,
Attend, ye persons all!
And preach to please the sinners,
If you would get a call.

Next came a spruce young dandy
Who wore his hair too long,
Another's coat was shabby,
And his voice not over strong;
And one New Haven student
Was worse than all those,
We couldn't hear the sermon
For thinking of his nose.

Then, wearying of candidates,
We looked the country through,
'Mid doctors and professors,
To find one that would do.
And after much discussion
On who should bear the ark,
With tolerable agreement,
We fixed on Dr. Park.

Here then we thought it settled,
But were amazed to find
Our flattering invitation,
Respectfully declined;
We turned to Dr. Hopkins
To help us in the lurch,
Who strangely thought that college
Had claims above "our church."

Next we dispatched committees,
By twos and threes, to urge
The labors for a Sabbath
Of the Rev. Shallow Splurge.
He came—a marked sensation,
So wonderful his style,
Followed the creaking of his boots
As he passed up the aisle.

His tones were so affecting,
His gesture so divine,
A lady fainted in the hymn,
Before the second line.
And on that day he gave us,
In accents clear and loud,
The greatest prayer ever addressed
To an enlightened crowd.

He preached a double sermon,
And gave us angel's food,
On such a lovely topic,
"The joys of solitude."

All full of sweet descriptions,
Of flowers and pearly streams,
Of warbling birds and moon-lit groves
And golden sunset beams;

Of faith and true repentance,
He'nothing had to say,
He rounded all the corners,
And smoothed the rugged way;
Managed with great adroitness,
To entertain and please,
And leave the sinner's conscience
Completely at its ease.

Six hundred is the salary
We gave in former days,
We thought it very liberal,
And found it hard to raise;
But where we took the paper,
We had no need to urge,
To raise a cool two thousand
For the Rev. Shallow Splurge.

In vain were all our efforts,
We had no chance at all,
We found ten city churches
Had given him a call;
And he is prayerful waiting,
Was keeping all in tow,
But where they bid the highest,
'Twas whispered he would go.

And now, good Christian brothers,
We ask your earnest prayers
That God would send a shepherd,
To guide our church affairs:
With this clear understanding,
A man to meet our views
Must preach to please the sinners,
And fill the vacant pews.

A RECOGNITION OF MERIT.

MR. W. S. REICHARD, Secretary of the Executive Committee of Arrangements for the Annual Conference of the Brethren, held at Hagerstown, Md., May 28 to June 4, 1891, has written upon authority of the Committee the following letter to Mr. B. F. Bond, Division Passenger Agent of the Baltimore and Ohio Railroad Company, who represented that Company in perfecting arrangements for the transportation of Brethren to the Conference. Mr. Reichard's letter is dated at Hagerstown, Md., April 26, last, and reads as follows:

"It is with extreme pleasure that in summing up and closing our business as the Executive Committee of Arrangements for the Annual Conference of the German Baptists, or Brethren, held at Hagerstown, Md., May 28 to June 4, 1891, I am authorized, as Secretary of that Committee, to notify the officials of the Baltimore and Ohio Railroad that a vote of thanks has been extended to them for the thoroughly efficient and masterly manner in which your Company handled the Brethren and their families attending the Conference from points both on and off its System, both going and returning, and take pride in recommending the Baltimore and Ohio System to the Brethren at large, believing that their elegantly equipped train service, the courteous treatment of their gentlemanly officials and their prompt and rapid transit will give them comfort and satisfaction. Respectfully yours,
W. S. REICHARD,
Secretary.

Mr. Bond has acknowledged receipt of the letter with a kind and courteous note.

THE GRAVE OF THE INFIDEL COUNTESS.

WE have before us a photograph, just received from abroad, of a section of a grave-yard in Hanover. It is a winter scene apparently; the great trees are leafless, the sky dull and leaden, and an appreciable gloom has settled down over this "city of the dead." Directly in the foreground is a somewhat pretentious monument, composed of a huge block of granite, resting upon a square base of the same material, to which it is secured by heavy iron clamps, the whole thing built evidently with an idea of great permanency. Upon one of the sides is this most singular inscription, "This burial place, purchased to all eternity, must never be opened." But Nature has defied art, and wrenched the great blocks of stone asunder, and the monument that was to endure to obscurity is at present an unsightly ruin.

What is the history of this remarkable grave, with its strange inscription? Many years ago, there died in the City of Hanover a young Countess, of pronounced infidel proclivities. She denied the doctrine of the resurrection in toto, and perhaps in a vain effort to defy any supernatural power that she thought might have a possible existence, she ordered that her body should be laid beneath the solid, and, in her judgment, impregnable structure our picture represents. Her wishes were strictly carried out, and there seemed a reasonable expectation that the pile would remain intact for many generations at least, and the bones of the skeptical countess rest in the oblivion she desired. But it was strangely ordered otherwise. A tiny seed shared this woman's resting place, and in its resurrection might had burst its shell, sent its small roots into the ground, and slowly gathering strength and proportions with the years, had wrenched open its prison doors, severed in twain the massive granite slabs, and having reached the light had spread itself heavenward, until it has become a great tree. The people of Hanover regard it with almost a superstitious awe, and tell with bated breath the tale of the wicked Countess and her futile efforts to defeat God's laws.

"Write what thou seest, and send it unto the churches."

Church News solicited for this Department. If you have had a good meeting, send a report of it, so that others may rejoice with you. In writing give name of church, County and State. Be brief. Notes of Travel should be as short as possible. Land Advertisements are not solicited for this Department. We have an advertising page, and, if occasionary, will issue supplements.

A Report.

FOR the satisfaction of those who may be curious to know something about the nature of the answers that have been sent in response to my "Favor Asked," and for the purpose of showing, approximately, the condition of, and the interest taken in the singing in the congregations of our church, I make this report. This includes all the answers received to date, and it is not likely that any more will be sent in now.

Some of the letters received answered all the questions asked and others answered only some of them. The following are the churches heard from:

Rock River church, Franklin Grove, Ill.; Girard, Ill.; Ephrata, Pa.; Lititz, Pa.; Scalp Level, Pa.; Rockton, Pa.; Duncaneville, Pa.; Walnut Grove church, Johnstown, Pa.; Pioneer, Ohio; Covington, Ohio; Mahoning church, Columbiana, Ohio; New Philadelphia, Ohio; Lexington church, Samantha, Ohio; Ridgeway, Ind.; Pyrmont, Ind.; Dago, Ind.; Montgomery church, Hillsdale, Ind.; New Haven church, Sethton, Mich.; Mound church, Adrian, Mo.; Warrensburgh, Mo.; Brga, Mo.; Cherokee church, Monmouth, Kans.; Pleasant View church, Booth, Kans.; Ozawkie, Kans.; Scott Valley church, Westphalia, Kans.; Conway Springs church, Kans.; South English, Iowa; Garden Grove, Iowa; Maxwell, Iowa; Greene, Iowa; Panorá, Iowa; Lewistown, Minn.; Falls City, Nebr.; Rushville, Nebr.; Lado, Va.; Pipe Creek church, Linwood, Md.; Grater's Ford, Pa; Penn Run, Pa.

To the question as to when the last singing-school was taught in the respective congregations, these are the answers: "We never had a singing-school in our church," seven; "Twenty years ago," one; "Eighteen years ago," one; "Twelve years ago," one; "Eight years ago," two; "Six years

the Lord may prosper us in his cause and keep us humble. Bro. W. R. Dove is living here with his children, and I believe he is a worthy brother. He has done a good work, though he has seen hard times since he came here, two years ago, from West Virginia.—JOHN J. HOOVER, *April 25.*

A Sad Accident.

WITHIN a mile and one-half of North Beatrice church, there lives a farmer by the name of Baker. He had two sons at work in the field. The younger, fifteen years of age, was cutting corn-stalks. When last seen by his brother, he was walking behind the cutter. Soon afterward the team was seen running away and the boy fast in the knives. He was carried this way for at least a quarter of a mile. There were large gashes cut all over his body. He died a few minutes after being found. This is the third son the aged parents had killed by accident. One was kicked by a horse, the other accidentally hung himself. The youngest and well-beloved came to his end as stated. They need Christians' prayers. Funeral by Rev. Ingram and the writer.

J. E. YOUNG.

Beatrice, Nebr., April 29.

From Nocona, Texas.

WE are still endeavoring to push the work of the Lord in the far south, but not without discouragements, for we meet them here in their various forms, as in other places. But these things only remind us of the fallibility of man. We truly need the fervent prayers of the righteous, in the frontier work of the church, in order to get the work established. How many embarrassments and disappointments the frontier minister has to meet! I would that the Brotherhood might get some practical ideas of the hardships, trials, sacrifice and loneliness that must be endured! If the brethren had a knowledge of all this, prayers would be made without ceasing to the God of heaven to bless and prosper the work, and they would hold up the arms and hands of the brethren in the missionary fields.

HENRY BRUBAKER.

April 25.

DURING the year 1890 there were published in England 555 new books on Bible questions, while in the United States 467 books of the same character appeared. In 1891 there were 538 in England and 538 in the United States, all of them treating Scriptural questions, thus showing that the Bible is by no means losing its interest with the reading public.

Notes from Our Correspondents.

"As cold water to a thirsty soul, so is good news from a far country."

Salem, Ohio.—Our council-meeting yesterday passed off pleasantly. Brethren Jesse K. Brumbaugh and Adam Pfeifer represent this church at Annual Meeting, and Bro. Pfeifer and the writer at District Meeting.—*John H. Brumbaugh, May 6.*

Johnstown, Pa.—We have a fine Sunday-school on what is called the Benshoof Hill. Our prayer is that it may continue such. We have a prayer-meeting every Thursday night, which is well attended. We also have preaching every third Sunday. Two weeks ago from yesterday there were four baptized and yesterday one. Bro. Teeter and I have just finished the visit preparatory to our love-feast, which will be next Sunday. We had not less than twenty-five families on our route, and not one word of complaint was offered about any members or anybody else.—*L. R. Brallier.*

Yellow Creek, Pa.—The Hopewell congregation met in quarterly council the second Saturday in April, and decided to represent at District and Annual Meeting by letter. All other business was adjusted without a jar. We decided against the erection of an "Old Folks' Home."—*A. Steele, Clerk, May 5.*

Quick City, Mo.—I write to know if a "Brethren's Almanac," of 1877, can be had. Any one having one that he wishes to dispose of, will please send it to me at the above address and name price. I would like also to have an Almanac of 1853. It would not matter so much about this being a "Brethren's Almanac."—*T. D. Haisten, May 5.*

El Reno, Ok. Ter.—I wish to state that I am located near El Reno, Oklahoma Territory, and should there there be any isolated members living in this Territory who wish to have some preaching, they can obtain my services by giving me their address. My desire is to obey the command, "Go ye." I am only stopping here for the summer.—*M. M. Ennis, May 2.*

White Church, Ind.—There have been two more received by baptism since our last report,—both young men. May the Lord keep them steadfast in his doctrine! We have quite an interesting Sunday-school, with Bro. Ira Fisher as Superintendent. We use the Brethren's literature. May the Good Lord bless all in their work for his cause and to the good of souls, is our prayer!—*D. C. Campbell.*

Williamsport, Ind.—We held our first Communion here last Saturday evening. Everything passed off very pleasantly. Many from adjoining congregations were with us. Bro. Billheimer came to us March 26 and held a series of meetings, lasting a week or more. Bro. Billheimer who had one of his eyes treated last fall, has much improved in his eyesight. It is now better than it has been for some time. His work among us was very gladly received.—*Geo. McKinney.*

Wells County, Ind.—The members of the Walnut Level church held their quarterly council-meeting last Saturday, April 30. Everything passed off pleasantly. We read the MESSENGER with much pleasure, for in it we hear the glad tidings and good news of the entire Brotherhood. When we read of the many good sermons that are delivered and the precious souls that are turning their backs to the world, to travel that narrow road that leads from earth to heaven, it makes us feel that the Lord's work is going on.—*Malinda S. Studebaker, May 5.*

Ashland, Nebr.—The railroad lines, west of the Missouri River have made a rate of one fare for the round trip, but tickets will not be on sale after June 3, which, as you know, is not late enough. I have made application so that tickets will be still on sale June 4 yet (Saturday), with fair prospects of having the request granted. We are making arrangements for two special cars via the Burlington Route and B, C. R. & N., to go June 4, and arrive on the Annual Meeting grounds June 5. We would like as many to go with us as can.—*G. E. Whisler, May 7.*

Austin, Ark.—We left home April 28 and came here to do some mission work, and to visit the scattered members. We are holding meetings each evening with fair attendance and good attention. Here we met for the first time our dear brother, Chas. Delp, and wife, who came from Kansas to assist in building up a church. There are now eight members here. I hope more may come. Members with some capital can get cheap homes, near the railroad, where small fruit farming seems to be a good business. From here we go to Wellington, Kans., where we can be addressed until May 25.—*Jas. R. Gish, May 3.*

Arcadia, Ind.—We, the members of the Arcadia, Ind., church, met in our regular, quarterly council April 30. The business of the meeting was disposed of in a brotherly manner. We appointed our Communion for Oct. 6, at 2 P. M.—*Eliza Smeltzer, May 4.*

Rock Creek, Colo.—Our Sunday-school is moving along nicely, with good attendance and good interest in the study of the lesson. The masons are at work on the foundation of our new church-house, and will be ready for the carpenters by the last of next week. Our sick sisters are improving in health. May the GOSPEL MESSENGER still continue to do much good!—*A. C. Snowberger, Monte Vista, Colo., May 5.*

Aurelia, Iowa.—We had set our love-feast for June 4, and sent notice to the MESSENGER to that effect. Since then we concluded that this was so close to the time of Annual Meeting as to make it inconvenient for those wishing to attend Annual Meeting from here. We therefore changed the time from June 4 to June 18. Since our first date has already been published in the MESSENGER, will you kindly change it, so that none be misled? We earnestly invite all within reach to be with us at that time, especially eastern brethren, who may be traveling through Western Iowa after Annual Meeting.—*Norman S. Eby, May 8.*

Woolwine, Va.—Brethren C. D. Hylton and Harvey Weddle came to us on Sunday, May 1, and preached two sermons and baptized three. When an invitation was extended, three more came forward and desired to unite with the church, which makes nine accessions to the church this year. Only three of them have as yet been baptized, but the remainder will be waited on at the next meeting,—the first Sunday in June. Let all remember us in their prayers, that the good work may go on! We have much reason to rejoice at the upbuilding of God's kingdom in our midst.—*J. A. Hooker.*

Macoupin Creek, Ill.—This church met in quarterly council April 30. A fair number of members and officials were present; also many from adjoining churches. This was very pleasant and shows a spirit of Christian unity. The business all passed off pleasantly. We were made sorry to have to grant church letters to four very worthy members. May they add to the prosperity of the cause where they now labor! The church treasury and Missionary, Book and Tract Work were not forgotten. Delegates to Annual Meeting were elected, and other minor business was attended to. Some soul-stirring counsel was given by ministers from adjoining churches. May all prove effective and may the Lord bless every effort for good, is the writer's fervent prayer.—*Michael Flory, May 2.*

Pleasant Hill, Ill.—This church convened in council yesterday and transacted work of a varied character. There were six received by letter, but, sad to state, one precious soul had to be expelled. The other usual quarterly work met its due share of attention. At present our Sunday-school seems to be progressing finely; also two places for regular, stated public preaching and two weekly social meetings, where the young members are permitted to exercise in things pertaining to our holy religion. Our delegate and alternate in Annual Conference are brethren J. H. Brubaker and G. W. Gibson. At this council it was unanimously agreed to elect a brother to the ministry. The lot fell on our worthy brother, James Wirt. Bro. Wirt and wife were duly installed into their office. May they labor in their new position with that untiring zeal which their high and holy calling requires!—*R. F. Brubaker, May 8.*

the Lord may prosper us in his cause and keep us humble. Bro. W. R. Dove is living here with his children, and I believe he is a worthy brother. He has done a good work, though he has seen hard times since he came here, two years ago, from West Virginia.   JOHN J. HOOVER.
April 25.

A Sad Accident.

WITHIN a mile and one-half of North Beatrice church, there lives a farmer by the name of Bak-er. He had two sons at work in the field. The younger, fifteen years of age, was cutting corn-stalks. When last seen by his brother, he was walking behind the cutter. Soon afterward the team was seen running away and the boy fast in the knives. He was carried this way for at least a quarter of a mile. There were large gashes cut all over his body. He died a few minutes after being found. This is the third son of the aged par-ents had killed by accident. One was kicked by a horse, the other accidentally hung himself. The youngest and well-beloved came to his end as stated. They need Christians' prayers. Fu-neral by Rev. Ingram and the writer.
J. E. YOUNG.
Beatrice, Nebr., April 29.

From Nocona, Texas.

WE are still endeavoring to push the work of the Lord in the far south, but not without dis-couragement, for we meet them here in their various forms, as in other places. But these things only remind us of the fallibility of man. We truly need the fervent prayers of the right-eous, in the frontier work of the church, in order to get the work established. How many embar-rassments and disappointments the frontier min-ister has to meet! I would that the Brotherhood might get some practical ideas of the hardships, trials, sacrifice and loneliness that must be en-dured! If the brethren had a knowledge of all this, prayers would be made without ceasing to the God of heaven to bless and prosper the work, and they would hold up the arms and hands of the brethren in the missionary fields.
HENRY BRUBAKER.
April 25.

DURING the year 1890 there were published in England 555 new books on Bible questions, while in the United States 467 books of the same char-acter appeared. In 1891 there were 538 in Eng-land and 538 in the United States, all of them treating Scriptural questions, thus showing that the Bible is by no means losing its interest with the reading public.

Notes from Our Correspondents.

"As cold water to a thirsty soul, so is good news from a far country."

Salem, Ohio. — Our council-meeting yesterday passed off pleasantly. Brethren Jesse K. Brum-baugh and Adam Pfeifer represent this church at Annual Meeting, and Bro. Pfeifer and the writer at District Meeting.—John H. Brumbaugh, May 6.

Johnstown, Pa.—We have a fine Sunday-school on what is called the Benshoof Hill. Our prayer is that it may continue such. We have a prayer-meeting every Thursday night, which is well at-tended. We also have preaching every third Sunday. Two weeks ago from yesterday there were four baptized and yesterday one." Bro. Teeter and I have just finished the visit prepara-tory to our love-feast, which will be next Sunday. We had not less than twenty-five families on our route, and not one word of complaint was offered about any members or anybody else.—L. R. Bral-lier.

Yellow Creek, Pa.—The Hopewell congregation met in quarterly council the second Saturday in April, and decided to represent at District and Annual Meeting by letter. All other business was adjusted without a jar. We decided against the erection of an "Old Folks' Home."—A. Steele, Clerk, May 5.

Quick City, Mo.—I write to know if a "Brethren's Almanac," of 1877, can be had. Any one having one that he wishes to dispose of, will please send it to me at the above address and name price. I would like also to have an Almanac of 1853. It would not matter so much about this being a "Brethren's Almanac."—T. D. Heiston, May 3.

El Reno, Ok. Ter.—I wish to state that I am locat-ed near El Reno, Oklahoma Territory, and should there there be any isolated members living in this Territory who wish to have some preaching, they can obtain my services by giving me their address. My desire is to obey the command, "Go ye." I am only stopping here for the summer.—M. M. Ennis, May 2.

White Church, Ind.—There have been two more received by baptism since our last report,—both young men. May the Lord keep them steadfast in his doctrine! We have quite an interesting Sunday-school, with Bro. Ira Fisher as Superin-tendent. We use the Brethren's literature. May the Good Lord bless all in their work for his cause and to the good of souls, is our prayer!—D. C. Campbell.

Williamsport, Ind.—We held our first Communion here last Saturday evening. Everything passed off very pleasantly. Many from adjoining con-gregations were with us, Bro. Billheimer came to us March 26 and held a series of meetings, last-ing a week or more. Bro. Billheimer who had one of his eyes treated last fall, has much im-proved in his eyesight. It is now better than it has been for some time. His work among us was very gladly received.—Geo. McKinney.

Wells County, Ind.—The members of the Walnut Level church held their quarterly council-meet-ing last Saturday, April 30. Everything passed off pleasantly. We read the MESSENGER with much pleasure, for in it we hear the glad tidings and good news of the entire Brotherhood. When we read of the many good sermons that are de-livered and the precious souls that are turning their Backs to the world, to travel that narrow road that leads from earth to heaven, it makes us feel that the Lord's work is going on.—Malinda S. Studebaker, May 5.

Ashland, Nebr.—The railroad lines, west of the Missouri River have made a rate of one fare for the round trip, but tickets will not be on sale after June 3, which, as you know, is not late enough. I have made application so that tickets will be still on sale June 4 yet (Saturday), with fair prospects of having the request granted. We are making arrangements for two special cars via the Burlington Route and B, C. R. & N., to go June 4, and arrive on the Annual Meeting grounds June 5. We would like as many to go with us as can.—G. E. Whisler, May 7.

Austin, Ark.—We left home April 28 and came here to do some mission work, and to visit the scattered members. We are holding meetings each evening with fair attendance and good atten-tion. Here we met for the first time our dear brother, Chas. Delp, and wife, who came from Kansas to assist in building up a church. There are now eight members here. I hope more may come. Members with some capital can get cheap homes, near the railroad, where small fruit farm-ing seems to be a good business. From here we go to Wellington, Kans., where we can be ad-dressed until May 25.—Jas. R. Gish, May 3.

Arcadia, Ind.—We, the members of the Arcadia, Ind., church, met in our regular, quarterly coun-cil April 30. The business of the meeting was disposed of in a brotherly manner. We appoint-ed our Communion for Oct. 6, at 2 P. M.—Elias Smeltzer, May 4.

Rock Creek, Colo.—Our Sunday-school is moving along nicely, with good attendance and good in-terest in the study of the lesson. The masons are at work on the foundation of our new church-house, and will be ready for the carpenters by the last of next week. Our sick sisters are improving in health. May the GOSPEL MESSENGER still con-tinue to do much good!—A. C. Snowberger, Monte Vista, Colo., May 5.

Aurelia, Iowa.—We had set our love-feast for June 4, and sent notice to the MESSENGER to that effect. Since then we concluded that this was so close to the time of Annual Meeting as to make it inconvenient for those wishing to attend Annual Meeting from here. We therefore changed the time from June 4 to June 18. Since our first date has already been published in the MESSEN-GER, will you kindly change it, so that none be misled? We earnestly invite all within reach to be with us at that time, especially eastern brethren, who may be traveling through Western Iowa after Annual Meeting.—Norman S. Eby, May 8.

Woolwine, Va.—Brethren C. D. Hylton and Har-vey Weddle came to us on Sunday, May 1, and preached two sermons and baptized three. When an invitation was extended, three more came for-ward and desired to unite with the church, which makes nine accessions to the church this year. Only three of them have as yet been baptized, but the remainder will be waited on at the next meeting,—the first Sunday in June. Let all re-member us in their prayers, that the good work may go on! We have much reason to rejoice at the upbuilding of God's kingdom in our midst.—J. A. Hooker.

Macoupin Creek, Ill.—This church met in quarter-ly council April 30. A fair number of members and officials were present; also many from adjoin-ing churches. This was very pleasant and shows a spirit of Christian unity. The business all passed off pleasantly. We were made sorry to have to grant church letters to four very worthy members. May they add to the prosperity of the cause where they now labor! The church treas-ury and Missionary, Book and Tract Work were not forgotten. Delegates to Annual Meeting were elected, and other minor business was at-tended to. Some soul-stirring counsel was given by ministers from adjoining churches. May all prove effective and may the Lord bless every ef-fort for good, is the writer's fervent prayer.—Mi-chael Flory, May 2.

Pleasant Hill, Ill.—This church convened in coun-cil yesterday and transacted work of a varied character. There were six received by letter, but, sad to state, one precious soul had to be expelled. The other usual quarterly work met its due share of attention. At present our Sunday-school seems to be progressing finely; also two places for reg-ular, stated public preaching and two weekly so-cial meetings, where the young members are per-mitted to exercise in things pertaining to our holy religion. Our delegate and alternate in Annual Conference are brethren J. H. Brubaker and G. W. Gibson. At this council it was unanimously agreed to elect a brother to the ministry. The lot fell on our worthy brother, James Wirt. Bro. Wirt and wife were duly installed into their office. May they labor in their new position with that untiring zeal which their high and holy calling requires!—R. F. Brubaker, May 8.

Hill Top, Ark. — The Pilot Knob church met in council, April 23, at Bro. John Price's. Bro. M. V. Price was chosen as delegate to District Meeting. Bro. Price is an able expounder of the Gospel, and is laboring hard to build up a church here. May the Good Lord reward his labor! We decided to hold a lovefeast, the Lord willing, Sept. 10. We also decided to build a church near the above place, if we can raise the means. — *Samuel P. Anderson, April 23.*

Cana, Va. — Bro. C. D. Hylton came to us on Saturday, April 23, and preached six soul-stirring sermons. One precious soul came out on the Lord's side and was buried with Christ in baptism to walk in newness of life. Several more were seriously impressed, and seemed to be halting between two opinions. Our united prayers are, that they may choose to serve the Lord. We also re-organized our Sunday-school, by electing the same superintendent. — *Wm. Wisler, Clerk, April 29.*

Adrian, Mo. — The Mound church Missouri, met in quarterly council on Saturday, April 30. The manner in which the meeting was conducted, and the love shown for each other, undoubtedly give us reason to feel encouraged to push forward in the work of our Master. There were six received by letter. We welcome them among us. We have a very interesting Sunday-school, and I hope it may be so conducted as to be the means of doing much good. — *Hannah Blocher, May 2.*

Sawyer, Kans. — The Brethren of the Mingona congregation, Barber Co., met in quarterly council April 2. Everything was done with the best of feeling. We elected two delegates to the District Meeting, viz., brethren J. Shamberger and N. F. Brubaker. A proposition was made to divide the congregation and unanimously accepted. The line was drawn six miles south of the south line of Pratt County. April 23 the Brethren in Pratt County met and organized under the name of the Bethel church. We now number twenty-eight members from the ministers and one deacon. — *J. H. Miller.*

Monticello, Ind. — We are still moving along in our Christian work. Peace is reigning among us at the present time and, we hope, may so continue. We all feel somewhat sad, at present, on account of our elder, A. S. Culp, and family, moving to Harrison County, Ind. Bro. Culp was respected by all, and his labors are greatly missed among us here, but we pray that the Lord may bless him and his family in their new field of labor. Our Sunday-school was re-opened the second Sunday of April, with a larger attendance than for several summers past. Bro. Bert Bridge is the Superintendent. We held our quarterly church meeting May 23. We had very little business, and everything was disposed of

in a Christian way. Brethren J. A. Weaver and David Dilling were ordained to the eldership, to fill the vacancy made by Bro. A. S. Culp moving away. Bro. D. Dilling is our delegate to Annual Meeting. — *J. A. Weaver, April 28*

Love-feast Recalled. — Notice is hereby given that the love-feast of the Bear Creek church, Montgomery County, Ohio, appointed for May 14, has been recalled. — *Josiah Eby, Dayton, Ohio.* [The above came just one day after the last issue went to press, hence the delay of this notice. — Ed.]

Glendora, Cal. — H. C. Niman, formerly of Mt. Morris, Ill., was working near here, and boarded at my house almost one year. He went to bed well and hearty, but was found dead in bed next morning. An inquest was held and the disease was pronounced heart disease. Funeral by Eld. Peter Overholtzer, of Covina, Cal. Mr. Niman said that his people live near Mt. Morris, Ill. — *John Smeltzer.*

Great Bend, Kans. — Our love-feast of April 30 and May 1 was a pleasant and profitable one. Ministers from abroad were brethren A. W. Vaniman, J. N. Perry, James Paxton and Jonas Hertaler. There was also a number of members present from adjoining Districts. Meetings were held from Tuesday evening of the previous week, and closed on Sunday evening. Our duties were made plain, and it now remains with us to give the more earnest heed. Bro. A. W. Vaniman did the preaching. May the Lord bless our dear brother for his labors of love, is our prayer! — *Michael Keller, May 2.*

" What therefore God hath joined together, let not man put asunder."

HUSTON—BONEBRAKE. — At the residence of the bride's mother, Mrs. Syble Bonebrake, April 10, 1892, Mr. J Edward Huston and Miss Addie E. Bonebrake, both of South Bend, Ind.

HUSTON—ALBERTS. — At the residence of the undersigned, April 24, 1892, Mr. Winfield S. Huston and Miss Anna Alberts, both of St. Joseph County, Ind.

H. W. Krieghbaum.

DAVIS—COCHRAN. — At the residence of the bride's parents, Mr. and Mrs. Jos. H. Cochran, in Annelly, Harvey Co., Kans., April 28, 1892, by the undersigned, Mr. Schuyler Colfax Davis and Miss Cora Bertha Cochran.   L. Andes.

MOORE—FURREY. — At the residence of the undersigned, in Montague County, Texas, April 8, 1892, Mr. R. E. Moore and sister Lizzie Furrey, of Colorado.

Henry Brubaker.

" Blessed are the dead which die in the Lord."

HEATWOLE. — In the Beaver Creek congregation, Rockingham County, Va., March 25, 1892, Sarah C. Heatwole, daughter of Bro. Gabriel Long, aged 22 years, 1 month and 6 days.

HEATWOLE. — At the same place, March 31, 1892, Sally, infant of the above-named mother, aged 14 days.

BITTINGER. — At the home of her son, James Bittinger, near Roxburp of heart trouble, Annie Bitinger, aged 76 years, 11 months and 16 days. She was the mother of twelve children.   Daniel Bittinger.

ENNIS. — In the Landisville church, near Marion, Grant Co., Ind., April 12, 1892, Henry Ennis, aged 15 years, 11 months and 2 days. Although his voice is hushed to mortal ear, it is heard in the sweet Beulah land. Henry was brought-under conviction a few weeks before his death, and earnestly desired to be baptized, but was so suddenly snatched away by death, that it was neglected. The dear family have our sympathies. May all people take warning and attend to the one thing needful! Funeral services by Bro. Samuel Leckrone from Matt. 11: 27, 28, 29.

Mrs. Esther Dickey. .

CLICK. — In the same congregation, April 7, 1892, Bro. Abraham Click, aged 73 years, 3 months and 17 days. Funeral at Beaver Creek by the Brethren.

EAVY. — In the same congregation, April 26, 1892, friend Michael Envy, aged 38 years, 3 months and 1 day. Funeral services at Ottobine, by Rev. Dyke.   G. W. Wine.

WEIGLE. — Near Wellington, Kans., March 4, 1892, of spasms and brain fever, Margie Fay, infant child of Henry and Minnie Weigle, aged 5 months and 3 days. Services at the house.

Lizzie Weigle Fahnestock.

WOODARD. — In the Newton church, Harvey Co., Kans., March 10, 1892, sister Sarah J. Woodard, wife of Joel Woodard, aged about 53 years. Funeral services from Job 17: 11, in the Baptist church in Newton, by the undersigned, assisted by Rev. Sawin, of the Baptist church. Her remains were laid to rest in the Newton City Cemetery. Sister Woodard suffered considerably, beginning with *La Grippe*, which finally ended in paralysis.

STONER. — In Sedgwick, Harvey Co., Kans., March 16, 1892, sister Susan Stoner, wife of D. P. Stoner, aged 37 years, 4 months and 14 days. Sister Stoner leaves a husband and six children, — some rather small yet. She suffered much from a complication of diseases, beginning with *La Grippe*, and ending in paralysis. She bore her sufferings with Christian patience and was willing to be released from her earthly bondage at the Master's call. Several hours before her death she engaged in singing. Funeral services by the writer from Matt. 13: 47—50 and Heb. 4: 9-13, assisted by the Congregational minister in whose church-house the services were held. Her remains were laid to rest in the Brethren's cemetery, seven miles north of Sedgwick.   L. Andes.

CARNS. — In the Spring Creek church, Kosciusko Co., Ind., April 21, 1892, Bro. Henry Carns, aged 73 years and 5 days. Deceased was born in Westmoreland County, Pa., April 16, 1819, and moved to Kosciusko County, Ind., in 1845. He was united in matrimony to Sarah Waybright, April 16, 1845. Both united with the church some years ago and lived faithful till death. Seven children were given them. His wife and two children preceded him to the spirit world. Of the five remaining children, two are in the church. Funeral services by the writer from Num. 23: 10.   Daniel Snell.

MAGLEY. — In the Blue River church, Whitley Co., Ind., Feb. 19, 1892, Delpha Arminda Magley, aged 22 years, 1 month and 5 days. She was the daughter of Bro. Frederic and Elizabeth Magley. Funeral services by Eld. Leonard Hyre.

WORKMAN. — In the same church, Feb. 19, 1892, Abraham Workman, aged 78 years, 5 months and 5 days. Funeral services by Bro. Jacob Swihart and others.

C. K. Zumbrun.

ZELLARS. — In Chicago, Ill., Jan. 7, 1892, Samuel Zellars, aged 15 years, 3 months and 10 days. Services by the undersigned.

W. R. Miller.

HELTAU. — In the bounds of the Prairie Creek church, Wells Co., Ind., April 27, 1892, sister Lavina Heltau, aged 37 years, 1 month and 1 day. Deceased was anointed by the elders during her sickness. Funeral services from 2 Cor. 5: 1, 2, by the writer.

Daniel Shidelar.

CURLY. — In Kokomo, in the bounds of the Greentown church, Howard Co., Ind., at the residence of his daughter, Mrs. Mary Quinn, Wm. Curly, aged 72 years, 10 months and 21 days. Deceased was born in Dublin, Ireland, and came to this country when a young man. Funeral services by the writer, assisted by Rev. David Wack, of the Christian church. Text, Job 14: 14.

Abraham Caylor.

ZUG. — In the Tulpahocken church, Richland, Lebanon Co., Pa., April 12, 1892, Abraham Zug, aged 85 years and 5 days. He was born in Lexington, Lancaster Co., Pa., April 7, 1807. His father, Eld. Abraham Zug, preceded him to the spirit world 50 years, 8 months and 24 days, at the age of 69 years, 4 months and 12 days. He was married Feb. 28, 1832, to sister Anna Royer. Their union was blessed with four sons and five daughters. Funeral services by Brethren S. R. Zug and C. Bucher, from Ps. 90.   Michael Zug.

STOVER. — At Hagerstown, Md., Jan. 10, 1892, sister Mary (nee Royer) Stover, widow of Jacob Stover, aged 79 years, 5 months and 21 days. Sister Stover was born near Waynesborough, Pa., and united with the Brethren's church when about twenty years old. Funeral services by Eld. Nicholas Martin in Price's church. Interment in cemetery adjoining.   A. B. Barnhart.

WITTER. — Near North Manchester, Wabash Co., Ind., April 25, 1892, sister Martha, wife of Levi W. Witter and youngest daughter of Bro. Christian and sister Mary Frantz, aged 26 years, 8 months and 24 days. She leaves a husband and four small children. She united with the Brethren church in 1879. Funeral discourse by brethren Albert Wright and Samuel Leckrone, from 1 Thess. 4: 13.

Emma Frantz.

JOSEPH. — In the Yellow River congregation, Marshall County, Ind., April 12, 1892, Eliza Owen, infant son of John and Mancla Joseph, aged 1 year, 6 months and 16 days. Services by Bro. John H. Sellers, assisted by William R. Myers, from Matt. 19: 14.

SNYDER. — In the same congregation, April 3, 1892, of whooping cough, Gracie, infant daughter of Henry and Alice Snyder, aged about five weeks. Services by Bro. John H. Sellers, assisted by Martin A. Eisenhour, from Matt. 19: 14.

GANSHORN. — In the Camp Creek gation, Marshall County, Ind., April 22, 1892, Elza Owen, infant son of John and Ralph Leroy, infant son of Bro. John and sister Addie Ganshorn, aged 5 months and 24 days. Funeral services were conducted by Bro. John H. Sellers, assisted by Bro. John W. Shively, from Job 11: 28.   Charlie H. Sellers.

EAGLER. — In the Tippecanoe church, Kosciusko Co., Ind., John Eagler, aged about 56 years. He was an invalid for several years. Seven weeks before his death he united with the church by faith and baptism. Funeral services from Job 14: 10.

D. Rothenberger.

BEEGHLY. — In Waterloo, Iowa, March 24, 1892, sister Susan, wife of Bro. Marsh Beeghly, aged 60 years and 12 months. Sister Beeghly was of an amiable disposition, and although she suffered severely, she bore it all patiently. Funeral services were held in the Brethren church in the city, by Bro. Wm. Ikenberry and the writer, in the presence of a large congregation.

FORNEY. — Also, in the South Waterloo church, Iowa, April 18, 1892, Mary Forney, wife of Joseph Forney, deceased. The subject of this notice had united with the Progressives, as also had her husband. Her age was 78 years, 11 months and 15 days. The funeral services were held in the South Waterloo church by H. R. Holsinger and the writer.

J. A. Murray.

Bill Top, Ark. — The Pilot Knob church met in council, April 28, at Bro. John Price's. Bro. M. V. Price was chosen as delegate to District Meeting. Bro. Price is an able expounder of the Gospel, and is laboring hard to build up a church here. May the Good Lord reward his labor! We decided to hold a lovefeast, the Lord willing, Sept. 10. We also decided to build a church near the above place, if we can raise the means.— *Samuel P. Anderson, April 29.*

Cana, Va.—Bro C. D. Hylton came to us on Saturday, April 23, and preached six soul-stirring sermons. One precious soul came out on the Lord's side and was buried with Christ in baptism to walk in newness of life. Several more were seriously impressed, and seemed to be halting between two opinions. Our united prayers are, that they may choose to serve the Lord. We also re-organized our Sunday-school, by electing the writer Superintendent.— *Wm. Wisler, Clerk, April 29.*

Adrian, Mo.—The Mound church Missouri, met in quarterly council on Saturday, April 30. The manner in which the meeting was conducted, and the love shown for each other, undoubtedly give us reason to feel encouraged to push forward in the work of our Master. There were six received by letter. We welcome them among us. We have a very interesting Sunday-school, and I hope it may be so conducted as to be the means of doing much good.— *Hannah Blocher, May 2.*

Sawyer, Kans.—The Brethren of the Mingona congregation, Barber Co., met in quarterly council April 2. Everything was done with the best of feeling. We elected two delegates to the District Meeting, viz., brethren J. Shamberger and N. F. Brubaker. A proposition was made to divide the congregation and unanimously accepted. The line was drawn six miles south of the south line of Pratt County. April 23 the Brethren in Pratt County met and organized under the name of the Bethel church. We now number twenty-eight members with two ministers and one deacon.— *J. H. Miller.*

Monticello, Ind.—We are still moving along in our Christian work. Peace is reigning among us at the present time and, we hope, may so continue. We all feel somewhat sad, at present, on account of our elder, A. S. Culp, and family, moving to Harrison County, Ind. Bro. Culp was respected by all, and his labors are greatly missed among us here, but we pray that the Lord may bless him and his family in their new field of labor. Our Sunday-school was re-opened the second Sunday of April, with a larger attendance than for several summers past. Bro. Bert Bridge is the Superintendent. We held our quarterly church meeting May 23. We had very little business, and everything was disposed of

in a Christian way. Brethren J. A. Weaver and David Dilling were ordained to the eldership, to fill the vacancy made by Bro. A. S. Culp moving away. Bro. D. Dilling is our delegate to Annual Meeting.— *J. A. Weaver, April 28*

Love-feast Recalled.—Notice is hereby given that the love-feast of the Bear Creek church, Montgomery County, Ohio, appointed for May 14, has been recalled. — *Josiah Eby, Dayton, Ohio.* [The above came just one day after the last issue went to press, hence the delay of this notice.—EDR.]

Glendora, Cal.—H. C. Niman, formerly of Mt. Morris, Ill., was working near here, and boarded at my house almost one year. He went to bed well and hearty, but was found dead in bed next morning. An inquest was held and the disease was pronounced heart disease. Funeral by Eld. Peter Overholtzer, of Covina, Cal. Mr. Niman said that his people live near Mt. Morris, Ill.— *John Smeltzer.*

Great Bend, Kans.—Our love-feast of April 30 and May 1 was a pleasant and profitable one. Ministers from abroad were brethren A. W. Vaniman, J. N. Perry, James Paxton and Jonas Hertzler. There was also a number of members present from adjoining Districts. Meetings were held from Tuesday evening of the previous week, and closed on Sunday evening. Our duties were made plain, and it now remains with us to give the more earnest heed.— Bro. A. W. Vaniman did the preaching. May the Lord bless our dear brother for his labors of love, is our prayer! — *Michael Keller, May 2.*

MATRIMONIAL.

"What therefore God hath joined together, let not man put asunder."

HUSTON—BONEBRAKE.—At the residence of the bride's mother, Mrs. Syble Bonebrake, April 10, 1892, Mr. J Edward Huston and Miss Addie E. Bonebrake, both of South Bend, Ind.

H. W. KRIEGHBAUM.

HUSTON—ALBERTS. — At the residence of the undersigned, April 24, 1892, Mr. Winfield S. Huston and Miss Anna Alberts, both of St. Joseph County, Ind.

H. W. KRIEGHBAUM.

DAVIS—COCHRAN.—At the residence of the bride's parents, Mr. and Mrs. Jos. H. Cochran, in Annelly, Harvey Co., Kans., April 28, 1892, by the undersigned, Mr. Schuyler Colfax Davis and Miss Cora Bertha Cochran.

L. ANDES.

MOORE—FURREY.—At the residence of the undersigned, in Montague County, Texas, April 8, 1892, Mr. R. E. Moore and sister Lizzie Furrey, of Colorado.

HENRY BRUBAKER.

FALLEN ASLEEP.

"Blessed are the dead which die in the Lord."

HEATWOLE.—In the Beaver Creek congregation, Rockingham County, Va., March 25, 1892, Sarah C. Heatwole, daughter of Bro. Gabriel Long, aged 22 years, 1 month and 6 days.

HEATWOLE.—At the same place, March 31, 1892, Sally, infant of the above-named mother, aged 14 days.

BITTINGER.—At the home of her son, James Bittinger, near Roxbury, of heart trouble, Annie Bittinger, aged 76 years, 11 months and 16 days. She was the mother of twelve children.

DANIEL BITTINGER.

ENNIS.—In the Landisville church, near Marion, Grant Co., Ind., April 11, 1892, Henry Ennis, aged 13 years, 11 months and 2 days. Although his voice is hushed to mortal ear, it is heard in the sweet Beulah land. Henry was brought-under conviction a few weeks before his death, and earnestly desired to be baptized, but was so suddenly snatched away by death, that it was neglected. The dear family have our sympathies. May all people take warning and attend to the one thing needful! Funeral services by Bro. Samuel Leckrone from Matt. 11: 27, 28, 29.

MRS. ESTHER DICKEY.

CLICK.—In the same congregation, April 7, 1892, Bro. Abraham Click, aged 73 years, 3 months and 17 days. Funeral at Beaver Creek by the Brethren.

EAVY.—In the same congregation, April 16, 1892, friend Michael Eavy, aged 78 years, 3 months and 1 day. Funeral services at Ottobine, by Rev. Dyke. G. W. WINE.

WEIGLE. — Near Wellington, Kans., March 4, 1892, of spasms and brain fever, Margie Fay, infant child of Henry and Minnie Weigle, aged 5 months and 3 days. Services at the house.

LIZZIE WEIGLE FAHNESTOCK.

WOODARD.— In the Newton church, Harvey Co., Kans., March 10, 1892, sister Sarah J. Woodard, wife of Joel Woodard, aged about 53 years. Funeral services from Job 17: 11, in the Baptist church in Newton, by the undersigned, assisted by Rev. Sawin, of the Baptist church. Her remains were laid to rest in the Newton City Cemetery. Sister Woodard suffered considerably, beginning with *La Grippe,* which finally ended in paralysis.

STONER.— In Sedgwick, Harvey Co., Kans., March 16, 1892, sister Susan Stoner, wife of D. P. Stoner, aged 37 years, 4 months and 14 days. Sister Stoner leaves a husband and six children,—some rather small yet. She suffered much from a complication of diseases, beginning with *La Grippe,* and ending in paralysis. She bore her sufferings with Christian patience and was willing to be released from her earthly bondage at the Master's call. Several hours before her death she engaged in singing. Funeral services by the writer from Matt. 19: 47-50 and Heb. 4: 9-13, assisted by the Congregational minister in whose church-house the services were held. Her remains were laid to rest in the Brethren's cemetery, seven miles north of Sedgwick.

L. ANDES.

CARNS.—In the Spring Creek church, Kosciusko Co., Ind., April 21, 1892, Bro. Henry Carns, aged 73 years and 5 days. Deceased was born in Westmoreland County, Pa., April 16, 1819, and moved to Kosciusko County, Ind., in 1845. He was united in matrimony to Sarah Waybright, April 16, 1845. Both united with the church some years ago and lived faithful till death. Seven children were given them. His wife and two children preceded him to the spirit world. Of the five remaining children, two are in the church. Funeral services by the writer from Num. 23: 10. DANIEL SNELL.

MAGLEY.—In the Blue River church, Whitley Co., Ind., Feb. 19, 1892, Delphia Arminda Magley, aged 22 years, 1 month and 5 days. She was the daughter of Bro. Fredric and Elisabeth Magley. Funeral services by Eld. Leonard Hyre.

WORKMAN.—In the same church, Feb. 17, 1892, Abraham Workman, aged 76 years, 5 months and 5 days. Funeral services by Bro. Jacob Swihart and others.

C. K. ZUMBRUN.

ZELLARS.—In Chicago, Ill., Jan. 7, 1892, Samuel Zellars, aged 15 years, 3 months and 10 days. Services by the undersigned.

W. R. MILLER.

HELTAU.—In the bounds of the Prairie Creek church, Wells Co., Ind., April 27, 1892, sister Lavina Heltau, aged 37 years, 1 month and 1 day. Deceased was anointed by the elders during her sickness. Funeral services from 2 Cor. 5: 1, 2, by the writer.

DANIEL SHIDELER.

CURLY.—In Kokomo, in the bounds of the Greentown church, Howard Co., Ind., at the residence of his daughter, Mrs. Mary Quinn, Wm. Curly, aged 72 years, 10 months and 21 days. Deceased was born in Dublin, Ireland, and came to this country when a young man. Funeral services by the writer, assisted by Rev. David Wack, of the Christian church. Text, Job 14: 14.

ABRAHAM CAYLOR.

ZUG.—In the Tulpahocken church, Richland, Lebanon Co., Pa., April 12, 1892, Abraham Zug, aged 85 years and 5 days. He was born in Lexington, Lancaster Co., Pa., April 9, 1807. His father, Eld. Abraham Zug, preceded him to the spirit world 50 years, 8 months and 24 days, at the age of 69 years, 4 months and 12 days. He was married Feb. 28, 1832, to sister Anna Royer. Their union was blessed with four sons and five daughters. Funeral services by Brethren S. R. Zug and C. Bucher, from Ps. 90. MICHAEL ZUG.

STOVER.—At Hagerstown, Md., Jan. 10, 1891, sister Mary (nee Royer) Stover, widow of Jacob Stover, aged 79 years, 5 months and 21 days. Sister Stover was born near Waynesborough, Pa., and united with the Brethren's church when about twenty years old. Funeral services by Eld. Nicholas Martin in Price's church. Interment in cemetery adjoining. A. B. BARNHART.

WITTER.—Near North Manchester, Wabash Co., Ind., April 15, 1892, sister Martha, wife of Levi W. Witter and youngest daughter of Bro. Christian and sister Mary Frantz, aged 28 years, 8 months and 24 days. She leaves a husband and four small children. She united with the Brethren church in 1879. Funeral discourse by brethren Albert Wright and Samuel Leckrone, from 1 Thess. 4: 13.

EMMA FRANTZ.

JOSEPH.—In the Yellow River congregation, Marshall County, Ind., April 21, 1892, Elza Owen, infant son of John and Mancie Joseph, aged 1 year, 6 months and 16 days. Services by Bro. John H. Sellers, assisted by William R. Myers, from Matt. 19: 14.

SNYDER. — In the same congregation, April 3, 1892, of whooping cough, Gracie, infant daughter of Henry and Alice Snyder, aged about five weeks. Services by Bro. John H. Sellers, assisted by Martin A. Eisenhour, from Matt. 19: 14.

GANSHORN. — In the Camp Creek church, Kosciusko County, Ind., Ralph Leroy, infant son of Bro. John and sister Addie Ganshorn, aged 5 months and 24 days. Funeral services were conducted by Bro. John H. Sellars, assisted by Bro. John W. Shively, from John 11: 28. CHARLIE H. SELLERS.

EAGLER.—In the Tippecanoe church, Kosciusko Co., Ind., John Eagler, aged about 56 years. He was an invalid for several years. Seven weeks before his death he united with the church by faith and baptism. Funeral services from Job 14: 10.

D. ROTHENBERGER.

BEEGHLY.—In Waterloo, Iowa, March 24, 1892, sister Susan, wife of Bro. Martin Beeghly, aged 60 years and 11 months. Sister Beeghly was of an amiable disposition, and although she suffered severely, she bore it all patiently. Funeral services were held in the Brethren church in the city, by Bro. Wm. Ikenberry and the writer, in the presence of a large congregation.

FORNEY.—Also, in the South Waterloo church, Iowa, April 18, 1892, Mary Forney, wife of Joseph Forney, deceased. The subject of this notice had united with the Progressives, as also had her husband. Her age was 78 years, 11 months and 15 days. The funeral services were held in the South Waterloo church by H. R. Holsinger and the writer.

J. A. MURRAY.

Announcements.

DISTRICT MEETINGS.

May 17, at 8 A. M., District of Southern Ohio, in the Lexington church, Highland Co., Ohio. Buy your ticket to Highland, Lexington Village, on the Cincinnati and Marietta Railway; go by way of Cincinnati.

May 24 and 25. South-eastern District of Kansas, to be held with the Brethren of Neosho County, near Cedar-burgh, on the M. K. & T. R. R., one mile north, and 1¾ miles east of Galesburgh. Ministerial Meeting May 24.

LOVE-FEASTS.

May 10, 10:3 P. M., Panther Creek church, Woodford Co., Ill. Meetings to continue over Sunday.

May 20, at 10 A. M., Mississinewa church, Delaware Co., Ind., 3 miles west of Shideler. Those coming by rail should come to Shideler and inquire for the brethren.

May 20, at 10 A. M., Bethel church, Nebr.

May 21, at 3 P. M., Pleasant View church, Reno Co., Kans., 1¾ miles south-west of Booth.

May 21, at 3 P. M., McPherson, Kans.

May 21, Alberta church, Pa.

May 21 and 22, at 10 A. M., West Branch church, Ogle Co., Ill.

May 21, in the Bethel church, Thayer Co., Nebr.

May 27, at 4 P. M., Hopewell church, Bedford Co., Pa.

May 21, at 1:30 P. M., Aughwick church, Pa. Meetings are to continue next day, to be held in the Germany Valley church.

May 21, English Prairie church, Lagrange Co., Ind. A series of meetings will commence on Thursday previous to the Communion.

May 21, at 3 P. M., McPherson, Kans.

May 25, at 4 P. M., Turkey Creek congregation, at the Gravelton house, Elkhart Co., Ind.

May 26 and 27, at 10 A. M., Pine Creek, Ogle Co., Ill.

May 27, at 10 A. M., in the Killbuck church, nine miles west of Muncie, Ind.

May 27, at 3 P. M., in the Harlan congregation, four miles east of Harlan, Shelby Co., Iowa. Meetings to continue over Sunday.

July 27, at 4 P. M., Buck Creek church, Ind.

May 28, at 10 A. M., Hartford Church, Hartford City, Ind.

May 27 and 28, at 2 P. M., Lost Creek congregation, Juniata Co., Pa., at Goodwill.

May 21, at 3 P. M., Monticello church, Ind.

May 27, at 4 P. M., Pleasant Hill church, Jefferson Co., Iowa. Stop off at Libertyville.

May 28, at 2 P. M., Middle Creek congregation, Somerset Co., Pa.

May 28, in the North Manchester church, 2 miles west of the town of North Manchester, Ind.

May 28, at 2 P. M., Pleasant Valley church, Darke Co., Ohio. Meetings to continue over Sunday.

May 28, at 3 P. M., Landisville, Grant Co., Ind.

May 28, at 10 A. M., Rome congregation, Oak Grove house, Hancock Co., Ohio.

May 28 and 29, at 3 P. M., Lanark church, Carroll Co., Ill.

May 28 and 29, at 10 A. M., in the Rock River congregation, Ill., at the Franklin Grove meeting-house.

May 29, at 2 P. M., Des Moines Valley church, Polk Co., Iowa. The 10 and 11 o'clock trains will be met at Ankeny on the day of meeting.

May 31 and June 1, at 2 P. M., Hickory Grove church, O.

May 31 and June 1, at 2 P. M., Cherry Grove, Carroll Co., Ill.

May 31, at 4 P. M., in the Bauge church, Elkhart Co., Ind., three miles north-west of Wakarusa, Ind.

May 31, at 4 P. M., Oakland church, Darke Co., Ohio.

May 31 and June 1, at 2 P. M., Buffalo Valley church, Union Co., Pa.

June 1, in the Yellow Creek church, Elkhart Co., Ind., 7 miles south-west of Goshen.

June 1, at 4 P. M., Yellow Creek church, Elkhart Co., Ind.

June 1, at 4 P. M., South Beatrice church, Gage Co., Nebr. Those coming via U. P. R. R., stop at Holmesville; via the B. & M. R. R., should stop off at Beatrice; via the Rock Island R. R., should stop at Rockford.

June 1, at 4 P. M., at Flora, Ind. Train due here from the south at 10 A. M.

June 1, at 4 P. M., White church, Montgomery Co., Ind., 4½ miles west of Colfax, Ind.

June 2, at 10 A. M., Buck Creek, Franklin Co., Pa., at the Shank meeting-house, 1½ miles south of Greencastle.

June 2 and 3, at 1 P. M., Yellow Creek, Ill.

June 2, at 4 P. M., in the Pakalina church, Darke Co., Ohio.

June 2, at 4 P. M., Upper Fall Creek church, 2 miles east of Middletown, Henry Co., Ind.

June 2, at 10 A. M., Bel River church, Ind.

June 2, at 10 A. M., Cedar Lake congregation, near Corunna, Dekalb Co., Ind.

June 2 and 3, at 10 A. M., Astoria church, Ill.

June 2, at 2 P. M., in the Solomony church, at Lancaster, 3 miles south of Huntington, Ind.

June 2, Pakalina church, Ohio. Members will be met at New Madison and Clark's Station on the "Big Four R. R." by notifying Moses Hollinger, New Madison, Ohio.

June 2, at 4 P. M., in the Okaw church, Platt Co., Ill. Ministering brethren on their way to Annual Meeting, will please stop with us.

June 2, Tippecanoe church, Koshiokko Co., Ind.

June 3, at 2 P. M., Walnut Level church, Wells Co., Ind.

June 3, at 4 P. M., Blue Ridge church, Piatt Co., Ill.

June 6, at 10 A. M., Springfield congregation, Wawaka, Ind.

June 4 and 5, at 2 P. M., 2½ miles south-west of Summerfield, Kan.

June 4, at 5 P. M., Mound church, Bates Co., Mo.

June 4 and 5, at 2 P. M., Hickory Grove church, Carroll Co., Ill. Brethren going to Annual Meeting will please remember us.

June 6, at 2 P. M., Barberly church, W. Va.

June 4, at 10 A. M., Lick Creek church, Williams Co., Ohio, 2 mile south-west of Bryan.

June 6, at 2 P. M., Brownsville, Md.

June 6, at 3 P. M., Maple Valley church, Iowa.

June 6, at 5 P. M., 3½ miles north-east of Summerville, Ind.

June 6, at 5 P. M., Mound church, Bates Co., Mo.

June 7, West Conestogo church, at the Middle Creek house, Lancaster Co., Pa.

June 8, at 2 P. M., Ephrata, Pa., at the Mohler house.

June 8, Welsh Oak church, at the Pennville house, Lee Center Co., Pa.

June 11, 5½ miles North-west of Cabool, Mo.

June 11, at 2 P. M., Cornell church, Ill., on the Streator Branch of the Wabash R. R.

June 11 and 12, at 10 A. M., Greene church, Greene, Iowa. There will be preaching on Friday evening previous.

June 11, at 2 P. M., Quemahoning church, Somerset Co., Pa.

June 11, at 2 P. M., Kingsley church, four miles south-east of Kingsley, Iowa.

June 11, at 2 P. M., in the Mueller church, 2 miles west and 2 miles south of McPherson, Kans.

June 11, at 10 A. M., Hudson, Ill.

June 11, at 5 P. M., in the Bethel congregation, Koskiosko Co., Ind., at the Pleasant View Chapel, three miles east of Milford.

June 11, at 4 P. M., Camp Creek church, Kosciusko Co., Ind., 2 miles North of Etta Green. Those coming from the West at 10 M. and East at 2 P. M., will find conveyance to the church.

June 18, at the Cedar Meeting house, Cerisco, Stark Co., Ohio.

June 18, at 6 P. M., in the Eagle Creek church, Ohio. A series of meetings will be held in connection, beginning June 16.

June 11, at 10 A. M., in the west house, Thornapple church, Mich. Take the D. L. & N. R. R. from Grand Rapids, Mich., to Elmdale, where you will be met by notifying L. D. Fry, Elmdale, Mich.

June 11, Plum Creek church, Pa. A series of meetings is begun one week previous. Eld. S. H. Meyers is expected to be with us.

June 11, at 4 P. M., in the Shade Creek congregation, Somerset Co., Pa.

June 17 and 18, Dallas Center church, Iowa.

June 17, at 4 P. M., Yellow River congregation, Marshall Co., Ind.

June 18 and 19, Panther Creek, Dallas Co., Iowa.

June 18, at 10 A. M., South Waterloo church, Waterloo, Iowa.

June 18, Green Spring District, Seneca Co., Ohio.

June 25, at 10 A. M., at the Van Wert church, seven miles north-east of Van Wert, Ohio. Those coming by rail will be met at Van Wert, day before the meeting by notifying Jacob Heisland, or Joseph Longnecker, Wetzel, Ohio.

June 25 and 26, Indian Creek church, Polk Co., Iowa.

June 18, at 2 P. M., Brick church, Ten Mile congregation, about 10 miles South-east of Washington, Pa. There will be one week's meeting previous to the feast.

Annual Meeting at Cedar Rapids.

FOR the coming Conference at Cedar Rapids, June next, "THE IOWA ROUTE," Burlington, Cedar Rapids & Northern Ry., offers you unlimited accommodations, operating in connection with the Chicago, Rock Island & Pacific, and Rock Island and Peoria Rys., making good connections at Chicago and Peoria with all eastern lines; at Kansas City with all south-western lines; at Omaha, with all western lines. And in connection with the St. L. & N. W. R. R. at St. Louis, with south, south-eastern, and south-western lines, a system of through train service being operated from above points, assures you of a quick and pleasant journey. Special trains will be run from various points to accommodate the demand of the business. All trains stop at the Union Depot in Cedar Rapids. Those traveling via this route may be assured of first-class accommodations and courteous treatment. For further information, as to rates of fare, time of trains, etc., apply to any agent of the above-named lines, or to

J. E. HANNEGAN,
G. T. & P. A., B. C. R. & N. R'y.
Cedar Rapids, Iowa.

Gospel Chimes.

BY WM. BEERY.

A new edition of this deservedly-popular Sunday-school song-book has just been issued.

Bro. Beery has had a large experience in Sunday-school work, and the book which we offer to the Brethren, and the public in general, evinces the exercise of talent as well as good judgment. The religious purity of the hymns, contributed by sister Beery, adds much to the excellence of the book.

Price per single copy, 30 cts.; per dozen, by mail, $3.00; by express, $2.60. Lots of more than a dozen must be sent by express.

BRETHREN'S PUBLISHING CO.,
Or Huntington, Pa.   Mt. Morris Ill.

NOTICE!

NEVER since the meeting at Bismark Grove, Kans., have I attended an Annual Meeting, nor have I been represented at any Conference since then; but I will attend the Meeting at Cedar Rapids, Iowa, this year, not to sell medicine, nor to give medicine away, nor to advertise any medicine; but to enjoy the meeting and be accessible to those of my numerous correspondents, who desire to interview me.

No one else will represent me; but those who want to pay money, or order medicine from me should do so by mail and address,

DR. PETER FAHRNEY,
S. Hoyne Ave.,
Chicago, Ill.

CANCERS, TUMORS, ETC.

Successfully treated by Dr. G. N. Boteler, of Waynesborough, Pa., who is at last prepared for the last sixteen years. Dr. Boteler is a graduate of the University of Maryland, at Baltimore City. References given and correspondence solicited. Address, Dr. G. W. Boteler, Waynesborough, Pa.

CRUDEN'S COMPLETE CONCORDANCE

THIS excellent work, which we offer for sale to our readers, at the low price of $1.50 post-paid, is the only one of its kind that may be depended upon as being strictly reliable. Any verse in the Bible may be readily found by looking for any material word in the verse. Besides this there are given the significations of the principal words, by which their true, Scriptural meaning may be known. A full account of Jewish customs and ceremonies is given as well as a complete concordance of the proper names of the Bible and of the books called Apocrypha. Send all orders for the above work to this office

Announcements.

DISTRICT MEETINGS.

May 17, at 8 A. M., District of Southern Ohio, in the Lexington church, Highland Co., Ohio. Buy your ticket to Highland, Lexington Village, on the Cincinnati and Marietta Railway; go by way of Cincinnati.

May 24 and 25, South-eastern District of Kansas, to be held with the Brethren of Neosho County, near Galesburgh, on the M. K. & T. R. R., one mile north, and 1½ miles east of Galesburgh. Ministerial Meeting May 24.

LOVE-FEASTS.

May 20, at 3 P. M., Panther Creek church, Woodford Co., Ill. Meetings to continue over Sunday.

May 20, at 10 A. M., Mininniewa church, Delaware Co., Ind. 3 miles west of Shideler. Those coming by rail should come to Shideler and inquire for the brethren.

May 21, at 10 A. M., Bethel church, Nebr.

May 21, at 1 P. M., Pleasant View church, Reno Co., Kans. 7½ miles south-west of Beech.

May 21, at 5 P. M., McPherson, Kans.

May 21, at Altoona church, Pa.

May 21 and 22, at 10 A. M., West Branch church, Ogle Co., Ill.

May 21, in the Bethel church, Thayer Co., Nebr.

May 27, at 4 P. M., Hopewell church, Bedford Co., Pa.

May 21, at 2:30 P. M., Aughwick church, Pa. Meetings are to continue next day, to be held in the Germany Valley church.

May 21, English Prairie church, Lagrange Co., Ind. A series of meetings will commence on Thursday previous to the Communion.

May 21, at 3 P. M., McPherson, Kans.

May 25, at 4 P. M., Turkey Creek congregation, at the Gravelton house, Elkhart Co., Ind.

May 26 and 27, at 10 A. M., Pine Creek, Ogle Co., Ill.

May 27, at 10 A. M., in the Killbuck church, nine miles west of Muncie, Ind.

May 27, at 2 P. M., in the Harlan congregation, four miles east of Harlan, Shelby Co., Iowa. Meetings to continue over Sunday.

May 27, at 4 P. M., Buck Creek, Ind.

May 28, at 10 A. M., Hartford Church, Hartford City, Ind.

May 27 and 28, at 2 P. M., Loni Creek congregation, Juniata Co., Pa., at Goodwill.

May 27, at 4 P. M., Monticello church, Ind.

May 27, at 2 P. M., Pleasant Hill church, Jefferson Co., Iowa. Stop off at Libertyville.

May 28, at 4 P. M., Middle Creek congregation, Somerset Co., Pa.

May 28, in the North Manchester church, 2 miles west of the town of North Manchester, Ind.

May 28, at 2 P. M., Pleasant Valley church, Darke Co., Ohio. Meetings to continue over Sunday.

May 28, at 1 P. M., Landessville, Grant Co., Ind.

May 28, at 10 A. M., Rome congregation, Oak Grove house, Hancock Co., Ind.

May 28 and 29, at 5 P. M., Lanark church, Carroll Co., Ill.

May 28 and 29, at 10 A. M., in the Rock River congregation, Ill., at the Franklin Grove meeting-house.

May 29, at 2 P. M., Des Moines Valley church, Polk Co., Iowa. The 10 and 12 o'clock trains will be met at Ankeny on the day of meeting.

May 31 and June 1, at 2 P. M., Hickory Grove church, O.

May 31 and June 1, at 2 P. M., Cherry Grove, Carroll Co., Ill.

May 31, at 4 P. M., in the Bango church, Elkhart Co., Ind., three miles north-west of Wakarusa, Ind.

May 31, at 4 P. M., Oakland church, Darke Co., Ohio.

May 31 and June 1, at 2 P. M., Buffalo Valley church, Union Co., Pa.

June 1, in the Yellow Creek church, Elkhart Co., Ind., 7 miles south-west of Goshen.

June 1, at 4 P. M., Yellow Creek church, Elkhart Co., Ind.

June 1, at 2 P. M., South Beatrice church, Gage Co., Nebr. Those coming via U. P. R. R., stop at Holmesville; via the B. & M.·R. R., should stop off at Beatrice; via the Rock Island R. R., should stop at Rockford.

June 1, at 2 P. M., at Flora, Ind. Train due here from the south at 10 A. M.

June 2, at 4 P. M., White church, Montgomery Co., Ind., 4¾ miles west of Colfax, Ind.

June 2, at 10 A. M., Back Creek, Franklin Co., Pa., at the Shank meeting-house, 1½ miles north of Greencastle.

June 2 and 3, at 2 P. M., Yellow Creek, Ill.

June 2, at 2 P. M., in the Palestine church, Darke Co., at the Oakland house.

June 2, at 2 P. M., Upper Fall Creek church, 7 miles east of Middletown, Henry Co., Ind.

June 2, at 10 A. M., Eel River church, Ind.

June 2, at 10 A. M., Cedar Lake congregation, near Corunna, Dekalb Co., Ind.

June 2 and 3, at 10 A. M., Astoria church, Ill.

June 2, at 2 P. M., in the Salimony church, at Lancaster, 5 miles south of Huntington, Ind.

June 2, Palastine church, Ohio. Members will be met at New Madison and Clark's Station on the "Big Four R. R." by notifying Hiram Holsinger, New Madison, Ohio.

June 2, at 4 P. M., in the Okaw church, Piatt Co., Ill. Ministering brethren on their way to Annual Meeting, will please stop with us.

June 3, Tippecanoe church, Kosciusko Co., Ind.

June 3, at 2 P. M., Walnut Level church, Wells Co., Ind.

June 3, at 2 P. M., Blue Ridge church, Piatt Co., Ill.

June 4, at 10 A. M., Springfield congregation, Wawaka, Ind.

June 4 and 5, at 4 P. M., 6½ miles south-west of Summerfield, Kan.

June 4, at 5 P. M., Mound church, Bates Co., Mo.

June 4 and 5, at 2 P. M., Hickory Grove church, Carroll Co., Ill. Brethren going to Annual Meeting will please remember us.

June 4, at 2 P. M., Berkeley church, W. Va.

June 4, at 10 A. M., Lick Creek church, Williams Co., Ohio, 7 mile south-west of Bryan.

June 4, at 2 P. M., Brownsville, Md.

June 4, at 3 P. M., Maple Valley church, Iowa.

June 4, at 2 P. M., 3½ miles north-east of Summitville, Ind.

June 7, West Crossings church, at the Middle Creek house, Lancaster Co., Pa.

June 8, at 3 P. M., Ephrata, Pa., at the Mohler house.

June 8, White Oak church, at the Pennville house, Lancaster Co., Pa.

June 11, 5½ miles North-west of Cabool, Mo.

June 11, at 2 P. M., Cornell church, Ill., on the Streator Branch of the Wabash R. R.

June 11 and 12, at 10 A. M., Greene church, Greene, Iowa. There will be preaching on Friday evening previous.

June 11, at 4 P. M., Quemahoning church, Somerset Co., Pa.

June 11, at 3 P. M., Kingsley church, four miles south-east of Kingsley, Iowa.

June 11, at 2 P. M., in the Monitor church, 8 miles west of, 2 miles south of McPherson, Kans.

June 11, at 10 A. M., Hudson, Ill.

June 11, at 2 P. M., in the Bethel congregation, Kewanna, Cass, Ind., at the Pleasant View Chapel, three miles east of Milford.

June 13, at 4 P. M., Camp Creek church, Kosciusko Co., Ind., 4 miles North of Etna Green. Those coming from the West at 10 M. and East at 2 P. M., will find conveyance to the church.

June 18, at the Center Meeting house, Canton, Stark Co., Ohio.

June 18, at 6 P. M., in the Eagle Creek church, Ohio. A series of meetings will be held in connection, beginning June 16.

June 21, at 10 A. M., in the west house, Thornapple church, Mich. Take the D. L. & N. R. R. from Grand Rapids, Mich., to Elmdale, where you will be met by notifying L. D. Fry, Elmdale, Mich.

June 23, Plum Creek church, Pa. A series of meetings to begin one week previous. Eld. S. H. Meyers is expected to be with us.

June 10, at 4 P. M., in the Shade Creek congregation, Somerset Co., Pa.

June 15 and 16, Dallas Center church, Iowa.

June 15, at 4 P. M., Yellow River congregation, Marshall Co., Ind.

June 18 and 19, Panther Creek, Dallas Co., Iowa.

June 18, at 10 A. M., South Waterloo church, Waterloo, Iowa.

June 18, Green Spring District, Seneca Co., Ohio.

June 18 and 19 at 11 A. M., Middle Creek church, Nebraska Co., Iowa.

June 25, at 10 A. M., at the Van Wert church, seven miles north-east of Van Wert, Ohio. Those coming by rail will be met at Van Wert, day before the meeting by notifying Jacob Heistand, or Joseph Longanecker, Wettel, Ohio.

June 25 and 26, Indian Creek church, Polk Co., Iowa.

June 18, at 2 P. M., Brick church, Ten Mile congregation, about 10 miles South-east of Washington, Pa. There will be one week's meeting previous to the feast.

Annual Meeting at Cedar Rapids.

For the coming Conference at Cedar Rapids, June next, "THE IOWA ROUTE," Burlington, Cedar Rapids & Northern Ry., offers you unlimited accommodations, operating in connection with the Chicago, Rock Island & Pacific, and Rock Island and Peoria Rys., making good connections at Chicago and Peoria with all eastern lines; at Kansas City with all south-western lines; at Omaha, with all western lines. And in connection with the St. L., K. & N. W. R. R. at St. Louis, with south, south-eastern, and south-western lines, a system of through train service being operated from above points, secures you of a quick and pleasant journey. Special trains will be run from various points to accommodate the demand of the business. All trains stop at the Union Depot in Cedar Rapids. Those traveling via this route may be assured of first-class accommodations and courteous treatment. For further information, as to rates of fare, time of trains, etc., apply to any agent of the above-named lines, or to

J. E. HANNEGAN,
G. T. & P. A., B. C. R. & N. R'y.
Cedar Rapids, Iowa.

Gospel Chimes.

BY WM. BEERY.

A new edition of this deservedly-popular Sunday-school song-book has just been issued.

Bro. Beery has had a large experience in Sunday-school work, and the book which we offer to the Brethren, and the public in general, evinces the exercise of talent as well as good judgment. The religious purity of the hymns, contributed by sister Beery, adds much to the excellence of the book.

Price per single copy, 30 cts.; per dozen, by mail, $3.00; by express, $2.60. Lots of more than a dozen must be sent by express.

BRETHREN'S PUBLISHING CO.,
Or Huntingdon, Pa., Mt. Morris Ill.

NOTICE!

NEVER since the meeting at Bismark Grove, Kans, have I attended an Annual Meeting, nor have I been represented at any Conference since then; but I will attend the Meeting at Cedar Rapids, Iowa, this year, NOT to sell medicine, NOT to give medicine away, NOT to advertise any medicine; but to enjoy the meeting and be accessible to those of my numerous correspondents, who desire to interview me.

No one else will represent me; but those who want to pay money, or order medicine from me should do so by mail and address,

DR. PETER FAHRNEY,
112 S. Hoyne Ave.,
Chicago, Ill.

CANCERS, TUMORS, ETC.

Successfully treated by Dr. G. N. Buteler, of Waynesborough, Pa., where he has practiced for the last sixteen years. Dr. Buteler is a graduate of the University of Maryland, at Baltimore City. References given and correspondence solicited. Address, Dr. G. W. Buteler, Waynesborough, Pa.

CRUDEN'S COMPLETE CONCORDANCE

THIS excellent work, which we offer for sale to our readers, at the low price of $1.50 post-paid, is the only one of the kind that may be depended upon as being strictly reliable. Any versel in the Bible may be readily found by looking for any material word in the verse. Besides this there are given the significations of the principal words, by which their true, Scriptural meaning may be known. A full account of Jewish customs and ceremonies is given as well as a complete concordance of the proper names of the Bible and of the books called Apocrypha. Send all orders for the above work to this office.

→ESSAYS←

"Study to show thyself approved unto God; a workman that needeth not be ashamed, rightly dividing the Word of Truth."

"NOW I LAY ME DOWN TO SLEEP."

[This poem, written by a tramp, and left by him at the office of the Wichita (Kansas) *Eagle*, for publication, has met with a hearty approval at the hands of the critics.]

Near the camp-fire's flickering light,
In my blanket-bed I lie,
Gazing through the shades of night
At the twinkling stars on high;
O'er me spirits in the air
Silent vigils seem to keep,
As I breathe my childhood's prayer,
"Now I lay me down to sleep."

Sadly sighs the whip-poor-will
In the boughs of yonder tree;
Laughingly the dancing rill
Swells the midnight melody:
Foeman may be lurking near,
In the canyon dark and deep,
Low I breathe in Jesus' ear,
"I pray thee, Lord, my soul to keep."

'Mid those stars a face I see,
One the Savior called away,—
Mother, who, in infancy,
Taught my baby lips to pray;
Her sweet spirit hovers near,
In this lonely mountain-brake;
Take me to her, Savior dear,
"If I should die before I wake."

Fainter glows the flickering light,
As each ember slowly dies;
Plaintively the birds of night
Fill the air with sudden cries;
Over me they seem to cry,
"You must never more awake,"
Low I lisp, "If I should die,
I pray thee, Lord, my soul to take."
—*Selected by J. E. Blough.*

CHRISTIAN SELF-DENIAL.

BY D. E. PRICE.

In Two Chapters.—Chapter Two.

WE read in 1 Pet. 4: 1, "Forasmuch then as Christ hath suffered for us in the flesh, arm yourselves likewise with the same mind; for he that hath suffered in the flesh hath ceased from sin." When the Scriptures speak of suffering in the flesh, they undoubtedly do not mean the physical body, but the carnal mind, or our stubborn and rebellious dispositions by nature.

The question might arise, "What is the cross, and of what does it consist?" Literally speaking, a cross is two lines or bodies crossing each other at right angles. The Roman cross on which the Savior was crucified, was found of two beams, or pieces of wood, crossing each other; but our cross is somewhat different from that, for it is to be borne daily. To illustrate, we will suppose a man to be in very limited circumstances financially, scarcely able to support himself and family, but his neighbor has abundance; his granaries are stored with the good things of earth. He concludes he will go to his neighbor's barn and appropriate some of his grain to his and his family's use, but the Word of God crosses his pathway, and says, " *Thou shalt not steal.*" Now, if he takes up the cross and refrains from doing what he intended to do, he ceases from the sin of theft, because he does not do what he is tempted to do. When the thought enters the heart to do anything that is contrary to the Word of God, and we do not yield to the desire of the flesh, but bring the evil thought into subjection to God's Word, we are bearing the cross, we practice self-denial. For instance, we are naturally inclined to follow the fashions of the world, but the Word of the Lord says, "Be not conformed to this world." Again,

we are inclined to go to places of worldly amusements, but the Word of God says, "Ye are not of this world, but I have chosen you out of the world." Thus, by always submitting to the truth, though it *crosses* our pathway,—though it produces *self-denial,* we cease from sin, and "have a conscience void of offence toward God and man."

But what will be the result if we yield to the temptations or inclinations of the flesh, and do what the Gospel forbids? Let us take up the *cross* and make humble confession and ask forgiveness of the Lord, and whomsoever else we may have offended, and we have the *precious promise* that it will be forgiven. 1 John 1: 9. It is no doubt more of a cross to confess a fault, than to refrain from committing it; but the only remedy for our mistakes in life is, to make humble acknowledgment, in order to our restitution to the favor of God. Some one may be ready to say, "Do we not read, 'That whosoever looketh on a woman to lust after her, hath committed adultery with her already in his heart'?" Matt. 5: 28. Again, "Whosoever hateth his brother is a murderer, and ye know that no murderer hath eternal life abiding in him." John 3: 15. There is quite a difference between being tempted, and lusting after anything unlawful. We may be tempted to do wrong, but should bring the unlawful desire into subjection, instead of seeking opportunity of satisfying our unhallowed inclinations. Suppose a brother should be severely insulted by his fellow-man, and the temptation would enter his heart to take his life, and he would seek opportunity to carry out his purpose, but fail. The crime would be as great in the sight of the Lord as if he had committed the act; but suppose, before he got the opportunity to carry out his intentions, he is brought to see the heinousness of his crime; it will be much easier to repent at that time, than if he had committed the crime. He will have to thoroughly repeat of his sin before God, and desire and ask pardon, but since no human being knows anything of it, or has been affected by it, there is nothing more necessary. But supposing he committed the act, and secreted the body somewhere, and no one else knew what had become of it, can he repent in the same way? We think not. The only possible chance in such a case, if any, would be to reveal his crime to the church, and undergo the judgment of that body, and then deliver himself up to the civil authorities and undergo the judgment there, even if it should be death.

But there is another way in which we must bear the cross. We find some positive commands in the Bible that are repulsive to the flesh. To illustrate, we are commanded to "not *resist* evil, to *love* our enemies, do them *good* and *pray* for them." All of this is contrary to nature, or we are naturally inclined to neglect; hence, when our nature comes in contact with, or crosses, God's Word we must take up the cross, and keep in conformity with it, do what we are commanded to do, however repulsive it may be to our natural propensities. Then we cease from the sin of *omission.* I am afraid that many professors of Christianity have no higher sense of Christian duty than the prohibitory law, or that which God hath said we shall not do. I sometimes call them negative Christians. The ordinances of baptism and feet-washing are also repulsive to the carnal mind; and if we would yield to the natural inclinations of the flesh, we would not submit to the observance of them; but as soon as we bring that *stubborn* and *rebellious* spirit into subjection to God's Word, we cease from the sin of *neglect.* "How shall we escape if we *neglect* so great salvation?"

The flesh must be *crucified* through repentance toward God, and faith in the Lord Jesus Christ, and brought into death. "Therefore we are buried with him by baptism into death: that like as

Christ was raised up from the dead by the glory of the Father, even so we also should walk in newness of life. For if we have been planted together in the likeness of his death, we shall be also in the likeness of his resurrection: knowing this, that our old man is crucified with him, that the body of sin might be destroyed, that henceforth we should not serve sin. For he that is dead is freed from sin." Rom. 6: 4-7.

After our conversion we do not serve sin any more; but "the motions of sin are in our members," which brings about this continual warfare between the flesh and the spirit. But if we practice *self-denial* enough to hold the flesh in subjection, we shall be heirs of eternal life. Oh, that all, who profess the Christian name, would deny themselves of all ungodliness and worldly lusts, and live soberly, righteously, and godly in this present world! Then they could gladly "look for the blessed hope, and glorious appearing of the great God, and our Savior Jesus Christ," or, as Paul could say when he was about to take his departure from this world, 2 Tim. 4: 6-8, "For I am now ready to be offered, and the time of my departure is at hand. I have fought a good fight, I have finished my course, I have kept the faith; henceforth there is laid up for me a crown of righteousness, which the Lord, the righteous judge, shall give me at that day; and not to me only, but to all them also that love his appearing."

DRESS REFORM.

HOWEVER much intelligent women may yield to the tyranny of Fashion, they recognize the fact that comfort and health are the last things with which that fickle goddess concerns herself. Indeed they know, and long have known, that the modern dress of their sex is positively injurious in both these respects. They know it as formerly many good men at the South felt slavery to be wrong, and yet felt obliged to submit to it as to an irremediable evil.

It is pitiable that this should be so at the height of modern civilization, Christian enlightenment and physiological knowledge, when nearly three thousand years ago the women of Greece furnished the world with the highest ideal of the female form, clad in robes that gave freedom to every limb and the fullest play to every internal organ. Our all-wise Creator sought to protect the nobler vital organs, and at the same time to provide for their freest movement, by surrounding them with the ribs and giving these power to expand with every inhalation; but fashion seeks to defy the Almighty.

Beginning when the bones are soft and pliable, it insists on diminishing the capacity of the chest and its power of expansion. The result is that respiration is interfered with, the liver is badly crowded upon, sometimes, in fact, almost out in two, while the abdominal organs are forced into unnatural positions which lead almost inevitably to serious disorders.

But it is a satisfaction to know that women are realizing more and more the galling and sinful character of this servitude. Indeed, dress reform is already among the recognized movements of the age. Nor is it in the hands of "cranks," but in those of broad-minded women, who understand the necessary limits of the reform proposed.

The reform is gathering momentum both in England and in this country. It is something that the word and the idea are becoming everywhere familiar among us, and that practical measures are in progress for its success. The study of physiology in schools is helping it. Says the *Lancet:*

"The close relation between health and wholesome dress need hardly be insisted on. It is, therefore, most satisfactory to learn that a new

✦ESSAYS✦

"Study to show thyself approved unto God; a workman that needeth not to be ashamed, rightly dividing the Word of Truth."

"NOW I LAY ME DOWN TO SLEEP."

[This poem, written by a tramp, and left by him at the office of the Wichita (Kansas) *Eagle*, for publication, has met with a hearty approval at the hands of the critics.]

Near the camp-fire's flickering light,
In my blanket-bed I lie,
Gazing through the shades of night
At the twinkling stars on high;
O'er me spirits in the air
Silent vigils seem to keep,
As I breathe my childhood's prayer,
" Now I lay me down to sleep."

Sadly sighs the whip-poor-will
In the boughs of yonder tree;
Laughingly the dancing rill
Swells the midnight melody;
Foeman may be lurking near,
In the canyon dark and deep,
Low I breathe in Jesus' ear,
"I pray thee, Lord, my soul to keep."

'Mid those stars a face I see,
One the Savior called away,—
Mother, who, in infancy,
Taught my baby lips to pray;
Her sweet spirit hovers near,
In this lonely mountain-brake;
Take me to her, Savior dear,
" If I should die before I wake."

Fainter glows the flickering light,
As each ember slowly dies;
Plaintively the birds of night
Fill the air with sudden cries;
Over me they seem to cry,
" You must never more awake,"
Low I lisp, " If I should die,
I pray thee, Lord, my soul to take."

—Selected by J. E. Bjough.

CHRISTIAN SELF-DENIAL.

BY D. E. PRICE.

In Two Chapters.—Chapter Two.

WE read in 1 Pet. 4: 1, "Forasmuch then as Christ hath suffered for us in the flesh, arm yourselves likewise with the same mind; for he that hath suffered in the flesh hath ceased from sin." When the Scriptures speak of suffering in the flesh, they undoubtedly do not mean the physical body, but the carnal mind, or our stubborn and rebellious dispositions by nature.

The question might arise, "What is the cross, and of what does it consist?" Literally speaking, a cross is two lines or bodies crossing each other at right angles. The Roman cross on which the Savior was crucified, was found of two beams, or pieces of wood, crossing each other; but our cross is somewhat different from that, for it is to be borne daily. To illustrate, we will suppose a man to be in very limited circumstances financially, scarcely able to support himself and family, but his neighbor has abundance; his granaries are stored with the good things of earth. He concludes he will go to his neighbor's barn and appropriate some of his grain to his and his family's use, but the Word of God crosses his pathway, and says, " *Thou shalt not steal.*" Now, if he takes up the cross and refrains from doing what he intended to do, he ceases from the sin of theft, because he does not do what he is tempted to do. When the thought enters the heart to do anything that is contrary to the Word of God, and we do not yield to the desire of the flesh, but bring the evil thought into subjection to God's Word, we are bearing the cross, we practice self-denial. For instance, we are naturally inclined to follow the fashions of the world, but the Word of the Lord says, " Be not conformed to this world." Again,

we are inclined to go to places of worldly amusements, but the Word of God says, " Ye are not of this world, but I have chosen you out of the world." Thus, by always submitting to the truth, though it crosses our pathway,—though it produces *self-denial*, we cease from sin, and " have a conscience void of offence toward God and man."

But what will be the result if we yield to the temptations or inclinations of the flesh, and do what the Gospel forbids? Let us take up the cross and make humble confession and ask forgiveness of the Lord, and whomsoever else we may have offended, and we have the *precious promise* that it will be forgiven. 1 John 1: 9. It is no doubt more of a cross to confess a fault, than to refrain from committing it; but the only remedy for our mistakes in life is, to make humble acknowledgment, in order to our restitution to the favor of God. Some one may be ready to say, "Do we not read, ' That whosoever looketh on a woman to lust after her, hath committed adultery with her already in his heart' ?" Matt. 5: 28. Again, "Whosoever hateth his brother is a murderer, and ye know that no murderer hath eternal life abiding in him." John 3: 15. There is quite a difference between being tempted, and lusting after anything unlawful. We may be tempted to do wrong, but should bring the unlawful desire into subjection, instead of seeking opportunity of satisfying our unhallowed inclinations. Suppose a brother should be severely insulted by his fellow-man, and the temptation would enter his heart to take his life, and he would seek opportunity to carry out his purpose, but fail. The crime would be as great in the sight of the Lord as if he had committed the act; but suppose, before he got the opportunity to carry out his intentions, he is brought to see the heinousness of his crime; it will be much easier to repent at that time, than if he had committed the crime. He will have to thoroughly repent of his sin before God, and desire and ask pardon, but since no human being knows anything of it, or has been affected by it, there is nothing more necessary. But supposing he committed the act, and secreted the body somewhere, and no one else knew what had become of it, can he repent in the same way? We think not. The only possible chance in such a case, if any, would be to reveal his crime to the church, and undergo the judgment of that body, and then deliver himself up to the civil authorities and undergo the judgment there, even if it should be death.

But there is another way in which we must bear the cross. We find some positive commands in the Bible that are repulsive to the flesh. To illustrate, we are commanded to "not *resist* evil, to *love* our enemies, do them *good* and pray for them." All of this is contrary to nature, or we are naturally inclined to neglect; hence, when our nature comes in contact with, or crosses, God's Word we must take up the cross, and keep in conformity with it, do what we are commanded to do, however repulsive it may be to our natural propensities. Then we cease from the sin of *omission*. I am afraid that many professors of Christianity have no higher sense of Christian duty than the prohibitory law, or that which God hath said we shall not do. I sometimes call them negative Christians. The ordinances of baptism and feet-washing are also repulsive to the carnal mind; and if we would yield to the natural inclinations of the flesh, we would not submit to the observance of them; but as soon as we bring that *stubborn* and *rebellious* spirit into subjection to God's Word, we cease from the sin of *neglect*. "How shall we escape if we *neglect* so great salvation?"

The flesh must be *crucified* through repentance toward God, and faith in the Lord Jesus Christ, and brought into death. "Therefore we are buried with him by baptism into death: that like as

Christ was raised up from the dead by the glory of the Father, even so we also should walk in newness of life. For if we have been planted together in the likeness of his death, we shall be also in the likeness of his resurrection: knowing this, that our old man is crucified with him, that the body of sin might be destroyed, that henceforth we should not serve sin. For he that is dead is freed from sin." Rom. 6: 4–7.

After our conversion we do not serve sin any more; but " the motions of sin are in our members," which brings about this continual warfare between the flesh and the spirit. But if we practice *self-denial* enough to hold the flesh in subjection, we shall be heirs of eternal life. Oh, that all, who profess the Christian name, would deny themselves of all ungodliness and worldly lusts, and live soberly, righteously, and godly in this present world! Then they could gladly " look for the blessed hope, and glorious appearing of the great God, and our Savior Jesus Christ," or, as Paul could say when he was about to take his departure from this world, 2 Tim. 4: 6–8, "For I am now ready to be offered, and the time of my departure is at hand. I have fought a good fight, I have finished my course, I have kept the faith; henceforth there is laid up for me a crown of righteousness, which the Lord, the righteous judge, shall give me at that day; and not to me only, but to all them also that love his appearing."

DRESS REFORM.

HOWEVER much intelligent women may yield to the tyranny of Fashion, they recognize the fact that comfort and health are the last things with which that fickle goddess concerns herself. Indeed they know, and long have known, that the modern dress of their sex is positively injurious in both these respects. They know it as formerly many good men at the South felt slavery to be wrong, and yet felt obliged to submit to it as to an irremediable evil.

It is pitiable that this should be so at the height of modern civilization, Christian enlightenment and physiological knowledge, when nearly three thousand years ago the women of Greece furnished the world with the highest ideal of the female form, clad in robes that gave freedom to every limb and the fullest play to every internal organ. Our all-wise Creator sought to protect the nobler vital organs, and at the same time to provide for their freest movement, by surrounding them with the ribs and giving these power to expand with every inhalation; but fashion seems to defy the Almighty.

Beginning when the bones are soft and pliable, it insists on diminishing the capacity of the chest and its power of expansion. The result is that respiration is interfered with, the liver is badly crowded upon, sometimes, in fact, almost cut in two, while the abdominal organs are forced into unnatural positions which lead almost inevitably to serious disorders.

But it is a satisfaction to know that women are realizing more and more the galling and sinful character of this servitude. Indeed, dress reform is already among the recognized movements of the age. Nor is it in the hands of " cranks," but in those of broad-minded women, who understand the necessary limits of the reform proposed.

The reform is gathering momentum both in England and in this country. It is something that the word and the idea are becoming everywhere familiar among us, and that practical measures are in progress for its success. The study of physiology in schools is helping it. Says the *Lancet*:

" The close relation between health and wholesome dress need hardly be insisted on. It is, therefore, most satisfactory to learn that a new

tempts hitherto made to construct even a doubtful representation of its characteristics are based upon the trifling play of fancy." — *Christian Standard.*

THE SOUL.

BY CHAS. M. YEAROUT.

In Four Chapters.—Chapter Four.

"Souls are said to go to the grave, Pa. 39: 48, to be raised from the grave, Acts 2: 81."—*Ibid., page 56.* I am astonished that an editor, professing to be a Christian, would formulate, print, and send out such a fabrication of misrepresentations. I read Psalm 39 through, and find it has but thirteen verses in it and neither "souls," or "grave" are mentioned. I also read the second chapter of Acts, and find it has but forty-seven verses, and neither "souls," or "grave" are mentioned. I read in verse 27, "Because thou wilt not leave my soul in hell (hades), neither wilt thou suffer thine Holy One to see corruption." Hades, as I have already shown, is the place of departed souls, and cannot be made to mean the grave.

In Psalm 30: 3, we read, "O Lord, thou hast brought up my soul from the grave: thou hast kept me alive, that I should not go down to the pit." If this is what the editor intended to refer to, it is against him; for David says he was kept alive, and life cannot exist in the grave. Neither had he gone to the grave at that time. Why go back from 1,000 to 4,000 years to prove or oppose the immortality of the soul, when it was not brought to light fully until Christ revealed it in the New Testament? Try your hand in that, to prove that man is not in possession of an immortal principle,—eternal life. The soul is purified now by obeying the truth or Word of God. 1 Pet. 1: 22. The body will be purified at the second coming of Christ, (that is the bodies of the righteous; for the bodies of the wicked will never be purified.) Phil. 3: 20–21; 1 Cor. 15: 43, 44, 53, 54. There is not an intimation in the Christian Scriptures,—the last Will and Testament of God,—of the soul going to the grave or coming out of the grave. That is simply a theory of the materialists, who are striving hard to dispose of that noble, God-given attribute,—the soul,—and bring mankind upon a level with the brute creation. Nevertheless, the fact remains, and Christ has said it, that the child of God is in possession of "eternal life." To believe in the existence of the soul, and its immortality, is an innate principle, instilled into man by the Creator. It makes no difference how uncivilized, and barbarous the nations,—all believe in a future state of existence, and that death does *not* extinguish life. Nearly all eminent philosophers, both Christian and heathen, have and do believe in the immortality of the soul. Cicero says, "But if I err in believing that the souls of men are immortal, I willingly err; nor while I live would I wish to have this delightful error extorted from me; and if, after death, I shall feel nothing, as some minute philosophers think, I am not afraid, lest dead philosophers should laugh at me for the error."

One of the early Christian Fathers (Chrysostom, I believe, it was) was brought before the inquisitors and asked to recant, or renounce, his faith, with a threat that if he did not, they would kill him. His answer to them was "Ye cannot kill me; for I am dead, and my life is hid with Christ in God."

The Red Man in North America has this inherent principle firmly rooted in his being. The most wild and savage tribes devotedly cleave to the belief that death does *not* end all life. In their ignorance and superstition, when one of their number dies, they kill his pony beside the grave or burial place, for him to ride to the "better hunting ground," as they call the spirit world. His dogs are also killed and laid beside him on the outside. His gun, or munitions of war, are laid beside him, inside the enclosure. They do not bury their dead in the ground, but lay them on top of the ground, and an arched roof is built over them, either of stone or wood. When I used to pass the Indian burial grounds I wondered why so many animal skeletons of different species were among their dead. They informed me that these were for the use of the departed Indians, or warriors in the better hunting ground. They believe that at death they go immediately to a better country. Where did they get this belief, if it was not instilled into them by the Creative Power, since they have never been taught it by man?

The identity of the soul is demonstrated where limbs have been amputated. Persons, having severed limbs, can tell the exact position of the dismembered part or limb, though many miles intervene between the person and the severed member.

There was a case that came under my personal observation some years ago. A dear brother accidentally shot his left arm off, so it had to be taken out of the socket joint in the shoulder. This took place near Madison, Greenwood Co., Kans. The dismembered arm was placed in a small box, and buried in a cemetery. About two weeks after this, my brother was moved to the City of Emporia in Lyon County, about twenty miles from Madison, in order that he might have the immediate supervision and care of the attending physician. Bro. Eli Franks and my oldest brother were his nurses in Emporia. After he had been there for some time he complained of his lost arm being crooked, and hurting him. My older brother wrote to me to go and take up the arm, and straighten it, if crooked. So a man, by the name of James Tompson, and myself, went and took up the arm, and found it in the exact position complained of, lying in a half circle. Decomposition has already set in. We straightened the arm and hand, with the exception of the thumb, which was bent down in the palm of the hand. At that very minute my brother in Emporia, about twenty miles away, said, "My arm is now straightened, but my thumb is crooked, hanging down in my hand," showing the exact position with his right hand. I account for this through the affinity of the soul. Though the arm was severed and had begun to decompose, the soul was not severed, and to it the position of the missing arm was known.

The medical fraternity, with all their knowledge of the anatomy of man, cannot give a solution of this phenomenon, neither can the materialist. I could give many striking incidents, similar to the above. I have talked with many persons who have lost a hand, foot or leg, and they all bear testimony to about the same experience as above, though not so fully developed.

Great and marvelous are the works of God, and the immortal soul is his chief work. As a Son of God, man cannot die (be separated from God), or cease to exist.

Westphalia, Kans.

HOW WE MAY MAKE OUR PRAYERS MORE EFFECTUAL.

BY A. E. HARBAUGH.

PRIMITIVE Christianity does not have "patented" or "copyrighted" forms of religion. Christ (TRUTH) is the *only* foundation: "For other foundation can no man lay than that is laid, which is Jesus Christ." 1 Cor. 3: 11.

The work of the Holy Ghost is Divine Love winging Truth to our spiritual consciousness: "And when the day of Pentecost was fully come, they were all with one accord in one place. . . . And they were all filled with the Holy Ghost,—." Acts 2: 1–4.

John's baptism, in the Jordan was baptism "unto repentance." Christ's baptism was a baptism " with the Holy Ghost and *with* fire."

The purpose of the writer is to show how we may obtain UNCTION OF THE SPIRIT in our prayers. To realize that we are primitive Christians is to know we are one body. "Now ye are the body of Christ (the embodiment of Truth) and members in particular." 1 Cor. 12: 27. Please read the entire chapter. "When thou prayest, enter into thy closet, and when thou hast shut thy door, pray to thy Father which is in secret; and thy Father which seeth in secret shall reward thee openly." Matt. 6: 6. So spake Jesus. The closet typifies the sanctuary of the Spirit, whose door shuts out sinful sense, but opens to truth, life, and love. The Father in secret is unseen to the senses; but he knows all things, and rewards according to motives,—not according to speech.

Thoughts unspoken are not unknown to the Divine Mind. Desire is prayer; and no less can occur from trusting God with our desires, that they may be moulded and exalted before they transpire in word or deed. Do we pray to make ourselves better, or to benefit those who hear us,—to enlighten the ignorance (?) of the Infinite, or to be heard of men? *The desire that goes forth HUNGERING AFTER RIGHTEOUSNESS, is BLESSED* of our Father, and does not return unto us void. What we most need is the prayer of daily desire, —of deeds, not words. Asking that we may love God will never make us love Him; but the longing to be better, higher, and purer, expressed in daily watchfulness, and in striving to assimilate more of the divine character,—this will mould and fashion us anew. If we are not secretly yearning and openly striving for the accomplishment of all we ask, our prayers are "vain repetitions." If our petitions are sincere, we shall labor for what we ask, and be blessed.

The next and great step required by wisdom is the test of our sincerity. To this end we are placed under the stress of circumstances. Christians and sinners get their full award, but not always in this world. The followers of Christ must drink his cup of sorrows. Ingratitude and persecution will fill it to the brim; but God pours the riches of joy into the understanding and gives us strength according to our day. Sinners flourish as a green bay-tree; but looking farther, the Psalmist could see their end,—namely, destruction. God is not separate from the wisdom he bestows. The talent he gives we must improve. God is not influenced by man. The "Divine Ear" is not a personal sense, but the all-hearing and all-knowing Mind, to whom each word of man is known, and by whom it will be supplied. In the quiet sanctuary of earnest longings and demands, deny thyself, and resolve to take up the cross, and go forth with honest hearts, to work, watch and pray for wisdom, truth, and love. This prayer will be answered, inasmuch as we shall put our desires into practice. The Master's injunction is that we pray in secret, and let our lives attest the sincerity of our petitions. Are we really grateful for the good already received? Then we shall avail ourselves of the blessings we have, and thus be fitted to receive more. This expresses more gratitude than speech. Praying for humility, with whatever fervency of expression, does not always mean a desire for it. If we turn away from the poor, we are not ready to receive the reward of Him who blesses the poor. If *selfishness* has given place to LOVE, we shall reward our neighbor unselfishly and bless them that curse us.

Consistent prayer is the desire to do right. Prayer means that we will walk in the light, so far

tempts hitherto made to construct even a doubtful representation of its characteristics are based upon the trifling play of fancy." — *Christian Standard.*

THE SOUL.

BY CHAS. M. YEAROUT.

In Four Chapters.—Chapter Four.

"Souls are said to go to the grave, Ps. 39: 48, to be raised from the grave, Acts 2: 31."—*Ibid., page 56.* I am astonished that an editor, professing to be a Christian, would formulate, print, and send out such a fabrication of misrepresentations. I read Psalm 39 through, and find it has but thirteen verses in it and neither "souls," or "grave" are mentioned. I also read the second chapter of Acts, and find it has but forty-seven verses, and neither "souls," or "grave" are mentioned. I read in verse 27, "Because thou wilt not leave my soul in hell (hades), neither wilt thou suffer thine Holy One to see corruption." Hades, as I have already shown, is the place of departed souls, and cannot be made to mean the grave.

In Psalm 30: 3, we read, "O Lord, thou hast brought up my soul from the grave: thou hast kept me alive, that I should not go down to the pit." If this is what the editor intended to refer to, it is against him; for David says he was kept alive, and life cannot exist in the grave. Neither had he gone to the grave at that time. Why go back from 1,000 to 4,000 years to prove or oppose the immortality of the soul, when it was not brought to light fully until Christ revealed it in the New Testament? Try your hand in that, to prove that man is not in possession of an immortal principle,— eternal life. The soul is purified now by obeying the truth or Word of God. 1 Pet. 1: 22. The body will be purified at the second coming of Christ, (that is the bodies of the righteous; for the bodies of the wicked will never be purified.) Phil. 3: 20-21; 1 Cor. 15: 43, 44, 53, 54. There is not an intimation in the Christian Scriptures,—the last Will and Testament of God,—of the soul going to the grave or coming out of the grave. That is simply a theory of the materialists, who are striving hard to dispose of that noble, God-given attribute,—the soul,—and bring mankind upon a level with the brute creation. Nevertheless, the fact remains, and Christ has said it, that the child of God is in possession of "eternal life." To believe in the existence of the soul, and its immortality, is an innate principle, instilled into man by the Creator. It makes no difference how uncivilized, and barbarous the nations,—all believe in a future state of existence, and that death does *not* extinguish life. Nearly all eminent philosophers, both Christian and heathen, have and do' believe in the immortality of the soul. Cicero says, "But if I err in believing that the souls of men are immortal, I willingly err; nor while I live would I wish to have this delightful error extorted from me; and if, after death, I shall feel nothing, as some minute philosophers think, I am not afraid, lest dead philosophers should laugh at me for the error."

One of the early Christian Fathers (Chrysostom, I believe, it was) was brought before the inquisitors and asked to recant, or renounce, his faith, with a threat that if he did not, they would kill him. His answer to them was "Ye cannot kill me; for I am dead, and my life is hid with Christ in God."

The Red Man in North America has this inherent principle firmly rooted in his being. The most wild and savage tribes devotedly cleave to the belief that death does *not* end all life. In their ignorance and superstition, when one of their number dies, they kill his pony beside the grave

or burial place, for him to ride to the "better hunting ground," as they call the spirit world. His dogs are also killed and laid beside him on the outside. His gun, or munitions of war, are laid beside him, inside the enclosure. They do not bury their dead in the ground, but lay them on top of the ground, and an arched roof is built over them, either of stone or wood. When I used to pass the Indian burial grounds I wondered why so many animal skeletons of different species were among their dead. They informed me that these were for the use of the departed Indians, or warriors in the better hunting ground. They believe that at death they go immediately to a better country. Where did they get this belief, if it was not instilled into them by the Creative Power, since they have never been taught it by man?

The identity of the soul is demonstrated where limbs have been amputated. Persons, having severed limbs, can tell the exact position of the dismembered part or limb, though many miles intervene between the person and the severed member. There was a case that came under my personal observation some years ago. A dear brother accidentally shot his left arm off, so it had to be taken out of the socket joint in the shoulder. This took place near Madison, Greenwood Co., Kans. The dismembered arm was placed in a small box, and buried in a cemetery. About two weeks after this, my brother was moved to the City of Emporia in Lyon County, about twenty miles from Madison, in order that he might have the immediate supervision and care of the attending physician. Bro. Eli Franks and my oldest brother were his nurses in Emporia. After he had been there for some time he complained of his lost arm being crooked, and hurting him. My older brother wrote to me to go and take up the arm, and straighten it, if crooked. So a man, by the name of James Tompson, and myself, went and took up the arm, and found it in the exact position complained of, lying in a half circle. Decomposition has already set in. We straightened the arm and hand, with the exception of the thumb, which was bent down in the palm of the hand. At that very minute my brother in Emporia, about twenty miles away, said, "My arm is now straightened, but my thumb is crooked, hanging down in my hand," showing the exact position with his right hand. I account for this through the affinity of the soul. Though the arm was severed and had begun to decompose, the soul was not severed, and to it the position of the missing arm was known. The medical fraternity, with all their knowledge of the anatomy of man, cannot give a solution of this phenomenon, neither can the materialist. I could give many striking incidents, similar to the above. I have talked with many persons who have lost a hand, foot or leg, and they all bear testimony to about the same experience as above, though not so fully developed.

Great and marvelous are the works of God, and the immortal soul is his chief work. As a Son of God, man cannot die (be separated from God), or cease to exist.

Westphalia, Kans.

HOW WE MAY MAKE OUR PRAYERS MORE EFFECTUAL.

BY A. E. HARBAUGH.

PRIMITIVE Christianity does not have "patented" or "copyrighted" forms of religion. Christ (TRUTH) is the *only* foundation: "For other foundation can no man lay than that is laid, which is Jesus Christ." 1 Cor. 3: 11.

The work of the Holy Ghost is Divine Love winging Truth to our spiritual consciousness: "And when the day of Pentecost was fully come,

they were all with one accord in one place. . . . And they were all filled with the Holy Ghost,—." Acts 2: 1-4.

John's baptism in the Jordan was baptism "unto repentance." Christ's baptism was a baptism "with the Holy Ghost and *with* fire."

The purpose of the writer is to show how we may obtain UNCTION OF THE SPIRIT in our prayers. To realize that we are primitive Christians is to know we are one body. "Now ye are the body of Christ (the embodiment of Truth) and members in particular." 1 Cor. 12: 27. Please read the entire chapter. "When thou prayest, enter into thy closet, and when thou hast shut thy door, pray to thy Father which is in secret; and thy Father which seeth in secret shall reward thee openly." Matt. 6: 6. So spake Jesus. The closet typifies the sanctuary of the Spirit, whose door shuts out sinful sense, but opens to truth, life, and love. The Father in secret is unseen to the senses; but he knows all things, and rewards according to motives,—not according to speech.

Thoughts unspoken are not unknown to the Divine Mind. Desire is prayer; and no less can occur from trusting God with our desires, that they may be moulded and exalted before they transpire in word or deed. Do we pray to make ourselves better, or to benefit those who hear us,—to enlighten the ignorance (?) of the Infinite, or to be heard of men? *The desire that goes forth* HUNGERING AFTER RIGHTEOUSNESS, IS BLESSED of our Father, and does not return unto us void. What we most need is the prayer of daily desire, —of deeds, not words. Asking that we may love God will never make us love Him; but the longing to be better, higher, and purer, expressed in daily watchfulness, and in striving to assimilate more of the divine character,—this will mould and fashion us anew. If we are not secretly yearning and openly striving for the accomplishment of all we ask, our prayers are "vain repetitions." If our petitions are sincere, we shall labor for what we ask, and be blessed.

The next and great step required by wisdom is the test of our sincerity. To this end we are placed under the stress of circumstances. Christians and sinners get their full award, but not always in this world. The followers of Christ must drink his cup of sorrows. Ingratitude and persecution will fill it to the brim; but God pours the riches of joy into the understanding and gives us strength according to our day. Sinners flourish as a green bay-tree; but looking farther, the Psalmist could see their end,—namely, destruction. God is not separate from the wisdom he bestows. The talent he gives we must improve. God is not influenced by man. The "Divine Ear" is not a personal sense, but the all-hearing and all-knowing Mind, to whom each *want* of man is known, and by whom it will be supplied. In the quiet sanctuary of earnest longings and demands, deny thyself, and resolve to take up the cross, and go forth with honest hearts, to work, watch and pray for wisdom, truth, and love. This prayer will be answered, inasmuch as we shall put our desires into practice. The Master's injunction is that we pray in secret, and let our lives attest the sincerity of our petitions. Are we really grateful for the good already received? Then we shall avail ourselves of the blessings we have, and thus be fitted to receive more. This expresses more gratitude than speech. Praying for humility, with whatever fervency of expression, does not always mean a desire for it. If we turn away from the poor, we are not ready to receive the reward of Him who blesses the poor. If *selfishness* has given place to LOVE, we shall reward our neighbor unselfishly and bless them that curse us.

Consistent prayer is the desire to do right. Prayer means that we will walk in the light, *so far*

Missionary and Tract Work Department.

Organization of Missionary Committee.

DANIEL VANIMAN, Foreman, - - - McPherson, Kans.
D. L. MILLER, Treasurer, - - - Mt. Morris, Ill.
GALEN B. ROYER, Secretary, - - - Mt. Morris, Ill.

Organization of Book and Tract Work.

S. W. HOOVER, Foreman, - - - Dayton, Ohio.
S. BOCK, Secretary and Treasurer, - - Dayton, Ohio.

"THE BIBLE ALONE."

BY B. F. MOOMAW.

THIS has been the motto of our people from my earliest recollection, "The Bible, the whole Bible, and nothing but the Bible." By this we mean the letter and the spirit of the Bible,—not confined to the imperative commands alone, but to the sayings of Christ, and other inspired men of God as well. "Not every one that saith unto me Lord, Lord, shall enter into the kingdom of heaven; but he that doeth the will of my Father which is in heaven." "Therefore whosoever heareth these sayings of mine, and doeth them, I will liken him unto a wise man which built his house upon a rock." Matt. 7: 21-27.

Facts continually demonstrate that so strait is this gate, and so narrow is this way, "that few there be that find them," yet every one that seeketh findeth, and to him that knocketh the gate shall be opened. And though this way has its difficulties, and is painful to the flesh, yet it has its comforts with which a stranger intermeddleth not. The entrance is commonly more arduous than the farther progress to those who set out resolutely, and the hope of heaven, and the joy of the Holy Spirit combine to render it "the way of pleasantness and the path of peace." But to all who would tread this narrow way we would say, Beware of those who prophesy smooth things, who invent easier ways to heaven, and more congenial with corrupt nature. These beguile unstable souls, and prejudice them against the pure religion of Christ.

To say that the Bible alone doctrine is dangerous is a misnomer, and is painful to any one who is a believer of its divine inspiration. But to pretend to be so much devoted to the Bible alone, and then take up one or two points, and reach out and connect with them the tendencies and results according to your liking, and then ignore, ridicule, and condemn the same rule in connection with other things to which it just as forcibly applies, and is even supported by the literal application of the inspired volume, is inconsistent and unfair.

To illustrate we indite the following: "It is said that there is no thus saith the Lord against horse-racing or card playing." This is true, and to bring an action against a brother for doing either, we will fail to make a case of it, for want of a thus saith the Lord; but knowing the tendency and the inevitable, we can arrive at a conclusion, by putting into the list the violations of moral law, such as swearing, lying, drinking, gambling, cheating, levity, and waste of time, and general immorality which are all claimed to be expressly forbidden by God's Word,—"the Bible alone." This is far-reaching, if it is all true, and if it is, you have a clear case for ecclesiastical government, and you may safely act upon the authority of 1 Cor. 5, to "put away from you that wicked person."

I accept the application of this rule as to the points in question; it is in harmony with the Bible alone idea. But I cannot ignore it when it comes in connection with other things, just as much in line with the word and spirit of the Bible, whatever it may be upon which the affections are inordinately placed. For example: The adorning of the body is admitted to be one of the most prominent weaknesses of our human nature, and leads to sinful practices, such as superfluities, indecencies, exposing parts of the body in an unbecoming manner. It results in sinful indulgences in many ways, such as levity, waste of time, theatre-going, the trifling amusements, and the dance with the sexes combined, coming out of which they are not likely to be as pure as when they went in, and are in danger of drifting into the bawdy-house of ill-fame, the very place of the promotion of evil ways, and the fountain from which flows the stream of fashion, with its demoralising tendencies, and sinful practices, in many ways, so clearly forbidden in the Bible, and a proper subject for discipline. There is no one thing upon which the affections are so much inordinately placed. This is clear to every careful observer. The object is to attract the attention of others, and the tendency is to excite immoral desires, especially when encouraged by parents and pastors, by advertising that they relinquish all restriction in the question of dress, etc.

Painful as it is, yet it is true that when once started in that direction it goes on and on, and those of rising generations who, a few years ago, were baptized, and promised fidelity to the teachings of the Bible, and are now to be seen covered with superfluities from the crown to the floor, and the sad information now reaches us, that they now engage in some of the practices mentioned above, therefore the necessity of mortifying our members which are upon the earth, is the more apparent. "Fornication, uncleanness, inordinate affection, evil concupiscence and covetousness, which is idolatry," should be put far away from us. We are commanded, also, to put away from among us that wicked person, and as the last alternative, when admonition and exhortation fail to prevent the current, the fountain must be closed. To get discipline out of the way entirely, we are told that the use of it does not make us any better. I must take issue on this point.

Do we not see it clearly demonstrated that by the afflictions of God's Providence thousands are brought to Christ, and that we are made better men and better women in the same way? Do we not, when kind words and milder means fail to have the desired effect upon our children, resort to discipline, to accomplish our object in their reformation? In our church work, we have, in our experience, witnessed the same results, in the case of a brother who, from time to time, gave the church much trouble. Finally it was decided that the Apostolic remedy be applied, to "deliver such a one unto Satan for the destruction of the flesh that the spirit might be saved in the day of the Lord Jesus." It was done, and after awhile he applied for restoration, was restored, and never gave the church any trouble afterwards.

But we have been asked the question if the plain dress has not been idolized, and used to cover up meanness and immorality. It has no doubt been so used, but I want to say that in such cases the affections were not placed upon the plain dress, but upon the object that it was intended to conceal, and this was the idol, and not the dress. Again, we are sometimes told, that we are just as likely to become proud of plain clothes as we are of fashionable. If even this be true, then the proud are, comparatively, very few. But I fail to see it in that way, as it requires sacrifice and self-denial, and I am sure that our Heavenly Father, who enables us to make the sacrifice, is able to keep us from becoming proud of it.

While style in dress is not necessary to respectability, and plainness is a Christian virtue and entirely safe, why not encourage it and be sure to not encourage the opposite, either by precept or example? We see that in the second illustration we have all the argument in the spirit and tendency that is claimed for the first, and, more still, we have, in the literal text more substantial argument for the Bible alone doctrine. See Rom. 12: 1, "I beseech you, brethren, by the mercies of God, that ye present your bodies a living sacrifice, which is your reasonable service." The body, with the senses and organs, is the instrument of the carnal mind in executing its purposes, and gratifying its evil inclinations. When, therefore, the mind is made spiritual, the body should, in like manner, execute its holy purposes, and express its spiritual affections. "And be not conformed to the world, but be ye transformed by the renewing of your mind." In these things Christians must go entirely against the course of this world, and not conform to the fashions of mankind in general. "In all these things the reproach of Christianity is honorable, the want of it suspicious, and to be fashionable is to be unchristian." A serious regard to this would show us in what things we must not be conformed to the world.

Again, it is said that women should adorn themselves in modest apparel, with modesty and sobriety, and not with braided hair, or gold, or pearls, or costly array, but which becometh women professing godliness, with good works. The same sentiment is expressed in 1 Pet. 3: 1-5.

This is what I regard as Bible alone doctrine, and the same mode of interpretation is suitable in any and all questions,—questions upon which the affections are inordinately placed, and subject alike to discipline, when proved to be true beyond a rational doubt, and not till then.

If such cases are decided according to truth and equity, it is ratified in heaven, but a groundless sentence of excommunication cannot possibly make any alteration in a man's state or character, but must reflect seriously upon the court presiding. I know that I am regarded by those progressing in liberal ideas, as being an extremist, but I am not. My only object has, in my lifework with the church, been to use my influence (such as it is) to teach and practice the doctrine of "the Bible alone," to preserve the identity of the time-honored principles of the church, that I much love, to prevent its drifting into the current of the complex element of modern Christianity, and to maintain the honor of our blessed religion.

Bonsack's, Va.

PEOPLE generally fall on the side toward which they lean. It will therefore be wise for each person to pause and consider the way he is leaning. By always leaning towards the right, there is a chance of falling on the safe side.

Missionary and Tract Work Department.

"Upon the first day of the week, let every one of you lay by him in store as God hath prospered him, that there be no gatherings when I come."—1 Cor. 16: 2.

"Every man as he purposeth in his heart, so let him give. Not grudgingly or of necessity, for the Lord loveth a cheerful giver."—2 Cor. 9: 7.

HOW MUCH SHALL WE GIVE?

"Every man *according to his ability.*" "Every one *as God hath prospered him.*" "Every man, *according as he purposeth in his heart,* so let him give." "For if there be first a willing mind. It is accepted *according to that a man hath,* and not according to that he hath not."—2 Cor. 8: 12.

Organization of Missionary Committee.

DANIEL VANIMAN, Foreman, . . . McPherson, Kans.
D. L. MILLER, Treasurer, ... Mt. Morris, Ill.
GALEN B. ROYER, Secretary, ... Mt. Morris, Ill.

Organization of Book and Tract Work.

S. W. HOOVER, Foreman, ... Dayton, Ohio.
S. BOCK, Secretary and Treasurer, . . . Dayton, Ohio.

☞All donations intended for Missionary Work should be sent to GALEN B. ROYER, Mt. Morris, Ill.

☞All money for Tract Work should be sent to S. BOCK, Dayton, Ohio.

☞Money may be sent by Money Order, Registered Letter, or Drafts on New York or Chicago. Do not send personal checks, or drafts on interior towns, as it costs 25 cents to collect them.

☞Solicitors are requested to faithfully carry out the plan of Annual Meeting, that all our members be solicited to contribute at least twice a year for the Mission and Tract Work of the Church.

☞Notes for the Endowment Fund can be had by writing to the Secretary of either Work.

"THE BIBLE ALONE."

BY B. F. MOOMAW.

THIS has been the motto of our people from my earliest recollection, "The Bible, the whole Bible, and nothing but the Bible." By this we mean the letter and the spirit of the Bible,—not confined to the imperative commands alone, but to the sayings of Christ, and other inspired men of God as well. "Not every one that saith unto me Lord, Lord, shall enter into the kingdom of heaven; but he that doeth the will of my Father which is in heaven." "Therefore whosoever heareth these sayings of mine, and doeth them, I will liken him unto a wise man which built his house upon a rock." Matt. 7: 21–27.

Facts continually demonstrate that so strait is this gate, and so narrow is this way, "that few there be that find them," yet every one that seeketh findeth, and to him that knocketh the gate shall be opened. And though this way has its difficulties, and is painful to the flesh, yet it has its comforts with which a stranger intermeddleth not. The entrance is commonly more arduous than the farther progress to those who set out resolutely, and the hope of heaven, and the joy of the Holy Spirit combine to render it "the way of pleasantness and the path of peace." But to all who would tread this narrow way we would say, Beware of those who prophesy smooth things, who invent easier ways to heaven, and more congenial with corrupt nature. These beguile unstable souls, and prejudice them against the pure religion of Christ.

To say that the Bible alone doctrine is dangerous is a misnomer, and is painful to any one who is a believer of its divine inspiration. But to pretend to be so much devoted to the Bible alone, and then take up one or two points, and reach out and connect with them the tendencies and results according to your liking, and then ignore, ridicule, and condemn the same rule in connection with other things to which it just as forcibly applies, and is even supported by the literal application of the inspired volume, is inconsistent and unfair.

To illustrate we indite the following: "It is said that there is no thus saith the Lord against horse-racing or card playing." This is true, and to bring an action against a brother for doing either, we will fail to make a case of it, for want of a thus saith the Lord; but knowing the tendency and the inevitable, we can arrive at a conclusion, by putting into the list the violations of moral law, such as swearing, lying, drinking, gambling, cheating, levity, and waste of time, and general immorality which are all *claimed* to be expressly forbidden by God's Word,—"the Bible alone." This is far-reaching, if it is all true, and if it is, you have a clear case for ecclesiastical government, and you may safely act upon the authority of 1 Cor. 5, to "put away from you that wicked person."

I accept the application of this rule as to the points in question; it is in harmony with the Bible alone idea. But I cannot ignore it when it comes in connection with other things, just as much in line with the word and spirit of the Bible, whatever it may be upon which the affections are inordinately placed. For example: The adorning of the body is admitted to be one of the most prominent weaknesses of our human nature, and leads to sinful practices, such as superfluities, indecencies, exposing parts of the body in an unbecoming manner. It results in sinful indulgences in many ways, such as levity, waste of time, theatre-going, the trifling amusements, and the dance with the sexes combined, coming out of which they are not likely to be as pure as when they went in, and are in danger of drifting into the bawdy-house of ill fame, the very place of the promotion of evil ways, and the fountain from which flows the stream of fashion, with its demoralizing tendencies, and sinful practices, in many ways, so clearly forbidden in the Bible, and a proper subject for discipline. There is no one thing upon which the affections are so much inordinately placed. This is clear to every careful observer. The object is to attract the attention of others, and the tendency is to excite immoral desires, especially when encouraged by parents and pastors, by advertising that they relinquish all restriction in the question of dress, etc.

Painful as it is, yet it is true that when once started in that direction it goes on and on, and those of rising generations who, a few years ago, were baptized, and promised fidelity to the teachings of the Bible, and are now to be seen covered with superfluities from the crown to the floor, and the sad information now reaches us, that they now engage in some of the practices mentioned above, therefore the necessity of mortifying our members which are upon the earth, is the more apparent. "Fornication, uncleanness, inordinate affection, evil concupiscence and covetousness, which is idolatry," should be put far away from us. We are commanded, also, to put away from among us that wicked person, and as the last alternative, when admonition and exhortation fail to prevent the current, the fountain must be closed. To get discipline out of the way entirely, we are told that the use of it does not make us any better. I must take issue on this point.

Do we not see it clearly demonstrated that by the afflictions of God's Providence thousands are brought to Christ, and that we are made better men and better women in the same way? Do we not, when kind words and milder means fail to have the desired effect upon our children, resort to discipline, to accomplish our object in their reformation? In our church work, we have, in our experience, witnessed the same thing, in the case of a brother who, from time to time, gave the church much trouble. Finally it was decided that the Apostolic remedy be applied, to "deliver such a one unto Satan for the destruction of the flesh that the spirit might be saved in the day of the Lord Jesus." It was done, and after awhile he applied for restoration, was restored, and never gave the church any trouble afterwards.

But we have been asked the question if the plain dress has not been idolized, and used to cover up meanness and immorality. It has no doubt been so used, but I want to say that in such cases the affections were not placed upon the plain dress, but upon the object that it was intended to conceal, and this was the idol, and not the dress. Again, we are sometimes told, that we are just as likely to become proud of this be true, then the proud are, comparatively, very few. But I fail to see it in that way, as it requires sacrifice and self-denial, and I am sure that our Heavenly Father, who enables us to make the sacrifice, is able to keep us from becoming proud of it.

While style in dress is not necessary to respectability, and plainness is a Christian virtue and entirely safe, why not encourage it and be sure to not encourage the opposite, either by precept or example? We see that in the second illustration we have all the argument in the spirit and tendency that is claimed for the first, and, more still, we have, in the literal text more substantial argument for the Bible alone doctrine. See Rom. 12: 1, "I beseech you, brethren, by the mercies of God, that ye present your bodies a living sacrifice, which is your reasonable service." The body, with the senses and organs, is the instrument of the carnal mind in executing its purposes, and gratifying its evil inclinations. When, therefore, the mind is made spiritual, the body should, in like manner, execute its holy purposes, and express its spiritual affections. "And be not conformed to the world, but be ye transformed by the renewing of your mind." In these things Christians must go entirely against the course of this world, and not conform to the fashions of mankind in general. "In all these things the reproach of Christianity is honorable, the want of it suspicious, and to be fashionable is to be unchristian." A serious regard to this would show us in what things we must not be conformed to the world.

Again, it is said that women should adorn themselves in modest apparel, with modesty and sobriety, and not with braided hair, or gold, or pearls, or costly array, but which becometh women professing godliness, with good works. The same sentiment is expressed in 1 Pet. 3: 1–5.

This is what I regard as Bible alone doctrine, and the same mode of interpretation is suitable in any and all questions,—questions upon which the affections are inordinately placed, and subject alike to discipline, when proved to be true beyond a rational doubt, and not till then.

If such cases are decided according to truth and equity, it is ratified in heaven, but a groundless sentence of excommunication cannot possibly make any alteration in a man's state or character, but must reflect seriously upon the court presiding. I know that I am regarded by those progressing in liberal ideas, as being an extremist, but I am not. My only object has, in my life-work with the church, been to use my influence (such as it is) to teach and practice the doctrine of "the Bible alone," to preserve the identity of the time-honored principles of the church, that I so much love, to prevent its drifting into the current of the complex element of modern Christianity, and to maintain the honor of our blessed religion.

Bonsack's, Va.

PEOPLE generally fall on the side toward which they lean. It will therefore be wise for each person to pause and consider the way he is leaning. By always leaning towards the right, there is a chance of falling on the safe side.

The Gospel Messenger,

A Weekly at $1.50 Per Annum.

PUBLISHED BY

The Brethren's Publishing Co.

D. L. MILLER,	Editor.
J. H. MOORE,	Office Editor.
J. B. BRUMBAUGH, }	Associate Editors.
J. G. ROYER, }	
JOSEPH AMICK,	Business Manager.

ADVISORY COMMITTEE.

R. H. Miller, A. Hutchison, Daniel Bays.

☞ Communications for publication should be legibly written with black ink on one side of the paper only. Do not attempt to interline, or to put on one page what ought to occupy two.

☞ Anonymous communications will not be published.

☞ Do not mix business with articles for publication. Keep your communications on separate sheets from all business.

☞ Time is precious. We always have time to attend to business and to answer questions of importance, but please do not subject us to need less answering of letters.

☞ The MESSENGER is mailed each week to all subscribers. If the address is correctly entered on our list, the paper must reach the person to whom it is addressed. If you do not get your paper, write us, giving particulars.

☞ When changing your address, please give your former as well as your future address in full, so as to avoid delay and misunderstanding.

☞ Always remit to the office from which you order your goods, no matter from where you receive them.

☞ Do not send personal checks or drafts on interior banks, unless you send with them 25 cents each, to pay for collection.

☞ Remittances should be made by Post-office Money Order. Drafts on New York, Philadelphia or Chicago, or Registered Letters, made payable and addressed to "Brethren's Publishing Co., Mount Morris, Ill.," or "Brethren's Publishing Co., Huntingdon, Pa."

☞ Entered at the Post-office at Mount Morris, Ill., as second-class matter.

Mount Morris, Ill., - - - - May 24, 1892.

$1.00 pays for the MESSENGER from now until Dec. 31, 1892. Subscribe now!

BRO. DANIEL HAYS may now be addressed at Broadway, Virginia, instead of Moore's Store, as heretofore.

THE Western District of Pennsylvania will be represented on the Standing Committee by Bro. J. C. Johnson.

BRO. J. G. ROYER returned home last Wednesday, after an absence of several weeks among the churches in the East.

BRO. JAS. A. SELL has been elected as a member of the Standing Committee, to represent the Middle District of Pennsylvania, at the approaching Annual Meeting.

BRO. J. C. LAHMAN and wife have returned from Florida. We can expect them to remain with us during the summer. They report a pleasant sojourn in the land of oranges.

THE First District of West Virginia sends no papers to the Annual Meeting this year. Bro. Geo. S. Arnold will represent the District on the Standing Committee.

THE Northern District of Missouri is to be represented on the Standing Committee by Bro. C. H. Brown. Bro. B. B. Whitmer represents North-western Kansas and Colorado.

BRO. JACOB TROXEL, during his recent trip in Arkansas, was so much pleased with the country that he decided to make it his home, and, as soon as he can make arrangements, will move to Carlisle.

IN this issue will be found the closing chapter of Bro. D. E. Price's excellent article on "Christian Self-denial." It was written by request, and will doubtless prove interesting to our readers. It abounds in quotations from, and references to, that excellent work, entitled, "Church Entertainments," which should be in the hands of all our readers. It will be sent post-paid for 30 cents per copy.

ALL persons wishing to communicate with the Committee of Arrangements for Annual Meeting, after May 20, will please address J. S. Snyder, Secretary, care of Annual Meeting Box, Cedar Rapids, Iowa.

THE Brethren of the Coal Creek congregation, Fulton Co., Ill., have arranged to dedicate their new house May 23. Bro. Solomon Bucklew is expected to do the preaching. The new building is to be known as the Macedonian house.

OUR correspondents in the North write us of the very backward and wet spring, so that farmers cannot plant their crops. This is just the reverse of what it is in certain parts of the South, where it has not been so dry in fifty years.

WE had very unpleasant weather for our feast at Silver Creek, May 13, still the attendance was large and the interest good. On account of the rain, the attendance from the neighboring churches was not as large as usual.

LOOKING over the Minutes of the District Meeting of Nebraska, we notice that considerable business was before the meeting. One query goes to the Annual Meeting. Bro. J. J. Hoover serves the District on the Standing Committee.

AT the General Conference of the M. E. Church, Omaha, Nebr., a pointed resolution was introduced calling upon the publishers of *The Church* to cease the placing of sensational advertisements on the backs of Sunday-school books and other publications. It was referred to the committee on book concerns.

IT is commonly reported that the Mormons have abandoned polygamy. They are soon to have an opportunity of demonstrating their sincerity, as they have purchased an extensive tract of land in Mexico, on which to establish a large body of their people. As the laws of Mexico do not seem to forbid polygamy, it remains to be seen whether the abandoning of the vice in Utah was in good faith.

IN the report of Bro. J. C. Lahman's visit to Southern Florida, some weeks ago, a few mistakes occurred. He made mention of visiting "sister Wm. More." It should have been sister Martin C. Mohr. Bro. Neher, in that instance, should have been printed Bro. Huber. We are pleased to learn that these members are making an effort to have the Brethren's doctrine more fully known in that locality. They also have prospects of others settling among them in the near future.

MODERN religious work sometimes develops some peculiar freaks. During the recent General M. E. Conference at Omaha, Nebr., a long discussion was indulged in concerning the reception of fraternal delegates. It leaked out that the fraternal delegation from the South did not want to be received at the same time of the reception of another delegation because there was one colored man among them. So separate evenings had to be arranged for the reception of these delegations. This seems like children at play.

WE are informed of a very influential congregation that declined sending delegates to its District Meeting because it had no query to send. This was indeed a very lame excuse. Discussing and answering queries may be only a small part of the work before the meeting; and even if that were all, the congregation referred to ought to be represented and aid in the work. In fact we earnestly urge every congregation to see that she is properly represented at her District Meetings by delegates, if possible. We must not neglect our District Meetings.

IN this issue Bro. Daniel Vaniman tells us of a charming place to hold the Annual Meeting in California, in 1894. If we could manage to get the place to come to the Annual Meeting, instead of the meeting having to go to it, the question would be an easy one to decide.

THE Examining Committee of the Brethren's Tract Work will meet at Mt. Morris this week for the purpose of examining such matters as may be placed in their hands for the Tract Department. The Tract Committee also have in contemplation a thorough revision of all the tracts heretofore published, and thus labor to improve them as much as possible.

AN Ohio firm has bought the Tom Paine farm, comprising 600 acres, at New Rochelle, New York, the consideration being $105,000. The property will be utilized as a stock farm, with a one-mile trotting course. This trotting course is in keeping with the teachings of Tom Paine. Nothing is said in favor of an educational, religious or charitable institution.

THE Baltimore & Ohio Railroad Co., has very kindly sent to our ministers, clergyman's permits over their road. This kindness on the part of the B. & O., will be duly appreciated. This will enable our ministers to travel at a greatly reduced rate, and the permits will be available in connection with those issued by the C. B. & Q., for those who wish to visit us at Mt. Morris. With these permits, the journey may be broken at pleasure.

IT is said that Rider Haggard, the noted English traveler, and author of "King Solomon's Mines," wears a ring, once owned and worn by Pharaoh, king of Egypt, during the time of Moses. The ring has quite a history. Over 3,300 years ago Pharaoh was drowned in the Red Sea. After the custom of the Egyptians his body was embalmed, and carefully stored away for safe keeping. A few years ago it was found in an excellent state of preservation, and with it was the noted ring referred to.

IMMEDIATELY after the Annual Meeting, we shall arrange to collect and print in pamphlet form, all of the Minutes of the Annual Meeting since the year 1885. The pamphlet will be so indexed that it can be used in connection with the Classified Minutes, which contain all the decisions of the Annual Meeting prior to, and including, 1885. The price will be announced later. We hope to be prepared to take orders at the coming Annual Meeting. We also have in contemplation the publishing of a new edition of the Classified Minutes.

WE desire to call special attention to Bro. S. H. Myers' communication in regard to the prospects of building up a church in Washington City. It seems that we now have at least fifteen members there, with indications of still more to be found. We suggest that our Brethren in that part of the East give this matter special consideration, and do their utmost to locate a minister in the city, and have Him give his entire attention and time to the building up of a good, strong church. "We by all means ought to have a congregation in the capital of our Nation. In the times of the apostles there was a strong church at Rome, and why not also have a strong one at Washington City? We are glad Bro. Myers is giving this important consideration attention, and trust he will receive all needed encouragement. Those who know of members, or those favorable to our doctrine, living in the city may do well to either write Bro. Myers or see him at the Annual Meeting. By all means let us have a church at Washington.

The Gospel Messenger,

A Weekly at $1.50 Per Annum.

PUBLISHED BY

The Brethren's Publishing Co.

D. L. MILLER, ... Editor.
J. H. MOORE, ... Office Editor.
J. B. BRUMBAUGH, }
J. G. ROYER, } . . . . Associate Editors.
JOSEPH AMICK, ... Business Manager.

ADVISORY COMMITTEE.
R. H. Miller, A. Hutchison, Daniel Hays.

☞Communications for publication should be legibly written with black ink on one side of the paper only. Do not attempt to interline, or to put on one page what ought to occupy two.

☞Anonymous communications will not be published.

☞Do not mix business with articles for publication. Keep your communications on separate sheets from all business.

☞Time is piccious. We always have time to attend to business and to answer questions of importance, but please do not subject us to need less answering of letters.

☞The MESSENGER is mailed each week to all subscribers. If the address is correctly entatled on our list, the paper must reach the person to whom it is addressed. If you do not get your paper, write us, giving particulars.

☞When changing your address, please give your former as well as your future address in full, so as to avoid delay and misunderstanding.

☞Always remit to the office from which you order your goods, no matter from which you receive them.

☞Do not send personal checks or drafts on interior banks, unless you send with them 25 cents each, to pay for collection.

☞Remittances should be made by Post-office Money Order, Drafts on New York, Philadelphia or Chicago, or Registered Letters, made payable and addressed to "Brethren's Publishing Co., Mount Morris, Ill." or "Brethren's Publishing Co., Huntingdon, Pa."

☞Entered at the Post-office at Mount Morris, Ill., as second-class matter.

Mount Morris, Ill., - - - - May 24, 1892.

$1.00 pays for the MESSENGER from now until Dec. 31, 1892. Subscribe now!

BRO. DANIEL HAYS may now be addressed at Broadway, Virginia, instead of Moore's Store, as heretofore.

THE Western District of Pennsylvania will be represented on the Standing Committee by Bro. J. C. Johnson.

BRO. J. G. ROYER returned home last Wednesday, after an absence of several weeks among the churches in the East.

BRO. JAS. A. SELL has been elected as a member of the Standing Committee, to represent the Middle District of Pennsylvania, at the approaching Annual Meeting.

BRO. J. C. LAHMAN and wife have returned from Florida. We can expect them to remain with us during the summer. They report a pleasant sojourn in the land of oranges.

THE First District of West Virginia sends no papers to the Annual Meeting this year. Bro. Geo. S. Arnold will represent the District on the Standing Committee.

THE Northern District of Missouri is to be represented on the Standing Committee by Bro. C. H. Brown. Bro. B. B. Whitmer represents North-western Kansas and Colorado.

BRO. JACOB TROXEL, during his recent trip in Arkansas, was so much pleased with the country that he decided to make it his home, and, as soon as he can make arrangements, will move to Cerlisle.

In this issue will be found the closing chapter of Bro. D. E. Price's excellent article on "Christian Self-denial." It was written by request, and will doubtless prove interesting to our readers. It abounds in quotations from, and references to, that excellent work, entitled, "Church Entertainments," which should be in the hands of all our readers. It will be sent post-paid for 30 cents per copy.

ALL persons wishing to communicate with the Committee of Arrangements for Annual Meeting, after May 20, will please address J. S. Snyder, Secretary, care of Annual Meeting Box, Cedar Rapids, Iowa.

THE Brethren of the Coal Creek congregation, Fulton Co., Ill., have arranged to dedicate their new house May 22. Bro. Solomon Bucklew is expected to do the preaching. The new building is to be known as the Macedonian house.

OUR correspondents in the North write us of the very backward and wet spring, so that farmers cannot plant their crops. This is just the reverse of what it is in certain parts of the South, where it has not been so dry in fifty years.

WE had very unpleasant weather for our feast at Silver Creek, May 13, still the attendance was large and the interest good. On account of the rain, the attendance from the neighboring churches was not as large as usual.

LOOKING over the Minutes of the District Meeting of Nebraska, we notice that considerable business was before the meeting. One query goes to the Annual Meeting. Bro. J. J. Hoover serves the District on the Standing Committee.

AT the General Conference of the M. E. Church, Omaha, Nebr., a pointed resolution was introduced calling upon the publishers of The Church to cease the placing of sensational advertisements on the backs of Sunday-school books and other publications. It was referred to the committee on book concerns.

IT is commonly reported that the Mormons have abandoned polygamy. They are soon to have an opportunity of demonstrating their sincerity, as they have purchased an extensive tract of land in Mexico, on which to establish a large body of their people. As the laws of Mexico do not seem to forbid polygamy, it remains to be seen whether the abandoning of the vice in Utah was in good faith.

In the report of Bro. J. C. Lahman's visit to Southern Florida, some weeks ago, a few mistakes occurred. He made mention of visiting "sister Wm. More." It should have been sister Martin C. Mohr. Bro. Neher, in that instance, should have been printed Bro. Huber. We are pleased to learn that these members are making an effort to have the Brethren's doctrine more fully known in that locality. They also have prospects of others settling among them in the near future.

MODERN religious work sometimes develops some peculiar freaks. During the recent General M. E. Conference at Omaha, Nebr., a long discussion was indulged in concerning the reception of fraternal delegates. It leaked out that the fraternal delegation from the South did not want to be received at the same time of the reception of another delegation because there was one colored man among them. So separate evenings had to be arranged for the reception of these delegations. This seems like children at play.

WE are informed of a very influential congregation that declined sending delegates to its District Meeting because it had no query to send. This was indeed a very lame excuse. Discussing and answering queries may be only a small part of the work before the meeting; and even if that were all, the congregation referred to ought to be represented and aid in the work. In fact we earnestly urge every congregation to see that she is properly represented at her District Meetings by delegates, if possible. We must not neglect our District Meetings.

IN this issue Bro. Daniel Vaniman tells us of a charming place to hold the Annual Meeting in California, in 1894. If we could manage to get the place to come to the Annual Meeting, instead of the meeting having to go to it, the question would be an easy one to decide.

THE Examining Committee of the Brethren's Tract Work will meet at Mt. Morris this week for the purpose of examining such matters as may be placed in their hands for the Tract Department. The Tract Committee also have in contemplation a thorough revision of all the tracts heretofore published, and thus labor to improve them as much as possible.

AN Ohio firm has bought the Tom Paine farm, comprising 500 acres, at New Rochelle, New York, the consideration being $105,000. The property will be utilized as a stock farm, with a one-mile trotting course. This trotting course is in keeping with the teachings of Tom Paine. Nothing is said in favor of an educational, religious or charitable institution.

THE Baltimore & Ohio Railroad Co., has very kindly sent to our ministers, clergymen's permits over their road. This kindness on the part of the B. & O., will be duly appreciated. This will enable our ministers to travel at a greatly reduced rate, and the permits will be available in connection with those issued by the C. B. & Q., for those who wish to visit us at Mt. Morris. With these permits, the journey may be broken at pleasure.

IT is said that Rider Haggard, the noted English traveler, and author of "King Solomon's Mines," wears a ring, once owned and worn by Pharaoh, king of Egypt, during the time of Moses. The ring has quite a history. Over 3,300 years ago Pharaoh was drowned in the Red Sea. After the custom of the Egyptians his body was embalmed, and carefully stored away for safe keeping. A few years ago it was found in an excellent state of preservation, and with it was the noted ring referred to.

IMMEDIATELY after the Annual Meeting, we shall arrange to collect and print in pamphlet form, all of the Minutes of the Annual Meetings since the year 1885. The pamphlet will be so indexed that it can be used in connection with the Classified Minutes, which contain all the decisions of the Annual Meeting prior to, and including, 1885. The price will be announced later. We hope to be prepared to take orders at the coming Annual Meeting. We also have in contemplation the publishing of a new edition of the Classified Minutes.

WE desire to call special attention to Bro. S. H. Myers' communication in regard to the prospects of building up a church in Washington City. It seems that we now have at least fifteen members there, with indications of still more to be found. We suggest that our Brethren in that part of the East give this matter special consideration, and do their utmost to locate a minister in the city, and have him give his entire attention and time to the building up of a good, strong church. We by all means ought to have a congregation in the capital of our Nation. In the times of the apostles there was a strong church at Rome, and why not also have a strong one at Washington City? We are glad Bro. Myers is giving this important consideration attention, and trust he will receive all needed encouragement. Those who know of members, or those favorable to our doctrine, living in the city may do well to either write Bro. Myers or see him at the Annual Meeting. By all means let us have a church at Washington.

ANNUAL MEETING POWER.

CIRCUMSTANCES seem to suggest the propriety of a few remarks concerning the power possessed by the church of Christ upon the earth. It may be well to state, in the first place, that legislative power, or the power to make and enact laws, has never been delegated to the church, and any religious assembly that attempts to exercise this power is transcending her authority. The only power authorized to make laws, to govern the religious world, is that which is divine.

But unto the church has been given judicial and executive authority, which reaches no further, however, than the written law. The church may decide what is the meaning of the law, and then proceed to execute it. It is concerning the judicial duty and privilege of the church that we write at this time. By judicial authority is meant the interpretation and application of laws. This authority was exercised by the church in council at Jerusalem when she rendered her decision concerning circumcision.

We do not understand that the council referred to, either laid down a new principle or made a new law; it carefully looked into the law or principles already in existence, and rendered a decision accordingly. By a careful reading of Acts 15, it will be seen that the apostles appealed directly to the written word and the Holy Spirit, which influenced and guided them in their work. From the Old Scriptures they learned that the Lord would build again the tabernacle of David which had fallen down, and that the name of the Lord would be called upon by the Gentiles, showing that among them God had a people. Reference was made to the success of Peter at the house of Cornelius, as well as the preaching of Paul and Barnabas among the Gentiles, and also how the work had been sanctioned by the Holy Ghost. From these circumstances they drew conclusions which resulted in the decision rendered. To all the churches that decision became the rule, not because the council at Jerusalem so decided, but because it was found to be the will of God. This is the thought that we want to get clearly before our readers, namely, that the decision of a council does not make a thing right or wrong. The duty of a council is to deliberate, prayerfully and carefully, in order to ascertain what the teachings of the Scriptures are on the question under consideration, and then render a decision accordingly. Scriptural references should not be selected to fit the decision, but the decision should be shaped to fit the exact meaning of the Scriptures, and let the consequences fall where they may.

With God a thing is right or it is wrong, independent of the decision of any council, and in the judgment we are to be tried by what is in the mind of God, hence the importance of councils making a special effort to get the mind of God clearly embodied in all their decisions. It will, therefore, pay to take time to frame these decisions in order that the proper end may be gained. If a council should happen to make a decision that is contrary to the will of the Lord, we do not understand that a violation of that decision is displeasing to God in the least, nor will it, in any manner, in the judgment, stand against the one who happens to disregard it. But on the other hand, the church must render an account for making such a wrong decision, and especially for attempting to enforce it. Any one who will pause and consider the subject in this light, cannot help but realize what a grave responsibility is resting upon those who hold the power in our Annual Council. The hasty manner in which decisions are sometimes urged, on very important questions, leads us to fear that this responsibility is not realized to the extent that it should be by those who endeavor to push through the Conference their hastily-formed conclusions.

Let it not be inferred that a council is granted the privilege to make any decision she thinks proper, and that the Lord will sanction it. Councils may make any decision that is *right*, and it will be sanctioned by heaven, not because the *council* made it, but because it is *right* in the sight of God. Whenever we get the idea thoroughly fixed in our minds that the power is in the *right* and not in the *council*, we will be less liable to make mistakes, and be more careful about *searching* for the *right*.

On all questions, relating to the manner of spreading the Gospel, erecting of places of worship, and things of that character, the church is most assuredly left to exercise her best judgment, and her judgment may vary in different ages and under different circumstances. And even different methods may be right and acceptable at the same time. Matters of this class are largely matters of expediency and ought to cut no figure in the question of loyalty. But there is another class of questions, pertaining to the right or wrong of action, that deserve special attention. When one of these questions comes before the Annual Meeting for a decision, there are two chances of making mistakes. One is to permit that which the Scriptures forbid; and the other is to forbid that which the Scriptures do not oppose. Which is the greater mistake, we will not venture to say. If possible, both should be avoided. To wink at an evil and permit members unrebuked to run into sin, is to sanction the wrong. To forbid things that the Gospel does not, in some way, condemn is to usurp authority. Now, just how far to go in matters of this kind so as not to endorse or encourage sin, and at the same time not overstep her authority, is a very grave question for the church to consider. Looking at the subject from this stand-point, enables us to clearly understand that the Annual Meeting, or any other council, is responsible to God for her work, and it is her duty to study the limits of her authority with great care. We offer these remarks, not for the purpose of finding fault with the work of our Annual Meeting in the past, but with a view of urging that we assume not too much authority on the one hand or neglect our duty on the other. We are in an age where it is possible for us to err in either direction, hence the necessity of great caution and an entire submission to the will of God.   J. H. M.

THE GREEK NOT A DEAD LANGUAGE.

ELD. B. W. JOHNSON, in the "Querist's Department" of the *Christian Evangelist* gives some valuable information in regard to the Greek as a living language. We clip the following:

"There is a modern kingdom of Greece, and a people called Greeks. They are said to speak the Greek language. Is their language the same as that in which the New Testament was written? I have always heard it stated that the Greek was a dead language."

"The writer has in his possession several Greek daily newspapers, published in the City of Athens. He found, when in that city, that his knowledge of the Ancient Greek enabled him to read a modern Greek newspaper. The Greeks who learn to read their own language have no difficulty in reading the writings of Plato or Xenophon. Indeed, the modern Greek, after two thousand years have passed, can read his classics with less difficulty than we have in reading and understanding Chaucer, and even Edmund Spenser. Prof. John Stuart Blackie, of Edinburg University, one of the foremost Greek scholars of our times, says, 'The Greek is a living language, and as much alive as it ever was in the days when Socrates preached the gospel of reason in the streets of Athens, and St. Paul put to shame the wisdom of certain Epicurean and Stoic writings, standing on the hills of Mars, in front of the Parthenon. The notion that Greek is a dead language, and should be treated as such, arose, no doubt, from the insular ignorance of Englishmen.'"

WINE FOR COMMUNION PURPOSES.

THOSE who purchase at the drugstores wine for Communion occasions, will do well to consider the following, clipped from one of our most reliable exchanges:

"Once the writer had some conversation with a neighbor, who was a traveling agent for a wholesale liquor house, concerning some of the secrets of the liquor trade. He admitted that they could manufacture any brand of liquor called for by the use of alcohol and drugs, and could 'age' it so as to pass it off for old Bourbon, or brandy, or favorite foreign wines. 'Three days was time enough to make three year old Bourbon.' In this connection an article in the *Christian Intelligencer* is of interest to those Americans who make it a point to entertain their friends with high-priced, foreign wines. There is more French champagne used in America alone than is made in all France. There is a hundred times as much 'port wine' (so called from Oporto), sold and drank as can be made from all the grapes raised in the region of Oporto, including the whole Douro Valley. 'If the whole Douro Valley were a thousand miles long, instead of only sixty, it could not furnish grapes enough to produce all this ocean of port wine. The whole world is drinking wine out of the little handful of grapes grown on the banks of a small creek in Portugal.'

Madeira grows 30,000 barrels of wine yearly, and America alone drinks 50,000 barrels of Madeira wine! A Madeira wine, which few can tell from the genuine, is made in this country, at a profit of 500 per cent. By mixing with cider, rain water, sulphuric acid and other ingredients, California wine is made in New Jersey and sold at perhaps a thousand per cent. profit."

Why should we continue the use of these adulterated wines at the Lord's table, when the pure, unfermented juice of the grape is within the reach of all who will make the effort to procure it?

FULL REPORT We are arranging to publish a Full Report of the coming Annual Meeting, and hope to have it fully up to any of the Reports that have appeared in former years. We shall make a special effort to have it ready for mailing very shortly after the close of the Annual Meeting. We are now ready to book orders, and would be pleased to receive them as soon as possible. Remember that the first that come are the ones first served. Price, 25cts per copy, or $2.50 per dozen.

ANNUAL MEETING POWER.

CIRCUMSTANCES seem to suggest the propriety of a few remarks concerning the power possessed by the church of Christ upon the earth. It may be well to state, in the first place, that legislative power, or the power to make and enact laws, has never been delegated to the church, and any religious assembly that attempts to exercise this power is transcending her authority. The only power authorized to make laws, to govern the religious world, is that which is divine.

But unto the church has been given judicial and executive authority, which reaches no farther, however, than the written law. The church may decide what is the meaning of the law, and then proceed to execute it. It is concerning the judicial duty and privilege of the church that we write at this time. By judicial authority is meant the interpretation and application of laws. This authority was exercised by the church in council at Jerusalem when she rendered her decision concerning circumcision.

We do not understand that the council referred to, either laid down a new principle or made a new law; it carefully looked into the law or principles already in existence, and rendered a decision accordingly. By a careful reading of Acts 15, it will be seen that the apostles appealed directly to the written word and the Holy Spirit, which influenced and guided them in their work. From the Old Scriptures they learned that the Lord would build again the tabernacle of David which had fallen down, and that the name of the Lord would be called upon by the Gentiles, showing that among them God had a people. Reference was made to the success of Peter at the house of Cornelius, as well as the preaching of Paul and Barnabas among the Gentiles, and also how the work had been sanctioned by the Holy Ghost. From these circumstances they drew conclusions which resulted in the decision rendered. To all the churches that decision became the rule, not because the council at Jerusalem so decided, but because it was found to be the will of God. This is the thought that we want to get clearly before our readers, namely, that the decision of a council does not make a thing right or wrong. The duty of a council is to deliberate, prayerfully and carefully, in order to ascertain what the teachings of the Scriptures are on the question under consideration, and then render a decision accordingly. Scriptural references should not be selected to fit the decision, but the decision should be shaped to fit the exact meaning of the Scriptures, and let the consequences fall where they may.

With God a thing is right or it is wrong, independent of the decision of any council, and in the judgment we are to be tried by what is in the mind of God, hence the importance of councils making a special effort to get the mind of God clearly embodied in all their decisions. It will, therefore, pay to take time to frame these decisions in order that the proper end may be gained. If a council should happen to make a decision that is contrary to the will of the Lord, we do not understand that a violation of that decision is displeasing to God in the least, nor will it, in any manner, in the judgment, stand against the one who happens to disregard it. But on the other hand, the church must render an account for making such a wrong decision, and especially for attempting to enforce it. Any one who will pause and consider the subject in this light, cannot help but

realize what a grave responsibility is resting upon those who hold the power in our Annual Council. The hasty manner in which decisions are sometimes urged, on very important questions, leads us to fear that this responsibility is not realized to the extent that it should be by those who endeavor to push through the Conference their hastily-formed conclusions.

Let it not be inferred that a council is granted the privilege to make any decision she thinks proper, and that the Lord will sanction it. Councils may make any decision that is right, and it will be sanctioned by heaven, not because the council made it, but because it is right in the sight of God. Whenever we get the idea thoroughly fixed in our minds that the power is in the right and not in the council, we will be less liable to make mistakes, and be more careful about searching for the right.

On all questions, relating to the manner of spreading the Gospel, erecting of places of worship, and things of that character, the church is most assuredly left to exercise her best judgment, and her judgment may vary in different ages and under different circumstances. And even different methods may be right and acceptable at the same time. Matters of this class are largely matters of expediency and ought to cut no figure in the question of loyalty. But there is another class of questions, pertaining to the right or wrong of action, that deserve special attention. When one of these questions comes before the Annual Meeting for a decision, there are two chances of making mistakes. One is to permit that which the Scriptures forbid; and the other is to forbid that which the Scriptures do not oppose. Which is the greater mistake, we will not venture to say. If possible, both should be avoided. To wink at an evil and permit members unrebuked to run into sin, is to sanction the wrong. To forbid things that the Gospel does not, in some way, condemn is to usurp authority. Now, just how far to go in matters of this kind so as not to endorse or encourage sin, and at the same time not overstep her authority, is a very grave question for the church to consider. Looking at the subject from this stand-point, enables us to clearly understand that the Annual Meeting, or any other council, is responsible to God for her work, and it is her duty to study the limits of her authority with great care. We offer these remarks, not for the purpose of finding fault with the work of our Annual Meeting in the past, but with a view of urging that we assume not too much authority on the one hand or neglect our duty on the other. We are in an age where it is possible for us to err in either direction, hence the necessity of great caution and an entire submission to the will of God.   J. H. M.

THE GREEK NOT A DEAD LANGUAGE.

ELD. B. W. JOHNSON, in the "Querist's Department" of the *Christian Evangelist* gives some valuable information in regard to the Greek as a living language. We clip the following:

"There is a modern kingdom of Greece, and a people called Greeks. They are said to speak the Greek language. Is their language the same as that in which the New Testament was written? I have always heard it stated that the Greek was a dead language."

"The writer has in his possession several Greek daily newspapers, published in the City of Athens.

He found, when in that city, that his knowledge of the Ancient Greek enabled him to read a modern Greek newspaper. The Greeks who learn to read their own language have no difficulty in reading the writings of Plato or Xenophon. Indeed, the modern Greek, after two thousand years have passed, can read his classics with less difficulty than we have in reading and understanding Chaucer, and even Edmund Spenser. Prof. John Stuart Blackie, of Edinburg University, one of the foremost Greek scholars of our times, says, 'The Greek is a living language, and as much alive as it ever was in the days when Socrates preached the gospel of reason in the streets of Athens, and St. Paul put to shame the wisdom of certain Epicurean and Stoic writings, standing on the hills of Mars, in front of the Parthenon. The notion that Greek is a dead language, and should be treated as such, arose, no doubt, from the insular ignorance of Englishmen.'"

WINE FOR COMMUNION PURPOSES.

THOSE who purchase at the drugstores wine for Communion occasions, will do well to consider the following, clipped from one of our most reliable exchanges:

"Once the writer had some conversation with a neighbor, who was a traveling agent for a wholesale liquor house, concerning some of the secrets of the liquor trade. He admitted that they could manufacture any brand of liquor called for by the use of alcohol and drugs, and could 'age' it so as to pass it off for old Bourbon, or brandy, or favorite foreign wines. 'Three days was time enough to make three year old Bourbon.' In this connection an article in the *Christian Intelligencer* is of interest to those Americans who make it a point to entertain their friends with high-priced, foreign wines. There is more French champagne used in America alone than is made in all France. There is a hundred times as much 'port wine' (so called from Oporto), sold and drank as can be made from all the grapes raised in the region of Oporto, including the whole Douro Valley. 'If the whole Douro Valley were a thousand miles long, instead of only sixty, it could not furnish grapes enough to produce all this ocean of port wine. The whole world is drinking wine out of the little handful of grapes grown on the banks of a small creek in Portugal.'

Madeira grows 30,000 barrels of wine yearly, and America alone drinks 50,000 barrels of Madeira wine! A Madeira wine, which few can tell from the genuine, is made in this country, at a profit of 500 per cent. By mixing with cider, rain water, sulphuric acid and other ingredients, California wine is made in New Jersey and sold at perhaps a thousand per cent. profit."

Why should we continue the use of these adulterated wines at the Lord's table, when the pure, unfermented juice of the grape is within the reach of all who will make the effort to procure it?

FULL REPORT We are arranging to publish a Full Report of the coming Annual Meeting, and hope to have it fully up to any of the Reports that have appeared in former years. We shall make a special effort to have it ready for mailing very shortly after the close of the Annual Meeting. We are now ready to book orders, and would be pleased to receive them as soon as possible. Remember that the first that come are the ones first served. Price, 25cts per copy, or $2.50 per dozen.

reject the additional instructions in John 16: 23, 24? This is my "query." It is not for my own special benefit I ask this question, but some who are not members of the Brethren church have asked the reasons for our practice. What shall we answer them?
JOHN E. MOHLER.
Warrensburgh, Mo.

From the George's Creek Church, Fayette Co., Pa.

WE held our council-meeting on the last Saturday in April. Everything passed off pleasantly. The church unanimously agreed to hold our love-feast on the last Saturday and Sunday of the present month. All are cordially invited to attend our feast. We have several applicants for baptism before the feast.

Our church will be represented at District Meeting of the Western District of Pennsylvania, by delegates. Some papers will go there relative to the time of holding District Meeting. We will have one week's meeting before our feast.
ALPHEUS DEBOLT.
Masontown, Pa., May 9.

From the South River Church, Iowa.

I VISITED the little band of believers near Osceola, Iowa, April 30. They assembled in council, and with unanimous voice, chose brethren W. W. Folger, Jacob Keffer and W. Caskey as Trustees. They are also the building committee, with Bro. Folger as President, Bro. Keffer, Treasurer, and Bro. Caskey, Secretary. They appreciate the assistance given them by the "Church Erection and Missionary Committee;" also that given by neighboring congregations. They expect to have their house ready for use by Oct. 1. This organization was formerly known as the Irish Grove congregation, organized in Warren County, but the center of membership has moved West, until now they built their house near South River, in Madison County. They have, accordingly, decided to change the name from Irish Grove to South River congregation.

The heavy rain and consequent high waters and bad roads prevented the contemplated meetings, etc., so I returned home May 2, leaving the brethren with two applicants for baptism in the near future.
J. D. HAUGHTELIN.
Panora, Iowa.

Lower Stillwater, Ohio, Notes.

TO-DAY was our quarterly council for regular church business, and to prepare for District and Annual Meeting.

Considerable business was transacted. The spirit manifested in disposing of it was good. When such is the case, those having matters before the church cannot fail to see that the church has a regard for them, and is seeking their welfare in its requirements of them.

We send but one delegate to Annual Meeting this year on account of distance and expense, viz., Bro. John Smith. Our delegates to District Meeting are Bro. John Smith and the writer.

We are having Sunday-school at each house this summer. It continued evergreen in the Lower house, where the attendance is best. Brethren Wm. Bowser and W. W. Barnhart were to-day elected Associate Superintendents. We would again call attention to our Ministerial Meeting to be held in the Upper house, May 28.

There will be preaching on Friday evening previous, Saturday evening, Sunday, and perhaps Sunday evening at the same place.

We expect a good attendance from Southern Ohio, and would especially welcome those from other parts of the Brotherhood who can be with

us and assist us with their counsel and experience. The nearest station on C. H. & D. (old narrow gauge) is Kinsey's. Any one stopping off there, will be cared for by Bro. David Landis, who lives near station and church. Those stopping at Haines' will be cared for by brethren living near by. Those coming by Pan Handle or D. & U. branch of the Big Four Road, should stop at Trotwood, and enquire for John Smith or the writer. Brethren on their way to Annual Meeting should make a note of this.

This Meeting will be of general interest, and for the benefit of all.

By a careful reading and rereading of "Chrysostom and Bread-breaking" in No. 19, it will be found that, from the statement of the Fathers there quoted, the brethren and sisters fared alike, i. e., the bishops broke bread to both similarly. The equality of the sexes is that important work in all that is claimed by those who favor the deferred query on that point to come up at Annual Meeting.

Although late in reporting, we had a very interesting series of meetings in our Upper house, conducted by Bro. D. P. Shively, of Peru, Ind. One was baptized, and one reclaimed as part of the good result of the meeting.
L. A. BOOKWALTER.
Trotwood, Ohio, May 11.

"To worship God and obey his laws is the most reasonable thing that a man ever did; and not to do this is hence the most unreasonable course that one ever pursued. The pious fear of God is 'the beginning of wisdom.'"

Notes from Our Correspondents.

"As cold water to a thirsty soul, so is good news from a far country."

Naperville, Ill.—Our feast was indeed an enjoyable one. It was one of the most impressive feasts we have attended in a long while. The Chicago church was well represented at our feast. The members truly have our thanks. Come again! It makes us rejoice to see members coming from adjoining congregations. Bro. D. B. Brubaker, of Mt. Morris, was with us and officiated. Who will come among us next?—*S. B. Kuhn.*

Notice.—I want to say, once for all, that I am in no way connected with the Progressive church, never have been and never expect to be, as the German Baptist Brethren church is good enough for me to live in, and we believe, if we live out its principles, it will be good enough to die in. I take this method to answer all inquiring minds, as I saw that my name appears in the "Progressive Almanac," in the ministerial list, and the question has been asked if I knew about it. I hope my name will be dropped from the list, and appear there no more in the future.—*Jacob W. Keiser, Pioneer, Ohio.*

Fairview, Iowa.—The Brethren of the Fairview church, Appanoose County, Iowa, have just closed a very interesting little series of meetings, conducted by Bro. A. Hutchison, in which he gave us seven able and soul-cheering discourses. He left two applicants for baptism as the result of his labors. At the close of his meetings the church council was taken concerning a Communion Meeting and it was decided, the Lord willing, to have it on Saturday following Annual Meeting, June 11, 1892. A general invitation is extended, and especially to laboring brethren. We hope some of our Western brethren will make a note of this, and stop off to preach for us. Those passing over the Rock Island R. R., will stop off at Unionville, drop a card to Bro. Martin Replogle, and some one will meet them at the station.—*Daniel Zook.*

Pleasant Valley Church, Va.—Our love-feast May 7, was enjoyed by all the members in attendance. We had very good order, and hope many good impressions were made on the mixed multitude of outsiders.—*Martha Click.*

Roanoke, Ill. — Brethren and others, living in Woodford and adjoining Counties, are hereby notified that the Rock Island R. R., has arranged with other lines, centering at Peoria, for one fare for all attending Annual Meeting at Cedar Rapids, and that they will do all they can for the safety and pleasure of their patrons.—*Thomas Keiser, May 4.*

Rock Run Church, Ind.—The members of this church met in quarterly council May 14. There were about ninety members present. A considerable amount of business came before the meeting, but all was disposed of in love and union. There were three letters granted and two received. We chose Levi Weaver as delegate to Annual Meeting; I. L. Berkey, alternate. We decided to hold our love-feast June 22.—*R. W. Davenport.*

Good Hope Church, Colo.—We are still getting along nicely. Our Communion will occur June 12, the Lord willing, seven miles north-east of Holyoke. Our Sunday-school is doing well with A. B. VanDyke for Superintendent. We had seven additions by letter this spring. Among the number is one speaker in the second degree. We baptized three on Easter Sunday. Prospects are encouraging for more during the summer. We have much rain this spring. Small grain is doing well. Prospects are good for a good crop again.—*John S. Snowberger.*

Edna Mills, Ind.—The Middle Fork church, Clinton Co., Ind., held a Communion May 14. On account of the rainy weather, the attendance was small, but the order was good. Brethren John Metzger, John W. Metzger, D. C. Campbell, Daniel Dilling and Ira Fisher did the preaching. Our aged brother, John Metzger, officiated. May 16, at 9:30 A. M., we had preaching by the brethren. At 8:30 P. M. we had a children's meeting, conducted by brethren John Metzger and D. C. Campbell. At 7:30 Bro. John Metzger preached again.—*John E. Metzger, May 16.*

Gypsum, Kans.—The Abilene church had her love-feast at the Navarre meeting-house, and surely it was a feast of love to those who surrounded the Lord's table, and commemorated the death and suffering of our Savior. There were about 110 communicants. Ministering brethren from a distance were S Z Sharp, John Forney, C. Hope, Smith, Zigler, Bombough, Haugh, Coover, and George Wine. During the meetings we held an election for a minister, and the lot fell on Bro. Shatto who was properly installed. Bro. Manon was advanced to the second degree of the ministry. The weather was very inclement during the entire meeting.—*John J. Manon.*

Alfred, Kans.—The members of the Washington Creek church held their love-feast in connection with the Pleasant Grove church, meeting, as previously stated, May 7. The weather was somewhat unsettled, but we had a glorious meeting. Twelve ministers were present and 153 communed. Eld. Jesse Studabaker, from Anderson County, Kans., officiated. One young sister, who has been afflicted for some time, was anointed on Saturday at the church, by elders Jesse Studabaker and I. H. Crist. Bro. I. L. Hoover was advanced to the second degree of the ministry. On Sunday forenoon we had singing and preaching, and in the afternoon children's meeting and Sunday-school. Bro. I. H. Crist, from Johnson County, conducted the children's meeting. We had a large crowd and the very best of order.—*S. M. Miller.*

reject the additional instructions in John 16: 23, 24? This is my "query." It is not for my own special benefit I ask this question, but some who are not members of the Brethren church have asked the reasons for our practice. What shall we answer them?   JOHN E. MOHLER.
Warrensburgh, Mo.

From the George's Creek Church, Fayette Co., Pa.

WE held our council-meeting on the last Saturday in April. Everything passed off pleasantly. The church unanimously agreed to hold our love-feast the present month. All are cordially invited to attend our feast. We have several applicants for baptism before the feast.

Our church will be represented at District Meeting of the Western District of Pennsylvania, by delegates. Some papers will go there relative to the time of holding District Meeting. We will have one week's meeting before our feast.
                                ALPHEUS DEBOLT.
Masontown, Pa., May 9.

From the South River Church, Iowa.

I VISITED the little band of believers near Osceola, Iowa, April 30. They assembled in council, and with unanimous voice, chose brethren W. W. Folger, Jacob Keffer and W. Caskey as Trustees. They are also the building committee, with Bro. Folger as President, Bro. Keffer, Treasurer, and Bro. Caskey, Secretary. They appreciate the assistance given them by the "Church Erection and Missionary Committee;" also that given by neighboring congregations. They expect to have their house ready for use by Oct. 1. This organization was formerly known as the Irish Grove congregation, organized in Warren County, but the center of membership has moved West, until now they built their house near South River, in Madison County. They have, accordingly, decided to change the name from Irish Grove to South River congregation.

The heavy rain and consequent high waters and bad roads prevented the contemplated meetings, etc., so I returned home May 2, leaving the brethren with two applicants for baptism in the near future.   J. D. HAUGHTELIN.
Panora, Iowa.

Lower Stillwater, Ohio, Notes.

TO-DAY was our quarterly council for regular church business, and to prepare for District and Annual Meeting.

Considerable business was transacted. The spirit manifested in disposing of it was good. When such is the case, those having matters before the church cannot fail to see that the church has a regard for them, and is seeking their welfare in its requirements of them.

We send but one delegate to Annual Meeting this year on account of distance and expense, viz., Bro. John Smith. Our delegates to District Meeting are Bro. John Smith and the writer.

We are having Sunday-school at each house this summer. It continued evergreen in the Lower house, where the attendance is best. Brethren Wm. Bowser and W. W. Barnhart were to-day elected Associate Superintendents. We we would again call attention to our Ministerial Meeting to be held in the Upper house, May 28.

There will be preaching on Friday evening previous, Saturday evening, Sunday, and perhaps Sunday evening at the same place.

We expect a good attendance from Southern Ohio, and would especially welcome those from other parts of the Brotherhood who can be with

us and assist us with their counsel and experience. The nearest station on C. H. & D. (old narrow gauge) is Kinsey's. Any one stopping off there, will be cared for by Bro. David Landis, who lives near station and church. Those stopping at Haines' will be cared for by brethren living near by. Those coming by Pan Handle or D. & U. branch of the Big Four Road, should stop at Trotwood, and enquire for John Smith or the writer. Brethren on their way to Annual Meeting should make a note of this.

This Meeting will be of general interest, and for the benefit of all.

By a careful reading and rereading of "Chrysostom and Bread-breaking" in No. 19, it will be found that, from the statement of the Fathers there quoted, the brethren and sisters fared alike, i. e., the bishops broke bread to both similarly. The equality of the sexes in that important work is all that is claimed by those who favor the deferred query on that point to come up at Annual Meeting.

Although late in reporting, we had a very interesting series of meetings in our Upper house, conducted by Bro. D. P. Shively, of Peru, Ind. One was baptized, and one reclaimed as part of the good result of the meeting.
                            L. A. BOOKWALTER.
Trotwood, Ohio, May 11.

"To worship God and obey his laws is the most reasonable thing that a man ever did; and not to do this is hence the most unreasonable course that one ever pursued. The pious fear of God is 'the beginning of wisdom.'"

Notes from Our Correspondents.

"As cold water to a thirsty soul, so is good news from a far country."

Naperville, Ill.—Our feast was indeed an enjoyable one. It was one of the most impressive feasts we have attended in a long while. The Chicago church was well represented at our feast. The members truly have our thanks. Come again! It makes us rejoice to see members coming from adjoining congregations. Bro. D. E. Brubaker, of Mt. Morris, was with us and officiated. Who will come among us next?—*S. B. Kuhn.*

Notice.—I want to say, once for all, that I am in no way connected with the Progressive church, never have been and never expect to be, as the German Baptist Brethren church is good enough for me to live in, and we believe, if we live out its principles, it will be good enough to die in. I take this method to answer all inquiring minds, as I saw that my name appears in the "Progressive Almanac," in the ministerial list, and the question has been asked if I knew about it. I hope my name will be dropped from the list, and appear there no more in the future.—*Jacob W. Keiser, Pioneer, Ohio.*

Fairview, Iowa.—The Brethren of the Fairview church, Appanoose County, Iowa, have just closed a very interesting little series of meetings, conducted by Bro. A. Hutchison, in which he gave us seven able and soul-cheering discourses. He left two applicants for baptism as the result of his labors. At the close of his meetings the church council was taken concerning a Communion Meeting and it was decided, the Lord willing, to have it on Saturday following Annual Meeting, June 11, 1892. A general invitation is extended, and especially to laboring brethren. We hope some of our Western brethren will make a note of this, and stop off to preach for us. Those passing over the Rock Island R. R., will stop off at Unionville, drop a card to Bro. Martin Replogle, and some one will meet them at the station.—*Daniel Zook.*

Pleasant Valley Church, Va.—Our love-feast May 7, was enjoyed by all the members in attendance. We had very good order, and hope many good impressions were made on the mixed multitude of outsiders.—*Martha Click.*

Roanoke, Ill.—Brethren and others, living in Woodford and adjoining Counties, are hereby notified that the Rock Island R. R., has arranged with other lines, centering at Peoria, for one fare for all attending Annual Meeting at Cedar Rapids, and that they will do all they can for the safety and pleasure of their patrons.—*Thomas Keiser, May 4.*

Rock Run Church, Ind.—The members of this church met in quarterly council May 14. There were about ninety members present. A considerable amount of business came before the meeting, but all was disposed of in love and union. There were three letters granted and two received. We chose Levi Weaver as delegate to Annual Meeting; I. L. Berkey, alternate. We decided to hold our love-feast June 22.—*R. W. Davenport.*

Good Hope Church, Colo.—We are still getting along nicely. Our Communion will occur June 12, the Lord willing, seven miles north-east of Holyoke. Our Sunday-school is doing well with A. B. VanDyke for Superintendent. We had seven additions by letter this spring. Among the number is one speaker in the second degree. We baptized three on Easter Sunday. Prospects are encouraging for more during the summer. We have much rain this spring. Small grain is doing well. Prospects are good for a good crop again.—*John S. Snowberger.*

Edna Mills, Ind.—The Middle Fork church, Clinton Co., Ind., held a Communion May 14. On account of the rainy weather, the attendance was small, but the order was good. Brethren John W. Metzger, D. C. Campbell, Daniel Dilling and Ira Fisher did the preaching. Our aged brother, John Metzger, officiated. May 15, at 9:30 A. M., we had preaching by the brethren. At 3:30 P. M. we had a children's meeting, conducted by brethren John Metzger and D. C. Campbell. At 7:30 Bro. John Metzger preached again.—*John E. Metzger, May 16.*

Gypsum, Kans.—The Abilene church had her love-feast at the Navarre meeting-house, and surely it was a feast of love to those who surrounded the Lord's table, and commemorated the death and suffering of our Savior. There were about 110 communicants. Ministering brethren from a distance were S Z. Sharp, John Forney, C. Hope, Smith, Zigler, Bombough, Haugh, Coover, and George Wine. During the meetings we held an election for a minister, and the lot fell on Bro. Shatto who was properly installed. Bro. Manon was advanced to the second degree of the ministry. The weather was very inclement during the entire meeting.—*John J. Manon.*

Alfred, Kans.—The members of the Washington Creek church held their love-feast in connection with the Pleasant Grove church, meeting, as previously stated, May 7. The weather was somewhat unsettled, but we had a glorious meeting. Twelve ministers were present and 163 communed. Eld. Jesse Studebaker, from Anderson County, Kans., officiated. One young sister, who has been afflicted for some time, was anointed on Saturday at the church, by elders Jesse Studebaker and I. H. Crist. Bro. I. L. Hoover was advanced to the second degree of the ministry. On Sunday forenoon we had singing and preaching, and in the afternoon children's meeting and Sunday-school. Bro. I. H. Crist, from Johnson County, conducted the children's meeting. We had a large crowd and the very best of order.—*S. M. Miller.*

ADVERTISEMENTS.

Church Entertainments: Twenty Objections.

By Rev. B. Carradine, D. D. 12mo, 100 pp. Paper cover, 30 cents. A strong book in defense of its position, written by a powerful pen, presenting the most candid and scriptural arraignment of unwarrantable methods for money-raising in the Church. The spirit of the book is highly devotional and cannot fail to inspire the reader with its seriousness.

Brethren's Church Manual.

THIS is a small book, adapted to the wants of every member of the Church, and will be found especially useful to our ministers, deacons, Sunday-school officers and teachers And all who wish to be posted in the faith and practices of the church. Besides giving the faith, practices and duties of the church, it contains forms of Ordinations, Installings, Marriages, Burials, Prayers, etc. The work ends with a complete set of rules for conducting all kinds of public meetings, and is just the book every one interested in church work needs. Send for a copy. Only 30 cents for a copy, post-paid; per dozen, $3.00. Address Brethren's Publishing Co., Mt. Morris, Ill., or Huntingdon, Pa.

Excursions to California.

Excursions in charge of M. M. Eshelman, Immigration Agent, will leave Chicago over the "Santa Fe Route" Tuesdays, and Kansas City Wednesdays, during the year 1892, on dates as follows:

Chicago, January 26, February 23, March 22, April 26, May 24, June 28, July 26, August 23, September 27, October 25, November 22, December 27.

Kansas City, January 27, February 24, March 23, April 27, May 25, June 29, July 27, August 24, September 28, October 26, November 23, December 28.

Parties wishing to avail themselves of the privileges of these excursions, should write M. M. Eshelman, North Pomona, California, prior to the 15th of each month, and from the fifteenth to the end of the month, at 1090 Union Avenue (opposite Union Depot), Kansas City, Mo., stating when and where they wish to join one of these excursions, and he will give them full information, and if desired will reserve berths in Tourist Sleeping Car for them. Do not fail to write him; he will do you good. The rates will be as low as the lowest made to the Pacific Coast.

GEORGE L. McDONOUGH,
TRAVELING AGENT.

→PUBLICATIONS←

☞The following books, Sunday-school supplies, etc., are for sale by the BRETHREN'S PUBLISHING CO., Mt. Morris, Ill., or Huntingdon, Pa., to whom all orders should be addressed.

The Brethren's Quarterly.

For Sunday-school teachers and scholars this publication is of the greatest benefit. Look at our prices:

Single subscription, one year,	........35 cents.
Single subscription, per quarter,	....10 cents.
Three copies, per quarter,	........20 cents.
Eight copies, per quarter,	.........20 cents.
Twenty copies and over,	....4 cents each.

Hymn Books.

New Tune and Hymn Books.

Half leather, per copy, post-paid,	...........$ 75
Morocco, per copy, post-paid,	.... 1 00
Morocco, gilt edge, per copy, post-paid,	.... 1 25

Hymn Books.

Morocco, per copy, post-paid,	.........$ 75
Morocco, gilt edge, per copy post-paid,	... 85
Arabesque, per copy, post-paid,	 45
Fine Limp, per copy, post-paid,	 75
Fine Limp, gilt edge, per copy, post-paid,	... 85
German and English, per copy, post-paid,	... 75

Sunday-School Requisites.

The following list of things is needed in all Sunday schools:

Testaments, Flexible, red edge, per dozen,	...$1 00
Minute Books, each,	 40
Class Books, per dozen,	 75
S. S. Primers, with-fine engravings, per dozen,	... 70

New and Beautiful Sunday-School Cards.

"The Gem," 10 picture cards, each with Bible text, verse of hymn, &c., ... 35
250 Reward Tickets—verse of Scripture—red or blue ... 10

The Young Disciple.

THE YOUNG DISCIPLE is a neatly printed weekly, published especially for the moral benefit and religious instruction of our young folks.

Single copy, one year,	........$ 50
Six copies (the sixth to the agent),	..... 2 50
Ten copies,	.... 4 00

For Three Months or Thirteen Weeks.

10 copies to one address,	......$1 70
30 " " "	... 3 00
50 " " "	... 3 35
75 " " "	... 3 80
100 " " "	... 7 00

For Six Months or Twenty-Six Weeks.

20 copies to one address,	......$ 3 35
30 " " "	... 5 00
40 " " "	... 6 60
50 " " "	... 7 50
75 " " "	... 10 30
100 " " "	... 13 75

Our paper is designed for the Sunday-school and the home circle. We desire the name of every Sunday-school Superintendent in the Brotherhood, and want an agent in every church. Send for sample copies.

Seven Great Monarchies.—By George Rawlinson. In three volumes, cloth. Per volume, $1.00.

Mental Science and Methods of Mental Culture.—By Edward Brooks. Cloth, $1.75.

Manual of Jewish History and Literature.—By D. Cassel. Cloth, 75 cents.

Every Day Christian Life.—By F. W. Farrar. Cloth, 12mo, $1.25.

JAMES T. QUINLAN,

SHIPPING & COMMISSION MERCHANT

Wool, Hay, Grain and Gen'l Produce,

305 South Charles St.,

BALTIMORE, - - MD.

Juvenile Quarterly.

THIS is just the Quarterly for the little folks. Price, Three Copies, per Quarter, 20 Cents; 6 Copies, per Quarter, 25 Cents; 10 Copies and over, per Quarter, 3 Cents each.

Tract Work.

List of Publications for Sale,—Sent Postage Prepaid.

CLASS A.

No. 1, Golden Gleams or Family Chart, ... $ 85
No. 2 Diagram of Passover and Lord's Supper, per copy, ... 70

CLASS B.

Plain Family Bible, per copy, ... $2.70
Trine Immersion, Quinter, per copy, ... 1 25
Europe and Bible Lands, Miller, per copy, ... 1 50
Doctrine of the Brethren Defended, Miller, per copy, ... 1 60
Close Communion, West, per copy, ... 40
Missionary Hymn Book, per dozen, $1.00; per copy, ... 10

CLASS C—(TRACTS).

No. 1, The Brethren or Dunkards, per 100, $1.50 per copy, ... 03
No. 2, Path of Life, per 100, $4; per copy, ... 05
No. 3, How to Become a Child of God, per 100, $4; per copy, ... 05
No. 4, Conversion, per 100, $2.50; per copy, ... 03
No. 5, Water Baptism, per 100, $1.50; per copy, ... 45
No. 6, Single Immersion, per 100, $1; per copy, ... 01
No. 7, Sabbatism, per 100, $1.50; per copy, ... 02
No. 8, Trine Immersion Traced to the Apostles, per 100, $7; per copy, ... 08
No. 9, Sermon on Baptism, per 100, $6; per copy, ... 03
No. 10, Glad Tidings of Salvation, per 100, $1.50; per copy, ... 02
No. 11, Life of Eld. S. Weir (Colored), per 100, $4.50; per copy, ... 02
No. 12, Ten Reasons for Trine Immersion, per 100, $1; per copy, ... 01
No. 13, The Lord's Day and the Sabbath, per 100, $2.50; per copy, ... 03

CLASS D.

No. 1, The House We Live In, per 100, ... $ .45
No. 2, Plan of Salvation, per 100, ... 45
No. 3, Come Let Us Reason Together, per 100, ... 45
No. 4, How Shall I know What my Sins are Pardonded? per 100, ... 45
No. 5, Intemperance, per 100, ... 45
No. 6, Plain Dressing, per 100, ... 45
No. 7, Which is the Right Church? per 100, ... 45
No. 8, The House We Live In (Swedish), per 100, ... 45
No. 9, The House We Live In (Danish), per 100, ... 45
No. 10, Paul Wetzel's Reasons (German), per 100, ... 45
No. 11, Dinner, Stop, per 100, ... 45
No. 12, Faith, per 100, ... 45
No. 13, The Light House, per 100, ... 45
No. 14, Close Communion, per 100, ... 45
No. 15, The Truth Shall Make You Free, per 100, ... 45
No. 16, Modern Skepticism, per 100, ... 45
No. 17, Infant Baptism Weighed, etc., per 100, ... 45
No. 18, Repentance, per 100, ... 45
No. 19, Talk to R. R. Employees, etc., per 100, ... 45
No. 20, Life and Death, per 100, ... 45
No. 21, The House We Live In (German), per 100, ... 45
No. 22, The Prayer Covering, per 100, ... 45
No. 23, The Lord's Supper, per 100, ... 45
No. 24, Shall I Smoke or Affirm? per 100, ... 45
No. 25, Secret Societies, per 100, ... 45
No. 26, Church Entertainments, per 100, ... 45
No. 27, Conversion or the New Birth, per 100, ... 45
No. 28, The Bible Service of Feet-washing, per 100, ... 45
No. 29, Scriptural Communion, per 100, ... 45

CLASS E.

No. 1, Pause and Think, per 100, ... $ .20
No. 2, What Do We Need? per 100, ... 20
No. 3, Right or Wrong Way, per 100, ... 20
No. 4, Why Am I Not a Christian? per 100, ... 20
No. 5, Saving Words, per 100, ... 20
No. 6, Christ and War, per 100, ... 20
No. 7, The Bound of Peace, per 100, ... 20
No. 8, The Kiss of Charity, per 100, ... 20
No. 9, The Evils of Intemperance, per 100, ... 20
No. 10, The Lost Opportunity, per 100, ... 20
No. 11, Are You a Christian? per 100, ... 20
No. 12, Lying Among the Pots, per 100, ... 20
No. 13, A Personal Appeal, per 100, ... 20
No. 14, Gold and Costly Array, per 100, ... 20
No. 15, The Brethren's Card, per 100, ... 20
No. 16, The Whole Gospel Must Be Obeyed, per 100, ... 20

Bibles, Testaments, Hymn Books of all styles, at publishers' lowest retail prices, which will be furnished on application. Address:
BRETHREN'S BOOK & TRACT WORK,
DAYTON, OHIO.

CATHOLICS The errors and dangers of their system, with a plain statement of our real Scriptural position. A book of startling facts and forcible logic. Over 600 pages, illustrated. Cloth, $2.00; Leather, $2.50. "What to Read," our monthly magazine, one year free to every purchaser of a book. Liberal inducements to agents. Write for circulars and terms to Jas. M. Neff, Covington, Ohio.

Announcements.

DISTRICT MEETINGS.

May 17, at 8 A. M., District of Southern Ohio, in the Lexington church, Highland Co., Ohio. Buy your ticket to Highland, Lexington Village, on the Cincinnati and Marietta Railway; go by way of Cincinnati.

May 24 and 25. South-eastern District of Kansas, to be held with the Brethren of Neosho County, near Galesburgh, on the M. K. & T. R. R., one mile north, and 1½ miles east of Galesburgh. Ministerial Meeting May 24.

LOVE-FEASTS.

May 25, at 4 P. M., Turkey Creek congregation, at the Gravelton house, Elkhart Co., Ind.

May 26 and 27, at 10 A. M., Pine Creek, Ogle Co., Ill.

May 27, at 10 A. M., in the Killbuck church, nine miles west of Muncie, Ind.

May 27, at 8 P. M., in the Harlan congregation, four miles east of Harlan, Shelby Co., Iowa. Meetings to continue over Sunday.

day 27, at 4 P. M., Buck Creek church, Ind.

May 27, at 1 P. M., Hopewell church, Bedford Co., Pa.

May 27 and 28, at 2 P. M., Lost Creek congregation, Juniata Co., Pa., at Goodwill.

May 27, at 4 P. M., Monticello church, Ind.

May 27, at 4 P. M., Pleasant Hill church, Jefferson Co., Iowa. Stop off at Libertyville.

May 28, at 10 A. M., Hartford Church, Hartford City, Ind.

May 28, at 4 P. M., Middle Creek congregation, Somerset Co., Pa.

May 28, in the North Manchester church, a miles west of the town of North Manchester, Ind.

May 28, at 10 A. M., Pleasant Valley church, Darke Co., Ohio. Meetings to continue over Sunday.

May 28, at 2 P. M., Loudonville, Grant Co., Ind.

May 28, at 10 A. M., Roree congregation, Oak Grove house, Hancock Co., Ohio.

May 28 and 29, at 3 P. M., Lanark church, Carroll Co., Ill.

May 28 and 29, at 10 A. M., in the Rock River congregation, Ill., at the Franklin Grove meeting-house.

May 29, at 1 P. M., Des Moines Valley church, Polk Co., Iowa. The 20 and 10 o'clock trains will be met at Ankeny on the day of meeting.

May 31 and June 1, at 2 P. M., Hickory Grove church, O.

May 31 and June 1, at 1 P. M., Cherry Grove, Carroll Co., Ill.

May 31, at 4 P. M., in the Rouge church, Elkhart Co., Ind., three miles north-west of Wakarusa, Ind.

May 31 and June 1, at 10 A. M., Oakland church, Darke Co., Ohio.

May 31 and June 1, at 2 P. M., Buffalo Valley church, Union Co., Pa.

June 1, in the Yellow Creek church, Elkhart Co., Ind., 7 miles south-west of Goshen.

June 1, at 4 P. M., Yellow Creek church, Elkhart Co., Ind.

June 1, at 4 P. M., South Beatrice church, Gage Co., Nebr. Those coming via U. P. R. R., stop at Holmesville; via the B. & M. R. R., should stop off at Beatrice; via the Rock Island R. R., should stop at Rockford.

June 1, at 2 P. M., at Flora, Ind. Train due here from the south at 10 A. M.

June 2, at 4 P. M., White church, Montgomery Co., Ind., 4¾ miles west of Colfax, Ind.

June 2, at 10 A. M., Buck Creek, Franklin Co., Pa. at the Shank meeting-house, 1¾ miles south of Green, castle.

June 2 and 3, at 2 P. M., Yellow Creek, Ill.

June 2 and 3, at 2 P. M., in the Palatine church, Darke Co., Ohio.

June 2, at 2 P. M., Upper Fall Creek church, 4 miles east of Middletown, Henry Co., Ind.

June 2, at 2 P. M., Pleasant Valley church, Elkhart Co., Ind.

June 2, at 10 A. M., Eel River church, Ind.

June 2, at 10 A. M., Cedar Lake congregation, near Corunna, Dekalb Co., Ind.

June 2 and 3, at 10 A. M., Antioch church, Ill.

June 2, at 3 P. M., in the Saloway church, at Lonaconing, 3 miles south of Blatingston, Ind.

June 2, Palestine church, Ohio. Members will be met at Rose Madison and Cloa's Station on the " Big Four R. R." by notifying Moses Hollinger, New Madison, Ohio.

June 2, at 4 P. M., in the Cloas church, Platt Co., Ill. Ministering brethren on their way to Annual Meeting, will please stop with us.

June 2, Tippecanoe church, Kosciusko Co., Ind.

June 3, at 4 P. M., Walnut Level church, Wells Co., Ind.

June 3, at 4 P. M., Blue Ridge church, Platt Co., Ill.

June 4, at 10 A. M., Springfield congregation, Wabash, Ind.

June 2 and 3, at 4 P. M., 6½ miles south-west of Sommerfield, Kans.

June 4, at 5 P. M., Mound church, Bates Co., Mo.

June 4 and 5, at 2 P. M., Hickory Grove church, Carroll Co., Ill. Brethren going to Annual Meeting will please remember us.

June 4, at 11 P. M., Berkeley church, W. Va.

June 6, at 10 A. M., Lick Creek church, Williams Co., Ohio, 5 mile south-west of Bryan.

June 6, at 3 P. M., Maple Valley church, Iowa.

June 4, at 2 P. M., 3½ miles north-east of Summitville, Ind.

June 6, at 5 P. M., Mound church, Bates Co., Mo.

June 7, West Conestoga church, at the Middle Creek house, Lancaster Co., Pa.

June 6, at 1 P. M., Ephrata, Pa., at the Mohler house.

June 8, White Oak church, at the Penrsville house, Lancaster Co., Pa.

June 11, 3¾ miles North-west of Cabool, Mo.

June 11, at 2 P. M., Cornell church, Ill., on the Streator Branch of the Wabash R. R.

June 12 and 13, at 10 A. M., Greene church, Greene, Iowa. There will be preaching on Friday evening previous.

June 11, at 5 P. M., Quemahoning church, Somerset Co., Pa.

June 11, at 3 P. M., Kingsley church, four miles south-east of Kingsley, Iowa.

June 11, at 2 P. M., in the Member church, 8 miles west and a mile south of McPherson, Kans.

June 12, at 10 A. M., Hudson, Ill.

June 12, at 3 P. M., in the Bethel congregation, Kosciusko Co., Ind., at the Pleasant View Chapel, three miles east of Milford.

June 12, at 10 A. M., Belleville church, Kans.

June 17, St. Vrain church, Colo.

June 12 and 13, at 10 A. M., in the Richland church, Richland County, Ohio, six miles north of Mansfield.

June 27, at 4 P. M., North Beatrice church, Nebr.

June 12 and 13, Kiddy church, Woodbury Co., Iowa.

June 12, Fairview church, Iowa.

June 12, 10 A. M., at the west house, Thornapple church, Mich. Take the D. L. & N. R. R. from Grand Rapids, Mich., to Elmdale, where you will be met by notifying L. D. Fry, Elmdale, Mich.

June 12, Plum Creek church, Pa. A series of meetings to begin one week previous. Eld. S. H. Meyers is expected to be with us.

June 12, at 2 P. M., in the Shade Creek congregation, Somerset Co., Pa.

June 13, Good Hope church, Iowa; 2 miles north of Holyoke.

June 15, at 2 P. M., Camp Creek church, Kosciusko Co., Ind., 3 miles north of Etna Green. Those coming from the West at 10 M. and East at 2 P. M., will find conveyance at the church.

June 14 and 15, Dallas Center church, Iowa.

June 16, at 2 P. M., Pigeon River church, Ind.

June 17, at 4 P. M., Yellow River congregation, Marshall Co., Ind.

June 18, at the Corner Meeting house, Canton, Stark Co., Ohio.

June 18, at 5 P. M., in the Eagle Creek church, Ohio. A series of meetings will be held in connection, beginning June 16.

June 18 and 19, at 10 A. M., Iowa River church, Iowa.

June 18 and 19, Panther Creek, Dallas Co., Iowa.

June 18, South Waterloo church, Waterloo, Iowa.

June 18, Green Spring District, Seneca Co., Ohio.

June 18 and 19 at 11 A. M., Middle Creek church, Markloe Co., Iowa.

June 18, at 2 P. M., Brush church, Two Mile congregation, seven or nine South-east of Washington, Pa. There will be one week's meeting previous to the feast.

June 19, at 4 P. M., in the Rock Run church, Elkhart Co., Ind.

June 25, at 10 A. M., in the Van Wert church, seven miles north-east of Van Wert, Ohio. Those coming by rail will be met at Van Wert, day before the meeting by notifying Jacob Brunner, or Joseph Longanecker, Wetsel, Ohio.

June 25 and 26, Indian Creek church, Polk Co., Iowa.

Annual Meeting at Cedar Rapids.

For the coming Conference at Cedar Rapids, June next, "THE IOWA ROUTE," Burlington, Cedar Rapids & Northern Ry., offers you unlimited accommodation, operating in connection with the Chicago, Rock Island & Pacific, and Rock Island, and Peoria Rys., making good connections at Chicago and Peoria with all eastern lines at Kansas City with all south-western lines; at Omaha, with all western lines. And in connection with the St. L., K. P. N. W. R. R. at St. Louis, with south, south-eastern, and south-western lines, a system of through train service being operated from above points, so that you in a quick and pleasant journey. Special trains will be run from which station is accommodated the demand of this business. All train stop at the Union Depot in Cedar Rapids. Those traveling via this route may be assured of first-class accommodations and courteous treatment. For further information, as to rates of fare, time of trains, etc., apply to any agent of the above-named lines, or to

J. E. HANNEGAN,
G. T. & P. A., B. C. R. & N. Ry.
Cedar Rapids, Iowa.

Gospel Chimes.

BY WM. BEERY.

A new edition of this deservedly popular Sunday-school song-book has just been issued.

Bro. Beery has had a large experience in Sunday-school work, and the book which we offer to the Brethren and the public in general, evinces the exercise of talent as well as good judgment. The religious purity of the hymns, contributed by sister Beery, adds much to the excellence of the book.

Price per single copy, 65 cts.; per dozen, by mail, $2.50; by express, $2.50. Lots of more than a dozen must be sent by express.

BRETHREN'S PUBLISHING CO.,
Or Huntingdon, Pa. Mt. Morris Ill.

NOTICE!

NEVER since the meeting at Bismark Grove, Kans., have I attended an Annual Meeting, nor have I been represented at any Conference since then; but I will attend the Meeting at Cedar Rapids, Iowa, this year, sorry to tell medicine, nor to give medicine away, nor to advertise any medicine; but to enjoy the meeting and be accessible to those of my numerous correspondents, who desire to interview me.

No one else will represent me; but those who wish to pay money, or order medicine from me should do so by mail and address,

DR. PETER FAHRNEY,
112 S. Hoyne Ave.,
Chicago, Ill.

CANCERS, TUMORS, ETC.

Successfully treated by Dr. G. N. Boteler, of Waynesborough, Pa., where he has practiced for the last sixteen years. Dr. Boteler is a graduate of the University of Maryland, at Baltimore City. References given and consultation free. Address, Dr. G. W. Boteler, Waynesborough, Pa.

The Annual Meeting of German Baptist Brethren at Cedar Rapids, Iowa,
June 3 to 9 inclusive.

Tickets for the above meeting will be good going from May 28 to June 9, good to return till June 30.

THE ILLINOIS CENTRAL RAILROAD is the popular and direct route from Chicago to Cedar Rapids. Two First-class express trains, equipped with beautiful, free, reclining-chair cars; leave Chicago daily at 11.30 P. M. and 11.35 P. M., arriving at Cedar Rapids at 11 P. M. and 11 A. M.

A large number of the Brethren from the different Eastern States have already decided to take this favorite route.

Tickets will be on sale at all railroad coupon ticket offices in the East.

Don't fail to ask for tickets via the Illinois Central R R from Chicago.

For further detailed information write

A. J. McDONALL,
343 Broadway, Eastern Pass. Agt, I. C. R. R., New York.

Announcements.

DISTRICT MEETINGS.

May 17, at 8 A. M., District of Southern Ohio, in the Lexington church, Highland Co., Ohio. Buy your ticket to Highland, Lexington Village, on the Cincinnati and Marietta Railway; go by way of Cincinnati.

May 24 and 25, South-eastern District of Kansas, to be held with the Brethren of Neosho County, near Galesburgh, on the M. K. & T. R. R., one mile north, and 1½ miles east of Galesburgh. Ministerial Meeting May 24.

LOVE FEASTS.

May 25, at 4 P. M., Turkey Creek congregation, at the Gravelton house, Elkhart Co., Ind.

May 26 and 27, at 10 A. M., Pine Creek, Ogle Co., Ill.

May 27, at 2 A. M., in the Killbuck church, nine miles west of Muncie, Ind.

May 27, at 8 P. M., in the Harlan congregation, four miles east of Huslan, Shelby Co., Iowa. Meetings to continue over Sunday.

day 27, at 4 P. M., Buck Creek church, Ind.

May 27, at 4 P. M., Hopewell church, Bedford Co., Pa.

May 27 and 28, at 2 P. M., Lost Creek congregation, Juniata Co., Pa., at Goodwill.

May 28, at 4 P. M., Monticello church, Ind.

May 28, at 10 A. M., Pleasant Hill church, Jefferson Co., Iowa. Stop off at Libertyville.

May 28, at 10 A. M., Hartford Church, Hartford City, Ind.

May 28, at 4 P. M., Middle Creek congregation, Somerset Co., Pa.

May 28, in the North Manchester church, 2 miles west of the town of North Manchester, Ind.

May 28, at 2 P. M., Pleasant Valley church, Darke Co., Ohio. Meetings to continue over Sunday.

May 28, at 4 P. M., Landessville, Grant Co., Ind.

May 28, at 10 A. M., Rome congregation, Oak Grove house, Hancock Co., Ohio.

May 28 and 29, at 2 P. M., Loose2 church, Carroll Co., Ill.

May 28 and 29, at 10 A. M., in the Rock River congregation, Ill., at the Franklin Grove meeting-house.

May 29, at 2 P. M., Des Moines Valley church, Polk Co., Iowa. The 29 and 30 o'clock trains will be met at Ankeny on the day of meeting.

May 31 and June 1, at 2 P. M., Hickory Grove church, O.

May 31 and June 1, at 1 P. M., Cherry Grove, Carroll Co., Ill.

May 31, at 4 P. M., in the Bangs church, Elkhart Co., Ind., three miles north-west of Wabarusa, Ind.

May 31, at 4 P. M., Oakland church, Darke Co., Ohio.

May 31 and June 1, at 2 P. M., Buffalo Valley church, Union Co., Pa

June 1, in the Yellow Creek church, Elkhart Co., Ind., 2 miles south-west of Goshen.

June 1, at 4 P. M., Yellow Creek church, Elkhart Co., Ind.

June 1, at 2 P. M., South Beatrice church, Gage Co., Neb. Those coming via U. P. R. R., stop at Holmesville; via the B. & M. R. R., should stop off at Beatrice; via the Rock Island R. R., should stop at Rockford.

June 1, at 2 P. M., at Flora, Ind. Train due here from the south at 10 A. M.

June 2, at 4 P. M., White church, Montgomery Co., Ind., 4¾ miles west of Colfax, Ind.

June 2, at 10 A. M., Buck Creek, Franklin Co., Pa., at the Shank meeting-house, 1¾ miles south of Greencastle.

June 2 and 3, at 2 P. M., Yellow Creek, Ill.

June 2, at 2 P. M., in the Palestine church, Darke Co., Ohio.

June 2, at 2 P. M., Upper Fall Creek church, 2 miles east of Middletown, Henry Co., Ind.

June 2, at 5 P. M., Pleasant Valley church, Elkhart Co., Ohio.

June 2, at 10 A. M., Eel River church, Ind.

June 2, at 10 A. M., Cedar Lake congregation, near Corunna, Dekalb Co., Ind.

June 2 and 3, at 10 A. M., Astoria church, Ill.

June 2, at 5 P. M., in the Kalloway church, at Lancaster, 9 miles south of Huntington, Ind.

June 2, Palestine church, Ohio. Members will be met at New Madison and Clark's Station on the "Big Four R. R." by notifying Moses Hollinger, New Madison, Ohio.

June 2, at 4 P. M., in the Ottaw church, Pifle Co., Ill. Adjoining brethren are their way to Annual Meeting will please stop with us.

June 2, Tippecanoe church, Kosciusko Co., Ind.

June 3, at 2 P. M., Walnut Level church, Wells Co., Ind.

June 3, at 4 P. M., Blue Ridge church, Flint Co., Ill.

June 3, at 10 A. M., Springfield congregation, Waukee, Ind.

June 3 and 3, at 2 P. M., 675 miles south-east of Summerfield, Kans.

June 3, at 5 P. M., Mettot church, Butts Co., Mo.

June 3 and 3, at 2 P. M., Hickory Grove church, Carroll Co., Ill. Brethren going to Annual Meeting will please remember us.

June 3, at 2 P. M., Brinkley church, W. Va.

June 3, at 10 A. M., Lick Creek church, Williams Co., Ohio, 3 miles south-west of Bryan.

June 4, at 4 P. M., Maple Valley church, Iowa.

June 4, at 2 P. M., 3½ miles north-east of Summerville, Ind.

June 4, at 2 P. M., Mound church, Bates Co., Mo.

June 7, West Otter creek church, in the Middle Creek house, Louisiana Co., Pa.

June 6, at 2 P. M., Ephrata, Pa., at the Mohler house.

June 8, White Oak church, at the Prairie house, Lancaster Co., Pa.

June 10, 3½ miles North-west of Cabool, Mo.

June 10, at 2 P. M., Carroll church, Ill., in the Stamer house at the Walnut R. R.

June 10 and 11, at 10 A. M., Greene church, Greene, Iowa. There will be preaching on Friday evening previous.

June 11, at 2 P. M., Quemahoning church, Somerset Co., Pa.

June 11, at 2 P. M., Kingsley church, four miles south-east of Kingsley, Iowa.

June 11, at 2 P. M., in the Mumfor church, 5 miles east and 2 miles south of McPherson, Kans.

June 11, at 10 A. M., Hudson, Ill.

June 11, at 2 P. M., in the Bethel congregation, Rostraw lot Co., Ind., at the Pleasant View Chapel, three miles east of Milford.

June 11, at 5 P. M., Wyot church, Colo.

June 16 and 16, 11 10 A. M., in the Richland church Richland County, Ohio, six miles north of Mansfield.

June 13, at 2 P. M., North Beatrice church, Nebr.

June 22 and 23, Kimsly church, Woodbury Co., Iowa.

June 23, Fairview church, Iowa.

June 23, at 10 A. M., in the west house, Thornapple church, Mich. Take the D. L. & N. R. R. from Grand Rapids, Mich., to Kinsale, where you will be met by notifying L. D. Fry, Elmdale, Mich.

June 22, Plev Creek church, Pa. A series of meetings to begin one week previous. Eld. S. H. Meyers is expected to be with us.

June 25 and 26, 2 P. M., in the Shride Creek congregation, Somerset Co., Pa.

June 25, Good Hope church, Colo., 7 miles north of Holyoke.

June 25, at 4 P. M., Camp Creek church, Kosciusko Co., Ind., 2 miles North of Knox Creek. Those coming from the West at 10 M. and East at 2 P. M., will find conveyance at the church.

July 2 and 16, Dallas Center church, Iowa

July 16, at 2 P. M., Pigeon River church, Ind.

June 27, at 4 P. M., Yellow River congregation, Marshall Co., Ind.

June 27, at the Center Meeting house, Coshen, Stark Co., Ohio.

June 28, at 2 P. M., in the Eagle Creek church, Ohio. A series of meetings will be held in connection, beginning June 16.

June 28 and 29, at 10 A. M., Iowa River church, Iowa.

June 28, at 10 A. M., South Waterloo church, Waterloo, Iowa.

June 28, Green Spring District, Seneca Co., Ohio.

June 18 and 29 at 11 A. M., Middle Creek church, Mahaska Co., Iowa.

June 16, at 2 P. M., Brick church, Ten Mile congregation, about 3 miles South-east of Washington, Pa. There will be one week's meeting previous to the feast.

June 29 and 3 P. M., in Rock Rim church, Marshall Co., Ind.

June 22, at 4 P. M., Root timber church, east of Goshen at the Rock Run church, Ind.

June 22, at 10 A. M., in the Van Wert church, services in the north-east of Van Wert, Ohio. Those coming by rail will be met at Van Wert, day before the meeting by notifying Jacob Holsinger, or Joseph Longanecker, Wabash, Ohio.

June 29 and 30, at Indian Creek church, Polk Co., Iowa.

Annual Meeting at Cedar Rapids.

For the coming Conference at Cedar Rapids, June next, "THE IOWA ROUTE," Burlington, Cedar Rapids & Northern R'y, offers you unlimited accommodations, again in connection with the Chicago, Rock Island & Pacific, and Rock Island and Peoria R'ys, making good connections at Chicago and Peoria with all eastern lines; at Kansas City with all south-western lines; at Omaha with all western lines. And in connection with the St. L., K. & N. W. R. R. at St. Louis, with south, southeastern, and south-western lines, a system of through train service being operated from almost points, insures you of a quick and pleasant journey. Special trains will be run from certain points to accommodate the demand of the business. All trains stop at the Union Depot in Cedar Rapids. Those traveling via this route may be assured of first-class accommodations and excellent treatment. For further information, as to rates of fare, time of trains, etc., apply to any agent of the above-named lines, or to

J. E. HANNEGAN,
G. T. & P. A., B. C. R. & N. R'y,
Cedar Rapids, Iowa.

Gospel Chimes.

BY WM. BEERY.

A new edition of this deservedly-popular Sunday-school song book has just been issued.

Bro. Beery has had a large experience in Sunday-school work, and the book which we offer to the Brethren, and the public in general, evinces the exercise of talent as well as good judgment. The religious purity of the hymns, contributed by sister Beery, adds much to the excellence of the book.

Price per single copy, 25 cts.; per dozen, by mail, $2.50; by express, $2.30. Lots of more than a dozen must be sent by express.

BRETHREN'S PUBLISHING CO.,
Or Huntington, Pa.   Mt. Morris, Ill.

NOTICE!

NEVER since the meeting at Bismark Grove, Kans, have I attended an Annual Meeting, nor have I been represented at any Conference since then; but I will attend the Meeting at Cedar Rapids, Iowa, this year, not to sell medicine, nor to give medicine away, nor to advertise any medicine; but to enjoy the meeting and be accessible to those of my numerous correspondents, who desire to interview me.

No one else will represent me; but those who want to pay money, or order medicine from me should do so by mail and address,

DR. PETER FAHRNEY,
113 S. Hoyne Ave.,
Chicago, Ill.

CANCERS, TUMORS, ETC.

Successfully treated by Dr. G. N. Boteler, of Waynesboro, Pa., where he has practiced for the last fourteen years. Dr. Boteler is a graduate of the University of Maryland, at Baltimore City. References given and correspondence solicited. Address, Dr. G. N. Boteler, Waynesborough, Pa.

The Annual Meeting of German Baptist Brethren at Cedar Rapids, Iowa, June 3 to 9 inclusive.

Tickets for the above meeting will be good going from May 28 to June 9, good to return till June 30.

THE ILLINOIS CENTRAL RAILROAD is the popular and direct route from Chicago to Cedar Rapids. Two First class express trains, equipped with beautiful, free, reclining chair cars, leave Chicago daily at 1:30 P. M. and 11:35 P. M., arriving at Cedar Rapids at 11 P. M. and 11 A. M. A large number of the Brethren from the different Eastern States have already decided to take this favorite route.

Tickets will be on sale at all railroad coupon ticket offices in the East.

Don't fail to ask for tickets via the Illinois Central R. R. from Chicago.

For further detailed information write

A. J. McDONGALL,
Eastern Pass. Agt., I. C. R. R.,
343 Broadway,   New York

⊹ESSAYS⊹

"Study to show thyself approved unto God; a workman that needeth not be ashamed, rightly dividing the Word of Truth."

WRITE THEM A LETTER TO-NIGHT.

Don't go to the theatre, concert or ball,
But stay in your room to-night;
Deny yourself to the friends that call,
And a good, long letter write—
Write to the sad old folks at home,
Who sit, when the day is done,
With folded hands and downcast eyes
And think of the absent one.

Don't selfishly scribble, "Excuse my haste,
I've scarcely the time to write,"
Lest their brooding thoughts go wandering back
To many a by-gone night,
When they lost their needed sleep and rest,
And every breath was a prayer
That God would leave their delicate babe
To their tender love and care.

Don't let them feel that you've no more need
Of their love or counsel wise;
For the heart grows strongly sensitive
When age has dimmed the eyes—
It might be well to let them believe
You might never forget them, quite;
That you deem it a pleasure, when far away,
Long letters home to write.

Don't think that the young and giddy friends
Who make your pastime gay,
Have half the anxious thought for you
That the old folks have to-day.
The duty of writing do not put off;
Let sleep or pleasure wait,
Lest the letter for which they looked and longed
Be a day or an hour too late.
— *Selected.*

THE COVERING.—1 Cor. 11: 1-16.

BY JOHN E. MOHLER.

THE thoughts I wish to present in this article are the result of a careful investigation of the *arguments* Paul produces, favoring a special head-covering in times of religious worship.

If a particular head-covering in time of worship was a custom, intended to be perpetuated in the Christian church, the institution must have been founded upon a living principle,—not upon a local and transient custom. What are the facts in the case? Were Paul's reasons, for the duty he is defending, based upon the habits of surrounding heathen nations? If so, when their fashions changed, Paul's reasons were void; and if his reasons become void, the ordinance itself becomes useless. This cannot be, for Paul especially names the church as against those who oppose the institution, and he urges the disciples to continue in the ordinance delivered them.

In studying the order and nature of man's creation, we may discern an appropriate, symbolical meaning in long hair for woman, and short hair for man. "So God created man in his own image: . . . ." Gen. 1: 27. He also gave him dominion "over every living thing that moveth upon the earth." Man's place in the creation was that of a king or ruler. "Man is the image and glory of God," *i. e.*, the image, majesty, dominion and power shine forth most brightly in the man; therefore he ought to have his head uncovered.

"'But,' you ask, 'Is not the woman also created in the image of God?' We say, Yes. Considering the woman according to her specifical nature, she was created after the image of God in righteousness and true holiness, as well as the man, but then, considering the woman according to her personal relation to the man, she is not the image of God, because *dominion, which is the image of God,* (Italics mine) is man's privilege, and sub-

jection the woman's duty.'"—*J. M. Mohler* in *Gospel Messenger.*

Which person do we say appears to us with greater power, or more in the image of God,—he with covered or with uncovered head? Most surely the one with uncovered head. In the worship of God it is appropriate that man only should appear, as much as possible, in the proper relation to his Maker. Therefore the declaration of Paul, "A man indeed ought not to cover his head, forasmuch as he is the image and glory of God."

If an uncovered head,—unencumbered by anything apart from what health demands,—suggests Godlike power and freedom, a head with a covering, which is more than health demands, likewise suggests limited power, dependence and submission. This symbolical meaning of long hair is more readily grasped when we think of the hair as loosely flowing,—its natural condition. Some may reason that, if this view of the hair as a covering, is correct, why should Paul insist upon an artificial head-covering? The reason is plain. The hair belongs to the *natural* man and the woman. It has a specific meaning in *nature only.* In *creation* it had a meaning, and the *same* meaning applies to-day, and will continue without change until the end of the world. But Paul is speaking to the church of Christ; and the manner of appearing in worship, which he is trying to establish, applies only to the children of God. In the church, as in nature, the man is the head of the woman. In the church, as in the world, his nature is better fitted to carry the heavy burdens. Man's uncovered head remains in the church the same as in nature, inasmuch as in both, he is the image of God. As in nature, so in the church, is woman subject to man. To denote her relation to man in the church, as in nature, a veil is to be worn. Her *hair* cannot possibly signify her relation to the *church*, because the hair already has its office in *nature*. Nature was, is, and will, forever be *the same*; and therefore the meaning of her symbols cannot change.

Paul logically reasons that if a woman be not veiled "it is one and the same thing as if she were shaven." That is, if she wears no artificial veil in religious exercises, she may as well cut off her hair, for it is meaningless in the *church of Christ*. But if it is a *shame* for her to be shorn,—if she has respect to the laws of *nature*,—let her be consistent, and show respect *also* to the law of *Christ* by the use of a veil, in addition to her hair.

The artificial veil illustrates a living principle in our religion; and woman without it, in religious service, makes herself equal, in church authority, to man. She thus does indeed dishonor man as her head, God as her Creator, and herself as God's creature.

Since the distinction in authority between the sexes, in both nature and the church, is permanent, so also must the veils, which denote this distinction, be permanent.

Warrensburgh, Mo.

"IF YE FAINT NOT."

BY C. H. BALSBAUGH.

To a Ministering Brother under the Juniper Tree:—

ALMOST everybody gets into the despondent mood of the Tishbite once in a while. Nobody should, but nobody is constantly so identified with Jesus by faith, as to live the Christ-life instead of his own. Because Paul could write Gal. 2: 20 he could also write Acts 20: 24.

Without the former the latter would be an impossibility. Was Paul an anomaly, or a specimen of a class? "Be as I am, for I am as ye are, Gal. 4: 12. "How readest thou?" my brother. "Whatsoever things were written aforetime were written for our learning, that we through *patience* and *comfort* of the *Scriptures* MIGHT HAVE HOPE." Rom. 15: 4. When Paul was stoned, and dragged out of the city, supposed to be dead, he rose up, went into the city and preached as boldly as before. Acts 14: 19, 20, 21.

That is genuine Christian grit. You, my dear brother, have known nothing in your trials beyond 1 Cor. 10: 13. You have never tasted Heb. 10: 34, and Heb. 11: 36, 37, 38, and Heb. 12: 4. We have a very lame, limping, squeamish Christianity to-day; but blessed be God that there is even so much left. If we attend well to sacraments, honor, conventionalities, and keep in the bounds of tradition, we pass muster. But let us be put to the test of Matt. 5: 39, 40, 41, 42, 44, and Matt. 10: 37, 38, and 1 Pet. 2: 19, 20, 21, 23, and 4: 12, 13, 14, 16; and lo, we are flat on the back under the Juniper Tree, wishing ourselves dead, or "thinking some strange thing has happened unto us."

This is not to "fight the good fight, and lay hold on eternal life, and profess a good profession before many witnesses." 1 Tim. 6: 12. This is not to "endure hardness as a good soldier of Jesus Christ,'" and "make full proof of our ministry." 2 Tim. 2: 3, and 4: 5. This is to play Demas and John Mark. Tim. 4: 10; Acts 13: 13, and 15: 38.

There is awful solemnity in Luke 9: 62, especially to the ambassadors of Christ. "*Neither count I my life dear unto myself*," is the motto of the faithful evangelist of Jesus Christ. Acts 20: 24. "*For THY SAKE we are killed all the day long.*" Rom. 8: 36. For once, my dear brother, make your phylactery broad, and inscribe on it in Holy Ghost capitals, the last eight verses of the eighth chapter of Romans. Then will the present and future in Jude 24 be your inspiration and hope.

The same is true of Sunday-school Superintendents and teachers. How few are constrained by the love that "suffereth long, and beareth all things," and directed by the wisdom that knows how to adapt eternal principles to disintegrating circumstances. How ready we are to run along when the chariot is on the self-impelled, down-hill course, and just as ready to desert our post when the work must be pulled through impediments by prayer, patience, and self-sacrifice!

How few can suffer martyrdom for their loyalty to the cross, and then rise up out of their ashes and go to work more earnestly and faithfully than ever! Ah, my brother, the genuine apostolic succession is rare in these days. Faith in Jesus means the reincarnation, devotion, compassion, forbearance, and unflinching steadfastness of Jesus. A faltering Christ is a doomed world. And a laggard, self-complacent, time-serving church, is a weak, self-reliant, inefficient institution. There is a little church within the church that really keeps the pulse of the divine life from syncope.

If every member of the entire Brotherhood was so full of the love of Christ as to court the cross for the glory of God in the salvation of souls, would not Solomon's Song 6: 10, be gloriously fulfilled? Would not "He that sitteth in the heavens laugh," and Jesus "see of the travail of His soul and be satisfied?" Ps. 2: 4; Isa. 53: 11. What Sabbath-schools we would have! What Pentecostal prayer-meetings! What edifying sociables! What flaming family altars! What a mighty, harmonious, love-impelled co-working

✦ESSAYS✦

"Study to show thyself approved unto God; a workman that needeth not be ashamed, rightly dividing the Word of Truth."

WRITE THEM A LETTER TO-NIGHT.

Don't go to the theatre, concert or ball,
 But stay in your room to-night;
Deny yourself to the friends that call,
 And a good, long letter write—
Write to the sad old folks at home,
 Who sit, when the day is done,
With folded hands and downcast eyes
 And think of the absent one.

Don't selfishly scribble, " Excuse my haste,
 I've scarcely the time to write,"
Lest their brooding thoughts go wandering back
 To many a by-gone night,
When they lost their needed sleep and rest,
 And every breath was a prayer
That God would leave their delicate babe
 To their tender love and care.

Don't let them feel that you've no more need
 Of their love or counsel wise;
For the heart grows strongly sensitive
 When age has dimmed the eyes—
It might be well to let them believe
 You might never forget them, quite;
That you deem it a pleasure, when far away,
 Long letters home to write.

Don't think that the young and giddy friends
 Who make your pastime gay,
Have half the anxious thought for you
 That the old folks have to-day.
The duty of writing do not put off;
 Let sleep or pleasure wait,
Lest the letter for which they looked and longed
 Be a day or an hour too late.
     — *Selected.*

THE COVERING.—1 Cor. 11: 1-16.

BY JOHN E. MOHLER.

The thoughts I wish to present in this article are the result of a careful investigation of the *arguments* Paul produces, favoring a special head-covering in times of religious worship.

If a particular head-covering in time of worship was a custom, intended to be perpetuated in the Christian church, the institution must have been founded upon a living principle,—not upon a local and transient custom. What are the facts in the case? Were Paul's reasons, for the duty he is defending, based upon the habits of surrounding heathen nations? If so, when their fashions changed, Paul's reasons were void; and if his reasons become void, the ordinance itself becomes useless. This cannot be, for Paul especially names the church as against those who oppose the institution, and he urges the disciples to continue in the ordinance delivered them.

In studying the order and nature of man's creation, we may discern an appropriate, symbolical meaning in long hair for woman, and short hair for man. "So God created man in his own image: . . . ." Gen. 1: 27. He also gave him dominion "over every living thing that moveth upon the earth." Man's place in the creation was that of a king or ruler. "Man is the image and glory of God," *i. e.,* the image, majesty, dominion and power shine forth most brightly in the man; therefore he ought to have his head uncovered.

"'But,' you ask, 'Is not the woman also created in the image of God?' We say, Yes. Considering the woman according to her specifical nature, she was created after the image of God in righteousness and true holiness, as well as the man, but then, considering the woman according to her personal relation to the man, she is not the image of God, because *dominion, which is the image of God,* (italics mine) is man's privilege, and sub-

jection the woman's duty.'*"—J. M. Mohler* in *Gospel-Messenger.*

Which person do we say appears to us with greater power, or more in the image of God,—he with covered or with uncovered head? Most surely the one with uncovered head. In the worship of God it is appropriate that man only should appear, as much as possible, in the proper relation to his Maker. Therefore the declaration of Paul, "A man indeed ought not to cover his head, forsamuch as he is the image and glory of God."

If an uncovered head,—unencumbered by anything apart from what health demands,—suggests Godlike power and freedom, a head with a covering, which is more than health demands, likewise suggests limited power, dependence and submission. This symbolical meaning of long hair is more readily grasped when we think of the hair as loosely flowing,—its natural condition. Some may reason that, if this view of the hair as a covering, is correct, why should Paul insist upon an artificial head-covering? The reason is plain. The hair belongs to the *natural* man and the woman. It has a specific meaning in *nature only.* In *creation* it had a meaning, and the *same* meaning applies to-day, and will continue without change until the end of the world. But Paul is speaking to the church of Christ, and the manner of appearing in worship, which he is trying to establish, applies only to the children of God. In the church, as in nature, the man is the head of the woman. In the church, as in the world, his nature is better fitted to carry the heavy burdens. Man's uncovered head remains in the church the same as in nature, inasmuch as in both, he is the image of God. As in nature, so in the church, is woman subject to man. To denote her relation to man in the church, as in nature, a veil is to be worn. Her *hair* cannot possibly signify her relation to the *church,* because the hair already has its office in *nature.* Nature was, is, and will forever be *the same;* and therefore the meaning of her symbols cannot change.

Paul logically reasons that if a woman be not veiled "it is one and the same thing as if she were shaven." That is, if she wears no artificial veil in religious exercises, she may as well cut off her hair, for it is meaningless in the *church of Christ.* But if it is a *shame* for her to be shorn,—if she has respect to the laws of *nature,*—let her be consistent, and show respect *also* to the law of *Christ* by the use of a veil, in addition to her hair.

The artificial veil illustrates a living principle in our religion; and woman without it, in religious service, makes herself equal, in church authority, to man. She thus does indeed dishonor man as her head, God as her Creator, and herself as God's creature.

Since the distinction in authority between the sexes, in both nature and the church, is permanent, so also must the veils, which denote this distinction, be permanent.

Warrensburgh, Mo.

"IF YE FAINT NOT."

BY C. H. BALSBAUGH.

To a Ministering Brother under the Juniper Tree.—

Almost everybody gets into the despondent mood of the Tishbite once in a while. Nobody should, but nobody is constantly so identified with Jesus by faith, as to live the Christ-life instead of his own. Because Paul could write Gal. 2: 20 he could also write Acts 20: 24.

Without the former the latter would be an impossibility. Was Paul an anomaly, or a specimen of a class? "Be as I am, for I am as ye are," Gal. 4: 12. "How reachest thou?" my brother. "Whatsoever things were written aforetime were written for our learning, that we through *patience* and *comfort* of the *Scriptures* MIGHT HAVE HOPE." Rom. 15: 4. When Paul was stoned, and dragged out of the city, supposed to be dead, he rose up, went into the city and preached as boldly as before. Acts 14: 19, 20, 21.

That is genuine Christian grit. You, my dear brother, have known nothing in your trials beyond 1 Cor. 10: 13. You have never tasted Heb. 10: 34, and Heb. 11: 36, 37, 38, and Heb. 12: 4. We have a very lame, limping, squeamish Christianity to-day; but blessed be God that there is even so much left. If we attend well to sacraments, honor, conventionalities, and keep in the bounds of tradition, we pass muster. But let us be put to the test of Matt. 5: 39, 40, 41, 42, 44, and Matt. 10: 37, 38, and 1 Pet. 2: 19, 20, 21, 23, and 4: 12, 13, 14, 16; and lo, we are flat on the back under the Juniper Tree, wishing ourselves dead, or "thinking some strange thing has happened unto us."

This is not to "fight the good fight, and lay hold on eternal life, and profess a good profession before many witnesses." 1 Tim. 6: 12. This is not to "endure hardness as a good soldier of Jesus Christ," and "make full proof of our ministry." 2 Tim. 2: 3, and 4: 5. This is to play Demas and John Mark. Tim. 4: 10; Acts 13: 13, and 15: 38.

There is awful solemnity in Luke 9: 62, especially to the ambassadors of Christ. "*Neither count I my life dear unto myself,*" is the motto of the faithful evangelist of Jesus Christ. Acts 20: 24. "*For THY sake we are killed all the day long.*" Rom. 8: 36. For once, my dear brother, make your phylactery broad, and inscribe on it in Holy Ghost capitals, the last eight verses of the eighth chapter of Romans. Then will the present and future in Jude 24 be your inspiration and hope.

The same is true of Sunday-school Superintendents and teachers. How few are constrained by the love that "suffereth long, and beareth all things," and directed by the wisdom that knows how to adapt eternal principles to disintegrating circumstances. How ready we are to run along when the chariot is on the self-impelled, down-hill course; and just as ready to desert our post when the work must be pulled through impediments by prayer, patience, and self sacrifice!

How few can suffer martyrdom for their loyalty to the cross, and then rise up out of their ashes and go to work more earnestly and faithfully than ever! Ah, my brother, the genuine apostolic succession is rare in these days. Faith in Jesus means the reincarnation, devotion, compassion, forbearance, and unflinching steadfastness of Jesus. A faltering Christ is a doomed world. And a laggard, self-complacent, time-serving church, in a weak, self-reliant, inefficient institution. There is a little church within the church that really keeps the pulse of the divine life from syncope.

If every member of the entire Brotherhood was so full of the love of Christ as to court the cross for the glory of God in the salvation of souls, would not Solomon's Song 6: 10, be gloriously fulfilled? Would not "He that sitteth in the heavens laugh," and Jesus "see of the travail of His soul and be satisfied?" Ps. 2: 4; Isa. 53: 11. What Sabbath-schools we would have! What Pentecostal prayer-meetings! What edifying sociables! What flaming family altars! What a mighty, harmonious, love-impelled co-working

record, although he may not have written his Gospel until forty or fifty years after Pentecost. The old apostle Peter did not forget to record the supper in his second epistle 2: 13, for he speaks, in the Revised Translation of some who were spots in their love-feasts when they feast with them. Jude, also, in verse 12 of his epistle, says, "These are hidden rocks in your love-feasts when they feast with you," or "in your feasts of charity," as we have it in the Old Version.

Paul was so strict in his old days, that he would not admit a poor widow into the number, to be supported by the charitable funds of the church, unless she had washed the saints' feet, not strangers' feet, as some would have it. I must give you a few scraps of history, on this much-neglected, and much-abused subject. I will begin with Wm. Smith, of London, England, as he gives it in his "Bible Dictionary." He says, on page 488, referring to the apostolic age, "They thus united every day the *Agape* or love-feast with the Eucharist." He also says, farther on, on the same page, "At some point in the feast, those who were present, men and women sitting apart, would rise to salute each other with the holy kiss." He also says, "This practice did not confine itself to the personal disciples at Jerusalem, but was imported into the Greek church at Corinth."

I next give you Islay Burns, Professor of Church History, at the Free Church College, Glasgow. He speaks of the first three centuries of the Christian era. On page 55 he says, "The chief peculiar features were their assembling in private houses and upper chambers, their celebrating of the Eucharist at eventide, the common brotherly meal or love-feast. In moments of solemn Communion brother saluted brother, and sister saluted sister in a holy embrace and kiss." On page 258 this same writer says, "These feasts were first kept in private houses, and other places where the Christians met for the purpose of religious worship. After they built church-houses, these feasts were held within their walls. This practice was forbidden in the middle of the fourth century. The council of Laodicea enacted that love-feasts should not be celebrated in churches. "Then these were held under trees and other shelter, up to the seventh century." Much more testimony can be given, but let this suffice for honest men.

Paul has well said in 1 Cor. 5: 7, 8, "For even Christ our passover is sacrificed for us: therefore let us keep the feast.".

1. Because Christ kept it with the apostles.

2. The apostles kept it in the churches. Paul introduced it in the church at Corinth, and they kept it, for which he praised them (1 Cor. 11: 2). But afterwards they got into a disorder in holding this feast, "and one ate before other his own supper, and one was hungry, and another drunken, and shamed them that had no supper." See verses 20-25. In verse 33 he tells them when they come together to eat, to tarry one for another.

3. The churches kept these feasts for over 300 years, as we have seen above. But the Communion was never called the Lord's Supper by inspired men.

Abilene, Kans.

SPIRITUAL RELIGION.

BY GERTRUDE A. FLORY.

WE hear, from time to time, a great deal about "practical religion," yet of far more importance is spiritual religion, the basis of a godly life, without which no soul can please God nor inherit eternal life. A person may practice all the ordinances of God's house, and obey strictly the letter of the Gospel, and still be carnally minded. But a person, born of the Spirit of God, acts in accordance with the will and nature of God, and lives in harmony with the principles and spirit of the Gospel while he obeys also the form and doctrine. It takes but a glance to note the vast difference between these two characters. The former acts upon the conviction of duty, while the latter's obedience is the spontaneous outgrowth of a cleansed and purified heart, subject to the Spirit's guidings. His individualism is lost; and he is a new creature, fashioned after the likeness of Christ. James 1: 27 says, "Pure religion and undefiled before God and the Father is this, to visit the fatherless and widows in their affliction, and to keep himself unspotted from the world."

This language infers that religion is of deep and broad significance. It implies a work of love to our fellow-mortal, a surrender of self, a sympathy for sorrow and distress, a pure and holy life before God, an isolation and separation from the world. "Unspotted from the world," signifies a separation, so far removed that no stain can touch the separated; that he shall not come in contact with the world, in a manner to become contaminated therewith, or to carry away with him anything which has any semblance of the world; that he has no resemblance to the world in his appearance, or he would not be spotted by the world. We see that James makes a distinction between religion and the world, and draws the line to the plummet, yet in perfect harmony with the teachings of Christ and the apostles; "A peculiar people," Titus 2: 14; 1 Pet. 2: 9; "Separate," 2 Cor. 6: 17; "Not of the world," John 17: 14, 16. For popularity, self-glory and other selfish motives, persons may, in the name of religion, do a certain amount of work which has a religious appearance, and may be accepted as such; but there is not a vestige of spirit in it, because it lacks the divine seal that "everything shall be done to the honor and glory of God, the Father;" before whom religion must be pure and undefiled, and separate from every motive that has not Christ and the furtherance of his cause in view.

"God is a Spirit, and they that worship him must worship him in spirit and in truth." John 4: 24. In order to worship in spirit, we must first become spiritual; and before we can worship in the truth, we must know what truth is and abide in it. This gives us a true spirit, which is of the nature of God. Then those who would worship (or serve) God acceptably, must be God-like in nature. This happy condition cannot be acquired as we gain wealth and education,—by persistent appliance of physical and mental powers,—neither can one person bestow it upon another. It is the gift of God, and is obtainable only by a complete surrender of the carnal nature, which brings us into subjection to the Written Word, whose purifying influence makes us fit temples for the indwelling of the Holy Spirit, and leads us into all truth, working in us a spiritual religion, or a godly life. And he who is thus governed is true to God, true to the church, true to his fellow-men and true to himself. He does not say, "I love thee, Lord," and then prove that declaration a lie by the love of the world. He manifests by his actions; he does not say, "I I have the prosperity of the church at heart," and by word and deed dishonor the holy principles she has struggled hard for years to maintain; he does not press the sweet kiss of love upon his brother's lips, and turn about and smite him in the back with the sword of envy and jealousy; nor does he say to his soul, "O soul, I have made a covenant with the Lord Jesus Christ, thy Savior, to live in faithful obedience to his Word until death, and to give thee into his keeping against that day," and then turn away from the council of the Lord, and feed on the outskirts of the fold, where the flood-gates of temptation stand wide open. For "the fruit of the Spirit is in all goodness, and righteousness, and truth, love, joy, peace, longsuffering, gentleness, goodness, faith, meekness, temperance." Eph. 5: 9; Gal. 5: 22, 23.

When we see the Spirit's fruit crowning a formal obedience, we know there has been a spiritual planting and a spiritual growth, and we look for a spiritual life. See how beautifully and intricately the work of the Spirit is intertwined with our religious lives! O that we might more fully comprehend its wonder workings, and measure the height and depth of its grandeur, its sublimity, its holiness and power! It is a subject that should deeply concern every soul. How vast and far-reaching is its theme! Its flaming eloquence, how far beyond the compass of an uninspired pen! O how it burns and flashes in our inmost being, and leaps for utterance! God, give us lips of speech, and hearts of understanding, and eloquence of angels, that we may tell abroad the glory and beauty of a "life hid with Christ in God!" This is the secret of every true Christian attainment and endeavor. "This I say then, Walk in the Spirit, and ye shall not fulfill the lust of the flesh." Gal. 5: 16.

"Oh, blessed life!—the heart at rest
When all wildest tumultuous seems—
That trusts a higher will, and deems
That higher will, not mine, the best.

Oh, blessed life!—heart, mind and soul,
From self-born aims and wishes free,
In all at one with Deity,
And loyal to the Lord's control."

La Porte, Ind.

"THESE SIGNS SHALL FOLLOW THEM THAT BELIEVE."—Mark 16: 17-20.

BY S. N. M'CANN.

A CASUAL reading of the Inspired Record impresses us with the thought that much has been lost in miraculous power by unfaithfulness on the part of the Christian of this age and generation.

A more careful reading will convince us that nothing has been lost, but that we possess the same power to-day that any Christian possessed, since "that which is perfect is come." 1 Cor. 15: 10. "These signs shall follow." "And they went forth and preached every-where, the Lord working with them, and confirming the Word with signs following." Mark 16: 20. Here we have the power given, and a clear statement of its fulfillment in the apostles' work. A reason why it is fulfilled is also clearly stated, when the apostle says that these signs confirmed the Word.

Christ says, "I came down from heaven, not to do mine own will, but the will of him that sent me." John 6: 38. The apostles were eye-witnesses to all that Jesus did and said. Even Matthias was chosen from those that companied with Jesus at all times, for "of these men which have companied with us all the time, that the Lord Jesus went in and out among us, beginning from the baptism of John, unto the same day that he was taken up from us, must one be ordained to be a witness with us of his resurrection." Acts 1: 21, 22.

Jesus promised that these sayings should follow, and we find that they did follow, for the apostles spake with new tongues; though Paul was bitten by a viper, he felt no hurt; the sick were restored to health, and the dead raised by them that believed. Christ never promised that all who believed should be able to perform the signs promised, but he only said that the signs should follow, and as soon as the apostles went forth to preach, and God confirmed their work with signs, the promise was fulfilled. Paul says that Christ worked in him "through mighty

record, although he may not have written his Gospel until forty or fifty years after Pentecost. The old apostle Peter did not forget to record the supper in his second epistle 2: 13, for he speaks, in the Revised Translation of some who were spots in their love-feasts when they feast with them. Jude, also, in verse 12 of his epistle, says, "These are hidden rocks in your love-feasts when they feast with you," or "in your feasts of charity," as we have it in the Old Version.

Paul was so strict in his old days, that he would not admit a poor widow into the number, to be supported by the charitable funds of the church, unless she had washed the saints' feet, not strangers' feet, as some would have it. I must give you a few scraps of history, on this much-neglected, and much-abused subject. I will begin with Wm. Smith, of London, England, as he gives it in his "Bible Dictionary." He says, on page 488, referring to the apostolic age, "They thus united every day the *Agape* or love-feast with the Eucharist." He also says, farther on, on the same page, "At some point in the feast, those who were present, men and women sitting apart, would rise to salute each other with the holy kiss." He also says, "This practice did not confine itself to the personal disciples at Jerusalem, but was imported into the Greek church at Corinth."

I next give you Islay Burns, Professor of Church History, at the Free Church College, Glasgow. He speaks of the first three centuries of the Christian era. On page 55 he says, "The chief peculiar features were their assembling in private houses and upper chambers, their celebrating of the Eucharist at eventide, the common brotherly meal or love-feast. In moments of solemn Communion brother saluted brother, and sister saluted sister in a holy embrace and kiss." On page 258 this same writer says, "These feasts were first kept in private houses, and other places where the Christians met for the purpose of religious worship. After they built church-houses, these feasts were held within their walls. This practice was forbidden in the middle of the fourth century. The council of Laodicea enacted that love-feasts should not be celebrated in churches. "Then these were held under trees and other shelter, up to the seventh century."

Much more testimony can be given, but let this suffice for honest men.

Paul has well said in 1 Cor. 5: 7, 8, "For even Christ our passover is sacrificed for us: therefore let us keep the feast.".

1. Because Christ kept it with the apostles.

2. The apostles kept it in the churches. Paul introduced it in the church at Corinth, and they kept it, for which he praised them (1 Cor. 11: 2). But afterwards they got into a disorder in holding this feast, "and one ate before other his own supper, and one was hungry, and another drunken, and ashamed them that had no supper." See verses 20-25. In verse 33 he tells them when they come together to eat, to tarry one for another.

3. The churches kept these feasts for over 300 years, as we have seen above. But the Communion was never called the Lord's Supper by inspired men.

Abilene, Kans.

SPIRITUAL RELIGION.

BY GERTRUDE A. FLORY.

WE hear, from time to time, a great deal about "practical religion," yet of far more importance is spiritual religion, the basis of a godly life, without which no soul can please God nor inherit eternal life. A person may practice all the ordinances of God's house, and obey strictly the letter of the Gospel, and still be carnally minded. But a person, born of the Spirit of God, acts in accordance with the will and nature of God, and lives in harmony with the principles and spirit of the Gospel while he obeys also the form and doctrine. It takes but a glance to note the vast difference between these two characters. The former acts upon the conviction of duty, while the latter's obedience is the spontaneous outgrowth of a cleansed and purified heart, subject to the Spirit's guidings. His individualism is lost; for he is a new creature, fashioned after the likeness of Christ. James 1: 27 says, "Pure religion and undefiled before God and the Father is this, to visit the fatherless and widows in their affliction, and to keep himself unspotted from the world."

This language infers that religion is of deep and broad significance. It implies a work of love to our fellow-mortal, a surrender of self, a sympathy for sorrow and distress, a pure and holy life before God, an isolation and separation from the world. "Unspotted from the world," signifies a separation, so far removed that no stain can touch the separated; that he shall not come in contact with the world, in a manner to become contaminated therewith, or to carry away with him anything which has any semblance of the world; that he has no resemblance to the world in his appearance, or he would not be spotted by the world. We see that James makes a distinction between religion and the world, and draws the line to the plummet, yet in perfect harmony with the teachings of Christ and the apostles; "A peculiar people," Titus 2: 14; 1 Pet. 2: 9; "Separate," 2 Cor. 6: 17; "Not of the world," John 17: 14, 16. For popularity, self-glory and other selfish motives, persons may, in the name of religion, do a certain amount of work which has a religious appearance, and may be accepted as such; but there is not a vestige of spirit in it, because it lacks the divine seal that "everything shall be done to the honor and glory of God, the Father," before whom religion must be pure and undefiled, and separate from every motive that has not Christ and the furtherance of his cause in view.

"God is a Spirit, and they that worship him must worship him in spirit and in truth." John 4: 24. In order to worship in spirit, we must first become spiritual; and before we can worship in the truth, we must know what truth is and abide in it. This gives us a true spirit, which is of the nature of God. Then those who would worship (or serve) God acceptably, must be God-like in nature. This happy condition cannot be acquired as we gain wealth and education,—by persistent appliance of physical and mental powers,—neither can one person bestow it upon another. It is the gift of God, and is obtainable only by a complete surrender of the carnal nature, which brings us into subjection to the Written Word, whose purifying influence makes us fit temples for the indwelling of the Holy Spirit and leads us into all truth, working in us a spiritual religion, or a godly life. And he who is thus governed is true to God, true to the church, true to his fellow-men and true to himself. He does not say, "I love thee, Lord," and then prove that declaration a lie by the love of the world. He manifests by his actions; he does not say, "I have the prosperity of the church at heart," and by word and deed dishonor the holy principles she has struggled hard for years to maintain; he does not press the sweet kiss of love upon his brother's lips, and turn about and smite him in the back with the sword of envy and jealousy; nor does he say to his soul, "O soul, I have made a covenant with the Lord Jesus Christ, thy Savior, to live in faithful obedience to his Word until death, and to give thee into his keeping against that day," and then turn away from the council of the Lord, and feed on the outskirts of the fold, where the flood-gates of temptation stand wide open. For "the fruit of the Spirit is in all goodness, and righteousness, and truth, love, joy, peace, longsuffering, gentleness, goodness, faith, meekness, temperance." Eph. 5: 9; Gal. 5: 22, 23.

When we see the Spirit's fruit crowning a formal obedience, we know there has been a spiritual planting and a spiritual growth, and we look for a spiritual life. See how beautifully and intricately the work of the Spirit is intertwined with our religious lives! O that we might more fully comprehend its wonder workings, and measure the height and depth of its grandeur, its sublimity, its holiness and power! It is a subject that should deeply concern every soul. How vast and far-reaching is its theme! Its flaming eloquence, how far beyond the compass of an uninspired pen! O how it burns and flashes in our inmost being, and leaps for utterance! God, give us lips of speech, and hearts of understanding, and eloquence of angels, that we may tell abroad the glory and beauty of a "life hid with Christ in God!" This is the secret of every true Christian attainment and endeavor. "This I say then, Walk in the Spirit, and ye shall not fulfill the lust of the flesh." Gal. 5: 16.

> "Oh, blessed life!—the heart at rest
> When all without tumultuous seems—
> That trusts a higher will, and deems
> That higher will, not mine, the best.
>
> Oh, blessed life!—heart, mind and soul,
> From self-born aims and wishes free,
> In all at one with Deity,
> And loyal to the Lord's control."

La Porte, Ind.

"THESE SIGNS SHALL FOLLOW THEM THAT BELIEVE."—Mark 16: 17-20.

BY S. N. M'CANN.

A CASUAL reading of the Inspired Record impresses us with the thought that much has been lost in miraculous power by unfaithfulness on the part of the Christian of this age and generation.

A more careful reading will convince us that nothing has been lost, but that we possess the same power to-day that any Christian possessed, since "that which is perfect is come." 1 Cor. 15: 10. "These signs shall follow." "And they went forth and preached everywhere, the Lord working with them, and confirming the Word with signs following." Mark 16: 20. Here we have the power given, and a clear statement of its fulfillment in the apostles' work. A reason why it is fulfilled is also clearly stated, when the apostles says that these signs confirmed the Word.

Christ says, "I came down from heaven, not to do mine own will, but the will of him that sent me." John 6: 38. The apostles were eye-witnesses to all that Jesus did and said. Even Matthias was chosen from those that companied with Jesus at all times, for "of these men which have companied with us all the time, that the Lord Jesus went in and out among us, beginning from the baptism of John, unto the same day that he was taken up from us, must one be ordained to be a witness with us of his resurrection." Acts 1: 21, 22.

Jesus promised that these sayings should follow, and we find that they did follow, for the apostles spake with new tongues; though Paul was bitten by a viper, he felt no hurt; the sick were restored to health, and the dead raised by them that believed. Christ never promised that all who believed should be able to perform the signs promised, but he only said that the signs should follow, and as soon as the apostles went forth to preach, and God confirmed their work with signs, the promise was fulfilled. Paul says that Christ worked in him "through mighty

Missionary and Tract Work Department.

"Upon the first day of the week, let every one of you lay by him in store as God hath prospered him, that there be no gatherings when I come."—1 Cor. 16: 2.

"Every man as he purposeth in his heart, so let him give. Not grudgingly or of necessity, for the Lord loveth a cheerful giver."—2 Cor. 9: 7.

HOW MUCH SHALL WE GIVE?

"Every man *according to his ability*." "Every one *as God hath prospered him*." "Every man, *according as he purposeth in his heart*, so let him give." "For if there be first a willing mind, it is accepted *according to that a man hath, and* not according to that he hath not."—2 Cor. 8: 12.

Organization of Missionary Committee.

DANIEL VANIMAN, Foreman, - - McPherson, Kans.
D. L. MILLER, Treasurer, - - Mt. Morris, Ill.
GALEN B. ROYER, Secretary, - - Mt. Morris, Ill.

Organization of Book and Tract Work.

S. W. HOOVER, Foreman, - - Dayton, Ohio.
S. BOCK, Secretary and Treasurer, - - Dayton, Ohio.

☞All donations intended for Missionary Work should be sent to GALEN B. ROYER, Mt. Morris, Ill.
☞All money for Tract Work should be sent to S. BOCK, Dayton, Ohio.
☞Money may be sent by Money Order, Registered Letter, or Drafts on New York or Chicago. Do not send personal checks, or drafts on interior towns, as it costs 25 cents to collect them.
☞Solicitors are requested to faithfully carry out the plan of Annual Meeting, that all our members be solicited to contribute at least twice a year for the Mission and Tract Work of the Church.
☞Notes for the Endowment Fund can be had by writing to the Secretary of either Work.

THE ARK AND THE ANIMALS.

BY PROFESSOR HOWARD OSGOOD, D. D.

Is our age more skeptical or unbelieving than many that have gone before it? I do not believe it. On the other hand, I believe that the most careful, sober estimate will prove that there are more persons in the world now holding the Bible to be the veritable word of God and devoted to the most sincere service of Jesus Christ than in any previous age. Some persons are greatly troubled because so many learned men publish their want of faith in the Scriptures as the Word of God in the highest sense. But granting that these learned men are twice as numerous as they are, and that their volumes and articles are sold tenfold more than they are, yet they weigh and number very small compared to the other side of the account. Consider for a moment. The sales of the Bible every year by the British and by the American Bible Societies are millions of volumes beyond all the sales of books intended to discredit the Bible as the Word of God. Then come the great United Tract Societies of England and America, and the Tract and Book Societies of the denominations, with their millions of annual publications. There must be large life where so much good food is required every year. Some of the fruit of this life is seen in the annual addition to the Protestant churches of our land of over four hundred thousand persons. There are between ten millions and twelve millions of children in the Sunday-schools of our land. Every one of these agencies is increasing in power every year. The Bible societies print and sell more Bibles every year; the tract and book societies print and sell more tracts and books; the number of converts steadily increases, and the Sunday-schools multiply with the growing population. Have there ever been more blessings of God upon the mission fields? Look at the New Hebrides, New Guinea, the Telugus, the Congo. The wonders of grace seen there are as great as the world has ever beheld.

Surely the believer in the Bible as the very Word of God has no reason for fear or doubt when he looks at its triumphs, however he may sorrow that, at times, it seems to be "smitten in the house of its friends."

No age has been free from learned and able opponents of the Bible; from suggested difficulties of Bible statements that perplexed many; from the proclamation of discoveries in philosophy or common sense that would soon diminish faith in the Bible. It has been proclaimed that this century is marked by the discovery that Moses was not the author of the Pentateuch, and the main reasons to support this discovery are the contradictions, repetitions, impossibilities, etc., found in the Pentateuch. But this is no discovery of this century. Seventeen hundred years ago an author wrote: "How could Moses write that Moses died? And whereas, in the time after Moses, about five hundred years or thereabouts, it [the Pentateuch] is found lying in the temple which was built, and, after about five hundred years more, it is carried away, and being burned in the time of Nebuchadnozzar it is destroyed, and thus being written after Moses and often lost, even this shows the foreknowledge of Moses, because he, foreseeing its disappearance, did not write it; but they who wrote it, being convicted of ignorance through their not foreseeing its disappearance, were not prophets." He adds that there are false and blasphemous chapters which were interpolated into the Scriptures; there are misrepresentations of God, some things false and some true; the Scriptures are very uncertain, for there are many contradictions in them. This author says God alone is true, and he represents God truly. All this sounds strangely like the statements of some writers of the present day, and effectually disposes of the claim of the new discovery that Moses is not the author of the Pentateuch, as one of the triumphs of critical skill in our age.

Of late, in a circle where science is held as the supreme test, and nothing is to be accepted that cannot be demonstrated clearly, it has been asserted that the story of the ark is positively proved to be a fable, myth, legend, by the fact that it would be an absolute impossibility to place two of every known species of land animals in the space of the ark. This appears to some young persons a conclusive proof, coming from a scientific source.

But as it is a simple question of the multiplication table, there is no science at all in this "positive proof," as a candid infidel of high authority in natural science declares. The matter is so simple that even an outsider, like myself, may state it. The narrative of the making of the ark is, "This is how thou shalt make it: the length of the ark three hundred cubits, the breadth of it fifty cubits, and the height of it thirty cubits."

The length of the cubit has been settled by the comparison of numerous Egyptian, Babylonian, and other cubits of earliest times, by Oppert, Lepsius, Flinders, Petrie, and others, and especially by the conclusive work of Lehmann. It was between nineteen and twenty inches; but, in order to be on the entirely safe side, we will take it to be only eighteen inches. Then the surface of one deck of the ark would be 450 multiplied by .75 which equals 33,750 square feet.

Naturalists differ very largely as to the classification of species, the majority estimating from 1,200 to 1,600 species; but we will take the extremest estimate by a high authority, Wallace, in his "Distribution of Animals" (New-York, 1876), who gives 3,415,—that is, 290 species above the size of the sheep, 757 from the sheep to the rat; and 1,359 of the rats, bats, and shrews. Then with two of each species, 2,415 multiplied by 2, equals 4,830, and with seven of each of the ten species of clean animals, 70, we would have, as the highest estimate of all the land mammalia, 4,900, to be placed in the ark.

In order to learn what space would be required, we must ascertain the average size of these 2,415 species. There is no sort of difficulty in this, since the measurements of the species are as well known and familiar to naturalists as the species themselves. But, lest I may seem to venture upon ground that is beyond me, I have the very high authority of Professor Ward, of Rochester, in the statement that the average size of all land mammalia would be about that of the grey fox, or the common house cat. Any one can verify this by consultation of the special works giving the size of animals.

The ocean steamers carrying cattle most carefully from America to England, allow twenty square feet to each ox. If we allow one-fourth of that space, five square feet, for a cat, we shall be giving a superabundance of room; then 4,900, multiplied by 5, which equals 24,500 square feet of surface, would be ample to contain all the known species of animals at the highest estimate of their number. We have seen that one deck of the ark contained 33,750 square feet; 33,750—24,500 equals 9,250. All the species, then, could be placed on one deck of the ark, and still there would be one-third (123½ multiplied by 75) of that deck vacant.

Wallace estimates of birds, 10,087; of reptiles, 979; of lizards, 1,252; of insects (roughly), 100,000 species. If we again take the average of all these species, they could easily be placed on the 9,250 square feet not occupied by the mammalia.

If the ark had only one deck, two of each known species of land mammalia, birds, reptiles, lizards, and insects, could find abundant room there. But if we follow the majority of naturalists, and take, above their estimate, 1,700 as the number of species, then 1,700 multiplied by 2 equals 3,400, plus 70 equals 3,470, multiplied by 5, equals 17,350 square feet. As the deck contained 33,750 square feet, then two of each species of all the mammalia would find abundant room on one-half of the deck and six feet additional, leaving the remaining nearly one-half (219 multiplied by 75) for the birds, reptiles, lizards, insects. Leaving the ark, it is plain that any of the great ocean steamers, plying between New York and Liverpool, could place, with abundant room, two of each known species of land mammalia, and birds, reptiles, etc., on one of their decks.

These facts are so well known, and so easy to learn if one does not know them, that we ask, What claim has a man to scientific knowledge, or to a scientific spirit, who makes the statement that the scientific knowledge of the species of animals is a conclusive proof that they could not have been placed in the ark, and hence the narrative of the ark is a mere myth?

Only one deck of the ark has been spoken of, to show its ample space for all the known species. But no one, who has studied the subject, supposes that the ark had only one deck. The ark is said to have had "rooms [marg., nests] in it," and "lower, second, and third stories." From this it is concluded that the ark had three decks, for, as every waterman knows, a flatboat forty-five feet deep is an utter absurdity and impossibility.

Retaining the length, breadth, and depth, given for the ark, it must have been of the shape of a ship, as Napier, in his "Manufacturing Arts in Early Times," has shown. The decks of the ark, then, would have been less than 33,750 square feet; but not enough less to have hindered giving abundant room to all the animals. There would be ample room for the animals, for food for a year, and for Noah and his family.

There are enough questions about the Bible which our ignorance, or the necessary limits of our thinking, or prejudice, prevents our solving; but the question whether all the species of land mammalia, birds, etc., could be placed in a certain number of square feet, is so simple that it is an arithmetical, and not a scientific, problem.

Missionary and Tract Work Department.

"Upon the first day of the week, let every one of you lay by him in store as God hath prospered him, that there be no gatherings when I come."—1 Cor. 16: 2.

"Every man as he purposeth in his heart, so let him give. Not grudgingly or of necessity, for the Lord loveth a cheerful giver."—2 Cor. 9: 7.

HOW MUCH SHALL WE GIVE?

"Every man according to his ability." "Every one as God hath prospered him." "Every man, according as he purposeth in his heart, so let him give." "For if there be first a willing mind, it is accepted according to that a man hath, and not according to that he hath not."—2 Cor. 8: 12.

Organization of Missionary Committee.

DANIEL VANIMAN, Foreman,		McPherson, Kans.
D. L. MILLER, Treasurer,		Mt. Morris, Ill.
GALEN B. ROYER, Secretary,		Mt. Morris, Ill.

Organization of Book and Tract Work.

S. W. HOOVER, Foreman,		Dayton, Ohio.
S. BOCK, Secretary and Treasurer,		Dayton, Ohio.

☞ All donations intended for Missionary Work should be sent to GALEN B. ROYER, Mt. Morris, Ill.

☞ All money for Tract Work should be sent to S. BOCK, Dayton, Ohio.

☞ Money may be sent by Money Order, Registered Letter, or Drafts on New York or Chicago. Do not send personal checks, or drafts on interior towns, as it costs 15 cents to collect them.

☞ Solicitors are requested to faithfully carry out the plan of Annual Meeting, that all our members be solicited to contribute at least twice a year for the Mission and Tract Work of the Church.

☞ Notes for the Endowment Fund can be had by writing to the Secretary of either Work.

THE ARK AND THE ANIMALS.

BY PROFESSOR HOWARD OSGOOD, D. D.

Is our age more skeptical or unbelieving than many that have gone before it? I do not believe it. On the other hand, I believe that the most careful, sober estimate will prove that there are more persons in the world now holding the Bible to be the veritable word of God and devoted to the most sincere service of Jesus Christ than in any previous age. Some persons are greatly troubled because so many learned men publish their want of faith in the Scriptures as the Word of God in the highest sense. But granting that these learned men are twice as numerous as they are, and that their volumes and articles are sold tenfold more than they are, yet they weigh and number very small compared to the other side of the account. Consider for a moment. The sales of the Bible every year by the British and by the American Bible Societies are millions of volumes beyond all the sales of books intended to discredit the Bible as the Word of God. Then come the great United Tract Societies of England and America, and the Tract and Book Societies of the denominations, with their millions of annual publications. There must be large life where so much good food is required every year. Some of the fruit of this life is seen in the annual addition to the Protestant churches of our land of over four hundred thousand persons. There are between ten millions and twelve millions of children in the Sunday-schools of our land. Every one of these agencies is increasing in power every year. The Bible societies print and sell more Bibles every year; the tract and book societies print and sell more tracts and books; the number of converts steadily increases, and the Sunday-schools multiply with the growing population. Have there ever been more blessings of God upon the mission fields? Look at the New Hebrides, New Guinea, the Telugus, the Congo. The wonders of grace seen there are as great as the world has ever beheld.

Surely the believer in the Bible as the very Word of God has no reason for fear or doubt when he looks at its triumphs, however he may sorrow that, at times, it seems to be "smitten in the house of its friends."

No age has been free from learned and able opponents of the Bible; from suggested difficulties of Bible statements that perplexed many; from the proclamation of discoveries in philosophy or common sense that would soon diminish faith in the Bible. It has been proclaimed that this century is marked by the discovery that Moses was not the author of the Pentateuch, and the main reasons to support this discovery are the contradictions, repetitions, impossibilities, etc., found in the Pentateuch. But this is no discovery of this century. Seventeen hundred years ago an author wrote: "How could Moses write that Moses died? And whereas, in the time after Moses, about-five hundred years or thereabouts, it [the Pentateuch] is found lying in the temple which was built, and, after about five hundred years more, it is carried away, and being burned in the time of Nebuchadnezzar it is destroyed, and thus being written after Moses and often lost, even this shows the foreknowledge of Moses, because he, foreseeing its disappearance, did not write it; but they who wrote it, being convicted of ignorance through their not foreseeing its disappearance, were not prophets." He adds that there are false and blasphemous chapters which were interpolated into the Scriptures; there are misrepresentations of God, some things false and some true; the Scriptures are very uncertain, for there are many contradictions in them. This author says God alone is true, and he represents God truly. All this sounds strangely like the statements of some writers of the present day, and effectually disposes of the claim of the new discovery that Moses is not the author of the Pentateuch, as one of the triumphs of critical skill in our age.

Of late, in a circle where science is held as the supreme test, and nothing is to be accepted that cannot be demonstrated clearly, it has been asserted that the story of the ark is positively proved to be a fable, myth, legend, by the fact that it would be an absolute impossibility to place two of every known species of land animals in the space of the ark. This appears to some young persons a conclusive proof, coming from a scientific source.

But as it is a simple question of the multiplication table, there is no science at all in this "positive proof," as a candid "infidel of high authority in natural science declares. The matter is so simple that even an outsider, like myself, may state it.

The narrative of the making of the ark is, "This is how thou shalt make it: the length of the ark three hundred cubits, the breadth of it fifty cubits, and the height of it thirty cubits."

The length of the cubit has been settled by the comparison of numerous Egyptian, Babylonian, and other cubits of earliest times, by Oppert, Lepsius, Flinders, Petrie, and others, and especially by the conclusive work of Lehmann. It was between nineteen and twenty inches; but, in order to be on the entirely safe side, we will take it to be only eighteen inches. Then the surface of one deck of the ark would be 450 multiplied by .75 which equals 33,750 square feet.

Naturalists differ very largely as to the classification of species, the majority estimating from 1,200 to 1,600 species; but we will take the extremest estimate by a high authority, Wallace, in his "Distribution of Animals" (New York, 1876), who gives 2,415,—that is, 290 species above the size of the sheep, 757 from the sheep to the rat; and 1,359 of the rats, bats, and shrews. Then with two of each species, 2,415 multiplied by 2, equals 4,830, and with seven of each of the ten species of clean animals, 70, we would have, as the highest estimate of all the land mammalia, 4,900, to be placed in the ark.

In order to learn what space would be required, we must ascertain the average size of these 2,415

species. There is no sort of difficulty in this, since the measurements of the species are as well known and familiar to naturalists as the species themselves. But, lest I may seem to venture upon ground that is beyond me, I have the very high authority of Professor Ward, of Rochester, in the statement that the average size of all land mammalia would be about that of the grey fox, or the common house cat. Any one can verify this by consultation of the special works giving the size of animals.

The ocean steamers carrying cattle most carefully from America to England, allow twenty square feet to each ox. If we allow one-fourth of that space, five square feet, for a cat, we shall be giving a superabundance of room; then 4,900, multiplied by 5, which equals 24,500 square feet of surface, would be ample to contain all the known species of animals at the highest estimate of their number. We have seen that one deck of the ark contained 33,750 square feet; 33,750—24,500 equals 9,250. All the species, then, could be placed on one deck of the ark, and still there would be one-third (12⅓ multiplied by 75) of that deck vacant.

Wallace estimates of birds, 10,087; of reptiles, 970; of lizards, 1,252; of insects (roughly), 100,000 species. If we again take the average of all these species, they could easily be placed on the 9,250 square feet not occupied by the mammalia.

If the ark had only one deck, two of each known species of land mammalia, birds, reptiles, lizards, and insects, could find abundant room there. But if we follow the majority of naturalists, and take, above their estimate, 1,700 as the number of species, then 1,700 multiplied by 2 equals 3,400, plus 70 equals 3,470, multiplied by 5, equals 17,350 square feet. As the deck contained 33,750 square feet, then two of each species of all the mammalia would find abundant room on one-half of the deck and six feet additional, leaving the remaining nearly one-half (219 multiplied by 75) for the birds, reptiles, lizards, insects. Leaving the ark, it is plain that any of the great ocean steamers, plying between New York and Liverpool, could place, with abundant room, two of each known species of land mammalia, and birds, reptiles, etc., on one of their decks.

These facts are so well known, and so easy to learn if one does not know them, that we ask, What claim has a man to scientific knowledge, or to a scientific spirit, who makes the statement that the scientific knowledge of the species of animals is a conclusive proof that they could not have been placed in the ark, and hence the narrative of the ark is a mere myth?

Only one deck of the ark has been spoken of, to show its ample space for all the known species. But no one, who has studied the subject, supposes that the ark had only one deck. The ark is said to have had "rooms [marg., nests] in it," and "lower, second, and third stories." From this it is concluded that the ark had three decks, for, as every waterman knows, a flatboat forty-five feet deep is an utter absurdity and impossibility.

Retaining the length, breadth, and depth, given for the ark, it must have been of the shape of a ship, as Napier, in his "Manufacturing Arts in Early Times," has shown. The decks of the ark, then, would have been less than 33,750 square feet; but not enough less to have hindered giving abundant room to all the animals. There would be ample room for the animals, for food for a year, and for Noah and his family.

There are enough questions about the Bible which our ignorance, or the necessary limits of our thinking, or prejudice, prevents our solving; but the question whether all the species of land mammalia, birds, etc., could be placed in a certain number of square feet, is so simple that it is an arithmetical, and not a scientific, problem.

The Gospel Messenger,

A Weekly at $1.50 Per Annum.

PUBLISHED BY

The Brethren's Publishing Co.

D. L. MILLER,	. . . . .	Editor.
J. H. MOORE,	. . . . .	Office Editor.
J. B. BRUMBAUGH,	. . . . .	Associate Editors.
J. G. ROYER,	. . . . .	
JOSEPH AMICK,	. . . . .	Business Manager.

ADVISORY COMMITTEE.

R. H. Miller, A. Hutchison, Daniel Hays.

☞ Communications for publication should be legibly written with black ink on one side of the paper only. Do not attempt to interline, or to put on one page what ought to occupy two.

☞ Anonymous communications will not be published.

☞ Do not mix business with articles for publication. Keep your communications on separate sheets from all business.

☞ Time is precious. We always have time to attend to business and to answer questions of importance, but please do not subject us to need less answering of letters.

☞ The MESSENGER is mailed each week to all subscribers. If the address is correctly entered on our list, the paper must reach the person to whom it is addressed. If you do not get your paper, write us, giving particulars.

☞ When changing your address, please give your former as well as your future address in full, so as to avoid delay and misunderstanding.

☞ Always remit to the office from which you order your goods, no matter from where you receive them.

☞ Do not send personal checks or drafts on interior banks, unless you send with them 25 cents each, to pay for collection.

☞ Remittances should be made by Post-office Money Order, Drafts on New York, Philadelphia or Chicago, or Registered Letters, made payable and addressed to "Brethren's Publishing Co., Mount Morris, Ill.," or "Brethren's Publishing Co., Huntingdon, Pa."

☞ Entered at the Post-office at Mount Morris, Ill., as second-class matter.

Mount Morris, Ill., - - - - **May 31, 1892.**

$1.00 pays for the MESSENGER from now until Dec. 31, 1892. Subscribe now!

THE Brethren at Hickory Grove, Illinois, have deferred their feast until June 25 and 26, commencing at I P. M.

BY an oversight, the second number of Bro. John Forney's articles appears in this issue instead of the one intended to be published first.

A NUMBER of our members attended the feast at West Branch, May 21; and report an excellent feast with a good attendance. Bro. D. B. Eby officiated.

THE District Meeting for Southern Ohio, we learn, passed off very pleasantly. No papers go to the Annual Meeting. Bro. I. J. Rosenberger will represent the District on the Standing Committee.

MANY are writing Bro. John Zuck, Clarence, Iowa, concerning lodging arrangements at the Annual Meeting. This is a mistake. All applications for lodging should be addressed to W. D. Tisdale, 536 E. Ave., Cedar Rapids, Iowa.

BRO. C. HOLDERMAN will represent the Southern District of Missouri and Arkansas on the Standing Committee, while Bro. Wm. Davis represents the North-eastern District of Kansas. Both of these Districts send papers to the Annual Meeting.

BRO. PETER FAHRNEY, of Chicago, has favored us with a very interesting folio pamphlet, giving a history of the Fahrney family, together with much other valuable information. The frontis piece is an excellent representation of one of our ancient Brethren, being a well-executed engraving of Eld. Jacob Fahrney, M. D. The work is not only interesting, but it is of historical value. Bro. Fahrney expects to attend the Annual Meeting at Cedar Rapids, not for the purpose of selling medicine, but to enjoy the meeting. His valuable medicine has given him a world-wide reputation.

As usual, the MESSENGER will have an office on the Annual Meeting grounds, where we shall be pleased to meet any of our patrons, and will also be prepared to transact any business in our line. We shall have on hand a good supply of Hymn Books and Hymnals, and other books that we keep in stock. We hope to enjoy the pleasure of meeting many of our friends and patrons whom we have never met before, and also renew acquaintances of former years.

BRETHREN Edmund Forney and Geo. D. Zollers, members of the Mt. Morris College Advisory Committee, were with us last week again, looking after the religious and moral interest of the school. They have an important duty to perform, in this respect, and we are pleased to know that they are becoming greatly interested, as well as much concerned about the welfare of our growing educational work. Only those who take the time to look into the workings of our schools, can rightly judge of their merits and wants.

WE were both surprised and pleased to meet in Cedar Rapids, Iowa, last week, our brother, William Jonson, of Malmo, Sweden. While in Sweden last fall, we had our home for a short time with Bro. Jonson's father, who is a deacon in the Malmo church, and became well acquainted with our young brother. He left his home on the 5th inst., and reached Cedar Rapids on the 20th, the same day we arrived at that place. Our meeting was quite accidental and it seemed singular that our movements were so directed that we thus met as we did. We were glad to see our brother and to be able to recommend him to the care of the brethren at Cedar Rapids. He finds a temporary home with Bro. Tisdale and plenty of work on the Annual Meeting grounds.

WE have just published a new edition of the "Doctrine of the Brethren Defended," by Eld. R. H. Miller. This is unquestionably the best defense of our faith and practice that has ever appeared among us, and ought to be in the hands of our readers, especially should it be in the hands of all our ministers. On his death-bed, Bro. Miller requested that we take charge of the publishing of his book, and pay his wife for the use of the plates. This we have now done and our agreement is to merely clear expenses on this edition. Therefore we have reduced the price of the book from $1.50 to $1.25, or to ministers, $1.00. We trust our readers will avail themselves of this opportunity and procure a copy of this able defense of primitive Christianity. Agents wanted in every congregation. Send for special terms to agents.

THE Annual Meeting, proper, opens on Tuesday morning, June 7, but the Standing Committee will meet and organize on Friday morning before. A number of others are expected to arrive on Friday, but on Saturday the crowd will begin to come. This is usually a very pleasant day for meeting with old friends, and talking over the events of by-gone days. A number of trains usually arrive Sunday morning, bringing in large crowds. This is generally the day of big meetings, when our ablest ministers will strain their voices to make themselves heard over the vast assemblies, which gather to hear the preaching of the Word. Monday is the day for reunions. By this time all who attend are generally present and friends meet and mutually encourage and strengthen each other. This has usually been considered the most enjoyable day of the Meeting. On Tuesday morning the great Conference opens and business commences in real earnest. We hope to meet thousands of our readers there and renew and form acquaintances that may be for the encouragement of us all.

IN this issue will be found an excellent report from the church at Johnstown, Pa., showing that the Brethren at that place have been doing some good work, and, seemingly, have a bright prospect before them. The Western District of Pennsylvania has also petitioned the Annual Meeting to hold the Conference of 1893 at Johnstown.

THE AUTHORITY OF OUR ANNUAL CONFERENCE.

No body of people can associate and labor together in Christian work without having a well-defined plan of procedure, and an authoritative governing power. The importance of well-organized effort is recognized by all, and it is equally apparent that there can be no organized effort without a plan and properly-constituted authority. All attempts to carry on work, contrary to these principles, have resulted in failure, and the church is by no means an exception to the rule laid down in the foregoing propositions. By the church we have direct reference to the church of the Brethren, incorporated under the name of German Baptist Brethren.

Jesus Christ is the head of the church, and all power and authority is derived from him. The Gospel is the written constitution of the church and is the all-sufficient plan of salvation. It was made and ratified in the council-chambers of heaven, and no power on earth has authority to change, annul, or set aside a single iota of its provisions. The church accepts this in its fullest and broadest sense. The Bible and the Bible alone is her constitution and from THE BOOK she has her rule of faith and practice. In the atoning blood of Christ, and upon obedience from the heart to all the Master's commandments, not some of them, she bases her hopes of salvation. To this doctrine she has held from the first and the attempts of her critics to show that she does not adhere to the Bible alone, are not in accord with the facts in the case.

Holding to the Bible as her authority, she claims that the church is an organized body of believers, receiving from its Head the power of self-government, and that such government is separate and distinct from the state, having its own rules and regulations and that this derived power is ministerial and administrative. She has the right to adopt the best means in her wisdom, to carry out the grand principles of the Gospel. She has authority to make rules in harmony with the spirit of the Gospel for her own government. As she is commanded to teach all nations, she has the right to select ministers and teachers, ordain and send them out into the field to teach and preach the Word, and to recall and depose them, if they prove unfaithful. She has the right to settle questions referred to her, upon which differences of opinion obtain among her members, and to give advice upon such questions as concern her welfare upon which the Gospel is silent.

The question now arises, Where does the power rest? Is it in the ministers and teachers? Have they the right to govern the church, or does the power rest in the whole church, the entire body of believers? The church accepts the latter view as being in harmony with the Gospel. In practice she holds that each member of the church is a unit of power and all are equal before God; and that the will of a large majority should become the will of the whole body. This is absolutely necessary to the success of her work. A violation of this principle of self-government can result on-

The Gospel Messenger,

A Weekly at $1.50 Per Annum.

PUBLISHED BY

The Brethren's Publishing Co.

D. L. MILLER,	Editor.
J. H. MOORE,	Office Editor.
J. B. BRUMBAUGH, } J. G. ROYER, }	Associate Editors.
JOSEPH AMICK,	Business Manager.

ADVISORY COMMITTEE.

R. H. Miller, A. Hutchison, Daniel Hays.

☞Communications for publication should be legibly written with black ink on one side of the paper only. Do not attempt to interline, or to put on one page what ought to occupy two.

☞Anonymous communications will not be published.

☞Do not mix business with articles for publication. Keep your communications on separate sheets from all business.

☞Time is precious. We always have time to attend to business and to answer questions of importance, but please do not subject us to need less answering of letters.

☞The MESSENGER is mailed each week to all subscribers. If the address is correctly entered on our list, the paper must reach the person to whom it is addressed. If you do not get your paper, write us, giving particulars.

☞When changing your address, please give your former as well as your future address in full, so as to avoid delay and misunderstanding.

☞Always remit to the office from which you order your goods, no matter from where you receive them.

☞Do not send personal checks or drafts on interior banks, unless you send with them 25 cents each, to pay for collection.

☞Remittances should be made by Post-office Money Order, Drafts on New York, Philadelphia or Chicago, or Registered Letters, made payable and addressed to "Brethren's Publishing Co., Mount Morris, Ill.," or "Brethren's Publishing Co., Huntingdon, Pa."

☞Entered at the Post-office at Mount Morris, Ill., as second-class matter.

Mount Morris, Ill., ... May 31, 1892.

$1.00 pays for the MESSENGER from now until Dec. 31, 1892. Subscribe now!

THE Brethren at Hickory Grove, Illinois, have deferred their feast until June 25 and 26, commencing at 1 P. M.

BY an oversight, the second number of Bro. John Forney's articles appears in this issue instead of the one intended to be published first.

A NUMBER of our members attended the feast at West Branch, May 21; and report an excellent feast with a good attendance. Bro. D. B. Eby officiated.

THE District Meeting for Southern Ohio, we learn, passed off very pleasantly. No papers go to the Annual Meeting. Bro. I. J. Rosenberger will represent the District on the Standing Committee.

MANY are writing Bro. John Zuck, Clarence, Iowa, concerning lodging arrangements at the Annual Meeting. This is a mistake. All applications for lodging should be addressed to W. D. Tisdale, 89 E. Ave., Cedar Rapids, Iowa.

BRO. C. HOLDEMAN will represent the Southern District of Missouri and Arkansas on the Standing Committee, while Bro. Wm. Davis represents the North-eastern District of Kansas. Both of these Districts send papers to the Annual Meeting.

BRO. PETER FAHRNEY, of Chicago, has favored us with a very interesting folio pamphlet, giving a history of the Fahrney family, together with much other valuable information. The frontispiece is an excellent representation of one of our ancient Brethren, being a well-executed engraving of Eld. Jacob Fahrney, M. D. The work is not only interesting, but it is of historical value. Bro. Fahrney expects to attend the Annual Meeting at Cedar Rapids, not for the purpose of selling medicine, but to enjoy the meeting. His valuable medicine has given him a world-wide reputation.

As usual, the MESSENGER will have an office on the Annual Meeting grounds, where we shall be pleased to meet any of our patrons, and will also be prepared to transact any business in our line. We shall have on hand a good supply of Hymn Books and Hymnals, and other books that we keep in stock. We hope to enjoy the pleasure of meeting many of our friends and patrons whom we have never met before, and also renew acquaintances of former years.

BRETHREN Edmund Forney and Geo. D. Zollers, members of the Mt. Morris College Advisory Committee, were with us last week again, looking after the religious and moral interest of the school. They have an important duty to perform, in this respect, and we are pleased to know that they are becoming greatly interested, as well as much concerned about the welfare of our growing educational work. Only those who take the time to look into the workings of our schools, can rightly judge of their merits and wants.

WE were both surprised and pleased to meet in Cedar Rapids, Iowa, last week, our brother, William Jonson, of Malmo, Sweden. While in Sweden last fall, we had our home for a short time with Bro. Jonson's father, who is a deacon in the Malmo church, and became well acquainted with our young brother. He left his home on the 5th inst., and reached Cedar Rapids on the 20th, the same day we arrived at that place. Our meeting was quite accidental and it seemed singular that our movements were so directed that we thus met as we did. We were glad to see our brother and to be able to recommend him to the care of the brethren at Cedar Rapids. He finds a temporary home with Bro. Tisdale and plenty of work on the Annual Meeting grounds.

WE have just published a new edition of the "Doctrine of the Brethren Defended," by Eld. R. H. Miller. This is unquestionably the best defense of our faith and practice that has ever appeared among us, and ought to be in the hands of our readers, especially should it be in the hands of all our ministers. On his death-bed, Bro. Miller requested that we take charge of the publishing of his book, and pay his wife for the use of the plates. This we have now done and our aim is to merely clear expenses on this edition. Therefore we have reduced the price of the book from $1.50 to $1.25, or to ministers, $1.00. We trust our readers will avail themselves of this opportunity and procure a copy of this able defense of primitive Christianity. Agents wanted in every congregation. Send for special terms to agents.

THE Annual Meeting, proper, opens on Tuesday morning, June 7, but the Standing Committee will meet and organize on Friday morning before. A number of others are expected to arrive on Friday, but on Saturday the crowd will begin to come. This is usually a very pleasant day for meeting with old friends, and talking over the events of by-gone days. A number of trains usually arrive Sunday morning, bringing in large crowds. This is generally the day of big meetings, when our ablest ministers will strain their voices to make themselves heard over the vast assemblies, which gather to hear the preaching of the Word. Monday is the day for reunions. By this time all who attend are generally present and friends meet and mutually encourage and strengthen each other. This has usually been considered the most enjoyable day of the Meeting. On Tuesday morning the great Conference opens and business commences in real earnest. We hope to meet thousands of our readers there and renew and form acquaintances that may be for the encouragement of us all.

In this issue will be found an excellent report from the church at Johnstown, Pa., showing that the Brethren at that place have been doing some good work, and, seemingly, have a bright prospect before them. The Western District of Pennsylvania has also petitioned the Annual Meeting to hold the Conference of 1893 at Johnstown.

THE AUTHORITY OF OUR ANNUAL CONFERENCE.

No body of people can associate and labor together in Christian work without having a well-defined plan of procedure, and an authoritative governing power. The importance of well-organized effort is recognized by all, and it is equally apparent that there can be no organized effort without a plan and properly-constituted authority. All attempts to carry on work, contrary to these principles, have resulted in failure, and the church is by no means an exception to the rule laid down in the foregoing propositions. By the church we have direct reference to the church of the Brethren, incorporated under the name of German Baptist Brethren.

Jesus Christ is the head of the church and all power and authority is derived from him. The Gospel is the written constitution of the church and is the all-sufficient plan of salvation. It was made and ratified in the council-chambers of heaven, and no power on earth has authority to change, annul, or set aside a single iota of its provisions. The church accepts this in its fullest and broadest sense. The Bible and the Bible alone is her constitution, and from THE BOOK she has her rule of faith and practice. In the atoning blood of Christ, and upon obedience from the heart to all the Master's commandments, not some of them, she bases her hopes of salvation. To this doctrine she has held from the first and the attempts of her critics to show that she does not adhere to the Bible alone, are not in accord with the facts in the case.

Holding to the Bible as her authority, she claims that the church is an organized body of believers, receiving from its Head the power of self-government, and that such government is separate and distinct from the state, having its own rules and regulations and that this derived power is ministerial and administrative. She has the right to adopt the best means in her wisdom, to carry out the grand principles of the Gospel. She has authority to make rules in harmony with the spirit of the Gospel for her own government. As she is commanded to teach all nations, she has the right to select ministers and teachers, ordain and send them out into the field to teach and preach the Word, and to recall and depose them if they prove unfaithful. She has the right to settle questions referred to her, upon which differences of opinion obtain among her members, and to give advice upon such questions as concern her welfare upon which the Gospel is silent.

The question now arises, Where does the power rest? Is it in the ministers and teachers? Have they the right to govern the church, or does the power rest in the whole church, the entire body of believers? The church accepts the latter view as being in harmony with the Gospel. In practice she holds that each member of the church is a unit of power and all are equal before God; and that the will of a large majority should become the will of the whole body. This is absolutely necessary to the success of her work. A violation of this principle of self-government can result in

WE sometimes hear about "prayerless Christians." We doubt whether there are any prayerless Christians. Prayer is one of the very strongest indications of the Christian life. It is the breathing of the true Christian soul. We may as well look for a living man without breath, as to seek for a Christian who never pours out his heart to God in prayer. All Christians should not only have their fixed seasons of prayer in the family, but they should frequent the prayer closet. We need more praying people to call down the blessings of God upon humanity.

THE London Times makes some startling figures concerning the enormous quantities of liquors consumed in the United Kingdom of Great Britain. The total is over 891 for every man, woman and child in the Kingdom. With this amount the entire population could be well fed, comfortably clothed and liberally educated. Much the greater portion of this worse than wasted money is spent by the men, leaving the women and children proportionally to suffer. We certainly do not exaggerate when we state that this liquor business is the most stupendous and appalling evil upon the face of the globe.

THE love-feast season seems to suggest to us the propriety of a few remarks concerning the necessity of our members taking special-interest in these feasts of charity. We think that it is the duty of every member to appear at the Lord's Table on all occasions, when it is within reason to do so. Especially should they attend the feasts in their home congregations. Business cares and other things should be so shaped that members can, by all means, attend the feasts. It might be well if the ministers would preach occasionally on the importance of attending to the ordinances of the house of God. When members begin to neglect these ordinances, and become careless concerning the sacred institutions that the church is required to perpetuate, their spiritual condition begins to decline, and ere long they lose all interest for religion. By all means should their presence at these feasts be insisted upon. If there should be other obstacles in the way, they should be removed. There is no necessity whatever for members to spend months, and some even years, in an unreconciled state with their brethren. If they will yield to the spirit of Christ, all difficulties may be easily removed, and they can then approach the Lord's Table in love and sincerity.

SOME of our sisters write very approvingly of the plain bonnet, usually worn by our sisters. Well, our sisters must wear some kind of a head-dress, and the neat Quaker bonnet is about as becoming a head-dress for women professing godliness, as is likely to be found. We see no reason for dispensing with it. For our part we like it. Even fashionable people admire it, and there is no valid reason why our sisters should not be contented with it. True, Madam Fashion may not endorse it, but then, she has enough to do in the world without meddling with the affairs of Christian women. And by the way, it is not necessary for us to go to the fashionable world in search of becoming apparel for Christian people. It seems to us, that when we do get a good thing, we ought to have stability enough about us to cling to it. All the Bible demands, is that the people of God attire themselves in plain, becoming garments, excluding ornaments of all classes. This is not only Bible, but it is unquestionably good common sense. And there is neither good sense nor Bible, for the constant change of head-dress as dictated by Madam Fashion. There is one thing, however, that we cannot admire, and that is the way some of our sisters are changing their bonnets until they are about as fashionable in appearance as

what the world endorses. We hope our sisters will give this matter proper consideration, for the neat Quaker bonnet is not only becoming Christian women of all ranks, but it certainly is in keeping with the Bible principle of plainness, and every reasonable effort should be made to retain it in its present form. Let our sisters, as well as our brethren, look to look a little more like members and not so much like the world.

WE are again reminded that there is a demand for further remarks concerning the length of sermons. Ministers who preach over forty-five minutes, at their regular appointments, may do well to quietly consult some of their clear-headed members, respecting the desired length of a sermon. In that way they may possibly learn more than we are able to tell them. The length of a sermon often depends upon who preaches it, and who listens to it. A minister who understands his business, and will take a little good advice from his members, can generally tell about how long to preach. Our observation is that a well-informed minister can do his very best inside of about forty minutes.

CHRISTIAN ENDEAVOR SOCIETY.

Is it advisable, or allowable for brethren and sisters to form themselves into a "Christian Endeavor Society," allowing members of other denominations and people not belonging to any church to become members? I would like an answer to the above question as soon as possible. They claim that there is nothing in the pledge that we have not already pledged ourselves to in our baptismal vows. What do the Brethren think about it?　　　　　M. C. WEAVER.

ANSWER.

IF there is nothing more in the pledge than we have already responded to in our baptismal vows, we see no use in repeating the pledge. Hence that part of it is certainly useless. While we are decidedly in favor of any proper auxiliary that may prove beneficial to the cause of Christianity, we can see no good likely to result from a Christian Endeavor Society among our people, especially so if we are to unite with those of other faiths, and even unconverted people. This is being unequally yoked together with unbelievers, religiously, which is positively unscriptural. The simple fact that the society referred to, takes into its number and fellowship unconverted people, shows that it is not, strictly speaking, a Christian institution. It is probably adapted to the wants of the popular denominations, but it is far from being in keeping with the principles held by the Brethren, therefore we advise our people not to organize a society of that character.　　J. H. M.

INFORMATION DESIRED.

We are living in Peabody, Kans., a small town, surrounded by a great many different denominations, some of which are trying to work against the faith and practice of the Brethren. Yesterday the Baptist minister called on me. He soon began on feet-washing. I gave him John 13 to read. When he came to the fourteenth verse, where it says, "Ye also ought to wash one another's feet," he said that ought was not binding. But I tried in my weakness to prove to him that it was binding. Then he wanted to leave that subject, but said he was going to study that chapter more than he had ever done before. Then he went to the Lord's Supper. He claims the bread and wine constitute the Supper, and that we keep the Passover for the Lord's Supper. He said that was also all the supper the Lord instituted. I did the best I could with that, but he had to leave and left it unfinished, and said he was coming back again. Now, brethren, please give me a clear distinction between the Lord's Supper and the Passover. This minister knows but little about our faith and practice, and by your help we may prove things to him he never knew.　　ESTHER SHEPLER.

REMARKS.

THAT is right, sister. Stand up for the truth. The next time that minister tells you that

"ought" is not binding, refer him to Eph. 5: 28, where it says, "So ought men to love their wives as their own bodies." If this is not binding, we certainly do not understand the force of language. As a common sense way of getting at a point of this kind, it may be well to ask whether Christ and his disciples did not occupy safe ground while engaged in feet-washing? Most assuredly they did. Then, if we do as they did, and as Jesus says we ought to, are we not, with them, occupying ground equally safe? It should be borne in mind that there are no doubts about those being on the safe side of the question, who practice feet-washing, as commanded by Jesus. All the doubts are about those who do not so practice. It is, then, an important question to be settled, whether we in this life are to occupy questionable ground, or will we occupy that which is infallibly safe? For our part we prefer to do what Christ says we ought to do. This we know is both right and safe. No man who has practiced this rite through life, dies with a guilty conscience, so far as feet-washing is concerned. The guilty conscience, pertaining to feet-washing, will be found in the hearts of those, who, during life, refuse to do what the Master plainly tells them they ought to do.

Concerning the Lord's Supper, we remark that the bread and cup are never called the Lord's Supper in any part of the New Testament. And in Luke 22: 20 we read, "Likewise also the cup after supper, saying, This cup is the new testament in my blood, which is shed for you." This shows that the cup was no part of the supper, for Luke plainly says it was taken "after supper."

Jesus did not partake of the Jewish passover at the time he instituted the Communion, for the Jews did not eat the passover until the next evening. We might give you a further explanation concerning the difference between the passover and the supper that Jesus ate with his disciples, but in this issue will be found a good article on that subject, from the pen of Eld. John Forney, to be followed by another from the same pen next week.

Yet we add, that the word supper is from the Greek word deipnon, which means a full or regular meal, as much so as baptizo means a full immersion. A small bit of bread and a sip of wine can no more constitute a supper, than sprinkling or pouring can constitute baptism.

J. H. M.

A PROSPEROUS INDICATION.

IT seems to us that there has never been a period in the history of our Brotherhood when peace, love and union so generally prevailed throughout the church at large, as at the present time. So far as heard from, and we have heard from nearly all of them, all the District Meetings passed off very pleasantly, and the business transacted was of a very satisfactory character.

Before us are the Minutes of these Meetings, and their contents are indeed encouraging, on account of the attention given to the missionary cause. A few years ago one short paragraph told the story of only a feeble effort in the interest of spreading the Gospel, but now it requires whole pages to chronicle only a part of what is being accomplished in the missionary line in not a few of the Districts. This is indeed an encouraging feature in our Brotherhood, and shows a healthy growth in the right direction.

This growth has much to do with the health and prosperity of the general Brotherhood. It is

WE sometimes hear about "prayerless Christians." We doubt whether there are any prayerless Christians. Prayer is one of the very strongest indications of the Christian life. It is the breathing of the true Christian soul. We may as well look for a living man without breath, as to seek for a Christian who never pours out his heart to God in prayer. All Christians should not only have their fixed seasons of prayer in the family, but they should frequent the prayer closet. We need more praying people to call down the blessings of God upon humanity.

THE *London Times* makes some startling figures concerning the enormous quantities of liquors consumed in the United Kingdom of Great Britain. The total is over $91 for every man, woman and child in the Kingdom. With this amount the entire population could be well fed, comfortably clothed and liberally educated. Much the greater portion of this worse than wasted money is spent by the men, leaving the women and children proportionally to suffer. We certainly do not exaggerate when we state that this liquor business is the most stupendous and appalling evil upon the face of the globe.

THE love-feast season seems to suggest to us the propriety of a few remarks concerning the necessity of our members taking special interest in these feasts of charity. We think that it is the duty of every member to appear at the Lord's Table on all occasions, when it is within reason to do so. Especially should they attend the feasts in their home congregations. Business cares and other things should be so shaped that members can, by all means, attend the feasts. It might be well if the ministers would preach occasionally on the importance of attending to the ordinances of the house of God. When members begin to neglect these ordinances, and become careless concerning the sacred institutions that the church is required to perpetuate, their spiritual condition begins to decline, and ere long they lose all interest for religion. By all means should their presence at these feasts be insisted upon. If there should be other obstacles in the way, they should be removed. There is no necessity whatever for members to spend months, and some even years, in an unreconciled state with their brethren. If they will yield to the spirit of Christ, all difficulties may be easily removed, and they can then approach the Lord's Table in love and sincerity.

SOME of our readers write very approvingly of the plain bonnet, usually worn by our sisters. Well, our sisters must wear some kind of a head-dress, and the neat Quaker bonnet is about as becoming a head-dress for women professing godliness, as is likely to be found. We see no reason for dispensing with it. For our part we like it. Even fashionable people admire it, and there is no valid reason why our sisters should not be contented with it. True, Madam Fashion may not endorse it, but then, she has enough to do in the world without meddling with the affairs of Christian women. And by the way, it is not necessary for us to go to the fashionable world in search of becoming apparel for Christian people. It seems to us, that when we do get a good thing, we ought to have stability enough about us to cling to it. All the Bible demands, is that the people of God attire themselves in plain, becoming garments, excluding ornaments of all classes. This is not only Bible, but it is unquestionably good common sense. And there is neither good sense nor Bible, for the constant change of head-dress as dictated by Madam Fashion. There is one thing, however, that we cannot admire, and that is the way some of our sisters are changing their bonnets until they are about as fashionable in appearance as

what the world endorses. We hope our sisters will give this matter proper consideration, for the neat Quaker bonnet is not only becoming Christian women of all ranks, but it certainly is in keeping with the Bible principle of plainness, and every reasonable effort should be made to retain it in its present form. Let our sisters, as well as our brethren, seek to look a little more like members and not so much like the world.

WE are again reminded that there is a demand for further remarks concerning the length of sermons. Ministers who preach over forty-five minutes, at their regular appointments, may do well to quietly consult some of their clear-headed members, respecting the desired length of a sermon. In that way they may possibly learn more than we are able to tell them. The length of a sermon often depends upon who preaches it, and who listens to it. A minister who understands his business, and will take a little good advice from his members, can generally tell about how long to preach. Our observation is that a well-informed minister can do his very best inside of about forty minutes.

CHRISTIAN ENDEAVOR SOCIETY.

Is it advisable, or allowable for brethren and sisters to form themselves into a "Christian Endeavor Society," allowing members of other denominations and people not belonging to any church to become members? I would like an answer to the above question as soon as possible. They claim that there is nothing in the pledge that we have not already pledged ourselves to in our baptismal vows. What do the Brethren think about it?   M. C. WEAVER.

ANSWER.

IF there is nothing more in the pledge than we have already responded to in our baptismal vows, we see no use in repeating the pledge. Hence that part of it is certainly useless. While we are decidedly in favor of any proper auxiliary that may prove beneficial to the cause of Christianity, we can see no good likely to result from a Christian Endeavor Society among our people, especially so if we are to unite with those of other faiths, and even unconverted people. This is being unequally yoked together with unbelievers, religiously, which is positively unscriptural. The simple fact that the society referred to, takes into its number and fellowship unconverted people, shows that it is not, strictly speaking, a *Christian* institution. It is probably adapted to the wants of the popular denominations, but it is far from being in keeping with the principles held by the Brethren, therefore we advise our people not to organize a society of that character.   J. H. M.

INFORMATION DESIRED.

We are living in Peabody, Kans., a small town, surrounded by a great many different denominations, some of which are trying to work against the faith and practice of the Brethren. Yesterday the Baptist minister called on me. He soon began on feet-washing. I gave him John 13 to read. When he came to the fourteenth verse, where it says, "Ye also ought to wash one another's feet," he said that ought was not binding. But I tried in my weakness to prove to him that it was binding. Then he wanted to leave that subject, but said he was going to study that chapter more than he had ever done before. Then he went to the Lord's Supper. He claims the bread and wine constitute the Supper, and that we keep the Passover for the Lord's Supper. He said that was also all the supper the Lord instituted. I did the best I could with that, but he had to leave and left it unfinished, and said he was coming back again. Now, brethren, please give me a clear distinction between the Lord's Supper and the Passover. This minister knows but little about our faith and practice, and by your help we may prove things to him he never knew.   ESTHER SHEPLER.

REMARKS.

THAT is right, sister. Stand up for the truth. The next time that minister tells you that

"ought" is not binding, refer him to Eph. 5: 28, where it says, "So ought men to love their wives as their own bodies." If this is not binding, we certainly do not understand the force of language. As a common sense way of getting at a point of this kind, it may be well to ask whether Christ and his disciples did not occupy safe ground while engaged in feet-washing? Most assuredly they did. Then, if we do as they did, and as Jesus says we ought to, are we not, with them, occupying ground equally safe? It should be borne in mind that there are no doubts about those being on the safe side of the question, who practice feet-washing, as commanded by Jesus. All the doubts are about those who do not so practice. It is, then, an important question to be settled, whether we in this life are to occupy questionable ground, or will we occupy that which is infallibly safe? For our part we prefer to do what Christ says we ought to do. This we know is both right and safe. No man who has practiced this rite through life, dies with a guilty conscience, so far as feet-washing is concerned. The guilty conscience, pertaining to feet-washing, will be found in the hearts of those, who, during life, refuse to do what the Master plainly tells them they ought to do.

Concerning the Lord's Supper, we remark that the bread and cup are never called the Lord's Supper in any part of the New Testament. And in Luke 22: 20 we read, "Likewise also the cup after supper, saying, This cup is the new testament in my blood, which is shed for you." This shows that the cup was no part of the supper, for Luke plainly says it was taken "after supper."

Jesus did not partake of the Jewish passover at the time he instituted the Communion, for the Jews did not eat the passover until the next evening. We might give you a further explanation concerning the difference between the passover and the supper that Jesus ate with his disciples, but in this issue will be found a good article on that subject, from the pen of Eld. John Forney, to be followed by another from the same pen next week.

Yet we add, that the word supper is from the Greek word *deipnon*, which means a full or regular meal, as much as *baptizo* means a full immersion. A small bit of bread and a sip of wine can no more constitute a *supper*, than sprinkling or pouring can constitute baptism.
                                                  J. H. M.

A PROSPEROUS INDICATION.

IT seems to us that there has never been a period in the history of our Brotherhood when peace, love and union so generally prevailed throughout the church at large, as at the present time. So far as heard from, and as we have heard from nearly all of them, all the District Meetings passed off very pleasantly, and the business transacted was of a very satisfactory character.

Before us are the Minutes of these Meetings, and their contents are indeed encouraging, on account of the attention given to the missionary cause. A few years ago one short paragraph told the story of only a feeble effort in the interest of spreading the Gospel, but now it requires whole pages to chronicle only a part of what is being accomplished in the missionary line in not a few of the Districts. This is indeed an encouraging feature in our Brotherhood, and shows a healthy growth in the right direction.

This growth has much to do with the health and prosperity of the general Brotherhood. It is

community. I have heard people say, "Why do not those Dunkard preachers come back and cultivate what they have sown; their doctrine seems to suit us, but they never come back."

I have heard these remarks many times. The people of the world must have a guide, and if we have the best doctrine, we must go to work and some one will be held responsible. I think we have everything in our favor.

ROSS HALTERMAN.

From Muenster, Texas.

BRO. MOLSBEE came to the William's Creek church May 5. Owing to heavy rains, he could not fill any appointments until the 7th, the day of our council. We had a pleasant council. In considering where to hold District Meeting, it was decided to build a meeting-house and have it ready by August, the time for our District Meeting, provided we could get the means. The members subscribed $217. One lamb came back to the fold at the council and two were baptized on Monday. One more applicant intends to come back to the Father's house. Our brother had to go home in the midst of an interesting meeting. He preached seven sermons in all, with power and demonstration of the Spirit, and his efforts seemed to have a telling effect on saint and sinner. Many shed tears, and all were loth to give up the meetings and part with the brother. The church seems to be much encouraged, and manifests a commendable zeal. May we all realize that lively work for the Master will keep out trouble, and as the old William's Creek church has had her trials, we pray we all may keep our eyes on Jesus, and work in earnest for the advancement of his cause. We desire an interest in the prayers of the faithful, that this outpost may hold out faithful and give God all the glory.

A. W. AUSTIN.

May 13.

Railroad Arrangements for Annual Meeting.

On the "Big Four" Railroad we will have special cars, leaving Springfield and Dayton on the morning of June 4, and arriving at Chicago at 5:30 P. M. Spending several hours in the City, we will arrive at Cedar Rapids next morning. Passengers have their choice of route west of Chicago, yet this party will principally go over the Chicago, Milwaukee and St. Paul Railroad, which runs by Forreston, Ill., only twelve miles from Mt. Morris. We invite all along the line to join us on this route, and we will try to make it pleasant for all.

HENRY FRANTZ.

From Johnstown, Pa.

As secretary of this congregation, I feel it my duty to give to the readers of the MESSENGER a brief account of our church.

After the late division in our church it was decided by mutual agreement, that the "Progressives" should have the brick church which had been built at a cost of $10,000. Two-thirds of the membership having gone with the above-named faction, it only left us about 125 members.

We were then without a large church in which to hold our love-feasts, and therefore prepared to build a new house. With the united efforts and push of the brethren and sisters, we succeeded in again erecting a large house at Walnut Grove, about thirty minutes' walk from the City. The church labored hard, and finally succeeded in extricating themselves from the difficulties and trouble which had thickened around them.

The church, with its faithful elder and ministering brethren, began to prosper and has so continued.

During the year 1891 there were received into the church by letter about thirty; there were also a number received by baptism. During the year 1892 there have so far been received about twenty-five members, and our present membership is in the neighborhood of 350. We have six ministering brethren, including our elder, David Hildebrand.

We have five Sunday-schools. Our Sunday-school at Walnut Grove is the largest, and is carried on during the entire year. It is also in reality a Brethren's school, and uses the *Young Disciple* for general distribution, and also the *"Advanced"* and *Juvenile Quarterlies.* In this school only Brethren are employed as officers and teachers. We also conduct a Bible class at our Walnut Grove church once a week.

We held our regular, semi-annual love-feast May 8. We regret that many were unable to get seats, and could not commune, although we can seat about 250 members at our tables.

The District Meeting of the Western District of Pennsylvania also convened at our Walnut Grove church May 11. All the churches were fairly well represented. Bro. John Johnson was Moderator, and all business which came before way. It is said by many who attended the meeting, that it was one of the best meetings that they had held for years.

It was decided to hold a ministerial meeting every year after this, and to hold the first one this fall, in our church at Walnut Grove. No date has been set yet. Brethren William Shrock, Hermon Stahl and Daniel Walker were appointed to draw up a program and have the same published. All queries were settled.

The District Meeting asks for the Annual Meeting to be held at Johnstown, Pa., in 1893. It believes Johnstown offers as good facilities for holding Annual Meeting in 1893 as any other place in the Brotherhood. We offer city accommodations and privileges. The population of the city is 30,000. We have good railroads, both the Pennsylvania Railroad and the Baltimore and Ohio. The latter runs one hundred yards from the grounds. Electric cars run to the grounds. We have electric lights, abundant water and excellent grounds.

May God bless the work that has been done, and may we strive to accomplish still more for the good cause in the future! E. W. SHAFFER.

From Myrtle Point, Oregon.

OUR quarterly council occurred April 9. There was considerable business before the meeting; but all passed off very pleasantly. The time for holding our Communion meeting is July 8, at 2 P. M., and it was the request of the church that this notice be given, and an invitation extended to all brethren, traveling through this country, to try to be with us. Our Sunday-school was organized the first Sunday in April, with Bro. Perry Vandyke as Superintendent, and other needed officers. The school commences this spring with very flattering prospects. There seems to be a good interest both in and out of the church.

The health is good, with but few exceptions. There has been an aged brother, Benjamin Sears, staying here with the Brethren for about four years. He was a poor man, and was making his home among the Brethren. While at Bro. J. S. Root's, on April 7, he was, seemingly, in better health than usual. On the morning of the 8th, when Bro. John went to call him to breakfast, he found him dead in bed. An inquest was held. Bro. D. M. Brower, the physician, pronounced his trouble apoplexy. Bro. Sears had no relatives in this country. He was baptized in this church

nearly four years ago. He lived a very exemplary life. He said he had sought all through life for a people who obeyed all the commands, and he had about given up finding them, when, at last, he had his wishes gratified. His age was seventy-eight years. He was never married, but had some relatives in New Bedford, Mass., and, I think, some in Maryland. Funeral preached by the Brethren. THOMAS BARKLOW.

Myrtle Point, Oregon, May 8.

From the Wolf Creek Church, Ohio.

THE Wolf Creek church held her council April 29, preparatory to our love-feast. A full day's work was transacted in much harmony. Eld. J. Garber is our delegate to Annual Meeting. Our Communion, held May 12, was a feast of fat things. Elders T. Kreider, H. Frantz, J. Horning, and brethren D. Garber, J. H. Brumbaugh, W. Bowser and Barnhart labored for us with much acceptance.

The District Meeting of Southern Ohio was held May 17 in the Lexington church, Highland Co., Ohio. This is one of the scattered churches in the southern part of the State. It has had days of prosperity and adversity. Here Eld. Thomas Major and sister Sarah Major preached for many years. At present brethren J. E. and A. Ockerman labor for them. The meeting being held some distance from the main body of the Brethren, in the Miami Valley, and inconvenient to reach by rail, was not largely attended. Thirty-two out of thirty-five churches, however, were represented.

The meeting was organized by electing Eld. H. Frantz, Moderator; Eld. J. Stutsman, Reading Clerk, and I. J. Rosenberger, Writing Clerk. The following business was transacted:

1. The deferred business of last year,— the "Old Folks' Home,"—was again deferred one year.

2. The missionary report revealed the fact that money was accumulating in the treasury and some of the five mission points neglected. The sum of $248 is in the treasury, and five members have been received into the church. Bro. L. West has labored for the colored folks at several points and baptized ten, with three applicants, and borne the expense himself. The Moderator appointed three brethren, — S. Horning, Silas Gilbert and J. H. Brumbaugh,—to select a committee of five to formulate a plan to get our missionary work on better footing. Brethren J. Horning, I. J. Rosenberger, Quinter Calvert, J. C. Bright, B. Trout, constitute said committee.

3. This query, relating to 'Mutual Insurance,' was perplexing in its statements, and was referred back to the church.

4. This query asked permission that members might belong to the Law and Order League. This organization, involving the principle of secrecy and force, was not allowed.

5. This query asked that church certificates be considered invalid after a certain time. It was referred to former Minutes.

6. Two queries, referring to electioneering for the election of church officers and delegates, asked that a stop be put to the evil. The meeting gave an emphatic disapprobation of the practice, and decided that all who engage in it, or are influenced thereby, should lose their votes, and those who engage in it should be amenable to their congregations.

Eld. I. J. Rosenberger was chosen as delegate to Annual Meeting; alternate, Eld. J. Stutsman. Eld. Henry Gump was chosen on the Missionary Board.

Resolutions of thanks were tendered the neighborhood for its marked hospitality in caring for its visitors. The next meeting will be held in the

community. I have heard people say, "Why do not those Dunkard preachers come back and cultivate what they have sown; their doctrine seems to suit us, but they never come back."

I have heard these remarks many times. The people of the world must have a guide, and if we have the best doctrine, we must go to work and some one will be held responsible. I think we have everything in our favor.

        Ross Halterman.

From Muenster, Texas.

Bro. Molsbee came to the William's Creek church May 5. Owing to heavy rains, he could not fill any appointments until the 7th, the day of our council. We had a pleasant council. In considering where to hold District Meeting, it was decided to build a meeting-house and have it ready by August, the time for our District Meeting, provided we could get the means. The members subscribed $217. One lamb came back to the fold at the council and two were baptized on Monday. One more applicant intends to come back to the Father's house. Our brother had to go home in the midst of an interesting meeting. He preached seven sermons in all, with power and demonstration of the Spirit, and his efforts seemed to have a telling effect on saint and sinner. Many shed tears, and all were loth to give up the meetings and part with the brother. The church seems to be much encouraged, and manifests a commendable zeal. May we all realize that lively work for the Master will keep out trouble, and as the old William's Creek church has had her trials, we pray we all may keep our eyes on Jesus, and work in earnest for the advancement of his cause. We desire an interest in the prayers of the faithful, that this outpost may hold out faithful and give God all the glory.

        A. W. Austin.

May 13.

Railroad Arrangements for Annual Meeting.

On the "Big Four" Railroad we will have special cars, leaving Springfield and Dayton on the morning of June 4, and arriving at Chicago at 5:30 P. M. Spending several hours in the City, we will arrive at Cedar Rapids next morning. Passengers have their choice of route west of Chicago, yet this party will principally go over the Chicago, Milwaukee and St. Paul Railroad, which runs by Forreston, Ill., only twelve miles from Mt. Morris. We invite all along the line to join us on this route, and we will try to make it pleasant for all.   Henry Frantz.

From Johnstown, Pa.

As secretary of this congregation, I feel it my duty to give to the readers of the Messenger a brief account of our church.

After the late division in our church it was decided by mutual agreement, that the "Progressives" should have the brick church which had been built at a cost of $10,000. Two-thirds of the membership having gone with the above-named faction, it only left us about 125 members.

We were then without a large church in which to hold our love-feasts, and therefore prepared to build a new house. With the united efforts and push of the brethren and sisters, we succeeded in again erecting a large house at Walnut Grove, about thirty minutes' walk from the City. The church labored hard, and finally succeeded in extricating themselves from the difficulties and troubles which had thickened around them.

The church, with its faithful elder and ministering brethren, began to prosper and has so continued.

During the year 1891 there were received into the church by letter about thirty; there were also a number received by baptism. During the year 1892 there have so far been received about twenty-five members, and our present membership numbers in the neighborhood of 350. We have six ministering brethren, including our elder, David Hildebrand.

We have five Sunday-schools. Our Sunday-school at Walnut Grove is the largest, and is carried on during the entire year. It is also in reality a Brethren's school, and uses the *Young Disciple* for general distribution, and also the *"Advanced"* and *Juvenile Quarterlies*. In this school only Brethren are employed as officers and teachers. We also conduct a Bible class at our Walnut Grove church once a week.

We held our regular, semi-annual love-feast May 8. We regret that many were unable to get seats, and could not commune, although we can seat about 250 members at our tables.

The District Meeting of the Western District of Pennsylvania also convened at our Walnut Grove church May 11. All the churches were fairly well represented. Bro. John Johnson was Moderator, and all business which came before the meeting was transacted in a very satisfactory way. It is said by many who attended the meeting, that it was one of the best meetings that they had held for years.

It was decided to hold a ministerial meeting every year after this, and to hold the first one this fall, in our church at Walnut Grove. No date has been set yet. Brethren William Shrock, Herman Stahl and Daniel Walker were appointed to draw up a program and have the same published. All queries were settled.

The District Meeting asks for the Annual Meeting to be held at Johnstown, Pa, in 1893. It believes Johnstown offers as good facilities for holding Annual Meeting in 1893 as any other place in the Brotherhood. We offer city accommodations and privileges. The population of the city is 30,000. We have good railroads, both the Pennsylvania Railroad and the Baltimore and Ohio. The latter runs one hundred yards from the grounds. Electric cars run to the grounds. We have electric lights, abundant water and excellent grounds.

May God bless the work that has been done, and may we strive to accomplish still more for the good cause in the future! E. W. Shaffer.

From Myrtle Point, Oregon.

Our quarterly council occurred April 9. There was considerable business before the meeting, but all passed off very pleasantly. The time for holding our Communion meeting is July 8, at 2 P. M., and it was the request of the church that this notice be given, and an invitation extended to all brethren, traveling through this country, to try to be with us. Our Sunday-school was organized the first Sunday in April, with Bro. Perry Vandyke as Superintendent, and other needed officers. The school commences this spring with very flattering prospects. There seems to be a good interest both in and out of the church.

The health is good, with but few exceptions. There has been an aged brother, Benjamin Sears, staying here with the Brethren for about four years. He was a poor man, and was making his home among the Brethren. While at Bro. J. S. Root's, on April 7, he was, seemingly, in better health than usual. On the morning of the 8th, when Bro. John went to call him to breakfast, he found him dead in bed. An inquest was held. Bro. D. M. Brower, the physician, pronounced his trouble apoplexy. Bro. Sears had no relatives in this country. He was baptized in this church

nearly four years ago. He lived a very exemplary life. He said he had sought all through life for a people who obeyed all the commands, and he had about given up finding them, when, at last, he had his wishes gratified. His age was seventy-eight years. He was never married, but had some relatives in New Bedford, Mass., and, I think, some in Maryland. Funeral preached by the Brethren.   Thomas Barklow.

Myrtle Point, Oregon, May 8.

From the Wolf Creek Church, Ohio.

The Wolf Creek church held her council April 29, preparatory to our love-feast. A full day's work was transacted in much harmony. Eld. J. Garber is our delegate to Annual Meeting. Our Communion, held May 12, was a feast of fat things. Elders T. Kreider, H. Frantz, J. Horning, and brethren D. Garber, J. H. Brumbaugh, W. Bowser and Barnhart labored for us with much acceptance.

The District Meeting of Southern Ohio was held May 17 in the Lexington church, Highland Co., Ohio. This is one of the scattered churches in the southern part of the State. It has had days of prosperity and adversity. Here Eld. Thomas Major and sister Sarah Major preached for many years. At present brethren J. E. and A. Ockerman labor for them. The meeting being held some distance from the main body of the Brethren, in the Miami Valley, and inconvenient to reach by rail, was not largely attended. Thirty-two out of thirty-five churches, however, were represented.

The meeting was organized by electing Eld. H. Frantz, Moderator; Eld. J. Stutsman, Reading Clerk, and I. J. Rosenberger, Writing Clerk. The following business was transacted:

1. The deferred business of last year,—the "Old Folks' Home,"—was again deferred one year.

2. The missionary report revealed the fact that money was accumulating in the treasury and some of the five mission points neglected. The sum of $248 is in the treasury, and five members have been received into the church. Bro. L. West has labored for the colored folks at several points and baptized ten, with three applicants, and borne the expense himself. The Moderator appointed three brethren, — S. Horning, Silas Gilbert and J. H. Brumbaugh,—to select a committee of five to formulate a plan to get our missionary work on better footing. Brethren J. Horning, I. J. Rosenberger, Quinter Calvert, J. C. Bright, B. Trout, constitute that committee.

3. This query, relating to 'Mutual Insurance,' was perplexing in its statements, and was referred back to the church.

4. This query asked permission that members might belong to the Law and Order League. This organization, involving the principle of secrecy and force, was not allowed.

5. This query asked that church certificates be considered invalid after a certain time. It was referred to former Minutes.

6. Two queries, referring to electioneering for the election of church officers and delegates, asked that a stop be put to the evil. The meeting gave an emphatic disapprobation of the practice, and decided that all who engage in it, or are influenced thereby, should lose their votes, and those who engage in it should be amenable to their congregations.

Eld. I. J. Rosenberger was chosen as delegate to Annual Meeting; alternate, Eld. J. Stutsman. Eld. Henry Gump was chosen on the Missionary Board.

Resolutions of thanks were tendered the neighborhood for its marked hospitality in caring for its visitors. The next meeting will be held in the

Allen, Pa.—We had a very good Communion meeting at the Mohler meeting-house, in the Lower Cumberland church, Pa. Bro. Royer was with us. We were glad to get acquainted with him. Our Sunday-school is doing well, though not very large. We have an average of about forty-five scholars. — *J. Mihiesley, May 16.*

Phœnix, Arizona Ter.—I arrived in the Salt River Valley May 9. Since then I have been looking over the country. There are some brethren here now, and others are on the road. The Brethren have preaching every Sunday. There is government land here that can be taken as homestead, or under the desert act. I would be pleased to have brethren come and see us. I have decided to make this my future home. — *W. F. Gillett, May 14.*

Gratis, Ohio.—April 3 we met to re-organize our Sunday-school which adjourned last fall. Bro. Isaac Young was chosen to superintend the work, and a full corps of teachers and officers were elected. A teacher's meeting has been begun and the outlook is very encouraging. These meetings are certainly a great help to the Sunday-school work, if teachers will only take hold of the means. May we all seek to promote the Sunday-school cause!—*Jenny K. Petry, Secretary, May 3.*

Kansas Center Church, Kans. — Our love-feast occasion has just closed. It was a special season of rejoicing from the presence of the Lord. This was clearly manifested, as there were five young men who left the ranks of sin and were buried with Christ in baptism, to rise to walk in newness of life. The power of the Holy Spirit was clearly felt through the preaching of the Word. Eld. George Wise, of Olathe, Kans, officiated. Elders M. Keller, J. O. Brubaker, Daniel Dierdorff, Jonas Heitsler, and our aged elder, George Elliott, of Ellinwood, Kans, were with us and did their part well. Members from adjoining congregations were also present, which added much to our pleasure.—*Isaac S. Brubaker, Mitchell, Kans., May 17.*

Moscow, Idaho.—The good seed sown here seems to be doing well. We have a better attendance and more interest in our Sunday-school work this spring than ever before. Last Sunday, May 8, after the three o'clock services, we went to the water-side where one dear soul was buried with Christ in baptism. How good it is to start in the Master's cause while yet young! There will probably be two more baptized at our Communion, June 11. Eld. Hodgden goes to Oregon this week to help in church work there. He will be gone about three weeks. The harvest truly is plenteous, but the laborers are few. Pray ye, therefore, the Lord of the harvest, that he will send forth laborers into his harvest! — *J. U. O. Stiverson, May 10.*

Necona, Texas.—We rejoice with the dear members of Clay County, Texas. With two other loved ones, I went, April 30, to the above place, and on the same evening, commenced a protracted meeting.' From the start there was a good interest. As a result of ten days' meetings, six made confession of faith and were baptized. All were over thirty years of age, except one dear young brother. The prospects are truly encouraging. From indications there are others near the kingdom.—*Henry Brubaker, May 13.*

Glessied, Mo.—A few members met at Bro. Kelley's in council May 7. We felt it was good to be there, as everything that came before the meeting was disposed of in a Christian spirit. We have no resident minister, but are supplied with preaching by the Prairie View church, which is at a distance of about seventeen miles from here. We would be pleased if a minister could be induced to locate at or near Florence, as there is a good work to be done here. Land is very cheap. —*J. K. Miller.*

Spring Run, Pa.—Our Communion meeting, April 30, passed off very harmoniously. At our quarterly meeting, March 26, a soliciting, and also a locating committee were appointed. To-day a building committee was appointed for the purpose of building a meeting-house in Bratton Township, on the farm of Bro. Abraham Grassmyer. The house is very much needed on the south side of the Juniata River. Since Jan. 1 twenty-three have been received by baptism, and three by letter.—*Emma Bollinger, McVeytown, Pa.*

Sheldon, Iowa.—Last Sunday morning I boarded the train at Sheldon for Edna, Lyon Co., to fill an appointment in the Edna school-house, a small town on the Illinois Central Railroad. Here I found a flourishing Sunday-school, superintended by Bro. Wm. Leonard. At this place we have nine members. Here I found brother and sister A. Shrader, formerly of Franklin Grove, Lee Co., Ill. The people at Edna enjoy preaching. The house was well filled with eager listeners. Health in general is good. We have a great deal of rain.—*Tobias Myers.*

Lewistown, Pa. — Our Communion meeting occurred May 8 and 9, and we trust we all have been made to feel that it was good for us to be there, and renewed our covenant again. Ministering brethren with us were John Beaver, Abram Myers and John Swigart They gave us good instructions and encouraged us to press onward. We were made to rejoice to learn that some have been made willing to forsake the sinful pleasures of this world, and cast their lot with the people of God. Six in number have been added to the church within the last month, and there are still many precious souls out of the ark of safety, striv-

ing against better light and knowledge. We pray that they may soon see the beauty of the religion of Jesus Christ.—*Sarah Spanogle, May 14.*

Smithville, Ohio.—On Saturday, May 14, occurred our regular, quarterly council. Considerable business was disposed of to the satisfaction of nearly all present. Bro. Samuel Sprankle was with us, and presided over our meeting. Since our last writing one of our number has passed away. Our aged elder,—Bro. George Irvin,—has gone to his reward His voice is heard no more in our councils. At the close of our meeting one dear sister was received by baptism. Bro. F. B. Weimer was elected delegate to Annual Meeting.—*M. C Lichtenwalter, May 17.*

MATRIMONIAL.

"What therefore God hath joined together, let not man put asunder."

PELLMAN—SHELLENBERGER.—At the residence of Bro. Abraham Bennet, the bride's uncle, May 5, 1892, by the writer, Mr. Charles G. Pellman and sister Lizzie Shellenberger, all of Richfield, Juniata Co., Pa.
     S. S. Beaver.

MATHES—STRAYER. — At the residence of the bride's parents, May 11, 1892, by the undersigned, Mr. Albert Mathes, of Norton, Kans., and Miss Mary Strayer, of Rockwell City, Kans.   G. M. Throne.

PRICE—ATKINS.—At the home of the bride's father, in Phillips County, Kans., April 24, 1892, by the writer, Mr. William R. Price and sister Nancy E. Atkins.
     J. W. Jarbor.

→ FALLEN ASLEEP ←

"Blessed are the dead which die in the Lord."

MILLER.—At Altoona, Pa., of pneumonia, Sylvania, daughter of Abram and sister Charlotte Miller, aged 9 months and 13 days. Funeral services by the writer.
     D. S. Brallier.

HIMES. — At Dorrance, Kans., May 6, 1892, Bro. Levi Himes, aged 80 years, 6 months and 8 days. He came to Kansas twenty years ago.   Wm. B. Himes.

CRIPE.—In the Goshen church, Elkhart Co., Ind., Jan. 21, 1892, Bro. David M. Cripe, aged 70 years, 7 months and 24 days. Deceased was born in Montgomery, Ohio, May 27, 1821, and came to Elkhart County, Ind., with his parents, when quite young. He leaves a wife and two children. Funeral services conducted by Bro. Joseph Kolb, assisted by Bro. Neff, from 2 Cor. 5: 1.
     Wm. Livengelter.

DITCH.—In the Elkhart Valley church, in the City of Elkhart, Ind., April 30, 1892, Bro. Henry Ditch, aged 66 years, 7 months and 10 days. Text, 2 Cor. 5: 1, 10
     Jos. S. Kulp.

AUVIL.—At her residence in the Cove church, Bedford Co., W. Va., May 5, 1892, sister Mary Auvil, wife of Bro. Elias Auvil, aged 69 years and 8 months. She had for some time been a sufferer from heart disease. On the day of her death she was about her work as usual and had arranged for an extra day's work, but at 10 A. M. she dropped dead. She had, for forty-three years, been a member of the German Baptist church.
     A. C. Bowman.

SHIRA.—Also, in the same church, May 6, 1892, Eddie Jefferson, son of Anthony and Blanche Shira, aged 13 years, 11 months and 13 days. Funeral services by the writer, from John 11: 25, 26.
     A. B. Lichtenwalter.

ATKINS.—In the Pleasant View congregation, Phillips Co., Kans., April 13, 1892, sister Nancy Atkins, wife of friend S. J. Atkins, aged 56 years, 2 months and 11 days. She leaves a husband and nine children. Funeral services by the writer at their home. Text, 1 Sam. 20: 18, latter clause, and 1 Thess. 4: 13, 14.   J. W. Jarbor.

DIXON.—In Savanna, Carroll Co., Ill., May 4, 1892, Emma, daughter of Bro. Frank and sister Mary Dixon, aged 4 years, 11 months and 10 days. Her remains were brought to the Hickory Grove cemetery for interment. Funeral services were conducted by Eld. Geo. D. Zollen.   Lizzie Zollers.

LYDICK.—In the Manor congregation, Indiana County, Pa., Feb. 14, 1892, sister Frances, wife of friend Jacob Lydick, aged 49 years, 9 months and 26 days. Occasion improved by the writer from Mark 14: 8 and Rev. 7: 14.

FYOCK.—In the same vicinity, March 28, 1892, Lottie, infant daughter of friend Jacob C. and Rebecca Fyock, aged 9 months and 15 days. Funeral text, 2 Sam. 12: 23.
     Joseph Holsopple.

MITCHELL.—In the bounds of the New Hope church, Cherokee Co., Kans., March 16, 1892, Alonzo Mitchell, infant son of Geo. W. and C. Mitchell. He was not quite a year old. Funeral services by the writer and Mr. Tobias, of the U. B. Church. Text, Matt. 18: 3.

SMITH.—In the Ten Mile congregation, March 28, 1892, of *La Grippe*, Bro. Israel Smith, aged 77 years, 9 months and 12 days. He was a member of the Brethren or German Baptist church since 1842, and was one of the strong pillars of the church in the congregation in which he lived. Funeral sermon by F. M. Wood, minister of the Disciple church, from 2 Tim. 1: 10.
     Hannah Smith.

MURPHY.—Near McVeytown, in the Spring Run church, Mifflin Co., Pa., April 18, 1892, Bro. Philip Andrew Murphy, aged 55 years and 23 days. A singular coincidence is that he was born on Easter, March 26, 1837, and died on Easter. He leaves a wife and one son. Funeral sermon by Eld. Abraham Myers.   Emma Bollinger.

KEISER.—In the Panther Creek church, Woodford Co., Ill., April 11, 1892, Bro. Samuel Keiser, aged 80 years, 10 months and 16 days. Deceased was born in Page County, Va., in 1811. He remained there till 1876, when he moved to Illinois, where he spent his last days. He served as deacon in the Brethren church for about twenty years. He passed quietly into everlasting rest.
     G. R. Elles.

STUTSMAN.—In the Rock Run church, Ind., May 2, 1892, after a long illness, of jaundice, Bro. Jacob W. Stutsman, aged 47 years, 5 months and 12 days. Deceased was married May 21, 1865, to Mary Ann Miller. To them were born four sons and one daughter. After her death he married Barbara Hoffman in 1880.   R. W. Davenport.

WALES.—In the Newton church, Harvey Co., Kans., May 10, 1892, sister Catharine Wales, wife of Bro. John Wales, aged 85 years, 6 months and 25 days. She leaves a kind husband and one son, Albert B. Wales. Funeral services by the Brethren.
     Enoch Eby.

MOSSER.—In the German Settlement congregation, Preston Co., W. Va., May 3, 1892, sister Phebe Mosser (née Pike), wife of Bro. Henry Mosser, aged 21 years, 11 months and 24 days. Feb. 15, 1891, they were united in marriage. The funeral services were preached in the Brethren's church at Maple Spring by the writer, assisted by Bro. Jonas Pike.   Tobias S. Fike.

BLOUGH.—In the Quemahoning congregation, Somerset Co., Pa., May 6, 1892, Christena Blough, aged 87 years, 2 months and 4 days. She was the mother of ten children. She was a faithful member of the Brethren church for more than fifty years. Funeral services to a large congregation, by brethren E. J. Blough and S. P. Zimmerman.
     J. S. Zimmerman.

Allen, Pa.—We had a very good Communion meeting at the Mohler meeting-house, in the Lower Cumberland church, Pa. Bro. Royer was with us. We were glad to get acquainted with him. Our Sunday-school is doing well, though not very large. We have an average of about forty-five scholars.— J. Mihiesley, May 16.

Phoenix, Arizona Ter.—I arrived in the Salt River Valley May 9. Since then I have been looking over the country. There are some brethren here now, and others are on the road. The Brethren have preaching every Sunday. There is government land here that can be taken as homestead, or under the desert act. I would be pleased to have brethren come and see us. I have decided to make this my future home.— W. F. Gillett, May 14.

Gratis, Ohio.—April 3 we met to reorganize our Sunday-school which adjourned last fall. Bro. Isaac Young was chosen to superintend the work, and a full corps of teachers and officers were elected. A teacher's meeting has been begun and the outlook is very encouraging. These meetings are certainly a great help to the Sunday-school work, if teachers will only take hold of the means. May we all seek to promote the Sunday-school cause!—Jenny K. Petry, Secretary, May 3.

Kansas Center Church, Kans. — Our love-feast occasion has just closed. It was a special season of rejoicing from the presence of the Lord. This was clearly manifested, as there were five young men who left the ranks of sin and were buried with Christ in baptism, to rise to walk in newness of life. The power of the Holy Spirit was clearly felt through the preaching of the Word. Eld. George Wise, of Olathe, Kans., officiated. Elders M. Keller, J. O. Brubaker, Daniel Dierdorff, Jonas Hertzler, and our aged elder, George Elliott, of Ellinwood, Kans., were with us and did their part well. Members from adjoining congregations were also present, which added much to our pleasure.—Isaac S. Brubaker, Mitchell, Kans., May 17.

Moscow, Idaho.—The good seed sown here seems to be doing well. We have a better attendance and more interest in our Sunday-school work this spring than ever before. Last Sunday, May 8, after the three o'clock services, we went to the water-side where one dear soul was buried with Christ in baptism. How good it is to start in the Master's cause while yet young! There will probably be two more baptized at our Communion, June 11. Eld. Hodgden goes to Oregon this week to help in church work there. He will be gone about three weeks. The harvest truly is plenteous, but the laborers are few. Pray ye, therefore, the Lord of the harvest, that he will send forth laborers into his harvest!—J. U. G. Stiverson, May 10.

Necosa, Texas.—We rejoice with the dear members of Clay County, Texas. With two other loved ones, I went, April 30, to the above place, and on the same evening, commenced a protracted meeting. From the start there was a good interest. As a result of ten days' meetings, six made confession of faith and were baptized. All were over thirty years of age, except one dear young brother. The prospects are truly encouraging. From indications there are others near the kingdom.—Henry Brubaker, May 13.

Elmated, Ne.—A few members met at Bro. Kelley's in council May 7. We felt it was good to be there, as everything that came before the meeting was disposed of in a Christian spirit. We have no resident minister, but are supplied with preaching by the Prairie View church, which is at a distance of about seventeen miles from here. We would be pleased if a minister could be induced to locate at or near Florence, as there is a good work to be done here. Land is very cheap. —J. K. Miller.

Spring Run, Pa.—Our Communion meeting, April 30, passed off very harmoniously. At our quarterly meeting, March 26, a soliciting, and also a locating committee were appointed. To-day a building committee was appointed for the purpose of building a meeting-house in Bratton Township, on the farm of Bro. Abraham Grassmyer. The house is very much needed on the south side of the Juniata River. Since Jan. 1 twenty-three have been received by baptism, and three by letter.—Emma Bollinger, McVeytown, Pa.

Sheldon, Iowa.—Last Sunday morning I boarded the train at Sheldon for Edna, Lyon Co., to fill an appointment in the Edna school-house, a small town on the Illinois Central Railroad. Here I found a flourishing Sunday-school, superintended by Bro. Wm. Leonard. At this place we have nine members. Here I found brother and sister A. Shrader, formerly of Franklin Grove, Lee Co., Ill. The people at Edna enjoy preaching. The house was well filled with eager listeners. Health in general is good. We have a great deal of rain.—Tobias Myers.

Lewistown, Pa. — Our Communion meeting occurred May 8 and 9, and we trust we all have been made to feel that it was good for us to be there, and renewed our covenant again. Ministering brethren with us were John Beaver, Abram Myers and John Swigart They gave us good instructions and encouraged us to press onward. We were made, to rejoice to learn that some have been made willing to forsake the sinful pleasures of this world, and cast their lot with the people of God. Six in number have been added to the church within the last month, and there are still many precious souls out of the ark of safety, striving against better light and knowledge. We pray that they may soon see the beauty of the religion of Jesus Christ.—Sarah Spanogle, May 16.

Smithville, Ohio.—On Saturday, May 14, occurred our regular, quarterly council. Considerable business was disposed of to the satisfaction of nearly all present. Bro. Samuel Sprankle was with us, and presided over our meeting. Since our last writing one of our number has passed away. Our aged elder,—Bro. George Irvin,—has gone to his reward His voice is heard no more in our councils. At the close of our meeting one dear sister was received by baptism. Bro. F. B. Weimer was elected delegate to Annual Meeting. —M. C Lichtenwalter, May 17.

MATRIMONIAL.

"What therefore God hath joined together, let not man put asunder."

PELLMAN—SHELLENBERGER.—At the residence of Bro. Abraham Renner, the bride's uncle, May 5, 1892, by the writer, Mr. Charles G. Pellman and sister Lizzie Shellenberger, all of Richfield, Juniata Co., Pa.
S. S. Beaver.

MATHES—STRAYER. — At the residence of the bride's parents, May 11, 1892, by the undersigned, Mr. Albert Mathes, of Norton, Kans., and Miss Mary Strayer, of Rockwell City, Kans.   G. M. Throne.

PRICE—ATKINS.—At the home of the bride's father, in Phillips County, Kans., April 24, 1892, by the writer, Mr. William R. Price and sister Nancy E. Atkins.
J. W. Jarboe.

→ FALLEN ASLEEP ←

"Blessed are the dead which die in the Lord."

MILLER.—In Altoona, Pa., of pneumonia, Sylvania, daughter of Abram and sister Charlotte Miller, aged 9 months and 13 days. Funeral services by the writer.
D. S. Brallier.

HIMES.— At Dorrance, Kans., May 6, 1892, Bro. Levi Himes, aged 80 years, 6 months and 8 days. He came to Kansas twenty years ago.   Wm. B. Himes.

CRIPE.—In the Goshen church, Elkhart Co., Ind., Jan. 21, 1891, Bro. David M. Cripe, aged 70 years, 7 months and 24 days. Deceased was born in Montgomery, Ohio, May 27, 1821, and came to Elkhart County, Ind., with his parents, when quite young. He leaves a wife and ten children. Funeral services conducted by Bro. Joseph Kolb, assisted by Bro. Neff, from 2 Cor. 5: 1.
Wm. Lindofelter.

DITCH.—In the Elkhart Valley church, in the City of Elkhart, Ind., April 30, 1892, Bro. Henry Ditch, aged 66 years, 7 months and 10 days. Text, 2 Cor. 5: 1, 10
Jos, S. Kulp.

AUVIL.—At her residence in the Cove church, Barbour Co., W. Va., May 5. 1892, sister Mary Auvil, wife of Bro. Elias Auvil, aged 69 years and 6 months. Deceased had for some time been a sufferer from heart disease. On the day of her death she was about her work as usual and had arranged for an extra day's work, but at 10 A. M. she dropped dead. She had, for forty-three years, been a member of the German Baptist church.
A. C. Bowman.

SHIRA.—Also, in the same church, May 6, 1892, Eddie Jefferson, son of Anthony and Blanche Shira, aged 13 years, 11 months and 13 days. Funeral services by the writer, from John 11: 25, 26.
A. B. Lichtenwalter.

ATKINS.—In the Pleasant View congregation, Phillips Co., Kans., April 13, 1892, sister Nancy Atkins, wife of friend S. J. Atkins, aged 56 years, 2 months and 1 day. She leaves a husband and nine children. Funeral services by the writer at their home. Text, 1 Sam. 20: 18, latter clause, and 1 Thess. 4: 13, 14.   J. W. Jarboe.

DIXON.—In Savanna, Carroll Co., Ill., May 4, 1892, Emma, daughter of Bro. Frank and sister Mary Dixon, aged 4 years, 11 months and 10 days. Her remains were brought to the Hickory Grove cemetery for interment. Funeral services were conducted by Eld. Geo. D. Zollers. Lizzie Zollers.

LYDICK.—In the Manor congregation, Indiana County, Pa., Feb. 24, 1892, sister Frances, wife of friend Jacob Lydick, aged 49 years, 9 months and 26 days. Occasion improved by the writer from Mark 14: 8 and Rev. 7: 14.

FYOCK.—In the same vicinity, March 28, 1892, Lottie, infant daughter of friend Jacob C. and Rebecca Fyock, aged 9 months and 15 days. Funeral text, 2 Sam. 12: 23.
Joseph Holsopple.

MITCHELL.—In the bounds of the New Hope church, Cherokee Co., Kans., March 16, 1892, Alonzo Mitchell, infant son of Geo. W. and C. Mitchell. He was not quite a year old. Funeral services by the writer and Mr. Tobias, of the U. B. Church. Text, Matt. 18: 3.

SMITH.—In the Ten Mile congregation, March 28, 1892, of La Grippe, Bro. Israel Smith, aged 77 years, 9 months and 12 days. He was a member of the Brethren or German Baptist church since 1842, and was one of the strong pillars of the church in the congregation in which he lived. Funeral sermon by P. M. Wood, minister of the Disciple church, from 2 Tim. 1: 10.
Hannah Smith.

MURPHY.— Near McVeytown, in the Spring Run church, Mifflin Co., Pa., April 18, 1892, Bro. Philip Andrew Murphy, aged 55 years and 23 days. A singular coincidence is that he was born on Easter, March 26, 1837, and died on Easter. He leaves a wife and one son. Funeral sermon by Eld. Abraham Myers.   Emma Bollinger.

KEISER.—In the Panther Creek church, Woodford Co., Ill., April 11, 1892, Bro. Samuel Keiser, aged 80 years, 11 months and 16 days. Deceased was born in Page County, Va., in 1811. He remained there till 1876, when he moved to Illinois, where he spent his last days. He served as deacon in the Brethren church for about twenty years. He passed quietly into everlasting rest.
G. R. Eller.

STUTSMAN.—In the Rock Run church, Ind., May 2, 1892, after a long illness, of jaundice, Bro. Jacob W. Stutsman, aged 47 years, 5 months and 12 days. Deceased was married. After her death he married Barbara Hoffman in 1880.   R. W. Davenport.

WALES.—In the Newton church, Harvey Co., Kans., May 10, 1892, sister Catherine Wales, wife of Bro. John Wales, aged 85 years, 6 months and 25 days. She leaves a kind husband and one son, Albert B. Wales. Funeral services by the Brethren.
Enoch Eby.

MOSSER.— In the German Settlement congregation, Preston Co., W. Va., May 3, 1892, sister Phebe Mosser (nee Pike), wife of Bro. Henry Mosser, aged 21 years, 11 months and 24 days. Feb. 15, 1891, they were united in marriage. The funeral services were preached in the Brethren's church at Maple Spring, by the writer, assisted by Bro. Jesse Pike.   Tobias S. Fike.

BLOUGH.—In the Quemahoning congregation, Somerset Co., Pa., May 6, 1892, Christina Blough, aged 87 years, 5 months and 4 days. She was the mother of ten children. She was a faithful member of the Brethren church for more than fifty years. Funeral services to a large congregation, by brethren E. J. Blough and S. P. Zimmerman.
J. S. Zimmerman.

WE do not often give a personal endorsement to advertisements, but we are convinced that our townsman, Mr. Brayton, has a humane means of destroying the horns on cattle. Last week he showed us the skull of a calf five weeks old, which had been killed for veal, upon which a few drops of his "Horn Preventer" had been placed when it was a few days old. A slight depression on either side of the skull showed where the horns would have been if the "Preventer" had not been applied; otherwise, the skull is perfectly smooth. This method of producing hornless cattle must commend itself to the humane man. It is certainly much better than dehorning cattle after the horns have grown to a considerable size. It is painless and can be applied in a very short time and it does the work effectually. The merciful man is merciful to his beast and he will take that method of performing a necessary operation which will produce the least suffering. We have known Mr. Brayton for a number of years and believe he will do all he promises. This is not a paid advertisement and was written in the interest of what we believe to be a humane remedy. His advertisement will be found in another column.

Announcements.

LOVE-FEASTS.

June 1, in the Yellow Creek church, Elkhart Co., Ind., 7 miles south-west of Goshen.

June 1, at 4 P. M., Yellow Creek church, Elkhart Co., Ind.

June 1, at 4 P. M., South Beatrice church, Gage Co., Nebr. Those coming via U. P. R. R., stop at Holmesville; via the B. & M. R. R., should stop off at Beatrice; via the Rock Island R. R., should stop at Rockford.

June 1, at 2 P. M., at Flora, Ind. Train due here from the south at 10 A. M.

June 1, at 4 P. M., White church, Montgomery Co., Ind., 4½ miles west of Colfax, Ind.

June 2, at 10 A. M., Buck Creek, Franklin Co., Pa. at the Shank meeting-house, 7½ miles south of Greencastle.

June 2 and 3, at 2 P. M., Yellow Creek, Ill.

June 2, at 2 P. M., in the Palestine church, Darke Co., Ohio.

June 2, at 2 P. M., Upper Fall Creek church, 2 miles east of Middletown, Henry Co., Ind.

June 2, at 5 P. M., Pleasant Valley church, Elkhart Co., Ind.

June 2, at 10 A. M., Eel River church, Ind.

June 2, at 10 A. M., Cedar Lake congregation, near Corunna, Dekalb Co., Ind.

June 2 and 3, at 10 A. M., Astoria church, Ill.

June 2, at 3 P. M., in the Salimony church, at Lancaster, 5 miles south of Huntington, Ind.

June 2, Palestine church, Ohio. Members will be met at New Madison and Clark's Station on the "Big Four R. R." by notifying Moses Hollinger, New Madison, Ohio.

June 2, at 4 P. M., in the Okaw church, Piatt Co., Ill. Ministering brethren on their way to Annual Meeting, will please stop with us.

June 3, Tippecanoe church, Kosciusko Co., Ind.

June 3, at 2 P. M., Walnut Level church, Wells Co., Ind.

June 3, at 2 P. M., Blue Ridge church, Piatt Co., Ill.

June 4, at 10 A. M., Springfield congregation, Wawaka, Ind.

June 4 and 5, at 4 P. M., 6½ miles south-west of Summerfield, Kans.

June 4, at 5 P. M., Mound church, Bates Co., Mo.

June 6, at 2 P. M., Berkeley church, W. Va.

June 4, at 10 A. M., Lick Creek church, Williams Co., Ohio, 1 mile south-west of Bryan.

June 4, at 4 P. M., Brownsville, Md.

June 6, at 3 P. M., Maple Valley church, Iowa.

June 4, at 2 P. M., 3¾ miles south-east of Summitville, Ind.

June 4, at 5 P M., Mound church, Bates Co., Mo.

June 7, West Conestoga church, at the Middle Creek house, Lancaster Co., Pa,

June 8, at 1 P. M., Ephrata, Pa., at the Mohler house.

June 8, White Oak church, at the Pennville house, Lancaster Co., Pa.

June 11, 5½ miles North-west of Cabool, Mo.

June 11, at 2 P. M., Cornell church, Ill., on the Streator Branch of the Wabash R. R.

June 11 22nd 12, 10 10 A. M., Greene church, Greene, Iowa. There will be preaching on Friday evening previous.

June 11, at 4 P. M., Quemahoning church, Somerset Co., Pa.

June 11, at 4 P. M., in the Fairview church, Pa.

June 11, Longmont, Colo.

June 11, at 10 A. M., Bellville church, Republic Co., Kans.

June 11, at 3 P. M., Kingsley church, four miles southeast of Kingsley, Iowa.

June 11, at 2 P. M., in the Monitor church, 8 miles west and 2 miles south of McPherson, Kans.

June 11, at 10 A. M., Hudson, Ill.

June 11, at 10 A. M., Beltsville church, Kans.

June 11, at 2:5 P. M., in the Bethel congregation, Kosciusko Co., Ind., at the Pleasant View Chapel, three miles east of Milford

June 11, St. Vrain church, Colo.

June 11 and 12, 10 10 A. M, in the Richland church, Richland County, Ohio, six miles north of Mansfield.

June 11, at 1 P. M., North Beatrice church, Nebr.

June 11 and 12, Kindy church, Woodbury Co., Iowa.

June 11, Fairview church, Iowa,

June 11, at 10 A. M., in the west house, Thornapple church, Mich. Take the D. L. & N. R. R. from Grand Rapids, Mich., to Elmdale, where you will be met by notifying L. D. Fry, Elmdale, Mich.

June 11, at 10 A. M., Chippewa church, Wayne Co., Pa.

June 11, Plum Creek church, Pa. A series of meetings to begin one week previous. Eld. S. H. Meyers is expected to be with us.

June 11, at 4 P. M., Summit church, Somerset Co., Pa.

June 11, at 4 P. M., in the Shade Creek congregation, Somerset Co., Pa.

June 11, Good Hope church, Colo., 7 miles north of Holyoke.

June 11, at 4 P. M., Camp Creek church, Kosciusko Co., Ind., 4 miles North of Etna Green. These coming from the West at 11 M. and East at 2 P. M., will find conveyance to the church.

June 15 and 16, Dallas Center church, Iowa.

June 16, at 2 P. M., Pigeon River church, Ind.

June 17, at 4 P. M., Yellow River congregation, Marshall Co., Ind.

June 18, at the Center Meeting house, Canton, Stark Co., Ohio.

June 18, at 6 P. M., in the Eagle Creek church, Ohio. A series of meetings will be held in connection, beginning June 16.

June 18 and 19, 10 10 A. M., Iowa River church, Iowa.

June 18, at 2 P. M., Cebus church 4¾ miles south-west of Colfax and 3 miles north of Coldwater, Ohio.

June 18, at 1 P. M., Wad.m's Grove, Stephenson Co., Ill.

June 18 and 19, Panther Creek, Dallas Co., Iowa.

June 18, 10 10 A. M., South Waterloo church, Waterloo, Iowa.

June 18, Green Spring District, Seneca Co., Ohio.

June 18, at Level Dick's, th 10 miles south of Custer, Morton Co., Mich.

June 18 and 19, at 11 A. M., Middle Creek church, Mahaska Co., Iowa.

June 18, 10 10 A. M., Brick church, Ten Mile congregation, about 12 miles South-east of Washington, Pa. There will be one week's meeting previous to the feast.

June 19, at 4 P. M., in Rock Run church, Elkhart Co., Ind.

June 22, at 4 P. M., five miles south-east of Goshen, at the Rock Run church, Ind.

June 20 and 23, Coon River church, near Panora, Iowa.

June 25, at 10 A. M., at the Van Wert church, seven miles north-east of Van Wert, Ohio. Those com'ng by rail will be met at Van Wert, day before the meeting by notifying Jacob Heistand, or Joseph Longanecker, Wetzel, Ohio.

June 25 and 26, Indian Creek church, Polk Co., Iowa.

June 25 and 26, at 2 P. M., Hickory Grove, Ill.

Oct. 8, 10 2 P. M., Kaskaskia church, Fayette Co., Ill., ten miles south-west of Bacher City, Ill. Those coming by rail will be met at the above-named place by informing Granville Nevinger.

Annual Meeting at Cedar Rapids.

For the coming Conference at Cedar Rapids, June next, "THE IOWA ROUTE," Burlington, Cedar Rapids & Northern Ry., offers you unrivalled accommodations, operating in connection with the Chicago, Rock Island & Pacific, and Rock Island and Peoria Rys., making good connections at Chicago and Peoria with all eastern lines; at Kansas City with all south western lines; at Omaha, with western lines. And in connection with the St. L. K. & N. W. R. R. at St. Louis, with south, south-eastern and south-western lines, a system of through train service being operated from above points, assures you of a quick and pleasant journey. Special trains will be run from various points to accommodate the demands of the business. All trains stop at the Union Depot in Cedar Rapids. Those traveling via this route may be assured of first-class accommodations and courteous treatment. For further information, as to rates of fare, time of trains, etc., apply to any agent of the above-named lines, or to

J. E. HANNEGAN,
G. T. & P. A., B. C. R. & N. R'y.
Cedar Rapids, Iowa.

Gospel Chimes.

BY WM. BEERY.

A new edition of this deservedly-popular Sunday-school song-book has just been issued.

Bro. Beery has had a large experience in Sunday-school work, and the book which we offer to the Brethren, and the public in general, evinces the exercise of talent as well as good judgment. The religious purity of the hymns, contributed by sister Beery, adds much to the excellence of the book.

Price per single copy, 35 cts.; per dozen, by mail, $3.50; by express, $3.50. Lots of more than a dozen must be sent by express.

BRETHREN'S PUBLISHING Co.,
Or Huntingdon, Pa. Mt. Morris Ill.

A Good Living

may be made by energetic persons in selling farm and township rights for the HOLLINGER FENCE. Scarcely any effort is required to sell this fence, as it needs only to be seen to be appreciated. If you want to help others while helping yourself, be sure to sell the Hollinger Fence, for many have regretted that they did not know of it sooner. For the special accommodation of those who may wish to see our fence, we have constructed a sample fence convenient to the Annual Meeting grounds, at Cedar Rapids, and will give any information desired at 'our office, one block west of the Annual Meeting grounds. Come and see us, or if not at the Meeting, address the HOLLINGER FENCE CO., Covington, Ohio.

CANCERS, TUMORS, ETC.

Successfully treated by Dr. G. N. Botzler, of Waynesborough, Pa., where he has practiced for the last sixteen years. Dr. Botzler is a graduate of the University of Maryland, at Baltimore City. References given and correspondence solicited. Address, Dr. G. W. Botzler, Waynesborough, Pa.

The Annual Meeting of German Baptist Brethren at Cedar Rapids, Iowa, June 3 to 9 inclusive.

Tickets for the above meeting will be good going from May 28 to June 4, good to return till June 30.

THE ILLINOIS CENTRAL RAILROAD is the popular and direct route from Chicago to Cedar Rapids. Two First-class express trains, equipped with beautiful, free, reclining chair cars, leave Chicago daily at 11:30 P. M. and 11:35 P. M., arriving at Cedar Rapids at 11 P. M. and 11 A. M.

A large number of the Brethren from the different Eastern States have already decided to take this favorite route.

Tickets will be on sale at all railroad coupon ticket offices in the East.

DON'T FAIL to ask for tickets via the Illinois Central R R from Chicago.

For further detailed information write

A. J. MCDONGALL,
Eastern Pass. Agt., I. C. R. R.,
343 Broadway, New York.

We do not often give a personal endorsement to advertisements, but we are convinced that our townsman, Mr. Brayton, has a humane means of destroying the horns on cattle. Last week he showed us the skull of a calf five weeks old, which had been killed for veal, upon which a few drops of his "Horn Preventer" had been placed when it was a few days old. A slight depression on either side of the skull showed where the horns would have been if the "Preventer" had not been applied; otherwise, the skull is perfectly smooth. This method of producing hornless cattle must commend itself to the humane man. It is certainly much better than dehorning cattle after the horns gave grown to a considerable size. It is painless and can be applied in a very short time and it does the work effectually. The merciful man is merciful to his beast and he will take that method of performing a necessary operation which will produce the least suffering. We have known Mr. Brayton for a number of years and believe he will do all he promises. This is not a paid advertisement and was written in the interest of what we believe to be a humane remedy. His advertisement will be found in another column.

Announcements.

LOVE FEASTS.

June 1, in the Yellow Creek church, Elkhart Co., Ind., 3 miles south-west of Goshen.

June 1, at 1 P. M., Yellow Creek church, Elkhart Co., Ind.

June 1, at 1 P. M., South Beatrice church, Gage Co., Nebr. Those coming via U. P. R. R., stop at Holmesville; via the B. & M. R. R., should stop at Beatrice; via the Rock Island R. R., should stop at Rockford.

June 1, at 2 P. M., at Flora, Ind. Train leaves from the south at 10 A. M.

June 2, at 2 P. M., White church, Montgomery Co., Ind., 4½ miles west of Colfax, Ind.

June 2, at 10 A. M., Back Creek, Franklin Co., Pa. at the Shank meeting-house, 1¾ miles south of Greentastle.

June 2 and 3, at 2 P. M., Yellow Creek, Ill.

June 2, at 10 A. M., in the Palestine church, Darke Co., Ohio.

June 2, at 2 P. M., Upper Fall Creek church, 2 miles east of Middletown, Henry Co., Ind.

June 2, at 2 P. M., Pleasant Valley church, Elkhart Co., Ind.

June 3, at 10 A. M., Eel River church, Ind.

June 3, at 10 A. M., Cedar Lake congregation, near Corunna, Dekalb Co., Ind.

June 2 and 3, at 10 A. M., Astoria church, Ill.

June 7, at 3 P. M., in the Salimony church, at Lancaster, 3 miles south of Huntington, Ind.

June 2, Palestine church, Ohio. Members will be met at New Madison and Clark's Station via the "Big Four R. R." by notifying Moses Hollinger, New Madison, Ohio.

June 2, at 4 P. M., in the Ozaw church, Platt Co., Ill. Ministering brethren on their way to Annual Meeting, will please stop with us.

June 7, Tippecanoe church, Kosciusko Co., Ind.

June 3, at 2 P. M., Walnut Level church, Wells Co., Ind.

June 3, at 4 P. M., Blue Ridge church, Platt Co., Ill.

June 2, at 10 A. M., Springfield congregation, Wawaka, Ind.

June 2 and 3, at 4 P. M., 6½ miles south-west of Summerfield, Kans.

June 3 at 5 P. M., Mound church, Bates Co., Mo.

June 4, at 1 P. M., Berkey church, W. Va.

June 4, at 10 A. M., Lick Creek church, Williams Co., Ohio, 1 mile south-west of Bryan.

June 4, at 2 P. M., Brownsville, Md.

June 4, at 3 P. M., Maple Valley church, Iowa.

June 4, at 2 P. M., 3½ miles north-east of Summitville, Ind.

June 6, at 5 P. M., Mound church, Bates Co., Mo.

June 7, West Conestoga church, at the Middle Creek house, Lancaster Co., Pa.

June 8, at 1 P. M., Ephrata, Pa., at the Mohler house.

June 8, White Oak church, at the Penoville house, Lancaster Co., Pa.

June 10, 3½ miles north-west of Cabool, Mo.

June 10, at 2 P. M., Conestoga church, Ill., on the Streator Branch of the Wabash R. R.

June 11 and 12, at 10 A. M., Greene church, Greene, Iowa. There will be preaching on Friday evening previous.

June 11, at 6 P. M., Quemahoning church, Somerset Co., Pa.

June 11, at 2 P. M., in the Fairview church, Pa.

June 11, Longmont, Colo.

June 11, at 10 A. M., Belleville church, Republic Co., Kans.

June 11, at 3 P. M., Kingsley church, four miles south-east of Kingsley, Iowa.

June 11, at 2 P. M., in the Monitor church, 2 miles West and 2 miles south of McPherson, Kans.

June 11, at 10 A. M., Hudson, Ill.

June 11, at 10 A. M., Belleville church, Kans.

June 11, at 2 P. M., in the Bethel congregation, Kosciusko Co., Ind., at the Pleasant View Chapel, three miles east of Milford.

June 11, St. Vrain church, Colo.

June 11 and 12, at 10 A. M., in the Richland church, Richland County, Ohio, 2½ miles north of Mansfield.

June 11, at 4 P. M., North Beatrice church, Nebr.

June 11 and 12, Kintly church, Woodbury Co., Iowa.

June 11, Fairview church, Iowa.

June 11, at 10 A. M., in the west house, Thornapple church, Mich. Take the D. L. & N. R. R. from Grand Rapids, Mich., to Elmdale, where you will be met by notifying L. D. Fry, Elmdale, Mich.

June 11, at 10 A. M., Chippewa church, Wayne Co., Ohio.

June 12, Plum Creek church, Pa. A series of meetings to begin one week previous. Eld. S. H. Meyers is expected to be with us.

June 12, at 4 P. M., Summit church, Somerset Co., Pa.

June 12, at 4 P. M., in the Shade Creek congregation, Somerset Co., Pa.

June 14, Good Hope church, Colo., 7 miles north of Holyoke.

June 13, at 2 P. M., Camp Creek church, Kosciusko Co., Ind., 4 miles North of Etna Green. Those coming from the West at 12 M. and East at 2 P. M., will find conveyance to the church.

June 15 and 16, Dallas Center church, Iowa.

June 16, at 2 P. M., Pigeon River church, Ind.

June 17, at 4 P. M., Yellow River congregation, Marshall Co., Ind.

June 18, at the Cedar Meeting house, Carroll, Stark Co., Ohio.

June 18, at 5 P. M., in the Eagle Creek church, Ohio. A series of meetings will be held in connection, beginning June 16.

June 18 and 19, at 10 A. M., Iowa River church, Iowa.

June 18, at 2 P. M., Colfax church, 2½ miles south-west of Colfax and 3 miles north of Coldwater, Ohio.

June 18, at 2 P. M., World An's Grove, Stephenson Co., Ill.

June 18 and 19, Panther Creek, Dallas Co., Iowa.

June 18, at 10 A. M., South Waterloo church, Waterloo, Iowa.

June 18, Grass Spring District, Seneca Co., Ohio.

June 18, at Levi Dake's, in 10 miles south of Custer, Mason Co., Mich.

June 18 and 19, at 11 A. M., Middle Creek church, Mahaska Co., Iowa.

June 18, at 2 P. M., Brick church, Ten Mile congregation, about 10 miles south-east of Washington, Pa. There will be one week's meeting previous to the feast.

June 22, at 4 P. M., in Rock Run church, Elkhart Co., Ind.

June 22, at 2 P. M., five miles south-east of Goshen, at the Rock Run church, Ind.

June 20 and 21, Oboe River church, near Peoria, Iowa.

June 25, at 10 A. M., at the Van Wert church, seven miles north-east of Van Wert, Ohio. Those coming by rail will be met at Van Wert, day before the meeting by notifying Jacob Heistand, or Joseph Longanecker, Wetzel, Ohio.

June 25 and 26, Indian Creek church, Polk Co., Iowa.

June 25 and 26, at 2 P. M., Hickory Grove, Ill.

Oct. 7, at 2 P. M., Kaskaskia church, Fayette Co., Ill., ten miles south-west of Shobet City, Ill. Those coming by rail will be met at the above-named place by informing Granville Nevinger.

Annual Meeting at Cedar Rapids.

For the coming Conference at Cedar Rapids, June next, "THE IOWA ROUTE," Burlington, Cedar Rapids & Northern Ry., offers you unexcelled accommodations, especially in connection with the Chicago, Rock Island & Pacific, and Rock Island and Peoria Rys., making good connections at Chicago and Peoria with all eastern lines; at Kansas City with all south-western lines; at Omaha with all western lines. Also in connection with the St. L. K. & N. W. R. R. at St. Louis, with south, south-eastern, and south-western lines, a system of through trails service being operated from above points, assuring you of a quick and pleasant journey. Special trains will be run from various points to accommodate the demands of the business. All trains stop at the Union Depot in Cedar Rapids. Those traveling via this route may be assured of first-class accommodation and courteous treatment. For further information, as to rates of fare, time of trains, etc., apply to any agent of the above-named line, or to

J. E. HANNEGAN,
G. T. & P. A., B. C. R. & N. R'y.
Cedar Rapids, Iowa.

Gospel Chimes.

BY WM. BEERY.

A new edition of this deservedly-popular Sunday-school song-book has just been issued.

Bro. Beery has had a large experience in Sunday-school work, and the book which we offer to the Brethren, and the public in general, evinces the exercise of talent as well as good judgment. The religious purity of the hymns, contributed by sister Beery, adds much to the excellence of the book.

Price per single copy, 25 cts.; per dozen, by mail, $2.50; by express, $2.50. Lots of more than a dozen must be sent by express.

BRETHREN'S PUBLISHING CO.,
Or Huntingdon, Pa. Mt. Morris Ill.

A Good Living

may be made by energetic persons in selling farm and township rights for the HOLLINGER FENCE. Scarcely any effort is required to sell this fence, as it needs only to be seen to be appreciated. If you want to help others while helping yourself, be sure to sell the Hollinger Fence, for many have regretted that they did not know of it sooner. For the special accommodation of those who may wish to see our fence, we have constructed a sample fence convenient to the Annual Meeting grounds, at Cedar Rapids, and will give any information desired at our office, one block west of the Annual Meeting grounds. Come and see us, or if not at the Meeting, address the HOLLINGER FENCE CO., Covington, Ohio.

CANCERS, TUMORS, ETC.

Successfully treated by Dr. G. N. Boteler, of Waynesborough, Pa., where he has practiced for the last sixteen years. Dr. Boteler is a graduate of the University of Maryland, at Baltimore City. References given and correspondence solicited. Address, Dr. G. W. Boteler, Waynesborough, Pa. 9tf60

The Annual Meeting of German Baptist Brethren at Cedar Rapids, Iowa, June 3 to 9 inclusive.

Tickets for the above meeting will be good going from May 28 to June 4, good to return till June 30.

THE ILLINOIS CENTRAL RAILROAD is the popular and direct route from Chicago to Cedar Rapids. Two First-class express trains, equipped with beautiful, free, reclining chair cars, leave Chicago daily at 1:30 P. M. and 11:35 P. M., arriving at Cedar Rapids at 11 P. M. and 11 A. M.

A large number of the Brethren from the different Eastern States have already decided to take this favorite route.

Tickets will be on sale at all railroad coupon ticket offices in the East.

DON'T FAIL to ask for tickets via the Illinois Central R. R. from Chicago.

For further information write

A. J. McDONGALL,
Eastern Pass. Agt., I. C. R. R.,
343 Broadway, New York.

➺ESSAYS➻

"Study to show thyself approved unto God; a workman that needeth not be ashamed, rightly dividing the Word of Truth."

THE FIRST ROSE OF SUMMER.

BY J. S. MOHLER.

THE wintry winds have moaned
The death of flowers that bloomed,
And leaves that fell below
In graves of ice and snow.
All Nature crape has worn,
Since death her beauty 's shorn.
The songs of birds no more
Along this dismal shore
Were heard; but solemn lays,
Through cold and dreary days.
The funeral 's been so long,
We loathe its doleful song,
And long once more to hear
The wooded songsters cheer
The drooping heart along
The way to Father's home.
Inhale the balmy air
Of landscape, sweet and fair,
And smell the fragrant rose
In scented winds that blow.

A stranger 's at the door,
I've never seen before;
Her blushing, crimson cheeks
Behind her veil, just peep
With such a smiling face,
Adorned with heavenly grace.
From fairer climes has come
To gladden earthly homes.
The first of all her kind,
The rest are just behind,
A hearty welcome finds
In hearts of all mankind.

Oh lovely stranger! · Come
And dwell within my home;
So glad I feel you're here,
You're to my heart so dear,
And do not think me rude,
If I should seem to intrude,
By clinging close to thee,
And press thee close to me
In loving, warm embrace,
And kiss thy tender face.
My heart I can't restrain
On seeing thee again;
With joy it overflows
And drives away my woes.
So long my heart 's been sad,
When all in mourning clad,
I cannot tell how glad
Your coming me has made.
By grace hast come before
And opened wide the door
For all thy kin to come
And bless each sighing home.
I trust you'll with us stay
All through the summer day,
And smooth the thorny way
When grief upon us preys.
Come, lay within my breast,
In peaceful slumber rest,
And by thy cheek to mine;
My arms I'll round thee twine
And draw thee nearer still,
Thy love my heart to fill.
Thy breath, in fragrance sweet,
Makes happiness complete.

Merrill, Kans.

THE COVERING AGAIN.

BY C. H. BALSBAUGH.

Dear Sister:—

YOUR last, inclosing mine, is here. I am always glad to hear from you. Yet I was sad to hear of the new turn your mind is taking, relative to the covering of the head in worship. The reasons you assign for the non-wearing of the veil, are not referred to in the remotest manner in Paul's injunction to the Corinthian sisters. There is nothing essentially Mosaic about it. Its basis is independent of all dispensations. The require-

ment is asserted by Paul, to inhere in the essential nature and relations of our dual humanity. With all humility, and yet with all boldness, I challenge the most expert exegete to show that the apostle was in the faintest degree controlled by either Levitical or conventional considerations.

The reasons for a covering, found in 1 Cor. 11: 1-16, have been valid before the Mosaic Economy, and are as valid for America in the nineteenth century, as for Greece in the first. Why such reasons exist, and why they should have such significance, is a matter for polemical theology, a sphere for which I have neither time nor inclination. But the injunction is in the Inspired Record, and the reason assigned, and that will suffice for faith and humility and loyalty. The reproof administered by the apostle to those, who violate this divine arrangement, is severe, but not necessarily renunciative of the relationship which the covering and uncovering symbolize.

It was not a member of the Jewish Sanhedrim, but an apostle of the New Covenant, who said, that if a woman pray unto God uncovered, it is as great a shame, and as profound a violation of her constitutional relation, Godward and manward, as if she were shorn or shaven. I perfectly accord with you that the symbol is essentially only a symbol, and cannot possibly have any inherent efficacy. And no doubt the dying malefactor is the representative of a larger class than we know.

But when we are fully satisfied that the symbol is really such, appointed by God as expressive of a certain truth or fact, it would require a very peculiar combination of circumstances to justify its omission. Your covering is not more repugnant to those among whom you live and labor, than your feet-washing, and yet there are no such cardinal reasons given for the latter as for the former. God understands Himself, and it is better to believe and obey, than to bring our shallow reason into collision with His infinite understanding.

Union Deposit, Pa.

ANNUAL MEETING INFLUENCE, AND HOW IT SHOULD BE DIRECTED.

BY L. W. TEETER.

As the time of our great annual gathering is approaching, I am very much impressed with the thought of Annual Meeting influence,—what it should be, and how it ought to be directed.

The Annual Conference may be properly regarded as the head of the literal organization of the General Brotherhood. As such it properly administers to the particular organizations, advice, counsel, or discipline, according to their needs. It is, therefore, governmental in character, to every part of the great body,—the Brotherhood,—alike; (1) to State Districts; (2) to congregations; (3) to individual members.

Every department of business should be conducted in the most perfect manner, so that even the methods of doing the public business of the meeting would become a model for conducting business in the several District Meetings, and even in the council-meetings of congregations, so far as they are applicable.

There is no reason why all business of public bodies in the church should not be conducted similarly, that is, in accordance with the accepted rules and principles for conducting public business. If such were the practice in all our business meetings, there would not be the strangeness or awkwardness felt among us that there is, in participating in those meetings.

No unwholesome rule or method should be employed in any meeting,—not even in a congregation.

The Annual Meeting is often referred to as doing business in such and such a way. It should therefore be carefully conducted, so as to be a safe pattern for all meetings of a similar character.

THE PREACHING

Done at Annual Meetings, in all of the preaching sessions, should be in reference to the *principles* of general church work; because the congregations are generally largely made up of *leaders* in church work, and of those who are especially interested in the welfare of the church.

Give them something to take with them to their homes. Being set on fire themselves at Annual Meeting, they will go home and set the church afire where they live.

We might refer to instances where the work, done at Annual Meetings and District Meetings, has yielded a powerful influence upon ministers, and even upon private members, who carried home with them a determination to contend more earnestly and bravely for "the faith once delivered unto the saints," than they had ever done before. This proved, apparently, the salvation of certain congregations.

Preaching done in reference to principles, or outlines, of certain departments of general church work, is also just as interesting to the congregation at large, at Annual Meeting, if not more so, than any other kind of preaching, because a great many persons attend those meetings for the purpose of learning the character of our church work. Many go out of curiosity,—both of which classes will receive more benefits, that will develop to greater proportions in after life, than an ordinary sermon on a common subject, which a minister of any denomination might preach.

In fine, all the characteristics, peculiar to the Brethren church, should be made prominent in the course of the Annual Meeting preaching, as taught in the Gospel, and practiced by the church; for there is no opportunity to so universally scatter seeds of the Truth, at any time or place, than at those meetings.

THE SINGING

Done at Annual Meetings should be with a view wholly to improve, not the singing at Annual Meeting, but in our home congregations. How shall this be done to the best effect?

1. To gain the greatest benefit from Annual Meeting singing, it is important that the same book should be used there that is used in the congregations. (*a*) Because if a hymn or tune is used, and precious time and care are spent to learn it out of a book that is not used in the congregations at home, there is no advantage but the practice of the persons who do the singing at that time.

The time that may be used at Annual Meeting in singing is not sufficient to learn perfectly any tune or hymn, hence one is under necessity to buy such a book, and likely, when he returns home, he will be the only one who has such a book, which will make it impracticable for him to introduce his new hymns or tunes as congregational singing. He, therefore, loses the money paid for the book, his time in learning pieces, which he cannot use in the congregation, and he also loses the opportunity of learning something that he *could* use at home.

(*b*) Since the Brethren's Hymn Book and Hymnal are the recognized congregational singing books of the Brotherhood, those *alone* should be used at our Annual Meetings.

The greatest hindrance in Annual Meeting singing is the lack of books. Hence, to make the singing interesting, both at Annual Meeting and afterwards at home, each one should take with him a Hymnal or Hymn Book to Annual Meeting.

✦ESSAYS✦

"Study to show thyself approved unto God; a workman that needeth not to be ashamed, rightly dividing the Word of Truth."

THE FIRST ROSE OF SUMMER.

BY J. S. MOHLER.

Thᴇ wintry winds have moaned
The death of flowers that bloomed,
In graves of ice and snow.
All Nature crape has worn,
Since death her beauty 's shorn.
The songs of birds no more
Were heard; but solemn lays,
Through cold and dreary days.
The funeral 's been so long,
We loathe its doleful song,
And long once more to hear
The wooded songsters cheer
The drooping heart along
The way to Father's home.
Inhale the balmy air
Of landscape, sweet and fair,
And smell the fragrant rose
In scented winds that blow.

A stranger 's at the door,
I've never seen before;
Her blushing, crimson cheeks
Behind her veil, just peep
With such a smiling face,
Adorned with heavenly grace.
From fairer climes has come
To gladden earthly homes.
The first of all her kind,
The rest are just behind,
A hearty welcome finds
In hearts of all mankind.

Oh lovely stranger! · Come
And dwell within my home;
So glad I feel you're here,
You're to my heart so dear,
And do not think me rude,
If I should seem to intrude,
By clinging close to thee,
And press thee close to me
In loving, warm embrace,
And kiss thy tender face.
My heart I can't restrain
On seeing thee again;
With joy it overflows
And drives away my woes.
So long my heart 's been sad,
When all in mourning clad,
I cannot tell how glad
Your coming me has made.
By grace hast come before
And opened wide the door
For all thy kin to come
And bless each sighing home.
I trust you'll with us stay
All through the summer day,
And smooth the thorny way
When grief upon us preys.
Come, lay within my breast,
In peaceful slumber rest,
And lay thy cheek to mine;
My arms I'll round thee twine
And draw thee nearer still,
Thy love my heart to fill.
Thy breath, in fragrance sweet,
Makes happiness complete.

Morrill, Kans.

THE COVERING AGAIN.

BY C. H. BALSBAUGH.

Dear Sister:—

Your last, inclosing mine, is here. I am always glad to hear from you. Yet I was sad to hear of the new turn your mind is taking, relative to the covering of the head in worship. The reasons you assign for the non-wearing of the veil, are not referred to in the remotest manner in Paul's injunction to the Corinthian sisters. There is nothing essentially Mosaic about it. Its basis is independent of all dispensations. The require-

ment is asserted by Paul, to inhere in the essential nature and relations of our dual humanity. With all humility, and yet with all boldness, I challenge the most expert exegete to show that the apostle was in the faintest degree controlled by either Levitical or conventional considerations.

The reasons for a covering, found in 1 Cor. 11: 1–16, have been valid before the Mosaic Economy, and are as valid for America in the nineteenth century, as for Greece in the first. Why such reasons exist, and why they should have such significance, is a matter for polemical theology, a sphere for which I have neither time nor inclination. But the injunction is in the Inspired Record, and the reason assigned, and that will suffice for faith and humility and loyalty. The reproof administered by the apostle to those, who violate this divine arrangement, is severe, but not necessarily renunciative of the relationship which the covering and uncovering symbolize.

It was not a member of the Jewish Sanhedrim, but an apostle of the New Covenant, who said, that if a woman pray unto God uncovered, it is as great a shame, and as profound a violation of her constitutional relation, Godward and manward, as if she were shorn or shaven. I perfectly accord with you that the symbol is essentially only a symbol, and cannot possibly have any inherent efficacy. And no doubt the dying malefactor is the representative of a larger class than we know. But when we are fully satisfied that the symbol is really such, appointed by God as expressive of a certain truth or fact, it would require a very peculiar combination of circumstances to justify its omission. Your covering is not more repugnant to those among whom you live and labor, than your feet-washing, and yet there are no such cardinal reasons given for the latter as for the former. God understands Himself, and it is better to believe and obey, than to bring our shallow reason into collision with His infinite understanding.

Union Deposit, Pa.

ANNUAL MEETING INFLUENCE, AND HOW IT SHOULD BE DIRECTED.

BY L. W. TEETER.

As the time of our great annual gathering is approaching, I am very much impressed with the thought of Annual Meeting influence,—what it should be, and how it ought to be directed.

The Annual Conference may be properly regarded as the head of the literal organization of the General Brotherhood. As such it properly administers to the particular organizations, advice, counsel, or discipline, according to their needs. It is, therefore, governmental in character, to every part of the great body,—the Brotherhood,—alike; (1) to State Districts; (2) to congregations; (3) to individual members.

Every department of business should be conducted in the most perfect manner, so that even the methods of doing the public business of the meeting would become a model for conducting business in the several District Meetings, and even in the council-meetings of congregations, so far as they are applicable.

There is no reason why all business of public bodies in the church should not be conducted similarly, that is, in accordance with the accepted rules and principles for conducting public business. If such were the practice in all our business meetings, there would not be the strangeness or awkwardness felt among us that there is, in participating in those meetings.

No unwholesome rule or method should be employed in any meeting,—not even in a congregation.

The Annual Meeting is often referred to as doing business in such and such a way. It should therefore be carefully conducted, so as to be a safe pattern for all meetings of a similar character.

THE PREACHING

Done at Annual Meetings, in all of the preaching sessions, should be in reference to the *principles* of general church work; because the congregations are generally largely made up of *leaders* in church work, and of those who are especially interested in the welfare of the church.

Give them something to take with them to their homes. Being set on fire themselves at Annual Meeting, they will go home and set the church afire where they live.

We might refer to instances where the work, done at Annual Meetings and District Meetings, has yielded a powerful influence upon ministers, and even upon private members, who carried home with them a determination to contend more earnestly and bravely for "the faith once delivered unto the saints," than they had ever done before. This proved, apparently, the salvation of certain congregations.

Preaching done in reference to principles, or outlines, of certain departments of general church work, is also just as interesting to the congregation at large, at Annual Meeting, if not more so, than any other kind of preaching, because a great many persons attend those meetings for the purpose of learning the character of our church work. Many go out of curiosity,—both of which classes will receive more benefits, that will develop to greater proportions in after life, than an ordinary sermon on a common subject, which a minister of any denomination might preach.

In fine, all the characteristics, peculiar to the Brethren church, should be made prominent in the course of the Annual Meeting preaching, as taught in the Gospel, and practiced by the church; for there is no opportunity to so universally scatter seeds of the Truth, at any time or place, than at those meetings.

THE SINGING

Done at Annual Meetings should be with a view wholly to improve, not the singing at Annual Meeting, but in our home congregations. How shall this be done to the best effect?

1. To gain the greatest benefit from Annual Meeting singing, it is important that the same book should be used there that is used in the congregations. (*a*) Because if a hymn or tune is used, and precious time and care are spent to learn it out of a book that is not used in the congregations at home, there is no advantage but the practice of the persons who do the singing at that time.

The time that may be used at Annual Meeting in singing is not sufficient to learn perfectly any tune or hymn, hence one is under necessity to buy such a book, and likely, when he returns home, he will be the only one who has such a book, which will make it impracticable for him to introduce his new hymns or tunes as congregational singing. He, therefore, loses the money paid for the book, his time in learning pieces, which he cannot use in the congregation, and he also loses the opportunity of learning something that he *could* use at home.

(*b*) Since the Brethren's Hymn Book and Hymnal are the recognized congregational singing books of the Brotherhood, those *alone* should be used at our Annual Meetings.

The greatest hindrance in Annual Meeting singing is the lack of books. Hence, to make the singing interesting, both at Annual Meeting and afterwards at home, each one should take with him a Hymnal or Hymn Book to Annual Meeting.

All this was done in the same preparation day, in the which Jesus ate the passover. The preparation day in which the passover must be killed, is never called the feast day in which the passover must be eaten, therefore the Jews would not go into the judgment hall lest they should be defiled; but that they might eat the passover. John 18: 28; 19: 14, 31, 42.

My fifth reason is this: The Jews, themselves, declared that they would not take him on the feast day lest there be an uproar among the people. Matt. 26: 4, 5; Mark 14: 2.

I have now set before the reader the difference of time between the passover of the Mosaic law and the one that Jesus Christ instituted and placed between feet-washing and the Communion of the body and blood of Christ, as Paul calls it.

SYMPATHY.

BY ALICE GARBER.

CHRIST died the ignominious death on the cross and suffered untold agonies, and is now at the right hand of the Father, pleading in our behalf. He has suffered and can sympathise with us in our tribulations. True sympathy knows how to feel for another, and that is only from those who have gone through the same fiery trials.

Christ was, and yet is, through his Word, ever ready to give comfort to the broken-hearted. We can do much towards our fellow-men to alleviate the sorrows that oppress us. How much good a few words, spoken in sympathy, will do a poor, afflicted person, both spiritually and physically! Often a word to those who are "almost persuaded," when they need the most sympathy, love and kindness, will cause them to turn from the errors of their way and find the blessed consolation in a Crucified Redeemer.

A kind word to a poor sufferer will brighten their otherwise dull sky, and cause them to think more of the "love of Christ that passeth understanding," and a loving memory will ever enshrine that person. Let us try it!

Christ suffered so that he might sympathize with us, and do we not suffer so we can sympathize with others? I think that is one of the silver linings in the clouds of affliction.

A soul away from Christ needs our keenest sympathy, for what can be more pitiful or a sadder sight? We were all once just where they are now and therefore ought to have compassion on them, and try to win them by loving words. How dear to me are the words of a kind friend who came to me one night after church, and plead with me to give my heart to the Blessed Jesus. They are written on my heart never to be erased, and oh! how often does memory revert to the sympathy she expressed and, I know, felt for poor wretched me! Ofttimes, in sorrow, a single pressure of the hand speaks volumes. Let us not spare the grasp of the hand, and show more sympathy for all. Let us lift up the fallen and tell them that Jesus is MIGHTY to save.

South English, Iowa.

TEMPTING THE LORD.

BY S. D. SMITH.

"And they said unto Moses, Because there were no graves in Egypt, hast thou taken us away to die in the wilderness? wherefore hast thou dealt thus with us, to carry us forth out of Egypt? Is not this the word that we did tell thee in Egypt, saying, Let us alone, that we may serve the Egyptians? For it had been better for us to serve the Egyptians, than that we should die in the wilderness."—Ex. 14: 11, 12.

WHEN the Children of Israel left Egypt they thought they were to be free from bondage, but when they looked back and saw King Pharaoh with his army, following hard upon them, and with the Red Sea before them, they thought escape was impossible, and therefore uttered the above language. They knew that if they ever fell into the king's hands, their burden would be greater.

It is the same way with Satan. When we leave him and decide to follow Jesus, he will surely try to get us to think that religion will be a failure. He tells us that we cannot hold out until the end, tells us of 2 Pet. 2: 20, 22, and tries to discourage us in every way he can. In all these things let us take courage and bear in mind what Peter says in the foregoing chapter.

Let us read a little farther and see the way in which the Lord delivered his people. After they had said what they did, Moses' heart was touched and he cried unto the Lord for help. Why did Moses go to the Lord for help? Why did he not deliver them himself, like a great many of us might have done? Because he felt his weakness. He knew that the Lord had all power in heaven and on earth, and had said that he would be with them, and deliver them from their enemies. Can we not learn a very good lesson from what Moses did?

But is the time of temptation the only time to go to the Lord for help? "Watch and pray that ye enter not into temptation." Matt. 26: 41. Did the Lord help the Children of Israel out of their trouble? Yes, he not only delivered them, but destroyed their enemies, as he had told them. Jesus has made us the very same promise, but he will do nothing unless we make some effort ourselves. God helps those that help themselves.

After their deliverance, their sorrow turned to joy and they sang songs to the Lord. Ex. 15. But it was not long until they fell to murmuring again, when they could not find any water to drink. All those temptations came upon them that their faith might be tried. So are our temptations to try our faith.

Here the query might arise, Who tempts us? The Lord tempts no man, but temptations come upon us that we may grow stronger thereby. Rev. 7: 14.

Just as soon as the Israelites lost their faith, the Lord would allow something to occur, to remind them of the past and of him. It is precisely the same with us, to-day. All these things are for our benefit. Can we not learn to look at them from the right side and profit thereby? Why do we so often look at them in a wrong way? Because of self-righteousness and lack of faith.

The starting out of the Children of Israel, on their journey, is much like a person starting in a religious life. He must travel some little distance before he comes to the Red Sea,—the blood of Christ, or baptism. After that comes the travel through the wilderness of life. Here is that we must work, or travel, in order that we reach the Promised Land. Is the land, that the Children of Israel were to inherit, as grand or as fine a country as the one promised to us? Certainly not. Earth has no place that will compare with heaven.

After the Children of Israel crossed the Red Sea, the first thing that they were in need of was bread and water. The first thing that we need in the spiritual life is the Bread and Water of Life. It is also in this travel, or life, that we tempt the Lord so often. The last thing they had, or that we will have to contend with, is the river Jordan (or death). Can it be possible that just two persons out of the six hundred thousand that left Egypt ever entered the promised land? Matt. 20: 16 and 22: 14. The question that should come to us so forcibly is this: Am I tempting the Lord so much that he will not allow me to enter the promised land?

Sterling, Ohio, Jan. 25.

SICKNESS,—ITS CAUSES AND SPIRITUAL REMEDY.

BY GERTRUDE A. FLORY.

Is God responsible for all the diseases and deaths which occur in the human family? Think what thousands die in the prime of usefulness! and how our blooming youths fade and pass away, and how many go down to the tomb in babyhood! Is this all the work of Providence? Let us illustrate that thought: One frosty autumn morning a mother let her year old baby boy play out doors several hours, barefoot and clothed with only a thin gown. That same day he was taken with membranous croup and died. Several years afterward that mother cursed God in bitterness of heart for taking her baby from her. Another mother, in feeble health, time after time refused her tender husband's offer to secure hired help, and worked on,—entirely unable to work,—until she took her bed for the last time. Her puny babe lingered in pain for two weeks and then died. After suffering beyond endurance, the mother followed her babe, leaving her disconsolate husband with three other children, who needed a mother's care then, more than they had since they were babies in her arms. Of course, there were those who applauded the "ambition" that kept her at work when she was too feeble to work, and sympathetic friends remarked upon the strange Providence that takes a mother from the bosom of her family. But, did God do this? We must admit that there are mysterious incidents in which the hand of Providence is visible, but is it not time that we cease blaming Providence with human errors and carelessness of exposures and overwork? "Facts are stubborn things," and they are bitter things, too, when they point our sufferings and losses back to our neglect of duty; and here is where the causes of much of the sickness and death in our land should be traced, and not to the Divine Hand. God never willed that humanity should suffer such untold misery in the flesh!

Almost unconsciously we transgress the laws of nature. We eat too much and too freely of innutritious and injurious food, or work when we ought to rest, and rest when we ought to work, or rob the physical powers by excessive brain work and care and fretting, and thus leave our enfeebled bodies an easy prey to disease; or weakness may be so constitutional that disease follows as an inevitable result. From this latter conception it may readily be seen how one can be sick and yet be free from personal transgression.

In the beginning of time man lived to a ripe old age and "slept with his fathers," having known no physical disease. And God's design now, undoubtedly, is that man should live out his allotted time of "three score years and ten," then, at its close, fall asleep in death's embrace as painlessly and peacefully as a babe goes to sleep in its mother's arms at the close of day. But by the transgression of God's law sickness came among men and it has followed each generation down to the present, and will, no doubt, continue through succeeding generations until the glorious millennium shall drive out sin from our midst and usher in perpetual health.

God, looking down the vista of time, beheld the wants of his children, and when providing means for their spiritual health, provided for their physical health as well. This thought is beautifully illustrated by the example of the Godman, who not only forgave sins but cured the bodily infirmities too. O tell me not, that, to establish faith in his Omnipotence was the only motive that moved his great, loving heart when the palsied forms were laid at his feet and leprous hands were imploringly stretched out to him, and the beseech-

All this was done in the same preparation day, in the which Jesus ate the passover. The preparation day in which the passover must be killed, is never called the feast day in which the passover must be eaten, therefore the Jews would not go into the judgment hall lest they should be defiled; but that they might eat the passover. John 18: 28; 19: 14, 31, 42.

My fifth reason is this: The Jews, themselves, declared that they would not take him on the feast day lest there be an uproar among the people. Matt. 26: 4, 5; Mark 14: 2.

I have now set before the reader the difference of time between the passover of the Mosaic law and the one that Jesus Christ instituted and placed between feet-washing and the Communion of the body and blood of Christ, as Paul calls it.

SYMPATHY.

BY ALICE GARBER.

CHRIST died the ignominious death on the cross and suffered untold agonies, and is now at the right hand of the Father, pleading in our behalf. He has suffered and can sympathize with us in our tribulations. True sympathy knows how to feel for another, and that is only from those who have gone through the same fiery trials.

Christ was, and yet is, through his Word, ever ready to give comfort to the broken-hearted. We can do much towards our fellow-men to alleviate the sorrows that oppress us. How much good a few words, spoken in sympathy, will do a poor, afflicted person, both spiritually and physically! Often a word to those who are "almost persuaded," when they need the most sympathy, love and kindness, will cause them to turn from the errors of their way and find the blessed consolation in a Crucified Redeemer.

A kind word to a poor sufferer will brighten their otherwise dull sky, and cause them to think more of the "love of Christ that passeth understanding," and a loving memory will ever enshrine that person. Let us try it!

Christ suffered so that he might sympathize with us, and do we not suffer so we can sympathize with others? I think that is one of the silver linings in the clouds of affliction.

A soul away from Christ needs our keenest sympathy, for what can be more pitiful or a sadder sight? We were all once just where they are now and therefore ought to have compassion on them; and try to win them by loving words. How dear to me are the words of a kind friend who came to me one night after church, and plead with me to give my heart to the Blessed Jesus. They are written on my heart never to be erased, and oh! how often does memory revert to the sympathy she expressed and, I know, felt for poor wretched me! Ofttimes, in sorrow, a single pressure of the hand speaks volumes. Let us not spare the grasp of the hand, and show more sympathy for all. Let us lift up the fallen and tell them that Jesus is MIGHTY to save.

South English, Iowa.

TEMPTING THE LORD.

BY S. D. SMITH.

"And they said unto Moses, Because there were no graves in Egypt, hast thou taken us away to die in the wilderness? wherefore hast thou dealt thus with us, to carry us forth out of Egypt? Is not this the word that we did tell thee in Egypt, saying, Let us alone, that we may serve the Egyptians? For it had been better for us to serve the Egyptians, than that we should die in the wilderness."—Ex. 14: 11, 12.

WHEN the Children of Israel left Egypt they thought they were to be free from bondage, but when they looked back and saw King Pharaoh with his army, following hard upon them, and with the Red Sea before them, they thought escape was impossible, and therefore uttered the above language. They knew that if they ever fell into the king's hands, their burden would be greater.

It is the same way with Satan. When we leave him and decide to follow Jesus, he will surely try to get us to think that religion will be a failure. He tells us that we cannot hold out until the end, tells us of 2 Pet. 2: 20, 22, and tries to discourage us in every way he can. In all these things let us take courage and bear in mind what Peter says in the foregoing chapter.

Let us read a little farther and see the way in which the Lord delivered his people. After they had said when they did, Moses' heart was touched and he cried unto the Lord for help. Why did Moses go to the Lord for help? Why did he not deliver them himself, like a great many of us might have done? Because he felt his weakness. He knew that the Lord had all power in heaven and on earth, and had said that he would be with them, and deliver them from their enemies. Can we not learn a very good lesson from what Moses did?

But is the time of temptation the only time to go to the Lord for help? "Watch and pray that ye enter not into temptation." Matt. 26: 41. Did the Lord help the Children of Israel out of their trouble? Yes, he not only delivered them, but destroyed their enemies, as he had told them. Jesus has made us the very same promise, but he will do nothing unless we make some effort ourselves. God helps those that help themselves.

After their deliverance, their sorrow turned to joy and they sang songs to the Lord. Ex. 15. But it was not long until they fell to murmuring again, whose they could not find any water to drink. All those temptations came upon them that their faith might be tried. So are our temptations to try our faith.

Here the query might arise, Who tempts us? The Lord tempts no man, but temptations come upon us that we may grow stronger thereby. Rev. 7: 14.

Just as soon as the Israelites lost their faith, the Lord would allow something to occur, to remind them of the past and of him. It is precisely the same with us, to-day. All these things are for our benefit. Can we not learn to look at them from the right side and profit thereby? Why do we so often look at them in a wrong way? Because of self-righteousness and lack of faith.

The starting out of the Children of Israel, on their journey, is much like a person starting in a religious life. He must travel some little distance before he comes to the Red Sea,—the blood of Christ, or baptism. After that comes the travel through the wilderness of life. Here it is that we must work, or travel, in order that we reach the Promised Land. Is the land, that the Children of Israel were to inherit, as grand or as fine a country as the one promised to us? Certainly not. Earth has no place that will compare with heaven.

After the Children of Israel crossed the Red Sea, the first thing that they were in need of was bread and water. The first thing that we need in the spiritual life is the Bread and Water of Life. It is also in this travel, or life, that we tempt the Lord so often. The last thing they had, or that we will have to contend with, is the river Jordan (or death). Can it be possible that just two persons out of the six hundred thousand that left Egypt ever entered the promised land? Matt. 20: 16 and 23: 14. The question that should come to us so forcibly is this: Am I tempting the Lord so much that he will not allow me to enter the promised land?

Sterling, Ohio, Jan. 25.

SICKNESS,—ITS CAUSES AND SPIRITUAL REMEDY.

BY GERTRUDE A. FLORY.

Is God responsible for all the diseases and deaths which occur in the human family? Think what thousands die in the prime of usefulness! and how our blooming youths fade and pass away, and how many go down to the tomb in babyhood! Is this all the work of Providence? Let us illustrate that thought: One frosty autumn morning a mother let her year old baby boy play out doors several hours, barefoot and clothed with only a thin gown. That same day he was taken with membraneous croup and died. Several years afterward that mother cursed God in bitterness of heart for taking her baby from her. Another mother, in feeble health, time after time refused her tender husband's offer to secure hired help, and worked on,—entirely unable to work,—until she took her bed for the last time. Her puny babe lingered in pain for two weeks and then died. After suffering beyond endurance, the mother followed her babe, leaving her disconsolate husband with three other children, who needed a mother's care then, more than they had since they were babies in her arms. Of course, there were those who applauded the "ambition" that kept her at work when she was too feeble to work, and sympathetic friends remarked upon the strange Providence that takes a mother from the bosom of her family. But, did God do this? We must admit that there are mysterious incidents in which the hand of Providence is visible, but is it not time that we cease blaming Providence with human errors and carelessness of exposures and over-work? "Facts are stubborn things," and they are bitter things, too, when they point our sufferings and losses back to our neglect of duty; and here is where the causes of much of the sickness and death in our land should be traced, and not to the Divine Hand. God never willed that humanity should suffer such untold misery in the flesh!

Almost unconsciously we transgress the laws of nature. We eat too much and too freely of innutritious and injurious food, or work when we ought to rest, and fret when we ought to work, or rob the physical powers by excessive brain work and care and fretting, and thus leave our enfeebled bodies an easy prey to disease; or weakness may be so constitutional that disease follows as an inevitable result. From this latter conclusion it may readily be seen how one can be sick and yet be free from personal transgression.

In the beginning of time man lived to a ripe old age and "slept with his fathers," having known no physical disease. And God's design now, undoubtedly, is that man should live out his allotted time of "three score years and ten," then, at its close, fall asleep in death's embrace as painlessly and peacefully as a babe goes to sleep in its mother's arms at the close of day. But by the transgression of God's law sickness came among men and it has followed each generation down to the present, and will, no doubt, continue through succeeding generations until the glorious millennium shall drive out sin from our midst and usher in perpetual health.

God, looking down the vista of time, beheld the wants of his children, and when providing means for their spiritual health, provided for their physical health as well. This thought is beautifully illustrated by the example of the Godman, who not only forgave sins but cured the bodily infirmities too. O tell me not, that, to establish faith in his Omnipotence was the only motive that moved his loving heart when the palsied forms were laid at his feet and leprous hands were imploringly stretched out to him, and the beseech-

Missionary and Tract Work Department.

"Upon the first day of the week, let every one of you lay by him in store as God hath prospered him, that there be no gatherings when I come."—1 Cor. 16: 2.

"Every man as he purposeth in his heart, so let him give. Not grudgingly or of necessity, for the Lord loveth a cheerful giver."—2 Cor. 9: 7.

HOW MUCH SHALL WE GIVE?

"Every man *according to his ability*." "Every one *as God hath prospered him*." "Every man, *according as he purposeth in his heart*, so let him give." "For if there be first a willing mind, it is accepted *according to that a man hath*, and not according to that he hath not."—2 Cor. 8: 12.

Organization of Missionary Committee.

DANIEL VANIMAN, Foreman,   · · ·   McPherson, Kans.
D. L. MILLER, Treasurer,   · · ·   Mt. Morris, Ill.
GALEN B. ROYER, Secretary,   · · ·   Mt. Morris, Ill.

Organization of Book and Tract Work.

S. W. HOOVER, Foreman,   · · ·   Dayton, Ohio.
S. BOCK, Secretary and Treasurer,   · · ·   Dayton, Ohio.

☞ All donations intended for Missionary Work should be sent to GALEN B. ROYER, Mt. Morris, Ill.

☞ All money for Tract Work should be sent to S. BOCK, Dayton, Ohio.

☞ Money may be sent by Money Order, Registered Letter, or Drafts on New York or Chicago. Do not send personal checks, or drafts on interior towns, as it costs 25 cents to collect them.

☞ Solicitors are requested to faithfully carry out the plan of Annual Meeting, that all our members be solicited to contribute at least twice a year for the Mission and Tract Work of the Church.

☞ Notes for the Endowment Fund can be had by writing to the Secretary of either Work.

THE PURPOSE OF GOD.

BY A. HUTCHISON.

In Two Chapters.—Chapter One.

WE wish to notice this subject a little in the light of the Scriptures. We will examine it first from what we find in the Old Testament. In Eccl. 3: 17, we have the following words, "I said in mine heart, God shall judge the righteous and the wicked: for there is a time there, for every purpose, and for every work." Here, we have the matter of judgment set out in full colors, including the righteous and the wicked. This is in harmony with the purpose of God, and it perfectly accords with the following, "For we must all appear before the judgment seat of Christ; that every one may receive the things done in his body, according to that he hath done, whether it be good or bad." 2 Cor. 5: 10.

Again, we quote from Eccl. 8: 6, "Because to every purpose there is a time and judgment, therefore the misery of man is great upon him." Why is his misery so great? Simply, because he refuses to accept of the mercies of God, when they are offered to him. See the following, "Because I have called, and ye refused; I have stretched out my hand, and no man regarded; but ye have set at naught all my counsel, and would none of my reproof." Prov. 1: 24, 25. Now it is easy to see why man's calamity should be so great, and why the Lord should say, in verse 26, "I also will laugh at your calamity, and mock when your fear cometh," etc. Jesus wept, because of man's refusal to accept his proffered mercy. We must remember that our God is infinite in his attributes and characteristics.

What would you think of a judge, before whom you would arraign a man, if he would acquit him, when you know that the judge knew of the man's guilt? Would you not condemn the judge for doing injustice? Why, then, think about living in disobedience to God's law, and still expect his mercy to be dealt out to you? We must keep before our minds, the fact that God's purpose is unalterably fixed. Paul says, "If we believe not, yet he abideth faithful; he cannot deny himself." He cannot let mercy come upon the impenitent,—but upon the penitent his mercy must come, for this is in keeping with his purpose. "In every nation he that feareth him, and worketh righteousness, is accepted with him." Acts 10: 35.

God must bring every nation and every individual to his own terms,—and then it will be true, as stated in the Sacred Record, "I have sworn by myself, the Word is gone out of my mouth in righteousness, and shall not return, that unto me every knee shall bow, every tongue shall swear." Isa. 45: 23 This is in perfect keeping with what we find in Philpp. 2: 9-11. Next we will notice what is found in Rom. 8: 28-30, "And we know that all things work together for good to them that love God, to them who are called according to his purpose. For whom he did foreknow, he also did predestinate, to be conformed to the image of his Son," etc.

Now, let us notice, to whom this applies, and in what sense. And we shall apply it to the twelve apostles. Proof, "Moreover, whom he did predestinate, them he also called." And whom did he call? "And he goeth up into a mountain, and calleth unto him whom he would: and they came unto him, and he ordained twelve, that they should be with him," etc. Mark 3: 13, 14.

Now we have found twelve that he called. We will notice the next thing in order: "And whom he called, them he also justified." See John 17: 6, "I have manifested thy name unto the men which thou gavest me out of the world; thine they were, and thou gavest them me; and they have kept thy word." He clearly justifies them here,—for he says, they have kept the Father's words. "And whom he justified, them he also glorified." Again we refer you to John 17: 22, "And the glory which thou gavest me I have given them; that they may be one, even as we are one."

Thus we show that all that is contained in that case, is fully explained in the citations given, and all these references show that the twelve apostles were the ones to whom reference is made. They were predestined to be conformed to the image of Christ, in obedience to the will and purpose of the Father. We will call your attention to Eph. 1: 9, which reads thus: "Having made known unto us the mystery of his will, according to his good pleasure, which he hath purposed in himself."

The next thing now to be done is, to find the turning-point in this matter of predestination according to the purpose of God. For this purpose we ask you to consider the following: "In whom also we have obtained an inheritance, being predestinated according to the purpose of him who worketh all things after the counsel of his own will: that we should be to the praise of his glory, who first trusted in Christ." Eph. 1: 11, 12. Up to this point you will notice that the apostle uses the pronoun we, which we understood to apply to the twelve apostles, with Paul added, all of which comes under the purpose of God, in getting the condition of things brought up to a point, where free agency and free grace could be brought about.

Now notice the change, as set forth in the thirteenth verse, "In whom ye also trusted, after that ye heard the Word of Truth, the Gospel of your salvation: in whom also, after that ye believed, ye were sealed with that Holy Spirit of promise." In this case you will notice that the pronoun we is not used,—but ye instead. And Paul does not say the gospel of our salvation,—but of your salvation. Then you see the change from we to ye. We were predestinated according to the purpose of God, but you come in by virtue of the Gospel. Here is the turning-point when the purpose of God was completed, so that now, "in every nation he that feareth him and worketh righteousness, is accepted of him."

(To be continued.)

WOMAN.

BY SADIE BRALLIER NOFFSINGER.

IN the creation the young earth smiled in new-born loveliness. Majesty crowned hill and vale, ocean and rivulet. Birds sang in harmony; flowers bloomed in fragrance and profusion; whilst man, in dignity and grandeur, walked serene. Yet the beauty of that Paradise was incomplete until God placed within its midst the crowning glory,—woman.

Woman has not departed from her high station. To-day she is the acknowledged queen of all the earth,—the inspiration of poets, the pride of sculptors, the joy and higher life of man.

Her sphere is a sphere of unabating usefulness. She has capabilities and responsibilities as well as man. Like him, she has duties, and talents, and power, and· privileges. She has brilliant aims and glorious conquests, and in all the ordinary departments of life, she walks by man's side, his help-meet and his equal.

In the excellency of her virtues, she stands infinitely superior to man. Her influence covers a broader plane than his. Her endeavors reach farther than his. Her intuition is clearer than his. Her purposes are holier and more divine than his.

Man's ambition reaches out for riches and learning and power and fame. The highest object of woman is love. To this end she labors, and weeps, and offers continual sacrifice; and in this capacity are her ambition and integrity extolled. Behold the extent of her devotion, the fullness of her joy and excellence! How beautifully has a great writer said: "If there is one thing above every other for which I bless my mother, it is for teaching me that next to being an angel, the grandest thing possible for me was, to be *a woman!*"

Woman's nature is highly spiritual, refined, and sensitive in a superlative degree. In her are centered all the diviner graces, which keep her heart untainted, and draw her near unto the perfect mind of God. Her whole life is a reflection of ineffable beauty and glory, and because of the multitude of her virtues, is she nourished and adored by man.

Purity is a virtue that is very dear to woman's heart, and when it dies, she ceases to be a woman; for it is an essential, in the absence of which her womanhood cannot survive. As a helpless lamb in the dark wilderness, without a shepherd to guide, it is devoured, even so must woman die a violent death, unless she trusts in this sure protector to shield her from the dark snares of temptation.

Her mission it is to purify the morals of the coarser sex, and with her soul arrayed in this unblemished garment, how grandly and successfully does she perform her work! Her pure conversation and chaste examples have a refining influence over the mind and heart of man. She it is who must lift him to a higher plane of dignity, and, never swerving in her purpose, she braves limitless obstructions to conduct him thence. She even descends to the darkest institutions of degradation, and her purity protects her from danger and insult. Men pause in their depravity, rise, "and call her blessed."

And how beautiful is woman as a comforter! Who has not seen her kneel by the little sufferer's bed, and heard her breathe forth precious words which caused the fevered face to wreathe in smiles, and the throbbing pulse to grow calm again? Who has not heard the strong man, even, in wild spasms of delirium cry: "Bring my wife!" or, "I want my mother!" And when that financial stroke fell so heavily upon him, blasting his

Missionary and Tract Work Department.

"Upon the first day of the week, let every one of you lay by him in store, as God hath prospered him, that there be no gatherings when I come."—1 Cor. 16: 2.

"Every man as he purposeth in his heart, so let him give. Not grudgingly or of necessity, for the Lord loveth a cheerful giver."—2 Cor. 9: 7.

HOW MUCH SHALL WE GIVE?

"Every man *according to his ability*." "Every one *as God hath proshored him*." "Every man, *according as he purposeth in his heart*, so let him give." "For if there be first a willing mind, it is accepted *according to that a man hath*, and not according to that he hath not."—1 Cor. 8: 12.

Organization of Missionary Committee.

DANIEL VANIMAN, Foreman,   ·   ·   McPherson, Kans.
D. L. MILLER, Treasurer,   ·   ·   Mt. Morris, Ill.
GALEN B. ROYER, Secretary,   ·   ·   Mt. Morris, Ill.

Organization of Book and Tract Work.

S. W. HOOVER, Foreman,   ·   ·   ·   Dayton, Ohio.
S. BOCK, Secretary and Treasurer,   ·   ·   Dayton, Ohio.

☞All donations intended for Missionary Work should be sent to GALEN B. ROYER, Mt. Morris, Ill.

☞All money for Tract Work should be sent to S. BOCK, Dayton, Ohio.

☞Money may be sent by Money Order, Registered Letter, or Drafts on New York or Chicago. Do not send personal checks, or drafts on interior towns, as it costs 25 cents to collect them.

☞Solicitors are requested to faithfully carry out the plan of Annual Meeting, that all our members be solicited to contribute at least twice a year for the Mission and Tract Work of the Church.

☞Notes for the Endowment Fund can be had by writing to the Secretary of either Work.

THE PURPOSE OF GOD.

BY A. HUTCHISON.

In Two Chapters.—Chapter One.

WE wish to notice this subject a little in the light of the Scriptures. We will examine it first from what we find in the Old Testament. In Eccl. 3: 17, we have the following words, "I said in mine heart, God shall judge the righteous and the wicked: for there is a time there, for every purpose, and for every work." Here, we have the matter of judgment set out in full colors; including the righteous and the wicked. This is in harmony with the purpose of God, and is perfectly accords with the following, "For we, must all appear before the judgment seat of Christ; that every one may receive the things done in his body, according to that he hath, done, whether it be good or bad." 2 Cor. 5: 10.

Again, we quote from Eccl. 8: 6, "Because to every purpose there is a time and judgment, therefore the misery of man is great upon him." Why is his misery so great? Simply, because he refuses to accept of the mercies of God, when they are offered to him. See the following, "Because I have called, and ye refused; I have stretched out my hand, and no man regarded; but ye have set at naught all my counsel, and would none of my reproof." Prov. 1: 24, 25. Now it is easy to see why man's calamity should be so great, and why the Lord should say, in verse 26, "I also will laugh at your calamity, and mock when your fear cometh," etc. Jesus wept, because of man's refusal to accept his proffered mercy. We must remember that our God is infinite in his attributes and characteristics.

What would you think of a judge, before whom you would arraign a man, if he would acquit him, when you know that the judge knew of the man's guilt? Would you not condemn the judge for doing injustice? Why, then, think about living in disobedience to God's law, and still expect his mercy to be dealt out to you? We must keep before our minds, the fact that God's purpose is unalterably fixed. Paul says, "If we believe not, yet he abideth faithful; he cannot deny himself." He cannot let mercy come upon the impenitent,—but upon the penitent his mercy must come, for this is in keeping with his pur-

pose. "In every nation he that feareth him, and · worketh righteousness, is accepted with him." Acts 10: 35.

God must bring every nation and every individual to his own terms,—and then it will be true, as stated in the Sacred Record, "I have sworn by myself, the Word is gone out of my mouth in righteousness, and shall not return, that unto me every knee shall bow, every tongue shall swear." Isa. 45: 23 This is in perfect keeping with what we find in Philpp. 2: 9-11. Next we will notice what is found in Rom. 8: 28-30, "And we know that all things work together for good to them that love God, to them who are called according to his purpose. For whom he did foreknow, he also did predestinate, to be conformed to the image of his Son," etc.

Now, let us notice, to whom this applies, and in what sense. And we shall apply it to the twelve apostles. Proof, "Moreover, whom he did predestinate, them he also called." And whom did he call? "And he goeth up into a mountain, and calleth unto him whom he would: and they came unto him, and he ordained twelve, that they should be with him," etc. Mark 3: 13, 14.

Now we have found twelve that he called. We will notice the next thing in order: "And whom he called, them he also justified." See John 17: 6, "I have manifested thy name unto the men which thou gavest me out of the world: thine they were, and thou gavest them me; and they have kept thy word." He clearly justifies them here,—for he says, they have kept the Father's words. "And whom he justified, them he also glorified." Again we refer you to John 17: 22, "And the glory which thou gavest me I have given them; that they may be one, even as we are one."

Thus we show that all that is contained in that case, is fully explained in the citations given, and all these references show that the twelve apostles were the ones to whom reference is made. They were predestined to be conformed to the image of Christ, in obedience to the will and purpose of the Father. We will call your attention to Eph. 1: 9, which reads thus: "Having made known unto us the mystery of his will, according to his good pleasure, which he hath purposed in himself."

The next thing now to be done is, to find the turning-point in this matter of predestination according to the purpose of God. For this purpose we ask you to consider the following: "In whom also we have obtained an inheritance, being predestinated according to the purpose of him who worketh all things after the counsel of his own will: that we should be to the praise of his glory, who first trusted in Christ." Eph. 1: 11, 12. Up to this point you will notice that the apostle uses the pronoun we, which · we understood to apply to the twelve apostles, with Paul added, all of which comes under the purpose of God, in getting the condition of things brought up to a point, where free agency and free grace could be brought about. Now notice the change, as set forth in the thirteenth verse, "In whom ye also trusted, after that ye heard the Word of Truth, the Gospel of your salvation: in whom also, after that ye believed, ye were sealed with that Holy Spirit of promise." In this case, you will notice that the pronoun *we* is not used,—but *ye* instead. And Paul does not say the gospel of *our* salvation,—but of *your* salvation. Then you see the change from *we* to *ye*. We were predestinated according to the purpose of God, but you come in by virtue of the Gospel. Here is the turning-point when the purpose of God was completed, so that now, "in every nation he that feareth him and worketh righteousness, is accepted of him."

(*To be continued.*)

WOMAN.

BY SADIE BRALLIER NOFFSINGER.

IN the creation the young earth smiled in new-born loveliness. Majesty crowned hill and vale, ocean and rivulet. Birds sang in harmony; flowers bloomed in fragrance and profusion; whilst man, in dignity and grandeur, walked serene. Yet the beauty of that Paradise was incomplete until God placed within its midst the crowning glory,—woman.

Woman has not departed from her high station. To-day she is the acknowledged queen of all the earth,—the inspiration of poets, the pride of sculpture, the joy and higher life of man.

Her sphere is a sphere of unabating usefulness. She has capabilities and responsibilities as well as man. Like him, she has duties, and talents, and power, and· privileges. She ·has brilliant aims and glorious conquests, and in all the ordinary departments of life, she walks by man's side, his help-meet and his equal.

In the excellency of her virtues, she stands infinitely superior to man. Her influence covers a broader plane than his. Her endeavors reach farther than his. Her intuition is clearer than his. Her purposes are holier and more divine than his.

Man's ambition reaches out for riches and learning and power and fame. The highest object of woman is love. To this end she labors, and weeps, and offers continual sacrifice; and in this capacity are her ambition and integrity extolled. Behold the extent of her devotion, the fullness of her joy and excellence! How beautifully has a great writer said: "If there is one thing above every other for which I bless my mother, it is for teaching me that next to being an angel, the grandest thing possible for me was, to be a *woman!*"

Woman's nature is highly spiritual, refined, and sensitive in a superlative degree. In her are centered all the diviner graces, which keep her heart untainted, and draw her near unto the perfect mind of God. Her whole life is a reflection of ineffable beauty and glory, and because of the multitude of her virtues, is she nourished and adored by man.

Purity is a virtue that is very dear to woman's heart, and when it dies, she ceases to be a woman; for it is an essential, in the absence of which her womanhood cannot survive. As a helpless lamb in the dark wilderness, without a shepherd to guide, it is devoured, even so must woman die a violent death, unless she trusts in this sure protector to shield her from the dark snares of temptation.

Her mission it is to purify the morals of the coarser sex, and with her soul arrayed in this unblemished garment, how grandly and successfully does she perform her work! Her pure conversation and chaste examples have a refining influence over the mind and heart of man. She it is who must lift him to a higher plane of dignity, and, never swerving in her purpose, she braves limitless obstructions to conduct him thence. She even descends to the darkest institutions of degradation, and her purity protects her from danger and insult. Men pause in their depravity, rise, "and call her blessed."

And how beautiful is woman as a comforter! Who has not seen her kneel by the little sufferer's bed, and heard her breathe forth precious words which caused the fevered face to wreathe in smiles, and the throbbing pulse to grow calm again? Who has not heard the strong man, even, in wild spasms of delirium cry: "Bring my wife!" or, "I want my mother!" And when that financial stroke fell so heavily upon him, blasting his

The Gospel Messenger,

A Weekly at $1.50 Per Annum.

PUBLISHED BY

The Brethren's Publishing Co.

D. L. MILLER, ... Editor.
J. H. MOORE, ... Office Editor.
J. B. BRUMBAUGH, } . . . . . Associate Editors.
J. G. ROYER, }
JOSEPH AMICK, ... Business Manager.

ADVISORY COMMITTEE:
R. H. Miller, A. Hutchison, Daniel Hays.

☞Communications for publication should be legibly written with black ink on one side of the paper only. Do not attempt to interline, or to put on one page what ought to occupy two.

☞Anonymous communications will not be published.

☞Do not mix business with articles for publication. Keep your communications on separate sheets from all business.

☞Time is precious. We always have time to attend to business and to answer questions of importance, but please do not subject us to need less answering of letters.

☞The MESSENGER is mailed each week to all subscribers. If the address is correctly entered on our list, the paper must reach the person to whom it is addressed. If you do not get your paper, write us, giving particulars.

☞When changing your address, please give your former as well as your future address in full, so as to avoid delay and misunderstanding.

☞Always remit to the office from which you order your goods, no matter from where you receive them.

☞Do not send personal checks or drafts on interior banks, unless you send with them 15 cents each, to pay for collection.

☞Remittances should be made by Post-office Money Order, Drafts on New York, Philadelphia or Chicago, or Registered Letters, made payable and addressed to "Brethren's Publishing Co., Mount Morris, Ill.," or "Brethren's Publishing Co., Huntingdon, Pa."

☞Entered at the Post-office at Mount Morris, Ill., as second-class matter.

Mount Morris, Ill., - - - - June 7, 1892.

IT now looks as though we were going to have an unfavorable time for our Annual Meeting, as it has been raining for a week or more. But we hope for better weather.

BRETHREN D. F. Stouffer, and P. D. Fahrney, of Maryland; Geo. Bucher, of Pennsylvania; John Driver and S. H. Myers, of Virginia, gave us a pleasant call on their way to the Annual Meeting.

SISTER Florida Etter, of Cartersville, Va., who has frequently favored our readers with some of her communications, writes us, that, with her aged mother, she will soon move to Indiana, and will reside in Middletown, Henry County.

WE are in receipt of a letter from a brother who says he sent for a "Church Manual" some time ago, but forgot to enclose the money. He now sends the money but forgets to sign his name. If this meets his eye, he will please forward his name and the book will be sent. The letter was mailed in Michigan.

WE have been too greatly crowded with work, to give attention to the Querist Department for a few weeks. After the close of the Annual Meeting we hope to devote more time and attention to that department of the MESSENGER. Of the one hundred queries now on the hook we will be able to answer only the more important ones.

FULL REPORT

We are arranging to publish a Full Report of the coming Annual Meeting, and hope to have it fully up to any of the Reports that have appeared in former years. We shall make a special effort to have it ready for mailing very shortly after the close of the Annual Meeting. We are now ready to book orders, and would be pleased to receive them as soon as possible. Remember that the first that come are the ones first served. Price, 25cts per copy, or $2.50 per dozen.

MOODY is now on his way to the Land of Palestine. He thinks that a personal visit to the Holy Land will enable him to obtain a better knowledge of the Scriptures.

ANY one who wishes to make his minister a present of "The Doctrine of the Brethren Defended," can have it for that purpose for one dollar. Here is an opportunity of helping your ministers.

IT is our usual custom to drop out one number of the MESSENGER at the time of the Annual Meeting, hence there will be no paper next week. We close this issue and start to the Meeting. Our next issue will be dated June 21.

SISTER MARY A. EVANS, widow of Eld. James Evans, who died in Oklahoma Territory last year, is now located with her children at 751, 27th Ave. N. E. Minneapolis, Minn., and will be pleased to have any of our members call when passing through the city.

BRO. A. S. CULP, formerly of Monticello, Indiana, is now permanently located at Laconia, Harrison County, same State, where he has entered upon the work in earnest. He finds plenty to engage his attention and we trust he will succeed in building up a flourishing congregation.

THE Brethren of the Maple Grove church, Michigan, met with quite a misfortune in having the frame of their new meeting-house blown down, causing considerable damage to the timber, thus increasing the expense of the house, which will fall heavily on the members, as they are in limited circumstances.

OUR Eastern Editor, Bro. H. B. Brumbaugh, pleasantly surprised us June 2, by a short visit, while on his way to the place of Annual Meeting. Bro. Henry has been in the editorial harness for many years, but has lost none of his vigor and genial cheerfulness. We regret that he cannot be with us more frequently.

WORK on the Old Peoples' and Orphans' Home at Mt. Morris, is progressing nicely. The structure is a large two-story frame building, veneered with brick, containing a good basement and divided into about twenty-one rooms, admirably located and arranged for the comfort and convenience of the aged poor who are expected to make the "Home" their home. The trustees are aiming to have the building completed some time in August. It will be heated by steam and otherwise made as comfortable and home-like as possible. It is situated only a few blocks from the Chapel, and so afford very convenient church privileges.

PROBABLY, instead of urging solicitors, for missionary funds, to push their work with more energy, it would be far better to insist upon our ministers preaching more on the duty of giving. Solicitors will meet with but little difficulty in raising money in a congregation where the members are properly taught the Gospel of giving as the Lord has expressed them. It is just as necessary to preach this part of the Gospel as that which relates to the ordinances. Those who decline to teach their flocks aright concerning the duty of giving for the support of the Gospel, may well pause and ask themselves whether they have not shunned to declare the whole counsel of God to the members over which the Holy Ghost has made them overseers. It should not be considered what the members may think of this part of the Gospel, but the minister should ask himself whether it is not his duty to preach the Word. While it is the duty of the young ministers to preach this as well as other parts of the Gospel, still it will be more acceptable if the aged ministers lead off.

THE other day, when traveling in Iowa, a gentleman asked us about our coming Conference at Cedar Rapids. He said: "I notice in the papers you are called German Baptists. Do you conduct the business of your Conference in the German language?" We explained to him that English was used altogether. "Then," said he, "I presume your preaching is all in German." Again we explained, and at the close of the interview felt very strongly that our name is quite misleading.

So the Hebrew is to become a living language in the United States: "Two weekly papers, which have just been started in New York City, furnish food for interesting thought. One is issued in Hebrew and the other in Arabic. These are kindred tongues, both being of the Semitic family of languages, and they were spoken by kindred peoples, dwelling in Asia 4,000 years ago. More than 3,000 years ago they had embodied some of the most exalted literature the world has ever known. And now in this New World and new era they are to be made the vehicle of modern thought and of current events."

THE North-eastern District of Kansas has instructed her Mission Board to confer with the General Mission Board and Tract Work Committee, in regard to locating a minister in Kansas City. The idea of locating a minister in that city is certainly a good one and should be encouraged. As a church, we ought to make greater efforts to establish congregations in large cities. Such was a very notable characteristic of the apostolic church that is worthy of imitation in this or any other age. Probably the first church ever organized was at Jerusalem, the largest city in the Land of Palestine. Soon after that, a church was planted at Samaria, another city of considerable importance. Then follow a long list of cities, such as Antioch, Corinth, Philippi, Ephesus, Rome, etc., etc., where flourishing congregations were early established and proved great strongholds for the Christian cause in those ages. True, corruption was found in some of these congregations, but that we may expect until Satan is bound and cast into the bottomless pit. What we want to do, is to go every-where preaching the Gospel, in cities, in the rural districts, or wherever the people may be found. The Gospel is intended for all of them and it is our duty to get it to them.

"A PICTURE," recently published in these columns, has been the subject of considerable interest. We have received a number of letters concerning it and we are convinced that the principle set forth in the editorial is correct and that it meets a warm response in many hearts in our Brotherhood. In places, however, sight is being lost of the principles involved and the lesson intended to be taught, and an effort is made to fit the picture to some particular local case, and when it is found that it don't fit in all particulars, it is thought that we were not fully and correctly informed as to what we wrote about. By way of explanation we now say that the article was written not for local but for general application, and that the intention was to illustrate a principle and to teach a lesson to all who have need of it. If there is found a case in any local church, and, judging from the letters received, there is more than one in which the principle set forth is violated, it applies to that church, even if, in all particulars and details, it does not exactly fit the local case. Our aim is not to discuss cases and persons but principle. We meant to cast reflections upon no church but we did mean to use the picture to impress an important truth. We trust our brethren who have local cases, will accept this explanation. Forget your personal case and study the truth set forth in the article in question.

The Gospel Messenger,

A Weekly at $1.50 Per Annum.

PUBLISHED BY

The Brethren's Publishing Co.

D. L. MILLER,	· · · · ·	Editor.
J. H. MOORE,		Office Editor.
J. B. BRUMBAUGH,	· · · · ·	Associate Editors.
J. G. ROYER,		
JOSEPH AMICK,	· · · · ·	Business Manager.

ADVISORY COMMITTEE.
R. H. Miller, A. Hutchison, Daniel Hays.

☞ Communications for publication should be legibly written with black ink on one side of the paper only. Do not attempt to interline, or to put on one page what ought to occupy two.

☞ Anonymous communications will not be published.

☞ Do not mix business with articles for publication. Keep your communications on separate sheets from all business.

☞ Time is precious. We always have time to attend to business and to answer questions of importance, but please do not subject us to need-less answering of letters.

☞ The Messenger is mailed each week to all subscribers. If the address is correctly entered on our list, the paper must reach the person to whom it is addressed. If you do not get your paper, write us, giving particulars.

☞ When changing your address, please give your former as well as your future address in full, so as to avoid delay and misunderstanding.

☞ Always remit to the office from which you order your goods, no matter from where you receive them.

☞ Do not send personal checks or drafts on interior banks, unless you send with them 15 cents each, to pay for collection.

☞ Remittances should be made by Post-office Money Order, Drafts on New York, Philadelphia or Chicago, or Registered Letters, made payable and addressed to "Brethren's Publishing Co., Mount Morris, Ill.," or "Brethren's Publishing Co., Huntingdon, Pa."

☞ Entered at the Post-office at Mount Morris, Ill., as second-class matter.

Mount Morris, Ill.,   June 7, 1892.

IT now looks as though we were going to have an unfavorable time for our Annual Meeting, as it has been raining for a week or more. But we hope for better weather.

BRETHREN D. F. Stouffer, and P. D. Fahrney, of Maryland; Geo. Bucher, of Pennsylvania; John Driver and S. H. Myers, of Virginia, gave us a pleasant call on their way to the Annual Meeting.

SISTER Florida Etter, of Cartersville, Va., who has frequently favored our readers with some of her communications, writes us, that, with her aged mother, she will soon move to Indiana, and will reside in Middletown, Henry County.

WE are in receipt of a letter from a brother who says he sent for a "Church Manual" some time ago, but forgot to enclose the money. He now sends the money but forgets to sign his name. If this meets his eye, he will please forward his name and the book will be sent. The letter was mailed in Michigan.

WE have been too greatly crowded with work, to give attention to the Querist Department for a few weeks. After the close of the Annual Meeting we hope to devote more time and attention to that department of the MESSENGER. Of the one hundred queries now on the hook we will be able to answer only the more important ones.

FULL REPORT We are arranging to publish a Full Report of the coming Annual Meeting, and hope to have it fully up to any of the Reports that have appeared in former years. We shall make a special effort to have it ready for mailing very shortly after the close of the Annual Meeting. We are now ready to book orders, and would be pleased to receive them as soon as possible. Remember that the first that come are the ones first served. Price, 25cts per copy, or $2.50 per dozen.

MOODY is now on his way to the Land of Palestine. He thinks that a personal visit to the Holy Land will enable him to obtain a better knowledge of the Scriptures.

ANY one who wishes to make his minister a present of "The Doctrine of the Brethren Defended," can have it for that purpose for one dollar. Here is an opportunity of helping your ministers.

IT is our usual custom to drop out one number of the MESSENGER at the time of the Annual Meeting, hence there will be no paper next week. We close this issue and start to the Meeting. Our next issue will be dated June 21.

SISTER MARY A. EVANS, widow of Eld. James Evans, who died in Oklahoma Territory last year, is now located with her children at 751, 27th Ave, N. E. Minneapolis, Minn., and will be pleased to have any of our members call when passing through the city.

BRO. A. S. CULP, formerly of Monticello, Indiana, is now permanently located at Laconia, Harrison County, same State, where he has entered upon the work in earnest. He finds plenty to engage his attention and we trust he will succeed in building up a flourishing congregation.

THE Brethren of the Maple Grove church, Michigan, met with quite a misfortune in having the frame of their new meeting-house blown down, causing considerable damage to the timber, thus increasing the expense of the house, which will fall heavily on the members, as they are in limited circumstances.

OUR Eastern Editor, Bro. H. B. Brumbaugh, pleasantly surprised us June 2, by a short visit, while on his way to the place of Annual Meeting. Bro. Henry has been in the editorial harness for many years, but has lost none of his vigor and genial cheerfulness. We regret that he cannot be with us more frequently.

WORK on the Old Peoples' and Orphans' Home at Mt. Morris, is progressing nicely. The structure is a large two-story frame building, veneered with brick, containing a good basement and divided into about twenty-one rooms, admirably located and arranged for the comfort and convenience of the aged poor who are expected to make the "Home" their home. The trustees are aiming to have the building completed some time in August. It will be heated by steam and otherwise made as comfortable and home-like as possible. It is situated only a few blocks from the Chapel, so as to afford very convenient church privileges.

PROBABLY, instead of urging solicitors, for missionary funds, to push their work with more energy, it would be far better to insist upon our ministers preaching more on the duty of giving. Solicitors will meet with but little difficulty in raising money in a congregation where the members are properly taught the Gospel of giving as the Lord has prospered them. It is just as necessary to preach this part of the Gospel as that which relates to the ordinances. Those who decline to teach their flocks aright concerning the duty of giving for the support of the Gospel, may well pause and ask themselves whether they have not shunned to declare the whole counsel of God to the members over which the Holy Ghost has made them overseers. It should not be considered what the members may think of this part of the Gospel, but the minister should ask himself whether it is not his duty to preach the Word. While it is the duty of the young ministers to preach this as well as other parts of the Gospel, still it will be more acceptable if the aged ministers lead off.

THE other day, when traveling in Iowa, a gentleman asked us about our coming Conference at Cedar Rapids. He said: "I notice in the papers you are called German Baptists. Do you conduct the business of your Conference in the German language?" We explained to him that English was used altogether. "Then," said he, "I presume your preaching is all in German." Again we explained, and at the close of the interview felt very strongly that our name is quite misleading.

So the Hebrew is to become a living language in the United States: "Two weekly papers, which have just been started in New York City, furnish food for interesting thought. One is issued in Hebrew and the other in Arabic. These are kindred tongues, both being of the Semitic family of languages, and they were spoken by kindred peoples, dwelling in Asia 4,000 years ago. More than 3,000 years ago they had embodied some of the most exalted literature the world has ever known. And now in this New World and new era they are to be made the vehicle of modern thought and of current events."

THE North-eastern District of Kansas has instructed her Mission Board to confer with the General Mission Board and Tract Work Committee, in regard to locating a minister in Kansas City. The idea of locating a minister in that city is certainly a good one and should be encouraged. As a church, we ought to make greater efforts to establish congregations in large cities. Such was a very notable characteristic of the apostolic church that is worthy of imitation in this or any other age. Probably the first church ever organized was at Jerusalem, the largest city in the Land of Palestine. Soon after that, a church was planted at Samaria, another city of considerable importance. Then follow a long list of cities, such as Antioch, Corinth, Philippi, Ephesus, Rome, etc., etc., where flourishing congregations were early established and proved great strongholds for the Christian cause in those ages. True, corruption was found in some of these congregations, but that we may expect until Satan is bound and cast into the bottomless pit. What we want to do, is to go every-where preaching the Gospel, in cities, in the rural districts, or wherever the people may be found. The Gospel is intended for all of them and it is our duty to get it to them.

"A PICTURE," recently published in these columns, has been the subject of considerable interest. We have received a number of letters concerning it and we are convinced that the principle set forth in the editorial is correct and that it meets a warm response in many hearts in our Brotherhood. In places, however, sight is being lost of the principles involved and the lesson intended to be taught, and an effort is made to fit the picture to some particular local case, and when it is found that it don't fit in all particulars, it is thought that we were not fully and correctly informed as to what we wrote about. By way of explanation we now say that the article was written not for local but for general application, and that the intention was to illustrate a principle and to teach a lesson to all who have need of it. If there is found a case in any local church, and, judging from the letters received, there is more than one in which the principle set forth is violated, it applies to that church, even if, in all particulars and details, it does not exactly fit the local case. Our aim is not to discuss cases and persons but principles. We meant to cast reflections upon no church but we did mean to use the picture to impress an important truth. We trust our brethren who have local cases, will accept this explanation. Forget your personal case and study the truth set forth in the article in question.

THOSE who are looking forward to the time when a costly monument may mark their resting-place in mother earth, will do well to ponder what Prof. Drummond has well said: "Christ built no church, wrote no book, lent no money, erected no monuments; yet show me ten square miles anywhere on earth, without Christianity, where the life of man and the purity of woman are respected, and I will give up Christianity."

FROM what the St. Louis *Christian Advocate* says below, it would seem that the six months' probationary porch is destined to be a thing of the past. "The M. E. church is discussing the abolition of the probationary system and the admission of applicants at once to all the privileges of church Communion. We have found it to work admirably in our church and commend it to our brethren of the North. When a man has been genuinely converted, there is neither a Scriptural nor a common-sense reason for keeping him standing in the vestibule of the church for six months. The pastor should have large discretion in the matter, and in this, as in everything else, a preacher should have 90 per cent of serpent and 10 per cent of dove, as we heard a well-known preacher of this city say the other day."

LUTHER'S GOOD ADVICE.

ON a postal card Bro. S. N. McCann, who was at Dayton, Ohio, at the time he wrote, sends us the following:

"Here are a few words from Martin Luther that I consider worthy of imitation. He says, 'It is no pleasure to me that certain persons are styled after me, Lutherans. I have done all in my power to avoid their being called so. I only wish that they would diligently peruse the Bible and see what that tells them' (See Book of Good Examples, by John Frost, LL D, page 233.)

May we only 'diligently peruse the Bible' and be directed by its holy teaching."

BAPTISM AND CONVERSION.

THERE are three positions taken by the religious world with respect to baptism and its relationship to conversion. Which one is right?

1. Those who practice so-called infant baptism before conversion. The child, without reference to its own wish, or will, is held and water is applied to its forehead. The place where reason is expected to dwell is subjected to a treatment that is not reasonable. The preacher dips (immerses) his fingers in water, and after his fingers come up out of the water, they are placed on the child's forehead and held there until the baptismal formula is pronounced. The child knows not what is being done, neither do those who witness the act, for they go away, thinking the child has been baptized, when, in fact, the only baptism was the preacher's fingers. This is baptism before conversion, is it? It is an earnest of what is to be. It is baptized, "so they say," on the faith of the parents. This is one step by which it is consecrated to the Lord. Its recital to the child, when it comes to years of understanding, may have such force as to lead to its conversion to the Lord.

2. Many maintain that baptism follows conversion. They claim that it is not valid unless it does follow conversion. The sinner, they say, must be convicted of sin, be sorry for sin, repent and give his heart to Christ. The work wrought in his soul must be thorough. If the change wrought in his soul is complete and he can give satisfactory evidence of pardon and acceptance with God, he is a fit subject for baptism. Baptism, they claim, is not a factor in conversion, not a condition in order to pardon, and not a condition in or-

der to the gaining of heaven, but a declaration that conversion has been achieved, and that the subject is ready, by observance of the proper ordinance, to be brought into the visible church.

3. Another class, which in no sense is to be despised, claims that baptism neither precedes nor follows conversion to Christ. They claim that it is the final step in conversion. They say, "The converted man is saved; the converted man is free from condemnation; the converted man is a child of God; the converted man is in Christ; the converted man is born again, and is in the kingdom of God's dear Son." With much power they call on the Word of God to testify that not one of the foregoing blessings can be claimed by any one before his baptism into Christ.

REMARKS.—The above clear statement of the three positions on baptism and conversion is clipped from one of our Disciple exchanges. The third position is the one generally held by our Brethren. Conversion, it should be remembered, is the change from one state or condition to another. Christian conversion refers to the change the sinner must undergo to constitute him a Christian. It is the change from the kingdom of Satan to the kingdom of Christ. This process ends where baptism ends, baptism being the last act or duty connected with conversion. Conversion commences where faith commences, continues on through godly sorrow, repentance, and is consummated in the new birth, when the new creature is born of the water and of the Spirit into the kingdom of God. Being a new creature with a new heart, in a new and better kingdom, released from the burden of sin, he is permitted to enter upon a new life with higher and nobler aspirations, and it is his highest duty to make that new life a success.
J. H. M.

AN INTERESTING REPORT.

THE following is the tabulated report published by the North-eastern District of Kansas in their Minutes. We give it here in order to induce other Districts to adopt the same method:

CHURCHES	Elders	Ministers	Members	Baptisms	Appointments	Solicitors	Sunday-schools
Abilene	3	3	120	16	7	2	
Appanoose	1	5	120	20	6	1	
Chapman Creek	2	3	55	4	1		
Cotton-wood	1		10				
Herington	2	3	53		8		1
Morrill	2	1	40	2	1	2	
North Morrill	2	3	100	12	3	2	
Ozawkis	3	3	190	25	6	2	
Olathe	3	3	90	8	4	2	
Pleasant Grove		4	63	2	2	1	
Sabetha	1		33	1	3	1	
Soldier Creek	3	4		2	2	2	
Vermillion	1		16				
Wolf River	4		43	3	3	1	1
Washington	3		26	5			
Washington C	1		95	8	1	1	
Wade	1	1	35	6	2	2	
Total	31	43	1164	108	58	20	17

A glance at the report will show the strength of the District in membership, elders and ministers, and indicates just where this strength is located. It also shows what is being accomplished in additions, appointments, and the Sunday-school interest. We suggest the addition of a finance column, showing what the District is doing financially for the Lord's cause.

If the Minutes of all the State Districts would contain a similar report, it would enable the Annual Meeting Clerk to give a tabulated report, representing the entire Brotherhood, thus affording

us a great deal of information that we now have no way of obtaining.

CORRESPONDENCE.

"Write what thou seest, and send it unto the churches."

☞Church News solicited for this Department. If you have had a good meeting, send a report of it, so that others may rejoice with you. In writing give name of church, County and State. Be brief. Notes of Travel should be as short as possible. Land Advertisements are not solicited for this Department. We have an advertising page, and, if necessary, will issue supplements.

From Austin, Arkansas.

We arrived here from Wichita, Kans., April 25, after twenty-two days' travel by wagon. We had a very enjoyable trip. We like our new home very well, so far. Of course it is like any other country,—there is always something that a person likes and something they dislike. We cannot expect to find a place in this world that is perfect. We must learn to take the bitter with the sweet wherever we are.

We have had several meetings since we are here. The people seem to be very anxious to hear our doctrine and they pay very good attention to the Word preached. But here, as well as at other places, it is necessary to have the Gospel preached in its purity, as people are very easily led away by false doctrines; they depend too much on what the preacher says. Since I am here I feel as though we, as a church, are not yet doing what we ought to save sinners from the error of their ways. Now I want to say to our young ministers (and old ones too), where there are four or five at one place, Scatter out and open up new fields! Don't be afraid to venture out away from home! The Lord will stand by you if you are engaged in his work. Think of the many souls who are perishing daily for the Bread of Life.

There are many places where the Gospel has not yet been preached. The great Commission is, "Go into all the world. Preach the Gospel to every creature." Now, don't wait to have a personal invitation, but go!   CHARLES E. DELP.

From Wichita, Kans.

THE Wichita congregation held a love-feast in the city of Wichita, on the evening of May 14. We can truly say it was a good meeting. The ministers present were brethren S. Z. Sharp, Samuel Bowser and Levi Andes, with the home ministers. The brethren gave us some excellent instructions and admonitions. One pleasing and profitable feature of the meeting was the children's meeting on Lord's Day morning. Brethren Sharp, Bowser and Andes gave good instruction and counsel to the children. We thought this meeting not only did the children good, but it helped older ones. Through the perseverance of some of our sisters, we are having a good Sunday-school.

Our meetings are well attended, with a fine prospect, if we had a meeting-house of our own. Pray for us that the Lord may bless our labors here in Wichita.   WILLIAM JOHNSTON.
1538 Orange St., Wichita, Kans.

From La Porte, Ind.

AT our council, March 12, Bro. Daniel Shively, of New Paris, Ind., was present for the purpose of encouraging the missionary spirit, by stirring us up to a more lively sense of our duty in that line. Among the good things he dispensed, was a proposition to organize a Bible class in connection with our regular Sunday services. The church accepted the proposition, and next morning organized, with Bro. Shively in charge of the lesson. After concluding the Bible lesson, Bro. Shively

THOSE who are looking forward to the time when a costly monument may mark their resting-place in mother earth, will do well to ponder what Prof. Drummond has well said: "Christ built no church, wrote no book, lent no money, erected no monuments; yet show me ten square miles anywhere on earth, without Christianity, where the life of man and the purity of woman are respected, and I will give up Christianity."

FROM what the St. Louis Christian Advocate says below, it would seem that the six months' probationary porch is destined to be a thing of the past. "The M. E. church is discussing the abolition of the probationary system and the admission of applicants at once to all the privileges of church Communion. We have found it to work admirably in our church and commend it to our brethren of the North. When a man has been genuinely converted, there is neither a Scriptural nor a common-sense reason for keeping him standing in the vestibule of the church for six months. The pastor should have large discretion in the matter, and in this, as in everything else, a preacher should have 90 per cent of serpent and 10 per cent of dove, as we heard a well-known preacher of this city say the other day."

LUTHER'S GOOD ADVICE.

ON a postal card Bro. S. N. McCann, who was at Dayton, Ohio, at the time he wrote, sends us the following:

"Here are a few words from Martin Luther that I consider worthy of imitation. He says, 'It is no pleasure to me that certain persons are styled after me, Lutherans. I have done all in my power to avoid their being called so. I only wish that they would diligently peruse the Bible and see what that tells them' (See Book of Good Examples, by John Frost, LL. D, page 283.)

May we only 'diligently peruse the Bible' and be directed by its holy teaching."

BAPTISM AND CONVERSION.

THERE are three positions taken by the religious world with respect to baptism and its relationship to conversion. Which one is right?

1. Those who practice so-called infant baptism before conversion. The child, without reference to its own wish, or will, is held and water is applied to its forehead. The place where reason is expected to dwell is subjected to a treatment that is not reasonable. The preacher dips (immerses) his fingers in water, and after his fingers come up out of the water, they are placed on the child's forehead and held there until the baptismal formula is pronounced. The child knows not what is being done, neither do those who witness the act, for they go away, thinking the child has been baptized, when, in fact, the only baptism was the preacher's fingers. This is baptism before conversion, is it? It is an earnest of what is to be. It is baptized, "so they say," on the faith of the parents. This is one step by which it is consecrated to the Lord. Its recital to the child, when it comes to years of understanding, may have such force as to lead to its conversion to the Lord.

2. Many maintain that baptism follows conversion. They claim that it is not valid unless it does follow conversion. The sinner, they say, must be convicted of sin, be sorry for sin, repent and give his heart to Christ. The work wrought in his soul must be thorough. If the change wrought in his soul is complete and he can give satisfactory evidence of pardon and acceptance with God, he is a fit subject for baptism. Baptism, they claim, is not a factor in conversion, not a condition in order to pardon, and not a condition in or-

der to the gaining of heaven, but a declaration that conversion has been achieved, and that the subject is ready, by observance of the proper ordinance, to be brought into the visible church.

3. Another class, which in no sense is to be despised, claims that baptism neither precedes nor follows conversion to Christ. They claim that it is the final step in conversion. They say, "The converted man is saved; the converted man is free from condemnation; the converted man is a child of God; the converted man is in Christ; the converted man is born again, and is in the kingdom of God's dear Son." With much power they call on the Word of God to testify that not one of the foregoing blessings can be claimed by any one before his baptism into Christ.

REMARKS.—The above clear statement of the three positions on baptism and conversion is clipped from one of our Disciple exchanges. The third position is the one generally held by our Brethren. Conversion, it should be remembered, is the change from one state or condition to another. Christian conversion refers to the change the sinner must undergo to constitute him a Christian. It is the change from the kingdom of Satan to the kingdom of Christ. This process ends where baptism ends, baptism being the last act or duty connected with conversion. Conversion commences where faith commences, continues on through godly sorrow, repentance, and is consummated in the new birth, when the new creature is born of the water and of the Spirit into the kingdom of God. Being a new creature with a new heart, in a new and better kingdom, released from the burden of sin, he is permitted to enter upon a new life with higher and nobler aspirations, and it is his highest duty to make that new life a success.   J. H. M.

AN INTERESTING REPORT.

THE following is the tabulated report published by the North-eastern District of Kansas in their Minutes. We give it here in order to induce other Districts to adopt the same method:

CHURCHES	Elders	Ministers	Members	Baptisms	Appointments	Solicitors	Sunday-schools
Abilene	3	3	120	16	7	4	1
Appanoose	1	5	120	20	6	1	
Chapman Creek	2	3	55	4			
Cottonwood	1	1	16	4	1		
Herington	2	3	53		8		1
Morrill	1	2	40	9	2	1	
North Morrill	3	3	100	12	3	2	1
Ozawkie	3	3	190	25	6	2	1
Olathe	3	3	90	6	4	2	
Pleasant Grove	4	6	5	2	1		
Rock Creek	1	1	33		1	2	
Sabetha	1	2	45	2	2	1	
Soldier Creek	1	1	16				
Vermillion		4	43	3	3	1	1
Wolf River	1	2	25				
Washington	3	3	26		5		
Washington	1	2	95	8	1	1	
Wade	1	1	35	6	1	2	
Total	21	43	1164	108	58	20	17

A glance at the report will show the strength of the District in membership, elders and ministers, and indicates just where this strength is located. It also shows what is being accomplished in additions, appointments, and the Sunday-school interest. We suggest the addition of a finance column, showing what the District is doing financially for the Lord's cause.

If the Minutes of all the State Districts would contain a similar report, it would enable the Annual Meeting Clerk to give a tabulated report, representing the entire Brotherhood, thus affording

us a great deal of information that we now have no way of obtaining.

CORRESPONDENCE.

"Write what thou seest, and send it unto the churches."

☞Church News solicited for this Department. If you have had a good meeting, send a report of it, so that others may rejoice with you. In writing give name of church, County and State. Be brief. Notes of Travel should be as short as possible. Land Advertisements are not solicited for this Department. We have an advertising page, and, if necessary, will issue supplements.

From Austin, Arkansas.

We arrived here from Wichita, Kans., April 25, after twenty-two days' travel by wagon. We had a very enjoyable trip. We like our new home very well, so far. Of course it is like any other country,—there is always something that a person likes and something they dislike. We cannot expect to find a place in this world that is perfect. We must learn to take the bitter with the sweet wherever we are.

We have had several meetings since we are here. The people seem to be very anxious to hear our doctrine and they pay very good attention to the Word preached. But here, as well as at other places, it is necessary to have the Gospel preached in its purity, as people are very easily led away by false doctrines; they depend too much on what the preacher says. Since I am here I feel as though we, as a church, are not yet doing what we ought to save sinners from the error of their ways. Now I want to say to our young ministers (and old ones too), where there are four or five at one place, scatter out and open up new fields! Don't be afraid to venture out away from home! The Lord will stand by you if you are engaged in his work. Think of the many souls who are perishing daily for the Bread of Life.

There are many places where the Gospel has not yet been preached. The great Commission is, "Go into all the world. Preach the Gospel to every creature." Now, don't wait to have a personal invitation, but go!   CHARLES E. DELP.

From Wichita, Kans.

THE Wichita congregation held a love-feast in the city of Wichita, on the evening of May 14. We can truly say it was a good meeting. The ministers present were brethren S. Z. Sharp, Samuel Bowser and Levi Andes, with the home ministers. The brethren gave us some excellent instructions and admonitions. One pleasing and profitable feature of the meeting was the children's meeting on Lord's Day morning. Brethren Sharp, Bowser and Andes gave good instruction and counsel to the children. We thought this meeting not only did the children good, but it helped older ones. Through the perseverance of some of our sisters, we are having a good Sunday-school.

Our meetings are well attended, with a fine prospect, if we had a meeting-house of our own. Pray for us that the Lord may bless our labors here in Wichita.   WILLIAM JOHNSTON.
1538 Orange St., Wichita, Kans.

From La Porte, Ind.

AT our council, March 12, Bro. Daniel Shively, of New Paris, Ind., was present for the purpose of encouraging the missionary spirit, by stirring us up to a more lively sense of our duty in that line. Among the good things he dispensed, was a proposition to organize a Bible class in connection with our regular Sunday services. The church accepted the proposition, and next morning organized, with Bro. Shively in charge of the lesson. After concluding the Bible lesson, Bro. Shively

ing churches. The ministerial help was ample. The attendance was large, both by members and also by the spectators. Good order prevailed during the evening exercises. Our church house is large, and will secure room for many persons, but, notwithstanding, it would not contain all the spectators. Such Communion meetings are refreshing for the soul, and should remind us all of the duties which we owe to our Heavenly Father.

JOHN LONG.

May 24.

Some of my Thoughts on Railroad Men and Religion.

ONE of the things about which I have been thinking, is this: What other class of people, give as much money for the advancement of the subject of religion, as railroad men do? I have in my possession six half-fare permits. The lowest number is 4,617, and the highest 30,547. Now that means that number of ministers who have obtained half-fare permits from those companies, and over the highest number here given, I have already traveled out over six dollars on this one trip. Then, suppose every one will travel as much as six dollars in the course of the year, it would amount to the handsome sum of $237,282. This alone for one company, and six dollars per minister, is certainly very low. That means, that one company gives that much to the promotion of the cause of Christianity. Then think of all the different companies, what they are doing, and the aggregate certainly will foot up an immense sum, so that we may well inquire, Who is doing as much? All this, too, outside of what they do for our people at our Annual Meetings. Railroad men do not get their share of credit for what they are doing.   A. HUTCHISON.

McPherson, Kans.

From Franklin Grove, Ill.

THROUGH love-feast notices, previously given, for May 28, brethren and sisters from near and far, met to engage in another love-feast, and to many the occasion will be long remembered in connection with the solemn ceremonial rites of God's house. Bro. D. B. Senger was elected to the ministry and while the burden is a hard one for him to bear, he may have the full assurance that God's faithful ones will help him up before a throne of grace in prayer. Bro. S. C. Lehman was advanced to the full ministry and Bro. C. M. Suter to the second degree.

Brethren from a distance were, Daniel Wolf, of Maryland; E. Eby, of Kansas; I. D. Parker, of Ashland, Ohio; D. E. Brubaker, D. L. Miller, and others, of Mt. Morris. Nearly the entire membership of Sterling, with their minister, P. R. Keltner, also brethren Edmund Forney and Callo Fahrney, of Pine Creek, Ill., and others, that are not named in this report. May all the brethren and sisters have the assurance that their assistance was very much appreciated.   O. H. HAWBECKER.

School Interests.

I HAVE been expecting to see something from the pen of some of the different visiting brethren, on the propriety of a meeting of said respective Visiting Committees at the place and time of our Annual Conference, but so far have seen nothing. I therefore suggest that as many of the visitors be present at Annual Meeting as well can, and that a meeting be called at some suitable time and place during the week, for the purpose of considering points of interest, to both school and church, looking toward more humility and adherence to the general order of our beloved Brotherhood.

Much work on that line needs to be done, also in many local churches as well, and should be

done NOW. Let us call a halt and see. "They that feared the Lord spake often to one another, and the Lord hearkened, and heard it." "In the multitude of counsellors there is safety."

I am glad there is a request going up to Conference to define the duties of the Visiting Committees more fully. Their position is an extraordinary responsible one, and they need the aid of Conference to perform their work well. This question should be kept prominently before the mind of all: Shall the church control the school, or the school the church? The latter is measurably unavoidable and requires no more effort than sailing down stream; the former is barely possible, and, like sailing up the stream, more difficult. If the church never had a Herculean power to control before, she has it now. Schools are mighty in power; and can only be controlled by a greater, obtained through sackcloth and ashes.

ENOCH EBY.

Booth, Kans.

Actions Speak Louder than Words.

DID you ever think, brethren and sisters, that when you confessed Jesus your Savior, you contracted with him to fill a seat in his sanctuary? Do you remember that you promised, when opportunity permitted, you would meet him with the children of God? Have you ever disappointed him? Has your seat been found vacant, and that so often that the minister and the members do not miss you any more? Jesus has promised to be there and his promises are always filled. If we do not feel his presence when we meet in his house, it is because we do not possess his Spirit. Matt. 18: 20. "For where two or three are gathered together in my name, there am I in the midst of them." We may meet in the house of God and not meet in his name. We may have lost sight of Jesus, even in his sanctuary, and that because we do not attend regularly.

When we come home from a council-meeting we frequently see members appear to manifest an interest in the meeting by being very eager to know what actions were taken at the meeting. Sometimes we feel a little delicate in telling them, because of the criticisms that follow.

If we had as much interest in sacred assembly, as we have in things of less importance, many more of us would assemble and help to make good meetings. We sometimes hear members appear to manifest an interest by expressing themselves not satisfied with certain proceedings, saying, "It could have been done better." This may be so. I would just say to those, "Come to council-meeting." We have need of good counselors. When we fail to assemble together through neglect, we lose our interest in the church, we lose our zeal, our love to God and the people of God, and lastly we lose our heaven, because we fail to comply with the requirements of heaven. Heb. 10: 23-26. When we lose pleasure in the assembly of God's people, it shows a weakness of our faith; hence we will be counted among the faithless. When we have no pleasure in the assembly of God's people, we have no pleasure in God. "Actions speak louder than words." 1 John 4: 20. Hence God has no pleasure in us, and he will remove our names from the Lamb's book of life.

B. F. MILLER.

Sangerville, Va.

THE *Worker* mentions a preacher who said he was ashamed to ask the Lord to help him quit a habit like the use of tobacco. He says, "I resolved to quit and I quit." Of another it says: "We know another preacher, pure, pious and prayerful, who quit the tobacco years ago and who says 'A quid or a cigar has been all these long years and is now a temptation to me.' He makes it a matter of conscience and stays quit."

Beware of Evil Thoughts.

To feed the mind on evil thoughts is sure to deform the character and produce vile actions in the life. The secret indulgence in such bad mental food will make itself visible in deeds done "on the housetops." Should the lily, in selecting from the mud in which it grows, the material needed to produce its beautiful bloom, take up substance unfitted to its ends, the effect would appear in its unsightly shades and imperfect form.

In like manner, the man, who secretly cherishes the evil thoughts which are cast up from the mind, will reveal this habit to the world in his spirit and actions. Nor will his "judgment day" be limited to time, seeing that in the life after death, "God shall bring every work into judgment, with every secret thing, whether it be good, or whether it be evil." Know, therefore, O man, that when thou findest delight in evil thoughts, thou art playing with sparks, which are to thy sinful passions what lighted matches are to grains of powder, scattered on the porch of a magazine. They are deadly things, not to be trifled with, but should be resolutely driven from our presence.   SOLOMON SCHUBERT.

Alvada, Ohio.

From Warsaw, Ind.

OUR quarterly council took place May 28, at which time we had considerable business to transact. Owing to the vacancy, left by the death of Bro. R. H. Miller, it became necessary, according to the arrangements of the committee of 1888, sent from Annual Meeting, for the adjoining elders to fill the vacancy, with the approval of the church, which was done at this meeting. The important trust was conferred on Bro. A. H. Puterbaugh, in whom we, as a church, have much confidence, and have all reasons to believe that the cause will not suffer under his care. Our prayer is that God's blessings may rest upon him, and that he may ever be guided by the Spirit, and may guard his trust with that rigid care so essential to the prosperity of the cause.

A choice was also had for two brethren to fill the office of deacon. The lot fell on brethren John Johnson and Nathaniel Mauzy. We pray that they may ever prove faithful and efficient workers in the vineyard of the Lord.

Love and harmony prevailed throughout the meeting. Let all avail themselves of the opportunity of attending our church councils. Let nothing in the way of temporal affairs hinder our attendance. We certainly can work one day out of every three months in the interest of an eternal home, when we spend the rest in the interest of our earthly. Brethren, pray for us!

N. B. HEETER.

QUERIES AND ANSWERS.

(Concluded from first page.)

special customs of the people, about which the narratives are given. The fruit of the grape, or grape-juice, was, in those days, a common accompaniment of their feasts, as much so as tea and coffee now. Whether or not any *special* signification should be attached to this cup, we are not prepared to decide. We are inclined to believe, that not more significance should be attached to it than to any other part of the feast, or supper. That this feast was not the Jewish passover must be evident to all Bible students. As the lamb, used at this feast, was the antitype of Christ, and the legal time for killing it was the hour or time when Christ expired on the cross, this feast of Christ and his disciples was, of course, in advance

ing churches. The ministerial help was ample. The attendance was large, both by members and also by the spectators. Good order prevailed during the evening exercises. Our church house is large, and will secure room for many persons, but, notwithstanding, it would not contain all the spectators. Such Communion meetings are refreshing for the soul, and should remind us all of the duties which we owe to our Heavenly Father.

JOHN LONG.

May 24.

Some of my Thoughts on Railroad Men and Religion.

ONE of the things about which I have been thinking, is this: What other class of people, give as much money for the advancement of the subject of religion, as railroad men do? I have in my possession six half-fare permits. The lowest number is 4,617, and the highest 39,547. Now that means that number of ministers who have obtained half-fare permits from those companies, and over the highest number here given, I have already traveled out over six dollars on this one trip. Then, suppose every one will travel as much as six dollars in the course of the year, it would amount to the handsome sum of $237,282. This alone for one company, and six dollars per minister, is certainly very low. That means, that one company gives that much to the promotion of the cause of Christianity. Then think of all the different companies, what they are doing, and the aggregate certainly will foot up an immense sum, so that we may well inquire, Who is doing as much? All this, too, outside of what they do for our people at our Annual Meetings. Railroad men do not get their share of credit for what they are doing.

A. HUTCHISON.

McPherson, Kans.

: From Franklin Grove, Ill.

THROUGH love-feast notices, previously given, for May 28, brethren and sisters from near and far, met to engage in another love-feast, and to many the occasion will be long remembered in connection with the solemn ceremonial rites of God's house. Bro. D. B. Senger was elected to the ministry and while the burden is a hard one for him to bear, he may have the full assurance that God's faithful ones will hold him up before a throne of grace in prayer. Bro. S. C. Lehman was advanced to the full ministry and Bro. C. M. Suter to the second degree.

Brethren from a distance were, Daniel Wolf, of Maryland; E. Eby, of Kansas; I. D. Parker, of Ashland, Ohio; D. E. Brubaker, D. L. Miller, and others, of Mt. Morris. Nearly the entire membership of Sterling, with their minister, P. R. Keltner, also brethren Edmund Forney and Callo Fahrney, of Pine Creek, Ill., and others, that are not named in this report. May all the brethren and sisters have the assurance that their assistance was very much appreciated. O. H. HAWBECKER.

School Interests.

I HAVE been expecting to see something from the pen of some of the different visiting brethren, on the propriety of a meeting of said respective Visiting Committees at the place and time of our Annual Conference, but so far have seen nothing. I therefore suggest that as many of the visitors be present at Annual Meeting as well can, and that a meeting be called at some suitable time and place during the week, for the purpose of considering points of interest, to both school and church, looking toward more humility and adherence to the general order of our beloved Brotherhood.

Much work on that line needs to be done, also in many local churches as well, and should be

done NOW. Let us call a halt and see. "They that feared the Lord spake often one to another, and the Lord hearkened, and heard it." "In the multitude of counsellors there is safety."

I am glad there is a request going up to Conference to define the duties of the Visiting Committees more fully. Their position is an extraordinary responsible one, and they need the aid of Conference to perform their work well. This question should be kept prominently before the mind of all: Shall the church control the school, or the school the church? The latter is measurably unavoidable and requires no more effort than sailing down stream; the former is barely possible, and, like sailing up the stream, more difficult. If the church never had a Herculean power to control before, she has it now. Schools are mighty in power; and can only be controlled by a greater, obtained through sackcloth and ashes.

ENOCH EBY.

Booth, Kans.

Actions Speak Louder than Words.

DID you ever think, brethren and sisters, that when you confessed Jesus your Savior, you contracted with him to fill a seat in his sanctuary? Do you remember that you promised, when opportunity permitted, you would meet him with the children of God? Have you ever disappointed him? Has your seat been found vacant, and that so often that the minister and the members do not miss you any more? Jesus has promised to be there and his promises are always filled. If we do not feel his presence when we meet in his house, it is because we do not possess his Spirit. Matt. 18: 20. "For where two or three are gathered together in my name, there am I in the midst of them." We may meet in the house of God and not meet in his name. We may have lost sight of Jesus, even in his sanctuary, and that because we do not attend regularly.

When we come home from a council-meeting we frequently see members appear to manifest an interest in the meeting by being very eager to know what actions were taken at the meeting. Sometimes we feel a little delicate in telling them, because of the criticisms that follow.

If we had as much interest in sacred assembly, as we have in things of less importance, many more of us would assemble and help to make good meetings. We sometimes hear members appear to manifest an interest by expressing themselves not satisfied with certain proceedings, saying. "It could have been done better." This may be so. I would just say to those, "Come to council-meeting." We have need of good counselors. When we fail to assemble together through neglect, we lose our interest in the church, we lose our zeal, our love to God and the people of God, and lastly we lose our heaven, because we fail to comply with the requirements of heaven. Heb. 10: 23-26. When we lose pleasure in the assembly of God's people, it shows a weakness of our faith; hence we will be counted among the faithless. When we have no pleasure in the assembly of God's people, we have no pleasure in God. "Actions speak louder than words." 1 John 4: 20. Hence God has no pleasure in us, and he will remove our names from the Lamb's book of life.

B. F. MILLER.

Sangerville, Va.

THE *Worker* mentions a preacher who said he was ashamed to ask the Lord to help him quit a habit like the use of tobacco. He says, "I resolved to quit and I quit." Of another it says: "We know another preacher, pure, pious and prayerful, who quit the tobacco years ago and who says 'A quid or a cigar has been all these long years and is now a temptation to me.' He makes it a matter of conscience and stays quit."

Beware of Evil Thoughts.

To feed the mind on evil thoughts is sure to deform the character and produce vile actions in the life. The secret indulgence in such bad mental food will make itself visible in deeds done "on the housetops." Should the lily, in selecting, from the mud in which it grows, the material needed to produce its beautiful bloom, take up substance unfitted to its ends, the effect would appear in its unsightly shades and imperfect form.

In like manner, the man, who secretly cherishes the evil thoughts which are cast up from the mind, will reveal his habit to the world in his spirit and actions. "Nor will his" judgment day" be limited to time, seeing that in the life after death, "God shall bring every work into judgment, with every secret thing, whether it be good, or whether it be evil." Know, therefore, O man, that when thou findest delight in evil thoughts, thou art playing with sparks, which are to thy sinful passions what lighted matches are to grains of powder, scattered on the porch of a magazine. They are deadly things, not to be trifled with, but should be resolutely driven from our presence. SOLOMON SCHUBERT.

Alvada, Ohio.

From Warsaw, Ind.

OUR quarterly council took place May 28, at which time we had considerable business to transact. Owing to the vacancy, left by the death of Bro. R. H. Miller, it became necessary, according to the arrangements of the committee of 1888, sent from Annual Meeting, for the adjoining elders to fill the vacancy, with the approval of the church, which was done at this meeting. The important trust was conferred on Bro. A. H. Puterbaugh, in whom we, as a church, have much confidence, and have all reasons to believe that the cause will not suffer under his care. Our prayer is that God's blessings may rest upon him, and that he may ever be guided by the Spirit, and may guard his trust with that rigid care so essential to the prosperity of the cause.

A choice was also had for two brethren to fill the office of deacon. The lot fell on brethren John Johnson and Nathaniel Mauzy. We pray that they may ever prove faithful and efficient workers in the vineyard of the Lord.

Love and harmony prevailed throughout the meeting. Let all avail themselves of the opportunity of attending our church councils. Let nothing in the way of temporal affairs hinder our attendance. We certainly can work one day out of every three months in the interest of an eternal home, when we spend the rest in the interest of our earthly. Brethren, pray for us!

N. B. HERTER.

QUERIES AND ANSWERS.

(Concluded from first page.)

special customs of the people, about which the narratives are given. The fruit of the grape, or grape-juice, was, in those days, a common accompaniment of their feasts, as much so as tea and coffee now. Whether or not any special signification should be attached to this cup, we are not prepared to decide. We are inclined to believe, that not more significance should be attached to it than to any other part of the feast, or supper. That this feast was not the Jewish passover must be evident to all Bible students. As the lamb, used at this feast, was the antitype of Christ, and the legal time for killing it was the hour or time when Christ expired on the cross, this feast of Christ and his disciples was, of course, in advance

Lima, Ohio.—The ministerial meeting of the North-western District of Ohio will be held in the Sugar Ridge church, Putnam Co., Ohio, Oct. 5 and 6, 1892.—*David Byerly, May 16.*

West Dayton, Ohio.—Bro. Wm. Bowser, of Taylorsburg, Ohio, came to us on Sunday, May 15. He preached at 10:30 A. M.; also at 7:30 P. M. He did not fear to declare the Gospel in its primitive purity.—*Elmer Wombold, May 18.*

Wallace, Nebr.—We had our council-meeting several weeks ago. One, who had wandered away from the fold, was reclaimed. All business was pleasantly disposed of, in a brotherly way. We have a membership of eighteen members at present.—*Allen Ortps, May 22.*

St. Martin, Mo.—The members of the Prairie View church met in quarterly council May 14, 1892. There was very little business before the meeting, but all passed off harmoniously. We will try to have one series of meetings commence on the fourth Sunday in August. The members are generally well.—*W. W. Holsopple, May 17.*

Mulberry Grove, Ill.—We met in quarterly council May 7. There was but little business before the meeting, but all passed off very pleasantly. We decided to hold a series of meetings, and also a love-feast during the coming October. One sister was received by letter. Eld. Henry Lilligh was elected delegate to Annual Meeting.—*Ida M. Lilligh.*

Peru, Ind.—I left home May 18, to meet the other members of the committee, appointed by District Meeting of Middle Indiana to visit the Landesville church, Grant Co., Ind. The committee met with the church on the 19th. After investigating the troubles that had been existing there for some time, they made out their report, which, among other things, re-instated Bro. Saunders to full fellowship in the church. Our report was accepted by the church, and peace and union, we think, were fully restored, and we predict a brighter future for the church. We pray God's blessing to rest on the labor done, and upon all the true Israel of God.—*D. P. Shively.*

Friendsville, Ohio.—May 14, Bro. Edward Loomis, of New Philadelphia, Ohio, came to us and commenced a series of meetings on Sunday morning, May 15, and continued during the week, preaching, in all, nine sermons, with increased interest and attendance. As an immediate result, one applied for Christian baptism, and we feel that many more were near the kingdom and that the Word sown will spring up and yield a rich harvest for the Lord. We were much encouraged and built up in that most holy faith, which was once delivered to the saints. We have the blessed assurance that God's Word shall not return unto him void. —*Wm. P. Wertz, May 23.*

Mexico, Ind.—The members of the Mexico church have organized two Sunday-schools, which, I think, are in good working order. The one, at the Mexico church-house, is superintended by Bro. Frank Fisher, and has a very large number of scholars. The other at the Court church-house is superintended by Bro. Amos Andrews, and also has a large number of scholars. I think the Sunday-school is a benefit to our children, for they get wholesome instruction from God's Word, and it does not harm the older ones to take lessons. —*J. D. Arnest, Denver, Ind, May 23.*

Hermenton, La.—I will try to let you know something of our condition, here in the Sunny South. May 7 we had our love-feast, and it was truly a feast to our souls. This was my first feast and I can say that I am now more fully convinced than ever, that our doctrine is of Christ. I am partly isolated,—living at a distance of ten miles from Esterly. As I am crippled I cannot be with the members often, and in my loneliness you cannot know how dear the MESSENGER is to me; for, through God's blessing, it was the means of bringing me to the light I say, "Go on with the good work!"—*E. W. Pratt, May 15.*

North Manchester, Ind.—We met in council May 21, preparatory to the love-feast May 28. It was a most harmonious meeting. Not an unkind word was said. Love, union, and harmony prevailed. Much business came before the meeting, but all was disposed of in apparent satisfaction. We were rejoiced to see one dear sister come out on the side of the Lord, and receive Christian baptism. Four were also received by letter. The day following (Sunday), at our regular meeting, another dear sister concluded to forsake sin and serve the Lord. She was also gladly received by baptism, making six, in all, since our last report.—*D. C. Cripe, May 23.*

Girard, Ill.—The Bear Creek church, Christian Co., Ill., held its quarterly council May 14. There were but few members present on account of much rain, high waters and very muddy roads. Considerable business was attended to. This church was, at one time, quite strong, both in membership and ministerial talent. It was formerly the home of Eld. Owen Peters, and others, and also that of our lamented brother, A. Lear, and, lastly, our efficient elder, M. J. McClure. Western emigration has decreased this church very much, and it has now no resident minister, and but one deacon. The writer has charge of this band of faithful members, and also preaches for them on Saturday evening before each second Sunday; and also on Sunday and Sunday evening. Their Communion will be held Aug. 19, at 4 P. M. Eld. Granville Nevinger will be there and remain with them to hold a series of meetings.—*Michael Flory, May 24.*

St. Paul, Va.—May 14 that old soldier of the cross, Eld J, H. Slusher, accompanied by Jacob Hylton, came to us and preached four excellent sermons. Bro. Jacob, though young in the ministry, shows by his labors that he intends to be "a workman that needeth not to be ashamed." The Brethren's sermons were certainly very much appreciated by all who heard them.—*Wm. Wist-r, May 27.*

MATRIMONIAL.

"What therefore God hath joined together, let not man put asunder."

BURNS—WISE.—At the residence of the bride's parents, May 1, 1892, by the undersigned, Bro. Irvin S. Burns and sister Susan A. Wise, both of Wakarusa, Elkhart Co., Ind.   ALEXANDER MILLER.

SMITH—PARTON.—At the residence of the bride's parents, James W. Parton, Mr. Mathias Smith and Mary E. Parton, both of Lincoln County, Nebr. . J. K. SHIVELY.

DAVIS—STITT.—At the residence of Bro. Fred Burns, near Mansfield, Ill., May 18, 1892, Mr. John H. DaVis and Miss Nora M. Stitt.   M. J. McCLURE.

→ FALLEN ASLEEP ←

"Blessed are the dead which die in the Lord."

GRABILL.—In the Clear church, Pa., April 2, 1892, Mary Grabill, aged 71 years, 11 months and 27 days. J. L. HOLSINGER.

SCHWARTZ.—In the Libertyville congregation, Jefferson Co., Iowa, May 14, 1893, sister Elizabeth Schwartz, consort of Bro. Abram Schwartz, deceased, aged 81 years, 7 months and 25 days. Sister Schwartz was a faithful member of the church for many years. A few days before her death she was anointed. Funeral services by Bro. Abram Wolf.   JAMES GLOTFELTY.

FISHER.—In the Little TraVerse congregation, Emmet Co., Mich., Jan. —, 1892, C. D. Ernest, Infant son of Barbara and —— Fisher, aged 3 months. Barbara is a daughter of Bro. Isaac Hufford, of Clarion, Mich. ServIces by Eld. J. R. Stutsman from the words, "Suffer little children to come unto me, and forbid them not: for of such is the kingdom of God."   L. R. WILCOX.

EIKENBERRY.—In the Bachelor Run congregation, Carroll Co., Ind., April 16, 1892, Ella Eikenberry, aged 17 years, 7 months and 4 days. Sister Ella was a patient sufferer for two years. . Six weeks before she passed away she was baptized. Weak as she was, she wanted to obey her Master's will. The funeral services were conducted by Rev. Abe Flora and father Hamilton.

A FRIEND.

MARTIN.—In the La Motte church, Crawford Co., Ill., April 10, 1892, sister Sarah C. Martin, aged 61 years, 1 month and 16 days. She was the daughter of Peter L. and Magdalene Bright. She was married to John H. Martin, March 22, 1852. To them were born six children. Her husband and two daughters preceded her in death over twenty-five years. Funeral services by Jesse Stoner from Rev. 14:13.   A. A. STONER.

GAUBY.—In the Washington church, Washington Co., Kans., May 14, 1892, Leby M. Gauby, aged 1 year, 1 month and 13 days. Deceased is a son of John Gauby, formerly of Berks County, Pa. Funeral by the writer, from Luke 23: 28. HUMPHREY TALHELM.

GOCKLEY.—In the Olathe church, Kans., May 14, 1892, Anna Gockley, aged 21 years, 1 month and 16 days. She leaVes a widowed mother, six sisters and two brothers. Funeral in the Methodist church in Olathe, by the writer, assisted by the Presbyterian minister, from the words, " We do all fade as a leaf."   ISAAC H. CRIST.

SAYLER.—In the Middle Fork church, Clinton Co., Ind , May 16, 1892, sister Sarah J., widow of Eld. Sanford H. Sayler, aged 60 years, 10 months and 13 days. Funeral servIces May 17 in the Pleasant View church by elders John W. Metzger and Isaac Billheimer from 2 Cor. 5: 1, 2. Our sister, after being afflicted for twenty years, is now at rest.
    JOHN E. METZGER.

SEIDER.—In the Union church, Marshall Co., Ind., May 16, 1892, Bro. Jacob Seider, aged 50 years, 7 months and 10 days. Deceased was born in Baden, Germany, and came with his parents to America when quite young. He was married to Margaret Knisley Dec. 12, 1861 and united with the church May —, 1865. He leaVes a dear wife and five children. Funeral serVices by the writer from Rev. 22: 14.   DANIEL SNELL.

HOLSWORTH.—In the Chippewa Creek church, Mecosta Co., Mich., May 1, 1892, Matthew Holsworth, born in .Wittenberg, Germany, April 8, 1821. He was buried May 3.' He leaVes a companion and seven children. Funeral serVices conducted by the writer from Ps. 14 and Job 14: 14.
    WM. H. KRIEGH.

WOODRING.—In the bounds of the Slate Creek congregation, Sedgwick Co., Kans., May 11, 1892, sister Barbara Woodring, wife of Bro. W. D. Woodring, aged 65 years, 7 months and 5 days. Sister Woodring was born in Preble County, Ohio, Oct. 6, 1828. She united with W. D. Woodring in marriage July 4, 1851, and united with the church in 1866 She, with her husband, came to Kansas when it was quite a new country. She was the mother of nine children. Funeral serVices conducted by the writer.   WILLIAM JOHNSON.

CONRAD.—In the White church, Montgomery Co., Ind., May 16, 1892, Charles E. Conrad, son of Bro. William and sister Martha Conrad, aged 19 years, 1 month and 16 days. Disease, lockjaw, caused by a cut in the palm of the hand. Funeral services by the Brethren from Psalms 144: 3.
    D. C. CAMPBELL.

HOOVER.—In the South Waterloo congregation, Iowa, May 9, 1892, sister Elizabeth Hoover, aged 72 years, 7 months and 29 days. Her maiden name was Miller. She was married to Martin HooVer, Dec. 20, 1838. To this union thirteen children were born. Her disease was cancer in the head, from which she has been a great sufferer for seVeral years but bore her affliction patiently. Funeral services conducted by the brethren from Philipp. 1: 21.   S. H. MILLER.

BONE.—At her home in Sawyer, Berrien Co., Mich., May 15, 1892, sister Elizabeth Bone, wife of Bro. Isaac Bone, aged 54 years and 2 months. She leaVes a husband, two sisters and one brother. Funeral serVices May 18 by the undersigned. in the Congregational church at Sawyer, from Rev. 23: 6, in compliance with her dying request.
    THURSTON MILLER.

YOUNG.—In the Beatrice congregation, Gage Co., Nebr., May 4. 1892, Ruth A. Young, infant daughter of Bro. J. E. and sister Sadie Young, aged 3 months and 18 days. Funeral serVices by the writer.
    URIAS SNICK.

SHRADER.—In the bounds of the Osawkie church, Jefferson Co., Kans., George G. Shrader, infant son of Charles and Fanny Shrader. Funeral serVices by the Writer at McLouth.   DAVID KIMMEL.

STRAWH.—In the Old Folks' Home, near Mexico, Ind., May 17, 1892, Bro. David Gottlieb Strawh, aged 84 years, 2 months and 20 days. He was born in Friedensburg, Germany, and was a faithful member of the church for about forty years. Funeral serVices from Rev. 14: 13 by John Layr and Jacob Fisher.

Lima, Ohio.—The ministerial meeting of the North-western District of Ohio will be held in the Sugar Ridge church, Putnam Co., Ohio, Oct. 5 and 6, 1892.—*David Byerly, May 16.*

West Dayton, Ohio.—Bro. Wm. Bowser, of Taylorsburg, Ohio, came to us on Sunday, May 15. He preached at 10:30 A. M.; also at 7:30 P. M. He did not fear to declare the Gospel in its primitive purity.—*Elmer Wombold, May 18.*

Wallace, Nebr.—We had our council-meeting several weeks ago. One, who had wandered away from the fold, was reclaimed. All business was pleasantly disposed of, in a brotherly way. We have a membership of eighteen members at present.—*Allen Oripe, May 22.*

St. Martin, Mo.—The members of the Prairie View church met in quarterly council May 14, 1892. There was very little business before the meeting, but all passed off harmoniously. We will try to have our series of meetings commence on the fourth Sunday in August. The members are generally well.—*W. W. Holsopple, May 17.*

Mulberry Grove, Ill.—We met in quarterly council May 7. There was but little business before the meeting, but all passed off very pleasantly. We decided to hold a series of meetings, and also a love-feast during the coming October. One sister was received by letter. Eld. Henry Lilligh was elected delegate to Annual Meeting.—*Ida M. Lilligh.*

Peru, Ind.—I left home May 18, to meet the other members of the committee, appointed by District Meeting of Middle Indiana to visit the Landessville church, Grant Co., Ind. The committee met with the church on the 19th. After investigating the troubles that had been existing there for some time, they made out their report, which, among other things, re-instated Bro. Saunders to full fellowship in the church. Our report was accepted by the church. All peace and union, we think, were fully restored, and we predict a bright-er future for the church. We pray God's blessing to rest on the labor done, and upon all the true Israel of God.—*D. P. Shively.*

Friendsville, Ohio.—May 14, Bro. Edward Loomis, of New Philadelphia, Ohio, came to us and commenced a series of meetings on Sunday morning, May 15, and continued during the week, preaching, in all, nine sermons, with increased interest and attendance. As an immediate result, one applied for Christian baptism, and we feel that many more were near the kingdom and that the Word sown will spring up and yield a rich harvest for the Lord. We were much encouraged and built up in that most holy faith, which was once delivered to the saints. We have the blessed assurance that God's Word shall not return unto him void.—*Wm. P. Werts, May 23.*

Mexico, Ind.—The members of the Mexico church have organized two Sunday-schools, which, I think, are in good working order. The one, at the Mexico church-house, is superintended by Bro. Frank Fisher, and has a very large number of scholars. The other at the Court church-house is superintended by Bro. Amos Andrews, and also has a large number of scholars. I think the Sunday-school is a benefit to our children, for they get wholesome instruction from God's Word, and it does not harm the older ones to take lessons.—*J. D. Arnest, Denver, Ind., May 23.*

Hermeston, La.—I will try ot let you know something of our condition, here in the Sunny South. May 7 we had our love-feast, and it was truly a feast to our souls. This was my first feast and I can say that I am now more fully convinced than ever, that our doctrine is of Christ. I am partly isolated,—living at a distance of ten miles from Esterly. As I am crippled I cannot be with the members often, and in my loneliness you cannot know how dear the MESSENGER is to me; for, through God's blessing, it was the means of bringing me to the light I say, "Go on with the good work!"—*E. W. Prati, May 15.*

North Manchester, Ind.—We met in council May 21, preparatory to the love-feast May 28. It was a most harmonious meeting. Not an unkind word was said. Love, union, and harmony prevailed. Much business came before the meeting, but all was disposed of in apparent satisfaction. We were rejoiced to see one dear sister come out on the side of the Lord, and receive Christian baptism. Four were also received by letter. The day following (Sunday), at our regular meeting, another dear sister concluded to forsake sin and serve the Lord. She was also gladly received by baptism, making six, in all, since our last report.—*D. C. Cripe, May 23.*

Girard, Ill.—The Bear Creek church, Christian Co., Ill., held its quarterly council May 14. There were but few members present on account of much rain, high waters and very muddy roads. Considerable business was attended to. This church was, at one time, quite strong, both in membership and ministerial talent. It was formerly the home of Eld. Owen Peters, and others, and also that of our lamented brother, A. Lear, and, lastly, our efficient elder, M. J. Mc-Clure. Western emigration has decreased this church very much, and it has now no resident minister, and but one deacon. The writer has charge of this band of faithful members, and also preaches for them on Saturday evening before each second Sunday; and also on Sunday and Sunday evening. Their Communion will be held Aug. 19, at 4 P. M. Eld. Granville Nevinger will be there and remain with them to hold a series of meetings.—*Michael Flory, May 24.*

St. Paul, Va.—May 14 that old soldier of the cross, Eld J. H. Slusher, accompanied by Jacob Hylton, came to us and preached four excellent sermons. Bro. Jacob, though young in the ministry, shows by his labors that he intends to be "a workman that needeth not to be ashamed." The Brethren's sermons were certainly very much appreciated by all who heard them.—*Wm. Wisler, May 17.*

MATRIMONIAL.

"What therefore God hath joined together, let not man put asunder."

BURNS—WISE.—At the residence of the bride's parents, May 1, 1892, by the undersigned, Bro. Irvin S. Burns and sister Susan A. Wise, both of Wakarusa, Elkhart Co., Ind.
　　ALEXANDER MILLER.

SMITH—PARTON.—At the residence of the bride's parents, James W. Parton, Mr. Mathias Smith and Mary E. Parton, both of Lincoln County, Nebr.　J. K. SHIVELY.

DAVIS—STITT.—At the residence of Bro. Fred Burns, near Mansfield, Ill., May 18, 1892, Mr. John H. Davis and Miss Nora M. Stitt.　M. J. McCLURE.

✦ FALLEN ASLEEP. ✦

"Blessed are the dead which die in the Lord."

GRABILL.—In the Clear church, Pa., April 2, 1892, Mary Grabill, aged 71 years, 11 months and 17 days.　J. L. HOLSINGER.

SCHWARTZ.—In the Libertyville congregation, Jefferson Co., Iowa, May 14, 1892, sister Elizabeth Schwartz, consort of Bro. Abram Schwartz, deceased, aged 81 years, 7 months and 23 days. Sister Schwartz was a faithful member of the church for many years. A few days before her death she was anointed. Funeral services by Bro. Abram Wolf.　JAMES GLOTFELTY.

FISHER.—In the Little Traverse congregation, Emmet Co., Mich., Jan. —, 1892, C. D. Ernest, infant son of Barbara and —— Fisher, aged 3 months. Barbara is a daughter of Bro. Isaac Hofford, of Clarion, Mich. Services by Eld. J. R. Stutsman from the words, "Suffer little children to come unto me, and forbid them not; for of such is the kingdom of God."　L. B. WILCOX.

EIKENBERRY.—In the Bachelor Run congregation, Carroll Co., Ind., April 16, 1892, Ella Eikenberry, aged 17 years, 7 months and 4 days. Sister Ella was a patient sufferer for two years. Six weeks before she passed away she was baptized. Weak as she was, she wanted to obey her Master's will. The funeral services were conducted by Rev. Abe Flora and father Hamilton.
　　A FRIEND.

MARTIN.—In the La Motte church, Crawford Co., Ill., April 10, 1892, sister Sarah C. Martin, aged 61 years, 1 month and 16 days. She was the daughter of Peter L. and Magdalene Bright. She was married to John H. Martin, March 23, 1852. To them were born six children. Her husband and two daughters preceded her in death over twenty-five years. Funeral services by Jesse Stoner from Rev. 14: 13.　A. A. STONER.

GAUBY.—In the Washington church, Washington Co., Kans., May 14, 1892, Leby M. Gauby, aged 1 year, 1 month and 13 days. Deceased is a son of John Gauby, formerly of Berks County, Pa. Funeral by the writer, from Luke 23: 43.　HUMPHREY TALHELM.

GOCKLEY.—In the Olathe church, Kans., May 14, 1892, Anna Gockley, aged 21 years, 1 month and 15 days. She leaves a widowed mother, six sisters and two brothers. Funeral in the Methodist church in Olathe, by the writer, assisted by the Presbyterian minister, from the words, "We do all fade as a leaf."
　　ISAAC H. CRIST.

SAYLER.—In the Middle Fork church, Clinton Co., Ind., May 16, 1892, sister Sarah J., widow of Eld. Sanford H. Sayler, aged 60 years, 10 months and 13 days. Funeral services May 17 in the Pleasant View church by elders John W. Metzger and Isaac Billheimer from 1 Cor. 5: 1, 2. Our sister, after being afflicted for twenty years, is now at rest.
　　JOHN E. METZGER.

SEIDER.—In the Union church, Marshall Co., Ind., May 16, 1892, Bro. Jacob Seider, aged 50 years, 7 months and 10 days. Deceased was born in Baden, Germany, and came with his parents to America when quite young. He was married to Margaret Knisley Dec. 12, 1861 and united with the church May —, 1865. He leaves a dear wife and five children. Funeral services by the writer from Rev. 22: 14.　DANIEL SNELL.

HOLSWORTH.—In the Chippewa Creek church, Mecosta Co., Mich., May 1, 1892, Matthew Holsworth, born in Wittenberg, Germany, April 8, 1821. He was buried May 3. He leaves a companion and seven children. Funeral services conducted by the writer from Ps. 14 and Job 14: 14.
　　Wm. H. KRIEGH.

WOODRING.—In the bounds of the Slate Creek congregation, Sedgwick Co., Kans., May 11, 1892, sister Barbara Woodring, wife of Bro. W. D. Woodring, aged 63 years, 7 months and 5 days. Sister Woodring was born in Preble County, Ohio, Oct. 6, 1828. She united with W. D. Woodring in marriage May 4, 1851, and united with the church in 1866. She, with her husband, came to Kansas when it was quite a new country. She was the mother of nine children. Funeral services conducted by the writer.　WILLIAM JOHNSON.

CONRAD.—In the White church, Montgomery Co., Ind., May 16, 1892, Charles E. Conrad, son of Bro. William and sister Martha Conrad, aged 19 years, 1 month and 16 days. Disease, lockjaw, caused by a cut in the palm of the hand. Funeral services by the Brethren from Psalms 144: 3.
　　D. C. CAMPBELL.

HOOVER.—In the South Waterloo congregation, Iowa, May 19, 1892, sister Elizabeth Hoover, aged 72 years, 7 months and 19 days. Her maiden name was Miller. She was married to Martin Hoover, Dec. 20, 1838. To this union thirteen children were born. Her disease was cancer in the head, from which she has been a great sufferer for several years but bore her affliction patiently. Funeral services conducted by the brethren from Philipp. 1: 21.　S. H. MILLER.

BONE.—At her home in Sawyer, Berrien Co., Mich., May 15, 1892, sister Elizabeth Bone, wife of Bro. Isaac Bone, aged 54 years and 2 months. She leaves a husband, two sisters and one brother. Funeral services May 18 by the undersigned, in the Congregational church at Sawyer, from Ps. 23: 6, in compliance with her dying request.
　　THURSTON MILLER.

YOUNG.—In the Beatrice congregation, Gage Co., Nebr., May 4, 1892, Barb A. Young, infant daughter of Bro. J. E. and sister Sadie Young, aged 3 months and 18 days. Funeral services by the writer.
　　URIAS SHICK.

SHRADER.—In the bounds of the Osawkie church, Jefferson Co., Kans., George G. Shrader, infant son of Charles and Fanny Shrader. Funeral services by the writer at McLouth.　DAVID KIMMEL.

STRAWH.—In the Old Folks' Home, near Mexico, Ind., May 17, 1892, Bro. David Gottlieb Strawh, aged 84 years, 2 months and 20 days. He was born in Fridenburg, Germany, and was a faithful member of the church for about forty years. Funeral services from Rev. 14: 13 by John Layr and Jacob Fisher.

Announcements.

LOVE-FEASTS.

June 8, at 1 P. M., Ephrata, Pa., at the Mohler house.

June 8, White Oak church, at the Pennville house, Lancaster Co., Pa.

June 11, 3½ miles North-west of Cabool, Mo.

June 11, at 4 P. M., Cornell church, Ill., on the Strasser Branch of the Wabash R. R.

June 11 and 12, at 10 A. M., Greene church, Greene, Iowa. There will be preaching on Friday evening previous.

June 11, at 4 P. M., Quemahoning church, Somerset Co., Pa.

June 11, at 4 P. M., in the Fairview church, Pa.

June 11, Longmont, Colo.

June 11, at 10 A. M., Belleville church, Republic Co., Kans.

June 11, at 2 P. M., Kingsley church, four miles southeast of Kingsley, Iowa.

June 11, at 2 P. M., in the Monitor church, 8 miles west and 2 miles south of McPherson, Kans.

June 11, at 10 A. M., Hudson, Ill.

June 11, at 3 P. M., in the Bethel congregation, Kosciusko Co., Ind., at the Pleasant View Chapel, three miles east of Milford.

June 11, St. Vrain church, Colo.

June 11 and 12, at 10 A. M., in the Richland church, Richland County, Ohio, six miles north of Mansfield.

June 11, at 4 P. M., North Beatrice church, Nebr.

June 11 and 12, Kinsly church, Woodbury Co., Iowa.

June 11, Fairview church, Iowa.

June 11, at 10 A. M., in the well house, Thornapple church, Mich. Take the D. L. & N. R. R from Grand Rapids, Mich., to Elmdale, where you will be met by notifying L. H. Fry. Elmdale, Mich.

June 11, Plum Creek church, Pa. A series of meetings to begin one week previous. Eld. S. H. Meyers is expected to be with us.

June 11, at 4 P. M., Sumsuit church, Somerset Co., Pa.

June 11, at 4 P. M., in the Shade Creek congregation, Somerset Co., Pa.

June 11, Good Hope church, Colo., 7 miles north of Holyoke.

June 11, at 4 P. M., Camp Creek church, Kosciusko Co., Ind., 4 miles North of Etna Green. Those coming from the West at 10 M. and East at 2 P. M., will find conveyance to the church.

June 13 and 16, Dallas Center church, Iowa.

June 16, at 2 P. M., Figure River church, Ind.

June 17, at 4 P. M., Yellow River congregation, Marshall Co., Ind.

June 18, at the Center Meeting house, Canton, Stark Co., Ohio.

June 18, at 6 P. M., In the Eagle Creek church, Ohio. A series of meetings will be held in connection, beginning June 16.

June 18 and 19, at 10 A. M., Iowa River church, Iowa.

June 18, at 2 P. M., Cellus church, 4½ miles south-west of Cellus and 3 miles north of Coldwater, Ohio.

June 18, at 1 P. M., Weddam's Grove, Stephenson Co., Ill.

June 18 and 19, Panther Creek, Dallas Co., Iowa.

June 18, at 10 A. M., South Waterloo church, Waterloo, Iowa.

June 18, Green Spring District, Seneca Co., Ohio.

June 18, at Levi Dake's, three miles south of Custer, Mason Co., Mich.

June 18 and 19, at 11 A. M., Middle Creek church, Mahaska Co., Iowa.

June 18, at 2 P. M., Brick church, Ten Mile congregation, three miles Southeast of Washington, Pa. There will be one week's meeting previous to the feast.

June 18, at 10 A. M., in Wooster congregation, Wayne Co., Ohio, at George Heestand's, ½ mile east of Smithville Station.

June 24, at 4 P. M., in Rock Run church, Elkhart Co., Ind.

June 25, at 4 P. M., Rice Mills church, Cedar Co., Iowa.

June 25 and 26, Coon River church, near Panora, Iowa.

June 25, at 10 A. M., in the Tan Wert church, seven miles south-east of Van Wert, Ohio. Those coming by rail will be met at Van Wert, day before the meeting by notifying Jacob Heestand, or Joseph Longanecker. Wren, Ohio.

June 25 and 26, Indian Creek church, Polk Co., Iowa.

June 25 and 26, at 1 P. M., Hickory Grove, Ill.

June 25, at 5 P. M., Blue River church, Whitley Co., Ind.

Sept. 17, 24, 4 P. M., Indian Creek congregation, Fayette Co., Pa. Series of meetings to commence Aug. 27.

Oct. 7, at 2 P. M., Kaskaskia church, Fayette Co., Ill., two miles north-west of Brownstown, Ill. Those coming by rail will be met at the above-named place by informing Granville Nevinger.

LIFE AND SERMONS

— OF —

ELD. JAMES QUINTER.

THIS is a neatly-printed and well-bound volume of 426 pages, containing a well written biographical sketch of Eld. James Quinter and forty of his sermons.

The biographical part will be found quite interesting, instructive and impressive. No one can read an account of Bro. Quinter's life without feeling deeply and favorably impressed. The work shows how a poor orphan boy, by hard work, and faithfulness to his religious convictions, rose step by step, until he reached a field of usefulness and honor as broad as the Nation itself. Though dead, his good deeds and the impressive examples in piety, learning and simplicity will follow him for generations to come.

The Sermon Department contains many of his choice sermons, which will prove exceedingly interesting and profitable reading to all, and especially to our ministers and isolated members. We feel that this book will fill a long-felt want in our Brotherhood. Price, post-paid, $1.25.

BRETHREN'S PUBLISHING CO.,
Mt. Morris, Ill.

Alone with God

THIS manual of devotions, by J. H. Garrison, comprises a series of meditations with forms of prayer for private devotions, family worship and special occasions. It is one of the most useful, most needed, and best adapted books of the year, and therefore it is not strange that it is proving one of the most popular. In work of this kind its distinguished, gifted, pious and beloved author is at his best. This book is helpful to every minister, church official, and Sunday-school superintendent as well as every private member of the church in all ages. It has models of prayer, suitable for the service of the prayer-meeting, with its suggestions, meditations and instructions are pre-eminently calculated to be of service in preparation for the solemn duties that rest upon the active members. Cloth, 75 cents; morocco, $1.25. Address this office.

CRUDEN'S COMPLETE CONCORDANCE

THIS excellent work, which we offer for sale to our readers, at the low price of $1.50 post-paid, is the only one of the kind that may be depended upon as being strictly reliable. Any verse in the Bible may be read, if found by looking for any material word in the verse. Besides this there are given the significations of the principal words, by which their true Scriptural meaning may be known. A full account of the Jewish customs and ceremonies is given as well as a complete concordance of the proper names of the Bible and of the books called Apocrypha. Send all orders for the above work to this office.

Announcements.

LOVE-FEASTS.

June 8, at 1 P. M., Ephrata, Pa., at the Mohler house.

June 8, White Oak church, at the Pennville house, Lancaster Co., Pa.

June 10, 5¾ miles North-west of Colood, Mo.

June 11, at 2 P. M., Cornell church, Ill., on the Streator Branch of the Walnut R. R.

June 10 and 11, at 10 A. M., Greene church, Greene, Iowa. There will be preaching on Friday evening previous.

June 11, at 4 P. M., Quemahoning church, Somerset Co., Pa.

June 11, at 4 P. M., in the Fairview church, Pa.

June 11, Longmont, Colo.

June 11 and 12, at 10 A. M., Belleville church, Republic Co., Kans.

June 11, at 3 P. M., Kingsley church, four miles south-east of Kingsley, Iowa.

June 11, at 2 P. M., in the Monitor church, 5 miles west and 2 miles south of McPherson, Kans.

June 11, at 10 A. M., Hudson, Ill.

June 11, at 2 P. M., in the Bethel congregation, Kosciusko Co., Ind., at the Pleasant View Chapel, three miles east of Milford.

June 11, St. Vrain church, Colo.

June 11 and 12, at 10 A. M., in the Richland church, Richland County, Ohio, 2½ miles north of Mansfield.

June 11, at 4 P. M., North Beatrice church, Nebr.

June 11 and 12, Kinsly church, Woodbury Co., Iowa.

June 11, Fairview church, Iowa.

June 11, at 10 A. M., in the Root house, Thornapple church, Mich. Take the D. L. & N. R. R. from Grand Rapids, Mich., to Elmdale, where you will be met by notifying L. D. Fry, Elmdale, Mich.

June 11, Plum Creek church, Pa. A series of meetings to begin one week previous. Eld. S. H. Meyers is expected to be with us.

June 11, at 4 P. M., Summit church, Somerset Co., Pa.

June 11, at 4 P. M., in the Shade Creek congregation, Somerset Co., Pa.

June 11, Good Hope church, Colo., 7 miles north of Holyoke.

June 11, at 4 P. M., Camp Creek church, Kosciusko Co., Ind., 4 miles North of Etna Green. Those coming from the West at 10 M., and East at 2 P. M., will find conveyance to the church.

June 13 and 16, Dallas Center church, Iowa.

June 16, at 2 P. M., Pigeon River church, Ind.

June 17, at 4 P. M., Yellow River congregation, Marshall Co., Ind.

June 18, at the Center Meeting-house, Canton, Stark Co., Ohio.

June 18, at 6 P. M., in the Eagle Creek church, Ohio. A series of meetings will be held in connection, beginning June 16.

June 18 and 19, at 10 A. M., Iowa River church, Iowa.

June 21, at 2 P. M., Celina church, 4½ miles south-west of Celina and 3 miles north of Coldwater, Ohio.

June 18, at 2 P. M., Waddam's Grove, Stephenson Co., Ill.

June 18 and 19, Panther Creek, Dallas Co., Iowa.

June 18, at 10 A. M., South Waterloo church, Waterloo, Iowa.

June 18, Green Spring District, Seneca Co., Ohio.

June 18, at Levi Dilke's, three miles south of Custer, Mason Co., Mich.

June 18 and 19, at 11 A. M., Middle Creek church, Mahaska Co., Iowa.

June 18, at 2 P. M., Brick church, Ten Mile congregation, about 11 miles South-east of Washington, Pa. There will be one week's meeting previous to the feast.

June 18, 18, at 10 A. M., in Wooster congregation, Wayne Co., Ohio, at George Heestand's, ½ mile east of Smithville Station.

June 21, at 4 P. M., in Rock Run church, Elkhart Co., Ind.

June 21, at 5 P. M., five miles south-west of Goshen, at the Rock Run church, Ind.

June 21 and 25, Coon River church, near Panora, Iowa.

June 25, at 10 A. M., of the Van Wert church, 10 miles south-east of Van Wert, Ohio. Those coming by rail will be met at Van Wert, day before the meeting by notifying Jacob Halterman, or Joseph Longenecker, Wetzel, Ohio.

June 25 and 26, Indian Creek church, Polo Co., Iowa.

June 25 and 26, at 3 P. M., Hickory Grove, Ill.

June 25, at 2 P. M., Blue River church, Whitley Co., Ind.

Sept. 16, at 4 P. M., Kaskaskia church, Fayette Co., Pa. Series of meetings to commence Aug. 17.

Oct. 7, at 2 P. M., Kaskaskia church, Fayette Co., Ill., two miles south-west of Racine City, Ill. Those coming by rail will be met at the above-named place by informing Gervase Bevington.

LIFE AND SERMONS

— OF —

ELD. JAMES QUINTER.

This is a neatly-printed and well-bound volume of 426 pages, containing a well-written biographical sketch of Eld. James Quinter and forty of his sermons.

The biographical part will be found quite interesting, instructive and impressive. No one can read an account of Bro. Quinter's life without feeling deeply and favorably impressed. The work shows how a poor orphan boy, by hard work, and faithfulness to his religious convictions, rose step by step, until he reached a field of usefulness and honor as broad as the Nation itself. Though dead, his good deeds and the impressive examples in piety, learning and simplicity will follow him for generations to come.

The Sermon Department contains many of his choice sermons, which will prove exceedingly interesting and profitable reading to all, and especially to our ministers and isolated members. We feel that this book will fill a long-felt want in our Brotherhood. Price, post-paid, $1.25.

BRETHREN'S PUBLISHING CO.,
Mt. Morris, Ill.

Alone with God

This manual of devotions, by J. H. Garrison, comprises a series of meditations with forms of prayer for private devotions, family worship and special occasions. It is one of the most useful, most needed, and best adapted books of the year, and therefore it is not strange that it is proving one of the most popular. In work of this kind its distinguished, gifted, pious and beloved author is at his best. This book is helpful to every minister, church official, and Sunday-school superintendent as well as every private member of the church in all ages. It has models of prayer, suitable for the service of the prayer-meeting, while its suggestions, meditations and instructions are pre-eminently calculated to be of service in preparation for the solemn duties that rest upon the active members. Cloth, 75 cents; morocco, $1.25. Address this office.

CRUDEN'S

COMPLETE

CONCORDANCE

This excellent work, which we offer for sale to our readers, at the low price of $1.50 post-paid, is the only one of the kind that may be depended upon as being strictly reliable. Any verse in the Bible may be easily found by looking for any material word in the verse. Besides this there are given the significations of the principal words, by which their true, Scriptural meaning may be known. A full account of Jewish customs and ceremonies is given as well as a complete concordance of the proper names of the Bible and of the books called Apocrypha. Send all orders for the above work to this office.

EUROPE

AND

Bible Lands

A new edition of this deservedly popular work has recently been published. It retains all the excellencies of its predecessors, and with those who are interested in Bible study this work will always remain a favorite. Those who have read the ordinary book of travel will be surprised to find "Europe and Bible Lands" of thrilling interest for both old and young. The large number of books already sold, proves that the work is of more than ordinary merit.

A fair supply of the last edition of this work is still on hand. Those who have not yet secured a copy of the work should embrace this opportunity of securing it. Price, in fine cloth binding, only $1.50 per copy, post-paid. To agents who are prepared to push an active canvass of the work, we are prepared to give special inducements. Write us.

BRETHREN'S PUBLISHING CO.,
Mt. Morris, Ill.

Gospel Chimes.

BY WM. BEERY.

A new edition of this deservedly popular Sunday-school song book has just been issued.

Bro. Beery has had a large experience in Sunday-school work, and the book which we offer to the Brethren, and the public in general, evinces the exercise of talent as well as good judgment. The religious purity of the hymns contributed by sister Beery, adds much to the excellence of the book.

Price per single copy, 35 cts.; per dozen, by mail, $3.50; by express, $4.50. Lots of more than a dozen must be sent by express.

BRETHREN'S PUBLISHING CO.,
Or Huntingdon, Pa.   Mt. Morris, Ill.

CANCERS, TUMORS, ETC.

Successfully treated by Dr. C. N. Boeder, at Waynesborough, Pa., where he has practiced for the last sixteen years. Dr. Boeder is a graduate of the University of Maryland, at Baltimore City. References given and correspondence solicited. Address, Dr. C. W. Boeder, Waynesborough, Pa.

Sacred Geography and Antiquities.—A practical, helpful work for Bible students, ministers and Sunday-school teachers. Price, $2.85.

The Origin and Growth of Religion.—Hibbert Lectures. By T. W. R. Davids. Cloth, 600. $2.50.

Comic Work, or Bible Reader's Commentary on the New Testament.—By J. G. Butler. Two vols. 800, $2.00.

Popular Commentary on the New Testament.—Edited by Philip Schaff. Four volumes, 800. Matthew, Mark and Luke; $6.00. John and the Acts; $6.00. Romans to Philemon; $5.00. Hebrews to Revelation; $5.00.

The Annual Meeting of German Baptist Brethren at Cedar Rapids, Iowa,

June 3 to 9 inclusive.

Tickets for the above meeting will be good going from May 28 to June 4, good to return till June 30.

THE ILLINOIS CENTRAL RAILROAD is the popular and direct route from Chicago to Cedar Rapids. Two First-class express trains, equipped with beautiful, free, reclining chair cars, leave Chicago daily at 11:30 P. M. and 11:35 P. M., arriving at Cedar Rapids at 11 P. M. and 11 A. M.

A large number of the Brethren from the different Eastern States have already decided to take this favorite route.

Tickets will be on sale at all railroad coupon ticket offices in the East.

Don't fail to ask for tickets via the Illinois Central R. R. from Chicago.

For further detailed information write

A. J. McDONGALL,
Eastern Pass. Agt., I. C. R. R.,
343 Broadway,   New York.

ESSAYS

"Study to show thyself approved unto God; a workman that needeth not be ashamed, rightly dividing the Word of Truth."

THE CHRISTIAN HERO.

SELECTED BY FANNIE B. ZUG.

Live on the field of battle!
Be earnest in the fight;
Stand forth with manly courage,
And struggle for the right.

Watch on the field of battle!
The foe is every-where;
His fiery darts fly thickly,
Like lightning through the air.

Pray on the field of battle!
God works with those who pray;
His mighty arm can nerve us,
And make us win the day.

Die on the field of battle!
'Tis noble thus to die;
God smiles on valiant soldiers,—
Their record is on high.

Mankcin, Pa.

SEEING AND SEEING.

BY C. H. BALSBAUGH.

To the Widow and Family of Eld. R. H. Miller:—

WALKING with God, Enoch-like, is ever-growing likeness to God, naturally leading into immediate presence of God, resulting in everlasting fellowship with God. "Can two walk together *except they be agreed?*" Amos 3: 3. I have known man and wife to walk together through life, the one "defaming," the other "entreating;" the one in the "power of the resurrection," the other in the "bondage of corruption;" having many things common apparently, yet nothing in common really. Physically and in external domesticity, they walked together, while spiritually and in the deepest sense, they were as far apart as the antipodal eternities. So we can "walk in all the commandments and ordinances of the Lord," but not "blameless." To "walk as Jesus walked" is to walk in the purity and power and peace of the Holy Ghost. Ordinances are types of spiritual realities to all; but they are expressions of divine life and love only by those who have been born of God.

Nothing is more spontaneous and exultant than the manifestations of love. All concede to this. God *is* love, and the incoming of his life by faith in Jesus Christ takes away every trace of legality and bondage from our obedience, and refers salvation, from beginning to end, to the superabounding grace of God in Christ. We are not saved because we obey, but we obey because "we are his workmanship, created in Christ Jesus unto good works." Eph. 2: 10. To prepare a plea by our obedience for reconciliation with God, is as impossible as for "the blood of bulls and goats to take away sin." But by our loyalty we can maintain the position which grace confers. But the same faith that made the provisions of grace ours, must externalize itself in all the forms and works "which God hath before ordained that we should walk in them." Eph. 2: 10. Such, I believe, was the life of Eld. Robert H. Miller.

"He walked with God, and is not, for God took him." Gen. 5: 24. In his death you have lost much, but he has gained more. What was revealed to his faith here, is now an open vision. 1 Cor. 2: 9, 10. The seeing of 2 Cor. 3: 18, is now the beatific beholding of Rev. 22: 4. His "*life was hid* with Christ in God," and now he has personal rapture of the "far more exceeding and eternal weight of glory." 2 Cor. 3: 3; 2 Cor. 4: 17. His "reckoning" is now fruition. Rom. 8:

18. He was no soul-sleeping theorist while here, and now he has conscious verification of the sublime doctrine of Christ, that "God is not the God of the *dead*, but of the *living.*"

His was a capacious soul, and now he has all the facilities at hand to be "filled with all the fullness of God." Rev. 7: 15, 16, 17. No longer "through a glass darkly, but face to face." 1 Cor. 13: 12. He has reached the wonderful "THERE" of John 14: 3. "WHERE I AM," says Jesus, "THERE ye may be also." When you think of the loved companion, your faith must enter into "the Holiest of all" and behold him among those who have "washed their robes in the blood of the Lamb," and stand on the sea of glass, sweeping with Spirit-taught hearts and hands the golden harps of Redemption's full-chorused anthem.

Give your imagination the wings of the Jordanic Dove, and soar aloft into the empyrean of the home-gathered, and live in the realization of Col. 3: 1, 2 and Philpp. 3: 20, 21. Do not fail to apprehend the present tense of Heb. 12: 22, and include in the "are" all the upper-world glories and raptures unfolded in 22, 23, 24. There is your beloved husband and father, there you are anticipatively by faith, and there you will shortly all be personally, if you live steadfastly in 1 Pet. 1: 8, 9.

I saw Eld. Miller but once,—at our last Annual Conference. Once he wrote to me, while he was at Ashland. His was not great mental *culture* in the common acceptation of the word, but great native intellectual powers. His mind was preeminently analytic, and he saw correct inferences intuitively. He was a constitutional logician. All his writings reveal this. But it was his piety that gave him his true grandeur. He was verily a saint. He was swayed in thought, word and act by "the powers of the world to come." His face was written all over with the chirography of God.

When it was my honor and pleasure to stand a few minutes before that vast concourse at Hagerstown and testify for Jesus, Eld. Miller sat right before me, and gazed into my very soul with apparently intense interest. When I remarked that "Love is God's great name, expressive of his great nature, and that it is this name that he writes in the foreheads of all his children, by which they are known and read of all men," Bro. Miller sweetly smiled and nodded an emphatic recognition.

Such a life on earth is very God in the flesh,—the exemplification of 1 Cor. 13: 4-7. Such enshrining and manifestation of the Holy Ghost, God counts on for the evangelization of the world. Not flesh-circumcised law-breakers, but heart-circumcised law-fulfillers, are "the light of the world, and the salt of the earth." Rom. 2: 25-29. To boast in the letter, and "make a fair show in the flesh," and be sensitively scrupulous in the observance of all the types and shadows of religion, is not "the power of God unto salvation." To do all these things faithfully, and be what the Christian ritual symbolizes,—this is to walk with God, this is to see him with the open face of 2 Cor. 3: 18, this is to know Rom. 15: 13, as we know the very fact of our personality.

The wonderful, sadly-overlooked mediate seeing of Heb. 2: 9 is in the past with Eld. Miller. The more wonderful seeing and transfiguration of 1 John 3: 2, is now his ecstatic, ever-growing blessedness. He was meek, lowly, loving, useful while here; now he is "present with the Lord," sharing in all the beatitudes and glories of redemption, still waiting for the final "manifestation of the sons of God." Rom. 8: 19-23. "THEREFORE,"—for all of us that remain. Rom. 12: 1.

Union Deposit, Pa.

A FEW MORE THOUGHTS.

BY FLORIDA J. ETTER.

I WISH to add a few thoughts in regard to what sister G. A. Flory says about teaching the children. I often think, What responsibilities rest on parents! There are so many temptations laid before them, that it requires a great effort on the parents' part to turn their feet away from them. The mother's influence is really greater than the father's. A child generally comes to the mother for protection and advice, as well as whatever it needs. It is apt to look to her first. Parents should be very careful how they act before their children. They will take notice of things they say or do that one would least expect of them. I have heard children say things that would surprise me to think they would take notice of so young, and when found out, they got it from mother or father. A child may wander away, but never can it forget its mother. Mothers should always try to set a good example before the little ones, for they will try to pattern after them. I will give a brief sketch that I read a short time ago, headed, "Five Minutes for Prayer," which will come under the head of what has been written:

"There is a great deal to do in short winter mornings; two or three young children to be dressed, two or three older ones to be gotten off to school by nine o'clock, the usual work to be done, and a breakfast to be gotten for seven souls in perfect health, with normal appetites for food. Every minute was precious, and it seemed as though prayers would be crowded out. But the children had no father save their Heavenly Father, and their mother felt that they must daily touch his hand, hear his voice speaking to them from the Sacred Page, and join their voices in unison with the great voice of the Christian in saying the Lord's Prayer. So she said to them, 'I know time is precious, but we cannot omit our daily devotions. I will read short lessons, we shall have short prayers, for we are not heard for our much speaking, and we can certainly afford five minutes for prayers.' So the Bible was put on the table with the breakfast dishes, and when the meal was over, a portion of Scripture was read and some one of the children was called on to lead in prayer, or the mother led and all joined in repeating the Lord's Prayer.

"So the keynote for the day was struck and the standard of absolute right was held up before all the children from morning to morning. The usual singing with the organ was omitted, save on Saturday and Sunday mornings, while the school was in session. The younger children caught the refrain, and as soon as the meal was over, would begin to call out, 'Five minutes for prayers!' They were all accustomed to be called on, from the time they could talk, to ask the blessing at the table, to lead in prayer, whether guests were present or not. It was a part of their daily life to pray and ask for what they wanted."

So is the rush of life in these modern days, that family devotion in the morning is in danger of being crowded out. We can always frame plenty of excuses for neglecting this and other great duties. At night the children are tired and sleepy; we are broken down and sleepy too. In the morning we are too busy; no time to spare, but all must be hurry and flurry and worry all day, and we are in no frame of mind to worship. All of these excuses will do here, but how will they stand at the day of judgment?

Who is it that could not spare five minutes in the morning, or a while at night for family devotion? We cannot wonder at children going astray, when they never see father or mother bow

✦ESSAYS✦

THE CHRISTIAN HERO.

SELECTED BY FANNIE B. ZUG.

Live on the field of battle!
Be earnest in the fight;
Stand forth with manly courage,
And struggle for the right.

Watch on the field of battle!
The foe is every-where;
His fiery darts fly thickly,
Like lightning through the air.

Pray on the field of battle!
God works with those who pray;
His mighty arm can nerve us,
And make us win the day.

Die on the field of battle!
'Tis noble thus to die;
God smiles on valiant soldiers,—
Their record is on high.

Mankein, Pa.

SEEING AND SEEING.

BY C. H. BALSBAUGH.

To the Widow and Family of Eld. R. H. Miller:—

WALKING with God, Enoch-like, is ever-growing likeness to God, naturally leading into immediate presence of God, resulting in everlasting fellowship with God. "Can two walk together *except they be agreed?*" Amos 3: 3. I have known man and wife to walk together through life, the one "defaming," the other "entreating;" the one in the "power of the resurrection," the other in the "bondage of corruption;" having many things common apparently, yet nothing in common really. Physically and in external domesticity, they walked together, while spiritually and in the deepest sense, they were as far apart as the antipodal eternities. So we can "walk in all the commandments and ordinances of the Lord," but not "blameless." To "walk as Jesus walked" is to walk in the purity and power and peace of the Holy Ghost. Ordinances are types of spiritual realities to all; but they are expressions of divine life and love only by those who have been born of God.

Nothing is more spontaneous and exultant than the manifestations of love. All concede to this. God is love, and the incoming of his life by faith in Jesus Christ takes away every trace of legality and bondage from our obedience, and refers salvation, from beginning to end, to the superabounding grace of God in Christ. We are not saved because we obey, but we obey because "we are his workmanship, created in Christ Jesus unto good works." Eph. 2: 10. To prepare a plea by our obedience for reconciliation with God, is as impossible as for "the blood of bulls and goats to take away sin." But by our loyalty we can maintain the position which grace confers. But the same faith that made the provisions of grace ours, must externalize itself in all the forms and works "which God hath before ordained that we should walk in them." Eph. 2: 10. Such, I believe, was the life of Eld. Robert H. Miller.

"He walked with God, and is not, for God took him." Gen. 5: 24. In his death you have lost much, but he has gained more. What was revealed to his faith here, is now an open vision. 1 Cor. 2: 9, 10. The seeing of 2 Cor. 3: 18, is now the beatific beholding of Rev. 22: 4. His "*life* was hid with Christ in God," and now he has personal rapture of the "far more exceeding and eternal weight of glory." Col. 3: 3; 2 Cor. 4: 17. His "reckoning" is now fruition. Rom. 8;

18. He was no soul-sleeping theorist while here, and now he has conscious verification of the sublime doctrine of Christ, that "God is not the God of the *dead*, but of the *living*."

His was a capacious soul, and now he has all the facilities at hand to be "filled with all the fullness of God." Rev. 7: 15, 16, 17. No longer "through a glass darkly, but face to face." 1 Cor. 13: 12. He has reached the wonderful "THERE" of John 14: 3. "WHERE I AM," says Jesus, "THERE ye may be also." When you think of the loved companion, your faith must enter into "the Holiest of all" and behold him among those who have "washed their robes in the blood of the Lamb," and stand on the sea of glass, sweeping with Spirit-taught hearts and hands the golden harps of Redemption's full-chorused anthem.

Give your imagination the wings of the Jordanic Dove, and soar aloft into the empyrean of the home-gathered, and live in the realization of Col. 3: 1, 2 and Philpp. 3: 20, 21. Do not fail to apprehend the present tense of Heb. 12: 22, and include in the "are" all the upper-world glories and raptures unfolded in 22, 23, 24. There is your beloved husband and father, there you are anticipatively by faith, and there you will shortly all be personally, if you live steadfastly in 1 Pet. 1: 8, 9.

I saw Eld. Miller but once,—at our last Annual Conference. Once he wrote to me, while he was at Ashland. His was not great mental *culture* in the common acceptation of the word, but great native intellectual powers. His mind was preeminently analytic, and he saw correct inferences intuitively. He was a constitutional logician. All his writings reveal this. But it was his piety that gave him his true grandeur. He was verily a saint. He was swayed in thought, word and act by "the powers of the world to come." His face was written all over with the chirography of God.

When it was my honor and pleasure to stand a few minutes before that vast concourse at Hagerstown and testify for Jesus, Eld. Miller sat right before me, and gazed into my very soul with apparently intense interest. When I remarked that "Love is God's great name, expressive of his great nature, and that it is this name that he writes in the foreheads of all his children, by which they are known and read of all men," Bro. Miller sweetly smiled and nodded an emphatic recognition.

Such a life on earth is very God in the flesh,—the exemplification of 1 Cor. 13: 4-7. Such enshrining and manifestation of the Holy Ghost, God counts on for the evangelization of the world. Not flesh-circumcised law-breakers, but heart-circumcised law-fulfillers, are "the light of the world, and the salt of the earth." Rom. 2: 25-29. To boast in the letter, and "make a fair show in the flesh," and be sensitively scrupulous in the observance of all the types and shadows of religion, is not "the power of God unto salvation." To do all these things faithfully, and be what the Christian ritual symbolizes,—this is to walk with God, this is to see him with the open face of 2 Cor. 3: 18, this is to know Rom. 15: 13, as we know the very fact of our personality.

The wonderful, sadly-overlooked mediate seeing of Heb. 2: 9 is in the past with Eld. Miller. The more wonderful seeing and transfiguration of 1 John 3: 2, is now his ecstatic, ever-growing blessedness. He was meek, lowly, loving, useful while here; now he is "present with the Lord," sharing in all the beatitudes and glories of redemption, still waiting for the final "manifestation of the sons of God." Rom. 8: 19-23. "THEREFORE,"—for all of us that remain. Rom. 12: 1.

Union Deposit, Pa.

A FEW MORE THOUGHTS.

BY FLORIDA J. ETTER.

I WISH to add a few thoughts in regard to what sister G. A. Flory says about teaching the children. I often think, What responsibilities rest on parents! There are so many temptations laid before them, that it requires a great effort on the parents' part to turn their feet away from them. The mother's influence is really greater than the father's. A child generally comes to the mother for protection and advice, as well as whatever it needs. It is apt to look to her first. Parents should be very careful how they act before their children. They will take notice of things they say or do that one would least expect of them. I have heard children say things that would surprise me to think they would take notice of so young, and when found out, they got it from mother or father. A child may wander away, but never can it forget its mother. Mothers should always try to set a good example before the little ones; for they will try to pattern after them. I will give a brief sketch that I read a short time ago, headed, "Five Minutes for Prayer," which will come under the head of what has been written:

"There is a great deal to do in short winter mornings; two or three young children to be dressed, two or three older ones to be gotten off to school by nine o'clock, the usual work to be done, and a breakfast to be gotten for seven souls in perfect health, with normal appetites for food. Every minute was precious, and it seemed as though prayers would be crowded out. But the children had no father save their Heavenly Father, and their mother felt that they must daily touch his hand, hear his voice speaking to them from the Sacred Page, and join their voices in unison with the great voice of the Christian in saying the Lord's Prayer. So she said to them, 'I know time is precious, but we cannot omit our daily devotions. I will read short lessons, we shall have short prayers, for we are not heard for our much speaking, and we can certainly afford five minutes for prayers.' So the Bible was put on the table with the breakfast dishes, and when the meal was over, a portion of Scripture was read and some one of the children was called on to lead in prayer, or the mother led and all joined in repeating the Lord's Prayer.

"So the keynote for the day was struck and the standard of absolute right was held up before all the children from morning to morning. The usual singing with the organ was omitted, save on Saturday and Sunday mornings, while the school was in session. The younger children caught the refrain, and as soon as the meal was over, would begin to call out, 'Five minutes for prayers!' They were all accustomed to be called on, from the time they could talk, to ask the blessing at the table, to lead in prayer, whether guests were present or not. It was a part of their daily life to pray and ask for what they wanted."

So is the rush of life in these modern days, that family devotion in the morning is in danger of being crowded out. We can always frame plenty of excuses for neglecting this and other great duties. At night the children are tired and sleepy; we are broken down and sleepy too. In the morning we are too busy; no time to spare, but all must be hurry and flurry and worry all day, and we are in no frame of mind to worship. All of these excuses will do here, but how will they stand at the day of judgment?

Who is it that could not spare five minutes in the morning, or a while at night for family devotion? We cannot wonder at children going astray, when they never see father or mother bow

THE STATE OF THE SOUL AFTER DEATH.

BY HENRY BIBLER.

THE state of the soul after death is a subject which deeply interests every true child of God. The rejection of the coming again of Christ to receive the saints, and to judge the earth before the end of the world, and the losing sight of the distinctive importance, given to the resurrection in the New Testament, has given, in the common evangelical faith, and that which is sound in the main, an absolute character to the vague idea of going to heaven, exclusive of all other conceptions of happiness and glory. But the Scriptures speak too plainly of the Lord's coming and the resurrection of the saints, to allow the thought of going to heaven, when we die, to maintain the absorbing place it held in the minds of the pious. Strange to say, going to heaven is not spoken of in Scripture, unless in the one case of the thief upon the cross going to be with Christ in Paradise. Not that we do not go there, but the Scriptural thought is always going to Christ. Since he is in heaven, of course we go there; but being with Christ, not being in heaven, is what Scripture puts forward, and this is important as to the state of the spiritual affections. Christ is the object before the soul, according to the Word, not simply being happy in heaven, though we shall be happy, and in heaven. I speak of it only as characterizing our habits of thought. Poor human nature is apt to follow its own thoughts, not simply to receive the Word of God.

My object is to give a plain Scriptural statement and proof from Scripture that there is immediate happiness with Christ for the departed Christian. It is an intermediate state, and so, as to his position as a man is Christ's, though he be in glory. The departing Christian' waits for the resurrection of the body, and then only will he be in his final state in glory. Men speak of glorified spirits,—the Scriptures, never. The purpose of God as to us is, that we should be conformed to the image of his Son, that he may be first born among many brethren." It doth not yet appear what we shall be, but we know that when he shall appear, we shall be like him for we shall see him as he is." "As we have borne the image of the earthly, so also we shall bear the image of the heavenly." This was exhibited for a moment when Moses and Elias appeared in glory with Christ at the transfiguration. (See Rom. 8: 29; 1 John 3: 2; 1 Cor. 15: 49; Luke 9: 28-36.) This, and to be forever with the Lord, received to himself in the Father's house, is our eternal state of joy and glory. But this is our eternal state when Christ shall have come and received us to himself, raised or changed into his likeness, when our poor, earthly body shall have been fashioned like his glorious body. Philpp. 3: 21. "God hath wrought us now, already, for this selfsame thing, and given to us the earnest of his Spirit." 2 Cor. 5: 5.

To be with the Lord and like the Lord forever is our everlasting joy, and that is the fruit of God's love, who has made us his children and will bring us into the mansions prepared in our Father's house. Two things belong to us; first, to be like and with Christ himself and, secondly, to be blessed with all spiritual blessings in heavenly places in him. Redemption has made this ours, but we are not in possession.

The first point as regards being like Christ we have already spoken of, though, what has been cited there, introduces us with Scriptural authority to the second, "So shall we ever be with the Lord." But I add here other proofs of the second point, namely, that our portion is in heavenly places. It is distinctive of believers, who have believed and suffered with him. God, we are told, will gather together in one, under Christ, all things, both which are in heaven and which are on earth. Eph. 1: 10. So we read all things were created by Christ and for Christ. Col. 1: 16, 20. All things will be put under his feet as man. Heb. 2; 1 Cor. 15: 27, 28; Eph. 1: 22. But we read in Heb. 2: 7 that all things are not put under him. He sits now on the Father's throne, not on his own. Rev. 3: 21. God has said, "Sit at my right hand, till I make thine enemies thy footstool." He is, according to Heb. 10, still expecting, till his enemies be made his footstool.

The time will come when not only all things in heaven and earth will be reconciled (Col. 1: 26), but even things under the earth, infernal things, will be forced to recognize his power and authority. "Every knee shall bow to him and every tongue confess that Jesus Christ, the despised and rejected of men, is lord, to the glory of God the Father." Phil. 2: 10, 11.

For this we must wait, but in this gathering of all things in heaven and earth under one head,— Christ,—our part is in heavenly places; and as it is our portion now in spirit, so it will be our part in glory. Nor is there any real separation between these two. Of course we are not in glory now,—there is no need to insist on that; but that is our calling now, that which we are redeemed to and wrought for, and wait for.

Now we have the treasure in earthly vessels and groan, being burdened. When we are out of the body, groaning is over, and we are with Christ in joy. When he comes, we shall have a body suited to that heavenly place,—we shall be in glory. Thus, in Eph. 1: 3, "He hath blessed us with all spiritual blessings in heavenly places in Christ." In 2 Cor. 5: 1, we read: "We know that if our earthly house of this tabernacle were dissolved, we have a building of God, a house not made with hands, eternal in the heavens." Philpp. 3: 20 tells us, "Our conversation (citizenship—our relationship in life as Christians) is in heaven . . . where you have a high calling." The true force of the word is, "calling above," as may be seen in a Bible with margin. We are called to be up above there. So, in Heb. 6: 19, 20, we read that Christ is entered within the vail,—that is, heaven itself, as our forerunner. Heb. 3 tells us that we are partakers of the heavenly calling. As united to Christ by the Holy Ghost, we are sitting in heavenly places in Christ. We are not with him yet, but in him,—that is our place. So, when the Lord comes, he gathers indeed, as Son of man, out of his kingdom all things that offend, and them that do iniquity. Then the righteous shall shine forth as the sun in the kingdom of their Father. Moses and Elias not only are manifested in glory on earth to show the state of the saints in the kingdom, but they enter into the cloud,— God's dwelling-place, whence the Father's voice came.

All this has not told us in distinct statements what the intermediate state is, though it has shown us, as a general principle, where all our blessing is and what redemption has obtained for us. The God of all grace has called us to his eternal glory by Christ Jesus. Wondrous love, but an integral part of Christ's own glory, for what is a Redeemer without his redeemed?

The whole object of the epistle to the Hebrews is, to show that our portion is heavenly, in contrast with the Judaism which was and, when Israel is restored, will be earthly. They had a high-priest on earth, because God sat between the cherubim down here. Such a high-priest became us, —holy, harmless, undefiled, separate from sinners, made higher than the heavens. Why? Because our place and portion are with God there. All had to be suited to this: the excellence of the sacrifice and the service of the priest.

But how far does the Word of God show us our intermediate state between the time of our being in this tabernacle, in which we groan, and having it glorified when Christ comes and shall change our vile bodies and fashion them like his own glorious body?

Our citizenship, now and always, is in heaven. How far we enjoy it when we die is the only question,—more than here or less? God is not the God of the dead, but of the living; for all live unto him. Luke 20: 38. Though dead for this world, they are for him as alive as ever, and so for faith.

But it is alleged they sleep. There is no ground for this whatever. Stephen fell asleep,—that is he died. It was not his soul that fell asleep after death; those which sleep in Jesus shall God bring with him. 1 Thess. 4: 14, but those (verse 16) are dead in Christ. Some have fallen asleep, that is, died (1 Cor. 15: 6). This is the same word as "sleep in Jesus" in 1 Thess. 4, and "remaining to this present" in Corinthians. It is simply dying. It is a beautiful expression to show they had not at all ceased to exist, but would wake up again in the resurrection, as a man out of sleep. This is clearly determined in the case of Lazarus. John 11. A Christian's falling asleep is neither more nor less than dying; a soul's sleeping is a pure invention.

Paul knew that God had wrought him for glory and did not wish to die (be unclothed) as if weary, but that mortality might be swallowed up in life. Christians are always confident, knowing that whilst they are at home in the body, they are absent from the Lord. Life,—eternal life in Christ, —they have, but here it lives absent from the Lord in the earthen vessel. When it leaves the poor, earthen vessel, which makes it groan, being burdened, it will be present with the Lord. Is that better or worse? and where is he? Is it,—though it has already the Holy Ghost as the power of life,—the spirit of life in Christ Jesus, going to sleep, knowing nothing? Christ is our life, because he lives, we live. Have we lost our connection with him when we die? Does he sleep in us? Paul was in a strait betwixt two, to depart and be with Christ, which was far better, dying (mark what he is speaking of) gain, though living was Christ. That is, he, having the blessed joy of knowing Christ, was his life, and living entirely for him, so that it was worth his while to stay, yet he found it far better, again, to go to sleep and know nothing of Christ at all! Is it not perfectly evident that when he speaks of being with Christ, and of its being far better than serving him here, though that was worth while, he speaks of the joy of being there? Who would think, if I spoke of the satisfaction and gain of going to somebody and being with him, I meant I was going to be fast asleep, and not know I was there? The Lord's answer to the thief on the cross was, according to the whole tenor of the Gospel, "You shall, this self-same day, be with me in Paradise."

This, then, is the portion of the departed saint: to be with Christ in blessedness, absent from the body and present with the Lord. I am aware of the miserable subterfuge, used by the Seventh Day Adventists, and others, by which it is attempted to read it, "Verily I say unto you this day, Thou shalt be with me in paradise." It not only destroys the whole characteristic point of the passage, according to the tenor of the Gospel it is found in, but perverts the order of the passage, as it destroys its sense. "To-day" is at the beginning of the phrase to give it emphasis in answer to "When thou comest."

The wickedness of the Jews, as an instrument, fulfilled the promise in breaking his legs, as it did

THE STATE OF THE SOUL AFTER DEATH.

BY HENRY BIHLER.

The state of the soul after death is a subject which deeply interests every true child of God. The rejection of the coming again of Christ to receive the saints, and to judge the earth before the end of the world, and the losing sight of the distinctive importance, given to the resurrection in the New Testament, has given, in the common evangelical faith, and that which is sound in the main, an absolute character to the vague idea of going to heaven, exclusive of all other conceptions of happiness and glory. But the Scriptures speak too plainly of the Lord's coming and the resurrection of the saints, to allow the thought of going to heaven, when we die, to maintain the absorbing place it held in the minds of the pious. Strange to say, going to heaven is not spoken of in Scripture, unless in the one case of the thief upon the cross going to be with Christ in Paradise. Not that we do not go there, but the Scriptural thought is always going to Christ. Since he is in heaven, of course we go there; but being with Christ, not being in heaven, is what Scripture puts forward, and this is important as to the state of the spiritual affections. Christ is the object before the soul, according to the Word, not simply being happy in heaven, though we shall be happy, and in heaven. I speak of it only as characterizing our habits of thought. Poor human nature is apt to follow its own thoughts, not simply to receive the Word of God.

My object is to give a plain Scriptural statement and proof from Scripture that there is immediate happiness with Christ for the departed Christian. It is an intermediate state, and so, as to his position as a man is Christ's, though he be in glory. The departing Christian waits for the resurrection of the body, and then only will he be in his final state in glory. Men speak of glorified spirits,—the Scriptures, never. The purpose of God as to us is, that we should be conformed to the image of his Son, that he may be first born among many brethren." It doth not yet appear what we shall be, but we know that when he shall appear, we shall be like him for we shall see him as he is." "As we have borne the image of the earthly, so also we shall bear the image of the heavenly." This was exhibited for a moment when Moses and Elias appeared in glory with Christ at the transfiguration. (See Rom. 8: 29; 1 John 3: 2; 1 Cor. 15: 49; Luke 9: 28-36.) This, and to be forever with the Lord, received to himself in the Father's house, is our eternal state of joy and glory. But this is our eternal state when Christ shall have come and received us to himself, raised or changed into his likeness, when our poor, earthly body shall have been fashioned like his glorious body. Philpp. 3: 21. "God hath wrought us now, directly, for this selfsame thing, and given to us the earnest of his Spirit." 2 Cor. 5: 5.

To be with the Lord and like the Lord forever is our everlasting joy, and that is the fruit of God's love, who has made us his children and will bring us into the mansions prepared in our Father's house. Two things belong to us; first, to be like and with Christ himself and, secondly, to be blessed with all spiritual blessings in heavenly places in him. Redemption has made this ours, but we are not in possession.

The first point as regards being like Christ we have already spoken of, though, what has been cited there, introduces us with Scriptural authority to the second, "So shall we ever be with the Lord." But I add here other proofs of the second point, namely, that our portion is in heavenly places. It is distinctive of believers, who have believed and suffered with him. God, we are told, will gather together in one, under Christ, all things, both which are in heaven and which are on earth. Eph. 1: 10. So we read all things were created by Christ and for Christ. Col. 1: 16, 20. All things will be put under his feet as man. Read in Heb. 2: 7 that all things are not put under him. He sits now on the Father's throne, not on his own. Rev. 3: 21. God has said, "Sit at my right hand, till I make thine enemies thy footstool." He is, according to Heb. 10, still expecting, till his enemies be made his footstool.

The time will come when not only all things in heaven and earth will be reconciled (Col. 1: 26), but even things under the earth, infernal things, will be forced to recognize his power and authority. "Every knee shall bow to him and every tongue confess that Jesus Christ, the despised and rejected of men, is lord, to the glory of God the Father." Phil. 2: 10, 11.

For this we must wait, but in this gathering of all things in heaven and earth under one head,—Christ,—our part is in heavenly places; and as it is our portion now in spirit, so it will by our part in glory. Nor is there any real separation between these two. Of course we are not in glory now,—there is no need to insist on that; but that is our calling now, that which we are redeemed to and wrought for, and wait for.

Now we have the treasure in earthly vessels and groan, being burdened. When we are out of the body, groaning is over, and we are with Christ in joy. When he comes, we shall have a body suited to that heavenly place,—we shall be in glory. Thus, in Eph. 1: 3, "He hath blessed us with all spiritual blessings in heavenly places in Christ." In 2 Cor. 5: 1, we read: "We know that if our earthly house of this tabernacle were dissolved, we have a building of God, a house not made with hands, eternal in the heavens." Philpp. 3: 20 tells us, "Our conversation (citizenship—our relationship in life as Christians) is in heaven . . . where you have a high calling." The true force of the word is, "calling above," as may be seen in a Bible with margin. We are called to be up above there. So, in Heb. 6: 19, 20, we read that Christ is entered within the vail,—that is, heaven itself, as our forerunner. Heb. 3 tells us that we are partakers of the heavenly calling. As united to Christ by the Holy Ghost, we are sitting in heavenly places in Christ. We are not with him yet, but in him,—that is our place. So, when the Lord comes, he gathers indeed, as Son of man, out of his kingdom all things that offend, and them that do iniquity. Then the righteous shall shine forth as the sun in the kingdom of their Father. Moses and Elias not only are manifested in glory on earth to show the state of the saints in the kingdom, but they enter into the cloud,—God's dwelling-place, whence the Father's voice came.

All this has not told us in distinct statements what the intermediate state is, though it has shown us, as a general principle, where all our blessing is and what redemption has obtained for us. The God of all grace has called us to his eternal glory by Christ Jesus. Wondrous love, that an integral part of Christ's own glory, for what is a Redeemer without his redeemed? But, thou shalt be with me in paradise." Is not Thou shalt be with me in paradise. Why? Because our place and portion are with God there. All had to be suited to this: the excellence of the sacrifice and the service of the priest.

But how far does the Word of God show us our intermediate state between the time of our being in this tabernacle, in which we groan, and having it glorified when Christ comes and shall change our vile bodies and fashion them like his own glorious body?

Our citizenship, now and always, is in heaven. How far we enjoy it when we die is the only question,—more than here or there? God is not the God of the dead, but of the living; for all live unto him. Luke 20: 38. Though dead for this world, they are for him as alive as ever, and so for faith.

But it is alleged they sleep. There is no ground for this whatever. Stephen fell asleep,—that is he died. It was not his soul that fell asleep after death; those which sleep in Jesus shall God bring with him. 1 Thess. 4: 14, but these (verse 16) are dead in Christ. Some have fallen asleep, that is, died (1 Cor. 15: 6). This is the same word as "sleep in Jesus" in 1 Thess. 4, and "remaining to this present 'in Corinthians. It is simply dying. It is a beautiful expression to show they had not at all ceased to exist, but would wake up again in the resurrection, as a man out of sleep. This is clearly determined in the case of Lazarus. John 11. A Christian's falling asleep is neither more nor less than dying; a soul's sleeping is a pure invention.

Paul knew that God had wrought him for glory and did not wish to die (be unclothed) as if weary, but that mortality might be swallowed up in life. Christians are always confident, knowing that whilst they are at home in the body, they are absent from the Lord. Life,—eternal life in Christ, —they have, but here it lives absent 'from the Lord in the earthen vessel. When it leaves the poor, earthen vessel, which makes it groan, being burdened, it will be present with the Lord. Is that better or worse? and where is he? Is it,—though it has already the Holy Ghost as the power of life,—the spirit of life in Christ Jesus, going to sleep, knowing nothing? Christ is our life, because he lives, we live. Have we lost our connection with him when we die? Does he sleep in us? Paul was in a strait betwixt two, to depart and be with Christ, which was far better, dying (mark what he is speaking of) gain, though living was Christ. That is, he, having the blessed joy of knowing Christ, was his life, and living entirely for him, so that it was worth his while to stay, yet he found it far better, again, to go to sleep and know nothing of Christ at all! Is it not perfectly evident that when he speaks of being with Christ, and of its being far better than serving him here, though that was worth while, he speaks of the joy of being there? Who would think, if I spoke of the satisfaction and gain of going to somebody and being with him, I meant I was going to be fast asleep, and not know I was there? The Lord's answer to the thief on the cross was, according to the whole tenor of the Gospel, "Yet shall, this self-same day, be with me in Paradise."

This, then, is the portion of the departed saint: to be with Christ in blessedness, absent from the body and present with the Lord. I am aware of the miserable subterfuge, used by the Seventh Day Adventists, and others, by which it is attempted to read it, "Verily I say unto you this day, Thou shalt be with me in paradise." It not only destroys the whole characteristic point of the passage, according to the tenor of the Gospel it is found in, but perverts the order of the passage, as it destroys its sense. "To-day" is at the beginning of the phrase to give it emphasis in answer to "When thou comest."

The wickedness of the Jews, as an instrument, fulfilled the promise in breaking his legs, as it did

Missionary and Tract Work Department.

"Upon the first day of the week, let every one of you lay by him in store as God hath prospered him, that there be no gatherings when I come."—1 Cor. 16: 2.

"Every man as he purposeth in his heart, so let him give. Not grudgingly or of necessity, for the Lord loveth a cheerful giver."—2 Cor. 9: 7.

HOW MUCH SHALL WE GIVE?

"Every man according to his ability." "Every one as God hath prospered him." "Every man, according as he purposeth in his heart, so let him give." "For if there be first a willing mind, it is accepted according to that a man hath, and not according to that he hath not."—2 Cor. 8: 12.

Organization of Missionary Committee.

DANIEL VANIMAN, Foreman,	McPherson, Kans.
D. L. MILLER, Treasurer,	Mt. Morris, Ill.
GALEN B. ROYER, Secretary,	Mt. Morris, Ill.

Organization of Book and Tract Work.

S. W. HOOVER, Foreman,	Dayton, Ohio.
S. BOCK, Secretary and Treasurer,	Dayton, Ohio.

☞All donations intended for Missionary Work should be sent to GALEN B. ROYER, Mt. Morris, Ill.

☞All money for Tract Work should be sent to S. BOCK, Dayton, Ohio.

☞Money may be sent by Money Order, Registered Letter, or Drafts on New York or Chicago. Do not send personal checks, or drafts on interior towns, as it costs 25 cents to collect them.

☞Solicitors are requested to faithfully carry out the plan of Annual Meeting, that all our members be solicited to contribute at least twice a year for the Mission and Tract Work of the Church.

☞Notes for the Endowment Fund can be had by writing to the Secretary of either Work.

THE PURPOSE OF GOD.

BY A. HUTCHISON.

In Two Chapters.—Chapter Two.

IT seems that for every phase of this subject, God has his own way of meeting the demands of the case. When he wished to make an exhibition of his power before the Egyptians, and to have his name spread among the nations, he raised up a Pharaoh,—for it is so stated in the following words: "For the Scripture saith unto Pharaoh, Even for this same purpose have I raised thee up, that I might show my power in thee, and that my name might be declared throughout all the earth." Rom. 9: 17.

And again, when the redemption of the human family was to be wrought out, God sent forth his Son, made of woman, etc. In this part of the work he makes use of a woman, to give us 'the world's Redeemer. But when this Redeemer must be delivered into the hands of wicked men, to be crucified, that the purpose of God might be further brought about, he makes choice of Judas, and so Judas must perform his part, because it was necessary, according to the purpose of God, that Christ be crucified, and he must first be betrayed and delivered up. Failing to make the necessary distinction between the case of Judas and others, who are free, moral agents, is where the criticisms of the brethren come in, respecting the case of Judas, as given in an article of mine sometime ago. We must not place two or more persons on an equality, when one is free, and the other bound. I see nothing in the criticisms that would be at all difficult to meet.

Just accept the idea, that, in the execution of God's will and purpose, as respecting the great salvation of man, he must have agents, and you can easily see why Judas does not stand as on equal footing with the Brethren at Corinth, or any-where else. His case stands independent of all other cases, like the "thief on the cross." The thief was where he could do nothing, and therefore he was not required to do, what he had no power to do. Hence it is no use to try to settle the case of Judas, or of the thief, by comparing them with any other cases. Jesus said to the twelve, "Have not I chosen you twelve, and one

of you is a devil? He spake of Judas Iscariot, the son of Simon, for he it was that should betray him, being one of the twelve." John 6: 70, 71. The entire twelve were chosen of God, but not to do the part that Judas performed.

I mean just what I said, in the first place, that I wished to cut off the force of the criticism, and that we take the word of the Lord, as it is given in the Book, in some things, but in others it is changed, etc. Bro. West thinks that in avoiding the critic on one side, I will run into a trouble on the other side. That I expected. But the criticisms, thus far, have been very brotherly. Now, I hope, I will be properly understood, when I say, that I think the brethren fail to notice the purpose of God, running through this case, when they compare the case of Judas with any other case, or attempt to settle it by reasoning from a human stand-point. Jesus made choice of him; he washed his feet; all admit that he ate food with him, dipping in the same dish; he talked with him, while they were eating, about the traitor, and said unto him, "Thou hast said," which was true,—for Judas had gone to the chief priests, etc., two days before this, and made an agreement with them that he would deliver Jesus into their hands for thirty pieces of silver. All of this was perfectly familiar to Jesus. Then all we have to do in the case is to leave it stand as an independent case, so provided according to the purpose of God, and not try to reason it into a shape so as to make Judas on an equal plane with free moral agents, or that Jesus would violate a heaven-born principle, to have given to him the Bread of Communion and the Cup of Blessing.

I shall not insist that he did, but will say, we have nothing to lose if he did, and much to gain by not attempting to prove that he did not. I am not writing at random, neither am I wishing to provoke any controversy. I have many critics to meet. God's Word is my great dependence.

McPherson, Kans.

REMARKS.

Before reading the above article we had announced in No. 18, that the two articles in that issue would close the exchange of views concerning the number of persons present at the first Communion services in Jerusalem. Bro. H. has a very conservative way of weaving in a few thoughts on the same line. We beg, however, to suggest this thought. It was needful that Judas should have twelve witnesses to testify concerning him after his departure. For this purpose he selected eleven friends from the ranks of the righteous, and then permitted Satan to have one witness to make out the twelve.

Judas was selected because he was a devil, so that Satan might have a representative among the witnesses. After this Satan put it into the heart of Judas to betray his Master. In this manner the betrayal was brought about, Satan using Judas as the instrument. Just before hanging himself Judas went into the witness stand and testified, "I have betrayed innocent blood." Thus Satan's own witness comes out and testifies in favor of Christ's divinity.

To this we add the testimony of the other eleven, making a verdict in proof of his character by twelve men, and one of them from the ranks of Satan. No wonder the devils believe and tremble when their own favored witness, Judas, gave his dying testimony in defense of Jesus.

J. H. M.

I AM GOING TO HEAVEN.

THE following was communicated to Zion's Watchman by a lady who was an eye-witness to the pathetic incident:

At a station a little girl came aboard, carrying a little bundle under her arm. She came into the car and deliberately took a seat. She then commenced an eager scrutiny of faces, but all were strange to her. She appeared weary, and, placing her bundle for a pillow, she prepared to secure a little sleep. Soon the conductor came along, collecting tickets and fares. Observing him she asked if she might lie there. The gentlemanly conductor replied that she might, and then kindly asked for 'her ticket. She informed him that she had none, when the following conversation ensued, said the conductor:

"Where are you going?"

She answered, "I am going to heaven."

He asked again, "Who pays your fare?"

She then said, "Mister, does this railroad lead to heaven, and does Jesus travel on it?"

He answered, "I think not. Why did you think so?"

"Why, sir, before my ma died she used to sing to me of the heavenly railroad, and you looked so nice and kind I thought this was the road. My ma used to sing of Jesus on the heavenly railroad, and that He paid the fare for everybody, and that the train stopped at every station to take people on board; but my ma don't sing to me any more. Nobody sings to me now, and I thought I'd take the cars and go to ma. Mister, do you sing to your little girl about the railroad that goes to heaven? You have a little girl, haven't you?"

He replied, weeping, "No, my little dear, I have no little girl now. I had one once, but she died some time ago, and went to heaven?"

Again she asked, "Did she go over this railroad, and are you going to see her now?"

By this time many in the carriage were upon their feet, and most of them were weeping. An attempt to describe what I witnessed is almost futile. Some said, "God bless the little girl!" Hearing some persons use the word "angel," the little girl earnestly replied, "Yes, my ma used to say I would be an angel some time."

Addressing herself once more to the conductor, she asked him, "Do you love Jesus? I do; and if you love Him, He will let you ride to heaven on his railroad. I am going there, and I wish you would go with me. I know Jesus will let me into heaven when I get there, and he will let you in too, and everybody that will ride on his railroad—yes, all these people. Wouldn't you like to see heaven, and Jesus, and your little girl?"

These words, so innocently and pathetically uttered, brought a great gush of tears from all eyes, but most profusely from the eyes of the conductor. Some who were traveling on the heavenly road shouted aloud for joy.

She now asked the conductor, "Mister, may I lie here until we get to heaven?"

He answered, "Yes, dear, yes."

She then asked, "Will you wake me up then, so that I may see my ma, your little girl, and Jesus, for I do so much want to see them all."

The answer came in broken accents, but in words very tenderly spoken, "Yes, dear angel, yes. God bless you." "Amen!" was sobbed by more than a score of voices. Turning her eyes again upon the conductor, she interrogated him again:

"What shall I tell your little girl when I see her? Shall I say to her that I saw her pa on Jesus' railroad? Shall I?"

This brought a fresh flood of tears from all present, and the conductor kneeled by her side, and, embracing her, wept the reply he could not utter. At this juncture the brakesman called the name of the station. The conductor arose and requested him to attend to his (conductor's) duty at the station, for he was engaged. That was a precious place. I thanked God that I was a wit-

Missionary and Tract Work Department.

"Upon the first day of the week, let every one of you lay by him in store as God hath prospered him, that there be no gatherings when I come."—1 Cor. 16: 2.

"Every man as he purposeth in his heart, so let him give. Not grudgingly or of necessity, for the Lord loveth a cheerful giver."—2 Cor. 9: 7.

HOW MUCH SHALL WE GIVE?

"Every man according to his ability." "Every one as God hath prospered him." "Every man, according as he purposeth in his heart, so let him give." "For if there be first a willing mind, it is accepted according to that a man hath, and not according to that he hath not."—2 Cor. 8: 12.

Organization of Missionary Committee.

DANIEL VANIMAN, Foreman, - - McPherson, Kans.
D. L. MILLER, Treasurer, - - Mt. Morris, Ill.
GALEN B. ROYER, Secretary, - - Mt. Morris, Ill.

Organization of Book and Tract Work.

S. W. HOOVER, Foreman, - - Dayton, Ohio.
S. BOCK, Secretary and Treasurer, - - Dayton, Ohio.

☞All donations intended for Missionary Work should be sent to GALEN B. ROYER, Mt. Morris, Ill.

☞All money for Tract Work should be sent to S. BOCK, Dayton, Ohio.

☞Money may be sent by Money Order, Registered Letter, or Drafts on New York or Chicago. Do not send personal checks, or drafts on interior towns, as it costs 25 cents to collect them.

☞Solicitors are requested to faithfully carry out the plan of Annual Meeting, that all our members be solicited to contribute at least twice a year for the Mission and Tract Work of the Church.

☞Notes for the Endowment Fund can be had by writing to the Secretary of either Work.

THE PURPOSE OF GOD.

BY A. HUTCHISON.

In Two Chapters.—Chapter Two.

It seems that for every phase of this subject, God has his own way of meeting the demands of the case. When he wished to make an exhibition of his power before the Egyptians, and to have his name spread among the nations, he raised up a Pharaoh,—for it is so stated in the following words: "For the Scripture saith unto Pharaoh, Even for this same purpose have I raised thee up, that I might show my power in thee, and that my name might be declared throughout all the earth." Rom. 9: 17.

And again, when the redemption of the human family was to be wrought out, God sent forth his Son, made of woman, etc. In this part of the work he makes use of a woman, to give us the world's Redeemer. But when this Redeemer must be delivered into the hands of wicked men, to be crucified, that the purpose of God might be further brought about, he makes choice of Judas, and so Judas must perform his part, because it was necessary, according to the purpose of God, that Christ be crucified, and he must first be betrayed and delivered up. Failing to make the necessary distinction between the case of Judas and others, who are free, moral agents, is where the criticisms of the brethren come in, respecting the case of Judas, as given in an article of mine sometime ago. We must not place two or more persons on an equality, when one is free, and the other bound. I see nothing in the criticisms that would be at all difficult to meet.

Just accept the idea, that, in the execution of God's will and purpose, as respecting the great salvation of man, he must have agents, and you can easily see why Judas does not stand as on equal footing with the Brethren at Corinth, or any-where else. His case stands independent of all other cases, like the "thief on the cross." The thief was where he could do nothing, and therefore he was not required to do, what he had no power to do. Hence it is in no use to try to settle the case of Judas, or of the thief, by comparing them with any other cases. Jesus said to the twelve, "Have not I chosen you twelve, and one of you is a devil? He spake of Judas Iscariot, the son of Simon, for he it was that should betray him, being one of the twelve." John 6: 70, 71. The entire twelve were chosen of God, but not to do the part that Judas performed.

I mean just what I said, in the first place, that I wished to cut off the force of the criticism, and that we take the word of the Lord, as it is given in the Book, in some things, but in others it is changed, etc. Bro. West thinks that in avoiding the critic on one side, I will run into a trouble on the other side. That I expected. But the criticisms, thus far, have been very brotherly. Now, I hope, I will be properly understood, when I say, that I think the brethren fail to notice the purpose of God, running through this case, when they compare the case of Judas with any other case, or attempt to settle it by reasoning from a human stand-point. Jesus made choice of him; he washed his feet; all admit that he ate food with him, dipping in the same dish; he talked with him, while they were eating, about the traitor, and said unto him, "Thou hast said," which was true,—for Judas had gone to the chief priests, etc., two days before this, and made an agreement with them that he would deliver Jesus into their hands for thirty pieces of silver. All of this was perfectly familiar to Jesus. Then all we have to do in the case is to leave it·stand as an independent case, so provided according to the purpose of God, and not try to reason it into a shape so as to make Judas on an equal plane with free moral agents, or that Jesus would violate a heaven-born principle, to have given to him the Bread of Communion and the Cup of Blessing.

I shall not insist that he did, but will say, we have nothing to lose if he did, and much to gain by not attempting to prove that he did not. I am not writing at random, neither am I wishing to provoke any controversy. I have many critics to meet. God's Word is my great dependence.

McPherson, Kans.

REMARKS.

Before reading the above article we had announced in No. 13, that the two articles in that issue would close the exchange of views concerning the number of persons present ·at the first Communion services in Jerusalem. Bro. H. has a very conservative way of weaving in a few thoughts on the same line. We beg, however, to suggest this thought. It was needful that Jesus should have twelve witnesses to testify concerning him after his departure. For this purpose he selected eleven friends from the ranks of the righteous, and then permitted Satan to have one witness to make out the twelve.

Judas was selected because he was a devil, so that Satan might have a representative among the witnesses. After this Satan put it into the heart of Judas to betray his Master. In this manner the betrayal was brought about, Satan using Judas as the instrument. Just before hanging himself Judas went into the witness stand and testified, "I have betrayed innocent blood." Thus Satan's own witness comes out and testifies in favor of Christ's divinity.

To this we add the testimony of the other eleven, making a verdict in proof of his character by twelve men, and one of them from the ranks of Satan. No wonder the devils believe and tremble when their own favored witness, Judas, gave his dying testimony in defense of Jesus.　J. H. M.

I AM GOING TO HEAVEN.

The following was communicated to Zion's Watchman by a lady who was an eye-witness to the pathetic incident:

At a station a little girl came aboard, carrying a little bundle under her arm. She came into the car and deliberately took a seat. She then commenced an eager scrutiny of faces, but all were strange to her. She appeared weary, and, placing her bundle for a pillow, she prepared to secure a little sleep. Soon the conductor came along, collecting tickets and fares. Observing him she asked if she might lie there. The gentlemanly conductor replied that she might, and then kindly asked for 'her ticket. She informed him that she had none, when the following conversation ensued, said the conductor:

"Where are you going?"

She answered, "I am going to heaven."

He asked again, "Who pays your fare?"

She then said, "Mister, does this railroad lead to heaven, and does Jesus travel on it?"

He answered, "I think not. Why did you think so?"

"Why, sir, before my ma died she used to sing to me of the heavenly railroad, and you looked so nice and kind I thought this was the road. My ma used to sing of Jesus on the heavenly railroad, and that He paid the fare for everybody, and that the train stopped at every station to take people on board; but my ma don't sing to me any more. Nobody sings to me now, and I thought I'd take the cars and go to ma. Mister, do you sing to your little girl about the railroad that goes to heaven? You have a little girl, haven't you?"

He replied, weeping, "No, my little dear, I have no little girl now. I had one once, but she died some time ago, and went to heaven."

Again she asked, "Did she go over this railroad, and are you going to see her now?"

By this time many in the carriage were upon their feet, and most of them were weeping. An attempt to describe what I witnessed is almost futile. Some said, "God bless the little girl!" Hearing some persons use the word "angel," the little girl earnestly replied, "Yes, my ma used to say I would be an angel some time."

Addressing herself once more to the conductor, she asked him, "Do you love Jesus? I do; and if you love Him, He will let you ride to heaven on his railroad. I am going there, and I wish you would go with me. I know Jesus will let me into heaven when I get there, and he will let you in too, and everybody that will ride on his railroad—yes, all these people. Wouldn't you like to see heaven, and Jesus, and your little girl?"

These words, so innocently and pathetically uttered, brought a great gush of tears from all eyes, but most profusely from the eyes of the conductor. Some who were traveling on the heavenly road shouted aloud for joy.

She now asked the conductor, "Mister, may I lie here until we get to heaven?"

He answered, "Yes, dear, yes."

She then asked, "Will you wake me up then, so that I may see my ma, your little girl, and Jesus? for I do so much want to see them all."

The answer came in broken accents, but in words very tenderly spoken, "Yes, dear angel, yes. God bless you." "Amen!" was sobbed ·by more than a score of voices. Turning her eyes again upon the conductor, she interrogated him again:

"What shall I tell your little girl when I see her? Shall I say to her that I saw her pa on Jesus' railroad? Shall I?"

This brought a fresh flood of tears from all present, and the conductor kneeled by her side, and, embracing her, wept the reply he could not utter. At this juncture the brakeman called the name of the station. The conductor arose and requested him to attend to his (conductor's) duty at the station, for he was engaged. That was a precious place. I thanked God that I was a wit-

The Gospel Messenger,

A Weekly at $1.50 Per Annum.

PUBLISHED BY

The Brethren's Publishing Co.

D. L. MILLER,	· · · · ·	Editor.
J. H. MOORE,	· · · · ·	Office Editor.
J. B. BRUMBAUGH,		
J. G. ROYER,	· · · ·	Associate Editors.
JOSEPH AMICK,	· · · ·	Business Manager.

ADVISORY COMMITTEE.

R. H. Miller, A. Hutchison, Daniel Hays.

Mount Morris, Ill., · · · · June 21, 1892.

BRO. S. N. McCANN, one of the teachers in the Bridgewater School, spent several days in visiting the different departments of the College here last week. He reports that the outlook of the Bridgewater School is quite promising.

IF the editorial department of this issue lacks interest, it may be attributed to the excessive warm weather that has prevailed here since the Annual Meeting. Your office editor has not experienced such suffering from heat in ten years.

LAST Sunday Bro. Daniel Vaniman preached at West Branch, Bro. Isaac Frantz at Franklin Grove, Bro. L. W. Teeter at Polo, Bro. I. N. H. Beahm at Salem, and Bro. A. W. Vaniman in the College Chapel. All of these brethren spent several days with us, and we enjoyed their presence very much.

THE Brethren at Philadelphia have broken ground for an addition to their meeting-house. Bro. T. T. Myers, who is with us at present, says this will give them a seating capacity of over 600. The present capacity of the house is about 400, and this is often crowded.

JUST before making up this issue for the press, Brethren S. Z. Sharp, S. R. Zug and T. C. Denton came among us to visit a few days. Possibly there may be a score or more of others whom we have not yet met. We regret to learn that Bro. Sharp is not in good health, Bro. S. W. Hoover is also reported not well.

BRETHREN S. W. Hoover and S. Bock, of the Tract Work, Dayton, Ohio, were among the many guests who spent several days at the Mount, last week. They speak very encouragingly of the outlook of the Tract Department, and are preparing to put out even more and better Tracts than have ever before been given to our Brotherhood.

AMONG the seventy or more members who visited Mt. Morris after the Annual Meeting, were Bro. Benj. Neff and his son, James M. Neff. Bro. James prepares the lessons for our advanced *Quarterly*, and we are pleased to know that they are giving quite general satisfaction. His lessons for the Third Quarter will be found among the most interesting of the lessons he has yet prepared.

IN this issue we can mention the names of only a few of our visitors, who called on us during the Annual Meeting. For a few days Mt. Morris seemed almost like a little Annual Meeting. We hope the brethren and sisters enjoyed themselves while among us, and we wish to assure them that their calls were very much appreciated. We regret that the excessive warm weather rendered some of the meetings not so pleasant as they otherwise might have been, but we must learn to take the weather as the Lord gives it and be thankful for it. We trust that these Christian associations, which we have been permitted to enjoy, may prove mutually beneficial to us all.

ON another page of this issue will be found an interesting letter concerning the great famine in Russia, written by one who was an eye-witness of the sufferings, and has a thorough knowledge of the situation.

THE ANNUAL MEETING.

THE outlook for pleasant weather during the Annual Meeting was rather discouraging when we went to press with the last issue. It had then been raining all week, and continued until the morning of the 4th. This, however, did not seem to dampen the ardor of those who had arranged to attend. A score or more of visitors, from various parts of the East, had stopped off at the Mount. We enjoyed their presence very much, and would like to give a list of them, but space will not permit.

By noon on Saturday, over one hundred members and friends were at the depot, awaiting the special train put on by the B. C. R. & N. Co. Our entire company appreciated the favor very much. The train left Mt. Morris at 12:15. At Oregon, Polo, Milledgeville, and other places, our company was greatly increased until four cars were well filled.

All along the route we could see the effects of the recent, heavy rains. Not more than half the corn crop had been planted, and many fields were yet unplowed. On reaching Savanna, and passing down the east side of the Mississippi River, the result of the heavy rains over the great Northwest was clearly manifested. The river had overflowed the fertile bottom, inundating farms, and causing immense damages generally. Many stacks of hay, standing in the meadows, were half submerged. Some farm-houses were standing in the water up to the windows. We crossed the river at Clinton, and after a very pleasant ride, landed at Cedar Rapids about seven in the evening. A delightful ride of one mile, on the electric railway, brought us to the Annual Meeting grounds, located on the east side of the city.

Near the middle of the forenoon, the rain had ceased, the clouds broke away, the sun shone out brightly, and we had a delightful day of it. We found a number of members already assembled, and every train brought in hundreds more. A glance at the buildings and surroundings impressed us with the fact that the Committee of Arrangements had done its work well. The tract of ground selected was covered with a fine coat of grass, and sloping just enough to shed the water nicely. The large tabernacle is situated near a pleasant grove, which afforded a shady resting place. The building is well constructed, after the usual order of constructing such buildings for that purpose. The roof is made of boards, covered with water-proof paper, rendering it a safe shelter in time of rain. At one end is a long, elevated platform for the Standing Committee and aged members. The other part of the room is well seated, and a good portion set apart for the use of the delegates. The entire building is well lighted up with electricity, rendering it very pleasant for night meetings. The tabernacle, we should judge, will seat about 5,000 persons.

The other buildings,—such as Dining Hall, Lunch Room, Baggage Room, MESSENGER and Tract Offices, were constructed about as at other Annual Meetings, save that they are well covered with water-proof paper, rendering them good shelter in case of rain. The dining and restaurant departments are also well lighted by electricity. The cooking department is the same as

last year, and is presided over by the same man, who certainly understands his business. We find everything, connected with the departments, neatly and nicely arranged. The cooking is excellent, provision in great abundance, and well served. So far as we see, there is nothing to complain of. It is certainly a pleasure to enjoy such Christian hospitality.

All of these buildings were constructed by the Cedar Rapids Commercial Company, and turned over to the Committee of Arrangements for the use of the Annual Meeting, absolutely free. This includes the use of the electric lights, and the convenient water-works. For this excellent favor the Commercial Company deserves the thanks of our entire Brotherhood. So far as we know, it has not been excelled by any favors that our Annual Meeting has heretofore been permitted to enjoy. We again repeat, many thanks to the Commercial Company.

Cedar Rapids is quite a large place, having a population of near 25,000. The people kindly threw open their doors to thousands of our members and friends, so that we found excellent resting places and commendable Christian hospitality. We also trust that the conduct of all the members was such as to favorably impress those with whom they lodged. At present we have no church in the place, and only a few members. It seems to us that this would be an excellent time to open up a mission here, with a view of establishing a congregation, for it must appear evident that all our visiting and preaching has, in a measure, laid in the hearts of the people a foundation on which a skillful missionary might build successfully. The Committee of Arrangements, composed of brethren John Zuck, J. S. Snyder and George W. Hopwood, have performed their work well, for they laid all the plans for the construction of the buildings, and the arrangements in general, and are executing their part admirably, always on the alert to do a favor. Bro. W. D. Tisdale had his hands full, as foreman of the lodging committee, but seemed to find a place for each one in some part of the city.

A public school building, near at hand, was set apart for the use of the Standing Committee, who pronounced their accommodations quite good.

On Saturday evening, Bro. J. S. Flory, of Lordsburg, Cal., gave us a very interesting talk on witnessing for Christ. There were probably two thousand persons present at this meeting.

SUNDAY

Morning opened up delightfully, with the promise of a clear day. Hundreds had come in during the night, and the crowd was greatly increased. Arrangements had been made for our ministers to fill nearly all the pulpits in the city, hence many of them had important work to perform. From many of the citizens we learned that the preaching was very much appreciated by the various churches. It would seem that the Brethren made good impressions in both their manner of preaching as well as in their general deportment, and we know that the kindness shown towards us by the people of Cedar Rapids will be long remembered.

At the Tabernacle morning service Bro. Enoch Eby preached one of his characteristic sermons, taking for his subject Jesus Christ, the Foundation of the Church, which he interpreted means "the called out." All the members are called out from the world, and as an organization, are found-

MORE SYSTEM.

It is not necessary for our churches to trouble themselves materially about the salaried ministry system, in order to render their work more effectual and successful. With a little improvement, or, rather, with the exercise of a little more wisdom, we have one of the most practical systems of church government in this age, especially for the rural districts. It is a system that enables each congregation to care for, instruct and edify its own members on the most economical basis. And, by the way, economy lies at the basis of all important movements, religious, secular or educational. Any enterprise that requires an expenditure in excess of its income, must eventually fail, however skillfully managed otherwise.

All congregations must be governed, instructed and edified in order to preserve a healthy and growing condition. The growth is a necessity that the losses from deaths, removals and other causes may be replaced. If a congregation does not grow, final extinction is inevitable. To secure growth, the Gospel means of instructing and edifying must be steadily kept up, hence it is said, that the Lord gave some apostles, prophets, etc., "for the perfecting of the saints, for the work of the ministry, for the edifying of the body of Christ." Eph. 4: 12. We think we have the best-known means of doing this, if we only exercise as much wisdom about our spiritual affairs as we do concerning our secular matters.

By having the preaching in new fields, and at isolated points, done by regular evangelists, set apart for that purpose, the home ministers are all left free to exercise their talents in instructing and edifying the home congregations. If the elder will then use wisdom in having the preaching properly divided up between the ministers in his charge, so that every minister has his work, the labor of edifying and instructing will be far more effectually performed. By thus doing, each man will have his work and prepare himself for it. In congregations where the labor is properly divided as suggested, there is very little complaint about the quality of preaching which the home ministers furnish. And it is our candid conviction that nothing will do more to preserve our churches from the evils of the salaried ministry system, than a judicious handling of our ministerial force in the manner indicated in this article.

While the general run of our ministers may be deficient in education and training, they nevertheless possess a native ability and zeal that enables them to make their influence felt wherever they have anything like a chance to exercise and prepare themselves for the work. But where there are a half dozen or more in one congregation, and neither one knows anything about the work that he has to perform, there is very little inducement for him to prepare himself as a minister ought to be prepared when he undertakes to preach the Word. Therefore let us exercise all of our wisdom in allotting to every man his work, and we will hear very little concerning the salaried ministry among our people.

However, there always will be poor ministers among us, who need aid, and ungrateful indeed is the church that permits one of her poor, worn out ministers to come to want, after he has spent the best years of his life in her service. We will also need evangelists in the fields, and workers in our cities where the dividing up method of ministerial labor cannot be employed so effectually

as in the rural districts, and good-working congregations. For these purposes we can use our means, and accomplish a great work without the never-ceasing burden of a salaried ministry.

Any one who will carefully study our system of church government in the light of these suggestions, cannot help but realize that our system is indeed very wisely arranged, and will accomplish the desired end if wisely administered.   J. H. M.

CORRESPONDENCE.

"Write what thou seest, and send it unto the churches."

☞ Church News solicited for this Department. If you have had a good meeting, send a Report of it, so that others may rejoice with you. In writing give name of church, County and State. Be brief. Notes of Travel should be as short as possible. Land Advertisements are not solicited for this Department. We have an advertising page, and, if necessary, will issue supplements.

The Famine in Russia.

The following communication by Mr. Edgar, of Minneapolis, Minn., who was one of the distributors of the funds, in Russia, will, no doubt, be of interest to all. Those of our members who helped to raise the means, contributed by us, as a church, may rest assured that,—though they may never meet on earth those whom they befriended in a time of need,—the Master will give ample reward:

L. A. Plate,

    Mt. Morris, Ill.,

        My Dear Sir:—

            I returned from Russia day before yesterday, and found your two favors, May 2 and May 24, on my desk, awaiting my arrival. If you have any further funds for distribution to the famine sufferers, I will be very glad indeed to send it over to persons who I know are engaged in the work of relieving the sufferings of the unfortunate peasants of that country. I have the names of a number who would be only too glad to receive any aid that you can send them.

As to the need for help, I assure you that it most certainly exists, and will continue to exist for many months yet. I promised to give you a report of the peasants as I found them, which herewith please find as follows: I went to Russia, arriving there in time to meet the Missouri when she came into Libau, loaded with the American flour. We arranged in St. Petersburg a list of those to whom we were to send the food, and the Russian government gave us free transportation by rail, delivering the flour wherever we ordered it sent to the persons-whose names we had-on our list. After seeing the flour unloaded from the ship, loaded on the cars and despatched to the interior, I returned to St. Petersburg, went thence to Moscow, and put in ten days in the famine district myself, examining into the condition of the people and the various methods of relief in use.

As a result of my own experience, together with the information gleaned from various responsible sources, including letters from a number of the people who received portions of our flour, I have no hesitation in saying that the condition of the peasants is simply terrible. The governments affected by the famine are seventeen of the richest provinces of Russia. They lie along the Volga, and many of them are densely populated. The total population of these seventeen governments is something like 38,000,000. Unquestionably 20,000,000 of them have had to be supported by outside aid during this season. I have samples of bread which these poor people use when they run short of other food, which are simply terrible, surpassing any idea which you can conceive of wretched food. The government is giving a great deal of relief, which is administered through the Zemstvos to the people. All supplies

are contributed free of charge by the government, and every effort is being made and has been made since last November, to cope with the appalling calamity which has befallen the people. When you consider that 20,000,000 of people have had to be helped, some faint idea of the great effort to sustain them may be obtained. Special relief committees, local relief committees, and, above all, the efforts of the landed proprietors to save their ex-serfs from starvation, have enabled the population to pull through in the condition in which I found them.

I visited about twelve or fifteen villages, driving about the country in a troika, and the sights witnessed by me were certainly heart-rending.

The typhus is raging in nearly all the famine countries, and following close on the heels of starvation, superinduced by weakness of the system caused by lack of food, and by the dampness of the huts on account of lack of fuel. In many districts small-pox is also raging, and in several governments scurvy is very bad indeed. The horses have died off during the winter, so that comparatively few are left. The mortality among the children has been dreadful, and in short, while I could write hundreds of pages on this subject and still leave much which should be said, lack of room necessitates that I should be brief, and simply say in one word that the situation is unparalleled for wide-spread suffering and destitution in the history of the world. The present famine in Russia I do not believe is equalled by any famine that history speaks of, certainly not which is referred to in modern chronicles. The prospects for the future are very dark indeed at present. The people are living from hand to mouth, and any cessation in the relief work results in immediate hunger and starvation. There can be no new crop raised until August, and then, as far as I am able to judge, owing to the lack of seed, the poor condition of the horses, the sickness of the peasantry themselves, there is little reason to hope that the new crop will even be sufficient to maintain the people during the winter.

If you can send any more money to aid in the work of saving these poor creatures from death and lingering starvation, or to buy them suitable food to eat during the convalescence from typhus, you will be doing a most praiseworthy act. There is need for all the aid that we can send them. Such poverty as I witnessed in the famine districts of Russia is unheard of in any other country in the world. We have poor people in the United States, but nowhere in the world do poverty, hunger, disease and wretchedness exist, as they now exist in that portion of Russia. Do everything you can to urge contributions to be sent for the relief of suffering humanity, for you may rest assured that all we can send will be most gratefully received, and most judiciously used. If I can be of any service to you in this matter, in any way, please command me   W. C. Edgar.

Minneapolis, Minn., June 2.

All the funds now on hand have, in compliance with the above request, been forwarded to Mr. Edgar, and, accompanied by our prayers, we hope will do much good. Further contributions will be received at the Messenger office, properly acknowledged, and forwarded as above mentioned.

L. A. Plate.

Mt. Morris, Ill.

From North Manchester, Ind.

Our love-feast, held May 28, was evidently true to name in every sense of the term. Love, joy and happiness prevailed. A very large corps of able ministers was present, among whom was that aged veteran of the cross,—Eld. John Metz-

school, after which Eld. Nicholas Martin delivered a very able sermon to a crowded house. His theme was, "Invitation to the great Supper."

In the evening of May 8, about twenty-five brethren and sisters repaired to the home of Bro. Adam Baker (one of our ministers), whose wife is an invalid. There we engaged in the solemn services of God's house for her special benefit. Just twelve persons engaged in the services, and as we surrounded the Lord's Table, it reminded us of that "upper room" supper where also there were twelve present besides Christ. From the feeling manifested, he was indeed in our midst. Bro. Adam Baker and his afflicted companion need the prayers of the church in their affliction.

WM. A. ANTHONY.

Mexico Home.

[It is the custom to publish eulogies over the death of the great and learned, but the inspired penman turned aside from the usual order, and narrated the triumphant death of a Lazarus. It may be interesting to our readers to read a brief notice of one who passed from the "Old Peoples' Home" to the home of the saints above.—ED.]

It becomes our painful duty to chronicle the death of our much-esteemed brother, David Strawh, who died at the "Home," May 17, 1892, aged 84 years, 2 months and 20 days.

Uncle David, as we familiarly knew and called him, came to the Home from the Pipe Creek church, Dec. 26, 1889, and during a few months over two years' stay at the Home, won, by his kindness and inoffensive disposition, the love and esteem of all the family. The writer, as Superintendent, can say that he never gave either wife or myself an unkind word, but was always obliging, and appreciated any favor done to him. He was always industrious and very prompt in his duties. Along with his choring work, he had a little potato patch, which he always planted early and took great pains in tending. Just a few days before he died, he good-naturedly remarked to me about his potatoes excelling mine. His potatoes are looking nice, but whenever I see them, and then think that I shall never see him at work in them again, it makes me feel sad. He was up and around the morning on which he died, and did his usual morning work, after which he went to his room, and was resting upon his bed. At 11 o'clock I was in his room, to see him, and found him sleeping very easy and naturally, but before I had left the dinner-table, I was summoned to his room and found him dying. His desire was to die without much suffering, which desire God granted, for he took him without a groan or a struggle. His sudden death cast a gloom of sadness over the family, but we feel that our loss is his eternal gain.

One old sister, Lieucinda Leslie, is still in bed the most of her time. The other inmates are as well as commonly. FRANK FISHER.

Mexico, Ind., May 22.

From Burr Oak, Kansas.

THE Burr Oak church met in quarterly council May 28, 1892. All business was settled satisfactorily, and I am glad to say that the dark clouds have passed over our church, and as the sun begins to dawn upon us, it finds all in love and union.

Since our brother, John Hollinger, of Russell, has had charge of the church, we have found him to be a good shepherd over our little flock. While he was with us, he labored hard and faithfully, but by request the church relieved him of his charge, and it will now rest with our home ministers for the present.

Bro. Hollinger will ever be remembered, and our prayers are that the Lord will bless him while laboring in the cause of the Master.

ANNA KINZIE.

From Middletown, Ind.

THROUGH the mercies of God we landed safe at our new home, at Middletown, Ind., the evening of May 31. Surely it has been the work of our Master that we are here, as he has opened up the way, and prospered us in all our undertakings. I came here for the purpose of trying to better myself in his work. I remained where I was as long as I could hope for the better, but all my efforts proved futile, so the Lord granted that I should fill my mission elsewhere, and now not my will, but his be done.

We had meetings at our place, before we left, by Bro. J. M. Cline. I trust the good Lord will send a shepherd to take care of the flock we left behind. It caused us great sorrow to leave so many dear friends behind, but we are told to forsake all for the cause of the Blessed Master. We arrived here in time to attend a glorious love-feast at the Upper Fall Creek church, June 2, and formed some happy acquaintances. It was a feast long to be remembered.

Next day we held a social meeting, at which some friendly admonitions were given by brethren from other churches, which caused many of us to shed tears, feeling that we were almost in sight of the heavenly city. The Lord be praised for this blessed privilege! We are among strangers in the flesh, but not in spirit. Remember us at a throne of grace! FLORIDA J. ETTER.

June 4.

Missionary Report.

THE following is a report of the Home Mission of the North-western District of Ohio from March 27, 1891, to May 28, 1892:

Amount received,	$268 23
Amount expended,	223 41
Balance on hand,	$34 82

JACOB BROWN, Treas.

Bryan, Ohio.

From the Big Creek Church, Richland County, Illinois.

WE met in quarterly council June 3, at 1 P. M. Eld. John Harshbarger, of Martin's Creek, Wayne Co., Ill., was with us and presided over the meeting. All business passed off pleasantly and with a good feeling. Not very much business was before the meeting. The missionary work was remembered. Our love-feast was appointed for Nov. 5, 1892, commencing at 3 P. M. We would give a hearty welcome to some of the brethren and sisters to be with us at our feast, and would be glad if some of the brethren that aim to make a change in their location would come to see us and locate among us. Such as are in full faith, and willing to work with the church, we would welcome with us. We have a good church-house and about fifty members. We have a fairly good country for farming, here in this part of Illinois. Any one wishing to engage in fruit culture could do no better than to come to Southern Illinois. Further information of this country can be had by addressing me at Parkersburg, Ill., by private letter. J. M. FORNEY.

Parkersburg, Ill., June 5.

From Egion, W. Va.

THE Maple Spring church met in council-meeting June 4. There was not much business before

the meeting. The writer was chosen correspondent for the MESSENGER. We decided to hold our love-feast Sept. 3, if it is the Lord's will. Bro. E. T. Fike is our solicitor for the Book and Tract Work. We felt sorry that our aged elder, S. A. Fike, and his aged companion, could not be with us at our council, but we are glad to know that he has sufficiently improved in health to be up part of the time, and hope that he may soon be able to meet with us at the house of the Lord. He has been confined to his bed and room two months, and his sufferings were great. We have a social meeting once a week and singing every Sunday evening. Our Sunday-school convenes each Sunday, and we have meeting every two weeks at Maple Spring, and every two weeks at four different school-houses. This congregation is building a church-house at Brookside, W. Va. They expect to have it completed till fall.

RACHEL WEIMER.

The Annual Meeting.

IN making up this issue we have room only for the following clipping from the *Cedar Rapids Daily Republican:*

Yesterday's meeting (Monday), of the German Baptists was a revelation to the people of Cedar Rapids in the way of a religious gathering. It had been thought that the immense throng of Sunday must nearly measure the strength of attendance, but it was eclipsed by yesterday. All of the Sunday night trains brought in their additions as did those of yesterday morning, until fully 10,000 members of this organization must have been on the ground during the day. It was an earnest throng, full of the purposes that brought them together, but elements of pleasure were not wanting, as was evidenced on every hand. Many were the pleasant reunions that have taken place among the elder members, and many more are the new acquaintances made that will contribute not only to the joyousness of this but of future gatherings.

The meeting is being held in Central Park, about one mile from the Union depot. A better location could not have been chosen, as the ground is well adapted for the purpose, and beautiful groves surround them, adding not a little to the pleasures attendant upon the meeting. The electric cars run within a block of the grounds and are giving the visitors every possible advantage in the way of transportation. The tabernacle is a massive building and will seat five thousand persons. Near the tabernacle is the large dining hall that will accommodate one thousand people at each meal. There is also a large lunch counter where persons, who do not wish to get a full meal, can be accommodated. There is also a post-office building on the ground and an office near by which is used by the *Gospel Messenger* and the Book and Tract people. Among the visitors, the sentiment is very general that the city has acquitted itself nobly in the way of accommodations throughout and many are the compliments passed daily upon the management that has brought this about.

From Border, Kans.

BRO. Z. HENRICKS, of Grant County, Kans., came to us March 9, to hold a series of meetings. He preached six interesting sermons; then closed on account of bad weather. There were no additions, but quite an interest was manifested. He came to us again May 26 and preached one sermon, and on the morning of May 27 two precious souls gave their hearts to Jesus and were buried with him in baptism.

Bro. Henricks then went to the little band of Brethren at Progress, Colo., but returned to us on

school, after which Eld. Nicholas Martin delivered a very able sermon to a crowded house. His theme was, "Invitation to the great Supper."

In the evening of May 8, about twenty-five brethren and sisters repaired to the home of Bro. Adam Baker (one of our ministers), whose wife is an invalid. There we engaged in the solemn services of God's house for her special benefit. Just twelve persons engaged in the services, and as we surrounded the Lord's Table, it reminded us of that "upper room" supper where also there were twelve present besides Christ. From the feeling manifested, he was indeed in our midst. Bro. Adam Baker and his afflicted companion need the prayers of the church in their affliction.

WM. A. ANTHONY.

Mexico Home.

[It is the custom to publish eulogies over the death of the great and learned, but the inspired penman turned aside from the usual order, and narrated the triumphant death of a Lazarus. It may be interesting to our readers to read a brief notice of one who passed from the "Old Peoples' Home" to the home of the saints above.—ED.]

IT becomes our painful duty to chronicle the death of our much-esteemed brother, David Strawh, who died at the "Home," May 17, 1892, aged 84 years, 2 months and 20 days.

Uncle David, as we familiarly knew and called him, came to the Home from the Pipe Creek church, Dec. 26, 1889, and during a few months over two years' stay at the Home, won, by his kindness and inoffensive disposition, the love and esteem of all the family. The writer, as Superintendent, can say that he never gave either wife or myself an unkind word, but was always obliging, and appreciated any favor done to him. He was always industrious and very prompt in his duties. Along with his choring work, he had a little potato patch, which he always planted early and took great pains in tending. Just a few days before he died, he good-naturedly remarked to me about his potatoes excelling mine. His potatoes are looking nice, but whenever I see them, and then think that I shall never see him at work in them again, it makes me feel sad. He was up and around the morning on which he died, and did his usual morning work, after which he went to his room, and was resting upon his bed. At 11 o'clock I was in his room, to see him, and found him sleeping very easy and naturally, but before I had left the dinner-table, I was summoned to his room and found him dying. His desire was to die without much suffering, which desire God granted, for he took him without a groan or a struggle. His sudden death cast a gloom of sadness over the family, but we feel that our loss is his eternal gain.

One old sister, Lieacinda Leslie, is still in bed the most of her time. The other inmates are as well as commonly.

FRANK FISHER.

Mexico, Ind., May 22.

From Burr Oak, Kansas.

THE Burr Oak church met in quarterly council May 28, 1892. All business was settled satisfactorily, and I am glad to say that the dark clouds have passed over our church, and as the sun begins to dawn upon us, it finds all in love and union.

Since our brother, John Hollinger, of Russell, has had charge of the church, we have found him to be a good shepherd over our little flock. While he was with us, he labored hard and faithfully, but by request the church relieved him of his charge, and it will now rest with our home ministers for the present.

Bro. Hollinger will ever be remembered, and our prayers are that the Lord will bless him while laboring in the cause of the Master.

ANNA KINZIE.

From Middletown, Ind.

THROUGH the mercies of God we landed safe at our new home, at Middletown, Ind., the evening of May 31. Surely it has been the work of our Master that we are here, as he has opened up the way, and prospered us in all our undertakings. I came here for the purpose of trying to better myself in his work. I remained where I was as long as I could hope for the better, but all my efforts proved futile, so the Lord granted that I should fill my mission elsewhere, and now not my will, but his be done.

We had meetings at our place, before we left, by Bro. J. M. Cline. I trust the good Lord will send a shepherd to take care of the flock we left behind. It caused us great sorrow to leave so many dear friends behind, but we are told to forsake all for the cause of the Blessed Master. We arrived here in time to attend a glorious love-feast at the Upper Fall Creek church, June 2, and formed some happy acquaintances. It was a feast long to be remembered.

Next day we held a social meeting, at which some friendly admonitions were given by brethren from other churches, which caused many of us to shed tears, feeling that we were almost in sight of the heavenly city. The Lord be praised for this blessed privilege! We are among strangers in the flesh, but not in spirit. Remember us at a throne of grace! FLORIDA J. ETTER.

June 4.

Missionary Report.

THE following is a report of the Home Mission of the North-western District of Ohio from March 27, 1891, to May 28, 1892:

Amount received,	$358 23
Amount expended,	323 41
Balance on hand,	$34 82

JACOB BROWN, Treas.

Bryan, Ohio.

From the Big Creek Church, Richland County, Illinois.

WE met in quarterly council June 3, at 1 P. M. Eld. John Harshbarger, of Martin's Creek, Wayne Co., Ill., was with us and presided over the meeting. All business passed off pleasantly and with a good feeling. Not very much business was before the meeting. The missionary work was remembered. Our love-feast was appointed for Nov. 5, 1892, commencing at 3 P. M. We would give a hearty welcome to some of the brethren and sisters to be with us at our feast, and would be glad if some of the brethren that aim to make a change in their location would come to see us and locate among us. Such as are in full faith, and willing to work with the church, we would welcome with us. We have a good church-house and about fifty members. We have a fairly good country for farming, here in this part of Illinois. Any one wishing to engage in fruit culture could do no better than to come to Southern Illinois. Further information of this country can be had by addressing me at Parkersburg, Ill., by private letter. J. M. FORNEY.

Parkersburg, Ill., June 5.

From Eglon, W. Va.

THE Maple Spring church met in council-meeting June 4. There was not much business before

the meeting. The writer was chosen correspondent for the MESSENGER. We decided to hold our love-feast Sept. 3, if it is the Lord's will. Bro. E. T. Fike is our solicitor for the Book and Tract Work. We felt sorry that our aged elder, S. A. Fike, and his aged companion, could not be with us at our council, but we are glad to know that he has sufficiently improved in health to be up part of the time, and hope that he may soon be able to meet with us at the house of the Lord. He has been confined to his bed and room two months, and his sufferings were great. We have a social meeting once a week and singing every Sunday evening. Our Sunday-school convenes each Sunday, and we have meeting every two weeks at Maple Spring, and every two weeks at four different school-houses. This congregation is building a church-house at Brookside, W. Va. They expect to have it completed till fall.

RACHEL WEIMER.

The Annual Meeting.

IN making up this issue we have room only for the following clipping from the *Cedar Rapids Daily Republican:*

Yesterday's meeting (Monday), of the German Baptists was a revelation to the people of Cedar Rapids in the way of a religious gathering. It had been thought that the immense throng of Sunday must nearly measure the strength of attendance, but it was eclipsed by yesterday. All of the Sunday night trains brought in their additions as did those of yesterday morning, until fully 10,000 members of this organization must have been on the ground during the day. It was an earnest throng, full of the purposes that brought them together, but elements of pleasure were not wanting, as was evidenced on every hand. Many were the pleasant reunions that have taken place among the elder members, and many more are the new acquaintances made that will contribute not only to the joyousness of this but of future gatherings.

The meeting is being held in Central Park, about one mile from the Union depot. A better location could not have been chosen, as the ground is well adapted for the purpose, and beautiful groves surround them, adding not a little to the pleasures attendant upon the meeting. The electric cars run within a block of the grounds and are giving the visitors every possible advantage in the way of transportation. The tabernacle is a massive building and will seat five thousand persons. Near the tabernacle is the large dining hall that will accommodate one thousand people at each meal. There is also a large lunch counter where persons, who do not wish to get a full meal, can be accommodated. There is also a post-office building on the ground and an office near by which is used by the Gospel Messenger and the Book and Tract people. Among the visitors, the sentiment is very general that the city has acquitted itself nobly in the way of accommodations throughout and many are the compliments passed daily upon the management that has brought this about.

From Border, Kans.

BRO. Z. HENRICKS, of Grant County, Kans., came to us March 9, to hold a series of meetings. He preached six interesting sermons; then closed on account of bad weather. There were no additions, but quite an interest was manifested. He came to us again May 26 and preached one sermon, and on the morning of May 27 two precious souls gave their hearts to Jesus and were buried with him in baptism.

Bro. Henricks then went to the little band of Brethren at Progress, Colo., but returned to us on

Salomon's Creek, Ind.—The brethren and sisters met in quarterly council June 4. The annual visit reported all to be in the faith, but four who refused to walk with the children of God. There were 178 members reported in this congregation. The necessary preparation was made for the feast, to be held June 18. Bro. Lingafelter was again selected to lead the school at the large church. Brethren Davis Younce and Lemuel Hillery are on the sick list. But few are attending Annual Conference, on account of high water. Northern Indiana is having a wet and backward spring, and but little corn has been planted, and farmers are somewhat discouraged.—*L. A. Neff, June 6.*

Fredonia, Kans.—On the morning of May 10, Bro. John Waas (who lives with his father about four and one-half miles south of Fredonia), was in an old cellar where there was about two inches of water. He was subject to fits, and it is supposed he had a fit while there and fell face foremost and drowned. May 11 his remains were taken to the Merino school-house, and placed in the Rainbow cemetery. His funeral was preached by Eld. G. W. Studabaker, from 2 Sam. 14: 14, to a large crowd of sympathizing friends. His age was sixteen years, five months and twenty-nine days.—*J. W. Frisor, June 4.*

Matrimonial.

"What therefore God hath joined together, let not man put asunder."

KINSEL—HENRY.—At the residence of the bride's parents, near Holidaysburg, Blair Co., Pa., May 25, 1892, by the undersigned, Bro. Harry C. Kinsel, of Altoona, Pa., and sister Della K. Henry, of the same place.　　D. S. BRALLIER.

SHAULIS—BECK.—At the residence of the undersigned, March 20, 1892, McClelland Shaulis, of Westmoreland County, Pa., and Priscilla Beck, of Somerset County.

McCORKLE—PATTERSON.—At the same place, May 5, 1892, M. H. McCorkle, of Allegheny County, Pa., and Mary A. Patterson, of Westmoreland County.　　D. D. HORNER.

RHINE—PEEK.—At the bride's parents, near Catalpa, May 31, 1892, by the undersigned, Mr. James L. Rhine and Miss Amanda B. Peek, all of Gove County, Kans.
　　　　　　　　　　　　　　　　　　J. B. WERTZ.

McELROY—STONER.—At the bride's parents, Mr. A. L. Stoner's, June 2, 1892, by the undersigned, William C. McElroy and Katie B. Stoner, all of Quinter, Kans.
　　　　　　　　　　　　　　　　　　J. B. WERTZ.

DICK—ALBRIGHT.—At the residence of the bride's parents, Roaring Springs, Blair Co., Pa., May 21, 1892, by the undersigned, Mr. Plomer B. Dick and Miss Emma Albright, both of Roaring Springs, Blair Co., Pa.　MICHAEL CLAAR.

PELLMAN—SHELLENBERGER.—At the residence of the bride's uncle, Abram Bennet, May 5, 1892, by the undersigned, Mr. Charles G. Pellman and sister Lizzie M. Shellenberger, both of Richfield, Juniata Co., Pa.　S. S. DEAVER.

Fallen Asleep.

"Blessed are the dead which die in the Lord."

HARNISH.—In the Ozawkie church, Kans., May 21, 1892, John, son of Bro. Elias and sister Harnish, aged 6 years, 9 months and 6 days. He came in on the morning of the above date not feeling well, and soon after was taken with a chill, which resulted in congestion of the brain. Funeral services from 1 Cor. 15: 54, 55.

BROWN.—Also in the same congregation, May 25, 1892, Charley, son of Bro. Samuel and sister Sarah Brown, aged 10 years, 4 months and 21 days. The dear little boy also struggled with the same disease, and in less than two days he also was taken away. Funeral services from 1 Pet. 1: 24.
　　　　　　　　　　　　　　　　　　J. A. ROOT.

BARBER.—In the bounds of the North Solomon church, Osborne Co., Kans., May 14, 1892, Sophia, wife of J. L. Barber, aged 50 years, 9 months and 23 days. Funeral services to a large congregation of neighbors and friends by the writer.　　　　　　　　　　　　　J. S. LEERW.

DULL.—At Shady Grove, Pa., May 5, 1892, Bro. Peter Dull, aged 71 years, 10 months and 25 days. Deceased was a member of the River Brethren church. He was buried at Price's church. Funeral discourse by Eld. Geo. Winger and the writer from Rev. 14: 13.

BURGER.—In the Libertyville church, Jefferson Co., Iowa, May 23, 1892, Warren Burger, son of Bro. Joseph and sister Salinda Burger, aged 8 years, 7 months and 9 days. Warren was quite a favorite in the neighborhood, but God loved him and took him to himself. Funeral services held at the house by the writer.　　　　　　　　ABRAHAM WOLF.

THOMPSON.—In the Pine Creek church, Marshall Co., Ind., May 25, 1892, Mrs. Adaline Thompson, wife of David Thompson, aged 34 years, 7 months and 9 days. She was the daughter of Bro. John and sister France and leaves a husband, two children and many friends to mourn their loss. Services by Bro. Jacob Hilderbrand.　CLARA L. HILDERBRAND.

HOLLOWAY.—In the Pine Creek church, Ind., May 19, 1892, Wm. Holloway, aged 74 years, 11 months and 27 days. Deceased was born at Winchester, England, May 23, 1818. Deceased was a member of the Catholic church. Funeral services by Jacob Hilderbrand.　CLARA L. HILDERBRAND.

BUCK.—In the bounds of the Mexico church, Ind., at his home near Deadville, on Monday, Feb. 8, 1892, Bro. Michael Morris Buck, aged about 69 years. He was a faithful member of the Brethren church for many years. He was twice married to women of Christian character. His first wife, Mary Dillman, died five years ago. He was married since to Mrs. Mary Purvis. On account of sickness among the friends, the funeral sermon was deferred, but will be preached in the near future.　　　　　　　　L. D. WITTER.

BUCK.—In the same home, on Friday, Feb. 19, 1892, sister Mary M. Buck, wife of the above-named Michael Morris Buck. She was born Oct. 13, 1832, in Rockbridge County, Va. Her maiden name was Wilhelm. Dec. 25, 1848, she was married to Jesse Purvis, Sr., to whom she bore six children. In 1887 she was married to Morris Buck, and was a kind, loving and faithful companion to him.
　　　　　　　　　　　　　　　　　　L. D. WITTER.

REDENBO.—In the Hurricane Creek congregation, Bond Co., Ill., May 28, 1892, sister Dollie Redenbo, wife of Bro. Aaron Redenbo, aged 27 years, 8 months and 19 days. She leaves a husband, two children and a host of friends to mourn her loss. Funeral services by Bro. John Cripe at her home. Text, Rev. 14: 13, 14 and 15.　　　Wm. H. KETRING.

VANFORTH.—In Poland, Ohio, May 1, 1892, Rosa Ann Vanforth, aged 23 years, 6 months and several days. Disease, dropsy. She neglected the preparation for the future until sickness had come, and several weeks before her departure she was very anxious to be baptized, but owing to her great weakness this was not attended to. May this be a warning to others "not to neglect so great salvation." Funeral improved from Rom. 5: 1-5 by the writer.　　J. H. KURTZ.

RUHLMAN.—Near Poland, Ohio, May 15, 1892, sister Eliza Ruhlman, aged 59 years, 2 months and 10 days. She lived, apparently, a consistent Christian life until a few years ago when her health became impaired, and some time after that, she became insane. She seemed to be in much mental misery, until death came to her relief. Funeral occasion improved from John 16: 33 by Bro. J. F. Kahler, assisted by the writer.　　　　　　　　　　　　　　J. H. KURTZ.

PFOUTZ.—In the Bear Creek church, Montgomery Co., Ohio, May 18, 1892, Lewis R. Pfoutz, aged 72 years, 7 months and 11 days. Squire Pfoutz was born in Carroll County, Maryland, Oct. 6, 1819. When a lad he, with his parents, emigrated to Ohio. His parents were members of the German Baptist Brethren. Although he made no religious profession, yet he was kindly disposed to the Brethren and donated liberally to the good cause when occasion required. His wife,—a saintly old mother in Israel,—and five children survive him to mourn their loss. Funeral services by brethren J. W. Beeghly and L. A. Bookwalter from 1 Cor. 7: 29, 31. Subject, "Shortness of time and its improvement."
　　　　　　　　　　　　　　　　　　JOSIAH EBY.

MUMAW.—At Alberton, Md., May 17, 1892, sister Mattie M., wife of Bro. W. H. Mumaw, aged 43 years, 11 months and 29 days. Sister Mumaw was a faithful member of the church for twenty-five years and died in the triumphs of a living faith. She was the mother of twelve children, ten of whom, with their father, mourn their loss. Burial at Mt. Crawford, Va. Funeral services in the German Reform church by brethren S. F. Sanger and J. M. Kagey.
　　　　　　　　　　　　　　　　　　H. C. EARLY.

SARK.—In Wells County, Ind., May 20, 1892, Moses Sark, aged 71 years, 4 months and 30 days. Funeral services conducted by Bro. Samuel Neher from the words, "Man dieth and wasteth away, yea he giveth up the ghost and where is he?" Job 14: 10.　　　　　MALINDA S. STUDEBAKER.

NOFFSINGER.—Near Union City, Ind., in the Union City church, May 31, 1892, Mr. Edward Noffsinger, aged 24 years, 3 months and 14 days. He did not seem to realize his critical condition, but entertained strong hope of his recovery until a very short time before his death. When the writer arrived at his bedside, about one-half hour before he died, he requested to be baptized. In a few minutes he passed over into the spirit world. Funeral discourse by the writer from James 4: 14, "What is our life?"　　　W. K. SIMMONS.

EIKENBERRY.—In the Bachelor Run church, Carroll Co., Ind., April 16, 1892, sister Ella Eikenberry, aged 17 years 7 months and 4 days. She was a patient sufferer for two years, and said that she was willing to die and meet her father who protected her several years. She was loved and respected by all who knew her. She leaves a mother, four sisters, one brother and many sympathizing friends to mourn their loss. Funeral services by brethren A. J. Flora and Hiel Hamilton.　　　　　　　　　　　　D. H. NICCUM.

JENKINS.—At Redkey, Ind., May 1, 1892, aged 83 years, 8 months and 18 days. In 1832 he was joined in holy matrimony to Mary Ullum, with whom he lived until 1853, when death separated them. To this union were born seven children, two of whom have preceded him. He was married to Catherine Miller Nov. 20, 1853. To them were born six children; two of whom have gone before him. He leaves a wife, nine children and a host of relatives and friends. He has twenty-eight grandchildren and two great-grandchildren living. In 1857 he came to Indiana and settled near Emmettsville, Randolph County, where he lived until last October, when he moved to Redkey. His last illness was very brief, but he was resigned to the fate that was awaiting him. Funeral discourse by W. K. Simmons from Rev. 14: 13.

FRANTZ.—In the South Beatrice church, Gage Co., Nebr. May 29, 1892, Bro. John L. Frantz, aged 40 years, 10 months and 12 days. Funeral discourse by Eld. Henry Brubaker, of Nocona, Tex., from Rev. 14: 13, 13, to a large concourse of people. Bro. Frantz suffered with a long, lingering disease of the stomach, which seemed to baffle the skill of our best physicians. He bore his sufferings with Christian resignation. He leaves a loving companion and seven children. Sister Frantz and her bereaved family stand in need of the prayers and sympathies of all the children of God.
　　　　　　　　　　　　　　　　　　M. L. SPIRE.

SINES.—In the Oakland congregation, Garrett Co., Md., May 29, 1892, sister Sarah Catherine Sines, wife of Bro. Taylor Sines, aged 43 years, 3 months and 7 days. Sister Sines was sick only a few days and never able to speak a word from the time she was taken. Bro. Sines was away from home, at the time, in the Maple Grove church, Md., holding a series of meetings. He arrived home in time to see his wife breathing her last, but she did not recognize him. Bro. Sines is well known as an efficient worker in the ministry. He has lost a worthy companion, the children a true, Christian mother, and the church a worthy member. Funeral services by the writer, assisted by J. O. Thompson.　　JONAS FIKE.

SUMMERS.—At the residence of Bro. William Bashor, near Myers, Jo Daviess Co., Ill., April 29, 1892, sister Barbara Summers, *nee* Bauman, aged 84 years, 7 months and 14 days. Sister Summers was born of Amish parents, Sept. 15, 1807, in Somerset County, Pa. She was married in Ohio to John Summers about 1826, and moved to Indiana in 1890. She moved to Richland County, Wis., in 1855 and came to Jo Daviess County, Ill., in 1872. Her husband died in 1863. She had ten children, three of whom preceded her to the grave. She was a faithful member of the church for about forty-three years. She was an invalid for about twenty-four years, and for the last ten years was confined to her bed. She bore all her sufferings with Christian patience. Services conducted by the writer and brethren A. H. Lutz and Israel Stees from 1 Cor. 15: 20, 21, 22.　　　ALLEN BOYER.

CARBAUGH.—In the bounds of the Falling Spring congregation, sister Elisa A. Carbaugh, aged 63 years, 1 month and 16 days. Funeral discourse to a large congregation of sympathizing friends by the writer, assisted by Eld. Wm. C. Koontz from Ps. 35: 14, last clause. Interment in the Brown's Mill grave-yard.

SHANK.—At his residence, near Greencastle, May 17, 1892, Bro. Isaac R. Shank, aged 55 years and 11 months. Interment at the Hade church. Services from Job 14: 14 by the writer and Eld. Wm. C. Koontz, to a large assembly. Bro. Shank was a deacon, and faithful in the discharge of his duty until death. He lived in the Falling Spring church, all his life, with the exception of a few years when he resided near Alpena, Dakota. He died very suddenly. Having cut a small gash in his foot while making fence, he bled so profusely that he was unable to rally again. At the time of the division he, with one other deacon and the youngest minister (Wm. C. Koontz, now our elder) did much to uphold the interests of the church, so that to-day their number is larger than before the division.　　　　　　　Wm. A. ANTHONY.

BUSSARD.—At Peabody, Marion Co., Kans., May 26, 1892, Bro. John B. Bussard, aged 55 years, 1 month and 1 day. He was born in Frederick County, Md., April 27, 1837. In 1840 he, with his parents, moved to Elkhart County, Ind., where he remained until manhood. After his marriage to Maria Weyrich he moved to Michigan, where they lived for eleven years, after which they returned to Indiana, where his wife died about one year later. In 1891 he came to Peabody, Kans., where he remained until his death. Five children were given them, of whom four survive their parents. Bro. Bussard endured the pain with true Christian patience until the good Lord said: "It is enough." Services by the writer from 2 Cor. 13: 11.　　GEO. STRYCHER.

Solomon's Creek, Ind.—The brethren and sisters met in quarterly council June 4. The annual visit reported all to be in the faith, but four who refused to walk with the children of God. There were 173 members reported in this congregation. The necessary preparation was made for the feast, to be held June 18. Bro. Lingafelter was again selected to lead the school at the large church. Brethren Davis Younce and Lemuel Hillery are on the sick list. But few are attending Annual Conference, on account of high water. Northern Indiana is having a wet and backward spring, and but little corn has been planted, and farmers are somewhat discouraged.—*L. A." Neff, June 6.*

Fredonia, Kans.—On the morning of May 10, Bro. John Waas (who lives with his father about four and one-half miles south of Fredonia), was in an old cellar where there was about two inches of water. He was subject to fits, and it is supposed he had a fit while there and fell face foremost and drowned. May 11 his remains were taken to the Merino school-house, and placed in the Rainbow cemetery. His funeral was preached by Eld. G. W. Studebaker, from 2 Sam. 14: 14, to a large crowd of sympathizing friends. His age was sixteen years, five months and twenty-nine days.—*J. W. Priser, June 4.*

Matrimonial.

" What therefore God hath joined together, let not man put asunder."

KINSEL—HENRY.—At the residence of the bride's parents, near Holidaysburg, Blair Co., Pa., May 25, 1892, by the undersigned, Bro. Harry C. Kinsel, of Altoona, Pa., and sister Della K. Heafy, of the same place. D. S. BRALLIER.

SHAULIS—BECK.—At the residence of the undersigned, March 20, 1892, McClelland Shaulis, of Westmoreland County, Pa., and Priscilla Beck, of Somerset County.

McCORKLE—PATTERSON.—At the same place, May 5, 1892, M. H. McCorkle, of Allegheny County, Pa., and Mary A. Paterson, of Westmoreland County.   D. D. HORNER.

RHINE—PEEK.—At the bride's parents, near Catalpa, May 31, 1892, by the undersigned, Mr. James L. Rhine and Miss Amanda B. Peek, all of Gove County, Kans.
J. B. WERTZ.

McELROY—STONER.—At the bride's parents, Mr. A. L. Stoner's, June 2, 1892, by the undersigned, William C. McElroy and Katie B. Stoner, all of Quinter, Kans.
J. B. WERTZ.

DICK—ALBRIGHT.—At the residence of the bride's parents, Roaring Springs, Blair Co., Pa., May 11, 1892, by the undersigned, Mr. Plomer B. Dick and Miss Emma Albright, both of Roaring Springs, Blair Co., Pa.   MICHAEL CLAAR.

PELLMAN—SHELLENBERGER.—At the residence of the bride's uncle, Abram Benner, May 5, 1892, by the undersigned, Mr. Charles G. Pellman and sister Lizzie M. Shellenberger, both of Richfield, Juniata Co., Pa.   S. S. DEAVER.

Fallen Asleep.

" Blessed are the dead which die in the Lord."

HARNISH.—In the Ozawkie church, Kans, May 21, 1892, John, son of Bro. Elias and sister Harnish, aged 17 years, 9 months and 6 days. He came in on the morning of the above date not feeling well, and soon after was taken with a chill, which resulted in congestion of the brain. Funeral services from 1 Cor. 15: 54, 55.

BROWN.—Also in the same congregation, May 25, 1892, Charley, son of Bro. Samuel and sister Sarah Brown, aged 10 years, 4 months and 21 days. The dear little boy also struggled with the same disease, and in less than two days he also was taken away. Funeral services from 1 Pet 1: 24.
J. A. ROOT.

BARBER.—In the bounds of the North Solomon church, Osborne Co., Kans., May 24, 1892, Sophia, wife of J. L. Barber, aged 50 years, 9 months and 23 days. Funeral services to a large congregation of neighbors and friends by the writer.   J. S. LEHEW.

DULL.—At Shady Grove, Pa., May 5, 1892, Bro. Peter Dull, aged 71 years, 10 months and 25 days. Deceased was a member of the River Brethren church. He was buried at Price's church. Funeral discourse by Eld. Geo. Wingert and the writer from Rev. 14: 13.

BURGER.—In the Libertyville church, Jefferson Co., Iowa, May 23, 1892, Warren Burger, son of Bro. Joseph and sister Salinda Burger, aged 8 years, 7 months and 9 days. Warren was quite a favorite in the neighborhood, but God loved him and took him to himself. Funeral services held at the house by the writer.   ABRAHAM WOLF.

THOMPSON.—In the Pine Creek church, Marshall Co., Ind., May 25, 1892, Mrs. Adaline Thompson, wife of David Thompson, aged 34 years, 7 months and 9 days. She was the daughter of Bro. John and sister France and leaves a husband, two children and many friends to mourn their loss. Services by Bro. Jacob Hildebrand.   CLARA L. HILDERBRAND.

HOLLOWAY.—In the Pine Creek church, Ind., May 19, 1892, Wm. Holloway, aged 74 years, 11 months and 27 days. Deceased was born at Winchester, England, May 23, 1818. Deceased was a member of the Catholic church. Funeral services by Jacob Hildebrand.   CLARA L. HILDERBRAND.

BUCK.—In the bounds of the Mexico church, Ind., at his home near Deedsville, on Monday, Feb. 8, 1892, Bro. Michael Morris Buck, aged about 69 years. He was a faithful member of the Brethren church for many years. He was twice married to women of Christian character. His first wife, Mary Dillman, died five years ago. He was married since to Mrs. Mary Purvis. On account of sickness among the friends, the funeral sermon was deferred, but will be preached in the near future.   L. D. WITTER.

BUCK.—In the same home, on Friday, Feb. 19, 1892, sister Mary M. Buck, wife of the above-named Michael Morris Buck. She was born Oct. 13, 1831, in Rockbridge County, Va. Her maiden name was Wilhelm. Dec. 25, 1848, she was married to Jesse Purvis, Sr., to whom she bore six children. In 1887 she was married to Morris Buck, and was a kind, loving, and faithful companion to him.
L. D. WITTER.

REDENBO.—In the Hurricane Creek congregation, Bond Co., Ill., May 28, 1892, sister Dollie Redenbo, wife of Bro. Aaron Redenbo, aged 27 years, 8 months and 19 days. She leaves a husband, two children and a host of friends to mourn her loss. Funeral services by Bro. John Cripe at her home. Text, Rev. 14: 13, 14 and 15.   Wm. H. KETRING.

VANFORTH.—In Poland, Ohio, May 1, 1892, Ross Ann Vanforth, aged 33 years, 6 months and several days. Disease, dropsy. She neglected the preparation for the future until sickness had come, and several weeks before her departure she was very anxious to be baptized, but owing to her great weakness this was not attended to. May this be a warning to others " not to neglect so great salvation." Funeral improved from Rom. 5: 1-5 by the writer.   J. H. KURTZ.

RUHLMAN.—Near Poland, Ohio, May 15, 1892, sister Eliza Ruhlman, aged 59 years, 2 months and 10 days. She lived, apparently, a consistent Christian life until a few years ago when her health became impaired, and some time after that, she became insane. She seemed to be in much mental misery, until death came to her relief. Funeral occasion improved from John 16: 33 by Bro. J. P. Kahler, assisted by the writer.   J. H. KURTZ.

PFOUTZ.—In the Bear Creek church, Montgomery Co., Ohio, May 18, 1892, Lewis R. Pfoutz, aged 72 years, 7 months and 12 days. Squire Pfoutz was born in Carroll County, Maryland, Oct. 6, 1819. When a lad he, with his parents, emigrated to Ohio. His parents were members of the German Baptist Brethren. Although he made no religious profession, yet he was kindly disposed to the Brethren and donated liberally to the good cause when occasion required. His wife,—a saintly old mother in Israel,—and five children survive him to mourn their loss. Funeral services by brethren J. W. Beeghly and L. A. Bonkwalter from 1 Cor. 7: 29, 31. Subject, " Shortness of time and its improvement."
JOSIAH EBY.

MUMAW.—At Alberton, Md, May 17, 1892, sister Mattie M , wife of Bro. W. H. Mumaw, aged 43 years, 11 months and 12 days. Sister Mumaw was a faithful member of the church for twenty-five years and died in the triumphs of a living faith. She was the mother of twelve children, ten of whom survive her, with her husband, mourn their loss. Burial at Mt. Crawford, Va. Funeral services in the German Reform church by brethren S. F. Sanger and J. M. Kagey.
H. C. EARLY.

SARK.—In Wells County, Indiana, May 23, 1892, Moses Sark, aged 72 years, 4 months and 30 days. Funeral services conducted by Bro. Samuel Neher from the words, " Man dieth and wasteth away, yea he giveth up the ghost and where is he?" Job 14: 10.   MALINDA S. STUDEBAKER.

NOFFSINGER.—Near Union City, Ind., in the Union City church, May 21, 1892, Mr. Edward Noffsinger, aged 24 years, 2 months and 14 days. He did not seem to realize his critical condition, but entertained strong hope of his recovery until a very-short time before his death. When the writer arrived at his bedside, about one-half hour before he died, he requested to be baptized. In a few minutes he passed over into the spirit world. Funeral discourse by the writer from James 4: 14, " What is our life?"   W. K. SIMMONS.

EIKENBERRY.—In the Bachelor Run church, Carroll Co., Ind., April 16, 1892, sister Ella Eikenberry, aged 17 years, 7 months and 4 days. She was a patient sufferer for two years, and said that she was willing to die and meet her father who preceded her several years. She was loved and respected by all who knew her. She leaves a mother, four sisters, one brother and many sympathizing friends to mourn their loss. Funeral services by brethren A. J. Flora and Hiel Hamilton.   D. H. NICCUM.

JENKINS.—At Redkey, Ind., May 2, 1892, aged 83 years, 8 months and 18 days. In 1832 he was joined in holy matrimony to Mary Ullom, with whom he lived until 1851, when death separated them. To this union were born seven children, two of whom have preceded him. He was married to Catherine Miller Nov. 20, 1853. To them were born six children; two of whom have gone before him. He leaves a wife, nine children and a host of relatives and friends. He has twenty-eight grandchildren and two great-grandchildren living. In 1857 he came to Indiana and settled near Emmetsville, Randolph County, where he lived until last October, when he moved to Redkey. His last illness was very brief, but he was resigned to the fate that was awaiting him. Funeral discourse by W. K. Simmons from Rev. 14: 13.

FRANTZ.—In the South Beatrice church, Gage Co., Nebr., May 29, 1892, Bro. John L. Frantz, aged 40 years, 10 months and 12 days. Funeral discourse by Eld. Henry Brubaker, of Nocona, Texas, from Rev. 14: 12, 13, to a large concourse of people. Bro. Frantz suffered with a long, lingering disease of the stomach, which seemed to baffle the skill of our best physicians. He bore his sufferings with Christian resignation. He leaves a loving companion and seven children. Sister Frantz and her bereaved family stand in need of the prayers and sympathies of all the children of God.
M. L. SPIRE.

SINES.—In the Oakland congregation, Garrett Co., Md., May 29, 1892, sister Sarah Catharine Sines, wife of Bro. Taylor Sines, aged 43 years, 3 months and 2 days. Sister Sines was sick only a few days and never able to speak a word from the time she was taken. Bro. Sines was away from home, at the time, in the Maple Grove church, Md., holding a series of meetings. He arrived home in time to see his wife breathing her last, but she did not recognize him. Bro. Sines is well known as an efficient worker in the ministry. He has lost a worthy companion, the children a true, Christian mother, and the church a worthy member. Funeral services by the writer, assisted by J. O. Thompson.   JONAS FIKE.

SUMMERS.—At the residence of Bro. William Bashor, near Nora, Jo Daviess Co., Ill., April 29, 1892, sister Barbara Summers, nee Bauman, aged 84 years, 7 months and 14 days. Sister Summers was born of Amish parents, Sept. 15, 1807, in Somerset County, Pa. She was married in Ohio to John Summers about 1826, and moved to Indiana in 1850. She moved to Richland County, Wis, in 1855 and came to Jo Daviess County, Ill., in 1872. Her husband died in 1865. She had ten children, three of whom preceded her to the grave. She was a faithful member of the church for about forty-three years. She was an invalid for about twenty-four years, and for the last ten years was confined to her bed. She bore all her sufferings with Christian patience. Services conducted by the writer and brethren A. H. Lutz and Israel Stees from 1 Cor. 15: 20, 21, 22.   ALLEN ROYER.

CARBAUGH.—In the bounds of the Falling Spring congregation, sister Eliza A. Carbaugh, aged 63 years, 1 month and 16 days. Funeral discourse to a large congregation of sympathizing friends by the writer, assisted by Eld. Wm. C. Koontz from Ps. 35: 14, last clause. Interment in the Brown's Mill grave-yard.

SHANK.—At his residence, near Greencastle, May 27, 1892, Bro. Isaac R. Shank, aged 55 years and 11 months. Interment at the Hade church. Services from Job 14: 14 by the writer and Eld. Wm. C. Koontz, to a large assembly. Bro. Shank was a deacon, and faithful in the discharge of his duty until death. He lived in the Falling Spring church, all his life, with the exception of a few years when he resided near Alpena, Dakota. He died very suddenly. Having cut a small gash in his foot while making fence, he bled so profusely that he was unable to rally again. At the time of the division he, with one other deacon and the youngest minister (Wm. C. Koontz, now our elder) did much to uphold the interests of the church, so that to-day their number is larger than before the division.   WM. A. ANTHONY.

BUSSARD.—At Peabody, Marion Co., Kans, May 28, 1892, Bro. John B. Bussard, aged 55 years, 1 month and 1 day. He was born in Frederick County, Md., April 27, 1837. In 1840 he, with his parents, moved to Elkhart County, Indiana where he remained until manhood. After his marriage to Maria Weybright he moved to Michigan, where they lived for eleven years, after which they returned to Indiana, where his wife died about one year later. In 1891 he came to Peabody, Kans, where he remained until his death. Five children were given them, of whom four survive their parents. Bro. Bussard endured the pain with true Christian patience until the good Lord said: " It is enough." Services by the writer from 2 Cor. 13: 11.   GEO. STRYCKER.

Announcements.

LOVE-FEASTS.

June 20, at 4 P. M., in Rock Run church, Elkhart Co., Ind.

June 21, at 4 P. M., five miles southeast of Goshen, at the Rock Run church, Ind.

June 22 and 23, Coon River church, near Panora, Iowa.

June 25, at 10 A. M., Somfield, Mich.

June 25, at 2 P. M., Weeping Water church, Cass Co., Nebr.

June 25, at 10 A. M., at the Van Wert church, seven miles north-east of Van Wert, Ohio. Those coming by rail will be met at Van Wert, day before the meeting by notifying Jacob Holsind, or Joseph Longnecker, Wetzel, Ohio.

June 25 and 26, Indian Creek church, Polk Co., Iowa.

June 25 and 26, at 1 P. M., Hickory Grove, Ill.

June 28, at 3 P. M., Bear River church, Whitley Co., Ind.

July 1, at 2 P. M., in the Salem church, Mackley, Oregon.

Sept. 6, at 4 P. M., Indian Creek congregation, Fayett Co., Pa. Series of meetings to commence Aug. 27.

Sept. 28, at 10 A. M., Spring Creek church, Kosciusko Co., Ind.

Oct. 1, Maple Grove church, Norton Co., Kans.

Oct. 8, at 2 P. M., Kaskaskia church, Fayette Co., Ill., ten miles south-west of Becher City, Ill. Those coming by rail will be met at the above-named place by informing Granville Nevinger.

Nov. 5, at 3 P. M., Big Creek church, Richland Co., Ill., 3½ miles North-east of Parkersburg, Ill. Conveyances will be at the above place by informing J. M. Forney.

GOOD BOOKS FOR ALL

Any book in the market furnished at publishers' lowest retail price by the Brethren's Publishing Company, Mt. Morris, Ill. Special prices given when books are purchased in quantities. When ordering books, put on the list, if possible, give title, name of author, and address of publishers.

Sacred Geography and Antiquities.— A practical, helpful work for Bible students, ministers and Sunday-school teachers. Price, $2.00.

The Origin and Growth of Religion.—Hebert Lectures. By T. W. K. Davids. Cloth, $1.25.

Bible Work, the Bible Reader's Commentary on the New Testament.—By J. G. Butler. Two vols. 8vo, $6.00.

Popular Commentary on the New Testament.—Edited by Philip Schaff. Four volumes, 8vo. Matthew, Mark and Luke, $6.00; John and the Acts, $6.00; Romans to Philemon, $6.00; Hebrews to Revelation, $6.00.

The Life and Epistles of the Apostle Paul.—By W. J. Conybeare. Cloth, $2.00.

The Prince and the House of David.—By J. H. Ingraham. Cloth, $1.00.

The Great Events of History.—By W.F. Collier. Cloth, $1.00.

Trine Immersion.— A vindication of the apostolic form of Christian baptism. By Eld. James Quinter. A most complete and reliable work on the subject. Price, cloth, single copy, $1.25; leather, $1.75.

The Throne of David.—By J. H. Ingraham. Cloth, $1.50.

Josephus' Complete Works.— Large type, 1 vol, 8vo, illustrated with many steel and wood engravings. Library sheep, $3.00.

The Doctrine of the Holy Spirit.—By James H. Watson. Cloth, $1.00.

The New Testament Ministry.—By Wm. Smith. Cloth, $1.25.

The Path of Life.—An interesting tract for everybody. Price, 12 cents per copy; 100 copies, $8.00.

Smith's Bible Dictionary.— Edited by Peloubet. Cloth, $2.00; leather, $3.00.

Ante-Nicene Christian Library.—A collection of all the works of the Fathers of the Christian Church prior to the Council of Nice. Edited by Rev. Alexander Roberts, D. D., and James Donaldson, LL. D. Twenty-four vols. 8 vo. Per vol. $1.00.

The Old Testament History.—By William Smith. Cloth, $1.25.

True Method of Searching the Scriptures.—By Tabor Running. Paper, 25 cents.

Universalism Against Itself.—By Hall. One of the best books against Universalism. Price, $1.00.

Biblical Antiquities.—By John Nevin. Gives a condise account of Bible times and customs. Invaluable to all students of Bible subjects. Price, $1.50.

Quinter and McConnell Debate.—A debate on Trine Immersion, the Lord's Supper, and Feet-washing, between Eld. James Quinter (German Baptist) and Eld. N. A. McConnell (Christian) held at Dry Creek, Iowa, 1880. Price, $1.50.

Sabbatism.—By J. M. Habelman. Treats the Sabbath question, showing that the first day of the work is the day for assembling in worship. Price, in cloth, 50 cents; paper, 25 cents.

German and English Testaments.—American Bible Society Edition. Price, 60 cents.

Bunyan's Pilgrim's Progress.—An excellent edition of this good work, printed on good paper, finely illustrated with forty engravings, at the low price of $1.00 per copy.

Europe and Bible Lands.—By D. L. Miller. A book for the people—more comprehensive and thorough than many high-priced works. Price, cloth, $1.50; leather, $2.00.

Ecclesiastical History.—By Hurlbut. Bible Library. Cloth, $1.00.

Constitutional History.—By Mosheim. 4 vols. 8vo, $2.00.

Early Days of Christianity.—By F. W. Farrar. Author's edition, cloth, 2 vols, $1.50.

The Story of the Bible.— An excellent volume for old and young; will interest and instruct all those desiring a knowledge of the Scriptures. Price, $1.00.

The Bible (for Sunday-school Text-book.—By Alfred Holbrook. Cloth, 75 cents.

Origin of Single Immersion.—By Eld. James Quinter. Price, 3 copies, 5 cents; 40 copies, 25 cents; 100 copies, $2.00.

Campbell and Owen Debate.—Contains a complete investigation of the evidences of Christianity. Price, $1.50.

The Pillar of Fire.—By J. H. Ingraham. Cloth, $1.50.

Every Day Religion.—By James Freeman Clarke. Cloth, $1.50.

Faiths of the World.—A concise history of the great religious systems of the world. Cloth, 8vo, $2.00.

Webster's International Dictionary.—Latest edition. Write for special low prices.

Biblical Theology of the Old Testament.—By R. F. Watson. Cloth, $2.25.

The House We Live in—By David Vaughan. It gives a concise account of the birth and practice of the Brethren. Price, 10 copies, 60 cents.

The Holy Land and the Bible—By Cunningham Geikie. Cloth, $2.50.

A Summary of Biblical Antiquities.—By John W. Nevin. Cloth, $1.50.

Gospel Chimes.

BY WM. BEERY.

A new edition of this deservedly-popular Sunday-school song book has just been issued.

Bro. Beery has had a large experience in Sunday school work, and the book which we offer to the Brethren and the public in general, evinces the exercise of talent as well as good judgment. The religious purity of the hymns, contributed by sister Beery, adds much to the excellence of the book.

Price per single copy, 25 cts.; per dozen, by mail, $2.50; by express, $2.40. Lots of more than a dozen must be sent by express.

Brethren's Publishing Co.,

Or Huntingdon, Pa.   Mt. Morris Ill.

Alone with God

This manual of devotions, by J. H. Garrison, comprises a series of meditations, with forms of prayer for private devotions, family worship and special occasions. It is one of the most useful, most needed, and best adapted works of the year, and therefore it is not strange that it is proving one of the most popular. Its work of this kind is distinguished, gifted, pious and beloved author is at his best. This book is helpful to every minister, church official, and Sunday-school superintendent as well as every private member of the church in all ages. It has models of prayer, suitable for the service of the prayer-meeting, while its suggestions, meditations and instructions are pre-eminently calculated to be of service in preparation for the solemn duties that rest upon the active members. Cloth, 75 cents; morocco, $1.25. Address this office.

CANCERS, TUMORS, ETC.

Successfully treated by Dr. G. N. Butler, of Waynesborough, Pa., where he has practiced for the last sixteen years. Dr. Butler is a graduate of the University of Maryland, at Baltimore City. References given and correspondents solicited. Address, Dr. G. W. Butler, Waynesborough, Pa.

LIFE AND SERMONS

OF

ELD. JAMES QUINTER.

This is a neatly-printed and well-bound volume of 426 pages, containing a well-written biographical sketch of Eld. James Quinter and forty of his sermons.

The biographical part will be found quite interesting, instructive and impressive. No one can read an account of Bro. Quinter's life without feeling deeply and favorably impressed. The work shows how a poor orphan boy, by hard work, and faithfulness in his religious convictions, rose step by step, until he reached a field of usefulness and honor as broad as the Nation itself. Though dead, his good deeds and the impressive examples in piety, learning and simplicity will follow him for generations to come.

The Sermon Department contains many of his choice sermons, which will prove exceedingly interesting and profitable reading to all, and especially to our ministers and isolated members. We feel that the book will fill a long-felt want in our Brotherhood. Price, post-paid, $1.25.

Brethren's Publishing Co.,

Mt. Morris, Ill.

CRUDEN'S

COMPLETE

CONCORDANCE

This excellent work, which we offer for sale to our readers, at the low price of $1.50 post-paid, is the only one of the kind that may be depended upon as being strictly reliable. Any verse in the Bible may be readily found by looking for any material word in the verse. Besides this there are given the significations of the principal words, by which their true, Scriptural meaning may be known. A full account of Jewish customs and ceremonies is given as well as a complete concordance of the proper names of the Bible and of the books called Apocrypha. Send all orders for the above work to this office.

Announcements.

LOVE-FEASTS.

June 21, at 4 P. M., in Rock Run church, Elkhart Co., Ind.

June 22, at 2 P. M., five miles south-east of Goshen, at the Rock Run church, Ind.

June 22 and 23, Coon River church, near Panora, Iowa.

June 25, at 10 A. M., Sunfield, Mich.

June 25, at 2 P. M., Weeping Water church, Cass Co., Neb.

June 25, at 10 A. M., at the Van Wert church, seven miles north-east of Van Wert, Ohio. Those coming by rail will be met at Van Wert, day before the meeting by notifying Jacob Hufstand, or Joseph Longanecker, Wetzel, Ohio.

June 25 and 26, Indian Creek church, Polk Co., Iowa.

June 25 and 26, at 1 P. M., Hickory Grove, Ill.

June 28, at 2 P. M., Miss River church, Whitley Co., Ind.

July 1, at 2 P. d., in the Salem church, Medany, Oregon.

Sept. 6, at 2 P. M., Indian Creek congregation, Forest Co., Pa. Series of meetings to commence Aug. 27.

Sept. 28, at 10 A. M., Spring Creek church, Kosciusko Co., Ind.

Oct. 1, Maple Grove church, Norton Co., Kans.

Oct. 7-10 1 P. M., Kaskaskia church, Fayette Co., Ill., ten miles south-west of Bucher City, Ill. Those coming by rail will be met at the above-named place by informing Greenville Nevinger.

Nov. 5, at 3 P. M., Big Creek church, Richland Co., Ill., 3½ miles North-east of Parkersburg, Ill. Conveyances will be at the above place by informing J. M. Forney.

GOOD BOOKS FOR ALL

ANY book in the market furnished at publishers' lowest retail price by the Brethren's Publishing Company, Mt. Morris, Ill. Special prices given when books are purchased in quantities. When ordering books, not on our list, if possible give title, name of author and address of publishers.

Sacred Geography and Antiquities.—A practical helpful work for Bible students, ministers and Sunday-school teachers.—Price, $1.25.

The Origin and Growth of Religion.—Edwin Lewis.—By C. W. R. threvels. Cloth, 600; $1.25.

Bible Work, or Bible Reader's Commentary on the New Testament.—By J. G. Butler. Two volumes $2.50.

Popular Commentary on the New Testament.—Edited by Philip Schaff. Four volumes. 8vo. Matthew, Mark and Luke $6.00. John and the Acts $6.00. Romans to Philemon $6.00. Hebrews to Revelation $6.00.

The Life and Epistles of the Apostle Paul.—By W. J. Conybeare. Cloth, $2.00.

The Prince of the House of David.—By J. H. Ingraham. Cloth, $1.50.

The Great Events of History.—By W. F. Collier. Cloth, $1.25.

Trine Immersion.—A vindication of the apostolic form of Christian baptism. By Eld. James Quinter. A most complete and reliable work on the subject. Price, cloth, single copy, $1.25; leather, $1.75.

The Throne of David.—By J. H. Ingraham. Cloth, $1.50.

Josephus' Complete Works.—Large type, 1 vol. 8vo. Illustrated with many steel and wood engravings. Library sheep, $3.00.

The Doctrine of the Holy Spirit.—By James B. Walker. Cloth, $1.25.

The New Testament History.—By Wm. Smith. Cloth, $1.25.

The Path of Life.—An interesting tract for everybody. Price, 10 cents per copy; 100 copies, $6.00.

Smith's Bible Dictionary.—Edited by Peloubet. Cloth, $2.00; leather, $3.00.

Ante-Nicene Christian Library.—A collection of all the works of the Fathers of the Christian Church prior to the Council of Nice. Edited by Rev. Alexander Roberts, D. D., and James Donaldson, LL.D. Twenty-four vols. 8vo. Per vol., $3.00.

The Old Testament History.—By William Smith. Cloth, $1.25.

True Method of Searching the Scriptures.—By Talbot Romayn. Paper, 25 cents.

Universalism Against Itself.—By Hall. One of the best works against Universalism. Price, $1.00.

Biblical Antiquities.—By John Nevin. Gives a concise account of Bible times and customs, invaluable to all students of Bible subjects. Price, $1.00.

Quinter and McConnell Debate.—A debate on Trine Immersion, the Lord's Supper, and Feet-washing, between Eld. James Quinter (German Baptist) and Eld. N. A. McConnell (Christian) held at Dry Creek, Iowa, 1867. Price, $1.50.

Sabbatism.—By M. M. Eshelman. Treats the Sabbath question, showing that the first day of the week is the day for assembling in worship. Price, 10 cents; 15 copies, $1.10.

German and English Testaments.—American Bible Society Edition. Price, 60 cents.

Bunyan's Pilgrim's Progress.—An excellent edition of this good work, printed on good paper, finely illustrated with forty engravings, at the low price of $1.00 per copy.

Europe and Bible Lands.—By D. L. Miller. A book for the people, where comprehensive and thorough than many higher-priced works. Price, cloth, $1.50; leather, $2.00.

Ecclesiastical History.—By Ruddiman, John Libby Co. Cloth, $2.00.

Ecclesiastical History.—By Mosheim. 2 vols. 8vo. $4.00.

Early Days of Christianity.—By F. W. Farrar. Authors edition, cloth, 2 vols. $1.50.

The Story of the Bible.—An excellent volume for old and young; will interest and instruct all those desiring a knowledge of the Scriptures. Price, $3.00.

The Sunday-school Class-book.—For the use of Bible students and teachers. Cloth, 75 cents.

Origin of Single Immersion.—By Eld. James Quinter. Proves a single immersion as origin, a custom to-apostle, $1.00.

Campbell and Owen Debate.—Contains a complete investigation of the evidences of Christianity. Price, $1.50.

The Pillar of Fire.—By J. H. Ingraham. Cloth, $1.50.

Every Day Religion.—By James Freeman Clarke. Cloth, 12mo, $1.50.

Faiths of the World.—A concise history of the great religious systems of the world. Cloth, 8vo, $2.00.

Webster's International Dictionary.—Latest edition. Write for special low prices.

✦ESSAYS✦

"Study to show thyself approved unto God: a workman that needeth not be ashamed, rightly dividing the Word of Truth."

THE LIFE BEYOND.

BY J. S. MOHLER.

WHEN friends are cold in Death's embrace,
Corruption's work begun,
Despairing hope, and falt'ring faith
Would leave us all undone.

Once they could walk, and talk as we,
They're fallen by our side
The tongue, the eye, and list'ning ear
Are deaf, and dumb, and blind.

We ask ourselves, "Where have they gone?"
We miss them ev'ry day,
The vacant chair, and bed, and room
Would teach, They've gone to stay.

Go, ask the wind that swiftly blows
From regions far and near,
About your friends, they'll answer, No
Your friends have not been here.

Go, ask the rolling, mighty deep
Whose billows loudly roar,
We saw them not, their language speaks,
On this Plutonian shore.

Go, ask the sacred, silent tomb,
The brittle bones would say,
"Your friends once lived within our home
But, long since moved away."

Go, ask the mountains tow'ring high
Among the fleecy clouds,
They say that none have e'er passed by
That wore a mortal shroud.

Go, ask the sun, and moon, and stars,
Which way your friends have gone,
Their shining light would point afar—
The soul's eternal home.

And shall they live beyond this vale
Of sorrow, pain, and death,
A life that ne'er grows old, nor frail,
Nor gasps for fleeting breath?

A life that knows no anxious care
For raiment, meat, and drink,
No dangers lurking here and there,
As on this mortal brink.

A life that flows with purest love,
Unvexed forevermore
With envy, hatred, there above
Upon that peaceful shore.

A life that ever blooms with youth,
In glory like the sun;
Where not a face will seem uncouth
Though millions years have run.

The blooming flowers and grass would say,
"We once were pale, and dead,
Your friends will live again some day
And leave their silent bed."

The crawling worm beneath our feet
Is changed to nobler form,
Thus teaching us, we're not complete
Till resurrection's morn.

Our inmost soul doth testify
A life beyond the grave
Else why this fear, and dread to die
If there's no soul to save.

The Savior truly taught that "I
The resurrection Am."
For, as in Adam all must die,
In Christ they'll live again.

And will we then appear the same
In form as here below,
That when we meet our friends again
That we each other know?

Yes, we will know each other there
As saints the *Savior* knew,
When he beyond the grave appeared
And they his body viewed.

The print of nails in hands and feet,
The wound within his side,
All proved the very Christ indeed
The Jews had crucified.

As we the earthly image bear,
Its likeness is bestowed
Upon our heavenly image, fair,
And thus each other know.

The mother thus her darling babe
Will know and fondly clasp
Its angel form, in glory made
Within her arms at last.

What joy there'll be when saints will meet
With those they've loved before,
In fond embrace each other greet
And stay, to part no more.

Like millions suns around the throne
The saints will brightly shine,
No deaf, nor lame, nor blind, nor dumb,
Each perfect and divine.

With rapid wings this angel band
To living fountains led,
Will soar across the heavenly plains,
With living manna fed.

Or fly away to distant lands
The Father's message bear
To those oppressed, by wicked hands,
Escape for them prepare.

Or hover round the dying bed
Of saints, their spirits bear
Away from all that's mortal, dead,
To climes forever fair.

Or teach the millions infant minds
In Paradise, before
The greater happiness can find,
On that Elysian shore.

There all the powers of mind and heart,
Will find some sweet employ,
Kind words, and looks, and deeds impart,
In constant streams of joy.

No night, nor cloudy days are there,
Nor light of sun, or moon,
But clearer light from God, the Lamb,
Shines one eternal noon.

Ten thousand times ten thousand saints
And thousands, thousands more,
With harps from God, and sweetest strains
Of song, their Lord adore.

For great and marv'lous are thy works
And true are all thy ways
Thou King of saints; in heaven and earth,
Accept our grateful praise.

Morrill, Kans.

"THE ATONEMENT."—Lev. 16: 1.

BY J. K. MILLER.

IN the Jewish church, the Day of Atonement occurred annually on the tenth day of the seventh month. It is called a Sabbath in the Book of Leviticus.

The remembrance on this day of all the sins of the past year made it a fit season for deep humiliation, fasting and prayer. All the services at the Tabernacle were performed by the high-priest, and, as far as we can learn from the Scriptures and Jewish traditions, were conducted as follows: The high-priest first laid aside his priestly robe, bathed himself with water in the holy place, and put on his white linen garments.

Coming out of the Tabernacle, he first brought forward the sacrifices for himself and his family, which were provided at his own cost, viz., a young bullock for a sin-offering, and a ram for a burnt-offering. This part of the ceremony sets forth the imperfection of the priesthood, in the Jewish church, to actually atone for sin,—though he was sanctified by God, and clad in spotless white, yet he was only a type of the True Intercessor and eternal High-priest, who needeth not offer up sacrifices, first for his own sin, and then for ours, for this he did once, when he offered up himself upon the cross, and is now seated at the right hand of the throne of God, ever making intercession for us. The high-priest then led forward the victims for the people's sins which were provided at the public cost, namely a ram for a burnt-offering, and two young goats for a sin-offering. The latter two he presented before Jehovah at the door of the Tabernacle and cast lots upon them. The one lot was inscribed, "For Jehovah," the other, "For Azzel," or scape-goat."

The animals being thus prepared, the high-priest proceeded to offer the young bullock as a sin-offering for himself and his house. Having slain it at the altar, he took some of its blood, and, with a censer, filled with live coals from the altar, and a handful of *sweet incense*, he entered into the Most Holy Place and threw the incense on the coals before the ark, and then sprinkled the blood seven times before the mercy-seat. The use of the incense, with the blood, under the law typifies that prayer is necessary in connection with the blood of Christ, in the Christian church, to cleanse us from sin.

The goat "of Jehovah," was then slain as a sin-offering for the people, and the high-priest again went into the most holy place and performed the same ceremonies with its blood. Afterwards he took of the blood of both the sin-offerings and made an atonement for the holy place and all the furniture therein. When this was done, he next laid his hands upon the head of the scape-goat and confessed over it all the sins of the people, and sent it away by a fit person into a place without the camp, never to return. The two goats fitly illustrate the sin-offering of Christ, who, by his DEATH and RESURRECTION, took away the sin of the world and consigned it to oblivion. "For by one offering he hath perfected forever them that are sanctified, and removed our transgressions from us as far as the east is from the west." After the great ceremony for the remission of sins was completed, the high-priest laid off his linen garments, washed himself in water, and put on his golden robe, peculiar to his office, and offered two rams as a burnt-offering, one for himself, and the other for the people, dedicating himself and people anew to the Lord. The flesh of the sin-offerings was carried away and burned without the camp. This had its fulfillment in Christ bearing our sins upon Calvary's brow, and there being nailed to the rugged cross. The significance of all these pointed forward to the true atonement, not made by the blood of bulls and goats, but by the precious blood of Jesus Christ, the Son of God.

For a long time this *great scheme* of redemption was the mystery of all mysteries, and hence it is a history of successive wonders. The conception was more or less confirmed by every new development of God's great purpose, whether in type or prophecy. Such promises, as were given to Abraham, that in his seed all the nations of the earth should be blessed, and that the scepter should not depart from Judah until Shiloh should come, would greatly aid to enlist the feelings of all rational beholders. Hence we find that the holy angels became greatly interested in the sublime drama of human redemption. But still, up to the time of Christ's preaching, all was a mystery. The veil of the Temple had not yet been rent; the way into the "True Holy of Holies" had not yet been made manifest to any creature, and life and immortality had not yet been fully brought to light by the Gospel. Even the apostles of Christ were yet ignorant of the fact that their Master must suffer death, be buried and rise again the third day, according to the Scriptures.

But in the fullness of time the Great Antitype of all the sacrifices that were ever slain by divine appointment appeared on the cross, and as his flesh was torn and mangled for the sin of the world, the veil of the Temple was rent from top to bottom, and the way into the holiest of all

❖ESSAYS❖

"Study to show thyself approved unto God; a workman that needeth not to be ashamed, rightly dividing the Word of Truth."

THE LIFE BEYOND.

BY J. S. MOHLER.

When friends are cold in Death's embrace,
Corruption's work begun,
Despairing hope, and falt'ring faith
Would leave us all undone.

Once they could walk, and talk as we,
They're fallen by our side
The tongue, the eye, and list'ning ear
Are deaf, and dumb, and blind.

We ask ourselves, "Where have they gone?"
We miss them ev'ry day,
The vacant chair, and bed, and room
Would teach, They've gone to stay.

Go, ask the wind that swiftly blows
From regions far and near,
About your friends, they'll answer, No
Your friends have not been here.

Go, ask the rolling, mighty deep
Whose billows loudly roar,
We saw them not, their language speaks,
On this Plutonian shore.

Go, ask the sacred, silent tomb,
The brittle bones would say,
"Your friends once lived within our home
But, long since moved away."

Go, ask the mountains tow'ring high
Among the fleecy clouds,
They say that none have e'er passed by
That wore a mortal shroud.

Go, ask the sun, and moon, and stars,
Which way your friends have gone,
Their shining light would point afar—
The soul's eternal home.

And shall they live beyond this vale
Of sorrow, pain, and death,
A life that ne'er grows old, nor frail,
Nor gasps for fleeting breath?

A life that knows no anxious care
For raiment, meat, and drink,
No dangers lurking here and there,
As on this mortal brink.

A life that flows with purest love,
Unvexed forevermore
With envy, hatred, there above
Upon that peaceful shore.

A life that ever blooms with youth,
In glory like the sun;
Where not a face will seem uncouth
Though millions years have run.

The blooming flowers and grass would say,
"We once were pale, and dead,
Your friends will live again some day
And leave their silent bed."

The crawling worm beneath our feet
Is changed to nobler form,
Thus teaching us, we're not complete
Till resurrection's morn.

Our inmost soul doth testify
A life beyond the grave
Else why this fear, and dread to die
If there's no soul to save.

The Savior truly taught that "I
The resurrection Am."
For, as in Adam all must die,
In Christ they'll live again.

And will we then appear the same
In form as here below,
That when we meet our friends again
That we each other know?

Yes, we will know each other there
As saints the *Savior* knew,
When he beyond the grave appeared
And they his body viewed.

The print of nails in hands and feet,
The wound within his side,
All proved the very Christ indeed
The Jews had crucified.

As we the earthly image bear,
Its likeness is bestowed
Upon our heavenly image, fair,
And thus each other know.

The mother thus her darling babe
Will know and fondly clasp
Its angel form, in glory made
Within her arms at last.

What joy there'll be when saints will meet
With those they've loved before,
In fond embrace each other greet
And stay, to part no more.

Like millions suns around the throne
The saints will brightly shine,
No deaf, nor lame, nor blind, nor dumb,
Each perfect and divine.

With rapid wings this angel band
To living fountains led,
Will soar across the heavenly plains,
With living manna fed.

Or fly away to distant lands
The Father's message bear
To those oppressed, by wicked hands,
Escape for them prepare.

Or hover round the dying bed
Of saints, their spirits bear
Away from all that's mortal, dead,
To climes forever fair.

Or teach the millions infant minds
In Paradise, before
The greater happiness can find,
On that Elysian shore.

There all the powers of mind and heart,
Will find some sweet employ,
Kind words, and looks, and deeds impart,
In constant streams of joy.

No night, nor cloudy days are there,
Nor light of sun, or moon,
But clearer light from God, the Lamb,
Shines one eternal noon.

Ten thousand times ten thousand saints
And thousands, thousands more,
With harps from God, and sweetest strains
Of song, their Lord adore.

For great and marv'lous are thy works
And true are all thy ways
Thou King of saints; in heaven and earth,
Accept our grateful praise.

Morrill, Kans.

"THE ATONEMENT."—Lev. 16: 1.

BY J. E. MILLER.

In the Jewish church, the Day of Atonement occurred annually on the tenth day of the seventh month. It is called a Sabbath in the Book of Leviticus.

The remembrance on this day of all the sins of the past year made it a fit season for deep humiliation, fasting and prayer. All the services at the Tabernacle were performed by the high-priest, and, as far as we can learn from the Scriptures and Jewish traditions, were conducted as follows: The high-priest first laid aside his priestly robe, bathed himself with water in the holy place, and put on his white linen garments.

Coming out of the Tabernacle, he first brought forward the sacrifices for himself and his family, which were provided at his own cost, *viz.*, a young bullock for a sin-offering, and a ram for a burnt-offering. This part of the ceremony sets forth the imperfection of the priesthood, in the Jewish church, to actually atone for sin,—though he was sanctified by God, and clad in spotless white, yet he was only a type of the True Intercessor and eternal High-priest, who needeth not offer up sacrifices, first for his own sin, and then for ours, for this he did once, when he offered up himself upon the cross, and is now seated at the right hand of the throne of God, ever making intercession for us.

The high-priest then led forward the victims for the people's sins which were provided at the public cost, namely, a ram for a burnt-offering, and two young goats for a sin-offering. The latter two he presented before Jehovah at the door of the Tabernacle and cast lots upon them. The one lot was inscribed, "For Jehovah," the other, "For Azazel, or scape-goat."

The animals being thus prepared, the high-priest proceeded to offer the young bullock as a sin-offering for himself and his house. Having slain it at the altar, he took some of its blood, and, with a censer, filled with live coals from the altar, and a handful of *sweet incense*, he entered into the Most Holy Place and threw the incense on the coals before the ark, and then sprinkled the blood seven times before the mercy-seat. The use of the incense, with the blood, under the law typifies that prayer is necessary in connection with the blood of Christ, in the Christian church, to cleanse us from sin.

The goat "of Jehovah," was then slain as a sin-offering for the people, and the high-priest again went into the most holy place and performed the same ceremonies with its blood. Afterwards he took of the blood of both the sin-offerings and made an atonement for the holy place and all the furniture therein. When this was done, he next laid his hands upon the head of the scape-goat and confessed over it all the sins of the people, and sent it away by a fit person into a place without the camp, never to return. The two goats fitly illustrate the sin-offering of Christ, who, by his Death and Resurrection, took away the sin of the world and consigned it to oblivion. "For by one offering he hath perfected forever them that are sanctified, and removed our transgressions from us as far as the east is from the west." After the great ceremony for the remission of sins was completed, the high-priest laid off his linen garments, washed himself in water, and put on his golden robe, peculiar to his office, and offered two rams as a burnt-offering, one for himself, and the other for the people, dedicating himself and people anew to the Lord. The flesh of the sin-offerings was carried away and burned without the camp. This had its fulfillment in Christ bearing our sins upon Calvary's brow, and there being nailed to the rugged cross. The significance of all these pointed forward to the true atonement, not made by the blood of bulls and goats, but by the precious blood of Jesus Christ, the Son of God.

For a long time this *great scheme* of redemption was the mystery of all mysteries, and hence it is a history of successive wonders. The conception was more or less confirmed by every new development of God's great purpose, whether in type or prophecy. Such promises, as were given to Abraham, that in his seed all the nations of the earth should be blessed, and that the scepter should not depart from Judah until Shiloh should come, would greatly aid to enlist the feelings of all rational beholders. Hence we find that the holy angels became greatly interested in the sublime drama of human redemption. But still, up to the time of Christ's preaching, all was a mystery. The veil of the Temple had not yet been rent; the way into the "True Holy of Holies" had not yet been made manifest to any creature, and life and immortality had not yet been fully brought to light by the Gospel. Even the apostles of Christ were yet ignorant of the fact that their Master must suffer death, be buried and rise again the third day, according to the Scriptures.

But in the fullness of time the Great Antitype of all the sacrifices that were ever slain by divine appointment appeared on the cross, and as his flesh was torn and mangled for the sin of the world, the veil of the Temple was rent from top to bottom, and the way into the holiest of all

matter seemed to satisfy him that it was the Lord's will that he should endure it, and the Lord did hear his prayer, but did not answer it just according to Paul's will, but according to the divine will which was, "I will give you, Paul, grace sufficient to endure it in patience."

The remedy was sufficient to counteract all unpleasant feelings about it; so much so that he looked upon it as really a needed discipline, to keep him humble, "Lest I should be exalted above measure."

How slow we are to believe our adversities, afflictions, or trials, are often for our own good! Paul learned that lesson so well that he finally became so resigned that he even lost all desire to get rid of it. "Most gladly, therefore will I rather glory in my infirmities." Also, "Therefore I take pleasure in infirmities."

Oh, what a glorious change grace had wrought in his feelings! It brought him to rely upon the power of God, and this overcoming faith opened up a new revelation to him. "For when I am weak then am I strong." "My strength is made perfect in weakness." Thus, in spite of infirmities, in spite of Satan's messengers, one may, by the grace of God, attain to a happy experience in the religious life, and at last fall asleep in the triumphs of a glorious hope.

Tuhunga, Cal.

BABYLONIAN LIFE IN THE TIME OF NEBUCHADNEZZAR.

BY A. B. SAYCE.

THE oriental investigations of the last fifty years have extended our knowledge of civilized man and his works into a remote past, which, until recently, we regarded as buried in eternal oblivion. Legend has been replaced by historical truth, and in lieu of the speculations of the historians of a later age we are confronted with contemporary testimony.

With the daily life, and hopes, and beliefs of the ancient Egyptians, the paintings on the walls of graves and temples have long rendered us familiar; and now old Babylon, too, has risen from the dead, and although the red bas-reliefs of the Chaldeans are lost to us, we have, nevertheless, a mass of written records of the time of Nebuchadnezzar, which convey more precise information than any paintings possibly could.

The excavations in Babylon, undertaken in 1876, for the British Museum, led to the discovery of a great number of clay tablets, consisting for the most part, of closed accounts and records of business transactions. The number of these tablets sent to Europe and America can hardly fall short of thirty thousand. Most of these tablets were dug from the mounds which rise above the plain on the former site of the cities of Babylon and Lippara. Lippara, the present Abu Habba, is the spot where once stood Bit-Uri, "The House of Light" the Temple of the Sun-god, and it is here that the first discoveries were made by Hormuzd Bassam. In the last two years similar discoveries have been made in the ruins of Nissur, the ancient Nipur, and mainly through the American expedition. The treasures discovered here, however, belong rather to the first Babylonian dynasty, while the other discoveries are attributable to the time of Nebuchadnezzar and his successors.

For the elucidation of a number of these tablets we are indebted to the patience, the industry, and the keen insight of Dr. Strassmeier. The judicial expressions which occur in them were interpreted by Julius Oppert and F. C. Peyser. With the help of their translations, and those of Pater Strassmeier's published tablets, and others in my

own possession, and elsewhere in public and private collections, I will endeavor to picture, in outline, the life of a Babylonian citizen of the time of Nebuchadnezzar.

Babylon was, at that period, the centre of the world's commerce, the market for the sale and exchange of the wares of all nations, from China to the Mediterranean, from Africa to Kurdistan. Grecian soldiers served in the Babylonian army, and Tyre was exposed to a thirteen years' siege with the object of destroying its commerce and transferring the advantages to Babylon.

In forming an estimate of Babylonian people and their modes of thought, it is necessary to keep the essentially commercial spirit of the city well in view. Babylon had all the characteristics of a commercial city; wealth was the measure of respectability; trade was the most dignified pursuit; and even the princes of the royal house did not think it beneath their dignity to engage in it. For example, we find that Belshazzar, the son and heir of Nabunid, sold wool to a private man to the value of twenty silvermines, taking as security for the payment a lien on the purchaser's house. The contract is drawn in the usual style, and subscribed by six witnesses, and also by the priest, who drew up the document. Trade must have been in great repute among a people where the heir apparent to the throne could be a wool merchant, and bound by the same rules of trade as were his lowest subjects.

As might be expected, the military impulse was not very strong in a people so addicted to trade. In this respect Babylon presented a strong contrast to Assyria, whose power rested on its military organization. The kingdom of Babylon was only the work of a single genial man, and at his death it fell together like a card-house. When Cyrus moved his forces upon Babylon, Nebuchadnezzar and his advisers had no greater anxiety than to bring the gods into security in the head temple. Babylon surrendered without serious resistance, and the citizens submitted themselves to the conqueror without murmur, being well satisfied with the permission to buy and sell as heretofore. None of the records make the remotest hint that public or private life was in any way disturbed by the conquest.

The lending of money on interest was highly developed; the interest, usually at 20 per cent, was payable monthly and was well secured. Even the priests lent money both on private account and on behalf of the temple, and credit-giving was fenced in with so many restrictions that bankruptcy was hardly possible. Interest fluctuated with social and political conditions. There is a record of a case in which, during a famine, a patriotic money-lender absolved all his debtors of the interest due.

The national currency was the silvermine, containing sixty silvershekels and estimated at $45. The goldmine, rarely used, is estimated to have been worth more than eight times as much.

The value of the currency was originally determined by weight. It was cast in bars, perhaps also in rings. This form was found very inconvenient, and during Nebuchadnezzar's reign stamped coins of specific value were substituted for the bars. But we find also that prices were frequently fixed in dates and corn (grain). Dates and grain were very cheap, a quart of either being procurable for two cents. Domestic animals were dearer. We have the record of the sale of a donkey for $29 in 569 B. C., and in the twenty-fourth year of the king's reign we find that an ox for the service of the temple was bought for $9.75.

Clothing was very costly, especially if ornamented with a gold thread or with gems. Even a common camel-hair mantle was worth about $3.50. Wine, the beverage of the wealthy, was imported.

There is a record of a large cask sold for $8.25, and of five smaller casks, of the same brand, selling for $7.50. The poorer classes brewed a sort of beer from dates which was drunk extensively.

The Babylonians were not only great traders, but the country people prosecuted agriculture no less energetically. The village lands were all farmed out to contractors, who were responsible for the taxes, and for keeping the buildings in order, and who gave the land to be cultivated on shares.

Woman stood on the same plane as man, both socially and in the matter of civil rights. The civilization of the Babylonians was not Semitic, but Summerian; the Babylonians were a mixed race, and woman owed her position to Summerian custom, which placed woman at the head of the household while the Semitic people awarded her a subordinate position.

The Babylonians were not only pious, but superstitious; but among the educated classes the religion approached closely to a pure monotheism. Listen, for instance, to the following prayer of Nebuchadnezzar: "To Merodach my Lord have I prayed, I commenced to pray, and the words of my heart sought him out, and I said, O Eternal Ruler, Lord of all creatures—for the king whom thou lovest, whom thou callest by names that seem pleasing unto thee, thou makest his name honored, and watchest over him in the straight path. I, the Prince, that obey thee, I am the work of thy hands, thou hast created me, and given me dominion over many, all according to the goodness, O Lord, which thou diffusest over all. Awake in me a love for thy lofty majesty, let my heart be penetrated with awe for the divine majesty, give me all which in thy judgment is good for me, for it is thou alone who sustainest my life." These words of Nebuchadnezzar found an echo in many other documents, and afford some indication of what manner of men were Nebuchadnezzar and the Babylonians of his age.—*Literary Digest.*

"CHARITY BEGINS AT HOME."

BY S. N. M'CANN.

ONE hears this sentence so frequently quoted, especially one who solicits funds for any good work, that it seems as familiar as "Do good for evil," "Love your enemies," or "Lend, hoping for nothing."

"Charity begins at home" is equivalent to no charity by most persons, who use the expression. It is used for an excuse for not doing what, at heart, would otherwise be felt a duty to do.

The sentence is strictly true, and no one can extend charity abroad unless it first be found at home. Light where there is nothing but darkness is just as true as charity abroad, when there is none at home.

What is charity? Not the disposition to give; for Paul says, "Though I bestow all my goods to feed the poor, . . . and have not charity it profiteth me nothing." 1 Cor. 13:3. It is love,—pure, undefiled love. "Charity begins at home." Listen, oh, listen: "Love begins at home." *At* HOME, yes, right in the center of the home, your heart, brother; yours, sister.

You see if love does not begin at home, it does not begin at all. The divine principle first permeates our own natures completely, and in so doing sheds a halo of bliss into the home circle, the neighborhood, and the church.

Charity must begin at home, but it will not begin there unless we let it begin. When it once begins at home, it is like the woman's leaven hid in three measures of meal,—it keeps spreading and spreading until the whole is leavened. You

matter seemed to satisfy him that it was the Lord's will that he should endure it, and the Lord did hear his prayer, but did not answer it just according to Paul's will, but according to the divine will which was, "I will give you, Paul, grace sufficient to endure it in patience."

The remedy was sufficient to counteract all unpleasant feelings about it; so much so that he looked upon it as really a needed discipline, to keep him humble, "Lest I should be exalted above measure."

How slow we are to believe our adversities, afflictions, or trials, are often for our own good! Paul learned that lesson so well that he finally became so resigned that he even lost all desire to get rid of it. "Most gladly, therefore will I rather glory in my infirmities." Also, "Therefore I take pleasure in infirmities."

Oh, what a glorious change grace had wrought in his feelings! It brought him to rely upon the power of God, and this overcoming faith opened up a new revelation to him. "For when I am weak then am I strong." "My strength is made perfect in weakness." Thus, in spite of infirmities, in spite of Satan's messengers, one may, by the grace of God, attain to a happy experience in the religious life, and at last fall asleep in the triumphs of a glorious hope.

Tuhunga, Cal.

BABYLONIAN LIFE IN THE TIME OF NEBUCHADNEZZAR.

BY A. H. SAYCE.

THE oriental investigations of the last fifty years have extended our knowledge of civilized man and his works into a remote past, which, until recently, we regarded as buried in eternal oblivion. Legend has been replaced by historical truth, and in lieu of the speculations of the historians of a later age we are confronted with contemporary testimony.

With the daily life, and hopes, and beliefs of the ancient Egyptians, the paintings on the walls of graves and temples have long rendered us familiar; and now old Babylon, too, has risen from the dead, and although the red bas-reliefs of the Chaldeans are lost to us, we have, nevertheless, a mass of written records of the time of Nebuchadnezzar, which convey more precise information than any paintings possibly could.

The excavations in Babylon, undertaken in 1876, for the British Museum, led to the discovery of a great number of clay tablets, consisting for the most part, of closed accounts and records of business transactions. The number of these tablets sent to Europe and America can hardly fall short of thirty thousand. Most of these tablets were dug from the mounds which rise above the plain on the former site of the cities of Babylon and Lippara. Lippara, the present Abu Habba, is the spot where once stood Bit-Uri, "The House of Light" the Temple of the Sun-god, and it is here that the first discoveries were made by Hormuzd Bassam. In the last two years similar discoveries have been made in the ruins of Nisaur, the ancient Nipur, and mainly through the American expedition. The treasures discovered here, however, belong rather to the first Babylonian dynasty, while the other discoveries are attributable to the time of Nebuchadnezzar and his successors.

For the elucidation of a number of these tablets we are indebted to the patience, the industry, and the keen insight of Dr. Strassmeier. The judicial expressions which occur in them were interpreted by Julius Oppert and F. C. Peyser. With the help of their translations, and those of Pater Strassmeier's published tablets, and others in my own possession, and elsewhere in public and private collections, I will endeavor to picture, in outline, the life of a Babylonian citizen of the time of Nebuchadnezzar.

Babylon was, at that period, the centre of the world's commerce, the market for the sale and exchange of the wares of all nations, from China to the Mediterranean, from Africa to Kurdistan. Grecian soldiers served in the Babylonian army, and Tyre was exposed to a thirteen years' siege with the object of destroying its commerce and transferring the advantages to Babylon.

In forming an estimate of Babylonian people and their modes of thought, it is necessary to keep the essentially commercial spirit of the city well in view. Babylon had all the characteristics of a commercial city; wealth was the measure of respectability; trade was the most dignified pursuit; and even the princes of the royal house did not think it beneath their dignity to engage in it. For example, we find that Belshazzar, the son and heir of Nabonid, sold wool to a private man to the value of twenty silvermines, taking as security for the payment a lien on the purchaser's house. The contract is drawn in the usual style, and subscribed by six witnesses, and also by the priest, who drew up the document. Trade must have been in great repute among a people where the heir apparent to the throne could be a wool merchant, and bound by the same rules of trade as were his lowest subjects.

As might be expected, the military impulse was not very strong in a people so addicted to trade. In this respect Babylon presented a strong contrast to Assyria, whose power rested on its military organization. The kingdom of Babylon was only the work of a single genial man, and at his death it fell together like a card-house. When Cyrus moved his forces upon Babylon, Nebuchadnezzar and his advisers had no greater anxiety than to bring the gods into security in the head temple. Babylon surrendered without serious resistance, and the citizens submitted themselves to the conqueror without murmur, being well satisfied with the permission to buy and sell as heretofore. None of the records make the remotest hint that public or private life was in any way disturbed by the conquest.

The lending of money on interest was highly developed; the interest, usually at 20 per cent, was payable monthly and was well secured. Even the priests lent money both on private account and on behalf of the temple, and credit-giving was fenced in with so many restrictions that bankruptcy was hardly possible. Interest fluctuated with social and political conditions. There is a record of a case in which, during a famine, a patriotic money-lender absolved all his debtors of the interest due.

The national currency was the silvermine, containing sixty silverneckle and estimated at $45. The goldmine, rarely used, is estimated to have been worth more than eight times as much.

The value of the currency was originally determined by weight. It was cast in bars, perhaps also in rings. This form was found very inconvenient, and during Nebuchadnezzar's reign stamped coins of specific value were substituted for the bars. But we find also that prices were frequently fixed in dates and corn (grain). Dates and grain were very cheap, a quart of either being procurable for two cents. Domestic animals were dearer. We have the record of the sale of a donkey for $29 in 569 B. C., and in the twenty-fourth year of the king's reign we find that an ox for the service of the temple was bought for $9.75.

Clothing was very costly, especially if ornamented with a gold thread or with gems. Even a common camel-hair mantle was worth about $8.50. Wine, the beverage of the wealthy, was imported. There is a record of a large cask sold for $8.25, and of five smaller casks, of the same brand, selling for $7.50. The poorer classes brewed a sort of beer from dates which was drunk extensively.

The Babylonians were not only great traders, but the country people prosecuted agriculture, no less energetically. The village lands were all farmed out to contractors, who were responsible for the taxes, and for keeping the buildings in order, and who gave the land to be cultivated on shares.

Woman stood on the same plane as man, both socially and in the matter of civil rights. The civilization of the Babylonians was not Semitic, but Summerian; the Babylonians were a mixed race, and woman owed her position to Summerian custom, which placed woman at the head of the household while the Semitic people awarded her a subordinate position.

The Babylonians were not only pious, but superstitious; but among the educated classes the religion approached closely to a pure monotheism. Listen, for instance, to the following prayer of Nebuchadnezzar: "To Merodach my Lord have I prayed, I commenced to pray, and the words of my heart sought him out, and I said, O Eternal Ruler, Lord of all creatures—for the king whom thou lovest, whom thou callest by his name honored, and watchest over him in the straight path. I, the Prince, that obey thee, I am the work of thy hands, thou hast created me, and given me dominion over many, all according to the goodness, O Lord, which thou diffusest over all. Awake in me a love for thy lofty majesty, let my heart be penetrated with awe for the divine majesty, give me all which in thy judgment is good for me, for it is thou alone who sustainest my life." These words of Nebuchadnezzar found an echo in many other documents, and afford some indication of what manner of men were Nebuchadnezzar and the Babylonians of his age. —*Literary Digest.*

"CHARITY BEGINS AT HOME."

BY S. N. M'CANN.

ONE hears this sentence so frequently quoted, especially one who solicits funds for any good work, that it seems as familiar as a "Do good for evil," "Love your enemies," or "Lend, hoping for nothing."

"Charity begins at home" is equivalent to no charity by most persons, who use the expression. It is used for an excuse for not doing what, at heart, would otherwise be felt a duty to do.

The sentence is strictly true, and no one can extend charity abroad unless it first be found at home. Light where there is nothing but darkness is just as true as charity abroad, when there is none at home.

What is charity? Not the disposition to give, for Paul says, "Though I bestow all my goods to feed the poor, . . . and have not charity it profiteth me nothing." 1 Cor. 13: 3. It is love,—pure, undefiled love. "Charity begins at home." Listen, oh, listen: "Love begins at home." *At HOME*, yes, love is in the center of the home, your heart, brother; yours, sister.

You see if love does not begin at home, it does not begin at all. The divine principle first permeates our own natures completely, and in so doing sheds a halo of bliss into the home circle, the neighborhood, and the church.

Charity must begin at home, but it will not begin there unless we let it begin. When it once begins at home, it is like the woman's leaven hid in three measures of meal,—it keeps spreading and spreading until the whole is leavened. You

Missionary and Tract Work Department.

"Upon the first day of the week, let every one of you lay by him in store as God hath prospered him, that there be no gatherings when I come."—1 Cor. 16: 2.

"Every man as he purposeth in his heart, so let him give. Not grudgingly or of necessity, for the Lord loveth a cheerful giver."—2 Cor. 9: 7.

HOW MUCH SHALL WE GIVE?

"Every man according to his ability." "Every one as God hath prospered him." "Every man, according as he purposeth in his heart, so let him give." "For if there be first a willing mind, it is accepted according to that a man hath, and not according to that he hath not."—2 Cor. 8: 12.

Organization of Missionary Committee.

Daniel Vaniman, Foreman,	- - -	McPherson, Kans.
D. L. Miller, Treasurer,	- - -	Mt. Morris, Ill.
Galen B. Royer, Secretary,	- - -	Mt. Morris, Ill.

Organization of Book and Tract Work.

S. W. Hoover, Foreman,	- - -	Dayton, Ohio.
S. Bock, Secretary and Treasurer,	- -	Dayton, Ohio.

☞ All donations intended for Missionary Work should be sent to GALEN B. ROYER, Mt. Morris, Ill.

☞ All money for Tract Work should be sent to S. BOCK, Dayton, Ohio.

☞ Money may be sent by Money Order, Registered Letter, or Drafts on New York or Chicago. Do not send personal checks, or drafts on interior towns, as it costs 25 cents to collect them.

☞ Solicitors are requested to faithfully carry out the plan of Annual Meeting, that all our members be solicited to contribute at least twice a year for the Mission and Tract Work of the Church.

☞ Notes for the Endowment Fund can be had by writing to the Secretary of either Work.

"AS YE GO, PREACH."

BY N. D. UNDERHILL.

JESUS himself was an unlearned carpenter, yet he did not hesitate to preach the Gospel. Why? Because God was with him, in him, and round about him. Because he trusted in God for help and strength, for wisdom and power, yea, for all things. But some will say, "That has nothing to do with us. He was divine, we are human," etc. But is not Christ in us? If so, then God is in us. He in us and we in him. Jesus said, "Follow me."

Let us, then, follow him. Let us do as he did! He prayed often and earnestly to the Father, trusted fully in God and faithfully obeyed his will. If we would all do likewise, we should hear less excuses made for the comparatively small amount of work that is done in the world by the lay members of the church. Those twelve disciples were only human men, only common souls like the rest of us. Some of them were uneducated and had, until Jesus called them, been occupied in the humble occupations of life. Yet Jesus told them to "preach," to "heal the sick, cleanse the lepers, raise the dead, cast out devils." What an eloquent preacher Peter, the humble fisherman, became! What great good they all accomplished! It was because they obeyed the Lord's commandments and trusted in him for strength. He commanded them to "preach the Gospel to every creature." Luke 16: 15. He also commanded them to teach every creature who should receive their word, "to observe all things whatsoever he had commanded them." Matt. 28: 20. Does not this (every creature) include the laity? Does not the commandment, "Teaching them to observe all things," include preaching the Gospel? "As ye go, preach." We are all going some place,—all travelers on life's journey. We all have some influence, some talent, which, if we use, God will increase.

We all have some opportunities. We may have been interested in fishing, or in farming or in stock-growing, or carpentering, or in some other business, we may have been in the habit of talking about these things whenever we met our friends, for "out of the abundance of the heart the mouth speaketh." We may have been accustomed to gossip about the latest styles, or of our neighbors' private affairs, or of our gardens, flowers, fruits, chickens, calves, our horse-work, our business prospects, etc. But now we are called, we are chosen, we are sanctified. What! sanctified? Yes, set apart to the service of Jesus who hath purchased us with his own blood. Before we were lost, we were dead; but now we are redeemed, are saved. Ought not we, then, to give our lives to the service of our Redeemer who gave himself for us? If so, let us be careful how we speak, for he says, "Every idle word that men shall speak they shall give account thereof, in the day of judgment." Therefore it becomes us to put aside all foolish and vain conversation, jesting, worldly gossip, etc. But must we be silent? Were not our tongues given us for a purpose? Jesus says, "Preach." When? Not, when we get to our journey's end, but "as ye go." That includes all the time during which we are on our way from earth to heaven. There is a tendency among ministers to wait till they have an invitation. Jesus says, "Go." Let us not wait for a flattering invitation, but obey the Savior's command. Some are willing to preach in a house which has been built for the purpose, but Jesus said, "Go into all the world."

Some are willing to preach to an attentive audience of a good many hearers, but Christ and Philip were not above preaching to an audience of one. God never commanded his children to wait till the heathen built comfortable houses and got a good-sized congregation together, and then sent a polite invitation to some preacher to come and talk to them. Jesus never even said, "Go and preach the Gospel to all the churches of your own kind, and to some school-houses where you are well received, but "Go into all the world and preach the Gospel to every creature," and his promise was,—not worldly comfort, kindly reception, rest, ease, etc.,—but, "Lo, I am with you always, even to the end of the world."

Is not this promise sufficient for us? Jesus has promised to be with us always,—every-where, in persecutions and afflictions and distresses, as well as in prosperity and health. Then, why should we hesitate to speak a word for Jesus? When God called Moses to be a leader of his children, Moses, like many of us who are called now, began to make excuses, to tell the Lord that he (Moses) was not the man for the position, that the people would not listen to him, that he was not influential, not eloquent, but slow of speech, etc., but God replied, "Who hath made man's mouth?" "Now therefore go, and I will be with thy mouth, and teach thee what thou shalt say."

When Christ and the angels commanded the women at the sepulcher to go and tell the good news of the resurrection to the brethren, that they go into Galilee and there meet the Savior, those women might have declined, as some now do, saying, "Oh, I'm only a woman." "Oh, they won't believe me." "Oh, I can't, they'd think I was too forward," etc. They loved the Savior, and if we love him, we are willing and glad to keep his commandments. So they went "and told all these things unto the eleven and to all the rest." Luke 24: 9. True, the hearers did not believe them, but whose business was that? It is our duty to obey, and God will take care of the results.

Then, "as ye go, preach." You may, not have a house to preach in, but never mind. The woman of Samaria was converted by the side of a well. The eunuch of Ethiopia was converted on the road from Jerusalem to Gaza. God spoke to his people from a mountain-top, and so Christ preached by the seaside, in desert places, and every-where. He is, our perfect pattern,—why not do likewise? Why not go out into the highways and hedges, and bring in the guests to the King's banquet? Jesus says, "I am with you." Then, why do we hesitate? The daisies do not all blossom around the door of the church or school-house, but some are out on the broad prairies. So the precious souls are not all the attentive members of the church-going audience. There are many who never come to us, until we go to them, yet they are worth saving. Let us carry the good news to those who never hear it from the pulpit. Why not carry the Bread of Life to prison doors, and miserable hovels, to isolated ranches, and to the homes of the ungodly? If they do not believe us, all right, we've done our duty; we can safely leave the rest to God. If they do believe, we may be the means of saving a soul, and thus cover a multitude of sins. We are God's watchmen. If we do not warn the people, their sins will be laid to our account, but if we warn them, we at least deliver ourselves. Ezek. 33: 7, 8, 9. Jesus says, "Watch therefore," Matt. 24: 42; 25: 13; Mark 13: 35; Luke 21: 36; Acts 20: 31. The latter are Paul's words, as are also 1 Cor. 16: 13; 1 Thess. 5: 6; 2 Tim. 4: 5. Peter also says, "Watch." 1 Pet. 4: 7. Oh, let us all watch and pray, preach, teach and warn; that some may, through our diligence, learn the Truth, and flee from the wrath to come. .

The jewels do not all glitter in the ears and hair of wealthy women. Some are down in the mines of earth. So are some of Christ's precious jewels yet down in the very depths of darkness, misery, guilt and sin. Let us delve down after them; let us go where they are, for they will never come to us, but we may find one, which, when cleansed and polished, will sparkle and shine throughout eternity. As we go, let us preach the Blessed Gospel of salvation, for we are called out of the world, and we should not think and talk of worldly things, but of heavenly things. True, we have not all the same gifts. But let us use what we have to the glory of Jesus. We have not all the gift of prophecy, nor all the gift of healing, but there is something which we all can do. Because we are not all ordained ministers, we need not lean back on our easy cushions and say, "I wish somebody else would do so-and-so."

The preachers and elders can't do all of our work and theirs too. Most of them are doing all they can, but are we (the laity) doing all we can to lead souls to Christ? Why should the isolated members be idle? The world is perishing in ignorance. If God has placed you in an isolated field, apart from your fellow-servants, let your light shine. Some poor, hungry, wayfaring soul may be there, for whose salvation you are sent to that place. If you are the only member of Christ's body in your vicinity, why clamor for the other, more influential members to come and do what God has shown you to do. Get the people together and tell them of Jesus. If you can't get many, talk to a few; no matter, if it is only one, and a poor, little, humble, black slave at that. Tell all of Jesus' love:

Every-where there are souls hungering, thirsting, longing for the Bread of Life. Jesus says, "Feed my lambs." No matter where; let us speak a word for Jesus whenever and wherever we have an opportunity. That is what God made your mouth for, and he will be with you as long as you obey him. We must not get an idea that all those who follow not us, are following the enemy. Mark 9: 38-42. There are many true, honest, sincere believers in the various so-called churches, who really love the Savior and are trying to serve him. If we know the Truth better than they, it is our duty to instruct them. Not a few of the Brethren were converted from other

Missionary and Tract Work Department.

"Upon the first day of the week, let every one of you lay by him in store as God hath prospered him, that there be no gatherings when I come."—1 Cor. 16: 2.

"Every man as he purposeth in his heart, so let him give. Not grudgingly or of necessity, for the Lord loveth a cheerful giver."—2 Cor. 9: 7.

HOW MUCH SHALL WE GIVE?

"Every man according to his ability." "Every one as God hath prospered him." "Every man, according as he purposeth in his heart, so let him give." "For if there be first a willing mind, it is accepted according to that a man hath, and not according to that he hath not."—2 Cor. 8: 12.

Organization of Missionary Committee.

DANIEL VANIMAN, Foreman,   -   -   McPherson, Kans.
D. L. MILLER, Treasurer,   -   -   -   Mt. Morris, Ill.
GALEN B. ROYER, Secretary,   -   -   Mt. Morris, Ill.

Organization of Book and Tract Work.

S. W. HOOVER, Foreman,   -   -   -   Dayton, Ohio.
S. BOCK, Secretary and Treasurer,   -   Dayton, Ohio.

☞All donations intended for Missionary Work should be sent to GALEN B. ROYER, Mt. Morris, Ill.

☞All money for Tract Work should be sent to S. BOCK, Dayton, Ohio.

☞Money may be sent by Money Order, Registered Letter, or Drafts on New York or Chicago. Do not send personal checks, or drafts on interior towns, as it costs 25 cents to collect them.

☞Solicitors are requested to faithfully carry out the plan of Annual Meeting, that all our members be solicited to contribute at least twice a year for the Mission and Tract Work of the Church.

☞Notes for the Endowment Fund can be had by writing to the Secretary of either Work.

"AS YE GO, PREACH."

BY N. D. UNDERHILL.

JESUS himself was an unlearned carpenter, yet he did not hesitate to preach the Gospel. Why? Because God was with him, in him, and round about him. Because he trusted in God for help and strength, for wisdom and power, yea, for all things. But some will say, "That has nothing to do with us. He was divine, we are human," etc. But is not Christ in us? If so, then God is in us. He in us and we in him. Jesus said, "Follow me."

Let us, then, follow him. Let us do as he did! He prayed often and earnestly to the Father, trusted fully in God and faithfully obeyed his will. If we would all do likewise, we should hear less excuses made for the comparatively small amount of work that is done in the world by the lay members of the church. Those twelve disciples were only human men, only common souls like the rest of us. Some of them were uneducated and had, until Jesus called them, been occupied in the humble occupations of life. Yet Jesus told them to "preach," to "heal the sick, cleanse the lepers, raise the dead, cast out devils." What an eloquent preacher Peter, the humble fisherman, became! What great good they all accomplished! It was because they obeyed the Lord's commandments and trusted in him for strength. He commanded them to "preach the Gospel to every creature." Luke 16: 15. He also commanded them to teach every creature who should receive their word, "to observe all things whatsoever he had commanded them." Matt. 28: 20. Does not this (every creature) include the laity?" Does not the commandment, "Teaching them to observe all things," include preaching the Gospel? "As ye go, preach." We are all going some place,— all travelers on life's journey. We all have some influence, some talent, which, if we use, God will increase.

We all have some opportunities. We may have been interested in fishing, or in farming or in stock-growing, or carpentering, or in some other business, we may have been in the habit of talking about these things whenever we met our friends, for "out of the abundance of the heart the mouth speaketh." We may have been accustomed to gossip about the latest styles, or of our neighbors' private affairs, or of our gardens, flowers, fruits, chickens, calves, our horse-work, our business prospects, etc. But now we are called, we are chosen, we are sanctified. What! sanctified? Yes, set apart to the service of Jesus who hath purchased us with his own blood. Before we were lost, we were dead; but now we are redeemed, are saved. Ought not we, then, to give our lives to the service of our Redeemer who gave himself for us? If so, let us be careful how we speak, for he says, "Every idle word that men shall speak they shall give account thereof, in the day of judgment." Therefore it becomes us to put aside all foolish and vain conversation, jesting, worldly gossip, etc. But must we be silent? Were not our tongues given us for a purpose? Jesus says, "Preach." When? Not, when we get to our journey's end, but "as ye go." That includes all the time during which we are on our way from earth to heaven. There is a tendency among ministers to wait till they have an invitation. Jesus says, "Go." Let us not wait for a flattering invitation, but obey the Savior's command. Some are willing to preach in a house which has been built for the purpose, but Jesus said, "Go into all the world."

Some are willing to preach to an attentive audience of a good many hearers, but Christ' and Philip were not above preaching to an audience of one. God never commanded his children to wait till the heathen built comfortable houses and got a good-sized congregation together, and then sent a polite invitation to some preacher to come and talk to them. Jesus never even said; "Go and preach the Gospel to all the churches of your own kind, and to some school-houses where you are well received, but "Go into all the world and preach the Gospel to every creature," and his promise was,—not worldly comfort, kindly reception, rest, ease, etc.,—but, "Lo, I am with you always, even to the end of the world."

Is not this promise sufficient for us? Jesus has promised to be with us always,—every-where, in persecutions and afflictions and distresses, as well as in prosperity and health. Then, why should we hesitate to speak a word for Jesus? When God called Moses to be a leader of his children, Moses, like many of us who are called now, began to make excuses, to tell the Lord that he (Moses) was not the man for the position, that the people would not listen to him, that he was not influential, not eloquent, but slow of speech, etc., but God replied, "Who hath made man's mouth?" "Now therefore go, and I will be with thy mouth, and teach thee what thou shalt say."

When Christ and the angels commanded the women at the sepulcher to go and tell the good news of the resurrection to the brethren, that they go into Galilee and there meet the Savior, those women might have declined, as some now do, saying, "Oh, I'm only a woman." "Oh, they won't believe me." "Oh, I can't, they'd think I was too forward," etc. They loved the Savior, and if we love him, we are willing and glad to keep his commandments. So they went "and told all these things unto the eleven and to all the rest." Luke 24: 9. True, the hearers did not believe them, but whose business was that? It is our duty to obey, and God will take care of the results.

Then, "as ye go, preach." You may not have a house to preach in, but never mind. The woman of Samaria was converted by the side of a well. The eunuch of Ethiopia was converted on the road from Jerusalem to Gaza. God spoke to his people from a mountain-top, and so Christ preached by the seaside, in desert places, and every-where. He is our perfect pattern,—why not do likewise? Why not go out into the highways and hedges, and bring in the guests to the King's banquet? Jesus says, "I am with you." Then, why do we hesitate? The daisies do not all blossom around the door of the church or school-house, but some are out on the broad prairies. So the precious souls are not all the attentive members of the church-going audience. There are many who never come to us, until we go to them, yet they are worth saving. Let us carry the good news to those who never hear it from the pulpit. Why not carry the Bread of Life to prison doors, and miserable hovels, to isolated ranches, and to the homes of the ungodly? If they do not believe us, all right, we've done our duty; we can safely leave the rest to God. If they do believe, we may be the means of saving a soul, and thus cover a multitude of sins. We are God's watchmen. If we do not warn the people, their sins will be laid to our account, but if we warn them, we at least deliver ourselves. Ezek. 33: 7, 8, 9. Jesus says, "Watch therefore," Matt. 24: 42; 25: 13; Mark 13: 35; Luke 21: 36; Acts 20: 31. The latter are Paul's words, as are also 1 Cor. 16: 13; 1 Thess. 5: 6; 2 Tim. 4: 5. Peter also says, "Watch." 1 Pet. 4: 7. Oh, let us all watch and pray, preach, teach and warn; that some may, through our diligence, learn the Truth, and flee from the wrath to come.

The jewels do not all glitter in the ears and hair of wealthy women. Some are down in the mines of earth. So are some of Christ's precious jewels yet down in the very depths of darkness, misery, guilt and sin. Let us delve down after them; let us go where they are, for they will never come to us, but we may find one, which, when cleansed and polished, will sparkle and shine throughout eternity. As we go, let us preach the Blessed Gospel of salvation, for we are called out of the world, and we should not think and talk of worldly things, but of heavenly things. True, we have not all the same gifts. But let us use what we have to the glory of Jesus. We have not all the gift of prophecy, nor all the gift of healing, but there is something which we all can do. Because we are not all ordained ministers, we need not lean back on our easy cushions and say, "I wish somebody else would do so-and-so."

The preachers and elders can't do all of our work and theirs too. Most of them are doing all they can, but are we (the laity) doing all we can to lead souls to Christ? Why should the isolated members be idle? The world is perishing in ignorance. If God has placed you in an isolated field, apart from your fellow-servants, let your light shine. Some poor, hungry, wayfaring soul may be there, for whose salvation you are sent to that place. If you are the only member of Christ's body in your vicinity, why clamor for the other, more influential members to come and do what God has shown you to do. Get the people together and tell them of Jesus. If you can't get many, talk to a few; no matter if it is only one. Lead a poor, little, humble, black slave at that. Tell all of Jesus' love.

Every-where there are souls hungering, thirsting, longing for the Bread of Life. Jesus says, "Feed my lambs." No matter where; let us speak a word for Jesus whenever and wherever we have an opportunity. That is what God made your mouth for, and he will be with you as long as you obey him. We must not get an idea that all those who follow not us, are following the enemy. Mark 9: 38-42. There are many true, honest, sincere believers in the various so-called churches, who really love the Savior and are trying to serve him. If we know the Truth better than they, it is our duty to instruct them. Not a few of the Brethren were converted from other

The Gospel Messenger,

A Weekly at $1.50 Per Annum.

PUBLISHED BY

The Brethren's Publishing Co.

D. L. MILLER,	Editor.
J. H. MOORE,	Office Editor.
J. B. BRUMBAUGH,	
J. G. ROYER,	Associate Editors.
JOSEPH AMICK,	Business Manager.

ADVISORY COMMITTEE.

R. H. Miller, A. Hutchison, Daniel Hays.

☞ Communications for publication should be legibly written with black ink on one side of the paper only. Do not attempt to interline, or to put on one page what ought to occupy two.

☞ Anonymous communications will not be published.

☞ Do not mix business with articles for publication. Keep your communications on separate sheets from all business.

☞ Time is precious. We always have time to attend to business and to answer questions of importance, but please do not subject us to need less answering of letters.

☞ The MESSENGER is mailed each week to all subscribers. If the address is correctly entered on our list, the paper must reach the person to whom it is addressed. If you do not get your paper, write us, giving particulars.

☞ When changing your address, please give your former as well as your future address in full, so as to avoid delay and misunderstanding.

☞ Always remit to the office from which you order your goods, no matter from which you receive them.

☞ Do not send personal checks or drafts on interior banks, unless you send with them 25 cents each, to pay for collection.

☞ Remittances should be made by Post-office Money Order, Drafts on New York, Philadelphia or Chicago, or Registered Letters, made payable and addressed to "Brethren's Publishing Co., Mount Morris, Ill.," or " Brethren's Publishing Co., Huntingdon, Pa."

☞ Entered at the Post-office at Mount Morris, Ill., as second-class matter.

Mount Morris, Ill., · · · · June 28, 1892.

THE address of Jacob Bahr is changed from Lebanon, Oregon, to Isabel, Oregon.

A CARD from Eld. Samuel Murray informs us that he is enjoying usual health, and feels happy in his religious experience.

BRO. S. Z. SHARP spent several days at Mt. Morris, on his way home from the Conference. He has not fully recovered from the accident that happened to his foot last winter, and still walks by the aid of a cane.

BRO. LEVI H. EBY, who attended the feast at Waddam's Grove, this State, a few days ago, reports an excellent meeting and the church in a joyful and hopeful condition. Bro. Ezra Lutz was elected to the ministry.

BRO. J. G. ROYER returned from the Iowa River church, Iowa, last week. He reports some good meetings in addition to the love-feast, which passed very pleasantly. One made the good confession, and was baptized.

PEOPLE who give the devil no trouble are likely to have a smooth road to travel in this world. It is the man who turns the world upside down that has the battles of life to fight. Satan makes it rough for the man who interferes with his policy.

THE Tract Examining Committee meets at Dayton, Ohio, this week, to resume the examination of tracts, commenced at Mt. Morris before the Annual Meeting. The work is a very necessary one, and is being performed with great care, and will place our tracts in a much better shape than they have heretofore been.

The Worker, now published at Lexington, Ky., comes to our table greatly improved and enlarged. It contains an excellent story, how Dr. Bay, at the suggestion of his daughter, preached a strong sermon against the modern, ungodly ways of collecting money, and broke up the church festival planned for his church. Preachers need more of that kind of daughters.

A VERY interesting communication reaches us from Bro. Daniel B. Arnold, of Burlington, W. Va., just a little too late for this issue. It will appear next week.

AT the Annual Meeting every delegate had a printed copy of all the queries presented for discussion, thus enabling them to keep a run of the business, and vote understandingly on the questions when discussed. We found the plan an excellent one.

BRO. ABRAHAM BARNHART and wife, of Hagerstown, Md., gave us a short call on their return from the Annual Meeting. Bro. B. had arranged to stop a few days with the Brethren at Polo and Lanark. We regret that he could not remain with us longer.

AT the close of the Annual Meeting Bro. I. J. Rosenberger went to Garrison, Iowa, where he remained over Sunday, expecting to stop at Mt. Morris on his way home. But being tired out, and his wife not well, he returned directly to his home at Covington, Ohio, where he arrived the 14th.

WE must again remind our readers that we do not print poetry in connection with obituary notices. Some writers even request us to set up special hymns that were sung at the funeral of the deceased. Furthermore, such notices must be accompanied by the name of the writer.

LET all of our isolated members send for a copy of Bro. R. H. Miller's "Doctrine of the Brethren Defended," to lend to their neighbors. In this way they may do some excellent missionary work and lay the foundation for the establishing of a church. Here is an excellent opportunity to do good.

WE have a card from Bro. J. H. Oakerice, of Marshalltown, Iowa, stating that his daughter, Mary, who took sick at the Annual Meeting, had the diphtheria, but is not improving. He wishes this statement made for the information of many who knew of the circumstance while at Cedar Rapids.

IN writing up the report of the Annual Meeting, our aim has been to give such news and information as will not appear in the Full Report. We hope all of our readers will send for a copy of this Report, so as to fully inform themselves concerning the work of the Conference. Price, 25 cents, or $2.50 per dozen.

ONE of our correspondents writes us, that at a Communion meeting, where 250 members were at the tables, the services closed by 9:30. This is commendable, as feasts should not be continued to a late hour, if it be possible to avoid it. Great regard should be had for the comfort of those who are aged and feeble.

WE were fortunate enough in having our Annual Meeting just at the right time this year. The week before was so rainy that it would have been impossible to have conducted the service with satisfaction, or entertained the people with any degree of comfort. The week following the meeting was extremely uncomfortable on account of the great heat.

BRO. P. A. MOORE, of Woodford County, this State, who has spent considerable time in Southern California, has been with us several days, enjoying the many gatherings connected with our religious and educational work here. He is greatly interested in the work in Southern California, and thinks the foundation is laid for many strong churches on the Pacific Coast. He carries home with him three dozen Hymnals. He believes in good music in our churches, and plenty of it.

BRO. W. M. LYON, of Union Bridge, Md., has decided to change location, if he can secure a position as book-keeper, or something of the kind, in a city where his help in the ministry will be needed. Brethren, knowing of an opening for a man who can engage in both pursuits, may do well to correspond with Bro. Lyon.

BRO. W. I. T. HOOVER, lately elected to the ministry at Dayton, Ohio, came to Mt. Morris several days ago on a special mission. Thinking it not good for man to be alone, he has taken to himself sister Carrie Yundt for a life companion. We not only congratulate them, but we trust that they both will prove faithful workers in the vineyard of the Lord.

BRO. JOHN T. DRISKILL, of Snyder, Tex., writes that he is distributing, to good advantage, the many copies of the GOSPEL MESSENGER, sent him for that purpose. He further reports that one of our ministers might do a good work in that part of the State. It is to be hoped that the seed sown by the MESSENGER and tracts distributed, will be watered by an Apollos.

BRO. S. H. MYERS, who spent several days with us before and after the Conference, is encouraged over the outlook for establishing a mission point in Washington City. An effort will be made to secure a minister adapted to city work. It is now believed that there are about fifty members in the capital of our own nation, and it is certainly important that we also have an active minister there.

BRO. J. M. SNYDER, editor and publisher of the *Educator and Companion*, McPherson, Kans., gave us a very pleasant call on his way home from the Annual Meeting. Bro. Snyder is an earnest, hard-working editor, and furnishes a very interesting little paper. He is also the editor of the *Brüderbote*, the only German paper among our people. It deserves a much better patronage than it at present enjoys.

THOSE who wish to make appeals through the MESSENGER, for aid to erect meeting-houses, will understand by this why their appeals do not appear in print. We have learned by experience, that such public calls for help seldom result in securing much aid. The better way is to appeal directly to those who are acquainted with the circumstances, and not burden the paper with calls that will likely receive no attention whatever from the general public.

BRO. JOHN ZUCK, foreman of the Committee of Arrangements, writes as follows: " We have about canceled our bills made at last Annual Meeting, and will have some surplus funds left to go into the mission fund. Taking into consideration that we have no per cent from the railroads, much bad weather to keep people away, etc., we feel to be very thankful for the result. We hope that our dear brethren and sisters will throw over our mistakes the mantle of charity."

WE feel just a little lonesome since about three hundred visitors and students have left us. It makes quite a difference in the size of our meetings and Sunday-schools. We are indeed thankful for the associations that we have been permitted to enjoy with our brethren and their children, and trust that their sojourn in our midst has been for their good. The School closed the day we went to press with the last issue, and we could give no account of the exercises. The Commencement Exercises were both instructive and pleasant. Over fifty students graduated. The year has been quite a successful one for both the School and the church.

The Gospel Messenger,

A Weekly at $1.50 Per Annum.

PUBLISHED BY

The Brethren's Publishing Co.

D. L. MILLER, ... Editor.
J. H. MOORE, ... Office Editor.
J. B. BRUMBAUGH, } . . . . . Associate Editors.
J. G. ROYER, }
JOSEPH AMICK, . . . Business Manager.

ADVISORY COMMITTEE.
R. H. Miller, A. Hutchison, Daniel Hays.

☞Communications for publication should be legibly written with black ink on one side of the paper only. Do not attempt to interline, or to put on one page what ought to occupy two.

☞Anonymous communications will not be published.

☞Do not mix business with articles for publication. Keep your communications on separate sheets from all business.

☞Time is precious. We always have time to attend to business and to answer questions of importance, but please do not subject us to need less answering of letters.

☞The MESSENGER is mailed each week to all subscribers. If the address is correctly entered on our list, the paper must reach the person to whom it is addressed. If you do not get your paper, write us, giving particulars.

☞When changing your address, please give your former as well as your future address in full, so as to avoid delay and misunderstanding.

☞Always remit to the office from which you order your goods, no matter from where you receive them.

☞Do not send personal checks or drafts on interior banks, unless you send with them 25 cents each, to pay for collection.

☞Remittances should be made by Post-office Money Order, Drafts on New York, Philadelphia or Chicago, or Registered Letters, made payable and addressed to "Brethren's Publishing Co., Mount Morris, Ill.," or "Brethren's Publishing Co., Huntingdon, Pa."

☞Entered at the Post-office at Mount Morris, Ill., as second-class matter.

Mount Morris, Ill., ... June 28, 1892.

THE address of Jacob Bahr is changed from Lebanon, Oregon, to Isabel, Oregon.

A CARD from Eld. Samuel Murray informs us that he is enjoying usual health, and feels happy in his religious experience.

BRO. S. Z. SHARP spent several days at Mt. Morris, on his way home from the Conference. He has not fully recovered from the accident that happened to his foot last winter, and still walks by the aid of a cane.

BRO. LEVI H. EBY, who attended the feast at Waddam's Grove, this State, a few days ago, reports an excellent meeting and the church in a joyful and hopeful condition. Bro. Ezra Lutz was elected to the ministry.

BRO. J. G. ROYER returned from the Iowa River church, Iowa, last week. He reports some good meetings in addition to the love-feast, which passed very pleasantly. One made the good confession, and was baptized.

PEOPLE who give the devil no trouble are likely to have a smooth road to travel in this world. It is the man who turns the world upside down that has the battles of life to fight. Satan makes it rough for the man who interferes with his policy.

THE Tract Examining Committee meets at Dayton, Ohio, this week, to resume the examination of tracts, commenced at Mt. Morris before the Annual Meeting. The work is a very necessary one, and is being performed with great care, and will place our tracts in a much better shape than they have heretofore been.

The Worker, now published at Lexington, Ky., comes to our table greatly improved and enlarged. It contains an excellent story, how Dr. Bay, at the suggestion of his daughter, preached a strong sermon against the modern, ungodly ways of collecting money, and broke up the church festival planned for his church. Preachers need more of that kind of daughters.

A VERY interesting communication reaches us from Bro. Daniel B. Arnold, of Burlington, W. Va., just a little too late for this issue. It will appear next week.

AT the Annual Meeting every delegate had a printed copy of all the queries presented for discussion, thus enabling them to keep a run of the business, and vote understandingly on the questions when discussed. We found the plan an excellent one.

BRO. ABRAHAM BARNHART and wife, of Hagerstown, Md., gave us a short call on their return from the Annual Meeting. Bro. B. had arranged to stop a few days with the Brethren at Polo and Lanark. We regret that he could not remain with us longer.

AT the close of the Annual Meeting Bro. I. J. Rosenberger went to Garrison, Iowa, where he remained over Sunday, expecting to stop at Mt. Morris on his way home. But being tired out, and his wife not well, he returned directly to his home at Covington, Ohio, where he arrived the 14th.

WE must again remind our readers that we do not print poetry in connection with obituary notices. Some writers even request us to set up special hymns that were sung at the funeral of the deceased. Furthermore, such notices must be accompanied by the name of the writer.

LET all of our isolated members send for a copy of Bro. R. H. Miller's "Doctrine of the Brethren Defended," to lend to their neighbors. In this way they may do some excellent missionary work and lay the foundation for the establishing of a church. Here is an excellent opportunity to do good.

WE have a card from Bro. J. H. Cakerice, of Marshalltown, Iowa, stating that his daughter, Mary, who took sick at the Annual Meeting, had the diphtheria, but is not improving. He wishes this statement made for the information of many who knew of the circumstance while at Cedar Rapids.

IN writing up the report of the Annual Meeting, our aim has been to give such news and information as will not appear in the Full Report. We hope all of our readers will send for a copy of this Report, so as to fully inform themselves concerning the work of the Conference. Price, 25 cents, or $2.50 per dozen.

ONE of our correspondents writes us, that at a Communion meeting, where 250 members were at the tables, the services closed by 9:30. This is commendable, as feasts should not be continued to a late hour, if it be possible to avoid it. Great regard should be had for the comfort of those who are aged and feeble.

WE were fortunate enough in having our Annual Meeting just at the right time this year. The week before was so rainy that it would have been impossible to have conducted the service with satisfaction, or entertained the people with any degree of comfort. The week following the meeting was extremely uncomfortable on account of the great heat.

BRO. P. A. MOORE, of Woodford County, this State, who has spent considerable time in Southern California, has been with us several days, enjoying the many gatherings connected with our religious and educational work here. He is greatly interested in the work in Southern California, and thinks the foundation is laid for many strong churches on the Pacific Coast. He carries home with him three dozen Hymnals. He believes in good music in our churches, and plenty of it.

BRO. W. M. LYON, of Union Bridge, Md., has decided to change location, if he can secure a position as book-keeper, or something of the kind, in a city where his help in the ministry will be needed. Brethren, knowing of an opening for a man who can engage in both pursuits, may do well to correspond with Bro. Lyon.

BRO. W. I. T. HOOVER, lately elected to the ministry at Dayton, Ohio, came to Mt. Morris several days ago on a special mission. Thinking it not good for man to be alone, he has taken to himself sister Carrie Yundt for a life companion. We not only congratulate them, but we trust that they both will prove faithful workers in the vineyard of the Lord.

BRO. JOHN T. DRISKILL, of Snyder, Tex., writes that he is distributing, to good advantage, the many copies of the GOSPEL MESSENGER, sent him for that purpose. He further reports that one of our ministers might do a good work in that part of the State. It is to be hoped that the seed sown by the MESSENGER and tracts distributed, will be watered by an Apollos.

BRO. S. H. MYERS, who spent several days with us before and after the Conference, is encouraged over the outlook for establishing a mission point in Washington City. An effort will be made to secure a minister adapted to city work. It is now believed that there are about fifty members in the capital of our own nation, and it is certainly important that we also have an active minister there.

BRO. J. M. SNYDER, editor and publisher of the Educator and Companion, McPherson, Kans., gave us a very pleasant call on his way home from the Annual Meeting. Bro. Snyder is an earnest, hard-working editor, and furnishes a very interesting little paper. He is also the editor of the Brüderbote, the only German paper among our people. It deserves a much better patronage than it at present enjoys.

THOSE who wish to make appeals through the MESSENGER, for aid to erect meeting-houses, will understand by this why their appeals do not appear in print. We have learned by experience, that such public calls for help seldom result in securing much aid. The better way is to appeal directly to those who are acquainted with the circumstances, and not burden the paper with calls that will likely receive no attention whatever from the general public.

BRO. JOHN ZUCK, foreman of the Committee of Arrangements, writes as follows: "We have about canceled our bills made at last Annual Meeting, and will have some surplus funds left to go into the mission fund. Taking into consideration that we have no per cent from the railroads, much bad weather to keep people away, etc., we feel to be very thankful for the result. We hope that our dear brethren and sisters will throw over our mistakes the mantle of charity."

WE feel just a little lonesome since about three hundred visitors and students have left us. It makes quite a difference in the size of our meetings and Sunday-schools. We are indeed thankful for the associations that we have been permitted to enjoy with our brethren and their children, and trust that their sojourn in our midst has been for their good. The School closed the day we went to press with the last issue, and we could give no account of the exercises. The Commencement Exercises were both instructive and pleasant. Over fifty students graduated. The year has been quite a successful one for both the School and the church.

ANNUAL MEETING SELECTIONS.

[The following, clipped from the *Cedar Rapids Daily*, was crowded out of last issue. It will prove interesting reading to those who could not attend the Annual Meeting.]

MISSIONARY AND TRACT MEETING.

Held at 1:30 o'clock, S. W. Hoover, of Dayton, presiding. The first speaker was Eld. S. Z. Sharp, of McPherson, Kans. The subject assigned him was "Duties of Ministers to Preach Missionary Sermons and of Elders to Appoint Solicitors in their Churches."

The speaker referred to the commission of the Savior to the apostles as authority for sending out missionaries. The promise of the Savior's presence with his people "unto the end of the world," is coupled with the obedience to carry out this command following the commission, namely, "Teach them to observe all things whatsoever I have commanded you." Christ taught his disciples to go and preach to all nations. The church must teach the followers of the apostles the same thing. When the Gospel was established at Antioch as a kind of headquarters for the Gentile Christians, then the Holy Ghost said, "Separate unto me Barnabas and Paul unto the work whereunto I have called them." This work of separating or setting apart missionaries is yet entrusted to the church.

1 Cor. 16: 1 was quoted, as the duty of collecting means for the saints, and especially for the saints who preach the Gospel, was pointed out, and reference made to the duty enjoined upon every elder and congregation to appoint.

Elder H. B. Brumbaugh addressed the meeting from the topic, "Why should we give?" He advocated inculcating the habit of giving from a sense of pleasure afforded, rather than from a sense of duty. We are creatures subject to being trained, and if the members are trained to give, it will afford them pleasure.

The third speaker was Elder Enoch Eby, of Kansas. Subject, "The Duty of Churches to make Greater Effort to Secure Suitable Brethren for the Mission Field." He spoke, in substance, as follows: Paul laid down the rule to Timothy for proper qualifications of a Gospel preacher: "Study to show thyself approved unto God, a workman that needeth not to be ashamed, rightly dividing the word of truth." A man to be a successful teacher for any organization, must be well grounded in the principles held by said organization. How shall we get men capable of wielding the Sword of the Spirit effectively? Every man ought so to live that he would be eligible to the office of bishop, as these qualifications are given us by Paul. The church should encourage him in this, and every sister should so live as to have the qualifications of a bishop's wife. Let all the members do their duty on this line and there will be no scarcity of men. Secondly,—what is the duty of the church? The church is a school and ought to conduct its work as a school. It should have Bible meetings and all the members take part in teaching, and especially in praying; thus the church will see who possesses talent, and know whom to choose when elections are held. Let me say to you if you have men who have talent and do not need them at home, elect them any way, that they may work wherever they may be. Educate them especially in the knowledge of the Bible, then they will be prepared to defend the truth. When they are out from the thickly-settled churches and have not the great body of brethren and sisters, they will be able to stand alone. But in all you do, don't send out policy men to uphold the prejudices.

Fourth speaker: "The Use of Tracts in Missionary Work," by Elder Isaac Frantz. The mission-

ary cause is one of great importance, and is to enlighten the unenlightened, to bring men out of the dungeon of darkness into the glorious Gospel of the Son of God. The tract work is one of the best auxiliaries to this work. We should have the examining committee composed of men consecrated to God, and well versed in the letter and spirit of the Gospel. Tracts may be used to introduce the cause of Christ and enable men to read and study more critically, and arrive at a better knowledge of the truth than a mere preaching of the Word will enable them to. The American people are eminently a reading people, and the books that a man reads are a fair index to his character. Books mould thought, and if we place the doctrine in this manner before the people, we will mould thought for the church. One of the most important features is to place these doctrinal tracts in the homes of the members and educate our children in the doctrines of the church.

Had we the time we could tell you of many instances in which souls have been brought to Christ through the instrumentality of the work already done by the church in this department. Tracts meet the wants of the people where it is not practicable to preach; by this means we reach the invalid and the man in the foreign lands. Another beautiful feature of this work is that all may become preachers by sending out the Gospel in this way.

The fifth speaker was L. W. Teeter, of Hagerstown, Ind. The subject assigned him was, "The Importance of Continued Effort in Missionary and Tract Work." He said in substance that the work implied organization, that any work to be successful must be a well-organized work, and that this organization must be begun in the pockets of the members, that continued effort only will succeed in any calling or profession. We need not expect to succeed in spreading the Gospel with less effort than we put forth in pushing a secular calling to success. If we follow the example of these three men, Abraham, Christ, and Paul, there will be no such thing as fail in our work.

The sixth speaker was Eld. S. F. Sanger, of Bridgewater, Va., theme, "The Macedonian Call." The speaker made an eloquent plea for men to be sent to the weaker churches and places where they don't get to hear the Gospel as they do in our larger churches, and closed by saying that this would take sacrifice on our part, but that we promised God when we entered the church that we would follow him in all things and this is one of the requirements of the Gospel. Eld. Joseph Lahman then announced that a collection would be taken for missionary purposes, which was accordingly done, amounting to $262.35.

EDUCATIONAL MEETING.

After a recess of half an hour, the meeting was called to order at four o'clock, and S. Z. Sharp, President of McPherson College, Kans., and Moderator of the meeting, explained the object of the assembly and announced that J. G. Royer, President of Mt. Morris College, Illinois, would make the opening address. Prof. Royer gave a short report of the progress of the college over which he presides. He stated that the past year was the most prosperous in the history of the institution, and its future prospects were very encouraging. He then spoke of the relation of the church to its young members and advocated forbearance toward the weak and erring.

The next speaker on the program was President S. Z. Sharp, of the college at McPherson, Kansas. He gave a very encouraging report of that institution. The patronage of the church exceeded that of last year thirty per cent, and the entire number enrolled was 384, although only four years old.

He explained the relations of the schools to the church and the necessity of receiving the church's fostering care. The schools are not reformatories and are not expected to reform in a few months the incorrigible sons or daughters of parents who have failed in home training. Neither are they intended to train young and weak members in a few months when the church failed to train them in years. The church needs to become better acquainted with the work of the schools and not pass judgment hastily.

H. B. Brumbaugh, President of the college at Huntingdon, Pa., was the next speaker. He gave a good report of his institution. He referred to the increased patronage and especially to that from the church. He gave a very satisfactory report of the Bible work done at his institution which was also a commendable feature of the other colleges.

Prof. I. N. McCann, of Bridgewater college, Va., reported for the college with which he is connected. He advocated the importance of the church sustaining her schools. The result would be felt in ages to come. These schoo's are recognized as a power and the church can make them a power for good or evil.

Elder J. S. Flory, of Lordsburg, California, in the absence of any of the faculty from that school, made a short report.

He stated that their school was certainly in its infancy, as it was less than a year old. He reported that the result of their experiment was satisfactory to themselves beyond their expectations.

ORIGIN OF THE BIBLE.

In view of the attention of late given to the so-called "high criticism" the following from W. G. T. Shedd, D. D., stating the two general views of the origin of the Bible, may prove interesting as well as instructive to our readers:

"*First.*—That it is the production of a limited circle of contemporaneous authors, whose names and dates can, in general, be mentioned with reasonable certainty, and who were divinely inspired for the purpose of producing a book having infallible accuracy and authority.

"*Second.*—That it is the production of non-contemporaneous and utterly unknown editors, who gathered up oral traditions, from unknown and often mythical sources, and put them in the form in which they now appear. The first is the historical view, or that commonly held in ancient, medieval, and modern Christendom. The second is the fragmentary theory, and confined to individuals and schools in modern Christendom. According to the historical theory, the Pentateuch has Moses for its responsible and inspired author. According to the fragmentary theory, with the exception of a few parts, which, perhaps, may be ascribed to Moses, no man knows who wrote the Pentateuch, any more than where the sepulchre of Moses is. According to the historical theory, the four Gospels are inspired productions of four men, Matthew (Peter), Mark (Paul), Luke and John, who received and obeyed their Lord's commission to prepare his biography for use of the church in all time. According to the fragmentary theory, the four Gospels are the uninspired product of unknown persons, later than the apostles, who gathered up the traditions concerning Christ that were floating about in the church, and put them into their present shape. Such, briefly stated, is the substantial difference between the two theories. One ascribes the Bible to known and infallible authors; the other ascribes it to unknown and fallible editors.

"*First.*—The first objection to the fragmentary theory of the origin of the Scriptures is, that it is wholly modern.

ANNUAL MEETING SELECTIONS.

[The following, clipped from the *Cedar Rapids Daily*, was crowded out of last issue. It will prove interesting reading to those who could not attend the Annual Meeting.]

MISSIONARY AND TRACT MEETING.

Held at 1:30 o'clock, S. W. Hoover, of Dayton, presiding. The first speaker was Eld. S. Z. Sharp, of McPherson, Kans. The subject assigned him was "Duties of Ministers to Preach Missionary Sermons and of Elders to Appoint Solicitors in their Churches."

The speaker referred to the commission of the Savior to the apostles as authority for sending out missionaries. The promise of the Savior's presence with his people "unto the end of the world," is coupled with the obedience to carry out this command following the commission, namely, "Teach them to observe all things whatsoever I have commanded you." Christ taught his disciples to go and preach to all nations. The church must teach the followers of the apostles the same thing. When the Gospel was established at Antioch as a kind of headquarters for the Gentile Christians, then the Holy Ghost said, "Separate unto me Barnabas and Paul unto the work whereunto I have called them." This work of separating or setting apart missionaries is yet entrusted to the church.

1 Cor. 16: 1 was quoted, as the duty of collecting means for the saints, and especially for the saints who preach the Gospel, was pointed out, and reference made to the duty enjoined upon every elder and congregation to appoint.

Elder H. B. Brumbaugh addressed the meeting from the topic, "Why should we give?" He advocated inculcating the habit of giving from a sense of pleasure afforded, rather than from a sense of duty. We are creatures subject to being trained, and if the members are trained to give, it will afford them pleasure.

The third speaker was Elder Enoch Eby, of Kansas. Subject, "The Duty of Churches to make Greater Effort to Secure Suitable Brethren for the Mission Field." He spoke, in substance, as follows: Paul laid down the rule to Timothy for proper qualifications of a Gospel preacher: "Study to show thyself approved unto God, a workman that needeth not to be ashamed, rightly dividing the word of truth." A man to be a successful teacher for any organization, must be well grounded in the principles held by said organization. How shall we get men capable of wielding the Sword of the Spirit effectively? Every man ought so to live that he would be eligible to the office of a bishop, as these qualifications are given us by Paul. The church should encourage him in this, and every sister should so live as to have the qualifications of a bishop's wife. Let all the members do their duty on this line and there will be no scarcity of men. Secondly, what is the duty of the church? The church is a school and ought to conduct its work as a school. It should have Bible meetings and all the members take part in teaching, and especially in praying; thus the church will see who possesses talent, and know whom to choose when elections are held. Let me say to you if you have men who have talent and do not need them at home, elect them any way, that they may work wherever they may be. Educate them especially in the knowledge of the Bible, then they will be prepared to defend the truth. When they are cut from the thickly-settled churches and have not the great body of brethren and sisters, they will be able to stand alone. But in all you do, don't send out policy men to uphold the principles.

Fourth speaker: "The Use of Tracts in Missionary Work," by Elder Isaac Frantz. The mission-ary cause is one of great importance, and is to enlighten the unenlightened, to bring men out of the dungeon of darkness into the glorious Gospel of the Son of God. The tract work is one of the best auxiliaries to this work. We should have the examining committee composed of men consecrated to God, and well versed in the letter and spirit of the Gospel. Tracts may be used to introduce the cause of Christ and enable men to read and study more critically, and arrive at a better knowledge of the truth than a mere preaching of the Word will enable them to. The American people are eminently a reading people, and the books that a man reads are a fair index to his character. Books mould thought, and if we place the doctrine in this manner before the people, we will mould thought for the church. One of the most important features is to place these doctrinal tracts in the homes of the members and educate our children in the doctrines of the church.

Had we the time we could tell you of many instances in which souls have been brought to Christ through the instrumentality of the work already done by the church in this department. Tracts meet the wants of the people where it is not practicable to preach; by this means we reach the invalid and the man in the foreign lands. Another beautiful feature of this work is that all may become preachers by sending out the Gospel in this way.

The fifth speaker was L. W. Teeter, of Hagerstown, Ind. The subject assigned him was, "The Importance of Continued Effort in Missionary and Tract Work." He said in substance that the work implied organization, that any work to be successful must be a well-organized work, and that this organization must be begun in the pockets of the members, that continued effort only will succeed in any calling or profession. We need not expect to succeed in spreading the Gospel with less effort than we put forth in pushing a secular calling to success. If we follow the example of these three men, Abraham, Christ, and Paul, there will be no such thing as fail in our work.

The sixth speaker was Eld. S. F. Sanger, of Bridgewater, Va., theme, "The Macedonian Call." The speaker made an eloquent plea for men to be sent to the weaker churches and places where they don't get to hear the Gospel as they do in our larger churches, and closed by saying that this would take sacrifice on our part, but that we promised God when we entered the church that we would follow him in all things and this is one of the requirements of the Gospel. Eld. Joseph Lahman then announced that a collection would be taken for missionary purposes, which was accordingly done, amounting to $362.35.

EDUCATIONAL MEETING.

After a recess of half an hour, the meeting was called to order at four o'clock, and S. Z. Sharp, President of McPherson College, Kans., and Moderator of the meeting, explained the object of the assembly and announced that J. G. Royer, President of Mt. Morris College, Illinois, would make the opening address. Prof. Royer gave a short report of the progress of the college over which he presides. He stated that the past year was the most prosperous in the history of the institution, and its future prospects were very encouraging. He then spoke of the relation of the church to its young members and advocated forbearance toward the weak and erring.

The next speaker on the program was President S. Z. Sharp, of the college at McPherson, Kansas. He gave a very encouraging report of that institution. The patronage of the church exceeded that of last year thirty per cent, and the entire number enrolled was 384, although only four years old.

He explained the relations of the schools to the church and the necessity of receiving the church's fostering care. The schools are not reformatories and are not expected to reform in a few months the incorrigible sons or daughters of parents who have failed in home training. Neither are they intended to train young and weak members in a few months when the church failed to train them in years. The church needs to become better acquainted with the work of the schools and not pass judgment hastily.

H. B. Brumbaugh, President of the college at Huntingdon, Pa., was the next speaker. He gave a good report of his institution. He referred to the increased patronage and especially to that from the church. He gave a very satisfactory report of the Bible work done at his institution which was also a commendable feature of the other colleges.

Prof. I. N. McCann, of Bridgewater college, Va., reported for the college with which he is connected. He advocated the importance of the church sustaining her schools. The result would be felt in ages to come. These schools are recognized as a power and the church can make them a power for good or evil.

Elder J. S. Flory, of Lordsburg, California, in the absence of any of the faculty from that school, made a short report.

He stated that their school was certainly in its infancy, as it was less than a year old. He reported that the result of their experiment was satisfactory to themselves beyond their expectations.

ORIGIN OF THE BIBLE.

In view of the attention of late given to the so-called "high criticism" the following from W. G. T. Shedd, D. D., stating the two general views of the origin of the Bible, may prove interesting as well as instructive to our readers:

"*First.*—That it is the production of a limited circle of contemporaneous authors, whose names and dates can, in general, be mentioned with reasonable certainty, and who were divinely inspired for the purpose of producing a book having infallible accuracy and authority.

"*Second.*—That it is the production of non-contemporaneous and utterly unknown editors, who gathered up oral traditions, from unknown and often mythical sources, and put them in the form in which they now appear. The first is the historical view, or that commonly held in ancient, mediæval, and modern Christendom. The second is the fragmentary theory, and confined to individuals and schools in modern Christendom. According to the historical theory, the Pentateuch has Moses for its responsible and inspired author. According to the fragmentary theory, with the exception of a few parts, which, perhaps, may be ascribed to Moses, no man knows who wrote the Pentateuch, any more than where the sepulchre of Moses is. According to the historical theory, the four Gospels are inspired productions of four men, Matthew (Peter), Mark (Paul), Luke and John, who received and obeyed their Lord's commission to prepare his biography for use of the church in all time. According to the fragmentary theory, the four Gospels are the uninspired product of unknown persons, later than the apostles, who gathered up the traditions concerning Christ that were floating about in the church, and put them into their present shape. Such, briefly stated, is the substantial difference between the two theories. One ascribes the Bible to known and infallible authors; the other ascribes it to unknown and fallible editors.

"*First.*—The first objection to the fragmentary theory of the origin of the Scriptures is, that it is wholly modern.

ters who are willing to spend their time in the mission fields. May God bless you in your work! Stand by your poor ministers, preach about it, write and give us all the encouragement you can. I almost feel like giving up, when I see how little my advice is heeded in regard to the decisions of the District and Annual Meetings, in relation to pride and extravagance.　　JOHN BARNHART.

From Mondovi, Wash.

I ASK, Why can not the missionary committee place a good minister somewhere, near here, so that we can have regular meetings? Souls are worth as much here as elsewhere. Thousands are dying here, who never hear the Gospel preached in its primitive purity. How can we, as a church, excuse ourselves in the great day of accounts, for this neglect of fulfilling the commission, given by Christ, "Go, teach all nations," etc?

Will the lack of money excuse us? No; there is too much of that in the church to excuse us. Will the lack of true Gospel charity, to contribute to the cause of spreading the Gospel, excuse? Emphatically no, but it will be against us. Then, will the lack of ministers and elders excuse us? Certainly not.

There is too much talent and good material in the church, lying dormant for want of encouragement. It is said that talent is dormant because the Spirit does not call them. Here is a very sad mistake, yet I fear it may often happen. Christ, the head, says, "Go, teach all nations."

Because a good minister spends all his time, and bears his own expenses, and saves thousands of souls in foreign lands, is no excuse for the church to remain idle, as she did not send him. The reward is solely his. The ministers doing all the work, is no credit to the church, but is a credit only to those that do the work.

What, then, will serve as an anchor for the church? We answer, "More unity, more love, more charity and greater zeal for Christ and the spreading of his Gospel." Let every member be fitly joined in the body, and each one have enough of that true charity that will enable him to contribute freely of his goods for the spread of the Gospel. Let the ministers and others lay aside all hindrances and unite in the one Christian spirit, and put all the good talent in the church to work, and the church will soon be able to supply the world with ministers. SAMUEL FORNEY.

June 5.

The Work at Mt. Morris, Ill.

TIME passes on, and nothing marks its movement more distinctly for us at Mt. Morris, than the closing exercises of the College at this place. The list of exercises was began with the last prayer-meeting. The subject was, "Our Strength is from Above," based on the Scripture, "Without me ye can do nothing." The graduates did the principal part of the speaking, and many thoughts were dropped that, it is hoped, will remain long in the minds of the hearers.

On Friday and Saturday evenings the two literary societies gave their contest entertainments. These were conducted in such a manner as to render satisfaction to all present.

On Sunday morning we received some rich lessons from the life of Daniel, given by brethren A. W. Vaniman, of McPherson, and S. N. Mc. Cann, of Bridgewater. In the afternoon the Sunday-school had its usual class work, and at its close the primary department came in and reviewed the lessons of the quarter thus far passed. This was quite a pleasing part of the Sunday-school. In the evening Eld. J. G. Royer delivered a good sermon to the graduates on the sub-

ject of "Love." This was listened to by a large and appreciative audience.

On Monday morning "the class" gave what is called "Class Day Exercises," and in the afternoon the Sunday-school workers had a meeting. Excellent thoughts on the best method of conducting Sunday-schools, and the way to success in winning young hearts to Christ, were given. In the evening Bro. E. S. Young gave an illustrated talk on the tabernacle and its furniture, bringing out many useful and practical lessons. On Tuesday morning began the Commencement Exercises proper. During the forenoon we listened to speeches from the eleven graduates of the Academic Department, all laden with good thoughts and noble sentiments. In the afternoon session the four Seminary graduates delivered productions well worthy the many favorable commendations made of them. At the close of the afternoon session fifty-one diplomas were given to graduates from the several departments. In the evening the Alumni had a short session, after which Bro. D. L. Miller, upon many urgent requests, gave an illustrated talk on Palestine.

All the exercises were well attended, from the first to the last. We were favored by a number of visitors from other States, who had stopped on their return from Annual Meeting. We enjoyed their presence, and hope they were favorably impressed with our work and entertainment. In our school work here we do not claim perfection, but we are trying to do our best for God, the church, and the young people under our tuition. A visit from those interested in our church and its important auxiliary, the schools, is always encouraging, and we hope our brethren will come to see us again. And above all, brethren and sisters, inasmuch as an important work lies in our schools, we earnestly ask you to implore God to guide us and keep us in the way of truth and holiness. Pray for our schools, that they may be strong in the Lord.　　GALEN B. ROYER.

June 17.

From Cedar Rapids, Iowa.

SINCE the Annual Meeting one more has decided to unite with us, and has already acted upon his decision. He is a Frenchman, who came, some time ago, from France, and is descended from Roman Catholic parents. He was, until thirty-three years of age, practically unacquainted with the Bible, and was at one time a member of the Salvation Army, together with that old sister, who was baptized during our Conference. Later, he united with the Baptists, and, while yet a member in good standing of that church, was baptized at the Dry Creek church, June 12, thus uniting with our church.

He appears to be very zealous in the cause, and is very anxious to persuade other people, even the Roman Catholics, to come with us. For example, last Thursday evening he and I were walking on the street. He repeatedly referred to a Frenchman with whom he had been conversing, and after a while we came to his place (the place of the subject of our conversation). We entered, and the conversation began, I chiefly listening. Our brother spoke in plain terms as to what church he considered right. We closed by both of us inviting our friend to a little social meeting which began last Thursday evening, and probably will be continued for some time at Bro. Tisdale's and other places, if opportunity is given. Our friend said he would like to attend, if possible, and I am in hopes that he will. Now, to my surprise, when we got outside, I was informed that we had been talking to a Roman Catholic; but then it was, perhaps, all the better.

We, about ten in number, together with three or four others, met and had a very enjoyable season

of encouragement, and sister Wesson and brother Rödigne, our new members, expressed themselves as having derived great pleasure and consolation from their new condition and surroundings. They would like to see some active work done here, and it seems strange that some special effort should not be made. People have been aroused, and should now have a better opportunity of pursuing the course which many believe to be a very exemplary one. In fact I believe the people are generally well impressed with our ways as a church. Cannot something be done?

WALTER L. KLINCK.

June 18.

From the Belleville Church, Kans.

WE enjoyed another love-feast on June 11 and 12. Several brethren and sisters of other congregations assembled with us, and we had a good meeting.

Brethren Samuel Myers, Wm. R. Phillipi, and D. Smith, were the ministers that came to assist in the labors of love. Our elder, C. S. Holsinger, who lately moved among us, officiated, assisted by Bro. Myers. The weather being nice, there was a good representation of our members, and a large congregation of others, both Saturday night and Sunday. We had a children's meeting on Sunday morning. Our Sunday-school is getting along nicely. We are using the *Brethren's Quarterlies* this summer. We have had six additions to the church by letter this spring.

LOUISA J. WILLIAMS.

June 14.

From the Saginaw Church, Mich.

OUR council took place June 11, at which time all business passed off pleasantly. The church is in love and union, and although we are not increasing fast, yet we feel that the Lord is with us. Last November Bro. John Felthouse, of Indiana, held a two weeks' meeting at our church. The members were much encouraged and two souls were added to the church, one an afflicted sister that has been suffering for two years. Soon after she requested to be anointed, and our elder, D. Chambers, was called, and anointed her. She is still with us, and to-day, June 12, we were encouraged to see her at church,—the first time for about one year. Hopes of her recovery are now entertained. We also held another two weeks' meeting, conducted by my father, David Baker, at one of our meeting points, eleven miles from the main body of the church. A good interest prevailed, with large and attentive congregations, but on account of poor health he was obliged to close the meetings. At this place we have three members. At our last council three were received by letter, making four since our last writing. We have an interesting Sunday-school, with a good attendance. Our Communion was appointed for Oct. 1 and 2.　　LEVI BAKER.

"THERE are thousands of lives, no incident in one of which can be used to illustrate any particular truth or assist in any particular cause, the sum total of each one of which is unanswerable argument for the right. We do not need to be waiting for a little social meeting which began passage in your life be so conspicuous as to arrest any man's attention, let your character, as a whole, make an impression for the truth. Let its weight, however little, press every one it touches away from the wrong and into the right."

"WOULD that the days of our human autumn were so calmly grand, as gorgeously hopeful, as the days that lead the aging year down to the grave of winter!"

ters who are willing to spend their time in the mission fields. May God bless you in your work! Stand by your poor ministers, preach about it, write and give us all the encouragement you can. I almost feel like giving up, when I see how little my advice is heeded in regard to the decisions of the District and Annual Meetings, in relation to pride and extravagance. JOHN BARNHART.

From Mondovi, Wash.

I ASK, Why can not the missionary committee place a good minister somewhere, near here, so that we can have regular meetings? Souls are worth as much here as elsewhere. Thousands are dying here, who never hear the Gospel preached in its primitive purity. How can we, as a church, excuse ourselves in the great day of accounts, for this neglect of fulfilling the commission, given by Christ, "Go, teach all nations," etc? Will the lack of money excuse us? No; there is too much of that in the church to excuse us. Will the lack of true Gospel charity, to contribute to the cause of spreading the Gospel, excuse? Emphatically no, but it will be against us. Then, will the lack of ministers and elders excuse us? Certainly not.

There is too much talent and good material in the church, lying dormant for want of encouragement. It is said that talent is dormant because the Spirit does not call them. Here is a very sad mistake, yet I fear it may often happen. Christ, the Head, says, "Go, teach all nations."

Because a good minister spends all his time, and bears his own expenses, and saves thousands of souls in foreign lands, is no excuse for the church to remain idle, as she did not send him. The reward is solely his. The ministers doing all the work, is no credit to the church, but is a credit only to those that do the work.

What, then, will serve as an anchor for the church? We answer, "More unity, more love, more charity and greater zeal for Christ and the spreading of his Gospel." Let every member be fitly joined in the body, and each one have enough of that true charity that will enable him to contribute freely all his goods for the spread of the Gospel. Let the ministers and others lay aside all hinderances and unite in the one Christian spirit, and put all the good talent in the church to work, and the church will soon be able to supply the world with ministers. SAMUEL FORNEY.
June 5.

The Work at Mt. Morris, Ill.

TIME passes on, and nothing marks its movement more distinctly for us at Mt. Morris, than the closing exercises of the College and Bible. The list of exercises was begun with the last prayer-meeting. The subject was, "Our Strength is from Above," based on the Scripture, "With out me ye can do nothing." The graduates did the principal part of the speaking, and many thoughts were dropped that, it is hoped, will remain long in the minds of the hearers.

On Friday and Saturday evenings the two literary societies gave their contest entertainments. These were conducted in such a manner as to render satisfaction to all present.

On Sunday morning we received some rich lessons from the life of Daniel, given by brethren A. W. Vaniman, of McPherson, and S. N. McCann, of Bridgewater. In the afternoon the Sunday-school had its usual class work, and at its close the primary department came in and reviewed the lessons of the quarter thus far passed. This was quite a pleasing part of the Sunday-school. In the evening Eld. J. G. Royer delivered a good sermon to the graduates on the subject of "Love." This was listened to by a large and appreciative audience.

On Monday morning "the class" gave what is called "Class Day Exercises," and in the afternoon the Sunday-school workers had a meeting. Excellent thoughts on the best method of conducting Sunday-schools, and the way to success in winning young hearts to Christ, were given. In the evening Bro. E. S. Young gave an illustrated talk on the tabernacle and its furniture, bringing out many useful and practical lessons. On Tuesday morning began the Commencement Exercises proper. During the forenoon we listened to speeches from the eleven graduates of the Academic Department, all laden with good thoughts and noble sentiments. In the afternoon session the four Seminary graduates delivered productions well worthy the many favorable commendations made of them. At the close of the afternoon session fifty-one diplomas were given to graduates from the several departments. In the evening the Alumni had a short session, after which Bro. D. L. Miller. upon many urgent requests, gave an illustrated talk on Palestine.

All the exercises were well attended, from the first to the last. We were favored by a number of visitors from other States, who had stopped on their return from Annual Meeting. We enjoyed their presence, and hope they were favorably impressed with our work and entertainment. In our school work here we do not claim perfection, but we are trying to do our best for God, the church, and the young people under our tuition. A visit from those interested in our church and its important auxiliary, the schools, is always encouraging, and we hope our brethren will come to see us again. And above all, brethren and sisters, inasmuch as an important work lies in our schools, we earnestly ask you to implore God to guide us and keep us in the way of truth and holiness. Pray for our schools, that they may be strong in the Lord. GALEN B. ROYER.
June 17.

From Cedar Rapids, Iowa.

SINCE the Annual Meeting one more has decided to unite with us, and has already acted upon his decision. He is a Frenchman, who came, some time ago, from France, and is descended from Roman Catholic parents. He was, until thirty-three years of age, practically unacquainted with the Bible, and was at one time a member of the Salvation Army, together with that old sister, who was baptized during our Conference. Later, he united with the Baptists, and, while yet a member in good standing of that church, was baptized at the Dry Creek church, June 12, thus uniting with our church.

He appears to be very zealous in the cause, and is very anxious to persuade other people, even the Roman Catholics, to come with us. For example, last Thursday evening he and I were walking on the street. He repeatedly referred to a Frenchman with whom he had been conversing, and after a while we came to his place (the place of the subject of our conversation). We entered, and the conversation began, I chiefly listening. Our brother spoke in plain terms as to what church he considered right. We closed by both of us inviting our friend to a little social meeting which began last Thursday evening, and probably will be continued for some time at Bro. Tisdale's and other places, if opportunity is given. Our friend said he would like to attend, if possible, and I am in hopes that he will. Now, to my surprise, when we got outside, I was informed that we had been talking to a Roman Catholic; but then it was, perhaps, all the better.

We, about ten in number, together with three or four others, met and had a very enjoyable season

of encouragement, and sister Wesson and brother Rödigue, our new members, expressed themselves as having derived great pleasure and consolation from their new condition and surroundings. They would like to see some active work done here, and it seems strange that some special effort should not be made. People have been aroused, and should now have a better opportunity of pursuing the course which many believe to be a very exemplary one. In fact I believe the people are generally well impressed with our ways as a church. Cannot something be done?
WALTER L. KLINCK.
June 18.

From the Belleville Church, Kans.

WE enjoyed another love-feast on June 11 and 12. Several brethren and sisters of other congregations assembled with us, and we had a good meeting.

Brethren Samuel Myers, Wm. R. Phillipi, and D. Smith, were the ministers that came to assist in the labors of love. Our elder, C. S. Holsinger, who lately moved among us, officiated, assisted by Bro. Myers. The weather being nice, there was a good representation of our members, and a large congregation of others, both Saturday night and Sunday. We had a children's meeting on Sunday morning. Our Sunday-school is getting along nicely. We are using the *Brethren's Quarterlies* this summer. We have had six additions to the church by letter this spring.
LOUISA J. WILLIAMS.
June 14.

From the Saginaw Church, Mich.

OUR council took place June 11, at which time all business passed off pleasantly. The church is in love and union, and although we are not increasing fast, yet we feel that the Lord is with us. Last November Bro. John Felthouse, of Indiana, held a two weeks' meeting at our church. The members were much encouraged and two souls were added to the church, one an afflicted sister that has been suffering for two years. Soon after she requested to be anointed, and our elder, D. Chambers, was called, and anointed her. She is still with us, and to-day, June 12, we were encouraged to see her at church,—the first time for about one year. Hopes of her recovery are now entertained. We also held another two weeks' meeting, conducted by my father, David Baker, at one of our meeting points, eleven miles from the main body of the church. A good interest prevailed, with large and attentive congregations, but on account of poor health he was obliged to close the meetings. At this place we have three members. At our last council three were received by letter, making four since our last writing. We have an interesting Sunday-school, with a good attendance. Our Communion was appointed for Oct. 1 and 2. LEVI BAKER.

"THERE are thousands of lives, no incident in one of which can be used to illustrate any particular truth or assist in any particular cause, the sum total of each one of which is unanswerable argument for the right. If no special passage in your life be so conspicuous as to arrest any man's attention, let your character, as a whole, make an impression for the truth. Let its weight, however little, press every one it touches away from the wrong and into the right."

"WOULD that the days of our human autumn were so calmly grand, as gorgeously hopeful, as the days that lead the aging year down to the grave of winter!"

A Sad Occurrence.—When we came home from the Annual Meeting we were informed of the death of Miss Mary Willetts by drowning in a pool of water near by. She arose at one o'clock in the night, and threw herself into the water where it was about eight feet deep. It was supposed that she was somewhat demented. She was the daughter of J. F. Willetts, the national lecturer of the Farmer's Alliance. She leaves six sisters, two brothers and a father and mother to mourn her untimely death. Funeral services were conducted by the writer.—*David Kimmel, McLouth, Kans.*

Linganore, Md.—We held our quarterly council May 21, at the Pleasant Hill church, in the Bush Creek congregation. Elders E. W. Stoner, Solomon Stoner and E. Bruner were present with us. All business was disposed of in a Christian spirit. Bro. S. H. Utz was ordained to the eldership, and Bro. W. T. Miller was advanced to the second degree of the ministry. We also held a very pleasant and enjoyable Communion meeting June 1. The attendance was large and the behavior very good. Bro. Kolb, of Rocky Ridge, officiated. Bro. Bricker and son, brethren Joseph Utz and John Smith were the ministers from abroad.—*M. E. Ecker, June 13.*

North Webster, Ind.—The Tippecanoe church, Kosciusko Co., Ind., held a series of meetings from May 29 to June 2. Bro. J. V. Felthouse did the preaching. May 27 was our quarterly council. All business passed off harmoniously. June 2 we held our love-feast. The ministerial aid was ample, and all seemed to enjoy the meeting. The rainy weather was against us. The congregations were not as large as they would have been under more favorable circumstances, but we trust some good has been done. We thank the Lord and take courage.—*Daniel Rothenberger, June 11.*

Pioneer, Ohio.—The Communion meeting of the Silver Creek church occurred June 11, 1892. Ministers present from a distance were brethren John Felthouse, Jeremiah Gump and Henry Steckley. Bro. John Felthouse officiated. It was a feast long to be remembered by all present, on account of the outpouring of the Holy Spirit upon us. We were made to rejoice by seeing one dear soul come boldly out from the ranks of Satan, and present himself for Christian baptism. Oh, how do saints rejoice when sinners ask for admittance into the church militant here below! Angels in heaven also rejoice when sinners turn to God. On Sunday morning we assembled in a Sabbath-school capacity, and had the brethren talk to the children, which all appeared to appreciate very much. We hope it will find lodgment in well-cultivated hearts and bear good fruit.—*J. W. Keiser.*

McPherson, Kans.—I am now at work in the town of Maxwell, Iowa, and am expected to remain here till June 24; then to attend the Indian Creek love-feast, on the 26th. After that my course will be homeward, hoping to be at home by June 28. Rest, at least for a little while, seems to be an actual necessity. I will aim to work some in Kansas until about the first of September, when I hope to be able to make out a program for the fall and winter. Brethren should remember, however, that I can be at but one place at a time, and please do not hurry me from place to place too rapidly. If your application cannot be met at once, do not get discouraged. I expect to work when the Lord is ready to help, and not to leave a work, when it is well begun, and go some, where else to begin again. We have had too much work lost that way already.—*A. Hutchison, June 13.*

Mansfield, Ill.—Our love-feast in the Blue Ridge church was held June 3. The ministering brethren that were with us were J. W. Metzger, Dan. Stoner, and —— Atchison. Bro. Stoner and Bro. Atchison stayed with us over Sunday and preached three interesting discourses. We enjoyed a feast of love indeed, and were made to rejoice to know that two were willing to join in with the Lord's children. Many precious souls are still out of the ark of safety, and we pray that they may soon see the beauty of the religion of Jesus Christ. We have a very large and interesting Sunday-school. It is prospering nicely and, we trust, will continue in that way.—*Bertha E. Barnhart, June 14.*

Purchase Line, Pa.—The brethren and sisters of the Manor congregation, Pa., met in church council June 4, preparatory to the love-feast. Everything passed off pleasantly, with one exception. Our love-feast, held June 9, was soul-cheering to all who are hungering and thirsting after righteousness. The order was much better than on former occasions. Brethren from abroad were elders Geo. Hanawalt and David Hildebrand. They labored faithfully for us. During their stay Bro. Joseph Holsopple was ordained to the eldership, and Bro John W. Fyock was called to the ministry. Amidst a great deal of solemnity and many tears, they were placed in their offices. God grant that they may be faithful, and that the church stand by them, and lift up their hands, for the strongest need help. May we bear one another's burdens, and so fulfill the law of Christ. One brother returned to the fold after a long absence, and caused much rejoicing among God's children.—*Lizzie Fyock.*

Matrimonial.

"What therefore God hath joined together, let not man put asunder."

WILTFONG—YODER.—At the residence of the bride's parents, Mr. and Mrs. S. F. Yoder, June 1, 1892, by the undersigned, Mr. Hiram E. Wiltfong, of Montior, McPherson Co., Kans., and Mrs. Emma Yoder, of Mitchell, Rice Co., Kans. ISAAC S. BRUBAKER.

Fallen Asleep.

"Blessed are the dead which die in the Lord."

RITTER.—In the Tippecanoe church, Kosciusko Co., Ind., May 24, 1892, Tidia Ritter, wife of Samuel Ritter, aged 38 years, 8 months and 21 days. She leaves a husband and nine children. Funeral services from John 17: 3 to a large concourse of people.

CRIPE.—At the same place, June 1, 1892, sister Lidda Ann (Hamman) Cripe, wife of Noah Cripe, aged 61 years, 3 months and 27 days. Her husband and six children survive her. Funeral services from Isa. 38: 1.
DANIEL ROTHENBERGER.

LATSHAW.—In the Middle Fork church, Ind., June 8, 1892, of consumption, sister Hannah, wife of Bro. Jeremiah Latshaw, aged 35 years, 4 months and 8 days. She leaves a husband and two children. Funeral services by Eld. Isaac Billheimer, assisted by Amos A. Neher, from Rev. 14: 13.
JOHN E. METZGER.

GERKEY.—In the Thornapple church, Mich., Jan. 31, 1891, sister Catharine Gerkey, aged 77 years, 1 month and 27 days.

GERKEY.—In the same church, Feb. 10, 1892, Bro. Henry Gerkey, aged 73 years, 6 months and 4 days.

The subjects of the above notice were both born in Dauphin County, Pa. While young, they, with their parents, emigrated to Ohio. They were married Nov. 26, 1840. They united with the Brethren in their young days, and remained with the church of their choice to the end. The funeral services by the Brethren from Job 14: 14.
S. M. SMITH.

SHANER.—In the Montgomery church, Pa., May 13, 1891, sister Mary Shaner, wife of Bro. Jeremiah Shaner, aged 37 years, 9 months and several days. She leaves a companion and eight children. L. A. SPICHER.

KELLEY.—In the Sandy church, Columbiana Co., Ohio, May 13, 1892, sister Susan Kelley, wife of Bro. Alpheus Kelley, aged 33 years, 7 months and 10 days. She was a member of the Brethren church, and leaves a husband and a large family of children. Funeral services by S. B. Stuckey and the writer. A. SHIVELY.

CHIDESTER.—In the Round Mountain church, Ark., Feb. 5, 1892, of *La Grippe*, Oscar Chidester, aged 21 years and 2 months. He was a member of the Brethren church for over six years. Services by Bro. Wimer.

CHIDESTER.— In the same family, June 10, 1892, —— Chidester, father of the above, aged about 60 years. Funeral services by Bro. Wimer. DELIAN CHIDESTER.

KAGEN.—At Mt. Jackson, Va., sister Barbara Kagen, aged about 81 years. Her funeral services were conducted at the Cedar Grove church. Her remains were then laid to rest in the cemetery near by. She united with the Brethren in her thirteenth year, where she lived and died an exemplary member.

MILLER.—In the same place, June 7, 1892, sister Catharine Miller (*nee* Fox), in her forty-eighth year. Her funeral and burial services took place at Cedar Grove. She leaves eight children and a husband. She was a consistent member of the Brethren church. Both funerals conducted by the writer. B. W. Neff.

HARNISH.—In the Dorrance arm of the church, Russell Co., Kans., June 3, 1892, Bro. Frank H. Harnish, son of Bro. Jacob and sister Susan Harnish, aged 19 years, 5 months and 21 days. Over one year ago he got a swelling on his knee and the doctors amputated the limb. As soon as he got well enough, he was baptized, and went to school all winter. Then he took sick and died. Funeral services were conducted by Bro. John Hollinger and the writer.
JOHN NEWCOMER.

HAYNES.—In Grant County, Ind., Feb. 13, 1892, John Haynes, aged 72 years, 10 months and 29 days. He was born in Roanoke County, Va., March 14, 1819, and was married to Sophia Mattox, in Roanoke County, Va., May 24, 1837. He was a member of the Brethren church for about forty-three years, and lived an exemplary life. He was the father of thirteen children. Funeral services by the writer.
N. W. CRUMRINE.

KNICELY.—In the Cook's Creek church, Va., Elizabeth C. Knicely, aged 21 years, 6 months and 3 days. Funeral service by Rev. J. W. Click, of Bridgewater, from Job 14: 10. She leaves a husband, and two little boys too young to realize what they have lost. She was a member of the German Baptist church. ELIZABETH C. MOWBRAY.

BYERS.—In Montavi, Washington, May 17, 1892, Lydia A., wife of John C. Byers, and daughter of Samuel and Sabina Forney, aged 26 years, 3 months and 21 days.
SAMUEL FORNEY.

WEYBRIGHT.—In the Lower Stillwater church, Montgomery Co., Ohio, June 5, 1891, of typhoid fever, sister Nancy Weybright, wife of Jacob Weybright, deceased, aged 59 years, 4 months and 12 days. Her funeral services were held in the Fairview meeting-house and conducted by brethren Jesse Kinsey, Bookwalter and the writer.
JOHN H. BRUMBAUGH.

The Gospel Messenger

A Sad Occurrence.—When we came home from the Annual Meeting we were informed of the death of Miss Mary Willetts by drowning in a pool of water near by. She arose at one o'clock in the night, and threw herself into the water where it was about eight feet deep. It was supposed that she was somewhat demented. She was the daughter of J. F. Willetts, the national lecturer of the Farmer's Alliance. She leaves six sisters, two brothers and a father and mother to mourn her untimely death. Funeral services were conducted by the writer.—*David Kimmel, McLouth, Kans.*

Linganore, Md.—We held our quarterly council May 21, at the Pleasant Hill church, in the Bush Creek congregation. Elders E. W. Stoner, Solomon Stoner and E. Bruner were present with us. All business was disposed of in a Christian spirit. Bro. S. H. Utz was ordained to the eldership, and Bro. W. T. Miller was advanced to the second degree of the ministry. We also held a very pleasant and enjoyable Communion meeting June 1. The attendance was large and the behavior very good. Bro. Kolb, of Rocky Ridge, officiated. Bro. Bricker and son, brethren Joseph Utz and John Smith were the ministers from abroad.—*M. E. Ecker, June 13.*

North Webster, Ind.—The Tippecanoe church, Kosciusko Co., Ind., held a series of meetings from May 29 to June 2. Bro. J. V. Felthouse did the preaching. May 27 was our quarterly council. All business passed off harmoniously. June 2 we held our love-feast. The ministerial aid was ample, and all seemed to enjoy the meeting. The rainy weather was against us. The congregations were not as large as they would have been under more favorable circumstances, but we trust some good has been done. We thank the Lord and take courage.—*Daniel Rothenberger, June 11.*

Pioneer, Ohio.—The Communion meeting of the Silver Creek church occurred June 11, 1892. Ministers present from a distance were brethren John Felthouse, Jeremiah Gump and Henry Steckley. Bro. John Felthouse officiated. It was a feast long to be remembered by all present, on account of the outpouring of the Holy Spirit upon us. We were made to rejoice by seeing one dear soul come boldly out from the ranks of Satan, and present himself for Christian baptism. Oh, how do saints rejoice when sinners ask for admittance into the church militant here below! Angels in heaven also rejoice when sinners turn to God. On Sunday morning we assembled in a Sabbath-school capacity, and had the brethren talk to the children, which all appeared to appreciate very much. We hope it will find lodgment in well-cultivated hearts and bear good fruit.—*J. W. Keiser.*

McPherson, Kans.—I am now at work in the town of Maxwell, Iowa, and am expected to remain here till June 24; then to attend the Indian Creek love-feast, on the 25th. After that my course will be homeward, hoping to be at home by June 28. Rest, at least for a little while, seems to be an actual necessity. I will aim to work some in Kansas until about the first of September, when I hope to be able to make out a program for the fall and winter. Brethren should remember, however, that I can be at but one place at a time, and please do not hurry me from place to place too rapidly. If your application cannot be met at once, do not get discouraged. I expect to work when the Lord is ready to help, and not to leave a work, when it is well begun, and go somewhere else to begin again. We have had too much work lost that way already.—*A. Hutchison, June 13.*

Mansfield, Ill.—Our love-feast in the Blue Ridge church was held June 3. The ministering brethren that were with us were J. W. Metzger, Dan. Stoner, and —— Atchison. Bro. Stoner and Bro. Atchison stayed with us over Sunday and preached three interesting discourses. We enjoyed a feast of love indeed, and were made to rejoice to know that two were willing to join in with the Lord's children. Many precious souls are still out of the ark of safety, and we pray that they may soon see the beauty of the religion of Jesus Christ. We have a very large and interesting Sunday-school. It is prospering nicely and, we trust, will continue in that way.—*Bertha E. Barnhart, June 14.*

Purchase Line, Pa.—The brethren and sisters of the Manor congregation, Pa., met in church council June 4, preparatory to the love-feast. Everything passed off pleasantly, with one exception. Our love-feast, held June 9, was soul-cheering to all who are hungering and thirsting after righteousness. The order was much better than on former occasions. Brethren from abroad were elders Geo. Hanawalt and David Hildebrand. They labored faithfully for us. During their stay Bro. Joseph Holsopple was ordained to the eldership, and Bro John W. Fyock was called to the ministry. Amidst a great deal of solemnity and many tears, they were placed in their offices. God grant that they may be faithful, and that the church stand by them, and lift up their hands, for the strongest need help. May we bear one another's burdens and so fulfill the law of Christ. One brother returned to the fold after a long absence, and caused much rejoicing among God's children.—*Lizzie Fyock.*

Matrimonial.

"What therefore God hath joined together, let not man put asunder."

WILTFONG—YODER.—At the residence of the bride's parents, Mr. and Mrs. S. F. Yoder, June 1, 1892, by the undersigned, Mr. Hiram E. Wiltfong, of Monitor, McPherson Co., Kans., and Mrs. Emma Yoder, of Mitchell, Rice Co., Kans.

ISAAC S. BRUBAKER.

Fallen Asleep.

"Blessed are the dead which die in the Lord."

RITTER.—In the Tippecanoe church, Kosciusko Co., Ind., May 24, 1892, Tildia Ritter, wife of Samuel Ritter, aged 38 years, 8 months and 22 days. She leaves a husband and nine children. Funeral services from John 17: 3 to a large concourse of people.

CRIPE.—At the same place, June 1, 1892, sister Lidda Ann (Hamman) Cripe, wife of Noah Cripe, aged 61 years, 3 months and 27 days. Her husband and six children survive her. Funeral services from Isa. 38: 1.

DANIEL ROTHENBERGER.

LATSHAW.—In the Middle Fork church, Ind., June 8, 1892, of consumption, sister Hannah, wife of Bro. Jeremiah Latshaw, aged 35 years, 4 months and 8 days. She leaves a husband and two children. Funeral services by Eld. Isaac Billheimer, assisted by Amos A. Neher, from Rev. 14: 12.

JOHN E. METZGER.

GERKEY.—In the Thornapple church, Mich., Jan. 31, 1892, sister Catharine Gerkey, aged 77 years, 1 month and 27 days.

GERKEY.—In the same church, Feb. 10, 1892, Bro. Henry Gerkey, aged 73 years, 6 months and 4 days.

The subjects of the above notice were both born in Dauphin County, Pa. While young, they, with their parents, emigrated to Ohio. They were married Nov. 26, 1840. They united with the Brethren in their young days, and remained with the church of their choice to the end. The funeral services by the Brethren from Job 14: 14.

S. M. SMITH.

SHANER.—In the Montgomery church, Pa., May 13, 1892, sister Mary Shaner, wife of Bro. Jeremiah Shaner, aged 37 years, 9 months and several days. She leaves a companion and eight children.

L. A. SPICHER.

KELLEY.—In the Sandy church, Columbiana Co., Ohio, May 13, 1892, sister Susan Kelley, wife of Bro. Alpheus Kelley, aged 33 years, 7 months and 10 days. She was a member of the Brethren church, and leaves a husband and a large family of children. Funeral services by S. B. Stuckey and the writer.

A. SHIVELY.

CHIDESTER.—In the Round Mountain church, Ark., Feb. 5, 1892, of *La Grippe*, Oscar Chidester, aged 21 years and 2 months. He was a member of the Brethren church for over six years. Services by Bro. Wimer.

CHIDESTER.—In the same family, June 10, 1892, —— Chidester, father of the above, aged about 60 years. Funeral services by Bro. Wimer.

DELIAH CHIDESTER.

KAGEN.—At Mt. Jackson, Va., sister Barbara Kagen, aged about 81 years. Her funeral services were conducted at the Cedar Grove church. Her remains were then laid to rest in the cemetery near by. She united with the Brethren in her thirteenth year, where she lived and died an exemplary member.

MILLER.—In the same place, June 7, 1892, sister Catharine Miller (*nee* Fox), in her forty-eighth year. Her funeral and burial services took place at Cedar Grove. She leaves eight children and a husband. She was a consistent member of the Brethren church. Both funerals conducted by the writer.

B. W. NEFF.

HARNISH.—In the Dorrance arm of the church, Russell Co., Kans., June 3, 1892, Bro. Frank H. Harnish, son of Bro. Jacob and sister Susan Harnish, aged 19 years, 5 months and 21 days. Over one year ago he got a swelling on his knee and the doctors amputated the limb. As soon as he got well enough, he was baptized, and went to school all winter. Then he took sick and died. Funeral services were conducted by Bro. John Hollinger and the writer.

JOHN NEWCOMER.

HAYNES.—In Grant County, Ind., Feb. 13, 1892, John Haynes, aged 72 years, 10 months and 29 days. He was born in Roanoke County, Va., March 14, 1819, and was married to Sophia Mattox, in Roanoke County, Va., May 24, 1837. He was a member of the Brethren church for about forty-three years, and lived an exemplary life. He was the father of thirteen children. Funeral services by the writer.

N. W. CRUMBINE.

KNICELY.—In the Cook's Creek church, Va., Elizabeth C. Knicely, aged 21 years, 6 months and 3 days. Funeral service by Rev. J. W. Olick, of Bridgewater, from Job 14: 10. She leaves a husband, and two little boys too young to realize what they have lost. She was a member of the German Baptist church.

ELIZABETH C. MOWBRAY.

BYERS.—At Mondovi, Washington, May 17, 1892, Lydia A., wife of John C. Byers, and daughter of Samuel and Sabina Forney, aged 26 years, 3 months and 21 days.

SAMUEL FORNEY.

WEYBRIGHT.—In the Lower Stillwater church, Montgomery Co., Ohio, June 5, 1892, of typhoid fever, sister Nancy Weybright, wife of Jacob Weybright, deceased, aged 59 years, 4 months and 12 days. Her funeral services were held in the Fairview meeting-house and conducted by brethren Jesse Kinsey, Bookwalter and the writer.

JOHN H. BRUMBAUGH.

The Gospel Messenger

Is the recognized organ of the German Baptist or Brethren's church, and advocates the form of doctrine taught in the New Testament and pleads for a return to apostolic and primitive Christianity.

It recognizes the New Testament as the only infallible rule of faith and practice, and maintains that Faith toward God, Repentance from dead works, Regeneration of the heart and mind, baptism by Trine Immersion for remission of sins unto the reception of the Holy Ghost by the laying on of hands, are the means of adoption into the household of God,—the church militant.

It also maintains that Feet-washing, as taught in John 13, both by example and command of Jesus, should be observed in the church.

That the Lord's Supper, instituted by Christ and as universally observed by the apostles and the early Christians, is a full meal, and, in connection with the Communion, should be taken in the evening or after the close of the day.

That the Salutation of the Holy Kiss, or Kiss of Charity, is binding upon the followers of Christ.

That War and Retaliation are contrary to the spirit and self-denying principles of the religion of Jesus Christ.

That the principle of Plain Dressing and of Non-conformity to the world, as taught in the New Testament, should be observed by the followers of Christ.

That the Scriptural duty of Anointing the Sick with Oil, in the Name of the Lord, James 5: 14, is binding upon all Christians.

It also advocates the church's duty to support Missionary and Tract Work, thus giving to the Lord for the spread of the Gospel and for the conversion of sinners.

In short, it is a vindicator of all that Christ and the apostles have enjoined upon us, and aims, amid the conflicting theories and discords of modern Christendom, to point out ground that all must concede to be infallibly safe.

☞ The above principles of our Fraternity are set forth on our "Brethren's Envelopes." Use them! Price, 15 cents per package; 40 cents per hundred.

Announcements.

LOVE-FEASTS.

July 2, at 2 P. d., in the Salem church, Machray, Oregon.

Sept. 1, at 6 P. M., Sugar Creek church, Sangamon County, Ill., 2 miles east of Auburn, Ill.

Sept. 6, at 4 P. M., Indian Creek congregation, Fayet's Co., Pa. Series of meetings to commence Aug. 27.

Sept, 9, at 10 A. M., Monroe County church, Iowa.

Sept. 24, at 5 P. M., in La Porte church, La Porte, Ind. Trains will be met in the forenoon and early afternoon of the day of meeting.

Sept. 28, at 10 A. M., Spring Creek church, Kosciusko Co., Ind.

Oct. 1, at 2 P. M., Okaw church, Crawford Co., Kans.

Oct. 1, at 2 P. M., Pokagon church, Dowagiac, Cass Co., Mich.

Oct. 1, at 2 P. M., Logan church, near DeGraf, Ohio.

Oct. 1, Maple Grove church, Norton Co., Kans.

Oct. 7, at 2 P. M., Kaskaskia church, Fayette Co., Ill., ten miles south-west of Teutober City, Ill. Those coming by rail will be met at the above-named place by informing Granville Nevinger.

Oct. 8, Swan Creek congregation, Ohio, 3½ miles west of Delta, Ohio.

Nov. 1, at 5 P. M., Big Creek church, Richland Co., Ill., 3½ miles North-east of Parkersburg, Ill. Conveyances will be at the above place by informing J. M. Forney.

Announcements.

LOVE-FEASTS.

July 1, at 2 P. d., in the Salem church, Macleay, Oregon.

Sept. 1, at 4 P. M., Sugar Creek church, Sangamon County, Ill., a mile east of Auburn, Ill.

Sept. 6, at 4 P. M., Indian Creek congregation, Fayet's Co., Pa. Series of meetings to commence Aug. 27.

Sept. 9, at 10 A. M., Monroe County church, Iowa.

Sept. 24, at 5 P. M., in La Porte church, La Porte, Ind. Trains will be met in the forenoon and early afternoon of the day of meeting.

Sept. 28, at 10 A. M., Spring Creek church, Kosciusko Co., Ind.

Oct. 1, at 4 P. M., Osage church, Crawford Co., Kans.

Oct. 1, at 2 P. M., Pokagon church, Dowagiac, Cass Co., Mich.

Oct. 1, at 4 P. M., Logan church, near DeGraff, Ohio.

Oct. 1, Maple Grove church, Norton Co., Kans.

Oct. 7, at 2 P. M., Kaskaskia church, Fayette Co., Ill., ten miles south-west of Fa.her City, Ill. Those coming by rail will be met at the above-named place by informing Grenville Nevinger.

Oct. 8, Swan Creek congregation, Ohio, 2½ miles west of Deire, Ohio.

Nov. 5, at 2 P. M., Big Creek church, Richland Co., Ill., 3M miles North-east of Parkersburg, Ill. Conveyances will be at the above place by in orning J. M. Forney.

GOOD BOOKS FOR ALL.

Any book in the market furnished at publishers' lowest retail price by the Brethren's Publishing Company, Mt. Morris, Ill. *Special prices* given when books are purchased in quantities. When ordering books, not on our list, if possible give title, name of author, and address of publisher.

The Throne of David.—By J. H. Ingraham. Cloth, $1.50.

Josephus' Complete Works.—Large type, 1 vol. 8vo. Illustrated with many steel and wood engravings. Library sheep, $3.00.

The Doctrine of the Holy Spirit.—By James B Walker. Cloth, $1.25.

The New Testament History.—By Wm. Smith. Cloth, $1.25.

The Path of Life.—An interesting tract for everybody. Price, 10 cents per copy; 100 copies, $6.00.

Smith's Bible Dictionary.—Edited by Peloubet. Cloth, 12.00 leather, $3.00.

Ante-Nicene Christian Library.—A collection of all the works of the Fathers of the Christian Church prior to the Council of Nicæa. Edited by Rev. Alexander Roberts, D. D., and James Donaldson. LL. D. Twenty-four vols. 8vo. Per vol., $3.00.

Sacred Geography and Antiquities.—A practical, helpful work for Bible students, ministers and Sunday-school teachers. Price, $2.00.

The Origin and Growth of Religion.—Hibbert Lectures. By T. W. R. Davids. Cloth, 8vo, $2.50.

Bible Work, or Bible Reader's Commentary on the New Testament.—By J. G. Butler, Two vols. 8vo, $6.00.

Popular Commentary on the New Testament.—Edited by Philip Schaff. Four volumes. 8vo. Matthew, Mark and Luke $6.00. John and the Acts $6.00. Romans to Philemon $6.00. Hebrews to Revelation $6.00.

The Life and Epistles of the Apostle Paul.—By W. J. Conybeare. Cloth, $2.00.

The Prince of the House of David.—By J. H. Ingraham. Cloth, $1.50.

The Great Events of History.—By W.H. Collier. Cloth, $2.25.

Trine Immersion.—A vindication of the apostolic form of Christian baptism. By Eld. James Quinter. A most complete and reliable work on the subject. Price, cloth, single copy, $1.25; leather, $1.75.

The Old Testament History.—By William Smith. Cloth, $1.25.

Trine Method of Searching the Scriptures.—By Tal. bat Fasting. Paper, 15 cents.

Universalism Against Itself.—By Hall. One of the best works against Universalism. Price, $1.00.

Biblical Antiquities.—By John Nevin. Gives a concise account of Bible rites and customs; invaluable to all students of Bible subjects. Price, $1.50.

Quinter and McConnell Debate.—A debate on Trine Immersion, the Lord's Supper, and Feet-washing, between Eld. James Quinter (German Baptist) and Eld. N. A. McConnell (Christian) held at Dry Creek, Iowa, 1867. Price, $1.50.

Sabbatism.—By M. M. Eshelman. Treats the Sabbath question, showing that the first day of the week is the day for assembling in worship. Price, in cost a'11 copies, $6.00.

The Story of the Bible.—An excellent volume for old and young; will interest and instruct all those desiring a knowledge of the Scriptures. Price, $2.00.

Biblical Theology of the Old Testament—By R. F. Weidner. Cloth, $2.25.

The House We Live In.—By Daniel Vannian. It gives a concise account of the faith and practice of the Brethren. Price, 100 copies, 60 cents.

The Holy Land and the Bible—By Cunningham Geikie. Cloth, $2.75.

A Summary of Biblical Antiquities.—By John W. Nevin. Cloth, $1.50.

German and English Testaments—American Bible Society Edition. Price, 60 cents.

Early Days of Christianity.—By F. W. Farrar. Author's edition, cloth, 12mo, $1.25.

Every Day Religion.—By James Freeman Clark. Cloth, 12mo, $1.25.

Father's the World.—A concise history of the great religious systems of the world. Cloth, 8vo, $2.00.

Europe and Bible Lands.—By D. L. Miller. A book for the people,—most comprehensive, and thorough than many higher-priced works. Price, cloth, $1.50; leather, $2.00.

The Pillar of Fire—By J. H. Ingraham. Cloth, $1.50.

The Bible the Sunday-school Text-book.—By Alfred Holborn. Cloth, 75 cents.

Origin of Single Immersion.—By Eld. James Quinter. Price, 2 copies, 5 cents; 12 copies, 25 cents; 50 copies, $1.00.

Campbell and Owen Debate.—Contains a complete investigation of the evidences of Christianity. Price, $1.50.

Ecclesiastical History.—By Eusebius. Bohn Library. Cloth, $2.00.

Gospel Chimes.

BY WM. BEERY.

A new edition of this deservedly-popular Sunday-school song-book has just been issued.

Bro. Beery has had a large experience in Sunday-school work, and the book which we offer to the Brethren, and the public in general, evinces the exercise of talent as well as good judgment. The religious purity of the hymns, contributed by sister Beery, adds much to the excellence of the book.

Price per single copy, 25 cts.; per dozen, by mail, $2.50; by express, $2.50. Lots of more than a dozen must be sent by express.

BRETHREN'S PUBLISHING CO.,
Or Huntingdon, Pa.   Mt. Morris Ill.

Alone with God.

THIS manual of devotions, by J. H. Garrison, comprises a series of meditations with forms of prayer for private devotions, family worship and special occasions. It is one of the most useful, most needed, and best adapted books of the year, and therefore it is not strange that it is proving one of the most popular. In work of this kind its distinguished, gifted, pious and beloved author is at his best. This book is helpful to every minister, church official, and Sunday-school superintendent, as well as every private member of the church in all ages. It has models of prayer, suitable for the service of the prayer-meeting, while its suggestions, meditations and instructions are pre-eminently calculated to be of service in preparation for the solemn duties that rest upon the active members. Cloth, 75 cents; morocco, $1.25. Address this office.

CANCERS, TUMORS, ETC.

Successfully treated by Dr. G. N. Deister, of Waynesborough, Pa., where he has practiced for the last sixteen years. Dr. Deister is a graduate of the University of Maryland, at Baltimore City. References given and correspondence solicited. Address, Dr. G. W. Deister, Waynesborough, Pa.   9180

LIFE AND SERMONS
—OF—
ELD. JAMES QUINTER.

THIS is a neatly-printed and well-bound volume of 426 pages, containing a well-written biographical sketch of Eld. James Quinter and forty of his sermons.

The biographical part will be found quite interesting, instructive and impressive. No one can read an account of Bro. Quinter's life without feeling deeply and favorably impressed. The work shows how a poor orphan boy, by hard work, and faithfulness to his religious convictions, rose step by step, until he reached a field of usefulness and honor as broad as the Nation itself. Though dead, his good deeds and the impressive examples in piety, learning and simplicity will follow him for generations to come.

The Sermon Department contains many of his choice sermons, which will prove exceedingly interesting and profitable reading to all, and especially to our ministers and isolated members. We feel that this book will fill a long-felt want in our Brotherhood. Price, post-paid, $1.25.

BRETHREN'S PUBLISHING CO.,
Mt. Morris, Ill.

✦ESSAYS✦

"Study to show thyself approved unto God; a workman that needeth not be ashamed, rightly dividing the Word of Truth."

MY LIFE ON THE OCEAN WAVE, MY HOME ON THE ROLLING DEEP.

BY GEO. D. ZOLLERS.

Again on mental wings I soar
Where ocean billows rise and roar,
Where tempests wild in anger sweep,
And spend their fury on the deep.
Once more I merge in ocean life,
And view the elements of strife;
Once more the sailor's burdens bear,
And all his midnight perils share.
Those nights of darkness on the deep,
I ever shall in mem'ry keep,
To aid me on the sea of time,
Till moored within the port divine.
Of Zion's ship I am aboard;
Her Captain's name is Christ the Lord.
We hope to land on Canaan's shore,
Where foaming surges beat no more.
How many similar things there be,
On this and on the natural sea;
Which similar points I will unfold,
Ere yet my ocean story 's told.
We meet the weather foul and fair,
And calms and storms, as well are there;
By furious winds we, too, are driven,
While steering on our way to heaven.
Can I a solace thus afford,
To some poor drooping hearts aboard,
Till we've outlived this ocean strife
And reached the port of end'em life?
Shall veteran sailors on the sea
Encounter storms with bravery?
And will the Christian mariner sleep,
Where sin's destructive billows sweep?
O Christian, wake, no rest for thee!
Dark clouds are lowering o'er the sea;
The lightnings flash, the thunders roll,
Stretch every nerve to save thy soul!

"BELIEVEST THOU THIS?"—John 11: 26.

BY C. H. BALSBAUGH.

To a Despairing Sister:—

This interrogation is the pivot of salvation. The *this* has its thousandfold repetitions. "Believest thou this? and *this?* and THIS?" And so on *ad infinitum*. And the answer is equally manifold. "Said I not unto thee, that if thou wouldest *believe*, thou shouldest see the glory of God?" Verse 40. Believing is seeing. There is an inner beholding which is salvation, possible only to faith. The *seeing* of Matt. 5: 8, and the *being* of 1 John 4: 17, last clause, are identical.

You vehemently protest that you *believe* all that is contained in the Scriptures, and especially that "Jesus died for our sins," and is our "advocate with the Father," and yet you have no peace. This is a self-evident contradiction. It is not possible for any to "*believe* with the heart unto righteousness," and not have "the *peace of* God, which passeth all understanding." Rom. 10: 10, and Philpp. 4: 7. These things are as vitally connected as the Persons in the Holy Trinity. God *cannot be just* in withholding peace from a believer. Rom. 3: 26, and 1 John 1: 9.

Works and grace are *opposites*, as grounds of salvation. Grace and faith are *complements*. Rom. 3: 27, 28, and 4: 4, 5, 6. You believe without reserve, in the sense of mental acceptance or credence; but you manifestly do not believe at all in the Gospel sense, *viz.*, by personal appropriation of "all the fullness of God," treasured up in Jesus for the depraved, guilty soul.

I meet with many who believe the whole Word, according to the letter, and who scrupulously attend to religious duties, and who bind themselves conscientiously to various self-imposed obligations, but they confess they have no peace, and no certainty of their acceptance in all the beatitudes of life everlasting. This is the old Law under Christian forms, with all the bondage and weariness of the pre-christian dispensation. In Gal. 5: 1, we have the vernacular of the Holy Ghost economy. In John 3: 16, 18, and Rom. 5: 1, and 1 John 5: 4, we have the testimony of that apprehension of Jesus, which, in the essential nature of things, can be granted only to faith.

You have been many years in the church, and have been as faithful in the discharge of your duties as any sister I know, and yet you have never enjoyed the assurance that the righteousness of God in Christ has been imputed to you. Why? The Scripture gives emphatic answer, and your letters give abundant corroboration. "*Because* YOU SOUGHT IT NOT BY FAITH, *but by works*." Rom. 9: 32.

Works are a necessary and spontaneous expression of our reconciliation and loyalty; but grace rules them absolutely out of account in the sphere of imputed righteousness. "If righteousness came by the law," if salvation is by works, in the sense of restored relationship, "then Christ is dead in vain." Gal. 2: 21; Eph. 2: 8, 9. In Rom. 4: 16, we see the plummet of God sunk to the bottom of this ocean of mystery, so that the feeblest mind can see how grace comprehends the All of God, and how faith must be its perfect counterpart. Gaze on this truth till it fills the whole horizon of your soul.

Just as soon as you can believe that all the satisfaction that the Godman rendered to the Supreme Majesty of the universe, *is* FOR YOU, as distinctly, directly, and personally, as if you were the only sinner on the earth, that moment will you have "peace *with* God," and "the peace *of* God."

If you live a century, yes, a millennium, in the most perfect obedience that it is possible for the most devoted soul to offer, in expectation of abiding peace from that cause, you are invariably doomed to disappointment. Your works are all right, commanded by divine authority; but you give them a position in your mind in relation to the divine righteousness, which God assigns to the works of Christ alone. Hence, you have no peace, and cannot have.

There is enough in Christ to satisfy God; and "*all the fullness of the Godhead* in him," is for the BANKRUPT SINNER. The faith that accepts this, is the faith that "works out its own salvation with fear and trembling." The faith that accepts Jesus, is the faith that loves and obeys Jesus. The faith that knows the blessed mystery of Rom. 5: 1, 2, is the faith that never falters in "walking even as he also walked." 1 John 2: 6.

You think God is dreadful angry with you because "you are so miserable, and have no rest of soul day or night." The only thing God has against you, is that you do not believe his testimony concerning his Son, and are all the time looking for a reason of salvation in your imperfect endeavors, instead of his faultless obedience and spotless righteousness.

God has raised Jesus from the dead to convince heaven and earth and hell, that he has fulfilled every jot and tittle of the Eternal Law. Death could not hold him, because he met its stroke with a life that was superior to all claims of the last enemy. For *us* he died, but rose in his inherent right to all prerogatives of Deity. And that same Jesus sits to-day at the right of God as *your* Advocate.

"Believest thou this?" What is his plea there? As mighty and righteous as God himself can offer. See how the Holy Ghost states it: "Who shall lay any thing to the charge of God's elect? It is God that justifieth. Who is he that condemneth? It is Christ that died, yea rather, that is risen again, who is even at the right hand of God, who also maketh intercession for us." Rom. 8: 33, 34.

"Believest thou this?" There are no types on earth large enough to print this glorious concentrated Gospel according to St. Paul, in the capitals of the Upper World Record, and the blessed realization of faith. Let go self, bad self and good self, and determine to know nothing but Jesus Christ and him crucified. 1 Cor. 2: 2.

Can you not believe that 1 Pet. 1: 8 is for *you?* For whom do you suppose 1 Tim. 1: 15 was written, *if* not for *you?* Did Jesus exclude *you* from his world-wide "ALL" in Matt. 11: 28? Will you dare to say that John 6: 37, means everybody but that poor, wretched, self-condemned soul in Kansas? Were he to stand visibly before you this hour, and assure you with his own mouth that John 15: 13, *is meant* SPECIALLY FOR YOU, would you *believe* him? Is not his veracity unchangeable? Could his love be more real and his word more infallible to-day, than when he spoke these words in the night of his faithful, sin-bearing Gethsemane agony? "Come unto me; I will give you rest." Believe in me; I will give you everlasting life. "Behold, what manner of love." "Heaven is love, not that we loved God, but that he loved us, and sent his Son to be a propitiation for our sins." 1 John 4: 10.

"Believest thou this?" Earth nor hell can keep you from Philpp. 4: 4, if you believe that *you* are included in the "WHOSOEVER" of John 3: 15. Let not the devil rob you of your faith in the love that is deep enough to bleed and die for you on the accursed cross, mighty enough to conquer death and hell, and true enough to plead for you to this very moment.

Union Deposit, Pa.

THE FOUNDATION.

BY B. F. MASTERSON.

"Upon this rock I will build my church; and the gates of hell shall not prevail against it."—Matt. 16: 18.

We are most deeply impressed by viewing things in contrast. Thus the value of light is most evident, when contrasted with darkness; health, when contrasted with sickness; hope, when contrasted with despair.

We wish to place in direct contrast the things that will pass away, and the things that will remain. The prophet Isaiah placed in striking contrast the stability of the salvation of God, and the perishable things that are seen. "Lift up your eyes to the heavens, and look upon the earth beneath: for the heavens shall vanish away like smoke, and the earth shall wax old like a garment, and they that dwell therein shall die in like manner: but my salvation shall be forever, and my righteousness shall not be abolished." Isa. 51: 6.

Our attention is first called to the heavens. He that is versed in the science of astronomy can form some idea of the distances and magnitudes of the heavenly bodies, the vast spaces which surround them, and the rapidity of their motions. When the Psalmist made them the subject of contemplation, he was affected with the skill and the power manifested in their formation and said: "When I consider the heavens, the work of thy fingers, the moon and the stars, which thou hast ordained."

Great as the bulk of the earth seems to us, it is but small, when compared with the bulks of some of the other planets, but notwithstanding the amazing magnitude, they shall vanish like smoke.

Man cleaves tenaciously to this world, and claims it as his home, and could he remain to en-

❖ESSAYS❖

"Study to show thyself approved unto God; a workman that needeth not be ashamed, rightly dividing the Word of Truth."

MY LIFE ON THE OCEAN WAVE, MY HOME ON THE ROLLING DEEP.

BY GEO. D. ZOLLERS.

Again on mental wings I soar
Where ocean billows rise and roar,
Where tempests wild in anger sweep,
And spend their fury on the deep.
Once more I merge in ocean life,
And View the elements of strife;
Once more the sailor's burdens bear,
And all his midnight perils share.
Those nights of darkness on the deep,
I eVer shall in mem'ry keep,
To aid me on the sea of time,
Till moored within the port diVine.
Of Zion's ship I am aboard;
Her Captain's name is Christ the Lord.
We hope to land on Canaan's shore,
Where foaming surges beat no more.
How many similar things there be,
On this and on the natural sea;
Which similar points I will unfold,
Ere yet my ocean story 's told.
We meet the weather foul and fair,
And calms and storms, as well ara there;
By furious winds we, too, are driVen,
While steering on our way to heaVen.
Can I a solace thus afford,
To some poor drooping hearts aboard,
Till we'Ve outlived this ocean strife
And reached the port of end'ess life?
Shall Veteran sailors on the sea
Encounter storms with braVery?
And will the Christian mariner sleep,
Where sin's destructive billows sweep?
O Christian, wake, no rest for thee!
Dark clouds are lowering o'er the sea;
The lightnings flash, the thunders roll,
Stretch eVery nerVe to saVe thy soul!

"BELIEVEST THOU THIS?"—John 11: 26.

BY C. H. BALSBAUGH.

To a Despairing Sister:—

This interrogation is the pivot of salvation. The *this* has its thousandfold repetitions. "Believest thou this? and *this?* and THIS?" And so on *ad infinitum.* And the answer is equally manifold. "Said I not unto thee, that if thou wouldest *believe,* thou shouldest see the glory of God?" Verse 40. Believing is seeing. There is an inner beholding which is salvation, possible only to faith. The *seeing* of Matt 5: 8, and the *being* of 1 John 4: 17, last clause, are identical.

You vehemently protest that you *believe* all that is contained in the Scriptures, and especially that "Jesus died for our sins," and is our "advocate with the Father," and yet you have no peace. This is a self-eVident contradiction. It is not possible for any to "*believe* with the heart unto righteousness," and not have "the *peace of* God, which passeth all understanding." Rom. 10: 10, and Philpp. 4: 7. These things are as vitally connected as the Persons in the Holy Trinity. God *cannot be just* in withholding peace from a believer. Rom. 3: 26, and 1 John 1: 9.

Works and grace are *opposites*, as grounds of salvation. Grace and faith are *complements.* Rom. 3: 27, 28, and 4: 4, 5, 6. You believe without reserve, in the sense of mental acceptance or credence; but you manifestly do not believe at all in the Gospel sense, *viz.,* by personal appropriation of "all the fullness of God," treasured up in Jesus for the depraved, guilty soul.

I meet with many who believe the whole Word, according to the letter, and who scrupulously attend to religious duties, and who bind themselves conscientiously to various self-imposed obliga-

tions, but they confess they have no peace, and no certainty of their acceptance in all the beatitudes of life everlasting. This is the old Law under Christian forms, with all the bondage and weariness of the pre-christian dispensation. In Gal. 5: 1, we have the vernacular of the Holy Ghost economy. In John 3: 16, 18, and Rom. 5: 1, and 1 John 5: 4, we have the testimony of that apprehension of Jesus, which, in the essential nature of things, can be granted only to faith.

You have been many years in the church, and have been as faithful in the discharge of your duties as any sister I know, and yet you have never enjoyed the assurance that the righteousness of God in Christ has been imputed to you, Why? The Scripture gives emphatic answer, and your letters give abundant corroboration. "*Because* you sought it not by faith, *but by works.*" Rom. 9: 32.

Works are a necessary and spontaneous expression of our reconciliation and loyalty; but grace rules them absolutely out of account in the sphere of imputed righteousness. "If righteousness came by the law," if salvation is by works, in the sense of restored relationship, "then Christ is dead in vain." Gal. 2: 21; Eph. 2: 8, 9. In Rom. 4: 16, we see the plummet of God sunk to the bottom of this ocean of mystery, so that the feeblest mind can see how grace comprehends the All of God, and how faith must be its perfect counterpart. Gaze on this truth till it fills the whole horizon of your soul.

Just as soon as you can believe that all the satisfaction that the Godman rendered to the Supreme Majesty of the universe, *is* for you, as distinctly, directly, and personally, as if you were the only sinner on the earth, that moment will you have "peace *with* God," and "the *peace of* God."

If you live a century, yea, a millennium, in the most perfect obedience that it is possible for the most devoted soul to offer, in expectation of abiding peace from that cause, you are invariably doomed to disappointment. Your works are all right, commanded by divine authority; but you give them a position in your mind in relation to the divine righteousness, which God assigns to the works of Christ alone. Hence, you have no peace, and cannot have.

There is enough in Christ to satisfy God; and "*all the fullness of the Godhead in him,*" is for the BANKRUPT SINNER. The faith that accepts this, is the faith that "works out its own salvation with fear and trembling." The faith that accepts Jesus, is the faith that loves and obeys Jesus. The faith that knows the blessed mystery of Rom. 5: 1, 2, is the faith that never falters in "walking even as he also walked." 1 John 2: 6.

You think God is dreadful angry with you because "you are so miserable, and have no rest of soul day or night." The only thing God has against you, is that you do not believe his testimony concerning his Son, and are all the time looking for a reason of salvation in your imperfect endeavors, instead of his faultless obedience and spotless righteousness.

God has raised Jesus from the dead to convince heaven and earth and hell, that he has fulfilled every jot and tittle of the Eternal Law. Death could not hold him, because he met its stroke with a life that was superior to all claims of the last enemy. For us he died, but rose in his inherent right to all prerogatives of Deity. And that same Jesus sits to-day at the right of God as *your* Advocate.

"Believest thou this?" What is his plea there? As mighty and righteous as God himself can offer. Seé how the Holy Ghost states it: "Who shall lay any thing to the charge of God's elect? It is God that justifieth. Who is he that

condemneth? It is Christ that died, yea rather, that is risen again, who is even at the right hand of God, who also maketh intercession for us." Rom. 8: 33, 34.

"Believest thou this?" There are no types on earth large enough to print this glorious concentrated Gospel according to St. Paul, in the capitals of the Upper World Record, and the blessed realization of faith. Let go self, bad self and good self, and determine to know nothing but Jesus Christ and him crucified. 1 Cor. 2: 2.

Can you not believe that 1 Pet. 1: 8 is for you? For whom do you suppose 1 Tim. 1: 15 was written, if not for you? Did Jesus exclude you from his world-wide "ALL" in Matt. 11: 28? Will you dare to say that John 6: 37, means everybody but that poor, wretched, self-condemned soul in Kansas? Were he to stand visibly before you this hour, and assure you with his own mouth that John 15: 13, *is meant* SPECIALLY FOR YOU, would you *believe* him? Is not his veracity unchangeable? Could his love be more real and his word more infallible to-day, than when he spoke these words in the night of his faithful, sin-bearing Gethsemane agony? "Come unto me; I will give you rest." Believe in me; I will give you everlasting life. "Behold, what manner of love." "Heaven is love, not that we loved God, but that he loved us, and sent his Son to be a propitiation for our sins." 1 John 4: 10.

"Believest thou this?" Earth nor hell can keep you from Philpp. 4: 4, if you believe that *you* are included in the "WHOSOEVER" of John 3: 15. Let not the devil rob you of your faith in the love that is deep enough to bleed and die for you on the accursed cross, mighty enough to conquer death and hell, and true enough to plead for you to this very moment.

Union Deposit, Pa.

THE FOUNDATION.

BY R-T. MASTERSON.

"Upon this rock I will build my church; and the gates of hell shall not prevail against it."—Matt. 16: 18.

We are most deeply impressed by viewing things in contrast. Thus the value of light is most evident, when contrasted with darkness; health, when contrasted with sickness; hope, when contrasted with despair.

We wish to place in direct contrast the things that will pass away, and the things that will remain. The prophet Isaiah placed in striking contrast the stability of the salvation of God, and the perishable things that are seen. "Lift up your eyes to the heavens, and look upon the earth beneath: for the heavens shall vanish away like smoke, and the earth shall wax old like a garment, and they that dwell therein shall die in like manner: but my salvation shall be forever, and my righteousness shall not be abolished." Isa. 51: 6.

Our attention is first called to the heavens. He that is versed in the science of astronomy can form some idea of the distances and magnitudes of the heavenly bodies, the vast spaces which surround them, and the rapidity of their . motions. When the Psalmist made them the subject of contemplation, he was affected with the skill and the power manifested in their formation and said: "When I consider the heavens, the work of thy fingers, the moon and the stars, which thou hast ordained."

Great as the bulk of the earth seems to us, it is but small, when compared with the bulks of some of the other planets, but notwithstanding the amazing magnitude, they shall vanish like smoke.

Man cleaves tenaciously to this world, and claims it as his home, and could he remain to en-

is celebrated by our American people as the Day of Independence.

While the seventh day Sabbath represented to the Israelites deliverance from Egyptian bondage and the rest that God promised them in Canaan, so the Resurrection Day, or first day, represents to those, who live under the New Covenant, deliverance from sin and from death, and promises to us eternal rest and deliverance.

This change was necessary when the priesthood being changed there must of necessity also be a change of the law. Heb. 7: 12 Then, when our Savior made the one offering for sins and delivered himself and us from the power of death, the new order or covenant is in force, and the apostle could say, "We enter into the holiest by a new and living way." Heb. 10: 20.

The disciples observed this day from its beginning. (See John 20: 19-26; Acts 20: 7.)

Kearney, Nebr.

MEET ME THERE.

SELECTED BY D. F. STOUFFER.

On the happy golden shore,
Where the faithful part no more,
When the storms of life are o'er,
    Meet me there;
Where the night dissolves away,
Into pure and perfect day,
I am going home to stay,
    Meet me there.

CHORUS.

Meet me there, meet me there,
Where the tree of life is blooming,
    Meet me there;
When the storms of life are o'er,
On the happy golden shore,
Where the faithful part no more,
    Meet me there.

Here our fondest hopes are vain,
Dearest ties are rent in twain,
But in heaven no throb of pain,
    Meet me there;
By the river sparkling bright,
In the city of delight,
Where our faith is lost in sight,
    Meet me there.—CHO.

Where the harps of angels ring,
And the blest forever sing
In the city of our King,
    Meet me there;
Where in sweet communion blend,
Heart with heart and friend with friend,
In a world that ne'er shall end,
    Meet me there.—CHO.

Beaverdam, Md.

OUR SINGING.

BY DAVID W. CRIST.

"I will sing with the spirit, and I will sing with the understanding also."—1 Cor. 14: 15.

NOTICE, here, how emphatically Paul declares his manner of singing! Can we not learn a good lesson from this plain, emphatic declaration? Certainly, we should desire to sing as the inspired apostle did. If we only could get that "I will" of Paul into our cold hearts! I fear, brethren, that we are much too careless in our singing.

In our regular worship, when a minister rises to open the meeting, he says, "Let us sing as the apostle directs; with the spirit and with the understanding also." So familiar are these words that we turn a heedless ear to what is said; hence, our singing lacks both spirit and understanding. Even though we hear it repeated almost weekly, and it seems old and worn-out to us, it should, nevertheless, be a new, living, stirring admonition to us. Yet, though we are told often how to sing, how carelessly we do sing!

On Sabbath morning we assemble at our regular place of meeting for worship. A crowd has gathered and still more are coming, and, as the time for opening has not quite arrived, some one suggests that we sing a hymn. The hymn is selected, some brother leads off in tune, and all voices ring melodiously together in song, and perhaps the spirit and understanding are doing their proper work. But now there is a halt. Some one is coming, and before we are aware of it, all eyes are turning to see who it is. Our singing may continue, but what of the spirit and understanding? Ah! I fear they are largely gone.

Sometimes we sing without so much as thinking of what the language expresses. When we just consider for a moment, we can only exclaim, "How coldly, how spiritless, and how void of understanding we do sing!"

Once, while in a singing class, not as a scholar, but rather a visitor; I was very strikingly impressed with the teacher's directions on a certain chorus. The chorus was, "I love Jesus; yes I do, I do love Jesus," etc. The teacher told us to sing as though we loved Jesus with all our might. Could he have said anything more appropriate! Should we not have more such training in our singing-classes?

I believe, if we were instructed to have a little more spirit in our singing, and to understand more perfectly what we sing, instead of having so many lessons on pitch and length of tones, loudness or softness of tones, etc., that God would be more truly honored, praised and glorified by our singing.

Paul, who is the author of our text, says to his Ephesian brethren, "And be not drunk with wine, wherein is excess; but be filled with the Spirit; speaking to yourselves in psalms and hymns and spiritual songs, singing and making melody in your heart to the Lord." Eph. 5: 18, 19.

Brethren, do we make melody in our hearts to the Lord? If we do, the Lord's ear is ever open to hear it. If we would only make more melody in our hearts, instead of having our minds diverted by other things, I believe our singing would be more pleasing to God, and I am sure we would praise him much more truly and reverently.

When we sing, our words should be the outflow of the very inmost parts of the soul. If we really wish to imitate the apostle in singing, and if we would more acceptably worship God in song, we should, in all our practice,—whether in our classes, on our farms, in our shops, stores, or factories,—always have the spirit and the understanding. Let us make this our rule, and then, when we come to the house of the Lord, it will be easy and natural for us to pour out from our hearts, through the lips, our heartiest songs of praise to God.

Timberville, Va.

A WARNING TO THE CHURCH.

SELECTED BY ELIZA J. M'GAUGHAY.

EVEN as there is no *surer* way of putting out a fire than by pouring cold water upon it, so is there no *surer* way of quenching the Holy Spirit than by rejecting and despising his revelations and promptings through the Written Word to us. Yet it is a fact, strange indeed, yet constantly noticeable, that whilst the only religion which the world believes in at all, is a life of *complete consecration* to God, and whilst the world makes no allowance for the defects of those who profess to belong to Christ,—yet the advocacy of such a life often moves the scorn of the church.

Holiness is sneered at as the sentimental dream of weak-minded people, or it is the hobby of a few foolish persons who are always teaching impossible doctrines. My brother, even if the teacher be ever so ignorant and unlearned about a thousand things, is it not much more likely that the Blessed Spirit is in the voice which urges us to get nearer to God, and to be more like Him, than in the voice which bids us not to trouble about these things, and to be content as we are? God has called us, and is calling us unto holiness; (holiness means healthy, whole, holy). "He that despiseth, despiseth not man, but God."

Or, again, the Holy Spirit may set before us these further possibilities of grace, the richer things of the Gospel, and may at once begin to associate them with the failings of some unhappy professor, who was slack in his dealings; slovenly or conceited, or ill-tempered and unlovely; well, is not that the reason for which the world rejects the Gospel of God's grace? And we know that none can avoid the terrible responsibility of rejecting the Gospel by any such excuses. He that despiseth, extends his scorn to God. There is a flippant and scornful way in which many people turn from the subject, saying, "I don't believe in perfection." Well, if we believe in imperfection, depend upon it, according to our faith it shall be unto us.

But what is the degree of imperfection which the church tolerates? Here is a religious man who has misrepresented some matter, and you are indignant that a man who calls himself a Christian should do such a thing. Say! you don't believe in *perfection.* This man pretended to be a Christian, and he robbed you; dreadful, was it not? But why be angry; you don't believe in perfection. This man says he is a Christian, and he is proud and harsh, and you think that a man who is a member of the church ought to be very different. Why? You don't believe in perfection. Ah, but you *do,*—everybody does, when it applies to *other* people.

It is only a cloak and apology for our own failings, that we keep these convenient limits of our belief. And think you we can shape God's will, and measure his grace by our belief? There is but one way of safety for us; it is to give ourselves right up to the claims of God in Christ Jesus, and to the power of his grace.

"He that rejecteth;" "quench not the Spirit;" "despise not." These words set before us the figure of Esau, who despised his birthright, and for a mess of pottage, bartered the high-calling and his relationship to Christ. For a present and passing indulgence, he let go the golden future and all its glory and high privilege. This is the way in which the church most frequently and most terribly quenches the Spirit,—despising the calling of God. When these great purposes of Christ are heard,—and yet, as if not heard, they kindle no desire; there is no enthusiasm awakened; they are not met by any ambition to be Christ-like.

We profess to be Christ's soldiers and servants, purchased by his blood, and going onward into his presence; yet we do not make his service the great purpose of our lives; we do not surrender *everything* to it,—that place is kept for business or some pleasure. Is not this to despise our calling and quench the Spirit? Where society, gain, honor, position, pleasures, the most trivial, have more charm for us than the presence and good pleasure of our Savior Jesus Christ,—is not that to despise our birthright and to be like Esau of old?

Again, there is another terrible possibility of evil here, one of the very worst that can befall any one. To see these things of God, these revelations of his will concerning us; to have all the better self standing up within the soul and saying, "There, that is what you ought to be, and what, in your best moments, you longed to be,"—then some secret sins, or some silly fear, some

is celebrated by our American people as the Day of Independence.

While the seventh day Sabbath represented to the Israelites deliverance from Egyptian bondage and the rest that God promised them in Canaan, so the Resurrection Day, or first day, represents to those, who live under the New Covenant, deliverance from sin and from death, and promises to us eternal rest and deliverance.

This change was necessary when the priesthood being changed there must of necessity also be a change of the law. Heb. 7: 12 Then, when our Savior made the one offering for sins and delivered himself and us from the power of death, the new order or covenant is in force, and the apostle could say, "We enter into the holiest by a new and living way." Heb. 10: 20.

The disciples observed this day from its beginning. (See John 20: 19-26; Acts 20: 7.)
Kearney, Nebr.

MEET ME THERE.

SELECTED BY D. F. STOUFFER.

On the happy golden shore,
Where the faithful part no more,
When the storms of life are o'er,
　　Meet me there;
Where the night dissolves away,
Into pure and perfect day,
I am going home to stay,
　　Meet me there.

CHORUS.

Meet me there, meet me there,
Where the tree of life is blooming,
　　Meet me there;
When the storms of life are o'er,
On the happy golden shore,
Where the faithful part no more,
　　Meet me there.

Here our fondest hopes are vain,
Dearest ties are rent in twain,
But in heaven no throb of pain,
　　Meet me there;
By the river sparkling bright,
In the city of delight,
Where our faith is lost in sight,
　　Meet me there,—Cho.

Where the harps of angels ring,
And the blest forever sing
In the city of our King,
　　Meet me there;
Where in sweet communion blend,
Heart with heart and friend with friend,
In a world that ne'er shall end,
　　Meet me there,—Cho.

Beavoale, Md.

OUR SINGING.

BY DAVID W. CRIST.

"I will sing with the spirit, and I will sing with the understanding also."—1 Cor. 14: 15.

NOTICE, here, how emphatically Paul declares his manner of singing! Can we not learn a good lesson from this plain, emphatic declaration? Certainly, we should desire to sing as the inspired apostle did. If we only could get that "I will" of Paul into our cold hearts! I fear, brethren, that we are much too careless in our singing.

In our regular worship, when a minister rises to open the meeting, he says, "Let us sing as the apostle directs; with the spirit and with the understanding also." So familiar are these words that we turn a heedless ear to what is said; hence, our singing lacks both spirit and understanding. Even though we hear it repeated almost weekly, and it seems old and worn-out to us, it should, nevertheless, be a new, living, stirring admonition to us. Yet, though we are told often how to sing, how carelessly we do sing!

On Sabbath morning we assemble at our regular place of meeting for worship. A crowd has gathered and still more are coming, and, as the time for opening has not quite arrived, some one suggests that we sing a hymn. The hymn is selooked, some brother leads off in tune, and all voices ring melodiously together in song, and perhaps the spirit and understanding are doing their proper work. But now there is a halt. Some one is coming, and before we are aware of it, all eyes are turning to see who it is. Our singing may continue, but what of the spirit and understanding? Ah! I fear they are largely gone.

Sometimes we sing without so much as thinking of what the language expresses. When we just consider for a moment, we can only exclaim, "How coldly, how spiritless, and how void of understanding we do sing!"

Once, while in a singing class, not as a scholar, but rather a visitor; I was very strikingly impressed with the teacher's directions on a certain chorus. The chorus was, "I love Jesus; yes I do, I do love Jesus," etc. The teacher told us to sing as though we loved Jesus with all our might. Could he have said anything more appropriate? Should we not have more such training in our singing-classes?

I believe, if we were instructed to have a little more spirit in our singing, and to understand more perfectly what we sing, instead of having so many lessons on pitch and length of tones, loudness or softness of tones, etc., that God would be more truly honored, praised and glorified by our singing.

Paul, who is the author of our text, says to his Ephesian brethren, "And be not drunk with wine, wherein is excess; but be filled with the Spirit; speaking to yourselves in psalms and hymns and spiritual songs, singing and making melody in your heart to the Lord." Eph. 5: 18, 19.

Brethren, do we make melody in our hearts to the Lord? If we do, the Lord's ear is ever open to hear it. If we would only make more melody in our hearts, instead of having our minds diverted by other things, I believe our singing would be more pleasing to God, and I am sure we would praise him much more truly and reverently.

When we sing, our words should be the outflow of the very inmost parts of the soul. If we really wish to imitate the apostle in singing, and if we would more acceptably worship God in song, we should, in all our practice,—whether in our classes, on our farms, in our shops, stores, or factories,—always have the spirit and the understanding. Let us make this our rule, and then, when we come to the house of the Lord, it will be easy and natural for us to pour out from our hearts, through the lips, our heartiest songs of praise to God.
Timberville, Va.

A WARNING TO THE CHURCH.

SELECTED BY ELIZA J. M'GAUGHAY.

EVEN as there is no *surer* way of putting out a fire than by pouring cold water upon it, so is there no *surer* way of quenching the Holy Spirit than by rejecting and despising his revelations and promptings through the Written Word to us. Yet it is a fact, strange indeed, yet constantly noticeable, that whilst the only religion which the world believes in at all, is a life of *complete consecration* to God, and whilst the world makes no allowance for the defects of those who profess to belong to Christ,—yet the advocacy of such a life often moves the scorn of the church.

Holiness is sneered at as the sentimental dream of weak-minded people, or it is the hobby of a few foolish persons who are always teaching impossible doctrines. My brother, even if the teacher be ever so ignorant and unlearned about a thousand things, is it not much more likely that the Blessed Spirit is in the voice which urges us to get nearer to God, and to be more like Him, than in the voice which bids us not to trouble about these things, and to be content as we are? God has called us, and is calling us unto holiness; (holiness means healthy, whole, holy). "He that despiseth, despiseth not man, but God."

Or, again, the Holy Spirit may set before us these further possibilities of grace, the richer things of the Gospel, and may at once begin to associate them with the failings of some unhappy professor, who was slack in his dealings; slovenly or conceited, or ill-tempered and unlovely; well, is not that the reason for which the world rejects the Gospel of God's grace? And we know that none can avoid the terrible responsibility of rejecting the Gospel by any such excuses. He that despiseth, extends his scorn to God. There is a flippant and scornful way in which many people turn from the subject, saying, "I don't believe in perfection." Well, if we believe in imperfection, depend upon it, according to our faith it shall be unto us.

But what is the degree of imperfection which the church tolerates? Here is a religious man who has misrepresented some matter, and you are indignant that a man who calls himself a Christian should do such a thing. Say! you don't believe in *perfection*. This man pretended to be a Christian, and he robbed you; dreadful, was it not? But why be angry; you don't believe in perfection. This man says he is a Christian, and he is proud and harsh, and you think that a man who is a member of the church ought to be very different. Why? You don't believe in perfection. Ah, but you do,—everybody does, when it applies to *other* people.

It is only a cloak and apology for our own failings, that we keep these convenient limits of our belief. And think you we can shape God's will, and measure his grace by our belief? There is but one way of safety for us; it is to give ourselves right up to the claims of God in Christ Jesus, and to the power of his grace.

"He that rejecteth;" "quench not the Spirit;" "despise not." These words set before us the figure of Esau, who despised his birthright, and for a mess of pottage, bartered the high-calling and his relationship to Christ. For a present and passing indulgence, he let go the golden future and all its glory and high privilege. This is the way in which the church most frequently and most terribly quenches the Spirit,—despising the calling of God. When these great purposes of Christ are heard,—and yet, as if not heard, they kindle no desire; there is no enthusiasm awakened; they are not met by any ambition to be Christ-like.

We profess to be Christ's soldiers and servants, purchased by his blood, and going onward into his presence; yet we do not make his service the great purpose of our lives; we do not surrender *everything* to it,—that place is kept for business or some pleasure. Is not this to despise our calling and quench the Spirit? Where society, gain, honor, position, pleasures, the most trivial, have more charm for us than the presence and good pleasure of our Savior Jesus Christ,—is not that to despise our birthright and to be like Esau of old?

Again, there is another terrible possibility of evil here, one of the very worst that can befall any one. To see these things of God, these revelations of his will concerning us; to have all the setting up within the soul and saying, "There, that is what you ought to be, and what, in your best moments, you longed to be,"—then some secret sins, or some silly fear, some

Missionary and Tract Work Department.

"Upon the first day of the week, let every one of you lay by him in store as God hath prospered him, that there be no gatherings when I come."—1 Cor. 16: 2.

"Every man as he purposeth in his heart, so let him give. Not grudgingly or of necessity, for the Lord loveth a cheerful giver."—2 Cor. 9: 7.

HOW MUCH SHALL WE GIVE?

"Every man *according to his ability.*"   "Every *one as God hath prospered him.*"   "Every man, *according as he purposeth in his heart,* so let him give."   "For if there be first a willing mind, it is accepted *according to that a man hath,* and not according to that he hath not."—2 Cor. 8: 12.

Organization of Missionary Committee.

DANIEL VANIMAN, Foreman,   -   -   McPherson, Kans.
D. L. MILLER, Treasurer,   -   -   Mt. Morris, Ill.
GALEN B. ROYER, Secretary,   -   -   Mt. Morris, Ill.

Organization of Book and Tract Work.

S. W. HOOVER, Foreman,   -   -   -   Dayton, Ohio.
S. BOCK, Secretary and Treasurer,   -   -   Dayton, Ohio.

☞All donations intended for Missionary Work should be sent to GALEN B. ROYER, Mt. Morris, Ill.
☞All money for Tract Work should be sent to S. BOCK, Dayton, Ohio.

☞Money may be sent by Money Order, Registered Letter, or Drafts on New York or Chicago. Do not send personal checks, or drafts on interior towns, as it costs 25 cents to collect them.

☞Solicitors are requested to faithfully carry out the plan of Annual Meeting, that all our members be solicited to contribute at least twice a year for the Mission and Tract Work of the Church.

☞Notes for the Endowment Fund can be had by writing to the Secretary of either Work.

RELIGION OF FREEMASONRY AND SECRET SOCIETIES.

BY FRANCIS ATWOOD (ADAPTED).

[The writer we understand has been in thirteen degrees of Masonry, and ought to know what he is writing about.—ED.]

SECRET societies are one of the characteristics of the age in which we now live. In the directory of Chicago there are reported over one thousand lodges. How many churches? Only three hundred, counting everything that pretends to be religious. There are probably, take the United States over, four lodges to every church.

The Masons, in this country, number six hundred thousand, the Odd Fellows, nearly as many, Knights of Pythias, a quarter of a million, and scores of others of like nature, some claiming good objects, composed mostly of men, and all of them taking money by hundreds of thousands from the earnings of the people.

Certainly, secret societies are, in their magnitude, one of the forces of this world, affecting our lives for good or evil, and the public services they hold, the literature they publish, and the testimony of conscientious men, who joined them in ignorance, saw the folly and have come forth, bearing witness against them, afford guidance to any man who honestly desires to know the truth concerning them, and to act as Christian duty requires.

While the names, rituals, etc., of these many organizations differ, the principle is the same. You cannot condemn one and justify any other. Even a secret temperance order involves the essential principles of Freemasonry and one who is a faithful member of the one, cannot be a consistent enemy of the other.

Of course, nearly all have a semblance of religion and this fact may appear very pleasantly to some. Look closer, my brother. Take Freemasonry,—the model-mother of all the rest, and you find chaplains, priests, and many have an altar,—one has a baptismal service, where even infants of members are baptized, to grow up and into the lodge! The burial services intimate that he who belongs to the order and died, is sure of an eternity of happiness, because he was a member of the Mason's lodge and kept his dues paid up. An ordinary Mason will tell you that the

man who lives up to his Masonic obligations, is sure of heaven! "Masonry is a good enough religion for me!" Now turn to Mackey's Lexicon of Freemasonry, page 369, "All ceremonies of our order are prefaced and terminated by prayer because Masonry is a religious institution."

Daniel Sickes, a noted New York Mason, says, in his notes on the third degree, "We now find man complete in morality and intelligence, with a state of religion added to insure him the protection of the Deity, and to guard him against ever going astray. These three degrees thus form a perfect and harmonious whole, nor can we conceive that anything can be suggested more, which the soul of man requires."—*Freemason's Monitor, Pages 97, 98.*

We, who are more conversant with the order know that the Mason's Lodge is non-Christian, and even anti-Christian. No Christian has any business with the titles and regalia they use; the religion of the Lord Jesus Christ is humble, serving and aspires to be useful to others, while Masonry is proud, vain and loves display. The higher (?) in the order a man stands, the more vain titles, the more decorations, feathers and collars he is entitled to wear. What a heaven of a "Grand Lodge above" he must expect!

A man who unites with the church must profess sorrow for sin, love for God and fellow-man and a desire to live a holy life. A man may become a Mason, who takes the oath and pays his initiation fee. The prayerless, godless, profane, drunken members of a lodge do not break their covenant if they continue in their evil ways. In fact, they are proud of saying that pirates, savages, robbers and murderers are members of the lodge in good and regular standing.

Christians, Jews, Mohammedans, Buddhists, Parsees, Confucians and Pagans are eligible to Freemasonry. Turn to Mackey, page 402, "The religion of Freemasonry is pure theism, on which its different members may engraft their own peculiar opinions; but they dare not introduce them into the lodge or to connect their truth or falsehood with the truth of Masonry." You may believe in a God, but don't dare to connect Jesus Christ with the truth (?) of Freemasonry! Christian, have you a right to belong to such an organization? The ritual once contained a recognition of our Savior, but this interfered with the universal character of Freemasonry, and was stricken out. Chase's "Digest of Masonic Law," pages 207, 208, says, "The Jews, the Chinese, the Turks each reject either the Old or the New Testament or both, and yet we see no good reason why they should not become Masons. In fact, Blue Lodge Masonry has nothing whatever to do, with the Bible. It is not founded on the Bible. If it was, it would not be Masonry. It would be something else."

If it be true that Masonry is a religion, what religion is it? Not Christian certainly, and hence it is a false, idolatrous religion, and the hundreds of thousands of men who are forsaking the prayer-meeting, profaning the Sabbath, neglecting their Bibles, and attending to their lodges, are in danger of losing their souls (and "ye cannot serve two masters"). They are simply heathen worshipers in a Christian land.

Either the men of our nation must become separated from these secret, pagan religions, or our nation must cease to be Christian and, ceasing to be Christian, go down in utter darkness. If it is a duty to convert the heathen, they are at your doors,—neighbors and friends who are putting time and money to heathenism, which, in two years' time, would, if used aright, send the "Gospel to every creature."

Our land cannot exist half heathen and half Christian; and God save our young men to Chris-

tianity and sweep the last secret order from the face of the earth.

THE EVANGELIZATION OF THE WORLD.

BY LEAH REPLOGLE.

IN Matt. 28: 19, we have the parting words of Jesus, "Go ye into all the world, and preach the Gospel to every creature." This commission was given to the disciples of Christ. The Lord might have committed this work to angels; no doubt they would have been glad to accept it, but He was pleased to confer this honor upon his people, and they ought to accept it gratefully. With the promise of Christ's abiding presence, the disciples ought to be willing to go anywhere. He does not only go with his people, but he goes before them, and opens the way for them. "He openeth and no man shutteth."

Some of the open fields are ready for the harvest. In India, China, and Japan they have already a foretaste of the Bread of Life, and are loudly calling for more. Africa is beckoning for help; they say, "Come and give us what you have." They do not comprehend what it is, but they realize that it is something better than they have, and they feel the need of it. Shall we refuse to give it? A similar voice comes from the islands of the sea, and from many smaller divisions of the Continents. From every part of the globe we hear the "Macedonian cry." Oh, brethren and sisters, can we listen to the calls unmoved? We can not excuse ourselves by sending the Bible to them, for the Gospel is to be *preached* to every creature, the nations are to be *taught, so* wherever the Bible goes the disciples of Christ must go and preach it.

The Gospel must be preached to every creature; because Christ died for all. He purchased, with his own blood, the redemptive right of every creature. He has provided everything for the salvation of those people, and now he only asks us to go and tell them about it, that they may have a chance to accept it. If they reject it, they alone are responsible. The disciple is responsible only for the teaching; the result he may safely leave with God.

We are not commanded to bring the whole world to Christ, but we *are* commanded to offer Christ to the whole world. The command to go, is not only imperative, but it is urgent. "The time is at hand," "Behold I come quickly." This Gospel of the kingdom must first be preached among all nations, and then shall the end be." Jesus is here speaking of his coming to set up his millennial kingdom; but he expressly says, This Gospel must first be preached to the world. He wants his disciples to gather unto of all kingdoms, and nations, and tongues, and people, subjects for his kingdom. He must have representatives from all the governments upon the earth, for he is King of kings, and Lord of lords.

Oh, brethren and sisters, what are we doing in this great work? Again I say, the command is urgent, Jesus will soon come again; this work must be done before he comes. If we do not go to work, it will in some way be done by others, and we will have no part in it.

The next thought is, What can we do for missions? This is an important question. We can not all go into foreign countries to preach, but we all can do something. There are many reasons why those who *can* go, *should* go soon, but we can not speak of this now.

First, we must get into sympathy with Jesus; we must seek such a oneness with him, that his interests will be *our* interests. Then we will have his love, and his sympathy, and we will be impelled to seek the salvation of the heathen for his

Missionary and Tract Work Department.

"Upon the first day of the week, let every one of you lay by him in store, as God hath prospered him, that there be no gatherings when I come."—1 Cor. 16: 2.

"Every man as he purposeth in his heart, so let him give. Not grudgingly or of necessity, for the Lord loveth a cheerful giver."—2 Cor. 9: 7.

HOW MUCH SHALL WE GIVE?

"Every man *according to his ability.*" "Every one *as God hath prospered him.*" "Every man, *according as he purposeth in his heart,* so let him give." "For if there be first a willing mind, it is accepted *according to that a man hath,* and not according to that he hath not."—2 Cor. 8: 12.

Organization of Missionary Committee.

DANIEL VANIMAN, Foreman, · · · McPherson, Kans.
D. L. MILLER, Treasurer, · · · Mt. Morris, Ill.
GALEN B. ROYER, Secretary, · · · Mt. Morris, Ill.

Organization of Book and Tract Work.

S. W. HOOVER, Foreman, · · · Dayton, Ohio.
S. BOCK, Secretary and Treasurer, · · Dayton, Ohio.

☞ All donations intended for Missionary Work should be sent to GALEN B. ROYER, Mt. Morris, Ill.

☞ All money for Tract Work should be sent to S. BOCK, Dayton, Ohio.

☞ Money may be sent by Money Order, Registered Letter, or Drafts on New York or Chicago. Do not send personal checks, or drafts on interior towns, as it costs 25 cents to collect them.

☞ Solicitors are requested to faithfully carry out the plan of Annual Meeting, that all our members be solicited to contribute at least twice a year for the Mission and Tract Work of the Church.

☞ Notes for the Endowment Fund can be had by writing to the Secretary of either Work.

RELIGION OF FREEMASONRY AND SECRET SOCIETIES.

BY FRANCIS ATWOOD (ADAPTED).

[The writer we understand has been in thirteen degrees of Masonry, and ought to know what he is writing about.—ED.]

SECRET societies are one of the characteristics of the age in which we now live. In the directory of Chicago there are reported over one thousand lodges. How many churches? Only three hundred, counting everything that pretends to be religious. There are probably, take the United States over, four lodges to every church.

The Masons, in this country, number six hundred thousand, the Odd Fellows, nearly as many, Knights of Pythias, a quarter of a million, and scores of others of like nature, some claiming good objects, composed mostly of men, and all of them taking money by hundreds of thousands from the earnings of the people.

Certainly, secret societies are, in their magnitude, one of the forces of this world, affecting our lives for good or evil, and the public services they hold, the literature they publish, and the testimony of conscientious men, who joined them in ignorance, saw the folly and have come forth, bearing witness against them, afford guidance to any man who honestly desires to know the truth concerning them, and to act as Christian duty requires.

While the names, rituals, etc., of these many organizations differ, the principle is the same. You cannot condemn one and justify any other. Even a secret temperance order involves the essential principles of Freemasonry and one who is a faithful member of the one, cannot be a consistent enemy of the other.

Of course, nearly all have a semblance of religion and this fact may appear very pleasantly to some. Look closer, my brother. Take Freemasonry,—the model-mother of all the rest, and you find chaplains, priests, and many have an altar,—one has a baptismal service, where even infants of members are baptized, to grow up and into the lodge! The burial services intimate that he who belongs to the order and died, is sure of an eternity of happiness, because he was a member of the Mason's lodge and kept his dues paid up. An ordinary Mason will tell you that the man who lives up to his Masonic obligations, is sure of heaven! "Masonry is a good enough religion for me!" Now turn to Mackey's Lexicon of Freemasonry, page 369, "All ceremonies of our order are prefaced and terminated by prayer because Masonry is a religious institution."

Daniel Sickes, a noted New York Mason, says, in his notes on the third degree, "We now find man complete in morality and intelligence, with a state of religion added to insure him the protection of the Deity, and to guard him against ever going astray. These three degrees thus form a perfect and harmonious whole, nor can we conceive that anything can be suggested more, which the soul of man requires."—*Freemason's Monitor, Pages 97, 98.*

We, who are more conversant with the order *know* that the Mason's Lodge is non-Christian, and even anti-Christian. No Christian has any business with the titles and regalia they use; the religion of the Lord Jesus Christ is humble, serving and aspires to be useful to others, while Masonry is proud, vain and loves display. The higher (?) in the order a man stands, the more vain titles, the more decorations, feathers and collars he is entitled to wear. What a heaven of a "Grand Lodge above" he must expect!

A man who unites with the church must profess sorrow for sin, love for God and fellow-man and a desire to live a holy life. A man may become a Mason, who takes the oath and pays his initiation fee. The prayerless, godless, profane, drunken members of a lodge do not break their covenant if they continue in their evil ways. In fact, they are proud of saying that pirates, savages, robbers and murderers are members of the lodge in good and regular standing.

Christians, Jews, Mohammedans, Buddhists, Parsees, Confucians and Pagans are eligible to Freemasonry. Turn to Mackey, page 402, "The religion of Freemasonry is pure theism, on which its different members may engraft their own peculiar opinions; but they are not permitted to introduce them into the lodge or to connect their truth or falsehood with the truth of Masonry." You may believe in a God, but don't dare to connect Jesus Christ with the truth (?) of Freemasonry! Christian, have you a right to belong to such an organization? The ritual once contained a recognition of our Savior, but this interfered with the universal character of Freemasonry, and was stricken out. Chase's "Digest of Masonic Law," pages 207, 208, says, "The Jews, the Chinese, the Turks each reject either the Old or the New Testament or both, and yet we see no good reason why they should not become Masons. In fact, Blue Lodge Masonry has nothing whatever to do, with the Bible. It is not founded on the Bible. If it was, it would not be Masonry. It would be something else."

If it be true that Masonry is a religion, what religion is it? Not Christian certainly, and hence it is a false, idolatrous religion, and the hundreds of thousands of men who are forsaking the prayer-meeting, profaning the Sabbath, neglecting their Bibles, and attending to their lodges, are in danger of losing their souls (and "ye cannot serve two masters"). They are simply heathen worshipers in a Christian land.

Either the men of our nation must become separated from these proud, Pagan religions, or our nation must cease to be Christian and, ceasing to be Christian, go down in utter darkness. If it is a duty to convert the heathen, they are at your doors,—neighbors and friends who are putting time and money to heathenism, which, in two years' time, would, if used aright, send the "Gospel to every creature."

Our land cannot exist half heathen and half Christian; and God save our young men to Christianity and sweep the last secret order from the face of the earth.

THE EVANGELIZATION OF THE WORLD.

BY LEAH REPLOGLE.

IN Matt. 28: 19, we have the parting words of Jesus, "Go ye into all the world, and preach the Gospel to every creature." This commission was given to the disciples of Christ. The Lord might have committed this work to angels; no doubt they would have been glad to accept it, but He was pleased to confer this honor upon his people, and they ought to accept it gratefully.   with the promise of Christ's abiding presence, the disciples ought to be willing to go anywhere. He does not only go with his people, but he goes before them, and opens the way for them. "He openeth and no man shutteth."

Some of the open fields are ready for the harvest. In India, China, and Japan they have already a foretaste of the Bread of Life, and are loudly calling for more. Africa is beckoning for help; they say, "Come and give us what you have." They do not comprehend what it is, but they realize that it is something better than they have, and they feel the need of it. Shall we refuse to give it? A similar voice comes from the islands of the sea, and from many smaller divisions of the Continents. From every part of the globe we hear the "Macedonian cry." Oh, brethren and sisters, can we listen to the calls unmoved? We can not excuse ourselves by sending the Bible to them, for the Gospel is to be *preached* to every creature, the nations are to be *taught,* so wherever the Bible goes the disciples of Christ must go and preach it.

The Gospel must be preached to every creature; because Christ died for all. He purchased, with his own blood, the redemptive right of every creature. He has provided everything for the salvation of those people, and now he only asks us to go and tell them about it, that they may have a chance to accept it. If they reject it, they alone are responsible. The disciple is responsible only for the teaching; the result he may safely leave with God.

We are not commanded to bring the whole world to Christ, but we *are* commanded to offer Christ to the whole world. The command to go, is not only imperative, but it is urgent. "The time is at hand," "Behold I come quickly." This Gospel of the kingdom must first be preached among all nations, and then shall the end be." Jesus is here speaking of his coming to set up his millennial kingdom; but he expressly says, This Gospel must first be preached to all the world. He wants his disciples to gather out of all kingdoms, and nations and tongues, and people, subjects for his kingdom. He must have representatives from all the governments upon the earth, for he is King of kings, and Lord of lords.

Oh, brethren and sisters, what are we doing in this great work? Again I say, the command is urgent, Jesus will soon come again; this work must be done before he comes. If we do not go to work, it will in some way be done by others, and we will have no part in it.

The next thought is, What can we do for missions? This is an important question. We cannot all go into foreign countries to preach, but we cannot all stay at something. There are many reasons why those who *can* go, *should* go soon, but we can not speak of this now.

First, we must get into sympathy with Jesus; we must seek such a oneness with him, that his interests will be *our* interests. Then we will have his love, and his sympathy, and we will be impelled to seek the salvation of the heathen for his

The Gospel Messenger,

A Weekly at $1.50 Per Annum.

PUBLISHED BY

The Brethren's Publishing Co.

D. L. MILLER, ... Editor.
J. H. MOORE, ... Office Editor.
J. B. BRUMBAUGH,⎫
J. G. ROYER,   ⎬ . . . . Associate Editors.
JOSEPH AMICK, ... Business Manager.

ADVISORY COMMITTEE.
R. H. Miller, A. Hutchison, Daniel Hays.

☞Communications for publication should be legibly written with black ink on one side of the paper only. Do not attempt to interline, or to put on one page what ought to occupy two.

☞Anonymous communications will not be published.

☞Do not mix business with articles for publication. Keep your communications on separate sheets from all business.

☞Time is precious. We always have time to attend to business and to answer questions of importance, but please do not subject us to read less answering of letters.

☞The MESSENGER is mailed each week to all subscribers. If the address is correctly entered on our list, the paper must reach the person to whom it is addressed. If you do not get your paper, write us, giving particulars.

☞When changing your address, please give your former as well as your future address in full, so as to avoid delay and misunderstanding.

☞Always remit to the office from which you order your goods, no matter from where you receive them.

☞Do not send personal checks or drafts on interior banks, unless you send with them 25 cents each, to pay for collection.

☞Remittances should be made by Post-office Money Order, Drafts on New York, Philadelphia or Chicago, or Registered Letters, made payable and addressed to "Brethren's Publishing Co., Mount Morris, Ill.," or "Brethren's Publishing Co., Huntingdon, Pa."

☞Entered at the Post-office at Mount Morris, Ill., as second-class matter.

Mount Morris, Ill., ... July 5, 1892.

BRO. D. E. BRUBAKER is laboring among the churches in Wisconsin.

BRO. L. H. EBY thinks of spending the summer among the churches in Iowa.

BRO. M. M. SHERRICK is spending his vacation at Lanark, Ill., and will assist in the preaching of the Word.

BRO. JOHN J. HOOVER, of Carleton, Nebr., is for the present located at Rocky Ford, Colo., where he should be addressed.

AT the close of the feast at Solomon's Creek, Ind., five came out on the Lord's side and were received into the church by confession and baptism.

BRO. S. N. McCANN is continuing his sojourn with the brethren and sisters of Southern Ohio. He was at the feast at Covington on the 17th, and did very acceptable preaching.

ON his return from Cedar Rapids, Bro. J. S. Flory spent one Lord's Day with the Brethren in Chicago, and preached for them. From there he returned to his home at Lordsburg, Cal.

BRO. ROYER'S "Vacation Talks" No. 1, did not reach our desk in time to occupy space on the editorial page in this issue, but it will be found among the Correspondence. We have No. 2 on the book for next week.

LAST week Bro. Solomon Buckley was engaged in preaching the Word at the Coal Creek church, Ill. When last heard from, two had been received into the church by confession and baptism, with prospects of more to follow.

IT is truly encouraging to witness the interest our Brethren are taking in the children. This is seen in our Sunday-school work and also in the attempts to instruct the little ones at children's meetings. It is a department of work that well deserves our attention as well as the best talent we can command.

A SPECIAL District Meeting for Southern Indiana is called to meet in the Arcadia congregation, Hamilton County, Ind., Sept. 1, for the purpose of arranging for the Annual Meeting of 1893. See special notice in this issue.

THE sum of $91,000,000 is spent each year in the United States for admission to theaters alone. Many of the so-called Christian people help to swell that enormous sum. We hope that not a dollar for that purpose comes from our people.

IF people would just pause and think, that they have two ears and only one tongue, they might be induced to tell only half they hear, and it would probably be best if they would form the habit of telling only the best half. The other half will do more good if it is not told.

THE Baptist Year Book, for that religious body, reports 160,247 received into fellowship by baptism, during the year 1891, and 42,396 expelled, showing that more than one-fourth of those received did not remain faithful. This is probably the result of work in most churches generally.

THE Moravian church stands first in missionary enterprise of all denominations, and the United Presbyterians, of Scotland, second. The Brethren would probably stand next if each and every member would pay the little sum of fifty cents a year, recommended by our Conference.

WRITING from Sterling, Ill., under date of June 27, Bro. P. R. Keltner says: "One was added to our little band Sunday, June 26, by baptism; also one who had wandered away was reclaimed, causing us to rejoice and take courage. May we have grace and strength to do the work that lies before us."

BRO. W. B. STOVER, who spent several days with us just after the Annual Meeting, reports the outlook in Germantown, Pa., reasonably encouraging. There is quite an increase in the size of the congregation, and the interest is growing. We hope to see the efforts continued, and a strong congregation re-established at this place of sacred memory.

THERE is one feature connected with the feasts, reported by Bro. Daniel B. Arnold, in this issue, that we heartily commend, and that is the holding of a series of meetings prior to love-feasts. It not only prepares the members for the solemn occasion, but it is often the means of bringing sinners to Christ. We feel to recommend and encourage the practice.

BRO. GRANT MAHAN,—at one time an efficient employee of the MESSENGER office, but last year professor at the College in this place,—left New York, June 14, on the steamer Spree, for Germany. He is accompanied by his wife, and it is their intention to spend some time at the University of Leipsic, for the further study of languages. The best wishes of all follow our brother and sister, in their endeavors to gain knowledge.

THE Asiatic cholera is raging to an alarming extent in Persia, with probabilities of its spreading to other countries. Nothing seemingly is being done to stay its ravages. The Mohammedans believe the pestilence is sent to remind them of the neglect of their religious duties. They go through the streets, among the unburied bodies, bewailing their sins. The disease has already reached some of the Russian border towns, and now threatens the famine-stricken districts. If not soon checked, it will reach Europe without question, and may possibly pass to the United States.

BRO. D. B. GIBSON, after mentioning that the members in the vicinity of Milmine, Illinois, returned from Cedar Rapids in good health, says, "The last Annual Meeting was the best one we ever attended. Thank the Lord."

SOME one who wants to know whether there are any members at San Antonia or Weimar, Texas, fails to give either his name or address. We wish everybody would learn to give their name and address when writing to this office.

THE correspondents, who do not find in the MESSENGER their carefully-prepared description of the country they wish to bring before the public, will please bear in mind, that this is not a real estate journal. We aim to confine our matter to subjects of a religious interest as much as possible, believing that secular matters should be published in secular papers.

THE unprecedented, heavy rains of late, in this part of the State, have caused considerable damage to property in various ways. On account of high waters and wash-outs along railroads, we were cut off from direct communication with Chicago for several days, and our mails from all directions were greatly hindered. Many communications intended for this issue reach e l us too late, and must go over till next week. The irregularity of the mails have caused some delay in our Full Report. We hope, however, to be able to mail it very soon.

OUR politicians are much concerned about our coast defense. The best coast defense this, or any other nation, can have, is to be well shod with the preparation of the Gospel. In this age of civilization it is all the defense needed. The nations of Europe are crushing the very life out of their subjects, by the enormous expense required to keep up their great standing armies and coast defenses. Aside from a little national pride, and a good deal of selfishness, there are no reasons whatever, for such enormous burdens. We are glad other people, besides our own, are beginning to throw their influence on the side of universal peace, and labor to discountenance and discourage war on every hand.

WHEN one reads the daily reports of the great party conventions, where the delegates vie with each other in their loud and long cries and cheers in the interest of their respective candidates, he is reminded of the scene, mentioned in Acts 19: 34, when the people, "all with one voice about the space of two hours cried out, Great is Diana of the Ephesians." The longest time any of the convention parties has yet been able to keep up the noise has been about the space of twenty-five minutes. The Ephesians in this heathenish custom are still ahead of our political conventions. And by the way, what business has a humble Christian in such gatherings!

Is it Gospel for a mixed assembly, at Sunday-school, to close by all saying the Lord's prayer in concert, standing?

THERE are two postures in prayer. One is kneeling and the other is standing. Preference should be given to kneeling. It seems much more appropriate. Standing may be resorted to when kneeling is not practicable. At our love-feast we stand in prayer, because it is not convenient to kneel. As Sunday-schools are generally held where it is convenient to kneel, it is hardly advisable to train the children to stand during prayer. In this as well as other things, it will be found wise to train the children in the way they are expected to go, and when they get older they will not depart from it. Let all things be done to the edification of the church, and be careful that no offense is given.

The Gospel Messenger,

A Weekly at $1.50 Per Annum.

PUBLISHED BY

The Brethren's Publishing Co.

D. L. MILLER,	. . . . .	Editor.
J. H. MOORE,	. . . . .	Office Editor.
J. B. BRUMBAUGH,	}	Associate Editors.
J. G. ROYER,		
JOSEPH AMICK,	. . . .	Business Manager.

ADVISORY COMMITTEE:

R. H. Miller, A. Hutchison, Daniel Hays.

☞Communications for publication should be legibly written with black ink on one side of the paper only. Do not attempt to interline, or to put on one page what ought to occupy two.

☞Anonymous communications will not be published.

☞Do not mix business with articles for publication. Keep your communications on separate sheets from all business.

☞Time is precious. We always have time to attend to business and to answer questions of importance, but please do not subject us to needless answering of letters.

☞The MESSENGER is mailed each week to all subscribers. If the address is correctly entered on our list, the paper must reach the person to whom it is addressed. If you do not get your paper, write us, giving particulars.

☞When changing your address, please give your former as well as your future address in full, so as to avoid delay and misunderstanding.

☞Always remit to the office from which you order your goods, no matter from where you receive them.

☞Do not send personal checks or drafts on interior banks, unless you send with them 25 cents each, to pay for collection.

☞Remittances should be made by Post-office Money Order, Drafts on New York, Philadelphia or Chicago, or Registered Letters, made payable and addressed to "Brethren's Publishing Co., Mount Morris, Ill.," or "Brethren's Publishing Co., Huntingdon, Pa."

☞Entered at the Post-office at Mount Morris, Ill., as second-class matter.

Mount Morris, Ill., ... July 5, 1892.

BRO. D. E. BRUBAKER is laboring among the churches in Wisconsin.

BRO. L. H. EBY thinks of spending the summer among the churches in Iowa.

BRO. M. M. SHERRICK is spending his vacation at Lanark, Ill., and will assist in the preaching of the Word.

BRO. JOHN J. HOOVER, of Carleton, Nebr., is for the present located at Rocky Ford, Colo., where he should be addressed.

AT the close of the feast at Solomon's Creek, Ind., five came out on the Lord's side and were received into the church by confession and baptism.

BRO. S. N. McCANN is continuing his sojourn with the brethren and sisters of Southern Ohio. He was at the feast at Covington on the 17th, and did very acceptable preaching.

ON his return from Cedar Rapids, Bro. J. S. Flory spent one Lord's Day with the Brethren in Chicago, and preached for them. From there he returned to his home at Lordsburg, Cal.

BRO. ROYER'S "Vacation Talks" No. 1, did not reach our desk in time to occupy space on the editorial page in this issue, so it will be found among the Correspondence. We have No. 2 on the hook for next week.

LAST week Bro. Solomon Buckley was engaged in preaching the Word at the Coal Creek church, Ill. When last heard from, two had been received into the church by confession and baptism, with prospects of more to follow.

IT is truly encouraging to witness the interest our Brethren are taking in the children. This is seen in our Sunday-school work and also in the attempts to instruct the little ones at children's meetings. It is a department of work that well deserves our attention as well as the best talent we can command.

A SPECIAL District Meeting for Southern Indiana is called to meet in the Arcadia congregation, Hamilton County, Ind., Sept. 1, for the purpose of arranging for the Annual Meeting of 1893. See special notice in this issue.

THE sum of $91,000,000 is spent each year in the United States for admission to theaters alone. Many of the so-called Christian people help to swell that enormous sum. We hope that not a dollar for that purpose comes from our people.

IF people would just pause and think, that they have two ears and only one tongue, they might be induced to tell only half they hear, and it would probably be best if they would form the habit of telling only the best half. The other half will do more good if it is not told.

THE Baptist Year Book, for that religious body, reports 160,247 received into fellowship by baptism, during the year 1891, and 42,896 expelled, showing that more than one-fourth of those received did not remain faithful. This is probably the result of work in most churches generally.

THE Moravian church stands first in missionary enterprise of all denominations, and the United Presbyterians, of Scotland, second. The Brethren would probably stand next if each and every member would pay the little sum of fifty cents a year, recommended by our Conference.

WRITING from Sterling, Ill., under date of June 27, Bro. P. R. Keltner says: "One was added to our little band Sunday, June 26, by baptism; also one who had wandered away was reclaimed, causing us to rejoice and take courage. May we have grace and strength to do the work that lies before us."

BRO. W. B. STOVER, who spent several days with us just after the Annual Meeting, reports the outlook in Germantown, Pa., reasonably encouraging. There is quite an increase in the size of the congregation, and the interest is growing. We hope to see the efforts continued, and a strong congregation re-established at this place of sacred memory.

THERE is one feature connected with the feasts, reported by Bro. Daniel B. Arnold, in this issue, that we heartily commend, and that is the holding of a series of meetings prior to love-feasts. It not only prepares the members for the solemn occasion, but it is often the means of bringing sinners to Christ. We feel to recommend and encourage the practice.

BRO. GRANT MAHAN,—at one time an efficient employee of the MESSENGER office, but last year professor at the College in this place,—left New York, June 14, on the steamer Spree, for Germany. He is accompanied by his wife, and it is their intention to spend some time at the University of Leipsic, for the further study of languages. The best wishes of all follow our brother and sister, in their endeavors to gain knowledge.

THE Asiatic cholera is raging to an alarming extent in Persia, with probabilities of its spreading to other countries. Nothing seemingly is being done to stay its ravages. The Mohammedans believe the pestilence is sent to remind them of the neglect of their religious duties. They go through the streets, among the unburied bodies, bewailing their sins. The disease has already reached some of the Russian border towns, and now threatens the famine-stricken districts. If not soon checked, it will reach Europe without question, and may possibly pass to the United States.

BRO. D. B. GIBSON, after mentioning that the members in the vicinity of Milmine, Illinois, returned from Cedar Rapids in good health, says, "The last Annual Meeting was the best one we ever attended. Thank the Lord."

SOME one who wants to know whether there are any members at San Antonio or Weimar, Texas, fails to give either his name or address. We wish everybody would learn to give their name and address when writing to this office.

THE correspondents, who do not find in the MESSENGER their carefully-prepared description of the country they wish to bring before the public, will please bear in mind, that this is not a real estate journal. We aim to confine our matter to subjects of a religious interest as much as possible, believing that secular matters should be published in secular papers.

THE unprecedented, heavy rains of late, in this part of the State, have caused considerable damage to property in various ways. On account of high waters and wash-outs along railroads, we were cut off from direct communication with Chicago for several days, and our mails from all directions were greatly hindered. Many communications intended for this issue reached us too late, and must go over till next week. The irregularity of the mails have caused some delay in our Full Report. We hope, however, to be able to mail it very soon.

OUR politicians are much concerned about our coast defense. The best coast defense this, or any other nation, can have, is to be well shod with the preparation of the Gospel. In this age of civilization it is all the defense needed. The nations of Europe are crushing the very life out of their subjects, by the enormous expense required to keep up their great standing armies and coast defenses. Aside from a little national pride, and a good deal of selfishness, there are no reasons whatever, for such enormous burdens. We are glad other people, besides our own, are beginning to throw their influence on the side of universal peace, and labor to discountenance and discourage war on every hand.

WHEN one reads the daily reports of the great party conventions, where the delegates vie with each other in their loud and long cries and cheers in the interest of their respective candidates, he is reminded of the scene, mentioned in Acts 19: 34, when the people, "all with one voice about the space of two hours cried-out, Great is Diana of the Ephesians." The longest time any of the convention parties has yet been able to keep up the noise has been about the space of twenty-five minutes. The Ephesians in this heathenish custom are still ahead of our political conventions. And by the way, what business has a humble Christian in such gatherings!

Is it Gospel for a mixed assembly, at Sunday-school, to close by all saying the Lord's prayer in concert, standing?

THERE are two postures in prayer. One is kneeling and the other is standing. Preference should be given to kneeling. It seems much more appropriate. Standing may be resorted to when kneeling is not practicable. At our love-feast we stand in prayer, because it is not convenient to kneel. As Sunday-schools are generally held where it is convenient to kneel, it is hardly advisable to train the children to stand during prayer. In this as well as other things, it will be found wise to train the children in the way they are expected to go, and when they get older they will not depart from it. Let all things be done to the edification of the church, and be careful that no offense is given.

MORALS OF DRESS.

The editor of the *Christian Standard* knows how to handle a very important question without gloves. He says:

However we may think of it, dress and manners are not simply matters of taste. They are matters of morals and religion, and Christians ought not to accept the rules and regulations set by leaders of fashion, without regard to these higher considerations. To give allegiance to arbitrary laws in these things, which are decreed by people whose lives are often shockingly immoral, is the most slavish sort of conformity to this world. The adornment of a meek and quiet spirit is of great price in the sight of God, but how many "girls of the period," even of those who are members of the church, are consciously striving to put on this adornment?

How many Christian mothers give as much thought to such adorning of their daughters as they do to "the putting on of apparel" in the latest and most stylish modes. Society at present does not foster the precious "meek and quiet spirit." It is ostentatious and boisterous. Young men run to legs and lungs more than formerly, and young women seem to strive to be mannish. If you will study the matter in places of public resort you will see the truth of this. Not many days since we were in a post-office where some forty persons were waiting for the mail to be distributed. Pretty much all sorts of people were represented, but there was one well-dressed young lady who *would* monopolize all attention. In a loud and metallic voice she was constantly pouring out crude remarks and lame witicisms, to the admiration of her set and the annoyance of the others.

On another recent occasion, in a place equally public, half a dozen misses, whose ages would probably have averaged the supposedly unlucky thirteen, were as garrulous, noisy and generally obstreperous as a half-drunken saloon crowd. And the conversation, or, rather, the chatter and clatter, was made up of bicycle and baseball talk, liberally interlarded with slang. They were all, we believe, daughters of Christian parents (one of them the daughter of a preacher) and several of them members of the church. We may be over-squeamish about these things, but it seemed to us that there was not much trace of the meek and quiet spirit,—the delicious maidenly reserve and modesty,—which is the chief ornament in God's estimation. Are we striving to bring up our children in the nurture and admonition of the Lord? Fathers and mothers,—fathers especially, and mothers most especially,—think of this.

THE HOLY KISS.

An outsider asked me why we did not greet one another with a holy kiss. I was unable to give a satisfactory answer. He said it was a straight command. See Rom. 16: 16; 1 Cor. 16: 20; 2 Cor. 13: 12; 1 Thess. 5: 26, and 1 Pet. 5: 14 says: Great one another with a kiss of charity. Will you be kind enough to give some light to an inquirer? W. H. Hickox.

In a time and country in which it was customary to greet friends with a kiss, it was quite natural that it should be enjoined that it should be a holy kiss, a kiss of true, brotherly love, and not a mere formality. But kissing itself as a form of greeting is hardly enjoined as a Christian institution. It was a custom to greet in this way, and while the custom prevailed it was to be sanctified as an expression of true Christian regard. But this will not be satisfactory to those who regard it as a Christian rite. "Let every one be fully persuaded in his own mind."—*Christian Standard*.

Certainly, every one should be fully persuaded in his own mind to obey from the heart the form of doctrine delivered by Paul and Peter to the saints. If he does this, he will most assuredly obey this as well as other commands.

UNFERMENTED WINE.—HOW TO MAKE IT.

Select good, ripe grapes. After separating them from the stems, wash clean, then press the juice out any way you please. Strain the juice, heat and can it the same as fruit. Take the same care of it that you do of canned fruit. It will keep for years. We use glass fruit cans. They are cheap and easily managed.

Another way is to first heat the grapes before pressing. Then heat the juice and can the same as suggested above. This is the way we make it for family use, for we find it to be an excellent beverage in the family, and it is no more intoxicating than milk. It should be used within a day or two after the can is opened, especially if the weather is not very cool, otherwise it will spoil the same as canned fruit. Any one, who knows how to can and care for canned fruit, can make and care for unfermented wine. We believe that it is the only wine that should be encouraged for our Communion services. It is not only the "fruit of the vine," commended by the Savior, but it is absolutely harmless, and will neither produce nor lead to drunkenness.

With a clear conscience we can recommend it to others for the "stomach's sake," and it is the only wine we would recommend for that purpose. We also have our grave doubts whether Paul would recommend any other to Timothy. You will find it a good wine for weddings. In fact it is the only wine we would allow at a wedding we had control of. This must have been the class of wine made by Jesus at the wedding in Cana of Galilee. He certainly had the power to make it, and he lost no opportunity of doing good when there was an occasion for it. J. H. M.

CORRESPONDENCE.

"Write what thou seest, and send it unto the churches."

☞ Church News solicited for this Department. If you have had a good meeting, send a report of it, so that others may rejoice with you. In writing give name of church, County and State. Be brief. Notes of Travel should be as short as possible. Land Advertisements are not solicited for this Department. We have an advertising page, and, if necessary, will issue supplements.

Refreshing Seasons.

We have had a glorious season of Communions again. The first one was held at the Pine church May. 7 and 8. Eld. Jeremiah Thomas, of West Virginia labored for us very acceptably. It was truly a feast of pleasure to the people of God. Two were baptized in this congregation one week after the feast.

Next came the feast at Knobley, May 21 and 22. Bro. Jonas Fike, of Eglon, West Virginia, did most of the preaching here and also held a series of meetings at this place during the week before the feast. As an immediate result one was baptized and the church much encouraged. Bro. Jonas is a faithful expounder of the Gospel, "rightly dividing the Word of Truth."

Next was the feast in our home church at Beaver Run, June 4 and 5. Eld. I. W. Abernathy, of Western Maryland, held a series of meetings for us during the week prior to the feast. Although Bro. Isaac was suffering from the effects of a cold, yet he labored earnestly and zealously, and the church manifested a commendable interest. Nine were baptized, and one reclaimed. This was one of the most pleasant feasts ever held at this place. Immediately afterwards, Bro. Abernathy was taken down to the Tearcoat congregation, to hold a series of meetings for them prior to their feast. Here the rainy weather interfered considerably; still meetings were held during the week, and as a result, one was baptized, and one reclaimed. The feast at this place, June 11 and 12, was also very enjoyable. Bro. Abernathy then returned home and our best wishes go with him. We feel impressed with the fact that our series of meetings are generally too short. Especially was this the case at Beaver Run. There was also a love-feast held June 11 and 12, in a new meeting-house, recently built in the west end of our congregation. Bro. Z. Annon, had promised to attend this feast and preach for us, but from some cause he did not come, so home talent from surrounding churches was utilized. This feast will be long remembered, as it was the first ever held at this place. One was recently baptized here.
Daniel B. Arnold.
Burlington, W. Va., June 16.

Christianity Begets Honesty.

There was a time in the history of the church, when honesty reigned in her midst. It is said that during the reign of King Alfred the Great, pocket-books, laid in the streets, would be perfectly safe. I have heard father say that, in his young days, a note among neighbors was a rare thing, but to-day we cannot trust our brother in the church without a note and good security. These things ought not so to be. Where true Christianity exists, honesty will prevail. When salvation came to Zaccheus, he said, "If I have taken anything from any man by false accusation I restore it to him fourfold."

This was true repentance-under the Mosaic Law. Jesus said unto him, "This day is salvation come to this house." If we, then, have the love of God reigning in our hearts, we will surely deal with our fellow-men on a square and equitable basis, for Christ says, "Whatsoever ye would that men should do to you, do ye even so to them."

Man, as a general thing, would like to have every cent that is due him. Many Christian professors, sad to say, can only be compelled by the laws of the land, to pay their honest dues. Christ says, "A good tree cannot bring forth evil fruit." Again he says, "He that climbeth up any other way is a thief and a robber."

Real honesty is one of the main principles of true Christianity, and yet there are many who profess to be Christians, who must be bound by the law before they will pay what they owe. True Christianity will prompt a man to pay the last cent that he owes without note or bond, and I think that is the only Christianity that will ever enter through the gates into heaven. Remember Ananias and Sapphira who kept back part of the price of their possession. But Peter said, "Ananias, why hath Satan filled thine heart to lie to the Holy Ghost and to keep back part of the price of the land? Thou hast not lied unto men, but unto God." The man that professes to be a Christian and will not pay his honest debts, is standing on the same ground that Ananias and Sapphira occupied; he is pretending to have what he has not. Such are professors, and not possessors. "Clouds they are without water, carried about of winds; trees whose fruit withereth, without fruit, twice dead, plucked up by the roots; raging waves of the sea, foaming out their shame; wandering stars, to whom is reserved the blackness forever." Jude 12, 13. J. W. Harold.
Higgin, Nebr.

MORALS OF DRESS.

THE editor of the *Christian Standard* knows how to handle a very important question without gloves. He says:

However we may think of it, dress and manners are not simply matters of taste. They are matters of morals and religion, and Christians ought not to accept the rules and regulations set by leaders of fashion, without regard to these higher considerations. To give allegiance to arbitrary laws in these things, which are decreed by people whose lives are often shockingly immoral, is the most slavish sort of conformity to this world. The adornment of a meek and quiet spirit is of great price in the sight of God, but how many "girls of the period," even of those who are members of the church, are consciously striving to put on this adornment?

How many Christian mothers give as much thought to such adorning of their daughters as they do to "the putting on of apparel" in the latest and most stylish modes. Society at present does not foster the precious "meek and quiet spirit." It is ostentatious and boisterous. Young men run to legs and lungs more than formerly, and young women seem to strive to be mannish. If you will study the matter in places of public resort you will see the truth of this. Not many days since we were in a post-office where some forty persons were waiting for the mail to be distributed. Pretty much all sorts of people were represented, but there was one well-dressed young lady who *would* monopolize all attention. In a loud and metallic voice she was constantly pouring out crude remarks and lame witticisms, to the admiration of her set and the annoyance of the others.

On another recent occasion, in a place equally public, half a dozen misses, whose ages would probably have averaged the supposedly unlucky thirteen, were as garrulous, noisy and generally obstreperous as a half-drunken saloon crowd. And the conversation, or, rather, the chatter and clatter, was made up of bicycle and baseball talk, liberally interlarded with slang. They were all, we believe, daughters of Christian parents (one of them the daughter of a preacher) and several of them members of the church. We may be over-squeamish about these things, but it seemed to us that there was not much trace of the meek and quiet spirit,—the delicious maidenly reserve and modesty,—which is the chief ornament in God's estimation. Are we striving to bring up our children in the nurture and admonition of the Lord? Fathers and mothers,—fathers especially, and mothers most especially,—think of this.

THE HOLY KISS.

An outsider asked me why we did not greet one another with a holy kiss. I was unable to give a satisfactory answer. He said it was a straight command. See Rom. 16: 16; 1 Cor. . 16: 20; 2 Cor. 13: 12; 1 Thess. 5: 26, and 1 Pet. 5: 14 says, Greet one another with a kiss of charity. Will you be kind enough to give some light to an inquirer? W. H. HICKOX.

IN a time and country in which it was customary to greet friends with a kiss, it was quite natural that it should be enjoined that it should be a holy kiss, a kiss of true, brotherly love, and not a mere formality. But kissing itself as a form of greeting is hardly enjoined as a Christian institution. It was a custom to greet in this way, and while the custom prevailed it was to be sanctified as an expression of true Christian regard. But this will not be satisfactory to those who regard

it as a Christian rite. "Let every one be fully persuaded in his own mind."—*Christian Standard.*

Certainly, every one should be fully persuaded in his own mind to obey from the heart the form of doctrine delivered by Paul and Peter to the saints. If he does this, he will most assuredly obey this as well as other commands.

UNFERMENTED WINE,—HOW TO MAKE IT.

SELECT good, ripe grapes. After separating them from the stems, wash clean, then press the juice out any way you please. Strain the juice, heat and can it the same as fruit. Take the same care of it that you do of canned fruit. It will keep for years. We use glass fruit cans. They are cheap and easily managed.

Another way is to first heat the grapes before pressing. Then heat the juice and can the same as suggested above. This is the way we make it for family use, for we find it to be an excellent beverage in the family, and it is no more intoxicating than milk. It should be used within a day or two after the can is opened, especially if the weather is not very cool, otherwise it will spoil the same as canned fruit. Any one, who knows how to can and care for canned fruit, can make and care for unfermented wine. We believe that it is the only wine that should be encouraged for our Communion services. It is not only the "fruit of the vine," commended by the Savior, but it is absolutely harmless, and will neither produce nor lead to drunkenness.

With a clear conscience we can recommend it to others for the "stomach's sake," and it is the only wine we would recommend for that purpose. We also have our grave doubts whether Paul would recommend any other to Timothy. You will find it a good wine for weddings. In fact it is the only wine we would allow at a wedding we had control of. This must have been the class of wine made by Jesus at the wedding in Cana of Galilee. He certainly had the power to make it, and he lost no opportunity of doing good when there was an occasion for it.   J. H. M.

CORRESPONDENCE.

"Write what thou seest, and send it unto the churches."

☞ Church News solicited for this Department. If you have had a good meeting, send a report of it, so that others may rejoice with you. In writing give name of church, County and State. Be brief. Notes of Travel should be as short as possible. Land Advertisements are not enlisted for this Department. We have an advertising page, and, if necessary, will issue supplements.

Refreshing Seasons.

WE have had a glorious season of Communions again. The first one was held at the Pine church May, 7 and 8. Eld. Jeremiah Thomas, of West Virginia labored for us very acceptably. It was truly a feast of pleasure to the people of God. Two were baptized in this congregation one week after the feast.

Next came the feast at Knobley, May 21 and 22. Bro. Jonas Fike, of Eglon, West Virginia, did most of the preaching here and also held a series of meetings at this place during the week before the feast. As an immediate result one was baptized and the church much encouraged. Bro. Jonas is a faithful expounder of the Gospel, "rightly dividing the Word of Truth."

Next was the feast in our home church at Beaver Run, June 4 and 5. Eld. I. W. Abernathy, of Western Maryland, held a series of meetings for us during the week prior to the feast. Although Bro. Isaac was suffering from the effects of a cold,

yet he labored earnestly and zealously, and the church manifested a commendable interest. Nine were baptized, and one reclaimed. This was one of the most pleasant feasts ever held at this place. Immediately afterwards, Bro. Abernathy was taken down to the Tearcoat congregation, to hold a series of meetings for them prior to their feast. Here the rainy weather interfered considerably; still meetings were held during the week, and as a result, one was baptized, and one reclaimed. The feast at this place, June 11 and 12, was also very enjoyable. Bro. Abernathy then returned home and our best wishes go with him. We feel impressed with the fact that our series of meetings are generally too short. Especially was this the case at Beaver Run. There was also a love-feast held June 11 and 12, in a new meeting-house, recently built in the west end of our congregation. Bro. Z. Annon, had promised to attend this feast and preach for us, but from some cause he did not come, so home talent from surrounding churches was utilized. This feast will be long remembered, as it was the first ever held at this place. One was recently baptized here.

DANIEL B. ARNOLD.

Burlington, W. Va., June 16.

Christianity Begets Honesty.

THERE was a time in the history of the church, when honesty reigned in her midst. It is said that during the reign of King Alfred the Great, pocket-books, laid in the streets, would be perfectly safe. I have heard father say that, in his young days, a note among neighbors was a rare thing, but to-day we cannot trust our brother in the church without a note and good security. These things ought not so to be. Where true Christianity exists, honesty will prevail. When salvation came to Zaccheus, he said, "If I have taken anything from any man by false accusation I restore it to him fourfold."

This was true repentance under the Mosaic Law. Jesus said unto him, "This day is salvation come to this house." If we, then, have the love of God reigning in our hearts, we will surely deal with our fellow-men on a square and equitable basis, for Christ says, "Whatsoever ye would that men should do to you, do ye even so to them."

Man, as a general thing, would like to have every cent that is due him. Many Christian professors, sad to say, can only be compelled by the laws of the land, to pay their honest dues. Christ says, "A good tree cannot bring forth evil fruit." Again he says, "He that climbeth up any other way is a thief and a robber."

Real honesty is one of the main principles of true Christianity, and yet there are many who profess to be Christians who must be bound by the law before they will pay what they owe. True Christianity will prompt a man to pay the last cent that he owes without note or bond, and I think that is the only Christianity that will ever enter through the gates into heaven. Remember Ananias and Sapphira who kept back part of the price of their possession. But Peter said, "Ananias, why hath Satan filled thine heart to lie to the Holy Ghost and to keep back part of the price of the land? Thou hast not lied unto men, but unto God." The man that professes to be a Christian and will not pay his honest debts, is standing on the same ground that Ananias and Sapphira occupied; he is pretending to have what he has not. Such are professors, and not possessors. "Clouds they are without water, carried about of winds; trees whose fruit withereth, without fruit, twice dead, plucked up by the roots; raging waves of the sea, foaming out their shame; wandering stars, to whom is reserved the blackness forever." Jude 12, 13.   J. W. HAROLD.

Higgin, Nebr.

winter months must be prepared and stewed under personal supervision. Even the meat, which is in all cases mutton, can only be gotten in the bulk. One's ingenuity is taxed in order to serve it differently that it may not become a weariness.

The household cares are not confined to the kitchen. Even in non-christian lands one must be clothed if he would be in his right mind. You know not what a care it is to have a seamstress in the house, although by right of experience she bears her title, but what is it to have a woman, who has no idea of anything beyond that of fastening two edges of cloth together, and that in a rough way. Even after the clothes are made there is the trouble of getting them clean. The housewife does not care to send them to the stream and have them beaten, so she must take a woman, stand over her or sit by her until the garments are hung out upon the line, and then she must persevere through the ironing. Time will show the patient teaching of these missionaries, and those who come in future years will reap the benefits. The Mission circle is always small, and there are not the diversions which are at home, a rest from the home cares,—no lectures, no readings unless by personal effort. Meeting daily the same few people, and exchanging ideas with them,—ideas become in course of years monotonous. There is inspiration in the contact with men of the world. No place is the latest book so appreciated as in far-away lands. No place are letters more prized, no place are little evidences of thoughtfulness more cherished. It is not enough for us to pay salary to our missionaries. We owe them more. Let us remember them at Christmas, at Easter, on their own birthday. There is much discouragement, there are burdens which those at home may lighten. The sure sympathy of the ladies of the Missionary society is stimulating and encouraging. It makes us feel that their interest extends beyond the ways and means of raising money.

Christian work of any kind brings its own reward in the doing of it. Foreign work is not an exception. It brings a daily joy to the worker.

First impressions of Missionary life in Persia have been exceedingly pleasant.

Oroomiah seems to be a favored spot. The workers are delightful people; its climate is sunshiny, its scenery rugged and picturesque. "Every prospect pleases, only man is vile." The efforts of those at home, yoked with the purpose of those here, are gradually working the change. The world for Christ.   H. M. GRIFFITH.

Vacation Talks with our Students.

NUMBER ONE.—HOME.

WHY everything so quiet about the Old Sandstone? Where the many merry melodious voices wont to be heard in the halls, on the campus, and in the morning chapel song and responsive Scripture reading? Where all those youthful, joyous souls? Echo reverberates along the empty halls, "They have gone home." Home! How sweet, how tender, how sacred and holy the word! Here are father, mother, brother, sister, companions,—all the heart loves. It represents the Eden of our earth. It comprehends all the joy and blessedness our fondest hopes can realize. I hope, my young friends, the sacred associations and inspirations of home prove refreshing to your souls as springs of living water. The word home is itself typical of comfort, love, sympathy, and all the other qualities which constitute the delights of social life. The social well-being of society rests on our homes. The success of our schools and colleges with their long train of far-reaching results rests upon our homes; and the foundation stones of our homes are woman's care and devotion. A good mother is everything in the home. God bless the young mothers of the coming homes!

A poet has said, " 'Tis home where the heart is." He means, home is where the heart is congenial. Not every place which is called home is home. The world is full of staying places, but not so full of homes. There is many a palace where people live and shine and smile, but are far away from home; because love and sympathy do not enter into the seasoning of the words spoken, and the otherwise sumptuous meals prepared. In their stead we may find impatience, coarseness, reproach and slander lurking like birds of prey in a dove cot.

Wherever these dwell, home is driven far away. When they come in at one door, home goes out at the other. The name of the Lord be praised, that on leaving our school home, you dear young friends could go to Christian homes. Christian homes because the dear ones dwelling there are of the family of him who left his heavenly home to provide means by which he may be admitted into our earthly homes; or, rather admit our earthly homes into that part of his family now upon the earth. Pleasing thought, that as a result of his divine favor resting upon our homes, streams of purity, health and happiness flow from them.

What a preaching of righteousness to the surrounding community,—a righteousness imbued with the power of God! What a means of promoting the purity of the church, and advancing the interests of our holy religion! God help each one of you to promote the welfare of your homes during your vacation!   J. G. ROYER.

Mt. Morris, Ill.

From Cedar Rapids, Iowa.

OUR Annual Conference at Cedar Rapids was not as largely attended as some have been, on account of the rainy weather, but we rejoice to know that our brethren and sisters, who came, were as one united family, showing a spirit of enterprise and brotherly love. All our people and members of our city churches were much strengthened, encouraged and built up by this powerful influence and Christian effort. This meeting was only a foretaste of what we shall enjoy if we prove faithful.

One brother remarked that he enjoyed the services and singing so much he forgot he had a home here on earth. We could say *amen* to this. It was soul-inspiring. We met many dear friends whom we had not seen for years, and were sorry we could not visit more with them. We were kept quite busy, sitting those who had made application for baptism. Bro. Isaac Frantz baptized three converts in the pure waters of the Cedar River. They came out rejoicing and thanking God for sending the Annual Meeting to Cedar Rapids. Many more were willing to accept this Gospel principle, but it was thought best to give them a little more time to read the New Testament and see if those things were so. Thus the good work goes on.

On Sunday, one young man walked seven miles out to our church to be baptized. This shows an earnest faith. We held our first prayer-meeting at our house, Thursday evening, June 16. It was the first one ever held by our people in Cedar Rapids. We were greatly edified and encouraged at this meeting. We do ask an interest in your prayers. We trust the good work may go on. We have arranged to have prayer-meeting every Thursday evening at our house for the present. Efforts are being made for preaching here every Sunday morning and evening. If any brother or sister should be passing through our city we invite them to stop with us.
          M. E. TISDALE.

Echoes from the Highway.

MAY 31 sixteen brethren, sisters and friends boarded the train for a trip eastward. It is hardly necessary to say our trip was indeed a pleasant one. The accommodations of the Santa Fe Road are such that as one family we live, eat and sleep in the car, with comfort and pleasure. The evening of the fourth day we arrived at Kansas City, and those going to Cedar Rapids soon left for that City, where we arrived on Saturday before noon. Of all Annual Meetings we ever attended, the one at Cedar Rapids was the most enjoyable. Evidently there is progress in the right direction. The members of our beloved Fraternity are seemingly becoming more uniform in living out the principles of the Gospel. We can readily notice an improved disposition to aspire to a higher degree of piety, and to live out the characteristics of that pure and undefiled religion, so beautifully expressed, where the spirit of love, union and harmony prevails. Where self-well is sacrificed, and obedience to the peculiarities of the church is the rule, along with all the distinctive features of the true, Christian religion, a marked advancement will assuredly be the result.

Leaving Cedar Rapids after the close of the Conference, we went to Chicago, and on Sunday preached in the church where the Brethren hold their meetings. The members in the City seem to be alive in the good work, and realize the importance of living out what they preach. There is a prospect that soon they will have a church-house of their own there. Then they will enjoy much better advantages for church work.

We also visited Rockford, Ill., which is in a fine section of country. The place itself is a great manufacturing centre. So far as we know only two members live there. They feel lonely, owing to the want of associations of kindred spirits.

Leaving Chicago Tuesday evening, we arrived at Kansas City next morning, where, according to previous arrangements, we met brother and sister Miller. Together we came on to Lordsburg. Prof. E. A. Miller will take charge of the Brethren's school here the ensuing collegiate year. The prospects for a good attendance are very encouraging, and it is the purpose of those brethren who have the school under their management, to run it in a way that it will meet the approval of the brethren in general, and to the satisfaction of the patrons in particular.

The closing exercises of the college were creditable to the school, and well spoken of by the large attendance, so far as we have heard. There were twelve graduates in the commercial department.   J. S. FLORY.

Lordsburg, Cal.

From Tearcoat, W. Va.

OUR love-feast is in the past. Bro. Isaac Abernathy, of Wilson's Mills, Grant Co., W. Va., came to us on Sunday evening, June 5. We believe Bro. Abernathy to be an earnest worker for the cause of Christ. Night meetings were held each evening during the week. The weather was very rainy, and the congregations were small, yet we hope the good seed sown may bring forth a copious harvest. On Saturday morning, June 11, the brethren and sisters met at the church for baptism. One precious soul was made willing to join in with the people of God. On the evening of the same day, just before the Communion services, one aged brother, who had withdrawn from

winter months must be prepared and stewed under personal supervision. Even the meat, which is in all cases mutton, can only be gotten in the bulk. One's ingenuity is taxed in order to serve it differently that it may not become a weariness.

The household cares are not confined to the kitchen. Even in non-christian lands one must be clothed if he would be in his right mind. You know not what a care it is to have a seamstress in the house, although by right of experience she bears her title, but what is it to have a woman, who has no idea of anything beyond that of fastening two edges of cloth together, and that in a rough way. Even after the clothes are made there is the trouble of getting them clean. The housewife does not care to send them to the stream and have them beaten, so she must take a woman, stand over her or sit by her until the garments are hung out upon the line, and then she must persevere through the ironing. Time will show the patient teaching of these missionaries, and those who come in future years will reap the benefits. The Mission circle is always small, and there are not the diversions which are at home, a rest from the home cares,—no lectures, no readings unless by personal effort. Meeting daily the same few people, and exchanging ideas with them,—ideas become in course of years monotonous. There is inspiration in the contact with men of the world. No place is the latest book so appreciated as in far-away lands. No place are letters more prized, no place are little evidences of thoughtfulness more cherished. It is not enough for us to pay salary to our missionaries. We owe them more. Let us remember them at Christmas, at Easter, on their own birthday. There is much discouragement, there are burdens which those at home may lighten. The sure sympathy of the ladies of the Missionary society is stimulating and encouraging. It makes us feel that their interest extends beyond the ways and means of raising money.

Christian work of any kind brings its own reward in the doing of it. Foreign work is not an exception. It brings a daily joy to the worker. First impressions of Missionary life in Persia have been exceedingly pleasant.

Ooroomiah seems to be a favored spot. The workers are delightful people; its climate is sunshiny, its scenery rugged and picturesque. "Every prospect pleases, only man is vile." The efforts of those at home, yoked with the purpose of those here, are gradually working the change. The world for Christ. **H. M. GRIFFITH.**

Vacation Talks with our Students.

NUMBER ONE.—HOME.

WHY everything so quiet about the Old Sandstone? Where the many merry melodious voices wont to be heard in the halls, on the campus, and in the morning chapel song and responsive Scripture reading? Where all those youthful, joyous souls? Echo reverberates along the empty halls, "They have gone home." Home! How sweet, how tender, how sacred and holy the word!

Here are father, mother, brother, sister, companions,—all the heart loves. It represents the Eden of our earth. It comprehends all the joy and blessedness our fondest hopes can realize. I hope, my young friends, the sacred associations and inspirations of home prove refreshing to your souls as springs of living water. The word home is itself typical of comfort, love, sympathy, and all the other qualities which constitute the delights of social life. The social well-being of society rests on our homes. The success of our schools and colleges with their long train of far-reaching results rests upon our homes; and the foundation stones of our homes are woman's care and devotion. A good mother is everything in the home. God bless the young mothers of the coming homes!

A poet has said, "'Tis home where the heart is." He means, home is where the heart is congenial. Not every place which is called home is home. The world is full of staying places, but not so full of homes. There is many a palace where people live and shine and smile, but are far away from home; because love and sympathy do not enter into the seasoning of the words spoken, and the otherwise sumptuous meals prepared. In their stead we may find impatience, coarseness, reproach and slander lurking like birds of prey in a dove cot.

Wherever these dwell, home is driven far away. When they come in at one door, home goes out at the other. The name of the Lord be praised, that on leaving our school home, you dear young friends could go to Christian homes. Christian homes because the dear ones dwelling there are of the family of him who left his heavenly home to provide means by which he may be admitted into our earthly homes; or, rather admit our earthly homes into that part of his family now upon the earth. Pleasing thought, that as a result of his divine favor resting upon our homes, streams of purity, health and happiness flow from them.

What a preaching of righteousness to the surrounding community,—a righteousness imbued with the power of God! What a means of promoting the purity of the church, and advancing the interests of our holy religion! God help each one of you to promote the welfare of your homes during your vacation! **J. G. ROYER.**
Mt. Morris, Ill.

From Cedar Rapids, Iowa.

OUR Annual Conference at Cedar Rapids was not as largely attended as some have been, on account of the rainy weather, but we rejoice to know that our brethren and sisters, who came, were as one united family, showing a spirit of enterprise and brotherly love. All our people and members of our city churches were much strengthened, encouraged and built up by this powerful influence and Christian effort. This meeting was only a foretaste of what we shall enjoy if we prove faithful.

One brother remarked that he enjoyed the services and singing so much he forgot he had a home here on earth. We could say amen to this. It was soul-inspiring. We met many dear friends whom we had not seen for years, and were sorry we could not visit more with them. We were kept quite busy, aiding those who had made application for baptism. Bro. Isaac Frantz baptized three converts in the pure waters of the Cedar River. They came out rejoicing and thanking God for sending the Annual Meeting to Cedar Rapids. Many more were willing to accept this Gospel principle, but it was thought best to give them a little more time to read the New Testament. We trust the good work may go on. Thus the good work goes on.

On Sunday, one young man walked seven miles out to our church to be baptized. This shows an earnest faith. We held our first prayer-meeting at our house, Thursday evening, June 16. It was the first one ever held by our people in Cedar Rapids. We were greatly edified and encouraged at this meeting. We do ask an interest in your prayers. We trust the good work may go on. We have arranged to have prayer-meeting every Thursday evening at our house for the present. Efforts are being made for preaching here every Sunday morning and evening. If any

brother or sister should be passing through our city we invite them to stop with us. **M. E. TISDALE.**

Echoes from the Highway.

MAY 31 sixteen brethren, sisters and friends boarded the train for a trip eastward. It is hardly necessary to say our trip was indeed a pleasant one. The accommodations of the Santa Fe Road are such that as one family we live, eat and sleep in the car, with comfort and pleasure. The evening of the fourth day we arrived at Kansas City, and those going to Cedar Rapids soon left for that City, where we arrived on Saturday before noon. Of all Annual Meetings we ever attended, the one at Cedar Rapids was the most enjoyable. Evidently there is progress in the right direction. The members of our beloved Fraternity are seemingly becoming more uniform in living out the principles of the Gospel. We can readily notice an improved disposition to aspire to a higher degree of piety, and to live out the characteristics of that pure and undefiled religion, so beautifully expressed, where the spirit of love, union and harmony prevails. Where self-will is sacrificed, and obedience to the peculiarities of the church is the rule, along with all the distinctive features of the true, Christian religion, a marked advancement will assuredly be the result.

Leaving Cedar Rapids after the close of the Conference, we went to Chicago, and on Sunday preached in the church where the Brethren hold their meetings. The members in the City seem to be alive in the good work, and realize the importance of living out what they preach. There is a prospect that soon they will have a churchhouse of their own there. Then they will enjoy much better advantages for church work.

We also visited Rockford, Ill., which is in a fine section of country. The place itself is a great manufacturing centre. So far as we know only two members live there. They feel lonely, owing to the want of associations of kindred spirits.

Leaving Chicago Tuesday evening, we arrived at Kansas City next morning, where, according to previous arrangements, we met brother and sister Miller. Together we came on to Lordsburg. Prof. E. A. Miller will take charge of the Brethren's school here the ensuing collegiate year. The prospects for a good attendance are very encouraging, and it is the purpose of those brethren who have the school under their management, to run it in a way that it will meet the approval of the brethren in general, and to the satisfaction of the patrons in particular.

The closing exercises of the college were creditable to the school, and well spoken of by the large attendance, so far as we have heard. There were twelve graduates in the commercial department. **J. S. FLORY.**
Lordsburg, Cal.

From Tearcoat, W. Va.

OUR love-feast is in the past. Bro. Isaac Abernathy, of Wilson's Mills, Grant Co., W. Va., came to us on Sunday evening, June 5. We believe Bro. Abernathy to be an earnest worker for the cause of Christ. Night meetings were held each evening during the week. The weather was very rainy, and the congregations were small, yet we hope the good seed sown may bring forth a copious harvest. On Saturday morning, June 11, the brethren and sisters met at the church for baptism. One precious soul was made willing to join in with the people of God. On the evening of the same day, just before the Communion services, one aged brother, who had withdrawn from

Ashland, Ohio.—Since last report another precious soul was received into church fellowship by baptism, at Maple Grove, Ohio. There is room for more. Come along, friends, we will try to do you good!—*David Snyder, June 16.*

Notice to the Members of the North-eastern District of Ohio.—Notice is hereby given that the next District Meeting of North-eastern Ohio will be held, the Lord willing, in the "Owl Creek" church, Knox County, Ohio. Further notice will be given at the proper time.- *Jacob Mishler, Clerk, Mogadore, Ohio, June 21.*

Soldier River Church, Iowa.—We had our regular meeting June 18 and 19. Bro. Moses Dierdorff was with us. He preached two splendid sermons, and I hope there was much good done by them. We had a very fair congregation, and good attention was given to the Word preached.—*Hester A. Stevens, Modale, Iowa.*

Hassell, Iowa.—We, the brethren and sisters of the above-named church decided in council to hold a Communion meeting July 9, commencing at 4 P. M. Meetings are to continue over Sunday. We extend a cordial invitation to the dear brethren and sisters of the surrounding churches, and especially ministering brethren, to be with us. Those who come by rail, will be met at Dumont or Hassell.—*Mary C. Allen.*

Bunker Hill, Ind.—We, the members of the Santa Fe church, held our quarterly church-meeting on Thursday, June 16. All business was transacted with the best of feeling, and, we hope, in Christian love. We appointed our Communion for Oct. 5, commencing at 10 A. M., six miles south of Peru, two miles east of Bunker Hill, and one mile north of Loree, Miami County, Ind. We also decided, at our December church-meeting, to hold a series of meetings this season, and secured Bro. Lewis W. Teeter to do the preaching.—*Jacob J. Fox, June 21.*

Cabool, Mo.—Our love-feast was a very pleasant and interesting one. There was good order and good interest. No one was present from adjoining churches. In the evening, just before the feast, two were received into the church by baptism. May God bless them, and enable them to be bright and shining lights in his church! There were others at the meeting, who were much interested, and some are counting the cost. Thus, by our continued effort, one by one they are brought into the church. May God help us to labor on!—*J. J. Troxel, June 21.*

Wakarusa, Ind.—The Yellow Creek church, Ind., enjoyed an agreeable surprise on Sunday, May 29. At the close of the morning services we were again called to order. Many faces were made to beam with joy, on hearing that another soul had fully made up her mind to come out on the Lord's side. We wish that such surprises might more frequently take place. Our love-feast was held June 1, at which time about four hundred communicants took part in its spiritual refreshments. We feel to thank the young people for their good behavior. God will bless them for it!—*Irvin S. Burns, June 21.*

Beatrice, Nebr.—Ben Ford, a young man of twenty-three summers, was cleaning a revolver last Sunday, that had been in use for four or five years. Afterward he hung it on a nail in the room, near the door. In the evening he stopped in the door and laid his hand on it and snapped it. It discharged, and he fell and never spoke a word afterward, but lived several hours. The exact way the tragedy occurred is not known; but it is another of those careless accidents with a gun. He had only been married three weeks. His funeral services were conducted by the writer from Ps. 89: 47.—*J. E. Young.*

Literary Notices.

"John G. Whittier, the Poet of Freedom." By Wm Sloane Kennedy. Cloth, 12mo, 330 pp. With portrait, $1: 50. New York, London, and Toronto: Funk & Wagnalls Company.

This is an entertaining and instructive book, full of history and interspersed with quotations from the poems and ballads of Whittier. To read this biography is like sauntering through a romantic country, some land like that through which the castled Rhine meanders, with history looking down at you over the shoulder of each hill, and with a romance in every dapple of the river. It should find a place in all family or circulating libraries. It is a valuable contribution to the annals of American literature and to the history of our country. The "poet of Freedom" still lives; and though he die, he must still live on dearer than ever in the literature, memories, and hearts of his countrymen.

"Biblical Commentary on the Prophecies of Isaiah." By Franz Delitzsch, D. D., Professor of Theology in the University of Leipzig. Authorized translation from the third edition. By the Rev. James Denney, B. D. In two volumes. Vol. II., 8vo, cloth, 496 pp. $3.50. Funk & Wagnalls Company, New York, Toronto, and London.

The volume just issued of this masterful Commentary, completes the work. The first volume, which we noticed in these columns last year, was well received, and called forth strong commendations from the religious press and students in theology. Indeed the name of Delitzsch was sufficient to warrant that. The Prophecies of Isaiah have always held a foremost place among the Sacred Books, and the scholars of the Church have given to them the most devout consideration and enlightened investigation. This Commentary takes immediate rank among the greatest studies of the Messianic Prophet. If you have not the first volume, you should send for it.

"The Preacher's Complete Homiletic Commentary on the Old Testament," (with critical and exegetical notes). By twenty distinguished homilists. Vol. I., Genesis. By Rev. J. S. Exell, M. A., and Rev. T. H. Leale, A. K. C. Cloth, 8vo, 747 pp, $3. New York: Funk & Wagnalls Company.

This is the first volume of an extensive work of twenty volumes on the Old Testament, printed from imported plates, obtained from the publishers in London, where the entire work has been issued after years of preparation. In this great Commentary, by various authors, is found a sermon outline, or homiletic suggestion, on every paragraph or verse of the Old Testament that can be turned to use in the preparation of a sermon. Abundant choice selections of illustration, etc., from many eminent sources, other than the authors of the volumes, are also given. Except in some introductory, critical, and explanatory notes preceding each chapter, no foreign words, such as Hebrew or Greek, are used. The type is large and clear, and the books are convenient to handle.

Considering the exhaustive character of this Commentary, inasmuch as it opens up for homiletic use, every available verse or paragraph of the Old Testament that can be turned into use for homiletical purposes, it is impossible to overestimate its importance. We regard this as one of the very best works that has yet been sent us for review. It is certainly a remarkable work, and will be highly prized by those who are so fortunate as to possess it.

Fallen Asleep.

"Blessed are the dead which die in the Lord."

KANDALL.—In the Santa Fe church, Ind., Jan. 26, 1892, Bro. Joseph Kandall, aged 76 years and 8 months. Funeral services by brethren D S. Caylor and Joseph Rife, of Somerset, assisted by friend Sprowel.

COX.—Also in the same place, May 7, 1892, Bro. Samuel D. Cox, aged 70 years, 7 months and 8 days. Funeral services by the writer, assisted by friend Sprowel from Heb. 13: 14, to a large congregation. JACOB J. FOX.

CAPPER.—Near Glen Easton, W. Va., June 9. 1891, Mrs. Margaret Capper, wife of John Capper, aged 53 years, 9 months and 11 days. Services by the writer, from the words, "The Master is come, and calleth for thee." John 11: 28. ANDREW CHAMBERS.

SHAFFER.—In the Quemahoning church, Pa., June 6, 1892, Milton Shaffer, son of William and Catharine Shaffer, aged 1 year, 1 month and 8 days. The infant son of the above parents died on the same day. Both of these children were buried in one grave. Funeral services by Bro. Jacob P. Spicher and the writer, in the Lutheran church at Casebeer's. JOHN J. DARR.

RAIRIGH.—In the Woodland church, Mich., sister Sarah, wife of Eld. Isaiah Rairigh, aged 49 years, 6 months and 23 days. Sister Rairigh leaves four children, two sons, two daughters and a kind husband. She was a loving companion,

---

a kind mother, a zealous worker in the church, and a loved and respected neighbor. Funeral services improved by Bro. Benj. Fryfogle, of the Sunfield church, Mich., and the home ministry from Rev. 13: 12, 13. JOHN M. SMITH.

HILL.—Near Bealisville, Washington Co., Pa., March 31, 1892, Ray, son of Harvey and Ellen Hill, aged 3 years and 7 months. The little sufferer was taken with convulsions in the morning and passed away the evening of the same day. Funeral services by Rev. Humes from Matt. 19: 14. REBECCA B. GRABLE.

BOLINGER.—In the Sugar Creek church, Whitley Co., Ind., June 3. 1892, Sophia (Mohler) Bolinger, aged 48 years, months and 29 days. She united with the Brethren church in her youth, and her life has been one of devotion and faithfulness. She was married to R. B. Bolinger Oct. 4, 1864. Unto this union were born six children, four daughters and two sons. Funeral services by the writer from Job 14: 14, to a large congregation of sympathizing friends.

WARD.—In the Appanoose church, Franklin Co., Kans., June 13, 1892, Clarence Benjamin, son of Bro. W. S. and sister Sarah Ward, aged 11 years, 9 months and 13 days. Funeral services improved by the Brethren from 2 Tim. 1: 10. JAMES T. KUEFIE.

SHOTTS.—In the Pigeon River congregation, in Steuben Co., Ind., Feb. 8, 1892, sister Christena Shotts, wife of Eld. Michael Shotts, aged 67 years, 5 months and 28 days. Deceased suffered at times intensely from rheumatism, for the space of about five years. At last she contracted *La Grippe*, which ended her days. Through her long and severe suffering, she bore her afflictions with Christian fortitude. Bro. Michael is the only one left of the family. Funeral services from 2 Tim. 4: 6, 7, 8, by Bro. Peter Long and the writer. N. H. SHUTT.

HUMBERT.—In the Bachelor Run church, Carroll Co., Ind., June 9, 1892, sister Catharine Humbert, aged 75 years, 1 month and 7 days. Funeral services by the Brethren. D. H. NICCUM.

GEHARDUS.—Near Damascus, Oregon, June 10, 1892, Anna Margret Gehardus, aged 54 years. Deceased was born in Westphalia, Germany. Funeral services by the writer. J. A. ROYER.

MATTHEWS.—At East Liberty, Pa., (stock-yards) May 28, 1892, Solomon Matthews, aged about 51 years. Deceased was killed while crossing the net-work of tracks at the above-named place. He was struck and instantly killed by an express train. The back of his head was knocked off; left shoulder and jaw broken; left limb broken. The family was notified by telegram on Sunday morning, and the oldest son went at once to take charge of the remains, and arrived at home May 30. The home of the deceased was near Bealisville, Washington Co., Pa. He was a stock dealer, and had taken his usual weekly load to the markets. He leaves a wife, two sons and two daughters (all grown except the youngest son, aged 6 years). Funeral services at Bealisville. REBECCA B. GRABLE.

The Gospel Messenger

Is the recognized organ of the German Baptist or Brethren's church, and advocates the form of doctrine taught in the New Testament and pleads for a return to apostolic and primitive Christianity.

It recognizes the New Testament as the only infallible rule of faith and practice, and maintains that Faith toward God, Repentance from dead works, Regeneration of the heart and mind, baptism by Trine Immersion for remission of sins unto the reception of the Holy Ghost by the laying on of hands, are the means of adoption into the household of God,—the church militant.

It also maintains that Feet-washing, as taught in John 13, both by example and command of Jesus, should be observed in the church.

That the Lord's Supper, instituted by Christ and as universally observed by the apostles and the early Christians, is a full meal, and, in connection with the Communion, should be taken in the evening or after the close of the day.

That the Salutation of the Holy Kiss, or Kiss of Charity, is binding upon the followers of Christ.

That War and Retaliation are contrary to the spirit and self-denying principles of the religion of Jesus Christ.

That the principle of Plain Dressing and of Non-conformity to the world, as taught in the New Testament, should be observed by the followers of Christ.

That the Scriptural duty of Anointing the Sick with Oil, in the Name of the Lord, James 5: 14, is binding upon all Christians.

It also advocates the church's duty to support Missionary and Tract Work, thus giving to the Lord for the spread of the Gospel and for the conversion of sinners.

In short, it is a Vindicator of all that Christ and the apostles have enjoined upon us, and seeks, amid the conflicting theories and discords of modern Christendom, to point out ground that all must concede to be infallibly safe.

☞ The above principles of our Fraternity are set forth on our "Brethren's Envelopes." Use them! Price, 15 cents per package; 40 cents per hundred.

Ashland, Ohio.—Since last report another precious soul was received into church fellowship by baptism, at Maple Grove, Ohio. There is room for more. Come along, friends, we will try to do you good!—*David Snyder, June 16.*

Notice to the Members of the North-eastern District of Ohio.—Notice is hereby given that the next District Meeting of North-eastern Ohio will be held, the Lord willing, in the "Owl Creek" church, Knox County, Ohio. Further notice will be given at the proper time.—*Jacob Mishler, Clerk, Mogadore, Ohio, June 21.*

Soldier River Church, Iowa.—We had our regular meeting June 18 and 19. Bro. Moses Dierdorff was with us. He preached two splendid sermons, and I hope there was much good done by them. We had a very fair congregation, and good attention was given to the Word preached.—*Hester A. Stevens, Modale, Iowa.*

Hassell, Iowa.—We, the brethren and sisters of the above-named church decided in council to hold a Communion meeting July 9, commencing at 4 P. M. Meetings are to continue over Sunday. We extend a cordial invitation to the dear brethren and sisters of the surrounding churches, and especially ministering brethren, to be with us. Those who come by rail, will be met at Dumont or Hansell.—*Mary C. Allen.*

Bunker Hill, Ind.—We, the members of the Santa Fe church, held our quarterly church-meeting on Thursday, June 16. All business was transacted with the best of feeling, and we hope, in Christian love. We appointed our Communion for Oct. 5, commencing at 10 A. M., six miles south of Peru, two miles east of Bunker Hill, and one mile north of Loree, Miami County, Ind. We also decided, at our December church-meeting, to hold a series of meetings this season, and secured Bro. Lewis W. Teeter to do the preaching.—*Jacob J. Fox, June 21.*

Cabool, Mo.—Our love-feast was a very pleasant and interesting one. There was good order and good interest. No one was present from adjoining churches. In the evening, just before the feast, two were received into the church by baptism. May God bless them, and enable them to be bright and shining lights in his church! There were others at the meeting, who were much interested, and some are counting the cost. Thus, by our continued effort, one by one they are brought into the church. May God help us to labor on!—*J. J. Troxel, June 21.*

Wakarusa, Ind.—The Yellow Creek church, Ind, enjoyed an agreeable surprise on Sunday, May 29. At the close of the morning services we were again called to order. Many faces were made to beam with joy, on hearing that another soul had fully made up her mind to come out on the Lord's side. We wish that such surprises might more frequently take place. Our love-feast was held June 1, at which time about four hundred communicants took part in its spiritual refreshments. We feel to thank the young people for their good behavior. God will bless them for it!—*Irvin S. Burns, June 21.*

Beatrice, Nebr.—Ben Ford, a young man of twenty-three summers, was cleaning a revolver last Sunday, that had been in use for four or five years. Afterward he hung it on a nail in the room, near the door. In the evening he stopped in the door and laid his hand on it and snapped it. It discharged, and he fell and never spoke a word afterward, but lived several hours. The exact way the tragedy occurred is not known; but it is another of those careless accidents with a gun. He had only been married three weeks. His funeral services were conducted by the writer from Ps. 89: 47.—*J. E. Young.*

Literary Notices.

"*John G. Whittier, the Poet of Freedom.*" By Wm Sloane Kennedy. Cloth, 12mo, 330 pp. With portrait, $1.50. New York, London, and Toronto: Funk & Wagnalls Company.

This is an entertaining and instructive book, full of history and interspersed with quotations from the poems and ballads of Whittier. To read this biography is like sauntering through a romantic country, some land like that through which the castled Rhine meanders, with history looking down at you over the shoulder of each hill, and with a romance in every ripple of the river. It should find a place in all family or circulating libraries. It is a valuable contribution to the annals of American literature and to the history of our country. The "poet of Freedom" still lives; and though he die, he must still live on dearer than ever in the literature, memories, and hearts of his countrymen.

"*Biblical Commentary on the Prophecies of Isaiah.*" By Franz Delitzsch, D. D., Professor of Theology in the University of Leipsig. Authorized translation from the third edition. By the Rev. James Denney, B. D. In two Volumes. Vol. II., 8vo, cloth, 496 pp. $3.50. Funk & Wagnalls Company, New York, Toronto, and London.

The volume just issued of this masterful Commentary, completes the work. The first volume, which we noticed in these columns last year, was well received, and called forth strong commendations from the religious press and students in theology. Indeed the name of Delitzsch was sufficient to warrant that. The prophecies of Isaiah have always held a foremost place among the Sacred Books, and the scholars of the Church have given to them the most devout consideration and enlightened investigation. This Commentary takes immediate rank among the greatest studies of the Messianic Prophet. If you have not the first volume, you should send for it.

"*The Preacher's Complete Homiletic Commentary on the Old Testament,*" (with critical and exegetical notes.) By twenty distinguished homilists. Vol. I., Genesis. By Rev. J. S. Exell, M. A., and Rev. T. H. Leale, A. K. C. Cloth, 8vo, 747 pp., $3. New York: Funk & Wagnalls Company.

This is the first volume of an extensive work of twenty volumes on the Old Testament, printed from imported plates, obtained from the publishers in London, where the entire work has been issued after years of preparation. In this great Commentary, by various authors, is found a sermon outline, or homiletic suggestion, on every paragraph or verse of the Old Testament that can be turned to use in the preparation of a sermon. Abundant choice selections of illustration, etc., from many eminent sources, other than the authors of the volumes, are also given. Except in some introductory, critical, and explanatory notes preceding each chapter, no foreign words, such as Hebrew or Greek, are used. The type is large and clear, and the books are convenient to handle.

Considering the exhaustive character of this Commentary, inasmuch as it opens up for homiletic use, every available verse or paragraph of the Old Testament that can be turned into use for homiletical purposes, it is impossible to overestimate its importance. We regard this as one of the very best works that has yet been sent us for review. It is certainly a remarkable work, and will be highly prized by those who are so fortunate as to possess it.

Fallen Asleep.

"Blessed are the dead which die in the Lord."

KANDALL.—In the Santa Fe church, Ind., Jan. 26, 1892, Bro. Joseph Kandall, aged 76 years and 8 months. Funeral services by brethren D. S. Caylor and Joseph Rife, of Somerset, assisted by friend Sprowel.

COX—Also in the same place, May 7, 1892, Bro. Samuel D. Cox, aged 70 years, 7 months and 8 days. Funeral services by the writer, assisted by friend Sprowel from Heb. 13: 14. to a large congregation. JACOB J. FOX.

CAPPER.—Near Glen Easton, W. Va., June 9. 1892, Mrs. Margaret Capper, wife of John Capper, aged 53 years, 9 months and 11 days. Services by the writer, from the words, "The Master's come, and calleth for thee." John 11: 28. ANDREW CHAMBERS.

SHAFFER.—In the Quemahoning church, Pa., June 6, 1892, Milton Shaffer, son of William and Catharine Shaffer, aged 1 year, 1 month and 8 days. The infant son of the above parents died on the same day. Both of these children were buried in one grave. Funeral services by Bro. Jacob F. Spicher and the writer, in the Lutheran church at Casebeer's. JOHN J. DARR.

RAIRIGH.—In the Woodland church, Mich., sister Sarah, wife of Eld. Isaiah Rairigh, aged 49 years, 6 months and 23 days. Sister Rairigh leaves four children, two sons, two daughters and a kind husband. She was a loving companion,

a kind mother, a zealous worker in the church, and a loved and respected neighbor. Funeral services improved by Bro. Benj. Fryfogle, of the Sunfield church, Mich., and the home ministry from Rev. 13: 12, 13. JOHN M. SMITH.

HILL.—Near Beallsville, Washington Co., Pa., March 31, 1892, Ray, son of Harvey and Ellen Hill, aged 3 years and 7 months. The little sufferer was taken with convulsions in the morning and passed away the evening of the same day. Funeral services by Rev. Humes from Matt. 19: 14. REBECCA B. GRABLE.

BOLINGER.—In the Sugar Creek church, Whitley Co., Ind., June 3. 1892, Sophia (Mohler) Bolinger, aged 48 years, 9 months and 29 days. She united with the Brethren church in her youth, and her life has been one of devotion and faithfulness. She was married to R. B. Bolinger Oct. 4, 1864. Unto this union were born six children, four daughters and two sons. Funeral services by the writer from Job 14: 14, to a large congregation of sympathizing friends. J. H. SHUTT.

WARD.—In the Appanoose church, Franklin Co., Kans., June 13, 1892, Clarence Benjamin, son of Bro. W. S. and sister Sarah Ward, aged 11 years, 9 months and 13 days. Funeral services improved by the Brethren from 2 Tim. 1: 10. JAMES T. KINSEY.

SHOTTS.—In the Pigeon River congregation, in Steuben Co., Ind., Feb. 8, 1892, sister Christena Shotts, wife of Eld. Michael Shotts, aged 67 years, 5 months and 28 days. Deceased suffered at times intensely from rheumatism, for the space of about five years. At last she contracted *La Grippe*, which ended her days. Through her long and severe suffering, she bore her afflictions with Christian fortitude. Bro. Michael is the only one left of the family. Funeral services from 2 Tim. 4: 6, 7, 8, by Bro. Peter Long and the writer. D. H. NICCUM.

HUMBERT.—In the Bachelor Run church, Carroll Co., Ind., June 9, 1892, sister Catharine Humbert, aged 75 years, 1 month and 7 days. Funeral services by the Brethren. J. A. ROYER.

GERARDUS.—Near Damascus, Oregon, June 10, 1892, Anna Margret Gerardus, aged 54 years. Deceased was born in Westphalia, Germany. Funeral services by the writer. J. A. ROYER.

MATTHEWS.—At East Liberty, Pa., (stock-yards) May 28, 1892, Solomon Matthews, aged about 51 years. Deceased was killed while crossing the net-work of tracks at the above-named place. He was struck and instantly killed by an express train. The back of his head was knocked off; left shoulder and jaw broken; left limb broken. The family was notified by telegram on Sunday morning, and the oldest son went at once to take charge of the remains, and arrived at home May 30. The home of the deceased was near Beallsville, Washington Co., Pa. He was a stock dealer, and had taken his usual weekly load to the markets. He leaves a wife, two sons and two daughters (all grown except the youngest son, aged 6 years). Funeral services at Beallsville. REBECCA B. GRABLE.

The Gospel Messenger

Is the recognized organ of the German Baptist or Brethren's church, and advocates the form of doctrine taught in the New Testament and pleads for a return to apostolic and primitive Christianity.

It recognizes the New Testament as the only infallible rule of faith and practice, and maintains that Faith toward God, Repentance from dead works, Regeneration of the heart and mind, baptism by Trine Immersion for remission of sins unto the reception of the Holy Ghost by the laying on of hands, are the means of adoption into the household of God,—the church militant.

It also maintains that Feet-washing, as taught in John 13, both by example and command of Jesus, should be observed in the church.

That the Lord's Supper, instituted by Christ and as universally observed by the apostles and the early Christians, is a full meal, and, in connection with the Communion, should be taken in the evening or after the close of the day.

That the Salutation of the Holy Kiss, or Kiss of Charity, is binding upon the followers of Christ.

That War and Retaliation are contrary to the spirit and self-denying principles of the religion of Jesus Christ.

That the principle of Plain Dressing and of Non-conformity to the world, as taught in the New Testament, should be observed by the followers of Christ.

That the Scriptural duty of Anointing the Sick with Oil, in the Name of the Lord, James 5: 14, is binding upon all Christians.

It also advocates the church's duty to support Missionary and Tract Work, thus giving to the Lord for the spread of the Gospel and for the conversion of sinners.

In short, it is a vindicator of all that Christ and the apostles have enjoined upon us, and aims, amid the conflicting theories and discords of modern Christendom, to point out ground that all must concede to be infallibly safe.

☞ The above principles of our Fraternity are set forth on our "Brethren's Envelopes." Use them! Price, 15 cents p'r package; 40 cents per hundred.

Announcements.

LOVE-FEASTS.

Sept. 2, at 4 P. M., Sugar Creek church, Sangamon County, Ill., 5 miles east of Auburn, Ill.

Sept. 6, at 4 P. M., Indian Creek congregation, Fayette Co., Pa. Series of meetings to commence Aug. 27.

Sept. 9, 10 10 A. M., Monroe County church, Iowa.

Sept. 17, 10 2 P. M., Bethel congregation at the Bethlehem meeting-house, Holt Co., Mo. For any information address Jos. Andes, Mound City, Holt Co., Mo.

Sept. 24, at 5 P. M., in La Porte church, La Porte, Ind. Trains will be met in the forenoon and early afternoon of the day of meeting.

Sept. 24, at 3 P. M., Martin's Creek church, Wayne Co., Ill.

Sept. 28, 10 10 A. M., Spring Creek church, Kosciusko Co., Ind.

Sept. 30, at 2 P. M., Milmine church, Piatt Co., Ill.

Oct. 1, 10 - 7 M., Sugar Creek church, Allen Co., Ohio.

Oct. 1, at 2 P. M., Osage church, Crawford Co., Kans.

Oct. 1, at 5 P. M., Pokagon church, Dowagiac, Cass Co., Mich.

Oct. 1, at 4 P. M., Logan church, near DeGraff, Ohio.

Oct. 1, Maple Grove church, Norton Co., Kans.

Oct. 7, at 2 P. M., Raskaskia church, Fayette Co., Ill., ten miles south-west of Brother City, Ill. Those coming by rail will be met at the above-named place by informing Granville Nevinger.

Oct. 7, 10 10 A. M., Sugar Creek, Richland Co., Ill.

Oct. 8 and 9, at 2 P. M., Arnold's Grove, Ill.

Oct. 8, 10 10 A. M., Dry Creek church, Linn Co., Iowa, one mile west of Robins Station.

Oct. 6, at 2 P. M., Spring Creek church, in the Keith's church-house, eleven miles south-west of Reece, Kans.

Oct. 8, Swan Creek congregation, Ohio, 3½ miles west of DePu, Ohio.

Nov. 5, at 2 P. M., Big Creek church, Richland Co., Ill., 3½ miles North-east of Parkersburg, Ill. Conveyances will be at the above place by informing J. M. Forney.

The First Three Christian Centuries. — By Islay Burns. Cloth. $1.25.

GOOD BOOKS FOR ALL.

ANY book in the market furnished at publishers' lowest retail price by the Brethren's Publishing Company, Mt. Morris, Ill., *Special prices* given when books are purchased in quantities. When ordering books, not on our list, if possible give title, name of author, and address of publishers.

The Throne of David.—By J. H. Ingraham. Cloth, $1.50.

Josephus' Complete Works.—Large type, 1 vol. 8vo. Illustrated with many steel and wood engravings. Library sheep, $3.00.

The Doctrine of the Holy Spirit. — By James H. Walker. Cloth, $1.25.

The New Testament History.— By Wm. Smith. Cloth, $1.25.

The Path of Life.—An interesting tract for everybody. Price, 10 cents per copy; 100 copies, $6.00.

Smith's Bible Dictionary. — Edited by Peloubet. Cloth, $2.00; leather. $3.00.

Ante-Nicene Christian Library.—A collection of all the works of the Fathers of the Christian Church prior to the Council of Nice. Edited by Rev. Alexander Roberts, D. D., and James Donaldson, LL. D. Twenty-four vols. 8 vo. Per vol., $3.00.

Sacred Geography and Antiquities.— A practical, helpful work for Bible students, ministers and Sunday-school teachers. Price, $2.25.

The Origin and Growth of Religion.—Hibbert Lectures. By T. W. R. Davids. Cloth, 8vo. $2.50.

Bible Work, or Bible Reader's Commentary on the New Testament.—By J. G. Butler. Two vols. 8vo, $10.00.

Popular Commentary on the New Testament.—Edited by Philip Schaff. Four volumes, 8vo. Matthew, Mark and Luke: $6.00. John and the Acts: $6.00. Romans to Philemon: $5.00. Hebrews to Revelation: $5.00.

The Life and Epistles of the Apostle Paul.—By W. J. Coneybeare. Cloth, $2.00.

The Prince of the House of David.—By J. H. Ingraham. Cloth, $1.50.

The Great Events of History.— By W. F. Collier. Cloth, $2.25.

Trine Immersion.—A vindication of the apostolic form of Christian baptism. By Eld. James Quinter. A most complete and reliable work on the subject." Price, cloth, single copy, $1.25; leather, $1.75.

The Old Testament History.—By William Smith. Cloth, $1.25.

True Method of Searching the Scriptures.—By Talbot Fanning. Paper, 15 cents.

Universalism Against Itself.—By Hall. One of the best works against Universalism. Price, $1.00.

Biblical Antiquities.—By John Nevin. Gives a concise account of Bible times and customs; invaluable to all students of Bible subjects. Price, $1.50.

Quinter and McConnell Debate.—A debate on Trine Immersion, the Lord's Supper, and Feet-washing, between Eld. James Quinter (German Baptist) and Eld. N. A. McConnell (Christian) held at Dry Creek, Iowa, 1867. Price, $1.50.

Sabbatism.—By M. M. Eshelman. Treats the Sabbath question, showing that the first day of the week is the day for assembling in worship. Price, 10 cents; 15 copies, $1.00.

The Story of the Bible. — An excellent volume for old and young; will interest and instruct all those desiring a knowledge of the Scriptures. Price, $1.00.

Biblical Theology of the Old Testament.—By R. F. Weidner. Cloth, $2.25.

The House We Live in.—By Daniel Vanbman. It gives a concise account of the faith and practice of the Brethren. Price, 100 copies, 60 cents.

The Holy Land and the Bible.—By Cunningham Geikie. Cloth, $2.75.

A Summary of Biblical Antiquities.—By John W. Nevin. Cloth, $1.50.

German and English Testaments.—American Bible Society Edition. Price, 60 cents.

Early Days of Christianity.—By F. W. Farrar. Author's edition. cloth. 12mo. $1.50.

Every Day Religion.—By James Freeman Clarke. Cloth, 12mo, $1.50.

Faiths of the World.—A concise history of the great religious systems of the world. Cloth, 8vo, $2.00.

Europe and Bible Lands.—By D. L. Miller. A book for the people,—more comprehensive and thorough than many higher-priced works. Price, cloth, $1.50; leather, $2.00.

The Pillar of Fire.—By J. H. Ingraham. Cloth, $1.50.

The Bible the Sunday-school Text-book.—By Alfred Holborn. Cloth, 75 cents.

Origin of Single Immersion.—By Eld. James Quinter. Price, 3 copies, 5 cents: 12 copies, 15 cents; 50 copies, $1.00.

Campbell and Owen Debate. — Contains a complete investigation of the evidences of Christianity. Price, $1.50.

Ecclesiastical History.—By Eusebius. Bohn Library. Cloth, $2.00.

Gospel Chimes.

BY WM. BEERY.

A new edition of this deservedly popular Sunday-school song-book has just been issued.

Bro. Beery has had a large experience in Sunday-school work, and the book which we offer to the Brethren, and the public in general, evinces the exercise of talent as well as good judgment. The religious purity of the hymns, combined by sister Beery, adds much to the excellence of the book.

Price per single copy, 25 cts.; per dozen, by mail, $2.50; by express, $2.50. Lots of more than a dozen must be sent by express.

BRETHREN'S PUBLISHING CO.,
Or Huntingdon, Pa.   Mt. Morris Ill.

Alone with God.

THIS manual of devotions, by J. H. Garrison, comprises a series of meditations with forms of prayer for private devotions, family worship and special occasions. It is one of the most useful, most needed, and best adapted books of the year, and therefore it is not strange that it is proving one of the most popular. In work of this kind its distinguished, gifted, pious and beloved author is at his best. This book is helpful to every minister, church official, and Sunday-school superintendent, as well as every private member of the church in all ages. It has models of prayer, suitable for the service of the prayer-meeting, while its suggestions, meditations and instructions are pre-eminently calculated to be of service in preparation for the solemn duties that rest upon the active members. Cloth, 75 cents; morocco, $1.25. Address this office.

EUROPE
AND
Bible Lands

A new edition of this deservedly popular work has recently been published. It retains all the excellencies of its predecessors, and with those who are interested in Bible study this work will always remain a favorite. Those who have read the ordinary book of travel will be surprised to find "Europe and Bible Lands" of thrilling interest for both old and young. The large number of books, already sold, proves that the work is of more than ordinary merit.

A fair supply of the last edition of this work is still on hand. Those who have not yet secured a copy of the work should embrace this opportunity of securing it. Price, in fine cloth binding, only $1.50 per copy, post-paid. To agents who are prepared to push an active canvass of the work, we are prepared to give special inducements. Write us.

BRETHREN'S PUBLISHING CO.,
Mt. Morris, Ill.

CRUDEN'S
COMPLETE
CONCORDANCE

THIS excellent work, which we offer for sale to our readers, at the low price of $1.50 post-paid, is the only one of the kind that may be depended upon as being strictly reliable. Any verse in the Bible may be readily found by looking for any material word in the Verse. Besides this there are given the significations of the principal words, by which their true, Scriptural meaning may be known. A full account of Jewish customs and ceremonies is given as well as a complete concordance of the proper names of the Bible and of the books called Apocrypha. Send all orders for this above work to this office.

Announcements.

LOVE-FEASTS.

Sept. 3, at 4 P. M., Sugar Creek church, Sangamon County, Ill., 9 miles east of Auburn, Ill.

Sept. 6, at 3 P. M., Indian Creek congregation, Fayette Co., Pa. Series of meetings to commence Aug. 27.

Sept. 9, at 10 A. M., Monroe County church, Iowa.

Sept. 17, at 2 P. M., Bethel congregation at the Bethlehem meeting-house, Holt Co., Mo. For any information address Jno. Andes, Mound City, Holt Co., Mo.

Sept. 24, at 3 P. M., in La Porte church, La Porte, Ind. Those will be met in the forenoon and early afternoon of the day of meeting.

Sept. 24, at 3 P. M., Martin's Creek church, Wayne Co., Ill.

Sept. 28, at 10 A. M. Spring Creek church, Kosciusko Co., Ind.

Sept. 30, at 2 P. M., Milledge church, Piatt Co., Ill.

Oct. 1, at 1 P. M., Sugar Creek church, Allen Co., Ohio.

Oct. 1, at 2 P. M., Osage church, Crawford Co., Kans.

Oct. 1, at 5 P. M., Pokagon church, Dowagiac, Cass Co., Mich.

Oct. 1, at 4 P. M., Logan church, near DeGraff, Ohio.

Oct. 1, Maple Grove church, Norton Co., Kans.

Oct. 7, at 2 P. M., Kaskaskia church, Fayette Co., Ill., ten miles south-west of Brother City, Ill. Those coming by rail will be met at the above-named place by informing Granville Nevinger.

Oct. 7, at 10 A. M., Sugar Creek, Whitley Co., Ind.

Oct. 8 and 9, at 2 P. M., Arnold's Grove, Ill.

Oct. 8, at 10 A. M., Dry Creek church, Linn Co., Iowa, one mile west of Robins Station.

Oct. 6, at 3 P. M., Spring Creek church, in the Keith's church-house, eleven miles south-west of Reece, Kans.

Oct. 8, South Creek congregation, Ohio, 3¾ miles west of Delta, Ohio.

Nov. 5, at 3 P. M., Big Creek church, Richland Co., Ill., 3¾ miles South-east of Parkersburg, Ill. Conveyance will be at the above place by informing J. M. Forney.

The First Three Christian Centuries. — By Islay Burns. Cloth, $1.25.

GOOD BOOKS FOR ALL.

ANY book in the market furnished at publishers' lowest retail price by the Brethren's Publishing Company, Mt. Morris, Ill. *Special prices* given when books are purchased in quantities. When ordering books, not on our list, if possible give title, name of author, and address of publishers.

The Throne of David.—By J. H. Ingraham. Cloth, $1.50.

Josephus' Complete Works.—Large type, 1 vol. 8vo. Illustrated with many steel and wood engravings. Library sheep, $3.00.

The Doctrine of the Holy Spirit.—By James B. Walker. Cloth, $1.25.

The New Testament History.—By Wm. Smith. Cloth, $1.25.

The Path of Life.—An interesting tract for everybody. Price, 10 cents per copy; 100 copies, $6.00.

Smith's Bible Dictionary.— Edited by Peloubet. Cloth, $2.00; leather, $3.00.

Ante-Nicene Christian Library.—A collection of all the works of the Fathers of the Christian Church prior to the Council of Nice. Edited by Rev. Alexander Roberts, D. D., and James Donaldson, LL. D. Twenty-four vols. 8 vo. Per vol., $3.00.

Sacred Geography and Antiquities.—A practical, helpful work for Bible students, ministers and Sunday-school teachers. Price, $2.25.

The Origin and Growth of Religion.—Hibbert Lectures. By T. W. R. Davids. Cloth, 8vo, $2.50.

Bible Work, or Bible Reader's Commentary on the New Testament.—By J. G. Butler. Two. vols. 8vo, $10.00.

Popular Commentary on the New Testament.—Edited by Philip Schaff. Four volumes, 8vo. Matthew, Mark and Luke; $6.00. John and the Acts; $6.00. Romans to Philemon; $6.00. Hebrews to Revelation; $5.00.

The Life and Epistles of the Apostle Paul.—By W. J. Conybeare. Cloth, $1.00.

The Prince of the House of David.—By J. H. Ingraham. Cloth, $1.50.

The Great Events of History.—By W. F. Collier. Cloth, $1.25.

Trine Immersion.—A vindication of the apostolic form of Christian baptism. By Eld. James Quinter. A most complete and reliable work on the subject." Price, cloth, single copy, $1.25; leather, $1.75.

The Old Testament History.—By William Smith. Cloth, $1.25.

True Method of Searching the Scriptures.—By Daniel Fanning. Paper, 15 cents.

Universalism Against Itself.—By Hall. One of the best works against Universalism. Price, $1.00.

Biblical Antiquities.—By John Nevin. Gives a concise account of Bible times and customs; invaluable to all students of Bible subjects. Price, $1.50.

Quinter and McConnell Debate.—A debate on Trine Immersion, the Lord's Supper, and Feet-washing, between Eld. James Quinter (German Baptist) and Eld. N. A. McConnell (Christian) held at Dry Creek, Iowa, 1867. Price, 8vo, $1.50.

Sabbatism.—By M. M. Eshelman. Treats the Sabbath question, showing that the first day of the week is the day for assembling in worship. Price, 10 cents; 15 copies, $1.00.

The Story of the Bible. — An excellent volume for old and young; will interest and instruct all those desiring a knowledge of the Scriptures. Price, $1.00.

Biblical Theology of the Old Testament.—By R. F. Weidner. Cloth, $1.25.

The House We Live In.—By Daniel Vaniman. It gives a concise account of the faith and practice of the Brethren. Price, 100 copies, 60 cents.

The Holy Land and the Bible.—By Cunningham Geikie. Cloth, $1.75.

A Dictionary of Biblical Antiquities.—By John W. Nevin. Cloth, $1.50.

German and English Testaments.—American Bible Society Edition. Price, 60 cents.

Early Days of Christianity.—By F. W. Farrar. Author's edition, cloth, $1.50.

Every Day Religion.—By James Freeman Clarke. Cloth, 12mo, $1.50.

Paths of the World.—A concise history of the great religious systems of the world. Cloth, 8vo, $2.00.

Europe and Bible Lands.—By D. L. Miller. A book for the people,—more comprehensive and thorough than many higher-priced works. Price, cloth, $1.50; leather, $2.00.

The Pillar of Fire.—By J. H. Ingraham. Cloth, $1.50.

The Bible, the Sunday-school Text-book.—By Alfred Holborn. Cloth, 75 cents.

Origin of Single Immersion.—By Eld. James Quinter. Price, 2 copies, 5 cents; 12 copies, 25 cents; 50 copies, $1.00.

Campbell and Owen Debate. — Contains a complete Investigation of the evidences of Christianity. Price, $1.50.

Ecclesiastical History.—By Eusebius. Bohn Library. Cloth, $2.00.

Gospel Chimes.

BY WM. BEERY.

A new edition of this deservedly-popular Sunday-school song-book has just been issued.

Bro. Beery has had a large experience in Sunday-school work, and the book which we offer to the Brethren, and the public in general, evinces the exercise of talent as well as good judgment. The religious purity of the hymns, contributed by sister Beery, adds much to the excellence of the book.

Price per single copy, 25 cts.; per dozen, by mail, $2.50; by express, $2.50. Lots of more than a dozen must be sent by express.

BRETHREN'S PUBLISHING CO.,
Or Huntingdon, Pa.   Mt. Morris Ill.

Alone with God.

THIS manual of devotions, by J. H. Garrison, comprises a series of meditations with forms of prayer for private devotions, family worship and special occasions. It is one of the most useful, most needed, and best adapted books of the year, and therefore it is not strange that it is proving one of the most popular. In work of this kind its distinguished, gifted, pious and beloved author is at his best. This book is helpful to every minister, church official, and Sunday-school superintendent, as well as every private member of the church in all ages. It has models of prayer, suitable for the service of the prayer-meeting, while its suggestions, meditations and instructions are pre-eminently calculated to be of service in preparation for the solemn duties that rest upon the active members. Cloth, 75 cents; morocco, $1.25. Address this office.

EUROPE AND Bible Lands

A new edition of this deservedly popular work has recently been published. It retains all the excellencies of its predecessors, and with those who are interested in Bible study this work will always remain a favorite. Those who have read the ordinary book of travel will be surprised to find "Europe and Bible Lands" of thrilling interest for both old and young. The large number of books, already sold, proves that the work is of more than ordinary merit.

A fair supply of the last edition of this work is still on hand. Those who have not yet secured a copy of the work should embrace this opportunity of securing it. Price, in fine cloth binding, only $1.50 per copy, post-paid. To agents who are prepared to push an active canvass of the work, we are prepared to give special inducements. Write us. BRETHREN'S PUBLISHING CO.,
Mt. Morris. Ill

CRUDEN'S
COMPLETE
CONCORDANCE

THIS excellent work, which we offer for sale to our readers, at the low price of $1.50 post-paid, is the only one of the kind that may be depended upon as being strictly reliable. Any verse in the Bible may be readily found by looking for any material word in the verse. Besides this there are given the significations of the principal words, by which their true, Scriptural meaning may be known. A full account of Jewish customs and ceremonies is given as well as a complete concordance of the proper names of the Bible and of the books called Apocrypha. Send all orders for the above work to this office

---

* Study to show thyself approved unto God, a workman that needeth not be ashamed, rightly dividing the Word of Truth.

WORK AND LOVE.

BY GERTRUDE A. FLORY.

Work, O, work! The burdens of sin
Souls noble and great are crushing;
Work, O, work! Till the *Light* shines in,
All sinning and sorrow hushing;
Work, till the world with that Light is ablaze,
And souls in sweet freedom echo its praise.

Love, O, love! There are aching hearts
For affection vainly pleading;
Love, O, love! Hatred's poison darts
Pierce hearts that are sore and bleeding;
Withhold not from these love's balm and repose;
To each is measured its portion of woes.

Work, O, work! The harvest is great,
And reapers are faint and weary;
Work, O, work! Pause not to await
A task more genial and cheery;
Soon will be falling the damp dew of night:
Leave not a sheaf for the mildew and blight!

Love, O, love! Let its streams flow on
To win all hearts with its sweetness;
Love, O, love! The immortal dawn
Will measure its full completeness;
Its volumes of bliss; its raptures untold;
Its riches more valued than pearls and gold.

Work bravely on! The day at length
In welcome rest sweetly closes;
Love with thy heart, soul, mind and strength
Till love in the Fountain reposes.
Rich will the recompense be of employ,
Ceaseless the glory and endless the joy!

La Porte, Ind.

WATCHMAN, WHAT OF THE NIGHT!

BY WILLIAM HOLSINGER.

"The watchman said, The morning cometh, and also the night."—Isaiah 21: 12.

"Lord, wilt thou at this time restore again the kingdom to Israel?"—Acts 1: 6.

"Son of man, I have made thee a watchman unto the house of Israel: therefore hear the word at my mouth, and give warning from me."—Ezek. 3: 17.

"Watch ye therefore: for ye know not when the master of the house cometh, at even, or at midnight, or at the cock-crowing, or in the morning: Lest coming suddenly he find you sleeping. And what I say unto you I say unto all, Watch."—Mark 13: 35-37.

THE Scriptures are of peculiar significance at this time, and it seems that they are somewhat differently understood by different persons; hence I will try to call attention to what, to my mind, is taught in the above texts.

A watchman is one set apart to keep the people informed of what is going on around them, and to give timely warning if any signs of danger are manifest. In Acts 1: 6 the people ask concerning the restoration of the kingdom to ISRAEL. It seems they understood that this was the mission of Jesus. They thought they had his own words as proof to that effect. Matt. 19: 28; Luke 22: 30.

Jesus had told them of many things that would come to pass, and even told them that the day, when he would do this, was not known by any man, nor the angels in heaven, neither did he himself know. From this it appears that their hope and comfort was that he would soon restore the kingdom, and they would be seated on thrones to judge (or rule) the twelve tribes of Israel. Jesus told them, "It is not for you to know the times or the seasons, which the Father hath put in his own power. But ye shall receive power, after that the Holy Ghost is come upon you." Acts 1: 7-8. After the day of Pentecost the disciples went out to preach the Gospel of the kingdom, and it seems that in their preaching they taught the doctrine of the return of Jesus to restore the kingdom to Israel. We learn that the early Christians held the belief that Jesus would soon come, and hence there were those who claimed to be the Christ, but they were "false Christs." All along these false Christs appeared, and thus kept in the mind of the believers the fact that Jesus had foretold these things, and given warning to his followers not to be deceived by them.

Jesus tells us of many things that were to come to pass before that time, and, by carefully studying his Word, none need be deceived by those who set the time in advance of prophetic time. Jesus says, "Search the Scriptures." John 5: 39. When the prophet, like in a panoramic view, sees these things from his time to the close of the Gentile rule brought before him, he is told that these things are sealed till the time of the end. Dan. 12. "In the time of the end knowledge will be increased." Then, if about A. D. 1000, some would say that Christ would come, they would only need be told that they were then in darkness (Dark Ages). Gross darkness covered the earth. In Paul's day there were things in the way. Among other things "except there come a falling away at first, and the man of sin be revealed, the son of perdition." Down to May, 1790, this one prominent sign that Jesus had given had not yet come to pass. Then the sun was darkened, and the moon did not give her light. Just shortly before this, the great tribulation upon the saints had ceased. Again, on Nov. 13, 1833, the great meteoric shower took place. This probably was the fulfillment of what Jesus had in mind when he said, "The stars shall fall from heaven." I would call particular attention to what Jesus tells his disciples. Matt. 24; Mark 13; Luke 21; also Matt. 25: 1, 14.

It seems that there is a waiting time implied, and plainly given in the parable of the ten virgins, and if there had been no time set or given for the coming until he did come, none could, or would know, when to go out to meet him. But when it seemed that the time was fulfilled, when he would come,—even the day and hour given,— a given number of those, looking for him, went out to meet him at a certain time, and while he tarried, they all slumbered and slept. At last the cry came, "Behold the bridegroom cometh; go ye out to meet him." "And they that were ready went in with him to the marriage; and the door was shut." Matt. 25: 10. "So likewise ye when ye shall see all these things, know that it is near, even at the doors." Matt. 24: 33.

Have the signs been fulfilled, as foretold by the prophets,—Christ and the apostles? I think that about all have, down to the very closing events of the coming Bridegroom.

Has the seal of Dan. 12: 4 been opened? If we look out into the world, we see the things just as they were shown him, and as they were to mark the "time of the end." "Many shall run to and fro, and knowledge shall be increased."

The increase of knowledge among men in the present century is unparalleled in the annals of history. The means for travel, commerce and communication are almost beyond comparison with the former centuries.

"And as he sat upon the Mount of Olives, the disciples came unto him privately saying, Tell us, when shall these things be?" ("Their house left desolate," "There shall not be left one stone upon another, that shall not be thrown down,"— of the Temple) "and what shall be the sign of thy coming?" — "And Jesus answered, Many shall come in my name,—saying I am Christ." "Ye shall hear of wars and rumors of wars;" "Nation shall rise against nation, kingdom against kingdom, famines, pestilences and earthquakes.

Many afflictions and trials shall come upon the saints,—and this Gospel of the kingdom shall be preached in all the world "for a witness unto all nations."

This seems to span the time of the Gentiles. Verses 16 to 20 gives us the destruction of Jerusalem which has been literally fulfilled. Verses 21 to 29 seem to reach to the time when the last day signs were to appear, "Immediately after the tribulation of those days shall the sun be darkened and the moon shall not give her light". This was fulfilled May 19, 1780. "And the stars shall fall from heaven." This was fulfilled Nov. 13, 1833. "And the powers of the heavens shall be shaken." We know that governments, powers, principalities,—both Political and Ecclesiastical,—have been wonderfully shaken within the present century, or since the darkening of the sun.

Dear readers, let us all be careful as to whether we are bearing testimony with and for Jesus, or against him. In conclusion, I will quote these words: "Who then is a *faithful* and *wise servant* whom his Lord hath made *ruler over his* HOUSEHOLD, *to give them meat in* DUE *season?*" "Blessed is that servant whom his Lord when he cometh shall find so doing. Verily I say unto you, that he shall make him ruler over all his goods. But and if that evil servant shall say in his heart, My lord delayeth his coming; and shall begin to smite his fellow servants, and to eat and drink with the drunken; the lord of that servant shall come in a day when he looketh not for him, and in an hour that he is not aware of, and shall cut him asunder, and appoint him his portion with the hypocrites: there shall be weeping and gnashing of teeth. Matt. 24: 46-51.

Rosedale, Kans.

GODLINESS.

BY MARY M. COX.

"Exercise thyself rather unto godliness. For bodily exercise profiteth little: but godliness is profitable unto all things, having the promise of the life that now is, and that which is to come."—2 Tim. 4: 7, 8.

WE all know the value of bodily exercise, for it gives both health and strength to our bodies, yet the apostle tells Timothy that, compared with godliness, it profiteth little. How important it is, then, that we exercise ourselves unto godliness! Bodily exercise is profitable in this life only, while godliness is profitable both in this life and that which is to come.

A child cannot grow to maturity fully developed, without proper exercise. If we sit idly down, after having become children of God, and do nothing, we will never reach true Christian manhood or womanhood. We must have godly exercise to fully develop our Christian character. Without godly exercise we soon die spiritually, so to speak. But how are we know what God would have us to do in order to exercise ourselves unto godliness? If we go to one minister, he inquire of him what we must do to be saved, he may possibly tell us that all we have to do is simply to believe in Christ and accept him as our Savior. Another will tell us that we are saved by works. One says that baptism is not one of the conditions of salvation, and another says that we cannot be saved without baptism, and so on.

The more we talk with men in regard to our salvation, the more we are mystified, and the only safe course for us to pursue is to ask wisdom of God, who giveth liberally and upbraideth not. If we really desire to serve and obey God, we must study his Word carefully and prayerfully, and he will undoubtedly give us understanding.

❖ESSAYS❖

Study to show thyself approved unto God; a workman that needeth not to be ashamed, rightly dividing the Word of Truth.

WORK AND LOVE.

BY GERTRUDE A. FLORY.

Work, O, work! The burdens of sin
Souls noble and great are crushing;
Work, O, work! Till the *Light* shines in,
All sinning and sorrow hushing;
Work, till the world with that Light is ablaze,
And souls in sweet freedom echo its praise.

Love, O, love! There are aching hearts
For affection vainly pleading;
Love, O, love! Hatred's poison darts
Pierce hearts that are sore and bleeding;
Withhold not from these love's balm and repose;
To each is measured its portion of woes.

Work, O, work! The harvest is great,
And reapers are faint and weary;
Work, O, work! Pause not to await
A task more genial and cheery!
Soon will be falling the damp dew of night;
Leave not a sheaf for the mildew and blight!

Love, O, love! Let its streams flow on
To win all hearts with its sweetness;
Love, O, love! The immortal dawn
Will measure its full completeness;
Its volumes of bliss; its raptures untold!
Its riches more valued than pearls and gold.

Work bravely on! The day at length
In welcome rest sweetly closes;
Love with thy heart, soul, mind and strength
Till love in the Fountain reposes.
Rich will the recompense be of employ,
Ceaseless the glory and endless the joy!

La Porte, Ind.

WATCHMAN, WHAT OF THE NIGHT!

BY WILLIAM FOLSINGER.

"The watchman said, The morning cometh, and also the night."—Isaiah 21: 12.

"Lord, wilt thou at this time restore again the kingdom to Israel?"—Acts 1: 6.

"Son of man, I have made thee a watchman unto the house of Israel: therefore hear the word at my mouth, and give warning from me."—Ezek. 3: 17.

"Watch ye therefore: for ye know not when the master of the house cometh, at even, or at midnight, or at the cock-crowing, or in the morning: Lest coming suddenly he find you sleeping. And what I say unto you I say unto all, Watch."—Mark 13: 35-37.

The Scriptures are of peculiar significance at this time, and it seems that they are somewhat differently understood by different persons; hence I will try to call attention to what, to my mind, is taught in the above texts.

A watchman is one set apart to keep the people informed of what is going on around them, and to give timely warning if any signs of danger are manifest. In Acts 1: 6 the people ask concerning the restoration of the kingdom to Israel. It seems they understood that this was the mission of Jesus. They thought they had his own words as proof to that effect. Matt. 19: 28; Luke 22: 30.

Jesus had told them of many things that would come to pass, and even told them that the day, when he would do this, was not known by any man, nor the angels in heaven, neither did he himself know. From this it appears that their hope and comfort was that he would soon restore the kingdom, and they would be seated on thrones to judge (or rule) the twelve tribes of Israel. Jesus told them, "It is not for you to know the times or the seasons, which the Father hath put in his own power. But ye shall receive power, after that the Holy Ghost is come upon you." Acts 1: 7-8. After the day of Pentecost the disciples went out to preach the Gospel of the kingdom, and it seems that in their preaching

they taught the doctrine of the return of Jesus to restore the kingdom to Israel. We learn that the early Christians held the belief that Jesus would soon come, and hence there were those who claimed to be the Christ, but they were "false Christs." All along these false Christs appeared, and thus kept in the mind of the believers the fact that Jesus had foretold these things, and given warning to his followers not to be deceived by them.

Jesus tells us of many things that were to come to pass before that time, and, by carefully studying his Word, none need be deceived by those who set the time in advance of prophetic time. Jesus says, "Search the Scriptures." John 5: 39. When the prophet, like in a panoramic view, sees these things from his time to the close of the Gentile rule brought before him, he is told that these things are sealed till the time of the end. Dan. 12. "In the time of the end knowledge will be increased." Then, if about A. D. 1000, some would say that Christ would come, they would only need be told that they were then in darkness (Dark Ages). Gross darkness covered the earth. In Paul's day there were things in the way. Among other things "except there come a falling away at first, and the man of sin be revealed, the son of perdition."

Down to May, 1780, this one prominent sign that Jesus had given had not yet come to pass. Then the sun was darkened, and the moon did not give her light. Just shortly before this, the great tribulation upon the saints had ceased. Again, on Nov. 13, 1833, the great meteoric shower took place. This probably was the fulfillment of what Jesus had in mind when he said, "The stars shall fall from heaven." I would call particular attention to what Jesus tells his disciples. Matt. 24; Mark 13; Luke 21; also Matt. 25: 1, 14.

It seems that there is a waiting time implied, and plainly given in the parable of the ten virgins, and if there had been no time set or given for the coming until he did come, none could, or would know, when to go out to meet him. But when it seemed that the time was fulfilled, when he would come,—even the day and hour given,—a given number of those, looking for him, went out to meet him at a certain time, and while he tarried, they all slumbered and slept. At last the cry came, "Behold the bridegroom cometh; go ye out to meet him." "And they that were ready went in with him to the marriage; and the door was shut." Matt. 25: 10. "So likewise ye when ye shall see all these things, know that it is near, even at the doors." Matt. 24: 33.

Have the signs been fulfilled, as foretold by the prophets,—Christ and the apostles? I think that about all have, down to the very closing events of the coming Bridegroom.

Has the seal of Dan. 12: 4 been opened? If we look out into the world, we see the things just as they were shown him, and as they were to mark the "time of the end." "Many shall run to and fro, and knowledge shall be increased."

The increase of knowledge among men in the present century is unparalleled in the annals of history. The means for travel, commerce and communication are almost beyond comparison with the former centuries.

"And as he sat upon the Mount of Olives, the disciples came unto him privately saying, Tell us, when shall these things be?" ("Their house left desolate," "There shall not be left one stone upon another, that shall not be thrown down,"—of the Temple) "and what shall be the sign of thy coming?" —"And Jesus answered, Many shall come in my name,—saying I am Christ." "Ye shall hear of wars and rumors of wars;" "Nation shall rise against nation, kingdom

against kingdom, famines, pestilences and earthquakes.

Many afflictions and trials shall come upon the saints,—and this Gospel of the kingdom shall be preached in all the world "for a witness unto all nations."

This seems to span the time of the Gentiles. Verses 16 to 20 gives us the destruction of Jerusalem which has been literally fulfilled. Verses 21 to 29 seem to reach to the time when the last day signs were to appear, "Immediately after the tribulation of those days shall the sun be darkened and the moon shall not give her light." This was fulfilled May 19, 1780. "And the stars shall fall from heaven." This was fulfilled Nov. 13, 1833. "And the powers of the heavens shall be shaken." We know that governments, powers, principalities,—both Political and Ecclesiastical,—have been wonderfully shaken within the present century, or since the darkening of the sun.

Dear readers, let us all be careful as to whether we are bearing testimony with and for Jesus, or against him. In conclusion, I will quote these words: "Who then is a *faithful* and *wise* servant whom his Lord hath made *ruler over his* household, *to give them meat in* due *season?*" "Blessed is that servant whom his Lord when he cometh shall find so doing. Verily I say unto you, that he shall make him ruler over all his goods. But and if that evil servant shall say in his heart, My lord delayeth his coming; and shall begin to smite his fellow servants, and to eat and drink with the drunken; the lord of that servant shall come in a day when he looketh not for him, and in an hour that he is not aware of, and shall cut him asunder, and appoint him his portion with the hypocrites: there shall be weeping and gnashing of teeth." Matt. 24: 45-51.

Rosedale, Kans.

GODLINESS.

BY MARY M. COX.

"Exercise thyself rather unto godliness. For bodily exercise profiteth little: but godliness is profitable unto all things, having the promise of the life that now is, and that which is to come."—2 Tim. 4: 7, 8.

We all know the value of bodily exercise, for it gives both health and strength to our bodies, yet the apostle tells Timothy that, compared with godliness, it profiteth little. How important it is, then, that we exercise ourselves unto godliness! Bodily exercise is profitable in this life only, while godliness is profitable both in this life and that which is to come.

A child cannot grow to maturity fully developed, without proper exercise. If we sit idly down, after having become children of God, and do nothing, we will never reach true Christian manhood or womanhood. We must have godly exercise to fully develop our Christian character. Without godly exercise we soon die spiritually, so to speak. But how are we know what God would have us to do in order to exercise ourselves unto godliness? If we go to one minister, and inquire of him what we must do to be saved, he may possibly tell us that all we have to do is simply to believe in Christ and accept him as our Savior. Another will tell us that we are saved by works. One says that baptism is not one of the conditions of salvation, and another says that we cannot be saved without baptism, and so on.

The more we talk with men in regard to our salvation, the more we are mystified, and the only safe course for us to pursue is to ask wisdom of God, who giveth liberally and upbraideth not.

If we really desire to serve and obey God, we must study his Word carefully and prayerfully, and he will undoubtedly give us understanding,

New Jerusalem, not made with hands, eternal in the heavens.

132 Fern Cliff Ave., Springfield, Ohio.

NOMINAL RELIGION.

BY T. A. ROBINSON.

PERSONS may be regular in outward forms of religion, and yet destitute of its spirit,—without an effectual change. Such cannot escape the judgment of God. God abhors indifference in religion no less than he does infidelity or open immorality. The more indifferent men become in religion, the more self-confident they are. The latter means Christ out and self in,—all nominal, no spirit, no love, no Christ and no reality in religion. I mean by this the religion of-Christ, for the world is full of religions, but there is only one that is heaven-born,—Christ-begotten, pure and undefiled. James says it is "unspotted from the world," or requires us to keep so.

Do we have this religion? Have we love for God's Holy Zion, enough to counteract the worldly desire for fashion, pride and the so-called social entertainments of the churches in modern Christendom? I look and wonder, Where is the Christ in them? It appears to be dark and formal from the desk to the door, from head to foot, from pastor to laity. I pause and wonder if, were Paul to come into their midst, he would not say as he did to the people at Mars' Hill, "Ye worship ye know not what." If John, the revelator, were to visit them at their grab parties or festivals, could he not truly address them as he did the church in Sardis: "Thou hast a name that thou livest, and art dead"? Rev. 3: 1. Would he tell them as he did the church of the Laodiceans, that they are neither "cold nor hot, but lukewarm"? Rev. 3: 14. Does this not represent our popular churches of to-day,—a little of Christ and a little of the world? It takes only a little transforming of Satan into light to make it take with the masses; too much Christ spoils all for them. There are many good, honest people among them (and my heart bleeds for them), but honesty in practicing an error does not make the error right, neither will it save us in the end. Paul thought he was doing God's service in persecuting the people of God, and was honest and sincere in the work. Finally, however, he found his error, he had to repent; then he changed. I hope all those who are honest will do likewise,—come out from among them, saith the Lord. Ye, laity, be not deceived! Leave the blind guides, who are after the fleece and not your soul! Take God's Word as your guide, and not man's!

The Law may not condemn because of ignorance, but it is not ignorance when we close our eyes on God's commands, and turn a deaf ear to the truth of the Gospel. It is willful blindness of the heart and not of mind only. Darkness is chosen rather than light, because the deeds are evil. Ye say ye love Christ, but in works ye deny him. "Ye have a form of godliness, but deny the power thereof." Ye claim to have come in at the door, when, really ye have climbed up another way. What does Christ say will be the fate in the end? "Ye shall seek to enter in but shall not be able." Sad fate indeed!

Is it true, as has been said, that the world is becoming more Christ-like? Does a mere profession of religion make the world more Christlike? If so, we are progressing; if not I fear we are retrograding, for it is one thing to profess, and quite another thing to possess. I became heart-faint, in pondering over the sinful ways of man, and especially those who claim to be in Christ and walk with the world. When I take a view of Christendom, from the ministry to the laity, I am almost made to ask, Was Christ divided? Has he died in vain? One might so conclude from the way we hear the Word explained. Man's opinion is taking the place of God's Word to-day. Paul says, "Let God be truth and every man a liar." Dare a man of God to-day speak out against the evil works, carried on by popular Christianity? Is he not denominated ignorance or fanaticism, and far behind the times? Thank the Lord we have a few citizens of Zion, who are not afraid to cry out aloud, and spare not. Dear Brethren, let us stand for God and shun not to declare the whole counsel of God. Let us hold aloft the banner of the cross till the last foe is vanquished, or till Shiloh comes.

Media, Kans., March 14.

WAS JUDAS A FREE MORAL AGENT?

BY JOHN E. MOHLER.

IN No. 24 of the GOSPEL MESSENGER, our dear brother Hutchison seems to take the view that Judas was not a free moral agent in the sense that the apostles were. For two reasons I do not see how he can consistently hold this idea.

1. It is not clearly supported by the Scriptures.
2. Its acceptance involves us in inextricable difficulties.

This view is not supported by the Scriptures because, (1) It contradicts the blessed words, "Whosoever will, let him take the water of life freely," and kindred Scriptures. (2) It relieves Judas of the awful responsibility of his crime, thus conflicting with Christ's condemnation of Judas, in Matt. 26: 24.

Such a position involves us in difficulties, for it indirectly supports the doctrine of predestination. If we admit that Judas was not free, Pharaoh was not free, etc., and the mind naturally asks, Who else is not free? Where is the limit? When we admit that one single person was not free, morally, then we cannot define with whom bondage ends, just as when we admit that obedience to one command of Christ is not essential, we cannot say what is essential. "God's purpose," in the case of Judas, does not affect our reasoning, for he has always purposes of more or less magnitude to work out, and every living being contributes to this end. If we free Judas from responsibility, by making him only a means of working out God's purpose, then the vilest sinner may take refuge behind "God's purpose," and sustain his evil course.

Judas was simply a very obedient servant to his master, Satan, just as the apostles were very obedient to their Master, Christ. I write this in the interest of what I believe to be Truth, and I hope our dear brother will so consider these thoughts.

Warrensburgh, Mo.

CHRISTIAN WORSHIP.

BY H. A. STAHL.

IT is the duty of every one to worship God in spirit and in truth. The material and local ideas of God, which many of the Jews entertained, cannot be tolerated in Christian, spiritual worship. Christianity, unencumbered by many forms and ceremonies, disconnected from the peculiarities of time and place, requires that we should draw near to God with reverence and bow in our spirits before the majesty of his throne.

In order to do this there must be a quickening in our spirits. Thus the Ephesians were quickened into newness of life. They,once were dead in trespasses and sins. They walked according to the way of the world. They bowed in idolatry to the prince of darkness and became children of wrath. Thus it was with all who are Christians. "But God who is rich in mercy, for his great love wherewith he loved us, even·when we were dead in sins, has quickened us together with Christ (by grace ye are saved), and hath raised us up togeth. er with Christ, and made us sit together in heav. only places in Christ Jesus." Eph. 2: 4–6.

Thus Christian worship must be the pulsation of the human spirit with the divine. It must take up the thoughts and the attention with divine things. It is not merely coming to the church and engaging in the forms of worship. How many worship God in solemn mockery! They worship with their lips while their hearts are far from him. While they are in prayer, their spirits are engaged in something else. While they are seated under the sound of the Gospel, they are laying their plans about something else than the truth, which is proclaimed out of God's Word. This they call worship. They return from the church fairly well pleased with themselves that they have put the preacher under special obligation for paying·such a compliment to their presence. This they call going to. church. But this is not worshiping God in spirit. There were some such in ancient time to whom God said, "When ye come to appear before me, who hath required this at your hand, to tread my courts? Bring no more vain oblations; incense is an abomination unto me; the new moons and sabbaths, the calling of assemblies, I cannot away with; it is iniquity, even the solemn meeting." Isa. 1: 12, 13.

The spirit, the soul, the rational part of man, that which is immortal and immaterial, must be engaged in our devotions, or it is not Christian, spiritual worship.

The great tendency of the human mind, as far as the worship of God is concerned, is, to take up and be satisfied with the externals as the mere forms of worship rather than with its internal life. We must have the form, but then we must not forget that the power, the spiritual life, to be communicated, is, after all, the great object of divine worship. This may have furnished a reason to the author of Christianity, why he connected with it so few ceremonies and outward forms. Christianity was to be different from Judaism. The former was to possess, in reality, what was merely foreshadowed by the latter. Hence Christianity was so painful to the Jews who were so long accustomed to an almost endless routine of ceremonies, mostly introduced by tradition. It was necessary that Christianity should be preceded by Judaism in order that its spirituality might be gradually instilled into the race. But as the Jews lost sight of the spiritual import of their symbols and were employed with that rather than what was symbolized by them, so the Christian may lose the spiritual import of God's worship and be satisfied, or put himself off with a few empty ceremonies and call this spiritual worship. "But be not deceived; God is not mocked." When we enter into his worship we must do it with a proper frame of mind. Our attention, our feelings, our whole soul must be absorbed in the divine exercise.

> "O for a heart to praise my God!
>   A heart from sin set free;
>   A heart that always feels the blood
>   So freely shed for me."

My dear reader, no one is so exalted as when he lies in the dust before God and loses himself in reverence for his Maker. But what want of reverence is there in much that is called Christian worship! What profane handling of sacred things! What irreverence is seen in God's house! Some will not even so much as kneel in prayer; they will remain seated and merely bow their

New Jerusalem, not made with hands, eternal in the heavens.

192 Fern Cliff Ave., Springfield, Ohio.

NOMINAL RELIGION.

BY T. A. ROBINSON.

PERSONS may be regular in outward forms of religion, and yet destitute of its spirit,—without an effectual change. Such cannot escape the judgment of God. God abhors indifference in religion no less than he does infidelity or open immorality. The more indifferent men become in religion, the more self-confident they are. The latter means Christ out and self in,—all nominal, no spirit, no love, no Christ and no reality in religion. I mean by this the religion of Christ, for the world is full of religions, but there is only one that is heaven-born,—Christ-begotten, pure and undefiled. James says it is "unspotted from the world," or requires us to keep so.

Do we have this religion? Have we love for God's Holy Zion, enough to counteract the worldly desire for fashion, pride and the so-called social entertainments of the churches in modern Christendom? I look and wonder, Where is the Christ in them? It appears to be dark and formal from the desk to the door, from head to foot, from pastor to laity. I pause and wonder if, were Paul to come into their midst, he would not say as he did to the people at Mars' Hill, "Ye worship ye know not what." If John, the revelator, were to visit them at their grab parties or festivals, could he not truly address them as he did the church in Sardis: "Thou hast a name that thou livest, and art dead"? Rev. 3: 1. Would he tell them as he did the church of the Laodiceans, that they are neither "cold nor hot, but lukewarm"? Rev. 3: 14. Does this not represent our popular churches of to-day,—a little of Christ and a little of the world? It takes only a little transforming of Satan into light to make it take with the masses; too much Christ spoils all for them. There are many good, honest people among them (and my heart bleeds for them), but honesty in practicing an error does not make the error right, neither will it save us in the end. Paul thought he was doing God's service in persecuting the people of God, and was honest and sincere in the work. Finally, however, he found his error, he had to repent; he changed. I hope all those who are honest will do likewise,—come out from among them, saith the Lord. Ye, laity, be not deceived! Leave the blind guides, who are after the fleece and not your soul! Take God's Word as your guide, and not man's!

The Law may not condemn because of ignorance, but it is not ignorance when we close our eyes on God's commands, and turn a deaf ear to the truth of the Gospel. It is willful blindness of the heart and not of mind only. Darkness is chosen rather than light, because the deeds are evil. Ye say ye love Christ, but in works ye deny him. "Ye have a form of godliness, but deny the power thereof." Ye claim to have come in at the door, when, in fact, ye have climbed up another way. What does Christ say will be the fate in the end? "Ye shall seek to enter in but shall not be able." Sad fate indeed!

Is it true, as has been said, that the world is becoming more Christ-like? Does a mere profession of religion make the world more Christlike? If so, we are progressing; if not I fear we are retrograding, for it is one thing to profess, and quite another thing to possess. I became heart-faint, in pondering over the sinful ways of man, and especially those who claim to be in Christ and walk with the world. When I take a view of Christendom, from the ministry to the laity, I am almost made to ask, Was Christ divided? Has he died in vain? One might so conclude from the way we hear the Word explained. Man's opinion is taking the place of God's Word to-day. Paul says, "Let God be truth and every man a liar." Dare a man of God to-day speak out against the evil works, carried on by popular Christianity? Is he not denominated ignorance or fanaticism, and far behind the times? Thank the Lord we have a few citizens of Zion, who are not afraid to cry out aloud, and spare not. Dear Brethren, let us stand for God and shun not to declare the whole counsel of God. Let us hold aloft the banner of the cross till the last foe is vanquished, or till Shiloh comes.

Media, Kans., March 14.

WAS JUDAS A FREE MORAL AGENT?

BY JOHN R. MOHLER.

IN No. 24 of the GOSPEL MESSENGER, our dear brother Hutchison seems to take the view that Judas was not a free moral agent in the sense that the apostles were. For two reasons I do not see how he can consistently hold this idea.

1. It is not clearly supported by the Scriptures.
2. Its acceptance involves us in inextricable difficulties.

This view is not supported by the Scriptures because, (1) It contradicts the blessed words, "Whosoever will, let him take the water of life freely," and kindred Scriptures. (2) It relieves Judas of the awful responsibility of his crime, thus conflicting with Christ's condemnation of Judas, in Matt. 26: 24.

Such a position involves us in difficulties, for it indirectly supports the doctrine of predestination. If we admit that Judas was not free, Pharaoh was not free, etc., and the mind naturally asks, Who else is not free? Where is the limit? When we admit that one single person was not free, morally, then we cannot define with whom bondage ends, just as when we admit that obedience to one command of Christ is not essential, we cannot say what is essential. "God's purpose," in the case of Judas, does not affect our reasoning, for he has always purposes of more or less magnitude to work out, and every living being contributes to this end. If we free Judas from responsibility, by making him only a means of working out God's purpose, then the vilest sinner may take refuge behind "God's purpose," and sustain his evil course.

Judas was simply a very obedient servant to his master, Satan, just as the apostles were very obedient to their Master, Christ. I write this in the interest of what I believe to be Truth, and I hope our dear brother will so consider these thoughts.

Warrensburgh, Mo.

CHRISTIAN WORSHIP.

BY H. A. STAHL.

IT is the duty of every one to worship God in spirit and in truth. The material and local ideas of God, which many of the Jews entertained, cannot be tolerated in Christian, spiritual worship. Christianity, unencumbered by many forms and ceremonies, disconnected from the peculiarities of time and place, requires that we should draw near to God with reverence and bow in our spirits before the majesty of his throne.

In order to do this there must be a quickening in our spirits. Thus the Ephesians were quickened into newness of life. They once were dead in trespasses and sins. They walked according to the way of the world. They bowed in idolatry to the prince of darkness and became children of wrath. Thus it was with all who are Christians. "But God who is rich in mercy, for his great love wherewith he loved us, even when we were dead in sins, has quickened us together with Christ (by grace ye are saved), and hath raised us up together with Christ, and made us sit together in heavenly places in Christ Jesus." Eph. 2: 4-6.

Thus Christian worship must be the pulsation of the human spirit with the divine. It must take up the thoughts and the attention with divine things. It is not merely coming to the church and engaging in the forms of worship. How many worship God in solemn mockery! They worship with their lips while their hearts are far from him. While they are in prayer, their spirits are engaged in something else. While they are seated under the sound of the Gospel, they are laying their plans about something else than the truth, which is proclaimed out of God's Word. This they call worship. They return from the church fairly well pleased with themselves that they have put the preacher under special obligation for paying such a compliment to their presence. This they call going to church. But this is not worshiping God in spirit. There were some such in ancient time to whom God said, "When ye come to appear before me, who hath required this at your hand, to tread my courts? Bring no more vain oblations; incense is an abomination unto me; the new moons and sabbaths, the calling of assemblies, I cannot away with; it is iniquity, even the solemn meeting." Isa. 1: 12, 13.

The spirit, the soul, the rational part of man, that which is immortal and immaterial, must be engaged in our devotions, or it is not Christian, spiritual worship.

The great tendency of the human mind, as far as the worship of God is concerned, is, to take up and be satisfied with the externals as the mere forms of worship rather than with its internal life. We must have the form, but then we must not forget that the power, the spiritual life, to be communicated, is, after all, the great object of divine worship. This may have furnished a reason to the author of Christianity, why he connected with it so few ceremonies and outward forms. Christianity was to be different from Judaism. The former was to possess, in reality, what was merely foreshadowed by the latter. Hence Christianity was so painful to the Jews who were so long accustomed to an almost endless routine of ceremonies, mostly introduced by tradition. It was necessary that Christianity should be preceded by Judaism in order that its spirituality might be gradually instilled into the race. But as the Jews lost sight of the spiritual import of their symbols and were employed with that rather than what was symbolized by them, so the Christian may lose the spiritual import of God's worship and be satisfied, or put himself off with a few empty ceremonies and call this spiritual worship. "But be not deceived; God is not mocked." When we enter into his worship we must do it with a proper frame of mind. Our attention, our feelings, our whole soul must be absorbed in the divine exercise.

> "O for a heart to praise my God!
>   A heart from sin set free;
> A heart that always feels the blood
>   So freely shed for me."

My dear reader, when no one is so exalted as when he lies in the dust before God and loses himself in reverence for his Maker. But what want of reverence is there in much that is called Christian worship! What profane handling of sacred things! What irreverence is seen in God's house! Some will not even so much as kneel in prayer; they will remain seated and merely bow their

Missionary and Tract Work Department.

"Upon the first day of the week, let every one of you lay by him in store as God hath prospered him, that there be no gatherings when I come."—1 Cor. 16: 2.

"Every man as he purposeth in his heart, so let him give. Not grudgingly or of necessity, for the Lord loveth a cheerful giver."—2 Cor. 9: 7.

HOW MUCH SHALL WE GIVE?

"Every man *according to his ability.*" "Every one *as God hath prospered him.*" "Every man, *according as he purposeth in his heart, so let him give.*" "For if there be first a willing mind, it is accepted according to that a man hath, and not according to that he hath not."—2 Cor. 8: 12.

Organization of Missionary Committee.

DANIEL VANIMAN, Foreman, - - McPherson, Kans.
D. L. MILLER, Treasurer, - - - Mt. Morris, Ill.
GALEN B. ROYER, Secretary, - - Mt. Morris, Ill.

Organization of Book and Tract Work.

S. W. HOOVER, Foreman, - - - Dayton, Ohio.
S. BOCK, Secretary and Treasurer, - Dayton, Ohio.

☞All donations intended for Missionary Work should be sent to GALEN B. ROYER, Mt. Morris, Ill.

☞All money for Tract Work should be sent to S. BOCK, Dayton, Ohio.

☞Money may be sent by Money Order, Registered Letter, or Drafts on New York or Chicago. Do not send personal checks, or drafts on interior towns, as it costs 25 cents to collect them.

☞Solicitors are requested to faithfully carry out the plan of Annual Meeting, that all our members be solicited to contribute at least twice a year for the Mission and Tract Work of the Church.

☞Notes for the Endowment Fund can be had by writing to the Secretary of either Work.

THE BIBLE LOST, BUT FOUND AGAIN.

BY LANDON WEST.

THE treatment that the Word of God has received from the people of this world is shameful and startling, for it has been forbidden by nations, banished by rulers and burned by priests; but, with all this, its worst treatment was for a people to have it in possession, promise to obey it, and then neglect it so far as to lose the only copy of it the world had, and yet think all the while that they had it at hand, and were loyal to its teaching. But such is the history of God's Word.

In Deut 31: 9, 30 the reader will find the Word of the Lord to Moses, which said: "Thou shalt read this law before all Israel in their hearing;" "at the end of every seven years, the year of release" (verses 10 and 11), that "all people with them, men, women and children, and strangers, may hear and fear the Lord your God, and observe to do all the words of the law," "and that their children may hear and learn to fear the Lord your God as long as ye live in the land beyond Jordan."

The same day Moses wrote his song, and taught it to the children of Israel. Verse 22; 32: 1, 43. This reading was given by Moses to all the people as his farewell address, east of the Jordan, and 1451 years before Christ. His charge to the Levites was: "Take this book of the law, and put it in the side of the ark of the covenant of the Lord your God, that it may be there for a witness against thee." 31: 26.

Then Moses gave charge to all the people of Israel, and said: "Set your hearts unto all the words which I testify among you this day, which ye shall command your children to observe to do, all the words of this law. For it is not a vain thing for you; because it is your life: and through this thing ye shall prolong your days in the land, whither ye go over Jordan to possess it." 32: 46, 47. He then blessed Israel, and departed to obtain a view of the land and to die. Chapter 34.

In Joshua 8: 34, 35, in the same year (1451 B. C.), we find a second reading, by Joshua, to all the people, men, women and little ones and to the strangers. But who would have thought that this duty, so pleasant and so instructive, besides so full of promises, even of life itself, should now, be neglected for hundreds of years? But it is true; for we hear nothing more of it, only what the priests said about the law, till the reign of Josiah,—827 years afterward.

Money and lands, war and pride, with lust, fine houses, and wives, and concubines, had so fully taken up the minds of kings and priests, and people, that this simple means of giving light to the people, was lost sight of, and the Book of God was buried in the silver of the temple treasury, which had now become a banking-house.

But the light broke forth again with a flame. In 624 B. C., Josiah sent Shaphan, the scribe, to the temple, and to Hilkiah, the high-priest, to get a report of all the silver then in the house of the Lord, and, in their effort to make a fine showing of the money collected in God's house, behold you, they found the *lost Bible,* and the copy of God's Law was again brought to light. 2 Kings 22: 8. The priest gave it to the scribe, Shaphan, and reading it, he came to the king, and after making a report of the money found, told him that they had also found the Book of God, and he read it before the king.

So alarming were the words spoken, and so vast the oversight, made by both kings and priests, and for so long a time, that the king rent his clothes. The silver was forgotten, and he, seeing the situation, sent for the high-priest and others, and these called upon Huldah, the prophetess of the Lord, for a message,—another message from heaven. It was given them, and a fearful one it was. The king sent and called all the elders of Judah and Jerusalem, both small and great, to meet, and again, the third time, all the words of the covenant were read to all the people. 23: 1, 2. But it was too late to reform. "The Lord said, I will remove Judah out of my sight." Verse 27. Is it any wonder that Isaiah, seventy-four years before the finding of God's Book, should have said: "They trust in vanity, and speak lies; we wait for light, but we walk in darkness. We grope for the wall like the blind, and we grope as if we had no eyes: we stumble at noonday as in the night." See Isa. 59: 4-10.

No wonder he speaks of "gross darkness" having fallen on the people (60: 2) when the Key of Knowledge had been lost for generations. . Brethren, do not overlook the fact that all this darkness occurred in the days of scholars and education, and that, too, when there was a college within sight of the temple, where God's Book and the witness against their nation, lay hid and silent in the dust and silver in the Lord's house. 22: 14.

Had the Book of God been read to all the people but once in a century, it would have saved the Book from being lost, and would have saved the nation, but to have read it each seven years, as commanded, would have given them 118 readings from Joshua to Josiah, and would have kept the light ablaze before all the people. David and Solomon, in their reign of eighty years, could have enjoyed at least eleven readings, and lost no good thing by it, but alas, a fine house for the Lord, fine houses for themselves, fine women and fine children so completely blinded their eyes that this secret of their nation's life (Deut. 32: 46, 47) and the light and wealth of their people was forgotten.

These things need not to have prevented the reading of the Law, but its reading would most assuredly have prevented so many wives, and, of course, so many wicked children. It would have made both of them better kings and better men, and there would have been a better nation. Prov. 14: 34. It would certainly have prevented the saying, "Has God cast away his people?"—"for they would not then have been cast away." Rom. 11: 1. The eleven readings by David and Solomon would have done more for God's name and for his people, than a score of temples.

The fourth and last reading of the Law was not had until the days of Nehemiah and Ezra, the prophet, B. C. 445, and 179 years after the reading by Josiah. Neh. 8. Jerusalem and its first and richest temple had been destroyed by the Babylonians; its people had been taken captive, and there, for seventy years, had mourned their city's desolation. They had returned again by the decree of Cyrus the Great, had rebuilt the city, and a second temple, amidst much persecution, was also built.

When Nehemiah at Suss, in the service of the king of Persia, heard of the situation, he came up to Jerusalem to rebuild the wall, which was completed in fifty-two days, amid fightings against their enemies and deception amongst their own people. But the work, though great, was done, "for the people had a mind to work," though some, like we see now, "put not their neck to the work of the Lord." Neh. 3: 5 and 4: 6. After numbering the people, of whom there were 49,942, and collecting the donations, made in gold, silver and sacred garments, "the people all gathered together as one man into the street that was before the water gate; and they spake unto Ezra the scribe to bring the book of the law of Moses, which the Lord had commanded to Israel." Neh. 8: 1.

Here again, on the first day of the seventh month, and 445 years B. C., Ezra brought the Law before the people, men, women and children. And when he had opened the Book, all the people stood up, and there, in the street, and from morning till noon, they stood, and were attentive to the reading of the Law. "And all the people wept when they heard the words of the law." And when Ezra blessed the Lord, the great God, all the people said, Amen, Amen, with lifting up their hands: and they bowed their heads, and worshipped the Lord with their faces to the ground." Verses 6, 10. The people came again on the second day, and so on, day by day for seven days, and he read to the people the Book of the law of God." Verse 18.

We notice here that the people called for the reading of the Law, and they manifested much zeal and patience in standing, day after day, in the street, to hear it read, but we hear no more of it being read to them afterward. When our Savior came and taught them 475 years afterward, the Jews, then alive and serving in the temple, with the scribes and teachers, knew very little of what Moses had given them in the Law, and what they named they had perverted from its correct meaning.

The reason is plain: The Word of God was not read every seven years, and the people got only what the priests said it taught. The priests did not like the labor of reading to the people, nor to take the time, for it was so much easier to tell it to the people. But they did not tell it all, for reading it in full would have condemned both kings and priests, hence, to save themselves and to save time and labor, they told some of God's Word and their traditions with it, which soon exceeded the Bible, both in bulk and importance, and the nation was blind, with blind guides to lead them. Turn to Matt. 15, and see what Jesus says of their teaching. No wonder he said, "Search the Scriptures" (John 5: 39), for they had hid it from the people and were ignorant of it themselves, and, like it is now, they depended too much upon what other men said about the Bible. Thus they took away the Key of Knowledge. Luke 11: 52. But had the Word been read every seven years, it would have given 212 readings till the baptism of Jesus, and would have saved cities, towns, temples, kings, prophets,

Missionary and Tract Work Department.

"Upon the first day of the week, let every one of you lay by him in store as God hath prospered him, that there be no gatherings when I come."—1 Cor. 16:2.

"Every man as he purposeth in his heart, so let him give. Not grudgingly or of necessity, for the Lord loveth a cheerful giver."—2 Cor. 9:7.

HOW MUCH SHALL WE GIVE?

"Every man *according to his ability.*" "Every one *as God hath prospered him.*" "Every man, *according as he purposeth in his heart,* so let him give." "For if there be first a willing mind, it is accepted *according to that a man hath,* and not according to that he hath not."—2 Cor. 8:12.

Organization of Missionary Committee.

DANIEL VANIMAN, Foreman,   - McPherson, Kans.
D. L. MILLER, Treasurer,   - Mt. Morris, Ill.
GALEN B. ROYER, Secretary,   - Mt. Morris, Ill.

Organization of Book and Tract Work.

S. W. HOOVER, Foreman,   - Dayton, Ohio.
S. BOCK, Secretary and Treasurer, - Dayton, Ohio.

☞All donations intended for Missionary Work should be sent to GALEN B. ROYER, Mt. Morris, Ill.

☞All money for Tract Work should be sent to S. BOCK, Dayton, Ohio.

☞Money may be sent by Money Order, Registered Letter, or Drafts on New York or Chicago. Do not send personal checks, or drafts on interior towns, as it costs 25 cents to collect them.

☞Solicitors are requested to faithfully carry out the plan of Annual Meeting, that all our members be solicited to contribute at least twice a year for the Mission and Tract Work of the Church.

☞Notes for the Endowment Fund can be had by writing to the Secretary of either Work.

THE BIBLE LOST, BUT FOUND AGAIN.

BY LANDON WEST.

THE treatment that the Word of God has received from the people of this world is shameful and startling, for it has been forbidden by nations, banished by rulers and burned by priests; but, with all this, its worst treatment was for a people to have it in possession, promise to obey it, and then neglect it so far as to lose the only copy of it the world had, and yet think all the while that they had it at hand, and were loyal to its teaching. But such is the history of God's Word.

In Deut 31: 9, 30 the reader will find the Word of the Lord to Moses, which said: "Thou shalt read this law before all Israel in their hearing;" "at the end of every seven years, the year of release" (verses 10 and 11), that "all people with them, men, women and children, and strangers, may hear and fear the Lord your God, and observe to do all the words of the law," "and that their children may hear and learn to fear the Lord your God as long as ye live in the land beyond Jordan."

The same day Moses wrote his song, and taught it to the children of Israel. Verse 22; 32: 1, 43. This reading was given by Moses to all the people as his farewell address, east of the Jordan, and 1451 years before Christ. His charge to the Levites was: "Take this book of the law, and put it in the side of the ark of the covenant of the Lord your God, that it may be there for a witness against thee." 31: 26.

Then Moses gave charge to all the people of Israel, and said: "Set your hearts unto all the words which I testify among you this day, which ye shall command your children to observe to do, all the words of this law. For it is not a vain thing for you; because it is your life: and through this thing ye shall prolong your days in the land, whither ye go over Jordan to possess it." 32: 46, 47. He then blessed Israel, and departed to obtain a view of the land and to die. Chapter 34.

In Joshua 8: 34, 35, in the same year (1451 B. C.), we find a second reading, by Joshua, to all the people, men, women and little ones and to the strangers. But who would have thought that this duty, so pleasant and so instructive, besides so full of promises, even of life itself, should now be neglected for hundreds of years? But it is true; for we hear nothing more of it, only what the priests said about the law, till the reign of Josiah,—827 years afterward.

Money and lands, war and pride, with lust, fine houses, and wives, and concubines, had so fully taken up the minds of kings and priests, and people, that this simple means of giving light to the people, was lost sight of, and the Book of God was buried in the silver of the temple treasury, which had now become a banking-house.

But the light broke forth again with a flame. In 624 B. C., Josiah sent Shaphan, the scribe, to the temple, and to Hilkiah, the high-priest, to get a report of all the silver then in the house of the Lord, and, in their effort to make a fine showing of the money collected in God's house, behold you, they found the *lost Bible,* and the copy of God's Law was again brought to light. 2 Kings 22: 8. The priest gave it to the scribe, Shaphan, and reading it, he came to the king, and after making a report of the money found, told him that they had also found the Book of God, and he read it before the king.

So alarming were the words spoken, and so vast the oversight, made by both kings and priests, and for so long a time, that the king rent his clothes. The silver was forgotten, and he, seeing the situation, sent for the high-priest and others, and these called upon Huldah, the prophetess of the Lord, for a message,—another message from heaven. It was given them, and a fearful one it was. The king sent and called all the elders of Judah and Jerusalem, both small and great, to meet, and again, the third time, all the words of the covenant were read to all the people. 23: 1, 2. But it was too late to reform. "The Lord said, I will remove Judah out of my sight." Verse 27. Is it any wonder that Isaiah, seventy-four years before the finding of God's Book, should have said: "They trust in vanity, and speak lies; we wait for light, but we walk in darkness. We grope for the wall like the blind, and we grope as if we had no eyes: we stumble at noonday as in the night." See Isa. 59: 4-10.

No wonder he speaks of "gross darkness" having fallen on the people (60: 2) when the Key of Knowledge had been lost for generations. Brethren, do not overlook the fact that all this darkness occurred in the days of scholars and education, and that, too, when there was a college within sight of the temple, where God's Book and the witness against their nation, lay hid and silent in the dust and silver in the Lord's house. 22: 14.

Had the Book of God been read to all the people but once in a century, it would have saved the Book from being lost, and would have saved the nation, but to have read it each seven years, as commanded, would have given them 118 readings from Joshua to Josiah, and would have kept the light ablaze before all the people. David and Solomon, in their reign of eighty years, could have enjoyed at least eleven readings, and lost no good thing by it, but alas, a fine house for the Lord, fine houses for themselves, fine women and fine children so completely blinded their eyes that this secret of their nation's life (Deut. 32: 46, 47) and the light and wealth of their people was forgotten.

These things need not to have prevented the reading of the Law, but its reading would most assuredly have prevented so many wives, and, of course, so many wicked children. It would have made both of them better kings and better men, and there would have been a better nation. Prov. 14: 34. It would certainly have prevented the saying, "Has God cast away his people?"—"for they would not then have been cast away." Rom. 11; 1. The eleven readings by David and Solomon would have done more for God's name and for his people, than a score of temples.

The fourth and last reading of the Law was not had until the days of Nehemiah and Ezra, the prophet, B. C. 445, and 179 years after the reading by Josiah. Neh. 8. Jerusalem and its first and richest temple had been destroyed by the Babylonians; its people had been taken captive, and there, for seventy years, had mourned their city's desolation. They had returned again by the decree of Cyrus the Great, had rebuilt the city, and a second temple, amidst much persecution, was also built.

When Nehemiah at Susa, in the service of the king of Persia, heard of the situation, he came up to Jerusalem to rebuild the wall, which was completed in fifty-two days, amid fightings against their enemies and deception amongst their own people. But the work, though great, was done, "for the people had a mind to work," though some, like we see now, "put not their neck to the work of the Lord." Neh. 3: 5 and 4: 6. After numbering the people, of whom there were 49,942, and collecting the donations, made in gold, silver and sacred garments, "the people all gathered together as one man into the street that was before the water gate; and they spake unto Ezra the scribe to bring the book of the law of Moses, which the Lord had commanded to Israel." Neh. 8: 1.

Here again, on the first day of the seventh month, and 445 years B. C., Ezra brought the Law before the people, men, women and children. And when he had opened the Book, all the people stood up, and there, in the street, and from morning till noon, they stood and were attentive to the reading of the Law. "And all the people wept when they heard the words of the law." And when Ezra blessed the Lord, the great God, all the people said, Amen, Amen, with lifting up their hands: and they bowed their heads, and worshipped the Lord with their faces to the ground." Verses 6, 10. The people came again on the second day, and so on, day by day for seven days, and he read to the people the Book of the law of God." Verse 18.

We notice here that the people called for the reading of the Law, and they manifested much zeal and patience in standing, day after day, in the street, to hear it read, and we hear no more of it being read to them afterward. When our Savior came and taught them 475 years afterward, the Jews, then alive and serving in the temple, with the scribes and teachers, knew very little of what Moses had given them in the Law, and what they named they had perverted from its correct meaning.

The reason is plain: The Word of God was not read every seven years, and the people got only what the priests said it taught. The priests did not like the labor of reading to the people, nor to take the time, for it was so much easier to tell it to the people. But they did not tell it all, for reading it in full would have condemned both kings and priests, hence, to save themselves and to save time and labor, they told some of God's Word and their traditions with it, which soon exceeded the Bible, both in bulk and importance, and the nation was blind, with blind guides to lead them. Turn to Matt. 15, and see what Jesus says of their teaching. No wonder he said, "Search the Scriptures" (John 5: 39), for they had hid it from the people and were ignorant of it themselves, and, like it is now, they depended too much upon what other men said about the Bible. Thus they took away the Key of Knowledge. Luke 11: 52. But had the Word been read every seven years, it would have given 212 readings till the baptism of Jesus, and would have saved cities, towns, temples, kings, prophets,

The Gospel Messenger,

A Weekly at $1.50 Per Annum.

PUBLISHED BY

The Brethren's Publishing Co.

D. L. MILLER,	· · · · ·	Editor.
J. H. MOORE,	· · · · ·	Office Editor.
J. B. BRUMBAUGH,	}	Associate Editors.
J. G. ROYER,	}	
JOSEPH AMICK,	· · · · ·	Business Manager.

ADVISORY COMMITTEE.

L. W. Teeter, A. Hutchison, Daniel Hays.

☞Communications for publication should be legibly written with black ink on one side of the paper only. Do not attempt to interline, or to put on one page what ought to occupy two.

☞Anonymous communications will not be published.

☞Do not mix business with articles for publication. Keep your communications on separate sheets from all business.

☞Time is precious. We always have time to attend to business and to answer questions of importance, but please do not subject us to need less answering of letters.

☞The MESSENGER is mailed each week to all subscribers. If the address is correctly entered on our list, the paper must reach the person to whom it is addressed. If you do not get your paper, write us, giving particulars.

☞When changing your address, please give your former as well as your future address in full, so as to avoid delay and misunderstanding.

☞Always remit to the office from which you order your goods, no matter from where you receive them.

☞Do not send personal checks or drafts on interior banks, unless you send with them 25 cents each, to pay for collection.

☞Remittances should be made by Post-office Money Order, Drafts on New York, Philadelphia or Chicago, or Registered Letters, made payable and addressed to "Brethren's Publishing Co., Mount Morris, Ill.," or "Brethren's Publishing Co., Huntingdon, Pa."

☞Entered at the Post-office at Mount Morris, Ill., as second-class matter.

Mount Morris, Ill., · · · · July 12, 1892.

TWO sisters were baptized at Silver Creek, Sunday, July 3.

THE church at Blackberry, Henry County, Va., is arranging to build a new meeting-house.

BRO. JOHN A. MYERS reports two recently received into the Rock Creek church, Ill., by confession and baptism.

BRO. SAMUEL LEHMAN, of Franklin Grove, started east this week, for the purpose of spending some time with the churches in Pennsylvania.

BRETHREN J. G. ROYER and D. L. Miller are at Dayton, Ohio, with the Tract Examining Committee, perfecting the further examination of Tracts.

IT would seem that a number of new meeting-houses are to be erected this season. The Killback church, Ind., has also decided to erect a house of worship.

THOSE who want their love-feast notices kept standing, will please write them on a separate slip aside from their correspondence. Otherwise they may be overlooked.

THE Brethren held religious services in the Chapel at Mt. Morris, July 4. This is our custom, and we think it a very profitable way to spend the Fourth.

HIGH waters and other unavoidable circumstances have caused some delay in the ANNUAL Meeting Report, but we will be ready to mail it inside of a few days.

BRO. J. H. SLUSHER, of Floyd County, Va., has arranged to spend the greater part of this season in the field, if his health will permit. He has not been in good health for some time.

WE would like the names and addresses of all the Sunday-school Superintendents in the Brotherhood. Please write such names on a slip of paper or card, separate from all other business.

WE are informed that at the council-meeting, held in the Rock Creek church, Whiteside County, Ill., a few days ago, it was decided to organize the members at Sterling into a separate congregation.

MANY of our correspondents speak of their interesting Sunday-schools. We are glad to hear that so many schools are making a success of their work, and we hope to see them still increase in usefulness.

OUR correspondent says, that before and after the Annual Meeting, nearly a score of visiting ministers visited the English River congregation, Iowa. That was good. We know the members greatly appreciated it.

THE work of grace is quite apparent in the Ephratah church, Pa. Six recently confessed Christ and were baptized for the remission of sins. May the good work, already begun, continue in the hearts of the people!

THE Mexico church, Miami County, Ind., will erect a new church-house if they succeed in raising the money for the purpose. The congregation is a very large one, and will therefore require a building of considerable size.

BRO. E. S. YOUNG is spending a week or more in the vicinity of Canton, Ohio, among friends and relatives and doing some preaching, we presume. His brother, S. S. Young, and wife, also left here last week for the same place.

ELD. JOHN METZGER and his son, John W. Metzger, will shortly return to California. These brethren seem quite well pleased with their home on the Pacific Coast. They will be the means of strengthening the cause in that new field.

THE Brethren have arranged to hold regular services in Oregon, the County-seat of this County. Our first meeting was July 3, and was quite well attended, and the interest manifested was excellent. There are several members in the city, and a number of others who do not reside far away.

BRO. J. R. GISH and wife have been at Wellington, Kans., for some weeks. They go to Missouri this week, and from that State to their home at Stuttgart, Ark. Bro. Gish sticks to his southern field, and is putting in a crop of seed that may give the next generation an abundance of work to cultivate.

BRETHREN A. MOLSBEE and A. W. Austin recently visited Gainsville, Texas, and found a number of members who had been living away from the church for years. Probably there are scores of other cities where members may be found. Our missionaries on every hand have a great work before them.

BRO. JOHN E. MOHLER, of Warrensburgh, Mo., who occasionally favors us with an article for the MESSENGER, goes to Colorado Springs, Colo., this week for his health. He thinks of remaining till next spring. We hope he will not only enjoy the trip, but derive great benefit from his sojourn among the mountains.

WE rejoice to learn that a number of ministers are being elected and installed into office in various parts of the Brotherhood. This is an important work that in too many instances is sadly neglected. Our system of instructing and edifying the members requires a large number of preachers, and we should not permit the cause to suffer when there is plenty of available material. It is one thing to install men, but quite another to encourage and properly use them.

THE Brethren in Florida are rejoicing over the return of the rainy season, and now have excellent prospects for fair crops. While, we in the North, have suffered great losses on account of much rain, it has been their lot to pass through the dryest season known in that State for fifty years.

THE spreading of the Asiatic cholera is creating considerable excitement in all parts of Europe, and especially in Russia. It is rapidly approaching Moscow, and it will require the greatest possible vigilance upon the part of the different governments to prevent it from following the same course it did in 1831 and 1847.

THE Mission Board of Northern Missouri has entered upon its work in earnest, and hopes to have the co-operation of all the members, and especially the elders of that part of the State. Their labors are important, and we trust they will receive the necessary encouragement and wisdom to make the work a success.

MANY of our readers will remember Eld. E. K. Beeghly, of Waterloo, Iowa. In his day he was not only a strong man, but a man of considerable influence. He is now quite old and feeble, and cannot expect to remain in this world much longer. His aged wife passed over the river a few days ago. The separation was a sad one, but it will not be a long one.

How many of our ministers are preaching missionary sermons this year? It is the duty of each and every minister to preach this part of the Gospel as well as any other part. Any one who refuses to preach what the Scriptures teach on this subject, neglects to declare the whole counsel of God. Let every elder see to it that all parts of his charge are favored with an earnest talk on missionary work, at least once each year.

WE know of no better line of study at this time for brethren, preparing themselves for the ministry, than the Sunday-school course the remainder of the year. It begins with the first chapter of Acts, and continues to the council at Jerusalem, mentioned in the 15th chapter. The lessons are well selected and make up a very instructive and interesting course. Those who are not favorably situated for attending Sunday-schools, might do well to procure copies of the Brethren's Quarterlies, and, with the aid of other helps, pursue the course of study at home.

WE again call the attention of our agents, and all others doing business with us, to the instructions at the head of this page, in regard to sending personal checks. Please do not send personal checks under any circumstances; unless you send twenty-five cents extra to pay for collecting. Every personal check sent us costs twenty-five cents for collecting, and of course is that much loss to us. It is far better to send drafts on Chicago or New York. All personal checks received after this, unless accompanied by twenty-five cents for collection, will have to be returned. Please remember this.

BRO. MARTIN BUTERBAUGH writes us that there are at least twelve members at Springfield, Mo., without a minister. They are very anxious to have a minister locate with them. They have also commenced social meetings, and are engaged in the study of the Acts, and wish us to suggest some helps. We commend them for organizing a class, and we trust they will continue it. As helps in their line of study, we suggest the Brethren's Quarterly, as the lesson during the remainder of the year will be in the Acts. For price, see next to the last page of this issue. They will find this line of study both interesting and instructive.

The Gospel Messenger,

A Weekly at $1.50 Per Annum.

PUBLISHED BY

The Brethren's Publishing Co.

D. L. MILLER,	. . . . .	Editor.
J. H. MOORE,	. . . . .	Office Editor.
J. B. BRUMBAUGH,	. . . . .	Associate Editors.
J. G. ROYER,		
JOSEPH AMICK,	. . . . .	Business Manager.

ADVISORY COMMITTEE.

L. W. Teeter A. Hutchison, Daniel Hays.

☞Communications for publication should be legibly written with black ink on one side of the paper only. Do not attempt to interline, or to put on one page what ought to occupy two.

☞Anonymous communications will not be published.

☞Do not mix business with articles for publication. Keep your communications on separate sheets from all business.

☞Time is precious. We always have time to attend to business and to answer questions of importance, but please do not subject us to need less unravelling of letters.

☞The MESSENGER is mailed each week to all subscribers. If the address is correctly entitled on our list, the paper must reach the person to whom it is addressed. If you do not get your paper, write us, giving particulars.

☞When changing your address, please give your former as well as your future address in full, so as to avoid delay and misunderstanding.

☞Always Remit to the office from which you order your goods, no matter from where you receive them.

☞Do not send personal checks or drafts on interior banks, unless you send with them 25 cents each, to pay for collection.

☞Remittances should be made by Post-office Money Order, Drafts on New York, Philadelphia or Chicago, or Registered Letters, made payable and addressed to "Brethren's Publishing Co., Mount Morris, Ill.," or "Brethren's Publishing Co., Huntingdon, Pa."

☞Entered at the Post-office at Mount Morris, Ill., as second-class matter.

Mount Morris, Ill. - - - July 12, 1892.

TWO sisters were baptized at Silver Creek, Sunday, July 3.

THE church at Blackberry, Henry County, Va., is arranging to build a new meeting-house.

BRO. JOHN A. MYERS reports two recently received into the Rock Creek church, Ill., by confession and baptism.

BRO. SAMUEL LAHMAN, of Franklin Grove, started east this week, for the purpose of spending some time with the churches in Pennsylvania.

BRETHREN J. G. ROYER and D. L. Miller are at Dayton, Ohio, with the Tract Examining Committee, perfecting the further examination of Tracts.

IT would seem that a number of new meeting-houses are to be erected this season. The Killbuck church, Ind., has also decided to erect a house of worship.

THOSE who want their love-feast notices kept standing, will please write them on a separate slip aside from their correspondence. Otherwise they may be overlooked.

THE Brethren held religious services in the Chapel at Mt. Morris, July 4. This is our custom, and we think it a very profitable way to spend the Fourth.

HIGH waters and other unavoidable circumstances have caused some delay in the ANNUAL Meeting Report, but we will be ready to mail it inside of a few days.

BRO. J. H. SLUSHER, of Floyd County, Va., has arranged to spend the greater part of this season in the field, if his health will permit. He has not been in good health for some time.

WE would like the names and addresses of all the Sunday-school Superintendents in the Brotherhood. Please write such names on a slip of paper or card, separate from all other business.

WE are informed that at the council-meeting, held in the Rock Creek church, Whiteside County, Ill., a few days ago, it was decided to organize the members at Sterling into a separate congregation.

MANY of our correspondents speak of their interesting Sunday-schools. We are glad to hear that so many schools are making a success of their work, and we hope to see them still increase in usefulness.

OUR correspondent says, that before and after the Annual Meeting, nearly a score of visiting ministers visited the English River congregation, Iowa. That was good. We know the members greatly appreciated it.

THE work of grace is quite apparent in the Ephratah church, Pa. Six recently confessed Christ and were baptized for the remission of sins. May the good work, already begun, continue in the hearts of the people!

THE Mexico church, Miami County, Ind., will erect a new church-house if they succeed in raising the money for the purpose. The congregation is a very large one, and will therefore require a building of considerable size.

BRO. E. S. YOUNG is spending a week or more in the vicinity of Canton, Ohio, among friends and relatives and doing some preaching, we presume. His brother, S. S. Young, and wife, also left here last week for the same place.

ELD. JOHN METZGER and his son, John W. Metzger, will shortly return to California. These brethren seem quite well pleased with their home on the Pacific Coast. They will be the means of strengthening the cause in that new field.

THE Brethren have arranged to hold regular services in Oregon, the County-seat of this County. Our first meeting was July 3, and was quite well attended, and the interest manifested was excellent. There are several members in the city, and a number of others who do not reside far away.

BRO. J. R. GISH and wife have been at Wellington, Kans., for some weeks. They go to Missouri this week, and from that State to their home at Stuttgart, Ark. Bro. Gish sticks to his southern field, and is putting in a crop of seed that may give the next generation an abundance of work to cultivate.

BRETHREN A. MOLSBEE and A. W. Austin recently visited Gainsville, Texas, and found a number of members who had been living away from the church for years. Probably there are scores of other cities where members may be found. Our missionaries on every hand have a great work before them.

BRO. JOHN E. MOHLER, of Warrensburgh, Mo., who occasionally favors us with an article for the MESSENGER, goes to Colorado Springs, Colo., this week for his health. He thinks of remaining till next spring. We hope he will not only enjoy the trip, but derive great benefit from his sojourn among the mountains.

WE rejoice to learn that a number of ministers are being elected and installed into office in various parts of the Brotherhood. This is an important work that in too many instances is sadly neglected. Our system of instructing and edifying the members requires a large number of preachers, and we should not permit the cause to suffer when there is plenty of available material. It is one thing to install men, but quite another to encourage and properly use them.

THE Brethren in Florida are rejoicing over the return of the rainy season, and now have excellent prospects for fair crops. While, we in the North, have suffered great losses on account of much rain, it has been their lot to pass through the dryest season known in that State for fifty years.

THE spreading of the Asiatic cholera is creating considerable excitement in all parts of Europe, and especially in Russia. It is rapidly approaching Moscow, and it will require the greatest possible vigilance upon the part of the different governments to prevent it from following the same course it did in 1831 and 1847.

THE Mission Board of Northern Missouri has entered upon its work in earnest, and hopes to have the co-operation of all the members, and especially the elders of that part of the State. Their labors are important, and we trust they will receive the necessary encouragement and wisdom to make the work a success.

MANY of our readers will remember Eld. E. K. Beeghly, of Waterloo, Iowa. In his day he was not only a strong man, but a man of considerable influence. He is now quite old and feeble, and cannot expect to remain, in this world much longer. His aged wife passed over the river a few days ago. The separation was a sad one, but it will not be a long one.

HOW many of our ministers are preaching missionary sermons this year? It is the duty of each and every minister to preach this part of the Gospel as well as any other part. Any one who refuses to preach what the Scriptures teach on this subject, neglects to declare the whole counsel of God. Let every elder see to it that all parts of his charge are favored with an earnest talk on missionary work, at least once each year.

WE know of no better time of study at this time for brethren, preparing themselves for the ministry, than the Sunday-school course the remainder of the year. It begins with the first chapter of Acts, and continues to the council at Jerusalem, mentioned in the 15th chapter. The lessons are well selected and make up a very instructive and interesting course. Those who are not favorably situated for attending Sunday-schools, might do well to procure copies of the Brethren's Quarterlies, and, with the aid of other helps, pursue the course of study at home.

WE again call the attention of our agents, and all others doing business with us, to the instructions at the head of this page, in regard to sending personal checks. Please do not send personal checks under any circumstances, unless you send twenty-five cents extra to pay for collecting. Every personal check sent us costs twenty-five cents for collecting, and of course is that much loss to us. It is far better to send drafts on Chicago or New York. All personal checks received after this, unless accompanied by twenty-five cents for collection, will have to be returned. Please remember this.

BRO. MARTIN BUTERBAUGH writes us that there are at least twelve members at Springfield, Mo., without a minister. They are very anxious to have a minister locate with them. They have also commenced social meetings, and are engaged in the study of the Acts, and wish us to suggest some helps. We commend them for organizing a class, and we trust they will continue it. As helps in their line of study, we suggest the Brethren's Quarterly, as the lesson during the remainder of the year will be in the Acts. For price, see next to the last page of this issue. They will find this line of study both interesting and instructive.

SHALL WE SUPPORT OUR MINISTERS?

"How then shall they call on him in whom they have not believed? and how shall they believe in him of whom they have not heard? and how shall they hear without a preacher? And how shall they preach except they be sent? as it is written, How beautiful are the feet of them that preach the gospel of peace, and bring glad tidings of good things!"—Rom. 10: 14, 15.

"Who goeth a warfare any time at his own charges? who planteth a vineyard, and eateth not of the fruit thereof? or who feedeth a flock and eateth not of the milk of the flock? Say I these things as a man? or saith not the law the same also? For it is written in the law of Moses, Thou shalt not muzzle the mouth of the ox that treadeth out the corn. Doth God take care for oxen? Or saith he it altogether for our sakes? For our sakes, no doubt, this is written: that he that plougheth should plough in hope; and he that thresheth in hope should be partaker of his hope. If we have sown unto you spiritual things, is it a great thing if we shall reap your carnal things? Even so hath the Lord ordained that they which preach the gospel should live of the gospel."—1 Cor. 9: 2, 8, 9, 10, 11, 14.

"Let him that is taught in the word, communicate unto him that teacheth in all good things."—Gal. 6: 6.

GOD's words are very plain. He who preaches has a right to be supported, and to " be sent." It detracts from the feeling of reverence we should entertain for our ministers, to see them engaged, as I have seen, a coal-miner at his work six days and then preach on Sunday. A butcher and a minister combined in the same person seems to me radically wrong. "The feet of them that preach the gospel of peace" should not go that way six days in the week. He should not go on "the warfare" against sin and Satan, "on his own charges." He sows spiritual things and should not be compelled to sow carnal things but rather be supported of our carnal things and we of his spiritual (for I speak as a lay-member). ·

The "Lord ordained" it so. The minister is our servant, being the server of spiritual things, and he shall "live of the things of the temple," as did the old Jewish priests. I consider Gal. 6: 6 as a positive command to give our teachers, our ministers, our good things of earth, for bringing us " tidings of good things " of life eternal.

You may refer to Acts 20: 33 and say that early ministers supported themselves and at times I admit they did. Now read 2 Cor. 11: 8, 9, where Paul took wages to go as a missionary, and at Corinth they gave him naught.

A minister may have ten talents and have them naturally abiding in him, to labor six days and yet find time to do justice to his charge,—the young and rising generation, the weekly prayer-meeting, Sunday services, and at times pay his own expenses to neighboring places, carrying the "good tidings," but most of them are ordinary mortals as the rest of us. Give them at least a partial support; get them some books and say, "Here, study to show thyself a better workman and let us do your temporal things; be more of a shepherd and give more time to the Truth and the light of the Gospel we love to hear!" We, perhaps, don't see that, while Christ's Gospel never changes, the world does; and while we are the same fishers of men, we use different nets. It takes more study, more and closer walks with God in this sinful age, to fish successfully. The minister needs seven days in the week to use for Christ and then he rises above the clay of the world, is set apart, holy, consecrated, and we come to him and he serves us. He helps us get rid of our clay and leads us closer to God, for he is closer, or should be. I want to assist my minister and I wish we all did, and the church of the Brethren would the sooner conquer the world "for Christ and the church."   FRANCIS ATWOOD.

Edgerton, Wis.

REMARKS.

We have received, from ministers, a number of well-prepared articles on this subject that we did not think proper to publish, but here is one from a brother, who is not a minister, and no one can accuse him of being self-interested in this question only in a general way. The article also gave us occasion to offer a few thoughts which we think will be in harmony with the mind of a large majority of our Brethren.

Possibly there may be lawful avocations in life not suitable for ministers to engage in, and yet that depends very largely· upon the minister and his surroundings. We know a minister who went from the plow and grubbing hoe to the defense of the Gospel in a public discussion where he displayed ability, culture and scholarship second to none in the learned assembly. His avocation did not, in the least, detract from his influence, and the cause of Christianity in general, that such remarkable talent should have been used at the plow handle or grubbing hoe, when the most ordinary man could have done just as good service, and the minister a great deal better work preaching the Gospel. This is one place where our system can stand some improving to creditable advantage.

There are evils connected with the popular salaried ministry system which renders it not advisable that it should be adopted by the Brethren. To adopt the system would require a change in the form of our church government so radical, as to greatly endanger some of our principles as well as much of our simplicity. It will be wise for us to retain these well-tested principles, and, when possible, improve our practice where years of experience seem to call for improvement.

We admire our manner of calling brethren to the ministry, and believe it to be in perfect accord with the Gospel. This enables us to use a plurality of ministers in a manner that greatly edifies the church as well as exempts her from the burden of the salaried ministry system. While the preaching may not be as polished and as learned as that enjoyed by many other churches, it has, nevertheless, proven the means of making good, earnest and substantial Christians. As long as the ministers are not overburdened, the system has proven excellent, and we prefer to let well enough alone. These churches, however, ought to do a handsome thing in the way of donations towards the spreading of the Gospel elsewhere, and if they do not, it is probably for the want of proper instructions and training in Christian liberality.

Still, under this system, scores of ministers have been, and are yet, overburdened, and on the account of poverty their usefulness has been greatly crippled. Here is another point where our system needs improving, for it is neither justice nor Gospel that the minister should be burdened beyond reason, when the church is abundantly able to assist him.

In many instances this needed assistance has been rendered by our Brethren in former years, and the commendable practice should be continued whenever occasions demand it. This can be done without changing our present system, which seems so admirably adapted to the wants of the rural districts, but we maintain that any minister, who devotes his entire time and attention to the work of the church, should be wholly supported. The church is in need of, and is now using to good advantage, preachers who must devote their whole attention to the work over which they have been appointed. Among these are missionaries and those who have undertaken special city work. However much some may be opposed to supporting preachers, it has been found a necessity in some cases, as well as a sacred duty. Men in this age cannot do much missionary work unless they give it their entire attention. This has been fully demonstrated. And by experience we have found the same true in regard to most of the city work.

At this very time every State District ought to have in the field one good, hard-working evangelist who could devote his whole time and attention to missionary work at isolated points. And we trust the time is not far distant, when every District Meeting will consider it a duty to put a regular, consecrated evangelist in the field, and sustain him temporally. There may be other circumstances requiring churches to give substantial aid to ministers. This is a privilege and sometimes it becomes an imperative duty.

Large congregations have often secured the services of a minister by purchasing a farm for him, or giving him a partial support. This has been done in a number of instances. Some of the ablest and most substantial ministers we ever had among us have been assisted in this manner, and it resulted in good. It is a way of assisting ministers that we recommend, and there ought to be a good deal more of it done than there is. By helping the honest, hard-working minister, the church, in turn, is greatly blessed.

There are many other ways of helping and encouraging the preachers in their arduous and responsible duties, that will suggest themselves to the liberal-hearted ones, who are not willing to see the preacher bear the cross alone and all the church go free. It will thus be seen that we are decidedly in favor of wholly supporting those who devote their whole time and attention to the ministry. This is in keeping with the decision of our Annual Meeting of 1890, Art. 6, Sec. 4. It is also in harmony with the present practice of the church in the mission fields.

We are also in favor of keeping much of our best talent in the field and rendering assistance to the hard-working ministers who stand in need of help.

But we are not in favor of surrendering our free ministry system. It is a good thing and has done a grand work in the past and there is yet a great work in the future to be done by it. It has proven a success, especially in the rural districts.

       J. H. M.

CORRESPONDENCE.

"Write what thou seest, and send it unto the churches."

☞ Church News solicited for this Department. If you have had a good meeting, send a report of it, so that others may rejoice with you. In writing give name of church, County and State. Be brief. Notes of Travel should be as short as possible. Land Advertisements are not solicited for this Department. We have an advertising page, and, if necessary, will issue supplements.

Query Answered.

OUR brother, Y. D. Yoder, asks us to give, through the GOSPEL MESSENGER, an explanation of 1 Cor. 11: 21 where Paul says, "For in eating every one taketh before other his own supper and one is hungry and another is drunken." Then the brother says, "They must have had fermented wine or they could not have got drunk."

We gladly answer the query, as it is a matter of clearly understand these seemingly difficult passages. If we would take into consideration the fact that certain words to which we now confine

SHALL WE SUPPORT OUR MINISTERS?

"How then shall they call on him in whom they have not believed? and how shall they believe in him of whom they have not heard? and how shall they hear without a preacher? And how shall they preach except they be sent? as it is written, How beautiful are the feet of them that preach the gospel of peace, and bring glad tidings of good things!"—Rom. 10: 14, 15.

"Who goeth a warfare any time at his own charges? who planteth a vineyard, and eateth not of the fruit thereof? or who feedeth a flock and eateth not of the milk of the flock? Say I these things as a man? or saith not the law the same also? For it is written in the law of Moses, Thou shalt not muzzle the mouth of the ox that treadeth out the corn. Doth God take care for oxen? Or saith he it altogether for our sakes? For our sakes, no doubt, this is written: that he that plougheth should plough in hope; and he that thresheth in hope should be partaker of his hope. If we have sown unto you spiritual things, is it a great thing if we shall reap your carnal things? Even so hath the Lord ordained that they which preach the gospel should live of the gospel."—1 Cor. 9: 7, 8, 9, 10, 11, 14.

"Let him that is taught in the word, communicate unto him that teacheth in all good things."—Gal. 6: 6.

GOD'S words are very plain. He who preaches has a right to be supported, and to "be sent." It detracts from the feeling of reverence we should entertain for our ministers, to see them engaged, as I have seen, a coal-miner at his work six days and then preach on Sunday. A butcher and a minister combined in the same person seems to me radically wrong. "The feet of them that preach the gospel of peace" should not go that way six days in the week. He should not go on "the warfare" against sin and Satan, "on his own charges." He sows spiritual seed and should not be compelled to sow carnal things but rather be supported of our carnal things and we of his spiritual (for I speak as a lay-member).

The "Lord ordained" it so. The minister is our servant, being the server of spiritual things, and he shall "live of the things of the temple," as did the old Jewish priests. I consider Gal. 6: 6 as a positive command to give our teachers, our ministers, our good things of earth, for bringing us "tidings of good things" of life eternal.

You may refer to Acts 20: 33 and say that early ministers supported themselves and at times I admit they did. Now read 2 Cor. 11: 8, 9, where Paul took wages to go as a missionary, and at Corinth they gave him naught.

A minister may have ten talents and have them naturally abiding in him, to labor six days and yet find time to do justice to his charge,—the young and rising generation, the weekly prayer-meeting, Sunday services, and at times pay his own expenses to neighboring places, carrying the "good tidings," but most of them are ordinary mortals as the rest of us. Give them at least a partial support; get them some books and say, "Here, study to show thyself a better workman and let us do your temporal things; be more of a shepherd and give more time to the Truth and the light of the Gospel we love to hear!" We, perhaps, don't see that, while Christ's Gospel never changes, the world does; and while we are the same fishers of men, we use different nets. It takes more study, more and closer walks with God in this sinful age, to fish successfully. The minister needs seven days in the week to use for Christ and then he rises above the clay of the world, is set apart, holy, consecrated, and we come to him and he serves us. He helps us get rid of our clay and leads us closer to God, for he is older, or should be. I want to assist my minister and I wish we all did, and the church of the Brethren would the sooner conquer the world "for Christ and the church."   FRANCIS ATWOOD.

Edgerton, Wis.

REMARKS.

We have received, from ministers, a number of well-prepared articles on this subject that we did not think proper to publish, but here is one from a brother, who is not a minister, and no one can accuse him of being self-interested in this question only in a general way. The article also gave us occasion to offer a few thoughts which we think will be in harmony with the mind of a large majority of our Brethren.

Possibly there may be lawful avocations in life not suitable for ministers to engage in, and yet that depends very largely upon the minister and his surroundings. We know a minister who went from the plow and grubbing hoe to the defense of the Gospel in a public discussion where he displayed ability, culture and scholarship second to none in the learned assembly. His avocation did not, in the least, detract from his influence, and yet it was unfortunate for both the church and the cause of Christianity in general, that such remarkable talent should have been used at the plow handle or grubbing hoe, when the most ordinary man could have done just as good service, and the minister a great deal better work preaching the Gospel. This is one place where our system can stand some improving to creditable advantage.

There are evils connected with the popular salaried ministry system which renders it not advisable that it should be adopted by the Brethren. To adopt the system would require a change in the form of our church government so radical, as to greatly endanger some of our principles as well as much of our simplicity. It will be wise for us to retain these well-tested principles, and, when possible, improve our practice where years of experience seem to call for improvements.

We admire our manner of calling brethren to the ministry, and believe it to be in perfect accord with the Gospel. This enables us to use a plurality of ministers in a manner that greatly edifies the church as well as exempts her from the burden of the salaried ministry system. While the preaching may not be as polished and as learned as that enjoyed by many other churches, it has, nevertheless, proven the means of making good, earnest and substantial Christians. As long as the ministers are not overburdened, the system has proven excellent, and we prefer to let well enough alone. These churches, however, ought to do a handsome thing in the way of donations towards the spreading of the Gospel elsewhere, and if they do not, it is probably for the want of proper instructions and training in Christian liberality.

Still, under this system, scores of ministers have been, and are yet, overburdened, and on the account of poverty their usefulness has been greatly crippled. Here is another point where our system needs improving, for it is neither justice nor Gospel that the minister should be burdened beyond reason, when the church is abundantly able to assist him.

In many instances this needed assistance has been rendered by our Brethren in former years, and the commendable practice should be continued whenever occasions demand it. This can be done without changing our present system, which seems so admirably adapted to the wants of the rural districts, but we maintain that any minister, who devotes his entire time and attention to the work of the church, should be wholly supported. The church is in need of, and is now using to good advantage, preachers who must devote their whole attention to the work over which they have been appointed. Among these are missionaries and those who have undertaken special city work. However much some may be opposed to supporting preachers, it has been found a necessity in some cases, as well as a sacred duty. Men in this age cannot do much missionary work unless they give it their entire attention. This has been fully demonstrated. And by experience we have found the same true in regard to most of the city work.

At this very time every State District ought to have in the field one good, hard-working evangelist who could devote his whole time and attention to missionary work at isolated points. And we trust the time is not far distant, when every District Meeting will consider it a duty to put a regular, consecrated evangelist in the field, and sustain him temporally. There may be other circumstances requiring churches to give substantial aid to ministers. This is a privilege and sometimes it becomes an imperative duty.

Large congregations have often secured the services of a minister by purchasing a farm for him, or giving him a partial support. This has been done in a number of instances. Some of the ablest and most substantial ministers we ever had among us have been assisted in this manner, and it resulted in good. It is a way of assisting ministers that we recommend, and there ought to be a good deal more of it done than there is. By helping the honest, hard-working minister, the church, in turn, is greatly blessed.

There are many other ways of helping and encouraging the preachers in their arduous and responsible duties, that will suggest themselves to the liberal-hearted ones, who are not willing to see the preacher bear the cross alone and all the church go free. It will thus be seen that we are decidedly in favor of wholly supporting those who devote their whole time and attention to the ministry. This is in keeping with the decision of our Annual Meeting of 1890, Art. 6, Sec. 4. It is also in harmony with the present practice of the church in the mission fields.

We are also in favor of keeping much of our best talent in the field and rendering assistance to the hard-working ministers who stand in need of help.

But we are not in favor of surrendering our free ministry system. It is a good thing and has done a grand work in the past and there is yet a great work in the future to be done by it. It has proven a success, especially in the rural districts.

J. H. M.

CORRESPONDENCE.

"Write what thou seest, and send it unto the churches."

☞Church News solicited for this Department. If you have had a good meeting, send a report of it, so that others may rejoice with you. In writing give name of church, County and State. Be brief. Notes of Travel should be as short as possible. Land Advertisements are not solicited for this Department. We have an advertising page, and, if necessary, will issue supplements.

Query Answered.

OUR brother, Y. D. Yoder, asks us to give, through the GOSPEL MESSENGER, an explanation of 1 Cor. 11: 21 where Paul says, "For in eating every one taketh before other his own supper and one is hungry and another is drunken." Then the brother says, "They must have had fermented wine or they could not have got drunk."

We gladly answer the query, as it is a matter of importance to every believer in Christ, that we clearly understand these seemingly difficult passages. If we would take into consideration the fact that certain words to which we now confine

with his wife, has been lately admitted to the Home. Bro. David is suffering very much from dropsical affliction.

The Pipe Creek members, after their love-feast, remembered our old brethren and sisters at the Home in a way that was highly appreciated by the inmates.

Since our last writing some of our "Good Samaritan" neighbors have presented some nice presents. Bro. Michael Minnich received a very nice rocking-chair, which he enjoys very much.

An old brother brought a bolt of calico, wherewith to make dresses and aprons for the aged sisters. This came just right, and is much appreciated. A sister bought hats for the little boys, Charlie and Willie. They often mention the good sister's name and say they like her.

FRANK FISHER.

From "Ten Mile" Congregation, Washington Co., Pa.

OUR council-meeting, preceding our love-feast, at the Brick church was held June 11. Very little business came before the meeting preparatory to the love-feast, and on account of failing to get any ministerial help, our series of meetings was recalled for the present. Our love-feast was held June 18. We met for worship at 2 P. M. We were made to feel sad to see so many seats vacant, formerly occupied by our aged brethren. We truly feel our loss is their eternal gain. Though few in number, we had a soul-cheering little Communion for all who are hungering and thirsting after righteousness. One was taken into our church communion here by letter. Eld. J. C. Johnson, of Uniontown, Pa., arrived with his daughter just in time for "preparatory services," at 5 P. M. He officiated for us and did the preaching. Good order prevailed throughout the meeting, which in itself made us enjoy the exercises of the meeting better, and speaks commendation to the people of this neighborhood for the honor and respect shown to the worship of God.

On Sunday, June 19, we met again at 11 A. M., for worship. Bro. J. C. Johnson preached another very soul-stirring and cheering sermon to incite us to faithfulness and loyalty. On the whole we had a good meeting, and trust, like Paul, "to thank God and take courage." Acts 28: 15.

N. B. CHRISTNER.

Odell, Pa.

From Northern Missouri.

THE members of the Mission Board, of the Northern District of Missouri, met in the Whitesville congregation June 18, and perfected an organization by electing Joel Glick, Chairman; W. F. Dowis, Treasurer; the writer, Secretary.

We are authorized to take this method of notifying any members of the District, who may desire mission work, that their requests must be signed by two or more members, and that the request be sent to the Secretary as soon as possible, so that the work may be outlined to the best advantage. As we are not strong in this District, and the demand for the Bread of Life is urgent, it will require our united energy and liberal contribution to be able to meet the calls. We are glad to be able to state that here is a greater interest manifested here in the mission cause than ever before, and we hope to see it result in much good. The Board requests that any members, who may have any suggestions to offer, that would advance the mission cause, present them at the next meeting of the Board, which will occur Oct. 29, in the Whitesville congregation. In order to accomplish the greatest good, it is especially necessary that elders, ministers and the Mission Board work together.

We extend our thanks to the Whitesville

brethren for the courtesies shown us during the time of our organization. JOS. ANDES, Sec. of Mission Board.

Mound City, Mo.

Solomon's Creek Love-feast.

IN compliance with Eld. Daniel Shively's request, I attended the love-feast in his congregation (Solomon's Creek, Ind.), on the evening of June 18, which, in connection with the meetings on the following day, was a rich feast of good things of different kinds.

Notwithstanding the rainy afternoon, and the appearance of a wet evening for the feast, their large church-house was well filled with brethren, sisters and attentive spectators. The attendance of members from adjoining churches was not large on account of the rain, and many of their friends were hindered from the same cause. Good order prevailed during all the exercises, and a spirit of deep and joyful solemnity characterized the meeting through all the services.

The ministerial force from abroad was small, but enough for all purposes. W. R. Deeter, Lemuel Hillary, George Shively, Daniel Rothenberger, and some other ministers, were present to help to make it a good meeting.

Bro. Hillery is suffering much bodily affliction from a complication of ailments, principally heart disturbance, but his spiritual zeal suffers no abatement. My prayer is, that he may soon rally again physically, that he may resume his ministerial labors, that are so much needed. Bro. Davis Younce is again at his post. Though not strong bodily, he is just as willing and zealous as ever.

As soon after breakfast next morning, as the house could be put in order, the Sunday-school scholars took their seats, but, instead of the regular lesson exercises, a number of short addresses were given by brethren and sisters. This seemed to be a happy change for the little folks, if smiling faces and sparkling eyes were true indications of their feelings.

A short recess followed these exercises, after which preaching began. At the close of the meeting three humble applicants presented themselves for admission into the fold; two brethren by baptism, and one sister by restoration. It was arranged to meet at the creek for baptism at 5 P. M., where a large number gathered to witness the work. Two additional applicants presented themselves for baptism,—a mother and her son, the latter a deaf-mute, aged about twenty years. It was indeed an occasion for rejoicing to see Bro. Hiram Forney lead those four willing hearts down to their baptismal graves, one after another, each to arise to walk in newness of life. Many seemed to feel that their cup was full to overflowing.

From the water all returned to the church-house, where, until time for evening preaching, the walls of the Lord's house echoed with the soul-reviving songs of Zion. Such music! In very truth a "heavenly place in Christ Jesus." The singing gave evidence of much practice, and showed what could and ought to be done in that line in every congregation.

While listening to the well-trained voices, the following lines of long ago came to my mind:

> "Were it not for cheerful song,
> Life would lose its pleasure.
> We could not endure it long,
> Should we lose this treasure."

Next in order was an excellent discourse in defense of the inspiration of the Bible, and the infinitude of God, by Bro. George Shively. After the closing prayer came the parting hymn, and then the Solomon's Creek meetings were num-

bered with the past. Reluctantly the parting hand was given, with many pledges to meet again where

> "Congregations ne'er break up,
> And Sabbaths ne'er end."

I was pleased to notice a number at the Lord's table who are very young in years. One little sister told me her age was eight years, and the ages of two or three other sisters ranged from ten to twelve. There were also brethren there as young as thirteen years, who greeted me with the kiss of love. O the touch from lips of such innocents is inspiring, and I felt that I was among angels as well as men.

Now, in conclusion, let me "tell it to the churches" that these little sisters were not ashamed of their little caps, nor need they be, and I shall pray the Good Father to give them grace to hold out faithful to the end, and then a crown will be given them in that day. Amen.

THURSTON MILLER.

La Porte, Ind.

The Russian Sufferers.

THE following amounts have been received since last report, up to and including July 2. God bless the noble-hearted givers!

M. D. Peebler, Libertyville, Iowa,.......$	1 00
A sister, Pennsylvania,...................	2 00
Phineas L. Fike, Dobbin, W. Va.,......	1 00
John Weybright, New Paris, Ind.,......	10 00
J. J. Wassam, Alvin, Texas,............	2 00
Ella Williams, Funkstown, Md.,.......	2 00
Henry Balsbaugh, Harrisburg, Pa......	2 00
David Vansickel, Trotwood, Ohio,.....	1 00
Reuben Martin, Apple Creek, Ohio,...	2 00
Mrs. O. H. Elliot, Gambier, Ohio,......	2 00
Aaron Sollenberger and wife, Lisle, Ill.,..	2 00
One who loves suffering humanity, Roseville, Ohio,........................	10 00
M. E. Miller, Mt. Morris, Ill.,..........	2 00
A brother, Washington, D. C.,..........	1 00
Silas Hoover, Boynton, Pa.,.............	1 00
A sister, Ephratah, Pa.,.................	5 00
A. I. and Ruth Bowers, St. Joseph, Ill.,...	5 00
E. Peebler, Libertyville, Iowa,.........	1 00
A sister, Lancaster, Pa.,................	5 00
A brother and family, Nappanee, Ind.,...	3 50
D. B. Heiny and wife,..................	2 00
L. C. Klingman and wife,...............	2 00
Friend Abel Green,.....................	10
A brother,.............................	25
A brother,.............................	10
Frank Pence,...........................	25
Jasper Higginbotham,...................	25
A friend,..............................	5
A brother, Laurel Hill, Va.,............	1 00
John Heraby and wife, Warrensburgh, Mo.,...............................	5 00
Des Moines Valley and Indian Creek churches, Iowa, by A. E. West,.....	25 00
D. E. Cripe, Akron, Ind..............	1 00
J. F. Flory, Lemoore Cal.,..............	100 00
A sister, Harleysville, Pa.,..............	2 00
Monticello Missionary Meeting, Monticello, Ind.,........................	5 00
J. S. Feebler, Jennings, La.,............	2 00

A letter, received from Mr. Edgar, reports that the funds are being most carefully distributed to relieve the suffering, which is still very great. Mrs. Olga Novikoff, Novo-Alexandrofka, Government Tambov, Russia, who is personally distributing funds at present, has also charge of the funds collected in Great Britain, and entrusted to her by Mr. and Mrs. Wm. E. Gladstone. Her great devotion to the needy ones is universally known, and a guarantee of the best possible distribution. L. A. PLATE.

Mt. Morris, Ill.

with his wife, has been lately admitted to the Home. Bro. David is suffering very much from dropsical affliction.

The Pipe Creek members, after their love-feast, remembered our old brethren and sisters at the Home in a way that was highly appreciated by the inmates.

Since our last writing some of our "Good Samaritan" neighbors have presented some nice presents. Bro. Michael Minnich received a very nice rocking-chair, which he enjoys very much.

An old brother brought a bolt of calico, wherewith to make dresses and aprons for the aged sisters. This came just right, and is much appreciated. A sister bought hats for the little boys, Charlie and Willie. They often mention the good sister's name and say they like her.

FRANK FISHER.

From "Ten Mile" Congregation, Washington Co., Pa.

OUR council-meeting, preceding our love-feast, at the Brick church was held June 11. Very little business came before the meeting preparatory to the love-feast, and on account of failing to get any ministerial help, our series of meetings was recalled for the present. Our love-feast was held June 18. We met for worship at 2 P. M. We were made to feel sad to see so many seats vacant, formerly occupied by our aged brethren. We truly feel our loss is their eternal gain. Though few in number, we had a soul-cheering little Communion for all who are hungering and thirsting after righteousness. One was taken into our church communion here by letter. Eld. J. C. Johnson, of Uniontown, Pa., arrived with his daughter just in time for "preparatory services," at 5 P. M. He officiated for us and did the preaching. Good order prevailed throughout the meeting, which in itself made us enjoy the exercises of the meeting better, and speaks commendation to the people of this neighborhood for the honor and respect shown to the worship of God.

On Sunday, June 19, we met again at 11 A. M., for worship. Bro. J. C. Johnson preached another very soul-stirring and cheering sermon to incite us to faithfulness and loyalty. On the whole we had a good meeting, and trust, like Paul, "to thank God and take courage." Acts 28: 15.

N. B. CHRISTNER.

Odell, Pa.

From Northern Missouri.

THE members of the Mission Board, of the Northern District of Missouri, met in the Whitesville congregation June 18, and perfected an organization by electing Joel Glick, Chairman; W. F. Dowie, Treasurer; the writer, Secretary.

We are authorized to take this method of notifying any members of the District, who may desire mission work, that their requests must be signed by two or more members, and that the request be sent to the Secretary as soon as possible, so that the work may be outlined to the best advantage. As we are not strong in this District, and the demand for the Bread of Life is urgent, it will require our united energy and liberal contribution to be able to meet the calls. We are glad to be able to state that there is a greater interest manifested here in the mission cause than ever before, and we hope to see it result in much good. The Board requests that any members, who may have any suggestions to offer, that would advance the mission cause, present them at the next meeting of the Board, which will occur Oct. 29, in the Whitesville congregation. In order to accomplish the greatest good, it is especially necessary that elders, ministers and the Mission Board work together.

We extend our thanks to the Whitesville brethren for the courtesies shown us during the time of our organization.

JOS. ANDES, Sec. of Mission Board.

Mound City, Mo.

Solomon's Creek Love-feast.

IN compliance with Eld. Daniel Shively's request, I attended the love-feast in his congregation (Solomon's Creek, Ind.), on the evening of June 18, which, in connection with the meetings on the following day, was a rich feast of good things of different kinds.

Notwithstanding the rainy afternoon, and the appearance of a wet evening for the feast, their large church-house was well filled with brethren, sisters and attentive spectators. The attendance of members from adjoining churches was not large on account of the rain, and many of their friends were hindered from the same cause. Good order prevailed during all the exercises, and a spirit of deep and joyful solemnity characterized the meeting through all the services.

The ministerial force from abroad was small, but enough for all purposes. W. R. Deeter, Lemuel Hillery, George Shively, Daniel Rothenberger, and some other ministers, were present to help to make it a good meeting.

Bro. Hillery is suffering much bodily affliction from a complication of ailments, principally heart disturbance, but his spiritual zeal suffers no abatement. My prayer is, that he may soon rally again physically, that he may resume his ministerial labors, that are so much needed. Bro. Davis Younce is again at his post. Though not strong bodily, he is just as willing and zealous as ever.

As soon after breakfast next morning, as the house could be put in order, the Sunday-school scholars took their seats, but, instead of the regular lesson exercises, a number of short addresses were given by brethren and sisters. This seemed to be a happy change for the little folks, if smiling faces and sparkling eyes were true indications of their feelings.

A short recess followed these exercises, after which preaching began. At the close of the meeting three humble applicants presented themselves for admission into the fold; two brethren by baptism, and one sister by restoration. It was arranged to meet at the creek for baptism at 5 P. M., where a large number gathered to witness the work. Two additional applicants presented themselves for baptism,—a mother and her son, the latter a deaf-mute, aged about twenty years. It was indeed an occasion for rejoicing to see Bro. Hiram Forney lead those four willing hearts down to their baptismal graves, one after another, each to arise to walk in newness of life. Many seemed to feel that their cup was full to overflowing.

From the water all returned to the church-house, where, until time for evening preaching, the walls of the Lord's house echoed with the soul-reviving songs of Zion. Such music! In very truth a "heavenly place in Christ Jesus." The singing gave evidence of much practice, and showed what could and ought to be done in that line in every congregation.

While listening to the well-trained voices, the following lines of long ago came to my mind:

"Were it not for cheerful song,
Life would lose its pleasure.
We could not endure it long,
Should we lose this treasure."

Next in order was an excellent discourse in defense of the inspiration of the Bible, and the infinitude of God, by Bro. George Shively. After the closing prayer came the parting hymn, and then the Solomon's Creek meetings were num-

bered with the past. Reluctantly the parting hand was given, with many pledges to meet again where

"Congregations ne'er break up,
And Sabbaths never end."

I was pleased to notice a number at the Lord's table who are very young in years. One little sister told me her age was eight years, and the ages of two or three other sisters ranged from ten to twelve. There were also brethren there as young as thirteen years, who greeted me with the kiss of love. O the touch from lips of such innocents is inspiring, and I felt that I was among angels as well as men.

Now, in conclusion, let me "tell it to the churches" that these little sisters were not ashamed of their little caps, nor need they be, and I shall pray the Good Father to give them grace to hold out faithful to the end, and then a crown will be given them in that day. Amen.

THURSTON MILLER.

La Porte, Ind.

The Russian Sufferers.

THE following amounts have been received since last report, up to and including July 2. God bless the noble-hearted givers!

M. D. Peebler, Libertyville, Iowa,	$ 1 00
A sister, Pennsylvania,	2 00
Phineas L. Fike, Dobbin, W. Va.,	1 00
John Weybright, New Paris, Ind.,	10 00
J. J. Wassam, Alvin, Texas,	2 00
Ella Williams, Funkstown, Md.,	2 00
Henry Balsbaugh, Harrisburg, Pa.,	2 00
David Vansickel, Trotwood, Ohio,	1 00
Reuben Martin, Apple Creek, Ohio,	2 00
Mrs. O. H. Elliot, Gambier, Ohio,	2 00
Aaron Sollenberger and wife, Lisle, Ill.,	2 00
One who loves suffering humanity, Roseville, Ohio,	10 00
M. E. Miller, Mt. Morris, Ill.,	2 00
A brother, Washington, D. C.,	1 00
Silas Hoover, Boynton, Pa.,	1 00
A sister, Ephratah, Pa.,	5 00
A. I. and Ruth Bowers, St. Joseph, Ill.,	5 00
E. Feebler, Libertyville, Iowa,	1 00
A sister, Lancaster, Pa.,	4 00
A brother and family, Nappanee, Ind.,	3 50
D. B. Heiny and wife,	2 00
L. C. Klingman and wife,	2 00
Friend Abel Green,	10
A brother,	25
A brother,	10
Frank Pence,	25
Jasper Higginbotham,	25
A friend,	5
A brother, Laurel Hill, Va.,	1 00
John Hershy and wife, Warrensburgh, Mo.,	5 00
Des Moines Valley and Indian Creek churches, Iowa, by A. E. West,	25 00
D. E. Cripe, Akron, Ind.,	1 00
J. F. Flory, Lemoore Cal.,	100 00
A sister, Harleysville, Pa.,	2 00
Monticello Missionary Meeting, Monticello, Ind.,	5 00
J. S. Feebler, Jennings, La.,	2 00

A letter, received from Mr. Edgar, reports that the funds are being most carefully distributed to relieve the suffering, which is still very great. Mrs. Olga Novikoff, Novo-Alexandrofka, Government Tambov, Russia, who is personally distributing funds at present, has also charge of the funds collected in Great Britain, and entrusted to her by Mr. and Mrs. Wm. E. Gladstone. Her great devotion to the needy ones is universally known, and a guarantee of the best possible distribution.

L. A. PLATE.

Mt. Morris, Ill.

English Prairie, Ind.—The members of this church held their council-meeting last Saturday, June 25. All the business was adjusted in brotherly love and union. In connection with our other business, we held a collection for the sufferers in Russia, and the sum of $8.00 was collected, and will be forwarded by Bro. J. V. Felthouse.—*John Long, Brighton, Ind., June 27.*

Ladoga, Ind.—Our regular church council occurred June 11. A good deal of business was before the meeting. We were made sad because one young sister decided to walk with us no more. Oct. 7 was the time set for our Communion meeting, to begin at 2 o'clock in the afternoon. All are invited to be with us. We expect to hold a harvest-meeting at each of our four church-houses. We have two flourishing Sunday-schools. Bro. Merton J. Holsinger is Superintendent of the school at Bethel, and Bro. Samuel Stoner of the one at Mt. Pleasant. We use the Brethren's literature.—*Charity Himes, June 26.*

Freeburg, Ohio.—Bro. J. M. Mohler, of Lewistown, Pa., came to us on the evening of May 13, and remained with us till the evening of the 29th. He preached twenty sermons. Although the dark nights, muddy roads, and rainy evenings, were much against us, yet a small number wended their way through rain and mud to the house of worship, where Bro. Mohler preached the Word to us in such unmistakable terms, and with a zeal well worthy of the cause. When the weather was favorable, our large house was well filled with attentive listeners. There were no accessions at this place, but many are counting the cost. We trust that the good seed sown may be gathered ere long.—*S. B. Stuckey.*

Bethel, Holt Co., Mo.—The members met in regular quarterly council to-day. Eld. S. B. Shirkey, of Ray County, presided. The members present seem to be still in the faith of the General Brotherhood. Although matters of a somewhat serious nature came before the council, all business was handled in the Christian spirit of forbearance. We were made to rejoice by one soul making application for baptism. "The poor ye have with you always and ye can do them good, if ye will," was forcibly impressed by a matter which was brought to the notice of the members to-day. May we always be willing to do good to God's poor, especially the old and infirm! We decided to hold a Communion meeting Sept. 17, beginning at 2 P. M., at the Bethlehem meeting-house.—*Jos. Andes, June 25.*

Farnhamville, Iowa.—The members of the Farnhamville church rejoice to see that so many precious souls are tired of living in sin, and have resolved to own the cause of their Blessed Master. Last Lord's Day two dear souls were buried with Christ by baptism. Four weeks ago three others were baptized into Christ. This makes fourteen since last October. Thus we all see the good work go on, but we regret to see so many dear souls resist the prompting of the Spirit, and put off their salvation till a more convenient season. We met in council June 25. Eld. J. W. Trostle presided. We decided to hold our love-feast Sept. 10, and also thought it necessary to hold a choice for a deacon. The lot fell on Bro. E. H. Squires. He and his companion were duly installed in the order of the Brethren. We are in need of ministerial help. The harvest is ripe and the laborers are few. There is a fair chance for a good minister to build up a church. If any of our ministering brethren are thinking of changing their location, we should like to have them come and see our country, or write.—*A. M. White, June 27.*

New Sharon, Iowa.—The members of the Middle Creek church, Mahaska Co., Iowa, enjoyed a pleasant love-feast June 18 and 19. Several brethren and sisters of other congregations assembled with us, and we had a good meeting. Ministers from adjoining churches were J. S. Snyder, G. W. Hopwood and Isaac Barnhizer. They broke the Bread of Life to the satisfaction of all. Bro. L. S. Snyder officiated. We also held an election for a minister. The lot fell on Bro. P. P. Frederick, and we hope and pray that he may be a faithful laborer in the vineyard of the Lord. One sister returned to the fold again, thank the Lord.—*John Gable, June 26.*

Van Wert, Ohio.—The members of the above-named church met in quarterly council June 23, 1892. There was considerable business before the council, but all was pleasantly disposed of. One brother was received by letter and one was reclaimed, which act gave great joy to the little flock of brethren and sisters, and also to the angels in heaven. With some members of the adjoining church, we met again June 25, 1892, for Communion purposes. Though there were but forty-four members at the tables, the house was well filled with very quiet spectators, who maintained the best of order. This made the meeting pleasant, and the brethren and sisters were made to realize that not always with the largest congregations the most joy and happiness are to be had. If we meet with our hearts emptied of self, and full of Christ, believing that he is able to do all he has promised, he will bless us with every time. Bro. Harp, our minister, was advanced to the second degree at our council.—*Jonathan Hahn.*

Matrimonial.

"What therefore God hath joined together, let not man put asunder."

KNUDSON — WEIDNER.— At the residence of the bride's parents, June 1, 1892, by the writer, Mr. Newt. Knudson and sister Mary C. Weidner, all of Story County, Iowa.
J. L. THOMAS.

TEETER — REBERT.— At the residence of the undersigned officiating minister, June 21, 1852, Bro. Noah A. Teeter and sister Anna M. Rebert, of Dayton, Ohio.
W. C. TEETER.

Fallen Asleep.

"Blessed are the dead which die in the Lord."

FRADENBERG.—In the Salem church, Marion Co., Ill., after nine weeks of intense suffering, Jesse M. Fradenburg, aged 58 years, 10 months and 22 days. Bro. Fradenburg moved here from Kosciusko County, Ind., last March. Funeral services by Eld. Jacob Frederic.
S. S. FOUTZ.

BOWMAN.—In the Bear Creek church, Montgomery Co., Ohio, Catharine, wife of John J. Bowman, aged 55 years, 5 months and 23 days. She attended meeting on Sunday, and five days later, fell asleep. There remains a husband (who is a minister) and five children, who realize the loss they have sustained. Services by Eld. Geo. Holler and the writer from Ps. 17: 15, in the old Bear Creek church, to a large congregation.
D. M. GARVER.

ULERY.—In the Elkhart church, Elkhart Co., Ind., June 17, 1892, sister Mary Ulery, aged 75 years, 9 months and 5 days. She was anointed before she died. Funeral services by Bro. A. Neff, from these words, "For I am now ready to be offered, and the time of my departure is at hand." Sister Ulery's husband preceded her to the spirit world some years ago. He was a faithful deacon, and widely known over Northern Indiana as a careful worker in the church.
J. H. MILLER.

SCHRANTZ.—At his home in Stonington, Ill., June 24, 1892, Mr. Ephraim Schrantz. He was born near Lititz, Lancaster Co., Pa., Feb. 15, 1823, and removed with his parents to Ohio in 1835, where he was married in 1844 to Nancy Mohler, who survives him. Five children were born to them. He came to Christian County in 1866, and to Stonington in 1887. His funeral was conducted by Rev. A. J. Amerman at the Methodist church.
TROPHIE J. AMERMAN.

WRAY.—In the Burr Oak church, Kans., April 9, 1892, Emery Riley Wray, son of Bro. Samuel and sister Nettie Wray, aged 11 months and 6 days. Funeral services by C. S. Hillery.
S. A. DAOGETT.

OBER.—In the Manor congregation, Indiana Co., Pa., May 5, 1892, sister Catharine Ober, companion of Eld. David Ober, deceased, aged 71 years, 8 months and 4 days. Deceased was the mother of nine children, five of whom preceded her to the spirit world. Three daughters and one son remain, She was a member of the Brethren church for over 50 years, and lived a very humble, consistent life. She lost her eyesight about two years before she died, but the loss of her natural sight only strengthened her spiritually. Funeral occasion improved from Rev. 13: 14.

WISE.—In the same congregation, June 5, 1892, sister Rachel Wise, wife of Bro. John H. Wise, aged 31 years and 13 days. Funeral and interment at Taylorsville.
MARK MINSER.

MYERS.—Near Crawltown, York Co., Pa., April 27, 1892, Clara J. Myers, aged 20 years, 7 months and 15 days. Services by J. A. Long and D. H. Baker.

ZIEGLER.—Near Mummert's meeting-house, Adams Co., Pa., May 1, 1892, Bro. George Ziegler, aged 61 years, 7 months and 26 days. Services by J. A. Long and D. H. Baker.
MARK K. BAKER.

BERKEY.—June 24, of cholera infantum, son of Bro. Perry and sister Sarah Berkey, aged 7 months and 19 days. Funeral services conducted by Bro. J. Crume from Rom. 5: 15.
R. W. DAVENPORT.

HITCHCOCK.—In the Mansfield congregation, Mansfield, Mo., June 21, 1892, of paralysis, Bro. Z. Hitchcock, aged 79 years and 19 days. Funeral services by Bro. S. D. Rothrock, from Rev. 14: 13.
LIZZIE ROTHROCK.

BLOUGH.—In the Brother's Valley congregation, Somerset Co., Pa., May 24, 1892, sister Barbara Blough, widow of Eld. Jacob Blough, deceased, of near Berlin, Pa., aged 82 years and 14 days. Deceased died of low vitality, incident to old age. She was the mother of eleven children, seven sons and four daughters, all of whom survive her. She lived to see the fourth generation of her family. Funeral occasion improved by the home ministry, to a large congregation of relatives and friends.
J. J. BLAUCH.

REPLOGLE.—In the Fairview church, Appanoose Co., Iowa, of lung disease, June 20, 1892, sister Mary Replogle, aged 29 years, 1 month and 26 days. She was the youngest daughter of Bro. Martin and sister Anna Replogle, and a most exemplary sister. She was for many months a great sufferer, and early in her sickness she called for the elders of the church, and was anointed. Funeral services by Eld. D. Zook.
J. W. HAWN.

MILLER.—June 10, 1892, John Ross, son of Joseph and Lottie E. Miller, aged 1 year and 4 days. The cause of death was cholera infantum.

MILLER.—March 31, 1892, of pneumonia, Sylvia Edna, twin-sister of the above-named little boy, aged 9 months and 13 days. Side by side they now repose in their quiet grave in Oak Ridge cemetery. Services conducted from 2 Cor. 5: 1 by the writer.
D. S. BRALLIER.

The Gospel Messenger

Is the recognized organ of the German Baptist or Brethren's church, and advocates the form of doctrine taught in the New Testament and pleads for a return to apostolic and primitive Christianity.

It recognizes the New Testament as the only infallible rule of faith and practice, and maintains that Faith toward God, Repentance from dead works, Regeneration of the heart and mind, baptism by Trine Immersion for remission of sins unto the reception of the Holy Ghost by the laying on of hands, are the means of adoption into the household of God,—the church militant.

It also maintains that Feet-washing, as taught in John 13, both by example and command of Jesus, should be observed in the church.

That the Lord's Supper, instituted by Christ and as universally observed by the apostles and the early Christians, is a full meal, and, in connection with the Communion, should be taken in the evening or after the close of the day.

That the Salutation of the Holy Kiss, or Kiss of Charity, is binding upon the followers of Christ.

That War and Retaliation are contrary to the spirit and self-denying principles of the religion of Jesus Christ.

That the principle of Plain Dressing and of Non-conformity to the world, as taught in the New Testament, should be observed by the followers of Christ.

That the Scriptural duty of Anointing the Sick with Oil, in the Name of the Lord, James 5: 14, is binding upon all Christians.

It also advocates the church's duty to support Missionary and Tract Work, thus giving to the Lord for the spread of the Gospel and for the conversion of sinners.

In short, it is a vindicator of all that Christ and the apostles have enjoined upon us, and aims, amid the conflicting theories and discords of modern Christendom, to point out ground that all must concede to be infallibly safe.

The above principles of our Fraternity are set forth on our "Brethren's Envelopes." Use them! Price, 15 cents per package; 40 cents per hundred.

English Prairie, Ind.—The members of this church held their council-meeting last Saturday, June 25. All the business was adjusted in brotherly love and union. In connection with our other business, we held a collection for the sufferers in Russia, and the sum of $8.00 was collected, and will be forwarded by Bro. J. V. Felthouse.—*John Long, Brighton, Ind., June 27.*

Ladoga, Ind.—Our regular church council occurred June 11. A good deal of business was before the meeting. We were made sad because one young sister decided to walk with us no more. One sister united with the church by baptism. Oct. 7 was the time set for our Communion meeting, to begin at 2 o'clock in the afternoon. All are invited to be with us. We expect to hold a harvest-meeting at each of our four church-houses. We have two flourishing Sunday-schools. Bro. Merton J. Holsinger is Superintendent of the school at Bethel, and Bro. Samuel Stoner of the one at Mt. Pleasant. We use the Brethren's literature.—*Charity Himes, June 26.*

Freeburg, Ohio.—Bro. J. M. Mohler, of Lewistown, Pa., came to us on the evening of May 13, and remained with us till the evening of the 29th. He preached twenty sermons. Although the dark nights, muddy roads, and rainy evenings, were much against us, yet a small number wended their way through rain and mud to the house of worship, where Bro. Mohler preached the Word to us in such unmistakable terms, and with a zeal well worthy of the cause. When the weather was favorable, our large house was well filled with attentive listeners. There were no accessions at this place, but many are counting the cost. We trust that the good seed sown may be gathered ere long.—*S. B. Stuckey.*

Bethel, Holt Co., Mo.—The members met in regular quarterly council to-day. Eld. S. B. Shirkey, of Ray County, presided. The members present seem to be still in the faith of the General Brotherhood. Although matters of a somewhat serious nature came before the council, all business was handled in the Christian spirit of forbearance. We were made to rejoice by one soul making application for baptism. "The poor ye have with you always and ye can do them good, if ye will," was forcibly impressed by a matter which was brought to the notice of the meeting to-day. May we always be willing to do good to God's poor, especially the old and infirm! We decided to hold a Communion meeting Sept. 17, beginning at 2 P. M., at the Bethlehem meeting-house. —*Jos. Andes, June 25.*

Farnhamville, Iowa.—The members of the Farnhamville church rejoice to see that so many precious souls are tired of living in sin, and have resolved to own the cause of their Blessed Master. Last Lord's Day two dear souls were buried with Christ by baptism. Four weeks ago three others were baptized into Christ. This makes fourteen since last October. Thus we all see the good work go on, but we regret to see so many dear souls resist the prompting of the Spirit, and put off their salvation till a more convenient season. We met in council June 25. Eld. J. W. Trostle presided. We decided to hold our love-feast Sept. 10, and also thought it necessary to hold a choice for a deacon. The lot fell on Bro. E. H. Squires. He and his companion were duly installed in the order of the Brethren. We are in need of ministerial help. The harvest is ripe and the laborers are few. There is a fair chance for a good minister to build up a church. If any of our ministering brethren are thinking of changing their location, we should like to have them come and see our country, or write.—*A. M. White, June 27.*

New Sharon, Iowa.—The members of the Middle Creek church, Mahaska Co., Iowa, enjoyed a pleasant love-feast June 18 and 19. Several brethren and sisters of other congregations assembled with us, and we had a good meeting. Ministers from adjoining churches were J. S. Snyder, G. W. Hopwood and Isaac Barnhizer. They broke the Bread of Life to the satisfaction of all. Bro. L. S. Snyder officiated. We also held an election for a minister. The lot fell on Bro. P. P. Frederick, and we hope and pray that he may be a faithful laborer in the vineyard of the Lord. One sister returned to the fold again, thank the Lord.—*John Gable, June 28.*

Van Wert, Ohio.—The members of the above-named church met in quarterly council June 23, 1892. There was considerable business before the council, but all was pleasantly disposed of. One brother was received by letter and one was reclaimed, which act gave great joy to the little flock of brethren and sisters, and also to the angels in heaven. With some members of the adjoining church, we met again June 25, 1892, for Communion purposes. Though there were but forty-four members at the tables, the house was well filled with very quiet spectators, who maintained the best of order. This made the meeting pleasant, and the brethren and sisters were made to realize that not always with the largest congregations the most joy and happiness are to be had. If we meet with our hearts emptied of self, and full of Christ, believing that he is able to do all he has promised, he will be with us every time. Bro. Harp, our minister, was advanced to the second degree at our council.—*Jonathan Hahn.*

Matrimonial.

"What therefore God hath joined together, let not man put asunder."

KNUDSON—WEIDNER.—At the residence of the bride's parents, June 1, 1892, by the writer, Mr. Newt. Knudson and sister Mary C. Weidner, all of Story County, Iowa.

J. L. THOMAS.

TEETER—REBERT.—At the residence of the undersigned officiating minister, June 21, 1892, Bro. Noah A. Teeter and sister Anna M. Rebert, of Dayton, Ohio.

W. C. TEETER.

Fallen Asleep.

"Blessed are the dead which die in the Lord."

FRADENBERG.—In the Salem church, Marion Co., Ill., after nine weeks of intense suffering, Jesse M. Fradenburg, aged 58 years, 10 months and 22 days. Bro. Fradenburg moved here from Kosciusko County, Ind., last March. Funeral services by Eld. Jacob Frederic. S. S. FOUTZ.

BOWMAN.—In the Bear Creek church, Montgomery Co., Ohio, Catharine, wife of John J. Bowman, aged 55 years, 5 months and 23 days. She attended meeting on Sunday, and five days later, fell asleep. There remains a husband (who is a minister) and five children, who realize the loss they have sustained. Services by Eld. Geo. Holler and the writer from Ps. 17: 15, in the old Bear Creek church, to a large congregation. D. M. GARVER.

ULERY.—In the Elkhart church, Elkhart Co., Ind., June 17, 1892, sister Mary Ulery, aged 75 years, 9 months and 5 days. She was anointed before she died. Funeral services by Bro. A. Neff, from these words, "For I am now ready to be offered, and the time of my departure is at hand." Sister Ulery's husband preceded her to the spirit world some years ago. He was a faithful deacon, and widely known over Northern Indiana as a careful worker in the church.

J. H. MILLER.

SCHRANTZ.—At his home in Stonington, Ill., June 24, 1892, Mr. Ephraim Schrantz. He was born near Lititz, Lancaster Co., Pa., Feb. 15, 1823, and removed with his parents to Ohio in 1835, where he was married in 1844 to Nancy Mohler, who survives him. Five children were born to them. He came to Christian County in 1866, and to Stonington in 1887. His funeral was conducted by Rev. A. J. Amerman at the Methodist church.

TROPHIE J. AMERMAN.

WRAY.—In the Burr Oak church, Kans., April 9, 1892, Emery Riley Wray, son of Bro. Samuel and sister Nettie Wray, aged 11 months and 6 days. Funeral services by C. S. Hillery. S. A. DAGGETT.

OBER.—In the Manor congregation, Indiana Co., Pa., May 5, 1892, sister Catharine Ober, companion of Eld. David Ober, deceased, aged 71 years, 8 months and 4 days. Deceased was the mother of nine children, five of whom preceded her to the spirit world. Three daughters and one son remain. She was a member of the Brethren church for over 50 years, and lived a very humble, consistent life. She lost her eyesight about two years before she died, but the loss of her natural sight only strengthened her spiritually. Funeral occasion improved from Rev. 13: 14.

WISE.—In the same congregation, June 5, 1892, sister Rachel Wise, wife of Bro. John H. Wise, aged 31 years and 13 days. Funeral and interment at Taylorsville.

MARK MINSER.

MYERS.—Near Crawltown, York Co., Pa., April 27, 1892, Clara J. Myers, aged 20 years, 7 months and 15 days. Services by J. A. Long and D. H. Baker.

ZIEGLER.—Near Mummert's meeting-house, Adams Co., Pa., May 1, 1892, Bro. George Ziegler, aged 61 years, 7 months and 26 days. Services by J. A. Long and D. H. Baker. MARY K. BAKER.

BERKEY.—June 24, of cholera infantum, son of Bro. Perry and sister Sarah Berkey, aged 7 months and 19 days. Funeral services conducted by Bro. J. Crume from Rom. 5: 15. R. W. DAVENPORT.

HITCHCOCK.—In the Mansfield congregation, Mansfield, Mo., June 21, 1892, of paralysis, Bro. Z. Hitchcock, aged 79 years and 19 days. Funeral services by Bro. S. D. Rothrock, from Rev. 14: 13. LIZZIE ROTHROCK.

BLOUGH.—In the Brother's Valley congregation, Somerset Co., Pa., May 24, 1892, sister Barbara Blough, widow of Eld. Jacob Blough, deceased, of near Berlin, Pa., aged 82 years and 14 days. Deceased died of low vitality, incident to old age. She was the mother of eleven children, seven sons and four daughters, all of whom survive her. She lived to see the fourth generation of her family. Funeral occasion improved by the home ministry, to a large congregation of relatives and friends. J. J. BLAUCH.

REPLOGLE.—In the Fairview church, Appanoose Co., Iowa, of lung disease, June 20, 1892, sister Mary Replogle, aged 29 years, 1 month and 26 days. She was the youngest daughter of Bro. Martin and sister Anna Replogle, and a most exemplary sister. She was for many months a great sufferer, and early in her sickness she called for the elders of the church, and was anointed. Funeral services by Eld. D. Zook. J. W. HAWN.

MILLER.—June 20, 1892, John Ross, son of Joseph and Lottie E. Miller, aged 1 year and 2 days. The cause of death was cholera infantum.

MILLER.—March 31, 1892, of pneumonia, Sylvie Edna, twin-sister of the above-named little boy, aged 9 months and 13 days. Side by side they now repose in their quiet grave in Oak Ridge cemetery. Services conducted from 2 Cor. 5: 1 by the writer. D. S. BRALLIER.

The Gospel Messenger

Is the recognized organ of the German Baptist or Brethren's church, and advocates the form of doctrine taught in the New Testament and pleads for a return to apostolic and primitive Christianity.

It recognizes the New Testament as the only infallible rule of faith and practice, and maintains that Faith toward God, Repentance from dead works, Regeneration of the heart and mind, baptism by Trine Immersion for remission of sins unto the reception of the Holy Ghost by the laying on of hands, are the means of adoption into the household of God,—the church militant.

It also maintains that Feet-washing, as taught in John 13, both by example and command of Jesus, should be observed in the church.

That the Lord's Supper, instituted by Christ and as universally observed by the apostles and the early Christians, is a full meal, and, in connection with the Communion, should be taken in the evening or after the close of the day.

That the Salutation of the Holy Kiss, or Kiss of Charity, is binding upon the followers of Christ.

That War and Retaliation are contrary to the spirit and self-denying principles of the religion of Jesus Christ.

That the principle of Plain Dressing and of Non-conformity to the world, as taught in the New Testament, should be observed by the followers of Christ.

That the Scriptural duty of Anointing the Sick with Oil, in the Name of the Lord, James 5: 14, is binding upon all Christians.

It also advocates the church's duty to support Missionary and Tract Work, thus giving to the Lord for the spread of the Gospel and for the conversion of sinners.

In short, it is a vindicator of all that Christ and the apostles have enjoined upon us, and aims, amid the conflicting theories and discords of modern Christendom, to point out ground that all must concede to be infallibly safe.

☞ The above principles of our Fraternity are set forth on our "Brethren's Envelopes." Use them! Price, 15 cents per package; 40 cents per hundred.

EUROPE
AND
Bible Lands

A new edition of this deservedly popular
work has recently been published. It retains
all the excellencies of its predecessors, and
with those who are interested in Bible study
this work will always remain a favorite.
Those who have read the ordinary book of
travel will be surprised to find "Europe and
Bible Lands" of thrilling interest for both old
and young. The large number of books, already sold, proves that the work is of more
than ordinary merit.

A fair supply of the last edition of this
work is still on hand. Those who have not
yet secured a copy of the work should embrace this opportunity of securing it. Price,
in fine cloth binding, only $1.50 per copy,
post-paid. To agents who are prepared to
push an active canvass of the work, we are
prepared to give special inducements. Write
BRETHREN'S PUBLISHING CO.,
Mt. Morris, Ill.

A Look, a Word, a Sign!

A trifling incident, has changed the course
of many a life.

It is said that Voltaire, when five years old,
learned an infidel poem; and he was never
able to free himself from its effects. Scott,
the commentator, when despairing, read a
hymn of Dr. Watts', and was turned from a
life of idleness and sin to one of usefulness.
Cowper, about to drown himself, was carried
the wrong way by his driver and went home
to write: "God moves in a mysterious way."
"A kiss from my mother," said Benjamin
West, "made me a painter." When yet a
child he had drawn a rude sketch of an infant
sleeping in a cradle. His mother chanced to
see his childish production, and was so well
pleased with it that she took the young artist
in her arms, and rapturously kissed him.
That mark of maternal delight fixed his fate
for life.

We do not say that the circumstance made
the man, but that the man was adapted to the
circumstance; that, had it not been for the
little event, his life might have been like a
mighty river that loses motive power as it
spreads over a thousand fields; but the occasion of the turning point was like a great dam
that forced it into a channel where it rushed
on with restless force.

Hundreds of Young People

may have the occasion of leading to the turning point presented by spending *one cent* for a
postal, and telling us what their longings are.
We can not help you unless we know where
you are. *Write now.* Address;

J. G. ROYER,
Mt. Morris, Ill.

Be sure to mention this paper.

ESSAYS

"Study to show thyself approved unto God; a workman that needeth not be ashamed, rightly dividing the Word of Truth."

KEEP ME, O FATHER!

Keep me, O Father, safe by thy side,
My bark is so small, the ocean so wide,
The waters are dark, the billows are strong,
My bark is so frail, and the distance so long.

Oh, yes! the rough ocean of life is wide,
Wild are the surges and eager the tide;
Often the quicksands and whirlpools appear.
Keep me, O Father, as onward I steer.

Keep me, my Father; O stay near the oar,
Surges are dashing this side of the shore;
While terror and darkness steal over my soul,
And the foam-crested billows angrily roll.   .

The waters are dark; I feel the damp spray
Steal over my vision, obscuring the way.
Sea winds are moaning in cadence so wild,
Stay, O my Father, stay close to thy child.

Half-hidden rocks appear to my view,
Threatening my trail bark in ruin to strew;
And dear ones who once started out by my side,
Are stranded and gone with the angry tide.

But lo! in the distance a light-house appears,
Hushed are my sorrows, dried are my tears,
The Savior is guiding my boat to the shore,
Where surges and tempests shall come evermore.

Safe into the harbor I'm sailing to-day,
I fear not the rocks nor the sands in my way;
For Father is near—and I hear a still voice—
"Sorrow not, child, but always rejoice."

Then keep me, Father, keep hold of my hand,
Till safely I reach that beautiful land,
And sing where sorrows come nevermore,
Away on the fadeless, golden shore.

    —Selected.

IN "THE SLOUGH OF DESPOND."

BY C. H. BALSBAUGH.

My Dear Brother:—

Your troubled letter troubles me. Not that I think there is in it anything hard to answer, but you are too deep in the mire,—over your very eyes,—to see "the truth as it is in Jesus."

You open your letter with these pregnant words: "I have been reading and thinking a little, and now I find myself involved in a perfect labyrinth of doubt and uncertainty as to the authorship and authenticity of the Bible." This is very sad, but perfectly natural. You have been reading and thinking what you ought not, and hence your perplexity. You never would have got into this "labyrinth of doubt and uncertainty" had you not left "the simplicity that is in Christ," and stepped aside into the mazes of scientific speculation, and the so-called "higher criticism." This has done the work for you, as it has done for thousands of others. You will never get out of your "labyrinth" by a philosophical dissipation of your doubts, but by simple trust in the veracity of Jehovah. God is not going to condescend to answer the quibbles raised by those who walk after the flesh, and not in the spirit. He has given us a Book replete with enough of His wisdom and will and goodness to satisfy any reasonable soul of His existence · and truth and justice and paternity.

You ask, "How do we *know* there is a God, and that the Bible is true?" Do you *know* that *you are*, and that your word is veracious? How? If you answer my question in the simplest possible way, *yours* will also be answered. If God does not address Himself to our consciousness with as positive certainty as the fact of our own being, then step confidently into the ranks of agnosticism. God asserts as a "Memorial to all generations," "I AM." Let this suffice until it is demonstrated that the sacred volume is a fiction.

You ask, "Who would believe such stories as Moses and the burning bush, and Daniel in the lion's den, etc., if read elsewhere? Why credit them in the Bible?" This question answers itself and is a strong defense of the Divine Authorship of the Bible. The reason nobody would credit such statements in any other work is simply because they could not possibly be supported by the requisite historical adjuncts. The latter are as impregnable as the constellations, and so long as these are intact, I accept all the miraculous stories between the two lids of "the volume of the Book."

Then comes the question: "Why do science and the Bible differ as to the age and creation of the earth?" This I squarely and promptly deny. Let me see the antagonism between what is really science, and the declarations of the Holy Scriptures. There is no science among men so unsettled and unreliable as Geology. If all the speculative chaff is winnowed away, and nothing left but what admits of no doubt, it would be no more than a respectable primer. We are not to be frightened by the "oppositions of science *falsely so called.*" 1 Tim. 6: 20. Please dismiss forever the "profane and vain babblings" of those who seek to make matter to preach a better Gospel than its Author. Obey John 5: 39, and treat all skeptical works according to Acts 10: 19, 20. I know all that the most expert scientists have to say *against* the Bible, from the euphonious Tyndall, and the philosophical Spencer, down to the ribald, smutty Ingersoll. Delirious babble, all. "Vanity of vanities." "*Touch not* the unclean thing."

One whom you can trust with supreme confidence in life and death calls you, "*Come unto* ME, *I will give you* REST." Matt. 11: 28. "My sheep hear my voice, and I know them, and they follow me: and I give unto them eternal life; and they shall never perish." John 10: 27, 28. "*A stranger will* they *not follow*, BUT WILL FLEE FROM HIM." Verse 5. This is your only safety. Let the *hiding* of Col. 3: 3, be the constant realization and exemplification of John 15: 7. Then your "labyrinth" will be among the things that were. Then will you be astonished and ashamed that you could ever call in question either the wisdom, or the truth, or the love of your Gracious Father and Redeemer.

Then you ask these strange questions: "If the Bible is a perfect work from a Perfect Author, why can we fully understand so little of it? Why is it so written as to admit so many views? Why can we have several hundred sects, all composed of honest, intelligent persons, believing so differently, and all confident they are following Christ?"

My dear brother, you utterly misconceive the essential constitution of humanity and of divine revelation, and of the philosophy of life. Who differs more than these very scientists who have so much to prate about the discrepancies of the Bible, and the conflicting creeds of Christendom? What one builds up in the most oracular tone, another as confidently pulls down. In nothing are they more irreconcilably at variance than in the age of the world and the antiquity of man. It is not only astounding, but laughable how they stumble over each other, and fight ferociously for the validity of their shadowy guesses. If I could fully understand the Bible, I might well doubt its Divine Authorship. I have read many of the profoundest works ever written by man, but I have not yet found one which I did not comprehend.

The authors were human, and so was I, hence they could not surpass my appreciation. But when Jehovah puts *His* mind into a Book for the study of finite creatures, what more natural than that we should find heights we cannot scale, depths we cannot fathom, lengths and breadths we cannot explore. Thank God that the Bible is so full of mysteries which I cannot compass. And as to the disparity of views, it would be equally surprising, if so many little minds, occupying different angles, looking at an infinite object, would have the same conception of every point. The idea of the Holy Trinity, with all-inclusive relations, is not questioned by any evangelical church. The divergences all begin a step lower than the central fact. It is our vital connection with GOD through such faith as we can honestly exercise that determines character.

The Incarnate Word, "the hearing of faith," the illumination of the Spirit, must shape our life according to the capacity which the law of inheritance and environment will allow. Every soul is dealt with on the ground of its own personality. We may all do the same thing, and yet no two be the same. "In the *beginning was* the WORD. Note the verb *was*. The *beginning* did not begin IT. Neither will it *end*. The Bible is the Text Book of eternity, the meaning of its precepts and principles and institutions being deep and vast enough to engage all created intelligence forever.

You charge the New Testament with impossible and unreasonable demands. For instance: "Be harmless as doves." Connect John 17: 23, and Philpp. 4: 13, and dare to say that such sweetness of disposition is impracticable. That we have tigers and panthers and lions and "bulls of Bashan," and hawks and vultures in the church, disproves not the fact of a perfect man in Emmanuel, and of souls like Him, who are wholly swayed by his indwelling. You regard it as arrogant and absurd to pretend to "be perfect as our Father in heaven is perfect." Give yourself to God as really and absolutely as Jesus gave himself to humanity, and then utter your verdict as to this possibility. The Bible does not ask us to be infinite, either in capacity or character, but it does demand us to allow God such possession of us as to be perfectly human; then are we like God according to our nature and measure.

You imagine that James 2: 10 precludes all possibility of salvation. Law and commandment are not the same. A commandment has a commander back of it. One principle runs through all divine requirements. We cannot infringe the least without running counter to the principle that supports the universe. "Guilty of all" is simply a law without which there could be no government, human or divine. Eminently beneficent is such a provision.

You ask me whether I can refer you to any good books that will be helpful to you. Plenty of them, but I will not mention any at present. The Bible is the supreme Book, and will solve all your problems and scatter all your mists. Make it your counsellor exclusively under the tuition of the Holy Spirit. Throw science and metaphysics and guess-work overboard. "THY WORD IS TRUTH." It was all the weapon Jesus needed in His terrible conflict with the devil. "It is written," "*It is written,*" "IT IS WRITTEN." With this "Sword of the Spirit" you can hew all the Agags to pieces. ·

Your soul is in jeopardy, and your only hope is in believing where you cannot see. Jesus has given as indisputable evidence of his divinity by what He did, as you have of your humanity by writing to me. Let Heb. 4: 14, 15, 16, and 6: 13-20, be to you the whole Gospel. The historical Christ defies all criticism. · This admitted, the Personal Christ must be accepted in all His claims and prerogatives. He is a "chief corner stone, elect, precious: and he that *believeth* on

→✦ESSAYS✦←

" Study to show thyself approved unto God; a workman that needeth not be ashamed, rightly dividing the Word of Truth."

KEEP ME, O FATHER!

Keep me, O Father, safe by thy side,
My bark is so small, the Ocean so wide,
The waters are dark, the billows are strong,
My bark is so frail, and the distance so long.

Oh, yes! the rough Ocean of life is wide,
Wild are the surges and eager the tide;
Often the quicksands and whirlpools appear.
Keep me, O Father, as onward I steer.

Keep me, my Father; O stay near the oar,
Surges are dashing this side of the shore;
While terror and darkness steal over my soul,
And the foam-crested billows angrily roll.

The waters are dark; I feel the damp spray
Steal over my Vision, obscuring the way.
Sea winds are moaning in cadence so wild,
Stay, O my Father, stay close to thy child.

Half-hidden rocks appear to my view,
Threatening my frail bark in ruin to strew;
And dear ones who once started out by my side,
Are stranded and gone with the angry tide.

But lo! in the distance a light-house appears,
Hushed are my sorrows, dried are my tears,
The Savior is guiding my boat to the shore,
Where surges and tempests shall come nevermore.

Safe into the harbor I'm sailing to-day,
I fear not the rocks nor the sands in my way;
For Father's near—and I hear a still voice—
" Sorrow not, child, but always rejoice."

Then keep me, Father, keep hold of my hand,
Till safely I reach that beautiful land,
And sing where sorrows come nevermore,
Away on the fadeless, golden shore.

—*Selected.*

IN " THE SLOUGH OF DESPOND."

BY C H. BALSBAUGH.

My Dear Brother:—

Your troubled letter troubles me. Not that I think there is in it anything hard to answer, but you are too deep in the mire,—over your very eyes,—to see "the truth as it is in Jesus."

You open your letter with these pregnant words: " I have been reading and thinking a little, and now I find myself involved in a perfect labyrinth of doubt and uncertainty as to the authorship and authenticity of the Bible." This is very sad, but perfectly natural. You have been reading and thinking what you ought not, and hence your perplexity. You never would have got into this "labyrinth of doubt and uncertainty" had you not left "the simplicity that is in Christ," and stepped aside into the mazes of scientific speculation, and the so-called "higher criticism." This has done the work for you, as it has done for thousands of others. You will never get out of your "labyrinth" by a philosophical dissipation of your doubts, but by simple trust in the veracity of Jehovah. God is not going to condescend to answer the quibbles raised by those who walk after the flesh, and not in the spirit. He has given us a Book that unfolds enough of His wisdom and will and goodness to satisfy any reasonable soul of His existence·and truth and justice and paternity.

You ask, "How do we *know* there is a God, and that the Bible is true?" Do you *know* that *you are*, and that your word is veracious? How? If you answer my question in the simplest possible way, yours will also be answered. If God does not address Himself to our consciousness with as positive certainty as the fact of our own being, then step confidently into the ranks of agnosticism. God asserts as a "Memorial to all generations," "I AM." Let this suffice until it

is demonstrated that the sacred volume is a fiction.

You ask, "Who would believe such stories as Moses and the burning bush, and Daniel in the lion's den, etc., if read elsewhere? Why credit them in the Bible?" This question answers itself and is a strong defense of the Divine Authorship of the Bible. The reason nobody would credit such statements in any other work is simply because they could not possibly be supported by the requisite historical adjuncts. The latter are as impregnable as the constellations, and so long as these are intact, I accept all the miraculous stories between the two lids of "the volume of the Book."

Then comes the question: "Why do science and the Bible differ as to the age and creation of the earth?" This I squarely and promptly deny. Let me see the antagonism between what is really science, and the declarations of the Holy Scriptures. There is no science among men so unsettled and unreliable as Geology. If all the speculative chaff is winnowed away, and nothing left but what admits of no doubt, it would be no more than a respectable primer. We are not to be frightened by the "oppositions of science *falsely so called.*" 1 Tim. 6: 20. Please dismiss forever the "profane and vain babblings" of those who seek to make matter to preach a better Gospel than its Author. Obey John 5: 39, and trust all skeptical works according to Acts 19: 19, 20. I know all that the most expert scientists have to say *against* the Bible, from the euphonious Tyndall, and the philosophical Spencer, down to the ribald, smutty Ingersoll. Delirious babble, all. "Vanity of vanities." "*Touch not* the unclean thing."

One whom you can trust with supreme confidence in life and death calls you, "*Come unto me, I will give you REST.*" Matt. 11: 28. "My sheep hear my voice, and I know them, and they follow me: and I give unto them eternal life; and they shall never perish." John 10: 27, 28. "A stranger will they *not follow,* BUT WILL FLEE FROM HIM." Verse 5. This is your only safety. Let the *hiding* of Col. 3: 3, be the constant realization and exemplification of John 15: 7. Then your "labyrinth" will be among the things that were. Then will you be astonished and ashamed that you could ever call in question either the wisdom, or the truth, or the love of your Gracious Father and Redeemer.

Then you ask these strange questions: "If the Bible is a perfect work from a Perfect Author, why can we fully understand so little of it? Why is it so written as to admit so many views? Why can we have several hundred sects, all composed of honest, intelligent persons, believing so differently, and all confident they are following Christ?" My dear brother, you utterly misconceive the essential constitution of humanity and of divine revelation, and of the philosophy of life. Who differs more than these very scientists who have so much to prate about the discrepancies of the Bible, and the conflicting creeds of Christendom? What one builds up in the most oracular 'tone, another as confidently pulls down. In nothing are they more irreconcilably at variance than in the age of the world and the antiquity of man. It is not only astounding, but laughable how they stumble over each other, and fight ferociously for the validity of their shadowy guesses. If I could fully understand the Bible, I might well doubt its Divine Authorship. I have read many of the profoundest works ever written by man, but I have not yet found one which I did not comprehend.

The authors were human, and so was I, hence they could not surpass my appreciation. But when Jehovah puts *His* mind into a Book for the

study of finite creatures, what more natural than that we should find heights we cannot scale, depths we cannot fathom, lengths and breadths we cannot explore. Thank God that the Bible is so full of mysteries which I cannot compass, And as to the disparity of views, it would be equally surprising, if so many little minds, occupying different angles, looking at an infinite object, would have the same conception of every point. The idea of the Holy Trinity, with all-inclusive relations, is not questioned by any evangelical church. The divergences all begin a step lower than the central fact. It is our vital connection with God through such faith as we can honestly exercise that determines character.

The Incarnate Word, "the bearing of faith," the illumination of the Spirit, must shape our life according to the capacity which the law of 'inheritance and environment will allow. Every soul is dealt with on the ground of its own personality. We may all do the same thing, and yet no two be the same. "In the *beginning was* the WORD. Note the verb *was.* The *beginning* did not be. gin IT. Neither will it *end.* The Bible is the Text Book of eternity, the meaning of its precepts and principles and institutions being deep and vast enough to engage all created intelligence forever.

You charge the New Testament with impossible and unreasonable demands. For instance: "Be harmless as doves." Connect John 17: 23, and Philpp. 4: 13, and dare to say that such sweetness of disposition is impracticable. That we have tigers and panthers and lions and "bulls of Bashan," and hawks and vultures in the church, disproves not the fact of a perfect man in Emmanuel, and of souls like Him, who are wholly swayed by his indwelling. You regard it as arrogant and absurd to pretend to "be perfect as our Father in heaven is perfect." Give yourself to God as really and absolutely as Jesus gave himself to humanity, and then utter your verdict as to this possibility. The Bible does not ask us to be infinite, either in capacity or character, but it does demand us to allow God such possession of us as to be perfectly human; then are we like God according to our nature and measure.

You imagine that James 2: 10 precludes all possibility of salvation. Law and commandment are not the same. A commandment has a commander back of it. One principle runs through all divine requirements. We cannot infringe the least without running counter to the principle that supports the universe. "Guilty of all" is simply a law without which there could be no government, human or divine. Eminently beneficent is such a provision.

You ask me whether I can refer you to any good books that will be helpful to you. Plenty of them, but I will not mention any at present. The Bible is the supreme Book, and will solve all your problems and scatter all your mists. Make it your counsellor exclusively under the tuition of the Holy Spirit. Throw science and metaphysics and guess-work overboard. "THY WORD IS TRUTH." It was all the weapon Jesus needed in His terrible conflict with the devil. "It is written," "*It is written,*" "*IT IS WRITTEN.*" With this "Sword of the Spirit" you can hew all the Agags to pieces.

Your soul is in jeopardy, and your only hope is in believing where you cannot see. Jesus has given as indisputable evidence of his divinity by what He did, as you have of your humanity by writing to me. Let Heb. 4: 14, 15, 16, and 6: 13-20, be to you the whole Gospel. The historical Christ defies all criticism. This admitted, the Personal Christ must be accepted in all His claims and prerogatives. He is a "chief corner stone, elect, precious: and he 'that *believeth* on

pass the city. Their desire is to take Elisha captive. His servant sees and fears, wondering what they shall do. Elisha is unmoved by their sudden appearance. In the quiet slumbers of night they came upon the city and surrounded it. While Elisha sees the hosts of the Syrian army, he also sees an army which his servant seeth not. "They that be with us are more than they that be with them." We need the prayer for ourselves that Elisha offered for his servant. "Lord, open our eyes that we may see."

Oh, if, when the hosts of Satan are encompassed about us, we could look to God and see him in his strength supporting us! Though the Syrians be many and seem formidable that we could truthfully and assuredly say, "They that be with us are more than they that be with them."

It should be our daily prayer that we might see more and more of the beatitudes brought by his Word, and the strength given to us thereby; more of the matchless, boundless graciousness of his love to usward; more of the invincible and immutableness of the truthfulness of his promises; more of the infinite and perfect righteousness of the life of Christ; more opportunities for "heaping coals of fire" on the heads of enemies, and more fully realizing that he is our strength and shield, "a present help in every time of need."

This world is full of realities, which are to us but vagueness to our carnal sight, — realities which seem very uncertain to our finite comprehension; yea, realities invisible to weak, short-sighted humanity. Lord, open thou our eyes!

We need to see the hand of God displayed in the beauties of nature. We ought to see the certain result of careless and indifferent living; the inevitable result of negligence of duty.

We desire to see godliness and truth exemplified in our midst to be as real as the land and trees about us. We need to see and understand our surroundings, in order to improve the opportunities for doing good. We must have the guidance of the Spirit, that we may see poor, suffering humanity every-where, not as our brethren in flesh merely, but as children of God; heirs with Christ. We desire their eyes to be open, that they may see Christ as he is, the Lamb of God that taketh away the sin of the world; the Sun of Righteousness; the Bread and Water of Life; the Bright and Morning Star; the Lily and the Rose.

We must live in Christ if we desire to be able to talk of him. We need to see and feel the gloriousness of the joys, and the causes for the hopes of the Christian's life. Were our eyes more fully opened, we would have more faith, stronger courage, grander inspirations, higher and holier aspirations of a noble life, bringing a peace that truly passeth understanding. Lord, open thou our eyes!

Girard, Ill.

THE IMPORTANCE OF BEING READY FOR DEATH.

BY SARAH GRAHAM.

IF we would enjoy the blessedness of a home in heaven, when the cares and toils of this weary life are over, we should be ready, when we are called to leave this world, for there is no repentance beyond the grave. Christ says, "Therefore be ye also ready: for in such an hour as ye think not the Son of man cometh." There are many people who put off their coming to Christ, from time to time, and let opportunity after opportunity go by, until they are brought down to sickness and death, and then begin to realize that it is too late; that they should have prepared for death while they were in health and strength.

It is dangerous to wait until death is at the door, and then call upon God. We should be in readiness, for we know not when we shall be called into the presence of the Great Judge. In the twinkling of an eye we may be hurled into eternity. Therefore, if we would gain heaven and immortal glory, it is necessary to be ready when God calls us home. Again, it is necessary that we prepare for death in our youth, for the longer we live in sin, the harder it is to turn from sin.

To all who are unprepared, let me say, Give your heart to Jesus now; do not hesitate any longer! If you resist the Holy Spirit of God, it may depart and never again return, for "the Spirit of God will not always strive with man." "Behold now is the accepted time. Behold now is the day of salvation."

God is not willing that any should perish. He says, "Him that cometh to me, I will in no wise cast out." O what an awful thing it must be to be ushered into the presence of the Almighty God, only to be cast out forever!

"In that lone land of deep despair,
No Sabbath's heav'nly light shall rise,
No God regard your bitter pray'r,
No Savior call you to the skies."

Let us all be ready to meet God when he calls us, and we shall have an entrance into the City of the New Jerusalem, where we shall be happy forever; where we shall see all of our loved ones gone before, and where we shall see God, the Great Ruler of the Universe, with Jesus Christ at his right hand. His sacred head, once crowned with thorns, is now crowned with glory, and then, "Unto him that loved us, and washed us from our sins in his own blood, and hath made us kings and priests unto God his Father, to him be glory and dominion forever and ever."

Staunton, Va.

EIGHTEEN HUNDRED NINETY-THREE.

SELECTED BY JAMES R. GISH.

I WOULD not have you think me a crank, but I do, at times, give my thoughts full scope, and at this time they run into sacred numbers, and while considering them, I am surprised at the conclusion I arrive at. The genealogy of our Blessed Lord is divided into three parts of fourteen,— twice seven,—generations each, which, added together, make forty-two generations, which divides by three and by seven.

When Christ was born there came three wise men, and of their treasures they laid at his feet three parts, i. e., gold, frankincense and myrrh. When he was three times four, or four times three years old, he was about his Father's business, and after three days his parents found him in the temple. He was three times ten, or ten times three years old when he began to preach. There were three temptations set before him. He raised three persons from the dead. He often took but three of his disciples with him. In the transfiguration there appeared three. He prayed in the garden three times. He preached three years. The number of his disciples was four times three. He was sold for thirty pieces of silver. He told Peter he would deny him three times. He had three trials. His last words were three, "It is finished."

There were three crosses at the time of his death, and over him were written three languages. There was darkness for three hours. Three Mary's witnessed the scene. Christ was three days in the tomb. [May I not add that at the last supper Christ practiced and so established three things, the washing of the saints' feet, the eating of the Lord's Supper and the

Communion service, saying, "It ye know these things, happy are ye if ye do them." John 13; Matt. 26. Just before he ascended to heaven he ordained baptism in three actions, viz., into the name of the Father, and of the Son, and of the Holy Ghost. Matt. 28: 19.]

As said before, there were three wise men at his feet, who, with his own people, represented the whole world. [The first time Christ was acknowledged to be the Son of God, was at his baptism by John in the River of Jordan. Coming straightway up out of the water, the Spirit descended upon him. The Father said, "This is my beloved Son, in whom I am well pleased." The second time was at the transfiguration, when the Father said, "This is my beloved Son, hear ye him." The third time when he will be acknowledged to be the Son, will doubtless be when he comes to judge the world, "and will give to every man according as his works shall be."]

Let us reason without the fear of being called "crack-brains." Might not our Lord come in 1893? Are not the signs pointing that way? Was the whole world ever as it is now? Among the nations of the earth there never was such a state of things. But let us reason this way, not that we believe that it will come to pass, but that it might. The "World's Fair" should have been held this year, for it was 1492 when America was discovered, but something influences the minds of men to put it off until next year, 1893, and why? Well, it might be that 1892 was one year too soon for the advent of Christ, and that, when he comes, the world must be represented,— gathered into one city or country,—and why not America, why may not Chicago be the city where Christ will be acknowledged as the Lord, our King?

Again, I will call your attention to the sacred numbers. Eighteen hundred ninety-three is divisible by three, and we have as the quotient, 631. Then add 1893 from right to left, and we have 21, which divide by 3, and we have 7, or divide by 7 and we have 3. Now take the first quotient, 631; add it and we have 10; subtract 7, and we have a remainder of 3. Thus you will see that in all our work, 1893, we have 7 and 3 rising before us, so that, if there be anything in sacred numbers, 1893 seems a reasonable year for the coming of Christ our Lord. What I have written may turn your thoughts in the same direction, and you may be able to render the subject in a clearer light than I have done or am able to do.—*J. Wm. Pope, Pittsburg, Pa., in Word and Works.*

THE DOCTRINE PRESENTED BEFORE THE MINISTERIAL ASSOCIATION OF CEDAR RAPIDS, IOWA.

BY J. S. MOHLER.

DURING our late Annual Conference at Cedar Rapids, a request was made by the Ministerial Association of the City, that a brief outline of our doctrine be presented to them. This request, we think, was made from good motives, i. e., that they might have a clear conception of our views concerning the doctrine of salvation. Doubtless they, like others, had heard various and conflicting reports concerning us, as a religious people; besides this, to the people of Cedar Rapids we were comparatively unknown, in point of doctrine, hence the request for information from a source that they could rely upon as being correct.

The Association embraces about all the ministers of the City,—some fifteen,—who were present. Brethren J. H. Moore and J. G. Royer were assigned the duty of presenting our doctrine before the above Association. The Young Men's Christian Association Room was designated as

Missionary and Tract Work Department.

"Upon the first day of the week, let every one of you lay by him in store as God hath prospered him, that there be no gatherings when I come."—1 Cor. xvi. 2.

"Every man as he purposeth in his heart, so let him give. Not grudgingly or of necessity, for the Lord loveth a cheerful giver."—2 Cor. 9: 7.

HOW MUCH SHALL WE GIVE?

"Every man according to his ability." "Every one as God hath prospered him." "Every man, according as he purposeth in his heart, so let him give." "For if there be first a willing mind, it is accepted according to that a man hath, and not according to that he hath not."—2 Cor. 8: 12.

Organization of Missionary Committee.

DANIEL VANIMAN, Foreman,	McPherson, Kans.
D. L. MILLER, Treasurer,	Mt. Morris, Ill.
GALEN B. ROYER, Secretary,	Mt. Morris, Ill.

Organization of Book and Tract Work.

S. W. HOOVER, Foreman,	Dayton, Ohio.
S. BOCK, Secretary and Treasurer,	Dayton, Ohio.

☞All donations intended for Missionary Work should be sent to GALEN B. ROYER, Mt. Morris, Ill.

☞All money for Tract Work should be sent to S. BOCK, Dayton, Ohio.

☞Money may be sent by Money Order, Registered Letter, or Drafts on New York or Chicago. Do not send personal checks, or drafts on interior towns, as it costs 25 cents to collect them.

☞Solicitors are requested to faithfully carry out the plan of Annual Meeting, that all our members be solicited to contribute at least twice a year for the Mission and Tract Work of the Church.

☞Notes for the Endowment Fund can be had by writing to the Secretary of either Work.

MISSIONARY SECRETARY'S REPORT.

BELOW is given a correct report of the money received by the Secretary for the General Mission Fund, during April, May and June. This does not include the money received for European Poor Fund or the Russian Sufferers. Those who have contributed during these months should look over the report and see if the amount they sent is correctly reported, and if not, notify the Secretary immediately.

APRIL.

Beaver Creek church, Md., $4.25; H. C. Tate, Bennington, Kans., $1; Brethren Sunday-school at Woodberry, Md., $2.16; Elk Run church, Va., $4.35; A. B. Smith and wife, Saltillo, Nebr., $1.04; J. C. Peck and wife, Crete, Nebr., $1.04; Lanah Peck, Crete, Nebr., 52 cents; D. G. Couser and wife, Lincoln, Nebr., $1.04; George Funderburg, North Hampton, Ohio, $1; Brownsville church, Md., $9; Emily R. Stifler, Homestead, Pa., 50 cents; Jason A. G. Stifler, Homestead, Pa., 50 cents; Frankfort church, Ohio, $5; St. Vrain Sunday-school, Colo., $3.85; Jno. H. Miller, Glendora, Cal., $2.90; Mary Hall, Beallsville, Pa., 50 cents; Keelin Leonard, Aurelia, Iowa, $5.00; Upper Conawago church, Pa., $2.50; North-eastern Ohio, East Nimishillen church, $3.00; North-eastern Ohio, Chippewa church, $15.13; North-eastern Ohio, Black River church, $7.72; North-eastern Ohio, Black River Sunday-school, $2.40; North-eastern Ohio, Mt. Zion church, 50 cents; Hickory Grove church, Ohio, $4.50; Wallace church, Nebr., 50 cents; South Bend church, Ind., $3.25; Marsh Creek church, Pa., $12; a brother, Maryland, $5; Grundy County church, Iowa, $8.40; two-thirds of remaining proceeds of Annual Meeting of 1891, $540; Broad Run church, Md., $12.84; Pleasant Valley church, Tenn., $8; a sister, California, $4; Woodbury church, Pa., $199.25; David H. Baker and wife, Abbottstown, Pa., $1.00; Roaring Spring church, Pa., $11.69; Left Hand, Md., $30; Nancy Stanble, Indiana, 50 cents; Kate Stanble, Indiana, 50 cents; Gertie Stanble, Indiana, 15 cents; Esterly church, La., $4.72; South-eastern District of Kansas, $1.75; Dry Valley church, Pa., $2.72; Wolf Creek church, Ohio, $25.10; Amanda Harris, Mt. Morris, Ill., 35 cents; a brother in Christ, Nebraska, $1.55.

MAY.

Hannah Good, Belsano, Pa., 50 cents; D. A. Miller, Le Mars, Iowa, $1.84; new brother, Kansas, 50 cents; District of South-western Kansas and Southern Colorado, $19.66; Quemahoning church, Pa., $7.50; Anna Wolfe, Cardington, Mo., 50 cents; Christiana Moyer, Harleysville, Pa., $1; Eastern District of Pennsylvania, $64.77; Russell church, Kans., $6; East Arm Belleville church, Kans., $2.30; Covington church, Ohio, $26.80; West Otter Creek church, Ill., $10.30; Emery Miller, Goblesville, Ind., 50 cents; a sister, Goblesville, Ind., 50 cents; children of Belleville church, Kans., $1.85; John Shoemaker, Eads, Colo., $1; Beaver Creek church, Va., $5; George Weinand, York Springs, Pa., 50 cents; W. W. Folger, Osceola, Iowa, 50 cents; a sister, Carlisle, Pa., $20; Johnstown church, Pa., $17; a sister, Columbus, Ohio, 25 cents; Maggie Butterfield, Oak Grove, Tenn., $2; Tropico church, Cal., $6.47; D. D. Horner, Jones' Mill, Pa., $2; a sister in Sam's Creek church, Pa., $1; Pipe Creek church, Ind., $11.25; John Miller, Mt. Morris, Ill., $1; Donnel's Creek church, Ohio, $1.50; Upper Stillwater church, Ohio, $9.60; Jacob Hollinger, Ohio, 50 cents; Loramies church, Ohio, $1.81; Nocona church, Texas, $3.80.

JUNE.

Redbank church, Pa., $6; a sister at Annual Meeting, $1; Wm. Ogden, Unionville, Iowa, $1; Sam's Creek church, Md., $2; some members of Nettle Creek church, Ind., $5.30; Mr. and Mrs. Allen Whisler, Unionville, Iowa, $1; a brother, Elkhart, Ind., $1; two-thirds of collection at Annual Meeting, 1892, $244.55; James Culler, Louisville, Ohio, $1.25; John Fishburn, Overbrook, Kans., $5; sister and self, Dobbin, W. Va., $1; Amos Moomaw, Pleasantville, Iowa, $1; Maggie V. Frederick, Romans, Va., $2; Covina church, Cal., $6.48; Fannie Fogle, La Paz, Ind., 75 cents; Daniel Barrick, Byron, Ill., $2; English River church, Iowa, $13; South Waterloo church, Iowa, $40; a sister, 50 cents; a sister, Maryland, $2.50; a sister, New Sharon, Iowa, $1; Jno. B. Replogle; Woodbury, Pa., $5; a sister, $1; a sister, 50 cents, two sisters, West Virginia, $12; Cedar County church, Iowa, $8.85; Sanfield church, Mich., $1.70; Geo. S. Roland, Mountville, Pa., $10; Samuel F. Miller, West Alexandria, Ohio, 25 cents; Upper Codorus church, Pa., $5; Children's Mission, per Mary Gibson, $47.65; Amwell church, Pa., $8.96; Little Swatara church, Pa., $5; Middle Creek church, Pa., $9.25; a sister, Fowler, Cal., $1; sisters of West Dayton church, Ohio, $3.68; Ephratah Sunday-school, Pa., $4.11; Southern District of Illinois, $15.12; Sunday-school at Woodberry, Md., $2.24; D. J. Culler, Louisville, Ohio, 50 cents.

GALEN B. ROYER, Sec.

Mt. Morris, Ill.

WHO SHOULD PREACH THE WORD.

BY ELLA RAFFENSPERGER.

THIS need not be a question to the minds of any of God's children, as we are all preachers. There is neither male nor female, for ye are all one in Christ Jesus. Gal. 3: 21. This includes sisters. It includes all who have not only joined the church, but have had their understandings fully enlightened by being thoroughly converted to the religion of Jesus Christ, as it is possible to become church members without being born of the water and of the Spirit.

I fear there are too many men and women, who profess Christianity, and yet think this great work rests only on the ministry. There is a great responsibility also resting on the laity. May the time soon come, when all our brethren and sisters will improve their talents to the full extent, and

not lose one opportunity to speak for Jesus at home or abroad! The sins of omission are as great as the sins of commission.

When Jesus said, "Let your light so shine before men, that they may see your good works," etc., Matt. 5: 16, he spoke to both men and women. The elected ministers have an example in the latter part of Matt. 28. I will give some of the ways of how those should preach, who are not commanded to preach from the pulpit.

1. We must have clean hands, that the Gospel be not blamed.

2. A pure heart, that our prayers may be heard.

3. A wise head, for "knowledge is power."

4. A quick eye, to see golden opportunities.

5. A ready ear, to hear both God and man.

6. A guarded tongue, that we may speak aright.

7. Swift feet, that we may say, "Send me."

We may think if Jesus were here now, we would do as the holy women of old did. He has left us, but said, "Inasmuch as ye do it unto one of the least of these, ye do it unto me."

Dear brethren and sisters, what are we doing in and out of the church for the poor sinners? Do we visit the sick and poor, and assist in caring for them? While some can give such food and clothing for the body, those of us, who have not that to give, should be able to give them something for their souls. We cannot live always by bread alone, but we can by every word of God.

Do we encourage series of meetings by our presence? Please read an article in MESSENGER No. 18, of 1889, entitled, "Revival of Religion the Glory of the Church." I wish Bro. Jno. F. Driver would give many more such facts. They are worth publishing. Every brother and sister who is opposed to series of meetings, Sunday-schools and prayer-meetings, should not fail to read the MESSENGER every week. They will then see many of the good results from such meetings. If strangers come to our meetings and Sunday-schools, do we go to them and speak a word of encouragement, and invite them to come again? Do we ever give those people tracts? Perhaps they cannot be reached any other way.

Do we try to make peace where there is none? Do we go and tell our brother and sister their faults, if they trespass against us? Do those that are strong bear the infirmities of the weak and not please themselves? Do we take the beam out of our own eye, before trying to cast the mote out of our brother's eye? Do we suffer for well doing? Do we take part in family worship? Do we ask a blessing at the table, when it falls to our lot? Do we, at all times, show our faith by our works? Do we, as sisters, have our heads covered when we pray or prophesy? Do we do as 1 Tim. 2: 9 teaches? Do we attend services when the sun or moon does not shine?

Do the older brethren and sisters set an example, in all these things, to the younger ones? "Feed my lambs." Yes, we need the necessary food, and if we do not get fed at home, sometimes lambs go where they can get it without asking for it.

Now, dear brethren and sisters, since there are so many ways in which we can help preach the Word, let us be up and doing, for the night may come before we are ready, and then we would like to say as Paul said, "I have fought a good fight; I have finished my course; I have kept the faith. Henceforth there is laid up for me a crown of righteousness that fadeth not away."

Remember that the pleasure of doing good is the only pleasure that never wears out. Earnestness that tramples under foot hindrances, and makes things bend or break, will be to the person whose life work is winning souls to Christ, like the rod in Moses' hand. Let us sustain our faith by the power of God, as David did, by saying,

Missionary and Tract Work Department.

"Upon the first day of the week, let every one of you lay by him in store as God hath prospered him, that there be no gatherings when I come."—1 Cor. 16: 2.

"Every man as he purposeth in his heart, so let him give. Not grudgingly or of necessity, for the Lord loveth a cheerful giver."—2 Cor. 9: 7.

HOW MUCH SHALL WE GIVE?

"Every man according to his ability." "Every one as God hath prospered him." "Every man, according as he purposeth in his heart, so let him give." "For if there be first a willing mind, it is accepted according to that a man hath, and not according to that he hath not."—2 Cor. 8: 12.

Organization of Missionary Committee.

DANIEL VANIMAN, Foreman,   -   McPherson, Kans.
D. L. MILLER, Treasurer,   -   Mt. Morris, Ill.
GALEN B. ROYER, Secretary,   -   Mt. Morris, Ill.

Organization of Book and Tract Work.

S. W. HOOVER, Foreman,   -   Dayton, Ohio.
S. BOCK, Secretary and Treasurer,   -   Dayton, Ohio.

☞ All donations intended for Missionary Work should be sent to GALEN B. ROYER, Mt. Morris, Ill.

☞ All money for Tract Work should be sent to S. BOCK, Dayton, Ohio.

☞ Money may be sent by Money Order, Registered Letter, or Drafts on New York or Chicago. Do not send personal checks, or drafts on interior towns, as it costs 25 cents to collect them.

☞ Solicitors are requested to faithfully carry out the plan of Annual Meeting, that all our members be solicited to contribute at least twice a year for the Mission and Tract Work of the Church.

☞ Notes for the Endowment Fund can be had by writing to the Secretary of either Work.

MISSIONARY SECRETARY'S REPORT.

BELOW is given a correct report of the money received by the Secretary for the General Mission Fund, during April, May and June. This does not include the money received for European Poor Fund or the Russian Sufferers. Those who have contributed during these months should look over the report and see if the amount they sent is correctly reported, and if not, notify the Secretary immediately.

APRIL.

Beaver Creek church, Md., $4.25; H. C. Tate, Bennington, Kans., $1; Brethren Sunday-school at Woodberry, Md., $2.16; Elk Run church, Va., $4.35; A. B. Smith and wife, Saltillo, Nebr., $1.04; J. C. Peck and wife, Crete, Nebr., $1.04; Lanah Peck, Crete, Nebr., 52 cents; D. G. Couser and wife, Lincoln, Nebr., $1.04; George Funderburg, North Hampton, Ohio, $1; Brownsville church, Md., $9; Emily R. Stifler, Homestead, Pa., 50 cents; Jason A. G. Stifler, Homestead, Pa., 50 cents; Frankfort church, Ohio, $5; St. Vrain Sunday-school, Colo., $3.85; Jno. H. Miller, Glendora, Cal., $2.90; Mary Hall, Beallsville, Pa., 50 cents; Keelin Leonard, Aurelia, Iowa, $5.00; Upper Conewago church, Pa., $2.50; North-eastern Ohio, East Nimishillen church, $3.00; North-eastern Ohio, Chippewa church, $15.13; North-eastern Ohio, Black River church, $7.72; North-eastern Ohio, Black River Sunday-school, $2.40; North-eastern Ohio, Mt. Zion church, 50 cents; Hickory Grove church, Ohio, $4.50; Wallace church, Nebr., 50 cents; South Bend church, Ind., $3.25; Marsh Creek church, Pa., $12; a brother, Maryland, $5; Grundy County church, Iowa, $8.40; two-thirds of remaining proceeds of Annual Meeting of 1891, $540; Broad Run church, Md., $13.84; Pleasant Valley church, Tenn., $8; a sister, California, $4; Woodbury church, Pa., $199.25; David H. Baker and wife, Abbottstown, Pa., $1.00; Roaring Spring church, Pa., $11.69; Left Hand, Md., $20; Nancy Stanble, Indiana, 50 cents; Kate Stanble, Indiana, 50 cents; Gertie Stanble, Indiana, 15 cents; Esterly church, La., $4.72; South-eastern District of Kansas, $1.75; Dry Valley church, Pa., $2.72; Wolf Creek church, Ohio, $25.10; Amanda Harris, Mt. Morris, Ill., 35 cents; a brother in Christ, Nebraska, $1.55.

MAY.

Hannah Good, Belsano, Pa., 50 cents; D. A. Miller, Le Mars, Iowa, $1.64; new brother, Kansas, 50 cents; District of South-western Kansas and Southern Colorado, $19.66; Quemahoning church, Pa., $7.50; Anna Wolfe, Cardington, Mo., 50 cents; Christiana Moyer, Harleysville, Pa., $1; Eastern District of Pennsylvania, $64.77; Russell church, Kans., $6; East Arm Belleville church, Kans., $2.30; Covington church, Ohio, $26.80; West Otter Creek church, Ill., $10.30; Emery Miller, Goblesville, Ind., 50 cents; a sister, Goblesville, Ind., 50 cents; children of Belleville church, Kans., $1.85; John Shoemaker, Eads, Colo., $1; Beaver Creek church, Va., $5; George Weinand, York Springs, Pa., 50 cents; W. W. Folger, Osceola, Iowa, 50 cents; a sister, Carlisle, Pa., $20; Johnstown church, Pa., $17; a sister, Columbus, Ohio, 25 cents; Maggie Sutterfield, Oak Grove, Tenn., $2; Tropico church, Cal., $6.47; D. D. Horner, Jones' Mill, Pa., $2; a sister in Sam's Creek church, Pa., $1; Pipe Creek church, Ind., $11.95; John Miller, Mt. Morris, Ill., $1; Donnel's Creek church, Ohio, $1.50; Upper Stillwater church, Ohio, $9.60; Jacob Hollinger, Ohio, 50 cents; Loramies church, Ohio, $1.81; Nocona church, Texas, $3.80.

JUNE.

Redbank church, Pa., $6; a sister at Annual Meeting, $1; Wm. Ogden, Unionville, Iowa, $1; Sam's Creek church, Md., $2; some members of Nettle Creek church, Ind., $5.30; Mr. and Mrs. Allen Whisler, Unionville, Iowa, $1; a brother, Elkhart, Ind., $1; two-thirds of collection at Annual Meeting, 1892, $244.55; James Culler, Louisville, Ohio, $1.25; John Fishburn, Overbrook, Kans., $5; sister and self, Dobbin, W. Va., $1; Amos Moomaw, Pleasantville, Iowa, $1; Maggie V. Frederick, Romana, Va., $2; Covina church, Cal., $6.48; Fannie Fogle, La Paz, Ind., 75 cents; Daniel Barrick, Byron, Ill., $2; English River church, Iowa, $13; South Waterloo church, Iowa, $40; a sister, 50 cents; a sister, Maryland, $2.50; a sister, New Sharon, Iowa, $1; Jno. B. Replogle, Woodbury, Pa., $5; a sister, $1; a sister, 50 cents, two sisters, West Virginia, $12; Cedar County church, Iowa, $8.85; Sanfield church, Mich., $1.70; Geo. S. Roland, Mountville, Pa., $10; Samuel F. Miller, West Alexandria, Ohio, 25 cents; Upper Codorus church, Pa., $5; Children's Mission, per Mary Gibson, $47.65; Amwell church, Pa., $8.86; Little Swatara church, Pa., $5; Middle Creek church, Pa., $9.25; a sister, Fowler, Cal., $1; sisters of West Dayton church, Ohio, $3.68; Ephratah Sunday-school, Pa., $4.11; Southern District of Illinois, $15.12; Sunday-school at Woodberry, Md., $2.21; D. J. Culler, Louisville, Ohio, 50 cents.

GALEN B. ROYER, Sec.
Mt. Morris, Ill.

WHO SHOULD PREACH THE WORD.

BY ELLA RAFFENSPERGER.

THIS need not be a question to the minds of any of God's children, as we are all preachers. There is neither male nor female, for ye are all one in Christ Jesus. Gal. 3: 21. This includes sisters. It includes all who have not only joined the church, but have had their understandings fully enlightened by being thoroughly converted to the religion of Jesus Christ, as it is possible to become church members without being born of the water and of the Spirit.

I fear there are too many men and women, who profess Christianity, and yet think this great work rests only on the ministry. There is a great responsibility also resting on the laity. May the time soon come, when all our brethren and sisters will improve their talents to the full extent, and not lose one opportunity to speak for Jesus at home or abroad! The sins of omission are as great as the sins of commission.

When Jesus said, "Let your light so shine before men, that they may see your good works," etc., Matt. 5: 16, he spoke to both men and women. The elected ministers have an example in the latter part of Matt. 28. I will give some of the ways of how these should preach, who are not commanded to preach from the pulpit.

1. We must have clean hands, that the Gospel be not blamed.
2. A pure heart, that our prayers may be heard.
3. A wise head, for "knowledge is power."
4. A quick eye, to see golden opportunities.
5. A ready ear, to hear both God and man.
6. A guarded tongue, that we may speak aright.
7. Swift feet, that we may say, "Send me."

We may think if Jesus were here now, we would do as the holy women of old did. He has left us, but said, "Inasmuch as ye do it unto one of the least of these, ye do it unto me."

Dear brethren and sisters, what are we doing in and out of the church for the poor sinners? Do we visit the sick and poor, and assist in caring for them? While some can give such food and clothing for the body, those of us, who have not that to give, should be able to give them something for their souls. We cannot live always by bread alone, but we can by every word of God.

Do we encourage series of meetings by our presence? Please read an article in MESSENGER No. 18, of 1889, entitled, "Revivals of Religion the Glory of the Church." I wish Bro. Jno. F. Driver would give many more such facts. They are worth publishing. Every brother and sister who is opposed to series of meetings, Sunday-schools and prayer-meetings, should not fail to read the MESSENGER every week. They will then see many of the good results from such meetings. If strangers come to our meetings and Sunday-schools, do we go to them and speak a word of encouragement, and invite them to come again? Do we ever give those people tracts? Perhaps they cannot be reached any other way.

Do we try to make peace where there is none? Do we go and tell our brother and sister their faults, if they trespass against us? Do those that are strong bear the infirmities of the weak and not please themselves? Do we take the beam out of our own eye, before trying to cast the mote out of our brother's eye? Do we suffer for well doing? Do we take part in family worship? Do we ask a blessing at the table, when it falls to our lot? Do we, at all times, show our faith by our works? Do we, as sisters, have our heads covered when we pray or prophesy? Do we do as 1 Tim. 2: 9 teaches? Do we attend services when the sun or moon does not shine?

Do the older brethren and sisters set an example, in all these things, to the younger ones? "Feed my lambs." Yes, we need the necessary food, and if we do not get fed at home, sometimes lambs go where they can get it without asking for it.

Now, dear brethren and sisters, since there are so many ways in which we can help preach the Word, let us be up and doing, for the night may come before we are ready, and then we would like to say as Paul said, "I have fought a good fight; I have finished my course; I have kept the faith. Henceforth there is laid up for me a crown of righteousness that fadeth not away."

Remember that the pleasure of doing good is the only pleasure that never wears out. Earnestness that tramples under foot hindrances, and makes things bend or break, will be to the person whose life work is winning souls to Christ, like the rod in Moses' hand. Let us sustain our faith by the power of God, as David did, by saying;

The Gospel Messenger,

A Weekly at $1.50 Per Annum.

PUBLISHED BY

The Brethren's Publishing Co.

D. L. MILLER, · · · · · · · Editor.
J. H. MOORE, · · · · · · Office Editor.
J. B. BRUMBAUGH, }
J. G. ROYER, } · · · Associate Editors.
JOSEPH AMICK, · · · · · Business Manager.

ADVISORY COMMITTEE.

L. W. Teeter A. Hutchison, Daniel Hays.

☞Communications for publication should be legibly written with black ink on one side of the paper only. Do not attempt to interline, or to put on one page what ought to occupy two.

☞Anonymous communications will not be published.

☞Do not mix business with articles for publication. Keep your communications on separate sheets from all business.

☞Time is precious. We always have time to attend to business and to answer questions of importance, but please do not subject us to need less answering of letters.

☞The MESSENGER is mailed each week to all subscribers. If the address is correctly entered on our list, the paper must reach the person to whom it is addressed. If you do not get your paper, write us, giving particulars.

☞When changing your address, please give your former as well as your future address in full, so as to avoid delay and misunderstanding. Always remit to the office from which you order your goods, no matter from where you receive them.

☞Do not send personal checks or drafts on interior banks, unless you send with them 25 cents each, to pay for collection.

☞Remittances should be made by Post-office Money Order, Drafts on New York, Philadelphia or Chicago, or Registered Letters, made payable and addressed to "Brethren's Publishing Co., Mount Morris, Ill.," or "Brethren's Publishing Co., Huntingdon, Pa."

☞Entered at the Post-office at Mount Morris, Ill., as second-class matter.

Mount Morris, Ill., · · · July 19, 1892.

FIVE recently united with the Lower Cumberland church, Pa.

BRO. JACOB HOLLINGER, of Loramies, Ohio, has changed his address to Portland, Jay County, Ind.

BRO. M. KELLER reports three good, interesting meetings at Laurel, Kans., the last week in June, with an interesting awakening.

RELIABLE witnesses certify that a Baptist minister, of Danville, Ky., recently baptized seventy-eight persons in twenty-seven minutes.

THOSE who are greatly concerned about the origin of Children's Meetings, might read and consider Mark 10: 13–16 to good advantage.

THE Northern District of Iowa, Minnesota, and Southern Dakotas will hold its Ministerial Meeting with the South Waterloo church, Oct. 4.

UNDER date of July 7, Bro. W. B. Stover, of Germantown, Pa., writes, "Bro. T. T. Myers baptized a lady from Brooklyn, last Sunday. She goes home happy, with numerous tracts and fond hopes."

A GOOD meeting was held at Panora, Iowa, July 4th. The day before, eight were received into the church by confession and baptism. The work seems to be moving on encouragingly in that part of the Lord's vineyard.

A REPORT of church news, from one of the churches in Ohio, has to be declined because the writer failed to give his name in full. Writers will please not neglect this. An obituary is also declined for the same reason.

LOST.—At Cedar Rapids, during the Annual Meeting, copies of the Minutes from 1886 to 1891. They were stitched together, and had an index attached, and the name of D. L. Miller written thereon. Any one finding the package will please return the same to this office, and greatly oblige.

BRO. FRANK MYERS, of Mt. Carroll, Ill., recently visited the Prairie Queen church, Minn., and did some very acceptable preaching, which resulted in three accessions to the church, with prospects of more if he could have remained longer.

THOSE of our readers who think Bro. Balsbaugh in the habit of getting the feed too high for the common mind, will find it within their reach this week. The skeptic may have to stoop to get some of the ideas, and we hope, before he lays the paper aside, he will be on his knees.

IT is said that the saloons in Albany, N. Y., take in on an average of $15,000.00 a day. Most of that is the bread and clothing taken from poor children and wives. What a terrible monster this drink is! Were it banished from the land, what a happy country we would have!

THE good work at Esterly, La., seems to be progressing encouragingly. Two were received into the church by baptism July 4th. The church is now preparing to erect a meeting-house this coming fall. All this speaks well for the Brethren and their efforts in that part of the Great South.

A FRIEND at Harleysville, Pa., has donated $300.00 to the Missionary Endowment Fund, the interest of which is to be used for the spread of the Gospel in Denmark and Sweden. The deed is a commendable one, and might be imitated by others who desire to see the cause furthered in other lands.

THE Brethren in Denver, Colo., have made at least a good beginning in their work. They have raised the necessary means, rented a hall and will hold regular services and conduct a Sunday-school in the city. We trust that they will receive the necessary encouragement, and meet with success in their efforts.

BRO. P. H. BEERY, who has been in school work at Mt. Morris for three years, is now at Kalida, Ohio. He wishes to continue his work in the higher branches, but prefers to enter a college in some city where the Brethren can use him to a good advantage in the ministry. Brethren, knowing of an opportunity of that kind may do well to correspond with Bro. Beery.

THE Texas Siftings hits the nail squarely on the head when it says: "Rum makes trouble everywhere. There is great agitation in England because the government proposes to compensate liquor dealers for pecuniary loss in retiring from the business. But there is no talk of compensating families for the losses which the liquor traffic has inflicted upon them."

THE Christian Cynosure recently published an illustrated exposition of the signs, grips, pass-words and oaths of the Farmer's Alliance. A subscriber in Florida wrote thus to the editor: "I know it is correct, for I spent $50.00 in its den before I subscribed for the Cynosure." When others have that much to say, Brethren will do well to steer clear of the organization and rest contented in the church of Jesus Christ.

IT will not be necessary for our readers to send any more money for the Russian sufferers, as the Government has announced that a sufficient amount has been received to relieve the distress. The suffering has been indeed great, but the Christian world responded liberally, and has been the means of prolonging the lives of thousands who otherwise would have starved to death. Our Brethren have also responded nobly to the cries of the sufferers, and the blessings will be sure to follow.

ALL orders for the Report have now been filled, and we still have a number of copies left for those who have not yet sent in their orders. Those wishing copies will please let us hear from them soon. Price, 25 cents, or $2.50 per dozen. The Report is an important one and should be widely read by our Brethren.

DURING the warm days of summer, most Christians try to take things as easy as possible, and many of the ministers enjoy their vacations. But the devil works right along and never thinks of taking a vacation. His time is limited and he loses none of it, for he is always busy in trying to overcome what little good there is in the world.

AS the Young Disciple and Quarterlies are published at Mt. Morris, all orders for them and Sunday-school supplies, in order to receive prompt attention, should be sent directly to that office. All communications intended for the columns of the Young Disciple should also be addressed to Mt. Morris, as the paper is now edited at this place.

POSSIBLY there are some people who strain their eyes until they become almost totally blind, (spiritually), looking for motes in the eyes of others. While they may become experts in this line, they are almost sure to lose their own souls in the end, for he who spends all his precious time, looking at the faults of others, is sure to neglect his own.

THE Turks are getting quite particular about the hymns used by the Christian missionaries in their services. The hymn, "Jesus shall reign where'er the sun," is quite offensive. They demand that this hymn, and others of like character shall be suppressed. They think that Mohammed, the prophet, is the one entitled to this honor. But Jesus will reign nevertheless.

BRO. JACOB WITMORE, of Centre View, Mo., has decided to spend the coming winter preaching among the churches, as his health will not permit him to do frontier work. We hope the churches will give him plenty to do, as he is capable of preaching the Word with ability. His wife (who, by the way, is a sister to the lamented S. S. Bosserman) will accompany him.

SISTER SADIE BRALLIER NOFFSINGER reports an excellent Children's Meeting at the Walnut Grove church, near Johnstown, Pa., July 3. There were some in attendance from other congregations, and the little ones seem to have enjoyed the exercises. We should by no means neglect the little ones, and yet we should strive to retain in these meetings becoming Christian simplicity.

THE Brethren in Chicago have at last purchased a meeting-house that can now be regarded as their own. It is located on Hasting Street, No. 183, one and a half block south of 12th St, and a half block east of Ashland Avenue. Twelfth Street cars, down town, will pass within two blocks of the church. The house is to be dedicated the 24th of this month at 11 A. M., and a love-feast will be held in the evening of the same day. A cordial invitation is extended to such as desire to assemble and worship with the Brethren on that occasion. We are glad to announce the purchasing of the house, as it gives our Brethren a permanency that will add strength, and also afford them a suitable place to hold their meetings unmolested. This will indeed be a great satisfaction to them. The house formerly belonged to the German Baptists, and we understand that it is located in a very favorable part of the city. We hope to hear of good results from the work in that city.

The Gospel Messenger,

A Weekly at $1.50 Per Annum.

PUBLISHED BY

The Brethren's Publishing Co.

D. L. MILLER, ... Editor.

J. H. MOORE, ... Office Editor.

J. B. BRUMBAUGH, } . . . . . . Associate Editors.
J. G. ROYER, }

JOSEPH AMICK, ... Business Manager.

ADVISORY COMMITTEE.
L. W. Teeter A. Hutchison, Daniel Hays.

☞Communications for publication should be legibly written with 'black ink on one side of the paper only. Do not attempt to interline, or 'to put on our page what ought to occupy two.

☞Anonymous communications will not be published.

☞Do not mix business with articles for publication. Keep your communications on separate sheets from all business.

☞Time is precious. We always have time to attend to business and to answer questions of importance, but please do not subject us to need less answering of letters.

☞The MESSENGER is mailed each week to all subscribers. If the address is correctly entered on our list, the paper must reach the person to whom it is addressed. If you do not get your paper, write us, giving particulars.

☞When changing your address, please give your former as well as your future address in full, so as to avoid delay and misunderstanding.

☞Always remit to the office from which you order your goods, no matter from where you receive them.

☞Do not send personal checks or drafts on interior banks, unless you send with them 15 cents each, to pay for collection.

☞Remittances should be made by Post-office Money Order, Drafts on New York, Philadelphia or Chicago, or Registered Letters, made payable and addressed to "Brethren's Publishing Co., Mount Morris, Ill.," or "Brethren's Publishing Co., Huntingdon, Pa."

☞Entered at the Post-office at Mount Morris, Ill., as second-class matter.

Mount Morris, Ill., ... July 19, 1892.

FIVE recently united with the Lower Cumberland church, Pa.

BRO. JACOB HOLLINGER, of Loramies, Ohio, has changed his address to Portland, Jay County, Ind.

BRO. M. KELLER reports three good, interesting meetings at Laurel, Kans., the last week in June, with an interesting awakening.

RELIABLE witnesses certify that a Baptist minister, of Danville, Ky., recently baptized seventy-eight persons in twenty-seven minutes.

THOSE who are greatly concerned about the origin of Children's Meetings, might read and consider Mark 10: 13–16 to good advantage.

THE Northern District of Iowa, Minnesota, and Southern Dakota will hold its Ministerial Meeting with the South Waterloo church, Oct. 4.

UNDER date of July 7, Bro. W. B. Stover, of Germantown, Pa., writes, "Bro. T. T. Myers baptized a lady from Brooklyn, last Sunday. She goes home happy, with numerous tracts and fond hopes."

A GOOD meeting was held at Panora, Iowa, July 4th. The day before, eight were received into the church by confession and baptism. The work seems to be moving on encouragingly in that part of the Lord's vineyard.

A REPORT of church news, from one of the churches in Ohio, has to be declined because the writer failed to give his name in full. Writers will please not neglect this. An obituary is also declined for the same reason.

LOST.—At Cedar Rapids, during the Annual Meeting, copies of the Minutes from 1886 to 1891. They were stitched together, and had an index attached, and the name of D. L. Miller written thereon. Any one finding the package will please return the same to this office, and greatly oblige.

BRO. FRANK MYERS, of Mt. Carroll, Ill., recently visited the Prairie Queen church, Minn., and did some very acceptable preaching, which resulted in three accessions to the church, with prospects of more if he could have remained longer.

THOSE of our readers who think Bro. Balsbaugh in the habit of getting the feed too high for the common mind, will find it within their reach this week. The skeptic may have to stoop to get some of the ideas, and we hope, before he lays the paper aside, he will be on his knees.

IT is said that the saloons in Albany, N. Y., take in on an average of $15,000.00 a day. Most of that is the bread and clothing taken from poor children and wives. What a terrible monster this drink is! Were it banished from the land, what a happy country we would have!

THE good work at Esterly, La., seems to be progressing encouragingly. Two were received into the church by baptism July 4th. The church is now preparing to erect a meeting-house this coming fall, All this speaks well for the Brethren and their efforts in that part of the Great South.

A FRIEND at Harleysville, Pa., has donated $300.00 to the Missionary Endowment Fund, the interest of which is to be used for the spread of the Gospel in Denmark and Sweden. The deed is a commendable one, and might be imitated by others who desire to see the cause furthered in other lands.

THE Brethren in Denver, Colo., have made at least a good beginning in their work. They have raised the necessary means, rented a hall and will hold regular services and conduct a Sunday-school in the city. We trust that they will receive the necessary encouragement, and meet with success in their efforts.

BRO. P. H. BEERY, who has been in school work at Mt. Morris for three years, is now at Kalida, Ohio. He wishes to continue his work in the higher branches, but prefers to enter a college in some city where the Brethren can use him to a good advantage in the ministry. Brethren, knowing of an opportunity of that kind may do well to correspond with Bro. Beery.

THE Texas Siftings hits the nail squarely on the head, when it says: "Rum makes trouble everywhere. There is great agitation in England because the government proposes to compensate liquor dealers for pecuniary loss in retiring from the business. But there is no talk of compensating families for the losses which the liquor traffic has inflicted upon them."

THE Christian Cynosure recently published an illustrated exposition of the signs, grips, pass-words and oaths of the Farmer's Alliance. A subscriber in Florida wrote thus to the editor: "I know it is correct, for I spent $50.00 in its den before I subscribed for the Cynosure." When others have that much 'to say, Brethren will do well to steer clear of the organization and rest contented in the church of Jesus Christ.

IT will not be necessary for our readers to send any more money for the Russian sufferers, as the Government has announced that a sufficient amount has been received to relieve the distress. The suffering has been indeed great, but the Christian world responded liberally, and has been the means of prolonging the lives of thousands who otherwise would have starved to death. Our Brethren have also responded nobly to the cries of the sufferers, and the blessings will be sure to follow.

ALL orders for the Report have now been filled and we still have a number of copies left for those who have not yet sent in their orders. Those wishing copies will please let us hear from them soon. Price, 25 cents, or $2.50 per dozen. The Report is an important one and should be widely read by our Brethren.

DURING the warm days of summer, most Christians try to take things as easy as possible, and many of the ministers enjoy their vacations. But the devil works right along and never thinks of taking a vacation. His time is limited and he loses none of it, for he is always busy in trying to overcome what little good there is in the world.

AS the Young Disciple and Quarterlies are published at Mt. Morris, all orders for them and Sunday-school supplies, in order to receive prompt attention, should be sent directly to that office. All communications intended for the columns of the Young Disciple should also be addressed to Mt. Morris, as the paper is now edited at that place.

POSSIBLY there are some people who strain their eyes until they become almost totally blind (spiritually), looking for motes in the eyes of others. While they may become experts in this line, they are almost sure to lose their own soul in the end, for he who spends all his precious time, looking at the faults of others, is sure to neglect his own.

THE Turks are getting quite particular about the hymns used by the Christian missionaries in their services. The hymn, "Jesus shall reign where'er the sun," is quite offensive. They demand that this hymn, and others of like character shall be suppressed. They think that Mohammed the prophet, is the one entitled to this honor. But Jesus will reign nevertheless.

BRO. JACOB WITMORE, of Centre View, Mo., has decided to spend the coming winter preaching among the churches, as his health will not permit him to do frontier work. We hope the churches will give him plenty to do, as he is capable of preaching the Word with ability. His wife (who, by the way, is a sister to the lamented S. S. Bosserman) will accompany him.

SISTER SADIE BRALLIER NOFFSINGER reports an excellent Children's Meeting at the Walnut Grove church, near Johnstown, Pa., July 3. There were some in attendance from other congregations, and the little ones seem to have enjoyed the exercises We should by no means neglect the little ones and yet we should strive to retain in these meetings becoming Christian simplicity.

THE Brethren in Chicago have at last purchased a meeting-house that can now be regarded as their own. It is located on Hasting Street, No. 183, one and a half block south of 12th St., and a half block east of Ashland Avenue. Twelfth Street cars, down town, will pass within two blocks of the church. The house is to be dedicated the 24th of this month at 11 A. M., and a love-feast will be held in the evening of the same day. A cordial invitation is extended to such as desire to assemble and worship with the Brethren on that occasion. We are glad to announce the purchasing of the house, as it gives our Brethren a permanency that will add strength, and also afford them a suitable place to hold their meetings unmolested. This will indeed be a great satisfaction to them. The house formerly belonged to the German Baptists, and we understand that it is located in a very favorable part of the city. We hope to hear of good results from the work in that city.

QUERISTS' DEPARTMENT.

Is it right for a young man, who has not been elected to the ministry by the church, to set himself apart for that place? If it be right, what is the proper preparation, and where is the best place?　　　　　　　　A YOUNG BROTHER.

WE think it right and proper for any young brother to humbly prepare himself for the ministry; then he will be ready to enter upon the work when the Lord sees fit to call him through the church. If he prepares himself for the work, that will be setting himself apart as much as it is his privilege to do. He need not make it known that he is preparing himself for the ministry,—the Lord sees the heart,—but he can go quietly about his duties and preparations.

The way to prepare is to study, to show yourself approved unto God. First of all, be sure that you are a converted man in the true sense, then labor to be faithful in all the departments of life. There is nothing so valuable as a pure life, which is of itself a class of preaching that cannot be gainsaid. We advise, at least, a good English education. A thorough knowledge of the higher branches will be useful if you have the time and means to reach them. Above all studies, there is nothing like studying the Bible and the needs of humanity.

Any of the Brethren's Schools will be a good place for you to prepare yourself. But we advise you to enter into active Sunday-school work at once, and master every lesson. This will prove a valuable training to you.

While preparing yourself for the ministry, do not be afraid to work. The Lord knows where to find his servants when he wants them. He found Elisha at the plow-handle, Moses herding cattle, and David looking after his father's sheep. The apostles were busy men when they were found. Work and be contented. The Lord has no use for idle or whining men.

If you should never be called to the ministry, do not be discouraged. The Lord has use for a number of good men in the laity, and he may want to keep you there as long as you live. Remember that a man who is not a good, exemplary private member is not fit for the ministry. You may happen, with a good education, to be more useful in the laity than in the ministry. So prepare yourself for the work, be faithful and meek, and the Lord will see to the rest.

A man has been around here with maps of the Bible lands, giving lectures, claiming his object is to prove the authenticity of the Bible. He says it is claimed by some, that Moses never got into the Promised Land. He also says that Moses died in the Promised Land. Is this correct?　　　　　　A. MARYLAND.

Moses died on Mount Nebo, which was on the east side of the River Jordan, but not in the Promised Land. The Jordan was the eastern boundary of the land promised to the children of Israel. This land was never entered by Moses, but was seen by him from the top of Mount Nebo. This mountain was situated in the territory assigned to the tribe of Reuben, and for that reason some have been led to think that it was in the Promised Land. Of all those who came out of the land of Egypt, Caleb and Joshua were the only ones permitted to cross the Jordan and enter the land of Canaan. The others could not enter in because of unbelief. Heb. 3: 19.

The members here want to know what the decision of Annual Meeting is on feet-washing. The church has been following the double mode, and a part of the members want to practice the single. Does it take a unanimous, or a majority vote, to decide the question in a church council?
　　　　　　　　ISAAC RODEFFER.

Art. 6, of 1879, says, "We can see no better way to avoid such trouble than to follow the last decision of Annual Meeting, which is to the effect that churches had better not change unless it can be done by a unanimous consent. Where there is a small minority, it is better to persuade, if it can be done, than to force the minority to yield." It will thus be seen that changes of this kind cannot be made by a mere majority, but should be done by unanimous consent. And while it may seem unfair for a large majority to be held back by a small minority, it nevertheless affords an opportunity for the majority to display a rare degree of Christian charity towards those who are opposed to the change. In a large church, 200 members, at one time, voted for a change and 13 against it. The 13 refused to yield. The 200 said, "Rather than make trouble and have hard feelings, we will sacrifice our wishes and yield to the minority. "This great display of brotherly love, upon the part of the majority, so affected the minority that they felt mortified, and gave their consent for a change at the first opportunity. We have all passed through that trouble here years ago, and know that Christian forbearance is the better way. In the end it will result in a higher order of Christian charity that "suffereth long and is kind," "that seeketh not her own, is not easily provoked." 1 Cor. 13: 4, 5. Above all things, brethren, live in peace with one another, and when a change is made from the double to the single mode, let it be with the best of feelings.

What would be proper when a brother does not believe in raising or using tobacco, and by another is asked to assist him in setting the plants or raising a barn? Shall the brother, who does not believe in raising or using it, assist in the work against his own will, to save his brother from being offended at him for not helping to do the work?
　　　　　　　　JOSEPH A. EASTER.

In our judgment questions of this kind should be left to each member's conscience. His surroundings and circumstances may have much to do with his duties and privileges. His duty probably lies between these two Scriptures: "Let not your good be evil spoken of," Rom. 14: 16, and "Abstain from all appearance of evil." 1 Thess. 5: 22.

A skeptic wants to know why the Almighty ever placed Satan in the world to destroy his own flesh and blood? He adds, "Why can he not reform him or make him do right?" Would it be advisable to answer his questions? If so, how shall we answer?　　　　　　DAVID W. CRIST.

He might ask with equal reason, Why have fire that will burn fingers or destroy houses? Why have water that will drown people and inundate farms? Why have the sunshine that will prostrate workmen and dry up the vegetation? Why have a moon that will shine but half the night? The question asked by the skeptic is but one of a thousand on the same line. We have never paused to consider why Satan is placed here, but we are greatly concerned about keeping out of the place where he is going to be in the next world. We are not much interested in the reforming of Satan, but we are interested in our own reformation. If people will concern themselves more about matters of this kind, they may make life a success in spite of Satan, while, on the other hand, the study of the whys and wherefores of Satan may land them all in the same place. The best use Satan can be put to is to be resisted or avoided. Those who study to avoid Satan will be kept out of a multitude of evil places.　　J. H. M.

"WHEN a man's temper gets the best of him, it reveals the worst of him."

VACATION TALKS WITH OUR STUDENTS.

NUMBER THREE.—OUR DAUGHTERS.

MEN and women often forget each other, but everybody remembers mother. God has given mother a position so exalted that our infant eyes and arms are first uplifted to her. We cling to the very name in manhood, and almost worship it in old age. Her love never tires, and her waking, watchful eye is upon her daughter every-where. Even after the mother has gone to the beyond her spirit continues to hover over the daughter's affections and overshadows her pathway to draw her to herself in heaven.

There are homes where the mother cooks, sweeps, washes, irons, waits on the table, works in the garden, toils early and late, while the hopeful daughters, with hands soft and white, spend the morning lounging in bed, and the afternoon in making fashionable calls. Such daughters, be their intellectual attainments ever so scholarly, have never mastered "Honor thy father and mother,"—the first commandment with promise,—and some day must necessarily pay very dearly for the defects in their education. The relations between the mother and the daughter are very interesting, and when properly understood and fully met by the daughter, bring showers of blessings upon her head.

When, on visiting the home of a young woman, I learn that she is uniformly kind and respectful to her mother, that she is anxious for her welfare and happiness, that she is ever ready to be helpful to her mother, even if it should necessitate the employment of those soft white hands in making butter, picking berries, or putting up pickles during the cooler hours, and in plying the needle during the warmer hours of the day, I conclude that such student girl did not only stand among the first of her class in school, but that she is at the head of her class in the home as well. She has mastered and made a part of her education the discipline afforded by the lesson, "Honor thy mother." It was such a daughter to which Addison referred when he said, "I am charmed to see one of the most beauteous women the age has produced, kneeling to put on her father's slippers."

The daughter, who lends her energies to assist and comfort her mother, invariably is in grateful sympathy toward her wise and good father, and will study to anticipate his comfort and happiness. Such a daughter fails not to manifest her affection for her brothers and sisters by a readiness to perform little acts of love, lightening their trials and hiding their faults, thus strengthening the bond of kindred sympathy and affection in the home. Such a daughter, properly educated, prudently united with an uncrowned monarch of the plow,—a farmer's son with an honest heart, a good head, and a pair of willing hands,—may well be looked upon as the future hope of both the church and the state. Such union will give us country homes, with roses and honeysuckles trained to climb over them; with peace and plenty, love, and, above all, contentment reigning within, making the homes the paradises which heaven has left for the attainment of man upon earth.　　J. G. R.

"To a mind which justly estimates the weight of eternal things, it will appear a greater honor to have converted a sinner from the error of his ways, than to have wielded the thunder of a Demosthenes, or to have kindled the flame of a Cicero."

True, we have no worldly means, but we have Jesus, and the love of God at heart, and that is better than earthly riches.

To the brethren and sisters who contemplate a change in location, climate, etc., and who are in full sympathy with the General Brotherhood, after the pattern of Christ, I would say, Come and help us! Come, for Christ's sake.

Since I came, one week ago, one brother from Sidney, Nebr., rented several farms and will move here in the fall. There are now five members in this neighborhood, and if those Brethren, living at Eads, are still there, I would like to hear from them. If those in Pueblo, or any others in this part, see these lines they will please write me. If the Mission Board of South-western Kansas, and South-eastern Colorado, know of Brethren living anywhere near here they will please inform me. Let all, who can in any way help us, do so either by information contributed, or by preaching. By so doing we, as workers together, may gather into the garner of the Lord many sheaves of golden grain. The Lord help us all to do our duty while time is ours.

JOHN J. HOOVER.

July 4.

Some Suggestions Offered Relating to Annual Meeting.

OUR late Annual Meeting constitutes another interesting chapter in the history of the church. The brethren in charge, and the citizens of Cedar Rapids, who had taken upon them obligations relating to the Meeting, did their part well; we feel to commend them as "faithful stewards."

There is certainly a marked improvement in the manner of holding our Annual Meeting, and the manner of doing our business at present, to what there was years ago. For improvement, however, there yet is room. We name the following for future consideration:

1. The Meeting should be located on high, dry, rolling ground. The reason for this is too apparent to occupy space.

When the Meeting can be held on grounds with permanent buildings, it is desirable and safe, especially in case of inclement weather.

2. The sanitary condition of the Meeting deserves more attention. Drinks,—water, lemonade, coffee and tea,—should be prepared with great care. Meats should be allowed plenty of time for the animal heat to escape. I name this as one of the leading causes for much of the sickness at some of our Annual Meetings. A man of my acquaintance one time furnished the meat for a meeting. He insisted for more time for the meat to cool; the manager insisted otherwise. He furnished the meat as directed; and it was with difficulty that they provided for the number of their sick. My friend attributed the excessive amount of their sickness to the condition of their meats. It requires more time for meats to properly cool than most persons are aware of. All decaying matter should be carefully removed from the grounds. How much have the guests at some of our Annual Meetings been disturbed at the offensive odor arising from the ground after showers and warm sun!

This has been named again and again by physicians as the cause of much of the sickness at our Annual Meetings.

3. There has been a desire for years to free the Brethren from the burden of expense in holding Annual Meeting, and make the Meeting self-supporting. That point has been reached. The desire now is, to meet the expense of the Meeting, and have a dividend left for the Missionary and Tract Work. This surely would be no harm if reached in a legitimate way, but care must be exercised lest this zeal lead us to

sell our goods and our provisions above their par value, which would be extortion,—a grave sin. It is on this line direct that many of the popular churches, in their zeal to raise funds to meet their excessive expenses, have been led to sell their goods at their church fairs at extortionary prices. It would be well for us to take warning, and seek to profit by the mistakes of those around us, knowing that we are persons of like passions.

4. Much of the business of Annual Meeting is done too hurriedly. The distance that many brethren travel, and their expense, demand proper time for their business. Especially is this true of the work of Standing Committee. For the information of the reader I name, that Standing Committee went in session at 7: 30 A. M., and 1 P. M., with evening sessions continuing as late as 10: 30. There was only a short intermission for meals, and very little recreation. Hence the Committee was too tired and worn-out to do business properly. Since Annual Meeting I visited a church from which came a petition for a committee. Their long paper was read at a late hour. The Committee was dull, some were dozing (please don't criticise this or think it strange, for Christ could not get his disciples to watch or wait one hour; here the business compelled us to watch, wait and work several hours each evening). Had the Committee taken more time, called in the petitioners and had them explain the nature and importance of their case, my impression is that a Committee would have been granted. But the petition, when read, was found to be irregular, and on a motion it was easily voted down and dismissed. There are cases that neither the church, adjoining elders, nor a committee from District Meeting can settle. Their only resort is Annual Meeting. Due time should be given to hear their cause patiently.

Standing Committee ought to be free to enjoy the associations of Monday in the tabernacle. I, therefore, propose that Standing Committee meet on Thursday instead of Friday before Annual Meeting.

5. The growing feeling of apportioning the work of Annual Meeting, and the work of committees to different brethren, living in different parts, is productive of good results. Stereotyped names for certain church work is not the sentiment of the church, and should not be encouraged.   I. J. ROSENBERGER.

Covington, Ohio.

From the Rock Creek Church, Ill.

THE Brethren of the Rock Creek church met in council July 2, 1892, elders Edmund Forney and Levi Trostle, and the Foreman of the Missionary Board, Bro. Samuel Riddlesbarger, being present with us. The meeting was for the purpose of dividing the congregation. Bro. Geo. D. Zollers was to be here, but, on account of the inclemency of the weather and high water, he was only permitted to get close enough to look across, and see the meeting-house on the hill. He, however, came another way, though too late for the meeting. The subject of dividing the congregation was taken into consideration, and, with the best of feeling, and the unanimous consent of all present, it was decided to make Sterling a separate organization with the dividing line as follows: To commence at the north line of Whiteside County, running south on the township line between Gordon and Genesee till the line strikes the Elkhorn Creek. Follow the Elkhorn Creek south-west, till it empties into Rock River; follow the river south-west to the township line between Hume and Prophetstown. Running south on that line, all the territory east of this line in the County of Whiteside is to belong to the Sterling church.

It was further decided that July 16, elders Edmund Forney, George D. Zollers and Levi Trostle meet in council with the Brethren in Sterling, to more fully organize. Thus ended a very pleasant council-meeting. May the Lord bless the work! In the evening of the same day Bro. Edmund Forney preached a very wholesome sermon for us from Matt. 20. The day following being Lord's Day, Bro. Levi Trostle preached a very acceptable sermon from John 3, followed by Bro. Geo. D. Zollers, with very suitable words. Upon the whole it was a very pleasant meeting.

JOHN A. MYERS.

Malvern, Ill.

From Muenster, Texas.

I MET Bro. A. Molsbee at Muenster. Together we journeyed to Gainesville. Bro. Molsbee preached in the Christian people's house in the city on Friday night, June 10. We found a number of our own members in the city, who had been isolated so long that they had lost their interest in the church to some extent, but, on being with them for a short time, we could see the fire of zeal in the soul rekindled.

Among those we visited was Bro. J. S. Giesler and sister, formerly Branscomb, a sister to Bro. George A. Branscomb, now laboring in North Carolina. They have been in this State sixteen years. They left East Tennessee seventeen years ago. Bro. Giesler's parents died four years ago, a few miles south of the city.

After visiting in the city until evening, we drove five miles south to the home of D. G. Jackson, a member of the Christian church. This was a home indeed, and they all joined in with a dear old grandmother to make it home to us.

On Sunday morning Bro. Molsbee preached to a crowded audience at a school-house. This was the most interesting congregation I ever met. A great interest has been worked up by the GOSPEL MESSENGER. I could not help but think of what could be done with our paper and with our ministry. Our paper is awakening an interest wherever it goes, here in this country, and those who get it say they cannot keep it long enough to read it, especially in the City of Gainesville.

Our fields of labor are spreading. We think there ought to be a minister in the City of Gainesville. I need help here very much, but I am not able to do the work of the Lord that I see ought to be done. I am hardly able to support myself and family. I could not do it at all, if it were not for the continued sacrifice of my children to help me. God bless the work and send the help!

A. W. AUSTIN.

Echoes from the Highway.

THE Lordsburg members held their church council, preparatory to their love-feast, June 23. With but a few exceptions, the visiting brethren reported all the members to be in a healthy state of mind, spiritually, and willing to press on in the cause of the Blessed Master. One sad feature of the occasion was the request of three of the members to be relieved of further connection with the church. Some eight or ten letters of membership were handed in, and one granted. Thus it will be seen the church here, numerically, is still in a state of progress.

On Saturday, following the council, the feast was held in the spacious dining-hall of the College building. It was spoken of as one of the most enjoyable meetings of the kind ever held at that place. Eld. P. S. Myers, of Los Angeles, was present, and his labors of love were highly appreciated. Over one hundred members communed. On Sunday morning there was a very

True, we have no worldly means, but we have Jesus, and the love of God at heart, and that is better than earthly riches.

To the brethren and sisters who contemplate a change in location, climate, etc., and who are in full sympathy with the General Brotherhood, after the pattern of Christ, I would say, Come and help us! Come, for Christ's sake.

Since I came, one week ago, one brother from Sidney, Nebr., rented several farms and will move here in the fall. There are now five members in this neighborhood, and if those Brethren living at Eads, are still there, I would like to hear from them. If those in Pueblo, or any others in this part, see these lines they will please write me. If the Mission Board of South-western Kansas, and South-eastern Colorado, know of Brethren living anywhere near here they will please inform me. Let all, who can in any way help us, do so either by information contributed, or by preaching. By so doing we, as workers together, may gather into the garner of the Lord many sheaves of golden grain. The Lord help us all to do our duty while time is ours.

JOHN J. HOOVER.

July 4.

Some Suggestions Offered Relating to Annual Meeting.

OUR late Annual Meeting constitutes another interesting chapter in the history of the church. The brethren in charge, and the citizens of Cedar Rapids, who had taken upon them obligations relating to the Meeting, did their part well; we feel to commend them as "faithful stewards."

There is certainly a marked improvement in the manner of holding our Annual Meeting, and the manner of doing our business at present, to what there was years ago. For improvement, however, there yet is room. We name the following for future consideration:

1. The Meeting should be located on high, dry, rolling ground. The reason for this is too apparent to occupy space.

When the Meeting can be held on grounds with permanent buildings, it is desirable and safe, especially in case of inclement weather.

2. The sanitary condition of the Meeting deserves more attention. Drinks,—water, lemonade, coffee and tea,—should be prepared with great care. Meats should be allowed plenty of time for the animal heat to escape. I name this as one of the leading causes for much of the sickness at some of our Annual Meetings. A man of my acquaintance one time furnished the meat for a meeting. He insisted for more time for the meat to cool; the manager insisted otherwise. He furnished the meat as directed; and it was with difficulty that they provided for the number of their sick. My friend attributed the excessive amount of their sickness to the condition of their meats. It requires more time for meats to properly cool than most persons are aware of. All decaying matter should be carefully removed from the grounds. How much have the guests at some of our Annual Meetings been disturbed at the offensive odor arising from the ground after showers and warm sun!

This has been named again and again by physicians as the cause of much of the sickness at our Meetings.

3. There has been a desire for years to free the Brethren from the burden of expense in holding Annual Meeting, and make the Meeting self-supporting. That point has been reached. The desire now is, to meet the expense of the Meeting, with the profits, and have a dividend left for the Missionary and Tract Work. This surely would be no harm if reached in a legitimate way, but care must be exercised lest this zeal lead us to

sell our goods and our provisions above their par value, which would be extortion,—a grave sin. It is on this line direct that many of the popular churches, in their zeal to raise funds to meet their excessive expenses, have been led to sell their goods at their church fairs at extortionary prices. It would be well for us to take warning. Let us seek to profit by the mistakes of those around us, knowing that we are persons of like passions.

4. Much of the business of Annual Meeting is done too hurriedly. The distance that many brethren travel, and their expense, demand proper time for their business. Especially is this true of the work of Standing Committee. For the information of the reader I name, that Standing Committee went in session at 7: 30 A. M., and 1 P. M., with evening sessions continuing as late as 10: 30. There was only a short intermission for meals, and very little recreation. Hence the Committee was too tired and worn-out to do business properly. Since Annual Meeting I visited a church from which came a petition for a committee. Their long paper was read at a late hour. The Committee was dull, some were dozing (please don't criticise this or think it strange, for Christ could not get his disciples to watch or wait one hour; here the business compelled us to watch, wait and work several hours each evening). Had the Committee taken more time, called in the petitioners and had them explain the nature and importance of their case, my impression is that a Committee would have been granted. But the petition, when read, was found too long, and on a motion it was easily voted down and dismissed. There are cases that neither the church, adjoining elders, nor a committee from District Meeting can settle. Their only resort is Annual Meeting. Due time should be given to hear their cause patiently.

Standing Committee ought to be free to enjoy the associations of Monday in the tabernacle. I, therefore, propose that Standing Committee meet on Thursday instead of Friday before Annual Meeting.

5. The growing feeling of apportioning the work of Annual Meeting, and the work of committees to different brethren, living in different parts, is productive of good results. Stereotyped names for certain church work is not the sentiment of the church, and should not be encouraged.　I. J. ROSENBERGER.

Covington, Ohio.

From the Rock Creek Church, Ill.

THE Brethren of the Rock Creek church met in council July 2, 1892, elders Edmund Forney and Levi Trostle, and the Foreman of the Missionary Board, Bro. Samuel Riddlesberger, being present with us. The meeting was for the purpose of dividing the congregation. Bro. Geo. D. Zollers was to be here, but, on account of the inclemency of the weather and high water, he was only permitted to get close enough to look across, and see the meeting-house on the hill. He, however, came another way, though too late for the meeting. The subject of dividing the congregation was taken into consideration, and, with the best of feeling, and the unanimous consent of all present, it was decided to make Sterling a separate organization with the dividing line as follows: To commence at the north line of Whiteside county, running south on the township line between Gordon and Genesee till the line strikes the Elkhorn Creek. Follow the Elkhorn Creek south-west, till it empties into Rock River; follow the river south-west to the township line between Hume and Prophetstown. Running south on that line, all the territory east of this line in the County of Whiteside is to belong to the Sterling church.

It was further decided that July 16, elders Edmund Forney, George D. Zollers and Levi Trostle meet in council with the Brethren in Sterling, to more fully organize. Thus ended a very pleasant council-meeting. May the Lord bless the work! In the evening of the same day Bro. Edmund Forney preached a very wholesome sermon for us from Matt. 20. The day following being Lord's Day, Bro. Levi Trostle preached a very acceptable sermon from John 3, followed by Bro. Geo. D. Zollers, with very suitable words. Upon the whole it was a very pleasant meeting.

JOHN A. MYERS.

Malvern, Ill.

From Muenster, Texas.

I MET Bro. A. Molsbee at Muenster. Together we journeyed to Gainesville. Bro. Molsbee preached in the Christian people's house in the city on Friday night, June 10. We found a number of our own members in the city, who had been isolated so long that they had lost their interest in the church to some extent, but, on being with them for a short time, we could see the fire of zeal in the soul rekindled.

Among those we visited was Bro. J. S. Giesler and sister, formerly Branscomb, a sister to Bro. George A. Branscomb, now laboring in North Carolina. They have been in this State sixteen years. They left East Tennessee seventeen years ago. Bro. Giesler's parents died four years ago, a few miles south of the city.

After visiting in the city until evening, we drove five miles south to the home of D. G. Jackson, a member of the Christian church. This was a home indeed, and they all joined in with a dear old grandmother to make it home to us.

On Sunday morning Bro. Molsbee preached to a crowded audience at a school-house. This was the most interesting congregation I ever met. A great interest has been worked up by the GOSPEL MESSENGER. I could not help but think of what could be done with our paper and with our ministry. Our paper is awakening an interest wherever it goes, here in this country, and those who get it say they cannot keep it long enough to read it, especially in the City of Gainesville.

Our fields of labor are spreading. We think there ought to be a minister in the City of Gainesville. I need help here very much, but I am not able to do the work of the Lord that I see ought to be done. I am hardly able to support myself and family. I could not do it at all, if it were not for the continued sacrifice of my children to help me. God bless the work and send the help!

A. W. AUSTIN.

Echoes from the Highway.

THE Lordsburg members held their church council, preparatory to their love-feast, June 22. With but a few exceptions, the visiting brethren reported all the members to be in a healthy state of mind, spiritually, and willing to press on in the cause of the Blessed Master. One sad feature of the occasion was the request of three of the members to be relieved of further connection with the church. Some eight or ten letters of membership were handed in, and one granted. Thus it will be seen the church here, numerically, is still in a state of progress.

On Saturday, following the council, the feast was held in the spacious dining-hall of the College building. It was spoken of as one of the most enjoyable meetings of the kind ever held at that place. Eld. P. S. Myers, of Los Angeles, was present, and his labors of love were highly appreciated. Over one hundred members communed. On Sunday morning there was a very

Prairie Queen, Minn.—Bro. Frank Myers, of Mt. Carroll, Ill., came to us June 20, and preached for us till June 30. We were made to rejoice when three souls were made willing to join in with the children of God. Many precious souls are still outside out of the ark of safety, and we pray that they may soon see the beauty of the religion of Jesus Christ.—*Mary Broadwater, July 3.*

Mt. Repose, Ohio.—Our love-feast will occur Oct. 1, at 10 A. M., at the Stone Lick church. As we are but few in number we earnestly hope that the brethren and sisters will cheer us by their presence, hoping that ministers will heed Acts 8: 4, as at this place much is needed to build up the cause of the Master. I often wonder why it is some good evangelist does not call at our place. They surely would obtain a reward for faithful work.—*Lydia C. Leah, July 4.*

Egles, W. Va.—July 3 we met at the Maple Spring church for services. Bro. Jonas Fike preached for us from Rev. 20: 11, 12, 13, and all could say it was good to be there. We were glad to see our dear brother S. A. Fike and his wife with us once more at the house of the Lord. Some shed tears for joy when he entered the door to-day. It is three months since he last met with us. We hope that it is the Lord's will that he will be spared a few years longer, but he is now in his seventy-third year. Pray for him and for us all!—*Rachel Weimer.*

Custer, Mich.—Our Communion meeting in the Sugar Ridge church occurred June 18 and 19. It was well attended and seemed to be greatly enjoyed by all present. Brethren Isaac Rairigh and S. M. Smith, from the Thornapple church, and Wm. H. Kreigh, of Chippewa Lake, were with us. All enjoyed a feast long to be remembered. The little band of members is only seventeen in number. We surely had a foretaste of that time when Christ said he would gird himself and serve us. We need the prayers of the church, as we are left without a resident minister, this place being supplied by the Mission Board. Bro. Isaac Rairigh does the preaching.—*Israel Fisher, June 21.*

Matrimonial.

"What therefore God hath joined together, let not man put asunder."

FRITSCH—SNYDER.—At the residence of the bride's parents, Bro. and sister Snyder, June 28, 1892, by the undersigned, Mr. Fred Fritsch and Miss Cora Snyder, both of Canton, Stark Co., Ohio.   J. WEIRICH.

Fallen Asleep.

"Blessed are the dead which die in the Lord."

SCOTT.—In the bounds of the Howard church, Ind., June 27, 1892, Isabinda Scott, aged 77 years, 1 month and 10 days. She was born in Madison County, Kentucky. When eleven years old she moved with her parents to Indiana. When nineteen years of age she was united in marriage to William Scott, who died March 17, 1855. She was the mother of six children. Funeral occasion improved from 1 Cor. 5: 1, by the writer.   DANIEL BOCK.

KESSLER.—In the bounds of the Beaver Dam congregation, Fulton Co., Ind., Dec. 16, 1891, John M. Kessler, aged 73 years, 10 months and 16 days. He was born in Miami County, Ohio, Jan. 30, 1818. He was married to Melinda Herriman, of Ohio, April 8, 1838. She, with four children out of eight, survives him. He and his wife united with the church in early life and he died in the hope of immortal glory. Funeral services by Bro. John Stafford.

WEIKEL.—In the bounds of the Tower City church, Pa., June 18, 1892, sister Rebecca, wife of Amos Weikel and daughter of Bro. George Tobias, aged 28 years, 6 months and 2 days. Funeral services to a large congregation of neighbors and friends by the writer.   D. P. ZIEGLER.

TOMBAUGH.—In the Ten Mile congregation, Washington Co., Pa., at her home, May 15, 1892, sister Rachel Tombaugh, widow of Mathias Tombaugh (deceased), aged 85 years, 1 month and 13 days. Funeral services by the writer

in the Pigeon Creek church-house from Deut. 3: 25. In the death of sister Rachel the church suffers an irreparable loss. She was the mother of ten children, seven of whom are living. She had a stroke of palsy April 2, which prostrated her, and took from her the power of speech, which she never regained in this world, though she remained conscious to the last. She was anointed with oil in the name of the Lord a few weeks before her death, according to James 5.   N. B. CHRISTNER.

BALLINGER.—In the bounds of the Brick church, Floyd, Va., June 3, 1892, sister Martha Ballinger, aged 80 years, 5 months and 28 days. She was a consistent member of the Brethren church for twenty-nine years and departed in peace. Funeral services to a large concourse of people by Bro. Jacob Hylton and the writer, from Rev. 14: 13. and 2 Cor. 5: 1, selected by the family.   J. H. SLUSHER.

ABSHIRE.—In the Roann congregation, Wabash Co., Ind., June 19, 1892, Bro. Abraham Abshire, aged 92 years, 2 months and 28 days. He was born in Franklin County, Virginia, March 21, 1800, and united with the church in 1826, in which he lived unwavering until death. He was married to Hannah Neff, Feb. 21, 1827. There were born to them fourteen children. Bro. Abshire, with his family, left Virginia in 1836 and came to Preble County, Ohio. Thence, in 1841, he moved to Wabash County, Ind., where he and his companion lived up to the time of their death. His body was entombed by the side of his wife, who preceded him seventeen years. Funeral discourse by the brethren. Text from Ecc. 9: 8.   JOSEPH JOHN.

KEIM.—Also, near the same place, June 20, 1892, Mrs. Mary Jane, wife of Mr. Joseph Keim, aged 47 years, 3 months and 16 days. She was the mother of two sons who, with their father, were absent at the time. She went to settle a colony of honey bees, which turned on her, stinging her fatally. Husband and sons came to her assistance in time to hear her say, " The bees have stung me to death." Soon after that she expired. Funeral discourse by the Brethren. Interment in the Shiloh cemetery.   JOSEPH JOHN.

STOLER.—In the bounds of the Spring Creek church, June 11, 1892, Mrs. Anna Stoler, aged 89 years and 17 days. She had been a member of the Baptist church, and died at her daughter's, Mrs. Stoler's, near South Whitley, Ind. Services by the writer from Mark 13: 35-37.   LEWIS WORKMAN.

BRIGHT.—In Wolf Creek church, Montgomery Co., Ohio, June 22, 1892, of inflammation of the brain, Jesse Marion, son of John Calvin and Lizzie A. Bright, aged 4 years, 1 month and 28 days.   THE FATHER.

SPICHER.—In the Montgomery church, Pa., June 2, 1892, Mrs. Ettie Spicher, wife of Bro. Milan Spicher, aged 24 years, 8 months and 26 days. She leaves a large circle of friends and relatives to mourn their loss. Funeral services by Eld. Mark Mineer from Rev. 21: 4.

SPICHER.—Also in the same family, June 5, 1892, Pearl (infant daughter), aged 8 months and 17 days. Funeral by Mark Mineer from Isa. 40: 9, 10, 11.   L A. SPICHER.

WILLIAMS.—In the South Waterloo church, Iowa, June 2, 1892, sister Sarah J., wife of friend Isaac D. Williams, aged 33 years, 6 months and 25 days. She leaves a husband and three children to mourn their loss. She bore her affliction with Christian fortitude and died in the hope of eternal life. Funeral services conducted by the writer to a large concourse of sorrowing people from Rev. 14: 13.   S. H. MILLER.

BAUMAN.—At the home of his son, in Dillsburg, York Co., Pa., June 3, 1892, Jesse Bauman, aged 79 years, 1 month and 8 days. Services held at the house of his son, and burial at the Brooklyn meeting-house in Cumberland County, Pa. Services by the writer, assisted by the Rev. Darr, of the Presbyterian church, and brethren Henry Beelman and L. S. Mohler.   DANIEL LANDIS.

MYERS.—At his home in Bowmansdale, Cumberland Co., Pa., of heart trouble, June 22, 1892, Bro. George Myers, aged 36 years, 9 months and 10 days. Bro. George leaves a wife (a sister) and four daughters. Our brother had been ailing since January last. Thinking that his time was short, and wishing to obey in all things, he called for the brethren and was anointed. Funeral services and burial at the Baker meeting-house, near Churchtown, Cumberland Co., Pa. Services conducted by the home brethren from the text of his choice, "Set thy house in order, for thou shalt die and not live."   DANIEL LANDIS.

SHAFFER.—In the Shiloh congregation, Barbour Co., W. Va., June 6, 1892, sister Martha Shaffer, wife of Andrew Shaffer, aged 41 years, 11 months and 16 days. Deceased was a daughter of Bro. Peter Bolyard. She leaves a family of eight children. Funeral services from Rev. 14: 13 by Eld. Elias Anvil.   LEVI POLING.

BEACHLY.—In the South Waterloo church, Iowa, June 23, 1892, Sally, wife of Eld. Elias K. Beachly, aged 79 years, 3 months and 14 days. Sister Beachley was one of the pioneers of the South Waterloo church, and it can be truly

said of her that she was a mother in Israel. She leaves an aged husband and a large circle of relatives. Funeral services by Bro. I. M. Gibson, from 1 Cor. 15: 20.   S. H. MILLER.

WAREHAM.—In Pocahontas County, Iowa, March 28, 1892, Lillie, aged 7 years, 1 month and 19 days; March 31, Goldie, aged 9 years and 6 days; April 1, Russell, aged 5 years and 18 days; April 5, Bertie, aged 1 year, 8 months and 22 days. These children died of diphtheria, and were the children of Bro. William and sister Delilah Wareham. The grief-stricken parents were received into the church by baptism during our late Annual Meeting at Cedar Rapids, Iowa. The funeral services of the above children were held in the Methodist church, at Fonela, Iowa, June 26, 1892, by the writer, from Matt. 19: 13, 14.   S. H. MILLER.

SPEICHER.—At Waterloo, Iowa, June 20, 1892, from the effects of a railroad accident, Bro. Ephraim Speicher, aged 70 years. Funeral occasion improved by the Brethren.

HEETER.—In the .Yellow Creek church, Pa, May 19, 1892, sister Cora Heeter, wife of Thomas Heeter, aged 19 years, 5 months and 6 days. Not quite a year ago she was married. She leaves a husband, father, mother and two brothers. Funeral services by brethren L. L. Holsinger and C. L. Buck.   BARBARA HOLSINGER.

HECKMAN.—In the Spring Creek church, Kosciusko Co., Ind., June 6, 1892, Bro. Henry Heckman, aged 75 years and 17 days. Deceased was born in Clark County, Ohio, May 19, 1817, and came to Kosciusko Co., Ind., in 1858, where he remained until death. He was never married. Funeral services conducted by Bro. Gorman Heeter and others.   R. ROSS.

FRY.—In the Quemahoning church, Somerset Co., Pa, June 19, 1892, Bro. Daniel Fry, aged 74 years and 18 days. Deceased was a sufferer for seven years, but bore his sufferings with Christian patience, until he gently passed away. Funeral services by J. W. Blough and the writer.   S. P. ZIMMERMAN.

BOLLINGER.—In the Sugar Creek church, Ind., June 3, 1892, Sophia Bollinger, aged 48 years, 9 months and 29 days. She leaves a husband, four daughters and one son. Funeral services at Tunker, Ind. Interment in the Eberhart cemetery. Mother suffered for six years but bore it patiently unto the end; because her hopes were built on high.   EMMA KIMMEL.

HECKLER.—In the Indian Creek church, Montgomery Co., Pa., Elizabeth Yocum Heckler, aged 85 years and 3 months. Grandmother was " only waiting " for her summons and we feel that she is at rest. ELIZABETH H. DELP.

MURRAY.—At Pennsville, Pa., in the Fayette congregation, May 12, 1892, Katie Murray, aged 17 months. Services by the writer.

FREED.—Also at the same place, June 26, 1892, Robert Freed, aged 74 years, 5 months and 16 days. Friend Freed never made a profession of religion, but his wife is a member of the River Brethren church. Services by the writer.   H. S. MYERS.

446 THE GOSPEL MESSENGER. July 19, 1892.

Prairie Queen, Minn.—Bro. Frank Myers, of Mt. Carroll, Ill., came to us June 20, and preached for us till June 30. We were made to rejoice when three souls were made willing to join in with the children of God. Many precious souls are still outside out of the ark of safety, and we pray that they may soon see the beauty of the religion of Jesus Christ.—*Mary Broadwater, July 3.*

Mt. Repose, Ohio.—Our love-feast will occur Oct. 1, at 10 A. M., at the Stone Lick church. As we are but few in number we earnestly hope that the brethren and sisters will cheer us by their presence, hoping that ministers will heed Acts 8: 4, as at this place much is needed to build up the cause of the Master. I often wonder why it is some good evangelist does not call at our place. They surely would obtain a reward for faithful work.—*Lydia C. Lesh, July 4.*

Eglon, W. Va.—July 3 we met at the Maple Spring church for services. Bro. Jonas Fike preached for us from Rev. 20: 11, 12, 13, and all could say it was good to be there. We were glad to see our dear brother S. A. Fike and his wife with us once more at the house of the Lord. Some shed tears for joy when he entered the door to-day. It is three months since he last met with us. We hope that it is the Lord's will that he will be spared a few years longer, but he is now in his seventy-third year. Pray for him and for us all!—*Rachel Weimer.*

Custer, Mich.—Our Communion meeting in the Sugar Ridge church occurred June 18 and 19. It was well attended and seemed to be greatly enjoyed by all present. Brethren Isaac Rairigh and S. M. Smith, from the Thornapple church, and Wm. H. Kreigh, of Chippewa Lake, were with us. All enjoyed a feast long to be remembered. The little band of members is only seventeen in number. We surely had a foretaste of that time when Christ said he would gird himself and serve us. We need the prayers of the church, as we are left without a resident minister, this place being supplied by the Mission Board. Bro. Isaac Rairigh does the preaching.—*Israel Fisher, June 21.*

Matrimonial.

"What therefore God hath joined together, let not man put asunder."

FRITSCH—SNYDER.—At the residence of the bride's parents, Bro. and sister Snyder, June 28, 1892, by the undersigned, Mr. Fred Fritsch and Miss Cora Snyder, both of Canton, Stark Co., Ohio. J. WEIRICH.

Fallen Asleep.

"Blessed are the dead which die in the Lord."

SCOTT.—In the bounds of the Howard church, Ind., June 27, 1892, Isabinda Scott, aged 77 years, 4 months and 10 days. She was born in Madison County, Kentucky. When eleven years old she moved with her parents to Indiana. When nineteen years of age she was united in marriage to William Scott, who died March 17, 1855. She was the mother of six children. Funeral occasion improved from 2 Cor. 5: 1, by the writer. DANIEL BOCK.

KESSLER.—In the bounds of the Beaver Dam congregation, Fulton Co., Ind., Dec. 26, 1891, John M. Kessler, aged 73 years, 10 months and 26 days. He was born in Miami County, Ohio, Jan. 30, 1818. He was married to Melinda Herriman, of Ohio, April 8, 1838. She, with four children out of eight, survives him. He and his wife united with the church in early life and he died in the hope of immortal glory. Funeral services by Bro. John Stafford.

WEIKEL.—In the bounds of the Tower City church, Pa., June 18, 1892, sister Rebecca, wife of Amos Weikel and daughter of Bro. George Tobias, aged 28 years, 6 months and 2 days. Funeral services to a large congregation of neighbors and friends by the writer. D. P. ZIEGLER.

TOMBAUGH.—In the Ten Mile congregation, Washington Co., Pa., at her home, May 15, 1892, sister Rachel Tombaugh, widow of Mathias Tombaugh (deceased), aged 85 years, 1 month and 13 days. Funeral services by the writer in the Pigeon Creek church-house from Deut. 3: 25. In the death of sister Rachel the church suffers an irreparable loss. She was the mother of ten children, seven of whom are living. She had a stroke of palsy April 2, which prostrated her, and took from her the power of speech, which she never regained in this world, though she remained conscious to the last. She was anointed with oil in the name of the Lord a few weeks before her death, according to James 5.

N. B. CHRISTNER.

BALLINGER.—In the bounds of the Brick church, Floyd, Va., June 3, 1892, sister Martha Ballinger, aged 80 years, 5 months and 28 days. She was a consistent member of the Brethren church for twenty-nine years and departed in peace. Funeral services to a large concourse of people by Bro. Jacob Hylton and the writer, from Rev. 14: 13, and 2 Cor. 5: 1, selected by the family. J. H. SLUSHER.

ABSHIRE.—In the Roann congregation, Wabash Co., Ind., June 19, 1892, Bro. Abraham Abshire, aged 92 years, 2 months and 28 days. He was born in Franklin County, Virginia, March 21, 1800, and united with the church in 1826, in which he lived unwavering until death. He was married to Hannah Neff, Feb. 21, 1827. There were born to them fourteen children. Bro. Abshire, with his family, left Virginia in 1836 and came to Preble County, Ohio. Thence, in 1841, he moved to Wabash County, Ind., where he and his companion lived up to the time of their death. His body was entombed by the side of his wife, who preceded him seventeen years. Funeral discourse by the brethren. Text from Ecc. 9: 8.

JOSEPH JOHN.

KEIM.—Also, near the same place, June 20, 1892, Mrs. Mary Jane, wife of Mr. Joseph Keim, aged 47 years, 3 months and 18 days. She was the mother of two sons who, with their father, were absent at the time. She went to settle a colony of honey bees, which turned on her, stinging her fatally. Husband and sons came to her assistance in time to hear her say, "The bees have stung me to death." Soon after that she expired. Funeral discourse by the Brethren. Interment in the Shiloh cemetery. JOSEPH JOHN.

STOLER.—In the bounds of the Spring Creek church, June 11, 1892, Mrs. Anna Stoler, aged 89 years and 17 days. She had been a member of the Baptist church, and died at her daughter's, Mrs. Stoler's, near South Whitley, Ind. Services by the writer from Mark 13: 35-37.

LEWIS WORKMAN.

BRIGHT.—In Wolf Creek church, Montgomery Co., Ohio, June 22, 1892, of inflammation of the brain, Jesse Marion, son of John Calvin and Lizzie A. Bright, aged 4 years, 1 month and 28 days. THE FATHER.

SPICHER.—In the Montgomery church, Pa., June 2, 1892, Mrs. Ettie Spicher, wife of Bro. Milen Spicher, aged 24 years, 8 months and 28 days. She leaves a large circle of friends and relatives to mourn their loss. Funeral services by Eld. Mark Minser from Rev. 21: 4.

SPICHER.—Also in the same family, June 5, 1892, Pearl (infant daughter), aged 8 months and 27 days. Funeral by Mark Minser from Isa. 40: 9, 10, 11. L. A. SPICHER.

WILLIAMS.—In the South Waterloo church, Iowa, June 2, 1892, sister Sarah J., wife of friend Isaac D. Williams, aged 33 years, 6 months and 25 days. She leaves a husband and three children to mourn their loss. She bore her affliction with Christian fortitude and died in the hope of eternal life. Funeral services conducted by the writer to a large concourse of sorrowing people from Rev. 14: 13. S. H. MILLER.

BAUMAN.—At the home of his son, in Dillsburg, York Co., Pa., June 3, 1892, Jesse Bauman, aged 79 years, 1 month and 8 days. Services held at the house of his son, and burial at the Brooklyn meeting-house in Cumberland County, Pa. Services by the writer, assisted by the Rev. Barr, of the Presbyterian church, and brethren Henry Beelman and L. S. Mohler. DANIEL LANDIS.

MYERS.—At his home in Bowmansdale, Cumberland Co., Pa., of heart trouble, June 22, 1892, Bro. George Myers, aged 36 years, 9 months and 10 days. Bro. George leaves a wife (a sister) and four daughters. Our brother had been ailing since January last. Thinking that his time was short, and wishing to obey in all things, he called for the brethren and was anointed. Funeral services and burial at the Baker meeting-house, near Churchtown, Cumberland Co., Pa. Services conducted by the home brethren from the text of his choice, "Set thy house in order, for thou shalt die and not live."

DANIEL LANDIS.

SHAFFER.—In the Shiloh congregation, Barbour Co., W. Va., June 6, 1892, sister Martha Shaffer, wife of Andrew Shaffer, aged 40 years, 11 months and 26 days. Deceased was a daughter of Bro. Peter Bolyard. She leaves a family of eight children. Funeral services from Rev. 14: 13 by Eld. Elias Anvil. LEVI POLING.

BEACHLEY.—In the South Waterloo church, Iowa, June 23, 1892, Sally, wife of Eld. Elias K. Beachly, aged 79 years, 3 months and 14 days. Sister Beachley was one of the pioneers of the South Waterloo church, and it can be truly said of her that she was a mother in Israel. She leaves an aged husband and a large circle of relatives. Funeral services by Bro. I. M. Gibson, from 1 Cor. 15: 20.

S. H. MILLER.

WAREHAM.—In Pocahontas County, Iowa, March 28, 1892, Lillie, aged 7 years, 1 month and 19 days; March 31, Goldie, aged 9 years and 6 days; April 1, Russell, aged 5 years and 18 days; April 5, Bertie, aged 1 year, 8 months and 22 days. These children died of diphtheria, and were the children of Bro. William and sister Delilah Wareham. The grief-stricken parents were received into the church by baptism during our late Annual Meeting at Cedar Rapids, Iowa. The funeral services of the above children were held in the Methodist church, at Fonela, Iowa, June 26, 1892, by the writer, from Matt. 19: 13, 14. S. H. MILLER.

SPEICHER.—At Waterloo, Iowa, June 20, 1892, from the effects of a railroad accident, Bro. Ephraim Speicher, aged 70 years. Funeral occasion improved by the Brethren.

L. R. PEIFER.

HEETER.—In the Yellow Creek church, Pa., May 29, 1892, sister Cora Heeter, wife of Thomas Heeter, aged 19 years, 5 months and 6 days. Not quite a year ago she was married. She leaves a husband, father, mother and two brothers. Funeral services by brethren L. L. Holsinger and C. L. Buck. BARBARA HOLSINGER.

HECKMAN.—In the Spring Creek church, Kosciusko Co., Ind., June 6, 1892, Bro. Henry Heckman, aged 75 years and 17 days. Deceased was born in Clark County, Ohio, May 19, 1817, and came to Kosciusko Co., Ind., in 1858, where he remained until death. He was never married. Funeral services conducted by Bro. Gorman Heeter and others.

R. ROSS.

FRY.—In the Quemahoning church, Somerset Co., Pa., June 19, 1892, Bro. Daniel Fry, aged 74 years and 18 days. Deceased was a sufferer for seven years, but bore his sufferings with Christian patience, until he gently passed away. Funeral services by J. W. Blough and the writer.

S. P. ZIMMERMAN.

BOLLINGER.—In the Sugar Creek church, Ind., June 3, 1892, Sophia Bollinger, aged 48 years, 9 months and 29 days. She leaves a husband, four daughters and two sons. Funeral services at Tunker, Ind. Interment in the Eberhart cemetery. Mother suffered for six years but bore it patiently unto the end, because her hopes were built on high.

EMMA KIMMEL.

HECKLER.—In the Indian Creek church, Montgomery Co., Pa., Elizabeth Yocum Heckler, aged 83 years and 3 months. Grandmother was "only waiting" for her summons and we feel that she is at rest. ELIZABETH H. DELP.

MURRAY.—At Pennsville, Pa., in the Fayette congregation, May 12, 1892, Katie Murray, aged 17 months. Services by the writer.

FREED.—Also at the same place, June 26, 1892, Robert Freed, aged 74 years, 5 months and 26 days. Friend Freed never made a profession of religion, but his wife is a member of the River Brethren church. Services by the writer.

H. S. MYERS.

The Gospel Messenger

Is the recognized organ of the German Baptist or Brethren's church, and advocates the form of doctrine taught in the New Testament and pleads for a return to apostolic and primitive Christianity.

It recognizes the New Testament as the only infallible rule of faith and practice, and maintains that Faith toward God, Repentance from dead works, Regeneration of the heart and mind, baptism by Trine Immersion for remission of sins unto the reception of the Holy Ghost by the laying on of hands, are the means of adoption into the household of God,—the church militant.

It also maintains that Feet-washing, as taught in John 13, both by example and command of Jesus, should be observed in the church.

That the Lord's Supper, instituted by Christ and as universally observed by the apostles and the early Christians, is a full meal, and, in connection with the Communion, should be taken in the evening or after the close of the day.

That the Salutation of the Holy Kiss, or Kiss of Charity, is binding upon the followers of Christ.

That War and Retaliation are contrary to the spirit and self-denying principles of the religion of Jesus Christ.

That the principle of Plain Dressing and of Non-conformity to the world, as taught in the New Testament, should be observed by the followers of Christ.

That the Scriptural duty of Anointing the Sick with Oil, in the Name of the Lord, James 5: 14, is binding upon all Christians.

It also advocates the church's duty to support Missionary and Tract Work, thus giving to the Lord for the spread of the Gospel and for the conversion of sinners.

In short, it is a Vindicator of all that Christ and the apostles have enjoined upon us, and aims, amid the conflicting theories and discords of modern Christendom, to point out ground that all must concede to be infallibly safe.

☞ The above principles of our Fraternity are set forth on our "Brethren's Envelopes." Use them! Price, 15 cents per package; 40 cents per hundred.

Announcements.

LOVE-FEASTS.

July 16 and 17, Grand Junction, Iowa. Those coming on the North-western R. R., will stop off at Beaver; those on the Rock Island R. R., will stop off at Grand Junction. A series of meetings one week prior to feast.

Aug. 13, at 2 P. M., Ogan's Creek church, five miles south-east of North Manchester, Wabash Co., Ind.

Aug. 19, at 4 P. M., the Bear Creek church, Palmer, Ill.

Sept. 2, at 4 P. M., Sugar Creek church, Sangamon County, Ill., 2 miles east of Auburn, Ill.

Sept. 3, at 5 P. M., at Independence, Kans.

Sept. 3, at 10 A. M., Washington church, Kans., at Bro. Wm. R. Phillippi's residence, three miles south, and three and one-half miles west of Washington, Kans.

Sept. 3, at 3 P. M., Silver Creek church, Cowley Co., Kans.

Sept. 3, Mill Creek church, Adams Co., Ill.

Sept. 3 and 4, English River congregation, Keokuk Co., Iowa.

Sept. 6, at 4 P. M., Indian Creek congregation, Fayette Co., Pa. Series of meetings to commence Aug. 27.

Sept. 8, at 10 A. M., Monroe County church, Iowa.

Sept. 7 and 8, at 2 P. M., Scott Valley, Coffey Co., Kans., at the house of W. A. Smith, one mile east and five south of Waverly. A series of meetings to be held in connection with the feast.

Sept. 10 and 11, Farmbenville, Calhoun Co., Iowa. Series of meetings in connection, beginning one week previous.

Sept. 17, at 2 P. M., Bethel congregation, at the Bethlehem meeting-house, Holt Co., Mo. For any information address Jos. Andes, Mound City, Holt Co., Mo.

Sept. 24, at 5 P. M., in La Porte church, La Porte, Ind. Trains will be met in the forenoon and early afternoon of the day of meeting.

Sept. 21, at 3 P. M., Martin's Creek church, Wayne Co., Ill.

Sept. 24 and 25, at 3 P. M., Lanark church, Carroll Co., Ill.

Sept. 28, South Bend church, Ind.

Sept. 28, at 10 A. M., Spring Creek church, Kosciusko Co., Ind.

Sept. 29 and 30, at 1 P. M., Rock Creek, Whiteside Co., Ill.

Sept. 30, at 10 A. M., Nettle Creek church, near Hagerstown, Wayne Co., Ind.

Sept. 30, at 2 P. M., Milmine church, Piatt Co., Ill.

Oct. 1, at 2 P. M., Sugar Creek church, Allen Co., Ohio.

Oct. 1, at 5 P. M., Osage church, Crawford Co., Kans.

Oct. 1, at 5 P. M., Pokagon church, Dowagiac, Cass Co., Mich.

Oct. 1, at 4 P. M., Logan church, near DeGraff, Ohio.

Oct. 1 and 2, Saginaw church, Mich.

Oct. 1 and 2, at 1: 30 P. M., Walnut Valley congregation, Barton Co., Kans.

Oct. 1 and 2, at 3 P. M., Alleghany congregation, Grant Co., W. Va.

Oct. 3, Maple Grove church, Norton Co., Kans.

Oct. 1, at 10 A. M., Appanoose church, Kans.

Oct. 1, at 10 A. M., Eight Mile church, Ind., at the town of Markle.

Oct. 1 and 2, at 11 A. M., Riverside, Iowa. Those coming by rail will stop at Iowa Junction, on B. C. R. & N. R. R., where they will be met.

Oct. 1, at 10 A. M., Stone Lick church, Clermont Co., Ohio.

Oct. 1, at 10 A. M., in the Beaver Dam church, Kosciusko Co., Ind., near the town of Burket.

Oct. 1, at 2 P. M., Rosan church, Ind.

Oct. 6, at 3 P. M., Spring Creek church, in the Keith's church-house, eleven miles south-west of Rossoe, Kans.

Oct. 2 and 3, at 10 A. M., Shannon, Ill.

Oct. 7, Black River church, Van Buren Co., Mich. Brethren coming by rail will stop off at Bangor.

Oct. 7, at 2 P. M., Lodoga, Ind.

Oct. 7, at 2 P. M., Kaskaskia church, Fayette Co., Ill., ten miles south-west of Beecher City, Ill. Those coming by rail will be met at the above-named place by informing Granville Nevinger.

Oct. 7, at 10 A. M., Sugar Creek, Whitley Co., Ind.

Oct. 7, at 2 P. M., Raccoon Creek church, Montgomery Co., Ind., one and one-half miles north-west of Ladoga.

Oct. 8, at 2 P. M., Greentown church, at Greentown, Howard Co., Ind.

Oct. 8, at 3: 30 P. M., Maple Glen church, Somerset Co., Pa.

Oct. 8, at 4 P. M., in the Elkhart Valley church, Elkhart Co., Ind.

Oct. 8 and 9, at 1 P. M., Arnold's Grove, Ill.

Oct. 8, at 10 A. M., Dry Creek church, Linn Co., Iowa, one mile east of Robins Station.

Oct. 8, Swan Creek congregation, Ohio, 3½ miles west of Delta, Ohio.

Oct. 8, at 4 P. M., Washington Creek church, Douglas Co., Kans.

Oct. 14, at 2 P. M., Union church, Marshal Co., Ind., five miles west of Plymouth. Trains will be met at both Plymouth and Burr Oak.

Oct. 14, Union church, Plymouth, Marshall Co., Ind. This church would like to have some brother hold meeting a week or ten days after.

Oct. 19 and 20, at 10 A. M., Pigeon Creek church, Ill., at the Oak Grove meeting-house.

Oct. 21 and 22, at 2 P. M., Oasis church, Madison Co., Ind., 3½ miles east of Summitville.

Nov. 5, at 3 P. M., Big Creek church, Richland Co., Ill., 3½ miles North-east of Parkersburg, Ill. Conveyances will be at the above place by informing J. M. Forney.

GOOD BOOKS FOR ALL.

ANY book in the market furnished at publishers' lowest retail price by the Brethren's Publishing Company, Mt. Morris, Ill. *Special prices* given when books are purchased in quantities. When ordering books, not on our list, if possible give title, name of author, and address of publishers.

The Throne of David.—By J. H. Ingraham. Cloth. $1.50.

Homiletics and Pastoral Theology.—By W. G. T. Shedd. Cloth. $2.50.

Lectures on Preaching.—By Rev. Phillips Brooks. Cloth, 16mo. $1.50

Josephus' Complete Works.—Large type, 1 vol. 8vo. Illustrated with many steel and wood engravings. Library sheep. $3.00.

The Doctrine of the Holy Spirit.—By James B Walker. Cloth. $1.25.

The New Testament History.—By Wm. Smith. Cloth. $1.25.

The Path of Life.—An interesting tract for everybody. Price, 10 cents per copy; 100 copies, $6.00.

Smith's Bible Dictionary.— Edited by Peloubet. Cloth. $2.00; leather, $3.00.

Ante-Nicene Christian Library.—A collection of all the works of the Fathers of the Christian Church prior to the Council of Nicaea. Edited by Rev. Alexander Roberts, D. D., and James Donaldson, LL. D. Twenty-four vols. 8 vo. Per vol. $3.00.

Sacred Geography and Antiquities.— A practical, helpful work for Bible students, ministers and Sunday-school teachers. Price, $2.25.

The Origin and Growth of Religion.—Hibbert Lectures. By T. W. R. Davids. Cloth, 8vo, $2.50.

Bible Work, or Bible Reader's Commentary on the New Testament.—By J. G. Butler. Two vols. 8vo, $10.00.

Popular Commentary on the New Testament.—Edited by Philip Schaff. Four volumes, 8vo. Matthew, Mark and Luke: $6.00. John and the Acts: $6.00. Romans to Philemon: $5.00. Hebrews to Revelation: $5.00.

The Life and Epistles of the Apostle Paul.—By W. J. Conybeare. Cloth, $1.00.

The Prince of the House of David.—By J. H. Ingraham. Cloth, $1.50.

The Great Events of History.—By W. F. Collier. Cloth, $1.25.

Trine Immersion.— A vindication of the apostolic form of Christian baptism. By Eld. James Quinter. A most complete and reliable work on the subject. Price, cloth, single copy, $1.25; leather, $1.75.

The Old Testament History.—By William Smith. Cloth. $1.25.

Biblical Antiquities.—By John Nevin. Gives a concise account of Bible times and customs; invaluable to all students of Bible subjects. Price, $1.60.

Biblical Theology of the Old Testament.—By R. F. Weidner. Cloth. $1.25.

The Normal College.

THE Fall Term of fifteen weeks opens Sept. 12. For recommendations and inducements, we point you to the work that has been done and the success of its graduates. In proportion to the number of the graduates, no school in the country can show a better record. A good, solid, practical education is what you want, and this is what we propose to give. For special information, Catalogues and a *free* copy of the *Juniata Echo*, address H. B. Brumbaugh, President, or J. H. Brumbaugh, Principal, Huntingdon, Pa.   28tf

Two Harvest Excursions—Half Rates to the West

August 30 and September 27.

On these dates the *Burlington Route* will sell tickets from Chicago, Peoria and St. Louis to the farming districts of Nebraska, Colorado and Northern Kansas. Half rates will apply, and tickets will be good for twenty days. Nebraska in one year produced three hundred million bushels of corn, besides other grain, fruit and live-stock. Write for free pamphlets, maps, etc., to P. S. Eustis, G. P. A., Burlington, Route, Chicago, Ill.

EUROPE
AND
Bible Lands

A new edition of this deservedly popular work has recently been published. It retains all the excellencies of its predecessors, and with those who are interested in Bible study this work will always remain a favorite. Those who have read the ordinary book of travel will be surprised to find "Europe and Bible Lands" of thrilling interest for both old and young. The large number of books, already sold, proves that the work is of more than ordinary merit.

A fair supply of the last edition of this work is still on hand. Those who have not yet secured a copy of the work should embrace this opportunity of securing it. Price, in fine cloth binding, only $1.50 per copy, post-paid. To agents who are prepared to push an active canvass of the work, we are prepared to give special inducements. Write us. BRETHREN'S PUBLISHING CO.,

Mt. Morris, Ill.

Announcements.

LOVE FEASTS.

July 16 and 17, Grand Junction, Iowa. Those coming on the North-western R. R., will stop off at Beaver; those on the Rock Island R. R., will stop off at Grand Junction. A series of meetings one week prior to feast.

Aug. 13, at 2 P. M., Ogan's Creek church, five miles south-east of North Manchester, Wabash Co., Ind.

Aug. 19, at 4 P. M., the Bear Creek church, Sangamon County, Ill., 2 miles east of Auburn, Ill.

Sept. 2, at 5 P. M., at Independence, Kans.

Sept. 3, 10 to A. M Washington church, Kans., at Bro. Wm. R. Phillippi's residence, three miles south, and three and one-half miles west of Washington, Kans.

Sept. 3, at 10 P. M., Silver Creek church, Cowley Co., Kans.

Sept. 3, Mill Creek church, Adams Co. Ill.

Sept. 3 and 4, English River congregation, Keokuk Co., Iowa.

Sept. 4, at 4 P. M., Indian Creek congregation, Fayette Co., Pa. Series of meetings to commence Aug. 27.

Sept. 9, 10 10 A. M., Monroe County church, Iowa.

Sept. 7 and 8, at 2 P. M , Scott Valley, Coffey Co., Kans , at the house of W. A. Smith, one mile east and five south of Waverly. A series of meetings to be held in connection with the feast.

Sept. 10 and 11, Farrshonville, Calhoun Co., Iowa. Series of meetings in connection, beginning one week previous.

Sept. 17, at 2 P. M., Bethel congregation, at the Bethlehem meeting-house, Holt Co., Mo. For any information address Jos. Andes, Mound City, Holt Co., Mo.

Sept. 20, at 2 P. M., in La Porte church, La Porte, Ind. Trains will be met in the forenoon and early afternoon of the day of meeting.

Sept. 24, at 5 P. M., Martin's Creek church, Wayne Co., Ill.

Sept. 24 and 25, at 3 P. M., Loxash church, Carroll Co., Ill.

Sept. 28, South Bend church, Ind.

Sept. 28, at 10 A. M., Spring Creek church, Kosciusko Co., Ind.

Sept. 29 and 30, at 2 P. M., Rock Creek, Whiteside Co., Ill.

Sept. 30, at 10 A. M , Nettle Creek church, near Hagerstown, Wayne Co., Ind.

Sept. 30, at 2 P. M , Milmine church, Piatt Co., Ill.

Oct. 1, at 2 P. M., Sugar Creek church, Allen Co., Ohio.

Oct. 1, at 2 P. M., Osage church, Crawford Co., Kans.

Oct. 1, at 2 P. M., Pokagon church, Dowagiac, Cass Co., Mich.

Oct. 1, at 4 P. M., Logan church, near DeGraff, Ohio.

Oct. 1 and 2, Saginaw church, Mich.

Oct. 1 and 2, at 2: 30 P. M., Walnut Valley congregation, Barton Co., Kans.

Oct. 1 and 2, at 1 P. M., Alleghany congregation, Grant Co., W. Va.

Oct. 1, Maple Grove church, Norton Co., Kans.

Oct. 1, at 10 A. M., Appanoose church, Kans.

Oct. 1, at 10 A. M., Eight Mile church, Ind., at the town of Markle.

Oct. 1 and 2, at 11 A. M , Riverside, Iowa. Those coming by rail will stop at Iowa Junction, on B. C. R. & N. R. R., where they will be met.

Oct. 1, at 10 A. M., Sioux Lick church, Clermont Co., Ohio.

Oct. 6, at 10 A. M., in the Beaver Dam church, Kosciusko Co., Ind., near the town of Burket.

Oct. 5, at 2 P. M., Rosass church, Ind.

Oct. 6, at 2 P. M., Spring Creek church, in the Keith's church-house, eleven miles south-west of Rosass, Kans.

Oct. 6 and 7, at 10 A. M., Shannon, Ill.

Oct. 7, Black River church, Van Buren Co., Mich. Brethren coming by rail will stop off at Bangor.

Oct. 7, at 2 P. M., Ladoga, Ind.

Oct. 7, at 2 P. M., Kaskaskia church, Fayette Co., Ill., ten miles north-west of Fetcher City, Ill. Those coming by rail will be met at the above-named place by informing Granville Havinger.

Oct. 7, at 10 A. M., Sugar Creek, Whitley Co., Ind.

Oct. 7, at 2 P. M., Raccoon Creek church, Montgomery Co., Ind., one and one-half miles north-west of Ladoga.

Oct. 8, at 2 P. M., Greentown church, at Greentown, Howard Co., Ind.

Oct. 8, at 3: 30 P. M., Maple Glen church, Somerset Co., Pa.

Oct. 8, at 4 P. M., in the Elkhorn Valley church, Elkhart Co., Ind.

Oct. 8 and 9, at 2 P. M., Arnold's Grove, Ill.

Oct. 8, at 4 P. M., Dry Creek church, Linn Co., Iowa, one mile west of Robins Station.

Oct. 8, at 4 P. M., Swan Creek congregation, Ohio, 5½ miles west of Delta, Ohio.

Oct. 8, at 4 P. M., Washington Creek church, Douglas Co., Kans

Oct. 14, at 4 P. M., Union church, Marshal Co , Ind , five miles west of Plymouth. Trains will be met at both Plymouth and Burr Oak.

Oct. 14, Union church, Plymouth, Marshall Co., Ind. This church would like to have some brother hold meeting a week or ten days after.

Oct. 19 and 20, at 10 A. M , Pigeon Creek church, Ill., at the Oak Grove meeting-house.

Oct. 20, at 4 P. M., Oasis church, Madison Co., Ind., 3½ miles east of Summitville.

Nov. 5, at 3 P. M., Big Creek church, Richland Co., Ill., 3½ miles North-east of Parkersburg, Ill. Conveyances will be at the above place by informing J. M. Forney.

GOOD BOOKS FOR ALL.

ANY book in the market furnished at publishers' lowest retail price by the Brethren's Publishing Company, Mt. Morris, Ill. *Special prices* given when books are purchased in quantities. When ordering books, not on our list, if possible give title, name of author, and address of publishers.

The Throne of David.—By J. H. Ingraham. Cloth. $2.50.

Homiletics and Pastoral Theology.—By W. G. T. Shedd. Cloth, $2.50.

Lectures on Preaching.—By Rev. Phillips Brooks. Cloth, 16mo, $1.50

Josephus' Complete Works.—Large type, 1 vol. 8vo. Illustrated with many steel and wood engravings. Library sheep, $3.00.

The Doctrine of the Holy Spirit.—By James B. Walker. Cloth, $1.25.

The New Testament History.—By Wm. Smith. Cloth, $1.25.

The Path of Life.—An interesting tract for everybody. Price, 10 cents per copy; 100 copies, $6.00.

Smith's Bible Dictionary.— Edited by Peloubet. Cloth. $2.00; leather, $3.00.

Ante-Nicene Christian Library.—A collection of all the works of the Fathers of the Christian Church prior to the Council of Nicea. Edited by Rev. Alexander Roberts, D. D., and James Donaldson, LL. D. Twenty-four vols. 8 vo. Per vol., $3.00.

Sacred Geography and Antiquities.— A practical, helpful work for Bible students, ministers and Sunday-school teachers. Price, $2.25.

The Origin and Growth of Religion.—Hibbert Lectures. By T. W. R. Davids. Cloth, 8vo, $2.50.

Bible Work, or Bible Reader's Commentary on the New Testament.—By J. G. Butler. Two vols. 8vo, $10.00.

Popular Commentary on the New Testament.—Edited by Philip Schaff. Four volumes, 8vo. Matthew, Mark and Luke: $6.00. John and the Acts: $6.00. Romans to Philemon: $6.00. Hebrews to Revelation: $5.00.

The Life and Epistles of the Apostle Paul.—By W. J. Coneybeare. Cloth. $1.00.

The Prince of the House of David.—By J. H. Ingraham. Cloth, $1.25.

The Great Events of History.—By W.F. Collier. Cloth. $1.25.

Trine Immersion.— A vindication of the apostolic form of Christian baptism. By Eld. James Quinter. A most complete and reliable work on the subject. Price, cloth, single copy, $1.25; leather, $1.75.

The Old Testament History.—By William Smith. Cloth, $1.25.

Biblical Antiquities.—By John Nevin. Gives a concise account of Bible times and customs; invaluable to all students of Bible subjects. Price, $1.50.

Biblical Theology of the Old Testament.—By R. F. Weidner. Cloth, $2.25.

The Normal College.

THE Fall Term of fifteen weeks opens Sept. 12. For recommendations and inducements, we point you to the work that has been done and the success of its graduates. In proportion to the number of the graduates, no school in the country can show a better record. A good, solid, practical education is what you want, and this is what we propose to give.

For special information, Catalogues and a *free copy* of the *Juniata Echo*, address H. B. Brumbaugh, President, or J. H. Brumbaugh, Principal, Huntingdon, Pa. 28tf

---

Two Harvest Excursions—Half Rates to the West.

August 30 and September 27.

On these dates the *Burlington Route* will sell tickets from Chicago, Peoria and St. Louis to the farming districts of Nebraska, Colorado and Northern Kansas. Half rates will apply, and tickets will be good for twenty days. Nebraska in one year produced three hundred million bushels of corn, besides other grain, fruit and live-stock. Write for free pamphlets, maps, etc., to P. S. Eustis, G. P. A., Burlington, Route, Chicago, Ill.

EUROPE
AND
Bible Lands

A new edition of this deservedly popular work has recently been published. It retains all the excellencies of its predecessors, and with those who are interested in Bible study this work will always remain a favorite. Those who have read the ordinary book of travel will be surprised to find "Europe and Bible Lands" of thrilling interest for both old and young. The large number of books, already sold, proves that the work is of more than ordinary merit.

A fair supply of the best edition of this work is still on hand. Those who have not yet secured a copy of the work should embrace this opportunity of securing it. Price, in fine cloth binding, only $1.50 per copy, post-paid. To agents who are prepared to push an active canvass of the work, we are prepared to give special inducements. Write at once.

BRETHREN'S PUBLISHING CO.,
Mt Morris, Ill

CANCERS, TUMORS, ETC.

Successfully treated by Dr. G. N. Boteler, of Way near Borough, Pa., where he has practiced for the last sixteen years. Dr. Boteler is a graduate of the University of Maryland, at Baltimore City. References given and correspondence solicited. Address, Dr. G. W. Boteler, Waynesborough, Pa. 91tto

---

How It Is Done!

A seed-dealer stated that the first five years he was in business, he could not ascertain that he made anything, but he was learning. Before ten years he was clearing thousands each year. A friend of his was doing well in manufacturing ropes, but was dissatisfied because he was not getting rich fast enough. His friends advised him to

"Hang to the Ropes,"

but he would try something else. He traded his rope factory for a grist-mill, bought grain, and broke a bank by his large failure.

Some farmers conclude cows are most profitable. They purchase a herd, erect buildings and begin well; but it being a new business they do not succeed as they expected. The next year they sell their dairy and buy sheep. That year the price of wool is very low, and they hear that much money is made in raising tobacco. Thus they go on, changing from one to another, never succeeding in anything, because they do not

Stick to It.

The one who does stick to an honorable business will prosper in the end. This is always true. The same is true in securing an education. Every young man and woman may secure it,—can secure it. I know who is so, and

The First 300 Young People

who write me shall know *how* I know it is so. No matter how far you are away; write, you will never regret it. In writing, call attention to what I promise here. Address:

J. G. ROYER,
Mt. Morris, Ill.

Be sure to mention this paper.

✦ESSAYS✦

"Study to show thyself approved unto God; a workman that needeth not be ashamed, rightly dividing the Word of Truth."

GOD'S APPOINTMENTS.

THIS thing on which thy heart was set, this thing that cannot be,
This weary, disappointing day, that dawns, my friend, for thee;—
Be-comforted; God knoweth best, the God whose name is Love,
Whose tender care is evermore our passing lives above.
He sends thee disappointment? Well, then, take it from his hand.
Shall God's appointment seem less good than what thyself had planned?

'Twas in thy mind to go abroad. He bids thee stay at home?
Oh! happy home; thrice happy if to it thy guest he come.
'Twas in thy mind thy friend to see. The Lord says, "Nay, not yet."
Be confident; the meeting time thy Lord will not forget.
'Twas in thy mind to work for him. His will is, " Child! sit still;"
And surely 'tis thy blessedness to mind the Master's will.
Accept thy disappointment, friend, thy gift from God's own hand.
Shall God's appointment seem less good than what thyself had planned?

So, day by day and step by step, sustain thy failing strength,
From strength to strength, indeed, go on through all the journey's length.
God bids thee tarry now and then, forbear the weak complaint;
God's leisure brings the weary rest, and cordial gives the faint.
God bids thee labor, and the place is thick with thorn and brier;
But he will share the hardest task, until he calls thee higher.
So take each disappointment, friend; 'tis at thy Lord's command.
Shall God's appointment seem less good than what thyself had planned?

　　　　　　　　　—*Selected.*

PERSECUTION OF THE JEWS IN RUSSIA.

THE following is a short statement of the persecution of the Jews in Russia, prepared for publication by the Russo-Jewish Committee. It gives in a succinct form a complete summary of the laws affecting the Jews in Russia.

1. The Jews have long been compelled,—with certain exceptions only,—to reside within the fifteen provinces known as the "Pale of the Jewish Settlement." This, though a geographically large tract of country, contains comparatively few towns.

2. They may not live within fifty versts (about thirty-three miles) of the frontier. 'A large smuggling business is carried on by Russians, and the object of the law is to prevent Jews from participating in this profitable business. The effect, however, is to prevent them from carrying on legitimate trade with neighboring countries.

3. Under the May laws, which prohibit Jews from settling "outside the cities and towns," those settled in villages since May, 1882, are expelled therefrom and driven into the overcrowded towns of the Pale. Even "skilled artisans," heretofore allowed to reside anywhere, have been expelled from the villages of the Pale.

4. Under certain decisions of the Senate, interpreting the May Laws, Jews settled in villages before May, 1882, have the right of remaining there, but only provided they do not move therefrom. Few can earn a livelihood under such a condition; so the force of circumstances drives many who have the right to remain villagers into the towns of the Pale.

5. Many have been driven out of the villages who had been settled there before 1882, but whose names had not been inscribed as villagers. Others have been expelled because they had temporarily left the village and returned since 1882.

Many who had temporarily left on military duty have been similarly expelled.

6. Suburbs of towns and small towns have been in many cases officially declared-to come within the category of villages, and the Jews have been expelled therefrom.

7. Under the May Laws, Jews are prohibited from owning or holding on lease, or even managing land. Those, therefore, who have the right to remain villagers, in consequence of settlement before 1882, cannot find a livelihood, and the majority must therefore migrate to the overcrowded towns of the Pale.

8. Jews are, under the May Laws, not allowed to take a mortgage of land; so they are debarred from the ordinary security for loans on farms.

Skilled artisans and their families have hitherto been allowed to reside outside the Pale of Settlement, subject to certain conditions. Under recent rules the Guild-masters are required to examine Jews claiming residence in Russia proper; and if these are found inefficient in their trade, or not actually in work, or past work by reason of age, they are expelled and returned into the Pale of Settlement.

10. The definition of "skilled artisan " has been contracted for the purpose of excluding Jews. It has lately been declared that bakers, vinegar makers, glaziers, printers' compositors, and other workers in light occupations, are not artisans, and Jews carrying on these trades have been accordingly expelled from towns in Russia proper, and driven into the towns of the Pale.

11. Until lately Jews of all classes were allowed to reside in the Grand Duchy of Finland, and in Courland, which, though part of the Russian Empire, had constitutions of their own. These provinces having been lately included in Russia proper, large numbers of Jews, not being artisans or merchants of the first Guild, have been expelled and driven into the Pale. Widows of men, who resided in Riga (Courland), have, though natives of Riga, been expelled therefrom and driven into the Pale, the reason given being that their husbands were natives of the Pale, and would, if still living, have been sent there.

12. Jews have lately been also expelled in large numbers from certain important commercial centers outside the Pale, such as Rostoff on the Don, Tomsk, and other towns in Siberia, where, for commercial reasons, they have hitherto been allowed to settle; also from the Trans-Caspian-provinces, and from Batoum, and other Asiatic places formerly owned by Turkey. The numbers so expelled are very numerous. Those in the Trans-Caspian provinces have not been merely expelled, but have been convoyed into the Pale of Settlement by *étape*; that is, convoyed in gangs of prisoners on foot between 1,500 and 1,600 miles, halting on the way only in places where there are prisons. This has taken place during the present winter, one year ago, and it is reported that large numbers of the victims died on the journey. Those who reach their destination find, in the Pale, no manner of livelihood.

13. The result of all these expulsions is not only to deprive of their livelihood the persons expelled, who have to commence a new career in the Pale of Settlement, but also to injure the original inhabitants of the towns of the Pale, who have to sustain the competition of these new arrivals, to incur the burden of a crowd of pauperized people, and to find the house-space within limits that were already too contracted.

14. Besides expulsions from Russia proper into the Jewish Pale, a very large number of expulsions of foreign Jews have taken place, not only from Russia proper, but from the Pale itself. Under recent legislation no foreign Jew may reside in Russia, the exceptions being so rare as to

be ·scarcely worthy· of notice. Among those classed as foreign Jews are those inhabitants of Bessarabia, who, when that province was transferred to Russia under the Treaty of Berlin, neglected to register themselves as Russian citizens. All these are now expelled or prosecuted as alien vagrants or rogues and vagabonds (*brodyaga*). Any Jew, who is unable to prove the place of his birth, may be prosecuted in the same way; and, as registration was formerly a lax institution in Russia, prosecutions and expulsions of Jews as alien vagrants are of no rare occurrence.

15. Jews are not allowed to occupy any government or public appointment. They have accordingly been dismissed from railway and post-office service, from the posts of school-masters and from notarial offices. They may no longer be appointed doctors, or even veterinary surgeons in the army. Under a law made about a year ago, no Jew may become an advocate, though fully qualified by examination, without the special sanction of the Minister of the Interior, and, as a matter of fact, that sanction has not once been given. According to a recent report of the *Times* correspondent in Vienna, all Jewish advocates practicing in St. Petersburg and Moscow are to be expelled. No Jew may become an officer in the army, though bound to serve in the rank and file like all other Russians. The penalty of evading military service is higher for the Jew than for others. Notwithstanding many evasions, the Jews serve in the army beyond their due proportion. No Jew may serve in the navy.

16. The attainment by a Jew of the highest degree in any University Faculty entitles him to the privilege of residing outside the Pale. A large number of Jews have hitherto been candidates for university distinctions, but recent laws have limited admissions not only to the universities, but to the gymnasia, the proportion fixed four years ago, being ten per cent in the Pale, five per cent outside of it, and three per cent in St. Petersburg and Moscow. The injustice of this limitation in a place like Odessa, where one-third of the inhabitants are Jews, is obvious. The Jews are not allowed schools of their own. Baron Hirsch's proposal to give two millions sterling for establishing technical schools for Jews was rejected by the Russian government. In the special technical schools, built and endowed by certain rich Jews, the proportion of Jews admitted is limited in the same way as if they had been established by the government.

17. Jewish children attending the public schools are required to be present on the Jewish Sabbath, the law stating that "their entrance to such institutions serves as evidence that they and their parents are no longer bound to that exclusiveness which demands the severest observance of Saturday."

19. Jews are not allowed to engage in the mining industry, or to hold mining shares, or to act as agents for persons engaged in mining. If they already hold any mining shares, they must sell them within two years.

20. Those Jews who, as high graduates of a university, or as merchants of the first guild (men paying at least 1,000 roubles taxation annually), are allowed to reside outside the Pale may have no more than two Jewish *employees* in their service. A privileged Jew, who wished his aged parents to reside with him outside the Pale, had to register the one as his valet, and the other as his cook.

21. Jews are prohibited from forwarding goods, as agents or *employees*, from frontier custom houses to localities outside the Pale. There are numerous other laws tending to cramp the trading of Jews, both inside and outside the Pale. Even the merchant of the first guild, who is allowed to reside outside the Pale, is subject to

❖ESSAYS❖

GOD'S APPOINTMENTS.

This thing on which thy heart was set, this thing that can-
　not be,
This weary, disappointing day, that dawns, my friend, for
　thee;—
Be comforted; God knoweth best, the God whose name is
　Love,
Whose tender care is evermore our passing lives above.
He sends thee disappointment? Well, then, take it from his
　hand.
Shall God's appointment seem less good than what thyself
　had planned?

'Twas in thy mind to go abroad. He bids thee stay at home?
Oh! happy home; thrice happy if to it thy guest he come.
'Twas in thy mind thy friend to see. The Lord says, "Nay,
　not yet."
Be confident; the meeting time thy Lord will not forget.
'Twas in thy mind to work for him. His will is, "Child! sit
　still;"
And surely 'tis thy blessedness to mind the Master's will.
Accept thy disappointment, friend, thy gift from God's own
　hand.
Shall God's appointment seem less good than what thyself
　had planned?

So, day by day and step by step, sustain thy failing strength,
From strength to strength, indeed, go on through all the
　journey's length.
God bids thee tarry now and then, forbear the weak com-
　plaint;
God's leisure brings the weary rest, and cordial gives the
　faint.
God bids thee labor, and the place is thick with thorn and
　brier;
But he will share the hardest task, until he calls thee higher.
So take each disappointment, friend; 'tis at thy Lord's com-
　mand.
Shall God's appointment seem less good than what thyself
　had planned?
　　　　　　　　　　　　　　　　　—Selected.

PERSECUTION OF THE JEWS IN RUSSIA.

The following is a short statement of the persecution of the Jews in Russia, prepared for publication by the Russo-Jewish Committee. It gives
in a succinct form a complete summary of the
laws affecting the Jews in Russia.

1. The Jews have long been compelled,—with
certain exceptions only,—to reside within the fifteen provinces known as the "Pale of the Jewish Settlement." This, though a geographically
large tract of country, contains comparatively few
towns.

2. They may not live within fifty versts (about
thirty-three miles) of the frontier. A large
smuggling business is carried on by Russians,
and the object of the law is to prevent Jews from
participating in this profitable business. The
effect, however, is to prevent them from carrying
on legitimate trade with neighboring countries.

3. Under the May laws, which prohibit Jews
from settling "outside the cities and towns," those
settled in villages since May, 1882, are expelled
therefrom and driven into the overcrowded towns
of the Pale. Even "skilled artisans," heretofore
allowed to reside anywhere, have been expelled
from the villages of the Pale.

4. Under certain decisions of the Senate, interpreting the May Laws, Jews settled in villages
before May, 1882, have the right of remaining
there, but only provided they do not move therefrom. Few can earn a livelihood under such a
condition; so the force of circumstances drives
many who have the right to remain villagers into
the towns of the Pale.

5. Many have been driven out of the villages
who had been settled there before 1882, but
whose names had not been inscribed as villagers.
Others have been expelled because they had temporarily left the village and returned since 1892.

Many who had temporarily left on military duty
have been similarly expelled.

6. Suburbs of towns and small towns have been
in many cases officially declared to come within
the category of villages, and the Jews have been
expelled therefrom.

7. Under the May Laws, Jews are prohibited
from owning or holding on lease, or even managing land. Those, therefore, who have the right
to remain villagers, in consequence of settlement
before 1882, cannot find a livelihood, and the majority must therefore migrate to the overcrowded
towns of the Pale.

8. Jews are, under the May Laws, not allowed
to take a mortgage of land; so they are debarred
from the ordinary security for loans on farms.

Skilled artisans and their families have hitherto been allowed to reside outside the Pale of Settlement, subject to certain conditions. Under recent rules the Guild-masters are required. to examine Jews claiming residence in Russia proper;
and if these are found inefficient in their trade,
or not actually in work, or past work by reason of
age, they are expelled and returned into the Pale
of Settlement.

10. The definition of "skilled artisan" has been
contracted for the purpose of excluding Jews.
It has lately been declared that bakers, vinegar makers, glaziers, printers' compositors, and
other workers in light occupations, are not artisans, and Jews carrying on these trades have been
accordingly expelled from towns in Russia proper,
and driven into the towns of the Pale.

11. Until lately Jews of all classes were allowed to reside in the Grand Duchy of Finland,
and in Courland, which, though part of the Russian Empire, had constitutions of their own.
These provinces having been lately included in
Russia proper, large numbers of Jews, not being
artisans or merchants of the first Guild, have
been expelled and driven into the Pale. Widows
of men, who resided in Riga (Courland), have,
though natives of Riga, been expelled therefrom
and driven into the Pale, the reason given being
that their husbands were natives of the Pale, and
would, if still living, have been sent there.

12. Jews have lately been also expelled in large
numbers from certain important commercial centers outside the Pale, such as Rostoff on the Don,
Tomsk, and other towns in Siberia, where, for
commercial reasons, they have hitherto been allowed to settle; also from the Trans-Caspian
provinces, and from Batoum, and other Asiatic
places formerly owned by Turkey. The numbers
so expelled are very numerous. Those in the
Trans-Caspian provinces have not been merely
expelled, but have been convoyed into the Pale of
Settlement by étape; that is, convoyed in gangs
of prisoners on foot between 1,500 and 1,600
miles, halting on the way only in places where
there are prisons. This has taken place during
the present winter, one year ago, and it is reported that large numbers of the victims died on
the journey. Those who reach their destination
find, in the Pale, no manner of livelihood.

13. The result of all these expulsions is not only to deprive of their livelihood the persons expelled, who have to commence a new career in
the Pale of Settlement, but also to injure the
original inhabitants of the towns of the Pale, who
have to sustain the competition of the new arrivals, to incur the burden of a crowd of pauperized
people, and to find for them house-space within
limits that were already too contracted.

14. Besides expulsions from Russia proper into
the Jewish Pale, a very large number of expulsions of foreign Jews have taken place, not only
from Russia proper, but from the Pale itself.
Under recent legislation no foreign Jews may reside in Russia, the exceptions being so rare as to

be scarcely worthy of notice. Among those
classed as foreign Jews are those inhabitants of
Bessarabia, who, when that province was transferred to Russia under the Treaty of Berlin, neglected to register themselves as Russian citizens.
All these are now expelled or prosecuted as alien
vagrants or rogues and vagabonds (brodyags).
Any Jew, who is unable to prove the place of his
birth, may be prosecuted in the same way; and,
as registration was formerly a lax institution in
Russia, prosecutions and expulsions of Jews as
alien vagrants are of no rare occurrence.

15. Jews are not allowed to occupy any government or public appointment. They have accordingly been dismissed from railway and post-office
service, from the posts of school-masters and
from notarial offices. They may no longer be appointed doctors, or even veterinary surgeons in
the army. Under a law made about a year ago,
no Jew may become an advocate, though fully
qualified by examination, without the special
sanction of the Minister of the Interior, and, as a
matter of fact, that sanction has not once been
given. According to a recent report of the Times
correspondent in Vienna, all Jewish advocates
practicing in St. Petersburg and Moscow are to
be expelled. No Jew may become an officer in
the army, though bound to serve in the rank and
file like all other Russians. The penalty of evading military service is higher for the Jew than
for others. Notwithstanding many evasions, the
Jews serve in the army beyond their due proportion. No Jew may serve in the navy.

16. The attainment by a Jew of the highest
degree in any University Faculty entitles him to
the privilege of residing outside the Pale. A
large number of Jews have hitherto been candidates for university distinctions, but recent laws
have limited admissions not only to the universities, but to the gymnasia, the proportion fixed
four years ago, being ten per cent in the Pale,
five per cent outside of it, and three per cent in
St. Petersburg and Moscow. The injustice of
this limitation in a place like Odessa, where one-
third of the inhabitants are Jews, is obvious.
The Jews are not allowed schools of their own.
Baron Hirsch's proposal to give two millions
sterling for establishing technical schools for the
Jews was rejected by the Russian government.
In the special technical schools, built and endowed by certain rich Jews, the proportion of
Jews admitted is limited in the same way as if
they had been established by the government.

17. Jewish children attending the public schools
are required to be present on the Jewish Sabbath, the law stating that "their entrance to
such institutions serves as evidence that they and
their parents are no longer bound to that exclusiveness which demands the severest observance of
Saturday."

19. Jews are not allowed to engage in the mining industry, or to hold mining shares, or to act
as agents for persons engaged in mining. If
they already hold any mining shares, they must
sell them within two years.

20. Those Jews who, as high graduates of a
university, or as merchants of the first guild (men
paying at least 1,000 roubles taxation annually),
are allowed to reside outside the Pale may have no
more than two Jewish employees in their service.
A privileged Jew, who wished his aged parents to
reside with him outside the Pale, had to register
the one as his valet, and the other as his cook.

21. Jews are prohibited from forwarding goods,
as agents or employees, from frontier custom
houses to localities outside the Pale. There are
numerous other laws tending to cramp the trading of Jews, both inside and outside the Pale.
Even the merchant of the first guild, who is allowed to reside outside the Pale, is subject to

here, now there, now yonder, in the face of opposition and persecution, in the land all round about, some were seen coming to the front on the question, as a last resort, separating themselves from the church of their parents, from the church into which they had been born. 'Twas no little matter, this, for there was principle at stake. These are the people history calls the "Pietists."

The village of Schwarzenau was ruled by a mild count. Here liberty of conscience was granted, and here a portion of the neighboring Pietists fled. The secluded little village soon became extensively known, and the eyes of the surrounding cities looked harshly in that direction. Peace and harmony dwelt there, and they called each other brothers, but their views, in many respects, were quite dissimilar. Now the Pietists as such, were never a church, and those in Schwarzenau, although they had their religious meetings, felt keenly the want of a church-home in which they could enjoy all the Lord's appointments. And here men and women, from various parts of the country, formerly of different religious persuasions, were united in one desire, more fully to get into Christ, there to remain.

Giving themselves scrupulously to the study of the simple Word, they agreed to follow wheresoever the Truth would lead them. They met frequently and compared the result of their investigations. They sought with great diligence, their avowed purpose being to re-establish the faith and doctrine of the apostolic church. There seems to have been a goodly number engaged in the work at first, but like any extended race for some coveted prize, as the racers near the goal, the points become more clearly defined, and the fatigue becomes greater, until, one by one, a number of the contestants drop out of the race, so too, as time became somewhat extended, and point after point had become manifestly clear to them through the Word, one by one, a number dropped out of the race, some going back to the churches from which they came, and others elsewhere, until a much smaller number than the original, finally reached the coveted goal.

The principles upon which they worked are of exceeding interest. They laid aside all creeds and confessions of faith. They laid aside the church catechisms. They spent little time in the subtleties of speculative theology. They surrounded themselves with the most reliable church histories and with Bibles, and they spent much time in fasting and prayer.

For example take their candid disposal of the question of baptism. There were some fixed ideas held by the little company. But, history gives trine immersion as the uniform baptism during the first and second centuries, and as the prevailing custom for twelve centuries. When they could find no Scripture to disqualify that for truth, and when they had found much Scripture in support of that baptism, they adopted it exclusively, in the face of that fact that the taking of such a position would place them all as unbaptized before God.

In such a way were the principles and boundary lines of the new church mapped out. I will not speak further concerning doctrine now. To the thoughtful mind there may have appeared ere this the difficulty into which they were getting. Here was a little band of believers, anxiously desiring to go forward in the fulfillment of all righteousness, but where was the administrator of the holy ordinance of baptism? Again, we are told, they sought the guidance of the Lord, and again he manifested his presence. They cast lots, and the lot fell upon one of their number. That one was to baptize another, and that other should in turn baptize the one upon whom the

lot had fallen, then the remainder of the company, and that the church might not be given the name of any man, they mutually pledged themselves that not one of them should ever reveal who among them had first baptized. Surely, in that little company of eight, nine were present. I believe the Lord wrought mightily in the restorative movement.

One morning at an early hour, thus being prepared, eight souls might have been seen passing quietly along the streets of Schwarzenau, past the borders of the village, down upon the green banks of the river Eder. There, in solitude before God, with no other witnesses than heaven and the birds, they were buried with Christ in baptism. This was in 1708, and this marks the beginning of the Brethren Reformation. They left the baptismal waters happy, with the words of Jehovah ringing in their ears: "Be fruitful and multiply." Rapidly, too, they grew during those early years. The little village became alive with Bible readers and faithful ones. But these rays of heavenly sunshine seem to have been occasioned only by a rift of the passing clouds. Opposition burst forth upon them with all its evils, and after long years of endurance the spirit of emigration seized them, and they soon began establishing their peaceful homes within the borders of free America. Earnestly did those good men engage in the work which their hands found to do. Diligently did they labor to enlarge the borders of Zion. To them belongs the credit for first calling Washington "the father of his country," and while Robert Raikes was yet a child they had a well-regulated Sunday-school going. Marked piety and reverence for the Scriptures, and their peace principles, were distinguishing characteristics, and to-day, from New Jersey to California, from Michigan to Florida, can be found faithful congregations of her unassuming worshipers. Such, in few words, is the history of the rise of the Brethren church. May her future be as great as her principles deserve.

Philadelphia, Pa.

THE GORING OX.

BY WILLIAM PETERS.

"If an ox gore a man or a woman that they die: then the ox shall be surely stoned, and his flesh shall not be eaten; but the owner of the ox shall be quit. But if the ox were wont to push with his horn in time past, and it hath been testified to his owner, and he hath not kept him in, but that he hath killed a man or a woman; the ox shall be stoned, and his owner also shall be put to death."—Ex. 21: 28, 29.

This was a law, and the owner of the ox was the responsible party, when he knew that the ox would push with his horn. There is now an ox that is goring thousands that they die, and the question is, Do the people know it? If so, who is the responsible party? I believe that their responsibility is far-reaching as we shall see if we make a proper investigation.

The ox I wish to speak of is doing much damage to the human family financially, morally and religiously. He is known as "STRONG DRINK." He wounds millions annually, and kills thousands, and makes thousands of widows and orphans, causing misery and destruction in thousands of homes. Last, but not least, he is sinking innumerable souls lower than the grave each year.

Notwithstanding the terrible results that are seen and felt in thousands of homes, there are men of intelligence, and some, to their shame, professing to be followers of the Lord Jesus, who claim that men should be protected by law to deal out this curse of our American homes. And why? Because there is money in it. They want protection for the man, who, for the sake of money, deals out this curse, that maddens the brain of men, causes them to destroy their property, beat their wives and children, abuse their neighbors, and commit crimes that they would not do if sober. Will not our Christian people, with one heart and one voice, say, "The ox must be slain, and the thousands of women and children liberated and these wrongs avenged?" I hope and pray that the professing Christians will have the power to slay the ox. This will be done as soon as all the churches become fully awakened to their duty, and the ox will be banished from our land. There are professing Christians who claim that if it was not for the license law we could not keep up public expenses, and in the towns they could not keep up needed improvements. Who wants to meet such expenses with the price of blood and the sacrifice of souls? It seems to me that such persons love darkness rather than light, because their deeds are evil. Were it not for the goring ox there would be but little need for lock-ups, jails, penitentiaries, poor-houses and insane asylums. If there were no distilleries or saloons, how many of such institutions would there be? Not one-sixth. Even if there were just as many as there are, the money spent for strong drink would cover the expense of all, and leave a large surplus for the spread of the Gospel. If our towns had the money annually spent for whiskey, they could have better sidewalks and street lights, and still have enough to feed and clothe all the poor children in the towns. Something could even be left for the missionary cause, and all would be happier and better off in heart, to say nothing of the next. It cannot be denied but that every person does suffer more or less through the direful effects of the abominable rum traffic, financially, physically or mentally, for who has a heart so hard that it is not pained to see a father, brother or friend, who has been wounded and, perhaps, is dying from the goring of this ox, to say nothing of the sufferings of mothers and children?

Go to our jails, and you will find that nine-tenths of the prisoners are there because of crimes committed while under the influence of the "goring of the ox." Go to our state prisons, and you will find that a great majority of the crimes for which the convicts were sent there can be traced to the "goring of the ox." This is the school where many receive their first lesson in sin, and it is written within its dazzling walls that they are broken down. Will thousands more, yet unborn, be educated in the way that leads to death? Go to the poor-houses throughout our land and you will find that strong drink has his victims there.

Only he who can count the hairs of our heads can count the mighty hosts who have fallen through strong drink. Our many penal institutions are made necessary only by the saloon. Why not do away with saloons? Then the majority of those institutions might be dispensed with. Then the millions of dollars, which are spent for their support could be used to support the homes that are desolate, and the overplus could be used in building houses of worship, and in Christianizing the heathen.

Shame to that land that boasts of Christian civilization and yet will stain itself with a crime worse than barbarism, and bring other nations also under the bondage of the cruel tyrant, "Rum,"—the ox that gores!

I wish to present a few of the many evils of this curse to humanity which is destroying all that is noble in man, and degrading him below the brute creation, blighting the hopes of wives and children. Statistics show that tobacco and strong drink cost more than all the necessaries

here, now there, now yonder, in the face of opposition and persecution, in the land all round about, some were seen coming to the front on the question, as a last resort, separating themselves from the church of their parents, from the church into which they had been born. 'Twas no little matter, this, for there was principle at stake. These are the people history calls the "Pietists."

The village of Schwarzenau was ruled by a mild count. Here liberty of conscience was granted, and here a portion of the neighboring Pietists fled. The secluded little village soon became extensively known, and the eyes of the surrounding cities looked harshly in that direction. Peace and harmony dwelt there, and they called each other brothers, but their views, in many respects, were quite dissimilar. Now the Pietists as such, were never a church, and those in Schwarzenau, although they had their religious meetings, felt keenly the want of a church-house in which they could enjoy all the Lord's appointments. And here men and women, from various parts of the country, formerly of different religious persuasions, were united in one desire, more fully to get into Christ, there to remain.

Giving themselves scrupulously to the study of the simple Word, they agreed to follow wheresoever the Truth would lead them. They met frequently and compared the result of their investigations. They sought with great diligence, their avowed purpose being to re-establish the faith and doctrine of the apostolic church. There seems to have been a goodly number engaged in the work at first, but like any extended race for some coveted prize, as the racers near the goal, the points become more clearly defined, and the fatigue becomes greater, until, one by one, a number of the contestants drop out of the race, so too, as time became somewhat extended, and point after point had become manifestly clear to them through the Word, one by one, a number dropped out of the race, some going back to the churches from which they came, and others elsewhere, until a much smaller number than the original, finally reached the coveted goal.

The principles upon which they worked are of exceeding interest. They laid aside all creeds and confessions of faith. They laid aside the church catechisms. They spent little time in the subtleties of speculative theology. They surrounded themselves with the most reliable church histories and with Bibles, and they spent much time in fasting and prayer.

For example take their candid disposal of the question of baptism. There were some fixed ideas held by the company. But, history gives trine immersion as the uniform baptism during the first and second centuries, and as the prevailing custom for twelve centuries. When they could find no Scripture to disqualify that for truth, and when they had found much Scripture in support of that baptism, they adopted it exclusively, in the face of that fact that the taking of such a position would place them all as unbaptized before God.

In such a way were the principles and boundary lines of the new church mapped out. I will not speak further concerning doctrine now. To the thoughtful mind there may have appeared ere this the difficulty into which they were getting. Here was a little band of believers, anxiously desiring to go forward in the fulfillment of all righteousness, but where was the administrator of the holy ordinance of baptism? Again, we are told, they sought the guidance of the Lord, and again he manifested his presence. They cast lots, and the lot fell upon one of their number. That one was to baptize another, and that other should in turn baptize the one upon whom the

lot had fallen, then the remainder of the company, and that the church might not be given the name of any man, they mutually pledged themselves that not one of them should ever reveal who among them had first baptized. Surely, in that little company of eight, nine were present. I believe the Lord wrought mightily in the restorative movement.

One morning at an early hour, thus being prepared, eight souls might have been seen passing quietly along the streets of Schwarzenau, past the borders of the village, down upon the green banks of the river Eder. There, in solitude before God, with no other witnesses than heaven and the birds, they were buried with Christ in baptism. This was in 1708, and this marks the beginning of the Brethren Reformation. They left the baptismal waters happy, with the words of Jehovah ringing in their ears: "Be fruitful and multiply." Rapidly, too, they grew during those early years. The little villages became alive with Bible readers and faithful ones. But these rays of heavenly sunshine seem to have been occasioned only by a rift of the passing clouds. Opposition burst forth upon them with all its evils, and after long years of endurance the spirit of emigration seized them, and they soon began establishing their peaceful homes within the borders of free America. Earnestly did those good men engage in the work which their hands found to do. Diligently did they labor to enlarge the borders of Zion. To them belongs the credit for first calling Washington "the father of his country," and while Robert Raikes was yet a child they had a well-regulated Sunday-school going. Marked piety and reverence for the Scriptures, and their peace principles, were distinguishing characteristics, and to-day, from New Jersey to California, from Michigan to Florida, can be found faithful congregations of her unassuming worshipers. Such, in few words, is the history of the rise of the Brethren church. May her future be as great as her principles deserve.

Philadelphia, Pa.

THE GORING OX.

BY WILLIAM PETERS.

"If an ox gore a man or a woman that they die: then the ox shall be surely stoned, and his flesh shall not be eaten; but the owner of the ox shall be quit. But if the ox were wont to push with his horn in time past, and it hath been testified to his owner, and he hath not kept him in, but that he hath killed a man or a woman; the ox shall be stoned, and his owner also shall be put to death."—Ex. 21: 28, 29.

This was a law, and the owner of the ox was the responsible party, when he knew that the ox would push with his horn. There is now an ox that is goring thousands that they die, and the question is, Do the people know it? If so, who is the responsible party? I believe that their responsibility is far-reaching as we shall see if we make a proper investigation.

The ox I wish to speak of is doing much damage to the human family financially, morally and religiously. He is known as "Strong Drink." He wounds millions annually, and kills thousands, and makes thousands of widows and orphans, causing misery and destruction in thousands of homes. Last, but not least, he is sinking innumerable souls lower than the grave each year.

Notwithstanding the terrible results that are seen and felt in thousands of homes, there are men of intelligence, and some, to their shame, professing to be followers of the Lord Jesus, who claim that men should be protected by law to deal out this curse of our American homes. And why? Because there is money in it. They want protection for the man, who, for the sake of mon-

ey, deals out this curse, that maddens the brain of men, causes them to destroy their property, beat their wives and children, abuse their neighbors, and commit crimes that they would not do if sober. Will not our Christian people, with one heart and one voice, say, "The ox must be slain, and the thousands of women and children liberated and these wrongs avenged." I hope and pray that the professing Christians will have the power to slay the ox. This will be done as soon as all the churches become fully awakened to their duty, and the ox will be banished from our land. There are professing Christians who claim that if it was not for the license law we could not keep up public expenses, and in the towns they wants to meet such expenses with the price of blood and the sacrifice of souls? It seems to me that such persons love darkness rather than light, because their deeds are evil. Were it not for the goring ox there would be but little need for lock-ups, jails, penitentiaries, poor-houses and insane asylums. If there were no distilleries or saloons, how many of such institutions would there be? Not one-sixth. Even if there were just as many as there are, the money spent for strong drink would cover the expenses of all, and leave a large surplus for the spread of the Gospel. If our towns had the money annually spent for whiskey, they could have better sidewalks and street lights, and still have enough to feed and clothe all the poor children in the towns. Something could even be left for the missionary cause, and all would be happier and better off in this life, to say nothing of the next. It cannot be denied but that every person does suffer more or less through the direful effects of the abominable rum traffic, financially, physically or mentally, for who has a heart so hard that it is not pained to see a father, brother or friend, who has been wounded and, perhaps, is dying from the goring of this ox, to say nothing of the sufferings of mothers and children?

Go to our jails, and you will find that nine-tenths of the prisoners are there because of crimes committed while under the influence of the "goring of the ox." Go to our state prisons, and you will find that a great majority of the crimes for which the convicts were sent there can be traced to the "goring of the ox." This is the school where many receive their first lesson in sin, and it is written within its dazzling walls that they are broken down. Will thousands more, yet unborn, be educated in the way that leads to death? Go to the poor-houses throughout our land and you will find that strong drink has his victims there.

Only he who can count the hairs of our heads can count the mighty hosts who have fallen through strong drink. Our many penal institutions are made necessary only by the saloon. Why not do away with saloons? Then the majority of those institutions might be dispensed with. Then the millions of dollars, which are spent for their support could be used to support the homes that are desolate, and the overplus could be used in building houses of worship, and in Christianizing the heathen.

Shame to that land that boasts of Christian civilization and yet will stain itself with a crime worse than barbarism, and bring other nations also under the bondage of the cruel tyrant, "Rum,"—the ox that gores!

I wish to present a few of the many evils of this curse to humanity which is destroying all that is noble in man, and degrading him below the brute creation, blighting the hopes of wives and children. Statistics show that tobacco and strong drink cost more than all the necessaries

Missionary and Tract Work Department.

"Upon the first day of the week, let every one of you lay by him in store as God hath prospered him, that there be no gatherings when I come."—1 Cor. 16:2.

"Every man as he purposeth in his heart, so let him give. Not grudgingly or of necessity, for the Lord loveth a cheerful giver."—2 Cor. 9:7.

HOW MUCH SHALL WE GIVE?

"Every man according to his ability." "Every one as God hath prospered him." "Every man, according as he purposeth in his heart, so let him give." "For if there be first a willing mind, it is accepted according to that a man hath, and not according to that he hath not."—2 Cor. 8:12.

Organization of Missionary Committee.

DANIEL VANIMAN, Foreman,	McPherson, Kans.
D. L. MILLER, Treasurer,	Mt. Morris, Ill.
GALEN B. ROYER, Secretary,	Mt. Morris, Ill.

Organization of Book and Tract Work.

S. W. HOOVER, Foreman,	Dayton, Ohio.
S. BOCK, Secretary and Treasurer,	Dayton, Ohio.

☞All donations intended for Missionary Work should be sent to GALEN B. ROYER, Mt. Morris, Ill.

☞All money for Tract Work should be sent to S. BOCK, Dayton, Ohio.

☞Money may be sent by Money Order, Registered Letter, or Drafts on New York or Chicago. Do not send personal checks, or drafts on interior towns, as it costs 45 cents to collect them.

☞Solicitors are requested to faithfully carry out the plan of Annual Meeting, that all our members be solicited to contribute at least twice a year for the Mission and Tract Work of the Church.

☞Notes for the Endowment Fund can be had by writing to the Secretary of either Work.

BAPTISM IN INDIA.

[WE are anxious to keep our readers informed on the various phases of missionary work in different parts of the world, and for that reason clip the following article from the *Independent*. Since we are becoming much interested in the spread of the Gospel among the heathens, it may be well for us, as much as possible, to acquaint ourselves with the nature of the work and the obstacles to be overcome. This article will afford no small amount of information in that line. It is written by Geo. F. Pentecost, D. D., who is quite familiar with the work of missionaries in foreign fields.—ED.]

One of the serious difficulties, and at present burning questions in India, is that of Baptism. I mean, of course, in connection with the heathen converts. On the one hand, there is a great lament on the part of missionaries that the Hindus—the higher and highest caste Hindus—even when there is reason to believe that they have received Christ in the heart—*refuse* to submit to baptism; that is, a great many of them do, who otherwise confess and profess Christ as Savior and Lord. On the other hand, there are not a few missionaries who are crying out bitterly against what they denounce as hasty baptisms, which are being administered to thousands of low-caste Hindus, especially by the American Baptist and Methodist missionaries; though these so-called hasty baptisms are not confined in their administration to the American missionaries alone. Vast numbers are being baptized by the Church Missionary Society and United Presbyterian missionaries, and in some districts also by the Free Church and London Missionary Society missionaries. It is true, however, that the great majority of the multitudes of heathen, who are now openly confessing Christ, are to be found in connection with the several American missions at work in India. Whether it is because the American missionaries are more aggressive and direct in their methods, or more careless of the quality of their converts, is a question often debated. I am inclined to believe that it is owing to the more aggressive spirit and methods seen among our missionaries. I say this without meaning to suggest

a reflection upon the zeal and consecration of the English and Scotch missionaries. It is largely a question of training and theory.

The two theories upon which missions are conducted in India may be expressed in these two formulas: "First convert the heathen, and afterward teach or educate him." The other theory is: "First educate the heathen, and then convert him." This puts it sharply; but I believe these two theories lie at the back of the methods of missionary work in India. I wish to call attention, in order, to these two complaints: "Too many baptisms," "Too few baptisms."

Too many baptisms.—By this it is not to be understood that anybody is complaining that there are too many conversions, but that there are too many *hasty* baptisms,—that is, baptism is administered in too many cases where there is not sufficient evidence of spiritual life,—with the result that the churches are being crowded with baptized heathen instead of baptized believers. In respect to the heathen, almost all missionaries are agreed upon the principle of "believers' baptism."

The conservatives say that the thousands who are now being baptized are not converted, but are coming over to Christianity from other considerations than those spiritual ones which should precede a confession of faith. They say that it is not possible that whole villages and communities should be converted *en masse*; that if they are really converted or even moved by a genuine spiritual impulse, they are still too ignorant to be baptized, and should be kept under instruction for months, if not years, in order that the genuineness of their faith may be proved,—that knowledge may be added to their faith. In other words, that proved Christian character should be the qualification of church membership. It is alleged that in many cases there have been wholesale apostasies from among these hastily-baptized thousands. Now what is the answer to these criticisms?

First. That we have been preaching and testifying the Gospel in India, diligently, for half a century or more. That our mission schools have been enlightening the minds of the people in general. That the presence of the missionaries and the testimony of their godly lives, their unwearied benevolence, their practical godliness, have been making steadily toward the conversion of the people. That the manifest effect of the Gospel upon such as have been converted in the way of righteousness, cleanliness, and general progress in everything that betters the life that now is, and in the evident elevation of the moral life, has also done much toward convincing the people of the superiority of Christianity over Hinduism. That we have been praying day and night, and asking the people to pray for an outpouring of the Holy Spirit, and that we ought not to be surprised or unbelieving, now that we see this marvelous movement among the low-caste people, all over India, toward Christ and Christianity. That to refuse these people baptism, when they seek it with evident sincerity, would be to dishonor the Holy Spirit and contradict and deny the very Gospel we have preached. That the movement has been too spontaneous and general to be other than the work of the Spirit.

For it must be borne in mind that while the vast majority of these thousands, who are now being converted, are in connection with the American Methodist Mission in the North and North-west of India, and the American Baptist Mission in the South of India, the movement is not confined to these missions, but is clearly discernible in connection with the work of both the C. M. S., the L. M., and the Scotch F. C. Missions. I have already noted the criticism that many of these converts are influenced by purely worldly consid-

erations; e. g., the native Christians are better fed, better clothed, better cared for in sickness, and, in general, are more prosperous than their Hindu fellow-villagers. But are not these things witnesses for Christ? Does it militate against the work of the Holy Ghost that heathens are influenced toward Christ and Christianity by the improved temporal condition of the Christians?

Second. In regard to the objection that these thousands are unfitted for baptism and church membership, in that they are not only ignorant of the great doctrines of the Gospel,—or comparatively so,—but they are still weighted down with an old heathen life and many practices utterly inconsistent with Christian character. That in many cases they are mendacious, or at least, untruthful, in some cases they are immoral; they are often very untrustworthy, being deceitful, and even downright dishonest. Well, let us grant that in some, even in many, cases this is true. What then? We have only to read the Epistles of Ephesians and Colossians to discover that all these grave faults were present with those two churches, and merely characteristic more or less of all converts from heathenism; therefore the constant exhortation of the apostle to "put off the old man" and all his works, and to "put on the new man" and all his virtues. Eph. 4; Col. 3.

Is it not a mistake to expect that these poor heathen idolaters, who have inherited for a hundred generations all these evil tendencies, will, at a bound, clear themselves of them? Do we, who have had all the benefit of previous ethical training and the culture of Christian homes, find ourselves free from faults and blemishes, not to say grave and glaring sins, from the moment we confessed Christ and onward? Are there no sinners in our American and European Zion? That these thousands of new converts, just emerging out of heathenism, are to be carefully and diligently taught and trained in all Christian virtue, goes without saying; but when they come to us declaring their belief in Christ and their desire to become his followers, that we should forbid them until they have developed Christian character and proved themselves to be Christians, and not heathen, by works of righteousness, is utterly contrary to the whole spirit and genius of the Gospel.

Christ came into the world to call sinners and not the righteous to repentance. "The whole need not a physician, but the sick." I have not been idle or inattentive in the observation and study of the matter, and I am convinced that it would be a great mistake to refuse baptism to these thousands,—low caste though they be,—who are pressing forward for baptism. It is said that we have not the teachers to train and take care of them. True, most true, painfully true! Every mission station in India is shamefully undermanned. But may I venture to suggest in the emergency. whether it would not be wisdom and in a truer line of Gospel work, to release *some. of the hundreds of missionaries, now wholly devoted to the secular education of the heathen*, and set them to teaching and training these new converts.

Third. It is charged that hundreds, even thousands of these hastily-baptized converts apostatize,—go back to heathenism,—and that this is the worst possible testimony to the heathen millions in India. Even granting this to be the case (I am sure it is vastly exaggerated in statement), are we to baptize no converts until we are absolutely sure that they will continue steadfast to the end? Have we no back-sliders and apostates at home? Verily, there are shoals of them in all our home churches. Did the apostles baptize no heathen except those who persevered to the end? Do we not read that "All Asia fell away"? Certainly, reasonable care should be taken; but if we

The Gospel Messenger,

A Weekly at $1.50 Per Annum.

PUBLISHED BY

The Brethren's Publishing Co.

D. L. MILLER,	. . . . .	Editor.
J. H. MOORE,	. . . .	Office Editor.
J. B. BRUMBAUGH,	}	Associate Editors.
J. G. ROYER,	}	
JOSEPH AMICK,	. . . .	Business Manager.

ADVISORY COMMITTEE.
L. W. Teeter, A. Hutchison, Daniel Hays.

☞Communications for publication should be legibly written with black ink on one side of the paper only. Do not attempt to interline, or to put on one page what ought to occupy two.

☞Anonymous communications will not be published.

☞Do not mix business with articles for publication. Keep your communications on separate sheets from all business.

☞Time is precious. We always have time to attend to business and to answer questions of importance, but please do not subject us to need less answering of letters.

☞The Messenger is mailed each week to all subscribers. If the address is correctly entered on our list, the paper must reach the person to whom it is addressed. If you do not get your paper, write us, giving particulars.

☞When changing your address, please give your former as well as your future address in full, so as to avoid delay and misunderstanding.

☞Always remit to the office from which you order your goods, no matter from where you receive them.

☞Do not send personal checks or drafts on interior banks, unless you send with them 25 cents each, to pay for collection.

☞Remittances should be made by Post-office Money Order, Drafts on New York, Philadelphia or Chicago, or Registered Letters, made payable and addressed to "Brethren's Publishing Co., Mount Morris, Ill.," or "Brethren's Publishing Co., Huntingdon, Pa."

☞Entered at the Post-office at Mount Morris, Ill., as second-class matter.

Mount Morris, Ill., · · · · July 26, 1892.

SIX recently united with the Rock Creek church, Pa.

THE District Meeting for Texas will be held in the William's Creek church, Cook County, Aug. 12.

A WRITER has well said, that "religion is not running in debt for things you do not need, and then never pay for them."

A LEADING paper says that Satan has some hopes of the man who habitually blacks his shoes on Sunday. There is something here that will at least do to think about.

ANY one knowing of members living in Columbus, Ohio, will do a favor by communicating their names and addresses to J. S. Lawrence, 561 E. Spring Street of that place.

BRO. WM. H. ASHMORE, of Baltimore, Md., writes very encouragingly of their Sunday-school. The attendance is from 75 to 125, and all the teachers are members. The school uses a number of our *Quarterlies*, and commends them. We hope it will remain an "evergreen" school.

IT is to be regretted that the Brethren have not been able to erect the meeting-house at Lincoln, Nebr., for which some money had already been collected. But those having the matter in charge have loaned the money on hand, until a time when they will be prepared to build. The plan is a good one, but we hope the time is not far distant when the house will be erected.

THE State of Louisiana finds it necessary to take stringent measures to prevent a further spread of the leprosy, which has existed in the older settled parts for over one hundred years. At present there are about 250 lepers in the State, and about 30 of them are in the City of New Orleans. Efforts will likely be made to confine all those affected with the disease to a fixed locality, and in this manner it may be entirely stamped out in course of time.

IDLENESS is the devil's workshop, and the more people he can get to do nothing, the greater his success. Those who do nothing may rest assured that they are at least counted on Satan's side.

THE church at Abilene, Kans., is increasing in numbers. Nine were recently translated from the kingdom of this world into the kingdom of Jesus Christ, much to the comfort of the saints.

WRITING from Hudson, Ill., Thos. D. Lyon says: "We are having real pleasant weather. Wheat and oats crops good. Corn crop very short. Health very good. Our meetings are well attended, and the Sunday-school is quite interesting. So you see we have no reason to complain."

CORRECTIONS for the ministerial list in the Almanac are now coming in. That is right, brethren, send in your corrections written on a card or slip of paper, separate and apart from all other business, and they will be sure to receive proper attention. Let us have all the corrections as soon as possible.

BRO. H. C. EARLY, of Rockingham County, Va., is booked for a public discussion with a Disciple minister in West Virginia, to take place about the first of September, next. The five points to be debated are about the same as those discussed by R. H. Miller and Daniel Sommer, in Missouri, a few years ago.

A COMMUNICATION, just received from Texas, informs us that the Brethren are pushing the missionary work in that State, but their cry is for more ministers to enter their fields and sow the Gospel seed, and also help gather in the sheaves. When will we have ministers enough to fill all these urgent calls!

PURE religion is not going to church to show your clothes, or to see what other people wear, or to find fault with the preacher. It means to fear God and keep his commandments. He who does that will find so many opportunities for doing good, that he will have but little time to talk about the faults of others.

A SECULAR paper says that forty-six Congregational churches in Connecticut are without pastors. It seems that the pastors they desire cannot be had, while those they can get they do not want. Possibly they are too particular on both sides. Christianity stands greatly in need of a free ministry system that will feed the flock of God. Men, who will not preach without a salary, are not the kind of preachers the Lord wants. Then, on the other hand, a church that will not assist her needy preachers in their earnest struggle to save sinners, is by no means what churches should be.

THE Brethren in Washington and Idaho are still calling for more ministers. One writer says there are less than half a dozen of our ministers in both Washington and Idaho. Surely the field is a large one, and a great work might be done there if we only had the men to put into the field. And by the way, these far western points would be excellent places for some of our strong young men to show their zeal for the spreading of the Gospel. Possibly too many of them are seeking to settle where there are strong churches to stand by them in their work, and afford them all the benefits of culture and social enjoyments. While these advantages are pleasant, it should be remembered that the minister has a still higher calling, and that as much as possible he should go where he can accomplish the most good for lost humanity.

THE man who is constantly complaining about bad neighbors, has an excellent opportunity of showing what a good neighbor is. There is nothing that goes so far and speaks so forcibly as a good example. One good neighbor may encourage others to do what is right, and thus, by the example of one, scores may be influenced for good.

THE Salvation Army people are not unfrequently the subjects of remarks, but they generally prove themselves entirely equal to the occasion, as the following will show: "That bonnet would scare the devil himself!" said a would-be smart young man to a Salvation Army lass, recently. "Yes; that's what I wear it for, sir!" she replied.

A WEALTHY Baptist in Queensland, Australia, left his whole estate, valued at about $170,000, to the Queensland Baptist Association for evangelistic work. The courts have annulled the will on the ground of insufficient attestation and non-registration. This should serve as another warning to those who have property to give to charitable institutions, to turn it over to such institutions as much as possible while they are living. Wills are being broken by the score, and the property placed where the owners never intended it should be.

MUCH disappointment comes from people trying to be what the Lord never intended. To be good and useful is within the reach of all, but talent and riches are possessed by the few, and as a rule do not give the happiness often enjoyed by those in the common walks of life. Let those, in the humble paths of life, strive for the enjoyment to be found within their reach, and they will soon find themselves in possession of joys more lasting and comforting, than anything that may be realized in the higher and more responsible circles.

NEXT after the earth is the planet Mars. It is much smaller than the earth, and moves around the sun once in every twenty-three months. In shape and movements it greatly resembles the globe on which we live. On the fifth of August this planet will come within 35,000,000 miles of the earth. This occurs about every fifteen years, and on this occasion a thousand telescopes will be leveled at it, and the planet will be studied with the greatest of interest. It is said that the great Lick Telescope will magnify Mars to a size as if viewed at a distance of only a little over 17,000 miles. The public will await the report of the astronomers with great interest, for who is it, that is not more or less concerned about the heavenly bodies!

THERE is not that life and push in some of the Brethren churches there ought to be. There are doubtless several reasons for the unfortunate condition, and one of them is a lack of interest taken in our church literature. We would like to push the MESSENGER into every nook and corner of our Brotherhood, as we think it would be the means of stirring up a greater interest for the church and her work. We are told by our traveling ministers that they cannot help noticing the marked differences between the churches that read the MESSENGER and those that do not. We are told that those who read the paper are not only as well posted in the Bible as others, but seem to be greatly concerned about the doings of all parts of the Brotherhood, and love to talk of the church and her work. They seem to manifest an interest, indicating more zeal for the cause of Christianity. We trust that special efforts are being made to get the paper into every family, for we are sure that the more widely the paper is read, the more activity it will produce among the churches.

The Gospel Messenger,

A Weekly at $1.50 Per Annum.

PUBLISHED BY

The Brethren's Publishing Co.

D. L. MILLER,	Editor.
J. H. MOORE,	Office Editor.
J. B. BRUMBAUGH, } J. G. ROYER, }	Associate Editors.
JOSEPH AMICK,	Business Manager.

ADVISORY COMMITTEE.

L. W. Teeter, A. Hutchison, Daniel Hays.

☞Communications for publication should be legibly written with black ink on one side of the paper only. Do not attempt to interline, or to put on one page what ought to occupy two.

☞Anonymous communications will not be published.

☞Do not mix business with articles for publication. Keep your communications on separate sheets from all business.

☞Time is precious. We always have time to attend to business and to answer questions of importance, but please do not subject us to need less answering of letters.

☞The MESSENGER is mailed each week to all subscribers. If the address is subsctly entered on our list, the paper must reach the person to whom it is addressed. If you do not get your paper, write us, giving particulars.

☞When-changing your address, please give your former as well as your future address in full, so as to avoid delay and misunderstanding.

☞Always remit to the office from which your goods, no matter from which you receive them.

☞Do not send personal checks or drafts on interior banks, unless you send with them 25 cents each, to pay for collection.

☞Remittances should be made by Post-office Money Order, Drafts on New York, Philadelphia or Chicago, or Registered Letters, made payable and addressed to "Brethren's Publishing Co., Mount Morris, Ill.," or "Brethren's Publishing Co., Huntingdon, Pa."

☞Entered at the Post-office at Mount Morris, Ill., as second-class matter.

Mount Morris, Ill.,   • • • •   July 26, 1892.

SIX recently united with the Rock Creek church, Pa.

THE District Meeting for Texas will be held in the William's Creek church, Cook County, Aug. 12.

A WRITER has well said, that "religion is not running in debt for things you do not need, and then never pay for them."

A LEADING paper says that Satan has some hopes of the man who habitually blacks his shoes on Sunday. There is something here that will at least do to think about.

ANY one knowing of members living in Columbus, Ohio, will do a favor by communicating their names and addresses to J. S. Lawrence, 561 E. Spring Street of that place.

BRO. WM. H. ASHMORE, of Baltimore, Md., writes very encouragingly of their Sunday-school. The attendance is from 75 to 125, and all the teachers are members. The school uses a number of our Quarterlies, and commends them. We hope it will remain an "evergreen" school.

IT is to be regretted that the Brethren have not been able to erect the meeting-house at Lincoln, Nebr., for which some money had already been collected. But those having the matter in charge have loaned the money on hand, until a time when they will be prepared to build. The plan is a good one, but we hope the time is not far distant when the house will be erected.

THE State of Louisiana finds it necessary to take stringent measures to prevent a further spread of the leprosy, which has existed in the older settled parts for over one hundred years. At present there are about 250 lepers in the State, and about 30 of them are in the City of New Orleans. Efforts will likely be made to confine all those affected with the disease to a fixed locality, and in this manner it may be entirely stamped out in course of time.

IDLENESS is the devil's workshop, and the more people he can get to do nothing, the greater his success. Those who do nothing may rest assured that they are at least counted on Satan's side.

THE church at Abilene, Kans., is increasing in numbers. Nine were recently translated from the kingdom of this world into the kingdom of Jesus Christ, much to the comfort of the saints.

WRITING from Hudson, Ill., Thos. D. Lyon says: "We are having real pleasant weather. Wheat and oats crops good. Corn crop very short. Health very good. Our meetings are well attended, and the Sunday-school is quite interesting. So you see we have no reason to complain."

CORRECTIONS for the ministerial list in the Almanac are now coming in. That is right, brethren, send in your corrections written on a card or slip of paper, separate and apart from all other business, and they will be sure to receive proper attention. Let us have all the corrections as soon as possible.

BRO. H. C. EARLY, of Rockingham County, Va., is booked for a public discussion with a Disciple minister in West Virginia, to take place about the first of September, next. The five points to be debated are about the same as those discussed by R. H. Miller and Daniel Sommer, in Missouri, a few years ago.

A COMMUNICATION, just received from Texas, informs us that the Brethren are pushing the missionary work in that State, but their cry is for more ministers to enter their fields and sow the Gospel seed, and also help gather in the sheaves. When will we have ministers enough to fill all these urgent calls!

PURE religion is not going to church to show your clothes, or to see what other people wear, or to find fault with the preacher. It means to fear God and keep his commandments. He who does that will find so many opportunities for doing good, that he will have but little time to talk about the faults of others.

A SECULAR paper says that forty-six Congregational churches in Connecticut are without pastors. It seems that the pastors they desire cannot be had, while those they can get they do not want. Possibly they are too particular on both sides. Christianity stands greatly in need of a free ministry system that will feed the flock of God. Men, who will not preach without a salary, are not the kind of preachers the Lord wants. Then, on the other hand, a church that will not assist her needy preachers in their earnest struggle to save sinners, is by no means what church-es should be.

THE Brethren in Washington and Idaho are still calling for more ministers. One writer says there are less than half a dozen of our ministers in both Washington and Idaho. Surely the field is a large one, and a great work might be done there if we only had the men to put into the field. And by the way, these far western points would be excellent places for some of our strong young men to show their zeal for the spreading of the Gospel. Possibly too many of them are seeking to settle where there are strong churches to stand by them in their work, and afford them all the benefits of culture and social enjoyments. While these advantages are pleasant, it should be remembered that the minister has a still higher calling, and that as much as possible he should go where he can accomplish the most good for lost humanity.

THE man who is constantly complaining about bad neighbors, has an excellent opportunity of showing what a good neighbor is. There is nothing that goes so far and speaks so forcibly as a good example. One good neighbor may encourage others to do what is right, and thus, by the example of one, scores may be influenced for good.

THE Salvation Army people are not unfrequently the subjects of remarks, but they generally prove themselves entirely equal to the occasion, as the following will show: "That bonnet would scare the devil himself!" said a would-be smart young man to a Salvation Army lass, recently: "Yes; that's what I wear it for, sir!" she replied.

A WEALTHY Baptist in Queensland, Australia, left his whole estate, valued at about $170,000, to the Queensland Baptist Association for evangelistic work. The courts have annulled the will on the ground of insufficient attestation and non-registration. This should serve as another warning to those who have property to give to charitable institutions, to turn it over to such institutions as much as possible while they are living. Wills are being broken by the score, and the property placed where the owners never intended it should be.

MUCH disappointment comes from people trying to be what the Lord never intended. To be good and useful is within the reach of all, but talent and riches are possessed by the few, and as a rule do not give the happiness often enjoyed by those in the common walks of life. Let those, in the humble paths of life, strive for the enjoyment to be found within their reach, and they will soon find themselves in possession of joys more lasting and comforting, than anything that may be realized in the higher and more responsible circles.

NEXT after the earth is the planet Mars. It is much smaller than the earth, and moves around the sun once in every twenty-three months. In shape and movements it greatly resembles the globe on which we live. On the fifth of August this planet will come within 35,000,000 miles of the earth. This occurs about every fifteen years, and on this occasion a number of telescopes will be leveled at it, and the planet will be studied with the greatest of interest. It is said that the great Lick Telescope will magnify her to a size as if viewed at a distance of only a little over 17,000 miles. The public will await the report of the astronomers with great interest, for who is it, that is not more or less concerned about the heavenly bodies!

THERE is not that life and push in some of the Brethren churches there ought to be. There are doubtless several reasons for the unfortunate condition, and one of them is a lack of interest taken in our church literature. We would like to push the MESSENGER into every nook and corner of our Brotherhood, as we think it would be the means of stirring up a greater interest for the church and her work. We are told by our traveling ministers that they cannot help noticing the marked differences between the churches that read the MESSENGER and those that do not. We are told that those who read the paper are not only as well posted in the Bible as others, but seem to be greatly concerned about the doings of all parts of the Brotherhood, and love to talk of the church and her work. They seem to manifest an-interest, indicating more zeal for the cause of Christianity. We trust that special efforts are being made to get the paper into every family, for we are sure that the more widely the paper is read, the more activity it will produce among the churches.

VACATION TALKS WITH OUR STUDENTS.

NUMBER FOUR.—LOVE IN THE HOME.

HAPPINESS in the home may be made reciprocal only by mutual forbearance, mutual guidance, and mutual trust. "The loves of home" says an eminent author, "constitute the poetry of human life and are worth more than all the other social ties."

It is true that there are loves, and we should distinguish between love, as exhibited in the Bible, and other forms of its manifestations. Beginning at the bottom of the scale we find natural love, or animal passion, as the lowest form. Closely related to this is the love of food, drink and dress. Both are transient feelings, now very strong, then entirely absent. Both are heaven-given boons, if properly entertained and prudently guarded; but when not controlled both become lusts which destroy the well-being of the individual and the enjoyments of the home circle. Next higher comes that which affords mental pleasure and profit. It is known as love of books and intellectual association. While the development of this power should be strongly urged, young people should also remember that in this age of strife for intellectual superiority and scramble after riches, there is danger of becoming so intensely intellectual as to usurp Love's throne. One thrill of genuine, natural love in the soul will be of greater value to the young than any amount of money, or the most extensive mental culture without it. We plead for a continuance of good, honest, genuine, natural love, divinely directed.

Next in the ascent comes love of parents for children, and of home and family, or natural, brotherly love. This is higher because it is less selfish. It is partly native, but admits of development. Its culture should be sacredly cherished because of its close kinship to love in its highest form,—the love of God.

This highest form is *divine* in its origin. It is begotten in the soul by the Holy Spirit, and its manifestations are denominated the fruit of the Spirit. God-like in character, it is not a respecter of persons or surroundings. Its manifestations are affected neither by physical or mental differences, which may obtain among the members of the home circle, nor by surroundings of wealth and affluence. It takes note not so much of the external as of the internal and spiritual. Hence, it converts the hovel and the cottage into home as readily and truly as the mansion and the palace. The office of this form of love is to preside over man's lower forms of love, and by its sanctifying influences render them first pure, then easily controlled and full of good fruits. Happiness in the home, therefore, is rendered mutual to the extent that the several members composing the home circle succeed in making manifestations of the love of God mutual. In our efforts to accomplish this each should daily recall, "Without me ye can do nothing." Are you enjoying a happy home, my young friends, give God the glory; is yours an unhappy one, the blame lies within the home circle, and much of it may be in your own breast.

J. G. R.

"GOD gives us life at the rate of a single second of time at once. No other second comes until that is gone, so that we must make the best of the time we have by living a true life in it. God himself is in possession of a complete life, having what we think of as a past and as future, no less than the present. Therefore his life is eternal; ours is temporal."

CORRESPONDENCE.

Messages Dropped by the Way.

TRAVELING amongst the isolated, one can gather valuable matter for messages of encouragement. Some years ago an old couple, with their family, lived in Jefferson County, Iowa. The father was irreligious and especially prejudiced against the Dunkard people. However, after emigrating to Kansas and being located near a church less objectionable to him, the old gentleman attended, upon being told that a stranger of a strange denomination was to preach. After the sermon he said that was the kind of doctrine he had been waiting for. Hearing this, a brother, who lives in the same town, gave him some copies of the GOSPEL MESSENGER, telling him that the paper contained altogether the same doctrine. In these papers he became very much interested. About this time a very sad and fatal accident occurred among the relatives,—fatal, it was feared, to both soul and body. When the old brother, living in the place, was requested to call for us, to come and hold several meetings, with a visit from house to house, the result was that the aged father in his eightieth year, and the mother in her seventy-fourth, and a married son of about twenty-five years of age, were baptized, after having shown much fruit, meet for repentance.

Brethren and sisters, thus the Lord works, but not without means. The Lord said, "Go ye." A certain brother went. A hardened old sinner heard; faith came by hearing; hearing by the Word of God; he had a preacher, because he was sent. An old Aquilla turned out a white-winged messenger now and then, who brought the olive branch to the man of God, saying, "The turbulent waters are subsiding."

Passing farther out amongst the scattered children of light, I found where a little band of members had combined in an agreement with one another to locate a minister among them, even if it did cost certain ones $75, one of whom lives twenty miles from the supposed location. Oh, who is it that lives convenient to church privileges, and realizes what is meant by Macedonian cries, "We are hungering for the Bread of Life?"

C. C. ROOT.

Some of the Happenings of Northern Indiana.

JUNE 8 we had a very pleasant council-meeting in the Bethel church. Much business was transacted in the fear of the Lord. At the close of the meeting a dear one was received into the fold by baptism. June 11 we had a very pleasant feast. We were kindly remembered by ministers from surrounding churches. We had children's meeting and preaching next day to a well-filled house. Bro. Tobias Hoover, of Ohio, was with us and did good service for the Master. June 18 we met with the saints of the Solomon's Creek church in Communion services. Notwithstanding the rain, there was a large number of communicants, their big church being well filled. At the close of the meeting, next day, one was received by baptism and one restored, for which let us all praise God. Bro. Thurston Miller served us here. Bro. Lemuel Hillery was president, but, owing to poor health, was not able to do much preaching. June 22 we attended a feast in the Rock Run church. Their spacious house was well filled with communicants. A number

of ministers were here also from surrounding churches, who did good service. Three were added here,—two by baptism and one restored. This church has had its dark days, but they have passed away, and prosperity seems to crown their efforts.

We had a special council-meeting in the Bethel church June 25, at which time one was restored who had wandered from the fold. June 26 we attended regular meetings at Syracuse, at which one was received by baptism. Thus the good work moves onward. To the Lord be the praise, now and evermore!   W. R. DEETER.

At Home Again.

AFTER the close of our meetings in Maxwell, Iowa, several brethren and sisters started for the love-feast in the Indian Creek congregation. At this place we had one of those feasts which carries the mind to a higher plane. The attendance, both of members and others, was large. As it sometimes occurs on such occasions,—the members' children are left to run outside and have a general good time, as the children would call it. While their being crowded out is scarcely avoidable, because of the large gathering of people who wish to occupy a place in the house where they can see and hear, yet it becomes a question whether members could not have their children realize more of the sacredness of these services.

Children, if left to be their own rulers on such occasions, and not looked after by their parents, will soon regard the places of love-feasts as common play-grounds. Amusements for children are necessary, but they should be taught to select some other occasions for their sports and loud noise. We, who have charge of children, have much to do.

It sometimes happens that, when we preach just what others say is their "motto," we get more into our preaching than the mottoists want. The motto is, "The Bible, the whole Bible, and nothing but the Bible." But we have found out that there is a little too much in that wonderful Book to be accepted now. Strange as it may seem, but it is nevertheless true, that the most plainly-stated and clearly-defined parts of the Bible are the very parts that are ignored. Those who preach the whole of it have one consolation,—that their salvation does not depend upon the number which they induce to accept the truth, but upon their fidelity in delivering to the people a pure testimony. We must not cease our efforts because people do not receive and embrace the Truth. Jesus himself, and the faithful all the way down since, have failed to have all men receive the Truth. The Master said, "This Gospel of the kingdom shall be preached in all the world for a witness unto all nations, and then shall the end come." Matt. 24: 14. And since this matter of preaching the whole truth to all nations is left in the hands of the church, the claim that we set up certainly requires of us a united effort in that direction. We hope to see the day, when we, as a church, become fully aroused on that subject.

To those who are asking for a published program of my course and work for the fall and winter, I will here say, that I expect to remain in Kansas until the middle of September. Then I again take up the work in Iowa; beginning in Dallas Centre, Sept. 17. From that point I will visit other congregations in Iowa. My present arrangement is to spend as much as two months in Iowa, and then my course will be eastward, if my health will allow me to work in those States during the winter season. But do not expect me to go to labor where I cannot have my lodging near the place of work. This is a matter of necessity

VACATION TALKS WITH OUR STUDENTS.

NUMBER FOUR.—LOVE IN THE HOME.

HAPPINESS in the home may be made reciprocal only by mutual forbearance, mutual guidance, and mutual trust. "The loves of home" says an eminent author, "constitute the poetry of human life and are worth more than all the other social ties."

It is true that there are loves, and we should distinguish between love, as exhibited in the Bible, and other forms of its manifestations. Beginning at the bottom of the scale we find natural love, or animal passion, as the lowest form. Closely related to this is the love of food, drink and dress. Both are transient feelings, now very strong, then entirely absent. Both are heaven-given boons, if properly entertained and prudently guarded; but when not controlled both become lusts which destroy the well-being of the individual and the enjoyments of the home circle. Next higher comes that which affords mental pleasure and profit. It is known as love of books and intellectual association. While the development of this power should be strongly urged, young people should also remember that in this age of strife for intellectual superiority and scramble after riches, there is danger of becoming so intensely intellectual as to usurp Love's throne. One thrill of genuine, natural love in the soul will be of greater value to the young than any amount of money, or the most extensive mental culture without it. We plead for a continuance of good, honest, genuine, natural love, divinely directed.

Next in the ascent comes love of parents for children, and of home and family, or natural, brotherly love. This is higher because it is less selfish. It is partly native, but admits of development. Its culture should be sacredly cherished because of its close kinship to love in its highest form,—the love of God.

This highest form is divine in its origin. It is begotten in the soul by the Holy Spirit, and its manifestations are denominated the fruit of the Spirit. God-like in character, it is not a respecter of persons or surroundings. Its manifestations are affected neither by physical or mental differences, which may obtain among the members of the home circle, nor by surroundings of wealth and affluence. It takes note not so much of the external as of the internal and spiritual. Hence, it converts the hovel and the cottage into home as readily and truly as the mansion and the palace. The office of this form of love is to preside over man's lower forms of love, and by its sanctifying influences render them first pure, then easily controlled and full of good fruits. Happiness in the home, therefore, is rendered mutual to the extent that the several members composing the home circle succeed in making manifestations of the love of God mutual. In our efforts to accomplish this each should daily recall, "Without me ye can do nothing." Are you enjoying a happy home, my young friends, give God the glory; is yours an unhappy one, the blame lies within the home circle, and much of it may be in your own breast.

J. G. R.

"GOD gives us life at the rate of a single second of time at once. No other second comes until that is gone, so that we must make the best of the time we have by living a true life in it. God himself is in possession of a complete life, having what we think of as a past and as future, no less than the present. Therefore his life is eternal; ours is temporal."

CORRESPONDENCE.

"Write what thou seest, and send it unto the churches."

☞Church News solicited for this Department. If you have had a good meeting, send a Dspoiff of it, so that others may rejoice with you. In writing give name of church, County and State. Be brief. Notes of Travel should be as short as possible. Land Advertisements are not solicited for this Department. We have an advertising page, and, if necessary, will issue supplements.

Messages Dropped by the Way.

TRAVELING amongst the isolated, one can gather valuable matter for messages of encouragement. Some years ago an old couple, with their family, lived in Jefferson County, Iowa. They were irreligious and especially prejudiced against the Dunkard people. However, after emigrating to Kansas and being located near a church less objectionable to him, the old gentleman attended, upon being told that a stranger of a strange denomination was to preach. After the sermon he said that was the kind of doctrine he had been waiting for. Hearing this, a brother, who lives in the same town, gave him some copies of the GOSPEL MESSENGER, telling him that the paper contained altogether the same doctrine. In these papers he became very much interested. About this time a very sad and fatal accident occurred among the relatives,—fatal, it was feared, to both soul and body. When the old brother, living in the place, was requested to call for us, to come and hold several meetings, with a visit from house to house, the result was that the aged father in his eightieth year, and the mother in her seventy-fourth, and a married son of about twenty-five years of age, were baptized, after having shown much fruit, meet for repentance.

Brethren and sisters, thus the Lord works, but not without means. The Lord said, "Go ye." A certain brother went. A hardened old sinner heard; faith came by hearing; hearing by the Word of God; he had a preacher, because he was sent. An old Aquilla turned out a white-winged messenger now and then, who brought the olive branch to the man of God, saying, "The turbulent waters are subsiding."

Passing farther out amongst the scattered children of light, I found where a little band of members had combined in an agreement with one another to locate a minister among them, even if it did cost certain ones $75, one of whom lives twenty miles from the supposed location. Oh, who is it that lives convenient to church privileges, and realizes what is meant by Macedonian cries, "We are hungering for the Bread of Life?"

C. C. ROOT.

Some of the Happenings of Northern Indiana.

JUNE 3 we had a very pleasant council-meeting in the Bethel church. Much business was transacted in the fear of the Lord. At the close of the meeting a dear one was received into the fold by baptism. June 11 we had a very pleasant feast. We were kindly remembered by ministers from surrounding churches. We had children's meeting and preaching next day to a well-filled house. Bro. Tobias Hoover, of Ohio, was with us and did good service for the Master. June 18 we met with the saints of the Solomon's Creek church in Communion services. Notwithstanding the rain, there was a large number of communicants, their big church being well filled. At the close of the meeting, next day, four were received by baptism and one restored, for which let us all praise God. Bro. Thurston Miller served us here. Bro. Lemuel Hillery was present, but, owing to poor health, was not able to do much preaching. June 22 we attended a feast in the Rock Run church. Their spacious house was well filled with communicants. A number of ministers were here also from surrounding churches, who did good service. Three were added here,—two by baptism and one restored. This church has had its dark days, but they have passed away, and prosperity seems to crown their efforts.

We had a special council-meeting in the Bethel church June 25, at which time one was restored who had wandered from the fold. June 26 we attended regular meetings at Syracuse, at which one was received by baptism. Thus the good work moves onward. To the Lord be the praise, now and evermore! — W. R. DETER.

AFTER the close of our meetings in Maxwell, Iowa, several brethren and sisters started for the love-feast in the Indian Creek congregation. At this place we had one of those feasts which carries the mind to a higher plane. The attendance, both of members and others, was large. As it sometimes occurs on such occasions,—the members' children are left to run outside and have a general good time, as the children would call it. While their being crowded out is scarcely avoidable, because of the large gathering of people who wish to occupy a place in the house where they can see and hear, yet it becomes a question whether members could not have their children realize more of the sacredness of these services.

Children, if left to be their own rulers on such occasions, and not looked after by their parents, will soon regard the places of love-feasts as common play-grounds. Amusements for children are necessary, but they should be taught to select some other occasions for their sports and loud noise. We, who have charge of children, have much to do.

It sometimes happens that, when we preach just what others say is their "motto," we get more into our preaching than the mottoists want. The motto is, "The Bible, the whole Bible, and nothing but the Bible." But we have found out that there is a little too much in that wonderful Book to be accepted now. Strange as it may seem, but it is nevertheless true, that the most plainly-stated and clearly-defined parts of the Bible are the very parts that are ignored. Those who preach the whole of it have one consolation,—that their salvation does not depend upon the number which they induce to accept the truth, but upon their fidelity in delivering to the people a pure testimony. We must not cease our efforts because people do not receive and embrace the Truth. Jesus himself, and the faithful all the way down since, have failed to have all men receive the Truth. The Master said, "This Gospel of the kingdom shall be preached in all the world for a witness unto all nations, and then shall the end come." Matt. 24: 14. And since this matter of preaching the whole truth to all nations is left in the hands of the church, the claim that we set up certainly requires of us a united effort in that direction. We hope to see the day, when we, as a church, become fully aroused on that subject.

To those who are asking for a published program of my course and work for the fall and winter, I will here say, that I expect to remain in Kansas until the middle of September. Then I again take up the work in Iowa; beginning in Dallas Centre, Sept. 17. From that point I will visit other congregations in Iowa. My present arrangement is to spend as much as two months in Iowa, and then my course will be eastward, if my health will allow me to work in those States during the winter season. But do not expect me to go to labor where I cannot have my lodging near the place of work. This is a matter of necessity

To-day our large house was well filled with attentive listeners. At 10 A. M., we had song services. At 11 o'clock, "Liberty," both politically and spiritually, was presented forcibly by Bro. Eby.

Next we had a recess, refreshments, social chat, and then children's meeting. Brethren, it is a step forward in the right direction to let the children feel that they are objects of especial care by our Father in heaven.

After this, "God be with you till we shall meet again," then "Farewell," with an occasional, intruding tear.

How much better to celebrate the anniversary of American liberty thus, than in the manner most generally done!   J. D. HAUGHTELIN.

July 4.

Notes and Jottings.

MAY 19 wife and I started for Shideler, Ind., to attend the love-feast at said place May 20. We had a very pleasant meeting and good attendance. Ministerial aid was sufficient from other Districts. Solomon Blickenstaff remained with us over Sunday, and assisted in preaching and in a children's meeting, held on Sunday afternoon, which seemed to be enjoyed by all present. May 28 the second ministerial meeting was held in Southern Ohio. The meeting was pleasant, and we hope it may result in good. I feel sure it can, if we all try to work for the purity of the church and labor to spread the Gospel far and wide, and if we, as ministers, work close up to the Gospel in all its characteristics. Had the ministers adhered more closely to the Gospel, as understood by the Brotherhood, we never would have had as much trouble among the laity, in regard to indifference and the worldly pleasure in fashion and many other ways. Ministers sow the seed, but the laity gives it room in the heart to grow. My co-laborers, let us take warning and profit thereby, and let our appearance and everything else be in harmony with the simplicity of the Gospel!

On the morning of June 4 wife and I, in company with many other brethren and sisters, set out for Cedar Rapids, Iowa, where we arrived in due time to attend the services in the Tabernacle on Sunday morning. We remained till the close of the Conference, as is our custom. Would it not be well when a local church elects a delegate to go to Annual Meeting, to require him to remain at his post till the close of the business of the Meeting, unless hindered by sickness, and if he will not promise to do this, to send the alternate? One-fourth of the delegates to be absent the last day of the Meeting does not look right to me. The Meeting was pleasant, yet there was considerable difference between the way we conduct the business now and the way it was conducted twenty, or even ten, or five years ago. We are getting to be much more parliamentary and act much more by motions and seconds. I hope it is all for the better, but some of our older brethren, that are not used to that way of proceeding, seem to be entirely silent now. They are afraid they cannot stick to the motion and cannot express their mind in that way.

We arrived home June 11. Our son, Edward, and wife, were also in our company from Cedar Rapids. June 16 I left home to meet with the members of the Eagle Creek church, Ohio. We commenced meeting the same evening, and continued till the evening of the 26th, with very good attendance and attention. One was baptized and we hope others may consider well and act wisely before it is too late. The feast took place June 18. On account of a heavy rain at the hour of the commencement of the meeting, the attendance was not as large as usual, but they had a very pleasant, quiet feast, and trust we were all much built up and revived.

The old church in New Carlisle was taken down several weeks ago, and the walls of the basement are about completed. Brick-laying will soon commence, and we hope that by early fall the house will be ready for use. The members of the Christian church kindly offered us the use of their church while ours is in course of erection, and we are using that building at present. At our last meeting in that house, Bro. McCann preached. He also spoke at Forgy Station in the evening. He has, since then, returned to Virginia.

No preventing Providence, to-morrow we go to Oak Shade, a mission point, 125 miles distant. It is too far away to make a success. These isolated points need a resident-minister to take care of the lambs through the week, as well as on the Lord's Day. Then they could have preaching every Sunday.

When will the time come when we can have suitable brethren for all these places,—men that will go? It is so much more pleasant to go among the more favored places, that it is sometimes hard to get those places filled, even for a week at a time. I must close these "Jottings," or they will find their way into the waste-basket. I have been troubled somewhat with asthma since Annual Meeting. Were there not so much that needs our attention, both temporally and spiritnally, we would go to some northern climate a few months.   HENRY FRANTZ.

Lone Star Items.

THE Sunday-school of the Nocona church is fairly well attended. As it is held in an arbor, the weather frequently interferes. The weather has been very disagreeable quite often, on account of so much wind.

Eld. Henry Brubaker, wife and babe returned from their visit to Nebraska the last day of June. We were glad to see their pleasant faces among us again. Bro. B. was also at Annual Meeting, and on his return visited a few days with his son in Des Moines, Iowa.

July 2 the Nocona church met in quarterly council. Among other business, the church decided to hold a love-feast, and Aug. 27 was selected as the time, being two weeks after District Meeting. We would be glad if ministers would arrange to stay among us till our feast. Any Brethren, contemplating a visit to Texas, will please note the time of our District Meeting and our feast and try to be with us. A good representation from the churches of the District is desired. As I see no standing notice in the MESSENGER, I will here give the date and place again: Aug. 12, in the William's Creek church, Cook Co., Tex.

July 8, in company with Eld. Brubaker, wife and daughter, I went to the Pleasant Valley church, Clay Co., Tex. After a drive of about fifty miles we arrived at Bro. John Galawey's about sundown. Their quarterly council was held the following day. They decided to hold a feast Sept. 10, and also to hold a series of meetings, to commence about a week previous to the feast. Bro. Brubaker preached three very good sermons. We returned home on Monday, and found all well. This church has been without a minister for some time, consequently is under the care of the Mission Board. They feel encouraged and their future prospects are bright. There were six received by baptism in May, and there are others counting the cost. They are much in need of a resident minister. The District Mission Board has been trying to get a minister to locate, but so far has been unable to do so. Any minister that would like to move where there is a good chance for him to work for the Master, and also get a home cheap in a good country, would do well to correspond with the writer, or A. W. Austin, Secretary of Mission Board, Muenster, Tex. The Board would be glad to assist several good ministers to locate, and if they could get them, would be willing to see that they do not lack for the necessaries of life.

Eld. Abe Molsbee went to a new point last Saturday, in the southern part of Montague County, under the direction of the Mission Board. He reports good congregations. He is to start to Brath County. July 14, to hold a week's meetings, and go from there to Parker County, and preach a while for them. The harvest truly is great, and the laborers are few. Who will come over and help us? We see many Macedonian calls through the MESSENGER, and how many of them have to go unheeded?

Does Bro. Driskill, of Snyder, Scurry Co., Texas, know of any other members in that County? I suggest that correspondents always give the County with their Post-office address, so that they can be located when desired.   A. J. WINE.

Nocona, Montague Co., Tex., July 13.

From Johnson City, Tenn.

THE MESSENGER for July 5, is just to hand. and I am glad I have it, for it is certainly a very interesting number to me, from the fact that so much is said in it with reference to the music of the church. I certainly think much more should be written on this subject. Our people are a great singing people,—from a religious standpoint, however, rather than from a scientific stand-point. Not that the latter is not commendable, but that the former is *especially* so. This very thing gives us, as a church, the supreme basis for the highest possible musical development. Music, in the highest sense, is a thing of sentiment, dependent, of course, upon a proper physical and mental training, and with a pure, religious sentiment at the foundation, a very superior superstructure is made possible.

The editorial of J. H. M. consists of " words fitly spoken." The idea, however, advanced by some, that we can become efficient in this matter of singing without systematic and thorough training and disciplining of our powers in that direction, is very erroneous. None talk that way but those who do not know. That were all one with spiritual obedience and literal disobedience. That a theoretic and scientific knowledge of music is not the highest attainment, all will, or should, admit. Still, without this knowledge, one is certainly not well equipped for the higher attainments,—the higher, spiritual attainments,—which are made possible through these means. Reason without sentiment is dangerous, but sentiment without reason is more so. So, with Bro. M, I say, Let the teaching be done! Of course, it should be teaching, that will direct both head and heart aright. Anything else would not be teaching in Christian light. Again we say, Let the work be done! It is actually needed, and *greatly* needed.   J. HENRY SHOWALTER.

From the Scott Valley Church, Coffey Co., Kans.

WE are still doing what we can to advance the Master's cause. We have an interesting Sunday-school and Bible class every Sunday afternoon. Much interest is taken in the Bible class. I think it a great help in disseminating pure Bible doctrine. We had a very enjoyable Fourth this year. A large crowd of friends and neighbors met with us at sister Bouse's, where seats were prepared under the shade-trees in the yard. We

To-day our large house was well filled with attentive listeners. At 10 A. M., we had song services. At 11 o'clock, "Liberty," both politically and spiritually, was presented forcibly by Bro. Eby.

Next we had a recess, refreshments, social chat, and then children's meeting. Brethren, it is a step forward in the right direction to let the children feel that they are objects of especial care by our Father in heaven.

After this, "God be with you till we shall meet again," then "Farewell," with an occasional, intruding tear.

How much better to celebrate the anniversary of American liberty thus, than in the manner most generally done!   J. D. HAUGHTELIN.

July 4.

Notes and Jottings.

MAY 19 wife and I started for Shideler, Ind., to attend the love-feast at said place May 20. We had a very pleasant meeting and good attendance. Ministerial aid was sufficient from other Districts. Solomon Blickenstaff remained with us over Sunday, and assisted in preaching and in a children's meeting, held on Sunday afternoon, which seemed to be enjoyed by all present. May 28 the second ministerial meeting was held in Southern Ohio. The meeting was pleasant, and we hope it may result in good. I feel sure it can, if we all try to work for the purity of the church and labor to spread the Gospel far and wide, and if we, as ministers, work close up to the Gospel in all its characteristics. Had the ministers adhered more closely to the Gospel, as understood by the Brotherhood, we never would have had as much trouble among the laity, in regard to indifference and the worldly pleasure in fashion and many other ways. Ministers sow the seed, but the laity gives it room in the heart to grow. My co-laborers, let us take warning and profit thereby, and let our appearance and everything else be in harmony with the simplicity of the Gospel!

On the morning of June 4 wife and I, in company with many other brethren and sisters, set out for Cedar Rapids, Iowa, where we arrived in due time to attend the services in the Tabernacle on Sunday morning. We remained till the close of the Conference, as is our custom. Would it not be well when a local church elects a delegate to go to Annual Meeting, to require him to remain at his post till the close of the business of the Meeting, unless hindered by sickness, and if he will not promise to do this, to send the alternate? One-fourth of the delegates to be absent the last day of the Meeting does not look right to me. The Meeting was pleasant, yet there was considerable difference between the way we conduct the business now and the way it was conducted twenty, or even ten, or five years ago. We are getting to be much more parliamentary and act much more by motions and seconds. I hope it is all for the better, but some of our older brethren, that are not used to that way of proceeding, seem to be entirely silent now. They are afraid they cannot stick to the motion and cannot express their mind in that way.

We arrived home June 11. Our son, Edward, and wife, were also in our company from Cedar Rapids. June 16 I left home to meet with the members of the Eagle Creek church, Ohio. We commenced meeting the same evening, and continued till the evening of the 26th, with very good attendance and attention. One was baptized and we hope others may consider well and act wisely before it is too late. The feast took place June 18. On account of a heavy rain at the hour of the commencement of the meeting, the attendance was not as large as usual, but they

had a very pleasant, quiet feast, and trust we were all much built up and revived.

The old church in New Carlisle was taken down several weeks ago, and the walls of the basement for the new building are about completed. Bricklaying will soon commence, and we hope that by early fall the house will be ready for use. The members of the Christian church kindly offered us the use of their church while ours is in course of erection, and we are using that building at present. At our last meeting in that house, Bro. McCann preached. He also spoke at Forgy Station in the evening. He has, since then, returned to Virginia.

No preventing Providence, to-morrow we go to Oak Shade, a mission point, 125 miles distant. It is too far away to make a success. These isolated points need a resident minister to take care of the lambs through the week, as well as on the Lord's Day. Then they could have preaching every Sunday.

When will the time come when we can have suitable brethren for all these places,—men that will go? It is so much more pleasant to go among the more favored places, that it is sometimes hard to get these places filled, even for a week at a time. I must close these "Jottings," or they will find their way into the waste-basket. I have been troubled somewhat with asthma since Annual Meeting. Were there not so much that needs our attention, both temporally and spiritually, we would go to some northern climate a few months.   HENRY FRANTZ.

Lone Star Items.

THE Sunday-school of the Nocona church is fairly well attended. As it is held in an arbor, the weather frequently interferes. The weather has been very disagreeable quite often, on account of so much wind.

Eld. Henry Brubaker, wife and babe returned from their visit to Nebraska the last day of June. We were glad to see their pleasant faces among us again. Bro. B. was also at Annual Meeting, and on his return visited a few days with his son in Des Moines, Iowa.

July 2 the Nocona church met in quarterly council. Among other business, the church decided to hold a love-feast, and Aug. 27 was selected as the time, being two weeks after District Meeting. We would be glad if ministers would arrange to stay among us till our feast. Any Brethren, contemplating a visit to Texas, will please note the time of our District Meeting and our feast and try to be with us. A good representation from the churches of the District is desired. As I see no standing notice in the MESSENGER, I will here give the date and place again: Aug. 12, in the William's Creek church, Cook Co., Tex.

July 8, in company with Eld. Brubaker, wife and daughter, I went to the Pleasant Valley church, Clay Co., Tex. After a drive of about fifty miles we arrived at Bro. John Galaway's about sundown. Their quarterly council was held the following day. They decided to hold a feast Sept. 10, and also to hold a series of meetings, to commence about a week previous to the feast. Bro. Brubaker preached three very good sermons. We returned home on Monday, and found all well. This church has been without a minister for some time, consequently is under the care of the Mission Board. They feel encouraged and their future prospects are bright. There were six received by baptism in May, and there are others counting the cost. They are much in need of a resident minister. The District Mission Board has been trying to get a minister to locate, but so far has been un-

able to do so. Any minister that would like to move where there is a good chance for him to work for the Master, and also get a home cheap in a good country, would do well to correspond with the writer, or A. W. Austin, Secretary of Mission Board, Muenster, Tex. The Board would be glad to assist several good ministers to locate, and if they could get them, would be willing to see that they do not lack for the necessaries of life.

Eld. Abe Molsbee went to a new point last Saturday, in the southern part of Montague County, under the direction of the Mission Board. He reports good congregations. He is to start to Erath County, July 14, to hold a week's meetings, and go from there to Parker County, and preach a while for them. The harvest truly is great, and the laborers are few. Who will come over and help us? We see many Macedonian calls through the MESSENGER, and how many of them have to go unheeded?

Does Bro. Driskill, of Snyder, Scurry Co., Texas, know of any other members in that County? I suggest that correspondents always give the County with their Post-office address, so that they can be located when desired.   A. J. WINE.

Nocona, Montague Co., Tex., July 13.

From Johnson City, Tenn.

THE MESSENGER for July 5, is just to hand. and I am glad I have it, for it is certainly a very interesting number to me, from the fact that so much is said in it with reference to the music of the church. I certainly think much more should be written on this subject. Our people are a great singing people,—from a religious standpoint, however, rather than from a scientific stand-point. Not that the latter is not commendable, but that the former is *especially* so. This very thing gives us, as a church, the supreme basis for the highest possible musical development. Music, in the highest sense, is a thing of sentiment, dependent, of course, upon a proper physical and mental training, and with a pure, religious sentiment at the foundation, a very superior superstructure is made possible.

The editorial of J. H. M. consists of "words fitly spoken." The idea, however, advanced by some, that we can become efficient in this matter of singing without systematic and thorough training and disciplining of our powers in that direction, is very erroneous. None talk that way but those who do not know. That were all one with spiritual obedience and literal disobedience. That a theoretic and scientific knowledge of music is not the highest attainment, all will, or should, admit. Still, without this knowledge, one is certainly not well equipped for the higher attainments,—the higher, spiritual attainments,—which are made possible through these means. Reason without sentiment is dangerous, but sentiment without reason is more so. So, with Bro. M., I say, Let the teaching be done! Of course, it should be teaching, that will direct both head and heart aright. Anything else would not be teaching in Christian light. Again we say, Let the work be done! It is actually needed, and *greatly* needed.   J. HENRY SHOWALTER.

From the Scott Valley Church, Coffey Co., Kans.

WE are still doing what we can to advance the Master's cause. We have an interesting Sunday-school and Bible class every Sunday afternoon. Much interest is taken in the Bible class. I think it is a great help in disseminating pure Bible doctrine. We had a very enjoyable Fourth this year. A large crowd of friends and neighbors met with us at sister Bouse's, where seats were prepared under the shade trees in the yard. We

Tub, Pa.—Oct. 8, at 3:30 P. M., is the date appointed for the love-feast in the Maple Glen congregation, eight miles west from Railroad Station, at West Salisbury, Somerset Co., Pa. We expect to have preaching during the week prior to the feast, beginning on Saturday evening, Oct. 1, 1892, to be continued to the 9th.—*J. N. Davis, July 4.*

Knobnoster, Mo.—The Walnut Creek church met in quarterly council July 2. All business passed off very pleasantly. Our love-feast will be Oct. 1. We have arranged for one week's series of meetings, prior to the feast, commencing Saturday, Sept. 24. Our Sunday-school is progressing nicely, with an average attendance of sixty-four. The first quarter ended June 25. May we all be diligent workers in the Master's vineyard and instrumental in bringing souls to Christ—*Esther Cripe.*

Plymouth, Ind.—The brethren and sisters of the Union church met in quarterly council June 27. The church decided to hold a love-feast Oct. 14. One week's series of meetings will follow our love-feast. We will also have a series of meetings during the early winter, the Lord willing. Four have been added to our number since our last report,—one by baptism and three by letter. Our Sunday-school is in a very flourishing condition at present. We use the *Juvenile Quarterlies* for children.—*Laura Appelman.*

Ida, Kans.—I left home to go to the Brethren at Red Cloud, to hold some meetings for them. I met with earnest listeners and found the brethren and sisters to be full of zeal. Bro. Noah Wagoner is their minister. There are nineteen members there. Bro. William and sister Thomas, from Northern Illinois, moved there last spring, one mile due west of Red Cloud. Any of the brethren, passing through Red Cloud, are invited to stop off. Bro. Thomas, with the help of the Brethren and the offer of outsiders, will try to build a meeting-house this fall.—*Wm. Lugenbeel, June 25.*

Greentown, Ind.—Our quarterly council occurred June 18. All business was adjusted in a Christian manner, and, we hope, to the satisfaction of all. No doubt all felt as the elder remarked, that "it was good for us to be here." We are glad that our brethren and sisters here are taking a forward step, to help to bear one another's burdens by giving freely as God hath prospered them, for the spreading of the Gospel. Oct. 8, at 2 P. M., is the time appointed for our Communion. Bro. M. J. McClure will be with us, the Lord willing, and hold a series of meetings.—*A. J. Lantz.*

Lacon, Ill.—We, the members of the Pigeon Creek church, met in quarterly council July 9. Eld. Levi Trostle, of Franklin Grove, presided. The business was all adjusted in the best of Christian spirit, and, we believe, by the good admonitions of Eld. Trostle, the brethren and sisters were greatly encouraged, and are starting out with renewed zeal to labor more earnestly and zealously in the vineyard of the Lord.—*Sam. Henry, July 11.*

Harbor Springs, Mich.—The members of the Little Traverse church, Emmet Co., Mich., held their love-feast June 25. The weather was fine, and the meeting fairly attended. Twenty-seven members surrounded the tables of the Lord. Some were deprived of the privilege of assembling with us on account of sickness. May the Good Lord stand by them in the time of their affliction! Brethren J. R. Stateman and Isaac Hufford officiated. They did nobly in holding forth the ever-blessed Gospel. One more precious soul was received by baptism.—*L. B. Wilcox, July 6.*

Modale, Iowa.—The members of the Soldier River church had their regular meeting on Sunday, July 3. Bro. Sloatman was with us. He delivered a very good sermon. The large audience present were very well pleased with the discourse. May the good work go on!—*Hester A. Stevens, July 3.*

Arkansas City, Kans.—Sept. 3, at 5 A. M., a love-feast will be held in the Silver Creek church, Cowley Co., Kans., at the home of Samuel Anglemyer, eight miles south and three miles east of Winfield, and about eight miles north-east of Arkansas City. Those coming by rail will be met at either of the above-named places by informing Bro. O. Harader, at Arkansas City.—*Margaret E. Anglemyer, July 9.*

Mount Storm, W. Va.—July 2 our quarterly council was held in this congregation. It was entirely harmonious. There was no business before the meeting, only the "laying in store" as the Lord had prospered us. The writer was appointed correspondent and also agent for the MESSENGER, etc. The most pleasing feature of the meeting was the addition of five precious souls to the believers in Christ. We entreat them, as a father, to be faithful in the vineyard of the Lord. The crown is waiting.—*Raphael Baker, July 7.*

Mathias, W. Va.—Sunday, June 20, was the regular time for services at the Crab Run church (a branch of this church). At this meeting a young man sent in his application for membership, but being unable to attend. After the meeting the members were retained in council, relative to his reception. He was unanimously received. In the afternoon they met at the Halterman school-house, near his home, where brief services were held, after which they repaired to the water-side, where prayer was wont to be made. He was then buried in the liquid grave, and arose to walk in newness of life. Thus once more the saints on earth and the angels in heaven are made to rejoice. Saturday, July 2, occurred the church council of this church. Next day the regular services at the church were taken up by the funeral of a little child of brother S. W. and sister Sarah See.—*P. Braxton Fitzwater, July 7.*

Matrimonial.

" What therefore God hath joined together, let not man put asunder."

KULP—BRENNEMAN.—At the home of the groom, in Chester County, Pa., June 26, 1892, by the undersigned, Bro. Wm. W. Kulp, of the Coventry church, and sister Essie O. Brenneman, of Missouri. J. P. HETRIC.

GRIFFIN—SKIRVION.—At the residence of Grant Mumpower, near Baker's Ferry Bridge, Clackamas Co., Oregon, July 2, 1892, by the undersigned, D. Griffin and Susie Skirvion, both of Damascus, Oregon.
JOSIAH A. ROYER.

LAW—TADLOCK.—At the residence of the bride's sister, near Densmore, Norton Co., Kans., June 23, 1892, by Mr. J. C. Burton (United Brethren minister), Mr. Marchal Law, of Graham County, and Miss Amelia Tadlock, of Norton County, Kans. W. C. HRISEL.

HARNLY—WITMORE.—At 960 Fourth Avenue, New York City, July 8, 1892, by the undersigned, Bro. H. J. Harnly, of Auburn, Ill., and sister Sarah Witmore, of Centre View, Mo. T. T. MYERS.

DAVIS—MILLER.—At the residence of the undersigned, July 3, 1892, Joseph B. Davis and Annie K. Miller, of Westmoreland County, Pa. ISAIAH C. JOHNSON.

Fallen Asleep.

" Blessed are the dead which die in the Lord."

WILLIAMSON.—Near Bourbon, Ind., in the Yellow River congregation, June 15, 1892, sister Mary E. Williamson. She leaves a husband and three small children to mourn their loss. Funeral services conducted by Bro. S. P. Eversole and the writer. J. F. APPELMAN.

GARRETSON.—Near Todville, Iowa, July 5, 1892, Elsie M. Garretson, daughter of sister Rebecca Garretson, aged 15 years, 2 months and 24 days. Deceased was a walter in the dining-hall at our last Annual Meeting. She died from the effect of measles. Services by Bro. S. C. Miller from Job 14: 14, assisted by the brethren. J. K. MILLER.

SNIDEMAN.—In the Pipe Creek church, Ind., July 2, 1892, Bro. David Snideman, aged 87 years and 6 months. The deceased was born in Wurtemberg, Germany, Jan. 2, 1805. He came to Lancaster County, Pa., and was married to Sarah Myers, in 1830. He came to Indiana in an early day, and to Miami County in 1866. Bro. Snideman belonged to the church of the Brethren for forty-five years. His wife preceded him two years ago. Six children remain to mourn their loss. Funeral services at Pipe Creek church on Sunday following, by Bro. Daniel P. Shively, assisted by Bro. Daniel Bowser. W. R. DAILY.

ARMEY.—In the Eel River church, Kosciusko Co., Ind., near Silver Lake, June 8, 1892, of diphtheria, Ida Bell Armey, aged 10 years, 7 months and 18 days. Also, in the same family, June 10, 1892, Flora Armey, aged 5 years, 10 months and 20 days. They were regular attendants at our Sunday-school. Services by Bro. John Stafford, assisted by the writer. EMANUEL LEEKRONE.

SHOEMAKER.—In the same church, near Silver Lake, June 30, 1892, of consumption, Sarah Shoemaker, aged 28 years, 1 month and 26 days. She was baptized May 4, 1892, by the writer, and was anointed with oil June 7, 1892. On the evening of June 27, a few brethren and sisters held a Communion meeting at Bro. Shoemaker's house, of which she partook, and then peacefully passed away a few days later. She leaves a husband and one little boy. Services by Bro. John Stafford, assisted by the writer.

BOLLINGER.—At Essex, Iowa, July 6, 1892, Fanny Bollinger, daughter of Bro. Henry Royer, of Darke County, Ohio, aged 53 years, 5 months and 27 days. She was the mother of thirteen children, three of whom preceded her to the spirit land. Funeral services by the writer.
ISAAC BARTO.

BROWER.—In the Salem church, Marion Co., Oregon, sister Salome Brower, wife of Bro. David Brower, aged 73 years and 6 months. Funeral services by the writer from Heb. 11: 13 to a sympathizing congregation.
JOSEPH B. EARLY.

GWIN.—July 5, 1892, Edgar Jacob Gwin, infant son of Bro. Jacob N. and sister Jane Gwin, aged 6 months. Funeral services at the Brethren's church, July 6, by Eld. Sidney Hodgden. J. U. G. STIVERSON.

TOM.—In the Bethel church, Ind., May 31, 1892, sister Lucinda (Nine) Tom, wife of Geo. Tom, of dropsy of heart, after a protracted illness of several months, aged 49 years, 7 months and 14 days. She was the mother of ten children. Funeral services at the residence by the writer, from Rev. 14: 13. W. R. DEETER.

BURGET.—In the Lower Cumberland church, Pa., July 1, 1892, Bro. Samuel Burget, aged 51 years, 3 months and 17 days. Funeral discourse by the writer and Bro. Henry Beelman. J. B. GARVER.

The Gospel Messenger

Is the recognized organ of the German Baptist or Brethren's church, and advocates the form of doctrine taught in the New Testament and pleads for a return to apostolic and primitive Christianity.

It recognizes the New Testament as the only infallible rule of faith and practice, and maintains that Faith toward God, Repentance from dead works, Regeneration of the heart and mind, baptism by Trine Immersion for remission of sins unto the reception of the Holy Ghost by the laying on of hands, are the means of adoption into, the household of God,—the church militant.

It also maintains that Feet-washing, as taught in John 13: both by example and command of Jesus, should be observed in the church.

That the Lord's Supper, instituted by Christ and as universally observed by the apostles and the early Christians, is a full meal, and, in connection with the Communion, should be taken in the evening or after the close of the day.

That the Salutation of the Holy Kiss, or Kiss of Charity, is binding upon the followers of Christ.

That War and Retaliation are contrary to the spirit and self-denying principles of the religion of Jesus Christ.

That the principle of Plain Dressing and of Non-conformity to the world, as taught in the New Testament, should be observed by the followers of Christ.

That the Scriptural duty of Anointing the Sick with Oil, in the Name of the Lord, James 5: 14, is binding upon all Christians.

It also advocates the church's duty to support Missionary and Tract Work, thus giving to the Lord for the spread of the Gospel and for the conversion of sinners.

In short, it is a vindicator of all that Christ and the apostles have enjoined upon us, and aims, amid the conflicting theories and discords of modern Christendom, to point out ground that all must concede to be infallibly safe.

☞ The above principles of our Fraternity are set forth on our "Brethren's Envelopes." Use them! Price, 15 cents er package; 40 cents per hundred.

Tub, Pa.—Oct. 8, at 3:30 P. M., is the date appointed for the love-feast in the Maple Glen congregation, eight miles west from Railroad Station, at West Salisbury, Somerset Co., Pa. We expect to have preaching during the week prior to the feast, beginning on Saturday evening, Oct. 1, 1892, to be continued to the 9th.—*J. N. Davis, July 4.*

Knobnoster, Mo.—The Walnut Creek church met in quarterly council July 2. All business passed off very pleasantly. Our love-feast will be Oct. 1. We have arranged for one week's series of meetings, prior to the feast, commencing Saturday, Sept. 24. Our Sunday-school is progressing nicely, with an average attendance of sixty-four. The first quarter ended June 25. May we all be diligent workers in the Master's vineyard and instrumental in bringing souls to Christ!—*Esther Cripe.*

Plymouth, Ind.—The brethren and sisters of the Union church met in quarterly council June 27. The church decided to hold a love-feast Oct. 14. One week's series of meetings will follow our love-feast. We will also have a series of meetings during the early winter, the Lord willing. Four have been added to our number since our last report,—one by baptism and three by letter. Our Sunday-school is in a very flourishing condition at present. We use the *Juvenile Quarterlies* for children.—*Laura Appelman.*

Ida, Kans.—I left home to go to the Brethren at Red Cloud, to hold some meetings for them. I met with earnest listeners and found the brethren and sisters to be full of zeal. Bro. Noah Wagoner is their minister. There are nineteen members there. Bro. William and sister Thomas, from Northern Illinois, moved there last spring, one mile due west of Red Cloud. Any of the brethren, passing through Red Cloud, are invited to stop off. Bro. Thomas, with the help of the Brethren and the offer of outsiders, will try to build a meeting-house this fall.—*Wm. Lugenbeel, June 25.*

Greentown, Ind.—Our quarterly council occurred June 18. All business was adjusted in a Christian manner, and, we hope, to the satisfaction of all. No doubt all felt as the elder remarked, that "it was good for us to be here." We are glad that our brethren and sisters here are taking a forward step, to help to bear one another's burdens by giving freely as God hath prospered them, for the spreading of the Gospel. Oct. 8, at 2 P. M., is the time appointed for our Communion. Bro. M. J. McClure will be with us, the Lord willing, and hold a series of meetings.—*A. J. Lantz.*

Lacon, Ill.—We, the members of the Pigeon Creek church, met in quarterly council July 9. Eld. Levi Trostle, of Franklin Grove, presided. The business was all adjusted in the best of Christian spirit, and, we believe, by the good admonitions of Eld. Trostle, the brethren and sisters were greatly encouraged, and are starting out with renewed zeal to labor more earnestly and zealously in the vineyard of the Lord.—*Sam. Henry, July 11.*

Harbor Springs, Mich.—The members of the Little Traverse church, Emmet Co., Mich., held their love-feast June 25. The weather was fine, and the meeting fairly attended. Twenty-seven members surrounded the tables of the Lord. Some were deprived of the privilege of assembling with us on account of sickness. May the Good Lord stand by them in the time of their affliction! Brethren J. R. Stutsman and Isaac Hufford officiated. They did nobly in holding forth the ever-blessed Gospel. One more precious soul was received by baptism.—*L. B. Wilcox, July 6.*

Modale, Iowa.—The members of the Soldier River church had their regular meeting on Sunday, July 3. Bro. Sloatman was with us. He delivered a very good sermon. The large audience present were very well pleased with the discourse. May the good work go on!—*Hester A. Stevens, July 9.*

Arkansas City, Kans.—Sept. 3, at 5 A. M., a love-feast will be held in the Silver Creek church, Cowley Co., Kans., at the home of Samuel Anglemyer, eight miles south and three miles east of Winfield, and about eight miles north-east of Arkansas City. Those coming by rail will be met at either of the above-named places by informing Bro. C. Harader, at Arkansas City.—*Margaret E. Anglemyer, July 9.*

Mount Storm, W. Va.—July 2 our quarterly council was held in this congregation. It was entirely harmonious. There was no business before the meeting, only the "laying in store" as the Lord had prospered us. The writer was appointed correspondent and also agent for the MESSENGER, etc. The most pleasing feature of the meeting was the addition of five precious souls to the believers in Christ. We entreat them, as a father, to be faithful in the vineyard of the Lord. The crown is waiting.—*Raphael Baker, July 7.*

Mathias, W. Va.—Sunday, June 20, was the regular time for services at the Crab Run church (a branch of this church). At this meeting a young man sent in his application for membership, he being unable to attend. After the meeting the members were retained in council, relative to his reception. He was unanimously received. In the afternoon they met at the Halterman schoolhouse, near his home, where brief services were held, after which they repaired to the water-side, where prayer was wont to be made. He was then buried in the liquid grave, and arose to walk in newness of life. Thus once more the saints on earth and the angels in heaven are made to rejoice. Saturday, July 2, occurred the church council of this church. Next day the regular services at the church were taken up by the funeral of a little child of brother S. W. and sister Sarah See.—*P. Braxton Fitzwater, July 7.*

Matrimonial.

"What therefore God hath joined together, let not man put asunder."

KULP—BRENNEMAN.—At the home of the groom, in Chester County, Pa., June 26, 1892, by the undersigned, Bro. Wm. W. Kulp, of the Coventry church, and sister Essie O. Brenneman, of Missouri. J. P. HETRIC.

GRIFFIN—SKIRVION.—At the residence of Grant Mumpower, near Baker's Ferry Bridge, Clackamas Co., Oregon, July 2, 1892, by the undersigned, D. Griffin and Susie Skirvion, both of Damascus, Oregon.
JOSIAH A. ROYER.

LAW—TADLOCK.—At the residence of the bride's sister, near Densmore, Norton Co., Kans., June 23, 1892, by Mr. J. C. Burton (United Brethren minister), Mr. Marchal Law, of Graham County, and Miss Amelia Tadlock, of Norton County, Kans. W. C. HEISEL.

HARNLY—WITMORE.—At 260 Fourth Avenue, New York City, July 8, 1892, by the undersigned, Bro. H. J. Harnly, of Auburn, Ill., and sister Sarah Witmore, of Centre View, Mo. T. T. MYERS.

DAVIS—MILLER.—At the residence of the undersigned, July 3, 1892, Joseph B. Davis and Annie K. Miller, of Westmoreland County, Pa. ISAIAH C. JOHNSON.

Fallen Asleep.

"Blessed are the dead which die in the Lord."

WILLIAMSON.—Near Bourbon, Ind., in the Yellow River congregation, June 15, 1892, sister Mary E. Williamson. She leaves a husband and three small children to mourn their loss. Funeral services conducted by Bro. S. P. Eversole and the writer. J. F. APPELMAN.

GARRETSON.—Near Todville, Iowa, July 5, 1892, Elsie M. Garretson, daughter of sister Rebecca Garretson, aged 15 years, 2 months and 24 days. Deceased was a waiter in the dining-hall at our last Annual Meeting. She died from the effect of measles. Services by Bro. S. C. Miller from Job 14: 14, assisted by the brethren. J. K. MILLER.

SNIDEMAN.—In the Pipe Creek church, Ind., July 2, 1892, Bro. David Snideman, aged 87 years and 6 months. The deceased was born in Wurtemberg, Germany, Jan. 2, 1805. He came to Lancaster County, Pa., and was married to Sarah Myers, in 1830. He came to Indiana in an early day, and to Miami County in 1866. Bro. Snideman belonged to the church of the Brethren for forty-five years. His wife preceded him two years ago. Six children remain to mourn their loss. Funeral services at Pipe Creek church on Sunday following, by Bro. Daniel P. Shively, assisted by Bro. Daniel Bowser. W. B. DAILY.

ARMEY.—In the Eel River church, Kosciusko Co., Ind., near Silver Lake, June 8, 1892, of diphtheria, Ida Bell Armey, aged 10 years, 7 months and 18 days. Also, in the same family, June 10, 1892, Flora Armey, aged 5 years, 10 months and 20 days. They were regular attendants at our Sunday-school. Services by Bro. John Stafford, assisted by the writer.

SHOEMAKER.—In the same church, near Silver Lake, June 30, 1892, of consumption, Sarah Shoemaker, aged 28 years, 1 month and 26 days. She was baptized May 4, 1892, by the writer, and was anointed with oil June 7, 1892. On the evening of June 27, a few brethren and sisters held a Communion meeting at Bro. Shoemaker's house, of which she partook, and then peacefully passed away a few days later. She leaves a husband and one little boy. Services by Bro. John Stafford, assisted by the writer.
EMANUEL LECKRONE.

BOLLINGER.—At Essex, Iowa, July 6, 1892, Fanny Bollinger, daughter of Bro. Henry Royer, of Darke County, Ohio, aged 53 years, 5 months and 27 days. She was the mother of thirteen children, three of whom preceded her to the spirit land. Funeral services by the writer.
ISAAC BARTO.

BROWER.—In the Salem church, Marion Co., Oregon, sister Salome Brower, wife of Bro. David Brower, aged 73 years and 6 months. Funeral services by the writer from Heb. 11: 13 to a sympathizing congregation.
JOSEPH B. EARLY.

GWIN.—July 5, 1892, Edgar Jacob Gwin, infant son of Bro. Jacob N. and sister Jane Gwin, aged 6 months. Funeral services at the Brethren's church, July 6, by Eld. Sidney Hodgden. J. U. G. STIVERSON.

TOM.—In the Bethel church, Ind., May 31, 1892, sister Lucinda (Nine) Tom, wife of Geo. Tom, of dropsy of heart, after a protracted illness of several months, aged 49 years, 7 months and 14 days. She was the mother of ten children. Funeral services at the residence by the writer, from Rev. 14: 13. W. R. DEETER.

BURGET.—In the Lower Cumberland church, Pa., July 1, 1892, Bro. Samuel Burget, aged 51 years, 3 months and 17 days. Funeral discourse by the writer and Bro. Henry Beelman. J. B. GARVER.

The Gospel Messenger

Is the recognized organ of the German Baptist or Brethren's church, and advocates the form of doctrine taught in the New Testament and pleads for a return to apostolic and primitive Christianity.

It recognizes the New Testament as the only infallible rule of faith and practice, and maintains that Faith toward God, Repentance from dead works, Regeneration of the heart and mind, baptism by Trine Immersion for remission of sins unto the reception of the Holy Ghost by the laying on of hands, are the means of adoption into the household of God,—the church militant.

It also maintains that Feet-washing, as taught in John 13, both by example and command of Jesus, should be observed in the church.

That the Lord's Supper, instituted by Christ and as universally observed by the apostles and the early Christians, is a full meal, and, in connection with the Communion, should be taken in the evening or after the close of the day.

That the Salutation of the Holy Kiss, or Kiss of Charity, is binding upon the followers of Christ.

That War and Retaliation are contrary to the spirit and self-denying principles of the religion of Jesus Christ.

That the principle of Plain Dressing and of Non-conformity to the world, as taught in the New Testament, should be observed by the followers of Christ.

That the Scriptural duty of Anointing the Sick with Oil, in the Name of the Lord, James 5: 14, is binding upon all Christians.

It also advocates the church's duty to support Missionary and Tract Work, thus giving to the Lord for the spread of the Gospel and for the conversion of sinners.

In short, it is a vindicator of all that Christ and the apostles have enjoined upon us, and aims, amid the conflicting theories and discords of modern Christendom, to point out ground that all must concede to be infallibly safe.

☞ The above principles of our Fraternity are set forth on our "Brethren's Envelopes." Use them! Price, 15 cents per package; 40 cents per hundred.

Announcements.

LOVE-FEASTS.

Aug. 13, at 2 P. M., Ogan's Creek church, five miles south-east of North Manchester, Wabash Co., Ind.

Aug. 19, at 4 P. M., the Bear Creek church, Palmer, Ill.

Aug. 27 and 28, at 4 P. M., Solem, in Sandy Creek congregation, Preston Co., W. Va.

Aug. 27, at 4 P. M., Notona church, Montague Co., Tex.

Sept. 1, at 4 P. M., Sugar Creek church, Sangamon County, Ill., 4 miles east of Auburn, Ill.

Sept. 3, at 3 P. M., Rockton church, Pa.

Sept. 3, at 10 A. M., Mt. Etna church, Ind. Conveyances on Friday, Sept. 2, at Corning.

Sept. 3, at 2 P. M., at Independence, Kans.

Sept. 3, at 10 A. M., Washington church, Kans., at Bro. Wm. R. Phillippi's residence, three mile 1 south, and three and one-half miles west of Washington, Kans.

Sept. 3, at 5 P. M., Silver Creek church, Cowley Co., Kans.

Sept. 3, Mill Creek church, Adams Co., Ill.

Sept. 3 and 4, English River congregation, Keokuk Co., Iowa.

Sept. 6, at 4 P. M., Indian Creek congregation, Fayette Co., Pa. Series of meetings to commence Aug. 27.

Sept. 7 and 8, at 2 P. M., Scott Valley, Coffey Co., Kans, at the house of W. A. Smith, one mile east and five south of Waverly. A series of meetings to be held in connection with the feast.

Sept. 9, at 10 A. M., Monroe County church, Iowa.

Sept. 10 and 11, Farnhamville, Calhoun Co., Iowa. Series of meetings in connection, beginning one week previous.

Sept. 10 and 11, at 2 P. M., Sterling church, Sterling, Ill.

Sept. 17, at 2 P. M., Bethel congregation, at the Bethlehem meeting-house, Holt Co., Mo. For any information address Jas. Andes, Mound City, Holt Co., Mo.

Sept. 14, at 5 P. M., in La Porte church, La Porte, Ind. Trains will be met in the forenoon and early afternoon of the day of meeting.

Sept. 24, at 3 P. M., Martin's Creek church, Wayne Co., Ill.

Sept. 24 and 25, at 3 P. M., Lanark church, Carroll Co., Ill.

Sept. 26, South Bend church, Ind.

Sept. 28, at 10 A. M., Spring Creek church, Kosciusko Co., Ind.

Sept. 29 and 30, at 2 P. M., Rock Creek, Whiteside Co., Ill.

Sept. 30, at 4 P. M., Nettle Creek church, near Hagerstown, Wayne Co., Ind.

Sept. 30, at 2 P. M., Milmine church, Piatt Co., Ill.

Oct. 1, at 2 P. M., Sugar Creek church, Allen Co., Ohio.

Oct. 1 and 2, at 5 P. M., Berrien Congregation, Mich.

Oct. 1 and 2, at 10 A. M., West Branch church, Ill. One week's meeting previous to feast.

Oct. 1 and 2, at 2 P. M., near Ames, Boone Co., Iowa. Noon trains meet at Ames on Saturday.

Oct. 1 and 2, at 4 P. M., Osage church, Crawford Co., Kans.

Oct. 1, at 4 P. M., Logan church, near DeGraff, Ohio.

Oct. 1 and 2, Saginaw church, Mich.

Oct. 1 and 2, at 1: 30 P. M., Walnut Valley congregation, Barton Co., Kans.

Oct. 1 and 2, at 3 P. M., Alleghany congregation, Grant Co., W. Va.

Oct. 1, Maple Grove church, Norton Co., Kans.

Oct. 1, at 10 A. M., Appanoose church, Kans.

Oct. 1, at 10 A. M., Elgin Mile church, Ind., at the town of Markle.

Oct. 1 and 2, at 11 A. M., Riverdale, Iowa. Those coming by rail will stop at Iowa Junction, on B. C. R. & N. R. R., where they will be met.

Oct. 1, at 10 A. M., Stone Lick church, Clermont Co., Ohio.

Oct. 1 and 2, at 10 A. M., in the Beaver Dam church, Kosciusko Co., Ind., near the town of Burket.

Oct. 5, at 2 P. M., Rossen church, Ind.

Oct. 1, at 2 P. M., Spring Creek church, in the Kelsh's church-house, eleven miles south-west of Reece, Kans.

Oct. 6 and 7, at 10 A. M., Shannon, Ill.

Oct. 6, at 2 P. M., Arcadia church, Ind.

Oct. 7, Black River church, Van Buren Co., Mich. Brethren coming by rail will stop off at Bangor.

Oct. 7, at 2 P. M., Ladoga, Ind.

Oct. 7, at 2 P. M., Kaskaskia church, Fayette Co., Ill. 10 m by rail south-west of Beecher City, Ill. Those coming by rail will be met at the above-named place by ,informing Granville Nevinger.

Oct. 7, at 10 A. M., Sugar Creek, Whitley Co., Ind.

Oct. 7, at 2 P. M., Rossmon Creek church, Montgomery Co., Ind., one and one-half miles north west of Ladoga.

Oct. 1, at 4 P. M., Mississippi Creek church, Montgomery Co., Ill. Those coming by rail will be met at Farmersville, on Springfield Road, and at Girard, on St. Louis Road on morning of meeting.

Oct. 8 and 9, at 10 A. M., Woodland church, Pulton Co., Ill. A series of meetings one week previous to the feast, and to continue two weeks.

Oct. 8, at 2 P. M., North Star, Darke County, Ohio.

Oct. 8, at 2 P. M., Greentown church, at Greentown, Howard Co., Ind.

Oct. 8, at 3: 30 P. M., Maple Glen church, Somerset Co., Pa.

Oct. 8, at 1 P. M., in the Elkhart Valley church, Elkhart Co., Ind.

Oct. 8 and 9, at 1 P. M., Arnold's Grove, Ill.

Oct. 8, at 10 A. M., Dry Creek church, Linn Co., Iowa, one mile west of Robins Station.

Oct. 8, Swan Creek congregation, Ohio, 3½ miles west of Delta, Ohio.

Oct. 8, at 4 P. M., Washington Creek church, Douglas Co., Kans.

Oct. 14, at 4 P. M., Union church, Marshal Co., Ind., five miles west of Plymouth. Trains will be met at both Plymouth and Burr Oak.

Oct. 14, Union church, Plymouth, Marshall Co., Ind. This church would like to have some brother hold a meeting a week or ten days after.

Oct. 28, at 1 P. M., South Beatrice church, Gage Co., Nebr. Conveyances the day before meeting at B. & M. depot, in Beatrice; Rock Island depot, in Rockford; Union Pacific depot, in Holmesville.

Oct. 28, at 4 P. M., Walnut church, Marshall Co., Ind.

Oct. 29, at 2 P. M., Ozawkie church, Kans. A series of meetings to commence Oct. 10.

Oct. 29 and 30, at 10 A. M., Pigeon Creek church, Ill., at the Oak Grove meeting-house.

Oct. 30, at 2 P. M., Osck church, Madison Co., Ind., at 3½ miles east of Summitville.

Nov. 5, at 3 P. M., Hickory Grove church, Richland Co., Ill., 3½ miles North-east of Parkersburg, Ill. Conveyance will be at the above place by in'orming J. M. Forney.

The Normal College.

THE Fall Term of fifteen weeks opens Sept. 12. For recommendations and inducements, we point you to the work that has been done and the success of its graduates. In proportion to the number of the graduates, no school in the country can show a better record. A good, solid, practical education is what you want, and this is what we p'opose to give.

For special information, Catalogues and a *free copy* of the *Juniata Echo*, address H. B. Brumbaugh, President, or J. H. Brumbaugh, Principal, Huntingdon, Pa. 28tf

EUROPE AND Bible Lands

A new edition of this deservedly popular work has recently been published. It retains all the excellencies of its predecessors, and with those who are interested in Bible study this work will always remain a favorite. Those who have read the ordinary book of travel will be surprised to find "Europe and Bible Lands" of thrilling interest for both old and young. The large number of books, already sold, proves that the work is of more than ordinary merit.

A fair supply of the last edition of this is with us on hand. Those who have not yet secured a copy of the work should embrace this opportunity of securing it. Price, in fine cloth binding, only $1.50 per copy, post-paid. To agents who are prepared to push an active canvass of the work, we are prepared to give special inducements. Write us:

BRETHREN'S PUBLISHING CO.,
Mt. Morris, Ill.

--- THE ---
Doctrine of the Brethren Defended.

THIS work contains a complete exposition of the faith and practice of the Brethren, the Divinity of Christ, the Divinity of the Holy Spirit, Immersion, Feet-washing, the Lord's Supper, the Holy Kiss, Non-conformity, Secret Societies, etc. Price, per copy, cloth binding, $1.25. Address this office.

GOOD BOOKS FOR ALL.

ANY book in the market furnished at publishers' lowest retail price by the Brethren's Publishing Company, Mt. Morris, Ill.. *Special prices given when books are purchased in quantities.* When ordering books, not on our list, if possible give title, name of author, and address of publishers.

The Throne of David.—By J. H. Ingraham. Cloth, $1.50.

Homiletics and Pastoral Theology.—By W. G. T. Shedd. Cloth, $2.50.

Lectures on Preaching.—By Rev. Phillips Brooks. Cloth, 16mo. $1.50.

Josephus' Complete Works.—Large type, 1 vol. 8vo. Illustrated with many steel and wood engravings. Library sheep, $3.00.

The Doctrine of the Holy Spirit.—By James B Walker. Cloth, $1.25.

The New Testament History.—By Wm. Smith. Cloth, $1.25.

The Path of Life.—An interesting tract for everybody. Price, 20 cents per copy; 100 copies, $6.00.

Smith's Bible Dictionary.—Edited by Peloubet. Cloth, $2.00; leather, $3.00.

The Origin and Growth of Religion.—Hibbert Lectures. By T. W. R. Davids. Cloth, 8vo, $2.50.

The Old Testament History.—By William Smith. Cloth, $1.25.

The Great Events of History.—By W.F. Collier. Cloth, $1.25.

Biblical Theology of the Old Testament.—By R. F. Weidner. Cloth, $1.25.

The Prince of the House of David.—By J. H. Ingraham. Cloth, $1.50.

Biblical Antiquities.—By John Nevin. Gives a concise account of Bible times and customs; invaluable to all students of Bible subjects. Price, $1.50.

Bible Work, or Bible Reader's Commentary on the New Testament.—By J. G. Butler. Two vols. 8vo. $10.00.

Trine Immersion.—A vindication of the apostolic form of Christian baptism. By Eld. James Quinter. A most complete and reliable work on the subject. Price, cloth, single copy, $1.25; leather, $1.75.

The Life and Epistle of the Apostle Paul.—By W. J. Conybeare. Cloth, $1.00.

Sacred Geography and Antiquities.—A practical helpful work for Bible students, ministers and Sunday-school teachers. Price, $2.25.

Popular Commentary on the New Testament.—Edited by Philip Schaff. Four volumes, 8vo. Matthew, Mark and Luke: $6.00. John and the Acts, $6.00. Romans to Philemon: $6.00. Hebrews to Revelation: $5.00.

Ante-Nicene Christian Library.—A collection of all the works of the Fathers of the Christian Church prior to the Council of Nice. Edited by Rev. Alexander Roberts, D. D., and James Donaldson, LL. D. Twenty-four vols. 8 vo. Per vol. $3.00.

Bunyan's Pilgrim's Progress.—An excellent edition of this good work, printed on good paper, finely illustrated with forty engravings, at the low price of $1.00 per copy.

The House We Live In.—By Daniel Vaninian. It gives a concise account of the faith and practice of the Brethren. Price, 100 copies, 60 cents.

Family Bible, with Notes and Instructions.—Contains the harmony of the Gospels, Chronology, Maps, Tables of Weights and Measures, Family Record, eight elegant Illustrations, etc. Price, substantially bound, $4.50.

Good Words for Neighbors.

I want to say to the brethren and all readers of the MESSENGER, that I will sell single top-buggies and two-seated family carriages at greatly reduced prices. I will put forth every effort I possibly can, to have these buggies and carriages introduced in every locality. Reader, now is your time to buy a good, serviceable buggy or carriage, of any style you want, at a lower price than you can buy at wholesale. Brethren wanting plainly-finished buggies, can have them on short notice. I could give a number of testimonials of brethren that have purchased buggies and carriages of us this season, but space will not permit me to do so. Buggies are carefully crated and shipped at our risk. I pay all freight charges. All quotations answered and price given to all that will address me by letter. ABRAHAM E. WEAVER, Syracuse, Kosciusko Co., Ind.

Announcements.

LOVE-FEASTS.

Aug. 13, at 2 P. M., Ogan's Creek church, five miles south-east of North Manchester, Wabash Co., Ind.

Aug. 19, at 4 P. M., the Bear Creek church, Palmer, Ill.

Aug. 27 and 28, at 4 P. M., Salem, in Sandy Creek congregation, Preston Co., W. Va.

Aug. 27, at 4 P. M., Nocona church, Montague Co., Tex.

Sept. 2, at 6 P. M., Sugar Creek church, Sangamon County, Ill., 9 miles east of Auburn, Ill.

Sept. 2, at 3 P. M., Rockton church, Pa.

Sept. 2, 10 10 A. M., Mt. Etna church, Iowa. Conveyances on Friday, Sept. 1, at Corning.

Sept. 2, at 2 P. M., at Independence, Kans.

Sept. 2, 10 10 A. M., Washington church, Kans., at Bro. Wm. R. Phillippi's residence, three miles south, and three and one-half miles west of Washington, Kans.

Sept. 2, at 3 P. M., Silver Creek church, Cowley Co., Kans.

Sept. 2, Mill Creek church, Adams Co., Ill.

Sept. 2 and 4, English River congregation, Keokuk Co., Iowa.

Sept. 2, at 2 A. M., Indian Creek congregation, Fayette Co., Pa. Series of meetings to commence Aug. 27.

Sept. 7 and 8, at 2 P. M., South Valley, Colfay Co., Kans., at the house of W. A. Smith, one mile east and five south of Waverly. A series of meetings to be held in connection with the feast.

Sept. 9, at 10 A. M., Monroe County church, Iowa.

Sept. 10 and 11, Fernhamville, Calhoun Co., Iowa. Series of meetings in connection, beginning one week previous.

Sept. 10 and 11, at 2 P. M., Sterling church, Sterling, Ill.

Sept. 13, at 2 P. M., Bethel congregation, at the Bethlehem meeting-house, Holt Co., Mo. For any information address Jas. Andes, Mound City, Holt Co., Mo.

Sept. 12, at 5 P. M., in La Porte church, La Porte, Ind. Trains will be met in the forenoon and early afternoon of the day of meeting.

Sept. 14, at 3 P. M., Martin's Creek church, Wayne Co., Ill.

Sept. 14 and 25, at 2 P. M., Losank church, Carroll Co., Ill.

Sept. 16, South Bend church, Ind.

Sept. 16, at 10 A. M., Spring Creek church, Kosciusko Co., Ind.

Sept. 19 and 20, at 2 P. M., Rock Creek, Whiteside Co., Ill.

Sept. 20, at 10 A. M., Nettle Creek church, near Hagerstown, Wayne Co., Ind.

Sept. 30, at 2 P. M., Milmine church, Piatt Co., Ill.

Oct. 1, at 2 P. M., Sugar Creek church, Allen Co., Ohio.

Oct. 1, at 2 P. M., Berrien Congregation, Mich.

Oct. 1 and 2, 10 10 A. M., West Branch church, Ill. One week's meeting previous to feast.

Oct. 1 and 2, at 2 P. M., near Ames, Boone Co., Iowa. Noon train meet at Ames on Saturday.

Oct. 1, at 3 P. M., Osage church, Crawford Co., Kans.

Oct. 1, at 4 P. M., Logan church, near DeGraff, Ohio.

Oct. 1 and 2, Saginaw church, Mich.

Oct. 1 and 2, at 1: 30 P. M., Walnut Valley congregation, Barton Co., Kans.

Oct. 1 and 2, at 3 P. M., Alleghony congregation, Grant Co., W. Va.

Oct. 1, Maple Grove church, Norton Co., Kans.

Oct. 1, 10 10 A. M., Appanoose church, Kans.

Oct. 1, at 10 A. M., Eight Mile church, Ind., at the town of Mahalt.

Oct. 1 and 2, at 11 A. M., Riverside, Iowa. Those coming by rail will stop at Iowa Junction, on B. C. R. & N. R. R., where they will be met.

Oct. 2, at 10 A. M., Stone Lick church, Clermont Co., Ohio.

Oct. 3, 4 at 10 A. M., in the Beaver Dam church, Kosci., usko Co., Ind., near the town of Burket.

Oct. 5, at 2 P. M., Rearo church, Ind.

Oct. 6, at 5 P. M., Spring Creek church, in the Keith's church-house, eleven miles south-west of Rocco, Kans.

Oct. 6 and 7, at 10 A. M., Shannon, Ill.

Oct. 6, at 2 P. M., Arcadia church, Ind.

Oct. 7, Black River church, Van Buren Co., Mich. Brethren coming by rail will stop off at Bangor.

Oct. 7, at 2 P. M., Ludoga, Ind.

Oct. 7, at 2 P. M., Kaskaskia church, Fayette Co., Ill. ten miles south-west of Beecher City, Ill. Those coming by rail will be met at the above-named place by informing Granville Nevinger.

Oct. 7, at 10 A. M., Sugar Creek, Whitley Co., Ind.

Oct. 7, 10 2 P. M., Raccoon Creek church, Montgomery Co., Ind., one and one half miles north west of Ladoga.

Oct. 7, at 2 P. M., Marquis Creek church, Montgomery Co., Ill. Those coming by rail will be met at Farmersville, on Spring field Road, east at Girard, on St. Louis Road on morning of meeting.

Oct. 8 and 9, at 10 A. M., Woodland church, Fulton Co., Ill. A series of meetings one week previous to the feast, and to continue two weeks.

Oct. 8, at 2 P. M., North Star, Darke County, Ohio.

Oct. 8, at 2 P. M., Greentown church, at Greentown, Howard Co., Ind.

Oct. 8, at 3: 30 P. M., Maple Glen church, Somerset Co., Pa.

Oct. 8, at 2 P. M., in the Elkhart Valley church, Elkhart Co., Ind.

Oct. 8 and 9, at 1 P. M., Arnold's Grove, Ill.

Oct. 8, 10 10 A. M., Dry Creek church, Linn Co., Iowa, one mile west of Robins Station.

Oct. 8, Swan Creek congregation, Ohio, 3½ miles west of Delta, Ohio.

Oct. 8, at 2 P. M., Washington Creek church, Douglas Co., Kans.

Oct. 14, at 2 P. M., Union church, Marshall Co., Ind., five miles west of Plymouth. Trains will be met at both Plymouth and Burr Oak.

Oct. 14, Union church, Plymouth, Marshall Co., Ind. This church would like to have some brother hold a meeting a week or ten days after.

Oct. 28, at 2 P. M., South Beatrice church, Gage Co., Nebr. Conveyances the day before meeting at B. & M. depot, in Beatrice; Rock Island depot, in Rockford; Union Pacific depot, in Holmesville.

Oct. 28, at 4 P. M., Walnut church, Marshall Co., Ind.

Oct. 29, at 2 P. M., Ozywkie church, Kans. A series of meetings to commence Oct. 20.

Oct. 29 and 30, at 10 A. M., Pigeon Creek church, Ill., at the Oak Grove meeting-house.

Oct. 30, at 2 P. M., Oscle church, Madison Co., Ind., 3½ miles east of Summitville.

Nov. 5, at 3 P. M., Big Creek church, Richland Co., Ill., 3½ miles North-east of Parkersburg, Ill. Conveyance will be at the above place by informing J. M. Forney.

The Normal College.

THE Fall Term of fifteen weeks opens Sept. 12. For recommendations and inducements, we point you to the work that has been done and the success of its graduates. In proportion to the number of the graduates, no school in the country can show a better record. A good, solid, practical education is what you want, and this is what we propose to give.

For special information, Catalogues and a *free* copy of the *Juniata Echo*, address H. B. Brumbaugh, President, or J. H. Brumbaugh, Principal, Huntingdon, Pa. 28tf

---

EUROPE

AND

Bible Lands

A new edition of this deservedly popular work has recently been published. It retains all the excellencies of its predecessors, and with those who are interested in Bible study this work will always remain a favorite. Those who have read the ordinary book of travel will be surprised to find "Europe and Bible Lands" of thrilling interest for both old and young. The large number of books, already sold, proves that the work is of more than ordinary merit.

A fair supply of the last edition of this work is still on hand. Those who have not yet secured a copy of the work should embrace this opportunity of securing it. Price, in fine cloth binding, only $1.50 per copy, post-paid. To agents who are prepared to push an active canvass of the work, we are prepared to give special inducements. Write us.

BRETHREN'S PUBLISHING CO.,
Mt. Morris, Ill.

Good Words for Neighbors.

I want to say to the brethren and all readers of the MESSENGER, that I will sell single top-buggies and two-seated family carriages at greatly reduced prices. I will put forth every effort I possibly can, to have these buggies and carriages introduced in every locality. Reader, now is your time to buy a good, serviceable buggy or carriage, of any style you want, at a lower price than you can buy at wholesale. Brethren wanting plainly-finished buggies, can have them on short notice. I could give a number of testimonials of brethren that have purchased buggies and carriages of us this season, but space will not permit me to do so. Buggies are carefully crated and shipped at our risk. I pay all freight charges. All questions answered and prices given to all that will address me by letter.

ABRAHAM E. WEAVER,
Syracuse, Kosciusko Co., Ind.

THE

Doctrine of the Brethren Defended.

THIS Work contains a complete exposition of the faith and practice of the Brethren, the Divinity of Christ, the Divinity of the Holy Spirit, Immersion, Feet-washing, the Lord's Supper, the Holy Kiss, Non-conformity, Secret Societies, etc. Price, per copy, cloth binding, $1.25. Address this office.

GOOD BOOKS FOR ALL.

ANY book in the market furnished at publishers' lowest retail price by the Brethren's Publishing Company, Mt. Morris, Ill. *Special prices given when books are purchased in quantities.* When ordering books, not on our list, if possible give title, name of author, and address of publishers.

The Throne of David.—By J. H. Ingraham. Cloth, $1.50.

Homiletics and Pastoral Theology.—By W. G. T. Shedd. Cloth, $2.50.

Lectures on Preaching.—By Rev. Phillips Brooks. Cloth, 16mo, $1.50.

Josephus' Complete Works.—Large type, 1 vol. 8vo. Illustrated with many steel and wood engravings. Library sheep, $3.00.

The Doctrine of the Holy Spirit.—By James B Walker. Cloth, $1.25.

The New Testament History.—By Wm. Smith. Cloth, $1.25.

The Path of Life.—An interesting tract for everybody. Price, 10 cents per copy; 100 copies, $6.00.

Smith's Bible Dictionary.—Edited by Peloubet. Cloth, $2.00; leather, $3.00.

The Origin and Growth of Religion.—Hibbert Lectures. By T. W. R. Davids. Cloth, 8vo, $2.50.

The Old Testament History.—By William Smith. Cloth, $1.25.

The Great Events of History.—By WIF. Collier. Cloth, $1.25.

Biblical Theology of the Old Testament.—By R. F. Weidner. Cloth, $1.25.

The Princes of the House of David.—By J. H. Ingraham. Cloth, $1.50.

Biblical Antiquities.—By John Nevin. Gives a concise account of Bible times and continual invaluable to all students of Bible subjects. Price, $1.50.

Bible Work, or Bible Reader's Commentary on the New Testament.—By J. G. Butler. Two vols. 8vo. $12.00.

Trine Immersion.—A vindication of the apostolic form of Christian Baptism. By Eld. James Quinter. A most complete and reliable work on the subject. Price, cloth, single copy, $1.25; leather, $1.75.

The Life and Epistles of the Apostle Paul.—By W. J. Conybeare. Cloth, $1.00.

Sacred Geography and Antiquities.—A practical helpful work for Bible students, ministers and Sunday-school teachers. Price, $2.25.

Popular Commentary on the New Testament.—Edited by Philip Schaff. Four volumes, 8vo. Matthew, Mark and Luke: $6.00. John and the Acts: $6.00. Romans to Philemon: $5.00. Hebrews to Revelation: $5.00.

Ante-Nicene Christian Library.—A collection of all the works of the Fathers of the Christian Church prior to the Council of Nice. Edited by Rev. Alexander Roberts, D. D., and James Donaldson, LL. D. Twenty-four vols. 8 vo. Per vol., $3.00.

Bunyan's Pilgrim's Progress.—An excellent edition of this good work, printed on good paper, finely illustrated with forty engravings, at the low price of $1.00 per copy.

The House We Live In.—By Daniel Vaniman. It gives a concise account of the faith and practice of the Brethren. Price, 100 copies, 60 cents.

Family Bible, with Notes and Instructions.—Contains the harmony of the Gospels, Chronology, Maps, Tables of Weights and Measures, Family Record, eight elegant illustrations, etc. Price, substantially bound, $4.50.

ESSAYS

"Study to show thyself approved unto God: a workman that needeth not be ashamed, rightly dividing the Word of Truth."

THE UNFADING INHERITANCE.

BY J. S. MOHLER.

All things on earth must fade and die,—dissolve
Into their parts whence they were formed at first,
When God this planet rolled from off his hands,
And light and life to plants and creatures gave;
The grass in living green adorned, and flowers
In beauteous form arrayed, and scented rare;
And trees so fair, so tall they upward reach
Their longing arms to him who formed them thus;
The worms and reptiles crawling on the earth,
And beasts of low, and those of higher birth;
The birds of every hue,—of plumage fair,
With songs like morning stars, of heaven born,—
And man, the noblest work of all. In God's
Own likeness,—beauteous image,—nobly formed,
With mind like God's,—if not so great as his,—
He yet can think of all things, good or bad;
Of things above, or things beneath, or things
To come, and things passed by, just as he will;
And kings, and queens, and princes, lords, and all
The nobles, down to lowest ranks in life.
All these must fade and die. Divine decree.

And all man's works, like stubble soon will burn.
His buildings, towns, and cities large and grand;
The royal palace of the kings of earth,
And battlements with armored steel encased,
With monster guns the world in power defies.
The roads of steel, with iron steed of strength,
And mighty vessels on the ocean's wave,
The earth, its rocks, its hills and mountains large,
And all the seas and mighty oceans deep,
Of living creatures full, both small and great.
And all the elements around will melt
With fervent heat, when at Jehovah's word
Sulphurous fire from vaulted skies will fall
In furious storm, more fierce than loudest hail,
And fires volcanic, long suppressed and hid
In bowels of the earth, belch forth their flame,
As in the days of yore, when God in wrath,
On Sodom rained his fire of vengeance just.
Like oil to flame the watery worlds will burn.
A seething, fiery, liquid, flaming mass,
Whose lurid flames and rolling clouds of smoke
To heaven rise; a veil of blackness o'er
The sun. The moon in crimson hues like blood
Is seen, and stars to earth will fall like figs
From trees, when shaken by the mighty wind.

    And like a ball of fire
The earth, as quartz within the caldron pent
With fires around on every side, to melt
The mass of mixed ore; the dross remove,
The shining gold bring forth in brilliant form;
And thus the vaulted skies, God's caldron great,
In which the world to burn, its dross remove,
That all things pure may thus remain forever.
And when the fires have burned the dross away,
And made a molten mass of sea and land,
Then God will cause his Spirit move, as in
The days of old, when sea and land a mass
Of formless void together lay. His voice
Called forth the land from ocean's grasp away.
And thus God's cooling winds will blow upon
This burning globe, and bring from out anew,
As shining gold just from the mint of God,
To burn no more.

The earth made new and fashioned by the mould
Of heaven, made according to the Lord's
Design, will be most glorious to behold.
And then the seas will all have passed away;
A river pure and clear as crystal, free
From germs of foul disease, and full of life,
Will flow forever from the throne of God,
To which we all may come and drink and live.
The tree of life along its banks will grow
And bear its fruit each month, as ages roll;
Its leaves forever fair (where frosts ne'er come),
To heal the soul's disease for all distressed.
No rugged rocks nor gorges deep are there,
Nor mountains bare of grass, of trees, of flowers,
Or overgrown with thorns and thistles, weeds;
But lawns so smooth and green, o'er all are spread,
Where flowers of heavenly hues forever bloom,
And Sharon's lovely rose its fragrance sheds
Until the air of heaven 's all perfumed.

No cloudy days are there,
Nor vivid lightnings flash, nor thunders crash,
Nor storms of wind, nor rain, nor hail, nor snow,
Nor nights of darkness. But brighter light than
The sun and moon and stars will ever shine
From God, so pure and bright, and Christ the Lamb;
And music sweet forever roll from heaven's
Band of holy angels; songs of glory,
And, joined by all the saints around the throne,
Their hallelujahs loud will ring through all
The vast, extended vault of heaven's dome;
And music, such as mortal ears ne'er heard,—
How grand the scene will then appear! Anew
The earth in heavenly splendor formed! All filth
And dross, disease and death, all banished hence,
And fitting such a country is the city
Of God,—the New Jerusalem, like a
Bride adorned to meet her husband's love,
And coming down from God upon the earth,
With mansions well prepared by Jesus Christ.
A home supremely grand for all the saints,
With walls most glorious to behold, and gates
Of pearl more white than snow, are all around
Each side the city walls; its streets of pure
And shining gold that mortal eyes cannot
Behold. The sight could not endure and live.
For such a place of everlasting bliss
'Tis meet that that those who dwell therein be fit;
In bodies changed, and freed from cumbrous clay,
And fashioned like the Savior's glorious form
Beyond the dead.

Upon a throne of brilliant light sat One
Of visage so sublime, no mortal could
Upon him look and live. The rainbow's light
Around him shone, the Jasper Sea beneath,
Unfading glory shone around,—one who
On earth had walked and talked and ate with men,
And suffered hunger, thirst and pain, and wept
For pity o'er the sorrows of our race.
Betrayed, denied and mocked, condemned and slain,
Triumphant from the dead he rose, and him
Destroyed or overcame, who had the power
Of death. The keys of death and hell, he from
The devil's grasp did take, and ever holds.
Those keys he'll use,—unlock the prison-house
Of all are in their graves, and clothe the saints
With immortality and brightness like
The sun, in the Father's everlasting
Kingdom. Forever there with Christ to dwell,
No sorrow there can e'er intrude to mar
The joys of those who washed their robes and made
Them white as snow in their Redeemer's blood.
No pain will e'er be felt, nor crying there,
For God, through Christ, the cause of tears removed
From heaven, and death destroyed, and through
The resurrection, gave immortal life,—
A body glorious to his saints, who then
Can soar across unbounded plains of worlds
Celestial, or of worlds terrestrial,
With speed so quick, it's like the lightning's flash;
Perhaps some kindly message bears to souls
With grief oppressed, in some far distant world;

Or words of warning bring to those who God
Forget, and live to please their carnal sense.
Our limbs of hands and feet and wings will move
With ease, and pleasure to us give; and though
They upward soar, or either course millions
Miles, they never tire along the way, but
To do their Father's will, who gave them all
They have,—their life, their body, active wing,—
Is all their pleasure and their chief delight.
In this their love and joy is all complete.
And sin is banished far away without
The city walls, and hence no unclean thing
Can enter nor defile that holy place.

    And this inheritance
Is incorruptible and undefiled
And nevermore shall fade away, though years
And ages run their ample rounds along.
The light of God's eternal city shines
In all its glorious splendor as at first;
Our lives as fresh and young and beautiful
As in the resurrection morning's dawn,
And our associations there with angels
And saints of every age and clime are still
As dear, as peaceful, loving as before;
For love will then have found its native soil,
And, like the magnet, draws its kind around.
The Father, kind and careful, us protects;
The Son in fondness gently leads us on
To fountains clear and pleasures ever new.
May this unfading land of glory ours
Forever be!

Morrill, Kans.

NOT YET SATISFIED.

BY C. H. BALSBAUGH.

You have manifestly misapprehended my former articles on the opposite requirements for man and woman in prayer, respecting the treatment of their heads. I will say very little more on the subject, but refer you to a fresh study of what I have already written.

You have quite overlooked the utter impossibility of identifying the *natural* and the *prayer-covering* as represented in 1 Cor. 11: 6 and 15. In verse 14 the apostle turns to the man's *hair* as an *illustration* of his subject. In the fifteenth verse he does the same in relation to woman. Here is a clincher which no logician can unclinch. If the woman's long hair is the covering for worship, then the man's hair is that which must be removed during prayer. It is just as dishonorable for man to pray covered, as for woman to pray uncovered. Verses 4 and 5. It is easy for woman to *retain* her *hair* when she prays, but how is it in the case of man? When Paul deals the *natural* covering, he speaks of shame in the one case, and glory in the other; just as in the *prayer-covering* he had spoken of *dishonor* for both, if they disregarded these opposite observances indicative of their relation to God and each other.

Ah, my dear sister, here is a hard dilemma for those who contend that *Paul* commended the woman's *hair* for a *prayer-covering.* Nature serves very well for illustration, but this does not justify us in ignoring the thing illustrated. The figure in 1 Cor. 10: 31, does not annul the great fact in John 6: 53 to 58.

All that you say and quote about the abrogation of the Law, and the equality of man and woman in Christ, is beautifully and gloriously true, but it has not the slightest bearing on the point under consideration. If you, or any other person, can show the faintest allusion to the legal economy, or prevailing custom, in all that Paul says about the personal and dual relation of man and woman, and the treatment of their heads by which it is symbolized, I will be greatly obliged.

The Law was never abrogated as a matter of fact, for it is radical and eternal; but it was utterly done away in Christ as a direct medium of communication with God. Here lies the whole glorious secret of salvation by *grace.* There is not a syllable in the Decalogue that is not as valid to-day as when uttered on Mount Sinai. All the Levitical ceremonies were applications of those principles adapted to "the time then present." The dispensation has changed, but its cardinal truths are all embodied in the Gospel.

The righteousness which is imputed unto us by faith in Christ, was wrought out by him in his life of perfect obedience to the Law. While the *foundations* of the Holy City have in them the names of the twelve apostles of the Lamb, the *twelve gates* of pearl, through which every redeemed soul must enter, have on them *the names of the twelve tribes of the Children of Israel.* This reveals the perfect *blending* of the two dispensations in that which is fundamental and abiding.

Those two little inflexible monosyllables in 1 Cor. 11: 6, "not" and "also," have always proved insurmountable obstacles to those who attempt to convert the woman's hair into a prayer-covering. God's grammar is too much for the analysis of carnal logic. This is only one instance. We are all miserable bunglers in sacred orthography and interpretation. All of us know too little of the "Higher Criticism," which alone "makes wise unto salvation." The curriculum in God's university is found in 1 Cor. 2: 12; 1 John 2: 20, 27, and 5: 20.

ESSAYS

"Study to show thyself approved unto God; a workman that needeth not be ashamed, rightly dividing the Word of Truth."

THE UNFADING INHERITANCE.

BY J. S. MOHLER.

All things on earth must fade and die,—dissolve
Into their parts whence they were formed at first,
When God this planet rolled from off his hands,
And light and life to plants and creatures gave;
The grass in living green adorned, and flowers
In beauteous form arrayed, and scented rare;
And trees so fair, so tall they upward reach
Their longing arms to him who formed them thus;
The worms and reptiles crawling on the earth,
And beasts of low, and those of higher birth;
The birds of every hue,—of plumage fair,
With songs like morning stars, of heaven born,—
And man, the noblest work of all. In God's
Own likeness,—beauteous image,—nobly formed,
With mind like God's,—if not so great as his,—
He yet can think of all things, good or bad;
Of things above, or things beneath, or things
To come, and things passed by, just as he will;
And kings, and queens, and princes, lords, and all
The nobles, down to lowest ranks in life.
All these must fade and die. Divine decree.

And all man's works, like stubble soon will burn.
His buildings, towns, and cities large and grand;
The royal palace of the kings of earth,
And battlements with armored steel encased,
With monster guns the world in power defies.
The roads of steel, with iron steed of strength,
And mighty vessels on the ocean's wave,
The earth, its rocks, its hills and mountains large,
And all the seas and mighty oceans deep,
Of living creatures full, both small and great.
And all the elements around will melt
With fervent heat, when at Jehovah's word
Sulphurous fire from vaulted skies will fall
In furious storm, more fierce than loudest hail,
And fires volcanic, long suppressed and hid
In bowels of the earth, belch forth their flame,
As in the days of yore, when God in wrath,
On Sodom rained his fire of vengeance just.
Like oil to flame the watery worlds will burn, '
A seething, fiery, liquid, flaming mass,
Whose lurid flames and rolling clouds of smoke
To heaven rise; a veil of blackness o'er
The sun. The moon in crimson hues like blood
Is seen, and stars to earth will fall like figs
From trees, when shaken by the mighty wind.

        And like a ball of fire
The earth, as quartz within the caldron pent
With fires around on every side, to melt
The mass of mixed ore; the dross remove,
The shining gold bring forth in brilliant form;
And thus the vaulted skies, God's caldron great,
In which the world to burn, its dross remove,
That all things pure may thus remain forever.
And where the fires have burned the dross away,
And made a molten mass of sea and land,
Then God will cause his Spirit move, as in
The days of old, when sea and land a mass
Of formless void together lay. His voice
Called forth the land from ocean's grasp away.
And thus God's cooling winds will blow upon
This burning globe, and bring it forth anew,
As shining gold just from the mint of God,
To burn no more.

The earth made new and fashioned by the mould
Of heaven, made according to the Lord's
Design, will be most glorious to behold.
And then the seas will all have passed away;
A river pure and clear as crystal, free
From germs of foul disease, and full of life,
Will flow forever from the throne of God,
To which we all may come and drink and live.
The tree of life along its banks will grow
And bear its fruit each month, as ages roll;
Its leaves forever fair (where frosts ne'er come),
To heal the soul's disease for all distressed.
No rugged rocks nor gorges deep are there,
Nor mountains bare of grass, of trees, of flowers,
Or overgrown with thorns and thistles, weeds;
But lawns so smooth and green, o'er all are spread,
Where flowers of heavenly hues forever bloom,
And Sharon's lovely rose its fragrance sheds
Until the air of heaven 's all perfumed.

No cloudy days are there,
Nor vivid lightnings flash, nor thunders crash,
Nor storms of wind, nor rain, nor hail, nor snow,
Nor nights of darkness. But brighter light than
The sun and moon and stars will ever shine
From God, so pure and bright, and Christ the Lamb;
And music sweet forever roll from heaven's
Band of holy angels; songs of glory,
And, joined by all the saints around the throne,
Their hallelujahs loud will ring through all
The vast, extended vault of heaven's dome;
And music, such as mortal ears ne'er heard,—
How grand the scene will then appear! Anew
The earth in heavenly splendor formed! All filth
And dross, disease and death, all banished hence,
And fitting such a country is the city
Of God,—the New Jerusalem, like a
Bride adorned to meet her husband's love,
And coming down from God upon the earth,
With mansions well prepared by Jesus Christ.
A home supremely grand for all the saints,
With walls most glorious to behold, and gates
Of pearl more white than snow, are all around
Each side the city walls; its streets of pure
And shining gold that mortal eyes cannot
Behold. The sight could not endure and live.
For such a place of everlasting bliss
'Tis meet that that those who dwell therein be fit;
In bodies changed, and freed from cumbrous clay,
And fashioned like the Savior's glorious form
Beyond the dead.

Upon a throne of brilliant light sat One
Of visage so sublime, no mortal could
Upon him look and live. The rainbow's light
Around him shone, the Jasper Sea beneath,
Unfading glory shone around,—one who
On earth had walked and talked and ate with men,
And suffered hunger, thirst and pain, and wept
For pity o'er the sorrows of our race.
Betrayed, denied and mocked, condemned and slain,
Triumphant from the dead he rose, and him
Destroyed or overcame, who had the power
Of death. The keys of death and hell, he from
The devil's grasp did take, and ever holds.
Those keys he'll use,—unlock the prison-house
Of all are in their graves, and clothe the saints
With immortality and brightness like
The sun, in the Father's everlasting
Kingdom. Forever there with Christ to dwell,
No sorrow there can e'er intrude to mar
The joys of those who washed their robes and made
Them white as snow in their Redeemer's blood.
No pain will e'er be felt, nor crying there,
For God, through Christ, the cause of tears removed
From heaven, and death destroyed, and through
The resurrection, gave immortal life,—
A body glorious to his saints, who then
Can soar across unbounded plains of worlds
Celestial, or of worlds terrestrial,
With speed so quick, it 's like the lightning's flash;
Perhaps some kindly message bears to souls
With grief oppressed, in some far distant world;

Or words of warning bring to those who God
Forget, and live to please their carnal sense.
Our limbs of hands and feet and wings will move
With ease, and pleasure to us give; and though
They upward soar, or either course millions
Miles, they never tire along the way, but
To do their Father's will, who gave them all
They have,—their life, their body, active wing,—
Is all their pleasure and their chief delight.
In this their love and joy is all complete.
And sin is banished far away without
The city walls, and hence no unclean thing
Can enter nor defile that holy place.

        And this inheritance
Is incorruptible and undefiled
And nevermore shall fade away, though years
And ages run their ample rounds along.
The light of God's eternal city shines
In all its glorious splendor as at first;
Our lives as fresh and young and beautiful
As in the resurrection morning's dawn,
And our associations there with angels
And saints of every age and clime are still
As dear, as peaceful, loving as before;
For love will then have found its native soil,
And, like the magnet, draws like kind around.
The Father, kind and careful, us protects;
The Son in fondness gently leads us on
To fountains clear and pleasures ever new.
May this unfading land of glory ours
Forever be!

Morrill, Kans.

NOT YET SATISFIED.

BY C. H. BALSBAUGH.

You have manifestly misapprehended my former articles on the opposite requirements for man and woman in prayer, respecting the treatment of their heads. I will say very little more on the subject, but refer you to a fresh study of what I have already written.

You have quite overlooked the utter impossibility of identifying the *natural* and the *prayer*-covering as represented in 1 Cor. 11: 6 and 15. In verse 14 the apostle turns to the man's *hair* as an *illustration* of his subject. In the fifteenth verse he does the same in relation to woman. Here is a clincher which no logician can unclinch. If the woman's long hair is the covering for worship, then the man's hair is that which must be removed during prayer. It is just as dishonorable for man to pray covered, as for woman to pray uncovered. Verses 4 and 5. It is easy for woman to *retain* her *hair* when she prays, but how is it in the case of man? When Paul deals with the *natural* covering, he speaks of shame in the one case, and glory in the other; just as in the *prayer*-covering he had spoken of *dishonor* for both, if they disregarded these opposite observances indicative of their relation to God and each other.

Ah, my dear sister, here is a hard dilemma for those who contend that *Paul* commended the woman's *hair* for a *prayer*-covering. Nature serves very well for illustration, but this does not justify us in ignoring the thing illustrated. The figure in 1 Cor. 10: 31, does not annul the great fact in John 6: 53 to 58.

All that you say and quote about the abrogation of the Law, and the equality of man and woman in Christ, is beautifully and gloriously true, but it has not the slightest bearing on the point under consideration. If you, or any other person, can show the faintest allusion to the legal economy, or prevailing custom, in all that Paul says about the personal and dual relation of man and woman, and the treatment of their heads by which it is symbolized, I will be greatly obliged.

The Law was never abrogated as a matter of fact, for it is radical and eternal; but it was utterly done away in Christ as a direct medium of communication with God. Here lies the whole glorious secret of salvation by *grace*. There is not a syllable in the Decalogue that is not as valid to-day as when uttered on Mount Sinai. All the Levitical ceremonies were applications of those principles adapted to "the time then present." The dispensation has changed, but its cardinal truths are all embodied in the Gospel.

The righteousness which is imputed unto us by faith in Christ, was wrought out by him in his life of perfect obedience to the Law. While the *foundations* of the Holy City have in them the *names* of the twelve apostles of the Lamb, the *twelve gates* of pearl, through which every redeemed soul must enter, have on them the *names of the twelve tribes of the Children of Israel*. This reveals the perfect *blending* of the two dispensations in that which is fundamental and abiding.

Those two little inflexible monosyllables in 1 Cor. 11: 6, "not" and "also," have always proved insurmountable obstacles to those who attempt to convert the woman's hair into a prayer-covering. God's grammar is too much for the analysis of carnal logic. This is only one instance. We are all miserable bunglers in sacred orthography and interpretation. All of us know too little of the "Higher Criticism," which alone "makes wise unto salvation." The curriculum in God's university is found in 1 Cor. 2: 12; 1 John 2: 20, 27, and 5: 20.

TROUBLE.

BY B. F. MASTERSON.

"The sea and the waves roaring."—Luke 21: 25.

As I was standing on the beach of the Pacific Ocean, and saw the works of the Lord and his wonders in the deep, the waves rolling up into a swell, then dashing upon the shore, forming a hollow sound, I was impressed with the language of our Savior, "The sea and the waves roaring." Figuratively this pointed out the calamity that should befall Judea when the Jewish polity should be abolished, and Jerusalem should be destroyed. There was murder, famine, and pestilence within: fire and sword, and all the horrors of war without.

One that is overwhelmed with trouble is like a vessel, tossed by the waves of a raging sea. We, who have never been on the ocean, and sailed on a tempestuous deep, cannot conceive nor form an adequate idea of the terrific sight. When the sea, literally, runs mountain-high, and the vessel stands upon a sharp ridge, only to be dashed in a moment into the valley between it and a similar mountain, which appears to be flying in the midst of heaven; when she reels to-and-fro, and staggers like a drunken man, when sails and mast are an incumbrance, and the helm of no use, then all hope of safety is taken away. The experienced captain, the skillful pilot, and the hardy sailors then cry out, "We are lost; we are lost!"

We cannot realize the feelings of the disciples, when there arose a great tempest on the sea, insomuch that the ship was covered with waves. With what anxiety and earnestness they cried, "Lord save us, we perish!" Neither can we realize the joy and gratitude that filled the hearts of the horror-stricken, when he, who rules the raging sea, rebuked the same and there was a great calm. Well might the fourteen hundred thousand Jews, who dwelt in the City of Jerusalem, when encompassed by the Roman army, say with the Psalmist, "Thou hast afflicted me with all thy waves." Mothers snatched the food from their children's mouths to save their own lives. One woman, being stripped and plundered of all her goods and provisions, by the Roman soldiers, in hunger, rage, and despair, killed and boiled her own child, and had eaten half of it before being discovered. Men were deceived by impostors. False Christs and false prophets promised deliverance to those that would follow them to the desert. Many followed and were destroyed by the enemy. "Wherefore, if they shall say unto you, Behold he is in the desert, go not forth."

A false prophet declared to the people in the city, that God had commanded them to go up into the temple, and there they should receive signs of deliverance. A multitude of men, women and children went up accordingly, but, instead of deliverance, the building was set on fire by the Romans and 6,000 souls perished in the flames. "Behold, if they shall say he is in the secret chamber, believe it not." The storm was not stilled,—the waves did not cease. It was the judgment of God sent upon them for rejecting the Savior of the world. 1,357,660, besides many of every age and sex who were not reckoned, were destroyed, and only 97,000 remained alive, to be taken captive and dispersed over all the nations of the earth, while Jerusalem was trodden under foot by the Gentiles, as Christ had prophesied. Though there were many Christians in the city when the Roman armies encompassed it, the general of the Roman army unexpectedly and unaccountably raised the siege, and the Christians made their escape, taking heed to the warning of Christ. Luke 21: 20-23. "And when ye, shall see Jerusalem compassed with armies, ... then let them which are in Judea flee to the moun-

tains, and let them which are in the midst of it, depart out, and let not them that are in the countries, enter thereinto." They put their trust in the Savior, and could say with the Psalmist, "The Lord on high is mightier than the noise of many waters, yea, than the mighty waves of the sea. Thy testimonies are very sure." On the other hand, those that rejected him against themselves were destroyed. "The sea and the waves roaring."

The woman that had an issue of blood twelve years, and had suffered many things of many physicians, and had spent all that she had, but was no better, but rather grew worse, had, in her mind, waves of trouble rolling mountain high,—wretchedness, want, and despair. But when she heard of him whom the wind and the sea obey, she said, "If I may touch the hem of his garment, I shall be whole." "Daughter, thy faith has made the whole; go in peace." Then there was a calm. Can you realize the happiness and gratitude which filled that heart and spoke peace to the soul?

My heart goes out to those who are afflicted. Some have left their homes and loved ones to come to this healthful clime (California) for relief. Oh, the anxiety for that great treasure, health! Their loved ones in the East are anxiously waiting for a message, stating the result, but they came too late, and cannot recover. "The sea and the waves" may roar, but be not discouraged; look to Christ. Instead of touching his garment, you can touch his sympathies. "He that believeth in me, though he were dead, yet shall he live." There is a calm.

I hear one say, Oh, the hardships I have to encounter! Such a large family to provide for; I do not know how to make ends meet. My bark is on a troubled sea, the waves are roaring. God bless you. Do your duty; you are in good company. "The foxes have holes, the birds of the air have nests; but the Son of Man has not where to lay his head." "Peace, be still."

A brother said he was all broken up, he did not know what to do. No wonder! He was bereft of one with whom he shared the pleasures and troubles of life,—the mother of his children. Cheer up! The words of Jesus, full of comfort, sound along the line of ages, "I am the resurrection and the life." This means a reunion of the children of God beyond this vale of tears. It calms the troubled mind.

The waves of trouble rolled mountain-high in the widow's heart when her only son was snatched away by the cruel hands of death. But her heart was filled with gladness when Christ restored him to her alive. The most terrific storm that both men and women pass through on this ocean of life, is, when they are surrounded, yes, overwhelmed with the spirit of conviction—like Jerusalem, when surrounded by the Roman army. The confusion in the mind of the sinner is perhaps no less than it was then. The effect, in both cases, was produced by the same cause, rejecting the counsel of God against themselves. The temple was defiled and destruction followed.

"What, know ye not (says Paul), that your body is the temple of the Holy Ghost?" Again he says, "He that defileth the temple of God, him will God destroy." The sinner's bark is on the troubled sea; yes, just now reeling on the ridge of a wave mountain-high, and ready to be dashed in the deep, destruction staring him in the face. For once his stubborn heart is failing within him, and with the sturdy sailor he will cry, "I am lost, I am lost!" "The sea and the waves roaring." Like the Jews in the siege, he is ready to follow any one who will promise deliverance. The world abounds with such who say, "Lo, here is Christ." "Therefore, if he shall say, Behold the deliverer is in the desert, go not forth," for fear, like the

Jews, you will be overtaken by the enemy. Or, "Behold, he is in the secret chamber, believe it not." If you will enter you will meet with the same fate as did the 6,000 in Jerusalem. Believe in him whom the sea and the waves obey; in him whose voice brought the dead to life; who healed all manner of diseases; he upon whom the Spirit descended in the bodily shape of a dove; he whom God acknowledged in an audible voice as his only begotten Son; he who said, "He that believeth and is baptized shall be saved." Believe on him and there will be a great calm, indeed. In obedience to him follows the hope, "which we have as an anchor of the soul, both sure and steadfast, and which entereth into that within the vale, whither the forerunner hath for us entered, even Jesus."

It is claimed that Portland, Oregon, has one of the finest harbors in the world. It is thirty miles from the ocean. When the ships arrive at the mouth of the Columbia river, the anchor is cast, waiting for the tug-boat to guide them through the sand-bar (caused by the waves). Then they sail quietly up the peaceful river into the harbor. So with the child of God when about to pass from the ocean of life, through the sandbars, caused by the waves of trouble,—the anchor is cast and the Holy Spirit, by the Word, guides it safely through the bars into the peaceful river of death, and, finally, in the resurrection, will land it at the harbor of eternal bliss.

The prophet Isaiah says, "The wicked are like the troubled sea, when it cannot rest, whose water cast up mire and dirt. There is no peace, says my God, to the wicked." I read an account in the paper, that the vessel coming through Hell-gate into New York City reported a terrific storm on the Sound, all being delayed, and all very sea-sick. Surely the sinner, who has not only made himself miserable on the ocean of life, but ruined others by his evil influence (casting up mire and dirt), will have a stormy passage through the gate of death, and will have no good report to make on the other shore.

MY FATHER'S BUSINESS.

BY S. P. WEAVER.

"Wist ye not that I must be about my Father's business?"

THE above text is the language of Jesus when, at the age of twelve, he went with his parents to Jerusalem, to the feast of the Passover. When the feast was over and his parents started home, Jesus tarried behind, and after three days they found him sitting with the lawyers and doctors, the most learned men of that day, asking and answering questions. When reproved by his mother, his answer was, "Wist ye not that I must be about my Father's business?" Though but a child, we find him about his Father's business. His Father's business was to bring about a plan of redemption to save poor, fallen humanity. Jesus took it upon himself, to suffer and die for our sins that we might be brought into favor with God.

After this we find Jesus subject unto his parents. He grew in stature and in favor with God and man, until he became about thirty years of age. He then entered upon his mission, to attend to his Father's business, to accomplish the great work of redemption. No doubt, when between twelve and thirty years of age, he was also about his Father's business the same as when with the lawyers and doctors, for we learn that he was filled with wisdom, and the grace of God was upon him. Thus he grew in favor with God and man. At the age of thirty, on entering upon the great work, he first gives us an example of baptism. Going down into the river Jordan, he was baptized by his forerunner, John. Then the

TROUBLE.

BY B. F. MASTERSON.

"The sea and the waves roaring."—Luke 21: 25.

As I was standing on the beach of the Pacific Ocean, and saw the works of the Lord and his wonders in the deep, the waves rolling up into a swell, then dashing upon the shore, forming a hollow sound, I was impressed with the language of our Savior, "The sea and the waves roaring." Figuratively this pointed out the calamity that should befall Judea when the Jewish polity should be abolished, and Jerusalem should be destroyed. There was murder, famine, and pestilence within: fire and sword, and all the horrors of war without.

One that is overwhelmed with trouble is like a vessel, tossed by the waves of a raging sea. We, who have never been on the ocean, and sailed on a tempestuous deep, cannot conceive nor form an adequate idea of the terrific sight. When the sea, literally, runs mountain-high, and the vessel stands upon a sharp ridge, only to be dashed in a moment into the valley between it and a similar mountain, which appears to be flying in the midst of heaven; when she reels to-and-fro, and staggers like a drunken man, when sails and mast are an incumbrance, and the helm of no use, then all hope of safety is taken away. The experienced captain, the skillful pilot, and the hardy sailors then cry out, "We are lost; we are lost!"

We cannot realize the feelings of the disciples, when there arose a great tempest on the sea, insomuch that the ship was covered with waves. With what anxiety and earnestness they cried, "Lord save us, we perish!" Neither can we realize the joy and gratitude that filled the hearts of the horror-stricken, when he, who rules the raging sea, rebuked the same and there was a great calm. Well might the fourteen hundred thousand Jews, who dwelt in the City of Jerusalem, when encompassed by the Roman army, say with the Psalmist, "Thou hast afflicted me with all thy waves." Mothers snatched the food from their children's mouths to save their own lives. One woman, being stripped and plundered of all her goods and provisions, by the Roman soldiers, in hunger, rage, and despair, killed and boiled her own child, and had eaten half of it before being discovered. Men were deceived by impostors. False Christs and false prophets promised deliverance to those that would follow them to the desert. Many followed and were destroyed by the enemy. "Wherefore, if they shall say unto you, Behold he is in the desert, go not forth."

A false prophet declared to the people in the city, that God had commanded them to go up into the temple, and there they should receive signs of deliverance. A multitude of men, women and children went up accordingly, but, instead of deliverance, the building was set on fire by the Romans and 6,000 souls perished in the flames. "Behold, if they shall say he is in the secret chamber, believe it not." The storm was not stilled,—the waves did not cease. It was the judgment of God sent upon them for rejecting the Savior of the world. 1,357,660, besides many of every age and sex who were not reckoned, were destroyed, and only 97,000 remained alive, to be taken captive and dispersed over all the nations of the earth, while Jerusalem was trodden under foot by the Gentiles, as Christ had prophesied. Though there were many Christians in the city when the Roman armies encompassed it, the general of the Roman army unexpectedly and unaccountably raised the siege, and the Christians made their escape, taking heed to the warning of Christ. Luke 21: 20-22. "And when ye, shall see Jerusalem compassed with armies, ... then let them which are in Judea flee to the moun-

tains, and let them which are in the midst of it, depart out, and let not them that are in the countries, enter thereinto." They put their trust in the Savior, and could say with the Psalmist, "The Lord on high is mightier than the noise of many waters, yea, than the mighty waves of the sea. Thy testimonies are very sure." On the other hand, those that rejected him against themselves were destroyed. "The sea and the waves roaring."

The woman that had an issue of blood twelve years, and had suffered many things of many physicians, and had spent all that she had, but was no better, but rather grew worse, had, in her mind, waves of trouble rolling mountain high,—wretchedness, want, and despair. But when she heard of him whom the wind and the sea obey, she said, "If I may touch the hem of his garment, I shall be whole." "Daughter, thy faith has made the whole; go in peace." Then there was a calm. Can you realize the happiness and gratitude which filled that heart and spoke peace to the soul?

My heart goes out to those who are afflicted. Some have left their homes and loved ones to come to this healthful clime (California) for relief. Oh, the anxiety for that great treasure, health! Their loved ones in the East are anxiously waiting for a message, stating the result, but they cannot too late, and cannot recover. "The sea and the waves" may roar, but be not discouraged; look to Christ. Instead of touching his garment, you can touch his sympathies. "He that believeth in me, though he were dead, yet shall he live." There is a calm.

I hear one say, Oh, the hardships I have to encounter! Such a large family to provide for; I do not know how to make ends meet. My bark is on a troubled sea, the waves are roaring. God bless you. Do your duty; you are in good company. "The foxes have holes, the birds of the air have nests; but the Son of Man has not where to lay his head." "Peace, be still."

A brother said he was all broken up, he did not know what to do. No wonder! he was bereft of one with whom he shared the pleasures and troubles of life,—the mother of his children. Cheer up! The words of Jesus, full of comfort, sound along the line of ages, "I am the resurrection and the life." This means a reunion of the children of God beyond this vale of tears. It calms the troubled mind.

The waves of trouble rolled mountain-high in the widow's heart when her only son was snatched away by the cruel hands of death. But her heart was filled with gladness when Christ restored him to her alive. The most terrific storm that both men and women pass through on this ocean of life, is, when they are surrounded, yea, overwhelmed with the spirit of conviction—like Jerusalem, when surrounded by the Roman army. The confusion in the mind of the sinner is perhaps no less than it was then. The effect, in both cases, was produced by the same cause, rejecting the counsel of God against themselves. The temple was defiled and destruction followed.

"What, know ye not (says Paul), that your body is the temple of the Holy Ghost?" Again he says, "He that defileth the temple of God, him will God destroy." The sinner's bark is on the troubled sea; yes, just now reeling on the ridge of a wave mountain-high, and ready to be dashed in the deep, destruction staring him in the face. For once his stubborn heart is failing within him, and with the sturdy sailor he will cry, "I am lost, I am lost!" "The sea and the waves roaring." Like the Jews in the siege, he is ready to follow any one who will promise deliverance. The world abounds with such who say, "Lo, here is Christ." "Therefore, if he shall say, Behold the deliverer is in the desert, go not forth," for fear, like the

Jews, you will be overtaken by the enemy. Or, "Behold, he is in the secret chamber, believe it not." If you will enter you will meet with the same fate as did the 6,000 in Jerusalem. Believe in him whom the sea and the waves obey; in him whose voice brought the dead to life; who healed all manner of diseases; he upon whom the Spirit descended in the bodily shape of a dove; he whom God acknowledged in an audible voice as his only begotten Son; he who said, "He that believeth and is baptized shall be saved." Believe on him and there will be a great calm, indeed. In obedience to him follows the hope, "which we have as an anchor of the soul, both sure and steadfast, and which entereth into that within the vale, whither the forerunner hath for us entered, even Jesus."

It is claimed that Portland, Oregon, has one of the finest harbors in the world. It is thirty miles from the ocean. When the ships arrive at the mouth of the Columbia river, the anchor is cast, waiting for the tug-boat to guide them through the sand-bar (caused by the waves). Then they sail quietly up the peaceful river into the harbor. So with the child of God when about to pass from the ocean of life, through the sandbars, caused by the waves of trouble,—the anchor is cast and the Holy Spirit, by the Word, guides it safely through the bars into the peaceful river of death, and, finally, in the resurrection, will land it at the harbor of eternal bliss.

The prophet Isaiah says, "The wicked are like the troubled sea, when it cannot rest, whose water cast up mire and dirt. There is no peace, says my God, to the wicked." I read an account in the paper, that the vessel coming through Hell-gate into New York City reported a terrific storm on the Sound, all being delayed, and all very sea-sick. Surely the sinner, who has not only made himself miserable on the ocean of life, but ruined others by his evil influence (casting up mire and dirt), will have a stormy passage through the gate of death, and will have no good report to make on the other shore.

MY FATHER'S BUSINESS.

BY S. F. WEAVER.

"Wist ye not that I must be about my Father's business?"

THE above text is the language of Jesus when, at the age of twelve, he went with his parents to Jerusalem, to the feast of the Passover. When the feast was over and his parents started home, Jesus tarried behind, and after three days they found him sitting with the lawyers and doctors, the most learned men of that day, asking and answering questions. When reproved by his mother, his answer was, "Wist ye not that I must be about my Father's business?" Though but a child, we find him about his Father's business. His Father's business was to bring about a plan of redemption to save poor, fallen humanity. Jesus took it upon himself, to suffer and die for our sins that we might be brought into favor with God.

After this we find Jesus subject unto his parents. He grew in stature and in favor with God and man, until he became about thirty years of age. He then entered upon his mission, to attend to his Father's business, to accomplish the great work of redemption. No doubt, when between twelve and thirty years of age, he was also about his Father's business the same as when with the lawyers and doctors, for we learn that he was filled with wisdom, and the grace of God was upon him. Thus he grew in favor with God and man. At the age of thirty, on entering upon the great work, he first gives us an example of baptism. Going down into the river Jordan, he was baptized by his forerunner, John. Then the

Missionary and Tract Work Department.

"Upon the first day of the week, let every one of you lay by him in store as God hath prospered him, that there be no gatherings when I come."—1 Cor. 16:2.

"Every man as he purposeth in his heart, so let him give. Not grudgingly or of necessity, for the Lord loveth a cheerful giver."—2 Cor. 9:7.

HOW MUCH SHALL WE GIVE?

"Every man *according to his ability*." "Every one *as God hath prospered him*." "Every man, *according to he purposeth in his heart*, so let him give." "For if there be first a willing mind, it is accepted *according to that a man hath*, and not according to that he hath not."—2 Cor. 8:12.

Organization of Missionary Committee.

DANIEL VANIMAN, Foreman, · · · McPherson, Kans.
D. L. MILLER, Treasurer, · · · · Mt. Morris, Ill.
GALEN B. ROYER, Secretary, · · · · Mt. Morris, Ill.

Organization of Book and Tract Work.

S. W. HOOVER, Foreman, · · · · Dayton, Ohio.
S. BOCK, Secretary and Treasurer, · · Dayton, Ohio.

☞All donations intended for Missionary Work should be sent to GALEN B. ROYER, Mt. Morris, Ill.

☞All money for Tract Work should be sent to S. BOCK, Dayton, Ohio.

☞Money may be sent by Money Order, Registered Letter, or Drafts on New York or Chicago. Do not send personal checks, or drafts on interior towns, as it costs 25 cents to collect them.

☞Solicitors are requested to faithfully carry out the plan of Annual Meeting, that all our members be solicited to contribute at least twice a year for the Mission and Tract Work of the Church.

☞Notes for the Endowment Fund can be had by writing to the Secretary of either Work.

NEW THINGS.

BY W. M. LYON.

MUCH has been said and written concerning "new things" as applied to Christianity in the present age, and yet differences of opinion still exist, even among the best of people.

Christianity, strictly speaking, is the same in all ages. There are many kinds of religion, but there can be but one Christianity. This proposition is established upon the principle that we have but one Christ. Principles are from God, hence eternal, therefore unchangeable. Christianity is based upon certain divinely-established principles. Deviate from those principles, and you forfeit your claim to its possession.

Whence, then, arises the present divided state of professed Christendom? Are we not safe in answering that it is principally due to the misapplication of divine principles, the exercise of human judgment, separate and distinct from God's arrangement, man assuming the prerogative that belongs to God only?

Christianity is a system, perfect and complete within itself. This system, when properly applied to the wants and needs of the human family, cannot possibly fail to produce the desired results in every possible condition of life.

It is the *abuse* of this system that creates disorder and disunion of any kind. With these thoughts before the mind, let us make a practical application of our subject, with reference to the cause of Christianity, as represented by us to-day. Are we, as human agencies, professing to act in unison with the divine order, accomplishing the great purposes of God? It is to be feared that, in too many instances, we fail. Can we fail if backed by the power of the Omnipotent? To illustrate this idea, let us refer to the Sunday-school work. Many good-meaning people have opposed it, and still oppose it, upon the claim that it is a "*new thing*." What leads to this conclusion? Is it the result of a perfect understanding of the Christian system, or of the doctrine of Christ? In the majority of cases has it not been produced by improper influences, or imperfect training? Traced to the true cause, perhaps the correct answer would be, "Father never attended Sunday-school."

We too often fail in Christian work because we are not willing to admit that we have been mistaken. We don't like to "unlearn what we have learned amiss." We have committed ourselves, and we think it will detract from our dignity now to give up our fondly-cherished views, therefore we choose to sacrifice *principle* at the stake of public opinion. Sometimes it is very, very hard to say, "*I was mistaken*."

We are now living in an age in which we have to meet many issues that have never before presented themselves. *How* are we to meet them? To be successful, the battle must be fought upon Gospel principles. This must be admitted by all, and it involves a great deal. To meet new issues and new questions, and to properly dispose of them, it is sometimes necessary to adopt new methods and measures. Does this mean to repudiate any part of the Gospel system? By no means. It simply means a different application of the same principle, in order to meet the wants of the present age. Go back a few generations and we find no meeting-houses. Why? The age did not so much require them. Time moved on and now they are a necessity. The age demands them. The church adopts measures to meet the new requirements, no Gospel principle is violated, but a new application of the principle is made, and thereby the good work is perpetuated. In this case, the "*new thing*" (meeting-house) proved to be a good thing. Why? Because it was founded upon true principles, and it met the wants of the age. Brethren, let us work by this rule always. It means success every time.

In looking back over the history of the church, we readily notice that many rules and measures, that were adopted many years ago, have become almost, if not entirely, obsolete. Some have concluded because of this fact that we are drifting worldward. This is not necessarily so. We have always entertained the idea that it is always right to change when it brings us *nearer* the *truth*; otherwise, better stick to the old position. Let us, then, be open to conviction, and, if convinced that we are in error, let us not be too proud to yield.

After all, why not use as much wisdom in spiritual things as we do in temporal? Why does the farmer substitute the machinery and implements of modern times for those of a century ago? To throw away the new and return to the old would be lawful, but not expedient, not wise. Man cannot originate a single principle. He cannot add any improvement whatever to God's system of salvation; he has not the right to speak when God is silent, neither should he refuse to act when God speaks, but it becomes his imperative duty to utilize, in God's own way, in God's own time, and according to God's own wisdom, the time and the power granted through his infinite mercy and goodness.

Union Bridge, Md.

THE CHRISTIAN STANDARD OR PERFECTION.

BY S. N. M'CANN.

In Three Chapters.—Chapter One.

" Be ye therefore perfect, even as your Father which is in heaven is perfect."—Matt. 5: 48.

THIS command is fully obeyed, and absolute perfection is ours whenever we receive Jesus as our Savior, "For by one offering he hath perfected forever them that are sanctified." Heb. 10: 13. "By grace are ye saved through faith; and that not of yourselves: it is the gift of God: Not of works, lest any man should boast." Eph. 2: 8, 9. Saved, sanctified, perfected by God's free gift. Rom. 6: 23. We may bless God that our perfection does not depend upon our imperfect sacrifice, our cold and careless devotion, but upon God,

"Who hath saved us, and called us with an holy calling, not according to our works, but according to his own purpose and grace, which was given us in Christ Jesus before the world began." 2 Tim. 1: 9.

Our works, our devotions are only a manifestation of our love for "If a man love me, he will keep my words." John 14: 23. We must love Jesus for his abounding gifts of life, salvation, perfection, sanctification. We are saved "not by works of righteousness which we have done, but according to his mercy he saved us by the washing of regeneration and renewing of the Holy Ghost." Titus 3: 5.

If we are saved "by grace, then it is no more of works; otherwise grace is no more grace. But if it be of works, then it is no more grace: otherwise work is no more work. What then?" Every man who depends upon his works, hath not obtained salvation, but he who drops out of self into Christ hath obtained sanctification, hath obtained perfection, and the rest were blinded. Rom. 11: 6, 7.

The man who works in order to get sanctification, perfection, salvation is wholly blinded, for true Christian work is a natural result of those gracious gifts, and not a vain effort to obtain them by and through works. Abraham was justified by faith and not by works and so is every man that "believeth on him that justifieth the ungodly, his faith is counted for righteousness." Rom. 4: 1, 5.

Work naturally follows salvation, sanctification, justification, hence Abraham's faith led him through love to complete obedience, our faith is dead if it does not lead us the same way. James 2: 21–26.

Self lost in Christ and perfection is reached and every energy is put forth to bring the life up to the perfect model, Christ, who bears our sins and thereby takes away all fear.

We have absolute perfection in Christ, but relatively we are full of imperfection, weakness and sin, and our life must be a constant struggle, growing daily in grace, in holiness and in perfection. The sanctified, the perfected, the holy do not obey in order to escape hell, or to gain heaven, but because they love Jesus. John 14: 15, 21, 23, 24.

The true child of God is saved, he is perfect, he is sanctified, he is holy, else he is not ready to die, and he cannot and dare not say with Paul, "We know that, if our earthly house of this tabernacle were dissolved, we have a building of God, an house not made with hands, eternal in the heavens." 2 Cor. 5: 1.

Heaven belongs to the child of God because of his relationship, and he now works because he loves, not because he wants heaven.

Dear brother, if you are not ready to die, you had better get ready, for you may be called away without one moment's warning. All your obedience, all your sacrifices, will not avail without perfection, and perfection cannot be obtained by obedience. The harder you try to be perfect, the less of perfection you will see in yourself and you must give up in despair, but for the Blessed Jesus who saves, sanctifies, makes perfect, if you believe him, if you trust him. Trust and obedience is a joy; it is a source of happiness, for you know that heaven is yours.

You have lost the old spirit of bondage and fear that ever troubles the life of him who is not made perfect; and instead you have received the spirit of adoption whereby you cry, Abba, Father. Rom. 8: 15.

Sins of weakness and imperfection do not fill with fear, lost heaven's gates be closed upon us, but our love, and confidence, and faith, and trust, brings us right up to the BLESSED JESUS.

The Gospel Messenger,

A Weekly at $1.50 Per Annum.

PUBLISHED BY

The Brethren's Publishing Co.

D. L. MILLER,	Editor.
J. H. MOORE,	Office Editor.
J. B. BRUMBAUGH,	Associate Editors.
J. G. ROYER,	
JOSEPH AMICK,	Business Manager.

ADVISORY COMMITTEE:

L. W. Teeter, A. Hutchison, Daniel Hays.

☞Communications for publication be legibly written with black ink on one side of the paper only. Do not attempt to interline, or to put on one page what ought to occupy two.

☞Anonymous communications will not be published.

☞Do not mix business with articles for publication. Keep your communications on separate sheets from all business.

☞Time is precious. We always have time to attend to business and to answer questions of importance, but please do not subject us to needless answering of letters.

☞The MESSENGERS is mailed each week to all subscribers. If the address is correctly entered on our list, the paper must reach the person to whom it is addressed. If you do not get your paper, write us, giving particulars.

☞When changing your address, please give your former as well as your future address in full, so as to avoid delay and misunderstanding.

☞Always remit to the office from which you order your goods, no matter from where you receive them.

☞Do not send personal checks or drafts on interior banks, unless you send with them 25 cents each, to pay for collection.

☞Remittances should be made by Post-office Money Order, Drafts on New York, Philadelphia or Chicago, or Registered Letters, made payable and addressed to "Brethren's Publishing Co., Mount Morris, Ill.," or "Brethren's Publishing Co., Huntingdon, Pa."

☞Entered at the Post-office at Mount Morris, Ill. as second-class matter.

Mount Morris, Ill., · · · · · August 2, 1892.

THE Rock Creek church-house, Colorado, is to be dedicated Sept. 4.

BRO. J. G. ROYER is engaged in a series of meetings at Plattsburgh, Mo.

BRO. GEO. D. ZOLLERS, of Hickory Grove, preached twice in the chapel for us last Sunday.

THE Brethren at Naperville, Ill., report four additions to the church at that place since we last heard from them.

THERE are some very favorable indications for good in the old Germantown church, Pa. The prospects for additions soon seem to be encouraging.

BRO. A. W. VANIMAN, of McPherson, Kansas, spent a few days with us last week. He reports Kansas in a flourishing condition this year.

ONE of our correspondents, in this issue, states that Bro. J. S. Mohler, of Morrill, Kans., is expected to move to Colorado, possibly in or near the Rock Creek church.

THE Old People's Home at Booth, Kans., is nearing completion, and is likely to be ready for some inmates in the fall. The enterprise is a noble one, and we certainly do wish it God-speed.

FROM a communication, elsewhere in this issue, it will be seen that a congregation has been organized at Sterling, Ill. We trust the mission work in that city will increase, for we are confident that there are many in the place in sympathy with our people, who may yet be induced to unite with the church.

We were mistaken week before last, in stating that a "friend" from Harleysville, Pennsylvania, had sent $300.00 for the missionary endowment fund. It should have been "friend to the mission cause," and the amount was $403.00, instead of $300.00. The donor requested the with holding of his name. We hope to hear of more of these commendable gifts.

IN this issue we commence a series of articles on "Christian Perfection," by Bro. S. N. McCann. Unless very carefully read it will be misunderstood. The minds of many people are much confused on this perfection question, and it becomes necessary to investigate the subject with great care.

IN one of the articles, placed on the book for next issue, the writer suggests that a few of our good doctrinal tracts ought to be given to each newly-baptized member. The idea is a commendable one. But would it not be a good plan if all of our members would read more of these doctrinal tracts? It is very desirable to be well rooted and grounded in the truth.

THE late reports indicate that the fear, of a general cholera epidemic in the East, is somewhat subsiding. The disease is of a mild type, and may possibly be kept under control until it can be stamped out. Some cases in Paris have proven fatal, and created at first considerable uneasiness, but as the epidemic has not spread beyond the immediate locality where it first appeared, great hopes are entertained of its speedy departure.

THE CHICAGO CHURCH.

ON Sunday, July 24, the members in Chicago met to hold their first meeting in their own house, located at 183 Hasting Street, a half block East of Ashland Avenue.

The house is small but is well adapted to the present needs of the church in Chicago. It was purchased by the efforts of the Home Mission Board of Northern Illinois, seconded by the labor and help of the Chicago members, and by the aid of liberal-hearted members in various parts of the Brotherhood. It is but due to those who gave with such large-hearted liberality, to say that the members in Chicago are deeply grateful for what has been done to help them in the important work of organizing and building up a church in Chicago, which now claims a population of nearly a million and a half. God will bless the liberal donors.

At 9:30 A. M., on the day above named, we attended the Sunday-school which was enlarged by the attendance of a number of children in the neighborhood of the church. At 11 A. M., the hour appointed for the first preaching-service, the house was well filled, a number of visitors were present from other churches, the Naperville church being well represented. The ministers present, were brethren Jos. C. Lahman, of Mt. Morris, A. W. Vaniman, of McPherson, Kans., Jacob and Aaron Sollenberger, of the Naperville church, and the writer. It fell to our lot to talk to the people, which we did as God gave us ability. At the close of the forenoon services, it was announced that dinner would be served for all who desired to remain, and this was done. The visiting members and friends, a number of children from the neighborhood and not a few of the members of the Chicago church enjoyed a social meal together. At 3:30 P. M., Bro. Vaniman preached, giving us an excellent lesson from the life of Naaman, and in the evening at five o'clock, we met for the examination services. Then followed the observance of the ordinances of the house of the Lord.

About fifty members were seated at the tables, and a number of spectators were present. To many of them it was an object lesson, in obedience to the plain, simple commands of the Savior, that made a deep impression upon their minds. Although feet-washing and the Lord's Supper are as old as the law of Christ, yet to som present it was entirely new.

The feast was an enjoyable one. [W]e feel that the Spirit of the Lord was [with us] that it was good to be there. Especi[ally the] members of the Chicago church enj[oyed the meet]ing. For eight years this little band [has] struggled on, sometimes under [trial] and again cheered by rays of hope. [Now] have they changed their place of w[orship,] ball to hall, and now at last they fin[d a place of] their own. It is small, it is plain a[nd grow]ing in appearance, but it is a home [to them,] and if those, who helped in this good [work,] have been present at the first meet[ing and the] first love-feast, held in the new house, [they would] have felt that it is a blessed thing to [aid in the] work of the Lord.

The house is plainly furnished. [The sisters] worked hard to have all ready, and th[ey did it] well. One sister went to her old hom[e and] returned with between thirty and f[orty dollars] which had been given to her, to he[lp defray] the expenses of painting and fur[nishing the] house. A friend, who ought to be a h[ead for such] a handsome Bible for the use of [the church.] Others gave and worked, and have at [last] the desire of their hearts accompli[shed. They] now have a comfortable house to wor[ship in.]

In the future services will be [held and] church regular as follows: Sunday m[orning] Sunday-school; at 11 A. M., and [in the evening] preaching service. On Thursday eve[ning of each] week, prayer-meeting. To reach t[he place of] meeting, take the Twelfth Street cars [and go] down town roads to Ashland Avenue, [go north] a block and a half on the avenue [to Hasting] Street, and a half block east on He[sting Street] to the little church.

The building was purchased of [the] Baptists, and that name had been [painted on] the door. The Brethren to avoid m[istakes] wisely changed this and placed a nam[e that] will not be misleading. A cordial [welcome is] given to members and friends visiti[ng, who will] attend the services of the church. [All are] made welcome.

Those who have given pledges of [aid to the] writer, are now invited to forward the [same,] as the money is needed.

THE CONVERSION OF CORNE[LIUS.]

PAUL regarded himself as the chie[f of sinners.] Yet, by the power of God, he was co[nverted,] of Cornelius it may be said, that he [was an] unconverted man mentioned in th[e Bible.] We know him to have been a person [of good] qualities, for he was "a devout man, [one that] feared God with all his house, whic[h gave] alms to the people, and prayed to [God always."] Acts 10: 2. Such a higher order o[f man is] rare even in this enlightened age. [He was to] us was not a converted man in the N[ew Testament] sense, for the angel said unto him, "[Send men to] Joppa, and call for Simon, whose [surname is] Peter; who shall tell thee words, whe[reby thou and] all thy house shall be saved." Act[s 11:13, 14.] From this it may be seen that he [was not in a] saved state.

Cornelius was a Roman military of[ficer, station]ed at Cæsarea, in charge of a compa[ny of Roman] soldiers. He was a Gentile and yet [a man] having probably studied the Ol[d Testament,]

The Gospel Messenger,

A Weekly at $1.50 Per Annum.

PUBLISHED BY

The Brethren's Publishing Co.

D. L. MILLER,	. . . . .	Editor.
J. H. MOORE,	. . . . .	Office Editor.
J. B. BRUMBAUGH,	}	Associate Editors.
J. G. ROYER,		
JOSEPH AMICK,	. . . .	Business Manager.

ADVISORY COMMITTEE.

L. W. Teeter, A. Hutchison, Daniel Hays.

☞Communications for publication should be legibly written with black ink on one side of the paper only. Do not attempt to interline, or to put on one page what ought to occupy two.

☞Anonymous communications will not be published.

☞Do not mix business with articles for publication. Keep your communications on separate sheets from all business.

☞Time is precious. We always have time to attend to business and to answer questions of importance, but please do not subject us to need less answering of letters.

☞The MESSENGER is mailed each week to all subscribers. If the address is correctly entered on our list, the paper must reach the person to whom it is addressed. If you do not get your paper, write us, giving particulars.

☞When changing your address, please give your former as well as your future address in full, so as to avoid delay and misunderstanding.

☞Always remit to the office from which you order your goods, no matter from where you receive them.

☞Do not send personal checks or drafts on interior banks, unless you send with them 25 cents each, to pay for collection.

☞Remittances should be made by Post-office Money Order, Drafts on New York, Philadelphia or Chicago, or Registered Letters, made payable and addressed to "Brethren's Publishing Co., Mount Morris, Ill.," or "Brethren's Publishing Co., Huntingdon, Pa."

☞Entered at the Post-office at Mount Morris, Ill., as second-class matter.

Mount Morris, Ill., · · · · August 2, 1892.

THE Rock Creek church-house, Colorado, is to be dedicated Sept. 4.

BRO. J. G. ROYER is engaged in a series of meetings at Plattsburgh, Mo.

BRO. GEO. D. ZOLLERS, of Hickory Grove, preached twice in the chapel for us last Sunday.

THE Brethren at Naperville, Ill., report four additions to the church at that place since we last heard from them.

THERE are some very favorable indications for good in the old Germantown church, Pa. The prospects for additions soon seem to be encouraging.

BRO. A. W. VANIMAN, of McPherson, Kansas, spent a few days with us last week. He reports Kansas in a flourishing condition this year.

ONE of our correspondents, in this issue, states that Bro. J. S. Mohler, of Morrill, Kans., is expected to move to Colorado, possibly in or near the Rock Creek church.

THE Old People's Home at Booth, Kans., is nearing completion, and is likely to be ready for some inmates in the fall. The enterprise is a noble one, and we certainly do wish it God-speed.

FROM a communication, elsewhere in this issue, it will be seen that a congregation has been organized at Sterling, Ill. We trust the mission work in that city will increase, for we are confident that there are many in the place in sympathy with our people, who may yet be induced to unite with the church.

We were mistaken week before last, in stating that a "friend" from Harleysville, Pennsylvania, had sent $300.00 for the missionary endowment fund. It should have been "friend to the mission cause," and the amount was $403.00, instead of $300.00. The donor requested the with holding of his name. We hope to hear of more of these commendable gifts.

IN this issue we commence a series of articles on "Christian Perfection," by Bro. S. N. McCann. Unless very carefully read it will be misunderstood. The minds of many people are much confused on this perfection question, and it becomes necessary to investigate the subject with great care.

IN one of the articles, placed on the hook for next issue, the writer suggests that a few of our good doctrinal tracts ought to be given to each newly-baptized member. The idea is a commendable one. But would it not be a good plan if all of our members would read more of these doctrinal tracts? It is very desirable to be well rooted and grounded in the truth.

THE late reports indicate that the fear, of a general cholera epidemic in the East, is somewhat subsiding. The disease is of a mild type, and may possibly be kept under control until it can be stamped out. Some cases in Paris have proven fatal, and created at first considerable uneasiness, but as the epidemic has not spread beyond the immediate locality where it first appeared, great hopes are entertained of its speedy departure.

THE CHICAGO CHURCH.

ON Sunday, July 24, the members in Chicago met to hold their first meeting in their own house, located at 183 Hasting Street, a half block East of Ashland Avenue.

The house is small but is well adapted to the present needs of the church in Chicago. It was purchased by the efforts of the Home Mission Board of Northern Illinois, seconded by the labor and help of the Chicago members, and by the aid of liberal-hearted members in various parts of the Brotherhood. It is but due to those who gave with such large-hearted liberality, to say that the members in Chicago are deeply grateful for what has been done to help them in the important work of organizing and building up a church in Chicago, which now claims a population of nearly a million and a half. God will bless the liberal donors.

At 9:30 A. M., on the day above named, we attended the Sunday-school which was enlarged by the attendance of a number of children in the neighborhood of the church. At 11 A. M., the hour appointed for the first preaching-service, the house was well filled, a number of visitors were present from other churches, the Naperville church being well represented. The ministers present, were brethren Jos. C. Lahman, of Mt. Morris, A. W. Vaniman, of McPherson, Kans., Jacob and Aaron Sollenberger, of the Naperville church, and the writer. It fell to our lot to talk to the people, which we did as God gave us ability. At the close of the forenoon services, it was announced that dinner would be served for all who desired to remain, and this was done, the visiting members and friends, a number of children from the neighborhood and not a few of the members of the Chicago church enjoyed a social meal together. At 3:30 P. M., Bro. Vaniman preached, giving us an excellent lesson from the life of Naaman, and in the evening at five o'clock, we met for the examination services. Then followed the observance of the ordinances of the house of the Lord.

About fifty members were seated at the tables, and a number of spectators were present. To many of them it was an object lesson, in obedience to the plain, simple commands of the Savior, that made a deep impression upon their minds. Although feet-washing and the Lord's Supper are

---

as old as the law of Christ, yet to some who were present it was entirely new.

The feast was an enjoyable one. Indeed we feel that the Spirit of the Lord was with us, and that it was good to be there. Especially did the members of the Chicago church enjoy the meeting. For eight years this little band of members has struggled on, sometimes under dark clouds and again cheered by rays of hope. Many time, have they changed their place of worship from hall to hall, and now at last they find a house of their own. It is small, it is plain and unassuming in appearance, but it is a home nevertheless and if those, who helped in this good work, could have been present at the first meeting and the first love-feast, held in the new house, they would have felt that it is a blessed thing to give to the work of the Lord.

The house is plainly furnished. The members worked hard to have all ready, and they succeeded well. One sister went to her old home church and returned with between thirty and forty dollars which had been given to her, to help to defray the expenses of painting and furnishing the house. A friend, who ought to be a brother, gave a handsome Bible for the use of the church. Others gave and worked, and have at length seen the desire of their hearts accomplished. The now have a comfortable house to worship in.

In the future services will be held in the church regular as follows: Sunday morning, 9:30 Sunday-school; at 11 A. M., and 7:30 P. M. preaching service. On Thursday evening of each week, prayer-meeting. To reach the place of meeting, take the Twelfth Street cars on any of the down town roads to Ashland Avenue; walk south a block and a half on the avenue to Hastin Street, and a half block east on Hasting Street to the little church.

The building was purchased of the German Baptists, and that name had been placed above the door. The Brethren to avoid mistakes, very wisely changed this and placed a name there that will not be misleading. A cordial invitation is given to members and friends visiting Chicago to attend the services of the church. You will be made welcome.

Those who have given pledges of help to the writer, are now invited to forward their donations as the money is needed.   D. L. M.

THE CONVERSION OF CORNELIUS.

PAUL regarded himself as the chief of sinner Yet, by the power of God, he was converted. But of Cornelius it may be said, that he was the best unconverted man mentioned in the Scripture. We know him to have been a person of excellent qualities, for he was "a devout man, and one that feared God with all his house, which gave much alms to the people, and prayed to God always. Acts 10: 2. Such a higher order of religion is rare even in this enlightened age. Still Cornelius was not a converted man in the New Testament sense, for the angel said unto him, "Send men to Joppa, and call for Simon, whose surname is Peter; who shall tell thee words, whereby thou and all thy house shall be saved." Acts 11: 13, 14. From this it may be seen that he was not in a saved state.

Cornelius was a Roman military officer, stationed at Cæsarea, in charge of a company of Rome soldiers. He was a Gentile and yet very devout, having probably studied the Old Testament

CHRISTIAN ENDEAVOR MOVEMENT.

It is still fresh in the minds of thousands who read the Messenger, what a surprise our late Annual Conference was to the people, of Cedar Rapids, most of whom likely had never heard of the Brethren Church, prior to that meeting. They did not seem to understand where all the Dunkards came from, and yet the meeting was comparatively a small one. Recently the people of New York City have been equally astonished at the immense gathering of the Christian Endeavor society. The body, composed of young men and women, was started only a few years ago and now numbers nearly one and a half million members. In the way of popular Christianity they are astonishing the world. Of the Convention referred to, the *Independent* has this to say:

"For bigness the Christian Endeavor demonstration in this city last week was tremendous. If we can believe not only the reports of those in charge, who added up the figures of attendance, but also the ocular proof of enormous audiences and crowded streets and the uniform testimony of the newspapers, which have given pages to their reports, the anticipations of the number of those expected have been surpassed by the reality. The Madison Square Garden, with its 14,000 seats, has been crowded morning, afternoon and evening, and several of the largest churches in the city would be full at the same time, and then an audience of three or four thousand young men and women with badges would be gathered in the neighboring park. They have taken possession of the city; they have gone everywhere; their numbers and their ubiquity have astonished the reporters and the public.

In the character of the delegates the success of the demonstration has been tremendous. It was a peculiar crowd that filled the streets of New York. There were twenty-five or thirty thousand of them, and not one of them was arrested for drunkenness; none were seen standing up before a bar; scarcely any appeared on the streets with a cigar or cigaret in his mouth. There was no swearing, no disturbance of the peace; the judges of the police courts would not have known they were in town. It was a very different crowd from that which filled the streets of Minneapolis and Chicago a few weeks ago; a pure-minded, clean-mouthed, earnest-hearted body of young people, absolutely decent and respectable; more than that, honest and upright. Somebody said that thirty thousand cakes of clean soap had been rubbed against the dirty face of New York. They represented to the public what Christianity proposes to be to the country and to the world. They left behind them a good record. Christianity will have a better name in New York for their having been there."

It may not be amiss for the Brethren to pause and consider whether there is not a way of making more use of our young members than we are now doing. They certainly are a power for good if properly utilized in the great work entrusted to our charge. We need not encourage them to enter into a separate organization like the Endeavor association, but we ought to find work for them and labor to prepare them for it.

In the department of labor they ought to take an earnest part in all Sunday-school work. Here is a field where both brethren and sisters can work together, and each one perform an important part. In singing, both at church and Sunday-school,

they should be encouraged to take an active part, and special efforts should be made to have singing-schools for their training. This can be done at the social meetings, and it may be done in a special way. Then in all cities there is much that the young people may do in the way of distributing tracts, inducing young people to attend church, looking after the distressed, and visiting those who need encouragement. By giving our young people more work to do we not only help them to become more faithful, but they will become greatly interested in the church, and labor the harder to maintain the principles of the general Brotherhood. We insist upon a greater interest in this department of usefulness, believing that we can wisely utilize our young members to a much greater advantage than we are now doing. This would be the means of keeping them away from worldly amusements and save them from a thousand snares. In order to retain our young members in the church, and make them strong in Christ, we must give them something useful to do, so as to interest them, and occupy their attention and talent. This will develop them into strong men and women, rooted and grounded in the truth, and alive to every good work.   J. H. M.

VACATION TALKS WITH OUR STUDENTS.

NUMBER FIVE.—SEPARATIONS IN THE HOME.

These happy earthly homes are not long abiding. Children leave them to establish homes of their own, and by and by, father, mother, sister, brother,—all will be gathered to the great family beyond. So far as place is concerned, the "household of God" is at present divided. One department, the preparatory, is upon earth; the other, the higher or more advanced, is in heaven. All desire some day to enter the department in heaven.

According to the teachings of the Bible, none but such as have passed through the preparatory department shall be admitted into the department in heaven. Of those, only they who have been most thorough and faithful in their work, will be admitted into the heavenly without final examination. All others, together with all who never entered the preparatory department, must appear on final examination day.

At school it sometimes happens that some are not present on examination day. Not so when God calls to examination. All will be present. None will even be tardy on that day. All will be there promptly on time. There will be no delay because somebody is not ready to begin. No scratch-book will be left behind, no pencil forgotten. All will be ready. There will be no failures occasioned by any one having forgotten that upon which he is to be examined. Everything will be distinctly remembered. Different from examinations at school, where all books are put away, here the "books will be opened," and then the examination will proceed.

It has always been a problem to me, how any one who has never gone through the preparatory department, can expect to enter the higher. No one would presume to do so in our school. No one will do so on God's day of examination. How sad it will be for the members of the once happy family in that comfortable earthly home, to come to examination and there be separated,—separated forever. Many of you recall the painful experience, when your trunk, packed to come to school, was on the wagon, at the gate the driver waiting,

while you turned to take father by the hand and say farewell; and then felt mother's burning tears fall upon your cheeks as you kissed her good-by, and received her "God bless you and keep you safe, my daughter." That separation, although so painful, was but for a few months. Here the separation will be forever,—for eternity; and all because some of that once happy family were not brought into the preparatory department,—the church. Somebody will have to answer for those unhappy separations. The blame must rest somewhere.

How many scores, yea hundreds of young people in different parts of our beloved Fraternity are happy to-day, because of what the schools under the supervision of the Brethren have done for them. How many more might be equally as happy, as well as useful to the church, had timely steps been taken to bring them under similar influences. God speed the day when hundreds more will realize that to attend the Brethren's schools is wiser and cheaper, because it is infinitely better in the end than to be brought under the decoying influences of those largely-advertised schools of fashion and infidelity.   J. G. R.

CORRESPONDENCE.

"Write what thou seest, and send it unto the churches."

☞Church News solicited for this Department. If you have had a good meeting, send a report of it, so that others may rejoice with you. In writing give name of church, County and State. Be brief. Notes of Travel should be as short as possible. Land Advertisements are not solicited for this Department. We have an advertising page, and, if necessary, will issue supplements.

From Denver, Colo.

I have experienced being isolated from a church of my own faith, to some extent, but was only a short distance from home, where I was acquainted with people in the place; but this time it is different.

After the close of school at Mt. Morris in June, I started for this country where there is some of the most beautiful scenery in the world. I arrived here Saturday evening, July 25, at 6:15. It being late, I was unable to find where Bro. Geo. Long lived that evening, so I remained in the city over night. After breakfast I started out to look for Bro. Long, hoping to get to our meeting that day. I left the large and beautiful city to go four and one-half miles into the country, in the direction in which, I supposed, I would find the church, but the foot-hills to my right, then the mountains covered with beautiful wild flowers and green grass, and further in the distance the snow shining on the mountain tops as it does on our level plain in mid-winter, with the beautiful city to my left, I realized there was fourteen miles between the foot-hills and the city. I could not believe it to be so far. I did not know where to go, but went to some houses and inquired for the place. One man within half a mile of another, seemed to be a perfect stranger. I continued walking the entire day, looking at beautiful scenes and inquiring for the little red school-house, but I did not find it. I found out afterwards I was only a half mile from it.

I returned home, weary from my walk and thinking of the change from what I was accustomed to, for you, who have been at Mt. Morris, know we cannot miss "church" and "Sunday-school," at that place; besides, we are fed spiritually and feel bettered by living and being under the good instruction and kind care of the brethren of that place. Now to attend neither, seemed so strange to me.

I did not reach Bro. Long's place till the next Saturday evening, but shall not attempt to tell

CHRISTIAN ENDEAVOR MOVEMENT.

IT is still fresh in the minds of thousands who read the MESSENGER, what a surprise our late Annual Conference was to the people, of Cedar Rapids, most of whom likely had never heard of the Brethren Church, prior to that meeting. They did not seem to understand where all the Dunkards came from, and yet the meeting was comparatively a small one. Recently the people of New York City have been equally astonished at the immense gathering of the Christian Endeavor society. The body, composed of young men and women, was started only a few years ago and now numbers nearly one and a half million members. In the way of popular Christianity they are astonishing the world. Of the Convention referred to, the *Independent* has this to say:

"For bigness the Christian Endeavor demonstration in this city last week was ·tremendous. If we can believe not only the reports·of those in charge, who added up the 'figures of attendance, but also the ocular proof of enormous audiences and crowded streets and the uniform testimony of the newspapers, which have given pages to their reports, the anticipations of the number of those expected have been surpassed by the reality. The Madison Square Garden, with its 14,000 seats, has been crowded morning, afternoon and evening, and several of the largest churches in the city would be full at the same time, and then an audience of three or four thousand young men and women with badges would be gathered in the neighboring park. They have taken possession of the city; they have gone everywhere; their numbers and their ubiquity have astonished the reporters and the public.

In the character of the delegates the success of the demonstration has been tremendous. It was a peculiar crowd that filled the streets of New York. There were twenty-five or thirty thousand of them, and not one of them was arrested for drunkenness; none were seen standing up before a bar; scarcely any appeared on the streets with a cigar or cigaret in his mouth. There was no swearing, no disturbance of the peace; the judges of the police courts would not have known they were in town. It was a very different crowd from that which filled the streets of Minneapolis and Chicago a few weeks ago; a pure-minded, clean-mouthed, earnest-hearted body of young people, absolutely decent and respectable; more than that, honest and upright. Somebody said that thirty thousand cakes of clean soap had been rubbed against the dirty face of New York. They represented to the public what Christianity proposes to be to the country and to the world. They left behind them a good record. Christianity will have a better name in New York for their having been there."

It may not be amiss for the Brethren to pause and consider whether there is not a way of making more use of our young members than we are now doing. They certainly are a power for good if properly utilized in the great work entrusted to our charge. We need not encourage them to enter into a separate organization like the Endeavor association, but we ought to find work for them and labor to prepare them for it.

In the department of labor they ought to take an earnest part in all Sunday-school work. Here is a field where both brethren and sisters can work together, and each one perform an important part. In singing, both at church and Sunday-school, they should be encouraged to take an active part, and special efforts should be made to have singing-schools for their training. This can be done at the social meetings, and it may be done in a special way. Then in all cities there is much that the young people may do in the way of distributing tracts, inducing young people to attend church, looking after the distressed, and visiting those who need encouragement. By giving our young people more work to do we not only help them ·to become more faithful, but they will become greatly interested in the church, and labor the harder to maintain the principles of the general Brotherhood. We insist upon a greater interest in this department of usefulness, believing that we can wisely utilize our young members to a much greater advantage than we are now doing. This would be the means of keeping them away from worldly amusements and save them from a thousand snares. In order to retain our young members in the church, and make them strong in Christ, we must give them something useful to do, so as to interest them, and occupy their attention and talent. This will develop them into strong men and women, rooted and grounded in the truth, and alive to every good work.   J. H. M.

VACATION TALKS WITH OUR STUDENTS.

NUMBER FIVE.—SEPARATIONS IN THE HOME.

THESE happy earthly homes are not long abiding. Children leave them to establish homes of their own, and by and by, father, mother, sister, brother,—all will be gathered to the great family beyond. So far as place is concerned, the "household of God" is at present divided. One department, the preparatory, is upon earth; the other, the higher or more advanced, is in heaven. All desire some day to enter the department in heaven.

According to the teachings of the Bible, none but such as have passed through the preparatory department shall be admitted into the department in heaven. Of those, only they who have been most thorough and faithful in their work, will be admitted into the heavenly without final examination. All others, together with all who never entered the preparatory department, must appear on final examination day.

At school it sometimes happens that some are not present on examination day. Not so when God calls to examination. All will be present. None will even be tardy on that day. All will be there promptly on time. There will be no delay because somebody is not ready to begin. No scratch-book will be left behind, no pencil forgotten. ·All will be ready. There will be no failures occasioned by any one having forgotten that upon which he is to be examined. Everything will be distinctly remembered. Different from examinations at school, where all books are put away, here the "books will be opened," and then the examination will proceed.

It has always been a problem to me, how any one who has·never gone through the preparatory department, can expect to enter the higher. No one would presume to do so in our school. No one will do so on God's day of examination. How sad it will be for the members of the once happy family in that comfortable earthly home, to come to examination and there be separated,—separated forever. Many of you recall the painful experience, when your trunk, packed to come to school, was on the wagon, at the gate the driver waiting, while you turned to take father by the hand and say farewell; and then felt mother's burning tears fall upon your cheeks as you kissed her good-by, and received her "God bless you and keep you safe, my daughter." That separation, although so painful, was but for a few months. Here ·the separation will be forever,—for eternity; and all because some of that once happy family were not brought into the preparatory department,—the church. Somebody will have to answer for those unhappy separations. The blame must rest somewhere.

How many scores, yea hundreds of young people in different parts of our beloved Fraternity are happy to-day, because of what the schools under the supervision of the Brethren have done for them. How many more might be equally as happy, as well as useful to the church, had timely steps been taken to bring them under similar influences. God speed the day when ·hundreds more will realize that to attend the Brethren's schools is wiser and cheaper, because it is infinitely better in the end than to be brought under the decoying · influences of those largely-advertised schools of fashion and infidelity.   J. G. R.

CORRESPONDENCE.

"Write what thou seest, and send it unto the churches."

Church News solicited for this Department. If you have had a good meeting, send a report of it, so that others may rejoice with you. In writing give name of church, County and State. Be brief. Notes of Travel should be as short as possible. Land Advertisements are not solicited for this Department. We have an advertising page, and, if necessary, will issue supplements.

From Denver, Colo.

I HAVE experienced being isolated from a church of my own faith, to some extent, but was ·only a short distance from home, where I was acquainted with people in the place; but this time it is different.

After the close of school at Mt. Morris in June, I started for this country where there is some of the most beautiful scenery in the world. I arrived here Saturday evening, July 25, at 6:15. It being late, I was unable to find where Bro. Geo. Long lived that evening, so I remained in the city over night. After breakfast I started out to look for Bro. Long, hoping to get to our meeting that day. I left the large and beautiful city to go four and one-half miles into the country, in the direction in which, I supposed, I would find the church, but the foot-hills to my right, then the mountains covered with beautiful wild flowers and green grass, and farther in the distance the snow shining on the mountain tops as it does on our level plain in mid-winter, with the beautiful city to my left, I realized there was fourteen miles between the foot-hills and the city. I could not believe it to be so far. I did not know where to go, but went to some houses and inquired for the place. One man within half a mile of another, seemed to be a perfect stranger. ·I continued walking the entire day, looking at beautiful scenes and inquiring for the little red school-house, but I did not find it. I found out afterwards I was only a half mile from it.

I returned home, weary from my walk and thinking of the change from what I was accustomed to, for you, who have been at Mt. Morris, know we cannot miss "church" and "Sunday-school" at that place; besides, we are fed spiritually and feel bettered by living and being under the good instruction and kind care of the brethren of that place. Now to attend neither, seemed so strange to me.

I did not reach Bro. Long's place till the next Saturday evening, but shall not attempt to tell

Items from the City Field.

I AM glad for the increased interest manifested in our city work. The Lord bless the work in Philadelphia, Chicago, Kansas City, Lincoln, Denver, and all other cities, and grant that it may be clearly shown that the Gospel is adapted to the needs of city people even in this close of the nineteenth century. Christ calls as loudly to-day to enter the cities with his Blessed Gospel as he did eighteen hundred years ago. May his people now be true to his call!

Two weeks ago I baptized a lady from Brooklyn. She was in our city, visiting, and attended our services regularly. After the morning services, of the last Sunday she was with us, she said: "I want to be baptized. I can't be satisfied with any other than trine immersion." A few days later I had the pleasure of visiting her in her home. She was happy and said, "Though I am some distance from you, yours however, shall be my church home." She is hopeful that a church may be built up in Brooklyn. Do we not all hope so? I gave her a number of tracts, and will have more sent to her. May the Lord nourish the little branch in that large city!

As soon as a few members can be collected in a city, a good faithful minister should be located with them. Then they should have a convenient, inviting place of worship, in which to hold regular services. I think we have learned that only by well-directed, continued efforts, can we build up anywhere, and especially in the city.

One of our greatest needs now is men,—truly converted men, devoted and consecrated men, men who will put heart and soul into the work, men who are willing to make sacrifices and suffer, if need be, for the sake of Christ and his truth. Then, too, we need sympathy, practical sympathy, the sympathy of the whole church. Let us all help in the good work!

A short time ago, while in New York, I had the pleasure of attending the National Convention of the Christian Endeavor Society. The meeting was held in the Madison Square Garden, which has a seating capacity of about sixteen thousand. There were at times several large overflow meetings held, to accommodate those who could not be accommodated in the large room. The convention took strong grounds on the inspiration of the Bible. I was glad to notice the firmness of the thousands of young people in the belief of the authenticity of the Bible. Several State delegations also voted not to attend the World's Fair if it is opened on Sunday. Strong positions were also taken on the temperance question. Such a large body, representing a much larger body, will certainly be recognized, and its power will be felt in the disposition of these great questions.

Our new church annex will soon be under roof. This will give us ample and convenient room for Sunday-school work. I am thankful to God for the zeal and earnestness manifested by our dear city members, and for their willingness to provide room and convenience as the work demands. Our services are well attended. One more applied for baptism last Sunday.

The work at Germantown is progressing. Bro. Stover becomes more encouraged as he continues in the work. They will have several accessions soon. T. T. MYERS.

1610 N. 8th St., Philadelphia, Pa.

At Home Again.

As many others have said, our late Annual Meeting was to me the best I ever attended. The pleasant associations with old acquaintances, and also many new ones, and the soul-cheering song services, and the zeal-inspiring and faith-strengthening sermons, delivered in the Tabernacle, from time to time, by our faithful brethren, will always be a bright spot in our memory. Best of all, a Christian spirit and brotherly love characterized the whole deliberations of the Conference. Not one unkind word did we, hear, showing that all had respect for the opinions and feelings of others. This made us feel like the faithful old patriarch said, "Surely the Lord is in this place. This is none other than the house of God." It caused us to forget that we had a place we call home in this world.

After Annual Meeting we visited the church at Brooklyn, Iowa. This privilege we enjoyed very much. We met with them three times for worship. Our stay here was too short, but our arrangements would not permit a longer stay.

Next we went to the English River church, Iowa. Here we also had a very pleasant sojourn with relatives and members. We met nine times for worship in their commodious church-house. There was a good supply of ministers from other States. We also enjoyed two sessions of their flourishing Sunday-school. In the afternoon of June 26 we had meeting in their house at North English.

Next day we boarded the train for the memorable City of Cedar Rapids. We spent the afternoon pleasantly in the city, and at our place of lodging during the Meeting, close to the depot. At 10 P. M. we started for home, and, notwithstanding the heavy rains and dangerous traveling, the hand of a kind Father guided us safely, without delay. We stopped twenty-four hours at Winchester, Va., and arrived safe at home June 30 at 9 P. M. We found the loved ones enjoying the richest of God's blessing,—good health, which blessing we also enjoyed during our entire trip. G. W. WINE.

Ottobine, Va., July 19.

Church Organization at Sterling, Ill.

THE preparatory meeting to confer with the brethren of the Rock Creek church, Whiteside County, Ill., in reference to the congregational boundary lines, and their willingness to have the Sterling brethren, who belonged to this congregation, form a separate organization, has already been alluded to in a former number, hence we will not repeat that part of the work. Brethren Edmund Forney, Levi Trostle, and the writer met at Sterling July 16, according to previous arrangement.

Bro. Forney was appointed Moderator of the meeting. The first work was to appoint an elder to preside over the Sterling church, which resulted in the choice of Eld. Daniel Dierdorff. Bro. Ira Hoak was then appointed Clerk, and sister Della Keltner, Treasurer, to serve in this new organization. Some wholesome admonitions were given by the elders who officiated, relative to the unity, love, consistency, non-conformity to the world, and untiring diligence of the members. Elders Jacob Myers, Levi Raffensperger, and Bro. Samuel Riddlesperger, who has been a member of the District Mission Board for a number of years, were present. Meetings were held over Sunday with good attendance and interest. Bro. Peter Keltner is the resident minister in the Sterling church and he, with his companion, are ardently toiling under the influence of divine love that constrains them to make sacrifices for the cause of Christ.

It is a work of considerable magnitude to properly regulate and guard the many interests that relate to a church in the city, but the many self-sacrifices of the faithful minister and the faithful of his flock, will be abundantly rewarded in the crowning day, and although they may now be sowing the Gospel seed in tears, they will then come with rejoicing, "bringing their sheaves with them." May the dear church at Sterling be represented in glory, is our prayer.

GEO. D. ZOLLERS.

The Home in Kansas.

THE building for the Home is up, and will soon be ready for the plasterers. We expect to have it ready for the inmates late in the fall, providing we can get all the money subscribed. We hope that all our subscribers will pay in soon after our bountiful harvest with which the Lord has blessed us.

As we still need more help, we take this method of informing our dear brethren and sisters, every-where, that we will much appreciate, and thankfully receive, any donation you may feel like giving.

We feel, in a measure, out of place to press our worthy claims on our dear brethren and sisters. Soliciting has not been our line of work till now, in old age, hence a little unnatural; nevertheless, taking into consideration the object of the work, "a home for the homeless," the promise of the Bible, the blessings it brings to the poor who will enjoy it, and the reward to the donor both in this life and that which is to come, and that our solicitations will injure no one, but, if heeded, will bring blessings to all, we feel we are, in every sense of the word, in the line of duty to God and man. Who will respond and get the blessing, and finally the crown?

For example I refer to a sister in Northern Illinois, who, after a short conversation, relative to the Home, said, "I feel to do a little, but it is only a trifle," handing me what I supposed to be a one-dollar bill. When I opened, behold it was five. This put me to thinking. According to circumstances, there would have been at least eight or ten in that District as able to give ten, as she, five, but they do not feel as she did, and, of course, will lose the blessing, and I am sure that at the end of the year, she will not be any poorer.

If the Brotherhood in Kansas had as much wealth in proportion to their poor as some other States, we feel it would be an imposition to write as we do. Furthermore, could the wealthier portions of our Brotherhood realize this truth as we do, since we live here, we would expect a favorable response. The hearts of our brethren and sisters are tender, and can be touched with the feelings of our wants, if they are made sensible of them. Our motto is economy, comfort and durability. We have no personal interest in writing. We have spent some time in serving the Brotherhood without money and without price, in different ways, in our weak and imperfect way, and are still willing to do what we can, the few remaining days of our sojourn on earth, but our work, at this time, seems to be the completion of the Kansas Home, and we must have help to do it. Were we favored with means, as some are, we feel it would be our duty to finish it, or were we favored with a brother or two, like the Middle District of Indiana, and others, we would lay down our pen and rejoice, thank God and take courage.

Brethren and sisters, in Kansas especially, think of the Home while you are gathering your crop. The Lord has blessed us; he wants the Home finished, for he says, "Remember the poor."

The Trustees will meet at the Home, the Lord willing, Aug. 1, after which we expect to write again, and tell you what kind of furniture we will need to furnish rooms, etc. Sisters in different places expressed a desire to furnish bed-clothing,

Items from the City Field.

I AM glad for the increased interest manifested in our city work. The Lord bless the work in Philadelphia, Chicago, Kansas City, Lincoln, Denver, and all other cities, and grant that it may be clearly shown that the Gospel is adapted to the needs of city people even in this close of the nineteenth century. Christ calls as loudly to-day to enter the cities with his Blessed Gospel as he did eighteen hundred years ago. May his people now be true to his call!

Two weeks ago I baptized a lady from Brooklyn. She was in our city, visiting, and attended our services regularly. After the morning services, of the last Sunday she was with us, she said: "I want to be baptized. I can't be satisfied with any other than trine immersion." A few days later I had the pleasure of visiting her in her home. She was happy and said, "Though I am some distance from you, yours however, shall be my church home." She is hopeful that a church may be built up in Brooklyn. Do we not all hope so? I gave her a number of tracts, and will have more sent to her. May the Lord nourish the little branch in that large city!

As soon as a few members can be collected in a city, a good faithful minister should be located with them. Then they should have a convenient, inviting place of worship, in which to hold regular services. I think we have learned that only by well-directed, continued efforts, can we build up anywhere, and especially in the city.

One of our greatest needs now is men,—truly converted men, devoted and consecrated men, men who will put heart and soul into the work, men who are willing to make sacrifices and suffer, if need be, for the sake of Christ and his truth. Then, too, we need sympathy, practical sympathy, the sympathy of the whole church. Let us all help in the good work!

A short time ago, while in New York, I had the pleasure of attending the National Convention of the Christian Endeavor Society. The meeting was held in the Madison Square Garden, which has a seating capacity of about sixteen thousand. There were at times several large overflow meetings held, to accommodate those who could not be accommodated in the large room. The convention took strong grounds on the inspiration of the Bible. I was glad to notice the firmness of the thousands of young people in the belief of the authenticity of the Bible. Several State delegations also voted not to attend the World's Fair if it is opened on Sunday. Strong positions were also taken on the temperance question. Such a large body, representing a much larger body, will certainly be recognized, and its power will be felt in the disposition of these great questions.

Our new church annex will soon be under roof. This will give us ample and convenient room for Sunday-school work. I am thankful to God for the zeal and earnestness manifested by our dear city members, and for their willingness to provide room and convenience as the work demands. Our services are well attended. One more applied for baptism last Sunday.

The work at Germantown is progressing. Bro. Stover becomes more encouraged as he continues in the work. They will have several accessions soon.

T. T. MYERS.

1610 N. 8th St., Philadelphia, Pa.

At Home Again.

As many others have said, our late Annual Meeting was to me the best I ever attended. The pleasant associations with old acquaintances, and also many new ones, and the soul-cheering song services, and the zeal-inspiring and faith-strengthening sermons, delivered in the Tabernacle, from time to time, by our faithful brethren, will always be a bright spot in our memory. Best of all, a Christian spirit and brotherly love characterized the whole deliberations of the Conference. Not one unkind word did we hear, showing that all had respect for the opinions and feelings of others. This made us feel like the faithful old patriarch said, "Surely the Lord is in this place. This is none other than the house of God." It caused us to forget that we had a place we call home in this world.

After Annual Meeting we visited the church at Brooklyn, Iowa. This privilege we enjoyed very much. We met with them three times for worship. Our stay here was too short, but our arrangements would not permit a longer stay.

Next we went to the English River church, Iowa. Here we also had a very pleasant sojourn with relatives and members. We met nine times for worship in their commodious church-house. There was a good supply of ministers from other States. We also enjoyed two sessions of their flourishing Sunday-school. In the afternoon of June 26 we had meeting in their house at North English.

Next day we boarded the train for the memorable City of Cedar Rapids. We spent the afternoon pleasantly in the city, and at our place of lodging during the Meeting, close to the depot. At 10 P. M. we started for home, and, notwithstanding the heavy rains and dangerous traveling, the hand of a kind Father guided us safely, without delay. We stopped twenty-four hours at Winchester, Va., and arrived safe at home June 30 at 9 P. M. We found the loved ones enjoying the richest of God's blessing,—good health, which blessing we also enjoyed during our entire trip.

G. W. WINE.

Ottobine, Va., July 19.

Church Organization at Sterling, Ill.

THE preparatory meeting to confer with the brethren of the Rock Creek church, Whiteside County, Ill., in reference to the congregational boundary lines, and their willingness to have the Sterling brethren, who belonged to this congregation, form a separate organization, has already been alluded to in a former number, hence we will not repeat that part of the work. Brethren Edmund Forney, Levi Trostle, and the writer met at Sterling July 16, according to previous arrangement.

Bro. Forney was appointed Moderator of the meeting. The first work was to appoint an elder to preside over the Sterling church, which resulted in the choice of Eld. Daniel Dierdorff. Bro. Ira Hoak was then appointed Clerk, and sister Della Keltner, Treasurer, to serve in their new organization. Some wholesome admonitions were given by the elders who officiated, relative to the unity, love, consistency, non-conformity to the world, and untiring diligence of the members. Elders Jacob Myers, Levi Raffensperger, and Bro. Samuel Riddlesperger, who has been a member of the District Mission Board for a number of years, were present. Meetings were held over Sunday with good attendance and interest. Bro. Peter Keltner is the resident minister in the Sterling church and he, with his companion, are ardently toiling under the influence of divine love that constrains them to make sacrifices for the cause of Christ.

It is a work of considerable magnitude to properly regulate and guard the many interests that relate to a church in the city, but the many self-sacrifices of the faithful minister and the faithful of his flock, will be abundantly rewarded in the crowning day, and although they may now be sowing the Gospel seed in tears, they will then come with rejoicing, "bringing their sheaves with them." May the dear church at Sterling be represented in glory, is our prayer.

GEO. D. ZOLLERS.

The Home in Kansas.

THE building for the Home is up, and will soon be ready for the plasterers. We expect to have it ready for the inmates late in the fall, providing we can get all the money subscribed. We hope that all our subscribers will pay in soon after our bountiful harvest with which the Lord has blessed us.

As we still need more help, we take this method of informing our dear brethren and sisters, every-where, that we will much appreciate, and thankfully receive, any donation you may feel like giving.

We feel, in a measure, out of place to press our worthy claims on our dear brethren and sisters. Soliciting has not been our line of work till now, in old age, hence a little unnatural; nevertheless, taking into consideration the object of the work, "a home for the homeless," the promise of the Bible, the blessings it brings to the poor who will enjoy it, and the reward to the donor both in this life and that which is to come, and that our solicitations will injure no one, but, if heeded, will bring blessings to all, we feel we are, in every sense of the word, in the line of duty to God and man. Who will respond and get the blessing, and finally the crown?

For example I refer to a sister in Northern Illinois, who, after a short conversation, relative to the Home, said, "I feel to do a little, but it is only a trifle," handing me what I supposed to be a one-dollar bill. When I opened, behold it was five. This put me to thinking. According to circumstances, there would have been at least eight or ten in that District as able to give ten, as she, five, but they do not feel as she did, and, of course, will lose the blessing, and I am sure that at the end of the year, she will not be any poorer.

If the Brotherhood in Kansas had as much wealth in proportion to their poor as some other States, we feel it would be an imposition to write as we do. Furthermore, could the wealthier portions of our Brotherhood realize this truth as we do, since we live here, we would expect a favorable response. The hearts of our brethren and sisters are tender, and can be touched with the feelings of our wants, if they are made sensible of them. Our motto is economy, comfort and durability. We have no personal interest in writing. We have spent some time in serving the Brotherhood without money and without price, in different ways, in our weak and imperfect way, and are still willing to do what we can, the few remaining days of our sojourn on earth, but our work, at this time, seems to be the completion of the Kansas Home, and we must have help to do it. Were we favored with means, as some are, we feel it would be our duty to finish it, or were we favored with a brother or two, like the Middle District of Indiana, and others, we would lay down our pen and rejoice, thank God and take courage.

Brethren and sisters, in Kansas especially, think of the Home while you are gathering your crop. The Lord has blessed us; he wants the Home finished, for he says, "Remember the poor."

The Trustees will meet at the Home, the Lord willing, Aug. 1, after which we expect to write again, and tell you what kind of furniture we will need to furnish rooms, etc. Sisters in different places expressed a desire to furnish bed-clothing,

Union Center, Ind.—The brethren and sisters met in council June 11. Considerable business came before the meeting, but all passed off pleasantly. We decided to hold our love-feast Oct. 1. Since our last report four more have made the good confession.—*Alex. Miller.*

Dallas Center, Iowa.—Our meetings are now in the past. Bro. L. H. E'by was with us and preached four sermons. One soul was received by baptism. Many good lessons were given which we should all remember. May God bless his labors for good!—*Lulu McCs ne, July 15.*

Nextoe, Ind.—To d:y, after regular preaching, the church repaired to the river, where two applicants were baptized. They were a husband and wife. Two weeks ago to-day there were two orphan boys received by baptism in this church, aged twelve and fifteen years. May the Lord bless them in their undertaking, is our prayer.—*J. M. Replogle.*

Maple Grove, Wis.—We desire to express through the MESSENGER our sincere thanks to the General Missionary Committee for their donation of $300.00, to aid us in building a house of worship. We also received a donation of $44 from the Tippecanoe church, Kosciusko Co., Ind. Our house is not yet completed, but we hope to have it completed far enough to hold a love-feast in it this fall.—*A. Mock.*

Avery, Mo.—July 9, the brethren and sisters of the Spring Branch church met in quarterly council. The small amount of business that came before the meeting was disposed of with a Christian spirit and apparently to the satisfaction of all present. The members here have in contemplation the erection of a meeting-house. We desire an interest in the prayers of all the dear brethren and sisters.—*B. E. Breshears, July 15.*

Woodland Church, Ill.—Two were recently received into the church by baptism, and, we trust, more will follow soon. We have an interesting Sunday-school under the care of brethren John Baker and Emmert Eshelman as Superintendents. The young folks seem to take an active part in it, which we love to see. We have agreed to hold a members' meeting once a month, which, we think will be edifying to us all. Our Communion meeting is appointed for Oct. 8 and 9, commencing at 10 A. M. An invitation is given to all those who wish to be with us, especially ministering brethren. Our quarterly council will be in September.—*Lydia Waller, July 16.*

Stanley's, Va.—Saturday, July 2, brethren B. M. Kesler and Samuel Boon came to us. While they were with us, we met for the purpose of organizing a Sunday-school. We elected Bro. W. M. Wells, Superintendent. On Sunday morning we went to the school-house for Sunday-school. Our Sunday-school literature having failed to come, we had a Bible lesson that day. At 11 A. M., we had public preaching. Bro. Boon did most of the work. On Sunday evening he had to start home, and Bro. Kesler preached at Bro. Dillon's house at 4 P. M. Bro. Dillon's wife is afflicted, and is seldom allowed the privilege of going out to preaching. The second Sunday brethren Daniel Neff and Daniel Peters preached for us at 11 o'clock. Owing to the rains we had no more meetings, so they started for home on Monday morning. We have plenty of rain here. Crops are very good; corn especially.—*H. J. Wells, July 11.*

EWEN—HOYLE.—At the residence of the bride's parents, in Grant County, Kans., July 10, 1892, by the undersigned, friend Charles A. Ewen and Miss Ada O. Hoyle, all of Grant County, Kans.   Z. HENRICKS.

NILL—FOSDICK.—By the undersigned, at his residence, July 7, 1892, Mr. Noah Nill, and Miss Ettie Fosdick, both of Eaton, Ohio.   A. G. CROSSWHITE.

BASHORE—HAUGH.— At my residence in Dorrance, Russell Co., Kans., July 10, 1891, George H. Bashore, formerly of Dauphin County, Pa., now of Dickinson County, Kans., to sister Minerva Haugh, of Dickinson County, Kans.
                    JACOB HARNISH.

ASCHENBRENNER.—In the Boone River church, Iowa, July 10, 1892, George Aschenbrenner, aged 56 years, 8 months and 24 days. Funeral services by the writer from Rev. 14:13.   HARVEY IKENBERRY.

CLINE.—At Flora, Ind., July 5, 1892, Mary June Cline, aged 61 years, 11 months and 27 days. Funeral services by Eld. Hiel Hamilton and Rila Montgomery from 2 Tim. 4: 7, 8.   D. H. NICCUM.

BOWMAN.—Near Edgemont, Maryland, July 11, 1892, George Bowman, aged 88 years, 4 months and 1 day. Many days, but not for Christ. Services by Bro. Snyder and myself from Jas. 4: 14.   W. B. STOVER.

MAUST.—In the Root River church, Fillmore County, Minn., June 13, 1892, sister Amy E. Maust, daughter of Bro. Jonas and sister Franey Maust, aged 10 years, 4 months and 1 day. Funeral services by Bro. Joseph Ogg.
                    FRANK OGG.

BUCK.—In the Verdigris church, Lyon Co., Kans., Lydia Ethel, infant daughter of Bro. Darius and sister Harriet Buck, aged 1 year, 11 months and 14 days. Funeral services by Bro. George Garst, from Job 14: 14.
                    J. M. QUAKENBUSH.

BUTTERBAUGH.—In the Eel River church, Kosciusko Co., Ind., July 8, 1892, Bro. Daniel Butterbaugh, aged 51 years, 9 months and 23 days. Daniel was a deacon and his place will be hard to fill. He was united with him, and respectfully by all who knew him. His funeral took place July 10, at the Old Ulry church, and was the largest funeral ever held at that place. Services were conducted by brethren Samuel Leckrone and Leander Pottinger. He leaves a wife, three sons, and two daughters.   EMANUEL LECKRONE

CORRELL.—In the Maquoketa church, Iowa, June 10, 1892, Jacob Correll, aged 78 years, and 5 months. Deceased was born in Cumberland County, Pa., Jan. 17, 1815, and went to Wayne County, Ohio, in 1836. He was united in marriage to Catharine Floyd, in 1839, and moved to Clinton County, Iowa, in 1854. He lived near Elwood until the time of his death. This union was blessed with eight children. The funeral was conducted by Rev. Rodgers of the M. E. church, at Elwood.   JOSHUA SHULTZ.

SHOCK.—In the Maple Grove church, Chippewa Co., Wis., sister Lena Shock, wife of Adam Shock, (Jr.), aged 26 years, and 10 months. Disease, consumption. Sister Shock emigrated from Germany to Indiana, as an orphan girl, when about fifteen years of age, leaving her only three brothers behind, whom she had not heard from since. When seventeen years of age she ma'ried Adam Shock. Soon after she, with her husband, moved to this State, where she became a member of the church. In a'out three weeks after her death, the heart-broken husband had to lay away to rest their youngest child, three years old. Little Manda is now resting beside her mother. There are still left to him three other children.
                    ALMAN MOCK.

JOHNSON.—In the Verdigris church, Lyon Co., Kans., sister Mary. Francia, wife of Bro. Clark Johnson, aged 35 years, 9 months and 14 days. She leaves a husband and five children. She was, to all appearance, in usual health. On the morning of July 12, she did her washing, prepared dinner, and ate with the family. Thirty minutes later she was a corpse. She fell dead from her chair, prostrated by heat, and heart disease. Funeral services by Eld. Stouder, from Rev. 14: 12, 13   J. M. QUAKENBUSH.

KIRK.—In the Bethany congregation, Marion County, W. Va., sister Mollie Kirk, wife of Bro. D. W. Kirk, aged about 41 years. She leaves a husband and two children. Deceased gave birth to a child a few days previous to her death, but the little one was called to the land of spirits when about three days old. Sister Kirk was a member of the Brethren church about ten years. In her death her husband has lost an affectionate companion, her children a kind mother, the church a strong pillar. Funeral services by the writer, from John 11: 25, latter clause. In connection with the above, to preach the infant's funeral, Mark 10: 14, latter clause, was used.
                    Z. ANNON.

SANDERS.—In the Bethany congregation, Marion County, W. Va., March 22, 1892, sister Mary Jane, wife of Bro. John Sanders, aged 54 years, 6 months and 21 days. She was a consistent member of the church for about eighteen years. Funeral services by the writer, assisted by Bro G. W. Annon, from Rev. 14: 13. In her death the husband is bereft of a kind companion, the children of a pious mother, the church of a faithful Christian. A husband and five children are left. Four had closed over before.   Z. ANNON.

NEWTON.—In the Dry Creek congregation, near Robins, Iowa, July 12, 1892, Flora Wilson Newton, aged 37 years, 10 months and 15 days. Services conducted from Matt. 24: 44, by the writer, assisted by Eld. T. G. Snyder, to a large congregation of relatives and friends.   J. KURTZ MILLER.

KART.—In the Thornapple church, Mich., July 8, 1892, sister Anna Bark, daughter of Bro Samuel and sister Rachel Kart, aged 22 years, 11 months and 4 days. Funeral services conducted by the brethren from Job 17: 11.
                    S. M. SMITH.

BURNER.—In the Midland church, near Midland, Va., June 25, 1892, Bro. George C. Burner, aged 65 years, 3 months and 7 days.

BAKER.—In the same church, near Mannassas, Va., June 30, 1891, Bessie Virginia, daughter of Bro. Joseph Y. and Christiana Baker, aged 2 years, 6 months and 3 days.
                    ABRAHAM CONNER.

CASSIDY.—In the Montgomery congregation, Pa., May 18, 1892, Willard Orrin Cassidy, little son of friend Richard and Amanda Cassidy, aged 1 year, 3 months and 24 days. He was a bright and lovely child. His remains were laid to rest in the Montgomery cemetery, near the Montgomery church. Services conducted by Bro. William Walker.
                    N. J. RARIGH.

LYON.—At Laurel Dale, W. Va., June 13, 1892, Bro. Hiram Lyon, aged 63 years, 2 months and 6 days. Bro. Lyon has been a great sufferer for nearly ten years with kidney troubles. He united with the church soon after he was taken sick, and lived an exemplary life until the Lord removed him by death. He leaves a wife, three sons, and three daughters. Funeral discourse by the writer from Job 14: 14.
                    JOHN C. FRANZ.

CRISMAN.—Near Carthage, Mo., in the Spring River church, Jan. 13, 1891, Melvina Crisman, aged 71 years, 1 month and 1 day. She was a member of the Baptist church for many years. Funeral services by the writer and Bro. G. Gault.   CHRISTIAN HOLDEMAN.

BROWN.—Also in the same church, June 26, 1892, Mary Grace Brown, daughter of Amos and Sarah Brown, aged 10 months. Services by the writer from Matt. 19: 13-15.
                    CHRISTIAN HOLDEMAN.

DUNNING.—Also, in the same church, July 5, 1892, Bro. Solomon Dunning, aged 63 years, 6 months and 13 days. Bro. Dunning has suffered much with Bright's disease. Later on he took the billous fever, which seemed to be about broken when heart failure ended his life. He was a faithful deacon for a number of years, and leaves a wife and eight children. The funeral was conducted by the writer, assisted by Eld. G. Barnhart from 2 Tim. 4: 8-10.
                    CHRISTIAN HOLDEMAN.

The Gospel Messenger

Is the recognized organ of the German Baptist or Brethren's church, and advocates the form of doctrine taught in the New Testament and pleads for a return to apostolic and primitive Christianity.

It recognizes the New Testament as the only infallible rule of faith and practice, and maintains that Faith toward God, Repentance from dead works, Regeneration of the heart and mind, baptism by Trine immersion for remission of sins unto the reception of the Holy Ghost by the laying on of hands, are the means of adoption into the household of God, the church militant.

It also maintains that Feet-washing, as taught in John 13, both by example and command of Jesus, should be observed in the church.

That the Lord's Supper, instituted by Christ and as universally observed by the apostles and the early Christians, is a full meal, and, in connection with the Communion, should be taken in the evening or after the close of the day.

That the Salutation of the Holy Kiss, or Kiss of Charity, is binding upon the followers of Christ.

That War and Retaliation are contrary to the spirit and self-denying principles of the religion of Jesus Christ.

That the principle of Plain Dressing and of Non-conformity to the world, as taught in the New Testament, should be observed by the followers of Christ.

That the Scriptural duty of Anointing the Sick with Oil, in the Name of the Lord, James 5: 14, is binding upon all Christians.

It also advocates the church's duty to support Missionary and Tract Work, thus giving to the Lord for the spread of the Gospel and for the conversion of sinners.

In short, it is a vindicator of all that Christ and the apostles have enjoined upon us, and aims, amid the conflicting theories and discords of modern Christendom, to point out ground that all must concede to be infallibly safe.

☞ The above principles of our Fraternity are set forth on our "Brethren's Envelopes." Use them! Price, 15 cents per package; 40 cents per hundred.

Union Center, Ind.—The brethren and sisters met in council June 11 Considerable business came before the meeting, but all passed off pleasantly. We decided to hold our love-feast Oct. 1. Since our last report four more have made the good confession.—*Alex. Miller.*

Dallas Center, Iowa.—Our meetings are now in the past. Bro. L. H. Eby was with us and preached four sermons. One soul was received by baptism. Many good lessons were given which we should all remember. May God bless his labors for good!—*Lulu McCune, July 15.*

Mexico, Ind.—To day, after regular preaching, the church repaired to the river, where two applicants were baptized. They were a husband and wife. Two weeks ago to-day there were two orphan boys received by baptism in this church, aged twelve and fifteen years. May the Lord bless them in their undertaking, is our prayer.—*J. M. Replogle.*

Maple Grove, Wis.—We desire to express through the MESSENGER our sincere thanks to the General Missionary Committee for their donation of $200.00, to aid us in building a house of worship. We also received a donation of $44 from the Tippecanoe church, Kosciusko Co., Iud. Our house is not yet completed, but we hope to have it completed far enough to hold a love-feast in this fall.—*A. Mock.*

Avery, Mo.—July 9, the brethren and sisters of the Spring Branch church met in quarterly council. The small amount of business that came before the meeting was disposed of with a Christian spirit and apparently to the satisfaction of all present. The members here have in contemplation the erection of a meeting-house. We desire an interest in the prayers of all the dear brethren and sisters.—*B. E. Breshears, July 15.*

Woodland Church, Ill.—Two were recently received into the church by baptism, and, we trust, more will follow soon. We have an interesting Sunday-school under the care of brethren John Baker and Emmert Eshelman as Superintendents. The young folks seem to take an active part in it, which we love to see. We have agreed to hold a members' meeting once a month, which, we think will be edifying to us all. Our Communion meeting is appointed for Oct. 8 and 9, commencing at 10 A. M. An invitation is given to all those who wish to be with us, especially ministering brethren. Our quarterly council will be in September.—*Lydia Waller, July 16.*

Stanley's, Va.—Saturday, July 2, brethren B. M. Kesler and Samuel Boon came to us. While they were with us, we met for the purpose of organizing a Sunday-school. We elected Bro. W. M. Wells, Superintendent. On Sunday morning we went to the school-house for Sunday-school. Our Sunday-school literature having failed to come, we had a Bible lesson that day. At 11 A. M., we had public preaching. Bro. Boon did most of the work. On Sunday evening he had to start home, and Bro. Kesler preached at Bro. Dillon's house at 4 P. M. Bro. Dillon's wife is afflicted, and is seldom allowed the privilege of going out to preaching. The second Sunday brethren Daniel Naff and Daniel Peters preached for us at 11 o'clock. Owing to the rains we had no more meetings, so they started for home on Monday morning. We have plenty of rain here. Crops are very good; corn especially.—*B. J. Wells, July 11.*

Matrimonial.

"What therefore God hath joined together, let not man put asunder."

EWEN—HOYLE.—At the residence of the bride's parents, in Grant County, Kans., July 10, 1892, by the undersigned,

friend Charles A. Ewen and Miss Ada O. Hoyle, all of Grant County, Kans. Z. HENRICKS.

NILL—FOSDICK.—By the undersigned, at his residence, July 7, 1892, Mr. Noah Nill, and Miss Ettie Fosdick, both of Eaton, Ohio. A. G. CROSSWHITE.

BASHORE—HAUGH.—At my residence in Dorrance, Russell Co, Kans., July 10, 1892, George H. Bashore, formerly of Dauphin County, Pa., now of Dickinson County, Kans., to sister Minerva Haugh, of Dickinson County, Kans. JACOB HARNISH.

Fallen Asleep.

"Blessed are the dead which die in the Lord."

ASCHENBRENNER.—In the Boone River church, Iowa, July 10, 1892, George Aschenbrenner, aged 56 years, 8 months and 24 days. Funeral services by the writer from Rev. 14:13. HARVEY IKENBERRY.

CLINE.—At Flora, Ind., July 5, 1892, Mary Jane Cline, aged 61 years, 11 months and 27 days. Funeral services by Eld. Hiel Hamilton and Rila Montgomery from 1 Tim. 4: 7, 8. D. H. NICCUM.

BOWMAN.—Near Edgemont, Maryland, July 11, 1892, George Bowman, aged 88 years, 4 months and 1 day. Many days, but not for Christ. Services by Bro. Snyder and myself from Jas. 4: 14. W. B. STOVER.

MAUST.—In the Root River church, Fillmore County, Minn., June 13, 1892, sister Amy E. Maust, daughter of Bro. Jonas and sister Franey Maust, aged 20 years, 4 months and 1 day. Funeral services by Bro Joseph Ogg. FRANK OGG.

BUCK.—In the Verdigris church, Lyon Co., Kans., Lydia Ethel, infant daughter of Bro. Darius and sister Harriet Buck, aged 1 year, 11 months and 14 days. Funeral services by Bro. George Garst, from Job 14: 14. J. M. QUAKENBUSH.

BUTTERBAUGH.—In the Eel River church, Kosciusko Co., Ind , July 8, 1892, Bro. Daniel Butterbaugh, aged 57 years, 9 months and 23 days. Daniel was a deacon and his place will be hard to fill. He was mild and firm, and respected by all who knew him. His funeral took place July 10, at the Old Ulry church, and was the largest funeral ever held at that place. Services were conducted by brethren Samuel Leckrone and Leander Pottinger. He leaves a wife, three sons, and two daughters. EMANUEL LECKRONE.

CORRELL.—In the Maquoketa church, Iowa, June 10, 1892, Jacob Correll, aged 78 years, and 5 months. Deceased was born in Cumberland County, Pa., Jan. 17, 1815, and went to Wayne County, Ohio, in 1836. He was united in marriage to Catharine Floyd, in 1839, and moved to Clinton County, Iowa, in 1854. He lived near Elwood until the time of his death. This union was blessed with eight children. The funeral was conducted by Rev. Rodgers of the M. E. church, of Elwood. JOSHUA SHULTZ.

SHOCK.—In the Maple Grove church, Chippewa Co., Wis., sister Lena Shock, wife of Adam Shock, (Jr.), aged 36 years, and 10 months. Disease, consumption. Sister Shock emigrated from Germany to Indiana, as an orphan girl, when about fifteen years of age, leaving her only three brothers behind, whom she had not heard from since. When seventeen years of age she married Adam Shock. Soon after she, with her husband, moved to this State, where she became a member of the church. In a bout three weeks after her death, the heart-broken husband had to lay away to rest their youngest child, three years old. Little Manda is now resting beside her mother. There are still left to him three other children. ALMAN MOCK.

JOHNSON.—In the Verdigris church, Lyon Co., Kans., sister Mary. Francis, wife of Bro. Clark Johnson, aged 35 years, 9 months and 14 days. She leaves a husband and five children. She was, to all appearance, in usual health. On the morning of July 12, she did her washing, prepared dinner, and ate with the family. Thirty minutes later she was a corpse. She fell dead from her chair, prostrated by heat, and heart disease. Funeral services by Eld. Stouder, from Rev. 14: 12, 13. J. M. QUAKENBUSH.

KIRK.—In the Bethany congregation, Marion County, W. Va., sister Mollie Kirk, wife of Bro. D. W. Kirk, aged about 41 years. She leaves a husband and two children. Deceased gave birth to a child a few days previous to her death, but the little one was called to the land of spirits when about three days old. Sister Kirk was a member of the Brethren church about ten years. In her death her husband has lost an affectionate companion, her children a kind mother, the church a strong pillar. Funeral services by the writer, from John 11: 25, latter clause. In connection with the above, to preach the infant's funeral, Mark 10: 14, latter clause, was used. Z. ANNON.

SANDERS.—In the Bethany congregation, Marion County, W. Va., March 22, 1892, sister Mary Jane, wife of Bro.

John Sanders, aged 54 years, 6 months and 21 days. She was a consistent member of the church for about eighteen years. Funeral services by the writer, assisted by Bro G. W. Annon, from Rev. 14: 13 In her death the husband is bereft of a kind companion, the children of a pious mother, the church of a faithful Christian. A husband and five children are left. Four had crossed over before. Z. ANNON.

NEWTON.—In the Dry Creek congregation, near Robins, Iowa, July 12, 1892, Flora Wilson Newton, aged 27 years, 10 months and 15 days. Services conducted from Matt. 24: 44, by the writer, assisted by Eld. T. G. Snyder, to a large congregation of relatives and friends. J. KURTZ MILLER.

KART.—In the Thornapple church, Mich., July 8, 1892, sister Anna Burt, daughter of Bro Samuel and sister Rachel Kart, aged 22 years, 11 months and 4 days. Funeral services conducted by the brethren from Job 17: 11. S. M. SMITH.

BURNER—In the Midland church, near Midland, Va., June 25, 1892, Bro. George C. Burner, aged 65 years, 3 months and 7 days.

BAKER—In the same church, near Mannassea, Va., June 30, 1891, Bessie Virginia, daughter of Bro. Joseph Y. and Christiana Baker, aged 2 years, 6 months and 3 days. ABRAHAM CONNER.

CASSIDY.- In the Montgomery congregation, Pa., May 18, 1892, Willard Orrin Cassidy, little son of friend Richard and Amanda Cassidy, aged 1 year, 3 months and 24 days. He was a bright and lovely child. His remains were laid to rest in the Montgomery cemetery, near the Montgomery church. Services conducted by Bro. William Walker. N. J. RAIRIGH.

LYON.—At Laurel Dale, W. Va., June 13, 1892, Bro. Hiram Lyon, aged 63 years, 2 months and 6 days. Bro. Lyon has been a great sufferer for nearly ten years with kidney troubles. He united with the church soon after he was taken sick, and lived an exemplary life until the Lord removed him by death. He leaves a wife, three sons, and three daughters. Funeral discourse by the writer from Job 14:14. JOHN C. FRANZ.

CRISMAN.—Near Carthage, Mo., In the Spring River church, Jan. 13, 1891, Melvina Crisman, aged 71 years, 1 month and 1 day. She was a member of the Baptist church for many years. Funeral services by the writer and Bro. G. Gault. CHRISTIAN HOLDEMAN.

BROWN—Also in the same church, June 26, 1892, Mary Grace Brown, daughter of Amos and Sarah Brown, aged 10 months. Services by the writer from Matt. 19: 13-15. CHRISTIAN HOLDEMAN.

DUNNING.—Also, in the same church, July 5, 1892, Bro. Solomon Dunning, aged 63 years, 6 months and 13 days. Bro. Dunning has suffered much with Bright's disease. Latter on he took the billions fever, which seemed to be about broken when heart failure ended his life. He was a faithful deacon for a number of years, and leaves a wife and eight children. The funeral was conducted by the Writer, assisted by Eld. G. Barnhart from 2 Tim. 4: 8-10. CHRISTIAN HOLDEMAN.

The Gospel Messenger

Is the recognized organ of the German Baptist or Brethren's church, and advocates the form of doctrine taught in the New Testament and pleads for a return to apostolic and primitive Christianity.

It recognizes the New Testament as the only infallible rule of faith and practice, and maintains that Faith toward God, Repentance from dead works, Regeneration of the heart and mind, baptism by True Immersion for remission of sins unto the reception of the Holy Ghost by the laying on of hands, are the means of adoption into the household of God,—the church militant.

It also maintains that Feet-washing, as taught in John 13, both by example and command of Jesus, should be observed in the church.

That the Lord's Supper, instituted by Christ and as universally observed by the apostles and the early Christians, is a full meal, and, in connection with the Communion, should be taken in the evening or after the close of the day.

That the Salutation of the Holy Kiss, or Kiss of Charity, is binding upon the followers of Christ.

That War and Retaliation are contrary to the spirit and self-denying principles of the religion of Jesus Christ.

That the principle of Plain Dressing and of Non-conformity to the world, as taught in the New Testament, should be observed by the followers of Christ.

That the Scriptural duty of Anointing the Sick with Oil, in the Name of the Lord, James 5: 14, is binding upon all Christians.

It also advocates the church's duty to support Missionary and Tract Work, thus giving to the Lord for the spread of the Gospel and for the conversion of sinners.

In short, it is a vindicator of all that Christ and the apostles have enjoined upon us, and aims, amid the conflicting theories and discords of modern Christendom, to point out ground that all must concede to be infallibly safe.

☞ The above principles of our Fraternity are set forth on our "Brethren's Envelopes." Use them! Price, 15 cents pr package; 40 cents per hundred.

Announcements.

LOVE-FEASTS.

Aug. 13, at 2 P. M., Ogan's Creek church, five miles south-east of North Manchester, Wabash Co., Ind.

Aug. 19, at 4 P. M., the Beef Creek church, Palmer, Ill.

Aug. 27 and 28, at 4 P. M., Salem, in Surrey Creek congregation, Preston Co., W. Va.

Aug. 27, at 4 P. M., Notoma church, Montague Co., Tex.

Sept. 2, at 4 P. M., Sugar Creek church, Sangamon County, Ill., 2 miles east of Auburn, Ill.

Sept. 2, at 2 P. M., Rockton church, Pa.

Sept. 3, at 10 A. M., Mt. Etna church, Iowa. Conveyances on Friday, Sept. 2, at Corning.

Sept. 3, at 5 P. M., at Independence, Kans.

Sept. 3, at 10 A. M., Washington church, Kans., at Dr. Wm. R. Phillippy's residence, three and a half miles, and three and one-half miles west of Washington, Kans.

Sept. 3, at 5 P. M., Silver Creek church, Cowley Co., Kans.

Sept. 3, Mill Creek church, Adams Co., Ill.

Sept. 3 and 4, English River congregation, Keokuk Co., Iowa.

Sept. 3, at 2 P. M., in the Mt. Hope church, Logan Co., Oklahoma Territory.

Sept. 3 and 4, at 10 A. M., in the North Solomon church, six miles north of Portis, Kans.

Sept. 3, Sappa church, Furnas Co., Nebr.

Sept. 3 and 4, Rock Creek church, Colo. Dedication of church-house on Sunday, Sept. 4. Those coming by rail, stop off at Monte Vista.

Sept. 8, at 4 P. M., Indian Creek congregation, Fayette Co., Pa. Series of meetings to commence Aug. 27.

Sept. 7 and 8, at 2 P. M., Scott Valley, Colley Co., Kans., at the home of W. A. Smith, one mile east and five tenth of Waverly. A series of meetings to be held in connection with the feast.

Sept. 9, at 10 A. M., Monroe County church, Iowa.

Sept. 10 and 11, Farnhamville, Calhoun Co., Iowa. Series of meetings in connection, beginning one week previous.

Sept. 10 and 11, at 2 P. M., Sterling church, Sterling, Ill.

Sept. 17, at 2 P. M., Bethel congregation, at the Bethlehem meeting-house, Holt Co., Mo. For any information address Jas. Addam, Mound City, Holt Co., Mo.

Sept. 17, at 4 P. M., Oakley church, Macon Co., Ill.

Sept. 24, at 2 P. M., in La Porte church, La Porte, Ind. There will be meet in the forenoon and early after noon of the day of meeting.

Sept. 24, at 3 P. M., Martin's Creek church, Wayne Co., Ill.

Sept. 24 and 25, at 2 P. M., Lanark church, Carroll Co., Ill.

Sept. 24, at 5 P. M., Pokagon church, Dowagiac, Cass Co., Mich.

Sept. 28, South Bend church, Ind.

Sept. 28, at 10 A. M., Spring Creek church, Kosciusko Co., Ind.

Sept. 29 and 30, at 2 P. M., Rock Creek, Whiteside Co., Ill.

Sept. 30, 10 A. M., Nettle Creek church, Wayne Co., Ind.

Oct. 1, at 2 P. M., Sugar Creek church, Allen Co., Ohio.

Oct. 1, at 5 P. M., Berrien Congregation, Mich.

Oct. 1, and 2, at 10 A. M., West Branch church, Ill. One week's meeting previous to feast.

Oct. 1 and 2, at 2 P. M., near Ames, Boone Co., Iowa. Noon train meet at Ames on Saturday.

Oct. 1, at 2 P. M., Osage church, Crawford Co., Kans.

Oct. 1, at 4 P. M., Logan church, near DeGraff, Ohio.

Oct. 1 and 2, Saginaw church, Mich.

Oct. 1 and 2, at 11: 30 P. M., Walnut Valley congregation, Barton Co., Kans.

Oct. 1 and 2, at 2 P. M., Allegheny congregation, Grant Co., W. Va.

Oct. 1, Maple Grove church, Norton Co., Kans.

Oct. 1, at 10 A. M., Appanoose church, Kans.

Oct. 1, at 10 A. M., Eight Mile church, Ind., at the town of Markle.

Oct. 1, at 11 A. M., Riverside, Iowa. Those coming by rail will stop at Iowa junction, on R. C. R. & N. R. R., where they will be met.

Oct. 1, at 10 A. M., Stone Lick church, Clermont Co., Ohio.

Oct. 1, at 10 A. M., Chippewa congregation, Wayne Co., Ohio.

Oct. 1 at 2 P. M., in the Verdigris church, at Bro. S. S. Redman's. A series of meetings will commence Sept. 25.

Oct. 4, at 10 A. M., in the Beaver Dam church, Kosciusko Co., Ind., near the town of Burket.

Oct. 5, at 2 P. M., Rossa church, Ind.

Oct. 6, at 2 P. M., Spring Creek church, in the Keith's church-house, eleven miles south-west of Reece, Kans.

Oct. 6 and 7, at 10 A. M., Shannon, Ill.

Oct. 6, at 2 P. M., Astoria church, Ind.

Oct. 1, Black River church, Van Buren Co., Mich. Brethren coming by rail will stop off at Bangor.

Oct. 7, at 2 P. M., Ludoga, Ind.

Oct. 7, at 2 P. M., Kaskaskia church, Fayette Co., Ill. ten miles south-west of Beecher City, Ill. Those coming by rail will be met at the above-named place by informing Grailville Mevinger.

Oct. 7, at 10 A. M., Sugar Creek, Whitley Co., Ind.

Oct. 7, at 2 P. M., Raccoon Creek church, Montgomery Co., Ind., one and one-half miles north-west of Ladoga.

Oct. 7, at 4 P. M., Macoupin Creek church, Montgomery Co., Ill. Those coming by rail will be met at Fosterville, on Springfield Road, east of Girard, on St. Louis Road on morning of meeting.

Oct. 7 and 8, at 12: 30 A. M., Four Mile church, Union Co., Ind.

Oct. 8, at 2 P. M., B. that church, on North County line, Dryfer Co., Nebr. Stations Curleton, Davenport, Carlisle and Shickley.

Oct. 8, at 2 P. M., Bear Creek church, Portland, Ind. Those coming by rail will be met by notifying H. P. Garber.

Oct. 8 and 9, at 10 A. M., Woodland church, Fulton Co., Ill. A series of meetings one week previous to the feast, and to continue two weeks.

Oct. 8, at 2 P. M., North Star, Darke County, Ohio.

Oct. 8, at 1: 30 P. M., Maple Glen church, Somerset Co., Pa.

Oct. 8, at 2 P. M., in the Elkhart Valley church, Ind.

Oct. 8 and 9, at 2 P. M., Arnold's Grove, Ill.

Oct. 8, at 10 A. M., Dry Creek church, Linn Co., Iowa, one mile west of Robins Station.

Oct. 8, Swan Creek congregation, Ohio, 3¼ miles west of Delta, Ohio.

Oct. 8, at 4 P. M., Washington Creek church, Douglas Co., Kans.

Oct. 14, and 15, at 11 A. M. South Keokuk church, Keokuk Co., Iowa. Those coming by rail will be met at Ollie, by notifying Isaac Shelley or Isaac Brown. Those coming from the West will arrive at Ollie about 11:30 A. M., theirs from the East at 3 P. M.

Oct. 14, at 4 P. M., Union church, Marshall Co., Ind., five miles west of Plymouth. Train will be met at both Plymouth and Burr Oak.

Oct. 14, Union church, Plymouth, Marshall Co., Ind. This church would like to have some brother hold a calling a week or ten days after.

Oct. 18, at 2 P. M., South Beatrice church, Gage Co., Nebr. Conveyances the day before meeting at B. B. M. depot, in Beatrice; Rock Island depot, in Rockford; Union Pacific depot, in Holmesville.

Oct. 18, at 4 P. M., Walnut church, Marshall Co., Ind.

Oct. 18, at 10 A. M., in the Buck Creek church, Henry Co., Ind.

Oct. 19, at 2 P. M., Ozawkie church, Kans. A series of meetings to commence Oct. 10.

Oct. 19 and 30, at 10 A. M., Pigeon Creek church, Ill., at the Oak Grove meeting-house.

Oct. 20, at 2 P. M., Oasis church, Madison Co., Ind., 3¼ miles east of Summitville.

Nov. 5, at 3 P. M., Spring Creek church, Richland Co., Ill., 2¾ miles North-east of Parkersburg, Ill. Conveyances will be at the above place by informing J. M. Forney.

— THE —
Doctrine of the Brethren Defended.

THIS work contains a complete exposition of the faith and practice of the Brethren, the Divinity of Christ, the Divinity of the Holy Spirit, Immersion, Feet-washing, the Lord's Supper, the Holy Kiss, Non-conformity, Secret Societies, etc. Price, per copy, cloth binding, $1.25. Address this office.

GOOD BOOKS FOR ALL.

ANY book in the market furnished at publishers' lowest retail price by the Brethren's Publishing Company, Mt. Morris, Ill. *Special prices given when books are purchased in quantities.* When ordering books, not on our list, if possible give title, name of author, and address of publishers.

The Throne of David.—By J. H. Ingraham. Cloth, $1.50.

Homiletics and Pastoral Theology.—By W. G. T. Shedd. Cloth, $2.50.

Lectures on Preaching.—By Rev. Phillips Brooks. Cloth, 12mo, $1.50

Josephus' Complete Works.—Large type, 1 vol. 8vo. Illustrated with many steel and wood engravings. Library sheep, $3.00.

The Doctrine of the Holy Spirit.—By James B. Walker. Cloth, $1.25.

The New Testament History.—By Wm. Smith. Cloth, $1.25.

The Path of Life.—An interesting tract for everybody. Price, 10 cents per copy; 100 copies, $6.00.

Smith's Bible Dictionary.—Edited by Peloubet. Cloth, $2.00; leather, $3.00.

The Origin and Growth of Religion.—Hibbert Lectures. By T. W. R. Davids. Cloth, 8vo, $2.50.

The Old Testament History.—By William Smith. Cloth, $1.25.

The Great Events of History.—By W.F. Collier. Cloth, $1.25.

Biblical Theology of the Old Testament.—By R. F. Weidner. Cloth, $1.25.

The Prince of the House of David.—By J. H. Ingraham. Cloth, $1.50.

Biblical Antiquities.—By John Nevin. Gives a concise account of Bible times and customs; invaluable to all students of Bible subjects. Price, $1.50.

Bible Work, or Bible Reader's Commentary on the New Testament.—By J. G. Butler. Two vols. 8vo. $2.00.

Trine Immersion.—A vindication of the apostolic form of Christian baptism. By Eld. James Quinter. 8 vols. cloth and reliable work on the subject. Price, cloth, single copy, $1.25; leather, $1.75.

The Life and Epistles of the Apostle Paul.—By W. J. Conybeare. Cloth, $2.00.

Sacred Geography and Antiquities.—A practical, helpful work for Bible students, ministers and Sunday-school teachers. Price, $2.25.

Popular Commentary on the New Testament.—Edited by Philip Schaff. Four volumes, 8vo. Matthew, Mark and Luke: $6.00. John and the Acts, $6.00. Romans to Philemon: $6.00. Hebrews to Revelation: $5.00.

The House We Live In.—By Daniel Vaniman. It gives a concise account of the faith and practice of the Brethren. Price, 100 copies, 60 cents.

EUROPE
AND
Bible Lands

A new edition of this deservedly popular work has recently been published. It retains all the excellencies of its predecessors, and with those who are interested in Bible study this work will always remain a favorite. Those who have read the ordinary book of travel will be surprised to find "Europe and Bible Lands" of thrilling interest for both old and young. The large number of books, already sold, proves that the work is of more than ordinary merit.

A fair supply of the last edition of this work is still on hand. Those who have not yet secured a copy of the work should embrace this opportunity of securing it. Price, in fine cloth binding, only $1.50 per copy, post-paid. To agents who are prepared to push an active canvass of the work, we are prepared to give special inducements. Write us.

BRETHREN'S PUBLISHING CO., Mt. Morris, Ill.

Announcements.

LOVE-FEASTS.

Aug. 13, at 2 P. M., Ogan's Creek church, five miles south-east of North Manchester, Wabash Co., Ind.

Aug. 19, at 4 P. M., the Bear Creek church, Palmer, Ill.

Aug. 27 and 28, at 2 P. M., Salem, in Supply Creek congregation, Preston Co., W. Va.

Aug. 27, at 4 P. M., Notatin church, Methughe Co., Tex.

Sept. 1, at 4 P. M., Sugar Creek church, Sangamon County, Ill., 2 miles east of Auburn, Ill.

Sept. 3, at 3 P. M., Rockton church, Pa.

Sept. 3, at 10 A. M., Mt. Etna church, Iowa. Conveyances on Friday, Sept. 2, at Cutting.

Sept. 3, at 2 P. M., at Independence, Kans.

Sept. 3, at 10 A. M., Washington church, Kans., at Bro. Wm. R. Phillippi's residence, three miles south, and three and one-half miles west of Washington, Kans.

Sept. 3, at 5 P. M., Silver Creek church, Cowley Co., Kans.

Sept. 3, Mill Creek church, Adams Co., Ill.

Sept. 3 and 4, English River congregation, Keokuk Co., Iowa.

Sept. 3 at 2 P. M., in the Mt. Hope church, Logan Co., Oklahoma Territory. *

Sept. 3 and 4 at 10 A. M., in the North Solomon church, six miles north of Portis, Kans.

Sept. 3, Sappa church, Furnas Co., Nebr.

Sept. 3 and 4, Rock Creek church, Colo. Dedication of church-house on Sunday, Sept. 4. Those coming by rail, stop off at Monte Vista.

Sept. 6, at 2 P. M., Indian Creek congregation, Fayette Co., Pa. Series of meetings to commence Aug. 27.

Sept. 3 and 8, at 2 P. M., Scott Valley, Colby Co., Kans., at the house of W. A. Smith, one mile east and five south of Waverly. Those coming from the West will arrive at Ollie about 11:30 A. M.; those from the East at 3 P. M.

Sept. 9, at 10 A. M., Monroe County church, Iowa.

Sept. 10 and 11, Farbhansville, Calhoun Co., Iowa. Series of meetings in connection, beginning one week previous.

Sept. 10 and 11, at 2 P. M., Sterling church, Sterling, Ill.

Sept. 17, at 2 P. M., Bethel congregation, at the Bethlehem meeting-house, Holt Co., Mo. For any information, the address Jas. Aniel, Mound City, Holt Co., Mo.

Sept. 17, at 4 P. M., Oakley church, Macon Co., Ill.

Sept. 24, at 5 P. M., in La Porte church, La Porte, Ind. Trains will be met in the forenoon and early afternoon of the day of meeting.

Sept. 24, at 3 P. M., Martin's Creek church, Wayne Co., Ill.

Sept. 24, and 25, at 3 P. M., Lanark church, Carroll Co., Ill.

Sept. 28, South Bend church, Ind.

Sept. 28, at 10 A. M., Spring Creek church, Kosciusko Co., Ind.

Sept. 29 and 30, at 2 P. M., Rock Creek, Whiteside Co., Ill.

Sept. 30, at 10 A. M., Nettle Creek church, near Hagerstown, Wayne Co., Ind.

Sept. 30, at 3 P. M., Milledine church, Platt Co., Ill.

Oct. 1, at 2 P. M., Sugar Creek church, Allen Co., Ohio.

Oct. 1, at 3 P. M., Berrien Congregation, Mich.

Oct. 1 and 2, at 10 A. M., West Branch church, Ill. One week's meeting previous to feast.

Oct. 1 and 2, at 2 P. M., near Ames, Boone Co., Iowa. Noon trains meet at Ames on Saturday.

Oct. 1, at 2 P. M., Osage church, Crawford Co., Kans.

Oct. 1, at 2 P. M., Logan church, near DeGraff, Ohio.

Oct. 1 and 2, Saginaw church, Mich.

Oct. 1 and 2, at 1:30 P. M., Walnut Valley congregation, Butler Co., Kans.

Oct. 2 and 3, at 2 P. M., Allegheny congregation, Grant Co., W. Va.

Oct. 1, Maple Grove church, Norton Co., Kans.

Oct. 1, at 10 A. M., Appanoose church, Kans.

Oct. 1, at 10 A. M., Eight Mile church, Ind., at the town of Markle.

Oct. 1 and 2, at 11 A. M., Riverside, Iowa. Those coming by rail will stop at Iowa Junction, on B. C. R. & N. R. R., where they will be met.

Oct. 1, at 10 A. M., Stone Lick church, Clermont Co., Ohio.

Oct. 1, at 10 A. M., Chippewa congregation, Wayne Co., Ohio.

Oct. 1, at 2 P. M., in the Verdigris church, at Dec. S. S. Redman's. A series of meetings will commence Sept. 17.

Oct. 4, at 10 A. M., in the Beaver Dam church, Kosciusko Co., Ind., near the town of Burket.

Oct. 5, at 2 P. M., Spring Creek church, Ind.

Oct. 6, at 3 P. M., Montgomery Co., Ind., near the Keith's churchhouse, eleven miles south-west of Russa, Kans.

Oct. 6 and 7, at 10 A. M., Shannon, Ill.

Oct. 6, at 2 P. M., Arcadia church, Ind.

Oct. 7, Black River church, Van Buren Co., Mich. Brethren coming by rail will stop off at Bangor.

Oct. 7, at 2 P. M., Lodogo, Ind.

Oct. 7, 10 2 P. M., Kaskaskia church, Fayette Co., Ill. ten miles south-west of Beecher City, Ill. Those coming by rail will be met at the above-named place by informing Granville Nevinger.

Oct. 7, at 10 A. M., Sugar Creek, Whitley Co., Ind.

Oct. 5, at 2 P. M., Raccoon Creek church, Montgomery Co., Ind., one and one half miles south west of Ladoga.

Oct. 7, at 4 P. M., Marcoupin Creek church, Montgomery Co., Ill. Those coming by rail will be met at Farmersville, on Springfield Road, and at Girard, on St. Louis Road on morning of meeting.

Oct. 7 and 8, at 12:30 A. M., Four Mile church, Union Co., Ind.

Oct. 8, at 2 P. M., Bethel church, on North County line, Thayer Co., Nebr. Station: Carleton, Davenport, Carlisle and Shickley.

Oct. 8, at 10 A. M., Bear Creek church, Portland, Ind. Those coming by rail will be met by notifying H. P. Garber.

Oct. 8, at 2 P. M., Woodland church, Fulton Co., Ill. A series of meetings one week previous to the feast, and to continue two weeks.

Oct. 8, at 2 P. M., North Star, Darke County, Ohio.

Oct. 8, at 2 P. M., Greentown church, at Greentown, Howard Co., Ind.

Oct. 8, at 2:30 P. M., Maple Glen church, Somerset Co., Pa.

Oct. 8, at 2 P. M., in the Elkhart Valley church, Elkhart Co., Ind.

Oct. 8 and 9, at 1 P. M., Arnold's Grove, Ill.

Oct. 8, at 10 A. M., Dry Creek church, Linn Co., Iowa, one mile west of Robins Station.

Oct. 8, Swan Creek congregation, Ohio, 3½ miles west of Delta, Ohio.

Oct. 8, at 2 P. M., Washington Creek church, Douglas Co., Kans.

Oct. 14 and 15, at 11 A. M. Soul's Keokuk church, Keokuk Co., Iowa. Those coming by rail will be met at Ollie, by notifying Isaac Shelley or Isaac Brown. Those coming from the West will arrive at Ollie about 11:30 A. M.; those from the East at 3 P. M.

Oct. 14, at 2 P. M., Union church, Marshall Co., Ind, five miles west of Plymouth. Trains will be met at both Plymouth and Burr Oak.

Oct. 14, Union church, Plymouth, Marshall Co., Ind. This church would like to have some brother hold meeting a week or ten days after.

Oct. 28, at 2 P. M., South District church, Gage Co., Nebr. Conveyances the day before meeting at B. & M. depot, in Beatrice; Rock Island depot, in Rockford Union Pacific depot, in Holmesville.

Oct. 28, at 2 P. M., Walnut church, Marshall Co., Ind.

Oct. 28, at 10 A. M., in the Buck Creek church, Henry Co., Ind.

Oct. 29, at 2 P. M., Osawkie church, Kans. A series of meetings to commence 6 Oct. 22.

Oct. 29 and 30, at 10 A. M., Pigeon Creek church, Ill., at the Oak Grove meeting-house.

Oct. 29, at 2 P. M., Coal Creek, Madison Co., Ind., 2⅝ miles east of Stoneablville.

Nov. 5, at 3 P. M., Big Creek church, Richland Co., Ill., 3½ miles North-west of Parkersburg, Ill. Conveyances will be at the above place by informing J. M. Forney.

NOW READY

If you are unwell, I will mail you NINE DAYS' Trial Treatment of the famous AUSTRALIAN ELECTRO PILLS FREE, or FIFTY DAYS' treatment for $1.00. These pills for actual liquid remedies in quickly curing Liver, Kidney or Stomach Trouble, Constipation, Indigestion, Sick Headache, La Grippe and its after effects. I want our agent in every church. Special terms to those running the MESSENGER. Address, Dr. E. J. Worst, Ashland, Ohio.

WHAT

Is Band, a monthly magazine published in the interests of all lovers of good literature, 50 cts. per year. But as a SPECIAL INDUCEMENT I will send it one year for 35 cts. and give free a Handy and Reliable little Dictionary, containing 25,000 words and 300 pages. It will be sent in book subscription at once. Address: Jas. M. Neff, Covington, Ohio.

→✦ESSAYS✦←

" Study to show thyself approved unto God; a workman that needeth not be ashamed, rightly dividing the Word of Truth."

SHALL WE KNOW EACH OTHER THERE!

SELECTED BY NORA ARNOLD.

WHEN we hear the music ringing
  In the bright celestial dome—
When sweet angels' voices singing,
  Gladly bid us welcome home
To the land of ancient story,
  Where the spirit knows no care,
In that land of life and glory—
  Shall we know each other there?

When the holy angels meet us,
  As we go to join their band,
Shall we know the friends that greet us
  In that glorious spirit land?
Shall we see the same eyes shining
  On us as in days of yore?
Shall we feel the dear arms twining
  Fondly round us as before?

Yes, my earth-worn soul rejoices,
  And my weary heart grows light,
For the thrilling angels' voices
  And the angel faces bright,
That shall welcome us in heaven,
  Are the loved ones long ago;
And to them 'tis kindly given
  Thus their mortal friends to know.

Oh ye weary, sad, and tossed ones,
  Droop not, faint not by the way!
Ye shall join the loved and just ones
  In that land of perfect day.
Harp-strings, touched by angel fingers,
  Murmured in my rapturous ear;—
Evermore their sweet song lingers—
  " We SHALL know each other there."

Dayton, Ohio.

THE LIFE OF JOB.

BY S. F. PRICE.

"There was a man in the land of Uz, whose name was Job; and that man was perfect and upright, and one that feared God, and eschewed evil."—Job 1: 1.

Now it would appear that in this one verse is stated all that is necessary to prove that this man was lacking in nothing that would recommend him to favor and fellowship with God, his Creator and Preserver. "And there were born unto him seven sons and three daughters. His substance also was seven thousand sheep, and three thousand camels, and five hundred yoke of oxen, and five hundred she asses, and a very great household; so that this man was the greatest of all the men of the east." Job 1: 2, 3.

We learn by this last passage that he was immensely wealthy in this world's goods. He had a large family of children, who, it seems, were peaceable and happy, often meeting together, both brothers and sisters, at each other's houses, feasting and making merry with each other. Their father was very solicitous for them while they were thus engaged, and sent and sanctified them, and offered burnt offerings according to the number of them all, for fear they had cursed God in their hearts, or done something wrong while their hearts were merry. It does not seem possible that their pious old father could have been more zealous and careful and loving, not only to them, but also to his God.

"Now there was a day when the sons of God came to present themselves before the Lord, and Satan came also among them." The statement that Satan came with the sons of God seems, to us, a very strange affair, but the words of Holy Writ makes the statement, and we must accept it as true. During the time, God enters into a conversation with " his Satanic majesty," inquiring from whence he came. He answered the Lord and said, " From going to and fro in the earth, and from walking up and down in it,"—a very busy personage. And the Lord said unto Satan, " Hast thou considered my servant Job, that there is none like him in the earth, a perfect and upright man in every way, one that feareth God and escheweth evil?" Satan answered the Lord and said, " Doth Job fear God for nought?" "See thou hast hedged him about, and given him great possessions, and hast blessed the work of his hands, until his substance is increased in the land, but put forth thine hand now, and touch all that he hath and he will curse thee to thy face."

This bold and defiant declaration of the devil, it seems, ought to have merited his banishment from the presence of God without further debate. But the Lord gave his faithful servant, with all he had, over into the power of Satan, to do as seemed good to him, except he was not to take away his life. So Satan went forth from the presence of the Lord.

"And there was a day when his sons and daughters were eating and drinking wine in their eldest brother's house: And there came a messenger unto Job, and said, The oxen were ploughing, and the asses were feeding beside them: And the Sabeans fell upon them, and took them away; yes, they have slain the servants with the edge of the sword; and I only am escaped alone to tell thee. While he was yet speaking, there came also another, and said, The fire of God is fallen from heaven, and hath burned up the sheep, and the servants, and consumed them; and I only am escaped alone to tell thee. While he was yet speaking, there came also another, and said, The Chaldeans made out three bands, and fell upon the camels, and have carried them away, yea, and slain the servants with the edge of the sword; and I only am escaped alone to tell thee. While he was yet speaking, there came also another and said, Thy sons and thy daughters were eating and drinking wine in their eldest brother's house: And, behold, there came a great wind from the wilderness, and smote the four corners of the house, and it fell upon the young men, and they are dead." Job 1: 13-19.

Yesterday Job was in the possession of wealth, surrounded by friends and children; perfect before God; a righteous man in all his ways. To-day he is bereft of his children, his earthly possessions have vanished, and he is left alone. What does he do? He does not become discouraged, nor give vent to his grief in unavailing regrets, nor is he overcome with melancholy. "But he arose and rent his mantle, shaved his head, and fell down upon the ground and worshiped God, and said: "Naked came I into this world, and naked shall I go out of it again. I brought nothing with me into the world, and I shall take nothing out of it. The Lord gave and the Lord hath taken away; blessed be the name of the Lord."

In all his humiliation Job sinned not with his lips, but maintained his integrity. Then, as if this was not enough to test the virtues of the man, God permitted Satan to afflict his body with sore boils from the sole of his foot to his crown, so that he suffered excruciating pain night and day, but in all this Job maintained his integrity, although his wife advised him to " curse God and die."

Job not only loathed himself, but even his wife abhorred him. Now where are his friends who thronged him during his prosperity? They fled like a shadow; there are only three persons who still claimed to be his friends. When they came to comfort him, they only reproached him and accused him of some great sins as the cause of his afflictions and bereavements. Job's soul became vexed at their conversation, and although the patience of Job has become proverbial, yet he became tired of their endeavors to comfort him, and reasoned with them to show his innocence, breaking forth in language like this, " Miserable comforters are ye all. If your soul were in my soul's stead, I could heap up words against you, and shake mine head at you. But I would strengthen you with my mouth, and assuage your grief. Though I speak, my grief is not assuaged, for mine enemies have gnashed upon me with their teeth; and sharpened their eyes upon me, and gaped upon me, and smitten me upon the cheek reproachfully, and gathered themselves together against me. Surely God hath delivered me to the ungodly, and turned me over into the hands of the wicked." Job 16.

But in course of time God vindicated his servant, and rebuked those comforters and told them to offer up for themselves a burnt offering "and my servant Job shall pray for you: for I will accept him: lest I deal with you after your folly in that ye have not spoken of me the thing which is right, like my servant Job."

"Then the Lord turned the captivity of Job, when he prayed for those false friends, and gave Job twice as much as he had before in wealth, and another family of seven sons and three daughters, and in all the land were no women found, so fair as the daughters of Job. As soon as Job's afflictions ceased and prosperity again smiled upon him, then came unto him all his brethren, and sisters, and all they that had been his acquaintances before, and did eat bread in his house: and comforted him over all the evil that the Lord had brought upon him. So the Lord blessed the latter end of Job's life more than his beginning. After this Job lived a hundred and forty years, and saw his sons, and his son's sons, even to four generations. So Job died, being old and full of days." Job 42.

SONG SERVICE.

BY WM. DERRY.

PERHAPS there never was a time when the subject of having singing taught was more generally agitated than it is at this time. The churches all over the land are lamenting the low ebb to which the singing in their services has come. Sunday-schools and all other religious meetings are suffering for the want of good singing. The social circle is lacking the charm that good singing alone can supply.

The need of that part of the education of the young is universally felt, and the demand for teachers of singing in the public schools, in the churches, and Sunday-schools, is great, and is rapidly increasing. And, in order to help those who are already teaching and to prepare others for the work, there are being held, during the summer seasons, in different localities, what are called Normal Musical Institutes. These schools usually continue for from four to six weeks. Special attention is given to the theory of music, note reading, harmony, voice culture, and the study of church and Sunday-school music.

Those who read my report in the MESSENGER, of the answers received to "A Favor Asked," will remember that, so far as reported by the brethren and sisters, a very small proportion of the members can read even the character notes, and still a smaller number the round notes.

Now it need not be expected that congregational singing will survive unless something be done in the way of teaching the people to read music for singing purposes. It must be remembered that there is a great difference between learning to read music for singing purposes and learning to read it.

❖ESSAYS❖

" Study to show thyself approved unto God; a workman that needeth not to be ashamed, rightly dividing the Word of Truth."

SHALL WE KNOW EACH OTHER THERE?

SELECTED BY NORA ARNOLD.

When we hear the music ringing
    In the bright celestial dome—
When sweet angels' voices singing,
    Gladly bid us welcome home
To the land of ancient story,
    Where the spirit knows no care,
In that land of life and glory—
    Shall we know each other there?

When the holy angels meet us,
    As we go to join their band,
Shall we know the friends that greet us
    In that glorious spirit land?
Shall we see the same eyes shining
    On us as in days of yore?
Shall we feel the dear arms twining
    Fondly round us as before?

Yes, my earth-worn soul rejoices,
    And my weary heart grows light,
For the thrilling angels' voices
    And the angel faces bright,
That shall welcome us to heaven.
    Are the loved ones long ago;
And to them 'tis kindly given
    Thus their mortal friends to know.

Oh ye weary, sad, and tossed ones,
    Droop not, faint not by the way!
Ye shall join the loved and just ones
    In that land of perfect day.
Harp-strings, touched by angel fingers,
    Murmured in my rapturous ear;—
Evermore their sweet song lingers—
    " We shall know each other there."

Dayton, Ohio.

THE LIFE OF JOB.

BY S. F. PRICE.

"There was a man in the land of Uz, whose name was Job; and that man was perfect and upright, and one that feared God, and eschewed evil."—Job 1: 1.

Now it would appear that in this one verse is stated all that is necessary to prove that this man was lacking in nothing that would recommend him to favor and fellowship with God, his Creator and Preserver. "And there were born unto him seven sons and three daughters. His substance also was seven thousand sheep, and three thousand camels, and five hundred yoke of oxen, and five hundred she asses, and a very great household; so that this man was the greatest of all the men of the east." Job 1: 2, 3.

We learn by this last passage that he was immensely wealthy in this world's goods. He had a large family of children, who, it seems, were peaceable and happy, often meeting together, both brothers and sisters, at each other's houses, feasting and making merry with each other. Their father was very solicitous for them while they were thus engaged, and sent and sanctified them, and offered burnt offerings according to the number of them all, for fear they had cursed God in their hearts, or done something wrong while their hearts were merry. It does not seem possible that their pious old father could have been more zealous and careful and loving, not only to them, but also to his God.

"Now there was a day when the sons of God came to present themselves before the Lord, and Satan came also among them." The statement that Satan came with the sons of God seems, to us, a very strange affair, but the words of Holy Writ makes the statement, and we must accept it as true. During the time, God enters into a conversation with "his Satanic majesty," inquiring from whence he came. He answered the Lord and said, " From going to and fro in the earth, and from walking up and down in it,"—a very busy personage. And the Lord said unto Satan, "Hast thou considered my servant Job, that there is none like him in the earth, a perfect and upright man in every way, one that feareth God and escheweth evil?" Satan answered the Lord and said, "Doth Job fear God for nought?" "See thou hast hedged him about, and given him great possessions, and hast blessed the work of his hands, until his substance is increased in the land, but put forth thine hand now, and touch all that he hath and he will curse thee to thy face."

This bold and defiant declaration of the devil, it seems, ought to have merited his banishment from the presence of God without further debate. But the Lord gave his faithful servant, with all he had, over into the power of Satan, to do as seemed good to him, except he was not to take away his life. So Satan went forth from the presence of the Lord.

"And there was a day when his sons and daughters were eating and drinking wine in their eldest brother's house: And there came a messenger unto Job, and said, The oxen were ploughing, and the asses were feeding beside them: And the Sabeans fell upon them, and took them away; yea, they have slain the servants with the edge of the sword; and I only am escaped alone to tell thee. While he was yet speaking, there came also another, and said, The fire of God is fallen from heaven, and hath burned up the sheep, and the servants, and consumed them; and I only am escaped alone to tell thee. While he was yet speaking, there came also another, and said, The Chaldeans made out three bands and fell upon the camels, and have carried them away, yea, and slain the servants with the edge of the sword; and I only am escaped alone to tell thee. While he was yet speaking, there came also another and said, Thy sons and thy daughters were eating and drinking wine in their eldest brother's house: And, behold, there came a great wind from the wilderness, and smote the four corners of the house, and it fell upon the young men, and they are dead." Job 1: 13-19.

Yesterday Job was in the possession of wealth, surrounded by friends and children; perfect before God; a righteous man in all his ways. To-day he is bereft of his children, his earthly possessions have vanished, and he is left alone. What does he do? He does not become discouraged, nor give vent to his grief in unavailing regrets, nor is he overcome with melancholy. "But he arose and rent his mantle, shaved his head, and fell down upon the ground and worshiped God, and said: "Naked came I into this world, and naked shall I go out of it again. I brought nothing with me into the world, and I shall take nothing out of it. The Lord gave and the Lord hath taken away; blessed be the name of the Lord."

In all his humiliation Job sinned not with his lips, but maintained his integrity. Then, as if this was not enough to test the virtues of the man, God permitted Satan to afflict his body with sore boils from the sole of his foot to his crown, so that he suffered excruciating pain night and day, but in all this Job maintained his integrity, and his wife advised him to "curse God and die."

Job not only loathed himself, but even his wife abhorred him. Now where are his friends who thronged him during his prosperity? They fled like a shadow; there are only three persons who still claimed to be his friends. When they came to comfort him, they only reproached him and accused him of some great sins as the cause of his afflictions and bereavements. Job's soul became vexed at their conversation, and although the patience of Job has become proverbial, yet he became tired of their endeavors to comfort him, and reasoned with them to show his innocence, breaking forth in language like this, "Miserable comforters are ye all. If your soul were in my soul's stead, I could heap up words against you, and shake mine head at you. But I would strengthen you with my mouth, and assuage your grief. Though I speak, my grief is not assuaged, for mine enemies have gnashed upon me with their teeth; and sharpened their eyes upon me, and gaped upon me, and smitten me upon the cheek reproachfully, and gathered themselves together against me. Surely God hath delivered me to the ungodly, and turned me over into the hands of the wicked." Job 16.

But in course of time God vindicated his servant, and rebuked those comforters and told them to offer up for themselves a burnt offering "and my servant Job shall pray for you: for I will accept him: lest I deal with you after your folly in that ye have not spoken of me the thing which is right, like my servant Job."

"Then the Lord turned the captivity of Job, when he prayed for those false friends, and gave Job twice as much as he had before in wealth, and another family of seven sons and three daughters, and in all the land were no women found, so fair as the daughters of Job. As soon as Job's afflictions ceased and prosperity again smiled upon him, then came unto him all his brethren and sisters, and all they that had been his acquaintances before, and did eat bread in his house; and comforted him over all the evil that the Lord had brought upon him. So the Lord blessed the latter end of Job's life more than his beginning. After this Job lived a hundred and forty years, and saw his sons, and his son's sons, even to four generations. So Job died, being old and full of days." Job 42.

SONG SERVICE.

BY WM. DEERY.

Perhaps there never was a time when the subject of having singing taught was more generally agitated than it is at this time. The churches all over the land are lamenting the low ebb to which the singing in their services has come. Sunday-schools and all other religious meetings are suffering for the want of good singing. The social circle is lacking the charm that good singing alone can supply.

The need of that part of the education of the young is universally felt, and the demand for teachers of singing in the public schools, in the churches, and Sunday-schools, is great, and is rapidly increasing. And, in order to help those who are already teaching and to prepare others for the work, there are being held, during the summer seasons, in different localities, what are called Normal Musical Institutes. These schools usually continue for from four to six weeks. Special attention is given to the theory of music, note reading, harmony, voice culture, and the study of church and Sunday-school music.

Those who read my report in the Messenger, of the answers received to "A Favor Asked," will remember that as far as reported by the brethren and sisters, a very small proportion of the members can read even the character notes, and still a smaller number the round notes.

Now it need not be expected that congregational singing will survive unless something be done in the way of teaching the people to read music for singing purposes. It must be remembered that there is a great difference between learning to read music for singing purposes and learning to read it

to suppose that Christ will be more forbearing towards them then he was to Peter? He told Peter that if he washed not, he had no part with him. Are those, who refuse to wash, better than Peter was?

Oh, no, it is not the want of evidence to prove it. It is the simple determination on the part of men not to do it. And, generally, when men do not wish to do a thing, any excuse, be it ever so poor, seems to satisfy their minds. In this particular case men seem to be unusually easy to satisfy.

If man's salvation depends upon the *examples* and *commands* of their Savior, feet-washing is just as important as anything else in the Bible: And people that deliberately refuse to do this ordinance, simply refuse to obey their Lord and Master, Jesus Christ.—*Herald of Truth.*

THE MYSTERY OF GODLINESS.

BY A. HUTCHISON.

"And without controversy great is the mystery of godliness: God was manifest in the flesh, justified in the Spirit, seen of angels, preached unto the Gentiles, believed on in the world, received up into glory."—1 Tim. 3: 16.

1. Is it true that God was manifest in the flesh? We learn that "God was in Christ, reconciling the world unto himself." 2 Cor. 5: 19. Next we inquire how this was brought about. Paul answers in the following language: "But when the fullness of the time was come, God sent forth his Son, made of a woman, made under the law, to redeem them that were under the law, that we might receive the adoption of sons." Gal. 4: 4, 5.

Here we have Christ referred to, as the character in whom God was manifest in the flesh, and, as an additional proof, we notice what is further said of Christ, as to the spirit, which he manifested, etc. "But made himself of no reputation, and took upon him the form of a servant, and was made in the likeness of men." Philpp. 2: 7. Let these two references suffice to show that he was manifest in the flesh.

2. "Justified in the Spirit." Matt. 3: 16 says, "And Jesus, when he was baptized, went up straightway out of the water, and, lo, the heavens were opened unto him, and he saw the Spirit of God descending like a dove, and lighting upon him, and lo a voice from heaven, saying, This is my beloved Son, in whom I am well pleased." Here we have him justified in the Spirit, both by visible manifestations of the Spirit, and the voice from heaven, affirming that this is the Christ, the Son of God. We also have an additional testimony from John, the forerunner, saying, "I saw the Spirit descending from heaven like a dove, and it abode upon him. And I knew him not: but he that sent me to baptize with water the same said unto me, Upon whom thou shalt see the Spirit descending, and remaining on him, the same is he which baptizeth with the Holy Ghost. And I saw, and bear record that this is the Son of God." John 1: 32-34.

3. "Seen of angels." Matt. 4: 11 says, "Then the devil leaveth him, and, behold, angels came and ministered unto him." Mark · 1: 13 says, "And he was there in the wilderness forty days, tempted of Satan; and was with the wild beasts; and the angels ministered unto him." Here we have the proof, not only that he was seen of angels, but also that they ministered unto him.

4. "Preached unto the Gentiles." The first of the preaching to the Gentiles was by Peter, to Cornelius and those that were with him in his house, as recorded in Acts 10. It was such a mystery to Peter, that the Gentiles should have the blessings of the Gospel granted unto them,

that a miracle had to be wrought before him, to convince him of that fact. Even after he did go to the house of Cornelius, he was called to account by his Jewish brethren for doing so.

5. "Believed on in the world." Acts 11: 21 says, "And the hand of the Lord was with them: and a great number believed, and turned unto the Lord." We also offer the additional testimony of John as follows, "And many of the people believed on him, and said, When Christ cometh, will he do more miracles than these which this man hath done?" John 7: 31.

6. "Received up into glory." In Acts 1: 9 we have the following: "And when he had spoken these things, while they beheld, he was taken up; and a cloud received him out of their sight." Eph. 4: 10 says, "He that descended is the same also that ascended up far above all heavens, that he might fill all things." In addition to all the above we have the following on the line of the mystery, in the shape of testimony, in favor of Christ being the true Messiah. John says, "And there are three that bear witness in earth,—the Spirit, and the water, and the blood: and these three agree in one." 1 John 5: 8. We have already noticed how, and when, the Spirit testified at his baptism, and we here present another proof from 1 John 5: 6, which says, "This is · he that came-by water and blood, even Jesus Christ; not by water only, but by water and blood. And it is the Spirit that beareth witness, because the Spirit is truth." These three, you will notice, bear witness in earth that this is the Christ. The apostle says, they agree in one. They agree in Christ,—the Spirit at the time of his baptism, and the water and the blood, at his crucifixion, when his side was pierced, and forthwith came thereout blood and water. Hence the' three all agree in Christ, as being ·the Redeemer of the world.

Now, while all this may be mysterious, as applied to Christ, it is no less mysterious that doing just such things as are commanded in the Scriptures will purify a soul, defiled by sin. Even obedience to the letter or form of the command will not purify a soul from sin, unless the service be rendered in faith, "for without faith it is impossible to please God." What could be more mysterious than to have water applied to a man's feet, as a medium through which to benefit his soul? People sometimes say, that the washing of one another's feet is too simple. They say they can see no benefit in such a thing. Well, we inquire, is that any more mysterious, than to take a bit of bread and a sip of wine into the stomach as a means by which to benefit the spiritual man? These things, however mysterious, come under the head of godliness, because they are commanded of God.

"Great is the mystery of godliness." It is not within the reach of man's reasoning powers to attain to a satisfactory conclusion, as to why God made it necessary for man to do the particular things which he did. We can only accept the idea that God knew why, and that, in his arrangement for man, it was necessary. We may lay down our own will, and accept God's will instead. We accept the things which he has given as tests of our faith and spirit. He wishes to test us. When we come to the standard which the apostle sets up, we will come out on the safe side. That standard may be understood by reference to the following language: "Whether therefore ye eat, or drink, or whatsoever ye do, do all to the glory of God." 1 Cor. 10: 31. The Lord's ways are not man's ways. He has his methods, means, and ways, by which to bring his people up to a higher plane. The enemy has his ways and means also, through which to reach people, and induce them to walk as he would

have them do, and it seems to be a great mystery with many, why those who do not observe the ordinances, as given in the New Testament, can do such great things as they do. They say they do them, for they have seen them do wonderful things. I refer such persons to Rev. · 13: 13, 14. Speaking of the beast, the revelator says, "And he doeth great wonders, so that he maketh fire come down from heaven on the earth in the sight of men, and deceiveth them that dwell on the earth by the means of those miracles, which he had power to do in the ·sight of the beast," etc. Rev. 16: 14 says, "For· they are the spirits of devils, working miracles," etc. · · · · · · ! · McPherson, Kans.

ANOINTING THE SICK.

BY ELD. SAMUEL MURRAY.

"Is any sick among you? let him call for the elders of the church; and let them pray over him, anointing him with oil in the name of the Lord: and the prayer of faith shall save the sick, and the Lord shall raise him up; and if he have committed sins, they shall be forgiven him."—James 5: 14, 15.

Do the Brethren, as a church, believe this to be a command given by divine authority? If so, why is it not preached by our ministers and elders, the · same as any other command, such as baptism, feet-washing, etc? Many members get sick and die, no doubt, and never think of the anointing, just because it is not preached as it should be, for most assuredly, it is a command. I do not remember that I ever heard a brother preach it in public. I never preached it in public myself till last spring. It made people inquire into it. The next day I visited a young man, who was low with consumption. He told me some folks were there, the evening before, who said the anointing was not in the Bible. I read it for him. He said, "There it is plain enough," and requested me to mark it for him, his parents being Methodists. They had three of their preachers to pray and work with him till they induced him to say he was saved. Soon after he died.

I am fearful that some of our brethren claim that the anointing is not a command. The inspired apostle recommends it and tells us of the happy effects, and the glorious results therefrom. I am happy to know that there are many living witnesses to testify to these happy results, and I am one of them.

Some brethren have intimated, through the MESSENGER, that if the faith of the elders and sick is right, the sick would get well every time. I think ·that is claiming too much. I wonder what those brethren thought of Bro. R. H. Miller's case, and the brethren who did the anointing. ·Brethren, let us be careful and not challenge each other's faith. We know it is appointed for man once to die. If the anointing would keep people from dying, not many of the members of the Brethren church would die.

I will now very briefly give some of my fifty years' experience in the anointing,—I mean since I have assisted in the anointing. In that early day the Brethren advised the · sick not to take medicine when they were anointed, but this went out of use. In Ohio the Brethren often met with the attending doctors. With one exception they universally gave the Brethren the preference, and said, "Do your work first." I remember of quite a number who were anointed by my own hands, who improved from the start and are living yet,— one, a sister, who was anointed some twenty years ago. Two sisters, whom the doctors said could not get well, got better right away after the anointing, and have been healthier since then than they had been for a number of years before. · ·

to suppose that Christ will be more forbearing towards them than he was to Peter? He told Peter that if he washed not, he had no part with him. Are those, who refuse to wash, better than Peter was?

Oh, no, it is not the want of evidence to prove it. It is the simple determination on the part of men not to do it. And, generally, when men do not wish to do a thing, any excuse, be it ever so poor, seems to satisfy their minds. In this particular case men seem to be unusually easy to satisfy.

If man's salvation depends upon the *examples* and *commands* of their Savior, feet-washing is just as important as anything else in the Bible. And people that deliberately refuse to do this ordinance, simply refuse to obey their Lord and Master, Jesus Christ.—*Herald of Truth.*

THE MYSTERY OF GODLINESS.

BY A. HUTCHISON.

"And without controversy great is the mystery of godliness: God was manifest in the flesh, justified in the Spirit, seen of angels, preached unto the Gentiles, believed on in the world, received up into glory."—1 Tim. 3: 16.

1. Is it true that God was manifest in the flesh? We learn that "God was in Christ, reconciling the world unto himself." 2 Cor. 5: 19. Next we inquire how this was brought about. Paul answers in the following language: "But when the fullness of the time was come, God sent forth his Son, made of a woman, made under the law, to redeem them that were under the law, that we might receive the adoption of sons." Gal. 4: 4, 5.

Here we have Christ referred to, as the character in whom God was manifest in the flesh, and, as an additional proof, we notice what is further said of Christ, as to the spirit, which he manifested, etc. "But made himself of no reputation, and took upon him the form of a servant, and was made in the likeness of men." Philpp. 2: 7. Let these two references suffice to show that he was manifest in the flesh.

2. "Justified in the Spirit." Matt. 3: 16 says, "And Jesus, when he was baptized, went up straightway out of the water, and, lo, the heavens were opened unto him, and he saw the Spirit of God descending like a dove, and lighting upon him, and lo a voice from heaven, saying, This is my beloved Son, in whom I am well pleased." Here we have him justified in the Spirit, both by visible manifestations of the Spirit, and the voice from heaven, affirming that this is the Christ, the Son of God. We also have an additional testimony from John, the forerunner, saying, "I saw the Spirit descending from heaven like a dove, and it abode upon him. And I knew him not: but he that sent me to baptize with water, the same said unto me, Upon whom thou shalt see the Spirit descending, and remaining on him, the same is he which baptizeth with the Holy Ghost. And I saw, and bear record that this is the Son of God." John 1: 32-34.

3. "Seen of angels." Matt. 4: 11 says, "Then the devil leaveth him, and, behold, angels came and ministered unto him." Mark 1: 13 says, "And he was there in the wilderness forty days, tempted of Satan; and was with the wild beasts; and the angels ministered unto him." Here we have the proof, not only that he was seen of angels, but also that they ministered unto him.

4. "Preached unto the Gentiles." The first of the preaching to the Gentiles was by Peter, to Cornelius and those that were with him in his house, as recorded in Acts 10. It was such a mystery to Peter, that the Gentiles should have the blessings of the Gospel granted unto them,

that a miracle had to be wrought before him, to convince him of that fact. Even after he did go to the house of Cornelius, he was called to account by his Jewish brethren for doing so.

5. "Believed on in the world." Acts 11: 21 says, "And the hand of the Lord was with them: and a great number believed, and turned unto the Lord." We also offer the additional testimony of John as follows, "And many of the people believed on him, and said, When Christ cometh, will he do more miracles than these which this man hath done?" John 7: 31.

6. "Received up into glory." In Acts 1: 9 we have the following: "And when he had spoken these things, while they beheld, he was taken up; and a cloud received him out of their sight." Eph. 4: 10 says, "He that descended is the same also that ascended up far above all heavens, that he might fill all things." In addition to all the above we have the following on the line of the mystery, in the shape of testimony, in favor of Christ being the true Messiah. John says, "And there are three that bear witness in earth,—the Spirit, and the water, and the blood: and these three agree in one." 1 John 5: 8. We have already noticed how, and when, the Spirit testified at his baptism, and we here present another proof from 1 John 5: 6, which says, "This is he that came by water and blood, even Jesus Christ; not by water only, but by water and blood. And it is the Spirit that beareth witness, because the Spirit is truth." These three, you will notice, bear witness in earth that this is the Christ. The apostle says, they agree in one. They agree in Christ,—the Spirit at the time of his baptism, and the water and the blood, at his crucifixion, when his side was pierced, and forthwith came thereout blood and water. Hence the three all agree in Christ, as being the Redeemer of the world.

Now, while all this may be mysterious, as applied to Christ, it is no less mysterious that doing just such things as are commanded in the Scriptures will purify a soul, defiled by sin. Even obedience to the letter or form of the command will not purify a soul from sin, unless the service be rendered in faith, "for without faith it is impossible to please God." What could be more mysterious than to have water applied to a man's feet, as a medium through which to benefit his soul? People sometimes say, that the washing of one another's feet is too simple. They say they can see no benefit in such a thing. Well, we inquire, is that any more mysterious, than to take a bit of bread and a sip of wine into the stomach as a means by which to benefit the spiritual man? These things, however mysterious, come under the head of godliness, because they are commanded of God.

"Great is the mystery of godliness." It is not within the reach of man's reasoning powers to attain to a satisfactory conclusion, as to why God made it necessary for man to do the particular things which he did. We can only accept the idea that God knew why, and that, in his arrangement for man, it was necessary. We may lay down our own will, and accept God's will instead. We accept the things which he has given as tests of our faith and spirit. He wishes to test us. When we come to the standard which the apostle sets up, we will come out on the safe side. That standard may be understood by reference to the following language: "Whether therefore ye eat, or drink, or whatsoever ye do, do all to the glory of God." 1 Cor. 10: 31. The Lord's ways are not man's ways. He has his methods, means, and ways, by which to bring his people up to a higher plane. The enemy has his ways and means also, through which to reach people, and induce them to walk as he would

have them do, and it seems to be a great mystery with many, why those who do not observe the ordinance, as given in the New Testament, can do such great things as they do. They say they do them, for they have seen them do wonderful things. I refer such persons to Rev. 13: 13, 14. Speaking of the beast, the revelator says, "And he doeth great wonders, so that he maketh fire come down from heaven on the earth in the sight of men, and deceiveth them that dwell on the earth by the means of those miracles, which he had power to do in the sight of the beast," etc. Rev. 16: 14 says, "For they are the spirits of devils, working miracles," etc.

McPherson, Kans.

ANOINTING THE SICK.

BY ELD. SAMUEL MURRAY.

"Is any sick among you? let him call for the elders of the church; and let them pray over him, anointing him with oil in the name of the Lord: and the prayer of faith shall save the sick, and the Lord shall raise him up; and if he have committed sins, they shall be forgiven him."—James 5: 14, 15.

Do the Brethren, as a church, believe this to be a command given by divine authority? If so, why is it not preached by our ministers and elders, the same as any other command, such as baptism, feet-washing, etc? Many members get sick and die, no doubt, and never think of the anointing, just because it is not preached as it should be, for most assuredly, it is a command. I do not remember that I ever heard a brother preach it in public. I never preached it in public myself till last spring. It made people inquire into it. The next day I visited a young man, who was low with consumption. He told me some folks were there, the evening before, who said the anointing was not in the Bible. I read it for him. He said, "There it is plain enough," and requested me to mark it for him, his parents being Methodists. They had three of their preachers to pray and work with him till they induced him to say he was saved. Soon after he died.

I am fearful that some of our brethren claim that the anointing is not a command. The inspired apostle recommends it and tells us of the happy effects, and the glorious results therefrom. I am happy to know that there are many living witnesses to testify to these happy results, and I am one of them.

Some brethren have intimated, through the MESSENGER, that if the faith of the elders and sick is right, the sick would get well every time. I think that is claiming too much. I wonder what those brethren thought of Bro. R. H. Miller's case, and the brethren who did the anointing. Brethren, let us be careful and not challenge each other's faith. We know it is appointed for man once to die. If the anointing would keep people from dying, not many of the members of the Brethren church would die.

I will now very briefly give some of my fifty years' experience in the anointing.—I mean since I have assisted in the anointing. In that early day the Brethren advised the sick not to take medicine when they were anointed, but this went out of use. In Ohio the Brethren often met with the attending doctors. With one exception they universally gave the Brethren the preference, and said, "Do your work first." I remember of quite a number who were anointed by my own hands, who improved from the start and are living yet,—one, a sister, who was anointed some twenty years ago. Two sisters, whom the doctors said could not get well, got better right away after the anointing, and have been healthier since than than they had been for a number of years before.

Missionary and Tract Work Department.

"Upon the first day of the week, let every one of you lay by him in store as God hath prospered him, that there be no gatherings when I come."—1 Cor. 16: 2.

"Every man as he purposeth in his heart, so let him give. Not grudgingly or of necessity, for the Lord loveth a cheerful giver."—2 Cor. 9: 7.

HOW MUCH SHALL WE GIVE?

"Every man *according to his ability.*" "Every one *as God hath prospered him.*" "Every man, *according as he purposeth in his heart*, so let him *give.*" "For if there be first a willing mind, it is accepted *according to that a man hath*, and not according to that he hath not."—2 Cor. 8: 12.

Organization of Missionary Committee.

DANIEL VANIMAN, Foreman, - - McPherson, Kans.
D. L. MILLER, Treasurer, - - - Mt. Morris, Ill.
GALEN B. ROYER, Secretary, - - Mt. Morris, Ill.

Organization of Book and Tract Work.

S. W. HOOVER, Foreman, - - - Dayton, Ohio.
S. BOCK, Secretary and Treasurer, - Dayton, Ohio.

☞All donations intended for Missionary Work should be sent to Galen B. Royer, Mt. Morris, Ill.
☞All money for Tract Work should be sent to S. Bock, Dayton, Ohio.
☞Money may be sent by Money Order, Registered Letter, or Drafts on New York or Chicago. Do not send personal checks, or drafts on interior towns, as it costs 25 cents to collect them.
☞Solicitors are requested to faithfully carry out the plan of Annual Meeting, that all our members be solicited to contribute at least twice a year for the Mission and Tract Work of the Church.
☞Notes for the Endowment Fund can be had by writing to the Secretary of either Work.

THE CHRISTIAN STANDARD OR PERFECTION.

BY S. N. M'CANN.

In Three Chapters.—Chapter Two.

"Be ye therefore perfect, even as your Father which is in heaven is perfect."—Matt. 5: 48.

MORALITY A FRUITLESS FAILURE.

MORALITY is a good thing, it is a noble thing, but it can never give perfection. The moral man is a noble man, and true morality needs encouragement. It needs help. If we cannot get men to be Christians in deed and in truth, let us do the next best thing, get them to be good moral men. Morality makes good and noble citizens, good neighbors, good associates, good men in every sense of the word. If the teachings of the Bible never did more than to help raise the standard of morals and sustain true morality, it would do a noble work.

True morality forbids a man to do anything that he believes to be wrong. You find in the true moral man a strong advocate of justice. He would blush to stoop to many things that are done under the garb of religion. The true, moral man is virtuous. He hates even loose conversation, and he would be put to shame to be even found in company with those who engage in low, lustful joking and jesting, so prevalent in this age.

The moral man is a temperate man in eating, working, talking, dressing, and every-where else. The moral man is a better man,—far better than many professors of religion. If perfection was a result of good works, the moral man would as often have the victory as the real Christian. If perfection is a result of good works, Christ died in vain. The law of Moses,—the moral law,—is enough, and the moral man is holy and pure enough, if perfection is a result of our works. There is enough of the Divine nature in a man, especially when aided by the moral law, to bring about a good, moral life. We need nothing more to do that, but morality does not, nor can it, bring perfection. We cannot praise morality enough, for the moral man is the grandest and the noblest man that can be produced by the highest development of the good and noble in human character.

We have many men who profess Christianity who are not even moral men,—men who will cheat, misrepresent, and revel in licentious conversation and even worse, but they are wolves in sheep's clothing. While morality is a good thing it is not Christianity; it is not perfection; it does not give salvation. Morality is always an accompaniment of Christianity, it is always found in the true Christian, not in a warring condition, but in a growing one.

There are more people to-day IN THE CHURCH who are moral men,—NOTHING ELSE than moral men,—than there are real Christians. The moral man is a good man. He makes a good church member in any church. All churches are pleased when the moral man comes to them. The church, in some instances and in some ways, is bettered by the moral man coming to her, but the moral man is not bettered one tithe by coming to the church, unless he gets absolute and unqualified perfection.

Hundreds, yea thousands, of reckless sinners profess Christianity, come into the church, live under the name of Christians, when, in deed and in truth, they have only become good moral men. They could have been just as good, just as perfect, outside of the church as they are in it. Their profession has helped to make them better men, the world has been made better by them, but they are only moral men, and cannot be perfect, cannot be holy, cannot be sanctified, cannot be saved.

It is no task, no hardship, no real sacrifice for a good, moral man to be baptized, to wash feet, to wear plain clothes, to keep all the ordinances and ceremonies of the church, if he can be made to feel that they are necessary, but they will raise his morality but little, if any, and they cannot make him perfect. Our (the Dunkard church), to-day has many, many members who are strictly moral, NOTHING MORE; they are convinced that it is best to wear plain clothes, to wash feet and the like, but they have never known that perfect love that casts out fear, and compels the true child to obey. They obey in order to escape hell and to gain heaven, and not because they love Jesus.

Jesus would say to many of our brethren who have kept all these things from their youth up, "One thing thou lackest; if thou wilt be 'PERFECT,' sacrifice your riches for me; sacrifice your pride for me; sacrifice your wills, your all, for me, and you shall be PERFECT." Matt. 19: 20–21. Strict morality, strict conformity to every outward ordinance, cannot give · perfection. · Morality, whether under the garb of Christianity or not, is a complete, an absolute, an entire failure. There is no perfection in it; there is no life, no salvation in it. "We are all as an unclean thing, and all our righteousnesses are as filthy rags." Isa. 64: 6.

FAILURE, FAILURE, absolute and entire failure without perfection. Morality, while good and noble, cannot bring perfection. Strict morality, coupled with strict conformity to the Word, cannot bring perfection. We all fail in word and deed; we are imperfect; we make an entire failure but for Jesus.

Drop your wills into Jesus' great will; let him be Lord and Master, King and Ruler, and perfection is yours. Jesus in your stead, your life hid with Christ in God, and you are perfect.

Christ is as perfect as God. Christ stands for you, or in your stead; therefore you stand as perfect as God.

If you cannot prevail on men to be Christians, help them to become good moral men, but not under the cloak of religion.

Bridgewater, Va.

WERE THE TEN TRIBES LOST?

PELOUBET, in a recent comment on a Sabbath-school lesson, observes: "All the tribes were amalgamated together by the exile and return."

There is a measure of truth in the remark, and yet it is not strictly accurate. The Tribal boundaries were not reconstituted after, as they were impracticable during,—the Babylonish captivity. The territorial divisions of Canaan, made by lot, and resting upon a peculiar land tenure, in which Jehovah was recognized as Lord Paramount, and land held irreversibly in fee simple, and reverting every fifty years to original owners or their heirs, had much to do with the preservation of tribal identity. The suspension of this property arrangement for seventy years, must have led largely to the unification of the twelve into a single nation.

It is evident, however, that another peculiarity, the preservation, in the main, of the genealogical registers during the captivity and even down to our Lord's day, and the hope of return and of repossession, which never died out, may have, and doubtless did, operate, to prevent inter-marriage and to keep the tribes apart even in exile.

Sacred history shows that while the bulk of the returned exiles were from the two faithful tribes, Judah and Benjamin, some of all the tribes, chose to remain in Babylon, and every tribe was represented in the new settlers of Canaan. The Ten Tribes, as such, never were lost any more than the remaining two, one of which has given this people their present name.

The proof, as condensed from the larger treatise upon the subject by Dr. C. C. Jones, is as follows:

1. The Lord's purpose and promise, as announced by the prophets, secured the return of the twelve tribes.

2. It is unaccountable if any tribe was lost at that period, that there is no mention of their absence from the companies brought back by the patriotic and pious leaders, who were not slow to reprimand infidelity to the covenanted privileges in their people. No such complaint is recorded.

3. The Jews themselves have never admitted the fact of any such loss. There is no allusion to any loss of any one, much less of the greater number of the tribes in the Apocryphal books, in Josephus, Philo, or in any of the Rabbinical writings.

4. An analysis of the facts and statistics of the return, demonstrates the presence of members of all the tribes who came back to Palestine from Assyria. The figures show that outside of the returned exiles, identified as from Judah, Benjamin and Levi, there are 12,442 persons to be accounted for, who must have belonged to the remaining nine tribes.

5. That none of the tribes were lost, is proven by New Testament references to them as existent in our Lord's day. Anna, waiting in the temple for the consolation of Israel, is described as "of the tribe of Aser" (Asher).

The representatives of all the tribes are now to be found among that people of a wonderful past, and as wonderful a future, who, as Baalam long ago prophesied, although scattered to the four quarters of the earth, meeting us in every village and city of our land, still "dwell alone."—*Southwestern Presbyterian.*

TRACTS.

BY LAURA V. ULLOM.

WE have just received a package of tracts from the Book and Tract Work, such as "The Origin of Single Immersion," "Ten Reasons for Trine Immersion," "The Prayer Covering," "Plain Dressing," "The Bible Service of Feet-washing," etc.

We feel very grateful to those who supply the fund which makes it possible to send these helps to mission stations like this.

Our little church numbers twenty-seven, and our territory is large. We have four regular appointments, with twenty miles distance between

Missionary and Tract Work Department.

"Upon the first day of the week, let every one of you lay by him in store as God hath prospered him, that there be no gatherings when I come."—1 Cor. 16: 2.

"Every man as he purposeth in his heart, so let him give. Not grudgingly or of necessity, for the Lord loveth a cheerful giver."—2 Cor. 9: 7.

HOW MUCH SHALL WE GIVE?

"Every man *according to his ability.*" "Every one *as God hath prospered him.*" "Every man, *according as he purposeth in his heart*, so let him give." "For if there be first a willing mind. If is accepted *according to that a man hath*, and not according to that he hath not."—2 Cor. 8: 12.

Organization of Missionary Committee.

DANIEL VANIMAN, Foreman, · · · McPherson, Kans.
D. L. MILLER, Treasurer, · · · Mt. Morris, Ill.
GALEN B. ROYER, Secretary, · · · Mt. Morris, Ill.

Organization of Book and Tract Work.

S. W. HOOVER, Foreman, · · · Dayton, Ohio.
S. BOCK, Secretary and Treasurer, · · Dayton, Ohio.

☞All donations intended for Missionary Work should be sent to GALEN B. ROYER, Mt. Morris, Ill.

☞All money for Tract Work should be sent to S. BOCK, Dayton, Ohio.

☞Money may be sent by Money Order, Registered Letter, or Drafts on New York or Chicago. Do not send personal checks, or drafts on interior towns, as it costs 25 cents to collect them.

☞Solicitors are requested to faithfully carry out the plan of Annual Meeting, that all our members be solicited to contribute at least twice a year for the Mission and Tract Work of the Church.

☞Notes for the Endowment Fund can be had by writing to the Secretary of either Work.

THE CHRISTIAN STANDARD OR PERFECTION.

BY S. N. M'CANN.

In Three Chapters.—Chapter Two.

"Be ye therefore perfect, even as your Father which is in heaven is perfect."—Matt. 5: 48.

MORALITY A FRUITLESS FAILURE.

MORALITY is a good thing, it is a noble thing, but it can never give perfection. The moral man is a noble man, and true morality needs encouragement. It needs help. If we cannot get men to be Christians in deed and in truth, let us do the next best thing, get them to be good moral men. Morality makes good and noble citizens, good neighbors, good associates, good men in every sense of the word. If the teachings of the Bible never did more than to help raise the standard of morals and sustain true morality, it would do a noble work.

True morality forbids a man to do anything that he believes to be wrong. You find in the true moral man a strong advocate of justice. He would blush to stop to many things that are done under the garb of religion. The true, moral man is virtuous. He hates even loose conversation, and he would be put to shame to be even found in company with those who engage in low, lustful joking and jesting, so prevalent in this age.

The moral man is a temperate man in eating, working, talking, dressing, and every-where else. The moral man is a better man,—far better than many professors of religion. If perfection was a result of good works, the moral man would as often have the victory as the real Christian. If perfection is a result of good works, Christ died in vain. The law of Moses,—the moral law,—is enough, and the moral man is holy and pure enough, if perfection is a result of our works. There is enough of the Divine nature in a man, especially when aided by the moral law, to bring about a good, moral life. We need nothing more to do that, but morality does not, nor can it, bring perfection. We cannot praise morality enough, for the moral man is the grandest and the noblest man that can be produced by the highest development of the good and noble in human character.

We have many men who profess Christianity who are not even moral men,—men who will cheat, misrepresent, and revel in licentious conversation and even worse, but they are wolves in sheep's clothing. While morality is a good thing it is not Christianity; it is not perfection; it does not give salvation. Morality is always an accompaniment of Christianity, it is always found in the true Christian, not in a warring condition, but in a growing one.

There are more people to-day IN THE CHURCH who are moral men,—NOTHING ELSE then moral men,—than there are real Christians. The moral man is a good man. He makes a good church member in any church. All churches are pleased when the moral man comes to them. The church, in some instances and in some ways, is bettered by the moral man coming to her, but the moral man is not bettered one tithe by coming to the church, unless he gets absolute and unqualified perfection.

Hundreds, yea thousands, of reckless sinners profess Christianity, come into the church, live under the name of Christians, when, in deed and in truth, they have only become good moral men. They could have been just as good, just as perfect, outside of the church as they are in it. Their profession has helped to make them better men, the world has been made better by them, but they are only moral men, and cannot be perfect, cannot be holy, cannot be sanctified, cannot be saved.

It is no task, no hardship, no real sacrifice for a good, moral man to be baptized, to wash feet, to wear plain clothes, to keep all the ordinances and ceremonies of the church, if he can be made to feel that they are necessary, but they will raise his morality but little, if any, and they cannot make him perfect. Our (the Dunkard church), to-day has many, many members who are strictly moral, NOTHING MORE; they are convinced that it is best to wear plain clothes, to wash feet and the like, but they have never known that perfect love that casts out fear, and compels the true child to obey. They obey in order to escape hell and to gain heaven, and not because they love Jesus.

Jesus would say to many of our brethren who have kept all these things from their youth up, "One thing thou lackest; if thou wilt be 'PERFECT,' sacrifice your riches for me; sacrifice your pride for me; sacrifice your wills, your all, for me, and you shall be PERFECT." Matt. 19: 20-21. Strict morality, strict conformity to every outward ordinance, cannot give · perfection. · Morality, whether under the garb of Christianity or not, is a complete, an absolute, an entire failure. There is no perfection in it; there is no life, no salvation in it. "We are all as an unclean thing, and all our righteousnesses are as filthy rags." Isa. 64: 6.

FAILURE, FAILURE, absolute and entire failure without perfection. Morality, while good and noble, cannot bring perfection. Strict morality, coupled with strict conformity to the Word, cannot bring perfection. We all fail in word and deed; we are imperfect; we make an entire failure but for Jesus.

Drop your will into Jesus' great will; let him be Lord and Master, King and Ruler, and perfection is yours. Jesus in your stead, your life hid with Christ in God, and you are perfect.

Christ is as perfect as God. Christ stands for you, or in your stead; therefore you stand as perfect as God.

If you cannot prevail on men to be Christians, help them to become good moral men, but not under the cloak of religion.

Bridgewater, Va.

WERE THE TEN TRIBES LOST?

PELOUBET, in a recent comment on a Sabbath-school lesson, observes: "All the tribes were amalgamated together by the exile and return." There is a measure of truth in the remark, and yet it is not strictly accurate. The Tribal boundaries were not reconstituted after, as they were impracticable during, the Babylonian captivity. The territorial divisions of Canaan, made by lot, and resting upon a peculiar land tenure, in which Jehovah was recognized as Lord Paramount, and land held irreversibly in fee simple, and reverting every fifty years to original owners or their heirs, had much to do with the preservation of tribal identity. The suspension of this property arrangement for seventy years, must have led largely to the unification of the twelve into a single nation.

It is evident, however, that another peculiarity, the preservation, in the main, of the genealogical registers during the captivity and even down to our Lord's day, and the hope of return and of repossession, which never died out, may have, and doubtless did, operate, to prevent inter-marriage and to keep the tribes apart even in exile.

Sacred history shows that while the bulk of the returned exiles were from the two faithful tribes, Judah and Benjamin, some of all the tribes, chose to remain in Babylon, and every tribe was represented in the new settlers of Canaan. The Ten Tribes, as such, never were lost any more than the remaining two, one of which has given this people their present name.

The proof, as condensed from the larger treatise upon the subject by Dr. C. C. Jones, is as follows:

1. The Lord's purpose and promise, as announced by the prophets, secured the return of the twelve tribes.

2. It is unaccountable if any tribe was lost at that period, that there is no mention of their absence from the companies brought back by the patriotic and pious leaders, who were not slow to reprimand infidelity to the covenanted privileges in their people. No such complaint is recorded.

3. The Jews themselves have never admitted the fact of any such loss. There is no allusion to any loss of any one, much less of the greater number of the tribes in the Apocryphal books, in Josephus, Philo, or in any of the Rabbinical writings.

4. An analysis of the facts and statistics of the return, demonstrates the presence of members of all the tribes who came back to Palestine from Assyria. The figures show that outside of the returned exiles, identified as from Judah, Benjamin and Levi, there are 12,442 persons to be accounted for, who must have belonged to the remaining nine tribes.

5. That none of the tribes were lost, is proven by New Testament references to them as existent in our Lord's day. Anna, waiting in the temple for the consolation of Israel, is described as "of the tribe of Aser" (Asher).

The representatives of all the tribes are now to be found among that people of a wonderful past, and as wonderful a future, who, as Baalam long ago prophesied, although scattered to the four quarters of the earth, meeting us in every village and city of our land, still "dwell alone."—*Southwestern Presbyterian.*

TRACTS.

BY LAURA V. ULLOM.

WE have just received a package of tracts from the Book and Tract Work, such as "The Origin of Single Immersion," "Ten Reasons for Trine Immersion," "The Prayer Covering," "Plain Dressing," "The Bible Service of Feet-washing," etc.

We feel very grateful to those who supply the fund which makes it possible to send these helps to mission stations like this.

Our little church numbers twenty-seven, and our territory is large. We have four regular appointments, with twenty miles distance between

The Gospel Messenger,

A Weekly at $1.50 Per Annum.

PUBLISHED BY

The Brethren's Publishing. Co.

D. L. MILLER,	. . . . .	Editor.
J. H. MOORE,	. . . . .	Office Editor.
J. B. BRUMBAUGH,	}	
J. G. ROYER,	}	Associate Editors.
JOSEPH AMICK,	. . . . .	Business Manager.

ADVISORY COMMITTEE.

L. W. Teeter, A. Hutchison, Daniel Hays.

☞Communications for publication should be legibly written with black ink on one side of the paper only. Do not attempt to interline, or to put on one page what ought to occupy two.

☞Anonymous communications will not be published.

☞Do not mix business with articles for publication. Keep your communications on separate sheets from all business.

☞Time is precious. We always have time to attend to business and to answer questions of importance, but please do not subject us to read less answering of letters.

☞The MESSENGER is mailed each week to all subscribers. If the address is correctly entered on our list, the paper must reach the person to whom it is addressed. If you do not get your paper, write us, giving particulars.

☞When changing your address, please give your former as well as your future address in full, so as to avoid delay and misunderstanding.

☞Always remit to the office from which you order your goods, no matter from where you receive them.

☞Do not send personal checks or drafts on interior banks, unless you send with them 25 cents each, to pay for collection.

☞Remittances should be made by Post-office Money Order, Drafts on New York, Philadelphia or Chicago, or Registered Letters, made payable and addressed to "Brethren's Publishing Co., Mount Morris, Ill.," or "Brethren's Publishing Co., Huntingdon, Pa."

☞Entered at the Post-office at Mount Morris, Ill., as second-class matter.

Mount Morris, Ill., · · · · August 9, 1892.

THE appointment at the Chapel last Sunday morning was filled by Bro. S. I. Newcomer, of Lanark.

BRO. J. C. MURRAY, we learn, is booked for a series of meetings near Clarence, Iowa, the last of September.

WE learn that Bro Lemuel Hillery has purchased a home in Texas, and is preparing to locate in that State.

BRO. DANIEL VANIMAN gave us a short call last week. He is traveling in the interest of the General Mission Board.

THE Jews are having a synagogue built in Baltimore, and, by special arrangements with the carpenters, no work is done on Saturday, the Jewish Sabbath.

IN No. 27 of the MESSENGER, North Industry, Ohio, was given as the address of Noah Longanecker. It should have been Hartville, Starke County, Ohio.

MIDDLE INDIANA will hold her Ministerial Meeting at North Manchester, commencing Oct. 11, and continuing over the next day. The Brethren have a very interesting program.

IN the interest of pure, religious homes, Spurgeon one time uttered this beautiful sentence: "When the home is ruled according to God's Word, angels might be asked to stay a night with us, and they would not find themselves out of their element."

WE must beg those sending stamps to use greater care in folding them together, especially in warm weather. Before being placed in the envelope they should be folded with coarse, brown paper between each fold. Or the better way is, to wrap them in oiled paper, kept by grocery men for covering butter, being careful to have each fold separated by the paper. In this way they will never stick together. The amount we lose by stamps sticking together, in letters sent us, amounts to considerable during the year.

THERE is nothing to be gained by a man going around and boasting about what a great sinner he has been. It is far better for him to show, by a meek, Christian life, that the Lord can make out of a sinner who will repent of his sins and live a godly life in Christ Jesus.

BRO. DAVID MARKLEY, one of our ministers of Mt. Etna, Iowa, recently had the misfortune to have his barn, corn and new crop of hay burned. For a struggling minister, the loss will be keenly felt. A little help from some of his friends would be appreciated and will come in good play.

BRO. WM. R. MILLER, of Chicago, gave us a pleasant call last week, and preached in the Chapel Sunday evening. He reports the outlook in Chicago very encouraging at this time. The members greatly appreciate their place of worship, and now feel at home, since they have a house of their own.

WE now have a sister living in Brooklyn, New York. It is to be hoped that her presence and efforts there will some day result in a mission in that city. Everything must have a beginning, and if God is in the work, it is sure to prosper, however small. Brethren, pray and work for the success of these city missions.

IN this issue, Bro. J. S. Mohler speaks of a good opening at Topeka, Kans., for the preaching of the Gospel, there being about twenty members in that place. The demands upon our people are rapidly increasing, and, instead of us being influenced to preach the Word by the "Go ye," we are rather induced to work by the "Come ye."

IN addition to over two hundred languages, into which the Bible, or parts of it, has already been translated, nine new languages have been added to the Bible Society's list of editions during the past year. Four of these are African, two for the Russian empire, one for China, one for the West Indies, and one for the New Hebrides.

A WRITER suggests, that if, in the judgment, we must render an account for every idle word, may it not be possible that we will also have to account for some of our silence! While at times it may be wisdom to remain silent, there are other times when it is most assuredly our duty to speak out and let it be known that we are on the side of right.

A FEW interesting meetings have lately been held in Cedar Rapids, Iowa, with very favorable indications. The greatest obstacle in the way at present, is the want of a suitable house in which to hold services. Efforts are being made in that direction, and it is to be hoped that a house will be secured, and arrangements perfected for regular preaching.

THOSE who are so foolish as to conclude that religious services cannot be made a success without semi-worldly attractions to draw the people, may find food for thought in the following: "Mr. Spurgeon's career has settled several important points. He has proved that evangelical preaching can draw the greatest congregation in the world, and hold it for a life-time, and that it is possible to draw and hold the greatest congregation, without organ, band, choir, or painted windows. He has demonstrated, beyond all question, that the voluntary principle can be so worked as to sustain the greatest religious and benevolent institutions in full vigor; and he has vividly—almost sublimely—illustrated the divine election which chooses its own instruments, protects them in the face of all hostility, and brings obscurity to the point of world-wide renown. Mr. Spurgeon was ordained in a mountain apart."

WE are not in the habit of publishing commendations of our own work, as our readers all well know, but Mr. Yarnall's communication on another page, speaks so well for the part our contributors are performing, that we think it will be an encouragement to them, as we know it is to us, to read his excellent letter. The writer is a stranger to us, but we are glad to know that he so greatly enjoys the MESSENGER, and can speak so highly of its character.

THE Germantown church, Va., did a very prudent thing in electing two young brethren to the ministry recently, though she was blessed with six ministers before. But she has a large field to look after, and then it may be well to keep in mind the importance of more laborers in the vineyard of the Lord, and that more faithful young brethren should be called to the ministry. We need more young men so they can be trained while the older ones are yet with us.

THE story is told of a man who joined first one church, then another, and finally quit all, not being able to find a church suiting his notion. Not till on his death-bed did he realize where the trouble was. He had spent a whole life-time looking for a people who were models in their faith and practice, not once looking at his own heart to see whether it was right in the sight of God. The mistake of his life was in watching others instead of himself. Thousands are going to their graves unprepared for the judgment, for the same reason.

THE Disciples are having no small dissension over the use of the organ in church services. Eld. Sommer,—best known among us on account of his debate with Bro. R. H. Miller,—with other leading preachers, has taken a decided stand against the use of instrumental music in religious services. Concerning this controversy, a writer in the Gospel Advocate says: "As long as Campbell and Franklin lived, they opposed choirs and organs in the worship. Campbell refused to preach in a Presbyterian house in New Orleans unless the organ was kept quiet. Errott opposed the organ much of his life."

IT is astonishing how many mistakes occur in the ministerial list in our Almanac, just for the want of a little care upon the part our ministers. Recently we looked in the Almanac to learn the initials of one of our ministers living within thirty miles of Mt. Morris, and, to our surprise, his name was not in our list, though he has been in the ministry several years. More than likely there are many similar mistakes in regard to other names. We now suggest that everybody, especially the ministers, carefully examine the list, and write us concerning all mistakes that may be discovered. Write all corrections on a slip of paper, separate and apart from all other business.

WITH many regrets we can all look back on our past lives, and see where we have failed to make the best use of opportunities for performing good in behalf of others as well as ourselves. Would we wish to return to childhood, and try life over again? We would not if we could. While our mistakes have been many, they might have been more. While our sufferings and hardships in life may have been painful at times, they could have been worse. And while we may have failed to make the best possible use of past opportunities, still there were hundreds of chances of making still greater failures. Wisdom now teaches us to profit by our experience, and make still greater efforts in the future, knowing that, while the past cannot be changed, there is a possibility of rounding out the future in a manner that will, in a measure, atone for the mistakes of the past.

The Gospel Messenger,

A Weekly at $1.50 Per Annum.

PUBLISHED BY

The Brethren's Publishing. Co.

D. L. MILLER, ... Editor.
J. H. MOORE, ... Office Editor.
J. B. BRUMBAUGH, |
J. G. ROYER, | . . . . Associate Editors.
JOSEPH AMICK, ... Business Manager.

ADVISORY COMMITTEE.
L. W. Teeter, A. Hutchison, Daniel Hays.

☞Communications for publication should be legibly written with black ink on one side of the paper only. Do not attempt to interline, or to put on one page what ought to occupy two.
☞Anonymous communications will not be published.
☞Do not mix business with articles for publication. Keep your communications on separate sheets from all business.
☞Time is precious. We always have time to attend to business and to answer questions of importance, but please do not subject us to need less answering of letters.
☞The Messenger is mailed each week to all subscribers. If the address is correctly marked on our list, the paper must reach the person to whom it is addressed. If you do not get your paper, write us, giving particulars.
☞When changing your address, please give your former as well as your future address in full, so as to avoid delay and misunderstanding.
☞Always Remit to the office from which you order your goods, no matter from where you receive them.
☞Do not send personal checks or drafts on interior banks, unless you send with them 25 cents each, to pay for collection.
☞Remittances should be made by Post-office Money Order, Drafts on New York, Philadelphia or Chicago, or Registered Letters, made payable and addressed to "Brethren's Publishing Co., Mount Morris, Ill.," or " Brethren's Publishing Co., Huntingdon, Pa."
☞Entered at the Post-office at Mount Morris, Ill., as second-class matter.

Mount Morris, Ill., ... August 9, 1892.

THE appointment at the Chapel last Sunday morning was filled by Bro. S. I. Newcomer, of Lanark.

BRO. J. C. MURRAY, we learn, is booked for a series of meetings near Clarence, Iowa, the last of September.

WE learn that Bro Lemuel Hillery has purchased a home in Texas, and is preparing to locate in that State.

BRO. DANIEL VANIMAN gave us a short call last week. He is traveling in the interest of the General Mission Board.

THE Jews are having a synagogue built in Baltimore, and, by special arrangements with the carpenters, no work is done on Saturday, the Jewish Sabbath.

IN No. 27 of the MESSENGER, North Industry, Ohio, was given as the address of Noah Longanecker. It should have been Hartville, Starke County, Ohio.

MIDDLE INDIANA will hold her Ministerial Meeting at North Manchester, commencing Oct. 11, and continuing over the next day; The Brethren have a very interesting program.

IN the interest of pure, religious homes, Spurgeon one time uttered this beautiful sentence: "When the home is ruled according to God's Word, angels might be asked to stay a night with us, and they would not find themselves out of their element."

WE must beg those sending stamps to use greater care in folding them together, especially in warm weather. Before being placed in the envelope they should be folded with coarse, brown paper between each fold. Or the better way is, to wrap them in oiled paper, kept by grocery men for covering butter, being careful to have each fold separated by the paper. In this way they will never stick together. The amount we lose by stamps sticking together ,in letters sent us, amounts to considerable during the year.

THERE is nothing to be gained by a man going around and boasting about what a great sinner he has been. It is far better for him to show, by a meek, Christian life, what the Lord can make out of a sinner who will repent of his sins and live a godly life in Christ Jesus.

BRO. DAVID MARKLEY, one of our ministers of Mt. Etna, Iowa, recently had the misfortune to have his barn, corn and new crop of hay burned. For a struggling minister, the loss will be keenly felt. A little help from some of his friends would be appreciated and will come in good play.

BRO. WM. R. MILLER, of Chicago, gave us a pleasant call last week, and preached in the Chapel Sunday evening. He reports the outlook in Chicago very encouraging at this time. The members greatly appreciate their place of worship, and now feel at home, since they have a house of their own.

WE now have a sister living in Brooklyn, New York. It is to be hoped that her presence and efforts there will some day result in a mission in that city. Everything must have a beginning, and if God is in the work, it is sure to prosper, however small. Brethren, pray and work for the success of these city missions.

IN this issue, Bro. J. S. Mohler speaks of a good opening at Topeka, Kans., for the preaching of the Gospel, there being about twenty members in that place. The demands upon our people are rapidly increasing, and, instead of us being influenced to preach the Word by the "Go ye," we are rather induced to work by the "Come ye."

IN addition to over two hundred languages, into which the Bible, or parts of it, has already been translated, nine new languages have been added to the Bible Society's list of editions during the past year. Four of these are African, two for the Russian empire, one for China, one for the West Indies, and one for the New Hebrides.

A WRITER suggests, that if, in the judgment, we must render an account for every idle word, may it not be possible that we will also have to account for some of our silence! While at times it may be wisdom to remain silent, there are other times when it is most assuredly our duty to speak out and let it be known that we are on the side of right.

A FEW interesting meetings have lately been held in Cedar Rapids, Iowa, with very favorable indications. The greatest obstacle in the way at present, is the want of a suitable house in which to hold services. Efforts are being made in that direction, and it is to be hoped that a house will be secured, and arrangements perfected for regular preaching.

THOSE who are so foolish as to conclude that religious services cannot be made a success without semi-worldly attractions to draw the people, may find food for thought in the following: "Mr. Spurgeon's career has settled several important points. He has proved that evangelical preaching can draw the greatest congregation in the world, and hold it for a life-time, and that it is possible to draw and hold the greatest congregation, without organ, band, choir, or painted windows. He has demonstrated, beyond all question, that the voluntary principle can be so worked as to sustain the greatest religious and benevolent institutions in full vigor; and he has vividly—almost sublimely—illustrated the divine election which chooses its own instruments, protects them in the face of all hostility, and brings obscurity to the point of world-wide renown. Mr. Spurgeon was ordained in a mountain apart."

WE are not in the habit of publishing commendations of our own work, as our readers all well know, but Mr. Yarnall's communication on another page, speaks so well for the part our contributors are performing, that we think it will be an encouragement to them, as we know it is to us, to read his excellent letter. The writer is a stranger to us, but we are glad to know that he so greatly enjoys the MESSENGER, and can speak so highly of its character.

THE Germantown church, Va., did a very prudent thing in electing two young brethren to the ministry recently, though she was blessed with six ministers before. But she has a large field to look after, and then it may be well to keep in mind the importance of more laborers in the vineyard of the Lord, and that more faithful young brethren should be called to the ministry. We need more young men so they can be trained while the older ones are yet with us.

THE story is told of a man who joined first one church, then another, and finally quit all, not being able to find a church suiting his notion. Not till on his death-bed did he realize where the trouble was. He had spent a whole life-time looking for a people who were models in their faith and practice, not once looking at his own heart to see whether it was right in the sight of God. The mistake of his life was in watching others instead of himself. Thousands go to their graves unprepared for the judgment, for the same reason.

THE Disciples are having no small dissension over the use of the organ in church services. Eld. Sommer,—best known among us on account of his debate with Bro. R. H. Miller,—with other leading preachers, has taken a decided stand against the use of instrumental music in religious services. Concerning this controversy, a writer in the Gospel Advocate says: "As long as Campbell and Franklin lived, they opposed choirs and organs in the worship. Campbell refused to preach in a Presbyterian house in New Orleans unless the organ was kept quiet. Errott opposed the organ much of his life."

IT is astonishing how many mistakes occur in the ministerial list in our Almanac, just for the want of a little care upon the part our ministers. Recently we looked in the Almanac to learn the initials of one of our ministers living within thirty miles of Mt. Morris, and, to our surprise, his name was not in our list, though he has been in the ministry several years. More than likely there are many similar mistakes in regard to other names. We now suggest that everybody, especially the ministers, carefully examine the list, and write us concerning all mistakes that may be discovered. Write all corrections on a slip of paper, separate and apart from all other business.

WITH many regrets we can all look back on our past lives, and see where we have failed to make the best use of opportunities for performing good in behalf of others as well as ourselves. Would we wish to return to childhood, and try life over again? We would not if we could. While our mistakes have been many, they might have been more. While our sufferings and hardships in life may have been painful at times, they could have been worse. And while we may have failed to make the best possible use of past opportunities, still there were hundreds of chances of making still greater failures. Wisdom now teaches us to profit by our experience, and make still greater efforts in the future, knowing that, while the past cannot be changed, there is a possibility of rounding out the future in a manner that will, in a measure, atone for the mistakes of the past.

NOT TO COPY AFTER THE WORLD.

UNDER the above heading the editor of the *Zion's Watchman* (Methodist) gives his readers a plain talk on the necessity of Christians giving due attention to their personal appearance. He says: Jesus says, "That which is highly esteemed among men is abomination in the sight of God." Nothing is more highly esteemed among the high, the proud, the unregenerated men of the world, than fine and fashionable attire. Unless there is some very strong reason why we should follow the fashions of the world, it is well to stop and ask if this is not one of those things which is an abomination in the sight of God.

If we would be followers of the meek and lowly Lamb of God, we cannot follow the world, "For the friendship of the world is enmity with God. Whosoever therefore will be a friend of the world is the enemy of God." James 4: 4. There is no half-way ground. We cannot serve two masters; we cannot be the friend of both God and the world. "Choose you this day whom you will serve."

God has always warned his people against idolatry, and punished them for worshiping idols. Loving fashion and following her dictates is as much idolatry as the worship of Baal ever was. The child of God should have nothing to do with it. Paul commands us to "present our bodies a living sacrifice, holy, acceptable unto God." To do this our bodies must be made pure, presented unto God on the altar of his service, and if he accepts them, they are his forever. We can never get them back again, while we serve him. "Ye are not your own but are bought with a price."

If, then, our bodies belong to God, we have no right whatever to lend them to fashion, in order that she might make a display upon them of her gaudy array. If they are his, they must be clothed for him in humility.

THE COLORED POPULATION.

IT may be interesting to our readers to know the facts concerning the population and increase of the colored people in the United States.

"According to a late bulletin from the Census Bureau, the colored population of the United States numbers 7,638,360—an increase of 875,547 in the decade between 1880 and 1890. In 1880 it was returned at 6,752,813, which was an increase of 1,783,819, or nearly 36 per cent between 1870 and 1880. In explanation of this incredible increase the present report says: "The census of 1880 was grossly deficient in the Southern States, so much so as not only to give an exaggerated rate of increase of the population between 1870 and 1880 in the States, but to affect materially the rate of increase in the country at large." The increase from 1880 to 1890 is only 13.11 per cent, which does not indicate its more rapid increase than that of the whites. In 1850 the colored race constituted between one-fifth and one-sixth of the whole population; in 1860 a little less than one-sixth, in 1870 between one-sixth and seventh, in 1880 less than one-seventh, and in 1890 a little less than one-eighth, so that it will be seen that they are a decreasing element. The only States which have a larger colored population than white are South Carolina, Mississippi and Louisiana, and in them the figures are: South Carolina, whites 462,-008, colored 689,141; Mississippi, whites 544,851, colored 744,749; Louisiana, whites 558,395, colored 560,192." And even in these States the whites are increasing faster than the colored people. Taking the United States over, the net increase, during the last ten years, has been nearly 26 per cent, while the increase among the negroes has been a

little less than 12 per cent. It will thus be seen that the increase of the white race is more than twice as much as that of the colored race. These statistics also show that only a very small number of negroes leave the old slave States. They are wedded to the South, and are there to remain. Whatever is to be done for them, in the way of education and religious culture, must be done in the South. There is room for a grand work among them. Much has been done already, but there is more yet to be accomplished. And while the field is a very important one, and right at our doors, it is nevertheless beset with difficulties hard to be overcome.   J. H. M.

VACATION TALKS WITH OUR STUDENTS.

NUMBER SIX.—PREPARATIONS IN THE HOME.

LETTERS from all quarters bring word that many are making preparations to come to school. Could the secretaries of our other schools be heard from, they, no doubt, would give similar reports. Hundreds of young people are now preparing to leave home and go to school. Many of them leave the dear old home for the first time. Allow me to suggest that in the preparations made, the Bible be not forgotten, and that church members bring letters of membership. Of course each one will be supplied with sufficient clothing. This should be plain. As a church we profess to be a plain people. Our schools are mainly for the Brethren's children. It is desirable, therefore, that our schools maintain plainness; hence we urge all, who are preparing to attend the Brethren's schools, to avoid extravagance in dress; and we strongly solicit the co-operation of parents in our efforts to maintain a proper consistency in this respect. Superfluity in dress and the wearing of jewelry are not only forbidden in the Word of God, but they are considered injurious in every way. We hope parents will see that their children do not come burdened with these hinderances.

We are aware that, aside from comfort, the true notion of dress is to appear well in the sight of others. This desire is deeply rooted in human nature, and when properly regulated is not wrong. The Bible would not have us neglect our personal appearance. Religion promotes neatness, cleanliness and a proper attention to our external appearance as truly as it does to the internal virtues of the soul. But, while this is true, it is equally true that the wearing of gold and gay and costly apparel are not the outgrowth of the soul virtues represented in the Bible as being " in the sight of God of great price." Persons who spend so much time and money on personal decoration, give an unmistakable proof of a lack of excellence within, and of a vain effort to supply the want of real goodness within, by the feeble and silly aids of dress and ornamentation without.

Several years ago two young men entered a certain school, each wearing a fine silk hat, costly rings, and a heavy gold chain with charm in display. So far as ornamentation was concerned, they made a fine display, but, when the work of classification began, it was found that neither could perform an operation in long division correctly. Excellence within was wanting, both mental and religious. A lady appears in chapel in latest style of dress, wearing gold, and her hair put up in grand display; but when called upon to recite in class, she sighs, giving a staring look into space, followed by a blush that says to all in the room, "I can't recite; but don't you see what a

beauty I am?" In all such cases there is a lameness or want, both in head and heart,—especially in heart development.

While it is true that we have a class of men—the fop, who is excessively fond of display in dress, the desire for display is evidently much more general among women. If they knew how large a part of their display in dress is lost upon the other sex, they would not set so much store, or spend so much time upon it. Five out of every six of the best men do not appreciate the difference in the quality and color of silks, laces, and ribbons which seemingly appear so important in woman's eyes. It certainly is no credit to a man to be able to point out, with any degree of appreciation, the distinctions of style in female attire. His time is supposed to be employed to better advantage.

Every man, however, is interested in what constitutes the ornaments of the heart. He knows or ought to know what is meant by a "meek and quiet spirit," by a kind and gentle temper, by a pure and affectionate heart. Every man can appreciate the worth of these; and if our young women would permanently please our best young men, and above all, please God, they must seek to develop, as far as possible, these soul ornaments.

Plain, neat and modest dressing aids in the development of these graces in both sexes, while the anxiety to please and appear well, by keeping pace with the ever-fluctuating fashions, develops irritability, restlessness and impatience. Hence we urge again that, in your preparations to come to school, you study to appreciate plainness, neatness and propriety.   J. G. R.

CORRESPONDENCE.

"Write what thou seest, and send it unto the churches."

☞ Church News solicited for this Department. If you have had a good meeting, send a report of it, so that others may rejoice with you. In writing give name of church, County and State. Be brief. Notes of Travel should be as short as possible. Land Advertisements are not solicited for this Department. We have an advertising page, and, if necessary, will issue supplements.

Musings by the Way.

FRIENDS have, a number of times, enquired of me why they see no more of my " Musings by the Way" in the GOSPEL MESSENGER. I must reply, The fire has not ceased to burn; thought has been busy, though my pen remained idle. Perhaps, like Martha, I have been cumbered with many cares.

To-day, a beautiful June day, as I study the Sunday-school lesson, No. 13, I read the suggestive words of Hosea: "Then shall we know if we *follow on to know the Lord:* His going forth is prepared as the morning, and he shall come to us as the rain, as the latter and the former rain." Memory turns for me many pages,—yea more than two score, and I hear the voices of God's dear servants teaching me *how* to "follow on to know the Lord;" and now, while they rest from their labors, I live to bear testimony, that,—in the lasting impressions made upon my young heart,— their works do follow them. Sunday-school teachers, weary not of your work, teach the " Word " faithfully and prayerfully, and it shall bear fruit in the hearts and lives of your children, even as the early and the latter rain bring out the fruits of the earth.

Now to the dear ones in Christ, with whom we have worshiped formerly: Though we are separated, by faith we gather around the altar and drink of that Spiritual Rock, and "He shall be unto us, as the light of the morning, when the sun riseth, even a morning without clouds; as the ten-

NOT TO COPY AFTER THE WORLD.

UNDER the above heading the editor of the *Zion's Watchman* (Methodist) gives his readers a plain talk on the necessity of Christians giving due attention to their personal appearance. He says:

Jesus says, "That which is highly esteemed among men is abomination in the sight of God." Nothing is more highly esteemed among the high, the proud, the unregenerated men of the world, than fine and fashionable attire. Unless there is some very strong reason why we should follow the fashions of the world, it is well to stop and ask if this is not one of those things which is an abomination in the sight of God.

If we would be followers of the meek and lowly Lamb of God, we cannot follow the world, "For the friendship of the world is enmity with God. Whosoever therefore will be a friend of the world is the enemy of God." James 4: 4. There is no half-way ground. We cannot serve two masters; we cannot be the friend of both God and the world. "Choose you this day whom you will serve."

God has always warned his people against idolatry, and punished them for worshiping idols. Loving fashion and following her dictates is as much idolatry as the worship of Baal ever was. The child of God should have nothing to do with it. Paul commands us to "present our bodies a living sacrifice, holy, acceptable unto God." To do this our bodies must be made pure, presented unto God on the altar of his service, and if he accepts them, they are his forever. We can never get them back again, while we serve him. "Ye are not your own but are bought with a price."

If, then, our bodies belong to God, we have no right whatever to lend them to fashion, in order that she might make a display upon them of her gaudy array. If they are his, they must be clothed for him in humility.

THE COLORED POPULATION.

IT may be interesting to our readers to know the facts concerning the population and increase of the colored people in the United States.

"According to a late bulletin from the Census Bureau, the colored population of the United States numbers 7,638,360—an increase of 875,547 in the decade between 1880 and 1890. In 1880 it was returned at 6,752,813, which was an increase of 1,783,819, or nearly 36 per cent between 1870 and 1880. In explanation of this incredible increase the present report says: "The census of 1880 was grossly deficient in the Southern States, so much so as not only to give an exaggerated rate of increase of the population between 1870 and 1880 in the States, but to affect materially the rate of increase in the country at large." The increase from 1880 to 1890 is only 13.11 per cent, which does not indicate its more rapid increase than that of the whites. In 1850 the colored race constituted about one-fifth and one-sixth of the whole population; in 1860 a little less than one-sixth, in 1870 between one-sixth and seventh, in 1880 less than one-seventh, and in 1890 a little less than one-eighth, so that it will be seen that they are a decreasing element. The only States which have a larger colored population than white are South Carolina, Mississippi and Louisiana, and in them the figures are: South Carolina, whites 462,008, colored 689,141; Mississippi, whites 544,851, colored 744,749; Louisiana, whites 558,395, colored 560,192." And even in these States the whites are increasing faster than the colored people. Taking the United States over, the net increase, during the last ten years, has been nearly 25 per cent, while the increase among the negroes has been a

little less than 12 per cent. It will thus be seen that the increase of the white race is more than twice as much as that of the colored race. These statistics also show that only a very small number of negroes leave the old slave States. They are wedded to the South, and are there to remain. Whatever is to be done for them, in the way of education and religious culture, must be done in the South. There is room for a grand work among them. Much has been done already, but there is more yet to be accomplished. And while the field is a very important one, and right at our doors, it is nevertheless beset with difficulties hard to be overcome.   J. H. M.

VACATION TALKS WITH OUR STUDENTS.

NUMBER SIX.—PREPARATIONS IN THE HOME.

LETTERS from all quarters bring word that many are making preparations to come to school. Could the secretaries of our other schools be heard from, they, no doubt, would give similar reports. Hundreds of young people are now preparing to leave home and go to school. Many of them leave the dear old home for the first time. Allow me to suggest that in the preparations made, the Bible be not forgotten, and that church members bring letters of membership. Of course each one will be supplied with sufficient clothing. This should be plain. As a church we profess to be a plain people. Our schools are mainly for the Brethren's children. It is desirable, therefore, that our schools maintain plainness; hence we urge all, who are preparing to attend the Brethren's schools, to avoid extravagance in dress; and we strongly solicit the co-operation of parents in our efforts to maintain a proper consistency in this respect. Superfluity in dress and the wearing of jewelry are not only forbidden in the Word of God, but they are considered injurious in every way. We hope parents will see that their children do not come burdened with these hinderances.

We are aware that, aside from comfort, the true notion of dress is to appear well in the sight of others. This desire is deeply rooted in human nature, and when properly regulated is not wrong. The Bible would not have us neglect our personal appearance. Religion promotes neatness, cleanliness and a proper attention to our external appearance as truly as it does to the internal virtues of the soul. But, while this is true, it is equally true that the wearing of gold and gay and costly apparel are not the outgrowth of the soul virtues represented in the Bible as being " in the sight of God of great price." Persons who spend so much time and money on personal decoration, give an unmistakable proof of a lack of excellence within, and of a vain effort to supply the want of real goodness within, by the feeble and silly aids of dress and ornamentation without.

Several years ago two young men entered a certain school, each wearing a fine silk hat, costly rings, and a heavy gold chain with charm in display. So far as ornamentation was concerned, they made a fine display, but when the work of classification began, it was found that neither could perform an operation in long division correctly. Excellence within was wanting, both mental and religious. A lady appears in chapel in latest style of dress, wearing gold, and her hair put up in grand display; but when called upon to recite in class, she sighs, giving a staring look into space, followed by a blush that says to all in the room, "I can't recite, but don't you see what a

beauty I am?" In all such cases there is a lameness or want, both in head and heart,—especially, in heart development.

While it is true that we have a class of men—the fop, who is excessively fond of display in dress, the desire for display is evidently much more general among women. If they knew how large a part of their display in dress is lost upon the other sex, they would not set so much store, or spend so much time upon it. Five out of every six of the best men do not appreciate the difference in the quality and color of silks, laces, and ribbons which seemingly appear so important in woman's eyes. It certainly is no credit to a man to be able to point out, with any degree of appreciation, the distinctions of style in female attire. His time is supposed to be employed to better advantage.

Every man, however, is interested in what constitutes the ornaments of the heart. He knows or ought to know what is meant by a "meek and quiet spirit," by a kind and gentle temper, by a pure and affectionate heart. Every man can appreciate the worth of these; and if our young women would permanently please our best young men, and above all, please God, they must seek to develop, as far as possible, those soul ornaments.

Plain, neat and modest dressing aids in the development of these graces in both sexes, while the anxiety to please and appear well, by keeping pace with the ever-fluctuating fashions, develops irritability, restlessness and impatience. Hence we urge again that, in your preparations to come to school, you study to appreciate plainness, neatness and propriety.   J. G. R.

CORRESPONDENCE.

"Write what thou seest, and send it unto the churches."

☞Church News solicited for this Department. If you have had a good meeting, send a report of it, so that others may rejoice with you. In writing give name of church, County and State. Be brief. Notes of Travel should be as short as possible. Land Advertisements are not solicited for this Department. We have an advertising page, and, if necessary, will issue supplements.

Musings by the Way.

FRIENDS have, a number of times, enquired of me why they see no more of my "Musings by the Way" in the GOSPEL MESSENGER. I must reply, The fire has not ceased to burn; thought has been busy, though my pen remained idle. Perhaps, like Martha, I have been cumbered with many cares.

To-day, a beautiful June day, as I study the Sunday-school lesson, No. 13, I read the suggestive words of Hosea: "Then shall we know if we *follow on to know the Lord:* His going forth is prepared as the morning, and he shall come to us as the rain, as the latter and the former rain." Memory turns for me many pages,—yea more than two score, and I hear the voices of God's dear servants teaching me *how* to "follow on to know the Lord;" and now, while they rest from their labors, I live to bear testimony, that,—in the lasting impressions made upon my young heart, — their works do follow them. Sunday-school teachers, weary not of your work, teach the "Word" faithfully and prayerfully, and it shall bear fruit in the hearts and lives of your children, even as the early and the latter rain bring out the fruits of the earth.

Now to the dear ones in Christ, with whom we have worshiped formerly: Though we are separated, by faith we gather around the altar and drink of that Spiritual Rock, and "He shall be, unto us, as the light of the morning, when the sun riseth, even a morning without clouds; as the ten-

A Trip to the North-Western Part of Nebraska.

By order of the District Mission Board, I left home June 30. My first stop was with the Brethren of the Rush Valley church, in Sheridan County. I held meetings each evening during one week, and on Saturday evening, July 9, about twenty-three of the Father's children gathered around the Lord's table and enjoyed a pleasant Communion season together.

This church is under the care of Eld. David Bear. Here I also met Bro. Aaron M. Musselman, who was my neighbor at one time in Northern Illinois. Our many pleasant seasons in the Hickory Grove church, were called to memory again.

While here, one day, the Brethren made up a party, and I accompanied them on a visit to the Pine Ridge Agency on the Sioux Indian Reservation in South Dakota. There the government has erected some large buildings for schools, stores, hospitals, etc. By the courtesy of the officers we were escorted through the buildings and grounds, and saw many things to attract our notice regarding this peculiar people.

By a contract with these Indians, the government keeps them well supplied with all that is needful, and trains and teaches about 150 Indian boys and girls in all the sciences of civilized life. We notice that many among them still adhere to the customs of their wild life in the matter of dress, etc.

Leaving the Rush Valley, I proceeded westward about sixty miles, to Crawford, where there is a small band of members, living quite isolated, and without an organization. No preacher is nearer than about sixty miles. This little colony emigrated to this country from West Virginia. Among them is Bro. William Dove and family.

After laboring here one week, two made the good confession and were baptized. From here I returned eastward 150 miles into Cherry County, where a call was made for the Brethren to come and preach. This is a new field for the Brethren, but as the Word was held forth, they that gladly received his Word were baptized. We resorted to the water-side where prayer was made, and then, like Philip and the eunuch, we both went down into the water, where two were baptized. Not a brother or sister was present to assist or witness the scene, for there are none living within fifty miles that I know of. About twenty-five of the neighbors were present to look on. A friend remarked, "That is the way the Dunkards baptize in Virginia." For this new field I have a good prospect, and recommend it to the especial attention of the Mission Board.

From here I returned to the place called home, where I arrived about midnight of July 23, very warm and much fatigued, having traveled over 1,000 miles on this trip.   JESSE Y. HECKLER.
Elmwood, Nebr.

From Arcanum, Ohio.

JUNE 25, the brethren and sisters of the Ludlow church met for special Communion services. These services were characterized by several distinctive features. First, in being appointed and conducted expressly for the benefit of the home membership. Second, while over 300 communed, only two or three were present from neighboring churches. Third, as being the last service of the kind to be held in the old Pitsburgh meeting-house. While absolutely free from any selfish motive, it offered decided advantages, in point of labor, convenience, and spiritual edification, over the crowded and laborious conditions of large public Communion services. Of course no thought of dispensing with the regular public Communion should, for a moment, be entertained, but in addition to it, a service of the above character would certainly be commendable.

The work of rebuilding the Pitsburgh house is now in progress, and will be brought to completion as speedily as possible. During the time of building, Sunday-school and church-services will be held in the grove near by. The Sunday-schools of the District are enjoying a very fair degree of prosperity and it is to be hoped much good seed is being sown on good ground.   C. E. CULP.
July 29.

Treasurer's Report.

THE following is the report of Boys and Girl's Bible School for quarter ending June 30, 1892:

RECEIPTS.

Balance from last report,	$18 20
Error in last report,	1 00
Sister Ella Williams, Funkstown, Md.,	2 00
Sister Jane Eoglar, Linwood, Md.,	1 00
Sister Elizabeth Roop, Linwood, Md.,	5 00
Wm. P. Klein, through W. W. Kulp, Pottstown, Pa.,	2 00
A brother, through W. W. Kulp, Pottstown, Pa.,	3 00
Hannah Sager, Indian Creek Church, Iowa, per T. H. Higgs,	2 00
Indian Creek Sunday-school, Iowa, per T. H. Higgs,	86
Lord's Tenth,	5 66
Total,	$40 72

EXPENDITURES.

Taking scholars to love-feast,	14 30
Taking scholars to preaching,	1 14
Oil,	16
Bibles,	1 30
Rent,	21 00
Freight on tracts,	60
Total,	$38 50
Balance in bank,	$ 2 22

JAMES T. QUINLAN, Supt.
JOSEPH J. ELLIS, Sec'y.

Watch the Dates.

IN GOSPEL MESSENGER No. 28, page 486, we find an article, "Eighteen Hundred and Ninety-three," selected by Bro. J. R. Gish, from "Words and Works." I do not think J. W. Pope is a "crank," for his solution represents thought in sacred numbers, but I wish to show, according to dates, that he is mistaken. The year 1893, according to our calendar, will be the next one, but, in reality, this present year, 1892, is 1893; consequently next year, 1893, will be really 1897,—four years past Mr. Pope's calculation already, and no second coming of Christ yet.

Concerning the second advent of Christ, the following facts are of interest and may be helpful to all of our Brethren who are looking up dates for the birth of Christ.

"The date, December, B. C. 5, is now regarded as at least approximating the actual date upon which Jesus was born, but neither the year nor the month can be laid down with certainty. His birth is placed in B. C. 5, instead of A. D. 1, because of the error of Dionysius Exiguus in the sixth century, in assigning the nativity to the year 754, of the Roman era, instead of to 749 or 750; as he should have done. He began the present system of counting the years from Jesus' birth instead of from the date of the founding of Rome, and in the eighth century, Bede followed him in writing history, and Pepin and Charlemagne adopted it in State affairs, thus giving it currency, and at the same time perpetuating the error." It requires 104 years yet to complete the Christian era, that is, to make this present dispensation 2,000 years.   DAVID SNYDER.
Ashland, Ohio.

From Bonbrook, Va.

PURSUANT to appointment, the Germantown church met at the old brick house, July 16, together with the elders and brethren from adjoining congregations. At this council brethren L. D. Eikenberry and Mankin Flora were elected to the ministry. They received nearly the entire vote of the church assembled. Brethren J. W. Eikenberry and T. I. Peters were elected to the office of deacon.

The installation services, conducted by Eld. Daniel Peters, then took place. This church had six ministers before selecting the above-named brethren. We have, however, more work to do than we can manage, and we hope that the two young ministers will make good workers.

In every respect the meeting was one of the most harmonious ones that I ever attended. Two were recently baptized into this church. Our accessions are not so numerous as in some other places. We are holding our own fairly well. We have a large field here to work in. There is a great work to do in the South-eastern part of Virginia and North Carolina.   WM. ROBERSON.
July 25.

From Southern Ohio.

SOUTHERN Ohio held her Second Semi-Annual Ministerial Meeting May 28, at the upper house of the Lower Stillwater congregation, Montgomery County, Ohio. The first was held last fall. As the District Meeting was so far at one end of the District, it was thought good to have one again this spring. Then we decided to try it again this fall, so we get two a year.

Well, we had a good meeting. It was largely attended and the subjects selected were discussed in an interesting and instructive manner. Bro. McCann, of Bridgewater, Va., was present and helped us along. Eld. Jesse Stutsman was Foreman; Jonas Horning, Reading Clerk, and Jacob Coppock, Writing Clerk. They performed their duties very satisfactorily.

JOHN CALVIN BRIGHT.
New Lebanon, Ohio, July 26.

Receipts of General Missionary Committee for July, 1892.

A. A. Rotruck, Ridgeville, W. Va., 25 cents; N. A. Gray and wife, Higgins, Texas, $4; Wallace church, Nebraska, 35 cents; Susan Rothrock, Carlisle, Nebr., $6; The Lord's Tenth, Sabetha, Kans., $10; H. Baughman and wife, Pennsylvania, $1.04; S. Livingood and wife, Pennsylvania, $1; J. L. Saylor and wife, Pennsylvania, $1.04; W. H. Miller and wife, Pennsylvania, $1.05; Abbie Barron, Pennsylvania, 52 cents; Sadie Barron, Pennsylvania, 50 cents; Kate Johnson, Pennsylvania, 55 cents; May Miller, Pennsylvania, 52 cents; Ellen Musser, Pennsylvania, 52 cents; Nettle Creek church, Indiana, $20; Loraine church, Illinois, $3.50; Weeping Water church, Nebraska, $10.12; Mrs. Geo. Windle, Mt. Morris, Ill., $10; Sarah Musselman, New Carlisle, Ohio, 50 cents; Brethren's Sunday-school at Hudson, Ill., $3.26; Flat Rock church, North Carolina, $5.90; Back Creek church, Pennsylvania, $5; Coventry church, Pennsylvania, $36.55; Covina church, California, $4.45; Huntingdon church, Pennsylvania, $18; George Bosler, deceased, Ari, Ind., $10; Oakland

A Trip to the North-Western Part of Nebraska.

By order of the District Mission Board, I left home June 30. My first stop was with the Brethren of the Rush Valley church, in Sheridan County. I held meetings each evening during one week, and on Saturday evening, July 9, about twenty-three of the Father's children gathered around the Lord's table and enjoyed a pleasant Communion season together.

This church is under the care of Eld. David Bear. Here I also met Bro. Aaron M. Musselman, who was my neighbor at one time in Northern Illinois. Our many pleasant seasons in the Hickory Grove church, were called to memory again.

While here, one day, the Brethren made up a party, and I accompanied them on a visit to the Pine Ridge Agency on the Sioux Indian Reservation in South Dakota. There the government has erected some large buildings for schools, stores, hospitals, etc. By the courtesy of the officers we were escorted through the buildings and grounds, and saw many things to attract our notice regarding this peculiar people.

By a contract with these Indians, the government keeps them well supplied with all that is needful, and trains and teaches about 150 Indian boys and girls in all the sciences of civilized life. We notice that many among them still adhere to the customs of their wild life in the matter of dress, etc.

Leaving the Rush Valley, I proceeded westward about sixty miles, to Crawford, where there is a small band of members, living quite isolated, and without an organization. No preacher is nearer than about sixty miles. This little colony emigrated to this country from West Virginia. Among them is Bro. William Dove and family.

After laboring here one week, two made the good confession and were baptized. From here I returned eastward 150 miles into Cherry County, where a call was made for the Brethren to come and preach. This is a new field for the Brethren, but as the Word was held forth, they that gladly received his Word were baptized. We resorted to the water-side where prayer was made, and then, like Philip and the eunuch, we both went down into the water, where two were baptized. Not a brother or sister was present to assist or witness the scene, for there are none living within fifty miles that I know of. About twenty-five of the neighbors were present to look on. A friend remarked, "That is the way the Dunkards baptize in Virginia." For this new field I have a good prospect, and recommend it to the especial attention of the Mission Board.

From here I returned to the place called home, where I arrived about midnight of July 23, very warm and much fatigued, having traveled over 1,000 miles on this trip. JESSE Y. HECKLER.

Elmwood, Nebr.

From Arcanum, Ohio.

June 25, the brethren and sisters of the Ludlow church met for special Communion services. These services were characterized by several distinctive features. First, in being appointed and conducted expressly for the benefit of the home membership. Second, while over 300 communed, only two or three were present from neighboring churches. Third, as being the last service of the kind to be held in the old Pitsburgh meeting-house. While absolutely free from any selfish motive, it offered decided advantages, in point of labor, convenience, and spiritual edification, over the crowded and laborious conditions of large public Communion services. Of course no thought of dispensing with the regular public

---

Communion should, for a moment, be entertained, but in addition to it, a service of the above character would certainly be commendable.

The work of rebuilding the Pitsburgh house is now in progress, and will be brought to completion as speedily as possible. During the time of building, Sunday-school and church-services will be held in the grove near by. The Sunday-schools of the District are enjoying a very fair degree of prosperity and it is to be hoped much good seed is being sown on good ground.

C. E. CULP.

July 29.

Treasurer's Report.

The following is the report of Boys and Girl's Bible School for quarter ending June 30, 1892:

RECEIPTS.

Balance from last report,	$18 20
Error in last report,	1 00
Sister Ella Williams, Funkstown, Md.,	2 00
Sister Jane Engler, Linwood, Md.,	1 00
Sister Elizabeth Roop, Linwood, Md.,	5 00
Wm. P. Klein, through W. W. Kulp, Pottstown, Pa,	2 00
A brother, through W. W. Kulp, Pottstown, Pa,	3 00
Hannah Sager, Indian Creek Church, Iowa, per T. H. Higgs,	2 00
Indian Creek Sunday-school, Iowa, per T. H. Higgs,	86
Lord's Tenth,	5 66
Total,	$40 72

EXPENDITURES.

Taking scholars to love-feast,	14 30
Taking scholars to preaching,	1 14
Oil,	16
Bibles,	1 30
Rent,	21 00
Freight on tracts,	60
Total,	$38 50
Balance in bank,	$ 2 22

JAMES T. QUINLAN, Supt.
JOSEPH J. ELLIS, Sec'y.

Watch the Dates.

In GOSPEL MESSENGER No. 29, page 436, we find an article, "Eighteen Hundred and Ninety-three," selected by Bro. J. R. Gish, from "Words and Works." I do not think J. W. Pope is a "crank," for his solution represents thought in sacred numbers, but I wish to show, according to dates, that he is mistaken. The year 1893, according to our calendar, will be the next one, but, in reality, this present year, 1892, is 1896; consequently next year, 1893, will be really 1897,—four years past Mr. Pope's calculation already, and no second coming of Christ yet.

Concerning the second advent of Christ, the following facts are of interest and may be helpful to all of our Brethren who are looking up dates for the birth of Christ.

"The date, December, B. C. 5, is now regarded as at least approximating the actual date upon which Jesus was born, but neither the year nor the month can be laid down with certainty. His birth is placed in B. C. 5, instead of A. D. 1, because of the error of Dionysius Exiguus in the sixth century, in assigning the nativity to the year 754, of the Roman era, instead of to 749 or 750; as he should have done. He began the present system of counting the years from Jesus' birth instead of from the date of the founding of Rome, and in the eighth century, Bede followed him in writing history, and Pepin and Charlemagne

---

adopted it in State affairs, thus giving it currency, and at the same time perpetuating the error." It requires 104 years yet to complete the Christian era, that is, to make this present dispensation 2,000 years. DAVID SNYDER.

Ashland, Ohio.

From Bonbrook, Va.

PURSUANT to appointment, the Germantown church met at the old brick house, July 16, together with the elders and brethren from adjoining congregations. At this council brethren L. D. Eikenberry and Mankin Flora were elected to the ministry. They received nearly the entire vote of the church assembled. Brethren J. W. Eikenberry and T. I. Peters were elected to the office of deacon.

The installation services, conducted by Eld. Daniel Peters, then took place. This church had six ministers before selecting the above-named brethren. We have, however, more work to do than we can manage, and we hope that the two young ministers will make good workers.

In every respect the meeting was one of the most harmonious ones that I ever attended. Two were recently baptized into this church. Our accessions are not so numerous as in some other places. We are holding our own fairly well. We have a large field here to work in. There is a great work to do in the South-eastern part of Virginia and North Carolina. WM. ROBERSON.

July 23.

From Southern Ohio.

SOUTHERN Ohio held her Second Semi-Annual Ministerial Meeting May 28, at the upper house of the Lower Stillwater congregation, Montgomery County, Ohio. The first was held last fall. As the District Meeting was so far at one end of the District, it was thought good to have one again this spring. Then we decided to try it again this fall, so we get two a year.

Well, we had a good meeting. It was largely attended and the subjects selected were discussed in an interesting and instructive manner. Bro. McCann, of Bridgewater, Va., was present and helped us along. Eld. Jesse Stutsman was Foreman; Jonas Horning, Reading Clerk, and Jacob Coppock, Writing Clerk. They performed their duties very satisfactorily.

JOHN CALVIN BRIGHT.

New Lebanon, Ohio, July 26.

Receipts of General Missionary Committee for July, 1892.

A. A. Rotruck, Ridgeville, W. Va., 25 cents; N. A. Gray and wife, Higgins, Texas, $4; Wallace church, Nebraska, 35 cents; Susan Rothrock, Carlisle, Nebr., $6; The Lord's Tenth, Sabetha, Kans., $10; H. Baughman and wife, Pennsylvania, $1.04; S. Livingood and wife, Pennsylvania, $1; J. L. Saylor and wife, Pennsylvania, $1.04; W. H. Miller and wife, Pennsylvania, $1.06; Abbie Barron, Pennsylvania, 52 cents; Sadie Barron, Pennsylvania, 50 cents; Kate Johnson, Pennsylvania, 55 cents; May Miller, Pennsylvania, 52 cents; Ellen Musser, Pennsylvania, 52 cents; Nettie Creek church, Indiana, $20; Loraine church, Illinois, $3.50; Weeping Water church, Nebraska, $10.12; Mrs. Geo. Windle, Mt. Morris, Ill., $10; Sarah Musselman, New Carlisle, Ohio, 50 cents; Brethren's Sunday-school at Hudson, Ill., $3.26; Flat Rock church, North Carolina, $5.20; Back Creek church, Pennsylvania, $5; Coventry church, Pennsylvania, $38.55; Covina church, California, $4.45; Huntingdon church, Pennsylvania, $18; George Bosler, deceased, Ari, Ind., $10; Oakland

Oakley, Ill.—The Lord willing, we, the members of the Oakley church, Macon County, Ill., expect to begin a series of meetings on the evening of Sept. 3, to continue until the time of our Communion meeting, Sept. 28, at 4 P. M. We expect Bro. Solomon Bucklew with us during the meetings.—*A. L. Bingaman, July 23.*

Austin, Ark.—Through the liberality of Bro. James R. Gish, the GOSPEL MESSENGER is again a welcome visitor in our home and it is well read, as three families read it weekly. We believe it will be the means of doing some good. Here we are having very interesting meetings, with very large attendance and good attention.—*Ada S. Delp, July 15.*

Mooreland, Ind.—The members of the Buck Creek church, Henry County, Ind., held their quarterly council June 25. Considerable business came before the meeting but all was disposed of in a Christian spirit. We decided to hold a Communion Oct. 28. A collection was held for the Orphans' Home, amounting to $2.55. We also decided to hold a series of meetings. On Sunday following we re-organized our Sunday-school. Sister Dora Rhodes was chosen as Superintendent. We decided to continue with the *Brethren's Quarterly*, which we think should be used in every church in the Brotherhood.—*Isaac Wike.*

Fergy, Ohio.—Last Saturday, July 23, was the time for the quarterly council in the Donald's Creek church, Ohio. We had a pleasant meeting, and arranged to have a harvest meeting Aug. 18, at 2 P. M. May we thank the Lord as we ought, and may our actions express our gratitude in noble *deeds*, not only from the lips, but from the promptings of the heart, in discharging our duty to God and man, as the Lord has prospered us. We also appointed a special council for Aug. 24, to hear the report of the annual visit preparatory to a love-feast, which is appointed for Oct. 6, at 10 A. M., and which are all invited to attend.—*Henry Frantz.*

Merrill, Kans.—By request I went to Topeka on Saturday, July 23. We had services on Saturday evening, Sunday morning and evening. The services were well attended, and the interest excellent. After the morning services we repaired to the side of the beautiful Kaw, just below the city, where Bro. Isaac D. Halderman was baptized into Christ, to the joy of all present. This is the first fruits of the work at Topeka,—a city of nearly 50,000 inhabitants. There are scattered around through the city about twenty members. Arrangements are made for regular preaching every two weeks in the Oakland addition of the city. These appointments will be promptly filled. An excellent door seems to be opening for us there. May the Lord enable us to improve our opportunities to his honor and glory!—*J. S. Mohler, July 24.*

Homestead, Pa.—In GOSPEL MESSENGER, No. 28, in Secretary's report for April, read Jason A. G. Stifler of Rosemont, New Jersey, instead of Homestead, Pa. I came here Oct. 5, 1891, and have not met a brother or sister of our Fraternity in this town since I came. I distributed seventy-five copies of GOSPEL MESSENGER, sent me by Bro. Galen D. Boyer. The secular papers give details of this sad state of affairs here during the last month, since June 24. One would scarcely believe that people could become so infuriated in a land of religious liberty. Governor Pattison came last Tuesday and returned on Friday. About eight or ten thousand soldiers have been stationed here since Tuesday morning, July 12. God knows when this terrible affair will end. Oh, that God will soften the hearts of the cruel ones that caused it!—*Emily R. Stifler, July 24.*

Matrimonial.

" What therefore God hath joined together, let not man put asunder."

FLORY—TROBAUGH.—At Tuhunga, Los Angeles Co., Cal., June 19, 1892, by S. G. Lehmer, Bro. David P. Flory to Miss Fleta Trobaugh.

FLORY—STANCLIFF.—At Tuhunga, Los Angeles Co., Cal., June 19, 1892, by S. G. Lehmer, Bro. Charles A. Flory to Miss Mary Stancliff. The brethren named are the two younger sons of Bro. J. S. Flory.

MUTTON—GROVE.—By the undersigned, at his residence, No. 105 East Fifth St., Canton, Ohio, June 7, 1892, Mr. Charles A. Mutton, of Canton, Ohio, and sister Frances C. Grove, of the same place. WM. H. QUINN.

Fallen Asleep.

" Blessed are the dead which die in the Lord."

SPINKEL.—At Goblesville, Huntington Co., Ind., July 18, 1892, Anna Gertrude Spinkel, aged 3 years and 29 days. Deceased was an adopted child of Bro. and sister Spinkel. Funeral services by the undersigned. SAMUEL MURRAY.

STUTZMAN.—In Virginia, Gage Co., Nebr., of cholera infantum, Myrtle Anna, daughter of James and Mary Stutzman, aged 8 months and 13 days. Funeral services by Eld. Owen Peters, to a large congregation.
LUCINDA R. STUTZMAN.

FESLER.—In the Lower Deer Creek church, Carroll County, Ind., July 19, 1892, sister Matilda J. Fesler, aged 50 years, 10 months and 12 days. Funeral services by Bro. Hiel Hamilton from 2 Cor. 5: 1. S. H. BECHTELHEIMER.

ABBOT.—In the Portage church, Wood County, Ohio, infant son of Mr. and Mrs. Abbot, aged 19 days. Services conducted by the writer from Eccl. 3: 4. I. P. KRABILL.

EIKENBERRY.—In Union County, Ind., June 27, 1892, Daniel Eikenberry, aged 48 years, 5 months, and 26 days. Deceased was united in marriage to Elizabeth Brown, Feb. 2, 1865. To this union were born seven children, one of whom preceded him to the spirit world. His wife and six children survive him. He was a member of the German Baptist church fifteen years. Funeral services improved by the Brethren. CARVY TONEY.

ESHENBAUGH.—In the Lower Cumberland church, Pa., near West Fairview, Jan. 15, 1892, John Eshenbaugh, aged 78 years, 5 months and 19 days.

MORRETT.—Near Churchtown, Cumberland Co., Pa., July 2, 1892, Mrs. Michael Morrett, aged 69 years, 1 month and 20 days. DAVID NIKELY.

HART.—In the Blanchard church, Putnam County, Ohio, June 13, 1892, sister Surlinda V. Hart, daughter of Bro. Jacob and sister Helstind, and wife of Bro. Hiram Hart, aged 27 years, 3 months and 15 days. Funeral services by brethren John and Daniel Prowant. P. H. BERRY.

LECKRONE.—Near Silver Lake, Kosciusko Co., Ind., within the bounds of the Eel River church, July 8, 1892, Orpha Leckrone, daughter of Emanuel and Charlotte Leckrone, aged 10 years, 10 months and 19 days. Funeral services by Bro. John Stafford, assisted by Leander Pottinger. G. ULREY.

HELTZEL.—In the Woodland church, Fulton County, Ill., June 30, 1892, Bro. Jonas Heltzel, aged 74 years, 7 months and 5 days. Deceased was born in York County, Pa., and was married in 1836 to Mary Horner, to whom nine children were born. His wife preceded him to the spirit world about two years ago. Funeral services by brethren S. D. Hamm and John Baker.

FITZ.—In the same congregation, July 14, 1892, of consumption, sister Ellen, only daughter of Bro. Henry and sister Mary Fitz, aged 24 years, 5 months and 2 days. She united with the church about a year ago. Several weeks before her death she was anointed, after which she seemed much encouraged. Services conducted by brethren Cyrus Bucher and John Baker from Isa. 3: 10. LYDIA WALTER.

BOWSER.—At Canton, Ohio, April 5, 1892, Cora Bell, daughter of Bro. and sister Daniel Bowser, aged 13 years, 9 months and 1 day. She suffered for several weeks with diphtheria which resulted in blood poison. Services by Eld. Sam. uel Sprankle, assisted by the writer. WM. H. QUINN.

STUTSMAN.—In the Elkhart church, Elkhart County, Ind., July 22, 1892, sister Hannah Stutsman, aged 79 years, 8 months and 10 days. She was a great sufferer for years from a growth in her stomach, supposed to be a 'cancer. She could not take any food for twenty-two days previous to her death, and for months before could eat only a little. Funeral services by Bro. Joseph Kulp and the Writer.
J. H. MILLER.

WHEELER.—In the bounds of the Ten Mile congregation, Washington County, Pa., July 18, 1892, Mr. Daniel W. Wheeler, aged about 38 years. Friend Wheeler had left his home, on West Cherry Alley, Washington, Pa., on Monday, July 18, for Sistersville, W. Va., a distance of about twenty-four miles. He left to secure work in an oil well, near the above, named place. In walking over a trestle on the railroad near that place, he made a misstep and fell to the ground, and was instantly killed. His dead body was not found till on Tuesday morning, July 19, by the railroad section hands. He leaves a grief-stricken widow, and five young children. His remains were interred in the Pigeon Creek Cemetery July 20. Funeral services by the writer from Job 30: 23.
N. B. CHRISTNER.

GLICK.—At Pleasant Valley, Augusta Co., Va., May 14, 1892, of consumption, Joseph Glick, aged about 73 years. Services by elders LeVi Garber and S. F. Sanger. He leaves a companion, three daughters, one son, and a large circle of friends to mourn their loss. S. A. DRIVER.

LECKINGTON.—In the Newton church, Harvey County, Kans., May 24, 1892, Melva B. Leckington, infant daughter of Isaiah and sister Phianna Leckington, aged 2 years, 11 months and 20 days. JOHN WALSH.

FUNDERBURG.—In Clarke County, Ohio, June 27, 1892, Susanna Funderburg, aged 89 years, 2 months and 7 days. Deceased was born in Augusta County, Va., April 20, 1803. She was united in marriage to Michael Click, in January, 1822, and, with her husband, emigrated to Clarke County, Ohio, in the autumn of 1826. Oct. 28, 1838, by the death of Michael Click, she was left a widow. In 1839 she was married again, to David Funderburg who died Sept. 10, 1869. Her death was caused by old age. She was a church member about seventy years. Her funeral was conducted by Eld. Henry Frantz, from 2 Tim. 4: 6-8. H. H. ARNOLD.

MILLER.—In the Beaver Creek congregation, Rockingham, Va., June 3, 1892, of cancer, sister Polly, wife of Bro. George Miller, aged 74 years and 3 months. Funeral services by the brethren.

YOUNG.—In the Lunatic Asylum, at Stanton, Va., July 9, 1892, John A., son of Bro. John and sister Young, aged 76 years, 3 months and 11 days. Burial at Beaver Creek. Funeral services by the brethren.

MILLER.—In the same congregation, July 14, 1892, of cancer, sister Mary F., wife of Bro. Joseph Miller, late from Ohio, aged 38 years, 5 months and 18 days. Burial at Clover Hill. Funeral services by the brethren. She leaves an afflicted husband and five motherless children. G. W. WINE.

HUNT.—In the Honey Creek church, Nodaway County, Mo., Missouri Hunt. aged 43 years, 3 months, and 22 days. Deceased was married to Nathan S. Hunt, September 30, 1869. She was a member of the Freewill Baptist church for a number of years, but for the last eight years has been a consistent member of the Brethren church and of the Honey Creek congregation. Sister Hunt was sorely afflicted for the past nine months. During her sickness she was anointed, and expressed a living faith. Funeral services by Eld. J. E. Ellenberger. E. REDDICK.

Oakley, Ill.—The Lord willing, we, the members of the Oakley church, Macon County, Ill., expect to begin a series of meetings on the evening of Sept. 3, to continue until the time of our Communion meeting, Sept. 23, at 4 P. M. We expect Bro. Solomon Bucklew with us during the meetings.—*A. L. Bingaman, July 22.*

Austin, Ark.—Through the liberality of Bro. James R. Gish, the GOSPEL MESSENGER is again a welcome visitor in our home and it is well read, as three families read it weekly. We believe it will be the means of doing some good. Here we are having very interesting meetings, with very large attendance and good attention.—*Ada S. Delp, July 15.*

Mooreland, Ind.—The members of the Buck Creek church, Henry County, Ind., held their quarterly council June 25. Considerable business came before the meeting but all was disposed of in a Christian spirit. We decided to hold a Communion Oct. 28. A collection was held for the Orphans' Home, amounting to $2.55. We also decided to hold a series of meetings. On Sunday following we re-organized our Sunday-school. Sister Dora Rhodes was chosen as Superintendent. We decided to continue with the *Brethren's Quarterly*, which we think should be used in every church in the Brotherhood.—*Isaac Wike.*

Perry, Ohio.—Last Saturday, July 23, was the time for the quarterly council in the Donald's Creek church, Ohio. We had a pleasant meeting, and arranged to have a harvest meeting Aug. 13, at 2 P. M. May we thank the Lord as we ought, and may our actions express our gratitude in noble *deeds*, not only from the lips, but from the promptings of the heart, in discharging our duty to God and man, as the Lord has prospered us. We also appointed a special council for Aug. 24, to hear the report of the annual visit preparatory to a love-feast, which is appointed for Oct. 5, at 10 A. M., and which all are invited to attend.—*Henry Frantz.*

Morrill, Kans.—By request I went to Topeka on Saturday, July 23. We had services on Saturday evening, Sunday morning and evening. The services were well attended, and the interest excellent. After the morning services we repaired to the side of the beautiful Kaw, just below the city, where Bro. Isaac D. Halderman was baptized into Christ, to the joy of all present. This is the first fruits of the work at Topeka,—a city of nearly 50,000 inhabitants. There are scattered around through the city about twenty members. Arrangements are made for regular preaching every two weeks in the Oakland addition of the city. These appointments will be promptly filled. An excellent door seems to be opening for us there. May the Lord enable us to improve our opportunities to his honor and glory!—*J. S. Mohler, July 28.*

Homestead, Pa.—In GOSPEL MESSENGER, No. 28, in Secretary's report for April, read Jason A. G. Stifler of Rosemont, New Jersey, instead of Homestead, Pa. I came here Oct. 6, 1891, and have not met a brother or sister of our Fraternity in this town since I came. I distributed seventy-five copies of GOSPEL MESSENGER, sent me by Bro. Galen B. Royer. The secular papers give details of the sad state of affairs here during the last month, since June 24. One would scarcely believe that people could become so infuriated in a land of religious liberty. Governor Pattison came last Tuesday and returned on Friday. About eight or ten thousand soldiers have been stationed here since Tuesday morning, July 12. God knows when this terrible affair will end. Oh, that God will soften the hearts of the cruel ones that caused it!—*Emily R. Stifler, July 24.*

Matrimonial.

"What therefore God hath joined together, let not man put asunder."

FLORY—TROBAUGH.—At Tuhunga, Los Angeles Co., Cal., June 19, 1892, by S. G. Lehmer, Bro David P. Flory to Miss Fieta Trobaugh.

FLORY—STANCLIFF.—At Tuhunga, Los Angeles Co., Cal., June 19, 1892, by S. G. Lehmer, Bro. Charles A. Flory to Miss Mary Stancliff. The brethren named are the two youngest sons of Bro. J. S. Flory.

MUTTON—GROVE.—By the undersigned, at his residence, No. 103 East Fifth St., Canton, Ohio, June 7, 1892, Mr. Charles A. Mutton, of Canton, Ohio, and sister Frances C. Grove, of the same place. WM. H. QUINN.

Fallen Asleep.

"Blessed are the dead which die in the Lord."

SPINKEL.—At Goblesville, Huntington Co., Ind., July 18, 1892, Anna Gertrude Spinkel, aged 3 years and 29 days. Deceased was an adopted child of Bro and sister Spinkel. Funeral services by the undersigned. SAMUEL MURRAY.

STUTZMAN.—In Virginia, Gage Co., Nebr., of cholera infantum, Myrtle Anna, daughter of James and Mary Stutzman, aged 8 months and 13 days. Funeral services by Eld. Owen Peters, to a large congregation.
LUCINDA R. STUTZMAN.

FESLER.—In the Lower Deer Creek church, Carroll County, Ind., July 19, 1892, sister Matilda J. Fesler, aged 50 yeah, 10 months and 12 days. Funeral services by Bro. Hiel Hamilton from 2 Cor. 5: 1. S. H. BECHTELHEIMER.

ABBOT.—In the Portage church, Wood County, Ohio, infant son of Mr. and Mrs. Abbot, aged 19 days. Services conducted by the writer from Eccl. 3: 4. I. P. KRABILL.

EIKENBERRY.—In Union County, Ind., June 27, 1892, Daniel Eikenberry, aged 48 years, 5 months, and 26 days. Deceased was united in marriage to Elizabeth Brown, Feb. 2, 1865. To this union were born seven children, one of whom preceded him to the spirit world. His wife and six children survive him. He was a member of the German Baptist church fifteen years. Funeral services improved by the Brethren. CAREY TONEY.

ESHENBAUGH.—In the Lower Cumberland church, Pa., near West Fairview, Jan. 15, 1892, John Eshenbaugh, aged 78 years, 5 months and 19 days.

MORRETT.—Near Churchtown, Cumberland Co., Pa., July 2, 1892, Mrs. Michael Morrett, aged 69 years, 7 months and 20 days. DAVID NISSLY.

HART.—In the Blanchard church, Putnam County, Ohio, June 18, 1892, sister Surinda V. Hart, daughter of Bro. Jacob and sister Helstand, and wife of Bro. Hiram Hart, aged 27 years, 3 months and 15 days. Funeral services by brethren John and Daniel Provant. F. H. BERRY.

LECKRONE.—Near Silver Lake, Kosciusko Co., Ind., within the bounds of the Eel River church, July 13, 1892, Orpha Leck-One, daughter of Emanuel and Charlotte Leckrone, aged 20 years, 10 months and 19 days. Funeral services by Bro. John Stafford, assisted by Leander Pottinger.
G. ULREY.

HELTZEL.—In the Woodland church, Fulton County, Ill., June 30, 1892, Bro. Jonas Heltzel, aged 74 years, 7 months and 5 days. Deceased was born in York County, Pa., and was married in 1836 to Mary Hornet, to whom nine children were born. His wife preceded him to the spirit world about two years ago. Funeral services by brethren S. D. Hamm and John Baker.

FITE.—In the same congregation, July 14, 1892, of consumption, sister Ellen, only daughter of Bro. Henry and sister Mary Fite, aged 24 years, 5 months and 2 days. She united with the church about a year ago. Several weeks before her death she was anointed, after which she seemed much encouraged. Services conducted by brethren Cyrus Bucher and John Baker from Isa. 3: 10. LYDIA WALTER.

BOWSER.—At Canton, Ohio, April 5, 1892, Cora Bell, daughter of Bro. and sister Daniel Bowser, aged 13 years, 9 months and 1 day. She suffered for several weeks with diphtheria which resulted in blood poison. Services by Eld. Samuel Sprankle, assisted by the writer. WM. H. QUINN.

STUTSMAN.—In the Elkhart church, Elkhart County, Ind., July 22, 1892, sister Hannah Stutsman, aged 79 years, 8 months and 10 days. She was a great sufferer for years from a growth in her stomach, supposed to be a cancer. She could not take any food for twenty-two days, previous to her death, and for months before could eat only a little. Funeral services by Bro. Joseph Kulp and the writer.
J. H. MILLER.

WHEELER.—In the bounds of the Ten Mile congregation, Washington County, Pa., July 18, 1892, Mr. Daniel W. Wheeler, aged about 38 years. Friend Wheeler had left his home, on West Cherry Alley, Washington, Pa., on Monday, July 18, for Sistersville, W. Va., a distance of about twenty-four miles. He left to secure work in an oil well, near the above-named place. In walking over a trestle on the railroad near that place, he made a misstep and fell to the ground, and was instantly killed. His dead body was not found till on Tuesday morning, July 19, by the railroad section hands. He leaves a grief-stricken widow, and five young children. His remains were interred in the Pigeon Creek Cemetery July 20. Funeral services by the writer from Job 30: 23.
N. B. CHRISTNER.

GLICK.—At Pleasant Valley, Augusta Co., Va., May 14, 1892, of consumption, Joseph Glick, aged about 73 years. Services by elders Levi Garber and S. F. Sanger. He leaves a companion, three daughters, one son, and a large circle of friends to mourn their loss. S. A. DRIVER.

LECKINGTON.—In the Newton church, Harvey County, Kans., May 24, 1892, Melva B. Leckington, infant daughter of friend Samuel and sister Phianna Leckington, aged 2 years, 11 months and 20 days. JOHN WALKS.

FUNDERBURG.—In Clarke County, Ohio, June 27, 1892, Susanna Funderburg, aged 89 years, 2 months and 7 days. Deceased was born in Augusta County, Va., April 20, 1803. She was united in marriage to Michael Click, in January, 1821, and, with her husband, emigrated to Clarke County, Ohio, in the autumn of 1826. Oct. 28, 1838, by the death of Michael Click, she was left a widow. In 1839 she was married again, to David Funderburg who died Sept. 10, 1869. Her death was caused by old age. She was a church member about seventy years. Her funeral was conducted by Eld. Henry Frantz, from 2 Tim. 4: 6-8. H. H. ARNOLD.

MILLER.—In the Beaver Creek congregation, Rockingham, Va., June 3, 1892, of cancer, sister Polly, wife of Bro. George Miller, aged 74 years and 3 months. Funeral services by the brethren.

YOUNG.—In the Lunatic Asylum, at Stanton, Va., July 9, 1892, John A., son of Bro. John and sister Young, aged 26 years, 3 months and 11 days. Burial at Beaver Creek. Funeral services by the brethren.

MILLER.—In the same congregation, July 11, 1892, of cancer, sister Mary F., wife of Bro. Joseph Miller, late from Ohio, aged 38 years, 5 months and 18 days. Burial at Clover Hill. Funeral services by the brethren. She leaves an afflicted husband and five motherless children. G. W. WINE.

HUNT.—In the Honey Creek church, Nodaway County, Mo., Missouri Hunt aged 43 years, 3 months, and 22 days. Deceased was married to Nathan S. Hunt, September 20, 1869. She was a member of the Freewill Baptist church for a number of years, but for the last eight years has been a consistent member of the Brethren church and of the Honey Creek congregation. Sister Hunt was sorely afflicted for the past nine months. During her sickness she was anointed, and expressed a living faith. Funeral services by Eld. J. E. Ellenberger. E. REDDICK.

The Gospel Messenger

Is the recognized organ of the German Baptist or Brethren's church, and advocates the form of doctrine taught in the New Testament and pleads for a return to apostolic and primitive Christianity.

It recognizes the New Testament as the only infallible rule of faith and practice, and maintains that Faith toward God, Repentance from dead works, Regeneration of the heart and mind, baptism by Trine Immersion for remission of sins unto the reception of the Holy Ghost by the laying on of hands, are the means of adoption into the household of God,—the church militant.

It also maintains that Feet-washing, as taught in John 13, both by example and command of Jesus, should be observed in the church.

That the Lord's Supper, instituted by Christ and as universally observed by the apostles and the early Christians, is a full meal, and, in connection with the Communion, should be taken in the evening or after the close of the day.

That the Salutation of the Holy Kiss, or Kiss of Charity, is binding upon the followers of Christ.

That War and Retaliation are contrary to the spirit and self-denying principles of the religion of Jesus Christ.

That the principle of Plain Dressing and of Non-conformity to the world, as taught in the New Testament, should be observed by the followers of Christ.

That the Scriptural duty of Anointing the Sick with Oil, in the Name of the Lord, James 5: 14, is binding upon all Christians.

It also advocates the church's duty to support Missionary and Tract Work, thus giving to the Lord for the spread of the Gospel and for the conversion of sinners.

In short, it is a vindicator of all that Christ and the apostles have enjoined upon us, and aims, amid the conflicting theories and discords of modern Christendom, to point out ground that all must concede to be infallibly safe.

☞ The above principles of our Fraternity are set forth on our "Brethren's Envelopes." Use them! Price 15 cents per package; 40 cents per hundred.

Announcements.

LOVE-FEASTS.

Aug. 13, at 2 P. M., Ogan's Creek church, five miles south-east of North Manchester, Wabash Co., Ind.

Aug. 19, at 4 P. M., the Bear Creek church, Palmer, Ill.

Aug. 27 and 28, at 4 P. M., Salem, in Sandy Creek congregation, Preston Co., W. Va.

Aug. 27, at 4 P. M., Nocona church, Montague Co., Tex.

Sept. 1, at 4 P. M., Sugar Creek church, Sangamon County, Ill., 4 miles east of Auburn, Ill.

Sept. 2, at 2 P. M., Roskton church, Pa.

Sept. 3, at 2 P. M., at Sangerville, in the Beaver Creek congregation, Rockingham Co., Va.

Sept. 3, Round Mountain church, Ark.

Sept. 3, at 10 A. M., Mt. Etna church, Iowa. Conveyances on Friday, Sept. 2, at Corning.

Sept. 3, at 5 P. M., at Independence, Kans.

Sept. 3, at 10 A. M., Washington church, Kans., at Bro. Wm. R. Phillippi's residence, three miles south, and three and one-half miles west of Washington, Kans.

Sept. 3, at 2 P. M., Silver Creek church, Cowley Co., Kans.

Sept. 3, Mill Creek church, Adams Co., Ill.

Sept. 3 and 4, English River congregation, Keokuk Co., Iowa.

Sept. 3, at 2 P. M., in the Mt. Hope church, Logan Co., Oklahoma Territory.

Sept. 3 and 4, at 10 A. M., in the North Solomon church, six miles north of Portis, Kans.

Sept. 3, Sappa church, Furnas Co., Nebr.

Sept. 3 and 4, Rock Creek church, Colo. Dedication of church-house on Sunday, Sept. 4. Those coming by rail, stop off at Moore Vista.

Sept. 6, at 4 P. M., Indian Creek congregation, Fayette Co., Pa. Series of meetings to commence Aug. 27.

Sept. 7 and 8, at 1 P. M., Scott Valley, Cedar Co., Kans., at the house of W. A. Smith, one mile east and five south of Waverly. A series of meetings to be held in connection with the feast.

Sept. 8, at 10 A. M., Monroe County church, Iowa.

Sept. 10 and 11, Farmhamville, Calhoun Co., Iowa. Series of meetings in connection, beginning one week previous.

Sept. 10 and 11, at 5 P. M., Sterling church, Sterling, Ill.

Sept. 17, at 2 P. M., Bethel congregation, at the Bethlehem meeting-house, Holt Co., Mo. For any information address Jos. Andes, Mound City, Holt Co., Mo.

Sept. 17, at 2 P. M., Oakley church, Macon Co., Ill.

Sept. 24, at 3 P. M., Libertyville church, Jefferson Co., Iowa. Series of meetings to commence immediately after feast.

Sept. 24, at 4 P. M., Maple Grove church, 4 miles north of Ashland City, Ashland Co., Ohio.

Sept. 24, at 2 P. M., Fredonia church, Wilson Co., Kans.

Sept. 24, at 2 P. M., Clear Creek congregation, Huntington Co., Ind.

Sept. 24 and 25, 2 miles west of Tipton, Cedar Co., Iowa, beginning at 2 P. M. Ministers of Middle Iowa will please arrange to come to us from District Meeting at Garrison. Our meeting-house is at a distance of one mile from Buchanan on the L. C. R. & N. R. R.

Sept. 24, at 5 P. M., in La Porte church, La Porte, Ind. Trains will be met in the forenoon and early afternoon of the day of meeting.

Sept. 24, at 3 P. M., Martin's Creek church, Wayne Co., Ill.

Sept. 24 and 25, at 3 P. M., Lenark church, Carroll Co., Ill.

Sept. 24, at 5 P. M., Pokagon church, Dowagiac, Cass Co., Mich.

Sept. 24, at 5 P. M., at Wenger meeting-house, St. Joseph church, Ind.

Sept. 26, South Bend church, Ind.

Sept. 28, at 10 A. M., Spring Creek church, Kosciusko Co., Ind.

Sept. 29 and 30, at 1 P. M., Rock Creek church, Whiteside Co., Ill.

Sept. 29 and 30, at 10 A. M., Lower Fall Creek church, 3 miles south of Anderson. Those coming on train should arrive a John Hornack, Anderson, Ind.

Sept. 30, at 10 A. M., Nettle Creek church, near Hagerstown, Wayne Co., Ind.

Sept. 30, at 2 P. M., Milmine church, Piatt Co., Ill.

Oct. 1, at 2 P. M., Sugar Creek church, Allen Co., Ohio.

Oct. 1, at 5 P. M., Berrien Congregation, Mich.

Oct. 1 and 2, at 10 A. M., West Branch church, Ill. One week's meeting previous to feast.

Oct. 1 and 2, at 2 P. M., near Ames, Boone Co., Iowa. Meet bodies meet at Ames on Saturday.

Oct. 1, at 2 P. M., Osage church, Crawford Co., Kans.

Oct. 1, at 2 P. M., Logan church, near DeGraff, Ohio.

Oct. 1 and 2, Saginaw church, Mich.

Oct. 1 and 2, at 11:30 P. M., Walnut Valley congregation, Barton Co., Kans.

Oct. 1 and 2, at 3 P. M., Alleghany congregation, Great Co., W. Va.

Oct. 1, Maple Grove church, Norton Co., Kans.

Oct. 1, at 10 A. M., Appanoose church, Kans.

Oct. 1, at 10 A. M., Eight Mile church, Ind., at the town of Muncie.

Oct. 1 and 2, at 11 A. M., Riverside, Iowa. Those coming by rail will stop at Iowa Junction, on B. C. R. & N. R. R., where they will be met.

Oct. 1, at 10 A. M., Stone Lick church, Clermont Co., Ohio.

Oct. 1, at 10 A. M., Chippewa congregation, Wayne Co., Ohio.

Oct. 1, at 2 P. M., in the Verdigris church, at Bro. S. S. Redman's. A series of meetings will commence Sept. 25.

Oct. 1, Camp Creek church, Ill., at the church 7 miles south of Colchester. Those coming by train will please notify S. S. Hummer, and they will be met at the depot at Colchester, and conveyed to place of meeting.

Oct. 1, at 11 A. M., Belleville church, Kans.

Oct. 1, at 10 A. M., in the Beaver Dam church, Kosciusko Co., Ind., near the town of Burket.

Oct. 2, at 2 P. M., Rosen church, Ind.

Oct. 3 and 6, Dallas Centre church. A series of meetings by Bro. Hutchison will commence Sept. 17.

Oct. 6, at 10 A. M., Wabash church, 7 miles south of Wabash Ind.

Oct. 6, at 10 A. M., Donnel's Creek church, Clarke Co., Ohio, seven miles from New Carlisle, and the same distance from Fairy and Springfield. Those coming from the West will stop either at New Carlisle or Fairy, where they will be met on the evening of the 5th. Those from the North-east or South should stop at Springfield.

Oct. 6, at 2 P. M., Spring Creek church, in the Keith's church-house, eleven miles south-west of Reece, Kans.

Oct. 6 and 7, at 10 A. M., Shannon, Ill.

Oct. 6, at 2 P. M., Arcadia church, Ind.

Oct. 7, Black River church, Van Buren Co., Mich. Brethren coming by rail will stop off at Bangor.

Oct. 7, at 2 P. M., Ladoga, Ind.

Oct. 7, at 2 P. M., Kaskaskia church, Fayette Co., Ill., ten miles south-west of Bender City, Ill. Those coming by rail will be met at the above-named place by informing Grenville Nevinger.

Oct. 7, at 10 A. M., Sugar Creek, Whitley Co., Ind.

Oct. 7, at 2 P. M., Rossom Creek church, Montgomery Co., Ind., one and one half miles north-west of Ladoga.

Oct. 7, at 2 P. M., Maccopin Creek church, Montgomery Co., Ill. Those coming by rail will be met at Farmersville, on Springfield Road, and at Girard, on St. Louis Road on morning of meeting.

Oct. 7 and 8, at 10:30 A. M., Four Mile church, Union Co., Ind.

Oct. 8, at 4 P. M., Bethel church, on North County line, Thayer Co., Nebr. Stations: Carleton, Davenport, Carlisle and Shickley.

Oct. 8, at 10 A. M., Bear Creek church, Portland, Ind. Those coming by rail will be met by notifying H. P. Garber.

Oct. 8 and 9, at 10 A. M., Woodland church, Fulton Co., Ill. A series of meetings one week previous to the feast, and to continue two weeks.

Oct. 8, at 2 P. M., North Star, Darke County, Ohio.

Oct. 8, at 2 P. M., Greentown church, at Greentown, Howard Co., Ind.

Oct. 8, at 3:30 P. M., Maple Glen church, Somerset Co., Pa.

Oct. 8, at 4 P. M., in the Elkhart Valley church, Elkhart Co., Ind.

Oct. 8 and 9, at 4 P. M., Arnold's Grove, Ill.

Oct. 8, at 10 A. M., Dry Creek church, Lion Co., Iowa, one mile west of Robins Station.

Oct. 8, Swan Creek congregation, Ohio, 3½ miles west of Delta, Ohio.

Oct. 8 and 9, at 10 A. M., Washington Creek church, Douglas Co., Kans.

Oct. 8 and 9, 11:10 A. M., Pine Creek congregation, Ill.

Oct. 8 and 9, Bethel church, Pratt Co., Kans., in the town of Sawyer. Meeting to commence at 7 o'clock.

Oct. 29 and 30, at 11 A. M., South Keokuk church, Keokuk Co., Iowa. Those coming by rail will be met at Olie, by notifying Isaac Shelley or Isaac Brown. Those coming from the West will arrive at Olie about 11:30 A. M.; those from the East at 3 P. M.

Oct. 12, at 4 P. M., Union church, Marshal Co., Ind., five miles west of Plymouth. Trains will be met at both Plymouth and Burr Oak.

Oct. 12, Union church, Plymouth, Marshall Co., Ind. This church would like to have some brother hold meetings a week or ten days after.

Oct. 13 and 16, at 10 A. M., Grundy church, ten miles west of Grundy Centre, Grundy Co., Iowa.

Oct. 21, at 10 A. M., Kilbuck church, Delaware Co., Ind., nine miles west of Muncie.

Oct. 28, at 2 P. M., St. Joseph Valley church, St. Joseph Co., Ind., 3 miles north of South Bend.

Oct. 28, at 4 P. M., in the Pleasant Hill church, near Girard and Virden, Ill.

Oct. 28, at 2 P. M., South Beatrice church, Gage Co., Nebr. Conveyances the day before meeting at B. & M. depot, in Beatrice; Rock Island depot, in Rockford; Union Pacific depot, in Holmesville.

Oct. 28, at 4 P. M., Walnut church, Marshall Co., Ind.

Oct. 28, at 10 A. M., in the Buck Creek church, Henry Co., Ind.

Oct. 29, St. Vrain church, Longmont, Colo.

Oct. 29, at 2 P. M., Omwake church, Kans. A series of meetings to commence Oct. 20.

Oct. 29 and 30, at 10 A. M., Pigeon Creek church, Ill., at the Oak Grove meeting-house.

Oct. 29, at 2 P. M., Oasis church, Madison Co., Ind., 3½ miles east of Summitville.

Nov. 6. Walnut Creek church, Mo.

Nov. 5, at 3 P. M., Big Creek church, Richland Co., Ill., 3½ miles Northeast of Parkersburg, Ill. Conveyances will be at the above place by informing J. M. Forney.

--- THE ---

Doctrine of the Brethren Defended.

THIS work contains a complete exposition of the faith and practice of the Brethren, the Divinity of Christ, the Divinity of the Holy Spirit, Immersion, Feet-washing, the Lord's Supper, the Holy Kiss, Non-conformity. Secret Societies, etc. Price, per copy, cloth binding, $1.25. Address this office.

Dr. Wrightsman's Sovereign Balm of Life is prepared especially to assist the **SORROWS** of **MOTHERHOOD**. Every MOTHER ought to acquaint herself with this remedy. An honest preparation,—a boon to woman. Write for circulars and get full particulars. Address: D. B. SENGER & CO., Box 401, Franklin Grove, Ill.

GOOD BOOKS FOR ALL.

ANY book in the market furnished at publishers' lowest retail price by the Brethren's Publishing Company, Mt. Morris, Ill. *Special price* given when books are purchased in quantities. When ordering books, not on our list, if possible give title, name of author, and address of publishers.

The Throne of David.—By J. H. Ingraham. Cloth, $1.50.

Homiletics and Pastoral Theology.—By W. G. T. Sheild. Cloth, $2.50.

Lectures on Preaching.—By Rev. Phillips Brooks. Cloth, 2000, $1.50.

Josephus' Complete Works.—Large type, 1 vol. 8vo. Illustrated with many steel and wood engravings. Library sheep, $3.00.

Biblical Antiquities.—By John Nevin. Gives a concise account of Bible times and customs; invaluable to all students of Bible subjects. Price, $1.50.

Announcements.

LOVE-FEASTS.

Aug. 13, at 5 P. M., Ogan's Creek church, five miles south-east of North Manchester, Wabash Co., Ind.

Aug. 19, at 4 P. M., the Bear Creek church, Palmer, Ill.

Aug. 27 and 28, at 4 P. M., Salem, in Sandy Creek congregation, Preston Co., W. Va.

Aug. 27, at 4 P. M., Nocona church, Montague Co., Tex.

Sept. 1, at 3 P. M., Rockton church, Pa.

Sept. 3, at 2 P. M., at Saegerville, in the Beaver Creek congregation, Rockingham Co., Va.

Sept. 3, Round Mountain church, Ark.

Sept. 3, at 10 A. M., Mt. Etna church, Iowa. Conveyance on Friday, Sept. 2, at Corning.

Sept. 3, at 2 P. M., at Independence, Kans.

Sept. 3, at 10 A. M., Washington church, Kans., at Bro. Wm. R. Phillippi's residence, three miles south, and three and one-half miles west of Washington, Kans.

Sept. 3, at 1 P. M., Silver Creek church, Cowley Co., Kans.

Sept. 3, Mill Creek church, Adams Co., Ill.

Sept. 3 and 4, English River congregation, Keokuk Co., Iowa.

Sept. 3, at 4 P. M., in the Mt. Hope church, Logan Co., Oklahoma Territory.

Sept. 3 and 4, at 10 A. M., in the North Solomon church, six miles north of Portis, Kans.

Sept. 3, Sappa church, Furnas Co., Nebr.

Sept. 3 and 4, Rock Creek church, Colo. Dedication of church-house on Sunday, Sept. 4. Those coming by rail, stop off at Monte Vista.

Sept. 6, at 4 P. M., Indian Creek congregation, Fayette Co., Pa. Series of meetings to commence Aug. 27.

Sept. 7 and 8, at 2 P. M., Scott Valley, Colby Co., Kans., at the house of W. A. Smith, one mile east and five south of Waverly. A series of meetings to be held in connection with the feast.

Sept. 9, at 10 A. M., Monroe County church, Iowa.

Sept. 10 and 11, Farmhersville, Calhoun Co., Iowa. Series of meetings to commence, beginning one week previous.

Sept. 10 and 11, at 2 P. M., Bethel congregation, at the Bethlehem meeting-house, Holt Co., Mo. For any information address Jno. Arden, Mound City, Holt Co., Mo.

Sept. 13, at 4 P. M., Oakley church, Macon Co., Ill.

Sept. 13, at 3 P. M., Libertyville church, Jefferson Co., Iowa. Series of meetings to commence immediately after feast.

Sept. 14, at 2 P. M., Maple Grove church, 4 miles north of Ashland City, Ashland Co., Ohio.

Sept. 24, at 2 P. M., Fredonia church, Wilson Co., Kans.

Sept. 24, at 4 P. M., Clear Creek congregation, Huntington Co., Ind.

Sept. 24 and 25, 4 miles west of Tipton, Cedar Co., Iowa, beginning at 2 P. M. Ministers of Middle Iowa will please arrange to come to us from District Meeting at Garrison. Our meeting-house is at a distance of two miles from Buchanan on the B., C. R. & N. R. R.

Sept. 24, at 5 P. M., in La Porte church, La Porte, Ind. Trains will be met in the forenoon and early afternoon of the day of meeting.

Sept. 24, at 3 P. M., Martin's Creek church, Wayne Co., Ill.

Sept. 24 and 25, at 3 P. M., Lanark church, Carroll Co., Ill.

Sept. 24, at 5 P. M., Pokagon church, Dowagiac, Cass Co., Mich.

Sept. 27, at 5 P. M., at Wenger meeting-house, St. Joseph church, Ind.

Sept. 27, South Bend church, Ind.

Sept. 28, at 10 A. M., Spring Creek church, Kosciusko Co., Ind.

Sept. 29 and 30, at 2 P. M., Rock Creek, Whiteside Co., Ill.

Sept. 29 and 30, at 10 A. M., Lower Fall Creek church, 3 miles south of Anderson. Those coming on train should address John Rouse, R. Anderson, Ind.

Sept. 30, at 10 A. M., Nettle Creek church, near Hagerstown, Wayne Co., Ind.

Sept. 30, at 2 P. M., Milmine church, Piatt Co., Ill.

Oct. 1, at 2 P. M., Sugar Creek church, Allen Co., Ohio.

Oct. 1, at 3 P. M., Berrien Congregation, Mich.

Oct. 1 and 2, at 10 A. M., West Branch church, Ill. One week's meeting previous to feast.

Oct. 1 and 2, at 2 P. M., near Amos, Boone Co., Iowa. Noon trains meet at Amos on Saturday.

Oct. 1, at 4 P. M., Osage church, Crawford Co., Kans.

Oct. 1, at 4 P. M., Logan church, near DeGraff, Ohio.

Oct. 1 and 2, Saginaw church, Mich.

Oct. 1 and 2, at 1:30 P. M., Walnut Valley congregation, Barton Co., Kans.

Oct. 1, Maple Grove church, Norton Co., Kans.

Oct. 1, at 10 A. M., Appanoose church, Kans.

Oct. 1, at 10 A. M., Eight Mile church, Ind., at the town of Markle.

Oct. 1 and 2, at 11 A. M., Riverside, Iowa. Those coming by rail will stop at Iowa Junction, on R. C. R. & N. R. R., where they will be met.

Oct. 1, at 10 A. M., Stone Lick church, Clermont Co., Ohio.

Oct. 1, at 10 A. M., Chippewa congregation, Wayne Co., Ohio.

Oct. 1, at 2 P. M., in the Verdigris church, at Bro. S. S. Redman's. A series of meetings w ll commence Sept. 25.

Oct. 1, Camp Creek church, Ill., at the church 7 miles south of Colchester. Those coming by train will please notify S. S. Hummer, and they will be met at the depot at Colchester, and conveyed to place of meeting.

Oct. 1, at 10 A. M., Belleville church, Kans.

Oct. 1, at 2 P. M., in the Beaver Dam church, Kosciusko Co., Ind., near the town of Burket.

Oct. 1, at 2 P. M., Roann church, Ind.

Oct. 1 and 2, Dallas Centre church. A series of meetings by Bro. Hutchison will commence Sept. 17.

Oct. 1, at 10 A. M., Wabash church, 7 miles south of Wabash Ind.

Oct. 6, 10 A. M., Donnel's Creek church, Clarke Co., Ohio, seven miles from New Carlisle, and the same distance from Forg. and Springfield. Those coming from the West will stop either at New Carlisle or Springfield. We will be met on the evening of the 5th. Those from the North-east or South should stop at Springfield.

Oct. 6, at 3 P. M., Spring Creek church, in the Keith's church-house, eleven miles south-west of Fence, Kans.

Oct. 6 and 7, at 10 A. M., Shannon, Ill.

Oct. 6, at 2 P. M., Arcadia church, Ind.

Oct. 7, Black River church, Van Buren Co., Mich. Brethren coming by rail will stop at Bangor.

Oct. 7, at 2 P. M., Kaskaskia church, Fayette Co., Ill., ten miles south-east of Bleriber City, Ill. Those coming by rail will be met at the above-named place by informing Granville Nevinger.

Oct. 7, at 10 A. M., Sugar Creek, Whitley Co., Ind.

Oct. 7, at 2 P. M., Raccoon Creek church, Montgomery Co., Ind., one and one-half miles north-west of Ladoga.

Oct. 7, at 2 P. M., Macoupin Creek church, Montgomery Co., Ill. Those coming by r ll will be met at Farmersville, on Springfield Road, and at Girard, on St. Louis Road on morning of meeting.

Oct. 7 and 8, at 10:30 A. M., Four Mile church, Union Co., Ind.

Oct. 8, at 4 P. M., Bethel church, on North County line, Thayer Co., Nebr. Stationed Carleton, Davenport, Carlisle and Shickley.

Oct. 8, at 10 A. M., Bear Creek church, Portland, Ind. Those coming by r ll will be met by notifying H. P. Garber.

Oct. 8 and 2, at 10 A. M., Woodland church, Fulton Co., Ill. A series of meetings one week previous to the feast, and to continue two weeks.

Oct. 8, at 2 P. M., North Star, Darke County, Ohio.

Oct. 8, at 4 P. M., Greentown church, at Greentown, Howard Co., Ind.

Oct. 8, at 3:30 P. M., Maple Glen church, Somerset Co., Pa.

Oct. 8, at 4 P. M., in the Elkhart Valley church, Elkhart Co., Ind.

Oct. 8 and 9, at 2 P. M., Arnold's Grove, Ill.

Oct. 8, at 10 A. M., Dry Creek church, Linn Co., Iowa, one mile west of Robins Station.

Oct. 8, Swan Creek congregation, Ohio, 3½ miles west of Delta, Ohio.

Oct. 8, at 4 P. M., Washington Creek church, Douglas Co., Kans.

Oct. 8 and 9, at 10 A. M., Pine Creek congregation, Ill., in town of Sawyer. Meeting to commence at 10 o'clock.

Oct. 14 and 15, at 11 A. M., South Keokuk church, Keokuk Co., Iowa. Those coming by rail will be met at Olie, by notify ng Isaac Shelley or Jesse Brown. Those coming from the West will arrive at Olie about 11:30 A. M.; those from the East at 3 P. M.

Oct. 14, at 4 P. M., Union church, Marshall Co., Ind., five miles west of Plymouth. Trains will be met at both Plymouth and Barr Oak.

Oct. 14, Union church, Plymouth, Marshall Co., Ind. This church would like to have some brother hold meetings a week or ten days after.

Oct. 15 and 16, at 10 A. M., Grundy church, ten miles west of Grundy Centre, Grundy Co., Iowa.

Oct. 21, at 10 A. M., Killbuck church, Delaware Co., Ind. Some miles west of Muncie.

Oct. 28, at 3 P. M., St. Joseph Valley church, St. Joseph, Ind., 3 miles north of South Bend.

Oct. 28, at 4 P. M., in the Pleasant Hill church, near Girard and Virden, Ill.

Oct. 28, at 2 P. M., South Beatrice church, Gage Co., Nebr. Conveyances the day before meeting at B. & M. depot, in Beatrice; Rock Island depot, in Rockford; Union Pacific depot, in Holmesville.

Oct. 28, at 4 P. M., Walnut church, Marshall Co., Ind.

Oct. 28, at 10 A. M., in the Buck Creek church, Henry Co., Ind.

Oct. 29, St. Vrain church, Longmont, Colo.

Oct. 29, at 2 P. M., Osawkie church, Kans. A series of meetings to commence Oct. 22.

Oct. 29 and 30, at 10 A. M., Pigeon Creek church, Ill., at the Oak Grove meeting-house.

Oct. 29, at 2 P. M., Oasis church, Madison Co., Ind., 3½ miles east of Summitville.

Nov. 4, Walnut Creek church, Mo.

Nov. 5, at 3 P. M., Big Creek church, Richland Co., Ill., 3½ miles North-east of Parkersburg, Ill. Conveyances will be at the above place by informing J. M. Forney.

—— THE ——

Doctrine of the Brethren Defended.

This work contains a complete exposition of the faith and practice of the Brethren, the Divinity of Christ, the Divinity of the Holy Spirit, Immersion, Feet-washing, the Lord's supper, the Holy Kiss, Non-conformity, Secret Societies, etc. Price, per copy, cloth binding, $1.25. Address this office.

GOOD BOOKS FOR ALL.

Any book in the market furnished at publishers' lowest retail price by the Brethren's Publishing Company, Mt. Morris, Ill. *Special prices* given when books are purchased in quantities. When ordering books, not on our list, if possible give title, name of author, and address of publishers.

The Throne of David.—By J. H. Ingraham. Cloth, $1.50.

Homiletics and Pastoral Theology.—By W. G. T. Shedd. Cloth. $2.50.

Lectures on Preaching.—By Rev. Phillips Brooks. Cloth, 18mo, $1.50.

Josephus' Complete Works.—Large type, 1 vol. 8vo. Illustrated with many steel and wood engravings. Library sheep, $3.00.

Biblical Antiquities.—By John Nevin. Gives a concise account of Bible times and customs: invaluable to all students of Bible subjects. Price, $1.50.

Wolf's Business College.

A thorough school for training pupils in the Commercial Branches, Shorthand, Typewriting, Telegraphy, and Penmanship. The school for those who want a practical, useful education. Write for catalogue.

D. EILER WOLF, Principal, Hagerstown, Md.

The Normal College.

The Fall Term of fifteen weeks opens Sept. 12. For recommendations and inducements, we point you to the work that has been done and the success of its graduates. In proportion to the number of the graduates, no school in the country can show a better record. A good, solid, practical education is what you want, and this is what we propose to give. For special information, Catalogues and a free copy of the *Juniata Echo*, address H. B. Brumbaugh, President, or J. H. Brumbaugh, Principal, Huntingdon, Pa.

◆ESSAYS◆

"Study to show thyself approved unto God; a workman that needeth not be ashamed, rightly dividing the Word of Truth."

FORGIVE AND FORGET.

BY SADIE BRALLIER NOFFSINGER.

LET by-gones be by-gones; throw all your compassion
On her who is destined to sorrow and fret.
Strive not to remember her misdeeds and errors,
But like Christian parents, forgive and forget.

O, deal with her gently! Remember 'twas weakness
That caused her to enter the sin-gilded net.
Cease weeping, cease grieving, cease, cease your reproaches;
Believe me, 'tis well to forgive and forget.

Temptation assailed her and claimed her his victim;
He sullied her garment of virtue; and yet,
Although your weak daughter unguardedly yielded,
O, parents! you ought to forgive and forget.

The fair, dazzling walls of the vile and the sinful,
This poor Magdalene hath forsaken; now let
Your charity reach her. She'll yet be a woman,
If, God-like, you only forgive and forget.

Nay, frown not in anger,—withhold not the blessing,
Nor slay your affection with bitter regret.
Lo, humble and prostrate she sues for your pardon,
And still you refuse to forgive and forget!

Behold her repentance! In shame she kneels weeping!
Forbear ye, forbear ye her conscience to whet!
O, hear her wild wailing! your love she's imploring!
Stern parents, have mercy,—forgive and forget!

Drown, drown your hard feelings; through sin she hath suffered.
The blood of our Savior hath cancelled her debt;
But know ye, my friends, you shall never see Heaven,
Unless you can freely forgive and forget.

Johnstown, Pa.

MUSICAL INSTRUMENTS IN WORSHIP.

ELD. I. J. ROSENBERGER,

Dear Brother:—

PLEASE send me your reasons against the use of an organ in church or Sunday-school. Give all the Gospel or Old Testament authority. I need it just now. I know you have given the subject some thought, and I hope to hear from you soon.   A BROTHER.

ANSWER.

I am opposed to the use of musical instruments in worship, either in church or Sunday-schools. My reasons, briefly told, are as follows:

1. *The origin of musical instruments is such as does not commend their use in worship.* Unto Adam and Eve were born Cain, Abel and Seth. The sad, short history of Abel's life is well known. Of Seth's ancestors it is early said: "Then began men to call upon the name of the Lord." But of guilty Cain it is said: "He went out from the presence of the Lord." Of Cain's ancestors we have Lamech, the introducer of polygamy, and Jubal, the father or inventor of the harp and organ. As Cain had gone out a fugitive and a vagabond, no doubt his descendants inherited a portion of his great guilt. Having no God to worship, they sought these means, no doubt, as a balm for their sad and alienated condition, hence musical instruments did not originate with a Divine Mind, were not devised for worship, but are suited to the carnal mind. In the books of the Kings and Chronicles and in the Psalms, there is repeated reference to David's use of instruments of music, even in worship. "Moreover four thousand were porters; and four thousand praised the Lord with the instruments which I made, said David. 1 Chron. 23: 5. "And when the burnt offerings began, the song of the Lord began also with the trumpets, and with the instruments ordained by David king of Israel." 2 Chron. 29: 27; see also Ezra 3: 10.

The prophet Amos is a very clear commentator on this part of David's life. "Woe to them that are at ease in Zion, . . . that lie on beds of ivory, . . . that chant to the sound of the viol, and invent to themselves instruments of music, like David." Amos 6: 1-5.

While David did much that was praiseworthy, yet he committed some errors, and the prophet plainly defines that one of his mistakes is seen in his efforts to secure instruments of music with which to praise God. I have been confronted with this question: "Was not the frequent use of instruments of music, referred to especially in the Psalms, by divine sanction?" To this I reply, "It was by permission and not by divine sanction."

God permitted Israel to have a king, Moses suffered the writing of divorcements; but neither were by divine sanction or permission. This distinction should be regarded with care.

2. *References, made by several sacred writers, shows clearly that the use of musical instruments in worship was not by divine sanction.* In Job 21: 7-14 we read thus: "Wherefore do the wicked live? . . Their seed is established in their sight with them. . . . They send forth their little ones like a flock, and their children dance. They take the timbrel and harp, and rejoice at the sound of the organ. They spend their days in wealth. . . Therefore they say unto God, Depart from us."

The prophet Isaiah enunciated a number of woes upon the wicked. In Isa. 5: 12, he says: "The harp and the viol, the tabret and pipe, and wine, are in their feasts." Kind reader, how can the above dark allusions to the use of instruments of music be reconciled with God's approval? As evidence that the foregoing declarations are true, we refer to Dan. 3: 1-8, the dedication of the great image, set up by Nebuchadnezzar, in the plains of Dura. The royal mandate was: "At what time ye hear the sound of the cornet, flute, harp, sackbut, psaltery, dulcimer, and all kinds of music, ye fall down and worship the golden image that Nebuchadnezzar the king hath set up." Surely the use of musical instruments, as referred to in old time, is not commendable.

Isaiah, in speaking of desolated Tarshish, and of Tyre, in derision says, "Take an harp, go about the city, thou harlot that hast been forgotten, . . . that thou mayest be remembered." Isa. 23: 16. This text clearly shows that in their spiritual whoredom they associated instrumental music with their worship.

In the midst of Job's deep affliction he says, "My harp also is turned to mourning, and my organ into the voice of them that weep." Job 30: 31. In the hour of distress Job's musical instruments afforded him no comfort, hence they were not of God. If they were not *then*, how can they be of God *now?* Better give your time and means to that which will be comfort now, and prove "solid comfort when we die."

The Seer upon Patmos, in his apocalyptic vision, beheld the overthrow of mystic Babylon, the apostate church. Mystic Babylon is the history of ancient Babylon repeating itself. The literal and the mystic go together,—are similar. The prophecy is as follows: "Babylon the great is fallen, is fallen. . . . Thus with violence shall that great city Babylon be thrown down, . . . and the voice of harpers, and musicians, and of pipers, and trumpeters, shall be heard no more at all in thee." Rev. 18: 2, 21, 22. In both ancient and mystic Babylon, among the corruptions named was the use of musical instruments in their worship, which has ceased in ancient Babylon and will yet cease in mystic Babylon, for it is not-of God.

3. In the New Testament we are authorized to sing, and told how to sing (1 Cor. 14: 15) but no-where told how to play on the organ; hence, to move an organ into the house of God, as an auxiliary to his worship, is clearly adding to God's Word, and those who do so are violators, named in Rev. 22: 18. The apostle bids, "Let all things be done to edifying." 1 Cor. 14: 26. Edifying means "building up in Christian knowledge, instructing, improving the mind."—*Webster.* This a musical instrument cannot do. It cannot recite words, because it is dumb. Upon this point the apostle says, "And even things without life giving sound, whether pipe or harp, except they give a distinction in the sounds, how shall it be known what is piped or harped? . . . So likewise ye, except ye utter by the tongue words easy to be understood, how shall it be known what is spoken?" 1 Cor. 14: 7-9. To utter, to sing words by the tongue, is just what we are contending for. Instrumental music is used in theaters, drinking dens, and halls of vice, with the sole aim to collect and entertain the crowd, but in no sense does it edify. The idea of worshiping God with a machine is repulsive to reason, and dates back to Paganism and the corruptions of Judaism, hence should be strenuously avoided by all lovers of pure Christianity.

I hope these brief outlines may afford you the desired information. I remain as ever your brother.   I. J. ROSENBERGER.

REMARKS ON MATT. 6: 6.

BY NOAH LONGANECKER.

"But thou, when thou prayest, enter into thy closet, and when thou hast shut thy door, pray to thy Father which is in secret; and thy Father which seeth in secret shall reward thee openly."

CHRIST informs us in verse 5, that "hypocrites love to pray standing in the synagogues, and in the corners of the streets, that they may be seen of men."

Does Christ condemn prayers offered in synagogue, or on corners of streets? Surely not; for in 1 Tim. 2: 8, we read, "I will that men pray every where."

Does he condemn the standing posture in prayer at said places? Verily no; for in Mark 11: 25 we read, "When ye stand praying, forgive if ye have aught against any."

Their *motive*, "that they may be seen of men," is what Christ condemns. Christ does not condemn long prayers in Matt. 23: 14, but he strongly condemns the "*pretense*" for which they were offered. So, then, it is not the prayer that is long or short, the prayer made on the corners of streets, or in the synagogue, the prayer made when standing, sitting, lying, or kneeling, that is condemned. It is not the private or public prayer that is condemned by Christ. But in all these, when we pray to be heard or seen of men, Christ condemns.

We have made the above remarks to assist us in determining the true sense of "Enter into thy closet." Some say it is some private or secluded place, away from the public. Since we are to "pray every-where," can this be the true sense? We think not. "Enter into thy closet" is as binding in our public as in our private prayers.

"*When* thou prayest." Paul writes concerning this as follows: "Know ye not that your body is the temple of the Holy Ghost, which is in you?" 1 Cor. 6: 19. The heart is the *closet* of this temple, and there God looks. Prayer is the most secret intercourse of the soul with God. We should commune with God in our hearts. Short of looking to ourselves, or of entering into our own hearts, and praying from our hearts to God, our prayers are but hypocrisy. Our hearts must be closed to the honor, evil thoughts, etc., of the

✦ESSAYS✦

"Study to show thyself approved unto God: a workman that needeth not to be ashamed, rightly dividing the Word of Truth."

FORGIVE AND FORGET.

BY SADIE BRALLIER NOFFSINGER.

Let by-gones be by-gones; throw all your compassion
On her who is destined to sorrow and fret.
Strive not to remember her misdeeds and errors,
But like Christian parents, forgive and forget.

O, deal with her gently! Remember 'twas weakness
That caused her to enter the sin-gilded net. ·
Cease weeping, cease grieving, cease, cease your reproaches;
Believe me, 'tis well to forgive and forget.

Temptation assailed her and claimed her his victim;
He sullied her garment of virtue; and yet,
Although your weak daughter unguardedly yielded,
O, parents! you ought to forgive and forget.

The fair, dazzling walls of the jile and the sinful,
This poor Magdalene hath forsaken; now let
Your charity reach her. She'll yet be a woman,
If, God-like, you only forgive and forget.

Nay, frown not in anger,—withhold not the blessing,
Nor slay your affection with biter regret.
Lo, humble and prostrate she sues for your pardon,
And still you refuse to forgive and forget!

Behold her repentance! in shame she kneels weeping!
Forbear ye, forbear ye her conscience to whet!
O, hear her wild wailing! your love she's imploring!
Stern parents, have mercy,—*forgive and forget!*

Drown, drown your hard feelings; through sin she hath suffered.
The blood of our Savior hath cancelled her debt;
But know ye, my friends, you shall never see Heaven,
Unless you can freely forgive and forget.
Johnstown, Pa.

MUSICAL INSTRUMENTS IN WORSHIP.

Eld. I. J. Rosenberger,

Dear Brother:—

Please send me your reasons against the use of an organ in church or Sunday-school. Give all the Gospel or Old Testament authority. I need it just now. I know you have given the subject some thought, and I hope to hear from you soon.   A Brother.

ANSWER.

I am opposed to the use of musical instruments in worship, either in church or Sunday-schools. My reasons, briefly told, are as follows:

1. *The origin of musical instruments is such as does not commend their use in worship.* Unto Adam and Eve were born Cain, Abel and Seth. The sad, short history of Abel's life is well known. Of Seth's ancestors it is early said: "Then began men to call upon the name of the Lord." But of guilty Cain it is said: "He went out from the presence of the Lord." Of Cain's ancestors we have Lamech, the introducer of polygamy, and Jubal, the father or inventor of the harp and organ. As Cain had gone out a fugitive and a vagabond, no doubt his descendants inherited a portion of his great guilt. Having no God to worship, they sought these means, no doubt, as a balm for their sad and alienated condition, hence musical instruments did not originate with a Divine Mind, were not devised for worship, but are suited to the carnal mind. In the books of the Kings and Chronicles and in the Psalms, there is repeated reference to David's use of instruments of music, even in worship. "Moreover four thousand were porters; and four thousand praised the Lord with the instruments which I made, said David." 1 Chron. 23: 5. "And when the burnt offerings began, the song of the Lord began also with the trumpets, and with the instruments ordained by David king of Israel." 2 Chron. 29: 27; see also Ezra 3: 10.

The prophet Amos is a very clear commentator on this part of David's life. "Woe to them that are at ease in Zion, . . . that lie on beds of ivory, . . . that chant to the sound of the viol, and invent to themselves instruments of music, like David." Amos 6: 1–5.

While David did much that was praiseworthy, yet he committed some errors, and the prophet plainly defines that one of his mistakes is seen in his efforts to secure instruments of music with which to' praise God. I have been confronted with this question: "Was not the frequent use of instruments of music, referred to especially in the Psalms, by divine sanction?" To this I reply, "It was by permission and not by divine sanction."

God permitted Israel to have a king, Moses suffered the writing of divorcements; but neither were by divine sanction or permission. This distinction should be regarded with care.

2. *References, made by several sacred writers, shows clearly that the use of musical instruments in worship was not by divine sanction.* In Job 21: 7–14 we read thus: "Wherefore do the wicked live? . . Their seed is established in their sight with them. . . They send forth their little ones like a flock, and their children dance. They take the timbrel and harp, and rejoice at the sound of the organ. They spend their days in wealth. . . Therefore they say unto God, Depart from us."

The prophet Isaiah enunciated a number of woes upon the wicked. In Isa. 5: 12, he says: "The harp and the viol, the tabret and pipe, and wine, are in their feasts." Kind reader, how can the above dark allusions to the use of instruments of music be reconciled with God's approval? As evidence that the foregoing declarations are true, we refer to Dan. 3: 1–3, the dedication of the great image, set up by Nebuchadnezzar, in the plains of Dura. The royal mandate was: "At what time ye hear the sound of the cornet, flute, harp, sackbut, psaltery, dulcimer, and all kinds of music, ye fall down and worship the golden image that Nebuchadnezzar the king hath set up." Surely the use of musical instruments, as referred to in old time, is not commendable.

Isaiah, in speaking of desolated Tarshish, and of Tyre, in derision says, "Take an harp, go about the city, thou harlot that hast been forgotten, . . . that thou mayest be remembered." Isa. 23: 16. This text clearly shows that in their spiritual whoredom they associated instrumental music with their worship.

In the midst of Job's deep affliction he says, "My harp also is turned to mourning, and my organ into the voice of them that weep." Job 30: 31. In the hour of distress Job's musical instruments afforded him no comfort, hence they were not of God. If they were not *then*, how can they be of God *now?* Better give your time and means to that which will be comfort now, and prove "solid comfort when we die."

The Seer upon Patmos, in his apocalyptic vision, beheld the overthrow of mystic Babylon, the apostate church. Mystic Babylon is the history of ancient Babylon repeating itself. The literal and the mystic go together,—are similar. The prophecy is as follows: "Babylon the great is fallen, is fallen. . . . Thus with violence shall that great city Babylon be thrown down, . . . and the voice of harpers, and musicians, and of pipers, and trumpeters, shall be heard no more at all in thee." Rev. 18: 2, 21, 22. In both ancient and mystic Babylon, among the corruptions named was the use of musical instruments in their worship, which has ceased in ancient Babylon and will yet cease in mystic Babylon, for it is not of God.

3. In the New Testament we are authorized to sing, and told how to sing (1 Cor. 14: 15) but nowhere told how to play on the organ; hence, to move an organ into the house of God, as an auxiliary to his worship, is clearly adding to God's Word, and those who do so are violators, named in Rev. 22: 18. The apostle bids, "Let all things be done to edifying." 1 Cor. 14: 26. Edifying means "building up in Christian knowledge, instructing, improving the mind."—*Webster.* This a musical instrument cannot do. It cannot recite words, because it is dumb. Upon this point the apostle says, "And even things without life giving sound, whether pipe or harp, except they give a distinction in the sounds, how shall it be known what is piped or harped? . . . So likewise ye, except ye utter by the tongue words easy to be understood, how shall it be known what is spoken?" 1 Cor. 14: 7–9. To utter, to sing words by the tongue, is just what we are contending for. Instrumental music is used in theaters, drinking dens, and hells of vice, with the sole aim to collect and entertain the crowd, but in no sense does it edify. The idea of worshiping God with a machine is repulsive to reason, and dates back to Paganism and the corruptions of Judaism, hence should be strenuously avoided by all lovers of pure Christianity.

I hope these brief outlines may afford you the desired information. I remain as ever your brother.   I. J. Rosenberger.

REMARKS ON MATT. 6: 6.

BY NOAH LONGANECKER.

"But thou, when thou prayest, enter into thy closet, and when thou hast shut thy door, pray to thy Father which is in secret; and thy Father which seeth in secret shall reward thee openly."

Christ informs us in verse 5, that "hypocrites love to pray standing in the synagogues, and in the corners of the streets, that they may be seen of men."

Does Christ condemn prayers offered in synagogues, or on corners of streets? Surely not; for in 1 Tim. 2: 8, we read, "I will that men pray every where."

Does he condemn the standing posture in prayer at said places? Verily no; for in Mark 11: 25 we read, "When ye stand praying, forgive if ye have aught against any."

Their *motive*, "that they may be seen of men," is what Christ condemns. Christ does not condemn long prayers in Matt. 23: 14, but he strongly condemns the "*pretense*" for which they were offered. So, then, it is not the prayer that is long or short, the prayer made on the corners of streets, or in the synagogues, the prayer made when standing, sitting, lying, or kneeling, that is condemned. It is not the private or public prayer that is condemned by Christ. But in all these, when we pray to be heard or seen of men, Christ condemns.

We have made the above remarks to assist us in determining the true sense of "Enter into thy closet." Some say it is some private or secluded place, away from the public. Since we are to "pray every-where," can this be the true sense? We think not. "Enter into thy closet" is as binding in our public as in our private prayers.

"When thou prayest." Paul writes concerning this as follows: "Know ye not that your body is the temple of the Holy Ghost, which is in you?" 1 Cor. 6: 19. The heart is the *closet* of this temple, and there God looks. Prayer is the most secret intercourse of the soul with God. We should commune with God in our hearts. Short of looking to ourselves, or of entering into our own hearts, and praying from our hearts to God, our prayers are but hypocrisy. Our hearts must be closed to the honor, evil thoughts, etc., of the

PALESTINE.

BLEST land of Judea! Thrice hallow'd of song,
Where the hollest of memories pilgrim like throng,
In the shade of thy palms, by the shores of thy sea,
On the hills of thy beauty, my heart is with thee.

With the eye of a spirit I look on that shore,
Where pilgrim and prophet haVe linger'd before;
With the glide of a spirit I traVerse the sod
Made bright by the steps of the angels of God.

Blue sea of the hills! In my spirit I hear
Thy waters, Gennsaret, chime on my ear;
Where the Lowly and Just with the people sat down,
And thy spray on the dust of his sandals was thrown.

Beyond are Bethulla'-mountains of green,
And the desolate hills of the wild Gadarene;
And I pause on the goat-crags of Tabor to see
The gleam of thy waters, O dark Galilee!

Hark, a sound in the Valley! Where, swollen and strong,
Thy riVer, O Kishon, is sweeping along;
Where the Canaanite strove with Jehovah in vain,
And the torrent grew dark with the blood of the slain.

There down from his mountains, stern Zebulon came,
And Naphtali's stag, with his eye-balls of flame,
And the chariots of Jabin rolled harmlessly on,
For the arm of the Lord was Abinoam's son!

There sleep the still rocks, and the caVerns, which-rang
To the song which the beautiful prophetess sang,
When the PrinceSs of Issachar stood by her side,
And the shout of a host in Its triumph replied..

Lo, Bethlehem's hill-site before me is seen,
With the mountains around and the Valley between;
There rested the shepherds of Judah, and there
The song of the angels rose sweet in the air.

And Bethany's palm trees in beauty still throw
Their shadows at noon on the ruins below;
But where are the sisters who hastened to greet
The lowly Redeemer, and sit at his feet?

I tread where the Twelve in their wayfaring trod;
I stand where they stood with the chosen of God—
Where his blessings were heard and his lessons were taught,
Where the blind were restored, and the healing was wrought.

Oh, here with his flock the sad Wanderer came—
These hills he tolled oVer in grief ere the same—
The founts where he drank by the wayside still flow,
And the same airs are blowing which breathed on his brow.

And throned on her hills sits Jerusalem yet,
But the dust on her forehead, and chains on her feet;
For the crown of her pride to the mocker hath gone,
And the holy Shekinah is dark where it shone.

But wherefore this dream of the earthly abode
Of humanity, clothed in the brightness of God?
Were my spirit but turned from the outward and dim,
It could gaze, eVen now, on the presence of him!

Not in clouds and in terrors, but gentle as when,
In loVe and in meekness, he moVed among men;
And the voice which breathed peace to the waVes of the sea,
In the hush of my spirit would whisper to me!

And what if my feet may not tread where he stood,
Nor my ears hear the dashing of Galilee's flood,
Nor my eyes see the cross which he bowed him to bear,
Nor my knees press Gethsemane's garden of prayer.

Yet, loVed of the Father, thy spirit is near
To the meek, and the lowly, and penitent here;
And the Voice of thy loVe is the same, eVen now,
As at Bethany's tomb, or on Olivet's brow.

Oh, the outward hath gone!—but, in glory and power,
The spirit surviveth the things of an hour;
Unchanged, undecaying, its Pentecost flame
On the heart's secret altar is burning the same.

         John G. Whittier.

THE CHRISTIAN STANDARD OR PERFECTION.

BY S. N. M'CANN.

In Three Chapters.—Chapter Three.

"Be ye therefore perfect, eVen as your Father which Is in heaVen is perfect."—Matt. 5: 48.

WHILE we are perfect, pure, holy, being sanctified, our lives are in constant conflict with sin, weakness, imperfection, and unholiness. While our robes are washed and kept white in the blood of the Lamb, we are constantly soiling them with sin. We are absolutely perfect on one hand, Jesus being our righteousness (2 Cor. 5: 21), but

upon the other we are relatively imperfect, weakness and sin hindering our every effort to do good.

While we are perfect, being sanctified, it is by and through the foreordaining power of God who created us, "in Christ Jesus unto good works which God hath before ordained that we should walk in them." Eph. 2: 10.

Some might say if we are perfect, it is in vain to work and sacrifice, for we can grow no better, holier, or purer. Our perfection is wholly a matter of free grace, God granting it to us without merit on our part, the merit being all in our Mediator.

The standard cannot be raised, but we can bring our lives nearer and nearer to the standard by devoted effort. Our little sins and imperfections do not lower our standard of perfection, hence we have boldness to come to the throne of grace without fear, knowing that "God's grace" is sufficient for us. 2 Cor. 12: 9.

While our little sins and weaknesses do not lower our standard of perfection, they do lower our lives, and, if persisted in, they drive away our Mediator, and we lose our birth-right, and our lives fall back upon our own merit, or the poor merit of works. The drunkard, the liar, the thief, the highwayman, and the moral man, whether in the church or out of it, are alike under sin and condemnation. God's free grace will alike make all perfect, save all, sanctify all, as soon as they truly believe on Jesus, Acts 13: 39, but it will not alike set each man, and every one upon the same plane of development. Christ saves a man right where he finds him, and perfects him and then he aids him to rise, step by step, out of the lowest depths of sin into the pure and complete development of true Christian manhood. The man, who has fallen low into vice and immorality, is as perfect the moment he gets into Christ, as the good moral man is the moment he gets into Christ, but he will have years of hard struggling to bring his life up to as high a plane of development as the good, moral man starts with.

Receiving Christ does not transport one immediately into a plane of high, moral standing, but it saves, and the whole soul is bent upon bringing the life up to higher and higher degrees of development. Life's work ended and this struggle with sin and self ends. While there is life, there is progression, development,—a constant growth into a higher, a purer, and a holier being, but nothing in reference to the state of being.

The moral man accepts Christ; he is saved, and the battle with self begins, that he may rise higher and higher, and become more and more like his Divine image, Christ. His mistakes and failings may not be seen by the church or the world, but he feels them sorely, and struggles on, realizing that his only source of perfection is Christ. Life's best and purest efforts are so full of failure that victory would be hopeless, were it not for his state of adoption.

The vilest sinner may accept Christ, and be saved, sanctified, made perfect. The battle with self begins, that he may rise to higher and higher planes of development, and become more and more like his Divine Image, but this time the world and the church see the struggle, especially the imperfect-steps in the struggle, and poor human judgment is apt to pronounce the work a failure.

The development may be more rapid and the growth greater than in the "moral man" but the plane, on which the battle begins, is so much lower that many of the imperfections are seen even by human eyes and they pass judgment and cry, "Failure." If these imperfections make it a failure it is a failure all along the line, but, thanks be to Christ who is our perfection, life's battles are

but one continued series of development that the man may become more and more like unto his Divine image. He may be always perfect in Christ, yet ever imperfect in character, ever struggling with sin and failure, yet he will never fail, for Christ is our all. Perfect as God, yet ever growing more perfect; sanctified, yet ever growing more holy, is the great mystery of godliness, that makes every man in Christ Jesus a new creature, that makes old things to pass away, and all things to become new. 2 Cor. 5: 17.

May our lives overflow with love and praise because Jesus is ours; for having him we have all, now and evermore.

Bridgewater, Va.

WHY TEACH THAT JUDAS DID NOT COMMUNE?

BY JOHN E. MOHLER.

IN reading the several Scriptural accounts of the institution of the Communion, most everyone would get the idea that Judas, the traitor, partook of the emblems of Christ's broken body and shed blood, and this view is widely received in the religious world. If Luke's account is accepted, the matter is settled; but if, we reject Luke, then it remains doubtful. Surely, in a matter of so great weight, the inspired Gospel gives no uncertain sound. While it is true, salvation need not be affected either by the Communion or non-communion of Judas, yet here exists a favorite point of attack upon so-called close-communionists. To admit, our opponents think, that Judas, a devil, was permitted by Christ to commune at his table, is to deny the right of the church to exclude from the Communion anyone who desires to partake of the bread and wine. To meet this argument and to satisfy their ideas of propriety is, I suppose, why many hold that Judas did not commune. But, as afore said, if we regard each of the narratives as being strictly correct, Judas did commune. To thus view the several Gospel accounts I am sure all will admit as the safest, provided we do not thereby encounter insurmountable difficulties. Let us, by all means, try to accept the Scriptures in their simplicity, and then look out for the difficulties. Supposing we take the view that Judas did commune, as Luke says. Does this argue that Christ violated a "heaven-born principle" in administering to him the sacred emblems, or that the church has no right to hold her "close-communion" ideas? No! To prove the truth of my answer is the purpose of this article.

We notice that when Christ personally instituted a church ordinance, he invariably did so by setting the example himself. He did not merely describe the ceremonies, but with his followers, actually performed them as they should thereafter be observed by the church. For instance, he entered the baptismal waters; with his disciples he ate the Lord's Supper; with them he instituted the Communion *just as the church should observe it in memory of him.* This, I think, no one will deny, yet its careful analysis will admit of only one interpretation of Judas' part in the Communion, to wit: that he did commune. When we say that Christ designed the Eucharist to be kept as instituted, we know that there was nothing in the manner of its first observance which it were not possible for the church to perform, for what the church cannot do, Christ did not set as example.

He expected the church to follow him, therefore there was nothing in the ceremony beyond the power of the finite mind. Christ's divine knowledge of all men must not affect the choice of communicants, since the church is destitute of the knowledge of the thoughts and secret intents of the heart. The twelve communicants were judged just as the church must judge her mem-

PALESTINE.

BLEST land of Judea! Thrice hallow'd of song,
Where the holiest of memories pilgrim like throng,
In the shade of thy palms, by the shores of thy sea,
On the hills of thy beauty, my heart is with thee.

With the eye of a spirit I look on that shore,
Where pilgrim and prophet have linger'd before;
With the glide of a spirit I traverse the sod
Made bright by the steps of the angels of God.

Blue sea of the hills! In my spirit I hear
Thy waters, Genesaret, chime on my ear;
Where the Lowly and Just with the people sat down,
And thy spray on the dust of his sandals·was thrown.

Beyond are Bethulia's mountains of green,
And the desolate hills of the wild Gadarene;
And I pause on the goat-crags of Tabor to see
The gleam of thy waters, O dark Galilee!

Hark, a sound in the valley! Where, swollen and strong,
Thy river, O Kishon, is sweeping along;
Where the Canaanite strove with Jehovah in vain,
And the torrent grew dark with the blood of the slain.

There down from his mountains, stern Zebulon came,
And Naphtali's stag, with his eye-balls of flame,
And the chariots of Jabin rolled harmlessly on,
For the arm of the Lord was Abinoam's son!

There sleep the still rocks, and the caverns, which·rang
To the song which the beautiful prophetess sang,
When the Princess of Issachar stood by her side,
And the shout of a host in its triumph replied..

Lo, Bethlehem's hill-site before me is seen,
With the mountains around and the valley between;
There rested the shepherds of Judah, and there
The song of the angels rose sweet in the air.

And Bethany's palm-trees in beauty still throw
Their shadows at noon on the rules below;
But where are the sisters who hastened to greet
The lowly Redeemer, and sit at his feet?

I tread where the Twelve in their wayfaring trod;
I stand where they stood with the chosen of God—
Where his blessings were heard and his lessons were taught,
Where the blind were restored, and the healing was wrought.

Oh, here with his flock the sad Wanderer came—
These hills he toiled over in grief are the same—
The founts where he drank by the wayside still flow,
And the same airs are blowing which breathed on his brow.

And throned on her hills sits Jerusalem yet,
But the dust on her forehead, and chains on her feet;
For the crown of her pride to the mocker hath gone,
And the holy Shekinah is dark where it shone.

But wherefore this dream of the earthly abode
Of humanity, clothed in the brightness of God?
Were my spirit but turned from the outward and dim,
It could gaze, even now, on the presence of him!

Not in clouds and in terrors, but gentle as when,
In love and in meekness, he moved among men;
And the voice which breathed peace to the waves of the sea,
In the hush of my spirit would whisper to me!

And what if my feet may not tread where he stood,
Nor my ears hear the dashing of Galilee's flood,
Nor my eyes see the cross which he bowed him to bear,
Nor my knees press Gethsemane's garden of prayer.

Yet, loved of the Father, thy spirit is near
To the meek, and the lowly, and penitent here;
And the voice of thy love is the same, even now,
As at Bethany's tomb, or on Olivet's brow.

Oh, the outward bath gone!—but, in glory and power,
The spirit surviveth the things of an hour;
Unchanged, undecaying, its Pentecost flame
On the heart's secret altar is burning the same.

                                        John G. Whittier.

THE CHRISTIAN STANDARD OR PERFECTION.

BY S. N. M'CANN.

In Three Chapters.—Chapter Three.

"Be ye therefore perfect, even as your Father which is in heaven is perfect."—Matt. 5: 48.

WHILE we are perfect, pure, holy, being sanctified, our lives are in constant conflict with sin, weakness, imperfection, and unholiness. While our robes are washed and kept white in the blood of the Lamb, we are constantly soiling them with sin. We are absolutely perfect on one hand, Jesus being our righteousness (2 Cor. 5: 21), but

upon the other we are relatively imperfect, weakness and sin hindering our every effort to do good.

While we are perfect, being sanctified, it is by and through the foreordaining power of God who created us, "in Christ Jesus unto good works which God hath before ordained that we should walk in them." Eph. 2: 10.

Some might say if we are perfect, it is in vain to work and sacrifice, for we can grow no better, holier, or purer. Our perfection is wholly a matter of free grace, God granting it to us without merit on our part, the merit being all in our Mediator.

The standard cannot be raised, but·we can bring our lives nearer and nearer to the standard by devoted effort. Our little sins and imperfections do not lower our standard of perfection, hence we have boldness to come to the throne of grace without fear, knowing that " God's grace " is sufficient for us. 2 Cor. 12: 9.

While our little sins and weaknesses do not lower our standard of perfection, they do lower our lives, and, if persisted in, they drive away our Mediator, and we lose our birth-right, and our lives fall back upon our own merit, or the poor merit of works. The drunkard,·the liar, the thief, the highwayman, and the moral man, whether in the church or out of it, are alike under sin and condemnation. God's free grace will alike make all perfect, save all, sanctify all, as soon as they truly believe on Jesus, Acts 13: 39, but it will not alike set each man, and every one upon the same plane of development. Christ saves a man right where he finds him, and perfects him and then he aids him to rise, step by step, out of the lowest depths of sin into the pure and complete·development of true Christian manhood. The man, who has fallen low into vice and immorality, is as perfect the moment he gets into Christ, as the good moral man is the moment he gets into Christ, but he will have years of hard struggling to bring his life up to as high a plane of development as the good, moral man starts with.

Receiving Christ does not transport one immediately into a plane of high, moral standing, but it saves, and the whole soul is bent upon bringing the life up to higher and higher degrees of development. Life's work ended and this struggle with sin and self ends. While there is life, there is progression, development,—a constant growth into a higher, a purer, and a holier being, but nothing in reference to the state of being.

The moral man accepts Christ; he is saved and the battle with self begins, that he may rise higher and higher, and become more and more like his Divine image, Christ. His mistakes and failings may not be seen by the church or the world, but he feels them sorely, and struggles on, realising that his only source·of perfection is Christ. Life's best and purest efforts are so full of failure that victory would be hopeless, were it not for his state of adoption.

The vilest sinner may accept Christ, and be saved, sanctified, made perfect. The battle with self begins, that he may rise to higher and higher planes of development, and become more and more like his Divine Image, but this time the world and the church see the struggle, especially the imperfect steps in the struggle, and poor human judgment is apt to pronounce the work a failure.

The development may be more rapid and the growth greater than in the " moral man " but the plane, on which the battle begins, is so much lower that many of the imperfections are seen even by human eyes and they pass judgment and cry, " Failure." If these imperfections make it a failure it is a failure all along the line, but, thanks be to Christ who is our perfection, life's battles are

but one continued series of development that the man may become more and more like unto his Divine image. He may be always perfect in Christ, yet ever imperfect in character, ever struggling with sin and failure, yet he will never fail, for Christ is our all. Perfect as God, yet ever growing more perfect; sanctified, yet ever growing more holy, is the great mystery of godliness, that makes every man in Christ Jesus·a new creature, that makes old things to pass away, and all things to become new. 2 Cor. 5: 17.

May our lives overflow with love and praise because Jesus is ours; for having him we have all, now and evermore.

Bridgewater, Va.

WHY TEACH THAT JUDAS DID NOT COMMUNE?

BY JOHN E. MOHLER.

IN reading the several Scriptural accounts of the institution of the Communion, most everyone would get the idea that Judas, the traitor, partook of the emblems of Christ's broken body and shed blood, and this·view is widely received in the religious world. If Luke's account is accepted, the matter is settled; but if, we reject Luke, then it remains doubtful. Surely, in a matter of so great weight, the inspired Gospel gives no uncertain sound. While it is true, salvation need not be affected either by the Communion or non-communion of Judas, yet here exists a favorite point of attack upon so-called close·communionists. To admit, our opponents think, that Judas, a devil, was permitted by Christ to commune at his table, is to deny the right of the church to exclude from the Communion anyone who desires to partake of the bread and wine. To meet this argument and to satisfy their ideas of propriety is, I suppose, why many hold that Judas did not commune. But, as afore said, if we regard each of the narratives as being strictly correct, Judas did commune. To thus view the several Gospel accounts I am sure all will admit as the safest, provided we do not thereby encounter insurmountable difficulties. Let us, by all means, try to accept the Scriptures in their simplicity, and then look out for the difficulties. Supposing we take the view that Judas did commune, as Luke says. Does it appear that Christ violated a " heaven-born principle " in administering to him the sacred emblems, or that the church has no right to hold her "close-communion " ideas? No! To prove the truth of my answer is the purpose of this article.

We notice that when Christ personally instituted a church ordinance, he invariably did so by setting the example himself. He did not merely describe the ceremonies, but, with his followers, actually performed them as they should thereafter be observed by the church. For instance, he entered the baptismal·waters; with his disciples he ate the Lord's Supper; with them he instituted the Communion *just as the church should observe it in memory of him*. This, I think, no one will deny, yet its careful analysis will admit of only one interpretation of Judas' part in the Communion, to wit: that he did commune. When we say that Christ designed the Eucharist to be kept as instituted, we know that there was nothing in the manner of its first observance which it were not possible for the church to perform, for what the church *cannot* do, Christ did not set an example. He accepted the church to follow him, therefore there was nothing in the ceremony beyond the power of the finite mind. Christ's divine knowledge of all men must not affect the choice of communicants, since the church is destitute of the knowledge of the thoughts and secret intents of the heart. The twelve communicants were judged just as the church must judge her mem-

Missionary and Tract Work Department.

"Upon the first day of the week, let every one of you lay by him in store as God hath prospered him, that there be no gatherings when I come."—1 Cor. 16: 2.

"Every man as he purposeth in his heart, so let him give. Not grudgingly or of necessity, for the Lord loveth a cheerful giver."—2 Cor. 9: 7.

HOW MUCH SHALL WE GIVE?

"Every man *according to his ability*." "Every one *as God hath prospered him*." "Every man, *according as he purposeth in his heart*, so let him give." "For if there be first a willing mind, it is accepted *according to that a man hath*, and not according to that he hath not."—2 Cor. 8: 12.

Organization of Missionary Committee.

DANIEL VANIMAN, Foreman, · · McPherson, Kans.
D. L. MILLER, Treasurer, · · Mt. Morris, Ill.
GALEN B. ROYER, Secretary, · · Mt. Morris, Ill.

Organization of Book and Tract Work.

S. W. HOOVER, Foreman, · · · Dayton, Ohio.
S. BOCK, Secretary and Treasurer, · · Dayton, Ohio.

☞All donations intended for Missionary Work should be sent to GALEN B. ROYER, Mt. Morris, Ill.

☞All money for Tract Work should be sent to S. BOCK, Dayton, Ohio.

☞Money may be sent by Money Order, Registered Letter, or Drafts on New York or Chicago. Do not send personal checks, or drafts on interior towns, as it costs 25 cents to collect them.

☞Solicitors are requested to faithfully carry out the plan of Annual Meeting, that all our members be solicited to contribute at least twice a year for the Mission and Tract Work of the Church.

☞Notes for the Endowment Fund can be had by writing to the Secretary of either Work.

THE Friendly Islands to-day contain some 30,000 church members or more, while fifty years ago there was not a native to honor the name of Christ.

THE Samoan Islands have a population of about 30,000, who hold to the Christian faith. In the largest of these Islands there are not fifty families that do not have family worship.

IN New York City alone there are more ministers of the Gospel than in all the land of India, of which we sing in number 265 of the Hymnal. The souls of India are almost five times as many as those of the United States.

THE attention of one who is watching the movements of the times, is again and again called to the results of the labor and self-sacrifice of the missionary in foreign fields. When a heathen man once finds the Light of the world,—Jesus,—he has no other object in life than to serve him.

"HE who makes up his mind that he came into this world to do something, and then goes to work to do it, will be of service to mankind. He is the one who will make his mark among men. It may be a humble mark, but it will be well worth preserving. He will not be forgotten when his life is ended."

Two things are necessary to having a zeal for missions. The first, a knowledge of the Gospel, the second, a knowledge of the fields open for the Gospel plow, and the former is of easier access than the latter. The call of the unsaved is long and loud and continuous. "He that hath ears to hear, let him hear."

LET everyone quickly find his work and enter upon it at once. You preach a sermon—you give a tract—you hand a flower—you sing a song—you give a crutch to a lame man—you teach the Sabbath-school class—you make some cloth for a poor person—you pick a splinter from a child's finger. Do something! There is plenty to do—much of it is right at your door. Commence doing it now and keep at it.

THOUGH nearly all denominations are earnestly working in foreign fields, there is no want of room for preachers of the Gospel. Afghanistan has a population of six millions, and no missionary. Anam has five millions, and only Roman Catholics are yet in the field. Persia has one million, while Thibet has one to two millions.

WHEN a little heathen girl, who had given her heart to Jesus the best she knew how, came to die she told her mission teacher that she was going to heaven now and that she would wait just inside the door until he came. That was sufficient inspiration to any one not to become weary in well doing. Christ's words to Peter have never been recalled: "Feed my lambs."

THE secret desire of some of our young people to go into fields to work, which have been heretofore untouched, is a desire worthy the most careful cultivation. There are many fields not only new to our own people but new to any Christianity, and the zeal to occupy these for Christ is only a repetition of that which characterized the life of the great apostle of the Gentiles, an unbounded zeal to work, and care lest he should build on the foundation laid by some other worker.

ROBERT HALDANE, of Scotland, some years ago, sold certain lands of his and gave the entire proceeds to the cause of missions. At the present time the influence is such that travelers, passing by those farms, feel a certain impulse not to speak above a whisper, for they are passing sacred places. As the roar of the ocean tells us of vastness, as the thunder of the clouds tells us of power; as the grave tells us of death, so the former estates of Robert Haldane tell us of one man who considered his possessions not his own but Christ's.

EDUCATION.—ITS RELATION TO PREACHING.

· BY J. S. FLORY.

WE are conscious of the fact that this subject is one on which lengthy articles might be written with profit, but it is not our purpose to enter into an elaborate examination of the subject, but to give a few brief hints as we pass along.

No person can preach without education, for education is to learn about and understand things, but as to whether a preacher must first attain to a high standard of intellectual culture, before he can be a successful minister, is a matter of difference of opinion. In the world's history we find mention of many remarkable men of power in the pulpit, as elsewhere, who know but little about the higher grades of culture other than a limited knowledge of their mother tongue, coupled with a fervent spirituality. It is not presumable that their lack of intellectual culture was an advantage to them, unless we take the ground that more education would have engendered a spirit of vanity to the suppression of their otherwise successful traits. Wealth, to some men, is a disadvantage, when not properly used, so it is with intellectual culture, and it is on this line that we propose to pen a few thoughts.

Cultured minds of every kind are coming to the front in our church. There is a marked difference in the diction of our books and periodicals, and in the discourses of our brethren from the sacred stand. The same improvement on this line is very apparent to what it was twenty-five years ago. We should, by no means, look to this improvement with fears or distrust, but try to so appropriate every advantage that good will be the result. Head culture is all right to the men or woman

that has true heart culture, and if it be true that knowledge is power (no one can doubt it), we certainly must admit that a large store of knowledge, used aright, will result in a great power for good.

Of no better way do we know to avoid the dangers, some are so ready to apprehend, which may occur from an educated ministry, as to take warning from others. The popular churches of the day are lamenting, in many places, the lack of spirituality in their people and the stiff, cold, formal labors of their ministers. They tell us culture, in too many sermons, outweighs the subject, and the spirit of the truth is not driven home to the heart; also that in many cases a high-toned, intellectual sermon so mellows down the stern facts of God's Word as to cause it to become to the hearers a tame, ineffectual thing. The intellectual man, if not careful, will insensibly be drawn over on the lovely side of Christianity, use his sympathies in that direction, and neglect the sterner facts of God's dealings with the disobedient.

Culture becomes a hinderance when it eliminates from a subject the depth of spiritual meaning there is in it. Some one has said, "Culture is like fire,—a good servant but a bad master." Like every subject it has its extremes and he who will ignore it, as well as he who idolizes it, will be a failure in the ministry. Use it, as any other good thing, as not abusing it, and it will, by the grace of God, be a thing of usefulness and power. Eloquence, often the child of culture has its place for good when coming from the very depths of a truly regenerate heart. Where learning and eloquence meet to kiss each other, as in the saying of King David, they stir the soul as nothing else can.

The one great lesson for all learned men to "get by heart" is this: "Man looks at the head; God looks at the heart." To please man, let the head belch forth its wisdom but if your wish is to please God, let the streams of the fires of love never cease to flow from the altar of a heart fully consecrated to God. Remember, ye ministers of his, that an essay on a religious subject is one thing,—a sermon quite another. In these submission to the knowledge of the subject you may spin out an essay, but when it comes to preaching, if you want to reach the hearts of your hearers, let go the shafts of truth, as sent from a soul, alive with the Holy Spirit. Better pick for a place to hit, than for words to tickle the ear. Better say a few words that will make sinners think of themselves, than to speak an hour, only to make the people praise you.

Lordsburg, Cal.

FOR THE REMISSION OF SINS.

BY H. C. LUCAS.

"Then Peter said unto them, Repent, and be baptized every one of you in the name of Jesus Christ for the remission of sins, and ye shall receive the gift of the Holy Ghost."—Acts 2: 38.

DURING the present century there has been long and loud controversy as to the meaning of these words, used by the apostle on the day of Pentecost. It was an important occasion, and the apostle's use of the language quoted, was backed by the highest authority by which any one could speak, namely that received from the Son of God, to whom *all power* in heaven and in earth had been given.

Why did he use this language? To convey to those who heard him on that occasion, and to those who afterwards should read it from God's Book, the knowledge of what God, in his wisdom and love, has seen fit to require of all that would

Missionary and Tract Work Department.

"Upon the first day of the week, let every one of you lay by him in store as God hath prospered him, that there be no gatherings when I come."—1 Cor. 16: 2.

"Every man as he purposeth in his heart, so let him give. Not grudgingly or of necessity, for the Lord loveth a cheerful giver."—2 Cor. 9: 7.

HOW MUCH SHALL WE GIVE?

"Every man according to his ability." "Every one as God hath prospered him." "Every man, according as he purposeth in his heart, so let him give." "For if there be first a willing mind, it is accepted according to that a man hath, and not according to that he hath not."—2 Cor. 8: 12.

Organization of Missionary Committee.

DANIEL VANIMAN, Foreman, · · McPherson, Kans.
D. L. MILLER, Treasurer, · · Mt. Morris, Ill.
GALEN B. ROYER, Secretary, · · Mt. Morris, Ill.

Organization of Book and Tract Work.

S. W. HOOVER, Foreman, · · Dayton, Ohio.
S. BOCK, Secretary and Treasurer, · · Dayton, Ohio.

☞ All donations intended for Missionary Work should be sent to GALEN B. ROYER, Mt. Morris, Ill.

☞ All money for Tract Work should be sent to S. BOCK, Dayton, Ohio.

☞ Money may be sent by Money Order, Registered Letter, or Drafts on New York or Chicago. Do not send personal checks, or drafts on interior towns, as it costs at cents to collect them.

☞ Solicitors are requested to faithfully carry out the plan of Annual Meeting, that all our members be solicited to contribute at least twice a year for the Mission and Tract Work of the Church.

☞ Notes for the Endowment Fund can be had by writing to the Secretary of either Work.

THE Friendly Islands to-day contain some 30,000 church members or more, while fifty years ago there was not a native to honor the name of Christ.

THE Samoan Islands have a population of about 30,000, who hold to the Christian faith. In the largest of these Islands there are not fifty families that do not have family worship.

IN New York City alone there are more ministers of the Gospel than in all the land of India, of which we sing in number 265 of the Hymnal. The souls of India are almost five times as many as those of the United States.

THE attention of one who is watching the movements of the times, is again and again called to the results of the labor and self-sacrifice of the missionary in foreign fields. When a heathen man once finds the Light of the world,—Jesus,—he has no other object in life than to serve him.

"HE who makes up his mind that he came into this world to do something, and then goes to work to do it, will be of service to mankind. He is the one who will make his mark among men. It may be a humble mark, but it will be well worth preserving. He will not be forgotten when his life is ended."

Two things are necessary to having a zeal for missions. The first, a knowledge of the Gospel, the second, a knowledge of the fields open for the Gospel plow, and the former is of easier access than the latter. The call of the unsaved is long and loud and continuous. "He that hath ears to hear, let him hear."

LET everyone quickly find his work and enter upon it at once. You preach a sermon—you give a tract—you hand a flower—you sing a song—you give a crutch to a lame man—you teach the Sabbath-school class—you make some cloth for a poor person—you pick a splinter from a child's finger. Do something! There is plenty to do—much of it is right at your door. Commence doing it now and keep at it.

THOUGH nearly all denominations are earnestly working in foreign fields, there is no want of room for preachers of the Gospel. Afghanistan has a population of six millions, and no missionary. Anam has five millions, and only Roman Catholics are yet in the field. Persia has one missionary for every 800,000 souls, while Thibet has one to two millions.

WHEN a little heathen girl, who had given her heart to Jesus the best she knew how, came to die she told her mission teacher that she was going to heaven now and that she would wait just inside the door until he came. That was sufficient inspiration to any one not to become weary in well doing. Christ's words to Peter have never been recalled: " Feed my lambs."

THE secret desire of some of our young people to go into fields to work, which have been heretofore untouched, is a desire worthy the most careful cultivation. There are many fields not only new to our own people but new to any Christianity, and the zeal to occupy these for Christ is only a repetition of that which characterized the life of the great apostle of the Gentiles, an unbounded zeal to work, and care lest he should build on the foundation laid by some other worker.

ROBERT HALDANE, of Scotland, some years ago, sold certain lands of his and gave the entire proceeds to the cause of missions. At the present time the influence is such that travelers, passing by those farms, feel a certain impulse not to speak above a whisper, for they are passing sacred places. As the roar of the ocean tells us of vastness, as the thunder of the clouds tells us of power; as the grave tells us of death, so the former estates of Robert Haldane tell us of one man who considered his possessions not his own but Christ's.

EDUCATION.—ITS RELATION TO PREACHING.

· BY J. S. FLORY.

WE are conscious of the fact that this subject is one on which lengthy articles might be written with profit, but it is not our purpose to enter into an elaborate examination of the subject, but to give a few brief hints as we pass along.

No person can preach without education, for education is to learn about and understand things, but as to whether a preacher must first attain to a high standard of intellectual culture, before he can be a successful minister, is a matter of difference of opinion. In the world's history we find mention of many remarkable men of power in the pulpit, as elsewhere, who knew but little of the higher grades of culture other than a limited knowledge of their mother tongue, coupled with a fervent spirituality. It is not presumable that their lack of intellectual culture was an advantage to them, unless we take the ground that more education would have engendered a spirit of vanity to the suppression of their otherwise successful traits. Wealth, to some men, is a disadvantage, when not properly used, so it is with mind culture, and it is on this line that we propose to pen a few thoughts.

Cultured minds of every kind are coming to the front in our church. There is a marked difference in the diction of our books and periodicals, and in the discourses of our brethren from the sacred stand. The same improvement on this line is very apparent to what it was twenty-five years ago. We should, by no means, look to this improvement with fears or distrust, but try to so appropriate every advantage that good will be the result. Head culture is all right to the man or woman

that has true heart culture, and if it be true that knowledge is power (no one can doubt it), we certainly must admit that a large store of knowledge, used aright, will result in a great power for good.

Of no better way do we know to avoid the dangers, some are so ready to apprehend, which may occur from an educated ministry, as to take warning from others. The popular churches of the day are lamenting, in many places, the lack of spirituality in their people and the stiff, cold, formal labors of their ministers. They tell us culture, in too many sermons, outweighs the subject, and the spirit of the truth is not driven home to the heart; also that in many cases a high-toned, intellectual sermon so mellows down the stern facts of God's Word as to cause it to become to the hearers a tame, ineffectual thing. The intellectual man, if not careful, will insensibly be drawn over on the lovely side of Christianity, use his sympathies in that direction, and neglect the sterner facts of God's dealings with the disobedient.

Culture becomes a hinderance when it eliminates from a subject the depth of spiritual meaning there is in it. Some one has said, "Culture is like fire,—a good servant but a bad master." Like every subject it has its extremes and he who will ignore it, as well as he who idolizes it, will be a failure in the ministry. Use it, as any other good thing, as not abusing it, and it will, by the grace of God, be a thing of usefulness and power. Eloquence, often the child of culture has its place for good when coming from the very depths of a truly regenerate heart. Where learning and eloquence meet to kiss each other, as in the saying of King David, they stir the soul as nothing else can.

The one great lesson for all learned men to "get by heart" is this: "Man looks at the head; God looks at the heart." To please man, let the head belch forth its wisdom but if your wish is to please God, let the streams of the fires of love never cease to flow from the altar of a heart, fully consecrated to God. Remember, ye ministers of his, that an essay on a religious subject is one thing,—a sermon quite another. In tame submission to the knowledge of the subject you may spin out an essay, but when it comes to preaching, if you want to reach the hearts of your hearers, let go the shafts of truth, as sent from a soul, alive with the Holy Spirit. Better pick for a place to hit, than for words to tickle the ear. Better say a few words that will make sinners think of themselves, than to speak an hour, only to make the people praise you.

Lordsburg, Cal.

FOR THE REMISSION OF SINS.

BY H. C. LUCAS.

"Then Peter said unto them, Repent, and be baptized every one of you in the name of Jesus Christ for the remission of sins, and ye shall receive the gift of the Holy Ghost."—Acts 2: 38.

DURING the present century there has been long and loud controversy as to the meaning of these words, used by the apostle on the day of Pentecost. It was an important occasion, and the apostle's use of the language quoted, was backed by the highest authority by which any one could speak, namely that received from the Son of God, to whom *all power* in heaven and in earth had been given.

Why did he use this language? To convey to those who heard him on that occasion, and to those who afterwards should read it from God's Book, the knowledge of what God, in his wisdom and love, has seen fit to require of all that would

The Gospel Messenger,

A Weekly at $1.50 Per Annum.

PUBLISHED BY

The Brethren's Publishing Co.

D. L. MILLER,	. . . .	Editor.
J. H. MOORE,	. . . . . .	Office Editor.
J. B. BRUMBAUGH, } J. G. ROYER, }	. . . .	Associate Editors.
JOSEPH AMICK,	. . . . .	Business Manager.

ADVISORY COMMITTEE.

L. W. Teeter, A. Hutchison, Daniel Hays.

☞Communications for publication should be legibly written with black ink on one side of the paper only. Do not attempt to interline, or to put on one page what ought to occupy two.

☞Anonymous communications will not be published.

☞Do not mix business with articles for publication. Keep your communications on separate sheets from all business.

☞Time is precious. We always have time to attend to business and to answer questions of importance, but please do not subject us to need less answering of letters.

☞The MESSENGER is mailed each week to all subscribers. If the address is correctly entered on our list, the paper must reach the person to whom it is addressed. If you do not get your paper, write us, giving particulars.

☞When changing your address, please give your former as well as your future address in full, so as to avoid delay and misunderstanding.

☞Always remit to the office from which you order your goods, no matter from where you receive them.

☞Do not send personal checks or drafts on interior banks, unless you send with them 25 cents each, to pay for collection.

☞Remittances should be made by Post-office Money Order, Drafts on New York, Philadelphia or Chicago, or Registered Letters, made payable and addressed to "Brethren's Publishing Co., Mount Morris, Ill.," or "Brethren's Publishing Co., Huntingdon, Pa."

☞Entered at the Post-office at Mount Morris, Ill., as second-class matter.

Mount Morris, Ill., · · · · August 16, 1892.

BRO. J. J. EMMERT, of Mt. Carroll, writes us that his health is improving, so he can now attend the regular services. He also reports an interesting Sunday-school.

BY an oversight upon our part, the initials " S. B." were omitted at the bottom of items on the Missionary page of this issue. That part of the paper was printed before the mistake was noticed.

THE church at La Mars, Iowa, seems to be moving along very encouragingly. Five recently united with the church. The little congregation contemplates the building of a new meeting-house next fall.

BRO. D. E. BRUBAKER started to Canada last week, where he may possibly spend some months in the mission field. He will likely stop at Clarence, N. Y., a short time for the purpose of holding a few meetings.

THE State of Maine must be greatly in need of a few good missionaries. It is reported that nearly one-half of the people in the State do not attend church; and that there are nearly 70,000 children not in Sunday-school.

CHRYSOSTOM, the noted Christian orator, once said, "Nothing can be more chilling than the sight of a Christian who makes no effort to save others. Neither poverty, nor humble station, nor bodily infirmity can exempt men from the obligation of this great duty."

BRO. L. W. TEETER sends us the following special announcement to the churches of the Southern District of Indiana: "All the churches wishing to apply for the Annual Meeting of '93, should be prepared to make their applications at the Special District Meeting, previously announced, to be held at Arcadia Sept. 1, that the Committee on Location may decide on the time and route, to visit the several locations offered. This might greatly speed their work."

WE are pleased to see corrections for the Almanac ministerial list coming in so freely. It indicates attention upon the part of our readers. Let everybody examine the list, and report the mistakes. And especially do we suggest that each minister give the list his personal attention.

BRO. J. G. ROYER returned from Plattsburg, Mo., last week. He reports good meetings, the very best of interest to the Word preached, and a large attendance in spite of the warm weather and busy season. Four were received by baptism, with the promise of some returning who had wandered away. He was very much pleased with his trip.

THE Philadelphia *Ledger* says, "Probably the oldest known specimens of recorded language in the world to-day are the inscriptions on the door sockets and brick stamps found at Niffer, by the Babylonian Exploration Expedition of Pennsylvania, which has recently returned. The brick stamps, which are of yellow clay, about four by five inches, and an inch in thickness, bear the name and titles of King Sargon and his son Narim Sin, who lived about 3800 B. C."

PROF. A. H. SAYCE, while exploring in the Valley of the Nile, in the land of Egypt, has made a discovery that may throw some light on that part of Genesis, (14:18) which mentions Melchizedek as "King of Salem." In examining the geographical lists of Rameses II. and III., in reference to localities in Palestine, in both of these he finds the names of Salem or Jerusalem, Carmel of Judah, etc. This means that in the time of Moses, when Rameses III. was king, "Salem" and "Jerusalem" were names applied to the same place. We are thus enabled to understand that Melchizedek, in the days of Abraham, was King of Salem, which afterwards became known as Jerusalem. The same list mentions the Dead Sea under the name of "The Lake of Bethpana."

FOR several years our Annual Conference has taken some very decided steps against the use of tobacco, especially by our officials. A few have probably thought the Conference a little too radical, but further developments are likely to demonstrate the wisdom of the course pursued thus far. Recently the United States Senate appointed a committee to investigate one phase of the tobacco habit. Here is what the *Independent* has to say concerning the report of that committee:

"There is a Senate Committee on Epidemic Diseases, and that Committee had before it last week an unusual topic—that of cigarette smoking, and presented a report to the effect that the use of tobacco in any form is injurious to the physical constitution of man, and that cigarette smoking is more injurious, especially to youths, than the use of tobacco in any other form. The Committee says that Congress has no constitutional power to prohibit the manufacture or sale of cigarettes in the States, but express the hope that Congress will prohibit the importation from foreign countries of cigarettes and their manufacture and sale in the District of Columbia and in the Territories. Of course we do not expect any such bill to pass; in fact the Committee did not present one. But it is an expression of sound opinion, and legislature by States or municipalities would do some good. We notice that the proposition is downright prohibition; but we believe in prohibition."

When a habit is so alarming, in the evil consequences that may result from it, as to induce a secular law-making body to investigate and denounce it, certainly the church cannot, and ought not, content herself by merely winking at the evil. It is high time that she should even command all her incoming officers to abstain from its use, and most earnestly persuade others to become ensamples to the flock, and then unitedly labor to free the entire membership from this bodily, if not soul and mind polluting habit.

ONE of our exchanges says: "When you get a scolding letter, there are three courses open to you: You may answer it in the same tone, or you may give it a polite and Christian reply, or you may pitch it into the fire. The first of these courses is always wrong. Whether it is better to adopt the second or the third will depend on circumstances. Very frequently absolute silence will prove to be wise." We are thankful that we do not receive many scolding letters. We have a little pigeon-hole in which to keep them, and it is not yet one-fourth full. Kind letters we try to remember, but scolding ones we like to forget.

FROM a communication in this issue it will be observed that Bro. John Olsson has been doing some very successful missionary work beyond the Arctic Circle. We have on the hook another article from him, in which he gives an account of the organization of a church, and the holding of a love-feast in the land of "Midnight Sun." To us it would probably seem a little out of place to participate in the Lord's Supper in broad day-light; but in countries where nights are unknown during the summer months, such must be the practice of those who carry out the ordinances of the Lord's house. We hope to hear more of this little band of members who now occupy the extreme northern limits of our Brotherhood. Soon the long, cold winter will be upon them where, for months, the sun will hardly be seen. May the Lord bless and prosper them!

YEARS ago we became acquainted with the wives of two evangelists. They were both women of intelligence and piety. With their husbands they traveled a great deal, and spent much time with other families. One sister made herself generally useful where she chanced to stop. She did not disdain to aid the care-worn wife with her home work. She did this in order to relieve her sister as much as possible, and afford opportunities for conversations on religious subjects. If she had leisure, she read or entertained the little ones with religious stories and songs. The other sister never turned her hand to lighten the burden of anyone. She spent her time at crocheting or fancy needle work. She read little, but talked a good deal to the older children of the family about the latest fashion plates, or the last story in the popular magazines. Which of the two sisters was the model wife for the evangelist? We need not tell you, you know. All ministers' wives may read and ponder this story to good advantage.

ALL attempts to find the grave of Moses, the great Jewish law-giver, have proved a failure. Otherwise a grand monument would probably mark the spot. Nevertheless Albany, N. Y., says the Chicago *Journal*, "is soon to be adorned with a statue of Moses, showing him, with outstretched hands, summoning the wanderers in the wilderness of Judea to drink from the stream that flowed from the rock of Horeb, after he had struck it with his rod. The statue is the gift of the late Henry L. King, son of Rufus King, who bequeathed $350,000 for the purpose. This is the proper country in which to erect a statue to the great Jewish law-giver. It has proved to be the Promised Land of the Children of Israel. Here they are free to cherish the religion of their fathers; here prejudice does not keep them from gaining political power or social position; here prejudice is more likely to be for than against them. A city in America and not one in Palestine is the place for a statue of Moses." Moses, however, built his own monument when he wrote the first five books of the Bible. This is a monument more lasting than marble and of more value than the gold mines of Ophir.

The Gospel Messenger,

A Weekly at $1.50 Per Annum.

PUBLISHED BY

The Brethren's Publishing Co.

D. L. MILLER, • • • • • • • • • Editor.

J. H. MOORE, • • • • • • Office Editor.

J. B. BRUMBAUGH, | • • • Associate Editors.
J. G. ROYER, |

JOSEPH AMICK, • • • • • Business Manager.

ADVISORY COMMITTEE.

L. W. Teeter, A. Hutchison, Daniel Hays.

☞ Communications for publication should be legibly written with black ink on one side of the paper only. Do not attempt to interline, or to put on one page what ought to occupy two.

☞ Anonymous communications will not be published.

☞ Do not mix business with articles for publication. Keep your communications on separate sheets from all business.

☞ Time is precious. We always have time to attend to business and to answer questions of importance, but please do not subject us to need less answering of letters.

☞ The MESSENGER is mailed each week to all subscribers. If the address is collectly entered on our list, the paper must reach the person to whom it is addressed. If you do not get your paper, write us, giving particulars.

☞ When changing your address, please give your former as well as your future address in full, so as to avoid delay and misunderstanding.

☞ Always remit to the office from which you order your goods, no matter from which you receive them.

☞ Do not send personal checks or drafts on interior banks, unless you send with them 25 cents each, to pay for collection.

☞ Remittances should be made by Post-office Money Order, Drafts on New York, Philadelphia or Chicago, or Registered Letters, made payable and addressed to "Brethren's Publishing Co., Mount Morris, Ill." or "Brethren's Publishing Co., Huntingdon, Pa."

☞ Entered at the Post-office at Mount Morris, Ill., as second-class matter.

Mount Morris, Ill., • • • • August 16, 1892

BRO. J. J. EMMERT, of Mt. Carroll, writes us that his health is improving, so he can now attend the regular services. He also reports an interesting Sunday-school.

BY an oversight upon our part, the initials "S. B." were omitted at the bottom of items on the Missionary page of this issue. That part of the paper was printed before the mistake was noticed.

THE church at La Mars, Iowa, seems to be moving along very encouragingly. Five recently united with the church. The little congregation contemplates the building of a new meeting-house next fall.

BRO. D. E. BRUBAKER started to Canada last week, where he may possibly spend some months in the mission field. He will likely stop at Clarence, N. Y., a short time for the purpose of holding a few meetings.

THE State of Maine must be greatly in need of a few good missionaries. It is reported that nearly one-half of the people in the State do not attend church; and that there are nearly 70,000 children not in Sunday-school.

CHRYSOSTOM, the noted Christian orator, once said, "Nothing can be more chilling than the sight of a Christian who makes no effort to save others. Neither poverty, nor humble station, nor bodily infirmity can exempt men from the obligation of this great duty."

BRO. L. W. TEETER sends us the following special announcement to the churches of the Southern District of Indiana: "All the churches wishing to apply for the Annual Meeting of '93 should be prepared to make their applications at the Special District Meeting, previously announced, to be held at Arcadia Sept. 1, that the Committee on Location may decide on the time and route, to visit the several locations offered. This might greatly speed their work."

WE are pleased to see corrections for the Almanac ministerial list coming in so freely. It indicates attention upon the part of our readers. Let everybody examine the list, and report the mistakes. And especially do we suggest that each minister give the list his personal attention.

BRO. J. G. ROYER returned from Plattsburg, Mo., last week. He reports good meetings, the very best of interest to the Word preached, and a large attendance in spite of the warm weather and busy season. Four were received by baptism, with the promise of some returning who had wandered away. He was very much pleased with his trip.

THE Philadelphia Ledger says, "Probably the oldest known specimens of recorded language in the world to-day are the inscriptions on the door sockets and brick stamps found at Niffer, by the Babylonian Exploration Expedition of Pennsylvania, which has recently returned. The brick stamps, which are of yellow clay, about four by five inches, and an inch in thickness, bear the name and titles of King Sargon and his son Narim Sin, who lived about 3800 B. C."

PROF. A. H. SAYCE, while exploring in the Valley of the Nile, in the land of Egypt, has made a discovery that may throw some light on that part of Genesis, (14:18) which mentions Melchizedek as "King of Salem." In examining the geographical lists of Rameses II. and III., in reference to localities in Palestine, in both of these he finds the names of Salem or Jerusalem, Carmel of Judah, etc. This means that in the time of Moses, when Rameses III. was king, "Salem" and "Jerusalem" were names applied to the same place. We are thus enabled to understand that Melchizedek, in the days of Abraham, was King of Salem, which afterwards became known as Jerusalem. The same list mentions the Dead Sea under the name of "The Lake of Bethpana."

FOR several years our Annual Conference has taken some very decided steps against the use of tobacco, especially by our officials. A few have probably thought the Conference a little too radical, but further developments are likely to demonstrate the wisdom of the course pursued thus far. Recently the United States Senate appointed a committee to investigate one phase of the tobacco habit. Here is what the Independent has to say concerning the report of that committee:

"There is a Senate Committee on Epidemic Diseases, and that Committee had before it last week an unusual topic—that of cigarette smoking, and presented a report to the effect that the use of tobacco in any form is injurious to the physical constitution of man, and that cigarette smoking is more injurious, especially to youths, than the use of tobacco in any other form. The Committee says that Congress has no constitutional power to prohibit the manufacture or sale of cigarettes in the States, but express the hope that Congress will prohibit the importation from foreign countries of cigarettes and their manufacture and sale in the District of Columbia and in the Territories. Of course we do not expect any such bill to pass; in fact the Committee did not present one. But it is an expression of sound opinion, and legislature by States or municipalities would do some good. We notice that the proposition is downright prohibition; but we believe in prohibition."

When a habit is so alarming, in the evil consequences that may result from it, as to induce a secular law-making body to investigate and denounce it, certainly the church cannot, and ought not, content herself by merely winking at the evil. It is high time that she should even command all her incoming officers to abstain from its use, and most earnestly persuade others to become examples to the flock, and then unitedly labor to free the entire membership from this bodily, if not soul and mind polluting habit.

ONE of our exchanges says: "When you get a scolding letter, there are three courses open to you: You may answer it in the same tone, or you may give it a polite and Christian reply, or you may pitch it into the fire. The first of these courses is always wrong. Whether it is better to adopt the second or the third will depend on circumstances. Very frequently absolute silence will prove to be wise." We are thankful that we do not receive many scolding letters. We have a little pigeon-hole in which to keep them, and it is not yet one-fourth full. Kind letters we try to remember, but scolding ones we like to forget.

FROM a communication in this issue it will be observed that Bro. John Olsson has been doing some very successful missionary work beyond the Arctic Circle. We have on the hook another article from him, in which he gives an account of the organization of a church, and the holding of a love-feast in the land of "Midnight Sun." To us it would probably seem a little out of place to participate in the Lord's Supper in broad day-light; but in countries where nights are unknown during the summer months, such must be the practice of those who carry out the ordinances of the Lord's house. We hope to hear more of this little band of members who now occupy the extreme northern limits of our Brotherhood. Soon the long, cold winter will be upon them where, for months, the sun will hardly be seen. May the Lord bless and prosper them!

YEARS ago we became acquainted with the wives of two evangelists. They were both women of intelligence and piety. With their husbands they traveled a great deal, and spent much time with other families. One sister made herself generally useful where she chanced to stop. She did not disdain to aid the care-worn wife with her house work. She did this in order to relieve her sister as much as possible, and afford opportunities for conversations on religious subjects. If she had leisure, she read or entertained the little ones with religious stories and songs. The other sister never turned her hand to lighten the burden of anyone. She spent her time at crocheting or fancy needle work. She read little, but talked a good deal to the older children of the family about the latest fashion plates, or the last story in the popular magazines. Which of the two sisters was the model wife for the evangelist? We need not tell, you know. All ministers' wives may read and ponder this story to good advantage.

ALL attempts to find the grave of Moses, the great Jewish law-giver, have proved a failure. Otherwise a grand monument would probably mark the spot. Nevertheless Albany, N. Y., says the Chicago Journal, "is soon to be adorned with a statue of Moses, showing him, with outstretched hands, summoning the wanderers in the wilderness of Judea to drink from the stream that flowed from the rock of Horeb, after he had struck it with his rod. The statue is the gift of the late Henry L. King, son of Rufus King, who bequeathed $350,000 for the purpose. This is the proper country in which to erect a statue to the great Jewish law-giver. It has proved to be the Promised Land of the Children of Israel. Here they are free to cherish the religion of their fathers; here prejudice does not keep them from gaining political power or social position; here prejudice is more likely to be for than against them. A city in America and not one in Palestine is the place for a statue of Moses." Moses, however, built his own monument when he wrote the first five books of the Bible. This is a monument more lasting than marble and of more value than the gold mines of Ophir.

"2. Closely akin to this thought is the same apostle's statement, that 'the Holy Spirit himself beareth witness with our spirit that we are the children of God.' (Rom. 8: 16.) Not many of us, I apprehend, are willing to abide by a once popular interpretation of this passage, which limited the testimony of the Divine Spirit to the revelation of the terms of salvation, and the testimony of our spirits to the fact that we had complied with these terms. This interpretation may be right enough as far as it goes, but it does not strike deep enough to reach the full meaning of the apostle's language. After all, the highest evidence we can have of its right relation with God, is that which is borne to its own consciousness by both the divine and human spirits, that this new life which stirs within it is of God. There is that in our human nature which apprehends the divine, and the adaptation of Christ's religion to our needs, and its ability to satisfy the deepest longings of the human heart, produce the highest degree of certitude that it is divine, and that the presence of its effects within the sphere of our consciousness is the true mark of sonship. Whoso, by the grace of God, attains to this union with him, in Christ, through the Spirit, is no more tossed about by the shifting winds of doctrine, or by the changing currents of the latest criticism, but rests securely in that peace which is the correlation of the human with the divine.

"3. It is through the Spirit that we are freed from the yoke of legalism. 'But if ye are led by the Spirit, ye are not under the law.' Gal. 5: 18. 'The letter killeth, but the Spirit giveth life.' 2 Cor. 3: 6. 'Where the Spirit of the Lord is, there is liberty.' 2 Cor. 3: 17. Whether the condition of things in the early Church, which called out these statements of Paul, has anything parallel in the state of the Church to-day, let the wise and thoughtful reader judge. Let such also consider whether there be any relation between that bondage to the letter, which has not infrequently destroyed the life of inspired teaching and perverted its aim, and a neglect to give proper emphasis to the Scriptural doctrine of the Holy Spirit in his relation to the Christian.

"4. We are 'sealed,' or marked by the Holy Spirit, who is also the pledge to us of our future glorification. Paul assured the Corinthian Christians that it was God who had 'established' them in Christ and 'anointed' them, 'who also sealed us and gave us the earnest of the Spirit in our hearts.' A seal anciently, as now, was an official mark put upon any document to authenticate it. The Christian has a mark of character put upon him by the Holy Spirit, which is at once a true sign to the world of his discipleship, and an 'earnest' or pledge to him of complete glorification in due time. So also Paul to the Ephesians (1: 13, 14): 'Ye were sealed with the Holy Spirit of promise which is an earnest of our inheritance, unto the redemption of God's own possession, unto the praise of his glory.' What language could convey more clearly the thought that it is the Divine Spirit dwelling in the soul of the believer that stamps it with the divine likeness, and gives to him the assurance of the final and perfect redemption?

"5. Again, Christians are 'strengthened with power through his Spirit in the inward man.' (Eph. 3: 16). Thus strengthened they become 'rooted and grounded in love,' and 'strong to apprehend with all the saints what is the breadth, and length, and height, and depth, and to know the love of God which passes knowledge,' and may be 'filled unto all the fullness of God.' Here are indicated possibilities of Christian growth which amaze us, but the strength for such high achievement comes from the Spirit of God.

"6. From Paul's exhortation to the Ephesian saints, to 'keep the unity of the Spirit in the bond of peace,' we are justified in concluding that the Holy Spirit is the author of unity in the Church, and that it is only as we are guided by the Spirit, and bring forth the fruits thereof in our lives, that we can either maintain unity among ourselves, or promote it among others. In view of the prominence we have given to the plea of Christian unity, it would follow that we ought to give equal prominence to the mission and power of the Holy Spirit in Christian lives. It is more than probable that we have given an undue proportion of emphasis to the doctrinal basis of unity, to the neglect of what is even more vital,—the possession of the Spirit.

"7. By so much as prayer is of vital importance to Christian life and growth, ought we to value the aid of the Holy Spirit, for 'the Spirit helpeth our infirmities; for we know not what we should pray for as we ought; but the Spirit himself maketh intercession for us with groanings which cannot be uttered.' (Rom. 8: 26). Alas! how fruitless many of our prayers seem to be. They are only potent as they are born of the Spirit, who helpeth our infirmities. How thankful we should be that the Holy Spirit in his intercession for us interprets our inarticulate groaning! Prayerlessness is a sure sign of the absence of the Divine Spirit. Christ possessed the Spirit without measure, and behold how he prayed! It was while praying that he was transfigured in the presence of his disciples (Luke 9: 29). It is only through prayer that we are transfigured into his likeness.

"8. The supreme value of the gift of the Holy Spirit is shown by the fruit of the Spirit, which is declared to be, 'Love, joy, peace, long-suffering, kindness, goodness, faithfulness, meekness, temperance.' Gal. 5: 22, 23. What a cluster of heavenly graces! How they beautify character! What dignity and glory they give to human life! No wonder our Lord spoke of the gift of the Holy Spirit as the sum of all spiritual blessings: 'If ye, then, being evil,' said he, 'know how to give good gifts unto your children, how much more shall your Heavenly Father give the Holy Spirit to them that ask him.' (Luke 11: 13). In view of the infinite blessings which flow to the soul through the possession of the Holy Spirit, how precious is this promise of Christ!

"Who can estimate the possibilities in spiritual growth, in moral beauty, and in high achievement for human good, of a soul that opens up all its avenues to the influx of the Divine Spirit, and whose whole being becomes instinct and luminous with the life of God! And yet such sublime possibilities are open to every Christian through his relation to the Holy Spirit."

In our next we hope to consider more carefully the dispensation of the Spirit, a subject to which we have incidentally alluded in these articles.

J. H. M.

QUERISTS' DEPARTMENT.

In a conversation with an old elder some years ago, on the subject of antitypes, the subject of circumcision came up. He contended that, as a type, it referred to Christian baptism. I have always understood it to refer to the cleansing of the heart,—circumcise the foreskin of your heart. Please give us the antitype of circumcision and oblige. HIRAM BERKMAN.

CIRCUMCISION is not a type of Christian baptism in any sense. It was a Jewish rite, first enjoined upon Abraham, and afterwards upon all male descendants of Jewish families. The only prerequisites were that the child should be eight days old, and of Jewish descent, but no faith or confession, upon the part of the child, was, or could be, required. Circumcision was a seal, or sign, of the covenant made with Abraham, in

which God gave to him and his seed the promised land. The rite was limited to the males, thus applying to only a part of the race. Baptism is for both sexes, and for that reason cannot be typified by circumcision. By virtue of Christ's death upon the cross the Adamic sin has been atoned for, and all children now born into the world enter life in a saved state, and remain in that state until, by transfiguration, they depart from it. They then have an opportunity of repenting and entering through the door of baptism into the church.

This door is for both sexes. To the Jews the natural birth and not circumcision was the door into the Jewish Church. The natural birth is now the door into the saved state which all children enter who come into the world, but the spiritual birth is the door into the church militant. Each state or condition is entered by a birth, either natural or spiritual. Circumcision typifies nothing in the way of a Christian ordinance, rite or ceremony. Hence, among the sacraments, it has no antitype in the Christian system. Stephen, in his memorial address at Jerusalem, applies it, in a figure, to the heart and ears (Acts 7: 51), but nowhere is it applied to a Christian sacrament.

Why is the Lord's Prayer, as given by Matthew, the one almost universally adopted, or in practice, while Luke also gives it? DAVID W. CRIST.

Matthew gives the Lord's Prayer in full, while Luke gives it only in part. That is the reason for using it as given by Matthew.

What do we understand by Christ going into the temple and driving out those that sold and bought, and upset the tables? How shall we apply it now? J. SNAVELY, Sen.

An account of this circumstance may be found in Matt. 21: 12, 13, where it says: "And Jesus went into the temple of God, and cast out all them that sold and bought in the temple, and overthrew the tables of the money-changers, and the seats of them that sold doves, and said unto them, It is written, My house shall be called the house of prayer; but ye have made it a den of thieves."

By this we are to understand that the house of God is a house of prayer, a consecrated building, set apart for religious services, and should not be desecrated by church festivals, church fairs, church shows and entertainment parties, etc., of a semi-religious nature. Those who turn the house of God over to amusement, as is a very common practice of to-day, certainly violate the spirit as well as the letter of this lesson. We can keep these things out of our own places of worship, but have no right to enter other churches for that purpose as the Savior entered the temple. But the temple was his Father's temple, and Jesus had a right to cleanse it. The moral to us, as stated above, is in the 13th verse, which certainly requires us to regard God's house as the house of prayer.

What about an elder, or a minister, who moves away from a church where he is so much needed, and leaves the church almost, or entirely, without help in the ministry, he having no just cause for the move? T. H. H.

That is a privilege that all ministers enjoy, for which they are alone responsible to God, who sees the heart and will know best how to judge. Such moves may not always seem right, and possibly some of them are not advisable, but who knows by what power the minister is induced to change location! And who can tell what may not result from such changes! We, however, think it very unwise for a minister to move from a church where his labors are greatly needed and

"2. Closely akin to this thought is the same apostle's statement, that 'the Holy Spirit himself beareth witness with our spirit that we are the children of God.' (Rom. 8: 16.) Not many of us, I apprehend, are willing to abide by a once popular interpretation of this passage, which limited the testimony of the Divine Spirit to the revelation of the terms of salvation, and the testimony of our spirits to the fact that we had complied with these terms. This interpretation may be right enough as far as it goes, but it does not strike deep enough to reach the full meaning of the apostle's language. After all, the highest evidence the soul can have of its right relation with God, is that which is borne to its own consciousness by both the divine and human spirits, that this new life which stirs within it is of God. There is that in our human nature which apprehends the divine, and the adaptation of Christ's religion to our needs, and its ability to satisfy the deepest longings of the human heart, produce the highest degree of certitude that it is divine, and that the presence of its effects within the sphere of our consciousness is the true mark of sonship. Whoso, by the grace of God, attains to this union with him, in Christ, through the Spirit, is no more tossed about by the shifting winds of doctrine, or by the changing currents of the latest criticism, but rests securely in that peace which is the correlation of the human with the divine.

"3. It is through the Spirit that we are freed from the yoke of legalism. 'But if ye are led by the Spirit, ye are not under the law.' Gal. 5: 18. 'The letter killeth, but the Spirit giveth life.' 2 Cor. 3: 6. 'Where the Spirit of the Lord is, there is liberty.' 2 Cor. 3: 17. Whether the condition of things in the early Church, which called out these statements of Paul, has anything parallel in the state of the Church to-day, let the wise and thoughtful reader judge. Let such also consider whether there be any relation between that bondage to the letter, which has not infrequently destroyed the life of inspired teaching and perverted its aim, and a neglect to give proper emphasis to the Scriptural doctrine of the Holy Spirit in his relation to the Christian.

"4. We are 'sealed,' or marked by the Holy Spirit, who is also the pledge to us of our future glorification. Paul assured the Corinthian Christians that it was God who had 'established' them in Christ and 'anointed' them, 'who also sealed us and gave us the earnest of the Spirit in our hearts.' A seal anciently, as now, was an official mark put upon any document to authenticate it. The Christian has a mark of character put upon him by the Holy Spirit, which is at once a true sign to the world of his discipleship, and an 'earnest' or pledge to him of complete glorification in due time. So also Paul to the Ephesians (1: 13, 14): 'Ye were sealed with the Holy Spirit of promise which is an earnest of our inheritance, unto the redemption of God's own possession, unto the praise of his glory.' What language could convey more clearly the thought that it is the Divine Spirit dwelling in the soul of the believer that stamps it with the divine likeness, and gives to him the assurance of the final and perfect redemption?

"5. Again, Christians are 'strengthened with power through his Spirit in the inward man.' (Eph. 3: 16). Thus strengthened they become 'rooted and grounded in love,' and 'strong to apprehend with all the saints what is the breadth, and length, and height, and depth, and to know the love of God which passes knowledge,' and may be 'filled unto all the fullness of God.' Here are indicated possibilities of Christian growth which amaze us, but the strength for such high achievement comes from the Spirit of God.

"6. From Paul's exhortation to the Ephesian saints, to 'keep the unity of the Spirit in the bond of peace,' we are justified in concluding that the Holy Spirit is the author of unity in the Church, and that it is only as we are guided by the Spirit, and bring forth the fruits thereof in our lives, that we can either maintain unity among ourselves, or promote it among others. In view of the prominence we have given to the plea of Christian unity, it would follow that we ought to give equal prominence to the mission and power of the Holy Spirit in Christian lives. It is more than probable that we have given an undue proportion of emphasis to the doctrinal basis of unity, to the neglect of what is even more vital,—the possession of the Spirit.

"7. By so much as prayer is of vital importance to Christian life and growth, ought we to value the aid of the Holy Spirit, for 'the Spirit helpeth our infirmities; for we know not what we should pray for as we ought; but the Spirit himself maketh intercession for us with groanings which cannot be uttered.' (Rom. 8: 26) Alas! how fruitless many of our prayers seem to be. They are only potent as they are born of the Spirit, who helpeth our infirmities. How thankful we should be that the Holy Spirit in his intercession for us interprets our inarticulate groaning! Prayerlessness is a sure sign of the absence of the Divine Spirit. Christ possessed the Spirit without measure, and behold how he prayed! It was while praying that he was transfigured in the presence of his disciples (Luke 9: 29). It is only through prayer that we are transfigured into his likeness.

"8. The supreme value of the gift of the Holy Spirit is shown by the fruit of the Spirit, which is declared to be, 'Love, joy, peace, long-suffering, kindness, goodness, faithfulness, meekness, temperance.' Gal. 5: 22, 23. What a cluster of heavenly graces! How they beautify character! What dignity and glory they give to human life! No wonder our Lord spoke of the gift of the Holy Spirit as the sum of all spiritual blessings: 'If ye, then, being evil,' said he, 'know how to give good gifts unto your children, how much more shall your Heavenly Father give the Holy Spirit to them that ask him.' (Luke 11: 13). In view of the infinite blessings which flow to the soul through the possession of the Holy Spirit, how precious is this promise of Christ!

"Who can estimate the possibilities in spiritual growth, in moral beauty, and in high achievement for human good, of a soul that opens up all its avenues to the influx of the Divine Spirit, and whose whole being becomes instinct and luminous with the life of God! And yet such sublime possibilities are open to every Christian through his surrender to the Holy Spirit."

In our next we hope to consider more carefully the dispensation of the Spirit, a subject to which we have incidentally alluded in these articles.   J. H. M.

QUERISTS' DEPARTMENT.

In a conversation with an old elder some years ago, on the subject of antitypes, the subject of circumcision came up. He contended that, as a type, it referred to Christian baptism. I have always understood it to refer to the cleansing of the heart,—circumcise the foreskin of your heart. Please give us the antitype of circumcision and oblige. HIRAM BERKMAN.

CIRCUMCISION is not a type of Christian baptism in any sense. It was a Jewish rite, first enjoined upon Abraham, and afterwards upon all male descendants of Jewish families. The only prerequisites were that the child should be eight days old, and of Jewish descent, but no faith or confession, upon the part of the child, was, or could be, required. Circumcision was a seal, or sign, of the covenant made with Abraham, in which God gave to him and his seed the promised land. The rite was limited to the males, thus applying to only a part of the race. Baptism is for both sexes, and for that reason cannot be typified by circumcision. By virtue of Christ's death upon the cross the Adamic sin has been atoned for, and all children now born into the world enter life in a saved state, and remain in that state until, by transgression, they depart from it. They then have an opportunity of repenting and entering through the door of baptism into the church.

This door is for both sexes. To the Jews the natural birth and not circumcision was the door into the Jewish Church. The natural birth is now the door into the saved state which all children enter who come into the world, but the spiritual birth is the door into the church militant. Each state or condition is entered by a birth, either natural or spiritual. Circumcision typifies nothing in the way of a Christian ordinance, rite or ceremony. Hence, among the sacraments, it has no antitype in the Christian system. Stephen, in his memorial address at Jerusalem, applies it, in a figure, to the heart and ears (Acts 7; 51), but nowhere is it applied to a Christian sacrament.

Why is the Lord's Prayer, as given by Matthew, the one almost universally adopted, or in practice, while Luke also gives it?   DAVID W. CRIST.

Matthew gives the Lord's Prayer in full, while Luke gives it only in part. That is the reason for using it as given by Matthew.

What do we understand by Christ going into the temple and driving out those that sold and bought, and upset the tables? How shall we apply it now?   J. SNAVELY, SR.

An account of this circumstance may be found in Matt. 21: 12, 13, where it says: "And Jesus went into the temple of God, and cast out all them that sold and bought in the temple, and overthrew the tables of the money-changers, and the seats of them that sold doves, and said unto them, It is written, My house shall be called the house of prayer; but ye have made it a den of thieves."

By this we are to understand that the house of God is a house of prayer, a consecrated building, set apart for religious services, and should not be desecrated by church festivals, church fairs, church shows and entertainment parties, etc., of a semi-religious nature. Those who turn the house of God over to amusement, as is a very common practice of to-day, certainly violate the spirit as well as the letter of this lesson. We can keep these things out of our own places of worship, but have no right to enter other churches for that purpose as the Savior entered the temple. But the temple was his Father's temple, and Jesus had a right to cleanse it. The moral to us, as stated above, is in the 13th verse, which certainly requires us to regard God's house as the house of prayer.

What about an elder, or a minister, who moves away from a church where he is so much needed, and leaves the church almost, or entirely, without help in the ministry, he having no just cause for the move?   T. H. H.

That is a privilege that all ministers enjoy, for which they are alone responsible to God, who sees the heart and will know best how to judge. Such moves may not always seem right, and possibly some of them are not advisable, but who knows by what power the minister is induced to change location! And who can tell what may not result from such changes! We, however, think it very unwise for a minister to move from a church where his labors are greatly needed and

the final tribunal, when there can be no mistake in the judgment.　B. F. MOOMAW.

Bonsack's, Va.

A Trip to Lulea and the Midnight Sun Country in Northern Sweden.

PART ONE.

BY order of the Missionary Committee, I left my home June 10, for Lulea, to assist Eld. Hans Olsson, in the mission work. The evening before I left, three sisters were baptized at Wanneberga. All in our church were happy in Jesus when I left them. Good Pentecost meetings have been held in Hör and Wanneberga, and we had a good love-feast at my home, and a goodly number witnessed the sacred order.

On the day above mentioned, I left my home at 5 o'clock P. M., for Stockholm. This place I reached at 7 the next morning. A brother and a sister in the flesh met me at the depot, and they were much interested in showing me some of the sights of the city. Stockholm is, as you possibly know, the capital of Sweden, and is a very fine city, situated as it is, on many isles. Many small steam-boats carry the passengers from one street to another, across the rivers, which flow from Lake Malaren to the Baltic Sea.

Among the places of interest I visited, was the royal palace which is very fine. The rooms are arrayed in tapestry of gold, silks and velvets, and furnished in a very expensive manner, at a cost of millions of *kroners*. I could not help thinking of the heavenly mansions, in the city above, with the golden streets and pearly gates, all given us free through our Savior, Jesus Christ.

At 1 o'clock A. M., June 13, the large steamer "Pitea" left Stockholm for Lulea. We had a very nice voyage all the time. At 9 o'clock P. M., we reached Lundsvall, a new, fine town, 280 miles from Stockholm. The old town was totally burned in 1889.

We left Lundsvall at 1 o'clock A. M., June 14, and reached Lulea at 7 P. M., June 15. Lulea is about 400 miles north of Lundsvall. At present I am about 1,000 miles from my home.

Here we have, at present, no night at all. The sun goes down at 11 P. M., and rises at 12: 30 A. M. Lulea is a town with about 8,000 inhabitants. The town is mostly newly-built, with fine houses, all of them constructed of wood. In 1887, ninety-five houses in the old town were totally burned down.

Since I came here, we have had meetings every evening at 9 P. M., and twice each Sunday. The people here are very hard,—they don't attend meetings of this kind very much. We had large hand-bills printed and posted up every-where on the house walls. By them we told the people, that we one evening intended to preach about baptism; another, about feet-washing, etc. As a result, we had a fair attendance at the meetings. The first members were baptized here June 6, by Bro. H. Olsson,—a brother and a sister. The sister had waited for baptism during the latter part of the winter, because the ice, in all the lakes here is, during the winter, from four to five feet thick. The thermometer ranges between thirty and forty degrees below zero almost the whole winter. June 19 we had the joy of baptizing another sister here, and we hope some will come during this summer.

June 28 we took the northernmost train in the world for Gellivara, 120 miles from Lulea, partly to hold some meetings, which we were invited to hold, and partly to see the midnight sun, which is to be seen from the high mountain, "Dundret," in about six weeks. In Gellivara we held seven

---

good meetings. Many people came to hear,—both Swedes and Lapps had a chance to hear the true Gospel, and many tracts were given to them.

At 9 o'clock P. M., June 24, we commenced climbing up to the top of the above-named mountain, which we reached after two hours' walking. The mountain is about 3,000 feet above the sea. At 12 o'clock in the night, the sun was standing very high above the horizon. In the far West, 100 miles away, we could see the snow-covered mountain range, which separates Sweden and Norway. It was a beautiful sight, indeed. Although it was June 24, much snow was still lying on the mountain. In some places the snow came up to our knees.　JOHN OLSSON.

Lulea, Sweden, July 7.

(To be continued.)

From Le Mars, Iowa.

OUR dear brother, Wm. C. Hipes, came and preached for us last March, and returned again June 20. He has been preaching more or less for us until the present date, and baptized five. We believe others are near the kingdom. We believe this to be the way to do mission work,—stay at one place as long as circumstances require. Bro. Hipes has worked faithfully, and the Lord has blessed his labors in this part of God's heritage. Oh how I wish we had more like him in the field! His wife, sister Rebekah, usually travels with him, and surely is a great help to him in his labors of love. The brethren and sisters met with us at our place July 2, to commemorate the death and suffering of our Blessed Master. It was the first love-feast, held in these parts, and was a feast indeed, to our hungry souls, and as such will long be remembered. Brethren Hipes and Nicodemus were the ministers present. They did not shun to warn sinners, and to encourage and uphold the saints. We also had an Independence Day service. Bro. Hipes preached two sermons, showing how our world is falling into unbelief as people did in the days of Noah.

Our neighbors and friends were much pleased. Some said that it was the most pleasant "Fourth of July," they had ever spent, and decided that it must be kept up in the future. We believe this is the way to spend that day. Elders J. W. Trostle and Wm. Thomas were with us July 30, and organized our little band of eleven into a church, namely the Pleasant Prairie church. We hope we may be recognized in heaven, as well as on earth, by that name, for if we live pleasantly together here, surely we can be recognized by the way we live. The brethren remained over Sunday, and gave us much encouragement by their hearty admonitions. Now, that we have bright prospects before us, we heartily invite Brethren to come and settle here, and help us in this great work. We chose Bro. J. W. Trostle to take the oversight of our little church. We have one minister, and one deacon, but have room for many more, for our prairie is broad and uncultivated spiritually, though thickly populated.

We contemplate building a church-house in the near future, and hope to have it finished this fall. Any wishing to know more of our country, will do well to correspond with the writer. He will gladly answer any questions to inquirers by enclosing a stamp.　D. A. MILLER.

From Marlow, Indian Territory.

I LEFT my home June 1, for the Annual Meeting. After the Meeting was over, I, in company with several other members and friends, took the train for the Greene church, Iowa, where I attended the love-feast.

June 13, in company with Bro. John Moore and his son, Bro. Oscar Moore, we took the train for their home in Northern Minnesota. At that point several other members,—seven in all,—are living. We had a few meetings with them and tried to encourage them in the good work, but there is not very much encouragement for building up the cause there.

July 1 I boarded the train for Greene, where I remained one week. I had meetings through the week, in the stone church, each evening until Saturday, when, in company with several of the members, we went to the Franklin County church to attend their love-feast, which occurred July 9, and 10. It was a good meeting. Several ministers were present and took part in the exercises. Eld. Stephen Johnson, of Garrison, Iowa, officiated. Bro. W. F. Ikenberry was advanced to the second degree of the ministry. I remained with them and held a few meetings. Upon returning to Greene, the latter part of the week, I met Wm. Ikenberry, of Waterloo, who is working in the interest of the missionary cause. On Sunday, July 17, there were two appointments, one at the meeting-house, the other out in the country. I, with Bro. Harvey Eikenberry, one of the ministers, and a few others, attended the latter. Bro. Wm. Ikenberry preached in the meeting-house in town. In the afternoon, at 3:30, I gave them my last talk. Then came the sad farewell. It was in that congregation that I united with the church, and was put to the ministry.

July 18 at 1:15 A. M., I took the train for South-western Kansas, near where I formerly lived in No Man's Land. There I intended to visit brother and sister Groves, at Meade Center. Upon my arrival there, I found the old sister, but the old brother had gone to his reward only a few days before I arrived. The old sister is lonely and desires an interest in the prayers of the Brethren, that she may be kept from the evil. The brother was eighty-five years old.

After spending one day and night I started for the Cimarron Valley by private conveyance. There are only two members living in that part of the country. I met with them three times in public worship, and tried to encourage them to hold out faithful. Their corn is scorched by the hot winds, so that it will make nothing but fodder.

On Tuesday, July 26, I took the train for home. The hot winds have nearly taken the western part of Kansas and the western part of Oklahoma, so far as the corn crop is concerned. The wheat and oats are good, so far as I could see. I arrived home July 27 and found all well, for which we felt very thankful to the Giver of all good. I was gone two months to the day.

The drouth in this part has cut our crops short, but I will get a good half crop, twenty bushels of corn per acre. Next week I expect to go to our District Meeting.　ELIHU MOORE.

From the Tuscarawas Church, Stark Co., Ohio.

YOUR weekly visits have been faithfully greeting us, with their blessed articles of love, joy and encouragement, with its sad and sorrowful notices of loved ones passing away over to the other shore, and the faithful co-working of the Spirit of God and the church, in the success and blessed efforts of spreading the Gospel, and the ingathering of precious souls into the fold of Christ.

We are happy to echo from the East that the condition of the Tuscarawas church is peace, love and union. Our congregations have increased with interest. Our Sunday-school is well attend-

Eldorado, Ohio.—The Price's Creek church, Ohio, met in quarterly council this morning at 10 A. M., with brethren Tobias Orider, William Simmons, George Stump, and Moses Hollinger. Considerable business was disposed of with but little difficulty, and a general good feeling prevailed. Bro. Andrew Miller was elected to the ministry. Our love-feast was appointed for Aug. 4, beginning at 10 A. M.—*John S. Richards.*

West Dayton, Ohio.—To-day I attended our home service. Bro. W. I. T. Hoover addressed the congregation. Theme, "Victory." To-day I am thirty-five years of age. I feel that one-half of my life is gone, but I hope not the best half. At our council yesterday, our church permitted the holding of social meetings in our congregation. All the business was adjusted pleasantly, and may this spirit ever lead, guide, and direct our little West Dayton church.—*H. C. Butterbaugh.*

McComb, Ohio.—The Ministerial Meeting of the North-western District of Ohio, will be held in the Sugar Ridge church, Oct. 5 and 6. Those coming from the North or South, on the C. H. & D. R. R., will be met at Leipsic, Oct. 4; also on the morning of Oct. 5, by notifying David Lytle, at Spitzer, Ohio. Those coming from the East on the Nickle Plate R. R, will stop at McComb, and those from the West will stop at Townwood, where they will be met. Those coming over the Nickle Plate R. R must come the day before the meeting, as there is no morning train on that road. There will be a love-feast the evening before the meeting, commencing at 5: 30 o'clock.—*E. H. Rosenberger, Aug. 8*

Eglon, W. Va.—July 27, Bro. S. N. McCann, from Bridgewater, Va., preached for us from Gal. 6: 2, "Bear ye one another's burdens and so fulfill the law of Christ." On the following evening, July 28, he preached from Matt. 5: 48, " Be ye therefore perfect, even as your Father which is in heaven is perfect." Bro. McCann is not ashamed to declare the whole counsel of God. His stay was short, but very pleasant. July 31 we met for Sunday-school, and after that for children's meeting. The children came bright and happy, but there was one seat vacant. Little Dora Fike could not be there. The hand of affliction is laid heavily upon her. Bro. Tobias Fike talked to the children from Eccl. 12: 1, " Remember, now thy Creator in the days of thy youth;" also from Eph. 6: 1-3, " Children, obey your parents in the Lord, for this is right. Honor thy father and mother," etc. Bro. Fike gave us all a grand lesson.—*Rachel Weimer.*

Powder Valley, Colo.—Our members met in quarterly council July 16. Eld. G. W. Fesler was present and presided over the meeting. The church decided to hold a love-feast Sept. 10. All of our dear brethren and sisters, who can be with us, are cordially invited to do so. The church decided to hold one week's meetings prior to the feast. We expect Bro. S. M. Goughenour, of Elkhart, Iowa, to be with us during our meetings. Since our last report two have been received by baptism and two by letter. It has been our painful duty to withdraw fellowship from one who would not hear the church. Thomas Price, one of our dear aged brethren, was paralyzed July 27. He requested Eld. G. W. Fesler to anoint him, which was done July 30. He is still quite poorly, but our prayer is that the Lord may restore him to health. We are penning these few lines while sitting at his bedside to-night. We desire the prayers of all of God's dear children in our behalf, that we may do some good on the frontier.—*D. M. Click.*

Matrimonial.

" What therefore God hath joined together, let not man put asunder,".

GARNER—SANDS.—In Philadelphia, July 26, 1892, by the undersigned, Mr. William N. Garner, and sister Bertha L. Sands, both of this city.   T. T. MYERS.

ZIMMERMAN—CABLE.—By the undersigned, at the bride's home in Quemahoning congregation, Somerset County, Pa., July 31, 1892, Bro. J. S. Zimmerman, to sister Katie Cable.   E. J. BLOUGH.

Fallen Asleep.

" Blessed are the dead which die in the Lord."

JORDAN.—In the Saline Valley church, Kans., Ethel May, daughter of Albert and Stella Jordan, aged three months less three days. Funeral services by L. W. Fitzwater from John 16: 22.   MARTHA FITZWATER.

ZETTY.—In the Coshocton church, Coshocton County, Ohio, July 5, 1892, Margaret Zetty, aged 86 years, 8 months and 7 days. Meekly and patiently she bore her sufferings, which were severe and protracted. She was a member of the Brethren church for thirty-seven years. Her husband preceded her nineteen years to the spirit land. She was the mother of seven children, one of whom died in infancy. Funeral discourse based on 2 Cor. 5: 4.   E. LOOMIS.

WAIRING.—Within the bounds of the Coshocton church, Coshocton County, Ohio, June 19, 1892, sister Mary Wairing, aged 58 years, 3 months and 11 days. She was the mother of twelve children, three of whom preceded her to the spirit world. She leaves her husband and nine children. Funeral discourse by the writer.   E. LOOMIS.

SWARTZ.—At Elkhart, Ind., July 18, 1892, Charles E. Swartz, aged 32 years, 5 months and 14 days. On the day of his death he went to the river to bathe, and was drowned. Funeral services at his brother-in-law's, Eli Simmon's, in the bounds of the Pleasant Valley church, by the writer, from the words of the Savior, " Therefore be ye also ready.":—   C. SCHROCK.

SPROGLE.—In Philadelphia, July 18, 1892, of apoplexy, John L. Sprogle, aged 66 years. He was a son of Eld. John H. Sprogle, known to many of our Brethren as one of the pioneer preachers of Northern Illinois.   S. M. E.

KURTZ.—In the Falling Spring congregation, July 15, 1892, of membranous croup, Edith Catharine Kurtz, daughter of Bro. Jacob and sister Mary Kurtz, aged 8 years, 2 months and 10 days. Services by the writer and Eld. Wm. C. Koontz, from these words " Is it well with the child? And she answered, It is well." 2 Kings 4: 26. Interment at Brown's Mill.   WM. A. ANTHONY.

JOURNEY.—In the Sterling congregation, July 31, 1892, sister Jennie Journey, wife of Bro. Journey, aged 61 years. By request of the deceased, the funeral occasion was improved by the writer from Ps. 23.   P. R. KELTNER.

CLARK.—In the Juniata congregation, Webster County, Nebr., July 14, 1892, William Lewis Clark, youngest son of Bro. Lewis and sister Clark. Deceased was born Sept. 21, 1886. Funeral text, Phil. 1: 23, to a sympathizing congregation. Disease, measles. Funeral services by the writer.   J. I. KINDIG.

LECKINGTON.—In the Newton church, Harvey County, Kans., July 25, 1892, Oby Ota Leckington, infant daughter of friend Isaiah and sister Philanna Leckington, aged 5 months and 1 day. Disease, cholera infantum.   JOHN WALLIS.

COBLE.—In Ashland City, in the bounds of the Maple Grove church, Ashland Co., Ohio, Bro. Jesse M. Coble, aged 41 years, 10 months and 10 days. Funeral sermon by W. L. Desenberg.   DAVID SNYDER.

SHINN.—In the New Hope church, Cherokee County, Kans., Alva Newton, infant son of brother and sister Shinn, aged 3 months and 15 days. Services by the writer. Text, 1 Pet. 1: 24, 25.   A. B. LICHTENWALTER.

BROWN.—In the same church as above, William Ralness, and Lulu May Brown. The boy was 4 months and 1 day old, the girl 4 months and 3 days old. They were twins, and were buried in the same grave. The boy died in Indian Territory, the girl near Neutral, Kans. Services by the writer. Text, Luke 8: 52, latter clause.   A. B. LICHTENWALTER.

KOUP.—In the Lower Cumberland church, at Duncannon, Pa., Bro. Jacob Koup, aged 58 years, 6 months, and 24 days. Funeral services by the writer, assisted by Bro. D. P. Long. Bro. Koup leaves an afflicted, sorrowing widow. Several weeks before her husband's death, when he seemed to be well, her life was, by her friends, despaired of. Now he is gone, and she is still here, looking for the appearing of her Redeemer.   J. B. GARVER.

KINNEY.—In the Des Moines Valley church, June 13, 1892, Sarah E Kinney, infant daughter of Bro. George and sister Kinney, aged 4 months. Funeral services were held in the Indian Creek church-house, by Bro. A. Hutchison from Luke 18: 15.   JEFFERSON MATHIAS.

BLOKER.—In the bounds of the La Porte church, La Porte County, Ind., at the residence of sister Catharine Haiter (sister of the deceased), John Bloker, aged 63 years, 10 months and 28 days. Deceased was born in Buffalo, Erie Co., N. Y., Aug. 31, 1828. Funeral discourse by the undersigned from Job 14: 14.   THURSTON MILLER.

KING.—In the Camp Creek church, Ill., at the home of his son, J. S. King, July 23, 1892, Bro. Isaiah King, aged 76 years, 6 months and 28 days. The deceased was born in Kentucky, in 1816, and was married to Sarah J. Keltner in 1841. Eleven children were born to them, eight of whom survive to mourn the loss of a kind father. Two are members of the Brethren church. His wife preceded him about four years. The deceased was an old settler and well known. A large number of friends and neighbors attended the funeral. Services by the undersigned.   S. S. HUMMER.

GIRL.—In the bounds of the Oakley church, Macon County, Ill., July 21, 1892, of cholera infantum, Leandel, little son of friend William and Alice Girl, aged 1 year, 6 months and 14 days. Funeral occasion improved by the writer.   LIZZIE CRIPE.

DOVE.—At Oleau, Mo., July 19, 1892, of peritonitis, Julia M., beloved wife of Dr. J. D. F. Dove, and eldest daughter of W. C. and B. A. Wolfe, aged 25 years, 3 months and 20 days. Deceased was born in Cumberland County, Pa., April 9, 1867, and removed with her parents at an early age to Clinton County, Mo. At the age of thirteen, she united with the Brethren church, and lived a devoted Christian life up to her death. She leaves a husband and infant daughter. She was brought home for burial. Services were conducted by brethren D. D. Sell, J. E. Ellenberger, and J. G. Royer from Rev. 14: 13, " Blessed are the dead, who die in the Lord."   W. C. W.

CORNMAN.—In the (once so called) River Falls church, Pierce County, Wis., April 9, 1892, Bro ——Cornman, aged 91 years, 7 months and 4 days. He came from Illinois to Pierce county, Wis., a few years ago. Funeral services improved by the writer near Hatney, Wis, from 1 Pet. 1: 24.   SAMUEL CRIST.

HINKLE.—In Ashland City, in the bounds of the Maple Grove church, Ashland Co., Ohio, June 29, 1892, sister Elizabeth Hinkle, aged 75 years, 9 months and 18 days. Deceased was born in Lancaster County, Pa. Funeral sermon by Eld. George Worst.   DAVID SNYDER.

MYERS.—Near Sipesville, Somerset Co., Pa., July 31, 1892, Bro. Michael H. Myers, aged 45 years, 5 months and 18 days. On Monday, prior to his death, Bro Myers was in usual health, and worked in the harvest field, when, in the evening, he took suddenly ill, and by Thursday he passed quietly away, leaving a wife and one little boy. Bro. Myers was just recently called to the deacon's office. Funeral services at the Sipesville church, by the writer, assisted by Eld. Jacob Speicher from Matt 24: 44.   ROBERT T. HILL.

The Gospel Messenger

Is the Recognized organ of the German Baptist or Brethren's church, and advocates the form of doctrine taught in the New Testament and pleads for a return to apostolic and primitive Christianity.

It recognizes the New Testament as the only infallible Rule of faith and practice, and maintains that Faith toward God, Repentance from dead works, Regeneration of the heart and mind, baptism by Trine Immersion for remission of sins unto the reception of the Holy Ghost by the laying on of hands, are the means of adoption into the household of God,—the church militant.

It also maintains that Feet-washing, as taught in John 13, both by example and command of Jesus, should be observed by the church.

That the Lord's Supper, instituted by Christ and as universally observed by the apostles and the early Christians, is a full meal, and, in connection with the Communion, should be taken in the evening or after the close of the day.

That the Salutation of the Holy Kiss, or Kiss of Charity, is binding upon the followers of Christ.

That War and Retaliation are contrary to the spirit and self-denying principles of the religion of Jesus Christ.

That the principle of Plain Dressing and of Non-conformity to the world, as taught in the New Testament, should be observed by the followers of Christ.

That the Scriptural duty of Anointing the Sick with Oil, in the Name of the Lord, James 5: 14, is binding upon all Christians.

It also advocates the church's duty to support Missionary and Tract Work, thus giving to the Lord for the spread of the Gospel and for the conversion of sinners.

In short, it is a Vindicator of all that Christ and the apostles have enjoined upon us, and aims, amid the conflicting theories and discords of modern Christendom, to point out the ground that all must concede to be infallibly safe.

☞ The above principles of our Fraternity are set forth on our " Brethren's Envelopes." Use them! Price 15 cents per package; 40 cents per hundred.

Eldorado, Ohio.—The Price's Creek church, Ohio, met in quarterly council this morning at 10 A. M., with brethren Tobias Crider, William Simmons, George Stump, and Moses Hollinger. Considerable business was disposed of with but little difficulty, and a general good feeling prevailed. Bro. Andrew Miller was elected to the ministry. Our love-feast was appointed for Aug. 4, beginning at 10 A. M.—*John S. Richards.*

West Dayton, Ohio.—To-day I attended our home service. Bro. W. I. T. Hoover addressed the congregation. Theme, "Victory." To-day I am thirty-five years of age. I feel that one-half of my life is gone, but I hope not the best half. At our council yesterday, our church permitted the holding of social meetings in our congregation. All the business was adjusted pleasantly, and may this spirit ever lead, guide, and direct our little West Dayton church.—*H. C. Butterbaugh.*

McComb, Ohio.—The Ministerial Meeting of the North-western District of Ohio, will be held in the Sugar Ridge church, Oct. 5 and 6. Those coming from the North or South, on the C. H. & D. R. R., will be met at Leipsic, Oct. 4; also on the morning of Oct. 5, by notifying David Lytle, at Spitzer, Ohio. Those coming from the East on the Nickle Plate R. R., will stop at McComb, and those from the West will stop at Townwood, where they will be met. Those coming over the Nickle Plate R. R. must come the day before the meeting, as there is no morning train on that road. There will be a love-feast the evening before the meeting, commencing at 5: 30 o'clock.—*E. H. Rosenberger, Aug. 2.*

Eglon, W. Va.—July 27, Bro. S. N. McCann, from Bridgewater, Va., preached for us from Gal. 6: 2, "Bear ye one another's burdens and so fulfill the law of Christ." On the following evening, July 28, he preached from Matt. 5: 48, "Be ye therefore perfect, even as your Father which is in heaven is perfect." Bro. McCann is not ashamed to declare the whole counsel of God. His stay was short, but very pleasant. July 31 we met for Sunday-school, and after that for children's meeting. The children came bright and happy, but there was one seat vacant. Little Dora Fike could not be there. The hand of affliction is laid heavily upon her. Bro. Tobias Fike talked to the children from Eccl. 12: 1, "Remember, now thy Creator in the days of thy youth;" also from Eph. 6: 1-3, "Children, obey your parents in the Lord, for this is right Honor thy father and mother," etc. Bro. Fike gave us all a grand lesson.—*Rachel Weimer.*

Powder Valley, Colo.—Our members met in quarterly council July 16. Eld. G. W. Fesler was present and presided over the meeting. The church decided to hold a love-feast Sept. 10. All of our dear brethren and sisters, who can be with us, are cordially invited to do so. The church decided to hold one week's meetings prior to the feast. We expect Bro. S. M. Goughenour, of Elkhart, Iowa, to be with us during our meetings. Since our last report two have been received by baptism and two by letter. It has been our painful duty to withdraw fellowship from one who would not hear the church. Thomas Price, one of our dear aged brethren, was paralyzed July 27. He requested Eld. G. W. Fesler to anoint him, which was done July 30. He is still quite poorly, but our prayer is that the Lord may restore him to health. We are penning these few lines while sitting at his bedside to-night. We desire the prayers of all of God's dear children in our behalf, that we may do some good on the frontier.—*D. M. Click.*

Matrimonial.

GARNER—SANDS.—In Philadelphia, July 26, 1892, by the undersigned, Mr. William N. Garner, and sister Bertha L. Sands, both of this city.
T. T. Myers.

ZIMMERMAN—CABLE.—By the undersigned, at the bride's home in Quemahoning congregation, Somerset County, Pa., July 31, 1892, Bro. J. S. Zimmerman, to sister Katie Cable.
E. J. Blough.

Fallen Asleep.

JORDAN.—In the Saline Valley church, Kans., Ethel May, daughter of Albert and Stella Jordan, aged three months less three days. Funeral services by L. W. Flitwaltr from John 16: 22.
MARTHA FITZWATER.

ZETTY.—In the Coshocton church, Coshocton County, Ohio, July 5, 1892, Margaret Zetty, aged 86 years, 8 months and 7 days. Meekly and patiently she bore her sufferings, which were severe and protracted. She was a member of the Brethren church for thirty-seven years. Her husband preceded her nineteen years to the spirit land. She was the mother of seven children, one of whom died in infancy. Funeral discourse based on 2 Cor. 5: 4.
E. LOOMIS.

WAIRING.—Within the bounds of the Coshocton church, Coshocton County, Ohio, June 19, 1892, sister Mary Wairing, aged 58 years, 3 months and 11 days. She was the mother of twelve children, three of whom preceded her to the spirit world. She leaves her husband and nine children. Funeral discourse by the writer.
E. LOOMIS.

SWARTZ.—At Elkhart, Ind., July 18, 1892, Charles E. Swartz, aged 31 years, 5 months and 14 days. On the day of his death he went to the river to bathe, and was drowned. Funeral services at his brother-in-law's, Eli Simmon, in the bounds of the Pleasant Valley church, by the writer, from the words of the Savior, "Therefore be ye also ready."
C. SCHROCK.

SPROGLE.—In Philadelphia, July 18, 1892, of apoplexy, John L. Sprogle, aged 66 years. He was a son of Eld. John H. Sprogle, known to many of our Brethren as one of the pioneer preachers of Northern Illinois.
S. M. E.

KURTZ.—In the Falling Spring congregation, July 15, 1892, of membranous croup, Edith Catharine Kurtz, daughter of Bro. Jacob and sister Mary Kurtz, aged 8 years, 2 months and 10 days. Services by the writer and Eld. Wm. C. Koonts, from these words "Is it well with the child? And she answered, It is well." 2 Kings 4: 26. Interment at Brown's Mill.
WM. A. ANTHONY.

JOURNEY.—In the Sterling congregation, July 31, 1892, sister Jennie Journey, wife of Bro. Journey, aged 61 years. By request of the deceased, the funeral occasion was improved by the writer from Ps. 23.
P. R. KELTNER.

CLARK.—In the Juniata congregation, Webster County, Nebr., July 14, 1892, William Lewis Clark, youngest son of Bro. Lewis and sister Clark. Deceased was born Sept. 21, 1886. Funeral text, Phil. 11: 23, to a sympathizing congregation. Disease, measles. Funeral services by the writer.
J. I. KINDIG.

LECKINGTON.—In the Newton church, Harvey County, Kans., July 25, 1892, Oby Ota Leckington, infant daughter of friend Isaiah and sister Philanna Leckington, aged 4 months and 1 day. Disease, cholera infantum.
JOHN WALKS.

COBLE.—In Ashland City, in the bounds of the Maple Grove church, Ashland Co., Ohio, Bro. Jesse M. Coble, aged 41 years, 10 months and 10 days. Funeral sermon by W. L. Desenberg.
DAVID SNYDER.

SHINN.—In the New Hope church, Cherokee County, Kans., Alva Newton, infant son of brother and sister Shinn, aged 3 months and 15 days. Services by the writer. Text, 1 Pet. 1: 24, 25.
A. B. LICHTENWALTER.

BROWN.—In the same church as above, William Earnest, and Lulu May Brown. The boy was 4 months and 1 day old, the girl 4 months and 3 days old. They were twins, and were buried in the same grave. The boy died in Indian Territory, the girl near Neutral, Kans. Services by the writer. Text, Luke 8: 52, latter clause.
A. B. LICHTENWALTER.

KOUP.—In the Lower Cumberland church, at Duncannon, Pa., Bro. Jacob Koup, aged 58 years, 6 months, and 24 days. Funeral services by the writer, assisted by Bro. D. F. Long. Bro. Koup leaves an afflicted, sorrowing widow. Several weeks before her husband's death, when he seemed to be well, her life was, by her friends, despaired of. Now he is gone, and she is still here, looking for the appearing of her Redeemer.
J. B. GARVER.

KINNEY.—In the Des Moines Valley church, June 13, 1892, Sarah E Kinney, infant daughter of Bro. George and sister Kinney, aged 4 months. Funeral services were held in the Indian Creek church-house, by Bro. A. Hutchison from Luke 18: 15.
JEFFERSON MATHIAS.

BLOKER.—In the bounds of the La Porte church, La Porte County, Ind., at the residence of Sister Catharine Halter (sister of the deceased), John Bloker, aged 63 years, 10 months and 28 days. Deceased was born in Buffalo, Erie Co., N. Y., Aug. 31, 1828. Funeral discourse by the undersigned from Job 14: 14.
THURSTON MILLER.

KING.—In the Camp Creek church, Ill., at the home of his son, J. S. King, July 23, 1891, Bro. Isaiah King, aged 76 years, 6 months and 28 days. The deceased was born in Kentucky, in 1816, and was married to Sarah J. Keltner in 1841. Eleven children were born to them, eight of whom survive to mourn the loss of a kind father. Two are members of the Brethren church. His wife preceded him about four years. The deceased was an old settler and well known. A large number of friends and neighbors attended the funeral. Services by the undersigned.
S. S. Hummer.

GIRL.—In the bounds of the Oakley church, Macon County, Ill., July 21, 1892, of cholera infantum, Leander, little son of friend William and Alice Girl, aged 1 year, 6 months and 14 days. Funeral occasion improved by Bro. Adam Bingaman.
LIZZIE CRIPE.

DOVE.—At Olean, Mo., July 29, 1892, of peritonitis, Della M., beloved wife of Dr. J. D. F. Dove, and eldest daughter of W. C. and B. A. Wolfe, aged 25 years, 3 months and 20 days. Deceased was born in Cumberland County, Pa., April 9, 1867, and removed with her parents at an early age to Clinton County, Mo. At the age of thirteen, she united with the Brethren church, and lived a devoted Christian life up to her death. She leaves a husband and infant daughter. She was brought home for burial. Services were conducted by brethren D. D. Soll, J. E. Ellenberger, and J. G. Royer from Rev. 14: 13, "Blessed are the dead, who die in the Lord."
W. C. W.

CORNMAN.—In the (once so called) River Falls church, Pierce County, Wis., April 9, 1892, Bro.——Cornman, aged 91 years, 7 months and 4 days. He came from Illinois to Pierce County, Wis., a few years ago. Funeral services improved by the writer near Hersey, Wis., from 1 Pet. 1: 24.
SAMUEL CRIST.

HINKLE.—In Ashland City, in the bounds of the Maple Grove church, Ashland Co., Ohio, June 29, 1892, sister Elizabeth Hinkle, aged 75 years, 9 months and 18 days. Deceased was born in Lancaster County, Pa. Funeral sermon by Eld. George Worst.
DAVID SNYDER.

MYERS.—Near Sipesville, Somerset Co., Pa., July 21, 1892, Bro. Michael H. Myers, aged 45 years, 5 months and 28 days. On Monday, prior to his death, Bro. Myers was in usual health, and worked in the harvest field, when, in the evening, he took suddenly ill, and by Thursday he passed quietly away, leaving a wife and one little boy. Bro. Myers was just recently called to the deacon's office. Funeral services at the Sipesville church, by the writer, assisted by Eld. Jacob Speicher from Matt. 24: 44.
ROBERT T. HILL.

The Gospel Messenger

Is the recognized organ of the German Baptist or Brethren's church, and advocates the form of doctrine taught in the New Testament and pleads for a return to apostolic and primitive Christianity.

It recognizes the New Testament as the only infallible rule of faith and practice, and maintains that Faith toward God, Repentance from dead works, Regeneration of the heart and mind, baptism by Trine Immersion for remission of sins unto the reception of the Holy Ghost by the laying on of hands, are the means of adoption into the household of God,—the church militant.

It also maintains that Feet-washing, as taught in John 13, both by example and command of Jesus, should be observed in the church.

That the Lord's Supper, instituted by Christ and as universally observed by the apostles and the early Christians, is a full meal, and, in connection with the Communion, should be taken in the evening or after the close of the day.

That the Salutation of the Holy Kiss, or Kiss of Charity, is binding upon the followers of Christ.

That War and Retaliation are contrary to the spirit and self-denying principles of the religion of Jesus Christ.

That the principle of Plain Dressing and of Non-conformity to the world, as taught in the New Testament, should be observed by the followers of Christ.

That the Scriptural duty of Anointing the Sick with Oil, in the Name of the Lord, James 5: 14, is binding upon all Christians.

It also advocates the church's duty to support Missionary and Tract Work, thus giving to the Lord for the spread of the Gospel and for the conversion of sinners.

In short, it is a Vindicator of all that Christ and the apostles have enjoined upon us, and also, amid the conflicting theories and discords of modern Christendom, to point out ground that all must concede to be infallibly safe.

☞ The above principles of our Fraternity are set forth on our "Brethren's Envelopes." Use them! Price 15 cents per package; 40 cents per hundred.

Announcements.

MINISTERIAL MEETINGS.

Nov. 25, at 9 A. M., in the South-east District of Kansas, Ministerial Meeting in the Cedar Creek church, Montello, Anderson Co., Kans.

Nov. 2 and 3, Western District of Pennsylvania will hold their Ministerial Meeting in Walnut Grove, Johnstown church.

DISTRICT MEETINGS.

Oct. 7, at 9 A. M., District Meeting in the Crooked-Creek church, Washington Co., Iowa. Those coming by rail will be met at Keota, at 10 A. M. from the East, and at 6:05 P. M. from the West, by notifying D. P. Miller.

LOVE FEASTS.

Aug. 20, at 5 P. M., the Bear Creek church, Palmer, Ill.

Aug. 27 and 28, at 4 P. M., Salem, in Scioty Creek congregation, Preston Co., W. Va.

Aug. 27, at 4 P. M., Nettola church, Meelague Co., Tex.

Sept. 2, at 2 P. M., Sugar Creek church, Sangamon County, Ill., 2 miles east of Auburn, Ill.

Sept. 3, at 3 P. M., Rockton church, Pa.

Sept. 3, at 4 P. M., Sangerville, in the Beaver Creek congregation, Rockingham Co., Va.

Sept. 3, Round Mountain church, Ark.

Sept. 3, at 10 A. M., Mt. Etna church, Iowa. Conveyances on Friday, Sept. 2, at Corning.

Sept. 3, at 2 P. M., Independence, Kans.

Sept. 3, at 10 A. M., Washington church, Kans., at Bro. Wm. R. Phillippi's residence, three miles South, and three and one-half miles west of Washington, Kans.

Sept. 3, at 2 P. M., Silver Creek church, Cowley Co., Kans.

Sept. 3, Mill Creek church, Adams Co., Ill.

Sept. 3 and 4, English River congregation, Keokuk Co., Iowa.

Sept. 3, at 2 P. M., in the Mt. Hope church, Logan Co., Oklahoma Territory.

Sept. 3 and 4, at 10 A. M., in the North Solomon church, six miles north of Portis, Kans.

Sept. 3, Soppo church, Furnas Co., Nebr.

Sept. 3 and 4, Rock Creek church, Colo. Dedication of church-house on Sunday, Sept. 4. Those coming by rail, stop off at Mettle Vista.

Sept. 3, at 10:30 P. M., Sam's Creek church, Mo.

Sept. 3 and 4, Spring Creek church, Chickasaw Co., Iowa.

Sept. 3, Wyman Valley church, in Pleasant Valley school-house.

Sept. 6, at 2 P. M., Johnstown church, Walnut Grove, Pa., 2 miles south of B. & O. and P. R. R.

Sept. 6, at 4 P. M., Indian Creek congregation, Fayette Co., Pa. Series of meetings to commence Aug. 27.

Sept. 7 and 8, at 2 P. M., Sand Valley, Coffey Co., Kans., at the home of W. A. Smith, one mile east and five south of Waverly. A series of meetings to be held in connection with the feast.

Sept. 9, at 10 A. M., Mouroe County church, Iowa.

Sept. 10, at 3 P. M., Fairview church, Garrett Co., Md.

Sept. 10, Poudre Valley church, Colo.

Sept. 10 and 11, Farnhamville, Calhoun Co., Iowa. Series of meetings in connection, beginning one week previous.

Sept. 10 and 11, at 2 P. M., Sterling church, Sterling, Ill.

Sept. 17, at 2 P. M., Bethel congregation, at the Bethlehem meeting-house, Holt Co., Mo. For any information Bro. Amick, Mound City, Holt Co., Mo.

Sept. 17, at 10 A. M., Oakley church, Macon Co., Ill.

Sept. 17, at 3 P. M., Libertyville church, Jefferson Co., Iowa. Series of meetings to commence immediately after feast.

Sept. 24, at 4 P. M., Maple Grove church, 4 miles north of Ashland City, Ashland Co., Ohio.

Sept. 24, at 2 P. M., Prodoella church, Wilson Co., Kans.

Sept. 24, at 2 P. M., Chief Creek congregation, Huntington Co., Ind.

Sept. 24, at 2 P. M., Fredonia, Kans.

Sept. 24, at 3 P. M., Martin's Creek church, Wayne Co., Ill.

Sept. 24 and 25, 4 miles west of Tiplat, Cedar Co., Iowa, beginning at 2 P. M. Ministers of Middle Iowa will please arrange to come to us from District Meeting at Garrison. Our meeting-house is at a distance of two miles from Buchanan on the B., C. R. & N. R.

Sept. 24, at 5 P. M., in La Porte church, La Porte, Ind. Trains will be met in the forenoon and early afternoon of the day of meeting.

Sept. 24 and 25, at 3 P. M., Loturk church, Carroll Co., Ill.

Sept. 24, at 5 P. M., Pokagon church, Dowagiac, Cass Co., Mich.

Sept. 27, at 5 P. M., at Wenger meeting-house, St. Joseph church, Ind.

Sept. 28, South Bend church, Ind.

Sept. 28, at 10 A. M., Spring Creek church, Kosciusko Co., Ind.

Sept. 29 and 30, at 10 A. M., Lower Fall Creek church, 5 miles south of Anderson. Those coming on train should address John Dunsuck, Anderton, Ind.

Sept. 30, at 10 A. M., Nettle Creek church, near Hagerstown, Wayne Co., Ind.

Sept. 30, at 2 P. M., Mineba church, Platt Co., Ill.

Oct. 1, at 2 P. M., Sugar Creek church, Allen Co., Ohio.

Oct. 1, at 2 P. M., Bertium Congregation, Mich.

Oct. 1 and 2, at 10 A. M., West Branch church, Ill. One week's meeting previous to feast.

Oct. 1 and 2, at 2 P. M., near Amen, Boone Co., Iowa. Noon train meet at Amen on Saturday.

Oct. 1, at 2 P. M., Osage church, Crawford Co., Kans.

Oct. 1, at 4 P. M., Logon church, near Degraff, Ohio.

Oct. 1 and 2, Saginaw church, Mich.

Oct. 1 and 2, at 2:30 P. M., Walnut Valley congregation, Burton Co., Kans.

Oct. 1 and 2, at 3 P. M., Alleghany congregation, Grant Co., W. Va.

Oct. 1, Maple Grove church, Norton Co., Kans.

Oct. 1, at 10 A. M., Appanoose church, Kans.

Oct. 1, at 10 A. M., Eight Mile church, Ind., at the town of Metcia.

Oct. 1 and 2, at 11 A. M., Riverside, Iowa. Those coming by rail will stop at Iowa Junction, on the B. C. R. & R. R., where they will be met.

Oct. 1, at 10 A. M., Sioux Lick church, Clermont Co., Ohio.

Oct. 1, at 10 A. M., Chippewa congregation, Wayne Co., Ohio.

Oct. 1, at 1 P. M., in the Verdigris church, at Bro. S. S. Redman's. A series of meetings will commence Sept. 15.

Oct. 1, Camp Creek church, 14, at the church 7 miles south of Colchester. Those coming by train will please notify S. S. Hummer, and they will be met at the depot at Colchester, and conveyed to place of meeting.

Oct. 1, at 2 P. M., South Waterloo church, Waterloo, Iowa.

Oct. 1, at 10 A. M., Belleville church, Kans.

Oct. 1, at 3 P. M., Johnstown church, Pa., 3 miles north-east of Johnstown and 2 miles north of Mineral Point on the P. R. R.

Oct. 4, at 5:30 P. M., Sugar Ridge church, Ohio.

Oct. 6, at 10 A. M., in the Beaver Dam church, Kosciusko Co., Ind., near the town of Burket.

Oct. 5, at 2 P. M., Peach church, Ohio.

Oct. 5 and 6, Dallas Centre church. A series of meetings by Bro. Hutchison will commence Sept. 17.

Oct. 6, at 10 A. M., Wabash church, 7 miles south of Wabash Ind.

Oct. 6, at 2 P. M., at Mt. Joy meeting-house, in Jacob's Creek congregation, Westmoreland Co., Pa. Series of meetings to commence Oct. 1.

Oct. 6, at 10 A. M., Donnel's Creek church, Clarke Co., Ohio, seven miles from New Carlisle, and the same distance from Fottys and Springfield. Those coming from the West will stop either at New Carlisle or Fottys, where they will be met on the evening of the 5th. Those from the North-east or South should stop at Springfield.

Oct. 6, at 2 P. M., Spring Creek church, in the Keith's church-house, eleven miles south-west of Reece, Kans.

Oct. 6 and 7, at 10 A. M., Shannon, Ill.

Oct. 6, at 2 P. M., Arnoln church, Ind.

Oct. 7, Black River church, Van Buren Co., Mich. Brethren coming by rail will stop off at Bangor.

Oct. 7, at 2 P. M., Ledoga, Ind.

Oct. 7, at 2 P. M., Kaskaskia church, Fayette Co., Ill., ten miles south-west of Beecher City, Ill. Those coming by rail will be met at the above-named place by informing Granville Nevinger.

Oct. 8, at 10 A. M., Sugar Creek, Whitley Co., Ind.

Oct. 8, at 2 P. M., Raccoon Creek church, Montgomery Co., Ind., one and one-half miles north-west of Ladoga.

Oct. 8, at 4 P. M., Maumgin Creek church, Montgomery Co., Ind. Those coming by rail will be met at Putnamville, on Springfield Road, and at Girard, on St.-Louis Road on morning of meeting.

Oct. 7 and 8, at 10:30 A. M., Four Mile church, Union Co., Ind.

Oct. 8, at 2 P. M., Bethel church, on North County line, Thayer Co., Nebr. Stations: Carleton, Davenport, Carlisle and Shickley.

Oct. 8, at 2 P. M., Lamotte church, Crawford Co., Ill.

Oct. 8, at 3:30 P. M., Maple Glen church, Somerset Co., Pa.

Oct. 8, at 2 P. M., in the Elkhart Valley church, Elkhart Co., Ind.

Oct. 8 and 9, at 2 P. M., Arnold's Grove, Ill.

Oct. 8, at 10 A. M., Dry Creek church, Linn Co., Iowa, one mile west of Robins Station.

Oct. 8, Swan Creek congregation, Ohio, 2½ miles west of Delta, Ohio.

Oct. 8, at 2 P. M., Washington Creek church, Douglas Co., Kans.

Oct. 8 and 9, 10 A. M., Pine Creek congregation, Ill.

Oct. 8 and 9, Bethel church, Pratt Co., Kans., in the town of Sawyer. Meeting to commence at 2 o'clock.

Oct. 8, at 10 A. M., Briar Creek church, Portland, Ind. Those coming by rail will be met by notifying H. P. Garber.

Oct. 8 and 9, at 11 A. M., Woodland church, Fulton Co., Ill. A series of meetings one week previous to the feast, and to continue two weeks.

Oct. 8, at 2 P. M., North Star, Darke County, Ohio.

Oct. 8, at 2 P. M., Greentown church, at Greentown, Howard Co., Ind.

Oct. 8, at 11 A. M., Crooked Creek church, Washington Co., Iowa.

Oct. 8, at 2 o'clock, Deerance church, Kans.

Oct. 14, at 4 P. M., Union church, Marshall Co., Ind., five miles west of Plymouth. Trains will be met at both Plymouth and Bart.

Oct. 13 and 15, at 11 A. M., South Keokuk church, Keokuk Co., Iowa. Those coming by rail will be met at Olie, by notifying Isaac Shelley or Isaac Brower. Those coming from the West will arrive at Olie about 12:30 A. M.; those from the East at 3 P. M.

Oct. 14, Union church, Plymouth, Marshall Co., Ind. This church would like to have some brother hold meetings a week or ten days after.

Oct. 15, at 10 A. M., Rome church, Oak Grove house. Also harvest meeting at same place Aug. 13, at 10 A. M.

Oct. 15 and 16, at 10 A. M., Grundy church, ten miles west of Grundy Centre, Grundy Co., Iowa.

Oct. 20, at 2 P. M., Middle Fork church, Clinton Co., Ind.

Oct. 25, at 10 A. M., Kidder church, Mo.

Oct. 28, at 2:30 P. M., Salamonie church, Kans.

Oct. 28, at 5 P. M., St. Joseph Valley church, St. Joseph Co., Ind., 5 miles north of South Bend.

Oct. 28, at 4 P. M., in the Pleasant Hill church, near Girard and Virden, Ill.

Oct. 28, at 2 P. M., South Beatrice church, Gage Co., Nebr. Conveyances the day before meeting at B. B. depot, in Beatrice; Rock Island depot, in Rockford; Union Pacific depot, in Holmesville.

Oct. 28, at 2 P. M., Walnut church, Marshall Co., Ind.

Oct. 28, at 10 A. M., in the Buck Creek church, Henry Co., Ind.

Oct. 29, at 2 P. M., in Zion congregation, Page, Va.

Oct. 29, St. Vrain church, Longmont, Colo.

Oct. 29, at 2 P. M., Osawkie church, Kans. A series of meetings to commence Oct. 20.

Oct. 29 and 30, 10 A. M., Pigeon Creek church, Ill., at the Oak Grove meeting-house.

Oct. 29, at 2 P. M., Oak church, Madison Co., Ind., 3½ miles east of Summitville.

Nov. 2, Walnut Grove church, Mo.

Nov. 5, at 3 P. M., Big Creek church, Richland Co., Ill., 3½ miles North-east of Parkersburg, Ill. Conveyances will be at the above place by informing J. M. Forney.

Nov. 12, at 2 P. M., Cedar Creek church, Anderson Co., Kans.

Announcements.

MINISTERIAL MEETINGS.

Nov. 15, at 9 A. M., in the South-east District of Kansas, Ministerial Meeting in the Cedar Creek church, Montida, Anderson Co., Kans.

Nov. 1 and 2. Western District of Pennsylvania will hold their Ministerial Meeting at Walnut Grove, Johnstown church.

DISTRICT MEETINGS.

Oct. 7, at 9 A. M., District Meeting in the Crooked-Creek church, Washington Co., Iowa. Those coming by rail will be met at Keota, at 10 A. M. from the East, and at 6:05 P. M. from the West, by notifying D. P. Miller.

LOVE-FEASTS.

Aug. 13, at 4 P. M., the Bear Creek church, Palmer, Ill.

Aug. 27 and 28, at 2 P. M., Salem, in Sandy Creek congregation, Preston Co., W. Va.

Aug. 27, at 4 P. M., Romine church, Montague Co., Tex.

Sept. 1, at 4 P. M., Sugar Creek church, Sangamon County, Ill., 2 miles east of Auburn, Ill.

Sept. 2, at 3 P. M., Rockton church, Pa.

Sept. 3, at 2 P. M., at Sangerville, in the Beaver Creek congregation, Rockingham Co., Va.

Sept. 3, Round Mountain church, Ark.

Sept. 3, at 10 A. M., Mt. Etna church, Iowa. Conveyances on Friday, Sept. 2, at Corning.

Sept. 3, at 5 P. M., at Independence, Kans.

Sept. 3, at 10 A. M., Washington church, Kans., at Brother W. R. Phillippi's residence, three miles south, and three and one-half miles west of Washington, Kans.

Sept. 3, at 3 P. M., Silver Creek church, Cowley Co., Kans.

Sept. 3, at English River congregation, Keokuk Co., Iowa.

Sept. 3, at 10 A. M., in the Mt. Hope church, Logan Co., Oklahoma Territory.

Sept. 3 and 4, at 10 A. M., in the North Solomon church, six miles north of Portis, Kans.

Sept. 3, Sappa church, Pawnee Co., Nebr.

Sept. 3 and 4, Rock Creek church, Colo. Declination of church-houses on Sunday, Sept. 4. Those coming by rail stop off at Mesita Visita.

Sept. 3, at 11 2 P. M., Sam's Creek church, Mo.

Sept. 3 and 4, Spring Creek church, Chikkamaw Co., Iowa.

Sept. 3, Wyogan Valley church, at Pleasant Valley school-house.

Sept. 4, at 2 P. M., Johnstown church, Walnut Grove, Pa., 2 miles south of B. & O. and P. R. R.

Sept. 6, at 4 P. M., Scott Valley, Cabby Co., Kans., at the house of W. A. Smith, one mile east and five tenth of Waverly. A series of meetings to be held in connection with the feast.

Sept. 9, at 10 A. M., Monroe County church, Iowa.

Sept. 10, at 3 P. M., Fairview church, Garrett Co., Md.

Sept. 10, Fossite Valley church, Colo.

Sept. 10 and 11, Farnhamville, Calhoun Co., Iowa. Series of meetings in connection, beginning one week previous.

Sept. 10 and 11, at 3 P. M., Sterling church, Sterling, Ill.

Sept. 10, at 4 P. M., Bethel congregation, at the Bethlehem meeting-house, Holt Co., Mo. For any information address Jno. Ander, Mound City, Holt Co., Mo.

Sept. 10, at 3 P. M., Oakley church, Macon Co., Ill.

Sept. 13, at 3 P. M., Libertyville church, Jefferson Co., Iowa. Series of meetings to commence immediately after feast.

Sept. 14, at 2 P. M., Maple Grove church, 4 miles north of Ashland City, Ashland Co., Ohio.

Sept. 14, at 2 P. M., Fredonia church, Wilson Co., Kans.

Sept. 14, at 2 P. M., Chief Creek congregation, Hunting-ton Co., Ind.

Sept. 24, at 2 P. M., Fredonia, Kans.

Sept. 24, at 5 P. M., Martin's Creek church, Wayne Co., Ill.

Sept. 24 and 25, 4 miles west of Tipton, Cedar Co., Iowa, beginning at 2 P. M. Ministers of Middle Iowa will please arrange to come to us from District Meeting at Garrison. Our meeting-house is but a distance of two miles from Buchanan on the B. C. R. & N. R. R.

Sept. 24, at 5 P. M., in La Porte church, La Porte, Ind. Trains will be met in the sixteenth and early afternoon of the day of meeting.

Sept. 24 and 25, at 5 P. M., Lanark church, Carroll Co., Ill.

Sept. 24, at 5 P. M., Pokagon church, Dowagiac, Cass Co., Mich.

Sept. 27, at 5 P. M., at Wenger meeting-house, St. Joseph church, Ind.

Sept. 28, South Bend church, Ind.

Sept. 28, at 10 A. M., Spring Creek church, Kosciusko Co., Ind.

Sept. 29 and 30, at 1 P. M., Rock Creek, Whiteside Co., Ill.

Sept. 29 and 30, at 10 A. M., Lower Fall Creek church, 5 miles south of Anderson. Those coming on train should address John Bostwick, Anderson, Ind.

Sept. 30, at 10 A. M., Nettle Creek church, near Hagerstown, Wayne Co., Ind.

Sept. 30, at 2 P. M., Milledoe church, Platt Co., Ill.

Oct. 1, at 5 P. M., Sugar Creek church, Allen Co., Ohio.

Oct. 1, at 5 P. M., Berrien Congregation, Mich.

Oct. 1 and 2, at 5 P. M., West Branch church, Ill. One week's meeting previous to feast.

Oct. 1 and 2, at 2 P. M., near Ames, Boone Co., Iowa. Noon trains meet at Ames on Saturday.

Oct. 1, at 2 P. M., Osage church, Crawford Co., Kans.

Oct. 1, at 1 P. M., Logan church, near DeGraff, Ohio.

Oct. 1 and 2, Saginaw church, Mich.

Oct. 1 and 2, at 1: 30 P. M., Walnut Valley congregation, Butler Co., Kans.

Oct. 1, at 3 P. M., Allegheny congregation, Grant Co., W. Va.

Oct. 1, Maple Grove church, Norton Co., Kans.

Oct. 1, at 10 A. M., Appanoose church, Kans.

Oct. 1, at 10 A. M., Eight Mile church, Ind., at the town of Markle.

Oct. 1 and 2, at 10 A. M., Riverdale, Iowa. Those coming by rail will stop at Iowa Junction, on B. C. R. & N. R. R., where they will be met.

Oct. 1, at 10 A. M., Chippewa congregation, Wayne Co., Ohio.

Oct. 1, at 1 P. M., in the Verdigris church, at Bro. S. S. Redman's. A series of meetings will commence Sept. 25.

Oct. 1, Camp Creek church, Ill., at the church 7 miles south of Colchester. Those coming by train will please notify S. S. Hummer, and they will be met at the depot at Colchester, and conveyed to place of meeting.

Oct. 1, at 4 P. M., South Waterloo church, Waterloo, Iowa.

Oct. 1, at 12 A. M., Belleville church, Kans.

Oct. 1, at 3 P. M., Johnstown church, Pa., 1 miles north-east of Johnstown and 1 mile north of Mineral Point on the P. R. R.

Oct. 6, at 3: 30 P. M., Sugar Ridge church, Ohio.

Oct. 6, at 10 A. M., in the Pleasant Dale church, Koscinsko Co., Ind., near the town of Burket.

Oct. 6, at 2 P. M., Roann church, Ind.

Oct. 5 and 6, Dallas Centre church. A series of meetings by Bro. Hutchison will commence Sept. 17.

Oct. 6, at 10 A. M., Joy meeting-house, in Jacob's Creek congregation, Westmoreland Co., Pa. Series of meetings to commence Oct. 1.

Oct. 6, at 10 A. M., Dunnel's Creek church, Clarke Co., Ohio, seven miles from New Carlisle, and the same distance from Forgy and Springfield. Those coming from the West will stop either at New Carlisle or Forgy, where they will be met on the evening of the 5th. Those from the North-east or South should stop at Springfield.

Oct. 6, at 5 P. M., Spring Creek church, in the Keith's church-house, eleven miles north-west of Reece, Kans.

Oct. 6 and 7, at 10 A. M., Sharman, Ill.

Oct. 6, at 2 P. M., Arcadia church, Ind.

Oct. 7, Black River church, Van Buren Co., Mich. Brethren coming by rail will stop off at Bangor.

Oct. 7, at 2 P. M., Lodoga, Ind.

Oct. 7, at 2 P. M., Kaskaskia church, Fayette Co., Ill., ten miles south-west of Brother City, Ill. Those coming by rail will be met at the above-named place by informing Granville Nevinger.

Oct. 7, at 10 A. M., Sugar Creek, Whitley Co., Ind.

Oct. 7, at 2 P. M., Raccoon Creek church, Montgomery Co., Ind., one and one-half miles north-west of Ladoga.

Oct. 7, at 2 P. M., Monaughn Creek church, Montgomery Co., Ill. Those coming by rail will be met at Fairmontville, on Springfield Road, and at Girard, on St.-Louis Road on morning of meeting.

Oct. 7 and 8, at 10 A. M., Four Mile church, Union Co., Ind.

Oct. 8, at 4 P. M., Bethel church, on North County line, Thayer Co., Nebr. Stations: Carleton, Davenport, Catlette and Sockeley.

Oct. 8, at 2 P. M., Lametic church, Crawford Co., Ill.

Oct. 8, at 3: 30 P. M., Maple Glen church, Somerset Co., Pa.

Oct. 8, at 4 P. M., in the Elkhart Valley church, Elkhart Co., Ind.

Oct. 8 and 9, at 5 P. M., Arnold's Grove, Ill.

Oct. 8, at 10 A. M., Dry Creek church, Linn Co., Iowa, one mile west of Robins Station.

Oct. 8, Swan Creek congregation, Ohio, 3½ miles west of Delta, Ohio.

Oct. 8, at 4 P. M., Washington Creek church, Douglas Co., Kans.

Oct. 8 and 9, 1 10 A. M., Pine Creek congregation, Ill. in town o' Sawyer. Advising to commence at 2 o'clock.

Oct. 8, at 10 A. M., Bear Creek church, Portland, Ind. Those coming by rail will be met by notifying H. P. Garber.

Oct. 8 and 9, at 10 A. M., Woodland church, Fulton Co., Ill. A series of meetings one week previous to the feast, and to continue two weeks.

Oct. 8, at 5 P. M., North Star, Darke County, Ohio.

Oct. 8, at 1 A. M., Greentown church, at Greentown, Howard Co., Ind.

Oct. 8, at 2 o'clock, Durrance church, Kans.

Oct. 14, at 4 P. M., Union church, Marshal Co., Ind., five miles west of Plymouth. Trains will be met at both Plymouth and Burr Oak.

Oct. 14 and 15, at 11 A. M., South Keokuk church, Keokuk Co., Iowa. Those coming by rail will be met at Ollie, by notifying Isaac Shelley or Isaac Brown. Those coming from the West will arrive at Ollie about 11:30 A. M.; those from the East at 3 P. M.

Oct. 14, Union church, Plymouth, Marshall Co., Ind. This church would like to have some brother hold meetings a week or ten days after.

Oct. 15, at 10 A. M., Rome church, Oak Grove house. Also harvest meeting at same place Aug. 13, at 10 A. M.

Oct. 15 and 16, at 10 A. M., Grundy church, ten miles west of Grundy Centre, Grundy Co., Iowa.

Oct. 20, at 2 P. M., Middle Fork church, Clinton Co., Ind.

Oct. 21, at 10 A. M., Kilbuck church, Delaware Co., Ind., nine miles west of Muncie.

Oct. 28, at 3 P. M., St. Joseph Valley church, St. Joseph Co., Ind., 3 miles north of South Bend.

Oct. 28, at 2 P. M., in the Pleasant Hill church, near Girard and Virden, Ill.

Oct. 28, at 2 P. M., South Beatrice church, Gage Co., Nebr. Conveyances the day before meeting at B. & M. depot, in Beatrice; Rock Island depot, in Rockford; Union Pacific depot, in Holmesville.

Oct. 28, at 1 P. M., Walnut church, Marshall Co., Ind.

Oct. 28, at 10 A. M., in the Burk Creek church, Henry Co., Ind.

Oct. 29, at 2 P. M., Mt. Zion congregation, Page, Va.

Oct. 29, St. Vrain church, Longmont; Colo.

Oct. 29, at 2 P. M., Oakwide church, Kans. A series of meetings to commence Oct. 10.

Oct. 29 and 30, at 10 A. M., Pigeon Creek church, Ind., at the Oak Grove meeting-house.

Oct. 29, at 2 P. M., Oasis church, Madison Co., Ind., 3½ miles east of Summitville.

Nov. 5, at 3 P. M., Big Creek church, Richland Co., Ill., 3½ miles North-east of Parkersburg, Ill. Conveyances will be at the above place by informing J. M. Forney.

Nov. 24, at 3 P. M., Cedar Creek church, Anderson Co., Kans.

✦ESSAYS✦

"Study to show thyself approved unto God: a workman that needeth not to be ashamed, rightly dividing the Word of Truth."

HOUSE OF MANY MANSIONS.

SELECTED BY MARY MYERS.

O HOUSE of many mansions,
Thy doors are open wide,
And dear are all the faces
Upon the other side.
Thy portals they are golden,
And those who enter in
Shall know no more of sorrow,
Of weariness, of sin.

O house of many mansions,
My weary spirit waits
And longs to join the ransomed
Who enter through thy gates;
Who enter through thy portals,
The mansions of the blest;
Who come to then aweary,
And find in thee their rest.

Thy walls are not of marble,
O house not built with hands;
I sigh for thee while waiting
Within these border-lands.
I know that but in dying
Thy threshold is crossed o'er;
There shall be no more sorrow
In thy forevermore.

JUSTIFICATION BY FAITH.

BY J. L. SWITZER.

"How then can a man be justified with God? or how can he be clean that is born of a woman?"—Job 25: 4.

THIS is the language, not of Job, but of Bildad, and he further goes on to say that the stars are not pure in the sight of God, and "how much less man, that is a worm, and the son of man which is a worm." The reply that Job made to Bildad, on his "justification" catechism is grand. Please turn and read it in the following chapters.

Right here is the place to bring in squarely the direct and unequivocal reply to the text above,—the reply of Inspiration to the question of a feeble comforter. " Ye see then how that by works a man is justified, and not by faith only." James 2: 24. Turn back in this chapter and read on from verse 14, and then believe "justification by faith only," if you can reject James' letter as being inspired language.

It is natural for man, realizing his great imperfection, to seek some way of either justifying himself, or getting some one else to justify him. We are all disposed somewhat, like the lawyer in Luke 10: 29, and like lawyers and all other people generally are, to justify ourselves on technical grounds. In fact, nothing comes more natural than an attempt at justification, just as soon as we are convicted of wrong. How natural, too, to look to some one else for justification!

But the wicked cannot look to God for justification, for he says positively, "I will not justify the wicked," and a woe is pronounced upon those who do "justify the wicked for reward."

In this connection I would notice also that those that call evil good, and good evil; that put darkness for light, and light for darkness; that put bitter for sweet, and sweet for bitter; that are wise in their own eyes, and prudent in their own sight, have also a woe resting upon them,—justification or no justification. The wicked cannot look to themselves for justification, or their own mouth would condemn them. "Yet by his knowledge shall my righteous servant justify many; for he shall bear their iniquities." Isa. 53: 11.

Here comes in the key-note for the "faith alone" tune. How did Jesus bear our iniquities?

He died for us; and is the propitiation for the sins of the whole world, by his giving himself a ransom for many.

That's the way he justified us,—how, then, are we justified "by faith only?" "Being now justified by his blood," says Paul, " We shall be saved from wrath through him." By his blood 'and through him.

Mankind were sinners, but remission of sin is promised unto them. The agencies for that remission are all made accessible. The knowledge and proper application of these divine agencies are plainly given from heaven. Justification begins just as soon as the sinner begins to avail himself of those agencies. Thus the Prodigal was justified when he made the good resolution. He was justified still further when he retraced his steps. He was justified still further when he prayed to his Father for forgiveness. A man is justified in the sight of God for everything good that he DOES. He is condemned for everything bad that he DOES. Justification and condemnation stand in the Scripture exactly opposed to each other. One is right, the other wrong. One is righteousness, the other sin. There is nothing but DOING that has anything to do with our eternal happiness or misery. The idea of trying to get justification without DOING, or rather to get DOING out of justification, is extremely ridiculous and pernicious. When a man thinks a good thought, he does something. When a woman heaves a devotional sigh she does something. No worship can take place without an act of the mind, or heart, or body. Every act of mental or physical volition is an act. That act is under the control of the will, and the will is subject to the creature. Hence Christ says: "This is the work of God, that ye believe on him whom he hath sent." John 6: 29.

The idea held out to us by the "faith-alone" advocates is about this: "We are justified by what Christ did for us, long before we ever came into the world." But then, as this is Universalism, of course this is too much to believe; so Paul is hitched up to his unwilling load and made to translate us instantaneously from earth to heaven, —the moment we believe that Jesus Christ is the Son of God,—the moment we have faith. In that moment we are translated from darkness to light, from Satan to God, from hell to heaven.

And why? Because Paul says: "Having been justified by faith, we have peace with God through our Lord Jesus Christ;" and this they hitch with: "Not of works lest any man should boast."

Now Paul does of course say that we are not justified by the works of the Jewish Law, and that is as much as he really ever says anywhere about our being justified without works. He tells us that Abraham did right in believing God, that this was ascribed to him for righteousness, and that in the same way righteousness will be ascribed unto us if we believe in the Lord Jesus Christ, and hence, of course, we are justified in turning from unbelief to faith. This doctrine was very essential in that day when Christ was rejected of men, when the Jews refused him, and the Gentiles had not yet heard of him, for "without faith it is impossible to please God," and the great desideratum then was to get men to receive him.

I have not space to argue this further now. Suffice it to say, in conclusion, that "we are under law to Christ." That law is made up of simple "shalts" and "shalt nots." It nowhere demands a great swelling profusion of triple-geared adjectives, of meaning so dense and obscure as to stretch the imagination like a horse blanket. Neither is there some great momentous, hidden,

mysterious spirituality in the Word of God that is not accessible to all God's creatures.

Love God, believe God, obey God. When you fail, confess and repent.

Watch and pray. Let us hear the conclusion: "Fear God and keep his commandments, for this is the whole duty of man."

McCune, Kans.

MUSICAL INSTRUMENTS.

BY ENOCH EBY.

I WRITE this article by request, and partly from a sense of duty. I was credibly informed that it is rumored that a brother and I were at a certain brother's house in Ohio, and that my comrade played on the organ, and that I used the violin. The facts are I could not play if I would, and would not if I could. I was taught by strict Christian parents, hence taught that it was at best a vain amusement, and a wrong use of money, just as our Brotherhood always hereto regarded it. She has given no uncertain sound on this point. Nothing sacred is in instrumental music, hence you can get nothing sacred out of it. I rejoice in the thought that the church's record is on the side of the Bible, the only safe side in matters of religion, especially in matters of doubtful propriety.

Some of the speeches at our last Conference seemed to say, better not make a record that we know will be violated by many members. We fail to see it in that light. Let the record be clean, even if the membership is not. It may save some, but a corrupt record will help no one. We may have a good record, and yet a bad membership, but we cannot expect a good membership with a bad record.

It is a well-known fact that a number of religious bodies have trouble on this question, extending even to schisms, and our Brotherhood is, by no means, free. Sentiment is being moulded; the child is being educated at the family altar to love the very thing they dare not have in the church. The crisis is coming; it is pressing its claims upon our Sunday-school, into our schools, and surely will into the church. Would we not better stop and look around us, and ask what is best to do? We need much, if not all, of that money to carry on the work of the Lord, to build homes for the poor members and orphans, and to clothe, feed, and educate them.

Money spent in that way makes no trouble in this world or in the world to come, but when spent for musical instruments, it has made and does make trouble, in this world, and will likely in the world to come. The Lord asks, "Wherefore do ye spend money for that which is not bread?" Isa. 55: 2. Important question; the use of the instrument will bring no bread to body or soul; this being a fact, it becomes a question, whether a Christian can use anything he cannot glorify God with, as we are to do all to his glory. 1 Cor. 10: 31.

It may be said we have the unpopular side of this question, that it is too late now to write against it, and that the world and the church are using them. This we deeply deplore, but when sins and departures were brought among the Israelites in God's ancient church, till it caused the faithful prophets to weep and lament, and rend their garments, and pray to God in sackcloth and ashes, they were not to hold their peace, but "Cry aloud, spare not, lift up thy voice like a trumpet and show my people their transgressions, and the house of Jacob their sins." Isa. 58: 1. If men of renown led all Israel to err, and introduced vanity and idolatry until the judgments of God rested upon them, shall the press and the

✦ESSAYS✦

"Study to show thyself approved unto God; a workman that needeth not be ashamed, rightly dividing the Word of Truth."

HOUSE OF MANY MANSIONS.

SELECTED BY MARY MYERS.

O HOUSE of many mansions,
Thy doors are open wide,
And dear are all the faces
Upon the other side.
Thy portals they are golden,
And those who enter in
Shall know no more of sorrow,
Of weariness, of sin.

O house of many mansions,
My weary spirit waits
And longs to join the ransomed
Who enter through thy gates;
Who enter through thy portals,
The mansions of the blest;
Who come to thee aweary,
And find in thee their rest.

Thy walls are not of marble,
O house not built with hands;
I sigh for thee while waiting
Within these border-lands.
I know that but in dying
Thy threshold is crossed o'er;
There shall be no more sorrow
In thy forevermore.

JUSTIFICATION BY FAITH.

BY J. L. SWITZER.

"How then can a man be justified with God? or how can he be clean that is born of a woman?"—Job 25: 4.

THIS is the language, not of Job, but of Bildad, and he further goes on to say that the stars are not pure in the sight of God, and "how much less man, that is a worm, and the son of man which is a worm." The reply that Job made to Bildad, on his "justification" catechism is grand. Please turn and read it in the following chapters.

Right here is the place to bring in squarely the direct and unequivocal reply to the text above,—the reply of Inspiration to the question of a feeble comforter. "Ye see then how that by works a man is justified, and not by faith only." James 2: 24. Turn back in this chapter and read on from verse 14, and then believe "justification by faith only," if you can reject James' letter as being inspired language.

It is natural for man, realizing his great imperfection, to seek some way of either justifying himself, or getting some one else to justify him. We are all disposed somewhat, like the lawyer in Luke 10: 29, and like lawyers and all other people generally are, to justify ourselves on technical grounds. In fact, nothing comes more natural than an attempt at justification, just as soon as we are convicted of wrong. How natural, too, to look to some one else for justification!

But the wicked cannot look to God for justification, for he says positively, "I will not justify the wicked," and a woe is pronounced upon those who do "justify the wicked for reward."

In this connection I would notice also that those that call evil good, and good evil; that put darkness for light, and light for darkness; that put bitter for sweet, and sweet for bitter; that are wise in their own eyes, and prudent in their own sight, have also a woe resting upon them,—justification or no justification. The wicked cannot look to themselves for justification, or their own mouth would condemn them. "Yet by his knowledge shall my righteous servant justify many; for he shall bear their iniquities." Isa. 53: 11.

Here comes in the key-note for the "faith alone" tune. How did Jesus bear our iniquities?

He died for us; and is the propitiation for the sins of the whole world, by his giving himself a ransom for many.

That's the way he justified us,—how, then, are we justified "by faith only?" "Being now justified by his blood," says Paul, "We shall be saved from wrath through him." *By his blood* 'and *through him.*

Mankind were sinners, but remission of sin is promised unto them. The agencies for that remission are all made accessible. The knowledge and proper application of these divine agencies are plainly given from heaven. Justification begins just as soon as the sinner begins to avail himself of those agencies. Thus the Prodigal was justified when he made the good resolution. He was justified still further when he retraced his steps. He was justified still further when he prayed to his Father for forgiveness. A man is justified in the sight of God for everything good that he DOES. He is condemned for everything bad that he DOES. Justification and condemnation stand in the Scriptures exactly opposed to each other. One is right, the other wrong. One is righteousness, the other sin. There is nothing but DOING that has anything to do with our eternal happiness or misery. The idea of trying to get justification without DOING, or rather to get DOING out of justification, is extremely ridiculous and pernicious. When a man thinks a good thought, he *does* something. When a woman heaves a devotional sigh she *does* something. . No worship can take place without an act of the mind, or heart, or body. Every act of mental or physical volition is an *act.* That act is under the control of the will, and the will is subject to the creature. Hence Christ says: "This is the work of God, that ye *believe* on him whom he hath sent." John 6: 29.

The idea held out to us by the "faith-alone" advocates is about this: "We are justified by what Christ did for us, long before we ever came into the world." But then, as this is Universalism, of course this is too much to believe; so Paul is hitched up to his unwilling load and made to translate us instantaneously from earth to heaven, —the moment we believe that Jesus Christ is the Son of God,—the moment we have faith. In that moment we are translated from darkness to light, from Satan to God, from hell to heaven.

And why? Because Paul says: "Having been justified by faith, we have peace with God *through* our Lord Jesus Christ;" and this they hitch with: "Not of works lest any man should boast."

Now Paul does of course say that we are not justified by the works of the Jewish Law, *and that is as much as he really ever says anywhere about our being justified without works.* He tells us that Abraham *did right* in believing God, that this was ascribed to him for righteousness, and that in the same way righteousness will be ascribed unto us if we believe in the Lord Jesus Christ, and hence, of course, we are justified in turning from unbelief to faith. This doctrine was very essential in that day when Christ was rejected of men, when the Jews refused him, and the Gentiles had not yet heard of him, for "without faith it is impossible to please God," and the great desideratum then was to get men to receive him.

I have not space to argue this further now. Suffice it to say, in conclusion, that "we are under law to Christ." That law is made up of simple "shalts" and "shalt nots." It nowhere demands a great swelling profusion of triple-geared adjectives, of meaning so dense and obscure as to stretch the imagination like a horse blanket. Neither is there some great momentous, hidden,

mysterious spirituality in the Word of God that is not accessible to all God's creatures.

Love God, believe God, obey God. When you fail, confess and repent.

Watch and pray. Let us hear the conclusion: "Fear God and keep his commandments, for this is the whole duty of man."

McCune, Kans.

MUSICAL INSTRUMENTS.

BY ENOCH EBY.

I WRITE this article by request, and partly from a sense of duty. I was credibly informed that it is rumored that a brother and I were at a certain brother's house in Ohio, and that my comrade played on the organ, and that I used the violin. The facts are I could not play if I would, and would not if I could. I was taught by strict Christian parents, hence taught that it was at best a vain amusement, and a wrong' use of money, just as our Brotherhood always hereto regarded it. She has given no uncertain sound on this point. Nothing sacred is in instrumental music, hence you can get nothing sacred out of it. I rejoice in the thought that the church's record is on the side of the Bible, the only safe side in matters of religion, especially in matters of doubtful propriety.

Some of the speeches at our last Conference seemed to say, better not make a record that we know will be violated by many members. We fail to see it in that light. Let the record be clean, even if the membership is not. It may save some, but a corrupt record will help no one. We may have a good record, and yet a bad membership, but we cannot expect a good membership with a bad record.

It is a well-known fact that a number of religious bodies have trouble on this question, extending even to schisms, and our Brotherhood is, by no means, free. Sentiment is being moulded; the child is being educated at the family altar to love the very thing they dare not have in the church. The crisis is coming; it is pressing its claims upon our Sunday-school, into our schools, and surely will into the church. Would we not better stop, and look around us, and ask what is best to do? We need much, if not all, of that money to carry on the work of the Lord, to build homes for the poor members and orphans, and to clothe, feed, and educate them.

Money spent in that way makes no trouble in this world or in the world to come, but when spent for musical instruments, it has made and does make trouble, in this world, and will likely in the world to come. The Lord asks, "Wherefore do ye spend money for that which is not bread?" Isa. 55: 2. Important question; the use of the instrument will bring no bread to body or soul; this being a fact, it becomes a question, whether a Christian can use anything he cannot glorify God with, as we are to do all to his glory. 1 Cor. 10: 31.

It may be said we have the unpopular side of this question, that it is too late now to write against it, and that the world and the church are using them. This we deeply deplore, but when sins and departures were brought among the Israelites in God's ancient church, till it caused the faithful prophets to weep and lament, and rend their garments, and pray to God in sackcloth and ashes, they were not to hold their peace, but "Cry aloud, spare not, lift up thy voice like a trumpet and show my people their transgressions, and the house of Jacob their sins." Isa. 58: 1.

If men of renown led old Israel to err, and introduced vanity and idolatry until the judgments of God rested upon them, shall the press and the

Missionary and Tract Work Department.

"Upon the first day of the week, let every one of you lay by him in store as God hath prospered him, that there be no gatherings when I come."—1 Cor. 16: 2.

"Every man as he purposeth in his heart, so let him give. Not grudgingly or of necessity, for the Lord loveth a cheerful giver."—2 Cor. 9: 7.

HOW MUCH SHALL WE GIVE?

"Every man according to his ability." "Every one as God hath prospered him." "Every man, according as he purposeth in his heart, so let him give." "For if there be first a willing mind, it is accepted according to that a man hath, and not according to that he hath not."—2 Cor. 8: 12.

Organization of Missionary Committee.

DANIEL VANIMAN, Foreman, · · · McPherson, Kans.
D. L. MILLER, Treasurer, · · · · Mt. Morris, Ill.
GALEN B. ROYER, Secretary, · · · Mt. Morris, Ill.

Organization of Book and Tract Work.

S. W. HOOVER, Foreman, · · · · Dayton, Ohio.
S. BOCK, Secretary and Treasurer, · · Dayton, Ohio.

☞All donations intended for Missionary Work should be sent to GALEN B. ROYER, Mt. Morris, Ill.

☞All money for Tract Work should be sent to S. BOCK, Dayton, Ohio.

☞Money may be sent by Money Order, Registered Letter, or Drafts on New York or Chicago. Do not send personal checks, or drafts on interior towns, as it costs 15 cents to collect them.

☞Solicitors are requested to faithfully carry out the plan of Annual Meeting, that all our members be solicited to contribute at least twice a year for the Mission and Tract Work of the Church.

☞Notes for the Endowment Fund can be had by writing to the Secretary of either Work.

WHY ARE WE GROWING WORLDLY?

BY GRANT MAHAN.

PROBABLY no one doubts that we are growing worldly, though it is not at all likely that we all agree as to the reason why we are doing so. Several reasons might be found, but there is due in particular which we should consider very earnestly just now, for the future of the Church depends largely on the way we decide to act in the matter. We profess to believe in plain dressing, and yet if one looks at one of our congregations, particularly the younger members of it, can he help asking himself whether we really do believe in it? This does not apply to anyone of our congregations in particular, though some of them are worse, more fashionable, in their dress than others.

We go into a church and see in the congregation sisters with caps on their heads; under the caps are curls and frizzes in abundance; the remainder of the body is dressed in anything but a plain manner. The cap is a symbol of consecration to God, the rest of the dress shows consecration to the world and its fashions. How forcibly are we struck by Christ's words, "No man can serve two masters: for either he will hate the one, and love the other; or else he will hold to the one, and despise the other. Ye cannot serve God and mammon." And yet how many are trying to do this very thing! Will they be able to do so? Can they serve God and mammon? Can they enjoy all there is in this world and then have a right to the tree of life in the world to come? Are they the ones of whom it is written, "And God shall wipe away all tears from their eyes?"

The brethren are no better; the sisters are spoken of here because we can see the contrast between the church and the world better by looking at them. Members of both sexes wear gold, just as if it were not prohibited by the Bible; even a minister's wife can wear a gold watch. We are getting about as far from the simplicity of the Gospel as we well can. There are not very many things done by the people of the world that are not done by some of us. Of course we are not guilty of some of the grossest sins, at least, not

openly; but it would be well for us to find out just where we are. Are we living to promote the cause of Christ in the world, or are we living for the gratification of the lower and perishable part of our being? Not long ago I read the instructions of a monk to the members of a nunnery; they were written some time during the first half of the twelfth century. In one place he speaks thus: "As to clothing; you will especially avoid high-priced clothing, which is absolutely forbidden by the Gospel." We claim to be very much enlightened in this latter part of the nineteenth century, but in our practice we are behind this monk who wrote more than seven hundred and fifty years ago.

So much for the effect. What is the cause? But one class of persons will so depart from the Law of God, and they are those who have not consecrated themselves to him. There can be no doubt about this. And why are our members not consecrated? For some years it has seemed to me that we are too anxious to increase our number. To talk and preach and try to get people into the church is one of the best things we can do; but there is a very great danger of getting persons in who should be outside. If there is any one step taken which ought to receive thought and prayer, it is the step one takes when he comes into the church. He is not deciding a question for a day and for himself, but for eternity and for all who come in contact with him. To come into the church and promise to obey the Gospel in all points, and at the same time purpose in your heart not to obey them, is worse than remaining out of the church. And so persons want to be sure they are converted before taking this step. And ministers are often guilty of overpersuading, almost frightening people to get them into the church. This is all wrong; we don't want that kind of members.

It is a very pleasant thing to hold meetings and baptize a great many, but it is a really good thing to convert one soul. It sounds very well to say we have a large number of members, but in reality there is nothing in it. What are numbers before God? This compassing sea and land to make one convert, who is worse after than before conversion, is not God's work. This desire to have a large membership, the desire on the part of the preacher to be able to say and have it said of him, that he has brought a great many into the fold, is, it seems to me one reason why we are getting so much of the world in the church; and it is not the least reason either.

And why should we care for numbers? Are we any more sure of reaching heaven if we are in a company of a hundred thousand, than if we are in a company of one thousand? It is a great deal better to be a member of a body of ten who are righteous, than it is to be a member of a body of ten million who are unrighteous; it is better by far to be alone with God, than to be with all the world against him. If right made right, then we should be justified in trying to get on the side where there is the greatest number; but might never did and never will make right. Nothing is more contemptible than a body which has nothing but its might to sustain it.

We often speak of the progress we are making, and we are making progress; but is it all in the right direction? Some of it is good: we are more awake to missionary work, we are more in favor of developing our mental powers. But it is not all good. Can we get rid of the evil? Can we return to the old and tried principles of our fathers, or must we go on, and on, till there is no distinction between us and the world, as so many other churches have done? We can do better; will we?

GRANT MAHAN.

Halle, a. S., Germany.

HOME MISSION WORK.

(Report of the Speech given by John A. Cline on "Home Mission Work," at the Closing Exercises of the Bible Term of Bridgewater College.)

"HOW can we Obtain the Best Results in our Home Mission?" By results we mean the most work and the greatest good. By home missions we mean the outside work of our individual congregations, viz., where we can go and return the same day; outside of fifteen or twenty miles.

To obtain the most work and the greatest good in our home missions, we should locate ministers in the isolated places of our territories,—young men without family encumbrances,—who have the cause of the Master and the salvation of souls at heart.

The next best thing is for the ministers of each congregation to meet and lay off the territorial work, appoint, select, or elect one or more ont of their number to do the mission work for six or twelve months, or whatever time specified; to keep a correct record of the time engaged, number of sermons preached, expenses, number received into the church, and report at the next meeting after the specified time expires. They can re-appoint, select, or elect, for the next specified time, or others may take their places in the same way.

The church should bear their expenses and allow them something for the time they are out on mission work. This is the work of the church and not an individual work.

Brethren, well qualified for the work, who have the cause of the Master at heart, who are interested in the saving of souls, who will not shun to declare the whole Gospel, who will contend earnestly for the faith once delivered unto the saints, and the usages of the Brethren church, who have vim and push about them, and who are not afraid to tell the truth, should be sent out.

They should go into those isolated places, make appointments, preach, and visit from house to house, being supplied with tracts to distribute amongst the people, and thereby get into their good graces as much as possible. They should conduct themselves in such a manner as to win the confidence and respect of all, never talking slightingly or unkindly of other denominations.

They should be supplied with a number of little cards, having suitable Scriptural verses printed on them, to distribute amongst little children. Make a great deal of the children. Never slight them, but always talk with them and to them, and shake hands with them. If you treat them kindly and be sociable with them, they will love and never forget you. *Here lies* our success. Evangelists should always have prayer with the people before leaving the house, and on leaving, always invite them to attend meeting, especially the little folks.

They should stay in one neighborhood as long as is best or expedient, going into other localities and pushing the work; returning to the first place in about two weeks, when they will begin to reap fruits of their labors. Never stay too long at one place, and never be absent too long, because when an interest is worked up in those isolated places, the devil will soon make his appearance in the form of a roaring lion, or even in his angelic form,

The missionary will meet with various opinions and religions. He must be well posted in Scripture, to successfully meet critics and opposers. Always keep them right down to the Word of God. Give them to understand that our opinions and notions are no criterion, and that they will not stand the test unless based upon the Word of the Lord. When the Scripture is cited to many, in its simplicity and purity, they feel condemned, and not a few cry out, "Do you believe you are right and all others wrong?" "Do you believe

Missionary and Tract Work Department.

"Upon the first day of the week, let every one of you lay by him in store as God hath prospered him, that there be no gatherings when I come."—1 Cor. 16: 2.

"Every man as he purposeth in his heart, so let him give. Not grudgingly or of necessity, for the Lord loveth a cheerful giver."—2 Cor. 9: 7.

HOW MUCH SHALL WE GIVE?

"Every man according to his ability." "Every one as God hath prospered him." "Every man, according as he purposeth in his heart, so let him give." "For if there be first a willing mind, it is accepted according to that a man hath, and not according to that he hath not."—2 Cor. 8: 12.

Organization of Missionary Committee.

DANIEL VANIMAN, Foreman,	- -	McPherson, Kans.
D. L. MILLER, Treasurer,	- -	Mt. Morris, Ill.
GALEN B. ROYER, Secretary,	- -	Mt. Morris, Ill.

Organization of Book and Tract Work.

S. W. HOOVER, Foreman,	- -	Dayton, Ohio.
S. BOCK, Secretary and Treasurer,	- -	Dayton, Ohio.

☞All donations intended for Missionary Work should be sent to GALEN B. ROYER, Mt. Morris, Ill.

☞All money for Tract Work should be sent to S. BOCK, Dayton, Ohio.

☞Money may be sent by Money Order, Registered Letter, or Drafts on New York or Chicago. Do not send personal checks, or drafts on interior towns, as it costs 25 cents to collect them.

☞Solicitors are requested to faithfully carry out the plan of Annual Meeting, that all our members be solicited to contribute at least twice a year for the Mission and Tract Work of the Church.

☞Notes for the Endowment Fund can be had by writing to the Secretary of either Work.

WHY ARE WE GROWING WORLDLY?

BY GRANT MAHAN.

PROBABLY no one doubts that we are growing worldly, though it is not at all likely that we all agree as to the reason why we are doing so. Several reasons might be found, but there is one in particular which we should consider very earnestly just now, for the future of the Church depends largely on the way we decide to act in the matter. We profess to believe in plain dressing, and yet if one looks at one of our congregations, particularly the younger members of it, can he help asking himself whether we really do believe in it? This does not apply to anyone of our congregations in particular, though some of them are worse, more fashionable, in their dress than others.

We go into a church and see in the congregation sisters with caps on their heads; under the caps are curls and frizzes in abundance; the remainder of the body is dressed in anything but a plain manner. The cap is a symbol of consecration to God, the rest of the dress shows consecration to the world and its fashions. How forcibly are we struck by Christ's words, "No man can serve two masters: for either he will hate the one, and love the other; or else he will hold to the one, and despise the other. Ye cannot serve God and mammon." And yet how many are trying to do this very thing! Will they be able to do so? Can they serve God and mammon? Can they enjoy all there is in this world and then have a right to the tree of life in the world to come? Are they the ones of whom it is written, "And God shall wipe away all tears from their eyes?"

The brethren are no better; the sisters are spoken of here because we can see the contrast between the church and the world better by looking at them. Members of both sexes wear gold, just as if it were not prohibited by the Bible; even a minister's wife can wear a gold watch. We are getting about as far from the simplicity of the Gospel as we well can. There are not very many things done by the people of the world that are not done by some of us. Of course we are not guilty of some of the grossest sins, at least, not openly; but it would be well for us to find out just where we are. Are we living to promote the cause of Christ in the world, or are we living for the gratification of the lower and perishable part of our being? Not long ago I read the instructions of a monk to the members of a nunnery; they were written some time during the first half of the twelfth century. In one place he speaks thus: "As to clothing; you will especially avoid high-priced clothing, which is absolutely forbidden by the Gospel." We claim to be very much enlightened in this latter part of the nineteenth century, but in our practice we are behind this monk who wrote more than seven hundred and fifty years ago.

So much for the effect. What is the cause? But one class of persons will so depart from the Law of God, and they are those who have not consecrated themselves to him. There can be no doubt about this. And why are our members not consecrated? For some years it has seemed to me that we are too anxious to increase our number. To talk and preach and try to get people into the church is one of the best things we can do; but there is a very great danger of getting persons in who should be outside. If there is any one step taken which ought to receive thought and prayer, it is the step one takes when he comes into the church. He is not deciding a question for a day and for himself, but for eternity and for all who come in contact with him. To come into the church and promise to obey the Gospel in all points, and at the same time purpose in your heart not to obey them, is worse than remaining out of the church. And so persons want to be sure they are converted before taking this step. And ministers are often guilty of overpersuading, almost frightening people to get them into the church. This is all wrong; we don't want that kind of members.

It is a very pleasant thing to hold meetings and baptize a great many, but it is a really good thing to convert one soul. It sounds very well to say we have a large number of members, but in reality there is nothing in it. What are numbers before God? This compassing sea and land to make one convert, who is worse after than before conversion, is not God's work. This desire to have a large membership, the desire on the part of the preacher to be able to say and have it said of him, that he has brought a great many into the fold, is, it seems to me one reason why we are getting so much of the world in the church; and it is not the least reason either.

And why should we care for numbers? Are we any more sure of reaching heaven if we are in a company of a hundred thousand, than if we are in a company of one thousand? It is a great deal better to be a member of a body of ten who are righteous, than it is to be a member of a body of ten million who are unrighteous; it is better by far to be alone with God, than to have all the world against him. If might made right, then we should be justified in trying to get on the side where there is the greatest number; but might never did and never will make right. Nothing is more contemptible than a body which has nothing but its might to sustain it.

We often speak of the progress we are making, and we are making progress; but is it all in the right direction? Some of it is good: we are more awake to missionary work, we are more in favor of developing our mental powers. But it is not all good. Can we get rid of the evil? Can we return to the old and tried principles of our fathers, or must we go on, and on, till there is no distinction between us and the world, as so many other churches have done? We can do better; will we?

GRANT MAHAN.

Halle, a. S., Germany.

HOME MISSION WORK.

(Report of the Speech given by John A. Cline on "Home Mission Work," at the Closing Exercises of the Bible Term of Bridgewater College.)

"How can we Obtain the Best Results in our Home Mission?" By results we mean the most work and the greatest good. By home missions we mean the outside work of our individual congregations, viz., where we can go and return the same day; outside of fifteen or twenty miles.

To obtain the most work and the greatest good in our home missions, we should locate ministers in the isolated places of our territories,—young men without family encumbrances,—who have the cause of the Master and the salvation of souls at heart.

The next best thing is for the ministers of each congregation to meet and lay off the territorial work, appoint, select, or elect one or more out of their number to do the mission work for six or twelve months, or whatever time specified; to keep a correct record of the time engaged, number of sermons preached, expenses, number received into the church, and report at the next meeting after the specified time expires. They can re-appoint, select, or elect, for the next specified time, or others may take their places in the same way.

The church should bear their expenses and allow them something for the time they are out on mission work. This is the work of the church and not an individual work.

Brethren, well qualified for the work, who have the cause of the Master at heart, who are interested in the saving of souls, who will not shun to declare the whole Gospel, who will contend earnestly for the faith once delivered unto the saints, and the usages of the Brethren church, who have vim and push about them, and who are not afraid to tell the truth, should be sent out.

They should go into those isolated places, make appointments, preach, and visit from house to house, being supplied with tracts to distribute amongst the people, and thereby get into their good graces as much as possible. They should conduct themselves in such a manner as to win the confidence and respect of all, never talking slightingly or unkindly of other denominations.

They should be supplied with a number of little cards, having suitable Scriptural verses printed on them, to distribute amongst little children. Make a great deal of the children. Never slight them, but always talk with them and to them, and shake hands with them. If you treat them kindly and be sociable with them, they will love and never forget you. Here lies our success. Evangelists should always have prayer with the people before leaving the house, and on leaving, always invite them to attend meeting, especially the little folks.

They should stay in one neighborhood as long as is best or expedient, going into other localities and pushing the work; returning to the first place in about two weeks, when they will begin to reap fruits of their labors. Never stay too long at one place, and never be absent too long, because when an interest is worked up in these isolated places, the devil will soon make his appearance in the form of a roaring lion, or even in his angelic form,

The missionary will meet with various opinions and religions. He must be well posted in Scripture, to successfully meet critics and opposers. Always keep them right down to the Word of God. Give them to understand that our opinions and notions are no criterion, and that they will not stand the test unless based upon the Word of the Lord. When the Scripture is cited to many, in its simplicity and purity, they feel condemned, and not a few cry out, "Do you believe you are right and all others wrong?" "Do you believe

The Gospel Messenger,

A Weekly at $1.50 Per Annum.

PUBLISHED BY

The Brethren's Publishing Co.

D. L. MILLER,	Editor.
J. H. MOORE,	Office Editor.
J. B. BRUMBAUGH,	Associate Editors.
J. G. ROYER,	
JOSEPH AMICK,	Business Manager.

ADVISORY COMMITTEE.

L. W. Teeter, A. Hutchison, Daniel Hays.

☞Communications for publication should be legibly written with black ink on one side of the paper only. Do not attempt to interline, or to put on one page what ought to occupy two.

☞Anonymous communications will not be published.

☞Do not mix business with articles for publication. Keep your communications on separate sheets from all business.

☞Time is precious. We always have time to attend to business and to answer questions of importance, but please do not subject us to read less answering of letters.

☞The MESSENGER is mailed each week to all subscribers. If the address is correctly entered on our list, the paper must reach the person to whom it is addressed. If you do not get your paper, write us, giving particulars.

☞When changing your address, please give your former as well as your future address in full, so as to avoid delay and misunderstanding.

☞Always remit to the office from which you order your goods, no matter from where you receive them.

☞Do not send personal checks or drafts on interior banks, unless you send with them at cents each, to pay for collection.

☞Remittances should be made by Post-office Money Order, Drafts on New York, Philadelphia or Chicago, or Registered Letters, made payable and addressed to "Brethren's Publishing Co., Mount Morris, Ill.," or "Brethren's Publishing Co., Huntingdon, Pa."

☞Entered at the Post-office at Mount Morris, Ill., as second-class matter.

Mount Morris, Ill.,   -   **August 23, 1892.**

THERE are now said to be, in the United States, 97 religious denominations, while in Great Britain there are 257.

BRO. J. T. BRITTON, of Dalinsville, Va., has changed his address to Bristol Station, Prince Williams County, same State.

"HORACE GREELEY was once asked whether a man or a woman was superior. He said that depended on who the man or woman was."

DURING the heated season, many of our popular churches are closed. But we have yet to hear of the Brethren closing any of their houses of worship on account of the warm weather.

BRO. T. T. MEYERS, of Philadelphia, Pa., may now be addressed at 2029 N. 13 St. instead of his former address. One was recently baptized there and two in Germantown, with fair prospects of more. So writes Bro. W. B. Stover.

AT Butteville, Oregon, there is said to be a Congregational church composed entirely of women, officers and all; there being not one man connected with the little band. The number composing this rather strange congregation is ten.

IN a former issue we said that Bro. J. C. Murray was to commence a series of meetings at Clarence, Iowa, the last of September. We are now informed that the meetings will commence Sept. 3, and continue several weeks. Bro. Zook desires the members of other congregations to attend and enjoy the meetings also.

A COMET is now said to be approaching the earth, which will almost equal, in brilliancy, the great comet of 1858. It can now be seen in the eastern sky in the morning, with the aid of an ordinary opera glass. About the last of the month it will be a magnificent sight. Old timers say they could read by the light of the comet in 1858. All these wonders show the handiwork of God, and when we come to think, how little do we know of the works of God!

WE wish to caution our readers against sending us any queries involving a personal case. We are willing to answer queries of a general character, such as may be of interest to the general Brotherhood, but those that involve personal matters we aim to decline. Our object is to teach principles that may apply in general terms.

BRO. I. J. ROSENBERGER has arranged to commence a series of meetings at Bonnieville, Kentucky, Aug. 25. From there he goes to Hodgensville, the same State, to commence meetings Sept. 1, expecting to be at Lanark, Ill., Sept. 8. He reports a good harvest-meeting at Covington, Ohio, and $15 raised for the new meeting-house at Hollowtown, Highland Co., Ohio.

WHILE we are receiving a number of corrections for the Almanac, no one has yet sent in any communications for its pages. We would like to fill the reading pages with the very best of matter, and for that purpose solicit from our readers some of their very best thoughts or selections. Those feeling an interest in this matter will please give it early and prompt attention.

WE trust our correspondents will not insist on us returning declined articles. It is quite a task to go through a great pile of manuscript, searching for some article that may have been laid aside one or more years ago. We can seldom spare the time for a task of the kind. Writers who consider their articles too valuable to be lost, in case they are declined, should keep a copy of them.

THE daily press reports great suffering among the Mexicans on both sides of the Rio Grande. Many families have been living for days on what they could pick up. Many children have died. The relief committee is giving out only four pounds of corn to each person a week,—merely enough to keep soul and body together. Clothing as well as food is greatly needed. Whole families go about entirely nude.

IT is reported that a decided sensation has been caused in Jerusalem by the introduction of electric light into a new and flourishing flour-mill, lately started there by some German proprietors. The building in which the light has been introduced, is near to the supposed site of Calvary and close to the Damascus Gate. It need hardly be said that the Arabs and Jews are much puzzled to account for a light in a lamp in which there is no oil. Up to the present time, while gazing with wonder, they have been keeping at a respectful distance.

"WHAT a gauntlet the farmer runs in producing a crop of wheat! At every point, from the turning of the sod to the harvesting of the mature grain, he is beset with possibilities of failure. Even after the harvest, the golden sheaves may rot in the stack, and disappoint the hopes and labors of a year. But does the farmer, therefore, fold his hands and cease to work? Not at all. He has faith to believe that, in the long run, his intelligent and persistent endeavors will meet with success. Without this faith the world would be absolutely without bread in less than two seasons." The farmer has faith in what he is doing, but it is not faith alone, for he knows that faith alone is dead. He works, knowing that by works his faith is made manifest. It is in the raising of crops there is a divine as well a human part. The farmer, by works, performs the human part, and trusts God for the divine part. Just so in salvation. We must do what God commands of us, and he will perform the rest. But there are no uncertainties in the work of grace if we, in faith, do the part assigned to us. The blessings are sure to follow.

WE do most cheerfully recommend the following good piece of advice, clipped from one of our exchanges: "Use pure language, such as will not offend the most refined and delicate sensibilities; let it be chaste and elegant; always choose the plainest and easiest words that will clearly express your ideas, and never be so undignified as to allow yourself to use coarse or slang phrases. Avoid them as you would a pestilence, for a moral pestilence they are. Rhetoricians and other writers on Belles-Lettres have told us a great deal about the power of imagination over all language, but have told us little about the power of language over the imagination and taste, and yet their influence is reciprocal. If a corrupt imagination will prompt corrupt language, corrupt language will beget a corrupt imagination."

JUST before going to press we received the following from Bro. J. G. Royer, dated Aug. 15, at Flora, Ind.: "We (wife, Mertie and self) arrived here Saturday at 6 P. M. We found wife's father, C. H. Reiff, quite feeble. It is manifest that he cannot continue here long. He has lived to a ripe old age, being in his eighty-ninth year. The scenes of his boyhood, the old farm with its orchard, its lane, its stone fence, its spring and the willow that hung over it, are pictures fresh before his mind. It looks as if life's register were unrolled to the beginning and he about to take his exit from the stage at the point where he stepped upon it. At church yesterday, we met our esteemed brother, Heil Hamilton. He, too, is in his eighties. He is one of Indiana's pioneer ministers. In closing the meeting he said, 'My day and time brought me experiences of which many, who enjoy the religious privileges of to-day, know nothing.' Bro. Hamilton officiated at the installation to the ministry of our departed brother, R. H. Miller; also at the installation of your humble servant. Physically, he is feeble, but spiritually, 'as a shock of corn fully ripe.' Eternity alone will reveal the blessings enjoyed by the church, as a result of the labors and sacrifices made by such veterans of the cross, as our beloved brother Hamilton. God bless their hoary heads."

THE *Christian Evangelist* says: "The old days are about ended in Palestine. Jerusalem is to become a modern city. The scream of the locomotive is to be echoed from the Mount of Olives and the Hill of Evil Counsel. The railway from Joppa which has been in progress for two years, is completed from the sea to the foot of the mountains, and it is thought will reach Jerusalem by October. A French company is building the line at an estimated cost of about $1,500,000. The line from Jaffa to the foot of the mountains is already in a fairly good condition, but it has not yet been opened to traffic. The part to be finished is that which lies between the Jaffa plain and Jerusalem, and which will follow one of the valleys leading up towards Jerusalem from the south-west. The work will be difficult, but it offers no insurmountable obstacles. The length of the whole line will be 54 miles, or 17 miles longer than the present carriage road. When the line is completed, a branch will be made from Ramleh to Gaza, with the object of forming a junction with a line from Egypt. This line, which will run over a level plain, can be readily constructed, and will enable the traveler to go from Jerusalem to Alexandria or Cairo by rail. Another line, for which a concession has been secured, is to run from Haifa at the foot of Mount Carmel, on the bay of Acre, through the level depression opened to the Jordan by the plain of Esdraelon, and to continue from thence to Damascus. The nineteenth century is knocking at the gates of the East and will not be denied admittance."

The Gospel Messenger,

A Weekly at $1.50 Per Annum.

PUBLISHED BY

The Brethren's Publishing Co.

D. L. MILLER, ... Editor.

J. H. MOORE, ... Office Editor.

J. B. BRUMBAUGH, } Associate Editors.
J. G. ROYER, }

JOSEPH AMICK, - . . . Business Manager.

ADVISORY COMMITTEE.
L. W. Teeter, A. Hutchison, Daniel Hays.

☞Communications for publication should be legibly written with black ink on one side of the paper only. Do not attempt to interline, or to put on one page what ought to occupy two.

☞Anonymous communications will not be published.

☞Do not mix business with articles for publication. Keep your communications on separate sheets from all business.

☞Time is precious. We always have time to attend to business and to answer questions of importance, but please do not subject us to need less answering of letters.

☞The MESSENGER is mailed each week to all subscribers. If the address is correctly entered on our list, the paper must reach the person to whom it is addressed. If you do not get your paper, write us, giving particulars.

☞When changing your address, please give your former as well as your future address in full, so as to avoid delay and misunderstanding.

☞Always remit to the office from which you order your goods, no matter from where you receive them.

☞Do not send personal checks or drafts on interior banks, unless you send with them 25 cents each, to pay for collection.

☞Remittances should be made by Post-office Money Order, Drafts on New York, Philadelphia or Chicago, or Registered Letters, made payable and addressed to "Brethren's Publishing Co., Mount Morris, Ill.," or "Brethren's Publishing Co., Huntingdon, Pa."

☞Entered at the Post-office at Mount Morris, Ill., as second-class matter.

Mount Morris, Ill., - - - August 23, 1892.

THERE are now said to be, in the United States, 97 religious denominations, while in Great Britain there are 257.

BRO. J. T. BRITTON, of Dallasville, Va., has changed his address to Bristol Station, Prince Williams County, same State.

"HORACE GREELEY was once asked whether a man or a woman was superior. He said that depended on who the man or woman was."

DURING the heated season, many of our popular churches are closed. But we have yet to hear of the Brethren closing any of their houses of worship on account of the warm weather.

BRO. T. T. MEYERS, of Philadelphia, Pa., may now be addressed at 2029 N. 13 St. instead of his former address. One was recently baptized there and two in Germantown, with fair prospects of more. So writes Bro. W. B. Stover.

AT Butteville, Oregon, there is said to be a Congregational church composed entirely of women, officers and all; there being not one man connected with the little band. The number composing this rather strange congregation is ten.

IN a former issue we said that Bro. J. C. Murray was to commence a series of meetings at Clarence, Iowa, the last of September. We are now informed that the meetings will commence Sept. 3, and continue several weeks. Bro. Zook desires the members of other congregations to attend and enjoy the meetings also.

A COMET is now said to be approaching the earth, which will almost equal, in brilliancy, the great comet of 1858. It can now be seen in the eastern sky in the morning, with the aid of an ordinary opera glass. About the last of the month it will be a magnificent sight. Old timers say they could read by the light of the comet in 1858. All these wonders show the handiwork of God, and when we come to think, how little do we know of the works of God!

WE wish to caution our readers against sending us any queries involving a personal case. We are willing to answer queries of a general character, such as may be of interest to the general Brotherhood, but those that involve personal matters we aim to decline. Our object is to teach principles that may apply in general terms.

BRO. I. J. ROSENBERGER has arranged to commence a series of meetings at Bonnieville, Kentucky, Aug. 25. From there he goes to Hodgensville, the same State, to commence meetings Sept. 1, expecting to be at Lanark, Ill., Sept. 8. He reports a good harvest-meeting at Covington, Ohio, and $15 raised for the new meeting-house at Hollowtown, Highland Co., Ohio.

WHILE we are receiving a number of corrections for the Almanac, no one has yet sent in any communications for its pages. We would like to fill the reading pages with the very best of matter, and for that purpose solicit from our readers some of their very best thoughts of selections. Those feeling an interest in this matter will please give it early and prompt attention.

WE trust our correspondents will not insist on us returning declined articles. It is quite a task to go through a great pile of manuscript, searching for some article that may have been laid aside one or more years ago. We can seldom spare the time for a task of the kind. Writers who consider their articles too valuable to be lost, in case they are declined, should keep a copy of them.

THE daily press reports great suffering among the Mexicans on both sides of the Rio Grande. Many families have been living for days on what they could pick up. Many children have died. The relief committee is giving out only four pounds of corn to each person a week,—merely enough to keep soul and body together. Clothing as well as food is greatly needed. Whole families go about entirely nude.

IT is reported that a decided sensation has been caused in Jerusalem by the introduction of electric light into a new and flourishing flour-mill, lately started there by some German proprietors. The building in which the light has been introduced, is near to the supposed site of Calvary and close to the Damascus Gate. It need hardly be said that the Arabs and Jews are much puzzled to account for a light in a lamp in which there is no bil. Up to the present time, while gazing with wonder, they have been keeping at a respectful distance.

"WHAT a gauntlet the farmer runs in producing a crop of wheat! At every point, from the turning of the sod to the harvesting of the mature grain, he is beset with possibilities of failure. Even after the harvest, the golden sheaves may rot in the stack, and disappoint the hopes and labors of a year. But does the farmer, therefore, fold his hands and cease to work? Not at all. He has faith to believe that, in the long run, his intelligent and persistent endeavors will meet with success. Without this faith the world would be absolutely without bread in less than two seasons." The farmer has faith in what he is doing, but it is not faith alone, for he knows that faith alone is dead. He works, knowing that by works his faith is made manifest. In the raising of crops there is a divine as well a human part. The farmer, by works, performs the human part, and trusts God for the divine part. Just so in salvation. We must do what God commands of us, and he will perform the rest. But there are no uncertainties in the work of grace if we, in faith, do the part assigned to us. The blessings are sure to follow.

WE do most cheerfully recommend th lowing good piece of advice, clipped from of our exchanges: 'Use pure language, such a not offend the most refined and delicate se ities; let it be chaste and elegant; always the plainest and easiest words that will clear press your ideas, and never be so undignified allow yourself to use coarse or slang ph Avoid them as you would a pestilence, moral pestilence they are. Rhetoricians other writers on Belles-Lettres have told great deal about the power of imagination all language, but have told us little about the er of language over the imagination and and yet their influence is reciprocal. If a co imagination will prompt corrupt language, rupt language will beget a corrupt imaginat

JUST before going to press we received th lowing from Bro. J. G. Royer, dated Aug. 1 Flora, Ind.: "We (wife, Mertie and self) are here Saturday at 6 P. M. We found wife' ther, C. H. Reiff, quite feeble. It is manifes he cannot continue here long. He has lived ripe old age, being in his eighty-ninth year. scenes of his boyhood, the old farm with it chard, its lane, its stone fence, its spring an willow that hung over it, are pictures fresh b his mind. It looks as if life's register wer rolled to the beginning and he about to tak exit from the stage at the point where he ste upon it. At church yesterday, we met ou teemed brother, Heil Hamilton. He, too, is eighties. He is one of Indiana's pioneer m ters. In closing the meeting he said, 'My and time brought me experiences of which n who enjoy the religious privileges of to-day, nothing.' Bro. Hamilton officiated at the in lation to the ministry of our departed brothe H. Miller; also at the installation of your hu servant. Physically, he is feeble, but spirit 'as a shock of corn fully ripe.' Eternity will reveal the blessings enjoyed by the ch as a result of the labors and sacrifices ma such veterans of the cross, as our beloved bro Hamilton. God bless their hoary heads."

THE Christian Evangelist says: "The old are about ended in Palestine. Jerusalem is come a modern city. The scream of the loo tive is to be echoed from the Mount of Olives the Hill of Evil Counsel. The railway from pa which has been in progress for two year completed from the sea to the foot of the m ains, and it is thought will reach Jerusale October. A French company is building the at an estimated cost of about $1,500,000. The from Jaffa to the foot of the mountains is alr in a fairly good condition, but it has not yet opened to traffic. The part to be finished i which lies between the Jaffa plain and Jerus and which will follow one of the valleys le up towards Jerusalem from the south-west work will be difficult, but it offers no insurm able obstacles. The length of the whole line be 54 miles, or 17 miles longer than the pr carriage road. When the line is complet branch will be made from Ramleh to Gaza, the object of forming a junction with a line Egypt. This line, which will run over a plain, can be readily constructed, and will er the traveler to go from Jerusalem to Alexand Cairo by rail. Another line, for which a con sion has been secured, is to run from Haifa a foot of Mount Carmel, on the bay of Acre, thr the level depression opened to the Jordan by plain of Esdraelon, and to continue from th to Damascus. The nineteenth century is kn ing at the gates of the East and will not be de admittance."

QUERISTS' DEPARTMENT.

Why do the Brethren, in writing on the prayer-covering, say vail? Some of our sisters persist in wearing the Vail instead of the cap, and use what is said in the MESSENGER in defense of their practice. Paul says nothing about the Vail. He calls it a covering.   S. H.

THE Revised Version renders the term vail, and that is certainly the meaning of the Greek. In the Apostolic Age the prayer-covering was a vail, and of course that must be the one referred to by Paul. The vail, however, has gone out of use as a prayer-covering. It is worn now only for fashion and comfort. No one thinks of it as a prayer-covering only those who prefer to resemble the world in their appearance rather than the church. The cap is the only prayer-covering now in use as such. To substitute a fashionable article is not only unwise but shows a disregard for the wishes of the church, and a dangerous preference for the ways of the world. We do not understand that Paul meant to establish a particular kind of covering when he named the oriental vail. If he did, then we are all out of line in this respect, for neither do those who wear the plain cap, or those who use the fashionable vail appear as did the sisters of the first centuries. It is the principle we must seek to emphasize when considering the prayer question, and leave the application of the principle to the different ages and circumstances. In this age the plain cap is the prayer-covering that becometh women professing godliness, and our sisters should not hesitate to adopt it, and thus conform to the general wishes of the church. A sister who wears this covering is known to be in sympathy with the church, but one who ignores it is occupying doubtful ground, to say the least of it. Her pleading for the vail is probably more on account of it being fashionable—a plea that is unholy in its nature and evil in its tendency. Were the cap fashionable, there would be no plea for the vail whatever.

Will you please write an article on Spiritualism, and talking with departed spirits?   E. S.

We will leave others to write on the question referred to. We have no confidence whatever, in either the works or claims of the advocates of Spiritualism. If the departed spirits, so-called, would exhort the living to obey the church, and live holy lives, there might be some grounds for at least encouraging the claim, but as it is, we have long since come to the conclusion that the only spiritual influence connected with the whole system is furnished by Satan. Any one who will compare the works of spirit mediums with the teachings of the Scriptures, certainly cannot help realizing that they are not from the same source.

Why did Paul quit baptizing and say he thanked God that he baptized no more?   J. B.

The Scripture referred to reads thus: "Now this I say, that every one of you saith, I am of Paul; and I of Apollos; and I of Cephas; and I of Christ. Is Christ divided? was Paul crucified for you? or were ye baptized in the name of Paul? I thank God that I baptized none of you, but Crispus and Gaius; lest any should say that I had baptized in mine own name. And I baptized also the household of Stephanas: besides, I know not whether I baptized any other. For Christ sent me not to baptize, but to preach the gospel: not with wisdom of words, lest the cross of Christ should be made of none effect." 1 Cor. 1: 12–17. We do not infer from this that Paul ceased baptizing. He thanked God that he had, by his own hands, baptized so few of the members composing the church at Corinth. They

were divided in sentiment, some holding to one preacher and some to another. Seeing the church in this unfortunate condition, caused Paul to feel thankful that he had baptized such a small number of them, lest they might say that he had baptized in his own name. He was the means of leading them to Christ, for he had preached the Gospel to them most earnestly, but the baptizing was done by his co-laborers in the Gospel, the same as Jesus had his disciples to do for him. Paul was selected and sent out to preach the Gospel, while others attended to the baptizing, though with his own hands he did administer the rite to a few, as we learn from the quotation above and other instances. Tradition informs us that Paul was a small man and not very strong physically, and for that reason he probably had others to immerse his converts. Viewed in this light we may better understand why the apostle did so little baptizing.   J. H. M.

FORTUNE HUNTERS.

THE following, clipped from the Chicago Journal, if heeded, may save thousands of dollars to that class of readers who imagine that great fortunes await them in the Old World. We advise a careful reading of the article, and then be contented with what can be done in America,—the land of freedom and plenty:

"The English authorities have done a good thing for one class of American fools,—the class who get excited over an announcement that they are among the heirs to great estates abroad, and who imagine that they may secure a share of the property. William Lord Moore, who has made a business of gulling Americans by representing himself as the agent of some of these mythical estates, has been arrested, and, though he may not be convicted, a good result will have been attained in the exposure of his bare-faced mode of swindling.

"It may be said of these foreign estates, to which Americans imagine themselves the heirs, that estates do-not go begging abroad any more than they do here. All property in the old country is in the hands of some one who will fight to retain its possession, and the chances are a hundred to one that the right of the case would be with him or her. Big sums of cash awaiting the proper claimants do not lie in the bank of England or anywhere else, and the laws over there are pretty well executed and have done tolerably good justice up to date. A group of swindlers, familiar with the exaggeration of hope among foolish people, have originated these tales of estates awaiting claimants, and have been fattening upon the contributions of their dupes. There have been meetings in this country of the Smiths, Joneses, and Robinsons, all confident that,' by raising a certain sum for expenses, they could secure, eventually, millions in return. They have been but foolish people, deluded, generally, by designing knaves. The arrest, upon his own ground, of one of the swindling operators is a good thing for the American lambs. Some of them will read the news and reflect upon it."

FOR THE REMISSION OF SINS.

IN answer to the inquiry whether backsliders should not be rebaptized, since baptism is for the remission of sins, the editor of the Christian Standard gives the following clear answer:

"The New Testament teaches us that the penitent believer secures the forgiveness of sins and acceptance with God, through Jesus Christ, when he,

from the heart, comes to the obedience of faith in the ordinance of baptism. See Mark 16: 16; Acts 2: 38; Acts 22: 16; Rom. 6: 17, 18; Gal. 3: 26, 27. These passages indicate the conditions of becoming the children of God. That God does not forgive those who honestly come short of exact obedience, need not be asserted, and should not be. But the conditions named in the Scriptures referred to are the appointed conditions of pardon for the world of mankind. The New Testament makes no provision for the forgiveness of an apostate, one who has become an enemy of Jesus Christ after being a Christian. See Heb. 6: 1–8. For sinning or backsliding Christians there is forgiveness through confession and prayer. Who does not daily need this forgiveness? Speaking of Christians, it is written, "If we confess our sins, he is faithful and righteous to forgive us our sins, and to cleanse us from all unrighteousness." (1 John 1: 9.) Why should we wish to have any law but this, for the forgiveness of Christians when they go astray?"

FASHIONABLE WOMEN.

THE people who teach and practice plainness may glean no small amount of consolation from the following, clipped from Zion's Watchman:

"Fashion kills more than toil or sorrow. Obedience to fashion is a great transgression of the law of woman's nature, a greater injury to her physical and mental constitution than the hardships of poverty and neglect. The slave woman at her toil still lives and grows old, and sees two or three generations of her mistresses pass away. The washer-woman, with scarcely a ray of hope to cheer her in her toils, will live to see her fashionable 'sisters all 'extinct. The kitchen maid is hearty and strong, when her lady has to be nursed like a sick baby. It is a sad truth that fashion-pampered women are always worthless for all good ends of life; they have still less power or moral will, and quite as little energy. They are dolls formed in the hands of milliners to be fed to order. If they rear children, what are they? What do they amount to but real scions of old stock? Who ever heard of a fashionable woman's child exhibiting any virtue and power of mind for which it became eminent? Read the biographies of our great men and women. Not one of them had a fashionable mother."

CORRESPONDENCE.

"Write what thou seest, and send it unto the churches."

☞Church News solicited for this Department. If you have had a good meeting, send a report of it, so that others may rejoice with you, in writing give name of church, County and State. Be brief. Notes of Travel should be as short as possible. Land Advertisements are not solicited for this Department. We have an advertising page, and, if necessary, will issue supplements.

Echoes from the Highway.

ECHOES sometimes are of a surprising character; however, they are, as a rule, the effects of a cause. Another chapter in the experience of the church at Lordsburg has opened and closed. The mountain, so to speak, moved and brought forth ——. Well Æsop of fable fame was no fool when it came to painting human character. Though it be not Scripture yet it is true, all the same, that "birds of a feather will flock together." Disloyalty, the outgrowth of worldly-mindedness, according to the laws of gravitation, will find its level, materialize and fossilize. Such is history, as the pages of the past show, and so it will always be, we presume.

One act of the drama, bordering on the ludicrous, was that of a small man, having a lifting power of, say two hundred pounds, trying to captivate and carry away the foundation-stone, more ponderous than the bulwarks of Gibraltar, as

QUERISTS' DEPARTMENT.

Why do the Brethren, in writing on the prayer-covering, say vail? Some of our sisters persist in wearing the vail instead of the cap, and use what is said in the MESSENGER in defense of their practice. Paul says nothing about the vail. He calls it a covering. S. H.

THE Revised Version renders the term vail, and that is certainly the meaning of the Greek. In the Apostolic Age the prayer-covering was a vail, and of course that must be the one referred to by Paul. The vail, however, has gone out of use as a prayer-covering. It is worn now only for fashion and comfort. No one thinks of it as a prayer-covering only those who prefer to resemble the world in their appearance rather than the church. The cap is the only prayer-covering now in use as such. To substitute a fashionable article is not only unwise but shows a disregard for the wishes of the church, and a dangerous preference for the ways of the world. We do not understand that Paul meant to establish a particular kind of covering when he named the oriental vail. If he did, then we are all out of line in this respect, for neither do those who wear the plain cap, or those who use the fashionable vail appear as did the sisters of the first centuries. It is the principle we must seek to emphasize when considering the prayer question, and leave the application of the principle to the different ages and circumstances. In this age the plain cap is the prayer-covering that becometh women professing godliness, and our sisters should not hesitate to adopt it, and thus conform to the general wishes of the church. A sister who wears this covering is known to be in sympathy with the church, but one who ignores it is occupying doubtful ground, to say the least of it. Her pleading for the vail is probably more on account of it being fashionable—a plea that is unholy in its nature and evil in its tendency. Were the cap fashionable, there would be no plea for the vail whatever.

Will you please write an article on Spiritualism, and talking with departed spirits? E. S.

We will leave others to write on the question referred to. We have no confidence whatever, in either the works or claims of the advocates of Spiritualism. If the departed spirits, so-called, would exhort the living to obey the Gospel, and live holy lives, there might be some grounds for at least encouraging the claim, but as it is, we have long since come to the conclusion that the only spiritual influence connected with the whole system is furnished by Satan. Any one who will compare the works of spirit mediums with the teachings of the Scriptures, certainly cannot help realizing that they are not from the same source.

Why did Paul quit baptizing and say he thanked God that he baptized no more? J. B.

The Scripture referred to reads thus: "Now this I say, that every one of you saith, I am of Paul; and I of Apollos; and I of Cephas; and I of Christ. Is Christ divided? was Paul crucified for you? or were ye baptized in the name of Paul? I thank God that I baptized none of you, but Crispus and Gaius; lest any should say that I had baptized in mine own name. And I baptized also the household of Stephanas: besides, I know not whether I baptized any other. For Christ sent me not to baptize, but to preach the gospel: not with wisdom of words, lest the cross of Christ should be made of none effect." 1 Cor. 1: 12-17. We do not infer from this that Paul ceased baptizing. He thanked God that he had, by his own hands, baptized so few of the members composing the church at Corinth. They

were divided in sentiment, some holding to one preacher and some to another. Seeing the church in this unfortunate condition, caused Paul to feel thankful that he had baptized such a small number of them, lest they might say that he had baptized in his own name. He was the means of leading them to Christ, for he had preached the Gospel to them most earnestly, but the baptizing was done by his co-laborers in the Gospel, the same as Jesus had his disciples to do for him. Paul was selected and sent out to preach the Gospel, while others attended to the baptizing, though with his own hands he did administer the rite to a few, as we learn from the quotation above and other instances. Tradition informs us that Paul was a small man and not very strong physically, and for that reason he probably had others to immerse his converts. Viewed in this light we may better understand why the apostle did so little baptizing. J. H. M.

FORTUNE HUNTERS.

THE following, clipped from the Chicago Journal, if heeded, may save thousands of dollars to that class of readers who imagine that great fortunes await them in the Old World. We advise a careful reading of the article, and then be contented with what can be done in America,—the land of freedom and plenty:

"The English authorities have done a good thing for one class of American fools,—the class who get excited over an announcement that they are among the heirs to great estates abroad, and who imagine that they may secure a share of the property. William Lord Moore, who has made a business of gulling Americans by representing himself as the agent of some of these mythical estates, has been arrested, and, though he may not be convicted, a good result will have been attained in the exposure of his bare-faced mode of swindling.

"It may be said of these foreign estates, to which Americans imagine themselves the heirs, that estates do not go begging abroad any more than they do here. All property in the old country is in the hands of some one who will fight to retain its possession, and the chances are a hundred to one that the right of the case would be with him or her. Big sums of cash awaiting the proper claimants do not lie in the bank of England or anywhere else, and the laws over there are pretty well executed and have done tolerably good justice up to date. A group of swindlers, familiar with the exaggeration of hope among foolish people, have originated these tales of estates awaiting claimants, and have been fattening upon the contributions of their dupes. There have been meetings in this country of the Smiths, Joneses, and Robinsons, all confident that, by raising a certain sum for expenses, they could secure, eventually, millions in return. They have been but foolish people, deluded, generally, by designing knaves. The arrest, upon his own ground, of one of the swindling operators is a good thing for the American lambs. Some of them will read the news and reflect upon it."

FOR THE REMISSION OF SINS.

IN answer to the inquiry whether backsliders should not be rebaptized, since baptism is for the remission of sins, the editor of the Christian Standard gives the following clear answer:

"The New Testament teaches us that the penitent believer secures the forgiveness of sins and acceptance with God, through Jesus Christ, when he,

from the heart, comes to the obedience of faith in the ordinance of baptism. See Mark 16: 16; Acts 2: 38; Acts 22: 16; Rom. 6: 17, 18; Gal. 3: 26, 27. These passages indicate the conditions of becoming the children of God. That God does not forgive those who honestly come short of exact obedience, need not be asserted, and should not be. But the conditions named in the Scriptures referred to are the appointed conditions of pardon for the world of mankind. The New Testament makes no provision for the forgiveness of an apostate, one who has become an enemy of Jesus Christ after being a Christian. See Heb. 6: 1-8. For sinning or backsliding Christians there is forgiveness through confession and prayer. Who does not daily need this forgiveness? Speaking of Christians, it is written, "If we confess our sins, he is faithful and righteous to forgive us our sins, and to cleanse us from all unrighteousness." (1 John 1: 9.) Why should we wish to have any law but this, for the forgiveness of Christians when they go astray?"

FASHIONABLE WOMEN.

THE people who teach and practice plainness may glean no small amount of consolation from the following, clipped from Zion's Watchman:

"Fashion kills more than toil or sorrow. Obedience to fashion is a great transgression of the law of woman's nature, a greater injury to her physical and mental constitution than the hardships of poverty and neglect. The slave woman at her toil still lives and grows old, and sees two or three generations of her mistresses pass away. The washer-woman, with scarcely a ray of hope to cheer her in her toils, will live to see her fashionable sisters all extinct. The kitchen maid is hearty and strong, when her lady has to be nursed like a sick baby. It is a sad truth that fashion-pampered women are always worthless for all good ends of life; they have still less power or moral will, and quite as little energy. They are dolls formed in the hands of milliners to be fed to order. If they rear children, what are they? What do they amount to but real scions of old stock? Who ever heard of a fashionable woman's child exhibiting any virtue and power of mind for which it became eminent? Read the biographies of our great men and women. Not one of them had a fashionable mother."

CORRESPONDENCE.

*** Write what thou seest, and send it unto the churches."

☞ Church News solicited for this Department. If you have had a good meeting, send a report of it, so that others may rejoice with you. In writing give name of church, County and State. Be brief. Notes of Travel should be as short as possible. Land Advertisements are not solicited for this Department. We have an advertising page, and, if necessary, will issue supplements.

Echoes from the Highway.

ECHOES sometimes are of a surprising character; however, they are, as a rule, the effects of a cause. Another chapter in the experience of the church at Lordsburg has opened and closed. The mountain, so to speak; moved and brought forth ——. Well Æsop of fable fame was no fool when it came to painting human character. Though it be not Scripture yet it is true, all the same, that "birds of a feather will flock together." Disloyalty, the outgrowth of worldly-mindedness, according to the laws of gravitation, will find its level, materialize and fossilize. Such is history, as the pages of the past show, and so it will always be, we presume.

One act of the drama, bordering on the ludicrous, was that of a small man, having a lifting power of, say two hundred pounds, trying to captivate and carry away the foundation-stone, more ponderous than the bulwarks of Gibraltar, as

been great murderers: They don't think they are defiling their church with such nonsense.

The University building is a very large one. I was in the school halls and found them decorated in the finest style. The room in which the President lives was about in the same style as that which was to be seen in the royal palace in Stockholm. The University is divided into four parts, the Medical, the Theological, the Philosophical and the Law Department, and from this learned men are going out into the whole kingdom.

To-morrow I intend to go to Stockholm and from there direct to my home, which I hope to reach July 15, at noon. From my home I will send you my last letter for this time.

JOHN OLSSON.

Upsala, Sweden.

(*To be Continued.*)

Ministerial Meeting.

THE following is the programme for the Ministerial Meeting of Southern Ohio, to be held in the Wolf Creek church, Montgomery County, Ohio, Oct. 27, commencing at 8:30 A. M.:

1. "What Should be the Aims of a Revival, and how Attained?"—S. W. Hoover and A. G. Crosswhite.

2. "What is the Best Method of Teaching in our Sunday-schools?"—Jesse Stutzman and J W. Beeghley.

3. "How May we Best Cultivate the Spirit of Liberality in the Church?"—W. K. Simmons and A. S. Rosenberger.

4. "How Should the Pastoral Visit be Conducted? What is its Object?"—Jacob Garber, Wm. R. Murphy.

5. "How may the Flock be Fed and Strengthened?"—Henry Gump and S. Gilbert.

All the brethren and sisters are invited to attend and take part in the exercises.

By order of Committee,

JOHN CALVIN BRIGHT, Sec.

From the Aughwick Church, Pa.

JULY 30, at 2 o'clock, we held our harvest-meeting. By request, Bro. J. W. Wilt, of Altoona, was with us and preached an able sermon. He also preached for us Sunday morning and evening. At 3 o'clock, our usual hour for Sunday-school, he gave us an address which was full of instruction, and, while the greater portion of his remarks was directed to the children, he also gave many good suggestions to the older ones, showing the relationship that should exist between us and the Sunday-school, and to which some of us would do well to take heed. Our brother labored earnestly while with us, and we were made to feel much encouraged by his special words of encouragement. We trust that all of us will profit thereby, and, with renewed resolutions, may we work more earnestly in the cause of Christ!

At our last meeting we discussed the propriety of calling for the Ministerial Meeting, to be held in our congregation this fall. There was a unanimous vote in favor of having it, and we hope our request may be granted.   WALTER S. LONG.

Shirleysburg, Pa.

From South River, Iowa.

WE had a council-meeting Aug. 5, at which considerable business of importance came up for consideration. At the request of our elder, Bro. Lewis Kob, Bro. J. D. Haughtelin, of Panora, was called to our assistance. All business passed off pleasantly and satisfactorily. The next day we had a sermon and baptized one dear young sister. After attending a funeral we took the parting hand.

On account of pressing duties, and the inconvenient situation, Bro. Kob requested to be released from the oversight of the South River congregation. Though our associations have been mutually pleasant and satisfactory, his reasonable request was granted, and Bro. Haughtelin was chosen to take his place, which he accepted with the understanding that his co-laborers and neighboring elders should assist in the work. We hope the cause of the Master will continue to prosper, and that our labors together will be as pleasant and profitable in the future, as they have been in the past.   MEDA CASKEY.

Truro, Iowa.

From the Paradise Prairie Church, Oklahoma Territory.

THE members of this church have made arrangements to begin a series of meetings Aug. 14, to continue two weeks, when we will celebrate the holy ordinances of God's house for the first time, in this part of Oklahoma Territory. Bro. O. C. Root, of Kansas, will be with us to labor for us during these meetings. We are looking forward to these meetings with anticipations of a glorious revival here in our midst, and we are praying that the church may be strengthened and sinners converted. We extend an invitation to any of the brethren and sisters that can, to be with us and enjoy these meetings. We especially invite ministering brethren to this new country. There is a large field here to labor in, and so far only a few are at work. So far as we know, there are only five ministers in Oklahoma Territory, with one elder. There are many calls that must go unheeded. Many members are scattered all over this country who cannot get to meeting. They are living too far away from church privileges. When we hear the urgent calls for preaching by the dear lambs, and others, we are made to wonder where there are from two to five preachers, will not come to this field. We think this is a good country for anyone to live in. Crops of almost all kinds are good.

The great command, "Go ye," is, by many of our preachers, overlooked. They pay too little heed to the great commission. We hear much said of missionary work. One of the most successful ways to do mission work is to go to a new country and make it your home, and preach by example as well as by precept. We ask an interest in the prayers of the church every-where, that the cause of our Blessed Master may be built up here in Oklahoma, and that we may have a glorious refreshing from the presence of the Lord at our coming meeting.   JACOB APPLEMAN.

Clarkson, Oklahoma.

From the Mississinewa Church, Delaware Co., Ind.

ACCORDING to arrangements the brethren and sisters met Aug. 6, to transact such business as would come before the church. Although only a few, comparatively, were in attendance, everything passed off very pleasantly, without a contrary word. The time set for our fall love-feast is Sept. 30. Two brethren, G. L. Studebaker and Jacob Rarick, were chosen to represent us at the special District Meeting, to be held in the Arcadia church, preparatory to Annual Meeting, which is to be held in this district.

We were very pleasantly surprised during our council-meeting to see Bro. Daniel Vaniman, of McPherson, Kansas, step in, no one knowing he was about. He stayed with us over Sunday, preaching Sunday forenoon and Sunday night. He gave us two sound, practical sermons. Bro. Vaniman is on his way through Ohio to Pennsylvania, in the interest of the General Missionary

cause. The church has invited Bro. W. R. Deeter, of Milford, Ind., to be present at our feast.   CALVIN W. HOOKE.

New Corner, Ind., Aug. 8.

From Stilson, Iowa.

MUCH we feel the loss of our dear father, who has gone to his long home. While on his death-bed he said he would like to stay with us until we could get another minister, but finally he said, "I trust the Lord will send you a little David." Now we are left without a minister. Bro. Harvey Ikenberry came to us on Saturday, Aug. 6, and remained with us until Monday following. During his stay he preached three sermons. He had good attendance and also good attention. There were those present that were made to exclaim like Agrippa to Paul, "Almost thou persuadest me to be a Christian."

Brother Harvey has made arrangements to be with us every four weeks, beginning with Aug. 6. According to previous arrangements we will hold our love-feast Sept. 24 and 25. A hearty invitation is given to all. Come and enjoy the feast with us in our new church. The Lord willing we will dedicate our church Sept 18. Our preparatory council will occur Sept. 17. Those coming by rail from the East, will come to Britt on the M. L. and St. P. R. R. and take the Minneapolis and St. Louis R. R. for Stilson. Notify the writer when you will come and you will be provided for.

DANIEL ASCHENBRENNER.

Aug. 10.

Notice to the North-Eastern District of Ohio.

DEAR brethren and sisters, and especially the elders of the local churches that compose the District, I take this way of calling your attention to our missionary work, that should lie close to all of our hearts. There are some churches that are doing well, while some are on the background as yet. Let all feel that it is their duty to do something for the Lord. Please remember that I receive all the donations for the General Mission Work and also for the Book and Tract Work, and the Home Mission Funds. Be careful to state how much to each branch of the cause. Let all work to the same end. Elders and solicitors will please read the Minutes of our last District Meeting of Eastern Ohio, and they will see at once, what is required of each church for Home Mission. Now as the Good Lord has blessed you with the good of the land, let us all, as a church, rally along the line, and make a strong effort for the good cause. I will say this, Don't be afraid to give, fearing the donation will not be used properly. The Brethren will try to use it all to the best advantage for the cause, and to save souls. Have all your donations sent to me by Sept. 25, so that I may have time to make out my report for District Meeting. I hope all the churches will be well represented in my report. Let all the churches be well represented at District Meeting, and let all the delegates be on hand in good time. Then we will be sure of a good meeting.   SAMUEL SPRANKEL.

Massillon, Ohio, Aug. 10.

Private Love-Feasts.

WHY not have our love-feasts in a private way at the church, and just prepare such things as are needed for the Supper, the Communion, etc.? Let the brethren, sisters, and friends, who cannot go home for their meals from one service to another, bring a few meals along with them, just as other people when going to a woods meeting, or camp-meeting. Thus they could spend a day or two together. Those coming from a great dis-

been great murderers. They don't think they are defiling their church with such nonsense.

The University building is a very large one. I was in the school halls and found them decorated in the finest style. The room in which the President lives was about in the same style as that which was to be seen in the royal palace in Stockholm. The University is divided into four parts, the Medical, the Theological, the Philosophical and the Law Department, and from this learned men are going out into the whole kingdom.

To-morrow I intend to go to Stockholm and from there direct to my home, which I hope to reach July 15, at noon. From my home I will send you my last letter for this time.

JOHN OLSSON.

Upsala, Sweden.

(*To be Continued.*)

Ministerial Meeting.

THE following is the programme for the Ministerial Meeting of Southern Ohio, to be held in the Wolf Creek church, Montgomery County, Ohio, Oct. 27, commencing at 8:30 A. M.:

1. "What Should be the Aims of a Revival, and how Attained?"—S. W. Hoover and A. G. Crosswhite.

2. "What is the Best Method of Teaching in our Sunday-schools?"—Jesse Stutzman and J W. Beeghley.

3. "How May we Best Cultivate the Spirit of Liberality in the Church?"—W. K. Simmons and A. S. Rosenberger.

4. "How Should the Pastoral Visit be Conducted? What is its Object?"—Jacob Garber, Wm. R. Murphy.

5. "How may the Flock be Fed and Strengthened?"—Henry Gump and S. Gilbert.

All the brethren and sisters are invited to attend and take part in the exercises.

By order of Committee,

JOHN CALVIN BRIGHT, Sec.

From the Aughwick Church, Pa.

JULY 30, at 2 o'clock, we held our harvest-meeting. By request, Bro. J. W. Wilt, of Altoona, was with us and preached an able sermon. He also preached for us Sunday morning and evening. At 3 o'clock, our usual hour for Sunday-school, he gave us an address which was full of instruction, and, while the greater portion of his remarks was directed to the children, he also gave many good suggestions to the older ones, showing the relationship that should exist between us and the Sunday-school, and to which some of us would do well to take heed. Our brother labored earnestly while with us, and we were made to feel much encouraged by his special words of encouragement. We trust that all of us will profit thereby, and, with renewed resolutions, may we work more earnestly in the cause of Christ!

At our last meeting we discussed the propriety of calling for the Ministerial Meeting, to be held in our congregation this fall. There was a unanimous vote in favor of having it, and we hope our request may be granted. WALTER S. LONG.

Shirleysburg, Pa.

From South River, Iowa.

WE had a council-meeting Aug. 5, at which considerable business of importance came up for consideration. At the request of our elder, Bro. Lew. is Kob, Bro. J. D. Haughtelin, of Panora, was called to our assistance. All business passed off pleasantly and satisfactorily. The next day we had a sermon and baptized one dear young sister. After attending a funeral, we took the parting hand.

On account of pressing duties, and the inconvenient situation, Bro. Kob requested to be released from the oversight of the South River congregation. Though our associations have been mutually pleasant and satisfactory, his reasonable request was granted, and Bro. Haughtelin was chosen to take his place, which he accepted with the understanding that his co-laborers and neighboring elders should assist in the work. We hope the cause of the Master will continue to prosper, and that our labors together will be as pleasant and profitable in the future, as they have been in the past. MEDA CASKEY.

Truro, Iowa.

From the Paradise Prairie Church, Oklahoma Territory.

THE members of this church have made arrangements to begin a series of meetings Aug. 14, to continue two weeks, when we will celebrate the holy ordinances of God's house for the first time, in this part of Oklahoma Territory. Bro. O. C. Root, of Kansas, will be with us to labor for us during these meetings. We are looking forward to these meetings with anticipations of a glorious revival here in our midst, and we are praying that the church may be strengthened and sinners converted. We extend an invitation to any of the brethren and sisters that can, to be with us and enjoy these meetings. We especially invite ministering brethren to this new country. There is a large field here to labor in, and so far only a few are at work. So far as we know, there are only five ministers in Oklahoma Territory, with one elder. There are many calls that must go unheeded. Many members are scattered all over this country who cannot get to meeting. They are living too far away from church privileges. When we hear the urgent calls for preaching by the dear lambs, and others, we are made to wonder why some of our ministers, who are living in churches where there are from two to five preachers, will not come to this field. We think this is a good country for anyone to live in. Crops of almost all kinds are good.

The great command, "Go ye," is, by many of our preachers, overlooked. They pay too little heed to the great commission. We hear much said of missionary work. One of the most successful ways to do mission work is to go to a new country and make it your home, and preach by example as well as by precept. We ask an interest in the prayers of the church every-where, that the cause of our Blessed Master may be built up here in Oklahoma, and that we may have a glorious refreshing from the presence of the Lord at our coming meeting. JACOB APPLEMAN.

Clarkson, Oklahoma.

From the Mississinewa Church, Delaware Co., Ind.

ACCORDING to arrangements the brethren and sisters met Aug. 6, to transact such business as would come before the church. Although only a few, comparatively, were in attendance, everything passed off very pleasantly, without a contrary word. The time set for our fall love-feast is Sept. 30. Two brethren, G. L. Studebaker and Jacob Rarick, were chosen to represent us at the next District Meeting, to be held in the Arcadia church, preparatory to Annual Meeting, which is to be held in this district.

We were very pleasantly surprised during our council-meeting to see Bro. Daniel Vaniman, of McPherson, Kansas, step in, no one knowing he was about. He stayed with us over Sunday, preaching Sunday forenoon and Sunday night. He gave us two sound, practical sermons. Bro. Vaniman is on his way through Ohio to Pennsylvania, in the interest of the General Missionary

cause. The church has invited Bro. W. R. Deeter, of Milford, Ind., to be present at our feast. CALVIN W. HOOKE.

New Corner, Ind., Aug. 8.

From Stilson, Iowa.

MUCH we feel the loss of our dear father, who has gone to his long home. While on his death-bed he said he would like to stay with us until we could get another minister, but finally he said, "I trust the Lord will send you a little David." Now we are left without a minister. Bro. Harvey Ikenberry came to us on Saturday, Aug. 6, and remained with us until Monday following. During his stay he preached three sermons. He had good attendance and also good attention. There were those present that were made to exclaim like Agrippa to Paul, "Almost thou persuadest me to be a Christian."

Brother Harvey has made arrangements to be with us every four weeks, beginning with Aug. 6. According to previous arrangements we will hold our love-feast Sept. 24 and 25. A hearty invitation is given to all. Come and enjoy the feast with us in our new church. The Lord willing we will dedicate our church Sept. 18. Our preparatory council will occur Sept. 17. Those coming by rail from the East, will come to Britt on the M. L. and St. P. R. R. and take the Minneapolis and St. Louis R. R. for Stilson. Notify the writer when you will come and you will be provided for.

DANIEL ASCHENBRENNER.

Aug. 10.

Notice to the North-Eastern District of Ohio.

DEAR brethren and sisters, and especially the elders of the local churches that compose the District, I take this way of calling your attention to our missionary work, that should lie close to all of our hearts. There are some churches that are doing well, while some are on the background as yet. Let all feel that it is their duty to do something for the Lord. Please remember that I receive all the donations for the General Mission Work and also for the Book and Tract Work, and the Home Mission Funds. Be careful to state how much to each branch of the cause. Let all work to the same end. Elders and solicitors will please read the Minutes of our last District Meeting of Eastern Ohio, and they will see at once, what is required of each church for Home Mission. Now as the Good Lord has blessed you with the good of the land, let us all, as a church, rally along the line, and make a strong effort for the good cause. I will say this, Don't be afraid to give, fearing the donation will not be used properly. The Brethren will try to use it all to the best advantage for the cause, and to save souls. Have all your donations sent to me by Sept. 25, so that I may have time to make out my report for District Meeting. I hope all the churches will be well represented in my report. Let all the churches be well represented at District Meeting, and let all the delegates be on hand in good time. Then we will be sure of a good meeting. SAMUEL SPRANKEL.

Massillon, Ohio, Aug. 10.

Private Love-Feasts.

WHY not have our love-feasts in a private way at the church, and just prepare such things as are needed for the Supper, the Communion, etc.? Let the brethren, sisters, and friends, who cannot go home for their meals from one service to another, bring a few meals along with them, just as other people when going to a woods meeting, or camp-meeting. Thus they could spend a day or two together. Those coming from a great dis-

Peabody, Kans.—The Peabody church met in quarterly council, and everything passed off in peace and harmony, for which we feel to thank the Lord. We decided to hold a love-feast Oct. 8, commencing at 2 o'clock.—*Kate Yost, July 23.*

Waynesville, Mo.—The church here is in union. We are glad to see the young come flocking home. One little sister, aged fourteen years, was willing to go down to the water and was baptized July 24. We have Sunday-school every Sunday in the Brethren's meeting-house.—*Maria F. Burrow, Aug. 4.*

Union Deposit, Pa.—MESSENGER No. 30 is exceptionally good. Bro. McCann is on the right track and if his theology is also experience, he is to be heartily congratulated. PERFECTION *that ever goes on to* PERFECTION, is the true conception of God incarnate in the individual believer.—*C. H. Balsbaugh.*

Falling Springs, Pa.—To-day our quarterly council was held at the Hade church. Considerable business came before the council, but all was disposed of in a satisfactory manner and in a Christian spirit. Some business was deferred on account of those interested not being present.—*Will am C. Koontz, Aug. 6.*

Canton, Ill.—We expect to hold our love-feast at the Coal Creek church, Fulton County, Oct. 8. The District Meeting will also be held here, commencing Oct. 4. We should like to have some ministers come Oct 1, and be with us through the love-feast. They will be met at Canton and Norris by the undersigned or Bro. Bucklew.—*Benjamin Roh er.*

Literary Notices.

"A New Handbook of Prohibition Facts." By Wilbur F. Copeland. Flexible cloth covers; 128 pp., 3¼x6⅛ inches. Fifty cents. New York: Funk & Wagnalls Company.

Facts are the backbone of argument. The man who undertakes to convince his neighbor that the liquor business is a nuisance that must be suppressed, needs to have a convincing fact with which to checkmate each objection his neighbor raises.

The form is convenient, the type clear, the paper first-class, the binding substantial. These qualities make it a book every Prohibitionist should carry in his pocket, especially from now until election.

"The Columbian Historical Novels." A complete history of our country, from Columbus down to the present day, in the form of twelve complete stories. By John R. Musick. Issued bi-monthly. Now ready: Vol. I, Columbia, a Story of the Discovery of America, 351 pp. Vol. II, Estevan, a Story of the Spanish Conquests, 399 pp. Illustrated with full-page half-tone engravings and other illustrations. Cloth, 12mo, gold stamps, etc. Per vol., $1 50. New York, London, and Toronto: Funk & Wagnalls Company.

Here we have a truly interesting announcement. These two volumes, now ready, supply a contribution of great value to American educational and historical literature. The provision, "Duty first and pleasure afterwards," has received a new and special illustration in the Columbian Historical Novels. To the average American school-boy and school-girl, Columbia, like Sinbad's "Old Man of the Sea," is an ever-present burden. The sins of all the fathers, from Columbus to the Civil War, have been visited on the children of this generation, who have been compelled to learn events from well-intended but, practically, Dryasdust histories. Now all this is past; the chronicler of events has given place to the story-teller, and in the first Volume of this series we have a story of fascinating interest, in which the wooden Columbus of the treatises is replaced by a living, breathing actor on the page of history.

The second Volume, Estevan, covers the whole period of the conquest; treading the ground cleared by Prescott in his "Conquest of Peru." Estevan, a Spanish boy of noble family, is introduced to us in the first Volume. The story of his boyhood is a romantic one, and as a youth he accompanies Columbus on the Voyage of discovery. In the second Volume we recognize him at once as an old acquaintance, in whose fortunes we take a lively interest, and find him and his son after him, among the chief actors in the moving scenes of history.

Vol. III. St. Augustine: A Story of the Huguenots. Vol. IV. Pocahontas: A Story of Virginia. Vol. V. The Pilgrims:

A Story of Massachusetts. Vol. VI. A Century too Soon: A Story of Bacon's Rebellion. Vol. VII. The Witch of Salem: or, Credulity Run Mad. Vol. VIII. Braddock: A Story of the French and Indian Wars. Vol. IX Independence: A Story of the American Revolution. Vol. X. Sustained Honor: A Story of the War of 1812. Vol. XI. Humbled Pride: A Story of the Mexican War. Vol. XII. Union: A Story of the Great Rebellion, and of Events Down to the Present Day.

In lieu of a bare record of disconnected events, which the average reader finds so difficult to arrange systematically in his memory, we here have the story of individual lives; and we can follow these lives along lines on which the events arrange themselves in orderly sequence. It is not too much to say that a day devoted to each of these Volumes by the average reader will afford a more comprehensive and permanent grasp of the history of the times to which they relate, than is ordinarily acquired by years of study of the dry histories of the schools. The books are timely, valuable and important. The books are handsomely bound.

Matrimonial.

"What therefore God hath joined together, let not man put asunder."

WOLF—WOLFORD.—At the residence of the undersigned, Aug. 3, 1892, Mr. B. F. Wolf and Miss Sarah Wolford, all of Deep River, Poweshiek Co., Iowa.
ISAAC BARNHIZER.

MARKHAM—DOLMAN.—At my residence, Mishawaka, Ind., June 25, 1892, Bro. Delbert Markham and sister Mary Dolman, both of Elkhart County, Ind.
H. M. SCHWALM.

WEAVER—SUMMER.—At the residence of the bride's parents, July 31, 1892, by the undersigned, Mr. A. J. Weaver, of Carroll County, and Miss Mary Summer, of East Rochester, Columbiana Co., Ohio.
S. B. STUCKEY.

Fallen Asleep.

"Blessed are the dead which die in the Lord."

ALLEN.—At Deshler, Henry Co., Ohio, July 14, 1892, sister Susanna E. Allen, aged 39 years, 3 months and 25 days. Discourse by the writer.
DAVID LYTLE.

HYLTON.—In the Brick church, Floyd Co., Va., July 5, 1892, sister Elizabeth Hylton, aged 82 years, 4 months and 26 days. She was received by the church a few years ago as a candidate for baptism, but claimed to be not able, so she passed away in that condition. Her mind was very much impaired for some time before her death. Funeral services from John 5: 25, 28 by the writer, to many friends and relatives.
J. H. SLUSHER.

BROWN.—In the Elkhart church, Elkhart Co., Ind., Aug. 2, 1892, sister Jennie Brown, daughter of Eld. Daniel Riggle, aged 20 years, 3 months and 13 days. She united with the church recently. She leaves a husband and an infant. Her mother preceded her to the spirit world about one year ago. Funeral services by brethren Lemuel Hillery and A. L. Neff, from these words: "There is no discharge in that war." Eccl. 8: 8.
J. H. MILLER.

WEIMER.—In the Ligonier Valley congregation, Pa., July 31, 1892, Bro. William Weimer, aged 69 years and 28 days. Bro. Weimer lived in this neighborhood and brought up a large family, most of whom are married. About two years ago he decided to unite with the children of God, and has since been a very devoted servant of the Master. Funeral services by Eld. George Hanawalt.
BARBARA M. HANAWALT.

MITCHEL.—In the Mt. Zion congregation, Page Co., Va., July 10, 1892, Bro George Mitchel, aged about 80 years. He was born in London, and has been a citizen of our country for about forty years, and a faithful member of the Brethren church for about twenty years. Funeral services by the writer from Ps. 8: 3, 4.
MARTIN REYHORS.

FERREL.—In the Newport congregation, Page Co., Va., July 28, 1892, sister Barbara E. Ferrel, aged 59 years, 9 months and 15 days. She has been a faithful sister in the Brethren church for nearly five years. Funeral services by the writer from Rev. 14: 13.
MARTIN ROTHGEB.

CROSS.—In the Quemahoning church, Somerset Co., Pa., July 18, 1892, Bro. William C. Cross, aged 31 years, 10 months and 1 day. He leaves a wife and three children to mourn their loss. Funeral services by brethren Valentine Blough and R. T. Hull.
JOHN J. DARR.

WEDDLE.—Near Santos, Floyd Co., Va., July 23, 1892, Levi Weddle, aged 73 years and 10 months. He had been a member of the Brethren church for more than thirty-one years and had served as deacon for twenty-seven years. He was the father of eleven children. Funeral services by elders J. B. Hylton, C. D. Hylton and Jacob Hylton.
J. H. SLUSHER.

ULREY.—In the Fairview church, Tippecanoe Co., Ind., May 20, 1892, Bro. Samuel Ulrey, aged 58 years, 2 months and 4 days. In 1860 Bro. Ulrey was chosen to the office of deacon, and to the ministry in 1870, in which office he faithfully served until his death. The church greatly feels her loss which, we hope, was his eternal gain. He leaves a wife and one son; a wife, three sons and one daughter having preceded him to the spirit world Disease, epilepsy. He was in his usual health when he retired for the night, when one of the paroxysms seized him and he peacefully passed away. Services by Eld. Isaac Cripe, in the Fyrmont church. Interment in the Pyrmont cemetery.
J. W. VETTER.

CRIPE.—In the North Fork church, Carroll Co., Ind., Aug. 3, 1892, sister Eve Cripe, aged 59 years, 5 months and 23 days. Her maiden name was Neher. Nov. 3, 1849, she was married to Joseph Hufford, with whom she lived nearly twelve years She was the mother of seven children, three of whom preceded her to the home beyond. In December, 1879, she was married to William Cripe, with whom she lived nearly nine years. A few years ago she became afflicted with palsy, from which she suffered greatly. July 31 she called for the elders and was anointed with oil in the name of the Lord. She peacefully passed away at the home of her son-in-law, Andrew Wagoner. She leaves four children. Funeral services conducted by elders Solomon Blickenstaff and Isaac Cripe. Interment in the Hufford cemetery Aug. 4.
J. W. VETTER.

STAUFFER.—In the Baugo church, Wakarusa, Ind., June 23, 1892, sister Christina Stauffer (*nee* Sanders), aged 57 years, 8 months and 24 days. Funeral services by Bro. M. C. Murry and the home ministers.

STAUFFER.—In the same church, July 4, 1892, Mr. Charles Allen Stauffer, son of the above, aged 24 years, 5 months and seven days. Funeral services by Eld. John Metzler and the undersigned.
H. M. SCHWALM.

ROWLAND.—Near Dallas Centre, Iowa, Aug. 6, 1892, sister Susan, wife of Bro. John Rowland and daughter of George and Sarah Buterbaugh, aged 66 years, 4 months and 24 days. Disease, cancer of stomach. She leaves an aged husband, three sons and one daughter. Funeral services were held near her home, after which her remains were taken to her former home, near Lanark, Ill., for interment, where services were conducted by Bro. George D. Zollers from Heb. 4: 9.
GEO. B. ROYER.

STUDEBAKER.—In the bounds of the Hickory Grove church, Miami Co., Ohio, sister Naomi Studebaker, aged 47 years, 1 month and 4 days. Sister Studebaker was severely afflicted and a great sufferer, which she patiently bore for over two years. With a faint hope of relief, she submitted to a severe surgical operation from the effects of which she never revived. Funeral services were conducted by brethren Bennett Trout and D. S. Filbrum.
JACOB COPPOCK.

COSIER.—In the Oakland church, Darke Co., Ohio, Aug. 4, 1892, of paralysis, sister Nancy Cosier, wife of Mr. John Cosier, deceased, aged 80 years, 1 month and 15 days. Her funeral services were held in the Oakland meeting-house and conducted by brethren J. H. Christian and B. F. Honeyman, from Prov. 12: 28.
I. B. MILLER.

Peabody, Kans.—The Peabody church met in quarterly council, and everything passed off in peace and harmony, for which we feel to thank the Lord. We decided to hold a love-feast Oct. 8, commencing at 2 o'clock.—*Kate Yost, July 23.*

Waynesville, Mo.—The church here is in union. We are glad to see the young come flocking home. One little sister, aged fourteen years, was willing to go down to the water and was baptized July 24. We have Sunday-school every Sunday in the Brethren's meeting-house.—*Maria F. Burrow, Aug. 4.*

Union Deposit, Pa.—MESSENGER No. 30 is exceptionally good. Bro. McCann is on the right track and if his theology is also experience, he is to be heartily congratulated. PERFECTION *that ever goes on to* PERFECTION, is the true conception of God incarnate in the individual believer.—*C. H. Balsbaugh.*

Falling Springs, Pa.—To-day our quarterly council was held at the Hade church. Considerable business came before the council, but all was disposed of in a satisfactory manner and in a Christian spirit. Some business was deferred on account of those interested not being present.—*William C. Koontz, Aug. 6.*

Canton, Ill.—We expect to hold our love-feast at the Coal Creek church, Fulton County, Oct. 8. The District Meeting will also be held here, commencing Oct 4. We should like to have some ministers come Oct. 1, and be with us through the love-feast. They will be met at Canton and Norris by the undersigned or Bro. Bucklew.—*Benjamin Rohrer.*

Literary Notices.

"A New Handbook of Prohibition Facts." By Wilbur F. Copeland. Flexible cloth covers; 128 pp., 3½x6⅜ inches. Fifty cents. New York: Funk & Wagnalls Company.

Facts are the backbone of argument. The man who undertakes to convince his neighbor that the liquor business is a nuisance that must be suppressed, needs to have a convincing fact with which to checkmate each objection his neighbor raises.

The form is convenient, the type clear, the paper first-class, the binding substantial. These qualities make it a book every Prohibitionist should carry in his pocket, especially from now until election.

"The Columbian Historical Novels." A complete history of our country, from Columbus down to the present day, in the form of twelve complete stories. By John R. Musick. Issued bi-monthly. Now ready: Vol. I, Columbia, a Story of the Discovery of America, 351 pp. Vol. II., Estevan, a Story of the Spanish Conquests, 399 pp. Illustrated with full-page half-tone engravings and other illustrations. Cloth, 12mo, gold stamps, etc. Per vol., $1.50. New York, London, and Toronto: Funk & Wagnalls Company.

Here we have a truly interesting announcement. These two volumes, now ready, supply a contribution of great value to American educational and historical literature. The proverb, " Duty first and pleasure afterwards," has received a new and special illustration in the Columbian Historical Novels. To the average American school-boy and school-girl, Columbia, like Sinbad's "Old Man of the Sea," is an ever-present burden. The sins of all the fathers, from Columbus to the Civil War, have been visited on the children of this generation, who have been compelled to learn events from well-intended but, practically, dry-as-dust histories. Now all this is past; the chronicler of events has given place to the story teller, and in the first volume of this series we have a story of fascinating interest, in which the wooden Columbus of the treatises is replaced by a living, breathing actor on the stage of history.

The second volume, Estevan, covers the whole period of the conquest; treading the ground cleared by Prescott in his "Conquest of Peru." Estevan, a Spanish boy of noble family, is introduced to us in the first volume. The story of his boyhood is a romantic one, and as a youth he accompanies Columbus on the voyage of discovery. In the second volume we recognize him at once as an old acquaintance, in whose fortunes we take a lively interest, and find him and his son after him, among the chief actors in the moving scenes of history.

Vol. III. St. Augustine: A Story of the Huguenots. Vol. IV. Pocahontas: A Story of Virginia. Vol. V. The Pilgrims:

A Story of Massachusetts. Vol. VI. A Century too Soon: A Story of Bacon's Rebellion. Vol. VII. The Witch of Salem: or, Credulity Run Mad. Vol. VIII. Braddock: A Story of the French and Indian Wars. Vol. IX Independence: A Story of the American Revolution. Vol. X. Sustained Honor: A Story of the War of 1812. Vol. XI. Humbled Pride: A Story of the Mexican War. Vol. XII. Union: A Story of the Great Rebellion, and of Events Down to the Present Day.

In lieu of a bare record of disconnected events, which the average reader finds so difficult to arrange systematically in his memory, we here have the story of individual lives; and we can follow these lives along lines on which the events arrange themselves in orderly sequence. It is not too much to say that a day devoted to each of these volumes by the average reader will afford a more comprehensive and permanent grasp of the history of the times to which they relate, than is ordinarily acquired by years of study of the dry histories of the schools. The books are timely, valuable and important. The books are handsomely bound.

Matrimonial.

" What therefore God hath joined together, let not man put asunder."

WOLF—WOLFORD.—At the residence of the undersigned, Aug. 3, 1892, Mr. B. F. Wolf and Miss Sarah Wolford, all of Deep River, Poweshiek Co., Iowa.
ISAAC BARNHIZER.

MARKHAM—DOLMAN.—At my residence, Mishawaka, Ind., June 25, 1892, Bro. Delbert Markham and sister Mary Dolman, both of Elkhart County, Ind.
H. M. SCHWALM.

WEAVER—SUMMER.—At the residence of the bride's parents, July 31, 1892, by the undersigned, Mr. A. J. Weaver, of Carroll County, and Miss Mary Summer, of East Rochester, Columbiana Co., Ohio.
S. B. STUCKEY.

Fallen Asleep.

" Blessed are the dead which die in the Lord."

ALLEN.—At Deshler, Henry Co., Ohio, July 14, 1892, sister Susanna E. Allen, aged 39 years, 3 months and 25 days. Discourse by the writer.
DAVID LYTLE.

HYLTON.—In the Brick church, Floyd Co., Va., July 5, 1892, sister Elizabeth Hylton, aged 81 years, 4 months and 16 days. She was received by the church a few years ago as a candidate for baptism, but claimed to be not able, so she passed away in that condition. Her mind was very much impaired for some time before her death. Funeral services from John 5:25, 28 by the writer, to many friends and relatives.
J. H. SLUSHER.

BROWN.—In the Elkhart church, Elkhart Co., Ind., Aug. 3, 1892, sister Jennie Brown, daughter of Eld. Daniel Riggle, aged 20 years, 3 months and 13 days. She united with the church recently. She leaves a husband and an infant. Her mother preceded her to the spirit world about one year ago. Funeral services by brethren Lemuel Hilbey and A. L. Neff, from these words: "There is no discharge in that war." Eccl. 8: 8.
J. H. MILLER.

WEIMER.—In the Ligonier Valley congregation, Pa., July 31, 1892, Bro. William Weimer, aged 69 years and 28 days. Bro. Weimer lived in this neighborhood and brought up a large family, most of whom are married. About two years ago he decided to unite with the children of God, and has since been a very devoted servant of the Master. Funeral services by Eld. George Hanawalt.
BARBARA M. HANAWALT.

MITCHEL.—In the Mt. Zion congregation, Page Co., Va., July 10, 1892, Bro George Mitchel, aged about 80 years. He was born in London, and has been a citizen of our country for about forty years, and a faithful member of the Brethren church for about twenty years. Funeral services by the writer from Ps. 8: 3, 4.
MARTIN ROTHGEB.

FERREL.—In the Newport congregation, Page Co., Va., July 28, 1892, sister Barbara E. Ferrel, aged 72 years, 9 months and 15 days. She has been a faithful sister in the Brethren church for nearly five years. Funeral services by the writer from Rev. 14: 13.
MARTIN ROTHGEB.

CROSS.—In the Quemahoning church, Somerset Co., Pa., July 18, 1892, Bro. William C. Cross, aged 31 years, 4 months and 1 day. He leaves a wife and three children to mourn their loss. Funeral services by brethren Valentine Blough and R. T. Hull.
JOHN J. DARR.

WEDDLE.—Near Santos, Floyd Co., Va., July 23, 1892, Levi Weddle, aged 72 years and 10 months. He had been a member of the Brethren church for more than thirty-one years and had served as deacon for twenty-seven years. He was the father of eleven children. Funeral services by elders J. B. Hylton, C. D. Hylton and Jacob Hylton.
J. H. SLUSHER.

ULREY.—In the Fairview church, Th[...] May 10, 1892, Bro. Samuel Ulrey, aged [...] and 4 days. In 1860 Bro. Ulrey was chos[...] deacon, and to the ministry in 1870, in wh[...] fully served until his death. The church [...] which, we hope, was his eternal gain. He [...] one son; a wife, three sons and one daught[...] him to the spirit word Disease, epileps[...] usual health when he retired for the nigh[...] paroxysms seized him and he peacefully p[...] loss by Eld. Isaac Cripe, in the Pyrmont [...] in the Pyrmont cemetery.

CRIPE.—In the North Fork church, [...] Aug. 3, 1892, sister Eve Cripe, aged 59 ye[...] 23 days. Her maiden name was Neher. [...] was married to Joseph Hufford, with whom[...] twelve years She was the mother of sev[...] of whom preceded her to the home beyo[...] 1879, she was married to William Cripe, w[...] nearly nine years. A few years ago sh[...] with palsy, from which she suffered gre[...] called for the elders and was anointed wit[...] the Lord. She peacefully passed away at [...] son-in-law, Andrew Wagoner. She leav[...] Funeral services conducted by elders Sol[...] and Isaac Cripe. Interment in the Hufford[...]

STAUFFER.—In the Baugo church, [...] June 23, 1892, sister Christena Stauffer (ne[...] years, 8 months and 21 days. Funeral serv[...] Murry and the home ministers.

STAUFFER.—In the same church, J[...] Charles Allen Stauffer, son of the above, [...] months and seven days. Funeral service[...] Metzler and the undersigned.
H. [...]

ROWLAND.—Near Dallas Centre, Iow[...] sister Susan, wife of Bro. John Rowland [...] George and Sarah Buterbaugh, aged 66 year[...] 24 days. Disease, cancer of stomach. Sh[...] were held near her home, after which her rer[...] to her former home, near Lanark, Ill., for l[...] services were conducted by Bro. George D. 2[...]
G[...]

STUDEBAKER.—In the bounds of the [...] church, Miami Co., Ohio, sister Naomi Stud[...] years, 1 month and 4 days. Sister Studebak[...] afflicted and a great sufferer, which she pa[...] over two years. With a faint hope of relief, [...] a severe surgical operation from the effects of [...] or revived. Funeral services were conduc[...] Bennett Trout and D. S. Filbrum.
JA[...]

COSIER.—In the Oakland church, Darke [...] 4, 1892, of paralysis, sister Nancy Cosier, w[...] Cosier, deceased, aged 80 years, 1 month and[...] Funeral services were held in the Oakland me[...] conducted by brethren J. H. Christian and B. [...] from Prov. 12: 28.

The Gospel Messeng[...]

Is the recognized organ of the German Baptist or [...] and advocates the form of doctrine taught in the N[...] pleads for a return to apostolic and primitive Christia[...]

It recognizes the New Testament as the only infallib[...] practice, and maintains that Faith toward God, Rep[...] works, Regeneration of the heart and mind, baptism f[...] for remission of sins unto the reception of the Holy G[...] on of hands, are the means of adoption into the hous[...] church militant.

It also maintains that Feet-washing, as taught in J[...] ample and command of Jesus, should be observed in G[...]

That the Lord's Supper, instituted by Christ and [...] served by the apostles and the early Christians, is a [...] connection with the Communion, should be taken in [...] the close of the day.

That the Salutation of the Holy Kiss, or Kiss of [...] upon the followers of Christ.

That War and Retaliation are contrary to the spir[...] principles of the religion of Jesus Christ.

That the principle of Plain Dressing and of Non[...] world, as taught in the New Testament, should be o[...] lowers of Christ.

That the Scriptural duty of Anointing the Sick with[...] of the Lord, James 5: 14, is binding upon all Christian[...]

It also advocates the church's duty to support M[...] Work, thus giving to the Lord for the spread of the [...] conversion of sinners.

In short, it is a Vindicator of all that Christ and th[...] joined upon us, and aims, amid the conflicting theor[...] modern Christendom, to point out ground that all mu[...] faithful safe.

☞ The above principles of our Fraterni[...] on our " Brethren's Envelopes." Use them [...] per package; 40 cents per hundred.

Peabody, Kans.—The Peabody church met in quarterly council, and everything passed off in peace and harmony, for which we feel to thank the Lord. We decided to hold a love-feast Oct. 8, commencing at 2 o'clock.—*Kate Yost, July 23.*

Waynesville, Mo.—The church here is in union. We are glad to see the young come flocking home. One little sister, aged fourteen years, was willing to go down to the water and was baptized July 24. We have Sunday-school every Sunday in the Brethren's meeting-house.—*Maria F. Burrow, Aug. 4.*

Union Deposit, Pa.—MESSENGER No. 30 is exceptionally good. Bro. McCann is on the right track and if his theology is also experience, he is to be heartily congratulated. PERFECTION *that ever goes on to* PERFECTION, is the true conception of God incarnate in the individual believer.—*C. H. Balsbaugh.*

Falling Springs, Pa.—To-day our quarterly council was held at the Hade church. Considerable business came before the council, but all was disposed of in a satisfactory manner and in a Christian spirit. Some business was deferred on account of those interested not being present.—*Will·am C. Koonts, Aug. 6.*

Canton, Ill.—We expect to hold our love-feast at the Coal Creek church, Fulton County, Oct. 8. The District Meeting will also be held here, commencing Oct 4. We should like to have some ministers come Oct 1, and be with us through the love-feast. They will be met at Canton and Norris by the undersigned or Bro. Bucklew.—*Benjamin Roh·er.*

Literary Notices.

"A New Handbook of Prohibition Facts." By Wilbur F. Copeland. Flexible cloth covers; 128 pp., 3¼x6½ inches. Fifty cents. New York: Funk & Wagnalls Company.

Facts are the backbone of argument. The man who undertakes to convince his neighbor that the liquor business is a nuisance that must be suppressed, needs to have a convincing fact with which to checkmate each objection his neighbor raises.

The form is convenient, the type clear, the paper first-class, the binding substantial. These qualities make it a book every Prohibitionist should carry in his pocket, especially from now until election.

"The Columbian Historical Novels." A complete history of our country, from Columbus down to the present day, in the form of twelve complete stories. By John R. Musick. Issued bi-monthly. Now ready: Vol. I, Columbia, a Story of the Discovery of America, 351 pp. Vol. II, Estevan, a Story of the Spanish Conquests, 399 pp. Illustrated with full-page half-tone engravings and other illustrations. Cloth, 12mo, gold stamps, etc. Per vol., $1 50. New York, London, and Toronto: Funk & Wagnalls Company.

Here we have a truly interesting announcement. These two Volumes, now ready, supply a contribution of great value to American educational and historical literature. The proverb, " Duty first and pleasure afterwards," has received a new and special illustration in the Columbian Historical Novels. To the average American school-boy and school-girl, Columbia, like Sinbad's " Old Man of the Sea," is an ever-present burden. The sins of all the fathers, from Columbus to the Civil War, have been visited on the children of this generation, who have been compelled to learn events from well-intended but, practically, Dry-as-dust histories. Now all this is past; the chronicler of events has given place to the story-teller, and in the first Volume of this series we have a story of fascinating interest, in which the wooden Columbus of the treatises is replaced by a living, breathing actor on the page of history.

The second Volume, Estevan, covers the whole period of the conquest; treading the ground cleared by Prescott in his " Conquest of Peru." Estevan, a Spanish boy of noble family, is introduced to us in the first Volume. The story of his boyhood is a romantic one, and as a youth he accompanies Columbus on the Voyage of discovery. In the second Volume we recognize him at once as an old acquaintance, in whose fortunes we take a lively interest, and find him and his son after him, among the chief actors in the moving scenes of history.

Vol. III. St. Augustine: A Story of the Huguenots. Vol. IV. Pocahontas: A Story of Virginia. Vol. V. The Pilgrims;

A Story of Massachusetts. Vol. VI. A Century too Soon: A Story of Bacon's Rebellion. Vol. VII. The Witch of Salem: or, Credulity Run Mad. Vol. VIII. Braddock: A Story of the French and Indian Wars. Vol. IX. Independence: A Story of the American Revolution. Vol. X. Sustained Honor: A Story of the War of 1812. Vol. XI. Humbled Pride: A Story of the Mexican War. Vol. XII. Union: A Story of the Great Rebellion, and of Events Down to the Present Day.

In lieu of a bare record of disconnected events, which the average reader finds so difficult to arrange systematically in his memory, we here have the story of individual lives; and we can follow these lives along lines on which the events arrange themselves in orderly sequence. It is not too much to say that a day devoted to each of these volumes by the average reader will afford a more comprehensive and permanent grasp of the history of the times to which they relate, than is ordinarily acquired by years of study of the dry histories of the schools. The books are timely, valuable and important. The books are handsomely bound.

Matrimonial.

" What therefore God hath joined together, let not man put asunder."

WOLF—WOLFORD.—At the residence of the undersigned, Aug. 3, 1892, Mr. B. F. Wolf and Miss Sarah Wolford, all of Deep River, Poweshiek Co., Iowa.

ISAAC BARNHIZER.

MARKHAM—DOLMAN.—At my residence, Mishawaka, Ind., June 25, 1892, Bro. Delbert Markham and sister Mary Dolman, both of Elkhart County, Ind.

H. M. SCHWALM.

WEAVER—SUMMER.—At the residence of the bride's parents, July 31, 1892, by the undersigned, Mr. A. J. Weaver, of Carroll County, and Miss Mary Summer, of East Rochester, Columbiana Co., Ohio.

S. B. STUCKEY.

Fallen Asleep.

" Blessed are the dead which die in the Lord."

ALLEN.—At Deshler, Henry Co., Ohio, July 14, 1892, sister Susanna E. Allen, aged 39 years, 2 months and 25 days. Discourse by the writer.

DAVID LYTLE.

HYLTON.—In the Brick church, Floyd Co., Va., July 5, 1892, sister Elizabeth Hylton, aged 82 years, 4 months and 26 days. She was received by the church a few years ago as a candidate for baptism, but claimed to be not able, so she passed away in that condition. Her mind was very much impaired for some time before her death. Funeral services from John 5: 25, 28 by the writer, to many friends and relatives.

J. H. SLUSHER.

BROWN.—In the Elkhart church, Elkhart Co., Ind., Aug. 3, 1892, sister jennie Brown, daughter of Eld. Daniel Riggle, aged 20 years, 3 months and 13 days. She united with the church recently. She leaves a husband and an infant. Her mother preceded her to the spirit world about one year ago. Funeral services by brethren Lemuel Hillery and A. L. Neff, from these words: " There is no discharge in that war." Eccl. 8: 8.

J. H. MILLER.

WEIMER.—In the Ligonier Valley congregation, Pa., July 31, 1892, Bro. William Weimer, aged 69 years and 28 days. Bro. Weimer lived in the neighborhood and brought up a large family, most of whom are married. About two years ago he decided to unite with the children of God, and has since been a very devoted servant of the Master. Funeral services by Eld. George Hanawalt.

BARBARA M. HANAWALT.

MITCHEL.—In the Mt. Zion congregation, Page Co., Va., July 10, 1892, Bro George Mitchel, aged about 80 years. He was born in London, and has been a citizen of our country for about forty years, and a faithful member of the Brethren church for about twenty years. Funeral services by the writer from Ps. 8: 3, 4.

MARTIN ROTHGEB.

FERREL.—In the Newport congregation, Page Co., Va., July 28, 1892, sister Barbara E. Ferrel, aged 59 years, 9 months and 15 days. She has been a faithful sister in the Brethren church for nearly five years. Funeral services by the writer from Rev. 14: 13.

MARTIN ROTHGEB.

CROSS.—In the Quemahoning church, Somerset Co., Pa., July 18, 1892, Bro. William C. Cross, aged 31 years, 2 months and 1 day. He leaves a wife and three children to mourn their loss. Funeral services by brethren Valentine Blough and R. T. Hull.

JOHN J. DARR.

WEDDLE.—Near Santos, Floyd Co., Va., July 23, 1892, Levi Weddle, aged 59 years and 10 months. He had been a member of the Brethren church for more than thirty-one years and had served as deacon for twenty-seven years. He was the father of eleven children. Funeral services by elders J. B. Hylton, C. D. Hylton and Jacob Hylton.

J. H. SLUSHER.

ULREY.—In the Fairview church, Tippecanoe Co., Ind., May 20, 1892, Bro. Samuel Ulrey, aged 58 years, 2 months and 4 days. In 1860 Bro. Ulrey was chosen to the office of deacon, and to the ministry in 1870, in which office he faithfully served until his death. The church greatly feels her loss which, we hope, was his eternal gain. He leaves a wife and one son; a wife, three sons and one daughter having preceded him to the spirit word Disease, epilepsy. He was in his usual health when he retired for the night, when one of the paroxysms seized him and he peacefully passed away. Services by Eld. Isaac Cripe, in the Fairview church. Interment in the Pyrmont cemetery.

J. W. VETTER.

CRIPE.—In the North Fork church, Carroll Co., Ind., Aug. 3, 1892, sister Eve Cripe, aged 59 years, 5 months and 23 days. Her maiden name was Nehar. Nov. 3, 1849, she was married to Joseph Hufford, with whom she lived nearly twelve years. She was the mother of seven children, three of whom preceded her to the home beyond. In December, 1879, she was married to William Cripe, with whom she lived nearly nine years. A few years ago she became afflicted with palsy, from which she suffered greatly. July 31 she called for the elders and was anointed with oil in the name of the Lord. She peacefully passed away at the home of her son-in-law, Andrew Wagoner. She leaves four children. Funeral services conducted by elders Solomon Blickenstaff and Isaac Cripe. Interment in the Hufford cemetery Aug. 4.

J. W. VETTER.

STAUFFER.—In the Baugo church, Wakarusa, Ind., June 23, 1892, sister Christena Stauffer (*nee* Sanders), aged 57 years, 8 months and 22 days. Funeral services by Bro. M. C. Murry and the home ministers.

STAUFFER.—In the same church, July 4, 1892, Mr. Charles Allen Stauffer, son of the above, aged 24 years, 5 months and seven days. Funeral services by Eld. John Metzler and the undersigned.

H. M. SCHWALM.

ROWLAND.—Near Dallas Centre, Iowa, Aug. 6, 1892, sister Susan, wife of Bro. John Rowland and daughter of George and Sarah Buterbaugh, aged 66 years, 4 months and 24 days. Disease, cancer of stomach. She leaves an aged husband, three sons and one daughter. Funeral services were held near her home, after which her remains were taken to her former home, near Lanark, Ill., for interment, where services were conducted by Bro. George D. Zollers from Heb. 4: 9.

GEO. B. ROYER.

STUDEBAKER.—In the bounds of the Hickory Grove church, Miami Co., Ohio, sister Naomi Studebaker, aged 47 years, 1 month and 4 days. Sister Studebaker was severely afflicted and a great sufferer, which she patiently bore for over two years. With a faint hope of relief, she submitted to a severe surgical operation from the effects of which she never revived. Funeral services were conducted by brethren Bennett Trout and D. S. Filbrum.

JACOB COPPOCK.

COSIER.—In the Oakland church, Darke Co., Ohio, Aug. 4, 1892, of paralysis, sister Nancy Cosier, wife of Mr. John Cosier, deceased, aged 80 years, 1 month and 15 days. Her funeral services were held in the Oakland meeting-house and conducted by brethren J. H. Christian and B. F. Honeyman, from Prov. 12: 26.

I. B. MILLER.

Peabody, Kans.—The Peabody church met in quarterly council, and everything passed off in peace and harmony, for which we feel to thank the Lord. We decided to hold a love-feast Oct. 8, commencing at 2 o'clock.—*Kate Yost, July 23.*

Waynesville, Mo.—The church here is in union. We are glad to see the young come flocking home. One little sister, aged fourteen years, was willing to go down to the water and was baptized July 24. We have Sunday-school every Sunday in the Brethren's meeting-house.—*Maria F. Burrow, Aug. 4.*

Union Deposit, Pa.—MESSENGER No. 30 is exceptionally good. Bro. McCann is on the right track and if his theology is also experience, he is to be heartily congratulated. PERFECTION *that ever goes on to* PERFECTION, is the true conception of God incarnate in the individual believer.—*C. H. Balsbaugh.*

Falling Springs, Pa.—To-day our quarterly council was held at the Hade church. Considerable business came before the council, but all was disposed of in a satisfactory manner and in a Christian spirit. Some business was deferred on account of those interested not being present.—*William C. Koonts, Aug. 6.*

Canton, Ill.—We expect to hold our love-feast at the Coal Creek church, Fulton County, Oct. 3. The District Meeting will also be held here, commencing Oct. 4. We should like to have some ministers come Oct. 1, and be with us through the love-feast. They will be met at Canton and Norris by the undersigned or Bro. Bucklew.—*Benjamin Rohrer.*

Literary Notices.

"A New Handbook of Prohibition Facts." By Wilbur F. Copeland. Flexible cloth covers; 128 pp., 3½x6⅝ inches. Fifty cents. New York: Funk & Wagnalls Company.

Facts are the backbone of argument. The man who undertakes to convince his neighbor that the liquor business is a nuisance that must be suppressed, needs to have a convincing fact with which to checkmate each objection his neighbor raises.

The form is convenient, the type clear, the paper first-class, the binding substantial. These qualities make it a book every Prohibitionist should carry in his pocket, especially from now until election.

" The Columbian Historical Novels." A complete history of our country, from Columbus down to the present day, in the form of twelve complete stories. By John R. Musick. Issued bi-monthly. Now ready: Vol. I, Columbia, a Story of the Discovery of America, 351 pp. Vol. II., Estevan, a Story of the Spanish Conquests, 399 pp. Illustrated with full-page half-tone engravings and other illustrations. Cloth, 12mo, gold stamps, etc. Per vol., $1.50. New York, London, and Toronto: Funk & Wagnalls Company.

Here we have a truly interesting announcement. These two volumes, now ready, supply a contribution of great value to American educational and historical literature. The professor, "Duty first and pleasure afterwards," has received a new and special illustration in the Columbian Historical Novels. To the average American school-boy and school-girl, Columbia, like Sinbad's "Old Man of the Sea," is an ever-present burden. The sins of all the fathers, from Columbus to the Civil War, have been visited on the children of this generation, who have been compelled to learn events from well-intended but, practically, dry-as-dust histories. Now all this is past; the chronicler of events has given place to the story-teller, and in the first volume of his series we have a story of fascinating interest, in which the wooden Columbus of the treatises is replaced by a living, breathing actor on the page of history.

The second volume, Estevan, covers the whole period of the conquest; treading the ground cleared by Prescott in his "Conquest of Peru." Estevan, a Spanish boy of noble family, is introduced to us in the first volume. The story of his boyhood is a romantic one, and as a youth he accompanies Columbus on the Voyage of discovery. In the second volume we recognize him at once as an old acquaintance, in whose fortunes we take a lively interest, and find him and his son after him, among the chief actors in the moving scenes of history.

Vol. III. St. Augustine: A Story of the Huguenots. Vol. IV. Pocahontas: A Story of Virginia. Vol. V. The Pilgrims:

A Story of Massachusetts. Vol. VI. A Century 100 Soon: A Story of Bacon's Rebellion. Vol. VII. The Witch of Salem: or, Credulity Run Mad. Vol. VIII. Braddock: A Story of the French and Indian Wars. Vol. IX Independence: A Story of the American Revolution. Vol. X. Sustained Honor: A Story of the War of 1812. Vol. XI. Humbled Pride: A Story of the Mexican War. Vol. XII. Union: A Story of the Great Rebellion, and of Events Down to the Present Day.

In lieu of a bare record of disconnected events, which the average reader finds so difficult to arrange systematically in his memory, we here have the story of individual lives; and we can follow these lives along lines on which the events arrange themselves in orderly sequence. It is not too much to say that a day devoted to each of these volumes by the average reader will afford a more comprehensive and permanent grasp of the history of the times to which they relate, than is ordinarily acquired by years of study of the dry histories of the schools. The books are timely, valuable and important. The books are handsomely bound.

Matrimonial.

" What therefore God hath joined together, let not man put asunder."

WOLF—WOLFORD.—At the residence of the undersigned, Aug. 3, 1892, Mr. B. F. Wolf and Miss Sarah Wolford, all of Deep River, Poweshiek Co., Iowa.

ISAAC BARNHIZER.

MARKHAM—DOLMAN.—At my residence, Mishawaka, Ind., June 25, 1892, Bro. Delbert Markham and sister Mary Dolman, both of Elkhart County, Ind.

H. M. SCHWALM.

WEAVER—SUMMER.—At the residence of the bride's parents, July 31, 1892, by the undersigned, Mr. A. J. Weaver, of Carroll County, and Miss Mary Summer, of East Rochester, Columbiana Co., Ohio.

S. B. STUCKEY.

Fallen Asleep.

" Blessed are the dead which die in the Lord."

ALLEN.—At Deshler, Henry Co., Ohio, July 14, 1892, sister Susanna E. Allen, aged 39 years, 2 months and 25 days. Discourse by the writer.

DAVID LYTLE.

HYLTON.—In the Brick church, Floyd Co., Va., July 5, 1892, sister Elizabeth Hylton, aged 82 years, 4 months and 26 days. She was received by the church a few years ago as a candidate for baptism,- but claimed to be not able, so she passed away in that condition. Her mind was very much impaired for some time before her death. Funeral services from John 5: 25, 28 by the writer, to many friends and relatives.

J. H. SLUSHER.

BROWN.—In the Elkhart church, Elkhart Co., Ind., Aug. 3, 1892, sister Jennie Brown, daughter of Eld. Daniel Riggle, aged 20 years, 3 months and 13 days. She united with the church recently. She leaves a husband and an infant. Her mother preceded her to the spirit world about one year ago. Funeral services by brethren Lemuel Hillery and A. L. Neff, from these words: "There is no discharge in that war." Eccl. 8: 8.

J. H. MILLER.

WEIMER.—In the Ligonier Valley congregation, Pa., July 31, 1892, Bro. William Weimer, aged 69 years and 28 days. Bro. Weimer lived in this neighborhood and brought up a large family, most of whom are married. About two years ago he decided to unite with the children of God, and has since been a very devoted servant of the Master. Funeral services by Eld. George Hanawalt.

BARBARA M. HANAWALT.

MITCHEL.—In the Mt. Zion congregation, Page Co., Va., July 10, 1892, Bro George Mitchel, aged about 80 years. He was born in London, and has been a citizen of our country for about forty years, and a faithful member of the Brethren church for about twenty years. Funeral services by the writer from Ps. 8: 3, 4.

MARTIN ROTHGEB.

FERREL.—In the Newport congregation, Page Co., Va., July 28, 1892, sister Barbara E. Ferrel, aged 59 years, 9 months and 15 days. She has been a faithful sister in the Brethren church for nearly five years. Funeral services by the writer from Rev. 14: 13.

J. MARTIN NEHER.

CROSS.—In the Quemahoning church, Somerset Co., Pa., July 18, 1892, Bro. William C. Cross, aged 31 years, 4 months and 1 day. He leaves a wife and three children to mourn their loss. Funeral services by brethren Valentine Blough and R. T. Hull.

JOHN J. DARR.

WEDDLE.—Near Santos, Floyd Co., Va., July 23, 1892, Levi Weddle, aged 72 years and 10 months. He had been a member of the Brethren church for more than thirty-one years and had served as deacon for twenty-seven years. He was the father of eleven children. Funeral services by elders J. B. Hylton, C. D. Hylton and Jacob Hylton.

J. H. SLUSHER.

ULREY.—In the Fairview church, Tippecanoe Co., Ind., May 20, 1892, Bro. Samuel Ulrey, aged 58 years, 2 months and 4 days. In 1860 Bro. Ulrey was chosen to the office of deacon, and to the ministry in 1870, in which office he faithfully served until his death. The church greatly feels her loss which, we hope, was his eternal gain. He leaves a wife and one son; a wife, three sons and one daughter having preceded him to the spirit world Disease, epilepsy. He was in his usual health when he retired for the night, when one of the paroxysms seized him and he peacefully passed away. Services by Eld. Isaac Cripe, in the Pyrmont church. Interment in the Pyrmont cemetery.

J. W. VETTER.

CRIPE.—In the North Fork church, Carroll Co., Ind., Aug. 3, 1892, sister Eve Cripe, aged 59 years, 5 months and 23 days. Her maiden name was Nehor. Nov. 3, 1849, she was married to Joseph Hufford, with whom she lived nearly twelve years. She was the mother of seven children, three of whom preceded her to the home beyond. In December, 1879, she was married to William Cripe, with whom she lived nearly nine years. A few years ago she became afflicted with palsy, from which she suffered greatly. July 31 she called for the elders and was anointed with oil in the name of the Lord. She peacefully passed away at the home of her son-in-law, Andrew Wagoner. She leaves four children. Funeral services conducted by elders Solomon Blickenstaff and Isaac Cripe. Interment in the Hufford cemetery Aug. 4.

J. W. VETTER.

STAUFFER.—In the Baugo church, Wakarusa, Ind., Aug. 3, 1892, sister Christena Stauffer (*see* Sanders), aged 57 years, 8 months and 22 days. Funeral services by Bro. M. C. Murry and the home ministers.

STAUFFER.—In the same church, July 4, 1892, Mr. Charles Allen Stauffer, son of the above, aged 24 years, 5 months and seven days. Funeral services by Eld. John Metzler and the undersigned.

H. M. SCHWALM.

ROWLAND.—Near Dallas Centre, Iowa, Aug. 6, 1892, sister Susan, wife of Bro. John Rowland and daughter of George and Sarah Buterbaugh, aged 66 years, 4 months and 24 days. Disease, cancer of stomach. She leaves an aged husband, three sons and one daughter. Funeral services were held near her home, after which her remains were taken to her former home, near Lanark, Ill., for interment, where services were conducted by Bro. George D. Zollers from Heb. 4: 9.

GEO. B. ROYER.

STUDEBAKER.—In the bounds of the Hickory Grove church, Miami Co., Ohio, sister Naomi Studebaker, aged 47 years, 1 month and 4 days. Sister Studebaker was severely afflicted and a great sufferer, which she patiently bore for over two years. With a faint hope of relief, she submitted to a severe surgical operation from the effects of which she never revived. Funeral services were conducted by brethren Bennett Trout and O. S. Filbrun.

JACOB COPPOCK.

COSIER.—In the Oakland church, Darke Co., Ohio, Aug. 4, 1892, of paralysis, sister Nancy Cosier, wife of Mr. John Cosier, deceased, aged 80 years, 1 month and 15 days. Her funeral services were held in the Oakland meeting-house and conducted by brethren J. H. Christian and B. F. Honeyman, from Prov. 12: 28.

I. B. MILLER.

The Gospel Messenger

Is the recognized organ of the German Baptist or Brethren's church, and advocates the form of doctrine taught in the New Testament and pleads for a return to apostolic and primitive Christianity.

It recognizes the New Testament as the only infallible rule of faith and practice, and maintains that Faith toward God, Repentance from dead works, Regeneration of the heart and mind, baptism by Trine Immersion for remission of sins unto the reception of the Holy Ghost by the laying on of hands, are the means of adoption into the household of God,—the church militant.

It also maintains that Feet-washing, as taught in John 13, both by example and command of Jesus, should be observed in the church.

That the Lord's Supper, instituted by Christ and as universally observed by the apostles and the early Christians, is a full meal, and, in connection with the Communion, should be taken in the evening or after the close of the day.

That the Salutation of the Holy Kiss, or Kiss of Charity, is binding upon the followers of Christ.

That War and Retaliation are contrary to the spirit and self-denying principles of the religion of Jesus Christ.

That the principle of Plain Dressing and of Non-conformity to the world, as taught in the New Testament, should be observed by the followers of Christ.

That the Scriptural duty of Anointing the Sick with Oil, in the Name of the Lord, James 5: 14, is binding upon all Christians.

It also advocates the church's duty to support Missionary and Tract Work, thus giving to the Lord for the spread of the Gospel and for the conversion of sinners.

In short, it is a vindicator of all that Christ and the apostles have enjoined upon us, and also, amid the conflicting theories and discords of modern Christendom, to point out ground that all must concede to be infallibly safe.

☞ The above principles of our Fraternity are set forth on our "Brethren's Envelopes." Use them! Price 15 cents per package; 40 cents per hundred.

Announcements.

MINISTERIAL MEETINGS.

Oct. 4, in the Blue River Valley church, Butler Co., Nebr., at Bro. Jerry Keller's, ¾ mile west of Octavia. Missionary meeting day before. Trains due here from the East at 12: 20 P. M., from the West at 2: 26 P. M.

Nov. 25, at 9 A. M., in the South-east District of Kansas, Ministerial Meeting in the Cedar Creek church, Moul Ida, Anderson Co., Kans.

Nov. 2 and 3, Western District of Pennsylvania will hold their Ministerial Meeting at Walnut Grove, Johnstown church.

DISTRICT MEETINGS.

Oct. 7, 10 9 A. M., District Meeting in the Crooked Creek church, Washington Co., Iowa. Those coming by rail will be met at Keota, at or 2 A. M. from the East, and at 6:54 P. M. from the West, by notifying D. F. Miller.

LOVE FEASTS.

Aug. 27 and 28, at 2 P. M., Salem, in Sandy Creek congregation, Preston Co., W. Va.

Aug. 27, at 4 P. M., Nocona church, Montague Co., Tex.

Sept. 2, at 2 P. M., Sugar Creek church, Sangamon County, Ill., 2 miles east of Auburn, Ill.

Sept. 2, at 3 P. M., Rockton church, Pa.

Sept. 3, at 4 P. M., at Sangerville, in the Beaver Creek congregation, Rockingham Co., Va.

Sept. 3, at 4 P. M., Dunker Hill church, Ohio. Preaching to commence on Thursday, evening previous to the feast.

Sept. 3, Round Mountain church, Ark.

Sept. 3, at 10 A. M., Mt. Etna church, Iowa. Conveyances on Friday, Sept. 2, at Corning.

Sept. 3, at 4 P. M., at Independence, Kans.

Sept. 3, at 10 A. M., Washington church, Kans., at Bro. M. R. Phillippi's residence, three miles south, and three and one-half miles west of Washington, Kans.

Sept. 3, at 5 P. M., Silver Creek church, Cowley Co., Kans.

Sept. 3, Mill Creek church, Adams Co., Ill.

Sept. 3 and 4, Rock Creme church, Colo. Dedication of church-house on Sunday, Sept. 4. Those coming by rail, stop off at Monte Vista.

Sept. 3, and 4, English River congregation, Keokuk Co., Iowa.

Sept. 3, at 2 P. M., in the Mt. Hope church, Logan Co., Oklahoma Territory.

Sept. 3 and 4, at 10 A. M., in the North Solomon church, six miles north of Portis, Kans.

Sept. 3, Sappa church, Furnas Co., Nebr.

Sept. 3 and 4, Rock Creme church, Colo. Dedication of church-house on Sunday, Sept. 4. Those coming by rail, stop off at Monte Vista.

Sept. 3, at 2 P. M., Sam's Creek church, Ill.

Sept. 3 and 4, Spring Creek church, Chickasaw Co., Iowa.

Sept. 3, at 2 P. M., in Pleasant Valley school-house.

Sept. 3, at 2 P. M., Green Mount, Va.

Sept. 4, at 2 P. M., Johnstown church, Walnut Grove, Pa., 2 miles south of B. & O. and P. R. R.

Sept. 6, at 4 P. M., Indian Creek congregation, Fayette Co., Pa. Series of meetings to commence Aug. 27.

Sept. 9 and 10, at 2 P. M., Scott Valley, Cosley Co., Kans., at the house of W. A. Smith, one mile east and five south of Waverly. A series of meetings to be held in connection with the feast.

Sept. 9, at 10 A. M., Monroe County church, Iowa.

Sept. 10, at 3 P. M., Fairview church, Garrett Co., Md.

Sept. 10, at Pigeon Creek church-house, 9 miles east of Washington, Pa., commencing at 2 P. M.

Sept. 10, Poudre Valley church, Colo.

Sept. 10 and 11, Panhandle, Calhoun Co., Iowa. Series of meetings in connection, beginning one week previous.

Sept. 10 and 11, at 2 P. M., Sterling church, Sterling, Ill.

Sept. 17, at 2 P. M., Bethel congregation, at the Bethlehem meeting-house, Holt Co., Mo. For any information address Jos. Auden, Mound City, Holt Co., Mo.

Sept. 23, at 4 P. M., Oakley church, Macon Co., Ill.

Sept. 23, at 3 P. M., Libertyville church, Jefferson Co., Iowa. Series of meetings to commence immediately after feast.

Sept. 24, at 4 P. M., Maple Grove church, 4 miles north of Ashland City, Ashland Co., Ohio.

Sept. 24 and 25, at 10 A. M., Dutch River church, Stillson, Hancock Co., Iowa.

Sept. 24, at 2 P. M., Pleasant church, Wilson Co., Kans.

Sept. 24, at 2 P. M., Clear Creek congregation, Huntington Co., Ind.

Sept. 24, at 2 P. M., Martin's Creek church, Wayne Co., Ill.

Sept. 24 and 25, 4 miles west of Tipton, Cedar Co., Iowa, beginning at 2 P. M. Ministers of Midd'e Iowa will p'ease arrange to come in on State District Meeting at Garrison. Our meeting-house is at a distance of two miles from Buchanan on the B. C. R. & N. R. R.

Sept. 24, at 5 P. M., in La Porte church, La Porte, Ind. Trains will be met in the forenoon and early afternoon of the day of meeting.

Sept. 24 and 25, at 3 P. M., Loraine church, Carroll Co., Ill.

Sept. 24, at 5 P. M., Pokagon church, Dowagiac, Cass Co., Mich.

Sept. 27, at 2 P. M., at Wenger meeting-house, St. Joseph church, Ind.

Sept. 28, South Bend church, Ind.

Sept. 28, at 10 A. M., Spring Creek church, Kosciusko Co., Ind.

Sept. 29 and 30, at 2 P. M., Rock Creek, Whiteside Co., Ill.

Sept. 29 and 30, at 10 A. M., Lower Fall Creek church, 5 miles south of Anderson. Those coming on train should address John Rensack, Anderson, Ind.

Sept. 30, at 10 A. M., Nettle Creek church, near Hagerstown, Wayne Co., Ind.

Sept. 30, at 2 P. M., Mississinewa church, Delaware Co., Ind. Those coming by rail stop off at Shideler.

Sept. 30, at 2 P. M., Milmine church, Piatt Co., Ill.

Oct. 1, at 2 P. M., Sugar Creek church, Allen Co., Ohio.

Oct. 1, at 5 P. M., Berrien Congregation, Mich.

Oct. 1 and 2, at 10 A. M., West Branch church, Ill. One week's meeting previous to feast.

Oct. 1 and 2, at 2 P. M., near Ankeny, Scotts Co., Iowa. North train meet at Ames on Saturday.

Oct. 1, at 2 P. M., Turkey Creek congregation, Pawnee Co., Nebr. Those coming by rail will please give notice and they will be met at Du Bois.

Oct. 1 and 2, in the Blue River Valley church, Butler Co., Nebr., at Bro. Jerry Keller's, ¾ mile west of Octavia.

Oct. 1, at 4 P. M., Logan church, near DeGraff, Ohio.

Oct. 1, at 2 P. M., Saginaw church, Mich.

Oct. 1 and 2, at 10: 30 P. M., Walnut Valley congregation, Barton Co., Kans.

Oct. 1 and 2, at 2 P. M., Allegheny congregation, Grant Co., W. Va.

Oct. 1, Maple Grove church, Norton Co., Kans.

Oct. 1, at 10 A. M., Appanoose church, Kans.

Oct. 1, at 10 A. M., Eight Mile church, Ind., at the town of Mexico.

Oct. 1 and 2, at 11 A. M., Riverdale, Iowa. Those coming by rail will stop at Iowa Junction, on B. C. R. & N. R. R., where they will be met.

Oct. 1, at 10 A. M., State Lick church, Chetmont Co., Ohio.

Oct. 1, at 10 A. M., Chippewa congregation, Wayne Co., Ohio.

Oct. 1, at 2 P. M., in the Verdigris church, at Bro. S. S. Reimmitt's. A series of meetings will commence Sept. 25.

Oct. 1, Camp Creek church, Ill., at the church 2 miles south of Colchester. Those coming by train will please notify S. S. Hummer', and they will be met at the depot at Colchester, and conveyed to place of meeting.

Oct. 1, at 2 P. M., South Waterloo church, Waterloo, Iowa.

Oct. 1, at 10 A. M., Belleville church, Kans.

Oct. 1, at 2 P. M., Johnstown church, Pa., 3 miles north-east of Johnstown and 2 miles north of Mineral Point on the P. R. R.

Oct. 4, at 5: 30 P. M., Sugar Ridge church, Ohio.

Oct. 4, at 10 A. M., in the Beaver Dam church, Kosciusko Co., Ind., near the town of Burket.

Oct. 4, at 2 P. M., Price's Creek church, Preble Co., Ohio.

Oct. 5, at 2 P. M., Nyson church, Ind.

Oct. 5 and 6, Dallas Centre church. A series of meetings by Bro. Hutchison will commence Sept. 17.

Oct. 5, at 10 A. M., Satt's Fe church, Ind., 6 miles south of Peru, 2 miles east of Bunker Hill and 1 mile north of Loree.

Nov. 5 and 6, at 4 P. M., North Beatrice church, Gage Co., Nebr.

Oct. 6, at 2 P. M., Altoona church, Ind.

Oct. 6, at 10 A. M., Prairie Creek church, Ind.

Oct. 6, at 10 A. M., Cedar County church, Cedar Co., Mo., 3 miles north-east of Jerico, at Bro. H. Tingley's.

Oct. 6, at 10 A. M., Wabash church, 5 miles south of Wabash, Ind.

Oct. 6, at 10 A. M., Shannon, Ill.

Oct. 6, at 3 P. M. 10 Mo. Joy meeting-house; in Jacob's Creek congregation, Westmoreland Co., Pa. Series of meetings to commence Oct. 2.

Oct. 6, at 10 A. M., Donnel's Creek church, Clarke Co., Ohio, seven miles from New Carlisle, and the same distance from Forge and Springfield. Those coming from the West will stop either at New Carlisle or Forgy, where they will be met on the evening of the 5th. Those from the North-east or South should stop at Springfield.

Oct. 6, at 3 P. M., Spring Creek church, in the Keith's church-house, eleven miles south-west of Rosco, Kans.

Oct. 7, Black River church, Van Buren Co., Mich. Brethren coming by rail will stop off at Hartford.

Oct. 7, at 4 P. M., Yellow Creek congregation, Bedford Co., Pa.

Oct. 7, at 2 P. M., Lodega, Ind.

Oct. 7, at 2 P. M., Kaskaskia church, Fayette Co., Ill., ten miles south-west of Beecher City, Ill. Those coming by rail will be met at the above-named place by informing Granville Nevinger.

Oct. 7, at 2 P. M., Sugar Creek, Whitley Co., Ind.

Oct. 7, at 10 A. M., Panther Creek church, Woodford Co., Ill.

Oct. 7, at 2 P. M., Dunning's Creek congregation, Bedford Co., Pa.

Oct. 7, at 2 P. M., Raccoon Creek church, Montgomery Co., Ind., one and one-half miles north west of Ladoga.

Oct. 7, at 2 P. M., Macoupin Creek church, Montgomery Co., Ill. Those coming by rail will be met at Farmersville, on Springfield Road, and at Girard, on St. Louis Road on morning of meeting.

Oct. 7 and 8, at 10:30 A. M., Four Mile church, Union Co., Ind.

Oct. 8, at 2 P. M., Lamotte church, Crawford Co. Ill.

Oct. 8, at 3: 30 P. M., Maple Glen church, Somerset Co., Pa.

Oct. 8, at 2 P. M., in the Elkhart Valley church, Elkhart Co., Ind.

Oct. 8 and 9, at 2 P. M., Arnold's Grove, Ill.

Oct. 8, at 10 A. M., Dry Creek church, Linn Co., Iowa, one mile west of Robins Station.

Oct. 8, Swan Creek congregation, Ohio, 3½ miles west of Delta, Ohio.

Oct. 8, at 4 P. M., Washington Creek church, Douglas Co., Kans.

Oct. 8 and 9, at 10 A. M., Pine Creek congregation, Ill.

Oct. 8 and 9, Bethel church, Pratt Co., Kans., in the town of Sawyer. Meeting to commence at 2 o'clock.

Oct. 8, at 10 A. M. Bear Creek church, Christian, Fulton Co., Ill. A series of meetings one week previous to the feast, and to continue two weeks.

Oct. 8, at 2 P. M., North Star, Darke County, Ohio.

Oct. 8, at 2 P. M., Greentown church, at Greentown, Howard Co., Ind.

Oct. 8, at 11 A. M., Crooked Creek church, Washington Co., Iowa.

Oct. 8, at 10 o'clock, Durrance church, Kans.

Oct. 8, at 2 P. M., Bethel church, on North County line, Thayer Co., Nebr. Stations: Carleton, Davenport, Carlisle and Shickley.

Oct. 8, at 3 P. M., County Line church, Allen Co., Ohio.

Oct. 8, at 2 P. M., New Hope church, Cherokee Co., Kans., 2½ E. Lichtenwalter's, 35 miles east of Neutral Station.

Oct. 8, Peabody, Kans.

Oct. 8, at 3: 30 P. M., Quinter church, Covina, Cal.

Oct. 8, at 10 A. M., Brooklyn church, Iowa.

Oct. 8, at 10 A. M., Rock Chalk church, Kans., 5 miles north of Sabetha. Those coming by rail should notify E. Cober a week before, stating no arrangements can be made to take them to place of meeting.

Oct. 14, at 4 P. M., Maple Grove church, Maryland Co., Ind., five miles west of Plymouth. Trains will be met at both Plymouth and Burr Oak.

Oct. 14 and 15, at 11 A. M., South Keokuk church, Keokuk Co., Iowa. Those coming by rail will be met at Olive, by notify'ng James Shalley or Isaac Brown. Those coming from the West will arrive at Ollie about 12:30 A. M.; those from the East at 2 P. M.

Oct. 14, Union church, Plymouth, Marshall Co., Ind. Talk church would like to have some brother hold meetings a week or ten days after.

Oct. 15, at 10 A. M., Rome church, Oak Grove house. Also Harvest meeting at home place Aug. 13, at 10 A. M.

Oct. 15 and 16, at 10 A. M., Grundy church, ten miles west of Grundy Centre, Grundy Co., Iowa.

Oct. 20, at 2 P. M., Middle Fork church, Clinton Co., Ind.

Oct. 22, at 10 A. M., Kilbuck church, Delaware Co., Ind., nine miles west of Muncie.

Oct. 29, at 2 P. M., Pleasant Grove church, Douglas Co., Kans.

Oct. 28, at 3 P. M., St. Joseph Valley church, St. Joseph Co., Ind., 3 miles north of South Bend.

Oct. 28, at 2 P. M., in the Pleasant Hill church, near Girard and Virden, Ill.

Oct. 28, at 2 P. M., South Beatrice church, Gage Co., Nebr. Conveyances the day before meeting at B. & K. depot, in Beatrice; Rock Island depot, in Rock Bend; Union Pacific depot, in Holmesville.

Oct. 28, at 2 P. M., Walnut church, Marshall Co., Ind.

Oct. 29, at 10 A. M., in the Buck Creek church, Henry Co., Ind.

Oct. 29, at 2 P. M., Mt. Cart Congregation, Page, Va.

Oct. 29, St. Vrain church, Longmont, Colo.

Oct. 29, at 2 P. M., Osawkie church, Kans. A series of meetings to commence Oct. 10.

Oct. 29 and 30, at 10 A. M., at the Pigeon Creek church, Ill., at the Oak Grove meeting-house.

Oct. 29, at 2 P. M., Cedar church, Madison Co., Ind., 3½ miles east of Summitville.

Oct. 29 and 30, 10 A. M., Maria church, Pa.

Nov. 1, Walnut Creek church, Mo.

Nov. 3, at 3 P. M., Big Creek church, Richland Co., Ill., 3½ miles North-east of Parkersburg, Ill. Conveyances will be at the above place by informing J. M. Forney.

Nov. 24, at 3 P. M., Cedar Creek church, Anderson Co., Kans.

Announcements.

MINISTERIAL MEETINGS.

Oct. 2, in the Blue River Valley church, Butler Co., Nebr., at Bro. Jerry Keller's, ¼ mile west of Octavia. Ministerial meeting day before. Trains due here from the East at 12:10 P. M., from the West at 2:26 P. M.

Nov. 15, at 9 A. M., in the South-east District of Kansas, Ministerial Meeting in the Cedar Creek church, Montclair, Anderson Co., Kans.

Nov. 2 and 3: Western District of Pennsylvania will hold their Ministerial Meeting at Walnut Grove, Johnstown church.

DISTRICT MEETINGS.

Oct. 3, 11 9 A. M., District Meeting in the Crooked Creek church, Washington Co., Iowa. Those coming by rail will be met at Keota, at 10 A. M. from the East, and at 6:25 P. M. from the West, by notifying D. P. Miller.

LOVE-FEASTS.

Aug. 27 and 28, at 4 P. M., Salem, in Sandy Creek congregation, Preston Co., W. Va.

Aug. 27, at 4 P. M., Neosho church, McHoagle Co., Tenn.

Sept. 2, at 4 P. M., Sugar Creek church, Sangamon County, Ill., 2 miles east of Auburn, Ill.

Sept. 2, at 3 P. M., Madison church, Pa.

Sept. 3, 10 4 P. M., at Saegersville, in the Beaver Creek congregation, Rockingham Co., Va.

Sept. 3, Round Mountain church, Ark.

Sept. 3, 11 10 A. M., Mt. Etna church, Iowa. Conveyances on Friday, Sept. 2, at Corning.

Sept. 8, at 3 P. M., at Independence, Kans.

Sept. 3, 10 10 A. M., Washington church, Kans., at Bro. Wm. R. Phillippi's residence, three miles south, and three and one-half miles west of Washington, Kans.

Sept. 3, at 3 P. M., Silver Creek church, Cowley Co., Kans.

Sept. 3, Mill Creek church, Adams Co., Ill.

Sept. 3 and 4, English River congregation, Keokuk Co., Iowa.

Sept. 3, at 2 P. M., in the Mt. Hope church, Logan Co., Oklahoma Territory.

Sept. 3 and 4, 10 10 A. M., in the North Solomon church, six miles North of Portis, Kans.

Sept. 3, Sappa church, Furnas Co. Nebr.

Sept. 3 and 4, Rock Creek church, Colo. Dedication of church-house on Sunday, Sept. 4. Those coming by rail, stop off at Mottle Vista.

Sept. 3, at 2 P. M., Sam's Creek church, Md.

Sept. 3 and 4, Spring Creek church, Chickamaw Co., Iowa.

Sept. 3, Wayman Valley church, at Pleasant Valley schoolhouse.

Sept. 3, at 5 P. M., Greek Meadow, Va.

Sept. 3, at 2 P. M., Jonestown church, Walnut Grove, Pa., 1 mile south of B. & O. and P. R. R.

Sept. 6, at 4 P. M., Indian Creek congregation, Fayette Co., Pa. Series of meetings to commence Aug. 27.

Sept. 7 and 8, at 2 P. M., Scott Valley, Corley Co., Kans., at the home of W. A. Smith, one mile east and five tenth of Waverly. A series of meetings to be held in connection with the feast.

Sept. 9, at 10 A. M., Medrow County church, Iowa.

Sept. 10, at 7 P. M., Fairview church, Garrett Co., Md.

Sept. 10, 11 3 P. M., Pigeon Creek church-house, 4 miles east of Washington, Pa., commencing at 2 P. M.

Sept. 10, Poudre Valley church, Colo.

Sept. 10 and 11, Panhandle, Calhoun Co., Iowa. Series of meetings in connection, beginning one week previous.

Sept. 10, 11 2 P. M., Sterling church, Sterling, Ill.

Sept. 12, at 3 P. M., Bethel congregation, at the Brethren meeting-house, Holt Co., Mo. For any information address Jos. Amlot, Mound City, Holt Co., Mo.

Sept. 17, at 4 P. M., Oakley church, Macon Co., Ill.

Sept. 17, at 3 P. M., Libertyville church, Jefferson Co., Iowa. Series of meetings to commence immediately after feast.

Sept. 24, at 4 P. M., Maple Grove church, 4 miles north of Ashland City, Ashland Co., Ohio.

Sept. 24 and 25, 10 10 A. M., Bear River church, Stilson, Hancock Co., Iowa.

Sept. 24, at 3 P. M., Fredonia church, Wilson Co., Kans.

Sept. 24, at 4 P. M., Clear Creek congregation, Huntington Co., Ind.

Sept. 24, 25, at 3 P. M., Martin's Creek church, Wayne Co., Ill.

Sept. 21 and 22, 4 miles west of Tipton, Cedar Co., Iowa, beginning at 2 P. M. Ministers of Middle Iowa will please arrange to come to us from District Meeting at Garrison. Our meeting-house is at a distance of two miles from Buchanan on the B., C. R. & N. R. R.

Sept. 24, at 3 P. M., in La Porte church, La Porte, Ind. Trains will be met in the forenoon and early afternoon of the day of meeting.

Sept. 24 and 25, at 3 P. M., Lenark church, Carroll Co., Ill.

Sept. 24, at 3 P. M., Pokagon church, Dowagiac, Cass Co., Mich.

Sept. 27, at 3 P. M., at Wenger meeting-house, St. Joseph Co., Ind.

Sept. 28, South Bend church, Ind.

Sept. 28, 10 10 A. M., Spring Creek church, Kosciusko Co., Ind.

Sept. 29 and 30, at 2 P. M., Rock Creek, Whiteside Co., Ill.

Sept. 29 and 30, 10 10 A. M., Lower Fall Creek church, 2 miles south of Anderson. Those coming on train should address John Bosserde, Anderson, Ind.

Sept. 30, at 10 A. M., North Creek church, near Hagerstown, Wayne Co., Ind.

Sept. 30, 10 10 A. M., Mississinewa church, Delaware Co., Ind. Those coming by rail stop off at Shideler.

Sept. 30, at 2 P. M., Milmine church, Piatt Co., Ill.

Oct. 1, at 2 P. M., Sugar Creek church, Allen Co., Ohio.

Oct. 1, 10 6 P. M., Berrien congregation, Mich.

Oct. 1 and 2, 10 10 A. M., West Branch church, Ill. One week's meeting previous to feast.

Oct. 1 and 2, at 2 P. M., near Ames, Boone Co., Iowa. Noon train meets at Ames on Saturday.

Oct. 1, at 3 P. M., Turkey Creek congregation, Pawnee Co., Nebr. Those coming by rail will please give notice and they will be met at Dubois.

Oct. 1 and 2, in the Blue River Valley church, Butler Co., Nebr., at Bro Jerry Keller's, ¼ mile west of Octavia.

Oct. 1, 10 2 P. M., Osage church, Crawford Co., Kans.

Oct. 1, at 4 P. M., Logan church, near DeGraff, Ohio.

Oct. 1 and 2, Saginaw church, Mich.

Oct. 1 and 2, at 1:30 P. M., Walnut Valley congregation, Barton Co., Kans.

Oct. 1, at 4 P. M., Allegheny congregation, Grant Co., W. Va.

Oct. 1, Maple Grove church, Norton Co., Kans.

Oct. 1, at 10 A. M., Appanoose church, Kans.

Oct. 1, 10 10 A. M., Bright Mile church, Ind., at the town of Markle.

Oct. 1 and 2, 11 11 A. M., Riverside, Iowa. Those coming by rail will stop at Iowa Junction, on B. C. R. & N. R. R., where they will be met.

Oct. 1, 10 10 A. M., Stone Lick church, Clermont Co., Ohio.

Oct. 1, at 10 A. M., Chippewa congregation, Wayne Co., Ohio.

Oct. 1, at 2 P. M., in the Verdigris church, at Bro. S. S. Redman's. A series of meetings will commence Sept. 25.

Oct. 1, Camp Creek church, Ill., at the church 7 miles south of Colchester. Those coming by train will please notify S. S. Hummer, and they will be met at the depot at Colchester, and conveyed to place of meeting.

Oct. 1, at 2 P. M., Belleville church, Iowa.

Oct. 1, at 3 P. M., Johnstown church, Pa., 3 miles north-east of Johnstown and 2 miles north of Mineral Point on the P. R. R.

Oct. 1, at 2 P. M., Sugar Ridge church, Mo.

Oct. 1, at 10 A. M., in the Beaver Dam church, Kosciusko Co., Ind., near the town of Burket.

Oct. 1, at 2 P. M., Price's Creek church, Preble Co., Ohio.

Oct. 3, at 2 P. M., Rgann church, Ind.

Oct. 5 and 6, Dallas Centre church. A series of meetings by Bro. Hutchison will commence Sept. 17.

Oct. 6, at 10 A. M., Santa Fe church, Ind., 2 miles south of Peru, 2 miles east of Bunker Hill and 2 mile north of Loree.

Nov. 5 and 6, 11 2 P. M., North Beatrice church, Gage Co., Nebr.

Oct. 6, at 10 A. M., Arcadia church, Ind.

Oct. 6, at 10 A. M., Prairie Creek church, Ind.

Oct. 6, at 10 A. M., Cedar County church, Cedar Co., Mo., 3 miles north-east of Jerico, at Bro. M. Tingley's.

Oct. 6, at 10 A. M., Wabash church, 7 miles south of Wabash, Ind.

Oct. 6 and 7, at 10 A. M., Shannon, Ill.

Oct. 6, 6, at 3 P. M., 10 Joy meeting-house; 2 miles north-west of Parkersburg, Ill. Conveyances will be at the above place by informing J. M. Forney.

Oct. 6, at 10 A. M., Donnel's Creek church, Clark Co., Ohio, seven miles from New Carlisle, and the same distance from Forgy and Springfield. Those coming from the West will stop either at New Carlisle or Forgy, where they will be met on the evening of the 5th. Those from the North-east or South should stop at Springfield.

Oct. 6, at 3 P. M., Spring Creek church, in the Keith's church-house, eleven miles south-west of Reece, Kans.

Oct. 7, Black River church, Van Buren Co., Mich. Brethren coming by rail will stop off at Bangor.

Oct. 7, at 4 P. M., Yellow Creek congregation, Bedford Co., Pa.

Oct. 7, at 2 P. M., Ludega, Ind.

Oct. 7, at 2 P. M., Kaskaskia church, Fayette Co., Ill., ten miles south-west of Beecher City, Ill. Those coming by rail will be met at the above-named place by informing Granville Nevinger.

Oct. 7, at 10 A. M., Sugar Creek, Whitley Co., Ind.

Oct. 7, at 10:30 A. M., Panther Creek church, Woodford Co., Ill.

Oct. 7, at 4 P. M., Dunning's Creek congregation, Bedford Co., Pa.

Oct. 8, at 2 P. M., Raccoon Creek church, Montgomery Co., Ind., one and one-half miles north-west of Ladoga.

Oct. 7, at 4 P. M., Mammopin Creek church, Montgomery Co., Ill. Those coming by rail will be met at Farmersville, on Springfield Road, and at Girard, on St. Louis Road on morning of meeting.

Oct. 7 and 8, at 10:30 A. M., Four Mile church, Union Co., Ind.

Oct. 8, at 2 P. M., Lamotte church, Crawford Co. Ill.

Oct. 8, at 3:30 P. M., Maple Glen church, Somerset Co., Pa.

Oct. 8, at 4 P. M., in the Elkhart Valley church, Elkhart Co., Ind., 3 miles south of Goshen.

Oct. 8, at 2 P. M., Arnold's Grove, Ill.

Oct. 8, 10 10 A. M., Dry Creek church, Linn Co., Iowa, one mile west of Robins Station.

Oct. 8, Swan Creek congregation, Ohio, 3½ miles west of Delta, Ohio.

Oct. 8, at 4 P. M., Washington Creek church, Douglas Co., Kans.

Oct. 8 and 9, 11 10 A. M., Pine Creek congregation, Ill.

Oct. 8 and 9, Bethel church, Pawnee Co., Kans., in the town of Sawyer. Meeting to commence at 10 o'clock.

Oct. 8, at 10 A. M., Bear Creek church, Portland, Ind. Those coming by rail will be met by notifying H. P. Garber.

Oct. 8 and 9, at 10 A. M., Woodland church, Fulton Co., Ill. A series of meetings one week previous to the feast, and to continue two weeks.

Oct. 8, at 2 P. M., North Star, Darke County, Ohio.

Oct. 8, at 2 P. M., Greentown church, at Greentown, Howard Co., Ind.

Oct. 8, at 10 A. M., Crooked Creek church, Washington Co., Iowa.

Oct. 8, at 10 o'clock, Dardanon church, Kans.

Oct. 8, at 4 P. M., Bethel church, on North County line, Thayer Co., Nebr. Stations: Carleton, Davenport, Carlisle and Shickley.

Oct. 8, at 2 P. M., County Line church, Allen Co., Ohio.

Oct. 8, at 3 P. M., New Hope church, Cherokee Co., Kans., at A. B. Lichtenwalter's, ¾ mile east of Neutral Station.

Oct. 8, Peabody, Kans.

Oct. 8, at 3:30 P. M., Covina church, Covina, Cal.

Oct. 8, 11 1 A. M., Brooklyn church, Iowa.

Oct. 8, at 10 A. M., Rock Creek church, Kans., 3 miles north of Sabetha. Those coming by rail should notify E. Cober a week before coming, so arrangements can be made to take them to place of meeting.

Oct. 14, at 4 P. M., Union church, Marshall Co., Ind., five miles west of Plymouth. Trains will be met at both Plymouth and Burr Oak.

Oct. 15 and 16, at 10 A. M., South Keokuk church, Keokuk Co., Iowa. Those coming by rail will be met at Ollie, by notifying Isaac Shelley or Isaac Brown. Those coming from the West will strike the Milton about 10:30 A. M.; those from the East at 3 P. M.

Oct. 15, Union church, Plymouth, Marshall Co., Ind. This church would like to have some Brother hold meetings a week or ten days after feast.

Oct. 15, at 10 A. M., Rome church, Oak Grove house. Also harvest meeting at same place Aug. 13, at 10 A. M.

Oct. 15 and 16, at 2 P. M., Grundy church, ten miles west of Grundy Centre, Grundy Co., Iowa.

Oct. 20, at 2 P. M., Middle Fork church, Clinton Co., Ind.

Oct. 20, at 10 A. M., Killbuck church, Delaware Co., Ind., nine miles west of Muncie.

Oct. 21, at 2 P. M., Pleasant Grove church, Douglas Co., Kans.

Oct. 28, at 5 P. M., St. Joseph Valley church, St. Joseph Co., Ind., 3 miles north of South Bend.

Oct. 28, at 4 P. M., in the Pleasant Hill church, Cerro Gordo and Virden, Ill.

Oct. 28, at 2 P. M., South Beatrice church, Gage Co., Nebr. Conveyances the day before meeting at U. & M. depot, in Beatrice; Rock Island depot, in Rock-ford; Union Pacific depot, in Holmesville.

Oct. 28, at 2 P. M., Walnut church, Marshall Co., Ind.

Oct. 28, at 10 A. M., in the Buck Creek church, Henry Co., Ind.

Oct. 29, at 2 P. M., Mt. Zion congregation, Page, Va.

Oct. 29, at 2 P. M., Sylvis church, Longmont, Colo.

Oct. 29, at 2 P. M., Osawatomie church, Kans. A series of meetings to commence Oct. 20.

Oct. 29 and 30, at 10 A. M., Pigeon Creek church, Ill., at the Oak Grove meeting-house.

Oct. 29, 11 2 P. M., Oak Creek church, Madison Co., Ind., 3½ miles east of Summitville.

Nov. 4, at 2 P. M., 11 10 A. M., Hade church, Pa.

Nov. 4, Walnut Creek church, Mo.

Nov. 5, at 3 P. M., Big Creek church, Richland Co., Ill., 3¼ miles North-east of Parkersburg, Ill. Conveyances will be at the above place by informing J. M. Forney.

Nov. 24, at 3 P. M., Cedar Creek church, Anderson Co., Kans.

Lectures on Preaching.—By Rev. Phillips Brooks. Cloth, 12mo, $1.50.

Josephus' Complete Works.—Large 12mo, 1 vol. 8vo. Illustrated with many steel and wood engravings. Library sheep, $3.00.

--- THE ---

Doctrine of the Brethren Defended.

THIS work contains a complete exposition of the faith and practice of the Brethren, the Divinity of Christ, the Divinity of the Holy Spirit, Immersion, Feet-washing, the Lord's supper, the Holy Kiss, Non-conformity, Secret Societies, etc. Price, per copy, cloth binding, $1.25. Address this office.

❖ESSAYS❖

"Study to show thyself approved unto God; a workman that needeth not be ashamed, rightly dividing the Word of Truth."

FARMER MORRISON'S WIFE.

Down at the farm-house below the hill,
The blinds were closed, and the wheel was still.

The swirl of the stream and the blue-fly's drone
Troubled the preacher's voice alone,

Where, by the open door he stood,
And talked to the gathered neighborhood

Of Earth and Heaven, and the grave between,
The visible world and the world unseen;

Glancing aside, with solemn air,
To the dead who lay in her coffin there.

Every breath of the soft May breeze
Shook the blossoming lilac trees,

And sent a quiver of light and bloom
Into the hushed and darkened room.

It touched with a gleam the shadowed wall,
It flickered over the funeral pall,

And circled about the tremulous head
Of the nearest mourner beside the dead:

Farmer Morrison, old and gray,
Bent and helpless for many a day,

Up and down, with a dull surprise,
Restlessly wandered his sunken eyes,

Seeking, it seemed, in that crowded place,
The one familiar, missing face,

The face that, stony and set, lay hid
Just out of sight 'neath the coffin-lid.

Never a day, till the day she died,
Had the wife been gone from her husband's side:

Thus were the twain asunder reft,
The helpful taken, the helpless left.

And the preacher spoke to the people there
Of the Will divine, in his simple prayer:

The Lord, who giveth and taketh away—
Praised be the name of the Lord for aye!

Now, when the last amen was said,
And the mourners rose to follow the dead,

Farmer Morrison, gaunt and tall,
Stood up straight in the sight of all.

Suddenly steady of eye and limb,
While the people gazed aghast at him,

He laid his hand on the coffin-lid,
He stooped to kiss the face it hid,

Then, spent with that one strong, sudden breath,
Life's latest flicker went out in death.

Thus were the twain again made one;
Trial over and trouble done.

And the preacher said in his solemn speech:
"The way of the Lord man may not reach.

Lo! He hath given and taken again!
Praised be the name of the Lord! Amen."
—Sel.

"WE HAVE SEEN STRANGE THINGS TO-DAY."—
Luke 5: 26.

BY I. BENNETT TROUT.

In Two Parts.—Part Two.

In the first part we learned that when Christ appeared among men, it was a strange thing to them to see a being upon earth that was not only able to heal the body, but equally able to cure the sin-sick soul. We now wish to notice a few of the many strange things which exist to-day, and to draw some practical lessons from them, as we did from the previous lesson.

1. The experience of ages, since Christ was in the world in human form, having fully established his willingness to save sinners, is it not very strange that so few, comparatively speaking, come to him and learn to know him in the pardon of their sins, and to have the work of grace established in their hearts?

2. I frequently see members of the Brethren church, the church that we should all love dearly, taking one or more secular papers, and buying a great amount of cheap (?) literature, but you will find neither the GOSPEL MESSENGER nor any of our church literature in their homes. The GOSPEL MESSENGER always comes with good things on its pages. True I find (only a few however) some sentiments in it that I cannot subscribe to, but when I think of the magnitude of the task to keep its columns free from errors of any kind, and then consider the fact that each brother and sister feels the right to be heard, I can but praise and encourage the present management of the paper, and ask the blessings of God upon those who have the control of it.

3. Another strange thing to me is, that we have yet a few members surrounded with the blessings of God, living in the midst of church advantages, with Sunday-school and preaching every Lord's day, giving nothing towards Mission or Tract Work, and, what is even worse, they oppose those that do. It is like the watchman saying, "I will close the shutters to my light-house. If the poor, ship-wrecked mariner wishes any of the blessings to be obtained from this light, he must abandon the sea and climb to where I am." Sure it would require less oil and labor to keep such a system of lights on the rocks, but it would come far short of giving light to the sea or saving the lost. We need to-day aggressive workers,—an aggressive church,—not simply a church that is willing to admit seekers, but one that will search for them.

4 Our church forbids the raising and using of tobacco (see Art. 14, 1881, p. 298, Revised Minutes), yet some of our dear brethren indulge in its use; others raise, or have it grown upon their land. They sell it to others who use it. If some poor sinner that bought his tobacco of them comes to be received into the church, the church (those raising tobacco constituting a part of her numbers), advises him to quit using the weed (Art. 14, 1888). How does such a course appear? I can only explain as follows: I sell something (tobacco) to my neighbor, but advise him not to use it. In turn I receive his money, or, in other words, I virtually receive his money without giving value received to him. Is not this a strange thing seen in our "streets" to-day? Had we not all better practice the advice given by Annual Meeting, thereby uniting our efforts to crush this filthy practice, waste of money, out of the church and the world?

5. The council-meetings are the family gatherings of God's children, in order to look after the family interests, but it frequently occurs that members absent themselves to look after worldly affairs. There is something especially enjoyable where the family holds these reunions, and no child should be absent without lawful reason.

6. Is it not strange that, in face of all the commands to pray and give thanks, and notwithstanding all the blessings promised to those who obey, we have so many homes in which parents do not gather their children around the altar of prayer? Each of us demands the thanks of those upon whom we confer some favor. Is it reasonable to suppose that the Giver "of every good gift, and every perfect gift," will demand less of us?

7. It is certainly strange to see those who have united themselves to a church which practices plainness, as taught in the Gospel, still indulging in the improprieties and superfluities of dress, as though they belonged to some one of the modern churches that pay no attention to Jesus' commands in this line.

I recently attended a church-council, where there had been a number of requests that the members be admonished to keep within the bounds of the church's regulations as to dress.

We did the best we could to set before the members the necessity and benefits of uniform plainness. We tried to intersperse the admonition with Gospel reasons.

In the afternoon of the same day, the same stand was occupied by a brother minister, who, as to his personal appearance in dress, could not be recognized as a brother at all, being dressed in modern style, and fashionably-cut hair. I suppose that the members admonished, thought they had seen *strange things* that day. And when I considered the vows made when entering the church, and especially when ministers are installed, I must confess that I thought it not a little strange myself.

After services a sister of that congregation said, "He preaches real well, but it does me no good." She assigned as the reason the inconsistency of the faith of the church and his practice in his appearance. While I think that sister should have treasured up and put into practice the good lesson he gave us, yet I plainly see that, by his (the minister's) own disregard of the principles of the Gospel, as practiced by the Brethren, he lost his power to edify that sister.

How much better it would be, could we be loyal to the church! We should remember that uniform plainness is the best and safest practical barrier against superfluous dressing.

We will now leave the reader to seek out any other *strange things* existing to-day, and to improve his own life by abandoning the evils with which he is surrounded. We now name a few lessons to be learned from the above:

1. We should be more devoted to God and less devoted to self.

2. We should supply our families with the GOSPEL MESSENGER and other of our church literature.

3. We should give more freely to mission, tract, and church work.

4. We should not allow the filthy use of the weed to be encouraged or supported by our using or raising it.

5. We should be more interested in the prosperity of the church.

6. We should not neglect the family altar.

6. We, as ministers in the church, in order to do effectual work, must be representative members, ensamples to the flock. 1 Tim. 4: 12; Titus 2: 7, 8; 1 Pet. 5: 3.

New Carlisle, Ohio.

LIBERTY.

BY S. B. MILLER.

The law of liberty is perfect, because it fills all man's needs. We know of the law, but what is the liberty produced by it?

The Truth is the same yesterday, to-day and forever. It is true because it is eternally true. The plainness and simplicity of the word attest its divinity. The results from following this perfect law must be noticeable, for it raises a man above the human standard of perfection, and creates higher aims.

One of God's attributes is quality; man seeks QUANTITY. Every follower of Truth desires to attain to a higher life, a purer living, a more Christ-like character. He is progressive, for progress is a living principle. Development of character is self-development. Self-activity alone can produce growth. The doing of any work demands self-sacrifice. It is self-sacrifice to toil from morn till night to gain a livelihood for loved ones. 'Tis self-sacrifice to spend energy for the advancement and development of our fellow-men. A man's service should be more valuable than his possessions. The soul that overcomes self

THE GOSPEL MESSENGER.

THE PREACHER IN POLITICS.

In view of the fact that at least two among the more eminent preachers of the Brethren church have been influenced to, at least, divide their time between preaching the Gospel and engaging in politics, and as one of these has seen fit to defend his course through the columns of the *Evangelist*, I feel to say something to counteract the influence such example and teaching may have on our ministry and church. Since the two ministers alluded to above, belong to opposing political parties, it will not be surprising to hear from each of them, that there is a "depressing and threatening condition" in our public affairs, and that "our free institutions are at stake, and that the perpetuity of our American liberty and the American Republic are seriously threatened," unless the principles which they are championing respectively, will prevail at the polls. It would not be surprising to hear of other ministers equally talented and conscientious, espousing the cause of the other national parties, and devoting their time and energies in showing that the country can be saved only by electing them, the preachers, to office.

The political campaign just opening, will be one that will be contested with fierce energy, and for months the work of the church will be pushed into the background, to give room to the clash of contending political parties. The calm observer will notice that the present political campaign does not differ materially from former campaigns, and that nine-tenths of the leaders of all the parties, as they are at present constituted, have greater concern for the emolument of office, than the principle of government announced through their party platforms.

While I believe that a Christian should not neglect his citizenship, it is certainly deplorable to have him engage in this political contest to the neglect of his Christian duties, and to allow his partisan and selfish feelings to take such control of him as to look upon his brother in Christ as unworthy the name of Christian, because he does not entertain the same political view with himself.

I have lately been reading a book entitled, "Lectures on Preaching," by Matthew Simpson D. D. LL. D., a bishop in the M. E. church, which contains among the rest, a lecture entitled: "Is the Modern Pulpit a Failure?" In this appear several paragraphs on the ministers' behavior during a political campaign, which is so good and timely, that I beg leave to have it published in the *Evangelist* in this connection, as follows: "The minister should ever announce great principles which lie at the foundation of society—principles affecting the rights of man and the duties of the government. But, valuable as are these topics, they should be but occasional and incidental. Sometimes, passing from these broad principles, the minister suffers himself to use the pulpit to promote the interests of a favorite political measure, which inures to the benefit of a party, or to the aspirations of some individual. Such a course ever lowers the tone of the pulpit, and offends some of the congregation. It requires skill and tact and heroism to utter the high moral requirements of the law of God, and yet to avoid such declarations that in times of high party excitement may foster mere party or personal interests.

"Still worse is it when the minister allows himself to be personally drawn into a political canvass. Parties are nearly equally balanced, and those in the minority fancy that the personal influence of the preacher may turn a sufficient number of votes to make them triumphant. Hence they urge him to become a candidate. They dwell upon the great issues at stake. They tell him how greatly good men are needed in office, show him what a

vast work he may perform, and endeavor to show him that it is really his duty to accept the nomination. Sometimes, alas! he is persuaded to do so; he leaves his pulpit, engages in the canvass, mingles in political scenes, if not in intrigues, and is absorbed for the time being in the pending issues. These instances are comparatively rare, and the minister conscientiously believes he is doing right; yet my conviction is that the result is always disastrous, both to himself and to the church. It is disastrous to himself in that his *status* is lowered even in the estimation of his political friends. They selected him, not because they cared for him, but because he was an available candidate. They flattered him to use him, and they henceforth regarded him as a man that may be flattered and used. Had he declined the proffered nomination; had he said: 'I have but one work to do, I must preach Christ and him crucified,' he would have occupied a position of higher moral eminence. But by those outside of his own party, he is simply regarded as one who is ready to use his ministerial influence for the promotion of his personal ambition. If unsuccessful, years will pass away before he can regain the high moral influence which he once exerted. If successful, his thoughts are turned from the pulpit. The questions which he considers, the associations in which he mingles, and the applications for office and assistance constantly pressed upon him, divert his attention from that course of reading and that character of mental study which gave him efficiency and power in the pulpit. As the result, he either turns to his ministry at the close of his official period, a weaker and less efficient minister than before, or what is more likely, having embarked on the political stream, he is borne onward by the current, never to return again. Thus one whom God has called to the ministry, is to that extent, lost to the cause of Christ. But the most disastrous result is, that the public understand that those who profess to belong to God have no convictions as bind them to their work; that they are ready to exchange it for any position which they may consider more lucrative or more honorable.

"As one minister accepts such a nomination, the public infer, all would do so, if they were equally pressed; and hence that the ministry is regarded by the ministers themselves, not as a divine calling, but as an inferior position that they use as a stepping-stone to something higher. In this way the character of the ministry suffers immensely, while the individual, at the best, can be but slightly benefited.

"I have stated this case in its least objectionable form; much worse is it when a minister seeks a nomination; when he voluntarily abandons the pulpit to mingle in party strife. * * * Quite possible all these cases have their root in the lack of a clear conviction of a divine call to the ministry or of deep earnestness of spirit, for without earnestness a man accomplishes but little good. * * * All the causes to which I have alluded contribute to the inefficiency of the pulpit, and give some color of reason to those who proclaim the pulpit to be a failure."

Of course the eminent lecturer goes on to show that the pulpit is not a failure.

I wish that every minister in the Brethren church could read this book of lectures.—*E. L. Yoder, in the Brethren (Progressive) Evangelist.*

EXUBERANT PRIDE AND NON-CONFORMITY.

BY S. O. BARWICK.

IT is an evident fact that we are living in a land where haughty pride and Dame Fashion are reigning supreme, and now stands as one of the great

vices of mankind. Pride has dwelt within the mind and heart of man for so many generations that it has long since become a chronic and hereditary affection of the whole human family in some form.

To-day we find it in the homes and in the gambling resorts, in the churches, and in institutions of all descriptions, and its presence and impressions, like the air, is present every-where.

Its physiological actions are King Terror to humanity and venoms to the soul; it is a thief, seducer, and oppressor to the poor, and also an offense to the Lord of high heaven. For thus says the Lord: "Pride and arrogancy do I hate." We also read that "God resisteth the proud" and "scattereth them in the imagination of their heart," that "only by pride cometh contention and shame," and "he that is of a proud heart stirreth up strife," and before destruction the heart of man is haughty, and thus its evil consequence is, "man's pride shall bring him down." From the following we will observe that pride is classed as being one of the elements of sinfulness, as thefts, covetousness, wickedness, deceit, lasciviousness, an evil eye, blasphemy, pride, foolishness. All these evil things come from within, and defile man. "For all that is in the world, the lust of the flesh, and the lust of the eye, and the pride of life, is not of the Father, but is of the world.

We may scan the Scriptures from Genesis to Revelation, and we will observe that pride is the work of Satan, and belongs to the evil inclinations of nature, is a relative of carnality and not of spirituality, and is an abomination unto the Lord. When candidly considering superfluous pride, we most emphatically observe that it and non-conformity are incompatible with each other, and there is no religionist who is skillful enough to combine the two as being officinal according to the dispensatory of the Lord and Savior Jesus Christ. It is invariably a fact that haughty pride and Dame Fashion are the expression of Satan, while non-conformity is the expression of the Lord and his Son Jesus, and a symbol of the inward motives of man, and the pretending Christian who purposely neglects to keep his Gospel vessel filled, trimmed, and brightly burning, would do well entirely to discard his external expression, as from the expressions and deeds of man we may "righteously judge" him clear to the heart.

There is a wonderful expression in plain Gospel non-conformity, as it is a representation of the Lord and Savior, an object of worship, love and obedience. It is one of the many elements of Christianity, and it should be observed by the children of God as a *symbol* of humility and meekness, and not as being a Pharisaical hobby.

Bangs, puffs, brussels, plug-hats, etc, are the expressions of pride; they cannot represent non-conformity, and do not belong to the conscientious Christian, and, above all, there will be no such things in heaven to confuse the angels, but with a robe and crown of righteousness will they ever reign with the Lord and Savior.

I am sorry to say that it is claimed by some that there is nothing "in it," but let us see further. Let us consider the worth and weight of expression. When we see those with silvery locks and a furred physiognomy, we observe the expression of age, and it is an evident fact that life is fast fading away. Then, when we view the Western rangers with their weapons strapped to their sides, we observe the expression of cruelty, combativeness and destructiveness, to whatever might offend them.

Again, to obtain the expression of the riotous regulator we must observe him from the top of his hat to the toe of his shoes, and most emphatically his external expression is precisely in harmony with his internal motives, which is envy;

THE PREACHER IN POLITICS.

In view of the fact that at least two among the more eminent preachers of the Brethren church have been influenced to, at least, divide their time between preaching the Gospel and engaging in politics, and as one of these has seen fit to defend his course through the columns of the *Evangelist*, I feel to say something to counteract the influence such example and teaching may have on our ministry and church. Since the two ministers alluded to above, belong to opposing political parties, it will not be surprising to hear from each of them, that there is a "depressing and threatening condition" in our public affairs, and that "our free institutions are at stake, and that the perpetuity of our American liberty and the American Republic are seriously threatened," unless the principles which they are championing respectively, will prevail at the polls. It would not be surprising to hear of other ministers equally talented and conscientious, espousing the cause of the other national parties, and devoting their time and energies in showing that the country can be saved only by electing them, the preachers, to office.

The political campaign just opening, will be one that will be contested with fierce energy, and for months the work of the church will be pushed into the background, to give room to the clash of contending political parties. The calm observer will notice that the present political campaign does not differ materially from former campaigns, and that nine-tenths of the leaders of all the parties, as they are at present constituted, have greater concern for the emolument of office, than the principle of government announced through their party platforms.

While I believe that a Christian should not neglect his citizenship, it is certainly deplorable to have him engage in this political contest to the neglect of his Christian duties, and to allow his partisan and selfish feelings to take such control of him as to look upon his brother in Christ as unworthy the name of Christian, because he does not entertain the same political view with himself.

I have lately been reading a book entitled, "Lectures on Preaching," by Matthew Simpson D. D. LL. D., a bishop in the M. E. church, which contains among the rest, a lecture entitled: "Is the Modern Pulpit a Failure?" In this appear several paragraphs on the ministers' behavior during a political campaign, which is so good and timely, that I beg leave to have it published in the *Evangelist* in this connection, as follows: "The minister should ever announce great principles which lie at the foundation of society—principles affecting the rights of man and the duties of the government. But, valuable as are these topics, they should be but occasional and incidental. Sometimes, passing from these broad principles, the minister suffers himself to use the pulpit to promote the interests of a favorite political measure, which inures to the benefit of a party, or to the aspirations of some individual. Such a course ever lowers the tone of the pulpit, and offends some of the congregation. It requires skill and tact and heroism to utter the high moral requirements of the law of God, and yet to avoid such declarations that in times of high party excitement may foster mere party or personal interests.

"Still worse is it when the minister allows himself to be personally drawn into a political canvass. Parties are nearly equally balanced, and those in the minority fancy that the personal influence of the preacher may turn a sufficient number of votes to make them triumphant. Hence they urge him to become a candidate. They dwell upon the great issues at stake. They tell him how greatly good men are needed in office, show him what a

vast work he may perform, and endeavor to show him that it is really his duty to accept the nomination. Sometimes, alas! he is persuaded to do so; he leaves his pulpit, engages in the canvass, mingles in political scenes, if not in intrigues, and is absorbed for the time being in the pending issues. These instances are comparatively rare, and the minister conscientiously believes he is doing right; yet my conviction is that the result is always disastrous, both to himself and to the church. It is disastrous to himself in that his *status* is lowered even in the estimation of his political friends. They selected him, not because they cared for him, but because he was an available candidate. They flattered him to use him, and they henceforth regarded him as a man that may be flattered and used. Had he declined the proffered nomination; had he said: 'I have but one work to do, I must preach Christ and him crucified,' he would have occupied a position of higher moral eminence. But by those outside of his own party, he is simply regarded as one who is ready to use his ministerial influence for the promotion of his personal ambition. If unsuccessful, years will pass away before he can regain the high moral influence which he once exerted. If successful, his thoughts are turned from the pulpit. The questions which he considers, the associations in which he mingles, and the applications for office and assistance constantly pressed upon him, divert his attention from that course of reading and that character of mental study which gave him efficiency and power in the pulpit. As the result, he either turns to his ministry at the close of his official period, a weaker and less efficient minister than before, or what is more likely, having embarked on the political stream, he is borne onward by the current, never to return again. Thus one whom God has called to the ministry, is to that extent, lost to the cause of Christ. But the most disastrous result is, that the public understand that those who profess to belong to God have no convictions as bind them to their work; that they are ready to exchange it for any position which they may consider more lucrative or more honorable.

"As one minister accepts such a nomination, the public infer, all should do so, if they were equally pressed; and hence that the ministry is regarded by the ministers themselves, not as a divine calling, but as an inferior position that they use as a stepping-stone to something higher. In this way the character of the ministry suffers immensely, while the individual, at the best, can be but slightly benefited.

"I have stated this case in its least objectionable form; much worse is it when a minister seeks a nomination; when he voluntarily abandons the pulpit to mingle in party strife. * * * Quite possible all these cases have their root in the lack of a clear conviction of a divine call to the ministry or of deep earnestness of spirit, for without earnestness a man accomplishes but little good. * * * All the causes to which I have alluded contribute to the inefficiency of the pulpit, and give some color of reason to those who proclaim the pulpit to be a failure."

Of course the eminent lecturer goes on to show that the pulpit is not a failure.

I wish that 'every minister in the Brethren church could read this book of lectures.—*E. L. Yoder, in the Brethren (Progressive) Evangelist.*

EXUBERANT PRIDE AND NON-CONFORMITY.

BY S. O. BARWICK.

It is an evident fact that we are living in a land where haughty pride and Dame Fashion are reigning supreme, and now stands as one of the great

vices of mankind. Pride has dwelt within the mind and heart of man for so many generations that it has long since become a chronic and hereditary affection of the whole human family in some form.

To-day we find it in the homes and in the gambling resorts, in the churches, and in institutions of all descriptions, and its presence and impressions, like the air, is present every-where.

Its physiological actions are King Terror to humanity and venoms to the soul; it is a thief, seducer, and oppressor to the poor, and also an offense to the Lord of high heaven. For thus says the Lord: "Pride and arrogancy do I hate." We also read that "God resisteth the proud" and "scattereth them in the imagination of their heart," that "only by pride cometh contention and shame," and "he that is of a proud heart stirreth up strife," and before destruction the heart of man is haughty, and thus its evil consequence is, "man's pride shall bring him down." From the following we will observe that pride is classed as being one of the elements of sinfulness, as thefts, covetousness, wickedness, deceit, lasciviousness, an evil eye, blasphemy, pride, foolishness. All these evil things come from within, and defile man. "For all that is in the world, the lust of the flesh, and the lust of the eye, and the pride of life, is not of the Father, but is of the world.

We may scan the Scriptures from Genesis to Revelation, and we will observe that pride is the work of Satan, and belongs to the evil inclinations of nature, is a relative of carnality and not of spirituality, and is an abomination unto the Lord. When candidly considering superfluous pride, we most emphatically observe that it and non-conformity are incompatible with each other, and there is no religionist who is skillful enough to combine the two as being official according to the dispensatory of the Lord and Savior Jesus Christ. It is invariably a fact that haughty pride and Dame Fashion are the expression of Satan, while non-conformity is the expression of the Lord and his Son Jesus, and a symbol of the inward motives of man, and the pretending Christian who purposely neglects to keep his Gospel vessel filled, trimmed, and brightly burning, would do well entirely to discard his external expression, as from the expressions and deeds of man we may "righteously judge" him clear to the heart.

There is a wonderful expression in plain Gospel non-conformity, as it is a representation of the Lord and Savior, an object of worship, love and obedience. It is one of the many elements of Christianity, and it should be observed by the children of God as a symbol of humility and meekness, and not as being a Pharisaical hobby.

Bangs, puffs, brussels, ping-hats, etc., are the expressions of pride; they cannot represent non-conformity, and do not belong to the conscientious Christian, and, above all, there will be no such things in heaven to confuse the angels, but with a robe and crown of righteousness will they ever reign with the Lord and Savior.

I am sorry to say that it is claimed by some that there is nothing "in it," but let us see further. Let us consider the worth and weight of expression. When we see those with silvery looks and a furred physiognomy, we observe the expression of age, and it is an evident fact that life is fast fading away. Then, when we view the Western rangers with their weapons strapped to their sides, we observe the expression of cruelty, combativeness and destructiveness, to whatever might offend them.

Again, to obtain the expression of the riotous regulator we must observe him from the top of his hat to the toe of his shoes; and most emphatically his external expression is precisely in harmony with his internal motives, which is envy,

Missionary and Tract Work Department.

"Upon the first day of the week, let every one of you lay by him in store as God hath prospered him, that there be no gatherings when I come."—1 Cor. 16: 2.

"Every man as he purposeth in his heart, so let him give. Not grudgingly or of necessity, for the Lord loveth a cheerful giver."—2 Cor. 9: 7.

HOW MUCH SHALL WE GIVE?

"Every man *according to his ability.*" "Every one *as God hath prospered him.*" "Every man, *according as he purposeth in his heart,* so let him give." "For if there be first a willing mind, it is accepted *according to that a man hath,* and not according to that he hath not."—2 Cor. 8: 12.

Organization of Missionary Committee.

DANIEL VANIMAN, Foreman, - - McPherson, Kans.
D. L. MILLER, Treasurer, - - Mt. Morris, Ill.
GALEN B. ROYER, Secretary, - - Mt. Morris, Ill.

Organization of Book and Tract Work.

S. W. HOOVER, Foreman, - - Dayton, Ohio.
S. BOCK, Secretary and Treasurer, - - Dayton, Ohio.

☞All donations intended for Missionary Work should be sent to GALEN B. ROYER, Mt. Morris, Ill.

☞All money for Tract Work should be sent to S. BOCK, Dayton, Ohio.

☞Money may be sent by Money Order, Registered Letter, or Drafts on New York or Chicago. Do not send personal checks, or drafts on interior towns, as it costs 25 cents to collect them.

☞Solicitors are requested to faithfully carry out the plan of Annual Meeting, that all our members be solicited to contribute at least twice a year for the Mission and Tract Work of the Church.

☞Notes for the Endowment Fund can be had by writing to the Secretary of either Work.

DREAMING.

BY W. REED DUNROV.

I'm dreaming a dream of home to-night
  Of my childhood's home and mother;
And midst the twilight's deepening gloom,
  I can dream, and dream no other.

Above the hum of the busy street,
  I hear a slow sweet measure,
A fragment of a bed-time song,
  My memory's precious treasure.

Thro' all the years of my weary life,
  In its sweetest joys and fiercest pain,
Above all songs be they sad or gay,
  I hear that song sung o'er again.

The voice that sung it, lies hushed and still,
  The old home now, is far away,
And I alone, of the old home group,
  Remain to mourn, o'er that long past day.

Soon I, too, when my work is done,
  Will be laid in the silent grave,
But the memory of my mother's song,
  Has had power my soul to save.

FAITHFUL MEMBERS IN THE LAITY.

BY J. B. MILLER.

IT requires boldness upon the part of the child of God to be a faithful worker. "Having therefore, brethren, boldness to enter into the holiest by the blood of Jesus, by a new and living way, which he hath consecrated for us, through the vail, that is to say, his flesh; and *having* a high priest over the house of God; let us draw near with a true heart in full assurance of faith, having our hearts sprinkled from an evil conscience, and our bodies washed with pure water. Let us hold fast the profession of *our* faith without wavering; for he is faithful that promised; and let us consider one another to provoke unto love and to good works: not forsaking the assembling of ourselves together, as the manner of *some is;* but exhorting *one another:* and so much the more, as ye see the day approaching." Heb. 10: 19-25.

1. A Gospel boldness is required to make all of God's children efficient workers.

2. In order that this Gospel boldness may grow upon us, we must draw nigh to God. If we draw nigh to God he will draw nigh to us. James 4: 8.

3. We should not forsake the assembling of our-

selves together as the manner of some is. The Lord wants us, as his children, to be busily engaged while here on the earth. The ministers have their work, the deacons have their work, and so has the laity. The church is no place for idlers. The Savior was not pleased to see men outside of the church, engaged in idleness. Matt. 20. How much more zealous should they be, after they become members of his body. The Savior's visit to this earth was only about thirty-three years in length. In that short period of time he was busy, working the works of him who had sent him. Boldness means activity, courage, bravery, etc., hence the lay-members must be active and courageous in the work. To be a good Christian requires much *bravery.*

In order that the church will prosper in her work, all must put their shoulder to the wheel. Idleness in the church, like in the world, has its bad effects. Some men boast because they do nothing, and, like the Sioux Indians, they claim they need not work. "White man works; Indian hunts and sports over the plains, and then there is our good Uncle Sam feeds us, and why should we work?"

Such persons are of no use to society, they are intruders in the busy thoroughfare of every-day life. The church has such intruders who will occasionally join its number, to lie down and sleep their way to the grave. Jonah tried the project and was startled to hear the voice, "What meanest thou, O sleeper; arise, call upon thy God."

One of the contemptible things there is in modern society, is a lazy man. It is said the Turks say, "The devil tempts everybody, but the idle man tempts the devil."

Paul would have us know that if any would not work, neither should he eat. Paul saw some who would walk among them "disorderly, working not at all, but are busybodies." A lazy youth will make a lazy man, just as sure as a crooked sapling makes a crooked tree. I have seen some members who join the church, and then forget to act as good soldiers of the cross of Christ.

2. In order that this Gospel boldness may grow upon us, we must draw nigh to God. We must draw nigh to God, and he will draw nigh to us. James 4: 8.

The Law made nothing perfect, but the bringing in of a better hope did, by the which we draw nigh unto God. Heb. 7: 19. The lay-members can truthfully say, "There is a work for us to do." Members who join the church must expect to work for the Lord. Jesus says, "Him that cometh to me I will in no wise cast out." John 6: 37. All have a work assigned them. Church work, like our every-day work in life, will only prosper when we faithfully attend to it. A man on his farm will not prosper, unless he attends to his work in proper season. The merchant, the physician, must all be busy and not neglect their occupation. If they do, failures may be the result. In the same way must the child of God be busy.

3. "Not forsaking the assembling of ourselves together as the manner of some is." Some lay-members who are full of the Holy Spirit, and who have a zeal according to knowledge, and who have promised to live faithful until death, are ever ready to dedicate their whole life to the cause of Jesus. Such faithful workers will not forsake the house of the Lord. The prophet tells us to "forsake the foolish and live." Prov. 9: 6. "If his children forsake my law, and walk not in my judgments; if they break my statutes and keep not my commands; then will I visit their transgressions with the rod, and their iniquity with stripes." Ps. 89: 30-33.

David was very careful to warn the people not to forsake the law of God. There are some things

in this world the child of God has a right to *forsake.* The sinful pleasures of this world we *must* forsake, but not forsake the house of God. "And the spirit of God came upon Azariah, the son of Oded: and he went out to meet Asa, and said unto him, Hear ye me, Asa, and all Judah and Benjamin; the Lord is with you, while ye be with him; and if ye seek him, he will be found of you, but if ye forsake him, he will forsake you." 2 Chron. 15: 1, 2. A rich lesson can be obtained from the prophet. All Israel had wandered away and "were without the true God, and without a teaching priest, and without law," but when they "turned unto the Lord God of Israel and sought him, he was found of them." I fear that many of God's spiritual Israel have wandered away, and some may have been away "for a long season."

My dear brother and sister, have you, like Israel of old, wandered away, or, like Paul said, been forsaking the house of the Lord? We must "hold fast the profession of our faith without wavering, and let us consider one another to provoke unto love and to good works." So long as we can provoke each other to love and "good works," our faith will continually grow. If we can bear the "exhorting one another," and fully follow the instructions of the Scriptures, our seat will never be vacant at church. Let us do it so much the more as we see the day approaching.

Lay-members may get the idea that there is "no special use for us to attend all the appointments." As well might the school-boy claim that there is no use for him to attend school regularly. Such students never make very good scholars.

Dear brother, did you ever have an attack of that peculiar "Sunday *headache?*" I remember of some who claimed to have such headache on Sunday, but in the week you would never hear them complain. Such will excuse themselves, and not attend church. Others get a little headache, because they have to fast a couple hours, that they call *sick headache.*

Fasting is recommended by the Savior. Mark 2: 18, 19, 20. The last clause of verse 20, which reads: "And then shalt thou fast in those days," I would consider as a command, and why not fast a few hours while at church?

A council-meeting is the most interesting meeting we can attend. Those business meetings are our school-teachers. Such meetings are to all church members what an institute is to a school-teacher. Those teachers who fail to attend the institute, will lose more than double a day's wages, I wonder how much a lay-member (as well as all church officers) will lose, by neglecting or forsaking the house of God. Some lay-members claim that they have so far to go to church, but do not consider, that, if the minister is not present, there will be some *complaining.*

Ministers, deacons and lay-members should consider well how faithful they should be in all of the church work, faithful around the family altar, in the Sunday-school, in the Bible class, the regular appointments, and the church-councils, also to attend Communion service, the District Meeting and the General Conference.

Goshen, Ind.

SHEPHERDS AND THEIR FLOCKS IN THE EAST.

BY I. J. ROSENBERGER.

THE following is related by a traveler in Syria: "On approaching a grove in which there was a well for watering, we found a large herd of sheep resting. Pretty soon one of the shepherds started off, calling, '*Menah! Menah!*' and a portion of the flock immediately separated and followed the seemingly well-known voice. A second started,

Missionary and Tract Work Department.

"Upon the first day of the week, let every one of you lay by him in store as God hath prospered him, that there be no gatherings when I come."—1 Cor. 16: 2.

"Every man as he purposeth in his heart, so let him give. Not grudgingly or of necessity, for the Lord loveth a cheerful giver."—2 Cor. 9: 7.

HOW MUCH SHALL WE GIVE?

"Every man according to his ability." "Every one as God hath prospered him." "Every man, according as he purposeth in his heart, so let him give." "For if there be first a willing mind, it is accepted according to that a man hath, and not according to that he hath not."—2 Cor. 8: 12.

Organization of Missionary Committee.

DANIEL VANIMAN, Foreman, · McPherson, Kans.
D. L. MILLER, Treasurer, · · Mt. Morris, Ill.
GALEN B. ROYER, Secretary, · Mt. Morris, Ill.

Organization of Book and Tract Work.

S. W. HOOVER, Foreman, · · Dayton, Ohio.
S. BOCK, Secretary and Treasurer, · Dayton, Ohio.

☞All donations intended for Missionary Work should be sent to GALEN B. ROYER, Mt. Morris, Ill.

☞All money for Tract Work should be sent to S. BOCK, Dayton, Ohio.

☞Money may be sent by Money Order, Registered Letter, or Drafts on New York or Chicago. Do not send personal checks, or drafts on interior towns, as it costs 25 cents to collect them.

☞Solicitors are requested to faithfully carry out the plan of Annual Meeting, that all our members be solicited to contribute at least twice a year for the Mission and Tract Work of the Church.

☞Notes for the Endowment Fund can be had by writing to the Secretary of either Work.

DREAMING.

BY W. REED DUNROY.

I'm dreaming a dream of home to-night
Of my childhood's home and mother;
And midst the twilight's deepening gloom,
I can dream, and dream no other.

Above the hum of the busy street,
I hear a slow sweet measure,
A fragment of a bed-time song,
My memory's precious treasure.

Thro' all the years of my weary life,
In its sweetest joys and fiercest pain,
Above all songs be they sad or gay,
I hear that song sung o'er again.

The Voice that sung it, lies hushed and still,
The old home now, is far away,
And I alone, of the old home group,
Remain to mourn, o'er that long past day.

Soon I, too, when my work is done,
Will be laid in the silent grave,
But the memory of my mother's song,
Has had power my soul to save.

FAITHFUL MEMBERS IN THE LAITY.

BY J. H. MILLER.

IT requires boldness upon the part of the child of God to be a faithful worker. "Having therefore, brethren, boldness to enter into the holiest by the blood of Jesus, by a new and living way, which he hath consecrated for us, through the vail, that is to say, his flesh; and, having a high priest over the house of God; let us draw near with a true heart in full assurance of faith, having our hearts sprinkled from an evil conscience, and our bodies washed with pure water. Let us hold fast the profession of our faith without wavering; for he is faithful that promised; and let us consider one another to provoke unto love and to good works; not forsaking the assembling of ourselves together, as the manner of some is; but exhorting one another; and so much the more, as ye see the day approaching." Heb. 10: 19-25.

1. A Gospel boldness is required to make all of God's children efficient workers.

2. In order that this Gospel boldness may grow upon us, we must draw nigh to God. If we draw nigh to God he will draw nigh to us. James 4: 8.

3. We should not forsake the assembling of our-selves together as the manner of some is. The Lord wants us, as his children, to be busily engaged while here on the earth. The ministers have their work, the deacons have their work, and so has the laity. The church is no place for idlers. The Savior was not pleased to see men outside of the church, engaged in idleness. Matt. 20. How much more zealous should they be, after they become members of his body. The Savior's visit to this earth was only about thirty-three years in length. In that short period of time he was busy, working the works of him who had sent him. Boldness means activity, courage, bravery, etc., hence the lay-members must be active and courageous in the work. To be a good Christian requires much bravery.

In order that the church will prosper in her work, all must put their shoulder to the wheel. Idleness in the church, like in the world, has its bad effects. Some men boast because they do nothing, and, like the Sioux Indians, they claim they need not work. "White man works; Indian hunts and sports over the plains, and then there is our good Uncle Sam feeds us, and why should we work?"

Such persons are of no use to society, they are likewise in the busy thoroughfare of every-day life. The church has such intruders who will occasionally join its number, to lie down and sleep their way to the grave. Jonah tried the project and was startled to hear the voice, "What meanest thou, O sleeper; arise, call upon thy God."

One of the contemptible things there is in modern society, is a lazy man. It is said the Turks say, "The devil tempts everybody, but the idle man tempts the devil."

Paul would have us know that if any would not work, neither should he eat. Paul saw some who would walk among them "disorderly, working not at all, but are busybodies." A lazy youth will make a lazy man, just as sure as a crooked sapling makes a crooked tree. I have seen some members who join the church, and then forget to act as good soldiers of the cross of Christ.

2. In order that this Gospel boldness may grow upon us, we must draw nigh to God. We must draw nigh to God, and he will draw nigh to us. James 4: 8.

The Law made nothing perfect, but the bringing in of a better hope did, by the which we draw nigh unto God. Heb. 7: 19. The lay-members can truthfully say, "There is a work for us to do." Members who join the church must expect to work for the Lord. Jesus says, "Him that cometh to me I will in no wise cast out." John 6: 37. All have a work assigned them. Church work, like our every-day work in life, will only prosper when we faithfully attend to it. A man on his farm will not prosper, unless he attends to his work in proper season. The merchant, the physician, must all be busy and not neglect their occupation. If they do, failures may be the result. In the same way must the child of God be busy.

3. "Not forsaking the assembling of ourselves together as the manner of some is." Some lay-members who are full of the Holy Spirit, and who have a zeal according to knowledge, and who have promised to live faithful until death, are ever ready to dedicate their whole life to the cause of Jesus. Such faithful workers will not forsake the house of the Lord. The prophet tells us to "forsake the foolish and live." Prov. 9: 6. "If his children forsake my law, and walk not in my judgments; if they break my statutes and keep not my commands, then will I visit their transgressions with the rod, and their iniquity with stripes." Ps. 89: 30-33.

David was very careful to warn the people not to forsake the law of God. There are some things in this world the child of God has a right to forsake. The sinful pleasures of this world we must forsake, but not forsake the house of God. "And the spirit of God came upon Azariah, the son of Oded; and he went out to meet Asa, and said unto him, Hear ye me, Asa, and all Judah and Benjamin; the Lord is with you, while ye be with him; and if ye seek him, he will be found of you, but if ye forsake him, he will forsake you." 2 Chron. 15: 1, 2. A rich lesson can be obtained from the prophet. All Israel had wandered away and "were without the true God, and without a teaching priest, and without law," but when they "turned unto the Lord God of Israel and sought him, he was found of them." I fear that many of God's spiritual Israel have wandered away, and some may have been away "for a long season."

My dear brother and sister, have you, like Israel of old, wandered away, or, like Paul said, been forsaking the house of the Lord? We must "hold fast the profession of our faith without wavering, and let us consider one another to provoke unto love and to good works." So long as we can provoke each other to love and "good works," our faith will continually grow. If we can bear the "exhorting one another," and fully follow the instructions of the Scriptures, our seat will never be vacant at church. Let us do it so much the more as we see the day approaching.

Lay-members may get the idea that there is "no special use for us to attend all the appointments." As well might the school-boy claim that there is no use for him to attend school regularly. Such students never make very good scholars.

Dear brother, did you ever have an attack of that peculiar "Sunday headache?" I remember of some who claimed to have such headache on Sunday, but in the week you would never hear them complain. Such will excuse themselves, and not attend church. Others get a little headache, because they have to fast a couple hours, that they call sick headache.

Fasting is recommended by the Savior. Mark 2: 18, 19, 20. The last clause of verse 20, which reads: "And then shalt thou fast in those days," I would consider as a command, and why not fast a few hours while at church?

A council-meeting is the most interesting meeting we can attend. Those business meetings are our school-teachers. Such meetings are to all church members what an institute is to a school-teacher. Those teachers who fail to attend the institute, will lose much knowledge,—in value more than double a day's wages. I wonder how much a lay-member (as well as all church officers) will lose, by neglecting or forsaking the house of God. Some lay-members claim that they have so far to go to church, but do not consider, that, if the minister is not present, there will be some complaining.

Ministers, deacons and lay-members should consider well how faithful they should be in all of the church work, faithful around the family altar, in the Sunday-school, in the Bible class, the regular appointments, and the church-councils, also to attend Communion service, the District Meeting and the General Conference.

Goshen, Ind.

SHEPHERDS AND THEIR FLOCKS IN THE EAST.

BY I. J. ROSENBERGER.

THE following is related by a traveler in Syria: "On approaching a grove in which there was a well for watering, we found a large herd of sheep resting. Pretty soon one of the shepherds started off, calling, 'Menah! Menah!' and a portion of the flock immediately separated and followed the seemingly well-known voice. A second started,

The Gospel Messenger,

A Weekly at $1.50 Per Annum.

PUBLISHED BY

The Brethren's Publishing Co.

D. L. MILLER,	· · · · · ·	Editor.
J. H. MOORE,	· · · · · ·	Office Editor.
J. B. BRUMBAUGH,		
J. G. ROYER,		Associate Editors.
JOSEPH AMICK,	· · · · ·	Business Manager.

ADVISORY COMMITTEE.

L. W. Teeter, A. Hutchison, Daniel Hays.

☞Communications for publication should be legibly written with black ink on one side of the paper only. Do not attempt to interline, or to put on one page what ought to occupy two.

☞Anonymous communications will not be published.

☞Do not mix business with articles for publication. Keep your communications on separate sheets from all business.

☞Time is precious. We always have time to attend to business and to answer questions of importance, but please do not subject us to need less unraveling of letters.

☞The MESSENGER is mailed each week to all subscribers. If the address is correctly entered on our list, the paper must reach the person to whom it is addressed. If you do not get your paper, write us, giving particulars.

☞When changing your address, please give your former as well as your future address in full, so as to avoid delay and misunderstanding.

☞Always remit to the office from which you order your goods, no matter from where you receive them.

☞Do not send personal checks or drafts on interior banks, unless you send with them 25 cents each, to pay for collection.

☞Remittances should be made by Post-office Money Order, Drafts on New York, Philadelphia or Chicago, or Registered Letters, made payable and addressed to "Brethren's Publishing Co., Mount Morris, Ill.," or "Brethren's Publishing Co., Huntingdon, Pa."

☞Entered at the Post-office at Mount Morris, Ill., as second-class matter.

Mount Morris, Ill., · · · · August 30, 1892.

BRO. M. L. HAHN, of Bloomer, Ohio, should now be addressed at Lakeside, Ind.

THE Brethren of the Brookside church, W. Va., recently dedicated their new meeting-house and now have another in contemplation.

A LEARNED preacher, Edward Everett Hale, once said, "If people would only stop talking where they stop knowing, half the evils of life would come to an end."

BRO. J. S. FLORY'S name was unintentionally omitted from his article in last issue, entitled, "Echoes from the Highway." The mistake was not noticed until the entire issue was printed and mailed.

IT is said that out of a population of 4,774,409 in Sweden, only 810 are Roman Catholics. The intelligence of the Swedes is proverbial. It is a good place for intelligent and successful missionary work.

AT a Baptist Young People's Convention, in Troy, N. Y., a resolution was adopted, indorsing the plan to send out one hundred new missionaries and raise $1,000,000, and pledging the support of the young people in raising the fund. This shows a zeal for missionary work that should prompt us to do still more than we are now accomplishing.

LET it be borne in mind that the last Annual Meeting recommended the use of unfermented wine for Communion purposes, and it therefore becomes the duty of congregations to provide such wine for that purpose. In a former issue we gave instructions how to make and preserve the fresh juice of the grape, and it will be well for each congregation to appoint some one to look after the matter and see that unfermented wine is always kept on hand for Communion occasions. Churches that have used this class of wine speak very highly of it, and we all know that it is free from the evil tendencies, pertaining to the use of that which is intoxicating in its nature.

ONE of the great wants of the present age is converted preachers. Do not think strange of this. Jesus once said to a noted preacher, of three years' standing, "When thou art converted, strengthen thy brethren."

AFTER announcing their feast at Beaver Creek, Rockingham County, Va., Bro. G. W. Wine reports two applicants for baptism. Bro. S. A. Walker also writes that two recently united with the Wyandot church, Ohio. ·

BRO. W. L. ROSS writes that Bro. David Richards recently closed a series of meetings at New Hope, Jackson County, Indiana, with thirteen additions. Nine were baptized, three reclaimed, and one is yet to be baptized.

IT is stated that not even one member of the Jewish Conference uses tobacco in any form. That is good. We wish we could say that much of our Conference. But it is coming to that point just as fast as can well be expected.

THE paper known as the Ram's Horn, has very ingeniously as well as truthfully said, " The less religion there is in a church, the more oysters and ice cream it takes to run it." One does not need very much argument to be convinced of the truthfulness of this statement.

IT is to be regretted that some who write for the MESSENGER are so careless about quoting Scripture. They depend too much on memory. Every quotation ought to be verified by the Book. Sometimes articles must be declined just because the quotations are so incorrect that it requires more time to look up the quotations and correct them, than we can spare. By all means let us honor the Scriptures by quoting them correctly.

LAST Sunday was a busy day for the Mt. Morris ministers. Bro. J. G. Royer preached at Waddam's Grove, J. C. Lahman at Lanark, E. S. Young at Chicago, Simon Yundt at Salem, David Hollinger at Pleasant Grove, and Thomas Watkins at the Chapel in the morning. The evening appointment at the Chapel was filled by the Senior Editor, while your Office Editor was with the Brethren at Mt. Carroll.

. THE Asiatic cholera is moving westward, and now threatens Europe. The excessive heat there will greatly aid its spreading, and when it once gets under headway, no sanitary precaution will check it until it has run its course. Like all other pestilences, it thrives best in filth, especially when aided by hot weather. Great care will be taken to keep it from reaching this country. Cold weather, however, is death to it.

IT is not our aim at any time to call from other journals that which is evil, or misleading in its tendency, but with pleasure we do occasionally make extracts containing points worthy of note. In this issue will be found a very timely article of this class from the Brethren's (Progressive) Evangelist, headed, "The Preacher in Politics." At this time, when political excitement is beginning to run high, and people are thinking more about how they are going to vote; than they do about how they are going to live, it is well for all ministers to consider their high calling, and 'not suffer themselves to be enticed from the sacred desk by a little political glory, or a few almighty dollars.· The article, coming from the source it does, will likely do good, and it will at least encourage those who have long stood opposed to our people taking an active part in any of the political movements.

BRO. D. M. MILLER, of Milledgeville, Ill., is now in the mission field in Wisconsin, expecting to remain about six weeks, and, during that time, may attend three love-feasts in that part of the State. His field of labor is at Red Cedar, Chippewa Valley and Irvin Creek.

Too late for insertion elsewhere in this issue, we receive notice that the Brethren of the Kewanna congregation, Fulton County, Indiana, will dedicate their new house of worship Sept. 18, services to commence at 10:30 A. M. Bro. Daniel Shively is expected to deliver the dedicatory sermon.

A NUMBER of the State Districts will hold their District Meetings this fall. We hope to receive an early report from each of them. Permit us to suggest a careful sifting of all the matter intended for the Annual Meeting so as to give the General Conference as little work as possible in this line. We have decisions covering nearly every part of church government, and by the aid of these, and our experience of the past, we can probably unite in carrying out the apostolic order quite successfully. Our Annual Meeting decisions are not law in any sense, but simply the views of the General Brotherhood, and are well calculated to lead us to a better understanding of the Gospel. Hence we should have as few of these decisions as possible, and depend as largely upon the Scriptures as circumstances will permit. We thus avoid the enlarging of the Minutes and greatly lessen the work of the Conference.

WE wish that all the correspondents, appointed by the churches, would place after their names "Church Correspondent," when sending in their church news.· Occasionally we receive reports.of the same meeting from two or more writers, but prefer to give the "Church Correspondent" the preference. By observing this rule suggested, we will always be enabled to do this. We further suggest that these correspondents send in all news just as soon as possible. Churches that have not appointed correspondents ought to do so at once. In churches, where there are no correspondents, we hope some one will take the liberty of reporting, and attending to it promptly. We prefer short reports, and plenty of them. For this purpose the large postal cards may be used to good advantage. In using these cards, write plainly, and do not put more than about 100 words on one card. More words than that makes the writing too hard on the eyes of the compositors.

THE "reformatory movement," commenced by Alexander Campbell more than fifty years ago, has had an amazing growth. Commencing with a few organizations, and perhaps less than one hundred communicants, it has now reached nearly one million members, and among them are to be found some of the brightest minds in America. Heretofore they have stood well united, generally agreeing on the principles by which to be governed. But there now seem to be strong indications of a division among them, largely on account of the use of instrumental music in worship, and their missionary societies. By reading their papers one can hardly determine the possible result. A division, however, of this kind is to be greatly regretted. To say the least of it, such misfortunes put Christ to open shame. By all means let divisions be discouraged, especially over questions of that character. Possibly there may be other causes for the existing divisions in sentiment. If so, we have not observed them. We are watching the movements with considerable interest.

The Gospel Messenger,

A Weekly at $1.50 Per Annum.

PUBLISHED BY

The Brethren's Publishing Co.

D. L. MILLER,	Editor.
J. H. MOORE,	Office Editor.
J. B. BRUMBAUGH, } J. G. ROYER, }	Associate Editors.
JOSEPH AMICK,	Business Manager.

ADVISORY COMMITTEE.

L. W. Teeter, A. Hutchison, Daniel Hays.

Communications for publication should be legibly written with black ink on one side of the paper only. Do not attempt to interline, or to put on one page what ought to occupy two.

Anonymous communications will not be published.

Do not mix business with articles for publication. Keep your communications on separate sheets from all business.

Time is precious. We always have time to attend to business and to answer questions of importance, but please do not subject us to need less answering of letters.

The MESSENGER is mailed each week to all subscribers. If the address be correctly entered on our list, the paper must reach the person to whom it is addressed. If you do not get your paper, write us, giving particulars.

When changing your address, please give your former as well as your future address in full, so as to avoid delay and misunderstanding.

Always remit to the office from which you order your goods, no matter from where you receive them.

Do not send personal checks or drafts on interior banks, unless you send with them 25 cents each, to pay for collection.

Remittances should be made by Post-office Money Order, Drafts on New York, Philadelphia or Chicago, or Registered Letters, made payable and addressed to "Brethren's Publishing Co., Mount Morris, Ill.," or "Brethren's Publishing Co., Huntingdon, Pa."

Entered at the Post-office at Mount Morris, Ill., as second-class matter.

Mount Morris, Ill.,   -   -   -   August 30, 1892.

BRO. M. L. HAHN, of Bloomer, Ohio, should now be addressed at Lakeside, Ind.

THE Brethren of the Brookside church, W. Va., recently dedicated their new meeting-house and now have another in contemplation.

A LEARNED preacher, Edward Everett Hale, once said, "If people would only stop talking where they stop knowing, half the evils of life would come to an end."

BRO. J. S. FLORY'S name was unintentionally omitted from his article in last issue, entitled, "Echoes from the Highway." The mistake was not noticed until the entire issue was printed and mailed.

IT is said that out of a population of 4,774,409 in Sweden, only 810 are Roman Catholics. The intelligence of the Swedes is proverbial. It is a good place for intelligent and successful missionary work.

AT a Baptist Young People's Convention, in Troy, N. Y., a resolution was adopted, indorsing the plan to send out one hundred new missionaries and raise $1,000,000, and pledging the support of the young people in raising the fund. This shows a zeal for missionary work that should prompt us to do still more than we are now accomplishing.

LET it be borne in mind that the last Annual Meeting recommended the use of unfermented wine for Communion purposes, and it therefore becomes the duty of congregations to provide such wine for that purpose. In a former issue we gave instructions how to make and preserve the fresh juice of the grape, and it will be well for each congregation to appoint some one to look after the matter and see that unfermented wine is always kept on hand for Communion occasions. Churches that have used this class of wine speak very highly of it, and we all know that it is free from the evil tendencies, pertaining to the use of that which is intoxicating in its nature.

ONE of the great wants of the present age is converted preachers. Do not think strange of this. Jesus once said to a noted preacher, of three years' standing, "When thou art converted, strengthen thy brethren."

AFTER announcing their feast at Beaver Creek, Rockingham County, Va., Bro. G. W. Wine reports two applicants for baptism. Bro. S. A. Walker also writes that two recently united with the Wyandot church, Ohio.

BRO. W. L. Ross writes that Bro. David Richards recently closed a series of meetings at New Hope, Jackson County, Indiana, with thirteen additions. Nine were baptized, three reclaimed, and one is yet to be baptized.

IT is stated that not even one member of the Jewish Conference uses tobacco in any form. That is good. We wish we could say that much of our Conference. But it is coming to that point just as fast as can well be expected.

THE paper known as the *Ram's Horn*, has very ingeniously as well as truthfully said, "The less religion there is in a church, the more oysters and ice cream it takes to run it." One does not need very much argument to be convinced of the truthfulness of this statement.

IT is to be regretted that some who write for the MESSENGER are so careless about quoting Scripture. They depend too much on memory. Every quotation ought to be verified by the Book. Sometimes articles must be declined just because the quotations are so incorrect that it requires more time to look up the quotations and correct them, than we can spare. By all means let us honor the Scriptures by quoting them correctly.

LAST Sunday was a busy day for the Mt. Morris ministers. Bro. J. G. Royer preached at Waddam's Grove, J. C. Lahman at Lanark, E. S. Young at Chicago, Simon Yundt at Salem, David Hollinger at Pleasant Grove, and Thomas Watkins at the Chapel in the morning. The evening appointment at the Chapel was filled by the Senior Editor, while your Office Editor was with the Brethren at Mt. Carroll.

THE Asiatic cholera is moving westward, and now threatens Europe. The excessive heat there will greatly aid its spreading, and when it once gets under headway, no sanitary precaution will check it until it has run its course. Like all other pestilences, it thrives best in filth, especially when aided by hot weather. Great care will be taken to keep it from reaching this country. Cold weather, however, is death to it.

IT is not our aim at any time to cull from other journals that which is evil, or misleading in its tendency, but with pleasure we do occasionally make extracts containing points worthy of note. In this issue will be found a very timely article of this class from the *Brethren's* (Progressive) *Evangelist*, headed, "The Preacher in Politics." At this time, when political excitement is beginning to run high, and people are thinking more about how they are going to vote, than they do about how they are going to live, it is well for all ministers to consider their high calling, and not suffer themselves to be enticed from the sacred desk by a little political glory, or a few almighty dollars. The article, coming from the source it does, will likely do good, and will at least encourage those who have long stood opposed to our people taking an active part in any of the political movements.

BRO. D. M. MILLER, of Milledgeville, Ill., is now in the mission field in Wisconsin, expecting to remain about six weeks, and, during that time, may attend three love-feasts in that part of the State. His field of labor is at Red Cedar, Chippewa Valley and Irvin Creek.

Too late for insertion elsewhere in this issue, we receive notice that the Brethren of the Kewanna congregation, Fulton County, Indiana, will dedicate their new house of worship Sept. 18, services to commence at 10:30 A. M. Bro. Daniel Shively is expected to deliver the dedicatory sermon.

A NUMBER of the State Districts will hold their District Meetings this fall. We hope to receive an early report from each of them. Permit us to suggest a careful sifting of all the matter intended for the Annual Meeting so as to give the General Conference as little work as possible in this line. We have decisions covering nearly every part of church government, and by the aid of these, and our experience of the past, we can probably unite in carrying out the apostolic order quite successfully. Our Annual Meeting decisions are not law in any sense, but simply the views of the General Brotherhood, and are well calculated to lead us to a better understanding of the Gospel. Hence we should have as few of these decisions as possible, and depend as largely upon the Scriptures as circumstances will permit. We thus avoid the enlarging of the Minutes and greatly lessen the work of the Conference.

WE wish that all the correspondents, appointed by *the churches*, would place after their names "Church Correspondent," when sending in their church news. Occasionally we receive reports of the same meeting from two or more writers, but prefer to give the "Church Correspondent" the preference. By observing the rule suggested, we will always be enabled to do this. We further suggest that these correspondents send in all news just as soon as possible. Churches that have not appointed correspondents ought to do so at once. In churches, where there are no correspondents, we hope some one will take the liberty of reporting, and attending to it promptly. We prefer short reports, and plenty of them. For this purpose the large postal cards may be used to good advantage. In using these cards, write plainly, and do not put more than about 100 words on one card. More words than that makes the writing too hard on the eyes of the compositors.

THE "reformatory movement," commenced by Alexander Campbell more than fifty years ago, has had an amazing growth. Commencing with a few organizations, and perhaps less than one hundred communicants, it has now reached nearly one million members, and among them are to be found some of the brightest minds in America. Heretofore they have stood well united, generally agreeing on the principles by which to be governed. But there now seem to be strong indications of a division among them, largely on account of the use of instrumental music in worship, and their missionary societies. By reading their papers one can hardly determine the possible result. A division, however, of this kind is to be greatly regretted. To say the least of it, such misfortunes put Christ to open shame. By all means let divisions be discouraged, especially over questions of that character. Possibly there may be other causes for the existing divisions in sentiment. If so, we have not observed them. We are watching the movements with considerable interest.

CORRESPONDENCE.

"Write what thou seest, and send it unto the churches."

Church News solicited for this Department. If you have had a good meeting, send a report of it, so that others may rejoice with you. In writing give name of church, County and State. Be brief. Notes of Travel should be as short as possible. Land Advertisements are not solicited for this Department. We have an advertising page, and, if necessary, will issue supplements.

In a Catholic Church.

NOT many Sundays ago we started out for church, and by chance came to a, Catholic house of worship. It was the first experience of the kind for us. Many things must strike one when he attends Catholic services for the first time. One respect in which they differ very materially from most Protestant, and for the better too, is in the reverence shown God's house and service. We can learn something from every one; and here is a lesson we should all take to heart, for there is a sad lack of this in most churches. Of course we cannot always tell from the outside what there is on the inside; but of one thing we may be absolutely certain, if there is not reverence on the outside, there is none on the inside.

The Catholic goes into the house, kneels with his face toward the altar and makes the cross three times, once on the forehead, once on the lips and once on the heart; then he rises and takes a seat. But not all of them kneel on the floor when they enter. Some of them give the knees a little bend, make the crosses and then sit down. It is interesting and instructive to watch them, even if we do not believe in what they do. One thing very noticeable, here as elsewhere, is that the more a person has of this world's goods on him or about him the less his knees will bend. There are a few exceptions to this, but they only prove the rule. See some poor one coming in! kneeling is not enough; the body is almost prostrated, the crosses are made slowly and prayerfully. Some have little benches for kneeling, and some have cushions on them to protect the knees. There is a great deal of cushion-seeking nowadays, and it is not all done in the world, and by worldly people either; it comes right into God's house and takes a front seat. When we begin to think so much about what we are kneeling on the chances are that we are forgetting what we are kneeling for.

The priest comes down the aisle and sprinkles the so-called "holy" water on one side, and on the other as he goes back. How anxious they all are to have a drop of it fall on them, and how reverently they make the cross as he goes along. One drop struck me on the forehead, but of course it had no virtue for an unbeliever; if some faithful one could but have had it—the effect would have been the same on him, though he might have imagined differently.

The sermon was about the rich and the poor, what they have here and what they will have on the other side. Most of the members are poor, very poor. It is well if they can have a hope of something better in the hereafter; if they had not, life for them would not be worth living. To lead a from-hand-to-mouth existence all one's life is not just the thing any of us want to do; we prefer to have more. What 'rapture must the poor starved person of this world experience when he thinks of what may be his hereafter. He is capable of appreciating it, though his richer brother (?) sneers at him and his poverty. And what a consolation there is for him in the thought that heaven is intended for him, that it does not take money to make the pearly gates swing open, that the question put to each one by God is, What are you?-and not, What have you? Too often this is forgotten by us. When we get so low down that we sneer at a man because he is poor, and the name of those who do so is legion, we are far too low to ever catch even a glimpse of what there is in the mansions over there, unless it be as the rich man spoken of in the Bible caught a glimpse of it. All these thoughts come naturally to one when he is seated among the rich and the poor and watches their different ways of worshiping. One cannot always have the opportunity of sitting with both classes at once. Some people are so good that they do not want to sit in the same room, even for worship, with those who are not good, financially, as they are. Spirituality does not count, not even when they come before that Being who is no respecter of persons. If we are unwilling to worship with a poor man, or a red man, or a yellow man, or a black man in this world, how can we expect to get to heaven? Surely no one is foolish enough to believe that only rich white people will get there. Of course we have no split in our church on account of money as yet, but we need to be careful; sin begins to come in a long time before there is a division.

But to go back to the service. Across the aisle sit some old ladies. They count their beads and go over their prayers almost constantly. While each bead is held between the thumb and forefinger a prayer is said to some saint. How earnest they are, and yet how utterly useless, worse than useless it all is! How can they be content with praying to some man or woman who has long since returned to dust, who perhaps was a very poor saint while here on earth, when they should pray to the living God? What can the bones or dust of any man do? What is there that God cannot do? Why worship what was once the creature, but is now nothing, more than him who is the everliving Creator? We do not know, we cannot tell; but so it goes on year after year and century after century. Perhaps it will be so till the end of the world. But some one is to blame for it, some one will have to answer for it. The blame cannot all be put on the poor souls who know no better, who know no better simply because they have been taught no better. What ignorance and what superstition do we find in the Catholic church! But they are zealous. If we who are called Protestant had more zeal it is quite probable that they would have less superstition. Are we blameless, or shall we be held to answer for some of this? —GRANT MAHAN.

A Trip to the West with Some Observations.

I ARRIVED safely at home, from my late trip to Iowa, July 13. Many of our eastern folks were delayed on their way home, after the Annual Meeting, on account of high water west of Chicago, but I came through on schedule time.

I was one of a party of about forty (principally brethren and sisters), who took passage on the B. & O. R. R , at Somerset, Meyersdale and other points in Somerset County, Pa., May 30, for the Annual Meeting, and to visit relatives and friends. From Chicago we took the Illinois Central road. At Freeport a number of us stopped off to visit a few days at Lanark and Dixon. Most of our party proceeded to points in Iowa. We also made a short stop with Eld. D. M. Miller, of the Milledgeville congregation, whom we met again at South Waterloo. He is, apparently full of zeal for the cause of the church.

June 4, at 4:45 P. M., we took the train at Freeport for Cedar Rapids, where we arrived shortly before midnight. This proved an undesirable time for strangers to reach the place, especially as it was Saturday night. Although I had applied, and had been assigned a lodging-place for myself and several others, when we arrived there, the door refused to open for us. We were then taken to the First Congregational church, where we found rest. There were many comfortable cots provided, and most of them were occupied. In the apartment to which I was assigned, a young man, who professed to be a brother, kept up a disturbance that prevented many from sleeping until a policeman appeared and quieted him. Of course his conduct, as well as his appearance was against his profession. If he has formally joined the body of Christ, he openly offered reproach to the church, and to its Head.

I want to be understood that no blame rests on the Lodging Committee for the unpleasant experience our party had on that Saturday night, for I found Bro. Tisdale and the rest of the committee very anxious that everybody should have a comfortable place to lodge. It is expected that the committee who are to provide for the comforts and wants of those who come in contact with them at Annual Meeting, understand their duties, and show courtesy and patience toward all. However, they cannot be expected to give attention to more than one party, or one matter, at a time, nor can they meet every emergency that may arise, beyond reasonable forethought. It is, therefore, proper that we, who depend upon their services, likewise be courteous and show patience. On such occasions it is well to remember also that we cannot reasonably expect to receive the attention and consideration that we may receive at home. On this account we should beware of falling back upon our diguity, and of saying unpleasant things, when we are seemingly slighted. These rules of action hold good in our conduct toward table-waiters, as well as towards the various committees. But there are places nearer home where we may practice these rules frequently, and such practice will enable us to carry them out with a better grace at Annual Meetings, or similar occasions. I have not written to convey the idea that, in my judgment, these essentials have been lacking to any great extent, but rather that they may commend themselves more universally, and may be carried out more perfectly hereafter.

After attending Annual Meeting, visiting among friends in Iowa and elsewhere was in order. Nearly all of our traveling party extended their journey to Waterloo and its vicinity, and enjoyed the hospitality and Christian fellowship of the brethren and friends there. Somerset County is largely represented among the present residents of Black Hawk County, Iowa, and a large majority of the members of the South Waterloo congregation are natives of Somerset County, or the descendants of them. These include the Milles, Lichtys, Fikes, Buechleys, Mausts, Berkleys, Bloughs and many others. They have found this a goodly land, and have nearly all prospered in temporal things, and, apparently, in spiritual things also. They have had their trials, but, I trust, they have been purified. Of late they have not been forgetful of the Lord's work, and have shown their liberality toward the different departments of church work. Their method of raising the yearly contributions toward missionary, tract, and other more local work in the church, is different from that recommended by Annual Meeting some years ago, and with them the result is a larger contribution than the Annual Meeting plan asks of them.

Our traveling party had the pleasure, also, of attending the love-feast at the South Waterloo church, June 18. All things,—not excluding even the weather,—seemed to work together to make it a very pleasant feast indeed. Good order is always commendable in religious exercises, but more particularly when the sufferings and death of our Savior are to be commemorated.

CORRESPONDENCE.

"Write what thou seest, and send it unto the churches."

☞Church News solicited for this Department. If you have had a good meeting, send a report of it, so that others may rejoice with you. In writing give name of church, County and State. Be brief. Notes of Travel should be as short as possible. Land Advertisements are not solicited for this Department. We have an advertising page, and, if necessary, will issue supplements.

In a Catholic Church.

NOT many Sundays ago we started out for church, and by chance came to a Catholic house of worship. It was the first experience of the kind for us. Many things must strike one when he attends Catholic services for the first time. One respect in which they differ very materially from most Protestant, and for the better too, is in the reverence shown God's house and service. We can learn something from every one; and here is a lesson we should all take to heart, for there is a sad lack of this in most churches. Of course we cannot always tell from the outside what there is on the inside; but of one thing we may be absolutely certain, if there is not reverence on the outside, there is none on the inside.

The Catholic goes into the house, kneels with his face toward the altar and makes the cross three times, once on the forehead, once on the lips and once on the heart; then he rises and takes a seat. But not all of them kneel on the floor when they enter. Some of them give the knees a little bend, make the crosses and then sit down. It is interesting and instructive to watch them, even if we do not believe in what they do. One thing very noticeable, here as elsewhere, is that the more a person has of this world's goods on him or about him the less his knees will bend. There are a few exceptions to this, but they only prove the rule. See some poor one coming in! kneeling is not enough; the body is almost prostrated, the crosses are made slowly and prayerfully. Some have little benches for kneeling, and some have cushions on them to protect the knees. There is a great deal of cushion-seeking nowadays, and it is not all done in the world, and by worldly people either; it comes right into God's house and takes a front seat. When we begin to think so much about what we are kneeling on the chances are that we are forgetting what we are kneeling for.

The priest comes down the aisle and sprinkles the so-called "holy" water on one side, and on the other as he goes back. How anxious they all are to have a drop of it fall on them, and how reverently they make the cross as he goes along. One drop struck me on the forehead, but of course it had no virtue for an unbeliever; if some faithful one could but have had it—the effect would have been the same on him, though he might have imagined differently.

The sermon was about the rich and the poor, what they have here and what they will have on the other side. Most of the members are poor, very poor. It is well if they can have a hope of something better in the hereafter; if they had not, life for them would not be worth living. To lead a from-hand-to-mouth existence all one's life is not just the thing any of us want to do; we prefer to have more. What 'rapture must the poor starved person of this world experience when he thinks of what may be his hereafter. He is capable of appreciating it, though his rich or brother (?) sneers at him and his poverty. And there's a consolation there is for him in the thought that heaven is intended for him, that it does not take money to make the pearly gates swing open, that the question put to each one by God is, What are you?·and not, What have you? Too often this is forgotten by us. When we get so low down that we sneer at a man because he is poor, and the name of those who do so is legion, we are far too low to ever catch even a glimpse of what there is in the mansions over there, unless it be as the rich man spoken of in the Bible caught a glimpse of it. All these thoughts come naturally to one when he is seated among the rich and the poor and watches their different ways of worshiping. One cannot always have the opportunity of sitting with both classes at once. Some people are so good that they do not want to sit in the same room, even for worship, with those who are not good, financially, as they are. Spirituality does not count, not even when they come before that Being who is no respecter of persons. If we are unwilling to worship with a poor man, or a red man, or a yellow man, or a black man in this world, how can we expect to get to heaven? Surely no one is foolish enough to believe that only rich white people will get there. Of course we have no split in our church on account of money as yet, but we need to be careful: sin begins to come in a long time before there is a division.

But to go back to the service. Across the aisle sit some old ladies. They count their beads and go over their prayers almost constantly. While each bead is held between the thumb and forefinger a prayer is said to some saint. How earnest they are, and yet how utterly useless, worse than useless it all is! How can they be content with praying to some man or woman who has long since returned to dust, who perhaps was a very poor saint while here on earth, when they should pray to the living God? What can the bones or dust of any man do? What is there that God cannot do? Why worship what was once the creature, but is now nothing, more than him who is the everliving Creator? We do not know, we cannot tell; but so it goes on year after year and century after century. Perhaps it will be so till the end of the world. But some one is to blame for it, some one will have to answer for it. The blame cannot all be put on the poor souls who know no better, who know no better simply because they have been taught no better. ,What ignorance and what superstition do we find in the Catholic church! But they are zealous. If we who are called Protestants had more zeal it is quite probable that they would have less superstition. Are we blameless, or shall we be held to answer for some of this? GRANT MAHAN.

A Trip to the West with Some Observations.

I ARRIVED safely at home, from my late trip to Iowa, July 13. Many of our eastern folks were delayed on their way home, after the Annual Meeting, on account of high water west of Chicago, but I came through on schedule time.

I was one of a party of about forty (principally brethren and sisters), who took passage on the B. & O. R. R., at Somerset, Meyersdale and other points in Somerset County, Pa., May 30, for the Annual Meeting, and to visit relatives and friends. From Chicago we took the Illinois Central road. At Freeport a number of us stopped off to visit a few days at Lanark and Dixon. Most of our party proceeded to points in Iowa. We also made a short stop with Eld. D. M. Miller, of the Milledgeville congregation, whom we met again at South Waterloo. He is, apparently, full of zeal for the cause of the church.

June 4, at 4:45 P. M., we took the train at Freeport for Cedar Rapids, where we·arrived shortly before midnight. This proved an undesirable time for strangers to reach the place, especially as it was Saturday night. Although I had applied, and had been assigned a lodging-place for myself and several others, when we arrived there, the door refused to open for us. We were then taken to the First Congregational church, where we found rest. There were many comfortable cots provided, and most of them were occupied. In the apartment to which I was assigned, a young man, who professed to be a brother, kept up a disturbance that prevented many from sleeping until a policeman appeared and quieted him. Of course his conduct, as well as his appearance was against his profession. If he has formally joined the body of Christ, he openly offered reproach to the church, and to its Head.

I want to be understood that no blame rests on the Lodging Committee for the unpleasant experience our party had on that Saturday night, for I found Bro. Tisdale and the rest of them were too very anxious that everybody should have a comfortable place to lodge. It is expected that the committee who. are to provide for the comforts and wants of those who come in contact with them at Annual Meeting, understand their duties, and show courtesy and patience toward all. However, they cannot be expected to give attention to more than one party, or one matter, at a time, nor can they meet every emergency that may arise, beyond reasonable forethought. It is, therefore, proper that we, who depend upon their services, likewise be courteous and show patience. On such occasions it is well to remember also that we cannot reasonably expect to receive the attention and consideration that we may receive at home. On this account we should beware of falling back upon our dignity, and of saying unpleasant things, when we are seemingly slighted. These rules of action hold good in our conduct toward table-waiters, as well as towards the various committees. But there are places nearer home where we may practice these rules frequently, and such practice will enable us to carry them out with a better grace at Annual Meetings, or similar occasions. I have not written to convey the idea that, in my judgment, these essentials have been lacking to any great extent, but rather that they may commend themselves more universally, and may be carried out more perfectly hereafter.

After attending Annual Meeting, visiting among friends in Iowa and elsewhere was in order. Nearly all of our traveling party extended their journey to Waterloo and its vicinity, and enjoyed the hospitality and Christian fellowship of the brethren and friends there. Somerset County is largely represented among the present residents of Black Hawk County, Iowa, and a large majority of the members of the South Waterloo congregation are natives of Somerset County, or the descendants of them. These include the Millers. Lichtys, Fikes, Bueghleys, Mausts, Berkleys Bloughs and many others. They have found this a goodly land; and have nearly all prospered in temporal things, and, apparently, in spiritual things also. They have had their trials, but, I trust, they have thereby been purified. Of late they have not been forgetful of the Lord's work, and have shown their liberality toward the different departments of church work. Their method of raising the yearly contributions toward missionary, tract, and other more local work in the church, is different from that recommended by Annual Meeting some years ago, and with them the result is a larger contribution than the Annual Meeting plan asks of them.

Our traveling party had the pleasure, also, of attending the love-feast at the South Waterloo church, June 18. All things,—not excluding even the weather,—seemed to work together to make it a very pleasant feast indeed. Good order is always commendable in religious exercises, but more particularly when the sufferings and death of our Savior are to be commemorated.

mortal existence. She has long felt the anointing of the spirit and not long since has felt the cleansing power of "the anointing with oil" in the name of the Lord. We had prayer with the sick and she seemed much encouraged. As we view in our memory the words and expressions of our sister,—"Mother in Israel,"—the words of the poet come to our minds with double meaning,

"Only Waiting till the shadows
  Are a little longer groWn;
Only waiting till the glimmer
  Of the day's last beam is floWn;
Till the night of death has faded
  From the heart once full of day;
Till the stars of heav'n are breaking
  Through the twilight soft and gray."

At the Pleasant Grove church, Kans., a pleasant harvest-meeting was held on Saturday, Aug. 6, at 10 A. M., and a church council in the afternoon. A love-feast was appointed for Oct. 22, and a series of meetings will begin one week previous.   JAMES Z. GILBERT.

The New Song Book.

THE compiling of the new book for our song service is now a settled matter. All the necessary details have been published by the worthy foreman of the committee. I wish only to solicit all the sympathy, talent and help that is available to bring out a book that will be adapted to the wants of the church.

For my own part I enter upon the work with mingled feelings. To wander in the flowery fields of lyrical literature is indeed congenial to my feelings, and what talent the Lord may have entrusted to me in selecting hymns for his divine service, I lay upon his altar with no little degree of pleasure. But when my weak and imperfect ability is called upon to improve upon the work of our lamented brother Quinter, I touch the harp of Zion with a trembling hand. Yet, when I think how well he served his day and generation,

"Methinks I feel
  A stronger faith, a deeper zeal."

And to use his own language: "If the glory of the Redeemer's kingdom so require, let the change be made." We have but few, if any, among us who are gifted to put their thoughts in the rounded sentences of rythm, but there are some among us who can cull the gems from the various authors and their help is needed.

Bro. Miller struck the key-note when he quoted: "Let me make a nation's songs and I care not who makes their laws." The sentiments, that are put in the minds by the force of song, mould the character so that laws are useless, either because they are not needed, or because they fail to correct what bad songs have corrupted. Let us, therefore, have hymns that express and reflect Gospel truth and burn it into the soul. Let us have words and music that will linger in the heart, and haunt the guilty like the voice of conscience, bring peace and comfort to the mourner, inspire and quicken the believer, and cause the tides of rapture to overflow the flood-gates of the soul, till our heart can unite in the chorus that fell from angel lips to the mighty watchers on the balmy plains of Judea, and inspire them with a longing and ardent desire to stand with the victorious company on the glassy sea, amidst the glory of ten thousand sunsets, to sing in higher and sweeter strains the "song of Moses, the servant of God, and the song of the Lamb."

We want hymns that will not only express, but also produce a fervent devotion, and enter into the proper feelings and experience of a Christian. It would be hard to estimate the power of just one hymn upon the life of many individuals. Before our Savior passed into the bitter anguish of Gethsemane he sang a hymn with his disciples. Although unknown, the influence of it, coming

down the centuries, has cheered and comforted many a storm-tossed and suffering believer. The ever-listening heart of the devout catches the symphonies of that song as they float out in the midnight air just before the Savior's soul entered the dismal gloom of suffering in the vale of Kedron. Into the cadences of that song we cannot enter, but the association is sacredly sweet.

There are many of the new hymns of our day that are little better than "doggerel," and their influence is to be feared. The wildfire enthusiasm of the mourner's bench receives its fuel in the sentimental chorus, set to exciting music. If we do not want the mourner's bench in our church, we must leave the spirit of it out of our hymns.

We have brethren and sisters whose taste, judgment, and opportunities enable them to do good service in making selections for the new book. We want them to come to the front. Send in hymns to Mount Morris by the hundred, and prayers to heaven by the thousand, and your work will tell upon the generation yet to be, and though the lethean flood of years shall consign your name to cold oblivion here, your deeds will be treasured in the archives of eternity, and your reward will be great.

"We may never know while we labor here
  What the fruits of toil may be,
But when we shall stand on the golden heights
  We'll the gathered harVest see."
                                    JAS. A. SELL.
McKee's Gap, Pa.

From Circleville, Ohio.

I REACHED the city in the evening, Aug. 13, and met members from Frankfort and Washington Court-house, and also our brother and sister Lawrence, from Columbus. This gave us a representation of three cities and our town, with some also from the country, and two lately baptized. The feast was held that night, in a large church of the city, the property of the African Methodists, who have always been very kind to the Brethren. The exercises were much enjoyed by all present, though the attendance was not so great as is usual at our feasts here, on account of a camp-meeting going on at the Fair Grounds near the city, and, as we learned next day, the feast had not been announced to the people of the city, as had been requested and expected. By the urgent request of the Methodist pastor, Mr. Young, I went with some eight members to the Fair Grounds on Sunday, Aug. 14, and at 10 o'clock spoke of the common salvation, from Jude 3. While I am glad that salvation is provided in common for all men, I am sorry that it, like our liberty and many more of the blessings of God, has become so common to many that salvation, with all other blessings, is trampled under foot, without heeding them.

I remained and preached again for them at 3 P. M., while Bro. Carter, of Frankfort, preached in the city. I find, however, that Fair Grounds are not always the best places for preaching, although we had a good hall; but on the Fair Grounds, and near Fair times, people are like the stony ground, and the good seed is soon caught away.

Returning to the city, I spoke again at night, while Bro. James May gave the Word to the people on the Fair Grounds. Both meetings closed with the night service, but with a very different feeling toward them. Our people were pleased and happy, while our Methodist friends were vexed and discouraged, and the pastor told us next day: "The Dunkard Brethren are all the friends we have had. We had to pay for every-thing done for us save what they did, and we are worse off than before the meeting. It did not

pay expenses. Even our elder charged us eleven dollars for one day's work, and two other ministers charged twelve dollars for their work of one day."

From there I came to Washington Court-house Aug. 15. I held one meeting with the members at that point, and having a call to come to a new point, Jeffersonville, about twelve miles Northwest, Bro. Ayers and I went up to see them, and we learned that a number want the preaching, together with the doing of the Lord's Word. Arrangements are to be made to that effect at an early day. I reached Dayton on the night of the 17th.   LANDON WEST.

The Present Outlook in Russia.

WHILE we announced, some time since, that contributions would no more be needed for the famine sufferers in Russia, it will nevertheless be interesting to hear something from those unfortunate ones, and also those noble-hearted souls who, in spite of danger incurred by exposure to disease, etc., did a grand work for humanity by personally distributing, not only what was sent by others, but also of their own means.

Mrs. Olga Novikoff, to whom, by Mr Edgar, were sent some of the funds contributed by the Brethren, writes as follows:

Novo Alexandrofka, Gov't of Tambof,
District of Kosloff, Russia, July 31, 1892.
L. A. PLATE,
  Dear Sir:—

The sympathy, expressed not only in sonorous words, but in generous deeds, by the noble-hearted American people, is really splendid. You give a lesson to the world, worthy of a Christian nation.

Many thanks for your remittance. . . . We are now fighting with the results of our terrible famine, the CHOLERA, every-where surrounding us. We are honestly doing our best,—distributing every kind of help, medicine and meat, and preventing the ignorant peasants from eating and drinking unwholesome things. We cannot do more than our utmost! Thanks to your donations, our work is less difficult!

We are spending our-own private means for the building of barracks for the cholera patients and getting doctors and surgeons. One fact we shall never forget,—if we have done any effectual good, it has been, to a great extent, due to the noble-hearted Christians of America. The Lord bless you!
                          Gratefully Yours,
                                OLGA NOVIKOFF.

Mrs. Novikoff, besides spending almost her entire very large possessions for the relief of the needy ones, has met with a personal loss that should arouse the sympathy of all. Her beloved daughter, while engaged in caring for the sufferers from cholera and other diseases, was stricken down while yet in the bloom of youth, and is thus another sacrifice on the altar of humanity.

We, as a church, talk of sacrificing all for Christ. Do we mean it? Are we ready to do as much as those Russian ladies, less enlightened, perhaps, than we are, but willing to part with all, even their own lives, to alleviate the woes of suffering humanity?   L. A. PLATE.
Mt. Morris, Ill.

Chips from the Work-house.

ON the way eastward, to Pennsylvania, after leaving Mt. Morris, I had the privilege of attending Sunday-school and two preaching services with the brethren and sisters in their new meeting-house in Chicago, July 31. I attended social meetings in Cerro Gordo, Ill., Aug. 3; a church council in the Mississinewa church, near Shidelsr, Ind., Aug. 6. Next day I attended Sunday-school and two preaching services in the same church. Aug. 9, in company with some brethren, I looked over the grounds near Muncie, which are offered as a location to hold next Annual Meeting.

At Hagerstown I found some brethren who desire that the Annual Meeting should be held at

mortal existence. She has long felt the anointing of the spirit and not long since has felt the cleansing power of "the anointing with oil" in the name of the Lord. We had prayer with the sick and she seemed much encouraged. As we view in our memory the words and expressions of our sister,—"Mother in Israel,"—the words of the poet come to our minds with double meaning.

" Only waiting till the shadows
    Are a little longer grown;
Only waiting till the glimmer
    Of the day's last beam is flown;
Till the night of death has faded
    From the heart once full of day;
Till the stars of heav'n are breaking
    Through the twilight soft and gray."

At the Pleasant Grove church, Kans., a pleasant harvest-meeting was held on Saturday, Aug. 6, at 10 A. M., and a church council in the afternoon. A love-feast was appointed for Oct. 22, and a series of meetings will begin one week previous.   JAMES Z. GILBERT.

The New Song Book.

THE compiling of the new book for our song service is now a settled matter. All the necessary details have been published by the worthy foreman of the committee. I wish only to solicit all the sympathy, talent and help that is available to bring out a book that will be adapted to the wants of the church.

For my own part I enter upon the work with mingled feelings. To wander in the flowery fields of lyrical literature is indeed congenial to my feelings, and what talent the Lord may have entrusted to me in selecting hymns for his divine service, I lay upon his altar with no little degree of pleasure. But when my weak and imperfect ability is called upon to improve upon the work of our lamented brother Quinter, I touch the harp of Zion with a trembling hand. Yet, when I think how well he served his day and generation,

" Methinks I feel
    A stronger faith, a deeper zeal."

And to use his own language: "If the glory of the Redeemer's kingdom so require, let the change be made." We have but few, if any, among us who are gifted to put their thoughts in the rounded sentences of rythm, but there are some among us who can cull the gems from the various authors and their help is needed.

Bro. Miller struck the key-note when he quoted: "Let me make a nation's songs and I care not who makes their laws." The sentiments, that are put in the minds by the force of song, mould the character so that laws are useless, either because they are not needed, or because they fail to correct what bad songs have corrupted. Let us, therefore, have hymns that express and reflect Gospel truth and burn it into the soul. Let us have words and music that will linger in the heart, and haunt the guilty like the voice of conscience, bring peace and comfort to the mourner, inspire and quicken the believer, and cause the tides of rapture to overflow the flood-gates of the soul, till our heart can unite in the chorus that fell from angel lips to the mighty watchers on the balmy plains of Judea, and inspire them with a longing and ardent desire to stand with the victorious company on the glassy sea, amidst the glory of ten thousand sunsets, to sing in higher and sweeter strains the "song of Moses, the servant of God, and the song of the Lamb."

We want hymns that will not only express, but also produce a fervent devotion, and enter into the proper feelings and experience of a Christian. It would be hard to estimate the power of just one hymn upon the life of many individuals. Before our Savior passed into the bitter anguish of Gethsemane he sang a hymn with his disciples. Although unknown, the influence of it, coming down the centuries, has cheered and comforted many a storm-tossed and suffering believer. The ever-listening heart of the devout catches the symphonies of that song as they float out in the midnight air just before the Savior's soul entered the dismal gloom of suffering in the vale of Kedron. Into the cadence of that song we cannot enter, but the association is sacredly sweet.

There are many of the new hymns of our day that are little better than "doggerel," and their influence is to be feared. The wildfire enthusiasm of the mourner's bench receives its fuel in the sentimental chorus, set to exciting music. If we do not want the mourner's bench in our hymns, we must leave the spirit of it out of our hymns.

We have brethren and sisters whose taste, judgment, and opportunities enable them to do good service in making selections for the new book. We want them to come to the front. Send in hymns to Mount Morris by the hundred, and prayers to heaven by the thousand, and your work will tell upon the generation yet to be, and though the lethean flood of years shall consign your name to cold oblivion here, your deeds will be treasured in the archives of eternity, and your reward will be great.

" We may never know while we labor here
    What the fruits of toil may be,
But when we shall stand on the golden heights
    We'll the gathered harvest see."
                                    JAS. A. SELL.
McKee's Gap, Pa.

From Circleville, Ohio.

I REACHED the city in the evening, Aug. 13, and met members from Frankfort and Washington Court-house, and also our brother and sister Lawrence, from Columbus. This gave us a representation of three cities and one town, with some also from the country, and two lately baptized. The feast was held that night, in a large church of the city, the property of the African Methodists, who have always been very kind to the Brethren. The exercises were much enjoyed by all present, though the attendance was not so great as is usual at our feasts here, on account of a camp-meeting going on at the Fair Grounds near the city, and, as we learned next day, the feast had not been announced to the people of the city, as had been requested and expected. By the urgent request of the Methodist pastor, Mr. Young, I went with some eight members to the Fair Grounds on Sunday, Aug. 14, and at 10 o'clock spoke of the common salvation, from Jude 3. While I am glad that salvation is provided in common for all men, I am sorry that it, like our liberty and many more of the blessings of God, has become so common to many that salvation, with all other blessings, is trampled under foot, without heeding them.

I remained and preached again for them at 3 P. M., while Bro. Carter, of Frankfort, preached in the city. I find, however, that Fair Grounds are not always the best places for preaching, although we had a good hall; but on the Fair Grounds, and near Fair times, people are like the stony ground, and the good seed is soon caught away.

Returning to the city, I spoke again at night, while Bro. James May gave the Word to the people on the Fair Grounds. Both meetings closed with the night service, but with a very different feeling toward them. Our people were pleased and happy, while our Methodist friends were vexed and discouraged, and the pastor told us next day: "The Dunkard Brethren are all the friends we have had. We had to pay for everything done for us save what they did, and we are worse off than before the meeting. It did not

pay expenses. Even our elder charged us eleven dollars for one day's work, and two other ministers charged twelve dollars for their work of one day."

From there I came to Washington Court-house Aug. 15. I held one meeting with the members at that point, and having a call to come to a new point, Jeffersonville, about twelve miles Northwest, Bro. Ayers and I went up to see them, and we learned that a number want the preaching, together with the doing of the Lord's Word. Arrangements are to be made to that effect at an early day. I reached Dayton on the night of the 17th.   LANDON WEST.

The Present Outlook in Russia.

WHILE we announced, some time since, that contributions would no more be needed for the famine sufferers in Russia, it will nevertheless be interesting to hear something from those unfortunate ones, and also those noble-hearted souls who, in spite of danger incurred by exposure to disease, etc., did a grand work for humanity by personally distributing, not only what was sent by others, but also of their own means.

Mrs. Olga Novikoff, to whom, by Mr Edgar, were sent some of the funds contributed by the Brethren, writes as follows:

Novo Alexandrofka, Gov't of Tambof,
    District of Kosloff, Russia, July 31, 1892.
L. A. PLATE,
Dear Sir:—

The sympathy, expressed not only in sonorous words, but in generous deeds, by the noble-hearted American people, is really splendid. You give a lesson to the world, worthy of a Christian nation.

Many thanks for your remittance. . . . We are now fighting with the results of our terrible famine, the CHOLERA, every-where surrounding us. We are honestly doing our best,—distributing every kind of help, medicines and heat, and preventing the ignorant peasants from eating and drinking unwholesome things. We cannot do more than our utmost! Thanks to your donations, our work is less difficult! We are spending our own private means for the building of barracks for the cholera patients and getting doctors and surgeons. One fact we shall never forget,—If we have done any effectual good, it has been, to a great extent, due to the noble-hearted Christians of America. The Lord bless you!
                                    Gratefully Yours,
                                    OLGA NOVIKOFF.

Mrs. Novikoff, besides spending almost her entire very large possessions for the relief of the needy ones, has met with a personal loss that should arouse the sympathy of all. Her beloved daughter, while engaged in caring for the sufferers from cholera and other diseases, was stricken down while yet in the bloom of youth, and is thus another sacrifice on the altar of humanity.

We, as a church, talk of sacrificing all for Christ. Do we mean it? Are we ready to do as much as those Russian ladies, less enlightened, perhaps, than we are, but willing to part with all, even their own lives, to alleviate the woes of suffering humanity?   L. A. PLATE.
Mt. Morris, Ill.

Chips from the Work-house.

ON the way eastward, to Pennsylvania, after leaving Mt. Morris, I had the privilege of attending Sunday-school and two preaching services with the brethren and sisters in their new meeting-house in Chicago, July 31. I attended social meetings in Cerro Gordo, Ill., Aug. 3; a church council in the Mississinewa church, near Shideler, Ind., Aug. 6. Next day I attended Sunday-school and two preaching services in the same church. Aug. 9, in company with some brethren, I looked over the grounds near Muncie, which are offered as a location to hold next Annual Meeting.

At Hagerstown I found some brethren who desire that the Annual Meeting should be held at

Adrian, Mo.—Saturday, Aug. 7, the members of the Mound church met in quarterly council, and enjoyed a very pleasant meeting. Seemingly everything that came before the meeting was disposed of satisfactorily. By God's help may we continue to prosper!—*Hannah Blocher.*

Mohawk Valley, Ore.—Aug. 4 wife and I left home to visit isolated members, and hold some meetings. We met with two persons who say they formerly belonged to the Brethren, but had neglected to obtain letters of membership; another, who had with him proper credentials, established his membership among us. Aug. 7 one was added to the church by baptism, which caused great joy, especially to her aged parents.—*Jacob Bahr, Aug. 13.*

Harrod, Ohio.—The Brethren of the La Fayette church, Allen County, Ohio, will hold their love-feast Sept. 3, at 4 o'clock, and continue over Sunday. We also expect to have two weeks' series of meetings previous to our love-feast. Those coming by the Chicago and Erie R. R. should stop off at Harrod, and those coming by the Pittsburgh, Fort Wayne and Chicago R. R., should get off at La Fayette. Conveyances will be at either place.—*A. M. Baker, Aug. 9.*

Rock Run, Ind.—Our harvest-meeting was held Aug. 7. We met at 9:30 on that day for Sunday-school, which is an evergreen one, with an average attendance of seventy-five. At 10:30 Bro. Abraham Neff showed forth the goodness of God, from Nahum 1:7. We were made to feel that the Lord knows those that love and serve him. At 2 o'clock we had a missionary sermon from brethren Eli Roose and Levi Hoke. The collection was $2.40 for home and foreign mission. Aug. 13 was our quarterly church-council. It was a pleasant meeting and to the edification of all present.—*R. W. Davenport.*

Mt. Zion, Ind.—We, the Prairie Creek church, held our quarterly church-meeting on Saturday, Aug. 13. All business that came before the meeting passed off pleasantly. We decided to hold our love-feast Oct. 6. We have two flourishing Sunday-schools in our church district,—one at the Sugar Grove house, with Robert Campbell as Superintendent, and one at the Popejoy school-house with W. A. Popejoy as Superintendent. We have prayer-meetings regularly at each place each week. Our elder, G. W. Sala, is much afflicted,—so much so that his recovery is despaired of.—*John Minnich, Aug. 15*

Girard, Ill.—Our quarterly council, Aug. 6, passed off pleasantly, and considerable business was done. Though a very busy time, the members were nearly all there, which was very commendable. The writer's two co-laborers were elected as delegates to District Meeting. The Home Mission, General Mission, and the Book and Tract Work were remembered. Two were added by letter. After all the regular business was attended to, the church proceeded to hold an election for two deacons, and the lot fell on brethren Martin Brubaker, and B. G. Stead, who were duly installed. May they prove faithful to their high calling! Oct. 1 is the time to have a report of the annual visit. We hope that much good will be accomplished.—*Michael Flory, Aug. 19.*

Matrimonial.

WITMORE—BLOCHER.—At the residence of the bride's parents, Aug. 10, 1892, by Bro. G. W. Lentz, Bro. Ira Witmore, of Centre View, Mo., and sister Hannah Blocher, of Adrian, Mo. GRACE E. BLOCHER.

HADSELL—BAKER.—At the residence of Bro. B. M. Byers, of Glendale, Arizona, July 31, 1892, by Rev. Alford

Jilll, Bro. N. D. Hadsell, of Glendale, Arizona, formerly of California, to sister N. Baker, of the same place, but formerly of Canada. W. F. GILLETT.

Fallen Asleep.

"Blessed are the dead which die in the Lord."

WARD.—At Imlertown, Bedford Co., Pa., while away from home, Aug. 10, 1892, of cancer, Bro. David Ward, of Clear Ridge, same County, between 65 and 67 years of age. Discourse from 1 Thess. 4: 18, "Wherefore comfort one another with these words." JOHN BENNETT.

BROWN.—In the Wacandah church, Ray Co., Mo., July 28, 1892, Birtle Alice, daughter of Bro. Joseph and sister Lizzie Brown, aged 7 years, 6 months and 6 days. Funeral services at the Rockingham church, Aug. 14, by Bro. A. W. Vaniman, of McPherson, Kans. J. H. SHIREY.

MAUST.—At Preston, Minn., June 13, 1892, sister Amy Maust, youngest daughter of Bro. Jonas and sister Fanny Maust, aged 20 years, 4 months and 1 day. Deceased died of consumption. She had been failing fast for more than a year. She leaves a father, mother, three sisters, and two brothers. Funeral services by Bro. Joseph Ogg.
EMMA MAUST.

BOND.—In the bounds of the Meadow Branch church, in the City of Baltimore, of indigestion and liver trouble, Bro. Eli Bond, aged about 60 years. Brother Bond and wife were on a visit to their daughter, from their home in Washington City, when he took sick, and, after seven weeks of suffering, closed his eyes in death. Deceased leaves a wife, who is a sister, and five children. Aug. 9 his body was laid away in the family lot attached to the Baptist church at Black Rock. The occasion was improved by Eld. E. W. Stoner. Text, "To die is gain." R. A. STONER.

PARKER.—In the bounds of the Forest church, Wis., Aug. 5, 1892, sister Mary Parker, wife of Ezekiel Parker, and daughter of Thomas and Miley Patten, aged 36 years, 3 months and 17 days. She leaves a husband and nine children (an infant babe of seven days). Sister Mary has been a member of the Brethren church for thirteen years. On account of the aged parents being in ill health, the funeral services were postponed. Interment in the Pleasant Ridge cemetery. M. A. TURNER.

MENEAR.—In the bounds of the Lower Conawago church, Franklintown, York Co., Pa., July 26, 1892, Daniel Menear, aged 88 years. Services and interment at the Latimer meeting-house, Upper Conawago church, by the writer from 2 Cor. 5: 1-3. HENRY BEELMAN.

FIRESTONE.—In the Lower Conawago church, York County, Pa., July 29, 1892, sister Martha Firestone, aged 71 years, 1 month and 13 days. Deceased was the beloved wife of Bro. Aaron Firestone. She had gained the love and respect of all. She leaves a husband, three sons and one daughter. Services and interment at the Walgamoth meeting-house to a large concourse of people, from 1 Thess. 4: 13, 14, by Bro. Hezekiah Cook and the writer. HENRY BEELMAN.

WATT.—At the residence of his nephew, friend Nelson Watt, in the bounds of the South River congregation, Madison County, Iowa, Aug 4, 1892, Andrew F. Watt, aged 76 years, 8 months and 23 days. Friend Watt was born in Preble County, Ohio. In youth he embraced religion and united with the Presbyterian church. His wife preceded him to the spirit land about thirteen months. Funeral discourse by Bro. Lewis Kob from 2 Sam. 14: 14. MEDA CASKEY.

UMBAUGH.—In the Spring Creek church, Whitley County, Ind., Aug. 2, 1892, Sarah C. Umbaugh, aged 80 years, 8 months and 28 days. She leaves five children to mourn their loss. Her husband, Eld. Jonas Umbaugh, died about seven years ago. Funeral services by Bro. Jacob Snell, from John 13: 36. R. ROSS.

FRY.—In the Smith Fork congregation, Mo., July 26, 1892, sister Mary Elizabeth Fry, aged 51 years, 4 months and 11 days.

DOVE.—In the same congregation, Aug. 10, 1892, Della M., infant daughter of Dr. J. D. F. and sister Della M. Dove, aged 2 months and 6 days. Funeral services conducted by elders J. E. Ellenberger and A. K. Sell. G. M. ELLENBERGER.

WILTROUT.—In the Jacob's Creek congregation, Pa., July 27, 1892, Ellas Franklin Wiltrout, aged 38 years and 15 days. Services by the writer. H. S. MYERS.

NICKLOW.—At Pennaville, Pa., Aug. 9, 1892, Flora H. Nicklow, aged 9 months and 26 days. Services by the writer. H. S. MYERS.

BARR.—At his home, west of Lineville, Iowa, Dec. 12, 1891, Robert D. Barr, aged 74 years, 5 months and 26 days. He emigrated with his family from Ohio to Decatur County, Iowa, April, 1876, where he resided until his death. He was the father of twelve children, nine of whom, with his com-

panion (a dear sister), survive. Funeral services conducted by the writer. LEWIS M. KOB.

HYER.—In the Lower Miami church, Montgomery County, Ohio, May 7, 1892, sister Mary Hyer, aged 84 years, 6 months and 8 days. Deceased was born in Frederick County, Maryland, Aug. 29, 1807. She came to Montgomery County, Ohio, in 1828, and was married to Roody Hyer in 1831, which union was blest with six children, four of whom preceded her to the spirit world. Fourteen years ago her husband was called away and left her to travel the remainder of her journey alone. She was a faithful member of the Brethren church for many years. Funeral services at the Lower Miami church on Sunday following, by Bro. Daniel Garver. IRVIN F. HYER.

GNAGY.—In the Summit congregation, Somerset County, Pa., July 27, 1892, of old age, sister Caroline Gnagy, aged 86 years, 5 months and 6 days. She was the second wife of Bro. Christian Gnagy. He preceded her to the spirit world about twelve years. She was the mother of C. C. Musselman, who preceded her some time, and also of Eld. Hiram Musselman, who is still an active elder in the Shade congregation.

SMITH.—In the Mingona church, Barber County, Kans., July 28, 1892, sister Elizabeth, wife of Bro. Wm. Smith, aged 36 years, 7 months and 8 days. The sorrowing husband and six children remain to mourn their loss. She bore her long illness with Christian fortitude. Funeral services conducted by Joseph Glick, from the words: "Set thine house in order." JESSE SHAMBERGER.

CRIPE.—In the bounds of the Pleasant Hill congregation, Aug. 10, 1892, sister Catherine Cripe, aged 77 years and 12 days. Her remains were followed to their last resting-place, at the Pleasant Hill church, by a large procession. Funeral services conducted by the writer, from 1 Thess. 4: 14, assisted by S. B. Miller. MICHAEL FLORY.

HOLLOPETER.—At Rockton, Pa., July 16, 1892, of diptheria, Charlie, son of Mary and Henry Hollopeter, aged 10 years, 4 months and 3 days. Funeral discourse preached two weeks later, on Sunday, from Job 1: 21, "The Lord gave, and the Lord hath taken away," by Rev. Seiner of Luthersburgh. LIDDIE HOLLOPETER.

WILLIAMS.—In the Winona church, Winona County, Minn., June 26, 1892, Mary Williams, wife of Bro. E. P. Williams, aged about 64 years. She was a member of the Baptist church for many years, and lived an exemplary Christian life. Funeral services by Bro. D. Whetstone. ELLA A. LEWIS.

SNYDER.—In the Dry Creek church, near Robins, Iowa, Aug. 13, 1892, sister Nancy Snyder, aged 64 years, 3 months and 17 days. Sister Snyder lay sick a long time, but bore her afflictions patiently, trusting in the Lord unto the end. Funeral services by D. W. Miller, J. K. Miller and the writer.
JOHN ZUCK.

LAWRENCE.—In the bounds of the Pleasant Hill congregation, Ill., Aug. 6, 1892, infant son of Joseph and —— Lawrence, aged 9 months and 12 days. Funeral services and burial at MacDuquin Creek church, conducted by the writer, assisted by C. C. Gibson, from Matt. 18: 3. MICHAEL FLORY.

The Gospel Messenger

Is the recognized organ of the German Baptist or Brethren's church, and advocates the form of doctrine taught in the New Testament and pleads for a return to apostolic and primitive Christianity.

It recognizes the New Testament as the only infallible rule of faith and practice, and maintains that Faith toward God, Repentance from dead works, Regeneration of the heart and mind, baptism by Trine immersion for remission of sins unto the reception of the Holy Ghost by the laying on of hands, are the means of adoption into the household of God,—the church militant.

It also maintains that Feet-washing, as taught in John 13, both by example and command of Jesus, should be observed in the church.

That the Lord's Supper, instituted by Christ and as universally observed by the apostles and the early Christians, is a full meal, and, in connection with the Communion, should be taken in the evening or after the close of the day.

That the Salutation of the Holy Kiss, or Kiss of Charity, is binding upon the followers of Christ.

That War and Retaliation are contrary to the spirit and self-denying principles of the religion of Jesus Christ.

That the principle of Plain Dressing and of Non-conformity to the world, as taught in the New Testament, should be observed by the followers of Christ.

That the Scriptural duty of Anointing the Sick with Oil, in the Name of the Lord, James 5: 14, is binding upon all Christians.

It also advocates the church's duty to support Missionary and Tract Work, thus giving to the Lord for the spread of the Gospel and for the conversion of sinners.

In short, it is a vindicator of all that Christ and the apostles have enjoined upon us, and aims, amid the conflicting theories and discords of modern Christendom, to point out ground that all must concede to be infallibly safe.

☞ The above principles of our Fraternity are set forth on our "Brethren's Envelopes." Use them! Price 15 cents per package; 40 cents per hundred.

Adrian, Mo.—Saturday, Aug. 7, the members of the Mound church met in quarterly council, and enjoyed a very pleasant meeting. Seemingly everything that came before the meeting was disposed of satisfactorily. By God's help may we continue to prosper!—*Hannah Blocher.*

Mohawk Valley, Ore.—Aug. 4 wife and I left home to visit isolated members, and hold some meetings. We met with two persons who say they formerly belonged to the Brethren, but had neglected to obtain letters of membership; another, who had with him proper credentials, established his membership among us. Aug. 7 one was added to the church by baptism, which caused great joy, especially to her aged parents.—*Jacob Bahr, Aug. 13.*

Harrod, Ohio.—The Brethren of the La Fayette church, Allen County, Ohio, will hold their love-feast Sept. 3, at 4 o'clock, and continue over Sunday. We also expect to have two weeks' series of meetings previous to our love-feast. Those coming by the Chicago and Erie R. R. should stop off at Harrod, and those coming by the Pittsburgh, Fort Wayne and Chicago R R, should get off at La Fayette. Conveyances will be at either place. —*A. M. Baker, Aug. 9.*

Rock Run, Ind.—Our harvest-meeting was held Aug. 7. We met at 9: 30 on that day for Sunday-school, which is an evergreen one, with an average attendance of seventy-five. At 10:30 Bro. Abraham Neff showed forth the goodness of God, from Nahum 1: 7. We were made to feel that the Lord knows those that love and serve him. At 2 o'clock we had a missionary sermon from brethren Eli Roose and Levi Hoke. The collection was $22.40 for home and foreign mission. Aug. 13 was our quarterly church-council. It was a pleasant meeting and to the edification of all present.—*R. W. Davenport.*

El. Zion, Ind.—We, the Prairie Creek church, held our quarterly church-meeting on Saturday, Aug. 13. All business that came before the meeting passed off pleasantly. We decided to hold our love-feast Oct 6 We have two flourishing Sunday-schools in our church district,—one at the Sugar Grove house, with Robert Campbell as Superintendent, and one at the Popejoy school-house with W. A. Popejoy as Superintendent. We have prayer-meetings regularly at each place each week. Our elder, G. W. Sala, is much afflicted,—so much so that his recovery is despaired of. —*John Minnich, Aug. 15*

Girard, Ill.—Our quarterly council, Aug 6, passed off pleasantly, and considerable business was done. Though a very busy time, the members were nearly all there, which was very commendable. The writer's two co-laborers were elected as delegates to District Meeting. The Home Mission, General Mission, and the Book and Tract Work were remembered. Two were added by letter. After all the regular business was attended to, the church proceeded to hold an election for two deacons, and the lot fell on brethren Martin Brubaker, and B G. Stead, who were duly installed. May they prove faithful to their high calling! Oct. 1 is the time to have a report of the annual visit. We hope that much good will be accomplished.—*Michael Flory, Aug. 10.*

Matrimonial.

"What therefore God hath joined together, let not man put asunder."

WITMORE–BLOCHER.—At the residence of the bride's parents, Aug. 10, 1891, by Bro. G. W. Lentz, Bro. Ira Witmore, of Centre View, Mo., and sister Hannah Blocher, of Adrian, Mo.   GRACE E. BLOCHER.

HAUSELL–BAKER.—At the residence of Bro. S. M. Byers, of Glendale, Arizona, July 31, 1892, by Rev. Alford

Hiff, Bro. N. D. Hadsell, of Glendale, Arizona, formerly of California, to sister N. Baker, of the same place, but formerly of Canada.   W. F. GILLETT.

Fallen Asleep.

"Blessed are the dead which die in the Lord."

WARD.—At Imlertown, Bedford Co., Pa., while away from home, Aug. 10, 1892, of cancer, Bro. David Ward, of Clear Ridge, same County, between 65 and 67 years of age. Discourse from 1 Thess. 4: 18, "Wherefore comfort one another with these words."   JOHN BENNETT.

BROWN.—In the Wacandah church, Ray Co., Mo., July 28, 1892, Birtle Alice, daughter of Bro. Joseph and sister Lizzie Brown, aged 7 years, 6 months and 6 days. Funeral services at the Rockingham church, Aug. 14, by Bro. A. W. Vaniman, of McPherson, Kans.   J. H. SHIRKY.

MAUST.—At Preston, Minn., June 13, 1892, sister Amy Maust, youngest daughter of Bro. Jonas and sister Fanny Maust, aged 20 years, 4 months and 1 day. Deceased died of consumption. She had been failing fast for more than a year. She leaves a father, mother, three sisters, and two brothers. Funeral services by Bro. Joseph Ogg.
                              EMMA MAUST.

BOND.—In the bounds of the Meadow Branch church, in the City of Baltimore, of indigestion and liver trouble, Bro. Eil Bond, aged about 60 years. Brother Bond and wife were on a visit to their daughter, from their home in Washington City, when he took sick, and, after seven weeks of suffering, closed his eyes in death. Deceased leaves a wife, who is a sister, and five children. Aug. 9 his body was laid away in the family lot attached to the Baptist church at Black Rock. The occasion was improved by Eld. E. W. Stoner. Text, "To die is gain."   R. A. STONER.

PARKER.—In the bounds of the Forest church, Wis., Aug. 5, 1892, sister Mary Parker, wife of Ezekiel Parker, and daughter of Thomas and Miley Patten, aged 36 years, 3 months and 17 days. She leaves a husband and nine children (an infant babe of seven days). Sister Mary has been a member of the Brethren church for thirteen years. On account of the aged parents being in ill health, the funeral services were postponed. Interment in the Pleasant Ridge cemetery.   M. A. TURNER.

MENEAR.—In the bounds of the Lower Conawago church, Franklintown, York Co., Pa., July 26, 1892, Daniel Menear, aged 88 years. Services and interment at the Latimer meeting-house, Upper Conawago church, by the writer from 2 Cor. 5: 1-3.   HENRY BEELMAN.

FIRESTONE.—In the Lower Conawago church, York County, Pa., July 29, 1892, sister Martha Firestone, aged 71 years, 1 month and 13 days. Deceased was the beloved wife of Bro. Aaron Firestone. She had gained the love and respect of all. She leaves a husband, three sons and one daughter. Services and interment at the Walgamoth meeting-house to a large concourse of people, from 1 Thess. 4: 13, 14, by Bro. Hezekiah Cook and the writer.
                              HENRY BEELMAN.

WATT.—At the residence of his nephew, friend Nelson Watt, in the bounds of the South River congregation, Madison County, Iowa, Aug 4, 1892, Andrew F. Watt, aged 76 years, 6 months and 23 days. Friend Watt was born in Preble County, Ohio. In youth he embraced religion and united with the Presbyterian church. His wife preceded him to the spirit land about thirteen months. Funeral discourse by Bro. Lewis Kob from 2 Sam. 14: 14.   MEDA CASKEY.

UMBAUGH.—In the Spring Creek church, Whitley County, Ind., Aug. 2, 1892, Sarah C. Umbaugh, aged 80 years, 8 months and 26 days. She leaves five children to mourn their loss. Her husband, Eld. Jonas Umbaugh, died about seven years ago. Funeral services conducted by Bro. Jacob Snell, from John 13: 36.   R. ROSS.

FRY.—In the Smith Fork congregation, Mo., July 26, 1892, sister Mary Elizabeth Fry, aged 52 years, 4 months and 11 days.

In the same congregation, Aug. 10, 1892, Delia M., infant daughter of Dr. J. D. F. and sister Delia M. Dove, aged 2 months and 6 days. Funeral services conducted by elders J. E. Ellenbzger and A. K. Sell. G. M. ELLENBERGER.

WILTROUT.—In the Jacob's Creek congregation, Pa., July 17, 1892, Eliza Franklin Wiltrout, aged 38 years and 15 days. Services by the writer.   H. S. MYERS.

NICKLOW.—At Pennsville, Pa., Aug. 9, 1892, Flora H. Nicklow, aged 9 months and 26 days. Services by the writer.   H. S. MYERS.

BARR.—At his home, west of Lineville, Iowa, Dec. 19, 1891, Robert D. Barr, aged 74 years, 5 months and 16 days. He emigrated with his family from Ohio to Decatur County, Iowa, April, 1876, where he resided until his death. He was the father of twelve children, nine of whom, with his companion (a dear sister), survive. Funeral services conducted by the writer.   LEWIS M. KOB.

HYER.—In the Lower Miami church, Montgomery County, Ohio, May 7, 1892, sister Mary Hyer, aged 84 years, 6 months and 8 days Deceased was born in Frederick County, Maryland, Aug. 29, 1807. She came to Montgomery County, Ohio, in 1828, and was married to Roody Hyer in 1831, which union was blest with six children, four of whom preceded her to the spirit world Fourteen years ago her husband was called away and left her to travel the remainder of her journey alone. She was a faithful member of the Brethren church for many years. Funeral services at the Lower Miami church on Sunday following, by Bro. Daniel Garver.   IRVIN F. HYER.

GNAGY.—In the Summit congregation, Somerset County, Pa., July 27, 1892, of old age, sister Caroline Gnagy, aged 76 years, 5 months and 6 days She was the second wife of Bro. Christian Guagy. He preceded her to the spirit world about twelve years. Since then she had her home with our esteemed elder, Jost Gnagy (youngest son of Bro. Christian), Deceased was the mother of C. C. Musselman, who preceded her some time, and also of Eld. Hiram Musselman, who is still an active elder in the Shade congregation.

SMITH.—In the Mingona church, Barber County, Kans., July 28, 1892, sister Elizabeth, wife of Bro. Wm. Smith, aged 56 years, 7 months and 8 days. The sorrowing husband and six children remain to mourn their loss. She bore her long illness with Christian fortitude. Funeral services conducted by Joseph Glick, from the words: " Set thine house in order."   JESSE SHAMBERGER.

CRIPE.—In the bounds of the Pleasant Hill congregation, Aug. 10, 1892, sister Catherine Cripe, aged 77 years and 12 days. Her remains were followed to their last resting-place, at the Pleasant Hill church, by a large procession. Funeral services conducted by the writer, from 1 Thess. 4: 14, assisted by S. B. Miller.   MICHAEL FLORY.

HOLLOPETER.—At Rockton, Pa., July 16, 1892, of diptheria, Charlie, son of Mary and Henry Hollopeter, aged 10 years, 4 months and 5 days. Funeral discourse preached two weeks later, on Sunday, from Job 1: 21, " The Lord gave, and the Lord hath taken away," by Rev. Selner of Luthersburgh.
                              LIZZIE HOLLOPETER.

WILLIAMS.—In the Winona church, Winona County, Minn., June 26, 1892, Mary Williams, wife of Bro. E. F. Williams, aged about 64 years. She was a member of the Baptist church for many years, and lived an exemplary Christian life. Funeral services by Bro. D. Whetstone.

                              ELLA A. LEWIS.

SNYDER.—In the Dry Creek church, near Robins, Iowa, Aug. 13, 1892, sister Nancy Snyder, aged 64 years, 3 months and 17 days. Sister Snyder lay sick a long time, but bore her afflictions patiently, trusting in the Lord unto the end. Funeral services by D. W. Miller, J. K. Miller and the writer.
                              JOHN ZUCK.

LAWRENCE.—In the bounds of the Pleasant Hill congregation, Ill., Aug. 6, 1892, infant son of Joseph and —— Lawrence, aged 9 months and 12 days. Funeral services and burial at Macoupin Creek church, conducted by the writer, assisted by C. C. Gibson, from Matt. 18: 3.
                              MICHAEL FLORY.

The Gospel Messenger

Is the recognized organ of the German Baptist or Brethren's church, and advocates the form of doctrine taught in the New Testament and pleads for a return to apostolic and primitive Christianity.

It recognizes the New Testament as the only infallible rule of faith and practice, and maintains that Faith toward God, Repentance from dead works, Regeneration of the heart and mind, baptism by Trine immersion for remission of sins unto the reception of the Holy Ghost by the laying on of hands, are the means of adoption into the household of God,—the church militant.

It also maintains that Feet-washing, as taught in John 13, both by example and command of Jesus, should be observed in the church.

That the Lord's Supper, instituted by Christ and as universally observed by the apostles and the early Christians, is a full meal, and, in connection with the Communion, should be taken in the evening or after the close of the day.

That the Salutation of the Holy Kiss, or Kiss of Charity, is binding upon the followers of Christ.

That War and Retaliation are contrary to the spirit and self-denying principles of the religion of Jesus Christ.

That the principle of Plain Dressing and of Non-conformity to the world, as taught in the New Testament, should be observed by the followers of Christ.

That the Scriptural duty of Anointing the Sick with Oil, in the Name of the Lord, James 5: 14, is binding upon all Christians.

It also advocates the church's duty to support Missionary and Tract Work, thus giving to the Lord for the spread of the Gospel and for the conversion of sinners.

In short, it is a vindicator of all that Christ and the apostles have enjoined upon us, and aims, amid the conflicting theories and discords of modern Christendom, to point out ground that all must concede to be infallibly safe.

☞ The above principles of our Fraternity are set forth on our "Brethren's Envelopes." Use them! Price 15 cents per package; 40 cents per hundred.

Announcements.

MINISTERIAL MEETINGS.

Oct. 4, in the Blue River Valley church, Butler Co., Nebr., at Bro. Jerry Keller's, ¼ mile west of Octavia. Ministerial meeting day before. Trains due here from the East at 10:10 P. M., from the West at 1:26 P. M.

Nov. 15, at 9 A. M., in the South-east District of Kansas, Ministerial Meeting in the Cedar Creek church, Miami Ids., Anderson Co., Kans.

Nov. 1 and 2, Western District of Pennsylvania will hold their Ministerial Meeting in Walnut Grove, Johnstown church.

DISTRICT MEETINGS.

Sept. 12, Middle District of Iowa, in the Garrison church, Benton Co., Iowa.

Oct. 1, at 9 A. M., District of Northern Iowa, Minnesota and South Dakota, in the South Waterloo church, Black Hawk Co., Iowa.

Oct. 7, at 9 A. M., Southern District of Illinois, in the Coal's Creek church, Fulton Co., Ill.

Oct. 7, at 9 A. M., District Meeting in the Crooked Creek church, Washington Co., Iowa. Those coming by rail will be met at Keota, at 10 A. M. from the East, and at 6:40 P. M. from the West, by notifying D. P. Miller.

LOVE-FEASTS.

Sept. 17, at 10 A. M., Black River, Medina Co., Ohio.

Sept. 21, at 10 A. M., Coffnloe church, Bethiah Co., Iowa.

Sept. 23, at 4 P. M., Oakley church, Macon Co., Ill.

Sept. 23, at 3 P. M., Libertyville church, Jefferson Co., Iowa. Series of meetings to commence immediately after feast.

Sept. 24, 25, 9 the south-east of Battle Creek, Ida Co., Iowa. Those coming by rail should come to Battle Creek and notify J. N. Isenhouwer.

Sept. 24, at 3 P. M., Cherokee church, Cherokee Co., Kans., at Leonard Wolf's, 4 miles south-west of Mc-Clure, Kans.

Sept. 24 and 25, at 2 P. M., in the Chapman Creek congregation, Kans., 3 miles north and 2 miles east of Abilene, Kans.

Sept. 24, at 4 P. M., Maple Grove church, 4 miles north of Ashland City, Ashland Co., Ohio.

Sept. 24 and 25, at 10 A. M., Soon River church, Stillson, Hancock Co., Iowa.

Sept. 24, at 2 P. M., Fredonia church, Wilson Co., Kans.

Sept. 24, 25, at 2 P. M., Clear Creek congregation, Huntington Co., Ind.

Sept. 24, at 3 P. M., Martin's Creek church, Wayne Co., Ill.

Sept. 24 and 25, 4 miles west of Tipton, Cedar Co., Iowa, beginning at 2 P. M. Ministers of Midd-e Iowa will please arrange to come to us from District Meeting at Garrison. Our meeting-house is at a distance of two miles from Buchanan on the B., C. R. & N. R. R.

Sept. 24, at 2 P. M., in La Porte church, La Porte, Ind. Trains will be met in the afternoon and early afternoon of the day of meeting.

Sept. 24 and 25, at 3 P. M., Lenark church, Carroll Co., Ill.

Sept. 24, at 5 P. M., Portage church, Douglas, Cass Co., Mich.

Sept. 27, at 3 P. M., at Wenger meeting-house, St. Joseph Co., Ind.

Sept. 28, South Bend church, Ind.

Sept. 28, at 10 A. M., Spring Creek church, Kosciusko Co., Ind.

Sept. 29 and 30, at 2 P. M., Rock Creek, Whiteside Co., Ill.

Sept. 29, at 10 A. M., Somerset church, at the Verne meeting-house, Wabash Co., Ind.

Sept. 30 and 24, at 10 A. M., Lower Fall Creek church, 3 miles south of Anderson. Those coming no train should address John Bernack, Anderson, Ind.

Sept. 30, at 2 P. M., blue Creek church, Adams Co., Ind.

Sept. 30, at 2 P. M., Walnut church, Montgomery Co., Ind., 4½ miles west of Clinton.

Sept. 30, at 10 A. M., Nettle Creek church, near Hagerstown, Wayne Co., Ind.

Sept. 30, at 10 A. M., Mississinewa church, Delaware Co., Ind. Those coming by rail at 3 off on Shideler.

Sept. 30, at 2 P. M., Mineloe church, Hon Co., Ill.

Oct. 1, at 2 P. M., Beaver Creek, Rockingham, Va.

Oct. 1 and 2, at 2 P. M., Hamilton congregation, at the house of D. C. Hershman, 3½ miles south-west of Hamilton. Any coming by rail on Hannibal & St. Joseph R. R., will be met at Hamilton by notifying D. C. Hershman.

Oct. 1 and 2, Kingman church, Kingman Co., Kans., 2½ miles east and one half mile north of Cleveland.

Oct. 1, at 4 P. M., at the Falls City church, Ohio.

Oct. 1, at 3 P. M., Berrien congregation, Mich.

Oct. 1 and 2, at 10 A. M., West Branch church, Ill. One week's meeting previous to feast.

Oct. 1 and 2, at 2 P. M., near Ames, Boone Co., Iowa. Moon trains meet at Ames on Saturday.

Oct. 1 and 2, in the Blue River Valley church, Butler Co., Nebr., at Bro. Jerry Keller's, ¼ mile west of Octavia.

Oct. 1, at 2 P. M., Osage church, Crawford Co., Kans.

Oct. 1, at 2 P. M., Logan church, near DeGraff, Ohio.

Oct. 1 and 2, Saginaw church, Mich.

Oct. 1 and 2, at 1:30 P. M., Walnut Valley congregation, Barton Co., Kans.

Oct. 1, Maple Grove church, Norton Co., Kans.

Oct. 1, at 10 A. M., Appanoose church, Kans.

Oct. 1, at 10 A. M., Eight Mile church, Ind., at the town of Norfolk.

Oct. 1 and 2, at 11 A. M., Riverside, Iowa. Those coming by rail will stop at Iowa Junction, on B. C. R. & N. R. R., where they will be met.

Oct. 1, at 10 A. M., Stone Lick church, Clermont Co., Ohio.

Oct. 1, at 2 P. M., Chippewa congregation, Wayne Co., Ohio.

Oct. 1, at 2 P. M., in the Verdigris church, at Bro. S. S. Redman's. A series of meetings will commence Sept. 25.

Oct. 1, Camp Creek church, Ill., at the church 7 miles south of Colchester. Those coming by train will please notify J. S. Hummer, and they will be met at the depot at Colchester, and conveyed to place of meeting.

Oct. 1, at 4 P. M., South Waterloo church, Waterloo, Iowa.

Oct. 1, at 11 A. M., Belleville church, Kans.

Oct. 2, at 10 P. M., Johnstown church, Pa., 2 miles north-east of Johnstown and 2 miles north of Mineral Point on the P. R. R.

Oct. 2, at 6:30 at 2 P. M., Yellow Creek, Ill.

Oct. 2 and 3, at 4 P. M., Rock River congregation, at Franklin Grove, Ill.

Oct. 2, at 10 A. M., Springfield church, Summit Co., Ohio.

Oct. 4, at 5:30 P. M., Sugar Ridge church, Ohio.

Oct. 6, at 10 A. M., in the Beaver Dam church, Kosciusko Co., Ind., near the town of Burket.

Oct. 5, at 10 A. M., Price's Creek church, Preble Co., Ohio.

Oct. 5, at 2 P. M., Rossom church, Ind.

Oct. 3 and 6, Dallas Center church. A series of meetings by Bro. Hutchison will commence Sept. 17.

Oct. 5, at 10 A. M., Santa Fe church, Ind., 6 miles south of Peru, 2 miles east of Bunker Hill and 1 mile south of Loree.

Oct. 5, at 10 A. M., Arcadia church, Ind.

Oct. 5, at 10 A. M., Prairie Creek church, Ind.

Oct. 6, at 10 A. M., Cedar County church, Cedar Co., Mo., 3 miles north-east of Jerico, at Bro. H. Tingley's.

Oct. 6, at 10 A. M., Wabash church, 7 miles south of Wabash Ind.

Oct. 6 and 7, at 10 A. M., Shannon, Ill.

Oct. 6, at 2 P. M., at Mt. Joy meeting-house, in Jacob's Creek congregation, Westmoreland Co., Pa. Series of meetings to commence Oct 1.

Oct. 6, at 10 A. M., Donnel's Creek church, Clarke Co., Ohio, seven miles from New Carlisle, and the same distance from Fergo and Springfield. Those coming from the West will stop either at New Carlisle or Fergy, where they will be met on the evening of the 5th. Those from the North-east or South should stop at Springfield.

Oct. 6, at 3 P. M., Spring Creek church, in the Keith's church-house, eleven miles south-west of Roens, Kans.

Oct. 7, Block River church, Van Buren Co., Mich. Brethren coming by rail will stop off at Bangor.

Oct. 7, at 1 P. M., Yellow Creek congregation, Bedford Co., Pa.

Oct. 7, at 10 A. M., Panther Creek church, Woodford Co., Ill.

Oct. 7, at 2 P. M., Ladoga, Ind.

Oct. 7, at 2 P. M., Kaskaskia church, Fayette Co., Ill., ten miles south-west of Brother City, Ill. Those coming by rail will be met at the above-named place by informing Granville Nevinger.

Oct. 7, at 10 A. M., Sugar Creek, Whitley Co., Ind.

Oct. 7, at 2 P. M., Downing's Creek congregation, Bedford Co., Pa.

Oct. 7, at 2 P. M., Raccoon Creek church, Montgomery Co., Ind., one and one half miles north-west of Ladoga.

Oct. 7, at 4 P. M., Marsoplin Creek church, Montgomery Co., Ind. Those coming by rail will be met at Farmersville, on Springfield Road, and at Girard, on St. Louis Road on morning of meeting.

Oct. 7 and 8, at 10:30 A. M., Four Mile church, Union Co., Ind.

Oct. 8, at 2 P. M., Lamotte church, Crawford Co. Ill.

Oct. 8, at 3:30 P. M., Maple Glen church, Somerset Co., Pa.

Oct. 8, at 4 P. M., in the Elkhorn Valley church, Elkhart Co., Ind.

Oct. 8, at 10 A. M., three-fourths of a mile west of Dupont, Ohio.

Oct. 8, at 2 P. M., Salina Valley church, at friend Ananias and sister Horting's, 2 mile east and one-half mile north of Tescott, Ottowa Co., Kans.

Oct. 8, at 2 P. M., Clover Creek church, Blair Co., Pa.

Oct. 8 and 9, State Center church, Iowa.

Oct. 8, at 10 A. M., Portage church, Wood Co., Ohio.

Oct. 8 and 9, at 11 P. M., Arnold's Grove, Ill.

Oct. 8, at 10 A. M., Dry Creek church, Linn Co., Iowa, one mile west of Robins Station.

Oct. 8, Snow Creek congregation, Ohio, 3½ miles west of Delta, Ohio.

Oct. 8, at 4 P. M., Washington Creek church, Douglas Co., Kans.

Oct. 8 and 9, at 10 A. M., Pine Creek congregation, in the town of Sawyer. Meeting to commence at 2 o'clock.

Oct. 8, at 10 A. M., Beer Creek church, Portland, Ind. Those coming by rail will be met by notifying M. P. Garber.

Oct. 8 and 9, at 10 A. M., Woodland church, Fulton Co., Ill. A series of meetings one week previous to the feast, and to continue two weeks.

Oct. 8, at 2 P. M., North Star, Darke County, Ohio.

Oct. 8, at 2 P. M., Greentown church, at Greentown, Howard Co., Ind.

Oct. 8, at 10 A. M., Crooked Creek church, Washington Co., Iowa.

Oct. 8, at 10 o'clock, Dorrance church, Kans.

Oct. 8 and 9, at 10 A. M., Bethel church, on North County line, Thayer Co., Nebr. Stations: Carleton, Davenport, Carlisle and Shickley.

Oct. 8 and 9, at 2 P. M., County Line church, Allen Co., Ohio.

Oct. 9, at 3 P. M., New Hope church, Cherokee Co., Kans., at A. B. Lichtenwalter's, ½ mile east of Neutral Station.

Oct. 8, Peabody, Kans.

Oct. 8, at 3:30 P. M., Covina church, Covina, Cal.

Oct. 8, at 11 A. M., Brooklyn church, Iowa.

Oct. 8, at 10 A. M., Rock Creek church, Kans. 3 miles north of Sabetha. Those coming by rail should notify S. Coder a week before coming, as arrangements can be made to take them to place of meeting.

Oct. 14, at 4 P. M., Union church, Marshal Co., Ind., five miles west of Plymouth. Trains will be met at both Plymouth and Burr Oak.

Oct. 14, at 10 A. M., South Keokuk church, Keokuk Co., Iowa. Those coming by rail will be met at Ollie, by notify by Isaac Shidler or Isaac Brown. Those coming from the West will arrive at Ollie about 11:30 A. M.; those from the East at 3 P. M.

Oct. 14, Union church, Plymouth, Marshall Co., Ind. This church would like to have some Brother hold meetings a week or two days after.

Oct. 15, at 10 A. M., Rome church, Oak Grove house. Also harvest-meeting at same place Aug. 17, at 10 A. M.

Oct. 15 and 16, at 10 A. M., Grundy church, ten miles west of Grundy Center, Grundy Co., Iowa.

Oct. 20, at 2 P. M., Middle Fork church, Clinton Co., Ind.

Oct. 21, at 10 A. M., Kittock church, Delaware Co., Ind., nine miles west of Muncie.

Oct. 22, at 4 P. M., Pleasant Grove church, Douglas Co., Kans.

Oct. 22, at 2 P. M., St. Joseph Valley church, Joseph Co., Ind., 3 miles north of South Bend.

Oct. 28, at 2 P. M., in the Pleasant Hill church, near Girard and Virden, Ill.

Oct. 28, at 2 P. M., South Beatrice church, Gage Co., Nebr. Those coming day before meeting at B. & M. depot, in Beatrice; Rock Island depot, in Rockford; Union Pacific depot, in Hollenville.

Oct. 28, at 2 P. M., Walnut church, Marshall Co., Ind.

Oct. 29, at 10 A. M., in the Buck Creek church, Henry Co., Ind.

Oct. 29, at 2 P. M., Salem church, 4 miles south-east of Salem.

Oct. 29, at 2 P. M., Mt.-Clion congregation, Page, Va.

Oct. 29, St. Vrain church, Longmont, Colo.

Oct. 29, at 2 P. M., Ozawkie church, Kans. A series of meetings to commence Oct. 20.

Oct. 29, at 2 P. M., Yellow Creek church, Ill., at the Oak Grove meeting-house.

Oct. 29, at 2 P. M., Oasis church, Madison Co., Ind., 3½ miles east of Summitville.

Oct. 29 and 30, at 10 A. M., Made church, Pa.

Nov. 4, Walnut Creek church, Mo.

Nov. 8, at 2 P. M., at the Kansas Center church, 3 miles east of Lyons, Rice Co., Kans. A series of meetings to commence a week previous.

Nov. 5, at 3 P. M., Big Creek church, Richland Co., Ill., 3½ miles North-east of Parkersburg, Ill. Conveyance will be at the above place by informing J. M. Forney.

Nov. 5 and 6, at 4 P. M., North Beatrice church, Gage Co., Nebr.

Nov. 22, at 3 P. M., Cedar Creek church, Anderson Co., Kans.

Announcements.

MINISTERIAL MEETINGS.

Oct. 4, in the Blue River Valley church, Butler Co., Nebr., at Bro. Jerry Keller's, ½ mile east of Octavia. Ministerial meeting day before. Trains due here from the East at 10:10 P. M., from the West at 2:16 P. M.

Nov. 15-16 9 A. M., In the South-east District of Kansas, Ministerial Meeting in the Cedar Creek church, Mont Ida, Anderson Co., Kans.

Nov. 1 and 2, Western District of Pennsylvania will hold their Ministerial Meeting at Walnut Grove, Johnstown church.

DISTRICT MEETINGS.

Sept. 12, Middle District of Iowa, in the Garrison church, Benton Co., Iowa.

Oct. 3, 10 9 A. M., District of Northern Iowa, Minnesota and South Dakota, in the South Waterloo church, Black Hawk Co., Iowa.

Oct. 4, at 8 A. M., Southern District of Illinois, in the Cool's Creek church, Fulton Co., Ill.

Oct. 7, 10 9 A. M., District Meeting In the Crooked Creek church, Washington Co., Iowa. Those coming by rail will be met at Keota, at 10 A. M. from the East, and at 6:04 P. M. from the West, by notifying D. P. Miller.

LOVE FEASTS.

Sept. 17, at 10 A. M., Black River, Medina Co., Ohio.

Sept. 21, 10 10 A. M., Garrison church, Benton Co., Iowa.

Sept. 24, at 4 P. M., Oakley church, Macon Co., Ill.

Sept. 24, at 2 P. M., Libertyville church, Jefferson Co., Iowa. Series of meetings to commence immediately after feast.

Sept. 20, 4½ miles south-east of Battle Creek, Ida Co., Iowa. Those coming by rail should come to Battle Creek and notify J. H. Isenbarger.

Sept. 24, at 3 P. M., Cherokee church, Cherokee Co., Kans., at Leonard Wolf's, 4 miles south-west of Mc Cune, Kans.

Sept. 24 and 25, at 2 P. M., in the Chapman Creek congregation, Kans., 9 miles north and 1 miles east of Abilene, Kans.

Sept. 24, 11 2 P. M., Maple Grove church, 1 miles north of Ashland City, Ashland Co., Iowa.

Sept. 24, at 10 A. M., Boon River church, Stilson, Hancock Co., Iowa.

Sept. 24, at 2 P. M., Fredonia church, Wilson Co., Kans.

Sept. 24, at 1 P. M., Clear Creek congregation, Huntington Co., Ind.

Sept. 24, at 3 P. M., Martin's Creek church, Wayne Co., Ind.

Sept. 24 and 25, 4 miles west of Tipton, Cedar Co., Iowa, beginning at 2 P. M. Ministers of Middle Iowa will please arrange to come to us from District Meeting at Garrison. Our meeting-house is at a distance of two miles from Buchanan on the B., C. R. & N. R. R.

Sept. 24, at 5 P. M., in La Porte church, La Porte, Ind. Trains will be met in the forenoon and early afternoon of the day of meeting.

Sept. 26 and 27, at 3 P. M., Lanark church, Carroll Co., Ill.

Sept. 24, at 5 P. M., Pokagon church, Dowagiac, Cass Co., Mich.

Sept. 27, at 5 P. M., at Wenger meeting-house, St. Joseph church, Ind.

Sept. 28, South Bend church, Ind.

Sept. 28, at 10 A. M., Spring Creek church, Kosciusko Co., Ind.

Sept. 29 and 30, at 2 P. M., Rock Creek, Whiteside Co., Ill.

Sept. 29, at 10 10 A. M., Somerset church, at the Vernon meeting-house, Wabash Co., Ind.

Sept. 29 and 30, at 10 A. M., Lower Fall Creek church, 8 miles south of Anderson. Those coming on train should address John Botaack, Anderson, Ind.

Sept. 30, at 2 P. M., Ulro Creek church, Adams Co., Ind.

Sept. 30, 10 2 P M., Wolfe church, Montgomery Co., Ind., 4¾ east miles of Colfax.

Sept. 30, at 10 A. M., Nettle Creek church, near Hagerstown, Wayne Co., Ind.

Sept. 30, at 10 A. M., Mississinewa church, Delaware Co., Ind. Those coming by rail 11 p of at Shideler.

Sept. 30, at 2 P. M., Milmine church, Piatt Co., Ill.

Oct. 1, at 2 P. M., Beaver Creek, Rockingham, Va.

Oct. 1 and 2, at 2 P. M., Hamilton congregation, at the house of D. C. Hardman, 2½ miles south-west of Hamilton, Any coming by rail on Hannibal & St. Joseph R. R., will be met at Hamilton by notifying D. C. Hardman.

Oct. 1 and 2, Kingman church, Kingman Co., Kans., 2½ miles west and one half mile north of Cleveland.

Oct. 1, at 4 P. M., at the Falls City church, Nebr.

Oct. 1 and 2, 11 10 30 A. M., Seneca church, Seneca Co., Ohio, 1½ miles north of Bloomville.

Oct. 1, at 2 P. M., Sugar Creek church, Allen Co., Ohio.

Oct. 1, at 5 P. M., Berrien congregation, Mich.

Oct. 1 and 2, at 10 A. M., West Branch church, Ill. One week's meeting previous to feast.

Oct. 1 and 2, at 2 P. M., near Ames, Boone Co., Iowa. Noon trains meet at Ames on Saturday.

Oct. 1, at 3 P. M., Turkey Creek congregation, Pawnee Co., Nebr. Those coming by rail will please give notice and they will be met at Dubois.

Oct. 1 and 2, in the Blue River Valley church, Butler Co., Nebr., at Bro. Jerry Keller's, ½ mile west of Octavia.

Oct. 1, at 4 P. M., Coquaga church, Crawford Co., Kans.

Oct. 1, at 4 P. M., Logan church, near DeGraff, Ohio.

Oct. 1 and 2, Saginaw church, Mich.

Oct. 1 and 2, at 11 30 P. M., Walnut Valley congregation, Barton Co., Kans.

Oct. 1 and 2, at 2 P. M., Allegheny congregation, Grant Co., W. Va.

Oct. 1, Maple Grove church, Norton Co., Kans.

Oct. 1, at 10 A. M., Appanoose church, Kans.

Oct. 1, at 10 A. M., Eight Mile church, Ind., at the town of Markle.

Oct. 1 and 2, at 11 A. M., Walnut church, Ind. Those coming by rail will stop at Iowa Junction, on B. C. R. & N. R. R., where they will be met.

Oct. 1, at 10 A. M., Stone Lick church, Clermont Co., Ohio.

Oct. 1, at 10 A. M., Chippewa congregation, Wayne Co., Ohio.

Oct 1, at 2 P. M., in the Verdigris church, at Bro. S. S. Redman's. A series of meetings will commence Sept. 25.

Oct. 1, Camp Creek church, Ind., at the church 7 miles south of Colchester. Those coming by train will please notify S. S. Hummer, and they will be met at the depot at Colchester, and conveyed to place of meeting.

Oct. 1, at 1 P. M., South Waterloo church, Waterloo, Iowa.

Oct. 1, at 10 A. M., Belleville church, Kans.

Oct. 1, at 2 P. M., Johnstown church, Pa., 3 miles north-east of Johnstown and 2 miles north of Mineral Point on the P. R. R.

Oct. 1 and 2, at 1 P. M., Yellow Creek, Ill.

Oct. 2, at 10 A. M., Rock River congregation, at Franklin Grove, Ill.

Oct. 2, at 10 A. M., Springfield church, Summit Co., Ohio.

Oct. 2, at 2 30 P. M., Sugar Ridge church, Ohio.

Oct. 2, at 10 A. M., in the Beaver Dam church, Kosciusko Co., Ind., near the town of Bucket.

Oct. 2, at 10 A. M., Price's Creek church, Preble Co., Ohio.

Oct. 2, at 2 P. M., Rossen church, Ind.

Oct. 3 and 6, Dallas Center church. A series of meetings by Bro. Hutchison will commence Sept. 17.

Oct. 3, at 2 P. M., Santa Fe church, Ind., 6 miles south of Peru, 2 miles east of Bunker Hill and 1 mile north of Loree.

Oct. 6, at 2 P. M., Arcadia church, Ind.

Oct. 6, at 10 A. M., Prairie Creek church, Ind.

Oct. 6, at 10 A. M., Cedar County church, Cedar Co., Iowa, 3 miles north-west of Jerico, at Bro. H. Tingley's.

Oct. 6, at 10 A. M., Wabash church, 7 miles south of Wabash Ind.

Oct. 6 and 7, at 10 A. M., Shannon, Ill.

Oct. 6, at 3 P. M., at Mt. Joy meeting-house; in Jacob's Creek congregation, Westmoreland Co., Pa. Series of meetings to commence Oct. 1.

Oct. 6, at 10 A. M., Donnel's Creek church, Clarke Co., Ohio, seven miles from New Carlisle, and the same distance from Forgy and Springfield. Those coming from the West will stop either at New Carlisle or Forgy, where they will be met on the evening of the 5th. Those from the North-east or South should stop at Springfield.

Oct. 6, at 2 P. M., Spring Creek church, in the Keith's church-house, eleven miles south-east of Reece, Kans.

Oct. 7, Black River church, Van Buren Co., Mich. Brethren coming by rail will stop off at Bangor.

Oct. 7, at 2 P. M., Yellow Creek congregation, Bedford Co., Pa.

Oct. 7, at 10 A. M., Panther Creek church, Woodford Co. Ill.

Oct. 7, at 2 P. M., Ladoga, Ind.

Oct. 7, at 2 P. M., Raukavuia church, Fayette Co., Ill., ten miles south-west of Beecher City, Ill. Those coming by rail will be met at the above-named place by informing Granville Nevinger.

Oct. 7, at 10 A. M., Sugar Creek, Whitley Co., Ind.

Oct. 7, at 1 P. M., Dunning's Creek congregation, Bedford Co., Pa.

Oct. 7, at 2 P. M., Raccoon Creek church, Montgomery Co., Ind., one and one half miles north west of Ladoga.

Oct. 7, at 4 P. M., Mo-quin Creek church, Montgomery Co., Ill. Those coming by rail will be met at Farmersville, on Springfield Road, and at Girard, on St. Louis Road on morning of meeting.

Oct. 7 and 8, at 10 30 A. M., Poor Aile church, Union Co., Ind.

Oct. 8, at 2 P. M., Lamotte church, Crawford Co. Ill.

Oct. 8, at 3 30 P. M., Maple Glen church, Somerset Co., Pa.

Oct. 8, at 2 P. M., in the Elkhart Valley church, Elkhart Co., Ind.

Oct. 8, at 10 A. M., three-fourths of a mile west of Dupont, Ohio.

Oct. 8, at 1 P. M., Saline Valley church, at friend Arnald-sias and sister Herring's, 2 miles east and one-half mile north of Tescott, Ottawa Co., Kans.

Oct. 8, at 4 P. M., Clover Creek church, Blair Co., Pa.

Oct. 8 and 9, State Center church, Iowa.

Oct. 8, at 10 A. M., Portage church, Wood Co., Ohio.

Oct. 8 and 9, at 1 P. M., Arnold's Grove, Ill.

Oct. 8, at 10 A. M., Dry Creek church, Linn Co., Iowa, one mile west of Robins Station.

Oct. 8, Swan Creek congregation, Ohio, 3¾ miles west of Delta, Fulton Co.

Oct. 8, at 4 P. M., Washington Creek church, Douglas Co., Kans.

Oct. 8 and 9, at 10 A. M., Pine Creek congregation, Ill., in the town of Sawyer. Meeting to commence at 2 o'clock.

Oct. 8, at 10 A. M., Bear Creek church, Portland, Ind. Those coming by rail will be met by notifying B. P. Gerber

Oct. 8, at 10 A. M., Woodland church, Fulton Co., Ill. A series of meetings one week previous to the feast, and to continue two weeks.

Oct. 8, at 2 P. M., North Star, Darke County, Ohio.

Oct. 8, at 2 P. M., Greentown church, at Greentown, Howard Co., Ind.

Oct. 8, at 11 A. M., Crooked Creek church, Washington Co., Iowa.

Oct. 8, at 10 o'clock, Dorrance church, Kans.

Oct. 8, at 4 P. M., Bethel church, on North County line, Thayer Co., Nebr. Stations: Carleton, Davenport, Carlisle and Shickley.

Oct. 8, at 6 P. M., County Line church, Allen Co., Ohio.

Oct. 8, at 2 P. M., Maple church, Cherokee Co., Ill., 2 miles north of Neosho.

Oct. 8, at 2 P. M., Brooklyn church, Iowa.

Oct. 8, at 10 A. M., Rock Creek church, Kans., 3 miles north of Sabetha. Those coming by rail should notify E. Usher a week before coming, so arrangements can be made to take them to place of meeting.

Oct. 14, at 4 P. M., Union church, Marshall Co., Ind., five miles west of Plymouth. Trains will be met at both Plymouth and Burr Oak.

Oct. 14 and 15, at 11 A. M., South Keokuk church, Keokuk Co., Iowa. Those coming by rail to the post at Ollie, by notify-ing Samuel Shirky or Basil Bogue. Those coming from the West will arrive at Ollie about 12:30 A. M.; those from the East at 8 P. M.

Oct. 12, Union church, Plymouth, Marshall Co., Ind. This church would like to have some brother hold meetings a week or ten days after.

Oct. 15, at 10 A. M., Rome church, Oak Grove house. Also harvest-meeting at same place Aug. 13, at 10 A. M.

Oct. 15 and 16, at 10 A. M., Grundy church, ten miles west of Grundy Centre, Grundy Co., Iowa.

Oct. 22, at 2 P. M., Middle Fork church, Clinton Co., Ind.

Oct. 22, at 10 A. M., Killbuck church, Delaware Co., Ind., nine miles west of Muncie.

Oct. 22, at 4 P. M., Pleasant Grove church, Douglas Co., Kans.

Oct. 28, at 5 P. M., St. Joseph Valley church, St. Joseph Co., Ind., 3 miles north of South Bend.

Oct. 28, at 10 A. M., in the Pleasant Hill church, near Girard and Virden, Ill.

Oct. 28, at 2 P. M., South Beatrice church, Gage Co., Nebr. Conveyances the day before meeting at R. M. depot, in Beatrice; Rock Island depot, to Rockford; Union Pacific depot, to Holmesville.

Oct. 28, at 4 P. M., Walnut church, Marshall Co., Iowa.

Oct. 28, at 10 A. M., in the Buck Creek church, Henry Co., Ind.

Oct. 29, at 1 P. M., Salem church, a mile south-east of Salem.

Oct. 29, at 2 P. M., Mt.-Zion congregation, Page, Va.

Oct. 29, St. Vrain church, Longmont, Colo.

Oct. 29, at 2 P. M., Ozawkie church, Kans. A series of meetings to commence Oct. 22.

Oct. 29 and 30, at 10 A. M., Pigeon Creek church, Ill., at the Oak Grove meeting-house.

Oct. 29 and 30, at 10 A. M., Osals church, Madison Co., Ind., 1½ miles east of Summitville.

Oct. 29 and 30, at 10 A. M., Hade church, Pa.

Nov. 2, Walnut Grove church, Mo.

Nov. 5, at 2 P. M., at the Kansas Center church, 7 miles east of Lyons, Rice Co., Kans. A series of meetings to commence a week previous.

Nov. 5, at 2 P. M., Big Creek church, Richland Co., Ill., 3½ miles North-east of Parkersburg, Ill. Conveyances will be at the above place by informing J. M. Forney.

Nov. 5 and 6, at 4 P. M., North Beatrice church, Gage Co., Nebr.

Nov. 24, at 3 P. M., Cedar Creek church, Anderson Co., Kans.

ESSAYS

"Study to show thyself approved unto God ; a workman that needeth not be ashamed, rightly dividing the Word of Truth."

MARY AT THE CROSS.

Stood the Virgin Mother weeping
Near the cross, sad vigils keeping
O'er her Son there crucified;
Through her soul in sorrow moaning,
Racked with grief, with anguish groaning,
Pierced the sword as prophesied.

Ah! how doleful and dejected
Was that woman, the elected
Mother of the Holy One;
Who, with weeping and with grieving,
Stood there trembling, while perceiving
How they smote her peerless Son.

Who could see without emotion,
Christ's dear mother, all devotion,
Crushed beneath such misery?
Could one see her desolation,
Would he hush her lamentation
For her Son in agony?

For his wicked nation pleading,
She saw Jesus scourged, and bleeding
'Neath the smitings of the rod;
Saw her Son's meek resignation,
As he died in desolation,
Yielding up his soul to God.

Mother, fount of love's deep yearning,
I, thy weight of woe discerning,
Partner in thy tears would be;
May my heart with ardor glowing,
And with love to Christ outflowing,
Sympathize with him and thee.

Hear, pure mother, this petition—
Print the wounds of crucifixion
Deeply on my inmost heart.
With thy Son, the wounded, bleeding,
For me stooping, interceding,
Let me feel the scourge and smart.

Let me join thy lamentation,
Share thy sweet commiseration,
And through life a mourner be;
Near the cross, with thee abiding,
I would stand, with thee dividing
All the woes afflicting thee.

Virgin, virgins all excelling,
Make my heart, like thine, love's dwelling,
Let thy tortures rend my soul;
Let me share Christ's crucifying,
Let me feel his pangs of dying,
Let his sorrows o'er me roll.

May I suffer all his bruising;
Quaff the crimson liquid oozing
From the wounds of that dear Son.
Rapt with fervor and affection,
Grant me, Virgin, thy protection
When the Judgment is begun.

Let me by the cross be guarded;
By Christ's death from danger warded;
By his grace through life supplied.
Death the ties of earth may sever;
I shall live in Christ forever,
One of Eden's glorified.

—*Selected.*

THE ANCIENT THEN AND THE MODERN NOW.

Those who are lamenting so much over sin in high places, and troubling themselves so greatly because of the general lack of spirituality in the churches of the present, may possibly gather some comfort from the following comparison, which a writer in the *New Christian Quarterly* sees proper to make between the condition of the world in the time of Paul and the present generation. While we may not be able to say so much in behalf of the church, it is certainly evident that the world, as a whole, has greatly improved. The writer says:

"Mark again the Pagan system of morals. A religion, whose gods were monsters of depravity, could not be expected to promote morality among its adherents. Grossest vices received homage in

the Olympian divinities. Priests and worshipers sought to imitate the crimes supposed to have been committed by Jupiter, Bacchus, Venus or Mars. Shrines and temples were the scenes of every impurity, and the vilest iniquities were practiced as rites of religion. There was no call to virtue; no voice in behalf of morals. If the high places of religion were so foul, the theatre and the arena presented even a more horrible pollution. Here hundreds of thousands looked daily upon scenes of lust or of blood. Rome sat in her Circus Maximus and saw men, women and children torn by wild beasts, or savage gladiators destroy each other by thousands, without mercy. Trajan celebrated his Dacian victories with the butchery of 11,000 beasts, and on one occasion had 10,000 slaves engaged in mortal combat, and prolonged the spectacle 123 days. Under Nero even senators and well-born women appeared as combatants. These sanguinary contests were held all over the empire, and were witnessed by both sexes and all grades of society. Emperors studied the faces of the dying and watched with artistic delight the varying phases of agony, and hardly one of the Roman moralists raised his voice against the evil.

"If the public morals of the most civilized peoples were so depraved, what must have been the corruption of private life? What fearful facts are revealed to us of the debaucheries, obscenities and adulteries in the best circles of Rome! Drunkenness and gluttony, with its revolting practice even among Emperors and Roman matrons of disgorging food by artificial means to excite anew the appetite; destruction of weak and ill-formed children; and what was most hopeless of all, men like Cato, Sallust, Plato and Aristotle sanctioning these crimes! Turn from this to the incomparable morals taught by Christ, the matchless Exemplar, who alone of all beings could say of himself, 'Which of you shall convict me of sin?' Consider his sublime teaching, such as never man taught, illustrated in 'three short years of active life which has done more to regenerate and soften mankind than all the disquisitions of philosophers and all the exhortations of moralists!' Consider the beautiful code of morals, suited to all times and circumstances, classes and conditions, by highest motives of love bringing tens of thousands out of this state of vice and degradation through moral discipline to the practice of celestial virtues—the uplifting force of this age, yea, of all ages!

"Note again the position of slaves and women and children under the appalling conditions of Paganism. The slave was less cared for than the cattle of his master. The old Roman law condemned to death the man who killed a plowing ox, but the murderer of a slave went free. Crassus crucified 10,000 slaves at once. Augustus delivered 30,000 at one time for execution. Vedius Pollio fed his slaves to the lampreys in his fishponds. The condition of woman was little better than that of the slave. She was never the equal of man. She was bought like meat in the shambles. She had to share with other wives her husband. Marriage was merely a temporary connection, and the morality of married life was unknown. Impure love was honored by temples and gods, and woman was the chattel or the sport of man. Hesiod calls woman 'an accursed brood and the chief scourge of the human race,' while Socrates daily thanked the gods that he was born neither a slave nor a woman. Cicero rejected his wife that he might get the dowry of another, and Cato gave one of his wives as a present to a friend. Juvenal tells of a woman who had eight husbands in five years, and we are told of another woman who married her twenty-third husband, she being his twenty-first wife. As to children under the

heathen systems, infanticide was universal. The parent had entire discretion to preserve or destroy his offspring. They were drowned, suffered to die of cold or hunger, exposed to beasts or birds of prey, or cruelly choked to death in the cradle. What a contrast does Christianity present here. Slavery has been abolished to the ends of the earth! Save among a few tribes of savages in Central Africa, no man to-day is in bondage. The great truth uttered by Paul that God made of one blood all the nations of the earth, and, therefore that all men are brothers, was the ax laid at the root of this tree. Woman is no longer the inferior of man. On equal terms, in life-long union, to be sundered by but one crime, the man and the woman come together. Few names come down to us in all the splendid histories of Greece and Rome of women who gave luster to those pages. How incalculable is the multitude of those that under Christ have become illustrious! What a mighty revolution has been wrought by that Gospel which proclaims: 'Ye are all the children of God by faith which is in Christ Jesus; there is neither Jew nor Greek, slave nor freeman, male nor female, but ye are all one in Christ Jesus!' What dignity and sanctity have been given to marriage! What protection and purity to the home! What ennoblement and exaltation and high usefulness to mothers and wives and daughters that fear the Lord! Little children come into a new world under the Gospel. Rights of infancy are protected by highest sanctions of law. The Son of God commands those that rebuke them, 'Suffer little children to come unto me, and forbid them not,' and the highest expression of the new faith is declared illustrated in the spirit of a little child."

THE GOSPEL TRUMPET'S "THREE POINTS" EXAMINED.

BY CHAS. M. YEAROUT.

In Three Parts—Part One.

The editor of the *Gospel Trumpet*, in numbers 10 and 12, issues of March 8 and 17, 1892, pages 1 and 4, writes an article under the heading, "Three Points," viz, (1) "Trine Immersion," (2) "A Meal Called the Supper," (3) "Women's Head-covering."

The above papers were sent to me with a request that I reply to said article. I wrote a reply and sent an article on one point to the *Trumpet*, and asked the editor to give us a hearing. Inasmuch as he had attacked us without provocation, we demanded a hearing before his readers, but it seems he was afraid to let the true Gospel light shine in the *Trumpet*. My article was not published, nor was it returned, as I requested, if not published. By permission of the editors I will now reply through the MESSENGER. The *Trumpet* says:

"First, then, let us candidly appeal to the New Testament Scriptures, and to history, to find the origin of the practice of administering three dips in baptism. Matt. 28; 19, we may truthfully say, is the only passage in the Bible that can be adduced as anything like proof of the practice: 'Go ye, therefore, and teach all nations, baptizing them in the name of the Father, and of the Son, and of the Holy Ghost.' We admit that the text would very naturally furnish evidence that trine immersion was of divine origin, but it is equally true that it is perfectly capable of being otherwise interpreted, and there being no other text, and no symbolic elements that require its triune interpretation, the symbolism in the ordinance, and other facts, both Scriptural and historical, all preponderate in a single action."

I am glad that the *Trumpet* editor admits trine immersion is authorized by the Savior's own language, and I assert that the commission, when

✦ESSAYS✦

"Study to show thyself approved unto God ; a workman that needeth not be ashamed, rightly dividing the Word of Truth."

MARY AT THE CROSS.

Stood the Virgin Mother weeping
Near the cross, and vigils keeping
O'er her Son there crucified;
Through her soul in sorrow moaning,
Racked with grief, with anguish groaning,
Pierced the sword as prophesied.

Ah! how doleful and dejected
Was that woman, the elected
Mother of the Holy One;
Who, with weeping and with grieving,
Stood there trembling, while perceiving
How they smote her peerless Son.

Who could see without emotion,
Christ's dear mother, all devotion,
Crushed beneath such misery?
Could one see her desolation,
Would he hush her lamentation
For her Son in agony?

For his wicked nation pleading,
She saw Jesus scourged, and bleeding
'Neath the smitings of the rod;
Saw her Son's meek resignation,
As he died in desolation,
Yielding up his soul to God.

Mother, fount of love's deep yearning,
I, thy weight of woe discerning,
Partner in thy tears would be;
May my heart with ardor glowing,
And with love to Christ outflowing,
Sympathize with him and thee.

Hear, pure mother, this petition—
Print the wounds of crucifixion
Deeply on my inmost heart.
With thy Son, the wounded, bleeding,
For me stooping, interceding,
Let me feel the scourge and smart.

Let me join thy lamentation,
Share thy sweet commiseration,
And through life a mourner be;
Near the cross, with thee abiding,
I would stand, with thee dividing
All the woe afflicting thee.

Virgin, virgins all excelling,
Make my heart, like thine, love's dwelling,
Let thy tortures rend my soul;
Let me share Christ's crucifying,
Let me feel his pangs of dying,
Let his sorrows o'er me roll.

Mdy I suffer all his bruising;
Quaff the crimson liquid oozing
From the wounds of that dear Son.
Rapt with fervor and affection,
Grant me, Virgin, thy protection
When the Judgment is begun.

Let me by the cross be guarded;
By Christ's death from danger warded;
By his grace through life supplied.
Death the ties of earth may sever;
I shall live in Christ forever,
One of Eden's glorified.

                                  —Selected.

THE ANCIENT THEN AND THE MODERN NOW.

THOSE who are lamenting so much over sin in high places, and troubling themselves so greatly because of the general lack of spirituality in the churches of the present, may possibly gather some comfort from the following comparison, which a writer in the New Christian Quarterly sees proper to make between the condition of the world in the time of Paul and the present generation. While we may not be able to say so much in behalf of the church, it is certainly evident that the world, as a whole, has greatly improved. The writer says:

"Mark again the Pagan system of morals. A religion, whose gods were monsters of depravity, could not be expected to promote morality among its adherents. Grossest vices received homage in

the Olympian divinities. Priests and worshipers sought to imitate the crimes supposed to have been committed by Jupiter, Bacchus, Venus or Mars. Shrines and temples were the scenes of every impurity, and the vilest iniquities were practiced as rites of religion. There was no call to virtue; no voice in behalf of morals. If the high places of religion were so foul, the theatre and the arena presented even a more horrible pollution. Here hundreds of thousands looked daily upon scenes of lust or of blood. Rome sat in her Circus Maximus and saw men, women and children torn by wild beasts, or savage gladiators destroy each other by thousands, without mercy. Trajan celebrated his Dacian victories with the butchery of 11,000 beasts, and on one occasion had 10,000 slaves engaged in mortal combat, and prolonged the spectacle 123 days. Under Nero even senators and well-born women appeared as combatants. These sanguinary contests were held all over the empire, and were witnessed by both sexes and all grades of society. Emperors studied the faces of the dying and watched with artistic delight the varying phases of agony, and hardly one of the Roman moralists raised his voice against the evil.

"If the public morals of the most civilized peoples were so depraved, what must have been the corruption of private life? What fearful facts are revealed to us of the debaucheries, obscenities and adulteries in the best circles of Rome! Drunkenness and gluttony, with its revolting practice even among Emperors and Roman matrons of disgorging food by artificial means to excite anew the appetite; destruction of weak and ill-formed children; and what was most hopeless of all, men like Cato, Sallust, Plato and Aristotle sanctioning these crimes! Turn from this to the incomparable morals taught by Christ, the matchless Exemplar, who alone of all beings could say of himself. "Which of you shall convict me of sin?" Consider his sublime teaching, such as never man taught, illustrated in 'three short years of active life which has done more to regenerate and soften mankind than all the disquisitions of philosophers and all the exhortations of moralists!' Consider the beautiful code of morals, suited to all times and circumstances, classes and conditions, by highest motives of love bringing tens of thousands out of this state of vice and degradation through moral discipline to the practice of celestial virtues'—the uplifting force of this age, yes, of all ages!

"Note again the position of slaves and women and children under the appalling conditions of Paganism. The slave was less cared for than the cattle of his master. The old Roman law condemned to death the man who killed a plowing ox, but the murderer of a slave went free. Crassus crucified 10,000 slaves at once. Augustus delivered 30,000 at one time for execution. Vedius Pollio fed his slaves to the lampreys in his fishponds. The condition of woman was little better than that of the slave. She was never the equal of man. She was bought like meat in the shambles. She had to share with other wives her husband. Marriage was merely a temporary connection, and the morality of married life was unknown. Impure love was honored by temples and gods, and woman was the chattel or the sport of man. Hesiod calls woman 'an accursed brood and the chief scourge of the human race,' while Socrates daily thanked the gods that he was born neither a slave nor a woman. Cicero rejected his wife that he might get the dowry of another, and Cato gave one of his wives as a present to a friend. Juvenal tells of a woman who had eight husbands in five years, and we are told of another woman who married her twenty-third husband, she being his twenty-first wife. As to children under the

heathen systems, infanticide was universal. The parent had entire discretion to preserve or destroy his offspring. They were drowned, suffered to die of cold or hunger, exposed to beasts or birds of prey, or cruelly choked to death in the cradle. What a contrast does Christianity present here. Slavery has been abolished to the ends of the earth! Save among a few tribes of savages in Central Africa, no man to-day is in bondage. The great truth uttered by Paul that God made of one blood all the nations of the earth, and, therefore that all men are brothers, was the ax laid at the root of this tree. Woman is no longer the inferior of man. On equal terms, in life-long union, to be sundered by but one crime, the man and the woman come together. Few names come down to us in all the splendid histories of Greece and Rome of women who gave luster to those pages. How incalculable is the multitude of those that under Christ have become illustrious! What a mighty revolution has been wrought by that Gospel which proclaims: 'Ye are all the children of God by faith which is in Christ Jesus; there is neither Jew nor Greek, slave nor freeman, male nor female, but ye are all one in Christ Jesus!' What dignity and sanctity have been given to marriage! What protection and purity to the home! What ennoblement and exaltation and high usefulness to mothers and wives and daughters that fear the Lord! Little children come into a new world under the Gospel. Rights of infancy are protected by highest sanctions of law. The Son of God commands those that rebuke them, 'Suffer little children to come unto me, and forbid them not,' and the highest expression of the new faith is declared illustrated in the spirit of a little child."

THE GOSPEL TRUMPET'S "THREE POINTS" EXAMINED.

BY CHAS. M. YEAROUT.

In Three Parts.—Part One.

THE editor of the Gospel Trumpet, in numbers 10 and 12, issues of March 3 and 17, 1892, pages 1 and 4, writes an article under the heading, "Three Points," viz, (1) "Trine Immersion," (2) "A Meal Called the Supper," (3) "Women's Head-covering."

The above papers were sent to me with a request that I reply to said article. I wrote a reply and sent an article on one point to the Trumpet, and asked the editor to give us a hearing. Inasmuch as he had attacked us without provocation, we demanded a hearing before his readers, but it seems he was afraid to let the true Gospel light shine in the Trumpet. My article was not published, nor was it returned, as I requested, if not published. By permission of the editors I will now reply through the MESSENGER. The Trumpet says:

"First, then, let us candidly appeal to the New Testament Scriptures, and to history, to find the origin of the practice of administering three dips in baptism. Matt. 28: 19, we may truthfully say, is the only passage in the Bible that can be adduced as anything like proof of the practice: 'Go ye, therefore, and teach all nations, baptizing them in the name of the Father, and of the Son, and of the Holy Ghost.' We admit that the text would very naturally furnish evidence that trine immersion was of divine origin, but it is equally true that it is perfectly capable of being otherwise interpreted, and there being no other text, and no symbolic elements that require its trinne interpretation, the symbolism in the ordinance, and other facts, both Scriptural and historical, all preponderate in a single notion."

I am glad that the Trumpet editor admits trine immersion is authorised by the Savior's own language, and I assert that the commission, when

ing that they should immerse into the Father, and the Son, and the Holy Spirit, not into one name, for we are immersed for each name, into each person, not once, but thrice." ("Tertullian's Works," p. 659.)

Chrysostom says: "Christ delivered to his apostles 'one baptism' in three immersions of the body, when he said to them, 'Go teach all nations, baptizing them in the name of the Father, and of the Son, and of the Holy Spirit.'" ("Antiquities of the Christian Church," I, p. 540.)

Jerome, in commenting on Eph. 4: 5, says: "We are thrice dipped in water that the mystery of the Trinity may appear to be but one, and therefore, though we be thrice put under the water to represent the mystery of the Trinity, yet it is reputed but one baptism." ("Chrystal's History of the Modes of Baptism," pp. 72, 73.)

"Monulus informs us that trine immersion had always been with the church, and makes it just as old as the command to preach the Gospel." "The doctrine of our holy mother, the Catholic church, has always, my brethren, been with us, and doth still abide with us, and especially the article of baptism, and the trine immersion wherewith it is celebrated, our Lord having said, "Go ye, and baptize the Gentiles in the name of the Father, and of the Son, and of the Holy Spirit." (Works of Cyprian, I, p. 240.) "Catholic Church" here has reference to the general church, and not Roman Catholics. Monulus wrote about the year A. D. 256.

Clement, of Alexandria, was born about A. D. 150, and, in addressing the Christian church of his age, says: "Ye were conducted to a bath just as Christ was carried to the grave; and were thrice immersed." ("Wiberg on Baptism," p. 228. I quote the above facts from "Stein and Ray Debate.")

Justin Martyr wrote "An Apology for Christians." In this work he describes the doctrines and ordinances of the church of Christ; and on baptism has the following passage: "Then we bring them to some place where there is water, and they are baptized by the same way of baptism by which we were baptized; for they are washed in the water in the name of God the Father, Lord of all things; and of our Savior Jesus Christ, and of the Holy Spirit." ("Pengilly on Baptism," p. 150.)

From "Trine Immersion Traced to the Apostles," we have the following: "Justin Martyr was born A. D. 100; the same year that the apostle John died. Every ancient historian attributes trine immersion to the great commission given by Christ in Matt. 28: 19, and the Greeks in whose language the New Testament was first written, practice trine immersion to this day. The Western, or Latin church, practiced trine immersion until the council of Toledo, A. D. 633, when it was voted that only one immersion should be used in baptism, because the Arians practiced trine immersion."

My friend cannot find, in history or practice, where single backward immersion was practiced till nearly fifteen hundred years after Christ, hence fifteen hundred years too late for Christian baptism. It is an innovation brought into the church by those that were insubordinate to Christ and his heavenly teachings. Trine immersion is recognized the world over as Christian baptism. "Go ye therefore, and teach all nations, baptizing them into the name of the Father, and of the Son, and of the Holy Spirit."

"Good words do more than hard speeches; as the sunbeam, without any noise, made the traveler cast off his cloak, which all the blustering wind could not do, but only make him bind it closer to him."

OUR PRESENT AND FUTURE REST.

BY J. J. EMMERT.

" Come unto me all ye that labor and are heavy laden, and I will give you rest. Take my yoke upon you, and learn of me; for I am meek and lowly in heart; and ye shall find rest unto your souls."—Matt. 11: 28, 29.

In our Savior's words, as above quoted, we notice that he speaks of rest twice, or, as we might say, a first and a second rest. He then proceeds to show to whom those rests are accessible, and also upon what condition. Some maintain that the rest first spoken of is received by the sinner when he fully resolves to leave his sins, and, by sincere repentance toward God and faith in Christ, turns his face Zionward. They claim that he will then experience a change of heart, hence receives the rest spoken of.

This I consider unsafe, and, to a certain degree, misleading, for it savors, to some extent, of the popular and unscriptural view held by many. They maintain that, if the sinner feels the assurance within that he is accepted of God and that his sins are pardoned, baptism will be to him, not a means of pardon, but only an initiatory rite into the church visible.

I wish to find a location for the first rest spoken of, that is perfectly safe to rely upon, and in every respect tenable.

The Savior extends the invitation to such as labor and are heavy laden, which means such as feel the heavy load and weight of sin. Thus struggling under the load with a guilty conscience, the sinner becomes penitent, turns to God, and desires to be relieved of his load of sin. Jesus then says to him, "Come to me and I will give you rest." He can come only in the way the Lord has arranged for him, and that way was plainly stated by the apostle Peter on the day of Pentecost. He told how pardon can be obtained and the burden removed, by telling us, "Repent ye, therefore, and be baptized, every one of you in the name of Jesus Christ, for the remission of sins, and ye shall receive the gift of the Holy Ghost." Acts 2: 38.

The Lord always blesses in the act of obedience, but while the penitent remains unbaptized, he continues in disobedience, hence has no promise. But if he now follows Christ in the observance of baptism, as he has followed him in faith and repentance, he has the assurance that his sins are all forgiven; hence it is now only that he obtains a present rest.

Do we not all remember the happy day when we arose from the baptismal grave, with a consciousness of having followed Jesus in obedience, and, oh, how rested we felt!

In the Hebrews leaving Egypt, we have many beautiful types of our Christian journey. I will refer to but one, 1 Cor. 10: 1, 2. "Brethren, I would not that ye should be ignorant, how that all our fathers were under the cloud, and all passed through the sea; and were all baptized unto Moses in the cloud and in the sea." In the above we are told of the deliverance of Israel from their enemies, and it was not until they saw them destroyed that they had actual rest. So it is with the sinner. How he can rejoice when he knows that his sins are all pardoned!

We refer yet to the prodigal son, Luke 15. When he resolved to come home to the father's house, the father met him in the way as he was coming, fell on his neck and kissed him. He was clothed with rags, no shoes on his feet, and utterly destitute, just like the returning, penitent sinner, clothed with sin and undone. He wants to be saved, his father knows his good intentions when afar off, and welcomes him, but he has no rest until his old, filthy rags of sin are removed,

by obedience to Christ in baptism. He is received into the home circle, the church of Christ, and clothed with the new robe of righteousness. He now enjoys a present rest, having the assurance that he is the child of God.

The rest to the soul, or second rest spoken of, is a blessed, everlasting rest, that the faithful followers of Christ shall enjoy when the toils of life are over. But to obtain this rest we must take his yoke upon us, and learn of him. We must be meek and self-sacrificing, following him in filial love, in all the ordinances and commandments, in order to insure the blessedness of the promised everlasting rest to the soul.

Mt. Carroll, Ill.

LOVE—WHAT IT IS, AND WHAT IT DOES.

BY P. BRAXTON FITZWATER.

Love is the affection, existing between the sexes, parents, children, and friends. It is the connecting link of the universe. It unites the moral and spiritual universe, and binds it to the throne of God. It is the vital force or attraction, which unites or binds the "all" and "in all." It is the root of creation, the essence of God, the rudimental elements of the soul. It is, therefore, a divine gift,—a blessing which the Creator did not withdraw from his erring children, when they were driven from Paradise into a world of desolation and strife. He left it as an inseparable cord, by which to draw the human heart ever upward to a brighter home,—a heavenly Eden. Love is the very essence of Divine Law. To its presence we are indebted for all that is good and true in art and nature. It endows humanity with countless virtues, and throws a mystic veil over our many faults. Literature owes to love its choicest gems. Without that, it would be as a floating mass of immaterial substance.

It is true, love has been degraded to some extent, but true love never seeks to degrade its object. On the contrary, it magnifies every virtue, endows it with the divinest attributes, and guards its chastity or honor at the sacrifice of its own life. It heightens spirituality, awakens hope, strengthens faith, and enhances devotion. It quickens the perceptions, intensifies the sensibilities, and redoubles the memory. As bone and reason is to our physical and intellectual beings, so is love to our moral and spiritual existence.

Love is to the moral and spiritual universe what gravitation is to the natural world,—it brings all things to a common center; yet it must be exercised judiciously. The normal exercise of love insures the richest blessings of life, while the abnormal enkindles God's wrath, and brings us down to poverty and shame. The heart demands an object upon which to lavish the largeness of its affection. In the absence of all else, some object, either animate or inanimate, will receive this homage.

When we obey the laws of love, our pleasures and happiness are increased, and vice versa. But in order to make it contented and perfect, it must be earnest, reciprocated love. Love is an imperative duty imposed upon us as professing Christians, for "he that loveth not, knoweth not God, for God is love." Love "hopeth all things," and "endureth all things."

Love may be of different kinds, viz., parental, conjugal, fraternal, supernal, and filial. Parental love is that which exists between parents and children. It is the bond of union, which perfects the bliss of home, and makes it the dearest spot on earth. Conjugal love enhances the happiness of the human race. It was designed by the Almighty as a blessing to domestic life. Fraternal love is the tie that unites and predominates over

ing that they should immerse into the Father, and the Son, and the Holy Spirit, not into one name, for we are immersed for each name, into each person, not once, but thrice." ("Tertullian's Works," p. 659.)

Chrysostom says: "Christ delivered to his apostles 'one baptism' in three immersions of the body, when he said to them, 'Go teach all nations, baptizing them in the name of the Father, and of the Son, and of the Holy Spirit.'" ("Antiquities of the Christian Church," I, p. 540.)

Jerome, in commenting on Eph. 4: 5, says: "We are thrice dipped in water that the mystery of the Trinity may appear to be but one, and therefore, though we be thrice put under the water to represent the mystery of the Trinity,' yet it is reputed but one baptism." ("Chrystal's History of the Modes of Baptism," pp. 72, 73.)

Monulus informs us that trine immersion had always been with the church, and makes it just as old as the command to preach the Gospel." "The doctrine of our holy mother, the Catholic church, has always, my brethren, been with us, and doth still abide with us, and especially the article of baptism; and the trine immersion wherewith it is celebrated, our Lord having said, "Go ye, and baptize the Gentiles in the name of the Father, and of the Son, and of the Holy Spirit." (Works of Cyprian, I, p. 240.)

"Catholic Church" here has reference to the general church, and not Roman Catholics. Monulus wrote about the year A. D. 256.

Clement, of Alexandria, was born about A. D. 150, and, in addressing the Christian church of his age, says: "Ye were conducted to a bath just as Christ was carried to the grave; and were thrice immersed." ("Wiberg on Baptism," p. 228. I quote the above facts from "Stein and Ray Debate.")

Justin Martyr wrote "An Apology for Christians." In this work he describes the doctrines and ordinances of the church of Christ; and on baptism has the following passage: "Then we bring them to some place where there is water, and they are baptized by the same way of baptism by which we were baptized; for they are washed in the water in the name of God the Father, Lord of all things; and of our Savior Jesus Christ, and of the Holy Spirit." ("Pengilly on Baptism," p. 150.)

From "Trine Immersion Traced to the Apostles," we have the following: "Justin Martyr was born A. D. 100; the same year that the apostle John died. Every ancient historian attributes trine immersion to the great commission given by Christ in Matt. 28: 19, and the Greeks in whose language the New Testament was first written, practice trine immersion to this day. The Western, or Latin church, practiced trine immersion until the council of Toledo, A. D. 633, when it was voted that only one immersion should be used in baptism, because the Arians practiced trine immersion."

My friend cannot find, in history or practice, where single backward immersion was practiced till nearly fifteen hundred years after Christ, hence fifteen hundred years too late for Christian baptism. It is an innovation brought into the church by those that were insubordinate to Christ and his heavenly teachings. Trine immersion is recognized the world over as Christian baptism. "Go ye therefore, and teach all nations, baptizing them into the name of the Father, and of the Son, and of the Holy Spirit."

"Good words do more than hard speeches; as the sunbeam, without any noise, made the traveler cast off his cloak, which all the blustering wind could not do, but only make him bind it closer to him."

OUR PRESENT AND FUTURE REST.

BY J. J. EMMERT.

"Come unto me all ye that labor and are heavy laden, and I will give you rest. Take my yoke upon you, and learn of me; for I am meek and lowly in heart: and ye shall find rest unto your souls."—Matt. 11: 28, 29.

IN our Savior's words, as above quoted, we notice that he speaks of rest twice, or, as we might say, a first and a second rest. He then proceeds to show to whom these rests are accessible, and also upon what condition. Some maintain that this rest first spoken of is received by the sinner when he fully resolves to leave his sins, and, by sincere repentance toward God and faith in Christ, turns his face Zionward. They claim that he will then experience a change of heart, hence receives the rest spoken of.

This I consider unsafe, and, to a certain degree, misleading, for it savors, to some extent, of the popular and unscriptural view held by many. They maintain that, if the sinner feels the assurance within that he is accepted of God and that his sins are pardoned, baptism will be to him, not a means of pardon, but only an initiatory rite into the church visible.

I wish to find a location for the first rest spoken of, that is perfectly safe to rely upon, and in every respect tenable.

The Savior extends the invitation to such as labor and are heavy laden, which means such as feel the heavy load and weight of sin. Thus struggling under the load with a guilty conscience, the sinner becomes penitent, turns to God, and desires to be relieved of his load of sin. Jesus then says to him, "Come to me and I will give you rest." He can come only in the way the Lord has arranged for him, and that way was plainly stated by the apostle Peter on the day of Pentecost. He told how pardon can be obtained and the burden removed, by telling us, "Repent ye, therefore, and be baptized, every one of you in the name of Jesus Christ, for the remission of sins, and ye shall receive the gift of the Holy Ghost." Acts 2: 38.

The Lord always blesses in the act of obedience, but while the penitent remains unbaptized, he continues in disobedience, hence has no promise. But if he now follows Christ in the observance of baptism, as he has followed him in faith and repentance, he has the assurance that his sins are all forgiven; hence it is now only that he obtains a present rest.

Do we not all remember the happy day when we arose from the baptismal grave, with a consciousness of having followed Jesus in obedience, and, oh, how rested we felt!

In the Hebrews leaving Egypt, we have many beautiful types of our Christian journey. I will refer to but one, 1 Cor. 10: 1, 2. "Brethren, I would not that ye should be ignorant, how that all our fathers were under the cloud, and all passed through the sea; and were all baptized unto Moses in the cloud and in the sea." In the above we are told of the deliverance of Israel from their enemies, and it was not until they saw them destroyed that they had actual rest. So it is with the sinner. How he can rejoice when he knows that his sins are all pardoned!

We refer yet to the prodigal son, Luke 15. When he resolved to come home to the father's house, the father met him in the way as he was coming, fell on his neck and kissed him. He was clothed with rags, no shoes on his feet, and utterly destitute, just like the returning, penitent sinner, clothed with sin and undone. He wants to be saved, his father from the good intentions when afar off, and welcomes him, but he has no rest until his old, filthy rags of sin are removed,

by obedience to Christ in baptism. He is received into the home circle, the church of Christ, and clothed with the new robe of righteousness. He now enjoys a present rest, having the assurance that he is the child of God.

The rest to the soul, or second rest spoken of, is a blessed, everlasting rest, that the faithful followers of Christ shall enjoy when the toils of life are over. But to obtain this rest we must take his yoke upon us, and learn of him. We must be meek and self-sacrificing, following him in filial love, in all the ordinances and commandments, in order to insure the blessedness of the promised everlasting rest to the soul.

Mt. Carroll, Ill.

LOVE.—WHAT IT IS, AND WHAT IT DOES.

BY P. BRAXTON FITZWATER.

LOVE is the affection, existing between the sexes, parents, children, and friends. It is the connecting link of the universe, and binds it to the throne of God. It is the vital force or attraction, which unites or binds the "all" and "in all." It is the root of creation, the essence of God, the rudimental elements of the soul. It is, therefore, a divine gift,—a blessing which the Creator did not withdraw from his erring children, when they were driven from Paradise into a world of desolation and strife. He left it as an inseparable cord, by which to draw the human heart ever upward to a brighter home,—a heavenly Eden. Love is the very essence of Divine Law. To its presence we are indebted for all that is good and true in art and nature. It endows humanity with countless virtues, and throws a mystic veil over our many faults. Literature owes to love its choicest gems. Without that, it would be as a floating mass of immaterial substance.

It is true, love has been degraded to some extent, but true love never seeks to degrade its object. On the contrary, it magnifies every virtue, endows it with the divinest attributes, and guards its chastity or honor at the sacrifice of its own life. It heightens spirituality, awakens hope, strengthens faith, and enhances devotion. It quickens the perceptions, intensifies the sensibilities, and redoubles the memory. As bone and reason is to our physical and intellectual beings, so is love to our moral and spiritual existence.

Love is to the moral and spiritual universe what gravitation is to the natural world,—it brings all things to a common center; yet it must be exercised judiciously. The normal exercise of love insures the richest blessings of life, while the abnormal enkindles God's wrath, and brings us down to poverty and shame. The heart demands an object upon which to lavish the largeness of its affection. In the absence of all else, some object, either animate or inanimate, will receive this homage.

When we obey the laws of love, our pleasures and happiness are increased, and vice versa. But in order to make it contented and perfect, it must be earnest, reciprocated love. Love is an imperative duty imposed upon us as professing Christians, for "he that loveth not, knoweth not God; for God is love." Love "hopeth all things," and "endureth all things."

Love may be of different kinds, viz., parental, conjugal, fraternal, supernal, and filial. Parental love is that which exists between parents and children. It is the bond of union, which perfects the bliss of home, and makes it the dearest spot on earth. Conjugal love enhances the happiness of the human race. It was designed by the Almighty as a blessing to domestic life. Fraternal love is the tie that unites and predominates over

Missionary and Tract Work Department.

"Upon the first day of the week, let every one of you lay by him in store as God hath prospered him, that there be no gatherings when I come."—Cor. 16: x.

"Every man as he purposeth in his heart, so let him give. Not grudgingly or of necessity, for the Lord loveth a cheerful giver."—2 Cor. 9:7.

HOW MUCH SHALL WE GIVE?

"Every man according to his ability." "Every one as God hath prospered him." "Every man, according as he purposeth in his heart, so let him give." "For if there be first a willing mind, it is accepted according to that a man hath, and not according to that he hath not."—1 Cor. 8: 12.

Organization of Missionary Committee.

DANIEL VANIMAN, Foreman, · · · McPherson, Kans.
D. L. MILLER, Treasurer, · · · · Mt. Morris, Ill.
GALEN B. ROYER, Secretary, · · · · Mt. Morris, Ill.

Organization of Book and Tract Work.

S. W. HOOVER, Foreman, · · · · Dayton, Ohio.
S. BOCK, Secretary and Treasurer, · · · Dayton, Ohio.

☞All donations intended for Missionary Work should be sent to GALEN B. ROYER, Mt. Morris, Ill.

☞All money for Tract Work should be sent to S. BOCK, Dayton, Ohio.

☞Money may be sent by Money Order, Registered Letter, or Drafts on New York or Chicago. Do not send personal checks, or drafts on interior towns, as it costs 25 cents to collect them.

☞Solicitors are requested to faithfully carry out the plan of Annual Meeting, that all our members be solicited to contribute at least twice a year for the Mission and Tract Work of the Church.

☞Notes for the Endowment Fund can be had by writing to the Secretary of either Work.

SOME BREAKERS AHEAD.

BY C. E. ARNOLD.

In Four Parts, No. I.—Liberalism.

UNDER the above caption it is purposed, in a brief series of articles, to notice a few of the "breakers," which endanger the future progress of orthodox Christianity.

In this paper we direct our attention to what may be styled "Liberalism." Tracing the spiritual condition of the church from the ecclesiastical tyranny of Rome, in the Dark Ages, to the present time, we are deeply impressed with the marvelous growth of religious freedom. The liberty of conscience enjoyed to-day is not a direct product of the Reformation; for Calvin, one of the leading reformers, burnt Servetus for heresy, and one hundred and sixty persons died for their faith under the reign of the Protestant Queen Elizabeth. Even the liberty-loving Puritans banished Roger Williams from their colony because he did not worship as they did. Religious tolerance, indeed, began with the Reformation, has been growing ever since, and is growing still to-day, and we are proud of that Christian charity now exercised by one toward another of a different faith.

We must, however, guard against two erroneous tendencies, apparently, along this line. What observer has failed to notice how popular, in recent years, is becoming the opinion that all churches are equally safe to a person seeking salvation? This is not orthodox. On the other hand, we believe it indicates a condition of faith in which men "believe lies," "will not endure sound doctrine," and are "turned unto fables."

Neither does this looseness of faith indicate strength of character. That Christian charity which teaches me not to question the motives of a man whose faith is different from mine, also permits me to retain my own faith without disparaging my motives. The very fact that Christian charity prevails, ought to encourage men to have definite religious views and to stand by them. We sometimes hear men spoken of as broad and liberal-minded, when the truth is, they do not have back-bone enough to have opinions of their own, and to let the world know what they really do believe.

I once heard a young minister say that if his own church did not offer a suitable opening for him, he would preach for some other denomination. He was ready to preach almost anything, and yet I believe he had persuaded himself that he was sincere. This sentiment already largely prevails among the popular churches, and is rapidly gaining favor.

"Liberalism" is about to take a step even in advance of this. It is ready to accept good moral people, exercising a historical faith in Christ, as being really Christians. The Rev. S. D. McConnell, D. D., writing in the New World, says: "The number of good people, tried by all fair tests of goodness, who are unsound in doctrine, and hold aloof from church membership, is increasing at a rate which few realize." The doctor further claims that these people are in fact Christians, and that Christianity will, after a while, nominally include them.

We meet many people nowadays who are willing to risk their salvation upon a correct moral life. These people expect to merit salvation by their own good works. God is under obligations to them. They keep a debit and credit account with God and he is on the debtor side! They call this Christianity! If it deserves to be called religion at all, it is simply a form of popular deism, which practically denies the merits of the great fundamental principle of the Gospel of grace,—the atonement.

You will notice the authority, quoted above, says, "These people are tried by all fair tests of goodness." He would probably have said the same to the young Jewish ruler who had kept the commandments from his youth up, but Jesus said: "One thing thou lackest."

While many regard these liberal tendencies as evidences of real Christian progress, we believe them to be an appalling hindrance to the progress of pure Gospel faith. Certainly, this doctrine of liberalism, originating as it has within the churches, threatens to prove more harmful to the cause of the pure principles of the Gospel than the attacks of infidelity and skepticism from without.

Daleville, Va.

BE A SUNFLOWER.

BY NANCY D. UNDERHILL.

JUST a little way above our house, out of sight, round a hill, is a beautiful spot. On one side of the little stream (where I was baptized) is a grassy bank, with tall shade trees, full of sweet song birds and little bird nests. Just beyond is a great, beautiful bluff, where solid rocks stand higher than our house, and oh, so majestic! All around are beautiful and picturesque mountains. Over-head is the clear, blue sky, with its banks and islands of white, fleecy clouds, but the dearest sight of all is a bank of yellow sunflowers, just across the stream.

When I am tired, wearied, lonely, and discouraged, I leave my cares at the house and hasten away to this quiet spot, where the first thing that meets my eye is the bed of wild flowers which God has planted, watered and cared for till they have grown tall, strong and beautiful, swaying gently in the wind, but never breaking, never wilting, never closing, but ever looking toward the sun and reflecting his golden glory in their own little faces. They cannot speak, they can neither preach, sing, or make eloquent prayers. They cannot even work, yet they let their light shine, and that light cheers a weary soul and helps a tired mother to bear her burdens with patience, to speak gently to the little ones, to encourage the young companion who is with her, to do her duty day by day, to look on the bright side of life and offer praise to the "Giver of all good things."

Looking up, I behold the great and wonderful works of God in his mountains, cliffs and caves, and still higher I find peace when I look away in to the blue sky at a lovely white cloud, which I imagine resembles the one on which our beloved Savior was seen sitting. Rev. 14: 14; and I look earnestly to see him coming again with all his holy angels crowned with glory and coming in the clouds to claim his own. Oh, will I be found worthy to be caught up into the air to meet him then? Will you, beloved reader?

Beholding the beautiful golden flowers, I learn to be steadfast, even as they are, for they never faint or complain,—they just keep on shining, no matter whether any one sees them or not,—they shine on just the same, till frost comes and kills them. So let you and I, dear, humble ones, never be discouraged, but shine on till the frost of death comes. It may be we cannot preach, or sing, or make eloquent prayers, or even work, but we can smile. Thus we may cheer some weary soul and help them to glorify God. Let us, like the dear, golden blossoms, keep our faces ever turned toward the "Sun of Righteousness." At morning, at noon, and at night, yes, every hour and every moment of the day (Paul says, "Pray without ceasing") let us look to him who is altogether lovely. Then, indeed, shall we reflect his (golden) beauty in our small faces and his wonderful mercy and loveliness in our every-day lives.

Dear ones, you may not be able to stand high in the church, like a great shade-tree which shelters the weary traveler, or like the great strong rocks and bluffs which fill us with awe, as we look at them, nor like the great, majestic mountains, which tower so far above us, you may not even be a beautiful rose or a strawberry-vine, but never mind, God has use for you, or he would not have made you. If you cannot be great and grand, learned and eloquent, you may at least be a beautiful, cheerful, golden sunflower reflecting the loveliness of the sun every moment of your life.

Canon City, Colo.

THE CANAANITISH WOMAN.

BY ELIZABETH H. DELP.

"Poor Canaanitish mother
Mark how she strays with folded arms
And her head is bent in woe
She shuts her thoughts to joy, or charms,
No tear attempts to flow."

THE woman came to the Savior in her bitter need, to the Great Physician who alone could heal her daughter. She was a heathen and knew little of the true God. An idolator, she had gone to her gods for help, had sacrificed unto them, but they were impassive, unheeding; her agonized prayers fell on cold stone. As she made her way to the Savior, the throng of Israelites scorned her, she belonged to a people whom they regarded as "unclean."

In her extremity, when it seems as if there is neither refuge, nor help, no trouble like unto hers, there was wrought a miracle and a mystery of grace. She believes, and her faith is strong. It finds utterance in her earnest prayer to Christ, the "man of sorrows." Low at his feet she lay with the cry, "Lord help me." She must break his silence. When at length he speaks, accusing her of unfitness, she ratifies the charge and humbles herself still more. Though the Savior seems more merciless than the gods of her people, as he tells her the hard truth, that she is a "dog" instead of a child, this woman, whose heart-chords were quivering in pain for her daughter, freely admits that she is worthy of but a crumb, and with head bowed in the dust, worships our Lord. "Then Jesus answered and said unto her, O woman, great is thy faith; be it unto thee even as thou

Missionary and Tract Work Department.

"Upon the first day of the week, let every one of you lay by him in store as God hath prospered him, that there be no gatherings when I come."—1 Cor. 16: 2.

"Every man as he purposeth in his heart, so let him give. Not grudgingly or of necessity, for the Lord loveth a cheerful giver."—2 Cor. 9: 7.

HOW MUCH SHALL WE GIVE?

"Every man *according to his ability*." "Every one *as God hath prospered him*." "Every man, *according as he purposeth in his heart*, so let him give." "For if there be first a willing mind, it is accepted *according to that a man hath*, and not according to that he hath not."—2 Cor. 8: 12.

Organization of Missionary Committee.

DANIEL VANIMAN, Foreman, - - McPherson, Kans.
D. L. MILLER, Treasurer, - - Mt. Morris, Ill.
GALEN B. ROYER, Secretary, - - Mt. Morris, Ill.

Organization of Book and Tract Work.

S. W. HOOVER, Foreman, - - Dayton, Ohio.
S. BOCK, Secretary and Treasurer, - Dayton, Ohio.

☞ All donations intended for Missionary Work should be sent to Mt. Morris, Ill.
☞ All money for Tract Work should be sent to S. BOCK, Dayton, Ohio.
☞ Money may be sent by Money Order, Registered Letter, or Drafts on New York or Chicago. Do not send personal checks, or drafts on interior towns, as it costs 25 cents to collect them.
☞ Solicitors are requested to faithfully carry out the plan of Annual Meeting, that all our members be solicited to contribute at least twice a year for the Mission and Tract Work of the Church.
☞ Notes for the Endowment Fund can be had by writing to the Secretary of either Work.

SOME BREAKERS AHEAD.

BY C. E. ARNOLD.

In Four Parts, No. I.—Liberalism.

UNDER the above caption it is purposed, in a brief series of articles, to notice a few of the "breakers," which endanger the future progress of orthodox Christianity.

In this paper we direct our attention to what may be styled "Liberalism." Tracing the spiritual condition of the church from the ecclesiastical tyranny of Rome, in the Dark Ages, to the present time, we are deeply impressed with the marvelous growth of religious freedom. The liberty of conscience enjoyed to-day is not a direct product of the Reformation; for Calvin, and one of the leading reformers, burnt Servetus for heresy, and one hundred and sixty persons died for their faith under the reign of the Protestant Queen Elizabeth. Even the liberty-loving Puritans banished Roger Williams from their colony because he did not worship as they did. Religious tolerance, indeed, began with the Reformation, has been growing ever since, and is growing still to-day, and we are proud of that Christian charity now exercised by one toward another of a different faith.

We must, however, guard against *two* erroneous tendencies, apparently, along this line. What observer has failed to notice how popular, in recent years, is becoming the opinion that all churches are equally safe to a person seeking salvation? This is not orthodox. On the other hand, we believe it indicates a condition of faith in which men "believe lies," "will not endure sound doctrine," and are "turned unto fables."

Neither does this looseness of faith indicate strength of character. That Christian charity which teaches me not to question the *motives* of a man whose faith is different from mine, also permits me to retain my own faith without disparaging my motives. The very fact that Christian charity prevails, ought to encourage men to have definite religious views and to stand by them. We sometimes hear men spoken of as broad and liberal-minded, when the truth is, they do not have back-bone enough to have opinions of their own, and to let the world know what they really do believe.

I once heard a young minister say that if his own church did not offer a suitable opening for him, he would preach for some other denomination. He was ready to preach almost anything, and yet I believe he had persuaded himself that he was sincere. This sentiment already largely prevails among the popular churches, and is rapidly gaining favor.

"Liberalism" is about to take a step even in advance of this. It is ready to accept good moral people, exercising a historical faith in Christ, as being really Christians. The Rev. S. D. McConnell, D. D., writing in the *New World*, says: "The number of good people, tried by all fair tests of goodness, who are unsound in doctrine, and hold aloof from church membership, is increasing at a rate which few realize." The doctor farther claims that these people are in fact Christians, and that Christianity will, after a while, nominally include them.

We meet many people nowadays who are willing to risk their salvation upon a correct moral life. These people expect to *merit* salvation by their own good works. God is under obligations to them. They keep a debit and credit account with God and he is on the debtor side! They call this Christianity! If it deserves to be called religion at all, it is simply a form of popular deism, which practically denies the merits of the great fundamental principle of the Gospel of grace,—the atonement.

You will notice the authority, quoted above, says, "These people are tried by all fair tests of goodness." He would probably have said the same to the young Jewish ruler who had kept the commandments from his youth up, but Jesus said: "One thing thou lackest."

While many regard these liberal tendencies as evidences of real Christian progress, we believe them to be an appalling hindrance to the progress of pure Gospel faith. Certainly, this doctrine of liberalism, originating as it has within the churches, threatens to prove more harmful to the cause of the pure principles of the Gospel than the attacks of infidelity and skepticism from without.

Daleville, Va.

BE A SUNFLOWER.

BY NANCY D. UNDERHILL.

JUST a little way above our house, out of sight, round a hill, is a beautiful spot. On one side of the little stream (where I was baptized) is a grassy bank, with tall shade trees, full of sweet song birds and little bird nests. Just beyond is a great, beautiful bluff, where solid rocks stand higher than our house, and oh, so majestic! All around are beautiful and picturesque mountains. Over-head is the clear, blue sky, with its banks and islands of white, fleecy clouds, but the dearest sight of all is a bank of yellow sunflowers, just across the stream.

When I am tired, wearied, lonely, and discouraged, I leave my cares at the house and hasten away to this quiet spot, where the first thing that meets my eye is the bed of wild flowers which God has planted, watered and cared for till they have grown tall, strong and beautiful, swaying gently in the very "Lord help me." Low at his feet she lay with er closing, but ever looking toward the sun and reflecting his golden glory in their own little faces. They cannot speak, they can neither preach, sing, or make eloquent prayers. They cannot even work, yet they let their light shine, and that light cheers a weary soul and helps a tired mother to bear her burdens with patience, to speak gently to the little ones, to encourage the young companion who is with her, to do her duty day by day, to look on the bright side of life and offer praise to the "Giver of all good things."

Looking up, I behold the great and wonderful works of God in his mountains, cliffs and caves, and still higher I find peace when I look away in to the blue sky at a lovely white cloud, which I imagine resembles the one on which our beloved Savior was seen sitting, Rev. 14: 14; and I look earnestly to see him coming again with all his holy angels crowned with glory and coming in the clouds to claim his own. Oh, will I be found worthy to be caught up into the air to meet him then? Will you, beloved reader?

Beholding the beautiful golden flowers, I learn to be steadfast, even as they are, for they never faint or complain,—they just keep on shining, no matter whether any one sees them or not,—they shine on just the same, till frost comes and kills them. So let you and I, dear, humble ones, never be discouraged, but shine on till the frost of death comes. It may be we cannot preach, or sing, or make eloquent prayers, or even work, but we can smile. Thus we may cheer some weary soul and help them to glorify God. Let us, like the dear, golden blossoms, keep our faces ever turned toward the "Sun of Righteousness." At morning, at noon, and at night, yes, every hour and every moment of the day (Paul says, "Pray without ceasing") let us look to him who is altogether lovely. Then, indeed, shall we reflect his (golden) beauty in our small faces and his wonderful mercy and loveliness in our every-day lives.

Dear ones, you may not be able to stand high in the church, like a great shade-tree which shelters the weary traveler, or like the great strong rocks and bluffs which fill us with awe, as we look at them, nor like the great, majestic mountains, which tower so far above us, you may not even be a beautiful rose or a strawberry-vine, but never mind, God has use for you, or he would not have made you. If you cannot be great and grand, learned and eloquent, you may at least be a beautiful, cheerful, golden sunflower reflecting the loveliness of the sun every moment of your life.

Canon City, Colo.

THE CANAANITISH WOMAN.

BY ELIZABETH H. DELP.

" Poor Canaanitish mother
Mark how she strays with folded arms
And her head is bent in woe
She shuts her thoughts to joy, or charms,
No tear attempts to flow."

THE woman came to the Savior in her bitter need, to the Great Physician who alone could heal her daughter. She was a heathen and knew little of the true God. An idolator, she had gone to her gods for help, had sacrificed unto them, but they were impassive, unheeding; her agonized prayers fell on cold stone. As she made her way to the Savior, the throng of Israelites scorned her, she belonged to a people whom they regarded as "unclean."

In her extremity, when it seems as if there is neither refuge, nor help, no trouble like unto hers, there was wrought a miracle and a mystery of grace. She believes, and her faith is strong. It, finds utterance in her earnest prayer to Christ, the "man of sorrows." Low at his feet she lay with the cry, "Lord help me." She must break his silence. When at length he speaks, accusing her of unfitness, she ratifies the charge and humbles herself still more. Though the Savior seems more merciless than the gods of her people, as he tells her the hard truth, that she is a "dog" instead of a child, this woman, whose heart-chords were quivering in pain for her daughter, freely admits that she is worthy of but a crumb, and with head bowed in the dust, worships our Lord-"Then Jesus answered and said unto her, O woman, great is thy faith! be it unto thee even as thou

The Gospel Messenger,

A Weekly at $1.50 Per Annum.

PUBLISHED BY

The Brethren's Publishing Co.

D. L. MILLER,	. . . . .	Editor.
J. H. MOORE,	. . . . .	Office Editor.
J. B. BRUMBAUGH,	. . . .	Associate Editors.
J. G. ROYER,		
JOSEPH AMICK,	-	Business Manager.

ADVISORY COMMITTEE.

L. W. Teeter, A. Hutchison, Daniel Hays.

☞Communications for publication should be legibly written with black ink on one side of the paper only. Do not attempt to interline, or to put on one page what ought to occupy two.

☞Anonymous communications will not be published.

☞Do not mix business with articles for publication. Keep your communications on separate sheets from all business.

☞Time is precious. We always have time to attend to business and to answer questions of importance, but please do not subject us to need less answering of letters.

☞The Messenger is mailed each week to all subscribers. If the address is correctly entered on our list, the paper must reach the person to whom it is addressed. If you do not get your paper, write us, giving particulars.

☞When changing your address, please give your former as well as your future address in full, so us to avoid delay and misunderstanding.

☞Always remit to the office from which you order your goods, no matter from where you receive them.

☞Do not send personal checks or drafts on interior banks, unless you send with them 15 cents each, to pay for collection.

☞Remittances should be made by Post-office Money Order, Drafts on New York, Philadelphia or Chicago, or Registered Letters, made payable and addressed to "Brethren's Publishing Co., Mount Morris, Ill.," or "Brethren's Publishing Co., Huntingdon, Pa."

☞Entered at the Post-office at Mount Morris, Ill., as second-class matter.

Mount Morris, Ill.,   · · · ·   Sept. 6, 1892.

IN No. 33, we got J. F. Britton's name and address both wrong. His address is Bristoe, Prince William Co., Va., and the name as given above.

THE Thornapple church, Michigan, seems to be in a prosperous condition just at this time. A number recently united with the church, and other applicants are yet to be baptized.

A MAN can see to walk much better if he follows after the Gospel light instead of trying to walk in front of it. If the light is in the rear, our shadow is sure to trouble us. Keep the light in front and the shadow in the rear.

ONE of the largest schools in the world is at Cairo, Egypt. It is controlled by the Mohammedans, and is attended by eleven thousand pupils who study Mussulman law, history and theology. The school is a power for evil.

ON a brass plate in front of a large bank in New York may be found these words: "No Beggars or Peddlers Allowed to Enter this Door." Fortunately nothing of that kind will be found over the door that opens into heaven. Lazarus saw no such a notice when he was carried by the angels to Abraham's bosom.

IT is well enough for men to cry "Wolf, wolf!" when they know the wolf is coming, but for a minister to pursue this course to keep his flock constantly in a state of excitement, so they cannot enjoy the abundant pastures within their reach, is a sad mistake indeed. Possibly there are some preachers spending so much of their time sounding the alarm that they actually neglect to feed the flock of God over which the Holy Ghost has made them overseers. We believe in sounding the alarm when necessary, but have no sympathy with the preachers who are starving the Lord's sheep. If the sheep are well fed, and kept in good health, they will keep out of the way of the wolves to good advantage. It may be well for us all to remember that wolves sometimes devour the bell sheep, as well as the others.

IT is reported that Mexico has granted 100,000 acres of fertile land to another Mormon family, and that 500 families will emigrate to the new settlement.

THERE will be no Ministerial Meeting at the Blue River Valley church, Butler County, Nebraska, Oct. 4. But the District Meeting will be held there at that time. There will be a Missionary Meeting the day before.

BRO. C. S. HOLSINGER, now of Belleville, Kans., recently visited his former field of labor in Christian County, Illinois, having been called there on account of the sickness and death of his daughter-in-law. He returned the first of this month.

INTEREST in Bible study is by no means diminishing. In 1890, not less than 1,022 religious works were published in the United States and England, and a still greater number in 1891. This speaks well for the interest taken in Bible study.

IF any minister's name is left out of the Almanac, or any mistake is not corrected in the list, it will not be our fault, for we have called attention to this matter a number of times. This, however, is the last call, as the list must be closed up inside of ten days.

THOSE of our readers who permit any little hinderance to keep them away from church services, should read what Bro. S. C. Lehman has to say about a sister who has no use of her feet, but has to work her way to meeting on her knees, and then thanks God that it is no worse.

SOME of the districts are sending out very neat and well-arranged programs of their Ministerial Meetings. These printed programs will be found very convenient for use at the time of the meetings, and will also be useful to file. We would like to be favored with copies for filing away. We are also prepared to print programs for those who wish to favor us with their work.

THE Brethren at Mechanicstown, Frederick County, Maryland, dedicated their new meeting-houses Aug. 21. The meeting is reported to have been a very interesting one. Next week we publish a very interesting article concerning the dedicatory service, and also a history of the church at that place. We suggest that the history of other congregations might also be written up to a good advantage.

"THERE is no confidence to be placed in that man or woman whose thoughts dwell pleasurably on scenes of crime. The fact of their finding pleasure in such thoughts, evidences their own inward pollution. They are corrupt already in fact, however it may be in form. This is why bad books and bad publications of various kinds do so much harm; they poison the imagination, induce bad thoughts, which, little by little, gain on their victims till all within is moral pollution."

WHEN done with the right motive, the preaching of the Gospel is the most useful, soul-inspiring work ever undertaken by man. It is not only self-sacrificing in its very nature, but the tendency is to lift up, ennoble and benefit others. It is the broadest class of charity, reaching out to benefit not only the souls of men and women, but their bodies likewise, for that which elevates and purifies the soul, confers a similar blessing on the body. Mothers, who prepare their sons for the sacred work, as Hannah of old prepared Samuel, and wives who assist and encourage their husbands in the work of the ministry, become ministering angels, whose influence may be felt to the end of time.

THE Mormons are establishing a colony in North-western Canada, and many of the families from Utah will emigrate to that place. The wholesome law of this country makes the way of the transgressor hard, so far as it pertains to polygamy.

BRO. F. W. DOVE, of Jonesboro, Tenn., has moved with his family to Cabool, Texas County, Mo., for the purpose of making that his future home. He has had this change of location in view for some time, and while we regret to have him leave Tennessee, we feel confident that he has selected a field where his labors are very much needed, and will be appreciated. Texas County is in the southern part of the State, about fifty miles east of Springfield.

"NEARLY four million copies of the Bible, Testament, and portions of the Bible were distributed last year by the British and Foreign Bible Society of England. The increase in copies distributed over the previous year was 62,680. Since the publication of the "Penny" Testament in July, 1884, 5,000,668 copies have been issued. Through twenty-seven societies grants were made for 364 Bible women during the year, who read the Scriptures on an average to 18,742 native women every week. Nine new versions of the Bible were issued."

JUST what relation the Christian sustains to the things of this world, depends a good deal upon whether he belongs to the world or Christ. The early Christians found nothing too great a sacrifice for the cause of Christianity. To them everything else was simply secondary and used, if used at all, as a means to an end. Their property, as well as their talent and lives, was fully consecrated to the Lord. They made money and acquired property, but it was all with a view of advancing the cause of the Christian religion. While they mingled, to some extent, with the world, they were everywhere known as pronounced Christians who were in no manner ashamed of their religion. We need in this day to cultivate more of this consecrated spirit.

MINISTERS who stand before a congregation and say they have made no preparation whatever, and will speak only as the Lord puts words into their mouth, ought to remember that the Lord does not put words into the mouth of that kind of a preacher. The Lord has placed his words in the Bible, and it is the duty of the minister, by careful study, to get them into his head, and from there into his heart. Such a man the Lord can and will help to preach. But how can or how will he help a man to preach who does not make the Bible a study! You might as well talk of the man who neither sows nor reaps, having his garners well stored with grain. The Lord helps those who try to help themselves, in preaching as well as in other things. We believe in every minister preparing himself to preach. This he does by hard study, prayer and consecration. We do not mean that he must always prepare his sermons, for some of the best sermons ever preached were prompted by the impressions of the occasion, but he ought to study so as to know how to rightly divide and present the Truth when called on to do so. We have heard ministers say, "I have given the subject no thought, and must speak as liberty is given." From their talk one would judge that they had given the matter no thought. Such a course may be well enough when one is unexpectedly called upon to preach, but for a minister to have weeks in which to prepare himself for the occasion, and then say that he has made no preparation, is a species of negligence for which there is no excuse.

The Gospel Messenger,

A Weekly at $1.50 Per Annum.

PUBLISHED BY

The Brethren's Publishing Co.

D. L. MILLER,	Editor.
J. H. MOORE,	Office Editor.
J. B. BRUMBAUGH, J. G. ROYER,	Associate Editors.
JOSEPH AMICK,	Business Manager.

ADVISORY COMMITTEE.

L. W. Teeter, A. Hutchison, Daniel Hays.

Mount Morris, Ill., - - - - Sept. 6, 1892.

IN No. 33, we got J. F. Britton's name and address both wrong. His address is Bristoe, Prince William Co., Va., and the name as given above.

THE Thornapple church, Michigan, seems to be in a prosperous condition just at this time. A number recently united with the church, and other applicants are yet to be baptized.

A MAN can see to walk much better if he follows after the Gospel light instead of trying to walk in front of it. If the light is in the rear, our shadow is sure to trouble us. Keep the light in front and the shadow in the rear.

ONE of the largest schools in the world is at Cairo, Egypt. It is controlled by the Mohammedans, and is attended by eleven thousand pupils who study Mussulman law, history and theology. The school is a power for evil.

ON a brass plate in front of a large bank in New York may be found these words: "No Beggars or Peddlers Allowed to Enter this Door." Fortunately nothing of that kind will be found over the door that opens into heaven. Lazarus saw no such a notice when he was carried by the angels to Abraham's bosom.

IT is well enough for men to cry "Wolf, wolf!" when they know the wolf is coming, but for a minister to pursue this course to keep his flock constantly in a state of excitement, so they cannot enjoy the abundant pastures within their reach, is a sad mistake indeed. Possibly there are some preachers spending so much of their time sounding the alarm that they actually neglect to feed the flock of God over which the Holy Ghost has made them overseers. We believe in sounding the alarm when necessary, but have no sympathy with the preachers who are starving the Lord's sheep. If the sheep are well fed, and kept in good health, they will keep out of the way of the wolves to good advantage. It may be well for us all to remember that wolves sometimes devour the bell sheep, as well as the others.

IT is reported that Mexico has granted 100,000 acres of fertile land to another Mormon family, and that 500 families will emigrate to the new settlement.

THERE will be no Ministerial Meeting at the Blue River Valley church, Butler County, Nebraska, Oct. 4. But the District Meeting will be held there at that time. There will be a Missionary Meeting the day before.

BRO. C. S. HOLSINGER, now of Belleville, Kans., recently visited his former field of labor in Christian County, Illinois, having been called there on account of the sickness and death of his daughter-in-law. He returned the first of this month.

INTEREST in Bible study is by no means diminishing. In 1890, not less than 1,022 religious works were published in the United States and England, and a still greater number in 1891. This speaks well for the interest taken in Bible study.

IF any minister's name is left out of the Almanac, or any mistake is not corrected in the list, it will not be our fault, for we have called attention to this matter a number of times. This, however, is the last call, as the list must be closed up inside of ten days.

THOSE of our readers who permit any little hinderance to keep them away from church services, should read what Bro. S. C. Lehman has to say about a sister who has no use of her feet, but has to work her way to meeting on her knees, and then thanks God that it is no worse.

SOME of the districts are sending out very neat and well-arranged programs of their Ministerial Meetings. These printed programs will be found very convenient for use at the time of the meetings, and will also be useful to file. We would like to be favored with copies for filing away. We are also prepared to print programs for those who wish to favor us with their work.

THE Brethren at Mechanicstown, Frederick County, Maryland, dedicated their new meeting-house Aug. 21. The meeting is reported to have been a very interesting one. Next week we publish a very interesting article concerning the dedicatory service, and also a history of the church at that place. We suggest that the history of other congregations might also be written up to a good advantage.

"THERE is no confidence to be placed in that man or woman whose thoughts dwell pleasurably on scenes of crime. The fact of their finding pleasure in such thoughts, evidences their own inward pollution. They are corrupt already in fact, however it may be in form. This is why bad books and bad publications of various kinds do so much harm; they poison the imagination, induce bad thoughts, which, little by little, gain on their victims till all within is moral pollution."

WHEN done with the right motive, the preaching of the Gospel is the most useful, soul-inspiring work ever undertaken by man. It is not only self-sacrificing in its very nature, but the tendency is to lift up, ennoble and benefit others. It is the broadest class of charity, reaching out to benefit not only the souls of men and women, but their bodies likewise, for that which elevates and purifies the soul, confers a similar blessing on the body. Mothers, who prepare their sons for the sacred work, as Hannah of old prepared Samuel, and wives who assist and encourage their husbands in the work of the ministry, become ministering angels, whose influence may be felt to the end of time.

THE Mormons are establishing a colony in North-western Canada, and many of the families from Utah will emigrate to that place. The wholesome law of this country makes the way of the transgressor hard, so far as it pertains to polygamy.

BRO. F. W. DOVE, of Jonesboro, Tenn., has moved with his family to Cabool, Texas County, Mo., for the purpose of making that his future home. He has had this change of location in view for some time, and while we regret to have him leave Tennessee, we feel confident that he has selected a field where his labors are very much needed, and will be appreciated. Texas County is in the southern part of the State, about fifty miles east of Springfield.

"NEARLY four million copies of the Bible, Testament, and portions of the Bible were distributed last year by the British and Foreign Bible Society of England. The increase in copies distributed over the previous year was 63,680. Since the publication of the "Penny" Testament in July, 1884, 5,000,668 copies have been issued. Through twenty-seven societies grants were made for 364 Bible women during the year, who read the Scriptures on an average to 18,742 native women every week. Nine new versions of the Bible were issued."

JUST what relation the Christian sustains to the things of this world, depends a good deal upon whether he belongs to the world or Christ. The early Christians found nothing too great a sacrifice for the cause of Christianity. To them everything else was simply secondary and used, if used at all, as a means to an end. Their property, as well as their talent and lives, was fully consecrated to the Lord. They made money and acquired property, but it was all with a view of advancing the cause of the Christian religion. While they mingled, to some extent, with the world, they were everywhere known as pronounced Christians who were in no manner ashamed of their religion. We need in this day to cultivate more of this consecrated spirit.

MINISTERS who stand before a congregation and say they have made no preparation whatever, and will speak only as the Lord puts words into their mouth, ought to remember that the Lord does not put words into the mouth of that kind of a preacher. The Lord has placed his words in the Bible, and it is the duty of the minister, by careful study, to get them into his head, and from there into his heart. Such a man the Lord can and will help to preach. But how can or how will he help a man to preach who does not make the Bible a study? You might as well talk of the man who neither sows nor reaps, having his garners well stored with grain. The Lord helps those who try to help themselves, in preaching as well as in other things. We believe in every minister preparing himself to preach. This he does by hard study, prayer and consecration. We do not mean that he must always prepare his sermons, for some of the best sermons ever preached were prompted by the impressions of the occasion, but he ought to study so as to know how to rightly divide and present the Truth when called on to do so. We have heard ministers say, "I have given the subject no thought, and must speak as liberty is given." From their talk one would judge that they had given the matter no thought. Such a course may be well enough when one is unexpectedly called upon to preach, but for a minister to have weeks in which to prepare himself for the occasion, and then say that he has made no preparation, is a species of negligence for which there is no excuse.

QUERISTS' DEPARTMENT.

I would like to Inquire whether it is the duty of a brother who does not use tobacco to salute one who is filthy with it?
GEO. BRILHART.

PAUL says, "Salute all the brethren with a holy kiss." As long as a man is in the church he is entitled to the Christian greeting. If he is not in a condition for greeting he should certainly be admonished and labored with until he can be induced to remove the filthiness of the flesh. One who is not fit to be saluted is not fit to remain in the church, but it becomes the duty of the church to do her utmost to reform anyone who has been overcome by this unfortunate habit, and we think by proper effort all of them may be sufficiently reformed to be born with in Christian fellowship. Possibly there may be members who are too sensitive to the smell of tobacco to salute those who use it rather freely, and yet cannot be considered indecent. Perhaps a friendly Christian conversation between the parties would remove troubles. While we are decidedly opposed to the use of tobacco in any form, we are willing to suffer some unpleasantness, in order to work a reform in those who need our help and prayers in this respect. But one thing is certain, there is no use of any man using tobacco or anything else so as to make himself indecent or offensive.

Please explain (1) 1 Tim. 5: 9, "Let not a widow be taken into their number under threescore years old," etc. (2) Also, John 21: 15. "Simon, son of Jonas, lovest thou me more than these?"
JOHN SCHMIDT.

1. Reference is here made to widows who were to be entirely supported by the church. In order to be thus favored it was necessary that they possess certain qualifications, and be not less than sixty years old. Possibly they were assigned certain work in the church becoming their sex. We know that in the apostolic age, as well as in succeeding centuries, women did engage in duties of this kind. Paul mentions the women who labored with him in the Gospel. Philpp. 4: 3.

2. The meaning of the quotation is this: "Lovest thou me more than these disciples love me?" Just before the trial of Jesus, Peter had boasted thus: "Though all men shall be offended because of thee, yet will I never be offended." Matt. 26: 33. Only a few hours later Peter denied his Master three times, thus going back on his boasting. Instead of standing firmer than any of the other disciples, which he said he would do, he displayed less firmness than any of them. Hence the question put to him by Jesus was a searching reproof, though uttered in simple words. Peter had denied Jesus three times, and is now called on to confess him three separate times.

Matt. 19: 5, 6 reads thus: "And said, For this cause shall a man leave father and mother, and shall cleave to his wife: and they twain shall be one flesh. Wherefore they are no more twain, but one flesh. . What therefore God hath joined together, let not man put asunder."

1. Does the woman become the wife when the man cleaves to her? Or do the parties become one flesh when engaged, or united by God, or by the marriage ceremony?

2. If joined by the marriage ceremony, is one who is not a true follower of Christ, qualified to perform the marriage ceremony, consistent with the Gospel?

3. When do they become husband and wife in the sight of God?
JOHN F. LEHMAN.

The Gospel is silent concerning the manner of uniting man and woman in the bonds of holy matrimony, hence the act must be governed by civil law. So long as this law does not conflict with Gospel principles, and promotes morality and justice, it is our duty to govern ourselves accordingly. Hence

1. The man and woman become one flesh at the consummation of the marriage ceremony, but not before. Engagement does not constitute them man and wife either in the sight of God or the law. Engagement vows may be broken by mutual consent, but marriage vows remain sacred both in the sight of the law and the Gospel, more so in the sense of the Gospel than in the sense of the law. God joins together only where the marriage is legal. This is a puzzling question in the minds of those who think there is a joining together separate and apart from the process required by law. We hold to the view that God endorses any legal form of marriage that is in keeping with morality and the Christian religion. This form may vary in different ages, and in different countries.

2. The Gospel says nothing concerning the qualifications of those who should perform a marriage ceremony. While one, who is not a true follower of Christ, may be qualified to perform the ceremony, it certainly does seem more appropriate that it should be performed by one who is, at least, a professing Christian.

3. This is fully answered under No. 1.

What is the duty of the church, or the adjoining elders, where a minister, or elder, moves into a congregation, and does not hand in his letter of membership, and also does not attend meeting? Will you please withhold my name?

This question was referred to Bro. Enoch Eby. Here is his answer: "I would treat an elder just like any other member in a similar case, only I would have another elder present when the certificate is demanded, so if he did not come to the council, the reasons could be presented to the church. If the reasons for not handing in the certificate are thought not valid by the church, then the church, with the elder present, may report him back to the church giving the letter, stating the facts in the case. And if the reasons are not valid, and nothing but selfishness is in the way, it might be well to report him to one or two adjoining elders of the church giving him his letter."

We farther add, that if for any cause an elder, or anyone else, cannot hand in his certificate very soon after locating in another congregation, he should explain the situation to the officials at once. This will avoid unnecessary suspicion, and probably gain for him the sympathy, as well as the assistance of the members. There is nothing like being candid about such things. J H M

OLD TIME SINGING.

IN articles and items, that have appeared from time to time, we have urged our members to give more attention to religious singing, so as to improve that part of our worship. We may be mistaken, but it seems to us that in former years more attention was given to vocal music than at present. At least there is a possibility of it being greatly neglected among us, as it has certainly been by others. In the following from the Pacific Methodist, we can clearly see the result of this great neglect among the Methodists, who, at one time, were the greatest singers on this Continent:

"It is a shame—and almost a sin—that Methodist congregations are so generally deficient in singing. Their superior singing was once one of the chief attractions that drew the people to our churches. Now their shameful deficiency is one of the chief causes that keep them away. The change is as unaccountable as it is lamentable. Our

people pay no attention to vocal music, and, with the exception of one here and there whom nature has gifted with a faultless ear, there are none who can lead the worship of God in singing. A hymn and tune book has been issued by our publishing house—and admirably is it gotten up. But how many of our members can use it? Many of them can no more read note-music than they can decipher Egyptian hieroglyphics. Men and women, well educated in other respects, intelligent and refined, have had no musical culture whatever. From some inexplicable cause this important part of education has been wholly neglected. Such singing as we have in many of our congregations! In some the preacher must do all the singing. Woe to him if he cannot sing at all, as is some. times the case! Then, again, there are too many volunteer leaders. Several brethren will start at once in different keys, and struggle for the mastery until the strongest lungs conquer.

"There should be a singing-school in every society. This is according to primitive Methodism. The early Methodists outsang all the world. They paid attention to the subject. They knew how to sing. They sung with the Spirit, for they were religious; they sung with the understanding, for they took pains to learn."

There is an urgent necessity for agitating this question. Our people are decidedly in favor of congregational singing, and opposed to the use of instrumental music in our worship. The decided tendency of the age is for instrumental music in all song services. If we succeed in maintaining our congregational singing, we must make the teaching of vocal music a specialty among the rising generation of our own people at least. Let us take warning from what has befallen other denominations, and see if we cannot cultivate our musical talent to a degree that will permit us to sing with the spirit and understanding in a manner that will enable the world to feel it, as well as hear it. We are just as much in favor of good singing as we are of good preaching, and believe that the former is as essential to true worship as the latter. J. H. M.

BY degrees we are restoring some of the "lost arts." In some respects the ancients excelled us both in knowledge and skill. In Damascus 3,000 years ago, swords were made that could be folded up and placed in boxes like paper collars. When taken out they would become as straight as a yard-stick, and were so sharp and hard that they would cut hair or iron rods with equal success. The ancients also knew how to make tools of copper, greatly superior in quality and hardness to the best of modern steel implements. These, with other inventions, have long been classed with the "lost arts." Recently, however, a blacksmith, of Quebec, has made known the discovery of a method for hardening copper so that it can be employed in making the very finest of tools. "In his sensational lecture on 'The Lost Arts,' which Wendell Phillips delivered some thirty years ago, the statement was made that the builders of the great pyramids understood how to harden copper, and that the tools they employed for cutting the stones, used in the monuments along the Nile, were made of that metal. Wilkinson, the celebrated Egyptologist, made the same statement. The natives of Mexico and Peru made most of their utensils out of copper, and their cutting tools were equal to any of those found in Egypt and brought to the British museum. Some have argued from this that there must have been communication between the people of Egypt and those of Peru and Mexico." By thus bringing to light the knowledge of the ancient, and adding it to the discoveries of the

QUERISTS' DEPARTMENT.

I would like to inquire whether it is the duty of a brother who does not use tobacco to salute one who is filthy with it?
GEO. BRILHART.

PAUL says, "Salute all the brethren with a holy kiss." As long as a man is in the church he is entitled to the Christian greeting. If he is not in a condition for greeting he should certainly be admonished and labored with until he can be induced to remove the filthiness of the flesh. One who is not fit to be saluted is not fit to remain in the church, but it becomes the duty of the church to do her utmost to reform anyone who has been overcome by this unfortunate habit, and we think by proper effort all of them may be sufficiently reformed to be born with in Christian fellowship. Possibly there may be members who are too sensitive to the smell of tobacco to salute those who use it rather freely, and yet cannot be considered indecent. Perhaps a friendly Christian conversation between the parties would remove troubles. While we are decidedly opposed to the use of tobacco in any form, we are willing to suffer some unpleasantness, in order to work a reform in those who need our help and prayers in this respect. But one thing is certain, there is no use of any man using tobacco or anything else so as to make himself indecent or offensive.

Please explain (1) 1 Tim. 5: 9, "Let not a widow be taken into their number under threescore years old," etc. (2) Also, John 21: 15. "Simon, son of Jonas, lovest thou me more than these?" JOHN SCHMIDT.

1. Reference is here made to widows who were to be entirely supported by the church. In order to be thus favored it was necessary that they possess certain qualifications, and be not less than sixty years old. Possibly they were assigned certain work in the church becoming their sex. We know that in the apostolic age, as well as in succeeding centuries, women did engage in duties of this kind. Paul mentions the women who labored with him in the Gospel. Philpp. 4: 3.

2. The meaning of the quotation is this: "Lovest thou me more than these disciples love me?" Just before the trial of Jesus, Peter had boasted thus: "Though all men shall be offended because of thee, yet will I never be offended." Matt. 26: 33. Only a few hours later Peter denied his Master three times, thus going back on his boasting. Instead of standing firmer than any of the other disciples, which he said he would do, he displayed less firmness than any of them. Hence the question put to him by Jesus was a searching reproof, though uttered in simple words. Peter had denied Jesus three times, and is now called on to confess him three separate times.

Matt. 19: 5, 6 reads thus: "And said, For this cause shall a man leave father and mother, and shall cleave to his wife: and they twain shall be one flesh. Wherefore they are no more twain, but one flesh. What therefore God hath joined together, let not man put asunder."

1. Does the woman become the wife when the man cleaves to her? Or do the parties become one flesh when engaged, or united by God, or by the marriage ceremony?

2. If joined by the marriage ceremony, is one who is not a true follower of Christ, qualified to perform the marriage ceremony, consistent with the Gospel?

3. When do they become husband and wife in the sight of God? JOHN F. LEHMAN.

The Gospel is silent concerning the *manner* of uniting man and woman in the bonds of holy matrimony, hence the act must be governed by civil law. So long as this law does not conflict with Gospel principles, and promotes morality and justice, it is our duty to govern ourselves accordingly. Hence

1. The man and woman become one flesh at the consummation of the marriage ceremony, but not before. Engagement does not constitute them man and wife either in the sight of God or the law. Engagement vows may be broken by mutual consent, but marriage vows remain sacred both in the sight of the law and the Gospel, more so in the sense of the Gospel than in the sense of the law. God joins together only where the marriage is legal. This is a puzzling question in the minds of those who think there is a joining together separate and apart from the process required by law. We hold to the view that God endorses any legal form of marriage that is in keeping with morality and the Christian religion. This form may vary in different ages, and in different countries.

2. The Gospel says nothing concerning the qualifications of those who should perform a marriage ceremony. While one, who is not a true follower of Christ, may be qualified to perform the ceremony, it certainly does seem more appropriate that it should be performed by one who is, at least, a professing Christian.

3. This is fully answered under No. 1.

What is the duty of the church, or the adjoining elders, where a minister, or elder, moves into a congregation, and does not hand in his letter of membership, and also does not attend meeting? Will you please withhold my name?

This question was referred to Bro. Enoch Eby. Here is his answer: "I would treat an elder just like any other member in a similar case, only I would have another elder present when the certificate is demanded, so if he did not come to the council, the reasons could be presented to the church. If the reasons for not handing in the certificate are thought not valid by the church, then the church, with the elder present, may report him back to the church giving the letter, stating the facts in the case. And if the reasons are not valid, and nothing but selfishness is in the way, it might be well to report him to one or two adjoining elders of the church giving him his letter." E. E.

We further add, that if for any cause an elder, or anyone else, cannot hand in his certificate very soon after locating in another congregation, he should explain the situation to the officials at once. This will avoid unnecessary suspicion, and probably gain for him the sympathy, as well as the assistance of the members. There is nothing like being candid about such things. J H M

OLD TIME SINGING.

IN articles and items, that have appeared, from time to time, we have urged our members to give more attention to religious singing, so as to improve that part of our worship. We may be mistaken, but it seems to us that in former years more attention was given to vocal music than at present. At least there is a possibility of its being greatly neglected among us, as it has certainly been by others. In the following from the *Pacific Methodist*, we can clearly see the result of this great neglect among the Methodists, who, at one time, were the greatest singers on this Continent:

"It is a shame—and almost a sin—that Methodist congregations are so generally deficient in singing. Their superior singing was once one of the chief attractions that drew the people to our churches. Now their shameful deficiency is one of the chief causes that keep them away. The change is as unaccountable as it is lamentable. Our

people pay no attention to vocal music, and, with the exception of one here and there whom nature has gifted with a faultless ear, there are none who can lead the worship of God in singing. A hymn and tune book has been issued by our publishing house—and admirably is it gotten up. But how many of our members can use it? Many of them can no more read note-music than they can decipher Egyptian hieroglyphics. Men and women, well educated in other respects, intelligent and refined, have had no musical culture whatever. From some inexplicable cause this important part of education has been wholly neglected. Such singing as we have in many of our congregations! In some the preacher must do all the singing. Woe to him if he cannot sing at all, as is sometimes the case! Then, again, there are too many volunteer leaders. Several brethren will start at once in different keys, and struggle for the mastery until the strongest lungs conquer.

"There should be a *singing-school in every society*. This is according to primitive Methodism. The early Methodists outsung all the world. They paid attention to the subject. They knew how to sing. They sung with the Spirit, for they were religious; they sung with the understanding, for they took pains to learn."

There is an urgent necessity for agitating this question. Our people are decidedly in favor of congregational singing, and opposed to the use of instrumental music in our worship. The decided tendency of the age is for instrumental music in all song services. If we succeed in maintaining our congregational singing, we must make the teaching of vocal music a specialty among the rising generation of our own people at least. Let us take warning from what has befallen other denominations, and see if we cannot cultivate our musical talent to a degree that will permit us to sing with the spirit and understanding in a manner that will enable the world to *feel* it, as well as hear it. We are just as much in favor of good singing as we are of good preaching, and believe that the former is as essential to true worship as the latter. J. H. M.

By degrees we are restoring some of the "lost arts." In some respects the ancients excelled us both in knowledge and skill. In Damascus 3,000 years ago, swords were made that could be folded up and placed in boxes like paper collars. When taken out they would become as straight as a yard-stick, and were so sharp and hard that they would cut hair or iron rods with equal success. The ancients also knew how to make tools of copper, greatly superior in quality and hardness to the best of modern steel implements. These, with other inventions, have long been classed with the "lost arts." Recently, however, a blacksmith, of Quebec, has made known the discovery of a method for hardening copper so that it can be employed in making the very finest of tools. "In his sensational lecture on 'The Lost Arts,' which Wendell Phillips delivered some thirty years ago, the statement was made that the builders of the great pyramids understood how to harden copper, and that the tools they employed for cutting the stones, used in the monuments along the Nile, were made of that metal. Wilkinson, the celebrated Egyptologist, made the same statement. The natives of Mexico and Peru made most of their utensils out of copper, and their cutting tools were equal to any of those found in Egypt and brought to the British museum. Some have argued from this that there must have been communication between the people of Egypt and those of Peru and Mexico." By thus bringing to light the knowledge of the ancient, and adding it to the discoveries of the

and father. His wife and a number of children survive him. Bro. Shaffer filled his seat in the sanctuary only nine days before. This should remind us again that this is not our home.

Our aged brother, A. A. Weaver, who has been confined to his room over three years, is very low and suffering greatly. He may be near the end.

In all probability, this will be my last correspondence to the MESSENGER from this place, as we expect, the Lord willing, to start from Manassas, Va., the beginning of September. We expect to make that our future home. Brethren and sisters, pray for us that we may ever be faithful, and in the end receive a crown of life.

J. E. BLOUGH.

Scalp Level, Pa., Aug. 11.

[We hope to hear from Bro. Blough after reaching his new field of labor. We always appreciate his well-prepared articles.—ED.]

The Debate Failed.

SINCE it was published in the MESSENGER a few weeks ago that a discussion of several propositions, covering much the same ground as the Miller and Sommer debate, was agreed upon between a minister of the Christian Church (Campbellite), of West Virginia, and myself, I feel it due the MESSENGER readers to say.now that the debate failed.

Some time in April last, M. J. Walters, the above Campbellite minister, challenged our Brethren to discuss the points of difference between himself and us, whereupon a committee of brethren was appointed to consider the challenge, and if, in their judgment, a discussion of the questions involved seemed proper, arrangements should be made at once for the debate. The committee at once informed Mr. Walters that if he would present a certificate, showing good standing in his church as a minister, also a certificate officially endorsed by the people whom he serves, setting him forward as in their judgment possessing sufficient ability to do them justice in debate, his challenge would be considered. Mr. Walters answered both in person and by letter, saying that the credentials named would be forthcoming.' His leading members said the same thing. Accordingly, the committee considered the challenge and decided to accept it, and proceeded to arrange for the discussion. Propositions, time, etc., were agreed upon, but when the preliminary meeting was held four days before the discussion was expected to open, the fact was clearly revealed that Mr. Walters' people were afraid. They positively refused to furnish the certificate endorsing their man in point of ability. Whether they were afraid of this man only, or of their position, or both, may yet be shown.

As to Mr. Walters the fact is, as has been shown throughout the proceedings, that he is a man of considerable courage, but with the most ordinary ability. This may serve to some of us, at least, as an important lesson.   H. C. EARLY.

Meyerheoffer's Store, Va., Aug. 22.

The German Hymn Book.

THE undersigned Committee, appointed by the Annual Meeting of 1891, to revise, or compile a new German Hymn Book, for the use of the German part of our Brotherhood, hereby inform all those interested in the work, that they have delayed work on the same, until they see what disposition will be made of the English Hymn Book question. That being now decided in favor of a new book, we call on all brethren, interested, to send us propositions as to how they would like to have it; viz., which of the two books now generally used, should be taken as a guide, and what hymns they want stricken out. Mention book and number, also send us hymns from other collections, if

you have any that you would like to see in the new book, etc. Hymns so mentioned and sent may possibly be more closely examined than they would be if the committee's attention were not especially called to them. Immediate attention should be given to this, in order to hasten the work.

S. R. Zpg, Mastersonville, Pa.,
J. H. LONGENECKER, Palmyra, Pa.,
J. ALDINGER, York, Pa.,
Committee.

From the Van Wert Church, Ohio.

OUR harvest or thanksgiving meeting was held here Aug. 11, 1892, it being the first meeting of the kind ever held in this church. Brethren D. Provant, and D. Miller were the ministers present from abroad, also brethren Jacob Heistand and James Harp, our home ministers. The whole day was spent in worshiping the Lord. Thanksgiving and praise were offered to the Lord for his protecting care over the Van Wert church and for the brethren and sisters everywhere. We also thanked the Lord for the harvest that we have again received. Though it was not great, yet we have enough and to spare. It was, indeed, a soul-reviving meeting, which will long be remembered as the first meeting of the kind ever attended by some of the brethren and sisters, and we hope it will not be the last one to be held at this place. There was an offering given for the Home Mission.

ANTHONY COPP.

Upper Twin Creek Notes.

AUG. 8 grandmother Mary Maphis, late of Rockingham County Va., being in declining health, desired to be anointed according to James 5, and it was attended to by the brethren, to her great joy and satisfaction. She is being tenderly cared for at the home of her son, Joseph Coffman.

Aug. 18 Bro. Peter Slyder, who had passed his seventy-third year, was suddenly summoned from time to eternity while driving from his home to West Alexandria on the afternoon of Aug. 16, and was buried in the Eversole cemetery to-day.

Aug. 24 occurred the council-meeting at Sugar Hill. The visit reported the church to be in good condition with a few exceptions. It will be a pleasure to many to learn that peace is again restored, and that we have appointed a Communion, to be held at Wheatville, Nov. 8, beginning at 10 A. M. We feel much encouraged to-day and ask God's blessing upon our work, as well as the prayers of the Brotherhood in our behalf.

A. G. CROSSWHITE.

Gratis, Ohio, Aug. 24.

Lower Stillwater Notes.

OUR harvest meeting was held in our lower house, Aug. 6, at 3 P. M. The Book and Tract Committee, and the Mission Board of Southern Ohio, met at different places near us the same day. They finished their business in time to attend our meeting. This gave us a good attendance of ministers. Bro. David Filburn gave us an appropriate address, followed by Bro. Isaac Frantz.

Meetings of this kind afford excellent opportunities for instruction in Gospel husbandry. Strange as it may seem to people who acknowledge no man-made creed, but profess to follow the pure Word of God, we are yet in need of clearer teaching on this subject. As Christ came into the world for its benefit, so the church is here for the same purpose.

Aug. 10, we held our regular quarterly council in the upper house. The business passed off in a quiet and pleasant manner. Bro. Wm. Klepinger was ordained to the full ministry or eldership. May he realize in the fear of God that this means increased activity in the Lord's vineyard, more

care in dressing it, and in looking after the weak lambs of the fold.

We arranged to have two series of meetings next.winter; one in the lower house, to be held by Bro. D. S. Filburn, of Brandt, Ohio, Dec. 1, the other in the upper house by W. Q. Calvert, to begin about Feb. 4. Our Communion is appointed for Nov. 2, at 2 P. M., in the upper house. An invitation is extended to all of like precious faith to be with us at that time.

Bro M. G. Brumbaugh, of Huntingdon Pa., has been in Southern Ohio for some time, conducting Teachers' Institutes. He has also been doing some Gospel preaching in our churches. At our place, Aug. 21, he gave an earnest sermon from 1 Thess. 5: 5, "The children of light." In the evening, in the Wolf Creek church, he spoke from 1 Sam. 7: 12, "Ebenezer."

L. A. BOOKWALTER.

Trotwood, Ohio, Aug. 28, 1892.

Notes by the Way.

WIFE and I left our home at Franklin Grove, Ill., July 14, for our eastern trip. We arrived at Hagerstown on the B. and O. R. R. next day. Our first visit was in York County, Pa. We met with the Brethren on Sunday at the Bucher meeting-house, in the Codorus church, under the care of Elder Aaron Baugher. Here we had several meetings.

We next visited the Big Conawago church, under the care of Eld. Peter Brown. We spent several weeks in this church, attended seven meetings and visited relatives. Among the number were two aged aunts, one in her ninety-second, the other in her eighty-second year.

We next met with the Brethren at Gettysburg. We also had a few meetings with the Marsh Creek Brethren. This church is under the care of Eld. L. C. Pfoutz. On the way we took a view of the battle-ground. From there we returned to Hagerstown and attended one meeting at the Welsh Run meeting-house. This church is under the care of B. N. Martin. At this meeting we had the pleasure of listening to Bro. S. N. McCann, of Bridgewater, Va.

At this writing we are staying with sister Katie Strock in Franklin County, Pa., a sister in deed and truth. She has no use of her feet, and has walked on her knees for almost sixty years. She works her way to the meetings whenever she can. She says she thanks God that it is not any worse than it is. I am made to wonder how many of us, who have the use of all our limbs, would feel as she does, if that were our lot.

Next Sunday we expect to meet with the Brethren in the Back Creek church at the Brandt house, and in the afternoon at the Upton house. This church is under the care of brethren Daniel Miller and John Lehner. It is the place of my boyhood. Many of my associates have passed over the river since 1854. From here we expect to visit Waynesborough. There we will see the peach orchards, heavily laden with fruit. From there our next visit will be Washington, Baltimore and York. We expect to spend some time in York among brethren and relatives.

S. C. LEHMAN.

Cashtown, Pa., Aug. 20.

From Alfonte, Madison County, Ind.

AUG. 13 Eld. D. R. Richards and W. N. Collins started for Jackson County to attend a trial as witnesses. Before starting, the undersigned notified the New Hope church to announce meetings for Saturday night. Meetings commenced as announced and continued from the 13th to the 18th, being, in all, eight sermons. As an immediate result thirteen souls came out on the Lord's side,

and father. His wife and a number of children survive him. Bro. Shaffer filled his seat in the sanctuary only nine days before. This should remind us again that this is not our home.

Our aged brother, A. A. Weaver, who has been confined to his room over three years, is very low and suffering greatly. He may be near the end.

In all probability, this will be my last correspondence with the MESSENGER from this place, as we expect, the Lord willing, to start from Manassas, Va., the beginning of September. We expect to make that our future home. Brethren and sisters, pray for us that we may ever be faithful, and in the end receive a crown of life.

J. E. BLOUGH.

Scalp Level, Pa., Aug. 11.

[We hope to hear from Bro. Blough after reaching his new field of labor. We always appreciate his well-prepared articles.—ED.]

The Debate Failed.

SINCE it was published in the MESSENGER a few weeks ago that a discussion of several propositions, covering much the same ground as the Miller and Sommer debate, was agreed upon between a minister of the Christian Church (Campbellite), of West Virginia, and myself, I feel it due the MESSENGER readers to say now that the debate failed.

Some time in April last, M. J. Walters, the above Campbellite minister, challenged our Brethren to discuss the points of difference between himself and us, whereupon a committee of brethren was appointed to consider the challenge, and if, in their judgment, a discussion of the questions involved seemed proper, arrangements should be made at once for the debate. The committee at once informed Mr. Walters that if he would present a certificate, showing good standing in his church as a minister, also a certificate officially endorsed by the people whom he serves, setting him forward as in their judgment possessing sufficient ability to do them justice in debate, his challenge would be considered. Mr. Walters answered both in person and by letter, saying that the credentials named would be forthcoming. His leading members said the same thing. Accordingly, the committee considered the challenge and decided to accept it, and proceeded to arrange for the discussion. Propositions, time, etc., were agreed upon, but when the preliminary meeting was held four days before the discussion was expected to open, the fact was clearly revealed that Mr. Walters' people were afraid. They positively refused to furnish the certificate endorsing their man in point of ability. Whether they were afraid of this man only, or of their position, or both, may yet be shown.

As to Mr. Walters the fact is, as has been shown throughout the proceedings, that he is a man of considerable courage, but with the most ordinary ability. This may serve to some of us, at least, as an important lesson. H. C. EARLY.

Meyerhoeffer's Store, Va., Aug. 22.

The German Hymn Book.

THE undersigned Committee, appointed by the Annual Meeting of 1891, to revise, or compile a new German Hymn Book, for the use of the German part of our Brotherhood, hereby inform all those interested in the work, that they have delayed work on the same, until they see what disposition will be made of the English Hymn Book question. That being now decided in favor of a new book, we call on all brethren, interested, to send us propositions as to how they would like to have it; viz., which of the two books now generally used, should be taken as a guide, and what hymns they want stricken out. Mention book and number, also send us hymns from other collections, if

you have any that you would like to see in the new book, etc. Hymns so mentioned and sent may possibly be more closely examined than they would be if the committee's attention were not especially called to them. Immediate attention should be given to this, in order to hasten the work.

S. R. ZUG, Mastersonville, Pa.,
J. H. LONGENECKER, Palmyra, Pa.,
J. ALDINGER, York, Pa.,
Committee.

From the Van Wert Church, Ohio.

OUR harvest or thanksgiving meeting was held here Aug. 11, 1892, it being the first meeting of the kind ever held in this church. Brethren D. Provant, and D. Miller were the ministers present from abroad, also brethren Jacob Heistand and James Harp, our home ministers. The whole day was spent in worshiping the Lord. Thanksgiving and praise were offered to the Lord for his protecting care over the Van Wert church and for the brethren and sisters everywhere. We also thanked the Lord for the harvest that we have again received. Though it was not great, yet we have enough and to spare. It was, indeed, a soul-reviving meeting, which will long be remembered as the first meeting of the kind ever attended by some of the brethren and sisters, and we hope it will not be the last one to be held at this place. There was an offering given for the Home Mission.

ANTHONY CUPP.

Upper Twin Creek Notes.

AUG. 8 grandmother Mary Maphis, late of Rockingham County Va., being in declining health, desired to be anointed according to James 5, and it was attended to by the brethren; to her great joy and satisfaction. She is being tenderly cared for at the home of her son, Joseph Coffman.

Aug. 18 Bro. Peter Slyder, who had passed his seventy-third year, was suddenly summoned from time to eternity while driving from his home to West Alexandria on the afternoon of Aug. 16, and was buried in the Eversole cemetery to-day.

Aug. 24 occurred the council-meeting at Sugar Hill. The visit reported the church to be in good condition with a few exceptions. It will be a pleasure to many to learn that peace is again restored, and that we have appointed a Communion, to be held at Wheatville, Nov. 8, beginning at 10 A. M. We feel much encouraged to-day and ask God's blessing upon our work, as well as the prayers of the Brotherhood in our behalf.

A. G. CROSSWHITE.

Gratis, Ohio, Aug. 24.

Lower Stillwater Notes.

OUR harvest meeting was held in our lower house, Aug. 6, at 3 P. M. The Book and Tract Committee, and the Mission Board of Southern Ohio, met at different places near us the same day. They finished their business in time to attend our meeting. This gave us a good attendance of ministers. Bro. David Filburn gave us an appropriate address, followed by Bro. Isaac Frantz.

Meetings of this kind afford excellent opportunities for instruction in Gospel husbandry. Strange as it may seem to people who acknowledge no man-made creed, but profess to follow the pure Word of God, we are yet in need of clearer teaching on this subject. As Christ came into the world for its benefit, so the church is here for the same purpose.

Aug. 10, we held our regular quarterly council in the upper house. The business passed off in a quiet and pleasant manner. Bro. Wm. Klepinger was ordained to the full ministry or eldership. May he realize in the fear of God that this means increased activity in the Lord's vineyard, more

care in dressing it, and in looking after the weak lambs of the fold.

We arranged to have two series of meetings next winter; one in the lower house, to be held by Bro. D. S. Filburn, of Brandt, Ohio, Dec. 1, the other in the upper house by W. Q. Calvert, to begin about Feb. 4. Our Communion is appointed for Nov. 2, at 2 P. M., in the upper house. An invitation is extended to all of like precious faith to be with us at that time.

Bro M. G. Brumbaugh, of Huntingdon Pa., has been in Southern Ohio for some time, conducting Teachers' Institutes. He has also been doing some Gospel preaching in our churches. At our place, Aug. 21, he gave an earnest sermon from 1 Thess. 5: 5, "The children of light." In the evening, in the Wolf Creek church, he spoke from 1 Sam. 7: 12, "Ebenezer." L. A. BOOKWALTER.

Trotwood, Ohio, Aug. 22, 1892.

Notes by the Way.

WIFE and I left our home at Franklin Grove, Ill., July 14, for our eastern trip. We arrived at Hagerstown on the B. and O. R. R. next day. Our first visit was in York County, Pa. We met with the Brethren on Sunday at the Bucher meeting-house, in the Codorus church, under the care of Elder Aaron Baugher. Here we had several meetings.

We next visited the Big Conawago church, under the care of Eld. Peter Brown. We spent several weeks in this church, attended seven meetings and visited relatives. Among the number were two aged saints, one in her ninety-second, the other in her eighty-second year.

We next met with the Brethren at Gettysburg. We also had a few meetings with the Marsh Creek Brethren. This church is under the care of Eld. L. C. Pfouts. On the way we took a view of the battle-ground. From there we returned to Hagerstown and attended one meeting at the Welsh Run meeting-house. This church is under the care of B. N. Martin. At this meeting we had the pleasure of listening to Bro. S. N. McCann, of Bridgewater, Va.

At this writing we are staying with sister Katie Strock in Franklin County, Pa., a sister in deed and truth. She has no use of her feet, and has walked on her knees for almost sixty years. She works her way to the meetings whenever she can. She says she thanks God that it is not any worse than it is. I am made to wonder how many of us, who have the use of all our limbs, would feel as she does, if that were our lot.

Next Sunday we expect to meet with the Brethren in the Back Creek church at the Brandt house, and in the afternoon at the Upton house. This church is under the care of brethren Daniel Miller and John Lehner. It is the place of my boyhood. Many of my associates have passed over the river since 1854. From here we expect to visit Waynesborough. There we will see the peach orchards, heavily laden with fruit From there our next visit will be Washington, Baltimore and York. We expect to spend some time in York among brethren and relatives.

S. C. LEHMAN.

Cashtown, Pa., Aug. 20.

From Alfonte, Madison County, Ind.

AUG. 13 Eld. D. R. Richards and W. N. Collins started for Jackson County to attend a trial as witnesses. Before starting, the undersigned notified the New Hope church to announce meetings for Saturday night. Meetings commenced as announced and continued from the 19th to the 18th, being, in all, eight sermons. As an immediate result thirteen souls came out on the Lord's side,

Wade, Kans.—The Wade's Branch church met in council Aug. 13, at our meeting-house, near Wade. A fair representation of the members was present, and the meeting passed off in harmony. We decided to hold our Communion meeting Nov. 4, commencing at 2 P. M. A series of meetings will commence one week previous, if the Lord will.—*G. M. Lauver.*

Peru, Ind.—Our harvest-meeting in the Pipe Creek church occurred Aug. 20. Quite a number of brethren and sisters were present. Brethren Noah Fisher, Jacob Fox, and David Wolf were present, and labed to the interest of the meeting. Bro. Fisher preached an excellent sermon for us on Sunday. One was received by baptism since my last report.—*William B Dailey, Aug. 22.*

Lyons, Kans.—The members of the Kansas Center church met in quarterly council Aug. 6. All business before the meeting passed off pleasantly, and, we trust, in the fear of the Lord. We appointed our love-feast for Nov. 5; also decided to begin a series of meetings a week previous. We shall gladly receive all the help we can get, either from ministers or laymembers. May the Lord help us all to improve our opportunities for doing good!—*S. J. Dresher, Secretary.*

Elkhart, Ind.—We, the members of the Elkhart Valley church, held a very enjoyable harvest-meeting. We called Bro. J. C. Murray, of Nappanee, Ind., to labor for us. He was with us and gave us very good counsel. A number of the neighboring ministers were also with us. We think we had a very good meeting, and believe all could say it was good to be there. The brethren gave us Gospel truths, and we hope we will remember the lessons learned. May God help us all to be of more use to the church hereafter than we were in the past. We can be of use to the church by giving of the means with which God has blessed us. We have freely received, so let us give freely and cheerfully.—*S. C. Kindy.*

Battle Creek, Iowa.—A few members live in the south-western part of Ida County, Iowa. We belong to the Kingsley church, which is thirty-five miles from here. Bro Joseph Trostle is our elder. We have no speaker here, and we do not have much preaching. The Mission Board sends a preacher once a year. Bro. E B. Hoff has promised to be here after Sept. 15, and give us some meetings. We have appointed our love-feast for Sept. 24. If any brethren can come and assist us, we would be very glad. We have a good country and would like if some minister would move among us. I know they could do good. By addressing me at Battle Creek, Ida Co., Iowa, I will meet any who may desire to come. You can reach us via the Chicago & North-western R. R.—*J. H. Isinbarger.*

Wyandot, Ohio.—We, the members of the Wyandot church, met in council Aug. 20. There was not much business before the meeting, and all was adjusted in a Christian manner. The visiting brethren made their report, which showed that all are in love and union. Bro. Loose, our elder, was with us and preached on Saturday evening; also on Sunday at the church, and on Sunday evening at the house of Bro. Henry Keller. Bro. S. A. Walker was to be with us Aug. 7, to do some baptizing but that morning he was sent for to preach a funeral, so he could not come that day. He came however, Aug. 14. A meeting was appointed at Bro. Henry Keller's, after which two young sisters were buried with Christ in baptism. We ask the prayers of all, that there may be a great gathering of souls in this part of God's vineyard.—*Alverty Buxton, Aug. 22.*

Pipe Creek, Md.—The Pipe Creek church will hold a series of meetings commencing Sept. 28. Eld. George S Arnold is expected to be with us. The members of the Meadow Branch church will hold their Communion meeting on Saturday, Oct 1, at 1:30 P. M.—*E. W. Stoner.*

Jonathan Creek, Ohio.—Sunday, Aug 14, the Brethren of the Goshen congregation were made to rejoice that two more, who felt the need of Christian baptism, came out on the Lord's side. Let us all take courage and pray that the spirit of God may move still more mightily, and that many more may be gathered into the kingdom!—*Quincy Leckrone, Ziontown, Ohio.*

Matrimonial.

"What therefore God hath joined together, let not man put asunder."

HORNBERGER—STUTZ.—At the residence of the undersigned, July 28, 1892, Mr O. L. Hornberger and Miss Clara Stutz, both of Ashland County, Ohio. - I. D. Parker.

LEHMAN—SHOWALTER.—At the home of the bride's father, in the Mohican church, Wayne County, Ohio, by the undersigned, Aug. 16, 1892, Mr. Henry H. Lehman and sister Alice Showalter. I. D. Parker.

Fallen Asleep.

"Blessed are the dead which die in the Lord."

EASTERDAY.—In the Pipe Creek church, Ind., Aug. 16, 1892, Emma Elizabeth, twin daughter of brother Emmanuel and sister Maria Easterday, aged 11 months and 6 days Funeral services by Bro. Daniel P. Shively. W. B. Dailey.

PETRY.—In the Price's Creek church, El Dorado, Ohio, Aug. 14, 1892, Hattie Catharine, daughter of Michael M. and Catharine Petry, aged 10 years, 7 months and 19 days. She leaves four sisters, eight brothers, father, mother, and a host of friends to mourn their loss. She was visiting her brothers and sisters, and was taken sick at the home of her sister, Sophia Tillbury, Aug. 10, and lived till Aug. 14. During her four days' illness she suffered a great deal, but was very patient. Funeral services were held at her father's residence, conducted by Bro. Joseph Longanecker and Bro. A. G. Crosswhite from 1 Thess. 4:13-18.' Death was caused by a lemon seed which lodged in the bowels and produced inflammation. Minnie Kitterman.

BENTON.—Near Wyandot, Ohio, Aug. 5, 1892, sister Amanda J. Benton, aged 43 years, 5 months and 2 days. Funeral sermon by the undersigned from Philipp. 1:21. S. A. Walker.

WEAVER.—In the Ashland church, Ohio, at the home of her daughter, sister Weidler, Aug. 8, 1892, sister Eliza Weaver, aged 78 years, 10 months and 21 days. The deceased was the wife of Eld. Moses Weaver, who died in Michigan in 1879. She was born in Pennsylvania, Sept. 17, 1813, and was married to Moses Weaver in 1836. Both united with the church in 1849, came to Ohio in 1852, lived in Ashland County thirty years; in the Canton church, Stark County, Ohio; five years, and in Michigan five years. She was confined to her bed but two days and passed peacefully to the reward of a faithful, Christian life. The funeral service was conducted by T. S. Moherman, assisted by others of the home ministry. I. D. Parker.

HOBBS.—In the Saginaw church, Michigan, July 28, 1892, Levi A. Hobbs, infant son of Mr. Thomas and sister Mary Hobbs, aged 10 months. Death was caused by falling from a bed about nine inches from the floor Levi Baker.

NOFSINGER.—In the Panther Creek church, Woodford County, Ill., July 8, 1892, after much suffering, Bro. William Nofsinger, aged 65 years, 8 months and 9 days. Deceased was born in Botetourt County, Va., Oct. 30, 1826. Funeral services by the writer to a large audience from Rev. 14:13. Thos. Keiser.

GRIFFITH.—In the bounds of the Bethel church, Nebr., Aug. 15, 1892, John F. Griffith, aged 14 years, 6 months and 21 days. Deceased was the son of Bro. Andrew and Mrs. — Griffith. He was killed by the team running away With a riding-plow. Funeral service by the writer, assisted by the brethren, to a large congregation. E. S. Rothrock.

GRAHAM.—Near Staunton, Va, in the bounds of the Barren Ridge church, Aug. 12, 1892, Wingfield Scott Graham, aged 45 years, 5 months and 15 days. Father was a consistent member of the Brethren church for eighteen years. He leaves a companion and seven children. Funeral service by Rev. J. D. Donovan, of the United Brethren church, from Gen. 15:15. Sarah Graham.

DIVELY.—In the Clear church, Blair County, Pa., Aug. 17, 1892, sister Susanna Dively, wife of F. C. Dively, aged 41 years, 5 months and 10 days. Sister Dively leaves a husband and five children, three daughters and two sons. The one son is a babe but six days old. Sister Dively lived a consistent member of the church for twenty-three years. She suffered from asthma for seventeen years, but bore her suffering with Christian patience, and was willing to be released from her earthly bondage at the Master's call. Sister Dively never had an enemy in this world to my knowledge. Bro. F. C. Dively is a minister in the first degree and the deceased was a great help to him. Her remains were interred in the Clear cemetery. Funeral services were conducted by Bro. Michael Clear from Job 19:25-27, in the new meeting house, not yet finished. C. F. Lingenfelter.

HAYES.—In the Rock Creek church, Whiteside County, Ill., Aug. 10, 1892, of apoplexy, Martha E, wife of friend Wm. D. Hayes, aged 58 years, 10 months and 15 days. Funeral services by Bro. A. L. Grater, from these words, "If a man die, shall he live again?" John A. Myers.

DEETER.—In the Warrensburgh church, Johnson County, Mo., Aug. 13, 1892, of cholera infantum, Lola Ethel, little daughter of Bro. John and sister Rachel Deeter, aged 8 months and 18 days. Funeral services by our home minister. Mary Mohler.

DEETER.—In the Oakland church, Darke County, Ohio, Aug. 14, 1892, sister Jeannette Deeter, wife of Daniel Deeter, aged 38 years, 11 months and 3 days. She leaves a husband and three children Sister Deeter was afflicted with consumption for nearly two years. A few months before she died she called for the elders, to be anointed with oil in the name of the Lord. Her sickness she bore patiently. Funeral services were conducted by Bro. J. H. Christian and B. F. Honeyman, in the Harris Creek church. Interment in the Cable cemetery. J. G. Porter.

GOOD.—In the Van Wert church, Van Wert County, Ohio, Aug. 13, 1892, Losey Edith Good, daughter of Bro. Samuel D., and sister Mary E. Good, aged 8 months and 18 days. Funeral services conducted by Bro. Jacob Helstand. Anthony Cupp.

BASORE.—Near Trotwood, Montgomery County, Ohio, Aug. 9, 1892, Samuel Basore, aged 84 years, 10 months and 19 days. He was one of the pioneers of South-Western Ohio, having, with his parents, emigrated to this County when quite young. He was married to Lydia Fetters of this County, in 1831. From this union, eight of Whom survive. Funeral services by the Brethren. S. W. Hoover.

FAIR.—In the bounds of the English Prairie church, La Grange County, Ind., Aug. 17, 1892, Rachel Fair, aged 81 years, 9 months and 4 days. To her were born thirteen children, eight of whom survive. Funeral services from Ps. 92:12-14 by Bro. Peter Long, assisted by Bro. J. V. Felthouse and the writer. N. H. Shutt.

McCOLLOUGH.—In Rock Run church, Elkhart County, Ind., Aug. 11, 1892, sister Roxanna, wife of John McCollough, aged 59 years, 8 months and 22 days. Funeral services by Eld. Daniel Riggle assisted by Levi Hoke from Num. 23:10. She leaves a husband and three children to mourn their loss. M. N. Remsberger.

The Gospel Messenger

In the recognized organ of the German Baptist or Brethren's church, and advocates the form of doctrine taught in the New Testament and pleads for a return to apostolic and primitive Christianity.

It recognizes the New Testament as the only infallible rule of faith and practice, and maintains that Faith toward God, Repentance from dead works, Regeneration of the heart and mind, baptism by Trine Immersion for remission of sins unto the reception of the Holy Ghost by the laying on of hands, are the means of adoption into the household of God,—the church militant.

It also maintains that Feet-washing, as taught in John 13, both by example and command of Jesus, should be observed in the church.

That the Lord's Supper, instituted by Christ and as universally observed by the apostles and the early Christians, is a full meal, and, in connection with the Communion, should be taken in the evening or after the close of the day.

That the Salutation of the Holy Kiss, or Kiss of Charity, is binding upon the followers of Christ.

That War and Retaliation are contrary to the spirit and self-denying principles of the religion of Jesus Christ.

That the principle of Plain Dressing and of Non-conformity to the world, as taught in the New Testament, should be observed by the followers of Christ.

That the Scriptural duty of Anointing the Sick with Oil, in the Name of the Lord, James 5:14, is binding upon all Christians.

It also advocates the church's duty to support Missionary and Tract Work, thus giving to the Lord for the spread of the Gospel and for the conversion of sinners.

In short, it is a vindicator of all that Christ and the apostles have enjoined upon us, and aims, amid the conflicting theories and discords of modern Christendom, to point out ground that all must concede to be infallibly safe.

☞ The above principles of our Fraternity are set forth on our Brethren's Envelopes." Use them! Price 15 cents per package; 40 cents per hundred.

Wade, Kans.—The Wade's Branch church met in council Aug. 13, at our meeting-house, near Wade. A fair representation of the members was present, and the meeting passed off in harmony. We decided to hold our Communion meeting Nov. 4, commencing at 2 P. M. A series of meetings will commence one week previous, if the Lord will.—*G. M. Lauver.*

Peru, Ind.—Our harvest-meeting in the Pipe Creek church occurred Aug. 20. Quite a number of brethren and sisters were present. Brethren Noah Fisher, Jacob Fox, and David Wolf were present, and labored to the interest of the meeting. Bro. Fisher preached an excellent sermon for us on Sunday. One was received by baptism since my last report.—*William B Dailey. Aug. 22.*

Lyons, Kans.—The members of the Kansas Center church met in quarterly council Aug. 6. All business before the meeting passed off pleasantly, and, we trust, in the fear of the Lord. We appointed our love-feast for Nov. 5; also decided to begin a series of meetings a week previous. We shall gladly receive all the help we can get, either from ministers or laymembers. May the Lord help us all to improve our opportunities for doing good!—*S. J. Dresher, Secretary.*

Elkhart, Ind.—We, the members of the Elkhart Valley church, held a very enjoyable harvest-meeting. We called Bro. J. O. Murray, of Nappanee, Ind., to labor for us. He was with us and gave us very good counsel. A number of the neighboring ministers were also with us. We think we had a very good meeting, and believe all could say it was good to be there. The brethren gave us Gospel truths, and we hope we will remember the lessons learned. May God help us all to be of more use in the church hereafter than we were in the past. We can be of use to the church by giving of the means with which God has blessed us. We have freely received, so let us give freely and cheerfully.—*S. C. Kindy.*

Battle Creek, Iowa.—A few members live in the south-western part of Ida County, Iowa. We belong to the Kingsley church, which is thirty-five miles from here Bro Joseph Trostle is our elder. We have no speaker here, and we do not have much preaching. The Mission Board sends a preacher once a year. Bro. E B. Hoff has promised to be here after Sept 15, and give us some meetings. We have appointed our love-feast for Sept. 24. If any brethren can come and assist us, we would be very glad. We have a good country and would like if some minister would move among us. I know they could do good. By addressing me at Battle Creek, Ida Co, Iowa, I will meet any who may desire to come. You can reach us *via* the Chicago & North-western R. R.—*J. H. Isinbarger.*

Wyandot, Ohio.—We, the members of the Wyandot church, met in council Aug. 20. There was not much business before the meeting, and all was adjusted in a Christian manner. The visiting brethren made their report, which showed that all are in love and union. Bro. Loose, our elder, was with us and preached on Saturday evening; also on Sunday at the church, and on Sunday evening at the house of Bro. Henry Keller. Bro. S. A. Walker was to be with us Aug. 7, to do some baptizing but that morning he was sent for to preach a funeral, so he could not come that day. He came however, Aug. 14. A meeting was appointed at Bro. Henry Keller's, after which two young sisters were buried with Christ in baptism. We ask the prayers of all, that there may be a great gathering of souls in this part of God's vineyard.—*Alverty Buxton, Aug. 22.*

Pipe Creek, Md.—The Pipe Creek church will hold a series of meetings commencing Sept. 28. Eld. George S Arnold is expected to be with us. The members of the Meadow Branch church will hold their Communion meeting on Saturday, Oct 1, at 1:30 P. M.—*E. W. Stoner.*

Jonathan Creek, Ohio.—Sunday, Aug. 14, the Brethren of the Goshen congregation were made to rejoice that two more, who felt the need of Christian baptism, came out on the Lord's side. Let us all take courage and pray that the spirit of God may more still more mightily, and that many more may be gathered into the kingdom!—*Quincy Leckrone, Ziontown, Ohio.*

Matrimonial.

"What therefore God hath joined together, let not man put asunder."

HORNBERGER—STUTZ.—At the residence of the undersigned, July 28, 1892, Mr. O. L. Hornberger and Miss Clara Stutz, both of Ashland County, Ohio.   - I. D. PARKER.

LEHMAN—SHOWALTER.—At the home of the bride's father, in the Mohican church, Wayne County, Ohio, by the undersigned, Aug. 16, 1892, Mr. Henry H. Lehman and sister Alice Showalter.   I. D. PARKER.

Fallen Asleep.

"Blessed are the dead which die in the Lord."

EASTERDAY.—In the Pipe Creek church, Ind., Aug. 16, 1892, Emma Elizabeth, twin daughter of brother Emmanuel and sister Maria Easterday, aged 11 months and 6 days Funeral services by Bro. Daniel P. ShiVely. W. B. DAILEY.

PETRY.—In the Price's Creek church, El Dorado, Ohio, Aug. 14, 1892, Hattie Catharine, daughter of Michael M. and Catharine Petry, aged 10 years, 7 months and 19 days. She leaves four sisters, eight brothers, father, mother, and a host of friends to mourn their loss. She was Visiting her brothers and sisters, and was taken sick at the home of her sister, Sophia Tillbury, Aug. 10, and lived till Aug. 14. During her four days' illness she suffered a great deal, but was Very patient. Funeral services were held at her father's residence, conducted by Bro. Joseph Longanecker and Bro. A G. Cross-white from 1 Thess. 4:13-18.' Death was caused by a lemon seed which lodged in the bowels and produced inflammation.
                                                            MINNIE KITTERMAN.

BENTON.—Near Wyandot, Ohio, Aug. 5, 1892, sister Amanda J. Benton, aged 43 years, 5 months, and 2 days. Funeral sermon by the undersigned from Philipp. 1:21.
                                                            S. A. WALKER.

WEAVER.—In the Ashland church, Ohio, at the home of her daughter, sister Weldier, Aug. 8. 1892, sister Eliza Weaver, aged 78 years, 10 months and 21 days. The deceased was the wife of Eld. Moses WeaVer, who died in Michigan in 1879. She was born in Pennsylvania, Sept. 17, 1813, and was married to Moses WeaVer in 1836. Both united with the church in 1849, came to Ohio in 1852, lived in Ashland County thirty years; in the Canton church, Stark County, Ohio, five years, and in Michigan five years. She was confined to her bed but two days and passed peacefully to the reward of a faithful, Christian life. The funeral serVice was conducted by T. S. Moherman, assisted by others of the home ministry.
                                                            I. D. PARKER.

HOBBS.—In the Saginaw church, Michigan, July 28, 1892, Levi A. Hobbs, infant son of Mr. Thomas and sister Mary Hobbs, aged 10 months. Death was caused by falling from a bed about nine inches from the floor   LEVI BAKER.

NOFSINGER.—In the Panther Creek church, Woodford County, Ill., July 8, 1892, after much suffering, Bro. William Nofsinger, aged 65 years, 8 months and 9 days. Deceased was born in Botetourt County, Va., Oct. 30, 1826. Funeral services by the writer to a large audience from Rev. 14: 13.
                                                            Thos. Krisan.

GRIFFITH.—In the bounds of the Bethel church, Nebr., Aug. 15, 1892, John F. Griffith, aged 14 years, 6 months and 21 days. Deceased was the son of Bro. Andrew and Mrs. —— Griffith. He was killed by the team running away With a riding-plow. Funeral serVices by the writer, assisted by the brethren, to a large congregation.   E. S. ROTHROCK.

GRAHAM.—Near Staunton, Va., in the bounds of the Barren Ridge church, Aug. 12, 1892, Winfield Scott Graham, aged 45 years, 5 months and 15 days. Father was a consistent member of the Brethren church for eighteen years. He leaves a companion and seven children. Funeral serVices by Rev. J. D. Donovan, of the United Brethren church, from Gen. 15:15.   SARAH GRAHAM.

DIVELY.—In the Clear church, Blair County, Pa., Aug. 17, 1892, sister Susanna DiVely, wife of F. C. DiVely, aged 41 years, 5 months and 10 days. Sister DiVely leaVes a husband and five children, three daughters and two sons. The one son is a babe but six days old. Sister DiVely liVed a consistent member of the church for twenty-three years. She suffered from asthma for seVenteen years, but bore her suffering with Christian patience, and was willing to be released from her earthly bondage at the Master's call. Sister DiVely never had an enemy in this world to my knowledge. Bro. F. C. DiVely is a minister in the first degree and the deceased was a great help to him. Her remains were interred in the Clear cemetery. Funeral serVices were conducted by Bro. Michael Clear from Job 19: 25-27, in the new meeting house, not yet finished.   C. F. LINGENFELTER.

HAYES.—In the Rock Creek church, Whiteside County, Ill., Aug. 12, 1892, of apoplexy, Martha E., wife of friend Wm. D. Hayes, aged 58 years, 10 months and 15 days. Funeral serVices by Bro. A. L. Grater, from these Words, "If a man die, shall he liVe again?"   JOHN A. MYERS.

DEETER.—In the Warrensburgh church, Johnson County, Mo., Aug. 13, 1892, of cholera infantum, Lois Ethel, little daughter of Bro. John and sister Rachel Deeter, aged 8 months and 18 days. Funeral serVices by our home minister.   MARY MOHLER.

DEETER.—In the Oakland church, Darke County, Ohio, Aug. 14, 1892, sister Jeannette Deeter, wife of Daniel Deeter, aged 38 years, 11 months and 3 days. She leaVes a husband and three children Sister Deeter was afflicted with consumption for nearly two years. A few months before she died she called for the elders, to be anointed with oil in the name of the Lord. Her sickness she bore patiently. Funeral services were conducted by Bro. J. H. Christian and B. F. Honeyman, in the Harris Greek church. Interment in the Cable cemetery.   J. G. PORTER.

GOOD.—In the Van Wert church, Van -Wert County, Ohio, Aug. 10, 1892, Lorey Edith Good, daughter of Bro. Samuel D., and sister Mary E. Good, aged 8 months and 18 days. Funeral serVices conducted by Bro. Jacob Helstand.
                                                            ANTHONY CUFF.

BASORE.—Near Trotwpod, Montgomery County, Ohio, Aug. 9, 1892, Samuel Basore, aged 84 years, 10 months and 19 days. He was one of the pioneers of South-western Ohio, haVing, with his parents, emigrated to this County when quite young. He was married to Lydia Fetters of this County, in 1834. There were nine children (three sons and six daughters) born to this union, eight of whom surViVe. Funeral serVices by the Brethren.   S. W. HOOVER.

FAIR.—In the bounds of the English Prairie church, La Grange County, Ind., Aug. 17, 1892, Rachel Fair, aged 61 years, 9 months and 4 days. To her were born thirteen children, eight of whom surVive. Funeral serVices. from Ps. 90:12-14 by Bro. Peter Long, assisted by Bro. J. V. Felthous and the writer.   N. H. SHUTT.

McCOLLOUGH.—In Rock Run church, Elkhart County, Ind., Aug. 11, 1892, sister Rosanna, wife of John McCollough, aged 59 years, 8 months and 22 days. Funeral serVices by Eld. Daniel Riggle assisted by LeVi Hoke from Num. 23: 10. She leaVes a husband and three children to mourn their loss.
                                                            M. N. RENSBERGER.

The Gospel Messenger

Is the recognized organ of the German Baptist or Brethren's church, and adVocates the form of doctrine taught in the New Testament, and pleads for a return to apostolic and primitiVe Christianity.

It recognizes the New Testament as the only infallible rule of faith and practice, and maintains that Faith toward God, Repentance from dead works. Regeneration of the heart and mind, baptism by Trine Immersion for remission of sins unto the reception of the Holy Ghost by the laying on of hands, are the means of adoption into the household of God, the church militant.

It also maintains that Feet-washing, as taught in John 13. both by example and command of Jesus, should be observed in the church.

That the Lord's Supper, instituted by Christ and as universally observed by the apostles and the early Christians, is a full meal, and in connection with the Communion, should be taken in the eVening or after the close of the day.

That the Salutation of the Holy Kiss, or Kiss of Charity, is binding upon the followers of Christ.

That War and Retaliation are contrary to the spirit and self-denying principles of the religion of Jesus Christ.

That the doctrine of Plain Dressing and Non-conformity to the world, as taught in the New Testament, should be observed by the followers of Christ.

That the Scriptural duty of Anointing the Sick with Oil, in the Name of the Lord, James 5: 14, is binding upon all Christians.

It also adVocates the church's duty to support Missionary and Tract Work, thus giving to the Lord for the spread of the Gospel and for the conversion of sinners.

In short, it is a vindicator of all that Christ and the apostles have enjoined upon us, and aims, amid the conflicting theories and discords of modern Christendom, to point out ground that all must concede to be infallibly safe.

☞ The above principles of our Fraternity are set forth on our Brethren's EnVelopes." Use them! Price 15 cents per package; 40 cents per hundred.

Announcements.

MINISTERIAL MEETINGS.

Nov. 2 and 3: Western District of Pennsylvania will hold their Ministerial Meeting at Walnut Grove, Johnstown church.

Nov. 23, at 9 A. M., in the South-east District of Kansas, Ministerial Meeting in the Cedar Creek church, Mont Ida, Anderson Co., Kans.

LOVE-FEASTS.

Sept. 10 and 11, at 10 A. M., Johnsville church, Va.

Sept. 17, at 10 A. M., Black River, Medina Co., Ohio.

Sept. 21, at 10 A. M., Garrison church, Benton Co., Iowa.

Sept. 21, at 4 P. M., Oakley church, Macon Co., Ill.

Sept. 23, at 3 P. M., Libertyville church, Jefferson Co., Iowa. Series of meetings to commence immediately after feast.

Sept. 24, 4½ miles south-east of Battle Creek, Ida Co., Iowa. Those coming by rail should come to Battle Creek and notify J. H. Imbstweiger.

Sept. 24, at 3 P. M., Cherokee church, Cherokee Co., Kans., at Leonard Wolf's, 4 miles south-west of Marcus, Kans.

Sept. 24 and 25, at 1 P. M., in the Chapman Creek congregation, Kans., 9 miles north and 2 miles east of Abilene, Kans.

Sept. 24, at 1 P. M., Maple Grove church, 4 miles north of Ashland City, Ashland Co., Ohio.

Sept. 24 and 25, at 10 A. M., Boon River church, Stilson, Hancock Co., Iowa.

Sept. 24, at 1 P. M., Fredonia church, Wilson Co., Kans.

Sept. 24, at 2 P. M., Clear Creek congregation, Huntington Co., Ind.

Sept. 24, at 3 P. M., Martin's Creek church, Wayne Co., Ill.

Sept. 24 and 25, 4 miles west of Tipton, Cedar Co., Iowa, beginning at 2 P. M. Ministers of Middle Iowa will please arrange to come to us from District Meeting at Garrison. Our meeting-house is at a distance of two miles from Buchanan on the B., C. R. & N. R. R.

Sept. 24, at 2 P. M., La Porte church, La Porte, Ind. Trains will be met in the forenoon and early afternoon of the day of meeting.

Sept. 24 and 25, at 3 P. M., Lanark church, Carroll Co., Ill.

Sept. 24, at 5 P. M., Pokagon church, Dowagiac, Cass Co., Mich.

Sept. 24, at 10 A. M., Osceola church, Oak Grove meeting-house, St. Clair Co., Mo.

Sept. 24, at 10 A. M., Wyandot church, Ohio. Those coming by rail on the 23d to Upper Sandusky, O.

Sept. 27, at 5 P. M., at Wenger meeting-house, St. Joseph church, Ind.

Sept. 28, South Bend church, Ind.

Sept. 28 and 29, at 10 A. M., Upper Cumberland church, Pa.; at the Mottis Isle meeting-house. Those coming on the P. H. & R. R., stop at Honsdale.

Sept. 28, at 10 A. M., Spring Creek church, Kosciusko Co., Ind.

Sept. 29 and 30, at 1 P. M., Rock Creek, Whiteside Co., Ill.

Sept. 29, at 10 A. M., Union City church, Randolph Co., Ind., 1½ miles north of the City. Those coming by rail should notify W. K. Simmons, Union City, Ind.

Sept. 29, at 10 A. M., West Nimishillen church, Stark Co., Ohio, at the Pleasant Valley house. A series of meetings to be held nine or ten days previous.

Sept. 30, at 10 A. M. Somerset church, at the Vernon meeting-house, Wabash Co., Ind.

Sept. 30 and 30, at 10 A. M., Lower Fall Creek church, 5 miles south of Anderson. Those coming on train should address John Bossack, Anderson, Ind.

Sept. 30, at 2 P. M., Pine Creek church, Adams Co., Ind.

Sept. 30, at 2 P. M., White church, Montgomery Co., Ind., 2½ west miles of Colfax.

Sept. 30, at 10 A. M., Nettle Creek church, near Rogers, Wayne Co., Ind.

Sept. 30, at 10 A. M., Mineralmes church, Delaware Co., Ind. Those coming by rail stop off at Shideler.

Sept. 30, at 2 P. M., Milmine church, Piatt Co., Ill.

Oct. 1, at 1 P. M., Washington church, 3 miles east of Warsaw, Ind

Oct. 1, at 3 P. M., Beaver Creek, Rockingham, Va.

Oct. 1 and 2, at 2 P. M., Hamilton congregation, at the house of D. C. Hardman, 2½ miles south-west of Hamilton. Any coming by rail on Hannibal & St. Joseph R. R., will be met at Hamilton by notifying D. C. Hardman.

Oct. 1 and 2, Kingwin church, Klugman Co., Kans., 2½ miles west and one half mile north of Cleveland.

Oct. 1 at 4 P. M., at the Falls City church, Nebr.

Oct. 1 and 2, at 10 A. M., Seneca church, Seneca Co., Ohio, 1½ miles north of Bloomville.

Oct. 2, at 2 P. M., Sugar Creek church, Allen Co., Ohio.

Oct. 1, at 5 P. M., Berrien congregation, Mich.

Oct. 1 and 2, at 10 A. M., West Branch church, Ill. One week's meeting previous to feast

Oct. 1 and 2, at 2 P. M., near Ames, Boone Co., Iowa. Noon trains met at Ames on Saturday.

Oct. 1, at 3 P. M., Turkey Creek congregation, Pawnee Co., Nebr. Those coming by rail will please give notice and they will be met at Dubois.

Oct. 1 and 2, in the Blue River Valley church, Butler Co., Nebr., at Bro. Jerry Keller's, 8 miles west of Octavia.

Oct. 2, at 2 P. M., Osage church, Crawford Co., Kans.

Oct. 1 and 2 P. M., Logan church, near DeGraff, Ohio.

Oct. 1 and 2, Saginaw church, Mich.

Oct. 1 and 2, at 11 P. M., Walnut Valley congregation, Barton Co., Kans.

Oct. 1 and 2, at 3 P. M., Alleghany congregation, Grant Co., W. Va.

Oct. 2, Maple Grove church, Norton Co., Kans.

Oct. 2, at 10 A. M., Appanoose church, Kans.

Oct. 2, at 10 A. M., Bight Mile church, Ind., at the town of Markle.

Oct. 2 and 2, at 11 A. M., Riverside, Iowa. Those coming by rail will stop at Iowa Junction, on B. C. R. & N. R. R., where they will be met.

Oct. 2, at 10 A. M., Stone Lick church, Clermont Co., Ohio.

Oct. 2, at 10 A. M., Chippewa congregation, Wayne Co., Ohio.

Oct. 2, at 2 P. M., in the Verdigris church, at Bro. S. S. Redman's. A series of meetings will commence Sept. 25.

Oct. 2, Camp Creek church, Ind., at the church, 7 miles south of Coldwater. Those coming by train will please notify S. S. Hummer, and they will be met at the depot at Coldwater, and conveyed to place of meeting.

Oct. 2, at 4 P. M., South Waterloo church, Waterloo, Iowa.

Oct. 2, at 10 A. M., Belleville church, Kans.

Oct. 2, Flat Rock church, Va., at the Pleasant house.

Oct. 2, at 1:30 P. M., Maple Valley church, Iowa.

Oct. 2, at 3 P. M., Johnstown church, Pa., 3 miles north-west of Johnstown and a mile north of Mineral Point on the P. R. R.

Oct. 2 and 3, at 1 P. M., Yellow Creek, Ill.

Oct. 4 and 5, at 4 P. M., Rock River congregation, at Franklin Grove, Ill.

Oct. 4, at 10 A. M., Springfield church, Summit Co., Ohio.

Oct. 4, at 5:30 P. M., Sugar Ridge church, Ohio.

Oct. 4, at 10 A. M., in the Beaver Dam church, Kosciusko Co., Ind., near the town of Burket.

Oct. 4, at 10 A. M., Price's Creek church, Preble Co., Ohio.

Oct. 5, at 2 P. M., Wakenda church, Ray Co., Mo., at the Rockingham meeting-house.

Oct. 5, at 2 P. M., Roann church, Ind.

Oct. 5 and 6, Dallas Center church. A series of meetings by Bro. Hutchison will commence Sept. 17.

Oct. 5, at 10 A. M., Santa Fe church, Ind., 6 miles south of Peru, 2 miles east of Bunker Hill and 1 mile north of Loree.

Oct. 5, at 10 A. M., Prairie Creek church, Ind.

Oct. 6, at 10 A. M., Cedar County church, Cedar Co., Mo., 3 miles north-east of Jerico, at Bro. H. Tingley's.

Oct. 6, at 10 A. M., Walnut church, 7 miles south of Wabash Ind.

Oct. 6, at 10 A. M., Shannon, Ill.

Oct. 6, at 1 P. M., at Mt. Jay meeting-house, in Jacob's Creek congregation, Westmoreland Co., Pa. Series of meetings to commence Oct. 1.

Oct. 6, at 10 A. M., Donnel's Creek church, Clarks Co. Ohio, seven miles from New Carlisle, and the same distance from Terry and Springfield. Those coming from the West will stop either at New Carlisle or Forgy, where they will get on the evening of the 5th. Those from the North-east or South should stop at Springfield.

Oct. 6, at 3 P. M., Keith's church, in the Keith's church-house, eleven miles south-west of Bryan, Ohio.

Oct. 6, Montgomery church, Pa. A series of meetings will be held in connection with the feast.

Oct. 7, Back River church, Morris Co., Mo. Sections coming by rail will stop off at Bangor.

Oct. 7, at 2 P. M., Yellow Creek congregation, Bedford Co., Pa.

Oct. 7, at 10 A. M., Panther Creek church, Woodford, Ill.

Oct. 7, at 2 P. M., Ludlow, Ind.

Oct. 7, at 2 P. M., Kaskaskia church, Fayette Co., Ill. two miles south-west of Beecher City, Ill. Those coming by rail will be met at the above-named place by informing Granville Nevinger.

Oct. 7, at 10 A. M., Sugar Creek, Whitley Co., Ind.

Oct. 7, at 4 P. M., Dunning's Creek congregation, Bed ford Co., Pa.

Oct. 7, at 2 P. M., Raccoon Creek church, Montgomery Co., Ind., one and one half miles north-west of Ladoga.

Oct. 7, at 4 P. M., Mexapin Creek church, Montgomery Co., Ill. Those coming by rail will be met at Farmersville, on Springfield Road, and at Girard, on St. Louis Road on morning of meeting.

Oct. 7 and 8, at 10:30 A. M., Four Mile church, Union Co., Ind.

Oct. 7 and 8, at 3 P. M., Lost Creek church, Juniata Co., Pa., at Free Spring.

Oct. 7 and 8, at 1 P. M., Lamotte church, Crawford Co., Pa.

Oct. 8, at 3:30 P. M., Maple Glen church, Somerset Co., Pa.

Oct. 8, at 4 P. M., in the Elkhart Valley church, Elkhart Co., Ind.

Oct. 8, at 10 A. M., three fourths of a mile west of Dupont, Ohio.

Oct. 8, at 4 P. M., Saline Valley church, at friend Ausmus and Elder Hoffing's, 1 mile east and one-half mile north of Tescott, Ottawa Co., Kans.

Oct. 8, at 4 P. M., Clover Creek church, Blair Co., Pa.

Oct. 8 and 9, Table Grove church, Iowa.

Oct. 8, at 10 A. M., Portage church, Wood Co., Ohio.

Oct. 8 and 9, at 2 P. M., Arnold's Grove, Ill.

Oct. 8, at 10 A. M., Dry Creek church, Linn Co., Iowa, one mile west of Robins Station.

Oct. 8, at 4 P. M., Woodland church, at Greentown, Howard Co., Ind.

Oct. 8 and 9, at 10 A. M., Pine Creek congregation, Ind.

Oct. 8, at 2 P. M., Crooked Creek church, Washington Co., Iowa.

Oct. 8, at 4 P. M., Bethel church, near North County Line, Thayer Co., Nebr. Stations: Carleton, Davenport, Carlisle and Hebron.

Oct. 8, at 2 P. M., County Line church, Allen Co., Ohio.

Oct. 8, at 4 P. M., New Hope church, Cherokee Co., Kans., at A. R. Lichenwalter's, ¾ mile east of Neutral Station.

Oct. 8 and 9, Burr Oak church, Jewell Co., Kans.

Oct. 8 and 9, at 1 P. M., Easter church, at Red Lion, 3½ miles north-east of McCool Junction, York Co., Nebr.

Oct. 8, at 4 P. M., Fair View church, Ill.

Oct. 8 and 9, at 1 P. M., Perry congregation, in the Three Spring meeting-house, Perry Co., Pa., 2½ miles south of Blain.

Oct. 8 and 9, at 10 A. M., Root River church, Minnesota.

Oct. 8, at 2 P. M., Log Creek church, Caldwell Co., Mo., at the Oak Grove meeting-house.

Oct. 8, at Flat Rock church, Va.

Oct. 9, at 2 P. M., Woodbury church, Pa.

Oct. 14, at 3 P. M., Union church, Marshall Co., Ind., five miles west of Plymouth. Those wishing to be met both Plymouth and Burr Oak.

Oct. 14 and 15, at 10 A. M., South Keokuk church, Keokuk Co., Iowa. Those coming by rail will be met at Ollie, by notify 03 Isaac Shelley or Isaac Brown. Those coming from the West will arrive at Ollie about 11:30 A. M.; those from the East at 3 P. M.

Oct. 14, Union church, Plymouth, Marshall Co., Ind. This church would like to have some brother hold meetings a week or ten days after.

Oct. 15, at 10 A. M., Salem church, Ohio.

Oct. 15, at 2 P. M., Hickory church, Jackson Co., Ind. Any one coming to the meeting notify James Lapak, Seymour, Ind.

Oct. 15 and 16, Wine's church, Miss.

Oct. 15, at 4 P. M., in the Ridge church, Highland Co., Ohio. Meetings begin Thursday night previous.

Oct. 15, at 10 A. M., Rome church, Oak Grove house. Also harvest-meeting at same place Aug. 13, at 10 A. M.

Oct. 16 and 16, at 10 A. M., Grundy church, ten miles west of Grundy Centre, Grundy Co., Iowa.

Oct. 22, at 1 P. M., Hartford church, Ind., 1½ miles Run Hartford City.

Oct. 22 and 22, at 2 P. M., Panther Creek church, Dallas Co., Iowa.

Oct. 22, at 10 P. M., Middle Fork church, Clinton Co., Ind.

Oct. 22, at 10 A. M., Killbuck church, Delaware Co., Ind., nine miles west of Muncie.

Oct. 22, at 4 P. M., Pleasant Grove church, Douglas Co., Kans.

Oct. 23 and 25, at 2 P. M., Warrior's Mark church, Pa.

Oct. 27, at 2 P. M., Pleasant Dale church, Adams Co., Ind.

Oct. 28, at 5 P. M., St. Joseph Valley church, 3 miles north of South Bend.

Oct. 29, at 10 A. M., the Pleasant Hill church, near Girard and Virden, Ill.

Oct. 29, at 4 P. M., South Beatrice church, Gage Co., Nebr. Conveyances the day before meeting at B. M. depot, in Beatrice Rock Island depot, in Rockford. Union Pacific depot, in Holmesville.

Oct. 28, at 4 P. M., Walnut church, Marshall Co., Ind.

Oct. 28, at 10 A. M., in the Shuck Creek church, Henry Co., Ind.

Oct. 29, at 2 P. M., Salem church, 1 mile south-east of Selma.

Oct. 29, at 2 P. M., Elm congregation, Page, Va.

Oct. 29, St. Frain church, Longmont, Colo.

Oct. 29, at 2 P. M., Ozawkie church, Kans. A series of meetings to commence Oct. 22.

Oct. 29 and 30, at 10 A. M., Pigeon Creek church, Ill., at the Oak Grove meeting-house.

Oct. 29 and 30, at 2 P. M., Mack church, Ind.

Oct. 29 and 30, at 10 A. M., Mado church, Pa.

Oct. 29, at 10 A. M., Elkins Creek congregation, at Conway Springs, Sumner Co., Kans.

Oct. 29, at 10 A. M., Beaver Run church Mineral Co. W. Va.

Oct. 29, Honey Creek church, Mo. Come to Sheridan, North Co., Mo. Notify W. H. Clark, W. F. Denith, or E. Reddick and they will be met.

Announcements.

MINISTERIAL MEETINGS.

Nov. 1 and 2: Western District of Pennsylvania will hold their Ministerial Meeting at Walnut Grove church, Johnstown church.

Nov. 15, at 9 A. M., in the South-east District of Kansas, Ministerial Meeting in the Cedar Creek church, Mound Ida, Anderson Co., Kans.

LOVE-FEASTS.

Sept. 10 and 11, at 10 A. M., Johnsville church, Va.

Sept. 17, at 10 A. M., Black River, Medina Co., Ohio.

Sept. 17, at 10 A. M., Garrison church, Benton Co., Iowa.

Sept. 23, at 4 P. M., Oakley church, Macon Co., Ill.

Sept. 18, at 3 P. M., Libertyville church, Jefferson Co., Iowa. Series of meetings to commence immediately after feast.

Sept. 24, 1½ miles south-east of Battle Creek, Ida Co., Iowa. Those coming by rail should come to Battle Creek and notify J. H. Isenbourger.

Sept. 24, at 3 P. M., Cherokee church, Cherokee Co., Kans., at Leonard Wolf's, 4 miles north-west of Mc-Cune, Kans.

Sept. 24 and 25, at 2 P. M., in the Chapman Creek congregation, Kans., 3 miles north and 2 miles east of Abilene, Kans.

Sept. 24, at 4 P. M., Maple Grove church, 4 miles north of Ashland City, Ashland Co., Ohio.

Sept. 24 and 25, at 10 A. M., Boon River church, Stilson, Hancock Co., Iowa.

Sept. 20, at 2 P. M., Fredonia church, Wilson Co., Kans.

Sept. 27, at 10 A. M., Clear Creek congregation, Huntington Co., Ind.

Sept. 24, at 3 P. M., Martin's Creek church, Wayne Co., Ill.

Sept. 24 and 25, 4 miles west of Tipton, Cedar Co., Iowa, beginning at 2 P. M. Ministers of Middle Iowa will please arrange to come to us from District Meeting at Garrison. Our meeting-house is at a distance of two miles from Bethanna on the B., C. R. & N. R. R.

Sept. 24, at 3 P. M., in La Porte church, La Porte, Ind. Trains will be met in the forenoon and early afternoon of the day of meeting.

Sept. 24 and 25, at 3 P. M., Lanark church, Carroll Co., Ill.

Sept. 24, at 3 P. M., Pokagon church, Dowagiac, Cass Co., Mich.

Sept. 24, at 2 P. M., Osceola church, Oak Grove meeting-house, St. Clair Co., Mo.

Sept. 24, at 10 A. M., Wyandot church, Ohio. Those coming by rail to 5? a Bucyrus, Upper Sandusky, O.

Sept. 27, at 5 P. M., at Wenger meeting-house, St. Joseph church, Ind.

Sept. 28, South Bend church, Ind.

Sept. 28 and 29, at 10 A. M., Upper Cumberland church, Pa., at the Huntsdale meeting-house. Those coming on the P. R. R., stop at Huntsdale.

Sept. 28, at 10 A. M., Spring Creek church, Kosciusko Co., Ind.

Sept. 29 and 30, at 1 P. M., Rock Creek, Whiteside Co., Ill.

Sept. 29, at 10 A. M., Union City church, Randolph Co., Ind., 1½ miles north of the City. Those coming by rail should notify W. R. Simmons, Union City, Ind.

Sept. 29, at 10 A. M., West Nimishillen church, Stark Co., Ohio, at the Pleasant Valley house. A series of meetings to be held nine or ten days previous.

Sept 29, at 10 A. M., Somerset church, at the Vernon meeting-house, Wabash Co., Ind.

Sept. 29 and 30, at 10 A. M., Lower Fall Creek church, 4 miles south of Anderson. Those coming on train should address John Bowman, Anderson, Ind.

Sept 30, at 2 P. M., Pine Creek church, Adams Co., Ind.

Sept. 30, at 10 A. M., Walnut church, Montgomery Co., Ind.

Sept. 30, at 10 A. M., Nettle Creek church, near Hagerstown, Wagon Co., Ind.

Sept. 30, at 10 A. M., Mineralboro church, Delaware Co., Ind. Those coming by rail stop off at Shideler.

Sept. 30, at 2 P. M., Milmine church, Platt Co., Ill.

Oct. 1, at 3 P. M., Washington church, 3 miles east of Warsaw, Ind.

Oct. 1, at 2 P. M., Beaver Creek, Rockingham, Va.

Oct. 1 and 2, at 2 P. M., Hamilton congregation, at the house of D. C. Hardman, 1½ miles south-east of Hamilton. Any coming by rail on Hannibal & St. Joseph R. R., will be met in Hamilton by notifying D. C. Hardman.

Oct. 1 and 2, Kingston church, Kingston Co., Kans., 2½ miles west and one half mile north of Cleveland.

Oct. 1 and 2, at 10:30 A. M., Seneca church, Seneca Co., Ohio, 1½ miles north of Bloomville.

Oct. 1, at 2 P. M., Sugar Creek church, Allen Co., Ohio.

Oct. 1, at 5 P. M., Berrien congregation, Mich.

Oct. 1 and 2, at 10 A. M., West Branch church, Ill. One week's meeting previous to feast.

Oct. 1 and 2, at 2 P. M., near Ames, Boone Co., Iowa. Noon union met at Ames on Saturday.

Oct. 1, at 2 P. M., Turkey Creek congregation, Pawnee Co., Nebr. Those coming by rail will please give notice and they will be met at Dubois.

Oct. 1 and 2, in the Bear River Valley church, Butler Co., Nebr., at Dry Jerry Keller's, ¾ mile west of Octavia.

Oct. 1, at 2 P. M., Osage church, Crawford Co., Kans.

Oct. 1, at 4 P. M., Logan church, near DeGraff, Ohio.

Oct. 1 and 2, Saginaw church, Mich.

Oct. 1 and 2, at 11:30 P. M., Walnut Valley congregation, Barton Co., Kans.

Oct. 1 and 2, at 3 P. M., Allegheny congregation, Grant Co., W. Va.

Oct. 1, Maple Grove church, Norton Co., Kans.

Oct. 1, at 10 A. M., Appanoose church, Kans.

Oct. 1 and 2, at 2 A. M., Right Mile church, Ind., at the town of Marble.

Oct. 1 and 2, at 11 A. M., Riverside, Iowa. Those coming by rail will stop at Iowa Junction, on B. C. R. & N. R. R., where they will be met.

Oct. 1, at 10 A. M., Stone Lick church, Clermont Co., Ohio.

Oct. 1, at 10 A. M., Chippewa congregation, Wayne Co., Ohio.

Oct. 1, at 2 P. M., in the Verdigris church, at Bro. S. S. Redman's. A series of meetings will commence Sept. 25.

Oct. 1, Camp Creek church, Fla., at the church, 7 miles south of Coldwater. Those coming by train will please notify S. S. Hummer, and they will be met at the depot at Colchester, and conveyed to place of meeting.

Oct. 1, at 2 P. M., South Waterloo church, Waterloo, Iowa.

Oct. 1, at 10 A. M., Belleville church, Kans.

Oct. 1, Flat Rock church, Va., at the Pleasant house.

Oct. 1, at 10:30 P. M., Maple Valley church, Iowa.

Oct. 2, at 3 P. M., Johnstown church, Pa., 3 miles north-east of Johnstown and 2 miles north of Mineral Point on the P. R. R.

Oct. 1 and 2, at 1 P. M., Yellow Creek, Ill.

Oct. 2 and 3, at 4 P. M., Rock River congregation, at Franklin Grove, Ill.

Oct. 2, at 10 A. M., Springfield church, Summit Co., Ohio.

Oct. 2, at 3:30 P. M., Sugar Ridge church, Ohio.

Oct. 3, at 10 A. M., in the Beaver Dam church, Kosciusko Co., Ind., near the town of Burket.

Oct. 2, at 10 A. M., Price's Creek church, Preble Co., Ohio.

Oct. 2, at 10 A. M., Wakanda church, Ray Co., Mo., at the Rockingham meeting-house.

Oct. 3, at 2 P. M., Nason church, Ind.

Oct. 3 and 4, Dallas Centre church. A series of meetings by Bro. Hutchison will commence Sept. 27.

Oct. 5, at 10 A. M., Santa Fe church, Ind., 6 miles south of Peru, 2 miles east of Bunker Hill and 1 mile north of Loree.

Oct. 6, at 2 P. M., Arcadia church, Ind.

Oct. 6, at 10 A. M., Prairie Creek church, Ind.

Oct. 6, at 10:30 A. M., Cedar County church, Cedar Co., Mo., 3 miles north-east of Jerico, at Bro. H. Tingley's.

Oct. 6, at 10 A. M., Maple church, 3 miles south of Wabash, Ind.

Oct. 6 and 7, at 10 A. M., Shannon, Ill.

Oct. 6, at 3 P. M., at Mt. Joy meeting-house, in Jacob's Creek congregation, Westmoreland Co., Pa. Series of meetings to commence Oct. 1.

Oct. 6, at 10 A. M., Donnel's Creek church, Clarke Co., Ohio, seven miles from New Carlisle, and the same distance from Forgy and Springfield. Those coming from the West will stop either at New Carlisle or Forgy, where they will be met on the evening of the 5th. Those from the North-east or South should stop at Springfield.

Oct. 6, at 3 P. M., Spring Creek church, in Keith's church-house, eleven miles south-west of Reece, Kans.

Oct. 6, Montgomery church, Pa. A series of meetings will be held in connection with the feast.

Oct. 7, Black River church, Medina Co., Mich. Brethren coming by rail will stop off at Spencer.

Oct. 7, at 2 P. M., Yellow Creek congregation, Bedford Co., Pa.

Oct. 7, at 10 A. M., Panther Creek church, Woodford, Co. Ill.

Oct. 7, at 2 P. M., Lodoga, Ind.

Oct. 7, at 3 P. M., Keokuklia church, Fayette Co., Ill., ten miles south-west of Decatur City, Ill. Those coming by rail will be met at the above-named place by informing Granville Nevinger.

Oct. 7, at 2 P. M., Sugar Creek, Whitley Co., Ind.

Oct. 7, at 3 P. M., Donning's Creek congregation, Bedford Co., Pa.

Oct 7 at 3 P. M., Raccoon Creek church, Montgomery Co., Ind., one and one half miles north-west of Ladoga.

Oct. 7, at 1 P. M., Morrespin Creek church, Montgomery Co., Ind. Those coming by rail will be met at Farmersville, on Springfield Road, and at Girard, on St. Louis Road on morning of meeting.

Oct. 7 and 8, at 10:30 A. M., Four Mile church, Union Co., Ind.

Oct. 7 and 8, at 2 P. M., Lost Creek church, Juniata Co., Pa., at Free Spring.

Oct. 8 at 2 P. M., Lamotte church, Crawford Co. Ill.

Oct. 8, at 3:30 P. M., Maple Glen church, Somerset Co., Pa.

Oct. 8, at 4 P. M., in the Elkhart Valley church, Elkhart Co., Ind.

Oct. 8, at 10 A. M., three fourths of a mile west of Dorans, Ohio.

Oct. 8, at 2 P. M., Salina Valley church, 20 friend Angast and sister Herring's, 1 mile east and one-half mile north of Trescott, Ottawa Co., Kans.

Oct. 8, at 4 P. M., Clover Creek church, Blair Co., Pa.

Oct. 8 and 9, State Centre church, Iowa.

Oct. 8, at 10 A. M., Portage church, Wood Co., Ohio.

Oct. 8 and 9, at 1 P. M., Arnold's Grove, Ill.

Oct. 8, at 10 A. M., Dry Creek church, Linn Co., Iowa, one mile west of Robins Station.

Oct. 8, Swan Creek congregation, Ohio, 3¼ miles west of Delta, Ohio.

Oct. 8, at 2 P. M., Washington Creek church, Douglas Co., Kans.

Oct. 8 and 9, at 10 A. M., Pine Creek congregation, Ill.

Oct. 8 and 9, at 2 P. M., Bethel church, in North County line, Hayter Co., Nebr. Station: Carleton, Davenport, Carlisle and Shickley.

Oct. 8, at 2 P. M., County Line church, Cherokee Co., Kans., at A. R. Lichtenwalter's, ¾ mile east of Neutral Station.

Oct. 8, at 2 P. M., New Hope church, Cherokee Co., Kans., at A. R. Lichtenwalter's, ¾ mile east of Neutral Station.

Oct. 8, Peabody, Kans.

Oct. 8, at 3:30 P. M., Covina church, Covina, Cal.

Oct. 8, at 10 A. M., Brooklyn church, Iowa.

Oct. 8, at 10 A. M., Rock Creek church, Kans., 6 miles north of Sabetha. Those coming by rail should notify S. Cober a week before coming, so arrangements can be made to take them to place of meeting.

Oct. 8 and 9, Bear Oak church, Jewell Co., Kans.

Oct. 8 and 9, at 2 P. M., Elston church, at Red Lion, 1½ miles south-east of McCool Junction, York Co., Nebr.

Oct. 8, at 3 P. M., Fair View church, Ill.

Oct. 8, at 2 P. M., Perry congregation, in the Three Spring meeting-house, Perry Co., Pa 2 1½ miles south of Blain.

Oct. 8 and 9, at 10 A. M., Root River church, Minnesota.

Oct. 8, at 2 P. M., Log Creek church, Caldwell Co., Mo., at the Oak Grove meeting-house.

Oct. 8, at Flat Rock church, Va.

Oct. 8 and 9, at 4 P. M., Woodbury church, Pa.

Oct. 14, at 2 P. M., Union church, Marshal Co., Ind., at the Oak Grove meeting-house.

Oct. 14, at 2 P. M., Salem church, Ohio.

Oct. 14, New Hope church, Jackson Co., Ind. Any one coming to the meeting notify James Irquil, Seymour, Ind.

Oct. 15 and 16, at 3 P. M., in the Ridge church, Highland Co., Ohio. Meetings begin Thursday night previous.

Oct. 15, at 10 A. M., Rome church, Oak Grove house. Also harvest-meeting at same place Aug. 13, at 10 A. M.

Oct. 15 and 16, at 10 A. M., Gru-dy church, ten miles west of Grundy Centre, Grundy Co., Iowa.

Oct. 15, at 10:30 A. M., Hartford river b, Ind., 1½ miles from Hartford City.

Oct. 20 and 21, at 2 P. M., Panther Creek church, Dallas Co., Iowa.

Oct. 20, at 2 P. M., Middle Fork church, Clinton Co., Ind.

Oct. 27, at 10 A. M., Kilbuck church, Delaware Co., Ind., nine miles west of Muncie.

Oct. 27, at 2 P. M., Pleasant Grove church, Douglas Co., Kans.

Oct. 22 and 23, at 2 P. M., Warrior's Mark church, Pa.

Oct. 27, at 2 P. M., Pleasant Dale church, Adams Co., Ind.

Oct. 28, at 3 P. M., St. Joseph Valley church, St. Joseph Co., Ind., 3 miles north of South Bend.

Oct. 28, at 4 P. M., in the Pleasant Hill church, near Girard and Virden, Ill.

Oct. 29, at 10 A. M., Libertyville church, Gage Co., Nebr. Conveyance the day before meeting at B. R. depot, in Beatrice; Rock Island depot, in Rockford; Union Pacific depot, in Holmesville.

Oct. 29, at 4 P. M., Walnut church, Marshall Co., Ind.

Oct. 26, at 10 A. M., in the Buck Creek church, Henry Co., Va.

Oct. 29, at 4 P. M., Salem church, 4 miles south-east of Salem.

Oct. 29, at 2 P. M., Iron congregation, Page, Va.

Oct. 29, St. Vrain church, Longmont, Colo.

Oct. 29, at 10 A. M., Danville church, Kans. A series of meetings to commence Oct. 10.

Oct. 29 and 30, at 10 A. M., Pigeon Creek church, Ill., at the Oak Grove meeting-house.

Oct. 30, at 2 P. M., Eagle church, Madison Co., Ind., 5½ miles east of Summitville.

Oct. 29 and 30, at 10 A. M., Hickok church, Pa.

Oct. 29, at 2 P. M., Slate Creek congregation, at Conway Springs, Sumner Co., Kans.

Oct. 29, at 10 A. M., Beaver Run church Mineral Co. W. Va.

Oct. 29, Honey Creek church. Mo. Come to Sheridan, North Co'l Mo. Notify W. H. Clark, W. F. Dowie, or E. Reidick and they will be met.

Farm for Sale!

A farm, containing 75 acres, situated about six miles south-east of Polo, in the town of Pine Creek, Ogle Co., Ill., is offered for sale. It is the last residence of John Gantz, deceased, and is within one and one-half miles of the German Baptist Brethren church. This farm is under a high state of cultivation, and well stocked with all kinds of fruit, common to this climate. It will be sold at private sale. Address, John T. Gantz, Oregon, Ill., or call on Chas. Hildebrand, now residing on the farm. 3tf

For Sale!

One of the best improved 320 acre stock or grain farms in Gage Co., Nebr., 6 miles from Beatrice and 2 miles from good shipping point. Brethren church and community adjoining farm. For terms address Box 164, Pickrell, Nebr. 33tf

DISTRICT MEETINGS.

Sept. 27, Middle District of Iowa, in the Garrison church, Benton Co., Iowa.

Sept. 6, at 9 A. M., District of Northern Iowa, Minnesota and South Dakota, in the South Waterloo church, Black Hawk Co., Iowa.

Oct. 4, at 8 A. M., Southern District of Illinois, in the Cerro Gordo church, Piatt Co., Ill.

Oct. 4, in the Bear River Valley church, Butler Co., Nebr., at Dry Jerry Keller's, ¾ mile west of Octavia. Missionary meeting day before. Trains met the day previous by notifying D. P. M. Ship coming on Sunday.

Oct. 7, at 2 A. M., District Meeting in the Crooked Creek church, Washington Co., Iowa. Those coming by rail will be met at Kaota, at 10 A. M. from the King, and at 6:05 P. M. from the West, by notifying D. P. Miller.

✦ESSAYS✦

"Study to show thyself approved unto God; a workman that needeth not to be ashamed, rightly dividing the Word of Truth."

HIS COMING.

BY DR. BONAR.

They tell me a solemn story,
But it is not sad to me,
For in its sweet unfolding
My Savior's love I see.

They say that at any moment
The Lord of life may come
To lift me from the cloudland
Into the light of home.

They say I may have no warning,
I may not even hear
The rustle of his garments,
As he softly draweth near.

Suddenly in a moment,
Upon my ear may fall
The summons, "Loved, of our Master,
Answer the Master's call."

Perhaps he will come in the noontide
Of some bright, sunny day,
When with dear ones all around me,
My life seems bright and gay.

Pleasant must be the pathway,
Easy the shining road,
Up from the dimmer sunlight
Into the light of God.

Perhaps he will come in the stillness
Of the mild and quiet night,
When the earth is calmly sleeping,
'Neath the moonbeam's silvery light;

When the stars are softly shining
O'er the slumbering land and sea,
Perhaps in holy stillness
The Master will come for me.

"WHEREUNTO."—Col 1: 29.

BY C. H. BALSBAUGH.

To T. T. MYERS, OF PHILADELPHIA,
Beloved in Christ Jesus:—

WHY it is I know not, but I am prompted to write to you this morning. I have just been reading MESSENGER No. 30, which, by the way, is an exceptional number, and has been flooded with many thoughts which may not all be uttered, nor could if I would. It is so sublime a thing to be, and so inspiring to be endowed with such stupendous possibilities of evolution, and so unutterably solemn and awful to have our eternal destiny centered in our own will, that it is not surprising that in connection with the "joy unspeakable and full of glory" which necessarily attends faith, we should be admonished to "work out our own salvation with fear and trembling." 1 Pet. 1: 8; Philpp. 2: 12.

As individuals, we have a goal and a prize which taxes even all the Resources of Godhead to consummate. Not a soul could be saved had not Jehovah emptied the exchequer of heaven for our ransom. "Not with corruptible things as silver and gold were we redeemed from our vain conversation; but with the precious blood of Christ as of a Lamb without blemish and without spot." 1 Pet. 1: 18, 19. Is there one among us that "walks *worthy of the LORD*," in view of the end contemplated and the measures employed by "the Author of our salvation?"

The special function of the church has reference to the *world* to be *in God's stead* to the unsaved. 2 Cor. 5: 20. The church is indeed *His body, the fullness of* HIM *that filleth "all in all*," and "every joint" has its supply for its fellow, and "every part" maketh increase of the whole. Eph. 1: 22, 23, and 4: 16. But the words,

"*head over all to the church*," in the first passage, and "from whom" in the latter, are the key to all capability and endeavor in the individual, and in our corporate capacity. How to save souls is the great lesson to learn and the great work to achieve.

To "know no man after the flesh," to be free from "the rudiments of the world", and "the traditions of men," and live under "the powers of the world to come," and "*show forth the praises of* HIM who hath *called us out of darkness into His marvelous light*," is just the secret which very few know. 2 Cor. 5: 16; Col. 2: 20; Mark 7: 7, 8; Heb. 6: 5; 1 Pet. 2: 9. How to represent God to the world, how to keep up and express the Pentecostal endowment of power, is the great problem and office of the church.

Nothing is easier, and nothing has been more sadly verified again and again, than a misconception of the divine ideal of the Mystical Body, and the consequent loss of that power by which alone God's ends can be gained. We are just now slowly awakening out of a lonely stupor in relation to the true character and intent of religious symbols, and limits of human authority. The keys of the kingdom of heaven are not committed to the church to open and close with any but delegated authority. That life is more than meat, and the body more than raiment, and the spirit more than organization, are eternal truths that are only coming above the horizon of the minority of those who name the Name of Christ.

Did we know as Paul knew in Philpp. 3: 10, our congregational and District Councils would not be characterized by the puerilities which sometimes disfigure them. God's ends are great enough, and His measures are wise and ample enough to engage all our time and all our energies of body and soul. To "perfect holiness in the fear of God," and to magnetize and win others by the exhibition of the divine nature, and mutually enlarge our hearts for a fuller influx of the life and peace and glory of Emmanuel, will allow us neither time nor disposition to discuss and legislate about the minutiæ of scissors and needles, full beards, cropt hair, and the length and breadth and color of a capstring.

The only exercise of our carnalities, whether "the lust of the eyes, or the lust of the flesh, or the pride of life," is the very incarnation of Christ Himself. As the day advances to the meridian, and we apprehend the Godman more and more, conformity to Him in all things will be established correspondingly. The sun does not spring into the zenith with a bound. Imperceptibly the light shines by degrees unto the perfect day. Prov. 4: 18. But from the very genesis of the new life, it is "God manifest in the flesh" that claims and directs all the activities of our being.

An artificial conscience is one of the most serious calamities. Nothing is more helpless than the conscience. It is wholly at the mercy of environment and instruction from without. The *sense* of right is *innate*. But *what* is right must be *taught*. What direful evil has been wrought in this sphere! How total should be our adherence to divine revelation in the family, the Sunday-school, the ministry, and every-where! One of the greatest hindrances to a true conception of "the truth as it is in Jesus" is the spurious conscience that results from false training. To ignore our early belief is one of the impossibilities to millions.

How many there are in all churches, ours included, whose miseducated consciences bind them hopelessly to views and customs which have no more connection with the life of Christ in the soul, than a fly-blister is the natural outgrowth of the vitality of the human organization. To

stand in the full blaze of the Light of Jehovah-Jesus, and know neither father nor mother, kin nor creed, save as known by the illumination and authority of the Holy Ghost through the Word, is a rarity. The God-born must also be the God-nursed. I shudder when I think how utterly sincere we may be, and how utterly wrong.

How well we do to heed and exemplify Eph. 4: 31, 32. Commandments for the sake of law we find not in the Word of God. All externalities in religion express divine ideas which we will comprehend in no other way. The dress question in the Levitical economy is now the heritage of the church in the life with which she "adorns the doctrine of God, our Savior, in all things." The object lessons have changed, but not the great truths they illustrate. Christ and His salvation is the substance of all.

Now I will repeat my text: "WHEREUNTO I *also labor, striving according to His working which worketh* IN ME MIGHTILY." Unto what? "WHOM we *preach, warning every man, and teaching every man in all wisdom,* THAT WE MAY PRESENT EVERY MAN PERFECT IN CHRIST JESUS." God bless thee, my dear brother, and make thee "a workman that needeth not to be ashamed." 2 Tim. 2: 15. Let the great reality of Gal. 2: 20, absorb and utilize your whole being. When you think of your little flock, and of the great city full of sinners, let the solemn words of Christ's consecration inspire you to mighty devotion and self-sacrifice: "for their sakes I sanctify myself." John 17: 19.

When you are criticised, misrepresented, buffeted, your very motives questioned, and your name made a target for the shafts of ignorance, prejudice, and malice, "CONSIDER HIM." Heb. 12: 3. Ask the Holy Ghost to print 1 Pet. 4: 12, 13, fresh into your mind and heart every day.
Union Deposit, Pa.

THERE IS MUSIC IN THE AIR.

BY MRS. JOHN E. MOHLER.

THERE is more in that title than many generally suppose. The space out of doors is not thought of as a rare music box: an instrument inexpensive, and that all may enjoy alike. But, what is music? Webster says it is melody or harmony, a succession of sounds so modulated as to please the ear. Richter, of Leipsic, says materially the same.

Where do we find the true, sweet, beautiful, grand, *soul-touching* music? Is it to be found in conservatories, the opera house, halls, or other numerous places of popular entertainment? By no means. The *highest* order of music is found out of doors,—in the orchards, woods, meadows, and by silvery streams. All nature is one grand harmony of sounds. No one need go to the piano to hear a thunder-storm, either in the elements or in the domestic circle. Wait patiently and you will see the original,—of the first at least,—which is always finer than a copy. The same is true of "whispering leaves." Have you ever listened to the rustling of the leaves? They will always give you a series of selections, adapted to each season of the year. So it is with "running water notes," "splash of the boatswain's oar," "spinning-wheel songs," "cradle songs" innumerable.

Where will you find anything sweeter, more tender, than a mother's lullaby to her sleeping babe! Above all these sounds, of music and harmony, are the thousands of bird songs. Is there anything, excepting a well-trained human voice, to be compared with the song of birds? Their little bodies fairly vibrate, as they so beautifully trill out their songs. Well might our prima-don-

✦ESSAYS✦

"Study to show thyself approved unto God; a workman that needeth not to be ashamed, rightly dividing the Word of Truth."

HIS COMING.

BY DR. DOMAR.

They tell me a solemn story,
But it is not sad to me,
For in its sweet unfolding
My Savior's love I see.

They say that at any moment
The Lord of life may come
To lift me from the cloudland
Into the light of home.

They say I may have no warning,
I may not even hear
The rustle of his garments,
As he softly draweth near.

Suddenly in a moment,
Upon my ear may fall
The summons, "Loved, of our Master,
Answer the Master's call."

Perhaps he will come in the noontide
Of some bright, sunny day,
When with dear ones all around me,
My life seems bright and gay.

Pleasant must be the pathway,
Easy the shining road,
Up from the dimmer sunlight
Into the light of God.

Perhaps he will come in the stillness
Of the mild and quiet night,
When the earth is calmly sleeping,
'Neath the moonbeam's silvery light;

When the stars are softly shining
O'er the slumbering land and sea,
Perhaps in holy stillness
The Master will come for me.

"WHEREUNTO."—Col 1: 29.

BY C. H. BALSBAUGH.

To T. T. MYERS, of PHILADELPHIA,
Beloved in Christ Jesus:—

WHY it is I know not, but I am prompted to write to you this morning. I have just been reading MESSENGER No. 30, which, by the way, is an exceptional number, and has been flooded with many thoughts which may not all be uttered, nor could if I would. It is so sublime a thing *to be*, and so inspiring to be endowed with such stupendous possibilities of evolution, and so unutterably solemn and awful to have our eternal destiny centered in our own will, that it is not surprising that in connection with the "joy unspeakable and full of glory" which necessarily attends faith, we should be admonished to "work out our own salvation with fear and trembling." 1 Pet. 1: 8; Philipp. 2: 12.

As individuals, we have a goal and a prize which taxes even all the Resources of Godhead to consummate. Not a soul could be saved had not Jehovah emptied the exchequer of heaven for our ransom. "Not with corruptible things as silver and gold were we redeemed from our vain conversation; but with the precious blood of Christ as of a Lamb without blemish and without spot." 1 Pet. 1: 18, 19. Is there one among us that "walks *worthy of the* LORD," in view of the end contemplated and the measures employed by "the Author of our salvation?"

The special function of the church has reference to the *world* to be *in God's stead* to the unsaved. 2 Cor. 5: 20. The church is indeed *His body, the fullness of HIM that filleth "all in all,"* and "every joint" has its supply for its fellow, and "every part" maketh increase of the whole. Eph. 1: 22, 23, and 4: 16. But the words,

---

"*head over all to the church,*" in the first passage, and "from whom" in the latter, are the key to all capability and endeavor in the individual, and in our corporate capacity. How to save souls is the great lesson to learn and the great work to achieve.

To "know no man after the flesh," to be free from "the rudiments of the world", and "the traditions of men," and live under "the powers of the world to come," and "*show forth the praises of* HIM who hath *called us out of darkness into* HIS *marvelous light,*" is just the secret which very few know. 2 Cor. 5: 16; Col. 2: 20; Mark 7: 7, 8; Heb. 6: 5; 1 Pet. 2: 9. How to represent God to the world, how to keep up and express the Pentecostal enduement of power, is the great problem and office of the church.

Nothing is easier, and nothing has been more sadly verified again and again, than a misconception of the divine ideal of the Mystical Body, and the consequent loss of that power by which alone God's ends can be gained. We are just now slowly awakening out of a lonely stupor in relation to the true character and intent of religious symbols, and limits of human authority. The keys of the kingdom of heaven are not committed to the church to open and close with any but delegated authority. That life is more than meat, and the body more than raiment, and the spirit more than organization, are eternal truths that are only coming above the horizon of the minority of those who name the Name of Christ.

Did we know as Paul knew in Philpp. 3: 10, our congregational and District Councils would not be characterized by the puerilities which sometimes disfigure them. God's ends are great enough, and His measures are wise and ample enough to engage all our time and all our energies of body and soul. To "perfect holiness in the fear of God," and to magnetize and win others by the exhibition of the divine nature, and mutually enlarge our hearts for a fuller influx of the life and peace and glory of Emmanuel, will allow us neither time nor disposition to discuss and legislate about the minutiæ of scissors and needles, full beards, cropt hair, and the length and breadth and color of a capstring.

The only corrective of all carnalities, whether "the lust of the eyes, or the lust of the flesh, or the pride of life," is the very incarnation of Christ Himself. As the day advances to the meridian, and we apprehend the Godman more and more, conformity to Him in all things will be established correspondingly. The sun does not spring into the zenith with a bound. Imperceptibly the light shines by degrees unto the perfect day. Prov. 4: 18. But from the very genesis of the new life, it is "God manifest in the flesh" that claims and directs all the activities of our being.

An artificial conscience is one of the most serious calamities. Nothing is more helpless than the conscience. It is wholly at the mercy of environment and instruction from without. The *sense* of right is *innate.* But *what* is right must be *taught.* What direful evil has been wrought in this sphere! How total should be our adherence to divine revelation in the family, the Sunday-school, the ministry, and every-where! One of the greatest hindrances to a true conception of "the truth as it is in Jesus" is the spurious conscience that results from false training. To ignore our early belief is one of the impossibilities to millions.

How many there are in all churches, ours included, whose miseducated consciences bind them hopelessly to views and customs which have no more connection with the life of Christ in the soul, than a fly-blister is the natural outgrowth of the vitality of the human organization. To

---

stand-in the full blaze of the Light of Jehovah-Jesus, and know neither father nor mother, kin nor creed, save as known by the illumination and authority of the Holy Ghost through the Word, is a rarity. The God-born must also be the God-nursed. I shudder when I think how utterly sincere we may be, and how utterly wrong.

How well we do to heed and exemplify Eph. 4: 31, 32. Commandments for the sake of law we find not in the Word of God. All externalities in religion express divine ideas which we will comprehend in no other way. The dress question in the Levitical economy is now the heritage of the church in the life with which she "adorns the doctrine of God, our Savior, in all things." The object lessons have changed, but not the great truths they illustrate. Christ and His salvation is the substance of all.

Now I will repeat my text: "WHEREUNTO *I also labor, striving according to* HIS *working which worketh* IN ME MIGHTILY." Unto what? "WHOM we preach, *warning every man, and teaching every man in all wisdom,* THAT WE MAY PRESENT EVERY MAN PERFECT IN CHRIST JESUS." God bless thee, my dear brother, and make thee "a work man that needeth not to be ashamed." 2 Tim. 2: 15. Let the great reality of Gal. 2: 20, absorb and utilize your whole being. When you think of your little flock, and of the great city full of sinners, let the solemn words of Christ's consecration inspire you to mighty devotion and self-sacrifice: "for their sakes I sanctify myself." John 17: 19.

When you are criticised, misrepresented, buffeted, your very motives questioned, and your name made a target for the shafts of ignorance, prejudice, and malice, "CONSIDER HIM." Heb. 12: 3. Ask the Holy Ghost to print 1 Pet. 4: 12, 13, fresh into your mind and heart every day.

Union Deposit, Pa.

THERE IS MUSIC IN THE AIR.

BY MRS. JOHN R. MOHLER.

THERE is more in that title than many generally suppose. The space out of doors is not thought of as a rare music box: an instrument inexpensive, and that all may enjoy alike. But, what is music? Webster says it is melody or harmony, a succession of sounds so modulated as to please the ear. Richter, of Leipsic, says materially the same.

Where do we find the true, sweet, beautiful, grand, soul-touching music? Is it to be found in conservatories, the opera houses, halls, or other numerous places of popular entertainment? By no means. The *highest* order of music is found out of doors,—in the orchards, woods, meadows, and by silvery streams. All nature is one grand harmony of sounds. No one need go to the piano to hear a thunder-storm, either in the elements or in the domestic circle. Wait patiently and you will see the original,—of the first at least,—which is always finer than a copy. The same is true of "whispering leaves." Have you ever listened to the rustling of the leaves? They will always give you a series of selections, adapted to each season of the year. So it is with "running water notes," "splash of the boatswain's oar," "spinning-wheel songs," "cradle songs" innumerable.

Where will you find anything sweeter, more tender, than a mother's lullaby to her sleeping babe! Above all these sounds, of music and harmony, are the thousands of bird songs. Is there anything, excepting a well-trained human voice, to be compared with the song of birds? Their little bodies fairly vibrate, as they so beautifully trill out their songs. Well might our prima-don-

Lamb was not to be killed until the going down of the sun in the second evening, and it was impossible for them to eat the passover before it was killed.

I will first examine the editor's supper of a sip of wine and a crumb of bread. I assert there is not a resemblance of a supper about it, especially if taken before dinner. Supper, in the New Testament, means a full meal, taken in the evening or close of the day. It is taken from the Greek word *deipnon*. "Herod on his birthday made a supper (*deipnon*) to his lords." Mark 6: 21. "When thou makest a dinner (*ariston*) or a supper" (*deipnon*), Luke 14: 12. "A certain man made a great supper (*deipnon*), and bade many, and he sent his servants at supper time" (*Horai tou deipnon*) verses 16, 17. "Likewise also the cup after the supper" (*deipessai*). Luke 22: 20. "They made him a supper (*"deipnon*). John 12: 2. "And supper (*deipnon*) being ended." John 13: 2. "He riseth from supper" (*deipnon*) verse 4. "Which also leaned on his breast at supper" (*deipnoi*), John 21: 20. "Taketh before other his own supper" (*deipnon*), 1 Cor. 11: 2, "This is not to eat the Lord's Supper" (*Kuriakon deipnon*) verse 20. "Blessed are they which are called unto the Marriage Supper (*deipnon*) of the Lamb." Rev. 19: 9. It is very clear, from the above citations, that supper (*deipnon*) means a full meal, taken at night or the close of the day.

Dr. Seiss, in his work, entitled, "The Baptist System Examined," says, "What, then, is the meaning of *deipnon?* . . . It denotes a full meal, and that an evening meal. All authorities agree that it stands for the principal meal of the Greeks and Romans. Three names of meals occur in the Homeric writings in the following order: *Ariston, deipnon,* and *dorpon.* The Greeks of a latter age partook of three meals, called *akratisma, arision, deipnon.* The principal meal was the *deipnon.* It was usually eaten rather late in the day, frequently not before sunset. ("Smith's Antiquities," pp. 303, 304.) Dr. Hally says: "Long before the apostolic age, *deipnon* had become regularly and constantly the evening meal." French states the same thing. Hence all great entertainments were called *deipna,* and always occurred in the latter part of the day or at night. *Deipnon* means a full meal, a banquet, a plentiful supper, an ample repast, the principal and most abundant meal of the day, which occurred in the evening. . . . It is also to be observed that the Lord's Supper, or *deipnon,* was first instituted or celebrated at night. Not only the meaning of the word, which was chosen, described it, but the very hour of its appointment and observance connected the Lord's Supper with the evening,—the close of the day. According to the plain, evident, and well-established meaning of words, therefore, and sustained by circumstances, two things would be assigned to the sacramental *deipnon.* First, it must be a full and plenteous meal; second, it must be eaten in the evening. A fragment of bread, a half inch square, and a sip of wine that would scarcely fill a teaspoon, is not a *deipnon,* as the Greeks used the word, any more than sprinkling a few drops of water on a man's face is an immersion of him, neither do we eat our supper in the morning. It is as great a contradiction in terms and confusion of ideas to speak of supping in the morning, as to speak of plunging a man by pouring water upon him." Page 277.

Mr. Hubbard, of the M. E. church, in his "Treatise on Baptism," Part 2, Sec. 9 says, "But there is no reason, so far as the mere philology of the question is concerned, why we should use *baptizo* in its primitive sense, immerse, and not as uniformly use *deipnon* in its primitive sense of 'a

feast or banquet.' If we can obey the command to eat the 'Lord's Supper,' by eating a morsel of bread, and taking a sip of wine, analogy would teach us that we might obey the command to be 'baptized' by having a small quantity of water applied to us."

Both the above authorities are Pedobaptists, and neither observes a full meal for the Lord's Supper; but their knowledge of language teaches them the meaning of words. Our children manifest more wisdom in using the term supper, than many of the popular ministers. Jesus ate a meal with his apostles in conjunction with the Communion, composed in part of a liquid or soup; for they "dipped their hands into the dish." "He dipped a sop" or a little piece. Matt. 26: 23; Mark 14: 20; John 13: 26, 27. "Sop, anything steeped or dipped and softened in liquor, but chiefly something thus dipped in broth or liquid food, and intended to be eaten."—*Webster.*

Luke, John, and Paul, calls this meal supper, the Supper, the Lord's Supper. Luke 22: 20; John 13: 4; 21: 20; 1 Cor. 11: 20, 25. This Supper was eaten at the beginning of the fourteenth day of the month Abib,— just twenty-four hours before the legal time prescribed in the law for eating the Jewish Passover, which was to be eaten at the close of the fourteenth day of the month, or beginning of the fifteenth day. Ex. 12: 6; Lev. 23: 5; Num. 9: 3; 28: 16; Deut. 16: 16. "The Hebrews computed their day from evening to evening, according to the order taught in their law. Their Sabbath being the seventh day of the week, had its beginning at sunset on the day we call Friday, and continued till the next sunset, when the first day of the new week is in. Upon this point all authors agree." "From even unto even, shall ye celebrate your Sabbath." Lev. 23: 32. Christ sent the disciples on the evening of the thirteenth, to make the necessary preparation for the passover, procure a lamb, etc., which, as prescribed in the law, was not to be killed till the going down of the sun the following evening. Christ ate the Supper with his disciples at the close of the thirteenth, or beginning of the fourteenth, while the Jewish passover was not to be eaten till the close of the fourteenth, or beginning of the fifteenth. Christ's Supper was therefore eaten twenty-four hours before the legal time for eating the passover. Hence Christ did not eat the passover at all that year.

When Christ was brought before Pilate, the next day after he had instituted his Supper and Communion, "the Jews would not go into the judgment hall, lest they be defiled; but that they might eat the passover." John 18: 28. Christ was betrayed, arrested, tried, condemned, crucified, and buried, all on the preparation day. "When Pilate, therefore, heard that saying, he brought Jesus forth, and sat down in the judgment-seat, in a place that is called the pavement, but in the Hebrew, Gabbatha. And it was the preparation of the passover, and about the sixth hour." John 19: 13, 14, 31. "There laid they Jesus therefore, because of the Jews' preparation day, for the sepulchre was nigh at hand." Verse 42.

It does seem strange that a man, who professes to believe the Holy Scriptures, will teach that Jesus ate the Jewish passover, when the Gospel positively teaches that he was crucified and buried on the preparation day, hence, before the legal time, prescribed by the Eternal God for eating the passover. Had Christ eaten the Jewish passover at the beginning of the fourteenth day of the month, as my friend says he did, the Jews would not have needed false witnesses to condemn him to death, for such a violation of God's law would have been sufficient to put him to death. The Jewish passover is nowhere in God's Word

called supper or the Supper. "Now Jesus knowing before the feast of the passover (*pascha*), that his hour was come, that he should depart out of this world and unto the Father. And supper (*deipnon*) being done," etc. John 13: 1, 2. ("Emphatic Diaglott.")

What right has any man to call the Jewish passover supper, or to say that Jesus ate the passover when Jesus himself says, his time to depart out of the world had come before the passover? Christ was the antitype of which the paschal lamb was the type, and died on the cross at the very hour the paschal lamb should have been killed. The bread and cup (which my friend calls the Lord's Supper) is called the Communion of the blood and body of Christ, 1 Cor. 10: 16, but was never called supper, or Lord's Supper by Christ, or his apostles. A crumb of bread and a sip of wine does not constitute a supper in any sense of the word, nor would my friend recognize it as a supper at a hotel where he was personally interested.

Again my friend says: "The observers of this sectarian meal tell us that the passover is one thing, and the Lord's Supper another, and bread and wine still another; that the first expired with the law, and the latter two are in force in the Gospel. But we have found nothing of this middle feast, introduced by Christ, and furthermore we can prove positively that the bread and cup is the Lord's Supper, and that no eating of a meal, as a religious feast, is tolerated in the kingdom or church of God."

The editor makes some bold assertions as he goes along, but proves nothing, and I cannot take his assertions; for they conflict with the teachings of Christ and the apostles. I challenge him, or any other man, to prove from the Word of God that the bread and cup of Communion is the Lord's Supper. Christ ate a meal, a supper,— with his apostles, at the close of which the Communion was instituted. Matt. 26: 26; Luke 22: 20. The apostles had a meal, a love-feast (*agape*) that was observed in their day. (2 Pet. 2: 13; Jude 12.) "The Eucharist was at first united with a social meal. Both constituted a whole, representing the communion of the faithful with their Lord, and their brotherly communion with one another. Both together were called the Supper of the Lord." ("Neander's Church History," I, p. 325.)

These suppers or love-feasts were observed by the apostles and early Christians in connection with the Communion, as Christ instituted them, and gave them example. "They were first prohibited by the council of Laodicea about the middle of the fourth century." ("Dupin's Ecclesiastical History," I, p. 614; "Cave's Primitive Christianity," 168; "Bingham's Antiquities," I, p. 330; "Clarke's Comments" on Jude 12.)

Paul does not condemn the church at Corinth for eating a supper, or for bringing bountiful provisions together for a supper. "When ye come together, therefore, into one place, this is not to eat the Lord's Supper." 1 Cor. 11: 20. Why did they not eat the "Lord's Supper"? Because those that brought provisions for the supper, "ate their own supper," and the poor had nothing. Verse 21. They should have spread their provision on a common table, and sanctified the meal by prayer and thanksgiving, and tarried one for another till everything was ready. Then all should have partaken of the meal. Thus they would have eaten the Lord's Supper instead of their own supper. "Wherefore, my brethren, when ye come together to eat, tarry one for another," verse 33, but eat your own suppers at home. It is very evident that Paul was not finding fault with the eating of a full meal, or coming into one place to eat it, but, to the contrary,

Lamb was not to be killed until the going down of the sun in the second evening, and it was impossible for them to eat the passover before it was killed.

I will first examine the editor's supper of a sip of wine and a crumb of bread. I assert there is not a resemblance of a supper about it, especially if taken before dinner. Supper, in the New Testament, means a full meal, taken in the evening or close of the day. It is taken from the Greek word *deipnon*. "Herod on his birthday made a supper (*deipnon*) to his lords." Mark 6: 21. "When thou makest a dinner (*ariston*) or a supper" (*deipnon*), Luke 14: 12. "A certain man made a great supper (*deipnon*), and bade many, and he sent his servants at supper time" (*Horai tou deipnou*) verses 16, 17. "Likewise also the cup after the supper" (*deipesai*). Luke 22: 20. "They made him a supper ("*deipnon*). John 12: 2. "And supper (*deipnon*) being ended." John 13: 2. "He riseth from supper" (*deipnon*) verse 4. "Which also leaned on his breast at supper" (*deipnoi*), John 21: 20. "Taketh before other his own supper" (*deipnon*), 1 Cor. 11: 2, "This is not to eat the Lord's Supper" (*Kuriakon deipnon*) verse 20. "Blessed are they which are called unto the Marriage Supper (*deipnon*) of the Lamb." Rev. 19: 9. It is very clear, from the above citations, that supper (*deipnon*) means a full meal, taken at night or the close of the day.

Dr. Seiss, in his work, entitled, "The Baptist System Examined," says, "What, then, is the meaning of *deipnon*? . . . It denotes a full meal, and that an evening meal. All authorities agree that it stands for the principal meal of the Greeks and Romans. Three names of meals occur in the Homeric writings in the following order: *Ariston*, *deipnon*, and *dorpon*. The Greeks of a latter age partook of three meals, called *akratisma*, *ariston*, *deipnon*. The principal meal was the *deipnon*. It was usually eaten rather late in the day, frequently not before sunset. ("Smith's Antiquities," pp. 303, 304) Dr. Hally says: "Long before the apostolic age, *deipnon* had become regularly and constantly the evening meal." French states the same thing. Hence all great entertainments were called *deipna*, and always occurred in the latter part of the day or at night. *Deipnon* means a full meal, a banquet, a plentiful supper, an ample repast, the principal and most abundant meal of the day, which occurred in the evening. . . . It is also to be observed that the Lord's Supper, or *deipnon*, was first instituted or celebrated at night. Not only the meaning of the word, which was chosen, described it, but the very hour of its appointment and observance connected the Lord's Supper with the evening,—the close of the day. According to the plain, evident, and well-established meaning of words, therefore, and sustained by circumstances, two things would be assigned to the sacramental *deipnon*. First, it must be a full plenteous meal; second, it must be eaten in the evening. A fragment of bread, a half inch square, and a sip of wine that would scarcely fill a teaspoon, is not a *deipnon*, as the Greeks used the word, any more than sprinkling a few drops of water on a man's face is an immersion of him, neither do we eat our supper in the morning. It is as great a contradiction in terms and confusion of ideas to speak of supping in the morning, as to speak of plunging a man by pouring water upon him." Page 277.

Mr. Hubbard, of the M. E. church, in his "Treatise on Baptism," Part 2, Sec. 9 says, "But there is no reason, so far as the mere philology of the question is concerned, why we should use *baptizo* in its primitive sense, immerse, and not as uniformly use *deipnon* in its primitive sense of 'a feast or banquet.' If we can obey the command to eat the 'Lord's Supper,' by eating a morsel of bread, and taking a sip of wine, analogy would teach us that we might obey the command to be 'baptized' by having a small quantity of water applied to us."

Both the above authorities are Pedobaptists, and neither observes a full meal for the Lord's Supper; but their knowledge of language teaches them the meaning of words. Our children manifest more wisdom in using the term supper, than many of the popular ministers. Jesus ate a meal with his apostles in conjunction with the Communion, composed in part of a liquid or soup: for they "dipped their hands into the dish." "He dipped a sop" or a little piece. Matt. 26: 23; Mark 14: 20; John 13: 26, 27. "Sop, anything steeped or dipped and softened in liquor, but chiefly something thus dipped in broth or liquid food, and intended to be eaten."—*Webster*.

Luke, John, and Paul, calls this meal supper, the Supper, the Lord's Supper. Luke 22: 20; John 13: 4; 21: 20; 1 Cor. 11: 20, 25. This Supper was eaten at the beginning of the fourteenth day of the month Abib,— just twenty-four hours before the legal time prescribed in the law for eating the Jewish Passover, which was to be eaten at the close of the fourteenth day of the month, or beginning of the fifteenth day. Ex. 12: 6; Lev. 23: 5; Num. 9: 3; 28: 16; Deut. 16: 16. "The Hebrews computed their day from evening to evening, according to the order taught in their law. Their Sabbath being the seventh day of the week, had its beginning at sunset on the day we call Friday, and continued till the next sunset, when the first day of the new week is in. Upon this point all authors agree." "From even unto even, shall ye celebrate your Sabbath." Lev. 23: 32. Christ sent the disciples on the evening of the thirteenth, to make the necessary preparation for the passover, procure a lamb, etc., which, as prescribed in the law, was not to be killed till the going down of the sun the following evening. Christ ate the Supper with his disciples at the close of the thirteenth, or beginning of the fourteenth, while the Jewish passover was not to be eaten till the close of the fourteenth, or beginning of the fifteenth. Christ's Supper was therefore eaten twenty-four hours before the legal time for eating the passover. Hence Christ did not eat the passover at all that year.

When Christ was brought before Pilate, the next day after he had instituted his Supper and Communion, "the Jews would not go into the judgment hall, lest they be defiled; but that they might eat the passover." John 18: 28. Christ was betrayed, arrested, tried, condemned, crucified, and buried, all on the preparation day. "When Pilate, therefore, heard that saying, he brought Jesus forth, and sat down in the judgment-seat, in a place that is called the pavement, but in the Hebrew, Gabbatha. And it was the preparation of the passover, and about the sixth hour." John 19: 13, 14, 31. "There laid they Jesus therefore, because of the Jews' preparation day, for the sepulchre was nigh at hand." Verse 42.

It does seem strange that a man, who professes to believe the Holy Scriptures, will teach that Jesus ate the Jewish passover, when the Gospel positively teaches that he was crucified and buried on the preparation day, hence, before the legal time, prescribed by the Eternal God for eating the passover. Had Christ eaten the Jewish passover at the beginning of the fourteenth day of the month, as my friend says he did, the Jews would not have needed false witnesses to condemn him to death, for such a violation of God's law would have been sufficient to put him to death. The Jewish passover is nowhere in God's Word called supper or the Supper. "Now Jesus knowing before the feast of the passover (*pascha*), that his hour was come, that he should depart out of this world into the Father. And supper (*deipnon*) being done," etc. John 13: 1, 2. ("Emphatic Diaglott.")

What right has any man to call the Jewish passover supper, or to say that Jesus ate the passover when Jesus himself says, his time to depart out of the world had come before the passover? Christ was the antitype of which the paschal lamb was the type, and died on the cross at the very hour the paschal lamb should have been killed. The bread and cup (which my friend calls the Lord's Supper) is called the Communion of the blood and body of Christ, 1 Cor. 10: 16, but was never called supper, or Lord's Supper by Christ, or his apostles. A crumb of bread and a sip of wine does not constitute a supper in any sense of the word, nor would my friend recognize it as a supper at a hotel where he was personally interested.

Again my friend says: "The observers of this sectarian meal tell us that the passover is one thing, and the Lord's Supper another, and bread and wine still another; that the first expired with the law, and the latter two are in force in the Gospel. But we have found nothing of this middle feast, introduced by Christ, and furthermore we can prove positively that the bread and cup is the Lord's Supper, and that no eating of a meal, as a religious feast, is tolerated in the kingdom or church of God."

The editor makes some bold assertions as he goes along, but proves nothing, and I cannot take his assertions, for they conflict with the teachings of Christ and the apostles. I challenge him, or any other man, to prove from the Word of God that the bread and cup of Communion is the Lord's Supper. Christ ate a meal, a supper,— with his apostles, at the close of which the Communion was instituted. Matt. 26: 26; Luke 22: 20. The apostles had a meal, a love-feast (*agape*) that was observed in their day. (2 Pet. 2: 13; Jude 12) "The Eucharist was at first united with a social meal. Both constituted a whole, representing the communion of the faithful with their Lord, and their brotherly communion with one another. Both together were called ' the Supper of the Lord." ("Neander's Church History," 1, p. 325.)

These suppers or love-feasts were observed by the apostles and early Christians in connection with the Communion, as Christ instituted them, and gave them example. "They were first prohibited by the council of Laodicea about the middle of the fourth century." ("Dupin's Ecclesiastical History," 1, p. 514; "Cave's Primitive Christianity," 168; "Bingham's Antiquities," 1, p. 330; "Clarke's Comments" on Jude 12.)

Paul does not condemn the church at Corinth for eating a supper, or for bringing bountiful provisions together for a supper. "When ye come together, therefore, into one place, this is not to eat the Lord's Supper." 1 Cor. 11: 20. Why did they not eat the "Lord's Supper"? Because those that brought provisions for the supper, "ate their own supper," and the poor had nothing. Verse 21. They should have spread their provision on a common table, and sanctified the meal by prayer and thanksgiving, and tarried one for another till everything was ready. Then all should have partaken of the meal. Thus they would have eaten the Lord's Supper instead of their own supper. "Wherefore, my brethren, when ye come together to eat, tarry one for another." verse 33, but eat your own suppers at home. It is very evident that Paul was not finding fault with the eating of a full meal, or coming into one place to eat it, but, to the contrary,

Missionary and Tract Work Department.

"Upon the first day of the week, let every one of you lay by him in store as God hath prospered him, that there be no gatherings when I come."—1 Cor. 16:2.

"Every man as he purposeth in his heart, so let him give. Not grudgingly or of necessity, for the Lord loveth a cheerful giver."—2 Cor. 9:7.

HOW MUCH SHALL WE GIVE?

"Every man according to his ability." "Every one as God hath prospered him." "Every man, according as he purposeth in his heart, so let him give." "For if there be first a willing mind, it is accepted according to that a man hath, and not according to that he hath not."—2 Cor. 8:12.

Organization of Missionary Committee.

DANIEL VANIMAN, Foreman,   McPherson, Kans.
D. L. MILLER, Treasurer,   Mt. Morris, Ill.
GALEN B. ROYER, Secretary,   Mt. Morris, Ill.

Organization of Book and Tract Work.

S. W. HOOVER, Foreman,   Dayton, Ohio.
S. BOCK, Secretary and Treasurer,   Dayton, Ohio.

☞All donations intended for Missionary Work should be sent to GALEN B. ROYER, Mt. Morris, Ill.

☞All money for Tract Work should be sent to S. BOCK, Dayton, Ohio.

☞Money may be sent by Money Order, Registered Letter, or Drafts on New York or Chicago. Do not send personal checks, or drafts on interior towns, as it costs 25 cents to collect them.

☞Solicitors are requested to faithfully carry out the plan of Annual Meeting, that all our members be solicited to contribute at least twice a year for the Mission and Tract Work of the Church.

☞Notes for the Endowment Fund can be had by writing to the Secretary of either Work.

THE ELDERS OF THE CHURCH.

BY DANIEL HAYS.

IT has become a matter of concern with many to know what is really the New Testament meaning and use of the term "elder," as applied to church officers. What we want to know is, Does the term denote a distinct and specific office in the church? We know that the term "elder" was the title of an office in the Jewish synagogue; but while this is true, we must not omit the fact that the term *bishop*, with which the term *elder* is associated in the New Testament, was not in use among the Jews. They had elders, but no bishops. Then we cannot rely on any theory, drawn from the customs of the Jews in defining the New Testament meaning and use of the term. We will look at it in the light of the apostolic age, and let the Gospel be its own interpreter.

The first officers appointed by our Savior were called Apostles (*apo*, away, and *stello*, I send) because they were sent to preach the Gospel. The term was not, however, confined to the Twelve by the inspired writers. It was applied to Jesus Christ: "Wherefore, holy brethren, partakers of the heavenly calling, consider the Apostle and High Priest of our profession, Christ Jesus" (Heb. 3:1). It was used to designate Paul and Barnabas at Iconium: "And part held with the Jews, and part with the Apostles," Acts 14:4. Yet, in a limited sense, and when used to denote the office, it was used to designate the Twelve, and the Apostle to the Gentiles, to which office Paul was called.

The office of an Apostle embraced that of the bishopric, Acts 1:20, a term employed to denote the nature of the office from which Judas fell, and to which Matthias was appointed. A bishop is one to whom a charge has been given, and who is made an overseer, to superintend the work of the church. This function the Apostles exercised and held in their own hands at Jerusalem, until other local churches were regularly organized, and overseers were duly appointed to take charge of them. The Apostles were also called "elders." Peter, who was one of the Twelve, applies the term to himself in these words: "The elders which are among you I exhort, who am also an elder." 1

Pet. 5:1. John also uses the term in two of his epistles: "The elder unto the elect lady; the elder unto the well-beloved Gaius." The term "elder" does not denote the nature of the office, but rather the gravity of the work and maturity in life and attainment necessary to meet the responsibilities which the position involves. The word *elder* is the comparative degree of *old* which has, as its radical meaning, the sense of *grown up*. Then the comparative elder is a degree beyond maturity, and denotes one advanced, a senior, one having precedence from office, or rank. In the latter sense it is used by the sacred writers in the New Testament to denote official relation. The superlative degree is not used to designate official position in the church, for "one is your Master even Christ, and all ye are brethren." From 1 Tim. 5:17, we discover that, in addition to being a minister, an elder is a ruler. "Let the elders that rule well be counted worthy of double honor, especially they who labor in the word and doctrine." Then the office of elder is in advance of the ministry, the elder having a duty imposed upon him in addition to preaching, and the term ruler would indicate that he is one with the bishop, who is also a ruler, or overseer.

Does the Gospel warrant a church in having more than one elder? This question may be answered by producing either a precedent or rule from the inspired record. Paul "sent to Ephesus, and called the elders of the church." Acts 20:17. The church at Ephesus, then, had more than one elder. Again, may a church have more than one bishop? This question is fully answered in Philpp. 1:1, "Paul and Timotheus, the servants of Jesus Christ, to all the saints in Christ Jesus which are at Philipi, with the bishops and deacons." Then the church at Philippi had more than one bishop, as well as more than one deacon.

But the main question still is pending, and we hope to answer it approximately at least; and we approach it with another question: Is the elder a bishop? To answer this we refer to Acts 20:17-28, "And from Miletus he sent to Ephesus and called the elders of the church." "Take heed therefore unto yourselves and all the flock over the which the Holy Ghost hath made you overseers (bishops) to feed the church of God, which he hath purchased with his own blood." This proves that the elders of the church at Ephesus were bishops. It proves that there may be more than one bishop as well as more than one elder in a church. It stands as solid evidence against the idea entertained by some that the foreman among the elders alone is bishop. What we want is the usage of the Apostolic age. Let us not forget that there were bishops at Philippi as well as at Ephesus. What of the note appended to the Second Epistle to Timothy, stating that Timothy was ordained the first bishop of the church of the Ephesians? What of that appended to Titus, stating that Titus was ordained the first bishop of the Cretians? Accepting these as historical facts, they simply show that Timothy was the first bishop ordained at Ephesus, and that Titus was the first ordained in Crete, and that they were simply first among their equals in office. The same Gospel rule obtains among bishops as among others: "Likewise ye younger, submit yourselves unto the elder." Our Annual Meeting has recognized the same principle in every ordination, in making the ordained equal with the elders, except where age and experience would give them advantage. Furthermore, Paul instructed Titus "to set in order the things that are wanting, and ordain elders in every city, as I had appointed thee; if any be blameless, the husband of one wife, having faithful children, not accused of riot, or unruly. For a bishop must be blameless as the steward of

God. Titus 1:5-7. Here the terms "elder" and "bishop" are applied to the same person in the same office, and therefore must be synonymous. We, then, have two facts clearly settled: First, Acts 20:17-28 proves that "the elders of the church are bishops. Second, Titus 1:5-7, proves that an ordained elder is a bishop. This leads us to the Scriptural conclusion that "the elders of the church" are "ordained elders."

We have now reached the main question, and apparently the above may be regarded as an answer to it, fairly and Scripturally drawn. But because the idea prevails among many that the term "elder" may be applied to other church officers besides the bishops, would it be asking too much to have a single specific case produced in the New Testament, where the term "elder" is used to designate the office of minister, deacon, or any other official position, short of the full ministry? One unquestionable instance will suffice. It will give us ground to believe that it may be used in a general sense, and that the term is applicable to anyone beyond the laity. The church, however, has hesitated in giving the word such a hearing. The church, in her official decisions, has restricted the word to the ordained, or the bishopric.

One of the clearest and most discriminating decisions ever reached upon the matter in hand was made by the church as to who shall anoint the sick with oil in the name of the Lord. The standing decision of the church is that the sick should be anointed with oil by ordained elders, if they can be obtained, and if not, then by the next in office. This decision is not only in harmony with the Gospel, but it also agrees with certain clearly-defined principles of church government.

1. It decides that ordained elders fill the position in official standing, with the "elders of the church" of James 5:14.

2. It recognizes the truth that "helps" (1 Cor. 12:28) are necessary in every position in life.

3. That in the performance of any duty where a work may be done by appointment, or by delegation, "the younger should be subject to the elder."

Our main question, then, is virtually already decided. The elders of the church of James 5:14 are ordained elders. But ordained elders cannot be had under all circumstances. What then? The church says get the next in office. This has frequently been done, and God has blessed the work. Where two elders cannot be had, one elder takes a minister, and sometimes a deacon, as an assistant. Upon the same principle the "next in office" may anoint the sick by appointment of the elder when necessary. "But," says one, "why does James direct the sick to send for the elders of the church if others may also anoint?" In the absence of the Savior, did not the man, whose son was a lunatic, apply to the disciples, and did the Savior reprove them for their attempt to heal the young man? Did not Joshua address the sun as ruler of the day when he wanted an extension of time till night-fall? Every organization has its overseer, or ruler. In the absence of Christ the church is his representative to carry on his work. James directs the sick to send for the elders of the church because they are the overseers or rulers of the church; and in their absence, the "next in office" is their representative by their appointment and the order of the church.

Broadway, Va.

CITY MISSIONS.

BY S. Z. SHARP.

AT no other time in the history of our church has so much been said and done in regard to city missions as now. As a people, we are becoming

Missionary and Tract Work Department.

"Upon the first day of the week, let every one of you lay by him in store as God hath prospered him, that there be no gatherings when I come."—1 Cor. 16: 2.

"Every man as he purposeth in his heart, so let him give. Not grudgingly or of necessity, for the Lord loveth a cheerful giver."—2 Cor. 9: 7.

HOW MUCH SHALL WE GIVE?

"Every man *according to his ability*." "Every man *as God hath prospered him*." "Every man, *according as he purposeth in his heart*, so let him give." "For if there be first a willing mind, it is accepted *according to that a man hath,* and not according to that he hath not."—2 Cor. 8: 12.

Organization of Missionary Committee.

DANIEL VANIMAN, Foreman,	McPherson, Kans.
D. L. MILLER, Treasurer,	Mt. Morris, Ill.
GALEN B. ROYER, Secretary,	Mt. Morris, Ill.

Organization of Book and Tract Work.

S. W. HOOVER, Foreman,	Dayton, Ohio.
S. BOCK, Secretary and Treasurer,	Dayton, Ohio.

☞All donations intended for Missionary Work should be sent to GALEN B. ROYER, Mt. Morris, Ill.

☞All money for Tract Work should be sent to S. BOCK, Dayton, Ohio.

☞Money may be sent by Money Order, Registered Letter, or Drafts on New York or Chicago. Do not send personal checks, or drafts on interior towns, as it costs 25 cents to collect them.

☞Solicitors are requested to faithfully carry out the plan of Annual Meeting, that all our members be solicited to contribute at least twice a year for the Mission and Tract Work of the Church.

☞Notes for the Endowment Fund can be had by writing to the Secretary of either Work.

THE ELDERS OF THE CHURCH.

BY DANIEL HAYS.

IT has become a matter of concern with many to know what is really the New Testament meaning and use of the term "elder," as applied to church officers. What we want to know is, Does the term denote a distinct and specific office in the church? We know that the term "elder" was the title of an office in the Jewish synagogue; but while this is true, we must not omit the fact that the term *bishop*, with which the term *elder* is associated in the New Testament, was not in use among the Jews. They had elders, but no bishops. Then we cannot rely on any theory, drawn from the customs of the Jews in defining the New Testament meaning and use of the term. We will look at it in the light of the apostolic age, and let the Gospel be its own interpreter.

The first officers appointed by our Savior were called Apostles (*apo*, away, and *stello*, I send) because they were sent to preach the Gospel. The term was not, however, confined to the Twelve by the inspired writers. It was applied to Jesus Christ: "Wherefore, holy brethren, partakers of the heavenly calling, consider the Apostle and High Priest of our profession, Christ Jesus" (Heb. 3: 1). It was used to designate Paul and Barnabas at Iconium: "And part held with the Jews, and part with the Apostles," Acts 14: 4. Yet, in a limited sense, and when used to denote the office, it was used to designate the Twelve, and the Apostle to the Gentiles, which office Paul was called.

The office of an Apostle embraced that of the bishopric, Acts 1: 20, a term employed to denote the nature of the office from which Judas fell, and to which Matthias was appointed. A bishop is one to whom a charge has been given, and who is made an overseer, to superintend the work of the church. This function the Apostles exercised and held in their own hands at Jerusalem, until other local churches were regularly organized, and overseers were duly appointed to take charge of them. The Apostles were also called "elders." Peter, who was one of the Twelve, applies the term to himself in these words: "The elders which are among you I exhort, who am also an elder." 1

Pet. 5: 1. John also uses the term in two of his epistles: "The elder unto the elect lady; the elder unto the well-beloved Gaius." The term "elder" does not denote the nature of the office, but rather the gravity of the work and maturity in life and attainment necessary to meet the responsibilities which the position involves. The word *elder* in the comparative degree of *old* which has, as its radical meaning, the sense of *grown* up. Then the comparative elder is a degree beyond maturity, and denotes one advanced, a senior, one having precedence from office, or rank. In the latter sense it is used by the sacred writers in the New Testament to denote official relation. The superlative degree is not used to designate official position in the church, for "one is your Master even Christ, and all ye are brethren." From 1 Tim. 5: 17, we discover that, in addition to being a minister, an elder is a ruler. "Let the elders that rule well be counted worthy of double honor, especially they who labor in the word and doctrine." Then the office of elder is in advance of the ministry, the elder having a duty imposed upon him in addition to preaching, and the term ruler would indicate that he is one with the bishop, who is also a ruler, or overseer.

Does the Gospel warrant a church in having more than one elder? This question may be answered by producing either a precedent or rule from the inspired record. Paul "sent to Ephesus, and called the elders of the church." Acts 20: 17. The church at Ephesus, then, had more than one elder. Again, may a church have more than one bishop? This question is fully answered in Philpp. 1: 1, "Paul and Timotheus, the servants of Jesus Christ, to all the saints in Christ Jesus which are at Philipi, with the bishops and deacons." Then the church at Philippi had more than one bishop, as well as more than one deacon.

But the main question still is pending, and we hope to answer it approximately at least; and we approach it with another question: Is the elder a bishop? To answer this we refer to Acts 20: 17-28, "And from Miletus he sent to Ephesus and called the elders of the church." "Take heed therefore unto yourselves and all the flock over the which the Holy Ghost hath made you overseers (bishops) to feed the church of God, which he hath purchased with his own blood." This proves that the elders of the church at Ephesus were bishops. It proves that there may be more than one Bishop as well as more than one elder in a church. It stands as solid evidence against the idea entertained by some that the foreman among the elders alone is bishop. What we want is the usage of the Apostolic age. Let us not forget that there were bishops at Philippi as well as at Ephesus. What of the note appended to the Second Epistle to Timothy, stating that Timothy was ordained the first bishop of the church of the Ephesians? What of that appended to Titus, stating that Titus was ordained the first bishop of the Cretians? Accepting these as historical facts, they simply show that Timothy was the first bishop ordained at Ephesus, and that Titus was the first ordained in Crete, and that they were simply first among their equals in office. The same Gospel rule obtains among bishops as among others: "Likewise ye younger, submit yourselves unto the elder." Our Annual Meeting has recognized the same principle in every ordination, in making the ordained equal with the elders, except where age and experience would give them advantage.

Furthermore, Paul instructed Titus "to set in order the things that are wanting, and ordain elders in every city, as I had appointed thee; if any be blameless, the husband of one wife, having faithful children, not accused of riot, or unruly. For a bishop must be blameless as the steward of

God. Titus 1: 5-7. Here the terms "elder" and "bishop" are applied to the same person in the same office, and therefore must be synonymous. We, then, have two facts clearly settled: First, Acts 20: 17-28 proves that "the elders of the church are bishops. Second, Titus 1: 5-7, proves that an ordained elder is a bishop. This leads us to the Scriptural conclusion that "the elders of the church" are "ordained elders."

We have now reached the main question, and apparently the above may be regarded as an answer to it, fairly and Scripturally drawn. But because the idea prevails among many that the term "elder" may be applied to other church officers besides the bishops, would it be asking too much to have a single specific case produced in the New Testament, where the term "elder" is used to designate the office of minister, deacon, or any other official position, short of the full ministry? One unquestionable instance will suffice. It will give us ground to believe that it may be used in a general sense, and that the term is applicable to anyone beyond the laity. The church, however, has hesitated in giving the word such a bearing. The church, in her official decisions, has restricted the word to the ordained, or the bishopric.

One of the clearest and most discriminating decisions ever reached upon the matter in hand was made by the church as to who shall anoint the sick with oil in the name of the Lord. The standing decision of the church is that the sick should be anointed with oil by ordained elders, if they can be obtained, and if not, then by the next in office. This decision is not only in harmony with the Gospel, but it also agrees with certain clearly-defined principles of church government.

1. It decides that ordained elders fill the position in official standing, with the "elders of the church" of James 5: 14.

2. It recognizes the truth that "helps" (1 Cor. 12: 28) are necessary in every position in life.

3. That in the performance of any duty where a work may be done by appointment, or by delegation, "the younger should be subject to the elder."

Our main question, then, is virtually already decided. The elders of the church of James 5: 14 are ordained elders. But ordained elders cannot be had under all circumstances. What then? The church says get the next in office. This has frequently been done, and God has blessed the work. Where two elders cannot be had, one elder takes a minister, and sometimes a deacon, as an assistant. Upon the same principle the "next in office" may anoint the sick by appointment of the elder when necessary. "But," says one, "why does James direct the sick to send for the elders of the church if others may also anoint?" In the absence of the Savior, did not the man, whose son was a lunatic, apply to the disciples, and did the Savior reprove them for their attempt to heal the young man? Did not Joshua address the sun as ruler of the day when he wanted an extension of time till night-fall? Every organization has its overseer, or ruler. In the absence of Christ the church is his representative to carry on his work. James directs the sick to send for the elders of the church because they are the overseers or rulers of the church; and in their absence, the "next in office" is their representative by their appointment and the order of the church.

Broadway, Va.

CITY MISSIONS.

BY S. Z. SHARP.

AT no other time in the history of our church has so much been said and done in regard to city missions as now. As a people, we are becoming

The Gospel Messenger,

A Weekly at $1.50 Per Annum.

PUBLISHED BY

The Brethren's Publishing Co.

D. L. MILLER,	. . . . . .	Editor.
J. H. MOORE,	. . . . .	Office Editor.
J. B. BRUMBAUGH,	}	Associate Editors.
J. G. ROYER,	}	
JOSEPH AMICK,	. . . .	Business Manager.

ADVISORY COMMITTEE:

L. W. Teeter, A. Hutchison, Daniel Hays.

☞ Communications for publication should be legibly written with black ink on one side of the paper only. Do not attempt to interline, or to put on one page what ought to occupy two.

☞ Anonymous communications will not be published.

☞ Do not mix business with articles for publication. Keep your communications on separate sheets from all business.

☞ Time is precious. We always have time to attend to business and to answer questions of importance, but please do not subject us to need less answering of letters.

☞ The MESSENGER is mailed each week to all subscribers. If the address is correctly entered on our list, the paper must reach the person to whom it is addressed. If you do not get your paper, write us, giving particulars.

☞ When changing your address, please give your former as well as your future address in full, so as to avoid delay and misunderstanding.

☞ Always remit to the office from which you order your goods, no matter from where you receive them.

☞ Do not send personal checks or drafts on interior banks, unless you send with them 25 cents each, to pay for collection.

☞ Remittances should be made by Post-office Money Order, Drafts on New York, Philadelphia or Chicago, or Registered Letters, made payable and addressed to "Brethren's Publishing Co., Mount Morris, Ill.," or "Brethren's Publishing Co., Huntingdon, Pa."

☞ Entered at the Post-office at Mount Morris, Ill., as second-class matter.

Mount Morris, Ill., - - - - Sept. 13, 1892.

BRO. D. E. PRICE is with the Brethren in Fulton County, this week. We trust he will have a pleasant season of worship with them.

BRO. JAMES R. GISH reports five additions on the mission field in Arkansas. In his article this week he throws out a few practical hints, well worth considering.

BRO. HENRY FRANTZ is expected to commence a series of meetings at West Branch, seven miles from Mt. Morris, Sept. 24, and continue till over the feast, Oct. 1 and 2.

BRO. SILAS HOOVER writes that he is now engaged in a series of meetings in the Middle Creek church, Pa., with increasing congregations. This congregation is presided over by Bro. Josiah Berkley.

BRO. S. M. GOUGHNOUR recently preached for the Brethren in Denver, Colo., where he thinks the prospects for building up a church quite encouraging. He went from there to Fort Collins, to hold a few meetings.

THE late Government statistics show that there are now about 140 denominations in the United States. Of these there are fifteen different varieties of Methodists, fourteen of Baptists and twelve of Presbyterians.

WHAT do some of the members, who cannot afford to go a mile or two to attend meeting, think of some of the Brethren in the West who must travel thirty miles in order to attend religious services? How does the zeal compare?

WE hope to receive a short report from each of the 197 feasts announced in this issue. In congregations, where the church has appointed no correspondent, and where there is no one who usually reports for the MESSENGER, let the elder see to it, that a short report is furnished for publication. Do not wait a week or more, but if possible send in the report as soon as the feast is over. Let these reports be short and to the point,

BRETHREN Geo. D. Zollers and C. P. Rowland recently visited the scattered members at Lost Nation, Iowa, and report the church very much in need of ministerial help. Bro. Zollers' letter concerning this church, its prospects, etc., will appear next week.

ONE of our correspondents from the West says, "We have much to thank God for." This is certainly better than complaining. If people would think more about their blessings and not so much concerning their misfortunes, life would be much more pleasant for them.

THE Mission Board of Texas, etc., would like to locate a few ministers where they are needed, if they can be found. Here, probably, is a chance for a few hard-working ministers to make themselves eminently useful. See Bro. Austin's notice among the gleanings in this issue.

THE Brethren at Gillaspie's, Va., have great reasons to rejoice. Twenty recently united with the church by confession and baptism, and six were restored. With the one not yet baptized, this makes twenty-seven additions. There is power in the good old Gospel, if preached in faith and power.

BRO. E. R. BUCKEY, of Union Bridge, Md., writes very favorably of the project to locate a minister in Washington City, D. C. He thinks that, if a good minister should be located there, a strong church may eventually be established at the Capital. It is to be hoped that the undertaking will not only meet the approval of the Brethren generally, but that it will meet with commendable success.

THE Mt. Morris Index, which, by the way, is one of the most newsy local papers of which we have any knowledge, says: "A stroll through our town is enough to make old residents shout for joy. The new residences that are going up will astonish anyone. In spite of this fact twenty more houses could be rented inside one week's time if they were to be had. One great fault is, there are not workmen enough here to push things through."

PEOPLE who think nothing of pitching their tent towards some Sodom for the sole purpose of making money, will do well to study the history of Lot. He probably made money in the operation and gained no small amount of popularity, but in the end he lost everything he had made, lost his wife and sacrificed his own morality and reputation. The ruin was complete. On the other hand, Abraham preferred to dwell in the modest plains of Mamre, and there built an altar to the Lord. He made life a success. It always pays to dwell where an altar can be erected and maintained unto the Lord.

THE American Messenger says, "There are not less than eighteen Christian churches at the present time in Jerusalem, besides a number of mosques and synagogues. The Arabic, Anglo-Jewish, and German Protestant congregations have each a church. The Greek Catholics have each five, as also the Roman Catholics, while the American, Syrian, Coptic, and Abyssinian Christians have one each. There are twenty-nine convents, and of these fifteen are Greek, seven Roman, two Armenian, two Abyssinian, and one Syrian, and ten hospitals; three German, one of which is for adults, one for children, one for lepers; two English, one being for Jews, the other for eye diseases, four others are under Jewish superintendence, one under Roman, and one under Greek. The fourteen educational institutions are divided up into six Roman, five Protestant, two Jewish, and one American."

THE cholera is still raging in Asia, and also spreading in Europe to an alarming extent. In Hamburg, Germany, as many as 400 new cases, and 116 deaths are reported daily. Several other points are infected, and the possibility of it getting a foot-hold in the United States, is almost a foregone conclusion, though it is too late in the season to permit it spreading very much. A few cases have already appeared at the quarantine station near New York, having been brought over on vessels sailing from infected cities in Europe. Our authorities, however, are taking very vigorous measures to prevent it from getting a firm hold here, and we think they will succeed.

IN his article this week, Bro. Sharp shows that we are making at least some progress in city mission work. So far our efforts in that direction are encouraging, and duty seems to indicate that they should be continued with increased zeal. There is no reason why we should not have congregations in all the cities in the United States. In the early centuries there were churches in all the leading cities in the Roman Empire. The apostles did nearly all their preaching in cities, and as we pretend to preach the same doctrine so successfully held forth by them, we can see no reason why we should not also succeed. We have made a good beginning and it is to be hoped that no efforts will be spared in vigorously pushing the work in the future.

As one travels around, he hears some strange doctrine. That is what Bro. D. E. Brubaker thought when the learned minister in Clarence, N. Y., told his congregation that Job's wife was non compos mentis. Were we to locate the trouble, we should probably examine the mind of the preacher more closely than the mind of Job's wife. A mother who can stand the loss of a large family, the loss of all the property, cling to her husband during a distressing period of intense suffering, expressing but one doubt all that while, and then help him regain all his property, and as much more, and raise another family of daughters, the most fair and lovely in all the land, would hardly be suspicioned of insanity in any civilized age. A little more credit is probably due this woman than she is in the habit of receiving. Has any one thought to write up the history of Job's wife in the light here suggested, and in the light of certain well-arranged and clearly-stated facts which will appear in the Essay Department of next issue?

NEVER before in the history of the church have so many love-feast notices been published at one time as may be found in this issue. The number is now about 197, which added to the seventy or more that have been taken out during the last few weeks, show not far from 300 love-feast announcements for this fall. This speaks volumes for the peace, zeal and loyalty of our general Brotherhood. It indicates that nearly, if not quite, all the congregations are blessed by peace in their own ranks, and have a zeal that prompts them to commendable Christian activity. It also indicates a loyalty to the Gospel that is to be commended and encouraged. It furthermore implies that there is a decided growth among our people, not only in the way of zeal and Gospel loyalty, but in strength and denominational individuality. Every year marks a decided growth in this direction, and we look for a still greater development as the years go by. These feasts will not only be the means of once more bringing us nearer to God and one another, but they will impart renewed strength to those already in the church, and perhaps be instrumental in bringing hundreds more into the fold.

The Gospel Messenger,

A Weekly at $1.50 Per Annum.

PUBLISHED BY

The Brethren's Publishing Co.

D. L. MILLER,	Editor.
J. H. MOORE,	Office Editor.
J. B. BRUMBAUGH,	
J. G. ROYER,	Associate Editors.
JOSEPH AMICK,	Business Manager.

ADVISORY COMMITTEE:

L. W. Teeter, A. Hutchison, Daniel Hays.

☞Communications for publication should be legibly written with black ink on one side of the paper only. Do not attempt to interline, or to put on one page what ought to occupy two.

☞Anonymous communications will not be published.

☞Do not mix business with articles for publication. Keep your communications on separate sheets from all business.

☞Time is precious. We always have time to attend to business and to answer questions of importance, but please do not subject us to need less answering of letters.

☞The MESSENGER is mailed each week to all subscribers. If the address is correctly entered on our list, the paper must reach the person to whom it is addressed. If you do not get your paper, write us, giving particulars.

☞When changing your address, please give your former as well as your future address in full, so as to avoid delay and misunderstanding.

☞Always remit to the office from which you order your goods, no matter from where you receive them.

☞Do not send personal checks or drafts on interior banks, unless you send with them 25 cents each, to pay for collection.

☞Remittances should be made by Post-office Money Order, Drafts on New York, Philadelphia or Chicago, or Registered Letters, made payable and addressed to "Brethren's Publishing Co., Mount Morris, Ill.," or "Brethren's Publishing Co., Huntingdon, Pa."

☞Entered at the Post-office at Mount Morris, Ill., as second-class matter.

Mount Morris, Ill., - - - - Sept. 13, 1892.

BRO. D. E. PRICE is with the Brethren in Fulton County, this week. We trust he will have a pleasant season of worship with them.

BRO. JAMES R. GISH reports five additions on the mission field in Arkansas. In his article this week he throws out a few practical hints, well worth considering.

BRO. HENRY FRANTZ is expected to commence a series of meetings at West Branch, seven miles from Mt. Morris, Sept. 24, and continue till over the feast, Oct. 1 and 2.

BRO. SILAS HOOVER writes that he is now engaged in a series of meetings in the Middle Creek church, Pa., with increasing congregations. This congregation is presided over by Bro. Josiah Berkley.

BRO. S. M. GOUGHNOUR recently preached for the Brethren in Denver, Colo., where he thinks the prospects for building up a church quite encouraging. He went from there to Fort Collins, to hold a few meetings.

THE late Government statistics show that there are now about 140 denominations in the United States. Of these there are fifteen different varieties of Methodists, fourteen of Baptists and twelve of Presbyterians.

WHAT do some of the members, who cannot afford to go a mile or two to attend meeting, think of some of the Brethren in the West who must travel thirty miles in order to attend religious services? How does the zeal compare?

WE hope to receive a short report from each of the 197 feasts announced in this issue. In congregations, where the church has appointed no correspondent, and where there is no one who usually reports for the MESSENGER, let the elder see to it, that a short report is furnished for publication. Do not wait a week or more, but if possible send in the report as soon as the feast is over. Let these reports be short and to the point,

---

BRETHREN Geo. D. Zollers and C. P. Rowland recently visited the scattered members at Lost Nation, Iowa, and report the church very much in need of ministerial help. Bro. Zollers' letter concerning this church, its prospects, etc., will appear next week.

ONE of our correspondents from the West says, "We have much to thank God for." This is certainly better than complaining. If people would think more about their blessings and not so much concerning their misfortunes, life would be much more pleasant for them.

THE Mission Board of Texas, etc., would like to locate a few ministers where they are needed, if they can be found. Here, probably, is a chance for a few hard-working ministers to make themselves eminently useful. See Bro. Austin's notice among the gleanings in this issue.

THE Brethren at Gillaspie's, Va., have great reasons to rejoice. Twenty recently united with the church by confession and baptism, and six were restored. With the one not yet baptized, this makes twenty-seven additions. There is power in the good old Gospel, if preached in faith and power.

BRO. E. B. BUCKEY, of Union Bridge, Md., writes very favorably of the project to locate a minister in Washington City, D. C. He thinks that, if a good minister should be located there, a strong church may eventually be established at the Capital. It is to be hoped that the undertaking will not only meet the approval of the Brethren generally, but that it will meet with commendable success.

THE Mt. Morris Index, which, by the way, is one of the most newsy local papers of which we have any knowledge, says: "A stroll through our town is enough to make old residents shout for joy. The new residences that are going up will astonish anyone. In spite of this fact twenty more houses could be rented within one week's time if they were to be had. One great fault is, there are not workmen enough here to push things through."

PEOPLE who think nothing of pitching their tent towards some Sodom for the sole purpose of making money, will do well to study the history of Lot. He probably made money in the operation and gained no small amount of popularity, but in the end he lost everything he had made, lost his wife and sacrificed his own morality and reputation. The ruin was complete. On the other hand, Abraham preferred to dwell in the modest plains of Mamre, and there built an altar to the Lord. He made life a success. It always pays to dwell where an altar can be erected and maintained unto the Lord.

THE American Messenger says, "There are not less than eighteen Christian churches at the present time in Jerusalem, besides a number of mosques and synagogues. The Arabic, Anglo-Jewish, and German Protestant congregations have each a church. The Greek Catholics have each five, as also the Roman Catholics, while the American, Syrian, Coptic, and Abyssinian Christians have one each. There are twenty-nine convents, and of these fifteen are Greek, seven Roman, two Armenian, two Abyssinian, and one Syrian, and ten hospitals; three German, one of which is for adults, one for children, one for lepers; two English, one being for Jews, the other for eye diseases, four others are under Jewish superintendence, one under Roman, and one under Greek. The fourteen educational institutions are divided up into six Roman, five Protestant, two Jewish, and one American."

THE cholera is still raging in Asia, and also spreading in Europe to an alarming extent. In Hamburg, Germany, as many as 400 new cases, and 116 deaths are reported daily. Several other points are infected, and the possibility of it getting a foot-hold in the United States, is almost a foregone conclusion, though it is too late in the season to permit it spreading very much. A few cases have already appeared at the quarantine station near New York, having been brought over on vessels sailing from infected cities in Europe. Our authorities, however, are taking very vigorous measures to prevent it from getting a firm hold here, and we think they will succeed.

IN his article this week, Bro. Sharp shows that we are making at least some progress in city mission work. So far our efforts in that direction are encouraging, and duty seems to indicate that they should be continued with increased zeal. There is no reason why we should not have congregations in all the cities in the United States. In the early centuries there were churches in all the leading cities in the Roman Empire. The apostles did nearly all their preaching in cities, and as we pretend to preach the same doctrine so successfully held forth by them, we can see no reason why we should not also succeed. We have made a good beginning and it is to be hoped that no efforts will be spared in vigorously pushing the work in the future.

As one travels around, he hears some strange doctrine. That is what Bro. D. E. Brubaker thought when the learned minister in Clarence, N. Y., told his congregation that Job's wife was non compos mentis. Were we to locate the trouble, we should probably examine the mind of the preacher more closely than the mind of Job's wife. A mother who can stand the loss of a large family, the loss of all the property, cling to her husband during a distressing period of intense suffering, expressing but one doubt all that while, and then help him regain all his property, and as much more, and raise another family of daughters, the most fair and lovely in all the land, would hardly be suspicioned of insanity in any civilized age. A little more credit is probably due this woman than she is in the habit of receiving. Has any one thought to write up the history of Job's wife in the light here suggested, and in the light of certain well-arranged and clearly stated facts which will appear in the Essay Department of next issue?

NEVER before in the history of the church have so many love-feast notices been published at one time as may be found in this issue. The number is now about 197, which added to the seventy or more that have been taken out during the last few weeks, show not far from 300 love-feast announcements for this fall. This speaks volumes for the Brotherhood. It indicates that nearly, if not quite, all the congregations are blessed by peace in their own ranks, and have a zeal that prompts them to commendable Christian activity. It also indicates a loyalty to the Gospel that is to be commended and encouraged. It furthermore implies that there is a decided growth among our people, not only in the way of zeal and Gospel loyalty, but in strength and denominational individuality. Every year marks a decided growth in this direction, and we look for a still greater development as the years go by. These feasts will not only be the means of once more bringing us nearer to God and one another, but they will impart renewed strength to those already in the church, and perhaps be instrumental in bringing hundreds more into the fold,

CORRESPONDENCE.

"Write what thou seest, and send it unto the churches."

☞Church News solicited for this Department. If you have had a good meeting, send a report of it, so that others may rejoice with you. In writing give name of church, County and State. Be brief. Notes of Travel should be as short as possible. Land Advertisements are not solicited for this Department. We have an advertising page, and, if necessary, will issue supplements.

From the Upper Cumberland Church, Pa.

THE members met in quarterly council, at Green Spring church, Aug. 15, which was largely attended, showing quite an interest in church work, which, we think, all members of our Fraternity should manifest.

The most important question considered seemed to be the building of a church in Carlisle, the County-seat of Cumberland County, the central point of the Upper and Lower Cumberland District. There are some members living there without a place of worship. The Land Improvement Company offer the ground free for a church. It was decided to unite with the Brethren of the Lower Cumberland church to build the house, if they will do so. Their council has not yet occurred, and we hope they will well consider the needs of the members at Carlisle, who are without a place of worship. Oh think of the salvation of the poor souls that may be gained by hearing the Word preached in its purity! We also decided to hold a love-feast Sept. 28 and 29, at Huntsdale. All business passed off pleasantly. Love and union seemed to prevail. May we all try to work for the purity of the church, and may God's blessings attend the efforts of our dear ministers.

LEAH T. MILLER.

Oakville, Pa., Aug. 25.

From Woodbury, Pa.

THE Brethren of the Woodbury church held their harvest-meeting Aug. 14, at 10 o'clock A. M. The harvest-meeting was preceded by a very interesting children's meeting. Quite a number of children and older ones had assembled to hear what Bro. J. B. Fluke, who conducted these meetings, had to say to them, and, judging by the attention given by the little folks, Bro. Fluke's talk surely was interesting to them, and very profitable, if put to practice. Bro. Fluke also preached a very able harvest sermon, choosing for his subject, "Harvest," from which he presented to us very important thoughts. Among them was, that, since the Lord has blessed us with so bountiful a harvest, we should not forget that some of it should be given to him, and, as a result, $12 03 was donated to assist Bro. Quinlan in his Baltimore work.

We also had public preaching in the evening at 7:30 o'clock. The meetings were well attended and the best interest was given. The church met in council Aug. 20, which passed off pleasantly.

J. C. STAYER.

Aug. 23.

From Weaubleau, Mo.

BRO. David Bowman came to us Aug. 11, and held meetings at Onion Hill school-house till the 23rd, preaching only at night, and two Sundays at eleven o'clock. There were no immediate additions, but the members are much encouraged and built up in the most holy faith. We believe that if the work is properly followed up, many will be brought into the fold at this place, as several have expressed themselves favorable to the doctrine of the Brethren. It was thought best by Bro. Bowman to organize the members here into a church, and also to hold a love-feast at the close of the meetings. Aug. 24 was appointed for the council-meeting and love-feast. All members being will-

ing to organize, the first business of the meeting was the reading of church letters, and the reception of two by letter. As we had one deacon with us, he was received as such. The members thought best to elect another deacon, and the lot fell on the writer, who was duly installed. Our love-feast services commenced at seven o'clock. Twenty two members surrounded the Lord's table to commemorate the death and sufferings of our Lord and Savior Jesus Christ. We had an enjoyable meeting, long to be remembered by all present. Ministering brethren present were elders A. A. Killingsworth, Jacob Yost and Jacob Bowman. The latter officiated at our love-feast. The church at this place will be known as the Weaubleau church. Brethren, pray for us in this part of God's moral vineyard. God help the good work to go on every-where!

W. M. FLEMING.

Aug 25.

Dedication of the German Baptist Church of Mechanicstown, Frederick Co., Md

THE origin of the German Baptists in this County dates back to 1757, when Eld. Daniel Leatherman moved from Lancaster County, Pa. He selected for his home a tract of land, lying in the extreme northern end of Middletown Valley, known as the mountain farm, where he spent his remaining days, and where also rest his remains. Elder Daniel's grandson, Jacob Leatherman, became the pioneer preacher in that locality, where now the Upper and Lower Middletown Valley churches are located. Some time near the above date some Brethren from Pennsylvania passed through the eastern part of Frederick County, sowing the Gospel seed, from which have grown the Eastern Maryland churches. It is said that those brethren passed on to Blackwater, Va., then to North Carolina, preaching the Gospel and organizing churches as they went.

In the year 1772 Daniel Sayler, with his son Daniel, moved from the Conestoga church, Lancaster County, Pa., to Beaver Dam, Frederick County, Md. Young Daniel soon became a prominent minister of the Gospel, and soon after the first ordained elder of the once-famous church of Beaver Dam. Elders Sayler and Leatherman were the first heralds of the Gospel among the Brethren in the vicinity of Mechanicstown, first preaching in private houses, then in a union house. Later on they purchased a lot of ground in the town on which stood a venerable-looking school-house, in which they worshiped God, until last March, when it was torn down and the present structure erected. Elder Sayler made his missionary tour on horseback, while Eld. Leatherman chose the more safe way of a pedestrian. It is said that Bro. Jacob was an extraordinary walker. Mechanicstown is situated at the eastern base of the Blue Ridge Mountain, and noted for its healthy climate, pure air and good water. It is twelve miles from the original Leatherman home.

Eld Leatherman would leave his home on Sunday morning, walk to Mechanicstown, fill his appointment, and, after dinner, with staff in hand, recross the mountain, going by the foot-path. Elder Jacob Sayler succeeded the above brethren in preaching in Mechanicstown; then came Eld. D. F. Sayler.

The writer is now, with the assistance of his co-laborers, T. J. Kolb, F. C. Reuner and John R. Flohr, trying to follow the faithful old brethren in preaching the Gospel.

It became necessary to have better accommodations for preaching the Word, hence the necessity of building a more suitable house, which, through the mercies of God and the assistance of some of our adjoining churches, we were permitted to do. The dimensions of the house are 30 by 36 feet, and

14 feet high. This part is completed. We expect further on to attach a kitchen to the rear end, for love-feast purposes. The Mechanicstown meeting-house is located within the bounds of the Monocacy church, formerly presided over by Eld. D. P. Saylor. We are pleased to say that the house is not only built but also paid for. The dedication occurred Aug. 21. Eld. D. F. Stouffer, of Benevola, Washington County, Md., was with us and preached on Saturday evening on general doctrine. On Sunday morning he preached the dedication sermon to a full house of attentive and interested people, giving general satisfaction to all present.

In the evening Eld. J. F. Oller, of Waynesborough, Pa, who had responded to a call to assist in the work, preached an interesting sermon from the text, "God is faithful, by whom ye are called." The preaching throughout was impressive and well received by all present. The Lord willing, we expect to have preaching every second Sunday at 3 P. M., commencing with Sunday, Aug. 21. Ministers present at the dedication were elders. D. F. Stouffer, of Washington County, Md.; J. F. Oller, of Waynesborough, Pa.; Geo Leatherman and Silas Harp, of Middletown Valley; Samuel Myers, of Virginia; Dr. P. D. Fahrney, of Frederick City, Md., T. J. Kolb and John R. Flohr, of Monocacy church. There were also present at the meeting Rev. Z. Whitmore, of the Reformed Church of Mechanicstown, and Rev. Z. Miller, of the Evangelical Lutheran Church of Baltimore, Md.

D. R SAYLER.

Mechanicstown, Md.

From the Thornapple Church, Mich.

SINCE our last item from this branch of the body, we have had some accessions to our number. On Sunday, July 3, at our regular meeting, five were received by confession and baptism, and Aug 13, at our quarterly council, one more was added, and there are some applicants for baptism, near Fisher Station, at the West side of our district. Their baptism is to be attended to in the near future. Thus we are made to rejoice in the goodness of God. Those who have been received are all young in years and need the tender, fostering care of the church.

At our late council it was decided to hold a series of meetings this fall and winter at each of our two houses,—the first, at the east house, will probably be held the latter part of October.

Our love-feast was appointed to be held Nov. 12, at the east house. At our harvest-meeting, held on Saturday last, we were made glad by the presence of Eld. J. Katherman and wife, from Ohio. Bro. Jerry gave us an interesting and profitable sermon, both on Saturday and on Sunday morning at the regular meeting. Thus we are made to feel that the Good Lord is blessing his children and verifying his promises among us.

PETER B. MESSNER

Aug. 29.

From the Highways and Hedges.

SINCE our return from the West (July 12) we have been quite busy, visiting and holding meetings for and among the scattered members. Our first trip was south to a place in Arkansas County called Long Point. Bro. and sister Carpenter live near there. We had several meetings with fair attendance and very good attention. Returning home, our next trip was to St. Francis County, this State. Wife and I left home Aug. 6, and arrived at Palestine the same evening. We commenced meetings on Sunday, Aug. 7, and continued our services morning and night. We also made our annual visit, preparatory to our Communion season. Between times we had a council

CORRESPONDENCE.

"Write what thou seest, and send it unto the churches."

☞ Church News solicited for this Department. If you have had a good meeting, send a report of it, so that others may rejoice with you. In writing give name of church, County and State. Be brief. Notes of Travel should be as short as possible. Land Advertisements are not solicited for this Department. We have an advertising page, and, if necessary, will issue supplements.

From the Upper Cumberland Church, Pa.

THE members met in quarterly council, at Green Spring church, Aug. 15, which was largely attended, showing quite an interest in church work, which, we think, all members of our Fraternity should manifest.

The most important question considered seemed to be the building of a church in Carlisle, the County-seat of Cumberland County, the central point of the Upper and Lower Cumberland District. There are some members living there without a place of worship. The Land Improvement Company offer the ground free for a church. It was decided to unite with the Brethren of the Lower Cumberland church to build the house, if they will do so. Their council has not yet occurred, and we hope they will well consider the needs of the members at Carlisle, who are without a place of worship. Oh think of the salvation of the poor souls that may be gained by hearing the Word preached in its purity! We also decided to hold a love-feast Sept. 28 and 29, at Huntsdale. All business passed off pleasantly. Love and union seemed to prevail. May we all try to work for the purity of the church, and may God's blessings attend the efforts of our dear ministers.

LEAH T. MILLER.

Oakville, Pa., Aug. 25.

From Woodbury, Pa.

THE Brethren of the Woodbury church held their harvest-meeting Aug. 14, at 10 o'clock A. M. The harvest-meeting was preceded by a very interesting children's meeting. Quite a number of children and older ones had assembled to hear what Bro. J. B. Fluke, who conducted these meetings, had to say to them, and, judging by the attention given by the little folks, Bro. Fluke's talk surely was interesting to them, and very profitable, if put to practice. Bro. Fluke also preached a very able harvest sermon, choosing for his subject, "Harvest," from which he presented to us very important thoughts. Among them was, that, since the Lord has blessed us with so bountiful a harvest, we should not forget that some of it should be given to him, and, as a result, $12 03 was donated to assist Bro. Quinlan in his Baltimore work.

We also had public preaching in the evening at 7:30 o'clock. The meetings were well attended and the best attention was given. The church met in council Aug. 20, which passed off pleasantly. J. C. STAYER.

Aug. 23.

From Weaubleau, Mo.

BRO. David Bowman came to us Aug. 11, and held meetings at Onion Hill school-house till the 23rd, preaching only at night, and two Sundays at eleven o'clock. There were no immediate additions, but the members are much encouraged and built up in the most holy faith. We believe that if the work is properly followed up, many will be brought into the fold at this place, as several have expressed themselves favorable to the doctrine of the Brethren. It was thought best by Bro. Bowman to organize the members here into a church, and also to hold a love-feast at the close of the meetings. Aug. 24 was appointed for the council, meeting and love-feast. All members being will-

ing to organize, the first business of the meeting was the reading of church letters, and the reception of two by letter. As we had one deacon with us, he was received as such. The members thought best to elect another deacon, and the lot fell on the writer, who was duly installed. Our love-feast services commenced at seven o'clock. Twenty two members surrounded the Lord's table to commemorate the death and sufferings of our Lord and Savior Jesus Christ. We had an enjoyable meeting, long to be remembered by all present. Ministering brethren present were elders A. A. Killingsworth, Jacob Yost and Jacob Bowman. The latter officiated at our love-feast. The church at this place will be known as the Weaubleau church. Brethren, pray for us in this part of God's moral vineyard. God help the good work to go on every-where! W. M. FLEMING.

Aug. 25.

Dedication of the German Baptist Church of Mechanicstown, Frederick Co., Md.

THE origin of the German Baptists in this County dates back to 1757, when Eld. Daniel Leatherman moved from Lancaster County, Pa. He selected for his home a tract of land, lying in the extreme northern end of Middletown Valley, known as the mountain farm, where he spent his remaining days, and where also rest his remains. Elder Daniel's grandson, Jacob Leatherman, became the pioneer preacher in that locality, where now the Upper and Lower Middletown Valley churches are located. Some time near the above date some Brethren from Pennsylvania passed through the eastern part of Frederick County, sowing the Gospel seed, from which have grown the Eastern Maryland churches. It is said that those brethren passed on to Blackwater, Va., then to North Carolina, preaching the Gospel and organizing churches as they went.

In the year 1772 Daniel Sayler, with his son Daniel, moved from the Conestoga church, Lancaster County, Pa., to Beaver Dam, Frederick County, Md. Young Daniel soon became a prominent minister of the Gospel, and soon after the first ordained elder of the once-famous church of Beaver Dam. Elders Sayler and Leatherman were the first heralds of the Gospel among the Brethren in the vicinity of Mechanicstown, first preaching in private houses, then in a union house. Later on they purchased a lot of ground in the town on which stood a venerable-looking school-house, in which they worshiped God, until last March, when it was torn down and the present structure erected. Elder Sayler made his missionary tour on horseback, while Eld. Leatherman chose the more safe way of a pedestrian. It is said that Bro. Jacob was an extraordinary walker. Mechanicstown is situated at the eastern base of the Blue Ridge Mountain, and noted for its healthy climate, pure air and good water. It is twelve miles from the original Leatherman home. Eld Leatherman would leave his home on Sunday morning, walk to Mechanicstown, fill his appointment, and, after dinner, with staff in hand, recross the mountain, going by the foot-path. Elder Jacob Sayler succeeded the above brethren in preaching in Mechanicstown; then came Eld. D. F. Sayler.

The writer is now, with the assistance of his co-laborers, T. J. Kolb, F. C. Ronner and John R. Flohr, trying to follow the faithful old brethren in preaching the Gospel.

It became necessary to have better accommodations for preaching the Word, hence the necessity of building a more suitable house, which, through the mercies of God and the assistance of some of our adjoining churches, we were permitted to do. The dimensions of the house are 30 by 36 feet, and

14 feet high. This part is completed. We expect, further on to attach a kitchen to the rear end, for love-feast purposes. The Mechanicstown meeting-house is located within the bounds of the Monocacy church, formerly presided over by Eld. D. P. Saylor. We are pleased to say that the house is not only built but also paid for. The dedication occurred Aug. 21. Eld. D. F. Stouffer, of Benevola, Washington County, Md., was with us and preached on Saturday evening on general doctrine. On Sunday morning he preached the dedication sermon to a full house of attentive and interested people, giving general satisfaction to all present.

In the evening Eld. J. F. Oller, of Waynesborough, Pa., who had responded to a call to assist in the work, preached an interesting sermon from the text, "God is faithful, by whom ye are called." The preaching throughout was impressive and well received by all present. The Lord willing, we expect to have preaching every second Sunday at 3 P. M., commencing with Sunday, Aug. 21. Ministers present at the dedication were elders. D. F. Stouffer, of Washington County, Md.; J. F. Oller, of Waynesborough, Pa.; George Leatherman and Silas Harp, of Middletown Valley; Samuel Myers, of Virginia; Dr. P. D. Fahrney, of Frederick City, Md., T. J. Kolb and John R. Flohr, of Monocacy church. There were also present at the meeting Rev. Z. Whitmore, of the Reformed Church of Mechanicstown, and Rev. Z. Miller, of the Evangelical Lutheran Church of Baltimore, Md.

D. R SAYLER.

Mechanicstown, Md.

From the Thornapple Church, Mich.

SINCE our last item from this branch of the body, we have had some accessions to our number. On Sunday, July 3, at our regular meeting, five were received by confession and baptism, and Aug 13, at our quarterly council, one more was added, and there are some applicants for baptism, near Fisher Station, at the West side of our district. Their baptism is to be attended to in the near future. Thus we are made to rejoice in the goodness of God. Those who have been received are all young in years and need the tender, fostering care of the church.

At our late council it was decided to hold a series of meetings this fall and winter at each of our two houses,—the first, at the east house, will probably be held the latter part of October.

Our love-feast was appointed to be held Nov. 12, at the east house. At our harvest-meeting, held on Saturday last, we were much pleased by the presence of Eld. J. Kathermau and wife, from Ohio. Bro. Jerry gave us an interesting and profitable sermon, both on Saturday and on Sunday morning at the regular meeting. Thus we are made to feel that the Good Lord is blessing his children and verifying his promises among us.

PETER B. MESSNER.

Aug. 29.

From the Highways and Hedges.

SINCE our return from the West (July 12) we have been quite busy, visiting and holding meetings for and among the scattered members. Our first trip was south to a place in Arkansas County called Long Point. Bro. and sister Carpenter live near there. We had several meetings with fair attendance and very good attention. Returning home, our next trip was to St. Francis County, this State. Wife and I left home Aug. 6, and arrived at Palestine the same evening. We commenced meetings on Sunday, Aug. 7, and continued our services morning and night. We also made our annual visit, preparatory to our Communion season. Between times we had a council

Chips from the Work-house.

On arriving in Eastern Pennsylvania, the following churches were visited in order, and one or more meetings attended in each: Chiques, over five hundred members, under the care of S. R. Zug; Lancaster City church, about fifty members, also under the care of S. R. Zug; Mountville, about three hundred members, H. E. Light, elder in charge; White Oak, Benjamin Eby, elder, about four hundred members; West Conestoga, two hundred members, J. W. Hackman in charge; Ephratah, over four hundred members, Israel Wenger in charge; Conestoga, three hundred members, John Grabill in charge.

Here I had the privilege of meeting quite a number of the adjoining elders, and the church, in council. Bro. John Grabill was ordained to the eldership, and the church placed under his care. Bro. Jacob Pfoutz was advanced to the second degree, and Samuel Taylor elected to the deaconship. All were installed into their respective offices, and their wives as helpmeets, in the usual order. A more uniformly plain, more hospitable, sociable, and kind class of members I have never met in all my travels.

The congregations for preaching were well attended by the members, and the older people of the neighborhood, but with one exception very few young people were at the meeting, and very few young people are members of the church. When the question is asked, Where are they?—a correct answer would in many cases be sufficient to bring the tear to the parent's eye, and perhaps to make angels weep.

As there is no effect without a cause, common sense would say, Seek out the cause and find a remedy if possible. In these small territories (as they seem to a Western man), there are from two to five good meeting-houses in each church, owned by the church, and from one to two union houses besides, where meetings are also held by the Brethren. Some of them have Sunday-school, and some have not.

Why any one who loves the Lord and puts his trust in his Word should oppose teaching God's Word in Sunday-school, these "Chips" don't say. In the primitive church, during the days of the apostles, and in the centuries immediately after, when the church grew and prospered as never since, special attention was given to the children and young people, they being seated in front at the meetings, and a prayer and sermon especially adapted to the children was given first. Thus were the children and young people made to feel that the church was also for them. May we not learn a lesson from this primitive practice?

In traveling over the rich and well-cultivated country where land is worth from one to three hundred dollars per acre, one will see acres and acres of tobacco, and hear them tell how one may sell the tobacco from an acre of ground for from two to five hundred dollars. Large quantities of it are here, in the same County, made up into cigars, in which business many of the young people, ladies especially, and some of the Brethren's children included, are employed. These cigars you may follow out over this vast country in all directions and into foreign countries until, at last, they are puffed off into smoke, leaving the consumer the poorer, from five to forty cents per day, amounting in a life-time to enough to bring many sinners to Christ, and lay up much treasure in heaven, if consecrated to Christ. Tobacco smoked up in cigars or chewed up and spit away, never converted a single sinner nor encouraged a saint, nor made any one more Christ-like. This chewing and smoking never laid up treasures in heaven for the purchaser, nor for the fellow on the other end who has produced it and taken the con-

sumer's money for that which he knows is worth nothing to the consumer.

Well, these "Chips" will only say, Surely if the raiser, seller and the consumer would all take the advice of Annual Meeting and do neither, they would certainly be on the safe side.

These "Chips" are made in the large City of Philadelphia where, and also on the remainder of this trip, I hope to find more blocks from which to make more "Chips."   Daniel Vaniman. *McPherson, Kans.*

Special Notice to the Brotherhood in Kansas.

At the last meeting of the Trustees of the Kansas Home, Aug. 1, 1892, it was ascertained that we must solicit another time, about the same as we did before, in order to finish the necessary buildings, and have a small fund to start with, about the middle of March, 1893.

We thought it good to write this notice, so that the members could be prepared; as we hope there is a readiness to will, so there may be a performance also out of that which ye have, "for if there be first a willing mind, it will be accepted according to that a man hath, and not according to that he hath not." 2 Cor. 8: 12.

The house is up and the plasterers are at work. We expect to finish without delay, but will not open for inmates till about the middle of March next. Any donations in the way of furnishing the house will be gladly received. A brother and sister agree to furnish a room. By request we sent them the size of each room and the number. They made choice of No. 2, and agree to bring good furniture and put it in, ready for occupants. They live nearly one hundred miles away. Another brother sends nearly enough for a room, to use at our pleasure. Who is the next to follow the good example? Any amount of good furniture or bed clothing will be gladly and thankfully received. The Trustees decided, however, that we should have all iron bed-steads; further we have nothing to dictate. Should any wish to furnish a room, please drop me a card, and I will give you the size and number of each room. We have twelve bed-rooms, and besides that, sitting and dining-rooms, kitchen, and bath-rooms.

We hope the Brotherhood will not consider us extravagant. We have an eye to economy but also to durability and comfort in the use of the means. We cannot fully report the entire cost, as we get the work done principally by the day, but will report it to the several District Meetings of Kansas next spring, if the Lord permits. The Good Lord has given us another good harvest, so that we can easily finish the good work begun. Each church will bear from us during the fall and winter, either by solicitor or otherwise, as may be thought best. All this could be avoided if all former subscribers would renew the amount of their original subscription, and solicit the new members in their congregations, and send it in to the treasurer, A. F. Miller, Booth, Reno Co., Kansas. Each member should feel as much interested in this good work as the Trustees, as it is the work of the church in Kansas and not of a few members. We hope the Lord will help all to see it in that light, and we hope that all may feel to respond liberally, for God loveth a cheerful giver. Overseers of churches should especially feel interested, and stir up the members to duty. Any necessary explanation asked for, will be gladly given by mail.   Enoch Eby. *Booth, Kans., Aug. 29.*

To the Churches of Southern Illinois.

The committee, appointed by last District Meeting, would like to have a report of the delegates

from each church at next District Meeting, as to the number of poor they have, what it costs to keep them, and if they are properly cared for.

Unless we have such a report, or some means of ascertaining the condition of the poor, we do not know whether we need a Home or not.

Thinking this to be the surest way of getting a correct report, we kindly ask some one in each church to make a note of this and see that we have a full report.

By order of committee: Thos. Keiser,
                        Cyrus Bucher,
                        S. B. Miller.

From North Manchester, Ind.

Yesterday, Sept. 1, we held our regular quarterly council-meeting in the Manchester church. Considerable business came before the meeting, but all was disposed of in a most agreeable manner. A Christ's spirit prevailed. One of the most important features of the meeting was the ample preparation made for the entertainment of the brethren and sisters at the Ministerial Meeting, to be held Oct. 11 and 12, at the church-house, two miles west of North Manchester. Quite a number of church letters were granted to young members who expect to attend school at Mt. Morris.

Since our last report we held two thanksgiving harvest-meetings, — one at each church-house. One young brother was received by baptism. May God bless him!

The sum of $36.29 was contributed to the missionary fund.

The Treasurer's report shows considerable means in the treasury. Preparations are being made to hold a series of meetings the coming fall and winter. Eld. Silas Gilbert, of Ohio, is expected at the church-house west of town.
                                  D. C. Cripe.
Sept. 2.

Notes of Travel.

Elders J. W. Eller and P. S. Miller have just returned from John's Chapel, a newly-built church which was dedicated and given the above name, Aug. 28, 1892. The church is in a good working condition. By the aid of the District, the Chapel was paid for before the dedication and everything seems to be working for the Master's cause. Eleven dear souls have been added to the church since July 1, 1892, and there are two more applicants for baptism.

The church numbers about eighty members, including two young ministers who are earnestly contending for the faith once delivered unto the saints. This little band is under the care of the Peter's Creek elders.   C. E. Eller.

Echoes from the Highway.

Saturday, Aug 20, was our quarterly council at Tropico. Considerable business was before the meeting, which was attended to in the spirit of love. Saturday following was our love-feast in that church. It was a happy Communion and a season of sweet fellowship. About sixty members were present, including nine ministers. A choice was held for two deacons. The lot fell on our brethren Joseph Brickett and Aaron Wolfe. May the blessings and grace of God abound in their behalf that they may be qualified for their calling. The prospects of the Tropico congregation are improving. Bro. David Kuns and wife have returned to Lordsburg. Students are coming in, preparatory to starting in at the opening of the school term.   J. S. Flory.
Lordsburg, Cal, Aug. 29.

Chips from the Work-house.

On arriving in Eastern Pennsylvania, the following churches were visited in order, and one or more meetings attended in each: Chiques, over five hundred members, under the care of S. R. Zug; Lancaster City church, about fifty members, also under the care of S. R. Zug; Mountville, about three hundred members, H. E. Light, elder in charge; White Oak, Benjamin Eby, elder, about four hundred members; West Conestoga, two hundred members, J. W. Hackman in charge; Ephratah, over four hundred members, Israel Wenger in charge; Conestoga, three hundred members, John Grabill in charge.

Here I had the privilege of meeting quite a number of the adjoining elders, and the church, in council. Bro. John Grabill was ordained to the eldership, and the church placed under his care. Bro. Jacob Pfoutz was advanced to the second degree, and Samuel Taylor elected to the deaconship. All were installed into their respective offices, and their wives as helpmeets, in the usual order. A more uniformly plain, more hospitable, sociable, and kind class of members I have never met in all my travels.

The congregations for preaching were well attended by the members, and the older people of the neighborhood, but with one exception very few young people were at the meeting, and very few young people are members of the church. When the question is asked, Where are they?—a correct answer would in many cases be sufficient to bring the tear to the parent's eye, and perhaps to make angels weep.

As there is no effect without a cause, common sense would say, Seek out the cause and find a remedy if possible. In these small territories (as they seem to a Western man), there are from two to five good meeting-houses in each church, owned by the church, and from one to two union houses besides, where meetings are also held by the Brethren. Some of them have Sunday-school, and some have not.

Why any one who loves the Lord and puts his trust in his Word should oppose teaching God's Word in Sunday-school, these "Chips" don't say. In the primitive church, during the days of the apostles, and in the centuries immediately after, when the church grew and prospered as never since, special attention was given to the children and young people, they being seated in front at the meetings, and a prayer and sermon especially adapted to the children was given first. Thus were the children and young people made to feel that the church was also for them. May we not learn a lesson from this primitive practice?

In traveling over the rich and well-cultivated country where land is worth from one to three hundred dollars per acre, one will see acres and acres of tobacco, and hear them tell how one may sell the tobacco from an acre of ground for from two to five hundred dollars. Large quantities of it are here, in the same County, made up into cigars, in which business many of the young people, ladies especially, and some of the Brethren's children included, are employed. These cigars you may follow out over this vast country in all directions and into foreign countries until, at last, they are puffed off into smoke, leaving the consumer the poorer, from five to forty cents per day, amounting in a life-time to enough to bring many sinners to Christ, and lay up much treasure in heaven, if consecrated to Christ. Tobacco smoked up in cigars or chewed up and spit away, never converted a single sinner nor encouraged a saint, nor made any one more Christ-like. This chewing and smoking never laid up treasures in heaven for the purchaser, nor for the fellow on the other end who has produced it and taken the con-

sumer's money for that which he knows is worth nothing to the consumer.

Well, these "Chips" will only say, Surely if the raiser, seller and the consumer would all take the advice of Annual Meeting and do neither, they would certainly be on the safe side.

These "Chips" are made in the large City of Philadelphia where, and also on the remainder of this trip, I hope to find more blocks from which to make more "Chips."   DANIEL VANIMAN.

McPherson, Kans

Special Notice to the Brotherhood in Kansas.

At the last meeting of the Trustees of the Kansas Home, Aug. 1, 1892, it was ascertained that we must solicit another time, about the same as we did before, in order to finish the necessary buildings, and have a small fund to start with, about the middle of March, 1893.

We thought it good to write this notice, so that the members could be prepared; as we hope there is a readiness to will, so there may be a performance also out of that which ye have, "for if there be first a willing mind, it will be accepted according to that a man hath, and not according to that he hath not." 2 Cor. 8: 12.

The house is up and the plasterers are at work. We expect to finish without delay, but will not open for inmates till about the middle of March next. Any donations in the way of furnishing the house will be gladly received. A brother and sister agree to furnish a room. By request we sent them the size of each room and the number. They made choice of No. 2, and agree to bring good furniture and put it in, ready for occupants. They live nearly one hundred miles away. Another brother sends nearly enough for a room, to use at our pleasure. Who is the next to follow the good example? Any amount of good furniture or bed clothing will be gladly and thankfully received. The Trustees decided, however, that we should have all iron bed-steads; farther we have nothing to dictate. Should any wish to furnish a room, please drop me a card, and I will give you the size and number of each room. We have twelve bed-rooms, and besides that, sitting and dining-rooms, kitchen, and bath-rooms.

We hope the Brotherhood will not consider us extravagant. We have an eye to economy but also to durability and comfort in the use of the means. We cannot fully report the entire cost, as we get the work done principally by the day, but will report it to the several District Meetings of Kansas next spring, if the Lord permits. The Good Lord has given us another good harvest, so that we can easily finish the good work begun. Each church will hear from us during the fall and winter, either by solicitor or otherwise, as may be thought best. All this could be avoided if all former subscribers would renew the amount of their original subscription, and solicit the new members in their congregations, and send it in to the treasurer, A. F. Miller, Booth, Reno Co., Kansas. Each member should feel as much interested in this good work as the Trustees, as it is the work of the church in Kansas and not of a few members. We hope the Lord will help all to see it in that light, and we hope that all may feel to respond liberally, for God loveth a cheerful giver. Overseers of churches should especially feel interested, and stir up the members to duty. Any necessary explanation asked for, will be gladly given by mail.   ENOCH EBY.

Booth, Kans., Aug. 29.

To the Churches of Southern Illinois.

The committee, appointed by last District Meeting, would like to have a report of the delegates

from each church at next District Meeting, as to the number of poor they have, what it costs to keep them, and if they are properly cared for.

Unless we have such a report, or some means of ascertaining the condition of the poor, we do not know whether we need a Home or not.

Thinking this to be the surest way of getting a correct report, we kindly ask some one in each church to make a note of this and see that we have a full report.

By order of committee: THOS. KEIBER,
         CYRUS BUCHER,
         S. B. MILLER.

From North Manchester, Ind.

Yesterday, Sept. 1, we held our regular quarterly council-meeting in the Manchester church. Considerable business came before the meeting, but all was disposed of in a most agreeable manner. A Christian spirit prevailed. One of the most important features of the meeting was the ample preparation made for the entertainment of the brethren and sisters at the Ministerial Meeting, to be held Oct. 11 and 12, at the church house, two miles west of North Manchester. Quite a number of church letters were granted to young members who expect to attend school at Mt. Morris.

Since our last report we held two thanksgiving harvest-meetings,—one at each church-house. One young brother was received by baptism. May God bless him!

The sum of $36.29 was contributed to the missionary fund.

The Treasurer's report shows considerable means in the treasury. Preparations are being made to hold a series of meetings, the coming fall and winter. Eld. Silas Gilbert, of Ohio, is expected at the church-house west of town.

     D. C. CRIPE.

Sept. 2.

Notes of Travel.

Elders J. W. Eller and P. S. Miller have just returned from John's Chapel, a newly-built church which was dedicated and given the above name, Aug. 28, 1892. The church is in a good working condition. By the aid of the District, the Chapel was paid for before the dedication and everything seems to be working for the Master's cause. Eleven dear souls have been added to the church since July 1, 1892, and there are two more applicants for baptism.

The church numbers about eighty members, including two young ministers who are earnestly contending for the faith once delivered unto the saints. This little band is under the care of Peter's Creek elders.   C. E. ELLER.

Echoes from the Highway.

Saturday, Aug 20, was our quarterly council at Tropico. Considerable business was before the meeting, which was attended to in the spirit of love. Saturday following was our love-feast in that church. It was a happy Communion and a season of sweet fellowship. About sixty members were present, including nine ministers. A choice was held for two deacons. The lot fell on our brethren Joseph Brickett and Aaron Wolfe. May the blessings and grace of God abound in their behalf that they may be qualified for their calling. The prospects of the Tropico congregation are improving. Bro. David Kuns and wife have returned to Lordsburg. Students are coming in, preparatory to starting in at the opening of the school term.   J. S. FLORY.

Lordsburg, Cal, Aug. 26.

Kewanna, Ind.—The Brethren of the Kewanna congregation expect to dedicate their new house of worship three and one-half miles north-east of Kewanna, Fulton County, Sept. 18. Elder Daniel Shively, of Peru, will deliver the dedicatory sermon at 10:30. Brethren and sisters of adjoining congregations are cordially invited to be present.—*S. A. Blessing, Aug. 21.*

Broadway, Va.—Our visit council-meeting was held at the Linville Creek church, Aug. 26. Quite a number of brethren and sisters were present. We were richly admonished by Eld. Benjamin Miller and the home ministers. We feel to take new courage and live nearer God's Word. Our church seems to be moving along in love and union, with a few exceptions. A love-feast was appointed for Oct 1, commencing at 2 P. M.—*Fannie H. Zigler.*

Maxwell, Iowa.—The members of the Indian Creek church, Iowa, expect to meet in quarterly council Saturday, Sept. 3. We have but one minister here at present, who is kept busy filling the appointments each Sunday except the fifth. We feel a little encouraged to hear that there is talk of others intending to locate at this place. We have Sunday-school every Sunday, with sister Clara E. Baldwin, Superintendent. The attendance is as good as can be expected under the circumstances. The whooping-cough, which has been prevalent here since July, is on the decrease.—*Charlotte Mowen.*

Smithborough, Ill.—Aug. 20 the regular quarterly council was held in the Hurricane Creek church. Our elder, Henry Lilligh, was present with us, but, for some cause, no other minister was present. There was a fair attendance of members. All business was transacted with the best of feeling. At the May council the church decided to hold a series of meetings, beginning about Sept. 20, providing we could get some elder to conduct the meetings, but as we failed to get anyone at that time, the church decided to continue the effort and set the time for Oct. 1. We intend also to hold a Communion on that date. We had written to three different ministers to come and conduct the meetings in September, but none of them could come. How true the words of the Savior, "Truly the harvest is great, but the laborers are few." Then he says, "Pray ye therefore the Lord of the harvest that he may send forth more laborers."—*Cornelius Kessler, Aug. 28.*

Locke, Ind.—The harvest-meeting of the Union Center church was held at the Brick church, Aug. 20. A congregation assembled from this and adjoining congregations,—six congregations being represented. Ministerial help were, J. C. Murray, Daniel Shively, Levi Hoke, Wm Buzzard, S. P. Ebersole and P. Stuckman. In the forenoon we were well entertained by J. C. Murray, who gave us a discourse on the importance of thankfulness and praise to God, and how it should be done. He was followed with some remarks by Daniel Shively, after which an announcement was made that an applicant for baptism was present, which added much to the enjoyment of the occasion. Then the tables in the basement were spread with refreshments, thanks returned, and our bodily wants supplied in an orderly manner. Baptism was then administered by Daniel Shively, after which a missionary discourse was delivered by Lemuel Hillery. A few short addresses were given to the children by brethren Buzzard and Shively. Then a collection was taken up, amounting to $18.94. The day following we met again for Sunday-school and preaching, when we were addressed by Levi Hoke. Bless the Lord, O my soul, and forget not all his benefits!—*J. R. Miller, Aug. 24.*

Eglon, W. Va.—Aug. 27 had been appointed for our quarterly council. We had a very pleasant meeting. Much business came before the church, but all passed off satisfactory. A dear brother was baptized in the evening after the council. He was raised in the Omish faith. May he and his dear companion now walk together hand in hand in Christ, and be a light to the world. Brethren John A. Arnold and Samuel K. Fike were elected to the office of deacon. They will not be installed till our love-feast. Bro. Nathaniel Ogg, and wife, from Fillmore, Minn., are now with us visiting relatives. We are always glad to meet with those of like précious faith.—*Rachèl Weimer.*

Canton, Ill.—The District Meeting of the Southern District of Illinois will be held with the Cole Creek congregation, Fulton Co., Ill., commencing Tuesday morning, Oct. 4, at 9 A. M. Those coming from North-east should stop at the Norris Station. The first train arrives at 10 A. M; the other, at 6 P. M. Trains from the South and West arrive at 8 A. M., and 3:45 P. M. We will make arrangements to meet those who come. There will be no one met at Canton, as was stated in our first notice; unless we are especially notified. We would like very much to have some of the ministers to come on Saturday before, to preach for us over Sunday, and attend our love-feast, which will occur on the evening of the 3rd.—*S. Bucklew, Aug. 29.*

Matrimonial.

"What therefore God hath joined together, let not man put asunder."

SANGER—GRAYBILL.—At the residence of the bride's parents, Aug. 11, 1892, by Eld. Jonas Graybill, Bro. M. G. Sanger, of Basic City, Va., and sister Nina L. Graybill, of Brugh's Mill, Botetourt Co., Va. N. C. GRAYBILL.

RODGERS—VAN BUREN.—At the M. E. parsonage, in the town of Loyal, Clark Co., Wis., Aug. 15, 1892, Mr. Noel Rodgers and Miss Olive Van Buren.
T. D. VAN BUREN.

WOLFE—RHODES.—At the residence of the groom's parents, Aug. 28, 1892, by the undersigned, Bro. Wm H. Wolfe, of Cherokee County, Kans., and Miss Lillie B. Rhodes, of Crawford County, Kans. ANDREW NEHER.

Fallen Asleep.

"Blessed are the dead which die in the Lord."

EVANS.—At her home near Ayr, Nebr., of inflammation, Ida E. Evans, wife of Bro. P. G. Evans and daughter of M. Y. Snavely, aged 23 years, 5 months and 26 days. She was a Christian for eleven years. Funeral services at her home and also at her father's near Kearney, Nebr., by J. J. Kendig, after which she was laid to rest in the Kearney cemetery. She leaves a husband and two small children. KATE A. LYON.

FARROR.—In the Union City church, Aug. 21, 1892, sister Mary E. Farror, *nee* Cook, aged 38 years and 11 days. Sister Mary was a patient sufferer for months past. She was a faithful member in the church and a devoted wife. She leaves a husband and two small children. Funeral services by the Brethren from the following text: "There is therefore now no condemnation to them which are in Christ Jesus."
W. K. SIMMONS.

HEASTON.—In the South Beatrice church, Gage Co., Nebr., Aug. 23, 1892, of consumption, sister Margaret Matilda Heaston, aged 21 years, 10 months and 4 days. Deceased was the daughter of brother John and sister Maria Heaston. These parents have also buried two other daughters who died of the same disease, at about the same age. Both are members of this congregation. Funeral discourse by Eld. Owen Peters from Rev. 14:13. M. L. SPIRE.

ROYER.—Near Burr Oak, Jewell Co., Kans., Aug. 16, 1892, of brain fever, Ida May Royer, daughter of friend Harry and Bell Royer, aged 11 years, 8 months and 9 days. Funeral services by Eld Eli Renner. DIANA RENNER.

PROSSER.—At Dillsburgh, York Co., Pa., Aug. 12, 1892, George Roy, son of friends Isaac and Ella Prosser, aged 6 years, 11 months and 16 days. Funeral services by the writer. J. B. GARVER.

PLETCHER.—In the Maple Glen church, Somerset Co., Pa., Aug. 22, 1892, sister Elisabeth Pletcher, aged 80 years, 7 months and 2 days. Her aged husband preceded her a few years to the home beyond. Sister Pletcher had given to her ten children, forty-eight grandchildren and ten great-grandchildren. Two of her children preceded her to the home beyond. The deceased was a member of the church for sixty years. All her children belonged to the same church, except one that died in infancy. This devoted servant of the Master called for the elders Aug 7, and was anointed with oil in the name of the Lord. Funeral services from Matt. 11:28, 29, 30, by the writer and L. A. Peck. J. N. DAVIS.

FOUTS.—Near Guide Rock, Webster Co., Nebr., Aug. 27, 1892, Delilah, infant daughter of sister Ida and Bro. Jacob Fouts. Funeral services by the Brethren, assisted by the United Brethren minister. N. B. WAGONER.

BOWERSOX.—At her residence in Girard, Ill., sister Sarah Bowersox, aged 84 years, 10 months and 27 days. Deceased was born in Green County, Pa., in 1807. She emigrated to Ohio in 1818 and was married to Jacob Bowersox in 1829. This union was blessed with nine children, who are all living. Deceased united with the German Baptist Brethren church in 1850, and always lived a consistent life. Funeral conducted by Cullen C. Gibson, assisted by the writer and G. W. Gibson. MICHAEL FLORY.

SEERS.—In the bounds of the Greentown church, Howard Co., Ind., Aug. 17, 1892, sister Patsy Seers, supposed to be 108 years old. Funeral services by the writer from Heb. 4:9, "There remaineth therefore a rest to the people of God."
ABRAHAM CAYLOR.

WELLER.—In the Licking Creek church, Maryland, Aug. 16, 1892, sister Maria Weller, wife of Eld. Jacob Weller, aged 54 years, 8 months and several days. Deceased was born and raised near her late residence. She has been a consistent member of the church for a number of years. In the death of sister Weller the husband has lost a faithful companion, the children a kind and loving mother, and the church a faithful sister. She has been a sufferer for two years. During her sickness she called for the elders and was anointed. She was the mother of twelve children. Funeral services conducted by Bro. A. Mellott from 1 Pet. 1:22, to a large concourse of sorrowing friends and neighbors.
JACOB S. KELLER.

FAHRNEY.—In Quincy, Pa., Aug. 15, 1892, Bessie Violetta, daughter of Bro. Jacob and sister Cush Fahrney, aged 2 years, 7 months and 22 days. Funeral services from Mark 10:14, by the writer and Eld. J. F. Oller. Interment at Price's. WM. A. ANTHONY.

PETRY.—In the Price's Creek church, Preble Co., Ohio, Aug. 14, 1892, Hattie Catharine, daughter of Bro. Michael M., and sister Catharine Petry, aged 10 years, 7 months and 19 days. Funeral services by brethren Joseph Longanecker and A. G. Crosswhite. JOSEPH SHAFFER.

RANKARD.—In the Dry Fork church, Jasper Co., Mo., July 17, 1892, Charles Evert Rankard, infant son of friend George and Geneva Rankard, aged 7 months and 17 days. Funeral services by the writer, assisted by D. W. Teeter.
W. M. HARVEY.

The Gospel Messenger

Is the recognized organ of the German Baptist or Brethren's church, and advocates the form of doctrine taught in the New Testament and pleads for a return to apostolic and primitive Christianity.

It recognizes the New Testament as the only infallible rule of faith and practice, and maintains that Faith toward God, Repentance from dead works, Regeneration of the heart and mind, baptism by Trine Immersion for remission of sins unto the reception of the Holy Ghost by the laying on of hands, are the means of adoption into the household of God,—the church militant.

It also maintains that Feet-washing, as taught in John 13, both by example and command of Jesus, should be observed in the church.

That the Lord's Supper, instituted by Christ and as universally observed by the apostles and the early Christians, is a full meal, and, in connection with the Communion, should be taken in the evening or after the close of the day.

That the Salutation of the Holy Kiss, or Kiss of Charity, is binding upon the followers of Christ.

That War and Retaliation are contrary to the spirit and self-denying principles of the religion of Jesus Christ.

That the principle of Plain Dressing and of Non-conformity to the world, as taught in the New Testament, should be observed by the followers of Christ.

That the Scriptural duty of Anointing the Sick with Oil, in the Name of the Lord, James 5:14, is binding upon all Christians.

It also advocates the church's duty to support Missionary and Tract Work, thus giving to the Lord for the spread of the Gospel and for the conversion of sinners.

In short, it is a vindicator of all that Christ and the apostles have enjoined upon us, and aims, amid the conflicting theories and discords of modern Christendom, to point out ground that all must concede to be infallibly safe.

☞ The above principles of our Fraternity are set forth on our Brethren's Envelopes." Use them! Price 15 cents per package; 40 cents per hundred.

Kewanna, Ind.—The Brethren of the Kewanna congregation expect to dedicate their new house of worship three and one-half miles north-east of Kewanna, Fulton County, Sept. 18. Elder Daniel Shively, of Peru, will deliver the dedicatory sermon at 10:30. Brethren and sisters of adjoining congregations are cordially invited to be present.—*S. A. Blessing, Aug. 21.*

Broadway, Va.—Our visit council-meeting was held at the Linville Creek church, Aug. 26. Quite a number of brethren and sisters were present. We were richly admonished by Eld. Benjamin Miller and the home ministers. We feel to take new courage and live nearer God's Word. Our church seems to be moving along in love and union, with a few exceptions. A love-feast was appointed for Oct 1, commencing at 2 P. M.—*Fannie H. Zigler.*

Maxwell, Iowa.—The members of the Indian Creek church, Iowa, expect to meet in quarterly council Saturday, Sept. 3. We have but one minister here at present, who is kept busy filling the appointments each Sunday except the fifth. We feel a little encouraged to hear that there is talk of others intending to locate at this place. We have Sunday-school every Sunday, with sister Clara E. Baldwin, Superintendent. The attendance is as good as can be expected under the circumstances. The whooping-cough, which has been prevalent here since July, is on the decrease.—*Charlotte Mowen.*

Smithborough, Ill.—Aug. 20 the regular quarterly council was held in the Hurricane Creek church. Our elder, Henry Lilligh, was present with us, but, for some cause, no other minister was present. There was a fair attendance of members. All business was transacted with the best of feeling. At the May council the church decided to hold a series of meetings, beginning about Sept. 20, providing we could get some elder to conduct the meetings, but as we failed to get anyone at that time, the church decided to continue the effort and set the time for Oct. 1. We intend also to hold a Communion on that date. We had written to three different ministers to come and conduct the meetings in September, but none of them could come. How true the words of the Savior, "Truly the harvest is great, but the laborers are few." Then he says, "Pray ye therefore the Lord of the harvest that he may send forth more laborers."—*Cornelius Kessler, Aug. 28.*

Locke, Ind.—The harvest-meeting of the Union Center church was held at the Brick church. Aug. 20 A congregation assembled from this and adjoining congregations,—six congregations being represented. Ministerial help were, J. C. Murray, Daniel Shively, Levi Hoke, Wm Buzzard, S. P. Ebersole and P. Stuckman. In the forenoon we were well entertained by J. C. Murray, who gave us a discourse on the importance of thankfulness and praise to God, and how it should become. He was followed with some remarks by Daniel Shively, after which an announcement was made that an applicant for baptism was present, which added much to the enjoyment of the occasion. Then the tables in the basement were spread with refreshments, thanks returned, and our bodily wants supplied in an orderly manner. Baptism was then administered by Daniel Shively, after which a missionary discourse was delivered by Lemuel Hillery. A few short addresses were given to the children by brethren Buzzard and Shively. Then a collection was taken up, amounting to $18.94. The day following we met again for Sunday-school and preaching, when we were addressed by Levi Hoke. Bless the Lord, O my soul, and forget not all his benefits!—*J. R. Miller, Aug. 24.*

Iglee, W. Va.—Aug. 27 had been appointed for our quarterly council. We had a very pleasant meeting. Much business came before the church, but all passed off satisfactory. A dear brother was baptized in the evening after the council. He was raised in the Omish faith. May he and his dear companion now walk together hand in hand in Christ and be a light to the world. Brethren John A. Arnold and Samuel K. Fike were elected to the office of deacon. They will not be installed till our love-feast. Bro. Nathaniel Ogg, and wife, from Fillmore, Minn., are now with us visiting relatives. We are always glad to meet with those of like precious faith.—*Rachel Weimer.*

Canton, Ill.—The District Meeting of the Southern District of Illinois will be held with the Cole Creek congregation, Fulton Co., Ill., commencing Tuesday morning, Oct. 4, at 9 A. M. Those coming from North-east should stop at the Norris Station. The first train arrives at 10 A. M; the other, at 6 P. M. Trains from the South and West arrive at 8 A. M., and 8:45 P. M. We will make arrangements to meet those who come. There will be no one met at Canton, as was stated in our first notice, unless we are especially notified. We would like very much to have some of the ministers to come on Saturday before, to preach for us over Sunday, and attend our love-feast, which will occur on the evening of the 3rd.—*S Bucklew, Aug. 29.*

Matrimonial.

" What therefore God hath joined together, let not man put asunder."

SANGER—GRAYBILL—At the residence of the bride's parents, Aug. 11, 1892, by Eld. Jonas Graybill, Bro. M. G. Sanger, of Basic City, Va., and sister Nina L. Graybill, of Brugh's Mill, Botetourt Co, Va.　　N. C. GRAYBILL.

RODGERS—VAN BUREN—At the M. E. parsonage, in the town of Loyal, Clark Co., Wis., Aug. 13, 1892, Mr. Noel Rodgers and Miss Olive Van Buren.
　　T. D. VAN BUREN.

WOLFE—RHODES.—At the residence of the groom's parents, Aug. 18, 1892, by the undersigned, Bro. Wm H. Wolfe, of Cherokee County, Kans., and Miss Lillie B. Rhodes, of Crawford County, Kans.　　ANDREW NEHER.

Fallen Asleep.

" Blessed are the dead which die in the Lord."

EVANS.—At her home near Ayr, Nebr., of inflammation, Ida E. Evans, wife of Bro. P. G. Evans and daughter of M. Y. Snavely, aged 23 years, 5 months and 26 days. She was a Christian for eleven years. Funeral services at her home and also at her father's near Kearney, Nebr., by J. J. Kendig, after which she was laid to rest in the Kearney cemetery. She leaves a husband and two small children. KATE A. LYON.

FARROR.—In the Union City church, Aug. 21, 1892, sister Mary E. Farror, nee Cook, aged 38 years and 11 days. Sister Mary was a patient sufferer for months past She was a faithful member in the church and a devoted wife. She leaves a husband and two small children Funeral services by the Brethren from the following text: "There is therefore now no condemnation to them which are in Christ Jesus."
　　W. K. SIMMONS.

HEASTON.—In the South Beatrice church, Gage Co., Nebr., Aug. 13, 1892, of consumption, sister Margaret Matilda Heaston, aged 21 years, 10 months and 4 days. Deceased was the daughter of brother John and sister Maria Heaston. These parents have also buried two other daughters who died of the same disease, at about the same age. Both are members of this congregation. Funeral discourse by Eld. Owen Peters from Rev. 14: 13　　M. L. SPIRE.

ROYER.—Near Burr Oak, Jewell Co., Kans., Aug. 16, 1892, of brain fever, Ida May Royer, daughter of friend Harry and Bell Royer, aged 11 years, 8 months and 9 days. Funeral services by Eld Eli Renner. DIANA RENNER.

PROSSER.—At Dillsburgh, York Co., Pa., Aug. 13, 1892, George Roy, son of friends Isaac and Ella Prosser, aged 6 years, 11 months and 16 days. Funeral services by the writer. J. B. GARVER.

PLETCHER.—In the Maple Glen church, Somerset Co., Pa., Aug. 21, 1892, sister Elizabeth Pletcher, aged 80 years, 3 months and 2 days. Her aged husband preceded her a few years to the home beyond. Sister Pletcher had given to her ten children, forty-eight grandchildren and ten great-grandchildren. Two of her children preceded her to the home beyond. The deceased was a member of the church for sixty years. All her children belonged to the same church, except one that died in infancy. This devoted servant of the Master called for the elders Aug 7. and was anointed with oil in the name of the Lord. Funeral services from Matt. 11: 28, 29, 30, by the writer and L. A. Peck. J. N. DAVIS.

FOUTS.—Near Guide Rock, Webster Co., Nebr., Aug. 27, 1892, Delilah, infant daughter of sister Ida and Bro. Jacob Fouts. Funeral services by the Brethren, assisted by the United Brethren minister. N. B. WAGONER.

BOWERSOX.—At her residence in Girard, Ill., sister Sarah Bowersox, aged 84 years, 10 months and 27 days. Deceased was born in Green County, Pa, in 1807. She emigrated to Ohio in 1816 and was married to Jacob Bowersox in 1829. This union was blessed with nine children, who are all living. Deceased united with the German Baptist Brethren church in 1850, and always lived a consistent life. Funeral conducted by Cullen C. Gibson, assisted by the Writer and G. W. Gibson. MICHAEL FLORY.

SEERS.—In the bounds of the Greentown church, Howard Co., Ind., Aug. 17, 1892, sister Patsy Seers, supposed to be 108 years old. Funeral services by the writer from Heb. 4: 9, "There remaineth therefore a rest to the people of God." ABRAHAM CAYLOR.

WELLER.—In the Licking Creek church, Maryland, Aug. 16, 1892, sister Maria Weller, wife of Eld. Jacob Weller, aged 54 years, 8 months and several days. Deceased was born and raised near her late residence. She has been a consistent member of the church for a number of years. In the death of sister Weller the husband has lost a faithful companion, the children a kind and loving mother, and the church a faithful sister. She has been a sufferer for two years. During her sickness she called for the elders and was anointed. She was the mother of twelve children. Funeral services conducted by Bro. A. Mellott from 1 Pet. 1: 22, to a large concourse of sorrowing friends and neighbors.
　　JACOB S. KELLER.

FAHRNEY.—In Quincy, Pa., Aug. 15, 1892, Bessie Violetta, daughter of Bro. Jacob and sister Clara Fahrney, aged 2 years, 7 months and 22 days. Funeral services from Mark 10: 14, by the writer and Eld. J. F. Oller. Interment at Price's. WM. A. ANTHONY.

PETRY.—In the Price's Creek church, Preble Co., Ohio, Aug. 14, 1892, Hattie Catharine, daughter of Bro. Michael M., and sister Catharine Petry, aged 10 years, 7 months and 19 days. Funeral services by brethren Joseph Longanecker and A. G. Crosswhite. JOSEPH SHATZER.

RANKARD.—In the Dry Fork church, Jasper Co., Mo., July 17, 1892, Charles Evert Rankard, infant son of friend George and Geneva Rankard, aged 5 months and 17 days. Funeral services by the writer, assisted by D. W. Teeter.
　　W. M. HARVEY.

The Gospel Messenger

Is the Recognized organ of the German Baptist or Brethren's church, and discusses the forms of doctrine taught in the New Testament and pleads for a return to apostolic and primitive Christianity.

It recognizes the New Testament as the only infallible rule of faith and practice, and maintains that Faith toward God. Repentance from dead works, Regeneration of the heart and mind, baptism by Trine Immersion for remission of sins unto the Reception of the Holy Ghost by the laying on of hands, are the means of adoption into the household of God,—the church militant.

It also maintains that Feet-washing, as taught in John 13, both by example and command of Jesus, should be observed in the church.

That the Lord's Supper, instituted by Christ and as universally observed by the apostles and the early Christians, is a full meal, and, in connection with the Communion, should be taken in the evening or after the close of the day.

That the Salutation of the Holy Kiss, or Kiss of Charity, is binding upon the followers of Christ.

That War and Retaliation are contrary to the spirit and self-denying principles of the religion of Jesus Christ.

That the principle of Plain Dressing and of Non-conformity to the world, as taught in the New Testament, should be observed by the followers of Christ.

That the Scriptural duty of Anointing the Sick with Oil, in the Name of the Lord, James 5: 14, is binding upon all Christians.

It also advocates the church's duty to support Missionary and Tract Work, thus giving to the Lord for the spread of the Gospel and for the conversion of sinners.

In short, it is a vindication of all that Christ and the apostles have enjoined upon us, and aims, amid the conflicting theories and discords of modern Christendom, to point out ground that all must concede to be infallibly safe.

☞ The above principles of our Fraternity are set forth on our Brethren's Envelopes." Use them! Price 15 cents per package; 40 cents per hundred.

Announcements.

(Concluded from preceding page.)

DISTRICT MEETINGS.

Sept. 23 and 24, in Powell's Valley church, at Damascus, Clackamas Co., Oregon. Clackamas Station, on the Southern Pacific R. R., is the nearest railroad point. Passengers will please address Bro. J. A. Royer, Clackamas, Oregon, who will give them conveyance.

Oct. 6, 10 i A. M., North-eastern District of Ohio, in the Owl Creek church, Knox County. Delegates will stop off at Ankenytown on the B. and O. R. R. They should arrive the day before. Trains going north arrive at 10 A. M. and 3:15 P. M. Going south at 11:04 A. M., and 5:05 P. M., city time.

MINISTERIAL MEETINGS.

Sept. 22, in Powell's Valley church, at Damascus, Clackamas Co., Oregon.

Oct. 5. Ministerial Meeting in the Northern District of Indiana. Those coming by rail stop either at Nappanee or Goshen.

LOVE FEASTS.

Sept. 16, at 2 P. M., Ottawa church, in Forest Park, Ottawa, Kans.

Sept. 23, in Powell's Valley church, at Damascus, Clackamas Co., Oregon.

Sept. 24, at 2 P. M., the Valley Pike church, 1 mile s.uth of Mauertown, Shenandoah Co., Va.

Sept. 24, at 4 P. M., Okaw church, Piatt Co., Ill.

Sept. 24. Fairview church, Shelby Co., Mo. A series of meetings to follow the feast, which is to be held at Bro. C. Lapp's, 2 miles south of Cherry Box.

Sept. 24, at 1 P. M., Pleasant View church, Reno Co., Kans.

Sept. 27, 28, at 2 P. M., Howard church, Ridgeway, Ind.

Oct. 1 and 2, Montour, Idaho. Those coming by rail will be met at the depot by notifying J. U. G. Stiverson when they will arrive, and on what road.

Oct. 1, Hurricane Creek church, Bond Co., Ill.

Oct. 1, at 4 P. M., Albion Prairie church, Lawrence Co., Ill.

Oct. 6, at 10 A. M., Vermillion church, Kans. Members will be met in Beatrix and Summerfield on the 5th.

Oct. 8 and 9, at 2 P. M., Neosho County church, Kans.

Oct. 14, 10 10 A. M., Poplar Ridge church, 4 miles east of Defiance, Ohio.

Oct. 15, at 10 o'clock, Monter church, 3 miles east of Mendon, Ohio, on the Lake Erie and Western R. R., 11 miles south-west of Salina and 2 miles west of Cold Water, Ohio.

Oct. 15, at 11 A. M., Deep River church, Iowa. Any coming by rail, come to Deep River on the Northwestern. Notify J. J. Brower, Deep River, Iowa, or Boz S8, and you will be met at the train.

Oct. 22, at 2 P. M., Eden Valley congregation, Stafford Co., Kans., at Bro. J. N. Miller's.

Oct. 22, at 10 A. M., Eagle Creek church, Hancock Co., Ohio.

Oct. 22, at 2 P. M., Eden Valley, Kans.

Oct. 22 and 23, at 10 A. M., Iowa River church, Marshall Co., Iowa.

Oct. 28, at 2 A. M., Mineral Creek, Johnson Co., Mo.

Oct. 28, at 4 P. M., in the Spring Run church, 2½ miles north of McVeytown station, Mifflin Co., Pa.

Oct. 29, at 2 P. M., Lick Creek church, Owen Co., Ind.

Oct. No 21 at 3 P. M., Marsh Creek church, Adams Co., Pa.

Oct. 29, Slate Creek Church, Sumner Co., Kans.

Nov. 2, at 2 P. M., Lower Stillwater, near Trotwood, Ohio, at the upper house.

Nov. 3, at 2 P. M., Lower Deer Creek church, Carroll Co., Ind.

Nov. 4, Walnut Creek church, Mo.

Nov. 5, at 4 P. M., Summit Mills, Somerset Co., Pa.

Nov. 5, at 2 P. M., at the Kansas Center church, 3 miles east of Lyons, Rice Co., Kans. A series of meetings to commence a week previous.

Nov. 5, at 3 P. M., Big Creek church, Richland Co., Ill., 2½ miles Northeast of Parkersburg, Ill. Conveyances will be at the above place by informing J. M. Forney.

Nov. 5 and 6, at 4 P. M., North Beatrice church, Gage Co., Nebr.

Nov. 5, at 4 P. M., Monticello church, Ind.

Nov. 11, at 10 A. M., Thornapple church, Mich., at the east house.

Nov. 24, at 2 P. M., Cedar Creek church, Anderson Co., Kans.

Oct. 8, at 2 P. M., Naperville, Ill.

Nov. 5 at 5 P. M., Mount Pleasant meeting-house, Cottton church, Starke Co., Ohio.

Announcements.

(Concluded from preceding page.)

DISTRICT MEETINGS.

Sept. 23 and 24, In Powell's Valley church, at Damascus, Clackamas Co., Oregon. Clackamas Station, on the Southern Pacific R. R., is the nearest railroad point. Passengers will please address Bro. J. A. Royer, Clackamas, Oregon, who will give them conveyance.

Oct. 1, District Meeting of Northern Indiana in the Yellow Creek church.

Oct. 6, at 8 A. M., North-eastern District of Ohio, in the Owl Creek church, Knox County. Delegates will stop off at Ankenytown on the B. and O. R. R. They should arrive the day before. Trains going south arrive at 10:10 A. M. and 3:14 P. M., city time.

MINISTERIAL MEETINGS.

Sept. 20, In Powell's Valley church, at Damascus, Clackamas Co., Oregon.

Oct. 4, Ministerial Meeting in the Northern District of Indiana. Those coming by rail stop either at Nappanee or Goshen.

LOVE FEASTS.

Sept. 16, at 2 P. M., Ottawa church, in Forest Park, Ottawa, Kans.

Sept. 17, In Powell's Valley church, at Damascus, Clackamas Co., Oregon.

Sept. 24, at 2 P. M., the Valley Pike church, 1 mile south of Mauzrtown, Shenandoah Co., Va.

Sept. 24, at 4 P. M., Okaw church, Piatt Co., Ill.

Sept. 24, Fairview church, Shelby Co., Mo. A series of meetings to follow the feast, which is to be held at Bro. L. Lipp's, 2 miles south of Cherry Box.

Sept. 24, at 2 P. M., Pleasant View church, Reno Co., Kans.

Sept. 27, at 2 P. M., Howard church, Ridgeway, Ind.

Oct. 1 and 2, Mexico, Indiana. Those coming by rail will be met at the depot by notifying J. G. Stinebaugh when they will arrive, and on what road.

Oct. 1, Hurricane Creek church, Bond Co., Ill.

Oct. 1, at 4 P. M., Allison Prairie church, Lawrence Co., Ill.

Oct. 8, at 10 A. M., Vermillion church, Kans. Members will be met at Bessrie and Summerfield on the 7th.

Oct. 8 and 9, at 2 P. M., Neosho County church, Kans.

Oct. 14, at 10 A. M., Poplar Ridge church, 4 miles east of Defiance, Ohio.

Oct. 15, at 10 o'clock, Mercer church, 3 miles east of Mendon, Ohio, or the Lake Erie and Western R. R., 11 miles south-west of Salina and 4 miles west of Celt Water, Ohio.

Oct. 15, at 10 A. M., Deep River church, Iowa. Any coming by rail, come to Deep River on the North-western. Notify J. J. Brower, Deep River, Iowa, Box 76, and you will be met at the train.

Oct. 20, at 2 P. M., Eden Valley congregation, Stafford Co., Kans., at Bro. J. N. Miller's.

Oct. 22, at 10:30 A. M., Eagle Creek church, Hancock Co., Ohio.

Oct. 22, at 2 P. M., Eden Valley, Kans.

Oct. 22, at 10 A. M., Iowa River church, Marshall Co., Iowa.

Oct. 22, at 10 A. M., Mineral Creek, Johnson Co., Mo.

Oct. 26, at 2 P. M., in the Spring Run church, 2½ miles north of McVeytown station, Mifflin Co., Pa.

Oct. 29, at 2 P. M., Lick Creek church, Owen Co., Ind.

Oct. 30, at 10:30 P. M., Marsh Creek church, Adams Co., Pa.

Oct. 29, Slate Creek Church, Sumner Co., Kans.

Nov. 4, at 2 P. M., Lower Stillwater, near Trotwood, Ohio, at the upper house.

Nov. 5, at 2 P. M., Lower Deer Creek church, Carroll Co., Ind.

Nov. 6, Walnut Creek church, Mo.

Nov. 5, at 4 P. M., Summit Mills, Somerset Co., Pa.

Nov. 5, at 2 P. M., at the Kansas Center church, 3 miles east of Lyons, Rice Co., Kans. A series of meetings to commence a week previous.

Nov. 5, at 3 P. M., Big Creek church, Richland Co., Ill., 3¾ miles North-east of Parkersburg, Ill. Conveyances will be at the above place by informing J. M. Forney.

Nov. 5 and 6, at 2 P. M., North Beatrice church, Gage Co., Nebr.

Nov. 5, at 4 P. M., Montlcello church, Ind.

Nov. 17, at 10 A. M., Thornapple church, Mich., at the east house.

Nov. 24, at 3 P. M., Cedar Creek church, Anderson Co., Kans.

Oct. 1, at 3 P. M., Lost Creek church, Miami Co., Ohio.

Oct. 8, at 2 P. M., Naperville, Ill.

Nov. 5, at 5 P. M., Mount Pleasant meeting-house, Canton church, Starke Co., Ohio.

ESSAYS

"Study to show thyself approved unto God: a workman that needeth not be ashamed, rightly dividing the Word of Truth."

ISRAEL'S CAPTIVITY.

BY J. S. MOHLER.

WHEN Israel of old to their idols were turned,
And the wrath of the Lord in great fury had burned,
His care and protection He from them withdrew,
Their enemies came and their armies they slew.

Away into exile and bondage were led,
Their Temple was burned, their rulers were dead,
In sighing and sadness, in sorrow and shame
To the land of their captors in weariness came.

Their captors would taunt them to sing them a song
Of beautiful Zion, the land of their home,
But how could they sing in a land that was strange
When Zion was burned, and her people were slain.

Their harps on the willows in silence they hung,
Zion's songs among strangers could never be sung,
By Babylon's waters they thought of their ways
And wept, they had ever forsaken God's praise.

Thus now the children of God may depart—
Some idol may worship in depth of their heart,
Neglecting to guard the way to the soul
Till Satan them captures, in bondage will hold.

And then, in his power, he'll taunt them to sing
A song of sweet Zion, to gratify him,
But unto his kingdom they never belonged,
And as captives and strangers, can utter no song.

But when they return in their hearts to their King,
Rejoicing for gladness, they cheerfully sing
In praise to the Lord, who received them again,
While journeying through Emmanuel's land.

Morrill, Kans.

THE BAPTISM OF FIRE.

BY ISRAEL WEIMER.

"I INDEED baptize you with water unto repentance; but he that cometh after me is mightier than I, whose shoes I am not worthy to bear; he shall baptize you with the Holy Ghost and with fire."

To whom was this language addressed? John the Baptist was speaking to those whom he baptized, and then said they should be baptized with the Holy Ghost and with fire; hence the three baptisms were intended for the same individuals. To my mind we destroy the force of language by applying the baptism of the Holy Ghost to one person, and that of fire to another; hence the language is parallel to that in the commission, which commands us to baptize in the name of the Father, and of the Son, and of the Holy Ghost. If we have not proper baptism except in the three distinct names of the three distinct persons in the Godhead, neither can there be a complete baptism, except with the Holy Ghost and with fire. Isa. 4: 4 tells us there shall be a time "when the Lord shall have washed away the filth of the daughters of Zion and shall have purged the blood of Jerusalem from the midst thereof by the spirit of judgment and by the spirit of burning. This prophecy referred to the daughters of Zion,—those who worship God, his people. Isa. 44: 3, 4. "For I will pour out water upon him that is thirsty, and floods upon the dry ground. I will pour my spirit upon thy seed, and my blessing upon thine offspring. And they shall spring up as among the grass, as willows by the water courses." This language has reference to the same time and the same persons that were spoken of in Isa. 4: 4. It has reference to those who shall be purged and purified by the great purifying power of the great God. Mal. 3: 2, 3, 4 also says, "But who may abide the day of his coming? And who shall stand when he appeareth, for he is like a refiner's fire, and like fuller's soap. And he shall sit as a refiner and purifier of silver and he shall

purify the sons of Levi and purge them as gold and silver, that they may offer unto the Lord an offering in righteousness. Then shall the offering of Judah and Jerusalem be pleasant unto the Lord, as in the days of old, and as in former years."

Now, these cannot possibly be the wicked which shall be cast into the lake of fire, and as we all know that it takes fire to purify gold and silver, so the Lord will, as in a refiner's fire, purify his gold from the dross which afterward shall be cast into the lake of fire and brimstone. God is not this lake of fire, neither are the two fires similar. He is the purifying fire with which he will baptize his elect and with which he did baptize on the day of Pentecost. Acts 2: 3.

"And there appeared unto them cloven tongues like as of fire and it sat upon each of them." This is the fire to which John the Baptist had reference, when he said, "And with fire." This was the spiritual fire,—the fire that the Laodiceans lacked, and the fire of which we need more in the church. It is that love which prompts us to action.

Maysville, Grant Co., W. Va.

THE HISTORY OF JOB.

A WRITER in the *Christian Standard* gives the most complete history of Job that we have yet seen. In view of the fact that our Sunday-school lesson for a part of next year will be in the book of Job, something of this kind will prove interesting reading. We have condensed the article somewhat, and give the following:

THE DESCENT INTO EGYPT.

In the forty-sixth chapter of Genesis we learn that the "sons of Israel carried Jacob their father, and their little ones, and their wives, in the wagons which Pharaoh had sent to carry him." In the thirteenth verse is named Issachar, the ninth son of Jacob, and his four children—Tola, Phuvah, Job and Shimron. In 1 Chron. 7: 1, this same Job is called Jashub; and in Num. 26: 24, we learn that he was the founder of "the family of the Jashubites." The line of descent from Abraham is familiar to all—Abraham, Isaac, Jacob, Issachar, Job. The Septuagint version of Job, made about 280 years before Christ, concedes this Job to be the patient man.

THE CHILD JOB.

I assume that Job, being next to the younger in Issachar's family, was about four years old at the time of going to Egypt. I conclude, too, that at an early age he married and removed to Uz.

THE LAND OF ISHMAEL.

The land of Uz, to which Job removed, was that occupied by the descendants of Ishmael, east and south-east of Palestine, and is now known as Arabia. Ishmael was a descendant of the same stock as Job—from Abraham through Hagar. Here Job lived among the descendants of his great-great-grandfather, Abraham. This common ancestry was no doubt known, and it gave to Job a prestige among the Ishmaelites that at once placed him in the highest rank. Familiar with the traditions current in the family of his ancestors, with some probable knowledge of records, and possessing the merits of true manhood, he rapidly accumulated wealth; his 7,000 sheep, 3,000 camels, 500 yoke of oxen and 500 she asses made it necessary for him to have a "very great household" to look after the details of his estate and business. His seven sons and three daughters had grown out of childhood, for even the three sisters were called to feast with the sons (Job 1: 4). So devoted was Job that after these feastings he sanctified them

with burnt offerings "according to the number of them all." "For it may be," said Job, "that my sons have sinned." (Job 1: 5).

JOB'S FIRST AFFLICTION.

In those days of prosperity and devotion, Job probably was about sixty years old. Joseph was ruler in Egypt and an age of prosperity rested upon God's people every-where. But in one of those days of prosperity, when the sons of God came to present themselves before the Lord, "Satan came also among them." (Job 1: 6). Then came the arrangements to test Job's sincerity, resulting so grandly in the most glorious triumph that humanity ever achieved. Satan was first given permission to do as he wished with Job's substance, but was not to touch his person. As a result, in rapid succession, his oxen were stolen by the Sabeans, the sheep were burned up, the camels were stolen by the Chaldeans, and all the attendants, save the messengers alone, were slain. Then came the crowning, crushing intelligence that while all his children were feasting, a great wind came, crumbling the house in which they were assembled, and killing them all. But after all this 'he "worshiped," and exclaimed: "The Lord gave and the Lord hath taken away, blessed be the name of the Lord." (Job 1: 21).

JOB'S SECOND AFFLICTION.

Having failed in his efforts to cause Job to sin, Satan made another effort, and this time got permission to touch his person, but to spare his life. Job was promptly smitten with "sore boils from the sole of his foot unto his crown (Job 2: 7), so that he took "a potsherd to scrape himself withal, and he sat among the ashes." His wife reproved him for still holding fast to his integrity, and urged him to " renounce God and die " (Job 2: 9). To this Job replied in scorn: " What? shall we receive good at the hand of God, and shall we not receive evil? " In all this affliction he sinned not.

HIGHWAY TO RESTORED PROSPERITY.

He must have been at least sixty years old. "And after this Job lived 140 years, and saw his sons, and his son's sons, even four generations" (Job 42: 16). " And the Lord gave Job twice as much as he had before " (Job 42: 10). He had the full and practical sympathy of his friends and neighbors, and they gave him presents, and comforted him, and he was blessed more than formerly, for he acquired 14,000 sheep, 6,000 camels, 1,000 yoke of oxen and 1,000 she asses. He also had seven sons and three daughters; "And in all the land were no women found so fair as the daughters of Job " (Job 42: 15).

JOB AND MOSES.

Joseph died in Egypt, 1635 B. C., when Job was about seventy-five years old. Prosperity continued, wealth accumulated, children were born; but in Egypt had arisen a ruler, who "knew not Joseph," and the children of Israel were serving under task-masters. When Job was 139 years old (1571 B. C.) Moses was born; and for the next forty years, while Job was prosperous, Moses was being educated "in all the wisdom of the Egyptians, and he was mighty in his words and works." (Acts 7: 22). At forty, Moses fled to the land of Midian, at which time Job's age was about 179 years, yet a year younger than was Isaac at his death. The land of Midian was about midway to the land of Uz. If we suppose that Job was but sixty years old at the time of his affliction, and we add the 140 years of prosperity, then for 21 years he lived while Moses was in Midian. Moses may have visited Job during this time, but Job may have lived longer. Had he lived until the Exode, he would have been but 219 years old. These extra years may have been given him because of his

✦ESSAYS✦

"Study to show thyself approved unto God; a workman that needeth not be ashamed, rightly dividing the Word of Truth."

ISRAEL'S CAPTIVITY.

BY J. S. MOHLER.

When Israel of old to their idols were turned,
And the wrath of the Lord in great fury had burned,
His care and protection He from them withdrew,
Their enemies came and their armies they slew.

Away into exile and bondage were led,
Their Temple was burned, their rulers were dead,
In sighing and sadness, in sorrow and shame
To the land of their captors in weariness came.

Their captors would taunt them to sing them a song
Of beautiful Zion, the land of their home,
But how could they sing in a land that was strange
When Zion was burned, and her people were slain.

Their harps on the willows in silence they hung,
Zion's songs among strangers could never be sung,
By Babylon's waters they thought of their ways
And wept, they had ever forsaken God's praise.

Thus now the children of God may depart—
Some idol may worship in depth of their heart,
Neglecting to guard the way to the soul
Till Satan them captures, in bondage will hold.

And then, in his power, he'll taunt them to sing
A song of sweet Zion, to gratify him,
But unto his kingdom they never belonged,
And as captives and strangers, can utter no song.

But when they return in their hearts to their King,
Rejoicing for gladness, they cheerfully sing
In praise to the Lord, who received them again,
While journeying through Emmanuel's land.

Merrill, Kans.

THE BAPTISM OF FIRE.

BY ISRAEL WEIMER.

" I INDEED baptize you with water unto repentance; but he that cometh after me is mightier than I, whose shoes I am not worthy to bear; he shall baptize you with the Holy Ghost and with fire."

To whom was this language addressed? John the Baptist was speaking to those whom he baptized, and then said they should be baptized with the Holy Ghost and with fire; hence the three baptisms were intended for the same individuals. To my mind we destroy the force of language by applying the baptism of the Holy Ghost to one person, and that of fire to another, inasmuch as the language is parallel to that in the commission, which commands us to baptize in the name of the Father, and of the Son, and of the Holy Ghost. If we have not proper baptism except in the three distinct names of the three distinct persons in the Godhead, neither can there be a complete baptism, except with the Holy Ghost and with fire.

Isa. 4: 4 tells us there shall be a time "when the Lord shall have washed away the filth of the daughters of Zion and shall have purged the blood of Jerusalem from the midst thereof by the spirit of judgment and by the spirit of burning." This prophecy referred to the daughters of Zion,—those who worship God, his people. Isa. 44: 3, 4. "For I will pour out water upon him that is thirsty, and floods upon the dry ground. I will pour my spirit upon thy seed, and my blessing upon thine offspring. And they shall spring up as among the grass, as willows by the water courses." '

This language has reference to the same time and the same persons that were spoken of in Isa. 4: 4. It has reference to those who shall be purged and purified by the great purifying power of the great God. Mal. 3: 2, 3, 4 also says, "But who may abide the day of his coming? And who shall stand when he appeareth, for he is like a refiner's fire, and like fuller's soap. And he shall sit as a refiner and purifier of silver and he shall

purify the sons of Levi and purge them as gold and silver, that they may offer unto the Lord an offering in righteousness. Then shall the offering of Judah and Jerusalem be pleasant unto the Lord, as in the days of old, and as in former years."

Now, these cannot possibly be the wicked which shall be cast into the lake of fire, and as we all know that it takes fire to purify gold and silver, so the Lord will, as in a refiner's fire, purify his gold from the dross which afterward shall be cast into the lake of fire and brimstone. God is not this lake of fire, neither are the two fires similar. He is the purifying fire with which he will baptize his elect and with which he did baptize on the day of Pentecost. Acts 2: 3.

"And there appeared unto them cloven tongues like as of fire and it sat upon each of them." This is the fire to which John the Baptist had reference, when he said, "And with fire." This was the spiritual fire,—the fire that the Laodicean lacked, and the fire of which we need more in the church. It is that love which prompts us to action.

Maysville, Grant Co., W. Va.

THE HISTORY OF JOB.

A WRITER in the *Christian Standard* gives the most complete history of Job that we have yet seen. In view of the fact that our Sunday-school lesson for a part of next year will be in the book of Job, something of this kind will prove interesting reading. We have condensed the article somewhat, and give the following:—

THE DESCENT INTO EGYPT.

In the forty-sixth chapter of Genesis we learn that the "sons of Israel carried Jacob their father, and their little ones, and their wives, in the wagons which Pharaoh had sent to carry him." In the thirteenth verse is named Issachar, the ninth son of Jacob, and his four children—Tola, Phuvah, Job and Shimron. In 1 Chron. 7: 1, this same Job is called Jashub; and in Num. 26: 24, we learn that he was the founder of "the family of the Jashubites." The line of descent from Abraham is familiar to all—Abraham, Isaac, Jacob, Issachar, Job. The Septuagint version of Job, made about 280 years before Christ, concedes this Job to be the patient man.

THE CHILD JOB.

I assume that Job, being next to the younger in Issachar's family, was about four years old at the time of going to Egypt. I conclude, too, that at an early age he married and removed to Us.

THE LAND OF ISHMAEL.

The land of Uz, to which Job removed, was that occupied by the descendants of Ishmael, east and south-east of Palestine, and is now known as Arabia. Ishmael was a descendant of the same stock as Job—from Abraham through Hagar. Here Job lived among the descendants of his great-great-grandfather, Abraham. This common ancestry was no doubt known, and it gave to Job a prestige among the Ishmaelites that at once placed him in the highest rank. Familiar with the traditions current in the family of his ancestors, with some probable knowledge of records, and possessing the merits of true manhood, he rapidly accumulated wealth; his 7,000 sheep, 3,000 camels, 500 yoke of oxen and 500 she asses made it necessary for him to have a "very great household" to look after the details of his estate and business. His seven sons and three daughters had grown out of childhood, for even the three sisters were called to feast with the sons (Job 1:4). So devoted was Job that after these feastings he sanctified them

with burnt offerings "according to the number of them all." "For it may be," said Job, "that my sons have sinned." (Job 1:5).

JOB'S FIRST AFFLICTION.

In those days of prosperity and devotion, Job probably was about sixty years old. Joseph was ruler in Egypt and an age of prosperity rested upon God's people every-where. But in one of those days of prosperity, when the sons of God came to present themselves before the Lord, "Satan came also among them." (Job 1: 6). Then came the arrangements to test Job's sincerity, resulting so grandly in the most glorious triumph that humanity ever achieved. Satan was first given permission to do as he wished with Job's substance, but was not to touch his person. As a result, in rapid succession, his oxen were stolen by the Sabeans, the sheep were burned up, the camels were stolen by the Chaldeans, and all the attendants, save the messengers alone, were slain. Then came the crowning, crushing intelligence that while all his children were feasting, a great wind came, crumbling the house in which they were assembled, and killing them all. But after all this ' he "worshiped," and exclaimed: "The Lord gave and the Lord hath taken away, blessed be the name of the Lord." (Job 1: 21).

JOB'S SECOND AFFLICTION.

Having failed in his efforts to cause Job to sin, Satan made another effort, and this time got permission to touch his person, but to spare his life. Job was promptly smitten with " sore boils from the sole of his foot unto his crown (Job 2: 7), so that he took "a potsherd to scrape himself withal, and he sat among the ashes." His wife reproved him for still holding fast to his integrity, and urged him to " renounce God and die " (Job 2: 9). To this Job replied in scorn: " What? shall we receive good at the hand of God, and shall we not receive evil?" In all this affliction he sinned not.

HIGHWAY TO RESTORED PROSPERITY.

He must have been at least sixty years old. "And after this Job lived 140 years, and saw his sons, and his son's sons, even four generations" (Job 42: 16). "And the Lord gave Job twice as much as he had before " (Job 42: 10). He had the full and practical sympathy of his friends and neighbors, and they gave him presents, and comforted him, and he was blessed more than formerly, for he acquired 14,000 sheep, 6,000 camels, 1,000 yoke of oxen and 1,000 she asses. He also had seven sons and three daughters; "And in all the land were no women found so fair as the daughters of Job " (Job 42: 15).

JOB AND MOSES.

Joseph died in Egypt, 1635 B. C., when Job was about seventy-five years old. Prosperity continued, wealth accumulated, children were born; in Egypt had arisen a ruler, who "knew not Joseph," and the children of Israel were serving under task-masters. When Job was 189 years old (1571 B. C.) Moses was born; and for the next forty years, while Job was prosperous, Moses was being educated "in all the wisdom of the Egyptians, and he was mighty in his words and works." (Acts 7: 22). At forty, Moses fled to the land of Midian, at which time Job's age was about 179 years, yet a year younger than was Isaac at his death. The land of Midian was about midway to the land of Uz. If we suppose that Job was but sixty years old at the time of his affliction, and we add the 140 years of prosperity, then for 21 years he lived while Moses was in Midian. Moses may have visited Job during this time, but Job may have lived longer. Had he lived until the Exode, he would have been but 219 years old. These extra years may have been given him because of his

with the blessedness of being considered worthy to be allowed to enter that beautiful City, where the wicked cease from troubling and the weary are at rest. May all who read these lines forget the trials and temptations that are past and be encouraged to press forward toward the mark for the prize of the high calling of God, as it is in Christ Jesus.

"Should coming days be cold and dark,
We need not cease our singing;
That perfect rest, naught can molest,
Where golden harps are ringing."

Sweet Springs, Mo.

THE GOSPEL TRUMPET'S "THREE POINTS" EXAMINED.

BY CHAS. M. YEAROUT.

In Three Parts.—Part Three.

THE editor of the *Trumpet* says: "We will now take up this last point of the three. The Scripture treating on this matter is 1 Cor. 11: 2-16. The real subject here embraced is the question of wearing long or short hair, over which there had been some contention. For this the apostle reproves them, telling them that 'nature itself teaches' what is suitable in this respect, and that the church had no rigid custom or law governing in this matter, and that there was, therefore, no occasion for contention about it. But in connection with the teaching that the woman's hair was given her for a covering (verse 15), there is, we infer, from verse 5 and 6, also an allusion to the head covering that was worn by Jewish females and by orientals generally."

I wonder who told the editor that the church had no law or custom governing in this matter. His conclusions are far-fetched, and miss the facts in the case. The apostle does not say a word about Jewish or oriental customs. He is teaching a principle or fact, that "every man praying or prophesying having his head covered dishonoreth his head; but every woman that prayeth or prophesieth with her head uncovered, dishonoreth her head; for that is even all one as if she were shaven."

If she be not covered, let her ALSO CUT HER HAIR OFF. What becomes of your long hair then? What if the woman is bald-headed, as is the case with some? Others, perhaps, have lost their long hair though sickness and other causes. Are they to stand dishonored or disgraced for what they cannot help?

There is, perhaps, a greater cause for this covering than my friend is aware of. In the beginning man and woman were equal, and were created in the image of God. "And God said, Let us make man in our own image, after our likeness: and let them have dominion over the fish of the sea, and over the fowl of the air, and over the cattle, and over all the earth, and over every creeping thing that creepeth upon the earth. So God created man in his own image, in the image of God created he him; male and female created he them." Gen. 1: 26, 27; 5: 1, 2. "And Adam said, This is now bone of my bones, and flesh of my flesh: she shall be called Woman (*Isha*), because she was taken out of man (*Ish*). Therefore shall a man leave his father and his mother, and shall cleave unto his wife: and they shall be one flesh." Gen. 2: 23, 24; Matt. 19: 4, 5, 6. But men did not remain in this happy state in which God had placed them. The woman, being enticed by the serpent, transgressed the law of God,—partook of the forbidden tree and enticed her husband to do likewise, and as the result of this transgression the man was made lord over the woman. "Unto the woman he said, I will greatly multiply thy sorrow and thy conception; in sorrow shalt thou bring forth children; and thy desire shall be to thy hus-

band (marginal, subject to thy husband), and he shall rule over thee." Gen. 3: 16. "For Adam was first formed, then Eve. And Adam was not deceived, but the woman being deceived was in the transgression." 1 Tim. 2: 14; 2 Cor. 11: 3.

All was lost in the transgression of our first parents in the Garden of Eden; but, thanks be to God, what was lost in Adam was regained in Christ to every faithful child of God. "Behold the Lamb of God which taketh away the sin of the world." John 1: 29.

What was the sin of the world? Evidently it was the Adamic transgression. "Death reigned from Adam to Moses, even over them that had not sinned after the similitude of Adam's transgression; therefore as by the offence of one judgment came upon all men to condemnation; even so by the righteousness of one, the free gift came upon all men unto justification of life." Rom. 5: 14, 18. "Christ is the head of the body, the church." Col. 1: 18; Eph. 5: 23; 4: 15, 16. "For as many of you as have been baptized into Christ, have put on Christ. There is neither Jew nor Greek, there is neither bond nor free, there is neither male nor female; for ye are all one in Christ Jesus." Gal. 3: 27, 28. "For by one spirit are we all baptized into one body, whether we be Jews or Gentiles, whether we be bond or free; and have been all made to drink into one spirit." 1 Cor. 12: 13.

Christ is the spiritual husband of the church, hence the woman, praying unto God through Christ, her Spiritual Head veils (or hides) man her moral head out of the way. "For the man is not of the woman, but the woman of the man; neither was the man created for the woman, but the woman for the man. For this cause ought the woman to have power (*Exousian*), authority, on her head," 1 Cor. 11: 8-10, that she may, as a free woman in Christ Jesus, pray unto God through Christ, her Spiritual Head.

I maintain that every woman praying or prophesying without this power (*Exousian*) authority upon her head, dishonors Christ, and is under man, her ruler or lord. She was made such as a penalty for her transgression and disobedience. Therefore, whenever it is necessary and appropriate for man to have his head uncovered, it is necessary and appropriate for the woman to have her head covered. If she will not cover her head in time of prayer and prophesying, let her also cut her hair off, and thus dishonor, disgrace, her moral head,—men.

Man applies to husband only. (See Gen. 3: 16; Eph. 5: 22, 23). If, as some assert (my friend among them), this covering is worn as a signal of her subjection to man, her husband, why does the apostle only require it to be worn in time of prayer and prophesying? Why must she be subject to man only on such solemn occasions, when she is in the service and worship of her Spiritual Head,—Christ?

"Authority" does not mean subjection to man, but just to the opposite, man being veiled out of the way. The woman is restored to her Edenic state in her holy relationship to Christ and the heavenly family. She can converse with God in the silent closet or public assembly, and pour out her thanks and ascriptions of praise to God through Christ, without having to ask man for the privilege, having her "authority" to do so "on her head." The administering angels recognize this authority.

Again the editor says: "It is a question of veiling, and it is all a question of proper decorum, and the latter wholly depends upon existing customs and habits. These create men's and women's ideality and tastes. What is very proper in one part of the earth, would be very indecorous in another."

I would hate to charge the apostle with upholding Jewish customs and habits, because they happened to be in vogue at that time, and this doctrine of doing as you feel and think is unscriptural and dangerous. That the Jews had such a custom as Paul was contending for, I emphatically deny. The men sat in the house of worship with their hats or turbans on, and the women bareheaded. The Jews wear their hats in their synagogues to this day. Hence the apostle was condemning the Jewish custom instead of upholding it, as my friend would make us believe.

The editor says in regard to the angels: "Probably they were sent by some subtile foe to spy out something by which they could bring reproach on the cause of Christ, and it may have been because of such angels of deception that God's saints, though free from the hard yokes imposed by time-honored customs, should nevertheless not use their liberty in a way that might be turned into scandal. Hence they should have power on their heads. So Paul, the eminent, inspired apostle, taught the saints to conform to the customs of the world, lest they (the world) talk about you and scandalize you. Please read John 15: 18, 19; Rom. 12: 2; James 4: 4. Paul says: "He that will live godly in this world shall suffer persecution." Let us see what God's Word says about angels. "The angel of the Lord encampeth round about them that fear him, and delivereth them." Ps. 34: 7; Dan. 6: 22; 3: 28. Every child of God has a guardian angel, who goes with him, or her, through the uneven, checkered journey of life. These guardian angels are ever hovering around us during the busy scenes of life, and keep their watchful vigils during the silent slumbers of night. "Are they not all ministering spirits sent forth to minister for them who shall be heirs of salvation?" Heb. 1: 14; Matt. 18: 10.

The woman should have this covering,—authority,—on her head because of her administering angel. The world has nothing to do with it; let them ridicule it if they choose; it will not hurt us. "If ye were of the world it would love you."

The editor, in speaking of those who follow Paul's instructions, says, "It is a trick of the devil who is the author of all such yokes." He takes the Greek word *periboleion* 1 Cor. 11: 15, which is defined in *Young's Concordance* as "something cast around." *Robison's Lexicon* defines the word thus: "To cast around; to throw around," etc. All right; but *periboleion* is not the word the apostle uses to designate the prayer covering. "The original employs different words to represent the two coverings. The special covering is represented by *kalupto*, 'to cover a thing,' or 'to put over as a covering.' (See Liddell and Scott.) The word *kalupto*, designating the artificial covering, is used five times, while *periboleiou*, from *periballo*, designating the natural covering, is used but once. Why would the apostle use two different words meaning different things, to express the same thing? "This distinction is recognized by all leading commentators, as Scott, Godwyn, Gill, Hammond, Lightfoot, Pierce, Whitby, Shoatgen, Clark, Benson, Barnes, Patrick, Lowth, Arnold, Lowman and others." "It has been the universal custom of the church through all ages. The putting away of the woman's head covering is a modern departure. It prevailed among the Primitive Christians." (See "Cave's Primitive Christianity," p. 139; "Writings of Tertullian," 1, p. 195, etc.; 2, pp. 154-180). "But if any man seem to be contentious, we have no such custom as men worshiping God with their hats or turbans on, and the women bareheaded, neither have the churches of God such a custom as that."

Man,—husband,—is the head of the wife from a physical and moral stand-point, but Christ is the

with the blessedness of being considered worthy to be allowed to enter that beautiful City, where the wicked cease from troubling and the weary are at rest. May all who read these lines forget the trials and temptations that are past and be encouraged to press forward toward the mark for the prize of the high calling of God, as it is in Christ Jesus.

"Should coming days be cold and dark,
We need not cease our singing;
That perfect rest, naught can molest,
Where golden harps are ringing."

Sweet Springs, Mo.

THE GOSPEL TRUMPET'S "THREE POINTS" EXAMINED.

BY CHAS. M. YEAROUT.

In Three Parts.—Part Three.

THE editor of the *Trumpet* says: "We will now take up this last point of the three. The Scripture treating on this matter is 1 Cor. 11: 2-16. The real subject here embraced is the question of wearing long or short hair, over which there had been some contention. For this the apostle reproves them, telling them that 'nature itself teaches' what is suitable in this respect, and that the church had no rigid custom or law governing in this matter, and that there was, therefore, no occasion for contention about it. But in connection with the teaching that the woman's hair was given her for a covering (verse 15), there is, we infer, from verse 5 and 6, also an allusion to the head covering that was worn by Jewish females and by orientals generally."

I wonder who told the editor that the church had no law or custom governing in this matter. His conclusions are far-fetched, and miss the facts in the case. The apostle does not say a word about Jewish or oriental customs. He is teaching a principle or fact, that "every man praying or prophesying having his head covered dishonoreth his head; but every woman that prayeth or prophesieth with her head uncovered, dishonoreth her head; for that is even all one as if she were shaven."

If she be not covered, let her ALSO CUT HER HAIR OFF. What becomes of your long hair then? What if the woman is bald-headed, as is the case with some? Others, perhaps, have lost their long hair though sickness and other causes. Are they to stand dishonored or disgraced for what they cannot help?

There is, perhaps, a greater cause for this covering than my friend is aware of. In the beginning man and woman were equal, and were created in the image of God. "And God said, Let us make man in our own image, after our likeness: and let them have dominion over the fish of the sea, and over the fowl of the air, and over the cattle, and over all the earth, and over every creeping thing that creepeth upon the earth. So God created man in his own image, in the image of God created he him; male and female created he them." Gen. 1: 26, 27; 5: 1, 2. "And Adam said, This is now bone of my bones, and flesh of my flesh: she shall be called Woman (*Isha*), because she was taken out of man (*Ish*). Therefore shall a man leave his father and his mother, and shall cleave unto his wife: and they shall be one flesh." Gen. 2: 23, 24; Matt. 19: 4, 5, 6. But men did not remain in this happy state in which God had placed them. The woman, being enticed by the serpent, transgressed the law of God,—partook of the forbidden tree and enticed her husband to do likewise, and as the result of this transgression the man was made lord over the woman. "Unto the woman he said, I will greatly multiply thy sorrow and thy conception; in sorrow shalt thou bring forth children; and thy desire shall be to thy hus-

band (marginal, subject to thy husband), and he shall rule over thee." Gen. 3: 16. "For Adam was first formed, then Eve. And Adam was not deceived, but the woman being deceived was in the transgression." 1 Tim. 2: 14; 2 Cor. 11: 3.

All was lost in the transgression of our first parents in the Garden of Eden; but, thanks be to God, what was lost in Adam was regained in Christ to every faithful child of God. "Behold the Lamb of God which taketh away the sin of the world." John 1: 29.

What was the sin of the world? Evidently it was the Adamic transgression. "Death reigned from Adam to Moses, even over them that had not sinned after the similitude of Adam's transgression; therefore as by the offence of one judgment came upon all men to condemnation; even so by the righteousness of one, the free gift came upon all men unto justification of life." Rom. 5: 14, 18. "Christ is the head of the body, the church." Col. 1: 18; Eph. 5: 23; 4: 15, 16. "For as many of you as have been baptized into Christ, have put on Christ. There is neither Jew nor Greek, there is neither bond nor free, there is neither male nor female; for ye are all one in Christ Jesus." Gal. 3: 27, 28. "For by one spirit are we all baptized into one body, whether we be Jews or Gentiles, whether we be bond or free; and have been all made to drink into one spirit." 1 Cor. 12: 13.

Christ is the spiritual husband of the church, hence the woman, praying unto God through Christ, her Spiritual Head veils (or hides) man her moral head out of the way. "For the man is not of the woman, but the woman of the man; neither was the man created for the woman, but the woman for the man. For this cause ought the woman to have power (*Exousian*), authority, on her head," 1 Cor. 11: 8-10, that she may, as a free woman in Christ Jesus, pray unto God through Christ her Spiritual Head.

I maintain that every woman praying or prophesying without this power (*Exousian*) authority upon her head, dishonors Christ, and is under man, her ruler or lord. She was made such as a penalty for her transgressions and disobedience. Therefore, whenever it [is] necessary and appropriate for man to have his head uncovered, it is necessary and appropriate for the woman to have her head covered. If she will not cover her head in time of prayer and prophesying, let her also cut her hair off, and thus dishonor, disgrace, her moral head,—man.

Man applies to husband only. (See Gen. 3: 16; Eph. 5: 22, 23). If, as some assert (my friend among them), this covering is worn as a signal of her subjection to man, her husband, why does the apostle only require it to be worn in time of prayer and prophesying? Why must she be subject to man only on such solemn occasions, when she is in the service and worship of, her Spiritual Head,—Christ?

"Authority" does not mean subjection to man, but just to the opposite, man being veiled out of the way. The woman is restored to her Edenic state in her holy relationship to Christ and the heavenly family. She can converse with God in the silent closet or public assembly, and pour out her thanks and ascriptions of praise to God through Christ, without having to ask man for the privilege, having her "authority" to do so "on her head." The administering angels recognize this authority.

Again the editor says: "It is a question of veiling, and it is all a question of proper decorum, and the latter wholly depends upon existing customs and habits. These create men's and women's ideality and tastes. What is very proper in one part of the earth, would be very indecorous in another."

I would hate to charge the apostle with upholding Jewish customs and habits, because they happened to be in vogue at that time, and this doctrine of doing as you feel and think is unscriptural and dangerous. That the Jews had such a custom as Paul was contending for, I emphatically deny. The men sat in the house of worship with their hats or turbans on, and the women bareheaded. The Jews wear their hats in their synagogues to this day. Hence the apostle was condemning the Jewish custom instead of upholding it, as my friend would make us believe.

The editor says in regard to the angels: "Probably they were sent by some subtile foe to spy out something by which they could bring reproach on the cause of Christ, and it may have been because of such angels of deception that God's saints, though free from the hard yokes imposed by time-honored customs, should nevertheless not use their liberty in a way that might be turned into scandal. Hence they should have power on their heads. So Paul, the eminent, inspired apostle, taught the saints to conform to the customs of the world, lest they (the world) talk about you and scandalize you. Please read John 15: 18, 19; Rom. 12: 2; James 4: 4. Paul says: "He that will live godly in this world shall suffer persecution." Let us see what God's Word says about angels. "The angel of the Lord encampeth round about them that fear him, and delivereth them." Ps. 34: 7; Dan. 6: 22; 3: 28. Every child of God has a guardian angel, who goes with him, or her, through the uneven, checkered journey of life. These guardian angels are ever hovering around us during the busy scenes of life, and keep their watchful vigils during the silent slumbers of night. "Are they not all ministering spirits sent forth to minister for them who shall be heirs of salvation?" Heb. 1: 14; Matt. 18: 10.

The woman should have this covering,—authority,—on her head because of her administering angel. The world has nothing to do with it; let them ridicule it if they choose; it will not hurt us. "If ye were of the world it would love you."

The editor, in speaking of those who follow Paul's instructions, says, "It is a trick of the devil who is the author of all such yokes." He takes the Greek word *periboleiou* 1 Cor. 11: 15, which is defined in *Young's Concordance* as 'something cast around.' *Robison's Lexicon* defines the word thus: "To cast around; to throw around," etc. All right; but *periboleiou* is not the word the apostle uses to designate the prayer covering. "The original employs different words to represent the two coverings. The special covering is represented by *kalupto*, 'to cover a thing,' or 'to put over as a covering.' (See Liddell and Scott.) The word *kalupto*, designating the artificial covering, is used five times, while *periboleiou*, from *peribolo*, designating the natural covering, is used but once. Why would the apostle use two different words meaning different things, to express the same thing? "This distinction is recognized by all leading commentators, as Scott, Godwyn, Gill, Hammond, Lightfoot, Pierce, Whitby, Shestgen, Clark, Benson, Barnes, Patrick, Lowth, Arnold, Lowman and others." "It has been the universal custom of the church through all ages. The putting away of the woman's head covering is a modern departure. It prevailed among the Primitive Christians." (See "Cave's Primitive Christianity," p. 189; "Writings of Tertullian," 1, p. 195, etc.; 2, pp. 154-180). "But if any man seem to be contentious, we have no such custom as men worshiping God with their hats or turbans on, and the women bareheaded, neither have the churches of God such a custom as that."

Man,—husband,—is the head of the wife from a physical and moral stand-point, but Christ is the

Missionary and Tract Work Department.

"Upon the first day of the week, let every one of you lay by him in store as God hath prospered him, that there be no gatherings when I come."—1 Cor. 16: 2.

"Every man as he purposeth in his heart, so let him give. Not grudgingly or of necessity, for the Lord loveth a cheerful giver."—2 Cor. 9: 7.

HOW MUCH SHALL WE GIVE?

"Every man according to his ability." "Every one as God hath prospered him." "Every man, according as he purposeth in his heart, so let him give." "For if there be first a willing mind, it is accepted according to that a man hath, and not according to that he hath not."—2 Cor. 8: 12.

Organization of Missionary Committee.

DANIEL VANIMAN, Foreman,   McPherson, Kans
D. L. MILLER, Treasurer,   Mt. Morris, Ill.
GALEN B. ROYER, Secretary,   Mt. Morris, Ill.

Organization of Book and Tract Work.

S. W. HOOVER, Foreman,   Dayton, Ohio.
S. BOCK, Secretary and Treasurer,   Dayton, Ohio.

☞All donations intended for Missionary Work should be sent to GALEN B. ROYER, Mt. Morris, Ill.

☞All money for Tract Work should be sent to S. BOCK, Dayton, Ohio.

☞Money may be sent by Money Order, Registered Letter, or Drafts on New York or Chicago. Do not send personal checks, or drafts on interior towns, as it costs 25 cents to collect them.

☞Solicitors are requested to faithfully carry out the plan of Annual Meeting, that all our members be solicited to contribute at least twice a year for the Mission and Tract Work of the Church.

☞Notes for the Endowment Fund can be had by writing to the Secretary of either Work.

SOME BREAKERS AHEAD.

BY C. E. ARNOLD.

In Four Parts.

Number Three.—Higher Criticism of the Bible.

THERE exists in America an organization of men who call themselves "Christian Scientists," and whose purpose it is to show that there is much error in the Old Testament Scriptures. They claim that much of what has been so accredly regarded is simply Jewish tradition, without any reasonable claim to infallibility. They so regard the Genesis account of creation and the flood, the Book of Job, and portions of a number of the books of the Old Testament; and they deny that Moses was the author of the books called Pentateuch.

We cannot discuss here the methods of investigation by which these results have been reached. Suffice it to say that these methods are decidedly speculative, and cannot be relied upon to produce definite results. These so-called "Higher Critics," it will be found, are not practical men of common sense affairs; but they are men of one idea (popularly called cranks), who have conjured up a pet theory, and are trying to make everything conform thereto.

There is some inducement to promulgate these peculiar views, in the fact that such literature usually has an extensive sale, and brings its author a certain kind of notoriety.

Let us remember that these Higher Critics are in the church, and profess to be laboring to promote the cause of Christianity. If, then, their influence has been hurtful rather than helpful, they should at once quit their unhallowed business, or step within the pales of professed infidelity, where they can consistently promote the cause of the devil. But what are they doing? In the first place, they have lessened the reverence with which the Holy Scriptures have been regarded by those influenced by Higher Criticism. Some have been driven to serious doubt, and even to infidelity.

Again, they have dampened their own spiritual ardor, if they ever had it. Doctor Monhall, the great northern evangelist, says: "I personally know two theological professors in this country, who are prominent as Higher Critics, and who

have not been in their own churches on the Lord's Day to worship for several years, though they reside close by, and are at home three Sundays out of every four." Higher Criticism gives to its followers spiritual deadness, and leaves their religion a dry, husky shell, not worthy the name of religion.

Without reviewing the arguments in favor of Higher Criticism, is not the following position a safe one to take? If Jesus Christ, the "Son of the Living God," who spake as "never man spake," and the Holy Spirit, our "Teacher," sent to "guide you into all the Truth," revealed no error in the Old Testament Scriptures, is this not evidence, unmistakable and final to the Christian, that our Bible needs no criticism? Jesus, his disciples, and the early Christians all regarded the Old Testament Scriptures with the utmost reverence; and they quoted them and referred to them as authority in spiritual matters. Anything like an imputation of fraud or error to the Old Testament is entirely foreign to the whole spirit of the New Testament and its writers. Thirty-six of the books of the Old Testament have supplied quotations and allusions in the writings of the New.

Men of great spiritual power have always so credly regarded the divinity of the Scriptures. It is said that Spurgeon, with all his extensive knowledge, never found a single thing in the Bible which he could not believe.

Higher Criticism saps the very life and spirit out of Christianity and leaves it a lifeless formalism, "and whosoever is deceived thereby is not wise."

Daleville, Va.

LITTLE MISSIONARIES.

BY NANCY D. UNDERHILL.

CHILDREN naturally love Jesus, and want to serve him. They can serve him if they only know how. Little children make the very best of missionaries, yet we do not wish to discourage any of the big ones from doing the same things. Children, either big or little, should never be ashamed to pray, no matter what kind of people are in the same room; even if there are very wicked folks who laugh at you. Don't pay a bit of attention to them; just remember that it is God to whom you are talking, and we must be very careful what we say to God. We must be sure never to say anything in our prayer only what we really mean from the very bottom of our hearts, for he hears every word, and the Holy Spirit knows every thought.

Once a man and woman named Ananias and Sapphira, told a lie to the Holy Ghost and they fell dead immediately. They thought they were only deceiving a man whose name was Peter, but the Lord heard their false words and punished them. So, when we kneel to pray at night, or in the morning, or return thanks at the table, we must always remember that we are talking to God, and not man, and be just as true, honest, and respectful as we can, and then not apologize.

Very often a young Christian, scarcely out of the teens, will be asked by his comrades to return thanks, to lead in prayer, or even to lead a meeting. They should never refuse to comply with such a request, but show by their words and actions that it is no hard task to "come to Jesus" and to commune with, and work for, One who loves us. Jesus bore many sneers and much mockery for our sakes. Let us be brave enough to bear such things for him. When we pray we should tell God just what we think, but we must be very careful, first, to have only such thoughts in our hearts as will please him. If we don't

know anything else to say we can repeat the "Lord's Prayer," and it is the model prayer for all Christians, but we must not become angry at anyone when we do so.

If we don't know how to "return thanks," it is sufficient to say (with grateful, loving hearts) something like this, "Father in heaven, we thank thee for these blessings, and pray thee to make us more useful in thy vineyard. In Jesus' name, Amen."

When children show by their actions that they are not afraid to confess Jesus, anywhere, everywhere, and to do as he has taught us, they are sure to encourage some one else to serve him too. Let me say to the dear girls, when a young man uses profane language in your presence, and then says, "Oh excuse me," or, "I beg your pardon," it is always best to tell him that God is the offended party; that he had better present his petition to him.

Children can help their parents and others to serve the Lord by always being promptly on time at the table, and at family services, at Sunday-school and at prayers, whenever and wherever it is their duty to be, and by being always quiet, attentive and respectful. If the parent or teacher, who is expected to lead, should be suffering with a headache, it would be only polite for some young disciple of Christ to offer to read for them. Such little things do encourage one. But aside from these little home helps, there are many things which children can do, to help plant the Gospel in people's hearts. One way is to save their nickles or pennies, and send them to the Brethren's Book and Tract Work, Dayton, Ohio, for a package of tracts and leaflets. These they can give to the children at their day-school, and get them to read them by saying pleasantly, "Will you please read this message when you have leisure?" or, "Here is a letter for you; take and read it to your mother, please." The very small children can be interested by showing them the big letters at the top, and teaching them how to spell the words of the title, then get them to take it home to their parents, or older sister or brother, and ask them to read it out loud to the little ones. If you ever find an old Testament or Bible that some one has thrown away, you can make nice little tracts by cutting out certain portions of them,—the psalms for instance,—or the beatitudes, or other portions of the Sermon on the Mount, and many other selections, and pasting them in the middle of a smooth sheet of pink or blue paper (such as druggists use) leaving a good margin of the tinted paper on the outside, and having only a short psalm, or a few paragraphs on each sheet. If you are a good hand to pink the edges nicely, it will make them more attractive. You can name these tracts, "letters from heaven." You can either paint the title (if you can do it well) or cut the letters out of old papers and put them together for a title. Beautiful valentines can be made the same way, only it should be a folio or some fancy shape, and your mama or most any elderly Christian would help you to select suitable verses for each one you wished to send, and to decorate them nicely. When you want to send a package of flower seeds, or some other little thing, to a friend, wrap them in a tract. When your mother gives a lunch to anyone who is a stranger, or not a member of the church, get her to wrap it in a "GOSPEL MESSENGER," or Young Disciple.

Another way is to get people to subscribe for the GOSPEL MESSENGER and the Young Disciple. If you can learn of anyone who does not take the MESSENGER, tell them, and show them what a good, pure-toned paper it is, and what plain, coarse print, and tell them that everybody ought to take a religious paper in this enlightened day.

Missionary and Tract Work Department.

"Upon the first day of the week, let every one of you lay by him in store as God hath prospered him, that there be no gatherings when I come."—1 Cor. 16: 2.

"Every man as he purposeth in his heart, so let him give. Not grudgingly or of necessity, for the Lord loveth a cheerful giver."—2 Cor. 9: 7.

HOW MUCH SHALL WE GIVE?

"Every man *according to his ability.*" "Every one *as God hath prospered him.*" "Every man, *according as he purposeth in his heart, so let him give.*" "For if there be first a willing mind, it is accepted *according to that a man hath,* and not according to that he hath not."—2 Cor. 8: 12.

Organization of Missionary Committee.

DANIEL VANIMAN, Foreman,   McPherson, Kans.
D. L. MILLER, Treasurer,   ·   ·   Mt. Morris, Ill.
GALEN B. ROYER, Secretary,   ·   Mt. Morris, Ill.

Organization of Book and Tract Work.

S. W. HOOVER, Foreman,   ·   ·   Dayton, Ohio.
S. BOCK, Secretary and Treasurer,   Dayton, Ohio.

☞All donations intended for Missionary Work should be sent to GALEN B. ROYER, Mt. Morris, Ill.

☞All money for Tract Work should be sent to S. BOCK, Dayton, Ohio.

☞Money may be sent by Money Order, Registered Letter, or Drafts on New York or Chicago. Do not send personal checks, or drafts on interior towns, as it costs 25 cents to collect them.

☞Solicitors are requested to faithfully carry out the plan of Annual Meeting, that all our members be solicited to contribute at least twice a year for the Mission and Tract Work of the Church.

☞Notes for the Endowment Fund can be had by writing to the Secretary of either Work.

SOME BREAKERS AHEAD.

BY C. E. ARNOLD.

In Four Parts.

Number Three.—Higher Criticism of the Bible.

THERE exists in America an organization of men who call themselves "Christian Scientists," and whose purpose it is to show that there is much error in the Old Testament Scriptures. They claim that much of what has been so sacredly regarded is simply Jewish tradition, without any reasonable claim to infallibility. They so regard the Genesis account of creation and the flood, the Book of Job, and portions of a number of the books of the Old Testament; and they deny that Moses was the author of the books called Pentateuch.

We cannot discuss here the methods of investigation by which these results have been reached. Suffice it to say that these methods are decidedly speculative, and cannot be relied upon to produce definite results. These so-called "Higher Critics," it will be found, are not practical men of common sense affairs; but they are men of one idea (popularly called cranks), who have conjured up a pet theory, and are trying to make everything conform thereto.

There is some inducement to promulgate these peculiar views, in the fact that such literature usually has an extensive sale, and brings its author a certain kind of notoriety.

Let us remember that these Higher Critics are in the church, and profess to be laboring to promote the cause of Christianity. If, then, their influence has been hurtful rather than helpful, they should at once quit their unhallowed business, or step within the pales of professed infidelity, where they can consistently promote the cause of the devil. But what are they doing? In the first place, they have lessened the reverence with which the Holy Scriptures have been regarded by those influenced by Higher Criticism. Some have been driven to serious doubt, and even to infidelity.

Again, they have dampened their own spiritual ardor, if they ever had it. Doctor Munhall, the great northern evangelist, says: "I personally know two theological professors in this country, who are prominent as Higher Critics, and who

have not been in their own churches on the Lord's Day to worship for several years, though they reside close by, and are at home three Sundays out of every four." Higher Criticism gives to its followers spiritual deadness, and leaves their religion a dry, husky shell, not worthy the name of religion.

Without reviewing the arguments in favor of Higher Criticism, is not the following position a safe one to take? If Jesus Christ, the "Son of the Living God," who spake as "never man spake," and the Holy Spirit, our "Teacher," sent to "guide you into all the Truth," revealed no error in the Old Testament Scriptures, is this not evidence, *unmistakable* and *final* to the Christian, that our Bible *needs no criticism?* Jesus, his disciples, and the early Christians all regarded the Old Testament Scriptures with the utmost reverence; and they quoted them and referred to them as authority in spiritual matters. Anything like an imputation of fraud or error to the Old Testament is entirely foreign to the whole spirit of the New Testament and its writers. Thirty-six of the books of the Old Testament have supplied quotations and allusions in the writings of the New.

Men of great spiritual power have always sacredly regarded the divinity of the Scriptures. It is said that Spurgeon, with all his extensive knowledge, never found a single thing in the Bible which he could not believe.

Higher Criticism saps the very life and spirit out of Christianity and leaves it a lifeless formalism, "and whosoever is deceived thereby is not wise."

Daleville, Va.

LITTLE MISSIONARIES.

BY NANCY D. UNDERHILL.

CHILDREN naturally love Jesus, and want to serve him. They can serve him if they only know how. Little children make the very best of missionaries, yet we do not wish to discourage any of the big ones from doing the same things. Children, either big or little, should never be ashamed to pray, no matter what kind of people are in the same room; even if there are very wicked folks who laugh at you. Don't pay a bit of attention to them; just remember that it is GOD to whom you are talking, and we must be very careful what we say to God. We must be sure never to say anything in our prayer only what we really mean from the very bottom of our hearts, for he hears every word, and the Holy Spirit knows every thought.

Once a man and woman named Ananias and Sapphira, told a lie to the Holy Ghost and they fell dead immediately. They thought they were only deceiving a man whose name was Peter, but the Lord heard their false words and punished them. So, when we kneel to pray at night, or in the morning, or return thanks at the table, we must always remember that we are talking to GOD, and not man, and be just as true, honest, and respectful as we can, and then not apologize.

Very often a young Christian, scarcely out of the teens, will be asked by his comrades to return thanks, to lead in prayer, or even to lead a meeting. They should never refuse to comply with such a request, but show by their words and actions that it is no hard task to "come to Jesus" and to commune with, and work for, One who loves us. Jesus bore many sneers and much mockery for our sakes. Let us be brave enough to bear such things for him. When we pray we should tell God *just what we think,* but we must be very careful, first, to have only such thoughts in our hearts as will please him. If we don't

know anything else to say we can repeat the "Lord's Prayer," and it is the *model* prayer for all Christians, but we must not become angry at anyone when we do so.

If we don't know how to "return thanks," it is sufficient to say (with grateful, loving hearts) something like this, "Father in heaven, we *thank* thee for these blessings, and pray thee to make us more useful in thy vineyard. In Jesus' name, Amen."

When children show by their actions that they are not afraid to confess Jesus, anywhere, everywhere, and to do as he has taught us, they are sure to encourage some one else to serve him too. Let me say, to the dear girls, when a young man uses profane language in your presence, and then says, "Oh excuse me," or, "I beg your pardon," it is always best to tell him that *God* is the offended party; that he had better present his petition to him.

Children can help their parents and others to serve the Lord by always being promptly on time at the table, and at family services, at Sunday-school and at prayers, whenever and wherever it is their duty to be, and by being always quiet, attentive and respectful. If the parent or teacher, who is expected to lead, should be suffering with a headache, it would be only polite for some young disciple of Christ to offer to read for them. Such little things do encourage one. But aside from these little home helps, there are many things which children can do, to help plant the Gospel in people's hearts. One way is to save their nickles or pennies, and send them to the Brethren's Book and Tract Work, Dayton, Ohio, for a package of tracts and leaflets. These they can give to the children at their day-school, and get them to read them by saying pleasantly, "Will you please read this message when you have leisure?" or, "Here is a letter for you; take and read it to your mother, please." The very small children can be interested by showing them the big letters at the top, and teaching them how to spell the words of the title, then get them to take it home to their parents, or older sister or brother, and ask them to read it out loud to the little ones. If you ever find an old Testament or Bible that some one has thrown away, you can make nice little tracts by cutting out certain portions of them,—the psalms for instance,—or the beatitudes, or other portions of the Sermon on the Mount, and many other selections, and pasting them in the middle of a smooth sheet of pink or blue paper (such as druggists use) leaving a good margin of the tinted paper on the outside, and having only a short psalm, or a few paragraphs on each sheet. If you are a good hand to pink the edges nicely, it will make them more attractive. You can name these tracts, "letters from heaven." You can either paint the title (if you can do it well) or cut the letters out of old papers and put them together for a title. Beautiful valentines can be made the same way, only it should be a folio or some fancy shape, and your mama or most any elderly Christian would help you to select suitable verses for each one you wished to send, and to decorate them nicely. When you want to send a package of flower seeds, or some other little thing, to a friend, wrap them in a tract. When your mother gives a lunch to anyone who is a stranger, or not a member of the church, get her to wrap it in a "GOSPEL MESSENGER," or *Young Disciple.*

Another way is to get people to subscribe for the GOSPEL MESSENGER and the *Young Disciple.* If you can learn of anyone who does not take the MESSENGER, tell them, and show them what a good, pure-toned paper it is, and what plain, coarse print, and tell them that everybody ought to take a religious paper in this enlightened day.

The Gospel Messenger,

A Weekly at $1.50 Per Annum.

PUBLISHED BY

The Brethren's Publishing Co.

D. L. MILLER,	Editor.
J. H. MOORE,	Office Editor.
J. B. BRUMBAUGH, }	Associate Editors.
J. G. ROYER, }	
JOSEPH AMICK,	Business Manager.

ADVISORY COMMITTEE.

L. W. Teeter, A. Hutchison, Daniel Hays.

☞Communications for publication should be legibly written with black ink on one side of the paper only. Do not attempt to interline, or to put on one page what ought to occupy two.

☞Anonymous communications will not be published.

☞Do not mix business with articles for publication. Keep your communications on separate sheets from all business.

☞Time is precious. We always have time to attend to business and to answer questions of importance, but please do not subject us to send less answering of letters.

☞The MESSENGER is mailed each week to all subscribers. If the address is correctly entered on our list, the paper must reach the person to whom it is addressed. If you do not get your paper, write us, giving particulars.

☞When changing your address, please give your former as well as your future address in full, so as to avoid delay and misunderstanding.

☞Always remit to the office from which you order your goods, no matter from where you receive them.

☞Do not send personal checks or drafts on interior banks, unless you send with them 25 cents each, to pay for collection.

☞Remittances should be made by Post-office Money Order, Drafts on New York, Philadelphia or Chicago, or Registered Letters, made payable and addressed to "Brethren's Publishing Co., Mount Morris, Ill.," or "Brethren's Publishing Co., Huntingdon, Pa."

☞Entered at the Post-office at Mount Morris, Ill., as second-class matter.

Mount Morris, Ill.,   · · · ·   Sept. 20, 1892.

THE Mission Board for Northern Illinois will meet at Mt. Morris, next Monday, the 19th.

THE address of Bro. J. E. Blough is now changed from Scalp Level, Pa., to Manassas, Va.

THE cause of Christ seems to be prospering in the Sugar Creek church, Ohio. Not long since sixteen were added to that congregation.

BRO. O. D. HYLTON reports thirteen additions to the Pleasant Valley church, Floyd County, Va., being the result of meetings incidentally held.

THE Osborne church, Kansas, has a new meeting-house in contemplation. The church is reported to be in peace, and prospering in the Master's work.

WRITING from Casstown, Ohio, Bro. W. R. Murphy says, "Aug. 28 two dear sisters made the good confession, and were received into the church by baptism."

A NUMBER of the love-feast notices in this issue were received about two hours after the last issue was put on the press. That is why they did not appear last week.

IT is said that missionary work during the last one hundred years, has put the Bible within the reach of 500,000,000 people. This is less, however, than one-half of the population of the globe. There is still a mighty work to do.

CONCERNING Spurgeon's great "power" as a preacher, Dr. Cuyler says: "It lay in the combination of half a dozen great qualities. He was the master of a vigorous Saxon-English style—the style of Cobbett, and Bunyan, and the King James' Version of the Bible. He held the word of God *in solution*, and could quote almost any passage on the instant from memory. He was the 'man of one book,' and had the most implicit faith in every jot and tittle of God's inspired word. He preached it without defalcation or discount; and this prodigious faith made his preaching prodigiously tonic."

WE learn with regrets that the wife of Bro. Jas. A. Sell has been sick the greater part of the summer, thus requiring much of his attention at home. We are now glad to be informed that she is greatly improving.

A SPECIAL District Meeting for Southern Indiana was held at Arcadia, Sept. 1, and a Locating Committee appointed to select a location for the Annual Meeting of 1893, and report through the MESSENGER. We hope to hear from the Committee shortly.

WE like Bro. S. F. Sanger's way of announcing the Ministerial Meeting to be held at Bridgewater, Va., Dec. 29 and 30. He says, "Programs upon application." That is better than to publish the programs in the paper. We recommend this way to other Districts.

THE Brethren who attended the feast at Sterling, last Saturday evening, report an excellent meeting, though the rain kept many away who had counted on being present. A number of ministers were in attendance and rendered good service in the preaching of the Word.

IT is gratifying to learn of a church prospering like the Beaver Dam church, Md., has during the last few years. With a small handful of members and two officers, it has worked its way up to strength and usefulness. What has been done in one locality is at least possible in another.

OUR quarterly council, held in the Chapel last Saturday, passed off very pleasantly. A harvest-meeting was appointed to be held at the Silver Creek meeting-house, Saturday, Sept. 24, commencing at 10:30, and continuing over Sunday. The time for our fall love-feast will be announced later.

BRO. D. B. GIBSON is engaged in a series of meetings in the Mill Creek church, Adams Co., Ill. Four have already made the good confession. This is the congregation formerly presided over by Eld. Geo. Wolfe, a sketch of whose life is now in type and will appear in the Brethren's Almanac for 1893.

WHILE a large membership is very desirable at all of our feasts, it is nevertheless unfortunate when there is not room enough at the tables for all of them. Special efforts, however, should be made to find room for each one, as it is highly important that every member of the body of Christ should commune as often as circumstances will permit. Let none remain away from the table.

THE GOSPEL MESSENGER will be sent free from now to the end of the present year to all new subscribers for 1893. We would therefore suggest to our agents that they make a special effort to procure as many new names as possible with this inducement. At the various feasts will be excellent places to see the members who are not now taking the paper. With proper efforts the MESSENGER might be introduced into nearly every family in the Brotherhood. We hope our agents will not only call on all the members, but also those who are not members, especially members' children. Remember that the price of the paper is $1.50 a year, but those who subscribe now not only get to read the paper all of 1893, but the remainder of the present year. We make a similar offer for the *Young Disciple*, which is published weekly for 50 cents a year, but those who subscribe now will also receive it free the remainder of the year. It will be well for those having children to subscribe for both papers. $2.00 will pay for both of them from now until the end of 1893. We hope to receive a large list of new names under this offer.

BRO. HENRY FRANTZ, this week tells of a young sister who came twenty miles to be baptized. Some who see little or nothing in baptism, think that indeed a long journey for a little ceremony. But they should remember that the Savior traveled about sixty miles to be immersed, and he probably needed baptism as little as anyone who ever lived. Surely it is wise to follow his example.

A LEADING writer says, that the various religions of the world are the pictures of men seeking after God, and that the Gospel is a picture of God seeking after the people, to offer them life and forgiveness. We might suggest that much of the New Testament is a picture of converted men walking with God. God found the men, offered them forgiveness and life, and they accepted the terms proposed, and in the picture we see them walking in the path marked out for them. It is the part of wisdom for us to study this picture that we may learn to walk even as they walked.

IT is a wise and truthful saying, that, "It is not all gold that glitters." Strangers who occasionally occupy seats in a fashionable church, listening to the scholarly sermon and artistic music, and being virtually charmed by the seemingly befitting surroundings, would imagine that the greatest possible harmony must exist between those who perform the different parts of this delightful service. Could they but glance behind the curtain and see the discord, jealousy, hatred, and hard feelings that often exist between the different members of the choir, or other members, who in public play an important part in the service, they would be astonished at the amount of discord that may be covered for an hour by the mantle of popular charity. It glitters, but it is not gold.

THIS is indeed the season for love-feasts, when more preaching will probably be done than at any other time. How important it is that the Word be presented in a forcible, correct and creditable manner! Considering the amount of good that may be accomplished by preaching, it surely stands our ministers in hand to make special preparations for these occasions, so as to bring from the great Fountain of Truth, things both new and old. It is not all old, nor all new that we should seek to set before the people, but we certainly ought to be able each year to present enough interesting thought to make the preaching services edifying to the public. Though we may tell the same old story, yet we can, by proper efforts, add still more Scriptural information, so as to thus strengthen the knowledge as well as the faith of our members.

WE beg to call attention to the Sunday-school *Quarterlies* for the closing quarter of this year. The lessons are still in the Acts, and afford the most interesting line of study the Sunday-schools have enjoyed for some time. We prepare lessons for both the advanced and juvenile grades, and it affords us great pleasure to know that our efforts in this direction are greatly appreciated by our Sunday-school workers. With our people these schools have come to stay, and it will be wisdom in us to make the very best possible use of them. It is to be hoped that many of them will be kept up during the winter, even if the attendance happens to be small. Studying the Scriptures the year round will be found a great advantage to any community. Schools using our *Quarterlies* will do well to order early, as we are now prepared to fill all orders. In localities where the schools are not kept up, it would be advisable to continue the *Quarterlies* and study them at home, rather than miss any part of the regular course of study.

QUERISTS' DEPARTMENT.

Is it against the rules of the church to hold a union Sunday-school, in a Brethren's meeting-house, providing the Brethren have not strength to manage one? And what should the church do in case one member should refuse to submit?　　　　　　　　　　　　　　G. M. LAUVER.

It is advisable that our Brethren fully control the Sunday-schools in their own houses, and furnish the literature for the same. Occasionally, when the membership is too weak to conduct a properly-equipped school, it may be necessary to unite with others, but it should be with the distinct understanding that the school will not be required or encouraged to participate or indulge in the popular amusements and other things so distasteful to our Brethren. This is one of the situations in life when we should be as wise as serpents and as harmless as doves. In new fields we have had more or less experience in union Sunday-school work and know that it may sometimes be necessary. We hardly know just what to say in regard to a faithful, earnest brother who refuses to submit to an arrangement of the kind referred to. Were we in that brother's place we would enter that Sunday-school with all the energy and ability we could command; we would take charge of a class, if wanted, would talk to other members, urge them to take a class, and in that way demonstrate to the doubting one that a very weak church, by the help of God, and the united efforts of a few earnest members, can run a Brethren's Sunday-school. If we could not do that, then we would say to the Brethren, "Do the best you can, and we will stand by you and help you all we are able."

Where is the Ark of the Covenant containing the two tables of stone, Aaron's rod, and the pot of manna? Will it ever be found, or seen again?　　　A. NELSON GRAYBILL.

The Ark of the Covenant was placed in the new Temple when completed by Solomon. Dr. Schaff says, "It was probably burnt up in the destruction of Jerusalem by Nebuchadnezzar," for he burned the Temple after removing a part of the furniture and it seems that the Ark was not removed. If not burned, it was probably carried to Babylon, where it was utterly destroyed with that city, which is now, and long has been, in a complete state of ruin.

Please give me an explanation on Luke 10:36. Who is our neighbor? Some say Christ. Others say it is our nearest neighbor.　　　　　　　　　　　　　A. C. N.

In the lesson referred to, a lawyer, in order to entrap the Savior, asked what he must do to inherit eternal life. Jesus asked him to quote the law, which he did, saying, "Thou shalt love the Lord thy God with all thy heart, and with all thy soul, and with all thy strength, and with all thy mind; and thy neighbor as thyself." Jesus told him to do that and he should live. The lawyer, to justify himself, and to farther puzzle the Savior says, "And who is my neighbor?" To answer him Jesus narrates a little circumstance, of a man going from Jerusalem to Jericho, who fell among thieves, was robbed, beaten, and left half dead. A priest and Levite passed by the unfortunate man and offered no assistance, but a despised Samaritan, who chanced to pass that way, had pity on him and administered to his wants. The Savior now asks the lawyer, "Which now of these three, thinkest thou was neighbor unto him that fell among the thieves?" The illustration was so clear that the lawyer was compelled to say, "He that showed mercy on him" was the neighbor. The lesson to be learned here is this: The

one who does us good is our neighbor, whether he lives near by or far away. The day before writing this we witnessed a clear illustration of the thought of the Savior. A man's children were out riding in a spring-wagon. When some five miles from home the horse became frightened, ran into a fence, breaking the wagon and damaging the horse. A brother living near by, extricated the horse from the wire fence, placed things in as good shape as possible, hitched up to his own comfortable carriage, and kindly took the children and horse to their home. That brother was a very close neighbor, though he lived five miles away. This is the doctrine the Savior labored to impress upon the mind of the lawyer. Doing good, and showing mercy to the unfortunate, regardless of where they live, is the neighborly principle so clearly and forcibly set forth in the Gospel.

A friend wishes an explanation as to why we dip three times face forward when baptizing? Is it Gospel, and where do we find it?　　　　　　　　　　　JOSEPH MATCHETT.

Just before the Savior took his departure from the world, he gave his disciples this instruction in regard to the manner of baptizing: "Go ye therefore and teach all nations, baptizing them in the name of the Father, and of the Son, and of the Holy Ghost." Matt 28:19. This is the only instance in the New Testament where the exact manner of performing baptism is described, though it is frequently referred to in other parts of the Scriptures. One place it is called a burial, showing that it is immersion. At another place it is called "one baptism," thus demonstrating that there was but one way of performing the sacred rite in the times of the apostles. The expression, "Baptizing them in the name of the Father, and of the Son, and of the Holy Ghost," is called the baptismal formula, and means the same as saying, "Baptizing them in the name of the Father, and baptizing them in the name of the Son, and baptizing them in the name of the Holy Ghost." A similar expression will be found in Luke 23:38, where it says that the superscription placed on the cross over Jesus "was written over him in letters of Greek, and Latin, and Hebrew," meaning, of course, that the superscription was "written in Greek, and written in Latin, and written in Hebrew." It required three actions to write in the three languages, and it, in like manner, requires three actions to baptize a person into the three names mentioned in the formula. There are three persons in the Trinity, viz, Father, Son, and Holy Ghost. These three names are also found in the baptismal formula. To correspond with these we have the three actions in baptism. The three persons in the Trinity are called one. In like manner the three actions in baptism are called one baptism. Furthermore, single immersion was not invented till more than 300 years after the death of Christ. It was first introduced by a heretic named Eunomius. Baptism, being an act of obedience, should be performed by a forward action, for all acts of obedience are thus performed. Backward baptism is not yet 400 years old, having been introduced about the time of the Reformation. Our Brethren practice the threefold immersion because we regard that as the only mode taught in the Scriptures, and the only mode old enough to extend anything like near the apostolic age. Not wishing to use much space just now on this subject, we only add that John Wesley always preferred to use trine immersion, believing that to have been the apostolic method

of baptizing. Luther recommended the same mode. Dr. Wall, the great Pedobaptist historian, says, "The way of trine immersion, or plunging the head of the person three times into the water, was the general practice of all antiquity." Chrysostom, the most eminent Greek Christian scholar of antiquity, affirms, that "Christ delivered to his disciples one baptism in three immersions of the body, when he said to them, 'Go teach all nations, baptizing them in the name of the Father, and of the Son, and of the Holy Ghost.'" For further information on the apostolic method of baptizing, we refer you to Quinter's excellent work on "Trine Immersion," and "The Doctrine of the Brethren Defended," by R. H. Miller. Both of these works discuss the question in a very able manner.　　　　　　　　J. H. M.

A REMARKABLE DISCOVERY.

The _Christian Advocate_ says that a remarkable discovery has been made by Mr. F. J. Bliss, son of President Bliss, of the American Protestant College, at Beirut, of an actual letter of historical value, on a clay tablet, and in the Babylonian language and writing. It is 700 years older than the Moabite stone, and is the first discovery in Palestine of a written record which goes back of the time of David or even of Moses. Mr. Bliss discovered it while working under the direction of the English Palestine Exploration Fund, and it was found in a mound which represents the old city of Lachish, or perhaps the old city of Gath. It gives us a little glimpse of the disturbed condition of things in Palestine while the children of Israel were in bondage in Egypt, and it contains mention of a Zimrida, governor of Lachish, of whom we already had knowledge from the remarkable collection of tablets, also in the Babylonian writing, found four years ago at Telel-Amarna, in Egypt. The significance of this fragment can hardly be estimated, showing, as it does, that the Babylonian language and civilization had been known in Palestine long before the exodus, and it was not the Nile, but the Euphrates that gave its culture first to Syria and Phenicia.

"Blessed are the peace-makers," says Jesus. Kind words are peace-makers the world over. The thought is so beautifully expressed in the following lines:

> "One day a harsh word, rashly said,
>　Upon an evil journey sped,
> And like a sharp and cruel dart
>　It pierced a fond and loving heart,
>　It turned a friend into a foe,
>　And everywhere brought pain and woe.
>
> A kind word followed it one day,
>　Flew swiftl on its blessed way,
>　It healed the wound, it soothed the pain,
>　And friends of old were friends again;
>　It made the hate and anger cease,
>　And every-where brought joy and peace.

We are again requested to publish a recipe for making unfermented wine. Here it is. The process is so simple that anyone can understand it. Press the juice from clean, ripe grapes in any manner desired, either by heating or otherwise. Then strain, heat, and can the same as fruit. Care for it the same as regular canned fruit. Some cook the grapes a little before pressing out the juice; others do not. Either way will do. Wine, put up and properly cared for in this manner, will keep for years. It is the very thing for sacramental purposes, being the real, unadulterated "fruit of the vine," recommended by the Savior,

QUERISTS' DEPARTMENT.

Is it against the rules of the church to hold a union Sunday-school, in a Brethren's meeting-house, providing the Brethren have not strength to manage one? And what should the church do in case one member should refuse to submit?   G. M. LAUVER.

IT is advisable that our Brethren fully control the Sunday-schools in their own houses, and furnish the literature for the same. Occasionally, when the membership is too weak to conduct a properly-equipped school, it may be necessary to unite with others, but it should be with the distinct understanding that the school will not be required or encouraged to participate or indulge in the popular amusements and other things so distasteful to our Brethren. This is one of the situations in life when we should be as wise as serpents and as harmless as doves. In new fields we have had more or less experience in union Sunday-school work and know that it may sometimes be necessary. We hardly know just what to say in regard to a faithful, earnest brother who refuses to submit to an arrangement of the kind referred to. Were we in that brother's place we would enter that Sunday-school with all the energy and ability we could command; we would take charge of a class, if wanted, would talk to other members, urge them to take a class, and in that way demonstrate to the doubting one that a very weak church, by the help of God, and the united efforts of a few earnest members, can run a Brethren's Sunday-school. If we could not do that, then we would say to the Brethren, "Do the best you can, and we will stand by you and help you all we are able."

Where is the Ark of the Covenant containing the two tables of stone, Aaron's rod, and the pot of manna? Will it ever be found, or seen again?   A. NELSON GRAYBILL.

The Ark of the Covenant was placed in the new Temple when completed by Solomon. Dr. Schaff says, "It was probably burnt up in the destruction of Jerusalem by Nebuchadnezzar," for he burned the Temple after removing a part of the furniture and it seems that the Ark was not removed. If not burned, it was probably carried to Babylon, where it was utterly destroyed with that city, which is now, and long has been, in a complete state of ruin.

Please give me an explanation on Luke 10: 36. Who is our neighbor? Some say Christ. Others say it is our nearest neighbor.   A. C. N.

In the lesson referred to, a lawyer, in order to entrap the Savior, asked what he must do to inherit eternal life. Jesus asked him to quote the law, which he did, saying, "Thou shalt love the Lord thy God with all thy heart, and with all thy soul, and with all thy strength, and with all thy mind; and thy neighbor as thyself." Jesus told him to do that and he should live. The lawyer, to justify himself, and to farther puzzle the Savior says, "And who is my neighbor?" To answer him Jesus narrates a little circumstance, of a man going from Jerusalem to Jericho, who fell among thieves, was robbed, beaten, and left half dead. A priest and Levite passed by the unfortunate man and offered no assistance, but a despised Samaritan, who chanced to pass that way, had pity on him and administered to his wants. The Savior now asks the lawyer, "Which now of these three, thinkest thou was neighbor unto him that fell among the thieves?" The illustration was so clear that the lawyer was compelled to say, "He that showed mercy on him" was the neighbor. The lesson to be learned here is this: The

one who does us good is our neighbor, whether he lives near by or far away. The day before writing this we witnessed a clear illustration of the thought of the Savior. A man's children were out riding in a spring-wagon. When some five miles from home the horse became frightened, ran into a fence, breaking the wagon and damaging the horse. A brother living near by, extricated the horse from the wire fence, placed things in as good shape as possible, hitched up to his own comfortable carriage, and kindly took the children and horse to their home. That brother was a very close neighbor, though he lived five miles away. This is the doctrine the Savior labored to impress upon the mind of the lawyer. Doing good, and showing mercy to the unfortunate, regardless of where they live, is the neighborly principle so clearly and forcibly set forth in the Gospel.

A friend wishes an explanation as to why we dip three times face forward when baptizing? Is it Gospel, and where do we find it?   JOSEPH MATCHETT.

Just before the Savior took his departure from the world, he gave his disciples this instruction in regard to the manner of baptizing: "Go ye therefore and teach all nations, baptizing them in the name of the Father, and of the Son, and of the Holy Ghost." Matt 28: 19. This is the only instance in the New Testament where the exact manner of performing baptism is described, though it is frequently referred to in other parts of the Scriptures. One place it is called a burial, showing that it is immersion. At another place it is called "one baptism," thus demonstrating that there was but one way of performing the sacred rite in the times of the apostles. The expression, "Baptizing them in the name of the Father, and of the Son, and of the Holy Ghost," is called the baptismal formula, and means the same as saying, "Baptizing them in the name of the Father, and baptizing them in the name of the Son, and baptizing them in the name of the Holy Ghost." A similar expression will be found in Luke 23: 38, where it says that the superscription placed on the cross over Jesus "was written over him in letters of Greek, and Latin, and Hebrew," meaning, of course, that the superscription was "written in Greek, and written in Latin, and written in Hebrew." It required three actions to write in the three languages, and it, in like manner, requires three actions to baptize a person into the three names mentioned in the formula. There are three persons in the Trinity, viz , Father, Son, and Holy Ghost. These three names are also found in the baptismal formula. To correspond with these we have the three actions in baptism. The three persons in the Trinity are called one. In like manner the three actions in baptism are called one baptism. Furthermore, single immersion was not invented till more than 300 years after the death of Christ. It was first introduced by a heretic named Eunomius. Baptism, being an act of obedience, should be performed by a forward action, for all acts of obedience are thus performed. Backward baptism is not yet 400 years old, having been introduced about the time of the Reformation. Our Brethren practice the threefold immersion because we regard that as the only mode taught in the Scriptures, and the only mode old enough to extend anything like near the apostolic age. Not wishing to use much space just now on this subject, we only add that John Wesley always preferred to use trine immersion, believing that to have been the apostolic method

of baptizing. Luther recommended the same mode. Dr. Wall, the great Pedobaptist historian, says, "The way of trine immersion, or plunging the head of the person three times into the water, was the general practice of all antiquity." Chrysostom, the most eminent Greek Christian scholar of antiquity, affirms, that "Christ delivered to his disciples one baptism in three immersions of the body, when he said to them, 'Go teach all nations, baptizing them in the name of the Father, and of the Son, and of the Holy Ghost.' " For further information on the apostolic method of baptizing, we refer you to Quinter's excellent work on "Trine Immersion," and "The Doctrine of the Brethren Defended," by R. H. Miller. Both of these works discuss the question in a very able manner.   J. H. M.

A REMARKABLE DISCOVERY.

THE Christian Advocate says that a remarkable discovery has been made by Mr. F. J. Bliss, son of President Bliss, of the American Protestant College, at Beirut, of an actual letter of historical value, on a clay tablet, and in the Babylonian language and writing. It is 700 years older than the Moabite stone, and is the first discovery in Palestine of a written record which goes back of the time of David or even of Moses. Mr. Bliss discovered it while working under the direction of the English Palestine Exploration Fund, and it was found in a mound which represents the old city of Lachish, or perhaps the old city of Gath. It gives us a little glimpse of the disturbed condition of things in Palestine while the children of Israel were in bondage in Egypt, and it contains mention of a Zimrida, governor of Lachish, of whom we already had knowledge from the remarkable collection of tablets, dug up in the Babylonian writing, found four years ago at Tel-el-Amarna, in Egypt. The significance of this fragment can hardly be estimated, showing, as it does, that the Babylonian language and civilization had been known in Palestine long before the exodus, and not the Nile, but the Euphrates that gave its culture first to Syria and Phenicia.

"BLESSED are the peace-makers," says Jesus. Kind words are peace-makers the world over. The thought is so beautifully expressed in the following lines:

"One day a harsh word, rashly said,
Upon an evil journey sped,
And like a sharp and cruel dart
It pierced a fond and loving heart,
It turned a friend into a foe,
And everywhere brought pain and woe.

A kind word followed it one day,
Flew swift on its blessed way,
It healed the wound, it soothed the pain,
And friends of old were friends again;
It made the hate and anger cease,
And every-where brought joy and peace.

WE are again requested to publish a recipe for making unfermented wine. Here it is. The process is so simple that anyone can understand it. Press the juice from clean, ripe grapes in any manner desired, either by heating or otherwise. Then strain, heat, and can the same as fruit. Care for it the same as regular canned fruit. Some cook the grapes a little before pressing out the juice; others do not. Either way will do. Wine, put up and properly cared for in this manner, will keep for years. It is the very thing for sacramental purposes, being the real, unadulterated "fruit of the vine," recommended by the Savior,

working order. After Sunday-school we had a children's meeting. In the evening we addressed a fair audience. The prospects for building up a church here are quite encouraging. Since we were there last, four weeks ago, one more member has moved in, making five since last spring. The meetings are well attended, with marked interest. In our judgment, Brethren, looking for cheap homes, would do well here, it being a comparatively new country, and cheap homes can still be had. This is also a good fruit country. Fruit of all kinds is plenty this year. We saw an apple orchard, seven years old, loaded with the most perfect apples we ever saw; plum and peach trees are breaking down under their load.

The members here show a zeal in spiritual things that is very commendable. If all our members would give as liberally as this little band does, according to their means, there would be great abundance. They have desired that members, in harmony with the general usages of the church, locate there and help build up the good cause. For particulars address, Israel Fisher, Custer, Mason Co., Mich.   I. F. RAIRIGH.

From Beaver Dam, Md.

TO-DAY has been a day of rejoicing to the members of the Beaver Dam, Md., congregation. We had our church council after our annual visit. All were found to be in love and union; and the few matters of church business that came up were disposed of peacefully, and to the best interests of all. It was the largest and best-attended council-meeting we have had, since the building of our new meeting-house, ten years ago. All the brethren and sisters seemed to take an interest in what was done. I make it a point to attend all the church councils and this was the best council I ever attended.

Our love-feast is appointed for Oct. 8, at 10 A. M. To-day, after the meeting was over, we went down to the banks of the Beaver Dam, where two young people, a man and his wife, were baptized. What a noble decision we make when we decide to serve the Lord! These young people, in commencing a home life for themselves, could do nothing better than to bring Jesus into that home and their hearts. He will never fail them.

A few weeks ago an old man, eighty-seven years old, who had been a member of another denomination since his childhood, was not satisfied with his condition but came and asked to be baptized into the church. Amidst the rejoicing of the members he was received. So we are prospering and gradually increasing. After the division, twelve years ago, with but two deacons as officials, we started to build up a church. There was nothing behind us but faction and ruin, there was nothing before us but the help of Christ. Now we have three ministers in the second degree, five deacons and over one hundred members. This we never could have done but for the fact that Jesus Christ has never failed us. Dear brethren and sisters, pray for your brethren and sisters at Beaver Dam. They need your prayers that they may stand firm, and endure unto the end.

In this evening's hour, my mind reverts to a scene eighteen years ago, on the banks of the little stream that runs by the Rock River meeting-house in Illinois. It was the scene of my baptism. How glad I was that beautiful Sabbath morning! That was long years ago, and to-night I am far away from the little stream by the meeting-house. In that time I have made many mistakes and many failures. There is one truth that stands out clearly before me, and to which I can testify with the absolute knowledge that comes from experience,—Jesus Christ has never failed me.

     GEO. K. SAPPINGTON.

From Lost Nation, Iowa.

A SHORT time ago Bro. Collin Rowland and I concluded to visit the church at Lost Nation, Clinton County, Iowa. We held two meetings in a union house in the town of Lost Nation on Saturday evening, and Sunday at 2: 30 P. M. There was a fair attendance and good interest. We visited two families,—one living in, and the other near the above-named town, and when homeward bound, spent one night with the elder, Bro. Joshua Schults, who is the only resident minister, but who is prevented by sickness from acting in his ministerial office, and looking after the interests of his scattered flock. This was once a flourishing church, but the ministers who were once active there, have gone to other fields of labor, and we conclude that this portion of God's heritage is neglected. We see nothing to hinder the cause at Lost Nation from being revived, and we sincerely hope that the Mission Board who, I believe, have the supervising of the matter, will push the work and send ministers to preach in that declining part of our Fraternity. We suggested the propriety of holding a love-feast there this fall, to revive the members and build up the cause. Some years ago from fifty to one hundred members went from Illinois to their annual feast, when the church was yet in a flourishing condition. If the Mission Board of the Middle District of Iowa will arrange for a love-feast this fall, I believe a number of the Brethren from Illinois, will agree to be represented there.   GEORGE D. ZOLLERS.

Mt. Carroll, Ill.

Ministerial Meeting of North-western Ohio.

THE following is the program of the Brethren's Ministerial Meeting of the North-western District of Ohio, to be held in the Sugar Ridge church, Hancock County, Ohio, Oct. 5th and 6th, 1892.

1. "The Church, its Mission and Relation to its Ministers."—James McMullen; B. F. Sholty, Alternate.

2. "How Can we Best Succeed in Planting the Doctrine of the Bible in our Children?"—S. M. Loose; Christian Krabill, Alternate.

3. "The Bible Class, and Prayer-Meeting,— How to Conduct Them."—J. W. Chambers; D. D. Thomas, Alternate.

4. "Ministerial Habits,—in his Association, in the Church and in the Stand."—L. H. Dickey; Jacob Kintner, Alternate.

5. "How Can We Have the Order of the General Brotherhood, in Reference to Uniformity of Dress, more Generally Observed in our Churches?"— David Lytle; Adam Beelman, Alternate.

6. "How shall we Educate our Brethren that They may Become more Interested in the Missionary Work of the Church?"—George Sellers; Silas Weidman, Alternate.

7. "What will Inspire our Churches with more Earnestness and Zeal?"—Abednego Miller; John Krabill, Alternate.

8. "How can We, as Ministers, Make Our Work more Effectual and what are the Hinderances?"— Jacob Driver; Jacob Heistand, Alternate.

9. "The Sermon,—its Length, how to Prepare and how to Deliver it."—J. C. Witmore; David Berkeybile, Alternate.

10. "The Right Relation of each Member to the Body—the Church,—and how to Maintain that Relation."—Samuel Driver; J. B. Light, Alternate.

11. "How can we Improve our Present Method of Sunday-School Work, so as to more fully Implant the Doctrine of the Brethren in the Minds of the Young?"—S. A. Walker; Charlie Wilkins, Alternate.

Those coming on C. H. & D. R. R. will be met at Leipsic, Oct. 4, or morning of the meeting, by notifying David Lytle, at Townwood, Ohio. Those coming from the East on the Nickle Plate R. R. will be met at McComb or Shawtown the day before the meeting, by notifying E. H. Rosenberger at McComb, Ohio. Those coming from the West, on the Nickle Plate R. R., will be met at Townwood or Shawtown the day before the meeting. For further information inquire of the above-named parties.   DAVID BYERLY.

Lima, Ohio.

Notes by the Way.

AUG. 18 wife and I started for Oak Shade, a mission point in Southern Ohio. At Hope Town we met Bro. Jonas Horning and wife, also en route for the same place. We had preaching the same evening at Hope Town. Next morning we started for a fifteen-mile drive to reach Oak Shade. In an open vehicle, amid a rain-storm, and after enduring the discomfort of traveling over a hilly road, we reached the place about noon. We had preaching the same day at 3 P. M. On Saturday morning we repaired to the water, a distance of three miles. Nearly all of us went on foot. At length we came to where there was much water. Five precious souls were baptized. One young lady came twenty miles to be baptized. May they all be shining lights in the church! In the evening we gathered around the Communion table,— the first Communion ever held in this part of Ohio. Eleven sisters and seven brethren were present. The occasion seemed to be enjoyed by all present. None of those sisters had ever seen a sister but those living there, till this visit. Oh, what joy it was to meet those of like precious faith! Sisters, go out among the isolated sometimes. You can do more good than the minister. How hard it is to get some to go! It seems as though nearly all would rather go where there are large churches and the membership large. Sometimes we could do much more good to go out among the few.

The meetings were continued till over Sunday with good interest. On the morning of the 22nd we started at an early hour for Chillicothe, fifteen miles distant, where we arrived at 6: 30 P. M. There brother and sister Horning took the train for Dayton, while wife and I went to Columbus. We arrived home safely the same evening.

Aug. 27 we commenced a series of meetings at Somerville, Ohio, another mission point of our district. Bro. John H. Brumbaugh and I met with the people at this point at the time appointed. Good interest and attention were given during the entire meetings, which closed last night with a full house. After meeting was dismissed a woman said she and her husband wished to be baptized, which was done that morning. She came over from the Methodist church, and her husband from the Disciple church. May they be faithful in their new calling!

Here, as well as elsewhere, we could have found use for other brethren and sisters to help with their presence and also in singing. We should not forget these isolated places, but favor them by our presence. At several of the meetings not one sister was present, and sometimes very few brethren, as none came to our relief except those living there. Brethren and sisters, all along the line, will you please awaken to a sense of duty, while you have time to work?

On account of asthmatic trouble, I have not enjoyed a good night's rest for ten days or more. I expect to spend eight or ten days in Northern Michigan, hoping to receive some relief at least. I spent a week at Toronto, Canada, in July, which gave me much relief for the time being. Church work called me back too soon, to get the relief so much needed. For the benefit of those concerned

working order. After Sunday-school we had a children's meeting. In the evening we addressed a fair audience. The prospects for building up a church here are quite encouraging. Since we were there last, four weeks ago, one more member has moved in, making five since last spring. The meetings are well attended, with marked interest. In our judgment, Brethren, looking for cheap homes, would do well here, it being a comparatively new country, and cheap homes can still be had. This is also a good fruit country. Fruit of all kinds is plenty this year. We saw an apple orchard, seven years old, loaded with the most perfect apples we ever saw; plum and peach trees are breaking down under their load.

The members here show a zeal in spiritual things that is very commendable. If all our members would give as liberally as this little band does, according to their means, there would be great abundance. They have desired that members, in harmony with the general usages of the church, locate there and help build up the good cause. For particulars address, Israel Fisher, Custer, Mason Co., Mich.   I. F. Raibigh.

From Beaver Dam, Md.

To-day has been a day of rejoicing to the members of the Beaver Dam, Md., congregation. We had our church council after our annual visit. All were found to be in love and union; and the few matters of church business that came up were disposed of peacefully, and to the best interests of all. It was the largest and best-attended council-meeting we have had, since the building of our new meeting-house, ten years ago. All the brethren and sisters seemed to take an interest in what was done. I make it a point to attend all the church councils and this was the best council I ever attended.

Our love-feast is appointed for Oct. 8, at 10 A. M. To-day, after the meeting was over, we went down to the banks of the Beaver Dam, where two young people, a man and his wife, were baptized. What a noble decision we make when we decide to serve the Lord! These young people, in commencing a home life for themselves, could do nothing better than to bring Jesus into that home and their hearts. He will never fail them.

A few weeks ago an old man, eighty-seven years old, who had been a member of another denomination since his childhood, was not satisfied with his condition but came and asked to be baptized into the church. Amidst the rejoicing of the members he was received. So we are prospering and gradually increasing. After the division, twelve years ago, with but two deacons as officials, we started to build up a church. There was nothing behind us but faction and ruin, there was nothing before us but the help of Christ. Now we have three ministers in the second degree, five deacons and over one hundred members. This we never could have done but for the fact that Jesus Christ has never failed us. Dear brethren and sisters, pray for your brethren and sisters at Beaver Dam. They need your prayers that they may stand firm, and endure unto the end.

In this evening's hour, my mind reverts to a scene eighteen years ago, on the banks of the little stream that runs by the Rock River meeting-house in Illinois. It was the scene of my baptism. How glad I was that beautiful Sabbath morning! That was long years ago, and to-night I am far away from the little stream by the meeting-house. In that time I have made many mistakes and many failures. There is one truth that stands out clearly before me, and to which I can testify with the absolute knowledge that comes from experience,—Jesus Christ has never failed me.

           Geo. K. Sappington.

From Lost Nation, Iowa.

A short time ago Bro. Collin Rowland and I concluded to visit the church at Lost Nation, Clinton County, Iowa. We held two meetings in a union house in the town of Lost Nation on Saturday evening, and Sunday at 2:30 P. M. There was a fair attendance and good interest. We visited two families,—one living in, and the other near the above-named town, and this homeward bound, spent one night with the elder, Bro. Joshua Schultz, who is the only resident minister, but who is prevented by sickness from acting in his ministerial office, and looking after the interests of his scattered flock. This was once a flourishing church, but the ministers who were once active there, have gone to other fields of labor, and we conclude that this portion of God's heritage is neglected. We see nothing to hinder the cause at Lost Nation from being revived, and we sincerely hope that the Mission Board who, I believe, have the supervising of the matter, will push the work and send ministers to preach in that declining part of our Fraternity. We suggested the propriety of holding a love-feast there this fall, to revive the members and build up the cause. Some years ago from fifty to one hundred members went from Illinois to their annual feast, when the church was yet in a flourishing condition. If the Mission Board of the Middle District of Iowa will arrange for a love-feast this fall, I believe a number of the Brethren from Illinois, will agree to be represented there.   George D. Zollers.

Mt. Carroll, Ill.

Ministerial Meeting of North-western Ohio.

The following is the program of the Brethren's Ministerial Meeting of the North-western District of Ohio, to be held in the Sugar Ridge church, Hancock County, Ohio, Oct. 5th and 6th, 1892.

1. "The Church, its Mission and Relation to its Ministers."—James McMullen;. B. F. Sholty, Alternate.

2. "How Can we Best Succeed in Planting the Doctrine of the Bible in our Children?"—S. M. Loose; Christian Krabill, Alternate.

3. "The Bible Class, and Prayer-Meeting, How to Conduct Them."—J. W. Chambers; D. D. Thomas, Alternate.

4. "Ministerial Habits,—in his Association, in the Church and in the Stand."—L. H. Dickey; Jacob Kintner, Alternate.

5. "How Can We Have the Order of the General Brotherhood, in Reference to Uniformity of Dress, more Generally Observed in our Churches?"—David Lytle; Adam Beelman, Alternate.

6. "How shall we Educate our Brethren that They may Become more Interested in the Missionary Work of the Church?"—George Sellers; Silas Weidman, Alternate.

7. "What will Inspire our Churches with more Earnestness and Zeal?"—Abednego Miller; John Krabill, Alternate.

8. "How can We, as Ministers, Make Our Work more Effectual and what are the Hinderances?"—Jacob Driver; Jacob Heistand, Alternate.

9. "The Sermon,—its Length, how to Prepare and how to Deliver it."—J. C. Witmore; David Berkeyhile, Alternate.

10. "The Right Relation of each Member to the Body—the Church,—and how to Maintain that Relation."—Samuel Driver; J. B. Light, Alternate.

11. "How can we Improve our Present Method of Sunday-School Work, so as to more fully Implant the Doctrine of the Brethren in the Minds of the Young?"—S. A. Walker; Charlie Wilkins, Alternate.

Those coming on C. H. & D. R. R. will be met at Leipsic, Oct. 4, or morning of the meeting, by notifying David Lytle, at Townwood, Ohio. Those coming from the East on the Nickle Plate R. R. will be met at McComb or Shawtown the day before the meeting, by notifying E. H. Rosenberger at McComb, Ohio. Those coming from the West, on the Nickle Plate R. R., will be met at Townwood or Shawtown the day before the meeting. For further information inquire of the above-named parties.   David Byerly.

Lima, Ohio.

Notes by the Way.

Aug. 18 wife and I started for Oak Shade, a mission point in Southern Ohio. At Hope Town we met Bro. Jonas Horning and wife, also en route for the same place. We had preaching the same evening at Hope Town. Next morning we started for a fifteen-mile drive to reach Oak Shade. In an open vehicle, amid a rain-storm, and after enduring the discomfort of traveling over a hilly road, we reached the place about noon. We had preaching the same day at 3 P. M. On Saturday morning we repaired to the water, a distance of three miles. Nearly all of us went on foot. At length we came to where there was much water. Five precious souls were baptized. One young lady came twenty miles to be baptized. May they all be shining lights in the church! In the evening we gathered around the Communion table,—the first Communion ever held in this part of Ohio. Eleven sisters and seven brethren were present. The occasion seemed to be enjoyed by all present. None of those sisters had ever seen a sister but those living there, till this visit. Oh, what joy it was to meet those of like precious faith! Sisters, go out among the isolated sometimes. You can do more good than the minister. How hard it is to get some to go! It seems as though nearly all would rather go where there are large churches and the membership large. Sometimes we could do much more good to go out among the few.

The meetings were continued till over Sunday with good interest. On the morning of the 22nd we started at an early hour for Chillicothe, fifteen miles distant, where we arrived at 6:30 P. M. There brother and sister Horning took the train for Dayton, while wife and I went to Columbus. We arrived home safely the same evening.

Aug. 27 we commenced a series of meetings at Somerville, Ohio, another mission point of our district. Bro. John H. Brumbaugh and I met with the people at this point at the time appointed. Good interest and attention were given during the entire meetings, which closed last night with a full house. After meeting was dismissed a woman said she and her husband wished to be baptized, which was done that morning. She came over from the Methodist church, and her husband from the Disciple church. May they be faithful in their new calling!

Here, as well as elsewhere, we could have found use for other brethren and sisters to help with their presence and also in singing. We should not forget these isolated places, but favor them by our presence. At several of the meetings not one sister was present, and sometimes very few brethren, as none came to our relief except those living there. Brethren and sisters, all along the line, will you please awaken to a sense of duty, while you have time to work?

On account of asthmatic trouble, I have not enjoyed a good night's rest for ten days or more. I expect to spend eight or ten days in Northern Michigan, hoping to receive some relief at least. I spent a week at Toronto, Canada, in July, which gave me much relief for the time being. Church work called me back too soon, to get the relief so much needed. For the benefit of those concerned

Green Mount, Va.—Our feast at Green Mount was a pleasant occasion, and a large number of brethren and sisters assembled. Our large house was filled, so much so that some could not be seated around the tables. The ministerial force from adjoining churches was sufficient to make the meeting a feast to the soul. Four were added to this church by baptism during the past few weeks.—*Jacob A. Garber.*

Roann, Ind.—We, the members of the Roann church, met in quarterly council Sept. 3. What little business came before the meeting was disposed of in harmony. We were made glad to see Bro. Noah Fisher, of Mexico, Ind., step in. He assisted us very kindly in the work of the meeting. The spirit of liberal giving was nobly manifested among the saints. The church treasury was replenished. The mission work received its share, and the poor were remembered, etc. We met again the same day at 2:30 P. M., for a harvest-meeting. Bro. Noah Fisher gave us a very impressive talk on the occasion from Deut. 15:10. Two more,—man and wife,—were baptized since my last report.—*Joseph John, Sept. 5.*

Goshen, Ind.—Sept. 3 I met with the Brethren of the Berrien church, Mich., in a church-council. I had not met with this body of members for nine months, on account of my wife's illness. As her health has now improved, I was pleased to meet there in church work. I had the pleasure of meeting Bro. Thurston Miller at their meeting. At that council I offered my resignation, which was accepted, and Bro. Thurston Miller appointed instead. I see that in Southern Michigan and in Northern Indiana the apple crop is almost an entire failure. The wet weather in the spring has caused less fruit than for many years. Although in places vegetables are very scarce, yet we have enough to live on, and should praise the Lord.—*J. H. Miller, Goshen, Ind., Sept 12.*

Pipe Creek Church, Md.—To-day, Sept. 1, was our quarterly council. All business was disposed of pleasantly. We are sorry to report that one was disowned. The church decided to hold a children's meeting Sept. 25. This, so far as our knowledge goes, will be the first meeting of this kind in Eastern Maryland. We trust it will not be the last. What better thing can we do than to thus express our interest in behalf of the children,—prove to them that their efforts are appreciated? Neglect the children and we neglect the church. Let every effort be put forth to save the young people and thus perpetuate the church. Sept. 28, we expect Bro. Geo. S. Arnold, of West Virginia, to be with us, to commence a series of meetings. Brethren, do we want this meeting to be a success? If so, let each member bear in mind the fact that he, or she, is individually responsible. Work and pray.—*W. M. Lyon, Union Bridge, Md.*

Matrimonial.

" What therefore God hath joined together, let not man put asunder."

LONG—HOWELL.—Near Panora, Iowa, Aug. 28, 1892, by Bro. Moses Dierdorff, Bro. Clarence Long and sister Ella Howell, both of Coon River congregation.

J. D. HAUGHTELIN.

CARVER—BOWMAN.—At the residence of Bro. Noah and sister A. Bowman, Bro. Y. C. Carver, formerly of Kentucky, and sister Sarah H. Bowman, of Texas.

A. W. AUSTIN.

MUIR—MOHERMAN.—At the residence of Father Moherman, in the Ashland church, Ashland County, Ohio, by the undersigned, Aug 24, 1892, Bro. F. G. Muir, of McPherson College, Kans., and sister Amanda Moherman.

I. D. PARKER.

Fallen Asleep.

" Blessed are the dead which die in the Lord."

WEAVER.—In the Rock Run church, Elkhart County, Ind., of paralysis, Bro. Levi H. Weaver, aged 67 years, 5 months and 11 days. Bro. Weaver was born in Lancaster County, Pa., and moved with his parents to Wayne County, Ohio, when a boy seven years old. He united with the church about the year 1854, and was elected to the deacon's office soon after his conversion. About the year 1859 he was elected to the ministry, and was soon advanced to the second degree. He remained a faithful minister until his death. In 1865 he, with his family, moved to Elkhart County, Ind. Bro. Weaver in his daily walk did his loudest preaching. He was a safe counselor, and could be regarded as a true Christian worker. He leaves a wife and six children to mourn their loss. The church has lost a good, faithful worker. Peace to his ashes! J. H. MILLER.

BARNCORD.—In the Broadfording congregation, Md., Aug. 25, of consumption, sister Sallie Barncord, beloved wife of Bro. Jacob Barncord, aged 39 years, 8 months and some days. She was a member of the church for twelve years. She leaves a family of five children, three having preceded her to the heavenly land. Services by Bro. S. Foltz.

ANNIE HOLLINGER.

FIFER.—In the Wacandah church, Ray County, Mo., Aug. 28, 1892, little Bertha, only child of Bro. Frank and sister Anna Fifer, aged 8 months and 6 days. Funeral services by the Brethren. J. H. SHIRRY.

CROCKETT.—In the bounds of the Lebanon congregation, Linn County, Oregon, June 6, 1892 Sina N Crockett, wife of Bro. John Crockett, aged 26 years and 10 months. She leaves a husband and two children. Funeral services by M. M. Norton, assisted by J. B. Fitewaters

M. M. BASHOR.

NEWCOMER.—In the Dorrance church, Russell County, Kans., July 26, 1892, Eld. John Newcomer, aged 70 years, 6 months and 19 days. Funeral services by Bro. John Hollinger. Deceased had been ailing for several years with chronic dysentery, but was confined to his bed only about eight or ten days. JACOB HARMISH.

SANDERS.—July 23, 1892, Pearile, second daughter of Mrs. Arminta Sanders, aged 18 years and 28 days. Funeral services conducted by Eld. D. F. Hoover, at the Old church, two miles east of Middletown, where interment took place.

J. L. HOOVER.

MATHEWS.—Aug. 19, 1892, Bessie Virginia, daughter of friend Jacob and sister Mattie Mathews, aged 3 months and 1 day. Funeral service at Bethel by Eld. D. F. Hoover.

J. L. HOOVER.

NICHOLS.—Aug. 20, 1892, Bro. George Nichols, son of John and sister Martha Nichols, aged 35 years, 3 months and 6 days. He was married Sept. 11, 1878, to Ida L. Hill. Unto them were born six children. Bro. George united with the church when very young, and remained a faithful member until death. Funeral services at the Brethren church two miles east of Middletown, by Eld. D. F. Hoover, followed by interment in the cemetery adjoining. J. L. HOOVER.

SNYDER.—In the Jacob's Creek congregation, Pa., Jan. 30, 1892, Bro. David G. Snyder, aged 85 years, 7 months and 24 days. He was the oldest member of his congregation, and could remember of attending the Brethren's meetings in this congregation eighty years ago. The funeral service was held at the Mt. Joy church, Aug. 28, 1892, by brethren Samuel Eicher and the writer. H. S. MYERS.

ETLING.—Near Pennsville, Pa., Aug 10, 1892, Mrs. Catherine Etling, aged 81 years. Services by the writer.

H. S. MYERS.

ANDERSON.—In the Walnut Level church, Wells Co., Ind., Sept. 3, 1892, infant daughter of Mr. Anderson, aged 3 months and 5 days Funeral services conducted by Bro Samuel Neher from 2 Kings 4:26, latter clause.

MALINDA S. STUDEBAKER.

HAINES—In the Clear Creek congregation, Huntington Co., Ind., Sept 4, 1892, Ora Melvin Haines, aged 2 years, 1 months and 17 days. Services by the writer.

DORSEY HODGDEN.

WIKLE.—In the Lower Deer Creek church, Carroll County, Ind., Aug. 23, 1892, Bro. Jacob Wikle, aged 67 years, 7 months and 26 days. He leaves a wife, five children, one sister, and two brothers to mourn their loss. Funeral services conducted by Bro. A. J. Flory.

S. H. BECHTELHEIMER.

WILT.—In the Monroe congregation, Mo., Aug. 27, 1892, Bro. Jacob Wilt, born Nov. 30, 1814. Deceased leaves a family of five sons and five daughters, and a faithful sister to mourn their loss. Bro. Wilt was a consistent brother and a faithful deacon, always at his post, ready to perform his duty. Funeral services by John Tucker and the writer from 1 Cor. 15:19. CHRISTIAN LAPP.

THOMAS—In Markleysburg, Pa., Aug. 8, 1892, Michael C. Thomas, aged 55 years, 10 months and 20 Funeral services by Eld. John H. Myers and Bro. Samuel Umbell.

LINF.—At the same place, Aug. 15, 1892, Eltra Linf, 39 years, 7 months and 19 days. Funeral services by John H. Myers from Job 14:14.

FISHER.—At the same place, Aug. 15, 1892, Gracie len Fisher, aged 10 months and 25 days. Funeral serv by Eld. John H. Myers from 2 Sam. 12:23.

MARSHAL N. THOMAS

BALSBAUGH.—Aug. 11, 1892, Sarah, consort of John C. Balsbaugh. Her virgin name was Longenecker Her father was my mother's brother. Her maternal grandmother was my paternal grandfather's sister. She was born Aug. 13, 1824, and was a member of the Brotherhood 35 years. Her children numbered seven, three preceding to the spirit realm. Four followed her to the tomb with many tears. The bereaved husband mourns deeply but hopefully, expecting soon to rejoin her. The text for the occasion was John 14:1, 2, commented on by elders William Hertzler and David Bitter. Christ, the Picture of God, faith, the impulsive function, holiness, the condition of fellowship, and heaven, the grand, eternal fruition, were the themes considered.

C. H. BALSBAUGH.

BAUM.—In the Ashland church, Ohio, Aug. 31, 1892, Jacob Baum, aged 82 years, 9 months and 17 days. Deceased was born in Lancaster County, Pa., Nov. 14, 1809. He was a faithful member of the church for 33 years. He had eight sons and one daughter. Sister Baum and two sons preceded him to the spirit world. By strict adherence to the laws of God, he lived both long and well. Funeral at the Maumee church. Services by the writer and Eld. William Murray from Zech. 14:7, latter clause. I. D. PARKER

MYERS.—At the home of her daughter, Fannie E. Brumbaugh, of Grafton, Huntingdon Co., Pa., April 12, 1892, sister Elizabeth Myers, aged 90 years, 3 months and 12 days. Deceased was the widowed wife of Samuel Myers (deceased) of Furgeson's Valley, near McVeytown, Mifflin Co., Pa., where they lived for a long time, and raised a large and respectable family of ten children, six sons and four daughters. The surviving daughters are Susan Cochrane, of Kansas, and Fannie E., wife of Eld. Geo. Brumbaugh, of Grafton, Pa., with whom grandmother chose to make her last home on earth for a period of eight years, which turned out to be a scene of almost constant suffering and distress, owing to a cancerous affection of the head and throat. Through all these years of suffering she stood firm in the faith of the Christian religion, being a devoted member of the Brethren church for the greater part of her life. Previous to her death she expressed that after that event her body be taken back to the old home cemetery for interment, and in accordance with this request she was taken and laid by the side of her husband on the hill, back of the McVeytown church, near the old homestead. Funeral services were conducted by Eld. Geo. Swigart and Abraham Myers, of the home church. GEO. BRUMBAUGH.

SMITH.—In the Vermillion church, Kansas, of cholera infantum, Fanny Alberta, youngest child of Bro. James R. and sister Ladosa Smith. Funeral services by the brethren from 1 Thess. 14:14. A. Z. GATES

The Gospel Messenger

Is the recognized organ of the German Baptist or Brethren's church, and advocates the form of doctrine taught in the New Testament and pleads for a return to apostolic and primitive Christianity.

It recognizes the New Testament as the only infallible rule of faith and practice, and maintains that Faith toward God, Repentance from dead works, Regeneration of the heart and mind, baptism by Trine Immersion for remission of sins unto the reception of the Holy Ghost by the laying on of hands, are the means of adoption into the household of God,—the church militant.

It also maintains that Feet-washing, as taught in John 13, both by example and command of Jesus, should be observed in the church.

That the Lord's Supper, instituted by Christ and as universally observed by the apostles and the early Christians, is a full meal, and in connection with the Communion, should be taken in the evening or after the close of the day.

That the Salutation of the Holy Kiss, or Kiss of Charity, is binding upon the followers of Christ.

That War and Retaliation are contrary to the spirit and self-denied principles of the religion of Jesus Christ.

That the principle of Plain Dressing and of Non-conformity to the world, as taught in the New Testament, should be observed by the followers of Christ.

That the Scriptural duty of Anointing the Sick with Oil. In the Name of the Lord, James 5:14, is binding upon all Christians.

It also advocates the church's duty to support Missionary and Tract Work, thus giving to the Lord for the spread of the Gospel and for the conversion of sinners.

In short, it is a vindicator of all that Christ and the apostles have enjoined upon us, and aims, amid the conflicting theories and discords of modern Christendom, to point out ground that all must concede to be infallibly safe.

☞ The above principles of our Fraternity are set forth on our Brethren's Envelopes." Use them! Price 15 cents per package; 40 cents per hundred.

Green Mount, Va.—Our feast at Green Mount was a pleasant occasion, and a large number of brethren and sisters assembled. Our large house was filled, so much so that some could not be seated around the tables. The ministerial force from adjoining churches was sufficient to make the meeting a feast to the soul. Four were added to this church by baptism during the past few weeks.—*Jacob A. Garber.*

Roann, Ind.—We, the members of the Roann church, met in quarterly council Sept. 3. What little business came before the meeting was disposed of in harmony. We were made glad to see Bro. Noah Fisher, of Mexico, Ind., step in. He assisted us very kindly in the work of the meeting. The spirit of liberal giving was nobly manifested among the saints. The church treasury was replenished. The mission work received its share, and the poor were remembered, etc. We met again the same day at 2:30 P. M., for a harvest-meeting. Bro. Noah Fisher gave us a very impressive talk on the occasion from Deut. 15:10. Two more,—man and wife,—were baptized since my last report.—*Joseph John, Sept. 5.*

Goshen, Ind.—Sept 3 I met with the Brethren of the Barrien church, Mich., in a church-council. I had not met with this body of members for nine months, on account of my wife's illness. As her health has now improved, I was pleased to meet there in church work. I had the pleasure of meeting Bro. Thurston Miller at their meeting. At that council I offered my resignation, which was accepted, and Bro. Thurston Miller appointed instead. I see that in Southern Michigan and in Northern Indiana the apple crop is almost an entire failure. The wet weather in the spring has caused less fruit than for many years. Although in places vegetables are very scarce, yet we have enough to live on, and should praise the Lord.—*J. H. Miller, Goshen, Ind., Sept 12.*

Pipe Creek Church, Md.—To-day, Sept. 1, was our quarterly council. All business was disposed of pleasantly. We are sorry to report that one was disowned. The church decided to hold a children's meeting Sept. 25. This, so far as our knowledge goes, will be the first meeting of this kind in Eastern Maryland. We trust it will not be the last. What better thing can we do than to thus express our interest in behalf of the children,—prove to them that their efforts are appreciated? Neglect the children and we neglect the church. Let every effort be put forth to save the young people and thus perpetuate the church. Sept. 28, we expect Bro. Geo. S. Arnold, of West Virginia, to be with us, to commence a series of meetings. Brethren, do we want this meeting to be a success? If so, let each member bear in mind the fact that he, or she, is individually responsible. Work and pray.—*W. M. Lyon, Union Bridge, Md.*

Matrimonial.

"What therefore God hath joined together, let not man put asunder."

LONG—HOWELL.—Near Panora, Iowa, Aug. 28, 1892, by Bro. Moses Dierdorff, Bro. Clarence Long and sister Ella Howell, both of Coon River congregation.

J. D. HAUGHTELIN.

CARVER—BOWMAN.—At the residence of Bro. Noah and sister A. Bowman, Bro. Y. C. Carver, formerly of Kentucky, and sister Sarah H. Bowman, of Texas.

A. W. AUSTIN.

MUIR—MOHERMAN.—At the residence of Father Moherman, in the Ashland county, Ohio, by the undersigned, Aug 24, 1892, Bro. F. G. Muir, of McPherson College, Kans., and sister Amanda Moherman.

I. D. PARKER.

Fallen Asleep.

"Blessed are the dead which die in the Lord."

WEAVER.—In the Rock Run church, Elkhart County, Ind., of paralysis, Bro. Levi H. Weaver, aged 67 years, 5 months and 11 days. Bro. Weaver was born in Lancaster County, Pa., and moved with his parents to Wayne County, Ohio, when a boy seven years old. He united with the church about the year 1851, and was elected to the deacon's office soon after his conversion. About the year 1859 he was elected to the ministry, and was soon advanced to the second degree. He remained a faithful minister until his death. In 1885 he, with his family, moved to Elkhart County, Ind. Bro. Weaver to his daily walk did his loudest preaching. He was a safe counselor, and could be regarded as a true Christian worker. He leaves a wife and six children to mourn their loss. The church has lost a good, faithful worker. Peace to his ashes!   J. H. MILLER.

BARNCORD.—In the Broadfording congregation, Md, Aug. 25, of consumption, sister Sallie Barncord, beloved wife of Bro. Jacob Barncord, aged 39 years, 8 months and some days. She was a member of the church for twelve years. She leaves a family of five children, three having preceded her to the heavenly land. Services by Bro. S. Foltz.

ANNIE HOLLINGER.

FIFER.—In the Wacandah church, Ray County, Mo., Aug. 28, 1892, little Bertha, only child of Bro. Frank and sister Anna Fifer, aged 8 months and 6 days. Funeral services by the Brethren.   J. H. SHIRKY.

CROCKETT.—In the bounds of the Lebanon congregation, Linn County, Oregon, June 6, 1892 Sina N Crockett, wife of Bro. John Crockett, aged 26 years and 10 months. She leaves a husband and two children. Funeral services by M. M. Norton, assisted by J. B. Fitzwaters.

NEWCOMER.—In the Dorrance church, Russell County, Kans., July 26, 1892, John Newcomer, aged 70 years, 6 months and 19 days Funeral services by Bro. John Hollinger. Deceased had been ailing for several years with chronic dysentery, but was confined to his bed only about eight or ten days.   JACOB HARNISH.

SANDERS.—July 23, 1892, Pearlie, second daughter of Mrs. Arminta Sanders, aged 18 years and 28 days. Funeral services conducted by Eld. D. F. Hoover, at the Old church, two miles east of Middletown, where interment took place.

J. L. HOOVER.

MATHEWS.—Aug. 19, 1892, Bessie Virginia, daughter of friend Jacob and sister Mattie Mathews, aged 3 months and 1 day. Funeral service at Bethel by Eld. D. F. Hoover.

J. L. HOOVER.

NICHOLS.—Aug. 20, 1892, Bro. George Nichols, son of John and sister Martha Nichols, aged 33 years, 3 months and 6 days. He was married Sept. 11, 1878, to Ida L. Hill. Unto them were born six children. Bro. George united with the church when very young, and remained a faithful member until death. Funeral services at the Brethren church two miles east of Middletown, by Elder D. F. Hoover, followed by interment in the cemetery adjoining.   J. L. HOOVER.

SNYDER.—In the Jacob's Creek congregation, Pa., Jan. 30, 1892, Bro. David G. Snyder, aged 86 years, 7 months and 24 days. He was the oldest member of his congregation, and could remember of attending the Brethren's meetings in this congregation eighty years ago. The funeral service was held at the Mt. Joy church, Aug. 28, 1892, by brethren Samuel Eicher and the writer.   H. S. MYERS.

ETLING.—Near Pennsville, Pa., Aug. 10, 1891, Mrs. Catherine Etling, aged 82 years. Services by the writer.

H. S. MYERS.

ANDERSON.—In the Walnut Level church, Wells Co., Ind., Sept. 3, 1892, infant daughter of Mr. Anderson, aged 3 months and 5 days Funeral services conducted by Bro Samuel Neher from 2 Kings 4:26, latter clause.

MALINDA S. STUDEBAKER.

HAINES.—In the Clear Creek congregation, Huntingdon Co., Ind., Sept 4, 1892, Ora Melvin Haines, aged 1 month and 17 days. Services by the writer.

DORSEY HODGDEN.

WIKLE.—In the Lower Deer Creek church, Carroll County, Ind., Aug. 23, 1892, Bro. Jacob Wikle, aged 67 years, 5 months and 26 days. He leaves a wife, five children, one sister, and two brothers to mourn their loss. Funeral services conducted by Bro. A. J. Flory.

S. H. BECHTELHEIMER.

WILT.—In the Monroe congregation, Mo., Aug. 27, 1892, Bro. Jacob Wilt, born Nov. 30, 1814. Deceased leaves a family of five sons and five daughters, and a faithful sister to mourn their loss. Bro. Wilt was a consistent brother and a faithful deacon, always at his post, ready to perform his duty. Funeral services by John Tucker and the Writer from 1 Cor. 15:19.   CHRISTIAN LAPP.

THOMAS—In Markleysburg, Pa., Aug. 8, 1892, Michael C. Thomas, aged 55 years, 10 months and 21 days. Funeral services by Eld. John H. Myers and Bro. Samuel Umbell.

LINT—At the same place, Aug. 15, 1892, Ellen Lint, aged 79 years, 7 months and 19 days. Funeral services by Eld. John H. Myers from Job 14:14.

FISHER—At the same place, Aug. 15, 1891, Gracie Ellen Fisher, aged 10 months and 25 days. Funeral services by Eld. John H. Myers from 2 Sam. 12:23.

MARSHAL N. THOMAS.

BALSBAUGH.—Aug. 11, 1892, Sarah, consort of Eld. John C. Balsbaugh. Her virgin name was Longenecker. Her father was my mother's brother. Her maternal grandmother was my paternal grandfather's sister. She was born Aug. 15, 1824, and was a member of the Brotherhood 35 years. Her children numbered seven, three preceding her to the spirit realm. Four followed her to the tomb within many tears. The bereaved husband mourns deeply but hopefully, expecting soon to rejoin her. The text for the occasion was John 14:1, 2, commented on by elders William Hertzler and David Etter. Christ, the Picture of God, faith, the restorative function, holiness, the condition of fellowship, and longer, the grand, eternal fruition, were the themes considered.

C. H. BALSBAUGH.

BAUM.—In the Ashland church, Ohio, Aug. 31, 1892, Jacob Baum, aged 82 years, 9 months and 17 days. Deceased was born in Lancaster County, Pa., Nov. 14, 1809. He was a faithful member of the church for 33 years. He had two sons and one daughter. Sister Baum and two sons preceded him to the spirit world. By strict adherence to the laws of God, he lived both long and well. Funeral at the Mennonite church. Services by the writer and Eld. William Metz, from Zech. 14:7, latter clause.   I. D. PARKER.

MYERS.—At the home of her daughter, Fannie E. Brumbaugh, of Grafton, Huntingdon Co., Pa., April 12, 1892, sister Elisabeth Myers, aged 90 years, 3 months and 12 days. Deceased was the widowed wife of Samuel Myers (deceased) of Furgason's Valley, near McVeytown, Mifflin Co., Pa., where they lived for a long time, and raised a large and respectable family of ten children, six sons and four daughters. The surviving daughters are Susan Cochrane, of Kansas, and Fannie E., wife of Eld. Geo. Brumbaugh, of Grafton, Pa., with whom grandmother chose to make her last home on earth for a period of eight years, which turned out to be a scene of almost constant suffering and distress, owing to a catarrhal affection of the head and throat. Through all these years suffering she stood firm in the faith of the Christian religion, being a devoted member of the Brethren church for greater part of her life. Previous to her death she expressed that after that event her body be taken back to the old home cemetery for interment, and in accordance with this request she was taken and laid by the side of her husband on the hill, back of the McVeytown church, near the old homestead Funeral services were conducted by Eld. Geo. Swigart and Abraham Myers, of the home church. GEO. BRUMBAUGH.

SMITH.—In the Vermillion church, Kansas, of cholera infantum, Fanny Alberta, youngest child of Bro. James R. and sister Ladosa Smith. Funeral services by the brethren from 1 Thess. 14:14.   A. Z. GATES.

The Gospel Messenger

Is the recognized organ of the German Baptist or Brethren's church, and advocates the form of doctrine taught in the New Testament and pleads for a return to apostolic and primitive Christianity.

It recognizes the New Testament as the only infallible rule of faith and practice, and maintains that Faith toward God, Repentance from our works, Regeneration of the heart and mind, baptism by Trine Immersion for remission of sins unto the reception of the Holy Ghost by the laying on of hands, are the means of adoption into the household of God,—the church militant.

It also maintains that Feet-washing, as taught in John 13, both by example and command of Jesus, should be observed in the church.

That the Lord's Supper, instituted by Christ and as universally observed by the apostles and the early Christians, is a full meal, and in connection with the Communion, should be taken in the evening or after the close of the day.

That the Salutation of the Holy Kiss, or Kiss of Charity, is binding upon the followers of Christ.

That War and Retaliation are contrary to the spirit and self-denying principles of the religion of Jesus Christ.

That the principle of Plain Dressing and of Non-conformity to the world, as taught in the New Testament, should be observed by the followers of Christ.

That the Scriptural duty of Anointing the Sick with Oil, in the Name of the Lord, James 5:14, is binding upon all Christians.

It also advocates the church's duty to support Missionary and Tract Work, thus giving to the Lord for the spread of the Gospel and for the conversion of sinners.

In short, it is a vindicator of all that Christ and the apostles have enjoined upon us, and aims, amid the conflicting theories and discords of modern Christendom, to point out ground that all must concede to be infallibly safe.

The above principles of our Fraternity are set forth on our Brethren's Envelopes." Use them! Price 15 cents per package; 40 cents per hundred.

Announcements.

(Concluded from preceding page.)

DISTRICT MEETINGS.

Sept. 23 and 24, in Powell's Valley church, at Damascus, Clackamas Co., Oregon. Clackamas Station, on the Southern Pacific R. R., is the nearest railroad point. Passengers will please address Bro. J. A. Royer, Clackamas, Oregon, who will give them conveyance.

Oct. 6, District Meeting of Northern Indiana in the Yellow Creek church.

Oct. 6, at 6 A. M., North-eastern District of Ohio, in the Owl Creek church. Knox County. Delegates will stop off at Anke-ytown on the B and O. R. R. They should arrive the day before. Trains going north arrive at 10 A. M. and 3:15 P. M. Going south at 11:10 A. M., and 5:05 P. M., city time.

Oct. 14 and 15, Second District of West Virginia, at the Valley River church, Barbour Co., W. Va. Those coming by rail will stop off at Junior.

MINISTERIAL MEETINGS.

Sept. 21, in Powell's Valley church, at Damascus, Clackamas Co., Oregon.

Oct. 5, Ministerial Meeting in the Northern District of Indiana. Those coming by rail stop either at Nappanee or Goshen.

Oct. 5, Northern District of Indiana, in the Yellow Creek church.

LOVE FEASTS.

Sept. 16, at 2 P. M., Ottawa church, in Forest Park, Ottawa, Kans.

Sept. 23, in Powell's Valley church, at Damascus, Clackamas Co., Oregon.

Sept. 24, at 4 P. M., the Valley Pike church, 1 mile s. of Mauerstown, Shenandoah Co., Va.

Sept. 24, at 4 P. M., Okaw church, Piatt Co., Ill.

Sept. 24, Fairview church, Shelby Co., Mo. A series of meetings to follow the feast, which is to be held at Bro. C. Lapp's, 2 miles south of Cherry Box.

Sept. 24, at 2 P. M., Pleasant View church, Reno Co., Kans.

Sept. 27, at 2 P. M., Howard church, Ridgeway, Ind.

Sept. 30, at 10 A. M., Denton church, Marshall Co., Ind.

Sept. 30, at 2 P. M., Newton church, Ohio.

Oct. 1 and 2, at 2 P. M., Harlogton church, Dickenson Co., Kans.

Oct. 1, and 2, at 2 P. M., Union Center, 5 miles north-east of Nappanee, Ind.

Oct. 1 and 2, Moscow, Idaho. Those coming by rail will be met at the depot by notifying J. U. G. Stiverson when they will arrive, and on what road.

Oct. 1, Hurricane Creek church, Bond Co., Ill.

Oct. 1, at 4 P. M., Albion Prairie church, Lawrence Co., Ill.

Oct. 1, at 2 P. M., Lost Creek church, Miami Co., Ohio.

Oct. 1 and 2, Lower Conewago church, York Co., Pa.

Oct. 1, at 4 P. M., Lewi town congregation, in the Dry Valley meeting-house. A series of meetings the week previous.

Oct. 4, at 10 A. M., Salimony church, Huntington Co., Ind.

Oct. 6, at 2 P. M., at the Hillsburg church, Clinton Co., Ind. Anyone coming will be met at Hillsburg.

Oct. 7, at 4 P. M., Elkhart church, near Goshen, Ind.

Oct. 8, at 2 P. M., Mt. Vernon church, 6 miles south of Mt. Vernon at Bro. David Negere.

Oct. 8, in the Juniata congregation, Adams Co., Nebr. at the Evans church, 1½ miles south of Roseland, and 20 miles south and 2 west of Juniata.

Oct. 8, 4 at 4 P. M., Blue Ridge church, Piatt Co., Ill.

Oct. 8, at 10 A. M., Pleasant View church, Philips Co., Kans., 7 miles east and 6 miles south of Republic City, Nebr.

Oct. 8, at 2 P. M., Meyersdale, Pa.

Oct. 8, at Garber's church, Cook's Creek congregation, Rockingham Co., Va.

Oct. 8, at 2 P. M., Naperville, Ill.

Oct. 8, at 3 P. M., in the Lincoln church, at Twenty-seventh and H. Umridge Streets, in the City of Lincoln. A series of meetings to begin Oct. 5.

Oct. 8, at 10 A. M., Vermillion church, Kans. Members will be met at Beatrie and Summerfield on the 7th.

Oct. 8 and 9, at 4 P. M., Neosho County church, Kans.

Oct. 9, at 4 P. M., Brothers' Valley congregation, Somerset Co., Pa., at the Grove church, 1 mi'e north of Berlin. A week's meeting will be held previous to the feast.

Oct. 14, at 10 A. M., Poplar Ridge church, 4 miles east of Defiance, Ohio.

Oct. 15, at 2 P. M., Plymouth, Ind.

Oct. 15 and 16, at Sabetha, Kans.

Oct. 15, at 10 o'clock, Mercer church, 3 miles east of Mendon, Ohio, on the Lake Erie and Western R. R., 11 miles south-west of Salina and 4 miles west of Cold Water, Ohio.

Oct. 15, at 11 A. M., Deep River church, Iowa. Any coming by rail, come to Deep River on the North-western. Notify J. J. Brower, Deep River, Iowa, Box 55, and you will be met at the train.

Oct. 20, at 2 P. M., Eden Valley congregation, Stafford Co., Kans., at Bro. J. N. Miller's.

Oct. 22, at 10:30 A. M., Eagle Creek church, Hancock Co., Ohio.

Oct. 22 and 23, at 10 A. M., Iowa River church, Marshall Co., Iowa.

Oct. 27, at 10 A. M., Mineral Creek, Johnson Co., Mo.

Oct. 28, in the Greenwood church, Texas Co., Mo., 6 miles north-east of Cabool.

Oct. 29, at 2 P. M., in the Spring Run church, 7½ miles north of McVeytown station, Mifflin Co., Pa.

Oct. 29, at 2 P. M., Brownsville, Md.

Oct. 29, at 2 P. M., Liberty church, Olathe congregation, Kans.

Oct. 29, at 10 A. M., Shoal Creek church, Newton Co., Mo., 1 mile south of Grangeville. Those coming by rail will be met at Pierce City on the morning of the day before by notifying John Holderread, Ergo, Mo. Those coming to Purdy will be met on the morning of the 29th by notifying Leander Harader, Pioneer, Mo.

Oct. 29, at 2 P. M., Lick Creek church, Owen Co., Ind.

Oct. 29, at 1:30 P. M., Marsh Creek church, Adams Co., Pa.

Oct. 29, Slate Creek church, Sumner Co., Kans.

Nov. 2, at 2 P. M., Lower Stillwater, near Trotwood, Ohio, at the upper house.

Nov. 3, at 2 P. M., Lower Deer Creek church, Carroll Co., Ind.

Nov. 3, at 10 A. M., at the Bird-in-hand meeting-house, Conestoga congregation, Lancaster Co., Pa. A series of meetings will commence Oct. 29 at the Blue Ball meeting-house.

Nov. 4, at 2 P. M., in the bounds of the David's Creek church, Madison Co., Ohio, 4 miles north-west of London. Conveyance at London on the day of meeting for 10:15 A. M. train from the West.

Nov. 4, Walnut Creek church. Mo.

Nov. 5, at 1 P. M., Summit Mills, Somerset Co., Pa.

Nov. 5, at 2 P. M., in the Kansas Center church, 3 miles east of Lyons, Rice Co., Kans. A series of meetings to commence a week previous.

Nov. 5, at 3 P. M., Big Creek church, Richland Co., Ill., 3½ miles North-east of Parkersburg, Ill. Conveyance will be at the above place by informing J. M. Forney.

Nov. 5, at 5 P. M., Mount Pleasant meeting-house, Cass church, Saunders Co., Ohio.

Nov. 5 and 6, at 4 P. M., North Beatrice church, Gage Co., Nebr.

Nov. 5, at 4 P. M., Monticello chu ch, Ind.

Nov. 24, at 2 P. M., Thornapple church, Mich., at the east house.

Nov. 24, at 3 P. M., Cedar Creek church, Anderson Co., Kans.

Announcements.

(Concluded from preceding page.)

DISTRICT MEETINGS.

Sept. 23 and 24, in Powell's Valley church, at Damascus, Clackamas Co., Oregon. Clackamas Station, on the Southern Pacific R. R., is the nearest railroad point. Passengers will please address Bro. J. A. Royer, Clackamas, Oregon, who will give them conveyance.

Oct. 6, District Meeting of Northern Indiana in the Yellow Creek church.

Oct. 6, at 8 A. M , North-eastern District of Ohio, in the Owl Creek church. Knox County. Delegates will stop off at Ankeny town on the B and C. R. R. They should arrive the day before. Trains going north arrive at 10 A. M. and 3:13 P. M. Going south at 11:05 A. M., and 5:05 P. M., city time.

Oct. 14 and 15, Second District of West Virginia, in the Valley River church, Barbour Co., W. Va. Those coming by rail will stop off at Junior.

MINISTERIAL MEETINGS.

Sept. 20, in Powell's Valley church, at Damascus, Clackamas Co., Oregon.

Oct. 5, Ministerial Meeting in the Northern District of Indiana. Those coming by rail stop off at Nappanee or Goshen.

Oct. 5, Northern District of Indiana, in the Yellow Creek church.

LOVE FEASTS.

Sept. 16, at 4 P. M., Ottawa church, in Forest Park, Ottawa, Kans.

Sept. 23, in Powell's Valley church, at Damascus, Clackamas Co., Oregon.

Sept. 24, at 2 P. M., the Valley Pike church, 1 mile s. of Masterstown, Shenandoah Co , Va.

Sept. 24, at 4 P. M. Okaw church, Piatt Co., Ill.

Sept. 24, at 4 P. M., Fairview church, Shelby Co., Mo. A series of meetings to follow the feast, which is to be held at Bro. C. Lapp's, 4 miles south of Cherry Box.

Sept. 24, at 2 P. M , Pleasant View church, Reno Co., Kans.

Sept. 27, at 2 P. M., Howard church, Ridgeway, Ind.

Sept. 30, at 10 A. M., Dorman church, Marshall Co., Ind.

Sept. 30, at 2 P. M., Newton church, Ohio.

Oct. 1 and 2, at 2 P. M., Harrington church, Dickinson Co., Kans.

Oct. 1 and 2, at 2 P. M., Union Center, 5 miles north-east of Nappanee, Ind.

Oct 1 and 2, Moscow, Idaho. Those coming by rail will be met at the depot by notifying J. U. G. Stiverson when they will arrive, and on what road.

Oct. 1, Hurricane Creek church, Butel Co., Ill.

Oct. 1, at 4 P. M., Albion Prairie church, Lawrence Co ., Ind.

Oct. 1, at 4 P. M., Lost Creek church, Miami Co., Ohio.

Oct. 1 and 2, Lower Cumorings church, York Co., Pa.

Oct. 1, at 4 P. M., Lewd town congregation, in the Dry Valley meeting-house. A series of meetings the week previous.

Oct. 1, at 10 A. M., Salimony church, Huntington Co., Ind.

Oct. 1, at 2 P. M., at the Hillsbury church, Clinton Co., Ind. A-hymn coming will be met at Hillsburg.

Oct. 1, at 2 P. M., Elkhart church, near Goshen, Ind.

Oct. 1, at 2 P. M., Mt. Vernon church, 6 miles north of Mt. Vernon, at Bro. David Hagan.

Oct. 1, in the Jonarla congregation, Adams Co., Nebr. at Eureka church, 1½ miles south of Roseland, and 10 miles south and 1 west of Juniata.

Oct. 1, at 2 P. M., Blue Ridge church, Piatt Co., Ill.

Oct. 1, at 10 A, M,, Pleasant View church, Phillips Co., Kans., 4 miles east and 5 miles south of Republic City, Nebr.

Oct. 8, at 2 P. M., Meyersdale, Pa.

Oct. 8, at Garber's church, Cook's Creek congregation, Rockingham Co , Va.

Oct. 8, at 2 P. M., Naperville, Ill.

Oct. 8, at 2 P. M , in the Lincoln church, at Twenty-seventh and H.Streign Streets, in the City of Lincoln. A series of meetings to begin Oct. 5.

Oct. 8, at 10 A. M., Vermilion church, Kans. Members will be met at Bartin and Summerfield on the 7th.

Oct. 8 and 9, at 2 P. M , Neosho County church, Kans.

Oct. 9, at 4 P. M., Brothers' Valley congregation, Somerset Co., Pa., at the Grove church, 1 mile north of Berlin. A week's meeting will be held previous to the feast.

Oct. 14, at 10 A. M., Poplar Ridge church, 6 miles east of Defiance, Ohio.

Oct. 15 and 16, at Sabetha, Kans.

Oct. 15, at 10 o'clock, Mexico church, 3 miles east of Meadow, Ohio. on the Lake Erie and Western R. R., 10 miles south-west of Salina and 4 miles west of Cold Water, Ohio.

Oct. 15, at 11 A. M., Deep River church, Iowa. Any coming by rail, come 12 Deep River on the North-western. Notify J. J. Brower, Deep River, Iowa, Box 58, and you will be met at the train.

Oct. 20, at 2 P. M., Eden Valley congregation, Stafford Co., Kans., at Bro. J N. Miller's.

Oct. 22, at 2 and 30 A. M., Eagle Creek church, Hancock Co., Ohio.

Oct. 22, at 2 P. M., Eden Valley, Kans.

Oct. 22 and 23, at 10 A. M., Iowa River church, Marshall Co., Iowa.

Oct. 22, at 10 A. M., Mineral Creek, Johnson Co., Mo.

Oct. 22, in the Greenwood church, Texas Co., Mo., 8 miles north-east of Cabool.

Oct. 22, at 4 P. M., in the Spring Run church, 2½ miles north of McVeytown station, Mifflin Co., Pa.

Oct. 29, at 2 P. M., Brownsville, Md.

Oct. 29, at 2 P. M., Liberty church, Osatha congregation, Kans.

Oct. 29, at 10 A. M. Shoal Creek church, Newton Co., Mo., 1 mile south of Orangeville. Those coming by rail will be met at Platte City on the morning of the day before by notifying John Holderread, Ergo, Mo. Those coming to Purdy will be met on the morning of the 29th by notifying Leander Hufaker, Plainer, Mo.

Oct. 29, at 2 P. M., Lick Creek church, Owen Co., Ind.

Oct. 29, at 2:30 P. M., Marsh Creek church, Adams Co., Pa.

Oct. 29, Elkic Creek Church, Sumner Co., Kans.

Nov. 2, at 2 P. M., Lower Stillwater, near Trotwood, Ohio, at the upper house.

Nov. 2, at 2 P. M , Lower Deer Creek church, Carroll Co., Ind.

Nov. 3, at 10 A. M , at the Blind-in-hand meeting-house, Conestoga congregation, Lancaster Co., Pa. A series of meetings will commence Oct. 29 at the Blue Boil-meeting-house.

Nov. 4, at 2 P. M., in the bounds of the Donald's Creek church, Madison Co., Ohio, 6 miles north-west of Lofdale. Conveyance to Lawton on the day of meeting for 10:25 A. M. train from the West.

Nov. 5, Walnut Creek church, Mo

Nov. 5, at 2 P. M. Summit Mills, S merset Co , Pa.

Nov. 5, at 2 P. M., at the Kansas Center church, 3 miles east of Lyons, Rice Co , Kans. A series of meetings to commence a week previous.

Nov. 5, at 2 P. M., Big Creek church, Richland Co., Ill., 3½ miles North-east of Parkersburg, Ill. Conveyance will be at the above place by notifying J. M. Putney.

Nov.5 at 5 P M , Mt. Pleasant meeting-house, Garrison's church, Stefan Co , Ohio.

Nov. 5 and 6, at 4 P. M., North Beatrice church, Gage Co., Nebr.

Nov. 5, at 4 P M , Monticello church, Ind.

Nov. 10, at 10 A. M., Thornapple church, Mich., at the east house.

Nov. 24, at 3 P. M , Cedar Creek church, Anderson Co., Kans.

❖ESSAYS❖

"Study to show thyself approved unto God, a workman that needeth not to be ashamed, rightly dividing the Word of Truth."

BE PATIENT WITH THE LIVING.

SELECTED BY FANNIE H. ZIGLER.

DEAR friends, when you and I are gone
Beyond earth's weary labor,
When small our need of help or love
From comrade or from neighbor,
Past all the strife, the toil, the care,
Past all the sorrows, grief and sighing,
What do we gain, what do we lose,
Alas! by simply dying?

Then lips too chary for their praise
Will tell our merits over.
And eyes too blind our faults to see
Shall no defect discover.
Then hands that would not lift a stone,
When stones were thick to cumber,
Upon our graves will scatter flowers
When we unconscious slumber.

Dear friends, perchance both you and I,
Ere love is past forgiving,
Should take the earnest lesson home
"Be patient with the living."
To-day's repressed rebuke may save,
Our blinding tears to-morrow.
Then patience, e'en when keenest edged
May whet a nameless sorrow.

'Tis easy to be gentle when
Death's silence shames our clamor;
And easy to discern the best
Through memory's mystic glamour;
But wise it were for you and me
Ere love is past forgiving,
To take the tender lesson home
"Be patient with the living."

Broadway, Va.

UNBELIEF THE BESETTING SIN.

BY A. HUTCHISON.

THAT unbelief is the common besetment of us all, I think may be shown to a much greater extent than we, at first glance, would be willing to admit. When we look down deep into our own hearts, we find more unbelief than we were aware of, before such examination, and what is true of us, was largely true of those who preceded us, but we must not think that God will accommodate himself to our unbelief. Paul says, "If we believe not, yet he abideth faithful: he cannot deny himself." 2 Tim. 2: 13.

Here we are plainly informed that our want of faith will not affect the case with God. He must be true to himself. Then, again, we have the following question asked: "For what if some did not believe, shall their unbelief make the faith of God without effect? God forbid: yes, let God be true, but every man a liar." Rom. 3: 3, 4. When we think of that good man Moses, we would be almost ready to rebuke ourselves, if we were to be found harboring the thought that there was any unbelief about him. Yet the Lord tells us that unbelief was the cause of his failure to lead Israel into the promised land. See what he says, "And the Lord spake unto Moses and Aaron, because ye believed me not, to sanctify me in the eyes of the children of Israel, therefore ye shall not bring this congregation into the land which I have given them." Num. 20: 12. Here the Lord tells the identical thing which caused the failure. It was unbelief. If he had not been possessed with a lack of faith, he would have spoken to the rock in the presence of the people, and would have done so in the name of the Lord, and thus sanctified, or set up, God before the eyes of the children of Israel, as the great power which caused water to come out of a rock for their use.

It seems as if that (otherwise) faithful man was too weak in faith to speak to a rock, with a view of opening it, so that the blessed beverage (pure water) would come forth, and that, therefore, he smote the rock with a rod. Not only did he smite the rock, but said to the people, "Hear now, ye rebels; must we fetch you water out of this rock?" Num. 20: 10.

How would it be with us, think you, if we were commanded to speak to a rock with the promise of receiving water out of that rock? Do you not think that our faith would be a little too weak? But why falter at that case, more than when he promises us the remission of our sins, upon complying with the conditions upon which he gave us such a promise? All things being possible with God, it would be just as easy for him to open the rock and cause water to flow out of it, as to cause the waters of the Jordan, or the Red Sea to divide before the Israelites. Again, if we were called upon to receive thirty-nine stripes for our faith in Christ, we would likely conclude one such experience to be enough. If we did not abandon the faith altogether, we would likely be a little on our guard, as to where we let ourselves be known as friends of Jesus. Christ says, "Ye are my friends, if ye do whatsoever I command you." John 15: 14. Then we become his friends when we do his commandments. We would certainly be considered his enemies, if we do not keep his commands, and the greatest cause, if not the only cause, why people do not obey the commandments of Jesus, is unbelief alone. We all want the promises, but it seems often as if we would like to have the promises without obeying the commands. But this is not God's method of doing business. He gives man something to do, as a test of his faith, so that, when he proves faithful, God can confer upon the man the honor of the victory. "To him that overcometh will I grant to sit with me in my throne," etc. Rev. 3: 21. Here we can see that the Lord proposes to honor such as honor him. This honor is conferred only upon such as overcome and gain the victory by their fidelity to the trust committed to them.

Notice how we are to overcome. "For whatsoever is born of God overcometh the world, and this is the victory that overcometh the world, even our faith." 1 John 5: 4. In this reference we see the great need of looking well to our faith, for unbelief is the only thing that will cause a failure in the great conflict of salvation. We may even go so far as to observe all the ordinances of the house of the Lord in a formal manner, and still fail to gain the victory, because we do them not in faith, and whatsoever is not of faith is sin. On the other hand, we must not expect to reach the goal, or gain the victory by faith, without obeying the commands, because these are given as a medium through which to try our faith. If we, like the faithful Abraham of old, falter not through unbelief, we, too, will come off as victors. We can only expect to overcome by the blood of the Lamb, and when we obey from the heart that form of doctrine which has been delivered unto us, by Christ and the apostles, we then and there come to, and continue in, that relation with Christ which makes his blood avail for us.

O! how we ought to watch for that great and besetting sin,—unbelief! While we are watching along one lane or street, he may come in at another, where we possibly think there is no danger. Unbelief did his work in Eden, and he has been at his work day and night ever since. From the skill and tact with which he managed the case there, we may look for great cunning and artfulness now.

When we look at the great inducement that is held out to the faithful, it would seem as if every one would press toward the mark, for the prize. In Rev. 21: 7 we have the glorious promise, and the soul-cheering assurance from Jesus, our Leader and High-priest, that "he that overcometh shall inherit all things; and I will be his God, and he shall be my son."

We might institute the inquiry here, What can keep anyone, or all of us, from securing that grand inheritance? The answer is, Unbelief. The evil spirit cannot do it unless we yield to his influence. We have a very strong testimony along the line of unbelief in the following words, "Therefore the Lord heard this, and was wroth: so a fire was kindled against Jacob, and anger also came up against Israel; because they believed not in God, and trusted not in his salvation." Psa. 78: 21, 22. Unbelief seems to be the besetting sin now, as well as in the past. Therefore, "see that ye refuse not him that speaketh: for if they escaped not who refused him that spake on earth, much more shall not we escape, if we turn away from him that speaketh from heaven." Heb. 12: 25. Faith takes us up, unbelief down.

IDENTITY OF THE CHURCH.

BY JONATHAN NAHM.

MANY different things resemble each other,—some more and some less,—and yet they are not the same. At the present time, and in the age in which we live, most people content themselves with the idea that the church to which they belong is more like the apostolic church than any other. Blinded by this delusion they conclude that all is well, and that they will get to heaven.

Many people think if they belong to some church, they will be all right. Sometimes this delusion is carried so far, that saving provisions are made for many "good people" who never become members of any church. This has no more approbation in the Word of God than the other.

The law of identification requires that the thing identified must correspond in every respect with that to which it is claimed to be united. We will here make a very simple illustration. Your neighbor has his horse stolen from his stable, and the color of the horse is sorrel, and it has one glass eye, three white feet, white tail and mane. After awhile you think you have found your neighbor's horse, and you go over and say, "Neighbor, I have found your horse." "Well, I am very glad for the news; we will bring him home." Together we go to see the horse. The neighbor says, "That horse is like mine in every way, but he has no glass eye; so he is not my horse." Would he then try to take the horse? If he did, would there be a magistrate anywhere who would give judgment in his favor? Yet in church matters men seem to be more unwise than this, for they claim, as the church of God, many organizations differing in quite a number of important features, from the apostolic church.

There are churches to-day, wearing different names from the one established by Christ and his apostles, with additions and subtractions, alterations and modifications, and yet their members claim for themselves that they are the same. Of course, should they ever cease to claim that, then they would cease to command respect from intelligent people.

Now, in order to identify the church of God, let us turn to the New Testament and learn all the law of citizenship, required to enter the one body. In the first place the preaching of the Gospel must be done, then, on the part of the hearer, there must be a faith in the Gospel with

—◆ESSAYS◆—

" Study to show thyself approved unto God; a workman that needeth not be ashamed, rightly dividing the Word of Truth."

BE PATIENT WITH THE LIVING.

SELECTED BY FANNIE M. ZIGLER.

Dear friends, when you and I are gone
　Beyond earth's weary labor,
When small our need of help or love
　From comrade or from neighbor,
Past all the strife, the toil, the care,
　Past all the sorrows, grief and sighing,
What do we gain, what do we lose,
　Alas! by simply dying?

Then lips too chary for their praise
　Will tell our merits over,
And eyes too blind our faults to see
　Shall no defect discover.
Then hands that would not lift a stone,
　When stones were thick to cumber,
Upon our graves will scatter flowers
　When we unconscious slumber.

Dear friends, perchance both you and I,
　Ere love is past forgiving,
Should take the earnest lesson home
　"Be patient with the living."
To-day's repressed rebuke may save,
　Our blinding tears to-morrow.
Then patience, e'en when keenest edged
　May whet a nameless sorrow.

'Tis easy to be gentle when
　Death's silence shames our clamor;
And easy to discern the best
　Through memory's mystic glamour:
But wise it were for you and me
　Ere love is past forgiving,
To take the tender lesson home,
　"Be patient with the living."

Broadway, Va.

UNBELIEF THE BESETTING SIN.

BY A. HUTCHISON.

That unbelief is the common besetment of us all, I think may be shown to a much greater extent than we, at first glance, would be willing to admit. When we look down deep into our own hearts, we find more unbelief than we were aware of, before such examination, and what is true of us, was largely true of those who preceded us, but we must not think that God will accommodate himself to our unbelief. Paul says, "If we believe not, yet he abideth faithful: he cannot deny himself." 2 Tim. 2: 13.

Here we are plainly informed that our want of faith will not affect the case with God. He must be true to himself. Then, again, we have the following question asked: "For what if some did not believe, shall their unbelief make the faith of God without effect? God forbid: yea, let God be true, but every man a liar." Rom. 3: 3, 4. When we think of that good man Moses, we would be almost ready to rebuke ourselves, if we were to be found harboring the thought that there was any unbelief about him. Yet the Lord tells us that unbelief was the cause of his failure to lead Israel into the promised land. See what he says, "And the Lord spake unto Moses and Aaron, because ye believed me not, to sanctify me in the eyes of the children of Israel, therefore ye shall not bring this congregation into the land which I have given them." Num. 20: 12. Here the Lord tells the identical thing which caused the failure. It was unbelief. If he had not been possessed with a lack of faith, he would have spoken to the rock in the presence of the people, and would have done so in the name of the Lord, and thus sanctified, or set up, God before the eyes of the children of Israel, as the great power which caused water to come out of a rock for their use.

It seems as if that (otherwise) faithful man was too weak in faith to speak to a rock, with a view of opening it, so that the blessed beverage (pure water) would come forth, and that, therefore, he smote the rock with a rod. Not only did he smite the rock, but said to the people, "Hear now, ye rebels; must we fetch you water out of this rock?" Num. 20: 10.

How would it be with us, think you, if we were commanded to speak to a rock with the promise of receiving water out of that rock? Do you not think that our faith would be a little too weak? But why falter at that case, more than when he promises us the remission of our sins, upon complying with the conditions upon which he gave us such a promise? All things being possible with God, it would be just as easy for him to open the rock and cause water to flow out of it, as to cause the waters of the Jordan, or the Red Sea to divide before the Israelites. Again, if we were called upon to receive thirty-nine stripes for our faith in Christ, we would likely conclude one-such experience to be enough. If we did not abandon the faith altogether, we would likely be a little on our guard, as to where we let ourselves be known as friends of Jesus. Christ says, "Ye are my friends, if ye do whatsoever I command you." John 15: 14. Then we become his friends when we do his commandments. We would certainly be considered his enemies, if we do not keep his commands, and the greatest cause, if not the only cause, why people do not obey the commandments of Jesus, is unbelief alone. We all want the promises, but it seems often as if we would like to have the promises without obeying the commands. But this is not God's method of doing business. He gives man something to do, as a test of his faith, so that, when he proves faithful, God can confer upon the man the honor of the victory. "To him that overcometh will I grant to sit with me in my throne," etc. Rev. 3: 21. Here we can see that the Lord proposes to honor such as honor him. This honor is conferred only upon such as overcome and gain the victory by their fidelity to the trust committed to them.

Notice how we are to overcome. "For whatsoever is born of God overcometh the world, and this is the victory that overcometh the world, even our faith." 1 John 5: 4. In this reference we see the great need of looking well to our faith, for unbelief is the only thing that will cause a failure in the great conflict of salvation. We may even go so far as to observe all the ordinances of the house of the Lord in a formal manner, and still fail to gain the victory, because we do them not in faith, and whatsoever is not of faith is sin. On the other hand, we must not expect to reach the goal, or gain the victory by faith, without obeying the commands, because these are given as a medium through which to try our faith. If we, like the faithful Abraham of old, falter not through unbelief, we, too, will come off as victors. We can only expect to overcome by the blood of the Lamb, and when we obey from the heart that form of doctrine which has been delivered unto us, by Christ and the apostles, we then and there come to, and continue in, that relation with Christ which makes his blood avail for us.

Oh how we ought to watch for that great and besetting sin,—unbelief! While we are watching along one lane or street, he may come in at another, where we possibly think there is no danger. Unbelief did his work in Eden, and he has been at his work day and night ever since. From the skill and tact with which he managed the case there, we may look for great cunning and artfulness now.

When we look at the great inducement that is held out to the faithful, it would seem as if every one would press toward the mark, for the prize. In Rev. 21: 7 we have the glorious promise, and the soul-cheering assurance from Jesus, our Leader and High-priest, that "he that overcometh shall inherit all things; and I will be his God, and he shall be my son."

We might institute the inquiry here, What can keep anyone, or all of us, from securing that grand inheritance? The answer is, Unbelief. The evil spirit cannot do it unless we yield to his influence. We have a very strong testimony along the line of unbelief in the following words, "Therefore the Lord heard this, and was wroth; so a fire was kindled against Jacob, and anger also came up against Israel; because they believed not in God, and trusted not in his salvation." Psa. 78: 21, 22. Unbelief seems to be the besetting sin now, as well as in the past. Therefore, "see that ye refuse not him that speaketh: for if they escaped not who refused him that spake on earth, much more shall not we escape, if we turn away from him that speaketh from heaven." Heb. 12: 25. Faith takes us up, unbelief down.

IDENTITY OF THE CHURCH.

BY JONATHAN HAHN.

Many different things resemble each other,—some more and some less,—and yet they are not the same. At the present time, and in the age in which we live, most people content themselves with the idea that the church to which they belong is more like the apostolic church than any other. Blinded by this delusion they conclude that all is well, and that they will get to heaven.

Many people think if they belong to some church, they will be all right. Sometimes this delusion is carried so far, that saving provisions are made for many "good people" who never become members of any church. This has no more approbation in the Word of God than the other.

The law of identification requires that the thing identified must correspond in every respect with that to which it is claimed to be united. We will here make a very simple illustration. Your neighbor has his horse stolen from his stable, and the color of the horse is sorrel, and it has one glass eye, three white feet, white tail and mane. After awhile you think you have found your neighbor's horse, and you go over and say, "Neighbor, I have found your horse." "Well, I am very glad for the news; we will bring him home." Together we go to see the horse. The neighbor says, "That horse is like mine in every way, but he has no glass eye; so he is not my horse." Would he then try to take the horse? If he did, would there be a magistrate anywhere who would give judgment in his favor? Yet in church matters men seem to be more unwise than this, for they claim, as the church of God, many organizations differing in quite a number of important features, from the apostolic church.

There are churches to-day, wearing different names from the one established by Christ and his apostles, with additions and subtractions, alterations and modifications, and yet their members claim for themselves that they are the same. Of course, should they ever cease to claim that, then they would cease to command respect from intelligent people.

Now, in order to identify the church of God, let us turn to the New Testament and learn all the law of citizenship, required to enter the one body. In the first place the preaching of the Gospel must be done, then, on the part of the hearer, there must be a faith in the Gospel with

might present them faultless before the throne of heaven.

Oh how glorious must be the future eternal home of the eternal pilgrim! On those golden plains, beyond the river of death, rays of divine glory are beaming in full effulgence. There the Sun of Righteousness is shining in all his splendor, making eternity one constant noontide of untold glory and blessedness, a day without clouds. There our Immanuel shall be as the light of the morning when the sun riseth, even a morning without clouds. No gloom or darkness will ever overspread those blissful realms beyond the shores of time. The celestial world will always be irradiated by the glory of God, and the redeemed shall ever be in the gladsome sunshine of Infinite Love. In that bright home of pilgrims, the Savior will conduct his ransomed ones to living fountains of waters,—streams of immortal joys,—and God shall wipe away all tears. In the presence of Jesus there is fullness of joy; at his right hand there are pleasures for evermore. Eye hath not seen, nor ear heard, nor has the human heart ever conceived those things which God has prepared for them that love him. An exceeding and eternal weight of glory will crown every pilgrim who has found the happy shores of Immanuel's land. In the palace of the King of kings all will be perfectly blessed, and from that building of God there shall be no more going out, but we shall ever be with the Lord, enjoying his love.

Oh happy abode of Zion's pilgrims! Oh sweet and pleasant clime, where the balmy zephyrs of heaven refresh the weary soul; where there floweth not a tear; where there entereth not a pain; where death itself shall be swallowed up in victory! This is the heritage of them that fear the Lord.

But before our feet stand on the shores of the heavenly Canaan, we have to pass through a wilderness scene. This world is that wilderness, where Zion's pilgrims wander till they are taken home to glory. It is a thorny pathway that leads to the realms of eternal day, but, by the grace of God, the Christian is able to keep on in the good way with joy, till he passes through the wilderness and over Jordan, more than a conqueror through Jesus, and takes up his song of triumph amid the undying splendors of immortality. There are two prominent ideas in this, which deserve our consideration.

1. This world is a wilderness.

2. The Christian is a pilgrim here.

a. To every child of God this world with all its conceivable pleasures is nothing but a wilderness,—far from his father's house, far from that goodly land, which he so ardently longs to possess. This is the view which every saint takes of earth, and it is a just one. What the wilderness was to the children of Israel in their journey to the promised land, this decaying scene is to the believer in his progress heavenward. It is not his rest; it is not his home. On the contrary, it is a wilderness world of trouble from which he is coming up to the mansions above. The dark, rugged pathway lies through dangers and difficulties, which sometimes rise like mountains before the Christian pilgrim, and threaten to retard his march to the land of immortality. But it is a blessed consolation to know that Jesus guards the way to Zion; that he will suffer no evil to befall us; that even here, in this world of sorrow, all things shall work together for our good. The sorrow and bereavements of life render this earth a trying wilderness to the child of God. Here the winds of adversity and floods of sorrow sweep along our path, making us long to reach the blissful hill of Zion, where no chilling blasts annoy; where all is blooming with love and peace. Here

we are almost constantly distressed with difficulties, cares, pains, and griefs which render this a weary land.

It is sin that makes this world a wilderness to the saint. On account of sin in his heart he often faints and is ready to die; he feels that this is a valley of weeping, and longs to arrive at the borders of the wilderness, that he may cross into Canaan.

Besides all this, he has to encounter, in his journey, violent opposition from an ungodly, persecuting world. This makes him cry out with the Psalmist, " Woe is me, that I sojourn in Mesech, that I dwell in the tents of Kedar! My soul hath long dwelt with him that hateth peace." In the world there are fightings without, and fears within. How unlike the dark abode of sin and misery are those radiant mansions, far beyond the starry sky! There the wicked cease from troubling, and there the weary are at rest.

b. The Christian is a pilgrim here. He has only a temporary residence in this vale of tears. His abiding home in this world is where momentary ages are no more. Now he is on his journey to those fearless, blissful regions where he is to spend the ceaseless ages of eternity.

When the children of Israel were in the wilderness, they had no permanent residence, but were continually roving about from place to place, journeying to that goodly land which flowed with milk and honey, and which was then the glory of all lands,—a land of brooks of water, of fountains and depths that spring out of valleys and hills, a land of wheat, and barley, and vines, and fig-trees; a land of oil and honey. So the believer is a pilgrim on earth, with no continuing city nor certain place of abode, travelling through a dreary wilderness to that city which shines in the highest noon of glory; to that land of blessedness and immortality, where perennial streams of bliss issue from the eternal fountain of life to refresh the weary soul, and where we may freely eat of the fruit of the tree of life in the midst of the Paradise of God.

How impressive is the language of Moses to Hobab, in the wilderness: " We are journeying unto the place of which the Lord said, I will give it you." The hosts of Israel, instead of making their abode in the waste, howling wilderness, were marching forward to obtain possession of that land which the Lord sware unto their fathers, Abraham, Isaac and Jacob to give unto them and to their seed after them. Like those ancient pilgrims, we have a promised land in view, and onward is our motto. Instead of seeking our home and our happiness in a perishing world, we are passing on to that glorious kingdom which Jesus, in his boundless love, has gone to prepare for our reception, and which he has promised to bestow on all them that love him, for he says: " I appoint unto you a kingdom, as my Father hath appointed unto me; that ye may eat and drink at my table, in my kingdom, and sit on thrones, judging the twelve tribes of Israel. Again, " Fear not, little flock; for it is your Father's good pleasure to give you the kingdom."

So the Christian pilgrim, animated by such precious promises, has good hope, through grace, of gaining the happy shores of Canaan, of possessing the heavenly inheritance, of making his eternal abode in the courts of Paradise, and of sitting down with Abraham, Isaac, and Jacob in the kingdom of God.

With such glorious prospects in view, no wonder he should look upon earth as a barren, homeless world,—that he should feel like a stranger and a sojourner in it. No wonder that he should speed his earthly flight to reach the blissful skies.

We are entreated by a compassionate Savior to seek the better country. In the wilderness the

divine injunction to the children of Israel was to march forward to the land of promise. " And the Lord said unto Moses, Depart and go up hence, thou and the people which thou hast brought up out of the land of Egypt, unto the land which I sware unto Abraham, to Isaac, and to Jacob, saying, unto thy seed will I give it." The same solemn command, reminding us of our short pilgrimage on earth is sounding in our ears. It is the entreating voice of the Savior, calling us to forsake this present evil world, and to seek our portion in the fair realms of eternal day. It is a voice of compassion and love that says to us, " Arise ye and depart, for this is not your rest. Seek ye first the kingdom of God and his righteousness."

The Christian pilgrim obeys the divine injunction, sets forward on his journey, leaves the world, looks beyond this dying scene, gazes on the celestial Canaan, till its glories beam upon his soul, till he breathes the pure atmosphere of the upper world, till his ear hears the glorious melody of heaven, and his eye catches a glimpse of the king in his beauty, and the land that is afar off. " O," says the weary pilgrim, as onward he journeys with his eyes directed toward heaven, " In yonder glorious world is my rest and abiding home."

All the children of God who have ever traveled to the Canaan on high have acknowledged that they were strangers and pilgrims in this world. Of those ancient worthies who died in the faith, it is said they confessed that they were strangers and pilgrims on earth. To this band of shadows and death their views were not confined. No; they looked higher than earth. They desired a better country; wherefore God is not ashamed to be called their God; for he hath prepared for them a city. Of Abraham it is said that he sojourned in the land of promise, as in a strange country, dwelling in tabernacles with Isaac and Jacob, the heirs with him of the same promise; for he looked for a city which hath foundations, whose builder and maker is God. The earthly Canaan was but a type of the heavenly, and therefore the patriarchs, overlooking the passing scenes of this world, elevated their views to the true land of promise beyond the skies.

The believer's life is a progressive one. All the true followers of Jesus are daily advancing in their journey towards the realms of peace. They go on from strength to strength, through this wilderness scene, until every one of them appear before God. Their earnest endeavors are to get nearer heaven; hence, forgetting the things which are behind, and reaching forth unto those which are before, they press toward the mark for the prize of the high-calling of God in Christ Jesus. They are not satisfied with their present life in the wilderness. It has but little attraction for them. They are not conformed to the world. Their course is upward.

All Christians are coming up out of the wilderness. Every real Christian is making progress. If the sheep are on the shoulder of the shepherd, they are always getting nearer the fold. With some the shepherd takes long steps.

Dear brethren and sisters we should be advancing towards the heavenly Canaan every day. Let us not take up our abode here; we are journeying. Then let all our endeavors be to get on in our journey to heaven. We would say to all, as Moses did to Hobab, " We are journeying unto the place of which the Lord said, I will give it you. Come thou with us and we will do thee good; for the Lord hath spoken good concerning Israel."

Montioello, Ind.

" A PROMISE is a just debt, which should always be paid, for honesty and honor are its security."

Missionary and Tract Work Department.

"Upon the first day of the week, let every one of you lay by him in store as God hath prospered him, that there be no gatherings when I come."—1 Cor. 16: 2.

"Every man as he purposeth in his heart, so let him give. Not grudgingly or of necessity, for the Lord loveth a cheerful giver."—2 Cor. 9: 7.

HOW MUCH SHALL WE GIVE?

"Every man *according to his ability.*" "Every one *as God hath prospered him.*" "Every man, *according as he purposeth in his heart,* so let him give." "For if there be first a willing mind, it is accepted *according to that a man hath,* and not according to that he hath not."—2 Cor. 8: 12.

Organization of Missionary Committee.

DANIEL VANIMAN, Foreman,	McPherson, Kans.
D. L. MILLER, Treasurer,	Mt. Morris, Ill.
GALEN B. ROYER, Secretary,	Mt. Morris, Ill.

Organization of Book and Tract Work.

S. W. HOOVER, Foreman,	Dayton, Ohio.
S. BOCK, Secretary and Treasurer,	Dayton, Ohio.

☞All donations intended for Missionary Work should be sent to GALEN B. ROYER, Mt. Morris, Ill.

☞All money for Tract Work should be sent to S. BOCK, Dayton, Ohio.

☞Money may be sent by Money Order, Registered Letter, or Drafts on New York or Chicago. Do not send Personal checks, or drafts on interior towns, as it costs 25 cents to collect them.

☞Solicitors are requested to faithfully carry out the plan of Annual Meeting, that all our members be solicited to contribute at least twice a year for the Mission and Tract Work of the Church.

☞Notes for the Endowment Fund can be had by writing to the Secretary of either Work.

PREDESTINATION, TRINITY, BAPTISM.

BY C. H. BALSBAUGH.

Beloved Fellow-Pilgrim:—

YOUR pathetic letter is here. Just like thousands I have received before, full of the sorrows of earth, and fuller of the joy of the Lord and the hope of glory. Your widowhood only makes the presence and fidelity of the Celestial Bridegroom sweeter. Your six orphan children will only put renewed energy into your soul to train them faithfully and wisely for the glory of God here and forever. Amen and Amen.

I thank God that one more soul has escaped from the shackles of Calvinistic Predestination. It represents God as a "respecter of persons," and as giving us a Gospel full of perplexing and revolting contradictions. *God's* Predestination is consistent, and offers the grace of Christ to every soul on the earth. That a certain number were foreknown as the Elect, does not necessitate an arbitrary decree, or deny salvation to a single sinner. Omniscience, Omnipotence, and Righteousness give us a Predestination and Election which excludes only those who exclude themselves.

The *any,* of 2 Pet. 3: 9, is as comprehensive as the race. Do not fear, beloved, that any soul will be lost because God has so predestined apart from His Foreknowledge of that person's deliberate choice of sin and perdition. That God is a Trinity of Persons can no more be refuted than that He is Personal at all. To dispute about the *mode* of His Tri-Personal Being, is idle work. That the Lord our God is *one* Lord is a Biblical Truism. Mark 12: 29.

Monotheism is a necessity of Eternal Being. That He is in an incomprehensible sense a Trinity, is equally incontrovertible. The Son was *in the Jordan,* the Father addressed Him *from heaven,* and the Holy Ghost *descended upon Him from the Father.* This distinction is maintained throughout the New Testament. How One, we know just as little as how Three. "*Without controversy,* GREAT IS THE MYSTERY." 1 Tim. 3: 16. God in the flesh toiling and preaching, and wandering up and down Palestine is as really the Eternal One as the Father not in the flesh. The Holy Spirit as truly *came* as Jesus *went,* and His work is as personal and universal as that of Emmanuel.

Into that Trinity we are baptized. That there should be "one baptism" with three similar actions, is not any more incredible than that there should be one God and Three Persons. The formula in Matt. 28: 19, is not only very beautiful, but Divinely philosophical. Such a unity of Being, and such a division of functions as characterize the Economy of Redemption, is fitly symbolized by trine immersion. Nothing can be more in accordance with the radical principle of all Divine Dispensations. Single immersion is a typical denial of the Holy Trinity. The point which you wish especially elucidated is the burial into the death of Christ.

Your opponents press you with the interrogation, "Was Christ buried three times, and did he rise three times from the dead?" Does not Christ's answer to the Sadducees well fit this case? "Ye do err, not knowing the Scriptures, nor the power of God." Matt. 22: 29. I know not where to find a more fundamental, significant, and solemn passage of Scripture, than Rom. 6: 3, 4. It is the pivot of our Christian life. The question there is not as to backward or forward, once, twice, or thrice, but relates to the fact of our identification with Him in that solemn crisis of His history which constitutes our atonement. To be baptized into His death is the profoundest spiritual reality we can ever know. To be immersed once backward or thrice forward, is not *per se* to be baptized into His death. Only those who *by faith* stand in the relation to God which Christ's Propitiation effects, can be baptized into His death.

The contrary view is popery of the blackest type. Water makes no saints; but it symbolizes the fact of sainthood, and the mystery of Godliness by which they were made such. A more important question cannot be asked than "whether Christ was buried and rose three times," with a view to invalidate trine immersion. Nothing less than a Triune God *in Unity* of Being and end, could make such a death and reconciliation as can truly represent that unique fact.

Do not argue so much with your pastor and friends. The texts and facts herein stated are enough to upset all controversy on the points involved. Let your life be your irrefragable argument. Show them that Gal. 2: 20 is the beatitude and glory of your being. If they pronounce you lunatic, or on the verge of craziness, let your only answer be Acts 5: 41. The inebriation and insanity of Acts 2: 13, and 26: 24, are the highest glory and wisdom of human nature. Let everybody know that you *are* baptized unto *the death of Christ,* by the unimpeachable exemplification of Gal. 6: 14. These are the predestined ones, the "Elect of God."

Union Deposit, Pa.

THE ROOT OF OBEDIENCE.

BY W. M. LYON.

WHY do I obey? Let every professor of religion ask himself this question. All professed Christians claim to be obedient, submissive to God's Word.

There are two kinds of obedience,—voluntary and involuntary. Voluntary obedience only is acceptable with God. In the eyes of the civil law, involuntary obedience is placed on a level with the voluntary. Take away the civil law, and many who have been regarded as honest will prove themselves to the contrary. They are honest (?) from policy, not from principle. This opens up the most important part of our subject.

Prepare to locate yourself. Do you act from policy, or from principle? Is your obedience based on true-love to God? Is it voluntary or involuntary?

Referring to the order of plainness, as prescribed by our fraternity, a sister once made this remark: "I *know* that *I* would not dress as I do, if I thought I could get to heaven without it." I pitied her. Why? Because. her obedience was not the result of an abiding faith, rooted and grounded in the LOVE of GOD.

I believe there are thousands who are the subjects of the same delusion. Why is this? I fear it is largely the result of false teaching. A sickly, diseased, enemy-infested root manifests itself both in leaf and in fruit. The remedy in that case can only be effectually applied to the root, the place where the trouble is located. If the root, soil and environments are all right, we will have but little, if any, trouble about the leaves and fruit. The poet, Watts, was right when he said: "Love is the fountain whence all true obedience flows." "For this is the love of God, that we keep his commandments: and his commandments are not grievous." 1 John 5: 3.

His commandments are not grievous. What a world of meaning attaches itself to that word—*grievous!* For much obedience is of this grievous kind, compulsory, forced, without reward. Very little things sometimes have big meanings. I will go to the sisters for another illustration. More than once have I noticed at public worship in old, established places, where the membership is large, and the peculiar usages of the church generally known, the sisters remove their bonnets and exhibit the prayer-covering, which is to be admired and commended, but many of those same sisters, attending church at other places, where our doctrine is but little known, fail to make the same open confession, but keep their bonnets on as though they were ashamed. This makes one think. I wondered if the observance of this command was not grievous to them. I thought, "Why burn our candles while the sun shines, and put the bushel over them when it gets dark." If the cap were more needed in the one place than in the other, I should have given the preference to the latter, and not to the former.

True faith in Christ will produce entire submission and perfect obedience to the will of God in all things, just as naturally as the rising sun dispels darkness and produces daylight. If our obedience does not spring from this faith—"faith which worketh by love" (Gal. 5: 6), we cannot hope to inherit God's promises. To illustrate further: Bro. A gives a certain sum toward a work of charity, but if he does not do it willingly, voluntarily, what is the result? His money does others good, but he loses the blessing and reward. 2 Cor. 9: 7 explains why. With him it was a matter of necessity. So, if this, or any other part of our obedience is a matter of necessity, we lose our reward. The same rule that applied to Bro. A will also apply to any other duty. It will likewise apply to the keeping of the ordinances of God's house.

Many cling tenaciously to the strict observance of "the letter," tithing "mint and anise and cummin," while they may have "omitted the weightier matters of the law, judgment, mercy, and faith." Matt. 28: 23. How may we know this? "By their fruits." Their profession clamors for strict obedience, but their lives bear the knotty, ill-shaped fruit of unbelief, coldness, and indifference. How common it is for man to reverse the divine order and arrangement. Another illustration: We have heard ministers in arguing on the subject of feet-washing as a public ordinance, argue that its observance produced humility. This made us feel sad. If we understand God's arrange-

Missionary and Tract Work Department.

"Upon the first day of the week, let every one of you lay by him in store as God hath prospered him, that there be no gatherings when I come."—1 Cor. 16: 2.

"Every man as he purposeth in his heart, so let him give. Not grudgingly or of necessity, for the Lord loveth a cheerful giver."—2 Cor. 9: 7.

HOW MUCH SHALL WE GIVE?

"Every man according to his ability." "Every one as God hath prospered him." "Every man, according as he purposeth in his heart, so let him give." "For if there be first a willing mind, it is accepted according to that a man hath, and not according to that he hath not."—2 Cor. 8: 12.

Organization of Missionary Committee.

DANIEL VANIMAN, Foreman,   · · ·   McPherson, Kans.
D. L. MILLER, Treasurer,   · · ·   Mt. Morris, Ill.
GALEN B. ROYER, Secretary,   · · ·   Mt. Morris, Ill.

Organization of Book and Tract Work.

S. W. HOOVER, Foreman,   · · ·   Dayton, Ohio.
S. BOCK, Secretary and Treasurer,   · ·   Dayton, Ohio.

☞ All donations intended for Missionary Work should be sent to GALEN B. ROYER, Mt. Morris, Ill.

☞ All money for Tract Work should be sent to S. BOCK, Dayton, Ohio.

☞ Money may be sent by Money Order, Registered Letter, or Drafts on New York or Chicago. Do not send personal checks, or drafts on interior towns, as it costs 25 cents to collect them.

☞ Solicitors are requested to faithfully carry out the plan of Annual Meeting, that all our members be solicited to contribute at least twice a year for the Mission and Tract Work of the Church.

☞ Notes for the Endowment Fund can be had by writing to the Secretary of either Work.

PREDESTINATION, TRINITY, BAPTISM.

BY C. H. BALSBAUGH.

Beloved Fellow-Pilgrim:—

YOUR pathetic letter is here. Just like thousands I have received before, full of the sorrows of earth, and fuller of the joy of the Lord and the hope of glory. Your widowhood only makes the presence and fidelity of the Celestial Bridegroom sweeter. Your six orphan children will only put renewed energy into your soul to train them faithfully and wisely for the glory of God here and forever. Amen and Amen.

I thank God that one more soul has escaped from the shackles of Calvinistic Predestination. It represents God as a "respecter of persons," and as giving us a Gospel full of perplexing and revolting contradictions. *God's* Predestination is consistent, and offers the grace of Christ to every soul on the earth. That a certain number were foreknown as the Elect, does not necessitate an arbitrary decree, or deny salvation to a single sinner. Omniscience, Omnipotence, and Righteousness give us a Predestination and Election which excludes only those who exclude themselves.

The *any*, of 2 Pet. 3: 9, is as comprehensive as the race. Do not fear, beloved, that any soul will be lost because God has so predestined apart from His Foreknowledge of that person's deliberate choice of sin and perdition. That God is a Trinity of Persons can no more be refuted than that He is Personal at all. To dispute about the *mode* of His Tri-Personal Being, is idle work. That the Lord our God is *one* Lord is a Biblical Truism. Mark 12: 29.

Monotheism is a necessity of Eternal Being. That He is in an incomprehensible sense a Trinity, is equally incontrovertible. The Son was *in the Jordan*, the Father addressed Him *from heaven*, and the Holy Ghost *descended upon Him from the Father*. This distinction is maintained throughout the New Testament. How One, we know just as little as how Three. "*Without controversy*, GREAT IS THE MYSTERY." 1 Tim. 3: 16. God in the flesh toiling and preaching, and wandering up and down Palestine is as really the Eternal One as the Father not in the flesh. The Holy Spirit as truly *came* as Jesus *went*, and His

work is as personal and universal as that of Emmanuel.

Into this Trinity we are baptized. That there should be "one baptism" with three similar actions, is not any more incredible than that there should be one God and Three Persons. The formula in Matt. 28: 19, is not only very beautiful, but Divinely philosophical. Such a unity of Being, and such a division of functions as characterize the Economy of Redemption, is fitly symbolized by trine immersion. Nothing can be more in accordance with the radical principle of all Divine Dispensations. Single immersion is a typical denial of the Holy Trinity. The point which you wish especially elucidated is the burial into the death of Christ.

Your opponents press you with the interrogation, "Was Christ buried three times, and did he rise three times from the dead?" Does not Christ's answer to the Sadducees well fit this case? "Ye do err, not knowing the Scriptures, nor the power of God." Matt. 22: 29. I know not where to find a more fundamental, significant, and solemn passage of Scripture, than Rom. 6: 3, 4. It is the pivot of our Christian life. The question there is not as to backward or forward, once, twice, or thrice, but relates to the fact of our identification with Him in that solemn crisis of His history which constitutes our atonement. To be baptized into His death is the profoundest spiritual reality we can ever know. To be immersed once backward or thrice forward, is not *per se* to be baptized into His death. Only those who by *faith* stand in the relation to God which Christ's Propitiation effects, can be baptized into His death.

The contrary view is popery of the blackest type. Water makes no saints; but it symbolizes the fact of sainthood, and the mystery of Godliness by which they were made such. A more important question cannot be asked than "whether Christ was buried and rose three times," with a view to invalidate trine immersion. Nothing less than a Triune God in Unity of Being and end, could make such a death and reconciliation possible. And nothing less than trine immersion can truly represent that unique fact.

Do not argue so much with your pastor and friends. The texts and facts herein stated are enough to upset all controversy on the points involved. Let your life be your irrefragable argument. Show them that Gal. 2: 20 is the beatitude and glory of your being. If they pronounce you lunatic, or on the verge of craziness, let your only answer be Acts 5: 41. The inebriation and insanity of Acts 2: 13, and 26: 24, are the highest glory and wisdom of human nature. Let everybody know that you *are* baptized unto *the death of Christ*, by the unimpeachable exemplification of Gal. 6: 14. These are the predestined ones, the "Elect of God."

Union Deposit, Pa.

THE ROOT OF OBEDIENCE.

BY W. M. LYON.

WHY do I obey? Let every professor of religion ask himself this question. All professed Christians claim to be obedient, submissive to God's Word.

There are two kinds of obedience,—voluntary and involuntary. Voluntary obedience only is acceptable with God. In the eyes of the civil law, involuntary obedience is placed on a level with the voluntary. Take away the civil law, and many who have been regarded as honest will prove themselves to the contrary. They are honest (?) from policy, not from principle. This opens up the most important part of our subject.

Prepare to locate yourself. Do you act from policy, or from principle? Is your obedience based on true love to God? Is it voluntary or involuntary?

Referring to the order of plainness, as prescribed by our fraternity, a sister once made this remark: "I *know* that I would not dress as I do, if I thought I could get to heaven without it." I pitied her. Why? Because her obedience was not the result of an abiding faith, rooted and grounded in the LOVE of GOD.

I believe there are thousands who are the subjects of the same delusion. Why is this? I fear it is largely the result of false teaching. A sickly, diseased, enemy-infested root manifests itself both in leaf and in fruit. The remedy in that case can only be effectually applied to the root, the place where the trouble is located. If the root, soil and environments are all right, we will have but little, if any, trouble about the leaves and fruit. The poet, Watts, was right when he said: "Love is the fountain whence all true obedience flows." "For this is the love of God, that we keep his commandments: and his commandments are not grievous." 1 John 5: 3.

His commandments are not grievous. What a world of meaning attaches itself to that word—*grievous!* For such obedience is of this grievous kind, compulsory, forced, without reward. Very little things sometimes have big meanings. I will go to the sisters for another illustration. More than once have I noticed at public worship in old, established places, where the membership is large, and the peculiar usages of the church generally known, the sisters remove their bonnets and exhibit the prayer-covering, which is to be admired and commended, but many of those same sisters, attending church at other places, where our doctrine is but little known, fail to make the same open confession, but keep their bonnets on as though they were ashamed. This makes one think. I wondered if the observance of this command was not grievous to them. I thought, "Why burn our candles while the sun shines, and put the bushel over them when it gets dark." If the cap were more needed in the one place than in the other, I should have given the preference to the latter, and not to the former.

True faith in Christ will produce entire submission and perfect obedience to the will of God in all things, just as naturally as the rising sun dispels darkness and produces daylight. If our obedience does not spring from this faith—"faith which worketh by love" (Gal. 5: 6), we cannot hope to inherit God's promises. To illustrate further: Bro. A gives a certain sum toward a work of charity, but if he does not do it willingly, voluntarily, what is the result? His money does others good, but he loses the blessing and reward. 2 Cor. 9: 7 explains why. With him it was a matter of necessity. So, if this, or any other part of our obedience is a matter of necessity, we lose our reward. The same rule that applied to Bro. A will also apply to any other duty. It will likewise apply to the keeping of the ordinances of God's house.

Many cling tenaciously to the strict observance of "the letter" tithing "mint and anise and cummin," while they may have "omitted the weightier matters of the law, judgment, mercy, and faith." Matt. 23: 23. How may we know this? "By their fruits." Their profession clamors for strict obedience, but their lives bear the knotty, ill-shaped fruit of unbelief, coldness, and indifference. How common it is for man to reverse the divine order and arrangement. Another illustration: We have heard ministers in speaking on the subject of feet-washing as a public ordinance, argue that its observance produced humility. This made us feel sad. If we understand God's arrange-

The Gospel Messenger,

A Weekly at $1.50 Per Annum.

PUBLISHED BY

The Brethren's Publishing Co.

D. L. MILLER, ...   Editor.

J. H. MOORE, ...   Office Editor.

J. B. BRUMBAUGH, }   . . . . .   Associate Editors.
J. G. ROYER, }

JOSEPH AMICK, ...   Business Manager.

ADVISORY COMMITTEE.
L. W. Teeter, A. Hutchison, Daniel Hays.

☞ Communications for publication should be legibly written with black ink on one side of the paper only. Do not attempt to interline, or to put on one page what ought to occupy two.

☞ Anonymous communications will not be published.

☞ Do not mix business with articles for publication. Keep your communications on separate sheets from all business.

☞ Time is precious. We always have time to attend to business and to answer questions of importance, but please do not subject us to need less answering of letters.

☞ The MESSENGER is mailed each week to all subscribers. If the address is correctly entered on our list, the paper must reach the person to whom it is addressed. If you do not get your paper, write us, giving particulars.

☞ When changing your address, please give your former as well as your future address in full, so as to avoid delay and misunderstanding.

☞ Always remit to the office from which you order your goods, no matter from where you receive them.

☞ Do not send personal checks or drafts on interior banks, unless you send with them 25 cents each, to pay for collection.

☞ Remittances should be made by Post-office Money Order, Drafts on New York, Philadelphia or Chicago, or Registered Letters, made payable and addressed to "Brethren's Publishing Co., Mount Morris, Ill.," or "Brethren's Publishing Co., Huntingdon, Pa."

☞ Entered at the Post-office at Mount Morris, Ill., as second-class matter.

Mount Morris, Ill.,   -   -   -   Sept. 27, 1892.

CONSIDERABLE correspondence is crowded out of this issue, and must lay over till next week.

THE Brethren are preparing to build a meeting-house west of Salem, Ill., the coming fall and winter.

BRO. D. R. FREEMAN, of Union City, Ind., has returned to Star City, Pulaski County, where he may now be addressed.

BRO. I. J. ROSENBERGER is now in the midst of an interesting series of meetings at Lanark, Ill., expecting to continue till after their feast.

THE District Meeting for Texas and Oklahoma has elected Bro. Jacob Appleman to represent them on the Standing Committee next year.

THE meeting held by Bro. Silas Hoover in the Middle Creek church, Pa., proved quite a success in the way of members, as twelve were added by confession and baptism.

BRO. O. PERRY HOOVER is now at Greencastle, Ind., and may be addressed at Box 754. Those knowing of members living near that place, will please inform Bro. Hoover.

BRETHREN Lemuel Hillery and W. R. Deeter, we learn, are in the midst of a soul-stirring meeting in the Solomon's Creek church, Elkhart County, Ind. Two have already made the good confession.

THE Brethren in Sterling, Ill., were engaged all last, and a part of this week in an interesting series of meetings. The church seems to be moving along quite smoothly, with good prospects in the future.

OUR Brethren are opening up the evangelistic work early this season. Already reports are coming in of many additions to the church. Eight recently united with the church at Glensted, Mo., by confession and baptism. Other reports will be found in the Correspondence Department.

OUR readers may wonder where we will find room to publish a report from each of the nearly 400 love-feasts in the Brotherhood, this fall. If the reports are short, and to the point, we can make room for one hundred of them in one issue. We would like to send out one issue containing one hundred condensed reports of these glorious feasts, held by our Brethren in all parts of the Brotherhood. Let no feast remain unreported this season.

MOST of our readers are not aware of the value of the excellent little book we keep for sale, entitled, "Church Entertainments," or "Twenty Reasons" against modern church entertainments, fairs, festivals, etc. Bro. I. J. Rosenberger has sold twenty copies, and now orders two dozen more. Hundreds of them would be purchased and read if our people generally comprehended the strength and character of the work. Price, 30 cents, or $3.00 a dozen.

THE last issue of the MESSENGER contained 220 standing love-feast announcements, and a number were crowded out for the lack of room. We regretted this very much, but it could not be avoided. After this we will limit all standing love-feast announcements to two lines, which will enable us to insert all notices of the kind received to much better advantage. Those needing more than two lines to describe the location of their feast, can make the necessary explanations in department of "Notes from Correspondents."

IT was our misfortune to lay over several hours at Rochelle, Ill., last week while the County Fair was in progress. We say misfortune, for the more we see and hear of these County Fairs, the less do we think of them as suitable places for Christians to patronize by either their presence or their money. Horse-racing seems to be the leading feature of these annual gatherings, and usually brings together the least desirable part of our civilization, if civilization we can call it. We noticed that the saloons in town were all patronized and the occasion furnished its usual amount of profanity and other undesirable conduct. Possibly a few of our members might like to attend these gatherings, but it seems to us that if they would take into consideration their high calling as exemplary Christians, their own true sense of propriety would certainly teach them that the way these Fairs are now conducted, renders them very unsuitable places for people who profess to be the true followers of Christ.

THIS year the cholera has demonstrated its power for swiftness in its rapid movement from east to west. Not five months ago it started from India and Western China, and by the middle of July had reached Russia. Thence it spread swiftly through Europe, breaking out in Hamburg one month later. Within a week from that date, we find it in Antwerp, Paris and other places, with a few cases here and there in England. Aug. 31, the unwelcomed pestilence was knocking at the harbor of New York for admittance, and so persistent were its efforts, that by the 14th of this month it had secured a foothold in the City, and not less than six persons have already died of the dreaded disease. It is now too late in the season to do extensive damage, but it is in the United States nevertheless. It is estimated that the disease has already carried off 300,000 persons in Asia and Europe, but the number of new cases in all parts of the East seems to be steadily diminishing, and the world has probably seen the worst of the epidemic for this year. Since writing the above, reports from all parts of the world indicate that the epidemic is fast disappearing, and that the outlook at New York is quite hopeful, as no new cases exist.

THE Brethren in Oklahoma are certainly succeeding in the good work of the Lord. Twenty have recently united with one of the congregations in the Territory, with prospects of the work continuing. With such encouraging indications as given by Bro. Root, in this issue, it would doubtless be well to place several more active ministers in that field and push the work while the country is yet new, and before other churches get too strong a hold.

ONE of our agents writes us that some of the members do not pay up their subscriptions as they ought to, though they have now been reading the paper more than half the year. He suggests that those of our readers who have not yet settled with the agents, should do so at once, so the agents can settle up their accounts with us. The suggestion is a good one, and we hope that delinquent subscribers will heed it. We would like to settle with all of our agents before opening books for the new year, but this we cannot do, so long as those who have not yet paid, do not settle with the agents to whom they gave their subscription.

THIS is a good time to suggest to our elders the advisability of not extending our Communion services too far into the night. Ten and eleven o'clock is too late to keep feeble members at the table. Many of our members are old, and even feeble, and sometimes unwell; and some others have little children to care for; and it seems hardly fair that they should be required to remain up so very late in order to enjoy the feast when it is really not necessary. Sundown, or even a little before, at this season of the year, is a good time to commence the services, and, if proper care is taken, the feast may close about eight. Much depends upon the elders who officiate. Sometimes they become so absorbed in the duties of the occasion, that they wholly forget the comfort of others. Long exhortations or sermons at these times are generally neither edifying nor instructive. A few brief introductory remarks before each service is generally sufficient. These brief remarks, together with the reading of the Scriptures, the singing, prayers and ordinances, afford food enough for the mind and soul on any one occasion. "Let all things be done unto edifying." 1 Cor. 14: 26.

OCCASIONALLY some of our members, who perhaps have a better supply of zeal than knowledge, insist upon our churches patterning a little more after the popular churches in the way of a regular, supported ministry. While we feel that most of our ministers do not have as much substantial encouragement as they are entitled to, we still rejoice that we are not burdened and tormented like some of the churches of which we have knowledge. If these members only knew how many ice-cream suppers, oyster suppers, festivals, and other semi-worldly gatherings it requires to keep up the expenses of most of these popular churches, they would most assuredly pray God to deliver them from such a galling bondage. We have heard so much about the burdens of these popular churches that we have no desire whatever to encourage the introduction of any of their systems among us. If our people only knew it, we have, probably, with a little improvement, the best system in the world of supplying our churches with preaching. In some places it it probably abused, and therefore condemned, but wherever prudently carried out we have made our mark in the face of the very strongest opposition. Let us, therefore, seek to not only strengthen and simplify our present system, but also to extend it, especially in the rural districts. For most of our city work we will have to improve and modify, to some extent, but this need not interfere with work in general.

The Gospel Messenger,

A Weekly at $1.50 Per Annum.

PUBLISHED BY

The Brethren's Publishing Co.

D. L. MILLER,	Editor.
J. H. MOORE,	Office Editor.
J. B. BRUMBAUGH, }	Associate Editors.
J. G. ROYER, }	
JOSEPH AMICK,	Business Manager.

ADVISORY COMMITTEE.
L. W. Teeter, A. Hutchison, Daniel Hays.

☞Communications for publication should be legibly written with black ink on one side of the paper only. Do not attempt to interline, or to put on one page what ought to occupy two.

☞Anonymous communications will not be published.

☞Do not mix business with articles for publication. Keep your communications on separate sheets from all business.

☞Time is precious. We always have time to attend to business and to answer questions of importance, but please do not subject us to need less answering of letters.

☞The Messenger is mailed each week to all subscribers. If the address is correctly entered on our list, the paper must reach the person to whom it is addressed. If you do not get your paper, write us, giving particulars.

☞When changing your address, please give your former as well as your future address in full, so as to avoid delay and misunderstanding.

☞Always remit to the office from which you order your goods, no matter from where you receive them.

☞Do not send personal checks or drafts on interior banks, unless you send with them 25 cents each, to pay for collection.

☞Remittances should be made by Post-office Money Order, Drafts on New York, Philadelphia or Chicago, or Registered Letters, made payable and addressed to "Brethren's Publishing Co., Mount Morris, Ill.," or "Brethren's Publishing Co., Huntingdon, Pa."

☞Entered at the Post-office at Mount Morris, Ill., as second-class matter.

Mount Morris, Ill., - - - - Sept. 27, 1892.

CONSIDERABLE correspondence is crowded out of this issue, and must lay over till next week.

THE Brethren are preparing to build a meeting-house west of Salem, Ill., the coming fall and winter.

BRO. D. R. FREEMAN, of Union City, Ind., has returned to Star City, Pulaski County, where he may now be addressed.

BRO. I. J. ROSENBERGER is now in the midst of an interesting series of meetings at Lanark, Ill., expecting to continue till after their feast.

THE District Meeting for Texas and Oklahoma has elected Bro. Jacob Appleman to represent them on the Standing Committee next year.

THE meeting held by Bro. Silas Hoover in the Middle Creek church, Pa., proved quite a success in the way of members, as twelve were added by confession and baptism.

BRO. O. PERRY HOOVER is now at Greencastle, Ind., and may be addressed at Box 754. Those knowing of members living near that place, will please inform Bro. Hoover.

BRETHREN Lemuel Hillery and W. R. Deeter, we learn, are in the midst of a soul-stirring meeting in the Solomon's Creek church, Elkhart County, Ind. Two have already made the good confession.

THE Brethren in Sterling, Ill., were engaged all last, and a part of this week in an interesting series of meetings. The church seems to be moving along quite smoothly, with good prospects in the future.

OUR Brethren are opening up the evangelistic work early this season. Already reports are coming in of many additions to the church. Eight recently united with the church at Glenated, Mo., by confession and baptism. Other reports will be found in the Correspondence Department.

OUR readers may wonder where we will find room to publish a report from each of the nearly 400 love-feasts in the Brotherhood, this fall. If the reports are short, and to the point, we can make room for one hundred of them in one issue. We would like to send out one issue containing one hundred condensed reports of these glorious feasts, held by our Brethren in all parts of the Brotherhood. Let no feast remain unreported this season.

MOST of our readers are not aware of the value of the excellent little book we keep for sale, entitled, "Church Entertainments," or "Twenty Reasons" against modern church entertainments, fairs, festivals, etc. Bro. I. J. Rosenberger has sold twenty copies, and now orders two dozen more. Hundreds of them would be purchased and read if our people generally comprehended the strength and character of the work. Price, 30 cents, or $3.00 a dozen.

THE last issue of the MESSENGER contained 220 standing love-feast announcements, and a number were crowded out for the lack of room. We regretted this very much, but it could not be avoided. After this we will limit all standing love-feast announcements to two lines, which will enable us to insert all notices of the kind received to much better advantage. Those needing more than two lines to describe the location of their feast, can make the necessary explanations in department of "Notes from Correspondents."

IT was our misfortune to lay over several hours at Rochelle, Ill., last week while the County Fair was in progress. We say *misfortune*, for the more we see and hear of these County Fairs, the less do we think, of them as suitable places for Christians to patronize by either their presence or their money. Horse-racing seems to be the leading feature of these annual gatherings, and usually brings together the least desirable part of our civilization, if civilization we can call it. We noticed that the saloons in town were well patronized and the occasion furnished its usual amount of profanity and other undesirable conduct. Possibly a few of our members would like to attend these gatherings, but it seems to us that if they would take into consideration their high calling as exemplary Christians, their own true sense of propriety would certainly teach them that the way these Fairs are now conducted, renders them very unsuitable places for people who profess to be the true followers of Christ.

THIS year the cholera has demonstrated its power for swiftness in its rapid movement from east to west. Not five months ago it started from India and Western China, and by the middle of July had reached Russia. Thence it spread swiftly through Europe, breaking out in Hamburg one month later. Within a week from that date, we find it in Antwerp, Paris and other places, with a few cases here and there in England. Aug. 31, the unwelcomed pestilence was knocking at the harbor of New York for admittance, and so persistent were its efforts, that by the 14th of this month it had secured a foothold in the City, and not less than six persons have already died of the dreaded disease. It is now too late in the season to do extensive damage, but it is in the United States nevertheless. It is estimated that the disease has already carried off 300,000 persons in Asia and Europe, but the number of new cases in all parts of the East seems to be steadily diminishing, and the world has probably seen the worst of the epidemic for this year. Since writing the above, reports from all parts of the world indicate that the epidemic is fast disappearing, and that the outlook at New York is quite hopeful, as no new cases exist.

THE Brethren in Oklahoma are certainly succeeding in the good work of the Lord. Twenty have recently united with one of the congregations in the Territory, with prospects of the work continuing. With such encouraging indications as given by Bro. Root, in this issue, it would doubtless be well to place several more active ministers in that field and push the work while the country is yet new, and before other churches get too strong a hold.

ONE of our agents writes us that some of the members do not pay up their subscriptions as they ought to, though they have now been reading the paper more than half the year. He suggests that those of our readers who have not yet settled with the agents, should do so at once, so the agents can settle up their accounts with us. The suggestion is a good one, and we hope that delinquent subscribers will heed it. We would like to settle with all of our agents before opening books for the new year, but this we cannot do, so long as those who have not yet paid, do not settle, with the agents to whom they gave their subscription.

THIS is a good time to suggest to our elders the advisability of not extending our Communion services too far into the night. Ten and eleven o'clock is too late to keep feeble members at the table. Many of our members are old, and even feeble, and sometimes unwell; and some others have little children to care for; and it seems hardly fair that they should be required to remain up so very late in order to enjoy the feast when it is really not necessary. Sundown, or even a little before, at this season of the year, is a good time to commence the services, and, if proper care is taken, the feast may close about eight. Much depends upon the elders who officiate. Sometimes they become so absorbed in the duties of the occasion, that they wholly forget the comfort of others. Long exhortations or sermons at these times are generally neither edifying nor instructive. A few brief introductory remarks before each service is generally sufficient. These brief remarks, together with the reading of the Scriptures, the singing, prayers and ordinances, afford food enough for the mind and soul on any one occasion. "Let all things be done unto edifying." 1 Cor. 14: 26.

OCCASIONALLY some of our members, who perhaps have a better supply of zeal than knowledge, insist upon our churches patterning a little more after the popular churches in the way of a regular, supported ministry. While we feel that most of our ministers do not have as much substantial encouragement as they are entitled to, we still rejoice that we are not burdened and tormented like some of the churches of which we have knowledge. If these members only knew how many ice-cream suppers, oyster suppers, festivals, and other semi-worldly gatherings it requires to keep up the expenses of most of these popular churches, they would most assuredly pray God to deliver them from such a galling bondage. We have heard so much about the burdens of these popular churches that we have no desire whatever to encourage the introduction of any of their systems among us. If our people only knew it, we have, probably, with a little improvement, the best system in the world of supplying our churches with preaching. In some places it it probably abused, and therefore condemned, but wherever prudently carried out we have made our mark in the face of the very strongest opposition. Let us, therefore, seek to not only strengthen and simplify our present system, but also to extend it, especially in the rural districts. For most of our city work we will have to improve and modify, to some extent, but this need not interfere with work in general.

Is man naturally in possession of immortality? And do the righteous go to heaven at death, and the wicked to hell?
T. E. ADAMS.

THE body, of course, is not immortal, but in man there is a part that is immortal. Mention of this is made by Solomon: "Then shall the dust return to the earth as it was: and the spirit shall return to God who gave it." Eccl. 12: 7. This same immortal element was referred to by Christ when he said, "And fear not them which kill the body, but are not able to kill the soul; but rather fear him which is able to destroy both soul and body in hell." Matt. 10: 28. It will be observed that the soul is capable of living after the death of the body, and that, while the body returns to the earth, this soul, under the name of "spirit" returns to God who gave it. It will further be observed that the soul is an element which man has not sufficient power to destroy, though he may kill the body. Putting all these things together, unavoidably leads to the conclusion that man, from the beginning of his natural existence in this world, has in him an immortal part that came from God, and at the close of life returns to the source from whence it came. We recognize in man a twofold nature, the animal and the spiritual. The animal shows man's relation and connection with the earth. The spiritual nature is proof of man's connection with the Deity from which he sprang, for "we are the offspring of God" (Acts 17: 29), and occupy a position a little lower than the angels. To man, from God, has been transmitted this germ of immortality, which lives after the death of the body. Man being thus related to the Deity, must be regarded as having no connection whatever with the animal creation. He owes his origin to a higher source, and carries in his very feelings and aspirations convictions showing his relation to a higher order of being, and also his capabilities of reaching a still higher plane in life. Since men's origin is from above, the tendency of true culture upon his part is to make him still more like God from whence he came. In the narrative of the rich man and Lazarus, mentioned in Luke 16, we observe not only life after death, but consciousness and condition. The rich man lifted up his eyes in hell; i. e., in that part of the spirit world where the spirits of the wicked are retained until the second resurrection. The spirit of Lazarus was carried by angels to that part of the spirit land where the righteous spirits are comforted until the first resurrection. It was the place where Abraham was. We understand that the righteous do not enter the heavenly state until the close of the final judgment. In the flesh the just and unjust dwell together, and alike enjoy the blessings of earth. At death their spirits are separated, the wicked going to the abode of wicked spirits, and the righteous to the Paradise of holy spirits. Though far apart, the two localities are in sight of each other. We read of the rich man seeing Lazarus afar off. At the judgment there is a final and an everlasting separation. This settles the condition of both the righteous and the wicked for all eternity. It is then that the wicked shall enter upon a life of everlasting punishment, and the righteous a life of eternal enjoyment. We will here observe that the term hell, in Luke 16, where mention is made of the rich man lifting up his eyes in hell, is not a correct rendering. It should be hades, or the abode of the wicked spirits.

Am I permitted to ask a question on prophesying? I read in the MESSENGER much about prayer-covering, why not also call it a prophesying-covering, according to 1 Cor. 11: 5? What do you understand about prophesying, so frequently spoken of? Paul says "But if all prophesy, and there come in one that believeth not, or one unlearned, he is convinced of all, he is judged of all: and thus are the secrets of his heart made manifest; and so falling down on his face he will worship God, and report that God is in you of a truth." 1 Cor. 14: 24, 25 "Let the prophets speak two or three, and let the other judge." Verse 29. "For ye may all prophesy one by one, that all may learn, and all may be comforted. And the spirits of the prophets are subject to the prophets. For God is not the author of confusion, but of peace, as in all churches of the saints." Verses 31-33. Philip, the evangelist, had four daughters, virgins, which did prophesy. Acts 21: 8, 9. Please explain about this prophesying through the GOSPEL MESSENGER.
PETER FIKE.

"Prayer-covering" is no more, or no less a Scripture term than prophesying-covering. As our sisters exercise more in prayer than in prophesying, the idea of prayer-covering seems more suggestive, and for that reason it is probably used. The few sisters among us who engage in prophesying, usually have their heads covered, but since many engage in prayer without regard to Paul's instructions, it has led to much writing on the subject, as well as the use of the term prayer-covering. It, however, may very properly be called such. Prayer comes before prophesying. Prophesying, in these quotations, cannot refer to foretelling future events. It refers to speaking to edification and confort, and possibly, warning and instruction. In this class of religious exercises, all the members of the church were permitted to take part. Philip had four daughters who exercised enough in that line to occasion the writer of Acts to make special mention of them. The custom of thus prophesying among the sisters was prevalent enough to induce the apostle Paul to instruct them to cover their heads while thus engaged. From this we may infer that prophesying was quite general in the Christian church. It was also connected with prayer, hence we conclude that it was principally exercised in at their informal meetings. Philip's daughters must have enjoyed a more extended liberty, for they seemed to have made it a special part of their work. Also those sisters, who helped Paul in the Gospel, must have engaged in prophesying as a special work pertaining to their mission as helpers in the Gospel. Prophesying was also engaged in by men, for Paul teaches that they dishonor their heads if they pray or prophesy with their heads covered. We must therefore understand that it was a duty, as well as a privilege, suited to both sexes, and could be engaged in, in the public assembly of the saints. All these, as well as much more which might be mentioned, leads us to conclude that in the apostolic age, sisters, as help-meets in the Gospel, enjoyed privileges, and possibly exerted an influence in religious circles, somewhat in advance of what they do among us at present. The frequent and favorable mention of them in the New Testament would indicate this. It may be to our advantage to again study the New Testament in the light of a woman's influence and capabilities as a helper in religious work. In other churches she is wielding an influence that looks very much like revolutionizing creeds. While we need not pattern after others, we nevertheless cannot help observing in their ranks the elements of female power or influence which, only in a more developed stage, exists among us, and it will be wise in us to develop, train, and use it in the interest of pure Christianity. It is probable that our sisters greatly outnumber the brethren, and in voting can wield the greater power. Where health permits, they are more regular in their attendance of meetings, and listen to the preaching of the Word more attentively than the men; for while brethren often sleep during services, sisters are seldom seen sleeping. Sisters generally far exceed the brethren in their attendance upon the prayer-meeting services, and are usually more concerned about Sunday-school work. While this is not so noticeable among our people at present, the tendency of our schools and Sunday-school work is to render it still more noticeable, and, perhaps, before another generation, they will wield an influence that some of us are not dreaming of. This influence will be felt in our Sunday-schools, prayer-meetings, colleges, and in our literature. In these departments are openings for hundreds of trained sisters, where they can and will enter upon the work of moulding the next generation. The simple fact that the church is called a "mother," and that in the latter days she is represented as a "woman clothed with the sun," indicates, perhaps, a stronger female element in the church than we are in the habit of calculating on. These reflections, if followed out on this line, would doubtless lead to the adoption of measures calculated to encourage our sisters still more in the exercise of the prophesying privileges, so clearly granted them in the Gospel. The time is coming, and in some localities is probably here, when sisters, of proper training and consecration, will be in great demand for that department of religious work becoming their sex, zeal and special adaptation. Hence the propriety and wisdom of us giving this matter more attention.
J. H. M.

WHEN AND WHAT TO READ.

A WRITER in the Golden Censer has shown that the Bible may be made applicable to nearly, if not quite, every condition of life. Consider well, and preserve the following, which is clipped from that journal:

If you are impatient, sit down quietly and have a talk with Job.

If you are just a little strong-headed, go to see Moses.

If you are getting weak-kneed, take a look at Elijah.

If there is no song in your heart, listen to David.

If you are a policy man, read Daniel.

If you are getting sordid, spend a while with Isaiah.

If you feel spiritually chilly, get the beloved disciple to put his arms around you.

If your faith is below par, read Paul.

If you are getting lazy, watch James.

If you are losing sight of the future, climb up to Revelation and get a glimpse of the promised land.

A writer in the Independent, as well as the editor of the Evangelist, points out the rapid progress of the Russians, or rather of the Russian wing of the Eastern Church, in securing a foot-hold in Palestine. All through the long period of Mohammedan domination there has remained a considerable body of Christians in Syria, and, indeed, all over Western Asia, who are connected with the Eastern or Greek Church. These are met with in almost every city of Palestine and hold large establishments at Nazareth, Bethlehem, and Jerusalem. In addition to these the Russians

QUERISTS' DEPARTMENT.

Is man naturally in possession of immortality? And do the righteous go to heaven at death, and the wicked to hell?

T. E. ADAMS.

THE body, of course, is not immortal, but in man there is a part that is immortal. Mention of this is made by Solomon: "Then shall the dust return to the earth as it was: and the spirit shall return to God who gave it." Eccl. 12: 7. This same immortal element was referred to by Christ when he said, "And fear not them which kill the body, but are not able to kill the soul; but rather fear him which is able to destroy both soul and body in hell." Matt. 10: 28. It will be observed that the soul is capable of living after the death of the body, and that, while the body returns to the earth, this soul, under the name of "spirit" returns to God who gave it. It will further be observed that the soul is an element which man has not sufficient power to destroy, though he may kill the body. Putting all these things together, unavoidably leads to the conclusion that man, from the beginning of his natural existence in this world, has in him an immortal part that came from God, and at the close of life returns to the source from whence it came. We recognize in man a twofold nature, the animal and the spiritual. The animal shows man's relation and connection with the earth. The spiritual nature is proof of man's connection with the Deity from which he sprang, for "we are the offspring of God" (Acts 17: 29), and occupy a position a little lower than the angels. To man, from God, has been transmitted this germ of immortality, which lives after the death of the body. Man being thus related to the Deity, must be regarded as having no connection whatever with the animal creation. He owes his origin to a higher source, and carries in his very feelings and aspirations convictions showing his relation to a higher order of being, and also his capabilities of reaching a still higher plane in life. Since man's origin is from above, the tendency of true culture upon his part is to make him still more like God from whence he came. In the narrative of the rich man and Lazarus, mentioned in Luke 16, we observe not only life after death, but consciousness and condition. The rich man lifted up his eyes in hell; i. e., in that part of the spirit world where the spirits of the wicked are retained until the second resurrection. The spirit of Lazarus was carried by angels to that part of the spirit land where the righteous spirits are comforted until the first resurrection. It was the place where Abraham was. We understand that the righteous do not enter the heavenly state until the close of the final judgment. In the flesh the just and unjust dwell together, and alike enjoy the blessings of earth. At death their spirits are separated, the wicked going to the abode of wicked spirits, and the righteous to the Paradise of holy spirits. Though far apart, the two localities are in sight of each other. We read of the rich man seeing Lazarus afar off. At the judgment there is a final and an everlasting separation. This settles the condition of both the righteous and the wicked for all eternity. It is then that the wicked shall enter upon a life of everlasting punishment, and the righteous a life of eternal enjoyment. We will here observe that the term hell, in Luke 16, where mention is made of the rich man lifting up his eyes in hell, is not a correct rendering. It

should be hades, or the abode of the wicked spirits.

Am I permitted to ask a question on prophesying? I read in the MESSENGER much about prayer-covering, why not also call it a prophesying-covering, according to 1 Cor. 11: 5? What do you understand about prophesying, so frequently spoken of? Paul says "But if all prophesy, and there come in one that believeth not, or one unlearned, he is convinced of all, he is judged of all: and thus are the secrets of his heart made manifest; and so falling down on his face he will worship God, and report that God is in you of a truth." 1 Cor. 14: 24, 25. "Let the prophets speak two or three, and let the other judge." Verse 29. "For ye may all prophesy one by one, that all may learn, and all may be comforted. And the spirits of the prophets are subject to the prophets. For God is not the author of confusion, but of peace, as in all churches of the saints." Verses 31-33. Philip, the evangelist, had four daughters, virgins, which did prophesy. Acts 21: 8, 9. Please explain about this prophesying through the GOSPEL MESSENGER.

PETER FIKE.

"Prayer-covering" is no more, or no less a Scripture term than prophesying-covering. As our sisters exercise more in prayer than in prophesying, the idea of prayer-covering seems more suggestive, and for that reason it is probably used. The few sisters among us who engage in prophesying, usually have their heads covered, but since many engage in prayer without regard to Paul's instructions, it has led to much writing on the subject, as well as the use of the term prayer-covering. It, however, may very properly be called such. Prayer comes before prophesying. Prophesying, in these quotations, cannot refer to foretelling future events. It refers to speaking to edification and comfort, and possibly, warning and instruction. In this class of religious exercises, all the members of the church were permitted to take part. Philip had four daughters who exercised enough in that line to occasion the writer of Acts to make special mention of them. The custom of thus prophesying among the sisters was prevalent enough to induce the apostle Paul to instruct them to cover their heads while thus engaged. From this we may infer that prophesying was quite general in the Christian church. It was also connected with prayer, hence we conclude that it was principally exercised in at their informal meetings. Philip's daughters must have enjoyed a more extended liberty, for they seemed to have made it a special part of their work. Also those sisters, who helped Paul in the Gospel, must have engaged in prophesying as a special work pertaining to their mission as helpers in the Gospel. Prophesying was also engaged in by men, for Paul teaches that they dishonor their heads if they pray or prophesy with their heads covered. We must therefore understand that it was a duty, as well as a privilege, suited to both sexes, and could be engaged in, in the public assembly of the saints. All these, as well as much more which might be mentioned, leads us to conclude that in the apostolic age, sisters, as help-meets in the Gospel, enjoyed privileges, and possibly exerted an influence in religious circles, somewhat in advance of what they do among us at present. The frequent and favorable mention of them in the New Testament would indicate this. It may be to our advantage to again study the New Testament in the light of a woman's influence and capabilities as a helper in religious work. In other churches she is wielding an influence that looks very much like revolutionizing creeds. While we need not pattern after others, we nevertheless cannot help observing in their ranks the elements of female power or influence which, only in a more undeveloped stage, exists among us, and it will be wise in us to develop, train, and use it in the

interest of pure Christianity. It is probable that our sisters greatly outnumber the brethren, and in voting can wield the greater power. Where health permits, they are more regular in their attendance of meetings, and listen to the preaching of the Word more attentively than the men; for while brethren often sleep during services, sisters are seldom seen sleeping. Sisters generally far exceed the brethren in their attendance upon the prayer-meeting services, and are usually more concerned about Sunday-school work. While this is not so noticeable among our people at present, the tendency of our schools and Sunday-school work is to render it still more noticeable, and, perhaps, before another generation, they will wield an influence that some of us are not dreaming of. This influence will be felt in our Sunday-schools, prayer-meetings, colleges, and in our literature. In these departments are openings for hundreds of trained sisters, where they can and will enter upon the work of moulding the next generation. The simple fact that the church is called a "mother," and that in the latter days she is represented as a "woman clothed with the sun," indicates, perhaps, a stronger female element in the church than we are in the habit of calculating on. These reflections, if followed out on this line, would doubtless lead to the adoption of measures calculated to encourage our sisters still more in the exercise of the prophesying privileges, so clearly granted them in the Gospel. The time is coming, and in some localities is probably here, when sisters, of proper training and consecration, will be in great demand for that department of religious work becoming their sex, zeal and special adaptation. Hence the propriety and wisdom of us giving this matter more attention.

J. H. M.

WHEN AND WHAT TO READ.

A WRITER in the Golden Censer has shown that the Bible may be made applicable to nearly, if not quite, every condition of life. Consider well, and preserve the following, which is clipped from that journal:

If you are impatient, sit down quietly and have a talk with Job.

If you are just a little strong-headed, go to see Moses.

If you are getting weak-kneed, take a look at Elijah.

If there is no song in your heart, listen to David.

If you are a policy man, read Daniel.

If you are getting sordid, spend a while with Isaiah.

If you feel spiritually chilly, get the beloved disciple to put his arm around you.

If your faith is below par, read Paul.

If you are getting lazy, watch James.

If you are losing sight of the future, climb up to Revelation and get a glimpse of the promised land.

A writer in the Independent, as well as the editor of the Evangelist, points out the rapid progress of the Russians, or rather of the Russian wing of the Eastern Church, in securing a foot-hold in Palestine. All through the long period of Mohammedan domination there has remained a considerable body of Christians in Syria, and, indeed, all over Western Asia, who are connected with the Eastern or Greek Church. These are met with in almost every city of Palestine and hold large establishments at Nazareth, Bethlehem, and Jerusalem. In addition to these the Russians

From Pueblo we came to Colorado Springs, where we are at present writing. Here we met several of our associates in former years. To-day we are visiting our aged sister, Anna Funk, the widow of Bro. Daniel. She now keeps house with her two sons, Daniel and Harry, in this city, at No. 212, Rio Grande Street. They are both in business here. Harry is a member of the church. We have only met one member outside of this family, but have been informed that several others are living in the city. Here again great anxiety is manifested for the upbuilding of Christ's kingdom.

Some may wonder why I have not been preaching any during my travels. In explanation I would say that my health has been much impaired for some months and I was in hopes that a rest from home cares on the farm, together with the influence of the mountain air, might make a change for the better. So far I do not feel any improvement to speak of yet, but wife enjoys the trip well. I have been trying, in a quiet way, to work up something for the Master's cause. From here we expect to go to Denver. We have not set our time yet to start home.   H. R. TAYLOR.

Deep River, Iowa, Sept. 3.

From the Poudre Valley Church, Colo.

SEPTEMBER 3, Bro. S M. Goughenour and wife of Elkhart, Iowa, came to us, and preached for us each evening during the following week. We had large crowds and the best of feeling prevailed. None were quite ready to go with the people of God, but Felix-like, desired a more convenient season.

Our love-feast, on the evening of the 10th, was indeed a feast to the soul. About thirty-five members communed. Just as we were about to begin the examination exercises, Bro. H. R. Taylor and wife, of Deep River, Iowa, came to us very unexpectedly. We were glad to meet them, and have them aid us in the good work. Quite a number of our dear brethren and sisters, from Longmont, Colorado, cheered us by their presence. The scene was new to many, but the very best of order prevailed among the outsiders. Sunday, Sept. 11, we had children's meeting at 9:30, and afterwards public preaching by brethren H. R. Taylor and S. M. Goughenour, after which the latter left us for home. Many were the prayers which went with him. Meetings closed on Sunday night with a crowded house. Bro. Taylor left us on Monday.   D. M. CLICK.

From Elkhart, Iowa.

AT my last writing we were in Denver. Sept. 3 we left for Fort Collins, where we commenced meetings the same evening. We continued until their love-feast Sept. 10. Sept. 7 they held their church council. Eld. G. W. Fesler came and remained until after their feast. During these meetings we saw no visible fruits of our labors, but seldom have we seen a deeper interest taken in our meetings than at this place. A number of members were up from Longmont to their feast, also Bro. H. R. Taylor and wife, from Deep River, Iowa. This was the first love-feast ever held in this part of Colorado. We were made to think of what a change time will bring. Here, a few years ago, the soldiers were stationed for the safety of the few citizens. Now, in full view of the electric lights, we are holding our feast. Brethren and sisters, let us pray for each other and especially for the little band of members at Fort Collins and Denver. Sept. 11 we bade farewell to the dear members to return home, and a sad parting it was, but we are looking forward to a time when the faithful will not

have these sad partings. We arrived home safely on the morning of the 13th and found all well.   S. M. GOUGHENOUR.

Sept. 13.

Messages Dropped by the Way.

SOME of these messages should have been dropped in various parts of the Indian Territory, when I met some of the Father's children at Stillwater, some at Clarkson, and some at Crescent, all in Oklahoma. At Clarkson we held meetings two weeks previous to their love-feast, which was Aug. 27; then continued the meetings for some days afterward. At this place twenty souls were added to the faithful in the Lord. Only six of them were formerly acquainted with the Brethren. Seven are heads of families; seven are young brethren, and six are young sisters. Here about six or seven more were received by letter. A choice was held for two brethren to the ministry, the lot falling upon Bro. Nicholas Gripe and —— Gorham; and for deacon upon Bro. J. O. Neher. All were duly installed into their offices. May they all prove faithful in their high and holy calling, is my earnest prayer. These dear brethren and sisters, now numbering about fifty-five, are under the gentle but earnest care of Eld. Jacob Appleman, who resides in their midst. To his amicable and able work much of their success is to be attributed. Much more may yet be expected, as he is chosen by District Meeting to represent the District of Oklahoma and Texas on Standing Committee next year, and he is also the home missionary for Oklahoma by the same authority. Ananias Neher is a zealous brother in the first degree of the ministry.

September 3 we suspended this work for two days, and about thirty of us went to the love-feast in the Mt. Hope congregation, near Crescent City, where we met another band of dear and loving members, under the temporary care of brethren George Landis and M. M. Ennis, and when we presented to Eld. Appleman, of our company, thirteen dear souls that were baptized since he left home four days previous, and told him of five more who had not come with us, it must suffice to imagine the emotions of his hopeful soul, and also the joy of all the saints present. During this meeting one brother was added to their number, over which, perhaps, no one will rejoice more than Eld. John Wise, whose son-in-law he is.

I note the fact that during all this work in the Territory we had the presence and the assistance of our esteemed and aged brother, Martin Neher, whose acquaintance I have enjoyed for forty-five years. Now, as for the country, if seasons and crops continue in general as they were since the country opened, it will certainly prove a "goodly land" indeed. The good products of earth are enjoyed there in their perfection, in great profusion and at low prices.   C. C. ROOT.

Ozawkie, Kans, Sept. 13, 1892.

Final Report of Funds for Russian Sufferers.

IN order to give this final report, we have waited until all the amounts could be reported. The following closes our list:

A brother, Canada, $15.00; David Neff, Girard, Ill., $5.00; John Barnhart, Mansfield, Ill., $10.88; S. B. Kuhn, Naperville, Ill., $2.00; W. S. Price, Royer's Ford, Pa., $3.25; B. Beckone, Good's Mills, Va., $5.00; Geo. W. Eavey, Calhoun, Ill., $1.50; Waynesborough, church, Pa., by J. F. Oller, $22.00; Ramona, Kansas, Sunday-school collections, by O. O. Button, $28.43; Mary J. Baile, South Strabane, Pa., $2.00; mother and daughter, Box 3, Ladoga, Ind., $2.50; English

Prairie church, Mongo, Ind., $9.50; K... church, Fla., by J. I. Miller, $13.00; sister Reese, Fowler, Cal., $1.00; George Renner, ...field, Wash., $5.00; Midland church, Va... Abram Conner, $6.00; unknown, South Eng... Iowa, $1.00; J. F. Flory, Lemoore, Cal., $1.00, from a sympathizer, Baltimore, Md., $2.00; to two sisters, Harleysville, Pa., $3.00; J. S. ... Susan Metzger, Cerro Gordo, Ill., $5.00; R... abeth Frantz, Cerro Gordo, Ill., 25 cents; M... K. Good, Midvale, Pa., $2.00; Lizzie M. C... Kiracofe, Va., 50 cents; Susan Clapper, C... Ohio, $10.00; Mary A. Layman, Nuzums, W. ... 50 cents; J. B. Heiskill, Nuzums, W. Va... cents; Amos Hoffman, Nuzums, W. Va., $... D. W. Kirk, Nuzums, W. Va., $1.00; C. T... Nuzums, W. Va., 10 cents; Florence L... Nuzums, W. Va., 15 cents; Mary J. Reyn... Nuzums, W. Va., $1.00; Helen Cool, Nu... W. Va., 50 cents; Richard Springer, Nu... W. Va., 50 cents; A. C. Snowberger, Monla ... ta, Cal., $3.40; Plum Creek Sunday-school, ... strong County, Pa., $5.10; New Haven ch... Gratiot Co., Mich., $6.00; Mrs. Martha E... East Coventry, Pa., $1.00; Susie Teeter, I... thorn, Fla., $5.00.

After sending to Mr. Edgar all the funds ... hand, at the date of the last forwarding of ... to Russia, a few amounts were received too ... for the purpose originally intended. By the ... sent of the donors, we will pass the balance ... hand to the MESSENGER Poor Fund, and thus ... complish a good work for the cause of primit ... Christianity.   L. A. PLATT ...

Mount Morris, Ill.

Notes from the Second District of West Virginia

AUG. 26 I left home to visit the Rock Oak ... church, in West Virginia, about sixty-five mi... distant. I spent the night very pleasantly wi... Bro. Cochran and family, about eight or ni... miles from the place of meeting. Next morni... Aug. 27, in company with brother and sist... Cochran, we started to the place of meeting. ... Goose Neck we were met by our esteemed bro... er John Friedly, who is one of the elders. B... John is well stricken in years and is as a sh... ready to be garnered. I preached (including ... munion services) in all twelve sermons. Duri... our meetings there was the best of attention gi... to the Word preached. Two precious souls w... added to the church, and others seemed to be ... ously impressed. We hope that the seed ... will, in due time, bring a bountiful crop. I ... ed quite a number of families, and my effort... think, were not without an effect. The memb... ship is quite small in this church and badly ... commuted. Only twelve members, including my... communed. While at the table, I thought of ... "twelve" in that upper room at Jerusalem. ... Brethren here need to be visited by our minist... ing brethren often as the two elders,—breth... Friedly and Cochran,—both are old and it ... not be expected for them to labor as in th... younger days. Bro. Milton Czigans, a mini... lives about eighteen miles away, and should vi... and preach at this place as much as he coul... As a whole our meeting was a pleasant one. ... thing we felt sorry for,—our aged sis... Friedly was not able to attend meeting. Sh... about eighty years of age, and is feeble in bo... but strong in the Lord. At the last season ... worship around the altar with her, she ma... choice of hymn No. 766, "See the leaves aro... us falling," etc. We felt that it was good to w... upon the Lord.

Sept. 4 I was taken to the station by B... Friedly's son-in-law, William Hurst, and w... soon homeward bound. I arrived home in ...

From Pueblo we came to Colorado Springs, where we are at present writing. Here we met several of our associates in former years. To-day we are visiting our aged sister, Anna Fank, the widow of Bro. Daniel. She now keeps house with her two sons, Daniel and Harry, in this city, at No. 212, Rio Grande Street. They are both in business here. Harry is a member of the church. We have only met one member outside of this family, but have been informed that several others are living in the city. Here again great anxiety is manifested for the upbuilding of Christ's kingdom.

Some may wonder why I have not been preaching any during my travels. In explanation I would say that my health has been much impaired for some months and I was in hopes that a rest from home cares on the farm, together with the influence of the mountain air, might make a change for the better. So far I do not feel any improvement to speak of yet, but wife enjoys the trip well. I have been trying, in a quiet way, to work up something for the Master's cause. From here we expect to go to Denver. We have not set our time yet to start home. H. R. TAYLOR.

Deep River, Iowa, Sept. 3.

From the Poudre Valley Church, Colo.

SEPTEMBER 3, Bro. S. M. Goughenour and wife of Elkhart, Iowa, came to us, and preached for us each evening during the following week. We had large crowds and the best of feeling prevailed. None were quite ready to go with the people of God, but Felix-like, desired a more convenient season.

Our love-feast, on the evening of the 10th, was indeed a feast to the soul. About thirty-five members communed. Just as we were about to begin the examination exercises, Bro. H. R. Taylor and wife, of Deep River, Iowa, came to us very unexpectedly. We were glad to meet them, and have them aid us in the good work. Quite a number of our dear brethren and sisters, from Longmont, Colorado, cheered us by their presence. The scene was new to many, but the very best of order prevailed among the outsiders. Sunday, Sept. 11, we had children's meeting at 9:30, and afterwards public preaching by brethren H. R. Taylor and S. M. Goughenour, after which the latter left us for Iowa. Many were the prayers which went with him. Meetings closed on Sunday night with a crowded house. Bro. Taylor left us on Monday. D. M. CLICK.

From Elkhart, Iowa.

AT my last writing we were in Denver. Sept. 8 we left for Fort Collins, where we commenced meetings the same evening. We continued until their love-feast Sept. 10. Sept. 7 they held their church council. Eld. G. W. Fesler came and remained until after their feast. During these meetings we saw no visible fruits of our labors, but seldom have we seen a deeper interest taken in our meetings than at this place. A number of members were up from Longmont by their feast, also Bro. H. R Taylor and wife, from Deep River, Iowa. This was the first love-feast ever held in this part of Colorado. We were made to think of what a change time will bring. Here, a few years ago, the soldiers were stationed for the safety of the few citizens. Now, in full view of the electric lights, we are holding our feast. Brethren and sisters, let us pray for each other and especially for the little band of members at Fort Collins and Denver, Colorado. Sept. 11 we bade farewell to the dear members to return home, and a sad parting it was, but we are looking forward to a time when the faithful will not have these sad partings. We arrived home safely on the morning of the 13th and found all well. S. M. GOUGHENOUR.

Sept. 13.

Messages Dropped by the Way.

SOME of these messages should have been dropped in various parts of the Indian Territory, when I met some of the Father's children at Stillwater, some at Clarkson, and some at Crescent, all in Oklahoma. At Clarkson we held meetings two weeks previous to their love-feast, which was Aug. 27; then continued the meetings for some days afterward. At this place twenty souls were added to the faithful in the Lord. Only six of them were formerly acquainted with the Brethren. Seven are heads of families; seven are young brethren, and six are young sisters. Here about six or seven more were received by letter. A choice was held for two brethren to the ministry, the lot falling upon Bro. Nicholas Gripe and —— Gorham; and for deacon upon Bro. J. C. Neher. All were duly installed into their offices. May they all prove faithful in their high and holy calling, is my earnest prayer. These dear brethren and sisters, now numbering about fifty-five, are under the gentle but earnest care of Eld. Jacob Appleman, who resides in their midst. To his amicable and able work much of their success is to be attributed. Much more may yet be expected, as he is chosen by District Meeting to represent the District of Oklahoma and Texas on Standing Committee next year, and he is also the home missionary for Oklahoma by the same authority. Ananias Neher is a zealous brother in the first degree of the ministry.

September 3 we suspended this work for two days, and about thirty of us went to the love-feast in the Mt. Hope congregation, near Crescent City, where we met another band of dear and loving members, under the temporary care of brethren George Landis and M. M. Ennis, and when we presented to Eld. Appleman, of our company, thirteen dear souls that were baptized since he left home four days previous, and told him of five more who had not come with us, it must suffice to imagine the emotions of his hopeful soul, and also the joy of all the saints present. During this meeting one brother was added to their number, over which, perhaps, no one will rejoice more than Eld. John Wise, whose son-in-law he is.

I note the fact that during all this work in the Territory we had the presence and the assistance of our esteemed and aged brother, Martin Neher, whose acquaintance I have enjoyed for forty-five years. Now, as for the country, if seasons and crops continue in general as they were since the country opened, it will certainly prove a "goodly land" indeed. The good products of earth are enjoyed there in their perfection, in great profusion and at low prices. C. C. ROOT.

Ozawkie, Kans., Sept. 12, 1892.

Final Report of Funds for Russian Sufferers.

IN order to give this final report, we have waited until all the amounts could be reported. The following closes our list:

A brother, Canada, $15.00; David Neff, Girard, Ill., $5.00; John Barnhart, Mansfield, Ill., $10.88; S. B. Kuhn, Naperville, Ill., $2.00; W. S. Price, Royer's Ford, Pa., $3.25; B. Beckone, Quaker's Mills, Va., $5.00; Geo. W. Eavey, Calhoun, Ill., $1.50; Waynesborough, church, Pa., by J. F. Oller, $22.00; Ramona, Kansas, Sunday-school collections, by O. O. Button, $28.43; Mary J. Baile, South Strabane, Pa., $2.00; mother and daughter, Box 3, Ladoga, Ind., $3.50; English

Prairie church, Mongo, Ind., $9.50; Kool church, Fla., by J. I. Miller, $13.00; sister , Reese, Fowler, Cal., $1.00; George Renner, field, Wash., $5.00; Midland church, Va., Abram Conner, $6.00; unknown, South Engli Iowa, $1.00; J. F. Flory, Lemoore, Cal., $10.00 from a sympathizer, Baltimore, Md., $2.00; fr two sisters, Harleysville, Pa., $3.00; J. S. Susan Metzger, Cerro Gordo, Ill., $5.00; Eli abeth Frantz, Cerro Gordo, Ill., 25 cents; M K. Good, Midvale, Pa., $2.00; Lizzie M. G Kiracofe, Va., 50 cents; Susan Clapper, C Ohio, $10.00; Mary A. Layman, Nuzums, W. Va 50 cents; J. B. Heiskill, Nuzums, W. Va., cents; Amos Hoffman, Nuzums, W. Va., $1. D. W. Kirk, Nuzums, W. Va., $1.00; C. Tra Nuzums, W. Va., 10 cents; Florence L Nuzums, W. Va., 15 cents; Mary J. Reynol Nuzums, W. Va., $1.00; Helen Cool, Nuzum W. Va., 50 cents; Richard Springer, Nuzum W. Va., 50 cents; A. C. Snowberger, Monie V ta, Cal., $3.40; Plum Creek Sunday-school, Arm strong County, Pa., $5.10; New Haven churc Gratiot Co., Mich., $6.00; Mrs. Martha Hig East Coventry, Pa., $1.00; Susie Teeter, Has thorn, Fla., $5.00.

After sending to Mr. Edgar all the funds hand, at the date of the last forwarding of fun to Russia, a few amounts were received too lat for the purpose originally intended. By the sa sent of the donors, we will pass the balance an hand to the MESSENGER Poor Fund, and thus a complish a good work for the cause of primiti Christianity. L. A. PLATE

Mount Morris, Ill.

Notes from the Second District of West Virginia

AUG. 26 I left home to visit the Rock Ca church, in West Virginia, about thirty-five mile distant. I spent the night very pleasantly wit Bro. Cochran and family, about eight or nin miles from the place of meeting. Next mornin Aug. 27, in company with brother and sis Cochran, we started to the place of meeting. Goose Neck we were met by our esteemed bro er John Friedly, who is one of the elders. B John is well stricken in years and is as a she ready to be garnered. I preached (including the munion services) in all twelve sermons. Durin our meetings there was the best of attention give to the Word preached. Two precious souls we added to the church, and others seemed to be seri ously impressed. We hope that the seed so will, in due time, bring a bountiful crop. I wis ed quite a number of families, and my efforts, think, were not without an effect. The member ship is quite small in this church and badly sc tered. Only twelve members, including mysel communed. While at the table, I thought of th "twelve" in that upper room at Jerusalem. T Brethren here need to be visited by our ministe ing brethren often as the two elders,—brethre Friedly and Cochran,—both are old and it c not be expected for them to labor as in their younger days. Bro. Milton Caignes, a ministe lives about eighteen miles away, and should visi and preach at this place as much as he coul As a whole our meeting was a pleasant one. On thing we felt sorry for,—our aged siste Friedly was not able to attend meeting. She b about eighty years of age, and is feeble in bod but strong in the Lord. At the last season o worship around the altar with her, she mad choice of hymn No. 766, "See the leaves arou us falling," etc. We felt that it was good to wal upon the Lord.

Sept. 4 I was taken to the station by Br Friedly's son-in-law, William Hurst, and wa soon homeward bound. I arrived home in the

Dunlap, Kans.—The members of the Cottonwood church met in council at Emporia, Kans., Sept. 3, at which time four were added to the church by letter. The spirit of love was manifested for the church and each other. We decided to hold our love-feast at the home of S. J. Burnett, three miles north-west of Dunlap, Oct. 29 and 30.—*Addie Burnett, Sept. 9.*

Kidder, Mo.—The members of the Hamilton church met in council Aug. 20. There was not much business before the meeting, and all was adjusted in a Christian manner. The visiting brethren made their report, which showed that all are in love and union. Our council was held at the house of our aged sister Doll. By request of the aged sister, the fourth chapter of Luke was read. Our Mill Creek Sunday-school is still alive and our penny collection for the North Missouri Mission is also being continued.—*Henry Etter.*

Dupont, Ohio.—We, the members of Auglaize church, held a very enjoyable harvest-meeting. We called Bro. Jacob Heistand, of Wetzel, Ohio, to labor for us. He was with us and gave us three soul-reviving sermons. We hope we will remember the lessons learned. May God help us all to be of more use in the church hereafter than we ever were in the past! We can be of use to the church by giving a part of the means with which God has blessed us. After services we took up a collection for the benefit of the Home Mission and raised $3.33.—*I. A. Carnahan, Dupont, Ohio, Sept. 1.*

Harrisonville, Mo.—The Communion meeting of the Eight Mile church, Cass County, Mo., was held at Bro. Jacob Kircher's house on Saturday, Sept. 3. There was a good attendance, and everything passed off in order. Our elders, J. M. Mohler, and brethren Martin Mohler, John Hougendoogler, and Albert Smith were present. We had a good meeting. The brethren remained with us and preached on Sunday morning and evening to a small but attentive audience. We have twenty-two members, but no preacher. We would like if some minister would move into our community. We have a good farming country and good society.—*J. F. Kircher, Sept. 6.*

Baltic, Ohio.—The Sugar Creek church held her quarterly council on Thursday, Sept. 1. All business that came before the meeting passed off pleasantly. On Saturday, Sept. 3rd, a love-feast was held at Bunker Hill, in the same church. It was a pleasant feast. Eld. F. B. Weimer, of Wayne County, Ohio, was with us over Sunday and gave us a few good sermons. Different ones have asked me about the location of the Bunker Hill church. It is only a branch of the Sugar Creek church. We rejoice to say that sixteen have been added to the above-named church recently. May the Good Lord continue his blessings upon us, and upon all God's believing children!—*M. H Shutt, Sept. 5.*

Liberty, Ill.—Bro. D. B. Gibson came to us on Saturday before the last Sunday of August and began a series of meetings. Sept. 3 and 4 was our feast, which was very enjoyable. There were fifty communicants at the table. Other ministers from abroad were brethren Lapp, of Missouri and H. W. Strickler, of Lorain this County. They did good work, and I think all could say of a truth that it was good to be there. The meeting is still in progress and up to this time four have made the good confession. There is quite a shaking among the dry bones. The interest is good. Many more are near the kingdom. Mill Creek is coming out victorious by the help of the Lord against the mighty. The good work still goes on. Praise the Lord for his goodness to the children of men!—*T. B. Digman, Sept. 8.*

Minnesota City, Minn.—I am now at the above-named place, where I will remain over Sunday, then return to Dover on Monday, the 5th, and continue there for a time. After our return home, about Sept. 20, wife and I will, the Lord willing, start south for the fall and early winter work in southern Iowa and Northern Missouri. We earnestly desire the prayers of all God's children.—*Wm. C. Hipes, Sept. 2.*

Matrimonial.

"What therefore God hath joined together, let not man put asunder."

FREESE—GROVE.—At the residence of the officiating minister, W. H. Quinn, Sept. 6, 1892, Mr. Wm. Freese and Miss Wilda Grove, both of Canton, Ohio. W. H. QUINN.

ROYER—SUMMER.—At the residence of the officiating minister, W. H. Quinn, Aug. 13, 1892, Bro. William Royer and sister Cena Summer, both of Louisville, Stark County, Ohio. W. H. QUINN.

HAMMOND—BOWEN.—July 23., 1892, by Bro. Samuel E. Burket, Mr. Milton E. Hammond and Miss Jennie Bowen, both of Sevastopol, Ind.

LOUDENBECK—KEPNER.—By the undersigned, Sept. 13, 1892, Mr. Edward Loudenbeck of Chicago, and Miss Sadie Kepner, of Carson City, Mich. GEO. E. STONE.

Fallen Asleep.

"Blessed are the dead which die in the Lord."

BYERS.—In the Paint Creek church, Bourbon County, Kans., Sept. 5, 1892, of cancer of the stomach, Bro. William Byers, aged 68 years. He was a deacon. A. C. NUMER.

WORKMAN.—In the Danville church, Ohio, Aug. 1, 1892, sister Nannie, wife of Elmer Workman, aged 20 years and 15 days. Funeral services by Bro. D. M. Irvin, of Orrville, Ohio. C. J. WORKMAN.

HORN.—In the Danville church, Ohio, Aug. 16, 1892, Bro. Hardman Horn, aged 80 years and 1 month. Deceased has been a member of the Brethren church about forty years. He died at his brother's home near Mt. Vernon. His body was interred in the North Bend cemetery. Funeral services by the writer, assisted by Rev. Disney, of Mt. Vernon. C. J. WORKMAN.

DENNEY.—In the Lower Deer Creek church; Carroll County, Ind., Sept. 9, 1892, Nora Denney, aged 20 years, 11 months and 6 days. Funeral services by brethren Hiel Hamilton and A. J. Flory. S. H. BECHTELHEIMER.

UMPHLET.—In the Centre View church, Warrensburgh, Mo., Aug. 24, 1892, sister Laura Z. Umphlet, daughter of Bro. John and sister Mary Umphlet, aged 17 years, 2 months and 28 days. Sister Laura was taken very ill with typhoid fever Aug. 1. Feeling that her life was near its close, she was anointed in the name of the Lord on the sixth day of her illness. Funeral services by Bro Jacob Witmore from John 38:17. She was laid to rest in the Warrensburgh church cemetery.

UMPHLET.—In the same home, Aug. 26, 1892, of cholera infantum, Sadie Allie, little daughter of Bro. John and sister Esther Umphlet, aged 14 months and 23 days. Funeral services by Bro. Joseph Brubaker. Thus two more earthly ties have been severed to be united in heaven.
SUSIE BLOCHER.

BRYANT.—In the bounds of the Beaver Dam church, Ind., Sept. 3, 1892, Catharine (Doran) Bryant, widow of William Bryant (deceased), aged 66 years, 5 months and 1 day. She was the mother of fourteen children, seven of whom survive her. Funeral services by Bro. Samuel E. Burket from the text, "Prepare to meet thy God." Amos 4:12.

MILUM.—In the Roann church, Wabash Co., Ind., Aug. 5, 1892, of a protracted illness, Bro. John Milum, aged 53 years and 20 days. He leaves a dear companion, a sister, and three children to mourn the loss of one who was near and dear to them. A short time before he died he sent for the elders of the church and was anointed. Funeral services by the Brethren. JOSEPH JOHN.

McKEEVER.—Near Sinking Springs, Highland County, Ohio, April 19, 1892; Nancy Jane McKeever, aged 18 years, 11 months and 12 days. She was a member of the church for five years. While crossing a creek on a log, she fell off and was drowned. Her sudden death is another lesson that we should always be ready for the great change.
W. Q. CALVERT.

LANDIS.—Near Hollowtown,Highland Co., Ohio, Aug. 15, 1892, S. Monroe Landis, aged 50 years, 3 months and 13 days. Friend Landis was a man of good judgment, was industrious, and had many good traits. He leaves a wife, six children to mourn their loss. The wife and five of children are in the fold. Funeral services from James 4. W. Q. CALVERT.

HARRISON.—At the home of his parents in Floyd County, Va., Joseph Clark, son of Robert and Lucinda Harrison, aged 14 years. The cause of his death was brain ... Though he had been afflicted almost from infancy, he was model of patience. J. O. Boone.

MILLER.—In the Upper Stillwater church, Miami Co., Ohio, Aug. 29, 1892, sister Lydia Miller, aged 72 years, ... months and 25 days. Deceased was the widow of Abraham Miller, one of our ministers who died about fifteen years ... Funeral services by the writer, assisted by Tobias Crider. W. H. Boone.

HOOP.—In the Marble Furnace church, Adams Co., Ohio, July 15, 1892, of lung disease, Rebecca Ann Hoop, aged 30 years, 1 month and 19 days. For five years she enjoyed a place in the fold of Christ. She quietly fell asleep, having previously called for the anointing, saying that if it is the Lord's will, she was willing and ready to go. Funeral by Matt. 26:8. W. Q. CALVERT.

SIMMONS.—In the bounds of the May Hill church, Adams Co., Ohio, Sept. 4, 1892, Salome Simmons, aged ... years, 7 months and 24 days. For about 64 years she lived in the church here, and we trust she has gone to be in the church triumphant. Funeral services at her home by Philpp. 1:21. W. Q. CALVERT.

SWISSHELM.—At May Hill, Adams Co., Ohio, April ... 1892, Alfred Elsworth Swisshelm, aged 9 months and ... days. Little Alfred's mother, sister Lizzie Swisshelm, preceded her little son to the spirit land in January last. Their ... ther, and bereaved husband, since the death of his dear wife, wisely cast his lot with the people of God. We pray that Bro. Philip will be faithful and join wife and son in the better land. Funeral services from the words, "What is your life ...." W. Q. CALVERT.

ELLENBERGER.—At May Hill, Adams Co., Ohio, April 13, 1892, Mary Ellenberger, aged 67 years, 3 months and 28 days. Deceased was the wife of Bro. Joseph Ellenberger. For fifty years she had been a member of the Presbyterian church. She lived a devoted life to the faith she professed, was very kind and beautiful-tempered, and was loved and respected by all. She is sadly missed by neighbors and friends, but more by the four daughters and one son, and most of all by Bro. Joseph. Funeral from 1 Kings 2:2. W. Q. CALVERT.

BAYLOR.—In the Bethany congregation, Taylor Co., W. Va., July 9, 1892, A. J. Baylor, aged about 51 years. He leaves a wife and several children to mourn their loss. Friend Baylor was afflicted about three years. His wife, sister Baylor, was a daughter of Eld. Henry Wilson, who was killed at his home during the late war. Funeral services by the writer, assisted by Bro. G. W. Annon from Pa. 103:15, to a large concourse of sympathizing friends. Z. ANNON.

WAGAMAN.—In the Loudonville church, Ohio, Aug. 9, 1892, Goldie, daughter of Bro. Jacob and sister Mary Wagaman, aged 1 year and 8 months. Funeral services by the writer from Mark 10:14. DAVID BRUBAKER.

The Gospel Messenger

Is the recognized organ of the German Baptist or Brethren's church, and advocates the form of doctrine taught in the New Testament and pleads for a return to apostolic and primitive Christianity.

It recognizes the New Testament as the only infallible rule of faith and practice, and maintains that Faith toward God, Repentance from dead works, Regeneration of the heart and mind, baptism by Triune Immersion for remission of sins unto the reception of the Holy Ghost by the laying on of hands, are the means of adoption into the household of God,—the church militant.

It also maintains that Feet-washing, as taught in John 13, both by example and command of Jesus, should be observed in the church.

That the Lord's Supper, instituted by Christ and as universally observed by the apostles and the early Christians, is a full meal, and in connection with the Communion, should be taken in the evening or after the close of the day.

That the Salutation of the Holy Kiss, or Kiss of Charity, is binding upon the followers of Christ.

That War and Retaliation are contrary to the spirit and self-denying principles of the religion of Jesus Christ.

That the principle of Plain Dressing and of Non-conformity to the world, as taught in the New Testament, should be observed by the followers of Christ.

That the Scriptural duty of Anointing the Sick with Oil, in the Name of the Lord, James 5:14, is binding upon all Christians.

It also advocates the church's duty to support Missionary and Tract Work, thus giving to the Lord for the spread of the Gospel and for the conversion of sinners.

In short, it is a Vindicator of all that Christ and the apostles have enjoined upon us, and aims, amid the conflicting theories and discords of modern Christendom, to point out ground that all must concede to be faithfully safe.

The above principles of our Fraternity are set forth on our Brethren's Envelopes. Use them! Price 15 cents per package; 40 cents per hundred.

Dunlap, Kans.—The members of the Cottonwood church met in council at Emporia, Kans., Sept. 3, at which time four were added to the church by letter. The spirit of love was manifested for the church and each other. We decided to hold our love-feast at the home of S. J. Burnett, three miles north-west of Dunlap, Oct. 29 and 30.—*Addie Burnett, Sept. 9.*

Kidder, Mo.—The members of the Hamilton church met in council Aug. 20. There was not much business before the meeting, and all was adjusted in a Christian manner. The visiting brethren made their report, which showed that all are in love and union. Our council was held at the house of our aged sister Doll. By request of the aged sister, the fourth chapter of Luke was read., Our Mill Creek Sunday-school is still alive and our penny collection for the North Missouri Mission is also being continued.—*Henry Etter.*

Dupont, Ohio.—We, the members of Auglaize church, held a very enjoyable harvest-meeting. We called Bro. Jacob Heistand, of Wetzel, Ohio, to labor for us. He was with us and gave us three soul-reviving sermons. We hope we will remember the lessons learned. May God help us all to be of more use in the church hereafter than we ever were in the past! We can be of use to the church by giving a part of the means with which God has blessed us. After services we took up a collection for the benefit of the Home Mission and raised $3.33.—*I. A. Carnahan, Dupont, Ohio. Sept. 1.*

Harrisonville, Mo.—The Communion meeting of the Eight Mile church, Cass County, Mo, was held at Bro. Jacob Kircher's house on Saturday, Sept. 3. There was a good attendance, and everything passed off in order. Our elders, J. M. Mohler, and brethren Martin Mohler, John Hougendougler, and Albert Smith were present. We had a good meeting. The brethren remained with us and preached on Sunday morning and evening to a small but attentive audience. We have twenty-two members, but no preacher. We would like if some minister would move into our community. We have a good farming country and good society.—*J. F. Kircher, Sept. 6.*

Salida, Ohio.—The Sugar Creek church held her quarterly council on Thursday, Sept. 1. All business that came before the meeting passed off pleasantly. On Saturday, Sept. 3rd, a love-feast was held at Bunker Hill, in the same church. It was a pleasant feast. Eld. F. B. Weimer, of Wayne County, Ohio, was with us over Sunday and gave us a few good sermons. Different ones have asked me about the location of the Bunker Hill church. It is only a branch of the Sugar Creek church. We rejoice to say that sixteen have been added to the above-named church recently. May the Good Lord continue his blessings upon us, and upon all God's believing children!—*M. H. Shutt, Sept. 5.*

Liberty, Ill.—Bro. D. B. Gibson came to us on Saturday before the last Sunday of August and began a series of meetings. Sept. 3 and 4 was our feast, which was very enjoyable. There were fifty communicants at the table. Other ministers from abroad were brethren Lapp, of Missouri and H. W. Strickler, of Lorain this County. They did good work, and I think all could say of a truth that it was good to be there. The meeting is still in progress and up to this time four have made the good confession. There is quite a shaking among the dry bones. The interest is good. Many more are near the kingdom. Mill Creek is coming out victorious by the help of the Lord against the mighty. The good work still goes on. Praise the Lord for his goodness to the children of man!—*T. B. Digman, Sept 8.*

Minnesota City, Minn.—I am now at the above-named place, where I will remain over Sunday, then return to Dover on Monday, the 5th, and continue there for a time. After our return home, about Sept. 20, wife and I will, the Lord willing, start south for the fall and early winter work in southern Iowa and Northern Missouri. We earnestly desire the prayers of all God's children.—*Wm. C. Hipes, Sept. 2.*

Matrimonial.

"What therefore God hath joined together, let no man put asunder."

FREESE—GROVE—At the residence of the officiating minister, W. H. Quinn, Sept. 6, 1892, Mr. Wm. Freese and Miss Wilda Grove, both of Canton, Ohio. W. H. QUINN.

ROYER—SUMMER—At the residence of the officiating minister, W. H. Quinn, Aug. 13, 1892, Bro. William Royer and sister Cena Summer, both of Louisville, Stark County, Ohio. W. H. QUINN.

HAMMOND—BOWEN—July 23., 1892, by Bro. Samuel E. Burket, Mr. Milton E. Hammond and Miss Jennie Bowen, both of Sewatopol, Ind.

LOUDENBECK—KEPNER—By the undersigned, Sept. 13, 1892, Mr. Edward Loudenbeck of Chicago, and Miss Sadie Kepner, of Carson City, Mich. GEO. E. STONE.

Fallen Asleep.

"Blessed are the dead which die in the Lord."

BYERS.—In the Paint Creek church, Bourbon County Kans., Sept. 5, 1892, of cancer of the stomach, Bro. William Byers, aged 68 years. He was a deacon. A. C. NUMER.

WORKMAN.—In the DanVille church, Ohio, Aug. 1, 1892, sister Nannie, wife of Elmer Workman, aged 30 years and 15 days. Funeral services by Bro. D. M. Irvin, of Orrville, Ohio. C. J. WORKMAN.

HORN.—In the DanVille church, Ohio, Aug. 16, 1892, Bro. Hardman Horn, aged 80 years and 1 month. Deceased has been a member of the Brethren church about forty years. He died at his brother's home near Mt. Vernon. His body was interred in the North Bend cemetery. Funeral services by the writer, assisted by Rev. Disney, of Mt. Vernon. C. J. WORKMAN.

DENNEY.—In the Lower Deer Creek church, Carroll County, Ind., Sept 9, 1892, Nora Denney, aged 10 years, 11 months and 6 days. Funeral services by brethren Hiel Hamilton and A. J. Flory. S. H. BECHTELHEIMER.

UMPHLET.—In the Centre View church, Warrensburg, Mo., Aug. 24, 1892, sister Laura Z. Umphlet, daughter of Bro. John and sisl f Mary Umphlet, aged 17 years, 2 months and 28 days. Sister Laura was taken very ill with typhoid fever Aug. 1. Feeling that her life was near its close, she was anointed in the name of the Lord on the sixth day of her illness. Funeral services by Bro Jacob Wittmore from John 38:17. She was laid to rest in the Warrensburgh church cemetery.

UMPHLET.—In the same home, Aug. 26, 1892, of cholera infantum, Sadie Allie, little daughter of Bro. John and sister Esther Umphlet, aged 14 months and 23 days. Funeral services by Bro. Joseph Brubaker. Thus two more earthly ties have been severed to be united in heaven. SUSIE BLOCHER.

BRYANT.—In the bounds of the Beaver Dam church, Ind., Sept 5, 1892, Catharine (Dohn) Bryant, widow of William Bryant (deceased), aged 66 years, 5 months and 1 day. She was the mother of fourteen children, seven of whom survive her. Funeral services by Bro. Samuel E. Burket from the text, "Prepare to meet thy God." AMOS 4:12.

MILUM.—In the Roann church, Wabash Co., Ind., Aug. 5, 1892, of a protracted illness, Bro. John Milum, aged 53 years and 20 days. He leaves a dear companion, a sister, and three children to mourn the loss of one who was near and dear to them. A short time before he died he sent for the elders of the church and was anointed. Funeral services by the Brethren. JOSEPH JOHN.

McKEEVER.—Near Sinking Springs, Highland County, Ohio, April 19, 1892, Nancy Jane McKeever, aged 18 years, 11 months and 12 days. She was a member of the church for five years. While crossing a creek on a log, she fell off and was drowned. Her sudden death is another lesson that we should always be ready for the great change. W. Q. CALVERT.

LANDIS.—Near Hollowtown, Highland Co., Ohio, Aug. 25, 1892, S. Monroe Landis, aged 59 years, 3 months and 13 days. Friend Landis was a man of good judgment, was industrious, and had many good traits. He leaves a wife six children to mourn their loss. The wife and five of children are in the fold. Funeral services from James 4: W. Q. CALVERT.

HARRISON.—At the home of his parents in Frank County, Va., Joseph Clark, son of Robert and Lucinda H rison, aged 14 years. The cause of his death was brain fe Though he had been afflicted almost from infancy, he wa model of patience. J. O. Boone.

MILLER.—In the Upper Stillwater church, Miami C Ohio, Aug. 30, 1892, sister Lydia Miller, aged 72 year months and 25 days. Deceased was the widow of Abraha Miller, one of our ministers who died about fifteen years Funeral services by the writer, assisted by Tobias Crider. W. H. Boone.

HOOP.—In the Marble Furnace church, Adams Co Ohio, July 15, 1892, of lung disease, Rebecca Ann Hoop, a 39 years, 1 month and 19 days. For five years she enjoyed place in the fold of Christ. She quietly fell asleep, havi previously called for the anointing, saying that if it had Lord's will, she was willing and ready to go. Funeral M Matt. 28: 8. W. Q. CALVERT.

SIMMONS.—In the bounds of the May Hill churc Adams Co., Ohio, Sept. 4, 1892, Salome Simmons, aged years, 7 months and 24 days. For about 64 years she had the church here, and we trust she has gone to be a t church triumphant. Funeral services at her home by Philpp. 1: 21. W. Q. CALVERT.

SWISSHELM.—At May Hill, Adams Co., Ohio, April 1892, Alfred Swisshelm, aged 9 months and days. Little Alfred's mother, sister Lizzie Swisshelm, preceded her little son to the spirit land in January last. They then, and bereaved husband, since the death of his dear wi wisely cast his lot with the people of God. We pray he Bro. Philip will be faithful and join wife and son in the bea land. Funeral services from the words, "What is your like W. Q. CALVERT.

ELLENSBERGER.—At May Hill, Adams Co., Ohio, April 13, 1892, Mary Ellenberger, aged 67 years, 3 month and 28 days. Deceased was the wife of Bro. Joseph Ellenberger. For fifty years she had been a member of the Presbyterian church. She lived a devoted life to the faith she professed, was very kind and industrious, and was loved and respected by all. She is sadly missed by neighbors and friends, but more by the four daughters and one son, and most of all by Bro. Joseph. Funeral from 1 Kings 2: 2. W. Q. CALVERT.

BAYLOR.—In the Bethany congregation, Taylor Co., W. Va., July 9, 1892, A. J. Baylor, aged about 51 years. He leaves a wife and several children to mourn their loss. Friend Baylor was afflicted about three years. His wife, sister Baylor, was a daughter of Eld. Henry Wilson, who was killed at his home during the late war. Funeral services by the writer, assisted by Bro. G. W. Annon from Ps. 103:15,4 to a large concourse of sympathizing friends. Z. ANNON.

WAGAMAN.—In the Loudonville church, Ohio, Aug. 9 1892, Goldie, daughter of Bro. Jacob and sister Mary Wagaman, aged 1 year and 8 months. Funeral services by the writer from MARK 10:14. DAVID BRUBAKER.

The Gospel Messenger

Is the recognized organ of the German Baptist or Brethren's church and advocates the form of doctrine taught in the New Testament and pleads for a return to apostolic and primitive Christianity.

It recognizes the New Testament as the only infallible rule of faith and practice, and maintains that Faith toward God, Repentance from dead works, Regeneration of the heart and mind, baptism by Trine Immersion for remission of sins unto the reception of the Holy Ghost by the laying on of hands, are the means of adoption into the household of God,—the church militant.

It also maintains that Feet-washing, as taught in John 13, both by example and command of Jesus, should be observed in the church.

That the Lord's Supper, instituted by Christ and as universally observed by the apostles and the early Christians, is a full meal, and, in connection with the Communion, should be taken in the evening or after the close of the day.

That the Salutation of the Holy Kiss, or Kiss of Charity, is binding upon the followers of Christ.

That War and Retaliation are contrary to the spirit and self-denying principles of the religion of Jesus Christ.

That the principle of Plain Dressing and of Non-conformity to the world, as taught in the New Testament, should be observed by the followers of Christ.

That the Scriptural duty of Anointing the Sick with Oil, in the Name of the Lord, James 5: 14, is binding upon all Christians.

It also advocates the church's duty to support Missionary and Tract Work, thus giving to the Lord for the spread of the Gospel and for the conversion of sinners.

In short, it is a Vindicator of all that Christ and the apostles have enjoined upon us, and aims, amid the conflicting theories and discords of modern Christendom, to point out ground that all must concede to be faithfully safe.

☞ The above principles of our Fraternity are set forth on our Brethren's Envelopes." Use them! Price 15 cents per package; 40 cents per hundred.

Announcements.

(Concluded from preceding page.)

LOVE FEASTS.

Oct. 1, Union Center District, Elkhart Co., Ind.

Oct. 1, at 1:30 P. M., Meadow Branch church, Carroll Co., Md.

Oct. 1, at 2 P. M., Wolf River church, Brown Co., Kans. Those coming by rail on the C. R. O. & P. R. R., will be met at Purcell, or those coming on the Grand Island road will be met at Leoma by notifying Rufus Sawyer.

Oct. 8, at 2 P. M., Brick meeting-house, German church, Henry Co., Ia.

Oct. 8 and 9, Kingsley church, Woodbury Co., Iowa.

Oct. 8, at 2 P. M., at Navarre, in the Ablene church, Dickinson Co., Kans.

Oct. 8, at 10 A. M., Maumee church, Defiance Co., Ohio.

Oct. 8., at 4 P. M., Bolivar congregation, at the meeting-house in Garfield, Indiana Co., Pa.

Oct. 8, at 10 A. M., Mohican church, Ohio.

Oct. 9, at 3:30 P. M., Shade Creek congregation, Somerset Co., Pa.

Oct. 12, at 10 A. M., 12 miles south-west of Colfax and 4 miles west of Cold Water, Mercer Co., Ohio.

Oct. 12, at 2 P. M., Pyrmont, Ind.

Oct. 12, at 2 P. M., Upper Stillwater church, Ohio.

Oct. 14, at 10 A. M., Poplar Ridge church, 4 miles east of Defiance, Ohio.

Oct. 15 and 16, at Sabetha, Kans.

Oct. 15, at 11 A. M., Deep River church, Iowa. Any coming by rail, come to Deep River on the Northwestern. Notify J. J. Brower, Deep River, Iowa, Box 55, and you will be met at the train.

Oct. 15, at 10 A. M. 5 miles east of Mendon, Mercer Co., Ohio.

Oct. 15, at 4 P. M., Ligonier Valley congregation, at the meeting-house in Waterford, Westmoreland Co., Pa.

Oct. 15, at 5 P. M., Mahoning church, near Columbiana, Ohio.

Oct. 15, at 10 A. M., Woodland church, Mich.

Oct. 15, at 10 A. M., Locust Grove church, Md.

Oct. 15 and 16, at 2 P. M., Rock Grove church, Floyd Co., Iowa.

Oct. 15, at 10 A. M., Wichita church, near Kechi, Kans.

O.t. 15 and 16, at Lucey's Creek meeting-house, Greenland church, Grant Co., W. Va.

Oct. 15, at 2 P. M., Eden Valley congregation, Stafford Co., Kans., at Bro. J. N. Miller's.

Oct. 22, at 10:30 A. M., Eagle Creek church, Hancock Co., Ohio.

Oct. 22, at 2 P. M., Eden Valley, Kans.

Oct. 22 and 23, at 10 A. M., Iowa River church, Marshall Co., Iowa.

Oct. 22, at 10 A. M., New Haven church, Gratiot Co., Mich.

Oct. 22 and 23, Coon River, near Panora, Iowa.

Oct. 27 and 28, at 1 P. M., Chiques church, Lancaster Co., Pa., at the Green Tree meeting-house, 3 miles east of Elizabethtown, Pa.

Oct. 27, at 10 A. M., Mineral Creek, Johnson Co., Mo.

Oct. 28, in the Greenwood church, Texas Co., Mo., 6 miles north-west of Cabool.

Oct. 28, at 2 P. M., at the Spring Run church, 2½ miles north of McVeytown station, Mifflin Co., Pa.

Oct. 29, at 2 P. M., East McPherson church.

Oct. 29 and 30, Beaver Run, Mineral Co., W. Va.

Oct. 29, at 2 P. M., Brownsville, Md.

Oct. 29, at 10 A. M., Shoal Creek church, Newton Co., Mo., 2 mile south of Grangeville. Those coming by rail will be met at Pierce City on the morning of the day before by notifying John Holderread, Roys, Mo. Those coming to Purdy will be met on the morning of the 29th by notifying Leander Horseler, Pioneer, Mo.

Oct. 29, at 2 P. M., Liberty church, Olathe congregation, Kans.

Oct. 29, at 2 P. M., Lick Creek church. Owen Co., Ind.

Oct. 29, at 1:30 P. M., Marsh Creek church, Adams Co., Pa.

Oct. 29, Silos Creek Church, Sumner Co., Kans.

Nov. 1 and 2, at 11:30 P. M., Buffalo Valley church, Union Co., Pa.

Nov. 1, at the Mohler house; Ephrata, Pa.

Nov. 2 and 3, Bem Settlement, Hardy Co., W. Va.

Nov. 2, at 2 P. M., Lower Stillwater, near Trotwood, Ohio, at the upper house.

Nov. 3, at 10 A. M., Dry Fork church, Jasper, Jasper Co., Mo.

Nov. 3, at 2 P. M., Lower Deer Creek church, Carroll Co., Ind.

Nov. 3, at 10 A. M., at the Bird-in-hand meeting-house, Conestoga congregation, Lancaster Co., Pa. A series of meetings will commence Oct. 29 at the Eboe Ball meeting-house.

Nov. 4, at 2 P. M., in the bounds of the Donald's Creek church, Madison Co., Ohio, 4 miles north-west of London. Conveyance at London on the day of meeting for 10:15 A. M. train from the West.

Nov. 4, Walnut Creek church, Mo.

Nov. 5, at 10 A. M., Sunfield church, Mich.

Nov. 5, at 2 P. M., Lower Miami church, Montgomery Co., Ohio.

Nov. 5 and 6, Tearcoat, Hampshire Co., W. Va.

Nov. 5, at 4 P. M., Solomon's Creek congregation, Elkhart Co., Ind., 2 miles 10th-east of Milford Junction.

Nov. 5, at 2 P. M., Smith Fork church, Clinton Co., Mo. at the Walnut Grove meeting-house.

Nov. 5, at 2 P. M., Summit Mills, Somerset Co., Pa.

Nov. 5, at 2 P. M., at the Kansas Center church; 3 miles east of Lyons, Rice Co., Kans. A series of meetings to commence a week previous.

Nov. 5, at 3 P. M., Big Creek church, Richland Co., Ill., 2½ miles North-east of Parkersburg, Ill. Conveyance will be at the above place by informing J. M. Forney.

Nov. 5, at 3 P. M., Mount Pleasant meeting-house, Canton church, Starke Co., Ohio.

Nov. 5 and 6, at 4 P. M., North Beatrice church, Gage Co., Nebr.

Nov. 5, at 4 P. M., Monticello church, Ind.

Nov. 12, Salem church, Reno Co., Kans., 2 miles south and 3 mi'es west of Nickerson.

Nov. 12, at 2 P. M., Blackberry church, Henry Co., Va.

Nov. 22, at 10 A. M., Thornapple church, Mich., at the 10s1 house.

Nov. 26, at 3 P. M., Cedar Creek church, Anderson Co., Kans.

--- THE ---
Doctrine of the Brethren Defended.

THIS work contains a complete exposition of the faith and practice of the Brethren, the Divinity of Christ, the Divinity of the Holy Spirit, Immersion, Feet-washing, the Lord's Supper, the Holy Kiss, Non-conformity, Secret Societies, etc. Price, per copy, cloth binding, $1.25. Address this office.

O Jerusalem! Jerusalem!

WHAT could be more beautiful and touching than a picture of Christ as he stood upon Olivet looking down over the beloved but sinful city, with tears trickling down over his cheeks, his lips parted as he cries, "O Jerusalem! Jerusalem!" We have such a picture 12x16 inches, beautifully executed in colors. No one can gaze upon it without being moved. Given free with a year's subscription to "What to Read" at 50 cents. An agent wanted in every church and neighborhood. Address,

JAS. M. NEFF, Covington, Ohio.

Excursions to California.

EXCURSIONS in charge of M. M. Eshelman, Immigration Agent, will leave Chicago over the "Santa Fe Route" Tuesdays, and Kansas City Wednesdays, during the year 1892, on dates as follows:

Chicago, January 26, February 23, March 22, April 26, May 24, June 28, July 26, August 23, September 27, October 25, November 22, December 27.

Kansas City, January 27, February 24, March 23, April 27, May 25, June 29, July 27, August 24, September 28, October 26, November 23, December 28.

Parties wishing to avail themselves of the privilege of these excursions, should write M. M. Eshelman, North Pomona, California, prior to the 15th of each month, and from the fifteenth to the end of the month, address him at Union Avenue (opposite Union Depot), Kansas City, Mo., stating when and where they wish to join one of these excursions, and he will give them full information, and if desired will reserve berths in Tourist Sleeping Car for them. Do not fail to write him; he will do you good. The rates will be as low as the lowest made to the Pacific Coast.

GORDON L. MCDONAUGH,
Travelling Agent.

DANCERS, TUMORS, ETC.

Successfully treated by Dr. G. N. Boteler, of Waynesborough, Pa., where he has practiced for the last sixteen years. Dr. Boteler is a graduate of the University of Maryland, at Baltimore City. References given and correspondence solicited. Address, Dr. G. W. Boteler, Waynesborough, Pa.

GOOD BOOKS FOR ALL.

ANY book in the market furnished at publishers' lowest retail price by the Brethren's Publishing Company, Mt. Morris, Ill. *Special prices* given when books are purchased in quantities. When ordering books, not on our list, if possible give title, name of author, and address of publishers.

The Throne of David.—By J. H. Ingraham. Cloth. $1.50.

The Doctrine of the Holy Spirit.—By James B Walker. Cloth. $1.25.

The New Testament History?—By Wm. Smith. Cloth, $1.25.

The Path of Life.—An interesting tract for everybody; Price, 10 cents per copy; 100 copies, $6.00.

Smith's Bible Dictionary.— Edited by Peloubet. Cloth, $2.00; leather, $3.00.

The Origin and Growth of Religion.—Hibbert Lecture. By F. W. M. Davids. Cloth, 8vo, $2.50.

The Old Testament History.—By William Smith. Cloth, $1.25.

The Great Events of History.—By W.J.F. Collier. Cloth, $1.25.

Lectures on Preaching.—By Rev. Phillips Brooks. Cloth, 8100, $1.50.

The Story of the Bible.— An excellent volume for old and young; will interest and instruct all those desiring a knowledge of the Scriptures. Price, $1.00.

Announcements.

(Concluded from preceding page.)

LOVE FEASTS.

Oct. 1, Union Center District, Elkhart Co., Ind.

Oct. 1, at 2:30 P. M., Meadow Branch church, Carroll Co., Md.

Oct. 1, at 2 P. M., Wolf River church, Brown Co., Kans. Those coming by rail on the C. R. O. & P. R. R., will be met at Purcell, or those coming on the Grand Island road will be met at Leona by notifying Rufus Sawyer.

Oct. 8, at 4 P. M., Brick meeting-house, German church, Henry Co., Va.

Oct. 8 and 9, Kingsley church, Woodbury Co., Iowa.

Oct. 8, at 2 P. M., at Navarre, in the Abilene church, Dickinson Co., Kans.

Oct. 8, at 2 P. M., Bolivar congregation, at the meeting-house in Garfield, Indiana Co., Pa.

Oct. 8, at 10 A. M., Mohican church, Ohio.

Oct. 9, at 3:30 P. M., Shade Creek congregation, Somerset Co., Pa.

Oct. 10, at 10 A. M., 11 miles south-west of Colina and 4 miles east of Cold Water, Mercer Co., Ohio.

Oct. 12, at 2 P. M., Pyrmont, Ind.

Oct. 13, at 2 P. M., Upper Stillwater church, Ohio.

Oct. 14, at 10 A. M., Poplar Ridge church, 4 miles east of Defiance, Ohio.

Oct. 15 and 16, at Sabetha, Kans.

Oct. 15, at 11 A. M., Deep River church, Iowa. Any coming by rail, come to Deep River on the Northwestern. Notify J. J. Brower, Deep River, Iowa, Box 55, and you will be met at the train.

Oct. 15, at 10 A. M. 3 miles east of Mendon, Mercer Co., Ohio.

Oct. 15, at 4 P. M., Ligonier Valley congregation, at the meeting-house in Waterford, Westmoreland Co., Pa.

Oct. 15, at 5 P. M., Mahoning church, near Columbiana, Ohio.

Oct. 15, at 10 A. M., Woodland church, Mich.

Oct. 15, at 10 A. M., Locust Grove church, Md.

Oct. 15 and 16, at 2 P. M., Rock Grove church, Floyd Co., Iowa.

Oct. 15, at 10 A. M., Wichita church, near Kechi, Kans.

O. 15 and 16, at Lusty's Creek meeting-house, Greenland church, Grant Co., W. Va.

Oct. 22, at 2 P. M., Eden Valley congregation, Stafford Co., Kans., at Bro. J. N. Miller's.

Oct. 22, at 10:30 A. M., Eagle Creek church, Hancock Co., Ohio.

Oct. 22, at 2 P. M., Eden Valley, Kans.

Oct. 22 and 23, at 10 A. M., Iowa River church, Marshall Co., Iowa.

Oct. 22, at 10 A. M., New Haven church, Gratiot Co., Mich.

Oct. 22 and 23, Coon River, near Panora, Iowa.

Oct. 27 and 28, at 1 P. M., Chiques church, Lancaster Co., Pa., at the Green Tree meeting-house, 2 miles east of Elizabethtown, Pa.

Oct. 27, at 10 A. M., Mineral Creek, Johnson Co., Mo.

Oct. 28, in the Greenwood church, Texas Co., Mo., 6 miles north-west of Cabool.

Oct. 28, at 4 P. M., in the Spring Run church, 2½ miles north of McVeytown station, Mifflin Co., Pa.

Oct. 29, at 2 P. M., East McPherson church.

Oct. 29 and 30, Deaver Run, Mineral Co., W. Va.

Oct. 29, at 2 P. M., Brownsville, Md.

Oct. 29, at 10 A. M., Shoal Creek church, Newton Co., Mo., 1 mile south of Orangeville. Those coming by rail will be met at Pierce City on the morning of the day before by notifying John Holderread, Ergo, Mo. Those coming to Purdy will be met on the morning of the 29th by notifying Leander Harder, Pioneer, Mo.

Oct. 29, at 2 P. M., Liberty church, Olathe congregation, Kans.

Oct. 29, at 2 P. M., Lick Creek church, Owen Co., Ind.

Oct. 29, at 1:30 P. M., Marsh Creek church, Adams Co., Pa.

Oct. 29, Slim Creek Church, Sumner Co., Kans., Union Co., Pa.

Nov. 1, at the Mohler house, Ephrata, Pa.

Nov. 2 and 3, Bear Settlement, Hardy Co., W. Va.

Nov. 2, at 2 P. M., Lower Stillwater, near Trotwood, Ohio, at the upper house.

Nov. 3, at 10 A. M., Dry Fork church, Jasper, Jasper Co., Mo.

Nov. 3, at 2 P. M., Lower Deer Creek church, Carroll Co., Ind.

Nov. 3, at 10 A. M., at the Bird-in-hand meeting-house, Conestoga congregation, Lancaster Co., Pa. A series of meetings will commence Oct. 29 at the Blue Ball meeting-house.

Nov. 4, at 2 P. M., in the bounds of the Donald's Creek church, Madison Co., Ohio, 4 miles north-west of London. Conveyance at London on the day of meeting for 10:15 A. M. train from the West.

Nov. 4, Walnut Creek church, Mo.

Nov. 5, at 10 A. M., Sunfield church, Mich.

Nov. 5, at 2 P. M., Lower Miami church, Montgomery Co., Ohio.

Nov. 5 and 6, Turncoat, Hampshire Co., W. Va.

Nov. 5, at 4 P. M., Solomon's Creek congregation, Elkhart Co., Ind., 2 miles north-east of Milford Junction.

Nov. 5, at 2 P. M., Smith Fork church, Clinton Co., Mo., at the Walnut Grove meeting-house.

Nov. 5, at 2 P. M., Summit Mills, Somerset Co., Pa.

Nov. 5, at 2 P. M., at the Kansas Center church, 7 miles east of Lyons, Rice Co., Kans. A series of meetings to commence a week previous.

Nov. 5, at 2 P. M., Big Creek church, Richland Co., Ill., 1¼ miles North-east of Parkersburg, Ill. Conveyance will be at the above place by informing J. M. Forney.

Nov. 5, at 5 P. M., Mount Pleasant meeting-house, Canton church, Starke Co., Ohio.

Nov. 5 and 6, at 4 P. M., North Beatrice church, Gage Co., Nebr.

Nov. 5, at 2 P. M., Monticello church, Ind.

Nov. 12, Salem church, Reno Co., Kans., 2 miles south and 2 mi'es west of Nickerson.

Nov. 12, at 4 P. M., Blackberry church, Henry Co., Va.

Nov. 17, at 10 A. M., Thornapple church, Mich., at the east house.

Nov. 24, at 2 P. M., Cedar Creek church, Anderson Co., Kans.

— THE —
Doctrine of the Brethren Defended.

THIS work contains a complete exposition of the faith and practice of the Brethren, the Divinity of Christ, the Divinity of the Holy Spirit, Immersion, Feet-washing, the Lord's Supper, the Holy Kiss, Non-conformity, Secret Societies, etc. Price, per copy, cloth binding, $1.25. Address this office.

O Jerusalem! Jerusalem!

WHAT could be more beautiful and touching than a picture of Christ as he stood upon Olivet looking down over the beloved but sinful city, with tears trickling down over his cheeks, his lips parted as he cries, "O Jerusalem! Jerusalem!" We have such a picture 22x28 inches, beautifully executed in colors. No one can gaze upon it without being moved. Given free with a year's subscription to "What to Read" at 50 cents. An agent wanted in every church and neighborhood. Address,

JAS. M. NEFF, Covington, Ohio.

Excursions to California.

Excursions in charge of M. M. Eshelman, Immigration Agent, will leave Chicago over the "Santa Fe Route" Tuesdays, and Kansas City Wednesdays, during the year 1892, on dates as follows:

Chicago, January 26, February 23, March 22, April 26, May 24, June 28, July 26, August 23, September 27, October 25, November 22, December 27.

Kansas City, January 27, February 24, March 23, April 27, May 25, June 29, July 27, August 24, September 28, October 26, November 23, December 28.

Parties wishing to avail themselves of the privileges of these excursions, should write M. M. Eshelman, North Pomona, California, prior to the 15th of each month, and from the fifteenth to the end of the month, at some Union Avenue (opposite Union Depot), Kansas City, Mo., stating when and where they wish to join one of these excursions, and he will give them full information, and if desired will reserve berths in Tourist Sleeping Cars for them. Do not tell us write him; he will do you good. The rates will be as low as the lowest made to the Pacific Coast.

GORDON L. McDONAUGH,
Traveling Agent.

LOOK AT THIS.

The Monon Route still reducing rates and offering better accommodations than ever before.

Commencing April 15, the fare from Chicago to Louisville, New Albany, Cincinnati, Hamilton, and Dayton will be $5.50; to Indianapolis $3.50. Round trip tickets good ten days at double the one way rate.

Parlor and Dining cars on day trains; Pullman Sleepers and Compartment Cars on night trains. A special Sleeper is run for Indianapolis business.

See that your tickets read via the MONON ROUTE.

For rates, schedules, etc., apply at Depot, Dearborn Station, City Ticket Office, 232 Clark Street, or address, JAMES BARKER, G. P. A., Monon Block, Chicago, Ill.

DANCERS, TUMORS, ETC.

Successfully treated by Dr. O. H. Butzler, of Waynesborough, Pa., where he has practiced for the last sixteen years. Dr. Butzler is a graduate of the University of Maryland, at Baltimore City. References given and correspondence solicited. Address, Dr. O. W. Butzler, Waynesborough, Pa.

GOOD BOOKS FOR ALL.

ANY book in the market furnished at publishers' lowest retail price by the Brethren's Publishing Company, Mt. Morris, Ill. *Special prices* given when books are purchased in quantities. When ordering books, not on our list, if possible give title, name of author, and address of publishers.

The Throne of David—By J. H. Ingraham. Cloth, $1.50.

The Doctrine of the Holy Spirit.—By James B. Walker. Cloth, $1.25.

The New Testament History.—By Wm. Smith. Cloth, $1.25.

The Path of Life.—An interesting tract for everybody. Price, 20 cents per copy; 100 copies, $6.00.

Smith's Bible Dictionary. — Edited by Peloubet. Cloth, $2.00; leather, $3.00.

The Origin and Growth of Religion.—Hibbert Lectures. By T. W. R. Davids. Cloth, 800, $2.50.

The Old Testament History.—By William Smith. Cloth, $2.00.

The Great Events of History.—By W. F. Collier. Cloth, $1.25.

Lectures on Preaching.—By Rev. Phillips Brooks. Cloth, 12mo, $1.50.

The Story of the Bible. — An excellent volume for old and young; will interest and instruct all those desiring a knowledge of the Scriptures. Price, $3.00.

✦ESSAYS✦

"Study to show thyself approved unto God; a workman that needeth not to be ashamed, rightly dividing the Word of Truth."

THE GIFT RETURNED.

BY GERTRUDE A. FLORY.

"Suffer little children to come unto me, and forbid them not."

Go, blessed child, to Jesus go!
    He has the way unbarred
For stainless souls as white as snow,
    Like thine by sin unmarred.

The shining host in rapture wait
    To bear thee to their King:
They swing ajar the pearly gate
    And joyful welcome sing.

While rain and snow falls on the sod
    Above thy lowly bed,
Thy spirit side by side with God
    The golden way shall tread.

Thy smile and pretty way we miss;
    Thy loving kiss we crave;
But we would rob thee not of bliss
    To hold thee from the grave.

Beyond its mystic portal, thou
    Shalt dwell among his lambs,
With glory twining round thy brow,
    And in thy hands bright palms.

Thy happy voice to praises toned,
    Which spring from sweetest joy,
And peace in Jesus' love enthroned,
    Death never can destroy.

Then, go to Jesus' waiting arms!
    Grief shall not hold thee back!
Safe in his bosom from all harm
    For love thou shalt not lack.

La Porte, Ind.

GATHERING.—SCATTERING.

BY MARGARET PFEIFFER.

"He that is not with me is against me; and he that gathereth not with me scattereth abroad."—Matt. 12: 30.

IF we profess to be for Jesus, it is also necessary, or our full duty, to be gathering for him. This we can do in many ways, by our acts in defending and laboring for the cause of Christ, and keeping ourselves unspotted from the world. Jesus said, "Let your light so shine before men that they may see your good works, and glorify your Father which is in heaven." If men would as fervently seek after love and righteousness as they do after opinions, there would be no strife or dissension on earth, and we would be as children of one Father, and should need no law, for God is not served by any law, excepting by obedience, for the kingdom of God consisteth not in meat or drink, or in opinions, but in love and power.

We all have but one order, which is to stand still to the Lord and resign our will to him and suffer God's Spirit to rule and reign in us, according to his will. Thus we give to him again as his own fruits, or talents, that which he worketh and manifesteth in us. If we are not impelled by the full force of the love of God, there is discord of action and want of interest in the work of saving the souls of men.

If we are lacking in the spirit of love and zeal for the welfare of the church of Christ, there is consequently more scattering than gathering for Jesus Christ. Other interests beside the salvation of the soul will crowd religion back and make it a secondary matter, and the cause of Christ will suffer. Not being led entirely by the Holy Spirit causes us to stumble at a great many things, for if we teach the Scripture from our own wisdom, we are sure to fall into error, for being weak in the love of Christ and not fully trusting Christ for strength, we are more apt to scatter than to gather for Christ. How sad to find so many strong in their own strength, wisdom and opinion, and determined not to allow themselves to be corrected by the Word and Spirit of God! They will rather hold to their own opinions. Some adhere so much to the formalities of religion, that they lose sight of the spiritual life that comes from God, which is necessary above all things in gathering for Christ. If we are for Christ, our actions will show in our daily life the reality of the religion of Jesus Christ.

The work which Christ wants to be done is sadly neglected when people strive about religion and bring forward opinions of their own. If we spurn the robe of charity, we are liable to fall into error and often drag others with us, and we will be scattering abroad, instead of gathering for Christ. Let us not deceive ourselves with the vain hope that we are for Christ if all our actions and inclinations are worldly, for the Word says, "If any man love the world, the love of the Father is not in him, for all that is in the world, the lust of the flesh and the lust of the eyes and the pride of life, is not of the Father, but is of the world. And the world passeth away and the lust thereof: but he that doeth the will of God abideth forever."

It is a blessed life to live continually near the Lord Jesus. In our baptismal covenant we have promised to live for him. Let us be true to the covenant we have made, and practice good works, that the world can see that we are born of God and that they may glorify our Father in heaven, so that, when our day is spent, and the evening of life comes, it may be one of quiet, serene enjoyment. The reward of a spiritual life, nobly lived, comes only to those who, through an earnest desire to do their duty, are awake to and seize the many valuable opportunities that each day brings to all humanity.

Their observance or neglect affects not only our earthly existence, but our eternal life. The Word says, "He that saith I know God and keepeth not his commandments is a liar and the truth is not in him. But whoso keepeth his word, in him verily is the love of God perfected: hereby know we that we are in him. He that saith he abideth in him ought himself also so to walk even as he walked." "If we say that we have fellowship with him and walk in darkness, we lie and do not the truth. But if we walk in the light as he is in the light, we have fellowship one with another, and the blood of Jesus Christ his Son cleanseth us from all sin. If we confess our sins he is faithful and just to forgive us our sins."

Nappanee, Ind.

AN EXAMPLE.

BY J. S. FLORY.

"Be thou an example of the believers, in word, in conversation, in charity, in spirit, in faith, in purity."—1 Tim. 4: 12.

HERE we have Paul's idea of what a young man, starting out in youth to work for the Lord, ought to be. If it is applicable to young men, surely it ought to be expected of the older.

"An example of the believers." What a wonderful responsibility, yet grandly noble! "In word." Ah, yes, preach only the Word, lay aside self and all the fine blandishments of giddy-headedness that may mar the image of Christ, or dull the edge of the sword. Be an example in preaching the cross, as well as in living a life of thorough consecration to Christ.

"Example in conversation." Now, tongue, what are you going to do about this matter? Continue to run on in foolish jesting, and a little nonsense now and then, just to keep the old man lively, or will the bridle be so constructed as to hold it in subjection to the spirit of Christ within? Paul means to say, "Be sober, and take care of your words in conversation."

"An example in charity." Oh the wondrous power of love! To be an example of the believers in love, means the fullness of God within, that the God-life may shine all around. God is love,— love is God,—therefore that charity that is greatest of all else is the godliness of a God-regenerated soul, and as God is the supreme Ruler, and above all, the love that comes from him and is shed abroad in the heart, is a living power that goes out and shows itself to be greater in efficiency than anything else. In fact, as God is all powerful, so is this gift of God all powerful. Use it, my brother, or my sister, and see how it is the divining rod, that, in your hand used aright, will enable you to work miracles, change an enemy to a friend, a gross sinner to leave the error of his way and be transformed into a lamb-like saint. Ah, yes, love stamped upon the heart will come through, so that all men can read on the breast-plate of the armor, "HOLINESS TO THE LORD." Think of it, ye Christian soldiers, how you may be examples of the believers and never be ashamed to let anybody you meet know where you belong.

"An example in spirit." A live spirit, an active spirit, is in harmony with the spirit of the Blessed Master. A spirit that stirs up other spirits,—a real leaven spirit, that makes things lively around you,—active in the work of the Lord at home, in the social meetings, at the altar, and everywhere,—a spirit of meekness and Christian forbearance,—a spirit of peace and joy that shows the blessedness of the great hope that broods within; a happy spirit of sociability, as well as a spirit of sympathy for the suffering; a spirit that sheds sunshine all around.

"An example in faith." This is another of the grand factors that go to make up Christian character,—a faith that takes the all of Jesus right into it and holds on to him with an eternal grasp. Do you know that obedience is only faith ripened? It is so fully developed that the ripe fruit hangs in golden clusters on the tree of life. That is all obedience is. If you think you can pocket the fruit to feed the soul in eternity, you will be mistaken. Fruit severed from faith will rot, and send forth a stench like the unsanctified mauns of old. Obedience without faith will not do. Get genuine, saving faith! That is to appropriate Christ by faith to one's self as a personal Savior! You will then see how grandly the believer goes on in the way of obedience! He cannot go any other way, for Christ within moves the heart to obey; every beating pulse of the sanctified soul is in harmony with Christ and the Living Word. Oh, for such examples of the believers to stand up for God!

Last, but not least, the believer is to be an example in purity. It must come to this, or our lives will be a living lie. Without holiness no one shall see the Lord. "Be perfect, as I am perfect," says Jesus. Why not, if he was pure, and he reigns in our sanctified souls? It is usual for men and women to look for perfection in others,—they want them to be honest, truthful, temperate, kind, charitable, and all this, but as to themselves, they are poor, miserable, weak, short-sighted sinners. Now Paul did not want Timothy to confess to any such impurities, or, in other words, he wanted him to be of such a purity in his life, that he need make no such confession. In the name of all that is good, why hold up Christ as the Savior from our sins, and then go on growing all the time in a way that we confess we want him to save us IN our sins! Let us get on a higher plane, where we can rest assured the Christian life means a clean life,—a life of purity. Come out from the cesspools of the world, get far

THE GIFT RETURNED.

BY GERTRUDE A. FLORY.

"Suffer little children to come unto me, and forbid them not."

Go, blessed child, to Jesus go!
He has the way unbarred
For stainless souls as white as snow,
Like thine by sin unmarred.

The shining host in rapture wait
To bear thee to their King;
They swing ajar the pearly gate
And joyful welcome sing.

While rain and snow falls on the sod
Above thy lowly bed,
Thy spirit side by side with God
The golden way shall tread.

Thy smile and pretty way we miss;
Thy loving kiss we crave;
But we would rob thee not of bliss
To hold thee from the grave.

Beyond its mystic portal, thou
Shalt dwell among his lambs,
With glory twining round thy brow,
And in thy hands bright palms.

Thy happy voice to praises toned,
Which spring from sweetest joy,
And peace in Jesus' love enthroned,
Death never can destroy.

Then, go to Jesus' waiting arms!
Grief shall not hold thee back!
Safe in his bosom from all harm
For love thou shalt not lack.

La Porte, Ind.

GATHERING,—SCATTERING.

BY MARGARET PFEIFFER.

"He that is not with me is against me; and he that gathereth not with me scattereth abroad."—Matt. 12: 30.

If we profess to be for Jesus, it is also necessary, or our full duty, to be gathering for him. This we can do in many ways, by our acts in defending and laboring for the cause of Christ, and keeping ourselves unspotted from the world. Jesus said, "Let your light so shine before men that they may see your good works, and glorify your Father which is in heaven." If men would as fervently seek after love and righteousness as they do after opinions, there would be no strife or dissension on earth, and we would be as children of one Father, and should need no law, for God is not served by any law, excepting by obedience, for the kingdom of God consisteth not in meat or drink, or in opinions, but in love and power.

We all have but one order, which is to stand still to the Lord and resign our will to him and suffer God's Spirit to rule and reign in us, according to his will. Thus we give to him again as his own fruits, or talents, that which he worketh and manifesteth in us. If we are not impelled by the full force of the love of God, there is discord of action and want of interest in the work of saving the souls of men.

If we are lacking in the spirit of love and zeal for the welfare of the church of Christ, there is consequently more scattering than gathering for Jesus Christ. Other interests beside the salvation of the soul will crowd religion back and make it a secondary matter, and the cause of Christ will suffer. Not being led entirely by the Holy Spirit causes us to stumble at a great many things, for if we teach the Scripture from our own wisdom, we are sure to fall into error, for being weak in the love of Christ and not fully trusting Christ for strength, we are more apt to scatter than to gather for Christ. How sad to find so many strong in their own strength, wisdom and opinion, and determined not to allow themselves to be corrected by the Word and Spirit of God! They will rather hold to their own opinions. Some adhere so much to the formalities of religion, that they lose sight of the spiritual life that comes from God, which is necessary above all things in gathering for Christ. If we are for Christ, our actions will show in our daily life the reality of the religion of Jesus Christ.

The work which Christ wants to be done is sadly neglected when people strive about religion and bring forward opinions of their own. If we spurn the robe of charity, we are liable to fall into error and often drag others with us, and we will be scattering abroad, instead of gathering for Christ. Let us not deceive ourselves with the vain hope that we are for Christ if all our actions and inclinations are worldly, for the Word says, "If any man love the world, the love of the Father is not in him, for all that is in the world, the lust of the flesh and the lust of the eyes and the pride of life, is not of the Father, but is of the world. And the world passeth away and the lust thereof: but he that doeth the will of God abideth forever."

It is a blessed life to live continually near the Lord Jesus. In our baptismal covenant we have promised to live for him. Let us be true to the covenant we have made, and practice good works, that the world can see that we are born of God and that they may glorify our Father in heaven, so that, when our day is spent, and the evening of life comes, it may be one of quiet, serene enjoyment. The reward of a spiritual life, nobly lived, comes only to those who, through an earnest desire to do their duty, are awake to and seize the many valuable opportunities that each day brings to all humanity.

Their observance or neglect affects not only our earthly existence, but our eternal life. The Word says, "He that saith I know God and keepeth not his commandments is a liar and the truth is not in him. But whoso keepeth his word, in him verily is the love of God perfected: hereby know we that we are in him. He that saith he abideth in him ought himself also so to walk even as he walked." "If we say that we have fellowship with him and walk in darkness, we lie and do not the truth. But if we walk in the light as he is in the light, we have fellowship one with another, and the blood of Jesus Christ his Son cleanseth us from all sin. If we confess our sins he is faithful and just to forgive us our sins."

Nappanee, Ind.

AN EXAMPLE.

BY J. S. FLORY.

"Be thou an example of the believers, in word, in conversation, in charity, in spirit, in faith, in purity."—1 Tim. 4: 12.

Here we have Paul's idea of what a young man, starting out in youth to work for the Lord, ought to be. If it is applicable to young men, surely it ought to be expected of the older.

"An example of the believers." What a wonderful responsibility, yet grandly noble! "In word." Ah, yes, preach only the Word, lay aside self and all the fine blandishments of giddy-headedness that may mar the image of Christ, or dull the edge of the sword. Be an example in preaching the cross, as well as in living a life of thorough consecration to Christ.

"Example in conversation." Now, tongue, what are you going to do about this matter? Continue to run on in foolish jesting, and a little nonsense now and then, just to keep the old man lively, or will the bridle be so constructed as to hold it in subjection to the spirit of Christ within? Paul means to say, "Be sober, and take care of your words in conversation."

"An example in charity." Oh the wondrous power of love! To be an example of the believers in love, means the fullness of God within, that the God-life may shine all around. God is love,—love is God,—therefore that charity that is greatest of all else is the godliness of a God-regenerated soul, and as God is the supreme Ruler, and above all, the love that comes from him and is shed abroad in the heart, is a living power that goes out and shows itself to be greater in efficiency than anything else. In fact, as God is all powerful, so is this gift of God all powerful. Use it, my brother, or my sister, and see how it is the divining rod, that, in your hand used aright, will enable you to work miracles, change an enemy to a friend, a gross sinner to leave the error of his way and be transformed into a lamb-like saint. Ah, yes, love stamped upon the heart will come through, so that all men can read on the breast-plate of the armor, "Holiness to the Lord." Think of it, ye Christian soldiers, how you may be examples of the believers and never be ashamed to let anybody you meet know where you belong.

"An example in spirit." A live spirit, an active spirit, is in harmony with the spirit of the Blessed Master. A spirit that stirs up other spirits,—a real leaven spirit, that makes things lively around you,—active in the work of the Lord at home, in the social meetings, at the altar, and everywhere,—a spirit of meekness and Christian forbearance,—a spirit of peace and joy that shows the blessedness of the great hope that broods within; a happy spirit of sociability, as well as a spirit of sympathy for the suffering; a spirit that sheds sunshine all around.

"An example in faith." This is another of the grand factors that go to make up Christian character,—a faith that takes the all of Jesus right into it and holds on to him with an eternal grasp. Do you know that obedience is only faith ripened? It is so fully developed that the ripe fruit hangs in golden clusters on the tree of life. That is all obedience is. If you think you can pocket the fruit to feed the soul in eternity, you will be mistaken. Fruit severed from faith will rot, and send forth a stench like the unsanctified manna of old. Obedience without faith will not do. Get genuine, saving faith! That is to appropriate Christ by faith to one's self as a personal Savior! You will then see how grandly the believer goes on in the way of obedience! He cannot go any other way, for Christ within moves the heart to obey; every beating pulse of the sanctified soul is in harmony with Christ and the Living Word. Oh, for such examples of the believers to stand up for God!

Last, but not least, the believer is to be an example in purity. It must come to this, or our lives will be a living lie. Without holiness no one shall see the Lord. "Be perfect, as I am perfect," says Jesus. Why not, if he was pure, and he reigns in our sanctified souls? It is usual for men and women to look for perfection in others,—they want them to be honest, truthful, temperate, kind, charitable, and all this, but as for themselves, they are poor, miserable, weak, short-sighted sinners. Now Paul did not want Timothy to confess to any such impurities, or, in other words, he wanted him to be such a purity in his life, that he need make no such confession. In the name of all that is good, why hold up Christ as the Savior *from* our sins, and then go on growing all the time in a way that we confess we want him to save us *in* our sins! Let us get on a higher plane, where we can rest assured the Christian life means a clean life,—a life of purity. Come out from the cesspools of the world, get far

our children have books and papers that will keep them in sympathy with the efforts made for its prohibition.

By personal example, by books, by reading and by prayer, we may make an atmosphere that shall set and keep our households right on that great question. Only thus can we hope to save ourselves and those, whom God has given to be with us, from the tide that sweeps to destruction so many of the noblest and best.

WHAT POSITION ARE OUR SCHOOLS TO HOLD?

BY GRANT MAHAN.

THIS, it seems to me, is one of the most important questions we have to think about just now, and it will continue to be so for some years to come. What is to be the relation of our schools to the church? Are they to mould the church, or is the church to mould them? Neither should do all the moulding, but surely the church should do most of it. Each one must decide for himself which has done the more; but in my opinion the school has done more than it should. There is no doubt that in many respects the school influence has been for good, and there is just as little doubt that in some respects it has been for evil. Schools may be made a very great blessing, they may also be made a very great curse: all depends on their use.

It has not been very many months since some one said to me, "It is impossible for one to attend a large school and come in contact with the men there without becoming more liberal in his ideas." That word "liberal" is very unsatisfactory here, for it may mean a great many things. Each one will take it his own way and no two will get the same idea from it. Does it mean that we are to lose our faith in some of our principles? And if that is what is meant, in which must we lose faith? If it does not mean this, what does it mean? Some of those who were once members of our church, have attended school a little while and then gone to some other denomination. But they did not go because they were educated. We all know some who have done thus. There are more among us who will do the same thing and in the same way. And the sooner they take their departure the better it will be for the church; for as long as they are inside the church they will have opportunity to do harm, but when they are once outside they are comparatively harmless.

But does education make us lose faith in our principles? None of us can answer the question fully, for as yet none of us have been educated: some have made a beginning, but most of us cannot say so much for ourselves. And yet we can say how it seems to us. For my own part, I have never yet learned anything that made me lose faith in any one of the commands of our Master. His life and words are my highest ideal, and if we could but approximately live up to them we should not so often hear this talk about becoming more liberal. There is nothing else in all the world so grand, so beautiful as his words. If we had even a little bit of his spirit we should be very far from sitting in judgment on his sayings and casting away some of them. When we become infatuated with ourselves we begin to think what we don't know isn't worth knowing. If we would but put it the other way it would be very true.

If this idea is to become the general one, if we are to be taught by our schools that as we gain in knowledge we must lose in faith, then they are destined to be the greatest curse we have ever experienced. But such an idea is all wrong. Some of the wisest men, all the best men, who

ever lived have clung closely to God's Word. They all say there is nothing better, nothing that can bring more joy into the world than obedience to that Word. There is nothing in education that need make us doubt the truth of our principles. The doubt, wherever there is doubt, comes from the evil that is within us.

But all this does not settle the question about the influence of the school and the church upon each other. How far is the one to be influenced by the other? There can be no doubt that as we advance in intelligence our conceptions of God are higher. The Indian and the Chinaman are very low intellectually, and so they are spiritually. The Mohammedan conceives of no higher heaven than the one in which the passions of the flesh are gratified. As long as what we learn tends to give us these higher conceptions and causes us to love God and his Word more, so long we are safe in letting education influence us, so long may the church let herself be influenced by the schools. But when a change comes, when those who teach try to make us believe what is not the truth, when they want to have us take their word rather than God's, then we are not safe, then the church must not let herself be influenced by the school. Whatever happens we must hold fast to the truth. We are told not to believe even an angel if he tells us what is contrary to this. Whenever men begin to tell us that this is not essential, or that is not essential, that we need not have humility in our actions if we have it in our hearts, then it is time for us to avoid those men and their teaching, for we know they are wrong.

Some things have found their way into our midst which should never have been allowed among us; the only right thing for us to do is to try to get rid of them. We find these things more in our schools, or in our members who have attended other schools, than elsewhere. Perhaps it is because so many young people are thrown together and one does not like to be outdone by the other. If they were as eager to excel in goodness as they are in some other things great blessings would follow. And why should they not have a greater desire to be good than to make a show or make some one envious?

What is written here is not written because I am opposed to schools, far from it; but that we may be on our guard, that we may get the most possible good out of our schools and the least evil. In themselves they are not bad, and the effort should be to keep them from becoming so. It is for the church to watch with unceasing vigilance and remove even the appearance of evil. If this is done we can all rejoice because we have schools; if this is not done we shall surely be sorry that they were ever brought into our midst. No one is a greater friend of education than I am, but at the same time it cannot be forgotten that our principles are worth more than education. If by gaining the latter the former must be sacrificed, the latter had better not be gained. We can and we should enjoy the advantage of both, for the one is not antagonistic to the other.

CANNOT BE A MASON.

A WRITER in a late number of the *Cynosure* tells why he cannot be a Mason. Read his experience; it may possibly confirm some of our people in their opposition to secret societies. The writer says:

"My convictions are that I should write my experience in Masonry. I joined the lodge about nineteen years ago, a little before I was converted. A short time after I was converted I came in contact with Bro. James Sullivan, of South Locke. He asked if I was a Mason. I said I

was. He then asked me if I could live a Christian and walk with the lodge. I told him I saw nothing as yet to hinder me; when I did, I should leave it.

"Soon after this a brother Mason came along one lodge night, it being on prayer-meeting night, and asked me if I was going to the lodge. I replied: 'I can't leave the prayer-meeting for the lodge;' and then the Scripture came to me, 'Have no fellowship with the unfruitful works of darkness.' I was then a member of the M. E. church. The next thought was, how can I take the Communion cup from the hand of a Mason who had taken such awful oaths? Conviction came more and more as the light shone. I called for my demit in the lodge, and said: 'I will pay my dues and leave honorably.' They said, no we want you with us. For five years I lived in this way, they all this time urging me to return to the lodge. I then said: 'No, sir; give me a demit and I will give you five dollars.' They did so. I took my demit home and burned it. I never attended the lodge after I was converted. Since I left the lodge I have talked against it, and God has wonderfully blessed me in so doing. I suffered persecution from the church of which I was a member nine years, doing the best I could for God and humanity all this time. I then left the church and for nine years have had no church fellowship, but serving the best I could and where I could, sometimes going to the Wesleyans, sometimes to the Free Methodists; but neither one was very convenient.

"Last winter I was privileged, in an adjoining neighborhood, to attend a revival meeting held by Rev. V. M. Thompson. I found in him and his people a spirit that dare oppose wrong, and God wonderfully blessed them. I have found a church home with them. I intend to stand wher, ever God calls me, and renounce Masonry as he may dictate. Since I have thus decided I have never been able to see how a man can be a Christian and a Mason at the same time. May God have mercy on all who dare claim this! My convictions are, also, I can no longer raise barley to sell to brewers. If I do I am a partaker with them in this sin. Full and free salvation from sin is my privilege to live.—*John P. Van Syele, of Williamston, Mich.*

CORRESPONDENCE.

" Write what thou seest, and send it unto the churches."

☞Church News solicited for this Department. If you have had a good meeting, send a report of it, so that others may rejoice with you. In writing give name of church, County and State. Be brief. Notes of Travel should be as short as possible. Land Advertisements are not solicited for this Department. We have an advertising page, and, if necessary, will issue supplements.

Chips from the Work-house.

A VISIT to Philadelphia, North Philadelphia, Germantown, Norristown, and the three New Jersey churches has furnished timber for many Chips. The nice point is to make such Chips out of it as may be of some use. If this cannot be done, it were better left alone.

That all the above churches need help and encouragement is freely admitted by all with whom the writer had opportunity to converse about the situation. In New Jersey we held two preaching services with each one of the three churches, the members being as kind and hospitable as members can be. The old brethren who, years ago, frequently visited these far Eastern churches, have died off or gone westward with the march of empire, as have also some of their own number, until they feel somewhat forsaken by the large Brotherhood in the West. This causes some of them to feel rather neglected. They are not being visited by Western Brethren as much as desirable.

our children have books and papers that will keep them in sympathy with the efforts made for its prohibition.

By personal example, by books, by reading and by prayer, we may make an atmosphere that shall set and keep our households right on that great question. Only thus can we hope to save ourselves and those, whom God has given to be with us, from the tide that sweeps to destruction so many of the noblest and best.

WHAT POSITION ARE OUR SCHOOLS TO HOLD?

BY GRANT MAHAN.

THIS, it seems to me, is one of the most important questions we have to think about just now, and it will continue to be so for some years to come. What is to be the relation of our schools to the church? Are they to mould the church, or is the church to mould them? Neither should do all the moulding, but surely the church should do most of it. Each one must decide for himself which has done the more; but in my opinion the school has done more than it should. There is no doubt that in many respects the school influence has been for good, and there is just as little doubt that in some respects it has been for evil. Schools may be made a very great blessing, they may also be made a very great curse: all depends on their use.

It has not been very many months since some one said to me, "It is impossible for me to attend a large school and come in contact with the men there without becoming more liberal in his ideas." That word "liberal" is very unsatisfactory here, for it may mean a great many things. Each one will take it his own way and no two will get the same idea from it. Does it mean that we are to lose our faith in some of our principles? And if that is what is meant, in which must we lose faith? If it does not mean this, what does it mean? Some of those who were once members of our church, have attended school a little while and then gone to some other denomination. But they did not go because they were educated. We all know some who have done thus. There are more among us who will do the same thing and in the same way. And the sooner they take their departure the better it will be for the church; for as long as they are inside the church they will have opportunity to do harm, but when they are once outside they are comparatively harmless.

But does education make us lose faith in our principles? None of us can answer the question fully, for as yet none of us have been educated: some have made a beginning, but most of us cannot say so much for ourselves. And yet we can say how it seems to us. For my own part, I have never yet learned anything that made me lose faith in any one of the commands of our Master. His life and words are my highest ideal, and if we could but approximately live up to them we should not so often hear this talk about becoming more liberal. There is nothing else in all the world so grand, so beautiful as his words. If we had even a little bit of his spirit we should be very far from sitting in judgment on his sayings and casting away some of them. When we become infatuated with ourselves we begin to think what we don't know isn't worth knowing. If we would but put it the other way it would be very true.

If this idea is to become the general one, if we are to be taught by our schools that as we gain in knowledge we must lose in faith, then they are destined to be the greatest curse we have ever experienced. But such an idea is all wrong. Some of the wisest men, all the best men, who

ever lived have clung closely to God's Word. They all say there is nothing better, nothing that can bring more joy into the world than obedience to that Word. There is nothing in education that need make us doubt the truth of our principles. The doubt, wherever there is doubt, comes from the evil that is within us.

But all this does not settle the question about the influence of the school and the church upon each other. How far is the one to be influenced by the other? There can be no doubt that as we advance in intelligence our conceptions of God are higher. The Indian and the Chinaman are very low intellectually, and so they are spiritually. The Mohammedan conceives of no higher heaven than the one in which the passions of the flesh are gratified. As long as what we learn tends to give us these higher conceptions and causes us to love God and his Word. more, so long we are safe in letting education influence us, so long may the church let herself be influenced by the schools. But when a change comes, when those who teach try to make us believe what is not the truth, when they want to have us take their word rather than God's, then we are not safe, then the church must not let herself be influenced by the schools. Whatever happens we must hold fast to the truth. We are told not to believe even an angel if he tells us what is contrary to this. Whenever men begin to tell us that this is not essential, or that is not essential, that we need not have humility in our actions if we have it in our hearts, then it is time for us to avoid those men and their teaching, for we know they are wrong.

Some things have found their way into our midst which should never have been allowed among us; the only right thing for us to do is to try to get rid of them. We find these things more in our schools, or in our members who have attended other schools, than elsewhere. Perhaps it is because so many young people are thrown together and one does not like to be outdone by the other. If they were as eager to excel in goodness as they are in some other things great blessings would follow. And why should they not have a greater desire to be good than to make a show or make some one envious?

What is written here is not written because I am opposed to schools, far from it; but that we may be on our guard, that we may get the most possible good out of our schools and the least evil. In themselves they are not bad, and the effort should be to keep them from becoming so. It is for the church to watch with unceasing vigilance and remove even the appearance of evil. If this is done we can all rejoice because we have schools; if this is not done we shall surely be sorry that they were ever brought into our midst. No one is a greater friend of education than I am, but at the same time it cannot be forgotten that our principles are worth more than education. If by gaining the latter the former must be sacrificed, the latter had better not be gained. We can and we should enjoy the advantage of both, for the one is not antagonistic to the other.

CANNOT BE A MASON.

A WRITER in a late number of the *Cynosure* tells why he cannot be a Mason. Read his experience; it may possibly confirm some of our people in their opposition to secret societies. The writer says:

"My convictions are that I should write my experience in Masonry. I joined the lodge about nineteen years ago, a little before I was converted. A short time after I was converted I came in contact with Bro. James Sullivan, of South Locke. He asked if I was a Mason. I said I

was. He then asked me if I could live a Christian and walk with the lodge. I told him I saw nothing as yet to hinder me; when I did, I should leave it.

"Soon after this a brother Mason came along one lodge night, it being on prayer-meeting night, and asked me if I was going to the lodge. I replied: 'I can't leave the prayer-meeting for the lodge;' and then the Scripture came to me, 'Have no fellowship with the unfruitful works of darkness.' I was then a member of the M. E. church. The next thought was, how can I take the Communion cup from the hand of a Mason who had taken such awful oaths? Conviction came more and more as the light shone. I called for my demit in the lodge, and said: 'I will pay my dues and leave honorably.' They said, no we want you with us. For five years I lived in this way, they all this time urging me to return to the lodge. I then said: 'No, sir; give me a demit and I will give you five dollars.' They did so. I took my demit home and burned it. I never attended the lodge after I was converted. Since I left the lodge I have talked against it, and God has wonderfully blessed me in so doing. I suffered persecution from the church of which I was a member nine years, doing the best I could for God and humanity all this time. I then left the church and for nine years have had no church fellowship, but serving the best I could and where I could, sometimes going to the Wesleyans, sometimes to the Free Methodists; but neither one was very convenient.

"Last winter I was privileged, in an adjoining neighborhood, to attend a revival meeting held by Rev. V. M. Thompson. I found in him and his people a spirit that dare oppose wrong, and God wonderfully blessed them. I have found a church home with them. I intend to stand wherever God calls me, and renounce Masonry as he may dictate. Since I have thus decided I have never been able to see how a man can be a Christian and a Mason at the same time. May God have mercy on all who dare claim this! My convictions are, also, I can no longer raise barley to sell to brewers. If I do I am a partaker with them in this sin. Full and free salvation from sin is my privilege to live.—*John P. Van Sycle, of Williamston, Mich.*

CORRESPONDENCE.

"Write what thou seest, and send it unto the churches."

☞Church News solicited for this Department. If you have had a good meeting, send a report of it, so that others may rejoice with you. In writing give name of church, County and State. Be brief. Notes of Travel should be as short as possible. Land Advertisements are not solicited for this Department. We have an advertising page, and, if necessary, will issue supplements.

Chips from the Work-house.

A VISIT to Philadelphia, North Philadelphia, Germantown, Norristown, and the three New Jersey churches has furnished timber for many Chips. The nice point is to make such Chips out of it as may be of some use. If this cannot be done, it were better left alone.

That all the above churches need help and encouragement is freely admitted by all with whom the writer had opportunity to converse about the situation. In New Jersey we held two preaching services with each one of the three churches, the members being as kind and hospitable as members can be. The old brethren who, years ago, frequently visited these far Eastern churches, have died off or gone westward with the march of empire, as have also some of their own number, until they feel somewhat forsaken by the large Brotherhood in the West. This causes some of them to feel rather neglected. They are not being visited by Western Brethren as much as desirable.

Missionary and Tract Work Department.

"Upon the first day of the week, let every one of you lay by him in store as God hath prospered him, that there be no gatherings when I come."—Cor. 16: 2.

"Every man as he purposeth in his heart, so let him give. Not grudgingly or of necessity, for the Lord loveth a cheerful giver."—2 Cor. 9: 7.

HOW MUCH SHALL WE GIVE?

"Every man *according to his ability*." "Every one *as God hath prospered him*." "Every man, *according as he purposeth in his heart*, so let him give." "For if there be first a willing mind, it is accepted *according to that a man hath*, and not according to that he hath not."—2 Cor. 8: 12.

Organization of Missionary Committee.

DANIEL VANIMAN, Foreman,   McPherson, Kans.
D. L. MILLER, Treasurer,   -   Mt. Morris, Ill.
GALEN B. ROYER, Secretary,   -   Mt. Morris, Ill.

Organization of Book and Tract Work.

S. W. HOOVER, Foreman,   -   Dayton, Ohio.
S. BOCK, Secretary and Treasurer,   Dayton, Ohio.

☞All donations intended for Missionary Work should be sent to GALEN B. ROYER, Mt. Morris, Ill.

☞All money for Tract Work should be sent to S. BOCK, Dayton, Ohio.

☞Money may be sent by Money Order. Registered Letter, or Draft on New York or Chicago. Do not send personal checks, or drafts on interior towns, as it costs 25 cents to collect them.

☞Solicitors are requested to faithfully carry out the plan of Annual Meeting, that all our members be solicited to contribute at least twice a year for the Mission and Tract Work of the Church.

☞Notes for the Endowment Fund can be had by writing to the Secretary of either Work.

MISSIONARY ITEMS.

The Methodist missions of North India received more than fifteen thousand converts last year.

* * *

The increase of population in India every year is equal to half the entire population of the United States.

* * *

How many ministers have this thought regularly in their public prayers: "Lord, hasten the day when all men shall have heard the Gospel?" How many ought to?

* * *

There is a certain young brother in one of our large cities who occasionally goes out evenings to the neglected parts of that great center, and there with his music gathers about him quite an audience of quiet listeners. Then he takes up the Word, and there he preaches the Gospel.

* * *

Thirty-six chiefs in the Uganda country, Africa, have offered to build each a house and maintain a European missionary, if men will come and reside thus with them. Two are now occupied. They see the results of Christianity outward and even on account of that are willing to encourage it, even though the grace of God has not yet found abiding place in their own hearts.

* * *

To the Chinese there is no day of rest,—no Sunday,—but all days are alike profane. A rice dealer, one Wang, was some years ago happily converted to Christ. Then the question was at issue for him, for closing his business on Saturday night and not opening till Monday morning meant exceeding ridicule and loss of custom. He decided in the right however. Soon his trade began growing less and less until he was in straitened circumstances, but he was decided. However, a new trade began to seek him, and, with his honesty and integrity, a larger business than before was, in due time, in his hands. Wang is to-day preaching the Gospel to his benighted countrymen and, having retired from business, is using his fortune in the cause of missions.

How to secure information on mission work and its opportunities is often a question. To read the life of a missionary, gives much uninteresting matter, and all concerning the work at one place. Mission encyclopedias are expensive. The best we know is to read travels among the mission stations, and notes, of course. Such can be obtained. A Hindu answering the question, "Which of all mission methods do you fear the most?" said, "We do not greatly fear your schools, for we need not send our children; we do not fear your books, for we need not read them; we do not fear your preaching, for we need not hear it; but we dread your women and your doctors; for your doctors are winning our hearts, and your women are winning our homes; and when our hearts and our homes are won, what is there left us?"   W. S.

WHY SHOULD WE BE FIRST IN MISSIONS?

BY W. B. STOVER.

It may seem rather an unfortunate thing to ask a question concerning our being *first* in the mission field, when the fact of the case is that we have not, at the present time, one missionary among the millions of heathendom. The exceeding greatness of that latter expression, "millions of heathendom," can scarcely be comprehended. Take an apple, a foot in circumference, and let that represent the world. Now, cut out carefully a section measuring one inch on the outer surface, or, in other words, just one-third of a quarter. Hold up in one hand the little slice, the remainder of the apple in the other, and you have before you an approximate but fair representation of Protestant Christianity as it stands in numbers before the world.

When we look over the fields before us, we are almost dumb-struck. There is so much to do. God says, "Subdue it." Jesus says, "Go ye into all the world and preach the Gospel." We ought to be into the work with our sleeves rolled up. We ought to go into the work, away in, deeper than to the tops of our heads.

Fifty or sixty years ago there could have been found some excuses, possibly, for not being active and to the front, but to-day it is vastly different. We might find reason for not preaching the Gospel in Turkey to-day, because it is strictly against the law, but not so in most other lands. China has no more a great wall around her empire. Japan is an open scene of activity. India and Africa and the islands of the sea are open to the evangel of God. The inhabitants of some of these lands are verily saying, time and again, "Send us teachers. Your religion seems good." These things are such great truths that the light seems to be blinding. Other denominations are earnestly pushing into these fields all over the world. Are we?

We, who claim, with good and sufficient reason too, to have the primitive Christianity; we, who have *the Christ baptism*, and no substitute for it; we, who perpetuate the apostolic love-feast, or *deipnon*; we, who practice the lowly example of the Master in washing one another's feet; we, who urge the apostolic simplicity and hospitality; we, who claim to read the Word and understand it literally as little children; are we doing what we must do?

When we read, "Go ye into all the world," do we see it, do we understand it, do we go? But ought we to be desirous for numbers in the church? For the sake of numbers, no. For the sake of souls, for the sake of truth, for the sake of Christ, yes. For the love of souls, for the love of truth, for the love of Christ, emphatically yes. Sometimes we hear it said that the Gospel

was once preached to all nations and the heathen are so by matter of choice. When was that? What is the responsibility of good Queen Victoria for the inglorious deeds of King John, centuries ago? Ah, love impels us. The people now want the Gospel, and we ought to give it to them.

Where were our ancestors before foreign missions found them? The days of the week ought to be a constant reminder of the debt we owe. See the array of gods and goddesses. Sun, Moon, Tuisco, Woden, Thor, Friga, Saeter. The worship of these by *our fathers* was often accompanied by bloody, human sacrifices, as dark as any now found in darkest Africa, and yet we rejoice in our boasted wisdom, and stay in our pleasant homes rejoicing.

It will doubtless be conceded that we ought to be in the fields all over the world, bringing in the sheaves for the Master. But, more than that, we ought to be fully consistent, to be doing more than anybody else. We should be first in missions. And why?

We claim to put a literal interpretation upon the Word whenever common sense will permit, and we hold the New Testament as the creed of this dispensation. That is a good position. But when we read, "Go into all the world and preach the Gospel" in the New Testament, why don't we, literally, some at least, go?

Again, we are largely a rural people, and as such have learned the principles of economy from the days of our birth. Economy is a necessary qualification to a successful missionary. It is that, too, over which a heathen man can never stumble, thinking there is possibly financial advantages, in being a Christian. Money given for missionary purposes is always accompanied with the desire that it may do as much good as possible. Economy answers this in every respect.

Again, out in the labors of the heathen foreign fields, as well as on the frontier of fields nearer home, there is required a great deal of physical ability. It is no light task to travel horse-back or on foot all day and then preach, or to preach in the open air daily and nightly, and then answer questions of a puzzling nature afterwards, to endure the heat of a burning sun and the cool of chilly nights, and such like. But we, farmers, and sons and daughters of farmers, raised in the corn-field, potato-patch, and garden, used to working hard from early morn to late in the night, we ought to be, and we are, equal to the emergency.

Another strong point is our wealth. The nature of the case makes us so. Although "the laborer is worthy of his hire," our ministerial support is generally very meager. While our neighbors pay their preachers from four hundred dollars a year upward, we put that in our pockets usually, and are, of course, that much farther ahead in finance. If we give what others give, and then put equal to their ministers' salaries on top of that yet, you see, at once, we are, proportionately, ahead of our neighbors on giving to missions. The cause of missions is a good work and we certainly want to be zealous in good works. All persons, as far as wealth is concerned, have a right to expect of us that we be first in missions. Our belief concerning our doctrine requires us to be first in missions, and while there in life any how, when we do not live for others? For all persons these lines may be a fitting motto:

"I live for those who love me;
For those who know me true;
For the heaven that smiles above me,
And awaits my spirit too;
For the wrong that needs resistance,
For the cause that lacks assistance,
For the future in the distance,
For the good that I can do."

Missionary and Tract Work Department.

"Upon the first day of the week, let every one of you lay by him in store, as God hath prospered him, that there be no gatherings when I come."—1 Cor. 16: 2.

"Every man as he purposeth in his heart, so let him give. Not grudgingly or of necessity, for the Lord loveth a cheerful giver."—2 Cor. 9: 7.

HOW MUCH SHALL WE GIVE?

"Every man *according to his ability.*" "Every one *as God hath prospered him.*" "For if there be first a willing mind, it is accepted according *to that a man hath,* and not according to that he hath not."—2 Cor. 8: 12.

Organization of Missionary Committee.

DANIEL VANIMAN, Foreman, · · · McPherson, Kans.
D. L. MILLER, Treasurer, · · · Mt. Morris, Ill.
GALEN B. ROYER, Secretary, · · · Mt. Morris, Ill.

Organization of Book and Tract Work.

S. W. HOOVER, Foreman, · · · Dayton, Ohio.
S. BOCK, Secretary and Treasurer, · · · Dayton, Ohio.

☞All donations intended for Missionary Work should be sent to GALEN B. ROYER, Mt. Morris, Ill.

☞All money for Tract Work should be sent to S. BOCK, Dayton, Ohio.

☞Money may be sent by Money Order. Registered Letter, or Drafts on New York or Chicago. Do not send personal checks, or drafts on interior towns, as it costs 25 cents to collect them.

☞Solicitors are requested to faithfully carry out the plan of Annual Meeting, that all our members be solicited to contribute at least twice a year for the Mission and Tract Work of the Church.

☞Notes for the Endowment Fund can be had by writing to the Secretary of either Work.

MISSIONARY ITEMS.

The Methodist missions of North India received more than fifteen thousand converts last year.

* * *

The increase of population in India every year is equal to half the entire population of the United States.

* * *

How many ministers have this thought regularly in their public prayers: "Lord, hasten the day when all men shall have heard the Gospel?" How many ought to?

* * *

There is a certain young brother in one of our large cities who occasionally goes out evenings to the neglected parts of that great center, and there with his music gathers about him quite an audience of quiet listeners. Then he takes up the Word, and there he preaches the Gospel.

* * *

Thirty-six chiefs in the Uganda country, Africa, have offered to build each a house and maintain a European missionary, if men will come and reside thus with them. Two are now occupied. They see the results of Christianity outward and even on account of that are willing to encourage it, even though the grace of God has not yet found abiding place in their own hearts.

* * *

To the Chinese there is no day of rest,—no Sunday,—but all days are alike profane. A rice dealer, one Wang, was some years ago happily converted to Christ. Then the question was at issue for him, for closing his business on Saturday night and not opening till Monday morning meant exceeding ridicule and loss of custom. He decided in the right however. Soon his trade began growing less and less until he was in straitened circumstances, but he was decided. However, a new trade began to seek him, and, with his honesty and integrity, a larger business than before was, in due time, in his hands. Wang is to-day preaching the Gospel to his benighted countrymen and, having retired from business, is using his fortune in the cause of missions.

How to secure information on mission work and its opportunities is often a question. To read the life of a missionary, gives much uninteresting matter, and all concerning the work at one place. Mission encyclopedias are expensive. The best we know is to read travels among the mission stations, and notes, of course. Such can be obtained. A Hindu answering the question, "Which of all mission methods do you fear the most?" said, "We do not greatly fear your schools, for we need not send our children; we do not fear your books, for we need not read them; we do not fear your preaching, for we need not hear it; but we dread your women and your doctors; for your doctors are winning our hearts, and your women are winning our homes; and when our hearts and our homes are won, what is there left us?"   W. S.

WHY SHOULD WE BE FIRST IN MISSIONS?

BY W. B. STOVER.

It may seem rather an unfortunate thing to ask a question concerning our being *first* in the mission field, when the fact of the case is that we have not, at the present time, one missionary among the millions of heathendom. The exceeding greatness of that latter expression, "millions of heathendom," can scarcely be comprehended. Take an apple, a foot in circumference, and let that represent the world. Now, cut out carefully a section measuring one inch on the outer surface, or, in other words, just one-third of a quarter. Hold up in one hand the little slice, the remainder of the apple in the other, and you have before you an approximate but fair representation of Protestant Christianity as it stands in numbers before the world.

When we look over the fields before us, we are almost dumb-struck. There is so much to do. God says, "Subdue it." Jesus says, "Go ye into all the world and preach the Gospel." We ought to be into the work with our sleeves rolled up. We ought to go into the work, away in, deeper than to the tops of our heads.

Fifty or sixty years ago there could have been found some excuses, possibly, for not being active and to the front, but to-day it is vastly different. We might find reason for not preaching the Gospel in Turkey to-day, because it is strictly against the law, but not so in most other lands. China has no more a great wall around her empire. Japan is an open scene of activity. India and Africa and the islands of the sea are open to the evangel of God. The inhabitants of some of these lands are verily saying, time and again, "Send us teachers. Your religion seems good." These things are such great truths that the light seems to be blinding. Other denominations are earnestly pushing into these fields all over the world. Are we?

We, who claim, with good and sufficient reason too, to have the primitive Christianity; we, who have the Christ baptism, and no substitute for it; we, who perpetuate the apostolic love-feast, or *deipnon*; we, who practice the humble example of the Master in washing one another's feet; we, who urge the apostolic simplicity and hospitality; we, who claim to read the Word and understand it literally as little children; are we doing what we must do?

When we read, "Go ye into all the world," do we see it, do we understand it, do we go?

But ought we to be desirous for numbers in the church? For the sake of numbers, no. For the sake of souls, for the sake of truth, for the sake of Christ, yes. For the love of souls, for the love of truth, for the love of Christ, emphatically yes. Sometimes we hear it said that the Gospel

was once preached to all nations and the heathen are so by matter of choice. When was that? What is the responsibility of good Queen Victoria for the inglorious deeds of King John, centuries ago? Ah, love impels us. The people now want the Gospel, and we ought to give it to them.

Where were our ancestors before foreign missions found them? The days of the week ought to be a constant reminder of the debt we owe. See the array of gods and goddesses. Sun, Moon, Tuisco, Woden, Thor, Friga, Saeter. The worship of these by *our fathers* was often accompanied by bloody, human sacrifices, as dark as any now found in darkest Africa, and yet we rejoice in our boasted wisdom, and stay in our pleasant homes rejoicing.

It will doubtless be conceded that we ought to be in the fields all over the world, bringing in the sheaves for the Master. But, more than that, we ought to be fully consistent, to be doing more than anybody else. We should be first in missions. And why?

We claim to put a literal interpretation upon the Word whenever common sense will permit, and we hold the New Testament as the creed of this dispensation. That is a good position. But when we read, "Go into all the world and preach the Gospel" in the New Testament, why don't we, literally, some at least, go?

Again, we are largely a rural people, and as such have learned the principles of economy from the days of our birth. Economy is a necessary qualification to a successful missionary. It is that, too, over which a heathen man can never stumble, thinking there is possibly financial advantages, in being a Christian. Money given for missionary purposes is always accompanied with the desire that it may do as much good as possible. Economy answers this in every respect.

Again, out in the labors of the heathen foreign fields, as well as on the frontier of fields nearer home, there is required a great deal of physical ability. It is no light task to travel horse-back or on foot all day and then preach, or to preach in the open air daily and nightly, and then answer questions of a puzzling nature afterwards, to endure the heat of a burning sun and the cool of chilly nights, and such like. But we, farmers, and sons and daughters of farmers, raised in the corn-field, potato-patch, and garden, used to working hard from early morn to late in the night, we ought to be, and we are, equal to the emergency.

Another strong point is our wealth. The nature of the case makes us so. Although "the laborer is worthy of his hire," our ministerial support is generally very meager. While our neighbors pay their preachers from four hundred dollars a year upward, we put that in our pockets usually, and are, of course, that much farther ahead in finance. If we give what others give, and then put equal to their ministers' salaries on top of that yet, you see, at once, we are, proportionately, ahead of our neighbors on giving to missions. The cause of missions is a good work and we certainly want to be zealous in good works. All persons, as far as wealth is concerned, have a right to expect of us that we be first in missions. Our belief concerning our doctrine requires us to be first in missions, and what is there in life any how, when we do not live for others? For all persons these lines may be a fitting motto:

"I live for those who love me;
For those who know me true;
For the heaven that smiles above me,
And awaits my spirit too;
For the wrong that needs resistance,
For the cause that lacks assistance,
For the future in the distance,
For the good that I can do."

The Gospel Messenger,

A Weekly at $1.50 Per Annum.

PUBLISHED BY

The Brethren's Publishing Co.

D. L. MILLER,	Editor.
J. H. MOORE,	Office Editor.
J. B. BRUMBAUGH,	Associate Editors.
J. G. ROYER,	
JOSEPH AMICK,	Business Manager.

ADVISORY COMMITTEE.

L. W. Teeter, A. Hutchison, Daniel Hays.

Mount Morris, Ill.,   ·   ·   ·   **Oct. 4, 1892.**

BRO. J. R. ROYER reports two more additions to the Ephratah church, Pa.

BRO. P. R. WRIGHTSMAN, of Kansas, has been spending about two weeks in the vicinity of Lanark.

NEXT week the General Mission Board will meet at Mt. Morris, to transact such business as may come in its line.

BRO. I. M. GIBSON has been holding a very interesting series of meetings at Hudson, Ill. Four made the good confession and were baptized.

PEOPLE talk about joining the church of their choice. Would it not look a little better if they would talk about uniting with the church of the Lord's choice?

As relic after relic is unearthed in the Bible Lands, one hardly knows what to expect next. Dr. Grant Bey, a learned Egyptologist, has found what he considers to have been the seal of Amoz, the scribe, father of Isaiah, the prophet.

BRO. HENRY FRANTZ, of Ohio, who is now in the midst of a series of meetings at West Branch, seven miles north-west of Mt. Morris, gave us a pleasant call last week. We enjoyed his visit very much, and trust he can visit us again shortly.

IN a note accompanying one of his recent articles, Bro. Balsbaugh says: " *True faith never supersedes works;* but works may easily encroach on true faith. This has been the tendency of the human heart from the primal apostasy to this moment."

WE suggest it would be wise for the Sunday-schools, now using the *Young Disciple,* to have them continued whether the schools remain in session or not. They can be handed to the children at the close of the regular meetings. In this way the little folks could get much valuable reading matter very cheaply during the winter months, when they enjoy reading so well,

BRO. J. C. LAHMAN, who has been spending several weeks in Iowa, informs us that he had a pleasant trip among the churches. He attended the District Meeting of Middle Iowa, at Garrison, Sept. 22, and reports that five were received into the church at that time. The meetings are being continued by Bro. Hipes.

IT is not often that we chronicle the death of a member who passes into the second century of his life. On another page of this issue will be found an interesting biographical sketch of a brother whose life commenced only a few years after the birth of our nation. He lived long enough to have seen all the Presidents of the United States.

SOME people would think themselves very fortunate if they had just money enough to start a school, but after running it a few years they would probably regard themselves still more fortunate if they only had money enough to stop it. Men who have had years of experience in school finances will see a world of meaning in this paragraph.

THE *Octographic Review* says: "The more proud and stingy the church, the more oysters and soup it requires to keep up appearances. Such a church is dead and don't know it. A church that is not independent of the world, may be a club, a society of educated people, a band of stingy men and women; it is not the church of Christ."

BRO. H. B. PUTERBAUGH, one of the compositors of the MESSENGER office, is now at Eureka Springs, Ark., for his health. He writes that he is greatly improving and much encouraged. He expresses a desire to distribute any tracts or papers that the Brethren see proper to send him. We have no congregation in that section of the State, and he feels quite at a loss without religious associations.

IT is now estimated that Europe will have to import nearly 200,000,000 bushels of wheat this year to feed her people. The greater part of this must come from America, India, and Australia. And while this is true, there is enough fertile land in Europe "devoted to hunting parks for the nobility to raise double that amount of wheat, and while there are more than enough able-bodied men, in the prime of life, to sow and to reap it, who are kept in the idle savagery of camp and barrack life, there are, besides, choice acres enough devoted to the production of wine and beer to bear over 170,000,000 bushels of wheat; and enough men engaged in producing these drinks to raise and manufacture them into flour." We need not wonder that there is so much suffering in the land, when we see this great misuse of soil and fruit.

WHILE this is an age of reading, it is not necessary that we read everything that comes in our way, any more than that we should eat everything or anything that we can lay hands on. Always read with an object in view. One book or paper well read is worth a dozen carelessly read or indifferently perused. Select what you need most and then have the firmness to stick to it. This will not only give you strength to avoid unprofitable reading, but will greatly strengthen you in what you do read. Remember that the object of reading is to improve the mind as well as to afford intellectual enjoyment. It is well to select such food as will best serve the wants of the body and satisfy a properly-cultivated appetite. It is also equally well to exercise the same wisdom in the selection of reading matter, keeping constantly in view the welfare of our spiritual and intellectual parts.

OUR Brethren may rest assured that all intelligibly-written obituaries, received at this office, appear in the paper. Occasionally there is one minus the place or date of the death that cannot be published. If you do not find in the paper the notice you are interested in, you may be certain that we have either not received it, or there is some omission about it, rendering it impossible to get it in readable shape.

BRO. A. W. REESE, formerly of Warrensburgh, Mo., is, for the present, located at the National Military Home, Leavenworth County, Kans., as surgeon in charge of the Keeley Institute, for the treatment of the soldiers at that place. The position is a very important one, and Bro. Reese, as a physician of long experience, is certainly well qualified for that kind of work. Our readers would appreciate something from his pen occasionally.

MANY of our readers will remember Eld. Geo. Long, of Clarksville, Mich., who went off with the Old Order element several years ago. He gave us a short call last week, and seemed as happy to meet us as in former years, saying that we did not have a more earnest reader of the MESSENGER than he is. We were glad to meet him, and trust that he, as well as scores of others, will make up his mind to return to the old fold ere the Master calls.

IT will be a matter of great interest to all of the children, and older people too, perhaps, to learn that sister Lizzie Miller, wife of Bro. D. L. Miller, has consented to write a series of articles for the *Young Disciple,* giving an account of her trip across the ocean, her visits to Germany, Denmark, and the land of Palestine. These articles will be written especially for children, and will be found exceedingly interesting, hence we suggest that all those, having children old enough to read, subscribe for the *Young Disciple,* so as to afford the little ones an opportunity of reading these articles. The paper is published and mailed weekly; price, only 50 cents a year, and those who will send in their subscriptions now, will receive the paper the remainder of this year free. Those desiring to start in with the beginning of these articles, should send in their names immediately, as the publication of the articles will commence in about two weeks.

WE notice that one of our local churches has decided not to invite ministers to preach for them who are not in harmony with our non-conformity principles in their general appearance. It is indeed unfortunate that there should be an occasion for a resolution of this nature, and it is also equally unfortunate that ministers, who pledged themselves to faithfulness, should now disregard their vow, and undertake to inflict upon the church an example that she never would have agreed to at the time of receiving them into their office. In receiving ministers into their office, the church acts in good faith, and she has a right to expect, and even demand, an equal degree of sincerity upon the part of all of these ministers, and for any of them to willfully ignore this principle, shows a great lack of faithfulness to their vows that is sad to contemplate. While we believe there are not many cases of this character among us, still there are at least enough to produce serious apprehensions, and we would therefore earnestly urge all of our ministers to carefully and sincerely reconsider their sacred vows and pledges, and see whether they are now honestly carrying them out in the sight of both God and man, as they promised when received into their office.

The Gospel Messenger,

A Weekly at $1.50 Per Annum.

PUBLISHED BY

The Brethren's Publishing Co.

D. L. MILLER,	·	·	·	·	·	·	·	·	Editor.
J. H. MOORE,	·	·	·	·	·	·	·	Office Editor.
J. B. BRUMBAUGH,								
J. G. ROYER,	}	·	·	·	·	Associate Editors.
JOSEPH AMICK,	·	·	·	·	·	Business Manager.

ADVISORY COMMITTEE.

L. W. Teeter, A. Hutchison, Daniel Hays.

☞ Communications for publication should be legibly written with black ink on one side of the paper only. Do not attempt to interline, or to put on one page what ought to occupy two.

☞ Anonymous communications will not be published.

☞ Do not mix business with articles for publication. Keep your communications on separate sheets from all business.

☞ Time is precious. We always have time to attend to business and to unravel questions of importance, but please do not subject us to need less answering of letters.

☞ The Messenger is mailed each week to all subscribers. If the address is correctly entered on our list, the paper must reach the person to whom it is addressed. If you do not get your paper, write us, giving particulars.

☞ When changing your address, please give your former as well as your future address in full, so as to avoid delay and misunderstanding.

☞ Always remit to the office from which you order your goods, no matter from where you receive them.

☞ Do not send personal checks or drafts on interior banks, unless you send with them 25 cents each, to pay for collection.

☞ Remittances should be made by Post-office Money Order, Drafts on New York, Philadelphia or Chicago, or Registered Letters, made payable and addressed to "Brethren's Publishing Co., Mount Morris, Ill." or "Brethren's Publishing Co., Huntingdon, Pa."

☞ Entered at the Post-office at Mount Morris, Ill., as second-class matter.

Mount Morris, Ill.,   · · · · ·   Oct. 4, 1892.

Bro. J. R. Royer reports two more additions to the Ephratah church, Pa.

Bro. P. R. Wrightsman, of Kansas, has been spending about two weeks in the vicinity of Lanark.

Next week the General Mission Board will meet at Mt. Morris, to transact such business as may come in its line.

Bro. I. M. Gibson has been holding a very interesting series of meetings at Hudson, Ill. Four made the good confession and were baptized.

People talk about joining the church of their choice. Would it not look a little better if they would talk about uniting with the church of the Lord's choice?

As relic after relic is unearthed in the Bible Lands, one hardly knows what to expect next. Dr. Grant Bey, a learned Egyptologist, has found what he considers to have been the seal of Amos, the scribe, father of Isaiah, the prophet.

Bro. Henry Frantz, of Ohio, who is now in the midst of a series of meetings at West Branch, seven miles north-west of Mt. Morris, gave us a pleasant call last week. We enjoyed his visit very much, and trust he can visit us again shortly.

In a note accompanying one of his recent articles, Bro. Balsbaugh says: "True faith never supersedes works; but works may easily encroach on true faith. This has been the tendency of the human heart from the primal apostasy to this moment."

We suggest it would be wise for the Sunday-schools, now using the Young Disciple, to have them continued whether the schools remain in session or not. They can be handed to the children at the close of the regular meetings. In this way the little folks could get much valuable reading matter very cheaply during the winter months, when they enjoy reading so well.

Bro. J. C. Lahman, who has been spending several weeks in Iowa, informs us that he had a pleasant trip among the churches. He attended the District Meeting of Middle Iowa, at Garrison, Sept. 22, and reports that five were received into the church at that time. The meetings are being continued by Bro. Hipes.

It is not often that we chronicle the death of a member who passes into the second century of his life. On another page of this issue will be found an interesting biographical sketch of a brother whose life commenced only a few years after the birth of our nation. He lived long enough to have seen all the Presidents of the United States.

Some people would think themselves very fortunate if they had just money enough to start a school, but after running it a few years they would probably regard themselves still more fortunate if they only had money enough to stop it. Men who have had years of experience in school finances will see a world of meaning in this paragraph.

The Octographic Review says: "The more proud and stingy the church, the more oysters and soup it requires to keep up appearances. Such a church is dead and don't know it. A church that is not independent of the world, may be a club, a society of educated people, or a band of stingy men and women; it is not the church of Christ."

Bro. H. B. Puterbaugh, one of the compositors of the Messenger office, is now at Eureka Springs, Ark., for his health. He writes that he is greatly improving and much encouraged. He expresses a desire to distribute any tracts or papers that the Brethren see proper to send him. We have no congregation in that section of the State, and he feels quite at a loss without religious associations.

It is now estimated that Europe will have to import nearly 200,000,000 bushels of wheat this year to feed her people. The greater part of this must come from America, India, and Australia. And while this is true, there is enough fertile land in Europe "devoted to hunting parks for the nobility to raise double that amount of wheat, and while there are more than enough able-bodied men, in the prime of life, to sow and to reap it, who are kept in the idle savagery of camp and barrack life, there are, besides, choice acres enough devoted to the production of wine and beer to bear over 170,000,000 bushels of wheat; and enough men engaged in producing those drinks to raise and manufacture them into flour." We need not wonder that there is so much suffering in the land, when we see this great misuse of soil and fruit.

While this is an age of reading, it is not necessary that we read everything that comes in our way, any more than that we should eat everything or anything that we can lay hands on. Always read with an object in view. One book or paper well read is worth a dozen carelessly read or indifferently perused. Select what you need most and then have the firmness to stick to it. This will not only give you strength to avoid unprofitable reading, but will greatly strengthen you in what you do read. Remember that the object of reading is to improve the mind as well as to afford intellectual enjoyment. It is well to select such food as will best serve the wants of the body and satisfy a properly-cultivated appetite. It is also equally well to exercise the same wisdom in the selection of reading matter, keeping constantly in view the welfare of our spiritual and intellectual parts.

Our Brethren may rest assured that all intelligibly-written obituaries, received at this office, appear in the paper. Occasionally there is one minus the place or date of the death that cannot be published. If you do not find in the paper the notice you are interested in, you may be certain that we have either not received it, or there is some omission about it, rendering it impossible to get it in readable shape.

Bro. A. W. Reese, formerly of Warrensburgh, Mo., is, for the present, located at the National Military Home, Leavenworth County, Kans., as surgeon in charge of the Keeley Institute, for the treatment of the soldiers at that place. The position is a very important one, and Bro. Reese, as a physician of long experience, is certainly well qualified for that kind of work. Our readers would appreciate something from his pen occasionally.

Many of our readers will remember Eld. Geo. Long, of Clarksville, Mich., who went off with the Old Order element several years ago. He gave us a short call last week, and seemed as happy to meet us as in former years, saying that we did not have a more earnest reader of the Messenger than he is. We were glad to meet him, and trust that he, as well as scores of others, will make up his mind to return to the old fold ere the Master calls.

It will be a matter of great interest to all of the children, and older people too, perhaps, to learn that sister Lizzie Miller, wife of Bro. D. L. Miller, has consented to write a series of articles for the Young Disciple, giving an account of her trip across the ocean, her visits to Germany, Denmark, and the land of Palestine. These articles will be written especially for children, and will be found exceedingly interesting, hence we suggest that all those, having children old enough to read, subscribe for the Young Disciple, so as to afford the little ones an opportunity of reading these articles. The paper is published and mailed weekly; price, only 50 cents a year, and those who will send in their subscriptions now, will receive the paper the remainder of this year free. Those desiring to start in with the beginning of these articles, should send in their names immediately, as the publication of the articles will commence in about two weeks.

We notice that one of our local churches has decided not to invite ministers to preach for them who are not in harmony with our non-conformity principles in their general appearance. It is indeed unfortunate that there should be an occasion for a resolution of this nature, and it is also equally unfortunate that ministers, who disregard their vow, and undertake to inflict upon the church an example that she never would have agreed to at the time of receiving them into their office. In receiving ministers into their office, the church acts in good faith, and she has a right to expect, and even demand, an equal degree of sincerity upon the part of all of these ministers, and for any of them to willfully ignore this principle, shows a great lack of faithfulness to their vows that is sad to contemplate. While we believe there are not many cases of this character among us, still there are at least enough to produce serious apprehensions, and we would therefore earnestly urge all of our ministers to carefully and sincerely reconsider their sacred vows and pledges, and see whether they are now honestly carrying them out in the sight of both God and man, as they promised when received into their office.

QUERISTS' DEPARTMENT.

Is it right for a church to relieve a minister of his office, who has preached about thirty eight years in one section of country, without consulting him, or intimating that there is dissatisfaction with him? If the preacher is dissatisfied, what course should be taken? D. LEEDY.

ONE would hardly think that such a case could occur, but if it did, it is not right, but should be appealed to the elders. It is always best to refer questions of this character to some one acquainted with all the circumstances. Our answer must be in general terms only. It is difficult to understand how a thing of this kind could happen. We know it could not occur in any well-regulated congregation. No officer should be relieved of his office without the charges being made known to him if it be possible to reach him, and an opportunity granted for a fair trial. Possibly there might be some deviation from this rule in dealing with gross crimes of the worst and most public character. If the minister, who is relieved of his office, is not satisfied, he may call for a rehearing in the presence of adjoining elders. If satisfaction is not thus obtained, he can make a call at the District Meeting for a committee. We can do no more than answer what appears on the face of the query.

Is it according to the Gospel for ministers, at meeting, to line the hymns when we all have books? I think it spoils the singing. MARY ATWOOD.

This is one of the questions concerning which the Gospel is silent, leaving each congregation to do that which seems for the better. Paul says, "Let all things be done unto edifying." Whatever is most edifying to the congregation, would be advisable. For our part we line hymns only where there is a great scarcity of books. Where all or most of the people have books, we think it is not necessary.

Here is a question I would like you to answer. It is a command Christ gave to his disciples, and there is no attention paid to it now: "And into whatsoever house ye enter first say, Peace be to this house. And if the son of peace be there, your peace shall rest upon it: if not, it shall turn to you again." Luke 10: 5, 6 ELMIRA S. MOYER.

This, as well as much more of the same character, was special, and pertained wholly to the disciples sent to the lost sheep of the house of Israel only. It is like the command, "Salute no man by the way." It was for a special purpose, and does not apply to us, who act on the authority of the last commission, which requires us to go into all the world and preach the Gospel to every creature. While there are principles in the command, suggested by our querist, that we will do well to heed, the command itself must be regarded as special, and is therefore not applicable to the department of labor now assigned to us.

Is it right for our Brethren to unite with other denominations and have a Sunday school celebration and picnic? Z. AXSON.

Our Brethren have very prudently advised against us uniting with others in the present semi-worldly manner of holding these gatherings. The appearance is evil, on account of unbecoming things often connected therewith. Besides, it is offensive to many of the faithful, and probably does no good in the end. We should rather follow that which makes peace.

A brother marries a wife, supposing her first husband to be dead. Will the church have to prove that the former husband is living, or must the brother prove that he is dead? ALEX. MILLER.

If the brother is called into question for marrying a woman whose former husband may possibly be living, it would be proper for him to offer his evidence in defense of the man being dead. It would then be the duty of the church to find evidence to the contrary. After the evidence is in from both sides, the church may then render her decision, whether or not the former husband is dead. Of course the brother must be held as innocent until he is proven guilty.

When was funeral preaching first introduced? Is it only a custom, or is it a command? J. SNAVELY, SR.

We cannot tell when funeral preaching was first introduced. Possibly some of our readers can. It is simply a custom, and a very good one if not abused.

"But he that is least in the kingdom of God is greater than he." Luke 7: 28. How can he be less than he? JOHN SNAVELY, SR.

The meaning is this: He that is least in the kingdom of God is greater than John the Baptist.

"For the gifts and calling of God are without repentance?" Is it God or man that is referred to as being without repentance? S. S. ULERY.

We understand it to be God, in this instance, who is without repentance. The gifts and calling of God pertained to the electing of Israel as the chosen people, and the covenant made concerning them. Of this the Lord never repented; he is unchangeable, though the people, thus especially elected, proved unfaithful. The covenant still stands intact.

Please explain Hebrews 6: 16: "For men verily swear by the greater: and an oath for confirmation is to them an end to all strife." This seems to imply to swear, although we are commanded to "swear not at all." R. SANGER.

Paul is here writing of that which pertained to the former dispensation, when it was in keeping with God's law to confirm by an oath, but in this new and better dispensation the command for all time, and under all circumstances is, "Swear not at all." Keep in mind the two dispensations, and the question will be easily understood.

The verse referred to reads thus: "And except those days should be shortened, there should no flesh be saved: but for the elect's sake those days shall be shortened." The Savior is here speaking of the destruction of Jerusalem, which event took place A. D. 70, at which time the suffering was so great that parents ate their own children. It was necessary that those days of intense sufferings and great loss of life should be shortened, that the elect, the Jews, might not all be destroyed. The shortening of these days took place when God permitted Titus, with the Roman army, to enter Jerusalem, Sept. 12, A. D. 70, and take possession of the city. The temple had been burned July 15. While the siege was going on, which lasted nearly one year, the Jews were divided into contending factions, and thus weakened their own forces, and greatly increased their own suffering. J. H. M.

When, where, and how did the Lord shorten those days? Matt. 24: 22. A. N. GRATBILL.

---

ing England, one of our nearest commercial neighbors. It is only a step across the ocean to our great cities; thence it may be carried by the railroads throughout the land. It is a deathly disease; few escape. It is of short duration, still it gives people a chance to pray and call upon their God. Dangerous as it is, it does not take away their reason. Prepare for it! The President has issued a proclamation that all vessels must be quarantined before any passengers can land. Public sentiment is in his favor and will uphold him, whether it is lawful or not, and whether treaties are violated or not, because it is for the public safety. We want to be saved from the disease, and keep it far away from our homes and our families. We cannot spare them.

Supposing every ship that crosses the ocean carried some of these microbes, some hidden away on the person of passengers, some in their trunks and chests and some even in barrels, supposing the large cities of New York, Philadelphia, Chicago, etc, all had shops where they would keep the microbes for sale receiving their right or license from the government to do so, supposing every village had its shop, with the sign "Cholera for sale," supposing that even in the country, shops are put up to catch the farmer's boy, the only hope of the future city, supposing that the people of a town would rise up to stay the disease. The railroads would bring it in spite of law, carrying the microbes behind closed doors,—slyly, but surely, killing some with the dreadful disease. Supposing the great political parties were afraid to say anything against it, supposing the President would be afraid to stay the great evil by quarantine, supposing, if we took the disease and it killed us, we had no hope of heaven, supposing even ministers of the Gospel would be afraid to warn the people of its danger, and if missionaries were sent to foreign countries where the disease was not known, to teach them "Christ and him crucified," some one would slip some of these microbes on the same ship and kill the poor heathens! "O consistency, thou art a jewel."

While cholera kills its thousands, strong drink kills its ten thousands, brings woe, destruction, death, and hell, as the drunkard's doom. While we are afraid of the one which has not done us any harm and is far away, the other is at our door, ready any time to take our dear child, and kill body and soul. Oh! come, cholera, take my child, a follower of Jesus, rather than let my son a drunkard's grave. Help me to quarantine our homes! Call loud the proclamation; let every paper take up the cry! The disease has come; we get used to it, and though we see its ravages every day, we are powerless to stop it. CYRUS BUCHER.

Astoria, Ill.

From Glensted, Mo.

OUR series of meetings, conducted by Bro. C. Hope, of Kansas, began on Friday, Aug. 26. On Saturday following, elders Witmore and Hope being with us, we held our quarterly council. All business was transacted in a Christian spirit. Bro. W. W. Holsopple was advanced to the second degree of the ministry, and Bro. J. A. Bowman elected to the office of deacon.

Bro Witmore remained with us over Sunday, when he departed for his home, leaving Bro. Hope to continue the meetings, which were conducted with good interest throughout.

Our feast occurred September 6, and was indeed an enjoyable one, and the largest ever held here.

While the meetings were in progress, eight dear souls were made willing to follow the exam-

---

CORRESPONDENCE.

"Write what thou seest, and send it unto the churches."

☞ Church News solicited for this Department. If you have had a good meeting, send a report of it, so that others may rejoice with you. In writing give name of church, County and State. Be brief. Notes of Travel should be as short as possible. Land Advertisements are not solicited for this Department. We have an advertising page and, if necessary, will issue supplements.

Cholera, Cholera!

YES, it is coming. It started in Asia and has been slowly making its way across Europe, reach-

QUERISTS' DEPARTMENT.

Is it right for a church to relieve a minister of his office, who has preached about thirty eight years in one section of country, without consulting him, or intimating that there is dissatisfaction with him? If the preacher is dissatisfied, what course should be taken? D. LERDY.

ONE would hardly think that such a case could occur, but if it did, it is not right, but should be appealed to the elders. It is always best to refer questions of this character to some one acquainted with all the circumstances. Our answer must be in general terms only. It is difficult to understand how a thing of this kind could happen. We know it could not occur in any well-regulated congregation. No officer should be relieved of his office without the charges being made known to him if it be possible to reach him, and an opportunity granted for a fair trial. Possibly there might be some deviation from this rule in dealing with gross crimes of the worst and most public character. If the minister, who is relieved of his office, is not satisfied, he may call for a rehearing in the presence of adjoining elders. If satisfaction is not thus obtained, he can make a call at the District Meeting for a committee. We can do no more than answer what appears on the face of the query.

Is it according to the Gospel for ministers, at meeting, to line the hymns when we all have books? I think it spoils the singing. MARY ATWOOD.

This is one of the questions concerning which the Gospel is silent, leaving each congregation to do that which seems for the better. Paul says, "Let all things be done unto edifying." Whatever is most edifying to the congregation, would be advisable. For our part we line hymns only where there is a great scarcity of books. Where all or most of the people have books, we think it is not necessary.

Here is a question I would like you to answer. It is a command Christ gave to his disciples, and there is no attention paid to it now: "And into whatsoever house ye enter first say, Peace be to this house. And if the son of peace be there, your peace shall rest upon it: if not, it shall turn to you again." Luke 10: 5, 6 ELMIRA S. MOYER.

This, as well as much more of the same character, was special, and pertained wholly to the disciples sent to the lost sheep of the house of Israel only. It is like the command, "Salute no man by the way." It was for a special purpose, and does not apply to us, who act on the authority of the last commission, which requires us to go into all the world and preach the Gospel to every creature. While there are principles in the command, suggested by our querist, that we will do well to heed, the command itself must be regarded as special, and is therefore not applicable to the department of labor now assigned to us.

Is it right for our Brethren to unite with other denominations and have a Sunday school celebration and picnic? Z. ANNON.

Our Brethren have very prudently advised against us uniting with others in the present semi-worldly manner of holding these gatherings. The appearance is evil, on account of unbecoming things often connected therewith. Besides, it is offensive to many of the faithful, and probably does no good in the end. We should rather follow that which makes peace.

A brother marries a wife, supposing her first husband to be dead. Will the church have to prove that the former husband is living, or must the brother prove that he is dead? ALEX. MILLER.

If the brother is called into question for marrying a woman whose former husband may possibly be living, it would be proper for him to offer his evidence in defense of the man being dead. It would then be the duty of the church to find evidence to the contrary. After the evidence is in from both sides, the church may then render her decision, whether or not the former husband is dead. Of course the brother must be held as innocent until he is proven guilty.

When was funeral preaching first introduced? Is it Only a custom, or is it a command? J. SNAVELY, SR.

We cannot tell when funeral preaching was first introduced. Possibly some of our readers can. It is simply a custom, and a very good one if not abused.

"But he that is least in the kingdom of God is greater than he." Luke 7: 28. How can he be less than he?

The meaning is this: He that is least in the kingdom of God is greater than John the Baptist.

"FOR the gifts and calling of God are without repentance?" Is it God or man that is referred to as being without repentance? S. S. ULDAY.

We understand it to be God, in this instance, who is without repentance. The gifts and calling of God pertained to the electing of Israel as the chosen people, and the covenant made concerning them. Of this the Lord never repented; he is unchangeable, though the people, thus specially elected, proved unfaithful. The covenant still stands intact.

Please explain Hebrews 6: 16: "For men verily swear by the greater: and an oath for confirmation is to them an end to all strife." This seems to imply to swear, although we are commanded to "swear not at all." B. SANGER.

Paul is here writing of that which pertained to the former dispensation, when it was in keeping with God's law to confirm by an oath, but in this new and better dispensation the command for all time, and under all circumstances is, "Swear not at all." Keep in mind the two dispensations, and the question will be easily understood.

When, where, and how did the Lord shorten those days? Matt. 24: 22. A. N. GRAYBILL.

The verse referred to reads thus: "And except those days should be shortened, there should no flesh be saved: but for the elect's sake those days shall be shortened." The Savior is here speaking of the destruction of Jerusalem, which event took place A. D. 70, at which time the suffering was so great that parents ate their own children. It was necessary that those days of intense sufferings and great loss of life should be shortened, that the elect, the Jews, might not all be destroyed. The shortening of these days took place when God permitted Titus, with the Roman army, to enter Jerusalem, Sept 12, A. D. 70, and take possession of the city. The temple had been burned July 15. While the siege was going on, which lasted nearly one year, the Jews were divided into contending factions, and thus weakened their own forces, and greatly increased their own suffering. J. B. M.

CORRESPONDENCE.

"Write what thou seest, and send it unto the churches."

☞ Church News solicited for this Department. If you have had a good meeting, send a report of it, so that others may rejoice with you. In writing give name of church, County and State. Be brief. Notes of Travel should be as short as possible. Land Advertisements are not solicited for this Department. We have an advertising page, and, if necessary, will issue supplements.

Cholera, Cholera!

YES, it is coming. It started in Asia and has been slowly making its way across Europe, reaching England, one of our nearest commercial neighbors. It is only a step across the ocean to our great cities; thence it may be carried by the railroads throughout the land. It is a deathly disease; few escape. It is of short duration, still it gives people a chance to pray and call upon their God. Dangerous as it is, it does not take away their reason. Prepare for it! The President has issued a proclamation that all vessels must be quarantined before any passengers can land. Public sentiment is in his favor and will uphold him, whether it is lawful or not, and whether treaties are violated or not, because it is for the public safety. We want to be saved from the disease and keep it far away from our homes and our families. We cannot spare them.

Supposing every ship that crosses the ocean carried some of these microbes, some hidden away on the person of passengers, some in their trunks and chests and some even in barrels, supposing the large cities of New York, Philadelphia, Chicago, etc, all had shops where they would keep the microbes for sale receiving their right or license from the government to do so, supposing every village had its shop, with the sign "Cholera for sale," supposing that even in the country, shops are put up to catch the farmer's boy, the only hope of the future city, supposing that the people of a town would rise up to stay the disease. The railroads would bring it in spite of law, carrying the microbes behind closed doors,—slyly, but surely, killing some with the dreadful disease. Supposing the great political parties were afraid to say anything against it, supposing the President would be afraid to stay the great evil by quarantine, supposing, if we took the disease and it killed us, we had no hope of heaven, supposing even ministers of the Gospel would be afraid to warn the people of its danger, and if missionaries were sent to foreign countries where the disease was not known, to teach them "Christ and him crucified," some one would slip some of these microbes on the same ship and kill the poor heathens! "O consistency, thou art a jewel."

While cholera kills its thousands, strong drink kills its ten thousands, brings woe, destruction, death, and hell, as the drunkard's doom. While we are afraid of the one which has not done us any harm and is far away, the other is at our door, ready any time to take our dear child, and kill body and soul. Oh! come, cholera, take my child, a follower of Jesus, rather than let my son fill a drunkard's grave. Help us to quarantine our homes! Call loud the proclamation; let every paper take up the cry! The disease has come; we get used to it, and though we see its ravages every day, we are powerless to stop it.

CYRUS BUCHER.

Astoria, Ill.

From Olensted, Mo.

OUR series of meetings, conducted by Bro. C. Hope, of Kansas. began on Friday, Aug. 26 On Saturday following, elders Witmore and Hope being with us, we held our quarterly council. All business was transacted in a Christian spirit. Bro. W. W. Holsopple was advanced to the second degree of the ministry, and Bro. J. A. Bowman elected to the office of deacon.

Bro Witmore remained with us over Sunday, when he departed for his home, leaving Bro. Hope to continue the meetings, which were conducted with good interest throughout.

Our feast occurred September 6, and was indeed an enjoyable one, and the largest ever held here.

While the meetings were in progress, eight dear souls were made willing to follow the exam-

From the English River Congregation, Keokuk County, Iowa.

OUR quarterly council passed off pleasantly, and we hope profitably, Aug. 27. The annual visit had been made prior to this meeting. The brethren reported things favorable, with a general strong faith and good feeling among the children of Christ's kingdom. Arrangements were also completed for our approaching feast, which occurred Sept. 3 and 4, and was truly a feast to the soul. The representation of members was good. The weather was fair and the preaching edifying, so that sinners were warned, and saints nourished and built up in the most holy faith. Ministers from abroad were John Gable and S. P. Miller, from Mahaska County; J. C. Seibert, from Johnson County, and A. Sanger, from Washington County, all in Iowa.

This meeting was a busy time for our members, and strange ministers. It has always been our custom to begin such meetings at 11 o'clock A. M., and as this was our regular thanksgiving day, we had a thanksgiving sermon preached. After dinner the church held a choice for one brother to serve in the ministry, and another in the deacon's office. Immediately after the election we had installation services, which was truly a solemn occasion. The members then proceeded to the water, where two sin-burdened souls were buried beneath the liquid waves, we trust to walk in newness of life. They belong to the Crooked Creek congregation. Regular examination services were next in order, followed by the regular course on such occasions. Next morning we met for morning worship and breakfast. At 9 o'clock Bro. Sharp, a blind brother, and Bro. Seibert, talked to the children at a meeting appointed for them. A sermon at 10 A. M., and another at 4 P. M., closed our meeting, which will long be remembered. Five were added to this congregation by letter at our last council. May God add his blessing, especially upon those called to such responsible positions by the church.

PETER BROWER.

From the Highways and Hedges.

AUGUST 30 my faithful help-meet and I started by private conveyance across the country, about fifty miles North-west, near Austin, Ark., where we arrived after one and a half day's travel.

Sept. 1 I commenced meetings and continued each evening. I made the annual visit to the members, assisted by Bro. Chas. Delp. We found all in peace and love as far as we could ascertain. On Tuesday, Sept 6, we met in the evening to commemorate the suffering and death of Christ, and keep the ordinances as they were delivered unto us by the Lord, when he said, " I have given you an example that ye should do as I have done to you." So we did and had a very pleasant little meeting,—the first of the kind ever held in that neighborhood. We had a fair attendance and excellent attention. A number said, "That is according to the Scriptures, and we cannot deny it." Yet there were some who were trying to stir up all the opposition they could. If the devil could not get any one to help him, he would have taken a back seat long ago, but that same spirit still works in the children of disobedience.

On the evening of the seventh we preached on the subject of anointing, and closed our meetings at the New Hope meeting-house.

Sept. 8th we closed and made a visit to the Mineral Mountain Spring. This is quite a resort for invalids recovering from sickness and general debility. It is free for all. People go there and camp and stay as long as they like. The Spring is not improved.

Sept. 9 we moved our meetings to another place where we had three meetings. In all we held about ten meetings in that vicinity. One was baptized and others confessed they were convinced of the right Whether they will have the courage to take up the cross and follow Christ, is yet to be tested. May the Lord give them courage to follow his teaching! Here, at Austin, Ark., there are now nine members. It would be a great help to the cause if several families of good, working members would move there. They are much needed to help build up a church. Brethren who have a little means can buy the cheapest houses that I know of anywhere. Some small farms that were fairly well improved before the war, have been deserted and are lying uncultivated. Some eighty-acre farms can be bought for from three to four hundred dollars, that would make comfortable homes when properly improved. Plenty of wood and stone can be had near by.

If you come, don't expect to find good brick houses and everything in good order. If you have the nerve to work and a willing mind, here is your place. If you don't want to work, this is not your place. If you want to know exactly, come and see for yourself, for I have not the time to answer many letters, neither have I lived there to know the particulars. Bro. Chas. Delp is the minister there. He is a poor man and works for his living. If you want many questions answered, send twenty-five cents in stamps. Then he can take time to answer. Address him at Austin, Ark.

JAS R. GISH.

The New Mexico Home.

WE are pleased to introduce to our many friends the New Home for children. No doubt many who noticed Bro. Miller's proposition in the GOSPEL MESSENGER have wondered about its progress.

We are pleased to announce that Bro. Miller has nearly completed the carrying out of his proposition, in erecting a two-story frame house, 36 by 54 feet, with a basement under it of five rooms.

The first floor contains seven rooms, namely, the general reception room, dining-room, bright office room, Superintendent's sleeping-room, nurse and toilet room. The upper floor contains two large rooms,—one for boys and one for girls,—a servant room, and a tank and bath room combined, making six rooms in all. There is a large veranda on the north, east and west, which makes additional room, and adds much to its comfort.

While upon the whole, the house is neat and plain, its arrangements for convenience is an honor to its founder, and will be a blessing to the unfortunate homeless children. And we pray the good Lord that it may be an honor to the Brotherhood, which is the full desire and prayer of its founder. As Bro. Miller has been so liberal and charitable in building this home, we hope the same spirit may be caught by our brethren and sisters, to whom we look for means to furnish our home, and as we do not expect to make a personal solicitation, except in the immediate vicinity of the Home, we trust every member interested in the welfare of our home may feel this article to be a personal solicitation, and send us a gift to furnish our New Home. We must have money to properly furnish the rooms,—each one for its purpose,—and we trust our members will give this matter their careful consideration and send us some help. Send all funds to Bro Levi Miller, stating that it is for the New Home so that Bro. Miller will know to which fund to place it, as he is the treasurer for the Old Folks' Home also.

Bro. Miller expects to meet the Trustees Oct. 8, in the New Home and intends to turn it over to them at that time, after which it will be the property of the Middle District of Indiana.

Since then will be the property of so many churches, we propose that each church or congregation dedicate it to the Lord in their own way with such services as they may think proper. We would suggest that Oct. 9 be the day for dedication, and we trust that every member may dedicate it in prayer to the Lord. The Home shall be a *temporary* home for the *homeless child*.

FRANK FISHER.

From Louisville, Ky.

THE apostle says: "How can they hear without a preacher?" Rom. 10: 14. I say, " How shall the people in Louisville hear without a preacher? I hear you ask, "Is there no preacher in a large city like Louisville?" There is not a preacher of our faith in all Louisville. If we have the right faith and practice, as I think we have, and we know the people can't hear without a preacher, do we not need a preacher here?

Again in Rom. 10: 15 we read, "And how shall they preach unless they be sent?" Since we know that a preacher is needed here, and in order to have one, he must be sent. Who is ready to say, "Here am I, send me"? There are no members of our church here so far as I know, except myself. People seem to think me very odd.

I have not met anyone here that ever saw a Dunkard, and most of them never knew there was such a religion. I think if we had a preacher, who is sound in our faith, he might do a good work here. True, we have no church of our own, but I think a place to hold meetings could be obtained. The lady I live with was inquiring about our faith. I read her the article of our faith and practice, written by Bro. Miller for our Almanac. She said, "You practice feet-washing, do you?" I told her we did. She said she used to think that they ought to practice that, but they never did, and her preacher, who is a Disciple, said, that feet-washing was only to teach humility.

I visited the Baptist church last Sunday evening, and witnessed the baptism of a young lady. The preacher led the lady into the water, and, after reading some passages of Scripture, referring to baptism, and repeating the three names of the Trinity, he immersed her once, using the backward mode. As we baptize in a very different way, and know we are right, having Christ and his Word in our favor, should we not try to teach all nations and all people the right way?

LURENA E. CHAPPELL.

No. 516 Chestnut St., Louisville, Ky.

Annual Meeting Locating Committee.

ACCORDING to appointment, the Brethren of the Southern District of Indiana met in special council Sept. 1., at Arcadia, Hamilton County, to make arrangements for our coming Annual Meeting of 1893, by selecting the following-named brethren as a committee to locate said Annual Meeting: (1) Jacob Rife, Foreman; (2) Lewis J. Hooke, Secretary; (3) Solomon Blickenstaff, (4) John H. Caylor, (5) W. R. Harshberger, (6) Jacob Yost, (7) Daniel Book.

This Locating Committee is authorized by District Meeting, after selecting the place of our next Annual Meeting, to select a Committee of Arrangements, who shall take entire charge of the work. The Locating Committee is instructed to publish through the GOSPEL MESSENGER a notice of the location as soon as selected. LEWIS J. HOOKE.

New Corner, Ind., Sept. 8, 1892.

From the English River Congregation, Keokuk County, Iowa.

Our quarterly council passed off pleasantly, and we hope profitably, Aug. 27. The annual visit had been made prior to this meeting. The brethren reported things favorable, with a general strong faith and good feeling among the children of Christ's kingdom. Arrangements were also completed for our approaching feast, which occurred Sept. 3 and 4, and was truly a feast to the soul. The representation of members was good. The weather was fair and the preaching edifying, so that sinners were warned, and saints nourished and built up in the most holy faith. Ministers from abroad were John Gable and S. P. Miller, from Mahaska County; J. C. Seibert, from Johnson County, and A. Sanger, from Washington County, all in Iowa.

This meeting was a busy time for our members, and strange ministers. It has always been our custom to begin such meetings at 11 o'clock A. M., and as this was our regular thanksgiving day, we had a thanksgiving sermon preached. After dinner the church held a choice for one brother to serve in the ministry, and another in the deacon's office. Immediately after the election we had installation services, which was truly a solemn occasion. The members then proceeded to the water, where two sin-burdened souls were buried beneath the liquid waves, we trust to walk in newness of life. They belong to the Crooked Creek congregation. Regular examination services were next in order, followed by the regular course on such occasions. Next morning we met for morning worship and breakfast. At 9 o'clock Bro. Sharp, a blind brother, and Bro. Seibert, talked to the children at a meeting appointed for them. A sermon at 10 A. M., and another at 4 P. M., closed our meeting, which will long be remembered. Five were added to this congregation by letter at our last council. May God add his blessing, especially upon those called to such responsible positions by the church.

PETER BROWER.

From the Highways and Hedges.

August 30 my faithful help-meet and I started by private conveyance across the country, about fifty miles North-west, near Austin, Ark., where we arrived after one and a half day's travel.

Sept. 1 I commenced meetings and continued each evening. I made the annual visit to the members, assisted by Bro. Chas. Delp. We found all in peace and love as far as we could ascertain. On Tuesday, Sept. 6, we met in the evening to commemorate the suffering and death of Christ, and keep the ordinances as they were delivered unto us by the Lord, when he said, "I have given you an example that ye should do as I have done to you." So we did and had a very pleasant little meeting,—the first of the kind ever held in that neighborhood. We had a fair attendance and excellent attention. A number said, "That is according to the Scriptures, and we cannot deny it." Yet there were some who were trying to stir up all the opposition they could. If the devil could not get any one to help him, he would have taken a back seat long ago, but that same spirit still works in the children of disobedience.

On the evening of the seventh we preached on the subject of anointing, and closed our meetings at the New Hope meeting-house.

Sept. 8th we rested and made a visit to the Mineral Mountain Spring. This is quite a resort for invalids recovering from sickness and general debility. It is free for all. People go there and camp and stay as long as they like. The Spring is not improved.

Sept. 9 we moved our meetings to another place where we had three meetings. In all we held about ten meetings in that vicinity. One was baptized and others confessed they were convinced of the right. Whether they will have the courage to take up the cross and follow Christ, is yet to be tested. May the Lord give them courage to follow his teaching! Here, at Austin, Ark., there are now nine members. It would be a great help to the cause if several families of good, working members would move there. They are much needed to help build up a church. Brethren who have a little means can buy the cheapest houses that I know of anywhere. Some small farms that were fairly well improved before the war, have been deserted and are lying uncultivated. Some eighty-acre farms can be bought for from three to four hundred dollars, that would make comfortable homes when properly improved. Plenty of wood and stone can be had near by.

If you come, don't expect to find good brick houses and everything in good order. If you have the nerve to work and a willing mind, here is your place. If you don't want to work, this is not your place. If you want to know exactly, come and see for yourself, for I have not the time to answer many letters, neither have I lived there to know the particulars. Bro. Chas. Delp is the minister there. He is a poor man and works for his living. If you want many questions answered, send twenty-five cents in stamps. Then he can take time to answer. Address him at Austin, Ark.

JAS R. GISH.

The New Mexico Home.

We are pleased to introduce to our many friends the New Home for children. No doubt many who noticed Bro. Miller's proposition in the GOSPEL MESSENGER have wondered about its progress.

We are pleased to announce that Bro. Miller has nearly completed the carrying out of his proposition, in erecting a two-story frame house, 36 by 54 feet, with a basement under it of five rooms.

The first floor contains seven rooms, namely, the general reception room, dining-room, kitchen, office room, Superintendent's sleeping-room, nurse and toilet room. The upper floor contains two large rooms,—one for boys and one for girls,—a servant room, and a tank and bath room combined, making six rooms in all. There is a large veranda on the north, east and west, which makes additional room, and adds much to its comfort.

While upon the whole, the house is neat and plain, its arrangements for convenience is an honor to its founder, and will be a blessing to the unfortunate homeless children. And we pray the good Lord that it may be an honor to the Brotherhood, which is the full desire and prayer of its founder. As Bro. Miller has been so liberal and charitable in building this home, we hope the same spirit may be caught by our brethren and sisters, to whom we look for means to furnish our home, and as we do not expect to make a personal solicitation, except in the immediate vicinity of the Home, we trust every member interested in the welfare of our home may feel this article to be a personal solicitation, and send us a gift to furnish our New Home. We must have money to properly furnish the rooms,—each one for its purpose,—and we trust our members will give this matter their careful consideration and send us some help. Send all funds to Bro Levi Miller, stating that it is for the New Home so that Bro. Miller will know to which fund to place it, as he is the treasurer for the Old Folks' Home also.

Bro. Miller expects to meet the Trustees Oct. 8, in the New Home and intends to turn it over to them at that time, after which it will be the property of the Middle District of Indiana.

Since it then will be the property of so many churches, we propose that each church or congregation dedicate it to the Lord in their own way with such services as they may think proper. We would suggest that Oct. 9 be the day for dedication, and we trust that every member may dedicate it in prayer to the Lord. The Home shall be a *temporary* home for the *homeless child.*

FRANK FISHER.

From Louisville, Ky.

The apostle says: "How can they hear without a preacher?" Rom. 10: 14. I say, "How shall the people in Louisville hear without a preacher? I hear you ask, "Is there no preacher in a large city like Louisville?" There is not a preacher of our faith in all Louisville. If we have the right faith and practice, as I think we have, and we know the people can't hear without a preacher, do we not need a preacher here?

Again in Rom. 10: 15 we read, "And how shall they preach unless they be sent?" Since we know that a preacher is needed here, and in order to have one, he must be sent. Who is ready to say, "Here am I, send me"? There are no members of our church here so far as I know, except myself. People seem to think me very odd.

I have not met anyone here that ever saw a Dunkard, and most of them never knew there was such a religion. I think if we had a preacher, who is sound in our faith, he might do a good work here. True, we have no church of our own, but I think a place to hold meetings could easily be obtained. The lady I live with was inquiring about our faith. I read her the article of our faith and practice, written by Bro. Miller for our Almanac. She said, "You practice feet-washing, do you?" I told her we did. She said she used to think that they ought to practice that, but they never did, and her preacher, who is a Disciple, said, that feet-washing was only to teach humility.

I visited the Baptist church last Sunday evening, and witnessed the baptism of a young lady. The preacher led the lady into the water, and, after reading some passages of Scripture, referring to baptism, and repeating the three names of the Trinity, he immersed her once, using the backward mode. As we baptize in a very different way, and know we are right, having Christ and his Word in our favor, should we not try to teach all nations and all people the right way?

LURENA E. CHAPPELL.
No. 516 Chestnut St., Louisville, Ky.

Annual Meeting Locating Committee.

According to appointment, the Brethren of the Southern District of Indiana met in special council Sept. 1, at Arcadia, Hamilton County, to make arrangements for our coming Annual Meeting of 1893, by selecting the following-named brethren as a committee to locate said Annual Meeting: (1) Jacob Rife, Foreman; (2) Lewis J. Hooke, Secretary; (3) Solomon Blickenstaff, (4) John H. Caylor, (5) W. R. Harshberger, (6) Jacob Yost, (7) Daniel Book.

This Locating Committee is authorized by District Meeting, after selecting the place of our next Annual Meeting, to select a Committee of Arrangements, who shall take entire charge of the work. The Locating Committee is instructed to publish through the GOSPEL MESSENGER a notice of the location as soon as selected.

LEWIS J. HOOKE.
New Corner, Ind., Sept. 8, 1892.

Belleville, Kans.—Bro. Levi Saylor, of Marshalltown, Iowa, preached for us to-day. He gave us some good food for the soul. He is an earnest expounder of the Gospel. Our series of meetings will commence on the evening of Sept. 24, and one week from that time will be our love-feast meeting.—*Louisa J. Williams, Sept. 18.*

Burr Oak, Kans.—The Burr Oak church met in council to arrange for our love-feast which is Oct. 8. The visit was extended and we found all in love and union. Any of the brethren and sisters seeking homes in North-western Kansas, will do well to come this way. We expect to hold a series of meetings after the feast.—*Joel H. Kinzie, Sept. 18.*

Greene, Iowa.—Wife and I returned from Minnesota a few days ago. We now go to Garrison to attend the District Meeting of Middle Iowa. We commence a series of meetings near Sharon, Sept. 24. From there we go to Ollie, to hold another meeting; then to Darlington, Mo. We will likely remain in Missouri till the Holidays.—*William C. Hipes, Sept. 19.*

Mastersonville, Pa.—Our quarterly council was held at Elizabethtown, Sept. 12, and was largely attended. Quite an amount of business came before the meeting, which was adjusted in love and peace, and, we hope, with the approval of God. A few questions were deferred to a council to be held at the same place Sept. 26. Our love-feast was appointed for Oct. 27 and 28. One sister was reclaimed amid many tears of joy.—*John C. Zug, Sept. 13.*

Libertyville, Iowa.—Since our last report we held three meetings in Batavia. One dear soul, a young sister, was baptized. On Saturday, the 17th, was the time for our quarterly meeting, preparatory to our feast. At the close of the meeting it was made known that another sister desired to unite with the people of God, which was attended to at the close of the meeting. We think there are others standing near the church.—*Abraham Wolf, Sept. 13.*

Garden Grove, Iowa—The members of the Franklin church, Decatur Co., Iowa, met in church council Sept. 17. All business passed off pleasantly. Those present manifested a willingness to labor with the General Brotherhood. Our love-feast will be held, the Lord willing, Oct. 29. There will be a meeting the evening before. Bro. A. Wolf, of Jefferson Co., Iowa, is expected to be with us at that time and hold a series of meetings. One was received by baptism lately, and one restored to fellowship. May all prove faithful!—*Jemima Kob, Sept. 19.*

Turkey Creek, Ind.—Martin V. Shively, who recently attended school at Mt. Morris, and was suddenly and severely taken down with typhoid fever on Sunday, Sept. 4, requested on Monday night, Sept. 12, to be received into the church by baptism. The writer was called to administer the ordinance, assisted by Bro. Wm. Bossard. Bro. Martin is a son of Bro. Geo. B. Shively, whose wife is also sick with the same disease. At the present writing both are convalescing. The family invokes an interest in the prayers of God's children. There seems to be considerable sickness at present, but all things work together for good to them that fear the Lord.—*Daniel Wysong, Sept. 20.*

Matrimonial.

"What therefore God hath joined together, let not man put asunder."

CLARK–ROCKLEY.—At the residence of the bride's parents, Sept. 13, 1892, by the undersigned, Mr. J. C. Clark and sister Emma Rockley, both of Madison, Kans.
D. W. STOUDER.

ROCKLEY–PROVO.—At the residence of the groom's parents, Sept. 14, 1892, by the undersigned, Mr. S. F. Rockley and sister Susan Olive Provo, of Madison, Kans.
D. W. STOUDER.

WILCOX–PROVINS.—At the residence of the bride's parents, Sept. 8, 1892, by the undersigned, Mr. Ellsworth Wilcox, of Ohio, and Miss Alice, Provins, of German Township, Fayette County, Pa.
ALPHEUS DeBOLT.

ROOT–SMITH.—At the residence of the groom's parents, Sept 4, 1892, by the undersigned Jacob L. Root and sister Mary E. Smith, of Mingona, Barber Co., Kans.
JESSE SNAMBERGER.

KESSLER–LILLIGH.—At the home of the bride's father, Eld. Henry Lilligh, near Woburn, Bond County, Ill., Sept. 4, 1892, by Eld. D. B. Stugis, Bro. Alfred C. Kessler and sister Ida M. Lilligh.
CORNELIUS KESSLER.

Fallen Asleep.

" Blessed are the dead which die in the Lord."

HOLSAPPLE.—April 25, 1892, John D. Holsapple, aged 69 years, 10 months and 1 day. He was married to Maty Ann North, Nov. 5, 1848. There were born to them seven children. He leaves a companion and four children. Sunday evening he set up late and talked with his children. Then he went to bed in seemingly good health, but in the morning was found dead in bed. Funeral discourse by the writer, assisted by the Groff brethren.
H. C. LONGANECKER.

KINNY.—Near Yorkshire, Ohio, Sept. 11, 1892, of apoplexy, Harriet Kinney, wife of David Kinney, aged about 73 years. Three husbands preceded her to the spirit world. She leaves a husband. Funeral services by the writer from Deut 32: 15, at the United Brethren church, Yorkshire, Ohio.
H. C. LONGANECKER.

DAVIS.—Near New Weston, Ohio, Aug. 20, 1892, of hasty consumption, Henrietta Lavill Davis, aged 21 years, 11 months and 14 days. She leaves a husband and a small babe. Funeral services at the Holsapple church by the writer from Amos 4: 12, to a large and sympathetic congregation.
H. C. LONGANECKER.

DAVIS.—In the same family, Sept. 2, 1892, Flora A. Davis, infant child of the above lady, aged 1 month and 2 days. Funeral services at the same place of the above, Sept. 3, at 3 P. M., also by the writer.
H. C. LONGANECKER.

SCHECHTER.—In the Iowa River church, Marshall Co., Iowa, Sept. 6, 1892, Amelia Schechter, aged 81 years. Deceased was born in Washington County, Md., in 1810. She had a complicated disease, supposed by some to be cancer of the stomach. Her sufferings were great. It seemed to be her chief desire to depart this life and be at rest. Her children, whom she so often called for, met at her bed side. It was her request to be buried beside her husband in Polk County, where she was taken. Funeral services from Rev. 14: 13, by Bro. Henry Troup, of the Indian Creek church, followed by F. M. Wheeler, of the Iowa River church.
ELLEN NICHOLSON.

BOWMAN.—At Knob Creek, Washington County, Tenn., Aug. 24, 1892, Elizabeth, wife of David Bowman. She was a faithful member of the church, and leaves a husband and four children to mourn their loss. Funeral services from Rev. 14: 13 by J. B. Bowman, and G. C. Bowman, to a large crowd of relatives, brethren, sisters and friends.
GEO. C. BOWMAN.

MILLER.—At Kamela, Oregon, June 30, 1892, by a tree top falling on the back of his head, breaking his neck and shoulders, Arthur, son of Bro. LaBar Miller, aged 10 years, 11 months and 22 days. He was loved by all who knew him. He leaves a father, brother, and two sisters. His mother preceded him to the spirit land about eight years ago.
S. E. RENNER.

PRICE.—Aug. 22, 1892, Bro. Thomas Price, aged 76 years, 3 months and 11 days. Deceased was paralyzed about four weeks before his death, during which time he suffered greatly. He called for the elders of the church and was anointed, after which he expressed himself willing to leave this world. He joined the Brethren church in 1857, and served as a deacon. He was true to the cause he loved so dearly. He was the father of eight children, three of whom preceded him to the spirit world. He leaves an aged companion and five daughters to mourn their loss.
D. M. CLICK.

MARSIE.—In the Johnstown congregation, Pa., Sept. 19, 1892, Bro. Henry Marsie, aged 40 years, 5 months and 18 days.
DAVID HILDEBRAND.

WENRICK.—In the South Beatrice church, Gage County, Nebr., Sept. 13, 1892, sister Lydia Ann Wenrick, aged 65 years, 8 months and 13 days. Sister Wenrick was the wife of Bro. George Wenrick, who survives her. She was born in Center County, Pa., Jan. 4, 1827. She has been a patient sufferer and nearly helpless for many years. Funeral discourse by Bro. T. W. Graham, from 2 Tim. 4: 7, 8.
M. L. SPIRE.

OELLIG.—In the Woodbury church, Bedford Co., Pa., Aug. 30, 1892, sister Susan Oellig, wife of Dr. Charles Oellig, aged 73 years, 5 months and 11 days. Funeral services conducted by elders J. W. and G. W. Brumbaugh, and Henry Clappet, from John 14: 1.
J. C. STAYER.

KARN.—In the Roann church, Wabash Co., Ind., Sept 13, 1892, Bro. Samuel Karn, aged 82 years, 11 months and 3 days. Funeral services by the brethren from Rom. 6: 23.
JOSEPH JOHN.

SCHROCK.—In the Summit Mills church, Somerset Co., Pa., Sept. 10, 1892, Bro. Samuel Schrock, aged 70 years and 8 months. He was a consistent member of the Brethren church for a number of years. Funeral services by the writer and J. W. Peck.
JOEL GNAGEY.

BOLLINGER.—In the Centre church, Johnson Co., Mo., Sept. 9, 1892, George Melvin, infant son of Bro. Daniel and sister Lizzie Bollinger, aged 1 year, 9 months and 1 day. Services by Bro. —— Brubaker, of Warrensburgh.
IRA WITMORE.

ROBISON.—At the home of their grandparents, Seck and Jenny Eby Robison, near North Star, Ohio, the twin children of Harry and Ida Robison. Aloy C. Robison took suddenly sick on the evening of Sept. 3, with a strange disease. Twenty-four hours after, he peacefully passed away at the age of 7 months and 14 days. Eloy E. Robison watched his little mate pass away, after which, in a few moments, he also took suddenly sick, seemingly, with the same disease. Twenty-four hours later death came to him as a relief at the age of 7 months and 15 days. These babes were always in the best of health until the time of sickness and death. It was the strangest occurrence that ever came under my notice. Funeral services at the home of their grandparents by the writer from Job 23: 2.
H. C. LONGANECKER.

LIVENGOOD.—In the Middle Creek church, Somerset County, Pa., Sept. 14, 1892, Fern, infant daughter of Bro. Archie and sister Sarah Livengood, aged 5 months and 20 days. Funeral services from Mark 10: 14 by the writer.
H. A. STAHL.

CROWELL.—In Sharon congregation, Marion Co., Ill., Sept. 12, 1892, sister Jane Crowell, aged 78 years, 3 months and 16 days. Services at the residence by Rev. N. Crow, of the M. E. church. Some time ago she fell and broke her hip. She bore her affliction patiently until death relieved her.
JACOB HERSHBERGER.

SHANK.—At his residence, in Dallas Centre, Iowa, Sept. 10, 1892, after a few days' sickness, Eld. F. Shank, youngest son of Daniel S. Shank, aged 37 years and 2 days. He united with the German Baptist church when a young man, and has been a consistent member ever since. The funeral took place at the German Baptist church and cemetery, east of town, at 3 o'clock Sunday afternoon. Bro. R. F. McCune conducted the services from Matt 24: 4.
A. R. BURGHA.

HUBBARD.—Near Oshawa, Kans., Sept. 3, 1892, Tommy, infant son of Sigel and Ida Hubbard, aged 5 months. Funeral services by the writer.
JOS. N. MORROW.

MARKLE.—In Perry County, Pa., Sept. 2, 1892, Bro. John Markle, aged 89 years, 2 months and 17 days. He leaves a mother and four fifty years. Eleven children are living and one dead. Funeral services by the writer.
ISAAC EBY.

The Gospel Messenger

Is the recognized organ of the German Baptist or Brethren's church, and advocates the form of doctrine taught in the New Testament and pleads for a return to apostolic and primitive Christianity.

It recognizes the New Testament as the only infallible Rule of faith and practice, and maintains that Faith toward God, Repentance from dead works, Regeneration of the heart and mind, baptism by Trine Immersion for remission of sins unto the reception of the Holy Ghost by the laying on of hands, are the means of adoption into the household of God,—the church militant.

It also maintains that Feet-washing, as taught in John 13, both by example and command of Jesus, should be observed in the church.

That the Lord's Supper, instituted by Christ and as universally observed by the apostles and the early Christians, is a full meal, and, in connection with the Communion, should be taken in the evening or after the close of the day.

That the Salutation of the Holy Kiss, or Kiss of Charity, is binding upon the followers of Christ.

That War and Retaliation are contrary to the spirit and self-denying principles of the religion of Jesus Christ.

That the principle of Plain Dressing and of Non-conformity to the world, as taught in the New Testament, should be observed by the followers of Christ.

That the Scriptural duty of Anointing the Sick with Oil, in the Name of the Lord, James 5: 14, is binding upon all Christians.

It also advocates the church's duty to support Missionary and Tract Work, thus giving to the Lord for the spread of the Gospel and for the conversion of sinners.

In short, it is a vindicator of all that Christ and the apostles have enjoined upon us, and since, amid the conflicting theories and discords of modern Christendom, to point out ground that all must concede to be infallibly safe.

☞ The above principles of our Fraternity are set forth on our "Brethren's Envelopes." Use them! Price 15 cents per package; 40 cents per hundred.

Belleville, Kans.—Bro. Levi Saylor, of Marshalltown, Iowa, preached for us to-day. He gave us some good food for the soul. He is an earnest expounder of the Gospel. Our series of meetings will commence on the evening of Sept. 24, and one week from that time will be our love-feast meeting.—*Louisa J. Williams, Sept. 18.*

Burr Oak, Kans.—The Burr Oak church met in council to arrange for our love-feast which is Oct. 8. The visit was extended and we found all in love and union. Any of the brethren and sisters seeking homes in North-western Kansas, will do well to come this way. We expect to hold a series of meetings after the feast.—*Joel H. Kinzie, Sept. 18.*

Greene, Iowa.—Wife and I returned from Minnesota a few days ago. We now go to Garrison to attend the District Meeting of Middle Iowa. We commence a series of meetings near Sharon, Sept. 24. From there we go to Ollie, to hold another meeting; then to Darlington, Mo. We will likely remain in Missouri till the Holidays.—*William C. Hipes, Sept. 19.*

Hastersville, Pa.—Our quarterly council was held at Elizabethtown, Sept 12, and was largely attended. Quite an amount of business came before the meeting, which was adjusted in love and peace, and, we hope, with the approval of God. A few questions were deferred to a council to be held at the same place Sept. 26. Our love-feast was appointed for Oct. 27 and 28. One sister was reclaimed amid many tears of joy.—*John C. Zug, Sept. 13.*

Libertyville, Iowa.—Since our last report we held three meetings in Batavia. One dear soul, a young sister, was baptized. On Saturday, the 17th, was the time for our quarterly meeting, preparatory to our feast. At the close of the meeting it was made known that another sister desired to unite with the people of God, which was attended to at the close of the meeting. We think there are others standing near the church.—*Abraham Wolf, Sept. 20.*

Garden Grove, Iowa.—The members of the Franklin church, Decatur Co., Iowa, met in church council Sept. 17. All business passed off pleasantly. Those present manifested a willingness to labor with the General Brotherhood. Our love-feast will be held, the Lord willing, Oct. 29. There will be a meeting the evening before. Bro. A. Wolf, of Jefferson Co., Iowa, is expected to be with us at that time and hold a series of meetings. One was received by baptism lately, and one restored to fellowship. May all prove faithful!—*Jemima Kob, Sept. 19.*

Turkey Creek, Ind.—Martin V. Shively, who recently attended school at Mt. Morris, and was suddenly and severely taken down with typhoid fever on Sunday, Sept. 4, requested on Monday night, Sept. 12, to be received into the church by baptism. The writer was called to administer the ordinance, assisted by Bro. Wm. Bossard. Bro. Martin is a son of Bro. Geo. B. Shively, whose wife is also sick with the same disease. At the present writing both are convalescing. The family invokes an interest in the prayers of God's children. There seems to be considerable sickness at present, but all things work together for good to them that fear the Lord.—*Daniel Wysong, Sept. 20.*

Matrimonial.

"What therefore God hath joined together, let not man put asunder."

CLARK—ROCKLEY.—At the residence of the bride's parents, Sept. 13, 1892, by the undersigned, Mr. J. C. Clark and sister Emma Rockley, both of Madison, Kans.
D. W. STOUDER.

ROCKLEY—PROVO.—At the residence of the groom's parents, Sept. 14, 1892, by the undersigned, Mr. S. F. Rockley and sister Susan Olive Provo, of Madison, Kans.
D. W. STOUDER.

WILCOX—PROVINS.—At the residence of the bride's parents, Sept. 8, 1892, by the undersigned, Mr. Ellsworth Wilcox, of Ohio, and Miss Alice Provins, of German Township, Fayette County, Pa.
ALPHEUS DEBOLT.

ROOT—SMITH.—At the residence of the groom's parents, Sept 4, 1892, by the undersigned, Jacob L. Root and sister Mary E. Smith, of Mingona, Barber Co., Kans.
JASSE SHAMBERGER.

KESSLER—LILLIGH.—At the home of the bride's father, Eld. Henry Lilligh, near Woburn, Bond County, Ill., Sept. 4, 1892, by Eld. D. B. Sturgis, Bro. Alfred C. Kessler and sister Ida M. Lilligh.
CORNELIUS KESSLER.

Fallen Asleep.

"Blessed are the dead which die in the Lord."

HOLSAPPLE.—April 25, 1892, John D. Holsapple, aged 69 years, 10 months and 1 day. He was married to Mary Ann Norris, Nov. 5. 1846. There were born to them seven children. He leaves a companion and four children. Sunday evening he sat up late and talked with his children. Then he went to bed in seemingly good health, but in the morning was found dead in bed. Funeral discourse by the writer, assisted by the Groff brethren.
H. C. LONGANECKER.

KINNY.—Near Yorkshire, Ohio, Sept. 12, 1892, of apoplexy, Harriet Kinney, wife of David Kinney, aged about 73 years. Three husbands preceded her to the spirit world. She leaves a husband. Funeral services by the writer from Deut 33: 15, at the United Brethren church, Yorkshire, Ohio.
H. C. LONGANECKER.

DAVIS.—Near New Weston, Ohio, Aug. 30, 1892, of hasty consumption, Henrietta Levitt Davis, aged 21 years, 11 months and 14 days. She leaves a husband and a small babe. Funeral services at the Holsapple church by the writer from Amos 4: 12, to a large and sympathetic congregation.
H. C. LONGANECKER.

DAVIS.—In the same family, Sept. 2, 1892, Flora A. Davis, infant child of the above lady, aged 1 month and 3 days. Funeral services at the same place of the above, Sept. 3, at 3 P. M., also by the writer.
H. C. LONGANECKER.

SCHECHTER.—In the Iowa River church, Marshall Co., Iowa, Sept. 6, 1892, Amelia Schechter, aged 82 years. Deceased was born in Washington County, Md., in 1810. She had a complicated disease, supposed by some to be cancer of the stomach. Her sufferings were great. It seemed to be her chief desire to depart this life and be at rest. Her children, whom she so often called for, met at her bed side. It was her request to be buried beside her husband in Polk County, where she was taken. Funeral services from Rev. 14: 13, by Bro. Henry Troup, of the Indian Creek church, followed by F. M. Wheeler, of the Iowa River church.
ELLEN NICHOLSON.

BOWMAN.—At Knob Creek, Washington County, Tenn., Aug. 24, 1892, Elizabeth, wife of David Bowman. She was a faithful member of the church, and leaves a husband and four children to mourn her loss. Funeral services from Rev. 14: 13 by J. B. Bowman, and G. C. Bowman, to a large crowd of relatives, brethren, sisters and friends.
GEO. C. BOWMAN.

MILLER.—At Kamela, Oregon, June 30, 1892, by a trestle falling on the back of his head, breaking his neck and shoulders, Arthur, son of Bro. Luther Miller, aged 10 years, 11 months and 22 days. He was loved by all who knew him. He leaves a father, brother, and two sisters. His mother preceded him to the spirit land about eight years ago.
S. E. RENNER.

PRICE.—Aug. 23, 1892, Bro. Thomas Price, aged 76 years, 3 months and 11 days. Deceased was paralyzed about four weeks before his death, during which time he suffered great. ly. He called for the elders of the church and was anointed, after which he expressed himself willing to leave this world. He joined the Brethren church in 1857, and served as a deacon. He was true to the cause he loved so dearly. He was the father of eight children, three of whom preceded him to the spirit world. He leaves an aged companion and five daughters to mourn their loss.
D. M. CLICK.

MARSIE.—In the Johnstown congregation, Pa., Sept. 29, 1892, Bro. Henry Marsie, aged 40 years, 5 months and 18 days.
DAVID HILDEBRAND.

WENRICK.—In the South Beatrice church, Gage County, Neb., Sept. 17, 1892, sister Lydia Ann Wenrick, aged 65 years, 8 months and 13 days. Sister Wenrick was the wife of Bro. George Wenrick, who survives her. She was born in Center County, Pa., Jan. 4, 1827. She has been a patient sufferer and nearly helpless for many years. Funeral discourse by Bro. T. W. Graham, from 2 Tim. 4: 7, 8. M. L. SPIRE.

OELLIG.—In the Woodbury church, Bedford Co., Pa., Aug. 30, 1892, sister Susan Oellig, wife of Dr. Charles Oellig, aged 73 years, 5 months and 11 days. Funeral services conducted by elders J. W. and G. W. Brumbaugh, and Henry Clapper, from John 14: 1.
J. C. STAYER.

KARN.—In the Roann church, Wabash Co., Ind., Sept 13, 1892, Bro. Samuel Karn, aged 82 years, 11 months and 3 days. Funeral services by the brethren from Rom. 6: 23.
JOSEPH JOHN.

SCHROCK.—In the Summit Mills church, Somerset Co., Pa., Sept. 10, 1892, Bro. Samuel Schrock, aged 79 years and 4 months. He was a consistent member of the Brethren church for a number of years. Funeral services by the writer and J. W. Peck.
JOEL GNAGEY.

BOLLINGER.—In the Centre church, Johnson Co., Mo., Sept. 9, 1892, George Melvin, infant son of Bro. Daniel and sister Lizzie Bollinger, aged 1 year, 9 months and 1 day. Services by Bro. —— Brubaker, of Warrensburgh.
IRA WITMORE.

ROBISON.—At the home of their grandparents, Scot and Jenny Eby Robison, near North Star, Ohio, the twin children of Harry and Ida Robison. Aloy C. Robison took suddenly sick on the evening of Sept. 3, with a strange disease. Twenty-four hours after, he peacefully passed away at the age of 7 months and 14 days. Eloy E. Robison watched his little mate pass away, after which, in a few moments, he also took suddenly sick, seemingly, with the same disease. Twenty-four hours later death came to him as a relief at the age of 7 months and 15 days. These babes were always in the best of health until the time of sickness and death. It was the strangest occurrence that ever came under my notice. Funeral services at the home of their grandparents by the writer from Job 23: 2.
H. C. LONGANECKER.

LIVENGOOD.—In the Middle Creek church, Somerset County, Pa., Sept. 14, 1892, Fern, infant daughter of Bro. Archie and sister Sarah Livengood, aged 5 months and 20 days. Funeral services from Mark 10: 14 by the writer.
H. A. STAHL.

CROWELL.—In the Salem congregation, Marion Co., Ill., Sept. 12, 1892, sister Jane Crowell, aged 78 years, 3 months and 16 days. Services at the residence by Rev. N. Crow, of the M. E. church. Some time ago she fell and broke her hip. She bore her affliction patiently until death relieved her.
JACOB HERSHBERGER.

SHANK.—At his residence, in Dallas Centre, Iowa, Sept. 10, 1892, after a few days' sickness, Israel F. Shank, youngest son of Daniel S. Shank, aged 37 years and 2 days. He united with the German Baptist church when a young man, and has been a consistent member ever since. The funeral took place at the German Baptist church and cemetery, east of town, at 3 o'clock Sunday afternoon. Bro. R. F. McCune conducted the services from Matt. 24: 4.
A. R. BURGER.

HUBBARD.—Near Ottawa, Kans., Sept. 3, 1892, Tommy, infant son of Sigel and Ida Hubbard, aged 5 months. Funeral services by the writer.
JOS. N. MORROW.

MARKLE.—In Perry County, Pa., Sept. 3, 1892, Bro. John Markle, aged 69 years, 2 months and 12 days. He was a member for over fifty years. Eleven children are living and one dead. Funeral services by the writer.
ISAAC EBY.

The Gospel Messenger

Is the recognized organ of the German Baptist or Brethren's church, and advocates the form of doctrine taught in the New Testament and pleads for a return to apostolic and primitive Christianity.

It recognizes the New Testament as the only infallible rule of faith and practice, and maintains that Faith toward God, Repentance from dead works, Regeneration of the heart and mind, baptism by Trine Immersion for remission of sins unto the reception of the Holy Ghost by the laying on of hands, are the means of adoption into the household of God,—the church militant.

It also maintains that Feet-washing, as taught in John 13, both by example and command of Jesus, should be observed in the church.

That the Lord's Supper, instituted by Christ and as universally observed by the apostles and the early Christians, is a full meal, and, in connection with the Communion, should be taken in the evening or after the close of the day.

That the Salutation of the Holy Kiss, or Kiss of Charity, is binding upon the followers of Christ.

That War and Retaliation are contrary to the spirit and self-denying principles of the religion of Jesus Christ.

That the principle of Plain Dressing and of Non-conformity to the world, as taught in the New Testament, should be observed by the followers of Christ.

That the Scriptural duty of Anointing the Sick with Oil, in the Name of the Lord, James 5: 14, is binding upon all Christians.

It also advocates the church's duty to support Missionary and Tract Work, thus giving to all for the spread of the Gospel and for the conversion of sinners.

In short, it is a vindicator of all that Christ and his apostles have enjoined upon us, and aims, amid the conflicting theories and discords of modern Christendom, to point out ground that all must concede to be faithfully safe.

☞ The above principles of our Fraternity are set forth on our Brethren's Envelopes." Use them! Price 15 cents per package; 40 cents per hundred.

Announcements.

(Concluded from preceding page.)

LOVE FEASTS.

Oct. 8, at 4 P. M., Cedar Creek church, DeKalb Co., Ind.

Oct. 8 and 9, at 2 P. M., Kingsley church, Woodbury Co., Iowa.

Oct. 15, at 3 P. M., Mohoning church, near Columbiana, Ohio.

Oct. 15, at 3 P. M., Lohette church, Altamont, Labette Co., Kans.

Oct. 15, at 4:30 P. M., Silver Creek church, Ogle Co., Ill., at the College Chapel, Mt. Morris.

Oct. 15, Weeping Water church, Cass Co., Nebr.

Oct. 15, at 2 P. M., Hyndman, Pa.,

Oct. 20, Prairie View church, Scott Co., Kans.

Oct. 27, at 2 P. M., Bachelor's Run church, Carroll Co., Ind.

Oct. 28, at 4 P. M., Stony Creek church, 4 miles east of Noblesville, Hamilton Co., Ind.

Oct. 28, at 10 A. M., Lower Twin Creek church, Ingomar Station, Preble Co., Ohio.

Oct. 29 and 30, at 2 P. M., Paint Creek church, Bourbon Co., Kans.

Oct. 29 and 30, at 2 P. M., Wuddam's Grove, Ill.

Oct. 29, Franklin church, Decatur Co., Iowa.

Nov. 1 and 2, at 3:30 A. M., Ephrata, Pa.

Nov. 2, at 3:30 P. M., West Otter Creek church, Macoupin Co., Ill.

EUROPE
AND
Bible Lands

CANCERS, TUMORS, ETC.

GOOD BOOKS FOR ALL.

— THE —
Doctrine of the Brethren Defended.

O Jerusalem! Jerusalem!

Excursions to California.

LOOK AT THIS.

Church Entertainments: Twenty Objections.

Alone with God.

Farm for Sale!

Windsor European Hotel
TRIBUNE BLOCK,

Wolf's Business College.

Announcements.

(Concluded from preceding page.)

LOVE FEASTS.

Oct. 8, at 4 P. M., Cedar Creek church, DeKalb Co., Ind.

Oct. 8 and 9, at 2 P. M., Kingsley church, Woodbury Co., Iowa.

Oct. 15, at 5 P. M., Mahoning church, near Columbiana, Ohio.

Oct. 15, at 3 P. M., Labette church, Altamont, Labette Co., Kans.

Oct. 15, at 4: 30 P. M., Silver Creek church, Ogle Co., Ill., at the College Chapel, Mt. Morris.

Oct. 15, Weeping Water church, Cass Co., Nebr.

Oct. 15, at 2 P. M., Hyndman, Pa.

Oct. 20, Prairie View church, Scott Co., Kans.

Oct. 27, at 2 P. M., Bachelor's Run church, Carroll Co., Ind.

Oct. 28, at 4 P. M., Stony Creek church, 4 miles east of Noblesville, Hamilton Co., Ind.

Oct. 28, at 10 A. M., Lower Twin Creek church, Ingomar Station, Preble Co., Ohio.

Oct. 29 and 30, at 2 P. M., Paint Creek church, Bourbon Co., Kans.

Oct. 29 and 30, at 2 P. M., Waddam's Grove, Ill.

Oct.'29, Franklin church, Decatur Co., Iowa.

Nov. 1 and 2, at 9: 30 A. M., Ephrata, Pa.

Nov. 4, at 3: 30 P. M., West Otter Creek church, Macoupin Co., Ill.

EUROPE
AND
Bible Lands

A new edition of this deservedly popular work has again been published. It retains all the excellencies of its predecessors, and with those who are interested in Bible study this work will always remain a favorite. Those who have read the ordinary book of travel will be surprised to find "Europe and Bible Lands" of thrilling interest for both old and young. The large number of books, already sold, proves that the work is of more than ordinary merit.

A fair supply of the last edition of this work is still on hand. Those who have not yet secured a copy of the work should embrace this opportunity of securing it. Price, in fine cloth binding, only $1.50 per copy, post-paid. To agents who are prepared to push an active canvass of the work, we are prepared to give special inducements. Write us.

BRETHREN'S PUBLISHING CO.,
Mt. Morris, Ill.

DANCERS, TUMORS, ETC.

Successfully treated by Dr. G. N. Bixler, of Waynesborough, Pa., where he has practiced for the last sixteen years. Dr. Bixler is a graduate of the University of Maryland, at Baltimore City. References given and correspondence solicited. Address, Dr. G. W. Bixler, Waynesborough, Pa.

WHAT to Read, a monthly magazine published in the interests of all lovers of good literature, 50 cts. per year. But as a SPECIAL INDUCEMENT I will send it one year for 35 cts., and give free a Handy and Reliable little Dictionary, containing 30,000 words and 300 pages, to all who send in their subscription at once. Address: Jas. M. Neff, Covington, Ohio.

GOOD BOOKS FOR ALL.

ANY book in the market furnished at publishers' lowest retail price by the Brethren's Publishing Company, Mt. Morris, Ill. *Special prices* given when books are purchased in quantities. When ordering books, not on our list, if possible give title, name of author, and address of publishers.

The Throne of David.—By J. H. Ingraham. Cloth, $1.50.

The Doctrine of the Holy Spirit.—By James B Walker. Cloth, $1.25.

Homiletics and Pastoral Theology.—By W. G. T. Shedd. Cloth, $2.50.

The New Testament History.—By Wm. Smith. Cloth, $1.25.

The Old Testament History.—By William Smith. Cloth, $1.25.

The Great Events of History.—By W.P. Collier. Cloth, $1.25.

Lectures on Preaching.—By Rev. Phillips Brooks. Cloth, 16mo. $1.50.

The Path of Life.—An interesting tract for everybody. Price, 10 cents per copy; 100 copies, $6.00.

The Origin and Growth of Religion.—Hibbert Lectures. By T. W. R. Davids. Cloth, 8vo, $2.50.

Hours with the Bible.—By Cunningham Geikie. Old Testament Series—six volumes. Per volume, 90 cents.

Bible Work, or Bible Reader's Commentary on the New Testament.—By J. G. Butler. Two vols. 8vo, $10.00.

Biblical Antiquities.—By John Nevin. Gives a concise account of Bible times and customs; invaluable to all students of Bible subjects. Price, $1.50.

The Story of the Bible.—An excellent volume for old and young; will interest and instruct all those desiring a knowledge of the Scriptures. Price, $1.00.

Life on Wheels.—By J. S. Mohler. The idea of the book is to represent the way to heaven, by using the different terms connected with an ordinary railroad. Price, single copy, 10 cents.

Trine Immersion.—A vindication of the apostolic form of Christian baptism. By Eld. James Quinter. A most complete and reliable work on the subject. Price, cloth, single copy, $1.25; leather, $1.75.

Popular Commentary on the New Testament.—Edited by Philip Schaff. Four volumes, 8vo. Matthew, Mark and Luke; $6.00. John and the Acts; $6.00. Romans to Philemon; $5.00. Hebrews to Revelation; $5.00.

Doctrine of the Brethren Defended.

THIS work contains a complete exposition of the faith and practice of the Brethren, the Divinity and Christ, the Divinity of the Holy Spirit, Immersion, Feet-washing, the Lord's Supper, the Holy Kiss, Non-conformity, Secret Societies, etc. Price, per copy, cloth binding, $1.25. Address this office.

O Jerusalem! Jerusalem!

WHAT could be more beautiful and touching than a picture of Christ as He stood upon Olivet looking down over the beloved but sinful city, with tears trickling down over his cheeks, his lips parted as he cries, "O Jerusalem! Jerusalem!" We have such a picture 24x18 inches, beautifully executed in colors. No one can gaze upon it without being moved. Given free with a year's subscription to "What to Read" at 50 cents. An agent wanted in every church and neighborhood. Address, Jas. M. Neff, Covington, Ohio.

Excursions to California.

EXCURSIONS in charge of M. M. Eshelman, Immigration Agent, will leave Chicago over the "Santa Fe Route" Tuesdays, and Kansas City Wednesdays, during the year 1892, on dates as follows:

Chicago, January 26, February 23, March 22, April 26, May 24, June 28, July 26, August 23, September 27, October 18, November 22, December 27.

Kansas City, January 27, February 24, March 23, April 27, May 25, June 29, July 27, August 24, September 28, October 28, November 23, December 28.

Parties wishing to avail themselves of the privileges of these excursions, should write M. M. Eshelman, North Pomona, California, prior to the 25th of each month, and from the fifteenth to the end of the month, at 1090 Union Avenue (opposite Union Depot), Kansas City, Mo., stating when and where they wish to join one of these excursions, and he will give them full information, and if desired will reserve berths in Tourist Sleeping Car for them. Do not fail to write him; he will do you good. The rates will be as low as the lowest made to the Pacific Coast.

GEORGE L. McDONAUGH,
Traveling Agent.

Burlington
Route
C.B. & Q.R.R.

BEST LINE

BETWEEN

Chicago and St. Louis,

KANSAS CITY,

OMAHA, DENVER,

And All Points in

UTAH AND CALIFORNIA

P. S. EUSTIS,
Gen. Pass. Agt.,
CHICAGO, ILL.

LOOK AT THIS.

The Monon Route still reducing rates and offering better accommodations than ever before.

Commencing April 15, the fare from Chicago to Louisville, New Albany, Cincinnati, Hamilton, and Dayton will be $5.50; to Indianapolis $3.50. Round trip tickets good ten days at double the one way rate. Parlor and Dining cars on day trains; Pullman Sleepers and Compartment Cars on night trains. A special Sleeper is run for Indianapolis business.

See that your tickets read via the MONON ROUTE.

For rates, schedules, etc., apply at Depot, Dearborn Station, City Ticket Office, 232 Clark Street, or address, JAMES BARKER, G. P. A., Monon Block, Chicago, Ill.

Church Entertainments: Twenty Objections.

By Rev. B. Carradine, D. D. 12mo, 100 pp. Paper cover, 30 cents. A strong book in defense of its position, written by a powerful pen, presenting the most candid and scriptural arraignment of unwarrantable methods for money-raising in the Church. The spirit of the book is highly devotional and cannot fail to inspire the reader with its seriousness.

Alone with God.

THIS manual of devotions, by J. H. Garrison, comprises a series of meditations with forms of prayer for private devotions, family worship and special occasions. It is one of the most useful, most needed, and best adapted books of the year, and therefore it is not strange that it is proving one of the most popular. In work of this kind its distinguished, gifted, pious and beloved author is at his best. This book is helpful to every minister, church official, and Sunday-school superintendent, as well as every private member of the church in all ages. It has models of prayer, suitable for the service of the prayer-meeting, while its suggestions, meditations and instructions are pre-eminently calculated to be of service in preparation for the solemn duties that rest upon the active members. Cloth, 75 cents; morocco, $1.25. Address this office.

M. PHILLIPSON & SON,

Warsaw, Ind.,

Manufacturers of

PLAIN
CLOTHING
-- FOR --
BRETHREN.

WE make a specialty of PLAIN CLOTHING, put in good cloth and trimmings and make them up first-class in every way.

Complete catalogue of all kinds of clothing for men and boys, rules for self-measurement, tape-measure, and samples of cloth, from which Brethren's suits are made, will be sent to any address on receipt of six cents in stamps.

Dr. Wrightsman's Sovereign Balm of Life is prepared especially to acquaint herself with its method. An honest preparation, — a boon to woman. Write for circulars and get full particulars. Address: D. B. SENGER & CO., 800 xxx, Franklin Grove, Ill.

SORROWS of MOTHERHOOD

Every MOTHER ought to acquaint herself with its method.

Farm for Sale!

A farm, containing 78 acres, situated about six miles south-east of Polo, in the town of Pine Creek, Ogle Co., Ill., is offered for sale. It is the late residence of John Gnats, deceased, and is within one and one-half miles of the German Baptist Brethren church. This farm is under a high state of cultivation, and well stocked with all kinds of fruit, common to this climate. It will be sold at private sale. Address, John T. Gnats, Oregon, Ill., or call on Chas. Hildebrand, now residing on the farm.

NOW READY. If you are unwell, I will mail you NINE DAYS' Trial Treatment of the famous AUSTRALIAN ELECTRO PILLS FREE, or FIFTY DAYS' treatment for $1.00. These pills for extra liquid remedies in quickly curing Liver, Kidney or Stomach Trouble, Constipation, Indigestion, Sick Headache, *La Grippe* and its after effects. I want one *live* agent in every church. Special terms to those naming the MESSENGER. Address, Dr. K. J. Worst, Ashland, Ohio.

Windsor
European Hotel

TRIBUNE BLOCK,

145 to 155 Dearborn St. S. GREGSTEN, Prop'r.

Chicago, Ill.

This hotel is centrally located, and the most respectable House of its class in the City. The charges are moderate, varying in price from 75 cents to $2.50 per day, per person. Thompson's Restaurant underneath. First-class Passenger Elevator.

Wolf's Business College.

A thorough school for training pupils in the Commercial Branches, Shorthand, Typewriting, Telegraphy, and Penmanship. The school for those who want a practical, useful education. Write for catalogue.

D. ELMER WOLF, Principal,
Hagerstown, Md.

✦ESSAYS✦

"Study to show thyself approved unto God; a workman that needeth not be ashamed, rightly dividing the Word of Truth."

IN LIFE—NOT DEATH.

SELECTED BY AMELIA C. NOFZIGER.

SOMETIMES we think,
When hard words fall upon the waiting ear,
That were that friend, now living, cold and dead,
How different the tones that we should hear.
How kind the things that would of him be said,
For most hearts shrink
From speaking harshly of the dead.

In life—not death,
Hearts need fond words to help them on their way,
Need tender thoughts and gentle sympathy,
Caresses, pleasant looks to cheer each passing day,
Then hoard them not until they useless be,
In life—not death,
Speak kindly, *living hearts* need sympathy.

Oh, do not wait
Till death shall press the weary eye-lids down,
To yield forbearance! Let it daily fall,
With it a golden calmness comes this life to crown;
Joy springs from charity, friends, one and all,
Before too late,
O'er faults and frailties let this mantle fall.

What worth can be
Love's gentlest glances, or its fondest tone,
The sweetest fancies loving lips can say,
When this form silent lies, cold and alone,
Beneath some grass-grown knoll not far away,
Ah, give to me
Love's prompt defenses while in life I stay!

"STRONG CONSOLATION."—Heb. 6:18.

BY C. H. BALSBAUGH.

"The Elect Lady, whom I love in the Truth."—2 John 1.
To a Crippled Sister:—

IN the first discourse of Jesus in His Childhood's Home He said, "The Spirit of the Lord is upon Me, because He hath anointed Me to preach the *Gospel* to *the poor*." Luke 4:18. This is also my mission. "To heal the broken-hearted," is a bliss and a glory worthy of God. My correspondence reaches from Dan to Beersheba, and it seems as if I were specially called to minister to the "captive" and the "bruised" and the disconsolate. The great sinners, the great burden-bearers, the soul-torn, the body-tortured, the weepers in Zion, the bereaved, the harpless and hopeless—many of these seem instinctively to ask me to share their sorrows.

It is a sweet paradox to find our purest, highest joy in sympathy with Him who was pre-eminently "a man of sorrows, and acquainted with grief." Because I have been the "chief of sinners," and have drained to the dregs the bitter cup of wormwood, and have seen the awful Majesty of the Holy One of Eternity, and the ineffable Glory and ravishing Beauty of His Love on the Cross, He has given me something to say of the fullness, and freeness, and sweetness of His Grace to those whom His discipline has made ready for the "strong consolation" of His infinite pity and good will. 2 Cor. 1:3-7; Heb. 6:17-19. When God soothes and satisfies with His own Peace, "of whom shall we be afraid"? Ps. 29:1. As secure, as restful, as happy as God; this is the eternal issue of the Incarnation.

"*Comfort ye, comfort ye my people, saith your God.*" Isa. 40:1. This is the Mission of Jehovah, through Jesus and the Comforter, delegated medially to all who are constrained by the Love of Christ. "For God sent not His Son into the world to condemn the world, but that the world *through Him* might be *saved*." John 3:17. When His personal work on earth was accom-

plished, and he returned to His Father as our perpetual Advocate, He said, "I will pray the Father, and he shall give you *another Comforter*, that He may *abide with you forever*." And His office shall be to "*testify of* ME." "*He shall glorify* ME; He shall receive of MINE, and shall *show it unto you*," John 14:16; 15:26; 16:14. This Tri-personal office of the Holy Trinity, the saints are to exercise in relation to each other. "*Wherefore comfort' one another with these words.*" 1 Thess. 4:18.

What "words"? Here the door opens into "all the fullness of God." Here the boundless treasures of Jehovah are offered to our acceptance and dispensation. "The unsearchable riches of Christ" are ours to enjoy and communicate. To the saints "God would make known what is the riches of the Glory of this Mystery." "That ye should show forth the praises of Him who hath called you out of darkness into *His Marvelous Light*." "GOD IS LIGHT, AND IN HIM IS NO DARKNESS AT ALL." "*If we walk in the light as He is in the light.*" Eph. 3:8; Col. 1:27; 1 Pet. 2:9; 1 John 1:5, 7.

Oh, to be like God, live like God, act like God, feel like God! For this He became man, that we may see "God in the flesh," and "walk even as He also walked." 1 John 2:6. This is our "High Calling of God in Christ Jesus," the mark and the prize toward which we are unceasingly to press. Philpp. 3:14. This is to "receive the end of our faith, even the salvation of our souls," "rejoicing with joy unspeakable and full of Glory." 1 Pet. 1:8, 9. Is not this comfort enough to sweeten the most pungent cup of vinegar and gall ever held to the lips of a sorrow-smitten soul? Is not this glory enough to illuminate your isolation, and thrill your helpless, suffering body with the very Life and Blessedness of the Godman? Is not Rom. 8:17, 18, like a soul-and-body-filling draught - from the Crystal River? Was not 2 Cor. 4:17, written expressly to uplift, and gladden and feast such poor, pain-disciplined, firepurged disciples like you? Does not the voice of Jesus sound from every page of the Gospel, repeating His gracious valedictory of deathless Love?—"*Lo, I am with you alway,* EVEN UNTO THE END." Matt. 28:20. Such an assurance and experience immeasurably outweigh all the agonies and sorrows that can befall us in our probationary state.

In Christian sympathy my heart goes out to fulfill Gal. 6:2. To "yield our members as instruments of righteousness unto holiness," in quiet, patient, joyful suffering, demands superabounding grace. Rom. 6:13, 19; 5:3; 12:12; 2 Cor. 12:7-10. These are the ingredients in Christ's adhesive plaster for the painful malady which is distorting your body. Rheumatic and neuralgic twinges are severe sifters of the reality of our identification with Christ. Physical pain, especially when intense and protracted, reveals where our anchor is fastened, whether in the doctor and temporal interests, or in "Him who was in all points tempted like as we are," but committed Himself to Him "who was able to deliver Him from death." Heb. 4:15; 5:7; 1 Pet. 2:23.

Few are so centered in the All-sufficiency of our Elder Brother and Advocate, the All-providing grace of our Divine-Human Sin-Bearer and Body-Healer, as to have neither thought nor desire in case of sickness beyond James 5:14, 15; Rom. 12:1; 1 Thess. 5:23. Jesus is Jehovah Raphi for our physical ailments, no less than Jehovah Shalom for our souls. Ex. 15:26. Judges 6:24. "Your faith groweth exceedingly," "strong in faith, giving glory to God," are fine commendations when Providence calls us to believe and bear the impossible. 2 Thess. 1:3; Rom. 4:20. Little faith may keep us from drowning, while

strong faith will enable us to tread with confidence and serene joy the raging billows. Matt. 14:28-31. It is one of the rarest things to see a Christian committed absolutely to the grace of Christ in every exigency. There is efficacy in some medicines that may be made available in some pathological conditions.

Hygiene is far superior, both in the prevention and cure of disease. But "faith in God," as free from flaw as that enjoined in Mark 11:23, 24, is better than all colleges, doctors, and drugs. Having been a physician myself, I do not speak at random. When the body is kept as becometh a temple of the Holy Ghost, and we eat and drink to the glory of God, and covet neither life nor health for its own sake, but only that Christ may be magnified, we may safely commit ourselves to the all-wise and gracious Proprietor of body, soul, and Spirit. 1 Cor. 6:19, 20; 10:31; Luke 23:42; Philpp. 1:20. The motive of our restoration, as Christians, must be for the pleasure and honor of our Redeemer. 2 Cor. 5:15. Life is a curse to all eternity if it be not "hid with Christ in God." Col. 3:3. The *because* in John 14:19, and the so in John 4:17, must be complemental. We do not conceive how good our Heavenly Father is, and how holy and beautiful and great He wants to make us. Our selfishness and blindness and distrust are amazing! But "He heareth long with them." Luke 18:7. "The longsuffering of our Lord is salvation." 2 Pet. 3:15. "We are saved by hope." Rom. 8:24. But this hope is not only *in God*, but *God in us*. Heb. 6:18, 19; Col. 1:27. Whosoever hath this hope in him, purifieth himself, even as he is pure." 1 John 3:3. What drowsy, fitful, dubious Christians many of us are!

"See how long a letter I have written unto you with mine own hand" Gal. 6:11. Not too long, I trust. It is a charger piled with bread from Heaven, and will nourish your soul many days. It is even superior to the Tishbite's Angel-baked cakes. 1 Kings 19:5-8. Butter and honey are delicious; it is Immanuel's food. Isa. 7:14, 15. Of these Heavenly Dainties all His followers shall eat. See verse 22. With these sweets of the Upper Paradise I loaded and flavored my letter. Of my own I offer you nothing; it is insipid and innutritious. Hand it to others to read, and in this way be a home missionary. Sow seed which will yield a harvest of joy in the endless future. One tiny grain may multiply a hundredfold.

A word, in closing, with reference to your opportune stamps. I would demur at your liberality were it not that I commit all my literary expenses to the Lord. I am simple enough to believe that Philpp. 4:19, includes stamps and stationery. When I need, or how much I need, is known only to Him who owns all the gold and silver. I have the sense of a Divine Calling in my pen-ministry, and I do not want a penny from any-one save those who feel mightily "constrained by the love of Christ." My prayer and wrestling night- and day is that Philpp. 4:6, 7, 11, 13, 19, may be my God-endorsed autobiography.

Union Deposit, Pa.

THE WAYS OF SATAN.

BY QUINCY LECKRONE.

IT has always been the design of Satan to destroy the church of Christ, or the institution of God, by whatever means available. He first tries one plan, and if that does not succeed, he tries another. He made a mighty effort at the fountain head, to pollute the stream in its infancy, when he tempted Christ in the wilderness, but, when defeated, busied himself in devising anoth-

✦ESSAYS✦

" Study to show thyself approved unto God; a workman that needeth not be ashamed, rightly dividing the Word of Truth."

IN LIFE—NOT DEATH.

SELECTED BY AMELIA C. NOFZIGER.

Sometimes we think,
When hard words fall upon the waiting ear,
That were that friend, now living, cold and dead,
How different the tones that we should hear,
How kind the things that would of him be said,
For most hearts shrink
From speaking harshly of the dead.

In life—not death,
Hearts need fond words to help them on their way,
Need tender thoughts and gentle sympathy,
Caresses, pleasant looks to cheer each passing day,
Then hoard them not until they useless be,
In life—not death,
Speak kindly, *living hearts* need sympathy.

Oh, do not wait
Till death shall press the weary eye-lids down,
To yield forbearance! Let it daily fall,
With it a golden calmness comes this life to crown;
Joy springs from charity, friends, one and all,
Before too late,
O'er faults and frailties let this mantle fall.

What worth can be
Love's gentlest glances, or its fondest tone,
The sweetest fancies loving lips can say,
When this form silent lies, cold and alone,
Beneath some grass-grown knoll not far away,
Ah, give to me
Love's prompt defenses while in life I stay!

"STRONG CONSOLATION."—Heb. 6:18.

BY C. H. BALSBAUGH.

" The Elect Lady, whom I love in the Truth."—2 John 1.
To a Crippled Sister:—

In the first discourse of Jesus in His Childhood's Home He said, " The Spirit of the Lord is upon Me, because He hath anointed Me to preach the *Gospel to the poor.*" Luke 4:18. This is also my mission. " To heal the broken-hearted," is a bliss and a glory worthy of God. My correspondence reaches from Dan to Beersheba, and it seems as if I were specially called to minister to the " captive " and the " bruised " and the disconsolate. The great sinners, the great burden-bearers, the soul-torn, the body-tortured, the weepers in Zion, the bereaved, the harpless and hopeless—many of these seem instinctively to ask me to share their sorrows.

It is a sweet paradox to find our purest, highest joy in sympathy with Him who was pre-eminently " a man of sorrows, and acquainted with grief." Because I have been the " chief of sinners," and have drained to the dregs the bitter cup of wormwood, and have seen the awful Majesty of the Holy One of Eternity, and the ineffable Glory and ravishing Beauty of His Love on the Cross, He has given me something to say of the fullness, and freeness, and sweetness of His Grace to those whom His discipline has made ready for the " strong consolation " of His infinite pity and good will. 2 Cor. 1:3–7; Heb. 6:17–19. When God soothes and satisfies with His own Peace, " of whom shall we be afraid " ? Ps. 29:1. As secure, as restful, as happy as God; this is the eternal issue of the Incarnation.

" *Comfort ye, comfort ye my people, saith your God.*" Isa. 40:1. This is the Mission of Jehovah, through Jesus and the Comforter, delegated medially to all who are constrained by the Love of Christ. " For God sent not His Son into the world to condemn the world, but that the world *through Him* might be saved." John 3:17. When His personal work on earth was accom-

plished, and he returned to His Father as our perpetual Advocate, He said, " I will pray the Father, and he shall give you *another Comforter,* that He may *abide with you forever.*" And His office shall be to " *testify of Me.*" " *He shall glorify Me*; He shall receive of Mine, and shall *show it unto you,*" John 14:16; 15; 26; 16:14 This Tri-personal office of the Holy Trinity, the saints are to exercise in relation to each other. " *Wherefore comfort one another with these words.*" 1 Thess. 4:18.

What " words" ? Here the door opens into " all the fullness of God." Here the boundless treasures of Jehovah are offered to our acceptance and dispensation. " The unsearchable riches of Christ " are ours to enjoy and communicate. To the saints " God would make known what is the riches of the Glory of this Mystery." " That ye should show forth the praises of Him who hath called you out of darkness into *His Marvelous Light.*" " God is light, and in Him is no darkness at all." " *If we walk in the light as He is in the light.*" Eph. 3:8; Col. 1:27; 1 Pet. 2:9; 1 John 1:5, 7.

Oh, to be like God, live like God, act like God, feel like God! For this He became man, that we may see " God in the flesh," and " walk even as He also walked." 1 John 2:6. This is our " High Calling of God in Christ Jesus," the mark and the prize toward which we are unceasingly to press. Philpp. 3:14 This is to " receive the end of our faith, even the salvation of our souls," " rejoicing with joy unspeakable and full of Glory." 1 Pet. 1:8, 9. Is not this comfort enough to sweeten the most pungent cup of vinegar and gall ever held to the lips of a sorrow-smitten soul? Is not this glory enough to illuminate your isolation, and thrill your helpless, suffering body with the very Life and Blessedness of the Godman? Is not Rom. 8:17, 18, like a soul-and-body-filling draught - from the Crystal River? Was not 2 Cor. 4:17, written expressly to uplift, and gladden and feast such poor, pain-disciplined, firepurged disciples like you? Does not the voice of Jesus sound from every page of the Gospel, repeating His gracious valedictory of deathless Love?—" *Lo, I am with you alway,* even unto the end." Matt. 28:20. Such an assurance and experience immeasurably outweigh all the agonies and sorrows that can befall us in our probationary state.

In Christian sympathy my heart goes out to fulfill Gal. 6:2. To " yield our members as instruments of righteousness unto holiness," in quiet, patient, joyful suffering, demands superabounding grace. Rom. 6:13, 19; 5:8; 12:19; 2 Cor. 12:7-10. These are the ingredients in Christ's adhesive plaster for the painful malady which is distorting your body. Rheumatic and neuralgic twinges are severe afters of the reality of our identification with Christ. Physical pain, especially when intense and protracted, reveals where our anchor is fastened, whether in the doctor and temporal interests, or in " Him who was in all points tempted like as we are," but committed Himself to Him " who was able to deliver Him from death." Heb. 4:15; 5:7; 1 Pet. 2:23.

Few are so centered in the All-sufficiency of our Elder Brother and Advocate, the All-providing grace of our Divine-Human Sin-Bearer and Body-Healer, as to have neither thought nor desire in case of sickness beyond James 5:14, 15; Rom. 12:1; 1 Thess. 5:23. Jesus is Jehovah Raphi for our physical ailments, no less than Jehovah Shalom for our souls. Ex. 15:26. Judges 6:24. " Your faith groweth exceedingly," " strong in faith, giving glory to God," are fine commendations when Providence calls us to believe and bear the impossible. 2 Thess. 1:3; Rom. 4:20. Little faith may keep us from drowning, while

strong faith will enable us to tread with confidence and serene joy the raging billows. Matt 14:28-31. It is one of the rarest things to see a Christian committed absolutely to the grace of Christ in every exigency. There is efficacy in some medicines that may be made available in some pathological conditions.

Hygiene is far superior, both in the prevention and cure of disease. But "faith in God," as free from flaw as that enjoined in Mark 11:23, 24, is better than all colleges, doctors, and drugs. Having been a physician myself, I do not speak at random. When the body is kept as becometh a temple of the Holy Ghost, and we eat and drink to the glory of God, and covet neither life nor health for its own sake, but only that Christ may be magnified, we may safely commit ourselves to the all-wise and gracious Proprietor of body, soul, and Spirit. 1 Cor. 6:19, 20; 10:31; Luke 22:42; Philpp. 1:20. The motive of our restoration, as Christians, must be for the pleasure and honor of our Redeemer. 2 Cor. 5:15. Life is a curse to all eternity if it be not " hid with Christ in God." Col. 3:3. The *because* in John 14:19, and the *so* in 1 John 4:17, must be complemental. We do not conceive how good our Heavenly Father is, and how holy and beautiful and great He wants to make us. Our selfishness and blindness and distrust are amazing! But " He beareth long with them." Luke 18:7. " The longsuffering of our Lord is salvation." 2 Pet. 3:15. " We are saved by hope." Rom. 8:24 But this hope is not only in God, but *God in us.* Heb. 6:18, 19; Col. 1:27. Whosoever hath this hope in him, purifieth himself, even as he is pure." 1 John 3: 3. What drowsy, fitful, dubious Christians many of us are!

" See how long a letter I have written unto you with mine own hand " Gal. 6:11. Not too long, I trust. It is a charger piled with bread from Heaven, and will nourish your soul many days. It is even superior to the Tishbite's Angel-baked cakes. 1 Kings 19:5-8. Butter and honey are delicious; it is Immanuel's food. Isa. 7:14, 15. Of these Heavenly Dainties all His followers shall eat. See verse 22. With these sweets of the Upper Paradise I loaded and flavored my letter. Of my own I offer you nothing; it is insipid and innutritious. Hand it to others to read, and in this way be a home missionary. Sow seed which will yield a harvest of joy in the endless future. One tiny grain may multiply a hundredfold.

A word, in closing, with reference to your opportune stamps. I would demur at your liberality were it not that I commit all my literary expenses to the Lord. I am simple enough to believe that Philpp. 4:19, includes stamps and stationery. When I need, or how much I need, is known only to Him who owns all the gold and silver. I have the sense of a Divine Calling in my pen-ministry, and I do not want a penny from any one save those who feel mightily " constrained by the love of Christ." My prayer and wrestling night and day is that Philpp. 4:6, 7, 11, 13, 19, may be my God-endorsed autobiography.

Union Deposit, Pa.

THE WAYS OF SATAN.

BY QUINCY LECKRONE.

It has always been the design of Satan to destroy the church of Christ, or the institution of God, by whatever means available. He first tries one plan, and if that does not succeed, he tries another. He made a mighty effort at the fountain head, to pollute the stream in its infancy, when he tempted Christ in the wilderness, but, when defeated, busied himself in devising anoth-

LIVELY STONES.—1 Pet. 2: 5.

A SERMON BY W. M. LYON.

The author of the Christian religion is the source of all life. "He that hath the Son, hath life." 1 John 5: 12. He is the "Living Stone." Every one that receives Christ becomes a "new creature," a "lively stone" in God's great, spiritual temple. It is the Christ-life that constitutes the Christian. "Ye are the light of the world." Matt. 5: 14. Why? John 1: 4 answers the question: "In him was life, and the life was the LIGHT OF MEN." From our text we get this division:

I. The Church is Compared to a Building.
II. Each Member Forms a Part of this Building.
III. God Selects Proper Material.

I. The Church, a Building. In 2 Cor. 5: 1 we learn that there is prepared for the Christian "a building of God, a house not made with hands, eternal in the heavens." This agrees with the promise of Christ to his disciples, "In my Father's house are many mansions." John 14: 2. We see, then, that God not only has a building for his people here on the earth,—the church, —but has prepared a great temple in the spirit land where his saints may dwell with him forever and ever. We have, then, a building celestial, awaiting those who are willing first to abide with Christ in his building terrestrial. Of the latter we now speak particularly. Why is the church compared to a building?

(a) A building is composed of a variety of material and many different parts, yet all tend to the accomplishment of the same purpose. So in the church we have a variety of talent, and, in a certain sense, many different parts, but all are united so that the same great purpose is accomplished. That purpose, I may add, is the glory of God and the salvation of souls. The smallest piece in a building performs a very important part. How? Simply by filling its proper place. Displace it and it produces disorder.

How true this figure with regard to the church! If each member fill his or her appointed place, there is no discord, no schisms, no divisions, no strife, no envy, no malice, but all is peace, union, love and good will. What a blessed thing it is when this divine rule is practiced! It is Godlike. To be a lively stone in God's building is simply to find your appointed place, and then, by God's help, try to fill it. Am I filling my appointed place?

(b) A building affords protection. As in the material or physical, so in the spiritual. The church is the place appointed for man's spiritual protection. If he refuse to enter, he is without promise. He stands exposed to God's wrath. God has purchased his redemption by the sacrifice of his own Son, has instituted the church for his salvation, and yet poor, sinful, rebellious man stands off and says, "I desire to be saved, I desire divine protection, but I want to have my own way about it. I want to be saved outside of the church." A man in Liverpool wishes to go to New York. Free transportation is offered him on one of the best steamers, but he refuses to go. The steamer doesn't exactly suit him, neither does he like the captain very well, so he gives up the voyage, thinking that perhaps in a few years aerial navigation may be a success, and he likes that better. What do you think of such a man? Do we find such people to-day? Are there not thousands who are refusing to take passage on the good ship Zion, with excuses no better than the one alluded to? The ship is waiting, their transportation is free, but they are not ready. They want to sail to heaven "on flowery beds of ease."

"Whenever we get everything to suit us, then we'll go." They want protection, but God's church is not exactly the place for them, therefore they subject themselves to the awful storm that is coming when God's mercy will have passed, to give way for his retributive justice.

(c) A house is intended for occupancy. It is not erected simply to look at. Its exterior may be very beautiful, it may be built of the very best material, and the finest architectural skill may be employed in its erection, but it amounts to little, indeed, if it be not occupied. No one wants to build a house simply to "lean against," or to stand off and talk about. So God has intended his church for occupancy, so to speak. You may "lean toward the church" all you please, you may stand off and look upon it with respect and even admiration, but if you are not willing to make it your abiding place, make it your home by dwelling within its sacred precincts, you can lay no claim whatever to the divine promises. You are not a "living stone," and it is life you need, life you must have. This is heaven.

II. Each Member Forms a Part of this Building.—If you are not a "living stone," you really do not belong to God's spiritual temple, and have no part in it. "For they are not all Israel, which are of Israel." Rom. 9: 6. God does not propose to use dead material in his church. Where there is spiritual life there is activity, growth, development. Then, if this is to be applied individually, the rule will hold collectively.

Then, if a church or congregation does not show signs of life, is not active, growing, developing, it is because there are too many dead stones in it. This dead material checks the wheels of progress. The dead stones roll in the way of all active church work; they get in front of our missionaries, they close the doors against prayer-meetings, Sunday-schools and every other good work.

Many there are who claim to be a part of this spiritual temple, and yet they remain silent and inactive from year to year. They can not be lively stones. Christ, our Great Exemplar, the Living Stone who is become "the head of the corner," "went about doing good." Acts 10: 38.

If we have been made partakers of his divine nature, will we not also be similarly engaged? We are living stones because we are born of love, for "God is love." We move in harmony with God's will because we have the mind and spirit of Christ in us. Dead matter may exhibit signs of life, but God does not stop with signs and pretensions.

"Man looketh on the outward appearance, but the Lord looketh at the heart." 1 Sam. 16: 7. It is no trouble for a lifeless lump to go at a high rate of speed down an inclined plane, and the same mass, when once in motion, may continue to move for a long time, even on an ascending grade. So may it be in the church. Many, very many are influenced to do much that is commendable from a human stand-point which God will never accept. Why? Because they do not act from this living principle, they are not "lively stones;" what they do is simply the result of contact with others, the force of fashion or custom, as exhibited by a fellow-creature, hence no true charity, therefore no reward.

To be a "living stone" is to draw our life from Christ, the Rock of Salvation. It is to act from principle,—from true love to God. The Christian, the living stone, is a burden-bearer, and the greater part of his own burden is to bear other people's burdens. He thus fulfills the law of Christ. Gal. 6: 2. In fact, the true Christian lives principally for others,—not for himself.

This is Christ-like. He prays for the peace and prosperity of Zion, and his prayers are backed up by the power of a holy life. Not so is he who always tries to evade duty, who feels that his main concern is in himself. He may offer up beautiful prayers and make a great "show" of religion, but God does not recognize him. He is no part of God's temple because he lacks life. He is "dead while he liveth." God wants a living sacrifice. Rom. 12: 1.

III. The Selection of Material.—In architecture, this is by no means an unimportant feature. God looks well to that part. A very beautiful building may be erected from very poor material. The Divine Architect cannot be deceived. Human architects have often been deceived in their judgment of work and material. God sets his stamp of approval only on genuine material properly used. In God's building, strength and beauty are combined. "Finally, my brethren, be strong in the Lord, and in the power of his might." Eph. 6: 10. The life of the Christian is the spirit of the living God. Here is beauty.

The stone is an emblem of strength and durability. These are both essential characteristics. Many would have you believe that there is no beauty in religion. O, what a great mistake in judgment! Of religion it may be truly said,

"A thing of beauty, and a joy forever."

But this beauty is hidden from the natural man, or rather, "The natural man receiveth not the things of the spirit of God; for they are foolishness unto him; neither can he know them, because they are spiritually discerned." 1 Cor. 2: 14.

This cuts off the hope of the moralist. It is impossible for him to "offer up spiritual sacrifices, acceptable to God by Jesus Christ." He has not "tasted that the Lord is gracious." He cannot belong to the "holy priesthood," because Christ alone is the holiness of the believer, and he refuses to accept him as his personal Savior. He rejects sanctification because he is not willing to receive the "truth as it is in Jesus," therefore Christ is rejected, for he is the way, the Truth, and the LIFE." Lively stones only have the promise of being "built up a spiritual house." "Ye also, as living stones are built up a spiritual house." This implies perfect submission to Christ. The moral man would like to become a part of this spiritual house, but he proposes to do it by his own efforts, not being willing to acknowledge publicly that without Christ he can do nothing. John 15: 5. He would have God step over the line of his promises to accommodate him in his unbelief and self-righteousness. O, what an unreasonable demand!

Right here let me appeal to every professor of religion that he fall not into the same channel of unbelief. How many there are who claim to be the meek and humble followers of Christ, who are not willing to submit themselves wholly to the doctrine of Christ! By their actions such would virtually say, "I know that my Master has taught me thus and so, but it is a very poor teacher who can't afford to violate his own rules once in awhile to accommodate some of his wise (?) and obedient (?) scholars." O, what presumption! "Be not deceived; God is not mocked."

Let us not comfort ourselves with the thought that God will use us as material in his spiritual temple while we are filled with the spirit of unbelief and self-righteousness. Talk about consecration! What is consecration? It is simply to LET GOD USE YOU. I mean you, YOU, YOU! My brother, God can't use you, neither will he use you, while you are struggling to have your own way about matters. Your will must be swallowed up in Christ's will.

LIVELY STONES.—1 Pet. 2: 5.

A SERMON BY W. M. LYON.

THE author of the Christian religion is the source of all life. "He that hath the Son, hath life." 1 John 5: 12. He is the "Living Stone." Every one that receives Christ becomes a "new creature," a "lively stone" in God's great, spiritual temple. It is the Christ-life that constitutes the Christian. "Ye are the light of the world." Matt. 5: 14. Why? John 1: 4 answers the question: "In him was life, and the life was the LIGHT OF MEN." From our text we get this division:

I. The Church is Compared to a Building.

II. Each Member Forms a Part of this Building.

III. God Selects Proper Material.

I. The Church, a Building. In 2 Cor. 5: 1 we learn that there is prepared for the Christian "a building of God, a house not made with hands, eternal in the heavens." This agrees with the promise of Christ to his disciples, "In my Father's house are many mansions." John 14: 2. We see, then, that God not only has a building for his people here on the earth,—the church, —but has prepared a great temple in the spirit land where his saints may dwell with him forever and ever. We have, then, a building celestial, awaiting those who are willing first to abide with Christ in his building terrestrial. Of the latter we now speak particularly. Why is the church compared to a building?

(a) A building is composed of a variety of material and many different parts, yet all tend to the accomplishment of the same purpose. So in the church we have a variety of talent, and, in a certain sense, many different parts, but all are united so that the same great purpose is accomplished. That purpose, I may add, is the glory of God and the salvation of souls. The smallest piece in a building performs a very important part. How? Simply by filling its proper place. Displace it and it produces disorder.

How true this figure with regard to the church! If each member fill his or her appointed place, there is no discord, no schism, no divisions, no strife, no envy, no malice, but all is peace, union, love and good will. What a blessed thing it is when this divine rule is practiced! It is Godlike. To be a lively stone in God's building is simply to find your appointed place, and then, by God's help, try to fill it. Am I filling my appointed place?

(b) A building affords protection. As in the material or physical, so in the spiritual. The church is the place appointed for man's spiritual protection. If he refuse to enter, he is without promise. He stands exposed to God's wrath. God has purchased his redemption by the sacrifice of his own Son, has instituted the church for his salvation, and yet poor, sinful, rebellious man stands off and says, "I desire to be saved, I desire divine protection, but I want to have my own way about it. I want to be saved outside of the church." A man in Liverpool wishes to go to New York. Free transportation is offered him in one of the best steamers, but he refuses to go. The steamer doesn't exactly suit him, neither does he like the captain very well, so he gives up the voyage, thinking that perhaps in a few years aerial navigation may be a success, and he likes that better. What do you think of such a man? Do we find such people to-day? Are there not thousands who are refusing to take passage on the good ship Zion, with excuses no better than the one alluded to? The ship is waiting, their transportation is free, but they are not ready. They want to sail to heaven "on flowery beds of ease."

"Whenever we get everything to suit us, then we'll go." They want protection, but God's church is not exactly the place for them, therefore they subject themselves to the awful storm that is coming when God's mercy will have passed, to give way for his retributive justice.

(c) A house is intended for occupancy. It is not erected simply to look at. Its exterior may be very beautiful, it may be built of the very best material, and the finest architectural skill may be employed in its erection, but it amounts to little, indeed, if it be not occupied. No one wants to build a house simply to "lean against," or to stand off and talk about. So God has intended his church for occupancy, so to speak. You may "lean toward the church" all you please, you may stand off and look upon it with respect and even admiration, but if you are not willing to make it your abiding place, make it your home by dwelling within its sacred precincts, you can lay no claim whatever to the divine promises. You are not a "living stone," and it is life you need, life you must have. This is heaven.

II. Each Member Forms a Part of this Building.—If you are not a "living stone," you really do not belong to God's spiritual temple, and have no part in it. "For they are not all Israel, which are of Israel." Rom. 9: 6. God does not propose to use dead material in his church. Where there is spiritual life there is activity, growth, development. Then, if this is to be applied individually, the rule will hold collectively.

Then, if a church or congregation does not show signs of life, is not active, growing, developing, it is because there are too many dead stones in it. This dead material checks the wheels of progress. The dead stones roll in the way of all active church work; they get in front of our missionaries, they close the doors against prayer-meetings, Sunday-schools and every other good work.

Many there are who claim to be a part of this spiritual temple, and yet they remain silent and inactive from year to year. They can not be lively stones. Christ, our Great Exemplar, the Living Stone who is become "the head of the corner," "went about doing good." Acts 10: 38. If we have been made partakers of his divine nature, will we not also be similarly engaged? We are living stones because we are born of love, for "God is love." We move in harmony with God's will because we have the mind and spirit of Christ in us. Dead matter may exhibit signs of life, but God does not stop with signs and pretensions.

"Man looketh on the outward appearance, but the Lord looketh at the heart." 1 Sam. 16: 7. It is no trouble for a lifeless lump to go at a high rate of speed down an inclined plane, and the same mass, when once in motion, may continue to move for a long time, even on an ascending grade. So may it be in the church. Many, very many are influenced to do much that is commendable from a human stand-point which God will never accept. Why? Because they do not act from this living principle, they are not "lively stones;" what they do is simply the result of contact with others, the force of fashion or custom, as exhibited by a fellow-creature, hence no true charity, therefore, no reward.

To be a "living stone" is to draw our life from Christ, the Rock of Salvation. It is to act from principle,—from true love to God. The Christian, the living stone, is a burden-bearer, and the greater part of his own burden is to bear other people's burdens. He thus fulfills the law of Christ. Gal. 6: 2. In fact, the true Christian lives principally for others,—not for himself.

This is Christ-like. He prays for the peace and prosperity of Zion, and his prayers are backed up by the power of a holy life. Not so is he who always tries to evade duty, who feels that his main concern is in himself. He may offer up beautiful prayers and make a great "show" of religion, but God does not recognize him. He is no part of God's temple because he lacks life. He is "dead while he liveth." God wants a living sacrifice. Rom. 12: 1.

III. The Selection of Material.—In architecture, this is by no means an unimportant feature. God looks well to that part. A very beautiful building may be erected from very poor material. The Divine Architect cannot be deceived. Human architects have often been deceived in their judgment of work and material. God sets his stamp of approval only on genuine material properly used. In God's building, strength and beauty are combined. "Finally, my brethren, be strong in the Lord, and in the power of his might." Eph. 6: 10. The life of the Christian is the spirit of the living God. Here is beauty.

The stone is an emblem of strength and durability. These are both essential characteristics. Many would have you believe that there is no beauty in religion. O, what a great mistake in judgment! Of religion it may be truly said,

"A thing of beauty, and a joy forever."

But this beauty is hidden from the natural man, or rather, "The natural man receiveth not the things of the spirit of God; for they are foolishness unto him; neither can he know them, because they are spiritually discerned." 1 Cor. 2: 14.

This cuts off the hope of the moralist. It is impossible for him to "offer up spiritual sacrifices, acceptable to God by Jesus Christ." He has not "tasted that the Lord is gracious." He cannot belong to the "holy priesthood," because Christ alone is the holiness of the believer, and he refuses to accept him as his personal Savior. He rejects sanctification because he is not willing to receive the "truth as it is in Jesus," therefore Christ is rejected, for he is the way, the Truth, and the LIFE." Lively stones, only have the promise of being "built up a spiritual house." "Ye also, as lively stones are built up a spiritual house." This implies perfect submission to Christ. The moral man would like to become a part of this spiritual house, but he proposes to do it by his own efforts, not being willing to acknowledge publicly that without Christ he can do nothing. John 15: 5. He would have God step over the line of his promises to accommodate him in his unbelief and self-righteousness. O, what an unreasonable demand!

Right here let me appeal to every professor of religion that he fall not into the same channel of unbelief. How many there are who claim to be the meek and humble followers of Christ, who are not willing to submit themselves wholly to the doctrine of Christ! By their actions such would virtually say, "I know that my Master has taught me thus and so, but it is a very poor teacher who can't afford to violate his own rules once in a while to accommodate some of his wise (?) and obedient (?) scholars." O, what presumption! "Be not deceived; God is not mocked."

Let us not comfort ourselves with the thought that God will use us as material in his spiritual temple while we are filled with the spirit of unbelief and self-righteousness. Talk about consecration! What is consecration? It is simply to LET GOD USE YOU. I mean you, YOU! My brother, God can't use you, neither will he use you, while you are struggling to have your own way about matters. Your will must be swallowed up in Christ's will.

Missionary and Tract Work Department.

"Upon the first day of the week, let every one of you lay by him in store as God hath prospered him, that there be no gatherings when I come."—1 Cor. 16: 2.

"Every man as he purposeth in his heart, so let him give. Not grudgingly or of necessity, for the Lord loveth a cheerful giver."—2 Cor. 9: 7.

HOW MUCH SHALL WE GIVE?

"Every man according to his ability." "Every one as God hath prospered him." "Every man, according as he purposeth in his heart, so let him give." "For if there be first a willing mind, it is accepted according to that a man hath, and not according to that he hath not."—2 Cor. 8: 12.

Organization of Missionary Committee.

DANIEL VANIMAN, Foreman, · · McPherson, Kans.
D. L. MILLER, Treasurer, · · · Mt. Morris, Ill.
GALEN B. ROYER, Secretary, · · Mt. Morris, Ill.

Organization of Book and Tract Work.

S. W. HOOVER, Foreman, · · · Dayton, Ohio.
S. BOCK, Secretary and Treasurer, · · Dayton, Ohio.

☞ All donations intended for Missionary Work should be sent to GALEN B. ROYER, Mt. Morris, Ill.

☞ All money for Tract Work should be sent to S. BOCK, Dayton, Ohio.

☞ Money may be sent by Money Order, Registered Letter, or Drafts on New York or Chicago. Do not send personal checks, or drafts on interior towns, as it costs 25 cents to collect them.

☞ Solicitors are requested to faithfully carry out the plan of Annual Meeting, that all our members be solicited to contribute at least twice a year for the Mission and Tract Work of the Church.

☞ Notes for the Endowment Fund can be had by writing to the Secretary of either Work.

READING.

BY J. H. MILLER.

A MAN is known by the company he keeps. So may a man's character be known by the kind of books he reads. It is said the American are the greatest reading people in the world. Reading may be a temptation to draw the young mind away from good morals, or it may be an inducement to lead the mind to a higher plane in life. The test of this work is forced upon the mind mostly at the time of leaving the school room. At this stage of life, how careful parents should be to see that their children have good and wholesome literature.

How necessary it is that no novels and frightful story papers are presented to children! To read books that present false pictures of human life is dangerous to body and soul. People who give themselves to novel reading are generally nervous and sometimes dream frightful dreams.

The world is filled with all kinds of reading matter. In our travels we often have newsboys throw reading matter down on the seat and are invited to buy. They never hand me a novel, but always some religious book. They can generally tell who is a novel reader. Inferior books should be rejected. Why should one's life-time (which is short) be spent in reading something that will not elevate one's standing in life? Why should we bow down to puddles, when we can approach freely to the crystal fountain-heads of science and letters? Half of the reading these days is done at random,—simply scanned over,—to see what is in it. Some books like serpents, may sting, and not poison the body but poison the soul.

"One day a gentleman in India went into his library and took down a book from the shelf. As he did so, he felt a sting, a slight pain in his finger like the prick of a pin. He imagined that a pin had been stuck by some one carelessly in the cover of the book, but soon his finger began to swell, then his arm, and his whole body, and in a few days he died. It was not a pin among the books, but a small and deadly serpent."

There are many serpents among the books nowadays. They nestle among the pages of some of our most fascinating literature. They coil around the flowers whose perfume intoxicates the senses. We read, we are charmed with the story. Poisonous literature has a sting that poisons the soul. Beware of poisonous literature.

I remember some years ago of preaching in a certain place, and at the close of the meeting a book was handed me to read. Many of the same kind had been sold there some months before. I took the book, read it through, and returned it. The title was "The Age of Reason," by Thomas Paine. That book did much harm in that neighborhood. Many who bought it, never had read much in the Bible, and were led astray. I know of some young men who purchased it and were thereby made believers of the Bible. Some who are Bible-reading men, can read such books and will suffer no harm, but the floating class of society had better never look into such literature. It is like a man walking through a hedge of burrs to get one blackberry,—he will get more burrs than blackberries. Reading poisonous literature reminds me of the Irishman who saw for the first time a hornet's nest, and who was anxious to know who lived in there. He thumped with his fingers on the nest, but, to his sorrow, he found out the fact in the case when it was too late. Too many brilliant minds are stung with the devil's sting, and do not realize the pain and misery until it is too late.

Parents, guard well the reading matter that comes before your children. "Consider that what we carry to a book is always quite as important as what we receive from it. We may strike the keys of the best instrument, from earliest morn to latest night, but unless there be music in our soul, it can produce no harmony in us.

To an earnest, inquiring, self-poised mind, a good book is the "plectrum," by which our else silent lyres are struck. Master your reading, and never let it master you. Then it will serve you with an ever-increasing fidelity. Good books, as the years pass on, will help us to walk in the light as we are nearing the dismal waters of death. The books that will profit us most, must be of a kind that are calculated first, to inform the mind; second, to correct the head; third, to better the heart. Such books are of immense value. Of all the books in my library the Holy Bible stands first. It is the Book of books, of all the books ever written. No one contains so much instruction, and is so sublime and so grand as the Bible. How much of this noble book should be read to our children every day! They should become familiar with it, and taught from whence it came, its mission on earth, etc.

Resolve to read one chapter each day for one year, and explain to their minds its realities. Soon their young minds will see more of the wonderful works of God,—more wonderful than any picture of fiction that has been drawn by the finest pencillings of master minds.

In reading good books we should read to receive some profit. Many read too hurriedly, and like Philip, might ask the question, "Understandest thou what thou readest?"

We are living in a fast age. Reading, like everything else must be done in a hurry. The people of the present age want fast cars to ride on, fast steamers to cross the ocean, fast horses to run a race, fast writers to fill the world with books, papers, etc., and a great many are calling for fast preachers.

A noted man was heard to preach, "I work in a hurry; I sleep in a hurry; I expect to die in a hurry." He failed to tell his congregation whether he had any desire to go to heaven in a hurry, or whether he expected to be over his hurry at the close of life. Too much of the reading is done this way. We cannot too much appreciate the power of the press, or too much and deeply deprecate its abuses. How many of our young men have spent their hard earnings at a tavern, depot, saloon, or some place of vice, who ought to have been reading some good book! How many of our young ladies, who are spending much of their time in fine needle work, studying the latest fashion, or getting ready for a social ball (so called), are preparing to go and spend weeks or months on some excursion trip, spending money to no purpose! They would better prepare the mind by reading some good book. Many parents, who have not spent even ten dollars for books for their families, would have given thousands of dollars to reclaim a son or daughter, who had thoughtlessly fallen into temptation.

Take away the press, and the vast educating power of our schools and colleges will come to an end. Education is one of the great, propelling powers of the age, but how careful should parents be where they send their children, and under whose influence they come!

Some years ago I was holding a series of meetings, and at the close of an evening service, an elderly sister stepped up to the stand with her husband and invited me home. The sister remarked, "One thing I want to see you about concerning which I am much worried." After we arrived at their home she related to me a sad story. She would wring her hands, and her heart would swell with grief when she related the following: "We have but one child,—a boy who is grown. We gave him all the advantages of education, sent him to one of the best schools in the State. He was gone three years. At the close of that term he returned home. One evening he picked up the Bible, brought it to me, and laid that book upon my lap and remarked, 'Mother, do you believe all that book teaches?' 'Why not, my son?' 'Well, mother, I believe that book as all other books; a set of smart men have written it. For me to say that book came from God or those men who wrote it were inspired, or smarter than men who have written other books since then, I cannot do. I have books in my pocket whose writings are as intelligent or as well written as the Bible. More than that. I have men who treat upon science, such men as Robert Ingersoll and Thomas Paine, who tell us without a doubt, that the Bible is not a book of God. More than that, mother, our teacher at school teaches the same. Our teachers have the books of Paine and Ingersoll, and they agree with science and other studies.'"

Here is a sad story of a broken-hearted sister. She farther tells her troubles, "We had but one boy, and from the start we were too lenient. After we sent him to school we looked after his welfare morally as long as he went to the home and high-school, but after we sent him away to college, we never concerned ourselves about him until he returned home. Then it was too late."

I asked the question, "Why did you not send him to the Brethren's schools?" "We thought they were a little more expensive and so far away, but had we known this, we should never, never have sent him there. Now, Bro. Miller, will you not do all you can to turn him away from those infidel ideas?"

Here was a sad family, all because they did not look to the interest of the soul as well as the body. It was not education that made an infidel out of this young man but he was sent to the wrong school. This brother and sister owned a nice farm but would gladly have given up all, if they could have saved their son. Parents, look well to the interest of your children, and do not get the idea that you can save a few dollars by sending your children to some school not conducted by the Brethren.

Missionary and Tract Work Department.

"Upon the first day of the week, let every one of you lay by him in store as God hath prospered him, that there be no gatherings when I come."—1 Cor. 16: 2.

"Every man as he purposeth in his heart, so let him give. Not grudgingly or of necessity, for the Lord loveth a cheerful giver."—2 Cor. 9: 7.

HOW MUCH SHALL WE GIVE?

"Every man *according to his ability.*" "Every one *as God hath prospered him.*" "Every man, *according as he purposeth in his heart,* so let him give." "For if there be first a willing mind, it is accepted *according to that a man hath,* and not according to that he hath not."—2 Cor. 8: 12.

Organization of Missionary Committee.

DANIEL VANIMAN, Foreman, - - McPherson, Kans.
D. L. MILLER, Treasurer, - - Mt. Morris, Ill.
GALEN B. ROYER, Secretary, - - Mt. Morris, Ill.

Organization of Book and Tract Work.

S. W. HOOVER, Foreman, - - Dayton, Ohio.
S. BOCK, Secretary and Treasurer, - - Dayton, Ohio.

☞All donations intended for Missionary Work should be sent to GALEN B. ROYER, Mt. Morris, Ill.
☞All money for Tract Work should be sent to S. BOCK, Dayton, Ohio.
☞Money may be sent by Money Order, Registered Letter, or Drafts on New York or Chicago. Do not send personal checks, or drafts on interior towns, as it costs 25 cents to collect them.
☞Solicitors are requested to faithfully carry out the plan of Annual Meeting, that all our members be solicited to contribute at least twice a year for the Mission and Tract Work of the Church.
☞Notes for the Endowment Fund can be had by writing to the Secretary of either Work.

READING.

BY J. H. MILLER.

A MAN is known by the company he keeps. So may a man's character be known by the kind of books he reads. It is said the Americans are the greatest reading people in the world. Reading may be a temptation to draw the young mind away from good morals, or it may be an inducement to lead the mind to a higher plane in life. The test of this work is forced upon the mind mostly at the time of leaving the school room. At this stage of life, how careful parents should be to see that their children have good and wholesome literature.

How necessary it is that no novels and frightful story papers are presented to children! To read books that present false pictures of human life is dangerous to body and soul. People who give themselves to novel reading are generally nervous and sometimes dream frightful dreams. The world is filled with all kinds of reading matter. In our travels we often have newsboys throw reading matter down on the seat and are invited to buy. They never hand me a novel, but always some religious book. They can generally tell who is a novel reader. Inferior books should be rejected. Why should one's life-time (which is short) be spent in reading something that will not elevate one's standing in life? Why should we bow down to puddles, when we can approach freely to the crystal fountain-heads of science and letters? Half of the reading these days is done at random,—simply scanned over,—to see what is in it. Some books like serpents, may sting, and not poison the body but poison the soul.

"One day a gentleman in India went into his library and took down a book from the shelf. As he did so, he felt a sting, a slight pain in his finger like the prick of a pin. He imagined that a pin had been stuck by some one carelessly in the cover of the book, but soon his finger began to swell, then his arm, and his whole body, and in a few days he died. It was not a pin among the books, but a small and deadly serpent."

There are many serpents among the books nowadays. They nestle among the pages of some of our most fascinating literature. They coil around the flowers whose perfume intoxicates the senses. We read, we are charmed with the story. Poisonous literature has a sting that poisons the soul. Beware of poisonous literature.

I remember some years ago of preaching in a certain place, and at the close of the meeting a book was handed me to read. Many of the same kind had been sold there some months before. I took the book, read it through, and returned it. The title was "The Age of Reason," by Thomas Paine. That book did much harm in that neighborhood. Many who bought it, never had read much in the Bible, and were led astray. I know of some young men who purchased it and were thereby made believers of the Bible. Some who are Bible-reading men, can read such books and will suffer no harm, but the floating class of society had better never look into such literature. It is like a man walking through a hedge of burrs to get one blackberry,—he will get more burrs than blackberries. Reading poisonous literature reminds me of the Irishman who saw for the first time a hornet's nest, and who was anxious to know who lived in there. He thumped with his fingers on the nest, but, to his sorrow, he found out the fact in the case when it was too late. Too many brilliant minds are stung with the devil's sting, and do not realize the pain and misery until it is too late.

Parents, guard well the reading matter that comes before your children. "Consider that what we carry to a book is always quite as important as what we receive from it. We may strike the keys of the best instrument, from earliest morn to latest night, but unless there be music in our soul, it can produce no harmony in us.

To an earnest, inquiring, self-poised mind, a good book is the "plectrum," by which our else silent lyres are struck. Master your reading, and never let it master you. Then it will serve you with an ever-increasing fidelity. Good books, as the years pass on, will help us to walk in the light as we are nearing the dismal waters of death. The books that will profit us most, must be of a kind that are calculated first, to inform the mind; second, to correct the head; third, to better the heart. Such books are of immense value. Of all the books in my library the Holy Bible stands first. It is the Book of books, of all the books ever written. No one contains so much instruction, and is so sublime and so grand as the Bible. How much of this noble book should be read to our children every day! They should become familiar with it, and taught from whence it came, its mission on earth, etc.

Resolve to read one chapter each day for one year, and explain to their minds its realities. Soon their young minds will see some of the wonderful works of God,—more wonderful than any picture of fiction that has been drawn by the finest pencilings of master minds.

In reading good books we should read to receive some profit. Many read too hurriedly, and like Philip, might ask the question, "Understandest thou what thou readest?"

We are living in a fast age. Reading, like everything else must be done in a hurry. The people of the present age want fast cars to ride on, fast steamers to cross the ocean, fast horses to run a race, fast writers to fill the world with books, papers, etc., and a great many are calling for fast preachers.

A noted sermon was heard to preach, "I work in a hurry; I sleep in a hurry; I expect to die in a hurry." He failed to tell his congregation whether he had any desire to go to heaven in a hurry, or whether he expected to be over his hurry at the close of life. Too much of the reading is done this way. We cannot too much appreciate the power of the press, or too much and deeply deprecate its abuses. How many of our young men have spent their hard earnings at a tavern, depot, saloon, or some place of vice, who ought to have been reading some good book! How many of our young ladies, who are spending much of their time in fine needle work, studying the latest fashion, or getting ready for a social ball (so called), are preparing to go and spend weeks or months on some excursion trip, spending money to no purpose! They would better prepare the mind by reading some good book. Many parents, who have not spent even ten dollars for books for their families, would have given thousands of dollars to reclaim a son or daughter, who had thoughtlessly fallen into temptation.

Take away the press, and the vast educating power of our schools and colleges will come to an end. Education is one of the great, propelling powers of the age, but how careful should parents be where they send their children, and under whose influence they come!

Some years ago I was holding a series of meetings, and at the close of an evening service, an elderly sister stepped up to the stand with her husband and invited me home. The sister remarked, "One thing I want to see you about concerning which I am much worried." After we arrived at their home she related to me a sad story. She would wring her hands, and her heart would swell with grief when she related the following: "We have but one child,—a boy who is grown. We gave him all the advantages of education, sent him to one of the best schools in the State. He was gone three years. At the close of that term he returned home. One evening he picked up the Bible, brought it to me, and laid that book upon my lap and remarked, 'Mother, do you believe all that book teaches?' 'Why not, my son?' 'Well, mother, I believe that book as all other books; a set of smart men have written it. For me to say that book came from God or those men who wrote it were inspired, or smarter than men who have written other books since then, I cannot do. I have books in my pocket whose writings are as intelligent or as well written as the Bible. More than that, I have men who treat upon science, such men as Robert Ingersoll and Thomas Paine, who tell us without a doubt, that the Bible is not a book of God. More than that, mother, our teacher at school teaches the same. Our teachers have the books of Paine and Ingersoll, and they agree with science and other studies.'"

Here is a sad story of a broken-hearted sister. She further tells her troubles, "We had but one boy, and from the start we were too lenient. After we sent him to school we looked after his welfare morally as long as he went to the home and high-school, but after we sent him away to college, we never concerned ourselves about him until he returned home. Then it was too late."

I asked the question, "Why did you not send him to the Brethren's schools?" "We thought they were a little more expensive and so far away, but had we known this, we should never, never have sent him there. Now, Bro. Miller, will you not do all you can to turn him away from those infidel ideas?"

Here was a sad family, all because they did not look to the interest of the soul as well as the body. It was not education that made an infidel out of this young man but he was sent to the wrong school. This brother and sister owned a nice farm but would gladly have given up all, if they could have saved their son. Parents, look well to the interest of your children, and do not get the idea that you can save a few dollars by sending your children to some school not conducted by the Brethren.

The Gospel Messenger,

A Weekly at $1.50 Per Annum.

PUBLISHED BY

The Brethren's Publishing Co.

D. L. MILLER,	. . . . .	Editor.
J. H. MOORE,	. . . . .	Office Editor.
J. B. BRUMBAUGH,	. . . .	Associate Editors.
J. G. ROYER,		
JOSEPH AMICK,	. . . . .	Business Manager.

ADVISORY COMMITTEE.
L. W. Teeter, A. Hutchison, Daniel Hays.

☞ Communications for publication should be legibly written with black ink on one side of the paper only. Do not attempt to interline, or to put on one page what ought to occupy two.

☞ Anonymous communications will not be published.

☞ Do not mix business with articles for publication. Keep your communications on separate sheets from all business.

☞ Time is precious. We always have time to attend to business and to answer questions of importance, but please do not subject us to need less answering of letters.

☞ The MESSENGER is mailed each week to all subscribers. If the address is correctly entailed on our list, the paper must reach the person to whom it is addressed. If you do not get your paper, write us, giving particulars.

☞ When changing your address, please give your former as well as your future address in full, so as to avoid delay and misunderstanding.

☞ Always remit to the office from which you order your goods, no matter from where you receive them.

☞ Do not send personal checks or drafts on interior banks, unless you send with them 25 cents each, to pay for collection.

☞ Remittances should be made by Post-office Money Order, Drafts on New York, Philadelphia or Chicago, or Registered Letters, made payable and addressed to "Brethren's Publishing Co., Mount Morris, Ill.," or "Brethren's Publishing Co., Huntingdon, Pa."

☞ Entered at the Post-office at Mount Morris, Ill., as second-class matter.

Mount Morris, Ill., - - - - Oct. 11, 1892.

BRO. C. HOPE, we learn, is now engaged in a series of meetings near Warrensburgh, Mo.

BRO. C. C. ROOT is now booked for a series of meetings at the Kansas Centre church, Rice County, Kansas, to commence Oct. 1.

THE home ministers are conducting an interesting series of meetings at Libertyville, Iowa. Six have already made the good confession and united with the church.

BRO. SOLOMON BUCKLEW recently held a glorious meeting in the Oakland church, Illinois. The services were largely attended, and thirteen united with the church by confession and baptism.

THE Middle District of Iowa is preparing to put an evangelist in the field. That is right. Every District ought to keep an evangelist employed on the outskirts. There is room and work for hundreds.

IN this issue Bro. A. Flory gives our Sunday-school workers a lesson that will be well for them to heed. The suggestion offered will apply with special force to parents who are careless concerning the reading matter they furnish to their families.

WE are so greatly pressed with work at this time that we must ask a little forbearance upon the part of those who expect personal replies to their communications. We would like to reply immediately to all the letters addressed to us, but cannot always find time to do so.

TWENTY years ago the Italians wrested the temporal power from the pope. His power is almost daily decreasing, and there is a possibility of him being deprived of still more privileges. Not many years ago it was hardly safe to own a Bible in Italy. All this change has been brought about by circulating the Scriptures among the people. It is an easy matter to see that the Bible makes no promises for a pope.

THE surplus left from the last Annual Meeting is $447.00,—not as much as was realized from some former meetings, but as much as could be expected under the circumstances. Taking everything into consideration, the amount thus secured for the Missionary and Tract Work is quite encouraging.

MAKE it a rule to send us reports of your meetings just as soon as they are over. Do not wait ten or twelve days before writing a report of your feast or series of meetings. If possible, write the news the very next day and let us have it early. We want fresh news and plenty of it in a condensed form.

THE Brethren have dedicated their new house near Kewanna, Ind. The attendance was very large and the interest excellent. Not only was the house dedicated, but three souls consecrated themselves to the Lord, and many saints renewed their vows around the Lord's table at the first love-feast held in that community.

BRO. M. M. SHERRICK, one of the young ministers at this place, not thinking it good to continue life's journey alone, has taken to himself a wife in the person of sister Minnie Mae Buck. We not only wish them much happiness, but trust that they will prove efficient workers in the vineyard of the Lord. They have decided to locate at Lanark, where Bro. Sherrick is much needed in the ministry.

LATE statistics show that we are by no means rid of the Mormon difficulty. At present they number over 66,000 and the church is rapidly increasing. It is strange indeed that a church should have such an unholy origin, with a terrible record of crimes, and yet find adherents to a doctrine not only contrary to reason, but decidedly immoral and degrading in its tendency. But such is the case and the end is not yet reached.

THE feast at Franklin Grove was held last Tuesday evening. It was one of the most orderly meetings we ever attended. About 250 communed. The house is very large, yet every part of it was well filled. It is indeed a pleasure to attend a feast among these Brethren. The members are not only firmly rooted and grounded in the truth, but they seem to exercise as much judgment in the handling of their religious matters as they do in their secular affairs, which in this case means a good deal.

WE are asked to say what ought to be done with a minister among our people, who in council-meeting will defend members who have united with secret societies, saying that as the secret order is religious, there is certainly some good in it. Our Brethren have long held that it is unscriptural as well as unwise, for any of our members to unite with a secret organization, and ministers who openly oppose the church in this respect, show a disregard for the rules of the church, and, in our estimation, should be called to account. Paul instructed Timothy to commit the Word to none but faithful men, who shall be able to teach others also. 2 Tim. 2:2. A minister who defends secret societies, and justifies members who unite with them, has most assuredly betrayed his trust and proved himself as unfaithful in the teaching of the Word, which condemns every religious organization that is not Christian in its nature and management. The tendency of all secret organizations is to bleed the church of Christ, and take her means as well as her members, and use them for a purpose foreign to that intended by the founders of the Christian church, and any man, be he minister or layman, who encourages such work, is no friend to the principles held by the Brethren.

BRO. I. J. ROSENBERGER has just closed his meetings at Lanark. It is said to be one of the most soul-cheering series of meetings held in that place for many years. The attendance was large and the interest excellent. Nine so far have come out on the Lord's side.

IT is now too late to send in matter for the Almanac, as the work has already gone to press and will be ready for filling orders in a very short time. We think it will be greatly appreciated by our people, as it contains an unusual amount of interesting and valuable reading matter. We are now prepared to book orders. Price, 10 cents. Agents will please send for special terms. We hope that efforts will be made to place a copy in each family in the Brotherhood.

BRO. DANIEL VANIMAN, who has been spending some months among the churches in the East, is with us, attending the meeting of the General Mission Board. He has many interesting things to relate concerning his trip, and feels encouraged with the work in which he is engaged. He also spent last Lord's Day with the Brethren in Chicago, and is deeply impressed with the importance of the cause in that thriving city. He goes from here to his home at McPherson, Kans.

THE love-feast at West Branch, last Saturday evening, was one of those heavenly places in Christ Jesus so much appreciated by the children of God. It was the largest feast we ever saw at that place. Every available part of the large house was well filled, and the very best of order prevailed. There were members present from nearly every congregation in Northern Illinois, and among them about twenty-five ministers. Bro. Henry Frantz officiated. He had been with the church here one week, holding a most interesting series of meetings, and we must say that we never saw things in a better shape for a feast. Twelve have already been baptized, with prospects of more to follow.

IT is high time for our Brethren to guard carefully against some mistakes that too often occur in connection with protracted meetings. At least one-half of these meetings close too soon. About the time the work gets under good headway, the preacher must go to another place to commence another series of meetings, to meet with the same fate. Thus the work goes on the season through, much commenced, but very little finished. Now, it would be far better to hold fewer meetings and do thorough work. When an evangelist commences a series of meetings, let it be understood that his time is unlimited; he will then be permitted to continue his efforts as long as there are prospects of doing good. Let churches as well as the ministers keep this in mind, this season, and see if more cannot be accomplished.

WE must not so far forget the old Gospel landmarks as to undertake to eat the Lord's Supper at dinner time in the middle of the day, nor should we go to the other extreme and get into the habit of making an unusually late meal of it. The Lord's Supper should be eaten about supper time. This, by common consent, is near six o'clock in the evening. In order to carry out the letter of the Gospel, it is not necessary to have the supper any later than that hour. If this rule were carefully followed, we would have better order at our feasts, for they would close just about dark, or before the unruly spectators generally assemble. Congregations, that have adopted this method, find that they are permitted to conduct the love-feast services in a more orderly manner. We trust that the churches generally will give it due consideration.

The Gospel Messenger,

A Weekly at $1.50 Per Annum.

PUBLISHED BY

The Brethren's Publishing Co.

D. L. MILLER,	Editor.
J. H. MOORE,	Office Editor.
J. B. BRUMBAUGH,	
J. G. ROYER,	Associate Editors.
JOSEPH AMICK,	Business Manager.

ADVISORY COMMITTEE.

L. W. Teeter, A. Hutchison, Daniel Hays.

☞ Communications for publication should be legibly written with black ink on one side of the paper only. Do not attempt to interline, or to put on one page what ought to occupy two.

☞ Anonymous communications will not be published.

☞ Do not mix business with articles for publication. Keep your communications on separate sheets from all business.

☞ Time is precious. We always have time to attend to business and to answer questions of importance, but please do not subject us to read less answering of letters.

☞ The MESSENGER is mailed each week to all subscribers. If the address is correctly entered on our list, the paper must reach the person to whom it is addressed. If you do not get your paper, write us, giving particulars.

☞ When changing your address, please give your former as well as your future address in full, so as to avoid delay and misunderstanding.

☞ Always remit to the office from which you order your goods, no matter from whom you receive them.

☞ Do not send personal checks or drafts on interior banks, unless you send with them 25 cents each, to pay for collection.

☞ Remittances should be made by Post-office Money Order, Drafts on New York, Philadelphia or Chicago, or Registered Letters, made payable and addressed to "Brethren's Publishing Co., Mount Morris, Ill.," or "Brethren's Publishing Co., Huntingdon, Pa."

☞ Entered at the Post-office at Mount Morris, Ill., as second-class matter.

Mount Morris, Ill.,   · · · ·   Oct. 11, 1892.

BRO. C. HOPE, we learn, is now engaged in a series of meetings near Warrensburgh, Mo.

BRO. C. C. ROOT is now booked for a series of meetings at the Kansas Centre church, Rice County, Kansas, to commence Oct. 1.

THE home ministers are conducting an interesting series of meetings at Libertyville, Iowa. Six have already made the good confession and united with the church.

BRO. SOLOMON BUCKLEW recently held a glorious meeting in the Oakland church, Illinois. The services were largely attended, and thirteen united with the church by confession and baptism.

THE Middle District of Iowa is preparing to put an evangelist in the field. That is right. Every District ought to keep an evangelist employed on the outskirts. There is room and work for hundreds.

IN this issue Bro. A. Flory gives our Sunday-school workers a lesson that will be well for them to heed. The suggestion offered will apply with special force to parents who are careless concerning the reading matter they furnish to their families.

WE are so greatly pressed with work at this time that we must ask a little forbearance upon the part of those who expect personal replies to their communications. We would like to reply immediately to all the letters addressed to us, but cannot always find time to do so.

TWENTY years ago the Italians wrested the temporal power from the pope. His power is almost daily decreasing, and there is a possibility of him being deprived of still more privileges. Not many years ago it was hardly safe to own a Bible in Italy. All this change has been brought about by circulating the Scriptures among the people. It is an easy matter to see that the Bible makes no promises for a pope.

THE surplus left from the last Annual Meeting is $447.00,—not as much as was realized from some former meetings, but as much as could be expected under the circumstances. Taking everything into consideration, the amount thus secured for the Missionary and Tract Work is quite encouraging.

MAKE it a rule to send us reports of your meetings just as soon as they are over. Do not wait ten or twelve days before writing a report of your feast or series of meetings. If possible, write the news the very next day and let us have it early. We want fresh news and plenty of it in a condensed form.

THE Brethren have dedicated their new house near Kewanna, Ind. The attendance was very large and the interest excellent. Not only was the house dedicated, but three souls consecrated themselves to the Lord, and many saints renewed their vows around the Lord's table at the first love-feast held in that community.

BRO. M. M. SHERRICK, one of the young ministers at this place, not thinking it good to continue life's journey alone, has taken to himself a wife in the person of sister Minnie Mae Buck. We not only wish them much happiness, but trust that they will prove efficient workers in the vineyard of the Lord. They have decided to locate at Lanark, where Bro. Sherrick is much needed in the ministry.

LATE statistics show that we are by no means rid of the Mormon difficulty. At present they number over 66,000 and the church is rapidly increasing. It is strange indeed that a church should have such an unholy origin, with a terrible record of crimes, and yet find adherents to a doctrine not only contrary to reason, but decidedly immoral and degrading in its tendency. But such is the case and the end is not yet reached.

THE feast at Franklin Grove was held last Tuesday evening. It was one of the most orderly meetings we ever attended. About 250 communed. The house is very large, yet every part of it was well filled. It is indeed a pleasure to attend a feast among these Brethren. The members are not only firmly rooted and grounded in the truth, but they seem to exercise as much judgment in the handling of their religious matters as they do in their secular affairs, which in this case means a good deal.

WE are asked to say what ought to be done with a minister among our people, who in council-meeting will defend members who have united with secret societies, saying that as the secret order is religious, there is certainly some good in it. Our Brethren have long held that it is unscriptural as well as unwise, for any of our members to unite with a secret organization, and ministers who openly oppose the church in this respect, show a disregard for the rules of the church, and, in our estimation, should be called to account. Paul instructed Timothy to commit the Word to none but faithful men, who shall be able to teach others also. 2 Tim. 2:2. A minister who defends secret societies, and justifies members who unite with them, has most assuredly betrayed his trust and proved himself as unfaithful in the teaching of the Word, which condemns every religious organization that is not Christian in its nature and management. The tendency of all secret organizations is to bleed the church of Christ, and take her means as well as her members, and use them for a purpose foreign to that intended by the founders of the Christian church, and any man, be he minister or layman, who encourages such work, is no friend to the principles held by the Brethren.

BRO. I. J. ROSENBERGER has just closed his meetings at Lanark. It is said to be one of the most soul-cheering series of meetings held in that place for many years. The attendance was large and the interest excellent. Nine so far have come out on the Lord's side.

IT is now too late to send in matter for the Almanac, as the work has already gone to press and will be ready for filling orders in a very short time. We think it will be greatly appreciated by our people, as it contains an unusual amount of interesting and valuable reading matter. We are now prepared to book orders. Price, 10 cents. Agents will please send for special terms. We hope that efforts will be made to place a copy in each family in the Brotherhood.

BRO. DANIEL VANIMAN, who has been spending some months among the churches in the East, is with us, attending the meeting of the General Mission Board. He has many interesting things to relate concerning his trip, and feels encouraged with the work in which he is engaged. He also spent last Lord's Day with the Brethren in Chicago, and is deeply impressed with the importance of the cause in that thriving city. He goes from here to his home at McPherson, Kans.

THE love-feast at West Branch, last Saturday evening, was one of those heavenly places in Christ Jesus so much appreciated by the children of God. It was the largest feast we ever saw at that place. Every available part of the large house was well filled, and the very best of order prevailed. There were members present from nearly every congregation in Northern Illinois, and among them about twenty-five ministers. Bro. Henry Frantz officiated. He had been with the church here one week, holding a most interesting series of meetings, and we must say that we never saw things in a better shape for a feast. Twelve have already been baptized, with prospects of more to follow.

IT is high time for our Brethren to guard carefully against some mistakes that too often occur in connection with protracted meetings. At least one-half of these meetings close too soon. About the time the work gets under good headway, the preacher must go to another place to commence another series of meetings, to meet with the same fate. Thus the work goes on the season through, much commenced, but very little finished. Now, it would be far better to hold fewer meetings and do thorough work. When an evangelist commences a series of meetings, let it be understood that his time is unlimited; he will then be permitted to continue his efforts as long as there are prospects of doing good. Let churches as well as the ministers keep this in mind, this season, and see if more cannot be accomplished.

WE should not so far forget the old Gospel landmarks as to undertake to eat the Lord's Supper at dinner time in the middle of the day, nor should we go to the other extreme and get into the habit of making an unusually late meal of it. The Lord's Supper should be eaten about supper time. This, by common consent, is near six o'clock in the evening. In order to carry out the letter of the Gospel, it is not necessary to have the supper any later than that hour. If this rule were carefully followed, we would have better order at our feasts, for they would close just about dark, or before the unruly spectators generally assemble. Congregations, that have adopted this method, find that they are permitted to conduct the love-feast services in a more orderly manner. We trust that the churches generally will give it due consideration.

QUERISTS' DEPARTMENT.

"WHILE I was with them in the world, I kept them in thy name: those that thou gavest me I have kept and none of them is lost, but the son of perdition; that the Scripture might be fulfilled." John 17: 12 From what was Judas lost?
JOHN SNAVELY, Sen.

JUDAS lost just what every unconverted sinner must lose, viz, salvation in heaven. All the other apostles were saved, hence made their apostleship a success. Judas made an absolute failure, though he enjoyed the same privileges as the rest. His conversion, at any period in his life, may be doubted, for he was a devil (John 6: 70), and that probably from the beginning. When he selected Judas, Jesus knew that he was an unbeliever and that he would remain such, and finally betray him. (John 6: 64) He was, however, granted the same favors that the other apostles enjoyed. He heard the preaching of Jesus, saw his many miracles and was exposed to all the good influences of the Gospel, yet his heart grew only the harder and resulted in the loss of the crown, promised to all the faithful.

Will you please explain Lev. 14: 33-53? Can the leprosy be in a house and in the walls to-day, as mentioned in the above verses? L. B. WATSON.

Too many verses are mentioned to admit of being quoted in full. The reader will please turn to and read them. By the term leprosy, reference is probably made to a species of fungus, called dry rot, very common in houses in warm climates. When once established in a building it spreads with great rapidity, and often demolishes the most solid houses in a few years. Houses constructed of wood and mud were much exposed to its ravages. It often appeared on the stones. As houses in those days were sometimes constructed of rough stones, somewhat like common stone fences, without the use of mortar, stones could be removed from the walls and replaced by others, or the entire walls built be plastered over so as to cover the fungus growth. This growth is still found in some warm climates, and requires similar vigorous methods to remove or destroy it. The tendency of it may possibly be to produce disease, hence the necessity of persistent efforts to destroy it.

What is the extent of sin or evil, that would disqualify a member to go to the Communion table? Is it absolutely necessary to be in peace with all the members? N. B.

Any sin or evil unrepented of will disqualify a member for engaging in the Communion service. It is absolutely necessary for him to be at peace with all the members, so far as it lieth in his power to do so. Especially should he be in peace with the members of his own home congregation. Let a man examine himself. If there is anything wrong, let him bring himself into judgment, condemn the wrong, repent of his errors, and so let him eat. If, on approaching the table, he remembers that his brother has aught against him, let him first go and be reconciled to his brother. No man should approach the Lord's table which he is not in peace with God and his brethren.

If A. and B. go into a saloon together, is it consistent or in harmony with the Gospel, or the rules of the church, for A. to have B. brought before the church? What is the nature of the offense? H. P. CALLANDER.

A. should first repent of his own wrongdoing, make a humble confession of his fault and receive the forgiveness of the church. Then he should privately plead with B., urging him to do likewise. If he refuses to make a voluntary confession, then A. is at liberty to have him cited to the church council. This is in harmony with the Scripture, requiring one to remove the beam from his own eye before attempting to pick the mote out of his brother's eye. The offense is clearly a public one, and should be dealt with in the manner suggested.
J. H. M.

LETTER AND SPIRIT IN FEET-WASHING.

WILL you please give an explanation of the original for "towel?" The Savior girded himself with a towel. Why do the Brethren use an apron instead of a towel? Would not the towel be closer to the letter? Also why use a tub instead of a basin? J. H.

THE term towel is from the Greek *lention*, which Donnegan, in his Greek Lexicon defines, "A linen cloth, a towel." The meaning of the letter is fully met by the use of a cloth in any convenient form, especially that of an apron. The apron is probably preferable. The basin,—*neptee* in Greek,—was "a vessel for washing the hands or feet in." That is what a small tub is used for, hence the use of it also meets the demands of the letter. However, we must not give so much attention to the letter as to neglect the spirit. There is danger of doing that when we insist too strongly on the towel or basin without pausing to consider the application of the terms.

Our people have studied the letter of feet-washing until they have a most thorough knowledge of both the precept and the example. It is now advisable that we give the spirit special consideration, especially in our preaching on love-feast occasions. The virtue of feet-washing is in the spirit, for that maketh alive. One may have the letter in his practice and yet not the spirit. The tendency of that course is to kill. But one cannot have the spirit to profit without the letter. Having conformed to the letter in all points demanded by the law, we feast upon the spirit as one may feast upon well-prepared food. The more the mind thus dwells upon the spiritual import of the sacred institution, the greater the spiritual growth. Jesus says, "If ye know these things, happy are ye if ye do them." The term *know*, in this instance, means the closest possible union and relation; so close that our spirits attain to a oneness with the spiritual character of the service. Our spirits must become completely absorbed by the spirit that pervades the occasion.

On these occasions we are too greatly inclined to let our minds run too much in the direction of the letter, and often look to a certain point in the letter for the spirit, where Christ probably never intended us to look. For our part, we can see no spiritual import in the kind of towel or basin, but we do see a deep spiritual meaning in the humble act of washing and wiping one another's feet. It is at this point that we may look for the spirit with profit. So let us learn to engage in this solemn service with the spirit, and the understanding also. The field for spiritual development, in connection with this as well as all other ordinances, is probably unlimited. J. H. M.

THE PREACHER'S DREAM.

IT is related in an exchange that a preacher once dreamed that his church was a stage-coach at the foot of a hill, up which, in the absence of horse power, it fell to his lot to drag it. Some of his officers and members bade him be of good cheer, for they would all help. He should guide the tongue, some of them would turn the wheels, others push, and so, together, they should get it up the hill. For awhile the heavy coach moved slowly, but surely, up. After a time, however, its weight seemed to increase, till the preacher bringing the vehicle to a stand on the first ridge, and turning the tongue to prevent its slipping down, ran to see what was the matter. All the helpers, tired of turning wheels and pushing, had jumped into the coach and were sitting inside! It was nice, thought they, to ride while the preacher did all the pulling.

In how many churches to-day are the preachers doing all the hard work while the members take things easy! Will each member pause to think just how much he is doing; and what would become of the church if others did no more pulling! No one can afford to ride when there is such a great up-hill work. On a down-grade it is an easy matter for everybody to get in and ride to destruction. Do not let the preachers do the pulling and all the members go free. There is a work for everyone.

BY degrees the old Bible Lands are yielding up their immense treasures of information, hid for thousands of years. "Forty more rooms are being prepared in the great Gizeh Museum for the reception of the immense number of Egyptian antiquities, which are being unearthed. By November, there will be eighty rooms crowded with these relics of a long-gone past. There are now being brought to the museum thirteen large stone slabs, belonging to the ancient times of the Fifth and Sixth Dynasties. Some of these stones weigh twenty-one tons, and are closely covered with delicate carvings. Excavations are also being made at the site of the celebrated ancient temple of Memphis, from which wonderful discoveries are expected. These researches have for Christendom a double interest, as being curiosities in themselves, and as bearing testimony for or against the accuracy of the Old Testament narratives."

CORRESPONDENCE.

"Write what thou seest, and send it unto the churches."

[Church News solicited for this Department. If you have had a good meeting, send a report of it, so that others may rejoice with you. In writing give name of church, County and State. Be brief. Notes of Travel should be as short as possible. Land Advertisements are not solicited for this Department. We have an advertising page, and, if necessary, will issue supplements.]

From the Round Mountain Church, Ark.

AFTER the Annual Meeting Eld. Z Henricks, of South-western Kansas, stopped with us on his return, and preached some for us. Bro. Henricks and I went out into Madison County, a distance of thirty miles, where we held several meetings. A few members are living at that point. About a month later, Bro. Krouse, one of our deacons, and I, went to Boston Mountain, thirty miles away, where there is a small organized church, which was placed under my charge by last District Meeting. I held some meetings for them, and also held a council, in order to get them into working order. We also stopped at Brentwood, on our way going and coming, and held two meetings. Brother and sister Watts live there. After this we had over a week's work to do on our church-house in the way of ceiling and making benches, which we did before our Communion, Sept. 3. We now have our house ceiled and some benches made, and we are very thankful to those who assisted us to purchase the lumber.

Elders George Barnhart and Samuel Click came to us Sept. 1, and preached for us. Sept. 3 we had our Communion. We had a very good meeting and an enjoyable feast.

QUERISTS' DEPARTMENT.

"WHILE I was with them in the world, I kept them in thy name: those that thou gavest me I have kept and none of them is lost, but the son of perdition; that the Scripture might be fulfilled." John 17:12   From what was Judas lost?
                                                    JOHN SNAVELY, Sen.

JUDAS lost just what every unconverted sinner must lose, viz, salvation in heaven. All the other apostles were saved, hence made their apostleship a success. Judas made an absolute failure, though he enjoyed the same privileges as the rest. His conversion, at any period in his life, may be doubted, for he was a devil (John 6: 70), and that probably from the beginning. When he selected Judas, Jesus knew that he was an unbeliever and that he would remain such, and finally betray him. (John 6: 64) He was, however, granted the same favors that the other apostles enjoyed. He heard the preaching of Jesus, saw his many miracles and was exposed to all the good influences of the Gospel, yet his heart grew only the harder and resulted in the loss of the crown, promised to all the faithful.

Will you please explain Lev. 14:33-57? Can the leprosy be in a house and in the walls to day, as mentioned in the above verses?   L. B. WATSON.

Too many verses are mentioned to admit of being quoted in full. The reader will please turn to and read them. By the term leprosy, reference is probably made to a species of fungus, called dry rot, very common in houses in warm climates. When once established in a building it spreads with great rapidity, and often demolishes the most solid houses in a few years. Houses constructed of wood and mud were much exposed to its ravages. It often appeared on the stones. As houses in those days were sometimes constructed of rough stones, somewhat like common stone fences, without the use of mortar, stones could be removed from the walls and replaced by others, or the entire walls might be plastered over so as to cover the fungus growth. This growth is still found in some warm climates, and requires similar vigorous methods to remove or destroy it. The tendency of it may possibly be to produce disease, hence the necessity of persistent efforts to destroy it.

What is the extent of sin or evil, that would disqualify a member to go to the Communion table? Is it absolutely necessary to be in peace with all the members?   N. B.

Any sin or evil unrepented of would disqualify a member for engaging in the Communion service. It is absolutely necessary for him to be at peace with all the members, so far as it lieth in his power to do so. Especially should he be in peace with the members of his own home congregation. Let a man examine himself. If there is anything wrong, let him bring himself into judgment, condemn the wrong, repent of his errors, and so let him eat. If, on approaching the table, he remembers that his brother has aught against him, let him first go and be reconciled to his brother. No man should approach the Lord's table when he is not in peace with God and his brethren.

If A. and B. go into a saloon together, is it consistent or in harmony with the Gospel, or the rules of the church, for A. to have B. brought before the church? What is the nature of the offense?   H. P. CALLANDER.

A. should first repent of his own wrongdoing, make a humble confession of his fault and receive the forgiveness of the church. Then he should privately plead with B., urging him to do likewise. If he refuses to make a voluntary confession, then A. is at liberty to have him cited to the church council. This is in harmony with the Scripture,

requiring one to remove the beam from his own eye before attempting to pick the mote out of his brother's eye. The offense is clearly a public one, and should be dealt with in the manner suggested.
                                                    J. H M.

LETTER AND SPIRIT IN FEET-WASHING.

WILL you please give an explanation of the original for "towel?" The Savior girded himself with a towel. Why do the Brethren use an apron instead of a towel? Would not the towel be closer to the letter? Also why use a tub instead of a basin?   J. H.

THE term towel is from the Greek lention, which Donnegan, in his Greek Lexicon defines, "A linen cloth, a towel." The meaning of the letter is fully met by the use of a cloth in any convenient form, especially that of an apron. The apron is probably preferable. The basin,—neptee in Greek,—was "a vessel for washing the hands or feet in." That is what a small tub is used for, hence the use of it also meets the demands of the letter. However, we must not give so much attention to the letter as to neglect the spirit. There is danger of doing that when we insist too strongly on the towel or basin without pausing to consider the application of the terms.

Our people have studied the letter of feet-washing until they have a most thorough knowledge of both the precept and the example. It is now advisable that we give the spirit special consideration, especially in our preaching on love-feast occasions. The virtue of feet-washing is in the spirit, for that maketh alive. One may have the letter in his practice and yet not the spirit. The tendency of that course is to kill. But one cannot have the spirit to profit without the letter. Having conformed to the letter in all points demanded by the law, we feast upon the spirit as one may feast upon well-prepared food. The more the mind thus dwells upon the spiritual import of the sacred institution, the greater the spiritual growth. Jesus says, "If ye know these things, happy are ye if ye do them." The term know, in this instance, means the closest possible union and relation; so close that our spirits attain to a oneness with the spiritual character of the service. Our spirits must become completely absorbed by the spirit that pervades the occasion.

On these occasions we are too greatly inclined to let our minds run too much in the direction of the letter, and often look to a certain point in the letter for the spirit, where Christ probably never intended us to look. For our part, we can see no spiritual import in the kind of towel or basin, but we do see a deep spiritual meaning in the humble act of washing and wiping one another's feet. It is at this point that we may look for the spirit with profit. So let us learn to engage in this solemn service with the spirit, and the understanding also. The field for spiritual development, in connection with this as well as all other ordinances, is probably unlimited.   J. H. M.

THE PREACHER'S DREAM.

IT is related in an exchange that a preacher once dreamed that his church was a stage-coach at the foot of a hill, up which, in the absence of horse power, it fell to his lot to drag it. Some of his officers and members bade him be of good cheer, for they would all help. He should guide the tongue, some of them would turn the wheels, others push, and so, together, they should get it up the hill. For awhile the heavy coach moved

slowly, but surely, up. After a time, however, its weight seemed to increase, till the preacher bringing the vehicle to a stand on the first ridge, and turning the tongue to prevent its slipping down, ran to see what was the matter. All the helpers, tired of turning wheels and pushing, had jumped into the coach and were sitting inside! It was nice, thought they, to ride while the preacher did all the pulling.

In how many churches to-day are the preachers doing all the hard work while the members take things easy! Will each member pause to think just how much he is doing; and what would become of the church if others did no more pulling! No one can afford to ride when there is such a great up-hill work. On a down-grade it is an easy matter for everybody to get in and ride to destruction. Do not let the preachers do the pulling and all the members go free. There is a work for everyone.

By degrees the old Bible Lands are yielding up their immense treasures of information, hid for thousands of years. "Forty more rooms are being prepared in the great Gizeh Museum for the reception of the immense number of Egyptian antiquities, which are being unearthed. By November, there will be eighty rooms crowded with these relics of a long-gone past. There are now being brought to the museum thirteen large stone slabs, belonging to the ancient times of the Fifth and Sixth Dynasties. Some of these stones weigh twenty-one tons, and are closely covered with delicate carvings. Excavations are also being made at the site of the celebrated ancient temple of Memphis, from which wonderful discoveries are expected. These researches have for Christendom a double interest, as being curiosities in themselves, and as bearing testimony for or against the accuracy of the Old Testament narratives."

CORRESPONDENCE.

"Write what thou seest, and send it unto the churches."

☞ Church News solicited for this Department. If you have had a good meeting, send a report of it, so that others may rejoice with you. In writing give name of church, County and State. Be brief. Notes of Travel should be as short as possible. Land Advertisements are not enlisted for this Department. We have an advertising page, and, if necessary, will issue supplements.

From the Round Mountain Church, Ark.

AFTER the Annual Meeting Eld. Z Henricks, of South-western Kansas, stopped with us on his return, and preached some for us. Bro. Henricks and I went out into Madison County, a distance of thirty miles, where we held several meetings. A few members are living at that point. About a month later, Bro. Krouse, one of our deacons, and I, went to Boston Mountain, thirty miles away, where there is a small organized church, which was placed under my charge by last District Meeting. I held some meetings for them, and also held a council, in order to get them into working order. We also stopped at Brentwood, on our way going and coming, and held two meetings. Brother and sister Watts live there. After this we had over a week's work to do on our church-house in the way of ceiling and making benches, which we did before our Communion, Sept. 3. We now have our house ceiled and some benches made, and we are very thankful to those who assisted us to purchase the lumber.

Elders George Barnhart and Samuel Click came to us Sept. 1, and preached for us. Sept. 3 we had our Communion. We had a very good meeting and an enjoyable feast.

active elder but is now old and infirm, waiting and anxious to pass over and rest from his labors. Others who were in the strength and vigor of life, are now on the shady side of life. Bro. S. H. Miller and Wm. Ikenberry have charge, with other active helpers in the ministry.

I had the pleasure of attending a church-meeting and noticed that the sentiment of co-operation with the general Brotherhood was strongly developed. They are active in District work also. The field of Northern Iowa is large, extending into Minnesota. We had a fine meeting and then I left for Hudson, an out-lying part of the congregation, where I spent the second Sunday. After that I took the train to Waterloo. Next morning, after spending the night with Bro. Jonas Lichty, who has charge of the Waterloo congregation, I continued on to Garrison, Benton County, to attend their feast and also the District Meeting of Middle Iowa. The feast was held Sept. 21, and the District Meeting next day. I spent the night with Bro. Peter Forney, who is not enjoying good health, and contemplates a trip to the Pacific Coast and Arizona, if the Lord will.

On arriving at the place of worship I found a fair representation. We had an enjoyable feast and had the privilege, after services, of leading two young sisters into the liquid stream, to follow the example of the Blessed Savior. Next morning another one was baptized by Bro. Hipes, and in the evening, after a sermon by Bro. Hipes, two more sisters arose and expressed a desire for newness of life with the people of God.

The work of District Meeting was next proceeded with. After a few queries the District Mission Work was taken up. Bro. R. F. McCune was Moderator; Bro. Seibert, Reading Clerk, and Bro. Taylor, Writing Clerk. Business passed off pleasantly and much interest was manifested in the work, and provision was made for more successfully carrying forward the work in Middle Iowa. The report of the committee of last Annual Meeting was submitted and accepted. The surplus was ordered turned over to the General Mission fund. Bro. R. F. McCune was selected to represent the District on the Standing Committee at the next Annual Meeting. J. C. LAHMAN.

Echoes from Cedar County, Iowa.

OUR feast, held Sept 24 and 25, was a refreshing season of grace. Ministers with us were brethren J. C. Seibert, H. R. Taylor, and David Miller, who dealt out the Bread of eternal life to all present. We pray God's blessing upon them for their labors of love! One was received into the church by baptism and two by letter. This encouraged us to labor on in the furtherance of the Master's cause. We are glad to announce also that Bro. J. E. Keller, of Hope, Kans., has located with us and will move here in the spring to help bear forward the ark of the Lord. Others are contemplating coming to Cedar County. That is right, brethren, come and pitch your tents with us, and we will try to do you good. Eternity alone will tell how much good you may do us. This is a goodly land in which to dwell, and still there is room. We shall be glad to furnish information on application. Write us.

Eld. J. C. Murray, of Indiana, spent a few weeks with us during the early part of September, delivering a number of his most excellent, soul-cheering sermons. Although there were no accessions, Bro. Murray made some warm friends, and left many deep impressions which, we hope, will bear fruit to the saving of some precious souls here, who are near the kingdom. A few were almost persuaded to be Christians. We pray the Father to still draw them nearer to Je-

sus. Saints are praying, angels are watching. The hosts of sin are pressing hard, but thanks be to God, who giveth us the victory through our Lord Jesus Christ! JOHN ZOOK.
Clarence, Iowa.

District Meeting Notes.

WE attended the feast at Garrison, which was held the day previous to our District Meeting. It was a feast indeed. Eld. Joseph Lahman, of Mt. Morris, was present. The District Meeting was harmonious and the spirit of the Lord was manifested. Eld. Frank McCune was Moderator of the Meeting, and will also represent Middle Iowa on Standing Committee at our next Annual Meeting in Indiana.

A committee was appointed to incorporate the church of Middle Iowa.

The Home Mission work received a strong push forward. God bless the work!

Five were received by baptism at Garrison at these meetings. The Committee of Arrangements of last Annual Meeting made their final report and were released. They report a balance of over $100 in their hands for the General Mission Work.

We expect soon to have District evangelists in Middle Iowa.

We contemplate holding a Ministerial Meeting near Marshalltown, Iowa, in the near future. JOHN ZOOK.

From Denver, Colorado.

THE first series of meetings, ever held here by the Brethren, commenced on the evening of Sept. 16, at 8 P. M., and closed on the evening of the 23rd. At 10 A. M., Sept. 23, the ordinance of baptism was administered near Bro G. W. Long's residence to John Acroyd, formerly of Bristol, England. This baptism is the first in the City, but we have good reasons to believe that, had the meetings been continued for a fortnight, there would have been others, as there was much interest manifested, and some are near the kingdom.

Bro. J. S. Mohler did all the preaching except on Sunday night, when Bro. H. R. Taylor, of Iowa, preached for us before starting home on the day following, after spending several weeks in different parts of the State for the benefit of his health. He expressed himself as being much benefited by the trip, and highly pleased with the country, and the treatment he received from the brethren and others.

Bro. Mohler labored earnestly in preaching and visiting from house to house. As he had promised the Brethren at Longmont to be there by the 24th, he had to leave here just as the work was beginning to manifest itself, and would, we believe, have resulted in much immediate good for the church and precious souls.

Brethren, you who travel, why do you not finish a work before you leave it? Remember, a gap in the wall may not be for the best.

Our Sunday-school is prospering, and we expect to re-organize to-morrow for the winter, as we desire to make it an evergreen Sunday-school. Experience has taught the writer that it takes a little more diligence and patient endurance to succeed. Bro. Long has the work at heart. He leaves the street car and invites the children along the way, to come to Sunday-school. He gives them good papers and lesson helps to read. With such energy the school will certainly succeed.

We acknowledge the receipt of another dollar from the young folks of the St. Vrain church, also one dollar from Bro. D. Leedy, of Hygiene.

Brethren Leedy and Shrove made the church visit to most of the members last Monday, but the members being so much scattered, they did not get to see all of them. Bro. Leedy having to return home that day, it fell to the lot of the writer to visit some. All were willing to continue in the faith, and to labor with and for the church.

Some of the members have been deprived of the privilege of assembling with the Brethren in public worship, so that, in compliance with a request from sister Lindsey, of 557 South Tenth Street, lately of Chicago, Ill., there will be prayer-meeting at her residence next Tuesday evening, the Lord willing.

After a long search (they having changed residence) we found our old brother and sister Ohmert in quite unfavorable circumstances. May the Lord move his children to a greater diligence in looking after the wants of the needy and infirm, and may we all work while it is called to-day, for the night cometh wherein no man can work! H. H. WINGER.
Sept. 24.

Death of Bro. Jacob W. Hawn.

BRO. JACOB W. HAWN was born in Frederick County, Md., Dec. 4, 1830, and died at his home in the Fairview congregation, Appanoose County, Iowa, Sept. 11, 1892, aged 61 years 9 months and 7 days. Sept. 5, 1892, the deceased was working at a pond with his team and scraper. While thus engaged he was accidentally hurt in some way, which he was never able to fully explain, on account of having so much misery. On Sunday, the day before the accident, he preached a very able sermon, and little did we think, as our dear brother stood before us, apparently in perfect health, that in one short week he would be taking that last long sleep.

We greatly feel our loss, as Bro. Hawn was one of our active ministers upon whom fell much of the ministerial work. He has been a valiant soldier for Jesus, for a number of years, and was never unwilling to defend God's truth.

Funeral services Sept. 12, by Bro. Martin Esplogie, assisted by Bro. Daniel Zook, from Rev. 20: 6, "Blessed and holy is he that hath part in the first resurrection; on such the second death hath no power, but they shall be priests of God and of Christ, and shall reign with him a thousand years." H. A. WHISLER.

Chips from the Work-house.

ANOTHER curious custom connected with funerals is, for male relatives of the deceased to sit in church during the entire services, prayer and all, with their hats on. One is made to wonder who ever started such a custom as that. Surely not the Apostle Paul, for he says, "Every man praying or prophesying with his head covered dishonoreth his Head." 1 Cor. 11: 4. But then, perhaps, these people, in order to be consistent, will just refuse to pray on funeral occasions. No explanation has ever, to my knowledge, been given; and no apology made for it. Since it is connected with funeral customs, it is presumably just followed, whether there be any reason or common sense in it or not.

Another curious fact is, that good preachers are like good books in a well-kept library,—they have their day on the first shelf, because much wanted, but unless much revised and kept even with true progress, they will soon find themselves on a higher shelf, because less wanted. There, if they persist in kicking and making a noise to annoy those who are now on the first shelf, they will all the sooner find themselves on the top shelf where they will be much left alone.

active elder but is now old and infirm, waiting and anxious to pass over and rest from his labors. Others who were in the strength and vigor of life, are now on the shady side of life. Bro. S. H. Miller and Wm. Ikenberry have charge, with other active helpers in the ministry.

I had the pleasure of attending a church-meeting and noticed that the sentiment of co-operation with the general Brotherhood was strongly developed. They are active in District work also. The field of Northern Iowa is large, extending into Minnesota. We had a fine meeting and then I left for Hudson, an out-lying part of the congregation, where I spent the second Sunday. After that I took the train to Waterloo. Next morning, after spending the night with Bro. Jonas Lichty, who has charge of the Waterloo congregation, I continued on to Garrison, Benton County, to attend their feast and also the District Meeting of Middle Iowa. The feast was held Sept. 21, and the District Meeting next day. I spent the night with Bro. Peter Forney, who is not enjoying good health, and contemplates a trip to the Pacific Coast and Arizona, if the Lord will.

On arriving at the place of worship I found a fair representation. We had an enjoyable feast and had the privilege, after services, of leading two young sisters into the liquid stream, to follow the example of the Blessed Savior. Next morning another one was baptized by Bro. Hipes, and in the evening, after a sermon by Bro. Hipes, two more sisters arose and expressed a desire for newness of life with the people of God.

The work of District Meeting was next proceeded with. After a few queries the District Mission Work was taken up. Bro. B. F. McCune was Moderator; Bro. Seibert, Reading Clerk, and Bro. Taylor, Writing Clerk. Business passed off pleasantly and much interest was manifested in the work, and provision was made for more successfully carrying forward the work in Middle Iowa. The report of the committee of last Annual Meeting was submitted and accepted. The surplus was ordered turned over to the General Mission fund. Bro. R. F. McCune was selected to represent the District on the Standing Committee at the next Annual Meeting   J. C. LAHMAN.

Echoes from Cedar County, Iowa.

OUR feast, held Sept 24 and 25, was a refreshing season of grace. Ministers with us were brethren J. C. Seibert, H. R. Taylor, and David Miller, who dealt out the Bread of eternal life to all present. We pray God's blessing upon them for their labors of love! One was received into the church by baptism and two by letter. This encouraged us to labor on in the furtherance of the Master's cause. We are glad to announce also that Bro. J. E. Keller, of Hope, Kans., has located with us and will move here in the spring to help bear forward the ark of the Lord. Others are contemplating coming to Cedar County. That is right, brethren, come and pitch your tents with us, and we will try to do you good. Eternity alone will tell how much good you may do us. This is a goodly land in which to dwell, and still there is room. We shall be glad to furnish information on application Write us.

Eld. J. C. Murray, of Indiana, spent a few weeks with us during the early part of September, delivering a number of his most excellent, soul-cheering sermons. Although there were no accessions, Bro. Murray made some warm friends, and left many deep impressions which, we hope, will bear fruit to the saving of some precious souls here, who are near the kingdom. A few were almost persuaded to be Christians. We pray the Father to still draw them nearer to Je-

sus. Saints are praying, angels are watching. The hosts of sin are pressing hard, but thanks be to God, who giveth us the victory through our Lord Jesus Christ!   JOHN ZUCK.
Clarence, Iowa.

District Meeting Notes.

WE attended the feast at Garrison, which was held the day previous to our District Meeting. It was a feast indeed. Eld. Joseph Lahman, of Mt. Morris, was present. The District Meeting was harmonious and the spirit of the Lord was manifested. Eld. Frank McCune was Moderator of the Meeting and will also represent Middle Iowa on Standing Committee at our next Annual Meeting in Indiana.

A committee was appointed to incorporate the church of Middle Iowa.

The Home Mission work received a strong push forward. God bless the work!

Five were received by baptism at Garrison at these meetings The Committee of Arrangements of last Annual Meeting made their final report and were released. They report a balance of over $100 in their hands for the General Mission Work.

We expect soon to have District evangelists in Middle Iowa.

We contemplate holding a Ministerial Meeting near Marshalltown, Iowa, in the near future.
                                        JOHN ZUCK.

From Denver, Colorado.

THE first series of meetings, ever held here by the Brethren, commenced on the evening of Sept 16, at 8 P. M., and closed on the evening of the 23rd. At 10 A. M., Sept. 23, the ordinance of baptism was administered near Bro G. W. Long's residence to John Acroyd, formerly of Bristol, England. This baptism is the first in the City, but we have good reasons to believe that, had the meetings been continued for a fortnight, there would have been others, as there was much interest manifested, and some are near the kingdom.

Bro. J. S. Mohler did all the preaching except on Sunday night, when Bro. H. R. Taylor, of Iowa, preached for us before starting home on the day following, after spending several weeks in different parts of the State for the benefit of his health. He expressed himself as being much benefited by the trip, and highly pleased with the country, and the treatment he received from the brethren and others.

Bro. Mohler labored earnestly in preaching and visiting from house to house. As he had promised the Brethren at Longmont to be there by the 24th, he had to leave here just as the work was beginning to manifest itself, and would, we believe, have resulted in much immediate good for the church and precious souls.

Brethren, you who travel, why do you not finish a work before you leave it? Remember, a gap in the wall may not be for the best.

Our Sunday-school is prospering, and we expect to re-organize to-morrow for the winter, as we desire to make it an evergreen Sunday-school. Experience has taught the writer that it takes a little more diligence and patient endurance to succeed. Bro. Long has the work at heart. He leaves the street car and invites the children along the way, to come to Sunday-school. He gives them good papers and lesson helps to read. With such energy the school will certainly succeed.

We acknowledge the receipt of another dollar from the young folks of the St. Vrain church; also one dollar from Bro. D. Leedy, of Hygiene.

Brethren Leedy and Shrove made the church visit to most of the members last Monday, but the members being so much scattered, they did not get to see all of them. Bro. Leedy having to return home that day, it fell to the lot of the writer, or to visit some. All were willing to continue in the faith, and to labor with and for the church.

Some of the members have been deprived of the privilege of assembling with the Brethren in public worship, so that, in compliance with a request from sister Lindsey, of 557 South Tenth Street, lately of Chicago, Ill., there will be prayer-meeting at her residence next Tuesday evening, the Lord willing.

After a long search (they having changed residence) we found our old brother and sister Obmert in quite unfavorable circumstances. May the Lord move his children to a greater diligence in looking after the wants of the needy and infirm, and may we all work while it is called to-day, for the night cometh wherein no man can work!   H. H. WINGER.
Sept. 24.

Death of Bro. Jacob W. Hawn.

BRO. JACOB W. HAWN was born in Frederick County, Md., Dec. 4, 1830, and died at his home in the Fairview congregation, Appanoose County, Iowa, Sept. 11, 1892, aged 61 years 9 months and 7 days. Sept. 5, 1892, the deceased was working at a pond with his team and scraper. While thus engaged he was accidentally hurt in some way, which he was never able to fully explain, on account of having so much misery. On Sunday, the day before the accident, he preached a very able sermon, and little did we think, as our dear brother stood before us, apparently in perfect health, that in one short week he would be taking that last long sleep.

We greatly feel our loss, as Bro. Hawn was one of our active ministers upon whom fell much of the ministerial work. He has been a valiant soldier for Jesus, for a number of years, and was never unwilling to defend God's truth.

Funeral services Sept. 12, by Bro. Martin Esplogle, assisted by Bro. Daniel Zock, from Rev. 20: 6, "Blessed and holy is he that hath part in the first resurrection; on such the second death hath no power, But they shall be priests of God and of Christ, and shall reign with him a thousand years."   H. A WHISLER.

Chips from the Work-house.

ANOTHER curious custom connected with funerals is, for male relatives of the deceased to sit in church during the entire services, prayer and all, with their hats on. One is made to wonder why ever started such a custom as that. Surely not the Apostle Paul, for he says, "Every man praying or prophesying with his head covered dishonoreth his Head." 1 Cor. 11: 4. But then, perhaps, these people, in order to be consistent, will just refuse to pray on funeral occasions No explanation has ever, to my knowledge, been given and no apology made for it. Since it is connected with funeral customs, it is presumably just followed, whether there be any reason or common sense in it or not.

Another curious fact is, that good preachers are like good books in a well-kept library,—they have their day on the first shelf, because much wanted, but unless much revised and kept even with true progress, they will soon find themselves on a higher shelf, because less wanted. There, if they persist in kicking and making a noise to annoy those who are now on the first shelf, they will all the sooner find themselves on the top shelf where they will be much left alone.

Johnstown, Pa.—Last Sunday, Sept. 18, after church services, another dear soul, a colored lady, decided to forsake sin and walk with the people of God. We give God the glory, and pray that more may follow!—*Sadie Brallier Noffsinger.*

Burlington, W. Va.—Last Sunday another brother was added to the fold in the Beaver Run congregation, and several weeks ago three others were baptized here, though they live just outside the borders of this congregation.—*Geo. S. Arnold.*

Cana, Va.—Bro. Thomas Reed preached three sermons for us last Saturday and Sunday, and buried two precious souls in the liquid stream, to walk in newness of life. We number thirty-three members now. By request of our elder, the time of holding our Communion was changed from the fifth Saturday in October to the third Saturday in October, 1892.—*Wm. Wisler, Sept. 21.*

Rogersville, Ind.—The Back Creek church, Ind., held their quarterly council-meeting Sept. 24. Two members were received by letter. Not much business came before the meeting, and all present seemed to enjoy the services very much. The day following was the day for our regular appointment. In the evening the young folks were addressed from 1 Cor. 9: 26, 27.—*D. E. Rhodes, Sept. 26.*

La Place, Ill.—Sept. 5 Bro. M. J. McClure commenced a series of doctrinal sermons in the Okaw church, which continued one week. We had a large attendance and good order. Bro. Martin did excellent work. The church was much built up. The doctrine of the Brethren is built upon the rock and will stand the storms. The meetings will be continued by Bro. Michael Flory.—*E. F. Wolfe.*

Muenster, Texas.—In my correspondence on page 590 of the MESSENGER, I meant to say the Mission Board "*could* locate a number of ministers." I referred to the Mission Board of Texas, Oklahoma, and Indian Territory,—*not* to the General Mission Board. I did NOT intend to imply that the Board would support the work, but that we would assist to find homes and places for ministers to work.—*A. W. Austin, Sec, Sept. 20.*

Jeffersonville, Ohio.—I am now at Jeffersonville, Fayette Co., Ohio, and alone on new ground. I find, too, that people seem afraid to attend our meetings although everything is favorable for coming, and no other meetings to interfere. But I work on in hope of a better day, for two members of the Baptist church tell me they are ready to go with us, and others are near the door. I look for Bro. Carter, of Frankfort, to meet me to-night or to-morrow.—*Landon West.*

Libertyville, Iowa.—Our love-feast is now in the past. We had a very enjoyable meeting, for which we feel like praising the Lord. About one hundred members communed. Ministers present from other churches were brethren Berkman and Follis, of Monroe County, Iowa. One dear soul was received by baptism before the Communion. Since that time six dear souls have confessed Christ, to be buried with him in baptism. They are all young in years. Among them was the wife of this writer. Our meetings are still in progress, and are being conducted by the home ministry.—*W. N. Glotfelty, Sept. 28.*

Literary Notices.

PELOUBET'S SELECT NOTES.—The 1893 edition of this standard commentary on the International Lessons is announced for early publication by W. A. Wilde & Co., Boston. Its universal use in years past has proved its intrinsic worth to thousands of teachers and scholars, who have been materially helped in their Bible study, through its original and carefully-selected comments on the Sunday-school Lessons.

"LIGHT on the Story of Jonah" is the title of an exceedingly interesting little work, by H. Clay Trumbull. The author discusses the question from a rather new, as well as a novel stand point. John D. Wattles, Philadelphia, Publisher.

"Two Northfield Sermons,"—Moral Color-Blindness, and Our Duty of Making the Past a Success. These sermons were preached by H. Clay Trumbull, and are of great value, especially to the young. The one on Moral Color-Blindness is of special importance to everybody. John D. Wattles, Philadelphia, Publisher.

Fallen Asleep.

" Blessed are the dead which die in the Lord."

MUMMERT.—In the Bachelor's Run church, Carroll Co., Ind., Sept. 18, 1892, Mary Mummert, aged 73 years, 6 months and 6 days. Deceased was born in August, 1819, in York County, Pa. She was married to John Mummert about 57 years ago, who preceded her to his final rest eighteen years. They raised seven children. The funeral was preached by Eld. Hiel Hamilton from 2 Tim. 4: 7, 8, assisted by the brethren. · HENRY LANDIS.

ANDREWS.—In the bounds of the Marlow church, Chickasaw Nation, I. T., Sept. 6, 1892, infant daughter of Charles and Susie Andrews. The occasion was improved by the writer. ELIHU MOORE.

SURBER.—Sept. 19, 1891, Andrew Cleo Clinton Surber, son of friend Elmer and Corrilla Surber, aged 6 months and 9 days. Services conducted by Eld. Jesse Kinsey and the writer, from Isa. 40: 11. JOHN H. BRUMBAUGH.

LONG.—In the Cedar Creek church, Ind., Aug. 19, 1892, Aaron Long, youngest child of Levi and Margaret Long, aged 6 months and 19 days. Funeral services conducted by Bro. Jeremiah Gump from John 3: 7. S. O. STECKLY.

HARRISON.—In the Johnstown congregation, Johnstown, Pa., at her home in Walnut Grove, Sept. 8, 1892, sister Mary E. Harrison, aged 23 years, 9 months and 2 days. She has been a member of the church for seven years and was widely known and dearly loved by all. The funeral services were conducted by brethren Abraham Fyock and George Rairigh. E. W. SHAFFER.

MINK.—In the Middle Fork church, Clinton Co., Ind., Sept. 18, 1892, sister Hannah Mink, widow of Bro. Charles Mink, aged 81 years, 6 months and 8 days. She leaves seven children. Funeral services in the Pleasant View church, by Eld. Solomon Blickenstaff to a large congregation. JOHN E. METZGER.

STULTZ.—In the Lost River church, Va., Aug. 22, 1892, Bro. William Stultz, aged 58 years, 10 months and 2 days. He was a faithful deacon for many years. Funeral services by the writer, assisted by M. Moyer. L. D. CALDWELL.

WHETZEL.—In the bounds of the Lost River church, Va., Aug. 22, 1892, Mrs. Marion Whetzel, aged 82 years, 6 months and 9 days. Funeral services by L. D. Caldwell.

WHETZEL.—At her residence in Hardy County, W. Va., Sept. 4, 1892, sister Mary Whetzel, aged 72 years, 1 month and 20 days. Funeral services by L. D. Caldwell and others.

MILLER.—Sept. 7, 1892, Samuel Miller, aged 11 months and 16 days. Funeral services by the writer. JASPER BARNTHOUSE.

SCOT.—In the Markleysburg church, Pa., Sept. 8, 1892, sister Mary C. Scot, aged 25 years, 1 month and 1 day. Funeral services by the writer. The deceased did her Saturday's work, and died on Tuesday afternoon. JASPER BARNTHOUSE.

HALTERMAN.—At his home on Pevy Run, W. Va., Aug. 29, 1892, of consumption, Bro. Silas L. Halterman, aged 22 years, 7 months and 9 days. The deceased united with the church about two months before his death. Shortly before his death he called for the elders and was anointed with oil according to James 5: 14. Funeral services by Bro. Moses Moyer from Rev. 14: 13.

KIMMEL.—In the bounds of the Bush Creek church, Randolph Co., Ind., Sept. 12, 1892, Bro. Samuel Kimmel, aged 63 years, 9 months and 29 days. He belonged to the church for about eighteen years. Funeral services by the writer from Rev. 14: 13. SAMUEL NEHER.

LITTLE.—At her home in Cedar County, Iowa, Sept. 25, 1892, Mrs. Mary Little, wife of Joseph Little, aged 62 years, 4 months and 14 days. Her maiden name was Dollinger. She was born in Bedford County, Pa., and leaves a husband and nine children. All of them were present at the funeral, which was conducted by the writer at the Presbyterian church, Red Oak Grove. JOHN ZUCK.

SHAW.—In the Scott Valley church, Coffey Co., Kans., Bro. James H. Shaw, aged 58 years, 8 months and 12 days. Bro. Shaw and his wife moved from Illinois to this country

about twenty-five years ago, and united with the Brethren church about seventeen years ago. He was a faithful brother, a minister in the second degree, and a man of more than ordinary talent. He leaves a wife and a daughter to mourn their loss, but they need not mourn as those who have no hope. Funeral services conducted by Eld. Jesse Studebaker from Rev. 14: 12, 13. JARED COLBERT.

COTTERMAN.—In the Van Wert church, Van Wert Co., Ohio, Sept. 19, 1892, Washington Cotterman, aged 70 years, 10 months and 19 days. Deceased was born Dec. 1, 1811, in Berks County, Pa., and moved to Ohio with his parents in 1838. He was married to Rebecca Bolin April 10, 1845. Afterwards he was married to Rocksey Ann Ennis June 6, 1867. He was again married to Sarah E. Kimble, Aug. 4, 1881, with whom he lived until his death. He was the father of fifteen children. He was buried in the cemetery at the church. Funeral services by Bro. Jacob Helstand, Text, Eccl. 8: 12, 13. ANTHONY CUPP.

IKENBERRY.—In the Okaw church, Moultrie County, Ill., Aug. 16, 1892, Eldo, son of Bro. John and Mary Ikenberry, aged 6 years, 6 months and 14 days. Funeral services by brethren John Arnold and Daniel Mohler. E. F. WOLFE.

BROWER.—At Cuba, Putnam Co., Ohio, Aug. 30, 1892, sister Elizabeth Brower, wife of ex-postmaster Brockman Brower, aged 74 years and 11 months. Deceased was born near Carlisle, Pa., Sept. 30, 1817. She was the mother of thirteen children,—seven sons and six daughters. She administered maternal aid to four different families. She came to Putnam County with her first husband, Jonas Wisterman, in 1836, who died about 1851. June 7, 1853, she was married to Brockman Brower. She joined the German Baptist church at the age of nineteen, and was a faithful member until death. The funeral services were held in the Cuba church on Thursday, Sept. 1, by brethren John and Daniel Prowant, after which her remains were laid to rest in the family grave-yard, near Cuba. L. B. PROWANT.

GIPE.—In the Richland church, Richland County, Ohio, Sept. 6, 1892, Bro. Benjamin Gipe, aged 79 years, 5 months and 6 days. Bro. Gipe was born in Lancaster County, Pa., March 30, 1813. In 1837 he was united in marriage to Miss Elisabeth Connelly, who, with three sons and five daughters, is left alone. They resided in Lancaster County, Pa., for some years, then moved to Franklin County, same State. In 1851 they moved to Richland County, Ohio, where he lived at the time of his death. Funeral services conducted by Eld. James McMullen. MARY M. HELFER.

HAWKINS.—In the Pine Creek congregation, Ogle Co., Ill., in Woosung, Sept. 20, 1892, Wm. Roy Hawkins, aged 4 years, 6 months and 27 days. Ps. 103 was used on the occasion. EDMUND FORNEY.

BURNER.—In the Pine Creek congregation, Ogle Co., Ill., Sept. 10, 1892, Mallssa Jane Burner, wife of Bro. John Burner, aged 46 years, 11 months and 10 days. The occasion was improved from Rev. 14: 13. EDMUND FORNEY.

FAHRNEY.—In the Pine Creek congregation, Ogle Co., Ill., Sept. 7, 1892, near Polo, David Fahrney, aged 74 years, 9 months and 22 days. The occasion was improved from Ps. 90. EDMUND FORNEY.

The Gospel Messenger

In the recognized organ of the German Baptist or Brethren's church, and advocates the form of doctrine taught in the New Testament and pleads for a return to apostolic and primitive Christianity.

It recognizes the New Testament as the only infallible rule of faith and practice, and maintains that Faith toward God, Repentance from dead works, Regeneration of the heart and mind, Baptism by Trine Immersion for remission of sins unto the reception of the Holy Ghost by the laying on of hands, are the means of adoption into the household of God,—the church militant.

It also maintains that Feet-washing, as taught in John 13, both by example and command of Jesus, should be observed in the church.

That the Lord's Supper, instituted by Christ and as universally observed by the apostles and the early Christians, is a full meal, and, in connection with the Communion, should be taken in the evening or after the close of the day.

That the Salutation of the Holy Kiss, or Kiss of Charity, is binding upon the followers of Christ.

That War and Retaliation are contrary to the spirit and self-denying principles of the religion of Jesus Christ.

That the principle of Plain Dressing and of Non-conformity to the world, as taught in the New Testament, should be observed by the followers of Christ.

That the Scriptural duty of Anointing the Sick with Oil, in the Name of the Lord, James 5: 14, is binding upon all Christians.

It also advocates the church's duty to support Missionary and Tract Work, thus giving to the Lord for the spread of the Gospel and for the conversion of sinners.

In short, it is a vindicator of all that Christ and the apostles have enjoined upon us, and aims, amid the conflicting theories and discords of modern Christendom, to point out ground that all must concede to be lawfully safe.

☞The above principles of our Fraternity are set forth on our Brethren's Envelopes. Use them! Price 15 cents per package; 40 cents per hundred.

Johnstown, Pa.—Last Sunday, Sept. 18, after church services, another dear soul, a colored lady, decided to forsake sin and walk with the people of God. We give God the glory, and pray that more may follow!—*Sadie Brallier Noffsinger.*

Burlington, W. Va.—Last Sunday another brother was added to the fold in the Beaver Run congregation, and several weeks ago three others were baptized here, though they live just outside the borders of this congregation.—*Geo. S. Arnold.*

Cass, Va.—Bro. Thomas Reed preached three sermons for us last Saturday and Sunday, and buried two precious souls in the liquid stream, to walk in newness of life. We number thirty-three members now. By request of our elder, the time of holding our Communion was changed from the fifth Saturday in October to the third Saturday in October, 1892.—*Wm. Wisler, Sept. 21.*

Rogersville, Ind.—The Buck Creek church, Ind., held their quarterly council-meeting Sept. 24. Two members were received by letter. Not much business came before the meeting, and all present seemed to enjoy the services very much. The day following was the day for our regular appointment. In the evening the young folks were addressed from 1 Cor. 9: 26, 27.—*D. E. Rhodes, Sept. 26.*

La Place, Ill.—Sept. 5 Bro. M. J. McClure commenced a series of doctrinal sermons in the Okaw church, which continued one week. We had a large attendance and good order. Bro. Martin did excellent work. The church was much built up. The doctrine of the Brethren is built upon the rock and will stand the storms. The meetings will be continued by Bro. Michael Flory.—*E. F. Wolfe.*

Huaesler, Texas.—In my correspondence on page 590 of the MESSENGER, I meant to say the Mission Board "*could* locate a number of ministers." I referred to the Mission Board of Texas, Oklahoma, and Indian Territory,—*not* to the General Mission Board. I did NOT intend to imply that the Board would support the work, but that we would assist to find homes and places for ministers to work.—*A. W. Austin, Sec, Sept. 20.*

Jeffersonville, Ohio.—I am now at Jeffersonville, Fayette Co., Ohio, and alone on new ground. I find, too, that people seem afraid to attend our meetings although everything is favorable for coming, and no other meetings to interfere. But I work on in hope of a better day, for two members of the Baptist church tell me they are ready to go with us, and others are near the door. I look for Bro. Carter, of Frankfort, to meet me tonight or to-morrow.—*Landon West.*

Libertyville, Iowa.—Our love-feast is now in the past. We had a very enjoyable meeting, for which we feel like praising the Lord. About one hundred members communed. Ministers present from other churches were brethren Berkman and Follis, of Monroe County, Iowa. One dear soul was received by baptism before the Communion. Since that time six dear souls have confessed Christ, to be buried with him in baptism. They are all young in years. Among them was the wife of the writer. Our meetings are still in progress, and are being conducted by the home ministry.—*W. N. Glotfelty, Sept. 28.*

Literary Notices.

PELOUBET'S SELECT NOTES.—The 1893 edition of this standard commentary on the International Lessons is announced for early publication by W. A. Wilde & Co., Boston. Its universal use in years past has proved its intrinsic worth to thousands of teachers and scholars, who have been materially helped in their Bible study, through its original and carefully-selected comments on the Sunday-school Lessons.

"LIGHT on the Story of Jonah" is the title of an exceedingly interesting little work, by H. Clay Trumbull. The author discusses the question from a rather new, as well as a novel stand point. John D. Wattles, Philadelphia, Publisher.

"Two Northfield Sermons,"—Moral Color-Blindness, and Our Duty of Making the Past a Success. These sermons were preached by H. Clay Trumbull, and are of great value, especially to the young. The one on Moral Color-Blindness is of special importance to every body. John D. Wattles, Philadelphia, Publisher.

Fallen Asleep.

"Blessed are the dead which die in the Lord."

MUMMERT.—In the Bachelor's Run church, Carroll Co., Ind., Sept. 18, 1892, Mary Mummert, aged 73 years, 6 months and 6 days. Deceased was born in August, 1819, in York County, Pa. She was married to John Mummert about 57 years ago, who preceded her to his final rest eighteen years. They raised seven children. The funeral was preached by Eld. Hiel Hamilton from 2 Tim. 4: 7, 8, assisted by the brethren.   HENRY LANDIS.

ANDREWS.—In the bounds of the Marlow church, Chickasaw Nation, I. T., Sept. 6, 1892, infant daughter of Charles and Susie Andrews. The occasion was improved by the writer.   ELIHU MOORE.

SURBER.—Sept. 19, 1891, Andrew Cleo Clinton Surber, son of friend Elmer and Corrilla Surber, aged 6 months and 9 days. Services conducted by Eld. Jesse Kinsey and the writer, from Isa. 40: 11.   JOHN H. BRUMBAUGH.

LONG.—In the Cedar Creek church, Ind., Aug. 29, 1892, Aaron Long, youngest child of Levi and Margaret Long, aged 6 months and 19 days. Funeral services conducted by Bro. Jeremiah Gump from John 13: 7.   S. O. STECKLY.

HARRISON.—In the Johnstown congregation, Johnstown, Pa., at her home in Walnut Grove, Sept. 8, 1892, sister Mary E. Harrison, aged 23 years, 9 months and 2 days. She has been a member of the church for seven years and was widely known and dearly loved by all. The funeral services were conducted by brethren Abraham Fyock and George Rairigh.   E. W. SHAFFER.

MINK.—In the Middle Fork church, Clinton Co., Ind., Sept. 18, 1892, sister Hannah Mink, widow of Bro. Charles Mink, aged 81 years, 6 months and 8 days. She leaves seven children. Funeral services in the Pleasant View church, by Eld. Solomon Blickenstaff to a large congregation.   JOHN E. METZGER.

STULTZ.—In the Lost River church, Va., Aug. 22, 1892, Bro. William Stultz, aged 58 years, 10 months and 2 days. He was a faithful deacon for many years. Funeral services by the writer, assisted by M. Moyer.   L. D. CALDWELL.

WHETZEL.—In the bounds of the Lost River church, Va., Aug. 22, 1892, Mrs. Marion Whetzel, aged 82 years, 6 months and 9 days. Funeral services by L. D. Caldwell.

WHETZEL.—At her residence in Hardy County, W. Va., Sept. 4, 1892, sister Mary Whetzel, aged 72 years, 1 month and 20 days. Funeral services by L. D. Caldwell and others.

MILLER.—Sept. 7, 1892, Samuel Miller, aged 71 months and 16 days. Funeral services by the writer.   JASPER BARNTHOUSE.

SCOT.—In the Markleysburg church, Pa., Sept. 8, 1892, sister Mary C. Scot, aged 25 years, 1 month and 1 day. Funeral services by the writer. The deceased did her Saturday's work, and died on Tuesday afternoon.   JASPER BARNTHOUSE.

HALTERMAN.—At his home on Pevy Run, W. Va., Aug. 29, 1892, of consumption, Bro. Silas L. Halterman, aged 22 years, 7 months and 9 days. The deceased united with the church about two months before his death. Shortly before his death he called for the elders and was anointed with oil according to James 5: 14. Funeral services by Bro. Moses Moyer from Rev. 14: 13.

KIMMEL.—In the bounds of the Bush Creek church, Randolph Co., Ind., Sept. 12, 1892, Bro. Samuel Kimmel, aged 63 years, 2 months and 29 days. He belonged to the church for about eighteen years. Funeral services by the writer from Rev. 14: 13.   SAMUEL NEHER.

LITTLE.—At her home in Cedar County, Iowa, Sept. 25, 1892, Mrs. Mary Little, wife of Joseph Little, aged 60 years, 4 months and 14 days. Her maiden name was Dollinger. She was born in Bedford County, Pa., and leaves a husband and nine children. All of them were present at the funeral, which was conducted by the writer at the Presbyterian church, Red Oak Grove.

SHAW.—In the Scott Valley church, Coffey Co., Kans., Bro. James H. Shaw, aged 58 years, 8 months and 12 days. Bro. Shaw and his wife moved from Illinois to this country about twenty-five years ago, and united with the Brethren church about seventeen years ago. He was a faithful brother, a minister in the second degree, a man of more than ordinary talent. He leaves a wife and a daughter to mourn their loss, but they need not mourn as those who have no hope. Funeral services conducted by Eld. Jesse Studebaker from Rev. 14: 12, 13.   JARED COLBERT.

COTTERMAN.—In the Van Wert church, Van Wert Co., Ohio, Sept. 19, 1892, Washington Cotterman, aged 70 years, 10 months and 19 days. Deceased was born Dec. 1 1821, in Berks County, Pa., and moved to Ohio with his parents in 1836. He was married to Rebecca Bolin April 10, 1845. Afterwards he was married to Rocksey Ann Ennis June 6, 1867. He was again married to Sarah E. Kimble, Aug. 4, 1881, with whom he lived until his death. He was the father of fifteen children. He was buried in the cemetery at the church. Funeral services by Bro. Jacob Helstand. Text, Eccl. 8: 12, 13.   ANTHONY CUPP.

IKENBERRY.—In the Okaw church, Moultrie County, Ill., Aug. 16, 1892, Eldo, son of Bro. John and Mary Ikenberry, aged 6 years, 6 months and 14 days. Funeral services by brethren John Arnold and Daniel Mohler.   E. F. WOLFE.

BROWER.—At Cuba, Putnam Co., Ohio, Aug. 30, 1892, sister Elizabeth Brower, wife of ex-postmaster Brockman Brower, aged 74 years and 11 months. Deceased was born near Carlisle, Pa., Sept. 30, 1817. She was the mother of fourteen children,—seven sons and six daughters. She administered maternal aid to four different families. She came to Putnam County with her first husband, Jonas Wisterman, in 1836, who died about 1852. June 7, 1853, she was married to Brockman Brower. She joined the German Baptist church at the age of nineteen, and was a faithful member until death. The funeral services were held in the Cuba church on Thursday, Sept. 1, by brethren John and Daniel Prowant, after which her remains were laid to rest in the family grave-yard, near Cuba.   L. B. PROWANT.

GIPE.—In the Richland church, Richland County, Ohio, Sept. 6, 1892, Bro. Benjamin Gipe, aged 70 years, 5 months and 6 days. Bro. Gipe was born in Lancaster County, Pa., March 30, 1822. In 1837 he was united in marriage to Miss Elizabeth Connelly, who, with three sons and five daughters, is left alone. They resided in Lancaster County, Pa., for some years, then moved to Franklin County, same State. In 1851 they moved to Richland County, Ohio, where he lived at the time of his death. Funeral services conducted by Eld. James McMullen.   MARY M. HELFER.

HAWKINS.—In the Pine Creek congregation, Ogle Co., Ills, in Woosung, Sept. 20, 1892, Wm. Roy Hawkins, aged 4 years, 6 months and 27 days. Ps. 103 was used on the occasion.   EDMUND FORNEY.

BURNER.—In the Pine Creek congregation, Ogle Co., Ill., Sept. 10, 1892, Malissa Jane Burner, wife of Bro. John Burner, aged 46 years, 11 months and 10 days. The occasion was improved from Rev. 14: 13.   EDMUND FORNEY.

FAHRNEY.—In the Pine Creek congregation, Ogle Co., Ill., Sept. 7, 1892, near Polo, David Fahrney, aged 74 years, 9 months and 22 days. The occasion was improved from Ps. 90.   EDMUND FORNEY.

Announcements.

(Concluded from preceding page.)

LOVE-FEASTS.

Oct. 15, at 10 A. M., Wichita church, continuing over Sunday.

Oct. 22 and 23, at 10 A. M., South Merrill church, 2½ miles south-east of Merrill, Kans.

Oct. 15, at 10 A. M., Upper Fall Creek church, 2 miles east of Middletown, Ind.

Oct. 18, at 2 P. M., Pleasant Hill Church, near Virden and Girard, Ill.

Oct. 19, at 4 P. M., Fairview church, Blair Co., Pa.

Oct. 23, at 2 P. M., Lick Creek church, Williams Co., Ohio, 1 mile south-west of Bryan.

Oct. 27, Woodberry, Baltimore City, Md.

Oct. 29, Marrow church, 1¾ miles from Marrow, I. T.

Oct. 29 and 30, at 3 P. M., Fairview church, Kans.

Oct. 30, at 4 P. M., Roaring Spring, Pa.

Nov. 5, at 2 A. M., Greene church, Greene, Butler Co., Iowa.

Nov. 5, at 2 P. M., English Prairie church, Lagrange Co., Ind.

Nov. 5, at 4 P. M., Ridgely church, Caroline Co., Md.

Nov. 12, at 2 P. M., Fairview church, Douglas Co., Mo., 8 miles south of Mansfield.

EUROPE
AND
Bible Lands

A new edition of this deservedly popular work has again been published. It retains all the excellencies of its predecessors, and with those who are interested in Bible study this work will always remain a favorite. Those who have read the ordinary book of travel will be surprised to find "Europe and Bible Lands" of thrilling interest for both old and young. The large number of books, already sold, proves that the work is of more than ordinary merit.

A fair supply of the last edition of this work is still on hand. Those who have not yet secured a copy of the work should embrace this opportunity of securing it. Price, in fine cloth binding, only $1.50 per copy, post-paid. To agents who are prepared to push an active canvass of the work, we are prepared to give special inducements. Write

BRETHREN'S PUBLISHING CO.,
Mt. Morris, Ill.

CANCERS, TUMORS, ETC.

Successfully treated by Dr. G. N. Beisler, of Waynesborough, Pa., where he has practiced for the last sixteen years. Dr. Beisler is a graduate of the University of Maryland, at Baltimore City. References given and correspondence solicited. Address, Dr. G. W. Beisler, Waynesborough, Pa.

WHAT to Read, a monthly magazine published in the interests of all lovers of good literature, 50 cts. per year. But as a SPECIAL INDUCEMENT I will send it one year for 35 cts. and give free a Handy and Reliable little Dictionary, containing 30,000 words and 300 pages, to all who send in their subscription at once. Address: Jas. M. Neff, Covington, Ohio.

GOOD BOOKS FOR ALL.

Any book in the market furnished at publishers' lowest retail price by the Brethren's Publishing Company, Mt. Morris, Ill. *Special prices* given when books are purchased in quantities. When ordering books, not on our list, if possible give title, name of author, and address of publishers.

The Throne of David.—By J. H. Ingraham. Cloth, $2.50.

The Doctrine of the Holy Spirit.—By James B Walker. Cloth, $1.25.

Homiletics and Pastoral Theology.—By W. G. T. Shedd. Cloth, $2.50.

The New Testament History.]—By Wm. Smith. Cloth, $1.25.

The Old Testament History.—By William Smith. Cloth, $1.25.

The Great Events of History.—By W.F. Collier. Cloth, $1.25.

Lectures on Preaching.—By Rev. Phillips Brooks. Cloth, 16mo, $1.50.

The Path of Life.—An interesting tract for everybody. Price, 10 cents per copy; 100 copies, $6.00.

The Origin and Growth of Religion.—Hibbert Lectures. By T. W. R. Davids. Cloth, 8vo, $2.50.

Hours with the Bible.—By Cunningham Geikie. Old Testament Series—six volumes. Per volume, 90 cents.

Bible Work, or Bible Reader's Commentary on the New Testament.—By J. G. Butler. Two. vols. 8vo, $10.00.

Biblical Antiquities.—By John Nevin. Gives a concise account of Bible times and customs; invaluable to all students of Bible subjects. Price, $1.50.

The Story of the Bible.—An excellent volume for old and young; will interest and instruct all those desiring a knowledge of the Scriptures. Price, $1.00.

Life on Wheels.—By J. S. Mohler. The idea of the book is to represent the way to heaven, by using the different terms connected with an ordinary railroad. Price, single copy, 40 cents.

Trine Immersion.—A vindication of the apostolic form of Christian baptism. By Eld. James Quinter. A most complete and reliable work on the subject." Price, cloth, single copy, $1.25; leather, $1.75.

Popular Commentary on the New Testament.—Edited by Philip Schaff. Four volumes, 8vo. Matthew, Mark and Luke: $6.00. John and the Acts: $6.00. Romans to Philemon: $5.00. Hebrews to Revelation: $5.00.

— THE —
Doctrine of the Brethren Defended.

This work contains a complete exposition of the faith and practice of the Brethren, the Divinity of Christ, the Divinity of the Holy Spirit, Immersion, Feet-washing, the Lord's Supper, the Holy Kiss, Non-conformity, Secret Societies, etc. Price, per copy, cloth binding, $1.25. Address this office.

O Jerusalem! Jerusalem!

What could be more beautiful and touching than a picture of Christ as he stood upon Olivet looking down over the beloved but sinful city, with tears trickling down over his cheeks, his lips parted as he cries, "O Jerusalem! Jerusalem!" We have such a picture 22x28 inches, beautifully executed in colors. No one can gaze upon it without being moved. Given free with a year's subscription to "What to Read" at 50 cents. An agent wanted in every church and neighborhood. Address, Jas. M. Neff, Covington, Ohio.

Excursions to California.

Excursions in charge of M. M. Eshelman, Immigration Agent, will leave Chicago over the "Santa Fe Route" Tuesdays, and Kansas City Wednesdays, during the year 1892, on dates as follows:

Chicago, January 26, February 23, March 22, April 26, May 24, June 28, July 26, August 23, September 27, October 25, November 29, December 27.

Kansas City, January 27, February 24, March 23, April 27, May 25, June 29, July 27, August 24, September 28, October 26, November 30, December 28.

Parties wishing to avail themselves of the privileges of these excursions, should write M. M. Eshelman, North Pomona, California; prior to the 15th of each month, and from the fifteenth to the end of the month, at 1092 Union Avenue (opposite Union Depot), Kansas City, Mo., stating when and where they wish to join one of these excursions, and we will give them full information, and if desired will reserve berths in Tourist Sleeping Car for them. Do not fail to write him; he will do you good. The rates will be as low as the lowest made to the Pacific Coast.

GEORGE L. McDOUGALL, Traveling Agent.

LOOK AT THIS.

The Monon Route still reducing rates and offering better accommodations than ever before.

Commencing April 15, the fare from Chicago to Louisville, New Albany, Cincinnati, Hamilton, and Dayton will be $5.50; to Indianapolis $3.50. Round trip tickets good ten days at double the one way rate.

Parlor and Dining cars on day trains; Pullman Sleepers and Compartment Cars on night trains. A special Sleeper is run for Indianapolis business.

See that your tickets read via the MONON ROUTE.

For rates, schedules, etc., apply at Depot, Dearborn Station, City Ticket Office, 232 Clark Street, or address, JAMES BARKER, G. P. A., Monon Block, Chicago, Ill.

Church Entertainments: Twenty Objections.

By Rev. B. Calvadine, D. D. 12mo, 100 pp. Paper cover, 30 cents. A strong book in defense of its position, written by a powerful pen, presenting the most candid and scriptural arraignment of unwarrantable methods for money-raising in the Church. The spirit of the book is highly devotional and cannot fail to inspire the reader with its seriousness.

Alone with God.

This manual of devotions, by J. H. Garrison, comprises a series of meditations with forms of prayer for private devotions, family worship and special occasions. It is one of the most useful, most needed, and best adapted books of the year, and therefore it is not strange that it is proving one of the most popular. In work of this kind its distinguished, gifted, pious and beloved author is at his best. This book is helpful to every minister, church official, and Sunday-school superintendent, as well as every private member of the church in all ages. It has modes of prayer, suitable for the service of the prayer-meeting, while its suggestions, meditations and instructions are pre-eminently calculated to be of service in preparation for the solemn duties that rest upon the active members. Cloth, 75 cents; morocco, $1.25. Address this office.

Announcements.

(Concluded from preceding page.)

LOVE-FEASTS.

Oct. 15, at 10 A. M., Wichita church, continuing over Sunday.

Oct. 22 and 23, at 10 A. M., South Morrill church, 2½ miles south-east of Morrill, Kans.

Oct. 22, at 10 A. M., Upper Fall Creek church, 2 miles east of Middletown, Ind.

Oct. 28, at 4 P. M., Pleasant Hill Church, near Virden and Girard, Ill.

Oct. 29, at 1 P. M., Fairview church, Blair Co., Pa.

Oct. 29, at 4 P. M., Lick Creek church, Williams Co., Ohio, 1 mile south-west of Bryan.

Oct. 29, Woodberry, Baltimore City, Md.

Oct. 29, Marlow church, 1½ miles from Marlow, I. T.

Oct. 29 and 30, at 3 P. M., Fairview church, Kans.

Oct. 30, at 4 P. M., Roaring Spring, Pa.

Nov. 3, at 10 A. M., Greene church, Greene, Butler Co., Iowa.

Nov. 5, at 2 P. M., English Prairie church, Lagrange Co., Ind.

Nov. 8, at 2 P. M., Ridgely church, Caroline Co., Md.

Nov. 12, at 2 P. M., Fairview church, Douglas Co., Mo., 6 miles south of Mansfield.

EUROPE

AND

Bible Lands

A new edition of this deservedly popular work has again been published. It retains all the excellencies of its predecessors, and with those who are interested in Bible study this work will always remain a favorite. Those who have read the ordinary book of travel will be surprised to find "Europe and Bible Lands" of thrilling interest for both old and young. The large number of books, although sold, proves that the work is of more than ordinary merit.

A fair supply of the last edition of this work is still on hand. Those who have not yet secured a copy of the work should embrace this opportunity of securing it. Price, in fine cloth binding, only $1.50 per copy, post-paid. To agents who are prepared to push an active canvass of the work, we are prepared to give special inducements. Write

  BRETHREN'S PUBLISHING CO.,

      Mt. Morris, Ill.

CANCERS, TUMORS, ETC.

WHAT to Read, a monthly magazine published in the interests of all lovers of good literature, 30 cts. per year. But as a SPECIAL INDUCEMENT I will send it one year for 25 cts. and give free a Handy and Reliable little Dictionary, containing 30,000 words and 320 pages, to all who send in their subscription at once. Address: Jas. M. Neff, Covington, Ohio.

GOOD BOOKS FOR ALL.

ANY book in the market furnished at publishers' lowest retail price by the Brethren's Publishing Company, Mt. Morris, Ill. *Special prices* given when books are purchased in quantities. When ordering books, not on our list, if possible give title, name of author, and address of publishers.

The Throne of David.—By J. H. Ingraham. Cloth, $1.50.

The Doctrine of the Holy Spirit.—By James B Walker. Cloth, $1.25.

Homiletics and Pastoral Theology.—By W. G. T. Shedd. Cloth, $2.50.

The New Testament History.—By Wm. Smith. Cloth, $1.25.

The Old Testament History.—By William Smith. Cloth, $1.25.

The Great Events of History.—By W.F. Collier. Cloth, $1.25.

Lectures on Preaching.—By Rev. Phillips Brooks. Cloth, 1800, $1.50.

The Path of Life.—An interesting tract for everybody. Price, 10 cents per copy; 100 copies, $6.00.

The Origin and Growth of Religion.—Hibbert Lectures. By T. W. R. Davids. Cloth, 8vo, $2.50.

The Story of the Bible.—An excellent volume for old and young; will interest and instruct all those desiring a knowledge of the Scriptures. Price, $1.00.

Life on Wheels.—By J. S. Mohler. The idea of the book is to represent the way to heaven, by using the different terms connected with an ordinary railroad. Price, single copy, 40 cents.

Trine Immersion.—A vindication of the apostolic form of Christian baptism. By Eld. James Quinter. A most complete and reliable work on the subject.". Price, cloth, single copy, $1.25; leather, $1.75.

Popular Commentary on the New Testament.—Edited by Philip Schaff. Four volumes, 8vo. Matthew, Mark and Luke: $6.00. John and the Acts: $6.00. Romans to Philemon: $5.00. Hebrews to Revelation: $5.00.

--- THE ---

Doctrine of the Brethren Defended.

THIS work contains a complete exposition of the faith and practice of the Brethren, the Divinity of Christ, the Divinity of the Holy Spirit, Immersion, Feet-washing, the Lord's Supper, the Holy Kiss, Non-conformity, Secret Societies, etc. Price, per copy, cloth binding, $1.25. Address this office.

O Jerusalem! Jerusalem!

WHAT could be more beautiful and touching than a picture of Christ as he stood upon Olivet looking down over the beloved but sinful city, with tears trickling down over his cheeks, his lips parted as he cries, "O Jerusalem! Jerusalem!" We have such a picture most beautifully executed in colors. No one can gaze upon it without being moved. Given free with a year's subscription to "What to Read" at 30 cents. An agent wanted in every church and neighborhood. Address, Jas. M. Neff, Covington, Ohio.

Excursions to California.

Excursions in charge of M. M. Eshelman, Immigration Agent, will leave Chicago over the "Santa Fe Route"—Tuesdays, and Kansas City Wednesdays, during the year 1892, on dates as follows:

Chicago, January 26, February 23, March 22, April 26, May 24, June 28, July 26, August 23, September 27, October 25, November 22, December 27.

Kansas City, January 27, February 24, March 23, April 27, May 25, June 29, July 27, August 24, September 28, October 26, November 23, December 28.

Parties wishing to avail themselves of the privileges of these excursions, should write M. M. Eshelman, North Pomona, California, prior to the 15th of each month, and from the fifteenth to the end of the month, at 100 Union Avenue (opposite Union Depot), Kansas City, Mo., stating when and where they wish to join one of these excursions, and he will give them full information, and if desired will reserve berths in Tourist Sleeping Car for them. Do not fail to write him: he will do you good. The rates will be as low as the lowest made to the Pacific Coast.

    GEORGE L. McDONAUGH,

      Traveling Agent.

Church Entertainments: Twenty Objections.

By Rev. B. Carradine, D. D. 12mo, 100 pp. Paper cover, 30 cents. A strong book in defense of its position, written by a powerful pen, presenting the most candid and scriptural arraignment of unwarrantable methods for money-raising in the Church. The spirit of the book is highly devotional and cannot fail to inspire the reader with its seriousness.

Alone with God.

THIS manual of devotions, by J. H. Garrison, comprises a series of meditations with forms of prayer for private devotions, family worship and special occasions. It is one of the most useful, most needed, and best adapted books of the year, and therefore it is not strange that it is proving one of the best popular. In work of this kind its distinguished, gifted, pious and beloved author is at his best. This book is helpful to every minister, church official, and Sunday-school superintendent, as well as every private member of the church in all ages. It has models of prayer, suitable for the service of the prayer-meeting, while its suggestions, meditations and instructions are pre-eminently calculated to be of service in preparation for the solemn duties that rest upon the active members. Cloth, 75 cents; morocco, $1.25, Address this office.

✦ESSAYS✦

"Study to show thyself approved unto God; a workman that needeth not be ashamed, rightly dividing the Word of Truth."

OMNISCIENT.

BY GERTRUDE A. FLORY.

Thou seest me!
When rayless night my dwelling-place pervades,
Or night before the morning splendor fades.
"Darkness and light are both alike to thee."

Thou seest me!
As we-view pages of an open book
Or gaze through crystal waters in a brook—
Yes, deeper far than human eye can see!

Thou seest me!
Just as I am; a fleshly heart and vile
Warring against a heart that loves not guile.
O Searcher of hearts! view pityingly!

Thou seest me!
When jealousy my carnal nature moves,
While secret admiration clearly proves,
The greatness of another's ministry.

Thou seest me!
Revealing evil passions of the mind
Through flashing eyes, whose glances should be kind,
Reflecting only sweetest charity.

Thou seest me!
When angry and impassioned accents nip
The loving word just budding on the lip
Of Friendship's pure and cherished sympathy.

Thou seest me!
Groveling in sin and shackled by its coils;
Pursuing eagerly forbidden spoils,
Which please but for a day, then cease to be.

Thou seest me!
Bowing repentant at thy blessed feet,
Where all the raptures of the spirit meet
To crown the soul new-born in purity.

Thou seest me!
And tenderly o'erspreads thy sheltering wings
To shield from Satan's sharp and venomed stings.
O gracious love! O wondrous mystery!

Thou seest me!
By love subdued; subject to thee alone.
So mercy pleads for me before thy throne
And from the record strikes iniquity!

Thou seest me!
In joy and sorrow, peace and righteous strife,—
From the beginning to the end of life,—
E'en through the cycles of eternity.

Jehovah, Father, Christ, Redeemer, King!
O may each impulse, thought and act I bring
Stand in thy holy sight approvingly!

La Porte, Ind.

THE BROOK BESOR.

BY ELIZABETH H. DELP.

"But David pursued, he and four hundred men: for two hundred abode behind, which were so faint that they could not go over the brook Besor."—1 Sam. 30: 10.

David and his six hundred men went in pursuit of their enemies. So impetuous was the leader that one-third of his men were unable to go with him to battle, but at the brook Besor they remained, fainting, exhausted, while the remaining four hundred men marched steadily on till they came upon the Amalekites,—suddenly, as Robert Bruce and his Scotchmen surprised the revelers at Bannockburn, making the conflict sharp and decisive. David and his men were fighting for their wives and little children; this is enough to let us know that they would win the victory, or die on the field. It seems to me that of the two tasks, marching on to battle, or remaining by the brook Besor, the latter was the harder task, for these men, lying on the banks of the brook were stirred by the thought that their loved ones are in danger, and they could not aid them. They waited at Besor, bearing their pain, tortured by doubts, for there may have been some among them who did not fully believe the Word of the Lord, and they dreaded, lest only a few of their comrades might come back to tell the story of defeat and captivity.

Ye who are fainting to-day by the brook Besor, accept this promise, that "all things work together for good to those who love the Lord." One of the "all things" is your enforced thraldom, as you may consider it, in your bitter humiliation. You see your fellow-soldiers going forth to win victories for Christ that will be celebrated in heaven, while you must "tarry," sorrowing over hopes unrealized, and perhaps forgetting that "weeping may endure for a night, but joy cometh in the morning" to all who are faithful.

Besor means "cool brook." Its cool waters proved refreshing to the fainting soldiers, "tarrying by the stuff." This was but a little task, but so it is always, a little work will remain for us to do. What can we do for Christ, when we halt fainting by the wayside of life? We can do something "unto the least of these," for the strong pass them by as they hasten to battle. It is ours to comfort their hearts, illuminate their minds, and speed their feet in the narrow way, and thus, by our encouragement, they may be fitted to go forth with the strong. Not ease, but the humble tasks, done by weary hands, may be given us. To others may be committed the raging flames, the clanking chain, and quarternion vigilance. Their life is well illustrated by the figure of a warfare. They must fight against all the black catalogue of sins that have twined themselves into nature, or fixed their fangs securely into physical being; they are soldiers and athletes for Christ, and must be protected by the armor of our king. Those about them know little of the conflict they are waging; but in the archives of heaven it is recorded, and let those annals contain no compromise, no cringing before the enemy, but may there be all the color, light and illumination upon the picture of a victor, who vanquished sin by the power of the cross. The fainting two hundred had enlisted with hopes as bright, and hearts as brave as those who were "able to endure unto the end," and with what despair they must have submitted to their relentless, inevitable fate! It was an inglorious campaign for them, truly,—no less than the master of song, Milton, said out of the depths of a bitter experience,

"They also serve,
Who only stand and wait."

Let us be patient and wait upon the Lord. A perfect service of faith and trust is precious in his sight. There is always some stuff by the brook Besor, which is our especial charge. We may be fettered in some way by disease; he would have us suffer his will, let our light shine, and wait.

Not always do we come in for our share of the spoils here, for often the gorgeous garlands, the ovations of the multitudes, and the flashing splendors of luminous praise are all concentrated upon those who have overcome and taken the enemy, but the Lord seeth, and that is sufficient.

THE "KEELEY CURE."

BY DR. A. W. REESE.

Perhaps the very first thought that will arise in the mind of the reader is this: What is the "Keeley Cure?" It shall be the object of this sketch to explain. Quietly basking in the soft sunshine, far away on the prairies of Northern Illinois, lies a little, sleepy-looking town, called Dwight. It is in Livingston County, on the C. & A. R.; 73 miles from Chicago, and 209 miles from St. Louis. A few years ago people knew little about and cared less for the small, insignificant town of Dwight. It was emphatically a place

"To fortune and to fame unknown."

But suddenly a change came over the spirit of its dream, and Dwight, like Rip Van Winkle, started up from its long nap. It woke up to find itself famous. What Jerusalem is to the devout Jew, what Mecca is to the faithful son of Islam, so Dwight is to the 80,000 souls who have been redeemed from the bondage of strong drink,—. "The Holy City." It is a strange story, and yet an "over true tale." Dwight is the home of Dr. Leslie E. Keeley, an old United States Army Surgeon during the late civil war.

For many years his attention had been attracted to the wide-spread and ruinous evils of alcoholism, and its kindred curse,—the use of opium. He felt that all attempts to check these monster evils, by the use of moral suasion, had signally failed. His medical researches and investigations led him to the conclusion that alcoholism—inebriety,—was not so much a vice to be combatted by moral means, as a disease that might be cured by medicine, if the proper remedy could be found.

In support of his views he says: "It is as rational, from a medical point of view, to treat drunkenness by expostulation, pledge signing, reproaches, and legislation, as it formerly was to treat insanity by incantations, exhibition of the bones of saints, and the laying on of hands. A fair enumeration of the signatures of total abstinence pledges, and the relapses into drunken ways, has always shown a model balance sheet. The tears, the agony, the starvation, the social misery of the drunkard's family; the insanity, mental imbecility, and criminality of his progeny; as well as the overflowing penitentiaries, jails and poor-houses, and the millions of headless, dishonored drunkards' graves, are all powerless,—have always been powerless,—to cure the disease of drunkenness."

What a terrible picture is this! and yet, alas! alas! how true! This withering, blighting, dreadful curse, hanging like a dark funeral pall over thousands of once happy homes, led Doctor Keeley's mind to seek out a cure, which, under the blessing of God, he has been enabled to find.

He says, "During my army experience of four years, men frequently came under my notice, who, in spite of all they could do to avoid it, yet would invariably get drunk at every opportunity which presented itself. Frequent punishments were of no avail, for it seemed as if they had no power to control the appetite which mastered them. Filled with remorse, during sober intervals, they made good resolutions which were broken at the first temptation to gratify their insatiable desire for intoxicants."

The doctor (in his little pamphlet, from which the foregoing statements are selected) goes on to state how he set to work, earnestly and perseveringly, to find some reliable remedy for this terrible disease. When we try to realize the misery, ruin, and death, produced by alcoholic excess, in our own beloved land alone, we are filled with horror at the view. We estimate, in the United States, 100,000 victims go down to the drunkard's grave. It is estimated that 1,500,000 more are addicted to the excessive use of opium, and the great majority of these poor creatures are *women.* These are ghastly figures, and may well cause a shudder to the philanthropic heart.

At length the good doctor's long and weary labors met their reward. The Double Chloride of

ESSAYS

"Study to show thyself approved unto God; a workman that needeth not to be ashamed, rightly dividing the Word of Truth."

OMNISCIENT.

BY GERTRUDE A. FLORY.

Thou seest me!
When rayless night my dwelling-place pervades,
Or night before the morning splendor fades.
"Darkness and light are both alike to thee."

Thou seest me!
As we-view pages of an open book
Or gaze through crystal waters in a brook—
Yes, deeper far than human eye can see!

Thou seest me!
Just as I am; a fleshly heart and vile
Warring against a heart that loves not guile.
O Searcher of hearts! view pityingly!

Thou seest me!
When jealousy my carnal nature moves,
While secret admiration clearly proves,
The greatness of another's ministry.

Thou seest me!
Revealing evil passions of the mind
Through flashing eyes, whose glances should be kind,
Reflecting only sweetest charity.

Thou seest me!
When angry and impassioned accents nip
The loving word just budding on the lip
Of friendship's pure and cherished sympathy.

Thou seest me!
Groveling in sin and shackled by its coils;
Pursuing eagerly forbidden spoils,
Which please but for a day, then cease to be.

Thou seest me!
Bowing repentant at thy blessed feet,
Where all the raptures of the spirit meet
To crown the soul new-born in purity.

Thou seest me!
And tenderly o'erspreads thy sheltering wings
To shield from Satan's sharp and venomed stings.
O gracious love! O wondrous mystery!

Thou seest me!
By love subdued: subject to thee alone.
So mercy pleads for me before thy throne
And from the record strikes iniquity!

Thou seest me!
In joy and sorrow, peace and righteous strife,—
From the beginning to the end of life,—
E'en through the cycles of eternity.

Thou seest me!
Jehovah, Father, Christ, Redeemer, King!
O may each impulse, thought and act I bring
Stand in thy holy sight approvingly!

La Porte, Ind.

THE BROOK BESOR.

BY ELIZABETH H. DELP.

"But David pursued, he and four hundred men: for two hundred abode behind, which were so faint that they could not go over the brook Besor."—1 Sam. 30: 10.

DAVID and his six hundred men went in pursuit of their enemies. So impetuous was the leader that one-third of his men were unable to go with him to battle, but at the brook Besor they remained, fainting, exhausted, while the remaining four hundred men marched steadily on till they came upon the Amalekites,—suddenly, as Robert Bruce and his Scotchmen surprised the revelers at Bannockburn, making the conflict sharp and decisive. David and his men were fighting for their wives and little children; this is enough to let us know that they would win the victory, or die on the field. It seems to me that of the two tasks, marching on to battle, or remaining by the brook Besor, the latter was the harder task, for these men, lying on the banks of the brook were stirred by the thought that their loved ones are in danger, and they could not aid them. They waited at Besor, bearing their pain, tortured by doubts, for there may have been some among them who did not fully believe the Word of the Lord, and they dreaded, lest only a few of their comrades might come back to tell the story of defeat and captivity.

Ye who are fainting to-day by the brook Besor, accept this promise, that "all things work together for good to those who love the Lord." One of the "all things" is your enforced thraldom, as you may consider it, in your bitter humiliation. You see your fellow-soldiers going forth to win victories for Christ that will be celebrated in heaven, while you must "tarry," sorrowing over hopes unrealized, and perhaps forgetting that "weeping may endure for a night, but joy cometh in the morning" to all who are faithful.

Besor means "cool brook." Its cool waters proved refreshing to the fainting soldiers, "tarrying by the stuff." This was but a little task, but so it is always, a little work will remain for us to do. What can we do for Christ, when we halt fainting by the wayside of life? We can do something "unto the least of these," for the strong pass them by as they hasten to battle. It is ours to comfort their hearts, illuminate their minds, and speed their feet in the narrow way, and thus, by our encouragement, they may be fitted to go forth with the strong. Not ease, but the humble tasks, done by weary hands, may be given us. To others may be committed the raging flames, the clanking chain, and quarternion vigilance. Their life is well illustrated by the figure of a warfare. They must fight against all the black catalogue of sins that-have twined themselves into nature, or fixed their fangs securely into physical being; they are soldiers and athletes for Christ, and must be protected by the armor of our king. Those about them know little of the conflict they are waging; but in the archives of heaven it is recorded, and let those annals contain no compromise, no cringing before the enemy, but may there be all the color, light and illumination upon the picture of a victor, who vanquished sin by the power of the cross. The fainting two hundred had enlisted with hopes as bright, and hearts as brave as those who were "able to endure unto the end," and with what despair they must have submitted to their relentless, inevitable fate! It was an inglorious campaign for them, truly,—no less than the master of song, Milton, said out of the depths of a bitter experience,

"They also serve,
Who only stand and wait."

Let us be patient and wait upon the Lord. A perfect service of faith and trust is precious in his sight. There is always some stuff by the brook Besor, which is our especial charge. We may be fettered in some way by disease; he would have us suffer his will, let our light shine, and wait.

Not always do we come in for our share of the spoils here, for often the gorgeous garlands, the ovations of the multitudes, and the flashing splendors of luminous praise are all concentrated upon those who have overcome and taken the enemy, but the Lord seeth, and that is sufficient.

THE "KEELEY CURE."

BY DR. A. W. REESE.

PERHAPS the very first thought that will arise in the mind of the reader is this: What is the "Keeley Cure?" It shall be the object of this sketch to explain. Quietly basking in the soft sunshine, far away on the prairies of Northern Illinois, lies a little, sleepy-looking town, called Dwight. It is in Livingston County, on the C. & A. R. R., 73 miles from Chicago, and 209 miles from St. Louis. A few years ago people knew little about and cared less for the small, insignificant town of Dwight. It was emphatically a place

"To fortune and to fame unknown."

But suddenly a change came over the spirit of its dream, and Dwight, like Rip Van Winkle, started up from its long nap. It woke up to find itself famous. What Jerusalem is to the devout Jew, what Mecca is to the faithful son of Islam, so Dwight is to the 80,000 souls who have been redeemed from the bondage of strong drink,—. "The Holy City." It is a strange story, and yet an "over true tale." Dwight is the home of Dr. Leslie E. Keeley, an old United States Army Surgeon during the late civil war.

For many years his attention had been attracted to the wide-spread and ruinous evils of alcoholism, and its kindred curse,—the use of opium. He felt that all attempts to check these monster evils, by the use of moral suasion, had signally failed. His medical researches and investigations led him to the conclusion that alcoholism—inebriety,—was not so much a vice-to be combatted by moral means, as a disease that might be cured by medicine, if the proper remedy could be found.

In support of his views he says: "It is as rational, from a medical point of view, to treat drunkenness by expostulation, pledge signing, reproaches, and legislation, as it formerly was to treat insanity by incantations, exhibition of the bones of saints, and the laying on, of hands. A fair enumeration of the signatures of total abstinence pledges, and the relapses into drunken ways, has always shown a model balance sheet. The tears, the agony, the starvation, the social misery of the drunkard's family; the insanity, mental imbecility, and criminality of his progeny; as well as the overflowing penitentiaries, jails and poor-houses, and the millions of headless, dishonored drunkards' graves, are all powerless,—have always been powerless,—to cure the disease of drunkenness."

What a terrible picture is this! and yet, alas! alas! how true! This withering, blighting, dreadful curse, hanging like a dark funeral pall over thousands of once happy homes, led Doctor Keeley's mind to seek out a cure, which, under the blessing of God, he has been enabled to find. He says, "During my army experience of four years, men frequently came under my notice, who, in spite of all they could do to avoid it, yet would invariably get drunk at every opportunity which presented itself. Frequent punishments were of no avail, for it seemed as if they had no power to control the appetite which mastered them. Filled with remorse, during sober intervals, they made good resolutions which were broken at the first temptation to gratify their insatiable desire for intoxicants."

The doctor (in his little pamphlet, from which the foregoing statements are selected) goes on to state how he set to work, earnestly and perseveringly, to find some reliable remedy for this terrible disease. When we try to realize the misery, ruin, and death, produced by alcoholic excess, in our own beloved land alone, we are filled with horror at the view. Annually, in the United States, 100,000 victims go down to the drunkard's grave. It is estimated that 1,500,000 more are addicted to the excessive use of opium, and the great majority of these poor creatures are *women*. These are ghastly figures, and may well cause a shudder to the philanthropic heart.

At length the good doctor's long and weary labors met their reward. The Double Chloride of

What worse condition could we be in than to be asleep or dead in sin? It is bad enough for those outside of the church, who make no profession of religion, to be in sin, but it is much worse for those in the church and who make a profession. There is no escape from the consequence of sin except by repentance. It is needful for Christians to repent as often as they sin.

Do we always do this? I fear not. If we would always do so, there would be a greater ingathering of souls into the church, a greater increase of true vital piety among the members. There would be more light shed abroad in the world, and less ignorance of the Bible. If we thoroughly repent of a sin, we will not likely commit that same fault again. But if unrepented of, we are inclined to repeat it, and go on from bad to worse. As members, we need to grow in grace, so as to be able to withstand temptation and avoid all sin.

WHICH WAY ARE WE GOING?

BY A. FLORY.

THE prophet laments Israel's condition because they went backward and not forward. Jer. 7: 24. They were a rebellious and a stiff-necked people, and would not hearken unto the voice of the Lord, but they were continually breaking his laws. They made promises, but did not keep them.

This was very discouraging to Moses, so much so, that at one time he was willing to give up the contest. He says: "Yet now, if thou wilt, forgive their sin—; and if not, blot me, I pray thee, out of thy book which thou hast written." Ex. 32:32.

How is it with those who have the oversight of God's chosen people to-day? Do they not feel almost like Moses when they look at the condition of some of the congregations of our Brotherhood? Possibly the disobedient members of those congregations have not departed quite as far from the Written Word and order of the church as Israel did, but is there not sufficient cause for the elders of those churches to be greatly discouraged? We think there is, for the tendency to go back seems to be on the increase. Some, who united with the church while in their youthful days, ran well for a short time, but, as they advanced in age, they also increased in pride and fashion, until now it is not possible to distinguish some of them from the world. Those members, as well as all others, promised annually to hear the church and help to build up the cause of Christ. Possibly they do not realize their real condition. Remember, dear reader, God will hold us strictly to our promises, regardless of what we may think of the matter now, especially so when those promises are in harmony with the spirit of the Gospel, and for the benefit and support of the church. The wise man, Solomon, tells us that it is better not to vow than to vow and not pay. This fact was fully tested by Ananias and Sapphira. They promised to support the church when they mutually agreed to sell their possessions, and bring the price thereof to the apostles. They violated their vows and were struck dead. At this time the church does not require us to sell our farms, but it does ask every one of us to submit to its plain order of dress, as well as many other things. It is not possible to help build up the church and at the same time reject its counsels, for the church is the pillar and ground of the truth.

Some may tell us, that the Gospel does not say what the cut of our garments shall be. That is true. The same is true of Ananias and Sapphira. There is not one word laid down in the Bible, telling them to sell their possessions, notwithstanding they agreed to do so. For that reason the Brethren have adopted an order of dress. We are living among a people who are evermore changing their fashions and customs, therefore it is of vital importance to have an order. Notwithstanding all the efforts that the church has ever put forth, pride and fashion are continually increasing in some of the congregations. Is there no remedy for this growing evil? Or will it continue to get worse and worse until the salt will have lost its savor, and time will be no longer?

Is there not sufficient cause for the church to fall in line with the prophet and say, "O that my head were fountains of water, and my eyes fountains of tears, that I might weep day and night for the slain of the daughters of my people!" Jer. 9: 1.

Could not some one suggest a plan by which the work of Annual Meeting would be applied more generally, and made more effectual in the churches? Every brother and sister should think on this subject, in order, if possible, to find out which way we are going. Possibly we are going backward and not forward. Let us prepare to go forward in the ways of the Lord!

Meyerhoeffer's Store, Va.

BEHOLD, WHAT WEARINESS!—Mal. 1: 13.

BY W. M. LYON.

THEY have come to stay, and their name is "Legion." Their religion is of the irksome sort, —a wearisome employment,—a tiresome business. Through their carelessness and indifference, these Jewish priests profaned the holy altar and rendered God's sacrifices contemptible in the eyes of the people. They felt that they were overburdened with the process of purification for themselves, as well as the "nice inspection of the sacrifices" brought to them. The divine law was before them but they "snuffed at it," and said, "Behold, what a weariness is it!" God had called for offerings "without spot or blemish," (Lev. 22) but they had concluded that "the torn, the lame, the sick," would be good enough.

This "good enough" doctrine was condemned by God in that age and he still hates it. "Let well enough alone." This may do when man's spiritual interests are not involved, but if it has any reference whatever to the standard of duty, as set up by the Great Law-giver, then, "Let God be true, and every man a liar." Rom. 3: 4. "Woe to them that are at EASE IN ZION." Amos 6: 1.

Once-at ease in the church and then commences the cry, "What a weariness is it!" "This is good enough, and that is good enough;" (excepting when applied to laying up treasures on earth) "I am willing still to go on with my offerings and sacrifices (?) but you will have to let me off easy; please accept the torn, the lame, and the sick."

It is the easiest thing in the world to get tired of a thing that we don't enjoy, and to enjoy we must first possess; then lack of enjoyment means lack of possession. A pretty good way to test our religion, is it not? When I speak of enjoyment I mean that to which the Psalmist refers in Ps. 1: 2. When I think of this, it makes me wonder why any Christian should sleep during religious services. My brother, do you really enjoy your religion? If you do, you will not say, "What a weariness is it!" It will be no trouble then, to attend to every means of grace within your power. The prayer-meeting, Bible-class, Sunday-school, the preaching of God's Word, and especially the Communion seasons, these, all these, will be to you "as cold water to a thirsty soul." David says (Ps. 42: 1), "As the hart panteth after the water brooks, so panteth my soul after thee, O God."

That soul cannot weary that pants after its God. If we want to find God, let us seek those places where he has promised to meet us. "Let us not be weary in well doing." Gal. 6: 9. Following God is always well doing, but if we want to follow him, we must "walk by faith, not by sight" (2 Cor. 5: 7). If we want to walk by sight, then we will become "wearied and faint" in our minds. Heb. 12: 3. Then it is that God's commandments become "grievous." 1 John 5: 3. We want to begin the "whittling down" process, make the way easy, and come with our offering of "the torn," and the lame, and the sick."

The Gospel in Rom. 12: 1 is the Gospel in Lev. 22 unfolded and intensified. Nathaniel says, "Moses in the law did write of Jesus of Nazareth." John 1: 45. What do we find in all the rites and services of the Levitical economy, but so many pictures of the "truth as it is in Jesus?"

Brethren, what kind of offerings are we presenting before the Lord? Have we really and truly presented our bodies living sacrifices? Before we can do this, we must know by experience the full meaning of Ps. 51: 17, which says, "The sacrifices of God are a broken spirit; a broken and a contrite heart, O God, thou wilt not despise."

Modern Christianity says, "Let us make our own nice selection of duties. Do not burden us with the ordinances and commandments that were practiced among the primitive Christians. We belong to a more enlightened (?) age." Thus they would say to the world, "Come on with your offerings of 'the torn, the lame, and the sick.'"

And, brethren, while this is a sad truth, let us see to it that we do not act the same part before the world and before God. I greatly fear that to-day there are many, very many among us who depend principally upon external rites and forms for salvation. By this they say, "Here, Lord, I give myself away," but sometimes, when they have an opportunity to give, instead of giving themselves away, it turns out to be a very small fractional part, and in some cases not even enough to make a fraction. Those Jewish priests performed their work mechanically,—the heart was not in the work at all, hence they told the truth, when they said, "Behold, what a weariness is it!" No wonder they were satisfied with "the torn, the lame, and the sick."

Brethren, let us all get to work and test our offerings. Try them by this rule. See if they are sickly, torn, and lame. If so, we can easily locate the trouble. We have the remedy. Will we apply it?

Union Bridge, Md.

THE YOUNG MAN.

BY EMMA WATSON.

"Run, speak to this young man."—Zach. 2: 4.

How necessary it is for the children of God to be continually on the watch, so as to be able to run and speak to the young men who are about to enter into temptation! There are so many snares and pit-falls spread to entice their inexperienced and unwary mind and feet from home and Christian influence! Satan is certainly going about like a "roaring lion, seeking whom he may devour." He also has many agents employed, who, it seems, are so diligent in their master's work that they scarcely have time to

What worse condition could we be in than to be asleep or dead in sin? It is bad enough for those outside of the church, who make no profession of religion, to be in sin, but it is much worse for those in the church and who make a profession. There is no escape from the consequence of sin except by repentance. It is needful for Christians to repent as often as they sin. Do we always do this? I fear not. If we would always do so, there would be a greater ingathering of souls into the church, a greater increase of true vital piety among the members. There would be more light shed abroad in the world, and less ignorance of the Bible. If we thoroughly repent of a sin, we will not likely commit that same fault again. But if unrepented of, we are inclined to repeat it, and go on from bad to worse. As members, we need to grow in grace, so as to be able to withstand temptation and avoid all sin.

WHICH WAY ARE WE GOING?

- BY A. FLORY.

The prophet laments Israel's condition because they went backward and not forward. Jer. 7: 24. They were a rebellious and a stiff-necked people, and would not hearken unto the voice of the Lord, but they were continually breaking his laws. They made promises, but did not keep them.

This was very discouraging to Moses, so much so, that at one time he was willing to give up the contest. He says: "Yet now, if thou wilt, forgive their sin—; and if not, blot me, I pray thee, out of thy book which thou hast written." Ex. 32:32. How is it with those who have the oversight of God's chosen people to-day? Do they not feel almost like Moses when they look at the condition of some of the congregations of our Brotherhood? Possibly the disobedient members of those congregations have not departed quite as far from the Written Word and order of the church as Israel did, but is there not sufficient cause for the elders of those churches to be greatly discouraged? We think there is, for the tendency to go back seems to be on the increase. Some, who united with the church while in their youthful days, ran well for a short time, but, as they advanced in age, they also increased in pride and fashion, until now it is not possible to distinguish some of them from the world. Those members, as well as all others, promised annually to hear the church and help to build up the cause of Christ. Possibly they do not realize their real condition. Remember, dear reader, God will hold us strictly to our promises, regardless of what we may think of the matter now, especially so when those promises are in harmony with the spirit of the Gospel, and for the benefit and support of the church. The wise man, Solomon, tells us that it is better not to vow than to vow and not pay. This fact was fully tested by Ananias and Sapphira. They promised to support the church when they mutually agreed to sell their possessions, and bring the price thereof to the apostles. They violated their vows and were struck dead. At this time the church does not require us to sell our farms, but it does ask every one of us to submit to its plain order of dress, as well as many other things. It is not possible to help build up the church and at the same time reject its counsels, for the church is the pillar and ground of the truth.

Some may tell us, that the Gospel does not say what the cut of our garments shall be. That is true. The same is true of Ananias and Sapphira. There is not one word laid down in the Bi-

ble, telling them to sell their possessions, notwithstanding they agreed to do so. For that reason the Brethren have adopted an order of dress. We are living among a people who are evermore changing their fashions and customs, therefore it is of vital importance to have an order. Notwithstanding all the efforts that the church has ever put forth, pride and fashion are continually increasing in some of the congregations. Is there no remedy for this growing evil? Or will it continue to get worse and worse until the salt will have lost its savor, and time will be no longer?

Is there not sufficient cause for the church to fall in line with the prophet and say, "O that my head were fountains of water, and my eyes fountains of tears, that I might weep day and night for the slain of the daughters of my people!" Jer. 9: 1.

Could not some one suggest a plan by which the work of Annual Meeting would be applied more generally, and made more effectual in the churches? Every brother and sister should think on this subject, in order, if possible, to find out which way we are going. Possibly we are going backward and not forward. Let us prepare to go forward in the ways of the Lord! *Meyerhoeffer's Store, Va.*

BEHOLD, WHAT WEARINESS!—Mal. 1:13.

BY W. M. LYON.

They have come to stay, and their name is "Legion." Their religion is of the irksome sort, —a wearisome employment,—a tiresome business. Through their carelessness and indifference, these Jewish priests profaned the holy altar and rendered God's sacrifices contemptible in the eyes of the people. They felt that they were overburdened with the process of purification for themselves, as well as the "nice inspection of the sacrifices" brought to them. The divine law was before them but they "snuffed at it," and said, "Behold, what a weariness is it!" God had called for offerings "without spot or blemish," (Lev. 22) but they had concluded that "the torn, the lame, the sick," would be good enough

This "good enough" doctrine was condemned by God in that age and he still hates it. "Let well enough alone." This may do when man's spiritual interests are not involved, but if it has any reference whatever to the standard of duty, as set up by the Great Law-giver, then, "Let God be true, and every man a liar." Rom. 3: 4. "Woe to them that are at EASE IN ZION." Amos 6: 1.

Once-at ease in the church and then commences the cry, "What a weariness is it!" "This is good enough, and that is good enough;" (excepting when applied to laying up treasures on earth) "I am willing still to go on with my offerings and sacrifices (?) but you will have to let me off easy; please accept the torn, the lame, and the sick."

It is the easiest thing in the world to get tired of a thing that we don't enjoy, and to enjoy we must first possess; then lack of enjoyment means lack of possession. A pretty good way to test our religion, is it not? When I speak of enjoyment I mean that to which the Psalmist refers in Ps. 1: 2. When I think of this, it makes me wonder why any Christian should sleep during religious services. My brother, do you really enjoy your religion? If you do, you will not say, "What a weariness is it!" It will be no trouble then, to attend to every means of grace within your power. The prayer-meeting, Bible-class, Sunday-school, the preaching of God's Word, and especially the Communion seasons, these, all

these, will be to you "as cold water to a thirsty soul." David says (Ps. 42: 1), "As the hart panteth after the water brooks, so panteth my soul after thee, O God."

That soul cannot weary that pants after its God. If we want to find God, let us seek those places where he has promised to meet us. "Let us not be weary in well doing." Gal. 6: 9. Following God is always well doing, but if we want to follow him, we must "walk by faith, not by sight" (2 Cor. 5: 7). If we want to walk by sight, then we will become "wearied and faint" in our minds. Heb. 12: 3. Then it is that God's commandments become "grievous." 1 John 5: 3. We want to begin the "whittling down" process, make the way easy, and come with our offering of "the torn, and the lame, and the sick."

The Gospel in Rom. 12: 1 is the Gospel in Lev. 22 unfolded and intensified. Nathaniel says, "Moses in the law did write of Jesus of Nazareth." John 1: 45. What do we find in all the rites and services of the Levitical economy, but so many pictures of the "truth as it is in Jesus?"

Brethren, what kind of offerings are we presenting before the Lord? Have we really and truly presented our bodies living sacrifices? Before we can do this, we must know by experience the full meaning of Ps. 51: 17, which says, "The sacrifices of God are a broken spirit; a broken and a contrite heart, O God, thou wilt not despise."

Modern Christianity says, "Let us make our own nice selection of duties. Do not burden us with the ordinances and commandments that were practiced among the primitive Christians. We belong to a more enlightened (?) age." Thus they would say to the world, "Come on with your offerings of 'the torn, the lame, and the sick.'"

And, brethren, while this is a sad truth, let us see to it that we do not act the same part before the world and before God. I greatly fear that to-day there are many, very many among us who depend principally upon external rites and forms for salvation. By this they say, "Here, Lord, I give myself away," but sometimes, when they have an opportunity to give, instead of giving themselves away, it turns out to be a very small fractional part, and in some cases not even enough to make a fraction. Those Jewish priests performed their work mechanically,—the heart was not in the work at all, hence they told the truth, when they said, "Behold, what a weariness is it!" No wonder they were satisfied with "the torn, the lame, and the sick."

Brethren, let us all get to work and test our offerings. Try them by this rule. See if they are sickly, torn, and lame. If so, we can easily locate the trouble. We have the remedy. Will we apply it?
Union Bridge, Md.

THE YOUNG MAN.

BY EMMA WATSON.

"Run, speak to this young man."—Zech. 2:4.

How necessary it is for the children of God to be continually on the watch, so as to be able to run and speak to the young men who are about to enter into temptation! There are so many snares and pit-falls spread to entice their inexperienced and unwary mind and feet from home and Christian influence! Satan is certainly going about like a "roaring lion, seeking whom he may devour." He also has many agents employed, who, it seems, are so diligent in their master's work that they scarcely have time to

Missionary and Tract Work Department.

"Upon the first day of the week, let every one of you lay by him in store as God hath prospered him, that there be no gatherings when I come."—1 Cor. 16: 2.

"Every man as he purposeth in his heart, so let him give. Not grudgingly or of necessity, for the Lord loveth a cheerful giver."—2 Cor. 9: 7.

HOW MUCH SHALL WE GIVE?

"Every man *according to his ability*." "Every one *as God hath prospered him*." "Every man, *according as he purposeth in his heart*, so let him give." "For if there be first a willing mind, it is accepted *according to that a man hath*, and not according to that he hath not."—2 Cor. 8: 12.

Organization of Missionary Committee.

DANIEL VANIMAN, Foreman, . . . McPherson, Kans.
D. L. MILLER, Treasurer, . . . Mt. Morris, Ill.
GALEN B. ROYER, Secretary, . . . Mt. Morris, Ill.

Organization of Book and Tract Work.

S. W. HOOVER, Foreman, . . . Dayton, Ohio.
S. BOCK, Secretary and Treasurer, . . . Dayton, Ohio.

☞All donations intended for Missionary Work should be sent to GALEN B. ROYER, Mt. Morris, Ill.

☞All money for Tract Work should be sent to S. BOCK, Dayton, Ohio.

☞Money may be sent by Money Order, Registered Letter, or Drafts on New York or Chicago. Do not send personal checks, or drafts on interior towns, as it costs 25 cents to collect them.

☞Solicitors are requested to faithfully carry out the plan of Annual Meeting, that all our members be solicited to contribute at least twice a year for the Mission and Tract Work of the Church.

☞Notes for the Endowment Fund can be had by writing to the Secretary of either Work.

THE MISSIONARY'S DREAM.

BY W. B. STOVER.

Beside a leafy palm he lay,
His Bible in his hand;
His face was dark, his Saxon hair
Was mingling with the sand.
O'ercome by the heat and toil of the day,
He dreamed of a far-off land.

He thought a blessed day had come,
His labors all were o'er;
And Jesus' name was glorified,
As ne'er it was before;
And all the saints were gathered there,
From every clime and shore.

And there he saw adjoining him
All those now passing by,
Where Jesus stood in the midst of them,
Directing them on high;
And dealing out his starry crowns,
Fit emblems of the sky.

And as the happy saints received
A measure of reward,
He, standing near, within his heart
So oft and oft implored:—
The while forgetful of himself—
That he might help the Lord.

But Jesus turning quick replied
In loving words and true,
"Thy work is ever done, my child,
There's else for thee to do."
His eyes with joyous tears were filled,
His heart was fullness too.

He dreamed he saw his mother there,
And all the loving band
Of those whom years and years ago,
He gave the parting hand,
As he went far away from home
To preach in heathen land.

Again he saw the Bible church,
Where first he preached the Word,
Much larger now, together how
Before the Christ their Lord,
As each and each received his crown,
A part of his reward.

And joy of joys of all the world,
Full soul now fuller still,
A host of those from heathendom,
Obedient to his will
Stand now redeemed before the Lord—
Without him they were lost.

He thought 'twas heaven where he was,
While heaven others won,
His greatest joy was others' joy
Or service weekly done.
And when the host had crowned passed,
He stood with Christ alone.

Scarce deeming himself worthy there,
He heard such voices call,
And wondering, since he was not crowned,
I one to him would fall,
The Master placed upon his head
The brightest crown of all.

ARE WE INSURED?

BY MAGGIE A. NOFZIGER.

NOT long ago when in the City of Los Angeles, we were made to wonder what would be the end of all this hurry. Where are all these people going? What is the object of each? How many are there who know not the love of Jesus, and, again, how many are insured to enter the pearly gate, should the summons come now?

Oh, how thoughtless is poor humanity! How we travel on from day to day, seemingly as though there is no death, no judgment! But we realise that life is uncertain and death is certain, as we enter the limits of this great city and see a hearse slowly passing along. Some one has changed worlds. One more heart has ceased to beat. The question which first comes to us is: Had I been called would I have been prepared? Again, has this one who was called, taken out a policy from the King's Insurance Company,—the oldest, surest, and most reliable company in the world, the one which has been in successful operation for hundreds of years? Other companies may insure for this life; but, dear reader, have you ever stopped to think 'that this is the only company which can insure against the great conflagration, spoken of in 2 Pet. 3: 10, 13, the only company insuring against wreck while passing over the dark waters of the Jordan of death? Isa. 43: 2. "When thou passest through the waters, I will be with thee and through the rivers, they shall not overflow thee."

Blessed thought to the Christian, but to those who have not yet insured, what hope have you? Where are you standing to-night? What promise have you? Surely you can do no better than to invest in this company. It is not expensive and every one has an invitation. Turn to Acts 20: 21 and read one of the conditions of the policy: "Repentance toward God and faith in the Lord Jesus Christ." The one who is altogether lovely "the same yesterday, and to-day and forever." Well might we exclaim in the words of another, "My mind is overmatched in striving to comprehend his incomprehensible blessedness." Again we find another condition in John 10: 28, "And I give unto them eternal life, and they shall never perish, neither shall any man pluck them out of my hand." Brethren and sisters, do you ever grow weary? Do you at times feel almost ready to give up? Oh, think of this blessed promise and may we ever keep in mind that the purest Christian derives all his holy affections, and all his higher and heavenly aspirations from the president of this company,—the King of kings, for he is "able to do exceeding abundantly above all that we ask or think." Eph. 3: 20.

"'Mid the losses and the gains,
Mid the pleasures and the pains,
And the hopings and the fears,
And the restlessness of years,
We repeat this promise o'er,
We believe it more and more;
Bread upon the waters cast,
Shall be gathered at the last."

Lordsburg, Cal.

THE KEY TO YOUR BOY'S HEART.

A LADY writer in the *Sunday School Times* gives this sensible talk to mothers:

"You will say, perhaps, that Tom, as a boy, is cold and unresponsive, that you 'cannot get at him.' That is because you lost the key when he was warm and responsive. It was the most valuable of your possessions—the key to your boy's heart.' If you had realized this, you would have tried to keep it, doubtless. But your thoughts were bent upon buying a farm, building a house, putting money in the bank. The eager little fellow was not attended to with even common politeness when he was bursting with a desire to talk to you and with you. His boyish confidences did not interest you—you had far 'more important things' to attend to. His expanding activities were not given scope in the right and natural direction; his need for change, for fun, above all, for sympathy, was not appreciated.

"But do not think for a moment that there is no key because your boy's heart is closed to you. He is open with somebody, you may be sure—with somebody who will listen to him, feel with him, or pretend to. You would be glad to know the name of this intimate friend who has won your boy. Ten to one it is hidden from you jealously; it certainly is if the companionship be questionable. Nothing is so delightful to the emotional child as a chance to open himself freely to another. The girl-friend who listens, sympathizes, appears to feel, when your daughter confides in her, is the friend who is adored with boundless enthusiasm. She has the key that you have lost, and by its aid, reaches the secret places of your daughter's nature, and leads her as she will.

"The boy-friend who is 'good' to your son is the one who influences him. Every-where one sees mothers 'too busy' to attend to the eager, wistful hearts and minds that need to be fed, entertained, helped or comforted, as the case may be. The mother who would sacrifice herself to the last extreme to attend to the physical wants of her child, to make his little garments and feed him with dainty food, leaves the finer part to starve, till food (?) is picked up wherever it can be found. We have all seen repeatedly, on long railroad journeys, the mother absorbed in a book, while the little one at her side wears himself out with questions that are never answered. He is forced to sit for hours without the slightest entertainment; full of curiosity about the scenes through which he is passing, he has no one to explain them to him, and the ride, which should have been a joy and a charming lesson to him, is a bore. It is that kind of a mother who wonders, a few years later, why her boy does not care for her society; who listens and longs for his return in the late evening, and wonders where he is; who does not understand why he makes friends of certain boys whom he prefers and she does not approve of."

How much we owe to God for denying us so many gifts that we have longed for, but which would have proved our ruin! If we could always have our own way, we should be sure to destroy ourselves. God's love toward us is shown in his denials of our many unwise requests, as truly as in his answers to our fewer right prayers. Every one of us has reason to say:

"Not only for the gifts bestowed,
But more for what thou dost withhold,
I thank thee, Lord."

IF you reject Justice and Peace when they sue for acceptance, be assured that the cause of Peace and Justice will be avenged.

Missionary and Tract Work Department.

"Upon the first day of the week, let every one of you lay by him in store as God hath prospered him, that there be no gatherings when I come."—1 Cor. 16: 2.

"Every man as he purposeth in his heart, so let him give. Not grudgingly or of necessity, for the Lord loveth a cheerful giver."—2 Cor. 9: 7.

HOW MUCH SHALL WE GIVE?

"Every man according to his ability." "Every one as God hath prospered him." "Every man, according as he purposeth in his heart, so let him give." "For if there be first a willing mind, it is accepted according to that a man hath, and not according to that he hath not."—2 Cor. 8: 12.

Organization of Missionary Committee.

DANIEL VANIMAN, Foreman,   McPherson, Kans.
D. L. MILLER, Treasurer,   Mt. Morris, Ill.
GALEN B. ROYER, Secretary,   Mt. Morris, Ill.

Organization of Book and Tract Work.

S. W. HOOVER, Foreman,   Dayton, Ohio.
S. BOCK, Secretary and Treasurer,   Dayton, Ohio.

☞ All donations intended for Missionary Work should be sent to GALEN B. ROYER, Mt. Morris, Ill.

☞ All money for Tract Work should be sent to S. BOCK, Dayton, Ohio.

☞ Money may be sent by Money Order, Registered Letter, or Drafts on New York or Chicago. Do not send personal checks, or drafts on interior towns, as it costs 25 cents to collect them.

☞ Solicitors are requested to faithfully carry out the plan of Annual Meeting, that all our members be solicited to contribute at least twice a year for the Mission and Tract Work of the Church.

☞ Notes for the Endowment Fund can be had by writing to the Secretary of either Work.

THE MISSIONARY'S DREAM.

BY W. B. STOVER.

Beside a leafy palm he lay,
  His Bible in his hand;
His face was dark, his Saxon hair
  Was mingling with the sand.
O'ercome by the heat and toil of the day,
  He dreamed of a far-off land.

He thought a blessed day had come,
  His labors all were o'er;
And Jesus' name was glorified,
  As ne'er it was before;
And all the saints were gathered there,
  From every clime and shore.

And there he saw adjoining him
  All those now passing by,
Where Jesus stood in the midst of them,
  Directing them on high;
And dealing out his starry crowns,
  Fit emblems of the sky.

And as the happy saints received
  A measure of reward,
He, standing near, within his heart
  So oft and oft implored—
The while forgetful of himself—
  That he might help the Lord.

But Jesus turning quick replied
  In loving words and true,
"Thy work is ever done, my child,
  There's else for thee to do."
His eyes with joyous tears were filled,
  His heart was fullness too.

He dreamed he saw his mother there,
  And all the loving band
Of those whom years and years ago,
  He gave the parting hand,
As he went far away from home
  To preach in heathen land.

Again he saw the little church,
  Where first he preached the Word,
Much larger now, together bow
  Before the Christ their Lord,
As each and each received his crown,
  A part of his reward.

And joy of joys of all the world,
  Full soul now fuller still,
A host of those from heathendom,
  Obedient to his will
Stand now redeemed before the Lord—
  Without him they were lost.

He thought 'twas heaven where he was,
  While heaven others won,
His greatest joy was others' joy
  Or service meekly done.
And when the host had crowned passed,
  He stood with Christ alone.

Scarce deeming himself worthy there,
  He heard such voices call,
And wondering, since he was not crowned,
  If one to him would fall,
The Master placed upon his head
  The brightest crown of all.

ARE WE INSURED?

BY MAGGIE A. NOFZIGER.

NOT long ago when in the City of Los Angeles, we were made to wonder what would be the end of all this hurry. Where are all these people going? What is the object of each? How many are there who know not the love of Jesus, and, again, how many are insured to enter the pearly gate, should the summons come now?

Oh, how thoughtless is poor humanity! How we travel on from day to day, seemingly as though there is no death, no judgment! But we realize that life is uncertain and death is certain, as we enter the limits of this great city and see a hearse slowly passing along. Some one has changed worlds. One more heart has ceased to beat. The question which first comes to us is: Had I been called would I have been prepared? Again, has this one who was called, taken out a policy from the King's Insurance Company,—the oldest, surest, and most reliable company in the world, the one which has been in successful operation for hundreds of years? Other companies may insure for this life; but, dear reader, have you ever stopped to think that this is the only company which can insure against the great conflagration, spoken of in 2 Pet. 3: 10, 13, the only company insuring against wreck while passing over the dark waters of the Jordan of death? Isa. 43: 2. "When thou passest through the waters, I will be with thee and through the rivers, they shall not overflow thee."

Blessed thought to the Christian, but to those who have not yet insured, what hope have you? Where are you standing to-night? What promise have you? Surely you can do no better than to invest in this company. It is not expensive and every one has an invitation. Turn to Acts 20: 21 and read one of the conditions of the policy: "Repentance toward God and faith in the Lord Jesus Christ." The one who is altogether lovely "the same yesterday, and to-day and forever." Well might we exclaim in the words of another, "My mind is overmatched in striving to comprehend this incomprehensible blessedness." Again we find another condition in John 10: 28, "And I give unto them eternal life, and they shall never perish, neither shall any man pluck them out of my hand." Brethren and sisters, do you ever grow weary? Do you at times feel almost ready to give up? Oh, think of this blessed promise and may we ever keep in mind that the purest Christian derives all his holy affections, and all his higher and heavenly aspirations from the president of this company,—the King of kings, for he is "able to do exceeding abundantly above all that we ask or think." Eph. 3: 20.

"'Mid the losses and the gains,
  'Mid the pleasures and the pains,
  And the hopings and the fears,
  And the restlessness of years,
  We repeat this promise o'er,
  We believe it more and more;
  Bread upon the waters cast,
  Shall be gathered at the last."

Lordsburg, Cal.

THE KEY TO YOUR BOY'S HEART.

A LADY writer in the *Sunday School Times* gives this sensible talk to mothers:

"You will say, perhaps, that Tom, as a boy, is cold and unresponsive, that you 'cannot get at him.' That is because you lost the key when he was warm and responsive. It was the most valuable of your possessions—the key to your boy's heart. If you had realized this, you would have tried to keep it, doubtless. But your thoughts were bent upon buying a farm, building a house, putting money in the bank. The eager little fellow was not attended to with even common politeness when he was bursting with a desire, to talk to you and with you. His boyish confidences did not interest you—you had far 'more important things' to attend to. His expanding activities were not given scope in the right and natural direction; his need for change, for fun, above all, for sympathy, was not appreciated.

"But do not think for a moment that there is no key because your boy's heart is closed to you. He is open with somebody, you may be sure—with somebody who will listen to him, feel with him, or pretend to. You would be glad to know the name of this intimate friend who has won your boy. Ten to one it is hidden from you jealously; it certainly is if the companionship be questionable. Nothing is so delightful to the emotional child as a chance to open himself freely to another. The girl-friend who listens, sympathizes, appears to feel, when your daughter confides in her, is the friend who is adored with boundless enthusiasm. She has the key that you have lost, and by its aid, reaches the secret places of your daughter's nature, and leads her as she will.

"The boy-friend who is 'good' to your son is the one who influences him. Every-where one sees mothers 'too busy' to attend to the eager, wistful hearts and minds that need to be fed, entertained, helped or comforted, as the case may be. The mother who would sacrifice herself to the last extreme to attend to the physical wants of her child, to make his little garments and feed him with dainty food, leaves the finer part to starve, till food (?) is picked up wherever it can be found. We have all seen repeatedly, on long railroad journeys, the mother absorbed in a book, while the little one at her side wears himself out with questions that are never answered. He is forced to sit for hours without the slightest entertainment; full of curiosity about the scenes through which he is passing, he has no one to explain them to him, and the ride, which should have been a joy and a charming lesson to him, is a bore. It is that kind of a mother who wonders, a few years later, why her boy does not care for her society; who listens and longs for his return in the late evening, and wonders where he is; who does not understand why he makes friends of certain boys whom he prefers and she does not approve of."

How much we owe to God for denying us so many gifts that we have longed for, but which would have proved our ruin! If we could always have our own way, we should be sure to destroy ourselves. God's love toward us is shown in his denials of our many unwise requests, as truly as in his answers to our fewer right prayers. Every one of us has reason to say:

"Not only for the gifts bestowed,
But more for what thou dost withhold,
   I thank thee, Lord."

IF you reject Justice and Peace when they sue for acceptance, be assured that the cause of Peace and Justice will be avenged.

The Gospel Messenger,

A Weekly at $1.50 Per Annum.

PUBLISHED BY

The Brethren's Publishing Co.

D. L. MILLER, ... Editor.
J. H. MOORE, ... Office Editor.
J. B. BRUMBAUGH, } . . . . . . Associate Editors.
J. G. ROYER, }
JOSEPH AMICK, ... Business Manager.

ADVISORY COMMITTEE.
L. W. Teeter, A. Hutchison, Daniel Hays.

☞Communications for publication should be legibly written with black ink on one side of the paper only. Do not attempt to interline, or to put on one page what ought to occupy two."

☞"Anonymous communications will not be published.

☞Do not mix business with articles for publication. Keep your communications on separate sheets from all business.

☞"Time is precious. We always have time to attend to business and to answer questions of importance, but please do not subject us to need less answering of letters.

☞The MESSENGER is mailed each week to all subscribers. If the address is correctly entered on our list, the paper must reach the person to whom it is addressed. If you do not get your paper, write us, giving particulars.

☞When changing your address, please give your former as well as your future address in full, so as to avoid delay and misunderstanding.

☞Always remit to the office from which you order your goods, no matter from where you receive them.

☞Do not send personal checks or drafts on interior banks, unless you send with them 25 cents each, to pay for collection.

☞Remittances should be made by Post-office Money Order, Drafts on New York, Philadelphia or Chicago, or Registered Letters, made payable and addressed to "Brethren's Publishing Co., Mount Morris, Ill.," or "Brethren's Publishing Co., Huntingdon, Pa."

☞"Entered at the Post-office at Mount Morris, Ill., as second-class matter.

Mount Morris, Ill., - - - - Oct. 18, 1892.

BRO. GEO. W. HOPWOOD, of Deep River, Iowa, favored us with a short call last week. We regret that he could not remain longer.

BRO. P. A. MOORE and wife, of Roanoke, Ill., are preparing to return to California next week, with the intention of remaining eighteen months.

THE Hymn Book Committee meet in Mt. Morris the morning that this issue goes on the press. Hence we can say nothing concerning their work this week.

THE Brethren's Ministerial Meeting, for the Southern District of Pennsylvania, will be held in the Codorus church, York, Pa., Nov. 30th, Dec. 1st and 2nd. Send to Jacob Aldinger for a neatly-printed program.

IT is said that the noted Peter Cartwright once attended one of the Brethren's love-feasts in Illinois. At the close of the services a brother asked him what he thought of the meeting. He said, "Well, brother, if you let me alone, I will let you alone."

ENCOURAGING reports are coming in from the feasts in all parts of the Brotherhood. As a general thing the weather has been delightful, the health good and the attendance all that could be expected. Probably never before in the history of the church have there been so many love-feasts, and while the world has been preparing for its great gatherings for worldly display, our people have been gaining spiritual strength by feasting together in heavenly places. Not a few have been gathered into the fold, with a fair prospect of a general awakening all along the line. These feasts have been the means of much Christian grace, and should be followed by great efforts upon the part of all our churches, to labor for a special ingathering of souls, as well as for the further strengthening of the members. God has abundantly blessed us in many ways, and we should certainly show our appreciation by serving him and his cause more earnestly.

THOSE seeking the best arguments in defense of our faith and practice should send for a copy of "The Doctrine of the Brethren Defended," by Eld. R. H. Miller. Price $1.25. A copy of this excellent work should be in the hands of every minister in the Brotherhood.

BRO. J. G. ROYER who has just returned from Roanoke, Illinois, reports an enjoyable visit among the Brethren and some good meetings. He speaks very highly of the church at that place and commends the members for their zeal and steadfastness in the Lord's work.

BRO. I. J. ROSENBERGER spent one day with us last week. He was on his way home from the Lanark meetings. He reports an excellent series of meetings which resulted in ten additions instead of nine, as mentioned last week. The weather was delightful and the congregations very large, sometimes filling the house to overflowing. We enjoyed Bro. Rosenberger's call very much and hope to have him call again when passing this way.

AT our ministerial meetings the Brethren should always advocate that which is in perfect accord with our accepted faith and doctrine. It would be neither wise nor right to use these meetings as a place to sow seed that may sooner or later lead to discord. The committee on program should keep an eye on this point, for it is worthy of prayerful consideration. Questions of difference in our Brotherhood, as well as others that virtually belong to the Annual Meeting, should be studiously avoided.

WE understand that Bro. Henry Frantz has consented to return to West Branch this week and continue his series of meetings at that place. He did an excellent work while with the church a few weeks ago, but it was quite apparent that the meetings closed too soon, as the whole community seems to have been aroused. We suggest that it might be good to keep Bro. Frantz in Northern Illinois several months. There are a number of churches in which he could do a good and a much needed work. He should, however, spend not less than four weeks at each point. Our brethren should enter into these meetings in earnest and continue them long enough to insure good results.

MR. CHARLES N. CRITTENTON, of New York, is a man of immense wealth. He counts his dollars by the million, and yet he is overflowing with a religious zeal that is to be commended. He thought to redeem some of the girls from their life of shame. On one occasion he plead with one of the outcasts, exhorting her to forsake her life of degradation. At last he said to her, "Neither do I condemn thee; go and sin no more." The poor creature turned to him and said, "Where can I go?" All the night long, and for days, did Mr. Crittenton had that question ringing in his ears. He knew that every respectable door in that great city was closed against the unfortunate one. He resolved that he would establish a great institution to which these poor sinful outcasts could be sent out reformed. Thousands of dollars were set apart for this purpose. This was done nine years ago, and five hundred outcasts are yearly gathered into this institution, and three-fourths of them are redeemed. Mr. Crittenton has established similar institutions in other large cities, and is thereby showing what good may be accomplished by great wealth. It is encouraging to see men of immense fortune using their means to redeem suffering humanity.

FROM the Beaver City, Nebraska Tribune we learn that Bro. Geo. M. Miller, of that place, died very suddenly. He was a deacon in the church. He came to the State about five years ago, and was, at the time of his death, seventy-two years old.

WE learn that the District Meeting of Southern Illinois, held this year in Fulton County, passed off very pleasantly. The business was transacted in a very agreeable manner. We have not yet been informed who is to represent the District at the next Annual Meeting.

BRO. D. L. MILLER has about completed his arrangements to sail for the Bible Lands in November next. Bro. J. C. Lahman is making preparations to accompany him. We shall have more to say of this trip when all the arrangements are perfected and the parties ready to start.

THE Sunday-school at West Dayton, Ohio, collected during the last year, $180.00 more than was needed to defray the current expenses of the school. This amount was used in the way of helping to defray the expenses of a Sunday-school room, lately added to the meeting-house.

WE have just printed a new supply of Certificates of membership; bound in neat book form, each book containing fifty certificates with stub attached, price 50 cents by mail. This is perhaps the neatest supply of well-bound certificates that we have yet put out. Every congregation should have one of these books.

IN Northern Illinois love-feasts were held last week at Shannon, Arnold's Grove, Pine Creek, Yellow Creek and Naperville. So far as heard from, everything passed off very pleasantly. At Pine Creek the Brethren were engaged in a series of meetings before and after the feast. At present there are six applicants for baptism with an increased interest, and the meetings are being continued.

THE time set for the Special District Meeting of Northern Illinois is Oct. 18. The meeting will be held at Mt. Morris, and is designed to consider questions pertaining to the interest of the Old People's Home at this place. The Home is now about completed, and the Trustees are prepared to receive and care for such bodies, furniture, etc., as may be intended for the use of the Home. We announce this for the information of those who are preparing to donate something for the use of this charitable institution. We shall have more to say of the Home later.

FOR years we have been personally acquainted with an aged father in the church, who always has plenty of earnest friends around him. Wherever he goes, his presence is always welcomed, and his company enjoyed. He is not learned, nor is he eloquent, yet there is something about him that draws but never repels. Even strangers admire him. The secret of this power is a young heart. His steps and appearance indicate great age, but he is as polite and obliging as a well-trained young man of twenty. To his children, as well as his wife, he is as polite and gentle as though they were visitors from some favorite families. He never forgets to be polite, nor does he forget that he was once young. He never visits a family without politely noticing every member in the family, even the very small children. While he is not forward in pointing out the mistakes of others, his godly life, and the interest he takes in the welfare of others, have been the means of leading hundreds to forsake sin and lead consecrated lives.

The Gospel Messenger,

A Weekly at $1.50 Per Annum.

PUBLISHED BY

The Brethren's Publishing Co.

D. L. MILLER, ... Editor
J. H. MOORE, ... Office Editor.
J. B. BRUMBAUGH, } . . . . . Associate Editors.
J. G. ROYER, }
JOSEPH AMICK, ... Business Manager.

ADVISORY COMMITTEE.
L. W. Teeter, A. Hutchison, Daniel Hays.

Communications for publication should be legibly written with black ink on one side of the paper only. Do not attempt to interline, or to put on one page what ought to occupy two.

Anonymous communications will not be published.

Do not mix business with articles for publication. Keep your communications on separate sheets from all business.

Time is precious. We always have time to attend to business and to answer questions of importance, but please do not subject us to need less answering of letters.

The MESSENGER is mailed each week to all subscribers. If the address is correctly entered on our list, the paper must reach the person to whom it is addressed. If you do not get your paper, write us, giving particulars.

When changing your address, please give your former as well as your future address in full, so as to avoid delay and misunderstanding.

Always remit to the office from which you order your goods, no matter from where you receive them.

Devout send personal checks or drafts on interior banks, unless you send with them 25 cents each, to pay for collection.

Remittances should be made by Post-office Money Order, Drafts on New York, Philadelphia or Chicago, or Registered Letter, made payable and addressed to "Brethren's Publishing Co., Mount Morris, Ill.," or "Brethren's Publishing Co., Huntingdon, Pa."

Entered at the Post-office at Mount Morris. Ill. as second-class matter.

Mount Morris, Ill., ... Oct. 18, 1892.

BRO. GEO. W. HOPWOOD, of Deep River, Iowa, favored us with a short call last week. We regret that he could not remain longer.

BRO. P. A. MOORE and wife, of Roanoke, Ill., are preparing to return to California next week, with the intention of remaining eighteen months.

THE Hymn Book Committee meet in Mt. Morris the morning that this issue goes on the press. Hence we can say nothing concerning their work this week.

THE Brethren's Ministerial Meeting, for the Southern District of Pennsylvania, will be held in the Codorus church, York, Pa., Nov. 30th, Dec. 1st and 2nd. Send to Jacob Aldinger for a neatly-printed program.

IT is said that the noted Peter Cartwright once attended one of the Brethren's love-feasts in Illinois. At the close of the services a brother asked him what he thought of the meeting. He said, "Well, brother, if you let me alone, I will let you alone."

ENCOURAGING reports are coming in from the feasts in all parts of the Brotherhood. As a general thing the weather has been delightful, the health good and the attendance all that could be expected. Probably never before in the history of the church have there been so many love-feasts, and while the world has been preparing for its great gatherings for worldly display, our people have been gaining spiritual strength by feasting together in heavenly places. Not a few have been gathered into the fold, with a fair prospect of a general awakening all along the line. These feasts have been the means of much Christian grace, and should be followed by great efforts upon the part of all our churches, to labor for a special ingathering of souls, as well as for the further strengthening of the members. God has abundantly blessed us in many ways, and we should certainly show our appreciation by serving him and his cause more earnestly.

THOSE seeking the best arguments in defense of our faith and practice should send for a copy of "The Doctrine of the Brethren Defended," by Eld. R. H. Miller. Price $1.25. A copy of this excellent work should be in the hands of every minister in the Brotherhood.

BRO. J. G. ROYER who has just returned from Roanoke, Illinois, reports an enjoyable visit among the Brethren and some good meetings. He speaks very highly of the church at that place and commends the members for their zeal and steadfastness in the Lord's work.

BRO. I. J. ROSENBERGER spent one day with us last week. He was on his way home from the Lanark meetings. He reports an excellent series of meetings which resulted in ten additions instead of nine, as mentioned last week. The weather was delightful and the congregations very large, sometimes filling the house to overflowing. We enjoyed Bro. Rosenberger's call very much and hope to have him call again when passing this way.

AT our ministerial meetings the Brethren should always advocate that which is in perfect accord with our accepted faith and doctrine. It would be neither wise nor right to use these meetings as a place to sow seed that may sooner or later lead to discord. The committee on program should keep an eye on this point, for it is worthy of prayerful consideration. Questions of difference in our Brotherhood, as well as others that virtually belong to the Annual Meeting, should be studiously avoided.

WE understand that Bro. Henry Frantz has consented to return to West Branch this week and continue his series of meetings at that place. He did an excellent work while with the church a few weeks ago, but it was quite apparent that the meetings closed too soon, as the whole community seems to have been aroused. We suggest that it might be good to keep Bro. Frantz in Northern Illinois several months. There are a number of churches in which he could do a good and a much needed work. He should, however, spend not less than four weeks at each point. Our brethren should enter into these meetings in earnest and continue them long enough to insure good results.

MR. CHARLES N. CRITTENTON, of New York, is a man of immense wealth. He counts his dollars by the million, and yet he is overflowing with a religious zeal that is to be commended. He thought to redeem some of the girls from their life of shame. On one occasion he plead with one of the outcasts, exhorting her to forsake her life of degradation. At last he said to her, "Neither do I condemn thee; go and sin no more." The poor creature turned to him and said, "Where can I go?" All the night long, and for days, did Mr. Crittenton hear that question ringing in his ears. He knew that every respectable door in that great city was closed against the unfortunate one. He resolved that he would establish a great institution to which these poor sinful outcasts could be sent out reformed. Thousands of dollars were set apart for this purpose. This was done nine years ago, and five hundred outcasts are yearly gathered into this institution, and three-fourths of them are redeemed. Mr. Crittenton has established similar institutions in other large cities, and is thereby showing what good may be accomplished by great wealth. It is encouraging to see men of immense fortunes using their means to redeem suffering humanity.

FROM the Beaver City, Nebraska *Tribune* we learn that Bro. Geo. M. Miller, of that place, died very suddenly. He was a deacon in the church. He came to the State about five years ago, and was, at the time of his death, seventy-two years old.

WE learn that the District Meeting of Southern Illinois, held this year in Fulton County, passed off very pleasantly. The business was transacted in a very agreeable manner. We have not yet been informed who is to represent the District at the next Annual Meeting.

BRO. D. L. MILLER has about completed his arrangements to sail for the Bible Lands in November next. Bro. J. C. Lahman is making preparations to accompany him. We shall have more to say of this trip when all the arrangements are perfected and the parties ready to start.

THE Sunday-school at West Dayton, Ohio, collected during the last year, $180.00 more than was needed to defray the current expenses of the school. This amount was used in the way of helping to defray the expenses of a Sunday-school room, lately added to the meeting-house.

WE have just printed a new supply of Certificates of membership; bound in neat book form, each book containing fifty certificates with stub attached, price 50 cents by mail. This is perhaps the neatest supply of well-bound certificates that we have yet put out. Every congregation should have one of these books.

IN Northern Illinois love-feasts were held last week at Shannon, Arnold's Grove, Pine Creek, Yellow Creek and Naperville. So far as heard from, everything passed off very pleasantly. At Pine Creek the Brethren were engaged in a series of meetings before and after the feast. At present there are six applicants for baptism with an increased interest, and the meetings are being continued.

THE time set for the Special District Meeting of Northern Illinois is Oct. 18. The meeting will be held at Mt. Morris, and is designed to consider questions pertaining to the interest of the Old People's Home at this place. The Home is now about completed, and the Trustees are prepared to receive and care for such bedding, furniture, etc., as may be intended for the use of the Home. We announce this for the information of those who are preparing to donate something for the use of this charitable institution. We shall have more to say of the Home later.

FOR years we have been personally acquainted with an aged father in the church, who always has plenty of earnest friends around him. Wherever he goes, his presence is always welcomed, and his company enjoyed. He is not learned, nor is he eloquent, yet there is something about him that draws but never repels. Even strangers admire him. The secret of this power is a young heart. His steps and appearance indicate great age, but he is as polite and obliging as a well-trained young man of twenty. To his children, as well as his wife, he is as polite and gentle as though they were visitors from some favorite families. He never forgets to be polite, nor does he forget that he was once young. He never visits a family without politely noticing every member in the family, even the very small children. While he is not forward in pointing out the mistakes of others, his godly life, and the interest he takes in the welfare of others, have been the means of leading hundreds to forsake sin and lead consecrated lives.

SET TO THINKING.

LAST evening, Sept. 28, Eld. Daniel Vaniman, of McPherson, Kans., preached a plain and practical sermon in the College Chapel. It was listened to with close attention, and our people were much pleased with the earnest spirit of the speaker. Eld. Vaniman has been spending some time in the churches of Eastern Pennsylvania, and his mission was to get our people to think on the mission question. We were impressed with this phase of his mission. It is very important that Christians have proper things to occupy their minds, and certainly the spread of the Gospel and the conversion of souls is a very proper subject for thought. If our people would think more along this line, a greater work would be done for Christ. Nor is this all. There would be more purity of life, less selfishness, and a higher plane of Christian living. Observation bears us out in this statement. Go into a church where there is no interest in mission work, where the membership has not been thinking on the subject at all, and, as a general thing, you find that church on the decline spiritually. This is more apparent now than in former years. The mission work is now held up before our people, and those who have been thinking are now afforded an opportunity to become active. Those who have not been thinking are still on the background in the work, and, as a result, lack warmth of Christian zeal. The panacea for this condition of affairs is to get our people to think, and Eld. Vaniman's mission is, therefore, in our estimation a very good one. No amount of fault-finding or scolding will accomplish the work. Thought on the subject is what is needed, and if we had a dozen more -men in the field with similar motives and feelings, a great work would be done. Not only would there be a revival in the mission work, but in all departments of Christian labor.

We are glad to learn that a brother is willing to give himself to mission work in India. His move is in harmony with the commission and with the apostolic injunction, "Do good to all men." We never could see how we, as a church, could do our duty without trying to teach those in heathen lands, and longed for the time when an effort in this direction would be made. We are glad to know that our Bro. Vaniman is heartily in sympathy with the brother who is willing to give himself to the work, and is making some of our people think on the subject of foreign missions. May God speed the work!

There is still another subject upon which some of our people need to be set thinking, and that is on the support of our educational work. We suppose Bro. Vaniman has been trying to get some to thinking along that line too. Perhaps, first of all, some teaching is needed in reference to our school work. We find that many of our brethren think that when a school building is up and paid for, and a fair patronage is secured, then the project is a success. Some even think those connected with such institutions are making money. The reverse is true. Were it not that sacrifices are made all around, and the closest economy used, our schools could not live at all. In fact, any school that must depend for support on the income from students, is not in a position to do extended educational work. The most it can do, is preparatory work, and this is just the situation of our schools now. We know of some eight or ten young men who have left our schools and

gone to other colleges because they cannot be served in our own. Does some one ask, why? Simply because we do not have the means to carry on a regular college course. To do this, apparatus is needed, and additional teachers, which would be attended with a heavy expense. What is needed is an endowment fund, and our people need to be set thinking on this subject. Our schools cannot meet the wants of the church until this is obtained.

To start our young men and women in their educational work and then have them go to other colleges to finish up their work, will prove ruinous, and the sooner we look at this matter squarely, the better. We are becoming interested in mission work; we want the doctrines of the Bible, as we understand them, given to the world, but who is to do this work, and who are to be our future missionaries? Our young men, certainly. And are other colleges, with all their liberalism in doctrine, the best places to fit them for this great work? There is more needed than money to carry on our mission work. We will need men with apostolic zeal for this work, and, for our part, we are at present more concerned about the men than the money.

With this feeling we look upon our educational work as the most important matter for consideration. We repeat a statement already made in this form: *Our young men will be our missionaries within the next ten years.* Ponder this statement and then consider whether it is not important that our schools meet the demands of our young men. This cannot be done without an endowment fund. Where is this to come from? From our people who have means, of course.

Now can't we get our Brethren to think on this line? We are glad that some are beginning to think. Recently a brother told us he had been thinking about this matter and without solicitation gave us an endowment note of five hundred dollars, at four per cent, the face value of the note to be paid out of his estate at death. This brother is a man of moderate means and has a family too, but he was thinking along this line, and hence the result. I give this as an illustration of the result of thinking. There are those who could give five, ten, twenty, and, indeed, there may be a few among us who could give one hundred thousand dollars, if they could be made to think on the subject, and see its importance.

We are forcibly impressed with the thought that Bro. Vaniman is working in the right way. What our people need is to *think* on these things.

Recently we made a trip to an adjoining State in behalf of our school interests. We were in localities where ten years ago there would have been opposition to any effort of this kind. But we were received with marked kindness everywhere, and were encouraged in our work. Why this change? Simply because our brethren and sisters have been thinking These observations have engendered within us a more charitable feeling towards those who are slow in contributing to the educational and missionary work of the church. Let us do what we can, in a most kindly way, to get our people to think along these lines.

J. B. B.

WHAT OF OUR CHILDREN?

WE have, in late issues of the MESSENGER, had considerable said about our schools,—their relation to the church, their moulding influence

upon the church, and the consequent necessity of special educational training for our ministers.

Many good things have been said in those articles, but there has been nothing said as to what shall be done with our children in the meantime. God has given us children to be brought up for him,—for his church and service,—and I ask, What are we doing for them?

Another faithful summer's work has been done by them for us. Winter is approaching and we feel that our children ought, yea, must go to school. Where shall they go? Where will we send them?

Whatever moulding influence the church receives through our schools must necessarily come through our children. If schools exert an influence upon our children, what must be the character of the influence our children and the church, through the children, receive in attending those widely-advertised cheap schools of fashion and infidelity? What must be the moulding effect of that influence when those children return,—bring it home into the family and into the church? It will be very similar to sending a child to Russia to bring cholera home into the family and neighborhood. No parent would, for a moment, think of bringing cholera into the family, and yet how many allow, and others even encourage, their children to attend those schools of the world?

There was a time when we were under the necessity of sending our children to schools of the world, if they were to be sent at all, but that time is in the past. We now have Brethren's schools,—we have them in Virginia, Pennsylvania, Illinois, Kansas and California, and we may send our children to those schools. Our schools afford the necessary educational facilities at very reasonable expense.

What excuse shall we offer, then, for sending our children elsewhere? It is true, sacrifices of various kinds must be made to send them away from home to school. How necessary, then, that the sacrifices we make bring the best possible returns for our children, our families and our church! I would suggest that parents, who have children who ought to go to school, or who expect to go to school, do so much, *at least*, as to send to our Brethren's schools for their catalogues. There is not a school under the management of the Brethren, but that will cheerfully send much information *free of charge*, if it is simply asked for. It will cost but one cent to secure such information, and you can do no harm by asking for it. Are there obstacles in the way of sending your children to a Brethren's school this winter, state them fully, and I am sure the brethren will do all in their power to help remove them.

J. G. R.

CORRESPONDENCE.

" Write what thou seest, and send it unto the churches."

☞Church News solicited for this Department. If you have had a good meeting, send a report of it, so that others may rejoice with you. In writing give name of church, County and State. Be brief. Notes of Travel should be as short as possible. Land Advertisements are not solicited for this Department. We have an advertising page, and, if necessary, will issue supplements.

From the Dry Creek Church, Iowa.

BRO J. C. MURRAY, of Nappanee, Ind., was engaged to hold a series of meetings in this congregation this fall, and, according to previous arrangements, we assembled at the old church house Saturday evening, Sept. 17, for worship

SET TO THINKING.

LAST evening, Sept. 28, Eld. Daniel Vaniman, of McPherson, Kans., preached a plain and practical sermon in the College Chapel. It was listened to with close attention, and our people were much pleased with the earnest spirit of the speaker. Eld. Vaniman has been spending some time in the churches of Eastern Pennsylvania, and his mission was to get our people to think on the mission question. We were impressed with this phase of his mission. It is very important that Christians have proper things to occupy their minds, and certainly the spread of the Gospel and the conversion of souls is a very proper subject for thought. If our people would think more along this line, a greater work would be done for Christ. Nor is this all. There would be more purity of life, less selfishness, and a higher plane of Christian living. Observation bears us out in this statement. Go into a church where there is no interest in mission work, where the membership has not been thinking on the subject at all, and, as a general thing, you find that church on the decline spiritually. This is more apparent now than in former years. The mission work is now held up before our people, and those who have been thinking are now afforded an opportunity to become active. Those who have not been thinking are still on the background in the work, and, as a result, lack warmth of Christian zeal. The panacea for this condition of affairs is to get our people to think, and Eld. Vaniman's mission is, therefore, in our estimation a very good one. No amount of fault-finding or scolding will accomplish the work. Thought on the subject is what is needed, and if we had a dozen more men in the field with similar motives and feelings, a great work would be done. Not only would there be a revival in the mission work, but in all departments of Christian labor.

We are glad to learn that a brother is willing to give himself to mission work in India. His move is in harmony with the commission and with the apostolic injunction, "Do good to all men." We never could see how we, as a church, could do our duty without trying to teach those in heathen lands, and longed for the time when an effort in this direction would be made. We are glad to know that our Bro. Vaniman is heartily in sympathy with the brother who is willing to give himself to the work, and is making some of our people think on the subject of foreign missions. May God speed the work!

There is still another subject upon which some of our people need to be set thinking, and that is on the support of our educational work. We suppose Bro. Vaniman has been trying to get some to thinking along that line too. Perhaps, first of all, some teaching is needed in reference to our school work. We find that many of our brethren think that when a school building is up and paid for, and a fair patronage is secured, then the project is a success. Some even think those connected with such institutions are making money. The reverse is true. Were it not that sacrifices are made all around, and the closest economy used, our schools could not live at all. In fact, any school that must depend for support on the income from students, is not in a position to do extended educational work. The most it can do, is preparatory work, and this is just the situation of our schools now. We know of some eight or ten young men who have left our schools and

gone to other colleges because they cannot be served in our own. Does some one ask, why? Simply because we do not have the means to carry on a regular college course. To do this, apparatus is needed, and additional teachers, which would be attended with a heavy expense. What is needed is an endowment fund, and our people need to be set thinking on this subject. Our schools cannot meet the wants of the church until this is obtained.

To start our young men and women in their educational work and then have them go to other colleges to finish up their work, will prove ruinous, and the sooner we look at this matter squarely, the better. We are becoming interested in mission work; we want the doctrines of the Bible, as we understand them, given to the world, but who is to do this work, and who are to be our future missionaries? Our young men, certainly. And are other colleges, with all their liberalism in doctrine, the best places to fit them for this great work? There is more needed than money to carry on our mission work. We will need men with apostolic zeal for this work, and, for our part, we are at present more concerned about the men than the money.

With this feeling we look upon our educational work as the most important matter for consideration. We repeat a statement already made in this form: *Our young men will be our missionaries within the next ten years.* Ponder this statement and then consider whether it is not important that our schools meet the demands of our young men. This cannot be done without an endowment fund. Where is this to come from? From our people who have means, of course.

Now can't we get our Brethren to think on this line? We are glad that some are beginning to think. Recently a brother told us he had been thinking about this matter and without solicitation gave us an endowment note of five hundred dollars, at four per cent, the face value of the note to be paid out of his estate at death. This brother is a man of moderate means and has a family too, but he was thinking along this line, and hence the result. I give this as an illustration of the result of thinking. There are those who could give five, ten, twenty, and, indeed, there may be a few among us who could give one hundred thousand dollars, if they could be made to think on the subject, and see its importance.

We are forcibly impressed with the thought that Bro. Vaniman is working in the right way. What our people need is to *think* on these things. Recently we made a trip to an adjoining State in behalf of our school interests. We were in localities where ten years ago there would have been opposition to any effort of this kind. But we were received with marked kindness everywhere, and were encouraged in our work. Why this change? Simply because our brethren and sisters have been thinking. These observations have engendered within us a more charitable feeling towards those who are slow in contributing to the educational and missionary work of the church. Let us do what we can, in a most kindly way, to get our people to think along these lines.   J. B. B.

WHAT OF OUR CHILDREN?

WE have, in late issues of the MESSENGER, had considerable said about our schools,—their relation to the church, their moulding influence

upon the church, and the consequent necessity of special educational training for our ministers.

Many good things have been said in those articles, but there has been nothing said as to what shall be done with our children in the meantime. God has given us children to be brought up for him,—for his church and service,—and I ask, What are we doing for them?

Another faithful summer's work has been done by them for us. Winter is approaching and we feel that our children ought, yes, must go to school. Where shall they go? Where will we send them?

Whatever moulding influence the church receives through our schools must necessarily come through our children. If schools exert an influence upon our children, what must be the character of the influence our children and the church, through the children, receive in attending those widely-advertised cheap schools of fashion and infidelity? What must be the moulding effect of that influence when those children return,—bring it home into the family and into the church? It will be very similar to sending a child to Russia to bring cholera home into the family and neighborhood. No parent would, for a moment, think of bringing cholera into the family, and yet how many allow, and others even encourage, their children to attend those schools of the world?

There was a time when we were under the necessity of sending our children to schools of the world, if they were to be sent at all, but that time is in the past. We now have Brethren's schools,—we have them in Virginia, Pennsylvania, Illinois, Kansas and California, and we may send our children to those schools. Our schools afford the necessary educational facilities at very reasonable expense.

What excuse shall we offer, then, for sending our children elsewhere? It is true, sacrifices of various kinds must be made to send them away from home to school. How necessary, then, that the sacrifices we make bring the best possible returns for our children, our families and our church! I would suggest that parents, who have children who ought to go to school, or who expect to go to school, do so much, *at least*, as to send to our Brethren's schools for their catalogues. There is not a school under the management of the Brethren, but that will cheerfully send much information *free of charge*, if it is simply asked for. It will cost but one cent to secure such information, and you can do no harm by asking for it. Are there obstacles in the way of sending your children to a Brethren's school this winter, state them fully, and I am sure the brethren will do all in their power to help remove them.

     J. G. R.

CORRESPONDENCE.

"Write what thou seest, and send it unto the churches."

☞ Church News solicited for this Department. If you have had a good meeting, send a report of it, so that others may rejoice with you. In writing give name of church, County and State. Be brief. Notes of Travel should be as short as possible. Land Advertisements are not solicited for this Department. We have an advertising page, and, if necessary, will issue supplements.

From the Dry Creek Church, Iowa.

BRO J. C. MURRAY, of Nappanee, Ind., was engaged to hold a series of meetings in this congregation this fall, and, according to previous arrangements, we assembled at the old church-house Saturday evening, Sept. 17, for worship

Church Dedication Near Kewanna, Ind.

At the District Meeting of the Middle District of Indiana, held at Flora, Carroll County, April 1, 1891, a request was presented to the Meeting by the little band of brethren and sisters, residing in the mission field, near Kewanna, Fulton County, Ind., for aid to build a house of worship. District Meeting, after duly considering the request, decided to aid them to the amount of two hundred dollars, and also instructed the Mission Board to correspond with the General Missionary Committee, and request a donation from them also. This was done, the Board granting them two hundred dollars. The brethren and friends, in the vicinity of the location, also subscribed liberally, until we thought a sufficient amount was subscribed, with the above donations, to erect said building. I am glad to say the house is built, and the dedicatory services were held Sept. 18. The day was beautiful. The house was well filled and many could not be accommodated. Eld. D. P. Shively, of Peru, delivered the dedicatory address, taking as a text Heb. 10: 25. Many beautiful thoughts were presented from the Sacred Word. At the close, two precious souls came out from the world, desiring to cast their lot with the people of God.

At 4 P. M., we again met for examination services, preparatory to Communion. At night the house was densely crowded and many could not be accommodated, it being the first Communion ever held in that vicinity, as far as we know, and, indeed, it was a feast of love. In the morning we again met, and after the farewell talk by our loving brother, when we were about taking our leave, another dear one came out on the side of the Lord. The ministers present were brethren D. Bowser, D. P. Shively, Abram Terrell, John Hardsock, Henry and Noah Richrue, and the writer. Brethren John Snowberger and S. M. Aukerman, of the Mission Board, well known as active workers, in building the house, were also present. Bro. S. M. Aukerman is the treasurer of the Mission Board, and is also on the Building Committee. Several young sisters from the Deer Creek church added to the interest of the meeting by their presence, orderly conduct, and manner of dress. Several other brethren and sisters were there from Northern Indiana. The outlook at Kewanna is very good at present. We think many more are near the kingdom.

W. S. TONEY.

Walton, Ind.

From Salem, Oregon.

The District Meeting of Oregon, Washington, and Idaho, was held in the Powell's Valley church, Clackamas Co., Oregon, Sept. 23 and 24, preceded by the Ministerial Meeting on the 22nd. Considerable business came before the Meeting, all of which was disposed of in harmony, and a spirit as becometh brethren.

The missionary cause was considered at length, and provided for, in the consideration of which the old standard bearers of this part of the Pacific Coast manifested a determination to hand down to succeeding generations the heritage of Truth, as taught and practiced by the Brethren.

There were nine ministers present, representing a wide extent of territory.

The members, though scattered, manifest a zeal to be present upon such occasions and associate with those of like precious faith.

Three brethren and two sisters came a distance of 250 miles, 200 of which were covered by private conveyance.

One sister was present from the western part of the State of Washington. Bro. Allen Ives, formerly of Barr Oak, Jewell Co., Kans, was there from Eastern Washington.

On the evening of Sept. 23 a love-feast was held at the home of Bro. Franklin Day. About thirty members were present. There, in the cooling breezes, wafted down from the everlasting snows of Mt. Hood, the monarch of the Cascade Range, was held one of the quietest and most orderly Communions I ever attended.

J. F. EBERSOLE.

From the Pleasant Valley Church, Darke Co., Ohio.

JULY 30 we met for a thanksgiving meeting at the Jordan house. Bro. H. C. Longanecker, of North Star, Ohio, was with us. The different branches of our Missionary and Tract Work were remembered. I was much pleased with the spirit of the giving, as all seemed eager to do something. Our council-meetings, that occurred since, passed off pleasantly and the church is in peace. Our Sunday-schools have enjoyed excellent interest and increased attendance. We held two excellent children's meetings, one in connection with our feast, which was conducted by Bro. D. M. Garver, of Farmersville, Ohio, the other one in connection with our thanksgiving meeting, conducted by Bro. H. C. Longanecker. We have arranged for two series of meetings during the coming winter.

I am, at this writing, in the Woodland church, Ill., where I have held two meetings with large congregations. I expect to spend a month in this and the Astoria church, Ill. As I have left the farm and home interests, to spend the fall and winter laboring for the church, I earnestly crave an interest in the prayers of our dear Brotherhood, that our labors may prove to be for the advancement of the church and saving of souls.

SILAS GILBERT.

Astoria, Ill , Oct 3.

From Mount Hope Church, Oklahoma Territory.

Our love-feast, Sept. 3, was one long to be remembered. Our dear elder, Jacob Appleman, did some good preaching, and Eld. C. G. Root, of Ozawkie, Kans., officiated. More than fifty members communed. We had a good attendance and the best of order. Brethren Root and Appleman bade us farewell in order to fill an appointment at Paradise Prairie. Brethren M. M. Ennis and J. O. Brubaker remained several days, holding forth the Word. When taking their leave, the meeting was continued over Sunday by our noble minister, George W. Landis, assisted by J. W. Burns. As an immediate result of the meeting twelve were baptized and the little band was truly made to rejoice. We ask an interest in the prayers of all our Father's children that we may be able to live out our profession even here in this new country. Bro. J. O. Brubaker bought a home near the church, adding one more faithful minister to our number. May the good Lord ever be with his people!

J. A. LANDIS.

Crescent City, Oklahoma Ter.

Notes from Our Correspondents.

" As cold water to a thirsty soul, so is good news from a far country."

Muenster, Texas.—Can some one of the Brethren give me full name and address of Bro. Elliott, of Houston, Texas? I want the name soon.—*A. W. Austin, Oct. 6.*

Fredonia, Kans.—Notice is hereby given that, since N. Trapp has resigned his position as Secretary of the Mission Board of South-eastern Kansas, and the Board has appointed in his place, the evangelists will please take notice and send in their reports promptly.—*N. M. Horner, Secretary.*

Bearing Spring, Pa.—The good work is still going on. One more was received by baptism last Sunday, Sept. 25.—*J. R. Stayer, Sept. 27.*

North Manchester, Ind.—Last Sunday, at the close of our Sunday-school, one dear sister was received into the fold of Christ by confession and baptism. Give God the praise, and may his blessings ever rest upon her!—*D. C. Cripe, Oct. 8.*

Greene, Iowa.—The members of the Greene church, Greene, Iowa, contemplate holding a series of meetings, commencing Oct. 29, one week previous to our love-feast. Bro. Joseph Holder will be with us at that time, to conduct the meetings.—*J. D Shook, Oct. 10.*

Fredric, Iowa.—We, the Brethren of Monroe County, held our Communion Sept. 9. It was an enjoyable season to all present. Brethren present from a distance were A. Wolf, John Gable, and M. Myers, who gave us wise counsel. One was added to our fold a short time before the feast. Others have also expressed a desire to unite with us.—*Z. M. Follis.*

Collins, Mo.—Our series of meetings, commenced Sept. 10, continued up to the 24th, when we held our love-feast. It was a feast long to be remembered. Brethren J. M. and Martin Mohler, from Johnson County, were with us and preached for us Saturday and Sunday night. As an immediate result of our meetings five came out on the Lord's side and were baptized. They were all young in years. May the Lord help them that they may live faithful!—*E. W. Tracey.*

Naperville, Ill.—A love-feast was held in the Naperville church, Oct. 8. A goodly number participated in the exercises. One family was debarred from participating with us on account of their child having taken poison. Some hopes however, are entertained of its recovery. Bro. G. D. Zollers, of Mt. Carroll, Ill., the author of "Thrilling Incidents on Sea and Land," dealt out the Bread of Life to us on this occasion. The Lord reward him for his labors!—*S. B. Kuhn, Oct. 9.*

Franklin Grove, Ill.—We can certainly report that the love-feast, held at this place Oct. 4 and 5, was an enjoyable one. Owing to the favorable weather, our own members were nearly all present, and we also had a good representation from surrounding congregations. Bro. Moore, of the MESSENGER office, officiated. The Spirit of the Lord seemed to pervade the entire meeting, and it was truly a feast of love. Two (a young man and his wife) were recently received into this church by baptism. What a blessed resolve it would be, if, all young people, who start out in life to establish a home, would resolve to have God in their home!—*D B. Senger.*

Washington Church, Ind.—Our feast is now in the past and was indeed a happy one. The attendance was good and the order excellent. Truly, the Lord was with us! Many brethren and sisters came to the meeting from adjoining congregations, which added much to the enjoyment of the occasion. A good ministerial force was in attendance, and rendered efficient help. We acknowledge the labors of the following-named brethren: Daniel Wysong, Noah Shutt, John Stafford, Daniel Rothenberger, Gorman Heeter and Lewis Workman. This morning, at 9:30, we held a children's meeting, and at 10:30 we had preaching services. In both the brethren acquitted themselves nobly, giving much good advice and counsel. To-night Bro. Shutt holds forth the Word of Life. May God bless all the faithful in every good word and work!—*A. H. Puterbaugh, Oct. 2.*

Church Dedication Near Kewanna, Ind.

At the District Meeting of the Middle District of Indiana, held at Flora, Carroll County, April 1, 1891, a request was presented to the Meeting by the little band of brethren and sisters, residing in the mission field, near Kewanna, Fulton County, Ind., for aid to build a house of worship. District Meeting, after duly considering the request, decided to aid them to the amount of two hundred dollars, and also instructed the Mission Board to correspond with the General Missionary Committee, and request a donation from them also. This was done, the Board granting them two hundred dollars. The brethren and friends, in the vicinity of the location, also subscribed liberally, until we thought a sufficient amount was subscribed, with the above donations, to erect said building. I am glad to say the house is built, and the dedicatory services were held Sept. 18. The day was beautiful. The house was well filled and many could not be accommodated. Eld. D. P. Shively, of Peru, delivered the dedicatory address, taking as a text Heb. 10: 25. Many beautiful thoughts were presented from the Sacred Word. At the close, two precious souls came out from the world, desiring to cast their lot with the people of God.

At 4 P. M., we again met for examination services, preparatory to Communion. At night the house was densely crowded and many could not be accommodated, it being the first Communion ever held in that vicinity, as far as we know, and, indeed, it was a feast of love. In the morning we again met, and after the farewell talk by our loving brother, when we were about taking our leave, another dear one came out on the side of the Lord The ministers present were brethren D. Bowser, D. P. Shively, Abram Terrell, John Hardsock, Henry and Noah Richros, and the writer. Brethren John Snowberger and S. M. Aukerman, of the Mission Board, well known as active workers in building the house, were also present. Bro. S. M. Aukerman is the treasurer of the Mission Board, and is also on the Building Committee. Several young sisters from the Deer Creek church added to the interest of the meeting by their presence, orderly conduct, and manner of dress. Several other brethren and sisters were there from Northern Indiana. The outlook at Kewanna is very good at present. We think many more are near the kingdom.

W. S. TONEY.

Walton, Ind.

From Salem, Oregon.

The District Meeting of Oregon, Washington, and Idaho, was held in the Powell's Valley church, Clackamas Co., Oregon, Sept. 23 and 24, preceded by the Ministerial Meeting on the 22nd. Considerable business came before the Meeting, all of which was disposed of in harmony, and a spirit as becometh brethren.

The missionary cause was considered at length, and provided for, in the consideration of which the old standard bearers of this part of the Pacific Coast manifested a determination to hand down to succeeding generations the heritage of Truth, as taught and practiced by the Brethren.

There were nine ministers present, representing a wide extent of territory.

The members, though scattered, manifest a zeal to be present upon such occasions and associate with those of like precious faith.

Three brethren and two sisters came a distance of 250 miles, 200 of which were covered by private conveyance.

One sister was present from the western part of the State of Washington. Bro. Allen Ives, formerly of Burr Oak, Jewell Co., Kans, was there from Eastern Washington.

On the evening of Sept. 23 a love feast was held at the home of Bro. Franklin Day. About thirty members were present. There, in the cooling breeze, wafted down from the everlasting snows of Mt. Hood, the monarch of the Cascade Range, was held one of the quietest and most orderly Communions I ever attended.

J. F. EBERSOLE.

From the Pleasant Valley Church, Darke Co., Ohio.

JULY 30 we met for a thanksgiving meeting at the Jordan house. Bro. H. C. Longanecker, of North Star, Ohio, was with us. The different branches of our Missionary and Tract Work were remembered. I was much pleased with the spirit of the giving, as all seemed eager to do something. Our council-meetings, that occurred since, passed off pleasantly and the church is in peace. Our Sunday-schools have enjoyed excellent interest and increased attendance. We held two excellent children's meetings, one in connection with our feast, which was conducted by Bro. D. M. Garver, of Farmersville, Ohio, the other one in connection with our thanksgiving meeting, conducted by Bro. H. C. Longanecker. We have arranged for two series of meetings during the coming winter.

I am, at this writing, in the Woodland church, Ill., where I have held two meetings with large congregations. I expect to spend a month in this and the Astoria church, Ill. As I have left the farm and home interests, to spend the fall and winter laboring for the church, I earnestly crave an interest in the prayers of our dear Brotherhood, that our labors may prove to be for the advancement of the church and saving of souls.

SILAS GILBERT.

Astoria, Ill., Oct 3.

From Mount Hope Church, Oklahoma Territory.

Our love-feast, Sept. 3, was one long to be remembered. Our dear elder, Jacob Appleman, did some good preaching, and Eld. C. C. Root, of Ozawkie, Kans., officiated. More than fifty members communed. We had a good attendance and the best of order. Brethren Root and Appleman bade us farewell in order to fill an appointment at Paradise Prairie. Brethren M. M. Ennis and J. O. Brubaker remained several days, holding forth the Word. When taking their leave, the meeting was continued over Sunday by our home minister, George W. Landis, assisted by J. W. Buxna. As an immediate result of the meeting twelve were baptized and the little band was truly made to rejoice. We ask an interest in the prayers of all our Father's children that we may be able to live out our profession even here in this new country. Bro. J. O. Brubaker bought a home near the church, adding one more faithful minister to our number. May the good Lord ever be with his people!

J. A. LANDIS.

Crescent City, Oklahoma Ter.

Notes from Our Correspondents.

"*As cold water to a thirsty soul, so is good news from a far country.*"

Muenster, Texas. — Can some one of the Brethren give me full name and address of Bro. Elliott, of Houston, Texas? I want the name soon.—*A. W. Austin, Oct. 6.*

Fredonia, Kans. — Notice is hereby given that, since N. Trapp has resigned his position as Secretary of the Mission Board of South-eastern Kansas, and the Board has appointed the writer in his place, the evangelist will please take notice and send in their reports promptly.—*E. M. Horner, Secretary.*

Roaring Spring, Pa. — The good work is still going on. One more was received by baptism last Sunday, Sept. 25.—*J. R. Stayer, Sept. 27.*

North Manchester, Ind. — Last Sunday, at the close of our Sunday-school, one dear sister was received into the fold of Christ by confession and baptism. Give God the praise, and may his blessings ever rest upon her!—*D. C. Cripe, Oct. 8.*

Greene, Iowa. — The members of the Greene church, Greene, Iowa, contemplate holding a series of meetings, commencing Oct. 29, one week previous to our love-feast. Bro. Joseph Holder will be with us at that time, to conduct the meetings.—*J. D. Shook, Oct. 10.*

Fredric, Iowa. — We, the Brethren of Monroe County, held our Communion Sept. 9. It was an enjoyable season to all present. Brethren present from a distance were A. Wolf, John Gable, and M. Myers, who gave us wise counsel. One was added to our fold a short time before the feast. Others have also expressed a desire to unite with us.—*Z. M. Follis.*

Collins, Mo. — Our series of meetings, commenced Sept. 10, continued up to the 24th, when we held our love-feast. It was a feast long to be remembered. Brethren J. M. and Martin Mohler, from Johnson County, were with us and preached for us Sunday and Sunday night. As an immediate result of our meetings five came out on the Lord's side and were baptized. They were all young in years. May the Lord help them that they may live faithful!—*E. W. Tracey.*

Naperville, Ill. — A love-feast was held in the Naperville church, Oct. 8. A goodly number participated in the exercises. One family was debarred from participating with us on account of their child having taken poison. Some hopes however, are entertained of its recovery. Bro. G. D. Zollers, of Mt. Carroll, Ill., the author of "Thrilling Incidents on Sea and Land," dealt out the Bread of Life to us on this occasion. The Lord reward him for his labors!—*S. B. Kuhn, Oct. 9.*

Franklin Grove, Ill. — We can certainly report that the love-feast, held at this place Oct. 4 and 5, was an enjoyable one. Owing to the favorable weather, our own members were nearly all present, and we also had a good representation from surrounding congregations. Bro. Moore, of the MESSENGER office, officiated. The Spirit of the Lord seemed to pervade the entire meeting, and it was truly a feast of love. Two (a young man and his wife) were recently received into this church by baptism. What a blessed resolve it would be, if all young people, who start out in life to establish a home, would resolve to have God in their home!—*D. B. Senger.*

Washington Church, Ind. — Our feast is now in the past and was indeed a happy one. The attendance was good and the order excellent. Truly, the Lord was with us! Many brethren and sisters came to the meeting from adjoining congregations, which added much to the enjoyment of the occasion. A good ministerial force was in attendance, and rendered efficient help. We acknowledge the labors of the following-named brethren: Daniel Wysong, Noah Shutt, John Stafford, Gorman Heeter and Lewis Workman. This morning, at 9:30, we held a children's meeting, at 10:30 we had preaching services. In both the brethren acquitted themselves nobly, giving much good advice and counsel. Tonight Bro. Shutt holds forth the Word of Life. May God bless all the faithful in every good word and work!—*A. H. Puterbaugh, Oct. 2.*

Highland, Ohio.—The members of the Lexington church met in quarterly council Sept. 24. Considerable business was disposed of with a good feeling throughout. At this time the result of the annual visit was reported, which was favorable for having a love-feast Oct. 8, 1892.—*Leslie E. Ookerman.*

Clear Creek, Ind.—Previous to our Communion the annual visit was made. All were found to be in peace and union. We decided to hold a Communion which occurred Sept. 24. It was an occasion not soon forgotten. Bro. David Neff, of Roann, officiated. The attendance was large, nine churches including our own being represented. May the Lord prosper us in the future!—*H. Shock.*

Damascus, Oregon.—Our feast, District Meeting and Ministerial Meeting were pleasant seasons to all. Quite a number of members were assembled. The ministerial force was very strong. Eight ministers from other congregations were present. One of the number was our esteemed brother, Eld. Allen Ives, of Washington. The brethren did some able preaching while they were with us —*J. A. Royer, Clackamas, Oregon, Sept. 26.*

Avilla, Mo.—Our love-feast in the Spring River church, Jasper County, Mo., was a pleasant and an enjoyable meeting. About seventy members communed. Ministers from abroad were brethren Andrew Neher, S. Wimer, J. P. Baily and D. W. Stoner. A number of brethren were also present from adjoining churches. Bro. Neher officiated. The forenoon of next day was spent in farewell addresses, in which a number participated. Our prayer is that we may all be benefited thereby.—*Samuel Gault, Sept. 30.*

Ridgeway, Ind.—The Communion in the Howard church was held Sept. 27. We had a good attendance of members and a good supply of ministers, who ably defended the cause of Christ. We had a large congregation of friends, who were very attentive and kept good order. One young sister was received into the church by baptism last Sunday. The locating committee of next Annual Meeting will meet again Oct. 11, to decide on the location. They have been viewing the following named places: Richmond, Hagerstown Muncie, Frankfort and Kokomo.—*Geo. Brubaker, Oct. 3.*

Sabetha, Kans.—The Wolf River love-feast was a joyful meeting. Oct. 1 the members gathered at the meeting-house, and it was made known that there were some who wished to be baptized. Six dear souls were ready to be baptized. Brethren Wm. Murray and John Racus were elected to the office of deacon. May the Lord help them to be faithful! This church is without a minister. There is a good opening for some speaker to move in and help them. They have a good house of worship, a good country and a membership of thirty or thirty-five near railroad, etc.—*Archie VanDyke, Oct. 3.*

Talent, Oregon.—Our love-feast in the Rogue River church occurred Sept. 3. We had a good meeting. The house was well filled and the best of order prevailed. Bro. S. S. Barklow was with us and officiated. It was the first feast ever held here at Talent. Some of the spectators said it was the most solemn Communion they ever attended. Bro. David Brower has now settled among us and we would be glad if other members would come and settle here. Brother and sister Harmon have come here from Pomona, Cal. They formerly lived in Nora, Ill. We have a good climate; none too wet, good health, and water and good fruit in abundance. The church is moving along now in love and union.—*Susan M. Rhodes, Oct. 1.*

Birds, Ill.—The church at Allison Prairie, Illinois, held Communion services on Saturday, Oct. 1. A number of brethren and sisters from Lamotte Prairie, and a few from Richland County were present. Bro. John Harshbarger, of Jefferson County, officiated, aided by Bro Jacob Swinger, of Lamotte Prairie. Those who partook of the emblems of the flesh and blood of the Son of Man seemed to get the new life promised. Surely they have that promise.—*Frank M. Calvert*

Literary Notices.

LUCY LARCOM, an intimate friend of the poet Whittier, contributes to the October *New England Magazine*, a descriptive article, really a prose-poem, dealing with "The Ossipee Park," long the summer resort of Whittier. It is finely illustrated, with pictures taken specially for the purpose.

"The Acadian Province-by-the-Sea," is the attractive title of an interesting article in the October *New England Magazine* on the historic Province of Nova Scotia, so closely allied to American history, as the wilderness of the loyalist exodus at the close of the War of Independence.

The Hon. L. G. Power contributes a paper on the moot question, "The Whereabouts of Vinland," to the October *New England Magazine.*

Matrimonial.

"What therefore God hath joined together, let not man put asunder."

MOYER—DELP.—At the residence of the groom, in Hatfield, Pa., Sept. 3, 1892, by Rev. F. P. Cassel, Jonas S. Moyer, of Hatfield, and Mattie H. Delp, of Mainland, Pa.
ELIZABETH DELP.

BERRIAN—HAMMOND.—At the residence of Waldo Hubbard, Sept. 14, 1892, by the undersigned, James M. Berrian and Hattie L. Hammond, both of Clackamas County, Oregon.
J. A. ROYER.

Fallen Asleep.

"Blessed are the dead which die in the Lord."

SPITZER.—In the Midland congregation, Sept. 27, 1892, Bro. John W. Spitzer, aged 46 years and 10 months. He was buried at the Midland church. Funeral services by the writer.
M. G. EARLY.

HARDMAN.—In the Lebanon congregation, Linn County, Oregon, Aug. 6, 1892, sister Mary Ann Hardman, widow of Christian Hardman, aged 41 years. She was a member of the church for over twenty years, and served as deaconess about fourteen years. She was always faithful to her calling. Funeral by the Brethren.
M. M. BASHOR.

ZOOK.—At his home in Cedar County, Iowa, Sept. 30, 1892, Jacob Zook, aged 76 years, 1 month and 9 days. Bro. Zook was born in Preble County, Ohio, and was married to Elizabeth Goodwin Dec. 13, 1838. To them were born eleven children, three of whom preceded Bro. Zook to the spirit land. Sister Zook and eight children survive, all being present at the funeral. He was baptized in 1839, and chosen a deacon in 1857, thus giving over half a century to the service of the Master. His death was sudden. Funeral services by the writer, to a large gathering of sympathizing friends and neighbors.
JOHN ZUCK.

WRAY.—In the Roann church, Wabash County, Ind., Sept. 27, 1892, Bro. Dewit Wray, aged 41 years, 11 months and 22 days. Deceased, at the time of his death, was working in a gravel pit, when the bank gave way, completely covering him up. He leaves a dear companion (a sister) and five children to mourn the loss of one who was dear to them, and so much needed in his family. The funeral was conducted by the Brethren from Heb. 13: 14.
JOSEPH JOHN.

LEEDY.—At her home in Deedsville, Miami Co., Ind., Aug. 15, 1892, sister Rebecca Leedy, widow of Bro. S. M. Leedy, aged 60 years and 6 months. Sister Leedy was born in Montgomery County, Ohio, and came to Indiana with her parents, Wm. and Nancy Leedy, in 1839. Funeral services by Eld. Noah Fisher from Rev. 22: 14.
J. M. REPLOGLE.

KINZIE.—In Mexico, Ind., Sept. 27, 1892, at her son's, sister Mary Kinzie, aged 75 years, 5 months and 12 days. Funeral services by Jacob Fisher, assisted by Frank Fisher from Ps. 17: 15.
J. M. REPLOGLE.

LEIB.—In the Lower Cumberland church, near Boiling Springs, Pa., sister Elizabeth Leib, aged 71 years, 7 months and 23 days. Her husband preceded her to the spirit world nearly two years. Funeral services by elders Jacob Hollinger, Levi S. Mohler and the writer, from Heb. 4: 9.
HENRY BEELMAN.

MILLER.—In the Plum Creek congregation, Armstrong Co., Pa., Sept. 30, 1892, Bro. Wm. Miller, aged 64 years, 3 months and 27 days. He leaves a companion and six children to mourn their loss. He was a church member for thirty years, and a deacon for nineteen years. Our loss, we trust, is his great gain. Funeral from 2 Cor. 5: 1.
LEWIS KIMMEL.

BEERY.—Near Covington, Miami Co., Ohio, Sept. 23, 1892, Bro. S. D. Beery, aged 25 years and 4 months. Deceased was the son of A. S. and Margaret Beery. Parents, four brothers and four sisters survive. He was born in Hocking County, Ohio, May 23, 1867, entered the profession of teaching in early manhood, and after teaching one term, spent some time as a student in Mt. Morris College. He was a promising and talented young brother, and, so far as man can see, his death seemed untimely indeed. He was taken seriously ill April 1, 1892, and suffered severely with a complication of diseases much of the time, until released by death. Funeral by D. D. Wine, assisted by George Mohler.
JAMES M. NEFF.

VOGLESONG.—In the bounds of the Lower Cumberland church, Hogestown, Pa., Wm. Wayne Voglesong, only child of Benjamin E., and Rebecca J. Voglesong, aged 2 years, 9 months and 22 days. Funeral services by Bro. Levi S. Mohler, and the writer from 2 Kings 4: 26. HENRY BEELMAN.

GEORGE.—At Clay Hill, Pa., Aug. 26, 1892, Hiram Roy George, aged 3 months and 10 days. Services by the undersigned.
WM. A. ANTHONY.

GAUS.—Near Hartville, Ohio, Sept. 2, 1892, Margaret Gaus, aged 85 years, 10 months and 26 days. Deceased was born in Bologne, France, Oct. 20, 1806. She emigrated to America in 1824; and was married to Jonathan Gaus, Feb. 8, 1828. Her maiden name was Margaret Frantz. She was a widow twenty-one years, and was an earnest, active, faithful and consistent member of the German Baptist church for sixty years.
A. BRUMBAUGH.

FIKE.—In the State Center church, Iowa, Sept. 28, 1892, Bro. Abraham H. Fike, aged 71 years, 6 months and 24 days. The subject of this notice was born in Somerset County, Pa. He was married to Elizabeth Knagy in 1840. Twelve children blessed this union, seven of whom are living. He united with the church nearly forty years ago. Funeral discourse by the writer from Rev. 14: 13.
S. M. GOUGHNOUR.

BAKER.—At Roaring Springs, Pa., Sept. 24, 1892, Dollie May, daughter of brother David and sister —— Baker, aged 1 year and 10 months.
J. R. STAYER.

REFFNER.—At the same place, Maggie Alice, daughter of Michael and Katie Reffner, aged 10 months and 12 days. Funeral services of both were conducted by J. S. Holsinger, assisted by the writer.
J. R. STAYER.

KINSEL.—In West Dayton, Ohio, Sept. 15, 1892, of typhoid fever, Bro. David Kinsel, aged 35 years. The church has lost a noble Christian worker, the sister a loving companion, the little ones a dear father. May God grant this family the richest of his blessings in their time of sorrow. Funeral services by Bro. Daniel M. Garber, assisted by Bro. John Smith, from Ps. 17: 23.
ELMER WOMBOLD.

The Gospel Messenger

Is the recognized organ of the German Baptist or Brethren's church, and advocates the form of doctrine taught in the New Testament and pleads for a return to apostolic and primitive Christianity.

It recognizes the New Testament as the only infallible rule of faith and practice, and maintains that Faith toward God, Repentance from dead works, Regeneration of the heart and mind, baptism by Trine Immersion for remission of sins unto the reception of the Holy Ghost by the laying on of hands, are the means of adoption into the household of God,—the church militant.

It also maintains that Feet-washing, as taught in John 13, both by example and command of Jesus, should be observed in the church.

That the Lord's Supper, instituted by Christ and as universally observed by the apostles and the early Christians, is a full meal, and, in connection with the Communion, should be taken in the evening or after the close of the day.

That the Salutation of the Holy Kiss, or Kiss of Charity, is binding upon the followers of Christ.

That War and Retaliation are contrary to the spirit and self-denying principles of the religion of Jesus Christ.

That the principle of Plain Dressing and of Non-conformity to the world, as taught in the New Testament, should be observed by the followers of Christ.

That the Scriptural duty of Anointing the Sick with Oil, in the Name of the Lord, James 5: 14, is binding upon all Christians.

It also advocates the church's duty to support Missionary and Tract Work, thus giving to the Lord for the spread of the Gospel and for the conversion of sinners.

In short, it is a vindicator of all that Christ and the apostles have enjoined upon us, and aims, amid the conflicting theories and discords of modern Christendom, to point out ground that all must concede to be infallibly safe.

☞ "The above principles of our Fraternity are set forth on our Brethren's Envelopes." Use them! Price 15 cents per package; 40 cents per hundred.

Highland, Ohio.—The members of the Lexington church met in quarterly council Sept. 24. Considerable business was disposed of with a good feeling throughout. At this time the result of the annual visit was reported, which was favorable for having a love-feast Oct. 8, 1892.—*Leslie E. Ockerman.*

Clear Creek, Ind.—Previous to our Communion the annual visit was made. All were found to be in peace and union. We decided to hold a Communion which occurred Sept. 24. It was an occasion not soon forgotten. Bro. David Neff, of Roann, officiated. The attendance was large, nine churches including our own being represented. May the Lord prosper us in the future!—*H. Shook.*

Damascus, Oregon.—Our feast, District Meeting and Ministerial Meeting were pleasant seasons to all. Quite a number of members were assembled. The ministerial force was very strong. Eight ministers from other congregations were present. One of the number was our esteemed brother, Eld. Allen Ives, of Washington. The brethren did some able preaching while they were with us.—*J. A. Royer, Clackamas, Oregon, Sept. 26.*

Avilla, Mo.—Our love-feast in the Spring River church, Jasper County, Mo., was a pleasant and an enjoyable meeting. About seventy members communed. Ministers from abroad were brethren Andrew Neher, S. Wimer, J. P. Baily and D. W. Stoner. A number of brethren were also present from adjoining churches. Bro. Neher officiated. The forenoon of next day was spent in farewell addresses, in which a number participated. Our prayer is that we may all be benefited thereby.—*Samuel Gault, Sept. 30.*

Ridgeway, Ind.—The Communion in the Howard church was held Sept. 27. We had a good attendance of members and a good supply of ministers, who ably defended the cause of Christ. We had a large congregation of friends, who were very attentive and kept good order. One young sister was received into the church by baptism last Sunday. The locating committee of next Annual Meeting will meet again Oct. 11, to decide on the location. They have been viewing the following named places: Richmond, Hagerstown Muncie, Frankfort and Kokomo.—*Geo. Brubaker, Oct. 3.*

Sabetha, Kans.—The Wolf River love-feast was a joyful meeting. Oct. 1 the members gathered at the meeting-house, and it was made known that there were some who wished to be baptized. Six dear souls were ready to be baptized. Brethren Wm. Murray and John Racca were elected to the office of deacon. May the Lord help them to be faithful! This church is without a minister. There is a good opening for some speaker to move in and help them. They have a good house of worship, a good country and a membership of thirty or thirty-five near railroad, etc.—*Archie VanDyke, Oct. 3.*

Talent, Oregon.—Our love-feast in the Rogue River church occurred Sept. 3. We had a good meeting. The house was well filled and the best of order prevailed. Bro. S. S. Barklow was with us and officiated. It was the first feast ever held here at Talent. Some of the spectators said it was the most solemn Communion they ever attended. Bro. David Brower has now settled among us and we would be glad if other members would come and settle here. Brother and sister Harmon have come here from Pomona, Cal. They formerly lived in Nora, Ill. We have a good climate, not too wet, good health, and water and good fruit in abundance. The church is moving along now in love and union.—*Susan M. Rhodes, Oct. 1.*

Birds, Ill.—The church at Allison Prairie, Illinois, held Communion services on Saturday, Oct. 1. A number of brethren and sisters from Lamotte Prairie, and a few from Richland County were present. Bro. John Harshbarger, of Jefferson County, officiated, aided by Bro Jacob Swinger, of Lamotte Prairie. Those who partook of the emblems of the flesh and blood of the Son of Man seemed to get the new life promised. Surely they have that promise.—*Frank M. Calvert*

Literary Notices.

LUCY LARCOM, an intimate friend of the poet Whittier, contributes to the October *New England Magazine*, a descriptive article, really a prose-poem, dealing with "The Ossipee Park," long the summer resort of Whittier. It is finely illustrated, with pictures taken specially for the purpose.

"The Acadian Province-by-the-Sea," is the attractive title of an interesting article in the October *New England Magazine* on the historic Provinces of Nova Scotia, so closely allied to American history, as the wilderness of the loyalist exodus at the close of the War of Independence.

The Hon. L. G. Power contributes a paper on the moot question, "The Whereabouts of Vinland," to the October *New England Magazine.*

Matrimonial.

"What therefore God hath joined together, let not man put asunder."

MOYER—DELP.—At the residence of the groom, in Hatfield, Pa., Sept. 3. 1892, by Rev. F. P. Cassel, Jonas S. Moyer, of Hatfield, and Mattie H. Delp, of Mainland, Pa. ELIZABETH DELP.

BERRIAN—HAMMOND.—At the residence of Waldo Hubbard, Sept. 14, 1892, by the undersigned, James M. Berrian and Hattie L. Hammond, both of Clackamas County, Oregon. J. A. ROYER.

Fallen Asleep.

"Blessed are the dead which die in the Lord."

SPITZER.—In the Midland congregation, Sept. 27, 1892, Bro. John W. Spitzer, aged 46 years and 10 months. He was buried at the Midland church. Funeral services by the writer. M. G. EARLY.

HARDMAN.—In the Lebanon congregation, Linn County, Oregon, Aug. 6, 1892, sister Mary Ann Hardman, widow of Christian Hardman, aged 41 years. She was a member of the church for over twenty years, and served as deaconess about fourteen years. She was always faithful to her calling. Funeral by the Brethren. M. M. BASHOR.

ZOOK.—At his home in Cedar County, Iowa, Sept. 30, 1892, Jacob Zook, aged 76 years, 1 month and 9 days. Bro. Zook was born in Preble County, Ohio, and was married to Elizabeth Goodwin Dec. 13, 1838. To them were born eleven children, three of whom preceded Bro. Zook to the spirit land. Sister Zook and eight children survive, all being present at the funeral. He was baptized in 1839, and chosen a deacon in 1857, thus giving over half a century to the service of the Master. His death was sudden. Funeral services by the writer, to a large gathering of sympathizing friends and neighbors. JOHN ZUCK.

WRAY.—In the Roann church, Wabash County, Ind., Sept. 27, 1892, Bro. Dewitt Wray, aged 41 years, 11 months and 22 days. Deceased, at the time of his death, was worshiping in a gravel pit, when the bank gave way, completely covering him up. He leaves a dear companion (a sister) and five children to mourn the loss of one who was dear to them, and so much needed in his family. The funeral was conducted by the Brethren from Heb. 13:14. JOSEPH JOHN.

LEEDY.—At her home in Deedsville, Miami Co., Ind., Aug. 15, 1892, sister Rebecca Leedy, widow of Bro. S. M. Leedy, aged 60 years and 6 months. Sister Leedy was born in Montgomery County, Ohio, and came to Indiana with her parents, Wm. and Nancy Leedy, in 1839. Funeral services by Eld. Noah Fisher from Rev. 22: 14. J. M. REPLOGLE.

KINZIE.—In Mexico, Ind., Sept. 27, 1892, at her son's, sister Mary Kinzie, aged 75 years, 5 months and 12 days. Funeral services by Jacob Fisher, assisted by Frank Fisher from Ps. 17:15. J. M. REPLOGLE.

LEIB.—In the Lower Cumberland church, near Boiling Springs, Pa., sister Elizabeth Leib, aged 71 years, 7 months and 23 days. Her husband preceded her to the spirit world nearly two years. Funeral services by elders Jacob Hollinger, Levi S. Mohler and the writer, from Heb. 4:9. HENRY BEELMAN.

MILLER.—In the Plum Creek congregation, Armstrong Co., Pa., Sept. 30, 1892, Bro. Wm. Miller, aged 64 years, 3 months and 27 days. He leaves a companion and six children to mourn their loss. He was a church member for thirty years, and a deacon for nineteen years. Our loss, we trust, is his great gain. Funeral from 2 Cor. 5:1. LEWIS KIMMEL.

BEERY.—Near Covington, Miami Co., Ohio, Sept. 23, 1892, Bro. S. D. Beery, aged 25 years and 4 months. Deceased was the son of A. S. and Margaret Beery. Parents, four brothers and four sisters survive. He was born in Hocking County, Ohio, May 13, 1867, entered the profession of teaching in early manhood, and after teaching one term, spent some time as a student in Mt. Morris College. He was a promising and talented young brother, and, so far as man can see, his death seemed untimely indeed. He was taken seriously ill April 1, 1892, and suffered severely with a complication of diseases much of the time, until released by death. Funeral by D. D. Wine, assisted by George Mohler. JAMES M. NEFF.

VOGLESONG.—In the bounds of the Lower Cumberland church, Hogestown, Pa., Wm. Wayne Voglesong, only child of Benjamin E., and Rebecca J. Voglesong, aged 2 years, 9 months and 21 days. Funeral services by Bro. Levi S. Mohler, and the writer from 2 Kings 4:26. HENRY BEELMAN.

GEORGE.—At Clay Hill, Pa., Aug. 26, 1892, Hiram Roy George, aged 3 months and 10 days. Services by the undersigned. WM. A. ANTHONY.

GAUS.—Near Hartville, Ohio, Sept. 2, 1892, Margaret Gaus, aged 85 years, 10 months and 26 days. Deceased was born in Bologne, France, Oct. 20, 1806. She emigrated to America in 1824, and was married to Jonathan Gaus, Feb. 8, 1828. Her maiden name was Margaret Frantz. She was a widow twenty one years, and was an earnest, active, faithful and consistent member of the German Baptist church for sixty years. A. BRUMBAUGH.

FIKE.—In the State Center church, Iowa, Sept. 28, 1892, Bro. Abraham H. Fike, aged 71 years, 6 months and 24 days. The subject of this notice was born in Somerset County, Pa. He was married to Elizabeth Knagy in 1840. Twelve children blessed this union, seven of whom are living. He united with the church nearly forty years ago. Funeral discourse by the writer from Rev. 14:13. S. M. GOUGHNOUR.

BAKER.—At Roaring Springs, Pa., Sept. 24, 1892, Dollie May, daughter of brother David and sister — Baker, aged 1 year and 10 months. J. R. STAYER.

REFFNER.—At the same place, Maggie Alice, daughter of Michael and Katie Reffner, aged 10 months and 12 days. Funeral services of both were conducted by J. S. Holsinger, assisted by the writer. J. R. STAYER.

KINSEL.—In West Dayton, Ohio, Sept. 15, 1892, of typhoid fever, Bro. David Kinsel, aged 35 years. The church has lost a noble Christian worker, the sister a loving companion, the little ones a dear father. May God grant this family the richest of his blessings in their time of sorrow. Funeral services by Bro. Daniel M. Garber, assisted by Bro. John Smith, from Ps. 17:15. ELMER WORWOLD.

Announcements.

(Concluded from preceding page.)

LOVE-FEASTS.

Oct. 14, Rock Run church, 3 miles south-east of Goshen, Ind.

Oct. 27, at 2 P. M., Bethel church, 3 miles east of Milford, Ind.

Oct. 29, at 2 P. M., James Creek, Pa.

Oct. 29, at 2 P.M., Beaver Creek church, Greene Co., Ohio.

Oct. 29, at 2 P. M., Mulberry Grove church, Ill.

Oct. 29, at 10 A. M., Green Spring district, Seneca Co., Ohio.

Nov. 1, at 3 P. M., Monitor church, McPherson Co., Kans.

Nov. 3, at 4 P. M., Beech Grove church, Allout, Madison Co., Ind.

Nov. 4, at 10 A. M., Camden church, Jay Co., Ind.

Nov. 4, at 4 P. M., "Forks of Creek," arm of Saake Spring church, Bedford Co., Pa.

Nov. 4, at 10 A. M., Camden church, 7 miles north of Redkey, Jay Co., Ind.

Nov. 5, at 3: 30 P. M., Huntingdon, Pa.

Nov. 5, at 2 P. M., Springfield congregation, near Wawaka, Ind.

Nov. 5, at 2 P. M, Hopewell church, Bedford Co., Pa.

Nov. 5, at 3 P. M., Columbia City district, 1 mile west of Columbia City, Whitley Co., Ind.

Nov. 5, at 3 P. M., McPherson, Kans.

EUROPE
AND
Bible Lands

A new edition of this deservedly popular work has again been published. It retains all the excellencies of its predecessors, and with those who are interested in Bible study this work will always remain a favorite. Those who have read the ordinary book of travel will be surprised to find "Europe and Bible Lands" of thrilling interest for both old and young. The large number of books, already sold, proves that the work is of more than ordinary merit.

A fair supply of the last edition of this work is still on hand. Those who have not yet secured a copy of the work should embrace this opportunity of securing it. Price, in fine cloth binding, only $1.50 per copy, post-paid. To agents who are prepared to push an active canvass of the work, we are prepared to give special inducements. Write

BRETHREN'S PUBLISHING CO.,
Mt. Morris, Ill.

Reason and Revelation.—By. R. Milligan. Should be in the hands of every Bible student. Price, $2.00.

Trine Immersion.—A vindication of the apostolic form of Christian baptism. By Eld. James Quinter. A most complete and reliable work on the subject. Price, cloth, single copy, $1.25; leather, $1.75.

GOOD BOOKS FOR ALL.

ANY book in the market furnished at publishers' lowest retail price by the Brethren's Publishing Company, Mt. Morris, Ill. *Special prices given when books are purchased in quantities.* When ordering books, not on our list, if possible give title, name of author, and address of publishers.

The Throne of David.—By J. H. Ingraham. Cloth, $2.50.

The Doctrine of the Holy Spirit.—By James B Walker. Cloth, $1.25.

Homiletics and Pastoral Theology.—By W. G. T. Shedd. Cloth, $2.50.

The New Testament History.]— By Wm. Smith. Cloth, $1.25.

The Old Testament History.—By William Smith. Cloth, $1.25.

The Great Events of History.—By W.F. Collier. Cloth, $1.25.

Lectures on Preaching.—By Rev.* Phillips Brooks. Cloth, 16mo, $1.50.

The Path of Life.—An interesting tract for everybody. Price, 10 cents per copy; 100 copies, $6.00.

The Origin and Growth of Religion.—Hibbert Lectures. By T. W. R. Davids. Cloth, 8vo, $2.50.

Hours with the Bible.—By Cunningham Geikie. Old Testament Series—six volumes. Per volume, 90 cents.

Farm for Sale.

A desirable property located 1½ miles east of Mt. Morris, consisting of 185 acres of well-improved land. One of the finest country residences in Ogle County. For further particulars call on, or address,

ELIZABETH MIDDLEKAUFF,
4tf   Mt. Morris, Ill.

WONDERFUL "Story of the Gospels." It is a book just published. Everybody interested in Christianity should read it. It is a large 500-page quarto book of about 200 pages and 150 full-page engravings. It contains some of the most wonderful chapters in the world's history, the battles, sieges, marches, victories, defeats, heroism, observations, death of thousands of Christians to recover Jerusalem and the Holy Sepulchre from the hated Mohammedans. Described in thrilling interest and instruction. Agents wanted everywhere. Circular free. Address, J. M. NEFF, Covington, Ohio.

--- THE ---
Doctrine of the Brethren Defended.

THIS work contains a complete exposition of the faith and practice of the Brethren, the Divinity of Christ, the Divinity of the Holy Spirit, Immersion, Feet-washing, the Lord's Supper, the Holy Kiss, Non-conformity, Secret Societies, etc. Price, per copy, cloth binding, $1.25. Address this office.

O Jerusalem! Jerusalem!

WHAT could be more beautiful and touching than a picture of Christ in his stand upon Olivet looking down over the beloved but sinful city, with tears trickling down over his cheeks, his lips parted as he cries, " O Jerusalem! Jerusalem!" We have such a picture 11x18 inches, beautifully executed in colors. No one can gaze upon it without being moved. Given free with a year's subscription to "What to Read" at 30 cents. Address, in every church and neighborhood. Address, JAS. M. NEFF, Covington, Ohio.

Excursions to California.

EXCURSIONS in charge of M. M. Eshelman, Immigration Agent, will leave Chicago over the "Santa Fe Route" Tuesdays, and Kansas City Wednesdays, during the year 1892, on dates as follows:

Chicago: January 26, February 23, March 22, April 26, May 24, June 28, July 26, August 23, September 27, October 25, November 22, December 27.

Kansas City, January 27, February 24, March 23, April 27, May 25, June 29, July 27, August 24, September 28, October 26, November 23, December 28.

Parties wishing to avail themselves of the privileges of these excursions, should write M. M. Eshelman, North Pomona, California, prior to the 15th of each month, and from the Brethren to the end of the month, at 1090 Union Avenue (opposite Union Depot), Kansas City, Mo., stating when and where they wish to join one of these excursions, and he will give them full information, and if desired will reserve berths in Tourist Sleeping Car for them. Do not fail to write him; he will do you good. The cars will be as low as the lowest made to the Pacific Coast.

GEORGE L. McDONAUGH,
Traveling Agent.

Announcements.

(Concluded from preceding page.)

LOVE-FEASTS.

Oct. 14, Rock Run church, 3 miles south-east of Goshen. Ind.

Oct. 22, at 4 P. M., Bethel church, 3 miles east of Milford, Ind.

Oct. 29, at 2 P. M., James Creek, Pa.

Oct. 29, at 10 A. M., Beaver Creek church, Greene Co., Ohio.

Oct. 29, at 4 P. M., Mulberry Grove church, Ill.

Oct. 29, at 10 A. M., Green Spring district, Seneca Co., Ohio.

Nov. 1, at 3 P. M., Monitor church, McPherson Co., Kans.

Nov. 3, at 4 P. M., Beech Grove church, Akron, Madison Co., Ind.

Nov. 4, at 10 A. M., Camden church, Jay Co., Ind.

Nov. 4, at 4 P. M., " Forks of Creek," arm of Snake Spring church, Bedford Co., Pa.

Nov. 5, at 10 A. M., Camden church, 7 miles north of Redkey, Jay Co., Ind.

Nov. 5, at 3:30 P. M., Huntington, Pa.

Nov. 5, at 2 P. M., Springfield congregation, near Wawaka, Ind.

Nov. 5, at 4 P. M., Hopewell church, Bedford Co., Pa.

Nov. 5, at 3 P. M., Columbia City district, 1 mile west of Columbia City, Whitley Co., Ind.

Nov. 19, at 3 P. M., McPherson, Kans.

EUROPE
AND
Bible Lands

A new edition of this deservedly popular work has again been published. It retains all the excellencies of its predecessors, and with those who are interested in Bible study this work will always remain a favorite. Those who have used the ordinary book of travel will be surprised to find " Europe and Bible Lands " of thrilling interest for both old and young. The large number of books, already sold, proves that the work is of more than ordinary merit.

A fair supply of the last edition of this work is still on hand. Those who have not yet secured a copy of the work should embrace this opportunity of securing it. Price, in fine cloth binding, only $1.50 per copy, post-paid. To agents who are prepared to push an active canvass of the work, we are prepared to give special inducements. Write us.

BRETHREN'S PUBLISHING CO.,
Mt. Morris, Ill.

CANCERS, TUMORS, ETC.

Successfully treated by Dr. G. N. Buteler, of Waynesborough, Pa., where he has practiced for the last thirteen years. Dr. Buteler is a graduate of the University of Maryland, at Baltimore City. References given and correspondence solicited. Address, Dr. G. W. Butcler, Waynesborough, Pa.

Reason and Revelation.—By. R. Milligan. Should be in the hands of every Bible student. Price, $2.00.

Trine Immersion.—"A vindication of the apostolic form of Christian baptism. By Eld. James Quinter. A most complete and reliable work on the subject. Price, cloth, single copy, $1.25; leather, $1.75.

GOOD BOOKS FOR ALL.

ANY book in the market furnished at publishers' lowest retail price by the Brethren's Publishing Company, Mt. Morris, Ill. *Special prices* given when books are purchased in quantities. When ordering books, not on our list, if possible give this, name of author, and address of publishers.

The Throne of David.—By J. H. Ingraham. Cloth, $1.50.

The Doctrine of the Holy Spirit.—By James B Walker. Cloth, $1.25.

Homiletics and Pastoral Theology.—By W. G. T. Shedd. Cloth, $2.50.

The New Testament History.—By Wm. Smith. Cloth, $1.25.

The Old Testament History.—By William Smith. Cloth, $1.25.

The Great Events of History.—By W. F. Collier. Cloth, $1.25.

Lectures on Preaching.—By Rev. Phillips Brooks. Cloth, 18mo, $1.60.

The Path of Life.—An interesting tract for everybody. Price, 20 cents per copy; 100 copies, $6.00.

The Origin and Growth of Religion.—Hibbert Lectures. By T. W. R. Davids. Cloth, 8vo, $2.50.

Hours with the Bible.—By Cunningham Geikie. Old Testament Series—six volumes. Per volume, 90 cents.

Farm for Sale.

A desirable property located 1¼ miles east of Mt. Morris, consisting of 185 acres of well-improved land. One of the finest country residences in Ogle County. For further particulars call on, or address,

ELIZABETH MIDDLEKAUFF.
4tf   Mt. Morris, Ill.

WONDERFUL "Story of the ComBible." " 'a book just published. Everybody interested in Christianity should read it. It is a large 500 7½ inch book of about 600 pages and 100 full-page engravings. It contains some of the most wonderful chapters in the world's history, the births, sings, marches, victories, defeats, heroism, starvation, death of thousands of God's host to recover Jerusalem and the Holy Sepulchre from the hand of the Mohammedans. Unsurpassed in thrilling interest and instruction. Agents wanted every where. Circulars free. Address, J. M. Nert, Covington, Ohio.

--- THE ---
Doctrine of the Brethren Defended.

THIS work contains a complete exposition of the faith and practice of the Brethren, the Divinity of Christ, the Divinity of the Holy Spirit, Immersion, Feet-washing, the Lord's Supper, the Holy Kiss, Non-conformity, Secret Societies, etc. Price, per copy, cloth binding, $1.25. Address this office.

O Jerusalem! Jerusalem!

WHAT could be more beautiful and touching than a picture of Christ as he stood upon Olivet looking down over the beloved but sinful city, with tears trickling down over his cheeks, his lips parted as he cries, " O Jerusalem! Jerusalem!" We have such a picture 22x28 inches, beautifully executed in colors. No one can gaze upon it without being moved. Given free with a year's subscription to " What to Read " at 50 cents. An agent wanted in every church and neighborhood. Address,
JAS. M. NEFF, Covington, Ohio.

Excursions to California.

EXCURSIONS in charge of M. M. Eshelman, Immigration Agent, will leave Chicago over the " Santa Fe Route " Tuesdays, and Kansas City Wednesdays, during the year 1892, on dates as follows:

Chicago: January 26, February 23, March 22, April 26, May 24, June 28, July 26, August 23, September 27, October 25, November 22, December 27.

Kansas City, January 27, February 24, March 23, April 27, May 25, June 29, July 27, August 24, September 28, October 26, November 23, December 28.

Parties wishing to avail themselves of the privileges of these excursions, should write M. M. Eshelman, North Pomona, California, prior to the 15th of each month, and from the fifteenth to the end of the month, at 1059 Union Avenue (opposite Union Depot), Kansas City, Mo., stating when and where they wish to join one of these excursions, and he will give them full information, and if desired will reserve berths in Tourist Sleeping Car for them. Do not fail to write him; he will do you good. The rates will be as low as the lowest made by the Santa Fe to the Pacific Coast.

GEORGE L. McDONAUGH,
Traveling Agent.

LOOK AT THIS.

The Monon Route still reducing rates and offering better accommodations than ever before.

Commencing April 15, the fare from Chicago to Louisville, New Albany, Cincinnati, Hamilton, and Dayton will be $5.90; to Indianapolis $3.50. Round trip tickets good ten days at double the one way rate.

Parlor and Dining cars on day trains; Pullman Sleepers and Compartment Cars on night trains. A special Sleeper is run for Indianapolis business.

For rates, schedules, etc. apply at Depot, Dearborn Station, City Ticket Office, 232 Clark Street, or address, JAMES BARKER, G. P. A., Monon Block, Chicago, Ill.

Church Entertainments: Twenty Objections.

By Rev. B. Carradine, D. D. 12mo, 100 pp. Paper cover, 30 cents. A strong book in defense of its position, written by a powerful pen, presenting the most candid and scriptural arraignment of unwarrantable methods for money-raising in the Church. The spirit of the book is highly devotional and cannot fail to inspire the reader with its seriousness.

Alone with God.

THIS manual of devotions, by J. H. Garrison, comprises a series of meditations with forms of prayer for private devotions, family worship and special occasions. It is one of the most useful, most needed, and best adapted books of the year, and therefore it is not strange that it is proving one of the most popular. In work of this kind its distinguished, gifted, pious and beloved author is at his best. This book is helpful to every minister, church official, and Sunday-school superintendent, as well as every private member of the church in all ages. It has models of prayer, suitable for the service of the prayer-meeting, while its suggestions, meditations and instructions are pre-eminently calculated to be of service in preparation for the solemn duties that rest upon the active members. Cloth, 75 cents; morocco, $1.25. Address this office.

❖ESSAYS❖

"Study to show thyself approved unto God; a workman that needeth not be ashamed, rightly dividing the Word of Truth."

THE TWO BRIDES.

BY SADIE BRALLIER NOFFSINGER.

On a holy eve,
By an altar wide
With the one she loved
Stood a trusting bride.
A tear-drop gleamed
On her face so fair,
And a flowing veil
Hid her raven hair.
Thus, she calmly leaned
On the dear, strong arm
That should guard and shield
Her from pain and harm.
Deep within her soul
Fell a blessing new,
And a rapture thrilled
Her young being through,
As she spoke the words
Of love's vow, sublime,
And her pure heart laid
On its loved one's shrine.

The slow years passed on:
Lo, her eye was dim,
And she had ceased
To believe in him!
She no longer walked
With that love-blest praise
Through bright illusion
Of bridal days.
And the shipwrecked hope
Left its traces there
On the calm, sweet face,
And the raven hair.
Anon and wildly,
Yet anon in vain
Rose: "Oh, heart be still!
Oh, pain! Oh pain!"
Till there came an eve
When, beneath the shade
Of that old altar,
Her still form was laid.
While the choir chanted:
"Lo, all love is dearth!"
The grave closed over
The sad bride of earth.

On a holy eve
By an altar wide
With the one she loved,
Stood a trusting bride.
A tear-drop gleamed
On her face so fair,
And a snowy veil
Hid her golden hair.
Thus, she calmly leaned
On the dear, strong arm
That should guard and shield
Her from pain and harm.
Deep within her soul
Fell a blessing new,
And a rapture thrilled
Her young being through,
While she spoke the words
Of love's vow divine,
And her pure heart laid
On its loved one's shrine.

The swift years passed on:
In her place there stood
A beautiful type
Of blest womanhood.
Anon and anon
In her happy face
Were the wondrous charms
Of exalted grace.
Fairer her beauty
And sweeter, in sooth,
Than on that blest day
When she plighted her troth!
She sang of a Love
Which shielded her heart
From the deadly pangs
Of earth's bitter smart;
Nor ceased she the song
Till one eve, when laid
In the peaceful hush
Of that altar's shade,

And angels chanted
True love's sweet applaud
While heaven received
The glad bride of God.

Sept. 23.

A PRACTICAL OUTLINE OF CHURCH GOVERNMENT.

BY DANIEL HAYS.

No. II.—Its Authority.

AUTHORITY has been delegated to the church by our Lord in these words: "Verily I say unto you, Whatsoever ye shall bind on earth shall be bound in heaven; and whatsoever ye shall loose on earth shall be loosed in heaven." Matt. 18: 18. How to use this power is clearly defined in the Written Word which lays the individual member under equal obligation to "hear the church." The relation, which the church sustains to each of its members, as well as that of the members to each other and to the church, we will now consider.

The Gospel gives the church authority to teach the individual. The command, "Go ye, therefore, and teach all nations," not only gives authority to teach, but also lays the nations, with each individual among them, under obligations to receive the instruction. The apostles were commanded to teach all nations, and those whom they baptized they were to continue to teach. The first teaching was the ground-work for the teaching that followed baptism. It included the first principles,—faith, repentance, and baptism. If the first teaching be thorough, if it comprehend all the Gospel, the second teaching will be comparatively easy. The fact that a man in the church is ready and willing, even anxious to be instructed further in the way of life, is good evidence of his conversion. The teaching to be continued to the Christian in the church is authoritative and comprehensive: "Teaching them to observe all things whatsoever I have commanded you." Matt. 28: 20.

When an individual, under the teaching of the Word, is convinced of the necessity of faith, repentance and baptism, accepts the great principles of the doctrine of Christ, and is willing to be obedient to all the commands and precepts of the Gospel, before he is received into the church, he promises to receive counsel, as well as to give counsel. He thus gives his consent to be governed by the church, and to take counsel of his brethren. This consent every member has given to the church, and Christ has laid it down in his divine rule of trespass that when we reach the church in any case, we should hear the church. This we all consented to do; and this is government by consent of the governed. This is the mildest, the safest, the strongest of all forms of ruling. No one is bound who gives not his consent. No one is bound longer than he gives his consent. And the bond that holds the faithful together, is the bond of truth, the bond of love.

When a man enters the service of God, seemingly in good faith, accepts the Gospel as interpreted by the church, and promises to hear the church, then falls into a wayward life, proves obstinate, and takes a course of his own, the church is required by the Gospel rule of Christ to withdraw fellowship. This man made a promise and broke it. He was not God-like. God keeps all his promises to us. Our God is a covenant-keeping God. "Let us hold fast the profession of our faith without wavering; for he is faithful that promised." Heb. 10: 23.

Of the three departments of government, the church exercises two,—the executive and judicial,—but not the legislative power. Christ is our lawgiver, and the laws of the church are in the Gospel. The church, however, is clothed by Gospel precept and precedent with a clearly defined line of executive authority. This applies especially to all matter of discipline affecting the conduct of her members. Without a proper exercise of this function, the church would be entirely helpless in the hands of evil-doers. This is done, too, without the use of force of any kind. The words of Christ in Matt. 18: 17, "Let him be," is more potent than physical force, and its application is in entire harmony with the principle of love, justice and truth. The church moves on in her course in saving souls, and lets go the hand that falls back into the ways of a wicked world.

The executive work of the church is further seen in that she elects her own officers. This work was done by our Lord when he chose the twelve apostles, and afterward appointed seventy others and sent them "two and two before his face." The church bases its action upon the authority of Christ and the precedent of the apostles, as seen in Acts 1: 21, 26; 6: 5; 13: 3; 15: 22, and elects her ministers, ordains elders, and appoints delegates to carry forward her work by representation.

The judicial work of the church is an important and necessary one. The church is "the pillar and ground of the truth." It is the duty of the church to hold up the truth before the world, to explain it, to interpret the Scriptures. It is in the church that the ordinances are obeyed, the commands are obeyed. The church is the ground of the truth in precept and example. All matters of difference between members become questions of judicial inquiry. There is, in every council-meeting, more or less matter for investigation and judicial consideration. Acts 15 records the work and results of a general judicial council of the church. Paul, in 1 Cor. 5: 1, 7, directs the church in a judicial investigation of a case, and closes by directing the church to execute the sentence, reached by the investigation. Thus the two functions,—the judicial and the executive,—may be employed in a single council-meeting.

Questions may arise, concerning which there is no direct Scripture applying. The general principles of the Gospel will enable the church to determine such matters according to the spirit of the Gospel. There is not a sin, however insignificant in the estimation of the world, that will not receive a severe rebuke in the presence of the precept. "Abstain from all appearance of evil." The general principles of the Gospel, faith in, and obedience to, all the Gospel, non-resistance, non-swearing, non-conformity to the world, non-secretism, separation from the world, and union with God, fellowship with Christ, and communion with the Holy Spirit,—these form the basis by which the church is enabled to determine what is not in accordance with the will of God. "The lust of the flesh, and the lust of the eyes, and the pride of life, is not of the Father, but is of the world." It is not safe to give the reins of government, in any degree, over to the carnal nature of man. This must be kept in subjection, to guard the membership from wrongdoing, and to protect the borders of Zion from the encroachment of evil, the Great Head of the church designed to secure for his people. This is attained perfectly and harmoniously in church union which is the true basis of a Gospel union in faith and practice.

"THERE is no heaven attainable for a man who does not protect his home and family, and who does not live more for those who are dependent upon him than for himself."

"Study to show thyself approved unto God ; a workman that needeth not be ashamed, rightly dividing the Word of Truth."

THE TWO BRIDES.

BY SADIE BRALLIER NOFFSINGER.

On a holy eve,
By an altar wide
With the one she loved
Stood a trusting bride.
A tear-drop gleamed
On her face so fair,
And a flowing veil
Hid her raven hair.
Thus, she calmly leaned
On the dear, strong arm
That should guard and shield
Her from pain and harm.
Deep within her soul
Fell a blessing new,
And a rapture thrilled
Her young being through,
As she spake the words
Of love's vow, sublime,
And her pure heart laid
On its loved one's shrine.

The slow years passed on:
Lo, her eye was dim,
And she had ceased
To believe in him!
She no longer walked
With that love-blest praise
Through bright illusion
Of bridal days.
And the shipwrecked hope
Left its traces there
On the calm, sweet face,
And the raven hair.
Anon and wildly,
Yet anon in vain
Rose: "Oh, heart be still!
Oh, pain! Oh pain!"
Till there came an eve
When, beneath the shade
Of that old altar,
Her still form was laid.
While the choir chanted:
"Lo, all love is dearth!"
The grave closed over
The sad bride of earth.

On a holy eve
By an altar wide
With the one she loved,
Stood a trusting bride.
A tear-drop gleamed
On her face so fair,
And a snowy veil
Hid her golden hair.
Thus, she calmly leaned
On the dear, strong arm
That should guard and shield
Her from pain and harm.
Deep within her soul
Fell a blessing new,
And a rapture thrilled
Her young being through,
While she spoke the words
Of love's vow divine,
And her pure heart laid
On its loved one's shrine.

The swift years passed on :
In her place there stood
A beautiful type
Of blest womanhood.
Anon and anon
In her happy face
Were the wondrous charms
Of exalted grace.
Fairer her beauty
And sweeter, in sooth,
Than on that blest day
When she plighted her troth!
She sang of a Love
Which shielded her heart
From the deadly pangs
Of earth's bitter smart;
Nor ceased she the song
Till one eve, when laid
In the peaceful hush
Of that altar's shade.

And angels chanted
True love's sweet applaud
While heaven received
The glad bride of God.

Sep. 23.

A PRACTICAL OUTLINE OF CHURCH GOVERNMENT.

BY DANIEL HAYS.

No. II.—Its Authority.

AUTHORITY has been delegated to the church by our Lord in these words: "Verily I say unto you, Whatsoever ye shall bind on earth shall be bound in heaven; and whatsoever ye shall loose on earth shall be loosed in heaven." Matt. 18: 18. How to use this power is clearly defined in the Written Word which lays the individual member under equal obligation to "hear the church." The relation, which the church sustains to each of its members, as well as that of the members to each other and to the church, we will now consider.

The Gospel gives the church authority to teach the individual. The command, "Go ye, therefore, and teach all nations," not only gives authority to teach, but also lays the nations, with each individual among them, under obligations to receive the instruction. The apostles were commanded to teach all nations, and those whom they baptized they were to continue to teach. The first teaching was the ground-work for the teaching that followed baptism. It included the first principles,—faith, repentance, and baptism. If the first teaching be thorough, if it comprehend all the Gospel, the second teaching will be comparatively easy. The fact that a man in the church is ready and willing, even anxious to be instructed farther in the way of life, is good evidence of his conversion. The teaching to be continued to the Christian in the church is authoritative and comprehensive: "Teaching them *to observe all things* whatsoever I have commanded you." Matt. 28: 20.

When an individual, under the teaching of the Word, is convinced of the necessity of faith, repentance and baptism, accepts the great principles of the doctrine of Christ, and is willing to be obedient to all the commands and precepts of the Gospel, before he is received into the church, he promises to receive counsel, as well as to give counsel. He thus gives his consent to be governed by the church, and to take counsel of his brethren. This consent every member has given to the church, and Christ has laid it down in his divine rule of trespass that when we reach the church in any case, we should hear the church. This we all consented to do; and this is government by consent of the governed. This is the mildest, the safest, the strongest of all forms of ruling. No one is bound who gives not his consent. No one is bound longer than he gives his consent. And the bond that holds the faithful together, is the bond of truth, the bond of love.

When a man enters the service of God, seemingly in good faith, accepts the Gospel as interpreted by the church, and promises to hear the church, then falls into a wayward life, proves obstinate, and takes a course of his own, the church is required by the Gospel rule of Christ to withdraw fellowship. This man made a promise and broke it. He was not God-like. God keeps all his promises to us. Our God is a covenant-keeping God. "Let us hold fast the profession of our faith without wavering; for he is faithful that promised." Heb. 10: 23.

Of the three departments of government, the church exercises two,—the executive and judicial,—but not the legislative power. Christ is our lawgiver, and the laws of the church are

in the Gospel. The church, however, is clothed by Gospel precept and precedent with a clearly-defined line of executive authority. This applies especially to all matter of discipline affecting the conduct of her members. Without a proper exercise of this function, the church would be entirely helpless in the hands of evil-doers. This is done, too, without the use of force of any kind. The words of Christ in Matt. 18: 17, "*Let him be*," is more potent than physical force, and its application is in entire harmony with the principle of love, justice and truth. The church moves on in her course in saving souls, and lets go the hand that falls back into the ways of a wicked world.

The executive work of the church is further seen in that she elects her own officers. This work was done by our Lord when he chose the twelve apostles, and afterward appointed seventy others and sent them "two and two before his face." The church bases its action upon the authority of Christ and the precedent of the apostles, as seen in Acts 1: 21, 26; 6: 5; 13: 3; 15: 22, and elects her ministers, ordains elders, and appoints delegates to carry forward her work by representation.

The judicial work of the church is an important and necessary one. The church is "the pillar and ground of the truth." It is the duty of the church to hold up the truth before the world, to explain it, to interpret the Scriptures. It is in the church that the ordinances are kept, that the commands are obeyed. The church is the ground of the truth in precept and example. All matters of difference between members become questions of judicial inquiry. There is, in every council-meeting, more or less matter for investigation and judicial consideration. Acts 15 records the work and results of a general judicial council of the church. Paul, in 1 Cor. 5: 1, 7, directs the church in a judicial investigation of a case, and closes by directing the church to execute the sentence, reached by the investigation. Thus the two functions,—the judicial and the executive,—may be employed in a single council-meeting.

Questions may arise, concerning which there is no direct Scripture applying. The general principles of the Gospel will enable the church to determine such matters according to the spirit of the Gospel. There is not a sin, however insignificant in the estimation of the world; that will not receive a severe rebuke in the presence of the precept. "Abstain from all appearance of evil." The general principles of the Gospel, faith in, and obedience to, all the Gospel, non-resistance, non-swearing, non-conformity to the world, non-secretism, separation from the world, and union with God, fellowship with Christ, and communion with the Holy Spirit,—these form the basis by which the church is enabled to determine what is not in accordance with the will of God. "The lust of the flesh, and the lust of the eyes, and the pride of life, is not of the Father, but is of the world." It is not safe to give the reins of government, in any degree, over to the carnal nature of man. This must be kept in subjection, to guard the membership from wrong-doing, and to protect the borders of Zion from the encroachment of evil, the Great Head of the church designed to secure for his people. This is attained perfectly and harmoniously in church union which is the true basis of a Gospel union in faith and practice.

"THERE is no heaven attainable for a man who does not protect his home and family, and who does not live more for those who are dependent upon him than for himself."

perfect, eternal affirmation of the divine holiness was in the resurrection of the Godman. What can be more consistent than that the first day of the week should be the day that hallows all the rest?

A greater than the Pope is here. Christ alone is our Rest, and the first day of the week is our Sabbath, because on that day transpired the august transaction without which "we are yet in our sins." 1 Cor. 15: 17. "Let not your heart be troubled: YE BELIEVE IN GOD, BELIEVE ALSO IN ME." Jesus is God's and Man's eternal Sabbath.

Union Deposit, Pa.

CORRESPONDENCE.

"Write what thou seest, and send it unto the churches."

☞ Church News solicited for this Department. If you have had a good meeting, send a Report of it, so that others may rejoice with you. In writing give name of church, County and State. Be brief. Notes of Travel should be as short as possible. Land Advertisements are not solicited for this Department. We have an advertising page, and, if necessary, will issue supplements.

Notice.

THE churches of North-western Ohio will take notice that the Committee, to whom was intrusted the location of next District Meeting, have located the same in the Maumee District, Defiance County.

S. M. Loose, Moderator,
S. H. Dickey, Reading Clerk,
D. D. Thomas, Writing Clerk.

Notes from the Second District of West Virginia.

On Friday, Oct. 7, I boarded the train, in company with Bro. G. W. Annon and his daughter,—a young sister,—to attend a love-feast, which was to be held the next evening in Marion County, W. Va. When we boarded the train we found three of our brethren from Maryland, who had been invited to attend the feast,—Wm. T. Sines, I. O. Thompson and John Cross. The two former are ministers, and the latter a deacon. Bro. Thompson addressed us in the evening from Rom. 1: 16. He broke to us the Bread of Life in an acceptable manner. We had meeting on the 8th at two o'clock P. M., when Bro. Sines preached from Ps. 23: 1. We felt that it was good to wait upon the Lord.

By this time Bro. W. R. Murphy, from Ohio, had made his appearance. We were all glad to see him, as he once lived in our congregation. Brethren Sines, Thompson and Murphy did some good talking during examination and Communion services. Our house was crowded to such an extent as to be very uncomfortable to many of the spectators. Thirty were at the table. One commendable thing was that all were at the table. Next day, at 10:30, Bro. Sines preached from Zech. 8: 23. He told us many good things, and Bro. Murphy also made some appropriate remarks.

At the close of the meeting an invitation was given, when three precious souls made application for membership. At 3:30 we gathered at the river, where prayer was wont to be made. Then baptism was administered to those three precious souls. As we were leaving the water, two more were ready, who had applied some time previous. After the usual services, they were buried with Christ in baptism. The last two were husband and wife. Both went in together. The sister being baptized first, waited for her husband, and both came out together. Many said it was the most beautiful sight they ever saw. At night brother Thompson preached to the people, and the next day several of the brethren left for home, leaving Bro. Murphy to preach next night. Upon the whole, our meeting was a

pleasant one, and one long to be remembered. The members were much built up, and feel that others are near the kingdom: Come again, brethren, and let us fight for the Lord against the mighty. If the Lord will, I will start to District Meeting, Oct. 13, after which I will give your readers a few more notes. Z. Annon.

Thornton, W. Va., Oct. 11.

From Grundy Centre, Iowa.

AFTER enjoying a feast at our home church (the Lower Fall Creek, Ind.), Sept. 30, I boarded the train at Anderson, Ind., next day, at noon, for the South Waterloo church, Iowa, to be present at their feast, Oct. 1. I found it to be a feast indeed and in truth. Oct. 3 was their District Meeting, which was another enjoyable meeting. Oct. 4 was their Ministerial Meeting. At 3 P. M. of the same day I bade them all farewell, to come to the place where I am now writing, to hold a series of meetings. Yesterday, Oct. 6, I was called upon to preach the funeral of Susie Essig, daughter of Eld. H. Strickler, who had moved some four years ago to Texas. Deceased died Sept. 30, 1892, aged 29 years, 11 months, and 4 days; and was brought back here for interment. Judging from the large congregation that assembled upon the occasion, Susie was highly respected. Text, Rev. 4: 3.

From here I go to the Iowa River church, to their love-feast, Oct. 22, and from there to Franklin County, to hold a series of meetings till the love-feast at Greene, Iowa, Nov. 5. I expect, also, to hold a series of meetings for them. From that time on, further arrangements can be made as the Brethren see fit. Joseph Holder.

Harvest Meetings.

ON the first Sunday of August we held a harvest-meeting in the south part of the Cedar Lake church. Bro. J. C. Murray, of Nappanee, came to our assistance, and preached four soul-stirring sermons. Sunday morning he preached a thanksgiving sermon, and in the afternoon he preached a missionary sermon which caused the brethren and sisters to reach down into their pockets. We took up a collection, and got something over seven dollars for the spread of Christ's kingdom. On the first Sunday of September we had a harvest-meeting in our church-house near Corunna. Bro. I. L. Berkey, of Goshen, was with us and preached four good Gospel sermons. In the morning he preached a thanksgiving sermon, and in the afternoon a missionary sermon, after which we took up another collection at which we got over seven dollars, making, in all, over fourteen dollars for the mission cause. Last but not least, at each of our harvest-meetings there was one soul born into the kingdom of Christ. May God's love ever be with them! J. H. Elson.

Fairfield Centre, Ind.

From the Belleville Church, Kans.

OUR series of meetings, conducted by Bro. J. E. Young, of Beatrice, Nebr., closed last evening. He came into our midst Sept. 24. We feel that we had a good meeting. The members have been strengthened in their faith, and some, no doubt, have formed new resolutions, and will try to live a better Christian life in the future. During these meetings two young people made the good confession and were initiated into the fold by baptism. Our feast was held Oct. 1. There was a good representation of our members, and others, from different places. Thirteen ministers, including our home force, were present. Our aged brother, John Forney, of Abilene, was

with us. We rejoiced to meet him once more and hear his good counsel. Brethren Levi Saylor, A. M. Dickey, Samuel Henry, W. R. Phillippi, —— Myers and Eli Renner of adjoining churches were also present. Bro. Young officiated. At this meeting Bro. Albion Daggett was advanced to the second degree of the ministry, and Bro. Chester Daggett to the deacon's office. It was also decided, at our last council, to continue our Sunday-school through the winter. Some of our members are on the bed of affliction. Sister Gooch has returned home with but little improvement in her condition. Grandfather Hil-lery is very sick. The brittle thread of life is about broken. Louisa J. Williams.

Oct. 5.

From the Wacondah Church, Ray Co., Mo.

SEPT. 3 Bro. Jacob Witmore began a series of meetings at the Rockingham church, and continued until the evening of Sept. 21, preaching, in all, twenty-three sermons. The attendance was good throughout. On the second Sunday we had children's meeting before regular services. There were probably fifty children present. Our brother entertained them well, and the parents did not fail to get their share of the short talk. On the third Sunday, by request, he told why we did not take the Communion on the first day of the week, and in day-time. During these meetings four decided for the right, and were baptized. Sept. 29 was our council, preparatory to our love-feast. Bro. J. E. Ellenberger, of the Smith Fork congregation, was with us. Much more business than usual came before this meeting, but all was satisfactorily disposed of. Bro. Ellenberger preached two sermons for us, and was with us at our love-feast; also Eld. Daniel Sell, from the same congregation, and Bro. David Hardman, from Hamilton, Mo.

On the evening of our love-feast, one more was baptized. This sister lives near no other members, and is the first-fruits of our Brethren's labors in that neighborhood. One was also received by letter. This was one of the largest love-feasts, ever held at this church. About one hundred seventy-five members communed. On the day following, Bro. Geo. Clemens was advanced to the full ministry, and brethren Samuel Sandy, Walker Falls, and Isaac Early were chosen as deacons. Two young sisters were also received into office, they being the wives of ministers who were unmarried when elected to the ministry. J. H. Shirkey.

Notes and Jottings.

ON our visit to the Kentucky Mission, in the month of August, we were joined by Bro. A. S. Culp, who moved from Monticello, Ind., to Laco-nia, Ind., near the Ohio River, below Louisville, Ky. We were sorry to find two of our number proving unfaithful. Upon the part of the rest, their relation to the church continued to be a pleasure to them. One was baptized. Bro. Culp will assist us in that mission in the future. The attendance was larger than at any previous meeting. The evidence was, the more people learn and hear of the Brethren's doctrine, the more they love it.

On the evening of Sept. 8, we met our appointment at Lanark, Ill. We were encouraged to observe an early, prayerful concern in behalf of the meeting. As our manner is, we started day meetings at 2 P. M., to which they were unaccustomed, but the attendance was a surprise. Their feast was Sept. 24, in the midst of the series of meetings. Results thus far were, five baptized and differences adjusted, so that members sat at the Communion table who had not done so for some

perfect, eternal affirmation of the divine holiness was in the resurrection of the Godman. What can be more consistent than that the first day of the week should be the day that hallows all the rest?

A greater than the Pope is here. Christ alone is our Rest, and the first day of the week is our Sabbath, because on that day transpired the august transaction without which "we are yet in our sins." 1 Cor. 15: 17. "*Let not your heart be troubled:* YE BELIEVE IN GOD, BELIEVE ALSO IN ME." Jesus is God's and Man's eternal Sabbath.
Union Deposit, Pa.

CORRESPONDENCE.

"Write what thou seest, and send it unto the churches."

☞Church News solicited for this Department. If you have had a good meeting, send a report of it, so that others may rejoice with you. In writing give name of church, County and State. Be brief. Notes of Travel should be as short as possible. Land Advertisements are not solicited for this Department. We have no advertising page, and, if necessary, will issue supplements.

Notice.

THE churches of North-western Ohio will take notice that the Committee, to whom was intrusted the location of next District Meeting, have located the same in the Maumee District, Defiance County.

S. M. LOOSE, Moderator,
S. H. DICKEY, Reading Clerk,
D. D. THOMAS, Writing Clerk.

Notes from the Second District of West Virginia.

ON Friday, Oct. 7, I boarded the train, in company with Bro. G. W. Annon and his daughter,—a young sister,—to attend a love-feast, which was to be held the next evening in Marion County, W. Va. When we boarded the train we found three of our brethren from Maryland, who had been invited to attend the feast,—Wm. T. Sines, I. O. Thompson and John Cross. The two former are ministers, and the latter a deacon. Bro. Thompson addressed us in the evening from Rom. 1: 16. He broke to us the Bread of Life in an acceptable manner. We had meeting on the 8th at two o'clock P. M., when Bro. Sines preached from Ps. 23: 1. We felt that it was good to wait upon the Lord.

By this time Bro. W. R. Murphy, from Ohio, had made his appearance. We were all glad to see him, as he once lived in our congregation. Brethren Sines, Thompson and Murphy did some good talking during examination and Communion services. Our house was crowded to such an extent as to be very uncomfortable to many of the spectators. Thirty were at the table. One commendable thing was that all were at the table. Next day, at 10:30, Bro. Sines preached from Zech. 8: 23. He told us many good things, and Bro. Murphy also made some appropriate remarks.

At the close of the meeting an invitation was given, when three precious souls made application for membership. At 3:30 we gathered at the river, where prayer was wont to be made. Then baptism was administered to those three precious souls. As we were leaving the water, two more were ready, who had applied some time previous. After the usual services, they were buried with Christ in baptism. The last two were husband and wife. Both went in together. The sister being baptized first, waited for her husband, and both came out together. Many said it was the most beautiful sight they ever saw. At night brother Thompson preached to the people, and the next day several of the brethren left for home, leaving Bro. Murphy to preach next night. Upon the whole, our meeting was a pleasant one, and one long to be remembered. The members were much built up, and feel that others are near the kingdom: Come again, brethren, and let us fight for the Lord against the mighty. If the Lord will, I will start to District Meeting, Oct. 13, after which I will give your readers a few more notes.
Z. ANNON.
Thornton, W. Va., Oct. 11.

From Grundy Centre, Iowa.

AFTER enjoying a feast at our home church (the Lower Fall Creek, Ind.), Sept. 30, I boarded the train at Anderson, Ind., next day, at noon, for the South Waterloo church, Iowa, to be present at their feast, Oct. 1. I found it to be a feast indeed and in truth. Oct. 3 was their District Meeting, which was another enjoyable meeting. Oct. 4 was their Ministerial Meeting. At 3 P. M. of the same day I bade them all farewell, to come to the place where I am now writing, to hold a series of meetings. Yesterday, Oct. 6, I was called upon to preach the funeral of Susie Essig, daughter of Eld. H. Strickler, who had moved some four years ago to Texas. Deceased died Sept 30, 1892, aged 29 years, 11 months, and 4 days; and was brought back here for interment. Judging from the large congregation that assembled upon the occasion, Susie was highly respected. Text, Rev. 4: 3.

From here I go to the Iowa River church, to their love-feast, Oct. 22, and from there to Franklin County, to hold a series of meetings till the love-feast at Greene, Iowa, Nov. 5. I expect, also, to hold a series of meetings for them. From that time on, further arrangements can be made as the Brethren see fit.
JOSEPH HOLDER.

Harvest Meetings.

ON the first Sunday of August we held a harvest-meeting in the south part of the Cedar Lake church. Bro. J. C. Murray, of Nappanee, came to our assistance, and preached four soul-stirring sermons. Sunday morning he preached a thanksgiving sermon, and in the afternoon he preached a missionary sermon which caused the brethren and sisters to reach down into their pockets. We took up a collection and got something over seven dollars for the spread of Christ's kingdom. On the first Sunday of September we had a harvest-meeting in our church-house near Corunna. Bro. I. L. Berkey, of Goshen, was with us and preached four good Gospel sermons. In the morning he preached a thanksgiving sermon, and in the afternoon a missionary sermon, after which we took up another collection at which we got over seven dollars, making, in all, over fourteen dollars for the mission cause. Last but not least, at each of our harvest-meetings there was one soul born into the kingdom of Christ. May God's love ever be with them!
J. H. ELSON.
Fairfield Centre, Ind.

From the Belleville Church, Kans.

OUR series of meetings, conducted by Bro. J. E. Young, of Beatrice, Nebr., closed last evening. He came into our midst Sept. 24. We feel that we had a good meeting. The members have been strengthened in their faith, and some, no doubt, have formed new resolutions, and try to live a better Christian life in the future. During these meetings two young people made the good confession and were initiated into the fold by baptism. Our feast was held Oct. 1. There was a good representation of our members, and others, from different places. Thirteen ministers, including our home force, were present. Our aged brother, John Forney, of Abilene, was with us. We rejoiced to meet him once more and hear his good counsel. Brethren Levi Saylor, A. M. Dickey, Samuel Henry, W. R. Phillippi, —— Myers and Eli Renner of adjoining churches were also present. Bro. Young officiated. At this meeting Bro. Albion Daggett was advanced to the second degree of the ministry, and Bro. Chester Daggett to the deacon's office. It was also decided, at our last council, to continue our Sunday-school through the winter. Some of our members, are on the bed of affliction. Sister Gooch has returned home with but little improvement in her condition. Grandfather Hillery is very sick. The brittle thread of life is about broken.
LOUISA J. WILLIAMS.
Oct. 5.

From the Wacandah Church, Ray Co., Mo.

SEPT. 3 Bro. Jacob Witmore began a series of meetings at the Rockingham church, and continued until the evening of Sept. 21, preaching, in all, twenty-three sermons. The attendance was good throughout. On the second Sunday we had children's meeting before regular services. There were probably fifty children present. Our brother entertained them well, and the parents did not fail to get their share of the short talk. On the third Sunday, by request, he told why we did not take the Communion on the first day of the week, and in day-time. During these meetings four decided for the right, and were baptized. Sept. 29 was our council, preparatory to our love-feast. Bro. J. E. Ellenberger, of the Smith Fork congregation, was with us. Much more business than usual came before this meeting, but all was satisfactorily disposed of. Bro. Ellenberger preached two sermons for us, and was with us at our love-feast; also Eld. Daniel Sell, from the same congregation, and Bro. David Hardman, from Hamilton, Mo.

On the evening of our love-feast, one more was baptized. This sister lives near no other members, and is the first-fruits of our Brethren's labors in that neighborhood. One was also received by letter. This was one of the largest love-feasts, ever held at this church. About one hundred seventy-five members communed. On the day following, Bro. Geo. Clemens was advanced to the full ministry, and brethren Samuel Sandy, Walker Falls, and Isaac Early were chosen as deacons. Two young sisters were also received into office, they being the wives of ministers who were unmarried when elected to the ministry.
J. H. SHIRKEY.

Notes and Jottings.

ON our visit to the Kentucky Mission, in the month of August, we were joined by Bro. A. S. Culp, who moved from Monticello, Ind., to Laconia, Ind., near the Ohio River, below Louisville, Ky. We were sorry to find two of our number proving unfaithful. Upon the part of the rest, their relation to the church continued to be a pleasure to them. One was baptized. Bro. Culp will assist us in that mission in the future. The attendance was larger than at any previous meeting. The evidence was, the more people learn and hear of the Brethren's doctrine, the more they love it.

On the evening of Sept. 8, we met our appointment at Lanark, Ill. We were encouraged to observe an early, prayerful concern in behalf of the meeting. As our manner is, we started day meetings at 2 P. M., to which they were unaccustomed, but the attendance was a surprise. Their feast was Sept. 24, in the midst of the series of meetings. Results thus far were, five baptized and differences adjusted, so that members sat at the Communion table who had not done so for some

Missionary and Tract Work Department.

"Upon the first day of the week, let every one of you lay by him in store as God hath prospered him, that there be no gatherings when I come."—1 Cor. 16: 2.

"Every man as he purposeth in his heart, so let him give. Not grudgingly or of necessity, for the Lord loveth a cheerful giver."—2 Cor. 9: 7.

HOW MUCH SHALL WE GIVE?

"Every man according to his ability." "Every one as God hath prospered him." "Every man, according as he purposeth in his heart, so let him give." "For if there be first a willing mind, it is accepted according to that a man hath, and not according to that he hath not."—2 Cor. 8: 22.

Organization of Missionary Committee.

DANIEL VANIMAN, Foreman,   -   McPherson, Kans.
D. L. MILLER, Treasurer,   -   Mt. Morris, Ill.
GALEN B. ROYER, Secretary,   -   Mt. Morris, Ill.

Organization of Book and Tract Work.

S. W. HOOVER, Foreman,   -   Dayton, Ohio.
S. BOCK, Secretary and Treasurer,   -   Dayton, Ohio.

☞All donations intended for Missionary Work should be sent to GALEN B. ROYER, Mt. Morris, Ill.

☞All money for Tract Work should be sent to S. BOCK, Dayton, Ohio.

☞Money may be sent by Money Order, Registered Letter, or Drafts on New York or Chicago. Do not send personal checks, or drafts on interior towns, as it costs 25 cents to collect them.

☞Solicitors are requested to faithfully carry out the plan of Annual Meeting, that all our members be solicited to contribute at least twice a year for the Mission and Tract Work of the Church.

☞Notes for the Endowment Fund can be had by writing to the Secretary of either Work.

MISSIONARY ITEMS.

NOT very many days ago a certain subscription paper for missions was being circulated in one of our churches in Maryland; a bright little sister, eleven years old, had heard of that call, and her heart was moved to help. When the opportunity was presented she said to her kind father: "Papa, now I have altogether just ninety-five cents saved up. That's all the money I have, but if you think I can earn the other five cents until it is to be paid, why then I'll put down a dollar." Her father said, "I think you can," and her bright eyes sparkled as she saw her papa write her name next beneath his own, and for a $1.00.

* * *

One could not well conclude what the American people were like by a visit to the gold mines of California and critically looking upon the dwellers there. Neither can one rightly judge the make-up of well-to-do Chinese by the average laundryman of the cities. That man has sacrificed a good deal, and for his one object in the world,—to get money. The Chinese in China are said to be bright, industrious, inventive, and are often styled "The Yankees of the Orient," and with China's 400,000,000 souls open to missionary influence, it presents almost a world-field itself. God says, "Go." Do I say, "No"?

* * *

If a person should enter upon the work of missions to the heathen and die there, would he be more unfortunate than if he had died at home?

* * *

Which is better, on being severed from those of like precious faith for a greater or less time, to say: "I hope and pray that I may be able to hold out faithful;" or, to say: "I hope and pray that I may be able to win others to the faith"?

* * *

Hier ruhes dis Gebeine
A. M.
Geboren 1679; gestorben 1735.
alt 56 Jahre.

This is the inscription on a little old tombstone in the Charter Oak graveyard, about three blocks from the old mother church in Germantown. It is not known to many, near or far, yet the work of Alexander Mack is felt by us all. What effects it to us whether stone or wave, far or near, tells the story of our death, if the most possible good works in the least possible time is the story of our life? "Only remembered by what I have done," is better than all.

* * *

The Karens of Burmah are well worth a good deal of attention. There are several tribes and dialects among them. They are small of stature, of a quiet and peaceable disposition, and usually are engaged in agricultural pursuits. They are very superstitious however, and are worshipers of demons. But what is striking is the fact that they have traditions of the creation, of the flood and other historical points very much in harmony with the Bible narration. They also claim to have had the Scriptures formerly, but, somehow, they became lost. Their crowning tradition or expectation is that the truth would be restored to them by people of distant lands. Thousands of the Karens have accepted Christianity through the labors of missionaries.

* * *

The *Missionary Review* for October contains much valuable information concerning the Greek church as it is to-day. While they are often regarded as akin to the Catholics, they are, in fact, as different from them as the Catholics are from Protestants. While they have some very good things as a church, they are buried deep beneath the debris of cold, dead formalism.

* * *

A church in Boston pays $5,000 for ministerial services and $36 for missions.—*The Kingdom.* How does that compare with one of our churches at ——, which pays nothing for ministerial services and the same for missions?

* * *

In reading of missions, the word *zenana* is often met with. These zenanas are the apartments of the women of India. No woman of India may spend much of her time elsewhere than in her rooms,—virtually her prison cell. She may not live according to our idea of a woman's life, but is the servant to her lord, her husband, and would rather die than be seen of other men. A good idea of the zenana may be gotten from Johnson's and other encyclopedias. There is a great field for lady missionaries. The number of women shut up in zenanas in India is equal to two-thirds the population of the United States.

* * *

If a faithful, loving mother gives a son to the cause of missions, how much should a well-to-do neighbor give to equal the mother's offering?

* * *

The prayer to the Lord to raise up workers for the Master's vineyard cannot be prayed very long before you feel God's breath as he approaches and is about to use you, or prepare you for use. Try it.   S. B.

RECEIPTS OF GENERAL MISSIONARY COMMITTEE FOR SEPTEMBER, 1892.

Mary E Strauser, Lyons, Ind., $2.70; Keuka church, Fla., $6.74; a sister, 42 cents; Lamotte church, Ill., $2.60; Eli Cottrell, Pyrmont, Ind., $1; Covington church, Ohio, $29.49; a brother in Christ, Sidney, Nebr., $4.80; Astoria church, Ill., $3.40; Michael Weyand and wife, Somerset County, Pa., $1.00; J. O. Kimmel and wife, Somerset County, Pa., $1.00; Daniel Kimmel, 50 cents; J. Fike and wife, Somerset County, Pa., 50 cents; Mary C. Musser, Somerset County, Pa., 25 cents; Annie C. Musser, Somerset County, Pa., 25 cents; Amanda Beeghly, Somerset County, Pa., 25 cents; A. J. Beeghly, Somerset County, Pa., 25 cents; G. G. Cupp, Somerset County, Pa., 25 cents; Sarah E. Shober, Somerset County, Pa., 25 cents; Emma Walker, Somerset Co., Pa., 25 cents; a brother, Somerset County, Pa., 50 cents; West Dayton church, Ohio, $4; Okaw church, Ill., $12.50; Elkhart church, Ind., $6; Huntington church, Ind., $4; Ephratah Sunday-school, Pa., $4; Lost Creek church, Ohio, $1.50; E. N., Pa., $2; South Waterloo church, Iowa, $40; Bethel church, Ind., $5; Beatrice church, Nebr., 70 cents; Clover Creek church, Pa., $13.50; Lincoln church, Nebr., $1.65; a sister, Redfield, Kans., 50 cents; harvest-meeting at New Enterprise church, Pa., $32.73; Duncansville church, Pa., $11; Cedar Lake church, Ind., $3.55; Mingo church, Pa., $14; a devoted family, Indiana, $5.41; Waterloo church, Iowa, $8.32; Loon Creek S. S., Salimony church, Ind., $3.30; K. Leonard, Aurelia, Iowa, $1.00; harvest-meeting, Yellow River church, Ind., $26; Ephratah church, Pa., $25; Big Swatara church, Pa., $10; Northern District of Illinois, $141.49; Northeastern District of Ohio, $167.01; Southern District of Illinois, $13.28; Panther Creek church, Iowa, $6.50; two-thirds surplus from Annual Meeting of 1892, Cedar Rapids, Iowa, $298; interest from endowment notes, $10.00; interest from loans of mission fund, $15.00.

SUMMARY.

Receipts for September, '91...... $871 95
Receipts for September, '92...... 948 24
                                            ————
Increase,...................... $576 29
Total receipts to close of September,
  '91...................... $1688 05
Total receipts to close of September,
  '92...................... 3750 44
                                            ————
Increase for year,.............. $2067 39
Should any one have sent money for general missionary purposes which has not been herein acknowledged, please inform the Secretary immediately.   GALEN B. ROYER, Sec.

CHURCH GOVERNMENT.

BY M. R. BASHORE.

IT is just as important for an elder to study the workings of his church as it is for a father to study the different dispositions and temperaments of his children, in order to be successful in the government of his church. An elder must not only keep a close watch over his flock, but he must carefully study his own life and adapt himself accordingly, in order that he may succeed well, and, unless he does this, the result will be a failure. The love for the welfare of the church should be one of the leading and ruling characteristics of every elder, in order that the unity of the spirit and the prosperity of the church be maintained. Unless the officials, and laity as well, show due respect to their shepherd, the elder, and assist him in his labors, they will leave a heavy burden rest upon his shoulders, and, in a measure, make themselves responsible for the prosperity of the church.

Union and harmony should be one of the first considerations. From some cause we sometimes see dark clouds overshadow a church. Everything seems dark and gloomy, the love grows cold; the unity and prosperity of the church are lost sight of. Just why such a state of things does sometimes exist we hardly know, but when we make a close investigation and arrive at the cause, we find that either the officials have allowed a spirit of envy, hatred, or malice to get among them, or the elder has not been discharging his religious duties or obligations. Indeed, there is no lawful reason why an elder should not be successful in maintaining and retaining good govern-

Missionary and Tract Work Department.

"Upon the first day of the week, let every one of you lay by him in store as God hath prospered him, that there be no gatherings when I come."—1 Cor. 16: 2.

"Every man as he purposeth in his heart, so let him give. Not grudgingly or of necessity, for the Lord loveth a cheerful giver."—2 Cor. 9: 7.

HOW MUCH SHALL WE GIVE?

"Every man according to his ability." "Every one as God hath prospered him." "Every man, according as he purposeth in his heart, so let him give." "For if there be first a willing mind, it is accepted according to that a man hath, and not according to that he hath not."—2 Cor. 8: 12.

Organization of Missionary Committee.

DANIEL VANIMAN, Foreman,   McPherson, Kans.
D. L. MILLER, Treasurer,   -   -   Mt. Morris, Ill.
GALEN B. ROYER, Secretary,   -   Mt. Morris, Ill.

Organization of Book and Tract Work.

S. W. HOOVER, Foreman,   -   -   Dayton, Ohio.
S. BOCK, Secretary and Treasurer,   -   Dayton, Ohio.

☞All donations intended for Missionary Work should be sent to GALEN B. ROYER, Mt. Morris, Ill.

☞All money for Tract Work should be sent to S. BOCK, Dayton, Ohio.

☞Money may be sent by Money Order, Registered Letter, or Drafts on New York or Chicago. Do not send personal checks, or drafts on interior towns, as it costs 25 cents to collect them.

☞Solicitors are requested to faithfully carry out the plan of Annual Meeting, that all our members be solicited to contribute at least twice a year for the Mission and Tract Work of the Church.

☞Notes for the Endowment Fund can be had by writing to the Secretary of either Work.

MISSIONARY ITEMS.

NOT very many days ago a certain subscription paper for missions was being circulated in one of our churches in Maryland; a bright little sister, eleven years old, had heard of that call, and her heart was moved to help. When the opportunity was presented she said to her kind father: "Papa, now I have altogether just ninety-five cents saved up. That's all the money I have, but if you think I can save the other five cents until it is to be paid, why then I'll put down a dollar." Her father said, "I think you can," and her bright eyes sparkled as she saw her papa write her name next beneath his own, and for a $1.00.

* * *

One could not well conclude what the American people were like by a visit to the gold mines of California and critically looking upon the dwellers there. Neither can one rightly judge the make-up of well-to-do Chinese by the average laundryman of the cities. That man has sacrificed a good deal, and for his one object in the world,—to get money. The Chinese in China are said to be bright, industrious, inventive, and are often styled "The Yankees of the Orient," and with China's 400,000,000 souls open to missionary influence, it presents almost a world-field itself. God says, "Go." Do I say, "No"?

* * *

If a person should enter upon the work of missions to the heathen and die there, would he be more unfortunate than if he had died at home?

* * *

Which is better, on being severed from those of like precious faith for a greater or less time, to say: "I hope and pray that I may be able to hold out faithful;" or, to say: "I hope and pray that I may be able to win others to the faith"?

* * *

Hier ruhen die Gebeine
A. M.
Geboren 1679; gestorben 1755.
alt 56 Jahre.

This is the inscription on a little old tombstone in the Charter Oak graveyard, about three blocks from the old mother church in Germantown. It is not known to many, near or far, yet the work

---

of Alexander Mack is felt by us all. What effects it to us whether stone or wave, far or near, tells the story of our death, if the most possible good works in the least possible time is the story of our life? "Only remembered by what I have done," is better than all.

* * *

The Karens of Burmah are well worth a good deal of attention. There are several tribes and dialects among them. They are small of stature, are engaged in agricultural pursuits. They are very superstitious however, and are worshipers of demons. But what is striking is the fact that they have traditions of the creation, of the flood and other historical points very much in harmony with the Bible narration. They also claim to have had the Scriptures formerly, but, somehow, they became lost. Their crowning tradition or expectation is that the truth would be restored to them by people of distant lands. Thousands of the Karens have accepted Christianity through the labors of missionaries.

* * *

The *Missionary Review* for October contains much valuable information concerning the Greek church as it is to-day. While they are, often regarded as akin to the Catholics, they are, in fact, as different from them as the Catholics are from Protestants. While they have some very good things as a church, they are buried deep beneath the debris of cold, dead formalism.

* * *

A church in Boston pays $5,000 for ministerial services and $36 for missions.—*The Kingdom*. How does that compare with one of our churches at ——, which pays nothing for ministerial services and the same for missions?

* * *

In reading of missions, the word *zenana* is often met with. These zenanas are the apartments of the women of India. No woman of India may spend much of her time elsewhere than in her rooms,—virtually her prison cell. She may not live according to our idea of a woman's life, but is the servant to her lord, her husband, and would rather die than be seen of other men. A good idea of the zenana may be gotten from Johnson's and other encyclopedias. There is a great field for lady missionaries. The number of women shut up in zenanas in India is equal to two-thirds the population of the United States.

* * *

If a faithful, loving mother gives a son to the cause of missions, how much should a well-to-do neighbor give to equal the mother's offering?

* * *

The prayer to the Lord to raise up workers for the Master's vineyard cannot be prayed very long before you feel God's breath as he approaches and is about to use you, or prepare you for use. Try it.   S. B.

RECEIPTS OF GENERAL MISSIONARY COMMITTEE FOR SEPTEMBER, 1892.

Mary E. Strauser, Lyons, Ind., $2.70; Keuka church, Fla., $6.74; a sister, 42 cents; Lamotte church, Ill., $2.60; Eli Cottrell, Pyrmont, Ind., $1; Covington church, Ohio, $29.49; a brother in Christ, Sidney, Nebr., $4.80; Astoria church, Ill., $3.40; Michael Weyand and wife, Somerset County, Pa., $1.00; J. O. Kimmel and wife, Somerset County, Pa., $1.00; Daniel Kimmel, 50 cents; J. Fike and wife, Somerset County, Pa., 50 cents; Mary C. Musser, Somerset County, Pa., 25 cents; Annie C. Musser, Somerset County, Pa., 25 cents; Amanda Beeghly, Somerset County, Pa., 25 cents;

A. J. Beeghly, Somerset County, Pa., 25 cents; G. G. Capp, Somerset County, Pa., 25 cents; Sarah E. Shober, Somerset County, Pa., 25 cents; Emma Walker, Somerset Co., Pa., 25 cents; a brother, Somerset County, Pa., 50 cents; West Dayton church, Ohio, $4; Okaw church, Ill., $12.50; Elkhart church, Ind, $6; Huntington church, Ind., $4; Ephratah Sunday-school, Pa., $4; Lost Creek church, Ohio, $1.50; E. N., Pa., $2; South Waterloo church, Iowa, $40; Bethel church, Ind., $5; Beatrice church, Nebr., 70 cents; Clover Creek church, Pa., $13.50; Lincoln church, Nebr., $1.65; a sister, Redfield, Kans., 50 cents; harvest-meeting at New Enterprise church, Pa., $32.73; Duncansville church, Pa., $11; Cedar Lake church, Ind., $3.55; Mingo church, Pa., $14; a devoted family, Indiana, $5.41; Waterloo church, Iowa, $8.32; Loon Creek S. S., Salimony church, Ind., $3.20; K. Leonard, Aurelia, Iowa, $1.00; harvest-meeting, Yellow River church, Ind., $26; Ephratah church, Pa., $25; Big Swatara church, Pa., $10; Northern District of Illinois, $141.49; Northeastern District of Ohio, $167.01; Southern District of Illinois. $18.28; Panther Creek church, Iowa, $6.50; two-thirds surplus from Annual Meeting of 1892, Cedar Rapids, Iowa, $298; interest from endowment notes, $10.00; interest from loans of mission fund, $15.00.

· SUMMARY.

Receipts for September, '91,......$371 95
Receipts for September, '92,...... 948 24
                                        ————
Increase,............................$576 29

Total receipts to close of September, '91,........................$1688 05 '

Total receipts to close of September, '92,........................3750 44
                                        ————
Increase for year,............$2067 39

Should any one have sent money for general missionary purposes which has not been herein acknowledged, please inform the Secretary immediately.   GALEN B. ROYER, Sec.

CHURCH GOVERNMENT.

BY M. D. BASHORE.

IT is just as important for an elder to study the workings of his church as it is for a father to study the different dispositions and temperaments of his children, in order to be successful in the government of his church. An elder must not only keep a close watch over his flock, but he must carefully study his own life and adapt himself accordingly, in order that he may succeed well, and, unless he does this, the result will be a failure. The love for the welfare of the church should be one of the leading and ruling characteristics of every elder, in order that the unity of the spirit and the prosperity of the church be maintained. Unless the officials, and laity as well, show due respect to their shepherd, the elder, and assist him in his labors, they will leave a heavy burden rest upon his shoulders, and, in a measure, make themselves responsible for the prosperity of the church.

Union and harmony should be one of the first considerations. From some cause we sometimes see dark clouds overshadow a church. Everything seems dark and gloomy, the love grows cold; the unity and prosperity of the church are lost sight of. Just why such a state of things does sometimes exist we hardly know, but when we make a close investigation and arrive at the cause, we find that either the officials have allowed a spirit of envy, hatred, or malice to get among them, or the elder has not been discharging his religious duties or obligations. Indeed, there is no lawful reason why an elder should not be successful in maintaining and retaining good govern-

The Gospel Messenger,

A Weekly at $1.50 Per Annum.

PUBLISHED BY

The Brethren's Publishing Co.

D. L. MILLER,	. . . . . . Editor
J. H. MOORE,	. . . . . . Office Editor.
J. B. BRUMBAUGH,	. . . . Associate Editors.
J. G. ROYER,	
JOSEPH AMICK,	. . . . . Business Manager.

ADVISORY COMMITTEE.

L. W. Teeter, A. Hutchison, Daniel Hays.

☞Communications for publication should be legibly written with black ink on one side of the paper only. Do not attempt to interline, or to put on one page what ought to occupy two.

☞Anonymous communications will not be published.

☞Do not mix business with articles for publication. Keep your communications on separate sheets from all business.

☞Time is precious. We always have time to attend to business and to answer questions of importance, but please do not subject us to needless answering of letters.

☞The MESSENGER is mailed each week to all subscribers. If the address is correctly entered on our list, the paper must reach the person to whom it is addressed. If you do not get your paper, write us, giving particulars.

☞When changing your address, please give your former as well as your future address in full, so as to avoid delay and misunderstanding.

☞Always remit to the office from which you order your goods, no matter from where you receive them.

☞Do not send personal checks or drafts on interior banks, unless you send with them 25 cents each, to pay for collection.

☞Remittances should be made by Post-office Money Order. Drafts on New York, Philadelphia or Chicago, or Registered Letters, made payable and addressed to "Brethren's Publishing Co., Mount Morris, Ill.," or "Brethren's Publishing Co., Huntingdon, Pa."

☞Entered at the Post-office at Mount Morris, Ill., as second-class matter.

Mount Morris, Ill., - - - - Oct. 25, 1892.

AT the District Meeting, recently held in Butler County, Nebr., Bro. Urias Shick was elected a member of the Standing Committee.

BRO. C. C. ROOT is to commence his meetings in the Kansas Center church, Kansas, November 1, instead of Oct 1, as mentioned a few weeks ago.

THE Hymn Book Compiling Committee was in session several days last week, and we shall have something to say concerning its work in next issue.

BRO. W. G. COOK has been elected a member of the Standing Committee, to represent Northern Iowa, Minnesota and South Dakota at the next Annual Meeting.

BRO. JACOB P. MOOMAW, of Moomaw, Nebr., is preparing to move to Manvel, Texas, where a number of Brethren are locating in a comparatively new section of the country.

ELSEWHERE in this issue our readers may see what Bro. I. J. Rosenberger has to say of that excellent little book, entitled, "Church Entertainments." The more widely this work is read among our people, the stronger will be our convictions and sentiments against the modern semireligious entertainments that are proving the ruination of many churches.

MT. MORRIS was full of visitors last week. The Special District Meeting and love-feast brought them here from all parts of Northern Illinois. The District Meeting passed off very pleasantly. The churches were well represented and the business transacted was of a very important character. It pertained wholly to the Old People's Home. A full report of the business transacted at this meeting will appear in the MESSENGER next week, and it is very important that it should be read by all the members in the District. The spirit of the meeting was good and the presence of so many members very enjoyable. We trust it was a mutual benefit to all.

BRO. DANIEL VANIMAN has arranged to visit Southern California this week, on important business pertaining to the work of the Mission Board. His wife will accompany him.

BRO. LEVI TROSTLE reports one application for baptism, in the Pigeon Creek church, Marshall County, Ill. In company with Bro. D. E. Brubaker he expects to visit the church the 26th of this month.

WE must again remind our correspondents that we cannot spare space for Sunday-school reports in the MESSENGER. It is sufficient to make these reports before your own school, for they are only of local interest.

ALL communications intended for the MESSENGER office should be addressed "Brethren's Publishing Co., Mt. Morris, Ogle Co., Ill." Please remember this and do not address letters intended for the office any other way.

THE Brethren at Pine Creek, Ill., still continue their interesting series of meetings with encouraging prospects. So far eight have made application for membership in the church, with very favorable indications for more.

BRO. HENRY FRANTZ has returned to West Branch, Ill., and is now engaged in another interesting series of meetings at that place. The weather is delightful, the roads good and the attendance and interest excellent.

BRO. GEO. S. ARNOLD, of Mineral County, W. Va., was with us last week for the first time, and did some very appropriate talking during our meetings. In his own State he holds the position of County Superintendent of Public Instruction.

BRO. J. S. MOHLER'S stay with us last week was very short. He went from here to Pine Creek, to preach a few times for the Brethren and then returned to his home at Morrill, Kans. He thinks of spending the greater part of the fall and winter in the mission field.

ONE of our Brethren in the South speaks of holding meetings in a depot building and using the bales of hay for seats and pulpit. Some of our well-to-do members may think it a little strange, but, actually, these meetings are the most enjoyable services one can attend.

ELD. SOLOMON GARBER, of Cook's Creek, Rockingham County, Virginia, closed his eyes in death Sept. 12, at the advanced age of eighty-three years, but it seems no one has reported his death, and the above facts we glean from a card just received from Bro. S. N. McCann.

WE would regard it as quite a favor if our contributors would leave one inch blank at the top of each page of their manuscript, and write on one side of the sheet only. On receiving an article we prefer to staple the pages together at the top, and this we cannot do unless a good margin is left, as suggested.

OUR love-feast was held in the College Chapel last Saturday evening. The attendance was very large, the weather delightful and the order excellent. The services commenced at 4:30 P. M., closed at eight, and were impressive, instructive and edifying throughout. Bro. Geo. S. Arnold officiated. Very little talking was done during the feast, most of the time being spent in singing and meditating. Our ministerial force from a distance was ample indeed, and the good sermons the brethren delivered the next day, and the evenings following, were greatly appreciated. Three made the good confession and are awaiting the initiatory rite.

BRO. P. R. WRIGHTSMAN, who for the present is at Lanark, Ill., attended the feast here, remained with us over last Sunday, and preached a very impressive and instructive sermon to one of the largest audiences that has assembled in our Chapel for some months. His visit was very much appreciated.

JUST now a good deal of correspondence must necessarily be crowded back a little, but we hope to find room for all of it shortly. This will probably serve as another reminder for our correspondents to use great brevity. Let them make their reports short and interesting. We prefer short, fresh reports and plenty of them.

BRO. JAMES A. SELL, of Pennsylvania, sojourned with us several days last week. It is not generally known that he at one time served as Assistant Editor of the Christian Family Companion, the first weekly religious paper ever published among the Brethren. He is now in the prime of life, and we hope to see more from his pen in the MESSENGER. He went from here to Pine Creek, Ill.

BRO. D. E. BRUBAKER has returned from his mission to Canada and reports an open-hearted and hospitable people, eager to listen to the proclaiming of the truth, yet slow to practically accept the terms of salvation as we understand the Gospel to teach. The field is an important one and should by no means be neglected. Bro. Brubaker may for the present be addressed at Mt. Morris, Ill.

POSSIBLY our readers may think there is a good deal of business in this issue. Well, we do not often talk business, but when we do, we mean it. Then it takes business to run our business, and we say enough this week to do for a while. Hoping that our agents, as well as others, will aid us in procuring an increased number of subscribers, we now turn our attention more fully to the spiritual part of our very important work.

WHILE with us, Bro. L. W. Teeter favored us with one of his pleasant calls, which are always too short and too far between. He reports his work on the New Testament Notes as progressing, but not as rapidly as he would desire. He has just completed 1 Corinthians, and on his return home will commence on 2 Corinthians. It requires time and labor to complete a work of this class. Our readers should not look for it too soon.

BRO. D. M. MILLER, after seven weeks' work in the Wisconsin field has returned to his home at Milledgeville. He held meetings in three churches, attended three feasts and in other ways labored to the edification of the saints and the conversion of sinners. Five were added to the church by confession and baptism, with prospects of many others, and a great spiritual interest seems to have been aroused. He further reports that the Brethren in Wisconsin are full of zeal and deeply in sympathy with the work of the general Brotherhood.

THE eclipse of the sun which is to take place only a few hours after this issue is put on the press, demonstrates not only the uniform and accurate movement of the heavenly bodies, but the ability of man to calculate by figures just when these eclipses are to occur. The time was when such natural occurrences were regarded with superstitious awe, but we now look upon them as intelligent and instructive shadows, marking the lapse of time upon the dial of the universe. He who cannot see the hand of intelligence displayed in all these things, is most assuredly blind and cannot see afar off in the realm of nature as well as in that of revelation.

The Gospel Messenger,

A Weekly at $1.50 Per Annum.

PUBLISHED BY

The Brethren's Publishing Co.

D. L. MILLER,	Editor
J. H. MOORE,	Office Editor.
J. B. BRUMBAUGH,	Associate Editors.
J. G. ROYAN,	
JOSEPH AMICK,	Business Manager.

ADVISORY COMMITTEE.

L. W. Teeter, A. Hutchison, Daniel Hays.

☞Communications for publication should be legibly written with black ink on one side of the paper only. Do not attempt to interline, or to put on one page what ought to occupy two.

☞Anonymous communications will not be published.

☞Do not mix business with articles for publication. Keep your communications on separate sheets from all business.

☞Time is precious. We always have time to attend to business and to answer questions of importance, but please do not subject us to needless answering of letters.

☞The MESSENGER is mailed each week to all subscribers. If the address is correctly entered on our list, the paper must reach the person to whom it is addressed. If you do not get your paper, write us, giving particulars.

☞When changing your address, please give your former as well as your future address in full, so as to avoid delay and misunderstanding.

☞Always remit to the office from which you order your goods, no matter from where you receive them.

☞Do not send personal checks or drafts on interior banks, unless you send with them 25 cents each, to pay for collection.

☞Remittances should be made by Post-office Money Order, Drafts on New York, Philadelphia or Chicago, or Registered Letter, made payable and addressed to "Brethren's Publishing Co., Mount Morris, Ill.," or "Brethren's Publishing Co., Huntingdon, Pa."

☞Entered at the Post-office at Mount Morris, Ill., as second-class matter.

Mount Morris, Ill.,   -   -   -   Oct. 25, 1892.

AT the District Meeting, recently held in Butler County, Nebr., Bro. Urias Shick was elected a member of the Standing Committee.

BRO. C. C. ROOT is to commence his, meetings in the Kaneas Center church, Kansas, November 1, instead of Oct 1, as mentioned a few weeks ago.

THE Hymn Book Compiling Committee was in session several days last week, and we shall have something to say concerning its work in next issue.

BRO. W. G. COOK has been elected a member of the Standing Committee, to represent Northern Iowa, Minnesota and South Dakota at the next Annual Meeting.

BRO. JACOB P. MOOMAW, of Moomaw, Nebr., is preparing to move to Manvel, Texas, where a number of Brethren are locating in a comparatively new section of the country.

ELSEWHERE in this issue our readers may see what Bro. I. J. Rosenberger has to say of that excellent little book, entitled, "Church Entertainments." The more widely this work is read among our people, the stronger will be our convictions and sentiments against the modern semi-religious entertainments that are proving the ruination of many churches.

MT. Morris was full of visitors last week. The Special District Meeting and love-feast brought them here from all parts of Northern Illinois. The District Meeting passed off very pleasantly. The churches were well represented and the business transacted was of a very important character. It pertained wholly to the Old People's Home. A full report of the business transacted at this meeting will appear in the MESSENGER next week, and it is very important that it should be read by all the members in the District. The spirit of the meeting was good and the presence of so many members very enjoyable. We trust it was a mutual benefit to all.

BRO. DANIEL VANIMAN has arranged to visit Southern California this week, on important business pertaining to the work of the Mission Board. His wife will accompany him.

BRO. LEVI TROSTLE reports one application for baptism, in the Pigeon Creek church, Marshall County, Ill. In company with Bro. D. E. Brubaker he expects to visit the church the 26th of this month.

WE must again remind our correspondents that we cannot spare space for Sunday-school reports in the MESSENGER. It is sufficient to make these reports before your own school, for they are only of local interest.

ALL communications intended for the MESSENGER office should be addressed "Brethren's Publishing Co., Mt. Morris, Ogle Co., Ill." Please remember this and do not address letters intended for the office any other way.

THE Brethren at Pine Creek, Ill., still continue their interesting series of meetings with encouraging prospects. So far eight have made application for membership in the church, with very favorable indications for more.

BRO. HENRY FRANTZ has returned to West Branch, Ill., and is now engaged in another interesting series of meetings at that place. The weather is delightful, the roads good and the attendance and interest excellent.

BRO. GEO. S. ARNOLD, of Mineral County, W. VA., was with us last week for the first time, and did some very appropriate talking during our meetings. In his own State he holds the position of County Superintendent of Public Instruction.

BRO. J. S. MOHLER'S stay with us last week was very short. He went from here to Pine Creek, to preach a few times for the Brethren and then returned to his home at Morrill, Kans. He thinks of spending the greater part of the fall and winter in the mission field.

ONE of our Brethren in the South speaks of holding meetings in a depot building and using the bales of hay for seats and pulpit. Some of our well-to-do members may think it a little strange, but, actually, these meetings are the most enjoyable services one can attend.

ELD. SOLOMON GARBER, of Cook's Creek, Rockingham County, Virginia, closed his eyes in death Sept. 12, at the advanced age of eighty-three years, but it seems no one has reported his death, and the above facts we glean from a card just received from Bro. S. N. McCann.

WE would regard it as quite a favor if our contributors would leave one inch blank at the top of each page of their manuscript, and write on one side of the sheet only. On receiving an article we prefer to staple the pages together at the top, and this we cannot do unless a good margin is left, as suggested.

OUR love-feast was held in the College Chapel last Saturday evening. The attendance was very large, the weather delightful and the order excellent. The services commenced at 4:30 P. M., closed at eight, and were impressive, instructive and edifying throughout. Bro. Geo. S. Arnold officiated. Very little talking was done during the feast, most of the time being spent in singing and meditating. Our ministerial force from a distance was ample indeed, and the good sermons the brethren delivered the next day, and the evenings following, were greatly appreciated. Three made the good confession and are awaiting the initiatory rite.

BRO. P. R. WRIGHTSMAN, who for the present is at Lanark, Ill., attended the feast here, remained with us over last Sunday, and preached a very impressive and instructive sermon to one of the largest audiences that has assembled in our Chapel for some months. His visit was very much appreciated.

JUST now a good deal of correspondence must necessarily be crowded back a little, but we hope to find room for all of it shortly. This will probably serve as another reminder for our correspondents to use great brevity. Let them make their reports short and interesting. We prefer short, fresh reports and plenty of them.

BRO. JAMES A. SELL, of Pennsylvania, sojourned with us several days last week. It is not generally known that he at one time served as Assistant Editor of the Christian Family Companion, the first weekly religious paper ever published among the Brethren. He is now in the prime of life, and we hope to see more from his pen in the MESSENGER. He went from here to Pine Creek, Ill.

BRO. D. E. BRUBAKER has returned from his mission to Canada and reports an open-hearted and hospitable people, eager to listen to the proclaiming of the truth, yet slow to practically accept the terms of salvation as we understand the Gospel to teach. The field is an important one and should by no means be neglected. Bro. Brubaker may for the present be addressed at Mt. Morris, Ill.

POSSIBLY our readers may think there is a good deal of business in this issue. Well, we do not often talk business, but when we do, we mean it. Then it takes business to run our business, and we say enough this week to do for a while. Hoping that our agents, as well as others, will aid us in procuring an increased number of subscribers, we now turn our attention more fully to the spiritual part of our very important work.

WHILE here, Bro. L. W. Teeter favored us with one of his pleasant calls, which are always too short and too far between. He reports his work on the New Testament Notes as progressing, but not as rapidly as he would desire. He has just completed 1 Corinthians, and on his return home will commence on 2 Corinthians. It requires time and labor to complete a work of this class. Our readers should not look for it too soon.

BRO. D. M. MILLER, after seven weeks' work in the Wisconsin field has returned to his home at Milledgeville. He held meetings in three churches, attended three feasts and in other ways labored to the edification of the saints and the conversion of sinners. Five were added to the church by confession and baptism, with prospects of many others, and a great spiritual interest seems to have been aroused. He further reports that the Brethren in Wisconsin are full of zeal and deeply in sympathy with the work of the general Brotherhood.

THE eclipse of the sun which is to take place only a few hours after this issue is put on the press, demonstrates not only the uniform and accurate movement of the heavenly bodies, but the ability of man to calculate by figures just when these eclipses are to occur. The time was when such natural occurrences were regarded with superstitious awe, but we now look upon them as intelligent and instructive shadows, marking the lapse of time upon the dial of the universe. He who cannot see the hand of intelligence displayed in all these things, is most assuredly blind and cannot see afar off in the realm of nature as well as in that of revelation.

HOW TO BAPTIZE.

THE following, published by the *Christian Standard* over twenty years ago, is still interesting if it is old. The Dr. Tyng, referred to, was a learned minister of the Episcopal Church:

"Rev. Chrystal, an Episcopal clergyman at New York, who has been baptized in the Greek Church, and believes in immersion as the true mode of baptism, applied for the use of Rev. S. A. Corey's chapel, on Murray Hill. Last Sunday, while Mr. Chrystal was waiting for an interview with Mr. Corey, Dr. Tyng stepped in to see the chapel, as it really contests the palm with St. George's for gorgeous decoration. Mr. Corey mentioned that Mr. Chrystal was waiting for him in his study, and stated his purpose. Dr. Tyng said: 'You Baptists don't know how to baptize. You lead people down into the pool and immerse them face upward, filling their eyes, ears and mouth with water, and half strangling the candidate. Instead of that,' said the Doctor, 'you should do as they do at the East, where you profess to get your authority. This is the way to baptize,' said the Doctor getting down on his knees in the middle aisle. 'Let the candidate kneel, and you have but little way to place him under water. One hand should be placed on the forehead, and the other placed on the back of the head, and then the candidate gently pressed forward until the immersion is complete."

"It is well known that when Dr. Judson engaged himself to Fanny Forester, she was a Presbyterian. She was baptized by Dr. Judson in the church at Utica. He baptized her in the style described by Mr. Tyng, and it gave great scandal to the old line of Baptists. Dr. Judson defended the practice as Eastern and apostolic, and said it was the mode in which all the converts in Burmah were introduced into the church. It was an interesting sight to see old Dr. Tyng, down on his knees in a Baptist church, instructing a Baptist minister how to perform the peculiar ordinance of his denomination."

JOHN AND JESUS.

When did John, the forerunner, first know Jesus? See Matt. 3: 13–17; Mark 1: 9–11; Luke 3: 21–22; John 1: 31–34. According to Matthew it appears that John knew Jesus before baptism: but according to John's Gospel, Jesus seems not to have been known by John before the visible descent of the Spirit.   W. T. K.

JOHN and Jesus, doubtless, knew each other from boyhood. Their mothers were cousins. Shortly before the birth of John, Mary, the mother of Jesus, visited Elizabeth, the mother of John. It is more than likely that they did some visiting afterwards. It is quite probable that they frequently met in Jerusalem where they attended the passover year after year. Mary and Elizabeth were likely fast friends, for they were parents of children of whom they had every reason to expect much. There were remarkable miracles connected with the history of both children, and while Mary kept many things that she saw and heard in her heart, it is not unreasonable to presume that she and her cousin Elizabeth, had many interesting talks concerning the future of their two sons that they were raising. After John's parents died and he grew into manhood, it is likely that he had many serious thoughts concerning his cousin Jesus, who was living in the little village of Nazareth. It is to be presumed that his mother had related to him how an angel had appeared to Mary, informing her that she was to become the mother of the Messiah. She may have related to him the story of the angels appearing at the time of his birth, the visit

of the wise men of the east and many other remarkable occurrences connected with the early history of the child. All these things would awaken, in the mind of John, some very serious reflections. As he studied the Scriptures, and pondered over the incidents related to him by his mother, he could not help wondering if this cousin of his might not be the promised Messiah. Finally the Lord sent him to preach and prepare the way for the coming Messiah, telling him that the one upon whom he should see the Spirit descending and remaining, was the long-looked-for deliverer. Day after day John preached and baptized but did not see the Spirit descend on any one. More than likely his mind often reverted to Jesus. He knew him personally, but yet had no way of knowing for certain that he was the promised one; still he could not help but think that way. Finally he sees him coming. From what he knew of his early history, he felt so confident in his own mind that he was the Christ, that he regarded himself as unworthy to baptize him. But he consented to do so. Then came the Spirit that he was looking for. Not until that moment did he positively know that Jesus was the Messiah, though he may have suspected it for months. Prior to his baptism, John knew Jesus only personally, and yet imagined that there was something extraordinary in him, but he did not know him as the promised Messiah until he witnessed the descent of the Spirit upon him.   J. H. M.

OUR VISIT TO ROANOKE

IT is because our children and neighbors, and their children are not saved to the church, that congregations arrange to hold series of meetings, and ministers leave home, work, and their families, to labor in those meetings.

It was with this in view, that we began to labor for the Brethren of Roanoke, Ill., Oct. 1, and continued until the 7th. Nine sermons, one talk to the children, an election of a minister, advancing another, and an impressive and enjoyable love-feast comprised the public services of the week.

Here is the home of our dear brother, James R. Gish, but his love for far-away souls has led him to spend most of his time, for several years, in Arkansas and other South-west mission fields. The Lord give us scores more of men, who are willing to deny themselves of home comforts and social enjoyments, to go into the by-ways and gather in the prodigals not yet citizens of sinland!

Although the church at Roanoke has sent out a large number of ministers and lay-members to assist in building up the cause in the West, it is still alive and doing a commendable work. The ministry consists of Elders Geo. W. Gish and P. A. Moore, together with brethren Thomas Keiser, Caleb Brubaker and Geo. Eller. On account of Eld. Gish's feeble health, and brethren Moore and Keiser going to California, the burden of the ministerial labor rests almost exclusively upon the two young brethren; but with the many zealous brethren and sisters, which they have standing to their side, we predict prosperity for the church. This was our first visit to the Brethren of Roanoke. The kindness shown us, and their manifest love for the church, and zeal for the Master's cause, awakened inspiration which, we trust, will prove incentives to greater diligence and more complete consecration to the work of the Lord. The Lord bless all the interests of the Brethren at Roanoke!   J. G. R.

CORRESPONDENCE.

"Write what thou seest, and send it unto the churches."

☞Church News solicited for this Department. If you have had a good meeting, send a report of it, so that others may rejoice with you. In writing give name of church, County and State. Be brief. Notes of Travel should be as short as possible. Land Advertisements are not solicited for this Department. We have an advertising page, and, if necessary, will issue supplements.

Among the Churches in Iowa.

I LEFT my home near Bijou Hills, S. Dak., for Waterloo, Iowa, to attend the District Meeting of Northern Iowa, Minnesota and South Dakota. The South Waterloo church held their love-feast Oct. 1, beginning at 4 P. M. By the time services should begin, the large meeting-house of the Brethren was well filled, and a large representation of ministers from different parts of the District was present; also Bro. Holder, from the Southern District of Indiana. This was our first meeting with the dear brethren and sisters here. While we met many who were strangers in the flesh to us, we had somewhat of a spiritual acquaintance, hence, as usual, we find a home among the brethren and sisters and always enjoy the same. The abundance of Christian love here manifested by the members to us, made us enjoy the meeting and especially to again meet around the Lord's table so many of his dear children. For a few years our lot has been one of isolation from the pleasure of meeting so many brethren and sisters, hence our inner man was refreshed beyond measure.

Sunday morning all met to enjoy the well-conducted Sunday-school of the Brethren in the South Waterloo church. We had appropriate remarks by Bro. Holder, after which we again enjoyed the privilege of hearing from Bro. Holder on the subject of "Duty." The evening services were conducted by the writer and Bro. J. F. Ikenberry.

Monday morning, Oct. 3, at 9 A. M., the District Meeting of Northern Iowa, Minnesota and South Dakota was called to order by Eld. Tobias Meyers. By calling the roll of the churches, twenty-four delegates were found to be present. Permanent organization was effected by electing Eld. J. W. Trostle, Moderator; W. G. Cook, Writing Clerk; S. H. Miller, Reading Clerk. The queries were then called for and five were presented and properly disposed of. None were sent to Annual Meeting. The brotherly love that was manifested during all the sessions of this District Meeting was very commendable and left impressions evidently for good. The missionary spirit prevailing was indeed commendable.

By arrangements, made at the last District Meeting, and perfected later by the Brethren, we assembled again at 9 A. M., Oct. 4, in the capacity of a Ministerial Meeting. A large assembly was present. The organization was made permanent for the day and year by electing W. G. Cook, Moderator; S. H. Miller, Clerk. This was my first opportunity of meeting with the Brethren at a Ministerial Meeting, and I must say I was much encouraged by enjoying its benefits, and prayerfully commend them to the Brotherhood. All of the propositions in the program were to our instruction and encouragement. The brotherly love manifested during this entire meeting made it pleasant and profitable to be there. The sermons on Monday evening, by Bro. Murray, of Waterloo, Iowa, and Bro. Ikenberry, of Franklin County, were strong and effective. The entire session of this Meeting was one, I am pleased to look back upon with much pleasure, and if the proper motive is not lost sight of, will be the means of certainly uniting the ministry,—instructing and encouraging them. This we all stand in need of, especially those of us on

HOW TO BAPTIZE.

THE following, published by the *Christian Standard* over twenty years ago, is still interesting if it is old. The Dr. Tyng, referred to, was a learned minister of the Episcopal Church:

"Rev. Chrystal, an Episcopal clergyman at New York, who has been baptized in the Greek Church, and believes in immersion as the true mode of baptism, applied for the use of Rev. S. A. Corey's chapel, on Murray Hill. Last Sunday, while Mr. Chrystal was waiting for an interview with Mr. Corey, Dr. Tyng stepped in to see the chapel, as it really contests the palm with St. George's for gorgeous decoration. Mr. Corey mentioned that Mr. Chrystal was waiting for him in his study, and stated his purpose. Dr. Tyng said: 'You Baptists don't know how to baptize. You lead people down into the pool and immerse them face upward, filling their eyes, ears and mouth with water, and half strangling the candidate. Instead of that,' said the Doctor, 'you should do as they do at the East, where you profess to get your authority. This is the way to baptize,' said the Doctor getting down on his knees in the middle aisle. 'Let the candidate kneel, and you have but little way to place him under water. One hand should be placed on the forehead, and the other placed on the back of the head, and then the candidate gently pressed forward until the immersion is complete."

"It is well known that when Dr. Judson engaged himself to Fanny Forester, she was a Presbyterian. She was baptized by Dr. Judson in the church at Utica. He baptised her in the style described by Mr. Tyng, and it gave great scandal to the old 'line of Baptists.' Dr. Judson defended the practice as Eastern and apostolic, and said it was the mode in which all the converts in Burmah were introduced into the church. It was an interesting sight to see old Dr. Tyng, down on his knees in a Baptist church, instructing a Baptist minister how to perform the peculiar ordinance of his denomination."

JOHN AND JESUS.

When did John, the forerunner, first know Jesus? See Matt. 3: 13–17; Mark 1: 9–11; Luke 3: 21–22; John 1: 32–34. According to Matthew it appears that John knew Jesus before baptism; but according to John's Gospel, Jesus seems not to have been known by John before the visible descent of the Spirit. W. T. K.

JOHN and Jesus, doubtless, knew each other from boyhood. Their mothers were cousins. Shortly before the birth of John, Mary, the mother of Jesus, visited Elizabeth, the mother of John. It is more than likely that they did some visiting afterwards. It is quite probable that they frequently met in Jerusalem where they attended the passover year after year. Mary and Elizabeth were likely fast friends, for they were parents of children of whom they had every reason to expect much. There were remarkable miracles connected with the history of both children, and while Mary kept many things that she saw and heard in her heart, it is not unreasonable to presume that she and her cousin Elizabeth, had many interesting talks concerning the future of their two sons that they were raising. After John's parents died and he grew into manhood, it is likely that he had many serious thoughts concerning his cousin Jesus, who was living in the little village of Nazareth. It is to be presumed that his mother had related to him how an angel had appeared to Mary, informing her that she was to become the mother of the Messiah. She may have related to him the story of the angels appearing at the time of his birth, the visit of the wise men of the east and many other remarkable occurrences connected with the early history of the child. All these things would awaken, in the mind of John, some very serious reflections. As he studied the Scriptures, and pondered over the incidents related to him by his mother, he could not help wondering if this cousin of his might not be the promised Messiah. Finally the Lord sent him to preach and prepare the way for the coming Messiah, telling him that the one upon whom he should see the Spirit descending and remaining, was the long-looked-for deliverer. Day after day John preached and baptized but did not see the Spirit descend on any one. More than likely his mind often reverted to Jesus. He knew him personally, but yet had no way of knowing for certain that he was the promised one; still he could not help but think that way. Finally he sees him coming. From what he knew of his early history, he felt so confident in his own mind that he was the Christ, that he regarded himself as unworthy to baptize him. But he consented to do so. Then came the Spirit that he was looking for. Not until that moment did he positively know that Jesus was the Messiah, though he may have suspected it for months. Prior to his baptism, John knew Jesus only personally, and yet imagined that there was something extraordinary in him, but he did not know him as the promised Messiah until he witnessed the descent of the Spirit upon him. J B. M.

OUR VISIT TO ROANOKE.

IT is because our children and neighbors, and their children are not saved to the church, that congregations arrange to hold series of meetings, and ministers leave home, work, and their families, to labor in those meetings.

It was with this in view, that we began to labor for the Brethren of Roanoke, Ill., Oct. 1, and continued until the 7th. Nine sermons, one talk to the children, an election of a minister, advancing another, and an impressive and enjoyable love-feast comprised the public services of the week.

Here is the home of our dear brother, James R. Gish, but his love for far-away souls has led him to spend most of his time, for several years, in Arkansas and other South-west mission fields. The Lord give us scores more of men, who are willing to deny themselves of home comforts and social enjoyments, to go into the by-ways and gather in the prodigals not yet citizens of sinland!

Although the church at Roanoke has sent out a large number of ministers and lay-members to assist in building up the cause in the West, it is still alive and doing a commendable work. The ministry consists of Elders Geo. W. Gish and P. A. Moore, together with brethren Thomas Keiser, Caleb Brubaker and Geo. Eller. On account of Eld. Gish's feeble health, and brethren Moore and Keiser going to California, the burden of the ministerial labor rests almost exclusively upon the two young brethren; but with the many zealous brethren and sisters, which they have standing to their side, we predict prosperity for the church. This was our first visit to the Brethren of Roanoke. The kindness shown us, and their manifest love for the church, and zeal for the Master's cause, awakened inspiration which, we trust, will prove incentives to greater diligence and more complete consecration to the work of the Lord. The Lord bless all the interests of the Brethren at Roanoke! J. G. R.

CORRESPONDENCE.

"Write what thou seest, and send it unto the churches."

☞"Church News solicited for this Department. If you have had a good meeting, send a report of it, so that others may rejoice with you. In writing give name of church, County and State. Be brief. Notes of Travel should be as short as possible. Land Advertisements are not solicited for this Department. We have an advertising page, and, if necessary, will issue supplements.

Among the Churches in Iowa.

I LEFT my home near Bijou Hills, S. Dak., for Waterloo, Iowa, to attend the District Meeting of Northern Iowa, Minnesota, and South Dakota. The South Waterloo church held their love-feast Oct. 1, beginning at 4 P. M. By the time services should begin, the large meeting-house of the Brethren was well filled, and a large representation of ministers from different parts of the District was present; also Bro. Holder, from the Southern District of Indiana. This was our first meeting with the dear brethren and sisters here. While we met many who were strangers in the flesh to us, we had somewhat of a spiritual acquaintance, hence, as usual, we find a home among the brethren and sisters and always enjoy the same. The abundance of Christian love here manifested by the members to us, made us enjoy the meeting and especially to again meet around the Lord's table so many of his dear children. For a few years our lot has been one of isolation from the pleasure of meeting so many brethren and sisters, hence our inner man was refreshed beyond measure.

Sunday morning all met to enjoy the well-conducted Sunday-school of the Brethren in the South Waterloo church. We had appropriate remarks by Bro. Holder, after which we again enjoyed the privilege of hearing from Bro. Holder on the subject of "Duty." The evening services were conducted by the writer and Bro. J. F. Ikenberry.

Monday morning, Oct. 3, at 9 A. M., the District Meeting of Northern Iowa, Minnesota and South Dakota was called to order by Eld. Tobias Meyers. By calling the roll of the churches, twenty-four delegates were found to be present. Permanent organization was effected by electing Eld. J. W. Trostle, Moderator; W. G. Cook, Writing Clerk; B. H. Miller, Reading Clerk. The queries were then called for and five were presented and properly disposed of. None were sent to Annual Meeting. The brotherly love that was manifested during all the sessions of this District Meeting was very commendable and left impressions evidently for good. The missionary spirit prevailing was indeed commendable.

By arrangements, made at the last District Meeting, and perfected later by the Brethren, we assembled again at 9 A M., Oct. 4, in the capacity of a Ministerial Meeting. A large assembly was present. The organization was made permanent for the day and year by electing W. G. Cook, Moderator; B H Miller, Clerk. This was my first opportunity of meeting with the Brethren at a Ministerial Meeting, and I must say I was much encouraged by enjoying its benefits, and prayerfully commend them to the Brotherhood. All of the propositions in the program were to our instruction and encouragement. The brotherly love manifested during this entire meeting made it pleasant and profitable to be there. The sermons on Monday evening, by Bro. Murray, of Waterloo, Iowa, and Bro. Ikenberry, of Franklin County, were strong and effective. The entire session of this Meeting was one, I am pleased to look back upon with much pleasure, and if the proper motive is not lost sight of, will be the means of certainly uniting the ministry,—instructing and encouraging them. This we all stand in need of, especially those of us on

attention given them by strange ministers. It encourages them to greater activity in Sunday-school work and helps them to form new resolutions to do better in life. It also has its effect on the parents, helping them to more fully realize the responsibilities resting upon them, and to make greater efforts to discharge their duties, and try harder to bring them up in "the fear and admonition of the Lord." Visiting ministers were elders Wm. Davis, W. H. H. Sawyer and H. Talhelm, of Washington, Kans. The latter officiated.
—A. Z. GATES.
Oct. 10.

From Dallas Center, Iowa.

WE, the members of the Dallas Center church, have again had refreshing meetings. Bro. Hutchison, of Kansas, has been laboring for us for over two weeks, but his work now has closed, and he goes on to other churches. May the bread, cast upon the waters, be gathered in the future, if not at the present! As a result of his work, two were made to see their unsafe position, and united with the church, Oct. 5. One was a brother of the writer. May they ever be bright and shining lights to the world! Oct. 5 and 6 we held our fall love-feast. Several members from adjoining churches were with us. Often we are privileged to be at these places, but let us be careful how we spend our time and thoughts! We will all be accountable for the blessings which are given us from time to time.
ELLA ROYER.

Notes from Our Correspondents.

"As cold water to a thirsty soul, so is good news from a far country."

Back Creek, Pa.—The Lord willing, we will hold a series of meetings at the Upton meeting-house, beginning Oct. 22. Bro. H. C. Early, from Virginia, will be with us to preach for us.—*John Lehner.*

Modena, Mo.—Sept 28 Bro. Lewis M. Kob commenced a series of meetings and continued till Oct. 2. The congregations were large, and good interest was manifested. The Word of God was held forth in its fullness. Surely some seed fell on good ground, and ere many days will bring forth abundant fruit.—*Wm. Whitestine.*

Hamilton, Mo.—We, the members of the Hamilton congregation, held our love-feast Oct. 1 and 2, in Bro. D. C. Hardman's barn. About thirty members communed. Ministers present from adjoining churches were brethren J. E. Ellenberger, D. D. Sell, S. B Shirkey, and J. B. Sell, of Cameron. We had splendid weather for the occasion, and the best of order prevailed throughout the meetings.—*Lizzie Henricks.*

Upton, Pa.—The members of the Back Creek church are still moving onward. Oct. 2 one precious soul was received by baptism. Oct. 6 our love-feast occurred. On that occasion two more made the good confession and were baptized. On the whole our feast was a pleasant one. Elders David Long, Wm. Hertzler, N. Martin, and others, were present and gave us wholesome food for the soul. May God bless them for their labors of love!—*John Lehner, Oct. 10.*

McCool, Nebr.—Our love-feast in the Exeter church was held Oct. 8 and 9. About forty-two members communed. We had a large congregation. The order was good and one young man was baptized. Bro. Wine, from David City, Nebr., was with us and did good work for the Master. Our meeting was held in a tent, as we had no meeting-house sufficiently large to hold a feast in. The Lord be praised for his mercies!—*D. B. Heiny, Oct. 10.*

North Manchester, Ind.—The Ministerial Meeting, held in this church, closed yesterday, Oct. 12. The weather was fine, and the attendance quite large. Eld. David Neff was chosen Moderator, and W. S. Toney, Secretary. The deliberations were pleasant, instructive, and to the point. A committee was selected to make necessary arrangements for the next Meeting.—*D. C. Cripe, Oct. 13.*

Blue Creek, Ind.—Our love-feast occurred Sept. 30. One dear sister, who had left the fold and gone with the Progressive element, desired to come back to us again. Her request was granted with pleasure. Our ministerial force at the feast was good. Bro. Joseph Longanecker officiated. About forty members communed, including members from adjoining congregations. The Spirit of the Lord was with us.—*S. Fink.*

Silver Creek, Ohio.—We held our quarterly council Sept. 24. Everything passed off with a good feeling. We decided to have a love-feast Nov. 5, beginning at 10 A. M. Those coming on the Wabash R. R, should come to Kunkle, Ohio, and notify J. F. Throne, Pioneer, Ohio. Those coming on the Mackinaw R. R., should come to Alvordton, Ohio, and notify Mahlon Moyer, Primrose, Ohio, who will provide conveyance to place of meeting.—*Noah Long.*

Barry, Ill.—Bro. T. B. Digman commenced a series of meetings at our place Sept. 25, and continued till Oct. 5. One sister was baptized. She was a bright, a model Christian in the Baptist church, and was loved by all, but she was not satisfied with single immersion, so she came to our church and was baptized. Others say they are almost persuaded. We had good meetings, and felt sad when Bro. Digman preached his farewell sermon. He is going to Maryland. Bro. Lierly and Bro. C. Lucas preached for us on Sunday, Oct. 9.—*Eliza Mickey, Oct. 11.*

Lincoln, Kans.—Our love-feast in the Saline Valley church passed off pleasantly and was appreciated by many, especially the members. The attendance was good. On Sunday we had children's meeting,—the first in this congregation. Brethren J. S. Snyder, of McPherson, and John Humbarger, of Abilene, were with us and talked to the little folks. They also did all the preaching and gave many good words, which, I hope, may have their desired effect. Bro. J. S. Mohler is expected to hold a series of meetings in November.—*L. W. Fitzwater, Oct. 13.*

Germantown, Va.—Our love-feast occurred Oct. 8. It was quite enjoyable. The members, far and near, put forth a commendable zeal by their presence at the feast. There was a large number of members from other churches. Bro. T. C. Denton officiated. The order was all that could be desired. We have had, within the last few weeks, twelve accessions by baptism and two reclaimed. All of this, we think, may be attributed to the earnest efforts of the home ministry, though we are willing to give the Holy One the praise.—*Wm. Roberson.*

Osage, Kans.—Sept. 25 Bro. A. T. Heestand came to us and preached, in all, eight sermons. We had large crowds and the best of feelings prevailed. Two were made to say they were tired of sin. O how our hearts were made to leap for joy to see the young lambs cast their lot with the people of God! Our love-feast, on the evening of Oct. 1, was indeed a feast to the soul. Quite a number of our dear brethren and sisters from adjoining churches cheered us by their presence. On account of bodily afflictions Bro. Heestand left us Oct. 3. His work while with us was much appreciated. May the Lord continue to send his blessings to all!—*Pink Wolfe.*

Elkhart, Ind.—Sept. 24 was our quarterly council in the Elkhart Valley church. Considerable business came before the meeting, which was adjusted to the satisfaction of all, apparently. It was decided to build a church-house in the City of Elkhart, 40 by 60 feet, and we appointed a building committee, with instructions to build as soon as its means would justify. Said committee has decided to commence to build at once.—*J. L. Puterbaugh, Sept. 30.*

Akron, Ind.—Our Communion meeting in the Beaver Dam church, Kosciusko Co., Ind., Oct. 4, was a very pleasant occasion. The weather was agreeable. Many of our neighboring brethren and sisters met with us. The ministerial force from other churches consisted of brethren J. H. Wright, S. S. Ulery, S. Leckrone, L. Pottinger and Isaac Miller. Bro. Wright officiated. About 130 members communed. The house was crowded full, and we hope good impressions were made on some of those who closely watched the ordinances of the Lord's house.—*D. E. Cripe, Oct. 5.*

Brooklyn, Iowa.—Our feast was held Oct. 8. Our series of meetings commenced on the evening of Oct. 2 and continued over the feast. One was baptized. Eld. John Zuck preached for us during the meetings. Ministers present at the feast were, Eld. John Zuck, H. R. Taylor and S. P. Miller. Our meetings were largely attended. Our council-meeting occurred Oct. 4. Bro. Zuck was with us. Love, peace and union prevailed. Our late meetings, we think, were the best and most profitable we have ever held.—*J. S. Snyder, Oct. 12.*

Beaver Creek, Va.—Our corresponding secretary, G. W. Wine, requested me to give you a report of the result of our Communion meeting at the Beaver Creek church, Rockingham Co., Va, Oct. 1, as he is absent from home and had not the privilege of enjoying the feast. It was a feast indeed to the child of God. About 350 members communed. The ministering brethren present from other congregations wielded the Sword with power. We certainly ought not neglect to try to improve the future of our lives after attending such feasts. May the Lord help us so to do!—*A. A. Miller, Oct. 3.*

Centre Church, Ind.—We met in quarterly council after the annual visit was made, and all, except one, expressed themselves in love and union, and willing to labor for the interest of the church, and to the advancement of the cause of Christ. This means a great deal, and, we trust, all will do all they expressed themselves. We just closed a very interesting series of meetings, conducted by Bro. G. W. Lentz. He is young in years, but, by the help of God, he defended the cause nobly. One made the good confession and united with the church. We feel the church was built up, and we hope that all will make new resolves to do more for the Master, and thus all work together for one common interest.—*Ira Witmore.*

Colchester, Ill.—Our love-feast in the Camp Creek church was an enjoyable occasion. The attendance was large and the order commendable. Quite a number of members from adjoining congregations communed with us. Ministers from other congregations were, John Pool, H. W. Strickler, B. F. Britt and J. H. Baker. The latter preached for us a week previous to the feast. Bro. Baker's services were very acceptable. Although there were no immediate conversions, we believe good impressions were made. The church being in need of official assistance, decided to hold an election for two deacons. The choice fell on brethren Sherman Stuckey and Eli Kniesly. May they prove to be efficient workers in their calling!—*S. S. Hummer, Oct. 12.*

attention given them by strange ministers. It encourages them to greater activity in Sunday-school work and helps them to form new resolutions to do better in life. It also has its effect on the parents, helping them to more fully realize the responsibilities resting upon them, and to make greater efforts to discharge their duties, and try harder to bring them up in "the fear and admonition of the Lord." Visiting ministers were elders Wm. Davis, W. H. H. Sawyer and H. Talhelm, of Washington, Kans. The latter officiated.—A. Z. GATES.

Oct. 10.

From Dallas Center, Iowa.

WE, the members of the Dallas Center church, have again had refreshing meetings. Bro. Hutchison, of Kansas, has been laboring for us for over two weeks, but his work now has closed, and he goes on to other churches. May the bread, cast upon the waters, be gathered in the future, if not at the present! As a result of his work, two were made to see their unsafe position, and united with the church, Oct. 5. One was a brother of the writer. May they ever be bright and shining lights to the world! Oct. 5 and 6 we held our fall love-feast. Several members from adjoining churches were with us. Often we are privileged to be at these places, but let us be careful how we spend our time and thoughts! We will all be accountable for the blessings which are given us from time to time.

ELLA ROYER.

Notes from Our Correspondents.

"As cold water to a thirsty soul, so is good news from a far country."

Back Creek, Pa.—The Lord willing, we will hold a series of meetings at the Upton meeting-house, beginning Oct. 22. Bro. H. C. Early, from Virginia, will be with us to preach for us.—*John Lehner.*

Mohees, Mo.—Sept. 28 Bro. Lewis M. Kob commenced a series of meetings and continued till Oct. 2. The congregations were large, and good interest was manifested. The Word of God was held forth in its fullness. Surely some seed fell on good ground, and ere many days will bring forth abundant fruit.—*Wm. Whitestine.*

Hamilton, Mo.—We, the members of the Hamilton congregation, held our love-feast Oct. 1 and 2, in Bro. D. C. Hardman's barn. About thirty members communed. Ministers present from adjoining churches were brethren J. E. Ellenberger, D. D. Sell, S. B Shirkey, and J. B. Sell, of Cameron. We had splendid weather for the occasion, and the best of order prevailed throughout the meetings.—*Lizzie Henricks.*

Upton, Pa.—The members of the Back Creek church are still moving onward. Oct. 2 one precious soul was received by baptism. Oct. 6 our love-feast occurred. On that occasion two more made the good confession and were baptized. On the whole our feast was a pleasant one. Elders David Long, Wm. Hertzler, N. Martin, and others, were present and gave us wholesome food for the soul. May God bless them for their labors of love!—*John Lehner, Oct. 10.*

McCool, Nebr.—Our love-feast in the Exeter church was held Oct. 8 and 9. About forty-two members communed. We had a large congregation. The order was good and one young man was baptized. Bro. Wine, from David City, Nebr., was with us and did good work for the Master. Our meeting was held in a tent, as we had no meeting-house sufficiently large to hold a feast in. The Lord be praised for his mercies!—*D. B. Heiny, Oct. 10.*

North Manchester, Ind.—The Ministerial Meeting, held in this church, closed yesterday, Oct. 12. The weather was fine, and the attendance quite large. Eld. David Neff was chosen Moderator, and W. S. Toney, Secretary. The deliberations were pleasant, instructive, and to the point. A committee was selected to make necessary arrangements for the next Meeting.—*D. C. Cripe, Oct. 13.*

Blue Creek, Ind.—Our love-feast occurred Sept. 30. One dear sister, who had left the fold and gone with the Progressive element, desired to come back to us again. Her request was granted with pleasure. Our ministerial force at the feast was good. Bro. Joseph Longanecker officiated. About forty members communed, including members from adjoining congregations. The Spirit of the Lord was with us.—*S. Fink.*

Silver Creek, Ohio.—We held our quarterly council Sept. 24. Everything passed off with a good feeling. We decided to have a love-feast Nov. 5, beginning at 10 A. M. Those coming on the Wabash R. R., should come to Kunkle, Ohio, and notify J. F. Throne, Pioneer, Ohio. Those coming on the Mackinaw R. R., should come to Alvordton, Ohio, and notify Mahlon Moyer, Primrose, Ohio, who will provide conveyance to place of meeting.—*Noah Long.*

Barry, Ill.—Bro. T. B. Digman commenced a series of meetings at our place Sept. 25, and continued till Oct. 5. One sister was baptized. She was a bright, a model Christian in the Baptist church, and was loved by all, but she was not satisfied with single immersion, so she came to our church and was baptized. Others say they are almost persuaded. We had good meetings, and felt sad when Bro. Digman preached his farewell sermon. He is going to Maryland. Bro. Lierly, Oct. 2.—Bro. C. Lucas preached for us on Sunday, Oct. 9.—*Eliza Mickey, Oct. 11.*

Lincoln, Kans.—Our love-feast in the Saline Valley church passed off pleasantly and was appreciated by many, especially the members. The attendance was good. On Sunday we had children's meeting,—the first in this congregation. Brethren J. S. Snyder, of McPherson, and John Humbarger, of Abilene, were with us and talked to the little folks. They also did all the preaching and gave many good words, which, I hope, may have their desired effect. Bro. J. S. Mohler is expected to hold a series of meetings in November.—*L. W. Fitzwater, Oct. 13.*

Germantown, Va.—Our love-feast occurred Oct. 8. It was quite enjoyable. The members, far and near, put forth a commendable zeal by their presence at the feast. There was a large number of members from other churches. Bro. T. C. Denton officiated. The order was all that could be desired. We have had, within the last few weeks, twelve accessions by baptism and two reclaimed. All of this, we think, may be attributed to the earnest efforts of the home ministry, though we are willing to give the Holy One the praise.—*Wm. Roberson.*

Osage, Kans.—Sept. 25 Bro. A. I. Heestand came to us and preached, in all, eight sermons. We had large crowds and the best of feelings prevailed. Two were made to say they were tired of sin. O how our hearts were made to leap for joy to see the young lambs cast their lot with the people of God! Our love-feast, on the evening of Oct. 1, was indeed a feast to the soul. Quite a number of our dear brethren and sisters from adjoining churches cheered us by their presence. On account of bodily afflictions Bro. Heestand left us Oct. 3. His work while with us was much appreciated. May the Lord continue to send his blessings to all!—*Pink Wolfe.*

Elkhart, Ind.—Sept. 24 was our quarterly council in the Elkhart Valley church. Considerable business came before the meeting, which was adjusted to the satisfaction of all, apparently. It was decided to build a church-house in the City of Elkhart, 40 by 60 feet, and we appointed a building committee, with instructions to build as soon as its means would justify. Said committee has decided to commence to build at once.—*J. L. Puterbaugh, Sept. 30.*

Akron, Ind.—Our Communion meeting in the Beaver Dam church, Kosciusko Co., Ind., Oct. 4, was a very pleasant occasion. The weather was agreeable. Many of our neighboring brethren and sisters met with us. The ministerial force from other churches consisted of brethren J. H. Wright, S. S. Ulery, S. Leckrone, L. Pottinger and Isaac Miller. Bro. Wright officiated. About 130 members communed. The house was crowded full, and we hope good impressions were made on some of those who closely watched the ordinances of the Lord's house.—*D. E. Cripe, Oct. 5.*

Brooklyn, Iowa.—Our feast was held Oct. 8. Our series of meetings commenced on the evening of Oct. 2 and continued over the feast. One was baptized. Eld. John Zuck preached for us during the meetings. Ministers present at the feast were, Eld. John Zuck, H. R. Taylor and S. P. Miller. Our meetings were largely attended. Our council-meeting occurred Oct. 4. Bro. Zuck was with us. Love, peace and union prevailed. Our late meetings, we think, were the best and most profitable we have ever held.—*J. S. Snyder, Oct. 12.*

Beaver Creek, Va.—Our corresponding secretary, G. W. Wine, requested me to give you a report of the result of our Communion meeting at the Beaver Creek church, Rockingham Co., Va., Oct. 1, as he is absent from home and had not the privilege of enjoying the feast. It was a feast indeed to the child of God. About 350 members communed. The ministering brethren present from other congregations wielded the Sword with power. We certainly ought not neglect to try to improve the future of our lives after attending such feasts. May the Lord help us so to do!—*A. A. Miller, Oct. 3.*

Centre Church, Mo.—We met in quarterly council after the annual visit was made, and all, except one, expressed themselves in love and union, and willing to labor for the interest of the church, and to the advancement of the cause of Christ. This means a great deal, and, we trust, all will do all they expressed themselves. We just closed a very interesting series of meetings, conducted by Bro. G. W. Lentz. He is young in years, but, by the help of God, he defended the cause nobly. One made the good confession and united with the church. We feel the church was built up, and we hope that all will make new resolves to do more for the Master, and thus all work together for one common interest.—*Ira Wilmore.*

Colchester, Ill.—Our love-feast in the Camp Creek church was an enjoyable occasion. The attendance was large and the order commendable. Quite a number of members from adjoining congregations communed with us. Ministers from other congregations were, John Pool, H. W. Strickler, B. F. Britt and J. H. Baker. The latter preached for us a week previous to the feast. Bro. Baker's services were very acceptable. Although there were no immediate conversions, we believe good impressions were made. The church being in need of official assistance, decided to hold an election for two deacons. The choice fell on brethren Sherman Stuckey and Eli Knisely. May they prove to be efficient workers in their calling!—*S. S. Hummer, Oct. 12.*

New Enterprise, Pa.—Our semi-annual love-feast was held on Oct. 7. Our large house was filled with communicants and spectators. Bro. O. Myers, of Huntingdon, Pa, remained with us until the 9th, and preached several interesting sermons for us. We expect to commence a series of meetings Oct. 29, to continue several weeks if sufficient interest is manifested.—*Geo. S. Myers, Oct. 10.*

Eglon, W. Va.—Oct. 9 closed a week's series of meetings at the Maple Spring church. Our home brethren did the preaching. They held forth the Word of God with power. Saints were made to rejoice, and sinners to tremble. Two were made willing to follow their Savior, and at a late hour in the night they were baptized. They are both sisters. Our hearts were made to rejoice to see them come out on the Lord's side. We were glad that our aged brother, S. A. Fike, and wife, could be at all of our meetings but one.—*Rachel Weimer.*

Union Bridge, Md.—Eld. George S Arnold came to us Sept. 28, and remained with us until Oct. 10. In his mild, earnest and pleasant way he entreated the members and their children and friends to a higher and holier life, walk and conversation. I believe we all felt that we had good meetings and were loth to have the meetings close so soon, but the meeting of the Hymn Book Committee called him to Mount Morris Oct. 13, and we reluctantly gave him the parting hand. One, in the glory and strength of youthful womanhood, cast her lot with us, and was baptized Oct. 6. At the same time one, that had wandered from the fold, was reclaimed. There is joy in the presence of the angels when the exiles return from their wandering. May many more be induced to forsake the ways of sin!—*E. W. Stoner, Oct. 10.*

Plevna, Ind.—Sept. 10 Bro. J. H Miller, of Goshen, Ind., commenced a series of meetings in the Plevna church, and continued until the 25th, delivering, in all, nineteen sermons. Sept. 17 we met in church council. Everything passed off in love and harmony. Bro. Miller gave us an interesting talk, which gave us courage to press on to the mark of our high calling. On Sunday following we had a children's meeting, which will ever be remembered as one of the best meetings we ever attended. During these meetings there was the most favorable weather, with the exception of about two nights. The house was packed nearly every night with attentive listeners. Judging from the remarks made by some, Bro. Miller has left an impression that will set the people to thinking. As an immediate result, one dear young sister came out and was received by baptism.—*A. J. Lantz.*

Matrimonial.

"What therefore God hath joined together, let not man put asunder."

CARVER—AUSTIN.—At the residence of the bride's parents, Sept. 25, 1891, Bro. George Carver and sister Lottie E. Austin, both of the Walnut Creek church, Cooke Co., Tex. A. W. AUSTIN.

HOLSOPPLE—QUINTER.—At the home of the bride's mother, Oct. 5, 1892, by Eld. Joseph Holsopple, the father of the groom, Bro. Frank F. Holsopple, of the Amwell church, New Jersey, and sister Grace Quinter, daughter of the late Eld. James Quinter, of Huntingdon, Pa.

GARRETT—RIDDLESBERGER.—At the home of the bride's parents, near Quincy, Franklin Co., Pa., Oct. 4, 1892, by the undersigned, Bro. John W. Garrett, of Waynesborough, Franklin Co., Pa., and Miss Lizzie Riddlesberger, eldest daughter of Eld. Isaac Riddlesberger. WM. C. KOONTZ.

FUNK—GIBBEL.—At the residence of the bride's parents, San Jacinto, Cal., Oct. 2, 1892, by Eld. John Metzger, Bro. Samuel W. Funk, of Glendora, Cal., and sister Hettie A. Gibbel. FANNIE B. GIBBEL.

GUYER—BECHTEL.—At New Enterprise, Pa., Oct. 6, 1892, by the undersigned, Bro. Irvin S. Guyer and sister Minnie K. Bechtel, both of Bedford County, Pa. GEO. S. MYERS.

Fallen Asleep.

"Blessed are the dead which die in the Lord."

SMITH.—At Clay Hill, Pa., Aug. 30, 1892, Edith R. Smith, infant daughter of Welty and Nettie (nee Knepper) Smith, aged 1 year and 12 days. Funeral services at Mt. Zion from Matt. 18: 3, by the writer, assisted by Harry Good, of the Old Order Brethren. WM A. ANTHONY.

TOPPER.—In the Cedar Lake church, De Kalb Co., Ind., Oct. 2, 1892, of dysentery and brain fever, Anna May, infant daughter of Bro. John and sister Irena Topper, aged 4 months and 16 days. Funeral services from Matt. 18: 3, by Eld. James Barton, of the Cedar Lake church, assisted by Bro. David Cover, of Defiance, Ohio, at the United Brethren church, near Newville. Interment in the Hicksville cemetery, Hicksville, Ohio. J. H. TOPPER.

MOORE.—In the Linville Creek church, Rockingham Co., Va., Oct. 5, 1892, Bro. Reuben Moore, aged 75 years, 7 months and 29 days. Funeral services conducted by Bro. John P. Zigler and the writer from Philpp. 3: 21. DANIEL HAYS.

LAMISON.—Near Osborne, Mo., Aug. 27, 1892, Wealthy A. Lamison (nee Horton). Deceased was born in Bedford County, Pa., March 27, 1841. She was united in marriage to David M. Lamison, Aug. 10, 1865, and moved to Missouri April 6, 1877. ISAAC B. MILLER.

COPELAND.—In the Nettle Creek church, Wayne Co., Ind., June 5, 1892, of typhoid fever, Josie Bell, daughter of Bro Samuel and sister Ruth J. Copeland, aged 21 years, 8 months and 29 days. Josie was a kind, obedient and an affectionate daughter. Funeral services by Bro. B. F. Wissler and the writer from 1 Thess. 4: 13. ABRAHAM BOWMAN.

EIKENBERRY.—In the Nettle Creek church, Ind., Sept. 12, 1892, Marion Clinton, son of Bro. Baltzer and sister Lydia Eikenberry, aged 15 years, 11 months and 9 days. Jan. 27, 1891, he was married to Mary Jane Reed. For the most part of the last fifteen months he was confined to his bed with that dread disease, consumption. He leaves a wife, father and mother. Services by the writer, assisted by brethren L. W. Teeter and Lewis Kinsey. ABRAHAM BOWMAN.

EILER.—In the Nettle Creek church, Ind., Aug. 17, 1892, Daniel Eiler, aged 57 years, 10 months and 12 days. He leaves a companion and five children. He was the son of Samuel Eiler, Sen. While digging a well in which there were "damps," he was suffocated. Funeral services by Eld. Lewis Kinsey and the writer from 1 Sam. 20: 3. ABRAHAM BOWMAN.

WHITEHEAD.—In the Union Center church, near New Paris, Elkhart Co., Ind., May 14, 1892, Sarah E., wife of friend David Whitehead, aged 47 years, 10 months and 23 days. Deceased leaves a husband, six sons and four daughters. Although not in fellowship, she ever respected the humble principles of the church, and went far and near to wait on the sick. Services by Bro. Lemuel Hillery, assisted with a few opening remarks by Rev. Murray of the M. E. church, to one of the largest crowds ever witnessed here. J. O. CULLER.

HAINES.—In the Salem church, Ohio, Sept. 29, 1892, Orpha Susan Haines, only daughter of Bro. Elias and sister Aliha Haines, aged 11 months. Another angel has been added to the glory world. Funeral services by brethren Jesse Kinsey, Samuel Horning and the writer, from 1 Thess. 4: 13-18. JOHN H. BRUMBAUGH.

KINSEY.—In the bounds of the Silver Creek church, Williams Co., Ohio, at Fayette, Ohio, Sept. 10, 1892, Bro. Jacob Kinsey, aged 84 years, 10 months and 3 days. Bro. Kinsey had been a member of the church ever since my earliest recollection. Funeral services by Eld. B. F. Sholty and E. M. Rittenhouse. NOAH LONG.

SAMPSON.—In the bounds of the Silver Creek church, Williams Co., Ohio, at Alvordton, Ohio, Sept. 10, 1892, Victor W. Sampson, infant son of Mr. William and sister Mary Sampson, aged 1 year, 2 months and 1 day. It was their only child. Funeral services by Bro. E. M. Rittenhouse and Eld. B. F. Sholty. NOAH LONG.

SNELL.—At Longmont, Colo., Sept. 10, 1892, Jeffry Marshal Snell, aged 8 years, 1 month and 13 days. He and his brother were out throwing rocks with a sling. By accident his brother hit him, which caused instant death. Services by the writer on Sunday. G. W. FESLER.

MERRILL.—March 14, 1892, sister Elenor Merrill, born in Somerset County, Pa. She was preceded by her husband, John Merrill, thirty-three years. She was a consistent member of the Brethren church for about fifty-five years. She

was the mother of eleven children, three of whom preceded her to the spirit land. She was afflicted for many years with rheumatism, though she was able to go about. She bore it patiently, and was conscious to the last moment of her life. Funeral preached from Rev. 22: 14. DAVID M. MERRILL.

KIMBAL.—In the bounds of the Wacandah church, Ray Co., Mo., Sept. 8, 1892, Gracie Belle, infant daughter of Bro. James Kimbal, aged 2 months and 18 days. J. H. SHIREY.

SMITH.—In the Sugar Creek church, Allen Co., Ohio, Sept. 18, 1892, Solomon Smith, aged 74 years, 6 months and 26 days. The deceased leaves a faithful companion and five children. Funeral services by Eld. Samuel Driver.

BINKLEY.—In the Eagle Creek church, Hancock Co., Ohio, Sept. 20, 1892, Bro. Samuel Binkley, aged 60 years, 5 months and 18 days. Funeral services by Eld. Samuel Driver. DAVID BYERLY.

WARBLE.—In the bounds of the Lanark church, Ill., Oct. 5, 1892, sister Mary Catharine Warble, wife of Bro. Aaron Warble, aged 54 years, 4 months and 9 days. When about two years old she came with her parents from Chambersburgh, Pa., to Carroll County, Ill., in which County she has since resided. She was the mother of six children; united with the church early in life and lived a most exemplary and useful life. Funeral services by the writer. The body was laid to rest in the Lanark cemetery. J. H. M.

FRETS.—At his home in De Kalb County, Ind., Sept. 24, 1892, Jacob Frets, aged 80 years, 5 months and 8 days. He was a member of the church forty years. Funeral services conducted by Eld. James Barton. J. H. ELSON.

PALMER.—In the Cedar Lake church, De Kalb Co., Ind., July 12, 1892, Jacob S. Palmer, aged 81 years, 7 months and 1 day. Bro. Palmer was a faithful member of the church for many years. Last spring, at our Communion, he said that would be the last one for him to attend. Funeral services by Eld. Jacob Gump and James Barton. J. H. ELSON.

MILLER.—In the bounds of the Bethel church, Kansas, Sept. 5, 1892, Jonathan Miller, aged 80 years, 2 months and 11 days. Funeral discourse by Bro. Joseph Glick, assisted by the writer. N. F. BRUBAKER.

WILTROUT.—At McClure, Pa., Oct. 7, 1892, John Franklin, infant son of Jacob Wiltrout, aged 7 months and 9 days. Services by the writer. H. L. MYERS.

COSS.—In the Walnut Valley church, Butler Co., Kans., Oct. 3, 1892, Clifford Coss, son of friend L. B. and sister Ellen Coss, aged 7 years, 8 months and 7 days. Little Clifford has been a patient sufferer for almost his life time. Funeral discourse by M. Keller from 1 Thess. 4: 18. E. KELLER.

EBY.—Near Union, Cass Co., Mich., in the Elkhart district, Bro. Peter Eby, aged 72 years, 5 months and 14 days. Bro. Eby was born in Stark County, Ohio and moved to Indiana in 1838. Soon after that he moved to Cass County, Mich., where he lived until his death. He was a faithful deacon, and ready at all times to defend the doctrine of the Bible, as understood by the Brethren. The Eby family have a record reaching back to the middle of the sixteenth century, and extending over Canada and the States. Eld. Enoch Eby, of Kansas, is connected with the family. J. H. MILLER.

The Gospel Messenger

Is the recognized organ of the German Baptist or Brethren's church, and advocates the form of doctrine taught in the New Testament and pleads for a return to apostolic and primitive Christianity.

It recognizes the New Testament as the only infallible rule of faith and practice, and maintains that Faith toward God, Repentance from dead works, Regeneration of the heart and mind, baptism by Trine immersion for remission of sins unto the reception of the Holy Ghost by the laying on of hands, are the means of adoption into the household of God,—the church militant.

It also maintains that Feet-washing, as taught in John 13, both by example and command of Jesus, should be observed in the church.

That the Lord's Supper, instituted by Christ and as universally observed by the apostles and the early Christians, is a full meal, and, in connection with the Communion, should be taken in the evening or after the close of the day.

That the Salutation of the Holy Kiss, or Kiss of Charity, is binding upon the followers of Christ.

That War and Retaliation are contrary to the spirit and self-denying principles of the religion of Jesus Christ.

That the principle of Plain Dressing and of Non-conformity to the world, as taught in the New Testament, should be observed by the followers of Christ.

That the Scriptural duty of Anointing the Sick with Oil, in the Name of the Lord, James 5: 14, is binding upon all Christians.

It also advocates the church's duty to support Missionary and Tract Work, thus giving to the Lord for the spread of the Gospel and for the conversion of sinners.

In short, it is a Vindicator of all that Christ and his apostles have enjoined upon us, and aims, amid the conflicting theories and discords of modern Christendom, to point out ground that all must concede to be infallibly safe.

☞ The above principles of our Fraternity are set forth on our Brethren's Envelopes." Use them! Price 15 cents per package; 40 cents per hundred.

New Enterprise, Pa.—Our semi-annual love-feast was held on Oct. 7. Our large house was filled with communicants and spectators. Bro. O. Myers, of Huntingdon, Pa, remained with us until the 9th, and preached several interesting sermons for us. We expect to commence a series of meetings Oct. 29, to continue several weeks if sufficient interest is manifested.—*Geo. S. Myers, Oct. 10.*

Egion, W. Va.—Oct. 9 closed a week's series of meetings at the Maple Spring church. Our home brethren did the preaching. They held forth the Word of God with power. Saints were made to rejoice, and sinners to tremble. Two were made willing to follow their Savior, and at a late hour in the night they were baptized. They are both sisters. Our hearts were made to rejoice to see them come out on the Lord's side. We were glad that our aged brother, S. A. Fike, and wife, could be at all of our meetings but one.—*Rachel Weimer.*

Union Bridge, Md.—Eld. George S Arnold came to us Sept. 28, and remained with us until Oct. 10. In his mild, earnest and pleasant way he entreated the members and their children and friends to a higher and holier life, walk and conversation. I believe we all felt that we had good meetings and were loth to have the meetings close so soon. but the meeting of the Hymn Book Committee called him to Mount Morris Oct. 13, and we reluctantly gave him the parting hand. One, in the glory and strength of youthful womanhood, cast her lot with us, and was baptized Oct. 6. At the same time one, that had wandered from the fold, was reclaimed. There is joy in the presence of the angels when the exiles return from their wandering. May many more be induced to forsake the ways of sin!—*E. W. Stoner, Oct. 10.*

Plevna, Ind.—Sept. 10 Bro. J. H. Miller, of Goshen, Ind., commenced a series of meetings in the Plevna church, and continued until the 25th, delivering, in all, nineteen sermons. Sept. 17 we met in church council. Everything passed off in love and harmony. Bro. Miller gave us an interesting talk, which gave us courage to press on to the mark of our high calling. On Sunday following we had a children's meeting, which will ever be remembered as one of the best meetings we ever attended. During these meetings there was the most favorable weather, with the exception of about two nights. The house was packed nearly every night with attentive listeners. Judging from the remarks made by some, Bro. Miller has left an impression that will set the people to thinking. As an immediate result, one dear young sister came out and was received by baptism.—*A. J. Lantz.*

Matrimonial.

"What therefore God hath joined together, let not man put asunder."

CARVER—AUSTIN.—At the residence of the bride's parents, Sept. 25, 1892, Bro. George Carver and sister Lottie E. Austin, both of the William's Creek church, Cooke Co., Tex.
A. W. Austin.

HOLSOPPLE—QUINTER.—At the home of the bride's mother, Oct. 5, 1892, by Eld. Joseph Holsopple, the father of the groom, Bro. Frank F. Holsopple, of the Amwell church, New Jersey, and sister Grace Quinter, daughter of the late Eld. James Quinter, of Huntingdon, Pa.

GARRETT—RIDDLESBERGER.—At the home of the bride's parents, near Quincy, Franklin Co., Pa., Oct. 4, 1892, by the undersigned, Bro. John W. Garrett, of Waynesborough, Franklin Co., Pa., and Miss Lizzie Riddlesberger, eldest daughter of Eld. Isaac Riddlesberger. Wm. C. Koontz.

FUNK—GIBBEL.—At the residence of the bride's parents, San Jacinto, Cal., Oct. 2, 1892, by Eld. John Metzgar, Bro. Samuel W. Funk, of Glendora, Cal., and sister Nettie A. Gibbel.
Fannie B. Gibbel.

GUYER—BECHTEL.—At New Enterprise, Pa., Oct. 6, 1892, by the undersigned, Bro. Irvin S. Guyer and sister Minnie K. Bechtel, both of Bedford County, Pa.
Geo. S. Myers.

Fallen Asleep.

"Blessed are the dead which die in the Lord."

SMITH.—At Clay Hill, Pa., Aug. 30. 1892, Edith R. Smith, infant daughter of Welty and Nettie (nee Knepper) Smith, aged 1 year and 12 days. Funeral services at Mt. Zion from Matt. 18: 3, by the writer, assisted by Harry Good, of the Old Order Brethren. Wm A. Anthony.

TOPPER.—In the Cedar Lake church, De Kalb Co., Ind., Oct. 2, 1892, of dysentery and brain fever, Anna May, infant daughter of Bro. John and sister Irena Topper, aged 4 months and 28 days. Funeral services from Matt. 18: 3, by Eld. James Barton, of the Cedar Lake church, assisted by Bro. David Cover, of Defiance, Ohio, at the United Brethren church, near Newville. Interment in the Hicksville cemetery, Hicksville, Ohio. J. H. Topper.

MOORE.—In the Lisville Creek church, Rockingham Co., Va., Oct. 5, 1892, Bro. Reuben Moore, aged 75 years, 7 months and 29 days. Funeral services conducted by Bro. John P. Zigler and the writer from Philipp. 3: 21.
Daniel Hays.

LAMISON.—Near Osborne, Mo., Aug. 27, 1892, Wealthy A. Lamison (nee Horton). Deceased was born in Bedford County, Pa., March 27, 1841. She was united in marriage to David M. Lamison, Aug. 20, 1865, and moved to Missouri April 6, 1877. Isaac B. Miller.

COPELAND.—In the Nettle Creek church, Wayne Co., Ind., June 5, 1892, of typhoid fever, Josie Bell, daughter of Bro Samuel and sister Ruth J. Copeland, aged 21 years, 8 months and 29 days. Josie was a kind, obedient and an affectionate daughter. Funeral services by Bro. B. F. Wissler and the writer from 1 Thess. 4: 13. Abraham Bowman.

EIKENBERRY.—In the Nettle Creek church, Ind., Sept. 12, 1892, Marion Clinton, son of Bro. Baltzer and sister Lydia Eikenberry, aged 25 years, 11 months and 9 days. Jan. 27, 1891, he was married to Mary Jane Reed. For the most part of the last fifteen months he was confined to his bed with that dread disease, consumption. He leaves a wife, father and mother. Services by the writer, assisted by brethren L. W. Teeter and Lewis Kinsey. Abraham Bowman.

EILER.—In the Nettle Creek church, Ind., Aug. 17, 1892, Daniel Eiler, aged 57 years, 10 months and 12 days. He leaves a companion and five children. He was the son of Samuel Eiler, Sen. While digging a well in which there were "damps," he was suffocated. Funeral services by Eld. Lewis Kinsey and the writer from 1 Sam. 20: 3.
Abraham Bowman.

WHITEHEAD.—In the Union Center church, near New Paris, Elkhart Co., Ind., May 14, 1892, Sarah E., wife of friend David Whitehead, aged 47 years, 10 months and 23 days. Deceased leaves a husband, six sons and four daughters. Although not in fellowship, she ever respected the humble principles of the church, and went far and near to wait on the sick. Services by Bro. Lemuel Hilleiy, assisted with a few opening remarks by Rev. Murray of the M. E. church, to one of the largest crowds ever witnessed here.
J. O. Culler.

HAINES.—In the Salem church, Ohio, Sept. 29, 1892, Orpha Susan Haines, only daughter of Bro. Elias and sister Aldha Haines, aged 11 months. Another angel has been added to the glory world. Funeral services by brethren Jesse Kinsey, Samuel Horning and the writer, from 1 Thess. 4: 13-18. John H. Brumbaugh.

KINSEY.—In the bounds of the Silver Creek church, Williams Co., Ohio, Sept. 10, 1892, Bro. Jacob Kinsey, aged 84 years, 1 month and 3 days. Bro. Kinsey had been a member of the church ever since my earliest recollection. Funeral services by Eld. B. F. Shoily and B. M. Rittenhouse. Noah Long.

SAMPSON.—In the bounds of the Silver Creek church, Williams Co., Ohio, at Alvordton, Ohio, Sept. 10, 1892, victor W. Sampson, infant son of Mr. William and sister Mary Sampson, aged 1 year, 2 months and 1 day. It was their only child. Funeral services by Bro. B. M. Rittenhouse and Eld. B. F. Shoily. Noah Long.

SNELL.—At Longmont, Colo, Sept. 20, 1892, Jeffry Marical Snell, aged 8 years, 1 month and 13 days. He and his brother were out throwing rocks with a sling. By accident his brother hit him, which caused instant death. Services by the writer on Sunday. G. W. Fesler.

MERRILL.—Match 14, 1892, sister Eleonr Merrill, born in Somerset County, Pa. She was preceded by her husband, John Merrill, thirty-three years. She was a consistent member of the Brethren church for about fifty-five years. She was the mother of eleven children, three of whom preceded her to the spirit land. She was afflicted for many years with rheumatism, though she was able to go about. She bore it patiently, and was conscious to the last moment of her life. Funeral preached from Rev. 22: 14. David M. Merrill.

KIMBAL.—In the bounds of the Wacandah church, Ray Co., Mo., Sept. 8, 1892, Gracie Belle, infant daughter of Bro. James Kimbal, aged 2 months and 28 days. J. H. Shirky.

SMITH.—In the Sugar Creek church, Allen Co., Ohio, Sept. 18, 1892, Solomon Smith, aged 74 years, 6 months and 26 days. The deceased leaves a faithful companion and five children. Funeral services by Eld. Samuel Driver.
David Byerly.

BINKLEY.—In the Eagle Creek church, Hancock Co., Ohio, Sept. 20, 1892, Bro. Samuel Binkley, aged 60 years, 5 months and 18 days. Funeral services by Eld. Samuel Driver.
David Byerly.

WARBLE.—In the bounds of the Lanark church, Ill., Oct. 5, 1892, sister Mary Catharine Warble, wife of Bro. Aaron Warble, aged 54 years, 4 months and 9 days. When about two years old she came with her parents from Chambersburgh, Pa., to Carroll County, Ill., in which County she has since resided. She was the mother of six children; united with the church early in life and lived a most exemplary and useful life. Funeral services by the writer. The body was laid to rest in the Lanark cemetery. J. H. M.

FRETS.—At his home in De Kalb County, Ind., Sept. 24, 1892, Jacob Frets, aged 80 years, 5 months and 8 days. He was a member of the church forty years. Funeral services conducted by Eld. James Barton. J. H. Elson.

PALMER.—In the Cedar Lake church, De Kalb Co., Ind., July 12, 1892, Jacob S. Palmer, aged 81 years, 7 months and 1 day. Bro. Palmer was a faithful member of the church for many years. Last spring, at our Communion, he said that would be the last one for him to attend. Funeral services by Eld. Jacob Gump and James Barton. J. H. Elson.

MILLER.—In the bounds of the Bethel church, Kansas, Sept. 5, 1892, Jonathan Miller, aged 80 years, 2 months and 11 days. Funeral discourse by Bro. Joseph Glick, assisted by the writer. N. F. Brubaker.

WILTROUT.—At McClure, Pa., Sept. 7, 1892, John Franklin, infant son of Jacob Wiltrout, aged 7 months and 9 days. Services by the writer. H. L. Myers.

COSS.—In the Walnut Valley church, Barton Co., Kans., Oct. 3, 1892, Clifford Coss, son of friend L. B. and sister Ellen Coss, aged 7 years, 8 months and 7 days. Little Clifford has been a patient sufferer for almost his life time. Funeral discourse by M. Keller from 1 Thess. 4: 18. E. Keller.

EBY.—Near Union, Cass Co., Mich., in the Elkhart district, Bro. Peter Eby, aged 72 years, 5 months and 14 days. Bro. Eby was born in Stark County, Ohio and moved to Indiana in 1838. Soon after that he moved to Cass County, Mich., where he lived until his death. He was a faithful deacon, and ready at all times to defend the doctrine of the Bible, as understood by the Brethren. The Eby family have a record reaching back to the middle of the sixteenth century, and extending over Canada and the States. Eld. Enoch Eby, of Kansas, is connected with the family. J. H. Miller.

The Gospel Messenger.

Is the recognized organ of the German Baptist or Brethren's church, and advocates the form of doctrine taught in the New Testament and pleads for a return to apostolic and primitive Christianity.

It recognizes the New Testament as the only infallible rule of faith and practice, and maintains that Faith, toward God, Repentance from dead works, Regeneration of the heart and mind, baptism by Trine Immersion for remission of sins unto the reception of the Holy Ghost by the laying on of hands, are the means of adoption into the household of God,—the church militant.

It also maintains that Feet-washing, as taught in John 13, both by example and command of Jesus, should be observed in the church.

That the Lord's Supper, instituted by Christ and as universally observed by the apostles and the early Christians, is a full meal, and, in connection with the Communion, should be taken in the evening or after the close of the day.

That the Salutation of the Holy Kiss, or Kiss of Charity, is binding upon the followers of Christ.

That War and Retaliation are contrary to the spirit and self-denying principles of the religion of Jesus Christ.

That the principle of Plain Dressing and of Non-conformity to the world, as taught in the New Testament, should be observed by the followers of Christ.

That the Scriptural duty of Anointing the Sick with Oil, in the Name of the Lord, James 5: 14, is binding upon all Christians.

It also advocates the church's duty to support Missionary and Tract Work, thus giving to the Lord for the spread of the Gospel and for the conversion of sinners.

In short, it is a vindication of all that Christ and the apostles have enjoined upon us, and aims amid the conflicting theories and discords of modern Christendom, to point out ground that all must concede to be infallibly safe.

☞ The above principles of our Fraternity are set forth on our Brethren's Envelopes." Use them! Price 15 cents per package; 40 cents per hundred.

Announcements.

(Concluded from preceding page.)

LOVE-FEASTS.

Nov. 2 and 3, at 9.30 A. M., Myersville congregation, Pa., at the Salunga house.

Nov. 3, at 4 P. M., Cedar Lake, De Kalb, Ind.

Nov. 3, at 2 P. M., Frederick City, Md.

Nov. 5 Hickory Grove church, 1 mile west and 2 miles north of Kusahs, William Co., Ohio.

Dec. 8, at 2 P. M., Cerro Gordo, Ill.

Nov. 10, at 4 P. M., Bear Creek, Montgomery Co., Ohio.

Nov. 19, Altoona, Pa.

Nov. 25 and 26, Beatrice church, Neb.

Oct. 29, at 4 P. M., Elk Lick congregation, Somerset Co., Pa.

Farm for Sale.

A desirable property located 1¾ miles east of Mt. Morris, consisting of 185 acres of well-improved land. One of the finest country residences in Ogle County. For further particulars call on, or address,

ELIZABETH MIDDLEKAUFF,
4:1tf   Mt. Morris, Ill.

EUROPE
AND
Bible Lands

A new edition of this deservedly popular work has again been published. It retains all the excellencies of its predecessors, and with those who are interested in Bible study this work will always remain a favorite. Those who have read the ordinary book of travel will be surprised to find "Europe and Bible Lands" of thrilling interest for both old and young. The large number of books, already sold, proves that the work is of more than ordinary merit.

A fair supply of the last edition of this work is still on hand. Those who have not yet secured a copy of the work should embrace this opportunity of securing it. Price, in fine cloth binding, only $1.50 per copy, post-paid. To agents who are prepared to push an active canvass of the work, we are prepared to give special inducements. Write at   BRETHREN'S PUBLISHING CO.,
Mt. Morris, Ill.

DANCERS, TUMORS, ETC.

Successfully treated by Dr. G. M. Botcher, of Waynesborough, Pa., where he has practiced for the last sixteen years. Dr. Botcher is a graduate of the University of Maryland, at Baltimore City. References given and correspondence solicited. Address, Dr. G. W. Botcher, Waynesborough, Pa.   38t0

Reason and Revelation.—By. R. Milligan. Should be in the hands of every Bible student. Price, $2.00.

Trine Immersion.—A vindication of the apostolic form of Christian baptism. By Eld. James Quinter. A most complete and reliable work on the subject. Price, cloth, single copy, $1.25; leather, $1.75.

GOOD BOOKS FOR ALL.

Any book in the market furnished at publishers' lowest retail price by the Brethren's Publishing Company, Mt. Morris, Ill. *Special prices* given when books are purchased in quantities. When ordering books, not on our list, if possible give title, name of author, and address of publishers.

The Throne of David.—By J. H. Ingraham. Cloth, $1.50.

The Doctrine of the Holy Spirit.—By James B Walker. Cloth, $1.25.

Homiletics and Pastoral Theology.—By W. G. T. Shedd. Cloth, $2.50.

The New Testament History.§—By Wm. Smith. Cloth, $1.25.

The Old Testament History.—By William Smith. Cloth, $1.25.

The Great Events of History.—By W.F. Collier. Cloth, $1.25.

Lectures on Preaching.—By Rev. Phillips Brooks. Cloth, 12mo, $1.50.

The Path of Life.—An interesting tract for everybody. Price, 10 cents per copy; 100 copies, $6.00.

The Origin and Growth, of Religion.—Hibbert Lectures. By T. W. R. Davids. Cloth, 8vo, $2.50.

Hours with the Bible.—By Cunningham Geikie. Old Testament Series—six volumes. Per volume, 90 cents.

For Sale!

I have for sale a complete set of *Gospel Visitor, Primitive Christian,* and *Gospel Messenger,* from 1876 to 1891 included, bound in morocco, cloth sides; also *Young Disciple,* from 1881 to 1889, bound in morocco, cloth sides, three years in a book. The *Gospel Visitor* is bound in black roan, paper sides. For terms address J. W. King, Huntingdon, Pa.

WONDERFUL "Story of the Cross-
ades." is a book just published. Everybody
Interested in Christianity
should read it. It is a large 500×¼ inch book of about
500 pages and 100 full-page engravings. It contains some
of the most wonderful chapters in the world's history, the
thrilling siege, massacres, victories, defeat, heroism, starvation, death of thousands of Christians to recover Jerusalem and the Holy Sepulchre from the hated Mohammedans. Unsurpassed in thrilling interest and instruction. Agents wanted everywhere. Circulars free. Address, J. M. Mohr, Covington, Ohio.

THE
Doctrine of the Brethren Defended.

This work contains a complete exposition of the faith and practice of the Brethren, the Divinity of Christ, the Divinity of the Holy Spirit, Immersion, Feet-washing, the Lord's Supper, the Holy Kiss, Non-conformity, Secret Societies, etc. Price, per copy, cloth binding, $1.25. Address this office.

O Jerusalem! Jerusalem!

What could be more beautiful and touching than a picture of Christ as he stood upon Olivet looking down over the beloved but sinful city, with tears trickling down over his cheeks, his lips parted as he cries, " O Jerusalem! Jerusalem!" We have such a picture 22x28 inches, beautifully executed in colors. No one can gaze upon it without being moved. Given free with a year's subscription to " What to Read " at 50 cents. An agent wanted in every church and neighborhood. Address, JAS. M. NEFF, Covington, Ohio.

Excursions to California.

EXCURSIONS in charge of M. M. Eshelman, Immigration Agent, will leave Chicago over the "Santa Fe Route" Tuesdays, and Kansas City Wednesdays, during the year 1892, on dates as follows:

Chicago, January 26, February 23, March 22, April 26, May 24, June 28, July 26, August 23, September 27, October 25, November 22, December 27.

Kansas City, January 27, February 24, March 23, April 27, May 25, June 29, July 27, August 24, September 28, October 26, November 23, December 28.

Parties wishing to avail themselves of the privilege at these excursions, should write M. M. Eshelman, North Pomona, California, prior to the 25th of each month, and from the fifteenth to the end of the month, at 1090 Union Avenue (opposite Union Depot), Kansas City, Mo., stating when and where they wish to join one of these excursions, and he will give them full information, and if desired will reserve berths in Tourist Sleeping Car for them. Do not fail to write him; he will do you good. The rates will be as low as the lowest made to the Pacific Coast.

GEORGE L. McDOWAUGH,
Traveling Agent.

Church Entertainments: Twenty Objections.

By Rev. B. Carradine, D. D. 12mo, 100 pp. Paper cover, 30 cents. A strong book in defense of its position; written by a powerful pen, presenting the most candid and scriptural arraignment of unwarrantable methods for money-raising in the Church. The spirit of the book is highly devotional and cannot fail to inspire the reader with its seriousness.

Alone with God.

This manual of devotions, by J. H. Garrison, comprises a series of meditations with forms of prayer for private devotions, family worship and special occasions. It is one of the most useful, most needed, and best adapted books of the year, and therefore it is not strange that it is proving one of the most popular. In work of this kind its distinguished, gifted, pious and beloved author is at his best. This book is helpful to every minister, church official, and Sunday-school superintendent, as well as every private member of the church in all ages. It has models of prayer, suitable for the service of the prayer-meeting, while its suggestions, meditations and instructions are pre-eminently calculated to be of service in preparation for the solemn duties that rest upon the active members. Cloth, 75 cents; morocco, $1.25; Address this office.

Announcements.

(Concluded from preceding page.)

LOVE-FEASTS.

Nov. 2 and 3, at 9, 30 A. M., Myersville congregation, Pa., at the Salunga house.
Nov. 3, at 4 P. M., Cedar Lake, De Kalb, Ind.
Nov. 3, at 4 P. M., Frederick City, Md.
Nov. 3, Hickory Grove church, 2 mile west and 2 miles north of Kunkle, Williams Co., Ohio.
Dec. 6, at 2 P. M., Cerro Gordo, Ill.
Nov. 10, at 4 P. M., Bear Creek, Montgomery Co., Ohio.
Nov. 19, Altoona, Pa.
Nov. 25 and 26, Beatrice church, Nebr.
Oct. 29, at 2 P. M., Elk Lick congregation, Somerset Co., Pa.

Farm for Sale.

A desirable property located 1½ miles east of Mt. Morris, consisting of 185 acres of well-improved land. One of the finest country residences in Ogle County. For further particulars call on, or address,

ELIZABETH MIDDLEKAUFF,
4tf Mt. Morris, Ill.

EUROPE
AND
Bible Lands

A new edition of this deservedly popular work has again been published. It retains all the excellencies of its predecessors, and with those who are interested in Bible study this work will always remain a favorite. Those who have read the ordinary book of travel will be surprised to find "Europe and Bible Lands" of thrilling interest for both old and young. The large number of books, already sold, proves that the work is of more than ordinary merit.

A fair supply of the last edition of this work is still on hand. Those who have not yet secured a copy of the work should embrace this opportunity of securing it. Price, in fine cloth binding, only $1.50 per copy, post-paid. To agents who are prepared to push an active canvass of the work, we are prepared to give special inducements. Write .o. BRETHREN'S PUBLISHING Co.,
Mt. Morris, Ill.

CANCERS, TUMORS, ETC.

Successfully treated by Dr. G. N. Boteler, of Waynesborough, Pa., where he has practiced for the last sixteen years. Dr. Boteler is a graduate of the University of Maryland, at Baltimore City. References given and correspondence solicited. Address, Dr. G. W. Boteler, Waynesborough, Pa. 9ttc

Reason and Revelation.—By R. Milligan. Should be in the hands of every Bible student. Price, $1.00.

Trine Immersion.—A vindication of the apostolic form of Christian baptism. By Eld. James Quinter. A most complete and reliable work on the subject.°.° Price, cloth, single copy, $1.25; leather, $1.75.

GOOD BOOKS FOR ALL.

ANY book in the market furnished at publishers' lowest retail price by the Brethren's Publishing Company, Mt. Morris, Ill. *Special prices* given when books are purchased in quantities. When ordering books, not on our list, if possible give title, name of author, and address of publishers.

The Throne of David.—By J. H. Ingraham. Cloth, $1.50.
The Doctrine of the Holy Spirit.—By James B Walker. Cloth, $1.25.
Homiletics and Pastoral Theology.—By W. G. T. Shedd. Cloth, $2.50.
The New Testament History.‡—By Wm. Smith. Cloth, $1.25.
The Old Testament History.—By William Smith. Cloth, $1.25.
The Great Events of History.—By WiP. Collier. Cloth, $2.25.
Lectures on Preaching.—By Rev. Phillips Brooks. Cloth, 12mo, $1.50.
The Path of Life.—An interesting tract for everybody. Price, 10 cents per copy; 100 copies, $6.00.
The Origin and Growth of Religion.—Hibbert Lectures. By T. W. R. Davids. Cloth, 8vo, $2.50.
Hours with the Bible.—By Cunningham Geikie. Old Testament Series—six volumes. Per volume, 90 cents.

For Sale!

I have for sale a complete set of *Gospel Visitor, Primitive Christian, and Gospel Messenger*, from 1876 to 1891 included, bound in morocco, cloth sides; also *Young Disciple*, from 1881 to 1889, bound in morocco, cloth sides, three years in a book. The *Gospel Visitor* is bound in black rose, paper sides. For terms address J. W. King, Huntingdon, Pa.

WONDERFUL!
"Story of the Cru- cifixion" is a book just published. Everybody interested in Christianity should read it. It is a large quarto book of about 300 pages and 200 full-page engravings. It contains some of the most wonderful chapters in the world's history, the battles, sieges, marches, victories, defeats, heroism, sincerity, death of thousands of Christians to recover Jerusalem and the Holy Sepulchre from the hated Mohammedans. Unsurpassed in thrilling interest and instruction. Agents wanted everywhere. Circulars free. Address, J. M. Nave, Covington, Ohio.

--- THE ---
Doctrine of the Brethren Defended.

THIS work contains a complete exposition of the faith and practice of the Brethren, the Divinity of Christ, the Divinity of the Holy Spirit, Immersion, Feet-washing, the Lord's Supper, the Holy Kiss, Non-conformity, Secret Societies, etc. Price, per copy, cloth binding, $1.25 Address this office.

O Jerusalem! Jerusalem!

WHAT could be more beautiful and touching than a picture of Christ as he stood upon Olivet looking down over the beloved but sinful city, with tears trickling down over his cheeks, his lips parted as he cries, "O Jerusalem! Jerusalem!" We have such a picture 22x28 inches, beautifully executed in colors. No one can gaze upon it without being moved. Given free with a year's subscription to "What to Read" at 50 cents. An agent wanted in every church and neighborhood. Address, Jas. M. Nave, Covington, Ohio.

Excursions to California.

EXCURSIONS in charge of M. M. Kableman, Immigration Agent, will leave Chicago over the "Santa Fe Route" Tuesdays, and Kansas City Wednesdays, during the year 1890, on dates as follows:
Chicago, January 26, February 23, March 22, April 26, May 24, June 28, July 26, August 23, September 27, October 18, November 22, December 29.
Kansas City, January 27, February 24, March 23, April 27, May 25, June 29, July 27, August 24, September 28, October 26, November 29, December 30.
Parties wishing to avail themselves of the privileges of these excursions, should write M. M. Kableman, North Pomona, California, prior to the 15th of each month, and from the fifteenth to the end of the month, at 1030 Union Avenue (opposite Union Depot), Kansas City, Mo., stating when and where they wish to join one of these excursions, and he will there make full information, and if desired will reserve berths in Tourist Sleeping Car for them. Do not fail to write him; he will do you good. The rates will be as low as the lowest made to the Pacific Coast.

GEORGE L. McDONAUGH,
Traveling Agent.

Church Entertainments: Twenty Objections.

By Rev. B. Carradine, D. D. 12mo, 100 pp. Paper cover, 30 cents. A strong book in defense of its position, written by a powerful pen, presenting the most candid and scriptural arraignment of unwarrantable methods for money-raising in the Church. The spirit of the book is highly devotional and cannot fail to inspire the reader with its seriousness.

Alone with God.

THIS manual of devotions, by J. H. Garrison, comprises a series of meditations with forms of prayer for private devotions, family worship and special occasions. It is one of the most useful, most needed, and best adapted books of the year, and therefore it is not strange that it is proving one of the most popular. In work of this kind its distinguished, gifted, pious and beloved author is at his best. This book is helpful to every minister, church official, and Sunday-school superintendent, as well as every private member of the church in all ages. It has models of prayer, suitable for the service of the prayer-meeting, while its suggestions, meditations and instructions are pre-eminently calculated to be of service in preparation for the solemn duties that rest upon the active members. Cloth, 75 cents; morocco, $1.25. Address this office.

ESSAYS

"Study to show thyself approved unto God: a workman that shedeth not be ashamed, rightly dividing the Word of Truth."

IDLENESS.

BY EMILY PEARSON BAILEY.

IDLY lamenting want of time,
I ate and drank and went my way,
Dreaming of work that I would do
When came a more convenient day.

Unnoticed slipped the moments by,
The hours were numbered one by one,
Until the last-dropped from time's hand;
The day was passed and nothing done.

Some little good I might have wrought,
But I was blind and dull and vexed;
Attempting service my own way,
Was hindered, worried and perplexed.

Let me be honest. Did not I
Care more for ease and praise of men
Than others' weal and that "Well done,
A faithful servant hast thou been"?

So all my prayers are weak and void
And all my days go idly by,
While wasted time makes bitter moan;
Lord, at thy feet I'contrite lie.

And while my nothingness I own,
Thy parable I plead and cry,
"Cut me not off as cumbering earth,
But on me look with pitying eye;

"Quickened by love and power divine,
May my weak purposes grow strong,
That I be not cast out in shame
While others sing the harvest song."

THE UNRIGHTEOUS MAMMON.

BY DAVID E. CRIPE.

"I say unto you, Make to yourselves friends of the mammon of unrighteousness; that, when ye fail, they may receive you into everlasting habitations. If therefore ye have not been faithful in the unrighteous mammon, who will commit to your trust the true riches?"—Luke 16: 9-11.

IN the language of this text our Savior gives to his disciples a direct command concerning the use to be made of the mammon of unrighteousness,—a command that does not appear to be very generally understood and one that is, perhaps, still less observed by the people of our day.

Mammon is a Syrian word, signifying riches. Unrighteous in this sense does not mean wicked, but only not righteous, to distinguish it from the true riches or righteous riches. We would, then, understand that unrighteous mammon, as Luther's translation has it, or the mammon of unrighteousness, is neither more nor less than property,—worldly possessions,—which constitute the riches of this world.

The parable of the unfaithful steward, which immediately precedes this text, throws much light on this command, and especially upon the manner in which we are to obey it. The rich man's steward was accused of having wasted his lord's goods. Then his lord told him he could be steward no longer. This made the steward, who was about to be thrust out of home and employment, reflect what he could do to better his condition. He thought if he would do a kindness to others while he yet had the power, they, in turn, would befriend him when he was thrust out. For this reason he called to him his lord's debtors, the .only class he could now befriend, and forgave them a part of the debt they owed, not to himself but to his lord. Then, when he was poor and homeless, these debtors, whom he had befriended, would receive him into their houses. Thus he made unto himself friends by using his lord's goods, and his lord commended him for his wisdom. In like manner, Christ says, we should make to ourselves friends of the mammon of unrighteousness.

The earth and all it contains belongs to God, and man, in reality, owns nothing. "The earth is the Lord's and the fullness thereof." Man brings nothing into the world, he can produce nothing without using the material the Lord has provided; he can take nothing out of the world. Therefore it is clear that nothing belongs to him, and whatever riches he may call his own really belong to God, who has only entrusted them unto him for a little while, as unto a steward.

A steward is one who is entrusted with a rich man's property, to care for it or use it in the owner's absence, as the owners may direct. God has entrusted some of the riches of this world into our care, and has commanded us how we shall use them. We are accountable unto him for the use we make of these riches or goods. If we, like the steward in the parable, waste our Lord's goods, he will be displeased with us, and sooner or later will take our stewardship from us. If we "spend our money for that which is not bread, and our labor for that which satisfieth not," we are wasting our Lord's goods. If we spend money for decorating our homes with that which can do us no good, or for any apparel that is not necessary, or adorn our bodies with showy ornaments, jewels and flashy trinkets, as the savage does who knows no better, we are wasting our Lord's goods. If we spend money for that which can gratify only the "lust of the flesh, the lust of the eye, and the pride of life," we are surely wasting our Lord's goods. If we, like the man the Savior speaks of, tear down our barns to build greater, so we can store away and hoard that which' has been entrusted unto us, then, also, are we wasting our Lord's goods, and he will declare that we can be steward no longer.

When we find that we must give up our stewardship, must give up life with all our possessions, we can yet do as did the steward in the parable,—"make to ourselves friends of the mammon of unrighteousness." The German says, "Make to yourselves friends with the unrighteous mammon." The Revised Version says, "By means of the mammon." So we, by using the goods or riches that have been entrusted unto us, can minister to the wants of the poor and needy, and can assist in carrying on the work of preaching the Gospel to all mankind.

However, we should not put off doing good with the means our Lord has entrusted to us until we expect soon to give an account of our stewardship. We should use them now and all the time as the Lord directs. "If therefore ye have not been faithful in the unrighteous mammon, who will commit to your trust the true riches?" From this we learn that if we continually use these riches as the Lord directs, neither hoarding nor wasting them, he will then commit to our trust the true riches. If we prove ourselves faithful in these little things, using these temporal riches as the Lord directs, then he will bless us with the far greater riches of his grace,—will give us to eat of the heavenly manna, and to drink of the fountain of living waters that quenches all thirst.

By thus doing good as opportunity offers, we make unto ourselves friends with the unrighteous mammon, or worldly goods. We not only make friends of the poor and needy, and the alien, but we also win the friendship of Christ, for he has said, "Inasmuch as ye have done it unto one of the least of these, my brethren, ye have done it unto me." Then, when we fail, that is, when this world fails us and we come to die, these friends we have made,—Jesus and the godly poor we have befriended,—will receive us into everlasting habitations, into those mansions prepared for us from the foundation of the world.

Akron, Ind.

WEARING THE HARNESS.

BY J. B. MILLER.

A BROTHER related to me that some years ago he, with his wife, took the train for Annual Meeting. In order that the Brethren could all be together and no one to disturb them, they chartered two coaches and requested the conductor that no one should be allowed in the cars but members. The request was granted. As the coaches were filling up, the conductor stationed himself at one place, closing all doors but one, watching closely that no one entered but members. Presently the conductor saw a finely-dressed man enter the coach. He soon caught this gentleman by the arm saying, "Mister, I wish to inform you that those two coaches are exclusively for the Dunkard brethren."

The gentleman stood there speechless.

The conductor said, "This is one of our brethren."

The conductor said, "One of your brethren?"

"Yes, sir."

"Well sir, why don't he wear the harness?"

Poor man! He had his light hid under a bushel. How necessary it is that we wear the harness, and be what we profess, so the world may know where to place us. A railroad official is not ashamed of his uniform and is willing to wear the harness. How much more should the child of God let the world know where he belongs!

Goshen, Ind.

LEAKING VESSELS.

BY J. O. BARNHART.

"Therefore we ought to give the more earnest heed to the things which we have heard, lest at any time we should let them slip."—Heb. 2: 1.

IN being "born again, not of corruptible seed but incorruptible, by the Word of God which liveth and abideth forever," we "are delivered unto a doctrine." Rom. 6: 17. This doctrine is the doctrine of Christ, and is made up of principles for our faith, commands for our obedience, promises for our comfort, and cautions, admonitions and warnings for our daily guidance and instruction.

This doctrine of salvation "began to be spoken by the Lord, and was confirmed unto us by them that heard him." Heb. 2: 3. To the principles of this faith we are exhorted to "give the more earnest heed, lest at any time we should let them slip."

To do this we must be in earnest and not begin to follow the Master from sinister motives, for when it becomes known that we are only after the "loaves and fishes" we will find that what little labor we have bestowed is in vain, and that we are letting those principles slip, which seemingly have benefited us so little.

The word "slip" however, by the marginal reading is translated, "to run out as leaking vessels." This seems to me a very pointed application, and the one which will receive most consideration in this article. So again, as previously stated, we must be in earnest. Those who start out in a distrustful, half-hearted way, to follow the principles of this doctrine, saying, as many do, "I will see what there is in this religion of which I hear so much," or as the others say, "I fear I cannot hold out," will be almost certain to fail. One lacks faith and doubts God when he says, "Ye shall receive," the other is not earnest enough,—is not determined to know nothing but Jesus Christ and him crucified.

The person who begins however, with the determination to leave the world behind him, for

✦ESSAYS✦

"Study to show thyself approved unto God; a workman that abdeth not be ashamed, rightly dividing the Word of Truth."

IDLENESS.

BY EMILY PEARSON BAILEY.

IDLY lamenting want of time,
I ate and drank and went my way,
Dreaming of work that I would do
When came a more convenient day.

Unnoticed slipped the moments by,
The hours were numbered one by one,
Until the last dropped from time's hand;
The day was passed and nothing done.

Some little good I might have wrought,
But I was blind and dull and vexed;
Attempting service my own way,
Was hindered, worried and perplexed.

Let me be honest. Did not I
Care more for ease and praise of men
Than others' weal and that? Well done,
A faithful servant hast thou been"?

So all my prayers are weak and cold
And all my days go idly by,
While wasted time makes bitter moan;
Lord, at thy feet I contrite lie.

And while my nothingness I own,
Thy parable I plead and cry,
"Cut me not off as cumbering earth,
But on me look with pitying eye;

"Quickened by love and power divine,
May my weak purposes grow strong,
That I be not cast out in shame
While others sing the harvest song."

THE UNRIGHTEOUS MAMMON.

BY DAVID E. CRIPE.

"I say unto you, Make to yourselves friends of the mammon of unrighteousness; that, when ye fail, they may receive you into everlasting habitations. If therefore ye have not been faithful in the unrighteous mammon, who will commit to your trust the true riches?"—Luke 16: 9-11.

IN the language of this text our Savior gives to his disciples a direct command concerning the use to be made of the mammon of unrighteousness,—a command that does not appear to be very generally understood and one that is, perhaps, still less observed by the people of our day.

Mammon is a Syrian word, signifying riches. Unrighteous in this sense does not mean wicked, but only not righteous, to distinguish it from the true riches or righteous riches. We would, then, understand that unrighteous mammon, as Luther's translation has it, or the mammon of unrighteousness, is neither more nor less than property,—worldly possessions,—which constitute the riches of this world.

The parable of the unfaithful steward, which immediately precedes this text, throws much light on this command, and especially upon the manner in which we are to obey it. The rich man's steward was accused of having wasted his lord's goods. Then his lord told him he could be steward no longer. This made the steward, who was about to be thrust out of home and employment, reflect what he could do to better his condition. He thought if he would do a kindness to others while he yet had the power, they, in turn, would befriend him when he was thrust out. For this reason he called to him his lord's debtors, the only class he could now befriend, and forgave them a part of the debt they owed, not to himself but to his lord. Then, when he was poor and homeless, these debtors, whom he had befriended, would receive him into their houses. Thus he made unto himself friends by using his lord's goods, and his lord commended him for his wisdom. In like manner, Christ says, we should make to ourselves friends of the mammon of unrighteousness.

The earth and all it contains belongs to God, and man, in reality, owns nothing. "The earth is the Lord's and the fullness thereof." Man brings nothing into the world, he can produce nothing without using the material the Lord has provided; he can take nothing out of the world. Therefore it is clear that nothing belongs to him, and whatever riches he may call his own really belong to God, who has only entrusted them unto him for a little while, as unto a steward.

A steward is one who is entrusted with a rich man's property, to care for it or use it in the owner's absence, as the owners may direct. God has entrusted some of the riches of this world in to our care, and has commanded us how we shall use them. We are accountable unto him for the use we make of these riches or goods. If we, like the steward in the parable, waste our Lord's goods, he will be displeased with us, and sooner or later will take our stewardship from us. If we "spend our money for that which is not bread, and our labor for that which satisfieth not," we are wasting our Lord's goods. If we spend money for decorating our homes with that which can do us no good, or for any apparel that is not necessary, or adorn our bodies with showy ornaments, jewels and flashy trinkets, as the savage does who knows no better, we are wasting our Lord's goods. If we spend money for that which can gratify only the "lust of the flesh, the lust of the eye, and the pride of life," we are surely wasting our Lord's goods. If we, like the man the Savior speaks of, tear down our barns to build greater, so we can store away and hoard that which has been entrusted unto us, then, also, are we wasting our Lord's goods, and he will declare that we can be steward no longer.

When we find that we must give up our stewardship, must give up life with all our possessions, we can yet do as did the steward in the parable,—"make to ourselves friends of the mammon of unrighteousness." The German says, "Make to yourselves friends of the unrighteous mammon." The Revised Version says, "By means of the mammon." So we, by using the goods or riches that have been entrusted unto us, can minister to the wants of the poor and needy, and can assist in carrying on the work of preaching the Gospel to all mankind.

However, we should not put off doing good with the means our Lord has entrusted to us until we expect soon to give an account of our stewardship. We should use them now and all the time as the Lord directs. "If therefore ye have not been faithful in the unrighteous mammon, who will commit to your trust the true riches?" From this we learn that if we continually use these riches as the Lord directs, neither hoarding nor wasting them, he will then commit to our trust the true riches. If we prove ourselves faithful in these little things, using these temporal riches as the Lord directs, then he will bless us with the far greater riches of his grace,—will give us to eat of the heavenly manna, and to drink of the fountain of living waters that quenches all thirst.

By thus doing good as opportunity offers, we make unto ourselves friends with the unrighteous mammon, or worldly goods. We not only make friends of the poor and needy, and the alien, but we also win the friendship of Christ, for he has said, "Inasmuch as ye have done it unto one of the least of these, my brethren, ye have done it unto me." Then, when we fail, that is, when this world fails us and we come to die, these friends we have made,—Jesus and the godly poor we have befriended,—will receive us into everlasting habitations, into those mansions prepared for us from the foundation of the world.

Akron, Ind.

WEARING THE HARNESS.

BY J. H. MILLER.

A BROTHER related to me that some years ago he, with his wife, took the train for Annual Meeting. In order that the Brethren could all be together and no one to disturb them, they chartered two coaches and requested the conductor that no one should be allowed in the cars but members. The request was granted. As the coaches were filling up, the conductor stationed himself at one place, closing all doors but one, watching closely that no one entered but members. Presently the conductor saw a finely-dressed man enter the coach. He soon caught this gentleman by the arm saying, "Mister, I wish to inform you that those two coaches are exclusively for the Dunkard brethren."

The gentleman stood there speechless.

A brother standing near by remarked, "This is one of our brethren."

The conductor said, "One of your brethren?"

"Yes, sir."

"Well sir, why don't he wear the harness?"

Poor man! He had his light hid under a bushel. How necessary it is that we wear the harness, and be what we profess, so the world may know where to place us. A railroad official is not ashamed of his uniform and is willing to wear the harness. How much more should the child of God let the world know where he belongs!

Goshen, Ind.

LEAKING VESSELS.

BY J. O. BARNHART.

"Therefore we ought to give the more earnest heed to the things which we have heard, lest at any time we should let them slip."—Heb. 2: 1.

IN being "born again, not of corruptible seed but incorruptible, by the Word of God which liveth and abideth forever," we "are delivered unto a doctrine." Rom. 6: 17. This doctrine is the doctrine of Christ, and is made up of principles for our faith, commands for our obedience, promises for our comfort, and cautions, admonitions and warnings for our daily guidance and instruction.

This doctrine of salvation "began to be spoken by the Lord, and was confirmed unto us by them that heard him." Heb. 2: 3. To the principles of this faith we are exhorted to "give the more earnest heed, lest at any time we should let them slip."

To do this we must be in earnest and not begin to follow the Master from sinister motives, for when it becomes known that we are only after the "loaves and fishes" we will find that what little labor we have bestowed is in vain, and that we are letting those principles slip, which seemingly have benefited us so little.

The word "slip" however, by the marginal reading is translated," "to run out as leaking vessels." This seems to me a very pointed application, and the one which will receive most consideration in this article. So again, as previously stated, we must be in earnest. Those who start out in a distrustful, half-hearted way, to follow the principles of this doctrine, saying, as many do, "I will see what there is in this religion of which I hear so much," or as the others say, "I fear I cannot hold out," will be almost certain to fail. One lacks faith and doubts God when he says, "Ye shall receive," the other is not earnest enough,—is not determined to know nothing but Jesus Christ and him crucified."

The person who begins however, with the determination to leave the world behind him, for

CORRESPONDENCE.

"Write what thou seest, and send it unto the churches."

☞ Church News solicited for this Department. If you have had a good meeting, send a report of it, so that others may rejoice with you. In writing give name of church, County and State. Be brief. Notes of Travel should be as short as possible. Land Advertisements are not solicited for this Department. We have an advertising page, and, if necessary, will issue supplements.

From Knobnoster, Mo.

WIFE and I visited the Prairie View church, Morgan Co., Mo., to attend their love-feast Sept. 7. Next day, in company with Eld. David Bowman, of the Prairie View church, we started for Montgomery County, Mo., to hold meetings. There are fourteen members at this point, who are without a resident minister. Eld. David Bowman has this mission point in charge. Here we had forty-three meetings. We held two meetings at the same time, about three miles apart, with good attendance at each place. The outlook here is encouraging, if the work can be followed up as it should be. We also held a love-feast with the members. One that had wandered away returned to the fold again. From what we were able to learn, several are about ready to cast their lot with the Brethren.

While Bro. Bowman continued the meetings, wife and I went to Audrain County, to the hospitable home of our aged brother and sister Moomaw. Here we had five meetings in a school-house. Brother and sister Moomaw are the only members at this place. Here, also, is a favorable point for mission work. From here we went to the town of Mexico, Audrain Co., where we again met Bro. Bowman. Here, also, are two members, —sister Sanders and her daughter. Here the neighbors were invited in by sister Sanders, to hear us preach. Bro. Bowman's sermon seemed to be enjoyed by all present. From here we started home, where we arrived Oct. 5.

ISRAEL CRIPE.

From Walnut Valley Church, Kans.

THE church met in council Sept. 28, preparatory to a love-feast. The business before the meeting was all disposed of pleasantly. One dear young sister made application to be received into the church and was buried with Christ in baptism. Oct. 1 we met to celebrate the sufferings and death of our Blessed Redeemer. The meeting was one long to be remembered. Quietness and solemnity prevailed, and we have reason to believe that many good impressions were made, and that some are almost persuaded to join in with the children of God. Ministers present from other congregations were elders Moses Brubaker, S. Z. Sharp, W. B. Hines and James Paxton. On Sunday we met at 9:30 A. M., for children's meeting. The brethren gave the children an interesting talk and asked them some questions which pleased the children very much. At 11 A. M., Bro. Sharp gave us an excellent sermon on the subject of sacrificing, and portrayed to our minds the importance of sacrificing to the Lord.   S. P. WEAVER.

Heisler, Kans.

Pierced to Death.

GARRETT M., only child of brother and sister S. F. Henricks, residing at this place, met with a very sad and sudden death Oct. 11. About one o'clock little Garrett said to his mother, "I want to get a bouquet of flowers for my teacher." He then took a large pair of shears to cut the flowers. In running around the house with the shears in his hand, the boy stumbled and fell, his breast striking upon the point of the shears with such force as to drive them through the flesh into his lungs, severing the main artery. He got up, pulled the shears out, ran a short distance, and then dropped down dead.

His little cousin, Amy Hoover, who was waiting for him to gather the flowers, saw the accident, and notified the boy's mother, who at once ran out and carried her dead son to the house. A physician was summoned, but nothing could be done, as life was extinct. Brother and sister Henricks have the sympathy of all who knew them, and also have the precious promise of meeting him again in a better world than this.

Garrett M., was born June 11, 1885, and was, at the time of his death, seven years and four months old. The remains were taken to Plymouth, and the funeral services were conducted in the Union meeting-house, five miles west of Plymouth, where the interment took place. Services were conducted by the writer, from 2 Kings 4: 26.

H. W. KRIEGHBAUM.

South Bend, Ind., Oct. 14.

From the Kaskaskia Church, Fayette Co., Ill.

WE had a glorious meeting. Eld. Daniel Mohler, of Piatt County, Ill., commenced a protracted effort in our new church-house, Oct. 1, and continued until the 11th. He baptized four precious souls, and left five applicants, which were baptized the day following. These, with six more dear souls, who are tired of sin, will make fifteen additions in all. We closed the meetings Oct. 16 with a good attendance and some near the kingdom. Oct. 7 we held our feast, which will long be remembered. Bro. Mohler officiated, and was aided in the ministry by Eld. Jacob Ullery, Bro. —Younger, of La Place, Ill., and Bro. Allen Taylor, of Mulberry Grove, Ill. At this meeting we held an election for a deacon, the lot falling upon our esteemed brother M. W. Clayton, who, with his worthy companion, was duly installed into office. We now number sixty members, of whom fifty-six live within less than four miles of the church-house. Twenty-three of them are yet in their teens.   GRANVILLE NEVINGER.

Beecher City, Ill.

From Rosedale, Cambria Co., Pa.

AUG. 2 I came to Johnstown, Cambria Co., Pa., where I found my cousin and brother in Christ, William Ford, confined to his bed since May 30, and in a suffering condition. Wednesday evening Aug. 3, he called for the elders of the church and was anointed in the name of the Lord. Preaching and prayer-meeting were held in his sick chamber, and a love-feast was also held Sept. 5. With the exception of about a week he is still (Oct. 7) confined to his bed. I have visited a number of families of Brethren and attended Sunday-school, church, and prayer-meeting with them. I also attended one love-feast. I have greatly enjoyed these meetings after being isolated so much from the church. There are not any Brethren at Homestead. I have distributed our church literature there, so that it may, at least, be as crumbs cast upon the waters.

Twice I have visited Grandview cemetery, above Johnstown, where the unidentified dead of the Johnstown flood are buried, and also many that were identified. A beautiful monument was erected and dedicated May 31 last, to mark the spot, and a plain marble slab marks each grave. There are eight hundred slabs. There are two ways of reaching the elevated country to the cemetery,—up the "incline" on the electric cars, or up a beautiful drive-way. We ascended by the former. My heart ached as I passed over the ground and beheld the burial-place of that vast number that were so hastily ushered into eternity by that dreadful flood, and many were the tears that flowed while surviving friends related that sad tale to me. This was my first visit to Johnstown and vicinity since the flood. One would scarcely realize that but so short a time the town was almost wiped away.

In a few days I shall return to Homestead, if God permits, and shall continue to labor for the Master. May God send some one there, in the near future, to break the Bread of Life to the thousands of God's creatures that dwell there. Those who hunger and thirst after righteousness, may their souls be filled!   EMILY R. STIFLER.

Mission Work in Southern Indiana.

I LEFT home Oct. 7, to visit the New Hope church, Jackson County. Upon my arrival at Chestnut Ridge, I was met by Bro. Bedel and taken to the new church-house that had just been finished. It has been built by the members of that church, aided by a donation of $200.00 from the General Church Erection and Missionary Fund. Here I met Bro. David R. Richards, who had come the same morning. We had meetings the same evening and the next day we labored to set things in order that were wanting. All business was disposed of to the general satisfaction of the members present. We continued the meetings each evening and on Sunday until the 11th, when Bro. Richards, owing to illness, went home, leaving the writer and the home minister to conduct the meetings. One was baptized on the 12th. The same evening brethren Daniel Bock and David F. Hoover came to our assistance. They spoke the Word with power.

On the evening of Oct. 13 Bro. Samuel Younce, of Eaton, Ind., came to assist us. This made us feel to rejoice. The Communion was set for Oct. 14. It was a feast to the soul. The house was filled to overflowing, and there were many who could not get in. It was estimated that at least five hundred persons were in the house and yard. There were thirty-one members at the table of the Lord. All seemed to rejoice.

We continued meetings over Sunday. On Sunday, Oct. 16, the house was dedicated to the Lord. Bro. David F. Hoover preached the dedicatory sermon from 1 Kings 8: 29. After the sermon two dear souls came out on the Lord's side and were baptized. The meeting closed on Sunday night with increased interest and a full house. Monday morning Bro. James Allison, who is afflicted, was anointed. Then we took our leave for home. I left the other brethren at Indianapolis. There is a very good opening for an ingathering in the near future. There was a very earnest call for the Brethren to go to Jennings County, Ohio, to preach the Word of Life. Who will answer the call?

There are a few faithful members in Martin County, Ind., near Shoals, who are in need of preaching. Bro. H. Tranter, of Shoals, inquired of me, whether they were to have any missionaries and when. Will the Mission Board please answer his request?   ISAAC E. BRANSON.

Muncie, Ind., Oct. 18.

Working for the Master.

ON the night of Sept. 28 I was aroused from my slumber and notified that a man in the adjoining neighborhood wished to unite with the church, and desired me to baptize him, which work, assisted by Bro. M. A. Eisenhour, we performed at about 3 o'clock A. M., Sept. 24. On the same day the wife of the applicant, referred

CORRESPONDENCE.

"Write what thou seest, and send it unto the churches."

☞ Church News solicited for this Department. If you have had a good meeting, send a report of it, so that others may rejoice with you. In writing give name of church, County and State. Be brief. Notes of Travel should be as short as possible. Land Advertisements are not solicited for this Department. We have an advertising page, and, if necessary, will issue supplements.

From Knobnoster, Mo.

WIFE and I visited the Prairie View church, Morgan Co., Mo., to attend their love-feast Sept. 7. Next day, in company with Eld. David Bowman, of the Prairie View church, we started for Montgomery County, Mo., to hold meetings. There are fourteen members at this point, who are without a resident minister. Eld. David Bowman has this mission point in charge. Here we had forty-three meetings. We held two meetings at the same time, about three miles apart, with good attendance at each place. The outlook here is encouraging, if the work can be followed up as it should be. We also held a love-feast with the members. One that had wandered away returned to the fold again. From what we were able to learn, several are about ready to cast their lot with the Brethren.

While Bro. Bowman continued the meetings, wife and I went to Audrain County, to the hospitable home of our aged brother and sister Moomaw. Here we had five meetings in a school-house. Brother and sister Moomaw are the only members at this place. Here, also, is a favorable point for mission work. From here we went to the town of Mexico, Audrain Co., where we again met Bro. Bowman. Here, also, are two members, —sister Sanders and her daughter. Here the neighbors were invited in by sister Sanders, to hear us preach. Bro. Bowman's sermon seemed to be enjoyed by all present. From here we started home, where we arrived Oct. 5.

ISRAEL CRIPE.

From Walnut Valley Church, Kans.

THE church met in council Sept. 28, preparatory to a love-feast. The business before the meeting was all disposed of pleasantly. One dear young sister made application to be received into the church and was buried with Christ in baptism. Oct. 1 we met to celebrate the sufferings and death of our Blessed Redeemer. The meeting was one long to be remembered. Quietness and solemnity prevailed, and we have reason to believe that many good impressions were made, and that some are almost persuaded to join in with the children of God. Ministers present from other congregations were elders Moses Brubaker, S. Z. Sharp, W. B. Hines and James Paxton. On Sunday we met at 9:30 A. M., for children's meeting. The brethren gave the children an interesting talk and asked them some questions which pleased the children very much. At 11 A. M., Bro. Sharp gave us an excellent sermon on the subject of sacrificing, and portrayed to our minds the importance of sacrificing to the Lord.   S. P. WEAVER.

Heisler, Kans.

Pierced to Death.

GARRETT M., only child of brother and sister S. F. Henricks, residing at this place, met with a very sad and sudden death Oct. 11. About one o'clock little Garrett said to his mother, "I want to get a bouquet of flowers for my teacher." He then took a large pair of shears to cut the flowers. In running around the house with the shears in his hand, the boy stumbled and fell, his breast striking upon the point of the shears with such force as to drive them through the flesh into his lungs, severing the main artery. He got up, pulled the shears out, ran a short distance, and then dropped down dead.

His little cousin, Amy Hoover, who was waiting for him to gather the flowers, saw the accident, and notified the boy's mother, who at once ran out and carried her dead son to the house. A physician was summoned, but nothing could be done, as life was extinct. Brother and sister Henricks have the sympathy of all who knew them, and also have the precious promise of meeting him again in a better world than this.

Garrett M., was born June 11, 1885, and was, at the time of his death, seven years and four months old. The remains were taken to Plymouth, and the funeral services were conducted in the Union meeting-house, five miles west of Plymouth, where the interment took place. Services were conducted by the writer, from 2 Kings 4: 26.

H. W. KRIEGHBAUM.

South Bend, Ind., Oct. 14.

From the Kaskaskia Church, Fayette Co., Ill.

WE had a glorious meeting. Eld. Daniel Mohler, of Piatt County, Ill., commenced a protracted effort in our new church-house, Oct. 1, and continued until the 11th. He baptized four precious souls, and left five applicants, which were baptized the day following. These, with six more dear souls, who are tired of sin, will make fifteen additions in all. We closed the meetings Oct. 16 with a good attendance and some near the kingdom. Oct. 7 we held our feast, which will long be remembered. Bro. Mohler officiated, and was aided in the ministry by Eld. Jacob Ullery, Bro. Younger, of La Place, Ill., and Bro. Allen Taylor, of Mulberry Grove, Ill. At this meeting we held an election for a deacon, the lot falling upon our esteemed brother M. W. Clayton, who, with his worthy companion, was duly installed into office. We now number sixty members, of whom fifty-six live within less than four miles of the church-house. Twenty-three of them are yet in their teens.   GRANVILLE NEVINGER.

Beecher City, Ill.

From Rosedale, Cambria Co., Pa.

AUG. 2 I came to Johnstown, Cambria Co., Pa., where I found my cousin and brother in Christ, William Ford, confined to his bed since May 30, and in a suffering condition. Wednesday evening Aug. 3, he called for the elders of the church and was anointed in the name of the Lord. Preaching and prayer-meeting were held in his sick chamber, and a love-feast was also held Sept. 5. With the exception of about a week he is still (Oct. 7) confined to his bed. I have visited a number of families of Brethren and attended Sunday-school, church, and prayer-meeting with them. I also attended one love-feast. I have greatly enjoyed these meetings after being isolated so much from the church. There are not any Brethren at Homestead. I have distributed our church literature there, so that it may, at least, be as crumbs cast upon the waters.

Twice I have visited Grandview cemetery, above Johnstown, where the unidentified dead of the Johnstown flood are buried, and also many that were identified. A beautiful monument was erected and dedicated May 31 last, to mark the spot, and a plain marble slab marks each grave. There are eight hundred slabs. There are two ways of reaching the elevated country to the cemetery,—up the "incline" on the electric cars, or up a beautiful drive-way. We ascended by the former. My heart ached as I passed over the ground and beheld the burial-place of that vast number that were so hastily ushered into eternity by that dreadful flood, and many were the tears that flowed while surviving friends related that sad tale to me. This was my first visit to Johnstown and vicinity since the flood. One would scarcely realize that but so short a time the town was almost wiped away.

In a few days I shall return to Homestead, if God permits, and shall continue to labor for the Master. May God send some one there, in the near future, to break the Bread of Life to the thousands of God's creatures that dwell there. Those who hunger and thirst after righteousness, may their souls be filled!   EMILY R. STIFLER.

Mission Work in Southern Indiana.

I LEFT home Oct. 7, to visit the New Hope church, Jackson County. Upon my arrival at Chestnut Ridge, I was met by Bro. Bedel and taken to the new church-house that had just been finished. It has been built by the members of that church, aided by a donation of $200.00 from the General Church Erection and Missionary Fund. Here I met Bro. David R. Richards, who had come the same morning. We had meetings the same evening and the next day we labored to set things in order that were wanting. All business was disposed of to the general satisfaction of the members present. We continued the meetings each evening and on Sunday until the 11th, when Bro. Richards, owing to illness, went home, leaving the writer and the home minister to conduct the meetings. One was baptized on the 12th. The same evening brethren Daniel Bock and David F. Hoover came to our assistance. They spoke the Word with power.

On the evening of Oct. 13 Bro. Samuel Younce, of Eaton, Ind., came to assist us. This made us feel to rejoice. The Communion was set for Oct. 14. It was a feast to the soul. The house was filled to overflowing, and there were many who could not get in. It was estimated that at least five hundred persons were in the house and yard. There were thirty-one members at the table of the Lord. All seemed to rejoice.

We continued meetings over Sunday. On Sunday, Oct. 16, the house was dedicated to the Lord. Bro. David F. Hoover preached the dedicatory sermon from 1 Kings 8: 29. After the sermon two dear souls came out on the Lord's side and were baptized. The meeting closed on Sunday night with increased interest and a full house. Monday morning Bro. James Albinson, who is afflicted, was anointed. Then we took our leave for home. I left the other three brethren at Indianapolis. There is a very good opening for an ingathering in the near future. There was a very earnest call for the Brethren to go to Jennings County, Ohio, to preach the Word of Life. Who will answer the call?

There are a few faithful members in Martin County, Ind., near Shoals, who are in need of preaching. Bro. H. Tranter, of Shoals, inquired of me, whether they were to have any missionaries and when. Will the Mission Board please answer his request?   ISAAC E. BRANSON.

Muncie, Ind., Oct. 18.

Working for the Master.

ON the night of Sept. 23 I was aroused from my slumber and notified that a man in the adjoining neighborhood wished to unite with the church, and desired me to baptize him, which work, assisted by Bro. M. A. Eisenhour, we performed at about 3 o'clock A. M., Sept. 24. On the same day the wife of the applicant, referred

Missionary and Tract Work Department.

"Upon the first day of the week, let every one of you lay by him in store as God hath prospered him, that there be no gatherings when I come."—1 Cor. 16: 2.

"Every man as he purposeth in his heart, so let him give. Not grudgingly or of necessity, for the Lord loveth a cheerful giver."—2 Cor. 9: 7.

HOW MUCH SHALL WE GIVE?

"Every man *according to his ability.*" "Every one *as God hath prospered him.*" "Every man, *according as he purposeth in his heart,* so let him give." "For if there be first a willing mind, it is accepted *according to that a man hath,* and not according to that he hath not."—2 Cor. 8: 12.

Organization of Missionary Committee.

DANIEL VANIMAN, Foreman,	-	-	McPherson, Kans.
D. L. MILLER, Treasurer,	-	-	Mt. Morris, Ill.
GALEN B. ROYER, Secretary,	-	-	Mt. Morris, Ill.

Organization of Book and Tract Work.

| S. W. HOOVER, Foreman, | - | - | Dayton, Ohio. |
| S. BOCK, Secretary and Treasurer, | - | - | Dayton, Ohio. |

☞All donations intended for Missionary Work should be sent to GALEN B. ROYER, Mt. Morris, Ill.

☞All money for Tract Work should be sent to S. BOCK, Dayton, Ohio.

☞Money may be sent by Money Order, Registered Letter, or Drafts on New York or Chicago. Do not send personal checks, or drafts on interior towns, as it costs 25 cents to collect them.

☞Solicitors are requested to faithfully carry out the plan of Annual Meeting, that all our members be solicited to contribute at least twice a year for the Mission and Tract Work of the Church.

☞Notes for the Endowment Fund can be had by writing to the Secretary of either Work.

REPORT OF THE SPECIAL DISTRICT MEETING OF THE NORTHERN DISTRICT OF ILLINOIS.

Held at Mt. Morris, Ill., Oct. 18, 1892.

THE Meeting was called to order at 9 A. M., and the devotional exercises were conducted by Bro. Geo. Arnold, of W. Va., and Bro. Henry Frantz, of Ohio. The old officers took charge of the Meeting, and the roll was called. All the churches in the District were represented by delegates but three.

The trustees presented a plan for governing the Old Peoples' and Orphans' Home, which, with some modifications, made by the Meeting, was adopted. The plan is as follows:—

Plan for Governing the Old Peoples' and Orphans' Home of Northern Illinois.

(*a*) The Home, intended to accommodate the poor members and orphans from the Northern District of Illinois, is owned, controlled, and supported by said District, but may receive donations and bequests from any and all sources.

(*b*) Members who are pronounced church charges by the church, in which they hold their membership, are eligible to the Home. If a member has some property or money and wants to bequeath it to the Home, he can do so, and then make the Home his home for life.

(*c*) All applications must be made to the Superintendent, through the church wherein such member holds his membership, and such application must be signed by at least a majority of the officials, and the Superintendent is not to admit anyone without the consent of the Trustees, and the church sending inmates shall bear the expense to and from the Home. The Home pays no traveling expenses of inmates.

(*d*) The Trustees are the Custodians of all who need assistance in the District, and are empowered to give assistance to those who may be able to make a partial living, if in their judgment they can be supported cheaper away from the Home than in it.

(*e*) All applications for admission of orphan children shall be made to the Superintendent, by the friends or guardian having charge of such children, through the church in which they live. Children must be admitted subject to the disposal of the Trustees, who shall procure homes for them among the Brethren if possible, otherwise among honorable families.

(*f*) All persons must be cleansed of all contagious diseases before they can be admitted.

(*g*) It is expected that all inmates work to the extent that they are able.

(*h*) In case of sickness the Home secures medical aid, and in the event of death gives a respectable burial, but in case the friends desire to remove the remains, they can do so by paying the expenses.

(*i*) It shall be the duty of the churches sending inmates to the Home, to furnish them with a change of clothing.

(*j*) Churches making applications should always give the name of the person, the age, and, if disabled in any way, how.

(*k*) Form of application. Application for admittance to the Old Peoples' and Orphans' Home of Northern Illinois.

We, the members of........(name of church)........ have, in council decided that........(name of person, age and disability)........is a church charge, and as such we, the members of said church, make application for her (or his) admittance to the Home.

From the report of the churches it was ascertained that there would be ten applications for admission, as soon as the Home could be started.

A report of the financial condition of the Home was called for and the following was given by Joseph Amick for the treasurer:

Total amount of cash received to Oct. 18, 1892,....	$7,305 52
Total amount of cash expended to Oct. 18, 1892,....	6,538 52
Balance on hand,............................	$ 767 00

The report was accepted and the following committee was appointed to audit the books of the Trustees: D. B. Senger, Frank Myers, and W. R. Miller.

REPORT OF AUDITING COMMITTEE.

We, the committee appointed by special District Meeting at Mt. Morris, Ill., Oct. 18, 1892, to audit the treasurer's report of the Old People's and Orphans' Home of Mt. Morris, Ill., find the above account correct to this date, with a balance on hand of $767.00.

D. B. SENGER,
W. R. MILLER,
FRANK MYERS.

An application for admission from Iowa, and all similar ones, was referred to the Trustees.

Upon motion the Trustees were authorized to manage and control the Home. It was decided that the delegates, accompanied by Eld. Joseph Lahman, should visit the Home, and upon their return after noon intermission, the Home was accepted by the District, and the committee relieved. It was further decided that it was the sense of this Meeting that those churches which have not paid their apportionment to the Home be requested to do so now. Adjourned.

DANIEL DEARDORFF,
Moderator.

D. L. MILLER, Reading Clerk.

JOS. AMICK,
GALEN B. ROYER,
} Writing Clerks.

CHILDREN'S JUBILEE.

BY C. H. BALSBAUGH.

OCT. 9, 1892, is a day long to be remembered by this community. It was the anniversary of our Sunday-school children's meeting. The day was lovely, the concourse amazing, the order excellent, the interest apparently profound and sustained.

The leading speaker was Bro. Samuel H. Hertzler, of Elizabethtown, Pa., son of Eld. William Hertzler. He treated a triple theme. Parental obligation. Col. 3: 21; Eph. 6: 4. Filial obligation. Eph. 6: 1, and Col. 3: 20. The absoluteness and universality of the divine claim. Luke 10: 27, and 1 John 2: 12, 13, 14.

Many a father and mother had the mask of formality and delinquency torn off. Young people were shown the folly and sin and bitterness of compliance with the social iniquities of the day. And the children were helped to a vivid illustration of the necessity of early acquaintance with the Word of God, as the only security against the manifold snares and seductions of the devil.

He was followed by Bro. John H. Witmer in the same line of thought, with various impressive illustrations and forcible applications. The immense value of the Sunday-school was one of his special points. It is beyond computation. With energy he drove home the stupendous wickedness of tampering with temptation in any form. Many of our debauching social usages were stabbed to the core.

Our aged home preacher, Bro. David Smith, of Union Deposit, made a brave little speech in

German. He hit the nail fair on the head, and knocked pipe and quid, and cut-and-dry, many leagues beyond the boundaries of Israel. He testified nobly to the orthodoxy and benefits of the Sunday-school.

The singing was very sweet, like the blending of a "rushing mighty wind," with the many-tuned harmonies of children, youth, and hoary age. It was like the ravishing prelude of the Everlasting Song in the countless congregation of the upper Sanctuary.

May the entire church become more and more open to 2 Cor. 3: 18, and 4: 6, so that the family and Sunday-school may be the manifest embodiment of Eph. 3: 19. Is the "*But*" of Heb. 2: 9 really ours? Then why is not Philpp. 4: 13, and 2 Thess. 1: 11, 12, gloriously ours also? God has not revoked 1 Cor. 3: 21, 22, 23.

Union Deposit, Pa.

THE LITTLE COATS.

IN a recent issue of the *Independent*, Dr. Theodore L. Cuyler addresses an excellent letter to the Christian mothers of the land. The article is so full of meaning that we give it entire:

" 'His mother made him a little coat.' There is a home-touch of nature in this 'wee' passage from the second chapter of the Book of Samuel. Away back in those far-away lands and ages, there was a young wife whom the Lord blessed with an infant son, and her joy was overflowing. 'For this child I prayed'—exclaimed the devout Hannah—' and the Lord hath given me my petition. Therefore I have lent him to the Lord, and as long as he liveth, he shall be lent to the Lord.' This solemn vow of consecration was never broken. If all the good promises which Christian parents make to God when they present their children for baptism were as faithfully kept, then a very sacred rite would become—not a barren form, but a source of inestimable blessings.

"Hannah placed her little son Samuel in the care of the High-priest Eli in the house of the Lord at Shiloh. Moreover 'his mother made him a little coat,' and brought it to him when she came to offer her annual sacrifices. What sort of a garment could the wee tunic or mantle have been? We do not know exactly; but we may believe that so sensible a mother did not degrade her only child into a doll. I wish I could say as much of thousands of Christian parents in these days who overload their children with costly finery. As if God did not make a child beautiful enough without being tortured with the tongs and screws of fashion and disfigured with extravagant upholsterings! This folly strikes through into the child's heart, enduing it with pride and greed of admiration and vainglory. How can a child be taught humility and frugality and that best of all lessons, self-denial, while its graceful form is smothered under the artificial trappings of fopperies and frivolities? Self-indulgence is the besetting sin of the church in these days; and one of its seeds is planted early, when a child that has been nominally dedicated to God is degraded into an over-dressed doll.

"But this little coat which Hannah made for her only boy has a far deeper significance. In the Bible, clothing has a figurative meaning; Christianity is spoken of as a vesture, and believers are commanded to 'put on Christ,' so that whenever they are looked at, their godly character may be as visible as the garments they wear. In Heaven the saints are said to be clothed in white raiment, which has been washed to a celestial purity by atoning blood. It is not a mere pun to remind my readers that the word 'habit' is used to signify both a bodily dress and also the disposition of the mind toward good or evil. Mothers

Missionary and Tract Work Department.

"Upon the first day of the week, let every one of you lay by him in store as God hath prospered him, that there be no gatherings when I come."—1 Cor. 16: 2.

"Every man as he purposeth in his heart, so let him give. Not grudgingly or of necessity, for the Lord loveth a cheerful giver."—2 Cor. 9: 7.

HOW MUCH SHALL WE GIVE?

"Every man according to his ability." "Every one as God hath prospered him." "Every man, according as he purposeth in his heart, so let him give." "For if there be first a willing mind, it is accepted according to that a man hath, and not according to that he hath not."—2 Cor. 8: 12.

Organization of Missionary Committee.

DANIEL VANIMAN, Foreman,   McPherson, Kans.
D. L. MILLER, Treasurer,   Mt. Morris, Ill.
GALEN B. ROYER, Secretary,   Mt. Morris, Ill.

Organization of Book and Tract Work.

S. W. HOOVER, Foreman,   Dayton, Ohio.
S. BOCK, Secretary and Treasurer,   Dayton, Ohio.

☞ All donations intended for Missionary Work should be sent to GALEN B. ROYER, Mt. Morris, Ill.

☞ All money for Tract Work should be sent to S. BOCK, Dayton, Ohio.

☞ Money may be sent by Money Order, Registered Letter, or Drafts on New York or Chicago. Do not send personal checks, or drafts on interior towns, as it costs 15 cents to collect them.

☞ Solicitors are requested to faithfully carry out the plan of Annual Meeting, that all our members be solicited to contribute at least twice a year for the Mission and Tract Work of the Church.

☞ Notes for the Endowment Fund can be had by writing to the Secretary of either Work.

REPORT OF THE SPECIAL DISTRICT MEETING OF THE NORTHERN DISTRICT OF ILLINOIS.

Held at Mt. Morris, Ill., Oct. 18, 1892.

THE Meeting was called to order at 9 A. M., and the devotional exercises were conducted by Bro. Geo. Arnold, of W. Va., and Bro. Henry Frantz, of Ohio. The old officers took charge of the Meeting, and the roll was called. All the churches in the District were represented by delegates but three.

The trustees presented a plan for governing the Old Peoples' and Orphans' Home, which, with some modifications, made by the Meeting, was adopted. The plan is as follows:—

Plan for Governing the Old Peoples' and Orphans' Home of Northern Illinois.

(a) The Home, intended to accommodate the poor members and orphans from the Northern District of Illinois, is owned, controlled, and supported by said District, but may receive donations and bequests from any and all sources.

(b) Members who are pronounced church charges by the church, in which they hold their membership, are eligible to the Home. If a member has some property or money and wants to bequeath it to the Home, he can do so, and then make the Home his home for life.

(c) All applications must be made to the Superintendent, through the church wherein such member holds his membership, and such application must be signed by at least a majority of the officials, and the Superintendent is not to admit anyone without the consent of the Trustees, and the church sending inmates shall bear the expense to and from the Home. The Home pays no traveling expenses of inmates.

(d) The Trustees are the Custodians of all who need assistance in the District, and are empowered to give assistance to those who may be able to make a partial living, if in their judgment they can be supported cheaper away from the Home than in it.

(e) All applications for admission of orphan children shall be made to the Superintendent, by the friends or guardian having charge of such children, through the church in which they live. Children must be admitted subject to the disposal of the Trustees, who shall procure homes for them among the Brethren if possible, otherwise among honorable families.

(f) All persons must be cleansed of all contagious diseases before they can be admitted.

(g) It is expected that all inmates work to the extent that they are able.

(h) In case of sickness the Home secures medical aid, and in the event of death gives a respectable burial, but in case the friends desire to remove the remains, they can do so by paying the expenses.

(i) It shall be the duty of the churches sending inmates to the Home, to furnish them with a change of clothing.

(j) Churches making applications should always give the name of the person, the age, and, if disabled in any way, how.

(k) Form of application. Application for admittance to the Old Peoples' and Orphans' Home of Northern Illinois.

We, the members of........(name of church)........ have, in council decided that........(name of person, age and disability)........is a church charge, and as such we, the members of said church, make application for her (or his) admittance to the Home.

From the report of the churches it was ascertained that there would be ten applications for admission, as soon as the Home could be started.

A report of the financial condition of the Home was called for and the following was given by Joseph Amick for the treasurer:

Total amount of cash received to Oct. 18, 1892,.....$7,305 52
Total amount of cash expended to Oct. 18, 1892,.... 6,538 52
                                        —————
Balance on hand,.........................$ 767 00

The report was accepted and the following committee was appointed to audit the books of the Trustees: D. B. Senger, Frank Myers, and W. R. Miller.

REPORT OF AUDITING COMMITTEE.

We, the committee appointed by special District Meeting at Mt. Morris, Ill., Oct. 18, 1892, to audit the treasurer's report of the Old People's and Orphans' Home of Mt. Morris, Ill., find the above account correct to this date, with a balance on hand of $767.00.

                D. B. SENGER,
                W. R. MILLER,
                FRANK MYERS.

An application for admission from Iowa, and all similar ones, was referred to the Trustees.

Upon motion the Trustees were authorized to manage and control the Home. It was decided that the delegates, accompanied by Eld. Joseph Lahman, should visit the Home, and upon their return after noon intermission, the Home was accepted by the District, and the committee relieved. It was further decided that it was the sense of this Meeting that those churches which have not paid their apportionment to the Home be requested to do so now. Adjourned.

                DANIEL DEARDORFF,
D. L. MILLER, Reading Clerk.   Moderator.
JOS. AMICK,   ⎫
GALEN B. ROYER, ⎬ Writing Clerks.
          ⎭

CHILDREN'S JUBILEE.

BY C. H. BALSBAUGH.

OCT. 9, 1892, is a day long to be remembered by this community. It was the anniversary of our Sunday-school children's meeting. The day was lovely, the concourse amazing, the order excellent, the interest apparently profound and sustained.

The leading speaker was Bro. Samuel H. Hertzler, of Elizabethtown, Pa., son of Eld. William Hertzler. He treated a triple theme. Parental obligation. Col. 3: 21; Eph. 6: 4. Filial obligation. Eph. 6: 1, and Col. 3: 20. The absoluteness and universality of the divine claim. Luke 10: 27, and 1 John 2: 12, 13, 14.

Many a father and mother had the mask of formality and delinquency torn off. Young people were shown the folly and sin and bitterness of compliance with the social iniquities of the day. And the children were helped to a vivid illustration of the necessity of early acquaintance with the Word of God, as the only security against the manifold snares and seductions of the devil.

He was followed by Bro. John H. Witmer in the same line of thought, with various impressive illustrations and forcible applications. The immense value of the Sunday-school was one of his special points. It is beyond computation. With energy he drove home the stupendous wickedness of tampering with temptation in any form. Many of our debauching social usages were stabbed to the core.

Our aged home preacher, Bro. David Smith, of Union Deposit, made a brave little speech in

German. He hit the nail fair on the head, and knocked pipe and quid, and cut-and-dry, many leagues beyond the boundaries of Israel. He testified nobly to the orthodoxy and benefits of the Sunday-school.

The singing was very sweet, like the blending of a "rushing mighty wind," with the many-tuned harmonies of children, youth, and hoary age. It was like the ravishing prelude of the Everlasting Song in the countless congregation of the upper Sanctuary.

May the entire church become more and more open to 2 Cor. 3: 18, and 4: 6, so that the family and Sunday-school may be the manifest embodiment of Eph. 3: 19. Is the "But" of Heb. 2: 9 really ours? Then why is not Philpp. 4: 13, and 2 Thess. 1: 11, 12, gloriously ours also? God has not revoked 1 Cor. 3: 21, 22, 23.

Union Deposit, Pa.

THE LITTLE COATS.

IN a recent issue of the *Independent*, Dr. Theodore L. Cuyler addresses an excellent letter to the Christian mothers of the land. The article is so full of meaning that we give it entire:

"'His mother made him a little coat.' There is a home-touch of nature in this 'wee' passage from the second chapter of the Book of Samuel. Away back in those far-away lands and ages, there was a young wife whom the Lord blessed with an infant son, and her joy was overflowing. 'For this child I prayed'—exclaimed the devout Hannah—'and the Lord hath given me my petition. Therefore I have lent him to the Lord, and as long as he liveth, he shall be lent to the Lord.' This solemn vow of consecration was never broken. If all the good promises which Christian parents make to God when they present their children for baptism were as faithfully kept, then a very sacred rite would become—not a barren form, but a source of inestimable blessings.

"Hannah placed her little son Samuel in the care of the High-priest Eli in the house of the Lord at Shiloh. Moreover 'his mother made him a little coat,' and brought it to him when she came to offer her annual sacrifices. What sort of a garment could the wee tunic or mantle have been? We do not know exactly; but we may believe that so sensible a mother did not degrade her only child into a doll. I wish I could say as much of thousands of Christian parents in these days who overload their children with costly finery. As if God did not make a child beautiful enough without being tortured with the tongs and screws of fashion and disfigured with extravagant upholsterings! This folly strikes through into the child's heart, poisoning it with pride and greed of admiration and vainglory. How can a child be taught humility and frugality and that best of all lessons, *self-denial*, while its graceful form is smothered under the artificial trappings of fopperies and frivolities? Self-indulgence is the besetting sin of the church in these days; and one of its seeds is planted early, when a child that has been nominally dedicated to God is degraded into an over-dressed doll.

"But this little coat which Hannah made for her only boy has a far deeper significance. In the Bible, clothing has a figurative meaning; Christianity is spoken of as a vesture, and believers are commanded to 'put on Christ,' so that whenever they are looked at, their godly character may be as visible as the garments they wear. In Heaven the saints are said to be clothed in white raiment, which has been washed to a celestial purity by atoning blood. It is not a mere pun to remind my readers that the word 'habit' is used to signify both a bodily dress and also the disposition of the mind toward good or evil. Mothers

The Gospel Messenger,

A Weekly at $1.50 Per Annum.

PUBLISHED BY

The Brethren's Publishing Co.

D. L. MILLER, ... Editor
J. H. MOORE, ... Office Editor.
J. B. BRUMBAUGH, } . . . . . Associate Editors.
J. G. ROYER, }
JOSEPH AMICK, ... Business Manager.

ADVISORY COMMITTEE.
L. W. Terter, A. Hutchison, Daniel Hays.

☞Communications for publication should be legibly written with black ink on one side of the paper only. Do not attempt to interline or to put on one page what ought to occupy two.

☞Anonymous communications will not be published.

☞Do not mix business with articles for publication. Keep your communications on separate sheets from all business.

☞Time is precious. We always have time to attend to business and to answer questions of importance, but please do not subject us to need less answering of letters.

☞The MESSENGER is mailed each week to all subscribers. If the address is correctly entered on our list, the paper must reach the person to whom it is addressed. If you do not get your paper, write us, giving particulars.

☞When changing your address, please give your former as well as your future address in full, so as to avoid delay and misunderstanding.

☞Always remit to the office from which you obtain your goods, no matter from where you receive them.

☞Do not send personal checks or drafts on interior banks, unless you send with them 25 cents each, to pay for collection.

☞Remittances should be made by Post-office Money Order, Drafts on New York, Philadelphia or Chicago, or Registered Letters, made payable and addressed to "Brethren's Publishing Co., Mount Morris, Ill.," or "Brethren's Publishing Co., Huntingdon, Pa."

☞Entered at the Post-office at Mount Morris, Ill., as second-class matter.

Mount Morris, Ill., ... Nov. 1, 1892.

THERE were nine additions at the Pine Creek meeting, instead of eight, as reported last week.

THE feast in the Aughwick church, Pa., Nov. 1, is to commence at 2 P. M., instead of 4 P. M., as previously announced.

THE Kaskaskia church, Fayette Co., Ill., is increasing in numbers. Fifteen were recently added to the church by confession and baptism.

BRO. SOLOMON BUCKLEW, we learn, is engaged in a series of meetings at the meeting-house in the north end of the Woodland congregation, Ill.

OUR short series of meetings at Mt. Morris closed last Tuesday with six additions. Five were baptized and one is yet to receive the initiatory rite.

THE District Meeting for the Second District of West Virginia, we learn, passed off very pleasantly. Bro. D. J. Miller has been selected to represent the District on the Standing Committee.

THE happiest people in the world are those who help others. In turn they make friends who help them. Like begets like, the world over. Those who want friends must be friendly themselves.

WE have just printed for the Middle District of Iowa a well-prepared program of their Ministerial Meeting, to be held in the Iowa River church, Dec. 6 and 7. For copy of program, etc., address Bro. J. C. Seibert, Hill's Siding, Iowa.

ONE of our exchanges says: "The record of crime in our country increases at a fearful rate. True, as the population increases, the facilities for the transmission of news increase, and the disposition on the part of the secular press to gather and report such items increases; but still, so far as we can learn, the increase of crime is proportioned to all these, and crime, too, of the most flagrant character. Attention should be given to this matter and close investigation made, both as to the cause and the cure.

THIRTY members have been added to the Antioch church, Bedford County, Va., since last August. The cause seems to be prospering encouragingly in that part of the State.

IF we had to be judged by one another, the probability is that not one of us would be saved. But we have a Judge who knows mercy as well as justice, and we can freely trust him.

AT the late District Meeting in Southern Illinois Bro. D. B. Gibson was Moderator; Conrad Fitz, Reading Clerk, and Chas. Gibson, Writing Clerk. Bro. John Harshbarger will represent the District on the next Standing Committee.

BRO. SIDNEY HODGDEN will represent Oregon, Washington and Idaho on the Standing Committee at the next Annual Meeting. The District is composed of seven congregations and they were all represented at the late District Meeting but one. One of the congregations was represented by a sister.

BRO. D. M. MILLER, of Milledgeville, goes to Laurens, Pocahontas Co., Iowa, this week, to hold a series of meetings, and may remain several weeks. He reminds us that we should never say in print, "Church of my choice," but the "Lord's choice," saying that "choice implies variety, hence justifies denominational divisions."

OCCASIONALLY we find money folded in between the pages of manuscript intended for publication. This is a very unsafe way of doing, as manuscript is sometimes laid to one side for weeks before the editor can get time to examine it. Please remember and write your business matter on a sheet separate and apart from the matter intended for publication, and do not fail to give your name and address in each instance.

IT is remarkable how careless some people are about the letters sent to an office like this. A few days ago we received a letter mailed in Missouri. On opening it we found a blank sheet of white paper, but not one word in writing. A day later an envelope came from Virginia with not one thing in it, not even a piece of paper. From Oklahoma Territory comes a letter containing $1.50, but the contents of the letter shows that it was intended for some intimate friend instead of us. As there is nothing about any of these letters to indicate who they are from, they, of course, cannot be answered, and at least three persons will soon feel that there is something wrong with this office.

IN these columns we do not often refer to political questions, or to the contests of the different political parties, but at this time it seems but due to the good name of our church and people that the following statement be made. Eld. S. H. Bashor is a candidate for election to Congress in this Congressional District, and we are receiving inquiries from parties not acquainted with our people as to whether he is a member and a minister in our church. It is only right that we should say that Eld. Bashor is not, and has not been a member of the German Baptist Brethren (Dunkard) church for a number of years. The Dunkards do not take an active part in politics and do not approve of any of their members running for a political office. We wish it distinctly understood that the party here referred to has no connection whatever with our church. He is a member of the Progressive Brethren church, and if, in the conduct of his canvass for a seat in Congress, he lowers the dignity of the Christian ministry and brings reproach upon the church of which he is a member, our people should not bear the censure arising from his conduct.

"THE publication of the proceedings of the London Oriental Society will, this year, be looked for with some interest. It is said that important discoveries, bearing directly on Biblical history and chronology, have been made, both in Palestine and in Assyria. Thousands of the volumes of Nebuchadnezzar's library are being translated, and the appearance of the results may throw much light on the books of Kings and Daniel."

IT is said that the Sunday-school superintendent of a certain "Christian Church" asked a lady of the world to join that church. She responded thus: "I think you ought to be ashamed of yourself. You dance and call out for dances, you play cards, play crap, and drink whiskey, and you ought to be ashamed to ask me to join your church." Professing Christians, who ask others to come to the church might do well to first pause and see whether their own light is shining as it ought.

PRIMITIVE CHRISTIANITY.

NEVER before have we been prepared to give our readers such interesting and valuable matter as will likely appear in the MESSENGER during the next year. In addition to letters from the Seven Churches of Asia, the Land of Goshen, Mt. Sinai and other parts of Bible Lands, we have arranged for a series of well-prepared articles, setting forth Primitive Christianity, as understood and practiced by the Brethren. These articles will be prepared by some of our best writers and examined with great care. Some of the writers have already spent months on their part of the work. In all there will be about eighty articles, presented in nearly forty chapters. The following is a list of the greater part of the subjects that will be treated in the order in which they appear here:

1. "Our Reasons for Receiving the Bible as the Word of God, and Our only Rule of Faith and Practice." Giving the origin and a brief history of the Bible; clear proof of its inspiration and adaptation to man, and reasons for accepting it.

2. "The Law and the Gospel." The Old and New Covenants—Moses the lawgiver for the former, and Christ for the latter. Show the difference between the Law and the Gospel, and how we are now living under the Gospel and not under the Law.

3. "Christ the Head and Founder of the Church." Showing the Divinity and Sonship of Christ,—the long-promised Messiah; his death, burial, resurrection and ascension, now the head of the church and our Lawgiver.

4. "Man's Need of a Savior." Showing the fall of man from his pure state, his inability to rescue himself, and the necessity of the atonement.

5. "Faith." What it is, what it embraces and its necessity. What the sinner must believe in order to have salvation, and how faith without works is dead.

6. "Repentance." What it is, its design and necessity. Show what genuine Gospel repentance is, and what it accomplishes in the life and character of a sinner as a step in his salvation from sin.

7. "Baptism; Subjects and Design." Showing that it is a divine command, intended for those capable of understanding the Gospel, believing it and repenting of their sins, and not for innocent children. That, in connection with faith and repentance, it is for the remission of sins, being one of the conditions of pardon.

The Gospel Messenger,

A Weekly at $1.50 Per Annum.

PUBLISHED BY

The Brethren's Publishing Co.

D. L. MILLER,	. . . . .	Editor.
J. H. MOORE,	. . . . .	Office Editor.
J. B. BRUMBAUGH,		Associate Editors.
J. G. ROYER,		
JOSEPH AMICK,	. . . . .	Business Manager.

ADVISORY COMMITTEE.
L. W. Teeter, A. Hutchison, Daniel Hays.

☞Communications for publication should be legibly written with black ink on one side of the paper only. Do not attempt to interline or to put on one page what ought to occupy two.

☞Anonymous communications will not be published.

☞Do not mix business with articles for publication. Keep your communications on separate sheets from all business.

☞Time is precious. We always have time to attend to business and to answer questions of importance, but please do not subject us to needless unraveling of letters.

☞The MESSENGER is mailed each week to all subscribers. If the address is correctly entered on our list, the paper must reach the person to whom it is addressed. If you do not get your paper, write us, giving particulars.

☞When changing your address, please give your former as well as your future address in full, so as to avoid delay and misunderstanding.

☞Always remit to the office from which you order your goods, no matter from where you receive them.

☞Do not send personal checks or drafts on interior banks, unless you send with them 25 cents each, to pay for collection.

☞Remittances should be made by Post-office Money Order, Drafts on New York, Philadelphia or Chicago, or Registered Letters, made payable and addressed to "Brethren's Publishing Co., Mount Morris, Ill.," or "Brethren's Publishing Co., Huntingdon, Pa."

☞Edited at the Post-office at Mount Morris, Ill., as second-class matter.

Mount Morris, Ill., . . . Nov. 1, 1892.

THERE were nine additions at the Pine Creek meeting, instead of eight, as reported last week.

THE feast in the Aughwick church, Pa., Nov. 1, is to commence at 2 P. M., instead of 4 P. M., as previously announced.

THE Kaskaskia church, Fayette Co., Ill., is increasing in numbers. Fifteen were recently added to the church by confession and baptism.

BRO. SOLOMON BUCKLEW, we learn, is engaged in a series of meetings at the meeting-house in the north end of the Woodland congregation, Ill.

OUR short series of meetings at Mt. Morris closed last Tuesday with six additions. Five were baptized and one is yet to receive the initiatory rite.

THE District Meeting for the Second District of West Virginia, we learn, passed off very pleasantly. Bro. D. J. Miller has been selected to represent the District on the Standing Committee.

THE happiest people in the world are those who help others. In turn they make friends who help them. Like begets like, the world over. Those who want friends must be friendly themselves.

WE have just printed for the Middle District of Iowa a well-prepared program of their Ministerial Meeting, to be held in the Iowa River church, Dec. 6 and 7. For copy of program, etc., address Bro. J. C. Seibert, Hill's Siding, Iowa.

ONE of our exchanges says: "The record of crime in our country increases at a fearful rate. True, as the population increases, the facilities for the transmission of news increase, and the disposition on the part of the secular press to gather and report such items increases; but still, so far as we can learn, the increase of crime is proportioned to all these, and crime, too, of the most flagrant character. Attention should be given to this matter and close investigation made, both as to the cause and the cure.

THIRTY members have been added to the Antioch church, Bedford County, Va., since last August. The cause seems to be prospering encouragingly in that part of the State.

IF we had to be judged by one another, the probability is that not one of us would be saved. But we have a Judge who knows mercy as well as justice, and we can freely trust him.

AT the late District Meeting in Southern Illinois Bro. D. B. Gibson was Moderator; Conrad Fitz, Reading Clerk, and Chas. Gibson, Writing Clerk. Bro. John Harshbarger will represent the District on the next Standing Committee.

BRO. SIDNEY HODGDEN will represent Oregon, Washington and Idaho on the Standing Committee at the next Annual Meeting. The District is composed of seven congregations and they were all represented at the late District Meeting but one. One of the congregations was represented by a sister.

BRO. D. M. MILLER, of Milledgeville, goes to Laurens, Pocahontas Co., Iowa, this week, to hold a series of meetings, and may remain several weeks. He reminds us that we should never say in print, "Church of my choice," but the "Lord's choice," saying that "choice implies variety, hence justifies denominational divisions."

OCCASIONALLY we find money folded in between the pages of manuscript intended for publication. This is a very unsafe way of doing, as manuscript is sometimes laid to one side for weeks before the editor can get time to examine it. Please remember and write your business matter on a sheet separate and apart from the matter intended for publication, and do not fail to give your name and address in each instance.

IT is remarkable how careless some people are about the letters sent to an office like this. A few days ago we received a letter mailed in Missouri. On opening it we found a blank sheet of white paper, but not one word in writing. A day later an envelope came from Virginia with not one thing in it, not even a piece of paper. From Oklahoma Territory comes a letter containing $1.50, but the contents of the letter shows that it was intended for some intimate friend instead of us. As there is nothing about any of these letters to indicate who they are from, they, of course, cannot be answered, and at least three persons will soon feel that there is something wrong with this office.

IN these columns we do not often refer to political questions, or to the contests of the different political parties, but at this time it seems but due to the good name of our church and people that the following statement be made. Eld. S. H. Bashor is a candidate for election to Congress in this Congressional District, and we are receiving inquiries from parties not acquainted with our people as to whether he is a member and a minister in our church. It is only right that we should say that Eld. Bashor is not, and has not been a member of the German Baptist Brethren (Dunkard) church for a number of years. The Dunkards do not take an active part in politics and do not approve of any of their members running for a political office. We wish it distinctly understood that the party here referred to has no connection whatever with our church. He is a member of the Progressive Brethren church, and if, in the conduct of his canvass for a seat in Congress, he lowers the dignity of the Christian ministry and brings reproach upon the church of which he is a member, our people should not bear the censure arising from his conduct.

"THE publication of the proceedings of the London Oriental Society will, this year, be looked for with some interest. It is said that important discoveries, bearing directly on Biblical history and chronology, have been made, both in Palestine and in Assyria. Thousands of the volumes of Nebuchadnezzar's library are being translated, and the appearance of the results may throw much light on the books of Kings and Daniel."

IT is said that the Sunday-school superintendent of a certain "Christian Church" asked a lady of the world to join that church. She responded thus: "I think you ought to be ashamed of yourself. You dance and call out for 'dances, you play cards, play crap, and drink whiskey, and you ought to be ashamed to ask me to join your church." Professing Christians, who ask others to come to the church might do well to first pause and see whether their own light is shining as it ought.

PRIMITIVE CHRISTIANITY.

NEVER before have we been prepared to give our readers such interesting and valuable matter as will likely appear in the MESSENGER during the next year. In addition to letters from the Seven Churches of Asia, the Land of Goshen, Mt. Sinai and other parts of Bible Lands, we have arranged for a series of well-prepared articles, setting forth Primitive Christianity, as understood and practiced by the Brethren. These articles will be prepared by some of our best writers and examined with great care. Some of the writers have already spent months on their part of the work. In all there will be about eighty articles, presented in nearly forty chapters. The following is a list of the greater part of the subjects that will be treated in the order in which they appear here:

1. "Our Reasons for Receiving the Bible as the Word of God, and Our only Rule of Faith and Practice." Giving the origin and a brief history of the Bible; clear proof of its inspiration and adaptation to man, and reasons for accepting it.

2. "The Law and the Gospel." The Old and New Covenants—Moses the lawgiver for the former, and Christ for the latter. Show the difference between the Law and the Gospel, and how we are now living under the Gospel and not under the Law.

3. "Christ the Head and Founder of the Church." Showing the Divinity and Sonship of Christ,—the long-promised Messiah; his death, burial, resurrection and ascension, now the head of the church and our Lawgiver.

4. "Man's Need of a Savior." Showing the fall of man from his pure state, his inability to rescue himself, and the necessity of the atonement.

5. "Faith." What it is, what it embraces and its necessity. What the sinner must believe in order to have salvation, and how faith without works is dead.

6. "Repentance." What it is, its design and necessity. Show what genuine Gospel repentance is, and what it accomplishes in the life and character of a sinner as a step in his salvation from sin.

7. "Baptism; Subjects and Design." Showing that it is a divine command, intended for those capable of understanding the Gospel, believing it and repenting of their sins, and not for innocent children. That, in connection with faith and repentance, it is for the remission of sins, being one of the conditions of pardon.

WHAT OF OUR CHILDREN?

Number Two.

WHEN the Apostle commanded parents to "bring up their children in the nurture and admonition of the Lord" he meant that they should train them physically, mentally, and morally in such a manner as would be approved by the Lord.

An infant is a feeble and helpless object. Every member of his physical being needs to be developed and strengthened. While nature, in a measure, has provided for this in the ceaseless activity of childhood, the unwearied care of parents is also demanded. It is the duty of parents to see that their children have a suitable quantity of wholesome and nourishing food, regular and appropriate hours of sleep, and abundant recreation in pure air.

They should also early be taught to perform manual labor, and with due caution, to endure hardships. In a word their training should be such as will, if possible, develop for them, not only full grown, but symmetrical, vigorous, enduring bodies. The blessings of good health through life, depend much upon the parental care and training in childhood. Hence, parents who bring up their children delicately and indolently, with frail and feeble bodies, or, on the other hand, impose unsuitable tasks and crushing burdens upon them, or give them unwholesome food, inflict an injury upon their children which gold cannot recompense, nor tears recall;—an injury for which parents are responsible and for which they will be brought into judgment.

The child also brings with him into the world mental powers in embryo form. These are given him to be developed by proper use and exercise. In other words, the child was designed to be educated. Proper education is as needful for the child's mind as food and clothing are for his body, and the duty of providing for both devolves upon the parents. The divine command brings parents under obligation to do what they can—all they can for the intellectual culture and development of their children. Nothing can justify parental neglect in this important matter. True, parents may be so circumstanced that they cannot do all they would for their children; but they who think to substitute wealth for education, allowing their children to grow up in ignorance, inflict wrong upon their children for which there is neither excuse nor redemption.

Another summer is gone, and its harvests are gathered. Is any part of it due to our children? The part they took in plowing, planting, cultivating and gathering, afforded them ample facilities for physical culture and development; and their faithfulness in laboring for us aided materially in replenishing our coffers. What shall we do with the part which is, strictly speaking, due to them? Shall it be appropriated to adding additional acres? Shall it be spent in having a gay time in the social circles of the world, or had it better be spent in sending them to a school affording facilities for intellectual and spiritual training and development? Let us not neglect the mental and religious training of our children.   J. G. R.

"THERE is no fortune so good but that it may be reversed, and none so bad but it may be bettered. The sun that rises in clouds may set in splendor, and that which rises in pleasure may set in gloom."

CORRESPONDENCE.

"Write what thou seest, and send it unto the churches."

Church News solicited for this Department. If you have had a good meeting, send a report of it, so that others may rejoice with you, in writing give name of church, County and State. Be brief. Notes of Travel should be as short as possible. Land Advertisements are not solicited for this Department. We have an advertising page, and, if necessary, will issue supplements.

Notes from the Canada Mission Field.

AT the close of the meetings, at Clarence, N. Y., Aug. 21, I proceeded to Hespeler, Canada, where I arrived Aug. 23. From the above date to Sept. 9 I did quite an amount of fireside preaching,—i. e., visiting from house to house, distributing tracts, and talking of the "things concerning the kingdom of God." In some cases the great question of salvation can be brought closer home to the heart privately than in the public assembly.

Sept. 9 we commenced a series of meetings near Bro. John Cober's, three miles out from Hespeler, at a union meeting-house, and continued until the 18th. From thence I went to Markham, about twenty-five miles north of Toronto. Here, after a few more days of private mission work, we secured the use of a union house for a few nights,—from Sept. 27 to Oct. 2.

Oct. 4 I was conveyed from this point about thirty-five miles north-east to Lesakdale, by Bro. Samuel Horner. Here we found no opportunity to secure the use of a meeting-house, but, as in olden times, we held meetings in Bro. Hossack's private house.

Our meetings were usually well attended, considering the many other meetings, fairs, and stock shows. Then, too, the farmers were very busy threshing, etc. As usual, a number of dear souls were made to feel the great importance of salvation, but,—like the pleasure-loving Felix,—they concluded to await the "more convenient season," which, I am quite sure, will never come.

In my associations with the dear members in Canada, I found them, with a very little exception, all strong in the faith and earnestly contending for it.

It has been noticed that occasionally some of our ministers, and others, have availed themselves of the health-giving climate of Canada, during their vacations from the toils and busy cares of life, on "our side of the line." To all of such I am requested to say that when any of you come up here, remember that the dear brethren's "latch strings" are all out, and they will bid you welcome. And while you are spending a vacation up here, in this goodly land,—where there is a regular net-work of clear, sparkling lakes, pure, crystal rivers and brooks, and sweet, balsam-scented breezes, from the evergreen forests of the North,—be sure to visit those dear, isolated members. You may do them much good and cherish the good in their hearts, "while the days are going by."   D. E. BRUBAKER.

From the Yellow Creek Church, Ill.

OUR love-feast, which was held Oct. 4 and 5, is now among the things of the past. Ministering brethren from adjoining churches were David Price, Simon Yundt, Frank Myers, W. K. Moore, I. Stees, and Ezra Lutz. There was a goodly number of laymembers from other churches present. We were all built up and encouraged by the good instructions. One commendable feature of the meeting was the spirit of earnestness that was manifested throughout the entire meetings. According to previous arrangements, a choice was held for a brother to serve the church as deacon. The lot fell on Bro. John

---

Wingart, who was duly installed into office. The Lord enable and strengthen him to be faithful in discharging the duties connected with the office, that he may ever exemplify the religion of Christ in his walk and conversation!

We feel to rejoice in the God of our salvation that we can enjoy such refreshing seasons. May we ever consecrate "our lives" fully to his service, and thereby work out our soul's salvation with fear and trembling!   LEWIS E. KELTNER.   Oct. 10.

From Southern Illinois.

SEPT. 29 in company with my daughter Fannie, and B. F. Britt and wife, we started to the District Meeting in the Cole's Creek congregation, Fulton County, Ill., seventy-five miles distant. When we reached a distance of forty miles, we stopped with the Brethren in the Camp Creek church, McDonough County, to enjoy a feast with them on the evening of Sept. 1. At this place Bro. John Baker, of the Woodland church, had been holding meetings for several days. Much interest was taken in the meetings, and the Communion was one of the largest.

From here, in company with Bro. S. S. Hummer, two of his daughters, and Bro. Baker, we went to the place of District Meeting, where we enjoyed a rich feast on Monday evening with the brethren and sisters of this congregation, and the many who had come to take part in the District Meeting. This truly was a feast indeed, and long to be remembered.

On Tuesday morning, at nine o'clock, the meeting was called together by the usual order, and new officers chosen for the year. Eld. D. B. Gibson was chosen Moderator; Charles Gibson, Writing Clerk, Conrad Fitz, Reading Clerk. All matter that came before the Meeting was disposed of in a very pleasant manner, and without any manifestation of strife. This is as it should be.

This is the congregation in which Eld. Solomon Bucklew lives, and of which he has the oversight. All who attended this Meeting were well cared for and made comfortable, and feel to thank God that we have men and women who are qualified for every calling in the great Brotherhood.   H. W. STRICKLER.

From La Place, Ill.

ACCORDING to previous arrangements, Bro. Michael Flory came to the Okaw church, Sept. 10, and conducted a series of meetings, which closed Sept. 29. We were favored with good roads, good attendance, and excellent preaching, which stirred up the inner man of saint and sinner. Nine precious souls were gathered into the church by baptism, and more were near the kingdom.

Sept. 24 we celebrated the Lord's Supper. About 200 persons communed. Truly, God's children have enjoyment in this present life, as was manifested at this meeting. Sept. 26 the church met in council. Bro. Wm. Bingaman was elected to the ministry. These meetings closed with a lively interest, and will be remembered as an outpouring of the love of our Master.   E. F. WOLFE.

From the Manor Church, Md.

THROUGH a well directed train of an all-wise Providence, we were permitted to meet, according to previous arrangements, Oct. 8, to hold our semi-annual love-feast. Although it commenced raining about the hour of meeting, the attendance was large. About three hundred members surrounded the tables of the Lord. Of the above

WHAT OF OUR CHILDREN?

Number Two.

WHEN the Apostle commanded parents to "bring up their children in the nurture and admonition of the Lord" he meant that they should train them physically, mentally, and morally in such a manner as would be approved by the Lord.

An infant is a feeble and helpless object. Every member of his physical being needs to be developed and strengthened. While nature, in a measure, has provided for this in the ceaseless activity of childhood, the unwearied care of parents is also demanded. It is the duty of parents to see that their children have a suitable quantity of wholesome and nourishing food, regular and appropriate hours of sleep, and abundant recreation in pure air.

They should also early be taught to perform manual labor, and with due caution, to endure hardships. In a word their training should be such as will, if possible, develop for them, not only full grown, but symmetrical, vigorous, enduring bodies. The blessings of good health through life, depend much upon the parental care and training in childhood. Hence, parents who bring up their children delicately and indolently, with frail and feeble bodies, or, on the other hand, impose unsuitable tasks and crushing burdens upon them, or give them unwholesome food, inflict an injury upon their children which gold cannot recompense, nor tears recall;—an injury for which parents are responsible and for which they will be brought into judgment.

The child also brings with him into the world mental powers in embryo form. These are given him to be developed by proper use and exercise. In other words, the child was designed to be educated. Proper education is as needful for the child's mind as food and clothing are for his body, and the duty of providing for both devolves upon the parents. The divine command brings parents under obligation to do what they can—all they can for the intellectual culture and development of their children. Nothing can justify parental neglect in this important matter. True, parents may be so circumstanced that they cannot do all they would for their children; but they who think to substitute wealth for education, allowing their children to grow up in ignorance, inflict wrong upon their children for which there is neither excuse nor redemption.

Another summer is gone, and its harvests are gathered. Is any part of it due to our children? The part they took in plowing, planting, cultivating and gathering, afforded them ample facilities for physical culture and development; and their faithfulness in laboring for us aided materially in replenishing our coffers. What shall we do with the part which is, strictly speaking, due to them? Shall it be appropriated to adding additional acres? Shall it be spent in having a gay time in the social circles of the world, or had it better be spent in sending them to a school affording facilities for intellectual and spiritual training and development? Let us not neglect the mental and religious training of our children.   J. G. R.

"THERE is no fortune so good but that it may be reversed, and none so bad but it may be bettered. The sun that rises in clouds may set in splendor, and that which rises in pleasure may set in gloom."

CORRESPONDENCE.

"Write what thou seest, and send it unto the churches."

☞Church News solicited for this Department. If you have had a good meeting, send a report of it, so that others may rejoice with you. In writing give name of church, County and State. Be brief. Notes of Travel should be as short as possible. Land Advertisements are not solicited for this Department. We have an advertising page, and, if necessary, will issue supplements.

Notes from the Canada Mission Field.

AT the close of the meetings, at Clarence, N. Y., Aug. 21, I proceeded to Hespeler, Canada, where I arrived Aug. 23. From the above date to Sept. 9 I did quite an amount of fireside preaching,—i. e., visiting from house to house, distributing tracts, and talking of the "things concerning the kingdom of God." In some cases the great question of salvation can be brought closer home to the heart privately than in the public assembly.

Sept. 9 we commenced a series of meetings near Bro. John Cober's, three miles out from Hespeler, at a union meeting-house, and continued until the 18th. From thence I went to Markham, about twenty-five miles north of Toronto. Here, after a few more days of private mission work, we secured the use of a union house for a few nights,—from Sept. 27 to Oct. 2.

Oct. 4 I was conveyed from this point about thirty-five miles north-east to Leaskdale, by Bro. Samuel Horner. Here we found no opportunity to secure the use of a meeting-house, but, as in olden times, we held meetings in Bro. Hossack's private house.

Our meetings were usually well attended, considering the many other meetings, fairs, and stock shows. Then, too, the farmers were very busy threshing, etc. As usual, a number of dear souls were made to feel the great importance of salvation, but,—like the pleasure-loving Felix,—they concluded to await the "more convenient season," which, I am quite sure, will never come.

In my associations with the dear members in Canada, I found them, with a very little exception, all strong in the faith and earnestly contending for it.

It has been noticed that occasionally some of our ministers, and others, have availed themselves of the health-giving climate of Canada, during their vacations from the toils and busy cares of life, on "our side of the line." To all of such I am requested to say that when any of you come up here, remember that the dear brethren's "latch strings" are all out, and they will bid you welcome. And while you are spending a vacation up here, in this goodly land,—where there is a regular net-work of clear, sparkling lakes, pure, crystal rivers and brooks, and sweet, balsam-scented breezes, from the evergreen forests of the North,—be sure to visit those dear, isolated members. You may do them much good and cherish the good in their hearts, "while the days are going by."   D. E. BRUBAKER.

From the Yellow Creek Church, Ill.

OUR love-feast, which was held Oct. 4 and 5, is now among the things of the past. Ministering brethren from adjoining churches were David Price, Simon Yundt, Frank Myers, W. K. Moore, I. Stees, and Ezra Lutz There was a goodly number of laymembers from other churches present. We were all built up and encouraged by the good instructions. One commendable feature of the meeting was the spirit of earnestness that was manifested throughout the entire meetings. According to previous arrangements, a choice was held for a brother to serve the church as deacon. The lot fell on Bro. John

Wingart, who was duly installed into office. The Lord enable and strengthen him to be faithful in discharging the duties connected with his office, that he may ever exemplify the religion of Christ in his walk and conversation!

We feel to rejoice in the God of our salvation, that we can enjoy such refreshing seasons. May we ever consecrate "our lives" fully to his service, and thereby work out our soul's salvation with fear and trembling!   LEWIS E. KELTNER.
· Oct. 10.

From Southern Illinois.

SEPT. 29 in company with my daughter Fannie, and B. F. Britt and wife, we started to the District Meeting in the Cole's Creek congregation, Fulton County, Ill., seventy-five miles distant. When we reached a distance of forty miles, we stopped with the Brethren in the Camp Creek church, McDonough County, to enjoy a feast with them on the evening of Sept. 1. At this place Bro. John Baker, of the Woodland church, had been holding meetings for several days. Much interest was taken in the meetings, and the Communion was one of the largest.

From here, in company with Bro. S. S. Hummer, two of his daughters, and Bro. Baker, we went to the place of District Meeting, where we enjoyed a rich feast on Monday evening with the brethren and sisters of this congregation, and the many who had come to take part in the District Meeting. This truly was a feast indeed, and long to be remembered.

On Tuesday morning, at nine o'clock, the meeting was called together by the usual order, and new officers chosen for the year. Eld. D. B. Gibson was chosen Moderator; Charles Gibson, Writing Clerk, Conrad Fitz, Reading Clerk. All matter that came before the Meeting was disposed of in a very pleasant manner, and without any manifestation of strife. This is as it should be.

This is the congregation in which Eld. Solomon Bucklew lives, and of which he has the oversight. All who attended this Meeting were well cared for and made comfortable, and feel to thank God that we have men and women who are qualified for every calling in the great Brotherhood.   H. W. STRICKLER.

From La Place, Ill.

ACCORDING to previous arrangements, Bro. Michael Flory came to the Okaw church, Sept. 10, and conducted a series of meetings, which closed Sept. 29. We were favored with good roads, good attendance, and excellent preaching, which stirred up the inner man of saint and sinner. Nine precious souls were gathered into the church by baptism, and more were near the kingdom.

Sept. 24 we celebrated the Lord's Supper. About 200 persons communed. Truly, God's children have enjoyment in this present life, as was manifested at this meeting. Sept. 26 the church met in council. Bro. Wm. Bingaman was elected to the ministry. These meetings closed with a lively interest, and will be remembered as an outpouring of the love of our Master.   E. F. WOLFE.

From the Manor Church, Md.

THROUGH a well directed train of an all-wise Providence, we were permitted to meet, according to previous arrangements, Oct. 8, to hold our semi-annual love-feast. Although it commenced raining about the hour of meeting, the attendance was large. About three hundred members surrounded the tables of the Lord. Of the above

council, and to continue to the love-feast. The meetings were held in the evenings only, except on the intervening Sundays, when there were also forenoon services. The congregations were large and interesting, and, as an immediate result, ten dear souls were received by baptism, and two were reclaimed, making, in all, thirteen baptized and reclaimed from the council to the feast. We feel that our late meetings were the most profitable ever enjoyed by the church, at this place. Many parents were made to rejoice in seeing their dear children make the good resolve, and we trust the good seed sown may still continue to grow, and that others will be made to count the cost, and follow in the good work. May these young converts strive to overcome the tempter's snares by keeping the narrow way, wherein only the meek and humble can journey to the heavenly city.

Bro. Stahl is as yet quite young in the ministry, but notwithstanding he is a ready and forcible speaker, and his thoughts are expressed as though he meant them, and are in concise and comprehensive language. The spiritual food he serves can be easily digested by all hungering after righteousness.

Our love-feast, now in the past, will not soon be forgotten. It was the largest ever held at this place. Seventy-one members surrounded the tables of the Lord. The house was filled to its utmost capacity with friends and neighbors from quite a distance, to witness the Scriptural way in which our people celebrate the ordinances of God's house. The best of order prevailed throughout the services and feast, as well as at the meetings preceding it. The ministers from other congregations were, Eld. Joel Gnagey, H. A. Stahl and David Hochstettler. Eld. Gnagey officiated very satisfactorily.

Remarks like this were heard coming from the large crowd of lookers-on, "What a grand feast these people have!" "What a love-feast!" Yes, thank the Lord for it!   J. N. Davis.

Tub, Pa., Oct. 13.

Announcement.

By consent of the District Meeting of Southern Illinois, the ministers of the District are making arrangements to have a "Bible Term" in connection with the "Ministerial Meeting," which is to be held in the Pleasant Hill church, Dec. 20 and 21, 1892. Address your communications to the Foreman of the Committee of Arrangements, J. H. Brubaker, Virden, Ill.   Chas. Gibson,
Secretary of District Meeting.

Notes from Our Correspondents.

"As cold water to a thirsty soul, so is good news from a far country."

Fredric, Iowa.—Since our last report two more have been added to the Monroe County church by confession and baptism.—*J. M. Follis.*

Oak Level, Pa.—Five were baptized in our congregation since last report. We have arranged for a love-feast at Sharon, Oct. 30; also at Antioch, Nov. 5 and 6.—*B. E Kesler.*

Dallas Centre, Iowa.—Recently two who had left our church and gone with the Progressives, returned to the church,—"their home" as they expressed it,—during Bro. Hutchison's stay with us.—*Ella Royer, Oct. 18.*

Poplar Ridge, Ohio.—Our love-feast of Oct. 14 was a soul-refreshing feast to all present. Among those with us was old sister Arnold, the wife of Eld. John Arnold. Ministers present were elders Jeremiah Gump, C. Krabill, B. F. Sholty, John Provant, and others. Eld. Gump officiated.—*Simon Long, Jewell, Ohio.*

Boynton, Pa.—Sept. 24 I met with the saints near Lewistown, Pa, and remained with them over their love-feast Oct. 4. Two united with the church by baptism. The congregations continued to increase and the best of interest prevailed. My association with the saints will long be remembered.—*Silas Hoover.*

Sulphur Springs, Ind.—The ministers of the Southern District of Indiana are hereby notified that the programs for the Ministerial Meeting, to be held at Middletown, Dec. 6, 7, and 8, are ready for delivery. Ministers, who have not already been supplied, will write to the undersigned.—*D. F. Hoover, Oct. 19.*

Panther Creek, Ill.—Our feast was very enjoyable. All present seemed to enjoy it very much. Bro. J. G. Royer, of Mt. Morris, was with us one week, and did some most excellent preaching while here. We were sorry he could not remain longer. On the day he left, one was baptized. Bro. Royer, and Bro. Henry, of Lacon, were the only visiting ministers present at our feast.—*Geo. W. Gish.*

Ladoga, Ind.—Since my last report four have united with the church by baptism. Our love-feast was held Oct. 7. We were glad to have quite a number of brethren and sisters from other churches with us. Brother Isaac Billheimer, Bro. Fred Fessler, and Bro. D. C. Campbell were with us. Bro. Billheimer officiated. He remained over Sunday and held some very interesting meetings for us.—*Charity Himes, Oct. 14.*

Unionville, Iowa.—We held our love-feast Oct 8, which was quite an enjoyable meeting. The large church was filled to its utmost capacity. At our meeting yesterday we were made to rejoice at seeing two dear souls come out on the Lord's side. Brethren, who are laboring in the mission field, would be gladly received if they could come and hold some meetings for us. All communications will be answered by addressing the writer.—*W. H. Leavell, Oct. 17.*

Bradford, Ohio.—One more feast of the Upper Stillwater church is in the past. All certainly enjoyed it because it was full of the Spirit of God. The weather was pleasant and the crowd large. Over four hundred and fifty members communed. Our ministerial force numbered twenty-one, including the home brethren. I hope and pray it may long be remembered and the strength gained be employed in doing more for the Lord.—*S. D. Royer, Oct. 17.*

Waddam's Grove, Ill.—The Brethren of the above-named church met in council preparatory to our feast. All that was before us was adjusted in harmony and love. We decided to hold a series of meetings one week before the feast, commencing Oct. 23, at the Louisa meeting-house. We also expect to have meetings at Chelsea, on Saturday evening, and Sunday at 10:30, and to be continued at the Louisa meeting-house until the feast. Bro. Simon Yundt, of Mt. Morris, Ill., is expected to conduct all the above meetings.—*W. K. Moore, Oct. 14.*

Harlow, L. T.—Since I last wrote I made a trip down to the Coast,—Alvin or Manvel, Texas,—to take a look at that place. I found brethren Wm. Leaman, and J. J. Wassam busy at work, preparing to build their meeting-house which will be 36 by 42. Bro. Leaman, their minister, is a zealous worker in the cause of the Master. The work is progressing fairly in this part of the Master's vineyard. At our regular meeting yesterday two made application and were received by baptism in the presence of a very large crowd of spectators that came to witness our mode of baptizing for the first time.—*Elihu Moore.*

Bement, Ill.—Bro. I. M. Gibson commenced a series of meetings here Sept. 25, and closed Oct. 4. Two dear souls came out on the Lord's side. The people were very much interested in the doctrine of the Brethren. There are now nine of us and we feel much encouraged.—*Lizzie Traxler.*

Stuttgart, Ark.—We had our Communion meeting two miles south of Stuttgart, Oct. 1, at the Stuckey school-house. The crowd was not large, yet we had a very pleasant meeting. Being alone, all the labor devolved upon the writer. To-day we start to Laforge, Mo., to hold some meetings.—*Jas. R. Gish, Oct. 13.*

Belington, W. Va.—The District Meeting of the Second District of West Virginia, convened in the Valley River church Oct. 14 and 15. Considerable business was before the meeting but all passed off harmoniously. We expect, the Lord willing, to begin our series of meetings Nov. 12. Bro. Aaron Fike, of Eglon, W. Va., is expected to do the preaching.—*W. A. Gaunt, Oct. 18.*

Fairview, Iowa.—Our love-feast was held Oct. 8. Bro. Hiram Berkman, of the Monroe County church, officiated. The weather being pleasant, about sixty-five members were permitted to meet around the table of the Lord. Oct. 16, at our regular preaching services, two precious souls made known their willingness to walk with the people of God, and were received into the church by baptism.—*H. A. Whisler, Unionville, Iowa.*

Rock Run, Ind.—Oct. 14 and 15 will be days long to be remembered in the Rock Run church, Elkhart Co., Ind. Friday, Oct. 14 was our love-feast, which was indeed a feast for the soul. Rich, spiritual food was dealt out to us by our brethren A. L. Neff, George Swihart, Lemuel Hillery and others. Our dear young brother, Melvin Rensberger was elected to the ministry. May God's greatest blessing rest on and be with him in his new calling!—*Candace Hoover.*

Appanoose, Kans.—Our regular appointment for worship at the Appanoose church occurred Oct. 16. A interested audience had assembled and listened very attentively to the Word preached. After the services we repaired to the water-side, and seven dear souls were led into the liquid stream and buried with Christ in baptism to rise, we trust, to walk in newness of life. May they, with us, prove faithful, and in the end receive a crown at God's right hand, is our prayer!—*C. W. Shoemaker, Oct. 17.*

Verdigris church, Kans.—Bro. A. L. Pearsoll, of Junction City, came to us Sept. 24, one week before our Communion, and commenced a series of meetings, which was greatly enjoyed by all. Two dear souls made the good confession, and were baptized on Saturday, Oct. 1, before examination services. Brethren C. C. Gibson, Jesse Studebaker and Lewis Flack were the ministers present. We had a good meeting throughout. Brethren Adam Downing and J. A. Stouder were advanced to the second degree of the ministry. Our meetings closed Oct. 2.—*J. M. Quackenbush.*

Isabel, Oregon.—According to previous notice, Oct. 1, the members of the Mohawk Valley church, convened at the house of Bro. Jeremiah Cochell, to celebrate the suffering and death of our adorable Redeemer. Although the members are scattered over a tract of country more than fifty miles in extent, all but four were present, and participated in the Communion services. The attention and conduct of the lookers-on, as well as that of the members, is seldom, if ever, surpassed. Two brethren were chosen to fill the office of deacon. Eld. M. M. Bashor, of Sodaville, officiated.—*Jacob Bahr.*

council, and to continue to the love-feast. The meetings were held in the evenings only, except on the intervening Sundays, when there were also forenoon services. The congregations were large and interesting, and, as an immediate result, ten dear souls were received by baptism, and two were reclaimed, making, in all, thirteen baptized and reclaimed from the council to the feast. We feel that our late meetings were the most profitable ever enjoyed by the church at this place. Many parents were made to rejoice in seeing their dear children make the good resolve, and we trust the good seed sown may still continue to grow, and that others will be made to count the cost, and follow in the good work. May these young converts strive to overcome the tempter's snares by keeping the narrow way, wherein only the meek and humble can journey to the heavenly city.

Bro. Stahl is as yet quite young in the ministry, but notwithstanding he is a ready and forcible speaker, and his thoughts are expressed as though he meant them, and are in concise and comprehensive language. The spiritual food he serves can be easily digested by all hungering after righteousness.

Our love-feast, now in the past, will not soon be forgotten. It was the largest ever held at this place. Seventy-one members surrounded the tables of the Lord. The house was filled to its utmost capacity with friends and neighbors from quite a distance, to witness the Scriptural way in which our people celebrate the ordinances of God's house. The best of order prevailed throughout the services and feast, as well as at the meetings preceding it. The ministers from other congregations were, Eld. Joel Gnagey, H. A. Stahl and David Hochstettler. Eld. Gnagey officiated very satisfactorily.

Remarks like this were heard coming from the large crowd of lookers-on, "What a grand feast these people have!" "What a love-feast!" Yes, thank the Lord for it!   J. N. DAVIS.
Tub, Pa., Oct. 13.

Announcement.

By consent of the District Meeting of Southern Illinois, the ministers of the District are making arrangements to have a "Bible Term" in connection with the "Ministerial Meeting," which is to be held in the Pleasant Hill church, Dec. 20 and 21, 1892. Address your communications to the Foreman of the Committee of Arrangements, J. H. Brubaker, Virden, Ill.   CHAS. GIBSON,
Secretary of District Meeting.

Notes from Our Correspondents.

"As cold water to a thirsty soul, so is good news from a far country."

Fredric, Iowa.—Since our last report two more have been added to the Monroe County church by confession and baptism.—J. M. Follis.

Oak Level, Pa.—Five were baptized in our congregation since last report. We have arranged for a love-feast at Sharon, Oct. 30; also at Antioch, Nov. 5 and 6.—B. E Kesler.

Dallas Centre, Iowa.—Recently two who had left our church and gone with the Progressives, returned to the church,—"their home" as they expressed it,—during Bro. Hutchison's stay with us.—Ella Royer, Oct. 18.

Poplar Ridge, Ohio.—Our love-feast of Oct. 14 was a soul-refreshing feast to all present. Among those with us was old sister Arnold, the wife of Eld. John Arnold. Ministers present were elders Jeremiah Gump, C. Krabill, B. F. Sholty, John Provant, and others. Eld. Gump officiated.—Simon Long, Jewell, Ohio.

Boynton, Pa.—Sept. 24 I met with the saints near Lewistown, Pa, and remained with them over their love-feast Oct. 4. Two united with the church by baptism. The congregations continued to increase and the best of interest prevailed. My association with the saints will long be remembered.—Silas Hoover.

Sulphur Springs, Ind.—The ministers of the Southern District of Indiana are hereby notified that the programs for the Ministerial Meeting, to be held at Middletown, Dec. 6, 7, and 8, are ready for delivery. Ministers, who have not already been supplied, will write to the undersigned.—D. F. Hoover, Oct. 19.

Panther Creek, Ill.—Our feast was very enjoyable. All present seemed to enjoy it very much. Bro. J. G. Royer, of Mt. Morris, was with us one week, and did some most excellent preaching while here. We were sorry he could not remain longer. On the day he left, one was baptized. Bro. Royer, and Bro. Henry, of Lacon, were the only visiting ministers present at our feast.—Geo. W. Gish.

Ladoga, Ind.—Since my last report four have united with the church by baptism. Our love-feast was held Oct. 7. We were glad to have quite a number of brethren and sisters from other churches with us. Brother Isaac Billheimer, Bro. Fred Fessler, and Bro. D. C. Campbell were with us. Bro. Billheimer officiated. He remained over Sunday and held some very interesting meetings for us.—Charity Himes, Oct, 14.

Unionville, Iowa.—We held our love-feast Oct 8, which was quite an enjoyable meeting. The large church was filled to its utmost capacity. We had meeting yesterday we were made to rejoice at seeing two dear souls come out on the Lord's side. Brethren, who are laboring in the mission field, would be gladly received if they could come and hold some meetings for us. All communications will be answered by addressing the writer.—W. H. Leavell, Oct. 17.

Bradford, Ohio.—One more feast of the Upper Stillwater church is in the past. All certainly enjoyed it because it was full of the Spirit of God. The weather was pleasant and the crowd large. Over four hundred and fifty members communed. Our ministerial force numbered twenty-one, including the home brethren. I hope and pray it may long be remembered and the strength gained be employed in doing more for the Lord.—S. D. Royer, Oct. 17.

Waddam's Grove, Ill.—The Brethren of the above-named church met in council preparatory to our feast. All that was before us was adjusted in harmony and love. We decided to hold a series of meetings one week before the feast, commencing Oct. 28, at the Louisa meeting-house. We also expect to have meetings at Chelsea, on Saturday evening, and Sunday at 10:30, and to be continued at the Louisa meeting-house until the feast. Bro. Simon Yundt, of Mt. Morris, Ill., is expected to conduct all the above meetings.—W. K. Moore, Oct. 14.

Marlow, I. T.—Since I last wrote I made a trip to the Coast,—Alvin or Manvel, Texas,—to take a look at that place. I found brethren Wm. Loaman, and J. J. Wassam busy at work, preparing to build their meeting-house which will be 36 by 42. Bro. Leaman, their minister, is a zealous worker in the cause of the Master. The work is progressing fairly in this part of the Master's vineyard. At our regular meeting yesterday two made application and were received by baptism in the presence of a very large crowd of spectators that came to witness our mode of baptizing for the first time.—Elihu Moore.

Bement, Ill.—Bro. I. M. Gibson commenced a series of meetings here Sept. 25, and closed Oct. 4. Two dear souls came out on the Lord's side. The people were very much interested in the doctrine of the Brethren. There are now nine of us and we feel much encouraged.—Lizzie Traxler.

Stuttgart, Ark.—We had our Communion meeting two miles south of Stuttgart, Oct. 1, at the Stuckey school-house. The crowd was not large, yet we had a very pleasant meeting. Being alone, all the labor devolved upon the writer. To-day we start to Laforge, Mo., to hold some meetings.—Jas. R. Gish, Oct. 13.

Bellington, W. Va.—The District Meeting of the Second District of West Virginia, convened in the Valley River church Oct. 14 and 15. Considerable business was before the meeting but all passed off harmoniously. We expect, the Lord willing, to begin our series of meetings Nov. 12. Bro. Aaron Fike, of Eglon, W. Va., is expected to do the preaching.—W. A. Gaunt, Oct. 18.

Fairview, Iowa.—Our love-feast was held Oct. 8. Bro. Hiram Berkman, of the Monroe County church, officiated. The weather being pleasant, about sixty-five members were permitted to meet around the table of the Lord. Oct. 16, at our regular preaching services, two precious souls made known their willingness to walk with the people of God, and were received into the church by baptism.—H. A. Whisler, Unionville, Iowa.

Rock Run, Ind.—Oct. 14 and 15 will be days long to be remembered in the Rock Run church, Elkhart Co., Ind. Friday, Oct. 14 was our love-feast, which was indeed a feast for the soul. Rich, spiritual food was dealt out to us by our brethren A. L. Neff, George Swihart, Lemuel Hillery and others. Our dear young brother, Melvin Rensberger was elected to the ministry. May God's greatest blessing rest on and be with him in his new calling!—Candace Hoover.

Appanoose, Kans.—Our regular appointment for worship at the Appanoose church occurred Oct. 16. A interested audience had assembled and listened very attentively to the Word preached. After the services we repaired to the water-side, and seven dear souls were led into the liquid stream and buried with Christ in baptism to rise, we trust, to walk in newness of life. May they, with us, prove faithful, and in the end receive a crown at God's right hand, is our prayer!—C. W. Shoemaker, Oct. 17.

Verdigris Church, Kans.—Bro. A. L. Pearsoll, of Junction City, came to us Sept. 24, one week before our Communion, and commenced a series of meetings, which was greatly enjoyed by all. Two dear souls made the good confession, and were baptized on Saturday, Oct. 1, before examination services. Brethren C. C. Gibson, Jesse Studebaker and Lewis Flack were the ministers present. We had a good meeting throughout. Brethren Adam Downing and J. A. Stonder were advanced to the second degree of the ministry. Our meetings closed Oct. 2.—J. M. Quackenbush.

Isabel, Oregon.—According to previous notice, Oct. 1, the members of the Mohawk Valley church, convened at the house of Bro. Jeremiah Cochell, to celebrate the suffering and death of our adorable Redeemer. Although the members are scattered over a tract of country more than fifty miles in extent, all but four were present and participated in the Communion services. The attention and conduct of the lookers-on, as well as that of the members, is seldom, if ever surpassed. Two brethren were chosen to fill the office of deacon. Eld. M. M. Bashor, of Sodaville, officiated.—Jacob Bahr.

Johnstown, Pa.—Our love-feast, held north of town last Sunday, was largely attended and was, in all respects, a season of joy. We trust that all have been benefited.—*J. B. Noffsinger.*

Linwood, Md.—We have just closed a very interesting series of meetings at the Pipe Creek church. Bro. Geo. S Arnold, of Burlington, W. Va., was with us and held forth the Word with power. One precious soul was received by baptism, and one who had strayed away from the fold returned.—*Rachel A. Pfouts, Oct. 10.*

Literary Notices.

"**Social Laws for Girls.**" When a woman of such unquestionably high position in New York society as that occupied by Mrs. Burton Harrison consents to define the best and most careful social laws for girls, our young women can well afford to listen and remember. There is every indication for a most agreeable interest in the series of articles on "The Well-bred Girl in Society," which Mrs. Harrison will begin in the November issue of *The Ladies' Home Journal.* Mrs. Harrison, in his series, take up every phase of a girl's life in society, and point out to her principally the mistakes it is wisest for her to avoid.

"**The Columbian Historical Novels.**" Vol. III, St. Augustine; A Story of the Huguenots in America. By John R. Musick. 316 pp., with Index. Illustrated with twenty-two full-page half-tone engravings and other illustrations Cloth, $1.00, gold stamps, etc., $1.50. New York, London, and Toronto: Funk & Wagnalls Company.

The romantic charm with which John R. Musick succeeded in investing the first two volumes of the Columbian Historical Novels is admirably sustained in "St. Augustine," the third of the series. This work covers the period of the establishment of St. Augustine, the oldest town in the United States, the period corresponding to the Reformation in Europe and the fierce persecution of the early Reformers. The murder of the Huguenots, who had sought a home in Florida, constitutes the chief historical episode of the work.

The author, in the preface, calls attention to the fact that historians have paid very little attention to this period, or, at least, have given it but little space in their works. Very little can be learned from the great histories of the Huguenot influence exerted in Florida, and of the persecution that followed these devoted people even to the New World. This volume especially sets forth these almost unknown, or, at least unwritten facts. The illustrations are numerous and in keeping with the high character of the book. They lighten up the text with a graphic and striking influence, calculated more strongly to impress upon the memory the fact and fiction of the volume, both of which are alike good and wholesome for readers young or old.

"**The Miracles of Our Lord.**" Expository and Homiletic. By John Laidlaw, D. D., Professor of Theology, New College, Edinburgh. Cloth, 8vo, 384 pp., $1.75. New York and Toronto: Funk & Wagnalls Company.

In this present volume we have the latest contribution to the study of the miracles. The clergyman and the student, although he may have the standard works on the miracles, cannot afford to say: "I have no use for this work." We have here a connected expository view of the miracles, their relation to one another, and the lessons to be derived from them as a whole. The work is marked by competent scholarship, sound and cautious exegesis, homiletic tact, and a wonderful suggestiveness that will probably place it among the permanent books of reference upon this interesting and important subject.

It has been said: "Christianity rests upon the Miracles of the Gospel," and hence the altruist, the skeptic, the antagonist of Christianity has always endeavored to show the unreality of these works of Jesus, knowing full well that if the people were led to disbelieve in the miracles, it would not be long before they would disbelieve in the Miracle-worker.

"**The Resultant Greek Testament,**" exhibiting the text in which the majority of modern editors are agreed. By Richard Francis Weymouth, D. D, Fellow of University College, London. 8vo, cloth, 644 pp., $3. New York and Toronto: Funk & Wagnalls Company.

The main object of this edition of the Greek Testament is to enable the student to tell at a glance the different readings in the leading editions of the Testament. Dr. Weymouth's idea is not new. He has had two predecessors on the same field. One was Dr. Scrivener, who did not, however, attempt to construct a text, but reprinted Stephen's third edition of 1550, and put in foot-notes the various readings of Lachman, Tregelles, and Tischendorf. The other is the Cambridge Greek Testament in which a text is constructed, but on the basis of those of Tregelles and Tischendorf alone; when these two editions are at variance, a determining voice is assigned

the text of Stephen when it agrees with either of the other readings; and to Lachman only when the text of Stephen differs from both. It will be seen from the title page that in the book just lacked the critical authorities are more numerous. The editor has produced a text in which (roughly speaking) the majority of the authorities named agree. At the same time he has not merely counted names, but has weighed the reasons which may have influenced an editor in adopting any particular reading. We have here, then, the only edition of the Greek Testament in which can be seen at a glance what is the present state of the Greek text of the New Testament, as determined by the consensus of the most competent editors.

Matrimonial.

"*What therefore God hath joined together, let not man put asunder.*"

PILE—MILLER.—At the residence of the officiating minister, Robert T. Hull, Oct. 2, 1892, Mr. Hamilton H. Pile and sister Tillie Miller, both of Bakersville, Somerset Co., Pa. ROBERT T. HULL.

SHINEBARGER—ZINK.—At the Portage church, Oct. 8, 1892, by the undersigned, Mr. Henry A. Shinebarger and Maggie J. Zink. J. W. REZ.

Fallen Asleep.

"*Blessed are the dead which die in the Lord.*"

CHAPMAN.—In the bounds of the Panther Creek church, Dallas Co., Iowa, Bro. Frank L. Chapman, aged 23 years, 3 months and 16 days. Deceased united with the church when quite young, and suffered for almost three years. He often expressed a desire to go home and be at rest. He called for the elders and was anointed. He leaves a father, mother, two brothers and a sister. Funeral services were conducted by Spencer Beaver from Matt. 11: 28, 29. L. A. CROUSE.

BOLLINGER.—In La Grange, Ind, Oct. 7, 1892, Daniel Bollinger, aged 82 years, 5 months and 28 days." He was born April 10, 1810, in Lancaster County, Pa. He was married July 10 to Elizabeth Brown, who died in 1884. They had eight children,—five sons and three daughters. Funeral at Shipshewana church, conducted by Bro. B. F. Leer.
B. B. BOLLINGER.

CRIPE.—In the Lower Deer Creek church, Carroll Co., Ind., Oct. 5, 1892, Nora Etta, little twin daughter of Bro. Wm. and sister Elizabeth Cripe, aged 19 days. Funeral services by the Brethren. S. H. BECHTELHEIMER.

CRIPE.—In the same place, Oct. 11, 1892, Cora Etta Cripe, twin sister to the above, aged 25 days. Funeral services by the Brethren. S. H. BECHTELHEIMER.

McCLURE.—Oct. 7, 1892, Victor, infant-son of Bro. John and sister Sarah McClure, aged 3 months and 26 days. Funeral at the Pleasant Hill church, near Virden, Ill., and interment accompanied by the writer, assisted by Chas. C. Gibson. Text, Matt. 18: 3 MICHAEL FLORY.

HUFF.—In the Springfield church, near Wawaka, Ind., Sept. 29, 1892, Bro. Abram Huff, aged 76 years and 10 days. He was born in Tuscarawas County, Ohio, Sept. 19, 1816, and was married to Sophia Trowl in 1840. He came to Noble County, Ind., in 1846 and united with the Brethren church in 1843. He served as a deacon for nearly forty years and is missed very much, as his place was seldom vacant at the church. Funeral services by Eld. Christian Weaver, who was elected to the ministry the day Bro. Huff was elected deacon. Text, Rev. 14: 13. ADAM EBEY.

SELLERS.—In the Green Spring church, Seneca Co., Ohio, Oct. 7, 1892, Bro. Frederick Sellers, aged 73 years, 10 months and 13 days. At the time of his death, which was very sudden, he was visiting in Wood County with his youngest son. He ate a hearty dinner, and when nearly through, he seemed to be choking, and went to the well for a drink. His son, noticing his strange actions, went to his assistance, and got him back to the porch where he expired. He was a member of the Brethren church about forty-five years, and served as a deacon over thirty-five years. He leaves a wife and eight children. His remains were brought home the day after his death, and the funeral service was conducted by Eld. S. M. Loose, assisted by Bro. J. B. Light.
LIDA SELLERS.

PEARSON.—At Progress, Colo., Oct. 1, 1892, Nellie, infant daughter of friend John E. and sister Ada Pearson, aged 15 days. Her days on earth were few and full of pain. Services by Rev. Manchester of the Christian church. MINA WALKER.

SHROCK.—In the Swan Creek church, Fulton Co., Ohio, Oct. 8, 1892, Bro. Emanuel Shrock, aged 74 years, 1 month and 5 days. He was born in Somerset County, Pa., and moved to the above place thirty-five years ago. Funeral services by Eld. Perry McKinney. DAVID BERKEYBILE.

REES.—Near Jersey City, Ohio, Aug. 11, 1892, Ira Burton Rees, aged 14 years, 5 months and 24 days. Deceased was the son of Bro. J. W. and S. E. Rees. The funeral was preached at the house, all the rest of the family being sick at the time. Funeral services by J. C. Witmore and J. R. Kulbill. J. W. REES.

STIVERSON.—At Moscow, Idaho, Maud Bell, daughter of J. U. G. and Sarah Stiverson, aged 6 months and 23 days. Funeral sermon by the writer. SIDNEY HODGDEN.

SHOWALTER.—In the James Creek church, Huntingdon Co., Pa, Sept. 4, 1892, Bro. John A. Showalter, aged 30 years, 9 months and 3 days.

NORRIS.—Also in the same congregation, Sept. 19, 1892, sister Nancy Norris, aged 68 years, 2 months and 21 days. Funeral services by the undersigned. GEO. BRUMBAUGH.

MALEY.—At Rosedale, Cambria Co., Pa., Oct. 3, 1892, of inflammation of the brain, Olive M. Maley, aged 1 year, 8 months and 2 days. She was the only child of Annie, and grandchild of Bro. William and sister Susan Ford. She was sick only about ten days, but an intense sufferer. Funeral services by Bro. Ananias Myers from Matt. 19: 13, 14, Oct. 5, when the little body was consigned to the tomb in the Roshoff cemetery. EMILY R. STIFLER.

MALEY.—In the Johnstown (Walnut Grove) church, Cambria Co., Pa., Aug. 29, 1892, Bro. William Henry Maley, aged 40 years, 5 months and 18 days. He was a consistent member of the Brethren church He was attending to his duties at the large iron works at Johnstown, when an explosion occurred and he was burned amid the burning cinders. His entire body was badly burned. He was removed to the hospital where he expired in a few hours. He requested to be anointed, but expired before it could be attended to. He leaves a sorrowing widow, two step-daughters and two little sons. EMILY M. STIFLER.

KURTZ.—In the Union City church, Ind., Oct. 14, 1892, sister Elizabeth Kurtz (*nee* Royer), aged 80 years, 5 months and 19 days. She was married in 1831 and was the mother of eight children. She united with the church early in life. Funeral discourse by the Brethren to a large audience from John 11: 25, "I am the resurrection and the life; he that believeth in me, though he were dead, yet shall he live."
W. E. Stuckman.

MYERS.—In the bounds of the Rocky Ridge church, Md., Sept. 29, 1892, Annie Otelia, daughter of Bro. Joel and sister Mary Myers, aged 6 years, 11 months and 21 days. Little Lela was a great sufferer in her short life, but was so patient that she was loved by all who knew her. Interment in the Pipe Creek cemetery. Funeral services conducted by Bro. Thomas Kolb. RACHEL A. PFOUTS.

MILLER.—In the Swan Creek church, Delta, Ohio, Sept. 27, 1892, aged 51 years, 10 months and 14 days, Lydia J. Miller, formerly of Johnstown, Pa Seventeen years ago she moved to the above place. She was a great sufferer for three years. She called for the elders shortly before her death and was anointed with oil in the name of the Lord. Funeral by Eld. Perry McKinney, assisted by Bro. William McKinney.
D. BERKEYBILE.

The Gospel Messenger

Is the recognized organ of the German Baptist or Brethren's church, and advocates the form of doctrine taught in the New Testament and pleads for a return to apostolic and primitive Christianity.

It recognizes the New Testament as the only infallible rule of faith and practice, and maintains that Faith toward God, Repentance from dead works, Regeneration of the heart and mind, baptism by Trine Immersion for remission of sins unto the reception of the Holy Ghost by the laying on of hands, are the means of adoption into the household of God,—the church militant.

It also maintains that Feet-washing, as taught in John 13, both by example and command of Jesus, should be observed in the church.

That the Lord's Supper, instituted by Christ and as universally observed by the apostles and the early Christians, is a full meal, and, in connection with the Communion, should be taken in the evening or after the close of the day.

That the Salutation of the Holy Kiss, or Kiss of Charity, is binding upon the followers of Christ.

That War and Retaliation are contrary to the spirit and self-denying principles of the religion of Jesus Christ.

That the principle of Plain Dressing and of Non-conformity to the world, as taught in the New Testament, should be observed by the followers of Christ.

That the Scriptural duty of Anointing the Sick with Oil, in the Name of the Lord, James 5: 14, is binding upon all Christians.

It also advocates the church's duty to support Missionary and Tract Work, thus giving to the Lord for the spread of the Gospel and the conversion of sinners.

In short, it is a vindicator of all that Christ and the apostles have enjoined upon us, and aims, amid the conflicting theories and discords of modern Christendom, to point out ground that all must concede to be infallibly safe.

The above principles of our Fraternity are set forth on our Brethren's Envelopes.* Use them! Price 15 cents per package; 40 cents per hundred.

Johnstown, Pa.— Our love-feast, held north of town last Sunday, was largely attended and was, in all respects, a season of joy. We trust that all have been benefited.—*J. B. Noffsinger.*

Linwood, Md.—We have just closed a very interesting series of meetings at the Pipe Creek church. Bro. Geo. S Arnold, of Burlington, W. Va., was with us and held forth the Word with power. One precious soul was received by baptism, and one who had strayed away from the fold returned.—*Rachel A. Pfouts, Oct. 10.*

Literary Notices.

"Social Laws for Girls." When a woman of such unquestionably high position in New York society as that occupied by Mrs. Burton Harrison consents to define the best and most careful social laws for girls, our young women can well afford to listen and remember. There is every indication for a most agreeable interest in the series of articles on "The Weihbred Girl in Society," which Mrs. Harrison will begin in the November issue of *The Ladies' Home Journal.* Mrs. Harrison will, in this series, take up every phase of a girl's life in society, and point out to her principally the mistakes it is wisest for her to avoid.

"The Columbian Historical Novels." Vol. III, St. Augustine; A Story of the Huguenots in America. By John R. Musick. 316 pp. with Index. Illustrated with twenty-two full-page half-tone engravings and other illustrations. Cloth, 12mo, gold stamps, etc., $4.50 New York, London, and Toronto: Funk & Wagnalls Company.

The romantic charm with which John R. Musick succeeded in investing the first two volumes of the Columbian Historical Novels is admirably sustained in "St. Augustine," the third of the series. This work covers the period of the establishment of St. Augustine, the oldest town in the United States, the period corresponding to the Reformation in Europe and the fierce persecution of the early Reformers. The murder of the Huguenots, who had sought a home in Florida, constitutes the chief historical episode of the work.

The author, in the preface, calls attention to the fact that historians have paid very little attention to this period, or, at least, have given it but little space in their works. Very little can be learned from the great histories of the Huguenot influence exerted in Florida, and of the persecution that followed these devoted people even to the New World. This volume especially sets forth these almost unknown, or, at least unwritten facts. The illustrations are numerous and in keeping with the high character of the book. They lighten up the text with a graphic and striking influence, calculated more strongly to impress upon the memory the fact and fiction of the volume, both of which are alike good and wholesome for readers young or old.

"The Miracles of Our Lord." Expository and Homiletic. By John Laidlaw, D. D., Professor of Theology, New College, Edinburgh. Cloth, 8vo, 384 pp., $1.75. New York and Toronto: Funk & Wagnalls Company.

In this present volume we have the latest contribution to the study of the miracles. The clergyman and the student, although he may have the standard works on the miracles, cannot afford to say: "I have no use for this work." We have here a connected expository view of the miracles, their relation to one another, and the lessons to be derived from them as a whole. The work is marked by competent scholarship, sound and cautious exegesis, homiletic tact, and a wonderful suggestiveness that will probably place it among the permanent books of reference upon this interesting and important subject.

It has been said: "Christianity rests upon the Miracles of the Gospel," and hence the difficult, the skeptic, the antagonist of Christianity has always endeavored to show the unreality of these works of Jesus, knowing full well that if the people were led to disbelieve in the miracles, it would not be long before they would disbelieve in the Miracle-worker.

"The Resultant Greek Testament," exhibiting the text in which the majority of modern editors are agreed. By Richard Francis Weymouth, D. D., Fellow of University College, London. 8vo, cloth, 644 pp., $3. New York and Toronto: Funk & Wagnalls Company.

The main object of this edition of the Greek Testament is to enable the student to tell at a glance the different readings in the leading editions of the Testament. Dr. Weymouth's idea is not new. He has had two predecessors on the same field. One was Dr. Scrivener, who did not, however, attempt to construct a text, but reprinted Stephen's third edition of 1550, and put in foot-notes the various readings of Lachman, Tregelles, and Tischendorf. The other is the Cambridge Greek Testament in which a text is constructed, but on the basis of those of Tregelles and Tischendorf alone; when these two editions are at variance, a determining voice is allowed to the text of Stephen when it agrees with either of the other readings; and to Lachman only when the text of Stephen differs from both. It will be seen from the title page that in the book just issued the critical authorities are more numerous. The editor has produced a text in which (roughly speaking) the majority of the authorities named agree. At the same time he has not merely counted names, but has weighed the reasons which may have influenced an editor in adopting any particular reading. We have here, then, the only edition of the Greek Testament in which can be seen at a glance what is the present state of the Greek text of the New Testament, as determined by the consensus of the most competent editors.

Matrimonial.

"What therefore God hath joined together, let not man put asunder."

PILE—MILLER.—At the residence of the officiating minister, Robert T. Hull, Oct. 2, 1892, Mr. Hamilton H. Pile and sister Tillie Miller, both of Bakersville, Somerset Co., Pa. ROBERT T. HULL.

SHINEBARGER—ZINK.—At the Portage church, Oct. 8, 1892, by the undersigned, Mr. Henry A. Shinebarger and Maggie J. Zink. J. W. REZ.

Fallen Asleep.

"Blessed are the dead which die in the Lord."

CHAPMAN.—In the bounds of the Panther Creek church, Dallas Co. Iowa, Bro. Frank L. Chapman, aged 23 years, 3 months and 16 days. Deceased united with the church when quite young, and suffered for almost three years. He often expressed a desire to go home and be at rest. He called for the elders and was anointed. He leaves a father, mother, two brothers and a sister. Funeral services were conducted by Spencer Beaver from Matt. 11:28, 29. L. A. CROUSE.

BOLLINGER.—In La Grange, Ind, Oct. 7, 1892, Daniel Bollinger, aged 81 years, 3 months and 28 days. He was born April 10, 1810, in Lancaster County, Pa. He was married to Elizabeth Bown, who died in 1884. They had eight children,—five sons and three daughters. Funeral at Shepshewana church, conducted by Bro. B. F. Leer. B. B. BOLLINGER.

CRIPE.—In the Lower Deer Creek church, Carroll Co., Ind., Oct. 5, 1892, Nora Edie, little twin daughter of Bro. Wm. and sister Elizabeth Cripe, aged 13 days. Funeral services by the Brethren. S. H. BECHTELHEIMER.

CRIPE.—In the same place, Oct. 11, 1892, Cora Ella Cripe, twin sister to the above, aged 25 days. Funeral services by the Brethren. S. H. BECHTELHEIMER.

McCLURE.—Oct. 7, 1892, Victor, infant son of Bro. John and sister Sarah McClure, aged 3 months and 26 days. Funeral at the Pleasant Hill church, near Virden, Ill., and interment conducted by the writer, assisted by Chas. C. Gibson. Text, Matt 18:3 MICHAEL FLORY.

HUFF.—In the Springfield church, near WaWaka, Ind., Sept 29, 1892, Bro. Abram Huff, aged 76 years, and 10 days. He was born in Tuscarawas County, Ohio, Sept. 19, 1816, and was married to Sophia Trowl in 1840. He came to Noble County, Ind., in 1846 and united with the Brethren church in 1843. He served as a deacon for nearly forty years and is missed very much, as his place was seldom vacant at the church. Funeral services by Eld. Christian Weaver, who was elected to the ministry the day Bro. Huff was elected deacon. Text, Rev. 14: 13. ADAM EBEY.

SELLERS.—In the Green Spring church, Seneca Co., Ohio, Oct. 7, 1892, Bro. Frederick Sellers, aged 73 years, 10 months and 13 days. At the time of his death, which was very sudden, he was visiting in Wood County with his youngest son. He ate a hearty dinner, and then nearly through, he seemed to be choking, and went to the well for a drink. His son, noticing his strange actions, went to his assistance, and got him back to the porch where he expired. He was a member of the Brethren church about forty-five years, and served as a deacon over thirty-five years. He leaves a wife and eight children. His remains were brought home the day after his death, and the funeral services was conducted by Eld. S. M. Loose, assisted by Bro. J. B. Light. LIDA SELLERS.

PEARSON.—At Progress, Colo., Oct. 1, 1892, Nellie, infant daughter of friend John R. and sister Ada Pearson, aged 15 days. Her days on earth were few and full of pain. Services by Rev. Manchester of the Christian church. MINA WALKER.

SHROCK.—In the Swan Creek church, Fulton Co., Ohio, Oct. 8, 1892, Bro. Emanuel Shrock, aged 74 years, 1 month and 5 days. He was born in Somerset County, Pa., and moved to the above place thirty-five years ago. Funeral services by Eld. Perry McKinney. DAVID BERKEYBILE.

REES.—Near Jersey City, Ohio, Aug. 11, 1892, Ira Burton Rees, aged 14 years, 5 months and 24 days. Deceased was the son of Bro. J. W. and S. E. Rees. The funeral was preached at his house, all the rest of the family being sick at the time. Funeral services by J. C. Witmore and J. P. Krabill. J. W. REES.

STIVERSON.—At Moscow, Idaho, Maud Bell, daughter of J. U. G. and Sarah Stiverson, aged 6 months and 23 days. Funeral sermon by the writer. SIDNEY HODGDEN.

SHOWALTER.—In the James Creek church, Huntingdon Co., Pa., Sept. 4, 1892, Bro. John A. Showalter, aged 39 years, 9 months and 3 days.

NORRIS.—Also in the same congregation, Sept. 19, 1892, sister Nancy Norris, aged 68 years, 2 months and 21 days. Funeral services by the undersigned. GEO. BRUMBAUGH.

MALEY.—At Rosedale, Cambria Co., Pa., Oct. 3, 1892, of inflammation of the brain, Olive M. Maley, aged 1 year, 8 months and 2 days. She was the only child of Annie, and grandchild of Bro. William and sister Susan Ford. She was sick only about ten days, but an intense sufferer. Funeral services by Bro. Ananias Myers from Matt. 19: 13, 14, Oct. 5, when the little body was consigned to the tomb in the Bennshoff cemetery. EMILY R. STIFLER.

MALEY.—In the Johnstown (Walnut Grove) church, Cambria Co., Pa., Aug. 29, 1892, Bro. William Henry Maley, aged 40 years, 5 months and 18 days. He was a consistent member of the Brethren church. He was attending to his duties at the large iron works at Johnstown, when an explosion occurred and he was burned amid the burning cinders. His entire body was badly burned. He was removed to the hospital where he expired in a few hours. He requested to be anointed, but expired before it could be attended to. He leaves a sorrowing widow, two step-daughters and two little sons. EMILY R. STIFLER.

KURTZ.—In the Union City church, Ind., Oct. 14, 1891, sister Elizabeth Kurtz (nee Royer), aged 82 years, 5 months and 19 days. She was married in 1831 and was the mother of eight children. She united with the church early in life. Funeral discourse by the Brethren to a large audience from John 11:25, "I am the resurrection and the life; he that believeth in me, though he were dead, yet shall he live." W. K. SIMMONS.

MYERS.—In the bounds of the Rocky Ridge church, Md., Sept. 29, 1892, Annie Otelia, daughter of Bro. Joel and sister Mary Myers, aged 6 years, 11 months and 21 days. Little Lela was a great sufferer in her short life, but was so patient that she was loved by all who knew her. Interment in the Pipe Creek cemetery. Funeral services conducted by Bro. Thomas Kolb. RACHEL A. PFOUTE.

MILLER.—In the Swan Creek church, Delta, Ohio, Sept. 27, 1892, aged 51 years, 10 months and 14 days, Lydia I. Miller, formerly of Johnstown, Pa Seventeen years ago she moved to the above place. She was a great sufferer for three years. She called for the elders shortly before her death and was anointed with oil in the name of the Lord. Funeral by Eld. Perry McKinney, assisted by Bro. William McKinney. D. BERKEYBILE.

The Gospel Messenger

Is the recognized organ of the German Baptist or Brethren's church, and advocates the form of doctrine taught in the New Testament and pleads for a return to apostolic and primitive Christianity.

It recognizes the New Testament as the only infallible rule of faith and practice, and maintains that Faith toward God, Repentance from dead works, Regeneration of the heart and mind, baptism by Trine Immersion for remission of sins unto the reception of the Holy Ghost by the laying on of hands, are the means of adoption into the household of God,—the church militant.

It also maintains that Feet-washing, as taught in John 13, both by example and command of Jesus, should be observed in the church.

That the Lord's Supper, instituted by Christ and as universally observed by the apostles and the early Christians, is a full meal, and, in connection with the Communion, should be taken in the evening or after the close of the day.

That the Salutation of the Holy Kiss, or Kiss of Charity, is binding upon the followers of Christ.

That War and Retaliation are contrary to the spirit and self-denying principles of the religion of Jesus Christ.

That the principle of Plain Dressing and of Non-conformity to the world, as taught in the New Testament, should be observed by the followers of Christ.

That the Scriptural duty of Anointing the Sick with Oil, in the Name of the Lord, James 5: 14, is binding upon all Christians.

It also advocates the church's duty to support Missionary and Tract Work, thus giving to the Lord for the spread of the Gospel and for the conversion of sinners.

In short, it is a vindicator of all that Christ and the apostles have enjoined upon us, and aims, amid the conflicting theories and discords of modern Christendom, to point out ground that all must concede to be infallibly safe.

The above principles of our Fraternity are set forth on our Brethren's Envelopes." Use them! Price 15 cents per package; 40 cents per hundred.

Announcements.

(Concluded from preceding page.)

LOVE-FEASTS.

Nov. 8, at 10 A. M., Wheatville (Upper Twin) church, Preble Co., Ohio. R. R. Snieltns; West Alexandria and Eaton.

Nov. 8, Amwell church, Sergeantsville, N. J.

Nov. 11, at 4 P. M., Winnemac church, Beaver Creek meeting-house, 12 miles south-west of Winnemac.

✢ESSAYS✢

"Study to show thyself approved unto God; a workman that needeth not be ashamed, rightly dividing the Word of Truth."

THE RAIN STORM.

BY J. S. MOHLER.

THE heat and the drouth had smitten the land,
And drooping, the plants would mournfully stand;
And the leaves that grew on the loftiest trees
Would beseeching turn, inviting the breeze.

Not a whisper was heard from the musical bird,
Scarce a leaf on the plants or the trees was stirred;
All nature in silence would seemingly pray
That the breeze and the rain no longer delay.

A cloud in the distance is seen to arise,
Though small as a hand, soon covers the skies;
All jumbled together, the clouds in a throng,
In the fury of the storm come rolling along.

The God of the clouds has harnessed his steeds
To his chariot that run with hurricane speed,
Directing its course by the lightning's flash,
Its rumbling is heard by the thunder's crash.

Like a giant he came all over the land,
To the right and the left with the might of his hand;
He scattered the wind and the rain on the earth,
That suffered so long from the heat and the dearth.

As the storm in its fury was passing away,
The field of his conflict imploring lay
Weeping and smitten by the pitiless storm,
Forsaken and desolate, naked and torn.

But the sun, like a friend, looked over the cloud
That covered the earth with its darkening shroud,
And lifted the veil that so mournfully hung
From the face of the field so cruelly wrung.

And, reaching his arms over forest and field,
Embraced and kissed each plant that would yield,
And the drops of the rain, like tears on the leaves,
All glistened like gems as they swayed in the breeze.

He soothingly wipes away with his hand,
And causes rejoicing all over the land.
The rainbow of promise in a circle is spread
O'er the heavens,—its glory around us shed.

The birds of the forest now cheerily sing
To him who walketh on the wings of the wind,
And scatters his blessings with a bountiful hand
To all of his creatures that dwell in the land.

Morrill, Kans.

THY KINGDOM COME.

BY J. L. SWITZER.

SUPPOSE old Mother Eve, in the Garden of Eden, had known that there was a devil. Suppose she had known the nature and character of that devil. Suppose she had known that the snake that wooed her so charmingly was that devil,—do you think, under such conditions, she would have accepted the fruit and given also to Adam, that he might eat of it?

But if you think there is a possibility that even under these circumstances she still might have made choice of sin, let us suppose further. Suppose that she-had known that the 'eating of that fruit would blight every tree in the garden, that it would cause Adam and her to suffer and toil, and bring on them all the ills to which the human flesh is heir. Suppose she had known that it would cause Cain to kill Abel, that it would open the grave, that it would be the rod to smite the heart and cause it to burst forth with a continual, perpetual flood of sorrows and anguish. If she had known all these direful consequences to flow certainly from eating that fruit, do you think she would have done it?

A curious mother she would have been, truly, to do so. Now we have another important consideration right here. Mother Eve and Father Adam were at one end of human experience.

We are at the other,—or, at least, near the other end. All these things that were written afore-time were written for our LEARNING,—for our PROFIT,—that we may be THOROUGHLY FURNISHED UNTO ALL GOOD.

We certainly are very *great fools* if we don't avoid the pitfalls that Father Adam and Mother Eve, and Cain, and Judas Iscariot fell into.

We would be much more unwise than they because we have their calamity and all its direful consequences as a warning to us.

I was driving along in a procession once when I observed that one of the front wagons went down into a hole. Immediately the teams that were following turned aside and avoided the hole. They had profited by the experience of the one ahead.

We are all driving along the road of human experience. What stupendous folly it is to run into the same holes, where we know thousands of others before us have gone down to destruction! "Now all these things happened unto them for ensamples; *and are written for our admonition,* upon whom the ends of the world are come."—*Paul.*

I want to make this article rich and full,—overflowing, if possible,—with good to my fellow-men. In doing so I appeal to your plain judgment. One of the finest articles that has ever been published in the GOSPEL MESSENGER is in No. 89, written by Cyrus Bucher, of Astoria, Ill. It is fine because he appeals so naturally to our plain common sense, to notice the inconsistency of our Government, and of mankind in general, in going to great expense to keep out the microbes of cholera, while breeding, fostering, suckling, nurturing full-grown asps in our family, and disseminating them without a protest, to destroy the soul and the body too,—little brown jugs. Is the agency of the devil visible there? Answer according to your Christian good sense.

Answer another thing. Has the church legitimately any concern with these agencies that are destroying bodies and souls? What is the church placed in the world for? Is it to be a light? Is it to be a city down under the foot of the mountain or up on top of the hill?

Teaching is to emanate from the church. Who is it to go out to? Warnings are to emanate from the church. Good counsel is to flow from it. Watchmen are upon the walls to warn. Who are they to warn? We are to cry aloud and spare not. Who are we to cry to? See here: "Go ye therefore and teach all nations." "Repentance and remission of sins shall be preached among ALL NATIONS." "Preach the word to every creature." "Set ye up a standard in the land, blow the trumpet among the nations." "Cry aloud and spare not; lift up thy voice like a trumpet."

Has the church, legitimately, any concern with *national sins?* Who is the author of national, legislative sins? The devil. What are we to do with the devil? Paul says the devil is the author of spiritual wickedness in high places. It is one of his wiles. He says we should arm ourselves against him, and James says we shall "resist the devil" and make him flee. Did not all the prophets prophesy against national evils?

Did not the Savior and all the apostles,—save one,—together with John the Baptist, suffer martyrdom at the hands of political authorities for preaching against wickedness in high places?

Are we no longer to wrestle against principalities,—against powers? Are the vile edicts of government not to be spoken against, not to be resisted, ever to be dodged around by the valiant soldiers of the cross?

Are these national mistakes to be winked at as "friends of grace, to help us on to God"? No sir! No sir! No sir!

If we love our country, we will tell it of its faults and teach it how to correct them. If we are faithful soldiers of Jesus, we will meet sin with a holy and stern resistance, wherever found, wherever it emanates from, and we will not interpret Paul's language, when he says, "Let every soul be bjec unto the higher powers," to mean that we shall be subject to their sins, and leave their festering schemes of abomination and corruption go unrebuked. Whenever we have opportunity, 't is our duty to cast our influence,—all our influence,—the whole weight and power of our word and deed, and all the gentle pressure and the irresistible impulses f the power of the Spirit of God within us, in favor of means that run parallel to, and in harmony with, the perfections of the kingdom of heaven, which we are continually praying for, that it might come. By this means we show consistency to that prayer, and this other beautiful one, which implores that the kingdom of this world may speedily become the kingdom of our Lord Jesus Christ. If we make these prayers, we should work to this end. Let our beloved brethren think of these things!

OBJECT LESSONS.

BY J. S. FLORY.

BY all means we should not overlook the intent and purpose of God, 'n giving commandments and ordinances for observance under the Gospel Dispensation.

The simplicity that is in Christ (2 Cor. 11: 3) is, in this way, made more manifest and plain to our finite minds. Object lessons more readily impress the mind than lessons in theory only. Our educators of to-day are becoming more and more impressed with the idea that it is the better course to pursue with the expanding minds of our youth. Books, with appropriate object lessons, are on the increase. In almost all branches of learning this course is now being pursued. The Great Teacher of all teachers adopted this course nearly two thousand years ago. The plan has been in vogue, relative to the teaching of theology, all those years, and yet how slow the world is to learn! Yea, we might say how slow the professing Christian world is to learn the great, grand, impressive, God-ordained truths of the Gospel! Ignoring the practical lessons, taught by Christ under the object lesson -system, our would-be teachers of Bible truths seem to think all that is necessary now is theory. It is theory only, in regard to faith; theory only, in regard to hope; theory only, in regard to charity; really, theory only, in regard to the redemptive plan of salvation.

It is true, many illustrations and vivid imaginary pictures are drawn to stir up the sensitive feelings of the hearers, but in reality the grotesque and unsymmetrical burlesques, originating from the minds of our modern preachers, only tend to darken counsel, and cripple the faith once delivered to the saints.

"I fear," says Paul, "lest by any means, as the serpent beguiled Eve, through his subtilty, so your minds should be corrupted from the simplicity that is in Christ."

The influence that corrupted the mind of Eve was of such a nature as to cause her to aspire to a higher life, independent of entire obedience to God. The same influence is prevalent to-day. Only so you have the spirit of obedience, you shall not surely die, says the old dragon, notwithstanding it is positively declared that Christ is the author of salvation unto all them that obey him. By some means the corrupting influence has gone out that he is the author of salvation to all them that theoretically believe in him. Faith

❖ESSAYS❖

"Study to shew thyself approved unto God; a workman that needeth not to be ashamed, rightly dividing the Word of Truth."

THE RAIN STORM.

BY J. S. MOHLER.

The heat and the drouth had smitten the land,
And drooping, the plants would mournfully stand;
And the leaves that grew on the loftiest trees
Would beseeching turn, inviting the breeze.

Not a whisper was heard from the musical bird,
Scarce a leaf on the plants or the trees was stirred;
All nature in silence would seemingly pray
That the breeze and the rain no longer delay.

A cloud in the distance is seen to arise,
Though small as a hand, soon covers the skies;
All jumbled together, the clouds in a throng,
In the fury of the storm come rolling along.

The God of the clouds has harnessed his steeds
To his chariot that run with hurricane speed,
Directing its course by the lightning's flash,
Its rumbling is heard by the thunder's crash.

Like a giant he came all over the land,
To the right and the left with the might of his hand;
He scattered life wind and the rain on the earth,
That suffered so long from the heat and the dearth.

As the storm in its fury was passing away,
The field of his conflict imploring lay
Weeping and smitten by the pitiless storm,
Forsaken and desolate, naked and torn.

But the sun, like a friend, looked over the cloud
That covered the earth with its darkening shroud,
And lifted the veil that so mournfully hung
From the face of the field so cruelly wrung.

And, reaching his arms over forest and field,
Embraced and kissed each plant that would yield,.
And the drops of the rain, like tears on the leaves,
All glistened like gems as they swayed in the breeze.

He soothingly wipes away with his hand,
And causes rejoicing all over the land.
The rainbow of promise in a circle is spread
O'er the heavens,—its glory around us shed.

The birds of the forest now cheerily sing
To him who walketh on the wings of the wind,
And scatters his blessings with a bountiful hand
To all of his creatures that dwell in the land.

Merrill, Kans.

THY KINGDOM COME.

BY J. L. SWITZER.

Suppose old Mother Eve, in the Garden of Eden, had known that there was a devil. Suppose she had known the nature and character of that devil. Suppose she had known that the snake that wooed her so charmingly was that devil,—do you think, under such conditions, she would have accepted the fruit and given also to Adam, that he might eat of it?

But if you think there is a possibility that even under these circumstances she still might have made choice of sin, let us suppose farther. Suppose that she-had known that the eating of that fruit would blight every tree in the garden, that it would cause Adam and her to suffer and toil, and bring on them all the ills to which the human flesh is heir. Suppose she had known that it would cause Cain to kill Abel, that it would open the grave, that it would be the rod to smite the heart and cause it to burst forth with a continual, perpetual flood of sorrows and anguish. If she had known all these direful consequences to flow certainly from eating that fruit, do you think she would have done it?

A curious mother she would have been, truly, to do so. Now we have another important consideration right here. Mother Eve and Father Adam were at one end of human experience.

We are at the other,—or, at least, near the other end. All these things that were written afore-

time were written for our LEARNING,—for our PROFIT,—that we may be THOROUGHLY FURNISHED UNTO ALL GOOD.

We certainly are very *great fools if* we don't avoid the pitfalls that Father Adam and Mother Eve, and Cain, and Judas Iscariot fell into.

We would be much more unwise than they because we have their calamity and all its direful consequences as a warning to us.

I was driving along in a procession once when I observed that one of the front wagons went down into a hole. Immediately the teams that were following turned aside and avoided the hole. They had profited by the experience of the one ahead.

We are all driving along the road of human experience. What stupendous folly it is to run into the same holes, where we know thousands of others before us have gone down to destruction! "Now all these things happened unto them for ensamples; *and are written for our admonition,* upon whom the ends of the world are come."— *Paul.*

I want to make this article rich and full,—overflowing, if possible,—with good to my fellow-men. In doing so I appeal to your plain judgment. One of the finest articles that has ever been published in the GOSPEL MESSENGER is in No. 39, written by Cyrus Bucher, of Astoria, Ill. It is fine because he appeals so naturally to our plain common sense, to notice the inconsistency of our Government, and of mankind in general, in going to great expense to keep out the microbes of cholera, while breeding, fostering, suckling, nurturing full-grown asps in our family, and disseminating them without a protest, to destroy the soul and the body too,—little brown jugs. Is the agency of the devil visible there? Answer according to your Christian good sense.

Answer another thing. Has the church legitimately any concern with these agencies that are destroying bodies and souls? What is the church placed in the world for? Is it to be a light? . Is it to be a city under the foot of the mountain or up on top of the hill?

Teaching is to emanate from the church. Who is it to go out to? Warnings are to emanate from the church. Good counsel is to flow from it. Watchmen are upon the walls to warn. Who are they to warn? We are to cry aloud and spare not. Who are we to cry to? See here: "Go ye therefore and teach all nations." "Repentance and remission of sins shall be preached among ALL NATIONS." "Preach the word to every creature." "Set ye up a standard in the land, blow the trumpet among the nations." "Cry aloud and spare not; lift up thy voice like a trumpet."

Has the church, legitimately, any concern with *national sins?* Who is the author of national, legislative sins? The devil. What are we to do with the devil? Paul says the devil is the author of spiritual wickedness in high places. It is one of his wiles. He says we should· arm ourselves against him, and James says we shall "resist the devil" and make him flee. .Did not all the prophets prophesy against national evils?

Did not the Savior and all the apostles,—save one,—together with John the Baptist, suffer martyrdom at the hands of political authorities for preaching against wickedness in high places?

Are we no longer to wrestle against principalities,—against powers? Are the vile idiots of government not to be spoken against, not to be resisted, ever to be dodged around by the valiant soldiers of the cross?

Are these national mistakes to be winked at as "friends of grace, to help us on to God"? No sir! No sir! No sir!

If we love our country, we will tell it of its faults and teach it how to correct them. If we are faithful soldiers of Jesus, we will meet sin with a holy and stern resistance, wherever found, wherever it emanates from, and we will not interpret Paul's language, when he says, "Let every soul be bjee unto the higher powers," to mean that w e shall be subject to their' sins, and leave their festering schemes of abomination and corruption go unrebuked. Whenever we have opportunity, 't is our duty to cast our influence,— all our influence,—the whole weight and power of our word and deed, and all the gentle pressure and the irresistible impulses f the power of the Spirit of God within us, in favor of means that run parallel to, and in harmony with, the perfections of the kingdom of heaven, which we are continually praying for, that it might come. By this means we show consistency to that prayer, and this other beautiful one, which implores that the kingdoms of this world may speedily become the kingdom of our Lord Jesus Christ. If we make these prayers, we should work to this end. Let our beloved brethren think of these things!

OBJECT LESSONS.

BY J. S. FLORY.

By all means we should not overlook the intent and purpose of God, the giving commandments and ordinances for observance under the Gospel Dispensation.

The simplicity that is in Christ (2 Cor. 11: 3) is, in this way, made more manifest and plain to our finite minds. Object lessons more readily impress the mind than lessons in theory only. Our educators of to-day are becoming more and more impressed with the idea that it is the better course to pursue with the expanding minds of our youth. Books, with appropriate object lessons, are on the increase. In almost all branches of learning this course is now being pursued. The Great Teacher of all teachers adopted this course nearly two thousand years ago. The plan has been in vogue, relative to the teaching of theology, all those years, and yet how slow the world is to learn! Yes, we might say how slow the professing Christian world is to learn the great, grand, impressive, God-ordained truths of the Gospel! Ignoring the practical lessons, taught by Christ under the object lesson -system, our would-be teachers of Bible truths seem to think all that is necessary now is theory. It is theory only, in regard to faith; theory only, in regard to hope; theory only, in regard to charity; really, theory only, in regard to the redemptive plan of salvation.

It is true, many illustrations and vivid imaginary. pictures are drawn to stir up the sensitive feelings of the hearers, but in reality the grotesque and unsymmetrical burlesques, originating from the minds of our modern preachers, only tend to darken counsel, and cripple the faith once delivered to the saints.

"I fear," says Paul, "lest by any means, as the serpent beguiled Eve, through his subtilty, so your minds should be corrupted from the simplicity that is in Christ."

The influence that corrupted the mind of Eve was of such a nature as to cause her to aspire to a higher life, independent of entire obedience to God. The same influence is prevalent to-day. Only so you have the spirit of obedience, you shall not surely die, says the old dragon, notwithstanding it is positively declared that Christ is the author of salvation unto all them that *obey* him. By some means the corrupting influence has gone out that he is the author of salvation to all them that theoretically believe in him. Faith

CORRESPONDENCE.

" Write what thou seest, and send it unto the churches."

☞ Church News solicited for this Department. If you have had a good meeting, send a report of it, so that others may rejoice with you. In writing give name of church, County and State. Be brief. Notes of Travel should be as short as possible. Land Advertisements are not solicited for this Department. We have an advertising page, and, if necessary, will issue supplements.

Among the Brethren.

My last communication, Oct. 6, I closed at the house of brother and sister Ogg. The Root River church is cared for by Bro. Ogg. They previously had solicited me to attend their love-feast, Oct. 8 and 9. The evening of Oct. 7 we met in their comfortable house of worship. We had a sermon by Bro. Harvey Eikenberry. Next morning the writer addressed the people, and at 2:30 P. M., we had a sermon by Bro. J. F. Eikenberry. At 4:30 P. M. we met for examination services. In the evening services a goodly number of brethren and sisters participated. During this meeting the house could not give accommodation to all present. A large number had to remain outside. The writer officiated. The meeting closed before 9 P. M. Next day there was preaching at 10:30 A. M., after which dinner was given to all présent. We had preaching also at 2:30 and 7 P. M., to large and very attentive audiences. Thus closed the meetings in the Root River congregation. This was our first visit or acquaintance with the members of this congregation. It did me much good to again meet with my brethren and sisters, and enjoy a few meetings with them. For several years we have been working on the frontier, and have not often enjoyed the associations of brethren and sisters outside of our own organization, and the great love manifested by my dear brethren and sisters toward us made it one of the most pleasant seasons of our life in the Lord's service.

Oct. 10 Bro. Joseph Ogg kindly took Bro. Samuel D. Ogg, his son, now of Minneapolis, and myself, to Lime Springs, Iowa, where we took the train. Bro. Ogg went to Minneapolis, and I to Winnebago City, Minn., where I was met by my old acquaintance, Mr. and Mrs. R. H. Hervey, who kindly took me to their pleasant home and family. They live three and one-half miles nearly west from the city. Mr. and Mrs. Hervey sustained an entire loss, by cyclone, June 15, of all their buildings and contents. Very fortunate for them the entire family escaped unhurt, by discerning the approach of the storm. They ran to the side of its pathway, and uninjured could see the labor of eighteen years all swept away. Fortunately they carried a small cyclone insurance. I left at 6:58 A. M., on the Southern Minnesota for Sioux Falls, Dak., where I stopped off and visited some members who recently moved here from the Bijou Hills church. We were made glad to meet again our friends and dear sisters in the Lord's work. I arrived in Kimball, Oct. 16.   W. G. Cook.

Bijou Hills, Dak., Oct. 18.

Chips from the Work-house.

On Saturday, Oct. 22, I attended a Communion in the Eden Valley church, Stafford Co., Kans. The meeting was held in an open corn-crib, with a shed on one side, and along the end of it, made out of headerbeds, turned on edge, and covered with canvas, used in heading grain, with a quilt fastened at the top, and a weight at the bottom, for a door into it. The ground was covered with nice, clean wheat straw for a floor, and some loose lumber laid on eight inch tile, set on end, furnished seats for spectators. This structure was well filled with very quiet, attentive listen-

ers. Around one Communion table in the corn-crib, and another under this quaint-looking shed, gathered sixty-four brethren and sisters. Some of the sisters wore heavy shawls, and some of the brethren, the writer included, had over-coats on, because of the cool weather since the recent rains. The ministerial force included three home ministers, Bro. Harnish, from Russell County; brethren Keller and Boyd, from Barton; Eld. John Wise, from Sumner, and Daniel Vaniman, from McPherson County. All the members had their hearts filled with the love of Jesus, and the shed was well filled with spectators. It soon became quite comfortable. The meeting closed at 8:30, all feeling that we surely had a good meeting.

The next morning being Lord's Day, after breakfast for neighbors and all who desired it, there was a thirty minutes' song service, then a social meeting, in which liberty was given for any brother or sister to speak, it being understood that it would be well for no one to exceed ten minutes, in order to give as many as felt to speak a word of encouragement, an opportunity to do so. Thus we had ten well-packed speeches upon various themes of our holy religion, with an occasional verse of song between speeches.

All were thus edified and encouraged and helped in the divine life. It was at this meeting again demonstrated that good and profitable meetings may be held in great simplicity, when only the heart is well filled with the love of Christ, and when there is a disposition to work with God in forwarding the work of the Lord. It is evident that this church, under the efficient oversight of Eld. John Wise, is growing both in membership and efficiency. The home ministers also seem to be doing their part well. A sister, who has been appointed solicitor for the missionary work in the church, came around and handed the writer silver and nickels down in his pocket-book could hold, to forward where it would be most needed to build up the cause of the Master. It is a singular fact that in these poor western churches, many of whom have not a meeting-house to hold Communion in, with small houses to live in, and no barns of any consequence, they are so impressed with the idea of spreading the Gospel of Christ into the borders beyond, that it seems a pleasure to give, and, in every other way that they can, to help to enlarge the borders of Zion. The causes for their readiness to help in the Lord's work, above others in more favorable circumstances, will furnish a block for more Chips in the future.   Daniel Vaniman.

From Stilson, Iowa.

Our feast in the Boon River church, Hancock Co., Iowa, occurred Sept. 24 and 25. We were blessed with good ministerial aid. Six ministers were present, among them Wm. Ikenberry, the only elder present, who officiated at our meeting. There were other brethren and sisters with us from a distance, whom we had never seen before. We were glad to have them with us. On Saturday after the examination services we were made to rejoice to see an aged sister of seventy-eight years baptized. She had been a member of the Methodist church since her youth.

The dedication of our meeting-house occurred Sept. 18. A donation of $148.10 was received at that time. Wm. Ikenberry preached from these words, " My house is called the house of prayer." Our preparatory council was a pleasant one. Bro. Wm. Ikenberry was elected as delegate to the District Meeting. Our next quarterly council will be the third Saturday of December. Bro. J. L. Thomas, of Ames, Story Co., Iowa, commenced a series of meetings Oct. 14, which con-

tinued until our feast. We learn that Bro. Harvey Ikenberry will be with us Oct. 29. Our Sunday-school, which has been known as the Stilson Sunday-school, has been moved to our new meeting-house, and will hereafter be called the Boon River Sunday-school.

    Daniel Aschenbrenner.

Messages Dropped by the Way.

Being notified by a telegram of the death of our aged brother Cline, of Rossville, I set out Oct. 15, in time to fill the Brethren's appointments at Silver Lake. The message of the funeral being too late, the funeral service was deferred till the 20th. In the meantime meetings were held in Rossville, during the week. As an immediate result two precious souls were added to the church by baptism. Others are almost persuaded. A lady visiting here, who lives at No. 9339½ Martha St., Omaha, goes away, grieving the absence of her husband, as being her only excuse for not coming now. She gives her address, in hopes that Brethren may call and see her. Her name is Mrs. Melissa Westley.

Oct. 21 we closed the meetings at Rossville, and went ten miles to the love-feast, which was held for the benefit of the isolated and scattered members. Twenty-five members were present, to participate in the Communion. These represented the vicinities of six different post-offices. Bro. Jacob Keller, of Hope, Kans., officiated, and preached on Sunday forenoon and afternoon. Bro. Keller's remarks during the Communion services, the becoming appearance of the communicants, and the Gospel-like order of the exercises, produced such a season of quiet awe and attention as will cause the occasion to be one long to be remembered.   C. C. Root.

City Mission Work Among Children in Chicago.

In the winter of 1888 a statement was made in the Sunday-school class in the Library at Mt. Morris, that there were 18,000 persons in the City of Chicago, perfectly ignorant of the Bible and its Divine Author.

Never was a statement more startling,—18,000 people in this *beautiful, civilized,* Christianized land of America, and in the Garden City of the West, perfectly ignorant of our Divine Creator! *What a burning shame!*

This set me to thinking. The longer I thought of it, the less could I comprehend such a statement. Upon further inquiry, and in conversation with those acquainted with city life I was compelled to accept the statement as an absolute fact. A sudden impulse seized me. I longed to go at once and carry the Blessed Gospel to those benighted ones, but I knew there must be some definite plan to carry on such a work successfully; and with a hope to do mission work in the future I put forth renewed energy to the work then in hand.

In the early spring of 1891, I began to form a definite plan for city mission work among children. I read and meditated, I became more and more convinced that, to accomplish the *greatest good, we must begin with the children.* In them lies our only hope to permanently establish our church work in large cities where the membership is transient.

My experience in public school-work has proven, that if we gain the confidence and esteem of the children, it is not long until the parents become interested and desire an acquaintance with the teacher. So in this work. If we gather in the children, give them something interesting and instructive, win their love and confidence,

CORRESPONDENCE.

"Write what thou seest, and send it unto the churches."

☞Church News solicited for this Department. If you have had a good meeting, send a report of it, so that others may rejoice with you. In writing give name of church, County and State. Be brief. Notes of Travel should be as short as possible. Land Advertisements are not solicited for this Department. We have an advertising page, and, if necessary, will issue supplements.

Among the Brethren.

MY last communication, Oct. 6, I closed at the house of brother and sister Ogg. The Root River church is cared for by Bro. Ogg. They previously had solicited me to attend their love-feast, Oct. 8 and 9. The evening of Oct. 7 we met in their comfortable house of worship. We had a sermon by Bro. Harvey Eikenberry. Next morning the writer addressed the people, and at 2:30 P. M., we had a sermon by Bro. J. F. Eikenberry. At 4:30 P. M. we met for examination services. In the evening services a goodly number of brethren and sisters participated. During this meeting the house could not give accommodation to all present. A large number had to remain outside. The writer officiated. The meeting closed before 9 P. M. Next day there was preaching at 10:30 A. M., after which dinner was given to all present. We had preaching also at 2:30 and 7 P. M., to large and very attentive audiences. Thus closed the meetings in the Root River congregation. This was our first visit or acquaintance with the members of this congregation. It did me much good to again meet with my brethren and sisters, and enjoy a few meetings with them. For several years we have been working on the frontier, and have not often enjoyed the associations of brethren and sisters outside of our own organization, and the great love manifested by my dear brethren and sisters toward us made it one of the most pleasant seasons of our life in the Lord's service.

Oct. 10 Bro. Joseph Ogg kindly took Bro. Samuel D. Ogg, his son, now of Minneapolis, and myself, to Lime Springs, Iowa, where we took the train. Bro. Ogg went to Minneapolis, and I to Winnebago City, Minn., where I was met by my old acquaintance, Mr. and Mrs. R. H. Hervey, who kindly took me to their pleasant home and family. They live three and one-half miles nearly west from the city. Mr. and Mrs. Hervey sustained an entire loss, by cyclone, June 15, of all their buildings and contents. Very fortunate for them the entire family escaped unhurt, by discerning the approach of the storm. They ran to the side of its pathway, and uninjured could see the labor of eighteen years all swept away. Fortunately they carried a small cyclone insurance. I left at 6:58 A. M., on the Southern Minnesota for Sioux Falls, Dak., where I stopped off and visited some members who recently moved here from the Bijou Hills church. We were made glad to meet again our friends and dear sisters in the Lord's work. I arrived in Kimball, Oct. 16.   W. G. COOK.

Bijou Hills, Dak., Oct. 18.

Chips from the Work-house.

ON Saturday, Oct. 22, I attended a Communion in the Eden Valley church, Stafford Co., Kans. The meeting was held in an open corn-crib, with a shed on one side, and along the end of it, made out of headerbeds, turned on edge, and covered with canvas, used in heading grain, with a quilt fastened at the top, and a weight at the bottom, for a door into it. The ground was covered with nice, clean wheat straw for a floor, and some loose lumber laid on eight inch tile, set on end, furnished seats for spectators. This structure was well filled with very quiet, attentive listen-

ers. Around one Communion table in the corn-crib, and another under this quaint-looking shed, gathered sixty-four brethren and sisters. Some of the sisters wore heavy shawls, and some of the brethren, the writer included, had overcoats on, because of the cool weather since the recent rains. The ministerial force included three home ministers, Bro. Harnish, from Russell County; brethren Keller and Boyd, from Barton; Eld. John Wise, from Sumner, and Daniel Vaniman, from McPherson County. All the members had their hearts filled with the love of Jesus, and the shed was well filled with spectators. It soon became quite comfortable. The meeting closed at 8:30, all feeling that we surely had a good meeting.

The next morning being Lord's Day, after breakfast for neighbors and all who desired it, there was a thirty minutes' song service, then a social meeting, in which liberty was given for any brother or sister to speak, it being understood that it would be well for no one to exceed ten minutes, in order to give as many as felt to speak a word of encouragement, an opportunity to do so. Thus we had ten well-packed speeches upon various themes of our holy religion, with an occasional verse of song between speeches.

All were thus edified and encouraged and helped in the divine life. It was at this meeting again demonstrated that good and profitable meetings may be held in great simplicity, when only the heart is well filled with the love of Christ, and when there is a disposition to work with God in forwarding the work of the Lord. It is evident that the meeting, under the efficient oversight of Eld. John Wise, is growing both in membership and efficiency. The home ministers also seem to be doing their part well. A sister, who has been appointed solicitor for the missionary work in the church, came around and handed the writer silver and nickels more than his pocket-book could hold, to forward where it would be most needed to build up the cause of the Master. It is a singular fact that in these poor western churches, many of whom have not a meeting-house to hold Communion in, with small houses to live in, and no barns of any consequence, are so wrapped up with the idea of spreading the Gospel of Christ into the borders beyond, that it seems a pleasure to give, and, in every other way that they can, to help to enlarge the borders of Zion. The causes for their readiness to help in the Lord's work, above others in more favorable circumstances, will furnish a hint for some Chips in the future.   DANIEL VANIMAN.

From Stillson, Iowa.

OUR feast in the Boon River church, Hancock Co., Iowa, occurred Sept. 24 and 25. We were blessed with good ministerial aid. Six ministers were present, among them Wm. Ikenberry, the only elder present, who officiated at our meeting. There were other brethren and sisters with us from a distance, whom we had never seen before. We were glad to have them with us. On Saturday after the examination services we were made to rejoice to see an aged sister of seventy-eight years baptized. She had been a member of the Methodist church since her youth.

The dedication of our meeting-house occurred Sept. 18. A donation of $148.10 was received at that time. Wm. Ikenberry preached from these words, "My house is called the house of prayer." Our preparatory council was a pleasant one. Bro. Wm. Ikenberry was elected as delegate to the District Meeting. Our next quarterly council will be the third Saturday of December. Bro. J. L. Thomas, of Ames, Story Co., Iowa, commenced a series of meetings Oct. 14, which con-

tinued until our feast. We learn that Bro. Harvey Ikenberry will be with us Oct. 29. Our Sunday-school, which has been known as the Stilson Sunday-school, has been moved to our new meeting-house, and will hereafter be called the Boon River Sunday-school.

DANIEL ASCHENBRENNER.

Messages Dropped by the Way.

BEING notified by a telegram of the death of our aged brother Cline, of Rossville, I set out Oct. 15, in time to fill the Brethren's appointments at Silver Lake. The message of the funeral being too late, the funeral service was deferred till the 20th. In the meantime meetings were held in Rossville, during the week. As an immediate result two precious souls were added to the church by baptism. Others are almost persuaded. A lady visiting here, who lives at No. 2939½ Martha St., Omaha, goes away, grieving the absence of her husband, as being her only excuse for not coming now. She gives her address, in hopes that Brethren may call and see her. Her name is Mrs. Melissa Westley.

Oct. 21 we closed the meetings at Rossville, and went ten miles to the love-feast, which was held for the benefit of the isolated and scattered members. Twenty-five members were present, to participate in the Communion. These represented the vicinities of six different post-offices. Bro. Jacob Keller, of Hope, Kans., officiated, and preached on Sunday forenoon and afternoon. Bro. Keller's remarks during the Communion services, the becoming appearance of the communicants, and the Gospel-like order of the exercises, produced such a season of quiet awe and attention as will cause the occasion to be one long to be remembered.   C. C. ROOT.

City Mission Work Among Children in Chicago.

IN the winter of 1888 a statement was made in the Sunday-school class in the Library at Mt. Morris, that there were 18,000 persons in the City of Chicago, perfectly ignorant of the Bible and its Divine Author.

Never was a statement more startling,—18,000 people in this *beautiful, civilized, CHRISTIANIZED* land of America, and in the Garden City of the West, perfectly ignorant of our Divine Creator! *What a burning shame!*

This set me to thinking. The longer I thought of it, the less could I comprehend such a statement. Upon further inquiry, and in conversation with those acquainted with city life I was compelled to accept the statement as an absolute fact. A sudden impulse seized me. I longed to go at once and carry the Blessed Gospel to those benighted ones, but I knew there must be some definite plan to carry on such a work successfully; and with a hope to do mission work in the future I put forth renewed energy to the work then in hand.

In the early spring of 1891, I began to form a definite plan for city mission work among children. I read articles on the subject, and as I read and meditated, I became more and more convinced that, to accomplish the *greatest* good, *we* MUST *begin* with the children. In them lies our only hope to permanently establish our church work in large cities where the membership is transient.

My experience in public school-work has proven, that if we gain the confidence and esteem of the children, it is not long until the parents become interested and desire an acquaintance with the teacher. So in this work. If we gather in the children, give them something interesting and instructive, win their love and confidence,

Missionary and Tract Work Department.

| "Open the first day of the week, let every one of you lay by him in store as God hath prospered him, that there be no gatherings when I come."—1 Cor. 16: 2. | "Every man as he purposeth in his heart, so let him give. Not grudgingly or of necessity, for the Lord loveth a cheerful giver."—2 Cor. 9: 7. |

HOW MUCH SHALL WE GIVE?

"Every man *according to his ability*." "Every one *as God hath prospered him*." "Every man, *according as he purposeth in his heart*, so let him give." "For if there be first a willing mind, it is accepted *according to that a man hath*, and not according to that he hath not."—2 Cor. 8: 12.

Organization of Missionary Committee.

DANIEL VANIMAN, Foreman,	-	-	McPherson, Kans.
D. L. MILLER, Treasurer,	-	-	Mt. Morris, Ill.
GALEN B. ROYER, Secretary,	-	-	Mt. Morris, Ill.

Organization of Book and Tract Work.

| S. W. HOOVER, Foreman, | - | - | Dayton, Ohio. |
| S. BOCK, Secretary and Treasurer, | - | Dayton, Ohio. |

☞All donations intended for Missionary Work should be sent to GALEN B. ROYER, Mt. Morris, Ill.

☞All money for Tract Work should be sent to S. BOCK, Dayton, Ohio.

☞Money may be sent by Money Order, Registered Letter, or Drafts on New York or Chicago. Do not send personal checks, or drafts on interior towns, as it costs 25 cents to collect them.

☞Solicitors are requested to faithfully carry out the plan of Annual Meeting, that all our members be solicited to contribute at least twice a year for the Mission and Tract Work of the Church.

☞Notes for the Endowment Fund can be had by writing to the Secretary of either Work.

A PRACTICAL OUTLINE ON CHURCH GOVERNMENT.

BY DANIEL HAYS.

No. 3.—How Administered.

THE first lesson in Church Government, as given by our Lord, is put into the hands of the individual to be administered to himself. Matt. 18: 4, 6, 7, 8 and 10. If this were uniformly heeded, *i. e.*, each member govern himself, then the church would have no trouble with her membership. This, doubtless, was the purpose of Christ in thus instructing each one, as well as in the law of trespass, to relieve the church of all possible trouble. But "offenses" do come, and "trespasses" will occur, and our Lord provides for their removal by a rule the most effectual, brotherly and kind. Matt. 18: 15-17. This instructs each one of us how to proceed with a trespassing brother,—one who failed to govern himself. This is designed by the Savior, to restore the erring ones, and in such a way as will be most effectual and salutary to all concerned.

When, however, individual efforts fail, our Lord places it in the hands of the church, in common with all open violations of the Gospel. The church is an organized body, with deacons, ministers and elders, "for the perfecting of the saints, for the work of the ministry, for the edifying of the body of Christ." The officers of the church are the servants of the church, by means of which discipline is administered, order is maintained, the Gospel is preached, and the life is perpetuated.

DEACONS.—The office of deacon is an important one in the government of the church. Their special duty is to "disburse the alms of the church and serve tables." They are "helps," and serve the church as such in the yearly visit, visiting the sick, looking after offences by special direction of the elder, and in assisting the ministry in singing, reading the Scriptures, exhortation and prayer.

THE MINISTRY.—The material, of which the church is composed, largely depends upon a faithful preaching of the Gospel to the unconverted. Get men and women thoroughly converted, and you have good church members. Then it becomes the duty of the ministry to "feed the flock," that there be a growth "in grace and in the knowledge of the truth." The fact that we grow is proof that we live. The evidence of our conversion is that we are willing to take counsel, and to be instructed in all the commandments of God. Where there is a faithful presentation of the Gospel, there is a faithful, prosperous membership.

ELDERS.—The elder is one who has the spiritual oversight of the church, and whose duty it is, by the assistance of his co-laborers in the ministry, to preach the Gospel, administer the ordinances, and the government of the church. Paul makes it his duty to "hold fast the faithful word as he hath been taught," which brings him under obligations to transmit the doctrine of the church to the next generation. The church prospers where its government is prudently administered, hence the elders should be well informed in the principles of church government. Questions arise concerning church polity that the elder should be able to explain and to give the reason why. Another reason why an elder should be well informed in church government is because he is a leading factor in it. An elder himself, may do a wrong, and the church, with the adjoining elders has the right to bring him to account and correct the error. On the other hand, a church may be in error. Then it becomes the duty of the adjoining elders to go to that church and labor with that church to correct the error, and set things in order. By this arrangement the balance of power is preserved. Christ is the chief Shepherd, and Peter admonishes that elders "feed the flock of God," "taking the oversight, not by constraint but willingly; not for filthy lucre, but of a ready mind; neither as being lords over God's heritage, but being examples to the flock." 1 Pet. 5: 2, 3.

CHURCH COUNCIL.—The government of the church is not congregational. Each local church forms a part of one common Brotherhood. For a local church to act independent of other local churches, leads to a division in sentiment and practice. The government of the church is a unity, and has been so designed by Christ in order to preserve his people as one body in faith and practice. Our present arrangement of local church meetings, District and Annual Meetings has grown up as a matter of necessity with the extension of the Brotherhood. Each local church has a common tie to the District to which it belongs, and through the District Meeting to Annual Meeting. By representation the work of Annual Meeting is as much a part of the work of each member in the Brotherhood as is the work of the church where he resides. Every member, male and female, has a vote in church council. Every member has a right of trial before the church, and of a re-hearing with the assistance and consent of adjoining elders; and may secure a committee from District Meeting, or from Annual Meeting, when considered necessary. This makes the rights and privileges of our church government broader and higher than that of any other, not bound together by the bond of love and union. It is the love of the mother reaching out after her wayward children, and tenderly gathering them into the fold.

The church should be respected in her council meetings by all the members. This applies equally well to District and Annual Meeting. Without a general conference of all the local churches, the union of the church could not long be maintained. The Apostolic church had such a conference in Jerusalem, and the "decrees" made by the apostles and elders with the whole church, were delivered to the churches "to keep," and so they "were established in the faith and increased in numbers daily." Acts 15.

Then, with a faithful membership, a pure, consecrated ministry, and a devoted, self-sacrificing eldership, under the blessing of God, the peace, prosperity and glory of the church will be assured. To this end let us labor, to this end let us pray, till the church "look forth as the morning, fair as the moon, clear as the sun, and terrible as an army with banners."

Broadway, Va.

THE RUSSIAN MENNONITES.

BY S. Z. SHARP.

A FEW Sundays ago I accepted an invitation to attend a harvest thanksgiving meeting among the Russian Mennonites, about twenty miles south of McPherson, Kansas. I learned some things which I believe to be interesting to the readers of the MESSENGER. This class of Christians began to emigrate to America about eighteen years ago, on account of a threatened impressment into military service. They settled in Manitoba, Dakota, Nebraska, and Kansas, and some scattered in other States. Those in Kansas prospering more, financially, than those in Dakota, many moved to Kansas.

Their strict economy, industry, and freedom from the drinking habit so common among foreigners, makes them a very desirable class of citizens. Their well-cultivated farms, fine orchards and vineyards, good barns and fine horses and cattle, indicate their material prosperity.

They dress plainly. Their women mostly wear a handkerchief over their heads when they go from home, and at church they retain it over their caps, while some have, in a measure, departed from the ancient custom and lay aside the upper covering, retaining the black caps. Some of the younger members have gone a step farther and are satisfied with their hair done up in a net. None have gone so far as to deform their heads with bangs.

In common conversation they use the Low-Dutch dialect, or the Russian language, while in church service they use the true German. They maintain German schools at their own expense, and use the public money to pay the salaries of English teachers for their children. Scarcely any of the older ones speak English, hence I was obliged to address them in German. The occasion which brought me among them was a thanksgiving service for their bountiful harvest. At the close of the meeting a collection was taken for the benefit of the poor and $98.00 was contributed.

In doctrine, these people have many things in common with ourselves. They advocate non-swearing, non-resistance, non-conformity to the world, feet-washing and the holy kiss, but do not observe the Supper in connection with the Communion. They oppose infant baptism, and baptize by pouring or by immersion. Some have come so far as to practice immersion exclusively. They are not bound together by a general conference and the consequence is, that they are split into six divisions. This is a matter of much importance to our church. These divisions arose largely on account of the character or teaching of some prominent elder. They live among each other, and their church-houses are often only a few miles apart. In the settlement where I was, I found the following churches and the distinguishing characteristics, as given by one of their members:

1. The original church in form like the old Mennonites in America. They baptize in the house by pouring.

2. The Toevss church, very conservative in plainness of dress, and allowing no fine buggies

Missionary and Tract Work Department.

Organization of Missionary Committee.

DANIEL VANIMAN, Foreman, · · · McPherson, Kans.
D. L. MILLER, Treasurer, · · · Mt. Morris, Ill.
GALEN B. ROYER, Secretary, · · · Mt. Morris, Ill.

Organization of Book and Tract Work.

S. W. HOOVER, Foreman, · · · Dayton, Ohio.
S. BOCK, Secretary and Treasurer, · · · Dayton, Ohio.

A PRACTICAL OUTLINE ON CHURCH GOVERNMENT.

BY DANIEL HAYS.

No. 3.—How Administered.

THE first lesson in Church Government, as given by our Lord, is put into the hands of the individual to be administered to himself. Matt. 18: 4, 6, 7, 8 and 10. If this were uniformly heeded, i. e., each member govern himself, then the church would have no trouble with her membership. This, doubtless, was the purpose of Christ in thus instructing each one, as well as in the law of trespass, to relieve the church of all possible trouble. But "offenses" do come, and "trespasses" will occur, and our Lord provides for their removal by a rule the most effectual, brotherly and kind. Matt. 18: 15–17. This instructs each one of us how to proceed with a trespassing brother,—one who failed to govern himself. This is designed by the Savior, to restore the erring ones, and in such a way as will be most effectual and salutary to all concerned.

When, however, individual efforts fail, our Lord places it in the hands of the church, in common with all open violations of the Gospel. The church is an organized body, with deacons, ministers and elders, "for the perfecting of the saints, for the work of the ministry, for the edifying of the body of Christ." The officers of the church are the servants of the church, by means of which discipline is administered, order is maintained, the Gospel is preached, and the faith is perpetuated.

DEACONS.—The office of deacon is an important one in the government of the church. Their special duty is to "disburse the alms of the church and serve tables." They are "helps," and serve the church as such in the yearly visit, visiting the sick, looking after offences by special direction of the elder, and in assisting the ministry in singing, reading the Scriptures, exhortation and prayer.

THE MINISTRY.—The material, of which the church is composed, largely depends upon a faithful preaching of the Gospel to the unconverted. Get men and women thoroughly converted, and you have good church members. Then it becomes the duty of the ministry to "feed the flock," that there be a growth "in grace and in the knowledge of the truth." The fact that we grow is proof that we live. The evidence of our conversion is that we are willing to take counsel, and to be instructed in all the commandments of God. Where there is a faithful presentation of the Gospel, there is a faithful, prosperous membership.

ELDERS.—The elder is one who has the spiritual oversight of the church, and whose duty it is, by the assistance of his co-laborers in the ministry, to preach the Gospel, administer the ordinances, and the government of the church. Paul makes it his duty to "hold fast the faithful word as he hath been taught," which brings him under obligations to transmit the doctrine of the church to the next generation. The church prospers where its government is prudently administered, hence the elders should be well informed in the principles of church government. Questions arise concerning church polity that the elder should be able to explain and to give the reason why. Another reason why an elder should be well informed in church government is because he is a leading factor in it. An elder himself, may do a wrong, and the church, with the adjoining elders has the right to bring him to account and correct the error. On the other hand, a church may be in error. Then it becomes the duty of the adjoining elders to go to that church and labor with that church to correct the error, and set things in order. By this arrangement the balance of power is preserved. Christ is the chief Shepherd, and Peter admonishes that elders "feed the flock of God," "taking the oversight, not by constraint but willingly; not for filthy lucre, but of a ready mind; neither as being lords over God's heritage, but being examples to the flock." 1 Pet. 5: 2, 3.

CHURCH COUNCIL.—The government of the church is not congregational. Each local church forms a part of one common Brotherhood. For a local church to act independent of other local churches, leads to a division in sentiment and practice. The government of the church is a unity, and has been so designed by Christ in order to preserve his people as one body in faith and practice. Our present arrangement of local church meetings, District and Annual Meetings has grown up as a matter of necessity with the extension of the Brotherhood. Each local church has a common tie to the District to which it belongs, and through the District Meeting to Annual Meeting. By representation the work of Annual Meeting is as much a part of the work of each member in the Brotherhood as is the work of the church where he resides. Every member, male and female, has a vote in church council. Every member has a right of trial before the church, and of a re-hearing with the assistance and consent of adjoining elders; and may secure a committee from District Meeting, or from Annual Meeting, when considered necessary. This makes the rights and privileges of our church government broader and higher than that of any other, not bound together by the bond of love and union. It is the love of the mother reaching out after her wayward children, and tenderly gathering them into the fold.

The church should be respected in her councilmeetings by all the members. This applies equally well to District and Annual Meeting. Without a general conference of all the local churches, the union of the church could not long be maintained. The Apostolic church had such a conference in Jerusalem, and the "decrees" made by the apostles and elders with the whole church, were delivered to the churches "to keep," and so they "were established in the faith and increased in numbers daily." Acts 15.

Then, with a faithful membership, a pure, consecrated ministry, and a devoted, self-sacrificing eldership, under the blessing of God, the peace, prosperity and glory of the church will be assured. To this end let us labor, to this end let us pray, till the church "look forth as the morning, fair as the moon, clear as the sun, and terrible as an army with banners."

Broadway, Va.

THE RUSSIAN MENNONITES.

BY S. Z. SHARP.

A FEW Sundays ago I accepted an invitation to attend a harvest thanksgiving meeting among the Russian Mennonites, about twenty miles south of McPherson, Kansas. I learned some things which I believe to be interesting to the readers of the MESSENGER. This class of Christians began to emigrate to America about eighteen years ago, on account of a threatened impressment into military service. They settled in Manitoba, Dakota, Nebraska, and Kansas, and some scattered in other States. Those in Kansas prospering more, financially, than those in Dakota, many moved to Kansas.

Their strict economy, industry, and freedom from the drinking habit so common among foreigners, makes them a very desirable class of citizens. Their well-cultivated farms, fine orchards and vineyards, good barns and fine horses and cattle, indicate their material prosperity.

They dress plainly. Their women mostly wear a handkerchief over their heads when they go from home, and at church they retain it over their caps, while some have, in a measure, departed from the ancient custom and lay aside the upper covering, retaining the black caps. Some of the younger members have gone a step farther and are satisfied with their hair done up in a net. None have gone so far as to deform their heads with bangs.

In common conversation they use the Low-Dutch dialect, or the Russian language, while in church service they use the true German. They maintain German schools at their own expense, and use this public money to pay the salaries of English teachers for their children. Scarcely any of the older ones speak English, hence I was obliged to address them in German. The occasion which brought me among them was a thanksgiving service for their bountiful harvest. At the close of the meeting a collection was taken for the benefit of the poor and $98.00 was contributed.

In doctrine, these people have many things in common with ourselves. They advocate non-swearing, non-resistance, non-conformity to the world, feet-washing and the holy kiss, but do not observe the Supper in connection with the Communion. They oppose infant baptism, and baptize by pouring or by immersion. Some have come so far as to practice immersion exclusively.

They are not bound together by a general conference and the consequence is, that they are split into six divisions. This is a matter of much importance on account of the character or teaching of some prominent elder. They live among each other, and their church-houses are often only a few miles apart. In the settlement where I was, I found the following churches and their distinguishing characteristics, as given by one of their members:

1. The original church in form like the old Mennonites in America. They baptize in the house by pouring.

2. The Toeves church, very conservative in plainness of dress, and allowing no fine buggies

The Gospel Messenger,

A Weekly at $1.50 Per Annum.

PUBLISHED BY

The Brethren's Publishing Co.

D. L. MILLER,	. . . .	Editor
J. H. MOORE,	. . . .	Office Editor.
J. B. BRUMBAUGH,	. . . .	Associate Editors.
J. G. ROYER,		
JOSEPH AMICK,	. . . .	Business Manager.

ADVISORY COMMITTEE.

L. W. Teeter, A. Hutchison, Daniel Hays.

☞Communications for publication should be legibly written with black ink on one side of the paper only. Do not attempt to interline, or to put on one page what ought to occupy two.

☞Anonymous communications will not be published.

☞Do not mix business with articles for publication. Keep your communications on separate sheets from all business.

☞Time is precious. We always have time to attend to business and to answer questions of importance, but please do not subject us to need less answering of letters.

☞The MESSENGER is mailed each week to all subscribers. If the address is correctly entered on our list, the paper must reach the person to whom it is addressed. If you do not get your paper, write us, giving particulars.

☞When changing your address, please give your former as well as your future address in full, so as to avoid delay and misunderstanding.

☞Always remit to the office from which you order your goods, no matter from where you receive them.

☞Do not send personal checks or drafts on interior banks, unless you send with them 25 cents each, to pay for collection.

☞Remittances should be made by Post-office Money Order, Drafts on New York, Philadelphia or Chicago, or Registered Letters, made payable and addressed to "Brethren's Publishing Co., Mount Morris, Ill.," or "Brethren's Publishing Co., Huntingdon, Pa."

☞Entered at the Post-office at Mount Morris, Ill., as second-class matter.

Mount Morris, Ill., ... Nov. 8, 1892.

THE address of Bro. P. F. Oupp is now changed from Griffin, Pa., to Listie, same State.

WE are now out of the "Church Manual," and can fill no more orders until a new edition is printed.

THE first love-feast ever held in Lancaster City, Pa., is appointed for Nov. 6. The cause seems to be progressing favorably there.

BRO. GEO. W. GIBSON, of Girard, Illinois, has decided to locate in the Indian Creek church, Iowa. He expects to make the change next March.

IN sister Lizzie Fahnestock's communication in No. 41 of the MESSENGER, the number of sermons preached by Bro. Hope should have been seventeen instead of seven.

CONSIDERABLE business came before the District Meeting of Southern Iowa, Oct. 7. One query goes to the Annual Meeting. Bro. John Gable has been chosen to represent the District on the Standing Committee.

THERE are probably scores of women in the church who spend days embroidering the napkins in which they propose to wrap for burial their unimproved talents. Reader, are you one of them? God knows.

BRO. ENOCH EBY writes that he is kept quite busy in church work and is from home most of the time. He reports the churches in Kansas in an encouraging condition. He promises us some more articles as soon as he can find time to prepare them.

WE suggest that it is hardly necessary to name all the ministers who attend this or that feast. It is probably sufficient to mention who officiated, or those from a distance. By omitting these long lists of names found in some of the reports, much space might be saved so as to make room for more notes. For the want of room thirty or more reports are crowded out of this issue and must lay over until next week.

IT is now fully settled that the next Annual Meeting will be held at Muncie, Delaware Co., Ind., a place of over 11,000 inhabitants and strong railroad facilities.

NOVEMBER 24 will be our National Thanksgiving Day. We have many things to thank the Lord for this year, and it would be well for all the churches to assemble in their places of worship and hold religious services.

A GOOD work has been performed in the Pleasant Grove congregation, Kans., where Bro. Isaac H. Crist recently held a series of meetings that resulted in fifteen additions to the church, with prospects of several more.

BRO. D. M. MILLER reports that he is having good meetings at Laurens, Iowa, with the very best of attention and interest. He speaks very highly of the country and people, and thinks it would be a good place to build up a church of solid material.

IT is said that the armies of the civilized nations of the world number 3,600,000 men. Besides the loss of their time and labor they cost at least $1,000 a year for each soldier, and that amounts to $3,600,000,000. What a waste of energy and money!

BRO. D. B. GIBSON closed his meetings at Mt. Vernon, Ill., Oct. 29, with quite an interest and six additions, with more near the kingdom. It is to be regretted that the meetings did not continue longer. His next point is with the Brethren at Loraine, Adams Co., Ill.

BRO. BALSBAUGH requests the following correction, which we make here: "Not creed but life is the test before God. See Acts 19: 34, 35. In No. 42, current volume, in the article, 'The Christian Sabbath,' in sixth line of second paragraph, instead of Baptist read PAPIST."

THE minister who can interest and make the children understand him, may rest assured that he has the ear of all the grown-up people too. It is always easier to pick an apple from the ground than from the top of the tree. Place the feed low. The sheep as well as the lambs can get it there.

NEVER before, in the history of our publishing business, have we received so many encouraging reports from the churches in all parts of the Brotherhood. Perhaps there never has been a fall when there were so many love-feasts. Add to this the hundreds of additions reported and we certainly have cause for rejoicing.

IT is said that in Canada a saloon-keeper is not permitted to hold a municipal office of any kind. It ought to be that way in the United States. Yea, more, he ought not to be allowed to vote. And it would be better still if he were not allowed to live in the country at all. But in the world to come there will be a place where he cannot enter, and there will also be another place where he will have to stay.

A FEW days ago Bro. Galen B. Royer, Secretary of the General Mission Board, showed us a letter that will do to imitate. It read about thus: "Enclosed please find draft for four hundred dollars, half for the Danish Mission and the other half for the General Mission Fund.' A brother." We are left to conjecture who sent it, and we even prefer not to conjecture. But it would be well to think that we have that kind of members in all parts of the Brotherhood. Members, who prefer not to let the left hand know what good the right hand is doing, have a chance to imitate this brother.

IN a few instances we have published more than one report of the same meeting. This, of course, was not intentional, but we cannot possibly remember them all and thus avoid the repetitions. We wish it could be so that only one report of a meeting would be sent. With a little arrangement upon the part of correspondents, living in the same locality, this might be done.

A BROTHER who has just read the Quinter and McConnell Debate on Trine Immersion, etc., for the first, came into the office the other day with a copy of the work in his hand, and said, "That is one of the best books I ever read, and every member ought to have a copy." We think so too, and can fill orders at $1.50 per copy. Parties desiring the book should order it soon.

WE do not care to meddle with the voting business but we must say that the man who attends church regularly and prays for temperance, and then goes to the polls and votes for license, may be called a Christian at church but his actions at the polls do not show it. If he can serve two masters at one time, he may be safe. If not, then he is on the same road the saloon-keeper is traveling, and every Bible reader knows where that road leads to.

WRITING from the Falling Spring church, Franklin Co., Pa., Bro. W. A. Anthony says: "Rejoice with us. On Sunday, at our regular meeting at Brown's Mill, five were baptized and on Friday next four more are to be baptized. There seems to be quite a stir among the people. Bro. Silas Hoover is to be with us on Nov. 26 and preach a week for us." LATER.—In all, ten have been baptized.

WHAT is it that some people cannot think about? Who says a congregation can be too poor to hold a love-feast? Then, again, who says a congregation can be too poor to raise money for the missionary cause? These questions are well answered in the "Chips from the Work-house" this week. It is a pity that some rich congregations do not have the same zeal for the spread of the Gospel that is found in some of the poor churches.

THERE is one thing we would like to get out of the minds of a few people, and that is this: When we carefully answer a query, do not concern yourself about who or what case the query or answer may possibly refer to, but study the principle contained in the answer. If the principles laid down in our answers are not correct, we would like to be advised of it, but as for the case, please give yourselves not the least concern. There are no personalities in any of our queries. We receive scores that are personal but we do not answer them in the MESSENGER. Our object in all of our writing is to tell the truth as best we understand it and rise above personalities.

IT is maintained by some of the papers that the new Mississippi dram-shop act is one of the severest liquor laws ever passed by any Legislature in the United States. The Wine and Spirit Gazette, which is supposed to know something about it, admits this and says: A liquor-dealer can do business only in the front part of his shop, and it is a misdemeanor for him to put up a screen. If he is convicted of selling adulterated liquor, he may be imprisoned from one year to five years. It will cost him $500 and six months in the penitentiary to allow a game of chance to be played in his shop; and indictments against him cannot be thrown out for defect of form. In cities the license is $1,200; in towns, $900; and in country, $600. A minor is not permitted even to come inside the door.

The Gospel Messenger,

A Weekly at $1.50 Per Annum.

PUBLISHED BY

The Brethren's Publishing Co.

D. L. MILLER,		Editor
J. H. MOORE,		Office Editor.
J. B. BRUMBAUGH,	}	Associate Editors.
J. G. ROYER,	}	
JOSEPH AMICK,		Business Manager.

ADVISORY COMMITTEE.

L. W. Teeter, A. Hutchison, Daniel Hays.

☞Communications for publication should be legibly written with black ink on one side of the paper only. Do not attempt to interline, or to put on one page what ought to occupy two.

☞Anonymous communications will not be published.

☞Time is precious. We always have time to attend to business and to answer questions of importance, but please do not subject us to need less answering of letters.

☞The MESSENGER is mailed each week to all subscribers. If the address is correctly entered on our list, the paper must reach the person to whom it is addressed. If you do not get your paper, write us, giving particulars.

☞When changing your address, please give your former as well as your future address in full, so as to avoid delay and misunderstanding.

☞Always remit to the office from which you order your goods, no matter from where you receive them.

☞Do not send personal checks or drafts on interior banks, unless you send with them 15 cents each, to pay for collection.

☞Remittances should be made by Post-office Money Order. Drafts on New York, Philadelphia or Chicago, or Registered Letters, made payable and addressed to "Brethren's Publishing Co., Mount Morris, Ill.," or "Brethren's Publishing Co., Huntingdon, Pa."

☞Entered at the Post-office at Mount Morris, Ill., as second-class matter.

Mount Morris, Ill., ・ ・ ・ ・ ・ Nov. 8, 1892.

THE address of Bro. P. F. Cupp is now changed from Griffin, Pa., to Listie, same State.

WE are now out of the "Church Manual," and can fill no more orders until a new edition is printed.

THE first love-feast ever held in Lancaster City, Pa., is appointed for Nov. 6. The cause seems to be progressing favorably there.

BRO. GEO. W. GIBSON, of Girard, Illinois, has decided to locate in the Indian Creek church, Iowa. He expects to make the change next March.

IN sister Lizzie Fahnestock's communication in No. 41 of the MESSENGER, the number of sermons preached by Bro. Hope should have been seventeen instead of seven.

CONSIDERABLE business came before the District Meeting of Southern Iowa, Oct. 7. One query goes to the Annual Meeting. Bro. John Gable has been chosen to represent the District on the Standing Committee.

THERE are probably scores of women in the church who spend days embroidering the napkins in which they propose to wrap for burial their unimproved talents. Reader, are you one of them? God knows.

BRO. ENOCH EBY writes that he is kept quite busy in church work and is from home most of the time. He reports the churches in Kansas in an encouraging condition. He promises us some more articles as soon as he can find time to prepare them.

WE suggest that it is hardly necessary to name all the ministers who attend this or that feast. It is probably sufficient to mention who officiated, or those from a distance. By omitting these long lists of names found in some of the reports, much space might be saved so as to make room for more notes. For the want of room thirty or more reports are crowded out of this issue and must lay over until next week.

IT is now fully settled that the next Annual Meeting will be held at Muncie, Delaware Co., Ind., a place of over 11,000 inhabitants and strong railroad facilities.

NOVEMBER 24 will be our National Thanksgiving Day. We have many things to thank the Lord for this year, and it would be well for all the churches to assemble in their places of worship and hold religious services.

A GOOD work has been performed in the Pleasant Grove congregation, Kans., where Bro. Isaac H. Crist recently held a series of meetings that resulted in fifteen additions to the church, with prospects of several more.

BRO. D. M. MILLER reports that he is having good meetings at Laurens, Iowa, with the very best of attention and interest. He speaks very highly of the country and people, and thinks it would be a good place to build up a church of solid material.

IT is said that the armies of the civilized nations of the world number 3,600,000 men. Besides the loss of their time and labor they cost at least $1,000 a year for each soldier, and that amounts to $3,600,000,000. What a waste of energy and money!

BRO. D. B. GIBSON closed his meetings at Mt. Vernon, Ill., Oct. 29, with quite an interest and six additions, with more near the kingdom. It is to be regretted that the meetings did not continue longer. His next point is with the Brethren at Loraine, Adams Co., Ill.

BRO. BALSBAUGH requests the following correction, which we make here: "Not creed but life is the test before God. See Acts 19: 34, 35. In No. 42, current volume, in the article, 'The Christian Sabbath,' in sixth line of second paragraph, instead of *Baptist* read PAPIST."

THE minister who can interest and make the children understand him, may rest assured that he has the ear of all the grown-up people too. It is always easier to pick an apple from the ground than from the top of the tree. Place the feed low. The sheep as well as the lambs can get it there.

NEVER before, in the history of our publishing business, have we received so many encouraging reports from the churches in all parts of the Brotherhood. Perhaps there never has been a fall when there were so many love-feasts. Add to this the hundreds of additions reported and we certainly have cause for rejoicing.

IT is said that in Canada a saloon-keeper is not permitted to hold a municipal office of any kind. It ought to be that way in the United States. Yea, more, he ought not to be allowed to vote. And it would be better still if he were not allowed to live in the country at all. But in the world to come there will be a place where he cannot enter, and there will also be another place where he will have to stay.

A FEW days ago Bro. Galen B. Boyer, Secretary of the General Mission Board, showed us a letter that will do to imitate. It read about thus: "Enclosed please find draft for four hundred dollars, half for the Danish Mission and the other half for the General Mission Fund. A brother." We are left to conjecture who sent it, and we even prefer not to conjecture, for it would be well to think that we have that kind of members in all parts of the Brotherhood. Members, who prefer not to let the left hand know what good the right hand is doing, have a chance to imitate this brother.

IN a few instances we have published more than one report of the same meeting. This, of course, was not intentional, but we cannot possibly remember them all and thus avoid the repetitions. We wish it could be so that only one report of a meeting would be sent. With a little arrangement upon the part of correspondents, living in the same locality, this might be done.

A BROTHER who has just read the Quinter and McConnell Debate on Trine Immersion, etc., for the first, came into the office the other day with a copy of the work in his hand, and said, "That is one of the best books I ever read, and every member ought to have a copy." We think so too, and can fill orders at $1.50 per copy. Parties desiring the book should order it soon.

WE do not care to meddle with the voting business but we must say that the man who attends church regularly and prays for temperance, and then goes to the polls and votes for license, may be called a Christian at church but his actions at the polls do not show it. If he can serve two masters at one time, he may be safe. If not, then he is on the same road the saloon-keeper is traveling, and every Bible reader knows where that road leads to.

WRITING from the Falling Spring church, Franklin Co., Pa., Bro. W. A. Anthony says: "Rejoice with us. On Sunday, at our regular meeting at Brown's Mill, five were baptized and on Friday next four more are to be baptized. There seems to be quite a stir among the people. Bro. Silas Hoover is to be with us on Nov. 26 and preach a week for us." LATER.—In all, ten have been baptized.

WHAT is it that some people cannot think about? Who says a congregation can be too poor to hold a love-feast? Then, again, who says a congregation can be too poor to raise money for the missionary cause? These questions are well answered in the "Chips from the Work-house" this week. It is a pity that some rich congregations do not have the same zeal for the spread of the Gospel that is found in some of the poor churches.

THERE is one thing we would like to get out of the minds of a few people, and that is this: When we carefully answer a query, do not concern yourself about who or what case the query or answer may possibly refer to, but study the *principle* contained in the answer. If the *principles* laid down in our answers are not correct, we would like to be advised of it, but as for the case, please give yourselves not the least concern. There are no personalities in any of our queries. We receive scores that are personal but we do not answer them in the MESSENGER. Our object in all of our writing is to tell the truth as best we understand it and rise above personalities.

IT is maintained by some of the papers that the new Mississippi dram-shop act is one of the severest liquor laws ever passed by any Legislature in the United States. The *Wine and Spirit Gazette*, which is supposed to know something about it, admits this and says: A liquor-dealer can do business only in the front part of his shop, and it is a misdemeanor for him to put up a screen; If he is convicted of selling adulterated liquor, he may be imprisoned from one year to five years. It will cost him $500 and six months in the penitentiary to allow a game of chance to be played in his shop; and indictments against him cannot be thrown out for defeat of form. In cities the license is $1,200; in towns, $900; and in country, $600. A minor is not permitted even to come inside the door.

THE OLD TESTAMENT

Was originally written in the Hebrew, the language of the Jews. Until the time of Joshua the first five books of the Bible, known as the Pentateuch,—a Greek word meaning *the fivefold book*,—was all the known written Word of God. It was written on carefully-prepared skins of animals, known as parchment, and the five books of the law composed one continuous roll. The writing, which was done by scribes, was begun and completed, probably, in the days of the wandering in -the wilderness. Other books were written and added to the ˙Pentateuch until the list was completed with addition of the prophecy of Malachi, 420 years before the birth of Christ. The length of time which elapsed between the writing of the law and the last book of the Bible was 1,070 years. Thus it took over 1,000 years to write the Old Testament.

About 420 years before Christ, and forty years after the return of the Jews from Babylon under Ezra, the books of the Old˙ Testament were collected into one book, and a completed list was made of them. This was done during the lives of the prophets Haggai, Zechariah and Malachi. After the death of the last-named prophet the spirit of prophecy ceased. Josephus, speaking of the Old Testament says, that from that time down to his own day, A. D. 80, "No one dared to˙ add, take away, or alter anything."

During the long period of time which elapsed while the books of the Old Testament were being written, the Hebrew underwent many marked changes. From this fact Dr. Osborn draws the following argument of the authenticity of the book: Had the Bible been the composition of an impostor, he would have used the Hebrew known at the time he lived, his work would have contained the style, ideas and meanings of the time he wrote, and there would have been traces of unity of style. But instead of this we find changes in style, new expressions, characteristic of the time when the particular book was written, peculiar additions, and uses of the words and letters, appearance of new idioms and grammatical forms from Genesis to the latest prophecies. These facts are the certain signs of progressive ages, and are so characteristic of the language of the Old Testament, that, to the Hebrew scholar of the present time, they indicate the age in which the book was written, and sometimes suggest the historic contents of the book composed in that style of Hebrew. The Hebrew itself frequently vindicates the genuineness and determines the age of the book. After a careful examination of this ground, our author says, "It is impossible intelligently to believe any charge of forgery against the Hebrew originals."

The Old Testament was the Scripture referred to and quoted from by our Savior and his apostles. With the exception of Ruth, Chronicles, Ezra, Nehemiah, Songs of Solomon, Lamentations, Obadiah, Nahum, and Zephaniah, all the books of the Old are quoted from, or referred to in the New Testament. The Old Testament was held by Christ and his apostles as inspired of God. If we accept the New Testament as the Gospel of Jesus Christ, the inspired Word of God, all controversy as to the Old ceases because it was accepted by Christ.   D. L. M.

MOST of the shadows that cross our path through life are caused by standing in our own light.

WHAT OF OUR CHILDREN?

Number Three.

THE command "Bring them up in the nurture and admonition of the Lord," should remind all parents that Paul knew that the eternal destiny of the child is placed, in a very important sense, into the hands of the parents. Some· have thought and even said that parents ought not to mould the religious belief of the child; that the child should be left to do this for himself, and on his own responsibility. It might as reasonably be argued that parents should neglect the care of the child's body and intellect. How cruel we should consider that parent who- would allow his child to grow up without having made an effort to cure a limb which had been broken! Is a deformed limb more to be dreaded than a bad character?

Parents are under obligation to give their children instruction, and cause them to be instructed in religion. I know it is said that the parents may be themselves in error, and so may mislead their child. Suppose they be in error, the fault is not the child's, but the parent's. It is the business of the parents to avail themselves of all the means God has put within their reach to know the truth, and then teach the ·child. The parents' decision on this subject involve the future happiness or misery, not only of their own soul, but also that of the child.

The parents are, therefore, under every solemn obligations to teach, and cause their child to be taught, its duties to God and to man,—to place the child under such discipline and instruction that he may become acquainted with the Lord,— a discipline which will develop in the child a spirit of piety or right feeling towards God. If the Bible enjoins anything upon parents, it is the duty of endeavoring, to train up their children in the ways of religion, making this life the great object and purpose to prepare them for heaven.

If it be asked, *In what way may* this be done?—we answer, By inculcating, directly, the doctrines of the Bible. This should be done just as anything else, which the parent regards highly valuable, is done. If the parents love God, his Word, and his church, as some love money, honor or power, there will be very little danger that the child will grow up to dislike or even neglect the church. Such parents will endeavor to eradicate, as far as possible, wrong propensities in their child. They will watch with ceaseless vigilance the first appearance of obstinacy, vanity, pride and kindred vices. They will endeavor to root out all such by kindly showing that God abhors those evil propensities, and that his Word condemns them. The parents will not fail to exhibit to the child, in the most inviting manner, the beauties of those virtues which should take the place of the vices.

Parents can inflict no greater unkindness upon their children than to allow them to grow up with their evil habits uncorrected. Parents should also see that their children are not led astray by those under whose instruction they are placed. It is because of this danger that we invariably advise parents to send their children, if sent away from home, to Brethren's schools. It matters not whether or not they belong to the church. They should, if possible, attend the Brethren's schools. It will always be the cheapest in the end.   J. G. R.

CORRESPONDENCE.

"Write what thou seest, and send it unto the churches."

☞Church News solicited for this Department. If you have had a good meeting, send a report of it, so that others may rejoice with you. In writing give name of church, County and State. Be brief. Notes of Travel should be as short as possible. Land Advertisements are not solicited for this Department. We have an advertising page, and, if necessary, will issue supplements.

From Mahassas, Va.

WE started at Scalp Level, Sept. 3, by wagons for Virginia. Near Bedford we were joined by Bro. Ephraim Seese and family, and together we journeyed till Sept. 9, about 9 P. M. ˙Bro. Conrad Seese and family did not get ready to come along, but came two weeks afterwards.

We were blessed with a favorable week for traveling, and we were also fortunate in securing good lodging-places every night. Including four of our friends, who returned again, there were twenty-five persons, yet all stood the trip well and enjoyed it. We passed over a part of Somerset, Bedford, Fulton and Franklin Counties, Pa. After that we went through Hagerstown, Md., and crossed the Potomac at Brunswick on the ferry-boat. The scenery along the road was varied and interesting. We passed the Bull Run battle-ground, and now live within sight of Fort Beauregard.

The next morning after our arrival the neighbors came to welcome us and see if they could help us. We have been here a month, and so far we are well satisfied with the change. The people are clever and hospitable and are glad to see Northern folks move in and help ·improve the country. Though Virginia is the oldest State, it is behind some of the Northern and Western States in improvements. It has not fully recovered from the ravages of the late war, but it boasts of a beautiful climate, short, mild˙ winters, long·˙ summers, and a productive soil, free from stone. Manassas is but thirty-three miles from the nation's capital, and therefore has good markets.

We find a Brethren church here (the Midland), composed of loyal, zealous members. It is the only one east of the mountains, and has an almost boundless territory. It has two˙ houses for Communion meetings,—one at Midland, and the other near Nokesville. Besides this there is a body of members living in Madison County, about sixty miles west, who also have a meeting-house. They also hold regular meetings in four or five school-houses. The ·fall ·lovefeast will be held at Midland, Nov. 5. If any of our ministers from the North can be with us, they will be welcome.

Bro. Sandy, of Ohio, is expected to hold a series of meetings prior to the feast. Two brethren have recently been baptized at Midland. One of them died since. We have been to meeting four times and I have preached twice. Remember us in your prayers!   J. E. BROWN.

Oct. 10.

From Moscow, Idaho.

OUR feast at Moscow occurred Oct. 1. ·We had a soul-refreshing meeting. Two precious souls were baptized,· and the church very much encouraged. Directly after the meeting we went to Waverly, sixty-five miles north of Moscow, and about thirty miles south of Spokane, where there is a little body of faithful brethren and sisters. Here I commenced meetings on Tuesday night, and continued through the week. On Saturday we met for Communion services. We had a ·most excellent attendance throughout. Methodist friends opened their house for us, and the United Brethren dismissed their meeting to attend ours. This increased the congregation to a full house. The people gave marked attention

singing and speaking by the school. We met again at 2:30 P. M. for services, after which we repaired to the waterside, to administer baptism to an aged father and mother, who had long since been just outside the pales of the church. May their last days be their happiest, is our prayer!

Bro. Wysong remained and preached for us until Oct. 20, when he took his leave from us for other fields of labor. He left many good impressions with us, and may God bless his labors! Our aged elder, Jacob Shively, has recently retired from the oversight of our church, leaving us entirely without an elder.　　　LAURA APPELMAN.

· Plymouth, Ind., Oct. 24.

"WITHOUT earnestness no man is ever great, or does really great things. He may be the cleverest of men; he may be brilliant, entertaining, popular; but he will want weight. No soul-moving picture was ever painted that had not in it a depth of shadow."

Notes from Our Correspondents.

"As cold water to a thirsty soul, so is good news from a far country."

Sand Ridge, Ohio.—Bro. J. J. Rosenberger has just closed a short but very interesting series of meetings in this church. The members were much built up, and some have promised to return, who have wandered away. We had five additions by baptism. May the sentiment of Psalm 23 ever be theirs!—C. E. Burns, Leipsic, Ohio, Oct. 25.

Nora Springs, Iowa.—The Rock Grove church love-feast, held Oct. 15 and 16, will long be remembered. Ministers present were elders J. F. Eikenberry, Wm. Ikenberry and Wm. H. Eikenberry. Our aged brother, Wm. Workman, has built an addition to our meeting-house which makes it more convenient than in former years. He also made needed improvements in the speaker's stand. For all this he has our thanks.—G. M. Noah.

Hansell, Iowa.—The meetings at the Grundy church are now past. Five precious souls became willing to serve the Lord. The love-feast at that place was one long to be remembered. From here I went to the Iowa River love-feast, which was another of those refreshing showers from the presence of the Lord. Here we met many members from different Counties of Iowa, with whom we had never met before. I am now in Franklin County, Iowa, and will stay here till the feast at Greene, Nov. 5, then go there.—Joseph Holder, Oct. 25.

Mohican, Ohio.—Our love-feast was held Oct. 8, at 10 A. M. We had the best of order and attention. One precious soul was baptized in the afternoon before the feast. We also had plenty of ministerial help. Eight ministers were present from different churches, and Bro. N. Longanecker officiated. On Sunday morning we had a social meeting, at which brethren and sisters were called upon to speak. The many good and encouraging remarks will not soon be forgotten.—Nancy A. Fackler, Oct. 11.

Neutral, Kans.—The love-feast of the New Hope church was held Oct. 8. We had a good meeting. We received two members by letter. The ministers that came to the feast were brethren —— Harvey, C. Holderman, N. Trapp, H. Shideler and S. Edgecomb. They labored for us earnestly. On Sunday morning, after the feast, it was made known that an old sister, who has been quite feeble for some time, wanted to be anointed. So, at about 9:30 a fair congregation gathered in the tent, and the rite of anointing was performed by Bro. Holderman in the public assembly. Bro. Harvey officiated at the feast.—A. B. Lichtenwalter, Oct. 19.

Pyrmont, Ind.—We are at the close of a series of meetings, begun Oct. 8. Our love-feast closed Oct. 13 and an election was held for one speaker and two deacons. Bro. D. C. Campbell is proclaiming glad tidings to all who obey. The result is that ten were baptized. May God enable us, through his Son, to obey his saving Gospel!—E. Cottrell, Oct. 20.

Ministerial Meeting, Southern District of Indiana.—The Upper Fall Creek church, where the Ministerial Meeting of the District is to be held in December, has changed the place of holding the Meeting from the church-house in Middletown, to the "Old church," two miles east of Middletown. Parties can now take their choice of stopping-places, either Honey Creek or Middletown.—D. F. Hoover, Writing Clerk.

Edna Mills, Ind.—Our Communion was held Oct. 20. The attendance was good. Quite a number of members from other congregations were present and enjoyed the meeting with us. Ministers present from a distance were L. T. Holsinger, H. Keim, D. Wysong, D. F. Hoover, D. C. Campbell and D. Bock. We had splendid order and good preaching, and the members present nearly all communed. Taking it as a whole, I believe it was one of the best Communions I ever attended in our church.—John E. Metzger, Oct. 21.

Hyndman, Pa.—At our late love-feast the following ministers were present: J. W. Miller, W. T. Sines, Samuel Richey and C. G. Lint. We were much built up and encouraged by the brethren's good instructions from the Word of Life. We are a small band of workers at this place, with a membership of about thirty-two. We have two ministers in the first degree and one deacon. We belong to the Meyersdale church. Ministering brethren, passing this way in their travels, are cordially invited to preach for us.—Thomas Harden, Oct. 21.

Notice to Solicitors.—As the new form of notes are to take the place of the old, we request you to collect the interest on all notes. When taken up, and new ones given, send all to the missionary treasurer, R. F. Brubaker, Virden, Ill., Box 343. We also earnestly request you to go to work with that zeal and earnestness which the noble enterprise deserves, in soliciting your territories. Let each one canvass the field thoroughly, no difference what objections may be filed, and the Lord will bless you abundantly.—R. F. Brubaker.

Lancaster, Pa.—Yesterday the Brethren of Lancaster held a council, at which Bro. T. F. Imler and wife, formerly of Waynesborough, Pa., handed in their certificates of membership. There was also a deacon elected. It was decided to hold a love-feast on Sunday, Nov 6, 1892. This will be the first love-feast ever held in this city. We are now in better working order, and do hope we may all appreciate this great blessing conferred upon us, and that our efforts may redound to the honor and glory of God!—A. J. Evans, Oct. 20.

Sawyer, Kans.—The love-feast of the Bethel church, Pratt Co., passed off pleasantly. Bro. John Wise, of Conway Springs, preached one week before the feast. We hope the good seed sown will bring forth its fruit in due season. The ministers present at the feast were brethren Wise, Smith, Bowser, Shamberger and A. F. Miller. Bro. Miller officiated. There was a choice held for two deacons. The lot fell on Jacob Blickenstaff and David Ginder. We hope they will be faithful to their calling. Bro. Daniel Gilbert and wife, Bro. Jacob Brubaker and wife, and Bro. Ezra Brubaker and wife, all of Illinois, were present. In all there were sixty-three at the table.—J. H. Miller, Oct. 20.

Notice.—The Committee on Arrangements for the next Ministerial Meeting for North-western District of Ohio is now ready to receive invitations from the local churches that desire the Meeting next year. It also solicits appropriate subjects and queries for program. Let all invitations, subjects and queries be sent to the undersigned by May 1, 1893.—J. W. Chambers, Sec Aivada, Ohio.

Iowa River, Iowa.—The feast at the Iowa River church, Oct. 22, will not soon be forgotten. These meetings should give us much strength and hope as we journey onward. A good many of our brethren and friends from a distance met with us, and we hope they will come again. Ministers present were brethren David Holder, Charles Garner and Stephen Johnson. Bro. Holder officiated. There were four baptized, — three on Sunday afternoon and one on Monday forenoon.—Ellen Nicholson, Oct. 25.

Pleasant Grove, Kans.—Oct. 15 I went to visit the above church, and continued meetings each evening until the 24th. On the evening of the 22nd was their Communion which was one of the most interesting we ever attended. During the meetings the Lord blessed the prayers and labors of the faithful with fifteen baptisms, three applicants and promises of more coming soon. The meetings closed with a growing interest. We will now remain with the family and home members until Nov. 12, when, if the Lord will, I commence a meeting in South Park.—Isaac P. Oriel Gardner, Kans., Oct. 25.

Clarion, Iowa.—We are located two and one-half miles east and 2 miles south of Clarion. There are no members near here, so far as we know, but there are several families living here, from Cerro Gordo, Ill., that are acquainted with our people and speak favorably of them. We are in the territory of the Boon River church, which, we are informed, is about twenty miles north, in Hancock County. We have held one meeting and have made arrangements to have meetings every two weeks at our school-house. The people are kind and sociable, and prospects seem favorable for building up a church.—Jefferson Mathis.

Salem, Oregon.—The members of the Salem church are still permitted to enjoy showers of heavenly manna. Brethren J. B. Early and J. R. Ebersole, lately from Missouri, are our ministers and are doing all they can, but the field is much too large to do justice to the work before then. We have members living in three Counties and there is plenty of room for three or four more ministers here in Marion County alone. We are often made to wonder why so few members seek homes in this goodly land,—a land where rain and crops never fail, where the climate is very mild and health good. We earnestly invite more ministers to come here to live among us.—J. L. Lehman, Oct. 16.

Lindside, W. Va.—Our love-feast of Oct. 15 and 16 was a glorious and soul-reviving feast. Many brethren and sisters were with us from other points. Ministering brethren were George Graybill, P. S. Miller, J. Gresso, A. Duncan and I. Argabright. Brethren Graybill and Miller did most of the preaching which was very interesting. Bro. Miller preached on Sunday, night and Monday following, and he certainly held forth the Word of God with great power. There were no additions to the church, but we believe some are counting the cost. We feel strengthened and encouraged to press forward in the good work. Although there are but few of us here, yet we are not discouraged. Could we have more such good meetings, we believe much good could be done.—Lena B. Fleshman.

singing and speaking by the school. We met again at 2:30 P. M. for services, after which we repaired to the waterside, to administer baptism to an aged father and mother, who had long since been just outside the pales of the church. May their last days be their happiest, is our prayer! Bro. Wysong remained and preached for us until Oct. 20, when he took his leave from us for other fields of labor. He left many good impressions with us, and may God bless his labors! Our aged elder, Jacob Shively, has recently retired from the oversight of our church, leaving us entirely without an elder.

LAURA APPELMAN.

Plymouth, Ind., Oct. 24.

"WITHOUT earnestness no man is ever great, or does really great things. He may be the cleverest of men; he may be brilliant, entertaining, popular; but he will want weight. No soul-moving picture was ever painted that had not in it a depth of shadow."

Notes from Our Correspondents.

"As cold water to a thirsty soul, so is good news from a far country."

Sand Ridge, Ohio.—Bro. J. J. Rosenberger has just closed a short but very interesting series of meetings in this church. The members were much built up, and some have promised to return, who have wandered away. We had five additions by baptism. May the sentiment of Psalm 23 ever be theirs!—*C. E. Burns, Leipsic, Ohio, Oct. 25.*

Nora Springs, Iowa.—The Rock Grove church love-feast, held Oct. 15 and 16, will long be remembered. Ministers present were elders J. F. Eikenberry, Wm. Ikenberry and Wm. H. Eikenberry. Our aged brother, Wm. Workman, has built an addition to our meeting-house which makes it more convenient than in former years. He also made needed improvements in the speaker's stand. For all this he has our thanks.—*G. M. Noah.*

Hansell, Iowa. — The meetings at the Grundy church are now past. Five precious souls became willing to serve the Lord. The love-feast at that place was one long to be remembered. From here I went to the Iowa River love-feast, which was another of those refreshing showers from the presence of the Lord. Here we met many members from different Counties of Iowa, with whom we had never met before. I am now in Franklin County, Iowa, and will stay here till the feast at Greene, Nov. 5, then go there.—*Joseph Holder, Oct. 25.*

Mohican, Ohio.—Our love-feast was held Oct. 8, at 10 A. M. We had the best of order and attention. One precious soul was baptized in the afternoon before the feast. We also had plenty of ministerial help. Eight ministers were present from different churches, and Bro. N. Longaneck-er officiated. On Sunday morning we had a social meeting, at which brethren and sisters were called upon to speak. The many good and encouraging remarks will not soon be forgotten.—*Nancy A. Fackler, Oct. 11.*

Neutral, Kans.—The love-feast of the New Hope church was held Oct. 8. We had a good meeting. We received two members by letter. The ministers that came to the feast were brethren Harvey, C. Holderman, N. Trapp, H. Shideler and S. Edgecomb. They labored for us earnestly. On Sunday morning, after the feast, it was made known that an old sister, who has been quite feeble for some time, wanted to be anointed. So, at about 9:30 a fair congregation gathered in the tent, and the rite of anointing was performed by Bro. Holderman in the public assembly. Bro. Harvey officiated at the feast.—*A. B. Lichtenwalter, Oct. 19.*

Pyrmont, Ind.—We are at the close of a series of meetings, begun Oct. 8. Our love-feast closed Oct. 13 and an election was held for one speaker and two deacons. Bro. D. C. Campbell is proclaiming glad tidings to all who obey. The result is that ten were baptized. May God enable us, through his Son, to obey his saving Gospel!—*E. Cottrell, Oct. 20.*

Ministerial Meeting, Southern District of Indiana.—The Upper Fall Creek church, where the Ministerial Meeting of the District is to be held in December, has changed the place of holding the Meeting from the church-house in Middletown, to the "Old church," two miles east of Middletown. Parties can now take their choice of stopping-places, either Honey Creek or Middletown.—*D. F. Hoover, Writing Clerk.*

Edna Mills, Ind.—Our Communion was held Oct. 20. The attendance was good. Quite a number of members from other congregations were present and enjoyed the meeting with us. Ministers present from a distance were L. T. Holsinger, H. Keim, D. Wysong, D. F. Hoover, D. C. Campbell and D. Bock. We had splendid order and good preaching, and the members present nearly all communed. Taking it as a whole, I believe it was one of the best Communions I ever attended in our church.—*John E. Metzger, Oct. 21.*

Hyndman, Pa.—At our late love-feast the following ministers were present: J. W. Miller, W. T. Sines, Samuel Richey and C. G. Lint. We were much built up and encouraged by the brethren's good instructions from the Word of Life. We are a small band of workers at this place with a membership of about thirty-two. We have two ministers in the first degree and one deacon. We belong to the Meyersdale church. Ministering brethren, passing this way in their travels, are cordially invited to preach for us.—*Thomas Harden, Oct. 21.*

Notice to Solicitors.—As the new form of notes are to take the place of the old, we request you to collect the interest on all notes. When taken up and new ones given, send all to the missionary treasurer, R. F. Brubaker, Virden, Ill., Box 342. We also earnestly request you to go to work with that zeal and earnestness which the noble enterprise deserves, in soliciting your territories. Let each one canvass the field thoroughly, no difference what objections may be filed, and the Lord will bless you abundantly.—*R. F. Brubaker.*

Lancaster, Pa.—Yesterday the Brethren of Lancaster held a council, at which Bro. T. F. Imler and wife, formerly of Waynesborough, Pa., handed in their certificates of membership. There was also a deacon elected. It was decided to hold a love-feast on Sunday, Nov 6, 1892. This will be the first love-feast ever held in this city. We are now in better working order, and do hope we may all appreciate this great blessing conferred upon us, and that our efforts may redound to the honor and glory of God!—*A. J. Evans, Oct. 20.*

Sawyer, Kans. — The love-feast of the Bethel church, Pratt Co., passed off pleasantly. Bro. John Wise, of Conway Springs, preached one week before the feast. We hope the good seed sown will bring forth its fruit in due season. The ministers present at the feast were brethren Wise, Smith, Bower, Shamberger and A. F. Miller. Bro. Miller officiated. There was a choice held for two deacons. The lot fell on Jacob Blickenstaff and David Ginder. We hope they will be faithful to their calling. Bro. Daniel Gilbert and wife, Bro. Jacob Brubaker and wife, and Bro. Ezra Brubaker and wife, all of Illinois, were present. In all there were sixty-three at the table.—*J. H. Miller, Oct. 20.*

Notice.—The Committee on Arrangements for the next Ministerial Meeting for North-western District of Ohio is now ready to receive invitations from the local churches that desire the Meeting next year. It also solicits appropriate subjects and queries for program. Let all invitations, subjects and queries be sent to the undersigned by May I, 1893.—*J. W. Chambers, &c. Alvada, Ohio.*

Iowa River, Iowa.—The feast at the Iowa River church, Oct. 22, will not soon be forgotten. These meetings should give us much strength and hope as we journey onward. A good many of our brethren and friends from a distance met with us and we hope they will come again. Ministers present were brethren David Holder, Charles Garner and Stephen Johnson. Bro. Holder officiated. There were four baptized,—three on Sunday afternoon and one on Monday forenoon.—*Ellen Nicholson, Oct. 25.*

Pleasant Grove, Kans.—Oct. 15 I went to visit the above church, and continued meetings each evening until the 24th. On the evening of the 22d was their Communion which was one of the most interesting we ever attended. During the meetings the Lord blessed the prayers and labors of the faithful with fifteen baptisms, three applicants and promises of more coming soon. The meetings closed with a growing interest. We now remain with the family and hold meetings until Nov. 12, when, if the Lord will, I commence a meeting in South Park.—*Isaac H. Crist, Gardner, Kans., Oct. 25.*

Clarion, Iowa.—We are located two and one-half miles east and 2 miles south of Clarion. There are no members near here, so far as we know, but there are several families living here, from Oak Gordo, Ill., that are acquainted with our people and speak favorably of them. We are in the territory of the Boon River church, which, we are informed, is about twenty miles north, in Hancock County. We have held one meeting and have made arrangements to have meetings every two weeks at our school-house. The people are kind and sociable, and prospects seem favorable for building up a church.—*Jefferson Mathis.*

Salem, Oregon. — The members of the Salem church are still permitted to enjoy showers of heavenly manna. Brethren J. B. Early and J. R. Ebersole, lately from Missouri, are our ministers and are doing all they can, but the field is much too large to do justice to the work before them. We have members living in three Counties and there is plenty of room for three or four more ministers here in Marion County alone. We are often made to wonder why so few members and homes in this goodly land,—a land where rain and crops never fail, where the climate is very mild and health good. We earnestly invite more ministers to come here to live among us.—*J. B. Lehman, Oct. 16.*

Lindside, W. Va.—Our love-feast of Oct. 15 and 16 was a glorious and soul-reviving feast. Many brethren and sisters were with us from other points. Ministering brethren were George Garbill, P. S. Miller, J. Gresso, A. Duncan and J. Argabright. Brethren Graybill and Miller did most of the preaching which was very interesting. Bro. Miller preached on Sunday night and Monday following, and he certainly held forth the Word of God with great power. There were no additions to the church, but we believe some are counting the cost. We feel strengthened and encouraged to press forward in the good work. Although there are but few of us here, yet we are not discouraged. Could we have more such good meetings, we believe much good could be done.—*Lena B. Fleshman.*

Washington, D. C.—I have on hand a "Critical Commentary and Paraphrase on the Old and New Testament, and Apocrypha," by Patrick, Lowth, Arnold, Whitley and Lowman, in four large volumes, which I will sell at $1.00 per volume." The entire work contains about 4,500 pages and is well bound and in fair condition.—W. M. Lyon, 303 Sixth St., S E.

Nebraska Notice.—The churches of the District of Nebraska will please take notice that there is now due about sixty or more dollars, unpaid, that has accrued from the Annual Meeting Committee, sent to Sidney, Nebraska, also two State District representatives to same place. All the churches, therefore, that have not sent in their quota for paying said expenses, will please send in at your earliest convenience. Send to your treasurer, Wm. A. Gish, Juniata, Adams Co., Nebr.

Warrensburgh, Mo.—The council, preceding our love-feast, was held on Thursday, Oct. 6, and was a very harmonious and pleasant meeting. Our love-feast occurred Oct. 14, at 10 A. M. The evening services were held an hour earlier in order to avoid the crowd that usually gathers on such occasions, and is a great annoyance. The meeting was well attended by members from the surrounding churches and was very enjoyable. Bro. Dell, of Nebraska, was with us, and our dear brother Hope held a two weeks' meeting for us, terminating at the feast. We were very sorry to part with him. May God's blessing ever rest upon him! As an immediate result of the meetings, one was baptized and one reclaimed.—A. A. Roop, Oct. 23.

Virden, Ill.—Oct. 22 the members of the Pleasant Hill church convened in council, preparatory to the Communion. The annual visit was reported and indicated love and harmony, in the main, prevailing. One was received by letter. The mission solicitor received the new blank form of endowment notes. The pastoral visit was encouraged. Brethren Daniel Shively, of Indiana, and John Eller, of Virginia, with other ministers from abroad, were present and assisted greatly in the council, giving us good and needed counsel. The first mentioned brother began a series of meetings in the evening, and delivered three sermons, one yesterday at the close of the Sunday-school, and again at night to large and attentive audiences, holding forth the Word in demonstration of the Spirit and power, creating, at this stage of the meeting, a commendable interest.—James Wirt, Oct. 24.

Alvada, Ohio.—On Saturday, Oct. 15, it was the happy privilege of the brethren and sisters of the Rome congregation once more to enjoy a love-feast together. A large delegation from abroad were present and enjoyed the sacred services with us. We thank the Lord for their presence, and for the loving words of encouragement. The voice of the church was taken for a minister. The lot fell on Bro. James Deary. We also advanced Bro. J. W. Chambers to the second degree of the ministry. At the close of the afternoon services a dear one of about ten summers, from the Sugar Ridge church, Ohio, was received into church fellowship by the sacred ordinance of baptism. This little sister previously wrote us, saying, "I have made up my mind to serve the Lord and want to be baptized." I was impressed with the thought, Oh, how great a work these faithful little lambs of the fold do for Jesus! Nearly their whole life can be consecrated to God! Bro. W. F. England, wife, and little daughter, remained with us until Tuesday, Oct. 18. Bro. England preached for us on Sunday and Monday evenings to attentive audiences, that were well entertained.—Maggie Dickey, Oct. 20.

Ollie, Iowa.—We are now in the midst of a glorious meeting at this place. One has been baptized and we have three more applicants to be baptized to-morrow. There are others very near the kingdom. There is no resident minister at this place. Bro. John Gable, of New Sharon, Iowa, has the oversight.—Wm. C. Hipes, Oct. 21.

Crimora Station, Va.—Bro. D. C. Flory, of Virginia, came to the Forest Chapel church Oct. 2 and conducted a children's meeting, which closed our Sunday-school for this season. The same evening, at 7 o'clock, he commenced a series of meetings which continued each evening until Saturday about 11 A. M., when we met at the water-side, where one dear sister was baptized. At 2 o'clock was the time for our love-feast. About fifty members surrounded the tables. Sunday forenoon Bro. I. M. Cline preached an interesting discourse to a full house of earnest listeners, and at 7 P. M. Bro. D. C. Flory delivered an excellent sermon.—S. F. Sorogham.

Centropolis, Kans.—Last Sunday, Oct. 16, was our regular appointment at the water-side. There was a large crowd present, and after services we repaired to the water-side, where seven dear souls were buried with Christ in baptism. This caused much joy among God's children, and especially the mother, whose two daughters and two sons, and their wives, were of the number baptized. Five of those baptized are now members of the Washington Creek church and living near the outskirts of the church. Our prayer is, that they may be shining lights to the church, that others may see their good works, and thereby be made willing to accept Christ.—James T. Kinzie, Oct. 20.

Nevada, Mo.—The feast in the Nevada church, Vernon County, Mo., occurred Oct. 1, and was truly a feast to those who were prepared to enjoy it. Ministers present were Geo. Barnhart, Samuel Wimer, Wm. Stockmire, John Stump and John Crume. They dealt out the Word faithfully. One young man made the good confession and was baptized. One minister and two deacons were elected and duly installed into their offices. The lot fell on Bro. Eli Leslie for minister and brethren Daniel Leslie and Riley Stump for deacons. They, with their companions, were all faithful workers in the social prayer-meeting and Bible class, hence we may expect them to be equally efficient in general church work.—S. Click, Oct. 20.

Hudson, Ill.—Our second series of meetings at Hudson, Ill., commenced on Sunday, Oct. 9, and closed Oct. 16. Bro. I. M. Gibson, of Roanoke, Va., did the preaching and the impressions made will yet bring fruit to God's glory and honor. As an immediate result three made the good profession and were baptized while others were almost persuaded. Bro. Gibson announced seven days in advance that he would preach upon "Trine Immersion," which called out a very large audience. A minister came a long distance to hear the sermon. He listened very attentively to the arguments which, by the way, were the most logical and convincing that we have yet heard from any source. On the Sunday he closed the text was Rev. 12: 1,—the church clothed with the sun of righteousness, the moon under her feet and the crown of twelve stars upon her head.—Thos. D. Lyon.

Matrimonial.

"What therefore God hath joined together, let not man put asunder."

SHATTO—BAKER.—At the residence of the undersigned, Oct. 12, 1892, by the undersigned, John Shatto and Viola Baker, both of Morris County, Kans. J. E. KELLER.

Fallen Asleep.

"Blessed are the dead which die in the Lord."

WENT.—At Rockwell City, Kans., Oct. 16, 1892, infant son of Frederic and Margaret Went. The occasion was improved from James 4: 14. G. M. THRONE.

FOUTZ.—In the Lower Deer Creek church, Carroll Co., Ind., Oct. 15, 1892, sister Barbara Foutz, aged 82 years, 7 months and 25 days. Deceased was born Dec. 20, 1809, in Mifflin County, Pa. Funeral services at the Paint Creek church by brethren Hiel Hamilton and Jacob Cripe from Rev. 14: 13, with very appropriate remarks.
S. H. BECHTELHEIMER.

OLFIELD.—In the Crooked Creek congregation, Washington Co., Iowa, Bro. Paul Olfield, aged 67 years, 4 months and 11 days. Funeral services by Eld. Samuel Flory.
D. P. MILLER.

DOUGHERTY.—In Lewistown, Pa., Sept. 21, 1892, sister Eliza Jordan Dougherty, aged 79 years, 6 months and 10 days. SARAH SPANGDLE.

TAWYER.—In the Panther Creek church, Woodford Co., Ill., Sept. 14, 1892, sister Barbara, wife of Bro. Jeremiah Tawyer, aged 66 years, 7 months and 20 days. She was a faithful member of the church of the Brethren for about thirty years. She leaves a faithful husband, four sons and two daughters to mourn their loss. Services at Panther Creek on Sunday, Oct. 16, to a very large concourse of people by the home brethren. G. W. GISH.

PALMER.—In the North Solomon church, Ind., Oct. 11, 1892, Lucy Emma, daughter of Bro. James and sister Phebe Palmer, aged 9 years and 16 days. P. LANDIS.

LAYTON.—In the Hopewell church, Bedford Co., Pa., Oct. 17, 1892, Joseph Lenard Layton, aged 1 month and 24 days. Funeral services by the writer from Matt. 18: 3.
D. S. CLAPPER.

MARTIN.—Near Inwood, Ind., Mabel, daughter of Charles L. and Emma Martin, aged 2 months and 4 days. Services by M. A. Eisenhour. JOHN E. JOSEPH.

SNYDER.—In the Yellow River church, Ind., Oct. 17, 1892, Mary, wife of — Snyder, aged 31 years, 1 month and 24 days. Services by Eld. John H. Sellers from Isa. 38: 1, "Set thine house in order for thou shalt die and not live."
JOHN E. JOSEPH.

JOHNSON.—In the Baugo church, Elkhart Co., Ind., Oct. 15, 1892, sister Jemima Johnson, aged 74 years, 7 months and 10 days. Funeral services by Eld. John Metzler.

GREEN.—In the same church, St. Joseph Co., Ind., Oct. 18, 1892, sister Elizabeth Green, aged 28 years, 5 months and 29 days. She leaves a husband and two daughters. One son preceded her to the spirit world. Funeral services by Eld. John Metzler and the writer. H. M. SCHALWM.

CLINE.—At Rossville, Kans., Oct. 9, 1892, of dropsy, Bro. Wm. H. Cline, aged 78 years, 6 months and 1 day. Deceased was baptized June 21. Ten days prior to his death he was anointed with oil in the name of the Lord, according to James 5: 14. C. C. ROOT.

The Gospel Messenger

In the recognized organ of the German Baptist or Brethren's church, and advocates the form of doctrine taught in the New Testament and pleads for a return to apostolic and primitive Christianity.

It recognizes the New Testament as the only infallible rule of faith and practice, and maintains that Faith toward God, Repentance from dead works, Regeneration of the heart and mind, baptism by Trine Immersion for remission of sins unto the reception of the Holy Ghost by the laying on of hands, are the means of adoption into the household of God,—the church militant.

It also maintains that Feet-washing, as taught in John 13, both by example and command of Jesus, should be observed in the church.

That the Lord's Supper, instituted by Christ and as universally observed by the apostles and the early Christians, is a full meal, and, in connection with the Communion, should be taken in the evening or after the close of the day.

That the Salutation of the Holy Kiss, or Kiss of Charity, is binding upon the followers of Christ.

That War and Retaliation are contrary to the spirit and self-denying principles of the religion of Jesus Christ.

That the principle of Plain Dressing and of Non-conformity to the world, as taught in the New Testament, should be observed by the followers of Christ.

That the Scriptural duty of Anointing the Sick with Oil, in the Name of the Lord, James 5: 14, is binding upon all Christians.

It also advocates the church's duty to support Missionary and Tract Work, thus giving to the Lord for the spread of the Gospel and for the conversion of sinners.

In short, it is a vindicator of all that Christ and the apostles have enjoined upon us, and aims, amid the conflicting theories and discords of modern Christendom, to point out ground that all must concede to be infallibly safe.

The above principles of our Fraternity are set forth on our Brethren's Envelopes." Use them! Price 15 cents per package; 40 cents per hundred.

Washington, D. C.—I have on hand a "Critical Commentary and Paraphrase on the Old and New Testament and Apocrypha," by Patrick, Lowth, Arnold, Whitley and Lowman, in four large volumes, which I will sell at $1.00 per volume. The entire work contains about 4,500 pages and is well bound and in fair condition.—*W. M. Lyon, 303 Sixth St., S. E.*

Nebraska Notice.—The churches of the District of Nebraska will please take notice that there is now due about sixty or more dollars, unpaid, that has accrued from the Annual Meeting Committee, sent to Sidney, Nebraska, also two State District representatives to same place. All the churches, therefore, that have not sent in their quota for paying said expenses, will please send in at your earliest convenience. Send to your treasurer, Wm. A. Gish, Juniata, Adams Co., Nebr.

Warrensburgh, Mo.—The council, preceding our love-feast, was held on Thursday, Oct. 6, and was a very harmonious and pleasant meeting. Our love-feast occurred Oct. 14, at 10 A. M. The evening services were held an hour earlier in order to avoid the crowd that usually gathers on such occasions, and is a great annoyance. The meeting was well attended by members from the surrounding churches and was very enjoyable. Bro. Dell, of Nebraska, was with us, and our dear brother Hope held a two weeks' meeting for us, terminating at the feast. We were very sorry to part with him. May God's blessing ever rest upon him! As an immediate result of the meetings, one was baptized and one reclaimed.—*A. A. Roop, Oct. 23.*

Virden, Ill.—Oct. 22 the members of the Pleasant Hill church convened in council, preparatory to the Communion. The annual visit was reported and indicated love and harmony, in the main, prevailing. One was received by letter. The mission solicitor received the new blank form of endowment notes. The pastoral visit was encouraged. Brethren Daniel Shively, of Indiana, and John Eller, of Virginia, with other ministers from abroad, were present and assisted greatly in the council, giving us good and needed counsel. The first mentioned brother began a series of meetings in the evening, and delivered three sermons, one yesterday at the close of the Sunday-school, and again at night to large and attentive audiences, holding forth the Word in demonstration of the Spirit and power, creating, at this stage of the meeting, a commendable interest.—*James Wirt, Oct. 24.*

Alvada, Ohio.—On Saturday, Oct. 15, it was the happy privilege of the brethren and sisters of the Rome congregation once more to enjoy a love-feast together. A large delegation from abroad were present and enjoyed the sacred services with us. We thank the Lord for their presence, and for the loving words of encouragement. The voice of the church was taken for a minister. The lot fell on Bro. James Deary. We also advanced Bro. J. W. Obambers to the second degree of the ministry. At the close of the afternoon services a dear one of about ten summers, from the Sugar Ridge church, Ohio, was received into church fellowship by the sacred ordinance of baptism. This little sister previously wrote us, saying, "I have made up my mind to serve the Lord and want to be baptized." I was impressed with the thought, Oh, how great a work these faithful little lambs of the fold do for Jesus! Nearly their whole life can be consecrated to God! Bro. W. F. England, wife, and little daughter, remained with us until Tuesday, Oct. 18. Bro. England preached for us on Sunday and Monday evenings to attentive audiences, that were well entertained.—*Maggie Dickey, Oct. 20.*

Ollie, Iowa.—We are now in the midst of a glorious meeting at this place. One has been baptized and we have three more applicants to be baptized to-morrow. There are others very near the kingdom. There is no resident minister at this place. Bro. John Gable, of New Sharon, Iowa, has the oversight.—*Wm. C. Hipes, Oct. 21.*

Crimora Station, Va.—Bro. D. C. Flory, of Virginia, came to the Forest Chapel church Oct. 2 and conducted a children's meeting, which closed our Sunday-school for this season. The same evening, at 7 o'clock, he commenced a series of meetings which continued each evening until Saturday about 11 A. M., when we met at the water-side, where one dear sister was baptized. At 2 o'clock was the time for our love-feast. About fifty members surrounded the tables. Sunday forenoon Bro. I. M. Cline preached an interesting discourse to a full house of earnest listeners, and at 7 P. M. Bro. D. C. Flory delivered an excellent sermon.—*S. F. Sorogham.*

Centropolis, Kans.—Last Sunday, Oct. 16, was our regular appointment at the church. There was a large crowd present, and after services we repaired to the water-side, where seven dear souls were buried with Christ in baptism. This caused much joy among God's children, and especially the mother, whose two daughters and two sons, and their wives, were of the number baptized. Five of those baptized are now members of the Washington Creek church and two lived near the outskirts of the church. Our prayer is, that they may see their good works, and thereby be made willing to accept Christ.—*James T. Kinzie, Oct. 20.*

Nevada, Mo.—The feast in the Nevada church, Vernon County, Mo., occurred Oct. 1, and was truly a feast to those who were prepared to enjoy it. Ministers present were Geo. Barnhart, Samuel Wimer, Wm. Stockmire, John Stump and John Crume. They dealt out the Word faithfully. One young man made the good confession and was baptized. One minister and two deacons were elected and duly installed into their offices. The lot fell on Bro. Eli Leslie for minister and brethren Daniel Leslie and Riley Stump for deacons. They, with their companions, were all faithful workers in the social prayer-meeting and Bible class, hence we may expect them to be equally efficient in general church work.—*S. Click, Oct. 20.*

Hudson, Ill.—Our second series of meetings at Hudson, Ill., commenced on Sunday, Oct. 9, and closed Oct. 16. Bro. I. M. Gibson, of Roanoke, Va., did the preaching and the impressions made will yet bring fruit to God's glory and honor. As an immediate result three- made the good profession and were baptized while others were almost persuaded. Bro. Gibson announced seven days in advance that he would preach upon "Trine Immersion," which called out a very large audience. A minister came a long distance to hear the sermon. He listened very attentively to the arguments which, by the way, were the most logical and convincing that we have yet heard from any source. On the Sunday he closed the text was Rev. 12: 1,—the church clothed with the sun of righteousness, the moon under her feet and the crown of twelve stars upon her head.—*Thos. D. Lyon.*

Matrimonial.

" What therefore God hath joined together, let not man put asunder."

SHATTO—BAKER.—At the residence of the undersigned, Oct. 13, 1892, by the undersigned, John Shatto and Viola Baker, both of Morris County, Kans. J. E. KELLER.

Fallen Asleep.

" Blessed are the dead which die in the Lord."

WENT.—At Rockwell City, Kans., Oct. 16, 1892, infant son of Frederic and Margaret Went. The occasion was improved from James 4: 14. G. M. THRONE.

FOUTZ.—In the Lower Deer Creek church, Carroll Co., Ind., Oct. 15, 1892, sister Barbara Foutz, aged 82 years, 9 months and 24 days. Deceased was born Dec. 20, 1809, in Mifflin County, Pa. Funeral services at the Paint Creek church by brethren Hiel Hamilton and Jacob Cripe from Rev. 14: 13, with very appropriate remarks.
S. H. BECHTELHEIMER.

OLFIELD.—In the Crooked Creek congregation, Washington Co., Iowa, Bro. Paul Olfield, aged 67 years, 4 months and 11 days. Funeral services by Eld. Samuel Flory.
D. P. MILLER.

DOUGHERTY.—In Lewistown, Pa., Sept. 21, 1892, sister Eliza Jordan Dougherty, aged 79 years, 6 months and 10 days. SARAH SPANOGLE.

TAWYER.—In the Panther Creek church, Woodford Co., Ill., Sept. 14, 1892, sister Barbara, wife of Bro. Jeremiah Tawyer, aged 66 years, 7 months and 20 days. She was a faithful member of the church of the Brethren for about thirty years. She leaves a faithful husband, four sons and two daughters to mourn their loss. Services at Panther Creek on Sunday, Oct. 16, to a very large concourse of people by the home brethren. G. W. GISH.

PALMER.—In the North Solomon church, Ind., Oct. 11, 1892, Lucy Emma, daughter of Bro. James and sister Phebe Palmer, aged 9 years and 16 days. P. LAROS.

LAYTON.—In the Hopewell church, Bedford Co., Pa., Oct. 17, 1892, Joseph Lenard Layton, aged 1 month and 24 days. Funeral services by the writer from Matt. 18: 3.
D. S. CLAPPER.

MARTIN.—Near Inwood, Ind., Mabel, daughter of Charles L. and Emma Martin, aged 2 months and 4 days. Services by M. A. Eisenhour. JOHN E. JOSEPH.

SNYDER.—In the Yellow River church, Ind., Oct. 17, 1892, Mary, wife of —— Snyder, aged 31 years, 1 month and 24 days. Services by Eld. John H. Sellers from Isa. 38: 1, " Set thine house in order for thou shalt die and not live."
JOHN E. JOSEPH.

JOHNSON.—In the Baugo church, Elkhart Co., Ind., Oct. 15, 1892, sister Jemima Johnson, aged 74 years, 7 months and 10 days. Funeral services by Eld. John Metzler.

GREEN.—In the same church, St. Joseph Co., Ind., Oct. 18, 1892, sister Elizabeth Green, aged 28 years, 5 months and 29 days. She leaves a husband and two daughters. One son preceded her to the spirit world. Funeral services by Eld. John Metzler and the writer. H. M. SCHALWM.

CLINE.—At Rossville, Kans., Oct. 9, 1892, of dropsy, Bro. Wm. H. Cline, aged 78 years, 6 months and 1 day. Deceased was baptized June 21. Ten days prior to his death he was anointed with oil in the name of the Lord, according to James 5: 14. C. C. ROOT.

The Gospel Messenger

Is the recognized organ of the German Baptist or Brethren's church and advocates the form of doctrine taught in the New Testament and pleads for a return to apostolic and primitive Christianity.

It recognizes the New Testament as the only infallible rule of faith and practice, and maintains that Faith toward God, Repentance from dead works, Regeneration of the heart and mind, baptism by Trine Immersion for remission of sins unto the reception of the Holy Ghost by the laying on of hands, are the means of adoption into the household of God,—the church militant.

It also maintains that Feet-washing, as taught in John 13, both by example and command of Jesus, should be observed in the church.

That the Lord's Supper, instituted by Christ and as universally observed by the apostles and the early Christians, is a full meal, and in connection with the Communion, should be taken in the evening or after the close of the day.

That the Salutation of the Holy Kiss, or Kiss of Charity, is binding upon the followers of Christ.

That War and Retaliation are contrary to the spirit and self-denying principles of the religion of Jesus Christ.

That the principle of Plain Dressing and of Non-conformity to the world, as taught in the New Testament, should be observed by the followers of Christ.

That the Scriptural duty of Anointing the Sick with Oil, in the Name of the Lord, James 5: 14, is binding upon all Christians.

It also advocates the church's duty to support Missionary and Tract Work, thus giving to the Lord for the spread of the Gospel and for the conversion of sinners.

In short, it is a vindicator of all that Christ and the apostles have enjoined upon us, and aims, amid the conflicting theories and discords of modern Christendom, to point out ground that all must concede to be infallibly safe.

☞ The above principles of our Fraternity are set forth on our Brethren's Envelopes." Use them! Price 15 cents per package; 40 cents per hundred.

Announcements.

MINISTERIAL MEETINGS.

Nov. 25, at 2 A. M., in the South-east District of Kansas, Ministerial Meeting in the Cedar Creek church, Montida, Anderson Co., Kans.

LOVE-FEASTS.

Nov. 8, at 10 A. M., Wheatville (Upper Twin) church, Preble Co., Ohio. R. R. Station: West Alexandria and Eaton.

Nov. 8, at 2 P. M., Ridgely church, Caroline Co., Md.

Nov. 10, at 4 P. M., Bear Creek, Montgomery Co., Ohio.

Nov. 11, at 4 P. M., Winnemac church, Beaver Creek meeting-house, 14 miles south-west of Winnemac.

Nov. 12, at 2 P. M., Fairview church, Douglas Co., Mo., 6 miles south of Mansfield.

Nov. 12, Salem church, Reno Co., Kans., 2 miles south and 3 miles west of Nickerson.

Nov. 12, at 4 P. M., Blackberry church, Henry Co., Va.

Nov. 12, at 10 A. M., Thornapple church, Mich., at the east house.

Nov. 19, at 3 P. M., McPherson, Kans.

Nov. 19, Altoona, Pa.

Nov. 21, at 3 P. M., Cedar Creek church, Anderson Co., Kans.

Nov. 23 and 26, Beatrice church, Nebr.

Dec. 8, at 2 P. M., Cerro Gordo, Ill.

Church Entertainments: Twenty Objections.

By Rev. B. Carradine, D. D. 12mo, 100 pp. Paper cover, 30 cents. A strong book in defense of its position, written by a powerful pen, presenting the most candid and scriptural arraignment of unwarrantable methods for money-raising in the Church. The spirit of the book is highly devotional and cannot fail to inspire the reader with its seriousness.

For Sale!

Having a desire to devote more time to church work, I offer one quarter section of choice farm land for sale. This farm has a good house, barn, fences, well, and a nice spring. It is situated 3½ miles south of the Brethren's meeting-house in Shannon, Ill. It is also within one mile of a good creamery. I also offer 50 head of registered Short Horn Cattle, 15 males and 35 females, — choice individuals at a very low price. Address for particulars, D. Rowland, Lanark, Ill.

--- THE ---

Doctrine of the Brethren Defended.

THIS work contains a complete exposition of the faith and practice of the Brethren, the Divinity of Christ, the Divinity of the Holy Spirit, Immersion, Feet-washing, the Lord's Supper, the Holy Kiss, Non-conformity, Secret Societies, etc. Price, per copy, cloth binding, $1.25. Address this office.

For Sale!

I have for sale a complete set of *Gospel Visitor*, *Primitive Christian*, and *Gospel Messenger*, from 1876 to 1891 included, bound in morocco, cloth sides; also *Young Disciple*, from 1881 to 1889, bound in morocco, cloth sides, three years in a book. The *Gospel Visitor* is bound in black roan, paper sides. For terms address J. W. King, Huntingdon, Pa.

EUROPE
AND
Bible Lands

A new edition of this deservedly popular work has again been published. It retains all the excellencies of its predecessors, and with those who are interested in Bible study this work will always remain a favorite. Those who have read the ordinary book of travel will be surprised to find "Europe and Bible Lands" of thrilling interest for both old and young. The large number of books, already sold, proves that the work is of more than ordinary merit.

A fair supply of the last edition of this work is still on hand. Those who have not yet secured a copy of the work should embrace this opportunity of securing it. Price, in fine cloth binding, only $1.50 per copy, post-paid. To agents who are prepared to push an active canvass of the work, we are prepared to give special inducements. Write us. BRETHREN'S PUBLISHING Co.,
Mt. Morris, Ill.

Alone with God.

THIS manual of devotions, by J. H. Garrison, comprises a series of meditations with forms of prayer for private devotions, family worship and special occasions. It is one of the most useful, most needed, and best adapted books of the year, and therefore it is not strange that it is proving one of the most popular. Its work of this kind its distinguished, gifted, pious and beloved author is at his best. This book is helpful to every minister, church official, and Sunday-school superintendent, as well as every private member of the church in all ages. It has models of prayer, suitable for the service of the prayer-meeting, while its suggestions; meditations and instructions are pre-eminently calculated to be of service in preparation for the solemn duties that rest upon the active members. Cloth, 75 cents; morocco, $1.25. Address this office.

Farm for Sale.

A desirable property located 1¼ miles east of Mt. Morris, consisting of 185 acres of well-improved land. One of the finest country residences in Ogle County. For further particulars call on, or address,
ELIZABETH MIDDLEKAUFF,
Mt. Morris, Ill.

Excursions to California.

Excursions in charge of M. M. Eshelman, Immigration Agent, will leave Chicago over the "Santa Fe Route" Tuesdays, and Kansas City Wednesdays, during the year 1892, on dates as follows:

Chicago, January 22, February 23, March 22, April 26, May 24, June 28, July 26, August 23, September 27, October 25, November 22, December 28.

Kansas City, January 27, February 24, March 23, April 27, May 25, June 29, July 27, August 24, September 28, October 26, November 23, December 28.

Parties wishing to avail themselves of the privileges of these excursions, should write M. M. Eshelman, North Fonseca, California, prior to the 15th of each month, and from the fifteenth to the end of the month, at 1019 Union Avenue (opposite Union Depot), Kansas City, Mo., stating when and where they wish to join one of these excursions, and he will give them full information, and it desired will reserve berths in Tourist Sleeping Car for them. Do not fail to write him; he will do you good. The rates will be as low as the lowest made to the Pacific Coast.

GEORGE L. McDONAUGH,
Traveling Agent,

✦ESSAYS✦

"Study to show thyself approved unto God; a workman that needeth not to be ashamed, rightly dividing the Word of Truth."

TO A DYING MISSIONARY.

BY H. PEARSON.

"He is dying, he is dying."
　From the South the message came,
And the winds around me sighing
　Whispered mournfully his name.

Then my heart with sorrow bleeding
　Could not curb its bitter pain,
Could not stop the question speeding
　Swiftly to the weary brain.

Must the golden bowl be shattered,
　When with truths of wisdom filled,
Truths that patiently were gathered,
　And by arduous labor tilled?

You, who tell the Savior's story,
　Lift us to the mercy throne,
Must you in your·noonday glory
　Sleep beneath the church-yard stone?

Thus in silence long I pondered
　Problems that I could not solve.
And my soul in·darkness wandered
　By etern'ty's mystic gulf.

Till a melancholy singing
　Woke me from my reverie.
In a cage beside me swinging
　Birdie sang its melody.

In the prison house it shivered,
　As it poured the magic strains,
Beat against the bars and quivered
　Longing for the woods and plains.

Pity moved me, and its prison
　Wide I opened.　You are free!
Seek the sun in beauty risen,
　Warble by the glittering sea.

Oh how joyfully it drifted
　Out into the endless blue;
With a heavenly music gifted,
　Sang and vanished from my view.

But it left the room so dreary
　That I wished it back again
From the woodlands bright and cheery.
　Oh how selfish I was then!

Now my soul, no longer frightened,
　Looked into the mystic gloom;
Saw the problems as they brightened—
　Saw them solved beyond the tomb.

Fight the battle; fight it bravely,
　Ere to death the spirit yields.
Fear not; Christ will lead you safely
　To the ever-blooming fields.

Cawnoy, Kans.

IN HIS FOOTSTEPS.—1 Pet. 2: 21.

BY C. H. BALSBAUGH.

THE footprints of Emmanuel seem to be visible to some eyes only in the ordinances. The whole of religion is summed up in many minds in baptism, feet-washing, Lord's Supper, and plain dress. God forbid that I should say one word against any of these, but we may have them all, and yet not be Christians, as many instances, past and present, sadly testify. Christianity is life, the very life of Christ, who is "GOD *manifest in the flesh.*" Baptism has no more power to wash away sin than to change an Ethiopian into a Caucasian. "The blood of Jesus Christ cleanseth from all sin." 1 John 1: 7. Immersion is a vivid symbol of this great fact and is enjoined by Divine Authority both as an objective representation of the personal application of the Atonement and as a test of our loyalty. And so of all externals in religion. We need them as helps both from God manward, and from man Godward. But the "footsteps" of Jesus are deeper. "Looking unto Jesus" is looking unto God. His love, his trust, his sacrifice must be ours. "He was in the *form* of God and thought it *not robbery* to be *equal* with God; but made himself of *no reputation,* and took upon himself the *form* of a *servant,* and was made in the likeness of men." This it would seem would be humiliation enough; but it was only the condition to the·utter descent and self-immolation in which his purpose and our hope culminate. "Being found in fashion as a man, he humbled himself and became obedient unto death, even the death of the cross." Philpp. 2: 5–8. Now we have the high, Divine import of Peter's urgent exhortation to follow the steps of the August Exemplar. "Even hereunto were ye called; because Christ also suffered for us, leaving us an example, that ye should follow his steps." "Let this mind be in you, which was also in Christ Jesus."

To·be baptized is as easy as to wash our hands before breakfast. But to live as this burial with Christ unto death signifies, is as hard as to die with Christ on the cross. To wash feet, literally, is like any other pedal ablution for the removal of "the filth of the flesh." But to wash feet in the Christian sense is to purge the church thoroughly from the abominable leaven that is forever striving to work its way to the most conspicuous position, and asking for seats at the right and left of the King of kings in the Supernal glory. Fearfully patent is it that numbers among us wash feet at every love-feast, and advertise themselves all the year round that they walk according to Philpp. 3: 18, 19. "He that saith he abideth in him ought himself also so to walk, even as he walked." 1 John 2: 6.

He walked from heaven to earth, from glory to shame, from Nazareth to Bethabara, from Jordan to the wilderness, then into all the fidelities of his prophetic office, and then into the deeper, darker ordeal of his priestly function, and lastly "led captivity captive, ascended on high, and gave gifts unto men." Eph. 4: 8. Our baptism is not worth talking about if it does not pledge us to the exemplification of all that the death of Christ is designed to secure. To refer to our initiation as evidence of our membership in the body of Christ, while we refuse to spend time and money and ease for the extension of the redemption of the cross to the ends of the earth, is a practical demonstration that your baptism is become unbaptism. Rom. 2: 25. The heathen have as valid a claim to the salvation achieved by the cross of Christ as any of us. We are not a whit more urgently enjoined to be baptized than to go into all the world and preach the Gospel to every creature. Our reluctance to evangelize the world only betrays our misapprehension of the essential nature and purpose of Christianity. The church exists for this very end, to make known the riches of the glory of the mystery of the cross among the Gentiles. Col. 1: 27. Conservatism is sure sure to dwarf and kill if it be not also progressive even to the death of the cross. This is the lesson for our time, as for all time, that the self-sacrifice of Jesus is to be perpetuated in his disciples, so that what he began in Palestine may reach over all latitudes and longitudes. We need more prayer, more profound self-emptying, more genuine Brotherhood, more absolute consecration, and a larger, fuller baptism of the Holy Spirit than we have had hitherto. If we are ready, God is always waiting to fulfil Eph. 3: 20. Our only excuse is, the terms of the cross are too rigid, too self-annihilating, leave no room for anything but the glory of God at the expense of all that the flesh holds dear. Philpp. 3: 7, 8. Who will accept salvation, and dedicate body, and soul, and purse to its extension in heathen lands and wherever people sit "in the region and shadow of death"? Where are those who are risen with Christ and seek those things which are above, where Christ sitteth at the right hand of God," whose "affections are set" on the imperishable realities for which ".Christ endured the cross, despising the shame"? Col. 3: 1, 2; Heb. 12: 2. Who is ready to "go forth unto him without the camp, bearing his reproach"? Heb. 13: 13. Whether we joyfully enter into the purpose and work of Jesus, or selfishly and fatally decline, let us be sure of this, that unto the church has "God committed the word of reconciliation," and that on our fidelity rests the salvation of millions of souls. The "*go*" of Matt. 28: 19, is as imperative to-day as the authority and love of God can make it.

Union Deposit, Pa.

A STUDY OF ΒΑΠΤΙΖΕΙ .

BY O. PERRY HOOVER.

THE word "baptize" is the Anglicised form of the Greek ΒΑΠΤΙΖΕΙΝ, which is used sixty-six times in the New Testament . Sixty-two times it is translated "baptize," twice "wash," and twice applied to John the Baptist. An older word *bapto* is used four times and translated "dip." *Baptizo* is the frequentative form from *bapto;* the ending *izo* emphasizes the action contained in *bapto.*

In this study we desire to present the original meaning of ΒΑΠΤΙΖΕΙΝ. Denominational controversy has so confused the true meaning, that its force is lessened. English readers generally apply it to the ordinance of baptism alone, which leads to misunderstanding because the daily use is not felt.

Words change in meaning sometimes so far as to lose the original altogether, *e. g.,* "tragedy" in the original of the drama, meant a goat-song, as "comedy" meant a village-song. But in the entire range of Greek literature ΒΑΠΤΙΖΕΙΝ has kept its original meaning. The word was as common among the Greeks as dip, sink, plunge, or overwhelm is with us. ΒΑΠΤΙΖΕΙΝ always expressed the same idea,—whether ludicrous or solemn, profane or sacred. · Extending over a period of 1,500 years or more, the word was used with the same ground-meaning by poets, rhetoricians, philosophers and historians; by writers on farming, medicine and theology; in romance, orations, odes and sermons; by Pagan, Jewish, and Christian writers.

The ground-meaning is to immerse, immerge, submerge, to dip, to plunge, to overwhelm and to sink. In profane literature this meaning was applied " to dip (baptize) wool in dye;" "steel in fire;" "heated iron in water for tempering"; "a cup in water for drinking" ; "to sink (baptize) a ship" ; "to drown (baptize) an animal"; "to besmear (baptize) the hand in blood"; "to thrust (baptize) the sword in an enemy's breast"; "to dip (baptize) sliced turnips in brine for salad."

Polybius and Plutarch use ΒΑΠΤΙΖΕΙΝ of sinking ships; Aristotle of sea-weed, exposed by ebb-tide; Strabo of Alexander's army marching in water waist deep; Diodorus of a defeated army drowned by a swollen stream. Josephus uses it to describe the drowning of the boy Aristobulus. Chrysostom, discoursing on the paralytic, let down through the roof, says, "But here no such thing is to be seen . . . no steel plunged in *baptisomenon* nor flowing blood." Josephus, again, speaking of Simion's suicide, says, "He thrust (*ebaptise*) the whole sword into his own neck."

The above examples are given to show the literal use of ΒΑΠΤΙΖΕΙΝ. The same fundamental idea is found in the figurative use, meaning·to

+ESSAYS+

"Study to show thyself approved unto God; a workman that needeth not to be ashamed, rightly dividing the Word of Truth."

TO A DYING MISSIONARY.

BY M. PEARSON.

"HE is dying, he is dying."
From the South the message came,
And the winds around me sighing
Whispered mournfully his name.

Then my heart with sorrow bleeding
Could not curb its bitter pain,
Could not stop the question speeding
Swiftly to the weary brain.

Must the golden bowl be shattered,
When with truths of wisdom filled,
Truths that patiently were gathered,
And by arduous labor tilled?

You, who tell the Savior's story,
Lift us to the mercy throne,
Must you in your noonday glory
Sleep beneath the church-yard stone?

Thus in silence long I pondered
Problems that I could not solve,
And my soul in darkness wandered
By eternity's mystic gulf.

Till a melancholy singing
Woke me from my reverie.
In a cage beside me swinging
Birdie sang his melody.

In the prison house it shivered,
As it poured the magic strains,
Beat against the bars and quivered
Longing for the woods and plains.

Pity moved me, and its prison
Wide I opened. You are free!
Seek the sun in beauty risen,
Warble by the glittering sea.

Oh how joyfully it drifted
Out into the endless blue;
With a heavenly music gifted,
Sang and vanished from my view.

But it left the room so dreary
That I wished it back again
From the woodlands bright and cheery.
Oh how selfish I was then!

Now my soul, no longer frightened,
Looked into the mystic gloom;
Saw the problems as they brightened—
Saw them solved beyond the tomb.

Fight the battle; fight it bravely,
Ere to death the spirit yields.
Fear not; Christ will lead you safely
To the ever-blooming fields.

Conway, Kans.

IN HIS FOOTSTEPS.—1 Pet. 2: 21.

BY C. H. BALSBAUGH.

THE footprints of Emmanuel seem to be visible to some eyes only in the ordinances. The whole of religion is summed up in many minds in baptism, feet-washing, Lord's Supper, and plain dress. God forbid that I should say one word against any of these, but we may have them all, and yet not be Christians, as many instances, past and present, sadly testify. Christianity is life, the very life of Christ, who is "GOD *manifest in the flesh*." Baptism has no more power to wash away sin than to change an Ethiopian into a Caucasian. "The blood of Jesus Christ cleanseth from all sin." 1 John 1: 7. Immersion is a vivid symbol of this great fact and is enjoined by Divine Authority both as an objective representation of the personal application of the Atonement and as a test of our loyalty. And so of all externals in religion. We need them as helps both from God manward, and from man Godward. But the "footsteps" of Jesus are deeper. "Looking unto Jesus" is looking unto God. His love, his trust, his sacrifice must be ours. "He was in the *form* of God and thought it *not robbery* to be equal with God; but made himself of *no reputation*, and took upon himself the *form* of a *servant*, and was made in the likeness of men." This it would seem would be humiliation enough; but it was only the condition to the utter descent and self-immolation in which his purpose and our hope culminate. "Being found in fashion as a man, he humbled himself and became obedient unto death, even the death of the cross." Philpp. 2: 5-8. Now we have the high, Divine import of Peter's urgent exhortation to follow the steps of the August Exemplar. "Even hereunto were ye called; because Christ also suffered for us, leaving us an example, that ye should follow his steps." "Let this mind be in you, which was also in Christ Jesus."

To be baptized is as easy as to wash our hands before breakfast. But to live as this burial with Christ unto death signifies, is as hard as to die with Christ on the cross. To wash feet, literally, is like any other pedal ablution for the removal of "the filth of the flesh." But to wash feet in the Christian sense is to purge the church thoroughly from the abominable leaven that is forever striving to work its way to the most conspicuous position, and asking for seats at the right and left of the King of kings in the Supernal glory. Fearfully patent is it that numbers among us wash feet at every love-feast, and advertise themselves all the year round that they walk according to Philpp. 3: 18, 19. "He that saith he abideth in him ought himself also so to walk, even as he walked." 1 John 2: 6.

He walked from heaven to earth, from glory to shame, from Nazareth to Bethabara, from Jordan to the wilderness, then into all the fidelities of his prophetic office, and then into the deeper, darker ordeal of his priestly function, and lastly "led captivity captive, ascended on high, and gave gifts unto men." Eph. 4: 8. Our baptism is not worth talking about if it does not pledge us to the exemplification of all that the death of Christ is designed to secure. To refer to our initiation as evidence of our membership in the body of Christ, while we refuse to spend time and money and ease for the extension of the redemption of the cross to the ends of the earth, is a practical demonstration that your baptism is become unbaptism. Rom. 2: 25. The heathen have as valid a claim to the salvation achieved by the cross of Christ as any of us. We are not a whit more urgently enjoined to be baptized than to go into all the world and preach the Gospel to every creature. Our reluctance to evangelize the world only betrays our misapprehension of the essential nature and purpose of Christianity. The church exists for this very end, to make known the riches of the glory of the mystery of the cross among the Gentiles. Col. 1: 27. Conservatism is sure sure to dwarf and kill if it be not also progressive even to the death of the cross. This is the lesson for our time, as for all time, that the self-sacrifice of Jesus is to be perpetuated in his disciples, so that what he began in Palestine may reach over all latitudes and longitudes. We need more prayer, more profound self-emptying, more genuine Brotherhood, more absolute consecration, and a larger, fuller baptism of the Holy Spirit than we have had hitherto. If we are ready, God is always waiting to fulfil Eph. 3: 20. Our only excuse is, the terms of the cross are too rigid, too self-annihilating, leave no room for anything but the glory of God at the expense of all that the flesh holds dear. Philpp. 3: 7, 8. Who will accept salvation, and dedicate body, and soul, and purse to its extension in heathen lands and wherever people sit "in the region and shadow of death"? Where are those who are risen with Christ and seek those things which are above, where Christ sitteth at the right hand of God," whose "affections are set" on the imperishable realities for which ".Christ endured the cross, despising the shame"? Col. 3: 1, 2; Heb. 12: 2. Who is ready to "go forth unto him without the camp, bearing his reproach"? Heb. 13: 13. Whether we joyfully enter into the purpose and work of Jesus, or selfishly and fatally decline, let us be sure of this, that unto the church has "God committed the word of reconciliation," and that on our fidelity rests the salvation of millions of souls. The "*go*" of Matt. 28: 19, is as imperative to-day as the authority and love of God can make it.

Union Deposit, Pa.

A STUDY OF APTIZEI.

BY O. PERRY HOOVER.

THE word "baptize" is the Anglicised form of the Greek BAPTIZEIN, which is used sixty-six times in the New Testament. Sixty-two times it is translated "baptize," twice "wash," and twice applied to John the Baptist. An older word *bapto* is used four times and translated "dip." *Baptizo* is the frequentative form from *bapto;* the ending *izo* emphasizes the action contained in *bapto.*

In this study we desire to present the original meaning of BAPTIZEIN. Denominational controversy has so confused the true meaning, that its force is lessened. English readers generally apply it to the ordinance of baptism alone, which leads to misunderstanding because the daily use is not felt.

Words change in meaning sometimes so far as to lose the original altogether, e. g., "tragedy" in the original of the drama, meant a goat-song, as "comedy" meant a village-song. But in the entire range of Greek literature BAPTIZEIN has kept its original meaning. The word was as common among the Greeks as dip, sink, plunge, or overwhelm is with us. BAPTIZEIN always expressed the same idea,—whether ludicrous or solemn, profane or sacred. Extending over a period of 1,500 years or more, the word was used with the same ground-meaning by poets, rhetoricians, philosophers and historians; by writers on farming, medicine and theology; in romance, orations, odes and sermons; by Pagan, Jewish, and Christian writers.

The ground-meaning is to immerse, immerge, submerge, to dip, to plunge, to overwhelm and to sink. In profane literature this meaning was applied " to dip (baptize) wool in dye;" "steel in fire;" "heated iron in water for tempering"; "a cup in water for drinking"; "to sink (baptize) a ship"; "to drown (baptize) an animal"; "to besmear (baptize) the hand in blood"; "to thrust (baptize) the sword in an enemy's breast"; "to dip (baptize) sliced turnips in brine for salad."

Polybius and Plutarch use BAPTIZEIN of sinking ships; Aristotle of sea-weed, exposed by ebb-tide; Strabo of Alexander's army marching in water waist deep; Diodorus of a defeated army drowned by a swollen stream. Josephus used it to describe the drowning of the boy Aristobulus. Chrysostom, discoursing on the paralytic, let down through the roof, says, "But here no such thing is to be seen . . . . no steel plunged in *baptisomenon* nor flowing blood." Josephus, again, speaking of Simion's suicide, says, "He thrust (*ebaptise*) the whole sword into his own neck."

The above examples are given to show the literal use of BAPTIZEIN. The same fundamental idea is found in the figurative use, meaning to

CORRESPONDENCE.

"Write what thou seest, and send it unto the churches."

☞Church News solicited for this Department. If you have had a good meeting, send a report of it, so that others may rejoice with you. In writing give name of church, County and State. Be brief. Notes of Travel should be as short as possible. Land Advertisements are not solicited for this Department. We have an advertising page, and, if necessary, will issue supplements.

From the Falling Spring Church, Franklin County, Pa.

OUR love-feast, held at the Hade church Oct. 29 and 30, was a good meeting, although the weather was very cold and stormy. On Saturday morning Bro. Wm. Hertzler, of Lancaster County, spoke very feelingly; judging by the attention he received, to the satisfaction of all. His text is found in Acts 2: 41. After dinner Bro. H. C. Early, from Virginia, preached to a crowded house from Matt. 16: 18, taking for his theme "The Church." We received an abundance of food for the soul. The solemn services of the evening were conducted by Bro. J. F. Oller, of Waynesborough, Pa. Bro. Oller has borne the heat and burden of many days. He has lost none of his zeal for the Master, but is working with increased zeal, feeling that, at best, his time is short to labor here in the vineyard of the Lord. Our elder, Wm. O. Koonts, remarked that he has been in this congregation a long time, but that this was the largest feast, in his recollection, that was ever held in this congregation. Not only was it the largest, but one of the most edifying. We elected two deacons. The lot fell on brethren Jacob Zug and Harry Stamy, two faithful brethren. Our prayer is that they may be sustained by grace divine, and that they may magnify their sacred office. Bro. Wm. Hertzler then preached from Col. 3: 1 to a large congregation. Brethren Nicholas Martin, John Lehner, Daniel Miller, Benjamin Price, Daniel Baker, Joseph Neibert, J. D. Garner, Abraham Rowland, John Fogiesauger, and others, also gave us words of encouragement.

Thus ended another Communion season in the old Falling Spring church. In the evening we had three love-feasts to hold at the homes of our aged brethren who are not able to leave home. Bro. Wm. C. Koonts went to Bro. Adam Baker's with the brethren and sisters and held one for the benefit of Bro. Baker's companion, who has been afflicted for some years. Bro. Isaac Riddlesberger went to Bro. Jacob Fahl's, to hold one for the benefit of sister Fahl, and the writer was sent to Bro. Jacob Benedict's, to hold a feast for the benefit of brother Jacob and sister Benedict, who are both past their threescore years and ten, and who seemingly stand on the verge of eternity. Sister Harshman, who lives quite near, was there also. She has attained the remarkable age of eighty-five years. It was a scene long to be remembered to see those aged brethren and sisters surround the Lord's table, and engage in the holy ordinance of God's house, which blessings they enjoyed so often in their younger days, but now are, to a certain extent, deprived of. It was pleasant to see the grandfather, son and grand-daughters all surround the table with us, and engage in the solemn services. Thus closed a day or scene in our life, that we can look back to with pleasure and profit.　WM. A. ANTHONY.

From the Jonathan Creek Church, Perry Co., Ohio.

THE members of the above church commenced a series of meetings Oct. 22. Bro. Wm. Dessenberg, of Ashland, Ohio, did the preaching. He is a workman that needeth not to be ashamed, rightly dividing the Word of Truth. Although there were no accessions, Bro. Dessenberg made some

warm friends, and left many deep impressions, which, we hope, will bear fruit to the saving of some precious souls here, who are near the kingdom. On Saturday evening, Oct. 29, we held our Communion. Quite a number communed, and Eld. I. D. Parker officiated. The large number of friends present deserve praise for their honorable deportment. Truly, this meeting was one that will not soon be forgotten, and while we feel to rejoice in the God of our salvation, that we can enjoy such refreshing seasons, let us remember the many hungry souls that are starving for the Bread and Water of Life. Let us not only remember them, but be willing to lend a helping hand in any way we can do them good.

Our meetings closed on Sunday evening, Oct. 30, with the best of interest, and we hope, by the many good instructions given us, we may consecrate our lives anew in the Master's cause. May we ever be found on the side of right, and thereby work out our soul's salvation with fear and trembling!　MYRA LECKRON.

Glenford, Ohio, Nov. 3.

Lower Stillwater Notes.

TWO were baptized since our last report. Our council, preparatory to the love-feast, was held Oct. 26. All matter coming before the meeting, was amicably adjusted.

On the following day the Ministerial Meeting for Southern Ohio convened in the Wolf Creek church. It was well attended and much interest was manifested. Our love-feast, Nov. 2, was well attended. The ministry and members from surrounding churches remembered us with their presence and assistance.

Our Sunday-schools have closed for the season, but we trust this will not be understood to mean that Scripture study shall cease, neither do we mean that the children shall be forgotten. We have arranged to have the *Young Disciple* distributed to them each week, at the meetings or otherwise.

If parents were more interested in the mental and spiritual welfare of their children, the future might yield a bountiful harvest to the church and great glory and honor to God.

Many spend money for trifles which do not benefit, and are often injurious to the children, but when it comes to subscribing for a good paper or book, suited to feed the young mind, they suddenly become very economical.

L. A. BOOKWALTER.

Trotwood, Ohio, Nov. 4.

On the Way.

OCT. 15 wife and I met with the Brethren of the Shipshewana church, where I commenced a series of meetings. On account of much sickness and three deaths in the neighborhood, our meetings were not largely attended. The political excitement ran high, and even some who called themselves members allowed themselves to be carried away by excitement. "Straws show which way the wind blows." "The lust of the flesh, the lust of the eye, and the pride of life is not of the Father." "From the abundance of the heart the mouth speaketh." The Lord might say, "When will my people refrain from evil?" "Be ye a separate people." "Be ye not unequally yoked together with unbelievers." "Broad is the road and wide is the gate." I was made to wonder if those, who were so eager to mix the world and religion together, ever thought that would be, perhaps, as difficult to do as to mix water and oil. "We cannot serve God and mammon." One sister was reclaimed and one person, seventy-five years of age, baptized.

At the close of the meeting the brethren had a feast, and a *feast* indeed, it was. This is a good way to close a series of meetings. Young converts may thereby receive so much spiritual strength. Brethren John Kurtz, Noah Shutt, O. Shrock and J. Hoover were with us.

J. H. MILLER.

From Baltimore City.

OUR love-feast, Saturday, Oct. 29, was the largest ever held in Woodberry by our Brethren. About one hundred and twenty members communed. We are gradually increasing in number and, we trust, in strength also. Brethren and sisters from far and near enjoyed the feast with us, and all, apparently, were strengthened and encouraged in their spiritual warfare. We have been greatly benefited by hearing eight good sermons, preceding our love-feast. We think it profitable to hold a series of meetings before love-feast, as it better prepares us to examine ourselves, that we may be welcome guests at the table of our Lord and Master.

Our elder, E. W. Stoner, of Union Bridge, Md., began the series of meetings Saturday evening, Oct. 22. Bro. Albert Hollinger, of Pennsylvania, arrived Oct. 26, and continued the meetings until Sunday night, Oct. 30.

Monday evening, Oct. 31, we enjoyed another love-feast in Bro. Stallar's house, at Timonium, about sixteen miles from here, on the N. C. R. R., held for the special benefit of Bro. Stallar, who was unable to leave home on account of sickness. Eld. Uriah Bixler, of Westminster, Md., officiated, assisted by Bro. John A. Smith, of Woodberry, Baltimore. Sixteen brethren and sisters were present, and a number of neighbors, who had never witnessed the ordinances of God's house performed. All seemed to enjoy the little love-feast very much. We were made to think of Christ's great promise in Matt. 18: 20, "For where two or three are gathered together in my name, there am I in the midst of them."

We rejoice that one precious soul, who had strayed away from the fold of God, has promised to return, and another has asked an interest in our prayers. Brethren, let us all pray for her, that she may return before it is forever too late. We were sorry that our meetings could not be continued longer, as there seemed to have been an interest aroused, but Bro. Hollinger's health did not permit him to remain. We hope our ministering brethren will not forget us when they have an opportunity to visit Baltimore City. More preaching is wanted, and more needed in the cities. Come, we will welcome you. We feel encouraged in our city work. Some members are moving in from other places. Bro. W. H. Moomaw, of Virginia, is moving in this week.

We have formed a Bible class, to meet weekly. Subjects to be considered are those contained in the *Brethren's Quarterly*, preceding each lesson in Sunday-school. The purpose of this meeting is, to better qualify us, as teachers, to impart wholesome food to the young minds confided to our care. We trust that this class may be continued until Christ calls us home. May we receive wisdom and knowledge from our Divine Instructor, to so conduct the class that it may answer its design to the fullest extent, and prove an honor to our God. And may godly love abound in every heart. We ask an interest in the prayers of all our Brethren.　JOHN S. GEISER.

Woodberry, Baltimore City, Md.

From Everett, Pa.

A MEETING was held in the Southern end of the Hopewell congregation, by Eld. Silas Hoover, in

CORRESPONDENCE.

"Write what thou seest, and send it unto the churches."

☞Church News solicited for this Department. If you have had a good meeting, send a report of it, so that others may rejoice with you. In writing give name of church, County and State. Be brief. Notes of Travel should be as short as possible. Land Advertisements are not solicited for this Department. We have an advertising page, and, if necessary, will issue supplements.

From the Falling Spring Church, Franklin County, Pa.

OUR love-feast, held at the Hade church Oct. 29 and 30, was a good meeting, although the weather was very cold and stormy. On Saturday morning Bro. Wm. Hertzler, of Lancaster County, spoke very feelingly; judging by the attention he received, to the satisfaction of all. His text is found in Acts 2: 41. After dinner Bro. H. C. Early, from Virginia, preached to a crowded house from Matt. 16: 18, taking for his theme "The Church." We received an abundance of food for the soul. The solemn services of the evening were conducted by Bro. J. F. Oller, of Waynesborough, Pa. Bro. Oller has borne the heat and burden of many days. He has lost none of his zeal for the Master, but is working with increased zeal, feeling that, at best, his time is short to labor here in the vineyard of the Lord. Our elder, Wm. C. Koontz, remarked that he has been in this congregation a long time, but that this was the largest feast, to his recollection, that was ever held in this congregation. Not only was it the largest, but one of the most edifying. We elected two deacons. The lot fell on brethren Jacob Zug and Harry Stamy, two faithful brethren. Our prayer is that they may be sustained by grace divine, and that they may magnify their sacred office. Bro. Wm. Hertzler then preached from Col. 3: 1 to a large congregation. Brethren Nicholas Martin, John Lehner, Daniel Miller, Benjamin Price, Daniel Baker, Joseph Neibert, J. D. Garner, Abraham Rowland, John Foglesanger, and others, also gave us words of encouragement.

Thus ended another Communion season in the old Falling Spring church. In the evening we had three love-feasts to hold at the homes of our aged brethren who are not able to leave home. Bro. Wm. C. Koontz went to Bro. Adam Baker's with the brethren and sisters and held one for the benefit of Bro. Baker's companion, who has been afflicted for some years. Bro. Isaac Riddlesberger went to Bro. Jacob Fahl's, to hold one for the benefit of sister Fahl, and the writer was sent to Bro. Jacob Benedict's, to hold a feast for the benefit of brother Jacob and sister Benedict, who are both past their threescore years and ten, and who seemingly stand on the verge of eternity. Sister Harshmar, who lives quite near, was there also. She has attained the remarkable age of eighty-five years. It was a scene long to be remembered to see those aged brethren and sisters surround the Lord's table, and engage in the holy ordinance of God's house, which blessings they enjoyed so often in their younger days, but now are, to a certain extent, deprived of. It was pleasant to see the grandfather, son and granddaughters all surround the table with us, and engage in the solemn services. Thus closed a day or scene in our life, that we can look back to with pleasure and profit.   WM. A. ANTHONY.

From the Jonathan Creek Church, Perry Co., Ohio.

THE members of the above church commenced a series of meetings Oct. 22. Bro. Wm. Dessenberg, of Ashland, Ohio, did the preaching. He is a workman that needeth not to be ashamed, rightly dividing the Word of Truth. Although there were no accessions, Bro. Dessenberg made some warm friends, and left many deep impressions, which, we hope, will bear fruit to the saving of some precious souls here, who are near the kingdom. On Saturday evening, Oct. 29, we held our Communion. Quite a number communed, and Eld. I. D. Parker officiated. The large number of friends present deserve praise for their honorable deportment. Truly, this meeting was one that will not soon be forgotten, and while we feel to rejoice in the God of our salvation, that we can enjoy such refreshing seasons, let us remember the many hungry souls that are starving for the Bread and Water of Life. Let us not only remember them, but be willing to lend a helping hand in any way we can do them good.

Our meetings closed on Sunday evening, Oct. 30, with the best of interest, and we hope, by the many good instructions given us, we may consecrate our lives anew in the Master's cause. May we ever be found on the side of right, and thereby work out our soul's salvation with fear and trembling!   MYRA LECKRON.

Glenford, Ohio, Nov. 3.

Lower Stillwater Notes.

Two were baptized since our last report. Our council, preparatory to the love-feast, was held Oct. 26. All matter coming before the meeting, was amicably adjusted.

On the following day the Ministerial Meeting for Southern Ohio convened in the Wolf Creek church. It was well attended and much interest was manifested. Our love-feast, Nov. 2, was well attended. The ministry and members from surrounding churches remembered us with their presence and assistance.

Our Sunday-schools have closed for the season, but we trust this will not be understood to mean that Scripture study shall cease, neither do we mean that the children shall be forgotten. We have arranged to have the *Young Disciple* distributed to them each week, at the meetings or otherwise.

If parents were more interested in the mental and spiritual welfare of their children, the future might yield a bountiful harvest to the church and great glory and honor to God.

Many spent money for trifles which do not benefit, and are often injurious to the children, but when it comes to subscribing for a good paper or book, suited to feed the young mind, they suddenly become very economical.

L. A. BOOKWALTER.

Trotwood, Ohio, Nov. 4.

On the Way.

OCT. 15 wife and I met with the Brethren of the Shipshewana church, where I commenced a series of meetings. On account of much sickness and three deaths in the neighborhood, our meetings were not largely attended. The political excitement ran high, and even some who called themselves members allowed themselves to be carried away by excitement. "Straws show which way the wind blows." "The lust of the flesh, the lust of the eye, and the pride of life is not of the Father." "From the abundance of the heart the mouth speaketh." The Lord might say, "When will my people refrain from evil?" "Be ye a separate people." "Be ye not unequally yoked together with unbelievers." "Broad is the road and wide is the gate." I was made to wonder if those, who were so eager to mix the world and religion together, ever thought that would be, perhaps, as difficult to do as to mix water and oil. "We cannot serve God and mammon." One sister was reclaimed and one person, seventy-five years of age, baptized.

At the close of the meeting the brethren had a feast, and a *feast* indeed, it was. This is a good way to close a series of meetings. Young converts may thereby receive so much spiritual strength. Brethren John Kurtz, Noah Shutt, C. Shrock and J. Hoover were with us.

J. H. MILLER.

From Baltimore City.

OUR love-feast, Saturday, Oct. 29, was the largest ever held in Woodberry by our Brethren. About one hundred and twenty members communed. We are gradually increasing in number and, we trust, in strength also. Brethren and sisters from far and near enjoyed the feast with us, and all, apparently, were strengthened and encouraged in their spiritual warfare. We have been greatly benefited by hearing eight good sermons, preceding our love-feast. We think it profitable to hold a series of meetings before love-feast, as it better prepares us to examine ourselves, that we may be welcome guests at the table of our Lord and Master.

Our elder, E. W. Stoner, of Union Bridge, Md., began the series of meetings Saturday evening, Oct. 22. Bro. Albert Hollinger, of Pennsylvania, arrived Oct. 26, and continued the meetings until Sunday night, Oct. 30.

Monday evening, Oct. 31, we enjoyed another love-feast in Bro. Stallar's house, at Timonium, about sixteen miles from here, on the N. C. R. R., held for the special benefit of Bro. Stallar, who was unable to leave home on account of sickness. Eld. Uriah Bixler, of Westminster, Md., officiated, assisted by Bro. John A. Smith, of Woodberry, Baltimore. Sixteen brethren and sisters were present, and a number of neighbors, who had never witnessed the ordinances of God's house performed. All seemed to enjoy the little love-feast very much. We were made to think of Christ's great promise in Matt. 18: 20, "For where two or three are gathered together in my name, there am I in the midst of them."

We rejoice that one precious soul, who had strayed away from the fold of God, has promised to return, and another has asked an interest in our prayers. Brethren, let us all pray for her, that she may return before it is forever too late. We were sorry that our meetings could not be continued longer, as there seemed to have been an interest aroused, but Bro. Hollinger's health did not permit him to remain. We hope our ministering brethren will not forget us when they have an opportunity to visit Baltimore City. More preaching is wanted, and more needed in the cities. Come, we will welcome you. We feel encouraged in our city work. Brethren are moving in from other places. Bro. W. H. Moomaw, of Virginia, is moving in this week.

We have formed a Bible class, to meet weekly. Subjects to be considered are those contained in the *Brethren's Quarterly*, preceding each lesson in Sunday-school. The purpose of this meeting is, to better qualify us, as teachers, to impart wholesome food to the young minds confided to our care. We trust that this class may be continued until Christ calls us home. May we receive wisdom and knowledge from our Divine Instructor, to so conduct the class that it may answer its design to the fullest extent, and prove an honor to our God. And may godly love abound in every heart. We ask an interest in the prayers of all our Brethren.   JOHN S. GEISER.

Woodberry, Baltimore City, Md.

From Everett, Pa.

A MEETING was held in the Southern end of the Hopewell congregation, by Eld. Silas Hoover, in

Missionary and Tract Work Department.

"Upon the first day of the week, let every one of you lay by him in store as God hath prospered him, that there be no gatherings when I come."—1 Cor. 16: 2.

"Every man as he purposeth in his heart, so let him give. Not grudgingly or of necessity, for the Lord loveth a cheerful giver."—2 Cor. 9: 7.

HOW MUCH SHALL WE GIVE?

"Every man according to his ability." "Every one as God hath prospered him." "Every man, according as he purposeth in his heart, so let him give." "For if there be first a willing mind, it is accepted according to that a man hath, and not according to that he hath not."—2 Cor. 8: 12.

Organization of Missionary Committee.

DANIEL VANIMAN, Foreman, · · · McPherson, Kans.
D. L, MILLER, Treasurer, · · · · Mt. Morris, Ill.
GALEN B. ROYER, Secretary, · · · Mt. Morris, Ill.

Organization of Book and Tract Work.

S. W. HOOVER, Foreman, · · · · Dayton, Ohio.
S. BOCK, Secretary and Treasurer, · · Dayton, Ohio.

☞All donations intended for Missionary Work should be sent to GALEN B. ROYER, Mt. Morris, Ill.

☞All money for Tract Work should be sent to S. BOCK, Dayton, Ohio.

☞Money may be sent by Money Order, Registered Letter, or Drafts on New York or Chicago. Do not send personal checks, or drafts on interior towns, as it costs 25 cents to collect them.

☞Solicitors are requested to faithfully carry out the plan of Annual Meeting, that all our members be solicited to contribute at least twice a year for the Mission and Tract Work of the Church.

☞Notes for the Endowment Fund can be had by writing to the Secretary of either Work.

TO COLORADO AND RETURN.

BY J. S. MOHLER.

In the following narrative, descriptive of our journey, we have nothing in view but to please and instruct the readers of the MESSENGER relative to things temporal, and spiritual, as they seemed to us along our line of travel, believing that a brief statement of our experience and observation would make fair reading.

Monday, Aug. 29, we started westward over the St. Joseph & Grand Island R. R., to Grand Island, Nebr. All along the route, the growing corn, and immense stacks of wheat gave evidence of the abundant harvest. As we neared Grand Island, the coaches became much crowded with soldiers of the late war, who intended to hold a reunion at the above place, to fight their battles over again, and to keep green, in their memories, the hardships endured, the dangers they were exposed to, and exhibit the scars of many a hard-fought battle.

And, in tenderness tell
Of their comrades, who fell.

While meditating on those things, we thought of the great reunion of the soldiers of the cross in heaven, when the mighty conflict with the wicked one, and with sin, is forever over, when the last battle will have been fought, and we are retired from service with victory inscribed on the banner of the cross; when they shall come from the East, and from the West, and from the North, and from the South, and sit down in the kingdom of heaven, and tell of the conflicts here below, of their doubts, and their fears, and their final triumph, and exultingly sing of their great victory, and the unfading glory of heaven forever spread out before them.

At Grand Island we boarded the Union Pacific train for Denver, Colo. This is a most excellent road, smooth as a floor, and straight as an arrow, with scarcely a cut or fill worth mentioning, from Grand Island to Denver, a distance of over four hundred miles. This line is finely equipped and well patronized.

As we neared Denver, the eastern range of the Rocky Mountains was clearly seen, though distant from fifty to sixty miles. Immense quantities of snow could be seen, Long's Peak, like a mighty giant, towered far above,—over 14,000 feet in height.

As we entered the city, we were sensibly impressed with its magnitude, by the dense clouds of smoke and steam that hung over it. There was the clatter of many trains and the screaming of scores of engines. Of the magnificence of its buildings and the activity of its citizens we will have more to say in a subsequent chapter.

(*To be continued.*)

SIMPLICITY.

BY J. S. FLORY.

It was the late Mr. Spurgeon, if I mistake not, who said, "One of the prominent evils of the ministry is affectation and ostentation." We have abundant evidence that he was right.

Nobody was ever converted to God through such means, or if they were, it was in spite of the unfavorable influence. Once I had a man, called a brother, say to me that when he went to preach, one thing embarrassed him, and that was, he had reason to think the people could not comprehend and appreciate his sermons. It is needless to say he sought pastures new. About all the "starch" a man wants, to insure success in the ministry, is to stand stiff for the truth. If a man wants to help humanity up to a higher plane of life, he must get down low enough so he can push him up. A man walking on stilts is a poor help to lead a child. A lame or crippled man needs some one to stoop down and get strong arms beneath him. Like the Blessed Master, he became weak and humble that he might raise the fallen. Servants must not make choice of the position or work, but do the bidding of their Master. Even if lords, let them become as servants. Character is more important than silly mannerism. Simple modesty, adorned with Christian grace, is worth more than all the stiff formalism ever invented by the genius of man. A truly simple man, with an honest heart, can fly more readily than an angel without wings.

BE TEMPERATE IN ALL THINGS.

BY J. H. SLUSHER.

Men and women lecture, preach, pray and write against intemperance,—the partaking of intoxicating drink to excess,—until one would almost think there were no intemperance save in drinking. But in the Word of God we learn that we are to be temperate in *all* things. If we follow the wholesome teachings and examples of the meek and lowly Redeemer, we will be temperate in *all* our actions.

Intemperance has long been admitted to be one of our greatest evils. Many men, in eloquent speeches, have pictured to us what intemperance has done, what it is doing, and what it will do unless its course is, in some way, staid. Our feelings have not only been stirred by reading or hearing of the disastrous effects, produced by intemperance, but we have been eye-witnesses of some of its effects. We are led to pity the poor outcast, as he staggers along the street. We pity his family, for it is destitute of the necessaries of life.

When we talk of intemperance, we should remember that the intemperate person is not only he who staggers along the street and highway, but there are many others who are guilty of intemperate acts in other respects, though they despise the very appearance of the cup, and endeavor to stay the onward tide of intemperance. To abstain from fermented liquor is not enough to make us temperate. The excessive use of anything is implied in the term. It is our duty to be temperate in *everything*.

In all our intercourse with the world, we should cultivate this habit, if we wish to add comfort to our pilgrimage. We are pilgrims traveling through a wilderness. With sad hearts we look upon the many who have gone down to a drunkard's grave, but we seldom think of those who have engaged in other intemperate acts. Thousands of men and women, who could have been a blessing to society and the church, have, by intemperate acts, been hastened into eternity. They might yet, had they been temperate, been living, and wielding a powerful influence in the world. We lament that so many die from the effects of intoxicants. If we only knew it, many more die from *other* intemperate acts.

One of the principal things of which we are guilty, is the impairing of our health,—that great boon of life. Especially is this the case with those who are so very eager to obtain knowledge and the riches of the world. We are so constituted, both physically and mentally, that we need *moderate* labor as well as recreation. Many persons who ought to stand in the front ranks, to Christianize the people, and scarcely able to accomplish anything in the great work. They may have the ability, so far as education is concerned, but they have not the strength of body to put into action the power of the mind. Thus they stand as wrecks in society. In this class are even some ministers who ought to stand upon the walls of Zion, beating back the foe of the church. The church needs them. Humanity calls for their aid, but alas, they are, to some extent, paralyzed!

Persons of this class we see every day, with a heart in the work of the Lord, but no strength to perform the work. We find them every-where. They wonder why it is that life is so miserable. They do not stop to think that they may have brought it upon themselves, and that they are, to a certain extent, responsible for their condition.

The Divine Decree has gone forth, "Do all to the honor and glory of God!" If any person, in any way, injures himself by intemperate acts, it is a moral wrong, and a sin against God. We need temperate men and women. We mean *temperate in everything*. Such people are the mainspring of society. They are the ones who perform the work. Oh that we might have more such temperate persons to perform great and glorious things for the Lord of Hosts!

It is an indisputable fact, that our old Brethren, who lived thirty and forty years ago, were in all things more temperate men than we are. They used the precious gifts of God, in this world, as not abusing them. If we, in this fast age of the world, would only follow their examples a little more closely, we would certainly be more temperate in all things. May the Lord help us all to consider well this great question!

"Great God subdue this vicious thirst
This love to vanity and dust,
Cure this vile fever of the mind
And fill our souls with joys refined."

Falconer's, Va.

WHAT ONE SISTER DID.

BY A SISTER.

As many of our sisters think and say, "I wish I could do something in the line of church work,—something for the Lord," I want to tell you what one dear sister did. A minister was holding a series of meetings in the congregation of which she was a member; and where the brethren were preparing to reward him for his

Missionary and Tract Work Department.

Organization of Missionary Committee.

Organization of Book and Tract Work.

TO COLORADO AND RETURN.

BY J. S. MOHLER.

In the following narrative, descriptive of our journey, we have nothing in view but to please and instruct the readers of the MESSENGER relative to things temporal and spiritual, as they seemed to us along our line of travel, believing that a brief statement of our experience and observation would make fair reading.

Monday, Aug. 29, we started westward over the St. Joseph & Grand Island R. R., to Grand Island, Nebr. All along the route, the growing corn, and immense stacks of wheat gave evidence of the abundant harvest. As we neared Grand Island, the coaches became much crowded with soldiers of the late war, who intended to hold a reunion at the above place, to fight their battles over again, and to keep green, in their memories, the hardships endured, the dangers they were exposed to, and exhibit the scars of many a hard-fought battle.

> And, in tenderness tell
> Of their comrades, who fell.

While meditating on these things, we thought of the great reunion of the soldiers of the cross in heaven, when the mighty conflict with the wicked one, and with sin, is forever over, when the last battle will have been fought, and we are retired from service with victory inscribed on the banner of the cross; when they shall come from the East, and from the West, and from the North, and from the South, and sit down in the kingdom of heaven, and tell of the conflicts here below, of their doubts, and their fears, and their final triumph, and exultingly sing of their great victory, and the unfading glory of heaven forever spread out before them.

At Grand Island we boarded the Union Pacific train for Denver, Colo. This is a most excellent road, smooth as a floor, and straight as an arrow, with scarcely a cut or fill worth mentioning, from Grand Island to Denver, a distance of over four hundred miles. This line is finely equipped and well patronized.

As we neared Denver, the eastern range of the Rocky Mountains was clearly seen, though distant from fifty to sixty miles. Immense quantities of snow could be seen, Long's Peak, like a mighty giant, towered far above, over 14,000 feet in height.

As we entered the city, we were sensibly impressed with its magnitude, by the dense clouds of smoke and steam that hung over it. There was the clatter of many trains and the screaming of scores of engines. Of the magnificence of its buildings and the activity of its citizens we will have more to say in a subsequent chapter.

(*To be continued.*)

SIMPLICITY.

BY J. S. FLORY.

IT was the late Mr. Spurgeon, if I mistake not, who said, "One of the prominent evils of the ministry is affectation and ostentation." We have abundant evidence that he was right.

Nobody was ever converted to God through such means, or if they were, it was in spite of the unfavorable influence. Once I had a man, called a brother, say to me that when he went to preach, one thing embarrassed him, and that was, he had reason to think the people could not comprehend and appreciate his sermons. It is needless to say he sought pastures new. About all the "starch" a man wants, to insure success in the ministry, is to stand stiff for the truth. If a man wants to help humanity up to a higher plane of life, he must get down low enough so he can push him up. A man walking on stilts is a poor help to lead a child. A lame or crippled man needs some one to stoop down and get strong arms beneath him. Like the Blessed Master, he became weak and humble that he might raise the fallen. Servants must not make choice of the position or work, but do the bidding of their Master. Even if lords, let them become as servants. Character is more important than silly mannerism. Simple modesty, adorned with Christian grace, is worth more than all the stiff formalism ever invented by the genius of man. A truly simple man, with an honest heart, can fly more readily than an angel without wings.

BE TEMPERATE IN ALL THINGS.

BY J. H. GLUSHER.

MEN and women lecture, preach, pray and write against intemperance,—the partaking of intoxicating drink to excess,—until one would almost think there were no intemperance save in drinking. But in the Word of God we learn that we are to be temperate in *all* things. If we follow the wholesome teachings and examples of the meek and lowly Redeemer, we will be temperate in *all* our actions.

Intemperance has long been admitted to be one of our greatest evils. Many men, in eloquent speeches, have pictured to us what intemperance has done, what it is doing, and what it will do unless its course is, in some way, staid. Our feelings have not only been stirred by reading or hearing of the disastrous effects, produced by intemperance, but we have been eye-witnesses of some of its effects. We are led to pity the poor outcast, as he staggers along the street. We pity his family, for it is destitute of the necessaries of life.

When we talk of intemperance, we should remember that the intemperate person is not only he who staggers along the street and highway, but there are many others who are guilty of intemperate acts in other respects, though they despise the very appearance of the cup, and endeavor to stay the onward tide of intemperance. To abstain from fermented liquor is not enough to make us temperate. The excessive use of anything is implied in the term. It is our duty to be temperate in *everything*.

In all our intercourse with the world, we should cultivate this habit, if we wish to add comfort to our pilgrimage. We are pilgrims traveling through a wilderness. With sad hearts we look upon the many who have gone down to a drunkard's grave, but we seldom think of those who have engaged in other intemperate acts. Thousands of men and women, who could have been a blessing to society and the church, have, by intemperate acts, been hastened into eternity. They might yet, had they been temperate, been living, and wielding a powerful influence in the world. We lament that so many die from the effects of intoxicants. If we only knew it, many, more die from *other* intemperate acts.

One of the principal things of which we are guilty, is the impairing of our health,—that great boon of life. Especially is this the case with those who are so very eager to obtain knowledge and the riches of the world. We are so constituted, both physically and mentally, that we need *moderate* labor as well as recreation. Many persons who ought to stand in the front ranks, to Christianize the people, are scarcely able to accomplish anything in the great work. They may have the ability, so far as education is concerned, but they have not the strength of body to put into action the power of the mind. Thus they stand as wrecks in society. In this class are even some ministers who ought to stand upon the walls of Zion,—beating back the foe of the church. The church needs them. Humanity calls for their aid, but alas, they are, to some extent, paralyzed!

Persons of this class we see every day; with a heart in the work of the Lord, but no strength to perform the work. We find them every-where. They wonder why it is that life is so miserable. They do not stop to think that they may have brought it upon themselves, and that they are, to a certain extent, responsible for their condition.

The Divine Decree has gone forth, "Do all to the honor and glory of God!". If any person, in any way, injures himself by intemperate acts, it is a moral wrong, and a sin against God. We need temperate men and women. We mean *temperate in everything.* Such people are the mainspring of society. They are the ones who perform the work. Oh that we might have more such temperate persons to perform great and glorious things for the Lord of Hosts!

It is an indisputable fact, that our old Brethren, who lived thirty and forty years ago, were in all things more temperate men than we are. They used the precious gifts of God, in this world, as not abusing them. If we, in this fast age of the world, would only follow their examples a little more closely, we would certainly be more temperate in all things. May the Lord help us all to consider well this great question!

> "Great God subdue this vicious thirst
> This love to vanity and dust,
> Cure this vile fever of the mind
> And fill our souls with joys refined."

Falconer's, Va.

WHAT ONE SISTER DID.

BY A SISTER.

As many of our sisters think and say, "I wish I could do something in the line of church work,—something for the Lord," I want to tell you what one dear sister did. A minister was holding a series of meetings in the congregation of which she was a member, and where the brethren were preparing to reward him for his

The Gospel Messenger,

A Weekly at $1.50 Per Annum.

PUBLISHED BY

The Brethren's Publishing Co.

D. L. MILLER,	. . . . . .	Editor
J. H. MOORE,	. . . . .	Office Editor.
J. B. BRUMBAUGH,	}	Associate Editors.
J. G. ROYER,	}	
JOSEPH AMICK,	. . . . . .	Business Manager.

ADVISORY COMMITTEE.

L. W. Teeter, A. Hutchison, Daniel Hays. .

☞ Communications for publication should be legibly written with black ink on one side of the paper only. Do not attempt to interline, or to put on one page what ought to occupy two.

☞ Anonymous communications will not be published.

☞ Do not mix business with articles for publication. Keep your communications on separate sheets from all business.

☞ Time is precious. We always have time to attend to business and to answer questions of importance, but please do not subject us to need less unraveling of letters.

☞ The MESSENGER is mailed each week to all subscribers. If the address is correctly entered on our list, the paper must reach the person to whom it is addressed. If you do not get your paper, write us, giving particulars.

☞ When changing your address, please give your former as well as your future address in full, so as to avoid delay and misunderstanding.

☞ Always remit to the office from which you order your goods, no matter from where you receive them.

☞ Do not send personal checks or drafts on interior banks, unless you send with them 25 cents each, to pay for collection.

☞ Remittances should be made by Post-office Money Order, Drafts on New York, Philadelphia or Chicago, or Registered Letter, made payable and addressed to " Brethren's Publishing Co., Mount Morris, Ill.," or " Brethren's Publishing Co., Huntingdon, Pa."

☞ Entered at the Post-office at Mount Morris, Ill., as second-class matter.

Mount Morris, Ill., - - - - Nov. 15, 1892.

BRO. H. C. EARLY reports an interesting ten days' meeting in the Upton church, Pa., with six additions so far, and prospects of others.

JOHN WESLEY once said, " I have two silver spoons at London and two at Bristol. I shall not buy any more whilst so many poor want bread."

BRO. J. J. WASSAM, of Manvel, Tex., would like to correspond with a brother who is a physician by profession, and another who is a blacksmith.

BRO. JOSEPH BEAM should be addressed at Ligonier, Westmoreland Co., Pa., Box 303. From some cause it seems his address is not given correctly in the Almanac.

BRETHREN, please do not jest about sacred things. Sacred things belong to God, and we should speak of them with all due reverence, as though we were in his presence.

EIGHTEEN recently united with the church at Nappanee, Ind. Reports equally encouraging are coming in from many parts of the Brotherhood. This is an unusual year for the ingathering of souls.

SOME of our members delay one month before sending in reports of their feasts and other meetings. Please do not do that, but send in the reports as soon as possible. We like our news to be fresh.

Do learn to be patient as you pass through this world. It is the only time you will be permitted to pass through the world and it is important that you leave a good record behind. Do not be impatient when the good things come to you slowly or in small particles. Remember that to some people they never come at all in this life. Much happiness can often be extracted from small things. Then learn to embrace the little opportunities of doing good as they occur to you daily. He who has a few happy moments daily, and does a few kind acts daily will soon forget the shadows of life and think more and more of the sunshine.

TWENTY-ONE have united with the church at Everett, Pa., during the summer and fall. At a meeting, recently held by Bro. Silas Hoover, a number came out on the Lord's side. There is general rejoicing in the community.

THE District Meeting of Nebraska sends no queries to the Annual Meeting, but petitions that the Conference may be held in that State sometime in the near future. Bro. Urias Shick will represent the District on the Standing Committee.

WRITING from Manassas, Va., Bro. Abram Connor says: " The Midland church is in the midst of a glorious meeting at the Midland house. Seven have made the good choice and more are near the church. Bro. Jacob D. Sandy, of Ohio, is doing the preaching."

BRO. I. J. ROSENBROCK, we presume, is now in the midst of a series of meetings at Cerro Gordo, Ill. Were we to venture any advice we would say to him what we would like to say to every evangelist in the Brotherhood, viz., do not close the meeting too soon, but make the work a success if it takes all winter.

IN reply to a number of inquiries we will say that the Brethren's meeting-house in Chicago is No. 183 Hastings Street. We should judge it to be about four miles south-west of the Union depot, in a very pleasant part of the city. Services are held each Sunday morning and evening. Members and friends who stop over Sunday in the city, should attend these services.

IT is common,—too common,—for people to defer giving for a good cause until they have a surplus over and above what they need themselves. As most people never reach that point in life, they go to their grave without having benefited the unfortunate,—the very ones who need help. Men who give only of their surplus do not realize the satisfaction to the heart, arising from cheerful giving.

FOR weeks the MESSENGER has been running over with good news from all sections of the Brotherhood, and the reports are still coming in. We call special attention to " Notes from our Correspondents." These notes are brief and to the point, and are worthy of imitation by all those who send in church news. This is getting to be the most interesting department in the paper, and we would like if more of our correspondents would study this style of brevity. Long reports are not interesting, as a general thing. It is better to send short reports and write oftener. If there is any good news, let us have it for this department. If you have any bad news, keep it at home. The object of the MESSENGER is to instruct, edify and encourage.

SINCE we can neither know nor change the future, why should we worry over it? It is far better to do the best we can for the present, and in that manner prepare for the future. To worry over troubles that may possibly never come, is to waste both time and strength on that which has no real existence. We should learn to meet and overcome the obstacles in life and in the meantime gain strength for possible future emergencies. The future will open to us fast enough,—as fast as we can take care of it. We need not waste our energies, trying to lift the veil that no one has yet been permitted to look beyond. In most instances it takes all our resources to provide for the present. What would we do, had we the great future yet opened to us? A God may look into and provide for a long future, but man must be contented to know the present, and he does well if he properly understands that.

THE following statement shows the sources from which the money came to purchase the Chicago meeting-house:

Collected and paid by D. L. Miller, Outside of the State District,	$ 791 50
D. L. Miller,	100 00
General Missionary Committee,	500 00
Amount raised and contributed by the Chicago members,	639 00
Total,	$2,030 50

WE are in receipt of the program of the Ministerial Meeting, to be held in the Maple Grove church, Ohio, Nov. 17. The subjects are well selected. We notice that Bro. I. D. Parker is booked for a sermon on Church Government. His views on that subject are not only sound, but easily understood. . We wish he would write them out for the MESSENGER. We assure him that they would be appreciated by our readers.

IT might be well for those who can do so, to send twenty-five cents or more to the Brethren's Tract Work, Dayton, Ohio, for samples of good tracts, from which to select suitable ones to keep on hand and circulate among the neighbors. In this way every member can become a missionary in his own immediate neighborhood, and know just what he is doing and where his money is being applied. Do not be afraid of spending a few dollars each year trying to save souls.

SOME men will spend more money for spite than for religion, and, in that way, show how greatly the evil in them predominates over the good. The man who, out of ill feelings, spends ten dollars to keep his neighbor from joining fence with him, and then gives only twenty-five cents for the spread of the Gospel, most assuredly proves that he is willing to do forty times as much for the works of the flesh as he does for the good of the spirit. He may not like to be told of it in that way, but it is the truth, nevertheless.

BRETHREN D. L. Miller and J. C. Lahman took their departure from Mt. Morris last Tuesday en route for the Bible Lands. They sail from New York the last of the week, and by the time this issue reaches most of our subscribers, the two brethren will be far out on the ocean. They preached their farewell sermons in the Chapel last Sunday, Bro. Lahman conducting the services in the morning and Bro. Miller in the evening. Their wives do not accompany them but remain at their homes in Mt. Morris. We hope to have a letter from Bro. Miller in time for the next issue.

IN this age of missionary work, when every preacher expects pay for every item of work done away from home, it is more than possible that numbers may fall short of their individual duty as ministers. The preacher who will not preach the Gospel, unless he sees a few almighty dollars waiting for him, is not the man whom the Lord would select to make an apostle of. In missionary enterprise the church has doubtless taken higher ground than that occupied by our old fathers, but, as individuals, our ministers may possibly be falling below them in self-sacrifice, especially is this likely in our large and well-supplied churches. Every minister should make some personal sacrifice, not for the sake of the sacrifice, but for the sake of souls. This he can do, and will do, if he is a consecrated minister. Let us sustain our missionaries and evangelists, and, if possible, put more of them in the field, but our personal and individual duties as ministers should, by no means, be neglected. If, in addition to our present missionary system, we would sacrifice and labor as did our ancient preachers, we would probably accomplish vastly more than we are now doing.

The Gospel Messenger,

A Weekly at $1.50 Per Annum.

PUBLISHED BY

The Brethren's Publishing Co.

D. L. MILLER, ... Editor
J. H. MOORE, ... Office Editor.
J. B. BRUMBAUGH,
J. G. ROYER, } . . . . . Associate Editors.
JOSEPH AMICK, ... Business Manager.

ADVISORY COMMITTEE.
L. W. Teeter, A. Hutchison, Daniel Hays. .

☞ Communications for publication should be legibly written with black ink on one side of the paper only. Do not attempt to interline, or to put on one page what ought to occupy two.

☞ Anonymous communications will not be published.

☞ Do not mix business with articles for publication. Keep your communications on separate sheets from all business.

☞ Time is precious. We always have time to attend to business and to answer questions of importance, but please do not subject us to need less answering of letters.

☞ The MESSENGER is mailed each week to all subscribers. If the address is correctly entitled on our list, the paper must reach the person to whom it is addressed. If you do not get your paper, write us, giving particulars.

☞ When changing your address, please give your former as well as your future address in full, so as to avoid delay and misunderstanding.

☞ Always remit to the office from which you order your goods, no matter from where you receive them.

☞ Do not send personal checks or drafts on interior banks, unless you send with them 25 cents each, to pay for collection.

☞ Remittances should be made by Post-office Money Order, Drafts on New York, Philadelphia or Chicago, or Registered Letters, made payable and addressed to "Brethren's Publishing Co., Mount Morris, Ill.," or "Brethren's Publishing Co., Huntingdon, Pa."

☞ Entered at the Post-office at Mount Morris, Ill., as second-class matter.

Mount Morris, Ill., - - - - Nov. 15, 1892.

BRO. H. C. EARLY reports an interesting ten days' meeting in the Upton church, Pa., with six additions so far, and prospects of others.

JOHN WESLEY once said, "I have two silver spoons at London and two at Bristol. I shall not buy any more whilst so many poor want bread."

BRO. J. J. WASSAM, of Marvel, Tex., would like to correspond with a brother who is a physician by profession, and another who is a blacksmith.

BRO. JOSEPH BEAM should be addressed at Ligonier, Westmoreland Co., Pa., Box 303. From some cause it seems his address is not given correctly in the Almanac.

BRETHREN, please do not jest about sacred things. Sacred things belong to God, and we should speak of them with all due reverence, as though we were in his presence.

EIGHTEEN recently united with the church at Nappanee, Ind. Reports equally encouraging are coming in from many parts of the Brotherhood. This is an unusual year for the ingathering of souls.

SOME of our members delay one month before sending in reports of their feasts and other meetings. Please do not do that, but send in the reports as soon as possible. We like our news to be fresh.

Do learn to be patient as you pass through this world. It is the only time you will be permitted to pass through the world and it is important that you leave a good record behind. Do not be impatient when the good things come to you slowly or in small particles. Remember that to some people they never come at all in this life. Much happiness can often be extracted from small things. Then learn to embrace the little opportunities of doing good as they occur to you daily. He who has a few happy moments daily, and does a few kind acts daily will soon forget the shadows of life and think more and more of the sunshine.

TWENTY-ONE have united with the church at Everett, Pa., during the summer and fall. At a meeting, recently held by Bro. Silas Hoover, a number came out on the Lord's side. There is general rejoicing in the community.

THE District Meeting of Nebraska sends no queries to the Annual Meeting, but petitions that the Conference may be held in that State sometime in the near future. Bro. Urias Shick will represent the District on the Standing Committee.

WRITING from Manassas, Va., Bro. Abram Connor says: "The Midland church is in the midst of a glorious meeting at the Midland house. Seven have made the good choice and more are near the church. Bro. Jacob D. Sandy, of Ohio, is doing the preaching."

BRO. I. J. ROSENBERGER, we presume, is now in the midst of a series of meetings at Cerro Gordo, Ill. Were we to venture any advice we would say to him what we would like to say to every evangelist in the Brotherhood, viz., do not close the meeting too soon, but make the work a success if it takes all winter.

IN reply to a number of inquiries we will say that the Brethren's meeting-house in Chicago is No. 183 Hastings Street. We should judge it to be about four miles south-west of the Union depot, in a very pleasant part of the city. Services are held each Sunday morning and evening. Members and friends who stop over Sunday in the city, should attend these services.

IT is common,—too common,—for people to defer giving for a good cause until they have a surplus over and above what they need themselves. As most people never reach that point in life, they go to their grave without having benefited the unfortunate,—the very ones who need help. Men who give only of their surplus do not realize the satisfaction to the heart, arising from cheerful giving.

FOR weeks the MESSENGER has been running over with good news from all sections of the Brotherhood, and the reports are still coming in. We call special attention to "Notes from our Correspondents." These notes are brief and to the point, and are worthy of imitation by all those who send in church news. This is getting to be the most interesting department in the paper, and we would like if more of our correspondents would study this style of brevity. Long reports are not interesting, as a general thing. It is better to send short reports and write oftener. If there is any good news, let us have it for this department. If you have any bad news, keep it at home. The object of the MESSENGER is to instruct, edify and encourage.

SINCE we can neither know nor change the future, why should we worry over it? It is far better to do the best we can for the present, and in that manner prepare for the future. To worry over troubles that may possibly never come, is to waste both time and strength on that which has no real existence. We should learn to meet and overcome the obstacles in life and in the mean-time gain strength for possible future emergencies. The future will open to us fast enough,—as fast as we can take care of it. We need not waste our energies, trying to lift the veil that no one has yet been permitted to look beyond. In most instances it taxes all our resources to provide for the present. What would we do, had we the great future yet opened to us? A God may look into and provide for a long future, but man must be contented to know the present, and he does well if he properly understands that.

THE following statement shows the sources from which the money came to purchase the Chicago meeting-house:

Collected and paid by D. L. Miller, Outside of the State District,	$ 791 50
D. L. Miller,	100 00
General Missionary Committee,	500 00
Amount raised and contributed by the Chicago members,	639 00
Total,	$3,030 50

WE are in receipt of the program of the Ministerial Meeting, to be held in the Maple Grove church, Ohio, Nov. 17. The subjects are well selected. We notice that Bro. I. D. Parker is booked for a sermon on Church Government. His views on that subject are not only sound, but easily understood. We wish he would write them out for the MESSENGER. We assure him that they would be appreciated by our readers.

IT might be well for those who can do so, to send twenty-five cents or more to the Brethren's Tract Work, Dayton, Ohio, for samples of good tracts, from which to select suitable ones to keep on hand and circulate among the neighbors. In this way every member can become a missionary in his own immediate neighborhood, and know just what he is doing and where his money is being applied. Do not be afraid of spending a few dollars each year trying to save souls.

SOME men will spend more money for spite than for religion, and, in that way, show how greatly the evil in them predominates over the good. The man who, out of ill feelings, spends ten dollars to keep his neighbor from joining fence with him, and then gives only twenty-five cents for the spread of the Gospel, most assuredly proves that he is willing to do forty times as much for the works of the flesh as he does for the good of the spirit. He may not like to be told of it in that way, but it is the truth, nevertheless.

BRETHREN D. L. Miller and J. C. Lahman took their departure from Mt. Morris last Tuesday en route for the Bible Lands. They sail from New York the last of the week, and by the time this issue reaches most of our subscribers, the two brethren will be far out on the ocean. They preached their farewell sermons in the Chapel last Sunday, Bro. Lahman conducting the services in the morning and Bro. Miller in the evening. Their wives do not accompany them but remain at their homes in Mt. Morris. We hope to have a letter from Bro. Miller in time for the next issue.

IN this age of missionary work, when every preacher expects pay for every item of work done away from home, it is more than possible that numbers may fall short of their individual duty as ministers. The preacher who will not preach the Gospel, unless he sees a few almighty dollars waiting for him, is not the man whom the Lord would select to make an apostle of. In missionary enterprise the church has doubtless taken higher ground than that occupied by our old fathers, but, as individuals, our ministers may possibly be falling below them in self-sacrifice, especially is this likely in our large and well-supplied churches. Every minister should make some personal sacrifice, not for the sake of the sacrifice, but for the sake of souls. This he can do, and will do, if he is a consecrated minister. Let us sustain our missionaries and evangelists, and, if possible, put more of them in the field, but our personal and individual duties as ministers should, by no means, be neglected. If, in addition to our present missionary system, we would sacrifice and labor as did our ancient preachers, we would probably accomplish vastly more than we are now doing.

Convent. While searching the library, he discovered in the corner of the room a box used for rubbish. In this box he noticed some parchment leaves, and his practical eye at once saw that the writing was in the old Greek capitals, and that it was a part of the Old Testament written at a very early period. It proved to be a part of the now famous copy of the Scriptures, but he was able to find at that time only a few leaves. In 1854 he made another trip to Sinai, but failed to discover the coveted treasure. Finally, in 1859, fifteen years after his first trip, Tischendorf succeeded in gaining from the Russian Government financial aid and moral support, which enabled him to visit Sinai again. He reached the place January 31, 1859, and began his search for the missing leaves; but he searched in vain, until the afternoon of February 4, when the steward of the Monastery called his attention to a manuscript which he had laid away. To the great joy of the German scholar it proved to be the missing manuscript,—an entire copy of the New Testament and a part of the Old. His long search was rewarded. After many perplexities and great difficulties he was enabled to make a copy of the manuscript, and finally succeeded in placing the original in the Library at St. Petersburg, Russia, where it still remains. We now have photographic copies of the original.

This valuable manuscript contains twenty-six books of the Old Testament, all of the New, and the Epistle of Barnabas, with a part of the Epistle of Hermas. It is justly regarded by scholars as the most important manuscript copy of the New Testament now known to exist. Tischendorf rendered valuable service to Christianity by his discovery, and in his persistent efforts to secure this copy of the Scriptures, his name will be associated with the New Testament until the end shall come.

Other valuable manuscripts of the Scripture are to be found in the great libraries of the Old World, notably one at Rome in the Vatican library; one in the library of the British Museum in London, and one in the library at Paris. Others might be referred to, but let this suffice. If we make a record of all the manuscript copies of the New Testament, written in the old Greek capitals from the second to the fifth century, which are now preserved in our libraries, we have of the four Gospels, fifty-six copies; the Acts, fourteen copies; the general Epistles, six copies; Paul's Epistles, fifteen copies, and of Revelations, five copies. Of the cursive or running hand manuscript, none of which are older than the tenth century, there are nearly 1,000 copies of the New Testament, and as many more of the various books and Epistles of the Gospel. These copies were all made after the tenth century, for it was not until that date that the running hand was used. In all writings prior to that time, the capitals were used, each letter being formed separately.

COPIES OF THE SCRIPTURES MADE BY ORDER OF CONSTANTINE, THE FIRST CHRISTIAN EMPEROR OF ROME.

Eusebius, Bishop of the church of Cesarea, wrote a life of Constantine in four books, from A. D. 306 to A. D. 337, and gives an account of the care of the Emperor for the Scriptures. Eusebius was a warm, personal friend of the Emperor and was held in high esteem by him. The following passage, quoted from the writings of

Eusebius, gives valuable testimony as to the manuscript copies of the Scriptures:

"Ever careful for the welfare of the *Churches of God*, the Emperor addressed me personally in a letter on the means of *providing copies of the Inspired Oracles*. His letter, which related to the providing of copies of the Scriptures for reading in the churches, was to the following purport:

Victor Constantine, Maximus Augustus to Eusebius:

It happens, through the faVoring of God our SaVior, that great numbers haVe united themselVes to the Most Holy Church in the City which is called by my name. It seems, therefore, highly requisite, since that city is rapidly advancing in prosperity in all other respects, that the number of churches should also be increased. Do you therefore receiVe with all readiness my determination on this behalf. I haVe thought it expedient to instruct your prudence to order *fifty copies of the Sacred Scriptures*, the provision and use of which you know to be most needful for the instruction of the church, to be written on prepared parchment, in a legible manner, and in a commodious and portable form, by transcribers thoroughly practiced in their art. The procurator of the diocese has also receiVed instructions by letter from our clemency to be careful to furnish all things necessary for the preparation of such copies; and it will be for you to take special care that they be completed with as little delay as possible. You haVe authority also, in Virtue of this letter, to use *two of the public carriages for their conveyance*, by which arrangement the copies, when fairly written, will most easily be forwarded for *my personal inspection*; and one of the deacons of your church may be intrusted with this serVice, who, on his arriVal here, shall experience my liberality. God preserVe you, beloVed brother!

"Such were the Emperor's commands, which were followed by the immediate execution of the work itself, which was sent him in magnificent and elaborate volumes of a threefold and fourfold form. This fact is attested by another letter, which the Emperor wrote in acknowledgment."

Here we have an account of the preparation of fifty copies of the Scriptures, two hundred years after they were written. This shows that as early as A. D. 306 the Scriptures existed in manuscript form, and that no doubt was held by the Emperor as to their authenticity and authority. Tischendorf was of the opinion that the valuable copy discovered at Mount Sinai was one of the copies ordered by Constantine, and that it was presented to the Convent by its founder, the Emperor Justinian. There can be but little doubt that some of the Ancient "Uncial" Manuscripts, which have come down to us, were made by Eusebius at the instance of Constantine.   D. L. M.

CORRESPONDENCE.
"Write what thou seest, and send it unto the churches."

☞ Church News solicited for this Department. If you haVe had a good meeting, send a report of it, so that others may rejoice with you. In writing giVe name of church, County and State. Be brief. Notes of Travel should be as short as possible. Land Advertisements are not solicited for this Department. We have an adVertising page, and, if necessary, will issue supplements.

From the Verdigris Church, Kans.

We met in council Sept. 24, preparatory to our love-feast. A series of meetings, conducted by Bro. Pearsoll, commenced that evening, and continued until Oct. 2. Our brother gave us many good admonitions, which were applicable to all of us.

The meetings closed with two applicants; both were young in years, and we hope they may ever be led by the Spirit of Christ.

On Saturday evening the Brethren met to commemorate the sufferings and death of our adorable Redeemer. It was a feast to our hungry souls. Brethren C. C. Gibson, Jesse Studebaker, and Lewis Flack were also with us. Bro. Gibson officiated. Some spoke of the meeting as being one of the most enjoyable feasts they ever attended.

I prize the MESSENGER Very highly because I am thus put into communication with the saints all over this broad land of ours. The spiritual strength one derives from it can be realized only by those who, in their isolation, have experienced the benefit.

On Saturday, Oct. 8, in company with Bro. J. M. Quackenbush and family, we started en route for our West Creek appointment,—a distance of about thirty miles. Here we had two meetings, on Saturday evening, and Sunday at eleven. We came home Monday, the 11th, feeling encouraged to labor more faithfully for the cause of the Master.   JAS. A. STOUDER.

Madison, Kans., Oct. 22.

From Virginia.

The Antioch church, Bedford Co., Va., held her Communion Oct. 15, 1892. The weather was delightful. At 3 o'clock P. M., the services began, with the home ministry and Eld. Samuel Crumpacker and Addison Dove, of the Botetourt church, present. Eld. Crumpacker officiated. Eighty members communed. It was one of the best meetings we ever attended. The spectators maintained good order and attention. We have learned long since that to have good order at such meetings, we must begin and close early, so that those who love darkness rather than light do not have so much time to disturb us. Supper need not be put off until 9 o'clock at night, but is better, on such occasions, at 6 o'clock.

Next morning brethren Crumpacker and Dove conducted the closing exercises of the Sunday-school. Some were added to the church, making thirty in all since August. We feel to rejoice. A few years ago the doctrine of the Brethren was not known here.   J. A. B. HERSHBERGER.

To the Middle District of Iowa.

Pursuant to decision of District Meeting, Sept. 22, 1892, your committee, John Zuck, H. R. Taylor and G. W. Hopwood, met in church council in the Brethren's meeting-house, near Lost Nation, Clinton Co., Iowa, Oct. 27, with the members of that congregation, and Bro. John Gable, of Mahaska County, Iowa. The meeting was opened with the usual devotional exercises, after which John Zuck was chosen Foreman, and H. R. Taylor, Secretary. Brethren John Gable and G. W. Hopwood were appointed as a committee to go aside, that each member present might come before them, that the standing of the members in relation to each other and to the church might be ascertained, and to learn their wishes in regard to other things pertaining to the church.

Our aged and much afflicted brother, Eld. Joshua Schultz, requested the church to call another elder to their assistance. The unanimous choice of the church was that Eld. John Zuck, of Clarence, Iowa, take charge of them.

We succeeded in obtaining a deed for the land on which the meeting-house stands. Hitherto it was only leased. The desire of the members is that the meeting-house remain where it is for the present. The sum of $26.50 was raised that day for the use of the church in preparing for their Communion, which was held the following Saturday evening. All the members present seemed to be in union and ready for Communion, but, sad to learn, some were not present and had decided not to walk with the church any longer. We rejoiced to see others return to the church that had wandered away.

This church once numbered probably over one hundred members, but a sad change has taken place. It is the opinion of the members there

an enjoyable occasion. The subjects as indicated by the programme, were all discussed in an able and creditable manner, showing careful study in the preparation of their work. Many brethren participated in the discussion, taking a deep interest in the entire meeting.

During the month of August two precious souls were received by baptism. Oct. 8 the writer attended the love-feast at the Auglaize Chapel, Ohio. It was a feast long to be remembered. We lived in this church five years, so it seemed home-like to us, to meet with them again.

Oct. 15, wife, daughter and I attended the love-feast at Oak Grove, Hancock Co., Ohio. This was certainly a feast of love.

Bro. I. J. Rosenberger commenced a series of meetings at this place Oct. 19 and closed Oct. 25. Five were added to the church by confession and baptism. This makes eight since Aug. 1.
　　　　　　　　　　　　　　D. W. C. Rau.
McComb, Ohio.

Notes from Our Correspondents.

"As cold water to a thirsty soul, so is good news from a far country."

Burnett, O. ?.—Two more precious souls came out on the Lord's side and were buried with Christ in baptism. Will not some dear brother respond to the Macedonian call and help us here?—*Henry Troxel.*

Monte Vista, Colo.—We are still trying to work in the interest of our Master's cause. Our last quarterly council, which occurred the last of September, passed off very pleasantly. We have Sunday-school, preaching service and social meeting in our church each Lord's Day, and have appointed our love-feast for Nov. 26.—*A. C. Snowberger, Oct. 30.*

Brownsville Church, Md.—Our love-feast of Oct. 29 was a good meeting. The single mode of feet-washing was observed. About 300 members communed. Eld. David Long officiated. A dear brother was baptized during the intermission between examination and evening services. At this feast some communed for the first time, and some perhaps for the last. There is a blessedness that follows the observance of these ordinances that the world knows not of.—*Geo. W. Kaetzel, Oct. 30.*

Everett, Pa.—Recently we met for services in a church-house in the town of Everett, near my home,—a house which we have the use of for a short time. Here we baptized one brother and reclaimed one. We have been holding meetings in this place during the summer in my barn, part of the time, and at other times in the grove, and have been having good congregations all summer. Quite an interest has seemingly been awakened in this place among the people. We have baptized and reclaimed six, which is encouraging. We need a meeting-house at this place. There is a good opening here and railroad facilities are good.—*D. S. Clopper.*

Marsh Creek Church, Pa.—An enjoyable love-feast was held here recently. The weather and roads being favorable, by noon of Oct. 29 a large representation from neighboring churches was on the grounds. Elders from abroad were Solomon Stoner, Peter Brown, David Neisley, and several other ministers whose presence was much appreciated. Bro. A. D. Taylor was elected to the responsible office of deacon. He, with his wife, were duly installed. We trust this choice was dictated by the Lord, and that they may use the office of deacon well, and purchase to themselves a good degree and great boldness in the faith. One precious soul was received by baptism, and one by letter.—*B. F. Kittinger.*

Middleton, Mich.—Our love-feast in the New Haven church was held Oct. 22. The meetings were very enjoyable. We were glad to see so many present from surrounding churches. Bro. Isaiah Rairigh officiated. Most excellent order prevailed, and the weather was very pleasant.—*Wm. P. Bosserman, Oct. 27.*

Middletown, Ind.—The love-feast of Oct. 25, at the Upper Fall Creek church, was greatly enjoyed. I also attended one at the Lower Fall Creek and Buck Creek. All were feasts to be long remembered. We met with Bro. Henry Frantz and wife, from Ohio, which was a happy surprise. Good order prevailed at each place.—*Florida Etter, Oct. 29.*

Greene, Iowa.—Oct. 30 closed a series of meetings at Franklin County, Iowa, with a crowded house, and the very best of interest. Here, like at a great many other places, we closed too soon, in order to meet other arrangements. I am now at Greene. The interest is growing each evening, and we anticipate a glorious meeting by the time their feast will take place, which is appointed for Nov. 5. I can truly say for Iowa that the harvest is great, but the laborers few.—*Joseph Holder, Nov. 3.*

Green Spring, Ohio.—The members of the Green Spring church, Seneca Co., Ohio, in company with loved ones from adjoining districts, enjoyed, on the evening of Oct. 29, a peaceful, quiet, interesting, beneficial, soul-inspiring love-feast. About ninety members communed. The ministerial force was ample. The Word of Life was dealt out in simplicity and power. Two more were received by confession and baptism. Two brethren were elected to fill the office of deacon. May all prove faithful in their high and holy calling, and to God be all the glory!—*J. B. Light, Oct. 31.*

Elkhart, Iowa.—Oct. 27 I left home on a mission of love to the Brethren of Decatur County, Iowa. I arrived at my destination next day, where I met Bro. Abraham Wolfe, of Libertyville, Iowa. In the evening we had preaching; also next morning at 11 A. M. In the evening their love-feast was held. Next morning we met again for preaching, after which our dear old brother, Wm. Stout, was anointed. We then repaired to the water where baptism was administered to one applicant. In the evening we met again for preaching, and next morning we met at the house of sister Caster, where sister McDonald, of Missouri, 85 years of age, was anointed. Thus closed another pleasant and, we trust, profitable love-feast. We arrived home Nov. 1, leaving Bro. Wolfe to continue the meetings.—*S. M. Goughnour.*

New Stark, Ohio.—The love-feast in the Eagle Creek church occurred Oct. 22. Eld. Samuel Driver officiated. Eld. E. Bosserman, of Michigan, and five of our adjoining ministers were with us and rendered valuable service during the meetings. The weather was fine and the surrounding churches were well represented. This is very encouraging to us, as we feel that we need the assistance of our neighboring churches. The feast was an enjoyable one throughout. About 170 members communed. One dear soul was baptized. On Sunday evening a little company of brethren and sisters gathered at the home of sister Frederick, where her son, Jesse, has been lying quite low for some months with Bright's disease. Bro. D. D. Thomas officiated in the Communion services. Although all present could not well commune, they seemed to enjoy the services very much, and especially was this true with our afflicted brother.—*J. R. Spacht, Oct. 31.*

Tippecanoe, Church, Ind.—Sept. 25, at our regular meeting two (husband and wife) were added to the church by confession and baptism. May they prove faithful, and may others follow! It affords much pleasure to God's children to have the neighbors join in with them.—*D. Rothenberger.*

Mendon, Ohio.—Our love-feast of Oct. 12, in the west end of our district, Mercer County, Ohio, was an enjoyable one and long to be remembered by all present. We had a good ministerial force and the Word was preached with power. One precious soul made a full surrender and was baptized.—*J. B. Detrick.*

Mt. Vernon, Ill.—Bro. D. B. Gibson came to our church Oct. 10 and held meetings each evening until Oct. 27. As a visible result of the meetings six were baptized,—one before our love-feast. Two of the number were children of the writer, and we have great reason to rejoice. Bro. Gibson did not shun to declare all the counsel of God. Sinners were made to tremble, and those that are in Christ were built up in that most holy faith.—*J. M. Angle, Oct. 27.*

Bradfording, Md.—Our love-feast was held Oct. 22, and was a very enjoyable meeting, and largely attended by both members and others. It was a feast to the soul. Eld. John Lehner officiated. Other ministering brethren from a distance were Eld. David Long and son, Daniel Wolf, William Anthony and others. Two precious souls were made willing to leave the ways of sin and turn to God in their old days. One was about eighty years of age.—*F. J. Neibert, Oct. 25.*

Mingona, Kans.—Our love-feast in the Mingona church, Barber County, Kans, was held Sept. 24. It was a pleasant and an enjoyable meeting. About twenty-six members communed. Bro. J. H. Shambarger's barn, where the love-feast was held, was well filled and the best of order prevailed. Bro. John Wise, of Conway Springs, Sumner County, was with us and officiated. We held a series of meetings preceding the feast, at the Mingona school-house, with good interest. Bro. Wise conducted the meetings. His sermons were edifying and soul-cheering.—*Jacob R. Root, Oct. 23.*

Greenwood Church, Mo.—Our council, preparatory to our love-feast, occurred Oct. 22. The day was inclement, yet a goodly number was present. Considering the nature of the business before the meeting, everything was disposed of in a satisfactory manner. At this meeting Eld. F. W. Dove and wife, of Tennessee, were received by letter. Our love-feast was held on the evening of Oct. 28. My wife being sick, she and I could not attend, but I learn they had a good meeting. A number of members were present from Douglas County, including some of their ministers. This added to the interest of our meeting.—*J. J. Troxel, Cabool, Mo., Oct. 30.*

Painter, Kans.—The members of the Prairie View church, appointed Oct. 22 as the time for their love-feast. Bro. Enoch Eby and Bro. Henricks were with us. We had preaching each evening up to the time of our love-feast. At our council-meeting on Friday afternoon we fully decided to build a meeting-house, the Lord willing. We were made to rejoice on Saturday when two dear young souls came out on the side of the Lord. On Sunday afternoon another precious soul was ready to follow Jesus. She is a lady of influence, and we truly believe she will be a good helper. Bro. Homer Ullom was advanced to the second degree of the ministry. We have had several visits from dear brethren and sisters this season, which cheers us much.—*Mary V. Harshbarger, Oct. 24.*

an enjoyable occasion. The subjects as indicated by the programme, were all discussed in an able and creditable manner, showing careful study in the preparation of their work. Many brethren participated in the discussion, taking a deep interest in the entire meeting.

During the month of August two precious souls were received by baptism. Oct. 8 the writer attended the love-feast at the Auglaize Chapel, Ohio. It was a feast long to be remembered. We lived in this church five years, so it seemed home-like to us, to meet with them again.

Oct. 15, wife, daughter and I attended the love-feast at Oak Grove, Hancock Co., Ohio. This was certainly a feast of love.

Bro. I. J. Rosenberger commenced a series of meetings at this place Oct. 19 and closed Oct. 25. Five were added to the church by confession and baptism. This makes eight since Aug. 1.

McComb, Ohio.　　　　　　D. W. C. Rau.

Notes from Our Correspondents.

"As cold water to a thirsty soul, so is good news from a far country."

Burnett, O. T.—Two more precious souls came out on the Lord's side and were buried with Christ in baptism. Will not some dear brother respond to the Macedonian call and help us here?—*Henry Trozel.*

Buena Vista, Colo.—We are still trying to work in the interest of our Master's cause. Our last quarterly council, which occurred the last of September, passed off very pleasantly. We have Sunday-school, preaching service and social meeting in our church each Lord's Day, and have appointed our love-feast for Nov. 26.—*A. C. Snowberger, Oct. 30.*

Brownsville Church, Md.—Our love-feast of Oct. 29 was a good meeting. The single mode of feet-washing was observed. About 300 members communed. Eld. David Long officiated. A dear brother was baptized during the intermission between examination and evening services. At this feast some communed for the first, time, and some perhaps for the last. There is a blessedness that follows the observance of these ordinances that the world knows not of.—*Geo. W. Kaelzel, Oct. 30.*

Everett, Pa.—Recently we met for services in a church-house in the town of Everett, near my home,—a house which we have the use of for a short time. Here we baptized one brother and reclaimed one. We have been holding meetings in this place during the summer in my barn, part of the time, and at other times in the grove, and have been having good congregations all summer. Quite an interest has seemingly been awakened in this place among the people. We have baptized and reclaimed six, which is encouraging. We need a meeting-house at this place. There is a good opening here and railroad facilities are good.—*D. S. Clopper.*

Marsh Creek Church, Pa.—An enjoyable love-feast was held here recently. The weather and roads being favorable, by noon of Oct. 29 a large representation from neighboring churches was on the grounds. Elders from abroad were Solomon Stoner, Peter Brown, David Netaley, and several other ministers whose presence was much appreciated. Bro. A. D. Taylor was elected to the responsible office of deacon. He, with his wife, were duly installed. We trust this choice was dictated by the Lord, and that they may use the office of deacon well, and purchase to themselves a good degree and great boldness in the faith. One precious soul was received by baptism, and one by letter.—*B. F. Kittinger.*

Middleton, Mich.—Our love-feast in the New Haven church was held Oct. 22. The meetings were very enjoyable. We were glad to see so many present from surrounding churches. Bro. Isaiah Rairigh officiated. Most excellent order prevailed, and the weather was very pleasant.—*Wm. P. Bosserman, Oct. 27.*

Middletown, Ind.—The love-feast of Oct. 25, at the Upper Fall Creek church, was greatly enjoyed. I also attended one at the Lower Fall Creek and Buck Creek. All were feasts to be long remembered. We met with Bro. Henry Frantz and wife, from Ohio, which was a happy surprise. Good order prevailed at each place.—*Florida Etter, Oct. 29.*

Greene, Iowa.—Oct. 30 closed a series of meetings at Franklin County, Iowa, with a crowded house, and the very best of interest. Here, like at a great many other places, we closed too soon, in order to meet other arrangements. I am now at Greene. The interest is growing each evening, and we anticipate a glorious meeting by the time their feast will take place, which is appointed for Nov. 5. I can truly say for Iowa that the harvest is great, but the laborers few.—*Joseph Holder, Nov. 3.*

Green Spring, Ohio.—The members of the Green Spring church, Seneca Co., Ohio, in company with loved ones from adjoining districts, enjoyed, on the evening of Oct. 29, a peaceful, quiet, interesting, beneficial, soul-inspiring love-feast. About ninety members communed. The ministerial force was ample. The Word of Life was dealt out in simplicity and power. Two more were received by confession and baptism. Two brethren were elected to fill the office of deacon. May all prove faithful in their high and holy calling, and to God be all the glory!—*J. B. Light, Oct. 31.*

Elkhart, Iowa.—Oct. 27 I left home on a mission of love to the Brethren of Decatur County, Iowa. I arrived at my destination next day, where I met Bro. Abraham Wolfe, of Libertyville, Iowa. In the evening we had preaching; also next morning at 11 A. M. In the evening their love-feast was held. Next morning we met again for preaching, after which our dear old brother, Wm. Stout, was anointed. We then repaired to the water where baptism was administered to one applicant. In the evening we met again for preaching, and next morning we met at the house of sister Caster, where sister McDonald, of Missouri, 85 years of age, was anointed. Thus closed another pleasant and, we trust, profitable love-feast. We arrived home Nov. 1, leaving Bro. Wolfe to continue the meetings.—*S. M. Goughnour.*

New Stark, Ohio.—The love-feast in the Eagle Creek church occurred Oct. 22. Eld. Samuel Driver officiated. Eld. B. Bosserman, of Michigan, and five of our adjoining ministers were with us and rendered valuable service during the meetings. The weather was fine and the surrounding churches were well represented. This is very encouraging to us, as we feel that we need the assistance of our neighboring churches. The feast was an enjoyable one throughout. About 170 members communed. One dear soul was baptized. On Sunday evening a little company of brethren and sisters gathered at the home of sister Frederick, where her son, Jesse, has been lying quite low for some months with Bright's disease. Bro. D. D. Thomas officiated in the Communion services. Although all present could not well commune, they seemed to enjoy the services very much, and especially was this true with our afflicted brother.—*J. R. Spacht, Oct. 31.*

Tippecanoe, Church, Ind.—Sept. 25, at our regular meeting two (husband and wife) were added to the church by confession and baptism. May they prove faithful, and may others follow! It affords much pleasure to God's children to have the neighbors join in with them.—*D. Rothenberger.*

Mendon, Ohio.—Our love-feast of Oct. 12, in the west end of our district, Mercer County, Ohio, was an enjoyable one and long to be remembered by all present. We had a good ministerial force and the Word was preached with power. One precious soul made a full surrender and was baptized.—*J. B. Detrick.*

Mt. Vernon, Ill.—Bro. D. B. Gibson came to our church Oct. 10 and held meetings each evening until Oct. 27. As a visible result of the meetings six were baptized,—one before our love-feast. Two of the number were children of the writer, and we have great reason to rejoice. Bro. Gibson did not shun to declare all the counsel of God. Sinners were made to tremble, and those that are in Christ were built up in that most holy faith.—*J. M. Angle, Oct. 27.*

Broadfording, Md.—Our love-feast was held Oct. 22, and was a very enjoyable meeting, and largely attended by both members and others. It was a feast to the soul. Eld. John Lehner, officiated. Other ministering brethren from a distance were Eld. David Long and son, Daniel Wolf, William Anthony and others. Two precious souls were made willing to leave the ways of sin and turn to God in their old days. One was about eighty years of age.—*F. J. Neibert, Oct. 25.*

Mingona, Kans.—Our love-feast in the Mingona church, Barber County, Kans, was held Sept. 24. It was a pleasant and an enjoyable meeting. About twenty-six members communed. Bro. J. H. Shambergar's barn, where the love-feast was held, was well filled and the best of order prevailed. Bro. John Wise, of Conway Springs, Sumner County, was with us and officiated. We held a series of meetings preceding the feast, at the Mingona school-house, with good interest. Bro. Wise conducted the meetings. His sermons were edifying and soul-cheering.—*Jacob R. Root, Oct. 23.*

Greenwood Church, Mo.—Our council, preparatory to our love-feast, occurred Oct. 22. The day was inclement, yet a goodly number was present. Considering the nature of the business before the meeting, everything was disposed of in a satisfactory manner. At this meeting Eld. F. W. Dove and wife, of Tennessee, were received by letter. Our love-feast was held on the evening of Oct. 28. My wife being sick, she and I could not attend, but I learn they had a good meeting. A number of members were present from Douglas County, including some of their ministers. This added to the interest of our meeting.—*J. J. Trozel, Cabool, Mo., Oct. 30.*

Palmter, Kans.—The members of the Prairie View church, appointed Oct. 22 as the time for their love-feast. Bro. Enoch Eby and Bro. Henricks were with us. We had preaching each evening up to the time of our love-feast. At our council-meeting on Friday afternoon we decided to build a meeting-house, the Lord willing. We had reason to rejoice on Saturday when two dear young souls came out on the side of the Lord. On Sunday afternoon another precious soul was ready to follow Jesus. She is a lady of influence, and we truly believe she will be a good helper. Bro. Homer Ullom was advanced to the second degree of the ministry. We have had several visits from dear brethren and sisters this season, which cheers us much.—*Mary V. Harshbarger, Oct. 24.*

Smithborough, Ill.—Last Wednesday evening brethren Javan Gibson and Joseph Jones, from Macoupin County, came to us and commenced a series of meetings, preaching every evening till Sunday night. The nights were dark and somewhat rainy, consequently the congregations were not very large, but the preaching was none the less interesting. While among us the brethren visited many of the families. This is a commendable way for our ministering brethren to do, for in this way they may gain some that otherwise would never be gathered into the fold.—*Cornelius Kessler, Oct. 25.*

Waynesville, Mo.—We held our love-feast on Tuesday evening Sept. 11. Brethren Barnhart and Jordan preached for us. Our meetings commenced on Saturday evening prior to the feast, and lasted until Wednesday evening after. Two dear souls came out on the Lord's side and we hope that more, in the near future, will turn their steps in the right direction. Bro. John Delaplain was advanced to the second degree of the ministry, and one deacon was elected. We hope the Lord will bless them in their work. We had fine weather and fair attendance at our meetings. —*Libbie Messenger.*

Accident, Md.—An interesting and soul-cheering series of meetings has just closed in the Bear Creek congregation. Bro. Valentine Blough, of Somerset Co., Pa., commenced a series of meetings Oct. 22, and continued until the 30th, delivering, in all, fourteen sermons, three of them in the German language. The members have been strengthened, and encouraged to live nearer to the foot of the cross, by the earnest appeals of our brother. May the Lord ever bless his labors of love to the good of the church, and the advancement of Christ's kingdom here on earth!—*Mary M. Biddinger, Oct 31.*

Peabody, Kans.—The Brethren of the Peabody church held their love-feast on the evening of Oct. 8. Brethren present from a distance were E. Eby, G. E. Studebaker and T. B. Young. The evening after the feast we commenced a series of meetings, which were kept up for two weeks. Bro. Alexander Miller, from Nappanee, Ind., did the preaching. Although there were no immediate accessions to the church, yet saints were encouraged to press onward and sinners were warned to flee the wrath to come. We hope the Word preached may be as bread cast upon the waters that may be gathered not many days hence.—*Katie Yost, Oct. 26.*

Mahoning, Ohio.—A series of meetings was held here by I. D. Parker in December of last year at Zion Hill. During those meetings six were added to the church, five baptized and one reclaimed. A series of meetings was held at the Bethel house last February by Bro. S. Sprankle. The preaching was good. We had good attention, and we hope lasting impressions were made, but we had no additions. A council-meeting was held at the Bethel house March 10. We agreed to build an addition to the Zion Hill house, suitable to hold Communion. A committee was appointed for that purpose. During the month of August, the annual visit was performed, and on Sept. 8 a council-meeting was held at the Zion Hill house. The building being nearly completed and all matters adjusted, it was agreed to have a Communion Oct. 15. At the time appointed the meeting was held, followed by a few other meetings. During these meetings four persons were baptized. All these meetings were pleasant and, we hope, profitable. Brethren Sprankle, Shively and John Kurtz were present, giving us wholesome instruction. May God's blessing be upon every effort to do good and to save souls!—*Jacob H. Kurtz.*

Mount Hope, Kans.—The brethren and sisters here are alive to the work of the Sunday-school. Ours is one of the evergreen schools. Having re-organized with Bro. J. H. Neher as Superintendent, we feel encouraged to continue to instruct the little ones. Brethren Brubaker and Irig, both ministers, having located here, is encouraging to the writer, seeing the harvest is indeed great, but the laborers are few. Brethren desiring to change locations, would do well to see our country before purchasing elsewhere. Mount Hope church is located eight miles north and four miles west of Guthrie, two miles north and four miles east of Crescent City, Oklahoma Ter. Homes may be had near the church.—*George W. Landis, Crescent City, Oklahoma Ter.*

Burnett, O. T.—It might be of interest to some to hear from us. We are not yet organized. Twelve members from the Owen's Prairie church, moved in here. We are much scattered, but have meetings regularly. We try, by the help of God, to hold forth the Word of Life, and, as a result, one precious soul came out on the Lord's side and was baptized. She was raised a Catholic, but when she heard the Brethren's doctrine, she saw her mistake, and was willing to cast her lot with the people of God. She has a husband and four children. The husband makes no profession. We would be glad for some missionary brother to give us a call and help us. We are poor, yet we would be glad to have some good brother come to our assistance.—*Henry Troxel.*

Literary Notices.

The Funk & Wagnalls Company have nearly ready a book on "English Compound Words and Phrases," by F. Horace Teall. Its main feature is a list of nearly 40,000 terms, originally made for guidance in the preparation of the "Standard Dictionary," now rapidly progressing. In its original form, this list was highly commended by many prominent educators and authors. Professor W. C. Wilkinson called it "a marvelously successful enterprise"; Dr. Leonard Woolsey Bacon expressed "satisfaction with the scientific spirit manifested"; and Gen. James Grant Wilson, Moses Coit Tyler, and E. Benjamin Andrews are among the many others who have expressed approval. The list has been very carefully revised and explained, and is now offered as a practical aid in determining word-forms, even for those who do not wish to write so many compounds as are indicated.

Matrimonial.

"What therefore God hath joined together, let not man put asunder."

SCHROCK—RAYMOND.—At my residence, near Listie, Somerset Co., Pa., Oct. 23, 1892, Bro. Irvin A. Schrock and Minerva Raymond, both of Friedens, Pa. P. F. CUPP.

Fallen Asleep.

"Blessed are the dead which die in the Lord."

GRABLE.—In the Neosho church, Neosho Co., Kans., of cholera infantum, Sadie Gertrude Grable, infant daughter of O. W. and sister Mary F. Grable, aged 2 months and 5 days. Funeral sermon by Eld. Sidney Hodgden, assisted by brethren M. O. Hodgden and A. I. Heestand. G. G. CRUMRINE.

HOSTETLER.—In the bounds of the La Porte church, Ind., Oct. 23, 1892, of brain fever, infant son of brother John and sister Sarah Hostetler, aged 17 months and 4 days. Funeral services by the writer, Oct. 24, at the residence. Interment in New Carlisle cemetery, St. Joseph Co., Ind.

THURSTON MILLER.

ESSIG.—At her home in Hartley, Texas, Sept. 30, 1892, of typhoid fever, Susan, wife of Gotlieb Essig, aged 29 years, 11 months and 4 days. The subject of this notice was the daughter of Henry and Maria Strickler, who emigrated from Illinois to Grundy County, Iowa, many years ago. Mrs. Essig, with her husband and family, moved to Texas in 1889, where they were living at the time of her death. The remains were brought to Grundy County, Iowa, for interment. She leaves a husband and two little children. Funeral services were conducted by Eld. Joseph Holder, of Indiana.

ALDA E. ALBRIGHT.

HALFHILL.—Near Pennsville, Pa., Oct. 24, 1892, Mrs. Maria Halfhill, aged 70 years and 6 days. Deceased was greatly respected in this community, for the many excellent traits of her character, and kindly deeds she has done, although she never made a public profession of religion. Services by the writer. H. S. MYERS.

HOPWOOD.—At Deep River, Iowa, Oct. 8, 1892, William Hopwood, aged 85 years, 2 months and 20 days. He united with the Brethren church in 1845. Soon afterwards he was elected to the deacon's office, in which he labored faithfully until he was called away. His wife preceded him nearly two years to the spirit world. Funeral services by Eld. Samuel Flory, of South English, Iowa, to a large audience. J. J. BROWER.

BERKEYBILE.—At her home in Cass County, Mo., Oct. 16, 1892, of convulsions, sister Millie Ann Berkeybile, aged 20 years, 9 months and 10 days. Deceased was the daughter of Eld. John and sister Rachel Hougendougler, and was married to Bro. E. E. Berkeybile Jan. 1, 1891. She was baptized last winter during the series of meetings conducted by Bro. G. Lentz in the Deep Water church, Mo. She leaves a husband and little infant son, father, mother, two brothers and four sisters. Funeral services Oct. 23, 1892, by Eld. J. M. Mohler, assisted by Bro. Isaac Dell, of Nebraska.

LIZZIE FAHNESTOCK.

EIKENBERRY.—In the bounds of the Labette church, Labette Co., Kans., Oct. 17, 1892, Susan Ala, daughter of Bro. Joel W. and sister Eikenberry, aged 12 years, 7 months and 28 days. Funeral services by the writer. N. TRAPP.

McCLAINE.—At her residence at Stear's Mill, in the bounds of the Cowanshannock congregation, Oct. 5, 1892, of consumption, Mrs. Virginia McClaine, aged 28 years, 5 months and 26 days. Two daughters survive the deceased. Mrs. McClaine's maiden name was Dickson. She was married to J. E. McClaine, who died Dec. 17, 1890, of the same disease, leaving her in charge of the two small children, now aged three and five years. Her remains were interred in the Lutheran cemetery. Funeral services by the writer from Amos 4: 12, last clause. ISAAC SECRIST.

COLLINS.—Near Sidney, Nebr., Oct. 12, 1892, Earl, infant son of Mr. and Mrs. R. L. Collins, aged 3 months.

ELLA L. SNAVELY.

EPPARD.—Oct. 16, 1892, Lara A. E. Epard, aged 1 year, 2 months and 28 days. The subject of this notice was an infant daughter of Bro. Samuel and sister Sallie Eppard. She lingered for three months under the hand of affliction, when she sweetly fell asleep in Jesus. Services by Eld. Hiram Branson from Rev. 14: 13. H. E. MILLSPAUGH.

EVANS.—In Syracuse, Ind., Sept. 8, 1892, sister Electa Evans, daughter of brother and sister Daniel Struby, aged 33 years, 10 months and 16 days. Feeling that her life was near its close, she was anointed in the name of the Lord. She was the mother of three children, two of whom preceded her to the spirit land. Funeral services by Bro. Davis Younce.

L. A. NEFF.

JORDAN.—At Staunton, Va., Sept. 14, 1892, Bro. W. J. Jordan, son of friend Peter C. and sister Lydia A. Jordan, aged 20 years, 4 months and 13 days. He united with the church before he was eighteen years of age. E. L. BROWER.

The Gospel Messenger

Is the recognized organ of the German Baptist or Brethren's church, and advocates the form of doctrine taught in the New Testament and pleads for a return to apostolic and primitive Christianity.

It recognizes the New Testament as the only infallible rule of faith and practice, and maintains that Faith toward God, Repentance from dead works, Regeneration of the heart and mind, baptism by Trine Immersion for remission of sins unto the reception of the Holy Ghost by the laying on of hands, are the means of adoption into the household of God,—the church militant.

It also maintains that Feet-washing, as taught in John 13, both by example and command of Jesus, should be observed in the church.

That the Lord's Supper, instituted by Christ and as universally observed by the apostles and the early Christians, is a full meal, and, in connection with the Communion, should be taken in the evening or after the close of the day.

That the Salutation of the Holy Kiss, or Kiss of Charity, is binding upon the followers of Christ.

That War and Retaliation are contrary to the spirit and self-denying principles of the religion of Jesus Christ.

That the principle of Plain Dressing and of Non-conformity to the world, as taught in the New Testament, should be observed by the followers of Christ.

That the Scriptural duty of Anointing the Sick with Oil, in the Name of the Lord, James 5: 14, is binding upon all Christians.

It also advocates the church's duty to support Missionary and Tract Work, thus giving to the Lord for the spread of the Gospel and for the conversion of sinners.

In short, it is a vindicator of all that Christ and the apostles have enjoined upon us, and aims, amid the conflicting theories and discords of modern Christendom, to point out ground that all must concede to be infallibly safe.

☞ "The above principles of our Fraternity are set forth on our Brethren's Envelopes." Use them! Price 15 cents per package; 40 cents per hundred.

Smithsborough, Ill.—Last Wednesday evening brethren Javan Gibson and Joseph Jones, from Macoupin County, came to us and commenced a series of meetings, preaching every evening till Sunday night The nights were dark and somewhat rainy, consequently the congregations were not very large, but the preaching was none the less interesting. While among us the brethren visited many of the families. This is a commendable way for our ministering brethren to do, for in this way they may gain some that otherwise would never be gathered into the fold.—*Cornelius Kessler, Oct. 25.*

Waynesville, Mo.—We held our love-feast on Tuesday evening Sept. 11. Brethren Barnhart and Jordan preached for us. Our meetings commenced on Saturday evening prior to the feast, and lasted until Wednesday evening after. Two dear souls came out on the Lord's side and we hope that more, in the near future, will turn their steps in the right direction. Bro. John Delaplain was advanced to the second degree of the ministry, and one deacon was elected. We hope the Lord will bless them in their work. We had fine weather and fair attendance at our meetings. —*Libbie Messenger.*

Accident, Md.—An interesting and soul-cheering series of meetings has just closed in the Bear Creek' congregation. Bro. Valentine Blough, of Somerset Co., Pa., commenced a series of meetings Oct. 22, and continued until the 30th, delivering, in all, fourteen sermons, three of them in the German language. The members have been strengthened, and encouraged to live nearer to the foot of the cross, by the earnest appeals of our brother. May the Lord ever bless his labors of love to the good of the church, and the advancement of Christ's kingdom here on earth!— *Mary M. Biddinger, Oct 31.*

Peabody, Kans.—The Brethren of the Peabody church held their love-feast on the evening of Oct. 8. Brethren present from a distance were E. Eby, G. E. Studebaker and T. B. Young. The evening after the feast we commenced a series of meetings, which were kept up for two weeks. Bro. Alexander Miller, from Nappanee, Ind., did the preaching. Although there were no immediate accessions to the church, yet saints were encouraged to press onward and sinners were warned to flee the wrath to come. We hope the Word preached may be as bread cast upon the waters that may be gathered not many days hence.— *Katie Yost, Oct. 26.*

Bahoring, Ohio.—A series of meetings was held here by I. D. Parker in December of last year at Zion Hill. During those meetings six were added to the church, five baptized and one reclaimed. A series of meetings was held at the Bethel house last February by Bro. S. Sprankle. The preaching was good. We had good attention, and we hope lasting impressions were made, but we had no additions. A council-meeting was held at the Bethel house March 10. We agreed to build an addition to the Zion Hill house, suitable to hold Communion. A committee was appointed for that purpose. During the month of August, the annual visit was performed, and on Sept 3 a council-meeting was held at the Zion Hill house. The building being nearly complete, ed and all matters adjusted, it was agreed to have a Communion Oct. 15. At the time appointed the meeting was held, followed by a few other meetings. During these meetings four persons were baptized. All these meetings were pleasant and, we hope, profitable. Brethren Sprankle, Shively and John Kurtz were present, giving us wholesome instruction. May God's blessing be upon every effort to do good and to save souls!—*Jacob H. Kurtz.*

Mount Hope, Kans.—The brethren and sisters here are alive to the work of the Sunday-school. Ours is one of the evergreen schools. Having re-organized with Bro. J. H. Neher as Superintendent, we feel encouraged to continue to instruct the little ones. Brethren Brubaker and Irig, both ministers, having located here, is encouraging to the writer, seeing the harvest is indeed great, but the laborers are few. Brethren desiring to change locations, would do well to see our country before purchasing elsewhere. Mount Hope church is located eight miles north and four miles west of Guthrie, two miles north and four miles east of Crescent City, Oklahoma Ter. Homes may be had near the church.—*George W. Landis, Crescent City, Oklahoma Ter.*

Burnett, O. T.—It might be of interest to some to hear from us. We are not yet organized. Twelve members from the Owen's Prairie church, moved in here. We are much scattered, but have meetings regularly. We try, by the help of God, to hold forth the Word of Life, and, as a result, one precious soul came out on the Lord's side and was baptized. She was raised a Catholic, but when she heard the Brethren's doctrine, she saw her mistake, and was willing to cast her lot with the people of God. She has a husband and four children. The husband makes no profession. We would be glad for some missionary brother to give us a call and help us. We are poor, yet we would be glad to have some good brother come to our assistance.—*Henry Trozel.*

Literary Notices.

The Funk & Wagnalls Company have nearly ready a book on " English Compound Words and Phrases," by F. Horace Teall. Its main feature is a list of nearly 40,000 terms, originally made for guidance in the preparation of the "Standard Dictionary," now rapidly progressing. In its original form, this list was highly commended by many prominent educators and authors. Professor W. C. Wilkinson called it "a marvelously successful enterprise "; Dr. Leonard Woolsey Bacon expressed "satisfaction With the scientific skill manifested"; and Gen. James Grant Wilson, Moses Colt Tyler, and E. Benjamin Andrews are among the many others who have expressed approval. The list has been Very carefully revised and explained, and is now offered as a practical aid in determining word-forms, even for those who do not wish to write so many compounds as are indicated.

Matrimonial.

" What therefore God hath joined together, let not man put asunder."

SCHROCK—RAYMOND.—At my residence, near Listie, Somerset Co., Pa., Oct. 23, 1892, Bro. Irvin A. Schrock and Minerva Raymond, both of Friedens, Pa.   P. F. Cupp.

Fallen Asleep.

" Blessed are the dead which die in the Lord."

GRABLE.—In the Neosho church, Neosho Co., Kans., of cholera infantum, Sadie Gertrude Grable, infant daughter of O. W. and sister Mary F. Grable, aged 2 months and 5 days. Funeral services by the writer, Oct. 24, at the residence. Interment in New Carlisle cemetery, St. Joseph Co., Ind.   G. G. Crumrine.

HOSTETLER.—In the bounds of the La Porte church, Ind., Oct. 23, 1892, of brain fever, infant son of brother John and sister Sarah Hostetler, aged 17 months and 4 days. Funeral services by the writer, Oct. 24, at the residence. Interment in New Carlisle cemetery, St. Joseph Co., Ind.   Thurston Miller.

ESSIG.—At her home in Hartley, Texas, Sept. 30, 1892, of typhoid fever, Susan, wife of Gottlieb Essig, aged 29 years, 11 months and 4 days. The subject of this notice was the daughter of Henry and Maria Strickler, who emigrated from Illinois to Grundy County, Iowa, many years ago. Mrs. Essig, with her husband and family, moved to Texas in 1889, where they were living at the time of her death. The remains were brought to Grundy County, Iowa, for interment. She leaves a husband and two little children. Funeral services were conducted by Eld. Joseph Holder, of Indiana.   Alda E. Albright.

HALFHILL.—Near Pennsville, Pa., Oct. 24, 1892, Mrs. Maria Halfhill, aged 70 years and 6 days. Deceased was greatly respected in this community, for the many excellent traits of her character, and kindly deeds she has done, although she never made a public profession of religion. Services by the writer.   H. S. Myers.

HOPWOOD.—At Deep River, Iowa, Oct. 8, 1892, William Hopwood, aged 85 years, 2 months and 10 days. He united with the Brethren church in 1845. Soon afterwards he was elected to the deacon's office, in which he labored faithfully until he was called away. His wife preceded him nearly two years to the spirit world. Funeral services by Eld. Samuel Flory, of South English, Iowa, to a large audience.   J.J. Brower.

BERKEYBILE.—At her home in Cass County, Mo., Oct. 16, 1892, of convulsions, sister Millie Ann Berkeybile, aged 20 years, 9 months and 10 days. Deceased was the daughter of Eld. John and sister Rachel Hougendougler, and was married to Bro. E. E. Berkeybile Jan. 1, 1891. She was baptized last winter during the series of meetings conducted by Bro. G. Lentz in the Deep Water church, Mo. She leaves a husband and little infant son, father, mother, two brothers and four sisters. Funeral services Oct. 23. 1892, by Eld. J. M. Mohler, assisted by Bro. Isaac Dell, of Nebraska.   Lizzie Fahnestock.

EIKENBERRY.—In the bounds of the Labette church, Labette Co., Kans., Oct. 17, 1891, Susan Ala, daughter of Bro.Joel W. and sister Eikenberry, aged 12 years, 7 months and 26 days. Funeral services by the writer.   N. Trapp.

McCLAINE.—At her residence at Stear's Mill, in the bounds of the Cowanshannock congregation, Oct. 5, 1892, of consumption, Mrs. Virginia McClaine, aged 28 years, 5 months and 26 days. Two daughters survive the deceased. Mrs. McClaine's maiden name was Dickason. She was married to J. E. McClaine, who died Dec. 17, 1890, of the same disease, leaving her in charge of the two small children, now aged three and five years. Her remains were interred in the Lutheran cemetery. Funeral services by the writer from Amos 4: 12, last clause.   Isaac Secrist.

COLLINS.—Near Sidney, Nebr., Oct. 12, 1892, Earl, infant son of Mr. and Mrs. R. L. Collins, aged 3 months.   Ella L. Snavely.

EPPARD.—Oct. 16, 1892, Lara A. E. Eppard, aged 1 year, 1 months and 28 days. The subject of this notice was an infant daughter of Bro. Samuel and sister Sallie Eppard. She lingered for three months under the hand of affliction, when she sweetly fell asleep in Jesus. Services by Eld. Hiram Branson from Rev. 14: 13.   H. E. Millspaugh.

EVANS.—In Syracuse, Ind., Sept. 8, 1892, sister Electa Evans, daughter of brother and sister Daniel Struby, aged 33 years, 10 months and 16 days. Feeling that her life was near its close, she was anointed in the name of the Lord. She was the mother of three children, two of whom preceded her to the spirit land. Funeral services by Bro. Davis Younce.   L. A. Naff.

JORDAN.—At Staunton, Va., Sept. 14, 1892, Bro. W. J. Jordan, son of friend Peter C. and sister Lydia A. Jordan, aged 30 years, 4 months and 13 days. He united with the church before he was eighteen years of age.   E. L. Brower.

The Gospel Messenger

Is the recognized organ of the German Baptist or Brethren's church, and advocates the form of doctrine taught in the New Testament and pleads for a return to apostolic and primitive Christianity.

It recognizes the New Testament as the only infallible rule of faith and practice, and maintains that Faith toward God, Repentance from dead works, Regeneration of the heart and mind, baptism by Trine Immersion for remission of sins unto the reception of the Holy Ghost by the laying on of hands, are the means of adoption into the household of God,—the church militant.

It also maintains that Feet-washing, as taught in John 13, both by example and command of Jesus, should be observed in the church.

That the Lord's Supper, instituted by Christ and as universally observed by the apostles and the early Christians, is a full meal, and, in connection with the Communion, should be taken in the evening or after the close of the day.

That the Salutation of the Holy Kiss, or Kiss of Charity, is binding upon the followers of Christ.

That War and Retaliation are contrary to the spirit and self-denying principles of the religion of Jesus Christ.

That the practice of Plain Dressing and of Non-conformity to the world, as taught in the New Testament, should be observed by the followers of Christ.

That the Scriptural duty of Anointing the Sick with Oil, in the Name of the Lord, James 5: 14, is binding upon all Christians.

It also advocates the church's duty to support Missionary and Tract Work, thus giving to the Lord for the spread of the Gospel and for the conversion of sinners.

In short, it is a vindicator of all that Christ and the apostles have enjoined upon us, and aims, amid the conflicting theories and discords of modern Christendom, to point out ground that all must concede to be infallibly safe.

☞ The above principles of our Fraternity are set forth on our Brethren's Envelopes. Use them! Price 15 cents per package; 40 cents per hundred.

Announcements.

MINISTERIAL MEETINGS.

Nov. 25, at 9 A. M., in the South-east District of Kansas, Ministerial Meeting in the Cedar Creek church, Mott Ida, Anderson Co., Kans.

Nov. 30, Dec. 1 and 2, Southern District of Pennsylvania. Ministerial Meeting in the East Codorus church, York, York Co., Pa.

Nov. 17, at 9 A. M., North-eastern District of Ohio, Ministerial Meeting, Maple Grove church, 4 miles north of Ashland, Ashland Co., Ohio.

LOVE-FEASTS.

Dec. 3. Good Hope church, at the Showberger school-house, 8 miles north-east of Holyoke, Phillips Co., Colo.

Nov. 19, at 3 P. M., McPherson, Kans.

Nov. 19, Altoona, Pa.

Nov. 22, at 2 P. M., Cedar Creek church, Anderson Co., Kans.

Nov. 25 and 26, Beatrice church, Nebr.

Dec. 8, at 2 P. M., Cerro Gordo, Ill.

Church Entertainments: Twenty Objections.

By Rev. B. Carradine, D. D. 12mo, 100 pp. Paper cover, 30 cents. A strong book in defense of its position, written by a powerful pen, presenting the most candid and scriptural arraignment of unwarrantable methods for money-raising in the Church. The spirit of the book is highly devotional and cannot fail to inspire the reader with its seriousness.

Close Communion.—By Landon West. Treats this important subject in a simple though conclusive manner. Price, 30 cents.

Companion to the Bible.—This valuable work is so full of instruction that it can not fail to be of great benefit to every Christian. Price, $1.25.

Dubbel's Cough and Croup Cure

Is a sure and quick cure for colds and especially for croup. It will cure any case of croup that a doctor can cure and with one-tenth the expense. It contains no dangerous drugs such as morphia, opium, chloral, etc., and is perfectly harmless. It is highly endorsed for La Grippe. Our Cough and Croup Cure is second to none, and we sell it on the strong guarantee, " No cure, no pay." We allow one-half the contents of the bottle to be tried and if the results are not satisfactory, return it to us or the agent of whom you purchased it. Your money will be refunded. Price, 25 cents per bottle. Agents wanted in every locality. We want 1,000 new agents till Jan. 1. To any person who secures us an agent who will offer two dozen at agents' rates we will give, as a present for securing the agent, the valuable book " Alone with God." Said book is advertised in the Gospel Messenger. Write for terms and circular.

Eld. P. D. Reid, Limestone, Tenn., writes April 6, '91: " Eld. Carthmod, whom I returned from a preaching tour in Virginia, I was run down from preaching and had contracted a very bad cold. I got a bottle of your Cough and Croup Cure from Bro. C. H. Diehl, of Jonesboro, Tenn. After taking half of it I was perfectly cured. For a cold or La Grippe I can certainly recommend it."

S. E. Dubbel & Co.,

Manufacturers and Proprietors,

Waynesboro, Franklin Co., Pa.

Also manufacturers of Red Thyme Pain Cure,—the medicine that proved to be such a blessing at the last Annual Meeting held at Cedar Rapids, Iowa.

For Sale!

Having a desire to devote more time to church work, I offer one quarter section of choice farm land for sale. This farm has a good house, barn, fences, well, and a nice spring. It is situated 3½ miles south of the Brethren's meeting-house in Shannon, Ill. It is also within one mile of a good creamery. I also offer 50 head of registered Short Horn Cattle, 15 males and 35 females, — choice individuals at a very low price. Address for particulars, D. Rowland, Lanark, Ill.

--- THE ---

Doctrine of the Brethren Defended.

THIS work contains a complete exposition of the faith and practice of the Brethren, the Divinity of Christ, the Divinity of the Holy Spirit, Immersion, Feet-washing, the Lord's Supper, the Holy Kiss, Non-conformity, Secret Societies, etc. Price, per copy, cloth binding, $1.25. Address this office.

For Sale!

I have for sale a complete set of *Gospel Visitor*, *Primitive Christian*, and *Gospel Messenger*, from 1876 to 1891 included, bound in morocco, cloth sides; also *Young Disciple*, from 1881 to 1889, bound in morocco, cloth sides, three years in a book. The *Gospel Visitor* is bound in black roan, paper sides. For terms address J. W. King, Huntingdon, Pa.

EUROPE
AND
Bible Lands

A new edition of this deservedly popular work has again been published. It retains all the excellencies of its predecessors, and with those who are interested in Bible study this work will always remain a favorite. Those who have read the ordinary book of travel will be surprised to find " Europe and Bible Lands " of thrilling interest for both old and young. The large number of books, already sold, proves that the work is of more than ordinary merit.

A fair supply of the last edition of this work is still on hand. Those who have not yet secured a copy of the work should embrace this opportunity of securing it. Price, in fine cloth binding, only $1.50 per copy, post-paid. To agents who are prepared to push an active canvass of the work, we are prepared to give special inducements. Write us. BRETHREN'S PUBLISHING CO., Mt. Morris, Ill.

CANCERS, TUMORS, ETC.

Successfully treated by Dr. G. N. Botsler, of Waynesborough, Pa., where he has practiced for the last thirteen years. Dr. Botsler is a graduate at the University of Maryland, at Baltimore City. References given and correspondence solicited. Address, Dr. G. W. Botsler, Waynesborough, Pa.

O Jerusalem! Jerusalem!

WHAT could be more beautiful and touching than a picture of Christ as he stood upon Olivet looking down over the beloved but sinful city, with tears trickling down over his cheeks, his lips parted as he cries, " O Jerusalem! Jerusalem!" We have such a picture 21×28 inches, beautifully executed in colors. No one can gaze upon it without being moved. Given free with a year's subscription to " What to Read " at 50 cents. An agent wanted in every church and neighborhood. Address, Jas. M. Nave, Covington, Ohio.

Alone with God.

THIS manual of devotions, by J. H. Garrison, comprises a series of meditations with forms of prayer for private devotions, family worship and special occasions. It is one of the most useful, most needed, and best adapted books of the year, and therefore it is not strange that it is proving one of the most popular. In work of this kind its distinguished, gifted, pious and beloved author is at his best. This book is helpful to every minister, church official, and Sunday-school superintendent, as well as every private member of the church in all ages. It has models of prayer, suitable for the service of the prayer-meeting, while its suggestions, meditations and instructions are pre-eminently calculated to be of service in preparation for the solemn duties that rest upon the active members. Cloth, 75 cents; morocco, $1.25. Address this office.

Farm for Sale.

A desirable property located 1½ miles east of Mt. Morris, consisting of 185 acres of well-improved land. One of the finest country residences in Ogle County. For further particulars call on, or address,

ELIZABETH MIDDLEKAUFF,
41tf
Mt. Morris, Ill.

Excursions to California.

Excursions in charge of M. M. Eshelman, Immigration Agent, will leave Chicago over the " Santa Fe Route " Tuesdays, and Kansas City Wednesdays, during the year 1898, on dates as follows:

Chicago, January 25, February 15, March 22, April 26, May 24, June 28, July 26, August 23, September 27, October 25, November 29, December 27.

Kansas City, January 27, February 24, March 23, April 27, May 26, June 29, July 27, August 24, September 28, October 26, November 23, December 28.

Parties wishing to avail themselves of the privilege of these excursions, should write to M. M. Eshelman, North Pomona, California, refer to the 15th of each month, and from the fifteenth to the end of the month, at 1090 Union Avenue (opposite Union Depot), Kansas City, Mo., stating when and where they wish to join one of these excursions, and he will give them full information, and if desired will reserve berths in Tourist Sleeping Car for them. Do not fail to write him; he will do you good. The rates will be as low as the lowest made to the Pacific Coast.

GEORGE L. McDONAUGH,
Traveling Agent,

LOOK AT THIS.

The Monon Route still reducing rates and offering better accommodations than ever before.

Commencing April 15, the fare from Chicago to Louisville, New Albany, Cincinnati, Hamilton, and Dayton will be $5.50; to Indianapolis $3.50. Round trip tickets good ten days at double the one way rate.

Parlor and Dining cars on day trains; Pullman Sleepers and Compartment Cars on night trains. A special Sleeper is run for Indianapolis business.

See that your tickets read via the MONON ROUTE.

For rates, schedules, etc., apply at Depot, Dearborn Station, City Ticket Office, 19 Clark Street, or address, JAMES BARKER, G. P. A., Monon Block, Chicago, Ill.

Wolf's Business College.

A thorough school for training pupils in the Commercial Branches, Shorthand, Typewriting, Telegraphy, and Penmanship. The school for those who want a practical, useful education. Write for catalogue.

D. ELMER WOLF, Principal,
Hagerstown, Md.

Announcements.

MINISTERIAL MEETINGS.

Nov. 25, at 9 A. M., in the South-east District of Kansas, Ministerial Meeting in the Cedar Creek church, Mont Ida, Anderson Co., Kans.

Nov. 30, Dec. 1 and 2, Southern District of Pennsylvania. Ministerial Meeting in the East Cordorus church, York, York Co., Pa.

Nov. 17, at 9 A. M., North-eastern District of Ohio, Ministerial Meeting, Maple Grove church, 4 miles north of Ashland, Ashland Co., Ohio.

LOVE-FEASTS.

Dec. 3, Good Hope church, at the Snowberger school-house, 8 miles north-east of Holyoke, Phillips Co., Cols.

Nov. 15, at 2 P. M., McPherson, Kans.

Nov. 19, Altoona, Pa.

Nov. 24, at 2 P. M., Cedar Creek church, Anderson Co., Kans.

Nov. 25 and 26, Beatrice church, Nebr.

Dec. 8, at 2 P. M., Cerro Gordo, Ill.

Church Entertainments: Twenty Objections.

By Rev. B. Carradine, D. D. 12mo, 100 pp. Paper cover, 30 cents. A strong book in defense of its position, written by a powerful pen, presenting the most candid and scriptural arraignment of unwarrantable methods for money-raising in the Church. The spirit of the book is highly devotional and cannot fail to inspire the reader with its seriousness.

Close Communion.—By Landon West. Treats this important subject in a simple though conclusive manner. Price, 50 cents.

Companion to the Bible.—This valuable work is so full of instruction that it can not fail to be of great benefit to every Christian. Price, $1.15.

For Sale!

Having a desire to devote more time to church work, I offer one quarter section of choice farm land for sale. This farm has a good house, barn, fences, well, and a nice spring. It is situated 2½ miles south of the Brethren's meeting-house in Shannon, Ill. It is also within one mile of a good creamery. I also offer 20 head of registered Short Horn Cattle, 15 males and 35 females,— choice individuals at a very low price. Address for particulars, D. Rowland, Lanark, Ill.

— THE —
Doctrine of the Brethren Defended.

THIS work contains a complete exposition of the faith and practice of the Brethren, the Divinity of Christ, the Divinity of the Holy Spirit, Immersion, Feet-washing, the Lord's Supper, the Holy Kiss, Non-conformity, Secret Societies, etc. Price, per copy, cloth binding, $1.25. Address this office.

For Sale!

I have for sale a complete set of *Gospel Visitor, Primitive Christian*, and *Gospel Messenger*, from 1856 to 1891 included, bound in morocco, cloth sides; also *Young Disciple*, from 1881 to 1889, bound in morocco, cloth sides, three years in a book. The *Gospel Visitor* is bound in black roan, paper sides. For terms address J. W. King, Huntingdon, Pa.

EUROPE
AND
Bible Lands

A new edition of this deservedly popular work has again been published. It retains all the excellencies of its predecessors, and, with those who are interested in Bible study this work will always remain a favorite. Those who have read the ordinary book of travel will be surprised to find "Europe and Bible Lands" of thrilling interest for both old and young. The large number of books, already sold, proves that the work is of more than ordinary merit.

A fair supply of the last edition of this work is still on hand. Those who have not yet secured a copy of the work should embrace this opportunity of securing it. Price, in fine cloth binding, only $1.50 per copy, post-paid. To agents who are prepared to push an active canvass of the work, we are prepared to give special inducements. Write us.

BRETHREN'S PUBLISHING CO.,
Mt. Morris, Ill.

CANCERS, TUMORS, ETC.

Successfully treated by Dr. G. N. Bender, of Waynesborough, Pa., where he has practiced for the last sixteen years. Dr. Bender is a graduate of the University of Maryland, at Baltimore City. References given and correspondence solicited. Address, Dr. G. W. Bender, Waynesborough, Pa.   9t60o

O Jerusalem! Jerusalem!

WHAT could be more beautiful and touching than a picture of Christ as he stood upon Olivet looking down over the beloved but sinful city, with tears trickling down over his cheeks, his lips parted as he cries, "O Jerusalem! Jerusalem!" We have such a picture 12x18 inches, beautifully executed in colors. He can can gaze upon it without being moved. Given free with a year's subscription to "What to Read" at 50 cents. An agent wanted in every church and neighborhood. Address,

Jas. M. Narr, Covington, Ohio.

Alone with God.

THIS manual of devotions, by J. H. Garrison, comprises a series of meditations with forms of prayer for private devotion, family worship and special occasions. It is one of the most useful, most needed, and best adapted books of the year, and therefore it is not strange that it is proving one of the most popular. In work of this kind its distinguished, gifted, pious and beloved author is at his best. This book is helpful to every minister, church official, and Sunday-school superintendent, as well as every private member of the church in all ages. It has models of prayer, suitable for the service of the prayer-meeting, while its suggestions, meditations and instructions are pre-eminently calculated to be of service in preparation for the solemn duties that rest upon the active members. Cloth, 75 cents; morocco, $1.25. Address this office.

Farm for Sale.

A desirable property located 1½ miles east of Mt. Morris, consisting of 183 acres of well-improved land. One of the finest country residences in Ogle County. For further particulars call on, or address,

ELIZABETH MIDDEKAUFF.
41tf   Mt. Morris, Ill.

Excursions to California.

EXCURSIONS in charge of M. M. Eshelman, Immigration Agent, will leave Chicago over the "Santa Fe Route" Tuesdays, and Kansas City Wednesdays, during the year 1899, on dates as follows:

Chicago, January 26, February 23, March 22, April 26, May 24, June 28, July 26, August 23, September 27, October 25, November 22, December 27.

Kansas City, January 25, February 24, March 23, April 27, May 25, June 29, July 27, August 24, September 28, October 26, November 23, December 28.

Parties wishing to avail themselves of the privileges of these excursions, should write M. M. Eshelman, North Pomona, California, prior to the 15th of each month, and from the fifteenth to the end of the month, at 1090 Union Avenue (opposite Union Depot), Kansas City, Mo., stating when and where they wish to join one of these excursions, and he will give them full information, and if desired will reserve berths in Tourist Sleeping Car for them. Do not fail to write him; he will do you good. The rates will be as low as the lowest made to the Pacific Coast.

GEORGE L. McDONAUGH,
Traveling Agent.

+ESSAYS+

* Study to show thyself approved unto God; a workman that needeth not to be ashamed, rightly dividing the Word of Truth.''

THANKSGIVING.

BY PHŒBE CARY.

O, MEN! grown sick with toil and care,
Leave for awhile the crowded mart;
O, women! sinking with despair,
Weary of limb and faint of heart,
Forget your cares to-day and come
As children back to childhood's home!

Follow again the winding rills;
Go to the places where you went,
When, climbing up the summer hills,
In their green lap, you sat, content;
And softly leaned your head to-rest
On nature's calm and peaceful breast.

Walk through the sere and fading wood,
So lightly trodden by your feet,
When all you knew of life was good,
And all you dreamed of life was sweet;
And let fond memory lead you back,
O'er youthful love's enchanted track.

Taste the ripe fruit of orchard boughs,
Drink from the mossy well once more;
Breathe fragrance from the crowded mows,
With fresh, sweet clover running o'er;
And count the treasures at your feet,
Of silver rye and golden wheat.

Go, sit beside the hearth again,
Whose circle once was glad and gay!
And if from out the precious chain
Some shining links have dropped away,
Then guard with tender heart and hand
The remnant of your household band.

Draw near the board with plenty spread.
And if in the accustomed place,
You see the father's reverent head,
Or mother's patient, loving face:
Whate'er your life may have of ill,
Thank God that there are left you still.

And though where home hath been, you stand
To-day in alien loneliness;
Though you may clasp no brother's hand,
And claim no sister's tender kiss.
Though with no friend or dear one nigh,
The past is all your company,—

Thank God for friends your life has known.
For every dear, departed day;
The blessed past is safe alone,—
God gives, but does not take away;
He only safely keeps above
For us the treasures that we love.

TALE-BEARING.

BY ANNIE B. BOWMAN.

OF all existing evils perhaps there is none greater than this. When we look around us and see with what apparent satisfaction it is entered into, and the zeal persons will manifest in circulating a new story or, perchance, elaborate on an old one, we are made to feel very sad indeed.

Habitual tale-bearers are never truthful. Here is where the evil becomes most apparent. "They say," and "It is rumored" are almost invariably the preface to an untruth. Let us, as a church, beware of them.

Tale-bearers cling to obnoxious, slanderous stories with wonderful tenacity, but touch very lightly the things that breathe of peace and love.

If only God's creatures could be made to realize the preverseness of such a course, for its effects are most appalling, and might truly be termed a terrible scourge, which not only enters the family circle and causes sorrow and distress there, but alienates entire neighborhoods, and even finds its way into the blessed church.

Oh, brethren and sisters, let me beseech you, not to be influenced by evil reports carried by idle tattlers.

You dare not risk your soul's safety, trying to keep abreast with that wonderful little piece of mechanism,—the tongue. This is a fictitious age and truly our authors are legion, and it may be, too, we ourselves feel an inclination to join the procession and add a story of our own. For instance, by way of trial, we polish off a piece of news just out; the bare facts are too plain; we will add a little fiction to make it more attractive, and, sure enough, before we are aware, we, too, are swallowed up in the whirlpool of insatiable fictitious tale-telling. But will such unreal stories bear God's test when he says, "Thou shalt not bear false witness"? Fiction cannot stand before such a verdict, hence we necessarily fall into judgment.

Life is too short,—far too earnest, to drift with such a tide. Besides we have no ears for rubbish, nor precious moments to spend pondering over trash. Let us, therefore, be engaged in acquiring that only which will tend to inspire pure morals, noble incentives, and lofty aspirations, for, in living to our utmost capabilities,—a true and Christian life,—can we ever hope to gain admission to that blissful realm which never fadeth away.

Harrisonburgh, Va.

THE BROAD WAY AND THE NARROW WAY.

BY J. W. KEISER.

THE broad road derives its name from the fact that it is the easiest to travel. Six thousand years ago this road was traveled by our foreparents, because they transgressed God's law in Eden. As years and centuries have rolled on, the broad way has been traversed by the human race, as it sped on more rapidly to destruction. The way becomes daily more hardened by the wickedness of a vain and gainsaying people. They rush headlong into sin and degradation, in spite of all God's people can do or say.

Not only does this way grow more slippery, but mankind reaches the end of the road sooner than in other years. To-day the average age of man is only about thirty years. The first man who traveled this way lived nine hundred and thirty years.

For six thousand years the race of mankind has been pursuing the broad way. Only a few, comparatively speaking, have tried to change their course and retrace their steps. Sin and death were brought into the world through the disobedience of our foreparents. Death was pronounced upon the human family, and not until the Gospel age was there a way of escape brought to light. In former ages rays of hope were dimly seen in types and shadows by a few, but life and immortality was not brought to light until the appearing of our Lord and Savior Jesus Christ. Although a way of escape has been made from the broad road to a path of life through the Gospel, the great mass of mankind will not heed the glad tidings of great joy because of their depraved nature, and will continue in sin until death overtakes them. Then they will have to reap the reward of the wicked.

The narrow way is fully described by Christ, when he says that because of the narrowness of this way many prefer to remain on the broad way. Jesus says, "Strait is the gate and narrow is the way that leadeth unto life, and few there be that find it."

When we consider this way, we must admit there are many dangers and difficulties. While we may not be able to discover all the secrets of life, we may safely say that the divine being, Jehovah, is the great fountain of life, from which all our supplies proceed. God, in his loving-

---

kindness and tender mercy, has prepared a way for his faithful children, and it is a straight and narrow way. It is too narrow for the human race to travel on in their carnal state. If we want to travel in this way, we must forsake sin and its allurements, and follow in the footsteps of our Lord and Master. Is it not passing strange that man, one of the masterpieces of God's creation, made only a little lower than the angels, should heed the council of the wicked one, and be driven from the glorious presence of his Creator, to revel in sin and wickedness all the days of his life, and bring death upon all his posterity? Death has passed upon all, for all have sinned.

Job says, "Yes, man giveth up the ghost and where is he?" Job 14: 10. "His sons come to honor and he knoweth it not, and they are brought low and he perceiveth it not of them." Job. 14: 21. "There is no work, nor device, nor knowledge, nor wisdom, in the grave where thou goest." Eccl. 9: 10. But since a ransom has been found; and since the death penalty has been paid by the Redeemer, man can again be restored to his beauty in the image of his Creator, when the sun of righteousness shall arise with healing in his wings. There is only one class of people who travel this narrow way. These are they who have had their robes washed and made white in the blood of the Lamb,—those whom John, the Revelator, saw in his vision on the lonely isle.

Then, if we want to travel this narrow way, we must daily be upon our guard. Is it not worth sacrificing a little of what the world calls pleasure, to travel on this narrow way? True, many times we meet with disappointments and trials by the way, but God has said, "My grace is sufficient for thee." Then, why doubt his word, and be plunged into woe and misery forever? Let us keep close to the side of Jesus, and when we come to the brink of the chilly river of death, he will accompany us across and land our souls in the shining portals of heaven.

Pioneer, Ohio.

THE SABBATH OF GOD:

BY C. H. BALSBAUGH.

Dear sister H——:

IT seems your Seventh Day neighbors are not satisfied with my former article on the Sabbath, and demur especially against what I intimated is essentially involved in their retention of the creative Sabbath. If they take time and care to study the previous article in the MESSENGER, they will find enough to sweep away their main defence in favor of their Sabbath. When they have attended fairly to the historical facts, and the insuperable chronological difficulties, they will need no further evidence that "Christ is the end" of all former dispensations.

Our first day Sabbath is no papal institution, as they assert, but has its origin and perpetuity wholly in the significance of the all-comprehending, all-culminating work of Christ. The rest of God in Christ is the consummation of his eternal purpose, counts infinitely more than the rest of the six creative days. The WORD that made the worlds, was made flesh and recreated all things new, and now proclaims the true rest in Him. This insistence of the Adventists on the primitive order of time is only another illustration of Luke 5: 39. The first century bears ample testimony to the struggle that disengaged the Jewish mind from their dispensational peculiarities. Human nature is still the same.

The obligations involved in Gal. 5: 3 apply with equal force to the Sabbath. The rejection of the day that emphasizes the resurrection as

✦ESSAYS✦

"Study to show thyself approved unto God; a workman that needeth not be ashamed, rightly dividing the Word of Truth."

THANKSGIVING.

BY PHŒBE CARY.

O, MEN! grown sick with toil and care,
  Leave for awhile the crowded mart;
O, WOMEN! sinking with despair,
  Weary of limb and faint of heart,
Forget your cares to-day and come
As children back to childhood's home!

Follow again the winding rills;
  Go to the places where you went,
When, climbing up the summer hills,
  In their green lap, you sat, content;
And softly leaned your head to rest
On nature's calm and peaceful breast-

Walk through the sere and fading wood,
  So lightly trodden by your feet,
When all you knew of life was good,
  And all you dreamed of life was sweet;
And let fond memory lead you back,
O'er youthful love's enchanted track.

Taste the ripe fruit of orchard boughs,
  Drink from the mossy well once more;
Breathe fragrance from the crowded mows,
  With fresh, sweet clover running o'er;
And count the treasures at your feet,
Of silver rye and golden wheat.

Go, sit beside the hearth again,
  Whose circle once was glad and gay;
And if from out the precious chain
  Some shining links have dropped away,
Then guard with tender heart and hand
The remnant of your household band.

Draw near the board with plenty spread,
  And if in the accustomed place,
You see the father's reverent head,
  Or mother's patient, loving face!
Whate'er your life may have of ill,
Thank God that these are left you still.

And though where home hath been, you stand
  To-day in alien loneliness;
Though you may clasp no brother's hand,
  And claim no sister's tender kiss.
Though with no friend or dear one nigh,
  The past is all your company,—

Thank God for friends your life has known.
  For every dear, departed day;
The blessed past is safe alone,—
  God gives, but does not take away;
He only safely keeps above
For us the treasures that we love.

TALE-BEARING.

BY ANNIE R. BOWMAN.

OF all existing evils perhaps there is none greater than this. When we look around us and see with what apparent satisfaction it is entered into, and the zeal persons will manifest in circulating a new story or, perchance, elaborate on an old one, we are made to feel very sad indeed.

Habitual tale-bearers are never truthful. Here is where the evil becomes most apparent. "They say," and "It is rumored" are almost invariably the preface to an untruth. Let us, as a church, beware of them.

Tale-bearers cling to obnoxious, slanderous stories with wonderful tenacity, but touch very lightly the things that breathe of peace and love.

If only God's creatures could be made to realize the preverseness of such a course, for its effects are most appalling, and might truly be termed a terrible scourge, which not only enters the family circle and causes sorrow and distress but then alienates entire neighborhoods, and even finds its way into the blessed church.

Oh, brethren and sisters, let me beseech you, not to be influenced by evil reports carried by idle tattlers.

You dare not risk your soul's safety, trying to keep abreast with that wonderful little piece of mechanism,—the tongue. This is a fictitious age and truly our authors are legion, and it may be, too, we ourselves feel an inclination to join the procession and add a story of our own. For instance, by way of trial, we polish off a piece of news just out; the bare facts are too plain; we will add a little fiction to make it more attractive, and, sure enough, before we are aware, we, too, are swallowed up in the whirlpool of insatiable fictitious tale-telling. But will such unreal stories bear God's test when he says, "Thou shalt not bear false witness"? Fiction cannot stand before such a verdict, hence we necessarily fall into judgment.

Life is too short,—far too earnest, to drift with such a tide. Besides we have no ears for rubbish, nor precious moments to spend pondering over trash. Let us, therefore, be engaged in acquiring that only which will tend to inspire pure morals, noble incentives, and lofty aspirations, for, in living to our utmost capabilities,—a true and Christian life,—can we ever hope to gain admission to that blissful realm which never fadeth away.

Harrisonburgh, Va.

THE BROAD WAY AND THE NARROW WAY.

BY J. W. KEISER.

THE broad road derives its name from the fact that it is the easiest to travel. Six thousand years ago this road was traveled by our fore-parents, because they transgressed God's law in Eden. As years and centuries have rolled on, the broad way has been traversed by the human race, as it sped on more rapidly to destruction. The way becomes daily more hardened by the wickedness of a vain and gainsaying people. They rush headlong into sin and degradation, in spite of all God's people can do or say.

Not only does this way grow more slippery, but mankind reaches the end of the road sooner than in other years. To-day the average age of man is only about thirty years. The first man who traveled this way lived nine hundred and thirty years.

For six thousand years the race of mankind has been pursuing the broad way. Only a few, comparatively speaking, have tried to change their course and retrace their steps. Sin and death were brought into the world through the disobedience of our foreparents. Death was pronounced upon the human family, and not until the Gospel age was there a way of escape brought to light. In former ages rays of hope were dimly seen in types and shadows by a few, but life and immortality was not brought to light until the appearing of our Lord and Savior Jesus Christ. Although a way of escape has been made from the broad road to a path of life through the Gospel, the great mass of mankind will not heed the glad tidings of great joy because of their depraved nature, and will continue in sin until death overtakes them. Then they will have to reap the reward of the wicked.

The narrow way is fully described by Christ, when he says that because of the narrowness of the way. Jesus says, "Strait is the gate and narrow is the way that leadeth unto life, and few there be that find it."

When we consider this way, we must admit there are many dangers and difficulties. While we may not be able to discover all the secrets of life, we may safely say that the divine being, Jehovah, is the great fountain of life, from which all our supplies proceed. God, in his loving-kindness and tender mercy, has prepared a way for his faithful children, and it is a straight and narrow way. It is too narrow for the human race to travel on in their carnal state. If we want to travel in this way, we must forsake sin and its allurements, and follow in the footsteps of our Lord and Master. Is it not passing strange that man, one of the masterpieces of God's creation, made only a little lower than the angels, should heed the council of the wicked one, and be driven from the glorious presence of his Creator, to revel in sin and wickedness all the days of his life, and bring death upon all his posterity? Death has passed upon all, for all have sinned.

Job says, "Yes, man giveth up the ghost and where is he?" Job 14: 10. "His sons come to honor and he knoweth it not, and they are brought low and he perceiveth it not of them." Job. 14: 21. "There is no work, nor device, nor knowledge, nor wisdom, in the grave where thou goest." Eccl. 9: 10. But since a ransom has been found, and since the death penalty has been paid by the Redeemer, man can again be restored to his beauty in the image of his Creator, when the sun of righteousness shall arise with healing in his wings. There is only one class of people who travel this narrow way. These are they who have had their robes washed and made white in the blood of the Lamb,—those whom John, the Revelator, saw in his vision on the lonely isle.

Then, if we want to travel this narrow way, we must daily be upon our guard. Is it not worth sacrificing a little of what the world calls pleasure, to travel on this narrow way? True, many times we meet with disappointments and trials by the way, but God has said, "My grace is sufficient for thee." Then, why doubt his word, and be plunged into woe and misery forever? Let us keep close to the side of Jesus, and when we come to the brink of the chilly river of death, he will accompany us across and land our souls in the shining portals of heaven.

Pioneer, Ohio.

THE SABBATH OF GOD.

BY C. H. BALSBAUGH.

Dear sister H——:

IT seems your Seventh Day neighbors are not satisfied with my former article on the Sabbath, and demur especially against what I intimated is essentially involved in their retention of the creative Sabbath. If they take time and care to study the previous article in the MESSENGER, they will find enough to sweep away their main defence in favor of their Sabbath. When they have attended fairly to the historical facts, and the insuperable chronological difficulties, they will need no further evidence that "Christ is the end" of all former dispensations.

Our first day Sabbath is no papal institution, as they assert, but has its origin and perpetuity wholly in the significance of the all-comprehending, all-culminating work of Christ. The rest of God in Christ is the consummation of His eternal purpose, counts infinitely more than the rest of the six creative days. The WORD that made the worlds, was *made flesh* and recreated all things new, and now proclaims the true rest in Him. This insistence of the Adventiste on the primitive order of time is only another illustration of Luke 5: 39. The first century bears ample testimony to the struggle that disengaged the Jewish mind from their dispensational peculiarities. Human nature is still the same.

The obligations involved in Gal. 5: 3 apply with equal force to the Sabbath. The rejection of the day that emphasizes the resurrection as

CORRESPONDENCE.

"Write what thou seest, and send it unto the churches."

☞"Church News solicited for this Department. If you have had a good meeting, send a report of it, so that others may rejoice with you. In writing give name of church, County and State. Be brief. Notes of Travel should be as short as possible. Land Advertisements are not solicited for this Department. We have an advertising page, and, if necessary, will issue supplements.

A Visit to Mineral and Hardy Counties, W. Va.

I LEFT home Oct. 26, to attend several love-feasts. In the evening of the same day I arrived at Romney where I was met by Bro. Wm. Arnold, who conveyed me to his home. After enjoying a pleasant night's rest we started to attend a love-feast at the Beaver Run church. Notwithstanding the unpleasant weather a large assembly gathered,—some to worship God, and others, no doubt, to see and be seen. We had a very pleasant and profitable feast, with the very best of order. Appointments having been made in the direction of the next feast in Hardy County,—about thirty miles farther west,—the Brethren kindly arranged that I should meet them promptly. Eld. D. B. Arnold was my right-hand man as we climbed the mountains that lay before us. Pause a moment and think, as you read what I am about to relate. We were faithfully drawn over these mountains by an old black horse named Selam, and, as stated by Eld. Arnold, has traveled at least 30,000 miles through cold and heat, wet and dry, in the service of the church. If there be a horse heaven, poor old "Selam" should have an indisputable right to the place.

But do not look too long at Selam and lose sight of his faithful master riding those many miles serving the church he loves, and loving the God he serves. While we were traveling through the mountains, we talked considerable about the Dunkard preachers, and while we talked I thought many things,—one thing being, if double honor is deserved by anyone it is the faithful Dunkard preacher, especially those who inhabit the hilly country of West Virginia.

The attendance at Hardy was small, but the meeting very enjoyable. A young man arose at this meeting with a desire to go with us to our Fatherland, and was at once received into the ranks.

From here I was taken by Bro. Flora to his home, twelve miles in the direction of another love-feast at the Tearcoat meeting-house. Nov. 5 we again met a large crowd of people. Political feeling being then at blood-heat, the meeting was threatened with disorder, but the exercises were marked throughout with the best of order. During the service we referred to the solid and sandy foundations. A lady, who was a very consistent member of another denomination, for many years, and whose husband is a deacon in the church of the Brethren, dreamed that night she was standing on one corner of a foundation and her husband on another and suddenly her corner began to sink, and she awoke to find it a dream. Her dream acted upon her much as Belshazzar's did upon him. She related her dream to Daniel, and in his interpretation of it she wept and concluded to place herself on a solid foundation. Just as the darkness of the evening covered the earth, she was led by the servant Daniel down into the stream and was baptized into Jesus Christ.

We then hastened to the Augusta church where we met a full house. After the sermon another lady arose in the congregation, desiring to be received. She was baptized on Monday morning, at which time I started for my home, arriving safely the same evening, for which I feel to say, Praise the Lord!

Benevola, Md., Nov. 9. D. F. STOUFFER.

From the Mission Field.

OCT. 22 Bro. A. J. Smith and the writer went about eighteen miles north-west of this place where there is an isolated brother and sister. We commenced meetings the same evening. Bro. Smith returned home next day. The writer continued over the next Sunday, preaching in all ten sermons, which seemed to be appreciated. One, that had wandered away from the fold, made application for re-instatement into the church. We explained to the people our faith and practice. This they admitted to be strictly evangelical. I believe much good can be done if the proper efforts were put forth. If any of the brethren find their hearts moved towards the isolated ones, drop a card to Bro. L. P. Donaldson, Everett, Mo., and you will be met at Archie, Mo. The people are very kind and have a warm feeling for the Brethren.

While I was there, I received a very urgent request for preaching at another point, northwest of a small station on the Missouri Pacific Branch, south from Pleasant Hill, called Lone Tree, where another isolated brother lives. If the Lord permits me, I will go there in the near future. Brethren, think of the lonely ones, but don't stop at thinking. W. H. MILLER.

Adrian, Bates Co., Mo.

From the Paint Creek Church, Bourbon Co., Kans.

ACCORDING to previous arrangements Bro. Heestand, of the Neosho church, commenced a series of meetings Oct. 23, and closed on Sunday evening, the 30th. On Saturday evening previous we assembled for love-feast services with a good attendance of members, and a crowded house of spectators. The best of order prevailed during the meetings. These meetings were well attended and the members, we trust, much built up in the cause of the Master. Although there were none added to the church, we trust, that, by the earnest labors of Bro. Heestand, impressions were made that will not soon be forgotten.

We have no resident minister. We are under the care of Eld. Samuel Click, of Nevada, Mo., who preached for us once a month. We would much like if some one, wanting to locate, would visit this place, as we think we have as good a country as many others who are well supplied with speakers. Anyone, traveling through this part of Kansas, should not forget the Paint Creek church, numbering about fifty members. The nearest railroad station is Redfield, Bourbon Co., Kans. J. B. BOLINGER.

From Jewell, Ohio.

HUSBAND and I left our home in Missouri, Nov. 3, for Ohio, on a mission tour, and also a visit among the relatives at our old home. We are now pleasantly situated among the Brethren in the Poplar Ridge church, Defiance Co., Ohio. The work has now begun and we are having attentive congregations. This is the first time I have had the opportunity of accompanying my husband in his field of labor, but I think I shall enjoy it. We find much work to be done, here as elsewhere, and we also feel the great responsibility resting on us. We hope we have the prayers of God's children, that the work undertaken may at least do some good.

For the information of many I will say that my maiden name is Bosserman, the sister of S. T. Bosserman, and the sister of Callie B. Teeter, (both deceased.)

On our visit among the different churches I would like to meet with those that are connected with the Bosserman family. I find many scattered here and there by that name, and they can all be traced to the same family, who, a few generations ago (three in number,—two brothers and one sister) came from Germany.

Address us until after Nov. 18, at Jewell, Ohio, after which, until Dec. 13, address DeGraff, Ohio, after that McComb, Ohio, until Jan. 1.

JACOB & AMANDA WITMORE.

Nov. 8.

Mt. Morris Bible Term.

As we are nearing the time of our Bible Term at Mt. Morris, I feel like taking the liberty to say something to urge our ministers to attend as far as possible our January Term. Only those who have been there before, feel the great importance and great need of attending again.

Every church ought to assist some of their ministers, so they might attend. Iowa alone ought to send fifty ministers to this coming Term. When we have such brethren as D. E. Price attend and enjoy themselves,—in fact forget their age,—we must come to the conclusion that it is good to be there. It has a tendency to unite us more closely in doctrine and church government, as well as on the ordinances.

Last winter there were at least forty ministers present, and the question was asked, "How many have taken the subject of anointing and preached a sermon from that subject?" No one had done so. It was surprising as we went over the first principles of the doctrine of Christ to see how careless we have been in the past, in regard to preaching for the anointing of the sick, nonconformity, etc.

That is not all. We learn how to conduct ourselves when we go out to hold meetings, and visit among the churches. I wish all could feel interested as much as some brethren who have donated as much as five thousand dollars to carry on the work.

If our churches could feel such an interest, we would have a large attendance at the coming Term. Please remember you have no tuition to pay. Your board and railroad fare are all the expenses you will have. Any information will be gladly given by the undersigned or by J. G. Royer, Mt. Morris, Ill. J. C. SEIBERT, Sec.

Hills Siding, Iowa, Oct. 31.

From Pleasant Dale, Ind.

WE, the members of the Pleasant Dale church, have enjoyed a soul-reviving series of meetings. Bro. D. S. Caylor, of Somerset, Wabash County, came to us on the third Saturday of October, and preached the Word with power one week previous to our love-feast. Our feast was held on the fourth Saturday of October and was very enjoyable. There was a number of brethren present from adjoining churches. Bro. D. S. Caylor officiated. During our meeting there was a choice held for a minister. The choice fell on Bro. Jacob Heller, a worthy and consistent brother. On Sunday morning before service Bro. Heller and companion were installed and the writer was advanced to the second degree of the ministry. Bro. Caylor remained and continued preaching the Word until the evening of Oct. 30. The same Sunday there were three precious souls added to the church by confession and baptism.

HOWARD J. BEAGLE.

From the Ozawkie Church, Kans.

BRO. CHAS. M. YEAROUT began a series of meetings Oct. 20, which he continued until the evening of Oct. 30 with increased interest to the close. The congregations were large throughout

CORRESPONDENCE.

"Write what thou seest, and send it unto the churches."

☞Church News solicited for this Department. If you have had a good meeting, send a report of it, so that others may rejoice with you. In writing give name of church, County and State. Be brief. Notes of Travel should be as short as possible. Land Advertisements are not solicited for this Department. We have an advertising page, and, if necessary, will issue supplements.

A Visit to Mineral and Hardy Counties, W. Va.

I LEFT home Oct. 28, to attend several love-feasts. In the evening of the same day I arrived at Romney where I was met by Bro. Wm. Arnold, who conveyed me to his home. After enjoying a pleasant night's rest we started to attend a love-feast at the Beaver Run church. Notwithstanding the unpleasant weather a large assembly gathered,—some to worship God, and others, no doubt, to see and be seen. We had a very pleasant and profitable feast, with the very best of order. Appointments having been made in the direction of the next feast in Hardy County,—about thirty miles farther west,—the Brethren kindly arranged that I should meet them promptly. Eld. D. B. Arnold was my right-hand man as we climbed the mountains that lay before us. Pause a moment and think, as you read what I am about to relate. We were faithfully drawn over these mountains by an old black horse named Selam, and, as stated by Eld. Arnold, has traveled at least 90,000 miles through cold and heat, wet and dry, in the service of the church. If there be a horse heaven, poor old "Selam" should have an indisputable right to the place.

But do not look too long at Selam and lose sight of his faithful master riding those many miles serving the church he loves, and loving the God he serves. While we were traveling through the mountains, we talked considerable about the Dunkard preachers, and while we talked I thought many things,—one thing being, if double honor is deserved by anyone it is the faithful Dunkard preacher, especially those who inhabit the hilly country of West Virginia.

The attendance at Hardy was small, but the meeting very enjoyable. A young man arose at this meeting with a desire to go with us to our Fatherland, and was at once received into the ranks.

From here I was taken by Bro. Flora to his home, twelve miles in the direction of another love-feast at the Tearcoat meeting-house. Nov. 5 we again met a large crowd of people. Political feeling being then at blood-heat, the meeting was threatened with disorder, but the exercises were marked throughout with the best of order. During the service we referred to the solid and sandy foundations. A lady, who was a very consistent member of another denomination, for many years, and whose husband is a deacon in the church of the Brethren, dreamed that night she was standing on one corner of a foundation and her husband on another and suddenly her corner began to sink, and she awoke to find it a dream. Her dream acted upon her much as Belshazzar's did upon him. She related her dream to Daniel, and in his interpretation of it she wept and concluded to place herself on a solid foundation. Just as the darkness of the evening covered the earth, she was led by the servant Daniel down into the stream and was baptized into Jesus Christ.

We then hastened to the Augusta church where we met a full house. After the sermon another lady arose in the congregation, desiring to be received. She was baptized on Monday morning, at which time I started for my home, arriving safely the same evening; for which I feel to say, Praise the Lord!

Benevola, Md., Nov. 9.   D. F. STOUFFER.

From the Mission Field.

OCT. 22 Bro. A. J. Smith and the writer went about eighteen miles north-west of this place where there is an isolated brother and sister. We commenced meetings the same evening. Bro. Smith returned home next day. The writer continued over the next Sunday, preaching in all ten sermons, which seemed to be appreciated. One, that had wandered away from the fold, made application for re-instatement into the church. We explained to the people our faith and practice. This they admitted to be strictly evangelical. I believe much good can be done if the proper efforts were put forth. If any of the brethren find their hearts moved towards the isolated ones, drop a card to Bro. L. P. Donaldson, Everett, Mo., and you will be met at Archie, Mo. The people are very kind and have a warm feeling for the Brethren.

While I was there, I received a very urgent request for preaching at another point, north-west of a small station on the Missouri Pacific Branch, south from Pleasant Hill, called Lone Tree, where another isolated brother lives. If the Lord permits me, I will go there in the near future. Brethren, think of the lonely ones, but don't stop at thinking.   W. H. MILLER.

Adrian, Bates Co., Mo.

From the Paint Creek Church, Bourbon Co., Kans.

ACCORDING to previous arrangements Bro. Heestand, of the Neosho church, commenced a series of meetings Oct. 23, and closed on Sunday evening, the 30th. On Saturday evening previous we assembled for love-feast services with a good attendance of members, and a crowded house of spectators. The best of order prevailed during the meetings. These meetings were well attended and the members, we trust, much built up in the cause of the Master. Although there were none added to the church, we trust, that, by the earnest labors of Bro. Heestand, impressions were made that will not soon be forgotten.

We have no resident minister. We are under the care of Eld. Samuel Click, of Nevada, Mo., who preached for us once a month. We would much like if some one, wanting to locate, would visit this place, as we think we have as good a country as many others who are well supplied with speakers. Anyone, traveling through this part of Kansas, should not forget the Paint Creek church, numbering about fifty members. The nearest railroad station is Redfield, Bourbon Co., Kans.   J. B. BOLINGER.

From Jewell, Ohio.

HUSBAND and I left our home in Missouri, Nov. 3, for Ohio, on a mission tour, and also a visit among the relatives at our old home. We are now pleasantly situated among the Brethren in the Poplar Ridge church, Defiance Co., Ohio. The work has now begun and we are having attentive congregations. This is the first time I have had the opportunity of accompanying my husband in his field of labor, but I think I shall enjoy it. We find much work to be done, here as elsewhere, and we also feel the great responsibility resting on us. We hope we have the prayers of God's children, that the work undertaken may at least do some good.

For the information of many I will say that my maiden name is Bosserman, the sister of S. T. Bosserman, and the sister of Callie B. Teeter, (both deceased.)

On our visit among the different churches I would like to meet with those that are connected with the Bosserman family. I find many scattered here and there by that name, and they can all be traced to the same family, who, a few generations ago (three in number,—two brothers and one sister) came from Germany.

Address us until after Nov. 18, at Jewell, Ohio, after which, until Dec. 13, address DeGraff, Ohio, after that McComb, Ohio, until Jan. 1.

JACOB & AMANDA WITMORE.

Nov. 8.

Mt. Morris Bible Term.

As we are nearing the time of our Bible Term at Mt. Morris, I feel like taking the liberty to say something to urge our ministers to attend as far as possible our January Term. Only those who have been there before, feel the great importance and great need of attending again.

Every church ought to assist some of their ministers, so they might attend. Iowa alone ought to send fifty ministers to this coming Term. When we have such brethren as D. E. Price attend and enjoy themselves,—in fact forget their age,—we must come to the conclusion that it is good to be there. It has a tendency to unite us more closely in doctrine and church government, as well as on the ordinances.

Last winter there were at least forty ministers present, and the question was asked, "How many have taken the subject of anointing and preached a sermon from that subject?" Not one had done so. It was surprising as we went over the first principles of the doctrine of Christ to see how careless we have been in the past, in regard to preaching for the anointing of the sick, non-conformity, etc.

That is not all. We learn how to conduct ourselves when we go out to hold meetings, and visit among the churches. I wish all could feel interested as much as some brethren who have donated as much as five thousand dollars to carry on the work.

If our churches could feel such an interest, we would have a large attendance at the coming Term. Please remember you have no tuition to pay. Your board and railroad fare are all the expenses you will have. Any information will be gladly given by the undersigned or by J. G. Royer, Mt. Morris, Ill.   J. C. SEIBERT, Sec.

Hills Siding, Iowa, Oct. 31.

From Pleasant Dale, Ind.

WE, the members of the Pleasant Dale church, have enjoyed a soul-reviving series of meetings. Bro. D. S. Caylor, of Somerset, Wabash County, came to us on the third Saturday of October, and preached the Word with power one week previous to our love-feast. Our feast was held on the fourth Saturday of October and was very enjoyable. There was a number of brethren present from adjoining churches. Bro. D. S. Caylor officiated. During our meeting there was a choice held for a minister. The choice fell on Bro. Jacob Heller, a worthy and consistent brother. On Sunday morning before services Bro. Heller and companion were installed and the writer was advanced to the second degree of the ministry. Bro. Caylor remained and continued preaching the Word until the evening of Oct. 30. The same Sunday there were three precious souls added to the church by confession and baptism.

HOWARD J. BEAGLE.

From the Ozawkie Church, Kans.

BRO. CHAS. M. YEAROUT began a series of meetings Oct. 20, which he continued until the evening of Oct. 30 with increased interest to the close. The congregations were large throughout

Missionary and Tract Work Department.

Organization of Missionary Committee.

DANIEL VANIMAN, Foreman, - - McPherson, Kans.
D. L. MILLER, Treasurer, - - - Mt. Morris, Ill.
GALEN B. ROYER, Secretary, - - Mt. Morris, Ill.

Organization of Book and Tract Work.

S. W. HOOVER, Foreman, - - - Dayton, Ohio.
S. BOCK, Secretary and Treasurer, - Dayton, Ohio.

THE CALL OF THE UNSAVED.

BY W. B. STOVER.

I LIVE in a well-furnished cottage
As happy as Christian can be,
But e'er and anon comes the thought of
The heathen across the sea.
I've leisure and books and the loved ones
And things just about as I will,
But the fullness of blessing condemns me
Because of the unsaved still.

I pray at morning and evening
For God to hasten the day
When all shall have heard of Jesus—
Salvation the good old way.
I give of my plenty a little,
And *go,* I hope, some others will,
Yet somehow I feel I don't answer
The call of the unsaved still.

There are many at home unconverted,
And the members need preachers too,
So why should I think to go elsewhere
When there's plenty at home to do?
But the heathen, ah, the heathen,
Who worship the gods of their will;
And the voice from the far-away land is
The call of the unsaved still.

The ripple of "sacred" waters,
The fall of rain from above,
The voice of the silent idol,
The absence of parental love,
The sad and downcast expression,
Souls longing great truths to fulfil,
All these seem to me so surely
The calls of the unsaved still.

I know our forefathers were heathen
And the very vilest of men,
And we would have been the same now
But for the foreign missions then.
To-day we're out of the darkness
And claim to do his will—
But can we unless we answer
The call of the unsaved still?

The call comes loud to me, louder,
As I sit in my rocking-chair
And think of the hopeless condition
Of the millions away over there.
And I pray the Lord for conviction,
His wishes to be my will,
That I may heartily answer
The call of the unsaved still.

November, 1892.

HARMONY.

BY A. HUTCHISON.

In Three Parts.—Part One.

WHEN we speak of harmony we mean agreement, and when the matter of salvation is under consideration it is of the greatest importance that we know with what we are in harmony. The simple fact that we are in full harmony with such as profess to be Christians does not, by any means, settle the question as to our salvation. In order that we may be assured of our safety, in the matter of salvation, we must know that we are in harmony with Jesus who is our Leader and our Savior. It matters not who else we may be yoked with, if we are not bearing the yoke of Christ we are in an unsaved state.

There is but one way for us to know whether we are so related to him as to bring salvation to us. We refer you to an apostle, to give you the key to that knowledge. He says, " We know that we have passed from death unto life, because we love the brethren." 1 John 3: 14. We hear persons talk a great deal about this Scripture, and how they are assured that they have passed from death unto life, because they love the brethren. But we inquire, How do you know that you do love the brethren? We are generally told, " We know it because we feel the love of our brethren and the love of God in our hearts. Well, we must remember that our hearts are not always in unison with God. Jeremiah, the prophet, says: " The heart is deceitful above all things and desperately wicked: who can know it?" Jer. 17: 9. And to still farther confirm what is here stated, we have Solomon, the wisest man, saying, " He that trusteth in his own heart is a fool." Prov. 28: 26.

Here it will be seen that it is very unsafe to depend upon our own hearts. Solomon continues in the same verse by saying, " But whoso walketh wisely he shall be delivered." Now, in order that we may know whether we are walking wisely and whether we are in harmony with Jesus, let us consult him on this line. He says, " Whosoever heareth these sayings of mine and doeth them, I will liken him unto a wise man which built his house upon a rock." Matt. 7: 24.

The wise man, then, is the one who acts in harmony with the Master. If there is no friction between us and him, that means salvation to us. A very significant question, however, which is enough to make every professor look carefully to his going, is the following: " And why call ye me Lord, Lord, and do not the things which I say?" Luke 6: 46. This question ought to stir us all up to a diligent review of our past life and of our present standing. We may conceive the idea that, because we wash our brethren's feet, and salute them with a kiss (though these be done only in a formal manner) that we are in perfect unison with God, but all these things may obtain in our outward life while our hearts are woefully "out of gear" with the divine life of our Master in other things. In music we must have all the parts brought into harmony with each other before we can have true melody, but each of the performers in music gives up his or her ideas of things and comes to the rule that is to govern in the case. Then, and then only, do we have true harmony and no grating to disturb our enjoyment. So it is with each of us,—we cannot afford to suppose, or guess, that we are working in harmony with the Captain of our salvation. The beloved apostle says, "And hereby do we know that we know him, if we keep his commandments." 1 John 2: 3.

Sometimes, however, we hear persons say that all they wish to know is to feel the love of God in their hearts, and we think that is good enough, if

---

we rightly comprehend what is meant by the love of God in the heart. A Scriptural idea of it is given thus, " By this we know that we love the children of God when we love God and keep his commandments. For this is the love of God that we keep his commandments." 1 John 5: 2, 3.

If the love of God, after this manner, is shed abroad in our hearts, we may begin to talk about being in harmony with God. Jesus plainly tells us, " If a man love me, he will keep my words." John 14: 23. This is just about what you would tell your child, if that child were to set up the claim that it loved you and yet was not disposed to obey you. You would say to it, " If you loved me, you would surely obey me."

Jesus has given us his commandments as a means by which to try our spirits, and if we have the spirit of our Master, we will most undoubtedly obey his words. If we have not the spirit of Christ we are none of his. Sad truth to be applied to anyone claiming to be a follower of Jesus! We have the blessed assurance in God's Word that we shall be happy if we know and do what Jesus has given us to do. On the other hand we have some pretty strong language against the false pretender. We will give you a sample in the following words, "He that saith I know him and keepeth not his commandments, is a liar and the truth is not in him." 1 John 2: 4. We do not understand the apostle to mean that such a man would not speak the truth in his fellow-man in the business affairs of life, but when he says, "He is a liar and the truth is not in him," he means to say that such a person is deceived in reference to the true relationship between himself and God. The words of the Lord is the truth that is not in him.

Jesus says, " If ye abide in me and my words abide in you, ye shall ask what ye will and it shall be done unto you." John 15: 7. This is the great test by which to determine whether we are in harmony with Jesus or not. He tells us that " He that rejoiceth me and receiveth not my words hath one that judgeth him: the word that I have spoken, the same shall judge him at the last day." John 12: 48.

We must remember that to be in harmony with Jesus means to antagonize the enemy of our souls at every point along the journey through life. The enemy well knows that his only time is now and his only chance is while we are in this tabernacle. For when we are no longer cumbered with this corruptible body, he can have no more dominion over us. He understands, too, that he can only gain the mastery over us by appealing to us through the lusts of the flesh. But we are so lovingly appealed to by the apostle that it seems as if we ought constantly to be on our guard. He says, " Dearly beloved, I beseech you as strangers and pilgrims, abstain from fleshly lusts which war against the soul." 1 Pet. 2: 11.

Here is our great danger, and we must also keep before our minds the fact that he will not attempt to get us to yield to any great sin at first. He will try us at first with little things. We all ought to commit to memory the following: "Take us the foxes, the little foxes, that spoil the vines: for our vines have tender grapes." Songs of Solomon 2: 15.

(*To be continued.*)

IS IT STEALING?

BY J. B. BRINEY.

THE next characteristic of the old man to be noticed, and which must also be put off, is stealing. To take that which belonged to another without compensation, was not regarded as a crime in some heathen communities. Among the

Missionary and Tract Work Department.

"Upon the first day of the week, let every one of you lay by him in store as God hath prospered him, that there be no gatherings when I come."—1 Cor. 16: 2.

"Every man as he purposeth in his heart, so let him give. Not grudgingly or of necessity, for the Lord loveth a cheerful giver."—2 Cor. 9: 7.

HOW MUCH SHALL WE GIVE?

"Every man according to his ability." "Every one as God hath prospered him." "Every man, according as he purposeth in his heart, so let him give." "For if there be first a willing mind, it is accepted according to that a man hath, and not according to that he hath not."—2 Cor. 8: 12.

Organization of Missionary Committee.

DANIEL VANIMAN, Foreman, - - McPherson, Kans.
D. L. MILLER, Treasurer, - - Mt. Morris, Ill.
GALEN B. ROYER, Secretary, - - Mt. Morris, Ill.

Organization of Book and Tract Work.

S. W. HOOVER, Foreman, - - Dayton, Ohio.
S. BOCK, Secretary and Treasurer, - Dayton, Ohio.

☞All donations intended for Missionary Work should be sent to GALEN B. ROYER, Mt. Morris, Ill.
☞All money for Tract Work should be sent to S. BOCK, Dayton, Ohio.
☞Money may be sent by Money Order, Registered Letter, or Drafts on New York or Chicago. Do not send personal checks, or drafts on interior towns, as it costs 25 cents to collect them.
☞Solicitors are requested to faithfully carry out the plan of Annual Meeting, that all our members be solicited to contribute at least twice a year to the Mission and Tract Work of the Church.
☞Notes for the Endowment Fund can be had by writing to the Secretary of either Work.

THE CALL OF THE UNSAVED.

BY W. B. STOVER.

I LIVE in a well-furnished cottage
  As happy as Christian can be,
But e'er and anon comes the thought of
  The heathen across the sea.
I've leisure and books and the loved ones
  And things just about as I will,
But the fullness of blessing condemns me
  Because of the unsaved still.

I pray at morning and evening
  For God to hasten the day
When all shall have heard of Jesus—
  Salvation the good old way.
I give of my plenty a little,
  And go, I hope, some others will,
Yet somehow I feel I don't answer
  The call of the unsaved still.

There are many at home unconverted,
  And the members need preachers too,
So why should I think to go elsewhere
  When there's plenty at home to do?
But the heathen, ah, the heathen,
  Who worship the gods of their will;
And the voice from the far-away land is
  The call of the unsaved still.

The ripple of "sacred" waters,
  The fall of rain from above,
The voice of the silent idol,
  The absence of parental love,
The sad and downcast expression,
  Souls longing great truths to fulfil,
All these seem to me as surely
  The calls of the unsaved still.

I know our forefathers were heathen
  And the very vilest of men,
And we would have been the same now
  But for the foreign missions then.
To-day we're out of the darkness
  And claim to do his will—
But can we unless we answer
  The call of the unsaved still?

The call comes loud to me, louder,
  As I sit in my rocking-chair
And think of the hopeless condition
  Of the millions away over there.
And I pray the Lord for conviction,
  His wishes to be my will,
That I may heartily answer
  The call of the unsaved still.
November, 1892.

HARMONY.

BY A. HUTCHISON.

In Three Parts.—Part One.

WHEN we speak of harmony we mean agreement, and when the matter of salvation is under consideration it is of the greatest importance that we know with what we are in harmony. The simple fact that we are in full harmony with such as profess to be Christians does not, by any means, settle the question as to our salvation. In order that we may be assured of our safety, in the matter of salvation, we must know that we are in harmony with Jesus who is our Leader and our Savior. It matters not who else we may be yoked with, if we are not bearing the yoke of Christ we are in an unsaved state.

There is but *one* way for us to know whether we are so related to him as to bring salvation to us. We refer you to an apostle, to give you the key to that knowledge. He says, "We know that we have passed from death unto life, because we love the brethren." 1 John 3: 14. We hear persons talk a great deal about this Scripture, and how they are assured that they have passed from death unto life, because they love the brethren. But we inquire, How do you know that you do love the brethren? We are generally told, "We know it because we feel the love of our brethren and the love of God in our hearts." Well, we must remember that our hearts are not always in unison with God. Jeremiah, the prophet, says: "The heart is deceitful above all things and desperately wicked: who can know it?" Jer. 17: 9. And to still farther confirm what is here stated, we have Solomon, the wisest man, saying, "He that trusteth in his own heart is a fool." Prov. 28: 26.

Here it will be seen that it is very unsafe to depend upon our own hearts. Solomon continues in the same verse by saying, "But whoso walketh wisely he shall be delivered." Now, in order that we may know whether we are walking wisely and whether we are in harmony with Jesus, let us consult him on this line. He says, "Whosoever heareth these sayings of mine and doeth them, I will liken him unto a wise man which built his house upon a rock." Matt. 7: 24.

The wise man, then, is the one who acts in harmony with the Master. If there is no friction between us and him, that means salvation to us. A very significant question, however, which is enough to make every professor look carefully to his going, is the following: "And why call ye me Lord, Lord, and do not the things which I say?" Luke 6: 46. This question ought to stir us all up to a diligent review of our past life and of our present standing. We may conceive the idea that, because we wash our brethren's feet, and salute them with a kiss (though these be done only in a formal manner) that we are in perfect unison with God, but all these things may obtain in our outward life while our hearts are woefully "out of gear" with the divine life of our Master in other things. In music we must have all the parts brought into harmony with each other before we can have true melody, but each of the performers in music gives up his or her ideas of things and comes to the rule that is to govern in the case. Then, and then only, do we have true harmony and no grating to disturb our enjoyment. So it is with each of us,—we cannot afford to suppose, or guess, that we are working in harmony with the Captain of our salvation. The beloved apostle says, "And hereby we do know that we know him, if we keep his commandments." 1 John 2: 3.

Sometimes, however, we hear persons say that all they wish to know is to feel the love of God in their hearts, and we think that is good enough, if we rightly comprehend what is meant by the love of God in the heart. A Scriptural idea of it is given thus, "By this we know that we love the children of God when we love God and keep his commandments." For this is the love of God that we keep his commandments." 1 John 5: 2, 3.

If the love of God, after this manner, is shed abroad in our hearts, we may begin to talk about being in harmony with God. Jesus plainly tells us, "If a man love me, he will keep my words." John 14: 23. This is just about what you would tell your child, if that child were to set up the claim that it loved you and yet was not disposed to obey you. You would say to it, "If you loved me, you would surely obey me."

Jesus has given us his commandments as a means by which to try our spirits, and if we have the spirit of our Master, we will most undoubtedly obey his words. If we have not the spirit of Christ we are none of his. Sad truth to be applied to anyone claiming to be a follower of Jesus! We have the blessed assurance in God's Word that we shall be happy if we know and do what Jesus has given us to do. On the other hand we have some pretty strong language against the false pretender. We will give you a sample in the following words, "He that saith I know him and keepeth not his commandments, is a liar and the truth is not in him." 1 John 2: 4. We do not understand the apostle to mean that such a man would not speak the truth to his fellowman in the business affairs of life, but when he says, "He is a liar and the truth is not in him," he means to say that such a person is deceived in reference to the true relationship between himself and God. The words of the Lord is the truth that is not in him.

Jesus says, "If ye abide in me and my words abide in you, ye shall ask what ye will and it shall be done unto you." John 15: 7. This is the great test by which to determine whether we are in harmony with Jesus or not. He tells us that "He that rejecteth me and receiveth not my words hath one that judgeth him: the word that I have spoken, the same shall judge him at the last day." John 12: 48.

We must remember that to be in harmony with Jesus means to antagonize the enemy of our souls at every point along the journey through life. The enemy well knows that his only time is now and his only chance is while we are in this tabernacle. For when we are no longer cumbered with this corruptible body, he can have no more dominion over us. He understands, too, that he can only gain the mastery over us by appealing to us through the lusts of the flesh. But we are so lovingly appealed to by the apostle that it seems as if we ought constantly to be on our guard. He says, "Dearly beloved, I beseech you as strangers and pilgrims, abstain from fleshly lusts which war against the soul." 1 Pet. 2: 11.

Here is our great danger, and we must also keep before our minds the fact that he will not attempt to get us to yield to any great sin at first. He will try us at first with little things. We all ought to commit to memory the following: "Take us the foxes, the little foxes, that spoil the vines: for our vines have tender grapes." Songs of Solomon 2: 15.

(To be continued.)

IS IT STEALING!

BY J. B. BRINNEY.

THE next characteristic of the old man to be noticed, and which must also be put off, is stealing. To take that which belonged to another without compensation, was not regarded as a crime in some heathen communities. Among the

The Gospel-Messenger,

A Weekly at $1.50 Per Annum.

PUBLISHED BY

The Brethren's Publishing Co.

D. L. MILLER,	Editor
J. H. MOORE,	Office Editor.
J. B. BRUMBAUGH, } J. G. ROYER, }	Associate Editors.
JOSEPH AMICK,	Business Manager.

ADVISORY COMMITTEE.
L. W. Teeter, A. Hutchison, Daniel Hays.

☞Communications for publication should be legibly written with black ink on one side of the paper only. Do not attempt to interline, or to put on one page what ought to occupy two.

☞Anonymous communications will not be published.

☞Do not mix business with articles for publication. Keep your communications on separate sheets from all business.

☞Time is precious. We always have time to attend to business and to answer questions of importance, but please do not subject us to need less answering of letters.

☞The MESSENGER is mailed each week to all subscribers. If the address is correctly entered on our list, the paper must reach the person to whom it is addressed. If you do not get your paper, write us, giving particulars.

☞When changing your address, please give your former as well as your future address in full, so as to avoid delay and misunderstanding.

☞Always remit to the office from which you order your goods, no matter from where you receive them.

☞Do not send personal checks or drafts on interior banks, unless you send with them 25 cents each, to pay for collection.

☞Remittances should be made by Post-office Money Order, Drafts on New York, Philadelphia or Chicago, or Registered Letters, made payable and addressed to "Brethren's Publishing Co., Mount Morris, Ill.," or "Brethren's Publishing Co., Huntingdon, Pa."

☞Entered at the Post-office at Mount Morris, Ill., as second-class matter.

Mount Morris, Ill., - - - - Nov. 22, 1892.

BRO. A. M. DICKEY, of Iowa, we learn, has decided to locate at McPherson, Kans.

FOR the want of room considerable correspondence and interesting church news must lay over until next week.

UNDER date of Nov. 14 Bro. J. L. Thomas, of Ames, Iowa, writes: "Yesterday at our regular appointment one was received by baptism."

BRO. HAYS' article on Church Government, No. 4, reached us too late for this issue. It will appear next week. It contains some excellent points.

NEXT week we will publish the semi-annual report of the Brethren's Book and Tract Work. The receipts during the last six months are quite encouraging.

THE Sunday-school at Mt. Morris has decided to take up a special collection on the Sunday prior to Thanksgiving, for the benefit of the mission work in Chicago.

BRO. D. P. MILLER, of Buchanan, Mich., requests a correction in his report of the feast at that place. The meeting was held Oct. 1, instead of Oct. 3, as reported.

A NEW YORK paper says: "While a deputy sheriff was moving the effects of Mrs. Halpin, an aged invalid, into the street, yesterday, for non-payment of rent, the woman, who was heart-broken, expired, kneeling in prayer."

THE Brethren at Mexico, Ind., are pushing the work on their much-needed new meeting-house, which they hope to have completed by Christmas. The new house has been under contemplation for several years and is now an absolute necessity, on account of the large and growing congregation. The old house is often too small to hold the people who attend the services. We not only commend the Brethren at Mexico for their wisdom in building a much larger and better house, but congratulate them on their success in keeping up their large congregation.

BRO. J. B. BRUMBAUGH, our Corresponding Editor, places an editorial on our desk just a little too late for this issue. It will appear on one of these pages next week.

BRO. H. C. EARLY's meeting, of which mention was made last week, closed the 7th with fifteen additions by confession and baptism, and the promise of others to come shortly.

THE District Meeting of Tennessee, etc., we learn, passed off very harmoniously. Bro. Henry Sheets, of North Carolina, will represent the District on the next Standing Committee.

BRO. LEMUEL HILLERY, who has not been in good health for some time, is now able to do some much-needed work. He is engaged in a series of meetings at the Pleasant Valley church, Ind.

THE Brethren at South Waterloo, Iowa, have just closed an excellent meeting with nine additions. Bro. D. A. Walker, of Pennsylvania, did the preaching. We learn that this church is in a prosperous condition.

THE Honey Creek church, Nodaway Co., Mo., is rejoicing over an excellent series of meetings, conducted by brethren C. H. Brown and J. E. Ellenberger. Fifteen came out on the Lord's side and were baptized.

BRO. PHILIP A. MOORE, of Roanoke, Ill., writes that he and his wife reached California in safety, after four days' travel, and are now enjoying what seems like summer weather. They may be addressed at Los Angeles.

BRO. ANDREW HUTCHISON has been placed in charge of the mission in Cedar Rapids, Iowa, and devotes all of his time to the work. We think the arrangement is a wise one and we hope it may result in great good.

IN London last Saturday it was as dark as midnight all day. The City was covered by a fog so dense that the electric lights proved insufficient to dispel the darkness. It was dangerous to even walk on the streets. The fog penetrated the houses, and every-where caused a feeling of distress.

WHEN gathering subscribers for the MESSENGER, we trust that our agents will not forget the Young Disciple. It is an illustrated weekly paper for the little folks, and should be in every family where there are children. Price, fifty cents a year. The list is rapidly increasing, and with a little effort on the part of our agents, it will increase still more.

IN this issue Bro. Daniel Vaniman tells of the largest donation yet received by the General Mission Board. It is in the nature of a large orange grove in California, valued at not less than fifty thousand dollars. It is a gift from Bro. Daniel Housof, whose name will go down to future generations as one of the most generous of brethren. It seems a little remarkable that some of the largest donations yet made to our missionary work, should come from comparatively new localities. The struggles on these fields seem, in some way, to develop the missionary spirit. What Bro. Houser has done should serve as an example for others. Had he made a will, it might have been set aside by the courts, as has been the case with hundreds of other wills. But, by making the transfer himself, he has the satisfaction of knowing that the property goes just where he wants it to go. We suggest that those who have property, which they intend to set apart for charitable purposes, make the transfer themselves; then they will know that it has been done right.

IN his fourth article on Church Government, Bro Daniel Hays has a paragraph which deserves the attention of every member. It reads thus: "Evil criticism is a source of discord among brethren. Bad, indeed, is his condition, who never sees a good quality in a man, and never fails to see a bad one."

THOSE who spend much time writing long, touching memoriams for the MESSENGER, could save themselves much trouble by observing that we do not publish that class of articles, though we receive scores of them. A well-written obituary, we think, is sufficient, excepting in case of a minister, whom we allow more liberty. A properly written obituary we never decline.

WE learn from the secular press that, during the feast near Philipsburgh, Ohio, about two hundred members were made sick by eating soup into which croton-oil had been maliciously poured. It seems that a deed of this kind would be about as mean a thing as one could be guilty of. The person who trifles with sacred things in that manner has a terrible account to settle in the judgment.

IN this issue will be found a short communication from our dear brother, S. S. Mohler, which will be appreciated by thousands, though they will regret to learn that our brother is still a great sufferer. Bro. Mohler has been a useful man among us, and he is greatly missed in the work of our general Brotherhood. It is to be hoped that he may yet be restored to health. For this may we most earnestly pray!

THE Christian Standard Publishing Company, Cincinnati, Ohio, proposes to publish a new edition of the celebrated Campbell and Rice Debate, in cloth, at $2.00 per copy, if one thousand copies can be vouched for. The book will contain about 800 pages. If any of our readers want a copy of this valuable work, let them immediately inform the publishers how many copies are wanted. Send no money, but pledges only. Your pledges must be sent before Dec. 1.

WE are now sending the MESSENGER on trial to hundreds whose names have been sent in by their friends. We hope they appreciate the paper and will consent to become permanent subscribers. The first of Bro. Miller's letters will be found in this issue, and as these letters will be continued, they will certainly prove an interesting feature of the paper. You can either send your subscriptions to us direct, or hand them to our agents. We prefer the latter where we have agents.

DURING their travels in the Old World, brethren D. L. Miller and J. C. Lahman may be addressed as follows: Until Dec. 10, I. B. Piazza Di Spagua, Rome, Italy, care of Thomas Cook & Son; until Feb. 1, 1893, Cairo, Egypt, care of Thomas Cook & Son; then, until March 10, Jerusalem, Syria, care of Thos. Cook & Son; then Ludgate Circus, London, England, care of Thos. Cook & Son. As they will be among strangers during their entire journey, letters from friends in America will be greatly appreciated. We therefore suggest that a number of our readers make it a point to write them a real good, newsy letter at least once in a month. While traveling in the land of Egypt, among the ruins of that once mighty kingdom, or climbing the mountain where Moses stood and received the Law, letters from dear ones on this side of the world will be to them "as cold water to a thirsty soul." For your letters use this paper and see that they do not weigh over one-half ounce. Remember that each letter should contain five cents postage. Always write your own name and address on the upper left hand corner.

The Gospel· Messenger,

A Weekly at $1.50 Per Annum.

PUBLISHED BY

The Brethren's Publishing Co.

D. L. MILLER, ... Editor
J. H. MOORE, ... Office Editor.
J. B. BRUMBAUGH, } . . . . . Associate Editors.
J. G. ROYER, }
JOSEPH AMICK, - . . . . Business Manager.

ADVISORY COMMITTEE.
L. W. Teeter, A. Hutchison, Daniel Hays.

☞Communications for publication should be legibly written with black ink on one side of the paper only. Do not attempt to interline, or to put on one page what ought to occupy two.

☞Anonymous communications will not be published.

☞Do not mix business with articles for publication. Keep your communications on separate sheets from all business.

☞Time is precious. We always have time to attend to business and to answer questions of importance, but please do not subject us to need less answering of letters.

☞The MESSENGER is mailed each week to all subscribers. If the address is correctly entered on our list, the paper must reach the person to whom it is addressed. If you do not get your paper, write us, giving particulars.

☞When changing your address, please give your former as well as your future address in full, so as to avoid delay and misunderstanding.

☞Always remit to the office from which you order your goods, no matter from where you receive them.

☞Do not send personal checks or drafts on interior banks, unless you send with them 25 cents each, to pay for collection.

☞Remittances should be made by Post-office Money Order, Drafts on New York, Philadelphia or Chicago, or Registered Letters, made payable and addressed to "Brethren's Publishing Co., Mount Morris, Ill.," or "Brethren's Publishing Co., Huntingdon, Pa."

☞Entered at the Post-office at Mount Morris, Ill., as second-class matter.

Mount Morris, Ill. - - - - Nov. 22, 1892.

BRO. A. M. DICKEY, of Iowa, we learn, has decided to locate at McPherson, Kans.

FOR the want of room considerable correspondence and interesting church news must lay over until next week.

UNDER date of Nov. 14 Bro. J. L. Thomas, of Ames, Iowa, writes: "Yesterday at our regular appointment one was received by baptism."

BRO. HAYS' article on Church Government, No. 4, reached us too late for this issue. It will appear next week. It contains some excellent points.

NEXT week we will publish the semi-annual report of the Brethren's Book and Tract Work. The receipts during the last six months are quite encouraging.

THE Sunday-school at Mt. Morris has decided to take up a special collection on the Sunday prior to Thanksgiving, for the benefit of the mission work in Chicago.

BRO. D. P. MILLER, of Buchanan, Mich., requests a correction in his report of the feast at that place. The meeting was held Oct. 1, instead of Oct. 3, as reported.

A NEW YORK paper says: "While a deputy sheriff was moving the effects of Mrs. Halpin, an aged invalid, into the street, yesterday, for nonpayment of rent, the woman, who was heart-broken, expired, kneeling in prayer."

THE Brethren at Mexico, Ind., are pushing the work on their much-needed new meeting-house, which they hope to have completed by Christmas. The new house has been under contemplation for several years and is now an absolute necessity, on account of the large and growing congregation. The old house is often too small to hold the people who attend the services. We not only commend the Brethren at Mexico for their wisdom in building a much larger and better house, but congratulate them on their success in keeping up their large congregation.

BRO. J. B. BRUMBAUGH, our Corresponding Editor, places an editorial on our desk just a little too late for this issue. It will appear on one of these pages next week.

BRO. H. C. EARLY'S meeting, of which mention was made last week, closed the 7th with fifteen additions by confession and baptism, and the promise of others to come shortly.

THE District Meeting of Tennessee, etc., we learn, passed off very harmoniously. Bro. Henry Sheets, of North Carolina, will represent the District on the next Standing Committee.

BRO. LEMUEL HILLERY, who has not been in good health for some time, is now able to do some much-needed work. He is engaged in a series of meetings at the Pleasant Valley church, Ind.

THE Brethren at South Waterloo, Iowa, have just closed an excellent meeting with nine additions. Bro. D. A. Walker, of Pennsylvania, did the preaching. We learn that this church is in a prosperous condition.

THE Honey Creek church, Nodaway Co., Mo., is rejoicing over an excellent series of meetings, conducted by brethren C. H. Brown and J. E. Ellenberger. Fifteen came out on the Lord's side and were baptized.

BRO. PHILIP A. MOORE, of Roanoke, Ill., writes that he and his wife reached California in safety, after four days' travel, and are now enjoying what seems like summer weather. They may be addressed at Los Angeles.

BRO. ANDREW HUTCHISON has been placed in charge of the mission in Cedar Rapids, Iowa, and devotes all of his time to the work. We think the arrangement is a wise one and we hope it may result in great good.

IN London last Saturday it was as dark as midnight all day. The City was covered by a fog so dense that the electric lights proved insufficient to dispel the darkness. It was dangerous to even walk on the streets. The fog penetrated the houses, and every-where caused a feeling of distress.

WHEN gathering subscribers for the MESSENGER, we trust that our agents will not forget the Young Disciple. It is an illustrated weekly paper for the little folks, and should be in every family where there are children. Price, fifty cents a year. The list is rapidly increasing, and with a little effort on the part of our agents, it will increase still more.

IN this issue Bro. Daniel Vaniman tells of the largest donation yet received by the General Mission Board. It is in the nature of a large orange grove in California, valued at not less than fifty thousand dollars. It is a gift from Bro. Daniel Housef, whose name will go down to future generations as one of the most generous of brethren. It seems a little remarkable that some of the largest donations yet made to our missionary work, should come from comparatively new localities. The struggles on these fields seem, in some way, to develop the missionary spirit. What Bro. Houser has done should serve as an example for others. Had he made a will, it might have been set aside by the courts, as has been the case with hundreds of other wills. But, by making the transfer himself, he has the satisfaction of knowing that the property goes just where he wants it to go. We suggest that those who have property, which they intend to set apart for charitable purposes, make the transfer themselves; then they will know that it has been done right.

IN his fourth article on Church Government, Bro Daniel Hays has a paragraph which deserves the attention of every member. It reads thus: "Evil criticism is a source of discord among brethren. Bad, indeed, is his condition, who never sees a good quality in a man, and never fails to see a bad one."

THOSE who spend much time writing long, touching memorials for the MESSENGER, could save themselves much trouble by observing that we receive scores of them. A well-written obituary, we think, is sufficient, excepting in case of a minister, when we allow more liberty. A properly written obituary we never decline.

WE learn from the secular press that, during the feast near Philipsburgh, Ohio, about two hundred members were made sick by eating soup into which croton-oil had been maliciously poured. It seems that a deed of this kind would be about as mean a thing as one could be guilty of. The person who trifles with sacred things in that manner has a terrible account to settle in the judgment.

IN this issue will be found a short communication from our dear brother, S. S. Mohler, which will be appreciated by thousands, though they will regret to learn that our brother is still a great sufferer. Bro. Mohler has been a useful man among us, and he is greatly missed in the work of our general Brotherhood. It is to be hoped that he may yet be restored to health. For this may we be most earnestly pray!

THE Christian Standard Publishing Company, Cincinnati, Ohio, proposes to publish a new edition of the celebrated Campbell and Rice Debate, in cloth, at $3.00 per copy, if one thousand copies can be vouched for. The book will contain about 800 pages. If any of our readers want a copy of this valuable work, let them immediately inform the publishers how many copies are wanted. Send no money, but pledges only. Your pledges must be sent before Dec. 1.

WE are now sending the MESSENGER on trial to hundreds whose names have been sent in by their friends. We hope they appreciate the paper and will consent to become permanent subscribers. The first of Bro. Miller's letters will be found in this issue, and as these letters will be continued, they will certainly prove an interesting feature of the paper. You can either send your subscriptions to us direct, or hand them to our agents. We prefer the latter where we have agents.

DURING their travels in the Old World, brethren D. L. Miller and J. C. Lahman may be addressed as follows: Until Dec. 10, I. B. Piazza Di Spagna, Rome, Italy, care of Thomas Cook & Son; until Feb. 1, 1893, Cairo, Egypt, care of Thomas Cook & Son; then, until March 10, Jerusalem, Syria, care of Thos. Cook & Son; then Ludgate Circus, London, England, care of Thos. Cook & Son. As they will be among strangers during their entire journey, letters from friends in America will be greatly appreciated. We therefore suggest that a number of our readers make it a point to write them a real good, newsy letter at least once in a month. While traveling in the land of Egypt, among the ruins of that once mighty kingdom, or climbing the mountain where Moses stood and received the Law, letters from dear ones on this side of the world will be to them "as cold water to a thirsty soul." For your letters use thin paper and see that they do not weigh over one-half ounce. Remember that each letter should contain five cents postage. Always write your own name and address on the upper left hand corner.

the year A. D. 70, when Barnabas wrote his epistle, there was a book extant, well known to Christians and of great authority among them, containing these words:

"MANY ARE CALLED, FEW CHOSEN."

Such a book is our present Gospel by Matthew, in which the text is twice found. Matt. 20: 16; 22: 14. And these words are to be found in no other book prior to the writing of Barnabas. Notice, too, that the author uses the words, "*It is written,*" the very phrase invariably used by the Jews when referring to the Scriptures. Christ used the same words in his temptation, "It is written, Thou shalt not tempt the Lord thy God." In addition to the above, Barnabas quotes many passages from the Gospel by Matthew. Among others, "Give to every one that asketh," Matt. 5: 42; "He came not to call the righteous, but sinners to repentance," Matt. 9: 13; Barnabas quoted from the Gospel by Matthew, just as surely as Dr. Thompson quoted from Beawulf, and as the Anti-Nicene Fathers quoted from Celsus.

We are in possession of an epistle, written by Clement, Bishop of Rome, who, some ancient writers assert, was the Clement to whom Paul refers in Philpp. 4: 3. This epistle is frequently spoken of by the Apostolic Fathers and acknowledged as authentic by all. Irenæus says: "It was written by Clement, who had seen the blessed apostles and conversed with them; who had the preaching of the apostles still sounding in his ears and their traditions before his eyes." The epistle was addressed to the church at Corinth, and Dionysius, Bishop of Corinth, was witness A. D. 170, that the epistle of Clement had been wont to be read in all the churches from ancient times. Clement, in his epistle, written about the close of the first century, quotes largely from the Gospels. Among others, the epistle contains the following valuable passages: "Especially remembering the words of the Lord Jesus which He spoke, teaching gentleness and long-suffering, for thus He spake: 'Be ye merciful that ye may obtain mercy; forgive that it may be forgiven you; as ye judge, so shall ye be judged; as ye are kind, so shall kindness be shown unto you; with what measure ye mete, with the same it shall · be measured unto you.'" Again, "Remember the words of the Lord Jesus, for he said: 'Woe to that man by whom offenses come; it were better for him that he had not been born, than that he should offend one of my elect; it were better for him that a mill-stone should be tied about his neck and that he should be drowned in the sea, than that he should offend one of my little ones!'" ("Apostolic Fathers," Edinburgh Edition, Chap. 13, page 16; compare also Matt. 6: 12–16; 7: 2 and 18; Luke 6: 36–38.) Here are quotations taken from the Gospels by Matthew and Luke, by an author who lived among the apostles and knew them personally. In quoting from the Gospel, he gives it as a matter about which there was no doubt or controversy. The language quoted, he says, are the words of the Lord Jesus. So generally was the Gospel by Matthew and Luke known and accepted among the apostles and disciples, that it was quoted as an end to all controversy. Again the only conclusion is, that when Clement wrote A. D. 98, he quoted from a copy of the Gospels by Matthew and Luke, and that such a book was in existence at that time.

Following Clement, we have Hermas named by Paul, Ignatius, Bishop of the church of Antioch,

thirty-seven years after Christ's ascension; Polycarp, Bishop of the church at Smyrna, who sat at the feet of St. John and who was burned at the stake A. D. 155; then, twenty years later, we have Justin Martyr, followed by Irenæus. All these were eminent Christians, who lived in the Apostolic Age and who wrote and quoted largely from the Gospel and the Epistles, and there is a close argument between the quotations and the New Testament, as we now have it. Indeed, so copious were the quotations made by the early church Fathers that the entire New Testament might be restored, even if we did not have the complete manuscript copies of A. D. 350. Irenæus, who was a disciple and student of Polycarp, gives the following testimony of the Scriptures, and this was written less than ninety years after the books of the New Testament were written. He says: "We have not received the knowledge of the way of our salvation by any other than those by whom the Gospel was brought to us, which Gospel they first preached and afterwards by the will of God committed to writing, that it might be for time to come the foundation and pillar of our faith. For after that our Lord rose from the dead, and they, the apostles, were endowed from above with the power of the Holy Ghost coming down upon them, they received a perfect knowledge of all things; Matthew, then among the Jews, wrote a Gospel in their own language, while Peter and Paul were preaching the Gospel at Rome and founding a church there; and after their exit, Mark, also the disciple and interpreter of Peter, delivered to us in writings the things that had been preached by Peter; and Luke, the companion of Paul, put down in a book the Gospel preached by Paul. Afterward John, the disciple of the Lord, who also leaned upon his breast, likewise published a Gospel while he dwelt at Ephesus in Asia." Here we might rest our case, but we give the

TESTIMONY OF UNBELIEVERS.

Celsus wrote against Christianity A. D. 176. He was a bitter opponent of the Christian religion. In his works, which are preserved in the writings of Origen, who wrote to refute them, Celsus makes more than eighty quotations from the New Testament. His whole argument proceeds upon the concession that the book he quoted from was in existence, that it was accepted as genuine and was held to be the Gospel of Jesus Christ. Had it been otherwise, how quickly and how gladly would this bitter opponent of Christianity have attacked the authenticity of the New Testament Scriptures. Here is the evidence of an unbeliever who wrote only seventy-six years after the death of the apostle John. Porphyry wrote A. D. 370, and was the most formidable opponent of Christianity in his time. He refers to Matthew, Mark, John, Acts and Galatians. There is in his writings no trace of a suspicion that the books were spurious. He held them to be what they purported, — the Gospel of Jesus Christ. Had there been the least shadow of doubt as to this, he would have attacked them at once at that point, for he did attack the Book of Daniel concerning the prophecy of the coming of Christ.

Hierocles wrote A. D. 303. He was President of Bithynia and a cruel persecutor of Christians. His writings are full of sarcasm, but he concedes the genuineness of the Gospels and seeks for contradictions, by which he aims to show that they are not inspired. He refers to six of the eight authors of the New Testament Scriptures.

Julian, the Emperor A. D. 361, quotes the Gospels, Acts, Romans, Corinthians and Galatians. His entire attack against Christianity assumes the genuineness and authenticity of the New Testament.

The facts here given are so conclusive of the authority and authenticity of the New Testament, that no one who examines them carefully can doubt. The quotations made by writers in the first, second and third centuries, show conclusively that the Gospel was then written and in book form, that it was held in high authority by the believers, and was quoted from as an end to·all controversy, and that the later copies, dating from A. D. 350, to which we now have access, are exact reproductions of the original. The invaluable testimony of pagan writers, who bitterly opposed the introduction of Christianity, also show that when they wrote the Sacred Book was in existence, and that it was held to be the Gospel of Jesus Christ. The entire line of evidence here given traces the New Testament with unerring certainty back to the days of the apostles when the book was written.

PROPHECY.

"Prophecy came not in old time by the will of man; but holy men of God spake as they were moved by the Holy Ghost." 2 Pet. 1: 21.

The truths of the Book of God rest for confirmation not alone on the evidence of its authenticity, for God has not left his people without a witness of the inspiration of the Bible. We are glad to know that the evidences here are just as strong and as convincing as are those already given. Upon prophecy and miracles we may well base our claim that the Bible is of divine origin, and that its precepts and commands are of supreme obligation to us. Prophecy is in itself a miracle. Only the divine and omniscient God can put aside the veil of the future and foretell the things that ·are surely to come to pass. Prophecy surely and unmistakably points out the hand of God in history. What seems to us a conflict, full of apparent discord and disorder, is seen, in the light of fulfilled prophecy and history, to be as a whole a grand and harmonious plan, in which the hand of the Almighty Controller of events is constantly visible,·and from which all chance is eliminated.

WHAT IS PROPHECY?

That "prophecy comes not by the will of man," is a statement that will be admitted by all, and it is equally true that it does come from God. No man, unaided by divine power, can look into the future and foretell ·what is to come to pass. Nothing is more surely settled than that the future is closed to human knowledge. Guesses we may all make, and by discerning the face of the sky, we may make a prediction as to the weather with some· degree of certainty; but this is not prophecy. The modern fortune-tellers, — to be found in our towns and cities and among the wandering gypsies, —with some knowledge of human nature, make shrewd guesses and extract the silver coins from their dupes; but they know nothing of the future. They can guess, and so can any of us; but guessing, even if it should hit, is as far from prophecy as the east is from the west. We may judge the future by the past, and with an accurate knowledge of human affairs, we may, with some degree of certainty, arrive at conclusions as to what the future will bring forth. History repeats itself, and like causes produce

the year A. D. 70, when Barnabas wrote his epistle, there was a book extant, well known to Christians and of great authority among them, containing these words:

"MANY ARE CALLED, FEW CHOSEN."

Such a book is our present Gospel by Matthew, in which the text is twice found. Matt. 20: 16; 22: 14. And these words are to be found in no other book prior to the writing of Barnabas. Notice, too, that the author uses the words, "It is written," the very phrase invariably used by the Jews when referring to the Scriptures. Christ used the same words in his temptation, "It is written, Thou shalt not tempt the Lord thy God." In addition to the above, Barnabas quotes many passages from the Gospel by Matthew. Among others, "Give to every one that asketh," Matt. 5: 42; "He came not to call the righteous, but sinners to repentance," Matt. 9: 13; Barnabas quoted from the Gospel by Matthew, just as surely as Dr. Thompson quoted from Seawulf, and as the Anti-Nicene Fathers quoted from Celsus.

We are in possession of an epistle, written by Clement, Bishop of Rome, who, some ancient writers assert, was the Clement to whom Paul refers in Philpp. 4: 3. This epistle is frequently spoken of by the Apostolic Fathers and acknowledged as authentic by all. Irenæus says: "It was written by Clement, who had seen the blessed apostles and conversed with them; who had the preaching of the apostles still sounding in his ears and their traditions before his eyes." The epistle was addressed to the church at Corinth, and Dionysius, Bishop of Corinth, was witness A. D. 170, that the epistle of Clement had been wont to be read in all the churches from ancient times. Clement, in his epistle, written about the close of the first century, quotes largely from the Gospels. Among others, the epistle contains the following valuable passages: "Especially remembering the words of the Lord Jesus which He spoke, teaching gentleness and long-suffering, for thus He spake: 'Be ye merciful that ye may obtain mercy; forgive that it may be forgiven you; as ye judge, so shall ye be judged; as ye are kind, so shall kindness be shown unto you; with what measure ye mete, with the same it shall be measured unto you.'" Again, "Remember the words of the Lord Jesus, for he said: 'Woe to that man by whom offenses come; it were better for him that he had not been born, than that he should offend one of my elect; it were better for him that a mill-stone should be tied about his neck and that he should be drowned in the sea, than that he should offend one of my little ones!'" ("Apostolic Fathers," Edinburgh Edition, Chap. 13, page 16; compare also Matt. 6: 12–15; 7: 2 and 18; Luke 6: 36–38.) Here are quotations taken from the Gospels by Matthew and Luke, by an author who lived among the apostles and knew them personally. In quoting from the Gospel, he gives it as a matter about which there was no doubt or contro-versy. The language quoted, he says, are the words of the Lord Jesus. So generally was the Gospel by Matthew and Luke known and accepted among the apostles and disciples, that it was quoted as an end to all controversy. Again the only conclusion is, that when Clement wrote A. D. 96, he quoted from a copy of the Gospels by Matthew and Luke, and that such a book was in existence at that time.

Following Clement, we have Hermas named by Paul, Ignatius, Bishop of the church at Antioch,

thirty-seven years after Christ's ascension; Polycarp, Bishop of the church at Smyrna, who sat at the feet of St. John and who was burned at the stake A. D. 155; then, twenty years later, we have Justin Martyr, followed by Irenæus. All these were eminent Christians, who lived in the Apostolic Age and who wrote and quoted largely from the Gospel and the Epistles, and there is a close argument between the quotations and the New Testament, as we now have it. Indeed, so copious were the quotations made by the early church Fathers that the entire New Testament might be restored, even if we did not have the complete manuscript copies of A. D. 350. Irenæus, who was a disciple and student of Polycarp, gives the following testimony of the Scriptures, and this was written less than ninety years after the books of the New Testament were written. He says: "We have not received the knowledge of the way of our salvation by any other than those by whom the Gospel was brought to us, which Gospel they first preached and afterwards by the will of God committed to writing, that it might be for time to come the foundation and pillar of our faith. For after that our Lord rose from the dead, and they, the apostles, were endowed from above with the power of the Holy Ghost coming down upon them, they received a perfect knowledge of all things; Matthew, then among the Jews, wrote a Gospel in their own language, while Peter and Paul were preaching the Gospel at Rome and founding a church there; and after their exit, Mark, also the disciple and interpreter of Peter, delivered to us in writings the things that had been preached by Peter; and Luke, the companion of Paul, put down in a book the Gospel preached by Paul. Afterward John, the disciple of the Lord, who also leaned upon his breast, likewise published a Gospel while he dwelt at Ephæsus in Asia." Here we might rest our case, but we give the

TESTIMONY OF UNBELIEVERS.

Celsus wrote against Christianity A. D. 176. He was a bitter opponent of the Christian religion. In his works, which are preserved in the writings of Origen, who wrote to refute them, Celsus makes more than eighty quotations from the New Testament. His whole argument proceeds upon the concession that the book he quoted from was in existence, that it was accepted as genuine and was held to be the Gospel of Jesus Christ. Had it been otherwise, how quickly and how gladly would this bitter opponent of Christianity have attacked the authenticity of the New Testament Scriptures. Here is the evidence of an unbeliever who wrote only seventy-six years after the death of the apostle John. Porphyry wrote A. D. 370, and was the most formidable opponent of Christianity in his time. He refers to Matthew, Mark, John, Acts and Galatians. There is in his writings no trace of a suspicion that the books were spurious. He held them to be what they purported, — the Gospel of Jesus Christ. Had there been the least shadow of doubt as to this, he would have attacked them at once at that point, for he did attack the Book of Daniel concerning the prophecy of the coming of Christ.

Hierocles wrote A. D. 303. He was President of Bithynia and a cruel persecutor of Christians. His writings are full of sarcasm, but he concedes the genuineness of the Gospels and seeks for contradictions, by which he aims to show that they are not inspired. He refers to six of the eight authors of the New Testament Scriptures.

Julian, the Emperor A. D. 361, quotes the Gospels, Acts, Romans, Corinthians and Galatians. His entire attack against Christianity assumes the genuineness and authenticity of the New Testament.

The facts here given are so conclusive of the authority and authenticity of the New Testament that no one who examines them carefully can doubt. The quotations made by writers in the first, second and third centuries, show conclusively that the Gospel was then written and in book form, that it was held in high authority by the believers, and was quoted from as an end to all controversy, and that the later copies, dating from A. D. 350, to which we now have access, are exact reproductions of the original. The invaluable testimony of pagan writers, who bitterly opposed the introduction of Christianity, also show that when they wrote the Sacred Book was in existence, and that it was held to be the Gospel of Jesus Christ. The entire line of evidence here given traces the New Testament with unerring certainty back to the days of the apostles when the book was written.

PROPHECY.

"Prophecy came not in old time by the will of man; but holy men of God spake as they were moved by the Holy Ghost." 2 Pet. 1: 21.

The truths of the Book of God rest for confirmation not alone on the evidence of its authenticity, for God has not left his people without a witness of the inspiration of the Bible. We are glad to know that the evidences here are just as strong and as convincing as are those already given. Upon prophecy and miracles we may well base our claim that the Bible is of divine origin, and that its precepts and commands are of supreme obligation to us. Prophecy is in itself a miracle. Only the divine and omniscient God can put aside the veil of the future and foretell the things that are surely to come to pass. Prophecy surely and unmistakably points out the hand of God in history. What seems to us a conflict, full of apparent discord and disorder, is seen, in the light of fulfilled prophecy and history, to be as a whole a grand and harmonious plan, in which the hand of the Almighty Controller of events is constantly visible, and from which all chance is eliminated.

WHAT IS PROPHECY?

That "prophecy came not by the will of man," is a statement that will be admitted by all, and it is equally true that it does come from God. No man, unaided by divine power, can look into the future and foretell what is to come to pass. Nothing is more surely settled than that the future is closed to human knowledge. Guesses we may all make, and by discerning the face of the sky, we may make a prediction as to the weather with some degree of certainty; but this is not prophecy. The modern fortune-tellers, — to be found in our towns and cities and among the wandering gypsies, —with some knowledge of human nature, make shrewd guesses and extract the silver coins from their dupes; but they know nothing of the future. They can guess, and so can any of us; but guessing, even if it should hit, is as far from prophecy as the east is from the west. We may judge the future by the past, and with an accurate knowledge of human affairs, we may, with some degree of certainty, arrive at conclusions as to what the future will bring forth. History repeats itself, and like causes produce

Notes from Our Correspondents.

"As cold water to a thirsty soul, so is good news from a far country."

Nora, Ill.—Our love-feast in the Waddam's Grove church was well attended. The ministers from other churches remembered us and did good preaching. Bro. Simon Yundt, of Mt. Morris, officiated. We also had one week's meetings before the feast. The brethren and sisters were much built up in the faith.—*W. K. Moore, Nov. 3.*

Mt. Repose, Ohio.—Our Communion, in the Stone Lick church, was a pleasant one. About thirty members communed. We had excellent ministerial assistance. Eld. Wm. Klepinger officiated. On Sunday, at 2 P. M., we had an enjoyable children's meeting. We expect to hold a series of meetings in the near future. May much good be done!—*Lydia C. Lesh.*

Macoupin Creek, Ill.—Our quarterly council was held Nov. 3. All business passed off pleasantly. Four were received by letter, one a deacon. Eld. James Buckley, of Texas, has just arrived with his family. We think he will locate in our territory. I expect, the Lord willing, to hold a series of meetings in the English River church, Iowa, Nov. 26.—*Michael Flory, Nov. 7.*

Smith Fork, Mo.—The Communion meeting, Nov. 5, was a pleasant one. On Saturday, at 2 P. M., we had preaching by Bro. S. B. Shirky, of the Rockingham congregation. About seventy members communed. Many were with us from other churches. On Sunday morning, owing to the unpleasant weather, many were kept away, but those who did assemble were ably instructed by brethren Henry Etter, and S. B. Shirky.—*Isaac B. Miller.*

Sterling, Kans.—I am very much pleased with the mission notice in No. 42, and think such a page for one year (or continually) might do more good than many solicitors. The feelings and sentiments of our people need cultivation and improvement to enable them to feel the importance of the great work before them, which must be felt before they will zealously enter into that work and do what they can easily perform.—*Jos. G. Calvert, Oct. 31.*

Arcadia Church, Ind.—According to previous arrangements Bro. J. C. Murray, of Nappanee, Ind., commenced a series of meetings Oct. 22, and continued to Nov. 1. Though there were no additions to the church, many good impressions were made. Our love-feast, of Oct. 6, was a pleasant one. Bro. Daniel Bowser officiated. We also received good admonitions from brethren J. H. Caylor, John McCarty and others. By doing we will be profited.—*Elias Smeltzer, Nov. 4.*

English Prairie Church, Ind.—Our love-feast, Nov. 5, was a pleasant one. Meetings were continued after the feast, until Sunday evening. The ministerial help was ample. Bro. W. R. Deeter officiated. One old brother, who had left the church some time since, was restored to the fold again. Bro. Adam Knub was chosen to the office of deacon. Bro. Deeter talked to the children before the forenoon services, which was of interest to old and young.—*John Long. Brighton, Ind., Nov. 7.*

Hartleton, Pa.—Our love-feast occurred Nov. 1 and 2. We had a series of meetings nine days before the feast. Bro. Spencer Beaver, from the Lost Creek church, did most of the preaching. He was assisted towards the last by Bro. Samuel J. Swigart, of Lewiston. It was the best and most refreshing series of meetings we have had for a long time. Seven young lambs were made willing to be received into the fold through the ordinance of baptism. This makes nine additions, so far, for this year.—*Adam Beaver, Nov. 4.*

Adrian, Mo.—Our church met in quarterly council. The business that came before the meeting was disposed of pleasantly. A series of meetings will commence Nov. 15. Bro. Hope is expected to preach for us.—*Diana Miller, Oct. 23.*

Harrisonburg, Va.—Our love-feast at the Garber church (Cook's Creek congregation) occurred Oct. 8 and was one long to be remembered by all. Eld. P. S. Miller, of Roanoke, Va., officiated. The spirit of the Lord seemed to pervade the entire meeting. It was one of the best ever held here.—*S. I. Bowman, Nov. 3.*

Crooked Creek Church, Iowa.—Bro. Stephen Miller, from Mahaska County, Iowa, came to us Oct. 19 and commenced meetings on the evening of the 20th. He preached eight sermons for us, by which saints were built up in their most holy faith and sinners warned to flee the wrath to come. As a result of the meetings, one dear sister came out on the Lord's side.—*D. E. Miller, Keota, Iowa.*

South Bend, Ind.—The members of the St. Joseph Valley church held their love-feast Oct. 28. About ninety brethren and sisters communed. There were representatives with us from eleven or twelve churches in the Brotherhood. Twelve ministers were with us,—four of them elders. Bro. H. W. Kreighbaum has the oversight of this church. Our dear brother, Frank Henricks, was elected to the ministry. One more,—a dear sister,—was willing to join in with the people of God, and was baptized a few weeks ago.—*Cannon Smith.*

Upton, Pa.—Eld. H. C. Early, from Rockingham County, Va., came to the Back Creek church, Oct. 22 and stayed until Nov. 7. He preached eighteen sermons, which were soul-reviving. As an immediate result fifteen precious souls were made willing to enter the flowing stream there to be baptized for the remission of their sins, to rise and walk in newness of life. One was reclaimed and two more expressed their desire to unite with us soon. Eight of those who were received are heads of families.—*John Lehner, Nov. 8.*

Morelock, Tenn.—The Tennessee District met in conference in the Valley church, Hawkins County, Tenn., Nov 4. The Meeting was opened by G. C. Bowman. Prayer was offered by the two oldest ministers present,—S. S. Sherfy and Joseph Wine. Bro. G. C. Bowman was chosen Moderator; S. J. Bowman, Reading Clerk; P. D. Reed, Writing Clerk. We had a very harmonious meeting. Business of great importance came before the Meeting. Preliminary steps were taken to establish a Brethren's School in the Tennessee District. Ministerial Meeting will be held during the Holidays. Bro. Henry Sheets, of North Carolina, will represent this District on Standing Committee at next Annual Meeting; Bro. John Brubaker alternate.—*P. M. Correll, Nov. 7.*

Laconia, Ind.—The members of the Harrison County church had their love-feast on the evening of Nov. 1. We had a good meeting and excellent order. The weather being somewhat unpleasant just previous to the meeting, kept many away, but all who did come, could be comfortably seated. This added much to the enjoyment of the meeting. Our home ministers commenced a series of meetings a week previous to our feast. On Wednesday evening Bro. David Dilling, of the Monticello church, Ind., met with us and labored earnestly for us until the following Wednesday evening, when we closed our meetings. The efforts of our brother were much appreciated. The attendance and order were good. One was added to the number of the faithful, during these meetings, and one a short time previous; both quite young in years.—*A. S. Culp, Nov. 6.*

Luray, Va.—Our love-feast at the Mt. Zion church is in the past, but will long be remembered. One was added to the church by baptism, which makes six additions recently. All were young in years, but we hope that, as time rolls on, they will make pillars in the church. Our church is in a very good condition spiritually.—*D. W. Strickler, Oct. 31.*

Woodbine, Va.—The Smith's River church held their love-feast Oct. 22. Elders C. D. Hylton, Harvey Weddle and Wm. H. Neff were present, together with several brethren in the ministry. They labored earnestly for the Master's cause. About seventy members were around the tables; Bro. Neff officiated. Several from adjoining congregations were present and their presence was much enjoyed. Brethren C. D. Hylton, Andrew Weddle and Wm. Elgin are now preaching south of us in a neighborhood where our Brethren have never been heard.—*J. A. Hooker, Oct. 28.*

Ridge Church, Ohio.—Our love-feast occurred Oct. 15. It was the most enjoyable one we have had for several years. Bro. Jonas Horning was present and officiated. Bro. Allen Ockerman, of the Lexington church, was present and did some good preaching. Quite a number of brethren and sisters were present from surrounding churches. All seemed to feel that it was good to be there. On the day following our feast an afflicted sister was reclaimed. We expect to hold a series of meetings some time during the early part of the winter. May the Lord enable us to win souls for Jesus.—*Albert P. Reed.*

Dillon's Mills, Va.—We had a pleasant love-feast at Bethlehem, Oct. 22. Over three hundred communicants surrounded the tables of the Lord. Bro. John B. Naff, of Roanoke County, officiated. We had good order, good preaching and a very large attendance. Next day, Nov. 6, I attended the love-feast at Antioch, where we also enjoyed the happy privilege of meeting with a large number of brethren and sisters from this and adjoining Counties. Bro. W. H. Naff, of Floyd County, officiated. Brethren Naff and I. W. H. Beahm delivered many good thoughts to a large, attentive congregation.—*Isaac Bowman, Nov. 6.*

Panora, Iowa.—Bro. Hutchison closed one week's series of meetings here last night. In his plain, fearless manner he presented the Bible testimony on "Prophecy," "Law," "Gospel," "Promises," "Duty," "Jesus," "The Church," "Mistakes," "Harmony," "Discord," and kindred subjects. Sinners were warned, believers strengthened and edified, and one baptized. Bro. Hutchison goes to the Harlan church from here, and then to Cedar Rapids. Our home ministers are now laboring among the isolated ones as follows: Brethren Fils and Diehl at Glidden, —— Deardorff at Modale, the writer at Dedham,—leaving brethren Myers and Brower to care for the work at home.—*J. D. Haughtelin, Nov 4.*

Garden Grove, Iowa.—Our Communion, held in the Franklin church, Decatur Co., Iowa, Oct. 29, passed off pleasantly. We had good order and attention. Eld. A. Wolf remained after the feast and preached for us each night except one, till Nov. 2, when he had to stop on account of ill health. The meetings were then continued by the home ministry, till the evening of Nov. 5, when it closed on account of rain. Two precious souls were made willing to take up the cross; one of them came fifteen miles to be received. May all prove faithful! Immediately after the sermon, Oct. 30, our elder, W. J. Stout, who is now seventy-seven years of age, and somewhat feeble, was anointed. The next morning a dear sister, Maria McDonnald, of Missouri, now eighty-five years of age, was anointed.—*Jemima Kob, Nov. 7.*

Notes from Our Correspondents.

"As cold water to a thirsty soul, so is good news from a far country."

Nora, Ill.—Our love-feast in the Waddam's Grove church was well attended. The ministers from other churches remembered us and did good preaching. Bro. Simon Yuedt, of Mt. Morris, officiated. We also had one week's meetings before the feast. The brethren and sisters were much built up in the faith.—*W. K. Moore, Nov. 8.*

Mt. Repose, Ohio.—Our Communion, in the Stone Lick church, was a pleasant one. About thirty members communed. We had excellent ministerial assistance. Eld. Wm. Klepinger officiated. On Sunday, at 2 P. M., we had an enjoyable children's meeting. We expect to hold a series of meetings in the near future. May much good be done!—*Lydia C. Lesh.*

Macoupin Creek, Ill.—Our quarterly council was held Nov. 3. All business passed off pleasantly. Four were received by letter, one a deacon. Eld. James Buckley, of Texas, has just arrived with his family. We think he will locate in our territory. I expect, the Lord willing, to hold a series of meetings in the English River church, Iowa, Nov. 26.—*Michael Flory, Nov. 7.*

Smith Fork, Mo.—The Communion meeting, Nov. 5, was a pleasant one. On Saturday, at 2 P. M., we had preaching by Bro. S. B. Shirky, of the Rockingham congregation. About seventy members communed. Many were with us from other churches. On Sunday morning, owing to the unpleasant weather, many were kept away, but those who did assemble were ably instructed by brethren Henry Etter, and S. B. Shirky.—*Isaac B. Miller.*

Sterling, Kans.—I am very much pleased with the mission notes in No. 42, and think such a page for one year (or continually) might do more good than many solicitors. The feelings and sentiments of our people need cultivation and improvement to enable them to feel the importance of the great work before them, which must be felt before they will zealously enter into that work and do what they can easily perform.—*Jos. G. Calvert, Oct. 31.*

Arcadia Church, Ind.—According to previous arrangements Bro. J. C. Murray, of Nappanee, Ind., commenced a series of meetings Oct. 22, and continued to Nov. 1. Though there were no additions to the church, many good impressions were made. Our love-feast, of Oct. 6, was a pleasant one. Bro. Daniel Bowser officiated. We also received good admonitions from brethren J. H. Caylor, John McCarty and others. By doing we will be profited.—*Elias Smeltzer, Nov. 4.*

English Prairie Church, Ind.—Our love-feast, Nov. 5, was a pleasant one. Meetings were continued after the feast, until Sunday evening. The ministerial help was ample. Bro. W. R. Deeter officiated. One old brother, who had left the church some time since, was restored to the fold again. Bro. Adam Kaub was chosen to the office of deacon. Bro. Deeter talked to the children before the forenoon services, which was of interest to old and young.—*John Long, Brighton, Ind, Nov. 7.*

Harleton, Pa.—Our love-feast occurred Nov. 1 and 2. We had a series of meetings nine days before the feast. Bro. Spencer Beaver, from the Lost Creek church, did most of the preaching. He was assisted towards the last by Bro. Samuel J. Swigart, of Lewiston. It was the best and most refreshing series of meetings we have had for a long time. Seven young lambs were made willing to be received into the fold through the ordinance of baptism. This makes nine additions, so far, for this year.—*Adam Beaver, Nov. 4.*

Adrian, Mo.—Our church met in quarterly council. The business that came before the meeting was disposed of pleasantly. A series of meetings will commence Nov. 15. Bro. Hope is expected to preach for us.—*Diana Miller, Oct. 23.*

Harrisonburg, Va.—Our love-feast at the Garber church (Cook's Creek congregation) occurred Oct. 8 and was one long to be remembered by all. Eld. P. S. Miller, of Roanoke, Va., officiated. The spirit of the Lord seemed to pervade the entire meeting. It was one of the best ever held here.—*S. I. Bowman, Nov. 3.*

Crooked Creek Church, Iowa.—Bro. Stephen Miller, from Mahaska County, Iowa, came to us Oct. 19 and commenced meetings on the evening of the 20th. He preached eight sermons for us, by which saints were built up in their most holy faith and sinners warned to flee the wrath to come. As a result of the meetings, one dear sister came out on the Lord's side.—*D. P. Miller, Keota, Iowa.*

South Bend, Ind.—The members of the St. Joseph Valley church held their love-feast Oct. 28. About ninety brethren and sisters communed. There were representatives with us from eleven or twelve churches in the Brotherhood. Twelve ministers were with us,—four of them elders. Bro. H. W. Kreighbaum has the oversight of this church. Our dear brother, Frank Henricks, was willing to join in with the people of God, and was baptized a few weeks ago.—*Cannon Smith.*

Upton, Pa.—Eld. H. C. Early, from Rockingham County, Va., came to the Back Creek church, Oct. 22 and stayed until Nov. 7. He preached eighteen sermons, which were soul-reviving. As an immediate result fifteen precious souls were made willing to enter the flowing stream there to be baptized for the remission of their sins, to rise and walk in newness of life. One was reclaimed and two more expressed their desire to unite with us soon. Eight of those who were received are heads of families.—*John Lehner, Nov. 8.*

Morelock, Tenn.—The Tennessee District met in conference in the Valley church, Hawkins County, Tenn, Nov 4. The Meeting was opened by G. C. Bowman. Prayer was offered by the two oldest ministers present,—S. S. Sherfy and Joseph Wine. Bro. G. C. Bowman was chosen Moderator; S. J. Bowman, Reading Clerk; P. D. Reed, Writing Clerk. We had a very harmonious meeting. Business of great importance came before the Meeting. Preliminary steps were taken to establish a Brethren's School in the Tennessee District. Ministerial Meeting will be held during the Holidays. Bro. Henry Sheets, of North Carolina, will represent this District on Standing Committee at next Annual Meeting; Bro. John Brubaker alternate.—*P. M. Correll, Nov. 7.*

Laconia, Ind.—The members of the Harrison County church had their love-feast on the evening of Nov. 1. We had a good meeting and excellent order. The weather being somewhat unpleasant just previous to the meeting, kept many away, but all who did come, could be comfortably seated. This added much to the enjoyment of the meeting. Our home ministers commenced a series of meetings a week previous to our feast. On Wednesday evening Bro. David Dilling, of the Monticello church, Ind., met with us and labored earnestly for us until the following Wednesday evening, when we closed our meetings. The efforts of our brother were much appreciated. The attendance and order were good. One was added to the number of the faithful, during these meetings, and one a short time previous; both quite young in years.—*A. S. Culp, Nov. 6.*

Luray, Va.—Our love-feast at the Mt. Zion church is in the past, but will long be remembered. One was added to the church by baptism, which makes six additions recently. All were young in years, but we hope that, as time rolls on, they will make pillars in the church. Our church is in a very good condition spiritually.—*D. W. Strickler, Oct. 31.*

Woodbine, Va.—The Smith's River church held their love-feast Oct. 22. Elders C. D. Hylton, Harvey Weddle and Wm. H. Neff were present, together with several brethren in the ministry. About seventy members were around the tables; Bro. Neff officiated. Several from adjoining congregations were present and their presence was much enjoyed. Brethren C. D. Hylton, Andrew Weddle and Wm. Elgin are now preaching south of us in a neighborhood where our Brethren have never been heard.—*J. A. Hooker, Oct. 28.*

Ridge Church, Ohio.—Our love-feast occurred Oct. 15. It was the most enjoyable one we have had for several years. Bro. Jonas Horning was present and officiated. Bro. Allen Ockerman, of the Lexington church, was present and did some good preaching. Quite a number of brethren and sisters were present from surrounding churches. All seemed to feel that it was good to be there. On the day following our feast an afflicted sister was reclaimed. We expect to hold a series of meetings some time during the early part of the winter. May the Lord enable us to win souls for Jesus.—*Albert P. Reed.*

Dillon's Mills, Va.—We had a pleasant love-feast at Bethlehem, Oct. 22. Over three hundred communicants surrounded the tables of the Lord. Bro. John B. Naff, of Roanoke County, officiated. We had good order, good preaching and a very large attendance. Next day, Nov. 6, I attended the love-feast at Antioch, where we also enjoyed the happy privilege of meeting with a large number of brethren and sisters from this and adjoining Counties. Bro. W. H. Naff, of Floyd County, officiated. Brethren Naff and I. W. H. Beahm delivered many good thoughts to a large, attentive congregation.—*Isaac Bowman, Nov. 6.*

Panora, Iowa.—Bro. Hutchison closed one week's series of meetings here last night. In his plain, fearless manner he presented the Bible testimony on "Prophecy," "Law," "Gospel," "Promises," "Duty," "Jesus," "The Church," "Mistakes," "Harmony," "Discord," and kindred subjects. Sinners were warned, believers strengthened and edified, and one baptized. Bro. Hutchison goes to the Harlan church from here, and then to Cedar Rapids. Our home ministers are now laboring among the isolated ones as follows: Brethren Fifa and Diehl at Glidden, —Deardorff at Modale, the writer at Dedham,—leaving brethren Myers and Brower to care for the work at home.—*J. D. Haughtelin, Nov 4.*

Garden Grove, Iowa.—Our Communion, held in the Franklin church, Decatur Co., Iowa, Oct. 29, passed off pleasantly. We had good order and attention. Eld. A. Wolf remained after the feast and preached for us each night except one, till Nov. 2, when he had to stop on account of ill health. The meetings were then continued by the home ministry, till the evening of Nov. 6, when it closed on account of rain. Two precious souls were made willing to take up the cross; one of them came fifteen miles to be received. May all prove faithful! Immediately after the sermon, Oct. 30, our elder, W. J. Stout, who is now seventy-seven years of age, and somewhat feeble, was anointed. The next morning a dear sister, Maria McDonnald, of Missouri, now eighty-five years of age, was anointed.—*Jemima Kob, Nov. 7.*

Fairview Church. Kans.—Our love-feast was a pleasant one. Eld. John S. Snowberger was here, and the church was dedicated to the Lord on Sunday morning. There were members present of other denominations, and many said it was the best sermon they ever heard on such occasion. Bro. John spoke of the abuse of God's house by the use of such things that desecrate it.—*John F. Cline.*

Purchase Line, Pa.—The brethren and sisters of the Manor congregation, Pa, met in church council Oct 29. All the business passed off pleasantly. One was received by letter. No preventing providence, we expect to begin a series of meetings in this congregation, in the Purchase Line meeting-house Dec. 24. Bro. Michael Claar, of Queen, Bedford County, is to do the preaching. We hope we will have a good and profitable meeting,—*Lizzie Fyock.*

Dunlap, Kans.—Bro. J. D. Trostle came to us Oct. 26, and preached three sermons to a small and attentive audience. On Saturday was our love-feast. Our hearts were cheered by the presence of dear brethren and sisters from adjoining churches. The church thought it necessary to elect a brother to the deacon's office, and Bro. R. M. Weddle was called to fill the office. Bro. G. W. Weddle was advanced to the second degree of the ministry. We held our feast in a tent. The weather was rather disagreeable, but the church was greatly encouraged to go forward in the discharge of her duty. About forty members communed. Six ministering brethren were present besides the home ministers. May God's blessings attend the efforts. —*Addie Burnell, Nov. 3.*

Boynton, Pa.—Eld. David Clapper, of the Hopewell church, Bedford Co., Pa., has changed his location, and has moved close to the town of Everett, at the south end of the congregation, and is doing some good church work. By his request I met with the members there on the evening of Oct 21, and had six meetings in a house, formerly owned by the colored people. During the meetings eight were baptized. We have five more applicants and one reclaimed. By diligence and care a prosperous church may be built up. At present I am engaged in a series of meetings in the Snake Spring Valley district, in what is called the Bement meeting-house, presided over by Eld. Jacob Koonts. So far two have made application for baptism.—*Silas Hoover, Nov. 4.*

Literary Notices.

OF undoubted interest and special value to all concerned in the study of criminals, to officers of the law, managers of penal and reformative institutions, pastors and preachers, lawyers, and the intelligent public in general, is a book on Criminology, soon to be issued by the Funk & Wagnalis Company. The book presents a psychological and scientific study of criminals with relation to psychical and physical types, etc. The author of the work is Dr. Arthur MacDonald, United States representative at the International Congress on Criminology at Brussels, Specialist in Criminology of the United States Bureau of Education, etc. Professor Cesare Lombroso, of the University of Turin, writes the Introduction. In an Appendix will be given an extensive and valuable Bibliography of the best books on crime, in the several languages. This Bibliography is said to be the most complete of its kind that has ever appeared in any language.

Matrimonial.

KINDY—ZIMMERMAN—At the residence of the bride's parents, Oct. 13, 1892, by Rev. W. W. Anderson, Bro. C. C. Kindy, of Loudonville, Ohio, and Miss Sadie Zimmerman, of Perrysville, Ohio. GOLDIE KINDY.

ROWLAND—RAIRIGH.—At the home of the bride's father, Oct. 30, 1892, by the writer, friend Albert Rowland, of Peabody, Marion Co., Kans., and sister Laura B. Rairigh, of Fred, Marion Co., Kans. GEO. STAYCKER.

CLAPPER—LANDES.—At the residence of Wm. H. Quinn, the officiating minister, Mr. Cyrus Clapper, of near Canton, Ohio, and sister Lizzie S. Landes, of Gettysburgh, Pa. WM. H. QUINN.

NONDORF—POAGE.—At the residence of the bride's parents, Oct. 16, 1892, Mr. Chas. Nondorf and Miss Viola May Poage, both of Republic County, Kans. CHAS. S. HILARY.

Fallen Asleep.

"Blessed are the dead which die in the Lord."

KEIM.—In Hawpatch, in the bounds of the Shipshewana church, Lagrange Co., Ind., Oct. 16, 1892, Sarah Keim, aged 42 years, 1 month and 16 days. Sister Keim was a faithful Christian and loved by all. She was anointed and then said she was ready to die. She had much to die for and nothing to live -for, as she was ready and prepared. Funeral services by the undersigned from Rev. 14: 13, assisted by Bro. B. Leer. J. L. BERKEY.

ARNOLD.—At Egion, W. Va., Oct. 28, 1892, Mary S. Arnold, wife of John A. Arnold and last daughter of Eld. S. A. Fike, aged 30 years, 6 months and 19 days. She leaves a dear companion and two children. By request of the deceased, Eld. Geo. S. Arnold, of Mineral County, W. Va., and Eld Isaac Abernathy, of Garrett.County, Md., were called to preach her funeral. Sister Arnold was sick not quite one week with inflammation of the bowels. She was anointed a few days before she died. Funeral text-from Rev. 22: 14. RACHEL WEIMER.

BERKLY.—In the South Waterloo church, Oct. 27, 1892, sister Sally Berkly, aged 85 years, 9 months and 5 days. She had been quite feeble for several years. She was truly a mother in Israel: Funeral services were conducted by Bro. D. Walker, of Somerset County, Pa., and the writer, in the presence of a large audience. J. A. MURRAY.

HUFF.—In the Price's Creek church, Ohio, Oct. 20, 1892, Bro. Daniel Hoff, aged 50 years, 11 months and 20 days. He leaves a dear companion, a sister and four children. Funeral services by brethren Jesse Stutsman and Joseph Longanecker from James 4: 14. GEORGE H. PETRY.

ORNDORF.—In the Salem congregation, Frederick Co., Va., Oct. 10. 1892, Jesse B. Orndorf, son of John A. and Rebecca Orndorf, aged 17 years, 1 month and 16 days. Funeral services by Abram Frantz, of Dawson, W. Va., assisted by W. Spiggie and the writer. DANIEL BAKER.

MYERS.—In the Monocacy church, Md., of diphtheria, Sept. 29, 1892, Anna Otelia, beloved daughter of brother Joel and sister Mary Myers, aged 6 years, 11 months and 21 days. Interment at Pipe Creek. Funeral services by the writer and Bro. Stoner. T. J. KOLB.

HINER.—In Clinton County, Ind., Oct. 17, 1892, David H. Hiner, aged 58 years and 28 days. Deceased leaves a wife, five children, twenty-six grandchildren and nine great grandchildren. He was born in Pendleton County, Virginia, and moved from Virginia to Indiana in 1847, where he lived until death. CATHARINE HINER.

ENFIELD—In Johnson County, Iowa, Oct. 30, 1892, Bro. Philip Enfield, aged 97 years, 7 months and 12 days. He was born in Somerset County, Pa., and united with the Brethren about fifty years ago. His wife is still living. Their wedded life was sixty-seven years. Twelve children were born to them. Funeral services at the Methodist church in Sharon Township. J. C. SEIBERT.

STEPHEN.—In the Fredonia church, Wilson Co., Kans., Sept. 18, 1892, Milla Pearl Stephen, aged 11 months and 25 days. Deceased was the daughter of Bro. J. W. and sister Melinda E. Stephen. Funeral services by Bro. Isaac Crist from 2 Sam. 12: 23. ELIZABETH STUDEBAKER.

PRICE.—In the bounds of the Berrien congregation, Mich., Sept. 10, 1892, James A. Price, aged 58 years and 15 days. Deceased united with the Brethren church about thirty years ago, but allowed himself to drift away from the church until last July, when he was received again into full fellowship and died in the triumphs of a living faith. Funeral services by the undersigned from Pr. 16: 11.

MILLER.—In the South Waterloo church, Black Hawk Co., Iowa, Oct. 26, 1892, Bro. Abraham A. Miller, aged 78 years, 2 months and 21 days. Bro. Miller was born in Somerset County, Pa., Aug. 5, 1814, and was married to Salome Forney, Nov. 13, 1836. To them were born fourteen children, seven of whom preceded Bro. Miller to the spirit land. Sister Miller and seven children survive him. He served as deacon for a number of years and was anointed by the elders some time previous to his death. He died of dropsy and heart trouble. Funeral services were conducted by Bro. Daniel Walker, assisted by Jonas Lichty. J. H. FIKE.

MILLER.—In the same congregation, Sept. 18, 1892, infant child of friend Philip Miller and wife. Text, " Suffer the little children to come unto me and forbid them not, for-of such is the kingdom of heaven."

LIVINGSTON.—Also, in the same congregation, Nov. 4, 1892, sister Sarah Livingston, aged 64 years and 28 days. She was received into church fellowship in the Brethren's church by baptism, and lived a consistent Christian life until the Master said, " It is enough: come up higher." Funeral text, Rev. 14: 13. Funeral services at the house. Burial in the Evangelical cemetery at Portage Prairie. D. P. MILLER.

ALBERT.—Sept. 26, 1892, Vinnona, daughter of C. C. and Ella Albert, aged 6 months and 16 days. Funeral services by the writer from Mark 10: 14. C. SCHROCK.

DARST.—At Dayton, Ohio, Oct. 26, 1892, of heart trouble, Mary Ethel Darst, daughter of Bro. Charles and sister Katie Darst, aged 10 years, 5 months and 15 days. Services by brethren S. W. Hoover and W. C. Teeter from 2 Thess. 2: 17. ELMER WOMBOLD.

ANGEL.—In the Tippecanoe church, Kosciusko Co., Ind., July 9, 1892, David Angel, aged 71 years, 1 month and 1 days. He was in faith with the Brethren but never identified himself with God's people. Funeral services in North Webster from Job 7: 17 to a large audience. DANIEL ROTHENBERGER.

HAMMAN.—At the same place, Sept. 1, 1892, July Ann Hamman, daughter of John and Abigail Hamman, aged 36 years and 29 days. Funeral services from Heb. 9: 27 to a large audience of sympathizing relatives and neighbors. DANIEL ROTHENBERGER.

RITTER.—At the same place, Sept. 22, 1892, Burta Ritter, son of Samuel Ritter, aged 4 months and 5 days. Funeral services from Ps. 89: 47. DANIEL ROTHENBERGER.

PHILLIPS.—Also at the same place, Oct. 17, 1892, sister Catharine (Spitler) Phillips, aged 52 years, 3 months and 7 days. She suffered intense pain much of her time, for the last six months of her life, but bore it patiently. Funeral services from Ps. 23: 4. DANIEL ROTHENBERGER.

MORNINGSTAR—In the Yellow Creek church, Elkhart Co., Ind., Oct. 8, 1892, Bro. Philip Morningstar, aged 60 years and 4 months. He leaves a wife and three sons to mourn their loss, which, we trust, is his eternal gain. Funeral services conducted by the writer from Rev. 14: 13, to a large concourse of sympathizing neighbors and friends. JOHN NUSSBAUM.

HERSHMAN.—In the Lower Cumberland church, Cumberland Co., Pa., Oct. 26, 1892, daughter of friend Oscar and Mary Hershman, aged 1 year, 8 months and 10 days. Funeral services by Levi Mohler from Matt. 18: 3.

STOUFFER—In the same church, Oct. 27, 1892, son of Bro. John Andrew (deceased) and sister Susan B. Stouffer, aged 15 years, 1 month and 26 days. Funeral services by Levi Mohler from John 11: 28. HETTIE E. GISELE.

ROWLAND.—In the Eel River congregation, Kosciusko Co., Ind., Oct. 6, 1892, Abram Rowland, aged 71 years, 6 months and 25 days. Deceased was born in Washington County, Pa., and when the death angel called was making preparations to attend a love feast in an adjoining congregation. The cause of his death has been attributed to heart failure. Funeral services by the writer. A. L. WRIGHT.

The Gospel Messenger

Is the recognized organ of the German Baptist or Brethren's church, and advocates the form of doctrine taught in the New Testament and pleads for a return to apostolic and primitive Christianity.

It recognizes the New Testament as the only infallible rule of faith and practice, and maintains that Faith toward God, Repentance from dead works, Regeneration of the heart and mind, baptism by Trine Immersion for remission of sins unto the reception of the Holy Ghost by the laying on of hands, are the means of adoption into the household of God,—the church militant.

It also maintains that Feet-washing, as taught in John 13, both by example and command of Jesus, should be observed in the church.

That the Lord's Supper, instituted by Christ and as universally observed by the apostles and the early Christians, is a full meal, and, in connection with the Communion, should be taken in the evening or after the close of the day.

That the Salutation of the Holy Kiss, or Kiss of Charity, is binding upon the followers of Christ.

That War and Retaliation are contrary to the spirit and self-denying principles of the religion of Jesus Christ.

That the principle of Plain Dressing and of Non-conformity to the world, as taught in the New Testament, should be observed by the followers of Christ.

That the Scriptural duty of Anointing the Sick with Oil, in the Name of the Lord, James 5: 14, is binding upon all Christians.

It also advocates the church's duty to support Missionary and Tract Work, thus giving to the Lord for the spread of the Gospel and for the conversion of sinners.

In short, it is a vindicator of all that Christ and the apostles have enjoined upon us, and aims, amid the conflicting theories and discords of modern Christendom, to point out ground that all must concede to be infallibly safe.

The above principles of our Fraternity are set forth on our Brethren's Envelopes. Use them! Price 15 cents per package; 40 cents per hundred.

Fairview Church. Kans.—Our love-feast was a pleasant one. Eld. John S. Snowberger was here, and the church was dedicated to the Lord on Sunday morning. There were members present of other denominations, and many said it was the best sermon they ever heard on such occasion. Bro. John spoke of the abuse of God's house by the use of such things that desecrate it.—*John F. Cline.*

Purchase Line, Pa.—The brethren and sisters of the Manor congregation, Pa., met in church council Oct 29. All the business passed off pleasantly. One was received by letter. No preventing providence, we expect to begin a series of meetings in this congregation, in the Purchase Line meeting-house Dec. 24. Bro. Michael Claar, of Queen, Bedford County, is to do the preaching. We hope we will have a good and profitable meeting.—*Lizzie Fyock.*

Dunlap, Kans.—Bro. J. D. Trostle came to us Oct 26, and preached three sermons to a small and attentive audience. On Saturday was our love-feast. Our hearts were cheered by the presence of dear brethren and sisters from adjoining churches. The church thought it necessary to elect a brother to the deacon's office, and Bro. R. M. Weddle was called to fill the office. Bro. G. W. Weddle was advanced to the second degree of the ministry. We held our feast in a tent. The weather was rather disagreeable, but the church was greatly encouraged to go forward in the discharge of her duty. About forty members communed. Six ministering brethren were present besides the home ministers. May God's blessings attend the efforts.—*Addie Burnett, Nov. 3.*

Boynton, Pa.—Eld. David Clapper, of the Hopewell church, Bedford Co., Pa., has changed his location, and has moved close to the town of Everett, at the south end of the congregation, and is doing some good church work. By his request I met with the members there on the evening of Oct 21, and had six meetings in a house, formerly owned by the colored people. During the meetings eight were baptized. We have five more applicants and one reclaimed. By diligence and care a prosperous church may be built up. At present I am engaged in a series of meetings in the Snake Spring Valley district, in what is called the Bement meeting-house, presided over by Eld. Jacob Koontz. So far two have made application for baptism.—*Silas Hoover, Nov. 4.*

Literary Notices.

OF undoubted interest and special value to all concerned in the study of criminals, to officers of the law, managers of penal and reformative institutions, pastors and preachers, lawyers, and the intelligent public in general, is a book on Criminology, soon to be issued by the Funk & Wagnalls Company. The book presents a psychological and scientific study of criminals with relation to psychical and physical types, etc. The author of the work is Dr. Arthur MacDonald, United States Representative at the International Congress on Criminology at Brussels, Specialist in Criminology of the United States Bureau of Education, etc. Professor Cesare Lombroso, of the University of Turin, writes the Introduction. In an Appendix will be given an extensive and valuable Bibliography of the best books on crime, in the several languages. This Bibliography is said to be the most complete of its kind that has ever appeared in any language.

Matrimonial.

"What therefore God hath joined together, let not man put asunder."

KINDY — ZIMMERMAN.—At the residence of the bride's parents, Oct. 13, 1892, by Rev. W. W. Anderson, Bro. C. C. Kindy, of Loudonville, Ohio, and Miss Sadie Zimmerman, of Perrysville, Ohio.   GOLDIE KINDY.

ROWLAND—RAIRIGH.—At the home of the bride's father, Oct. 30, 1892, by the writer, friend Albert Rowland, of Peabody, Marion Co., Kans., and sister Laura B. Rairigh, of Fred, Marion Co., Kans.   GEO. STRYCKER.

CLAPPER—LANDES.—At the residence of Wm. H. Quinn, the officiating minister, Mr. Cyrus Clapper, of near Canton, Ohio, and sister Lizzie S. Landes, of Gettysburgh, Pa.   WM. H. QUINN.

NONDORF—POAGE.—At the residence of the bride's parents, Oct. 16, 1892, Mr. Chas. Nondorf and Miss Viola May Poage, both of Republic County, Kans.
                              CHAS. S. HILARY.

Fallen Asleep.

"Blessed are the dead which die in the Lord."

KEIM.—In Hawpatch, in the bounds of the Shipshewana church, Lagrange Co., Ind., Oct. 26, 1892, Sarah Keim, aged 42 years, 1 month and 16 days. Sister Keim was a faithful Christian and loved by all. She was anointed and then said she was ready to die. She had much to do for and nothing to live for, as she was ready and prepared. Funeral services by the undersigned from Rev. 14: 12, 13, assisted by Bro. B. Leer.   I. L. BERKEY.

ARNOLD.—At Eglon, W. Va., Oct. 28, 1892, Mary S. Arnold, wife of John A. Arnold and last daughter of Eld. S. A. Fike, aged 30 years, 6 months and 19 days. She leaves a dear companion and two children. By request of the deceased, Eld. Geo. S. Arnold, of Mineral County, W. Va., and Eld Isaac Abernathy, of Garrett County, Md., were called to preach her funeral. Sister Arnold was sick not quite one week with inflammation of the bowels. She was anointed a few days before she died. Funeral text from Rev. 22: 14.
                              RACHEL WEIMER.

BERKLY.—In the South Waterloo church, Oct. 27, 1892, sister Sally Berkly, aged 85 years, 9 months and 5 days. She had been quite feeble for several years. She was truly a mother in Israel. Funeral services were conducted by Bro. D. Walker, of Somerset County, Pa., and the writer, in the presence of a large audience.   J. A. MURRAY.

HOFF.—In the Price's Creek church, Ohio, Oct. 20, 1892, Bro. Daniel Hoff, aged 50 years, 11 months and 20 days. He leaves a dear companion, a sister and four children. Funeral services by brethren Jesse Stutsman and Joseph Longanecker from James 4: 14.   GEORGE H. PETRY.

ORNDORF.—In the Salem congregation, Frederick Co., Va., Oct. 10, 1892, Jesse B. Orndorf, son of John A. and Rebecca Orndorf, aged 17 years, 1 month and 16 days. Funeral services by Abram Frantz, of Dawson, W. Va., assisted by W. Spiggle and the writer.   DANIEL BAKER.

MYERS.—In the Monocacy church, Md., of diphtheria, Sept. 29, 1892, Anna Otella, beloved daughter of brother Joel and sister Mary Myers, aged 6 years, 11 months and 21 days. Interment at Pipe Creek. Funeral services by the writer and Bro. S. Stoner.   T. J. KOLB.

HINER.—In Clinton County, Ind., Oct. 17, 1892, David H. Hiner, aged 78 years and 28 days. Deceased leaves a wife, five children, twenty-six grandchildren and nine great grandchildren. He was born in Pendleton County, Virginia, and moved from Virginia to Indiana in 1847, where he lived until death.   CATHARINE HINER.

ENFIELD.—In Johnson County, Iowa, Oct. 30, 1892, Bro. Philip Enfield, aged 97 years, 7 months and 12 days. He was born in Somerset County, Pa., and united with the Brethren about fifty years ago. His wife is still living. Their wedded life was sixty-seven years. Twelve children were born to them. Funeral services at the Methodist church in Sharon Township.   J. C. SEIBERT.

STEPHEN.—In the Fredonia church, Wilson Co., Kans., Sept. 18, 1892, Milla Pearl Stephen, aged 11 months and 25 days. Deceased was the daughter of Bro. J. W. and sister Melinda E. Stephen. Funeral services by Bro. Isaac Crist from 2 Sam. 12: 23.   ELIZABETH STUDEBAKER.

PRICE.—In the bounds of the Berrien congregation, Mich., Sept. 10, 1892, James A. Price, aged 58 years and 25 days. Deceased united with the Brethren church about thirty years ago, but allowed himself to drift away from the church until last July, when he was received again into full fellowship and died in the triumphs of a living faith. Funeral services by the undersigned from Ps. 16: 11.

MILLER.—In the South Waterloo church, Black Hawk Co., Iowa, Oct. 26, 1892, Bro. Abraham A. Miller, aged 78 years, 2 months and 12 days. Bro. Miller was born in Somerset County, Pa., Aug. 5, 1814, and was married to Salome Forney, Nov. 13, 1836. To them were born fourteen children, seven of whom preceded Bro. Miller to the spirit land. Sister Miller and seven children survive him. He served as deacon for a number of years and was anointed by the elders some three previous to his death. He died of dropsy and heart trouble. Funeral services were conducted by Bro. Daniel Walker, assisted by Jonas Lichty.   J. H. FIKE.

MILLER.—In the same congregation, Sept. 18, 1892, infant child of friend Philip Miller and wife. Text, "Suffer the little children to come unto me and forbid them not, for of such is the kingdom of heaven."

LIVINGSTON.—Also, in the same congregation, Nov. 4, 1892, sister Sarah Livingston, aged 64 years and 28 days, wife was received into church fellowship in the Brethren's church by baptism, and lived a consistent Christian life until the Master said, "It is enough; come up higher." Funeral text, Rev. 14: 13. Funeral services at the house. Burial in the Evangelical cemetery at Portage Prairie.
                              D. P. MILLER.

ALBERT.—Sept. 16, 1892, Vinnona, daughter of C. C. and Etta Albert, aged 6 months and 16 days. Funeral services by the writer from Mark 10: 14.   C. SCHROCK.

DARST.—At Dayton, Ohio, Oct. 16, 1892, of heart trouble, Mary Ethel Darst, daughter of Bro. Charles and sister Katie Darst, aged 10 years, 5 months and 15 days. Services by brethren S. W. Hoover and W. C. Teeter from 2 Thess. 2: 17.
                              ELMER WOMBOLD.

ANGEL.—In the Tippecanoe church, Kosciusko Co., Ind., July 9, 1892, David Angel, aged 71 years, 2 months and 2 days. He was in faith with the Brethren but never identified himself with God's people. Funeral services in North Webster from Job 7: 17 to a large audience.
                              DANIEL ROTHENBERGER.

HAMMAN.—At the same place, Sept. 1, 1892, July Ann Hamman, daughter of John and Abigail Hamman, aged 16 years and 29 days. Funeral services from Heb. 9: 27 to a large audience of sympathizing relatives and neighbors.
                              DANIEL ROTHENBERGER.

RITTER.—At the same place, Sept. 21, 1892, Burta Ritter, son of Samuel Ritter, aged 4 months and 5 days. Funeral services from Ps. 89: 47.   DANIEL ROTHENBERGER.

PHILLIPS.—Also at the same place, Oct. 17, 1892, sister Catharine (Spitler) Phillips, aged 52 years, 3 months and 7 days. She suffered intense pain much of her time, for the last six months of her life, but bore it patiently. Funeral services from Ps. 23: 4.   DANIEL ROTHENBERGER.

MORNINGSTAR.—In the Yellow Creek church, Elkhart Co., Ind., Oct. 8, 1892, Bro. Philip Morningstar, aged 60 years and 4 months. He leaves a wife and three sons to mourn their loss, which, we trust, is his eternal gain. Funeral services conducted by the writer from Rev. 14: 13, to a large concourse of sympathizing neighbors and friends.
                              JOHN NUSBAUM.

HERSHMAN.—In the Lower Cumberland church, Cumberland Co., Pa., Oct. 26, 1892, daughter of friend Oscar and Mary Hershman, aged 1 year, 8 months and 10 days. Funeral services by Levi Mohler from Matt. 18: 3.

STOUFFER.—In the same church, Oct 15, 1892, son of Bro. John Andrew (deceased) and sister Susan B. Stouffer, aged 15 years, 1 month and 26 days. Funeral services by Levi Mohler from John 11: 28.   HETTIE E. GIBBLE.

ROWLAND.—In the Eel River congregation, Kosciusko Co., Ind., Oct. 6, 1892, Abram Rowland, aged 70 years, 6 months and 25 days. Deceased was born in Washington County, Pa., and when the death angel called was making preparations to attend a love feast in an adjoining congregation. The cause of his death has been attributed to heart failure. Funeral services by the writer.   A. L. WRIGHT.

The Gospel Messenger

Is the recognized organ of the German Baptist or Brethren's church, and advocates the form of doctrine taught in the New Testament and pleads for a return to apostolic and primitive Christianity.

It recognizes the New Testament as the only infallible rule of faith and practice, and maintains that Faith toward God, Repentance from dead works, Regeneration of the heart and mind, baptism by Trine immersion for remission of sins unto the reception of the Holy Ghost by the laying on of hands, are the means of adoption into the household of God,—the church militant.

It also maintains that Feet-washing, as taught in John 13, both by example and command of Jesus, should be observed in the church.

That the Lord's Supper, instituted by Christ and as universally observed by the apostles and the early Christians, is a full meal, and, in connection with the Communion, should be taken in the evening or after the close of the day.

That the Salutation of the Holy Kiss, or Kiss of Charity, is binding upon the followers of Christ.

That War and Retaliation are contrary to the spirit and self-denying principles of the religion of Jesus Christ.

That the principle of Plain Dressing and of Non-conformity to the world, as taught in the New Testament, should be observed by the followers of Christ.

That the Scriptural duty of Anointing the Sick with Oil, in the Name of the Lord, James 5: 14, is binding upon all Christians.

It also advocates the church's duty to support Missionary and Tract Work, thus giving to the Lord for the spread of the Gospel and for the conversion of sinners.

In short, it is a vindicator of all that Christ and the apostles have enjoined upon us, and aims, amid the conflicting theories and discords of modern Christendom, to point out ground that all must concede to be infallibly safe.

The above principles of our Fraternity are set forth on our Brethren's Envelopes. Use them! Price 15 cents per package; 40 cents per hundred.

Announcements.

MINISTERIAL MEETINGS.

Nov. 27, at 2 A. M., In the South-east District of Kansas, Ministerial Meeting in the Cedar Creek church, Mont Ida, Anderson Co., Kans.

Nov. 30, Dec. 1 and 2, Southern District of Pennsylvania. Ministerial Meeting in the East Cordorus church, York Co., Pa.

Nov. 17, at 9 A. M., North-eastern District of Ohio, Ministerial Meeting, Maple Grove church, 4 miles north of Ashland, Ashland Co., Ohio.

LOVE-FEASTS.

Dec. 3. Good Hope church, at the Snowberger school-house, 8 miles north-east of Holyoke, Phillips Co., Colo.

Nov. 14, at 5 P. M., Cedar Creek church, Anderson Co., Kans.

Nov. 25 and 26, Beatrice church, Nebr.

Dec. 8, at 2 P. M., Cerro Gordo, Ill.

Dec. 31. Glendale, Maricopa Co., Ariz. Those coming by raft will be met by at Tempe by notifying T. J. Ehrsbine.

All for 55 Cents!

THE MONON ROUTE has added to its already-splendid equipment, two brand new dining cars, which are now in daily service on the fast day trains between Chicago and Louisville.

These cars are models of convenience, comfort, and beauty, and are operated on the a la carte plan, which means that a passenger can get anything he wants and pay only for what he gets. An elegant steak, with bread, butter, coffee or tea with cream, is served for only 55 cents.

Watch for MONON's new schedule to Florida.

Dubbel's Cough and Croup Cure

Is a sure and quick cure for coughs and especially for croup. It will cure any case of *croup* that a doctor can cure and with *one-tenth* the expense. It contains no dangerous drugs such as morphia, opium, chloral, etc., and is perfectly harmless. It is highly endorsed for *La Grippe*. Our Cough and Croup Cure is second to none, and we sell it on the strong guarantee, "No cure, no pay." We allow *one-half* the contents of the bottle to be used and if the results are not satisfactory, return it to us or the agent of whom you purchased. Your money will be refunded. Price, 25 cents per bottle. Agents wanted in every locality. We want 1,600 new agents till Jan. 1. To any person who secures us an agent who will order two dozen at agents' rates we will give, as a present for securing us agent, the valuable book "Alone with God." Said book is advertised in the GOSPEL MESSENGER. Write for terms and circulars.

Ed. P. D. Reid, Limestone, Tenn., writes April 6, '99: "Last Christmas, when I returned from a preaching tour in Virginia, I was run down from preaching and had contracted a very bad cold. I got a bottle of your Cough and Croup Cure from Bro. C. H. Diehl, of Jonesboro, Tenn. After using half of it I was perfectly cured. For a cold or *La Grippe* I can certainly recommend it.

S. E. Dubbel & Co.,

Manufacturers and Proprietors,

Waynesboro, Franklin Co., Pa.

Also manufacturers of Red Things Pain Cure,—the medicine that proved to be such a blessing at the late Annual Meeting held at Cedar Rapids, Iowa.

For Sale!

Having a desire to devote more time to church work, I offer one quarter section of choice farm land for sale. This farm has a good house, barn, fences, well, and a nice spring. It is situated 2½ miles south of the Brethren's meeting-house in Shannon, Ill. It is also within one mile of a good creamery. I also offer 30 head of registered Short Horn Cattle, 15 males and 35 females,— choice individuals at a very low price. Address for particulars, D. Rowland, Lanark, Ill.

---THE---
Doctrine of the Brethren Defended.

THIS work contains a complete exposition of the faith and practice of the Brethren, the Divinity of Christ, the Divinity of the Holy Spirit, Immersion, Feet-washing, the Lord's Supper, the Holy Kiss, Non-conformity, Secret Societies, etc. Price, per copy, cloth binding, $1.25 Address this office.

Popular Commentary on the New Testament.—Edited by Philip Schaff. Four volumes, 8vo. Matthew, Mark and Luke: $6.00. John and the Acts: $6.00. Romans to Philemon: $5.00. Hebrews to Revelation: $5.00.

EUROPE
AND
Bible Lands

A new edition of this deservedly popular work has again been published. It retains all the excellencies of its predecessors,-and with those who are interested in Bible study this work will always remain a favorite. Those who have read the ordinary book of travel will be surprised to find "Europe and Bible Lands" of thrilling interest for both old and young. The large number of books, already sold, proves that the work is of more than ordinary merit.

A fair supply of the last edition of this work is still on hand. Those who have not yet secured a copy of the work should embrace this opportunity of securing it. Price, in fine cloth binding, only $1.50 per copy, post-paid. To agents who are prepared to push an active canvass of the work, we are prepared to give special inducements. Write us.
BRETHREN'S PUBLISHING CO.,
Mt Morris, Ill.

CANCERS, TUMORS, ETC.

Successfully treated by Dr. G. M. Botsler, of Waynesborough, Pa., where he has practiced for the last sixteen years. Dr. Botsler is a graduate of the University of Maryland, at Baltimore City. References given and correspondence solicited. Address, Dr. G. W. Botsler, Waynesborough, Pa.

Brethren, Wanted

To sell Trees, vines, etc., in their own community during the winter, and earn good wages. Special offer now. Write for terms to McNary & Co, Nurserymen, Dayton, Ohio.

O Jerusalem! Jerusalem!

WHAT could be more beautiful and touching than a picture of Christ as he stood upon Olivet looking down over the beloved but sinful city, with tears trickling down over his cheeks, his lips parted as he cries, "O Jerusalem! Jerusalem!" We have such a picture 12x16 inches, beautifully colored in colors. No one can gaze upon it without being moved. Given free with a year's subscription to "What to Read" at 50 cents. An agent wanted in every church and neighborhood. Address,
Jas. M. Nevy, Covington, Ohio.

Alone with God.

THIS manual of devotions, by J. H. Garrison, comprises a series of meditations with forms of prayer for private devotions, family worship and special occasions. It is one of the most useful, most needed, and best adapted books of the year, and therefore it is not strange that it is proving one of the most popular. In work of this kind its distinguished, gifted, pious and beloved author is at his best. This book is helpful to every minister, church official, and Sunday-school superintendent, as well as every private member of the church in all ages. It has models of prayer, suitable for the service of the prayer-meeting, while its suggestions, meditations and instructions are pre-eminently calculated to be of service in preparation for the solemn duties that rest upon the active members. Cloth, 75 cents; morocco, $1.25. Address this office.

Farm for Sale.

A desirable property located 2¼ miles east of Mt. Morris, consisting of 185 acres of well-improved land. One of the finest country residences in Ogle County. For further particulars call on, or address,
ELIZABETH MIDDLEKAUFF,
Mt. Morris, Ill.

Excursions to California.

Excursions in charge of M. M. Eshelman, Immigration Agent, will leave Chicago over the "Santa Fe Route" Tuesdays, and Kansas City Wednesdays, during the year 1899, on dates as follows:

Chicago, January 26, February 22, March 22, April 26, May 24, June 28, July 26, August 23, September 27, October 25, November 22, December 27.

Kansas City, January 27, February 24, March 24, April 27, May 25, June 29, July 27, August 24, September 28, October 26, November 23, December 28.

Parties wishing to avail themselves of the privileges of these excursions, should write M. M. Eshelman, North Pomona, California, prior to the 15th of each month, and from the fifteenth to the end of the month, at 1050 Union Avenue (opposite Union Depot), Kansas City, Mo., stating when and where they wish to join one of these excursions, and he will give them full information, and if desired will reserve berths in Tourist Sleeping Car for them. Do not fail to write him; he will do you good. The miss will be as low as the lowest made to the Pacific Coast.

GEORGE L. McDONAVON,
Traveling Agent.

Church Entertainments: Twenty Objections.

By Rev. B. Carradine, D. D. 12mo, 100 pp. Paper cover, 30 cents. A strong book in defense of its position, written by a powerful pen, presenting the most candid and scriptural arraignment of unwarrantable methods for money-raising in the Church. The spirit of the book is highly devotional and cannot fail to inspire the reader with its seriousness.

Announcements.

MINISTERIAL MEETINGS.

Nov. 25, at 9 A. M., in the South-east District of Kansas, Ministerial Meeting in the Cedar Creek church, Mont Ida, Anderson Co., Kans.

Nov. 30, Dec. 1 and 2, Southern District of Pennsylvania, Ministerial Meeting in the East Cordorus church, York, York Co., Pa.

Nov. 17, at 9 A. M., North-eastern District of Ohio, Ministerial Meeting, Maple Grove church, 4 miles north of Ashland, Ashland Co., Ohio.

LOVE-FEASTS.

Dec. 3, Good Hope church, at the Snowberger school-house, 8 miles north-east of Holyoke, Phillips Co., Colo.

Nov. 24, at 5 P. M., Cedar Creek church, Anderson Co., Kans.

Nov. 25 and 26, Beatrice church, Nebr.

Dec. 3, at 2 P. M., Cerro Gordo, Ill.

Dec. 31, Glendale, Maricopa Co., Ariz. Those coming by rail will be met by an Tempe by notifying T. J. Kisenhise.

All for 55 Cents!

The MONON ROUTE has added to its already-splendid equipment, two brand new dining-cars, which are now in daily service on the fast day trains between Chicago and Louisville.

These cars are models of convenience, comfort, and beauty, and are operated on the à la carte plan, which means that a passenger can get anything he wants and pay only for what he gets. An elegant steak, with bread, butter, coffee or tea, with cream, is served for only 55 cents.

Watch for MONON'S new schedule to Florida.

Dubbel's Cough and Croup Cure

For Sale!

Having a desire to devote more time to church work, I offer one quarter section of choice farm land for sale. This farm has a good house, barn, fences, well, and a nice spring. It is situated 2½ miles south of the Brethren's meeting-house in Shannon, Ill. It is also within one mile of a good creamery. I also offer 50 head of registered Short Horn Cattle, 15 males and 35 females,—choice individuals at a very low price. Address for particulars, D. Rowland, Lanark, Ill.

--- THE ---
Doctrine of the Brethren Defended.

THIS work contains a complete exposition of the faith and practice of the Brethren, the Divinity of Christ, the Divinity of the Holy Spirit, Immersion, Feet-washing, the Lord's Supper, the Holy Kiss, Non-conformity, Secret Societies, etc. Price, per copy, cloth binding, $1.25. Address this office.

Popular Commentary on the New Testament.—Edited by Philip Schaff. Four volumes, 8vo. Matthew, Mark and Luke: $6.00. John and the Acts: $6.00. Romans to Philemon: $5.00. Hebrews to Revelation: $5.00.

EUROPE
AND
Bible Lands

A new edition of this deservedly popular work has again been published. It retains all the excellencies of its predecessors, and with those who are interested in Bible study this work will always remain a favorite. Those who have read the ordinary book of travel will be surprised to find "Europe and Bible Lands" of thrilling interest for both old and young. The large number of books, already sold, proves that the work is of more than ordinary merit.

A fair supply of the last edition of this work is still on hand. Those who have not yet secured a copy of the work should embrace this opportunity of securing it. Price, in fine cloth binding, only $1.50 per copy, post-paid. To agents who are prepared to push an active canvass of the work, we are prepared to give special inducements. Write us.
BRETHREN'S PUBLISHING CO.,
Mt. Morris, Ill.

CANCERS, TUMORS, ETC.

Successfully treated by Dr. G. M. Boteler, of Waynesborough, Pa., where he has practiced for the last sixteen years. Dr. Boteler is a graduate of the University of Maryland, at Baltimore City. References given and correspondence solicited. Address, Dr. G. W. Boteler, Waynesborough, Pa.

Brethren Wanted

To sell Trees, Vines, etc., in their own community during the winter, and earn good wages. Special offer now. Write for terms to McNary & Co., Nurserymen, Dayton, Ohio.

O Jerusalem! Jerusalem!

Alone with God.

THIS manual of devotions, by J. H. Garrison, comprises a series of meditations with forms of prayer for private devotions, family worship and special occasions. It is one of the most useful, most needed, and best adapted books of the year, and therefore it is not strange that it is proving one of the most popular. In work of this kind this distinguished, gifted, pious and beloved author is at his best. This book is helpful to every minister, church official, and Sunday-school superintendent, as well as every private member of the church in all ages. It has models of prayer, suitable for the service of the prayer-meeting, while its suggestions, meditations and instructions are pre-eminently calculated to be of service in preparation for the solemn duties that rest upon the active members. Cloth, 75 cents; morocco, $1.25. Address this office.

Farm for Sale.

A desirable property located 1¾ miles east of Mt. Morris, consisting of 185 acres of well-improved land. One of the finest country residences in Ogle County. For further particulars call on, or address,
ELIZABETH MIDDLEKAUFF,
Mt. Morris, Ill.

Excursions to California.

NOTICE!

I wish to inform the brethren that I will sell, from now until Jan. 1, 1893, single Top Buggies and Family Carriages at the lowest cash prices ever offered before. For prices write to Abraham E. Weaver, Syracuse, Kosciusko Co., Ind.

Church Entertainments: Twenty Objections.

By Rev. B. Carradine, D. D. 12mo, 100 pp. Paper cover, 30 cents. A strong book in defense of its position, written by a powerful pen, presenting the most candid and scriptural arraignment of unwarrantable methods for money-raising in the Church. The spirit of the book is highly devotional and cannot fail to inspire the reader with its seriousness.

Wolf's Business College.

A thorough school for training pupils in the Commercial Branches, Shorthand, Typewriting, Telegraphy, and Penmanship. The school for those who want a practical, useful education. Write for catalogue.
D. ELMER WOLF, Principal,
Hagerstown, Md.

✦ESSAYS✦

"Study to show thyself approved unto God: a workman that needeth not be ashamed, rightly dividing the Word of Truth."

ONE STEP MORE.

SELECTED BY SARAH PUTERBAUGH.

WHAT though before me it is dark,
Too dark for me to see;
I ask but light for one step more,
'Tis quite enough for me;
Each little humble step I take,
The gloom clears from the next;
So though 'tis very dark beyond,
I never am perplexed.

And if sometimes the mist hangs close,
So close I fear to stay,
Patient I wait a little while,
And soon it clears away.
I would not see my future,
For mercy veils it so
My present steps might harder be
Did I the future know.

It may be that my path is long,
Thorny and hard and steep;
And knowing this my attempt might fall
Through fear and terror deep.
It may be that it winds along,
A smooth and flowery way,
And seeing this I might despise
The journey of to-day.

Perhaps my path is very short,
My journey nearly done,
And I might tremble at the thought
Of ending it so soon.
Or, if I saw a weary length
Of road that I must wend,
Fainting, I'd say, "My feeble powers
Will fall me at the end."

And so I do not wish to see
My journey and its length,
Assured that through my Father's love
Each step will bring its strength,
Thus step by step I onward go,
Not looking far before;
Trusting that I shall always have
Light for just "one step more."

Philadelphia, Pa.

HARMONY.

BY A. HUTCHISON.

In Three Parts.—Part Two.

IN order that we may be successful in our Christian warfare we must learn to know the enemy's method of attack. The greatest military chieftains are not always the men who meet the enemy in open battle. Often the greatest victories are the result of tact in maneuvering, so as to cause confusion among those whom he would defeat. If confusion between the commander and his soldiers can be produced, then the antagonist has his work largely accomplished.

What is true in natural warfare is also true, to a very considerable extent, in the spiritual, and while our common enemy is represented as going about as a roaring lion, we must not fail to notice the nature of the lion. He is not always roaring. When he wants to catch his prey, he is not only quiet but crouches very low. He does not desire to be noticed until his victim is fully in his reach; then he pounces upon it without mercy.

God's people have ever had to guard against the intrusion of evil into their ranks, and the difficulty, frequently, comes from such as are associated with them as members of the same body. Paul speaks about a trouble that he had and he says it was "because of false brethren unawares brought in, who came in privily to spy out our liberty which we have in Christ Jesus, that they might bring us into bondage." Gal. 2: 4.

In this case the apostle tells how those parties came in, and he says that their object was,—"to spy out our liberty." They desired to bring the faithful into bondage. The apostle continues by saying, "To whom we gave place by subjection, no, not for an hour." That has the right ring! In harmony there is strength.

In the above-described case the lion came into the fold as a lamb, but when he had accomplished his purpose, he began first, to growl, and later, to roar. Having been in long enough to spy out the liberty of the Father's children, he now feels that he knows how to make his attack. Then he comes out boldly and roars with all the power he can command. The object seems to be, if possible, to sow discord among the sheep of the Lord's flock. Peter, in his second epistle, gives a very lucid description of such characters. He says, "But chiefly them that walk after the flesh in the lust of uncleanness and despise government." 2 Pet. 2: 10. Government means harmony. Then those characters don't like government because that means to lay down personal choice and render submission, as in Heb. 13: 17.

As proof of the fact that it is here where the trouble comes in, see what Peter further says in the verse above cited: "Presumptuous are they, self-willed; they are not afraid to speak evil of dignities." He farther continues his description in the following words: "Which have forsaken the right way and are gone astray." 2 Pet. 2: 15. Such have failed to take that good advice of Bro. Paul where he says, "Nevertheless, whereto we have already attained let us walk by the same rule, let us mind the same thing." Philpp. 3: 16. This course, pursued by a body of people, must result in harmony. The Savior said, "Take heed what ye hear." Mark 4: 24. No wonder that he gives such a caution when we consider the following: "But there were false prophets also among the people, even as there shall be false teachers among you who privily shall bring in damnable heresies," etc. "Many shall follow their pernicious ways, by reason of whom the way of truth shall be evil spoken of." 2 Pet. 2: 1, 2.

It is clear to every careful observer that, as long as the soldiers under the generalship of King Jesus, keep strictly to the word of command, no harm can befall them, but they must remember that he said, "What I say unto you I say unto all, Watch." What shall they watch for? Ans.— For just such as the following: "For when they speak great swelling words of vanity they allure through the lusts of the flesh, through much wantonness, those that were clean escaped from them who live in error." 2 Pet. 2: 18. Now you will observe that the charge to watch was given to the faithful.

Those who are spoken to, in the verse quoted above, were also of the faithful, for they were "clean escaped" from such as live in error. They don't tell those, who come with their "great swelling words" that they will be lost if they continue in their present course, but they "promise them liberty." 2 Pet. 2: 19. They try to make them believe that they can have liberty and be saved too.

All such is not liberty to the spirit, but to the flesh, for they appeal to them through the lusts of the flesh. We might inquire, What do such persons want when they thus speak to the faithful? We will let Paul tell us. He says, "Also of your own selves shall men arise, speaking perverse things to draw away disciples after them. Therefore watch and remember that by the space of three years I ceased not to warn every one night and day with tears." Acts 20: 30, 31.

There is no uncertainty in his answer. They want followers, and, instead of going out into the highways and hedges to convert the unsaved, they go among the faithful to secure followers. The apostle says they speak as they do to draw away disciples. Draw away from what? He is speaking about what shall take place in the church of Christ.

It is clear, then, that the effort to draw away disciples means to draw them away from the church. When they succeed in inducing any one to yield to their plea, they have to confess that they have nothing to promise them except liberty, and it is a pitiable case when it is all told, for it is clear that the liberty promised is only the liberty to do a little more as you please.

It does not require a man to be a Solomon, to know that when that kind of liberty is granted, the individuals will generally drift into the common current, and soon all their love for the self-denying advice of the Scriptures, and of the church, is drowned in the stream of worldly pleasures. Not unfrequently is Christ crucified unto such and put to an open shame, because, as soon as any one turns to the glittering toys of earth, and takes pleasure in the tinsel thereof, they are not in harmony with Jesus. We should not forget that he says, "Without me ye can do nothing."

After all, what have we gained by following any one beside him who gave his life a ransom for us? God has seen fit to organize a church in the world, and in that church he has provided a place for his creatures to work, and he has sanctified ordinances and elements to be employed in the prosecution of that work.

In our next we propose to show that the church has been trying faithfully to maintain these.

THE LOOM OF LIFE.

BY ELIZABETH H. DELP.

"My days are swifter than a weaver's shuttle."—Job 7: 6.

THE passing of days, the short years, and the centuries completed, all remind us that we are drawing near a measureless eternity. Our trite expression, "Time flies," is only another version of Job's thought. The weaver's shuttle, as it flies back and forth, truthfully symbolizes the flight of time, and it also brings to us other thoughts, "The hours perish and are laid to our charge." Happy are we, if we can look into the past, not mournfully, but with the feeling that it holds the best of which we are capable. In the days that are passing like a weaver's shuttle, we are weaving our life. The loom, upon which we are at work, may hold a coarse, colorless cloth, or it may be an exquisite fabric of fabulous worth. We are the weavers and, to some extent, the designers of our own pattern.

With indomitable energy we must sometimes put our task, seeing that our work is marred by our own heedlessness, or that, by our own willfulness, we have tangled the threads. Sometimes it is past unfaithfulness that has caused the present trouble. Then the only way is to unravel the past, and begin again, upon the strength of God's promise, "that whoso confesseth and forsaketh his sins shall have mercy." The blood of Christ will make white as snow the life-fabric that was stained with sin and marred with duties neglected. When all the disciples forsook the Savior and fled, and when Peter denied the Christ, until a look from the Savior revealed to him dark threads of unbelief and desertion; then, with tears, he rent them, and commenced anew, and wove a pattern of such clearness, boldness, and strength, that to-day we study to imitate it.

At the loom of sin, the shuttle flies swiftly, but the threads are torn and discolored, the fabric

❖ESSAYS❖

* Study to show thyself approved unto God: a workman that needeth not to be ashamed, rightly dividing the Word of Truth.

ONE STEP MORE.

SELECTED BY SARAH PUTERBAUGH.

WHAT though before me it is dark,
  Too dark for me to see;
I ask but light for one step more,
  'Tis quite enough for me;
The gloom clears from the next;
So though 'tis very dark beyond,
  I never am perplexed.

And if sometimes the mist hangs close,
  So close I fear to stay,
Patient I wait a little while,
  And soon it clears away.
I would not see my future,
  For mercy veils it so
My present steps might harder be
  Did I the future know.

It may be that my path is long,
  Thorny and hard and steep;
And knowing this my strength might fail
  Through fear and terror deep.
It may be that it winds along,
  A smooth and flowery way,
And seeing this I might despise
  The journey of to-day.

Perhaps my path is very short,
  My journey nearly done,
And I might tremble at the thought
  Of ending it so soon.
Or, if I saw a weary length
  Of road that I must wend,
Fainting, I'd say, "My feeble powers
  Will fall me at the end."

And so I do not wish to see
  My journey and its length,
Assured that through my Father's love
  Each step will bring its strength,
Thus step by step I onward go,
  Not looking far before;
Trusting that I shall always have
  Light for just "one step more."

Philadelphia, Pa.

HARMONY.

BY A. HUTCHISON.

In Three Parts—Part Two.

IN order that we may be successful in our Christian warfare we must learn to know the enemy's method of attack. The greatest military chieftains are not always the men who meet the enemy in open battle. Often the greatest victories are the result of tact in maneuvering, so as to cause confusion among those whom he would defeat. If confusion between the commander and his soldiers can be produced, then the antagonist has his work largely accomplished.

What is true in natural warfare is also true, to a very considerable extent, in the spiritual, and while our common enemy is represented as going about as a roaring lion, we must not fail to notice the nature of the lion. He is not always roaring. When he wants to catch his prey, he is not only quiet but crouches very low. He does not desire to be noticed until his victim is fully in his reach; then he pounces upon it without mercy.

God's people have ever had to guard against the intrusion of evil into their ranks, and the difficulty, frequently, comes from such as are associated with them as members of the same body. Paul speaks about a trouble that he had and he says it was "because of false brethren unawares brought in, who came in privily to spy out our liberty which we have in Christ Jesus, that they might bring us into bondage." Gal. 2: 4.

In this case the apostle tells how those parties came in, and he says that their object was,—" to spy out our liberty." They desired to bring the faithful into bondage. The apostle continues by saying, "To whom we gave place by subjection, no, not for an hour." That has the right ring! In harmony there is strength.

In the above-described case the lion came into the fold as a lamb, but when he had accomplished his purpose, he began first, to growl, and later, to roar. Having been in long enough to spy out the liberty of the Father's children, he now feels that he knows how to make his attack. Then he comes out boldly and roars with all the power he can command. The object seems to be, if possible, to sow discord among the sheep of the Lord's flock. Peter, in his second epistle, gives a very lucid description of such characters. He says, "But chiefly them that walk after the flesh in the lust of uncleanness and despise government." 2 Pet. 2: 10. Government means harmony. Then those characters don't like government because that means to lay down personal choice and render submission, as in Heb. 13: 17.

As proof of the fact that it is here where the trouble comes in, see what Peter further says in the verse above cited: "Presumptuous are they, self-willed; they are not afraid to speak evil of dignities." He farther continues his description in the following words: "Which have forsaken the right way and are gone astray." 2 Pet. 2: 15. Such have failed to take that good advice of Bro. Paul where he says, "Nevertheless, whereto we have already attained let us walk by the same rule, let us mind the same thing." Philpp. 3: 16.

This course, pursued by a body of people, must result in harmony. The Savior said, "Take heed what ye hear." Mark 4: 24. No wonder that he gives such a caution when we consider the following: "But there were false prophets also among the people, even as there shall be false teachers among you who privily shall bring in damnable heresies," etc. "Many shall follow their pernicious ways, by reason of whom the way of truth shall be evil spoken of." 2 Pet. 2: 1, 2.

It is clear to every careful observer that, as long as the soldiers under the generalship of King Jesus, keep strictly to the word of command, no harm can befall them, but they must remember that he said, "What I say unto you I say unto all, Watch." What shall they watch for? *Ans.*— For just such as the following: "For when they speak great swelling words of vanity they allure through the lusts of the flesh, through much wantonness, those that were clean escaped from them who live in error." 2 Pet. 2: 18. Now you will observe that the charge to watch was given to the faithful.

Those who are spoken to, in the verse quoted above, were also of the faithful, for they were "clean escaped" from such as live in error. They don't tell those, who come with their "great swelling words" that they will be lost if they continue in their present course, but they "promise them liberty." 2 Pet. 2: 19. They try to make them believe that they can have liberty and be saved too.

All such is not liberty to the spirit, but to the flesh, for they appeal to them through the lusts of the flesh. We might inquire, What do such persons want when they thus speak to the faithful? We will let Paul tell us. He says, "Also of your own selves shall men arise, speaking perverse things to draw away disciples after them. Therefore watch and remember that by the space of three years I ceased not to warn every one night and day with tears." Acts 20: 30, 31.

There is no uncertainty in his answer. They want followers, and, instead of going out into the highways and hedges to convert the unsaved, they go among the faithful to secure followers. The apostle says they speak as they do to draw away disciples. Draw away from what? He is speaking about what shall take place in the church of Christ.

It is clear, then, that the effort to draw away disciples means to draw them away from the church. When they succeed in inducing any one to yield to their plea, they have to confess that they have nothing to promise them except *liberty*, and it is a pitiable case when it is all told, for it is clear that the liberty promised is only the liberty to do a little more as you please.

It does not require a man to be a Solomon, to know that when that kind of liberty is granted, the individuals will generally drift into the common current, and soon all their love for the self-denying advice of the Scriptures, and of the church, is drowned in the stream of worldly pleasures. Not unfrequently is Christ crucified unto such and put to an open shame, because, as soon as any one turns to the glittering toys of earth, and takes pleasure in the tinsel thereof, they are not in harmony with Jesus. We should not forget that he says, "Without me ye can do nothing."

After all, what have we gained by following any one beside him who gave his life a ransom for us? God has seen fit to organize a church in the world, and in that church he has provided a place for his creatures to work, and he has sanctified ordinances and elements to be employed in the prosecution of that work.

In our next we propose to show that the church has been trying faithfully to maintain these.

THE LOOM OF LIFE.

BY ELIZABETH H. DELP.

" My days are swifter than a weaver's shuttle."—Job 7: 6.

THE passing of days, the short years, and the centuries completed, all remind us that we are drawing near a measureless eternity. Our trite expression, "Time flies," is only another version of Job's thought. The weaver's shuttle, as it flies back and forth, truthfully symbolizes the flight of time, and it also brings to us other thoughts, "The hours perish and are laid to our charge." Happy are we, if we can look into the past, not mournfully; but with the feeling that it holds the best of which we are capable. In the days that are passing like a weaver's shuttle, we are weaving our life. The loom, upon which we are at work, may hold a coarse, colorless cloth, or it may be an exquisite fabric of fabulous worth. We are the weavers and, to some extent, the designers of our own pattern.

With indomitable energy we must sometimes begin our task, seeing that our work is marred by our own heedlessness, or that, by our own willfulness, we have tangled the threads. Sometimes it is past unfaithfulness that has caused the present trouble. Then the only way is to unravel the past, and begin again, upon the strength of God's promise, "that whoso confesseth and forsaketh his sins shall have mercy." The blood of Christ will make white as snow the life-fabric that was stained with sin and marred with duties neglected. When all the disciples forsook the Savior and fled, and when Peter denied the Christ, until a look from the Savior revealed to him dark threads of unbelief and desertion; then, with tears, he rent them, and commenced anew, and wove a pattern of such clearness, boldness and strength, that to-day we study to imitate it.

At the loom of sin, the shuttle flies swiftly, but the threads are torn and discolored, the fabric

CORRESPONDENCE.

" Write what thou seest, and send it unto the churches."

☞Church News solicited for this Department. If you have had a good meeting, send a report of it, so that others may rejoice with you. In writing give names of church, County and State. Be brief. Notes of Travel should be as short as possible. Land Advertisements are not solicited for this Department. We have an advertising page, and, if necessary, will issue supplements.

From Greene, Iowa.

Nov. 1 Bro. Joseph Holder, of Indiana, commenced a series of meetings for us, which he continued until the 5th, the time of our love-feast, which will long be remembered by all who were permitted to be present. Bro. Holder officiated, assisted by a number of ministers from the adjoining churches. By request, the elders of the Northern Iowa, Minnesota and South Dakota District selected two elders to attend our feast and do church work. An election was held for two deacons. Bro. J. B. Shank was advanced to the second degree of the ministry, and Bro. Harvey Eikenberry ordained to the eldership. Brethren David Eikenberry and Wm. McRoberts were elected to the office of deacon. All were installed into their offices by elders J. Holder and Jonas Lichty. It was the most solemn scene ever witnessed on such an occasion. We pray that they will be faithful in their calling, and that the church will stand by them.

On Sunday following there was a children's meeting at 2 P. M., when our ministers gave us ten-minute talks of an interesting and edifying nature. The meetings then continued each evening with a good attendance, considering the weather, until the night of the 13th, when Bro. Holder closed with a good interest, and left for other fields of labor. One applied for baptism, while others seemed to be laboring under conviction, and said by their actions, When we have a more convenient season we will come.

J. F. EIKENBERRY.

From Lancaster, Pa.

WE held our love-feast Nov. 6. There was a large attendance and many were obliged to stand. I was told that some went away because there was no room inside. I hope it will not be long before we can accommodate all who may have a desire to witness the administration of the ordinances of God's house. We have a church-house, but it is too small and inconvenient for love-feasts, yet, through the good management of Bro. T. F. Imler, our resident minister, about eighty-five members found room enough to commune last Sunday. It was indeed a season of refreshing from the Lord. The occasion will be one long to be remembered, and we have been very much encouraged in the work of the Lord. The best of order prevailed and most all were favorably impressed. We felt glad to see so many of our adjoining ministers and brethren at the tables. We were assured that they were in sympathy with our efforts here, and hope we may see them often, as their associating and being with us will be a great help to our work.

We invite all ministering brethren traveling this way to stop off and give us a call. Anyone contemplating coming this way, will, by addressing Bro. T. F. Imler, 418 West Walnut Street, or the writer, be furnished all information desired.   A. J. EVANS.

Nov. 10.

From the Summit Mills Church, Somerset Co., Pa.

THE brethren and sisters of the above-named church decided on having two weeks' series of meetings,—one at the Crossroads meeting-house, and the other at the large meeting-house at Me-

chanicsburgh. Bro. Jeremiah Thomas, of Clifton Mills, Preston Co., W. Va., was chosen to do the preaching. The meeting began Oct. 22, and continued at the Crossroads till Friday, Oct. 28. On Saturday the brethren and sisters met in council at our large meeting-house. The same evening we met at the same place to hear the Gospel preached. Bro. Thomas told us many good things. His dear uncle, George Thomas, a brother to Eld. Jacob Thomas, came with him. We enjoyed their associations very much. We were blessed with pleasant weather, good attendance and excellent preaching. Six dear souls came out on the Lord's side. Nov. 5 we celebrated the Lord's Supper. A goodly number of members communed. On Sunday brethren Thomas and Joel Gnagey were called to preach the funeral of sister Malinda, wife of Solomon Gnagey, who died of typhoid fever. A few days previous to her death, she called for the elders, to be anointed. Bro. Thomas preached in all sixteen sermons.   MATILDA J. VOUGHT.

Nov. 9.

From Denver, Colo.

PERHAPS the readers of the MESSENGER will remember that some time last spring we asked all members, having relatives or friends living in Denver, to give us their address, that we might visit them and, if possible, get them to attend our meetings.

About March 1, 1892, by request of the Brethren, I began holding regular services in a school-house in the suburbs of the city, with an attendance of from fifteen to twenty-five, mostly Brethren and their children.

As the people in the vicinity of the school-house were principally Catholics, we could not hope to increase our audience very much, and the Brethren concluded to hire a hall in the city, and there hold their Sunday-school and church-services.

Since then they have prospered beyond their expectation. They now have a very promising Sunday-school, with an attendance of from forty to fifty. Perhaps half or more of the number are children, from six to twelve years of age, who live in the vicinity of the hall. It is pleasing to see their bright little faces as they come in and take their places in the class. I have talked with nearly all of them, and they say they love to come to our Sunday-school. The church attendance is also encouraging; new faces appear at nearly every meeting.

One has been baptized. He is an old man who had never before heard of our people. He is very earnest and devoted, and is distributing tracts over the city. We think we have reason to expect more additions soon.

Denver is a large city, and I believe we have as good a prospect for building up a large church here as in any city in the world, but you know the adage, "No excellence without labor." It will take labor and money to do it. The Brethren there are just as liberal and zealous as they can be, but are mostly in limited circumstances, and the burden is too heavy for them to bear. They must have help. Surely you will not let the cause, you lost so well, suffer for a few paltry dollars! I know you will not. There are thousands of souls perishing for the Bread of Life. Hundreds might be saved if we would all put our shoulders to the wheel and push together. Here is a chance for all to work in the Master's cause. Here is a chance for us to add stars to our crown.

Dear brother, dear sister, how do you know but that last dollar you spent for a parlor ornament, or table luxury, might not have saved a soul, had it been used in the Master's service.

I appeal to you in the name of him who died for you, that you do something for the Denver mission. If you can only give ten cents, give it in the name of Jesus. If you love him, manifest it by extending a helping hand to a perishing brother. Jesus loves sinners,—why should not we?

What they most need in Denver is a resident minister who can devote *all his time to the cause*. He needs to work seven days in a week, but he cannot do this and make his own living. He must be supported.

The Brethren there will not have much difficulty in getting the minister, when they have the means of support. Please send all contributions to Henry Hutton, 1535 Market St., Denver, and we guarantee they will be judiciously used. At present Bro. Fesler and myself are taking turns filling the appointment, which is on the first and third Sundays of each month.

I have not written this in my own interest. I am so situated, at present, that I could not make Denver my place of residence if I wished to, and were qualified for the place, which, I am free to confess, I am not.   D. H. WEAVER.

Longmont, Colo.

REMARKS. — We suggest that the Mission Board, in whose territory Denver is located, take this matter into consideration, and if help is needed let it be called for and used by the authority of the Board. Denver is a very promising field in which to make special efforts. Very little can be accomplished in any of the large cities without resident ministers who understand city work, and, to secure the needed aid to set the work afoot, the co-operation and direction of the District Board will be found necessary.—ED.

From Warrensburgh, Mo.

ABOUT two years ago we commenced holding monthly meetings at the Mason school-house,— a new point about seven miles North-east of Warrensburgh. On Sunday evening Oct. 16, Bro. Jacob Witmore, of Centre View, commenced a series of meetings at that point. He preached to the people two weeks in his plain, earnest way, awakening quite an interest. On Sunday following, we had one applicant for baptism. Bro. Witmore was obliged to leave us at that time, to meet engagements in Ohio. The home ministry continued the meetings, and on Thursday following we baptized four, and one more on Sunday. These six who were baptized, are all young people who have been members of other churches. Among them is the Superintendent of the Sunday-school (who is also teacher of the district school), the Assistant Superintendent, the Secretary, Assistant Secretary, and one of the teachers.

Nearly all the different churches are represented among the people of the neighborhood, but not enough of any one church to have regular meetings. Here, as in many other places, the people are tired of this "Prophesying for hire," and "Divining for money." We intend to hold meeting twice a month at this place hereafter, and hope, by the Lord's help, to establish his work among this people.   D. M. MOHLER.

Nov. 15.

On the Way.

NOV. 11 I met with the members of the Pine Creek church in a Communion service. The meeting was not so large as on former occasions, but a very interesting one. This church, like some others, has had dark clouds of sorrow, but now we think we see the mist rolling away, and love and fellowship are now made manifest. Eld. W.

CORRESPONDENCE.

"Write what thou seest, and send it unto the chutches."

☞"Church News solicited for this Department. If you have had a good meeting, send a report of it, so that others may rejoice with you. In writing give name of chulbh, County and State. Be brief. Notes of Travel should be as short as possible. Land Advertisements are not solicited for this Department. We have an advertising page, and, if necessary, will issue supplements.

From Greene, Iowa.

Nov. 1 Bro. Joseph Holder, of Indiana, commenced a series of meetings for us, which he continued until the 5th, the time of our love-feast, which will long be remembered by all who were permitted to be present. Bro. Holder officiated, assisted by a number of ministers from the adjoining churches. By request, the elders of the Northern Iowa, Minnesota and South Dakota District selected two elders to attend our feast and do church work. An election was held for two deacons. Bro. J. B. Shank was advanced to the second degree of the ministry, and Bro. Harvey Eikenberry ordained to the eldership. Brethren David Eikenberry and Wm. McRoberts were elected to the office of deacon. All were installed into their offices by elders J. Holder and Jonas Lichty. It was the most solemn scene ever witnessed on such an occasion. We pray that they will be faithful in their calling, and that the church will stand by them.

On Sunday following there was a children's meeting at 2 P. M., when our ministers gave us ten-minute talks of an interesting and edifying nature. The meetings then continued each evening with a good attendance, considering the weather, until the night of the 13th, when Bro. Holder closed with a good interest, and left for other fields of labor. Some applied for baptism, while others seemed to be laboring under conviction, and said by their actions, When we have a more convenient season we will come.

J. F. EIKENBERRY.

From Lancaster, Pa.

WE held our love-feast Nov. 6. There was a large attendance and many were obliged to stand. I was told that some went away because there was no room inside. I hope it will not be long before we can accommodate all who may have a desire to witness the administration of the ordinances of God's house. We have a church-house, but it is too small and inconvenient for love-feasts, yet, through the good management of Bro. T. F. Imler, our resident minister, about eighty-five members found room enough to commune last Sunday. It was indeed a season of refreshing from the Lord. The occasion will be one long to be remembered, and we have been very much encouraged in the work of the Lord. The best of order prevailed and most all were favorably impressed. We felt glad to see so many of our adjoining ministers and brethren at the tables. We were assured that they were in sympathy with our efforts here, and hope we may see them often, as their associating and being with us will be a great help to our work.

We invite all ministering brethren traveling this way to stop off and give us a call. Anyone contemplating coming this way, will, by addressing Bro. T. F. Imler, 418 West Walnut Street, or the writer, be furnished all information desired. A. J. EVANS.

Nov. 10.

From the Summit Mills Church, Somerset Co., Pa.

THE brethren and sisters of the above-named church decided on having two weeks' series of meetings,—one at the Crossroads meeting-house and the other at the large meeting-house at Me-

chanicsburgh. Bro. Jeremiah Thomas, of Clifton Mills, Preston Co., W. Va., was chosen to do the preaching. The meeting began Oct. 22, and continued at the Crossroads till Friday, Oct. 28. On Saturday the brethren and sisters met in council at our large meeting-house. The same evening we met at the same place to hear the Gospel preached. Bro. Thomas told us many good things. His dear uncle, George Thomas, a brother to Eld. Jacob Thomas, came with him. We enjoyed their associations very much. We were blessed with pleasant weather, good attendance and excellent preaching. Six dear souls came out on the Lord's side. Nov. 5 we celebrated the Lord's Supper. A goodly number of members communed. On Sunday brethren Thomas and Joel Gnagey were called to preach the funeral of sister Malinda, wife of Solomon Gnagey, who died of typhoid fever. A few days previous to her death, she called for the elders, to be anointed. Bro. Thomas preached in all sixteen sermons. MATILDA J. VOUGHT.

Nov. 9.

From Denver, Colo.

PERHAPS the readers of the MESSENGER will remember that some time last spring we asked all members, having relatives or friends living in Denver, to give us their address, that we might visit them and, if possible, get them to attend our meetings.

About March 1, 1892, by request of the Brethren, I began holding regular services in a school-house in the suburbs of the city, with an attendance of from fifteen to twenty-five, mostly Brethren and their children.

As the people in the vicinity of the school-house were principally Catholics, we could not hope to increase our audience very much, and the Brethren concluded to hire a hall in the city, and there hold their Sunday-school and church-services.

Since then they have prospered beyond their expectation. They now have a very promising Sunday-school, with an attendance of from forty to fifty. Perhaps half or more of the number are children, from six to twelve years of age, who live in the vicinity of the hall. It is pleasing to see their bright little faces as they come in and take their places in the class. I have talked with nearly all of them, and they say they love to come to our Sunday-school. The church attendance is also encouraging; new faces appear at nearly every meeting.

One has been baptized. He is an old man who had never before heard of our people. He is very earnest and devoted, and is distributing tracts over the city. We think we have reason to expect more additions soon.

Denver is a large city, and I believe we have as good a prospect for building up a large church here as in any city in the world, but you know the adage, "No excellence without labor." It will take labor and money to do it. The Brethren here are just as liberal and zealous as they can be, but are mostly in limited circumstances, and the burden is too heavy for them to bear. They must have help. Surely you will not let the cause, you love so well, suffer for a few paltry dollars! I know you will not. There are thousands of souls perishing for the Bread of Life! Hundreds might be saved if we would all put our shoulders to the wheel and push together. Here is a chance for all to work in the Master's cause. Here is a chance for us to add stars to our crown.

Dear brother, dear sister, how do you know but that last dollar your spent for a parlor ornament, or table luxury, might not have saved a soul, had it been used in the Master's service.

I appeal to you in the name of him who died for you, that you do something for the Denver mission. If you can only give ten cents, give it in the name of Jesus. If you love him, manifest it by extending a helping hand to a perishing brother. Jesus loves sinners,—why should not we?

What they most need in Denver is a resident minister who can devote *all his time to the cause.* He needs to work seven days in a week, but he cannot do this and make his own living. He must be supported.

The Brethren there will not have much difficulty in getting the minister, when they have the means of support. Please send all contributions to Henry Hutton, 1535 Market St., Denver, and we guarantee they will be judiciously used. At present Bro. Fesler and myself are taking turns filling the appointment, which is on the first and third Sundays of each month.

I have not written this in my own interest. I am so situated, at present, that I could not make Denver my place of residence if I wished to, and were qualified for the place, which, I am free to confess, I am not. D. H. WEAVER.

Longmont, Colo.

REMARKS.— We suggest that the Mission Board, in whose territory Denver is located, take this matter into consideration, and if help is needed let it be called for and used by the authority of the Board. Denver is a large city, and from what we can learn, is a very promising field in which to make special efforts. Very little can be accomplished in any of the large cities without resident ministers who understand city work, and, to secure the needed aid to set the work afoot, the co-operation and direction of the District Board will be found necessary.—ED.

From Warrensburgh, Mo.

ABOUT two years ago we commenced holding monthly meetings at the Mason school-house,— a new point about seven miles North-east of Warrensburgh. On Sunday evening Oct. 16, Bro. Jacob Witmore, of Centre View, commenced a series of meetings at that point. He preached to the people two weeks in his plain, earnest way, awakening quite an interest. On Sunday following, we had one applicant for baptism. Bro. Witmore was obliged to leave us at that time, to meet engagements in Ohio. The home ministry continued the meetings, and on Thursday following we baptized four, and one more on Sunday. These six who were baptized, are all young people who had been members of other churches. Among them is the Superintendent of the Sunday-school (who is also teacher of the district school), the Assistant Superintendent, the Secretary, Assistant Secretary, and one of the teachers.

Nearly all the different churches are represented among the people of the neighborhood, but not enough of any one church to have regular meetings. Here, as in many other places, the people are tired of this "Prophesying for hire," and "Divining for money." We intend to hold meeting twice a month at this place hereafter, and hope, by the Lord's help, to establish his work among this people. D. M. MOHLER.

Nov. 15.

On the Way.

Nov. 11 I met with the members of the Pine Creek church in a Communion service. The meeting was not so large as on former occasions, but a very interesting one. This church, like some others, has had dark clouds of sorrow, but now we think we see the mist rolling away, and love and fellowship are now made manifest. Eld. W.

Missionary and Tract Work Department.

"Upon the first day of the week, let every one of you lay by him in store as God hath prospered him, that there be no gatherings when I come."—1 Cor. 16: 2.

"Every man as he purposeth in his heart, so let him give. Not grudgingly or of necessity, for the Lord loveth a cheerful giver."—2 Cor. 9: 7.

HOW MUCH SHALL WE GIVE?

"Every man according to his ability." "Every one as God hath prospered him." "Every man, according as he purposeth in his heart, to let him give." "For if there be first a willing mind, it is accepted according to that a man hath, and not according to that he hath not."—2 Cor. 8: 12.

Organization of Missionary Committee.

DANIEL VANIMAN, Foreman, - - McPherson, Kans.
D. L. MILLER, Treasurer, - - - Mt. Morris, Ill.
GALEN B. ROYER, Secretary, - - Mt. Morris, Ill.

Organization of Book and Tract Work.

S. W. HOOVER, Foreman, - - - Dayton, Ohio.
S. BOCK, Secretary and Treasurer, - Dayton, Ohio.

☞All donations intended for Missionary Work should be sent to GALEN B. ROYER, Mt. Morris, Ill.

☞All money for Tract Work should be sent to S. BOCK, Dayton, Ohio.

☞Money may be sent by Money Order, Registered Letter, or Drafts on New York or Chicago. Do not send personal checks, or drafts on interior towns, as it costs 25 cents to collect them.

☞Solicitors are requested to faithfully carry out the plan of Annual Meeting, that all our members be solicited to contribute at least twice a year for the Mission and Tract Work of the Church.

☞Notes for the Endowment Fund can be had by writing to the Secretary of either Work.

MISSIONARY NOTES.

Go ye into all the world and preach the Gospel.—*Jesus.*

* * *

We need no more intellectual power so much, as the one unqualifiedly greatest want,—spiritual power.

* * *

In China to-day are nearly fifty thousand converts. *Come over and help us!* Four hundred million souls in the Chinese Empire!

* * *

What becomes of the heathen who die without the Gospel, is not so much a question as, What becomes of me, if I refuse to take it to them?

* * *

The Moravian church is more than half converts from heathendom. We will have some work to do before that can be said of ourselves.

* * *

After missionary Judson had worked for ten years, he had eighteen converts to show for it, but being asked by those at home about prospects, he replied, "Prospects! All right,—bright as the promises of God."

* * *

Sailing from New York to Calcutta, the cost is about $250 for one first-class passage. The expense of an American missionary in India usually amounts to about $600 a year, according to the calculation of the Baptist society.

* * *

The great hope for successful work in foreign missions is to get native preachers and teachers. They can enter into full sympathy with those for whom they are working, and can reach the heart more readily. The cost of supporting a native preacher in India is about seventy dollars a year, or less. In China it is probably still less than in India.

* * *

A ten-year-old boy in one of our eastern churches had sixteen cents saved for candy and a good time. Upon having an opportunity to help send the Gospel to the heathen,—to "all the world,"—his actions said earnestly, "If doing without candy helps little heathen boys to know the Gospel, I'll eat no candy while the world stands." Thus the fund was sixteen cents larger. "Men of the future are boys to-day."

Ten converts from heathendom more than once formed themselves into actual self-supporting churches. This is the way they say they did it, "We will each give one-tenth of our income, and we will call a minister to serve us, who is willing to live on a level with us, and he will have his ten-tenths, with one-tenth to give away like the rest of us."

* * *

A far-reaching point is hinted at by W. M. Taylor: "There is but one lake in the surface of the globe from which there is no outlet, and that is the Dead Sea, which receives much, but gives nothing. Such a lake is a perfect illustration of a church whose efforts all terminate on itself. Around it there will be desolation, and in it there will be no life."

* * *

The question often and rightly comes up, "How may I attain to spiritual highness and missionary zeal?" That Christ-like thirst for souls is so often only in the distance. The substance of the *how* is in two words,—"*Desire it.*" When you work, desire it. When you rest, desire it. When you eat, desire it. When you sleep, desire it. When you read, desire it. When you pray, desire it. When you talk, desire it. When you meditate, desire it. Let it be the desire of your heart *always*, and presently it will take possession of your soul; the Bible will be a new book, and the constraining power of your life will be LOVE.   S. B.

A PRACTICAL OUTLINE OF CHURCH GOVERNMENT.

BY DANIEL HAYS.

No. IV.—Its Applications.

1. WHEN a case is put into the hands of the church for decision, the church should fully understand the case, first, as it relates to the one, or more, concerned; second, as it relates to the Gospel.

2. No matter should be submitted to the church for decision before it is ready. No matter should be withheld from the church when it is ready.

3. When a charge is brought against an individual member, two deacons, under the direction of the elder, should investigate the case first, and then make a statement of the matter as they found it, before the church. It then becomes the property of the church.

4. An individual member should not present a charge against a member before the church. This is the duty of the officers of the church.

5. An elder should not undertake to do the work that belongs to the church in order to save the church trouble.

6. An elder should always aim to keep the church between himself and trouble.

7. An elder should not go on an investigating committee. This is the duty of the deacon.

8. When a matter is brought before the church, the elder should not take sides; he should stand aloof and above, and lead the church on to a proper decision.

9. When a matter is before the church, irrelevant matter and side issues should not be entertained. Long and tedious council-meetings, as a rule, are not productive of good.

10. To defer a matter for future consideration is safer and better than a hasty or untimely decision.

11. Each local church should transact business in harmony with the adjoining churches and the General Brotherhood.

12. The doctrines of non-conformity, non-resistance, non-swearing, etc., etc., are fundamental in the church, and no local church can consistently disregard any part of it.

13. A church will be more or less what the ministry make it. A minister, then, should preach the doctrine of the church.

14. An orderly church is one that walks according to the Gospel rule. A minister, then, should defend the order of the church and uphold her principles. Her principles are Gospel principles that have stood the test of the ages.

15. Every minister should be in sympathy with the doctrine and order of the church.

16. Every minister should be in sympathy with his co-laborers. There is work for all and room for all.

17. Each minister has his proper sphere; let him labor in it; and if he has not found it, let him labor to find it.

18. A united ministry insures a united church.

19. After all, self-government is the most difficult, for "he that is slow to anger is better than the mighty; and he that ruleth his spirit, than he that taketh a city." Prov. 16: 32.

20. It is the duty of every Christian to cultivate individual self-control.

21. He that would rule others should first learn to govern himself.

22. The nearer we draw together to God, the nearer we draw toward each other.

23. Society is made up of concessions. The church is the one true society, based upon equal rights and privileges.

24. Christ is the center,—the middle point in the church,—where all the members meet in union.

25. In matters of personal difference we should be willing to meet each other half-way, and at that middle point we will find Christ.

26. The bond of union is secured by daily, hourly self-denial.

27. He is the truly great man who can sacrifice self for the good of others, and then say nothing about it.

28. If we do a great or good action, we should let the action itself speak for us.

29. We lose nothing by self-denial. "The more a man denies himself, the more he shall obtain from God."

30. "In honor preferring one another," is a golden precept, and self-denial engraves it in living characters on the temple of fraternal love and Christian Brotherhood.

31. The tongue is an unruly member, and needs the bridle of self-restraint. "If any man offend not in word, the same is a perfect man, and able also to bridle the whole body." James 3: 2.

32. The counsel of the church, when properly directed and heeded, brings the whole membership under good discipline.

33. It is an easy matter to criticise the action of another, but not so easy to do the work any better yourself.

34. "Evil criticism" is a sower of discord among brethren. Bad, indeed is his condition who never sees a good quality in a man, and never fails to see a bad one.

35. Things and not persons should be the subjects of conversation,—"Finally, brethren, whatsoever things are true, whatsoever things are honest, whatsoever things are just, whatsoever things are pure, whatsoever things are lovely, whatsoever things are of good report; if there be any virtue, and if there be any praise, think on these things." Philpp. 4: 8.

36. A Christian should not, by improper conduct, set himself up as a target for evil criticism. A man of God should live above suspicion.

37. The church should rather encourage such a standard of purity in life and character in the membership as will place them above evil criticism, than try to check evil criticism itself. "Give none occasion to the adversary to speak reproachfully." 1 Tim. 5: 14.

Missionary and Tract Work Department.

"Upon the first day of the week, let every one of you lay by him in store as God hath prospered him, that there be no gatherings when I come."—1 Cor. 16: 2.

"Every man as he purposeth in his heart, so let him give. Not grudgingly or of necessity, for the Lord loveth a cheerful giver."—2 Cor. 9: 7.

HOW MUCH SHALL WE GIVE?

"Every man *according to his ability.*" "Every one as God hath prospered him." "Every man, *according as he purposeth in his heart,* so let him give." "For if there be first a willing mind, it is accepted *according to that a man hath,* and not according to that he hath not."—2 Cor. 8: 12.

Organization of Missionary Committee. *

DANIEL VANIMAN, Foreman, - - McPherson, Kans.
D. L. MILLER, Treasurer, - - - Mt. Morris, Ill.
GALEN B. ROYER, Secretary, - - Mt. Morris, Ill.

Organization of Book and Tract Work.

S. W. HOOVER, Foreman, - - - Dayton, Ohio.
S. BOCK, Secretary and Treasurer, - Dayton, Ohio.

☞All donations intended for Missionary Work should be sent to GALEN B. ROYER, Mt. Morris, Ill.

☞All money for Tract Work should be sent to S. BOCK, Dayton, Ohio.

☞Money may be sent by Money Order, Registered Letter, or Drafts on New York or Chicago. Do not send personal checks, or drafts on interior towns, as it costs 25 cents to collect them.

☞Solicitors are requested to faithfully carry out the plan of Annual Meeting, that all our members be solicited to contribute at least twice a year for the Mission and Tract Work of the Church.

☞Notes for the Endowment Fund can be had by writing to the Secretary of either Work.

MISSIONARY NOTES.

Go ye into all the world and preach the Gospel.—*Jesus.*

* * *

We need not more intellectual power so much, as the one unqualified greatest want,—spiritual power.

* * *

In China to-day are nearly fifty thousand converts. *Come over and help us!* Four hundred million souls in the Chinese Empire!

* * *

What becomes of the heathen who die without the Gospel, is not so much a question as, What becomes of me, if I refuse to take it to them?

* * *

The Moravian church is more than half converts from heathendom. We will have some work to do before that can be said of ourselves.

* * *

After missionary Judson had worked for ten years, he had eighteen converts to show for it, but being asked by those at home about prospects, he replied, "Prospects! All right,—bright as the promises of God."

* * *

Sailing from New York to Calcutta, the cost is about $250 for one first-class passage. The expense of an American missionary in India usually amounts to about $600 a year, according to the calculation of the Baptist society.

* * *

The great hope for successful work in foreign missions is to get native preachers and teachers. They can enter into full sympathy with those for whom they are working, and can reach the heart more readily. The cost of supporting a native preacher in India is about seventy dollars a year, or less. In China it is probably still less than in India.

* * *

A ten-year-old boy in one of our eastern churches had sixteen cents saved for candy and a good time. Upon having an opportunity to help send the Gospel to the heathen,—to "all the world,"—his actions said earnestly, "If doing without candy helps little heathen boys to know the Gospel, I'll eat no candy while the world stands." Thus the fund was sixteen cents larger. "Men of the future are boys to-day."

Ten converts from heathendom more than once formed themselves into actual self-supporting churches. This is the way they say they did it, "We will each give one-tenth of our income, and we will call a minister to serve us, who is willing to live on a level with us, and he will have his ten-tenths, with one-tenth to give away like the rest of us."

* * *

A far-reaching point is hinted at by W. M. Taylor: "There is but one lake in the surface of the globe from which there is no outlet, and that is the Dead Sea, which receives much, but gives nothing. Such a lake is a perfect illustration of a church whose efforts all terminate on itself. Around it there will be desolation, and in it there will be no life."

* * *

The question often and rightly comes up, "How may I attain to spiritual highness and missionary zeal?" That Christ-like thirst for souls is so often only in the distance. The substance of the *how* is in two words,—"*Desire it.*" When you work, desire it. When you read, desire it. When you eat, desire it. When you sleep, desire it. When you read, desire it. When you pray, desire it. When you talk, desire it. When you meditate, desire it. Let it be the desire of your heart *always,* and presently it will take possession of your soul; the Bible will be a new book, and the constraining power of your life will be LOVE.   S. B.

A PRACTICAL OUTLINE OF CHURCH GOVERNMENT.

BY DANIEL HAYS.

No. IV.—Its Applications.

1. WHEN a case is put into the hands of the church for decision, the church should fully understand the case, first, as it relates to the one, or more, concerned; second, as it relates to the Gospel.

2. No matter should be submitted to the church for decision before it is ready. No matter should be withheld from the church when it is ready.

3. When a charge is brought against an individual member, two deacons, under the direction of the elder, should investigate the case first, and then make a statement of the matter as they found it, before the church. It then becomes the property of the church.

4. An individual member should not present a charge against a member before the church. This is the duty of the officers of the church.

5. An elder should not undertake to do the work that belongs to the church in order to save the church trouble.

6. An elder should always aim to keep the church between himself and trouble.

7. An elder should not go on an investigating committee. This is the duty of the deacon.

8. When a matter is brought before the church, the elder should not take sides; he should stand aloof and above, and lead the church on to a proper decision.

9. When a matter is before the church, irrelevant matter and side issues should not be entertained. Long and tedious council-meetings, as a rule, are not productive of good.

10. To defer a matter for future consideration is safer and better than a hasty or untimely decision.

11. Each local church should transact business in harmony with the adjoining churches and the General Brotherhood.

12. The doctrines of non-conformity, non-resistance, non-swearing, etc., etc. are fundamental in the church, and no local church can consistently disregard any part of it.

---

13. A church will be more or less what the ministry make it. A minister, then, should preach the doctrine of the church.

14. An orderly church is one that walks according to the Gospel rule. A minister, then, should defend the order of the church and uphold her principles. Her principles are Gospel principles that have stood the test of the ages.

15. Every minister should be in sympathy with the doctrine and order of the church.

16. Every minister should be in sympathy with his co-laborers. There is work for all and room for all.

17. Each minister has his proper sphere; let him labor in it; and if he has not found it, let him labor to find it.

18. A united ministry insures a united church.

19. After all, self-government is the most difficult, for "he that is slow to anger is better than the mighty; and he that ruleth his spirit, than he that taketh a city." Prov. 16: 32.

20. It is the duty of every Christian to cultivate individual self-control.

21. He that would rule others should first learn to govern himself.

22. The nearer we draw together to God, the nearer we draw toward each other.

23. Society is made up of concessions. The church is the one true society, based upon equal rights and privileges.

24. Christ is the center,—the middle point in the church,—where all the members meet in union.

25. In matters of personal difference we should be willing to meet each other half-way, and at that middle point we will find Christ.

26. The bond of union is secured by daily, hourly self-denial.

27. He is the truly great man who can sacrifice self for the good of others, and then say nothing about it.

28. If we do a great or good action, we should let the action itself speak for us.

29. We lose nothing by self-denial. "The more a man denies himself, the more he shall obtain from God."

30. "In honor preferring one another," is a golden precept, and self-denial engraves it in living characters on the temple of fraternal love and Christian Brotherhood.

31. The tongue is an unruly member, and needs the bridle of self-restraint. "If any man offend not in word, the same is a perfect man, and able also to bridle the whole body." James 3: 2.

32. The counsel of the church, when properly directed and heeded, brings the whole membership under good discipline.

33. It is an easy matter to criticise the action of another, but not so easy to do the work any better yourself.

34. "Evil criticism" is a sower of discord among brethren. Bad, indeed is his condition who never sees a good quality in a man, and never fails to see a bad one.

35. Things and not persons should be the subjects of conversation,—"Finally, brethren, whatsoever things are true, whatsoever things are honest, whatsoever things are just, whatsoever things are pure, whatsoever things are lovely, whatsoever things are of good report; if there be any virtue, and if there be any praise, think on these things." Philpp. 4: 8.

36. A Christian should not, by improper conduct, set himself up as a target for evil criticism. A man of God should live above suspicion.

37. The church should rather encourage such a standard of purity in life and character in the membership as will place them above evil criticism, than try to check evil criticism itself. "Give none occasion to the adversary to speak reproachfully." 1 Tim. 5: 14.

The Gospel Messenger,

A Weekly at $1.50 Per Annum.

PUBLISHED BY

The Brethren's Publishing Co.

D. L. MILLER,	Editor
J. H. MOORE,	Office Editor.
J. B. BRUMBAUGH, } J. G. ROYER, }	Associate Editors.
JOSEPH AMICK,	Business Manager.

ADVISORY COMMITTEE.

L. W. Teeter, A. Hutchison, Daniel Hays.

☞Communications for publication should be legibly written with black ink on one side of the paper only. Do not attempt to interline, or to put on one page what ought to occupy two.

☞Anonymous communications will not be published.

☞Do not mix business with articles for publication. Keep your communications on separate sheets from all business.

☞Time is precious. We always have time to attend to business and to answer questions of importance, but please do not subject us to need less answering of letters.

☞The Messenger is mailed each week to all subscribers. If the address is correctly entered on our list, the paper must reach the person to whom it is addressed. If you do not get your paper, write us, giving particulars.

☞When changing your address, please give your former as well as your future address in full, so as to avoid delay and misunderstanding.

☞Always remit to the office from which you order your goods, no matter from where you receive them.

☞Do not send personal checks or drafts on interior banks, unless you send with them 25 cents each, to pay for collection.

☞Remittances should be made by Post-office Money Order, Drafts on New York, Philadelphia or Chicago, or Registered Letters, made payable and addressed to "Brethren's Publishing Co., Mount Morris, Ill.," or " Brethren's Publishing Co., Huntingdon, Pa."

☞Entered at the Post-office at Mount Morris, Ill., as second-class matter.

Mount Morris, Ill., - - - - **Nov. 29, 1892.**

By confession and baptism nine more were recently added to the church at Germantown, Va.

Bro. J. C. Witmore, we learn, is at Bellefontaine, Ohio this week, engaged in a series of meetings.

Bro. T. B. Digman, formerly of Liberty, Adams Co., Ill., may now be addressed at Mountain Lake Park, Md.

Bro. A. I. Mow, of Argos, Ind., has changed his field of labor. He may now be addressed at Palestine, St. Francis Co., Ark.

We understand that since the last Annual Meeting the Brethren's Tract Work has printed over three million pages of tracts.

Bro. John W. Eller, of Salem, Va., who recently held a two weeks' meeting in the Monitor church, Kans., is now engaged in a protracted effort at McPherson.

The time for the feast at Cerro Gordo, Ill., has been changed from Dec. 8 to Nov. 29. A telegram, announcing the change, was received a little too late for notice in the last issue.

Too-late for insertion elsewhere we receive notice that the feast at Pittsburg, Ohio will be held Dec. 3, commencing at 2 P. M. The new house will probably be finished by that time.

At the Mt. Morris Sunday-school last Sunday, a collection was taken up for the purpose of aiding the mission work among the children in Chicago. The amount raised was $13.03.

Can not our agents manage to get the Messenger into every family in the Brotherhood? Will not the elders and preachers unite in encouraging all the members to take the paper? By a united effort let us see what can be done. Let our agents call on every family. Then we want the names of all the congregations where the paper goes into every family where there are members.

Bro. Daniel Vaniman, who is yet in Southern California, is expected to remain in that State a month or more. He is booked for several sermons during the Special Bible Term at Mt. Morris next January.

On the afternoon of Nov. 17 we had our first taste of genuine winter weather for the season. The wind, snow and cold combined to make it anything but pleasant. It caused a longing for the Sunny South.

The feast at Chicago last Sunday evening is reported to have been a very pleasant gathering. About forty members communed. Two deacons were elected and the outlook for the church is encouraging.

We admire the preachers who want to die with their armor on, but we also like to see them keep up their study of the Word. As long as they are careful students of the Bible they do not need to think of retiring from the desk.

Bro. Lemuel Hillery of Indiana, started to Alvin, Texas, last Monday. We have not learned whether he intends to make the Lone Star State his future home, or is arranging to spend only the winter in that mild climate.

About 400 persons recently stood on the bank of the stream in the South Keokuk church, Iowa, and witnessed the baptism of eight persons in twelve minutes. The church at that place seems to be in a flourishing condition just now.

Speaking of bearing one another's burdens, one of our contributors thinks that the laity ought to carry at least the light end of the burden. This they can do by contributing of their abundance in aiding the minister in the arduous task of spreading the Gospel.

Most of our readers are aware that Alexander Campbell died nearly thirty years ago. His widow is still living hale and hearty at the advanced age of ninety. A writer, who recently met her, says from all appearances she may yet reach her one hundredth birthday.

The people in China, in their densely-populated districts, are often exposed to great calamities. Not long since Yellow River overflowed its banks, inundating a large tract of country, drowning about 5,000 people and throwing a million more upon the charity of the government.

Bro. J. G. Royer returned from New Enterprise, Pa., last week too late for us to say anything concerning his meetings. He reports excellent meetings, large congregations, the best of interest, and seventeen additions with prospects of many more. The meetings were continued by the home ministers.

There seems to be no let up to Bro. Jas. R. Gish's call for more ministers in Arkansas. We would like to see about a score of trusty ministers settle at different points in that State. There are plenty of places in the North where that number can be spared. We also have plenty of material to make more to fill their places here. Those who do respond to Bro. Gish's call should remember that he has very little or no use for men who give an uncertain sound in either their preaching, appearance or conduct. A strong, well-grounded church may possibly endure and counteract the unfavorable influence of a few preachers not wholly in sympathy with the regulations of the General Brotherhood, but to put such men on the mission field would be unwise in the extreme. Here is where our hard battles must be fought, and it is here that we must have trusty men.

Our nation is certainly blessed with an abundance this year. A few days ago ten thousand cars of wheat stood on the side tracks in Chicago because there was no place to unload them, all the elevators in the cities being full. The same was also true of the elevators in other large cities. A country with such a supply of food surely ought not to complain.

One of our brethren, in an article intended for the Messenger, suggests that we ought to have but one mode of feet-washing as we have but one mode of baptism. It is coming to that just as fast as the sentiment can be quietly moulded in favor of the present prevailing mode. Just have a little start; it commends itself to all who see it rightly observed, and in the course of a few years we will have but the one mode.

In a letter, recently received from Bro. Olsson, of Denmark, we learn they have been holding meetings at a new point called Stro. A love-feast was held there, and many who attended were solemnly impressed. Two applied for baptism which will be attended to soon. The Brethren are holding meetings at Hore also, and quite an interest is manifested. Bro. Swensen has sold his farm and is now located at Wanneberga. He is quite a help to the church at that place. Their new meeting-house will soon be finished and perhaps by Dec. 15 will be dedicated.

Bro. Enoch Eby, who succeeds in packing very much encouraging news in a small space, has an article on the book for next issue. He has just closed his sixty-fourth year, travels and preaches most of the time, is now booked for work until about the middle of January, thinks he ought to make up for lost time, and is thereby putting to shame hundreds who are "at ease in Zion," both in and out of the laity. Preachers may rest assured that they are not going to turn much of the world upside down while sitting around comfortable fires.

The National Commission for the World's Fair had the good sense to pass the following commendable rule by which the Fair is to be governed: "The Exposition shall be open for the admission of visitors during the six months, commencing May 1 and ending Oct. 30, 1893, on each day of the week—subject to such regulations hereinafter provided for—except the first day thereof, commonly called Sunday, and on said last mentioned day the said Exposition and the gates thereof shall be closed." It is gratifying to the Christian people of this land to know that some public respect is to be paid to the Lord's Day.

In next issue Bro. L. W. Teeter will explain the attitude of the Hymn Book Committee more fully. It seems that the Committee is somewhat misunderstood by some of our readers. In its investigations of its work, and the selection of hymns for the proposed New Hymn Book the Committee met with obstacles not foreseen, and did not wish to assume the responsibility of removing them. Read Bro. Teeter's article carefully next week, have a little patience, a good deal of faith, and at the next Annual Meeting be prepared to give the Committee further instructions if necessary, and in a short time you can have a book that will likely meet the wants of all. Do not be too hasty. Haste sometimes makes waste. It is no small matter to make a good hymn book, and a little delay now may save time and money in the end.

The Gospel Messenger,

A Weekly at $1.50 Per Annum.

PUBLISHED BY

The Brethren's Publishing Co.

D. L. MILLER,	Editor
J. H. MOORE,	Office Editor.
J. B. BRUMBAUGH,	Associate Editors.
J. G. ROYER,	
JOSEPH AMICK,	Business Manager.

ADVISORY COMMITTEE.
L. W. Teeter, A. Hutchison, Daniel Hays.

☞Communications for publication should be legibly written, with black ink on one side of the paper only. Do not attempt to interline, or to put on one page what ought to occupy two.

☞Anonymous communications will not be published.

☞Do not mix business with articles for publication. Keep your communications on separate sheets from all business.

☞Time is precious. We always have time to attend to business and to answer questions of importance, but please do not subject us to need less answering of letters.

☞The MESSENGER is mailed each week to all subscribers. If the address is correctly entered on our list, the paper must reach the person to whom it is addressed. If you do not get your paper, write us, giving particulars.

☞When changing your address, please give your former as well as your future address in full, so as to avoid delay and misunderstanding.

☞Always remit to the office from which you order your goods, no matter from where you receive them.

☞Do not send personal checks or drafts on interior banks, unless you send with them 25 cents each, to pay for collection.

☞Remittances should be made by Post-office Money Order, Drafts on New York, Philadelphia or Chicago, or Registered Letters, made payable and addressed to "Brethren's Publishing Co., Mount Morris, Ill.," or "Brethren's Publishing Co., Huntingdon, Pa."

☞Entered at the Post-office at Mount Morris, Ill., as second-class matter.

Mount Morris, Ill., - - - - **Nov. 29, 1892.**

By confession and baptism nine more were recently added to the church at Germantown, Va.

Bro. J. C. WITMORE, we learn, is at Bellefontaine, Ohio, this week, engaged in a series of meetings.

Bro. T. B. DIGMAN, formerly of Liberty, Adams Co., Ill., may now be addressed at Mountain Lake Park, Md.

Bro. A. I. MOW, of Argos, Ind., has changed his field of labor. He may now be addressed at Palestine, St. Francis Co., Ark.

We understand that since the last Annual Meeting the Brethren's Tract Work has printed over three million pages of tracts.

Bro. JOHN W. ELLER, of Salem, Va., who recently held a two weeks' meeting in the Monitor church, Kans., is now engaged in a protracted effort at McPherson.

The time for the feast at Cerro Gordo, Ill., has been changed from Dec. 8 to Nov. 29. A telegram, announcing the change, was received a little too late for notice in the last issue.

Too late for insertion elsewhere we receive notice that the feast at Pittsburg, Ohio will be held Dec. 3, commencing at 2 P. M. The new house will probably be finished by that time.

At the Mt. Morris Sunday-school last Sunday, a collection was taken up for the purpose of aiding the mission work among the children in Chicago. The amount raised was $13.03.

Can not our agents manage to get the MESSENGER into every family in the Brotherhood? Will not the elders and preachers unite in encouraging all the members to take the paper? By a united effort let us see what can be done. Let our agents call on every family. Then we want the names of all the congregations where the paper goes into every family where there are members.

Bro. DANIEL VANIMAN, who is yet in Southern California, is expected to remain in that State a month or more. He is booked for several sermons during the Special Bible Term at Mt. Morris next January.

On the afternoon of Nov. 17 we had our first taste of genuine winter weather for the season. The wind, snow and cold combined to make it anything but pleasant. It caused a longing for the Sunny South.

The feast at Chicago last Sunday evening is reported to have been a very pleasant gathering. About forty members communed. Two deacons were elected and the outlook for the church is encouraging.

We admire the preachers who want to die with their armor on, but we also like to see them keep up their study of the Word. As long as they are careful students of the Bible they do not need to think of retiring from the desk.

Bro. LEMUEL HILLERY of Indiana, started to Alvin, Texas, last Monday. We have not learned whether he intends to make the Lone Star State his future home, or is arranging to spend only the winter in that mild climate.

About 400 persons recently stood on the bank of the stream in the South Keokuk church, Iowa, and witnessed the baptism of eight persons in twelve minutes. The church at that place seems to be in a flourishing condition just now.

Speaking of bearing one another's burdens, one of our contributors thinks that the laity ought to carry at least the light end of the burden. This they can do by contributing of their abundance in aiding the minister in the arduous task of spreading the Gospel.

Most of our readers are aware that Alexander Campbell died nearly thirty years ago. His widow is still living hale and hearty at the advanced age of ninety. A writer, who recently met her, says from all appearances she may yet reach her one hundredth birthday.

The people in China, in their densely-populated districts, are often exposed to great calamities. Not long since Yellow River overflowed its banks, inundating a large tract of country, drowning about 5,000 people and throwing a million more upon the charity of the government.

Bro. J. G. ROYER returned from New Enterprise, Pa., last week too late for us to say anything concerning his meetings. He reports excellent meetings, large congregations, the best of interest, and seventeen additions with prospects of many more. The meetings were continued by the home ministers.

There seems to be no let up to Bro. Jas. R. Gish's call for more ministers in Arkansas. We would like to see about a score of trusty ministers settle at different points in that State. There are plenty of places in the North where that number can be spared. We also have plenty of material to make more to fill their places here. Those who do respond to Bro. Gish's call should remember that he has very little or no use for men who give an uncertain sound in either their preaching, appearance or conduct. A strong, well-grounded church may possibly endure and counteract the unfavorable influence of a few preachers not wholly in sympathy with the regulations of the General Brotherhood, but to put such men on the mission field would be unwise in the extreme. Here is where our hard battles must be fought, and it is here that we must have trusty men.

Our nation is certainly blessed with an abundance this year. A few days ago ten thousand cars of wheat stood on the side tracks in Chicago because there was no place to unload them, all the elevators in the cities being full. The same was also true of the elevators in other large cities. A country with such a supply of food surely ought not to complain.

One of our brethren, in an article intended for the MESSENGER, suggests that we ought to have but one mode of feet-washing as we have but one mode of baptism. It is coming to that just as fast as the sentiment can be quietly moulded in favor of the present prevailing mode. Just have a little patience and it will all come around right by and by. The most commendable way has a good start; it commends itself to all who see it rightly observed, and in the course of a few years we will have but one mode.

In a letter, recently received from Bro. Olsson, of Denmark, we learn they have been holding meetings at a new point called Siro. A love-feast was held there, and many who attended were solemnly impressed. Two applied for baptism which will be attended to soon. The Brethren are bold-ing meetings at Hore also, and quite an interest is manifested. Bro. Swensen has sold his farm and is now located at Wanneberga. He is quite a help to the church at that place. Their new meeting-house will soon be finished and perhaps by Dec. 15 will be dedicated.

Bro. ENOCH EBY, who succeeds in packing very much encouraging news in a small space, has an article on the hook for next issue. He has just closed his sixty-fourth year, travels and preaches most of the time, is now booked for work until about the middle of January, thinks he ought to have twenty years more to work for the Lord to make up for lost time, and is thereby putting to shame hundreds who are "at ease in Zion," both in and out of the laity. Preachers may rest assured that they are not going to turn much of the world upside down while sitting around comfortable fires.

The National Commission for the World's Fair had the good sense to pass the following commendable rule by which the Fair is to be governed: "The Exposition shall be open for the admission of visitors during the six months, commencing May 1 and ending Oct. 30, 1893, on each day of the week—subject to such regulations hereinafter provided for—except the first day thereof, commonly called Sunday, and on said last mentioned day the said Exposition and the gates thereof shall be closed." It is gratifying to the Christian people of this land to know that some public respect is to be paid to the Lord's Day.

In next issue Bro. L. W. Teeter will explain the attitude of the Hymn Book Committee more fully. It seems that the Committee is somewhat misunderstood by some of our readers. In its investigations of its work, and the selection of hymns for the proposed New Hymn Book the Committee met with obstacles not foreseen, and did not wish to assume the responsibility of removing them. Read Bro. Teeter's article carefully next week, have a little patience, a good deal of faith, and at the next Annual Meeting be prepared to give the Committee further instructions if necessary, and in a short time you can have a book that will likely meet the wants of all. Do not be too hasty. Haste sometimes makes waste. It is no small matter to make a good hymn book, and a little delay now may save time and money in the end.

ancient City of Tyre. At that time, Tyre was the great metropolis of the Levant,—the great commercial city of the East. Her sails whitened every port on the Mediterranean Sea, and her merchant princes grew rich in their trade with all parts of the known world. If you would know of the greatness of the city and of her wealth, read Ezek. 27.

When the city was at the height of its prosperity, these words were spoken against her: "Thus," saith the Lord God; "Behold, I am against thee, O Tyrus, and will cause many nations to come up against thee, as the sea causeth his waves to come up. And they shall destroy the walls of Tyrus, and break down her towers; I will also scrape her dust from her, and make her like the top of a rock. And I will make thee like the top of a rock; thou shalt be a place to spread nets upon; thou shalt be built no more, for I, the Lord, have spoken it, saith the Lord God." Ezek. 26.

It requires a revolution to destroy a great city,—the center of the commerce of nations. In 1884, New York City was destroyed by fire, but it was speedily rebuilt and became greater and larger than ever. In 1871, Chicago was burned with a great conflagration; but she rose, Phœnix-like, from her ashes, and to-day has a population of a million and a half of souls. These cities were the centers of trade and commerce, and it is difficult to blot out a city of this kind.

No doubt the merchants of Tyre thought the same of their great city, and scorned the words of the prophet. But the prophecy has been literally fulfilled. The city was destroyed and never rebuilt. More than two thousand years have passed away since Alexander the Great, conquered and destroyed the City of Tyre, and in doing so, scraped the earth from the old site of the city, and made it like the top of a rock. Thus the great conqueror fulfilled the words of the prophets. The City has never been rebuilt. Volney, in his "Ruined Cities," says: "The whole village of Tyre contains only fifty or sixty poor families who live obscurely on the produce of their little ground and a *trifling fishery*." Bruce describes Tyre as a "rock whereon fishers dry their nets." To-day Tyre is a considerable village; fishing is one of the occupations of the inhabitants, and as you walk along the shore of the sea you may see the fisherman spread their nets on the rocks to dry. How literally have the words of the prophet been fulfilled! What abundant evidence of the inspiration of the Book of God!

THE FALL OF BABYLON.

Babylon under the reign of Nebuchadnezzar was the metropolis of the world. The history of this great city is marvelous, and the fulfillment of prophecy, connected with its destruction, gives abundant evidence of the inspiration of the Bible. Two hundred and fifty years before the city fell, the prophet Isaiah said,—"Thus, saith the Lord to his anointed, to Cyrus, whose right hand I have holden, to subdue nations before him; and I will loose the loins of kings, to open before him the two-leaved gates; and the gates shall not be shut." Ancient history records the literal fulfillment of this prophecy; for notwithstanding the great walls of the city guarded them on all sides like mountains, yet the two-leaved gates were opened, Cyrus entered the city and the great Babylonian Empire vanished like "snow in the glance of the Lord."

The remarkable fulfillment of prophecy, in which the prophet named the general who is to accomplish the work of destruction, is without parallel in the divine record. Isaiah lived two hundred and fifty years before Herodotus, and it is not likely that the historians knew of the prophecies of the Hebrew Seer, but he confirms them in a most remarkable manner. Prophecy is history foretold; history is prophecy fulfilled.

But Babylon was the subject of many prophecies. Isaiah said: "And Babylon, the glory of kingdoms, the beauty of the Chaldeans' excellency, shall be as when God overthrew Sodom and Gomorrah. It shall never be inhabited, neither shall it be dwelt in from generation to generation, neither shall the Arabian pitch his tent there. But wild beasts of the desert shall lie there; and their houses shall be full of doleful creatures; and owls shall dwell there, and satyrs shall dance there. And the wild beasts of the islands shall cry in their desolate houses, and dragons in their pleasant palaces."

This indeed was a bold prophecy, but it has been fulfilled to the letter. To say that a great city like Babylon should never be inhabited, doubtless seemed like a silly tale to its people, but to-day the prophecy is history, and even the "Arabian does not pitch his tent there." The wandering Arab, on the plains of Arabia, or in the valleys of Syria spreads his tent where night overtakes him and lies down under its folds in safety; but when he nears Babylon, he times his journey to reach a Khan at the close of the day.

The shepherd, no less fearful than the Arab, leads his flock through the marshes to feed through the day, but returns to the fortified Khan ere sunset, thus confirming the prophetic words of Isaiah, "Neither shall shepherds make their folds there." In the fulfillment of the prophet's words, the ruins of Babylon have become a menagerie of wild beasts. Rauwolf, a German traveler, who visited the ruined city in the sixteenth century, says of the temple of Belus: "This tower is full of venomous animals that can only be approached during the winter months when they do not leave their holes." A Carmelite monk passed the ruins in 1657 and "heard the roaring of the lions, which from time to time answered one another from the opposite shores of the river to our no small terror." In December, 1881, Mr. Rich, English Consul at Bagdad, made excavations among the ruins of Belshazzar's palace and says: "There are many dens of wild beasts in various parts, in one of which I found the bones of sheep and other wild animals, and perceived a strong smell, like that of a lion. I also found quantities of porcupine quills; and in most of the cavities are numbers of owls and bats."

Layard in his notes, says: "In this section of country are to be found leopards, lynxes, wild cats, wolves, hyenas, jackals, deer, porcupine and other animals in vast numbers." Dr. Newman who visited Babylon in 1876, says: "A large lion was in the habit of coming from the Euphrates to a canal which I crossed on my way to Babylon, till he was shot by one of the Arabs. Captain Cowley, of the steamer on which I came up the Tigris, shot three lions, which had their lair on an island nearly opposite the ruined city."

Surely the words of Israel's greatest Seer have been fulfilled to the very letter, "But the wild beasts shall lie there."

We might continue these evidences, for the fulfillment of the prophecies concerning Egypt, Nineveh, Damascus, Jerusalem and other countries and cities is just as remarkable as are those to which we have referred, but to do so would be to write a volume. We rest our faith not on cunningly-devised fables, but upon a book proven by incontestable evidence to be the inspired Word of God. Christ himself appeals to the test of prophecy when he says: "And now I have told you before it came to pass, that when it is come to pass ye might believe." John 14: 29. And now, in the light of the fulfillment of not one but hundreds of prophecies, we believe.

OTHER EVIDENCES.

The remaining list of evidences, many in number and all strong in their character, each filling an important place in the completed proofs of the authenticity, the credibility and the inspiration of the Bible, can only be glanced at here.

The miracles performed by the founder of the Christian religion and his immediate followers, the remarkable rapidity with which Christianity spread over the world, meeting successfully the most formidable foes, the faith and devotion of the apostles and disciples of Christ, who submitted to the most cruel torture and suffered martyrdom rather than deny him in whom they believed, and the benefits growing out of the religion of Jesus Christ wherever it was properly developed, and its teachings fully observed, go to make up, with what has been given in the preceding pages, a mass of eternal evidence that defies successful contradiction.

Added to this are the internal proofs of the truth of the Book of God. Among them are the doctrines of the Gospel. For more than 1,800 years the teachings of Christ have been subjected to the closest scrutiny and the criticism of friend and foe, and the universal testimony is that for its pure, elevated morality, its adaptation to the wants of humanity, its grand benevolence, its uprightness, its most excellent teachings the Gospel stands before the world in its own light unequaled and unapproachable by the writings of men. There, above all, stands the holy and elevated character of the Founder of our faith. His pure life of self-sacrifice, his love for humanity, his gentleness, and with it his strength of character, his wonderful wisdom, all mark him in the most perfect sense as the "realized ideal of humanity."

Well might Rousseau say of him and his teachings,—"How petty are the books of the philosophers, with all their pomp, compared with the Gospel! Can it be that writings at once so sublime and so simple are the work of men? Is there anything in his character of enthusiast or ambitious sectary? What sweetness, what purity in his ways, what touching grace in his teachings! What loftiness in his maxims, what profound wisdom in his words! What presence of mind, what delicacy and aptness in his replies! What an empire over his passions! Where is the man, where is the sage, who knows how to act, to suffer and to die without weakness and without display? My friend, men do not invent like this; and the facts respecting Socrates, which no one doubts, are not so well attested as those about Jesus Christ. These Jews could never have struck this tone, or thought of this morality, and the Gospel has characteristics of truthfulness so grand, so striking, so perfectly inim-

ancient City of Tyre. At that time, Tyre was the great metropolis of the Levant,—the great commercial city of the East. Her sails whitened every port on the Mediterranean Sea, and her merchant princes grew rich in their trade with all parts of the known world. If you would know of the greatness of the city and of her wealth, read Ezek. 27.

When the city was at the height of its prosperity, these words were spoken against her: "Thus," saith the Lord God; "Behold, I am against thee, O Tyrus, and will cause many nations to come up against thee, as the sea causeth his waves to come up. And they shall destroy the walls of Tyrus, and break down her towers; I will also scrape her dust from her, and make her like the top of a rock. And I will make thee like the top of a rock; thou shalt be a place to spread nets upon; thou shalt be built no more, for I, the Lord, have spoken it, saith the Lord God." Ezek. 26.

It requires a revolution to destroy a great city,—the center of the commerce of nations. In 1884, New York City was destroyed by fire, but it was speedily rebuilt and became greater and larger than ever. In 1871, Chicago was burned with a great conflagration; but she rose, Phœnix-like, from her ashes, and to-day has a population of a million and a half of souls. These cities were the centers of trade and commerce, and it is difficult to blot out a city of this kind.

No doubt the merchants of Tyre thought the same of their great city, and scorned the words of the prophet. But the prophecy has been literally fulfilled. The city was destroyed and never rebuilt. More than two thousand years have passed away since Alexander the Great, conquered and destroyed the City of Tyre, and in doing so, scraped the earth from the old site of the city, and made it like the top of a rock. Thus the great conqueror fulfilled the words of the prophets. The City has never been rebuilt. Volney, in his "Ruined Cities," says: "The whole village of Tyre contains only fifty or sixty poor families who live obscurely on the produce of their little ground and a *trifling fishery*." Bruce describes Tyre as a "rock whereon fishers dry their nets." To-day Tyre is a considerable village; fishing is one of the occupations of the inhabitants, and as you walk along the shore of the sea you may see the fisherman spread their nets on the rocks to dry. How literally have the words of the prophet been fulfilled! What abundant evidence of the inspiration of the Book of God!

THE FALL OF BABYLON.

Babylon under the reign of Nebuchadnezzar was the metropolis of the world. The history of this great city is marvelous, and the fulfillment of prophecy, connected with its destruction, gives abundant evidence of the inspiration of the Bible. Two hundred and fifty years before the city fell, the prophet Isaiah said,—"Thus, saith the Lord to his anointed, to Cyrus, whose right hand I have holden, to subdue nations before him; and I will loose the loins of kings, to open before him the two-leaved gates; and the gates shall not be shut." Ancient history records the literal fulfillment of this prophecy; for notwithstanding the great walls of the city guarded them on all sides like mountains, yet the two leaved gates were opened, Cyrus entered the city and the great Babylonian Empire vanished like "snow in the glance of the Lord."

The remarkable fulfillment of prophecy, in which the prophet named the general who is to accomplish the work of destruction, is without parallel in the divine record. Isaiah lived two hundred and fifty years before Herodotus, and it is not likely that the historians knew of the prophecies of the Hebrew Seer, but he confirms them in a most remarkable manner. Prophecy is history foretold; history is prophecy fulfilled.

But Babylon was the subject of many prophecies. Isaiah said: "And Babylon, the glory of kingdoms, the beauty of the Chaldeans' excellency, shall be as when God overthrew Sodom and Gomorrah. It shall never be inhabited, neither shall it be dwelt in from generation to generation, neither shall the Arabian pitch his tent there. But wild beasts of the desert shall lie there; and their houses shall be full of doleful creatures; and owls shall dwell there, and satyrs shall dance there. And the wild beasts of the islands shall cry in their desolate houses, and dragons in their pleasant palaces."

This indeed was a bold prophecy, but it has been fulfilled to the letter. To say that a great city like Babylon should never be inhabited, doubtless seemed like a silly tale to its people, but to-day the prophecy is history, and even the "Arabian does not pitch his tent there." The wandering Arab, on the plains of Arabia, or in the valleys of Syria spreads his tent where night overtakes him and lies down under its folds in safety; but when he nears Babylon, he times his journey to reach a Khan at the close of the day.

The shepherd, no less fearful than the Arab, leads his flock through the marshes to feed through the day, but returns to the fortified Khan ere sunset, thus confirming the prophetic words of Isaiah, "Neither shall shepherds make their folds there." In the fulfillment of the prophet's words, the ruins of Babylon have become a menagerie of wild beasts. Rauwolf, a German traveler, who visited the ruined city in the sixteenth century, says of the temple of Belus: "This tower is full of venomous animals that can only be approached during the winter months when they do not leave their holes." A Carmelite monk passed the ruins in 1657 and "heard the roaring of the lions, which from time to time answered one another from the opposite shores of the river to our no small terror." In December, 1881, Mr. Rich, English Consul at Bagdad, made excavations among the ruins of Belshazzar's palace and says: "There are many dens of wild beasts in various parts, in one of which I found the bones of sheep and other wild animals, and perceived a strong smell, like that of a lion. I also found quantities of porcupine quills; and in most of the cavities are numbers of owls and bats."

Layard in his notes, says: "In this section of country are to be found leopards, lynxes, wild cats, wolves, hyenas, jackals, deer, porcupine and other animals in vast numbers." Dr. Newman who visited Babylon in 1876, says: "A large lion was in the habit of coming from the Euphrates to a canal which I crossed on my way to Babylon, till he was shot by one of the Arabs. Captain Cowley, of the steamer on which I came up the Tigris, shot three lions, which had their lair on an island nearly opposite the ruined city."

Surely the words of Israel's greatest Seer have been fulfilled to the very letter, "But the wild beasts shall lie there."

We might continue these evidences, for the fulfillment of the prophecies concerning Egypt, Nineveh, Damascus, Jerusalem and other countries and cities is just as remarkable as are those to which we have referred, but to do so would be to write a volume. We rest our faith not on cunningly-devised fables, but upon a book proven by incontestable evidence to be the inspired Word of God. Christ himself appeals to the test of prophecy when he says: "And now I have told you before it came to pass, that when it is come to pass ye might believe." John 14: 29. And now, in the light of the fulfillment of not one but hundreds of prophecies, we believe.

OTHER EVIDENCES.

The remaining list of evidences, many in number and all strong in their character, each filling an important place in the completed proofs of the authenticity, the credibility and the inspiration of the Bible, can only be glanced at here.

The miracles performed by the founder of the Christian religion and his immediate followers, the remarkable rapidity with which Christianity spread over the world, meeting successfully the most formidable foes, the faith and devotion of the apostles and disciples of Christ, who submitted to the most cruel torture and suffered martyrdom rather than deny him in whom they believed, and the benefits growing out of the religion of Jesus Christ wherever it was properly developed, and its teachings fully observed, go to make up, with what has been given in the preceding pages, a mass of eternal evidence that defies successful contradiction.

Added to this are the internal proofs of the truth of the Book of God. Among them are the doctrines of the Gospel. For more than 1,800 years the teachings of Christ have been subjected to the closest scrutiny and the criticism of friend and foe, and the universal testimony is that for its pure, elevated morality, its adaptation to the wants of humanity, its grand benevolence, its uprightness, its most excellent teachings the Gospel stands before the world in its own light unequaled and unapproachable by the writings of men. There, above all, stands the holy and elevated character of the Founder of our faith. His pure life of self-sacrifice, his love for humanity, his gentleness, and with it his strength of character, his wonderful wisdom, all mark him in the most perfect sense as the "realized ideal of humanity."

Well might Rousseau say of him and his teachings,—"How petty are the books of the philosophers, with all their pomp, compared with the Gospel! Can it be that writings at once so sublime and so simple are the work of men? Is there anything in his character of enthusiast or ambitious sectary? What sweetness, what purity in his ways, what touching grace in his teachings! What loftiness in his maxims, what profound wisdom in his words! What presence of mind, what delicacy and aptness in his replies! What an empire over his passions! Where is the man, where is the sage, who knows how to act, to suffer and to die without weakness and without display? My friend, men do not invent like this; and the facts respecting Socrates, which no one doubts, are not so well attested as those about Jesus Christ. These Jews could never have struck this tone, or thought of this morality, and the Gospel has characteristics of truthfulness so grand, so striking, so perfectly inim-

and, like Paul, "counted all things loss that he might gain Christ." He was not strong in body for some years, and after about six weeks' illness, during which he was patient and full of hope, he passed peacefully to his reward. It was our pleasure to assist the church under his care in several series of meetings, and shall ever be thankful that I could associate with one from whom I could learn so many lessons of meekness and true Christian piety. These were his greatest sermons, and they will live forever in the memory of all who came in contact with his devoted life.

He was always ready to lend a helping hand to the poor, and was a special friend of mission work in the church. He did not have a large estate, but left by will a portion to missionary work, teaching others by example to use the Lord's money for his cause.

The greater part of ministerial labor falls on his son, Bro. John Kahler, who is in the second degree of the ministry, as the other brethren in the ministry are engaged in home duties that interfere very much with the callings of a minister. We pray they may all do the best they can to carry forward to victory the work that Father Kahler has left resting upon them. Many ministers of North-eastern Ohio were present at the funeral services, conducted by the writer and Bro. Noah Longanecker, from the words, "At evening time it shall be light." Zech. 14: 7.

I. D. PARKER.

From the Cedar Lake Church, Ind.

OCT. 3 we had a pleasant love-feast in the Cedar Lake church, De Kalb Co., Ind. The attendance was not so large as on some former occasions. We had a good, quiet meeting. God's Holy Spirit seemed to pervade every heart. There were many good things said to encourage God's dear children. Bro. I. L. Berkey held a few meetings previous to the feast. He is a workman that need not be ashamed. Bro. H. H. Brallier officiated. Our meeting closed at 7:80. It is, we think, useless to protract a meeting until 9 and 10 o'clock. Short Communion services give the best result. May God's blessings rest on the faithful every-where. J. H. ELSON.

Fairfield Center, Ind., Nov. 8.

Notes from Our Correspondents.

"As cold water to a thirsty soul, so is good news from a far country."

McPherson, Kans.—Another of the students was received by baptism yesterday. Our Fall Term of school closes Nov. 21. We have been greatly blessed this year. To the Lord be all the praise.—S. Z. Sharp, Nov. 15

Red Bank Church, Pa.—We held our love-feast Oct. 15. Oct. 11 Bro. John C. Johnson came to our church and preached some good sermons. He remained with us till Oct. 16. One young sister was baptized. We had a enjoyable feast. We also remembered our home mission with over seven dollars.—J. A. Hetrick, Oakland, Pa.

Hctune, Kans.—The Cherokee church met in quarterly council Nov. 12. Not much business came before the meeting, but such as did, was disposed of in a kindly and satisfactory manner. Sister Clara Houseworth was appointed agent for the MESSENGER, and as correspondent for the church for one year. Bro. John Slifer was chosen as solicitor of funds for missionary and tract purposes. This church is in good working order. The members are in peace and love with one another.—L. Wolfe, Nov. 13.

Bourbon, Ind.—I wish to make a correction in my article, "Working for the Master," which appeared on page 676 of MESSENGER. I meant to say 7 A. M., instead of 3 A. M. In the same article it should read "after the feast" instead of "before the feast."—John Sellers, Nov. 7.

Germantown, Va.—Since my last report we have had nine more accessions by baptism and one more applicant. This makes twenty-one additions within the last five months, ranging in age from eleven to seventy years. The cause that we love seems to be tending upwards throughout our County.—Wm. Roberson, Nov. 13.

La Place, Ill.—Last Sunday the members of the Okaw church were made glad to receive a dear young sister into the church by baptism. Truly, she has forsaken all, as all the rest of her family are of another faith. We are attending meetings in the Cerro Gordo church at present, conducted by Bro. I. J. Rosenberger. Glorious meetings they are; it is good to be there.—E. F. Wolfe, Nov. 15.

Roaring Spring, Pa.—Oct. 23 we opened a series of meetings, which closed Oct. 30 with a love-feast. One of our home elders, Bro. G. W. Brumbaugh, did the preaching. He held forth the Word with power. During these meetings there were three received by letter, two reclaimed and one bapt'zed. Bro. J. B. Replogle officiated at our Communion which was largely attended.—J. R. Slayer, Oct. 31.

Kinzie, Ind.—We have closed a very interesting series of meetings in the Spring Creek church. It began Oct. 23 and, conducted by the home ministers, continued for two weeks. Bro. Daniel Snell did the preaching. He held forth the Word with power, to attentive congregations. One young sister came out on the Lord's side and was baptized. One sister united with the church in September. We are glad to see people come flocking home to Christ.—R. Ross.

Osawkie, Kans.—Will we not make a united effort to have the MESSENGER read in every household of our Brotherhood the coming year? Should we succeed, we bespeak for us a spiritual growth, which we so much need and must have, but to get it we must go to work in earnest. No one can read such a church paper without deriving much good from it. God bless our editors with much wisdom in their arduous labor. We are glad to report one more accession by baptism last Sunday after preaching.—J. A. Root, Nov. 17.

Beaver Dam, Ind.—Nov. 11 we held a special council. Brethren George Beigh and D. E. Cripe were elected to the office of deacon. May the Lord be with them and help them in the discharge of their official duty! Ministers from adjoining churches were present and gave us much wholesome council. May the Lord bless the work done, is our prayer! We are now holding a few meetings at the Brick church. One dear soul was baptized last Sunday. May he be the means of bringing others to the light of the Gospel!—S. E. Burket.

Pleasant Grove, Kans.—Bro. I. Crist, of Johnson County, Kans., commenced a series of meetings Oct. 15 and continued until the 24th. On the evening of the 22nd was our love-feast, which was a pleasant one. Next morning, at 10 o'clock, we had a children's meeting, and preaching afterward. At the close an invitation was given, and seventeen souls arose and came forward. Fifteen were baptized that evening. On Monday night one more came out, but was not baptized until the next Sunday. On that day one more came forward, making, in all, nineteen. Two were baptized in Johnson County, Kans.—J. W. Baker, Clerk.

Crawford, Nebr.—Bro. Jesse Y. Heckler came to us Nov. 4. We had a very interesting meeting that evening, and the evening following. The weather on Sunday being very unpleasant we had a very small congregation. Bro. Heckler presented the Truth in a powerful as well as attractive way.—J. G. Dove, Nov. 12.

Bear Creek Church, Ohio.—Our love-feast occurred Nov. 10. It was a pleasant one and seemed to be greatly enjoyed by all present. We were glad to see so many present from surrounding churches. We had a good ministerial force. Bro. Jacob Garber officiated. Most excellent order prevailed.—Josiah Eby, Nov. 13.

Pleasant Valley, Ind.—The members of the above church met in quarterly council Nov. 5. Love prevailed among all. We decided to hold a Communion Nov. 16. The weather being pleasant, we had a very good attendance. Bro. Hillery and wife were with us recently, visiting with sister Hillery's father, David Nihart, before going south for Bro. Hillery's health. Our dear brother preached seven sermons for us previous to our Communion services. We were much built up by his good instructions. — Levi E. Weaver, Nov. 17.

Midland, Va.—Oct. 29 Bro. Jacob Sandy, from Ohio, came to this place to hold a series of meetings, and continued until Nov. 8. During this time he gave us some soul-cheering sermons. He is a good worker, and not ashamed to declare the counsel of God. One precious soul was reclaimed, nine were received by baptism and many, more are seriously considering their case. Seven of the above are young. May God help them to live faithful! On the 5th was our Communion, which passed off pleasantly.—F. N. Weimer, Nov. 3.

Nora Springs, Iowa.—The meetings at Greece, Iowa, are now over. We closed with two applicants for baptism. Others are seriously counting the cost. Here, at the love-feast at Greene, there were two elected to the office of deacon. Bro. Shank was advanced to the second degree of the ministry. Bro. Harvey Eikenberry was ordained to the full ministry. Our prayer is that they may hold out faithful. I will remain here one week; then go to the Iowa River church. Soon after that I will bid adieu to Iowa and all those with whom I have formed acquaintance.—Jos. Holder, Nov. 15.

Locust Grove Church, Md.—Our love-feast, Oct. 15, was a very pleasant one. The attendance was very large, but the behavior not very commendable. Bro. Pfoutz officiated. We closed our Sunday-school Nov. 12. Bro. S. H. Utz and several sisters addressed the school. We were made glad by the presence of one of our former associates and Sunday-school scholars (Mollie Trostle, of Hope, Kans.), who spoke very impressively to the scholars. Several of the scholars memorized ten thousand verses, for which they were rewarded with Bibles, Testaments, etc.—M. E. Ecker, Linganore, Md., Nov. 16.

Union, Iowa.—Since our last report we had the pleasure of adding again one dear sister to the Salem church. We did the baptizing in the Stillwater River. Her husband put off coming for a "more convenient season." We hope he may soon soon see that "procrastination is the thief of time." We purpose commencing a series of meetings Nov. 19. Bro. Daniel Snell, of Indiana, will do the preaching. We appointed a Thanksgiving meeting for Nov. 24, as directed by the Chief Magistrate. We hope to report in our next the result of a good meeting in our church. Brethren, pray for us!—Jesse K. Brumbaugh, Nov. 15.

and, like Paul, "counted all things loss that he might gain Christ." He was not strong in body for some years, and after about six weeks' illness, during which he was patient and full of hope, he passed peacefully to his reward. It was our pleasure to assist the church under his care in several series of meetings, and shall ever be thankful that I could associate with one from whom I could learn so many lessons of meekness and true Christian piety. These were his greatest sermons, and they will live forever in the memory of all who came in contact with his devoted life.

He was always ready to lend a helping hand to the poor, and was a special friend of mission work in the church. He did not have a large estate, but left by will a portion to missionary work, teaching others by example to use the Lord's money for his cause.

The greater part of ministerial labor falls on his son, Bro. John Kahler, who is in the second degree of the ministry, as the other brethren in the ministry are engaged in home duties that interfere very much with the callings of a minister. We pray they may all do the best they can to carry forward to victory the work that Father Kahler has left resting upon them. Many ministers of North-eastern Ohio were present at the funeral services, conducted by the writer and Bro. Noah Longanecker, from the words, "At evening time it shall be light." Zech. 14: 7.

L. D. PARKER.

From the Cedar Lake Church, Ind.

Oct. 3 we had a pleasant love-feast in the Cedar Lake church, De Kalb Co., Ind. The attendance was not so large as on some former occasions. We had a good, quiet meeting. God's Holy Spirit seemed to pervade every heart. There were many good things said to encourage God's dear children. Bro. L. L. Berkey held a few meetings previous to the feast. He is a workman that need not be ashamed. Bro. H. H. Brallier officiated. Our meeting closed at 7:30. It is, we think, useless to protract a meeting until 9 and 10 o'clock. Short Communion services give the best result. May God's blessings rest on the faithful every-where. J. H. ELSON.

Fairfield Center, Ind., Nov 8.

Notes from Our Correspondents.

"As cold water to a thirsty soul, so is good news from a far country."

McPherson, Kans.—Another of the students was received by baptism yesterday. Our Fall Term of school closes Nov. 21. We have been greatly blessed this year. To the Lord be all the praise.—S. Z. Sharp, Nov. 15

Red Bank Church, Pa.—We held our love-feast Oct. 15. Oct. 11 Bro. John O. Johnson came to our church and preached some good sermons. He remained with us till Oct. 16. One young sister was baptized. We had a very enjoyable feast. We also remembered our home mission with over seven dollars.—J. A. Helrick, Oakland, Pa.

McCune, Kans.—The Cherokee church met in quarterly council Nov. 12. Not much business came before the meeting, but such as did, was disposed of in a kindly and satisfactory manner. Sister Clara Houseworth was appointed agent for the MESSENGER, and the writer as correspondent for the church for one year. Bro. John Slifer was chosen as solicitor of funds for missionary and tract purposes. This church is in good working order. The members are in peace and love with one another.—L. Wolfe, Nov. 13.

Bourbon, Ind.—I wish to make a correction in my article, "Working for the Master," which appeared on page 676 of MESSENGER. I meant to say 7 A. M., instead of 3 A. M. In the same article it should read "after the feast" instead of "before the feast."—John Sellers, Nov. 7.

Germantown, Va.—Since my last report we have had nine more accessions by baptism and one more applicant. This makes twenty-one additions within the last five months, ranging in age from eleven to seventy years. The cause that we love seems to be tending upwards throughout our County.—Wm. Roberson, Nov. 13.

La Place, Ill.—Last Sunday the members of the Okaw church were made glad to receive a dear young sister into the church by baptism. Truly, she has forsaken all, as all the rest of her family are of another faith. We are attending meetings in the Cerro Gordo church at present, conducted by Bro. I. J. Rosenberger. Glorious meetings they are; it is good to be there.—E. F. Wolfe, Nov. 15.

Roaring Spring, Pa.—Oct. 23 we opened a series of meetings, which closed Oct. 30 with a love-feast. One of our home elders, Bro. G. W. Brumbaugh, did the preaching. He held forth the Word with power. During these meetings there were three received by letter, two reclaimed and one bapt'zed. Bro. J. B. Replogle officiated at our Communion which was largely attended.—J. R. Slayer, Oct. 31.

Kinzie, Ind.—We have closed a very interesting series of meetings in the Spring Creek church. It began Oct. 23 and, conducted by the home ministers, continued for two weeks. Bro. Daniel Snell did the preaching. He held forth the Word with power, to attentive congregations. One young sister came out on the Lord's side and was baptized. One sister united with the church in September. We are glad to see people come flocking home to Christ.—R. Ross.

Ozawkie, Kans.—Will we not make a united effort to have the MESSENGER read in every household of our Brotherhood the coming year? Should we succeed, we bespeak for us a spiritual growth, which we so much need and must have, but to get it we must go to work in earnest. No one can read such a church paper without deriving much good from it. God bless our editors with much wisdom in their arduous labor. We are glad to report one more accession by baptism last Sunday after preaching.—J. A. Root, Nov. 17.

Beaver Dam, Ind.—Nov. 11 we held a special council. Brethren George Beigh and D. E. Cripe were elected to the office of deacon. May the Lord be with them and help them in the discharge of their official duty! Ministers from adjoining churches were present and gave us much wholesome council. May the Lord bless the work done, is our prayer! We are now holding a few meetings at the Brick church. One dear soul was baptized last Sunday. May he be the means of bringing others to the light of the Gospel!—S. E. Burket.

Pleasant Grove, Kans.—Bro. I. Crist, of Johnson County, Kans., commenced a series of meetings Oct. 15 and continued until the 24th. On the evening of the 22nd was our love-feast, which was a pleasant one. Next morning, at 10 o'clock, we had a children's meeting, and preaching afterward. At the close an invitation was given, and seventeen souls arose and came forward. Fifteen were baptized that evening. On Monday night one more came out, but was not baptized until the next Sunday. On that day one more came forward, making, in all, nineteen. Two were baptized in Johnson County, Kans.—J. W. Baker, Clark.

Crawford, Nebr.—Bro. Jesse Y. Heckler came to us Nov. 4. We had a very interesting meeting that evening, and the evening following. The weather on Sunday being very unpleasant we had a very small congregation. Bro. Heckler presented the Truth in a powerful as well as attractive way.—J. G. Dove, Nov. 12.

Bear Creek Church, Ohio.—Our love-feast occurred Nov. 10. It was a pleasant one and seemed to be greatly enjoyed by all present. We were glad to see so many present from surrounding churches. We had a good ministerial force. Bro. Jacob Garber officiated. Most excellent order prevailed.—Josiah Eby, Nov. 13.

Pleasant Valley, Ind.—The members of the above church met in quarterly council Nov. 5. Love prevailed among all. We decided to hold a Communion Nov. 16. The weather being pleasant, we had a very good attendance. Bro. Hillery and wife were with us recently, visiting with sister Hillery's father, David Nihart, before going south for Bro. Hillery's health. Our dear brother preached seven sermons for us previous to our Communion services. We were much built up by his good instructions. — Levi E. Weaver, Nov. 17.

Midland, Va.—Oct. 29 Bro. Jacob Sandy, from Ohio, came to this place to hold a series of meetings, and continued until Nov. 8. During this time he gave us some soul-cheering sermons. He is a good worker, and not ashamed to declare the counsel of God. One precious soul was reclaimed, nine were received by baptism and many, more are seriously considering their case. Seven of the above are young. May God help them to live faithful! On the 5th was our Communion, which passed off pleasantly.—F. N. Weimer, Nov. 9.

Nora Springs, Iowa.—The meetings at Greene, Iowa, are now over. We closed with two applicants for baptism. Others are seriously counting the cost. Here, at the love-feast at Greene, there were two elected to the office of deacon. Bro. Shank was advanced to the second degree of the ministry. Bro. Harvey Eikenberry was ordained to the full ministry. Our prayer is that they may hold out faithful. I will remain here one week; then go to the Iowa River church. Soon after that I will bid adieu to Iowa and all those with whom. I have formed acquaintance.—Jos. Holder, Nov. 15.

Locust Grove Church, Md.—Our love-feast, Oct. 15, was a very pleasant one. The attendance was very large, but the behavior not very commendable. Bro. Pfoutz officiated. We closed our Sunday-school Nov. 12. Bro. S. H. Utz and several sisters addressed the school. We were made glad by the presence of one of our former associates and Sunday-school scholars (Mollie Trostle, of Hope, Kans.), who spoke very impressively to the scholars. Several of the scholars memorized ten thousand verses, for which they were rewarded with Bibles, Testaments, etc.—M. E. Ecker, Linganore, Md., Nov. 16.

Union, Iowa.—Since our last report we had the pleasure of adding again one dear sister to the Salem church. We did the baptizing in the Stillwater River. Her husband put off coming for a "more convenient season." We hope he may soon soon see that "procrastination is the thief of time." We purpose commencing a series of meetings Nov. 19. Bro. Daniel Snell, of Indiana, will do the preaching. We appointed a Thanksgiving meeting for Nov. 24, as directed by the Chief Magistrate. We hope to report in our next the result of a good meeting in our church. Brethren, pray for us!—Jesse K. Brumbaugh, Nov. 15.

Grundy Centre, Iowa.—Our Sunday-school still continues and is large and interesting. We just closed a good meeting by Joseph Holder, of Indiana. Five united with the church.—*Ada M. Hoffa, Nov. 1.*

North Manchester, Ind.—At our regular meeting on Sunday, Nov. 6, one dear sister was received into church fellowship by confession and baptism. May God bless her and help her to hold out faithful!—*D. C. Cripe.*

Monticello Church, Ind.—Our feast, held Nov. 5, was an enjoyable one. The attendance was large and the best of order prevailed throughout. Bro. Noah Crumrine, of Wabash, Ind., officiated. Next day the ministers present encouraged the members in their Christian work. At the close of the services one young girl came out on the Lord's side. May the Lord, through his Spirit and Word, help her to hold out faithful!—*J. A. Weaver, Nov. 7.*

Cerro Gordo, Ill.—Yesterday, at our Sunday-school, a collection was taken to assist sister Alice Boone in her work of teaching the poor little boys and girls of Chicago. The collection amounted to $16 30. Surely she has undertaken a noble work and while she has the prayers of all interested in the mission work, we think help should be given in a financial way, in order to make it a success. Bro. I. J. Rosenberger will begin a series of meetings for us Nov. 10.—*Wm. Landis, Nov. 7.*

Greene, Iowa.—I have now been here one week. We had a soul-refreshing season Nov. 5 at their love-feast. At this feast one made the good choice, and others are deeply impressed. I will remain here till Nov. 15. Then I go to Nora Springs, Iowa, by the request of the Mission Board of Northern Iowa, and will remain there until the 24th, after which I will turn my face homeward. My prayer is that we may have good meetings while here. From here I go to Ohio, if the Lord will.—*Joseph Holder, Nov 8.*

Red Oak Ridge, W. Va.—Our Communion was held Oct. 8. Bro. George Grabill and Bro. George Hutchison were our ministers. About forty-three communicants were present. Our members are much scattered but the church still increases in numbers. We baptized four this summer. Bro. John Argabright, our minister, was advanced to the second degree and two brethren were elected to the office of deacon,—Isaac Hylton and James King. We have commenced to build a church here, but will hardly be able to finish it ourselves. Will not some of our able brethren visit our little congregation? Ada is our nearest railroad station. It is six miles from here.—*Cynthia J. Kahler, Nov. 2.*

Literary Notices.

"From the Pulpit to the Poor-house," is the rather ingenious title of an excellent volume of 200 pages, just from the press of Messrs. Hunt & Eaton, New York. Price, $1.00. The author, Rev. Jay Benson Hamilton, is indeed an interesting writer. He tells the story of the suffering ministers who, during their active ministry, receive hardly enough to keep soul and body together, and then when they get too old to preach must retire and almost starve. It is one of those works that one can hardly lay down until he gets to the end of the story. We read such books with profit.

"On the Rock," by D. R. Dungan, is the title of a religious romance issued by the Christian Publishing Company, St. Louis, Mo. Price in paper cover, 40 cents. It contains 398 well-printed pages, and is one of those volumes that any honest seeker after the truth may read with profit. The author is an ingenious reasoner, understands human nature thoroughly, has seemingly been raised in the field of controversy and knows how to play the different parts well. It is a book that is hard to lay down when once you commence reading it.

D. D. Merrill Co., Publishers, 44 & 45 Bible House, N. Y., favor us with a neatly-printed volume, "Little Comrade Mine," by Martha Burr Banks. Price, $1.00. The story is a good one for little folks.

The Christian Publishing Company, St. Louis, Mo., has just issued an excellent little volume entitled, "Moral Evil," by L. B. Wilkes. Price, 75 cents. The line of reasoning on election and endless punishment is not only new but forcible. Possibly some of our readers will remember L. B. Wilkes as the able Disciple minister who held a public discussion with Bro. Quinter in Macoupin County, this State, many years ago. The book is neat and well put up. The printing is excellent, and the contents will prove valuable to any one who will read the work with care.

Matrimonial.

"What therefore God hath joined together, let not man put asunder."

LEATHERMAN—FEASTER.—At the residence of the groom's parents, Oct. 19, 1892, by Bro. Peter Arnold, Wm. J. Leatherman and Miranda B. Feaster, both of Mineral County, W. Va. M. Jennie Bailey.

FOX—FOGLE.—At my residence, Nov. 6, 1892, by the writer, assisted by Bro. W. A. Anthony, Mr. William Oscar Fox and Miss Mary Elizabeth Fogle. T. J. Kolb.

KOLB—GARBER.—At the home of the bride's parents, near Uniontown, Carroll Co., Md., Nov. 1, 1892, by Eld. Solomon Stoner, Mr. William E. Kolb and Miss Jennie E. Garber. Rachel A. Pfoutz.

KING—POTE.—Nov. 2, 1892, by the undersigned, Mr. David L. King and Miss Sadie J. Pote, both of Baker's Summit, Pa. Jas. D. Brumbaugh.

MICHAEL—EVANS.—In the Wakenda church, Ray Co., Mo., Nov. 13, 1892, by Bro. S. B. Shirky, Mr. Allen Michael to sister Effie Evans. J. H. Shirky.

Fallen Asleep.

"Blessed are the dead which die in the Lord."

HOLMES.—In the Sugar Creek church, Holmes Co, Ohio, Feb. 25, 1892, Margaret, wife of David C. Holmes, aged 52 years, 11 months and 23 days. Funeral services by Bro. Peter Long from Indiana and the writer.

LOWER.—In the Sugar Creek church, Holmes Co., Ohio, March 18, 1892, John P. Lower, aged 80 years, 11 months and 17 days. Deceased came to Ohio in 1830 and was united in marriage to Christina Snyder in 1832. Ten children were born to them,—five sons and five daughters. Services by Rev. Weaver, of the M. E. church, and the writer.

RENNECKER.—In the Sugar Creek church, Ohio, April 1, 1897, Sylvan Lovell, son of Thomas and Emily Rennecker, aged 4 years, 4 months and 9 days. Little Sylvan suffered a great deal until consumption ended his life. Funeral services by Bro. S. J. Burger and the writer.

HOCHSTETTLER.—In the Sugar Creek church, Ohio, May 17, 1892, Thomas Paine, son of Daniel and Mary M. Hochstettler, aged 6 years, 10 months and 9 days. Funeral services by the writer.

GOTTSHALL.—In the Sugar Creek church, Ohio, July 2, 1892, Henry Gottshall, a member of the Mennonite church, aged 70 years, 2 months and 10 days. Funeral services by the writer and Rev. Wise in the town of New Bedford.

FRAUTCHEY.—In the Sugar Creek church, O., July 25, 1892, Lisette, wife of Joseph E. Frautchey, aged 21 years, 11 months and 30 days. Funeral services by the writer in the town of Ragersville, Ohio.

WIDDER.—Near New Comerstown, Ohio, Aug. 8, 1892, John Henry, son of Fred and Elizabeth Widder, aged 19 years, 6 months and 2 days. This young man dropped from the platform of an engine, and was picked up dead. Funeral by the writer and Rev. Palmer of the M. E. church to a large audience.

ROBBERTS.—In the Sugar Creek church, Ohio, Aug. 30, 1892, Elizabeth Robberts, aged 51 years, 11 months and 4 days. Her last days were marked by pain and suffering. Funeral by the writer to a large congregation in the town of Ragersville.

SWONGER.—In the Sugar Creek church, Ohio, Oct. 10, 1892, Clara A., wife of John Swonger, aged 28 years, 4 months and 14 days. She was joined in marriage to Mr Swonger, March 14, 1881. Five children were born to them. Funeral services by the writer. M. H. Shutt.

COBLE.—In Lindsey, Jefferson Co, Pa., June 13, 1892, of diphtheria, Elsie Ada, daughter of Bro. David and sister Maggie Coble, aged 11 years, 7 months and 13 days. Maggie Coble.

MOYER.—Oct. 4, 1892, of apoplexy, sister Christiana Moyer, aged 71 years, 3 months and 11 days. Sister Moyer had been attending a love-feast in the Springfield church, Bucks Co., Pa., and afterwards went to the residence of her nephew, Eld. Jonas H. Price, where she was overtaken with apoplexy, and died. Her remains were then taken to her home at the residence of her son-in-law, Bro. James Markley, at Mainland, Montgomery Co, Pa., where the funeral was held on the following Sunday. Brethren Jonas H. Price, of Richland Center, and T. T. Myers, of Philadelphia, spoke words of consolation to the bereaved at the house of mourning, and brethren H. A. Price and Jacob Booz followed in the German language at the Indian Creek meeting-house to a large concourse of relatives and friends. Jas. Y. Heckler.

BALLINGER.—In the Brick church, Floyd, Va., Sept. 4, 1892, Elizabeth R. Ballinger, the wife of Bro. Marion Ballinger, aged 53 years, 4 months and 10 days. She united with the church June, 1864. Funeral services from Rev. 14: 13 by Eld. H. P. Hylton and the writer. J. H. Slusher.

HYLTON.—In the Brick church, Floyd, Va., Aug. 11, 1892, of consumption, Bro. John B. Hylton, Jr, aged 46 years, 4 months and 11 days. He united with the Brethren church when quite young and was a consistent member. He leaves a widowed sister, seven sons, two of them members of the church, and one daughter. Services from 1 Pet. 4: 17, 18 by the Brethren. J. H. Slusher.

JEWETT.—At Janesville, Wis, Nov. 10, 1892, sister Amy, wife of Eugene Jewett, aged 31 years, 8 months and 16 days. The deceased was sick but a few days. A telegram brought the sad and unexpected news to her parents, brother Jacob and sister Julia A. Spangle, Wolcott, Ind., that Amy was dead. Her remains were brought home and the funeral held in the M. E. church, of Wolcott. Bro. M. L. Hahn, assisted by Bro. J. T. Dobbins, preached from the words, "I will not leave you comfortless." John 14: 18. Cyrus Wallick.

FITZWATER.—In the Wakenda church, Ray Co., Mo., Oct. 30, 1892, of typhoid fever, Dora, daughter of Bro. John and sister —— Fitzwater, aged 11 years. J. H. Shirky.

RAUMAKER.—Near Richland, Keokuk Co., Iowa, Oct. 24, 1892, of heart failure, Harrison G., son of friend Henry and Ellie Raumaker, of Mt. Ayr, Kans., aged 4 years, 3 months and 15 days. Funeral discourse by the writer in the Brethren church, near Ollie, to a large congregation. Wm. C. Hipes.

CALDWELL.—In the bounds of the Verdigris church, Kans., Nov. 6, 1892, Dow Frank Caldwell, aged 3 years, 3 months and 7 days. Deceased was the son of W. H. and Melvina Caldwell, and died of membraneous croup. Funeral services by the undersigned. D. W. Stouder.

STULL.—In the Sandy church, in Homeworth, Ohio, Nov. 7, 1892, Johnnie, son of friend Uriah and Mary A. Stull, aged 26 days. Services by the writer. Eli Stroup.

BURK.—In the bounds of the Rome church, in Wharton, Wyandot Co., Ohio, sister Sarah Wolfe Burk, aged 66 years, 9 months and 9 days. Funeral services by the undersigned in the M. E. church, assisted by the minister of that church. Silas Weidman.

The Gospel Messenger

Is the recognized organ of the German Baptist or Brethren's church, and advocates the form of doctrine taught in the New Testament and pleads for a return to apostolic and primitive Christianity.

It recognizes the New Testament as the only infallible rule of faith and practice, and maintains that Faith toward God, Repentance from dead works, Regeneration of the heart and mind, baptism by Trine Immersion for remission of sins unto the reception of the Holy Ghost by the laying on of hands, are the means of adoption into the household of God,—the church militant.

It also maintains that Feet-washing, as taught in John 13, both by example and command of Jesus, should be observed in the church.

That the Lord's Supper, instituted by Christ and as universally observed by the apostles and the early Christians, is a full meal, and, in connection with the Communion, should be taken in the evening or after the close of the day.

That the Salutation of the Holy Kiss, or Kiss of Charity, is binding upon the followers of Christ.

That War and Retaliation are contrary to the spirit and self-denying principles of the religion of Jesus Christ.

That the principle of Plain Dressing and of Non-conformity to the world, as taught in the New Testament, should be observed by the followers of Christ.

That the Scriptural duty of Anointing the Sick with Oil, in the Name of the Lord, James 5: 14, is binding upon all Christians.

It also advocates the church's duty to support Missionary and Tract Work, thus giving to the Lord for the spread of the Gospel and for the conversion of sinners.

In short, it is a Vindicator of all that Christ and the apostles have enjoined upon us, and aims, amid the conflicting theories and discords of modern Christendom, to point out ground that all must concede to be infallibly safe.

☞ "The above principles of our Fraternity are set forth on our Brethren's Envelopes." Use them! Price 15 cents per package; 40 cents per hundred.

Grundy Centre, Iowa.—Our Sunday-school still continues and is large and interesting. We just closed a good meeting by Joseph Holder, of Indiana. Five united with the church.—*Ada M. Hoffa, Nov. 1.*

North Manchester, Ind.—At our regular meeting on Sunday, Nov. 6, one dear sister was received into church fellowship by confession and baptism. May God bless her and help her to hold out faithful!—*D. C. Cripe.*

Monticello Church, Ind.—Our feast, held Nov. 5, was an enjoyable one. The attendance was large and the best of order prevailed throughout. Bro. Noah Crumrine, of Wabash, Ind., officiated. Next day the ministers present encouraged the members in their Christian work. At the close of the services one young girl came out on the Lord's side. May the Lord, through his Spirit and Word, help her to hold out faithful!—*J. A. Weaver, Nov. 7.*

Cerro Gordo, Ill.—Yesterday, at our Sunday-school, a collection was taken to assist sister Alice Boone in her work of teaching the poor little boys and girls of Chicago. The collection amounted to $16 30. Surely she has undertaken a noble work and while she has the prayers of all interested in the financial way, in order to make it a success. Bro. I. J. Rosenberger will begin a series of meetings for us Nov. 10.—*Wm. Landis, Nov. 7.*

Greene, Iowa.—I have now been here one week. We had a soul-refreshing season Nov. 5 at their love-feast. At this feast one made the good choice, and others are deeply impressed. I will remain here till Nov. 15. Then I go to Nora Springs, Iowa, by the request of the Mission Board of Northern Iowa, and will remain there until the 24th, after which I will turn my face homeward. My prayer is that we may have good meetings while here. From here I go to Ohio, if the Lord will.—*Joseph Holder, Nov 8.*

Red Oak Ridge, W. Va.—Our Communion was held Oct. 8. Bro. George Grabill and Bro. George Hutchison were our ministers. About forty-three communicants were present. Our members are much scattered but the church still increases in numbers. We baptized four this summer. Bro. John Argabright, our minister, was advanced to the second degree and two brethren were elected to the office of deacon,—Isaac Hylton and James King. We have commenced to build a church here, but will hardly be able to finish it ourselves. Will not some of our able brethren visit our little congregation? Ada is our nearest railroad station. It is six miles from here.—*Cynthia J. Kahler, Nov. 2.*

Literary Notices.

"From the Pulpit to the Poor-house," is the rather ingenious title of an excellent volume of 200 pages, just from the press of Messrs. Hunt & Eaton, New York. Price, $1.00. The author, Rev. Jay Benson Hamilton, is indeed an interesting writer. He tells the story of the suffering minister who, during their active ministry, receive hardly enough, to keep soul and body together, and then when they get too old to preach must retire and almost starve. It is one of those works that one can hardly lay down until he gets to the end of the story. We read such books with profit.

"On the Rock," by D. R. Dungan, is the title of a religious romance issued by the Christian Publishing Company, St. Louis, Mo. Price in paper cover, 40 cents. It contains 398 well-printed pages, and is one of those volumes that any honest seeker after the truth may read with profit. The author is an ingenious reasoner, understands human nature thoroughly, has seemingly been raised in the field of controversy and knows how to play the different parts well. It is a book that is hard to lay down when once you commence reading it.

D. D. Merrill Co., Publishers, 44 & 45 Bible House, N. Y., favor us with a neatly-printed volume, "Little Comrade Mine," by Martha Burr Banks. Price, $1 00. The story is a good one for little folks.

The Christian Publishing Company, St. Louis, Mo., has just issued an excellent little volume entitled, "Moral Evil," by L. B. Wilkes. Price, 75 cents. The line of reasoning on election and endless punishment is not only new but forcible. Possibly some of our readers will remember L. B. Wilkes as the able Disciple minister who held a public discussion with Bro. Quinter in Macoupin County, this State, many years ago. The book is neat and well put up. The printing is excellent, and the contents will prove valuable to any one who will read the work with care.

Matrimonial.

"What therefore God hath joined together, let not man put asunder."

LEATHERMAN—FEASTER.—At the residence of the groom's parents, Oct. 19, 1892, by Bro. Peter Arnold, Wm. J. Leatherman and Miranda B. Feaster, both of Mineral County, W. Va.   M. Jennie Bailey.

FOX—FOGLE—At my residence, Nov. 6, 1892, by the writer, assisted by Bro. W. A. Anthony, Mr. William Oscar Fox and Miss Mary Elizabeth Fogle.   T. J. Kolb.

KOLB—GARBER.—At the home of the bride's parents, near Uniontown, Carroll Co., Md., Nov. 1, 1891, by Eld. Solomon Stoner, Mr. William E. Kolb and Miss Jennie E. Garber.   Rachel A. Foutz.

KING—POTE.—Nov. 2, 1892, by the undersigned, Mr. David L. King and Miss Sadie J. Pote, both of Baker's Summit, Pa.   Jas. D. Brumbaugh.

MICHAEL—EVANS.—In the Wakenda church, Ray Co., Mo., Nov. 13, 1892, by Bro. S. B. Shirky, Mr. Allen Michael to sister Effie Evans.   J. H. Shirky.

Fallen Asleep.

"Blessed are the dead which die in the Lord."

HOLMES.—In the Sugar Creek church, Holmes Co., Ohio, Feb. 25, 1892, Margaret, wife of David C. Holmes, aged 52 years, 11 months and 23 days. Funeral services by Bro. Peter Long from Indiana and the writer.

LOWER.—In the Sugar Creek church, Holmes Co., Ohio, March 18, 1892, John P. Lower, aged 80 years, 11 months and 17 days. Deceased came to Ohio in 1830 and was united in marriage to Christina Snyder in 1831. Ten children were born to them,—five sons and five daughters. Services by Rev. Weaver, of the M. E. church, and the writer.

RENNECKER.—In the Sugar Creek church, Ohio, April 1, 1892, Sylvan Lovell, son of Thomas and Emily Rennecker, aged 4 years, 4 months and 9 days. "Little Sylvan suffered a great deal until consumption ended his life." Funeral services by Bro. S. J. Burger and the writer.

HOCHSTETTLER.—In the Sugar Creek church, Ohio, May 17, 1892, Thomas Paine, son of Daniel and Mary M. Hochstettler, aged 6 years, 10 months and 9 days. Funeral services by the writer.

GOTTSHALL.—In the Sugar Creek church, Ohio, July 3, 1892, Henry Gottshall, a member of the Mennonite church, aged 70 years, 3 months and 10 days. Funeral services by the writer and Rev. Wise in the town of New Bedford.

FRAUTCHEY.—In the Sugar Creek church, O., July 25, 1892, Lisette, wife of Joseph E. Frautchey, aged 31 years, 11 months and 30 days. Funeral services by the writer in the town of Ragersville, Ohio.

WIDDER.—Near New Comerstown, Ohio, Aug. 8, 1892, John Henry, son of Fred and Elizabeth Widder, aged 19 years, 6 months and 2 days. This young man dropped from the platform of an engine, and was picked up dead. Funeral by the writer and Rev. Palmer of the M. E. church to a large audience.

ROBBERTS.—In the Sugar Creek church, Ohio, Aug. 30, 1892, Elizabeth Robberts, aged 51 years, 11 months and 4 days. Her last days were marked by pain and suffering. Funeral by the writer to a large congregation in the town of Ragersville.

SWONGER.—In the Sugar Creek church, Ohio, Oct. 10, 1892, Clara A., wife of John Swonger, aged 28 years, 4 months and 14 days. She was joined in marriage to Mr. Swonger, March 14, 1881. Five children were born to them. Funeral services by the writer.   M. H. Shutt.

COBLE.—In Lindsey, Jefferson Co., Pa., June 13, 1892, of diphtheria, Elsie Ada, daughter of Bro. David and sister Maggie Coble, aged 11 years, 7 months and 13 days.   Maggie Coble.

MOYER.—Oct. 4, 1892, of apoplexy, sister Christiana Moyer, aged 71 years, 3 months and 11 days. Sister Moyer had been attending a love-feast in the Springfield church, Bucks Co., Pa., and afterwards went to the residence of her nephew, Eld. Jonas H. Price, where she was overtaken with apoplexy, and died. Her remains were then taken to her home at the residence of her son-in-law, Bro. James Markley, at Mainland, Montgomery Co., Pa., where the funeral was held on the following Sunday. Brethren Jonas H. Price, of Richland Center, and T. T. Myers, of Philadelphia, spoke words of consolation to the bereaved at the house of mourning, and brethren H. A. Price and Jacob Boon followed in the German language at the Indian Creek meeting-house to a large concourse of relatives and friends. Jas. Y. Heckler.

BALLINGER.—In the Brick church, Floyd, Va., Sept. 4, 1892, Elizabeth R. Ballinger, the wife of Bro. Marion Ballinger, aged 53 years, 4 months and 10 days. She united with the church June, 1864. Funeral services from Rev. 14: 13 by Eld. H. F. Hylton and the writer.   J. H. Slusher.

HYLTON.—In the Brick church, Floyd, Va., Aug. 11, 1892, of consumption, Bro. John B. Hylton, Jr., aged 46 years, 4 months and 11 days. He united with the Brethren church when quite young and was a consistent member. He leaves a widowed sister, seven sons, two of them members of the church, and one daughter. Services from 1 Pet. 4: 17, 18 by the Brethren.   J. H. Slusher.

JEWETT.—At Janesville, Wis., Nov. 10, 1892, sister Amy, wife of Eugene Jewett, aged 31 years, 8 months and 16 days. The deceased was sick but a few days. A telegram brought the sad and unexpected news to her parents, brother Jacob and sister Julia A. Spangle, Wolcott, Ind., that Amy was dead. Her remains were brought home and the funeral held in the M. E. church, of Wolcott. Bro. M. L. Hahn, assisted by Bro. J. T. Dobbins, preached from the words, "I will not leave you comfortless." John 14: 18.   Cyrus Wallick.

FITZWATER.—In the Wakenda church, Ray Co., Mo., Oct. 30, 1892, of typhoid fever, Dora, daughter of Bro. John and sister — Fitzwater, aged 11 years.   J. H. Shirky.

RAUMAKER.—Near Richland, Keokuk Co., Iowa, Oct. 24, 1892, of heart failure, Harrison G., son of friend Henry and Ellie Raumaker, of Mt. Ayr, Kans., aged 4 years, 3 months and 15 days. Funeral discourse by the writer in the Brethren church, near Ollie, to a large congregation. Wm. C. Hipes.

CALDWELL.—In the bounds of the Verdigris church, Kans., Nov. 6, 1892, Dow Frank Caldwell, aged 3 years, 3 months and 7 days. Deceased was the son of W. H. and Melvina Caldwell, and died of membraneous croup. Funeral services by the undersigned.   D. W. Stouder.

STULL.—In the Sandy church, in Homeworth, Ohio, Nov. 7, 1892, Johnnie, son of friend Uriah and Mary A. Stull, aged 26 days. Services by the writer.   Eli Stroup.

BURK.—In the bounds of the Rome church, in Wharton, Wyandot Co., Ohio, sister Sarah Wolfe Burk, aged 66 years, 9 months and 9 days. Funeral services by the undersigned in the M. E. church, assisted by the minister of that church.   Silas Weidman.

The Gospel Messenger

Is the recognized organ of the German Baptist or Brethren's church, and advocates the form of doctrine taught in the New Testament and pleads for a return to apostolic and primitive Christianity.

It recognizes the New Testament as the only infallible rule of faith and practice, and maintains that Faith toward God, Repentance from dead works, Regeneration of the heart and mind, baptism by Trine Immersion for remission of sins unto the reception of the Holy Ghost by the laying on of hands, are the means of adoption into the household of God,—the church militant.

It also maintains that Feet-washing, as taught in John 13, both by example and command of Jesus, should be observed in the church.

That the Lord's Supper, instituted by Christ and as universally observed by the apostles and the early Christians, is a full meal, and, in connection with the Communion, should be taken in the evening or after the close of the day.

That the Salutation of the Holy Kiss, or Kiss of Charity, is binding upon the followers of Christ.

That War and Retaliation are contrary to the spirit and self-denying principles of the religion of Jesus Christ.

That the principle of Plain Dressing and of Non-conformity to the world, as taught in the New Testament, should be observed by the followers of Christ.

That the Scriptural duty of Anointing the Sick with Oil, in the Name of the Lord, James 5: 14, is binding upon all Christians.

It also advocates the church's duty to support Missionary and Tract Work, thus giving to the Lord for the spread of the Gospel and for the conversion of sinners.

In short, it is a vindicator of all that Christ and the apostles have enjoined upon us, and aims, amid the conflicting theories and discords of modern Christendom, to point out ground that all must concede to be infallibly safe.

☞ The above principles of our Fraternity are set forth on our Brethren's Envelopes." Use them! Price 15 cents per package; 40 cents per hundred.

Announcements.

MINISTERIAL MEETINGS.

Nov. 25, at 9 A. M., in the South-east District of Kansas, Ministerial Meeting in the Cedar Creek church, Mont Ida, Anderson Co., Kans.

Nov. 30, Dec. 1 and 2, Southern District of Pennsylvania, Ministerial Meeting in the East Cordorus church, York, York Co., Pa.

Nov. 17, at 9 A. M., North-eastern District of Ohio, Ministerial Meeting, Maple Grove church, 4 miles north of Ashland, Ashland Co., Ohio.

LOVE-FEASTS.

Dec. 3, Good Hope church, at the Snowberger school-house, 8 miles north-east of Holyoke, Phillips Co. Colo.

Nov. 24. at 3 P. M., Cedar Creek church, Anderson Co., Kans.

Nov. 25 and 26, Beatrice church, Nebr.

Nov 29, at 2 P. M., Coon Creek, Ill.

Dec 3. Gird in Mani apa Co Ariz. Those coming by r 1 will be met by 11 Tempe by notifying T. J. S—, 50

For Sale!

Having a desire to devote more time to church work, I offer one quarter section of choice farm land for sale. This farm has a good house, barn, fences, well, and a nice spring. It is situated 2½ miles south of the Brethren's meeting-house in Shannon, Ill. It is also within one mile of a good creamery. I also offer 30 head of registered Short Horn Cattle, 15 males and 15 females,—choice individuals at a very low price. Address for particulars, D. Rowland, Lanark, Ill.

EUROPE
AND
Bible Lands

deservedly popular
It retains all
and with
such rich
Those
and
copy of the work should immediately of securing it. Price.
only $1.00 per copy.

Mt. Morris, Ill.

GOOD BOOKS FOR ALL.

Any book in the market furnished at publishers' lowest retail price by the Brethren's Publishing Company, Mt. Morris, Ill. Special prices given when books are purchased in quantities. When ordering books, not on our list, if possible give title, name of author, and address of publishers.

Webster's International Dictionary.—Latest edition. Write for special low prices.

Teaching and Teachers.—By H. Clay Trumbull. Just the book for a live Sunday-school teacher. Cloth, $1.25.

Josephus' Complete Works.—Large type, 1 vol. 8vo. Illustrated with many steel and wood engravings. Library sheep, $3.00.

The House We Live In.—By Daniel Vaniman. It gives a concise account of the faith and practice of the Brethren. Price, 100 copies, 60 cents.

Bunyan's Pilgrim's Progress.—An excellent edition of this good work, printed on good paper, finely illustrated with forty engravings, at the low price of $1.00 per copy.

Classified Minutes of Annual Meeting.—A work of rare interest for all who desire to be well informed in the church work, from the early days of our Brethren until the present. Price, cloth, $1.50; leather, $2.00.

Ante-Nicene Christian Library.—A collection of all the works of the Fathers of the Christian Church prior to the Council of Nice. Edited by Rev. Alexander Roberts, D. D., and James Donaldson, LL. D. Twenty-four vols. 8 vo. Per vol. $3.00.

Church Entertainments: Twenty Objections.

By Rev. B. Carradine, D. D. 12mo, 100 pp. Paper cover, 30 cents. A strong book in defense of its position, written by a powerful pen, presenting the most candid and scriptural arraignment of unwarrantable methods for money-raising in the Church. The spirit of the book is highly devotional and cannot fail to inspire the reader with its seriousness.

— THE —
Doctrine of the Brethren Defended.

This work contains a complete exposition of the faith and practice of the Brethren, the Divinity of Christ, the Divinity of the Holy Spirit, Immersion, Feet-washing, the Lord's Supper, the Holy Kiss, Non-conformity, Secret Societies, etc. Price, per copy, cloth binding, $1.25. Address this office.

WONDERFUL "Story of the Crusades" is a book just published. Everybody interested in Christianity should read it. It is a large gem in each book of about 300 pages and 100 full-page engravings. It contains some of the most wonderful chapters in the world's history, the battles, sieges, marches, victories, defeats, heroism, starvation, death of thousands of Christians to recover Jerusalem and the Holy Sepulchre from the hated Mohammedans. Unsurpassed in thrilling interest and instruction. Agents wanted every-where. Circulars free. Address, J. M. Nave, Covington, Ohio.

Dubbel's Cough and Croup Cure

It is a sure and quick cure for coughs and especially for croup. It will cure any case of croup that a doctor can cure and with one-tenth the expense. It contains no dangerous drugs such as morphia, opium, chloral, etc., and is perfectly harmless. It is highly endorsed for La Grippe. Our Cough and Croup Cure is second to none, and we sell it on the strong guarantee, "No cure, no pay." We allow one-half the contents of the bottle to be used and if the results are not satisfactory, return it to us or the agent of whom you purchased it. Your money will be refunded. Price, 25 cents per bottle. Agents wanted in every locality. We want 1,000 new agents at once. To any patient who becomes an agent who will offer two doses at almost cost we will give, as a present for boosting the agent, the valuable book "Alone with God." Said book is advertised on the Gospel Messenger. Write for terms and circular.

Eld. P. D. Reed, Lanark, writes April 6, '92:—"Last Christmas, when I returned from a preaching tour in Virginia, I was run down from preaching and had contracted a very bad cold. I got a bottle of your Cough and Croup Cure from Bro. C. H. Diehl, of Jonesboro, Tenn. After using half of it I was perfectly cured. For a cold or La Grippe I can certainly recommend it.

S. H. Dubbel & Co.,

Manufacturers and Proprietors,

Waynesboro, Franklin Co., Pa.

Also manufacturers of Red Thyme Pain Cure,—the medicine that proved to be such a blessing at the late Annual Meeting held at Cedar Rapids, Iowa.

Alone with God.

This manual of devotions, by J. M. Garrison, comprises a series of meditations with forms of prayer for private devotions, family worship and special occasions. It is one of the most useful, most needed, and best adapted books of the year, and therefore it is not strange that it is proving one of the most popular. In work of this kind its distinguished, gifted, pious and beloved author is at his best. This book is helpful to every minister, church official, and Sunday-school superintendent, as well as every private member of the church in all ages. It has models of prayer, suitable for the service of the prayer-meeting, while its suggestions, meditations and instructions are pre-eminently calculated to be of service in preparation for the solemn duties that rest upon the active members. Cloth, 75 cents; morocco, $1.25. Address this office.

O Jerusalem! Jerusalem!

What could be more beautiful and touching than a picture of Christ as he stood upon Olivet looking down over the beloved but sinful city, with tears trickling down over his cheeks, his lips parted as he cries, "O Jerusalem! Jerusalem!" We have such a picture size 18 inches, beautifully executed in colors. No one can gaze upon it without being moved. Given free with a year's subscription to "What to Read" at 50 cents. An agent wanted in every church and neighborhood. Address, Jas. M. Nave, Covington, Ohio.

Excursions to California.

Excursions in charge of M. M. Eshelman, Immigration Agent, will leave Chicago over the "Santa Fe Route" Tuesdays, and Kansas City Wednesdays, during the year 1892, on dates as follows:

Chicago, January 19, February 23, March 22, April 26, May 24, June 28, July 26, August 23, September 27, October 25, November 22, December 27.

Kansas City, January 20, February 24, March 23, April 27, May 25, June 29, July 27, August 24, September 28, October 26, November 23, December 28.

Parties wishing to avail themselves of the privileges of these excursions, should write M. M. Eshelman, Rochester, California, prior to the 15th of each month, and from the fifteenth to the end of the month, at 1050 Union Avenue (opposite Union Depot), Kansas City, Mo., stating when and where they wish to join one of these excursions, and he will give them full information, and if desired will reserve berths in Tourist Sleeping Car for them. Do not fail to write him; he will do you good. Our aim will be as low as the lowest made to the Pacific Ocean.

George L. McDonough,
Traveling Agent.

Announcements.

MINISTERIAL MEETINGS.

Nov. 25, at 9 A. M., in the South-east District of Kansas, Ministerial Meeting in the Cedar Creek church, Mont Ida, Anderson Co., Kans.

Nov. 30, Dec. 1 and 2, Southern District of Pennsylvania Ministerial Meeting in the East Codorus church, York, York Co., Pa.

Nov. 17, at 9 A. M., North-eastern District of Ohio, Ministerial Meeting, Maple Grove church, 4 miles north of Ashland, Ashland Co., Ohio.

LOVE-FEASTS.

Dec. 3, Good Hope church, at the Snowberger schoolhouse, 8 miles north-east of Holyoke, Phillips Co. Colo.

Nov. 14, at 3 P. M., Cedar Creek church, Anderson Co., Kans

Nov. 25 and 26, Beatrice church, Nebr.

Dec. 3, Oil and 26 Meet upon Co. Ariz Those coming by rail will be met by us Tempe by notifying T. J. Esterlie.

For Sale!

Having a desire to devote more time to church work, I offer one quarter section of choice farm land for sale. This farm has a good house, barn, fences, well, and a nice spring. It is situated 2½ miles south of the Brethren's meeting-house in Shannon, Ill. It is also within one mile of a good creamery. I also offer 50 head of registered Short Horn Cattle, 15 males and 35 females,— choice individuals at a very low price. Address for particulars, D. Rowland, Lanark, Ill.

EUROPE

AND

Bible Lands

... avowedly popular ... It retains all ...

... the last edition of this ... on hand. Those who have not ... a copy of the work should em... ... opportunity of securing it. Price, ... only $1.00 per copy.

Mt. Morris, Ill.

✦ESSAYS✦

"Study to show thyself approved unto God; a workman that needeth not be ashamed, rightly dividing the Word of Truth."

A GLANCE INTO THE FUTURE.

BY GERTRUDE A. FLORY.

The Vision.

BETWEEN the harvest of the wheat and corn,
Into the vision-world my soul was borne:
The day was closing and the twilight fair
With an inspiring rapture filled the air.

Hushed was every sound; sacred seemed the spot;
The former world and cares were all forgot:
So blessed was the silence and the grace
Which like celestial calm suffused the place.

The evening dusk was falling darkly down
When lo! a mystical and golden wave,
Like sunlight, swept across an open grave
Within a stubble field all bare and brown.

Transfixed with wonder, there, I gazing stood
Till a soft footstep broke the quietude.
He, who from all the world had kept apart
The dearest love and tenderest of my heart,

Came bringing my deceased and feeble form,
Made useless by the ravages of storm,
And placed it in the grave, then heaped the sands
Upon it with his own beloved hands.

His countenance wore not a trace of grief,
But lingering there were emblems of relief.
A cherished friend looked on my new-made tomb
And smiled as if it were with flowers abloom.

Above my lifeless body lying there,
None sang a requiem, nor breathed a prayer,
Nor mourned that I had journeyed from the earth
Where I had been esteemed of little worth

When he, who claimed my best and earliest love,
Toward our broken home his footsteps turned,
I ran before him as a fledgling dove
While rapture in my unbound spirit burned.

My joyous feet so lightly touched the sod
I moved unheard, unseen, yet, so as God,
My soul was jubilant in sweet surprise!
The mortal veil was taken from my eyes.

Thus evermore with loved ones round my home,
My happy spirit should unhindered roam,
Disturbed not that none missed me from my place
And Time, my memory would soon deface.
　　　If it were true!

Ah, when this fleeting life shall close on earth
Will I have been as infants at their birth,
Who for the ministry of loving hands
Return no love, fulfill no law's demands?

If it were true, that after death I'd be
As one who lived for self—apart from Thee,
O God! would this warm heart with rapture beat
As lightly pressed the sod my spirit feet?

In that strange world could I contentment find
Had I ne'er spoken words consoling, kind;
Nor rocks had smitten, that its flowing cleft
Might issue streams of balm for those bereft;

If in no memory I was enshrined
By blessings from a sympathetic mind,
Could I be happy? O Eternal God!
Are such dark records hid beneath the sod?

Ah, could this ardent, loving nature rest
If never once a soul its warmth had blest?
Or could these hands be folded in repose
Had they not lightened poverty's stern woes?

O! if these feet on errands never ran
To help and cheer a struggling fellow-man,
They would the grave's sealed door wide open force
And strive to run a nobler, wiser course.

For they could never rest in peace and know
They never hastened to console a woe,
Nor lift a burden from a troubled mind,
Nor o'er a stranded life love's ivy twined.

But if in worthy toil my powers were spent
As downward to the darkened tomb I went,
I should be happy as a sinless child,
Nor care that men above my grave had smiled.

Because those smiles should then be gleams of joy
That I had passed unto divine employ,
And my glad soul, unfettered from its clay,
Should travel not again earth's sin-strewn way.

La Porte, Ind.

PRIMITIVE CHRISTIANITY, AS UNDERSTOOD AND PRACTICED BY THE BRETHREN.

[We invite careful and intelligent criticism on all the articles published under this head. Criticisms on language, facts and arguments will be in order, and should be sent to the author of the article to which they refer.]

BY A. W. REESE.

Faith.

"But without faith it is impossible to please him: for he that cometh to God must believe that he is, and that he is a rewarder of them that diligently seek him."—Heb. 11: 6.

Part One.

THE chief corner-stone of Christianity is *faith!* It is the beginning, the middle, and the end of the system. It is the solid *foundation* upon which the grand superstructure,—"the whole building, fitly framed together," rests. "Without faith it is impossible to please God! This is the very *first step* towards the kingdom of heaven. "He that cometh to God must *believe* that *he is!*" What more reasonable,—what more logical,—than this?. Without this preliminary exercise of the mind, no step towards salvation will,—indeed, can be,—made.

"He that believeth and is baptized shall be saved!" These conditions, or terms, are immutable,—inexorable. The man that will not, or does not, comply with these conditions is *lost.* Lost through all time! Lost in sight of the cross! Lost through the boundless cycles of eternity! There can be no question about this. "He that believeth not shall be damned." There is no hope for the unbeliever,—no escape from the wrath of God. Unbelief is the culminating sin, because it includes all other sins. It rivals the "unpardonable sin," because it rejects the very means by which only man can be saved. All the powers in the wide universe of God cannot save the man who *will not believe.* God himself cannot save the unbeliever, because he has so declared in his immutable Word. We see, then, how the very issues of life and death are involved in the question of *faith.*

It is of vital importance, therefore, that we understand what faith is, in the Bible sense of that term. If we turn to Heb. 11: 1, we will find the Scriptural definition of the word *faith.* "Now faith is the substance of things hoped for, the evidence of things not seen." In short, faith cohesists in *seeing the unseen.* If we consult the standard exponents of the English language,—our mother tongue,—we find the definition of the word "substance" as follows: "Something underlying the outward manifestation of things,—the hidden foundation, that upon which the essence, or cause, of the visible phenomena is built,—that which is real, in contradistinction to that which is apparent." We see, then, that faith does not *necessarily* carry with it the idea of actual *knowledge,* and yet, correct knowledge of the truth is essential to all genuine Christian faith.

Like hope, faith is an exercise of the mind outside and independent of knowledge, *per se.* "For what a man seeth (knoweth) what doth he yet hope for?" This would be idle indeed. Further, faith does not cavil at the *improbabilities* of the case, nor does it lean upon any knowledge of the implied *facts* presented to the mind. Faith does not stop to reason with the *possibilities* of the problem involved. Faith does not call in the aid of human science to see whether the Scriptures harmonize with the speculations of man. Faith does not hesitate to accept what God declares, whether that declaration is sustained by *evidence* or not.

In the long line of illustrious examples furnished in Heb. 11, we see how clearly the foregoing ideas of faith are carried out. Let us consider, for a brief period, the history of some of these noble exemplars of the Christian faith.

"Abraham, when he was called to go out into a place which he should after receive for an inheritance, obeyed, and he went out, not knowing whither he went." When he was called to offer up Isaac, the beloved son of his declining years,—that son in whom were the promises of God concerning Israel, he *obeyed,* without a protest,—without a murmur,—without a doubt. Abraham did not *know* that God would stay the uplifted knife,—that God, at the very last moment of that supreme trial of mortal faith, would arrest the fatal stroke and provide another sacrifice in place of the devoted lad. Abraham did not *know* this, but his *faith* in the promise of God was so *strong* that, concerning Isaac, it would be fulfilled, though God should raise him from the dead. So it is recorded of Abraham in another place, that he "believed God, and it (his faith) was accounted unto him for righteousness, and he was called the friend of God."

"By faith Noah, being warned of things not seen as yet (having no actual knowledge of the impending deluge), moved with fear, prepared an ark," etc., etc. The case of Noah is a remarkable one. There was no precedent in the experience of the human race. What more unreasonable—what so improbable—what, indeed, so *impossible* in the light of human reason—what so absurd, when weighed in the balance of science, as the predicted flood? What! shall the "windows of heaven be opened,"—the "fountains of the great deep be broken up,"—the rain, in mighty torrents, descend upon the earth for forty consecutive days and as many nights,—the incessant roar of tempestuous waves commingling in terrific strife, which as

　　"The footsteps of a dreadful God
　　　Marching upon the storm
　　In vengeance seemed——"

until the tallest peaks of earth's loftiest mountains shall disappear beneath the waves? No eye of man had looked upon a scene like this.

A picture of such sublime horror had never entered the imagination of man. We may well suppose that the people of that day, the learned scientists as well as the illiterate crowd, scoffed at the warning of God. Doubtless they ridiculed Noah as they saw the pious old man, day by day, patiently at work on the Ark. No doubt they regarded him as a religious fanatic, and pitied his delusion as to the approaching "storm."

Again, we see that "Moses, when he was come to years, refused to be called the son of Pharaoh's daughter," etc., etc., and that it was *by faith* that he was induced to adopt this remarkable course.

National Military Home, Kans.

WHAT SHALL I DO?

BY JAS. M. NEFF.

LET's talk a little about this question, "What shall I do to be saved?" Never has a question of more profound importance forced itself upon the consideration of men and women; and never has a question received so small an amount of prayerful, unprejudiced attention in proportion to that which it demands. Yesterday, to-day and all the time; here, there and everywhere, in all conditions and under all circumstances should the question be asked, re-asked and asked again: "What shall I do to be saved?"

How is it? Can there be but one answer to this question? No; there are many. A number of different answers may be given to this question,

✦ESSAYS✦

"Study to show thyself approved unto God; a workman that needeth not to be ashamed, rightly dividing the Word of Truth."

A GLANCE INTO THE FUTURE.

BY GERTRUDE A. FLORY.

The Vision.

BETWEEN the harvest of the wheat and corn,
Into the vision-world my soul was borne:
The day was closing and the twilight fair
With an inspiring rapture filled the air.

Hushed was every sound; sacred seemed the spot;
The former world and cares were all forgot:
So blessed was the silence and the grace
Which like celestial calm suffused the place.

The evening dusk was falling darkly down
When lo! a mystical and golden wave,
Like sunlight, swept across an open grave
Within a stubble field all bare and brown.

Transfixed with wonder, there, I gazing stood
Till a soft footstep broke the quietude.
He, who from all the world had kept apart
The dearest love and tenderest of my heart,

Came bringing my deceased and feeble form,
Made useless by the ravages of storm,
And placed it in the grave, then heaped the sands
Upon it with his own beloved hands.

His countenance wore not a trace of grief,
But lingering there were emblems of relief.
A cherished friend looked on my new-made tomb
And smiled as if it were with flowers abloom.

Above my lifeless body lying there,
None sang a requiem, nor breathed a prayer,
Nor mourned that I had journeyed from the earth
Where I had been esteemed of little worth

When he, who claimed my best and earliest love,
Toward our broken home his footsteps turned,
I ran before him as a fledgling dove
While rapture in my unbound spirit burned.

My joyous feet so lightly touched the sod
I moved unheard, unseen, yet, so as God,
My soul was jubilant in sweet surprise:
The mortal veil was taken from my eyes.

Thus evermore with loved ones round my home,
My happy spirit should unhindered roam,
Disturbed not that none missed me from my place
And Time, my memory would soon deface.
If it were true!

Ah, when this fleeting life shall close on earth
Will I have been as infants at their birth,
Who for the ministry of loving hands
Return no love, fulfill no law's demands?

If it were true, that after death I'd be
As one who lived for self—apart from Thee,
O God! would this warm heart with rapture beat
As lightly pressed the sod my spirit feet?

In that strange world could I contentment find
Had I ne'er spoken words consoling, kind;
Nor rocks had smitten, that its flowing cleft
Might issue streams of balm for those bereft;

If in no memory I was enshrined
By blessings from a sympathetic mind,
Could I be happy? O Eternal God!
Are such dark records hid beneath the sod?

Ah, could this ardent, loving nature rest
If never once a soul its warmth had blest?
Or could these hands be folded in repose
Had they not lightened poverty's stern woes?

O! if these feet on errands never ran
To help and cheer a struggling fellow-man,
They would the grave's sealed door wide open force
And strive to run a nobler, wiser course.

For they could never rest in peace and know
They never hastened to console a woe,
Nor lift a burden from a troubled mind,
Nor o'er a stranded life love's ivy twined.

But if in worthy toil my powers were spent
As downward to the darkened tomb I went,
I should be happy as a sinless child,
Nor care that men above my grave had smiled.

Because those smiles should then be gleams of joy
That I had passed unto divine employ,
And my glad soul, unfettered from its clay,
Should travel not again earth's sin-strewn way.
La Porte, Ind.

PRIMITIVE CHRISTIANITY, AS UNDERSTOOD AND PRACTICED BY THE BRETHREN.

[We invite careful and intelligent criticism on all the articles published under this head. Criticisms on language, facts and arguments will be in order, and should be sent to the author of the article to which they refer.]

BY A. W. REESE.

Faith.

"But without faith it is impossible to please him: for he that cometh to God must believe that he is, and that he is a rewarder of them that diligently seek him."—Heb. 11: 6.

Part One.

THE chief corner-stone of Christianity is *faith!* It is the beginning, the middle, and the end of the system. It is the solid *foundation* upon which the grand superstructure,—"the whole building, fitly framed together," rests. "Without faith it is impossible to please God! This is the very *first* step towards the kingdom of heaven. "He that cometh to God must *believe* that *he* is!". What more reasonable,—what more logical,—than this?. Without this preliminary exercise of the mind, no step towards salvation will,—indeed, can be,—made.

"He that believeth and is baptized shall be saved!" These conditions, or terms, are immutable,—inexorable. The man that will not, or does not, *comply* with these conditions is *lost*. Lost through all time! Lost in sight of the cross! Lost through the boundless cycles of eternity! There can be no question about this. "He that believeth not shall be damned.". There is no hope for the unbeliever,—no escape from the wrath of God. Unbelief is the culminating sin, because it includes all other sins. It rivals the "unpardonable sin," because it rejects the very means by which only man *can* be saved. All the powers in the wide universe of God cannot save the man who *will not believe*. God himself cannot save the unbeliever, because he has so declared in his immutable Word. We see, then, how the very issues of life and death are involved in the question of *faith*.

It is of vital importance, therefore, that we understand what faith is, in the Bible sense of that term. If we turn to Heb. 11: 1, we will find the Scriptural definition of the word *faith*. "Now faith is the substance of things hoped for, the evidence of things not seen." In short, faith consists in *seeing* the *unseen*. If we consult the standard exponents of the English language,—our mother tongue,—we find the definition of the word "substance" as follows: "Something underlying the outward manifestation of things,—the hidden foundation, that upon which the essence, or cause, of the visible phenomena is built,—that which is real, in contradistinction to that which is apparent." We see, then, that faith does not *necessarily* carry with.it the idea of actual *knowledge*, and yet, correct knowledge of the truth is essential to all genuine Christian faith.

Like *hope*, faith is an exercise of the mind outside and independent of knowledge, *per se*. "For what a man seeth (knoweth) what doth he yet hope for?" This would be idle indeed. Further, faith does not cavil at the *improbabilities* of the case, nor does it lean upon any knowledge of the implied *facts* presented to the mind. Faith does not stop to reason with the *possibilities* of the problem involved. Faith does not call in the aid of human science to see whether the Scriptures harmonize with the speculations of man. Faith does not hesitate to accept what God declares, whether that declaration is sustained by *evidence* or not.

In the long line of illustrious examples furnished in Heb. 11, we see how clearly the foregoing ideas of faith are carried out. Let us consider, for a brief period, the history of some of those noble exemplars of the Christian faith.

"Abraham, when he was called to go out into a place which he should after receive for an inheritance, obeyed, and he went out, not knowing whither he went." When he was called to offer up Isaac, the beloved son of his declining years,—that son in whom were the promises of God concerning Israel, he *obeyed*, without a protest,—without a murmur,—without a doubt. Abraham did not *know* that God would stay the uplifted knife,—that God, at the very last moment of that supreme trial of mortal faith, would arrest the fatal stroke and provide another sacrifice in place of the devoted lad. Abraham did not *know* this, but his *faith* in the promise of God was so *strong* that, concerning Isaac, it would be fulfilled, though God should raise him from the dead. So it is recorded of Abraham in another place, that he "believed God, and it (his faith) was accounted unto him for righteousness, and he was called the friend of God."

"By faith Noah, being warned of things not seen as yet (having no actual knowledge of the impending deluge), moved with fear, prepared an ark," etc., etc. The case of Noah is a remarkable one. There was no precedent in the experience of the human race. What more unreasonable—what so improbable—what, indeed, so *impossible* in the light of human reason—what so absurd, when weighed in the balance of science, as the predicted flood? What! shall the "windows of heaven be opened,"—the "fountains of the great deep be broken up,"—the rain, in mighty torrents, descend upon the earth for forty consecutive days and as many nights,—the incessant roar of tempestuous waves commingling in terrific strife, which as

"The footsteps of a dreadful God
Marching upon the storm
In vengeance seemed——"

until the tallest peaks of earth's loftiest mountains shall disappear beneath the waves? No eye of man had looked upon a scene like this.

A picture of such sublime horror had never entered the imagination of man. We may well suppose that the people of that day, the learned scientists as well as the illiterate crowd, scoffed at the warning of God. Doubtless they ridiculed Noah as they saw the pious old man, day by day, patiently at work on the Ark. No doubt they regarded him as a religious fanatic, and pitied his delusion as to the approaching "storm."

Again, we see that "Moses, when he was come to years, refused to be called the son of Pharaoh's daughter," etc., etc., and that it was *by faith* that he was induced to adopt this remarkable course.
National Military Home, Kans.

WHAT SHALL I DO?

BY JAS. M. NEFF.

LET us talk a little about this question, "What shall I do to be saved?" Never has a question of more profound importance forced itself upon the consideration of men and women; and never has a question received so small an amount of prayerful, unprejudiced attention in proportion to that which it demands. Yesterday, to-day and all the time; here, there and everywhere, in all conditions and under all circumstances should the question be asked, re-asked and asked again: "What shall I do to be saved?"

How is it? Can there be but one answer to this question? No; there are many. A number of different answers may be given to this question,

as a guide in the selection of proper things to eat. From a physiological standpoint we have no fault to find with the tongue. In its proper use we have displayed in it the wisdom of the Great Mechanic who never made a machine that "would not work."

Notwithstanding the fact that the tongue is so wonderful and so indispensable to our physical well-being, the Bible says some very bad things about it. "Even so the tongue is a little member and boasteth great things." "And the tongue is a fire, a world of iniquity." "For every kind of beasts, and of birds, and of serpents, and of things in the sea, is tamed and hath been tamed of mankind: but the tongue can no man tame; it is an unruly evil, full of deadly poison." See James 3.

What shall we do about our tongues, then, if they are so bad? Jesus says, "If thy right hand offend thee, cut it off and cast it from thee." What! should we then, cut out our tongues and cast them from us? No, the Bible tells us of a better plan: "Behold we put bits in the horses' mouths, that they may obey us; and we turn about the whole body." We can bridle our tongues. They are not safe unless we do so. But we must be sure to have the bridles to fit closely, otherwise we may not be able to guide them properly. When a tongue is well bridled, it will "speak evil of no man." It will not engage in unchaste conversation. It will not speak anything that does not "become sound doctrine." It will not quarrel. It will always tell the truth. One great man had his tongue so well bridled that it is said of him that he always spoke the right word at the right place and at the right time. "If any man among you seem to be religious and bridleth not his tongue, but deceiveth his own heart, this man's religion is vain." James 1: 26.

Dayton, Ohio.

CORRESPONDENCE.

"Write what thou seest, and send it unto the churches."

☞Church News solicited for this Department. If you have had a good meeting, send a report of it, so that others may rejoice with you. In writing give name of church, County and State. Be brief. Notes of Travel should be as short as possible. Land Advertisements are not solicited for this Department. We have an advertising page, and, if necessary, will issue supplements.

Glorious Meetings in Eastern Virginia.

BRO. JACOB D. SANDY, of Ohio, commenced a series of meetings in the Midland church, Oct. 29. On the same day our council, preparatory to the love-feast, was held. Very little business came before the meeting. All the members were in peace and harmony. The meetings continued for ten days in the Midland house. Nov. 5 nine dear souls were buried with Christ in baptism. One brother was also reclaimed. Our love-feast, Nov. 5, was a very enjoyable one. During the night services the house was crowded. The labor devolved upon Bro. Sandy and the home ministry. This was the first feast we ever attended in Virginia, and we enjoyed it indeed.

Nov. 10 the meetings were moved to the Valley View house, where they continued until the 17th, when they were moved to the Cannon Branch school-house, about 2½ miles west of Manassas, where they continued until Nov. 24. Nov. 20 three were baptized, and, on Thanksgiving Day eight more were willing to be led into the liquid stream. We had a glorious Thanksgiving meeting. The whole audience was moved to tears, to see so many dear ones forsaking sin. Others were made to weep because their children were not in the number to be baptized. Bro. Sandy preached thirty-two sermons, and the good these meetings have done cannot be estimated. As a visible result twenty were added by baptism, one reclaimed, and the membership was much re-

vived. Quite a number are near the church. Several of those baptized are pupils of the writer. All are unmarried but three. One is a traveling book-seller, and, at one time, was an Adventist missionary, but when he chanced to learn of our church and doctrine, he wished to unite with us. Brethren and sisters, let us remember these young converts in our prayers, and may God help those who are almost persuaded to come soon, for we have no assurance of our life. Bro. Sandy is but young in the ministry, but is an earnest worker and strong advocate of the distinctive principles of the church. May God go with him wherever he goes!

We are still well pleased with our new home, and would invite others to come. Bro. H. W. Herring, of Somerset County, Pa., has lately bought a farm here and brethren Cyrus and Elmer Walker, of Somerset County, Pa., are here now, looking for farms.   J. E. BLOUGH.

Manassas, Va., Nov. 25.

Wayside Notes.

WE left Moscow Oct. 13 for a short visit to our former home in Kansas. We arrived safely after five days and four nights. Our son Dorsey, from Huntington, Ind., met us. We had not seen him for a number of years. If the meeting of loved ones here affords such comfort and pleasure, what must the meeting be over there! The brethren soon made arrangements for a series of meetings, which continued about two weeks. We had a most glorious meeting. One was baptized and one restored. After the close of meetings, our son went east while self and wife went to the Far West. We stopped at Denver and had two meetings with the Brethren there. We also were at their Sunday-school. We found a zealous little band of workers in this great city. They very much need a resident minister. The brethren from Longmont come occasionally and preach for them, but to make the work successful, it is necessary that a minister locate among them. I see no reason why a large church should not be built up in this great city, if the proper efforts were put forth. We left Denver Nov. 14, for Moscow. We were detained somewhat on account of wrecks and land-slides, but arrived safely Nov. 18.

At this time our faith is good. With the prayers of the faithful we hope to accomplish a good work for the Lord. The greatest difficulty we have to contend with is the large field we have to cultivate. Our visits are far apart and the devil is always active, ready to pluck the good seed from the heart, but we must continue the sowing and God will give the increase.

On our arrival we found the Brethren active in the work, having an evergreen Sunday-school, social meeting, and preaching every Sunday. At this writing we are having much rain and mud.

                                        SIDNEY HODGDEN.

Moscow, Idaho, Nov. 22.

A Visit to the Churches.

THE Pleasant View feast, in Reno County, was small on account of a busy time. A brother should have been baptized, but, because of a misunderstanding, it was delayed till one week later.

Oct. 1, at the Cannon church in Kingman County, Bro. Samuel Bowser was ordained to the eldership, and Jacob Bowser advanced to the second degree in the ministry.

Oct. 8 a feast was held near Peabody, Marion County. There, wife returned home and I went to Sidney, Nebr., on committee work, as authorized by the last General Conference. The Grand Prairie church was dissatisfied with the work of the previous District Meeting. Our labor of love

among them seemed to be appreciated, and gave general satisfaction to all who heard the investigation. At this place a resident elder, full of the Holy Ghost, and an able minister of the New Testament, is greatly needed. A good work could be done. There is plenty of material here of which to build a large spiritual house,—a habitation for God through the Spirit.

From here I went to Scott County, Kans., where we enjoyed another feast with this little "Philadelphia" church. Bro. Homer Ullom was advanced to the second degree of the ministry. One brother and two sisters were added by baptism. Those dear members are laboring faithfully and hopefully, both spiritually and temporally. They should have help in their large field, Bro. D. Vaniman and wife might stop with them one or two weeks on their return from California.

I then returned home and after two days, wife and I went to the East McPherson church to a feast Oct. 29. Here we had the pleasure of meeting brethren J. W. Eller, of Virginia, Josiah Berkley, of Pennsylvania, and A. W. Dickey, of Iowa. This church desired two of her ministering brethren to be ordained to the eldership. But as the one felt himself too unworthy, only Bro. F. H. Bradley had hands laid on him. We then took our leave and came direct to the Monitor church, in the western part of McPherson Co., to enjoy the fellowship of the saints around the table, Nov. 1. The three above-named brethren were present on this occasion to administer the Bread of Life. The next day we went to Lyons, Rice County, expecting to keep the feast with the brethren and sisters in the Kansas Center church, Nov. 5. Here we found Bro. C. C. Root engaged in a series of meetings. The next day we met in council, but did not get through with the business, consequently a few of the members could not enjoy the good feast that the rest of us did. We, however, reviewed a lesson we learned years ago,—not to leave business of such importance till on the verge of a love-feast; as it often interferes with somebody's enjoyment. Bro. Eller remained at Monitor, to hold a few meetings, but followed in time to enjoy the feast here also. Then he returned to his post again, and Bro. C. C. Root continued the work at Kansas Center.

We returned home and remained one day; then went to the Salem church, Reno County, and labored in the interest of the Kansas Home.

Nov. 12 we enjoyed another feast of fat things. Thus ended my 64th year and I felt it would be a good time to cross the river now, after such a continuous feast, if my Father thought best, but his ways are not mine, or rather my ways are not his. Viewing it from another standpoint, I should have twenty years more for the cause, to make up lost time.

All the above feasts were well attended and plenty of ministerial help was at hand. Everything we could ask for, contributed to make them enjoyable. There seems to be a general feeling to march forward, and invade the ranks of the enemy, who, with the least permission, will interfere, and sow his seed of pride and discord.

The home members decided, that, upon my return, I should aid in holding a series of meetings, commencing next week. The length of time will be governed by the interest. Our time is all engaged till about the middle of January if the good Lord grants health and strength, which, so far, has been remarkably good, for which we praise his holy name.

Young ministering brethren, quit you like men, be strong in the Lord. Work while you are vigorous; when you come to threescore and ten, your life will seem like a blank to you, compared to what remains to be done.

as a guide in the selection of proper things to eat. From a physiological standpoint we have no fault to find with the tongue. In its proper use we have displayed in it the wisdom of the Great Mechanic who never made a machine that "would not work."

Notwithstanding the fact that the tongue is so wonderful and so indispensable to our physical well-being, the Bible says some very bad things about it. "Even so the tongue is a little member and boasteth great things." "And the tongue is a fire, a world of iniquity." "For every kind of beasts, and of birds, and of serpents, and of things in the sea, is tamed and hath been tamed of mankind: but the tongue can no man tame; it is an unruly evil, full of deadly poison." See James 3. What shall we do about our tongues, then, if they are so bad? Jesus says, "If thy right hand offend thee, cut it off and cast it from thee." What! should we, then, cut out our tongues and cast them from us? No, the Bible tells us of a better plan: "Behold we put bits in the horses' mouths, that they may obey us; and we turn about the whole body." We can bridle our tongues. They are not safe unless we do so. But we must be sure to have the bridles to fit closely, otherwise we may not be able to guide them properly. When a tongue is well bridled, it will "speak evil of no man." It will not engage in unchaste conversation. It will not speak anything that does not "become sound doctrine." It will not quarrel. It will always tell the truth. One great man had his tongue so well bridled that it is said of him that he always spoke the right word at the right place and at the right time. "If any man among you seem to be religious and bridleth not his tongue, but deceiveth his own heart, this man's religion is vain." James 1: 26.

Dayton, Ohio.

CORRESPONDENCE.

"Write what thou seest, and send it unto the churches."

☞Church News solicited for this Department. If you have had a good meeting, send a report of it, so that others may rejoice with you. In writing give name of church, County and State. Be brief. Notes of Travel should be as short as possible. Land Advertisements are not solicited for this Department. We have an advertising page, and, if necessary, will issue supplements.

Glorious Meetings in Eastern Virginia.

BRO. JACOB D. SANDY, of Ohio, commenced a series of meetings in the Midland church, Oct. 29. On the same day our council, preparatory to the love-feast, was held. Very little business came before the meeting. All the members were in peace and harmony. The meetings continued for ten days in the Midland house. Nov. 5 nine dear souls were buried with Christ in baptism. One brother was also reclaimed. Our love-feast, Nov. 5, was a very enjoyable one. During the night services the house was crowded. The labor devolved upon Bro. Sandy and the home ministry. This was the first feast we ever attended in Virginia, and we enjoyed it indeed.

Nov. 10 the meetings were moved to the Valley View house, where they continued until the 17th, when they were moved to the Cannon Branch school-house, about 2½ miles west of Manassas, where they continued until Nov. 20. Nov. 20 three were baptized, and on Thanksgiving Day eight more were willing to be led into the liquid stream. We had a glorious Thanksgiving meeting. The whole audience was moved to tears, to see so many dear ones forsaking sin. Others were made to weep because their children were not in the number to be baptized. Bro. Sandy preached thirty-two sermons, and the good these meetings have done cannot be estimated. As a visible result twenty were added by baptism, one reclaimed, and the membership was much re-

vived. Quite a number are near the church. Several of those baptized are pupils of the writer. All are unmarried but three. One is a traveling book-seller, and, at one time, was an Adventist missionary, but when he chanced to learn of our church and doctrine, he wished to unite with us. Brethren and sisters, let us remember these young converts in our prayers, and may God help those who are almost persuaded to come soon, for we have no assurance of our life. Bro. Sandy is but young in the ministry, but is an earnest worker and strong advocate of the distinctive principles of the church. May God go with him wherever he goes!

We are still well pleased with our new home, and would invite others to come. Bro. H. W. Herring, of Somerset County, Pa., has lately bought a farm here and brethren Cyrus and Elmer Walker, of Somerset County, Pa., are here now, looking for farms.   J. E. BLOUGH.

Manassas, Va., Nov. 25.

Wayside Notes.

WE left Moscow Oct. 13 for a short visit to our former home in Kansas. We arrived safely after five days and four nights. Our son Dorsey, from Huntington, Ind., met us. We had not seen him for a number of years. If the meeting of loved ones here affords such comfort and pleasure, what must the meeting be over there! The brethren soon made arrangements for a series of meetings, which continued about two weeks. We had a most glorious meeting. One was baptized and one restored. After the close of meetings, our son went east while self and wife went to the Far West. We stopped at Denver and had two meetings with the Brethren there. We also were at their Sunday-school. We found a zealous little band of workers in this great city. They very much need a resident minister. The brethren from Longmont come occasionally and preach for them, but to make the work successful, it is necessary that a minister locate among them. I see no reason why a large church should not be built up in this great city, if the proper efforts were put forth. We left Denver Nov. 14, for Moscow. We were detained somewhat on account of wrecks and land-slides, but arrived safely Nov. 18.

At this time our health is good. With the prayers of the faithful we hope to accomplish a good work for the Lord. The greatest difficulty we have to contend with is the large field we have to cultivate. Our visits are far apart and the devil is always active, ready to pluck the good seed from the heart, but we must continue the sowing and God will give the increase.

On our arrival we found the Brethren active in the work, having an evergreen Sunday-school, social meeting, and preaching every Sunday. At this writing we are having much rain and mud.

SIDNEY HODGDEN.

Moscow, Idaho, Nov. 22.

A Visit to the Churches.

THE Pleasant View feast, in Reno County, was small on account of a busy time. A brother should have been baptized, but, because of a misunderstanding, it was delayed till one week later.

Oct. 1, at the Communion in Kingman County, Bro. Samuel Bowser was ordained to the eldership, and Jacob Bowser advanced to the second degree in the ministry.

Oct. 8 a feast was held near Peabody, Marion County. There, wife returned home and I went to Sidney, Nebr., on committee work, as authorized by the last General Conference. The Grand Prairie church was dissatisfied with the work of the previous District Meeting. Our labor of love

among them seemed to be appreciated, and gave general satisfaction to all who heard the investigation. At this place a resident elder, full of the Holy Ghost, and an able minister of the New Testament, is greatly needed. A good work could be done. There is plenty of material here of which to build a large spiritual house,—a habitation for God through the Spirit.

From here I went to Scott County, Kans., where we enjoyed another feast with this little "Philadelphia" church. Bro. Homer Ullom was advanced to the second degree of the ministry. One brother and two sisters were added by baptism. Those dear members are laboring faithfully and hopefully, both spiritually and temporally. They should have help in their large field, Bro. D. Vaniman and wife might stop with them one or two weeks on their return from California.

I then returned home and after two days, wife and I went to the East McPherson church to a feast Oct. 29. Here we had the pleasure of meeting brethren J. W. Eller, of Virginia, Josiah Berkley, of Pennsylvania, and A. W. Dickey, of Iowa. This church desired two of her ministering brethren to be ordained to the eldership. But as the one felt himself too unworthy, only Bro. F. H. Bradley had hands laid on him. We then took our leave and came direct to the Monitor church, in the western part of McPherson Co., to enjoy the fellowship of the saints around the table, Nov. 1. The three above-named brethren were present on this occasion to administer the Bread of Life. The next day we went to Lyons, Rice County, expecting to keep the feast with the brethren and sisters in the Kansas Center church, Nov. 5. Here we found Bro. C. C. Root engaged in a series of meetings. The next day we met in council, but did not get through with the business, consequently a few of the members could not enjoy the good feast that the rest of us did. We, however, reviewed a lesson we learned years ago,—not to leave business of such importance till on the verge of a love-feast, as it often interferes with somebody's enjoyment. Bro. Eller remained at Monitor, to hold a few meetings, but followed in time to enjoy the feast here also. Then he returned to his post again, and Bro. C. C. Root continued the work at Kansas Center.

We returned home and remained one day; then went to the Salem church, Reno County, and labored in the interest of the Kansas Home.

Nov. 12 we enjoyed another feast of fat things. Thus ended my 64th year and I felt it would be a good time to cross the river now, after such a continuous feast, if my Father thought best, but his ways are not mine, or rather my ways are not his. Viewing it from another standpoint, I should have twenty years more for the cause, to make up lost time.

All the above feasts were well attended and plenty of ministerial help was at hand. Everything we could ask for, contributed to make them enjoyable. There seems to be a general feeling to march forward, and invade the ranks of the enemy, who, with the least permission, will interfere, and sow his seed of pride and discord.

The home members decided, that, upon my return, I should aid in holding a series of meetings, commencing next week. The length of time will be governed by the interest. Our time is all engaged till about the middle of January if the good Lord grants health and strength, which, so far, has been remarkably good, for which we praise his holy name.

Young ministering brethren, quit you like men, be strong in the Lord. Work while you are vigorous; when you come to threescore and ten, your life will seem like a blank to you, compared to what remains to be done.

Missionary and Tract Work Department.

> "Upon the first day of the week, let every one of you lay by him in store as God hath prospered him, that there be no gatherings when I come."—1 Cor. 16: 2.

> "Every man as he purposeth in his heart, so let him give. Not grudgingly or of necessity, for the Lord loveth a cheerful giver."—2 Cor. 9: 7.

HOW MUCH SHALL WE GIVE?

"Every man *according to his ability*." "Every *one as God hath prospered him*." "Every man, *according as he purposeth in his heart*, so let him give." "For if there be first a willing mind, it is accepted *according to that a man hath*, and not according to that he hath not."—2 Cor. 8: 12.

Organization of Missionary Committee.

DANIEL VANIMAN, Foreman, - - McPherson, Kans.
D. L. MILLER, Treasurer, - - Mt. Morris, Ill.
GALEN B. ROYER, Secretary, - Mt. Morris, Ill.

Organization of Book and Tract Work.

S. W. HOOVER, Foreman, - - - Dayton, Ohio.
S. BOCK, Secretary and Treasurer, - Dayton, Ohio.

☞ All donations intended for Missionary Work should be sent to GALEN B. ROYER, Mt. Morris, Ill.

☞ All money for Tract Work should be sent to S. BOCK, Dayton, Ohio.

☞ Money may be sent by Money Order, Registered Letter, or Drafts on New York or Chicago. Do not send personal checks, or drafts on interior towns, as it costs 25 cents to collect them.

☞ Solicitors are requested to faithfully carry out the plan of Annual Meeting, that all our members be solicited to contribute at least twice a year for the Mission and Tract Work of the Church.

☞ Notes for the Endowment Fund can be had by writing to the Secretary of either Work.

DO THEY PRAY FOR ME AT HOME?

SELECTED BY MARY V. HARSHBARGER.

Do they pray for me at home?
Do they ever pray for me,
When I ride the dark sea-foam,
When I cross the stormy sea?
Oh how oft in foreign lands,
As I see the bended knee,
Comes the thought at twilight hour,
Do they ever pray for me?

Do they pray for me at home,
When the summer birds appear?
Do they pray for me the while,
That my path may be less drear?
At the home of early youth,
Do they place the vacant chair,
Where my heart so oft returns
To the loved gathered there?

Do they pray for me at home,
When the winds of winter blow?
Do they pray for me with love,
As they watch the winter snow?
In the season's chilly cold,
Are their hearts for me still warm?
Am I cherished still of old,
Through the beating of the storm?

Painter, Kans.

"TRACTS AND TRACT WORK."

WE have been almost silent in these columns for the greater portion of the time since our last Annual Conference. We hope, however, that this has not been regarded as an indication of idleness or indifference upon our part in this important line of the Master's work. All has moved along fairly well, the circumstances considered. Shortly before the commencement of the present tract year, May 1, and pending revision, provided for the year previous, we had a large edition of tracts printed to carry us over this period. These, during the interim and up to this time, have mostly been sent out and distributed in various parts of the country,—large numbers from house to house.

Willing hearts and hands have voluntarily come forward and taken hold of the work, and with such earnestness, too, and spirit, that we almost feared our available stock would become exhausted before we should be able to get out a quantity of the new. But this has all happily been overcome, and, in consequence, we now have a large edition of the revised, in all, twenty-five different titles, printed and ready for general circulation.

However long and painfully dormant lay the more hopeful missionary spirit of our Brethren, and, I may say, Fraternity, in years gone by, we nevertheless, as such, now have much, very much to be thankful for, not enjoyed then, and to encourage us to move on in the good cause with increased vigor and zeal; especially as we note the steadily-growing interest, everywhere being taken in and developed by our people, both in our home work and home and foreign missions. It is all the more gratifying still, for this very reason, that in all lines of fruitful endeavor, so far as it affects the development of systematized efforts, we may understandingly and with zeal, move on toward the further and more complete observance of Matt. 28: 19, 20. Then, too, the more substantial elements of wakeful missionary endeavor are constantly bringing many new and strong workers, full of nerve and spirit into the ranks. These, added to those already in the field, time after time, will enable the "Work" to daily sow the "good seed of life" more and more widely among the people than ever before.

The work of revision and getting out all new electrotypes, together with the work of printing an edition of some four hundred thousand copies, or a total of over three million pages of reading matter, has not been a small work, but has required much particular labor, time and expense. Our tracts are now all printed on good white paper in long primer type, which makes the reading easy, and also presents a neat and tasty appearance.

The Revising Committee have spared no pains to make their work efficient, and great improvements have been made in every way. The literary style and character of each tract will, at least, compare favorably with the best religious literature in the land. And when it comes to the most essential and valuable part of the Brethren's tracts,—their high standard, stanch and uncompromising character of the doctrines of the New Testament Scriptures, as our only rule of faith and practice, and the clear and concise manner in which the various subjects are treated and the principles and examples of Christ are set forth,—pure, fresh and full,—they appear without competition or parallel in tract publications.   H.

OUR TRIP TO COLORADO AND RETURN.

BY J. S. MOHLER.

ARRIVING at Denver Tuesday morning, Aug. 30, at 7:30, we were met at the depot by Bro. F. Shrove and conveyed to his house, about four miles in the country. Here we were kindly cared for till evening, when he brought us to the depot again, in time for our train to Monte Vista,—distant from Denver, south-west, 268 miles. To reach our destination, we had to cross the eastern range of the Rocky Mountains. On reaching the summit the cold increased to such an extent, that fires were built in the coaches to keep us warm. The grade, in places, is so steep that two engines were required to move the train, and then could go but slowly.

Emerging from Poncha Pass, we entered the famous San Luis Valley. The scenic display of the valley is magnificent. The valley itself is fifty miles wide by two hundred miles in length. It is bounded on the east by the Eastern range of the Rocky Mountains; on the north and north-west by the Western range; on the south by the *Sangre de Christo* range, and on the south-west by the Mountains of New Mexico. The Rio Grande River heads far up in the mountains of eternal snows, and runs through this valley nearly its entire length, about central, affording most excellent facilities for irrigation.

The readers of the MESSENGER will pardon me for digressing a little from my direct line of travel, in order to give a brief description of the resources and improvements of this valley.

Its altitude is 7,500 feet and is very healthy for nearly all lung diseases. The nights are invariably cool. Fruits, such as berries of all varieties, do well in the valley, but for apples, peaches and grapes, the frosts are too frequent, occurring about ten months in a year. The people, however, are well supplied with all kinds of fruit from New Mexico, at prices quite reasonable.

All vegetables do well except the vines, such as pumpkins, melons, cucumbers, etc., on account of frost. Wheat, oats and barley do exceedingly well. For corn the weather is too cool. Alfalfa grows to perfection, and so does the native grass, which embraces about half a dozen kinds of the wild varieties. It is very nutritious. Stock-raising is easy and profitable, on account of the unlimited supply of mountain range. Irrigation is far on the way. The wells in the valley are all Artesian, affording large reservoirs of clear water, which are well stocked with fish. The Denver and Rio Grande railroad runs through the entire valley, dividing at Alamosa,—one division bearing north, the other south-west to the Santa Fe. Society is good. School-houses abound, and churches are being built. The people, generally, are of an enterprising character. On account of the large mining population, the markets for all kinds of produce are good.

This short description of the San Luis Valley is not written in the interest of any party, but merely as a matter of history. Persons desiring to move there should go and see for themselves.

On Wednesday morning, Aug. 31, I arrived at Monte Vista, where Bro. A. C. Snowberger met me and conveyed me to the hospitable home of friend and sister Heilman. The same evening we commenced meetings and continued till Sunday, Sept. 11. During this time we held a love-feast and dedicated the church. The church is organised and under the care of Eld. George Fessler, of Longmont. Brethren Snowberger and Larick are resident ministers, and are doing good work. They have a good Sunday-school in the church, and a prayer-meeting, as well as appointments elsewhere. The future of the church there seems promising. While there were no accessions at this meeting, we need not feel discouraged, as the work there is comparatively new, and the people nearly all strangers to the doctrine. Thus continuous work is required before an inroad can be made into the strongholds of the enemy.

Their church-house is completed and is a neat, plain structure 26 by 40 feet in size. It is all paid for, except a small balance, which the members there thought they could easily defray.

The number of members there, as yet, is quite small. I believe it is about the same as those saved in Noah's Ark, of which the world has been peopled. But, so far as we could discern, they are bright and shining lights in that community, which cannot fail to tell for the cause in course of time. We were kindly received and entertained by members and friends while there, and when the time of parting came, we were loth to part. About all the members accompanied us to the train, bidding us an affectionate farewell till we would meet again.

(*To be continued.*)

WRITE the "Tract Work" for our new catalogue and price list. Also for descriptive catalogue and prices of "International" series Bibles and Testaments. Over two hundred styles and sizes.   E.

Missionary and Tract Work Department.

"Upon the first day of the week, let every one of you lay by him in store, as God hath prospered him, that there be no gatherings when I come."—1 Cor. 16: 2.

"Every man as he purposeth in his heart, so let him give. Not grudgingly or of necessity, for the Lord loveth a cheerful giver."—2 Cor. 9: 7.

HOW MUCH SHALL WE GIVE?

"Every man *according to his ability.*" "Every one *as God hath prospered him.*" "Every man, *according as he purposeth in his heart,* so let him give." "For if there be first a willing mind, it is accepted *according to that a man hath,* and not according to that he hath not."—2 Cor. 8: 12.

Organization of Missionary Committee.

DANIEL VANIMAN, Foreman,	McPherson, Kans.
D. L. MILLER, Treasurer,	Mt. Morris, Ill.
GALEN B. ROYER, Secretary,	Mt. Morris, Ill.

Organization of Book and Tract Work.

S. W. HOOVER, Foreman,	Dayton, Ohio.
S. BOCK, Secretary and Treasurer,	Dayton, Ohio.

☞All donations intended for Missionary Work should be sent to GALEN B. ROYER, Mt. Morris, Ill.

☞All money for Tract Work should be sent to S. BOCK, Dayton, Ohio.

☞Money may be sent by Money Order, Registered Letter, or Drafts on New York or Chicago. Do not send personal checks, or drafts on interior towns, as it costs 25 cents to collect them.

☞Solicitors are requested to faithfully carry out the plan of Annual Meeting, that all our members be solicited to contribute at least twice a year for the Mission and Tract Work of the Church.

☞Notes for the Endowment Fund can be had by writing to the Secretary of either Work.

DO THEY PRAY FOR ME AT HOME!

SELECTED BY MARY V. HARNSBARGER.

Do they pray for me at home?
Do they ever pray for me,
When I ride the dark sea-foam,
When I cross the stormy sea?
Oh how oft in foreign lands,
As I see the bended knee,
Comes the thought at twilight hour,
Do they ever pray for me?

Do they pray for me at home,
When the summer birds appear?
Do they pray for me the while,
That my path may be less drear?
At the home of early youth,
Do they place the vacant chair,
Where my heart so oft returns
To the loved gathered there?

Do they pray for me at home,
When the winds of winter blow?
Do they pray for me with love,
As they watch the winter snow?
In the season's chilly cold,
Are their hearts for me still warm?
Am I cherished still of old,
Through the beating of the storm?

Painter, Kans.

"TRACTS AND TRACT WORK."

WE have been almost silent in these columns for the greater portion of the time since our last Annual Conference. We hope, however, that this has not been regarded as an indication of idleness or indifference upon our part in this important line of the Master's work. All has moved along fairly well, the circumstances considered. Shortly before the commencement of the present tract year, May 1, and pending revision, provided for the year previous, we had a large edition of tracts printed to carry us over this period. These, during the interim and up to this time, have mostly been sent out and distributed in various parts of the country,—large numbers from house to house.

Willing hearts and hands have voluntarily come forward and taken hold of the work, and with such earnestness, too, and spirit, that we almost feared our available stock would become exhausted before we should be able to get out a quantity of the new. But this has all happily been overcome, and, in consequence, we now have a large edition of the revised, in all, twenty-five different titles, printed and ready for general circulation.

However long and painfully dormant lay the more hopeful missionary spirit of our Brethren, and, I may say, Fraternity, in years gone by, we nevertheless, as such, now have much, very much to be thankful for, not enjoyed then, and to encourage us to move on in the good cause with increased vigor and zeal; especially as we note the steadily-growing interest, everywhere being taken in and developed by our people, both in our home work and home and foreign missions. It is all the more gratifying still, for this very reason, that in all lines of fruitful endeavor, so far as it affects the development of systematized efforts, we may understandingly and with zeal, move on toward the further and more complete observance of Matt. 28: 19, 20. Then, too, the more substantial elements of wakeful missionary endeavor are constantly bringing many new and strong workers, full of nerve and spirit into the ranks. These, added to those already in the field, time after time, will enable the "Work" to daily sow the "good seed of life" more and more widely among the people than ever before.

The work of revision and getting out all new electrotypes, together with the work of printing an edition of some four hundred thousand copies, or a total of over three million pages of reading matter, has not been a small work, but has required much particular labor, time and expense. Our tracts are now all printed on good white paper in long primer type, which makes the reading easy, and also presents a neat and tasty appearance.

The Revising Committee have spared no pains to make their work efficient, and great improvements have been made in every way. The literary style and character of each tract will, at least, compare favorably with the best religious literature in the land. And when it comes to the most essential and valuable part of the Brethren's tracts,—their high standard, staunch and uncompromising character of the doctrines of the New Testament Scriptures, as our only rule of faith and practice, and the clear and concise manner in which the various subjects are treated and the principles and examples of Christ are set forth,—pure, fresh and full,—they appear without competition or parallel in tract publications. B.

OUR TRIP TO COLORADO AND RETURN.

BY J. S. MOHLER.

ARRIVING at Denver Tuesday morning, Aug. 30, at 7:30, we were met at the depot by Bro. F. Shrove and conveyed to his house, about four miles in the country. Here we were kindly cared for till evening, when he brought us to the depot again, in time for our train to Monte Vista,—distant from Denver, south-west, 268 miles. To reach our destination, we had to cross the eastern range of the Rocky Mountains. On reaching the summit the cold increased to such an extent, that fires were built in the coaches to keep us warm. The grade, in places, is so steep that two engines were required to move the train, and then could go but slowly.

Emerging from Poncha Pass, we entered the famous San Luis Valley. The scenic display of the valley is magnificent. The valley itself is fifty miles wide by two hundred miles in length. It is bounded on the east by the Eastern range of the Rocky Mountains; on the north and north-west by the Western range; on the south by the *Sangre de Christo* range, and on the south-west by the Mountains of New Mexico. The Rio Grande River heads far up in the mountains of eternal snows, and runs through this valley nearly its entire length, about central, affording most excellent facilities for irrigation.

The readers of the MESSENGER will pardon me for digressing a little from my direct line of travel, in order to give a brief description of the resources and improvements of this valley.

Its altitude is 7,500 feet and is very healthy for nearly all lung diseases. The nights are invariably cool. Fruits, such as berries of all varieties, do well in the valley, but for apples, peaches and grapes, the frosts are too frequent, occurring about ten months in a year. The people, however, are well supplied with all kinds of fruit from New Mexico, at prices quite reasonable.

All vegetables do well except the vines, such as pumpkins, melons, cucumbers, etc., on account of frost. Wheat, oats and barley do exceedingly well. For corn the weather is too cool. Alfalfa grows to perfection, and so does the native grass, which embraces about half a dozen kinds of the wild varieties. It is very nutritious. Stock-raising is easy and profitable, on account of the unlimited supply of mountain range. Irrigation is far on the way. The wells in the valley are all Artesian, affording large reservoirs of clear water, which are well stocked with fish. The Denver and Rio Grande railroad runs through the entire valley, dividing at Alamosa,—one division bearing north, the other south-west to the Santa Fe. Society is good. School-houses abound, and churches are being built. The people, generally, are of an enterprising character. On account of the large mining population, the markets for all kinds of produce are good.

This short description of the San Luis Valley is not written in the interest of any party, but merely as a matter of history. Persons desiring to move there should go and see for themselves.

On Wednesday morning, Aug. 31, I arrived at Monte Vista, where Bro. A. C. Snowberger met me and conveyed me to the hospitable home of friend and sister Heilman. The same evening we commenced meetings and continued till Sunday, Sept. 11. During this time we held a love-feast and dedicated the church. The church is organized and under the care of Eld. George Fessler, of Longmont. Brethren Snowberger and Larick are resident ministers, and are doing good work. They have a good Sunday-school in the church, and a prayer-meeting, as well as appointments elsewhere. The future of the church there seems promising. While there were no accessions at this meeting, we need not feel discouraged, as the work there is comparatively new, and the people nearly all strangers to the doctrine. Thus continuous work is required before an inroad can be made into the strongholds of the enemy.

Their church-house is completed and is a neat, plain structure 26 by 40 feet in size. It is all paid for, except a small balance, which the members there thought they could easily defray.

The number of members there, as yet, is quite small. I believe it is about the same as those saved in Noah's Ark, of which the world has been peopled. But, so far as we could discern, they are bright and shining lights in that community, which cannot fail to tell for the cause in course of time. We were kindly received and entertained by members and friends while there, and when the time of parting came, we were loth to part. About all the members accompanied us to the train, bidding us an affectionate farewell till we would meet again.

(*To be continued.*)

WRITE the "Tract Work" for our new catalogue and price list. Also for descriptive catalogue and prices of "International" series Bibles and Testaments. Over two hundred styles and sizes. B.

The Gospel Messenger,

A Weekly at $1.50 Per Annum.

PUBLISHED BY

The Brethren's Publishing Co.

D. L. MILLER, ... Editor.
J. H. MOORE, ... Office Editor.
J. B. BRUMBAUGH, ... Associate Editors.
J. G. ROYER,
JOSEPH AMICK, ... Business Manager.

ADVISORY COMMITTEE.

L. W. Teeter, A. Hutchison, Daniel Hays.

☞ Communications for publication should be legibly written with black ink on one side of the paper only. Do not attempt to interline, or to put on one page what ought to occupy two.

☞ Anonymous communications will not be published.

☞ Do not mix business with articles for publication. Keep your communications on separate sheets from all business.

☞ Time is precious. We always have time to attend to business and to answer questions of importance, but please do not subject us to needless answering of letters.

☞ The MESSENGER is mailed each week to all subscribers. If the address is correctly entered on our list, the paper must reach the person to whom it is addressed. If you do not get your paper, write us, giving particulars.

☞ When changing your address, please give your former as well as your future address in full, so as to avoid delay and misunderstanding.

☞ Always remit to the office from which you order your goods, no matter from where you receive them.

☞ Do not send personal checks or drafts on interior banks, unless you send with them 25 cents each, to pay for collection.

☞ Remittances should be made by Post-office Money Order, Drafts on New York, Philadelphia or Chicago, or Registered Letters, made payable and addressed to "Brethren's Publishing Co., Mount Morris, Ill.," or "Brethren's Publishing Co., Huntingdon, Pa."

☞ Entered at the Post-office at Mount Morris, Ill., as second-class matter.

Mount Morris, Ill., ... Dec. 6, 1892.

BRO. J. S. MOHLER writes us that Bro. J. E. Young is engaged in a series of meetings in the North Morrill church, Kansas.

THIS week Bro. D. E. Brubaker is engaged in a series of meetings in the Roanoke church, Woodford County, Illinois, expecting to remain some ten days.

THE church near Stonewall, Va., known as the Valley District, has been blessed with nineteen additions during the summer and fall. Six of them came out quite recently.

THE Hopewell church, Bedford County, Pa., has many reasons to rejoice. Fifteen recently made the good confession during a series of meetings held by Bro. Silas Hoover.

ON Thanksgiving Day Bro. Jacob D. Sandy, of Ohio, closed a glorious series of meetings near Manassas, Virginia. Twenty united with the church by confession and baptism.

FROM the California Advance we learn that Bro. Daniel Vaniman was booked for a series of meetings in the Lordsburg College Chapel, at Lordsburg, commencing Nov. 27.

BRO. DANIEL STONER, of Pekin, Illinois, is preparing to move to Arkansas. We regret to see him leave Pekin, as it leaves that locality without a minister. But since he is going to change location we are glad that he is going where he is needed.

ON Thanksgiving morning we received a cablegram from Bro. D. L. Miller, stating that he and Bro. Lahman had reached Genoa, Italy, that morning, that they were both well and had a very pleasant voyage. We expect letters from them by the time we go to press with the next issue, and will soon commence publishing Bro. Miller's interesting articles of his travels. Our readers may expect something both profitable and interesting in these letters.

BRETHREN, we must again say, Do not wait so long before sending in reports of your meetings. Some correspondents delay a month. Please do not do this, but give us the news while it is fresh. We want the news fresh and short, and plenty of it.

IN the Russel church, Kansas, the ministers keep up the habit of preaching their yearly missionary sermons. As a consequence the members are imbued with the missionary spirit, and the solicitors have little trouble in raising needed missionary money.

UNDER date of Nov. 19, Bro. Geo. L. Studebaker writes, "At present I am with the Brethren in the Somerset church, Wabash Co., Ind. I came yesterday and expect to remain two weeks. Two were baptized in the Mississinewa church last Sunday, Nov. 13."

THE library in the British Museum, in London, contains 1,600,000 books. It is probably the largest library in the world save the celebrated National Library of France, which numbers at this time 2,500,000 volumes, and is the most valuable collection of books in existence.

BRO. DAVID PUTERBAUGH and wife, of East McPherson, Kansas, are spending some weeks among the churches in Northern Illinois. They gave us a pleasant call last week. They speak well of their western home and are hopeful of their work in the East McPherson church.

WE are receiving some encouraging reports from the Thanksgiving meetings, held by the Brethren in different parts of the Brotherhood. Collections were taken up for different charitable purposes, and at some places a number came out on the Lord's side. At one Thanksgiving meeting eight were baptized.

Do not spend time wishing for the return of former days, or yearning to live life over again. Those days can never return, and if they did, they might contain more dark clouds and painful incidents than we now think. There are plenty of good days in the future, if we will only strive to make the best use of them.

MR. A. VANDERWERKER, of Brooklyn, New York, is probably more nice than wise. He has issued circulars, giving four reasons for objecting to the use of one or two cups at the Communion table. He thinks it not decent for so many to sip from one cup, especially the last ones. Then he suggests that it may be the means of spreading disease. He would have one little cup for each communicant. Our impression is that when people once get so nice (?), the Communion will be of but little, if any, benefit to them. Paul says, "The cup which we bless;" not 400 cups. One cup will do for people who are of the same mind and of the same judgment.

OUR Thanksgiving meeting in the Chapel, last Thursday, was largely attended. We felt to give thanks unto the Lord for his abundant mercies bestowed upon us, for the bountiful harvest of the year, for our exemption from pestilences and calamities, for this land of perfect religious freedom, for rulers who are mindful enough of the Great God of heaven, to set apart a day of special thanksgiving, and especially for our deliverance from sin through Jesus Christ who has paid the debt for our redemption. A collection was taken up and $36.00 raised for home missionary work in Northern Illinois. This, added to the amount raised by the Sunday-school last Sunday, makes our thanksgiving offering over $53.28.

ALL of the tracts, now published by the Brethren's Tract Work, have been bound in a neat volume, and make a very respectable and valuable little book. In this manner the tracts will be preserved in permanent book form, and will serve as an important reference when one desires to read up on any of the subjects treated in the tracts. Price, 75 cents by mail. It may be ordered from this office.

BRO. GEO. W. GISH, of Woodford County, Ill., spent several days with us last week. He is one of the old pioneers in the church work of the Far West. It is interesting to meet these aged brethren and converse with them about their history and the struggles of the past. The present generation knows little of what our aged fathers had to endure when they planted the standard of Christianity on these wild western prairies.

NOT long since a congregation was requested to send for Bro. —— to hold a series of meetings. Some brother objected, saying, "We have had him twice, and the last time he was here he preached the same sermons he did the first time, using the same text in each instance." The reason for objecting to the minister was a good one in this age, and we mention it only to serve as a reminder to ministers, that in preaching variety is both essential and commendable.

IN all of our writing for the press, as well as in all of our speaking for Jesus, let neither the pen nor the tongue give an uncertain sound. If we are not thoroughly rooted and grounded in the truth, so that we can be depended upon at all times, let us pray God to increase our faith and establish our hearts that we be not easily moved by the cunning devices of either man or Satan. This is an age in which the hearts of men are being tried, and it is important that all Christians be thoroughly established.

A BROTHER who lives nine miles from the church, is confined to his room most of the time with consumption, feels very lonely and sad because none of the brethren visit him. He says brother A. used to come to see him, but he is now dead. We have it that this sick brother lives "nine miles" from the church. Perhaps he lives next door neighbor to many of our readers. Let the members in each church look him up, and then ponder well the reasons given for excluding some from heaven,—"I was sick and ye visited me not."

IN their preaching as well as in their writing there is a tendency upon the part of some to deal almost exclusively with the external. They preach and write much about plainness of appearance, etc., but do not encourage the higher order of heart religion. By no means should we neglect the external, neither should we fail to guard all due attention to the inner man of the heart. We sometimes think that if our Brethren would study and preach more about the true Christian graces, and how to develop a higher order of Christian character, that it might possibly enable them to treat the external duties with more power and skill. Without heart religion there can be no true manifestation of religion, Hence the importance of a real heart conversion in the start. Furthermore, for one to have all the external appearance of a brother, and then seem altogether like a man of the world in everything else is most assuredly a detriment to the cause that we are advocating. We want to teach our members to walk closer to God, and to cultivate all the inward as well as the outward graces necessary to make of them Christians that will give the church influence as well as purity.

The Gospel Messenger,

A Weekly at $1.50 Per Annum.

PUBLISHED BY

The Brethren's Publishing Co.

D. L. MILLER,	Editor.
J. H. MOORE,	Office Editor.
J. B. BRUMBAUGH,	
J. G. ROYER,	Associate Editors.
JOSEPH AMICK,	Business Manager.

ADVISORY COMMITTEE.
L. W. Teeter, A. Hutchison, Daniel Hays.

☞ Communications for publication should be legibly written with black ink on one side of the paper only. Do not attempt to interline, or to put on one page what ought to occupy two.

☞ Anonymous communications will not be published.

☞ Do not mix business with articles for publication. Keep your communications on separate sheets from all business.

☞ Time is precious. We always have time to attend to business and to answer questions of importance, but please do not subject us to need less answering of letters.

☞ The MESSENGER is mailed each week to all subscribers. If the address is correctly entered on our list, the paper must reach the person to whom it is addressed. If you do not get your paper, write us, giving particulars.

☞ When changing your address, please give your former as well as your future address in full, so as to avoid delay and misunderstanding.

☞ Always remit to the office from which you order your goods, no matter from where you receive them.

☞ Do not send personal checks or drafts on interior banks, unless you send with them 15 cents each, to pay for collection.

☞ Remittances should be made by Post-office Money Order, Drafts on New York, Philadelphia or Chicago, or Registered Letters, made payable and addressed to "Brethren's Publishing Co., Mount Morris, Ill.," or "Brethren's Publishing Co., Huntingdon, Pa."

☞ Entered at the Post-office at Mount Morris, Ill., as second-class matter.

Mount Morris, Ill., ... Dec. 6, 1892.

BRO. J. S. MOHLER writes us that Bro. J. E. Young is engaged in a series of meetings in the North Morrill church, Kansas.

THIS week Bro. D. E. Brubaker is engaged in a series of meetings in the Roanoke church, Woodford County, Illinois, expecting to remain some ten days.

THE church near Stonewall, Va., known as the Valley District, has been blessed with nineteen additions during the summer and fall. Six of them came out quite recently.

THE Hopewell church, Bedford County, Pa., has many reasons to rejoice. Fifteen recently made the good confession during a series of meetings held by Bro. Silas Hoover.

ON Thanksgiving Day Bro. Jacob D. Sandy, of Ohio, closed a glorious series of meetings near Manassas, Virginia. Twenty united with the church by confession and baptism.

FROM the *California Advance* we learn that Bro. Daniel Vaniman was booked for a series of meetings in the Lordsburg College Chapel, at Lordsburg, commencing Nov. 27.

BRO. DANIEL STONER, of Pekin, Illinois, is preparing to move to Arkansas. We regret to see him leave Pekin, as it leaves that locality without a minister. But since he is going to change location we are glad that he is going where he is needed.

ON Thanksgiving morning we received a cable-gram from Bro. D. L. Miller, stating that he and Bro. Lahman had reached Genoa, Italy, that morning, that they were both well and had a very pleasant voyage. We expect letters from them by the time we go to press with the next issue, and will soon commence publishing Bro. Miller's interesting articles of his travels. Our readers may expect something both profitable and interesting in these letters.

BRETHREN, we must again say, Do not wait so long before sending in reports of your meetings. Some correspondents delay a month. Please do not do this, but give us the news while it is fresh. We want the news fresh and short, and plenty of it.

IN the Russel church, Kansas, the ministers keep up the habit of preaching their yearly missionary sermons. As a consequence the members are imbued with the missionary spirit, and the solicitors have little trouble in raising needed missionary money.

UNDER date of Nov. 19, Bro. Geo. L. Studebaker writes, "At present I am with the Brethren in the Somerset church, Wabash Co., Ind. I came yesterday and expect to remain two weeks. Two were baptized in the Mississinewa church last Sunday, Nov. 13."

THE library in the British Museum, in London, contains 1,600,000 books. It is probably the largest library in the world save the celebrated National Library of France, which numbers at this time 2,500,000 volumes, and is the most valuable collection of books in existence.

BRO. DAVID PUTERBAUGH and wife, of East McPherson, Kansas, are spending some weeks among the churches in Northern Illinois. They gave us a pleasant call last week. They speak well of their western home and are hopeful of their work in the East McPherson church.

WE are receiving some encouraging reports from the Thanksgiving meetings, held by the Brethren in different parts of the Brotherhood. Collections were taken up for different charitable purposes, and at some places a number came out on the Lord's side. At one Thanksgiving meeting eight were baptized.

Do not spend time wishing for the return of former days, or yearning to live life over again. Those days can never return, and if they did, they might contain more dark clouds and painful incidents than we now think. There are plenty of good days in the future, if we will only strive to make the best use of them.

MR. A. VANDERWERKER, of Brooklyn, New York, is probably more nice than wise. He has issued circulars, giving four reasons for objecting to the use of one or two cups at the Communion table. He thinks it not decent for so many to sip from one cup, especially the last ones. Then he suggests that it may be the means of spreading disease. He would have one little cup for each communicant. Our impression is that when people once get so nice (?), the Communion will be of but little, if any, benefit to them. Paul says, "The cup which we bless;" not 400 cups. One cup will do for people who are of the same mind and of the same judgment.

OUR Thanksgiving meeting in the Chapel, last Thursday, was largely attended. We felt to give thanks unto the Lord for his abundant mercies bestowed upon us, for the bountiful harvest of the year, for our exemption from pestilences and calamities, for this land of perfect religious freedom, for rulers who are mindful enough of the Great God of heaven, to set apart a day of special thanksgiving, and especially for our deliverance through Jesus Christ who has paid the debt for our redemption. A collection was taken up and $36.00 raised for home missionary work in Northern Illinois. This, added to the amount raised by the Sunday-school last Sunday, makes our thanksgiving offering over $53.28.

ALL of the tracts, now published by the Brethren's Tract Work, have been bound in a neat volume, and make a very respectable and valuable little book. In this manner the tracts will be preserved in permanent book form, and will serve as an important reference when one desires to read up on any of the subjects treated in the tracts. Price, 75 cents by mail. It may be ordered from this office.

BRO. GEO. W. GISH, of Woodford County, Ill., spent several days with us last week. He is one of the old pioneers in the church work of the Far West. It is interesting to meet these aged brethren and converse with them about their history and the struggles of the past. The present generation knows little of what our aged fathers had to endure when they planted the standard of Christianity on these wild western prairies.

NOT long since a congregation was requested to send for Bro. —— to hold a series of meetings. Some brother objected, saying, "We have had him twice, and the last time he was here he preached the same sermons he did the first time, using the same text in each instance." The reason for objecting to the minister was a good one in this age, and we mention it only to serve as a reminder to ministers, that in preaching variety is both essential and commendable.

IN all of our writing for the press, as well as in all of our speaking for Jesus, let neither the pen nor the tongue give an uncertain sound. If we are not thoroughly rooted and grounded in the truth, so that we can be depended upon at all times, let us pray God to increase our faith and establish our hearts that we be not easily moved by the cunning devices of either man or Satan. This is an age in which the hearts of men are being tried, and it is important that all Christians be thoroughly established.

A BROTHER who lives nine miles from the church, and is confined to his room most of the time with consumption, feels very lonely and sad because none of the brethren visit him. He says brother A. used to come to see him, but he is now dead. We have it that this sick brother lives "nine miles" from the church. Perhaps he lives next door neighbor to many of our readers. Let the members in each church look him up, and then ponder well the reasons given for excluding some from heaven,—"I was sick and ye visited me not."

IN their preaching as well as in their writing there is a tendency upon the part of some to deal almost exclusively with the external. They preach and write much about plainness of appearance, etc., but do not encourage the higher order of heart religion. By no means should we neglect the external, neither should we fail to give all due attention to the inner man of the heart. We sometimes think that if our Brethren would study and preach more about the true Christian graces, and how to develop a higher order of Christian character, that it might possibly enable them to treat the external duties with more power and skill. Without heart religion there can be no true manifestation of religion. Hence the importance of a real heart conversion in the start. Furthermore, for one to have all the external appearance of a brother, and then seem altogether like a man of the world in everything else is most assuredly a detriment to the cause that we are advocating. We want to teach our members to walk closer to God, and to cultivate all the inward as well as the outward graces necessary to make of them Christians that will give the church influence as well as purity.

OUR VISIT TO THE EAST.

NEW ENTERPRISE is a village in Bedford County, Pa., situated in one end of what is known as "The Cove." The valley contains an area of about 150 square miles and is entirely enclosed by mountains. Over one thousand of the present inhabitants of the valley are members of the Brethren church. Many flourishing churches in the West have been planted by brethren who came from this valley, while many a hillside is studded with marble slabs marking the graves of those who once aided in bearing aloft the banner of the Blessed Master, but have long since gone to their reward. The dawn of eternity alone will reveal the results of the influences for good, set to work by the humble followers of Jesus whose earthly homes were in "The Cove."

On Saturday evening, Oct. 29, we began a series of meetings with the Brethren of New Enterprise and continued until Nov. 15. From the beginning the meetings were well attended and the best of attention given to the Word preached. By the end of the first week it was manifest that the Spirit was at work, and during the second week fifteen precious souls were saved to the family of God militant. All but one were young people, and all were members of the Sunday-school. We regretted very much that other duties compelled us to leave at this stage of the meetings, as it was evident that others were seriously considering the propriety of taking up the cross. The meetings were, however, continued by the home brethren and we are happy to know that others have accepted their Savior. We hope many more will do so.

In the earlier part of the meetings the sympathies of the community were called out in favor of Eld. Joseph Replogle and family on account of the sudden death of their eight-year-old daughter. She came home from school unwell, and grew worse but was not considered dangerously ill by the family. Bro. Replogle himself has been afflicted both physically and mentally for some time. Weary and care-worn sister Replogle and family lay down to rest. On waking up they found that the spirit of little Sadie had gone to the beyond.

" How short is human life! the very breath
Which frames my words, accelerates my death."

The church at New Enterprise had her dark days during the division, the marks of which remain in the form of a small congregation of those who would no longer walk with us. With a full corps of officers, a large and live Sunday-school and prayer-meeting, together with the good will and sympathies of those who are looking in, we feel assured of the future prosperity of the church at New Enterprise. Our visit was a very pleasant one and, we trust, profitable as well. The Lord bless all the dear brethren and sisters whose love and kindness we so much enjoyed while among them.　　　　J. G. R.

CORRESPONDENCE.

" Write what thou seest, and send it unto the churches."

☞Church News solicited for this Department. If you have had a good meeting, send a report of it, so that others may rejoice with you. In writing give name of church, County and State. Be brief. Notes of Travel should be as short as possible. Land Advertisements are not solicited for this Department. We have an advertising page, and, if necessary, will issue supplements.

From North Michigan.

ON the evening of Nov. 3 we boarded the train at Clarkesville, where we met Eld. Isaiah Rair-igh, en route for Grand Rapids. Upon our arrival we were met by our esteemed brother, A. T. Morrison, and his two daughters (who are members). They took us to their home, where we enjoyed a pleasant talk on religious topics. Next morning we boarded the train for our mission post at Custer, Mason County, where we met with the little band of members in council the same afternoon. We found there was a unanimous desire to have an election for a deacon. Instead of one there were two elected,—brethren Israel Fisher and Jacob Mahler. These brethren, with their wives, were duly installed. Our prayer is that they may prove faithful in their important office! We remained here till the morning of Nov. 7. During our stay with them Bro. Isaiah preached four sermons. We then started for Traverse City, a distance of ninety miles north. The day was very gloomy and rainy. Upon our arrival we found our friend (now a brother), John Leeee, awaiting us. He took us to his home, a distance of eight miles, over some very rolling country. It was in behalf of this family we had come. The GOSPEL MESSENGER was sent to him by his brother, from the Thornapple church, and by reading it he became convicted and wanted to unite with us. We found his wife also deeply interested, and after we had set before them our faith and practice, all through, and tried to give Scriptural reasons for all, and especially on immersion, she (the wife) said she was also ready to go into the water.

After a season of prayer, we retired at a late hour. The next morning, at an early hour, we made the necessary arrangements. Though the morning was cold and the ground covered with snow, in the twilight we started for the water,—a distance of one and one-half miles,—where we found a beautiful little stream. Here they were buried beneath the liquid wave. Though our number was only six, the scene, with its surroundings, was very solemn and impressive. After the baptism we bade the newly-baptized ones farewell and turned our faces homeward, where we arrived at 8 P. M., and found all well.

I. F. RAIRIGH.

BIBLE DEPARTMENT MT. MORRIS COLLEGE.

Second Term.—Jan. 3 to March 21, 1893.

COURSE OF STUDY.

I. *Old Testament History.*—Pentateuch Completed.

1. LEVITICUS.—Worship, sacrifice and priesthood.

2. NUMBERS.—Marshaling of the Lord's hosts and their victorious march to Canaan.

3. DEUTERONOMY.—The law made emphatic by repetition.

4. Special outline of Mosaic Law.

II. *Old Testament History.*—Prophecy.

1. Historical view of books of the prophets.

2. Hebrew prophecy.

3. Predictive prophecy.

4. Primitive Messianic ideas.

5. Messianic prophecy in the Mosaic Age.

6. Messianic prophecy in the Davidic period.

7. Messianic ideas of the early prophets.

8. Study of the book of Isaiah by outline.

III. *New Testament History.*

1. Book of Hebrews by outline; (a) comparison of the two covenants; (b) New Testament Mediator, as Son above all other mediators of revelation and redemption; (c) Jesus Christ as Eternal Priestly King, the Counterpart of Melchisedec; (d) preeminence of the New Covenant mediated through Jesus Christ.

(2) Books of 1st and 2nd Corinthians by outline; (a) unwarranted divisions in the church; (b) teachings on morality; (c) bestowment of spiritual gifts; (d) certainty of the resurrection; (e) Paul's account of his conduct towards the Corinthians; (f) his fidelity and encouragement; (g) condition of activity at Corinth; (h) Paul's claim and proof of apostleship.

IV. *Church History.*—Reformation.

1. General character of Reformation.

2. Rise and decline of papal hierarchy.

3. Causes of ecclesiastical revolution prior to the sixteenth century.

4. Luther and German Reformation to the diet of Augsburg.

5. Reformation of the Scandinavian kingdom.

6. John Calvin and Genevan Reformation.

7. Reformation in France.

8. Reformation in Netherlands.

9. Reformation in England and Scotland.

10. Reformation in Italy and Spain.

11. Struggles of Protestantism.

12. Protestant Reformation.

V. *Chautauqua Sunday-school Normal Course.*

1. Bible studies.

(a) Old Testament as a preparation for the Christian church; (1) a divine religion given to man; (2) development of divine religion in the life of chosen people.

(b) Old Testament as a preparation for Christ; (1) sacrifices and types; (2) kingdom and the prophets.

(c) New Testament of the manifestation of Christ; (1) facts in life of Christ, and order in which they should be taught; (2) the doctrines of Christ; (3) relation of facts to the doctrine.

(d) New Testament as a revelation of the Christian church; (1) its essential elements; (2) its history in the New Testament; (3) progress of doctrine in the New Testament; (4) doctrine in the Acts and epistles.

VI. *Sermons and Lectures.*

There will be a sermon or lecture every evening during the month of January.

1. Progress of Revelation.

(a) Canon of Scripture.

(b) Hebrew prophecies.

(c) Sacrifices.

2. The Church.

(a) As to place; (1) local; (2) general; (3) militant; (4) triumphant.

(b) As to doctrine; (1) baptism; (2) Lord's Supper.

(c) As to government. Relation of church to Annual Conference.

(d) As to mission work; (1) Gospel authority for mission work; (2) relation of church to mission work; (3) qualifications of missionaries; (4) present mission field and how to cultivate it.

(e) As to the ministry; (1) call and preparation; (2) relation of the minister to the church; (a) ambassador; (b) pastor; (c) steward; (d) elder; (3) ministers' relation to (a) Sunday-school; (b) prayer-meetings; (c) mission work; (4) ministers' inner life; (5) ministers' outer life as manifested (a) in house of God; (b) in business; (c) in neighborhood.

3. Tabernacle and events in the Savior's life, as illustrated by lantern views.

GENERAL INFORMATION.

1. The course of instruction is entirely practical and adapted to the wants of nearly every class of Bible students.

OUR VISIT TO THE EAST.

NEW ENTERPRISE is a village in Bedford County, Pa., situated in one end of what is known as "The Cove." The valley contains an area of about 150 square miles and is entirely enclosed by mountains. Over one thousand of the present inhabitants of the valley are members of the Brethren church. Many flourishing churches in the West have been planted by brethren who came from this valley, while many a hillside is studded with marble slabs marking the graves of those who once aided in bearing aloft the banner of the Blessed Master, but have long since gone to their reward. The dawn of eternity alone will reveal the results of the influences for good, set to work by the humble followers of Jesus whose earthly homes were in "The Cove."

On Saturday evening, Oct. 29, we began a series of meetings with the Brethren of New Enterprise and continued until Nov. 15. From the beginning the meetings were well attended and the best of attention given to the Word preached. By the end of the first week it was manifest that the Spirit was at work, and during the second week fifteen precious souls were saved to the family of God militant. All but one were young people, and all were members of the Sunday-school. We regretted very much that other duties compelled us to leave at this stage of the meetings, as it was evident that others were seriously considering the propriety of taking up the cross. The meetings were, however, continued by the home brethren and we are happy to know that others have accepted their Savior. We hope many more will do so.

In the earlier part of the meetings the sympathies of the community were called out in favor of Eld. Joseph Replogle and family on account of the sudden death of their eight-year-old daughter. She came home from school unwell, and grew worse but was not considered dangerously ill by the family. Bro. Replogle himself has been afflicted both physically and mentally for some time. Weary and care-worn sister Replogle and family lay down to rest. On waking up they found that the spirit of little Sadie had gone to the beyond.

" How short is human life! the very breath
Which frames my words, accelerates my death."

The church at New Enterprise had her dark days during the division, the marks of which remain in the form of a small congregation of those who would no longer walk with us. With a full corps of officers, a large and live Sunday-school and prayer-meeting, together with the good will and sympathies of those who are looking in, we feel assured of the future prosperity of the church at New Enterprise. Our visit was a very pleasant one and, we trust, profitable as well. The Lord bless all the dear brethren and sisters whose love and kindness we so much enjoyed while among them.

J. G. R.

CORRESPONDENCE.

Write what you need, and send it unto the churches."

Church News solicited for this Department. If you have had a good meeting, send a report of it, so that others may rejoice with you. In writing give name of church, County and State. Be brief. Notes of Travel should be as short as possible. Land Advertisements are not solicited for this Department. We have an advertising page, and, if necessary, will issue supplements.

From North Michigan.

ON the evening of Nov. 3 we boarded the train at Clarkesville, where we met Eld. Isaiah Rair-

igh, en route for Grand Rapids. Upon our arrival we were met by our esteemed brother, A. T. Morrison, and his two daughters (who are members). They took us to their home, where we enjoyed a pleasant talk on religious topics. Next morning we boarded the train for our mission post at Custer, Mason County, where we met with the little band of members in council the same afternoon. We found there was a unanimous desire to have an election for a deacon. Instead of one there were two elected,—brethren Israel Fisher and Jacob Mahler. These brethren, with their wives, were duly installed. Our prayer is that they may prove faithful in their important office! We remained here till the morning of Nov. 7. During our stay with them Bro. Isaiah preached four sermons. We then started for Traverse City, a distance of ninety miles north. The day was very gloomy and rainy. Upon our arrival we found our friend (now a brother), John Leese, awaiting us. He took us to his home, a distance of eight miles, over some very rolling country. It was in behalf of this family we had come. The GOSPEL MESSENGER was sent to him by his brother, from the Thornapple church, and by reading it he became convicted and wanted to unite with us. We found his wife also deeply interested, and after we had set before them our faith and practice, all through, and tried to give Scriptural reasons for all, and especially on immersion, she (the wife) said she was also ready to go into the water.

After a season of prayer, we retired at a late hour. The next morning, at an early hour, we made the necessary arrangements. Though the morning was cold and the ground covered with snow, in the twilight we started for the water,—a distance of one and one-half miles,—where we found a beautiful little stream. Here they were buried beneath the liquid wave. Though our number was only six, the scene, with its surroundings, was very solemn and impressive. After this baptism we bade the newly-baptized ones farewell and turned our faces homeward, where we arrived at 8 P. M., and found all well.

I. F. RAIRIGH.

BIBLE DEPARTMENT MT. MORRIS COLLEGE.

Second Term.—Jan. 3 to March 21, 1893.

COURSE OF STUDY.

I. *Old Testament History.*—Pentateuch Completed.
   1. LEVITICUS.—Worship, sacrifice and priesthood.
   2. NUMBERS.—Marshaling of the Lord's hosts and their victorious march to Canaan.
   3. DEUTERONOMY.—The law made emphatic by repetition.
   4. Special outline of Mosaic Law.
II. *Old Testament History.*—Prophecy.
   1. Historical view of books of the prophets.
   2. Hebrew prophecy.
   3. Predictive prophecy.
   4. Primitive Messianic ideas.
   5. Messianic prophecy in the Mosaic Age.
   6. Messianic prophecy in the Davidic period.
   7. Messianic ideas of the early prophets.
   8. Study of the book of Isaiah by outline.
III. *New Testament History.*
   1. Book of Hebrews by outline; (a) comparison of the two covenants; (b) New Testament Mediator, as Son above all other mediators of revelation and redemption; (c) Jesus Christ as Eternal Priestly King, the Counterpart of Melchisedec; (d) preeminence of the New Covenant mediated through Jesus Christ.

   (2) Books of 1st and 2nd Corinthians by outline; (a) unwarranted divisions in the church; (b) teachings on morality; (c) bestowment of spiritual gifts; (d) certainty of the resurrection; (e) Paul's account of his conduct towards the Corinthians; (f) his fidelity and encouragement; (g) condition of activity at Corinth; (h) Paul's claim and proof of apostleship.
IV. *Church History.*—Reformation.
   1. General character of Reformation.
   2. Rise and decline of papal hierarchy.
   3. Causes of ecclesiastical revolution prior to the sixteenth century.
   4. Luther and German Reformation to the diet of Augsburg.
   5. Reformation of the Scandinavian kingdom.
   6. John Calvin and Genevan Reformation.
   7. Reformation in France.
   8. Reformation in Netherlands.
   9. Reformation in England and Scotland.
   10. Reformation in Italy and Spain.
   11. Struggles of Protestantism.
   12. Protestant Reformation.
V. *Chautauqua Sunday-school Normal Course.*
   1. Bible studies.
      (a) Old Testament as a preparation for the Christian church; (1) a divine religion given to man; (2) development of divine religion in the life of chosen people.
      (b) Old Testament as a preparation for Christ; (1) sacrifices and types; (2) kingdom and the prophets.
      (c) New Testament the manifestation of Christ; (1) facts in life of Christ, and order in which they should be taught; (2) the doctrines of Christ; (3) relation of facts to the doctrine.
      (d) New Testament as the revelation of the Christian church; (1) its essential elements; (2) its history in the New Testament; (3) progress of doctrine in the New Testament; (4) doctrine in the Acts and epistles.
VI. *Sermons and Lectures.*
   There will be a sermon or lecture every evening during the month of January.
   1. Progress of Revelation.
      (a) Canon of Scripture.
      (b) Hebrew prophecies.
      (c) Sacrifices.
   2. The Church.
      (a) As to place; (1) local; (2) general; (3) militant; (4) triumphant.
      (b) As to doctrine; (1) baptism; (2) Lord's Supper.
      (c) As to government. Relation of church to Annual Conference.
      (d) As to mission work; (1) Gospel authority for mission work; (2) relation of church to mission work; (3) qualifications of missionaries; (4) present mission field and how to cultivate it.
      (e) As to the ministry; (1) call and preparation; (2) relation of the minister to the church; (a) ambassador; (b) pastor; (c) steward; (d) elder; (3) ministers' relation to (a) Sunday-school; (b) prayer-meetings; (c) mission work; (4) ministers' inner life; (5) ministers' outer life as manifested (a) in house of God; (b) in business; (c) in neighborhood.
   3. Tabernacle and events in the Savior's life, as illustrated by lantern views.

GENERAL INFORMATION.

1. The course of instruction is entirely practical and adapted to the wants of nearly every class of Bible students.

immersion by the twelve apostles in six hours and twelve minutes.— MARY HEILMAN. *Nov. 13.*

Removing the Body.

ON the morning of Nov. 2, I started for Dorrance, Kans., to assist Mother Newcomer in bringing the dead body of Father John Newcomer east. Father Newcomer died in July, of which mention was made in the MESSENGER. He moved to Kansas about fifteen years ago, and has been older of the Dorrance church from that time until the good Lord said, "It is enough; come up higher." I arrived there Saturday morning, Nov. 5. On Sunday morning we had the happy privilege of meeting brother Trostle. In the evening we started for Dorrance, where we arrived next morning and found mother in good health. On Monday evening we had the privilege of meeting with the members at the Dorrance meeting-house. Brother Keller has been conducting a series of meetings here for eight or ten days. One precious soul came out on the Lord's side. We were told that others were almost persuaded. On Wednesday morning, Nov. 9, mother and I started with father's' remains for the East. Many of the brethren accompanied us to the station. We arrived at home on Friday evening. On Saturday afternoon we met with some of the brethren and sisters at the Ridge grave-yard, to deposit the body of Father Newcomer beside that of his first companion, Barbara Shoemaker.   W. M. FOGLESONGER.
Shippensburg, Pa.

Notes from Our Correspondents.

"As cold water to a thirsty soul, so is good news from a far country."

Los Angeles, Cal.—We arrived here Nov. 18. We met with the members in Tropico for worship Saturday and Sunday afternoon Nov. 20 and 21. We found them all still working for the Lord. The weather here is lovely. Our address will be Redondo, Cal.—*P. A. and Clarenda Moore.*

Meyersdale, Pa.—I met with the Brethren at the Greenville church, Meyersdale congregation, Somerset Co., Pa., on the evening of Sept. 10, and continued till the 18th, preaching, in all, eleven sermons. As an immediate result there were nine additions by baptism. Give God the praise!—*D. H. Walker.*

Weiser, Ark.—The Brethren at this place had a good time of refreshing in the cause of our Master. Bro. J. R. Gish came to us Oct. 27 and labored for us till Nov. 7. One precious soul was made willing to be buried with Christ in baptism, and we think there are others almost ready to make that good choice.—*Sarah Coyn, Nov. 18.*

Mansfield, Mo.—Our love-feast occurred Nov. 12 and 13. A large number was at the feast. One dear soul was baptized in the morning before the love-feast. The weather was enjoyable, and we had the very best of order. Brethren J. T. Mason, F. W. Dove and others were with us. Bro. J. T. Mason officiated. It will be a meeting long to be remembered by many of us.—*Lizzie Robertson.*

Nodaln, Iowa.—The members of the Soldier River church held their regular meeting Nov. 20. Bro. Samuel Sloatman was with us. We were glad to hear the true Word preached. There was quite a number present and good attention was given while our brother was talking to us. I pray that the good work may go on, and that there may be some good done here yet.—*Hester A. Stevens, Nov. 24.*

Johnstown, Pa.—Our series of meetings, conducted by Bro. Brice Sell, began Nov. 5, and closed Nov. 20. Bro. Sell shunned not to declare the Gospel of the Living God. Saints were built up in the most holy faith, and though there were no immediate accessions, we have reason to believe that much good has been done in the name of Jesus.—*Sadie Brallier Noffsinger, Nov. 25.*

Mulberry Grove, Ill.—We, the members of the Mulberry Grove church, held our love-feast Oct. 29. We had an enjoyable meeting. Eld. Michael Flory and wife, of Girard, were present. Bro. Flory officiated. Nov. 12 we held our quarterly council. Although there were but few present, all business passed off quietly and in good order. If the Lord will, we expect to commence a series of meetings Jan. 14.—*Ida M. Kessler.*

Adrian, Mo.—The Mound church met in quarterly council Nov. 5. All business was transacted in love and Christian courtesy. All felt it was good to be there. We have an evergreen Sunday-school with good workers and an able body of officials. We meet each Sunday at 10 A. M. Bro. Hope is now with us, holding a series of meetings the result of which we will report later. Remember us at a throne of grace!—*Albert J. Smith.*

Glensted, Mo.—The members of Prairie View church met in quarterly council on Saturday, Nov. 5. The business which came before the meeting was transacted satisfactory to all. The church is in a prosperous condition and steadily moving on, with bright prospects for its future. One of our ministers,—Bro. Holsopple,—was deprived of meeting with us on account of illness, but the members, generally, were present.—*Anna Bowman, Nov. 13.*

Wyman, Ark.—Nov. 3 I attended the feast in the Dry Fork church, Jasper Co., Mo. It was a good one. Here I met Bro. Samuel Edgecomb, who, with myself, remained one week after the feast. Wm. Harvey is the elder of the Dry Fork church. We expect him here in December, to hold a series of meetings for us. Nov. 19 I am to go into Indian Territory, fifteen miles south of Fort Smith. I will write when I return.—*Samuel Weimer, Nov. 15.*

Lexington Church, Ohio.—A number of brethren, sisters and friends gathered at the church-house on the above date for Thanksgiving services. Ministers present were J. E. and Allen Ockerman. The meeting consisted of singing, Scripture-reading and talking. At the close of the meeting a collection was taken to increase the missionary funds of the home treasury. Throughout it was an enjoyable occasion. We trust much good may be done.—*Leslie Ockerman, Nov. 24.*

Eglon, W. Va.—Nov. 5 Bro. J. O. Thompson preached at the Brookside church. The next morning,—Sunday,—he preached at the Maple Spring church. Nov. 13 we met at the latter place at 9 A. M. for Sunday-school, and in the afternoon and evening Bro. S. A. Sisler preached for us. Nov. 20 brethren Jonas and Tobias Fike were with us, and on Thanksgiving Day we met again for worship. Brethren Aaron and Moses Fike did the preaching.—*Rachel Weimer.*

Boynton, Pa.—I commenced a series of meetings in the Hopewell church, Bedford Co., Pa., presided over by Eld. Henry Clapper, on the evening of Nov. 12, and continued until the evening of the 21st. As an immediate result twelve were baptized and we have three more applicants. The meeting was one of good attention to the Word spoken. May they all prove shining lights in the church, and may a silent yet convincing power go out that may lead others to the Savior.—*Silas Hoover, Nov. 22.*

Talent, Ore.—To-day we heard a good sermon on baptism by our dear old brother, David Brower. One dear sister was then baptized. This was the first one ever baptized here at Talent by the Brethren and we hope her companion will soon follow her example.—*Susan M. Rhodes, Nov. 20.*

Washington, D. C.—Please state in GOSPEL MESSENGER that whoever may have friends or relatives living in this City, and who desire me to look after their spiritual welfare, will notify me, giving address, etc. We are now holding meetings regularly every Sunday, at the Odd Fellows' Hall on Eighth St., S. E., at 11 A. M. and 7:30 P. M. We have social meetings every Thursday evening at houses of members and friends.—*W. M. Lyon, 308 Sixth St., S. E.*

Ministerial Meeting.—The Ministerial Meeting of the Western District of Maryland, will be held at the Broad Fording meeting-house, in the Welsh Run congregation, Dec. 30 and 31, 1892. All are invited to attend, and especially our co-laborers in the ministry. A program can be had by addressing the undersigned. Any one coming by rail will please notify the undersigned by postal, and arrangements will be made to take them to the place of meeting.—*W. S Reichard, Hagerstown, Md., Nov. 18.*

Baltimore, Md.—Sunday, Nov. 20, two more precious souls were received into the fold of Christ through baptism, administered by Bro. Samuel Utz, of New Market, Md. May they ever walk in newness of life and let their lights shine in accordance with Matt. 5: 16. Bro. Wm. H. Franklin, of Sam's Creek, Md., preached for us in the morning and evening. He also gave us a very interesting and encouraging talk in Sunday-school in the afternoon. Come again, brethren; we appreciate your visits.—*John S. Geiser, Woodberry, Md.*

Mt. Jackson, Va.—By the request of the Brethren I began a series of meetings Oct. 24, at what is known as the Willow Grove school-house. The weather was pleasant and the interest excellent throughout the meetings which closed on the evening of Oct. 30. As an immediate result eleven dear souls were received by baptism, and we have three more applicants. One of the applicants was since received. The members seemed much encouraged and I hope that our labors, as well as theirs, may accomplish much good.—*B. W. Neff, Mt. Jackson, Va.*

Russell, Kans.—The members of the Russell church are in love and union. We keep up our yearly missionary sermons to a good effect. At our last missionary meeting we got over $14. It does not require much work, by that means, for the solicitors to collect money. I leave home Dec. 1, to go to Gove County; then to Thomas County, then to Sherman County, then to Cheyenne County, then to Wallace County. It is my purpose to more fully establish the mission work in North-western Kansas. The Mission Board feels like pushing the work, to win souls to Christ.—*John Hollinger, Nov. 17.*

Oak Hill Church, Va.—Oct. 22 we held our love-feast, which was a pleasant one. On Sunday evening Bro. Frantz commenced a series of meetings and continued till Oct. 30, preaching, in all, nine sermons. Seven were received by baptism. Saints were made to rejoice and sinners to tremble. Bro. Frantz is an earnest worker and his return to us will be much appreciated. Bro. D. F. Stouffer, of Maryland, conducted a series of meetings recently. He preached, in all, eight soul-stirring sermons. As a result two were baptized. One more made application at the close of the services. We had a soul-cheering meeting.—*Wm. Peters.*

immersion by the twelve apostles in six hours and twelve minutes. MARY HEILMAN.

Nov. 13.

Removing the Body.

ON the morning of Nov. 2, I started for Dorrance, Kans., to assist Mother Newcomer in bringing the dead body of Father John Newcomer east. Father Newcomer died in July, of which mention was made in the MESSENGER. He moved to Kansas about fifteen years ago, and has been elder of the Dorrance church from that time until the good Lord said, "It is enough; come up higher." I arrived there Saturday morning, Nov. 5. On Sunday morning we had the happy privilege of meeting brother Trostle. In the evening we started for Dorrance, where we arrived next morning and found mother in good health. On Monday evening we had the privilege of meeting with the members at the Dorrance meeting-house. Brother Keller has been conducting a series of meetings here for eight or ten days. One precious soul came out on the Lord's side. We were told that others were almost persuaded. On Wednesday morning, Nov. 9, mother and I started with father's remains for the East. Many of the brethren accompanied us to the station. We arrived at home on Friday evening. On Saturday afternoon we met with some of the brethren and sisters at the Ridge grave-yard, to deposit the body of Father Newcomer beside that of his first companion, Barbara Shoemaker. W. M. FOGLESONGER.

Shippensburg, Pa.

Notes from Our Correspondents.

"As cold water to a thirsty soul, so is good news from a far country."

Los Angeles, Cal.:—We arrived here Nov. 18. We met with the members in Tropico for worship Saturday night and Sunday afternoon Nov. 20 and 21. We found them all still working for the Lord. The weather here is lovely. Our address will be Redondo, Cal.—*P. A. and Clarenda Moore.*

Meyersdale, Pa.—I met with the Brethren at the Greenville church, Meyersdale congregation, Somerset Co., Pa., on the evening of Sept. 10, and continued till the 18th, preaching, in all, eleven sermons. As an immediate result there were nine additions by baptism. Give God the praise!—*D. H. Walker.*

Weiser, Ark.—The Brethren at this place had a good time of refreshing in the cause of our Master. Bro. J. B. Gish came to us Oct. 27 and labored for us till Nov. 7. One precious soul was made willing to be buried with Christ in baptism, and we think there are others almost ready to make that good choice.—*Sarah Coyn, Nov. 18.*

Russellville, Mo.—Our love-feast occurred Nov. 12 and 13. A large number was at the feast. One dear soul was baptized in the morning before the love-feast. The weather was enjoyable, and we had the very best of order. Brethren J. T. Mason, F. W. Dove and others were with us. Bro. J. T. Mason officiated. It will be a meeting long to be remembered by many of us.—*Lizzie Robertson.*

Mcdale, Iowa.—The members of the Soldier River church held their regular meeting Nov. 20. Bro. Samuel Sloatman was with us. We were glad to hear the true Word preached. There was quite a number present and good attention was given while our brother was talking to us. I pray that the good work may go on, and that there may be some good done here yet.—*Hester A. Stevens, Nov. 24.*

Johnstown, Pa.—Our series of meetings, conducted by Bro. Brice Sell, began Nov. 5, and closed Nov. 20. Bro. Sell shunned not to declare the Gospel of the Living God. Saints were built up in the most holy faith; and though there were no immediate accessions, we have reason to believe that much good has been done in the name of Jesus.—*Sadie Brallier Noffsinger, Nov. 25.*

Mulberry Grove, Ill.—We, the members of the Mulberry Grove church, held our love-feast Oct. 29. We had an enjoyable meeting. Eld. Michael Flory and wife, of Girard, were present. Bro. Flory officiated. Nov. 12 we held our quarterly council. Although there were but few present, all business passed off quietly and in good order. If the Lord will, we expect to commence a series of meetings Jan. 14.—*Ida M. Kessler.*

Adrian, Mo.—The Mound church met in quarterly council Nov. 5. All business was transacted in love and Christian courtesy. All felt it was good to be there. We have an evergreen Sunday-school with good workers and an able body of officials. We meet each Sunday at 10 A. M. Bro. Hope is now with us, holding a series of meetings the result of which we will report later. Remember us at a throne of grace!—*Albert J. Smith.*

Glensted, Mo.—The members of Prairie View church met in quarterly council on Saturday, Nov. 5. The business which came before the meeting was transacted satisfactorily to all. The church is in a prosperous condition and steadily moving on, with bright prospects for its future. One of our ministers,—Bro. Holsopple,—was deprived of meeting with us on account of illness, but the members, generally, were present.—*Anna Bowman, Nov. 12.*

Wyman, Ark.—Nov. 3 I attended the feast in the Dry Fork church, Jasper Co., Mo. It was a good one. Here I met Bro. Samuel Edgecomb, who, with myself, remained one week after the feast. Wm. Harvey is the elder of the Dry Fork church. We expect him here in December, to hold a series of meetings for us. Nov. 19 I am to go into Indian Territory, fifteen miles south of Fort Smith. I will write when I return.—*Samuel Weimer, Nov. 15.*

Lexington Church, Ohio.—A number of brethren, sisters and friends gathered at the church-house on the above date for Thanksgiving services. Ministers present were J. E. and Allen Ockerman. The meeting consisted of singing, Scripture-reading and talking. At the close of the meeting a collection was taken to increase the missionary funds of the home treasury. Throughout it was an enjoyable occasion. We trust much good may be done.—*Leslie Ockerman, Nov. 24.*

Eglon, W. Va.—Nov. 5 Bro. J. O. Thompson preached at the Brookside church. The next morning,—Sunday,—he preached at the Maple Spring church. Nov. 13 we met at the latter place at 9 A. M. for Sunday-school, and in the afternoon and evening Bro. S. A. Sisler preached for us. Nov. 20 brethren Jonas and Tobias Fike were with us, and on Thanksgiving Day we met again for worship. Brethren Aaron and Moses Fike did the preaching.—*Rachel Weimer.*

Boynton, Pa.—I commenced a series of meetings in the Hopewell church, Bedford Co., Pa., presided over by Eld. Henry Clapper, on the evening of Nov. 12, and continued until the evening of the 21st. As an immediate result twelve were baptized and we have three more applicants. The meeting was one of good attention to the Word spoken. May they all prove shining lights in the church, and may a silent yet convincing power go out that may lead others to the Savior.—*Silas Hoover, Nov. 22.*

Talent, Ore.—To-day we heard a good sermon on baptism by our dear old brother, David Brower. One dear sister was then baptized. This was the first one ever baptized here at Talent by the Brethren and we hope her companion will soon follow her example.—*Susan M. Rhodes, Nov. 20.*

Washington, D. C.—Please state in GOSPEL MESSENGER that whoever may have friends or relatives living in this City, and who desire me to look after their spiritual welfare, will notify me, giving address, etc. We are now holding meetings regularly every Sunday, at the Odd Fellows' Hall on Eighth St., S. E., at 11 A. M. and 7:30 P. M. We have social meetings every Thursday evening at houses of members and friends.—*W. M. Lyon, 808 Sixth St., S. E.*

Ministerial Meeting.—The Ministerial Meeting of the Western District of Maryland, will be held at the Broad Fording meeting-house, in the Welsh Run congregation, Dec. 30 and 31, 1892. All are invited to attend, and especially our co-laborers in the ministry. A program can be had by addressing the undersigned. Any one coming by rail will please notify the undersigned by postal, and arrangements will be made to take them to the place of meeting.—*W. S. Reichard, Hagerstown, Md., Nov. 18.*

Baltimore, Md.—Sunday, Nov. 20, two more precious souls were received into the fold of Christ through baptism, administered by Bro. Samuel Utz, of New Market, Md. May they ever walk in newness of life and let their lights shine in accordance with Matt. 5: 16. Bro. Wm. H. Franklin, of Sam's Creek, Md., preached for us in the morning and evening. He also gave us a very interesting and encouraging talk in Sunday-school in the afternoon. Come again, brethren; we appreciate your visits.—*John S. Geiser, Woodberry, Md.*

Mt. Jackson, Va.—By the request of the Brethren I began a series of meetings Oct. 24, at what is known as the Willow Grove school-house. The weather was pleasant and the interest excellent throughout the meetings which closed on the evening of Oct. 30. As an immediate result eleven dear souls were received by baptism, and we have three more applicants. One of the applicants was once received. The members seemed much encouraged and I hope that our labors, as well as theirs, may accomplish much good.—*B. W. Neff, Mt. Jackson, Va.*

Russell, Kans.—The members of the Russell church are in love and union. We keep up our yearly missionary sermons to a good effect. At our last missionary meeting we got over $14. It does not require much work, by that means, for the solicitors to collect money. I leave home Dec. 1, to go to Gove County; then to Thomas County, then to Sherman County; then to Cheyenne County, then to Wallace County. It is my purpose to more fully establish the mission work in North-western Kansas. The Mission Board feels like pushing the work, to win souls to Christ.—*John Hollinger, Nov. 17.*

Oak Hill Church, Va.—Oct. 22 we held our love-feast, which was a pleasant one. On Sunday evening Bro. Frantz commenced a series of meetings and continued till Oct. 30, preaching, in all, nine sermons. Seven were received by baptism. Saints were made to rejoice and sinners to tremble. Bro. Frantz is an earnest worker and his return to us will be much appreciated. Bro. D. F. Stouffer, of Maryland, conducted a series of meetings recently. He preached, in all, eight soul-stirring sermons. As a result two were baptized. One more made application at the close of the services. We had a soul-cheering meeting.—*Wm. Peters.*

Literary Notices.

"English Compound Words and Phrases." A reference list, with statement of principles and rules. By F. Horace Teall, author of "The Compounding of English Words," and department editor of Funk & Wagnalls' Standard Dictionary. Cloth, 8vo, 311 pp. $2.50. New York, London, and Toronto: Funk & Wagnalls Company.

This book will prove a valuable aid to writers, printers, teachers, and in fact, to all sorts of people, including business men, correspondents, and others who wish to write clearly and correctly the English language. This book is unique, treating a phase of language that is a continual source of annoyance, and giving in shape for instant use the decisions of the author as to form, together with guiding rules based upon a close, careful, and scientific study of the subject.

Mr. Teall is the first scholar, so far as we know, who has made a detailed comparative and inductive study of the compound forms found in our literature, and who has formulated the principles therein exemplified. His work shows extreme care throughout and provides a ready answer, from his practical point of view, for any question as to compounding or non-compounding of words.

The principles and rules evolved by Mr. Teall from usage are here stated and applied in a list of 40,000 terms, this list being the main feature of the book.

It is claimed that all the rules and forms set down are indicated by weight of usage, and that most of the forms actually predominate in practice, and this claim is, no doubt, justified. Quite a number of the terms included are not defined in the dictionaries, and yet they are all in common use.

"Bible Lesson Books for 1893," published by the Christian Publishing Co., St. Louis, Mo. The series consists of the following volumes, fully covers every department of the school, and perfectly meets every want: "The Lesson Primer," for the little ones of the primary class; single copy, 20 cents. "The Lesson Mentor" for the boys and girls of the junior classes; single copy, 25 cents. "The Lesson Helper" for the young people of the senior class; single copy, 35 cents. "The Lesson Commentary" for teachers and advanced pupils; single copy, $1.00.

The authors, B. W. Johnson, editor of *Christian Evangelist*, author of "The People's New Testament," "Commentary on John," "Vision of the Ages," etc., and W. W. Dowling, editor of *Our Young Folks, Sunday-school Evangelist, The Little Ones*, author of "The Bible Hand-book," "The Helping Hand," "The Guide Book," "The Christian Psalter," etc., who, by universal consent, occupy the foremost rank as Sunday-school writers and instructors, and Bible commentators, have given these volumes their best thought and most careful attention.

Considering the size, style of printing and binding, and the superior quality of the contents, these Lesson Annuals are the cheapest books of their class ever printed. Nothing but the immense patronage that they enjoy enables us to furnish the books at such low rates.

Any of these publications may be ordered from the Messenger office. We especially recommend "The Lesson Commentary."

"The New Christian Quarterly." Christian Publishing Co., St. Louis, Mo., publishers. J. H. Garrison and B. W. Johnson, editors. Price, $2.00 per annum, or 50 cents per copy. The first year of this excellent quarterly is now completed. We have had the pleasure of reading it the entire year. We regard it as the ablest journal coming to our table. To our some of the articles are worth the price of any number of the publications. Their leading religious topics of the day are handled in a masterly manner and yet so simple as to be within the comprehension of the ordinary reader. To us the article entitled "The Levitical Code," by Thomas Munell, is the most satisfactory production we have yet seen in defense of Moses as the author of the Pentateuch. There are many other articles, which we prize just as highly but cannot take space to mention. We are glad that the publication is to be continued for it is one of the journals that we do not want to be without.

Matrimonial.

"What therefore God hath joined together, let not man put asunder."

MONINGER—ZOLLARS.—At the residence of the bride's parents, Oct. 19, 1892, by Rev. Smith, pastor of the M. E. church, Hillsborough, Pa., Mr. Grant Meninger and Miss Mary R. Zollars, both of near Odell, Pa.
N. B. CHRISTNER.

TENNANT—REYNOLDS.—At my residence, Sept. 4, 1892, by the writer, Mr. Otho J. Tennant and Miss Kate Reynolds, both of near Washington, Pa.
N. B. CHRISTNER.

GARBER—LANE.—At the residence of the bride's parents, Oct. 27, 1892, by the undersigned, Mr. Samuel R. Garber and sister Annie M. Lane, both of South Strabane, Pa.
N. B. CHRISTNER.

SUMMY—TUCKER.—At my residence, Oct. 10, 1892, by the undersigned, Mr. Leonard Summy and Effie Tucker, all of Kosciusko County, Ind. JOHN STAFFORD.

BLOCHER—HINES.—At the residence of the bride's parents, Oct. 27, 1892, by the undersigned, Bro. John Blocher and sister Minnie Hines, all of Kosciusko County, Ind.
JOHN STAFFORD.

Fallen Asleep.

"Blessed are the dead which die in the Lord."

DICKEY.—In the Middle Creek church, Somerset Co., Pa., Nov. 11, 1892, Bro. David Dickey, aged 66 years, 3 months and 7 days. He was born in Adams County, Pa., and moved to Fayette County years ago, where he died. Funeral services by the writer. H. A. STAHL.

CAMERER.—At Roaring Spring, Pa., Oct. 11, 1892, Lizzie Camerer, daughter of John and —— Camerer, aged 13 years, 11 months and 24 days. J. R. STAYER.

BEAVER.—At Clay Hill, Pa., Oct. 14, 1892, of diphtheretic croup, Mary Ellen Beaver, aged 5 years, 2 months and 19 days. Funeral services improved by the writer and Eld. Wm C. Koontz. WM. A. ANTHONY.

HECKMAN.—In the Baugo church, Elkhart Co., Ind., sister Sarah Heckman (*nee* Leonard), aged 84 years and 1 month. She united with the German Baptist Brethren about fifty-five years ago and always lived a consistent Christian life. She was born near Roann, North Carolina. Funeral services by Eld. John Metzler, assisted by Bro. Joseph Culp and the writer. H. M. SCHWALM.

HETRICK.—At the residence of his son, M. N. Hetrick, near Oakland, in the Red Bank church, Pa., Sept. 6, 1892, Bro. John Hetrick, aged 78 years, 6 months and 24 days. He was a member of the church for fifty years. He was the father of nineteen children of whom five are dead. He was married twice. His first wife was Catharine Reedy; his second a Mrs. Anthony,—both members of the church. His funeral text was Job 5: 26, "Thou shalt come to thy grave in a full age, like as a shock of corn cometh in in his season." Funeral discourse by the Rev. Sparks, of the Free Will Baptist church. J. A. HETRICK.

BOOKER.—In the Ludlow church, Darke Co., Ohio, Sept. 4, 1892, sister Rebecca, wife of Bro. Jacob Booker, aged 52 years, 10 months and 1 day. She was a faithful member of the Brethren church. Services at the Painter Creek house by Jesse Stuteman and the writer from Job 16: 22.
TOBIAS KREIDER.

KINSEY.—In Arcanum, Ohio, at her son in-law's, Nov. 8, 1892, Susan Boyer Kinsey, aged 80 years, 7 months and 24 days. Deceased was born in Montgomery County, Md., March 14, 1812. Her parents emigrated to Ohio in 1823. She was married to Jacob Kinsey Sept. 6, 1832. To this union were born ten daughters and three sons. Sister Kinsey was a pious, faithful Christian for fifty-six years. Funeral services Nov. 10, conducted by Bro. John Smith and the writer. S. W. HOOVER.

LONG.—In the Brother's valley congregation, Somerset Co., Pa., Nov. 2, 1892, Mary, infant daughter of Bro. Levi and sister Lizzie Long, aged about three weeks. Funeral services conducted by the undersigned. S. P. RIEMAN.

TRENT.—In the Bachelor Run church, Carroll Co., Ind., Nov. 9, 1892, Bro. Jeremiah Trent, aged 68 years, 4 months and 9 days. Deceased leaves a wife, one son and three daughters. He has been a member of the Brethren church about forty-seven years. Funeral services by brethren Hiel Hamilton and Abram Flory. DAVID H. NICCUM.

FRY.—In the Garrison church, Benton Co., Iowa, Nov. 14, 1892, sister Christina Fry (*nee* Dilger), aged 39 years, 7 months and 3 days. She was a consistent member of the Brethren church from her youth. She was the mother of nine children. Six children (the babe but eight months old), with her husband, Bro. Daniel, are left to mourn their loss. The occasion was improved by the writer and S. Johnson from 1 Pet. 1: 24. PETER FORNEY.

WOOD.—In the bounds of the Warrensburgh church, Mo., Nov. 14, 1892, of diphtheria, Alfred F., stepson of Bro. George, and son of sister Mollie Ford, aged 4 years, 5 months and 24 days. D. M. MOHLER.

SNYDER.—At Greenville, Darke Co., Ohio, Nov. 14, 1892, of stomach trouble, sister Nancy Snyder, wife of George Snyder, aged 68 years, 11 months and 22 days. Funeral services by Eld. Resin Stephens, Moses Hollinger and George Stump, from Rev. 14: 12, 13 at the West Branch church, in the Palestine district, after which the remains were interred in the cemetery near by. D. E. BOSSERMAN.

TRAVERSE.—At the Pine Creek church, Ill., Nov. 11, 1892, Catharine Traverse, aged 74 years, 4 months and 7 days. Funeral services by the writer. EDMUND FORNEY.

BRUBAKER.—At Girard, Ill., Nov. 13, 1892, sister Lizzie, wife of Moses Brubaker, aged 50 years, 5 months and 10 days. She leaves a sorrowing husband and four children. She was at church in the forenoon, came home, ate a hearty dinner, and in fifteen minutes after was dead. She united with the Brethren church in early life and lived a consistent and exemplary life. Her remains were followed to their last resting-place by a very large procession. Funeral conducted by the writer. Text, Rev. 14: 12, 13, assisted by Bro. Javan Gibson. MICHAEL FLORY.

HILDEBRAND.—In the bounds of the English River congregation, Iowa Co., Iowa, Nov. 2, 1892, sister Elisabeth, wife of friend Samuel Hildebrand, aged 71 years, 10 months and 6 days. Sister Elisabeth united with the church in her youth and proved faithful until death. PETER BROWER.

HENNINGER.—In the Cherokee church, Cherokee Co., Kans., Oct. 16, 1892, of old age, Elisabeth Henninger, aged 92 years, 7 months and 14 days. She was born in the City of Philadelphia, Pa., March 12, 1800. Funeral services by the Brethren. LEONARD WOLFE.

WALKER.—In the Montgomery church, Pa., Sept. 23, 1892, of typhoid malaria and congestion of the lungs, Bro. Wm. G. Walker, aged 40 years, 3 months and 23 days. The church has lost a faithful deacon, the sister a loving companion, the children a dear father. Our loss, we trust, is his great gain. Interment in the Brethren's cemetery.
LYDIA A. SPICHER.

MILTON.—In the Harrison County church, Ind., Nov. 16, 1892, Charles J. Milton, son of sister Milton (who is living in widowhood), aged 21 years, 5 months and 18 days. He had expressed a desire to unite with the church if he gained bodily strength to do so. Sister Milton has the sympathy of all as this was her only child. Funeral services by the writer.
A. S. CULP.

KEITH.—In the Mansfield congregation, Douglas Co., Mo., of typhoid fever, Bennie Keith, son of James and Elisabeth Keith, aged 20 years and 20 days. Funeral services by brethren J. T. Mason and F. W. Dove.
LIZZIE ROBERTSON.

STOUFFER.—In the Berkeley church, Berkeley County, W. Va., Rebecca R., wife of Bro. John B. Stouffer, aged 61 years, 5 months and 17 days. She died very suddenly. She was a member of the Baptist church. Funeral services by Rev. I. W. Hundley. JOHN BRINDLE.

PUTERBAUGH.—In the Pipe Creek church, Ind., Nov. 5, 1892, Bro. David Puterbaugh, aged 74 years, 4 months and 27 days. The deceased was born in Miami County, Ohio, June 8, 1817. He came to Cass County, Ind., in 1841 and settled on the farm where he died. He was united in marriage to Mary McCullough March 25, 1841. Bro. Puterbaugh united with the Brethren in 1844, and lived an upright and Christian life. He was the father of nine children. Funeral services by Bro. Jacob Fisher from 2 Tim. 4: 6, 7, 8, to a large and attentive audience. W. B. DAILEY.

The Gospel Messenger

Is the recognized organ of the German Baptist or Brethren's church, and advocates the form of doctrine taught in the New Testament and pleads for a return to apostolic and primitive Christianity.

It recognizes the New Testament as the only infallible rule of faith and practice, and maintains that Faith toward God, Repentance from dead works, Regeneration of the heart and mind, baptism by Trine Immersion for remission of sins unto the reception of the Holy Ghost by the laying on of hands, are the means of adoption into the household of God,—the church militant.

It also maintains that Feet-washing, as taught in John 13, both by example and command of Jesus, should be observed in the church.

That the Lord's Supper, instituted by Christ and as universally observed by the apostles and the early Christians, is a full meal, and, in connection with the Communion, should be taken in the evening or after the close of the day.

That the Salutation of the Holy Kiss, or Kiss of Charity, is binding upon the followers of Christ.

That War and Retaliation are contrary to the spirit and self-denying principles of the religion of Jesus Christ.

That the principle of Plain Dressing and of Non-conformity to the world, as taught in the New Testament, should be observed by the followers of Christ.

That the Scriptural duty of Anointing the Sick with Oil, in the Name of the Lord, James 5: 14, is binding upon all Christians.

It also advocates the church's duty to support Missionary and Tract Work, thus giving to the Lord for the spread of the Gospel and for the conversion of sinners.

In short, it is a vindicator of all that Christ and the apostles have enjoined upon us, and aims, amid the conflicting theories and discords of modern Christendom, to point out ground that all must concede to be infallibly safe.

☞ The above principles of our Fraternity are set forth on our Brethren's Envelopes." Use them! Price 15 cents per package; 40 cents per hundred.

Literary Notices.

"English Compound Words and Phrases." A reference list, with statement of principles and rules. By F. Horace Teall, author of "The Compounding of English Words," and department editor of Funk & Wagnalls' Standard Dictionary. Cloth, 8vo, 311 pp. $2.50. New York, London, and Toronto: Funk & Wagnalls Company.

This book will prove a valuable aid to writers, printers, teachers, and in fact to all sorts of people, including business men, correspondents, and others who wish to write clearly and correctly the English language. This book is unique, treating a phase of language that is a continual source of annoyance, and giving in shape for instant use the decisions of the author as to form, together with guiding rules based upon a close, careful, and scientific study of the subject.

Mr. Teall is the first scholar, so far as we know, who has made a detailed comparative and inductive study of the compound forms found in our literature, and who has formulated the principles therein exemplified. His work shows extreme care throughout and provides a ready answer, from his practical point of view, for any question as to compounding or not compounding of words.

The principles and rules evolved by Mr. Teall from usage are here stated and applied in a list of 40,000 terms, this list being the main feature of the book.

It is claimed that all the rules and forms set down are indicated by weight of usage, and that most of the forms actually predominate in practice, and this claim is, no doubt, justified. Quite a number of the terms included are not defined in the dictionaries, and yet they are all in common use.

"Bible Lesson Books for 1893," published by the Christian Publishing Co., St. Louis, Mo. The series consists of the following volumes, fully covers every department of the school, and perfectly meets every want: "The Lesson Primer," for the little ones of the primary class; single copy, 20 cents. "The Lesson Mentor" for the boys and girls of the junior classes; single copy, 25 cents. "The Lesson Helper" for the young people of the senior class; single copy, 35 cents. "The Lesson Commentary" for teachers and advanced pupils; single copy, $1.00.

The authors, B. W. Johnson, editor of *Christian Evangelist*, author of "The People's New Testament," "Commentary on John," "Vision of the Ages," etc., and W. W. Dowling, editor of *Our Young Folks, Sunday-school Evangelist, The Little Ones*, author of "The Bible Hand-book," "The Helping Hand," "The Guide Book," "The Christian Psalter," etc., who, by universal consent, occupy the foremost rank as Sunday-school writers and instructors, and Bible commentators, have given these volumes their best thought and most careful attention.

Considering the size, style of printing and binding, and the superior quality of the contents, these Lesson Annuals are the cheapest books of their class ever printed. Nothing but the immense patronage that they enjoy enables us to furnish the books at such low rates.

Any of these publications may be ordered from the MESSENGER office. We especially recommend "The Lesson Commentary."

"The New Christian Quarterly." Christian Publishing Co., St. Louis, Mo., publishers. J. H. Garrison and B. W. Johnson, editors. Price, $2.00 per annum, or 50 cents per copy. The first year of this excellent quarterly is now completed. We have had the pleasure of reading it the entire year. We regard it as the ablest journal coming to our table. To us some of the articles are worth the price of any number of the publication. The leading religious topics of the day are handled in a masterly manner and yet so simple as to be within the comprehension of the ordinary reader. To us the article entitled "The Levitical Code," by Thomas Munell, is the most satisfactory production we have yet seen in defense of Moses as the author of the Pentateuch. There are many other articles, which we prize just as highly but cannot take space to mention. We are glad that the publication is to be continued for it is one of the journals that we do not want to be without.

Matrimonial.

"What therefore God hath joined together, let not man put asunder."

MONINGER—ZOLLARS.—At the residence of the bride's parents, Oct. 19, 1892, by Rev. Smith, pastor of the M. E. church, Hillsborough, Pa., Mr. Grant Moninger and Miss Mary R. Zollars, both of near Odell, Pa.

N. B. CHRISTNER.

TENNANT—REYNOLDS.—At my residence, Sept. 4, 1892, by the writer, Mr. Otho J. Tennant and Miss Kate Reynolds, both of near Washington, Pa.

N. B. CHRISTNER.

GARBER—LANE.—At the residence of the bride's parents, Oct. 27, 1892, by the undersigned, Mr. Samuel R. Garber and sister Annie M. Lane, both of South Strabane, Pa.

N. B. CHRISTNER.

SUMMY—TUCKER.—At my residence, Oct. 20, 1892, by the undersigned, Mr. Leonard Summy and Effie Tucker, all of Kosciusko County, Ind. JOHN STAFFORD.

BLOCHER—HINES.—At the residence of the bride's parents, Oct. 27, 1892, by the undersigned, Bro. John Blocher and sister Minnie Hines, all of Kosciusko County, Ind.

JOHN STAFFORD.

Fallen Asleep.

"Blessed are the dead which die in the Lord."

DICKEY.—In the Middle Creek church, Somerset Co., Pa., Nov. 11, 1892, Bro. David Dickey, aged 66 years, 3 months and 7 days. He was born in Adams County, Pa., and moved to Fayette County years ago, where he died. Funeral services by the writer. H. A. STAHL.

CAMERER.—At Roaring Spring, Pa., Oct. 11, 1892, Lizzie Camerer, daughter of John and —— Camerer, aged 13 years, 11 months and 24 days. J. R. STAYER.

BEAVER.—At Clay Hill, Pa., Oct. 14, 1892, of diphtheretic croup, Mary Ellen Beaver, aged 5 years, 2 months and 19 days. Funeral services improved by the writer and Eld. Wm C. Koontz. WM. A. ANTHONY.

HECKMAN.—In the Baugo church, Elkhart Co., Ind., sister Sarah Heckman (*nee* Leonard), aged 84 years and 1 month. She united with the German Baptist Brethren about fifty-five years ago and always lived a consistent Christian life. She was born near Roann, North Carolina. Funeral services by Eld. John Metzler, assisted by Bro. Joseph Culp and the writer. H. M. SCHWALM.

HETRICK.—At the residence of his son, M. N. Hetrick, near Oakland, in the Red Bank church, Pa., Sept. 6, 1892, Bro. John Hetrick, aged 78 years, 6 months and 24 days. He was a member of the church for fifty years. He was the father of nineteen children of whom five are dead. He was married twice. His first wife was Catharine Reedy; his second a Mrs. Anthony,—both members of the church. His funeral text was Job 5: 26, "Thou shalt come to thy grave in a full age, like as a shock of corn cometh in in his season." Funeral discourse by the Rev. Sparks, of the Free Will Baptist church. J. A. HETRICK.

BOOKER.—In the Ludlow church, Darke Co., Ohio, Sept. 4, 1892, sister Rebecca, wife of Bro. Jacob Booker, aged 52 years, 10 months and 1 day. She was a faithful member of the Brethren church. Services at the Painter Creek house by Jesse Stutsman and the writer from Job 16: 22.

TOBIAS KREIDER.

KINSEY.—In Arcanum, Ohio, at her son in-law's, Nov. 8, 1892, Susan Boyer Kinsey, aged 80 years, 7 months and 24 days. Deceased was born in Montgomery County, Md., March 14, 1812. Her parents emigrated to Ohio in 1813. She was married to Jacob Kinsey Sept. 6, 1832. To this union were born ten daughters and three sons. Sister Kinsey was a pious, faithful Christian for fifty-six years. Funeral services Nov. 10, conducted by Bro. John Smith and the writer. S. W. HOOVER.

LONG.—In the Brother's Valley congregation, Somerset Co., Pa., Nov. 2, 1892, Mary, infant daughter of Bro. Levi and sister Lizzie Long, aged about three weeks. Funeral services conducted by the undersigned. S. F. RIEMAN.

TRENT.—In the Bachelor Run church, Carroll Co., Ind., Nov. 9, 1892, Bro. Jeremiah Trent, aged 68 years, 4 months and 9 days. Deceased leaves a wife, one son and three daughters. She has been a member of the Brethren church about forty-seven years. Funeral services by brethren Hiel Hamilton and Abram Flory. DAVID H. NICCUM.

FRY.—In the Garrison church, Benton Co., Iowa, Nov. 14, 1892, sister Christina Fry (*nee* Dilger), aged 39 years, 7 months and 3 days. She was a consistent member of the Brethren church from her youth. She was the mother of nine children. Six children (the babe but eight months old), with her husband, Bro. Daniel, are left to mourn their loss. The occasion was improved by the writer and S. Johnson from 1 Pet. 1: 24. PETER FORNEY.

WOOD.—In the bounds of the Warrensburgh church, Mo., Nov. 14, 1892, of diphtheria, Alfred F., stepson of Bro. George, and son of sister Mollie Ford, aged 4 years, 5 months and 24 days. D. M. MOHLER.

SNYDER.—At Greenville, Darke Co., Ohio, Nov. 14, 1892, of stomach trouble, sister Nancy Snyder, wife of George Snyder, aged 68 years, 11 months and 22 days. Funeral services by Eld. Rezin Stephens, Moses Hollinger and George Stump, from Rev. 14: 12, 13 at the West Branch church, in the Palestine district, after which the remains were interred in the cemetery near by. D. E. BOSSERMAN.

TRAVERSE.—At the Pine Creek church, Ill., Nov. 11, 1892, Catharine Traverse, aged 74 years, 4 months and 7 days. Funeral services by the writer. EDMUND FORNEY.

BRUBAKER.—At Girard, Ill., Nov. 13, 1892, sister Lizzie, wife of Moses Brubaker, aged 50 years, 5 months and 20 days. She leaves a sorrowing husband and four children. She was at church in the forenoon, came home, ate a hearty dinner, and in fifteen minutes after was dead. She united with the Brethren church in early life and lived a consistent and exemplary life. Her remains were followed to their last resting-place by a very large procession. Funeral conducted by the writer. Text, Rev. 14: 12, 13, assisted by Bro. Javan Gibson. MICHAEL FLORY.

HILDEBRAND.—In the bounds of the English River congregation, Iowa Co., Iowa, Nov. 2, 1892, sister Elizabeth, wife of friend Samuel Hildebrand, aged 71 years, 10 months and 6 days. Sister Elizabeth united with the church in her youth and proved faithful until death. PETER BROWER.

HENNINGER.—In the Cherokee church, Cherokee Co., Kans., Oct. 26, 1892, of old age, Elizabeth Henninger, aged 92 years, 7 months and 14 days. She was born in the City of Philadelphia, Pa., March 12, 1800. Funeral services by the Brethren. LEONARD WOLFE.

WALKER.—In the Montgomery church, Pa., Sept. 23, 1892, of typhoid malaria and congestion of the lungs, Bro. Wm. G. Walker, aged 40 years, 3 months and 23 days. The church has lost a faithful deacon, the sister a loving companion, the children a dear father. Our loss, we trust, is his great gain. Interment in the Brethren's cemetery.

LYDIA A. SPICHER.

MILTON.—In the Harrison County church, Ind., Nov. 16, 1892, Charles J. Milton, son of sister Milton (who is living in widowhood), aged 21 years, 6 months and 18 days. He had expressed a desire to unite with the church if he gained bodily strength to do so. Sister Milton has the sympathy of all as this was her only child. Funeral services by the writer.

A. S. CULP.

KEITH.—In the Mansfield congregation, Douglas Co., Mo., of typhoid fever, Bennie Keith, son of James and Elizabeth Keith, aged 20 years and 20 days. Funeral services by brethren J. T. Mason and F. W. Dove.

LIZZIE ROBERTSON.

STOUFFER.—In the Berkeley church, Berkeley County, W. Va., Rebecca R., wife of Bro. John B. Stouffer, aged 61 years, 5 months and 17 days. She died very suddenly. She was a member of the Baptist church. Funeral services by Rev. I. W. Hundley. JOHN BRINDLE.

PUTERBAUGH.—In the Pipe Creek church, Ind., Nov. 5, 1892, Bro. David Puterbaugh, aged 74 years, 4 months and 27 days. The deceased was born in Miami County, Ohio, June 8, 1817. He came to Cass County, Ind., in 1841 and settled on the farm where he died. He was united in marriage to Mary McCullough March 25, 1841. Bro. Puterbaugh united with the Brethren in 1844, and lived an upright and Christian life. He was the father of nine children. Funeral services by Bro. Jacob Fisher from 2 Tim. 4: 6, 7, 8, to a large and attentive audience. W. B. DAILEY.

The Gospel Messenger

Is the recognized organ of the German Baptist or Brethren's church, and advocates the form of doctrine taught in the New Testament and pleads for a return to apostolic and primitive Christianity.

It recognizes the New Testament as the only infallible rule of faith and practice, and maintains that Faith toward God, Repentance from dead works, Regeneration of the heart and mind, baptism by Trine Immersion for remission of sins unto the reception of the Holy Ghost by the laying on of hands, are the means of adoption into the household of God,—the church militant.

It also maintains that Feet-washing, as taught in John 13, both by example and command of Jesus, should be observed in the church.

That the Lord's Supper, instituted by Christ and as universally observed by the apostles and the early Christians, is a full meal, and, in connection with the Communion, should be taken in the evening or after the close of the day.

That the Salutation of the Holy Kiss, or Kiss of Charity, is binding upon the followers of Christ.

That War and Retaliation are contrary to the spirit and self-denying principles of the religion of Jesus Christ.

That the principle of Plain Dressing and of Non-conformity to the world, as taught in the New Testament, should be observed by the followers of Christ.

That the Scriptural duty of Anointing the Sick with Oil, in the Name of the Lord, James 5: 14, is binding upon all Christians.

It also advocates the church's duty to support Missionary and Tract Work, thus giving to the Lord for the spread of the Gospel and for the conversion of sinners.

In short, it is a vindicator of all that Christ and the apostles have enjoined upon us, and aims, amid the conflicting theories and discords of modern Christendom, to point out ground that all must concede to be infallibly safe.

☞ The above principles of our Fraternity are set forth on our Brethren's Envelopes." Use them! Price 15 cents per package; 40 cents per hundred.

Announcements.

LOVE-FEASTS.

Dec. 31, Glendale, Maricopa Co., Ariz. Those coming by rail will be met by at Tempe by notifying T. J. Kinzulus.

--- THE ---

Doctrine of the Brethren Defended.

THIS work contains a complete exposition of the faith and practice of the Brethren, the Divinity of Christ, the Divinity of the Holy Spirit, Immersion, Feet-washing, the Lord's Supper, the Holy Kiss, Non-conformity, Secret Societies, etc. Price, per copy, cloth binding, $1.25. Address this office.

For Sale!

Having a desire to devote more time to church work, I offer one quarter section of choice farm land for sale. This farm has a good house, barn, fences, well, and a nice spring. It is situated 8½ miles south of the Brethren's meeting-house in Shannon, Ill. It is also within one mile of a good creamery. I also offer 50 head of registered Short Horn Cattle, 15 males and 35 females, — choice individuals at a very low price. Address for particulars, D. Rowland, Lanark, Ill.

━━━❖ESSAYS❖━━━

* Study to show thyself approved unto God: a workman that needeth not be ashamed, rightly dividing the Word of Truth."

THE EARTH IS THE LORD'S AND THE FULLNESS THEREOF.

BY J. S. MOHLER.

The mountains and hills, and the valleys below,
The fountains and rivers as onward they flow,
Making fertile the plains wheresoever they go,
"The earth is the Lord's and the fulness thereof."

And ocean's deep waves o'er us proudly would roll
By the hand of Omnipotence held in control,
All teeming with creatures, the timid and bold,
"The earth is the Lord's and the fulness thereof."

The beasts of the forest as wildly they roam,
And those of the field for the comfort at home,
Wherever they range under heaven's high dome,
"The earth is the Lord's and the fulness thereof."

The fowls of the air as they happily soar
All over the land to its furthermost shore,
In notes and songs their Creator adore,
"The earth is the Lord's and the fullness thereof."

The sheaves so well laden with grain from the field,
And golden the fruit that the orchard doth yield,
The garden its tribute in bounty reveals,
"The earth is the Lord's and the fullness thereof."

The jewels of silver and jewels of gold,
And stones that in beauty are grand to behold,
Their value in numbers has never been told,
"The earth is the Lord's and the fullness thereof."

And man in the image of God has been wrought,
By Jesus our Savior has dearly been bought,
The way, and the truth, and the life has been taught,
"The earth is the Lord's and the fullness thereof."

All glory to God who dwelleth on high,
And ruleth the earth, the sea, and the sky,
His children he hears in their pitiful cry,
" And opens his hands ev'ry want to supply!

Merrill, Kans.

PRIMITIVE CHRISTIANITY, AS UNDERSTOOD AND PRACTICED BY THE BRETHREN.

[We invite careful and intelligent criticism on all the articles published under this head. Criticisms on language, facts and arguments will be in order, and should be sent to the author of the article to which they refer.]

BY A. W. REESE.

Faith.

" But without faith it is impossible to please him: for he that cometh to God must believe that he is, and that he is a rewarder of them that diligently seek him."—Heb. 11: 6.

Part Two.

LET us consider, for a few moments, what Moses *relinquished* when he "refused to be called the son of Pharaoh's daughter." He cast away, as a mere bauble, a kingly crown! That was a strange thing for a sensible man to do, especially if he possessed a spark of human ambition.

More than this, it was no *ordinary* throne that Moses refused. The monarchs of that day were endowed with autocratic power. They had absolute control of the services, treasure, and even the very lives of their subjects. " Whom they would they slew, and whom they would they kept alive! " Egypt was the most splendid, the most powerful, and the wealthiest kingdom in that age of the world. Its monarch was the greatest of all the mighty rulers of ancient times. His court was distinguished by all the pomp, splendor and pageantry that the most abundant wealth could bestow. All this grandeur, wealth, power, luxury, ease, influence, adulation, homage, and worldly honor Moses threw away when he "refused to be called the son of Pharaoh's daughter." What did he gain, or accept, in return for this astonishing renunciation, — for this strange sacrifice of all those things that captivate the affections of men? He deliberately "chose rather to suffer affliction with the people of God, than to enjoy the pleasures of sin for a season."

Who were these "people of God?" Slaves! Outcasts! Pariahs! A people trodden under the iron heel of a cruel and pitiless despotism! A people whose abject and servile degradation had no equal on the face of the earth, a people groaning under the bitter yoke of a bondage worse than death. O, what a strange choice! More than this: "Esteeming the reproach of Christ greater riches than the treasures of Egypt." What is recorded of the treasures of that wonderful land?

We can form some faint conception of the vast wealth of that great empire when we bear in mind that special *cities* had to be built in which to stow away the immense treasures belonging to Egypt. All this Moses forfeited when he refused to be called the son of Pharaoh's daughter, for that son was the "heir apparent" to the Egyptian throne.

What was the cause that influenced Moses to do this? Faith! It is declared that "by faith" Moses made this extraordinary choice. It is also declared that "he had respect unto the recompense of reward," the' hope of glory made manifest unto him, not by sight, not by knowledge, but *by faith.*

Perhaps there can be found no more striking example of the subject under consideration than that of Naaman, the great captain of the Syrian host. Let us call attention first to the *humble instrumentality* by which the astounding results, in this remarkable case, were procured. Simply the chance remark of a little captive Jewish maid serving the wife of Naaman: "Would God my Master were with the prophet in Samaria, for he would recover him of his leprosy! "

Let us consider the character and station of the man in question. An illustrious warrior, a laureled chieftain, "foremost captain of his time," covered with the glittering decorations of his rank, the proud insignia of his military renown, high in the esteem and confidence of the great monarch whom he served, and of whose serried hosts he was commander-in-chief.

And, moreover, these high honors were worthily bestowed, for the Divine Record declares that Naaman was a mighty man, honorable, — a man of valor. Naaman was not the creature of accident or mere official favor. He was a man of high character, of a rare degree of merit. He had "achieved greatness" in the profession of arms. This great warrior stood next, in rank and power, to the mighty monarch of Syria himself. What more could human ambition desire? Surely if worldly honors and distinction could secure happiness, Naaman's cup was full to the very brim. But alas! the Divine Record completes the recital of all this rank, station, and power with these terrible words: "*But he was a leper*" ! ! A leper! The subject of a foul, disgusting, loathsome, *incurable* disease! A malady so contagious, so dreaded, so abhorred of all mankind as to fix the seal of banishment on its wretched and unhappy victim! A disorder so shocking to the sight and so repulsive in all its features -as to shut out the poor sufferer from the companionship and the sympathy of his fellow-men. A leper! What were power, rank, station, honor to him? The leper was doomed! There was no hope of relief! Never since creation's dawn had the leper been healed! The loathsome malady had defied all human skill in all the ages of the world. The leper was lost!

No ray of hope glimmered through the thick darkness of his long night of horror

" That had no mOrn beyOnd it,
And no star!"

How startling, then, the words of the little Jewish maid! How the great monarch's heart must have been stirred within him! We can well imagine the glad surprise, the letter to the king of

Israel, the preparations for the momentous journey, the gorgeous equipage of Naaman, the magnificent retinue, the regal escort, the magnificent presents to the Jewish king (whose value has been variously estimated at from *fifty* to one hundred *thousand dollars*). We can also understand the consternation and the dismay of the king of Israel at the astounding demand of the Syrian monarch. Behold, I send Naaman, my servant, that you should recover him of his leprosy! No wonder that the Jewish king, in his terror and dismay, rent his garments and the despairing cry rose to his trembling lips: " Am I God, to kill and to make alive, that this man sendeth one to be recovered of his leprosy? Behold how he seeketh a quarrel with me." But Elisha, the prophet of God, comes to the relief of the distracted king, "Send him to me." Naaman, at the head of his princely cortege, moves on. The gorgeous cavalcade passes before the prophet's humble abode.

Never before had such pomp and pageantry honored the prophet's door. There, in his lordly chariot, sat the great commander of the Syrian hosts! a man of stern and iron mould, a man at the menace of whose hand

" Realms were chilled with fear
And armies musketed at the sign! as When
Clouds rise on clouds before the rainy East!
Gray captains leading bands of veteran men
. And fiery youths to be the vulture's feast!"

But the prophet of God, seemingly unimpressed by the high rank of his illustrious visitor, and strangely insensible to the bewildering splendor of his equipage, declining with a quiet dignity his imperial gifts, did not come out to do the great man suitable honor. He sent a messenger, a servant, a menial, with the simple command, " Go ' wash seven times in Jordan, and thou shalt be clean!" No higher insult could have been offered to such a man as Naaman. No wonder that the astounded warrior cried out, "Behold, I thought he would come out!" What more natural and fitting the occasion, indeed, than this? Not only *come out*, but that he would "stand, uncovered too, in the presence of this mighty man and further, that he would "call on the name of the Lord his God," and that "he would strike his hand over the place and recover the leper!" Surely this would have been the proper way to proceed in accordance with the rank and dignity of the great man who had come to be cured. No wonder, in this view, that Naaman "turned away in a rage." No wonder that, in the pride of his heart, he cried out, "Are not Abana and Pharpar, rivers of Damascus, better than all these waters of Israel, may I not wash in them and be clean?"

O how like proud, rebellious *man* that is! The means were too simple, too common, too plebeian to suit the ideas of this proud and haughty leader of the Syrian hosts. He proposed to *improve* on the *prophet's* plan. He suggested a more respectable, a more aristocratic way! And that idea is still a good deal in vogue in these "last days."

So Naaman "turned away in a rage." He intended to have his own way about the matter, and how *like* man that is! But wiser councils prevailed. "My father!" (a term of great respect) if the prophet had bid thee do some great thing, wouldst thou not have done it? How much rather when he saith to thee, Wash and be clean?" That was sensible advice on the part of the subordinates of the great magnate who had come all the way from Syria to be cured of a disease that had, hitherto, defied the skill of all preceding ages. But the remedy,—ah, it was too simple! It was not great enough for the great man! Ah! to do some *great* thing! What a sympathetic chord that strikes in the carnal heart! Man wants to do some great thing ' but he does not want to · do

❖ESSAYS❖

THE EARTH IS THE LORD'S AND THE FULLNESS THEREOF.

BY J. S. MOHLER.

The mountains and hills, and the valleys below,
The fountains and rivers as onward they flow,
Making fertile the plains wheresoever they go,
"The earth is the Lord's and the fulness thereof."

And ocean's deep waves o'er us proudly would roll
By the hand of Omnipotence held in control,
All teeming with creatures, the timid and bold,
"The earth is the Lord's and the fullness thereof."

The beasts of the forest as wildly they roam,
And those of the field for the comfort of home,
Wherever they range under heaven's high dome,
"The earth is the Lord's and the fullness thereof."

The fowls of the air as they happily soar
All over the land to its furthermost shore,
In notes and songs their Creator adore,
"The earth is the Lord's and the fullness thereof."

The sheaves so well laden with grain from the field,
And golden the fruit that the orchard doth yield,
The garden its tribute in bounty reveals,
"The earth is the Lord's and the fullness thereof."

The jewels of silver and jewels of gold,
And stones that in beauty are grand to behold,
Their value in numbers has never been told,
"The earth is the Lord's and the fullness thereof."

And man in the image of God has been wrought,
By Jesus our Savior has dearly been bought,
The way, and the truth, and the life has been taught,
"The earth is the Lord's and the fullness thereof."

All glory to God who dwelleth on high,
And ruleth the earth, the sea, and the sky,
His children he hears in their pitiful cry,
"And opens his hands ev'ry want to supply!

Morrill, Kans.

PRIMITIVE CHRISTIANITY, AS UNDERSTOOD AND PRACTICED BY THE BRETHREN.

[We invite candid and intelligent criticism on all the articles published under this head. Criticisms on language, facts and arguments will be in order, and should be sent to the author of the article to which they refer.]

BY A. W. REESE.

Faith.

"But without faith it is impossible to please him: for he that cometh to God must believe that he is, and that he is a rewarder of them that diligently seek him."—Heb. 11: 6.

Part Two.

Let us consider, for a few moments, what Moses *relinquished* when he "refused to be called the son of Pharaoh's daughter." He cast away, as a mere bauble, a kingly crown! That was a strange thing for a sensible man to do, especially if he possessed a spark of human ambition.

More than this, it was no *ordinary* throne that Moses refused. The monarchs of that day were endowed with autocratic power. They had absolute control of the services, treasure, and even the very lives of their subjects. "Whom they would they slew, and whom they would they kept alive!" Egypt was the most splendid, the most powerful, and the wealthiest kingdom in that age of the world. Its monarch was the greatest of all the mighty rulers of ancient times. His court was distinguished by all the pomp, splendor and pageantry that the most abundant wealth could bestow. All this grandeur, wealth, power, luxury, ease, influence, adulation, homage, and worldly honor Moses threw away when he "refused to be called the son of Pharaoh's daughter." What did he gain, or accept, in return for this astonishing renunciation, — for this strange sacrifice of all those things that captivate the affections of men? He deliberately "chose rather to suffer affliction with the people of God, than to enjoy the pleasures of sin for a season."

Who were these "people of God?" Slaves! Outcasts! Pariahs! A people trodden under the iron heel of a cruel and pitiless despotism! A people whose abject and servile degradation had no equal on the face of the earth, a people groaning under the bitter yoke of a bondage worse than death. O, what a strange choice! More than this: "Esteeming the reproach of Christ greater riches than the treasures of Egypt." What is recorded of the treasures of that wonderful land?

We can form some faint conception of the vast wealth of that great empire when we bear in mind that special *cities* had to be built in which to store away the immense treasures belonging to Egypt. All this Moses forfeited when he refused to be called the son of Pharaoh's daughter, for that son was the "heir apparent" to the Egyptian throne.

What was the cause that influenced Moses to do this? Faith! It is declared that "by faith" Moses made this extraordinary choice. It is also declared that "he had respect unto the recompense of reward," the hope of glory made manifest unto him, not by sight, not by knowledge, but *by faith*.

Perhaps there can be found no more striking example of the subject under consideration than that of Naaman, the great captain of the Syrian host. Let us call attention first to the *humble instrumentality* by which the astounding results, in this remarkable case, were procured. Simply the chance remark of a little captive Jewish maid serving the wife of Naaman: "Would God my Master were with the prophet in Samaria, for he would recover him of his leprosy!"

Let us consider the character and station of the man in question. An illustrious warrior, a laureled chieftain, "foremost captain of his time," covered with the glittering decorations of his rank, the proud insignia of his military renown,— high in the esteem and confidence of the great monarch whom he served, and of whose serried hosts he was commander-in-chief.

And, moreover, these high honors were worthily bestowed, for the Divine Record declares that Naaman was a mighty man, honorable,—a man of valor. Naaman was not the creature of accident or mere official favor. He was a man of high character, of a rare degree of merit. He had "achieved greatness" in the profession of arms.

This great warrior stood next, in rank and power, to the mighty monarch of Syria himself. What more could human ambition desire? Surely if worldly honors and distinction could secure happiness, Naaman's cup was full to the very brim. But alas! the Divine Record completes the recital of all this rank, station, and power with these terrible words: "*But he was a leper*" !! A leper! The subject of a foul, disgusting, loathsome, in-*curable* disease! A malady so contagious, so dreaded, so abhorred of all mankind as to fix the seal of banishment on its wretched and unhappy victim! A disorder so shocking to the sight and so repulsive in all its features as to shut out the poor sufferer from the companionship and the sympathy of his fellow-men. A leper! What were power, rank, station, honor to him? The leper was doomed! There was no hope of relief! Never since creation's dawn had the leper been healed! The loathsome malady had defied all human skill in all the ages of the world. The leper was lost!

No ray of hope glimmered through the thick darkness of his long night of horror

"That had no morn beyond it,
And no star!"

How startling, then, the words of the little Jewish maid! How the great monarch's heart must have been stirred within him! We can well imagine the glad surprise, the letter to the king of

Israel, the preparations for the momentous journey, the gorgeous equipage of Naaman, the magnificent retinue, the regal escort, the magnificent presents to the Jewish king (whose value has been variously estimated at from *fifty to one hundred thousand dollars*). We can also understand the consternation and the dismay of the king of Israel at the astounding demand of the Syrian monarch: Behold, I send Naaman, my servant, that you should recover him of his leprosy! No wonder that the Jewish king, in his terror and dismay, rent his garments and the despairing cry rose to his trembling lips: "Am I God, to kill and to make alive, that this man sendeth one to be recovered of his leprosy? Behold how he seeketh a quarrel with me." But Elisha, the prophet of God, comes to the relief of the distracted king, "Send him to me." Naaman, at the head of his princely cortege, moves on. The gorgeous cavalcade pauses before the prophet's humble abode.

Never before had such pomp and pageantry honored the prophet's door. There, in his lordly chariot, sat the great commander of the Syrian hosts! a man of stern and iron mould, a man at the menace of whose hand

"Realms were chilled with fear
And armies mustered at the sign! as when
Clouds rise on clouds before the rainy East!
Gray captains leading-bands of veteran men
And fiery youths to be the Vulture's feast!"

But the prophet of God, seemingly unimpressed by the high rank of his illustrious visitor, and strangely insensible to the bewildering splendor of his equipage, declining with a quiet dignity his imperial gifts, did not come out to do the great man suitable honor. He sent a messenger, a servant, a menial, with the simple command, "Go wash seven times in Jordan, and thou shalt be clean!" No higher insult could have been offered to such a man as Naaman. No wonder that the astounded warrior cried out, "Behold, I thought he would come out!" What more natural and fitting the occasion, indeed, than that the renowned prophet would "stand," *uncovered* too, in the presence of this mighty man and further, that he would "call on the name of the Lord his God," and that "he would strike his hand over the place and recover the leper!" Surely this would have been the proper way to proceed in accordance with the rank and dignity of the great man who had come to be cured. No wonder, in this view, that Naaman "turned away in a rage." No wonder that, in the pride of his heart, he cried out, "Are not Abana and Pharpar, rivers of Damascus, better than all these waters of Israel, may I not wash in them and be clean?"

O how like proud, rebellious *man* that is! The means were too simple, too common, too plebeian to suit the ideas of this proud and haughty leader of the Syrian hosts. He proposed to *improve* on the *prophet's* plan. He suggested a more respectable, a more aristocratic way! And that idea is still a good deal in vogue in these "last days."

So Naaman "turned away in a rage." He intended to have his own way about the matter, and how *like* man that is! But wiser councils prevailed. "My father!" (a term of great respect) if the prophet had bid thee do some great thing, wouldst thou not have done it? How much rather when he saith to thee, Wash and be clean?" That was sensible advice on the part of the subordinates of the great magnate who had come all the way from Syria to be cured of a disease that had, hitherto, defied the skill of all preceding ages. But the remedy,—ah, it was too simple! It was not great enough for the great man! Ah! to do some *great* thing! What a sympathetic chord that strikes in the carnal heart! Man wants to do some great thing· but he does not want to do

The true church is taught by Christ, the Great Head of the church, to teach the people and to baptize believers by trine immersion, as taught in Matt. 28: 19. They are to observe all things. Included in this is feet-washing, the Lord's Supper, the Communion, the holy kiss, etc. These are some of the fruits by which we can know the true church. "By this shall all men know that ye are my disciples, if ye have love one for another."

From the foregoing, it can easily be seen in what church the Lord's people are to be found. Then, having come so far with Jesus and the apostles, let us go on to perfection, bearing the cross, despising the shame, and the crown will be ours.

Cameron, Mo.

MEMBERS IN SECRET SOCIETIES.

BY GRANT MAHAN.

EVERY little while we hear of trouble in some congregation because some member wishes to cling to his society. The only thing for those who do not believe in secret societies to do is to try for a reasonable time to convince the one who has gone astray; and if they can not do this there is nothing left for them but to cut the said member off.

This may seem harsh, it may appear to some to be unjust, and yet it is the only safe way, the only way in which the church can be kept free from this contamination. At times a member who works well and faithfully in Sunday school and prayer meeting, and wherever else occasion may offer, comes in question. What is to be done then? Is an influential, a hard-working member to be cut off merely because he belongs to some secret society? Yes; a thousand times yes.

There are some persons who seem to think it more necessary to compromise with a member who happens to have money or influence than with some one who has not; and one can't feel sure that this spirit is not sometimes shown when action is taken. If any difference in treatment of members is allowable it should not be this difference. There is a great deal more reason for bearing with the weaknesses of the weak than those of the strong. A strong member has no occasion to stumble because of the action of some weak one; but how can the weak one keep from stumbling because of the wrong action of the strong one?

And then too it is sometimes urged that by disowning some well-to-do person the church will lose influence in that locality. Rather the contrary is true. Just think of it for a moment. Is it better to have a church that relies on money, on members who have money, for influence, or to have a church that relies on principle, a church that is willing to stand by its principles no matter what happens? For the man who is a Christian at heart, who wishes to see the cause of truth and righteousness advance in the world, there can be but one answer to the above question. Any thought of compromise is unworthy of a Christian. The church professes to stand outside of and above worldly considerations, and rightly so; for the Leader has said, "Ye are not of the world."

The church does not need to take these things into consideration; nay, more: as soon as the church begins to rely for influence on any of the things of this world, just that soon she begins to lose in spiritual power; but as long as she relies on God for her strength, just that long will God bless and prosper her, and no longer. Most of the readers of the paper are familiar with the history of Asa and the words of Hanani the prophet:

"Because thou hast relied on the king of Syria, and not relied on the Lord thy God." How can one professing Christianity read these words without thinking of them, without taking them home to himself and asking himself, On what am I relying? Or how can he read Christ's words without doing the same thing? If there is any one thing taught in the New Testament, it is other-worldliness, it is that the followers of the Master are not to be governed by the motives that govern the people of the world. And yet it is very hard, apparently, for many of those who profess to be children of God to do as he tells them to do. But if they do not do so, what assurance have they of being accepted by him in the last great day?

And if those who belong to these societies would but look at their case squarely and honestly surely they would see how inconsistent they are. They profess to love the Lord with all their soul, mind and strength; and yet they cling closer to an institution of the world than they do to the church; in a great many cases where the matter comes to a test they give up the latter in order that they may keep the former. This is a very good reason why every one should be made to decide between the two, and that as soon as possible after he tries to belong to both at the same time. If his heart is with the church, he will forsake his society; if his heart is not with the church, he ought not to be in the church. There is no use letting a society draw a man from the church, and that is why it is better to make him decide at once. It is easier to give up a society 'when one has first joined than it is after he has attended its meetings for years. If these persons choose to leave us when the choice is given them of leaving the society or us, we can say with John: "They went out from us, but they were not of us; for if they had been of us, they would no doubt have continued with us."

There is no desire to be harsh, there is no desire to be hasty or unjust, but there is a most solemn desire to keep the church free from anything and everything that can make her lose her spiritual strength in any degree. She can't be kept too pure, too free from the world. She has need of all the spirituality at her disposal if the forces that make for evil are to be overcome by her. The great thing to do is to decide whether a thing is of the world (and in the case in question there is not the slightest doubt that it is of the world); then read John: "Love not the world, neither the things that are in the world. If any man love the world, the love of the Father is not in him. For all that is in the world, the lust of the flesh, and the lust of the eyes, and the pride of life, is not of the Father, but is of the world. And the world passeth away, and the lust thereof: but he that doeth the will of God abideth forever." Why should any one, especially after he has been converted and joined the church, hesitate to give up the world? Why should he insist on clinging to worldly institutions when he knows that his so doing destroys the peace of the church and is sure to bring evil upon him in the end? Can any one who does this give one good reason for doing it?

Halle, Germany.

"A STRONG temperance sermon was delivered by an unfortunate woman of Cape Girardeau, Mo., before her husband in a bar-room. Setting a covered dish, which she had brought with her, upon the table, she said: 'Presuming, husband, that you are too busy to come home to dinner, I have brought you yours,' and disappeared. With a forced laugh he invited his friend to dine with him, but on removing the cover from the dish, found only a slip of paper, on which was written: 'I hope you will enjoy your meal; it is the same your family have at home.'"

CORRESPONDENCE.

"Write what thou seest, and send it unto the churches."

☞Church News solicited for this Department. If you have had a good meeting, send a report of it, so that others may rejoice with you. In writing give name of church, County and State. Be brief. Notes of Travel should be as short as possible. Land Advertisements are not solicited for this Department. We have an advertising page, and, if necessary, will issue supplements.

From Double Pipe Creek, Carroll Co., Md.

OUR love-feast was held in the Rocky Ridge house Nov. 5 and 6. It was a very interesting meeting. Brethren Wm. Anthony, David Ausherman, Joseph Long, and others, were with us. The meeting was a large one and some very good food was dealt out to saint and sinner. Bro. Joseph Long, of Pennsylvania, commenced a series of meetings at our Double Pipe Creek house on the evening of Nov. 6 and continued till the evening of the 15th. There were no additions. Bro. Long deals out good and wholesome food, that will bring good results in due time.

At our third quarterly council it was decided to call one brother to the ministry and one to the deacon's office. The time was set for Thanksgiving Day, Nov. 24, at Rocky Ridge. Elders Wm. Franklin and Samuel Utz were present. The lot fell upon John S. Weybright for minister, and upon Preston Duvall for deacon. Circumstances being such that only Bro. Duvall was present, the installation was postponed until some indefinite time, when the work may be finished. Those elected are young and worthy brethren. We hope to see them make themselves useful, as the church is in need of young, active brethren. After services we resorted to the river where one was baptized. Others are counting the cost and we hope that they will soon follow.

SAMUEL WEYBRIGHT.

Our Trip to Colorado and Return.

ON Sunday evening, Sept. 11, we bade farewell to the members of the Rock Creek church, at Monte Vista, and started on our return trip. At midnight we arrived at Salida, and were met at the depot by Bro. Frey and taken to his home, about a mile outside the town, where we lodged for the remainder of the night. In the morning we made an effort to obtain a church in which to hold some meetings. As I failed in my effort, and as Bro. Frey was busily engaged just then, I concluded to pursue my journey. After a season of devotional exercises with his family, and commending them to the grace of God, we took the train at noon for Canyon City. As we neared the city, we passed the Royal Gorge of the Arkansas. The Gorge is about ten miles long. The scenery is exceedingly grand and awe-inspiring. As the train slowed up, the passengers crowded the platforms of the coaches and down the steps, and threw their heads back to see the top of the gorge if possible. From the bed of the river to the top is a solid wall that reaches to the clouds. One cannot help but feel the *mightiness* of the AL-MIGHTY when beholding his wonderful works. In comparison, our train and its mighty engine dwindled down to mere playthings and man to a feeble grasshopper.

At Canyon City we were met by Mr. and Mrs. Ewing, and conveyed to their home and lodged for the night. Next day they conveyed us to the home of sister Underhill, distant from Canyon City about twelve miles. The road is very mountainous. It took us from about 9 A. M. to 3 P. M., to make the trip.

Perhaps a brief description of the place and surroundings, where sister Underhill lives, would be interesting reading for the MESSENGER family. Sister Underhill lives in a cottage built against

The true church is taught by Christ, the Great Head of the church, to teach the people and to baptize believers by trine immersion, as taught in Matt. 28: 19. They are to observe *all things*. Included in this is feet-washing, the Lord's Supper, the Communion, the holy kiss, etc. These are some of the fruits by which we can know the true church. "By this shall all men know that ye are my disciples, if ye have love one for another."

From the foregoing, it can easily be seen in what church the Lord's people are to be found. Then, having come so far with Jesus and the apostles, let us go on to perfection, bearing the cross, despising the shame, and the crown will be ours.

Cameron, Mo.

MEMBERS IN SECRET SOCIETIES.

BY GRANT MAHAN.

EVERY little while we hear of trouble in some congregation because some member wishes to cling to his society. The only thing for those who do not believe in secret societies to do is to try for a reasonable time to convince the one who has gone astray; and if they can not do this there is nothing left for them but to cut the said member off.

This may seem harsh, it may appear to some to be unjust, and yet it is the only safe way, the only way in which the church can be kept free from this contamination. At times a member who works well and faithfully in Sunday school and prayer meeting, and wherever else occasion may offer, comes in question. What is to be done then? Is an influential, a hard-working member to be cut off merely because he belongs to some secret society? Yes; a thousand times yes.

There are some persons who seem to think it more necessary to compromise with a member who happens to have money or influence than with some one who has not; and one can't feel sure that this spirit is not sometimes shown when action is taken. If any difference in treatment of members is allowable it should not be this difference. There is a great deal more reason for bearing with the weaknesses of the weak than those of the strong. A strong member has no occasion to stumble because of the action of some weak one; but how can the weak one keep from stumbling because of the wrong action of the strong one?

And then too it is sometimes urged that by disowning some well-to-do person the church will lose influence in that locality. Rather the contrary is true. Just think of it for a moment. Is it better to have a church that relies on money, on members who have money, for influence, or to have a church that relies on principle, a church that is willing to stand by its principles no matter what happens? For the man who is a Christian at heart, who wishes to see the cause of truth and righteousness advance in the world, there can be but one answer to the above question. Any thought of compromise is unworthy of a Christian. The church professes to stand outside of and above worldly considerations, and rightly so; for the Leader has said, "Ye are not of the world."

The church does not need to take these things into consideration; nay, more: as soon as the church begins to rely for influence on any of the things of this world, just that soon she begins to lose in spiritual power; but as long as she relies on God for her strength, just that long will God bless and prosper her, and no longer. Most of the readers of the paper are familiar with the history of Asa and the words of Hanani the prophet:

"Because thou hast relied on the king of Syria, and not relied on the Lord thy God." How can one professing Christianity read these words without thinking of them, without taking them home to himself and asking himself, On what am *I relying?* Or how can he read Christ's words without doing the same thing? If there is any one thing taught in the New Testament, it is other-worldliness, it is that the followers of the Master are not to be governed by the motives that govern the people of the world. And yet it is very hard, apparently, for many of those who profess to be children of God to do as he tells them to do. But if they do not do so, what assurance have they of being accepted by him in the last great day?

And if those who belong to these societies would but look at their case squarely and honestly surely they would see how inconsistent they are. They profess to love the Lord with all their soul, mind and strength; and yet they cling closer to an institution of the world than they do to the church; in a great many cases where the matter comes to a test they give up the latter in order that they may keep the former. This is a very good reason why every one should be made to decide between the two, and that as soon as possible after he tries to belong to both at the same time. If his heart is with the church, he will forsake his society; if his heart is not with the church, he ought not to be in the church. There is no use letting a society draw a man from the church, and that is why it is better to make him decide at once. It is easier to give up a society when one has first joined than it is after he has attended its meetings for years. If these persons choose to leave us when the choice is given them of leaving the society or us, we can say with John: "They went out from us, but they were not of us; for if they had been of us, they would no doubt have continued with us."

There is no desire to be harsh, there is no desire to keep the church free from any thing and every thing that can make her lose her spiritual strength in any degree. She can't be kept too pure, too free from the world. She has need of all the spirituality at her disposal if the forces that make for evil are to be overcome by her. The great thing to do is to decide whether a thing is of the world (and in the case in question there is not the slightest doubt that it is of the world); then read John: "Love not the world, neither the things that are in the world. If any man love the world, the love of the Father is not in him. For all that is in the world, the lust of the flesh, and the lust of the eyes, and the pride of life, is not of the Father, but is of the world. And the world passeth away, and the lust thereof: but he that doeth the will of God abideth forever." Why should any one, especially after he has been converted and joined the church, hesitate to give up the world? Why should he insist on clinging to worldly institutions when he knows that his so doing destroys the peace of the church and is sure to bring evil upon him in the end? Can any one who does this give one good reason for doing it?

Halle, Germany.

"A STRONG temperance sermon was delivered by an unfortunate woman of Cape Girardeau, Mo., before her husband in a bar-room. Setting a covered dish, which she had brought with her, upon the table, she said: 'Presuming, husband, that you are too busy to come home to dinner, I have brought you yours,' and disappeared. With a forced laugh he invited his friend to dine with him, but on removing the cover from the dish, found only a slip of paper, on which was written: 'I hope you will enjoy your meal; it is the same your family have at home.'"

CORRESPONDENCE.

"Write what thou seest, and send it unto the churches."

☞ Church News solicited for this Department. If you have had a good meeting, send a report of it, so that others may rejoice with you. In writing give name of church, County and State. Be brief. Notes of Travel should be as short as possible. Land Advertisements are not solicited for this Department. We have an advertising page, and, if necessary, will issue supplements.

From Double Pipe Creek, Carroll Co., Md.

OUR love-feast was held in the Rocky Ridge house Nov. 5 and 6. It was a very interesting meeting. Brethren Wm. Anthony, David Aush- erman, Joseph Long, and others, were with us. The meeting was a large one and some very good food was dealt out to saint and sinner. Bro. Joseph Long, of Pennsylvania, commenced a series of meetings at our Double Pipe Creek house on the evening of Nov. 6 and continued till the evening of the 15th. There were no additions. Bro. Long deals out good and wholesome food, that will bring good results in due time.

At our third quarterly council it was decided to call one brother to the ministry and one to the deacon's office. The time was set for Thanksgiving Day, Nov. 24, at Rocky Ridge. Elders Wm. Franklin and Samuel Uts were present. The lot fell upon John S. Weybright for minister, and upon Preston Duvall for deacon. Circumstances being such that only Bro. Duvall was present, the installation was postponed until some indefinite time, when the work may be finished. Those elected are young and worthy brethren. We hope to see them make themselves useful, as the church is in need of young, active brethren. After services we resorted to the river where one was baptized. Others are counting the cost and we hope that they will soon follow.

SAMUEL WEYBRIGHT.

Our Trip to Colorado and Return.

ON Sunday evening, Sept. 11, we bade farewell to the members of the Rock Creek church, at Monte Vista, and started on our return trip. At midnight we arrived at Salida, and were met at the depot by Bro. Frey and taken to his home, about a mile outside the town, where we lodged for the remainder of the night. In the morning we made an effort to obtain a church in which to hold some meetings. As I failed in my effort, and as Bro. Frey was busily engaged just then, I concluded to pursue my journey. After a season of devotional exercises with his family, and commending them to the grace of God, we took the train at noon for Canyon City. As we neared the city, we passed the Royal Gorge of the Arkansas. The Gorge is about ten miles long. The scenery is exceedingly grand and awe-inspiring. As the train slowed up, the passengers crowded the platforms of the coaches and down the steps, and threw their heads back to see the top of the gorge if possible. From the bed of the river to the top is a solid wall that reaches to the clouds. One cannot help but feel the *mightiness* of the AL- MIGHTY when beholding his wonderful works. In comparison, our train and its mighty engine dwindled down to mere playthings and man to a feeble grasshopper.

At Canyon City we were met by Mr. and Mrs. Ewing, and conveyed to their home and lodged for the night. Next day they conveyed us to the home of sister Underhill, distant from Canyon City about twelve miles. The road is very mountainous. It took us from about 9 A. M. to 3 P. M., to make the trip.

Perhaps a brief description of the place and surroundings, where sister Underhill lives, would be interesting reading for the MESSENGER family. Sister Underhill lives in a cottage built against

Missionary and Tract Work Department.

"Upon the first day of the week, let every one of you lay by him in store as God hath prospered him, that there be no gatherings when I come."—1 Cor. 16: 2.

"Every man as he purposeth in his heart, so let him give. Not grudgingly or of necessity, for the Lord loveth a cheerful giver."—2 Cor. 9:7.

HOW MUCH SHALL WE GIVE?

"Every man according to his ability." "Every one as God hath prospered him." "Every man, according as he purposeth in his heart, so let him give." "For if there be first a willing mind, it is accepted according to that a man hath, and not according to that he hath not."—2 Cor. 8: 12.

Organization of Missionary Committee.

DANIEL VANIMAN, Foreman,	-	McPherson, Kans.
D. L. MILLER, Treasurer,	-	Mt. Morris, Ill.
GALEN B. ROYER, Secretary,	-	Mt. Morris, Ill.

Organization of Book and Tract Work.

S. W. HOOVER, Foreman,	-	Dayton, Ohio.
S. BOCK, Secretary and Treasurer,	-	Dayton, Ohio.

☞All donations intended for Missionary Work should be sent to GALEN B. ROYER, Mt. Morris, Ill.

☞All money for Tract Work should be sent to S. BOCK, Dayton, Ohio.

☞Money may be sent by Money Order, Registered Letter, or Drafts on New York or Chicago. Do not send personal checks, or drafts on interior towns, as it costs 25 cents to collect them.

☞Solicitors are requested to faithfully carry out the plan of Annual Meeting, that all our members be solicited to contribute at least twice a year for the Mission and Tract Work of the Church.

☞Notes for the Endowment Fund can be had by writing to the Secretary of either Work.

THE CHILDREN'S MISSION.

BY MARY M. GIBSON.

Dear Children:—

We almost feel as though we have been neglecting you, as we have not written you for so long. I believe I get as anxious to write, as you do, to hear from me. We have learned of late that some have been anxiously looking for a letter, so we feel to delay no longer. It seems to have become a second nature to us, to write and to hear. We are glad that our missives are appreciated and perused by some at least. We only give you that which God gives us, hence you should give God the praise for all. We are glad that he prompts us not to be negligent toward you, for it is concerning his kingdom that we should feel deeply interested. When we realize that the souls of the children are at stake, we should arise with a mighty effort for their salvation.

Many, yes many, are going the downward road to ruin. Are we now ready and willing that none should die and perish in their sins? Some of you have chosen the good part. Be like Mary of old,—do not let it be taken away from you. Times may come when you feel discouraged, but hold on a little longer,—the darkest clouds have their silvery lining. You can fight the battle through, as the faithful ones will wear the brightest crowns in the end. I dare say. there are but few (if any) who profess the name of Jesus, but have their dark hours and trials, and are striving hard to endure as good soldiers of the cross. This is to try our faith in Jesus. The enemy is going forth as a roaring lion, seeking whom he may devour. God grant that it may not be those who have named the name of Jesus. Our souls are of too great a value to let the enemy of souls get the upper hand of us. Life is real and earnest, and is worth living well, for it will endure unto eternity, whether for good or for evil. May we count the cost!

I have more family duties to attend to recently, consequently my writing to you may not be so frequently but I shall try, by the help of God, to be just as punctual in the future as in the past. The greatest thing is, to be perfectly contented with that which the Lord provides for us. This will help us to exercise our Christian graces. We sometimes feel a desire for a more excellent way, but God has said, "Not so," by placing us just where we are, that we might live it out, well pleasing in his sight. When he sees fit, he will bid us come up higher even in this life, and that at some time when we are the least expecting it.

It is no disgrace to crave the higher callings. There are steps and degrees here, before we are qualified for higher ones. The first step is to know that we love Jesus, and prepare ourselves to enter the fold of Christ by baptism. This proves we have first sought the kingdom of heaven and its righteousness, and are now ready to have the other things that are promised to be added unto us. We have learned, too, dear children, that some of the older ones appreciate and are interested in the work. For this we should feel very thankful, for they are likely to become co-workers with us. We must not, by any means, become exalted in our work, for God might then take it away from us. Let it make us more humble and contrite in heart, and be glad that he counts us worthy creatures of his, to do his will, whatsoever it may be, with singleness of heart.

I have just perused a loving letter from sister Clara E. Baldwin. We formed a warm attachment for each other at our last Annual Meeting. She is one of the workers among the children. God is ever mindful of all we do for him, even to the cup of cold water, if given in Jesus' name. This, indeed, should inspire us to the higher degrees in life. There is no standing in life so high as to be a true child of God. This will truly make us kind, loving, sympathetic and merciful to all of God's creation.

We need not hope for glory and honor if we neglect Christ's kingdom while here in this life. I am happy to inform you that our "Children's Mission" is increasing. The amount already exceeds that of last year's report. This is good news, and will gladden the hearts of all that are deeply concerned about their Father's business.

We read of many children's meetings now and then. We have often wondered why our elders and Superintendents do not give them a chance, at that time, to put in a donation. I have been at children's meetings, where, after the close of the meeting, some would come and slip their donation into my hand gladly. Children, you will have to do likewise. You need not be afraid that any one will refuse to take your offering. They know that it takes our time, talents and pennies to carry on the work of the Lord. Let us not be as the idle or scornful, but do his will to the glory and honor of God, in Jesus' name, so that, at his coming, we may be weighed in his balances and not found wanting.

Virden, Ill., Box 421.

THE IDEAL SUNDAY-SCHOOL.

BY JOHN CALVIN BRIGHT.

At our late ministerial meeting a young minister gave a beautiful description of what constitutes an ideal Sunday-school. It was so good and instructive that we think it should be spread everywhere.

What constitutes the ideal Sunday-school? First, the older should give it the benefit of his experience and presence. He should enter into the work with a zeal becoming an overseer of the flock. He should attend all the sessions that it is possible for him to attend, and give it encouragement in every lawful way. What is true of the elder, is true of all the ministers and deacons in the church. They should take hold of the work after the same manner that the faithful elder does. They should bring their families to the school too. The little folks, the older members of the family, and, if possible, the hired help,—all should take an active part in the exercises. The older members should copy close after the faithful official members. None are too old to help the school, nor are they too old to enjoy it, or be helped by it. Let them bring their families, too. Let them all be there on time, enjoy the opening exercises, and help to make them interesting.

The younger members will, in that way, find it easy to take up their part of the labor, and make the school a grand success. Here they will find a field of labor suited to their capacity, and broad enough for all to labor together. Let nothing hinder them from performing their part of the work. Let the Master's work be first, and last, and all the time.

The Superintendent should give the school much thought, and prayer, and preparation. He should be punctual, courteous, and active. He should give each one his appropriate place and work. The teachers should be after the same pattern. Nothing but a special providence of God should keep them from meeting their classes at the appointed hour. The entire work should be done with an eye single to the glory of God, the welfare of Zion and the salvation of souls.

It is a mistake for the officials to take no part in the work, just as it would be a mistake for them to have one themselves. It is also a sad mistake for either the parents to go without the children, or the children to go without the parents. Let all be perfectly joined together in the same mind, speak the same thing, and learn the same lessons from God's Word.

REPORT OF MINISTERIAL MEETING.

BY NEUBEN SHROYER.

The Ministerial Meeting of North-eastern District of Ohio was held in the Maple Grove church, Nov. 17, 1892. On the preceding evening Eld. I. D. Parker delivered a sermon on Church Government. His arguments were able and had the right ring. We are confident that Bro. Parker has done much good by giving his attention to the important subject, and hope he will arrange his sermons on the subject for publication in the MESSENGER.

On the morning of Nov. 17 the program that had been arranged was carried out.

On the topic, "What is Necessary to Hold a Successful Protracted Meeting," the following was brought out: It should be a *revival* meeting, a coming to *life*. To effect a revival, we must have the Lord with us. There must be a united effort on the part of the church. Music is necessary; all should sing. The minister should feel a deep sense of the responsibility resting upon him, and the magnitude of the work. . Earnestness and sincerity, coupled with continued prayer will bring about a successful protracted meeting.

Upon the topic, "What is the Minister's Duty to the Church," the following thoughts were advanced: He should preach the Word; be instant in season and out of season. He should *study* to show himself approved unto God. He should exhort and rebuke with all long-suffering and doctrine. He should visit the members of the church, should be an *example* to the flock. He should have the welfare of the church at heart, be a servant of the church. He should inquire into the spiritual conditions of his members, etc.

"What is the Duty of the Church to the Ministry," brought out the following: The duty of the church to the minister is to encourage him by expressions of tender regard, by an apprecia-

Missionary and Tract Work Department.

"Upon the first day of the week, let every one of you lay by him in store as God hath prospered him, that there be no gatherings when I come."—1 Cor. 16: 2.

"Every man as he purposeth in his heart, so let him give. Not grudgingly or of necessity, for the Lord loveth a cheerful giver."—2 Cor. 9: 7.

HOW MUCH SHALL WE GIVE?

"Every man *according to his ability.*" "Every one *as God hath prospered him.*" "Every man, *according as he purposeth in his heart,* so let him give." "For if there be first a willing mind, it is accepted *according to that a man hath,* and not according to that he hath not."—1 Cor. 8: 12.

Organization of Missionary Committee.

DANIEL VANIMAN, Foreman, - - - McPherson, Kans.
D. L. MILLER, Treasurer, - - - Mt. Morris, Ill.
GALEN B. ROYER, Secretary, - - - Mt. Morris, Ill.

Organization of Book and Tract Work.

S. W. HOOVER, Foreman, - - - Dayton, Ohio.
S. BOCK, Secretary and Treasurer, - - Dayton, Ohio.

☞All donations intended for Missionary Work should be sent to GALEN B. ROYER, Mt. Morris, Ill.

☞All money for Tract Work should be sent to S. BOCK, Dayton, Ohio.

☞Money may be sent by Money Order, Registered Letter, or Drafts on New York or Chicago. Do not send personal checks, or drafts on interior towns, as it costs 25 cents to collect them.

☞Solicitors are requested to faithfully carry out the plan of Annual Meeting, that all our members be solicited to contribute at least twice a year for the Mission and Tract Work of the Church.

☞Notes for the Endowment Fund can be had by writing to the Secretary of either Work.

THE CHILDREN'S MISSION.

BY MARY M. GIBSON.

Dear Children:—

WE almost feel as though we have been neglecting you, as we have not written you for so long. I believe I get as anxious to write, as you do, to hear from me. We have learned of late that some have been anxiously looking for a letter, so we feel to delay no longer. It seems to have become a second nature to us, to write and to hear. We are glad that our missives are appreciated and perused by some at least. It gives us encouragement to write again. We only give you that which God gives us, hence you should give God the praise for all. We are glad that he prompts us not to be negligent toward you, for it is concerning his kingdom that we should feel deeply interested. When we realize that the souls of the children are at stake, we should arise with a mighty effort for their salvation.

Many, yea many, are going the downward road to ruin. Are we now ready and willing that none should die and perish in their sins? Some of you have chosen the good part. Be like Mary of old,—do not let it be taken away from you. Times may come when you feel discouraged, but hold on a little longer,—the darkest clouds have their silvery lining. You can fight the battle through, as the faithful ones will wear the brightest crowns in the end. I dare say. there are but few (if any) who profess the name of Jesus, but have their dark hours and trials, and are striving hard to endure as good soldiers of the cross. This is to try our faith in Jesus. The enemy is going forth as a roaring lion, seeking whom he may devour. God grant that it may not be those who have named the name of Jesus. Our souls are of too great a value to let the enemy of souls get the upper hand of us. Life is real and earnest, and is worth living well, for it will endure unto eternity, whether for good or for evil. May we count the cost!

I have more family duties to attend to recently, consequently my writing to you may not be so frequently but I shall try, by the help of God, to be just as punctual in the future as in the past. The greatest thing is, to be perfectly contented with that which the Lord provides for us. This will help us to exercise our Christian graces. We sometimes feel a desire for a more excellent way, but God has said, "Not so," by placing us just where we are, that we might live it out, well pleasing in his sight. When he sees fit, he will bid us come up higher even in this life, and that at some time when we are the least expecting it.

It is no disgrace to crave the higher callings. There are steps and degrees here, before we are qualified for higher ones. The first step is to know that we love Jesus, and prepare ourselves to enter the fold of Christ by baptism. This proves we have first sought the kingdom of heaven and its righteousness, and are now ready to have the other things that are promised to be added unto us. We have learned, too, dear children, that some of the older ones appreciate and are interested in the work. For this we should feel very thankful, for they are likely to become co-workers with us. We must not, by any means, become exalted in our work, for God might then take it away from us. Let it make us more humble and contrite in heart, and be glad that he counts us worthy creatures of his, to do his will, whatsoever it may be, with singleness of heart.

I have just perused a loving letter from sister Clara E. Baldwin. We formed a warm attachment for each other at our last Annual Meeting. She is one of the workers among the children. God is ever mindful of all we do for him, even to the cup of cold water, if given in Jesus' name. This, indeed, should inspire us to the higher degrees in life. There is no standing in life so high as to be a true child of God. This will truly make us kind, loving, sympathetic and merciful to all of God's creation.

We need not hope for glory and honor if we neglect Christ's kingdom while here in this life. I am happy to inform you that our "Children's Mission" is increasing. The amount already exceeds that of last year's report. This is good news, and will gladden the hearts of all that are deeply concerned about their Father's business.

We read of many children's meetings now and then. We have often wondered why our elders and Superintendents do not give them a chance, at that time, to put in a donation. I have been at children's meetings, where, after the close of the meeting, some would come and slip their donation into my hand gladly. Children, you will have to do likewise. You need not be afraid that any one will refuse to take your offering. They know that it takes our time, talents and pennies to carry on the work of the Lord. Let us not be as the idle or scornful, but do his will to the glory and honor of God, in Jesus' name, so that, at his coming, we may be weighed in his balances and not found wanting.

Virden, Ill., Box 421.

THE IDEAL SUNDAY-SCHOOL.

BY JOHN CALVIN BRIGHT.

AT our late ministerial meeting a young minister gave a beautiful description of what constitutes an ideal Sunday-school. It was so good and instructive that we think it should be spread everywhere.

What constitutes the ideal Sunday-school? First, the older should give it the benefit of his experience and presence. He should enter into the work with a zeal becoming an overseer of the flock. He should attend all the sessions that it is possible for him to attend, and give it encouragement in every lawful way. What is true of the elder, is true of all the ministers and deacons in the church. They should take hold of the work after the same manner that the faithful elder does. They should bring their families to the school too. The little folks, the older members of the family, and, if possible, the hired help,—all should take an active part in the exercises. The older members should copy close after the faithful official members. None are too old to help the school, nor are they too old to enjoy it, or be helped by it. Let them bring their families, too. Let them all be there on time, enjoy the opening exercises, and help to make them interesting.

The younger members will, in that way, find it easy to take up their part of the labor, and make the school a grand success. Here they will find a field of labor suited to their capacity, and broad enough for all to labor together. Let nothing hinder them from performing their part of the work. Let the Master's work be first, and last, and all the time.

The Superintendent should give the school much thought, and prayer, and preparation. He should be punctual, courteous, and active. He should give each one his appropriate place and work. The teachers should be after the same pattern. Nothing but a special providence of God should keep them from meeting their classes at the appointed hour. The entire work should be done with an eye single to the glory of God, the welfare of Zion and the salvation of souls.

It is a mistake for the officials to take no part in the work, just as it would be a mistake for them to have one themselves. It is also a sad mistake for either the parents to go without the children, or the children to go without the parents. Let *all* be perfectly joined together in the same mind, speak the same thing, and learn the same lessons from God's Word.

REPORT OF MINISTERIAL MEETING.

BY REUBEN SHROYER.

THE Ministerial Meeting of North-eastern District of Ohio was held in the Maple Grove church, Nov. 17, 1892. On the preceding evening Eld. I. D. Parker delivered a sermon on Church Government. His arguments were able and had the right ring. We are confident that Bro. Parker has done much good by giving his attention to the important subject, and hope he will arrange his sermons on the subject for publication in the MESSENGER.

On the morning of Nov. 17 the program that had been arranged was carried out.

On the topic, "What is Necessary to Hold a Successful Protracted Meeting," the following was brought out: It should be a *revival* meeting, a coming to *life.* To effect a revival, we must have the Lord with us. There must be a united effort on the part of the church. Music is necessary; all should sing. The minister should feel a deep sense of the responsibility resting upon him, and the magnitude of the work. Earnestness and sincerity, coupled with continued prayer will bring about a successful protracted meeting.

Upon the topic, "What is the Minister's Duty to the Church," the following thoughts were advanced: He should preach the Word; be instant in season and out of season. He should *study* to show himself approved unto God. He should exhort and rebuke with all long-suffering and doctrine. He should visit the members of the church, should be an *example* to the flock. He should have the welfare of the church at heart, be a servant of the church. He should inquire into the spiritual conditions of his members, etc.

"What is the Duty of the Church to the Ministry," brought out the following: The duty of the church to the minister is to encourage him by expressions of tender regard, by an apprecia-

The Gospel Messenger,

A Weekly at $1.50 Per Annum.

PUBLISHED BY

The Brethren's Publishing Co.

D. L. MILLER,	Editor.
J. H. MOORE,	Office Editor.
J. B. BRUMBAUGH,	Associate Editors.
J. G. ROYER,	
JOSEPH AMICK,	Business Manager.

ADVISORY COMMITTEE.

L. W. Teeter, A. Hutchison, Daniel Hays.

Communications for publication should be legibly written with black ink on one side of the paper only. Do not attempt to interline, or to put on one page what ought to occupy two.

Anonymous communications will not be published.

Do not mix business with articles for publication. Keep your communications on separate sheets from all business.

Time is precious. We always have time to attend to business and to answer questions of importance, but please do not subject us to need-less answering of letters.

The MESSENGER is mailed each week to all subscribers. If the address is correctly entered on our list, the paper must reach the person to whom it is addressed. If you do not get your paper, write us, giving particulars.

When changing your address, please give your former as well as your future address in full, so as to avoid delay and misunderstanding.

Always remit to the office from which you order your goods, no matter from where you receive them.

Do not send personal checks or drafts on interior banks, unless you send with them 25 cents each, to pay for collection.

Remittances should be made by Post-office Money Order, Drafts on New York, Philadelphia or Chicago, or Registered Letters, made payable and addressed to "Brethren's Publishing Co., Mount Morris, Ill.," or "Brethren's Publishing Co., Huntingdon, Pa."

Entered at the Post-office at Mount Morris, Ill., as second-class matter.

Mount Morris, Ill., • • • • **Dec. 13, 1892.**

BRO. JACOB HOLLINGER, of Noble County, Ind., informs us that his address is now Wawaka instead of Albion.

THE MESSENGER last week contained over one hundred articles, reports, and items, in addition to the obituary and literary notices.

NEVER get on the devil's side of the fence and then pray the Lord to help you. If you want help from above keep on the Lord's-side.

BRO. JOHN M. MOHLER recently closed an excellent meeting in the West Conestoga church, Pa., with eleven additions by confession and baptism.

BRETHREN Samuel Lehman, of Franklin Grove, and Thomas Keiser, of Roanoke, Ill., have decided to spend the present winter in California, and are probably in the State ere this.

BRO. HENRY BALSBAUGH, of Harrisburg, Pa., is in the habit of sending the MESSENGER as a donation to a few worthy persons each year. He says he will do likewise next year. This is commendable.

THERE are now thought to be more Jews in the world than at any former time. They also possess more wealth than at any previous time. Their great wealth makes them a power in the world.

THAT was a sensible writer who wrote, "I am tired of seeing all the flowers at weddings and funerals; we need a few in between." There are people who never think of giving a flower to one whom they should love most, but as soon as they are dead can cover the coffin with the most lovely flowers. All this is for mere show. If flowers are expressions of love and tender regards, let them be used while there is life, that they be enjoyed. For our part we prefer the tokens of kindness while living that we may feel and know in the living heart what it is to love and to be loved. Flowers were made for the living, not for the dead.

THERE are said to be three thousand spoken languages in the world. The Bible has been translated into about two hundred of them. This enables nearly two-thirds of the people on the globe to read the Word of God.

ONLY one more issue and the present volume of the MESSENGER closes. How time does fly! We are one year nearer our long home. Soon the volume that contains the record of our lives will be closed to be opened only at the judgment.

THE home ministers at Shannon, Ill., have been engaged in an interesting series of meetings for several days. They expected some help this week and may continue the meetings at least the remainder of this week.

A MAN in Jasper County, Indiana, thinking that he had faith sufficient to enable him to take up serpents and they would do him no harm, tried it on a rattlesnake, which bit him and ended his life. Faith was not intended for use in that way.

TRAIN up a child in the way that he should not go, and when he is old he will most assuredly not depart from it. This may serve as a lesson to parents who are training their little ones in the ways of fashion more than the ways of Christianity.

BRO. C. C. ROOT, of Ozawkie, Kans., requests that all those who paid him for the Brethren's Almanac will please drop him a card, as he has lost his diary containing a list of the names. He will return postals with the Almanacs.

BRO. HUTCHISON, who is now at Cedar Rapids, Iowa, is arranging to be at Mt. Morris the first of January, with a view of enjoying the Bible Term. That is good, but the Bible Term will also have the pleasure of enjoying Bro. Hutchison.

AT a public meeting, recently held in Chicago, a public speaker pointed out the fact that of the 50,000 persons yearly arrested in that city for some misdemeanor, liquor was the direct cause of nine-tenths of the arrests. Banish the saloons and you destroy the great breeders of crime.

THE comet has come and gone. It did not come very close to the earth, but it has departed for parts unknown. For a few weeks the timid were more or less alarmed, fearing that the celestial visitor would strike the earth and we would be no occasion for alarm. Even in case of a collision between this earth and a comet, little would be experienced aside from a grand meteoric display and some unpleasant odor in our atmosphere. People who are prepared to go to heaven need not be alarmed at an occasional visit from one of these celestial travelers.

BRO. H. CLARK, Sheridan, Mo., writes that the members at that place would like a minister to locate with them and are willing to render him some very substantial assistance. They want a man who understands the Gospel, can preach it to the edification and instruction of the people, and is in full sympathy with the faith and practice of the church. Their demand is a reasonable one and no minister should apply for the place who does not know himself to be in accord with their views. We have little sympathy for ministers who are willing to receive assistance from the church and then deliberately disregard her faith and practice, and teach others to do likewise. There is a growing demand for ministers sound in the faith, well rooted and grounded in the doctrine, and for such substantial assistance may be found in many localities.

THE oldest church building in the United States is the church of San Miguel, erected at Santa Fe, New Mexico, seventy-seven years before the landing of the pilgrims on Plymouth Rock, twenty years before the founding of St. Augustine, Fla., and fifty-three years after the landing of Columbus.

WHEN we commenced reading Bro. D. F. Stoutfer's "Visit to Powell's Fort," found in this issue, we decided to cut him short about one-half. But his walk up that huge mountain, and his graphic description of the grand view from nature's aerial pulpit, not made with hands, proved so interesting that we decided to give the article entire. It will be appreciated by all lovers of mountain scenery.

PRESIDENT HARPER, of the Chicago University, in a recent address has seen proper to discourage the formation of secret societies, believing that whatever of good is aimed at in these societies may be gained by other means, free from the objections of secrecy, of rigid exclusiveness and of antagonism to the democratic spirit, such as belongs to the true scholarship, the best manhood, the noblest citizenship.

THE first Monday evening in each month the ministers in this congregation, including the ministers who attend school here, have a very interesting ministerial meeting. One hour is spent on some subject of special interest to the minister and his work. At our last meeting we had up this question: "The best Method of Conducting a Series of Meetings." Many interesting points were brought out, and the meeting, doubtless, proved very profitable to all those present. Our next meeting will be the first Monday evening in January, the evening before the Bible Term opens.

RECENTLY a brother had occasion to stop off at a wayside station, awaiting the arrival of another train. While he and other brethren and sisters passed the time in pleasant conversation, two gentlemen near by were gazing with some astonishment at the little group of members. Apparently the gentlemen were members of the legal profession and presently one of them asked: "Who are those people?" The answer was: "They are Dunkards,—a people that do not believe in going to law." After some study the first speaker said: "Well, they are wise; they can save a great deal of money by it."

WE are just in receipt of a long article from Bro. D. L. Miller, mailed at Genoa, Italy, Nov. 24. It will appear in our next issue and will prove exceedingly interesting. We now expect articles from him quite frequently, describing a portion of country of which many of our readers have read but little. These letters will prove not only interesting but profitable to all of those who are so fortunate as to be readers of the MESSENGER. We suggest that our agents everywhere make good use of this important feature in gathering subscribers for the MESSENGER. In this way hundreds of others might be induced to subscribe and become permanent readers of the paper. In almost every congregation there are families where the paper is never read and the members know but little of the doings of the Brotherhood, and of course are not so interested in her various departments of work. We throw out these suggestions to agents and others, who are thoroughly interested in our efforts, trusting that they will see the necessity and advantage of making still greater efforts to get the MESSENGER into all the families in the Brotherhood, as well as into other families, who may be favorably impressed by reading our church literature.

The Gospel Messenger,

A Weekly at $1.50 Per Annum.

PUBLISHED BY

The Brethren's Publishing Co.

D. L. MILLER,	. . . . .	Editor.
J. H. MOORE,	. . . . .	Office Editor.
J. B. BRUMBAUGH,	}	Associate Editors.
J. G. ROYER,	}	
JOSEPH AMICK,	. . . . .	Business Manager.

ADVISORY COMMITTEE.

L. W. Teeter, A. Hutchison, Daniel Hays.

☞ Communications for publication should be legibly written with black ink on one side of the paper only. Do not attempt to interline, or to put on one page what ought to occupy two.

☞ Anonymous communications will not be published.

☞ Do not mix business with articles for publication. Keep your communications on separate sheets from all business.

☞ Time is precious. We always have time to attend to business and to answer questions of importance, but please do not subject us to need less answering of letters.

☞ The MESSENGER is mailed each week to all subscribers. If the address is correctly entered on our list, the paper must reach the person to whom it is addressed. If you do not get your paper, write us, giving particulars.

☞ When changing your address, please give your former as well as your future address in full, so as to avoid delay and misunderstanding.

☞ Always remit to the office from which you order your goods, no matter from where you receive them.

☞ Do not send personal checks or drafts on interior banks, unless you send with them 25 cents each, to pay for collection.

☞ Remittances should be made by Post-office Money Order, Drafts on New York, Philadelphia or Chicago, or Registered Letters, made payable and addressed to "Brethren's Publishing Co., Mount Morris, Ill.," or "Brethren's Publishing Co., Huntingdon, Pa."

☞ Entered at the Post-office at Mount Morris, Ill., as second-class matter.

Mount Morris, Ill.,   · · · ·   Dec. 13, 1892.

BRO. JACOB HOLLINGER, of Noble County, Ind., informs us that his address is now Wawaka instead of Albion.

THE MESSENGER last week contained over one hundred articles, reports, and items, in addition to the obituary and literary notices.

NEVER get on the devil's side of the fence and then pray the Lord to help you. If you want help from above keep on the Lord's side.

BRO. JOHN M. MOHLER recently closed an excellent meeting in the West Conestoga church, Pa., with eleven additions by confession and baptism.

BRETHREN Samuel Lehman, of Franklin Grove, and Thomas Keiser, of Roanoke, Ill., have decided to spend the present winter in California, and are probably in the State ere this.

BRO. HENRY BALSBAUGH, of Harrisburg, Pa., is in the habit of sending the MESSENGER as a donation to a few worthy persons each year. He says he will do likewise next year. This is commendable.

THERE are now thought to be more Jews in the world than at any former period. They also possess more wealth than at any previous time. Their great wealth makes them a power in the world.

THAT was a sensible writer who wrote, "I am tired of seeing all the flowers at weddings and funerals; we need a few in between." There are people who never think of giving a flower to the one whom they should love most, but as soon as they are dead can cover the coffin with the most lovely flowers. All this is for mere show. If flowers are expressions of love and tender regards, let them be used while there is life, that they be enjoyed. For our part we prefer the tokens of kindness while living that we may feel and know in the living heart what it is to love and to be loved. Flowers were made for the living, not for the dead.

THERE are said to be three thousand spoken languages in the world. The Bible has been translated into about two hundred of them. This enables nearly two-thirds of the people on the globe to read the Word of God.

ONLY one more issue and the present volume of the MESSENGER closes. How time does fly! We are one year nearer our long home. Soon the volume that contains the record of our lives will be closed to be opened only at the judgment.

THE home ministers at Shannon, Ill., have been engaged in an interesting series of meetings for several days. They expected some help this week and may continue the meetings at least the remainder of this week.

A MAN in Jasper County, Indiana, thinking that he had faith sufficient to enable him to take up serpents and they would do him no harm, tried it on a rattlesnake, which bit him and ended his life. Faith was not intended for use in that way.

TRAIN up a child in the way that he should not go, and when he is old he will most assuredly not depart from it. This may serve as a lesson to parents who are training their little ones in the ways of fashion more than the ways of Christianity.

BRO. C. C. ROOT, of Ozawkie, Kans., requests that all those who paid him for the Brethren's Almanac will please drop him a card, as he has lost his diary containing a list of the names. He will return postals with the Almanac.

BRO. HUTCHISON, who is now at Cedar Rapids, Iowa, is arranging to be at Mt. Morris the first of January, with a view of enjoying the Bible Term. That is good, but the Bible Term will also have the pleasure of enjoying Bro. Hutchison.

AT a public meeting, recently held in Chicago, a public speaker pointed out the fact that of the 50,000 persons yearly arrested in that city for some misdemeanor, liquor was the direct cause of nine-tenths of the arrests. Banish the saloons and you destroy the great breeders of crime.

THE comet has come and gone. It did not come very close to the earth, but it has departed for parts unknown. For a few weeks the timid were more or less alarmed, fearing that the celestial visitor would strike the earth and work no little woe. In all likelihood there has been no occasion for alarm. Even in case of a collision between this earth and a comet, little would be experienced aside from a grand meteoric display and some unpleasant odor in our atmosphere. People who are prepared to go to heaven need not be alarmed at an occasional visit from one of these celestial travelers.

BRO. H. CLARK, Sheridan, Mo., writes that the members at that place would like a minister to locate with them and are willing to render him some very substantial assistance. They want a man who understands the Gospel, can preach it to the edification and instruction of the people, and is in full sympathy with the faith and practice of the church. Their demand is a reasonable one and no minister should apply for the place who does not know himself to be in accord with their views. We have little sympathy for ministers who are willing to receive assistance from the church and then deliberately disregard her faith and practice, and teach others to do likewise. There is a growing demand for ministers sound in the faith, well rooted and grounded in the doctrine, and for such substantial assistance may be found in many localities.

THE oldest church building in the United States is the church of San Miguel, erected at Santa Fe, New Mexico, seventy-seven years before the landing of the pilgrims on Plymouth Rock, twenty years before the founding of St. Augustine, Fla., and fifty-three years after the landing of Columbus.

WHEN we commenced reading Bro. D. F. Stouffer's "Visit to Powell's Fort," found in this issue, we decided to cut him short about one-half. But his walk up that huge mountain, and his graphic description of the grand view from nature's eternal pulpit, not made with hands, proved so interesting that we decided to give the article entire. It will be appreciated by all lovers of mountain scenery.

PRESIDENT HARPER, of the Chicago University, in a recent address has seen proper to discourage the formation of secret societies, believing that whatever of good is aimed at in these societies may be gained by other means, free from the objections of secrecy, of rigid exclusiveness and of antagonism to the democratic spirit, such as belongs to the true scholarship, the best manhood, the noblest citizenship.

THE first Monday evening in each month the ministers in this congregation, including the ministers who attend school here, have a very interesting ministerial meeting. One hour is spent on some subject of special interest to the minister and his work. At our last meeting we had up this question: "The best Method of Conducting a Series of Meetings." Many interesting points were brought out, and the meeting, doubtless, proved very profitable to all those present. Our next meeting will be the first Monday evening in January, the evening before the Bible Term opens.

RECENTLY a brother had occasion to stop off at a wayside station, awaiting the arrival of another train. While he and other brethren and sisters passed the time in pleasant conversation, two gentlemen near by were gazing with some astonishment at the little group of members. Apparently the gentlemen were members of the legal profession and presently one of them asked: "Who are those people?" The answer was: "They are Dunkards,—a people that do not believe in going to law." After some study the first speaker said: "Well, they are wise; they can save a great deal of money by it."

WE are just in receipt of a long article from Bro. D. L. Miller, mailed at Genoa, Italy, Nov. 24. It will appear in our next issue and will prove exceedingly interesting. We now expect articles from him quite frequently, describing a portion of country of which many of our readers have read but little. These letters will prove not only interesting but profitable to all of those who are so fortunate as to be readers of the MESSENGER. We suggest that our agents everywhere make good use of this important feature in gathering subscribers for the MESSENGER. In this way hundreds of others might be induced to subscribe and become permanent readers of the paper. In almost every congregation there are families where the paper is never read and the members know but little of the doings of the Brotherhood, and of course are not so interested in her various departments of work. We throw out these suggestions to agents and others, who are thoroughly interested in our efforts, trusting that they will see the necessity and advantage of making still greater efforts to get the MESSENGER into all the families in the Brotherhood, as well as into other families, who may be favorably impressed by reading our church literature.

LITTLE THINGS.—Prov. 30.

In this world we judge of the greatness or smallness of things by comparison. Were it not for the faculty of comparison, the words big and little would have no meaning to us. In making our comparisons we compare things of a kind. When I say the largest apple, I draw a comparison between the apple I speak of and other apples. If I should compare an apple with a house, as to size, I would render the comparison worthless. Notice that our comparisons are made between things that have form, size, weight, color, and distances, heights, depths, etc., etc.

Our natural disposition to draw comparisons has led us to draw comparisons between moral actions. We speak of little sins, of little or white lies. We also speak of little acts of kindness, little actions of benevolence. Now I doubt if there is such a thing as comparison between right and wrong. A thing is right or it is wrong, and, if wrong, it has only one quality, and that is the quality of wrong. If a statement is made to deceive, it is an untruth and a lie, and the quality of little or white does not attach to it. It is an untruth.

There is a good deal of this kind of lying going on in the world. In the world, did I say? Better change that and say it is to be found in the church. It leads us to invite people to come to see us, simply because it is the proper thing to do, and when, at the same time, we would rather they would not come. I need not pursue this farther. I only want to say that an untruth is an untruth, and lying is sinful always and under all circumstances.

In the same way we compare good actions. We talk about little acts of kindness. I doubt much if the speech is right. An act of kindness has in it the quality of goodness, and in the sight of God, the cup of cold water and the widow's mite are not little things, but great as is every act of goodness done by man. And how glad we should be that God's rule of comparison is not like ours! If it were, the millions of Rockafeller in the Endowment of the Chicago University, or Stanford's twenty million for the school in California would so dwarf the dollars given to build up our school at this place that they would be so covered up as to never be found.

But God counts the mites. When the rich Pharisee, with slow and measured tread, and with dignified air, walked up the aisle of the temple and cast into the treasury a handful of gold, giving of his great abundance, he doubtless felt that he was great in giving, and, according to man's method of estimating greatness, he was right. But, behold the poor widow, with bowed head and trembling step, go up to the box, and she drops in but a farthing. Poverty stricken, she gives of her living, and the Son of God says she has given more than all the rest. Strange comparison from human standpoint. But God does not see things as we see them. He looks on the inside, we on the outside. We judge of the seen, he of the unseen.

The wise man calls our attention to four things that are little upon the earth, and asks us to consider them, because of their exceeding wisdom. Solomon was a student of natural history and learned wisdom from the animal creation. "The ants are a people not strong, yet they prepare their meat in the summer."

Here we have a lesson of industry. The same writer says, "Go to the ant, thou sluggard, and learn wisdom." An ant is very small, and not strong, but her storehouse is filled in the summer, the time for gathering in. Life is the summer, and we are to learn wisdom from the ant by preparing for the winter of death. Will we learn wisdom from the ant, for the Bible says she is exceedingly wise.

"The conies are but a feeble folk, yet make they their homes in the rocks." The coney is a small animal having something of the nature of our rabbits. They are shy, meek, non-resisting animals, and manifest their wisdom by building their houses in the rocks. We may learn wisdom from the coney in meekness. What is meekness? "The meek shall inherit the earth." Their wisdom is also manifest in building among the rocks,—a place of safety. Among the inaccessible rocks of the mountains these little animals are to be found. As Christians we need to build on the Rock. But we may rejoice that the Rock of Ages was cleft for us, and we may hide in the cleft. Hiding thus in the "Rock that is higher than I," we manifest the wisdom of the coney. Can we not thus hide away from the enemy of our souls?

The locusts have no kings, yet they go forth in bands. Those who know something of the grasshoppers, know how they go forth in bands without leaders. Without a king they accomplish their purpose. We ought surely to learn wisdom from the locust, and stand together a united band. What we need more than all else is union in Christ. Breaking the band results in disunion, separation and destruction. We need to be united. We cannot all have our own way, but we must bear with each other, and thus strengthen the band of union.

"The spider taketh hold with her hands and is found in kings' houses." It is the lesson of taking hold, of doing something, instead of standing idly by. It is said that Satan always finds some work for idle hands to do, and how true this is! The idle Christian will not long remain idle. If he is not at work for the Lord, he will soon be at work for the world. My brother, my sister, would you be found in the end in the king's house? Then take hold with your hands, and you will but show the wisdom of the spider.

D. L. M.

THE LOVE-FEAST IN CHICAGO.

This was not only a feast of spiritual good to the membership, but a more than ordinarily impressive scene to the lookers-on. The services of the day consisted of the Sunday-school and preaching in the morning, the installation of two deacons in the afternoon, and the love-feast and Communion services in the evening. The attendance at all these services was good, although the house at no time was crowded. The ministers present were brethren W. R. Miller and Edward Frantz, residing in the city, C. P. Rowland, of the Mission Board, and the writer. About forty participated in the Communion services, while others sat in solemn silence beholding, as some expressed it, a scene, solemn, impressive and inviting.

Brethren Wm. Shively and Geo. Miller were the ones appointed and installed as deacons. They are both young brethren, but active in the work of the church, both being teachers in the Sunday-school. May the Lord enable them so to use the office as to purchase to themselves great boldness in the faith which is in Christ Jesus!

At the close of the Sunday-school it was our privilege to talk to the children of the Brethren's mission school, in charge of sister Alice Boone. There is a small room in the rear end of the church, and a small cottage back of the church. The cottage is partly occupied by sister Boone as her home, while the remainder, and the room at the rear end of the church, are occupied by the school. Although the school is but a few months old, about fifty children receive instruction in the several classes. These children are gathered in from the streets, washed and combed, and then instructed free of charge. While the work is a noble one, let me assure you, dear reader, it is one of labor, patience, love and trust.

Sister Boone did not come to Chicago with a fortune to spend upon these neglected street children of the city. Neither could the brethren of the infant church in the city promise her large sums from their coffers, for our church is not made up of the "rich in this world," but having received, while at Mt Morris College, an inspiration to become a city missionary, sister Boone asked the church in Chicago to give her the use of those rooms in which to begin the work. The church did so, and proposed to assist to the extent of her ability. Thus far the Lord has prospered the work beyond the expectations of its most sanguine friends. Let his name be praised for it!

The work is carried on entirely by means of voluntary contributions, and, by way of explanation, we wish to say that a committee of three responsible brethren have charge of the funds contributed, and will make a report of all monies received, and the purposes to which it is appropriated. Persons desiring to help the good work along, may do so by sending their contributions to Andrew Emmert, 651 South Ashland Ave., Chicago.   J. G. R.

CORRESPONDENCE.

"Write what thou seest, and send it unto the churches."

Church News solicited for this Department. If you have had a good meeting, send a report of it, so that others may rejoice with you. In writing give name of church, County and State. Be brief. Notes of Travel should be as short as possible. Land Advertisements are not solicited for this Department. We have an advertising page, and, if necessary, will issue supplements.

Some Thoughts by the Way.

As we journey along, down the stream of life, many thoughts pass through the mind. I am made to wonder why the fashions of this world can travel so much faster, and meet with so much more favor, than the plain truths of God's Word. That which comes from Paris seems to have a great many more friends than that which comes from heaven. Is that because Paris is so much nearer to us than heaven? We all seem to have a desire to go to heaven after awhile. But are we going to patronize Paris now, and then go to heaven after we can no longer enjoy the things of this world?

If we expect to reach heaven when we die, consistency would say that we ought to show our friendship now. Well, after all, it is no very difficult problem to determine why the worldly fashion gets on so much more rapidly. The secret of it is that everybody, with few exceptions, gives it a push. Now, if even all the professing class would as faithfully help on the Lord's cause, how much more might be done for the cause which so many of us claim to love!

At our love-feast about eighty members communed. The order certainly was commendable. The house was full of spectators. Brother and sister Hope, accompanied by Bro. Dell, then left us for Adrian, Bates Co., Mo., where Bro. Hope will conduct a series of meetings. During our meetings three precious souls were gathered into the fold. After Bro. Hope left, Bro. Joseph Brubaker, formerly from Nebraska, continued a few evenings until it became necessary to close on account of bad weather, and thus ended a good meeting.   ESTHER CRIPE.

Nov. 19.

A Still Small Voice.

THE home ministers have been holding meetings for about ten days, with encouraging interest. We have had no strong winds to rend the mountains, and break in pieces the rocks (hard hearts) but we had a little fire, and we see the still small voice at work, calling and saying, "What doest thou here, sinner?" 1 Kings 19: 11.

But we are grieved, and much perplexed to see the work and devices of the devil. We have long since learned that while the Christians sleep, he will sow tares, and when the Christian wakes and goes to work, he changes his tactics. When the sinner cries, "Lord Jesus, have mercy," he or his agents will cry, "Hold your peace," or he may call a worldly gathering to keep him from the worship of God. The poet says:

"He has a thousand treacherous arts,
To practice on the mind."

We are not able to decide yet who will be the victor. Our efforts will be continued a little longer if the Lord will.

The Kansas Home is nearing completion, so far as pertains to the house, but we must have a small barn, water-tank and pipes, cistern, heating apparatus, etc., as well as furniture which will cost still more money. In order to avoid answering letters for information, how and where to send to, we here say, Bro. A. F. Miller and I have the same address, and both live near the Home. Send to either anything you feel to donate. Whatever will contribute to the comfort of the inmates, will be thankfully received. We want various kind of fruit trees, shrubbery and small fruits of the best kind. Should any feel to send us a donation in the spring, we would be very glad. Each one sending a little, would fill the space, and make the hearts of the aged glad.

We fondly hope our frequent lines in reference to our Home will not become monotonous. We cannot travel as fast as those who have small Districts and much wealth. We have the entire State, and only limited means, and can best reach our brethren through the paper.

The Trustees have not yet decided on the day for the dedication services, and the opening of the Home for inmates, but expect it to be about March 1, 1893. The Trustees will meet again on the first Monday in March.   ENOCH EBY.

From Summit Church, Pa.

BRO. D. B. ARNOLD, of Burlington, W. Va., commenced a series of meetings in the Summit church, two and one-half miles north-east of Somerset, Pa., on Saturday evening, Nov. 19, and closed on Monday evening, Nov. 28. He preached fourteen sermons in all. On Thanksgiving Day he delivered a very practical and appropriate discourse for the occasion. He gave prominence to the idea that thanksgiving on this day should not be a mere lip service, but should be manifested in such a substantial way that we may remember the unfortunate ones among us with our free-will offerings, so that they thereby may have cause for thanksgiving. His text on this occasion was 1 Thess. 3: 9, first part of verse. His sermons indicate that he is a zealous minister, who shuns not to declare the whole counsel of God.

Disagreeable weather and bad roads caused small congregations most of the time during the meetings. There were no additions by baptism, but we trust Bro. Arnold's labors were not in vain. Those in the church were admonished to greater activity in the spiritual life, while the unregenerated were warned of their perilous condition, and the danger of delay in neglecting the great salvation, and to secure it, the present,—now,—is the accepted time.

When the Lord shall gather in the great harvest, Bro. Arnold will, if he continues faithful as he has been, doubtless be among the husbandmen who will come bearing many precious sheaves. May the Lord grant much grace unto his faithful ministers, as well as unto those to whom they minister the words of truth and life!

JOHN D. BAER.

Friedens, Pa., Nov. 30.

Notes from Our Correspondents.

"As cold water to a thirsty soul, so is good news from a far country."

Clear Church, Pa.—We expect to commence a meeting for the Brethren at Purchase Line, Indiana County, Pa., in the near future, and to continue for several weeks. May God crown our work with success.—*Michael Claar.*

Covington, Ohio.—On Thanksgiving Day we had an interesting meeting. The minister did not have time enough to tell all the good things the Lord is doing for us. At the close of the services we had a collection to promote the Lord's cause.—*Jacob S. Mohler, Nov. 30.*

Red Cedar, Wis.—Dec. 3 the members of the Chippewa Valley church convened for church council. All business was disposed of satisfactorily. We decided to hold a series of meetings in the near future. We expect Bro. Van Buren, of the Maple Grove church to be with us. May we ever be found faithful!—*Katie Joyce, Dec. 4.*

Hermitage, Va.—Bro. David Kindig, of Virginia, came to the Barren Ridge church and commenced a series of meetings Oct. 23, which he continued for two weeks. Oct. 30 two young sisters came out on the Lord's side and were baptized. Our love-feast occurred Nov. 5. Two more were baptized in the morning before the feast.—*Joann E. Zarick.*

South River Church, Iowa.—The dedication of our new meeting-house took place Nov. 24 at 11 A. M. At 6 o'clock P. M., we had our Communion meeting. Bro. Isaac Barto officiated. Bro. Lewis Kob remained with us over Sunday, preaching some excellent sermons. It gives us spiritual strength to have the Bread of Life given to us so bountifully.—*Meda Caskey.*

West Dayton, Ohio.—Nov. 6 Bro. Isaac Frantz, of Pleasant Hill, Ohio, preached for us at 10:30; also at 7:30 P. M. Nov. 20 Bro. Jacob Coppock, of Tippecanoe City, Ohio, came to us and gave us two good lessons from Divine Truth. Nov. 24, on the National Thanksgiving Day, Bro. O. P. Hoover, of Greencastle, Ind., improved the occasion; also Nov. 21, at 10:30 A. M., and 7:30 P. M. Dec. 4 Bro. I. J. Rosenberger, of Covington, Ohio, began a series of meetings. Three were received by letter Dec. 4. Pray for our success in the city, and the upbuilding of Christ's kingdom.—*Elmer Wombold, Dec. 5.*

Dorrance Church, Kansas.—Bro. Jacob Kelier, of Dickinson County, Kans., commenced a series of meetings on the evening of Oct. 29, and continued until the evening of Nov. 8. During this time he preached some able sermons on doctrinal points. One precious soul was received by baptism, and we trust there was some good seed sown in the hearts of others.—*W. J. Long.*

Mcgester, Texas.—On our visiting the City of Gainesville we concluded that some good could be done there by one of our ministers settling in the town, or near by. In our humble judgment this would be a rich field. The MESSENGER has been going from house to house, and sowing seed. Tracts have also been circulated thoroughly. The question is, Who will go?—*A. W. Austin, Secretary of Mission Board of Texas, Nov. 30.*

Indian Creek Church, Iowa.—Bro. S. H. Miller, of Waterloo, Iowa, commenced a series of meetings in the Brethren's meeting-house Nov. 19, and continued till the evening of the 29th. On account of sickness, gloomy weather and dark nights, the meetings were not so well attended, but Bro. Miller made earnest appeals to those yet out of the church. He also admonished the members to put on the whole armor of God. There were no additions to the church, but we believe lasting impressions were made.—*Thos. H. Higgs, Nov. 30.*

Mt. Vernon, S. Dak.—I did not have the privilege of worshiping with the brethren and sisters on Thanksgiving Day, as I am living in an isolated place. Nevertheless I am glad to say that I did not forget to return thanks unto our Heavenly Father for his goodness, love and mercy, bestowed upon us during the past year. I am living in a lonely place, where I have now resided for over one year, and have not seen a member in all that time, but the more I see of the world, the more I try to serve my God, for he has done so much for me.—*Rosa Whitmer, Nov. 24.*

Kewanee Church, Ind.—The members of this church have been much revived during the series of meetings, held here by Bro. Daniel P. Shively and Bro. Fisher. The meetings commenced Nov. 12 and continued until Nov. 27. The Brethren held forth the Word with power. There were no additions. We feel that the seed sown will yet grow and bring much fruit. The church held a choice for a minister. The lot fell on Bro. S. A. Blessing. The church also advanced Bro. Henry Ritzius to the second degree of the ministry. We are in love and union.—*L. F. Miller.*

South English, Iowa.—The English River church, Iowa, met in regular quarterly council Nov. 26. Considerable business came before the meeting, for the furtherance of Christ's kingdom. All was harmoniously disposed of. A manifestation of God's spirit seemed to pervade the meeting. Bro. Daniel Niswander not being installed at our Communion meeting, was solemnly installed into the deacon's office. One was added by letter. Bro. Michael Flory, from Illinois, is with us at present, holding meetings. — *Peter Brower, Nov. 29.*

Laurens, Iowa.—The Stony Lake church commenced a series of meetings on Monday, Nov. 28. Bro. D. M. Miller, of Milledgeville, Ill., held forth the Word in its power. Although there were no accessions to the church, many were made to think of their way. Bro. Miller presented the Truth in such plainness that it will not be easily shook off. Some are not far from the kingdom and we hope they will not put off the important work too long. The members were much built up to press onward to the prize. Come again, Bro. Miller.—*J. W. Butterbaugh, Dec. 1.*

At our love-feast about eighty members communed. The order certainly was commendable. The house was full of spectators. Brother and sister Hope, accompanied by Bro. Dell, then left us for Adrian, Bates Co., Mo., where Bro. Hope will conduct a series of meetings. During our meetings three precious souls were gathered into the fold. After Bro. Hope left, Bro. Joseph Brubaker, formerly from Nebraska, continued a few evenings until it became necessary to close on account of bad weather, and thus ended a good meeting. ESTHER CRIPE.

Nov. 19.

A Still Small Voice.

THE home ministers have been holding meetings for about ten days, with encouraging interest. We have had no strong winds to rend the mountains, and break in pieces the rocks (hard hearts) but we had a little fire, and we see the still small voice at work, calling and saying, "What doest thou here, sinner?" 1 Kings 19: 11.

But we are grieved, and much perplexed to see the work and devices of the devil. We have long since learned that while the Christians sleep, he will sow tares, and when the Christian wakes and goes to work, he changes his tactics. When the sinner cries, "Lord Jesus, have mercy," he or his agents will cry, "Hold your peace," or he may call a worldly gathering to keep him from the worship of God. The poet says:

"He has a thousand treacherous arts,
To practice on the mind."

We are not able to decide yet who will be the victor. Our efforts will be continued a little longer if the Lord will.

The Kansas Home is nearing completion, so far as pertains to the house, but we must have a small barn, water-tank and pipes, cistern, heating apparatus, etc., as well as furniture which will cost still more money. In order to avoid answering letters for information, how and where to send to, we here say, Bro. A. F. Miller and I have the same address, and both live near the Home. Send to either anything you feel to donate. Whatever will contribute to the comfort of the inmates, will be thankfully received. We want various kind of fruit trees, shrubbery and small fruits of the best kind. Should any feel to send us a donation in the spring, we would be very glad. Each one sending a little, would fill the space, and make the hearts of the aged glad.

We fondly hope our frequent lines in reference to our Home will not become monotonous. We cannot travel as fast as those who have small Districts and much wealth. We have the entire State, and only limited means, and can best reach our brethren through the paper.

The Trustees have not yet decided on the day for the dedication services, and the opening of the Home for inmates, but expect it to be about March 1, 1893. The Trustees will meet again on the first Monday in March. ENOCH EBY.

From Summit Church, Pa.

BRO. D. B. ARNOLD, of Burlington, W. Va., commenced a series of meetings in the Summit church, two and one-half miles north-east of Somerset, Pa., on Saturday evening, Nov. 19, and closed on Monday evening, Nov. 28. He preached fourteen sermons in all. On Thanksgiving Day he delivered a very practical and appropriate discourse for the occasion. He gave prominence to the idea that thanksgiving on this day should not be a mere lip service, but should be manifested in such a substantial way that we may remember the unfortunate ones among us with our free-will offerings, so that they thereby may have cause for thanksgiving. His text on this occasion was 1 Thess. 3: 9, first part of verse. His sermons indicate that he is a zealous minister, who shuns not to declare the whole counsel of God.

Disagreeable weather and bad roads caused small congregations most of the time during the meetings. There were no additions by baptism, but we trust Bro. Arnold's labors were not in vain. Those in the church were admonished to greater activity in the spiritual life, while the unregenerated were warned of their perilous condition, and the danger of delay in neglecting the great salvation, and to secure it, the present,—*now*,—is the accepted time.

When the Lord shall gather in the great harvest, Bro. Arnold will, if he continues faithful as he has been, doubtless be among the husbandmen who will come bearing many precious sheaves. May the Lord grant much grace unto his faithful ministers, as well as unto those to whom they minister the words of truth and life!

JOHN D. BARR.

Friedens, Pa., Nov. 30.

Notes from Our Correspondents.

"As cold water to a thirsty soul, so is good news from a far country."

Claar Church, Pa.—We expect to commence a meeting for the Brethren at Purchase Line, Indiana County, Pa., in the near future, and to continue for several weeks. May God crown our work with success.—*Michael Claar.*

Covington, Ohio.—On Thanksgiving Day we had an interesting meeting. The minister did not have time enough to tell all the good things the Lord is doing for us. At the close of the services we had a collection to promote the Lord's cause.—*Jacob S. Mohler, Nov. 30.*

Red Cedar, Wis.—Dec. 3 the members of the Chippewa Valley church convened for church council. All business was disposed of satisfactorily. We decided to hold a series of meetings in the near future. We expect Bro. Van Buren, of the Maple Grove church to be with us. May we ever be found faithful!—*Katie Joyce, Dec. 4.*

Hermitage, Va.—Bro. David Kindig, of Virginia, came to the Barren Ridge church and commenced a series of meetings Oct. 23, which he continued for two weeks. Oct. 30 two young sisters came out on the Lord's side and were baptized. Our love-feast occurred Nov. 5. Two more were baptized in the morning before the feast.—*Joann E. Zarick.*

South River Church, Iowa.—The dedication of our new meeting-house took place Nov. 24 at 11 A. M. At 6 o'clock P. M., we had our Communion meeting. Bro. Isaac Barto officiated. Bro. Lewis Kob remained with us over Sunday, preaching some excellent sermons. It gives us spiritual strength to have the Bread of Life given to us so bountifully.—*Meda Caskey.*

West Dayton, Ohio.—Nov. 6 Bro. Isaac Frantz, of Pleasant Hill, Ohio, preached for us at 10:30; also at 7:30 P. M.. Nov. 20 Bro. Jacob Coppock, of Tippecanoe City, Ohio, came to us and gave us two good lessons from Divine Truth. Nov. 24, on the National Thanksgiving Day, Bro. O. P. Hoover, of Greencastle, Ind., improved the occasion; also Nov. 21, at 10:30 A. M, and 7:30 P. M. Dec. 4 Bro. I. J. Rosenberger, of Covington, Ohio, began a series of meetings. Three were received by letter Dec. 4. Pray for our success in the city, and the upbuilding of Christ's kingdom.—*Elmer Wombold, Dec. 5.*

Dorrance Church, Kansas.—Bro. Jacob Keller, of Dickinson County, Kans., commenced a series of meetings on the evening of Oct. 29, and continued until the evening of Nov. 8 During this time he preached some able sermons on doctrinal points. One precious soul was received by baptism, and we trust there was some good seed sown in the hearts of others.—*W. J. Long.*

Muenster, Texas.—On our visiting the City of Gainesville we concluded that some good could be done there by one of our ministers settling in the town, or near by. In our humble judgment this would be a rich field. The MESSENGER has been going from house to house, and sowing seed. Tracts have also been circulated thoroughly. The question is, Who will go?—*A. W. Austin, Secretary of Mission Board of Texas, Nov. 30.*

Indian Creek Church, Iowa.—Bro. S. H. Miller, of Waterloo, Iowa, commenced a series of meetings in the Brethren's meeting-house Nov. 19, and continued till the evening of the 29th. On account of sickness, gloomy weather and dark nights, the meetings were not so well attended, but Bro. Miller made earnest appeals to those yet out of the church. He also admonished the members to put on the whole armor of God. There were no additions to the church, but we believe lasting impressions were made.—*Thos. B. Higgs, Nov. 30.*

Mt. Vernon, S. Dak.—I did not have the privilege of worshiping with the brethren and sisters on Thanksgiving Day, as I am living in an isolated place. Nevertheless I am glad to say that I did not forget to return thanks unto our Heavenly Father for his goodness, love and mercy, bestowed upon us during the past year. I am living in a lonely place, where I have now resided for over one year, and have not seen a member in all that time, but the more I see of the world, the more I try to serve my God, for he has done so much for me.—*Rosa Whitmer, Nov. 24.*

Kewanee Church, Ind. — The members of this church have been much revived during the series of meetings, held here by Bro. Daniel P. Shively and Bro. Fisher. The meetings commenced Nov. 12 and continued until Nov. 27. The Brethren held forth the Word with power. There were no additions. We feel that the seed sown will yet grow and bring much fruit. The church held a choice for a minister. The lot fell on Bro. S. A. Blessing. The church also advanced Bro. Henry Ritzius to the second degree of the ministry. We are in love and union.—*L. F. Miller.*

South English, Iowa.—The English River church, Iowa, met in regular quarterly council Nov. 26. Considerable business came before the meeting, for the furtherance of Christ's kingdom. All was harmoniously disposed of. A manifestation of God's spirit seemed to pervade the meeting. Bro. Daniel Niswander not being installed at our Communion meeting, was solemnly installed into the deacon's office. One was added by letter. Bro. Michael Flory, from Illinois, is with us at present, holding meetings. — *Peter Brower, Nov. 29.*

Laurens, Iowa.—The Stony Lake church commenced a series of meetings on Monday, Nov. 28. Bro. D. M. Miller, of Milledgeville, Ill., held forth the Word in its power. Although there were no accessions to the church, many were made to think of their way. Bro. Miller presented the Truth in such plainness that it will not be easily shook off. Some are not far from the kingdom and we hope they will not put off the important work too long. The members were much built up to press onward to the prize. Come again, Bro. Miller.—*J. W. Butterbaugh, Dec. 1.*

Literary Notices.

"Christian Science" unmasked. By Rev. W. T. Hogg.

"Ecclesiastical Amusements." By Rev. E. P. Marvan, with introduction by Drs. Hall and Crosby.

"Secret Societies: Are They Right or Wrong? Are They a Blessing or a Curse?" An address by B. Carradine, D. D.

The above publications are put up in neat pamphlet form, and published by A. W. Hall, Syracuse, N. Y. All of them are well worth reading, and the latter in particular,—it makes a strong point against secret societies, and should be widely circulated.

"Timely Topics," Political, Biblical, Ethical, Practical. Discussed by college presidents, professors, and eminent writers of our times. E. B. Treat, New York, publishers. Price, $1.50.

The work is a neatly-bound volume of 360 pages, and discusses live issues in a learned and logical manner. For well-arranged information on a wide range of fresh topics the volume will prove of great value to the student.

"Six Song Services," with connective reading, designed for special religious services. By Philip Phillips and Son. Square 12mo, manilla, 70 pp. Per copy, 20 cents; dozen, $2; hundred, $15. New York, London, and Toronto: Funk & Wagnalls Company.

Here is something new and attractive. The services with words, music, etc., are arranged topically, as follows: (1) Christ in Song; (2) Salvation in Song; (3) Thanksgiving in Song; (4) Children's Services in Song; (5) Temperance in Song; (6) Christmas in Song.

"Peloubet's Select Notes," by Rev. Dr. F. N. & M. A. Peloubet. 310 pages. Illustrated, cloth, 12mo. Price, $1.25 Boston, W. A. Wilde & Co.

This Commentary on the International Sunday-school Lessons for 1893, like its eighteen predecessors, bears evidence of the widest research on the part of its compilers into every field of Christian literature. Its exhaustive quotations, excellent suggestions to teachers, helpful anecdotes, and admirable notes, wonderfully illumine the Scripture text and impress upon the mind the salient points of each lesson.

The library references are particularly full and a great convenience to the busy worker, who desires to study in detail from original sources, of the times, places, personages, and secular, as well as the sacred, history of the events and peoples mentioned in the lessons. In authentic colored maps, appropriate original illustrations, and general mechanical make up, the present volume excels all previous issues, and this is praise enough.

"Study of the Model Life" The various aspects of Christ considered in a series of essays by Rev. Burdett Hart, D. D. E. B. Treat, New York, publisher. Price, $1.25.

The author brings out, in a beautiful manner, the soul nature of the great Teacher Jesus, showing the tendency of his life to soften the disposition of the races. Nor does he, in any manner, neglect the divinity, everywhere present in his life. The book throughout is forcible, instructive, and the style elegant.

The four illustrations are fine. The frontispiece is the best representation of our idea of Jesus we have ever seen. The expression of the face is grand and inspiring. But the Commemorative Feast, intended to represent the last Supper, is hardly excusable in this enlightened age. Jesus and the twelve are seated around a very small table on which there is a single glass half filled with wine, while the Savior holds in his left hand a loaf of bread in the act of blessing it. Every Bible reader knows that the little company on that memorable occasion *reclined* at a table on which was a full meal. The book is neatly printed, well bound, and contains 288 pages. The work is a good one.

Matrimonial.

"What therefore God hath joined together, let not man put asunder."

JONES—HEISZ.—At the residence of the undersigned, near Belleville, Kans., Nov. 21, by the writer, Mr. Wm. A. Jones and Miss Mary C. Heisz, both of Courtland, Republic Co., this State. C. S. Hilary.

HARSHMAN—ELLMAKER.—At the residence of the bride's parents, Mr. Amos Ellmaker's, Sterling, Ill., Nov. 23, 1892, by the undersigned, Mr. Alfred Harshman and Miss Emma G. Ellmaker. P. R. Keltner.

KIRKWOOD—BRUMBAUGH.—At the bride's residence, Grafton, Pa., Nov. 10, 1892, John M. L. Kirkwood, of Pittsburg, Pa., and Elma A., daughter of Eld. George Brumbaugh. H. B. B.

BROWN—PUDERBAUGH.—At the Brethren's church, Ozawkie, Kans., Oct. 9, 1892, by the undersigned, Emmanuel Brown and sister Clara Belle Puderbaugh.

BROWN—ROOT.—At the same time and place, Bro. Elsie E. Brown and sister Fanny E. Root, all of Ozawkie, Kans. A. Puderbaugh.

Fallen Asleep.

"Blessed are the dead which die in the Lord."

OELLIG.—In Woodbury, Pa., Aug. 30, 1892, sister Susan Oellig, wife of Bro. Charles S. Oellig, aged 73 years, 5 months and 11 days. Sister Oellig was a daughter of Frederick Wertz. She was born and raised in Quincy Township, Franklin Co., Pa. In 1842 she came to Woodbury, and in the fall of the same year she married Dr. Charles S. Oellig. In the fall of 1843 she united with the Brethren church, and has since lived a devoted Christian life. She was the mother of eight children, three of whom preceded her to the spirit world. By request of the deceased the funeral services were conducted by Eld. G. W. and J. W. Brumbaugh and J. B. Miller at the Replogle church from the words, "Let not your hearts be troubled." Her remains were interred in the Keagy cemetery. J. C. Stayer.

BOETTCHER.—In Plattsburgh, Mo., Nov. 11, 1892, Mrs. Frederick Boettcher, aged 75 years, 5 months and 9 days. Deceased was born at Poehlde, Germany. She came to America with her husband and children in 1854. After living a short time in Cincinnati, Ohio, and a few years in Kentucky, she came to Missouri about 1857. With her husband she united with the Brethren church near Plattsburgh, during the summer of 1870, and lived faithful until her death. She attended the Communion meeting which was held Nov. 5, at the Smith Fork church, and on the road going home, with one of her old neighbors, she became quite chilly from riding in the night air. She then took sick and was sick about two weeks. The Sunday after the Communion she was very sick. On Friday night afterwards she passed quietly away at the home of Henry Lohman. Her funeral was preached by Bro. J. E. Ellenberger. Isaac B. Miller.

NEWCUMER.—In the bounds of the Iowa River church, Iowa, Oct. 28, 1892, sister Lydia, the only child of Bro. Joseph and sister Mary Newcumer, aged 13 years and 9 months. Funeral services by the writer, assisted by Bro. Levi Saylor, to a very large audience. Stephen Johnson.

BISHOP.—Near Bernina, Iowa, Nov. 3, 1892, the daughter of Mr. and Mrs. Bishop, aged 2 years and a few days. Funeral services at the family residence by the writer. S. P. Miller.

PETRES.—Near Bernina, Iowa, Nov. 7, 1892, the son of Mr. and Mrs. Petres, aged 2 years and a few days. Funeral services by the writer at the M. E. church, at Peoria, Iowa. S. P. Miller.

STOUT.—Near Bernina, Iowa, Nov. 16, 1892, the son of Mr. and Mrs. W. I. Stout, aged 3 years, 4 months and 27 days. Funeral services at Peoria, in the M. E. church, by the writer. S. P. Miller.

MORRIS.—At Morelock, Tenn., Nov. 15, 1892, Bro. Levi Morris, aged about 65 years. On the morning of Nov. 15 he, in company with two of his grandsons, went to the mountain to make boards. In a short time he complained of his head, then of his breast and back. He managed to get to a house near by, where he died before medical aid, or even his family, could reach him. He was a consistent member of the Brethren church for many years and leaves a wife and six children,—five sons and one daughter. P. M. Correll.

CEARFOSS.—At Hagerstown, Md., Nov. 21, 1892, Lillie Victoria, daughter of Bro. Charles W. and sister Katie A. Cearfoss, aged 2 months and 13 days. Little Lillie suffered intensely during her short life, but is now in the bright world beyond. Barbara Martin.

STOCKMAN.—In the Irvin Creek church, Wis., Oct. 24, 1892, infant daughter of friend James and Amy Stockman, aged about 11 months. Funeral services by the writer from Luke 18: 15-17.

KECH.—In the same place, Nov. 11, 1892, Mary Kech, wife of friend Archibald Kech, aged 50 years lacking six days. Funeral services by the writer from Rev. 14: 13. Samuel Crist.

MAPES.—In the Sugar Ridge church, Hancock Co., Ohio, Nov. 26, 1892, Eli, son of sister Clarissa and friend Wayne Mapes, aged 12 years, 9 months and 9 days. Funeral services by the writer from Jer. 15: 9. E. H. Rosenberger.

MORTON.—Oct. 30, 1892, sister Elvina Morton, aged 61 years, 2 months and 17 days. Funeral occasion improved by Eld. W. B. Sell and the writer. C. Harader.

CAYLOR.—In the Ottawa church, Kans., sister Susannah Caylor, aged 55 years, 9 months and 29 days. The deceased leaves a companion, who is a brother, and five children to mourn their loss; also a little motherless grandson, who was dependent on her care. Funeral services by the writer in the M. E. church, at Peoria, Kans., from 2 Cor. 5: 1. Jos. N. Morrow.

CARMICHAEL.—At the Lochiel boarding-house, Harrisburgh, Pa., Nov. 2, 1892, sister Susannah Carmichael, aged 82 years, 4 months and 26 days. For many years she was a consistent member. Services by the writer. J. B. Garver.

CLARK.—In the Beaver Run church, Mineral Co., W. Va., Nov. 12, 1892, Bro. Hendricks Clark, aged 73 years, 1 month and 10 days. He was afflicted for several years. He united with the church about ten years ago, and since then has lived an exemplary life. Funeral services were conducted by Bro. Geo. S. Arnold, assisted by Eld. D. B. Arnold, from Acts 24: 15.

NISWONGER.—In the Ludlow church, Darke Co., Ohio, Aug. 20, 1892, Bro. David Niswonger, aged 58 years, 3 months and 25 days. Deceased was strangely and severely afflicted nearly eighteen months, but bore all with remarkable patience and Christian fortitude. He was a faithful deacon in the church and a highly-respected citizen of the community. His faithful companion and eight children remain. Funeral services by brethren Jesse Stutsman and Tobias Kreider. C. E. Culp.

HARTER.—In the Nettle Creek church, Ind., Oct. 13, 1892, of cancer, sister Elizabeth Harter, aged 64 years, 11 months and 10 days. She was the wife of Bro. Levi Harter, who preceded her in death a little over three years. She leaves three children. Funeral services by Eld. Lewis Kinsey and the writer from Heb. 11: 16. Abraham Bowman.

JAMES.—In the bounds of the Sterling church, Whiteside Co., Ill., Nov. 24, 1892, Mrs. Mary James, aged 49 years and 20 days. Deceased was born in Cambria County, Pa. Her mother and sister met their death in the great disaster at Johnstown a few years ago. Funeral by the writer in the Rock Falls M. E. church, to a large and sympathizing congregation. P. R. Keltner.

PRICE.—In the Ephratah church, Lancaster Co., Pa., Nov. 26, 1892, Wm. Price, aged 70 years, 8 months and 2 days. He was ailing about two years. Last week he had a stroke of paralysis which resulted in his death. He was widely known and highly esteemed. He was elected to the ministry when twenty-seven years of age and proved a good, willing worker. Services by our home preachers and brethren Gibble and George Bucher from 2 Cor. 5: 1. Jacob Keller.

SHEETS.—In the bounds of the Walnut church, Marshall Co., Ind., Nov. 18, 1892, Elva N., daughter of Bro. Winfield and sister Betty Sheets, aged 11 years, 8 months and 6 days. Services were conducted by Bro. John R. Miller from Matt. 18: 3. Myrta I. Swihart.

BOONE.—In the Kansas Center church, Rice Co., Kans., Nov. 1, 1892, Edith Myrtle, daughter of Robert and Arrennah Boone, aged 4 years, 4 months and 23 days. Funeral services conducted by Bro. Enoch Eby. S. J. Dresher.

PATERSON.—In the Bachelor Run church, Carroll Co., Ind., Oct. 19, 1892, of typhoid fever, Malinda F. Paterson, daughter of friend William H. and sister Catharine J. Cline, aged 28 years, 6 months and 11 days. She leaves a mother, one brother, one sister and two little children. Funeral by Bro. Abram Flory. David H. Niccum.

The Gospel Messenger

Is the recognized organ of the German Baptist or Brethren's church, and advocates the form of doctrine taught in the New Testament and pleads for a return to apostolic and primitive Christianity.

It recognizes the New Testament as the only infallible rule of faith and practice, and maintains that Faith toward God, Repentance from dead works, Regeneration of the heart and mind, baptism by Trine Immersion for remission of sins unto the reception of the Holy Ghost by the laying on of hands, are the means of adoption into the household of God,—the church militant.

It also maintains that Feet-washing, as taught in John 13, both by example and command of Jesus, should be observed in the church.

That the Lord's Supper, instituted by Christ and as universally observed by the apostles and the early Christians, is a full meal, and, in connection with the Communion, should be taken in the evening or after the close of the day.

That the Salutation of the Holy Kiss, or Kiss of Charity, is binding upon the followers of Christ.

That War and Retaliation are contrary to the spirit and self-denying principles of the religion of Jesus Christ.

That the principle of Plain Dressing and of Non-conformity to the world, as taught in the New Testament, should be observed by the followers of Christ.

That the Scriptural duty of Anointing the Sick with Oil, in the Name of the Lord, James 5: 14, is binding upon all Christians.

It also advocates the church's duty to support Missionary and Tract Work, thus giving to the Lord for the spread of the Gospel and for the conversion of sinners.

In short, it is a Vindicator of all that Christ and the apostles have enjoined upon us, and aims, amid the conflicting theories and discords of modern Christendom, to point out ground that all must concede to be infallibly safe.

☞ "The above principles of our Fraternity are set forth on our Brethren's Envelopes." Use them! Price 15 cents per package; 40 cents per hundred.

Literary Notices.

" Christian Science " unmasked. By Rev. W. T. Hogg.
" Ecclesiastical Amusements." By Rev. E. P. Mairn,
with introduction by Drs. Hall and Crosby.

. " Secret Societies: Are They Right or Wrong? Are They
a Blessing or a Curse? " An address by B. Carradine, D. D.

The above publications are put up in neat pamphlet form,
and published by A. W. Hall, Syracuse, N. Y. All of them
are well worth reading, and the latter in particular,—it
makes a strong point against secret societies, and should be
widely circulated.

"Timely Topics," Political, Biblical, Ethical, Practical.
Discussed by college presidents, professors, and eminent writers of our times. E. B. Treat, New York, publishers. Price,
$1.50.

The work is a neatly-bound volume of 360 pages, and discusses live issues in a learned and logical manner. For well-
arranged information on a wide range of fresh topics the volume will prove of great value to the student.

" Six Song Services," with connective reading, designed
for special religious services. By Philip Phillips and Son.
Square 12mo, manilla, 30 pp. Per copy, 20 cents; dozen, $2;
hundred, $15. New York, London, and Toronto: Funk &
Wagnalls Company.

Here is something new and attractive. The services with
words, music, etc., are arranged topically, as follows: (1)
Christ in Song; (2) Salvation in Song; (3) Thanksgiving in
Song; (4) Children's Services in Song; (5) Temperance in
Song; (6) Christmas in Song.

" Peloubet's Select Notes," by Rev. Dr. F. N. & M. A. Peloubet. 310 pages. Illustrated, cloth, 12mo. Price, $1.25
Boston, W. A. Wilde & Co.

This Commentary on the International Sunday-school Lessons for 1893, like its eighteen predecessors, bears evidence of
the widest research on the part of its compilers into every
field of Christian literature. Its exhaustive quotations, excellent suggestions to teachers, helpful anecdotes, and admirable notes, wonderfully illumine the Scripture text- and impress upon the mind the salient points of each lesson.

The library references are particularly full and a great convenience to the busy worker, who desires to study in detail
from original sources, of the times, places, personages, and
secular, as well as the sacred, history of the events and peoples mentioned in the lessons. In authentic colored maps,
appropriate original illustrations, and general mechanical
make up, the present volume excels all previous issues, and
this is praise enough.

" Study of the Model Life." The various aspects of Christ
considered in a series of essays by Rev. Burdett Hart, D. D.
E. B. Treat, New York, publisher. Price, $1.25.

The author brings out, in a beautiful manner, the soul nature of the great Teacher Jesus, showing the tendency of his
life to soften the disposition of the races. Nor does he, in
any manner, neglect the divinity, everywhere present in his
life. The book throughout is forcible, instructive, and the
style elegant.

The four illustrations are fine. The frontispiece is the best
representation of our idea of Jesus we have ever seen. The
expression of the face is grand and inspiring. But the Commemorative Feast, intended to represent the last Supper, is
hardly excusable in this enlightened age. Jesus and the
twelve are seated around a very small table on which there is
a single glass half filled with wine, while the Savior holds in
his left hand a loaf of bread in the act of blessing it. Every
Bible reader knows that the little company on that memorable occasion reclined at a table on which was a full meal.
The book is neatly printed, well bound, and contains 288 pages. The work is a good one.

Matrimonial.

" What therefore God hath joined together, let not
man put asunder."

*JONES—HEISZ.—At the residence of the undersigned,
near Belleville, Kans., Nov. 21, by the writer, Mr. Wm. A.
Jones and Miss Mary C. Heisz, both of Courtland, Republic
Co., this State.   C. S. HILARY.

. HARSHMAN—ELLMAKER.—At the residence of the
bride's parents, Mr. Amos Ellmaker's, Sterling, Ill., Nov. 23,
1892, by the undersigned, Mr. Alfred Harshman and Miss
Emma G. Ellmaker.   P. R. KELTNER.

. KIRKWOOD—BRUMBAUGH.—At the bride's resi-
dence, Quincy, Pa., Nov. 10, 1892, John M. L. Kirkwood, of
Pittsburg, Pa., and Elma A., daughter of Eld. George Brumbaugh.   H. B. B.

. BROWN—PUDERBAUGH.—At the Brethren's church,
Osawkie, Kans., Oct. 9, 1892, by the undersigned, Emmanuel
Brown and sister Clara Belle Puderbaugh.

BROWN—ROOT.—At the same time and place, Bro. Elsie E. Brown and sister Fanny E. Root, all of Osawkie, Kans.
    A. PUDERBAUGH.

Fallen Asleep.

" Blessed are the dead which die in the Lord."

OELLIG.—In Woodbury, Pa., Aug. 30, 1892, sister Susan
Oellig, wife of Bro. Charles S. Oellig, aged 73 years, 5
months and 11 days. Sister Oellig was a daughter of Frederick Wertz. She was born and raised in Quincy Township,
Franklin Co., Pa. In 1842 she came to Woodbury, and in
the fall of the same year she married Dr. Charles S. Oellig.
In the fall of 1843 she united with the Brethren church, and
has since lived a devoted Christian life. She was the mother
of eight children, three of whom preceded her to the spirit
world. By request of the deceased the funeral services were
conducted by Eld. G. W. and J. W. Brumbaugh and J. B.
Miller at the Replogle church from the words, " Let not your
hearts be troubled." Her remains were interred in the Keagy
cemetery.   J. C. STAYER.

BOETTCHER.—In Plattsburgh, Mo., Nov. 11, 1892, Mrs.
Frederick Boettcher, aged 73 years, 5 months and 9 days. Deceased was born at Poehide, Germany. She came to America with her husband and children in 1854. After living a
short time in Cincinnati, Ohio, and a few years in Kentucky,
she came to Missouri about 1857. With her husband she
united with the Brethren church near Plattsburgh, during the
summer of 1870, and lived faithful until her death. She attended the Communion meeting which was held Nov. 5, at
the Smith Fork church, and on the road going home, with
one of her old neighbors, she became quite chilly from riding
in the night air. She then took sick and was sick about two
weeks. The Sunday after the Communion she was very
sick. On Friday night afterwards she passed quietly away at
the house of Henry Lohman. Her funeral was preached by
Bro. J. E. Ellenberger.   ISAAC B. MILLER.

NEWCUMER.—In the bounds of the Iowa River church,
Iowa, Oct. 18, 1892, sister Lydia, the only child of Bro. Joseph and sister Mary Newcumer, aged 13 years and 9 months.
Funeral services by the writer, assisted by Bro. Levi Saylor,
to a very large audience.   STEPHEN JOHNSON.

BISHOP.—Near Bernina, Iowa, Nov. 3, 1892, the daughter of Mr. and Mrs. Bishop, aged 2 years and a few days.
Funeral services at the family residence by the writer.
    S. P. MILLER.

PETRES.—Near Bernina, Iowa, Nov. 7, 1892, the son of
Mr. and Mrs. Petres, aged 2 years and a few days. Funeral
services by the writer at the M. E. church, at Peoria, Iowa.
    S. P. MILLER.

STOUT.—Near Bernina, Iowa, Nov. 16, 1892, the son of
Mr. and Mrs. W. I. Stout, aged 3 years, 4 months and 27
days. Funeral services at Peoria, in the M. E. church, by
the writer.   S. P. MILLER.

MORRIS.—At Morelock, Tenn., Nov. 15, 1892, Bro. Levi
Morris, aged about 65 years. On the morning of Nov. 15 he,
in company with two of his grandsons, went to the mountain
to make boards. In a short time he complained of his head,
then of his breast and back. He managed to get to a house
near by, where he died before medical aid, or even his family,
could reach him. He was a consistent member of the Brethren church for many years and leaves a wife and six children,—five sons and one daughter.   P. M. CORRELL.

·CEARFOSS.—At Hagerstown, Md., Nov. 21, 1892, Lillie
Victoria, daughter of Bro. Charles W. and sister Kalie A.
Cearfoss, aged 5 months and 13 days. Little Lillie suffered
intensely during her short life, but is now in the bright world
beyond.   BARBARA MARTIN.

STOCKMAN.—In the Irvin Creek church, Wis., Oct. 24,
1892, infant daughter of friend James and Amy Stockman,
aged about 11 months. Funeral services by the writer from
Luke 18: 15-17.

KECH.—In the bounds, Nov. 11, 1892, Mary Kech,
wife of friend Archibald Kech, aged 50 years lacking six days.
Funeral services by the writer from Rev. 14: 13.
    SAMUEL CRIST.

MAPES.—In the Sugar Ridge church, Hancock Co., Ohio,
Nov. 26, 1892, Eli, son of sister Clarinca and friend Wayne
Mapes, aged 12 years, 9 months and 9 days. Funeral servic-
es by the writer from Jer. 15: 9.   E. H. ROSENBERGER.

MORTON.—Oct. 30, 1892, sister Elvina Morton, aged 62
years, 2 months and 17 days. Funeral occasion improved by
Eld. W. B. Sell and the writer.   C. HARADER.

CAYLOR.—In the Ottawa church, Kans., sister Susannah Caylor, aged 55 years, 9 months and 29 days. The deceased leaves a companion, who is a brother, and five children
to mourn their loss; also a little motherless grandson, who
was dependent on her care. Funeral services by the writer
in the M. E. church, at Peoria, Kans., from 2 Cor. 5: 1.
    JOS. N. MORROW.

CARMICHAEL.—At the Lochiel boarding-house, Harrisburgh, Pa., Nov. 2, 1892, sister Susannah Carmichael, aged
82 years, 4 months and 26 days. For many years she was a
consistent member. Services by the writer.
    J. B. GARVER.

CLARK.—In the Beaver Run church, Mineral Co., W.
Va., Nov. 12, 1892, Bro. Hendricks Clark, aged 73 years, 1
month and 10 days. He was afflicted for several years. He
united with the church about ten years ago, and since then
has lived an exemplary life. Funeral services were conducted by Bro. Geo. S. Arnold, assisted by Eld. D. B. Arnold,
from Acts 24: 15.

NISWONGER.—In the Ludlow church, Darke Co.,
Ohio, Aug. 20, 1892, Bro. David Niswonger, aged 58 years, 3
months and 25 days. Deceased was strangely and severely
afflicted nearly eighteen months, but bore all with remarkable
patience and Christian fortitude. He was a faithful deacon
in the church and a highly-respected citizen of the community. His faithful companion and eight children remain. Funeral services by brethren Jesse Stutsman and Tobias Kreider.   C. E. COLE.

HARTER.—In the Nettle Creek church, Ind., Oct. 13,
1892, of cancer, sister Elizabeth Harter, aged 64 years, 11
months and 10 days. She was the wife of Bro. Levi Harter,
who preceded her in death a little over three years. She
leaves three children. Funeral services by Eld. Lewis Kinsey and the writer from Heb. 11: 16.   ABRAHAM BOWMAN.

JAMES.—In the bounds of the Sterling church, Whiteside
Co., Ill., Nov. 24, 1892, Mrs. Mary-James, aged 49 years and
20 days. Deceased was born in Cambria County, Pa. Her
mother and sister met their death in the great disaster at
Johnstown a few years ago. Funeral by the writer in the
Rock Falls M. E. church, to a large and sympathizing congregation.   P. R. KELTNER.

PRICE.—In the Ephratah church, Lancaster Co., Pa.,
Nov. 26, 1892, Wm. Price, aged 70 years, 8 months and 2
days. He was ailing about two years.. Last week he had a
stroke of paralysis which resulted in his death.. He was widely known and highly esteemed. He was elected to the ministry when twenty-seven years of age and proved a good,
willing worker. Services by our home preachers and brethren Gibble and George Bucher from 2 Cor. 5: 1.
    JACOB KELLER.

SHEETS.—In the bounds of the Walnut church, Marshall Co., Ind., Nov. 18, 1892, Elva N., daughter of Bro. Winfield and sister Betty Sheets, aged 11 years, 8 months and 6
days. Services were conducted by Bro. John R. Miller from
Matt. 18: 3.   MYRTA I. SWIHART.

BOONE.—In the Kansas Center church, Rice Co., Kans.,
Nov. 1, 1892, Edith Myrtle, daughter of Robert and Arrennah Boone, aged 4 years, 4 months and 23 days. Funeral
services conducted by Bro. Enoch Eby.   S. J. DRESSLER.

PATERSON.—In the Bachelor Run church, Carroll Co.,
Ind., Oct. 19, 1892, of typhoid fever, Malinda F. Paterson,
daughter of friend William H. and sister Catharine J. Clice,
aged 28 years, 6 months and .11 days. She leaves a mother,
one brother, one sister and two little children. Funeral by
Bro. Abram Flory.   DAVID H. NICCUM.

The Gospel Messenger

Is the recognized organ of the German Baptist or Brethren's church,
and advocates the form of doctrine taught in the New Testament and
pleads for a return to apostolic and primitive Christianity.

It recognizes the New Testament as the only infallible rule of faith and
practice, and maintains that Faith toward God, Repentance from dead
works, Regeneration of the heart and mind, baptism by Trine Immersion
for remission of sins unto the reception of the Holy Ghost by the laying
on of hands, are the means of adoption into the household of God,—the
church militant.

It also maintains that Feet-washing, as taught in John 13, both by example and command of Jesus, should be observed in the church.

That the Lord's Supper, instituted by Christ and as universally observed by the apostles and the early Christians, is a full meal, and, in
connection with the Communion, should be taken in the evening or after
the close of the day.

That the Salutation of the Holy Kiss, or Kiss of Charity, is binding
upon the followers of Christ.

That War and Retaliation are contrary to the spirit and self-denying
principles of the religion of Jesus Christ.

That the principle of Plain Dressing and of Non-conformity to the
world, as taught in the New Testament, should be observed by the followers of Christ.

That the Scriptural duty of Anointing the Sick with Oil, in the Name
of the Lord, James 5: 14, is binding upon all Christians.

It also advocates the church's duty to support Missionary and Tract
Work, thus giving to the Lord for the spread of the Gospel and for the
conversion of sinners.

In short, it is a Vindicator of all that Christ and the apostles have or-
joined upon us, and aims, amid the conflicting theories and discords of
modern Christendom, to point out ground that all must concede to be in-
faithly safe.

☞ The above principles of our Fraternity are set forth
on our Brethren's Envelopes." Use them! Price 15 cents
per package; 40 cents per hundred.

Announcements.

LOVE-FEASTS.

Dec. 31, Glendale, Maricopa Co., Ariz. Those coming by rail will be met by at Tempe by notifying T. J. Elsenbise.

For Sale!

Having a desire to devote more time to church work, I offer one quarter section of choice farm land for sale. This farm has a good house, barn, fences, well, and a nice spring. It is situated 2½ miles south of the Brethren's meeting-house in Shannon, Ill. It is also within one mile of a good creamery. I also offer 50 head of registered Short Horn Cattle, 15 males and 35 females, — choice individuals at a very low price. Address for particulars, D. Rowland, Lanark, Ill.

Tract-Work.

List of Publications for Sale.—Sent by Mail or Express, Prepaid

CLASS A.

Golden Gleams or Light of Life, per copy,	$ .85

CLASS B.

Plain Family Bible, per copy,	$4 50
Trine Immersion, Quinter, per copy,	1 25
Life and Sermons, Quinter, per copy,	1 25
Europe and Bible Lands, Miller, per copy,	1 50
Doctrine of the Brethren Defended, Miller, per copy,	1 50
Close Communion, West, per copy,	40
Classified Minutes of Annual Meeting, per copy,	1 75
Brethren's Tracts and Pamphlets, neatly bound in Book, Vol. 1, 494 pages, per copy,	75

HYMNALS.

Half Leather, per copy,	$ 75
Morocco, per copy,	1 00
Morocco, gilt edge, per copy,	1 25

HYMN BOOKS.

Morocco, per copy,	$ 75
Morocco, gilt-edge, per copy,	85
Arabesque, per copy,	40
Fine Limp, per copy,	45
Fine Limp, gilt-edge, per copy,	85

CLASS C. (Tracts.)

REVISED AND IMPROVED.

	Per 100.	Per copy.
The Brethren or Dunkards,	$1 50	$0 01
Path of Life,	4 00	01
Single Immersion,	1 00	08
Trine Immersion traced to the Apostles,	6 00	08
Christian Baptism,	2 00	03
Salvation or Safe Ground,	6 00	01
The Sabbath and the Lord's Day,	3 50	04
Secret Societies Incompatible with Christianity,	1 50	03

CLASS D.

The tracts in this class at 60 cents per 100, contain eight pages.

	Per 100.
House We Live In,	$0 60
Come Let Us Reason Together,	60
The Atoning Blood of Christ,	40
Intemperance,	40
Plain Dressing,	60
Which is the Right Church,	60
Close Communion Examined,	60
House We Live In (Swedish,)	60
House We Live In (Danish,)	40
The Light House,	60
Close Communion,	60
Modern Skepticism,	40
House We Live In (German,)	60
The Proper Covering,	60
The Lord's Supper,	60
The Bible Service of Feet-Washing,	60
Communion,	40
Are Christians Allowed to Swear?	40

CLASS E.

	Per 100.
Why Am I Not a Christian?	20
Christ and War,	20
Gold and Costly Array,	20
The Brethren's Card,	

We also print Family and Teacher's Bibles and Testaments, all styles and sizes, Hymnals and Hymn Books. *Send for our catalogue and price list.*

BRETHREN'S BOOK & TRACT WORK,
DAYTON, OHIO.

→ESSAYS←

"Study to show thyself approved unto God; a workman that needeth not be ashamed, rightly dividing the Word of Truth."

THE DEPARTING YEAR.

BY SADIE BRALLIER NOFFSINGER.

Lo thou art passing, with slow step, but surely,
Hoary of head and dejected of mien,
Into the shadows. We watch and know truly
Protests are futile and struggles in vain.
Droopeth thy brow; and each pulse beateth faster.
Fadeth thy breath; and each heart throbbeth wild.
Fleeth thy strength and abateth thy courage,
'Neath the dread import of truth unbeguiled.

Lo, thou art dying nor yet do we mourn thee.
In thy departure our hearts but rejoice.
Joyful we kneel by thy side, and thanksgiving
Render to Heaven with uplifted voice.
Sweet were the ties which in wrath thou hast sundered;
Dear were the joys which thy foul breath hath slain;
Lofty the hopes which thy cruel hand captured;
Yet in thy death we may find them again.

True, thou wert fair; and we welcomed thy presence,
Hailing thy advent with pen and with song;
Tuning our harps to the voice of thy laughter,—
Bidding our hearts their loud praises prolong.
Lo! soon were hushed the sweet carols of music;
Soon our gay harps on the willows were hung;
Thistles and thorns were strewn over our pathway,
And a long year of sad mourning begun.

Oh, we have wept! for our feet faint and weary
Traveled anon in the valley of fears.
And our poor hearts, sad and torn, oft seemed truly,
Even transformed into fountains of tears.
Vain was the struggle to rise from our bondage;
Vain our endeavors to flee from thy breath.
Sore have we sighed, and full wearily walked,
Hoping and praying for peace in thy death.

Still do we weep! for the sad recollection
Of the fond treasures our lives held most dear,
Mocketh our sorrow and filleth our beings
With a deep sense of its loneliness drear.
Dark is the night and its gloom settles o'er us.
Panteth our heart, and we long for the dawn.
Light breaketh now! A grave opens before us!
Lo, thou art passing! We pray thee, pass on!

Johnstown, Pa.

PRIMITIVE CHRISTIANITY, AS UNDERSTOOD AND PRACTICED BY THE BRETHREN.

[We invite careful and intelligent criticism on all the articles published under this head. Criticism on language, facts and arguments will be in order, and should be sent to the author of the article to which they refer.]

BY A. W. REESE.

Faith.

"But without faith it is impossible to please him; for he that cometh to God must believe that he is, and that he is a rewarder of them that diligently seek him."—Heb. 11: 6.

Part Three.

LET us take another example, — that of the blind man, recorded in John 9. A man *born* blind,—congenital blindness,—a hopeless case; one beyond the reach of human skill or aid! Never since the world began had it been heard that a man *born* blind had been restored to sight. A pitiable object! A common pauper sitting, dejected and lonely, by the public highway! A poor, blind beggar! Jesus passed by, saw him in this distressful state, had compassion on him and restored his sight.

Observe, now, the *simplicity* of the *means* employed by the Son of God. He spat on the ground, made clay of the spittle, anointed the eyes of the blind man with the clay, and said unto him, "Go wash in the pool of Siloam, (which is by interpretation Sent)." "He went his way, therefore, and washed, and came seeing."

This is a most remarkable narrative. An humble pauper,—perhaps an outcast,—sits by a public highway; a blind beggar,—blind from his birth,—hopeless, helpless, dependent upon public charity for his daily morsel of bread, is unexpectedly accosted by a comparative stranger, "a man that is called Jesus," a man of humble birth and parentage like himself, and, by the simplest means in the world, is restored to sight. And, moreover, "this man Jesus" does not present himself with great pomp, or with the *prestige* of a great name. He is comparatively obscure, "a friend of publicans and sinners,"—a sort of *itinerant preacher,*—wandering about the country on foot, attended by a small lot of strolling fishermen, who regard "this man Jesus" as a prophet, or teacher sent from God, while, on the other hand, the Pharisees and doctors of the law, with the great majority of the people, regard "this man Jesus" as an impostor, a blasphemer, and a person every way worthy of death.

This man Jesus, passing by with his disciples, or proselytes, accosts the blind man and undertakes his *cure!* How does he proceed? A good deal like a Hindoo juggler, or an Indian "medicine man"! He spat on the ground, made clay of the spittle, anointed the blind man's eyes, and tells him to go wash in the pool of Siloam.

Now, what more seemingly *absurd* than this performance, in reason's eye? Science might well turn up her haughty nose at "nonsense" like this. Men of thoughtful, investigating minds, might well smile at the *credulity* that could place any reliance in such means for the cure of *any* disorder, much less so formidable a case as that of a man *born* blind. Popular skepticism might well ask, "What healing virtue, or power, in this simple clay,—this ointment made with human spittle?"

Not only might science shake her doubtful head, but might not these suggestions, naturally, present themselves to the mind of the beggar himself? "Why go to the *Siloam* pool? Was there ever a case of blindness cured by going there, by washing in its waters? What is there in this common clay,—this human saliva,—to open the eyes of the blind?"

These would be *natural* suggestions,—such as might be *expected* to rise in the mind, and their usual effect would be to induce doubt, hesitation, indecision, and skepticism in the end. Yet, in spite of such misgivings, we read with wonder, that "he went his way, therefore, and washed, and came seeing." Now, what induced this blind beggar, in the face of all human reason, and in defiance of all human experience, to *do* this thing? What strange, mysterious influence induced such conduct on his part?

The recognized laws of mental philosophy offer no solution for the exercise of a credulity like this. It cannot be ascribed to mental imbecility, or hallucination, because the subsequent interviews between this man and the unbelieving Pharisees prove him to have been remarkably *acute* and a person of no mean ability. Nor could it have been a *hallucination,* because he could not be deceived, either as to his former condition, or as to his subsequent restoration to sight.

How, then, shall we explain the conduct of this man? Simply by the word *faith.* "Thy faith hath made thee whole!" How? By a simple *exercise* of the *mind* without any corresponding *action* on his part? By no *means* used? O no! he must *obey* the word. He must *go* to the pool of Siloam. Is that all? O no! he must *wash* in that pool when he gets there. It took all this,—as well as the ointment of clay,—to constitute the *faith* necessary to his *cure.* Why could he not have gone down to the *Jordan,* like Naaman, and have washed there for a cure? Simply because "the man Jesus" did not tell him to go there. Christ told him to do a *certain thing,* and his faith accepted that thing, and, without stopping to ask a single question, or to reason about the "why's and wherefore's" of the case, he went and did the thing commanded to be done,—hence the *cure.* Obedience being "the evidence of things not seen,"—the *test* of *faith!*

Unbelief, on the other hand, stops to reason, to question, to quibble, to doubt, to suggest. God commands a certain thing, and that, too, in the plainest language possible to be used, and instead of *doing* just that certain thing,—nothing more, nothing less,—men want to do *something* else that *they* think will do equally as *well,* if not a little better, than the thing that God commands. But these are not the processes of genuine faith. The quintessence of faith is to *know* and to *do* the will of God,—to *obey* his Word. Take the case of the man with the *withered* hand. Here was a sad affliction,—a hand shrunken, useless,—devoid of sensation and the power of motion, lifeless as a stick of wood!

In the temple, on that memorable Sabbath day, Jesus said to this man, "Stretch forth thy hand." What an idea! Say *this* to a man who had no more power of motion in that hand than if it were the stiff, cold hand of a corpse! Well might that man have replied, "Sir, do you come hither to mock my distress? I have no power to stretch forth that hand!" And would not all human science have sustained this position? But no! without a moment's hesitation, he obeyed the command. He stretched forth his withered hand, and *it was made whole like unto the other.*

What cured the blind man? The ointment of clay? The washing in the pool of Siloam? Did his *faith* cure him? No; "the man called Jesus" cured him,—restored his sight. The power of God did the work, but *faith* was the *instrument* through which that work was done. If the blind man had lacked *faith* in "the man called Jesus," he would not have gone to the pool of Siloam, nor washed therein; and failing to *do* these things, he would *not* have *received his sight.* If the man with the withered hand had made *no effort* to stretch forth that hand, he would not have been cured. And without *faith* in "the man called Jesus," he would have made no effort. And why should he?

National Military Home, Kans.

"MY BELOVED IS MINE, AND I AM HIS."—

Sol. Song 2: 16.

BY C. H. BALSBAUGH.

Dear Sister in Christ Jesus:—

How deep, how pure, how divine, how pure this relationship is, we need eternity to unfold. Christ has redeemed us, loves us, keeps us, sanctifies us by His own eternal life, and therefore we are one in Him. Matt. 12: 49, 50. With "our life hid with Christ in God," our souls are knit together in the very bond that makes the Holy Trinity a unit. Where God dwells, there all forms and vestiges of selfishness must vanish. The cross shows how unselfish God is.

Religion is not theology or opinion, or tradition, or creed, or church, but "*God manifest in the flesh.*" The indwelling Christ must shape all our thoughts, aspirations, enjoyments, words and actions. The church in general is so busy with forms and customs and propositions, and external movements and aggressions, that we have lost sight of the very essence of Christianity,—the life of God in sacrifice, and the beauty of holiness, and the glory of self-forgetting love for human weal. I get thousands of letters from all parts of the Brotherhood, full of startling revelations and hard questions and amazing misapprehensions of the purpose of God in Christ; but how few testify to the joyous, personal relation-

✦ESSAYS✦

"Study to show thyself approved unto God; a workman that needeth not be ashamed, rightly dividing the Word of Truth."

THE DEPARTING YEAR.

BY SADIE BRALLIER NOFFSINGER.

Lo thou art passing, with slow step, but surely,
  Hoary of head and dejected of mien,
Into the shadows. We watch and know truly
  Protests are futile and struggles In vain.
Droopeth thy brow; and each pulse beateth faster.
  Fadeth thy strength and abateth thy courage,
Fleeth thy strength and abateth thy courage,
  'Neath the dread import of truth unbeguiled.

Lo, thou art dying nor yet do we mourn thee.
  In thy departure our hearts but rejoice.
Joyful we kneel by thy side, and thanksgiving
  Render to Heaven with uplifted voice.
Sweet were the ties which in wrath thou hast sundered;
  Dear were the joys which thy foul breath hath slain;
Lofty the hopes which thy cruel hand captured;
  Yet in thy death we may find them again.

True, thou wert fair; and we welcomed thy presence,
  Hailing thy advent with pen and with song;
Tuning our harps to the voice of thy laughter,—
  Bidding our hearts their loud praises prolong.
Lo! soon were hushed the sweet carols of music;
  Soon our gay harps on the willows were hung;
Thistles and thorns were strewn over our pathway,
  And a long year of sad mourning begun.

Oh, we have wept! for our feet faint and weary
  Traveled anon in the Valley of fears.
And our poor hearts, sad and torn, oft seemed truly,
  Even transformed Into fountains of tears.
Vain was the struggle to rise from our bondage;
  Vain our endeavors to flee from thy breath.
Sore have we sighed, and full wearily waited,
  Hoping and praying for peace in thy death.

Still do we weep! for the sad recollection
  Of the fond treasures our lives held most dear,
Mocketh our sorrow and filleth our beings
  With a deep sense of its loneliness drear.
Dark is the night and its gloom settles o'er us.
  Panteth our heart, and we long for the dawn.
Light breaketh now! A grave opens before us!
  Lo, thou art passing! We pray thee, pass on!
Johnstown, Pa.

PRIMITIVE CHRISTIANITY, AS UNDERSTOOD AND PRACTICED BY THE BRETHREN.

[We invite careful and intelligent criticism on all the articles published under this head. Criticisms on language, facts and arguments will be in order, and should be sent to the author of the article to which they refer.]

BY A. W. REESE.

Faith.

"But without faith it is impossible to please him: for he that cometh to God must believe that he is, and that he is a rewarder of them that diligently seek him."—Heb. 11: 6.

Part Three.

LET us take another example,—that of the blind man, recorded in John 9. A man born blind,—congenital blindness,—a hopeless case: one beyond the reach of human skill or aid! Never since the world began had it been heard that a man born blind had been restored to sight. A pitiable object! A common pauper sitting, dejected and lonely, by the public highway! A poor, blind beggar! Jesus passed by, saw him in this distressful state, had compassion on him and restored his sight.

Observe, now, the *simplicity* of the *means* employed by the Son of God. He spat on the ground, made clay of the spittle, anointed the eyes of the blind man with the clay, and said unto him, "Go wash in the pool of Siloam, (which is by interpretation Sent)." "He went his way, therefore, and washed, and came seeing."

This is a most remarkable narrative. An humble pauper,—perhaps an outcast,—sits by a public highway; a blind beggar,—blind from his birth,—hopeless, helpless, dependent upon public charity for his daily morsel of bread, is unexpectedly accosted by a comparative stranger, "a man that is called Jesus," a man of humble birth and parentage like himself, and, by the simplest means in the world, is restored to sight. And, moreover, "this man Jesus" does not present himself with great pomp, or with the *prestige* of a great name. He is comparatively *obscure*, "a friend of publicans and sinners,"—a sort of *itinerant preacher*,—wandering about the country on foot, attended by a small lot of strolling fishermen, who regard "this man Jesus" as a prophet, or teacher sent from God, while, on the other hand, the Pharisees and doctors of the law, with the great majority of the people, regard "this man Jesus" as an impostor, a blasphemer, and a person every way worthy of death.

This man Jesus, passing by with his disciples, or proselytes, accosts the blind man and undertakes his *cure!* How does he proceed? A good deal like a Hindoo juggler, or an Indian "medicine man"! He spat-on the ground, made clay of the spittle, anointed the blind man's eyes, and tells him to go wash in the pool of Siloam.

Now, what more seemingly *absurd* than this performance, in reason's eye? Science might well turn up her haughty nose at "nonsense" like this. Men of thoughtful, investigating minds, might well smile at the *credulity* that could place any reliance in such means for the cure of *any* disorder, much less so formidable a case as that of a man *born* blind. Popular skepticism might well ask, "What healing virtue, or power, in this simple clay,—this ointment made with human spittle?"

Not only might *science* shake her doubtful head, but might not these suggestions, naturally, present themselves to the mind of the beggar himself? "Why go to the *Siloam* pool? Was there ever a case of blindness cured by going there, by washing in its waters? What is there in this common clay,—this human saliva,—to open the eyes of the blind?"

These might be *natural* suggestions,—such as might be *expected* to rise in the mind, and their usual effect would be to induce doubt, hesitation, indecision, and skepticism in the end. Yet, in spite of such misgivings, we read with wonder, that "he went his way, therefore, and washed, and came seeing." Mine, what induced this blind beggar, in the face of all human reason, and in defiance of all human experience, to do this thing? What strange, mysterious influence induced such conduct on his part?

The recognized laws of mental philosophy offer no solution for the exercise of a credulity like this. It cannot be ascribed to mental imbecility, or hallucination, because the subsequent interviews between this man and the unbelieving Pharisees prove him to have been remarkably *acute* and a person of no mean ability. Nor could it have been a *hallucination*, because he could not be deceived, either as to his former condition, or as to his subsequent restoration to sight.

How, then, shall we explain the conduct of this man? Simply by the word *faith.* "Thy faith hath made thee whole! How? By a simple *exercise* of the *mind* without any corresponding *action* on his part? By no *means* used? O no! he must obey the word. He must *go* to the pool of Siloam. Is that all? O no! he must *wash* in that pool when he gets there. It took all this,— as well as the ointment of clay,—to constitute the *faith* necessary to his *cure.* He must not have gone down to the *Jordan*, like Naaman, and have washed there for a cure? Simply because "the man Jesus" did not tell him to go there. Christ told him to do a *certain* thing, and his faith accepted that thing, and, without stopping to ask a single question, or to reason about the "why's and wherefore's" of the case, he went and did the thing commanded to be done,—hence the *cure.* Obedience being "the *evidence* of things not seen,"—the *test* of *faith!*

Unbelief, on the other hand, stops to reason, to question, to quibble, to doubt, to suggest. God commands a certain thing, and that, too, in the plainest language possible to be used, and instead of *doing* just that certain thing,—nothing more, nothing less,—men want to do *something* else that *they* think will do equally as *well*, if not a little better, than the thing that God commands.

But these are not the *processes* of genuine faith. The quintessence of faith is *to know* and *to do* the will of God,—*to obey* his Word. Take the case of the man with the *withered* hand. Here was a sad affliction,—a hand shrunken, useless,—devoid of sensation and the power of motion, lifeless as a stick of wood!

In the temple, on that memorable Sabbath day, Jesus said to this man, "Stretch forth thy hand." What an idea! Say *this* to a man who had no more power of motion in that hand than if it were the stiff, cold hand of a corpse! Well might that man have replied, "Sir, do you come hither to mock my distress? I have no power to stretch forth that hand!" And would not all human science have sustained this position? But no! without a moment's hesitation, he obeyed the command. He stretched forth his withered hand, and *it was made whole like unto the other.*

What cured the blind man? The ointment of clay? The washing in the pool of Siloam? Did his *faith* cure him? No; "the man called Jesus" *cured* him,—restored his sight. The power of God did the *work*, but *faith* was the *instrument* through which that work was done. If the blind man had lacked *faith* in "the man called Jesus," he would not have gone to the pool of Sil-o...; washed therein; and failing to do these things, he would *not* have *received his sight.* If the man with the withered hand had made *no effort* to stretch forth that hand, he would not have been cured. And without *faith* in "the man called Jesus," he would have made no effort. And why should he?

National Military Home, Kans.

"MY BELOVED IS MINE, AND I AM HIS."—

Sol. Song 2: 16.

BY C. H. BALSBAUGH.

Dear Sister in Christ Jesus:—

How deep, how dear, how divine, how pure this relationship is, we need eternity to unfold. Christ has redeemed us, loves us, keeps us, sanctifies us by His own eternal life, and therefore we are one in Him. Matt. 12: 49, 50. With "our life hid with Christ in God," our souls are knit together in the very bond that makes–the Holy Trinity a unit. Where God dwells, there all forms and vestiges of selfishness must vanish. The cross shows how unselfish God is.

Religion is not theology or opinion, or tradition, or creed, or church, but "*God manifest in the flesh.*" The indwelling Christ must shape all our thoughts, aspirations, enjoyments, words and actions. The church in general is so busy with forms and customs and propositions, and external movements and aggressions, that we have lost sight of the very essence of Christianity,—the life of God in sacrifice, and the glory of holiness, and the glory of self-forgetting love for human weal. I get thousands of letters from all parts of the Brotherhood, full of startling revelations and hard questions and amazing misapprehensions of the purpose of God in Christ; but how few testify to the joyous, personal relation-

tained from a good book? All boys like tools. Give them saws, hammers, planes, awls and all sorts of useful tools. Let them learn to work, and thus make use of the time which God has given them. Give the girls pretty work boxes or baskets, filled with suitable materials for their pleasure, instruction and use. If Polly or Johnny loves to write, give them a writing-desk, a pretty box of stationery, a tablet, a fountain pen, or inkstand, or pen and paper rack. Give the four-year-old a set of alphabet blocks.

Have you a friend of whom you know almost nothing? Well, give him or her a year's subscription to some religious paper,—the GOSPEL MESSENGER for instance, or if it is a child, the Young Disciple. If you live where nuts of all kinds are abundant, and you haven't much money, gather in the fall a bushel or two of nuts to send to the children who live away out West, where nuts don't grow. If you are just a penniless boy or girl yourself, save up your Sunday-school papers for a year, bind them into a book and send to some less-favored child. Save your lesson cards and tickets the same way. When you are contemplating a visit, just think if there isn't some poor, despised, neglected soul, who would be delighted beyond measure if you should only go over and spend half a day (or a whole one) with them, and then go where you think your presence would do the most good. If you live in the country, and know of some poor widow, or invalid, or other poor, struggling, hard-working soul in the city, take them a turkey or chicken, or something that will prove useful to the family. But if you are a city resident, and your friends live in the country, ask them to come in and visit you, and when they come, don't act as though you were ashamed of them, but give them a chance to see and enjoy all they can. Take them to church, introduce them to your friends. If you are much more wealthy than your pastor, don't forget him and his faithful helpmeet. If he is so poor that he must walk to his several appointments, why could not several well-to-do folks put together and procure for him a horse and buggy? If he is a young, aspiring man, earnestly striving for an education to make him more useful in God's service, give him something that will help him in that way.

If you can't give to everybody you love, give to one poor soul something which will gladden the heart and cause a thought of Jesus. Do not try to give valuable presents to persons more wealthy than yourself. Give of your means to bless the poor, but to those who have far more means than yourself, if you feel that you ought to give them something, let it be some nice little thing that your hands have made,—a painting, a poem, a bouquet, a picture frame, some useful and pretty article of household use, or of apparel,—anything that you can do neatly and well. This they will prize, because your loving heart has guided your dear hands to do it for them.

Very often a little round piece of gold with the picture of an eagle on it will be quite as useful to a poor pastor, a widow, an invalid, an aged and infirm parent or friend, or any other needy person, as a costly album, cane, or other gift. "He that hath pity on the poor, lendeth to the Lord."

"THE worth of a thing is seen in the work it produces. Can you think of any good works that come from liquor-drinking? Does it make a man wiser, better, happier, or more useful? Does it give him fine clothes, good books, a noble character, and a good home? If it does none of these things for a man, shall we give the intoxicating bowl to our lips?"

ODE TO THE CLOSING YEAR.

BY M. M. SHERRICK.

THE day is dark, While o'er and o'er
I con a lesson of the years,
Whose speeding cycles evermore
ReVive alternate hopes and tears.

Old Year, we loVe thee for thyself;
For the full fruitage thou has brought,
For riches Which are more than pelf—
The gracious deed, the noble thought.

We loVe thee for the hopes of Spring—
Thy resurrection morn, when all
The cerements broke and eVerything
Awoke, in answer to thy call.

We bless thee for the summer days
That waxed and waned o'er freemen's soil,
When all the bright, eternal ways
Were open to the sons of toil.

And now beneath thy naked boughs,
We walk among the withered leaVes
And listen to thy wind which, like
A Wandering spirit, broods and grieVes.

The birds of passage all haVe flown
To warmer climes and sunnier skies,
While in the Woodland's depth alone
Is heard the lone crow's Wanton cries.

Old Year, that, passing from our sight,
Dost leaVe us in uncertain gloom,
And wrapping round us deep and white,
The Virgin raiment of the tomb.

Say, Wilt thou at some future day,
Beyond the bound and sense of pain,
With garlands of the Spring array
Thyself, and come to us again?

Our hearts are burdened and distressed
To hear the hurrying of thy feet,
To see thee passing to thy rest—
A whirling storm thy winding sheet.

Old Year, with bowed and reVerent head,
We stand amid the gathering gloom
That shrouds the hall-Ways of the dead,
And watch thee passing to the tomb.

And didst thou neVer mutual ties,
Thou, too, hast reunited friends
Where sacred friendship never dies,
Where halloWed service neVer ends.

We toiled with thee from strength to strength,
And learned the way from faith to faith,
Thrice conquering sin, we feel at length
That we shall triumph oVer death.

Old Year, with bowed and reVerent head,
We stand amid the gathering gloom
That shrouds the hall-ways of the dead,
And bless thee passing to the tomb.

JUDGE NOT, BUT SHED ABROAD THE LIGHT.

BY SOLOMON SCHUBERT.

ABOVE all things we should be slow to harshly judge our fellow-men. We know not what lies behind the screen; what battles are being, or have been, fought in that soul, what inheritance of criminal impulses, of vice, of selfishness or of hatred may have been bequeathed him by his parents, in what foul, immoral atmosphere he has passed many days or years, or what great temptations may have visited him. We know not but that, if we had been in his place, we might have sinned far more than he.

Our mission is not to judge, nor yet to selfishly ignore the erring. It is to patiently, kindly and bravely seek to lead them into a higher life. Let us show them we have faith in them, that they are our brothers, that they can attain the noblest heights, and that we will aid them.

Where this humane and civilized course has been pursued, a large per cent of the erring ones in every condition of moral retrogression have been lifted to a higher plane and made a blessing to society. Whenever we place ourselves in the offender's place, our judgment is immediately tempered, and we are better able to understand our simple duty.

CORRESPONDENCE.

"Write what thou seest, and send it unto the churches."

☞ Church News solicited for this Department. If you haVe had a good meeting, send a report of it, so that others may rejoice with you. In writing give name of church, County and State. Be brief. Notes of Travel should be as short as possible. Land AdVertisements are not solicited for this Department. We haVe an adVertising page, and, if necessary, will issue supplements.

From Gardner, Kans.

NOV. 27 I left home to attend the council in the Ottawa church. We had a very pleasant meeting. In the business of this new organization the members adhere to Rom. 12: 11, and in one hour all matters, brought before the church, were disposed of. One sister was restored to fellowship. One of our members was recently removed by death.

Bro. T. A. Robinson met me at Ottawa, where we held meetings a few days. Much interest was manifested during the services and by faithfulness and unity on the part of the members, we predict an ingathering of souls.

Feeling a deep interest in the cause at Ottawa, permit me to again call attention to the good country and cheap, improved farms. Loyal members will meet with a kind reception both in the country and city. We left sister Fannie A. Morrow suffering with inflammatory rheumatism, which confines her to her home. I then returned home from Ottawa, and am now suffering with a severe cold.

I expect to confine my work to our home church during December. After that I will again take the field, if the Lord will. Bro. J. H. Neher, of Mc-Oune, Kans., is now in our congregation, holding meetings near Olathe. Dec. 20 Bro. John Sherfy will begin a series of meetings at our churchhouse near Gardner. Nearly one hundred members have been received by baptism in North-eastern Kansas since Oct. 1. May the good work continue, and while we gain in numbers, may we all grow in true vital piety.   ISAAC H. Crist.
Dec. 10.

From Palestine, Ark.

WE have been in Arkansas since the night of Dec. 18. On Sunday after we arrived, we attended the Brethren's Bible Class at 11 A. M., and spoke to the members and friends at 7 P. M. On Thanksgiving Day we had services, morning and evening. Since then we spoke each evening, except two, when it rained. In all seventeen discourses were delivered, one by Eld. Jas. K. Gish. The members seem much revived, and rejoice to have church privileges. Some of the friends here are much interested in this work of life, and we have confidence that the work done here is not done in vain. God will give the increase.

A dear young minister, from Indiana, has written us that he has some thought of coming to us to help in the work. May our Father confirm his resolution, and speed its fulfillment, is our humble prayer! We now start to Stuttgart, where we hope, by the Father's grace and blessings, to pursue our service to him.

We were happily disappointed when we got here, to find so many loving hearts, hungry souls, and a country with so much better improvements and advantages than we expected.

We feel a little ashamed that we did not sooner heed the urgent cry for help, and submit to God's requirements. We, too, earnestly hope that many in the North and East, who are chosen to be ministers, but are now standing idly by, will raise their courage and be remiss no longer. Sell your personal effects, pay your debts and come where your humblest labors will be appreciated and encouraged. Here you may realize the divine blessing which follows devoted labor

tained from a good book? All boys like tools. Give them saws, hammers, planes, awls and all sorts of useful tools. Let them learn to work, and thus make use of the time which God has given them. Give the girls pretty work boxes or baskets, filled with suitable materials for their pleasure, instruction and use. If Polly or Johnny loves to write, give them a writing-desk, a pretty box of stationery, a tablet, a fountain pen, or ink-stand, or pen and paper rack. Give the four-year-old a set of alphabet blocks.

Have you a friend of whom you know almost nothing? Well, give him or her a year's subscription to some religious paper,—the GOSPEL MESSENGER for instance, or if it is a child, the Young Disciple. If you live where nuts of all kinds are abundant, and you haven't much money, gather in the fall a bushel or two of nuts to send to the children who live away out West, where nuts don't grow. If you are just a penniless boy or girl yourself, save up your Sunday-school papers for a year, bind them into a book and send to some less-favored child. Save your lesson cards and tickets the same way. When you are contemplating a visit, just think if there isn't some poor, despised, neglected soul, who would be delighted beyond measure if you should only go over and spend half a day (or a whole one) with them, and then go where you think your presence would do the most good. If you live in the country, and know of some poor widow, or invalid, or other poor, struggling, hard-working soul in the city, take them a turkey or chicken, or something that will prove useful to the family. But if you are a city resident, and your friends live in the country, ask them to come in and visit you, and when they come, don't act as though you were ashamed of them, but give them a chance to see and enjoy all they can. Take them to church, introduce them to your friends. If you are much more wealthy than your pastor, don't forget him and his faithful helpmeet. If he is so poor that he must walk to his several appointments, why could not several well-to-do folks put together and procure for him a horse and buggy? If he is a young, aspiring man, earnestly striving for an education to make him more useful in God's service, give him something that will help him in that way.

If you can't give to everybody you love, give to one poor soul something which will gladden the heart and cause a thought of Jesus. Do not try to give valuable presents to persons more wealthy than yourself. Give of your means to bless the poor, but to those who have far more means than yourself, if you feel that you ought to give them something, let it be some nice little thing that your hands have made,—a painting, a poem, a bouquet, a picture frame, some useful and pretty article of household use, or of apparel,—anything that you can do neatly and well. This they will prize, because your loving heart has guided your dear hands to do it for them.

Very often a little round piece of gold with the picture of an eagle on it will be quite as useful to a poor pastor, a widow, an invalid, an aged and infirm parent or friend, or any other needy person, as a costly album, cane, or other gift. "He that hath pity on the poor, lendeth to the Lord."

"THE worth of a thing is seen in the work it produces. Can you think of any good works that come from liquor-drinking? Does it make a man wiser, better, happier, or more useful? Does it give him fine clothes, good books, a noble character, and a good home? If it does none of these things for a man, shall we give the intoxicating bowl to our lips?"

ODE TO THE CLOSING YEAR.

BY M. M. SHERRICK.

THE day is dark, while o'er and o'er
  I con a lesson of the years,
Whose speeding cycles evermore
  Revive alternate hopes and tears.

Old Year, we love thee for thyself;
  For the full fruitage thou has brought,
For riches which are more than pelf—
  The gracious deed, the noble thought.

We love thee for the hopes of Spring—
  Thy resurrection morn, when all
The cerements broke and everything
  Awoke, in answer to thy call.

We bless thee for the summer days
  That waxed and waned o'er freemen's soil,
When all the bright, eternal ways
  Were open to the sons of toil.

And now beneath thy naked boughs,
  We walk among the withered leaves
And listen to thy wind which, like
  A wandering spirit, broods and grieves.

The birds of passage all have flown
  To warmer climes and sunnier skies,
While in the woodland's depth alone
  Is heard the lone crow's wanton cries.

Old Year, that, passing from our sight,
  Dost leave us in uncertain gloom,
And wrapping round us deep and white,
  The virgin ralment of the tomb;

Say, wilt thou at some future day,
  Beyond the bound and sense of pain,
With garlands of the Spring array
  Thyself, and come to us again?

Our hearts are burdened and distressed
  To hear the hurrying of thy feet,
To see thee passing to thy rest—
  A whirling storm thy winding sheet.

Old Year, with bowed and reverent head,
  We stand amid the gathering gloom
That shrouds the hall-ways of the dead,
  And watch thee passing to the tomb.

And didst thou sever mutual ties,
  Thou, too, hast reunited friends
Where sacred friendship never dies,
  Where hallowed service never ends.

We toiled with thee from strength to strength,
  And learned the way from faith to faith,
Thrice conquering sin, we feel at length
  That we shall triumph over death.

Old Year, with bowed and reverent head,
  We stand amid the gathering gloom
That shrouds the hall-ways of the dead,
  And bless thee passing to the tomb.

JUDGE NOT, BUT SHED ABROAD THE LIGHT.

BY SOLOMON SCHUBERT.

ABOVE all things we should be slow to harshly judge our fellow-men. We know not what lies behind the screen; what battles are being, or have been, fought in that soul, what inheritance of criminal impulses, of vice, of selfishness or of hatred may have been bequeathed him by his parents, in what foul, immoral atmosphere he has passed many days or years, or what great temptations may have visited him. We know not but that, if we had been in his place, we might have sinned far more than he.

Our mission is not to judge, nor yet to selfishly ignore the erring. It is to patiently, kindly and bravely seek to lead them into a higher life. Let us show them we have faith in them, that they are our brothers, that they can attain the noblest heights, and that we will aid them.

Where this humane and civilized course has been pursued, a large per cent of the erring ones in every condition of moral retrogression have been lifted to a higher plane and made a blessing to society. Whenever we place ourselves in the offender's place, our judgment is immediately tempered, and we are better able to understand our simple duty.

CORRESPONDENCE.

" Write what thou seest, and send it unto the churches."

☞Church News solicited for this Department. If you have had a good meeting, send a report of it, so that others may rejoice with you. In writing give name of church, County and State. Be brief. Notes of Travel should be as short as possible. Land Advertisements are not solicited for this Department. We have an Advertising page, and, if necessary, will issue supplements.

From Gardner, Kans.

NOV. 27 I left home to attend the council in the Ottawa church. We had a very pleasant meeting. In the business of this new organization the members adhere to Rom. 12: 11, and in one hour all matters, brought before the church, were disposed of. One sister was restored to fellowship. One of our members was recently removed by death.

Bro. T. A. Robinson met me at Ottawa, where we held meetings a few days. Much interest was manifested during the services and by faithfulness and unity on the part of the members, we predict an ingathering of souls.

Feeling a deep interest in the cause at Ottawa, permit me to again call attention to the good country and cheap, improved farms. Loyal members will meet with a kind reception both in the country and city. We left sister Fannie A. Morrow suffering with inflammatory rheumatism, which confines her to her home. I then returned home from Ottawa, and am now suffering with a severe cold.

I expect to confine my work to our home church during December. After that I will again take the field, if the Lord will. Bro. J. H. Neher, of McCune, Kans., is now in our congregation, holding meetings near Olathe. Dec. 22 Bro. John Sherfy will begin a series of meetings at our church-house near Gardner. Nearly one hundred members have been received by baptism in North-eastern Kansas since Oct. 1. May the good work continue, and while we gain in numbers, may we all grow in true vital piety.   ISAAC H. CRIST.

Dec. 10.

From Palestine, Ark.

WE have been in Arkansas since the night of Dec. 18. On Sunday after we arrived, we attended the Brethren's Bible Class at 11 A. M., and spoke to the members and friends at 7 P. M. On Thanksgiving Day we had services, morning and evening. Since then we spoke each evening, except two, when it rained. In all seventeen discourses were delivered, one by Eld. Jas. R. Gish. The members seem much revived, and rejoice to have church privileges. Some of the friends here are much interested in this work of life, and we have confidence that the work done here is not done in vain. God will give the increase.

A dear young minister, from Indiana, has written us that he has some thought of coming to us to help in the work. May our Father confirm his resolution, and speed its fulfillment, is our humble prayer! We now start to Stuttgart, where we hope, by the Father's grace and blessings, to pursue our service to him.

We were happily disappointed when we got here, to find so many loving hearts, hungry souls, and a country with so much better improvements and advantages than we expected.

We feel a little ashamed that we did not sooner heed the urgent cry for help, and submit to God's requirements. We, too, earnestly hope that many in the North and East, who are chosen to be ministers, but are now standing idly by, will raise their courage and be remiss no longer. Sell your personal effects, pay your debts and come where your humblest labors will be appreciated and encouraged. Here you may realize the divine blessing which follows devoted labor

All things are his, both in the realm of grace and in the realm of nature. In this world the Christian may have a foretaste of heaven. Here rich feasts are provided for him, and as he investigates, new beauties, new wonders are ever unfolded to him.

RECEIPTS OF GENERAL MISSIONARY COMMITTEE FOR NOVEMBER, 1892.

A brother, Ill., $4; Aunt Etta, Bremen, Ind., $1; a brother in Christ, Sidney, Nebr., $2.70; William's Creek church, Tex., $13 50; John C. and Mary E. Franz, $5; Mr. and Mrs. Slater, Flagg Centre, Ill., $1.25; Wolf Creek church, Ohio, $19.05; Good Hope church, Kans., $1.00; J. E. Gnagey, Accident, Md., $10; Marsh Creek church, Pa., $3.60; two sisters, Oklahoma, $2; Tropico church, Cal., $3.20; Loramie's church, Ohio, $3.30; Stony Creek S. S., Ind., $4.05; Monitor church, Kans., $2; Harriet Reed, Easton, W. Va., $10; O. W. Reed, Easton, W. Va., $1; M. W. Reed, Easton. W. Va., $10; H. Clara Reed, Easton, W. Va., $2; Mrs. Lizzie Barndollar, Everett, Pa., $5; Mrs. Margaret Calhoun, Everett, Pa., $5; Lafayette church, Ohio, $2.57; Pleasant Hill S. S., Ind. $1.90; Grundy County church, Iowa, $13.50; a sister, Pa., 75 cents; a brother and family, Louisville, Ohio, $2.00; Long Meadow church of Beaver's Creek congregation, Md., $5.36; Broadfording church of Welsh Run congregation, Md., $3.75; J. T. Dobbins, Wolcott, Ind., $1; Mary Replogle, deceased, Unionville, Iowa, $5; Exeter church, Nebr., $3; Lafayette church, Ohio, $3.60; Luther Petry, Atlanta, Ga., $1.75; a brother, Minneapolis, Kans., $1.04; a brother and sister, Liberty, Ohio, $5; G. W. Fandler, Bellevue, Idaho, $1; Lizzie A. Hope, Mandon, N. Dak., $1.06; Mrs. Abram Hook, Mowerville, Pa., 60 cents; Mineral Creek church, Mo., $6.50; Libertyville church, Iowa, $5; Lick Creek church, Ohio, $13; a sister in Christ, Philadelphia, Pa., $1; J. Henry and Emma Showalter, Johnson City, Tenn., $2.00; Middle Fork church, Ind., $13.57. Interest from endowment notes, $10.75; interest from loans of mission fund, $2.63; interest from loans of endowment fund, $52 50.

SUMMARY.

Receipts for November, 1891,.... $177 53
Receipts for November, 1892,.... $664 47
　　　　　　　　　　　　　　　　—————
　Increase,.......................... $486 94
Total receipts for year to close of
　Nov. 30, '91.............. $2,644 89
Total receipts for year to close of
　Nov. 30, '92.............. $5,186 81
　　　　　　　　　　　　　　　　—————
　Increase,.......................... $2,541 92

THE INTERIOR OF THE EARTH.

PROF. R. E. Thompson, S. T. D, in The Sunday School Times says:

"In the discussion of the future of our planet, there is a frequent reference to the supposition that the center of the earth is 'a sea of molten fire,' which may break out any day in a destructive flood. This supposed fact is appealed to in theological discussions connected with the Second Advent, and applied by way of parable to the social condition of the race. It is said that at any moment these fires might break forth to the ruin of the fair fabric of the globe. Also that in moral matters we are treading upon the thin crust of conventional proprieties and restraints, which may give way at any moment and plunge us into ruin.

"What are the facts? It is true that as we go down toward the earth's center, we find everywhere a higher degree of heat than on the surface, and that when we have reached a great depth, the heat becomes nearly unbearable. It is safe to assume that if we went farther, we should find such a heat as would make animal and vegetable life impossible. It also is true that at various points on the surface of the globe we observe violent eruptions, which pour forth great masses of molten material, sometimes to such an extent as to build up whole islands, Iceland being the most notable instance of this. It also is true that these eruptions resemble each other so much in their manner and in the volcanic material they cast up, as to suggest a common cause at work at points so distant from each other as Iceland, Java, and Sicily.

"This, however, does not necessitate the opinion that the interior of the earth is 'a sea of molten fire.' If it were so, Sir William Thomson has shown, by the operation of such a fluid mass, the outer crust, even though that were as rigid as steel, would have been first drawn out of its spheroidal shape by the strain the fluid contents would occasion, and then would have been burst into fragments during its passage round its orbit. And this even if the crust were two or three hundred miles in thickness.

"That the center of the earth is at a very high degree of heat is hardly open to doubt. Evidently we live on a planet which has been cooled off superficially, while the interior still retains the degree of heat which once characterized the whole. But a very high degree of heat does not necessitate a molten condition. In order to melt, a heated body must be set free from superincumbent pressure, as in order to burn, it must be brought into contact with a supply of oxygen. The center of the earth, therefore, may be as solid, dark, and destitute of incandescence, as any part of its surface, and yet possess a degree of heat which would produce melting and incandescence on the surface.

"This is the view now generally taken of the earth's interior. Under the pressure of the superincumbent crust, which has cooled off, the interior can neither incandesce nor melt. But if at any point and in any way this pressure should be removed, a small part of the interior will melt at once, and pour itself upward to the surface through the vent thus furnished. But nothing less than the destruction of the present crust could bring the whole earth into that condition; and when it attained to it, it would begin afresh to cool off into a firm crust, under which the process of melting would be again restrained.

"There is yet another theory of volcanic action, which is held by some scientific men. It is that in the interior strata are found great masses of metal like sodium, which ignite at once when brought into contact with water. It is alleged that volcanoes are almost confined to the points where sea and land touch each other, or to the open sea. It is supposed, therefore, that the percolation of water downward has reached those deposits, and has produced a disturbance by violent eruptions. This is the chemical theory of volcanic eruption, and it has the advantage of explaining why volcanic action is so constant in certain places, why it always appears near the water-line, and why volcanic action has ceased entirely in districts where it once was prevalent. In such areas the chemical process is complete.

"It is noteworthy that, while heat increases as we pass downward, it increases very irregularly, being less at some deeper points on the same line of descent than at points nearer the surface."

"WHY."

BY FANNY MORROW.

Why will people, who claim to be thoughtful reasoners, say they believe Jesus Christ to have been a Good Man, a Perfect Example, a Medium of Light and Wisdom to the people of this world and also that he taught the best, the most perfect code of morals, ever given to the human family, and yet declare they cannot believe in his divinity? This class of people profess to believe in the immortality of the soul. They say the wisest thing a man can do in this world is to prepare for the future life. According to the wisdom of this world they are seeking after truth and light, but refuse to believe the God-given light of Truth. Why do they not see that, if Christ was a good man, he must have been what he claimed to be.

Let us examine his own testimony concerning himself. In Matt. 3 we read of Christ's baptism. A voice from heaven said, "This is my beloved Son in whom I am well pleased." In Matt. 16, Simon Peter said, "Thou art the Christ, the Son of the Living God." Jesus answered, "Blessed art thou, Simon Bar-Jonah. Flesh and blood hath not revealed it unto thee, but my Father which is in heaven." In the first case Christ does not deny, and in the latter he affirms the assertion.

In John 5 we learn that the Jews sought to stone Christ because he made himself equal with God. In John 10 Jesus says, speaking to the fault-finding Jews, "Say ye of him whom the Father sanctified and sent into the world, Thou blasphemest because I said, I am the Son of God?"

Dear reader, we will ask you to carefully consider the following: Did you ever hear of any human being having an existence prior to his earthly life? Christ said, "Before Abraham was I am." And again, "I came down from heaven; what and if ye shall see the Son of man ascending, up where He was before?" He also offered this prayer, "O Father, glorify thou me with thine own self with the glory which I had with thee before the world was." So, by the very words of the Christ, we prove he had an existence prior to his earthly life, and upon that ground he was equal to God.

Why is it that people who would be shocked to call Christ an impostor, will, in the face of such evidence, say they cannot believe in his divinity? Here is still more testimony. John says, "In the beginning was the Word and the Word was with God, and the Word was God." In John was life, and the life was the light of men."

In the above quotation, the personal pronoun him must refer to Word for its antecedent, so, then, Word represents a person, NOT a book, or any other object. Very plain it seems, that Word in this place means Christ. He says, in John 8, "I am the light of the world. He that followeth me, need not walk in darkness but shall have the light of life." Why, O why, cannot all, who desire life everlasting, follow Christ as he declares the way? Then none need walk in darkness.

People who would never think of insulting an honest man by telling him they could not believe the half he told them, can pick flaws in the Written Word, and want to believe only a part. They say they believe God is a wise and beneficent Being, who would not cast man upon the sea of life without a guide or compass. They admit the Bible to be that compass, pointing man to heaven, yet they choose to believe and obey only a part of that Bible.

I ask, would an allwise God give any unnecessary rules or imperfect commands? Why will frail, fallible man try to change or improve upon the inspired Word of God?

Ottawa, Kans.

"There is no greater mistake than to suppose that Christians can impress the world by agreeing with it. It is not conformity that we want; it is not being able to beat the world in its own way; but it is to stand apart from and above it, and to produce the impression of a holy and separate life,"

privileges are for

s of safety. And is! To how many used in this world al But here is "a w from the heat ones is as a storm

ty. Dangers may his people only at eigning may menod's elect. They ions of Satan, safe re incident to hur. We are taught fear; because fear is not made perthose things that iction of the Master which he deshe shall be sub-

conferred upon the iosen generation. nd foreigners but and of the houseve all the rights children. A free e is not compelled prisoner confined ors are not barred out at pleasure. aving once entered ons of the Gospel, What boundless le to him! What y be his! What nfolded to him as o the mysteries of on! Here, indeed, the soul, the most

—he need not comod, as revealed by ire, as seen in the i beneath, speak to n of God. To him t God; and the firork. To him the iands, proclaiming , both on the sea il, cultured Christh. Kindness and d. Harmony and ere, too, the cultipasture,—food for out and find past.

Christ, and if
or its god some-
the Bible; there-
from Mt. Sinai,
a Christ,
between Masonry
on the spirit of

S PEOPLE

ter, he shall be saved,
."—John 10:9.

and advantage of
may be said with
,—that it is much
profitable unto all
life that now is,
truly the child of
privileges are for-

e of safety. And
is! To how many
ceed in this world
al But here is "a
w from the heat
ones is as a storm

ty. Dangers may
his people only at
signing may men-
od's elect. They
ions of Satan, safe
re inclined to hu-
r. We are taught
fear; because fear
is not made per-
those things that
action of the Mas-
fter which he de-
she shall be sub-

onferred upon the
hosen generation.
nd foreigners but
and of the house-
ave all the rights
children. A free
e is not compelled
prisoner confined
ors are not barred
out at pleasure.
aving once entered
ons of the Gospel,
What boundless
ble to him! What
ay be his! What
unfolded to him as
o the mysteries of
on! Here, indeed,
the soul, the meat

—he need not con-
oil, as revealed by
ors, as seen in the
a beneath, speak to
n of God. To him
d God; and the fir-
ork. To him the
hands, proclaiming
, both on the sea
al, cultured Chris-
sh. Kindness and
d. Harmony and
ere, too, the culti-
pastore,—food for
ent and find past-

All things are his

All things are his, both in the realm of grace
and in the realm of nature. In this world the
Christian may have a foretaste of heaven. Here
rich feasts are provided for him, and as he investigates, new beauties, new wonders are ever unfolded to him.

RECEIPTS OF GENERAL MISSIONARY COMMIT-TEE FOR NOVEMBER, 1892.

A brother, Ill., $4; Aunt Etta, Bremen, Ind., $1;
a brother in Christ, Sidney, Nebr., $2.70; Will-
iam's Creek church, Tex., $12.50; John C. and
Mary E. Franz, $5; Mr. and Mrs. Slater, Flagg
Centre, Ill., $1.25; Wolf Creek church, Ohio, $12.-
05; Good Hope church, Kans, $1.00; J. E. Gnag-
ey, Accident, Md., $10; Marsh Creek church, Pa.,
$3.50; two sisters, Oklahoma, $2; Tropico church,
Cal., $6.20; Loramie's church, Ohio, $3.80; Stony
Creek S. S., Ind., $4.05; Monitor church, Kans.,
$2; Harriet Reed, Easton, W. Va., $10; O. W.
Reed, Easton, W. Va., $1; M. W. Reed, Easton,
W. Va., $10; H. Clara Reed, Easton, W. Va., $2;
Mrs. Lizzie Barndollar, Everett, Pa., $5; Mrs.
Margaret Calhoun, Everett, Pa., $5; Lafayette
church, Ohio, $2.57; Pleasant Hill S. S., Ind.,
$1.90; Grundy County church, Iowa, $13.50; a sis-
ter, Pa., 75 cents; a brother and family, Louisville,
Ohio, $2.00; Long Meadow church of Beaver's
Creek congregation, Md., $5.36; Broadfording
church of Welsh Run congregation, Md., $8.75; J.
T. Dobbins, Wolcott, Ind., $1; Mary Replogle, de-
ceased, Unionville, Iowa, $5; Exeter church,
Nebr., $3; Lafayette church, Ohio, $3.60; Luther
Petry, Atlanta, Ga., $1.75; a brother, Minneapolis,
Kans., $1.04; a brother and sister, Liberty, Ohio,
$5; G. W. Fandler, Bellevue, Idaho, $1; Lizzie A.
Hope, Maudon, N. Dak., $1.05; Mrs. Abram Hook,
Mowerville, Pa., 60 cents; Mineral Creek church,
Mo., $8.50; Libertyville church, Iowa, $5; Lick
Creek church, Ohio, $13; a sister in Christ, Phila-
delphia, Pa., $1; J. Henry and Emma Showalter,
Johnson City, Tenn., $2.00; Middle Fork church,
Ind., $13.57. Interest from endowment notes,
$10.75; interest from loans of mission fund, $2.63;
interest from loans of endowment fund, $52.50.

SUMMARY.

Receipts for November, 1891,....	$177 53
Receipts for November, 1892,....	$684 47
Increase,..............................	$486 94
Total receipts for year to close of	
Nov. 30, '91,.............	$2,644 80
Total receipts for year to close of	
Nov. 30, '92,.............	$5,186 91
Increase,..............................	$2,541 92

THE INTERIOR OF THE EARTH.

PROF. R. E. Thompson, S. T. D., in *The Sunday
School Times* says:

"In the discussion of the future of our planet,
there is a frequent reference to the supposition
that the center of the earth is 'a sea of molten fire,'
which may break out any day in a destructive flood.
This supposed fact is appealed to in theological
discussions connected with the Second Advent,
and applied by way of parable to the social condition of the race. It is said that at any moment
these fires might break forth to the ruin of the
fair fabric of the globe. Also that in moral matters we are treading upon the thin crust of conventional proprieties and restraints, which may
give way at any moment and plunge us into ruin.

"What are the facts? It is true that as we go
down toward the earth's center, we find every-
where a higher degree of heat than on the
surface, and that when we have reached a
great depth, the heat becomes nearly unbearable.
It is safe to assume that if we went farther, we
should find such a heat as would make animal and

vegetable life impossible. It also is true that at
various points on the surface of the globe we observe violent eruptions, which pour forth great
masses of molten material, sometimes to such an
extent as to build up whole islands, Iceland being
the most notable instance of this. It also is true
that these eruptions resemble each other so much
in their manner and in the volcanic material they
cast up, as to suggest a common cause at work at
points so distant from each other as Iceland, Java,
and Sicily.

"This, however, does not necessitate the opinion that the interior of the earth is 'a sea of molten fire.' If it were so, Sir William Thomson
has shown, by the operation of such a fluid mass,
the outer crust, even though that were as rigid as
steel, would have been first drawn out of its spheroidal shape by the strain the fluid contents would
occasion, and then would have been burst into
fragments during its passage round its orbit. And
this even if the crust were two or three hundred
miles in thickness.

"That the center of the earth is at a very high
degree of heat is hardly open to doubt. Evidently we live on a planet which has been cooled off
superficially, while the interior still retains the
degree of heat which once characterized the
whole. But a very high degree of heat does not
necessitate a molten condition. In order to melt, a
heated body must be set free from superincumbent
pressure, as in order to burn, it must be brought
into contact with a supply of oxygen. The center of the earth, therefore, may be as solid, dark,
and destitute of incandescence, as any part of its
surface, and yet possess a degree of heat which
would produce melting and incandescence on the
surface.

"This is the view now generally taken of the
earth's interior. Under the pressure of the superincumbent crust, which has cooled off, the interior
can neither incandesce nor melt. But if at any
point and in any way this pressure should be removed, a small part of the interior will melt at
once, and pour itself upward to the surface
through the vent thus furnished. But nothing
less than the destruction of the present crust could
bring the whole earth into that condition; and
when it attained to it, it would begin afresh to
cool off into a firm crust, under which the process
of melting would be again restrained.

"There is yet another theory of volcanic action,
which is held by some scientific men. It is that
in the interior strata are found great masses of
metal like sodium, which ignite at once when
brought into contact with water. It is alleged
that volcanoes are almost confined to the points
where sea and land touch each other, or to the
open sea. It is supposed, therefore, that the percolation of water downward has reached those deposits, and has produced a disturbance by violent
eruptions. This is the chemical theory of volcanic eruption, and it has the advantage of explaining why volcanic action is so constant in certain places, why it always appears near the water-
line, and why volcanic action has ceased entirely
in districts where it once was prevalent. In such
areas the chemical process is complete.

"It is noteworthy that, while heat increases as
we pass downward, it increases very irregularly,
being less at some deeper points on the same line
of descent than at points nearer the surface."

"WHY."

BY FANNY MORROW.

WHY will people, who claim to be thoughtful
reasoners, say they believe Jesus Christ to have
been a Good Man, a Perfect Example, a Medium
of Light and Wisdom to the people of this world

and also that he taught the best, the most perfect
code of morals, ever given to the human family,
and yet declare they cannot believe in his divinity? This class of people profess to believe in the
immortality of the soul. They say the wisest
thing a man can do in this world is to prepare for
the future life. According to the wisdom of this
world they are seeking after truth and light, but
refuse to believe the God-given light of Truth.
Why do they not see that, if Christ was a *good*
man, he must have been that he claimed to be.

Let us examine his own testimony concerning
himself. In Matt. 3 we read of Christ's baptism.
A voice from heaven said, "This is my beloved
Son in whom I am well pleased." In Matt. 16,
Simon Peter said, "Thou art the Christ, the Son
of the Living God." Jesus answered, "Blessed
art thou, Simon Bar-Jonah. Flesh and blood
hath not revealed it unto thee, but my Father
which is in heaven." In the first case Christ does
not deny, and in the latter he affirms the assertion.

In John 5 we learn that the Jews sought to
stone Christ because he made himself equal with
God. In John 10 Jesus says, speaking to the
fault-finding Jews, "Say ye of him whom the
Father sanctified and sent into the world, Thou
blasphemest, because I said, I am the Son of God?"

Dear reader, we will ask you to carefully consider the following: Did you ever hear of any
human being having an existence prior to this
earthly life? Christ said, "Before Abraham was
I am." And again, "I came down from heaven;
what and if ye shall see the Son of man ascending
up *where He was before?*" He also offered this
prayer, "O Father, glorify thou me with thine
own self with the glory which I had with thee before the world was." So, by the very words of the
Christ, we prove he had an existence prior to his
earthly life, and upon that ground he was equal
to God.

Why is it that people who would be shocked to
call Christ an impostor, will, in the face of such
evidence, say they cannot believe in his divinity?
Here is still more testimony. John says, "In the
beginning was the Word and the Word was with
God; and the Word was God. In him was life,
and the life was the light of men."

In the above quotation, the personal pronoun
him must refer to Word for its antecedent, so,
then, *Word* represents a person, NOT a book, or
any other object. Very plain it seems, that *Word*
in this place means Christ. He says, in John 8,
"I am the light of the world. He that followeth
me, need not walk in darkness but shall have the
light of life." Why, O why, cannot all, who desire life everlasting, follow Christ as he declares
the way? Then none need walk in darkness.

People who would never think of insulting an
honest man by telling him they could not believe
the half he told them, can pick flaws in the Written
Word, and want to believe only a part. They say
they believe God is a wise and beneficent Being,
who would not cast man upon the sea of life without a guide or compass. They admit the Bible to
be that compass, pointing man to heaven, yet
they choose to believe and obey only a part of
that Bible.

I ask, would an allwise God give any *unnecessary* rules or imperfect commands? Why will
frail, fallible man try to change or improve upon
the inspired Word of God?

Ottawa, Kans.

"THERE is no greater mistake than to suppose
that Christians can impress the world by agreeing
with it. It is not conformity that we want; it is
not being able to beat the world in its own way;
but it is to stand apart from and above it, and to
produce the impression of a holy and separate
life."

The Gospel Messenger,

A Weekly at $1.50 Per Annum.

PUBLISHED BY

The Brethren's Publishing Co.

D. L. MILLER,	Editor.
J. H. MOORE,	Office Editor.
J. B. BRUMBAUGH,	Associate Editors.
J. G. ROYER,	
JOSEPH AMICK,	Business Manager.

ADVISORY COMMITTEE.
L. W. Teeter, A. Hutchison, Daniel Hays.

☞ Communications for publication should be legibly written with black ink on one side of the paper only. Do not attempt to interline, or to put on one page what ought to occupy two.

☞ Anonymous communications will not be published.

☞ Do not mix business with articles for publication. Keep your communications on separate sheets from all business.

☞ Time is precious. We always have time to attend to business and to answer questions of importance, but please do not subject us to need less answering of letters.

☞ The MESSENGER is mailed each week to all subscribers. If the address is correctly entered on our list, the paper must reach the person to whom it is addressed. If you do not get your paper, write us, giving particulars.

☞ When changing your address, please give your former as well as your future address in full, so as to avoid delay and misunderstanding.

☞ Always remit to the office from which you order your goods, no matter from where you receive them.

☞ Do not send personal checks or drafts on interior banks, unless you send with them 25 cents each, to pay for collection.

☞ Remittances should be made by Post-office Money Order, Drafts on New York, Philadelphia or Chicago, or Registered Letters, made payable, and addressed to "Brethren's Publishing Co., Mount Morris, Ill.," or "Brethren's Publishing Co., Huntingdon, Pa."

☞ Entered at the Post-office at Mount Morris, Ill., as second-class matter.

Mount Morris, Ill., - - - - Dec. 20, 1892.

BRO. DANIEL VANIMAN is expected home from California this week. His trip has been full of interest and earnest work.

BRETHREN D. L. MILLER and J. C. Lahman may now be addressed at Cairo, Egypt, in care of Thomas Cook & Son. Each letter to this address will require five cents postage.

THE 4th of this month Bro. John Sherfy closed a series of meetings in the Cedar Creek church, Kans., with fifteen additions. Thirteen of them were by baptism. The other two were reclaimed.

BRO. H. R. TAYLOR, of Deep River, Iowa, writes that his health is much better than it was while in Colorado. He feels truly grateful to the members for the kindness shown him while with them.

BRO. ANDREW HUTCHISON closed his two weeks' meetings in Cedar Rapids with two additions. He is now at Garrison, Iowa, expecting to remain ten days or more, but was not well when last heard from.

THE Greenland church, Grant Co., W. Va., has been favored with a number of meetings for a month or more past, resulting in twenty-one additions to the church. The church is greatly revived and encouraged to continue in its good work.

THE feast at Mexico, Ind., is appointed for Dec. 28, commencing at 2 P. M. The Brethren expect to have their new house completed and ready to dedicate by the 18th. Bro. J. W. Wright is expected to hold a series of meetings there, commencing immediately after the feast.

THIS item of news from Bro. C. C. Root reads a little different from the general rule. We certainly do hope the MESSENGER will prove a great help to the converts: "I just closed a series of meetings in Pottawatomie County, Kans., with four additions by baptism and six subscribers to the GOSPEL MESSENGER, with good prospects for the opening of a good work there in the near future."

BRO. JOSEPH L. MYERS, of Yale Iowa, is now visiting among the churches in Northern Illinois. He is also preparing to attend the Bible Term.

BRO. H. C. EARLY has lately been doing some excellent preaching in the Antietam congregation, Pa. His meetings closed with eighteen additions to the church, and great rejoicing among the saints.

BRO. ALEXANDER MILLER, of Nappanee, Ind., gave us a short call last week. He was on his way home from an extended tour through Kansas and Nebraska. He seems very much pleased with the West.

WRITING from Oswego, Ind., under date of Dec. 8, Bro. A. H. Puterbaugh says, "We are gaining slowly in the Washington church. Two more were baptized recently. The future looks favorable for us."

PRIMITIVE Christianity is prospering in Northeastern Kansas encouragingly of late. About one-hundred have been added to the church since the first of October last, with indications of the ingathering continuing.

BRO. W. Q. CALVERT has just closed a two weeks' meeting at the Lost Creek church, Miami Co., Ohio. He is now engaged in a meeting at Dawson, Shelby County, same State, expecting to continue until Christmas.

BRO. D. E. BRUBAKER reports a pleasant visit with the Brethren at Roanoke, Ill., but on account of very muddy roads his meetings were not largely attended. He speaks very highly of the zeal and enterprise of the members in that congregation.

THE program of the Ministerial Meeting of Northern Illinois, to be held in the Arnold's Grove church, May 2, 1893, has been published and mailed to all the congregations in the District. Fifteen copies were mailed to each congregation, to be distributed among the ministers, and others interested in the work. Additional copies may be had on receipt of stamp.

MOST of our subscribers are procured by agents, who not only send in the names, but collect the money and settle the account with us. On receiving a list of names it is our custom to charge the whole amount to the agent sending the names, mark the names paid on the mailing galleys and then look to the agent for our pay. As the agent sends in money we give him credit. We also instruct agents to take no subscriptions for which they do not receive the cash, or are willing to stand good for. One of our good agents has had a sad experience however. After securing another person to take his place as agent, he writes: "I give up the work because of the very unpleasant duty of reminding the members that they have not paid their subscriptions for several years, and to-day one brother owes me for 1888, '89, '90, '91 and '92. He is able but slow." Probably we have one hundred agents who have to perform the unpleasant duty of reminding the members that their subscriptions are unpaid, and in scores of instances agents have lost money, for rather than see us lose so much, they pay it out of their own pockets. This way of treating agents is certainly not right; it is not honorable. A member who subscribes for a paper and receives it week after week ought to pay for it, and we trust that all who are yet indebted to agents for subscriptions, almanacs and books, will go to them and settle the account at once. That kind of a debt is just as much of a debt as any other. It is pleasant to act as agent where all the members pay up promptly, but where they do not, it is just the reverse.

BRO. B. F. MILLER has returned from his farm in Dakota, and may now be addressed at Dallas Centre, Iowa. He expects to spend the winter preaching in Iowa and Illinois.

ON a postal, under date of Dec. 5, Bro. Silas Hoover says, "I am at present engaged in a series of meetings at the Hade church, in the Falling Spring District, Franklin County, Pa. The congregations are large and increasing. Yesterday four were baptized."

AFTER reading sister Underhill's suggestions concerning suitable Christmas presents, do not forget to give your preacher some good books. Books he needs, and they will do him good. If they are the right kind of works, you will get the value of them back in his improved preaching. He charges you nothing for his preaching, though it often costs him both money and time,—it is a free gift, and it is no more than proper that you should in some way "give good gifts" unto him.

CHRISTMAS will soon be here. It is usually celebrated as the Savior's birthday. The popular belief is that he was born on that day. This belief may be correct, or it may not. At the time of the Savior's birth the shepherds were in the fields, watching over their flocks by night. In the Land of Palestine there is some winter, and shepherds do not remain out in the fields with their flocks that late in the season. They usually return to their homes in October. It is more than likely that the Savior was born sometime in October. But let that be as it may. Christmas will soon be here and we are glad of it. It is a day of general rejoicing in all Christian lands. On that day we give gifts one to another, and especially do we favor those of our kindred with presents. The habit is a good one, but we fear that it is greatly abused. More money is squandered on Christmas than any other day in the year. To give the little ones toys and other things suited to their age and enjoyment, tends to cheer their hearts and let into their little souls the sunshine of life. While they are children we may expect them to act as children, and we should treat them as such; but there is no necessity of running into the extravagance that characterizes most well-to-do families. The presenting of useful gifts at Christmas is in keeping with Christian privileges and propriety, but the tendency is to run into extravagance. This year our people will probably spend over $30,000 foolishly for Christmas presents, and during the entire year not give more than $10,000 to Jesus for preaching the Gospel. This shows how much greater hold foolishness has on our pocketbooks than the love of common humanity. The man who can spend one dollar for unnecessary presents, and then throw in thirty cents for the missionary cause, shows at once where his heart is. We often wait until the time of love-feasts for self-examination. Perhaps right now is as good a time as any for careful examination of our hearts, money purses, Christmas presents and our missionary contributions. Were all of our members to do this, more than likely our Mission Board would receive a few thousand dollars "conscience money."

A LOOK AT THE PAST.

THE year 1892 is drawing to a close. Only a few more days and the year will be ended, and the record of the same securely sealed. It was not possible for us to see the end from the beginning, but it is now within our power to review our actions during the year from the beginning to the

The Gospel Messenger,

A Weekly at $1.50 Per Annum.

PUBLISHED BY

The Brethren's Publishing Co.

D. L. MILLER, ... Editor.
J. H. MOORE, ... Office Editor.
J. B. BRUMBAUGH, } . . . . . Associate Editors.
J. G. ROYER, }
JOSEPH AMICK, ... Business Manager.

ADVISORY COMMITTEE.
L. W. Teeter, A. Hutchison, Daniel Hays.

☞Communications for publication should be legibly written with black ink on one side of the paper only. Do not attempt to interline, or to put on one page what ought to occupy two.

☞Anonymous communications will not be published.

☞Do not mix business with articles for publication. Keep your communications on separate sheets from all business.

☞Time is precious. We always have time to attend to business and to answer questions of importance, but please do not subject us to need less answering of letters.

☞The MESSENGER is mailed each week to all subscribers. If the address is correctly entered on our list, the paper must reach the person to whom it is addressed. If you do not get your paper, write us, giving particulars.

☞When changing your address, please give your former as well as your future address in full, so as to avoid delay and misunderstanding.

☞Always remit to the office from which you order your goods, no matter from where you receive them.

☞Do not send personal checks or drafts on interior banks, unless you send with them 25 cents each, to pay for collection.

☞Remittances should be made by Post-office Money Order, Drafts on New York, Philadelphia or Chicago, or Registered Letters, made payable and addressed to "Brethren's Publishing Co., Mount Morris, Ill.," or "Brethren's Publishing Co., Huntingdon, Pa."

☞Entered at the Post-office at Mount Morris, Ill., as second-class matter.

Mount Morris, Ill., - - - - Dec. 20, 1892.

BRO. DANIEL VANIMAN is expected home from California this week. His trip has been full of interest and earnest work.

BRETHREN D. L. MILLER and J. C. LEHMAN may now be addressed at Cairo, Egypt, in care of Thomas Cook & Son. Each letter to this address will require five cents postage.

THE 4th of this month Bro. John Sherfy closed a series of meetings in the Cedar Creek church, Kans., with fifteen additions. Thirteen of them were by baptism. The other two were reclaimed.

BRO. H. R. TAYLOR, of Deep River, Iowa, writes that his health is much better than it was while in Colorado. He feels truly grateful to the members for the kindness shown him while with them.

BRO. ANDREW HUTCHISON closed his two weeks' meetings in Cedar Rapids with two additions. He is now at Garrison, Iowa, expecting to remain ten days or more, but was not well when last heard from.

THE Green'and church, Grant Co., W. Va., has been favored with a number of meetings for a month or more past, resulting in twenty-one additions to the church. The church is greatly revived and encouraged to continue in its good work.

THE feast at Mexico, Ind., is appointed for Dec. 28, commencing at 2 P. M. The Brethren expect to have their new house completed and ready to dedicate by the 18th. Bro. J. W. Wright is expected to hold a series of meetings there, commencing immediately after the feast.

THIS item of news from Bro. C. C. Root reads a little different from the general rule. We certainly do hope the MESSENGER will prove a great help to the converts: "I just closed a series of meetings in Pottawatomie County, Kans., with four additions by baptism and six subscribers for the GOSPEL MESSENGER, with good prospects for the opening of a good work there in the near future."

BRO. JOSEPH L. MYERS, of Yale Iowa, is now visiting among the churches in Northern Illinois. He is also preparing to attend the Bible Term.

BRO. H. C. EARLY has lately been doing some excellent preaching in the Antietam congregation, Pa. His meetings closed with eighteen additions to the church, and great rejoicing among the saints.

BRO. ALEXANDER MILLER, of Nappanee, Ind., gave us a short call last week. He was on his way home from an extended tour through Kansas and Nebraska. He seems very much pleased with the West.

WRITING from Oswego, Ind., under date of Dec. 8, Bro. A. H. Puterbaugh says, "We are gaining slowly in the Washington church. Two more were baptized recently. The future looks favorable for us."

PRIMITIVE Christianity is prospering in Northeastern Kansas encouragingly of late. About one hundred have been added to the church since the first of October last, with indications of the ingathering continuing.

BRO. W. Q. CALVERT has just closed a two weeks' meeting at the Lost Creek church, Miami Co., Ohio. He is now engaged in a meeting at Dawson, Shelby County, same State, expecting to continue until Christmas.

BRO. D. E. BRUBAKER reports a pleasant visit with the Brethren at Roanoke, Ill., but on account of very muddy roads his meetings were not largely attended. He speaks very highly of the zeal and enterprise of the members in that congregation.

THE program of the Ministerial Meeting of Northern Illinois, to be held in the Arnold's Grove church, May 2, 1893, has been published and mailed to all the congregations in the District. Fifteen copies were mailed to each congregation, to be distributed among the ministers, and others interested in the work. Additional copies may be had on receipt of stamp.

MOST of our subscribers are procured by agents, who not only send in the names, but collect the money and settle the account with us. On receiving a list of names it is our custom to charge the whole amount to the agent sending the names, mark the names paid on the mailing galleys and then look to the agent for our pay. As the agent sends in money we give him credit. We also instruct agents to take no subscriptions for which they do not receive the cash, or are willing to stand good for. One of our good agents has had a sad experience however. After securing another person to take his place as agent, he writes: "I give up the work because of the very unpleasant duty of reminding the members that they have not paid their subscriptions for several years, and to-day one brother owes me for 1888, '89, '90, '91 and '92. He is able but slow." Probably we have one hundred agents who have to perform the unpleasant duty of reminding the members that their subscriptions are unpaid, and in scores of instances agents have lost money, for rather than see us lose so much, they pay it out of their own pockets. This way of treating agents is certainly not right; it is not honorable. A member who subscribes for a paper and receives it week after week ought to pay for it, and we trust that all who are yet indebted to agents for subscriptions, almanacs and books, will go to them and settle the account at once. That kind of a debt is just as much of a debt as any other. It is pleasant to act as agent where all the members pay up promptly, but where they do not, it is just the reverse.

BRO. B. F. MILLER has returned from his farm in Dakota, and may now be addressed at Dallas Centre, Iowa. He expects to spend the winter preaching in Iowa and Illinois.

ON a postal, under date of Dec. 5, Bro. Silas Hoover says, "I am at present engaged in a series of meetings at the Hade church, in the Falling Spring District, Franklin County, Pa. The congregations are large and increasing. Yesterday four were baptized."

AFTER reading sister Underhill's suggestions concerning suitable Christmas presents, do not forget to give your preacher some good books. Books he needs, and they will do him good. If they are the right kind of works, you will get the value of them back in his improved preaching. He charges you nothing for his preaching,—it is a free gift, and it is no more than proper that you should in some way "give good gifts" unto him.

CHRISTMAS will soon be here. It is usually celebrated as the Savior's birthday. The popular belief is that he was born on that day. This belief may be correct, or it may not. At the time of the Savior's birth the shepherds were in the fields, watching over their flocks by night. In the Land of Palestine there is some winter, and shepherds do not remain out in the fields with their flocks that late in the season. They usually return to their homes in October. It is more than likely that the Savior was born sometime in October. But let that be as it may. Christmas will soon be here and we are glad of it. It is a day of general rejoicing in all Christian lands. On that day we give gifts one to another, and especially do we favor those of one kindred with presents. The habit is good one, but we fear that it is greatly abused. More money is squandered on Christmas than any other day in the year. To give the little ones toys and other things suited to their age and enjoyment, tends to cheer their hearts and let into their little souls the sunshine of life. While they are children we may expect them to act as children, and we should treat them as such, but there is no necessity of running into the extravagance that characterizes most well-to-do families. The presenting of useful gifts at Christmas is in keeping with Christian privilege and propriety, but the tendency is to run into extravagance. This year our people will probably spend over $30,000 foolishly for Christmas presents, and during the entire year not give more than $10,000 to Jesus for preaching the Gospel. This shows how much greater hold foolishness has on our pocketbooks than the love of common humanity. The man who can spend one dollar for unnecessary presents, and then throw in thirty cents for the missionary cause, shows at once where his heart is. We often wait until the time of love-feasts for self-examination. Perhaps right now is as good a time as any for careful examination of our hearts, money purses, Christmas presents and our missionary contributions. Were all of our members to do this, more than likely our Mission Board would receive a few thousand dollars "conscience money."

A LOOK AT THE PAST.

THE year 1892 is drawing to a close. Only a few more days and the year will be ended, and the record of the same securely sealed. It was not possible for us to see the end from the beginning, but it is now within our power to review our actions during the year from the beginning to the

behind the western clouds, bathing sea and sky with the tints of red and gold, preparations were made to give the lifeless form to the waves. A platform was fastened to the side of the ship, and all the arrangements were completed. It was sad to think of this burial, and of the stricken hearts in that far-away New England home when the news should reach them of the death and burial of their only son. At the last moment the efforts of some of the passengers were successful. They guaranteed the payment of all expenses, the-body was embalmed and will be carried to Genoa, and then be sent back to New York.

This act of loving-kindness on the part of strangers makes our faith stronger in humanity. It is one of those acts so wholly unselfish and disinterested that comes only from a desire to obey the golden rule, and it shall in no wise lose its reward. And so, at the last moment, the sea was robbed of its prey, and the friends at home will have the sorrowful satisfaction of laying the body of their boy in the family tomb.

He was the only son and the only child; the joy of a mother's heart, the hope of a father's declining years, gone never to return again. In that home father and mother are waiting anxiously for news from their boy, and when the cable shall flash the news back from the shores of Spain, it will carry a sad, sad story, for to them

"The wind of the sea is the waft of death,
The waves are singing a song of woe;
By silent river, by moaning sea,
Long and vain shall the watching be;
Never again shall the sweet voice call,
Never the white hand rise and fall!"

We turn away from this sad picture with heart-felt sympathy for the stricken home. But the impression made by the sudden appearance of death in our midst left an impression upon all that will not soon be forgotten. Surely, in the midst of life, we are in death!

By planning our present trip to the "Bible Lands," we aimed to take the most direct route from New York to Port Said, Egypt. Instead of going to Northern Europe, we took a more southerly course which will carry us by the Azores Islands to the Strait of Gibraltar. Heretofore we have landed at Bremen, Germany, 52° North Latitude. On this trip we shall catch our first glimpse of the Eastern Continent when we sight Cape St. Vincent, the southern point of Portugal, fifteen degrees south of Bremen.

Two points are gained in taking this southern route. We gain time. We are anxious to spend as much of the winter and spring in Egypt and Palestine as possible. The other point, not so important but not to be overlooked, is, that by taking the southern route we escape the heavy winter storms of the North Atlantic. Having had an experience last December, as to what a winter hurricane on the ocean means, we have no desire to try another. Our curiosity in that direction has been more than satisfied.

At this writing, Nov. 21, having been at sea nine days, we can say that our anticipation of a pleasant voyage has thus far been fully realized. The weather has been delightfully pleasant. Sunshine and clear skies, with warm, balmy breezes have been the order of the days as they have gone by. It has been altogether one of the finest of our five Atlantic voyages. For two days we had the swells of the ocean, caused by a great storm that passed north of us, and we were liter-

ally "rocked in the cradle of the deep." Judging from the great, heaving swells that bore down upon us, the storm to the North must have been very severe. We were glad to escape with only two days of rocking and rolling.

When the swells were heaviest, we were standing on deck, looking over the rail at the dark waters below. A number of passengers, ladies mostly, were sitting in steamer chairs, ranged along and fastened to the inner and upper side of the deck. The chairs are made on the principle of an invalid's extension chair so that, when sitting down, one is in a half-reclining posture. The passengers were enjoying the refreshing evening breeze, and were protected by having heavy shawls or traveling blankets thrown over the lower part of the body. Suddenly a mighty swell bore down upon the ship and she rolled over until the deck stood at an angle of at least forty-five degrees. As a result the luckless passengers slid from their chairs down the inclined deck and piled up at the ship's railing. A good deal of screaming was heard, but fortunately no one was injured. After this incident the deck was very soon deserted.

Bro. Lahman proves to be a good seaman, having suffered very little from seasickness and seems to enjoy his first ocean voyage quite well. Barring the sad incident referred to at the beginning of our voyage, our journey thus far has been as pleasant as could be hoped for under the circumstances. We thank the Lord for his protecting care over us, and trust to him for a continuance of the blessings which we have thus far enjoyed.

To-day we cast anchor in the open roadstead off the Rock of Gibraltar, and our Atlantic voyage is ended. We have a thousand miles or less to sail on the Mediterranean before reaching Genoa, where we shall land, but here we pass from the Atlantic Ocean and sail upon the blue waters of the "Great Sea." No sooner is the anchor down than our ship is surrounded by small boats, laden with oranges, tangarines, figs and other semi-tropical fruits, and the venders call out in a jargon of English, Italian and Spanish, the price of their commodities they have for sale. At first it was a question with us as to how they were to reach the passengers who stood twenty feet above them on the deck of the ship. But the problem was soon solved. A rope was thrown up and caught by the would-be purchaser, a basket was attached, and the means of communication were at once established. The purchaser put his money into the basket, the boatman replaced it with the articles desired, and in this way a brisk trade was kept up for several hours. The Rock of Gibraltar, the strongest natural fortress in the world, is an immense cliff, composed of limestone, dense grey marble, and red sandstone, some three miles in length, 1,430 feet high, and about six miles in circumference. It fell into the hands of the English in 1704, and since then England has held the key to the Mediterranean Sea. In 1779 France and Spain besieged the Rock, and although they kept up the siege four years, were at last obliged to give it up. The garrison consists of five thousand men in times of peace, with quarters for a hundred thousand when necessity requires. A constant food supply for five years is stored away on the Rock. The hill-side is pierced with cave-like openings, from each of which the muzzle of a cannon is faintly discerned. On the highest point of the mountain is a bat-

tery of 100 ton guns. It requires 450 pounds of powder for a single charge for each of these monster implements of death and destruction.

On the west-side the rock stands on a narrow plateau, and on this and the sloping hill-side the town of Gibraltar is built. To the east the cliffs rise like giant walls from the sea. The entire aspect of the place is that of solitude and inaccessibility. It stands like a huge sentinel, keeping everlasting watch over the waters of the sea, nature's own impregnable fortress.

Hoisting anchor, we sail through the Straits with the guns of the rock frowning down upon us. To the south from ten to twenty miles away is the clearly-outlined coast of Africa where the Atlas Mountains raise a natural bulwark against the sea. Turning the point of the rock we have the coast of Spain laid out in panoramic view before us. All day we coast along these beautiful shores. The snow-covered heights of the Sierras glisten like great domes of silver in the bright sunlight. The sky is marvelously clear, and its blue tint is deepened in contrast with the darker waters of the sea. A gentle breeze, warmed by "Africa's burning sand" is borne lazily to us from the South, breaking the waters into myriads of ripples, which sparkle in the clear light of the sun, as if the diamonds of the world were set in the crest of each tiny wavelet. On such a sea, with such surroundings, one might sail on forever, forgetting the storms which lash the waters to fury and bring swift destruction to many hapless mariners. But as we write the sun drops into the western sea, leaving a pathway of glory behind him. The light fades away, the hills of Spain are seen only in dim outline as the darkness comes down over land and sea, and our day-dream is ended.

Two days and a half we sail along the shores of Spain, France, and Italy; the sea as smooth as glass, the weather most delightful, and then we cast anchor in the beautiful harbor of "Genova La Superba" as the Italians call the City of Genoa. The boat of the health officer comes alongside, and, upon hearing that we have had a death on board, says he must send the doctor to examine us in the morning. We are quarantined for the night. They remember that there were rumors of cholera at New York and are extra careful. As we have a clean bill of health we shall land early in the morning.

Here, with the close of our sea voyage, we close this letter. From Genoa we go to Rome, where we will spend a few weeks and then hurry on to Egypt. Our next letter will be from the Eternal City. We thank God and go on trusting in him.

D. L. M.

"FOUR THINGS COME NOT BACK:

The Spoken Word; the Sped Arrow; the Past Life, and the Neglected Opportunity."

EVERY one is amenable to God for the use he makes of his talents, his time, and his opportunities. We should improve them as those who must give account. Another year has passed away from us, and we are about to step into a new epoch of time. It is but right that we each ask, What have I done with the opportunities afforded me in the past year? Did I make hay while the sun shone? Did I gather roses while they bloomed? Those who properly improved opportunities as they came to them, may look back upon the work of the past year with some degree of satisfaction.

behind the western clouds, bathing sea and sky with the tints of red and gold, preparations were made to give the lifeless form to the waves. A platform was fastened to the side of the ship, and all the arrangements were completed. It was sad to think of this burial, and of the stricken hearts in that far-away New England home when the news should reach them of the death and burial of their only son. At the last moment the efforts of some of the passengers were successful. They guaranteed the payment of all expenses, the body was embalmed and will be carried to Genoa, and then be sent back to New York.

This act of loving-kindness on the part of strangers makes our faith stronger in humanity. It is one of those acts so wholly unselfish and disinterested that comes only from a desire to obey the golden rule, and it shall in no wise lose its reward. And so, at the last moment, the sea was robbed of its prey, and the friends at home will have the sorrowful satisfaction of laying the body of their boy in the family tomb.

He was the only son and the only child; the joy of a mother's heart, the hope of a father's declining years, gone never to return again. In that home father and mother are waiting anxiously for news from their boy, and when the cable shall flash the news back from the shores of Spain, it will carry a sad, sad story, for to them

"The wind of the sea is the waft of death,
The waves are singing a song of woe;
By silent river, by moaning sea,
Long and vain shall the watching be;
Never again shall the sweet voice call,
Never the white hand rise and fall!"

We turn away from this sad picture with heartfelt sympathy for the stricken home. But the impression made by the sudden appearance of death in our midst left an impression upon all that will not soon be forgotten. Surely, in the midst of life, we are in death!

By planning our present trip to the "Bible Lands," we aimed to take the most direct route from New York to Port Said, Egypt. Instead of going to Northern Europe, we took a more southerly course which will carry us by the Azores Islands to the Strait of Gibraltar. Heretofore we have landed at Bremen, Germany, 52° North Latitude. On this trip we shall catch our first glimpse of the Eastern Continent when we sight Cape St. Vincent, the southern point of Portugal, fifteen degrees south of Bremen.

Two points are gained in taking this southern route. We gain time. We are anxious to spend as much of the winter and spring in Egypt and Palestine as possible. The other point, not so important but not to be overlooked, is, that by taking the southern route we escape the heavy winter storms of the North Atlantic. Having had an experience last December, as to what a winter hurricane on the ocean means, we have no desire to try another. Our curiosity in that direction has been more than satisfied.

At this writing, Nov. 21, having been at sea nine days, we can say that our anticipation of a pleasant voyage has thus far been fully realized. The weather has been delightfully pleasant. Sunshine and clear skies, with warm, balmy breezes have been the order of the days as they have gone by. It has been altogether one of the finest of our Atlantic voyages. For two days we had the swells of the ocean, caused by a great storm that passed north of us, and we were literally "rocked in the cradle of the deep." Judging from the great, heaving swells that bore down upon us, the storm to the North must have been very severe. We were glad to escape with only two days of rocking and rolling.

When the swells were heaviest, we were standing on deck, looking over the rail at the dark waters below. A number of passengers, ladies mostly, were sitting in steamer chairs, ranged along and fastened to the inner and upper side of the deck. The chairs are made on the principle of an invalid's extension chair so that, when sitting down, one is in a half-reclining posture. The passengers were enjoying the refreshing evening breeze, and were protected by having heavy shawls or traveling blankets thrown over the lower part of the body. Suddenly a mighty swell bore down upon the ship and she rolled over until the deck stood at an angle of at least forty-five degrees. As a result the luckless passengers slid from their chairs down the inclined deck and piled up at the ship's railing. A good deal of screaming was heard, but fortunately no one was injured. After this incident the deck was very soon deserted.

Bro. Lahman proves to be a good seaman, having suffered very little from seasickness and seems to enjoy his first ocean voyage quite well. Barring the sad incident referred to at the beginning of our voyage, our journey thus far has been as pleasant as could be hoped for under the circumstances. We thank the Lord for his protecting care over us, and trust to him for a continuance of the blessings which we have thus far enjoyed.

To-day we cast anchor in the open roadstead off the Rock of Gibraltar, and our Atlantic voyage is ended. We have a thousand miles or less to sail on the Mediterranean before reaching Genoa, where we shall land, but here we pass from the Atlantic Ocean and sail upon the blue waters of the "Great Sea." No sooner is the anchor down than our ship is surrounded by small boats, laden with oranges, tangarines, figs and other semi-tropical fruits, and the venders call out in a jargon of English, Italian and Spanish, the price of their commodities they have for sale. At first it was a question with us as to how they were to reach the passengers who stood twenty feet above them on the deck of the ship. But the problem was soon solved. A rope was thrown up and caught by the would-be purchaser, a basket was attached, and the means of communication were at once established. The purchaser put his money into the basket, the boatman replaced it with the articles desired, and in this way a brisk trade was kept up for several hours. The Rock of Gibraltar, the strongest natural fortress in the world, is an immense cliff, composed of limestone, dense grey marble, and red sandstone, some three miles in length, 1,430 feet high, and about six miles in circumference. It fell into the hands of the English in 1704, and since then England has held the key to the Mediterranean Sea. In 1779 France and Spain besieged the Rock, and although they kept up the siege four years, were at last obliged to give it up. The garrison consists of five thousand men, in times of peace, with quarters for a hundred thousand when necessity requires. A constant food supply for five years is stored away on the Rock. The hill-side is pierced with cave-like openings, from each of which the muzzle of a cannon is faintly discerned. On the highest point of the mountain is a battery of 100 ton guns. It requires 450 pounds of powder for a single charge for each of these monster implements of death and destruction.

On the west-side the rock stands on a narrow plateau, and on this and the sloping hill-side the town of Gibraltar is built. To the east the cliffs rise like giant walls from the sea. The entire aspect of the place is that of solitude and inaccessibility. It stands like a huge sentinel, keeping everlasting watch over the waters of the sea, nature's own impregnable fortress.

Hoisting anchor, we sail through the Straits with the guns of the rock frowning down upon us. To the south from ten to twenty miles away is the clearly-outlined coast of Africa where the Atlas Mountains raise a natural bulwark against the sea. Turning the point of the rock we have the coast of Spain laid out in panoramic view before us. All day we coast along these beautiful shores. The snow-covered heights of the Sierras glisten like great domes of silver in the bright sunlight. The sky is marvelously clear, and its blue tint is deepened in contrast with the darker waters of the sea. A gentle breeze, warmed by "Africa's burning sand" is borne lazily to us from the South, breaking the waters into myriads of ripples, which sparkle in the clear light of the sun, as if the diamonds of the world were set in the crest of each tiny wavelet. On such a sea, with such surroundings, one might sail on forever, forgetting the storms which lash the waters to fury and bring swift destruction to many hapless mariners. But as we write the sun drops into the western sea, leaving a pathway of glory behind him. The light fades away, the hills of Spain are seen only in dim outline as the darkness comes down over land and sea, and our day-dream is ended.

Two days and a half we sail along the shores of Spain, France, and Italy; the sea as smooth as glass, the weather most delightful, and then we cast anchor in the beautiful harbor of "Genova La Superba" as the Italians call the City of Genoa. The boat of the health officer comes alongside, and, upon hearing that we have had a death on board, says he must send the doctor to examine us in the morning. We are quarantined for the night. They remember that there were rumors of cholera at New York and are extra careful. As we have a clean bill of health we shall land early in the morning.

Here, with the close of our sea voyage, we close this letter. From Genoa we go to Rome, where we will spend a few weeks and then hurry on to Egypt. Our next letter will be from the Eternal City. We thank God and go on trusting in him.

D. L. M.

"FOUR THINGS COME NOT BACK;"

The Spoken Word; the Sped Arrow; the Past Life, and the Neglected Opportunity."

EVERY one is amenable to God for the use he makes of his talents, his time, and his opportunities. We should improve them as those who must give account. Another year has passed away from us, and we are about to step into a new epoch of time. It is but right that we each ask, What have I done with the opportunities afforded me in the past year? Did I make hay while the sun shone? Did I gather roses while they bloomed? Those who properly improved opportunities as they came to them, may look back upon the work of the past year with some degree of satisfaction.

means the cowardly part that Pilate took in Christ's crucifixion. The apostle dwells with emphasis on Christ's resurrection; (verse 30-37) showing the ascending of Christ over David. While David saw corruption, Christ whom he now was preaching, saw no corruption. The apostle then proceeds with the following statement: "Be it known unto you, therefore, men and brethren, that through *this man* is preached unto *you* the forgiveness of sins. And by *him* all that believe are justified from all things, from which they could not be justified by the law of Moses." Verses 38, 39. This declaration must have fallen on their ears with the crushing weight of an avalanche.

3. The venerable apostle closes his address with a terrible prophetic warning, "Beware therefore, lest that come upon *you*, which is spoken of in the prophets; Behold, ye despisers, and wonder, and perish; for I work a work in your days, a work which ye shall in no wise believe, though a man declare it unto you." Verse 40, 41. The reader doubtless is familiar with the telling results of this, Paul's first effort in the missionary cause.

From the above we glean the following:

1. It is the duty of missionary workers to watchfully improve every opportunity to address the people on their great mission.

2. Missionaries should not "speak smooth things" nor "prophesy deceits," Isa. 30: 10, but present kindly the pointed, sharp, double-edged truth, keeping each point as Paul did,—supported by Scriptural texts.

3. Let our manner and life be the clearest proof that we are converted ourselves, and hence believe the doctrine we preach,—that we are willing to "count all things but loss that we might win Christ." I. J. ROSENBERGER.

The Lord's Cause in Cedar Rapids, Iowa.

PERHAPS you are ready to inquire, "Will it be a success?" Yes, it will, provided it receives the necessary help. If the right course is pursued, and the right thing is done, success must follow. Your correspondent has now been with the little band of faithful workers in this city for the past two weeks. While two weeks is too short a time to accomplish a great work in a place like this, the time is long enough to fully see what is necessary, in order that a good work may be wrought. There are a good many persons in the city, who are not in sympathy with the popular religion of this age. Something more common-place would be more in harmony with their feelings, and more fully meet the longings of their anxious hearts. These are persons, too, of excellent character. Brethren and sisters, shall these burdened and anxious people have a suitable place in which to meet and worship the true and living God? Will you not say, Yes? I feel fully warranted in saying, that, if you had been with us for the last two weeks, and witnessed the deep throbbing of the inquiring hearts, and the anxieties of the few members who are set for the defense of the Lord's cause in this city, you would say yes with all your heart.

What is absolutely necessary, is a good, substantial, plain house of worship, located in a suitable place in the city. Here, in what is called "Central Park," that is, that part of the City, between the place where the Tabernacle was located for the Annual Meeting last spring, and the College on the hill, as you go toward the Depot, near the street car line, would be a favorable location. I suggest the propriety of looking at this place, before building anywhere else.

Dear brethren, sisters and friends, do you not now call to mind how you enjoyed yourselves at this place last spring, at the Annual Meeting? I feel confident that you can call up many precious remembrances of kind friends whom you met here in this "Park." You are ready to say it was one of the best, if not the very best, meetings you ever attended.

Well, that is one side of the case. Do you not also remember, how earnestly and constantly the members and friends here, worked day and night, to make us comfortable and happy? Those in behalf of whom this article is written, are among the prominent ones who were so earnest in their efforts for the success of that meeting. Do you not feel that you ought to help them to a good house, in which to worship the true God? They are just as earnest now, in their efforts to sustain the cause of the Master in the city, as they were for our comfort then, but they are compelled to use a house, that is located in such an out-of-the-way place, that it is difficult to find, and very few can be induced to hunt for it. No other place can now be secured for love or money. I hope the Mission Board of this District will give the matter their early and prompt attention, so that the matter can be properly brought before the District, and the Brotherhood as well.

In conclusion I wish to say to one and all, Just think how easily you can furnish the means to make these anxious hearts happy. Perhaps you are ready to say, I cannot afford to give more than $5 or $10, and that would not go very far toward building a church in a city like Cedar Rapids. While all that may be strictly true, yet you should think again, that there may be a thousand or two that feel the same way, so let each one send in their five or ten dollars, less or more, and all of these sums will secure just what is necessary. Watch for the opportunity! These members here are in earnest about the work. Let every one come to the rescue of the Lord's cause in this city! A. HUTCHISON.

From Alpena, S. Dak.

ON Friday evening Nov. 11, I left Alpena for Aberdeen, S. Dak., a distance of 95 miles, to hold a series of meetings for the Brethren at Bro. Fulker's school-house, 3¼ miles south of Aberdeen. Upon arrival I found Bro. Fulker very sick. He went to Aberdeen Nov. 12, and on returning home, took a severe chill, which resulted in pleuro-pneumonia. He was a constant sufferer for over a week. On Sunday, Nov. 20, he closed his eyes in death. I commenced meetings on the evening of Nov. 12. Being alone in a strange place it took a few evenings to get up an interest. Bro. Fulker was much interested in the meetings and always expressed a desire to be present with us. After holding five meetings, Bro. W. W. Horning came to our aid. After holding two meetings more, with good interest, we deemed it prudent to discontinue on account of Bro. Fulker growing very ill. Bro. Horning and I remained until after Bro. Fulker was buried.

Nov. 23, in company with Bro. Horning, we went to his place, 30 miles farther North, where we resumed our meetings again. Both places are under the eldership of Bro. Horning. We held six meetings near Bro. Horning's in a school-house. The meetings were well attended and had excellent order. This proved to me that the people there were taught the way of the Lord. If we could have remained longer we might have had good results. On account of some promises made before them, I had to return to Alpena, to prepare to go to Iowa, to hold some meetings. My wife is now at Dallas Center, Iowa, waiting my arrival, to join her in the happy reunion with our dear children who live in and near Dallas Center. We have rented our farm in South Dakota and made sale of our stock and farming implements. Having retired from hard and close confinement on the farm, I am now willing to devote my time to the cause of Christ. I have served the church in Dakota to the best of my ability, during nearly nine years. I have seen rejoicing seasons in gathering souls to Christ. I was treated very lovingly during my stay by all of my Dakota brethren and friends, and as I now bid them farewell I leave them in God's care. At my new field of labor, I will be ready to serve any of the congregations that desire me to come and hold meetings. Wife and I do not expect to keep house for one year, therefore will try to visit some among the churches in Iowa and Illinois. Any of the local churches that desire me to hold some meetings for them, should address me at Dallas Center, Dallas Co., Iowa. ELD. B. F. MILLER.

Notes from Our Correspondents.

" As cold water to a thirsty soul, so is good news from a far country."

McPHERSON, KANS.—In my "McPherson Notes," in No. 48 of the MESSENGER, I meant to say, "Just a little over six years," instead of "two years."—*S. Z. Sharp.*

Washington Church, Ind.—One more dear soul was received into church fellowship on the second Sunday in November in the Washington church. May she ever be a bright and shining light in the church!—*H. H. Brallier.*

North English, Iowa.—Bro. Michael Flory, of Girard, Ill., came to us Nov. 27, and began preaching in our church here in town last evening. Three dear souls came forward and others are counting the cost.—*T. H. Mannen, Dec. 10.*

Wayside, Kansas.—Bro. Fogle has been holding meetings two miles west of Havanna one week. He baptized two yesterday after meeting,—a young man and his wife. One was baptized last spring at the same place. Bro. Fogle's earnest labors have not been in vain, and we rejoice with the angels.—*Mary E. Needels, Dec. 5.*

Lost Creek Church, Ohio.—A two weeks' series of meetings in the Lost Creek church, Miami County, Ohio, closed Dec. 4. We had quite a pleasant meeting, but no accessions. We trust that the Lord will bless the work of the meeting, that it may prove a blessing to some. Quite an interest was manifested.—*W. Q. Calvert, Dec. 8.*

Indian Creek Church, Iowa.—Dec. 3 was our quarterly council. The business that came before the meeting was disposed of very pleasantly. At that meeting the church appointed Dec. 9 as the time to elect two brethren to the ministry. The lot fell on brethren A. Flora and F. Hulse. It was a very solemn occasion.—*Thos. H. Higgs, Dec 9.*

Barren Ridge, Va.—The members of the Barren Ridge congregation, Augusta Co., Va., called S. D. Kendig, of Fishersville, Va., to hold a series of meetings for them. He commenced the meetings on the night of Oct. 23 and continued until our love-feast, Nov. 5 and 6. Four dear ones were received by baptism during the meetings. Thus ended another interesting and profitable meeting.—*E. L. Brower.*

Cedar Rapids, Iowa. — Bro. A. Hutchison just closed a two weeks' series of meetings Sunday evening with good interest. Two came out on the Lord's side. We feel to thank the Lord for the many blessings he has bestowed upon us. The members are filled with the missionary spirit. One dear sister, from Marion, gave us a thanksgiving offering of $5.00 for the work in Cedar Rapids. The Lord loves a cheerful giver.—*M. E. Tisdale.*

means the cowardly part that Pilate took in Christ's crucifixion. The apostle dwells with emphasis on Christ's resurrection; (verse 30-37) showing the ascending of Christ over David. While David saw corruption, Christ whom he now was preaching, saw no corruption. The apostle then proceeds with the following statement: "Be it known unto you, therefore, men and brethren, that through *this man* is preached unto you the forgiveness of sins. And by *him* all that believe are justified from all things, from which they could not be justified by the law of Moses." Verses 38, 39. This declaration must have fallen on their ears with the crushing weight of an avalanche.

3. The venerable apostle closes his address with a terrible prophetic warning, "Beware therefore, lest that come upon you, which is spoken of in the prophets; Behold, ye despisers, and wonder, and perish; for I work a work in your days, a work which ye shall in no wise believe, though a man declare it unto you." Verse 40, 41. The reader doubtless is familiar with the telling results of this, Paul's first effort in the missionary cause.

From the above we glean the following:

1. It is the duty of missionary workers to watchfully improve every opportunity to address the people on their great mission.

2. Missionaries should not "speak smooth things" nor "prophesy deceits," Isa. 30: 10, but present kindly the pointed, sharp, double-edged truth, keeping each point as Paul did,—supported by Scriptural texts.

3. Let our manner and life be the clearest proof that we are converted ourselves, and hence believe the doctrine we preach,—that we are willing to "count all things but loss that we might win Christ."   I. J. ROSENBERGER.

The Lord's Cause in Cedar Rapids, Iowa.

PERHAPS you are ready to inquire, "Will it be a success?" Yes, it will, provided it receives the necessary help. If the right course is pursued, and the right thing is done, success must follow. Your correspondent has now been with the little band of faithful workers in this city for the past two weeks. While two weeks is too short a time to accomplish a great work in a place like this, the time is long enough to fully see what is necessary, in order that a good work may be wrought. There are a good many persons in the city, who are not in sympathy with the popular religion of this age. Something more common-place would be more in harmony with their feelings, and more fully meet the longings of their anxious hearts. These are persons, too, of excellent character. Brethren and sisters, shall these burdened and anxious people have a suitable place in which to meet and worship the true and living God? Will you not say, Yes? I feel fully warranted in saying, that, if you had been with us for the last two weeks, and witnessed the deep throbbing of the inquiring hearts, and the anxieties of the few members who are set for the defense of the Lord's cause in this city, you would say yes with all your heart.

What is absolutely necessary, is a good, substantial, plain house of worship, located in a suitable place in the city. Here, in what is called "Central Park," that is, that part of the City, between the place where the Tabernacle was located for the Annual Meeting last spring, and the College on the hill, as you go toward the Depot, near the street car line, would be a favorable location. I suggest the propriety of looking at this place, before building anywhere else.

Dear brethren, sisters and friends, do you not now call to mind how you enjoyed yourselves at this place last spring, at the Annual Meeting? I feel confident that you can call up many precious remembrances of kind friends whom you met here in this "Park." You are ready to say it was one of the best, if not the very best, meetings you ever attended.

Well, that is one side of the case. Do you not also remember, how earnestly and constantly the members and friends here, worked day and night, to make us comfortable and happy? Those in behalf of whom this article is written, are among the prominent ones who were so earnest in their efforts for the success of that meeting. Do you not feel that you ought to help them to a good house, in which to worship the true God? They are just as earnest now, in their efforts to sustain the cause of the Master in the city, as they were for our comfort then, but they are compelled to use a house, that is located in such an out-of-the-way place, that it is difficult to find, and very few can be induced to hunt for it. No other place can now be secured for love or money. I hope the Mission Board of this District will give the matter their early and prompt attention, so that the matter can be properly brought before the District, and the Brotherhood as well.

In conclusion I wish to say to one and all, Just think how easily you can furnish the means to make these anxious hearts happy. Perhaps you are ready to say, I cannot afford to give more than $5 or $10, and that would not go very far toward building a church in a city like Cedar Rapids. While all that may be strictly true, yet you should think again, that there may be a thousand or two that feel the same way, so let each one send in their five or ten dollars, less or more, and all of these sums will secure just what is necessary. Watch for the opportunity! These members here are in earnest about the work. Let every one come to the rescue of the Lord's cause in this city!   A. HUTCHISON.

From Alpena, S. Dak.

ON Friday evening Nov. 11, I left Alpena for Aberdeen, S. Dak., a distance of 95 miles, to hold a series of meetings for the Brethren at Bro. Fulker's school-house, 2½ miles south of Aberdeen. Upon arrival I found Bro. Fulker very sick. He went to Aberdeen Nov. 12, and on returning home, took a severe chill, which resulted in pleuro-pneumonia. He was a constant sufferer for over a week. On Sunday, Nov. 20, he closed his eyes in death. I commenced meetings on the evening of Nov. 12. Being alone in a strange place it took 6 few evenings to get up an interest. Bro. Fulker was much interested in the meetings and always expressed a desire to be present with us. After holding five meetings, Bro. W. W. Horning came to our aid. After holding two meetings more, with good interest, we deemed it prudent to discontinue on account of Bro. Fulker growing very ill. Bro. Horning and I remained until after Bro. Fulker was buried.

Nov. 23, in company with Bro. Horning, we went to his place, 30 miles farther North, where we resumed our meetings again. Both places are under the eldership of Bro. Horning. We held six meetings near Bro. Horning's in a schoolhouse. The meetings were well attended and we had excellent order. This proved to me that the people there were taught the way of the Lord. If we could have remained longer we might have had good results. On account of some promises made before theirs, I had to return to Alpena, to prepare to go to Iowa, to hold some meetings. My wife is now at Dallas Center, Iowa, waiting my arrival, to join her in the happy reunion with our dear children who live in and near Dallas Center. We have rented our farm in South Dakota and made sale of our stock and farming implements. Having retired from hard and close confinement on the farm, I am now willing to devote my time to the cause of Christ. I have served the church in Dakota to the best of my ability, during nearly nine years. I have seen rejoicing seasons in gathering souls to Christ. I was treated very lovingly during my stay by all of my Dakota brethren and friends, and as I now bid them farewell I leave them in God's care. At my new field of labor, I will be ready to serve any of the congregations that desire me to come and hold meetings. Wife and I do not expect to keep house for one year, therefore will try to visit some among the churches in Iowa and Illinois. Any of the local churches that desire me to hold some meetings for them, should address me at Dallas Center, Dallas Co., Iowa.

ELD. B. F. MILLER.

Notes from Our Correspondents.

" As cold water to a thirsty soul, so is good news from a far country."

McPHERSON, KANS.—In my "McPherson Notes," in No. 48 of the MESSENGER, I meant to say, "Just a little over six years," instead of "two years."—*S. Z. Sharp.*

Washington Church, Ind.—One more dear soul was received into church fellowship on the second Sunday in November in the Washington church. May she ever be a bright and shining light in the church!—*H. H. Brallier.*

North English, Iowa.—Bro. Michael. Flory, of Girard, Ill., came to us Nov. 27, and began preaching in our church here in town last evening. Three dear souls came forward and others are counting the cost.—*T. H. Mannen, Dec. 10.*

Wayside, Kansas.—Bro. Fogle has been holding meetings two miles west of Havanna one week. He baptized two yesterday after meeting,—a young man and his wife. One was baptized last spring at the same place. Bro. Fogle's earnest labors have not been in vain, and we rejoice with the angels.—*Mary E. Needels, Dec. 5.*

Lost Creek Church, Ohio.—A two weeks' series of meetings in the Lost Creek church, Miami County, Ohio, closed Dec. 4. We had quite a pleasant meeting, but no accessions. We trust that the Lord will bless the work of the meeting, that it may prove a blessing to some. Quite an interest was manifested.—*W. Q. Calvert, Dec. 8.*

Indian Creek Church, Iowa.—Dec. 3 was our quarterly council. The business that came before the meeting was disposed of very pleasantly. At that meeting the church appointed Dec. 9 as the time to elect two brethren to the ministry. The lot fell on brethren A. Flora and F. Hulse. It was a very solemn occasion.—*Thos. H. Higgs, Dec. 9.*

Barren Ridge, Va.—The members of the Barren Ridge congregation, Augusta Co., Va., called E. D. Kendig, of Fishersville, Va., to hold a series of meetings for them. He commenced the meetings on the night of Oct. 23 and continued until our love-feast, Nov. 5 and 6. Four dear ones were received by baptism during the meetings. Thus ended another interesting and profitable meeting.—*E. L. Brower.*

Cedar Rapids, Iowa.—Bro. A. Hutchison just closed a two weeks' series of meetings Sunday evening with good interest. Two came out on the Lord's side. We feel to thank the Lord for the many blessings he has bestowed upon us. The members are filled with the missionary spirit. One dear sister, from Marion, gave us a thanksgiving offering of $5.00 for the work in Cedar Rapids. The Lord loves a cheerful giver.—*M. E. Tisdale.*

Panora, Iowa.—Bro. A. Brower, of Dale, and the writer held a few meetings with the isolated members of the Adair congregation with a growing interest. Bro. M. Herman is alone in the ministry here. There is a good opening here for an efficient minister. Visits from traveling ministers will be highly appreciated. Address Sylvester Noland, Casey, Iowa. Brethren Diehl and Fitz have gone to the Ministerial Meeting in Marshall County. Bro. Myers and wife are in Illinois. Bro. Deardorff and wife are in Kansas. So we are all busy.—*J. D. Haughtelin, Dec. 5.*

Washington Creek Church, Kans.—In a former report I stated that we thought of holding a series of meetings. While we have enjoyed the meetings, our Heavenly Father alone knows the good they have done. Nov. 2 Bro. Wm. Jarboe, of Phillips County, Kans., preached three sermons. Then Bro. Eli Miller, of Elkhart County, Ind., preached each evening for over two weeks, also on two Sundays. One Sunday we held a children's meeting. While we had no additions, yet some good will certainly result from our meetings as Bro. Miller did his part of the work faithfully.—*S. M. Miller, Alfred, Kans.*

St. Joseph, Mo.—By the request of my two sons I will say that they are members of the Christian (or Disciple) church, but are dissatisfied with their doctrine. They have been reading the GOSPEL MESSENGER and want some one to come and explain to them more fully the Brethren's faith. I try to do the best I can. There are four members living here in town, but we have no preaching. My sons are very anxious to understand the truths of the Bible. If any members or preachers pass through the city, we would be very glad to have them stop and see us. We may be found at 517 Sylvanie Street.—*S. J. Cook.*

Eglon, W. Va.—This church met in council Dec. 3. There was not much business before the meeting, and all passed off very nicely. It was pleasant to be there. We organized a home mission work, and also appointed the time for our series of meetings this winter. We want to begin a series of meetings at the Maple Spring church on Christmas, and one at Brookside a week before or a week after. We expect Bro. Jasper Barnthouse or Bro. W. A. Gaunt to do the preaching if we can get one of them. The next morning,—Sunday,—we met for Sunday-school and for meeting. Bro. Aaron Fike preached for us.—*Rachel Weimer, Cor. Sec.*

River, Ind.—In my former letter to the MESSENGER I forgot some things I had intended to say. At the Communion at Flora, Ind., during my recent trip, on meeting an aged elder, I remarked to him that he was looking quite well. He said, "Yes, I quit chewing tobacco seven years ago. My health is much better now, and I thank God that I got rid of the filthy weed. I often think of the time when you used to talk to me. I did not then believe that I could quit, but I have no appetite for it now." He said he often thought of writing to the MESSENGER of his experience, and requested me to write for him. Several years ago an aged brother, who had used tobacco nearly seventy years, told me that I should write to the MESSENGER that he had quit. He had tried several times but failed, but as soon as he got faith, it was no trouble for him to quit.—*Samuel Murray.*

Literary Notices.

"A Journey to Palestine." By Rev. B. Carradine, D. D. Publisher, A. W. Hall, Syracuse, N. Y. A neatly-printed and well-bound volume of 489 pages in which the author, in a most graphic manner, narrates his journey from the United States to the Land of Palestine. He visits England, Scotland and France. From Paris he travels through Germany and Switzerland, and then visits the noted places in Italy. Crossing the Mediterranean we find him in Egypt among the Pyramids, and next in the Holy Land visiting Jerusalem, the Jordan and other parts of the Bible Lands and describing each place in a most interesting manner. The work is well written, fairly illustrated, while the writer's style is excellent, being both entertaining and instructive.

Matrimonial.

"What therefore God hath joined together, let not man put asunder."

LEHMAN—BURKHOLDER.—At the residence of the bride's parents, in the Abilene congregation, Kans., Dec. 1, 1892, by the writer, Henry L. Lehman and sister Anna Burkholder, both of Jefferson Township, Dickinson Co., Kans.
J. E. KELLER.

HAGER—HOWELL.—At the residence of Bro. D. D. Hager, Nov. 29, 1892, by the writer, Bro. Alvin L. Hager and Miss Rosa D. Howell, both of Jefferson County, Ill.
O. Z. HICKS.

DOTY—TAYLOR.—Near Deep River, Iowa, Nov. 30, 1892, by the undersigned, Mr. Marion Doty and Miss Annie Taylor.
H. R. TAYLOR.

BRALLIER—DITTMAN.—At the residence of the bride's mother, Nov. 16, 1892, by Rev. F. P. Mayser, Mr. Harry Edwin Brallier, son of D. S. and S. O. Brallier, and Sue C. Dittman, daughter of Mrs. Dora Dittman, both of Lancaster, Pa.
D. S. BRALLIER.

BALDWIN—DEARDORFF.—At the residence of the bride's parents, Dec. 1, 1892, by Bro. Isaac Deardorff, Mr. Oscar Baldwin and sister Catharine Deardorff, both of Wabash County, Ind.
JOSEPH JOHN.

Fallen Asleep.

"Blessed are the dead which die in the Lord."

BENEDICK.—In the Falling Spring church, Franklin Co., Pa., Nov. 26, 1892, Bro. Jacob Benedick, at the advanced age of 82 years, 9 months and 25 days. He leaves an aged companion (a sister), and eight children. The subject of this notice was the father of eleven children, of whom three have preceded him to the other world. Funeral services by the writer and Wm. A. Anthony, from 2 Tim. 6: 7, 8.
WM. C. KOONTZ.

DICKEY.—In the Middle Creek church, Somerset Co., Pa., Nov. 11, 1892, Bro. David Dickey, aged 66 years, 3 months and 7 days. He was born in Adams County, Pa. When a boy he moved with his parents to Fayette County, where he lived until the time of his death. Funeral services by the writer.
H. A. STAHL.

BOSSERMAN.—In the New Haven church, Gratiot Co., Mich., Nov. 21, 1892, sister Lydia Bosserman, aged 44 years, 11 months and 16 days. Deceased leaves a husband, a little daughter, 7 years of age, three brothers, two sisters and ten stepchildren. Sister Bosserman united with the German Baptist church when only seventeen years of age and lived a consistent Christian life until her death. Funeral services conducted by Eld. Isaiah Raleigh from Phil. 1: 21.
GEO. E. STONE.

HALL.—Near Montezuma, Iowa, Nov. 28, 1892, Ethel Zell, daughter of William and Allie Hall. She was a child of more than ordinary abilities. Though only of a little more than ten summers, she realized her situation and said to her mother that she was going far away, never to come back again.
H. R. TAYLOR.

GOCHENOUR.—In the Claar church, Pa., Nov. 4, 1892, sister Sarah Gochenour, aged 74 years and 20 days. Funeral occasion improved by Bro. John L. Holsinger and the writer.
MICHAEL CLAAR.

BURKET.—In the same church, Nov. 28, 1892, Roy Burket, infant son of Bro. David and sister Elizabeth Burket, aged 1 year, 5 months and 26 days. Funeral sermon by the writer from 2 Kings 4: 26, "It is well."
MICHAEL CLAAR.

BURROWS.—In the Upper Deer Creek congregation, Cass Co., Ind., Nov. 9, 1892, Bro. Joseph Burrows, aged 70 years, 9 months and 11 days. He united with the Brethren church in 1871. Soon afterward he was elected to the office of deacon, in which he labored faithfully until his death. He was one of the strong pillars in the church. May his Christian life and good counsels ever live in the memory of his children and others. Funeral services by elders D. P. Shively and A. Rinehart.
W. S. TONEY.

LOCKE.—In Indian Territory, Sept. 6, 1892, Bro. Henry D. Locke. He was born in Kentucky, May 23, 1840. He was a member of the church of the Brethren about eighteen years and was highly respected by all.
SAMUEL WEIMER.

BONSALL.—Near Union Mills, Iowa, Aug. 9, 1892, Robinson Bonsall, aged 67 years, 9 months and 20 days. Funeral services by the writer.
S. P. MILLER.

KIRBY.—Near Union Mills, Iowa, Sept. 22, 1892, Agnes Kirby, aged 1 year, 2 months and 11 days. Funeral services in Union Mills, in the Christian church, by the writer.
S. P. MILLER.

HEIL.—Near New Sharon, Iowa, Oct. 27, 1892, infant son of Bro. Miles and sister Jennie Heil, aged about 1 year. Funeral services at their home by the writer.
S. P. MILLER.

LORIN.—In the Salem congregation, Marion Co., Ore., Nov. 19, 1892, Bro. Peter Lorin, aged 37 years and 7 months. A few years ago he moved up into the mountain for the benefit of his health, but realizing that his days here were but few, he left his mountain home for the valley, where, at the home of Bro. Bosler, he quietly breathed his last. Funeral services by the writer.
J. F. EBERSOLE.

HOLLAR.—In the Green Mount congregation, Rockingham County, Va., Nov. 6, 1892, Mary C. Hollar, beloved wife of Bro. Noah Hollar, aged 22 years, 5 months and 5 days. She was a faithful member of the German Baptist Brethren. She leaves a husband and two small children. Funeral text, Ps. 17: 15, "I shall be satisfied when I awake with thy likeness."
I. C. MYERS.

CORRELL.—In the bounds of the Chippewa church, Wayne Co., Ohio, sister Rebecca Ann Correll, aged 39 years, 6 months and 28 days. She was born in Wayne County, Ohio, and lived there until after the death of her parents, when she moved to the State of Iowa. Wishing to visit the old home, she came home with her brother and sister from Annual Meeting and visited with her friends until she was taken down with typhoid fever, and peacefully passed away on the above date. Funeral services held in the Beech Grove meeting-house by the Brethren.
F. B. WEIMER.

BROWER.—In Roann, Wabash Co., Ind., Dec. 3, 1892, Bro. Jacob Brower, aged 79 years, 7 months and 18 days. He lived a faithful member in the church for many years and was a bright, shining light to the world. Funeral discourse by Eld. David Neff from Ps. 23: 1, 4, to a large audience.
JOSEPH JOHN.

FIKE.—In Roann, Wabash Co., Ind., Nov. 26, 1892, Miss Elizabeth, daughter of friend Christian Fike, aged 26 years, 9 months and 14 days. This young lady, while working with the fire in the cook-stove, being alone in the house at the time, accidentally set her clothes on fire. Her clothes also set fire to the carpets. Close neighbors rushed to the scene, only to find poor Lizzie laboring in agonies of death. Four hours later death came to her relief. Her remains were taken to Chili and there interred. Funeral services conducted by brethren Frank and Jacob Fisher.
JOSEPH JOHN.

SCHNEIDER.—In the Locust Grove church, Frederick Co., Md., Nov. 24, 1892, of heart disease, Mr. Leopold Schneider, husband of sister Rosanna Schneider, aged 77 years and 20 days. Deceased was born in Germany in 1815. His remains were interred in the Locust Grove cemetery. Funeral services by Eld. E. Bruner, of Frederick. Text, Rev. 22: 14.
M. E. ECKER.

The Gospel Messenger

Is the recognized organ of the German Baptist or Brethren's church, and advocates the form of doctrine taught in the New Testament and pleads for a return to apostolic and primitive Christianity.

It recognizes the New Testament as the only infallible rule of faith and practice, and maintains that Faith toward God, Repentance from dead works, Regeneration of the heart and mind, baptism by Trine Immersion for remission of sins unto the reception of the Holy Ghost by the laying on of hands, are the means of adoption into the household of God,—the church militant.

It also maintains that Feet-washing, as taught in John 13, both by example and command of Jesus, should be observed in the church.

That the Lord's Supper, instituted by Christ and as universally observed by the apostles and the early Christians, is a full meal, and, in connection with the Communion, should be taken in the evening or after the close of the day.

That the Salutation of the Holy Kiss, or Kiss of Charity, is binding upon the followers of Christ.

That War and Retaliation are contrary to the spirit and self-denying principles of the religion of Jesus Christ.

That the principle of Plain Dressing and of Non-conformity to the world, as taught in the New Testament, should be observed by the followers of Christ.

That the Scriptural duty of Anointing the Sick with Oil, in the Name of the Lord, James 5: 14, is binding upon all Christians.

It also advocates the church's duty to support Missionary and Tract Work, thus giving to the Lord for the spread of the Gospel and for the conversion of sinners.

In short, it is a Vindicator of all that Christ and the apostles have enjoined upon us, and aims, amid the conflicting theories and discords of modern Christendom, to point out ground that all must concede to be infallibly safe.

☞ The above principles of our Fraternity are set forth on our Brethren's Envelopes." Use them! Price 15 cents per package; 40 cents per hundred.

Panora, Iowa.—Bro. A. Brower, of Dale, and the writer held a few meetings with the isolated members of the Adair congregation with a growing interest. Bro. M. Herman is alone in the ministry here. There is a good opening here for an efficient minister. Visits from traveling ministers will be highly appreciated. Address Sylvester Noland, Casey, Iowa. Brethren Diehl and Fitz have gone to the Ministerial Meeting in Marshall County. Bro. Myers and wife are in Illinois. Bro. Deardorff and wife are in Kansas. So we are all busy.—*J. D. Haughtelin, Dec. 5.*

Washington Creek Church, Kans.—In a former report I stated that we thought of holding a series of meetings. While we have enjoyed the meetings, our Heavenly Father alone knows the good they have done. Nov. 2 Bro. Wm. Jarboe, of Phillips County, Kans., preached three sermons. Then Bro. Eli Miller, of Elkhart County, Ind., preached each evening for over two weeks, also on two Sundays. One Sunday we held a children's meeting. While we had no additions, yet some good will certainly result from our meetings as Bro. Miller did his part of the work faithfully.—*S M. Miller, Alfred, Kans.*

St. Joseph, Mo.—By the request of my two sons I will say that they are members of the Christian (or Disciple) church, but are dissatisfied with their doctrine. They have been reading the GOSPEL MESSENGER and want some one to come and explain to them more fully the Brethren's faith. I try to do the best I can. There are four members living here in town, but we have no preaching. My sons are very anxious to understand the truths of the Bible. If any members or preachers pass through the city, we would be very glad to have them stop and see us. We may be found at 517 Sylvanie Street.—*S. J. Cook.*

Eglon, W. Va.—This church met in council Dec. 3. There was not much business before the meeting, and all passed off very nicely. It was pleasant to be there. We organized a home mission work, and also appointed the time for our series of meetings this winter. We want to begin a series of meetings at the Maple Spring church on Christmas, and one at Brookside a week before or a week after. We expect Bro. Jasper Barnthouse or Bro. W. A. Gaunt to do the preaching if we can get one of them. The next morning,—Sunday,—we met for Sunday-school and for meeting. Bro. Aaron Fike preached for us.—*Rachel Weimer, Cor. Sec.*

River, Ind.—In my former letter to the MESSENGER I forgot some things I had intended to say. At the Communion at Flora, Ind., during my recent trip, on meeting an aged elder, I remarked to him that he was looking quite well. He said, "Yes, I quit chewing tobacco seven years ago. My health is much better now, and I thank God that I got rid of the filthy weed. I often think of the time when you used to talk to me. I did not then believe that I could quit, but I have no appetite for it now." He said he often thought of writing to the MESSENGER of his experience, and requested me to write for him. Several years ago an aged brother, who had used tobacco nearly seventy years, told me that I should write to the MESSENGER that he had quit. He had tried several times but failed, but as soon as he got faith, it was no trouble for him to quit.—*Samuel Murray.*

Literary Notices.

"A Journey to Palestine." By Rev. B. Carradine, D. D. Publisher, A. W. Hall, Syracuse, N. Y. A neatly-printed and well-bound volume of 489 pages in which the author, in a most graphic manner, narrates his journey from the United States to the Land of Palestine. He visits England, Scotland and France. From Paris he travels through Germany and Switzerland, and then visits the noted places in Italy. Crossing the Mediterranean we find him in Egypt among the Pyramids, and next in the Holy Land visiting Jerusalem, the Jordan and other parts of the Bible Lands and describing each place in a most interesting manner. The work is well written, fairly illustrated, while the writer's style is excellent, being both entertaining and instructive.

Matrimonial.

"What therefore God hath joined together, let not man put asunder."

LEHMAN—BURKHOLDER.—At the residence of the bride's parents, in the Abilene congregation, Kans., Dec. 1, 1892, by the writer, Henry L. Lehman and sister Anna Burkholder, both of Jefferson Township, Dickinson Co., Kans.
J. E. KELLER.

HAGER—HOWELL.—At the residence of Bro. D. D. Hager, Nov. 29, 1892, by the writer, Bro. Alvin L. Hager and Miss Rosa D. Howell, both of Jefferson County, Ill.
O. Z. HICKS.

DOTY—TAYLOR.—Near Deep River, Iowa, Nov. 30, 1892, by the undersigned, Mr. Marion Doty and Miss Annie Taylor. H. R. TAYLOR.

BRALLIER—DITTMAN.—At the residence of the bride's mother, Nov. 16, 1892, by Rev. F. P. Mayser, Mr. Harry Edwin Brallier, son of D. S. and S. O. Brallier, and Sue C. Dittman, daughter of Mrs. Dora Dittman, both of Lancaster, Pa. D. S. BRALLIER.

BALDWIN—DEARDORFF.—At the residence of the bride's parents, Dec. 1, 1892, by Bro. Isaac Deardorff, Mr. Oscar Baldwin and sister Catharine Deardorff, both of Wabash County, Ind. JOSEPH JOHN.

Fallen Asleep.

"Blessed are the dead which die in the Lord."

BENEDICK.—In the Falling Spring church, Franklin Co., Pa., Nov. 26, 1892, Bro. Jacob Benedick, at the advanced age of 82 years, 9 months and 25 days. He leaves an aged companion (a sister), and eight children. The subject of this notice was the father of eleven children, of whom three have preceded him to the other world. Funeral services by the writer and Wm. A. Anthony, from 2 Tim. 6: 7, 8.
WM. C. KOONTZ.

DICKEY.—In the Middle Creek church, Somerset Co., Pa., Nov. 11, 1892, Bro. David Dickey, aged 66 years, 3 months and 7 days. He was born in Adams County, Pa. When a boy he moved with his parents to Fayette County, where he lived until the time of his death. Funeral services by the writer. H. A. STAHL.

BOSSERMAN.—In the New Haven church, Gratiot Co., Mich., Nov. 21, 1892, sister Lydia Bosserman, aged 44 years, 11 months and 16 days. Deceased leaves a husband, a little daughter, 7 years of age, three brothers, two sisters and ten stepchildren. Sister Bosserman united with the German Baptist church when only seventeen years of age and lived a consistent Christian life until her death. Funeral services conducted by Eld. Isaiah Rairigh from Phil. 1: 21.
GEO. E. STONE.

HALL.—Near Montezuma, Iowa, Nov. 28, 1892, Ethel Zell, daughter of William and Allie Hall. She was a child of more than ordinary abilities. Though only of a little more than ten summers, she realized her situation and said to her mother that she was going far away, never to come back again. H. R. TAYLOR.

GOCHENOUR.—In the Claar church, Pa., Nov. 4, 1892, sister Sarah Gochenour, aged 74 years and 20 days. Funeral occasion improved by Bro. John L. Holsinger and the writer.
MICHAEL CLAAR.

BURKET.—In the same church, Nov. 28, 1892, Roy Burket, infant son of Bro. David and sister Elizabeth Burket, aged 1 year, 5 months and 26 days. Funeral sermon by the writer from 2 Kings 4: 26, "It is well." MICHAEL CLAAR.

BURROWS.—In the Upper Deer Creek congregation, Cass Co., Ind., Nov. 9, 1892, Bro. Joseph Burrows, aged 70 years, 9 months and 11 days. He united with the Brethren church in 1871. Soon afterward he was elected to the office of deacon, in which he labored faithfully until his death. He was one of the strong pillars in the church. May his Christian life and good counsels ever live in the memory of his children and others. Funeral services by elders D. P. Shively and A. Rinehart. W. S. TONEY.

LOCKE.—In Indian Territory, Sept. 6, 1892, Bro. Henry D. Locke. He was born in Kentucky, May 23, 1840. He was a member of the church of the Brethren about eighteen years and was highly respected by all. SAMUEL WEIMER.

BONSALL.—Near Union Mills, Iowa, Aug. 9, 1892, Robinson Bonsall, aged 67 years, 9 months and 20 days. Funeral services by the writer. S. P. MILLER.

KIRBY.—Near Union Mills, Iowa, Sept. 22, 1892, Agnes Kirby, aged 1 year, 2 months and 11 days. Funeral services in Union Mills, in the Christian church, by the writer.
S. P. MILLER.

HEIL.—Near New Sharon, Iowa, Oct. 27, 1892, infant son of Bro. Miles and sister Jennie Heil, aged about 1 year. Funeral services at their home by the writer. S. P. MILLER.

LORIN.—In the Salem congregation, Marion Co., Ore., Nov. 19, 1892, Bro. Peter Lorin, aged 37 years and 7 months. A few years ago he moved up into the mountain for the benefit of his health, but realizing that his days here were but few, he left his mountain home for the valley, where, at the home of Bro. Bosler, he quietly breathed his last. Funeral services by the writer. J. F. EBERSOLE.

HOLLAR.—In the Green Mount congregation, Rockingham County, Va., Nov. 6, 1892, Mary C. Hollar, beloved wife of Bro. Noah Hollar, aged 22 years, 5 months and 5 days. She was a faithful member of the German Baptist Brethren. She leaves a husband and two small children. Funeral text, Ps. 17: 15, "I shall be satisfied when I awake with thy likeness." I. C. MYERS.

CORRELL.—In the bounds of the Chippewa church, Wayne Co., Ohio, sister Rebecca Ann Correll, aged 39 years, 6 months and 28 days. She was born in Wayne County, Ohio, and lived there until after the death of her parents, when she moved to the State of Iowa. Wishing to visit the old home, she came home with her brother and sister from Annual Meeting and visited with her friends until she was taken down with typhoid fever, and peacefully passed away on the above date. Funeral services held in the Beech Grove meeting-house by the Brethren. F. B. WEIMER.

BROWER.—In Roann, Wabash Co., Ind., Dec. 3, 1892, Bro. Jacob Brower, aged 79 years, 7 months and 18 days. He lived a faithful member in the church for many years and was a bright, shining light to the world. Funeral discourse by Eld. David Neff from Ps. 23: 1, 4, to a large audience.
JOSEPH JOHN.

FIKE.—In Roann, Wabash Co., Ind., Nov. 26, 1892, Miss Elizabeth, daughter of friend Christian Fike, aged 26 years, 9 months and 14 days. This young lady, while working with the fire in the cook-stove, being alone in the house at the time, accidentally set her clothes on fire. Her clothes also set fire to the carpets. Close neighbors rushed to the scene, only to find poor Lizzie laboring in agonies of death. Four hours later death came to her relief. Her remains were taken to Chili and there interred. Funeral services conducted by brethren Frank and Jacob Fisher. JOSEPH JOHN.

SCHNEIDER.—In the Locust Grove church, Frederick Co., Md., Nov. 24, 1892, of heart disease, Mr. Leopold Schneider, husband of sister Rosanna Schneider, aged 77 years and 20 days. Deceased was born in Germany in 1815. His remains were interred in the Locust Grove cemetery. Funeral services by Eld. E. Bruner, of Frederick. Text, Rev. 22: 14.
M. E. ECKER.

The Gospel Messenger

Is the recognized organ of the German Baptist or Brethren's church, and advocates the form of doctrine taught in the New Testament and pleads for a return to apostolic and primitive Christianity.

It recognizes the New Testament as the only infallible rule of faith and practice, and maintains that Faith toward God, Repentance from dead works, Regeneration of the heart and mind, baptism by Trine Immersion for remission of sins unto the reception of the Holy Ghost by the laying on of hands, are the means of adoption into the household of God,—the church militant.

It also maintains that Feet-washing, as taught in John 13, both by example and command of Jesus, should be observed in the church.

That the Lord's Supper, instituted by Christ and as universally observed by the apostles and the early Christians, is a full meal, and, in connection with the Communion, should be taken in the evening or after the close of the day.

That the Salutation of the Holy Kiss, or Kiss of Charity, is binding upon the followers of Christ.

That War and Retaliation are contrary to the spirit and self-denying principles of the religion of Jesus Christ.

That the principle of Plain Dressing and of Non-conformity to the world, as taught in the New Testament, should be observed by the followers of Christ.

That the Scriptural duty of Anointing the Sick with Oil, in the Name of the Lord, James 5: 14, is binding upon all Christians.

It also advocates the church's duty to support Missionary and Tract Work, thus giving to the Lord for the spread of the Gospel and for the conversion of sinners.

In short, it is a Vindicator of all that Christ and the apostles have enjoined upon us, and aims, amid the conflicting theories and discords of modern Christendom, to point out ground that all must concede to be infallibly safe.

☞ "The above principles of our Fraternity are set forth on our Brethren's Envelopes." Use them! Price 15 cents per package; 40 cents per hundred.

CPSIA information can be obtained
at www.ICGtesting.com
Printed in the USA
BVHW04*1423200918
528044BV00007B/269/P